Random House
Historical
Dictionary
of
American Slang

Random House
Historical
Dictionary
of
American Slang

Volume 1, A–G

J. E. Lighter, Editor

Assistant Editors

J. Ball

J. O'Connor

Random House   New York

Excerpts from the following works are from manuscript materials housed at the Kinsey Institute Collections, Bloomington, Indiana: "Sexual Vocabulary" by Henry N. Carey, "Jody Calls" by Paul Cameron, "Folklore of the U.S. Marine Corps" and "U.S.M.C. Marianas" Collection by Don Higginbotham, "Bawdy Elements in Ozark Folk Speech" and "Unprintable Songs from the Ozarks" by Vance Randolph, manuscript graffiti collection by John Del Torto, "Old American Ballads," "41st Fighter Squadron Songbook," and "Erotic Verse to 1955."

Grateful acknowledgment is made to the following for permission to print unpublished material:

Collin Baker, D. R. Ladd, and Thomas Robb: Excerpts from "CUSS: College Undergraduate Slang Survey" by Collin Baker, D. R. Ladd, and Thomas Robb, written at Brown University in 1968 under the supervision of Professor W. Nelson Francis. Reprinted by permission of the authors.

Dan Cragg: Excerpts from "Lexicon Militaris" by Dan Cragg and a personal letter to the author. Reprinted by permission of Dan Cragg.

Folklore Institute at Indiana University: Excerpts from various collections housed in the Folklore Archives at the Folklore Institute at Indiana University. Reprinted by permission.

University of Missouri—Columbia, Western Historical Manuscript Collection: Excerpts from the Peter Tamony Collection. Reprinted by permission of the University of Missouri—Columbia, Western Historical Manuscript Collection.

Charles Vandersee: Excerpts from "Dictionaries with Pockets for Change: An African American Cue," by Charles Vandersee. Paper presented at the annual meeting of the Modern Language Association, December, 1993. Reprinted by permission.

Library of Congress Cataloging-in-Publication Data

Historical dictionary of American slang / editor, J.E. Lighter
      p.   cm.
    Includes bibliographical references.
    ISBN 0-394-54427-7 (v. 1).
     1. English language—United States—Slang—Dictionaries.
    2. English language—United States—Obsolete words—Dictionaries.
    3. Americanisms—Dictionaries.
    I. Lighter, J. E. (Jonathan E.)
    PE2846.H57   1994
    427'.973'03—dc20   94-9721
                                    CIP

Manufactured in the United States of America

10 9 8 7 6 5 4 3 2

First Edition

New York   Toronto   London   Sydney   Auckland

CONTENTS

ACKNOWLEDGMENTS

The present volume was created not by the chief editor alone or with the aid of jovial blue genies or elfin leftenants. A surprising passel of idealistic ladies and gentlemen has encouraged with word and deed the editor in chief of this fascicle. The names of some of the most dedicated appear on the title page. Without their devoted and at times selfless aid there literally would have been no book at all.

But others have played an equally vital role, and I wish to record here my gratitude. Foremost among all friends of this dictionary has been John Hurt Fisher, Chaucerian scholar and lover of language, whose unflagging enthusiasm and confidence in this project over a period of twenty-plus years can never be repaid. When I lost heart, he didn't. It was he who suggested, with a mischievous twinkle, that *American Speech* might be interested in publishing an undergraduate's gleanings of slang for the edification of the learned.

In time it came to pass, but not without the deft hand of John Algeo, then editor of *American Speech*, who also ranks as one of the major abettors of this enterprise over many years, reaffirming his confidence on more than one crucial occasion. Richard W. Bailey paused in his seemingly unrelated labors to devote a lexicography session of the Modern Language Association to a discussion of an American slang lexicon. Frederic Cassidy of the *Dictionary of American Regional English* was present, and Sidney Landau, author of *Dictionaries*, was there too, and all three have been unstinting in their enthusiasm ever since. I extend sincerest thanks to all of them.

Were it not for the late Stuart Flexner, co-editor of the *Dictionary of American Slang* and former editor in chief at Random House Reference, the present lexicon would have gone a-glimmering down the vale of the might-have-been. Having waded through slang-fields himself, Stuart, my first editor at Random House, took a personal interest in this project and convinced all concerned that "the book" (we thought it would be just one volume in those days) needed to be published. He is sorely missed.

At Random House, and within its orbit, I thank Carol Braham, Mary Louise Byrd, Carole Cook, Trudy Nelson, Joyce O'Connor, Connie Padakis, James L. Rader, Anne D. Steinhardt, and especially Sol Steinmetz, for their editorial wisdom; Judy Kaplan, whose contributions to the accuracy of the book would be hard to overstate; Enid Pearsons for pronunciations as well as many other helpful suggestions; Robert Costello, former editor in chief of the Reference Department, who provided unflagging enthusiasm for this dictionary for nearly ten years; Mia McCroskey for keeping the project on track through thick and thin; Pat Ehresmann for actually producing the book; Catherine Fowler, Lenore Hauck, Phyllis Henrici, John L. Hornor, Michael Mellin, and Kenzi Sugihara on the executive level for sustaining interest in what must be to commercial publishing a somewhat unusual project; Ampersand Graphics, Ltd.; and Electric Ink, Ltd. (Karl Barndt, Kristen Barndt, and Lydia Ievins) for production and technical wizardry.

I would also like to extend special thanks to Jesse T. Sheidlower, my editor at Random House Reference, and project editor of this volume, for his exceptional assistance in getting this book done. Few editors faced with a project of this magnitude could have shown equal energy, ingenuity, and effectiveness in keeping it on schedule and on target. This resourceful lexicographer has re-edited almost every entry in the volume. As in-house editor, his name does not appear on the title page, but his extensive and invaluable contribution to this volume has been quite the equal of the Assistant Editors named there.

David L. Gold brought his seemingly omniscient eye to the etymologies, elucidating obscure connections and removing inaccuracies. I only regret that considerations of space prevented the full details of his research from being expressed.

Dan Cragg, warrior-sage, not to mention novelist, military historian, and co-author of *A Dictionary of Soldier Talk*, deserves many thanks for being a good guy who granted permission to quote from a long letter he wrote me about army slang, and also for putting up with a civilian's eccentric views on the subject. Better yet, Dan's quick thinking and lightning reflexes got the project flying again just as it was turning into an albatross.

Connie Eble, at the University of North Carolina, Chapel Hill, is one of the few professional linguists to write cogently on college slang. She gets a round of applause for generously sharing her collection of college slang, made over a period of nearly twenty years. Her forthcoming book on the subject—the first since 1856—will fill additional gaps in our knowledge.

Gerald Cohen, at the University of Missouri, Rolla, deserves the thanks of many for his discoveries regarding *shyster, smart aleck, Big Apple,* and other terms. He responded quickly to the general request I circulated for data. An impeccable scholar, he also edits *Comments on Etymology,* a publication that deserves a wider circulation.

Gershon Legman gets a bow both for his interest and for the courageous example he set many years ago of never expurgating or bowdlerizing collections of folklore. There was a time when few heeded this elementary scholarly imperative. Legman also supplied a microfilm of *The Stag Party* (1888) and leads to additional unique historical material.

Also at long distance, Robert Burchfield, editor of the four-volume supplement to the *OED,* more than once provided tremendous encouragement. Eric Partridge too expressed his enthusiasm long ago: his books were an early inspiration. Peter Tamony of San Francisco, a legend among scholars of the American language (and discoverer long ago of the earliest citation of *jazz*), cheerfully sent books and comments. And Randy Roberts generously provided access to the word treasures of the Tamony Collection

at the Ellis Library of the University of Missouri, Columbia.

Col. Albert F. Moe, USMC-ret., was collecting early examples of Navy and Marine Corps terms when we corresponded in the 1970's. His articles for *American Speech* on *gung ho, gyrene,* and *tell it to the marines* are models of scrupulous historical scholarship, and he set me right on a number of technical points.

Owen Lock and Joelle Del Burgo at Ballantine Books liked my dissertation and, assuming that "who says 'A' must say 'B through Z'," brought it to Stuart Flexner's attention.

Thanks also, for encouraging this work in its embryonic stages at New York University, to Christopher Collins, Allan F. Hubbell, Sumner Ives, Stephen Khinoy, Robert Kolker, and, at the Office of Sponsored Research, Ann M. Greenberg.

The following persons at the University of Tennessee, Knoxville, have actively and essentially kept the project alive, and it is a genuine pleasure to thank them all. Bain T. Stewart offered me an office and a job, and Percy G. Adams helped make sure that I did it. Henry Kratz, lexicographer and etymologist, scholar of medieval German and reviewer of Icelandic novels, stepped in at a critical moment to keep things on track. At a still more decisive moment, Jeffrey C. Sekula, George B. Hutchinson, and Michael A. Lofaro offered the opportunity to teach classes in American Studies. D. Allen Carroll gave his official stamp of approval to continued research on several occasions, as did Joseph B. Trahern, Jr., Sheadrick A. Tillman IV, and Clifton Woods III. Allen has been an especially strong supporter, as have Bethany Dumas and Thomas J. Heffernan. The trustees of the John C. Hodges Better English Fund voted me a subsistence grant at a time when English classes were unavailable. Without the efforts of the entire Research Administration of the University of Tennessee, Knoxville, and, at a much earlier date, the Office of Sponsored Programs of New York University, labor on this dictionary would have come to an abrupt halt. Yet the special diligence of Jane Perry, Lydia Petersson, Phyllis L. Tobler, and Carolyn M. Webb should not go unmentioned. Nor should the enthusiasm of the approximately eight hundred students who filled out slang questionnaires and that of the numerous graduate teaching assistants who took time to administer them.

Thanks to the staff of the University of Tennessee Libraries, particularly Paula T. Kaufman, Linda L. Phillips, Joe C. Rader, and the staff of Interlibrary Services, who were able to locate and provide many otherwise unobtainable sources.

Thanks also to my two undergraduate assistants of 1975–76, Mary Beth Calio and Sandra C. McGeohagan.

For their assistance in a thousand less specific but no less essential ways, my best thanks go also to Frank G. Bemis, Jr., and Kathie M. Bemis; Keith F. Blue; Susan Bolcar; Michael Brennan; Alvin G. Burstein; Robert Drake; Chad Hilton; Martin F. Kearney and Charlene Kearney; C. J. Mellor; Michael Montgomery; Anthony K. Moses; Steve Reddick and Vickie Reddick; Mary P. Richards; Norman J. Sanders; Cindy Schnebley and Jim Schnebley; William H. Shurr; Michael K. Smith; Jane Stanfield; and Leila Zogby.

Besides my genuine obligation to the National Endowment for the Humanities in Washington, D.C., of which more will be said anon, I wish also to thank two very kind and capable public servants at that agency, Donna Grace and Adrienne Lo.

I am indebted to Raven I. McDavid and Virginia McDavid; Allen Walker Read; David W. Maurer; Reinhold Aman, editor of *Maledicta: The International Journal of Verbal Aggression*; Charles D. Poe (for providing a number of useful citations); George Cheatham; Judy Moses; Andrea Shabsin; Dennis Diamonti; Dennis Ryan; Steve Widner; Guy Bailey; Eugene Young; Suzanne Greenfield; Andrew S. Allen; W. Nelson Francis; Collin Baker, Thomas Robb, and D. Robert Ladd (for permission to quote from *CUSS*, their unpublished collection of college slang from the late 1960's); Charles Vandersee (for permission to quote from his unpublished paper, "Dictio-naries with Pockets for Change: An African American Cue," presented at the annual meeting of the Modern Language Association, December, 1993); Leonard Zwilling; Ron Butters, current editor of *American Speech*; Edmund Wilson; Robert Chapman; and Laurence Urdang.

And the following institutions:

The New York Public Library, the Library of Congress, and the libraries of the following colleges and universities: New York University; Harvard College; Indiana University and the archives of its Folklore Institute; San Diego State University; University of Louisville; University of Kentucky; University of Texas; Kent State University; University of Connecticut; University of North Carolina; University of Virginia; Vanderbilt University; East Tennessee State University; Texas Technical University; Ohio State University; Mississippi State College; University of Alabama in Birmingham; Indiana State University in Terre Haute; Bowling Green State University; Carson-Newman College; Berry College; James Madison University; University of California at Los Angeles; Texas Agricultural and Mechanical College; Western Kentucky University; Southern Arkansas University; and Southern Illinois University at Carbondale.

And these additional libraries:

The Lawson McGhee Public Library, Knoxville, Tennessee; Richmond, Virginia, Public Library; Joint University Libraries, Nashville, Tennessee; Armor School Library, Fort Knox, Kentucky; Library of the Kinsey Institute; Library of the Seamen's Church Institute, New York City; and the Library of the Ohio State Historical Society.

This dictionary has been made possible in great measure by support from the National Endowment for the Humanities, an agency that deserves not only my thanks but also general acknowledgment for its support of research in the humanities that enhances the understanding of our culture and thus the quality of American life.

INTRODUCTION

Slang is the poetry of everyday life.
  —S. I. Hayakawa, *Language in Action*, 1941

Slang, *n.* The grunt of the human hog (*Pignoramus intolerabilis*) with an audible memory.
  —Ambrose Bierce, *The Devil's Dictionary*, 1911

I shall invent a new game; I shall write bits of slang and poetry on slips and give them to you to separate.
  —George Eliot, *Middlemarch*, 1871

What Is Slang?

Slang—however you define it—is a term that conveniently designates words and phrases diverging markedly in social ambiance, use, and style from those of the standard lexicon. Public and professional interest in slang has never been greater than it is today. The purpose of this and succeeding volumes is, through the use of established historical methods, to shed fresh light on the slang element in American English and, by so doing, to better our understanding of American English as a whole.

As a rough-and-ready label for an abstraction that, as our epigraphs suggest, encourages as much appreciation as dispraise, *slang* has frequently inspired discordant, sometimes antagonistic, definitions. The public employs the term as a simple synonym for a subjectively "bad" English, and it may well be that the word most often appears in the parental admonition "Don't use slang!" For close to two and a half centuries popular definitions of slang have embraced every variety of unconventional or unfamiliar English, from the lingo of felons to the language of philosophers. Yet no commonly accepted definition of slang has won much favor among linguists, who mostly regard the boundaries between slang and other levels of discourse as too insubstantial for analysis. And one can hardly blame them. For it is true that, taken together,

slang and its associated epithets *argot* and *cant* are in practice a terminological jumble, each frequently laden with negative overtones and each one ready to serve as a synonym of the others. Yet differing interpretations of the word *slang* do not come about because it designates an exterior phenomenon of ineffable or elusive qualities; they arise instead because the interpreters—dictionary makers, schoolteachers, and arbiters of diction—differ in their preconceptions about language, view language from varying angles, and examine it for very different purposes. Items as dissimilar as *snack bar, ain't, gentrification, sandwich, bikini, redcoat, date rape, motel,* and *wuss* have now and again been cited as slang or former slang by various commentators, as has the interjectional *say!* ("Oh, say, can you see by the dawn's early light...?"), a claim that, lumped with all the others, leaves the useful word *slang* with scarcely any meaning at all.

In deriving a definition of slang so as to limit the scope of the present work and to keep its contents as much of a piece as possible, we have tried to work within a judicious tradition established over the past hundred years by W. D. Whitney[1], James A. H. Murray, Henry Bradley, and others—lexicographers whose judgments rested upon a meticulous consideration of actual usage, which in lexicography is the only convincing evidence there is. We reject the practice that attaches the name of "slang" to whatever is new or popular in the way of language.

In this dictionary slang is conceived of in a rather limited way as a social and stylistic subset of the larger informal vocabulary of U.S. English. Slang may thus be briefly defined:

> an informal, nonstandard, nontechnical vocabulary composed chiefly of novel-sounding synonyms for standard words and phrases.

But a definition of slang that confines itself to stylistic traits such as these will necessarily remain inadequate. Slang has a vital social dimension as well: it turns up especially in the derisive speech play of youthful, raffish, or undignified persons and groups; and partly owing to this and partly because of the unconventional images slang often evokes, the use of slang often carries with it striking overtones of impertinence or irreverence, especially for idealized values and attitudes within the prevailing culture. Often too, the use of slang suggests, as standard speech cannot, an intimate familiarity with a referential object or idea (compare, for example, the difference between *professional dancer* and *hoofer*, *wait tables* and *sling hash*, *prison* and *the joint*, *beer* and *suds*, *intellectual* and *wonk*).

The use of slang also suggests something about the slangster's orientation to the interlocutor. It implies that the other person identifies fully with the speaker's attitudes. Thus, the English critic Walter Raleigh argued in the 1920's that "the strong vivid slang word cannot be counted on to do its work. It sets the hearer thinking, not on the subject of my speech, but on such irrelevant questions as the nature of my past education and the company I keep."[2]

Our abbreviated characterization of slang suggests something too about its chief rhetorical effect: the use of slang undermines the dignity of verbal exchange and charges discourse with an unrefined and often aggressive informality. It pops the balloon of pretense. There is often a raw vitality in slang, a ribald sense of humor and a flip self-confidence; there is also very often locker-room crudity and toughness, a tawdry sensibility. Whether slang's undignified tone communicates abrasive disrespect or a down-to-earth egalitarianism depends upon one's point of view. A trite misconception has it that the "nature of slang" is to assail dignity or taste or to "prove" that one somehow "belongs"; the truth is simply that, no matter what else the label is attached to, any word or phrase producing these particular effects is automatically classified as slang.

In fact, a truly unexpurgated collection of slang reminds us that the world of discourse, like the world of sense, is savage as well as sublime. For slang, romanticized as "the poetry of everyday life," has a regrettable side too, a side often stupidly coarse and provocative. The cultural focus of slang in Britain, America, Australia, and elsewhere as an adversary of dignity and taste has always inclined toward the ignoble. Certain subjects of enduring interest have been especially productive of English-language slang: physical sexuality; bodily functions; intoxication by liquor or drugs; sudden, energetic, or violent actions of various kinds; money; death; deception; criminal activity; weakness of mind or character; positive or sharply negative evaluations of people and things; and the derisive or contemptuous categorization of people of differing classes and groups—racial, ethnic, sexual, regional, socio-economic, occupational.

John Farmer and William Ernest Henley's *Slang and Its Analogues*, compiled in England mainly before 1890, is notable for its extensive lists of nonstandard synonyms for sex and alcohol. The Australians Keith Allan and Kate Burridge, discussing the current state of affairs in the Antipodes, declare flatly that "the degree of synonymy in the vocabulary for genitalia and copulation has no parallel elsewhere in the English lexicon."[3] Stuart Flexner and others have averred that the word having the most slang synonyms is probably *drunk*. We believe *drunk* comes in second to the sexual terms, and does so throughout the English-speaking world.

Yet those who might accept a sketch of the national character based on slang alone would do well to remember that that portrayal is only a caricature, which bears as much resemblance to everyday life as do the stories in underground comix or the lyrics of gangsta rap. An opposing picture of the real world could as well be evoked by reflecting upon the rich English vocabulary of faith and philanthropy. However, such a rendering would be no more accurate, though admittedly more reassuring.

We can see that slang varies in important ways from other modes of language and levels of discourse. While its specific characteristics vis-à-vis those of nonstandard and colloquial language, as well as those of dialect and jargon, will be discussed later (see Slang Distinguished From Other Levels of Discourse, p. xiv), we should add here that slang differs too from idiosyncratic wordplay and other nonce figuration in that it maintains a currency independent of its creator, the individual writer or speaker. And it is not inappropriate to point out here, in anticipation of a fuller discussion, that slang differs broadly from *dialect* (a regional or social variety of speech) and *jargon* (a vocabulary of technical terms). Persons who naturally speak the same dialect (Northern American English or Hispanic American English, for example) necessarily share a similar regional or cultural background. Those who share a jargon (like electricians, surgeons, executives, quilt makers, economists, fighter pilots, and lawyers) share training or expertise. But a shared slang is more likely to suggest mutually held antiestablishment attitudes, especially a sharpened disdain for convention or pretense.

The Mutability of the Slang Lexicon

The claim is often made that American slang effectively defies the historical treatment accorded to other classes of discourse by monuments like the *Dictionary of American Regional English* (*DARE*) and *The Oxford English Dictionary* (*OED*). It is said that slang is too fleeting or too trivial for serious attention; that documentation of individual slang terms is more or less impossible because slang appears infrequently in print or because slang changes almost overnight. The *OED*, however, the touchstone of English lexicography since the first fascicle was ready in 1884, has from the beginning incorporated as much slang as the great James A. H. Murray and succeeding editors could document sufficiently for inclusion. And although editors Frederic Cassidy and Joan Hall have intentionally forgone use of the slang label in *DARE*, probably eight to ten percent of the entries in that grand collection of regional dialect well fit the definition of slang offered here. Popular expectation notwithstanding, no dictionary of a living language can ever be all-inclusive, and much that one might call slang is indeed limited and ephemeral—as is much seriously intended "standard" terminology. Yet the sheer force of the data gathered for the first time in these volumes must dispel the notion that American slang is of insufficient interest or importance to merit historical investigation.

This dictionary treats of words and phrases that could sensibly be labeled *American slang*, now or in times past. Some current senses are obsolete or nearly so; yet the proportion of truly obsolete senses—no longer usable or recognizable by anybody—is surprisingly small. While slang expressions specially linked with entertainment fads or media scandals may be epidemic for a short time and then fade away, and while the fad idioms of high school cliques and other small, localized groups can come and go in a matter of days or weeks, the life of a slang term that has gained a toehold in popular speech is likely to be long, on a human if not always on a linguistic scale. *Twenty-three skiddoo*, of uncertain inspiration, had a brief but intense vogue about 1905; it is often given as an example of "dead" slang. Yet millions still recognize it, even if few would ever use it. Like much slang that has been declared officially dead, *twenty-three skiddoo* has simply passed from the nation's active into its passive vocabulary. It is still slang; it is just no longer in vogue.

Captain Francis Grose, compiler of the influential *Classical Dictionary of the Vulgar Tongue* in 1785, affords us even more apposite examples. He believed that "the late fashionable words *a bore* and *twaddle*" had vanished "without leaving a trace behind"; both are now Standard English. He also defined "to *hump*" as "once a fashionable word for copulation."[4] As for more recent times, it could not have been predicted in 1972 that the press would abstract the element *-gate* from *Watergate* to imply, in combination, any real or suspected scandal and cover-up, still less that such *-gate* combinations would still be productive and presumably amusing more than two decades later.

A relatively few slang terms, especially of eccentric or uncertain origin, have risen in educated esteem to the status of colloquial or Standard English. *Bamboozle, blimp, blizzard, buddy, crony, disc jockey, Dixie, doxy, flabbergast, flimflam, gadget, GI, hijack, hoodlum*, to be *into* (something of interest), *jazz, jeep, jitters, jukebox, mob, ogle, O.K., quiz, rogue, snob*, and *slang* itself are familiar examples, drawn from various centuries. The list could be greatly expanded, but the number of slang coinages that have approached literary status would remain small, considering the immensity of the English vocabulary.

In still fewer cases words once deemed fit for literary use have since become slang. This is especially true of several anatomical and scatological terms, including *ass*, *balls*, and *shit*, from the period of Middle English or before, when there was not yet any sense of a standard language. Some of these were the only words available for their referents in the language.[5] But now, based on their current associations, we feel it is entirely appropriate to consider these words—and indeed other terms sometimes considered "vulgar" or "obscene"—slang.

As the reader by now has gathered, slang even in a restricted sense is a rowdy category; its existence hinges entirely on its contrast with a cultivated standard lexicon. In other words, the recognition of slang, as well as the slang status of any word or phrase, stems entirely from the native speaker's perception of social and stylistic custom and nuance, conditioned by an awareness of a sanctioned standard from which slang is felt to deviate. Without the contrast of a recognized standard vocabulary, any basis for distinguishing slang from something else disappears. This is not to say that the entire populace must be equally discerning of that standard, still less that the lowest common denominator of taste be consulted when judging the status of a given expression. Public education and continual exposure to mass media have presumably sensitized all of us to verbal and stylistic nuance more thoroughly than could any phenomena of prior centuries, and so the slang effect remains salient, especially for those whose training or experience has encouraged them to attend closely to verbal nuance in general. We hope that users of this dictionary who are fluent in American English will agree that the entries defined in the following pages sufficiently match our stipulated and thoroughly heuristic definition of slang, and that most of what is left out does not.[6]

Slang Distinguished From Other Levels of Discourse

As we have observed, overmuch of the immense vocabulary of English has been loosely referred to as slang. Indeed, the grab-bag nature of the category, as popularly employed, led the psychologist Frank Sechrist to observe in 1913 that "slang represents characteristics that answer to the most contrary terms of qualitative description."[7] After taking into account the kinds of words and phrases that nonspecialists have classified as slang, one thinks of Alfred Kazin's recent facetious comment about New York (reported by Charles Kuralt on *CBS Sunday Morning*) that "there's nothing you can say about it that isn't true." This illogical state of affairs can be mitigated, however, at least for slang.

So far as we may intelligently do so, we should be careful to distinguish *slang* from certain other terms relating to style or to "levels of discourse." The most common of these are *standard, nonstandard,* and *substandard,* and *cant, jargon, colloquialism,* and *dialect.* To add to our difficulties, these words are neither entirely parallel nor fully complementary. Still less do they demarcate permanent or rigorously established boundaries.

For three hundred years the only English that professionals have deemed fit for all uses without apology has been Standard English. Though pedagogy often gives the impression that Standard English is somewhere engraved on stone tablets, never to be tampered with or fully understood, it is in fact an evolving set of conventions that are both consciously and unconsciously acquired. The very idea of Standard English brings with it strong expectations (and relatively stable limits) regarding orthography, grammar, vocabulary, pronunciation, and tone. Unlike the case of French or Italian, no specially convened academy of prestigious scholars has ever embarked on the largely pointless task of imposing official restrictive standards on English by formally condemning all but the most necessary and all of the most fashionable new developments. Nor did the idea of a standard vocabulary develop overnight. As we will see, it scarcely existed in English before 1500, and it did not become a matter of concern to learned critics for another two hundred years.

The conventions of Standard English usage have gradually altered to encourage greater concision and to accommodate more and more features of the spoken language. From the perspective of less than a century ago, Standard American English in the 1990's—exemplified in the pages of such popular but scrupulously edited publications as *The New York Times, The Washington Post, Time, National Geographic, Scientific American,* and *The New Yorker*—is less weighty, less staid, and less formal than ever before. At all times, however, its vocabulary has encompassed language almost universally familiar to well-educated persons; and such a vocabulary is the hallmark of a standard language. The technical vocabulary of recognized specialist fields—religion, music and the arts, literature, philosophy, law, government, medicine, science, engineering, navigation, and so forth—has also and inevitably been regarded as Standard English for as long as that phrase has had any meaning.

Virtually by definition, Standard English is the kind of vocabulary and usage that is taught in school and used in serious writing by even moderately painstaking professionals.[8] It is also worth pointing out what is not necessarily obvious to ordinary users of dictionaries, that a given "standard" locution is not necessarily the only proper way to express a particular idea. Although immediate stylistic considerations may favor one over the other, *car* and *automobile* are interchangeable, as are *is not* and *isn't*, adverbial *slow* and *slowly*, and innumerable other examples.

Necessarily the most inclusive sociostylistic label is *nonstandard.* It is also the easiest to describe. Nonstandard words and phrases are those that, though part of the enormous abstraction called the English language, are notably absent from edited Standard English prose. They may, of course, appear in dialogue or for special effect, and many are in unselfconscious everyday use among millions of native speakers. Take for example the notorious *ain't*, the Southern *y'all* and *might could*, the very general *as far as* ('as for, regarding'), and *irregardless.* Yet for an assortment of reasons, not all of them logically defensible, these are uses excluded from edited standard discourse. In the framework of standard versus nonstandard, slang clearly belongs to the latter category.

The more stigmatizing label *substandard* is sometimes applied to a limited number of usages that have become shibboleths among schoolteachers as presumed markers of ignorance or illiteracy. Common examples are *ain't, irregardless, infer* (in the sense 'to imply'), socially restricted regional forms such as *you'ns* and *hisn,* epenthetic pronunciations such as "*cock-a-roach*" and "*ath-a-lete*," the "present habitual" tense as in *they be fightin'*, a sudden narrative shift (at least outside of literature) into the historical present, syntactically illogical constructions such as *between you and I* or *me and her went to the show,* and others. Descriptive linguists find little use for the *substandard* label, which erroneously suggests that users of such expressions are too stupid to comprehend, use, or remember the corresponding standard form.

The label *colloquial* legitimately takes in some of both the standard and the nonstandard, terms that relate to acceptability in informative discourse that has been edited for clarity as well as for stability of tone. To call an expression a colloquialism, however, is to look at it from a quite different perspective, that of simple formality versus informality. Until very recently schoolteachers seemed bent on interpreting the *colloquial* label in dictionaries to mean much the same thing as *substandard*, and as a result many standard dictionaries have dispensed with it. The change, however, is unfortunate. *Informal,* the label that has generally supplanted *colloquial,* imparts a clearer message, but it is too imprecise. Informality in language encompasses both slang and colloquialism: all slang, therefore, is informal, but not all that is informal is slang. Slang, in fact, carries with it an even greater sense of opposition to "form" than does the merely colloquial. A *colloquialism,* as used here, is an expression more typical of the unstilted voice of daily conversation, and of writing intended to convey such a voice, than it is of formal, carefully edited prose. Most of the standard vocabulary is equally appropriate to both formal and colloquial styles. The colloquial, however, conveys an easygoing naturalness, that unselfconscious flexibility of style nowadays appropriate to most civilized uses of language outside of ceremonious or highly technical usage. It is a misconception that "standard" and "formal" English are always synonyms; indeed, owing to shifts in stylistic etiquette that began to take place before 1900, they have not been completely interchangeable for nearly a hundred years. Standard expressions (verbal contractions like *can't* and *won't* are good examples) are no more necessarily "formal" than informal idioms (*scarce as hen's teeth, mad as a hor-*

net, etc.) are necessarily "nonstandard." Colloquialisms in general are simply informal English. In this dictionary the *colloquial* label specifically designates informal terms that are not slang.

As a term in language study the word *dialect* refers to cohesive, chiefly regional and socioeconomic varieties of a language. *Dialectal* serves to characterize all major elements of speech: phonology, syntax, and lexicon. Of these, words and phrases ("lexical items") are by far the most likely to move into more general usage and thus lose their dialect status. This is exactly what has happened over the centuries to a good number of English words that are now universally known. Formerly dialectal words have made themselves at home at various levels of usage: prime examples are *chitlins, chop suey, fun, galore, heist, loch, mustang, pizza, schmooze, skedaddle, skirt, spook,* and *they* and *them.*

The three main regional dialects of American English now recognized are Northern, Southern, and Western. (The Midland dialect, stretching on older maps from Maryland to Texas, is now often considered to comprise subdialects of the other three.) There are additionally at least two conspicuous ethnic dialects spoken in varying degree by millions of Americans, namely Black English and Hispanic English, of which only the former has so far contribu d greatly to general slang. Differences among major American dialects are relatively small when compared with many of those elsewhere, for example the British Isles. By their very nature dialects of American English are chiefly identifiable by spoken features and by their social and regional distribution rather than by their representation in writing. To that extent dialectal forms are all informal; many—folk-level grammatical forms and pronunciations in particular—are also nonstandard. As Cassidy and others have noted, mobility, urbanization, and mass media are all eroding the regional differences in American English, though by no means so rapidly as observers once predicted. Significantly, these same influences are also among the most important factors favoring the creation and popularization of slang.

Cant, argot, and *jargon* too have often taken on confusing and overlapping meanings. *Cant,* a private language of the underworld, was the earliest form of nonstandard language to be condemned by critics, and will be discussed in more detail below. The phenomenon of cant appears to be common to all societies large enough to sustain a sizable criminal class. Cant is nowadays more likely to be called *argot* by American linguists, but sociologists use the latter term merely to designate any kind of subcultural vocabulary unfamiliar to most outsiders (as the *argot* of teenagers or of basketball players). Unlike the modern slang popularly associated with lawbreakers and broadcast far and wide in our popular culture, English cant in its ancient form and narrowest sense consisted primarily of made-up or altered words, often of Celtic or unknown origin. Unlike modern slang the ancient cant approaches the notion of an "antilanguage," as proposed by M. A. K. Halliday,[9] and certainly a "cryptolect," as described by Ian Hancock.[10] Altered by time, it retains a degree of currency in the British Isles and North America among Travelers, a traditionally itinerant people including the Roma (Gypsies) and other groups.[11]

The word *jargon* has developed almost as wide a range of meanings as has *slang,* but we will here restrict it to the technical terms peculiar to specific occupations and professions. Because the gratuitous use of recherché technical terms makes for an impenetrable opaqueness of style, writing instructors have come to condemn as jargon any bad prose inflated with obscurities and warped by contorted syntax; that is not the sense of the word intended. Jargon is, at bottom, Standard English that is unfamiliar beyond the limits of those specialized fields for which it provides the recognized standard vocabulary. Jargon consists of "terms of art," in the legal phrase, which is itself a good example of the use of jargon. A technical term that simply designates something—regardless of the term's etymology or the social status of those who use it—is properly considered jargon, not slang. Jargon, like Standard English, serves to indicate a referent, usually with great precision; while slang characterizes and often makes light of what is referred to, and nonslang synonyms are almost always readily available. Technical language develops among specialists for the purpose of cooperation; slang develops among associates for purposes of expressiveness, companionability and to some extent exclusivity.

It is the necessity of speaking and writing with precision that has led professions and hobbies to develop an extensive technical jargon, some of which becomes familiar to the general public: the army speaks of *LZs* and *MREs*, hospital staffs of everything from *phenol* to *PET scans*, construction crews of *I-beams* and *cherry pickers*, aviators of *tarmac* and *wind shear*, drama critics of the *mise-en-scène*, physicists of *superstrings*, philosophers of *ontology*, runners of *VO₂max*; and chefs debate what gives a fish stew the right to call itself a *bouillabaisse*. The more insouciant groups manage also to generate a body of rhetorically more forceful expressions that we call slang; compare the army's *FNG* and *FUBAR*, a hospital's *blade* and *gomer*, a construction crew's *bridge snake*, an aviator's *groundhog*, a runner's *hitting the wall*. Most slang, however, is not from easily identifiable fields; rather, it develops from obscure or unknown sources, from pursuits legal and otherwise, and from a variety of regional, ethnic, and socioeconomic vocabularies. Whatever its provenience, a slang expression always has the potential to emerge into wider currency, either slowly or quite rapidly, by word of mouth or through the mass media.

Slang in Its Cultural Environment

If we are to understand slang intelligently we must examine it within the general framework of productivity and linguistic innovation, qualities of human language that, unlike our notion of slang itself, are truly universal.

The *productive* property of language may be explained as follows. The linguistic resources of any functioning society are more than versatile—they are potentially infinite. All peoples can speak eloquently in their native tongues about any subject of interest. Even the Latin language, usually regarded as extinct, clings to a tenuous existence in the form of Modern Latin, which is maintained as the official vehicle of papal encyclicals within the Roman Catholic Church, its vocabulary regularly if artificially updated to

cover such post-Classical developments as motorcycles and wonder drugs—an indication of Latin's continued viability, if not its practicality, as a vehicle of contemporary thought.

All human languages are linguistic *systems;* and each of these independent systems of contrastive sound, structure, and meaning provides an inexhaustible framework for the expression of thought as well as for the creation or adoption of new words and meanings. But the framework itself is useless without the existence of people to bend it to their needs, both as individuals and as sharers in a common culture. The productivity of each language system relies entirely upon its living speakers. The element added by speakers of a language is the active participation of living, thinking minds in a preexisting but entirely abstract system. Living minds alone possess the power to transform language from a lifeless set of instructions into something much more profound: a dynamic entity or process continually evolving in unpredictable ways.

As any adult who tries to learn a second language discovers, linguistic systems vary greatly. Yet no language that we know of or can guess about is "primitive" in the sense of having a tiny, infertile vocabulary, or a structure that is somehow an obstacle to sophisticated thought. Quite the contrary: all languages are in principle infinitely flexible and adequate to the changing needs of their speakers and their societies. When the Apache language, for example, required a new vocabulary to name automobile parts, it didn't simply borrow terms from English; it quickly developed an automotive vocabulary from native elements, which is exactly what English had done.[12]

The speech of various small nomadic and agrarian cultures scattered across the world five thousand years ago developed incrementally into the international tongues of the present day. Their slow metamorphosis into systems perfectly suited to discuss notions of artificial intelligence, political philosophy, or the mass marketing of frozen orange juice occurred not because of any special virtues in the ancestor languages of English, Spanish, Arabic, Chinese, Russian, and the rest, but because all natural languages since before recorded history have had the fundamental ability to change and expand along with the societies that use them.

Thus, all living languages innovate in response to new developments and expand their vocabularies to encompass new ideas. But slang is not a simple synonym for lexical innovation, even at the level of nonstandard speech. Slang is lexical innovation within a particular cultural context.

Even linguists often take for granted the idea that slang is equally manifest in all languages and cultures. Such an assumption rests upon shaky foundations indeed. Like the innocent belief that all societies share a common sense of humor, the cliché that slang is as old as language, and that every language has its slang, stems largely from a naïve uniformitarian view of world cultures.[13] It rests too upon a failure to distinguish slang from other forms of wordplay and linguistic innovation. Anthropologists, for example, have written articles reporting on "slang" in languages as different from English—and from each other—as Hanunóo and Zuni, but the vocabularies and syntactical devices they identify function rather differently from the kinds of words and phrases that bear the *slang* label in English dictionaries. Figurative expressions that might sound like slang to us in literal translation are not necessarily perceived as such in the languages that employ them. The existence—the experience—of slang *as* slang requires the currency, within a language community, of quite specific sociolinguistic assumptions and expectations about stylistic norms and their nonobservance. Slang, therefore, conveys social and cultural associations that would be entirely foreign to nonliterate societies lacking both a standardized written language and a system of formal education to inculcate it.

Thus, the evidence from linguistic anthropology, incomplete as it is, strongly suggests that slang exists in literate, complex, heterogeneous cultures recognizing a standard usage whose primacy is upheld by a strong pedagogical tradition. Slang abounds in English, French, Spanish, Russian, and other modern Indo-European languages. The vocabulary of Roman comedy and satirical verse, much of which does not appear in serious Roman writing, suggests that slang existed in Popular Latin as well. In contrast, nonliterate societies appear not to judge varieties of *language* as either good or bad: what they do judge is the effectiveness of the individual *speaker*, particularly in a given context.[14] The correlation between slang and extended societies whose structure resembles our own comes from the interplay of several far from universal factors:

1. a written language that turns words into visual symbols, which can then be scrutinized as discrete entities;

2. public consciousness of a normative standard written usage and a consequent tendency to weigh language as "good" or "bad," "reputable" or "disreputable";

3. the existence of vocabularies widely associated with disesteemed social groups, subcultures, or countercultures;

4. sufficient interaction among mainstream speakers and these numerous subcultures to give prominence to a sizable vocabulary of antiestablishment or stylistically unorthodox expressions;

5. opportunity for that vocabulary to circulate more or less freely;

6. very importantly, enough resistance to change in standard usage to keep most such innovations from gaining formal acceptance (that is, from losing their bite) very quickly; and

7. crucially, a widespread habit among "respectable" speakers of emulating the "unrespectable," either by adopting the irreverent, symbolically potent vocabulary of the disesteemed or by developing parallel, irreverent locutions of their own, in a rhetorical climate felt to discourage this very habit.

Some Features of Slang

What is it exactly that differentiates slang from the standard vocabulary? Because most slang terms are simply old words given additional new meanings, slang cannot usually be distinguished on the basis of its formal ("morphemic") or grammatical ("syntactic") features.

The exceptions to this rule are few. There are a small number of morphological elements, in English typically suffixes, that are themselves regarded as slang: the productive suffix *-eroo*, for example, abstracted from *buckaroo* or *kangaroo* before 1930. There is occasional infixing, which sets an expletive into a longer word (*absogoddamlutely, fan-fucking-tastic, guarandamntee,* and *unfuckingbelievable* are among the most common; compare the similar use of tmesis in the common profane oath *Jesus H. Christ!*). There has also been the creation of semijocular rhyming compounds (*fuddy-duddy, killer-diller, legal eagle, nitty-gritty, super-duper,* etc.), a process not to be confused with Anglo-Australian "rhyming slang" of the *lump of lead* 'head' or *elephant trunk* 'drunk' variety, which despite popularity elsewhere has never held much appeal for Americans. Virtually unknown in the United States are the British phenomena of "back slang," which consciously reverses the spelling of words, such as *yob* 'boy' or *slop* (from *ecilop*) 'police', and "center slang," which resembles pig Latin in moving initial consonant clusters to the end of words, such as *(h)oolerfer* 'fool', *(h)atfler* 'hat', and *(h)evethee* 'thief'.

Popular coinages of obscure origin, like *flivver, skedaddle, spondulix, lollapalooza, bozo, beezer, gizmo, dweeb,* and *dork,* are almost universally perceived as slang, but the rare examples from learned professions (like *quark* and *googol*) are not, even when they exhibit a semihumorous aspect. Clipped words like *mob* and *flu* are often said especially to typify slang in English, but the corpus assembled here suggests that this is not really so. Some clippings fit our definition of slang while others do not, and perhaps it is pointless to debate whether *gin* (from *geneva,* itself from Dutch *genever* with no connection to the Swiss city) and *rum* (from *rumbustion* or *rumbullion,* both of unknown origin) were once slang (according to Mencken) or not (according to Murray). Nevertheless, though Swift and other eighteenth-century critics denounced all obviously shortened words as corruptions, many informal clippings have steadily made their way into the standard vocabulary, often through informal use among specialists or, in the present century, through their appearance in newspaper headlines where space is at a premium (*ad,* [*sports*] *fan, phone,* and *condo* are good examples).

But clipping alone will only make a word slang if the social and psychological associations are right: one is confident that *homo, nympho,* and *syph* will not soon rise to respectability.

Interestingly, a small number of apheretic clippings—which drop a stressed initial syllable (and sometimes the following unstressed syllable)—of common words, like *rette* 'cigarette', *rents* 'parents', and *za* 'pizza', have appeared over the past twenty-five years. From a historical point of view they are very eccentric, and it is this eccentricity, combined with the fact that they are used almost exclusively by teenagers, that makes them slang, not the fact that they are clippings. (Among the very few earlier, nonslang examples are *wig* from *periwig, bus* from *omnibus,* and *phone* from *telephone;* they came into wide colloquial use as short forms of familiar words. In contrast, aphetic forms, which, like *possum* and *squire,* drop an *unstressed* initial syllable, must nearly all have originated in colloquial speech and are not especially germane to our discussion.)

Odd pronunciation is even less a hallmark of American slang, but a few terms do owe their existence to deliberate, jocular mispronunciations: *anyhoo* 'anyhow', *automobubble* 'automobile', *divoon* 'divine', *fatigews* 'fatigues (military uniform)', *ossifer* 'officer', *garbazh* 'garbage', *Scandihoovian* 'Scandinavian', *au reservoir* 'au revoir', *maroon* 'moron', *nerts* 'nuts (in slang senses)', and others. Taken all together, such jocular pronunciations go to make up an almost imperceptible fraction of the slang lexicon.

If slang locutions differ only rarely from Standard English in form, structure, and pronunciation, the primary distinctions must lie elsewhere. We are left to examine the very broad area of meaning (semantics) to account for most of the distinction.

Semantics is one of the major theoretical fields of linguistic study. Yet because the very idea of "meaning" in the abstract resists quantification and definitive analysis, the study of semantics has perhaps produced fewer determinate answers than have investigations of more straightforward topics. One elementary concept, however, is that the totality of a word's meaning can be divided into two aspects, though the boundaries between them are indistinct. The first aspect is *denotation*. This refers to any one of the simple, more or less consciously recognized and objectively deducible senses of the word, the sort of meaning that would appear as a dictionary definition. Take the noun *cat*, for example. Its primary denotation is the familiar house pet. A secondary denotation is the lion, tiger, or other wild feline. If we turn to the verb *cat*, we find a technical sense: among sailors it denotes 'to raise (an anchor, as on a sailing vessel) and secure it to the cathead'. These and other denotations have long been Standard English, verifiable by their routine appearance in standard discourse.

A word's *connotations*, however, are harder to determine. In fact, they vary among speakers of a language, and they can even vary in the mind of an individual speaker. Connotations embrace all emotive and cognitive associations that a word brings to mind beyond its simple dictionary meaning. Because the connotations of most words are in principle infinite, it is a testament to the cultural integrity of a society that so many are held in common. For cat fanciers, the predominant connotations of the word *cat* are one thing; for cat haters, they are quite another. Those who feel neutral about cats will have correspondingly muted associations. And for any individual, the connotations will be quite specific, if not idiosyncratic: it is unlikely that any two people alive have precisely identical thoughts about cats.

One of the interesting things about connotations is that they tend to spill over from one denotation to another. It is difficult for anyone familiar with the usual sense of *cat* to avoid transferring some of its associations—favorable, unfavorable, neutral, or mixed—to less common denotations of the word, including those as far afield as the *catting* of an anchor up to the *cathead* 'a projecting timber or beam to which an anchor is secured'. Clearly, the transference of these connotations is quite preposterous, there being no apparent connection between house cats and the act of weighing anchor. And what about *CAT scans*? At this point we may seem to have digressed from our exploration of slang, but fundamental to the modern concept of slang is a widely shared sensitivity to its connotational as well as denotational incongruity, with the norms of standard discourse on the one hand and the limits of seriously intended metaphor on the other. The "cat" of *CAT scan*, from Computerized *A*xial *T*omography, is not even a metaphor: it is a diverting accident.

But contrast the standard senses of *cat* with one of its slang offshoots, 'a usually male performer or avid devotee of jazz or swing music'. There are ways of explaining this development—apparently narrowed from the earlier sense of 'a man'—but more important is the eccentricity of meaning, the incongruity in both denotation and connotation from the perspective of Standard English. The difference in tone is central. And here semantics begins to shade into social psychology. The slang effect is enhanced by the perception that these recent meanings of *cat* originated and spread well outside the social boundaries of educated discourse. In formalist terms, slang—like the poetry to which Hayakawa and George Eliot compared it in our epigraphs—works to defamiliarize reality, and the more it does so, the slangier it is. Thus, certain words and meanings are more likely to be slang at any given period than others, or are likely to remain slang longer.

Yet slanginess is not an immutable, inherent quality. As we have seen above (The Mutability of the Slang Lexicon, p. xiii), a slang term has the potential to rise to complete respectability. But it is an exaggeration to claim that today's slang is tomorrow's Standard English. Respectability must be preceded by changes in attitudes toward the slang word. The evidence in this dictionary suggests that a slang term is more likely either to remain slang or to fade entirely from use than it is to become Standard English. From the opposite perspective, any standard term—especially short, widely known nouns, verbs, adverbs, and adjectives ("content words")—may develop a slang sense or become part of a slang phrase.

But why do people use nonstandard forms at all? A standard language with a standard lexicon performs indispensable services: by eliminating most distractions and eccentricities, it makes possible the efficient communication of ideas. The linguist Paul Kay has described a standard written language as "autonomous" in nature;

that is, working independently of prior personal understandings between writer and reader, speaker and listener: "Autonomous speech is suited to the communication of novel, exact, emotionally neutral information to an unfamiliar addressee." The answer is that nonstandard forms exist because, as Kay explains, "autonomous speech [is] ideal for technical and abstract communication among strangers but inappropriate for the communication of immediate and emotionally laden content between intimates."[15]

The History of Slang

The Rise of Cant

The history of English since the Middle Ages shows that the vivid perception of slang and similar deviations from customary usage accompanied the rise of a highly conservative prescriptivism in English usage, chiefly after the Restoration of 1660. Prescriptivism developed as an attempt to restrict the rate of change in both spoken and written English. What evidence we have strongly suggests that before the late seventeenth century, which witnessed a dramatic rise in influential critical interest in English usage, scholars and English speakers in general found little occasion to reflect upon what linguists today call levels of discourse; that is, different stylistic levels of vocabulary linked to different kinds of social interaction. Until about 1420 truly formal (learned, serious, or official) writing was ordinarily done in Latin or French. The very idea of a specially cultivated "formal English" in the days after the Norman Conquest (1066), when the English language was little more than an underdog vernacular, would have been a gratuitous and perhaps ridiculous concept, and no medieval scholar was ever moved to urge its development. Chaucer's *Canterbury Tales* of 1387–1400 varies in tone, but the contrasts fall more naturally between the poetic and the conversational rather than between anything the age could have interpreted as "standard" and "nonstandard." (The fact that Chaucer used the word *bones* in "The Pardoner's Tale" as a synonym for *dice* [made of bone] does not imply that *bones* was slang in the fourteenth century; more-

over, the tone of the entire passage weighs heavily against such an interpretation.)

We know from writers like Chaucer, the twelfth-century William of Malmesbury, and the fifteenth-century printer William Caxton, that traveled Englishmen of the Middle Ages had an ear for regional differences in pronunciation, grammar, and to some extent vocabulary. Dialects other than one's own were doubtless regarded in the main as peculiar if not laughable (see Chaucer's "The Reeve's Tale"). But outside of the church and the law courts, functional literacy was rare before the seventeenth century, and before the eighteenth the reading public by and large had neither the theory nor the motivation to judge which variety of English might be "standard" or morally superior.

Not even the king's own usage—so far as it could be known—set a standard. We may reflect for a moment on one revealing example of semantic change so as to illustrate a real change in attitudes toward usage current at the end of the English Renaissance. The familiar phrase *the king's English* has its best known early manifestation in *The Merry Wives of Windsor* (1597–98); when Shakespeare wrote of "old abusing of Gods patience and the Kings English" (I iv), the abuse he meant was the employment of language for the unseemly purposes of invective and profane swearing, rather than the violation of some subtle principles of usage. But the phrase was employed earlier and more tellingly still in Thomas Wilson's attack on pretentious "inkhorn terms" in *The Arte of Rhetorique* (1553). The significance to Wilson of the "king's English" is far removed from the modern understanding of the phrase. Whereas today the expression signifies 'fastidious grammar and usage (supposedly "worthy of a king")', Wilson understood it instead as the everyday colloquial English of "most men":

Emong al other lessons, this should first be learned, that we never affect any straunge ynkehorne termes, but so speake as is commonly received: neither sekyng to be over fine, nor yet livyng over carelesse, usyng our speache as most men do....Some seke so farre for outlandishe Englishe, that thei forget altogether their mothers language. And I dare sware this, if some of their mothers were alive, thei were not able to tell, what thei say, and yet these fine Englishe clerkes, wil saie thei speake in their mother tongue, if a man should charge them for counterfeityng the kynges English.[16]

Broad distinctions of style and register are a fundamental aspect of language. There is plenty of evidence that such broad distinctions in English discourse were indeed identifiable to people of the Middle Ages. The surviving Old English poetry, including *Beowulf*, shows that poets and their patrons conceived of poetic language as more metaphorically and syntactically complex than everyday speech. Similarly, specialists in various occupations and pursuits insisted upon the proper use of technical terms: *The Boke of St. Albans*, by Dame Juliana Barnes (1486), a thorough treatise on hunting and hawking, has a section that specifies "the kyndeli termis that belong to hawkis" and cautions, for example, that a hawk has a "beke" not a "bille" and that "we shall say that hawkis doon *Eyer*, and not *brede* in the woodes. And we shall say that hawkys doon *draw* when they bere tymbering to their nestes, and nott they *beld* ne *make ther nestes*."[17] Equally certain is that clerics, scholars, and courtiers recognized occasional specific distinctions between ceremonial and everyday English throughout the later Middle Ages; the possibly "over fine" Sir Thomas Elyot, in a well-known passage in *The Boke Named the Governour* (1531), had urged upon nobles and gentles (though on no one else) a "cleane polite, perfectly and articulately pronounced" English.

But no one subscribed to an equally abstract notion, carried over from the study of Cicero and Virgil, of a polite English *vocabulary* founded either on taste or on canons of logic. Undoubtedly, fastidious persons would have been irritated by the occasional word that they regarded as obscene, affected, newfangled, or blasphemous. But no cultural or psychological stimulus existed for classifying English words as other than familiar or unfamiliar, technical or everyday, plain or ceremonial, offensive or not. It is notable that no general category remotely corresponding to our present notion of slang seems to have occurred to anyone before the sixteenth or seventeenth century.

Occasional examples of the latitude allowed to formal English in earlier times can be found in unlikely places. It has been estimated, for example, that Chaucer's *Canterbury Tales* contains two hundred separate oaths.[18] The exalted prose of the King James Bible (1611), now often held up as a paragon from which our late-twentieth-century English has precipitously declined, has at least two very striking examples of words now considered slang: Leviticus 21:20 gives us "[A man that] hath his stones broken," and in 2 Kings 18:27 we find "They may...drink their own piss with you." And in serious secular writing we have Randle Cotgrave's *Dictionary of the French and English Tongues* (also 1611), the earliest of French-English lexicons, which runs to eight hundred densely packed pages and boasts sixty thousand serious-minded entries drawn from every field of knowledge. At least one modern scholar has praised its "wit and richness of definition" as well as its "breadth and accuracy," all of which "go to make this one of the world's great books."[19] It thus surprises a modern learned sensibility to find among Cotgrave's magisterial pages the following item:

> *Cul de Cheval.* A small, and ouglie, fish, or excrescence of the Sea, resembling a mans bung-hole, and called, the red Nettle.

Presumably the common red sea anemone (*Actinia equina* or *A. mesembryanthemum*) is meant.

Pivotal to the concept of slang as an extensive maverick vocabulary—novel, perverse, and perniciously appealing, especially to the young and to the masses—was the discovery, before 1530, of a mystifying English criminal *cant*. This was the English analogue of the French *jobelin*, which François Villon, for its riddlishness and shock value, had already turned to poetic purposes by 1463, and of the German *Rotwelsch*, alluded to in the thirteenth century but revealed to the learned world in the *Liber Vagatorum* of ca1514: Martin Luther himself added a preface to the 1528 edition. Possibly thus alerted to the existence of foreign cant, Robert Copland (*The Hye Way to the Spyttel Hous*, perhaps as early as 1517), John Awdelay (*The Fraternitye of Vacabondes*, 1560), and Thomas Harman (*A Caveat or Warening, for Commen Cursetors*, 1567) had little difficulty in ferreting out and publishing exposés of cant in England.

Harman was, significantly enough, a justice of the peace and, like his glossarial predecessors, saw the use of cant by cheats and criminals as a menacing linguistic aid to knavery, a loathsome new kind of speech that he memorably condemned as a "leud, lousey language of...lewtering Lusks and lasy Lorrels,...bold, beastly, bawdy Beggars,...vaine Vacabondes" and a whole rampant "rowsey, ragged, rabblement of rakehelles." Yet the synonym *pedlyng Frenche*, recorded by Copland, indicates that the identity of cant as a register of native English was doubted, though it certainly bore no relationship to French. Albeit the chief difference between cant and other sorts of English lay in its baffling substitution of words like *dell* and *doxy* for 'girl' and *autem* for 'church', schoolmaster Elisha Coles, who first included cant in a general dictionary (his *English Dictionary* of 1676), seems to have regarded it as a foreign language; and until the latter part of the nineteenth century it was ignorantly believed to be identical with Romani. Its core vocabulary by 1550 probably did not exceed two hundred terms. Though itinerant and mendicant ranks had swelled during 1536–39, when Henry VIII suppressed the English religious houses and monasteries, fluent practitioners of cant probably numbered fewer than ten thousand speakers out of an English-speaking population of under four million.[20]

Harman's informants led him to the conclusion that English cant was not much older than the dissolution of the monasteries. This is unlikely. Though no proven examples of English cant prior to 1517 have ever been identified, at least some of the material collected by Harman, Awdelay, and Copland must have originated in the 1400's, if not earlier. Yet not until the sixteenth century did scholarship become aware of cant as something new and unsettling: a substantial renegade language, transgressing "without order or reason" the boundaries of sanctioned speech. Awareness of the existence of cant had far-ranging implications for English rhetoricians; it ultimately gave rise to the idea of a much broader but equally-to-be-condemned category of *slang*—a word that at one time was interchangeable with *cant* itself.

Cant to the Present Day

Since the end of the Augustan age in English literature, when eighteenth-century schoolmasters taught pupils to view decorum as an additional cardinal virtue, common usage has offhandedly used *slang* as a synonym for a casually conceived "bad English"—bad, that is, in point of behavior as well as of language. Critics of the late seventeenth century had similarly enlarged the sphere of the word *cant*, extending it from its original folk meaning of "an arcane vocabulary of itinerants and lawbreakers" into a loose synonym for all unapproved or "lawless" speech—quasi-learned as well as popular.

Criminal cant, insofar as it was known to the bloods of the age, seems to have enjoyed a minor vogue, at least in London, during the 1600's. Richard Brome's comedy *A Jovial Crew* (1641) put cant on the English stage for the first time. Beaumont and Fletcher followed suit in their *Beggars' Bush* (1647). The anonymously edited *A New Academy of Complements* (1669), intended as a sourcebook of clichés and light verse for tongue-tied swains, found room alongside sonnets by Shakespeare for a lengthy poem in cant, which includes the earliest known example of the word *hick*. (Such "canting poems and songs" began with Copland and continued to appear sporadically into the nineteenth century.) In 1688 Thomas Shadwell prepared a cant glossary to accompany his farce *The Squire of Alsatia*, where it is explicitly associated with "Rogues... Beggars, Gipsies, Thieves and Jayl-Birds." The opening scene is as apt today as it was then: a comic, bumptious youth, hearing cant from a gang of thugs, fervently declares it "quaint," "pretty," "admirable," "ingenious," and "neat," the language of "Wits," and immediately begins to emulate it. Despite the passage of three hundred years the spread of slang in our own age relies upon similar evaluations.

But the iniquitous diction of "thieves' Latin," as it was later called, was not the only perceived threat to "good English," a notion that began to take observable shape only in the decades after the Restoration. Indeed, although Caxton, nearing seventy, had lamented with nostalgia that "our langage now vsed varyeth ferre from that, which was vsed and spoken whan I was borne [*ca*1422],"[21] serious objections to specific lexical usages before the 1660's were almost nonexistent. Occasional complaints, such as Ben Jonson's ridicule of John Marston's use of *strenuous, retrograde,* and various other Latinate words, did not entirely reflect the temper of the times and, in that case at least, flowed from more than linguistic motives.[22] But by 1700, once English had finally supplanted Latin and French in their few remaining official functions, the concern of rhetoricians for its welfare intensified. This concern, moreover, turned away from the desirability of enlarging and elaborating the language to the perceived necessity of fixing and purifying it. English, it was said, had clearly entered its prime: unauthorized linguistic habits could lead only to weakness and eventual decay. Critics wished to see, in the days of Queen Anne, the enthronement of a fixed and regulated lexicon that would eliminate from educated currency all words of "spurious" origin. As seeds of potentially deleterious change, irregular vocabularies and disputable points of usage suddenly came under careful scrutiny.

For critics like Jonathan Swift, Richard Steele, and Daniel Defoe, novel popular speech of any kind, supported by no classical authority and defended by no learned advocate, was by its very nature corrupting, morally as well as intellectually. They abhorred such novelties. Except for the rarest and most compelling innovations, linguistic change itself came to be seen as an impediment to the smooth functioning of society. Indeed, in the preface to his *Dictionary* (1755) Samuel Johnson offered the remarkable opinion that the Elizabethan vocabulary of a hundred and fifty years before, which critics like Dryden and Defoe had lamented as inferior to French, was, quite the contrary, "perfect" and sufficient to express almost anything that would ever need to be thought:

> [E]very language has a time of rudeness antecedent to perfection.... From the authours which rose in the time of *Elizabeth,* a speech might be formed adequate to all the purposes of elegance. If the language of theology were extracted from *Hooker* and the translation of the Bible; the terms of natural knowledge from *Bacon;* the phrases of policy, war, and navigation from *Raleigh;* the dialect of poetry and fiction from

Spenser and *Sidney;* and the diction of common life from *Shakespeare,* few ideas would be lost to mankind, for want of *English* words, in which they might be expressed.

Ideally, the only acceptable new words would be those absolutely required by discoveries in science, technology, and exploration. But in Johnson's time even the established terms of humble but obviously essential industries were somehow below the salt. In explaining that "words must be sought where they are used," the great lexicographer rhetorically inquired, "[i]n what pages, eminent for purity, can terms of manufacture or agriculture be found?"

To all but the most requisite innovations eighteenth-century critics sweepingly applied the epithet of *cant.* Swift, in a celebrated letter to the Earl of Oxford (1712), identified the muddy springs of so-called cant as "coffee-houses" and "gaming ordinaries," its promoters as "young Men at the Universities," "illiterate Court-Fops," and "half-witted Poets." To the modern ear such complaints jumble together registers, modes of discourse, cultural levels, and expressive purposes that students of language have now learned to keep separate. In its subversion of taste and reason this undisciplined "low" speech rivaled the "barbarous" Latinisms (Wilson's "ynkehorne" English) manufactured by second-rate authors, such as *incrassate, proditorious, fallaciloquent, eruncate,* and *celsitude;* more than two thousand had been singled out and condemned by lexicographers even before Johnson.[23] Steele, in the *Tatler* (No. 12), had complained that the objectionable vocabulary of chocolate-house loungers was shifting every six months owing to the energies of "gamesters, banterers, biters, swearers and twenty new-born insects more." And in 1737 Benjamin Franklin put on the front page of the *Pennsylvania Gazette* a list of more than two hundred slangy expressions for drunkenness that he had collected from voluble tipplers, including the still-current *stew'd, jagg'd, boozy,* and *cock-ey'd.* But twenty years later the great Johnson, who realized better than most that language would inevitably change despite the dictates of taste and reason, still did not consider this level of vocabulary as deserving of serious attention. It was "fugitive cant...always in a state of increase or decay"; it could "not be regarded as any part of the durable materials of a language, and therefore must be suffered to perish with other things unworthy of preservation." The influential grammarians Bishop Lowth and Lindley Murray emphatically agreed. By 1800 they and other eighteenth-century rhetoricians had established for the first time, among pupils and schoolmasters alike, a key element in the social conceptualization of slang, namely, the "widespread consciousness of a relatively uniform 'correct' English."[24] Surfacing in general usage only in the 1750's and unlisted by Johnson, this odd word *slang* gradually came to replace the epithet *cant* in the educated vocabulary. Its story and that of various senses need not divert us here.[25] Suffice it to say that when, in 1828, after a hundred years of unprecedented academic anxiety about the purity of English diction, Noah Webster included the word *slang* in his *American Dictionary*, he knew the term merely as a generic designator of "low, vulgar unmeaning language." Yet it remains a felicitous chance that Webster's, the first standard dictionary in the world to be advertised as American, was also the first to make room for the word *slang* as a part of the recognized English vocabulary.

While a finicky attention to usage, quite exceeding the demands of clarity and grace, still has its defenders, eighteenth-century theories of language have been on the wane for some time. It is worth pointing out, however, that such theories, though faulty and framed in moralizing terms, were sincerely held and not, as has been claimed, designed solely to keep the lower classes in their place. The rhetoricians believed implicitly that language much resembled mathematics ("two negatives make a positive" was first promulgated at this time), that the language of Eden, imparted by God less than six thousand years earlier, had no inconsistencies or imperfections, and that every effort must be made to uphold—and to improve wherever possible—whatever inherent logic of syntax, vocabulary, and tradition kept modern English intact: the "collapse" of Imperial Latin into the mutually unintelligible and supposedly inferior Romance languages was never far from their minds. But by and large, later generations of scholars have proved less impatient than Swift, Johnson, and Webster in their judgment of words. Fortified by comparative philology and conversant with the

discoveries of new-word collectors like J. C. Hotten and John Bartlett, intellectuals of the late nineteenth century came to take a more moderate view of what was called slang, finally transforming the label into a less disdainful synonym for the nonstandard informal vocabulary, especially in its urban manifestations. Bartlett, from Massachusetts, published four editions of his trail-blazing *Americanisms* between 1848 and 1877. Johnson might have called its entire contents cant. Hotten, an Englishman who had lived briefly in America, produced the first slang dictionary (1859) that was more than a mere word list. It too went through several editions.

The Emergence of Slang in the United States

Unnoticed by either critics or lexicographers, new words and new senses of old words were creeping into the language from England's colonies in North America. By 1650, six small English-speaking colonies clung precariously to America's eastern seaboard, mostly in areas that had been conveniently cleared for them by centuries of Native American agriculture. The total colonial population: about 50,000, a disappointing turnout today at a single football game. By 1700 the English-speaking population in America possibly exceeded 250,000, about ten percent being African slaves, whose fluency in English must have varied greatly. The natural and cultural novelties of America had already begun to enlarge the English vocabulary, and Americanisms of the seventeenth and early eighteenth centuries are not hard to find. The standard histories of the language give numerous examples: we could mention *caribou, chinquapin, hickory, opossum, powwow, skunk, squash, sugar maple, blue jay, moccasin, raccoon,* and *bullfrog.*[26]

By way of contrast early Americanisms answering to our notion of slang are hard to identify. But likely seventeenth-century contenders are the New England *netop* 'friend' (borrowed from the Algonquians) and *kill-devil* 'strong West Indian rum'. (One is reminded of the Wright brothers' first powered flight from the Kill Devil Hill of Kitty Hawk, North Carolina, in 1903; the word even seems to have gone into French as *guildive*). In addition to whatever criminal lingo was transplanted by the roughly twenty thousand felons transported to America between 1619 and 1772, perhaps the most obvious slang terms of the age were anatomical. Not all have been discovered in early American sources, but they were current in Britain and thus undoubtedly known to colonists, the vast majority of whom came from the less refined strata of English society. Some terms are older, but most of these examples stem from the eighteenth century; a few, of course, are still current: *peepers*, *daylights*, and *ogles*, all meaning 'eyes'; *gob*, *chops*, *muzzle*, and *potato-trap* 'mouth'; *clapper* 'tongue'; *mug* and *phiz* 'face'; *snout*, *smeller*, and *beak* 'nose'; *block*, *mazzard*, *knowledge-box*, and *noddle* 'head', *daddle*, *fin*, *paw*, and *mauley* 'hand'; *breadbasket* 'belly'; *balls*, *stones*, and *cods* 'testicles'; *prick*, *cock*, *tool*, *hammer*, *tail*, *roger*, and *yard* 'penis'; *cunt*, *cunny*, *cat*, *tail*, *oven*, and *quim* 'vulva or vagina'; *bubs* and *bubbies* 'a woman's breasts'; *pins* 'legs'; and *trotters* 'feet'.

As any history of the language is bound to recognize, the upheavals of the nineteenth century—westward expansion, the Civil War and Abolition, and the unprecedented Northern urbanization that had begun by 1860—all left a bold and unmistakable legacy in the form of new idioms in American English. Less apparent is that slang took somewhat longer to come into its own. Other than the amateur philologist John Bartlett and his imitator, the Swedish immigrant and Confederate officer Maximilian Schele de Vere (*Americanisms*, 1871), for both of whom slang was only an incidental interest, few Americans bothered to collect slang. Learned comment on the subject rarely went beyond sweeping generalizations.

Yet among American writers as various as the poet Walt Whitman, the philologist W. D. Whitney, and the critic Brander Matthews, slang was coming to be seen as a misunderstood and generally benign linguistic presence. As the undisputed vox populi, an idea that would have appalled Swift, it replenished with fresh vocabulary a standard lexicon always on the edge of going stale. But most Victorian critics continued to define slang to include any informal usage that sounded new and could not be found in the by-then numerous glossaries of British dialects. Beginning with Whitney in 1875,[27] American writers

expressing a tolerance, even an appreciation, of slang typically took pains to evince also their discomfort at its novelty and "otherness," its tonal and connotational clashes with Standard English as well as with "old-fashioned" provincialisms and familiar illiteracies. In a mostly favorable article in *Harper's Monthly* (July, 1893) describing slang as "a collection of colloquialisms gathered from all sources," Brander Matthews reminded readers that it nevertheless bore "the bend sinister of illegitimacy." A few years later (1901) the Harvard professors James Bradstreet Greenough and George Lyman Kittredge pictured slang as the unwelcome guest in the halls of English, "a peculiar kind of vagabond language, always hanging on the outskirts of legitimate speech, but continually straying or forcing its way into the most respectable company."[28]

But a crucial distinction between these writers and the critics of the Age of Reason was that Matthews and his contemporaries usually appreciated the vivacity of such diction. Though they felt that little of it would ever succeed in slipping past the gatekeepers of Standard English, they also believed slang to be a vital part of any living language. In "Slang in America" (1885), Walt Whitman characteristically lavished praise on the subject, calling slang a "wholesome…attempt of common humanity to escape from bald literalism, and express itself illimitably."[29] Enthusiastically extending the notion of so-called slang to cover every kind of popular metaphor, Whitman boldly suggested that "slang, or indirection,… doubtless in pre-historic times gave the start to, and perfected, the whole immense tangle of the old mythologies." By the end of the century most philologists had concluded, albeit more reservedly than Whitman, that uncouth though it was, novel popular speech was vigorous and colorful, not to be encouraged yet interesting and appealing as a minor linguistic diversion and for the flamboyant light it could occasionally shed on the sense development of English words. Their leniency toward slang, however, took time to reach the level of popular writers on diction, some of whom continued to fulminate against slang and colloquialism well into the Prohibition era of the 1920's.

The situation in England was rather different: the Oxford anthropologist E. B. Tylor published a pioneering if moralizing essay, "The Philosophy of Slang," as early as 1874. John Farmer and William Ernest Henley's ambitious seven-volume *Slang and Its Analogues* began to appear in 1890. Like their predecessors, Farmer and Henley were not learned academics; they were word lovers with antiquarian interests. Farmer published new editions of Tudor drama, and Henley, a literary editor and poet, was the author of the well-known poem "Invictus." Farmer especially had the inspiration and patience to sift through popular literature and subliterature of all periods, and neither he nor Henley had to fear the scorn of professorial colleagues. There were many reasons behind the failure of nineteenth-century professors to give slang more than a passing glance. One was that, like Samuel Johnson, they disdained the material as too crude and too evanescent, a language of waste, riot, and wild companions. Indeed, as the contributions of Swift, Steele, Franklin, and others had indicated, slang was invented and passed around mainly in saloons and similar establishments. (Washington Irving in 1824 had correctly implicated carnivals and boxing matches as well.[30]) And there were more serious scholarly tasks at hand, such as the editing of medieval manuscripts and the reconstruction of lost languages. Disdain for slang as a subject of research was reinforced by a prejudice behind ivied walls, again following Johnson, that deplored most developments in American English as inelegant even when necessary. But there was another, less apparent reason for this neglect: the academics simply did not encounter nearly as much slang as have their descendants in the twentieth century. Although this dictionary shows that a great deal of U.S. slang was indeed current in the 1800's, particularly in the generation following the Civil War, there was much less of it at that time than there is now. It spread far more slowly, and little of it was familiar to a wide audience.

Why should this have been so? Well-known differences in popular writing styles are certainly a factor, but far more significant, and at a deeper level, are important demographic and technological considerations. First of all, the population of the United States in the mid nineteenth century, though sizable in comparison to the countries of Europe, was by present standards small and scattered: the twenty-three million Americans reported in the 1850 census were about equal in number to the combined present populations of the New York and Philadelphia metropolitan areas alone. (The two and a half million Americans of 1776, diffused from Georgia to what is now Maine, did not exceed in number the present population of Brooklyn, New York.) The geographical center of population, southwest of St. Louis in 1990, was five hundred miles to the east in 1850, near Charleston, (West) Virginia. The demographic concept of "conurbation," a huge city and its connected suburbs (cited from 1915 in *OED2*), was quite unknown, as was the interesting phrase "youth culture" (1962, coined as a title by Ernest A. Smith).[31]

Communications before the Civil War were slow: even the establishment of telegraph offices in the 1850's for the instant transmission of brief messages could not alter the fact that, before the existence of the telephone, fresh idioms, like all news, could ordinarily travel no faster than a galloping horse or, later, a thundering express train. About two hundred and sixty newspapers published thin, formally written daily editions in 1850. By 1910 there were ten times that number, the editions were thicker, and many of them carried the eccentric lingo of the daily comic strip, a popular art form dating only from the 1890's.

Stirrings in the United States and elsewhere of an insatiable public demand for novelty, information, and entertainment were evident even before 1910, and this demand led to a reciprocal explosion of mass media. A new phenomenon was the appearance before World War I of light, humorous, and often slangy fiction in truly popular mass-circulation periodicals aimed at a national, multiclass readership. One need only compare the style and contents of the *Saturday Evening Post* of 1917, for example, with those of *Harper's Monthly* of a generation earlier to see with crystal clarity the results of a stylistic revolution in American popular writing. (Mark Twain's *Huckleberry Finn* [1884], often cited as a turning point in fictional narrative, can hardly take all the credit for this.) The *Post*, claiming a paid circulation of two million by 1919, must have reached and directly influenced at least twice as many readers in that year alone.

In the groundbreaking *Dictionary of American Slang* (1960) Stuart Flexner estimated that half the entries in that book "could be traced directly to some forty-five general sub-groups of our culture," ranging alphabetically from "airplane pilots" to "unskilled factory workers." The number forty-five may be somewhat arbitrary, but Flexner's point is well taken: dozens of durable groups and subcultures, many of them creations of the twentieth century, have enlarged the sphere of American slang. The incursion of slang into the national pop consciousness, spearheaded by the humorist George Ade's series of "Fables in Slang," which began in 1897 and continued for a quarter century, is fully reflected in successive editions of H. L. Mencken's *American Language*. The first, published in 1919, spared fewer than ten pages for the discussion of slang; the fourth edition in 1936 devoted fifty-four, and the Supplement of 1948 provided an additional one hundred and fifty. The importance of slang in American English could no longer be doubted.

Expanding through the development of film, radio, television, and now computer networks, the communications explosion has inundated the language with new words and metaphors from innumerable and unexpected sources. And the stylistic revolution of eighty years ago has in fact increased its momentum, for the tone of all current mass media, spurred by the demands of competition, plunges on in the direction of the breezy, the startling, the tough-minded and terse—attitudes that slang is born to impart.

Influences on Slang: Military and Civilian

It is difficult to appreciate fully what is implied for the future of slang, as for American English as a whole, by the various demographic and technological changes that have reshaped America several times over since 1850 and with relentless force especially after 1900. Moreover, the transformation of the thirteen colonies from an agrarian frontier of chiefly English, West African, and Native American inhabitants into a transcontinental, urban-industrial, electronically bound, multiethnic mass society has wrought unimag-ined changes on the English vocabulary, as it has on the face of the earth itself. Let us focus on one easily delineated sociological phenomenon that has possibly outstripped all others in its impact on the acquisition and popularization of slang throughout America—military service.[32]

Military service—strengthened by wars and by thirty-five years of conscription—has shaped with particular effect the contours of modern American slang. Not that it has done so alone. The typical high school or college student may possibly utter more slang terms than the average person in military service. But many of the student expressions fall by the wayside as too adolescent or too esoteric for adult life. For various reasons related especially to perceptions of maturity and competence, recognizably adolescent slang is generally regarded as inappropriate in adult conversation. Unlike students, however, military veterans are not strongly dissuaded from employing in later life the slang, of whatever provenience, that they learned in the service: it is far less specific to age (the majority of service personnel being well out of their teens) and it is likely to be understood by many more people—the multitudes of other veterans and their families—as opposed to the small circles of high school cliques. And of course no special vocabulary has to be used on anything like a regular basis *by individuals* to gain a foothold in the language as a whole: the magic of a multiplicity of social networks and interlocking groups will do the job. As is true of most such questions involving popular diction, the studies that could shed real light on the matter remain to be done. Nevertheless, at this stage of our understanding, the nation's armed forces, at least until the end of the draft in 1973, appear to have been the single most important social nexus for the creation, exchange, and eventual dispersion throughout society of American slang in this century.

Consider, first, sheer numbers. The relatively brief U.S. participation in World War I (1917–18) expanded the armed forces to nearly five million men (and about eleven thousand women), a fortyfold increase over prewar levels. In the three adult generations since 1917, on the order of forty million Americans have seen military service, a population roughly five times that of the entire English-speaking world in 1750.

More to the point, these veterans—living and dead—represent more than a quarter of all adult American men alive during the past seventy-five years. The Veterans Administration, in fact, reports that "approximately 30 percent of all civilian males 18 years old and older were veterans on September 30, 1991."[33] Each veteran has communicated to family and friends at least a few words of the slang vocabulary—civilian and military alike—that he assimilated in military service. The familiar occurrence in all mass media and in various contexts, nearly half a century after the end of World War II, of terms like *snafu, GI, brass, flattop, chew out, boondocks, goof up, sweat it out, flyboy, blitz, foul up, shack up, chow, hit the sack, skivvies, buy it, sad sack, pissed off*—all of which gained most of their civilian currency during that war—alone suggests the impact of military service on the aggregate of the nation's slang.

Reportage following America's entrance into World War I quickly familiarized the reading public with slang widely current in British military circles, notably *Blighty, Huns, fed up*, and *cooties*. Innocuous lists of British army slang appeared in Arthur Guy Empey's best-selling *Over the Top* (1917) and in the columns of the popular *Literary Digest*. Even so, although journalism has often encouraged the spread of slang, the chief method of popularization has always been the shifting associational networks among individuals. Military service in this century has compelled the formation—temporarily but significantly—of countless new networks of individuals from every region and every class of society. While something similar happened during the Civil War, the enforced commingling of regional backgrounds was substantially less and the communications environment was far less conducive to the dispersion of slang, as of other neologisms, beyond face-to-face interaction. The total number of Civil War, Spanish-American War, and other veterans alive between 1865 and 1916 (less than two and a half million) in proportion to all Americans alive in that period (perhaps a hundred and thirty million) was just one in fifty-two, or about five percent of all male adults, one-fifth of the corresponding twentieth-century figure.[34] Insofar as we may gauge "sociocultural influence" of any kind, the modern veterans have had the opportunity to exert many times the

influence of the veterans of the Civil War, in terms of raw numbers alone.

And as vocabulary does not develop in a social or psychological vacuum, numbers are not the only issue. The extent and rapidity of social change in wartime is well known. Unquestionably, World War I was responsible for the spread of more American slang of all kinds than was possible in any previous two-year period. Because new words and meanings, like any social trend, can take time to spread, the public often learns about war slang only after hostilities have ceased. To take a purely military example, *doughboy*, current in the Army since the Mexican War (1846–48), suddenly attracted national attention in 1917–18. So did other now familiar examples, many of them of prewar origin but previously little known outside the armed forces: *leatherneck, gob, limey, Heinie, frog, birdman, chow, bump off, ammo, Big Bertha, foxhole, dogtag, brass hat*, and *buck private*.

World War II surpassed World War I in word production as well as in violence. By V-J Day American forces at home and abroad were double their 1918 levels, and the spread of slang had increased exponentially. To the World War II examples previously given, we might add *gyrene* 'a marine', confined before 1942 to the Navy and Marine Corps, but provably dating back, at least at Annapolis, to the 1890's. *Sweat it out*, an older regional phrase in the sense 'to endure with anxiety', first surged into national vogue via the World War II military for no very obvious reason: Mark Twain had used the current sense in *Tom Sawyer*, and it had appeared in print as early as 1865, with only rare printed appearances before 1944.

The Korean War contributed relatively little slang to the civilian vocabulary aside from *bug out, whirlybird, chopper*, and *skosh* 'a little bit', adopted from Japanese *sukoshi*. But the long and intensively reported Vietnam War popularized much that was, again, both old and new: *grunt, zap, gook, hootch, Charlie, waste* 'to kill', *Nam, the World, Hanoi Hilton*. The insulting *gook* is by far the oldest of these, in print as long ago as 1920 but confined largely to the armed forces for nearly fifty years.

Other components of slang use in the armed forces go deeper than mere numbers or the degree of simple geographical dislocation in service life. All the well-known social and psychological factors mentioned earlier that go into the creation and use of slang are present in military society to an extraordinary degree. Armed forces personnel, especially in this century, are socialized into a heightened if not always welcome sense of belonging to a large, diverse loose-knit but easily definable group (the infantry, enlisted men, the crew of a specific naval vessel, for example), especially as opposed to various other groups (nonaviators, nonparatroopers, nonmarines, commissioned officers, the enemy, all civilians). Plunged into the "total institution" of basic training, generally far from home; thrown into enforced close contact with numerous strangers; abused and ridiculed in ingenious, memorable terms by drill instructors; facing an uncertain and presumably violent future; roundly depersonalized and treated explicitly as an expendable instrument of command policy; and discomfited by the entire process, the trainee often begins to affect a casehardened (or, nowadays, *hard-core*) persona, chiefly among his comrades, but occasionally elsewhere as well. The point of this behavior is largely to "prove" through language, partly to others and partly to himself, that he is now free of mainstream (that is, civilian) social restraints. Much of this aggressive and amply documented form of self-presentation, not strictly confined to the military, turns conspicuously upon a cynical, macho style of speech in which slang plays a prominent role.[35]

From a different angle the discontents of service life have always led soldiers and sailors to grumble, another habit that encourages slang use. But our point here is simply that, for the past seventy-five years, fighting wars or preparing to do so has directly and indirectly encouraged more Americans to use more slang than has any other readily identifiable activity.

Nevertheless, though it may not spread far and wide quite as quickly, most slang originates outside of the military, among civilians following civilian pursuits. In addition to student slang (not very noticeable until the roaring twenties), we should mention some other interesting and important sources.

The extensive—and often caricatured—seafaring slang of the nineteenth century faded with the disappearance of commercial deep-water sail during the 1920's; few modern expressions have a nautical rather than a specifically naval origin.

The slang of the cowboy—whose numbers probably did not exceed twenty-five thousand between 1865 and 1890, the brief period of the great cattle drives—began reaching an eager general audience only after the turn of the century: the first cowboy novel worthy of the name was Owen Wister's lexically conservative *The Virginian* of 1902. So-called cowboy slang was greatly augmented in the twenties and thirties by Zane Grey and other fiction writers. Ernest Haycox, for example, popularized the now standard *gunslinger* among Western writers and readers. (We may doubt the term's credentials as a genuine product of the Old West: it did not see print until 1928.) *Cowpuncher* (hence later *cowpunch* and *cowpoke*) comes from the 1870's, *bronco-buster, bronc-fighter*, and *bronc-stomper* from a little later. If, as has been suggested, *dogey* 'a runted or motherless calf' is of West African origin—a similar word is used in Jamaica for short-legged fowl—it must go back to Texas in the slave era before the trail drives; of this, however, we have no direct evidence, and the origin of *dogey* remains uncertain.

The flamboyant style of sports reporting, replete with slang neologisms, has its ultimate roots in journalistic accounts by Pierce Egan and others of British prizefighting in the early nineteenth century; this style experienced an American renaissance, originally in baseball, before 1910. To this period we owe *bingle* 'a base hit', *southpaw* (simply "the left hand" in earlier use), *hurler, bush league*, and *bean ball*.

The Jazz Age got under way in 1917 with the phonographic release of "Livery Stable Blues" and "The Darktown Strutters' Ball," but it introduced little slang directly related to the music, a music whose unique amalgamation of African, European, and Spanish-American traits soon swept the world. The spectacular lexical exception was the new and respectable meaning of the formerly obscene word *jazz*, which, received by the majority of Americans as merely a new word to designate the music, was quickly destined to become Standard English. (The curious may ponder the likelihood that the four-letter word *jazz*, originally meaning 'to copulate with', may well have sprung from the nineteenth-century *jasm* or *jism* 'semen; vitality', itself of unknown origin.[36]) It was not until the swing era of the thirties and forties that the dictionary was imprinted with *jam session*, *(solid) sender*, *alligator*, *jive*, *killer-diller*, *hepcat*, *jitterbug*, and *square*. As is true of most subcultural vocabularies, most of these words had been in use among insiders before becoming national fads; others, often of questionable authenticity, were publicized by press agents and journalists. The jazz artist Louis Armstrong himself was credited by colleagues with introducing new senses of *dig* and *cat* into jazz speech, though precisely from where is not clear: they do not appear in earlier Black English and thus are unlikely to have developed from African words. (Nor does etymology support an African origin for *hep/hip*, *jitterbug*, or *O.K.*: early attestation in slavery times is lacking for each of these terms, as is a likely source from an influential parent language. Improbable as it may seem, the documentary evidence unearthed long ago by Allen Walker Read that *O.K.* originally abbreviated the facetious *oll korrect* is rock solid. Other researchers have had thirty years to controvert Read's findings but have not cogently done so.[37, 38])

Because relatively few black Americans (fewer than five percent) lived in crowded Northern cities by 1910, Black English had a late start as a salient influence on national slang. Little slang of any kind appears in the many volumes of testimony collected from elderly former slaves by WPA writers in the 1930's.[39] Not until the thirties, during the great northward migration of millions of black Southerners, can one observe a contribution of Black English and jazz slang to general slang, mainly through the popularity of swing bands like Cab Calloway's in major cities and the widespread dissemination of their recordings. But Black English became a major influence on slang only after the desegregation of the armed forces (1948–52), continued migration, and the popularization of black slang through all mass media, beginning at the height of the civil rights movement in the 1960's and continuing to the present day. We should point out that Black English words are not necessarily of African origin; many are rooted in Southern

regionalisms, are semantic shifts of Standard English words, or are of unknown origin. Doubtless of African-American origin are such terms as *badmouth*, *beat one's chops*, *cakewalk* 'an easy task', *chump change*, *dicty*, *dig* 'to see, enjoy, understand, etc.', *dis*, *funky*, *fox* 'an attractive woman', *gig* 'a job', *gutbucket* 'a style of jazz', *jive*, *juke joint*, *main man*, *nitty-gritty*, *ofay*, *salty* 'angry', *soul brother* (or *sister*), *wig out*, and *bad* and *cool* in senses with connotations of stylishness and quality. A few of these are now Standard American English, and all are abundantly documented in recent writing.

Robbins Burling and others have called attention to a seeming paradox in the widespread adoption of black slang by white speakers who would "rarely imitate black grammar or black pronunciation except in derision."[40] We believe this paradox can be explained as follows. Those bigoted whites who would imitate Black English only in derision are unlikely, except for the purpose of ridicule, to knowingly adopt Black English slang at all. Other whites take to black slang for various reasons. First, its novelty appeals to them, regardless of its ethnic origin; that is, they adopt it as they would any other slang. Second, some speakers, especially younger ones, may not recognize it as black slang in particular. Third, some may enjoy, possibly subconsciously, the vicarious identifications with big-city street life (compare the attraction of cant for Thomas Shadwell's seventeenth-century youth in Cant to the Present Day, p. xxiii). And fourth, they may predictably absorb new expressions from people they like, regardless of color, whether those people are friends, associates, or distant celebrities. For similar reasons blacks often adopt the slang of whites. Words, after all, are words, and as such have no ethnicity of their own.

The film industry, too, and show business in general, grew to impressive slang-disseminating proportions in the twenties, thirties, and forties. Much of that new slang vocabulary was spread at the time by way of the Broadway-based trade paper *Variety*, whose editors cultivated a reputation for slang and telegraphically occult headlines. ("Sticks Nix Hick Pix" [July 17, 1935, p. 1] was the prime example, often palely imitated, as by *Newsweek* in 1993, "Hip Lips Dis Yucky Flicks" [January 18, p. 65], but surpassed in New

York's *Cue* magazine, which entitled an article on *Variety* "Crix Nix Hix Pix" [August 1, 1936, p. 6].) Consider *turkey*, *flack*, *lay an egg* (or *a bomb*), *nabe*, *disc jockey*—all apparently products of the *Variety* staff.

Media interest has, of course, diffused underworld and prison terms ever since the days of Robert Copland in the early sixteenth century; popular interest in graphic accounts of criminality soared after the onset of Prohibition in 1920. The next dozen or so years led to the debut of numerous underworld terms in the general slang lexicon, notably *grifter*, *flatfoot*, *fence*, *gun moll*, *gunsel*, *torpedo*, *case (the joint)*, and *big shot*.

The half century since the end of World War II also saw contributions from the Beat and hippie movements, urban homosexuals, the drug subculture, citizens-band operators, and—heirs apparent to the military as the most important source of slang—students in the nation's myriad secondary schools and colleges. Although face-to-face interaction, especially in cities, has absolutely encouraged the diffusion of slang from these groups, the critical element for rapid rather than gradual dissemination has undoubtedly been media representations of such groups in both fictional and nonfictional form.

Some recent writers have asserted that groups notable for slang use—soldiers, students, convicts, and ethnic minorities—use slang largely because they lack political power. Such assertions are mainly circular and based on simple impressionism and shifting definitions of slang. We should suspend judgment on such claims. It has also been observed traditionally—though, again, impressionistically—that women use less slang than men. As long ago as 1868 the middle-class monthly *The Ladies' Repository*, aimed at a female audience, congratulated its readers that "if it were not for our women there would be danger of having our English smothered in slang. They seldom use it—a well-bred woman never uses it."[41] A century later Stuart Flexner, in his introduction to the *Dictionary of American Slang*, stated the proposition strongly:

Most American slang is created and used by males. Many types of slang words—including the taboo and strongly derogatory ones, those referring to sex, women, work, money, whiskey, politics, transportation, sports, and the like—refer primarily to male endeavor and interest. The majority of entries in this dictionary could be labeled "primarily masculine use."[42]

Though inconclusive in itself, the citational evidence in this dictionary, as well as the editor's own admittedly limited impressions, supports the hypothesis that American men in general have traditionally known and used a more extensive slang repertory than have women of the same socioeconomic class, especially upper- and middle-class women. (*Slang*, as used here, does not mean 'general informal or nonstandard language'. Common experience suggests that the speech of both sexes is comparably informal.) If this hypothesis proves true, Flexner's explanation could be a valid one: until the recent past, relatively few women were involved with exceptionally slang-productive activities and subcultures. Nor has the slang persona of flippancy, hyperbole, cynicism, and tough talk held much appeal for the class of suburban women that advertisers once stereotyped as "America's moms." Even so, countless anecdotal reports and one or two competent studies compel the belief that the situation has slowly been changing, particularly in the lessening of verbal taboos. The use of profanity and a few sexual and scatological terms once largely confined (we think) to masculine gatherings, while detectable after World War I in the familiar middle-class speech of both sexes, has burgeoned since World War II. Among themselves and among others, college women—no longer so middle-class as in previous generations—almost certainly have begun to affect a more "masculine" scatological speech style since Flexner wrote in 1960. For empirical evidence see our discussion of Cameron's study below.[43] Of course, an increased prominence of "dirty words" in anybody's vocabulary does not entail an increased familiarity with a larger slang lexicon. The interesting questions of "women and slang," "men and slang," "minorities and slang," "power and slang," etc., are complicated ones, and current "answers" rest mainly on unanalyzed assumptions. Careful investigation is required from more than one discipline.

Slang in Other English-speaking Countries

English is now geographically the most wide-spread language on earth, and the existence of a lexicon of American slang raises the compelling question of how that slang compares with the slang of other English-speaking parts of the world, notably Canada, the United Kingdom, Australia, and New Zealand. Like so many questions about language, this one is difficult to answer at all and impossible to answer completely. National slang vocabularies differ far more than do the national standard varieties. Though the influence of U.S. speech on Canada has been great, our northern neighbors appear to employ more identifiably British slang than we do. Eric Partridge guessed in 1933 that possibly twenty percent of Canadian slang was imported from Britain, but real studies have never been done on any of these topics. Perhaps more telling is that of thirty-two Canadian army terms of 1918 listed by Partridge, twenty-three apparently originated in the United States.[44] The great majority of World War II and postwar terms identified as Canadian in later editions of Partridge's *Dictionary of Slang and Unconventional English* were likewise current in the United States and appear to be Americanisms rather than Canadianisms.

Sidney J. Baker's collections of Australian and New Zealand slang and colloquialisms are a somewhat different matter. Here we find relatively few American terms. Undoubtedly, American influence on Australian slang has increased and will continue to do so thanks to the steady growth in transoceanic tourism and the power of Hollywood. Very little South Pacific English slang—and there is a lot of it—has been adopted in the United States, but that too is likely to increase.

Britain, of course, is the birthplace of English slang, and readers may be surprised at the number of items in this dictionary that appear to be of actual British origin. The ratio of such expressions to American slang in general is heaviest before about 1850. But perhaps there is a sampling error here, early American writers being generally wary of employing slang at all and

British models being readily available. Certainly, the three or four authentic glossaries of U.S. underworld lingo assembled between 1791 and 1859 are made up almost entirely of British terms. The very conservative Dr. Oliver Wendell Holmes assailed the slang he heard around Boston in the 1850's as "commonly the dish-water from the washings of English dandyism, schoolboy or full-grown, wrung out of a three-volume novel which had sopped it up, or decanted from the pictured urn of Mr. Verdant Green [eponymous hero of a comic novel of Oxford by "Cuthbert Bede" (Edward Bradley)], and diluted to suit the provincial climate."[45] Of course, Holmes could not be everywhere or hear everything: his element was the Harvard Medical School. But as proved by the dialect humorists of the 1830's and later, general American nonstandard usage, including slang, had already diverged from that of England. The newest developments were not only in the West, either. Perhaps the slangiest American books of the period were the Canadian Judge Thomas C. Haliburton's wildly popular "Sam Slick" series (1836–59), written in Yankee guise, and the bumpkin comedy *High Life in New York* (1843–44), by "Jonathan Slick, Esq.," actually Ann S. Stephens, a magazine editor and one of our first female humorists.

But certain vocabularies were still largely British—seafaring slang, for example. Even in the days before the Civil War, when Yankee ships such as *Great Republic* and *Sovereign of the Seas* dominated commerce, their crews, like their chanteys and come-all-ye's, hailed from both sides of the Atlantic. The fifteen-year-old Charles A. Abbey went to sea on the thousand-ton ship *Surprise*, bound from New York for Penang and Singapore in 1856. His diaries[46] of this and succeeding voyages before the mast until 1860 include a number of slang expressions of the period (*cast up accounts* 'to vomit', *prayer-book* 'a small holystone', *pipe (one's) eye* 'to weep', *bloody* 'damned', *hooker* 'sailing vessel', *buggered up* 'messed up', *Johnny Crapeau* 'a French vessel', *brick* 'an estimable fellow', etc.), many of which were of English origin. The parallel is inexact, but consider a more recent case: in the 250-word glossary of Royal Navy slang of World War II given from personal recollection by the Welsh sailor Tristan Jones,[47] barely five percent are known to have been current in the U.S. Navy in the same period, and only three terms had significant currency there (*dose* 'venereal disease', *sky pilot* 'chaplain', and *tin fish* 'torpedo'), all of them current in World War I or earlier.

Scrutiny of Partridge's *Dictionary of the Underworld* shows a comparable contrast between British and American criminal slang. Bias in reporting is probably insufficient to account for a decreasing overlap between the two in the past century and a quarter. For an extreme example, a cartoon in *Mad* magazine about 1960 alleged with tongue in cheek that English films now required American subtitles to explain spoken lines such as "It's crackers to slip a rozzer the dropsy in snide"—roughly, "It's crazy to pay off a police officer with counterfeit money." In broader perspective, comparison of the present lexicon with that of the eighth edition of Partridge's *Dictionary of Slang and Unconventional English* shows far more differences than similarities in the transatlantic slang vocabulary.

Early popularity of the Beatles seems to have given *fab* a durable if minor position in American teenage slang, but the laundry detergent *Fab* (a trademark) antedates 1964 (the year the Beatles hit U.S. soil) and has undoubtedly exerted a greater impact on American life. Most of the slang influence (as of cultural influence in general) now goes from West to East, but despite the unifying effects of motion pictures, syndicated television, overseas calls, junior years abroad, probes of Loch Ness, visits to Disney World, NATO maneuvers, LP's, CD's, and the "British invasion" of 1964–67, the British seem bent on going their own way.

Motives for Using Slang

We grow up speaking the language we hear around us; our accents and our use of grammar—standard or otherwise—feel so natural as to discourage spontaneous reflection or analysis. We are as unlikely to analyze our individual speech habits as we are to question our favorite colors. But the use of slang does seem to result from rhetorical decisions somewhat closer to consciousness than are many other stages in the production of utterances. To that extent it may

be possible to identify some of the motives for using slang.

Slang varies sufficiently to support almost any tendentious hypothesis to account for its use in psychological or sociological terms. From a Freudian perspective, then, one could find an oedipal motive behind its popularity. Jungians, on the other hand, could view slang as the repressed "shadow" or *anima/animus* of school-taught English. Older Marxists might regard much of slang as the true lexicon of the working class, an attempt of the politically marginalized to defy the hegemony of an imperialist linguistic standard. Going still further in this direction, followers of the postmodernist critic Michel Foucault could detect in some slang a pervasive "terrorist" code of dehumanizing and objectifying women and minorities. Such views would be entirely conjectural and, more to the point, rarely illuminating.

Sixty years ago Eric Partridge, perhaps the century's best-known collector of unconventional English, offered his choice of fifteen important impulses behind the use of slang. Many of these motives overlap; they run from "just for the fun of the thing" through various attempts at euphemism to a conscious desire for secrecy. Partridge also suggested that slang was sometimes used "to enrich the language," "to induce either friendliness or intimacy of a deep or a durable kind," or "to be 'in the swim'."[48] He also doubted—as do we—that the desire for "secrecy" is one of the most important motivations for using slang; rather, it is more of a "badge of distinction."[49]

But despite Partridge, not much genuine slang seems consciously created "to enrich the language." Neologisms seriously intended to fill gaps in the dictionary usually fall upon deaf ears or else turn into Standard English rather quickly without going through an identifiable slang phase (consider Horace Walpole's *serendipity* and Gelett Burgess's *blurb*). Others (George Bush's *voodoo economics*, for example) are meant as satire rather than as names for new concepts and, if effective, turn into recognizable allusions or Standard English clichés. Jocular neologisms of a very self-conscious kind, like the imaginative coinages of the cartoonist T. A. Dorgan

(1877–1929), the staff of *Variety* (notably Jack Conway [1888–1928]), and the columnist Walter Winchell (1897–1972), owe their birth partly to high spirits but chiefly to the coiner's forgivable desire to impress the public with his or her wit. Winchell's *Reno-vate* 'to travel to Reno, Nevada, for a quick divorce' is a good example: it is always associated with its creator and, from the point of view of lexicography, remains an idiosyncracy rather than slang. On the other hand, *making whoopee*, also coined by Winchell (about 1929), successfully entered the general slang vocabulary, aided immeasurably by a popular song of that name and *Whoopee!* (1930), the motion picture in which it was featured. In like manner author Raymond Chandler seems to have extended the meaning of the once rare term *shamus* from 'watchman or policeman' to 'detective, especially a private detective', a sense that, popularized by other writers, entered the general slang vocabulary from the mystery pulps about 1940 without being particularly associated with Chandler. Current hip-hop slang has leaped from obscurity via the popularity of performers who take pride in its dissemination: "I can take a phrase that's rarely heard,/Flip it, now it's a daily word."[50] As is true of expressions at all levels of language, lexical innovations are traceable only rarely to specific persons; the proportion of slang actually created by identifiable individuals is minute.

In many cases a vague sense of sodality within a loose-knit group or subculture (like that of teenagers or baseball players) seems to accompany and to account at least partially for the use of slang. Like the use of any special vocabulary, unselfconscious and accurate use of an identifiable group's slang both implies and contributes to a strong emotional allegiance to that group and its values. Perry Wolff's ironic war novel, *The Friend*, published in 1950, provides a nice example of the linguistic subtleties—not so subtle to those involved—that can divide subcultures. A weary combat soldier admonishes a self-serving war correspondent, "Don't call us GI Joes....Call us GI's or Joes, but not GI Joes"—the shorter forms being the enlisted man's self-referential terms of choice, the longer one owing much of its currency to a newspaper cartoon.[51] Likewise, certain speakers today may deride those who detect only a phonetic differ-

ence between *hip* and *hep*, or who believe it is sexist (or nonsexist for that matter) to refer to women as *guys*, or who disagree about the offensiveness of the word *crap*.

There are undoubtedly important psychological motives behind the use of slang that go beyond any we have mentioned so far. For example, the role of slang in what the psychologist Erving Goffman called "impression management" and "presentation of self" is potentially complex and has never been fully explored. One method of making a particular kind of impression is to express oneself in antiestablishment terms. Certainly the conscious use of slang enables children and adults alike to break the rules in a conspicuous but more or less permissible way—in this case rules of verbal behavior inflicted, perhaps long ago, by Mom, Dad, and Mrs. Grundy. To use a modern and most revealing idiom, thus to employ slang, or any nonstandard diction, is precisely "to throw the book away." South African teenagers in the 1980's reacted to a slang questionnaire with "astounding enthusiasm,...delight at being able to let go of linguistic inhibitions anonymously, and at the fact that some people are interested in the language of youth."[52] Others who have administered similar questionnaires in U.S. colleges have seen like reactions. Slang obviously has emotional charms that Standard English is perceived to lack.

For some speakers just the notion of slang has developed a certain mystique. They feel it to be, perhaps, a "truer" style of communication than what is being taught in school. "Correct English," said the George Eliot character in *Middlemarch*, as long ago as 1871, "is the slang of prigs who write history and essays." To be "hip," "fly," "with it," or "cool," however, is not to be a prig. By 1908, ironically with U.S. literacy rates and educational opportunities both slowly on the rise, Jack London's fictional alter ego, Martin Eden, was recoiling from "correct English" as an empty façade, a means of bourgeois control: informal language, including the nonstandard and the slang, was "real talk." Of course, Eden had been repeatedly humiliated by his college-educated, upper-crust inamorata, Ruth, in maddening dialogue such as this, which millions can still sympathize with:

"I can study by myself....You see yourself what I did with grammar. And I've learned much of other things—you would never dream how much. And I'm only getting started....I'm getting my first real feel of things now. I'm beginning to size up the situation—"

"Please don't say 'size up,' " she interrupted.

"To get a line on things," he hastily amended.

"That doesn't mean anything in correct English....Don't say, 'where I'm at'...[or 'people' for 'persons']."[53]

The view of Standard English as the enemy, encouraged by experiences like the above, has never been more widespread than it is today. This is the opposite of the neoclassic position of Johnson and Swift. Fearing that corruption of the language would enfeeble reason, eighteenth-century critics turned into zealots for regulation of every aspect of speech. But today, beleaguered by pretense, bombast, and propaganda, abused by amateur grammarians, and with reading skills in decline, much of the public now distrusts even the style and vocabulary of measured discourse. From the point of view of reason, this distrust is unfortunate, to put it mildly.

Just how common is slang in everyday speech? Certain items picked up and popularized by the mass media are self-evidently ubiquitous. Flexner in 1960 tentatively suggested that slang, broadly defined, "forms about 10 per cent of the words known" though not always used by "the average American."[54] Occasional estimates that as many as "25 per cent of the words we use most frequently are slang"[55] may be dismissed, if only because they usually understand "slang" to include colloquialisms, and seem to be mere guesses at that. Because of their methodological difficulties, studies of word frequency in speech are rarely attempted. However, Paul Cameron's ingenious study of Detroit speakers in the late sixties found (without attempting at all to do so) that so-called taboo words, which make up a significant part of slang, also play a surprisingly prominent role in the speech of society at large.[56]

Fashions have changed since the founding of Jamestown in 1607, but vulgarity has never been entirely absent from informal speech; indeed, it has often enough been cultivated. Jack London, clearly no prude, recalled "all the inconceivable filth" he had heard as a child in San Mateo, California, in the 1880's; except in delirium he "never dared utter such oaths."[57] The illustrator and Civil War veteran Dan Beard, on assignment for *Scribner's Magazine* in the lumber woods of Michigan in 1883, encountered among the shanty-boys "not just plain profanity...but terrible blasphemy, *carefully thought out and composed for the occasion*. Even the memory of it singes my naked soul."[58] Partly to discourage such nonsense, Beard later founded the Boy Scouts of America. Of the same period, the ex-cowpuncher Philip A. Rollins remembered that

men frequently were endearingly addressed with seeming curses and apparently scourging epithets....Where in the wide world, other than in the West, would grown men have ridden miles to engage in a competitive "cussing match," with a saddle for the prize, or a person held for as probably the State champion in blasphemy?[59]

Where indeed? Except for the part about riding miles, and presumably the saddle, Rollins (and Beard as well) might be describing a Scots "flyting" of 1500 or a battle of the "dozens" in 1990.[60]

In any event sociologist Cameron observes that, far from being strictly taboo, vulgarisms are "often *demanded* if one is to be 'one of the boys' at a party, or on an assembly line, or a comedian at night clubs." Although some speakers scrupulously avoid such language, he found that, overall, vulgarisms and profanity accounted for "8.1 per cent of the college, 12.7 per cent of the adult-leisure, and 3.5 per cent of the on-the-job samples! [Cameron's exclamation mark]" The workplace vulgarity rate was "about 1 per cent for white-collar proletarians; about 5 per cent for common service occupations, and around 10 per cent for blue-collar workers." According to Cameron's study, results of which should be more or less comparable to those presumably to be discovered in other big American cities and their suburbs, the words *shit, fuck, hell,* and *god damn* (treated as two separate words) are probably among the seventy-five most frequently uttered words in American English. In all three samples the excretory vocabulary was surpassed in frequency by the religiously profane and the sexual. In same-sex groups, the rate of vulgar language among college women did not differ appreciably from that among college men.[61] All this was a generation ago; would the results be very different today?

But verve is more central than vulgarity to the phenomenon of slang. The tolerance—in fact, the demand—of contemporary literature and journalism for a vigorous informal vocabulary, innocently trusted to be free of pretension and insincerity, leads us to expect that, in coming decades, more slang will achieve standard status more quickly than ever before. (So completely have the earlier stylistic expectations of readers changed that an undergraduate once inquired whether Hazlitt's well-known essay "On Familiar Style" [1822], which argued the importance of writing "without affectation," might not be a bold, ironic satire in the spirit of Swift's "Modest Proposal.") It may also be that in a future linguistic environment the entire notion of slang, as here set forth, will have little meaning: regional and subcultural expressions will always exist, but except for technical, scientific, legal, and diplomatic communications, whose very nature requires maximum precision for predictable results, it may well be that standard American writing will become so breezy and uninhibitedly informal that the label *slang* will itself become obsolete. Before that happened, the *slang* and *informal* labels would disappear from dictionaries completely. (To take some current examples: Merriam-Webster retains the label *slang* but long ago eliminated *colloquial*; as noted, *DARE* does not label slang; and Australia's important *Macquarie Dictionary* now labels all other-than-standard items as simply *colloquial*, proof altogether that lexicography is always an art and only marginally a science.) Dictionaries of the future—available in cyberspace editions—might mark instead the "formal" words only, that is, the technical and ceremonial vocabulary of "hard words" seldom encountered by the general populace. Except for the cyberspace, we should then be back to the situation that obtained in Cotgrave's and Thomas Wilson's day, when dignity in discourse was imparted chiefly by subject and occasion rather than by the elegant use or avoidance of individual expressions.

History of the Project

Research for this *Historical Dictionary of American Slang* had its inception in an idle moment in 1968, when the editor, who, thanks to a premium offer from a monthly book club, had been exposed at an unnaturally early age to the *Shorter Oxford English Dictionary*, mused in folly that it might be fun to collect and document American slang for about as far back as it went. That turned out to be pretty far, and, while slang sprints ahead regardless, the editor has found it necessary either to abjure his quarter century of collecting, storing, alphabetizing, inquiring, comparing, defining, justifying (and let's not forget lucubrating) or else to reconsider his original definition of "fun." That has been reconsidered, and the present work is the result.

Those who have read thus far may be fortified by the knowledge that the third and final volume of this dictionary will contain a full bibliographical accounting of all sources, published, filmed, broadcast, or in manuscript, that have furnished the dated citations to illustrate each defined sense of every entry herein. This list of sources now runs to about eight thousand titles, a large number; and one trusts that impending developments in the slang world will not necessitate the addition of many more before the somnolent letter *Z* is shaken and brought into the light.

We discovered very early on that, to paraphrase Johnson, words must be sought where they are found. Our bibliography is a true list of sources rather than a listing of all "works consulted." If the reader discovers there a disproportionate number from working-class and military life, various forms of adventure and misadventure, malice and mischief, it is because these—rather than the novels of Henry James and Edith Wharton—are the kinds of sources that have yielded the earliest and most numerous examples of American slang.

J.E.L.
Knoxville, Tennessee
January 1994

Notes

[1] Whitney's definition of slang in the *Century Dictionary* (1889–90) is perhaps the first comprehensive modern treatment of the term.

[2] *On Writers and Writing* (Edinburgh: Edinburgh Press, 1926), p. 20.

[3] *Euphemism and Dysphemism* (Oxford: Oxford University Press, 1991), p. 96.

[4] Eric Partridge, ed. (New York: Barnes and Noble, 1963), pp. 7, 197.

[5] Thomas W. Ross has provided an illuminating discussion of what monastic glossarists at the end of the Middle Ages regarded as "offensive language" (and, more interesting, what they didn't) in "Taboo-Words in Fifteenth-Century English," in Robert F. Yeager, ed., *Fifteenth-Century Studies* (Hamden, Conn.: Archon, 1984), pp. 137–60.

[6] For a survey of standard dictionary treatments of slang, see Connie C. Eble, "Slang: Variations in Dictionary Labeling Practices," in R. A. Hall, Jr., ed., *The Eleventh LACUS Forum 1984* (Columbia, S.C.: Hornbeam Press, 1985), pp. 294–302.

[7] Frank K. Sechrist, "The Psychology of Unconventional Language," in *The Pedagogical Seminary* XX (1913), pp. 413–59.

[8] Sidney I. Landau offers a most illuminating discussion of Standard English and other germane topics in *Dictionaries: The Art and Craft of Lexicography* (New York: Charles Scribner's Sons, 1984), pp. 174–225.

[9] In *Language as Social Semiotic* (London: Edward Arnold, 1978), pp. 165–82.

[10] "The Cryptolectal Speech of the American Roads," *American Speech*, LXI (1986), pp. 206–20.

[11] For an in-depth study of a remarkable cantlike cryptolect developed a century ago, chiefly for amusement, by the quite law-abiding citizens of Boonville, California, see Charles C. Adams, *Boontling: An American Lingo* (Austin, Tex.: University of Texas Press, 1971).

[12] K. H. Basso, "Semantic Aspects of Linguistic Acculturation," *American Anthropologist*, LXIX (1957), pp. 454–64.

[13] See, for example, Laura Bohannan, "Shakespeare in the Bush," *Natural History* (Aug.–Sept. 1966), pp. 28–33, an entertaining discussion of the reaction of the Tiv of Nigeria to the plot of *Hamlet*.

[14] P. Mühlhäusler, "Language and Communicational Efficiency: The Case of Tok Pisin," *Language and Communication*, II (1982), pp. 105–21.

[15] "Language Evolution and Speech Style," in Ben G. Blount and Mary Sanches, eds., *Sociocultural Dimensions of Language Change* (New York: Academic Press, 1977), pp. 21–33.

[16] Thomas J. Derrick, ed. (New York: Garland, 1982), pp. 325–26.

[17] The passage is most readily accessible in Robert M. Estrich and Hans Sperber, *Three Keys to Language* (New York: Rinehart, 1952), p. 19; emphasis added.

[18] Ralph Elliott, *Chaucer's English* (London: Deutsch, 1974), p. 262.

[19] Levy, quoted in William S. Woods's introduction to the reprint (New York: Columbia University Press, 1950), p. [v].

[20] Gertrude E. Noyes, "The Development of Cant Lexicography in England, 1566–1785," *Studies in Philology*, XXXVIII (1941), pp. 462–79.

[21] Prologue to his translation of *Eneydos*, in W. F. Bolton, ed., *The English Language: Essays...1490–1839* (Cambridge: Cambridge University Press, 1966), p. 2.

[22] Ben Jonson, *The Poetaster*, V iii.

[23] Many are on display in N. E. Osselton's *Branded Words* (Groningen, Netherlands: J. B. Wolters, 1958).

[24] James Milroy and Lesley Milroy, *Authority in Language* (London: Routledge, 1985), p. 36.

[25] See J. E. Lighter, "American Slang," in John Algeo, ed., *The Cambridge History of the English Language: American English* (Cambridge: Cambridge University Press), forthcoming.

[26] See especially H. L. Mencken, *The American Language*, ed. Raven McDavid, Jr., and David W. Maurer (New York: Knopf, 1963), pp. 110–42, and Thomas Pyles, *Words and Ways of American English* (New York: Random House, 1952), pp. 3–54. For a memorable and sobering picture of colonial conditions in general based on modern statistical research, turn to Robert V. Wells, *Revolutions in Americans' Lives* (Westport, Conn.: Greenwood, 1982), pp. 3–48.

[27] William Dwight Whitney, *The Life and Growth of Language* (repr. New York: D. Appleton, 1897).

[28] Greenough and Kittredge, *Words and Their Ways in English Speech* (New York: Macmillan, 1901).

[29] *North American Review*, Nov. 1885, pp. 431–35.

[30] "Tales of a Traveller," in Andrew B. Myers, ed., *Washington Irving: Bracebridge Hall*, etc. (New York: Library of America, 1991), pp. 507, 533.

[31] Smith, *American Youth Culture* (New York: Free Press of Glencoe [Macmillan], 1962).

[32] A few of the points in the following discussion were made earlier by Arthur M. Z. Norman, "Army Speech and the Future of American English," *American Speech*, XXXI (1956), pp. 107–12.

[33] *Annual Report of the Secretary of Veterans Affairs* (Washington, D.C.: U.S. Department of Veterans Affairs, 1991), p. 1.

[34] *Historical Statistics of the United States: Colonial Times to 1970*, Part II (Washington, D.C.: Bureau of the Census [1976]), pp. 1144–45.

[35] For concise sociological reports from World War II, see Henry Elkin, "Aggressive and Erotic Tendencies in Army Life," *American Journal of Sociology*, LI (1946), pp. 408–13, and Frederick Elkin, "The Soldier's Language," *ibid.*, pp. 414–22. See also H. H. Stern, "The Language of the German Service Man of World War II and the Nature of Slang," *German Life and Letters*, N.S. XII (1960), pp. 282–97.

[36] See for a discussion Alan P. Merriam and Fradley H. Garner, "Jazz—The Word," *Ethnomusicology*, XII (1968), pp. 373–96, and an amusing footnote by Raven McDavid, Jr.,

in Mencken, *The American Language*, p. 743.

[37] Read's evidence is most conveniently summarized by Raven McDavid, Jr., in Mencken, *The American Language*, pp. 169–75, where footnotes will also direct the *O.K.* aficionado to Read's own writings on the subject.

[38] For the well-publicized conjecture—unamplified by any professional linguist or lexicographer since its evulgation—that *O.K.* and other recent U.S. slang terms came from Africa, see David Dalby, "The African Element in American English," in *Rappin' and Stylin' Out*, ed. Thomas Kochman (Urbana: University of Illinois Press, 1972), pp. 170–86. This must be read in conjunction with Frederic G. Cassidy, "*OK—Is it African?*," *American Speech*, LVI (1981), pp. 269–73. Cassidy's answer is no, and all standard dictionaries concur.

[39] George P. Rawick, ed., *The American Slave: A Composite Autobiography* (Westport, Conn.: Greenwood Press, 1972–79), 41 vols.

[40] Robbins Burling, *English in Black and White* (New York: Holt, Rinehart & Winston, 1973), p. 87.

[41] Quoted in Kenneth Cmiel's valuable *Democratic Eloquence* (New York: Morrow, 1990), p. 129.

[42] Harold Wentworth and Stuart Berg Flexner, eds., *Dictionary of American Slang* (New York: Crowell, 1960), p. xii.

[43] Specialists with an interest in slang will find plenty to think about—though no slang—in James Milroy's "Social Network and Prestige Arguments in Sociolinguistics," in Kingsley Bolton and Helen Kwok, eds., *Sociolinguistics Today* (London: Routledge, 1992), pp. 147–62, and in Lesley Milroy's "New Perspectives in the Analysis of Sex Differentiation in Language," *ibid.*, pp. 163–78.

[44] *Slang To-day and Yesterday* (London: Routledge, 1933), pp. 292–93.

[45] *The Autocrat of the Breakfast Table* (1858; repr. ed. New York: Signet Classics, 1961), pp. 213–14.

[46] *Before the Mast in the Clippers*, H.A. Gosnell, ed. (New York: Derrydale Press, 1937).

[47] *Heart of Oak* (1984; repr. ed. New York: Bantam, 1986), pp. 231–39.

[48] *Slang To-day and Yesterday*, pp. 4–9.

[49] *Ibid.*, p. 146; this should be contrasted with Halliday's "antilanguage" and Hancock's "cryptolect," which are intended to exclude outsiders.

[50] "Eric B. & Rakim," "Follow the Leader," 1988.

[51] Perry Wolff, *The Friend* (1950; repr. ed. New York: Pocket Books, 1951), p. 112.

[52] Vivian de Klerk, "Slang: A Male Domain?" *Sex Roles*, XXII (1990), p. 590.

[53] Jack London, *Martin Eden*, Chapter 10.

[54] *Dictionary of American Slang*, p. viii.

[55] Vincent E. Barry and Douglas J. Soccio, *Practical Logic*, 3rd ed. (New York: Holt, Rinehart & Winston, 1988), p. 56.

[56] "Frequency and Kinds of Words in Various Social Settings," *Pacific Sociological Review*, XII (Fall, 1969), pp. 101–04.

[57] Jack London, *John Barleycorn* (London: Mills & Boon, 1914), p. 27.

[58] *Hardly a Man Is Now Alive* (New York: Doubleday, 1939), p. 309; emphasis added.

[59] *The Cowboy* (1922; repr. ed. New York: Ballantine, 1973), p. 77.

[60] For the former, see the quite mad "Flyting Betwixt Polwart and Montgomery" in Harriet Harvey Wood, ed., *James Watson's Choice Collection of Comic and Serious Scots Poems* (1706–11; repr. ed. Edinburgh: Scottish Text Society, 1977), Part III, pp. 1–32, and the discussion in Geoffrey Hughes, *Swearing* (Oxford: Blackwell, 1991), pp. 119–25. For the latter, see especially John Dollard, "The Dozens," *American Imago*, I (1939), pp. 3–25, and Roger D. Abrahams, "Playing the Dozens," *Journal of American Folklore*, LXXV (1962), pp. 209–20, both conveniently reprinted with invaluable commentary by Alan Dundes in his *Mother Wit from the Laughing Barrel* (Englewood Cliffs, N.J.: Prentice-Hall, 1973), pp. 277–309.

[61] And for a concentrated example of the use of vulgar language among college football scholars in Texas about 1965, with perceptive comments applicable to other groups as well, see Gary Shaw's memoir, *Meat on the Hoof* (1972; repr. ed. New York: Dell, 1973), pp. 189–90.

SELECT ANNOTATED BIBLIOGRAPHY

Adams, Ramon F. *Western Words: A Dictionary of the American West.* 2d ed. Norman: Univ. of Oklahoma Press, 1968. An informative collection, for a popular audience, of chiefly slang, colloquialisms, and technical jargon of the trans-Mississippi West. The frequently discursive definitions benefit from the author's extensive knowledge of the West and of the literature that has grown around it. A weakness of the book is its emphasis on colorful turns of speech that appear to have had very little currency.

Allen, Irving Lewis. *The Language of Ethnic Conflict: Social Organization and Lexical Culture.* New York: Columbia Univ. Press, 1983. A sociolinguistic analysis of multiethnic racial animosity in the United States as reflected in the large lexicon of American ethnic epithets. Suffers from an overreliance on uncritically assembled word lists such as those of Berrey and Van den Bark. Suggests that the continued use of pejorative terms by majority groups tends to encourage ethnic discrimination; minorities employ similar racial slurs as a psychological defense to redress social injustice.

Ayto, John, and John Simpson. *The Oxford Dictionary of Modern Slang.* Oxford: Oxford Univ. Press, 1992. Contains the twentieth-century slang included in the *Oxford English Dictionary,* 2d ed., with a number of additional terms, tersely defined, and brief, dated citations illustrating about eighty percent of the entries. The date of earliest occurrence known to the *OED2* editors is given, as are etymologies. A handy and unusually reliable slang dictionary covering well-attested slang of Great Britain, North America, and Australia, with a few terms from South Africa, Ireland, and New Zealand.

Barrère, Albert, and Charles G. Leland. *A Dictionary of Slang, Jargon, and Cant, Embracing English, American, and Anglo-Indian Slang, Pidgin English, Tinkers' Jargon, and Other Irregular Phraseology.* [Edinburgh:] Printed for subscribers only at the Ballantyne Press, 1889–90. 2 vols. Important for the extent of its coverage, but typically naive in its approach to etymologies and, although the widely traveled Leland was an American, disappointing in its limited treatment of U.S. slang. Many citations of usage are given; definitions, though full, are sometimes glib and moralizing, in the manner of much nineteenth-century cultural commentary.

Bartlett, John Russell. *Dictionary of Americanisms: A Glossary of Words and Phrases, Usually Regarded as Peculiar to the United States.* New York: Bartlett and Welford, 1848. The most influential nineteenth-century collection of Americanisms. A good number of the entries may be regarded as slang, and this element was notably increased by the time of the fourth and final edition in 1877. The introduction to the 1877 edition justifies the inclusion of "slang" (i.e., working-class colloquialisms) on the basis of its conspicuousness in the United States and its contributions to the growth of the general vocabulary.

"B.E., Gent." *A New Dictionary of the Terms Ancient and Modern of the Canting Crew, in its Several Tribes of Gypsies, Beggars, Thieves, Cheats, &c., with the Addition of Some Proverbs, Phrases, Figurative Speeches, &c....* London: Printed for W. Hawes at the Rose in Ludgate-Street [etc.], n.d. [1698–99]. The first in a long line of cant-and-slang dictionaries that extended through Grose and Hotten and, at one or two removes, to Farmer and Henley and to Partridge. Many unique (or uniquely early) entries. Though very brief, the definitions appear to be reliable. The identity of the compiler remains unknown.

Berger, Morroe. "Some Excesses of Slang Compilers." *American Speech* XXI (1946) 196–98. Points out the tendency of amateur glossarists to collect and publish jocular nonce terms as the everyday slang of groups such as jazz musicians and military servicemen. Important for its insistence on the exercise of critical judgment in the compilation of slang lexicons.

Berrey, Lester V., and Melvin Van den Bark. *The American Thesaurus of Slang: A Complete Reference Book of Colloquial Speech.* New York: Thomas Y. Crowell, 1942. The first and still the best comprehensive slang thesaurus, an astonishing grab bag of lexical material arranged according to topic and by field of endeavor, and including as much slang and near-slang as the editors and their undergraduate assistants could amass in a decade of collecting. Consultants such as David W. Maurer substantially added to the specialty sections. Though often misleading in its inclusion of ephemera, its very inclusiveness makes this an essential book in the study of American slang. A supplement of teenage and military slang was added in 1947, and the entire collection was integrated and expanded somewhat further in 1952.

Bradley, Henry. "Slang." *Encyclopaedia Britannica.* 11th ed., 1910. The earliest detailed overview of the entire subject by an outstanding scholar, one of the later editors of the *OED*. Emphasizes British slang, with some comments on slang and cant in French and other West European languages along with historical details. Still perhaps the best brief treatment, but expresses the erroneous though once common view that the essence of slang is the desire to conceal speech from outsiders.

Burke, W[illiam] J[eremiah]. *The Literature of Slang.* New York: The New York Public Library, 1939. Erudite, indispensable bibliography of writings on (and occasionally in) nonstandard English of all sorts, from 1517 to 1939. Contains annotated references to well over 2,000 books, articles, etc. The annotations, up to several hundred words in length, are frequently of great value and interest. An outstanding work. (Reprinted, Detroit: Gale, 1965.)

Cameron, Paul. "Frequency and Kinds of Words in Various Social Settings, or What the Hell's Going On?" *Pacific Sociological Review* XII (1969) 101–104. A carefully conducted study of the spoken frequency of individual words in everyday conversation in the Detroit area. The study revealed that so-called taboo words (profanity and coarse physiological terms) accounted for nearly ten percent of the total. Relatively minor differences were found in the frequency of usage between men and women of college age.

Chapman, Robert L. *New Dictionary of American Slang.* New York: Harper & Row, 1986. A complete revision of Wentworth and Flexner, 1975, with the addition of some new material along with definitions rewritten by Chapman, a professional lexicographer. Unfortunately, the dates of the numerous citations do not appear, and the useful bibliography has been dropped. The supplementary material in Wentworth and Flexner has also been jettisoned. Chapman has supplied a new preface, but the original preface by Flexner has also been retained.

Chapman, Robert L. *Thesaurus of American Slang.* Grand Rapids, etc.: Harper & Row, 1989. Hastily assembled from the above. Some usage notes, but no prefatory, introductory, or bibliographical material.

Clark, Thomas L. *The Dictionary of Gambling and Gaming.* Cold Spring, N.Y.: Lexik House, 1987. A dated source is identified for each definition in this solidly researched and thoroughly professional dictionary of American gamblers' idioms and technical terms. About 6,000 definitions are given. Includes an introduction and bibliography of over 200 sources.

Dickson, Paul. *Dickson's Baseball Dictionary.* New York: Facts on File, 1988. Designed for a popular audience, but includes much useful historical information as well as a bibliography and many dated citations.

Dumas, Bethany K., and Jonathan Lighter. "Is *Slang* a Word for Linguists?" *American Speech* LIII (1978) 5–17. Examines the various inconsistent ways in which linguists, lexicographers, and others have employed the word "slang." Suggests some essential social and rhetorical characteristics that define a slang vocabulary.

Drake, G. F. "The Social Role of Slang." In *Language: Social Psychological Perspectives*, 63–70. Edited by Howard Giles, W. P. Robinson, and P. M. Smith. Oxford: Pergamon Press, 1980. Argues that the use of slang can signal alienation as well as solidarity, often simultaneously, and that in-groups value their slang because it emphasizes their sense of distinctiveness.

Eble, Connie. *College Slang 101*. Georgetown, Conn.: Spectacle Lane Press, 1989. Though regrettably formatted by the publisher as "humor," this assemblage of slang and other student idiom from the University of North Carolina at Chapel Hill is meant to illustrate the operation of familiar linguistic processes in the creation of slang. Of perhaps greater interest are Eble's articles on the subject of college slang, chiefly in the annual volumes of *The LACUS Forum*, especially "Slang: Deviation or Norm" X (1984) 409–16; "Slang and Cultural Knowledge" XII (1986) 385–90; "Slang as Poetry" XIV (1988) 442–48; "The Ephemerality of American College Slang" XV (1988) 458–69; and "Slang: Etymology, Folk Etymology, and Multiple Etymology," *The SECOL Review* X (Spring 1986) 8–16.

Elting, Colonel John R., Sergeant-Major Dan Cragg, and Sergeant First Class Ernest L. Deal. *A Dictionary of Soldier Talk*. New York: Charles Scribner's Sons, 1984. The first unexpurgated dictionary of U.S. military vernacular, from the seventeenth century through the 1980's. Most of the modern entries are identified as slang. Aimed at a popular audience, the definitions are often discursive and always informative, and very few entries appear to be idiosyncratic items. Contains an "Appendix of Naval and Marine Terms."

Farmer, John Stephen, and William Ernest Henley. *Slang and Its Analogues Past and Present: A Dictionary, Historical and Comparative, of the Heterodox Speech of all Classes of Society for More Than Three Hundred Years. With Synonyms in English, French, German, Italian, etc...* [London, Edinburgh:] Printed for subscribers only, 1890–1904. 7 vols. By far the most ambitious and most carefully edited of pre-twentieth-century slang dictionaries, and of tremendous value, though rather amateurish by the professional standards of today. Over 100,000 dated (occasionally misdated) citations of British and American slang are included. Unexpurgated treatment of sexual and scatological vocabulary. Farmer was a prolific independent scholar known to posterity solely from his works on slang (English and French), his reprints of Tudor dramatic works, and a few other volumes. Henley was the well-known poet, author of "Invictus."

Farmer, John Stephen, and William Ernest Henley. *Dictionary of Slang and Its Analogues*. Introductions by G. Legman and Lee Revens. New Hyde Park, N.Y.: University Books, 1966. Facsimile reprint of the very rare revised first volume of the complete set, the only revised volume (1903–09) that Farmer published. A lengthy introduction—concerning sexual language in particular—by Legman, an outstanding authority on sexual attitudes and folklore, is linguistically lightweight but culturally of unusual interest.

Flexner, Stuart Berg. *I Hear America Talking: An Illustrated Treasury of American Words and Phrases*. New York: Van Nostrand Reinhold, 1976. A generous selection of characteristic and colorful American expressions from all levels of usage, including much slang. Encyclopedic articles and discursive definitions place the entries in their historical and cultural contexts. However, the dates of earliest usage, drawn from various sources, are frequently misleading.

Flexner, Stuart Berg. *Listening to America: An Illustrated History of Words and Phrases from Our Lovely and Splendid Past*. New York: Simon & Schuster, 1982. A sequel to the above, presented in the same popular format.

Folb, Edith. *Runnin' Down Some Lines*. Cambridge, Mass.: Harvard Univ. Press, 1980. An in-depth sociocultural examination of the nonstandard vocabulary of black teenagers in the Los Angeles inner city. Extremely thorough treatment, but does not always distinguish nonce terms from the core vocabulary.

Gold, Robert S. *A Jazz Lexicon*. New York: Alfred A. Knopf, 1964. A dictionary of jazz terms on historical principles. The first American attempt to apply this technique to a subcultural, largely slang, vocabulary. Extensive bibliography. Revised as *Jazz Talk* (Indianapolis and New York: Bobbs-Merrill, 1975).

Goldin, Hyman, Frank O'Leary, and Morris Lipsius. *Dictionary of American Underworld Lingo*. New York: Twayne, 1950. Compiled in a New York state prison in 1942 by Chaplain Goldin and two inmate associates. The definitions are models of conciseness and clarity, making this the most impressive of the popular specialized slang dictionaries.

Green, Jonathon. *The Dictionary of Contemporary Slang*. Briarcliff Manor, N.Y.: Stein and Day, 1984. About 13,000 entries briefly defined, drawn chiefly from about 300 sources which are listed in a bibliography. Attempts to cover British, North American, and Australian slang. Writing for a popular audience, the compiler claims to have "done [his] best to assimilate as much as possible in the time available." A companion volume, *The Slang Thesaurus* (London: Elm Tree Books), appeared in 1986.

Grose, Captain Francis. *A Classical Dictionary of the Vulgar Tongue*. London: S. Hooper, 1785. A collection of about 3,000 entries by a boon companion of Robert Burns. Indebted—as Grose readily admits—to earlier dictionaries of cant, Grose's was nonetheless the first lexicon to devote most of its attention to what we now call slang, much of it collected at first hand in taverns and at public spectacles. Editions revised and enlarged by Grose appeared in 1788 and 1796, and further enlargements came in 1811 (as *Lexicon Balatronicum*) and in 1823 (by the sports editor Pierce Egan). The 1796 edition has been edited with extensive annotations by Eric Partridge (New York: Barnes & Noble, 1963).

Hall, Benjamin H. *A Collection of College Words and Customs*. Rev. ed. Cambridge, Mass.: John Bartlett, 1856. Hall, a Harvard senior, was perhaps the first American to call attention to college vocabulary as a topic of interest. The revised edition of his book (which appeared originally in 1851) covers the slang and techni-

cal jargon of British and American colleges. It includes much historical information and a large number of illustrative citations.

[Hotten, John Camden]. *The Slang Dictionary, Etymological, Historical, and Anecdotal*. A new [i.e., 4th] edition. London: Chatto & Windus, 1874. An eclectic and very influential amateur attempt not only to define English slang terms but to put the entire subject in some historical and cultural perspective as well. The introduction and bibliography remain of interest, and about 5,000 entries are defined. Earlier editions appeared in 1859, 1860, and 1865. The 1887 edition was reprinted in 1972, with a new preface by J.D.A. Widdowson (Totowa, N.J.: Rowman and Littlefield).

Irwin, Godfrey. *American Tramp and Underworld Slang*. London: Scholartis Press, 1931. Although the compiler himself had been an itinerant before the First World War, the value of his book suffers from an apparent reliance on printed sources, especially glossaries published in *Dialect Notes* and *American Speech*. Has generally reliable definitions, but also the unreliable etymologies typical of amateur attempts in this direction. Irwin was an important source of information for Partridge's later *Dictionary of the Underworld* and for Wentworth and Flexner's *Dictionary of American Slang*.

Jay, Timothy. *Cursing in America: A Psycholinguistic Study of Dirty Language in the Courts, in the Movies, in the Schoolyards and on the Streets*. Philadelphia: J. Benjamins, 1992. A professional-level study applying socio- and psycholinguistic investigative methods to the subject of "taboo" vocabulary use in American English in the 1970's. Concludes that the standards of acceptable informal verbal behavior are far more liberal than is often assumed. Proposes a "Five-Stage Model of Anger" as it relates to the use of abusive language.

Kenyon, John S. "Cultural Levels and Functional Varieties of English." *College English* X (1948) 31–36. Suggests, as part of a general discussion, that slang represents a "cultural level" of usage rather than simply a stylistic resource.

Lewin, Esther, and Albert E. Lewin. *The Thesaurus of Slang: 150,000 Uncensored Contemporary Slang Terms, Common Idioms, and Colloquialisms Arranged for Quick and Easy Reference*. New York and Oxford: Facts on File, 1988. Comparable in size to Berrey and Van den Bark's thesaurus; much less informative but more up to date.

Lighter, Jonathan. "The Slang of the A.E.F. 1917–1919: An Historical Glossary." *American Speech* XLVII (1972) 5–142. Defines and illustrates with copious dated citations about 800 examples of slang more or less restricted to the U.S. Army and Marine Corps during World War I. The citations illustrate the time span of usage of each sense; many reappeared in the various *OED* Supplements. The data challenge the assumption that war slang is especially ephemeral. The bibliography lists about 800 sources.

Maitland, James. *The American Slang Dictionary*. Chicago: privately printed, 1891. The earliest general dictionary of U.S. "slang," defined as any nonstandard vocabulary. Maitland was a Chicago journalist whose work owes a great deal to Hotten.

Maurer, David W. *Language of the Underworld*. Collected and edited by Allan W. Futrell and Charles B. Wordell. Lexington Univ. Press of Kentucky, 1981. More than twenty articles and glossaries written and compiled over a period of fifty years by the century's principal authority on criminal slang and jargon. Valuable introduction (by Futrell), epilogue, and word index. Of equal sociolinguistic interest are Maurer's book-length monographs, *Whiz Mob* (Publication of the American Dialect Society, 1955) and *The Big Con* (Indianapolis: Bobbs-Merrill, 1940). Both monographs are unsurpassed efforts to integrate the study of subcultural vocabularies and behavior.

Partridge, Eric. *A Dictionary of Slang and Unconventional English*. Edited by Paul Beale. 8th ed. London: Macmillan, 1984. Partridge's magnum opus, updated by Beale after the compiler's death in 1980. The first edition appeared in 1936 and could be regarded as an abridgment, revision, and modernization of Farmer

and Henley; but Partridge added a great many new items and continued to do so throughout his life. Because it contains an enormous amount of information, not readily accessible elsewhere, *DSUE* has enjoyed a high reputation among writers and librarians; linguists and language historians hold it in less esteem. Covers mainly British and Australian slang but includes items of American origin. A vast, eclectic dictionary that includes cant and "unconventional" colloquialisms as well as slang. Each term is accompanied by either an estimate of its date of origin or, less frequently, the date of the earliest citation or the earliest citation itself. Despite serious flaws, including an overreliance on secondary sources, the book is a landmark in recent slang lexicography.

Partridge, Eric. *A Dictionary of the Underworld, British and American*. 3d ed. London: Macmillan, 1968. Partridge's best and most thoroughly researched work, yet it suffers from many of the same flaws as his general slang dictionary. This volume, which first appeared in 1949, covers the daunting mass of criminal argot ("cant") that has been recorded in English since the early sixteenth century. Often ludicrous etymologies, occasionally erroneous definitions, especially for U.S. material. Sufficiently wary readers, however, can compensate for these problems and will recognize the book's importance in its presentation of the earliest known citation for virtually every defined sense and its scrupulous enumeration of original sources for each.

Partridge, Eric. *Slang To-day and Yesterday*. London: George Routledge and Sons, 1933. The only full-length discussion of slang yet written. Restricts the label "slang" to intentionally unorthodox vocabulary and then examines the subject thoroughly, albeit from a now outdated perspective. Contains a wealth of information, not all of it demonstrably correct. Though it includes glossaries of British, Australian, and American slang, the treatment of U.S. material is inadequate, the definitions and dates of usage often misleading.

Rodgers, Bruce. *The Queens' Vernacular*. San Francisco: Straight Arrow, 1972. More than

8,000 items, most of dubious currency, collected from homosexual Americans and partially grouped according to referent. Indirectly suggests the great extent of idiosyncratic wordplay and nonce coinages in this—and presumably other—subcultures. The introduction asserts, without providing evidence, that "the people who use slang most…are the economically oppressed." The bibliography lists about seventy printed sources.

Sagarin, Edward. *The Anatomy of Dirty Words.* New York: Lyle Stuart, 1962. The first book-length discussion of the subject. Attempts to place "taboo" words in a current social-psychological context. The author's intuitive, anecdotal approach is strengthened by his interesting examples of actual usage.

Sechrist, Frank. "The Psychology of Unconventional Language." *The Pedagogical Seminary* XX (1913) 413–59. A wide-ranging if diffuse discussion of the individual and social-psychological functions of nonstandard vocabulary, broadly labeled as "slang." Emphasizes its origin in oral culture, independent of the attitudes inculcated by formal education. Notes that "slang" originates in various strata of society and that it plays a generally positive role in refreshing the power of the standard vocabulary. Examples are drawn from several languages. One of the earliest American sources to discuss slang in a favorable manner.

Spears, Richard A. *Slang and Euphemism: A Dictionary of oaths, curses, insults, sexual slang and metaphor, racial slurs, drug talk, homosexual lingo, and related matters.* 2d abridged [*sic;* i.e., "revised and expanded"] ed. New York: Signet, 1991. An idiosyncratic compilation, as described in the subtitle, of slang and non-slang, common and otherwise, from about 500 sources, most of them earlier glossaries and dictionaries. An attempt is made, in the manner of Partridge's *DSUE,* to date the period of usage of each sense. About 32,000 definitions are given, covering all of English from the Anglo-Saxon period. The informative introductory material makes clear that the compiler is aware of the many pitfalls of his approach. The first edition was published in 1981 (Middle Village, New York: Jonathan David).

Spears, Richard A. *The Slang and Jargon of Drugs and Drink.* Metuchen, N.J.: Scarecrow Press, 1986. Meticulously compiled if loosely edited dictionary of about 9,000 terms found in about 350 earlier dictionaries and glossaries, British and American. Lists of synonyms are also given. Sources are listed for each defined sense in the manner of Partridge's *Dictionary of the Underworld,* making this a useful reference for persons interested in comparing the contents of published collections.

Wentworth, Harold, and Stuart Berg Flexner. *Dictionary of American Slang.* 2d Supplemented [i.e., 3d] ed. New York: Thomas Y. Crowell, 1975. First published in 1960 and hailed as a "landmark in American lexicography" for its serious and relatively unexpurgated treatment of general slang. Junior editor Flexner was responsible for much of the editing and defining, as well as for the substantial preface and the linguistics-oriented appendix of word lists grouped conceptually and morphologically. Flexner's preface, reprinted several times in university textbooks (and again in Chapman's *NDAS*), places a broadly defined American slang in the context of general American culture. The dictionary's weaknesses—looseness of definition, unpredictable allocation of citations, and a certain historical naiveté—somewhat undercut its reliability. About 8,000 definitions are included, and there is an excellent bibliography.

Weseen, Maurice H. *Dictionary of American Slang.* New York: Thomas Y. Crowell, 1934. Arranged by field of interest, the vocabularies appear to have been drawn quite uncritically from mostly secondary sources. Brief definitions; no documentation, dates, or examples of usage.

Whitman, Walt. "Slang in America." *The North American Review* CXLI (1885) 431–35. Written in praise of "slang," which the poet Whitman defines mistily as "the lawless germinal element below all words and sentences, and behind all poetry…an attempt of common humanity to escape from bald literalism." Gives numerous examples of figurative language in popular speech. Notable as the earliest encomium to the American vernacular by a prominent literary artist.

Zwilling, Leonard. *A TAD Lexicon*, in *Etymology and Linguistic Principles* III, edited by Gerald Cohen. Rolla, Mo.: Gerald Cohen, 1993. An inclusive glossary of the innovative slang and nonce vocabulary found in the work of Thomas A. Dorgan ("TAD") (1877–1929), a nationally syndicated cartoonist of the early twentieth century whose comic art helped popularize a number of slang expressions, including *malarkey, hard-boiled,* and *kibitzer.* Informative introductory chapters, extensive dated citations from Dorgan's work, and cross references to the *OED* and other standard sources.

GUIDE TO THE DICTIONARY

Form and Order of Headwords

An entry always begins with the headword in boldface type. The headword is given in standard form and any exceptions are usually shown after the definition as variant forms. A headword can be followed immediately by a variant form if the variant is a common phonological or orthographical variant of the same lexeme. Examples:

defi or **defy**
-ass or **-assed**

For further discussion, see *Variant Forms*, below.

Entries are listed in strict alphabetical order. Words that have the same part of speech and the same spelling except for capitalization are ordered by decreasing number of capital letters. Example:

BAM *n.*
Bam *n.*
bam[1] *n.*
bam[2] *n.*

Superscript homograph numbers are assigned to headwords that have identical spellings and identical parts of speech but different etymological origins. Senses stemming from the same source but influenced by semantic development are typically treated under the same headword. For instance, all senses of the noun *dog* refer to the domesticated canid *Canis familiaris*. Since the sense 'the D model of any aircraft' derives from the use of *dog* as communications jargon for the letter 'D', this sense is listed under *dog*. On the other hand, the noun *gee* has several entirely different origins: one is a clipping of *grand* 'one thousand dollars', one is probably based on the French male given name *Guy*, and one is a borrowing from Hindustani *ghee*. Each of these has been considered a different word, and therefore identified by a different homograph number. (The noun *Gee*, a clipping and alteration of *Por-*

tuguese, is not numbered as a separate homograph because it is spelled with an initial capital.)

Homographs are ordered by the date of the earliest citation.

Headwords with the same spelling but different parts of speech are ordered as follows:

n.
pron.
adj.
adv.
prep.
conj.
v.
interj.
art.
bound forms:
   prefix.
   infix.
   suffix.
   comb. form.

While this practice differs from that usually followed in historical dictionaries, it allows a reader to find a desired part of speech without focusing on the historical development of forms. Notes discussing issues of development are provided where necessary.

For entries entirely in brackets, see the discussion at *Definitions*, below.

Pronunciations

The pronunciation immediately follows the headword and is given in a broad International Phonetic Alphabet (IPA) transcription enclosed in virgules (//). Pronunciations are given for a very small number of words, usually only when a feature such as stress or vowel length is notably different from the usual pronunciation of the word. Also, pronunciations are usually given for pronunciation spellings such as *b'hoy* and for facetious variants such as /gɑrˈbɑʒ/ for *garbage*.

No attempt has been made to represent pronunciations for nonstandard varieties of English.

Parts of Speech

Words are classified in this dictionary into the parts of speech listed above; however, pronouns, prepositions, conjunctions, and articles are extremely rare in slang and seldom occur in this dictionary. The part of speech is given immediately after the headword or after a pronunciation. The only other label used in this position is *n.pl.* to indicate plural nouns. Phrases are not labeled with part-of-speech designations.

Words that occasionally function as other parts of speech without any significant changes in meaning have this noted after the definition. For example:

dirty *adj.*....characterized by strong blues elements.... Also as adv.

In cases like these, where the changes in meaning result solely from differences in syntactic structure, a separate listing for the different part of speech is given only when justified by their frequency in the corpus.

Noun is used to classify all words with nominal function, including single words, compound or phrasal nouns, proper nouns, verbal nouns (when not treated under the verb), and nominalizations of verbs or verb phrases such as *goof-up*. When attributive use of a noun seems frequent, this is noted; if it is especially prevalent or if the meaning is notably different, this usage may be presented separately as an adjectival entry.

Verbs are not usually labeled for transitivity; in most cases, the definition and the illustrative citations make clear whether or not the verb takes an object. When a distinction is necessary but the structure of a definition makes this impossible, it is noted in a comment or as an internal comment before a part of the definition. Other parts of speech formed from verbs, such as agentive nouns, verbal nouns, or participial adjectives, are normally treated at the verb; they may or may not be explicitly shown.

Combining forms are bound forms that are words in their own right. Thus *-age* is given as a suffix but *-ass* is a combining form. This label is used sparingly; combining forms that function as infixes are labeled as infixes, and nouns with one sense functioning as a combining form usually have a comment "usu. used in combs." for that sense, rather than separating the sense into a new entry.

Etymologies

The etymology is in square brackets. It is placed immediately before the sections of an entry to which it applies, so that an etymology referring to an entire word will follow the part of speech, but an etymology referring to a single sense will follow the definition number for that sense. The etymology should not be confused with the discursive note (see discussion at *Discursive Notes*, below), which is also in square brackets but which follows the definition and does not normally cover etymological ground; when an etymological comment is quite long, the discussion has sometimes been moved to or extended into the discursive note.

The majority of slang words are formed by semantic shifts from Standard English words. Etymologies are not supplied for the standard words, since these may be found in general dictionaries. The slang senses are only discussed when the semantic connection to the standard word might be obscure.

References to other languages are kept to a minimum. Words clearly borrowed from another language are usually traced to that language only, and not to the ultimate source. In some cases analogues in other languages are given where a sense development seems unusual; in these cases it is made clear that the language may be a source of the English construction or that it merely provides an interesting parallel.

daylight *n.*....[cf. L *lumen* 'eye', lit. 'light']...an eye.

Field Labels

The field label appears in italics immediately before the definition. Note that the field label refers to the group, subculture, etc., of people who *use* the word, not necessarily to those to whom the word applies. Modifiers such as "Esp." or "Orig." may appear before a label, and one definition may have more than one label, such as "*Navy & USMC.*"

The decision to include field labels was made on the basis of citational evidence, and while in most cases this evidence is an accurate reflection of a word's range of use, the presence of a label should not imply that the word is used exclusively by the designated group, or that persons using such words have real ties to the designated group.

Definitions

Definition numbers (or letters) are given in bold-face type. Individual senses of a word are usually labeled with Arabic numerals; subdivisions of those senses are labeled with lowercase letters. In several complicated instances, an entry has been structured around a major division of senses. For example, the major senses of *bird* are divided into three groups: "senses referring especially to people," "senses referring to physical representations of birds or to the ability of flight," and "other senses." These major divisions are labeled with uppercase Roman numerals.

The degree of precision possible in sense division depends greatly on the amount of available evidence. If the evidence for one sense is slight, this definition may be run into an existing one, preceded by a word such as "(*hence*)" or "(*also*)," even if the senses are not very close. In other cases, it has been possible to carefully divide and define much more closely related senses simply because evidence was more abundant.

The reader should note that the overall context in addition to that provided in a citation has often facilitated the accurate placement of a citation, even though such placement may seem problematical at first glance.

Certain comments can appear before or within a definition, in parentheses. The most common of these, which show the relationship between two parts of a definition, are (*hence*), which indicates that the second meaning logically follows from the first; (*also*), which merely indicates that the second meaning is related to the first; and (*specif.*) and (*broadly*), which indicate respectively that the second meaning is a narrower or broader version of the first. Certain other comments, such as "(now *colloq.*)," "(*rare* in U.S.)," "(*trans.*)," and "(*hence*, as adj.),* can also appear internally when they affect only one part of the definition; their meanings are discussed elsewhere in this Guide.

In most cases, definitions are ordered by the date of the earliest citation. This also applies to lettered subdefinitions, but definitions are treated discretely. That is, if a word has definitions 1.a., 1.b., and 2, sense 1.b. will be later than sense 1.a., and sense 2 will be later than sense 1.a. but not necessarily later than sense 1.b. For dating purposes, bracketed citations (see discussion at *Citations*, below) are generally treated as relevant when they clearly point to the use under discussion. When a bracketed citation is simply an interesting parallel, it is discounted in the ordering of senses.

Because a strict historical presentation is the most accurate and the most helpful for the reader, very close relationships between senses are reflected by lettered subdivisions of definitions or by a breakdown within the definition itself. Since the sequence of senses was not always logical, it was preferable to let the citations speak for themselves, rather than to impose order where it may not belong.

There are two major exceptions to chronological treatment. In cases where one sense is almost certainly the original, but a secondary sense is attested earlier, the senses have been given in the assumed logical order, rather than the chronological one. There is usually a note such as "despite the evidence of the dates, this meaning is undoubtedly the original." (When the development is less clear, the definitions have been left in chronological order with a note added, such as "prob. the original sense.") In a few instances, words usually used in combination have their senses divided based on the part of speech with which they are combined. The order of senses follows the order given above for parts of speech.

A definition, or very rarely a whole entry, can appear entirely in brackets. Here the brackets indicate that the word or sense under discussion has never been in slang use in the United States. Usually this occurs either when a word or sense is attested only in British sources, but points to related uses in American slang (examples are *bung (one's) eye* s.v. BUNG, *v.* and FAKER, *n.*, 1), or when a sense has always been colloquial or dialectal but may have influenced the development of slang senses (an example is CHICKEN, 1.a.). There is always a note explaining the rationale behind the decision.

For the use of phrases within definitions, see discussion at *Phrases*, below.

Comments and Labels about Usage and Status

Certain definitions in this dictionary bear additional comments. These may consist of information about grammar, style, frequency, currency, and other aspects of usage. Most comments about usage are preceded by a dash, although others (such as "Now *S.E.*" or "*Joc.*") may be freestanding.

The abbreviation "usu.," meaning "almost always, though not inevitably," is used before a label to indicate that "mainstream standards" are flexible and are primarily based on situation and speaker-to-speaker relationships.

Ethnic and racial epithets are classic examples of the double lives led by some English words. What makes them epithets (or "slurs") is their willful use to demean or degrade. Yet, within the insulted groups, the same words may be used in mere derision or rough humor; in recent use, some terms, such as *dyke*, *nigger*, and *queer*, have been used self-referentially in an attempt to defuse their effect as epithets of hatred. It is such variation in intent and effect that warrants the use of "usu." with labels for these terms.

As used in this dictionary, "vulgar" carries the meaning 'coarsely offensive to mainstream standards of delicacy and taste'; the level of vulgarity can range from mild to extreme. Those entries marked "vulgar" usually refer to items of a sexual or scatological nature.

The words "derisively" and "contemptuously" are meant to convey their everyday meanings. "Derisively" implies an element of ridicule or banter that makes such terms less directly provocative than those entries marked as "contemptuous." Although many slang terms applied to human beings convey at least mild disrespect, only those senses conveying strong derision or contempt are so labeled. Labels are used only when the nature of the definition does not make its status clear; definitions of the sort "an idiot; fool" do not require labels such as "derisive" or "contemptuous."

The label "offensive" means that a term is likely to be considered offensive by the person, group, etc., to whom it refers. Used alone, it does not imply that any offense is intended by the person using the word. *Although the "offensive" label is not normally used for a word labeled as "derisive" or "contemptuous," such a word should be considered "offensive" nonetheless.* As with other labels, the "usu." has been applied to terms labeled "offensive" to account for the varying reception given to words by different individuals. Of course, the offensiveness lies in the context of the word's use rather than in the word itself.

Certain labels reflect the status of terms. A label of "Now *hist.*" indicates that as far as the editors can determine, a word is only used in historical contexts. This can mean that the referent of the word no longer exists (the *Blues* and the *Grays* of the Civil War, or the *flappers* of the Jazz Age) or that the word itself, while still remembered, is no longer in active use (the *Ameche* for a telephone, or a *flivver* for a cheap automobile). The "Now *hist.*" label does not mean that a word is rare or that it is no longer slang, although frequently used terms of this sort often become Standard English. This dictionary does not necessarily include recent citations for words labeled "Now *hist.*," but the label itself indicates that the word may still be used.

The label "*Joc.*" indicates that a word is considered humorous by the person using the word, but should not be regarded as inherently amusing. Some terms may be used jocularly, but can be offensive nonetheless; such words, when not labeled as derisive or contemptuous, will always be labeled as offensive as well.

The labels "Now *colloq.*" and "Now *S.E.*" are used for words that have shaken off their slang status. No systematic attempt has been made to supply recent citations for these terms. Such words should be regarded as being in reasonably frequent use unless otherwise indicated.

Labels of the sort "*Obs.*" or "*Rare*" are not shown when this information can be easily inferred from the citations. However, labels of the sort "*Obs.* [or *Rare*] in U.S." are used when there is evidence that a sense apparently obsolete or rare in America is still in use in Britain or Australia. These "obsolete" and "rare" labels do appear internally, to separate parts of definitions, since these distinctions are often difficult to determine from a quick glance at the citations.

Variant Forms

Variant forms, except for those given directly after the headword (see *Form and Order of Headwords*, above), are found immediately after the definition in several different formats. In this dictionary, a "variant form" is any form other than that given at the headword: a different spelling, a use as a different part of speech, and a derived form are all considered variants.

Different spellings appear in boldface type preceded by the word "Also." Only spellings with a reasonable currency are generally shown. The variety of spellings, especially for the early history of a word's use, for words not normally written down, or for words borrowed from other languages, can be great: *floozy*, for example, has *flusie, fluzie, floosie, fluzzy, flousie, floosey*, and *floozie* as variants. Since it is not the purpose of this dictionary to catalog all spelling variations of a word, these variants are not listed individually. Nor are cross references given at the different spellings. In most cases such an entry includes an "Also vars." label, which is the broadest label

used for variants. Conversely, relatively minor variants appear in the citations without comment. Variants for such aspects as differing hyphenation, capitalization, or presence or absence of periods in abbreviations are almost never listed.

For variant parts of speech, see the discussion at *Parts of Speech*, above. The form is "Also as adj." or the like.

A derived form is given after a definition rather than as a new entry when it has no large independent currency and when the derivation is quite clear. Such derived forms are shown in boldface immediately after the definition and are preceded by the word "Hence." Cross references to derived forms are not normally given.

bellyache *v.* [cf. syn. GRIPE] to whine or complain. Hence **bellyacher,** *n.*

cake-eater *n.* Esp. *Stu.* an effeminate fellow; sissy....Hence **cake-eating,** *adj.*

Greenland *n.* Ireland. Hence **Greenlander** an Irishman. *Joc.*

Discursive Notes

The discursive note, in square brackets, is usually the last element preceding the body of citations. It may cover a variety of subjects depending on the needs of an entry, including etymological material. The following examples represent typical discursive notes:

[Quots. ref. to WWII.]

[See *OED* for closely related S.E. senses not recorded here.]

[U.S. usage has app. arisen independently of 18th C. quots. given below.]

[Typical of the "Valley Girl" fad of 1982–83.]

[The sense intended in the 1840 quot. is not entirely clear.]

[Farmer & Henley *Slang* erroneously dates *1789 quot. as "1781."]

Cross References

Words that are treated elsewhere in this dictionary are shown in small capital type, followed by the part of speech when necessary and the definition number where possible; often a cross reference refers to several senses and it is not practical to specify every one. Example: Cf. CHICKEN, *n.*, 8.a.

Cross references to other senses of the same entry have the definition number in boldface type, in parentheses, with the word "above" or "below" to direct the reader to the proper spot. Example: quot. at (**4.a.**), above.

Phrases in cross references are given in italics, with the headword where the phrase is found given in small capitals. If the phrase is at the same entry, it will be followed by "above" or "below." Cross references normally cite only the base form of the phrase, even though variants for phrases are given at the actual entry. Examples: See *blow the gaff* s.v. GAFF. Cf. *dog it*, below.

Citations

Citations are ordered strictly chronologically. For a citation with a range of dates (see discussion at *Dating and Bibliographic Style*, below), the last date is the one used for ordering. Citations from the same year are ordered by exact date if this is available.

An asterisk (*) before the date indicates that a citation is from a non–North American source. An American book quoting British usage will have an asterisk, and an English book referring to an American usage or quoting an American author will not. The reader should also note that before *ca*1820, differences between British and American slang, as between British and American English in general, are far less marked (see the Introduction for a discussion of this issue).

In this dictionary American and Canadian English are not differentiated—neither variety has an asterisk (see the Introduction for a discussion of the relationship between Canadian and American slang). There is very little Canadian English in this dictionary; even the most notable exception—Thomas C. Haliburton—was writing in the voice of a Yankee.

A citation is placed in square brackets if it does not actually exemplify the slang use under discussion. The following are the most common reasons for a bracketed citation:

1. A citation has the same word as the slang sense but the relationship between the citation and the slang sense is unclear, or the bracketed example may be suspected of being poorly or erroneously defined in the original source. Example from the word *benny* 'a benefit or good thing of any sort; goodie':

[**1941** Kendall *Army & Navy Slang* 1: *A benny*....a break in formation during which a soldier can rest or smoke.]

2. A citation has the same word as the slang sense but in a different meaning. Example for a nonce usage of *goon* apparently unrelated to the later sense 'stupid person':

[**1921** F.L. Allen, in *Harper's Mag.* (Dec.)...122: A goon-ish style is one that reads as if it were the work of a goon. It is thick and heavy....It employs the words "youth" and "lad," likes the exclamation "lo!" [etc.].]

3. A citation is a possible allusion, or perhaps simply an interesting parallel, to a slang sense. Example from *geesefeathers* 'snow':

[**1912** in Truman *Dear Bess* 73: The heavenly geese are certainly shedding feathers around this neighborhood this morning.]

4. A citation exemplifies a use—perhaps a nonce use—closely related to the headword. Example from *China syndrome* 'a...meltdown of...a nuclear reactor':

[**1974** Widener *N.U.K.E.E.* 67: The core was in a run-away melt-down condition—the classic "China Accident."]

5. A citation is an unmistakable allusion to a slang sense without explicitly using the head-word. Example from *wrote the book* s.v. BOOK:

[**1906–07** Ade *Slim Princess* 52: "You have traveled a great deal?"..."Me and Baedeker and Cook wrote it."]

6. A citation is a euphemistic variant of a slang sense. Example from the slang phrase *the sweat off (one's) balls* s.v. BALL:

[**1928** Dahlberg *Bottom Dogs* 130: You're keepin' up the old homestead by the sweat of your groins.]

Dating and Bibliographic Style

The task of assigning a precise date to a text is often difficult. Even the seemingly straightforward case of a novel published only once has a number of complications: Was it written at an earlier time but not published for several years?

Was it written over a span of several years? Is a fictional character quoting an actual earlier source? Is the action set in an earlier period of which the author has personal experience?

The overriding concern has been to supply a date that most accurately reflects the time the word was written or recorded. In some cases the date of a citation will not agree with the publication date of a book. The bibliography in the final volume will be explicit about publication dates of books and dates of citations in those books, but the citations in the dictionary will only give the date of the citation and enough information about the title to allow the work to be tracked down. A number of different conventions have been adopted for determining the dating of a citation:

1. *Use of "in" in citations*

   When a citation is known to have originated earlier than the work in which it is found, the date of the citation will be followed by *in*, followed by the bibliographical reference to the work itself. The range of possibilities is very large: citations quoted from other historical dictionaries (**1821** in *OED*); citations quoted from historical works or other works of scholarship (**1846** in H.L. Gates, Jr. *Sig. Monkey* 93); letters or diary entries, or collections thereof; and so on.

   The author of a citation is usually not given if the source is a magazine or a historical dictionary. However, when an author being quoted is celebrated in his or her own right, the name is given before *in*, such as ***1739** H. Walpole, in *OED*, or **1940** Z.N. Hurston, in *Amer. Mercury*.

   If the source itself cites a date earlier than the publication date, but does not give the actual citation, the style is **1947** (cited in *W9*). If the source does give the actual citation but this dictionary does not give it, the style is **1927** in Partridge *DSUE* 21.

2. *Book written earlier than the publication date of the edition*

   Books published as current editions—that is, books that are not editions of earlier works,

later publications of historical memoirs, etc.—can sometimes be shown to have been written earlier than the publication date. For instance, the first edition of Mencken's *American Language* is dated 1918 in this dictionary, even though the publication date is 1919. The preface is dated January 1, 1919, and therefore the book as a whole must have been written before that. In most cases the difference will be only a year or two.

3. *Citations dated with a range of years*

   Some citations have a range of dates spanning a number of years, rather than a single date. For instance, James Joyce wrote *Ulysses* from 1914 to 1922; it is therefore cited as ***1914–22** Joyce *Ulysses*. An article published in a 1944 issue of *American Speech* discussing a research project that began in 1942 is cited as **1942–44** *AS*. Entries in the *Dictionary of American Regional English* often quote a number of examples from the *DARE* survey, which took place largely from 1965 to 1970; when quoting these examples they are cited as **1965–70** in *DARE*.

4. *Use of "a" and "ca," especially in citations*

   The abbreviation *a*, for Latin *ante* 'before', is used immediately before a date to indicate that the citation was written (or the event occurred) shortly before the date given, but it is not possible to be any more accurate. In all cases citations are dated no earlier than is defensible on the basis of evidence. In no case should *a* be assumed to refer to an indefinitely long period. For example, a non-historical dictionary such as *WNID3* may give a citation without giving the full source, so the only possible reference is *a*1961 in *WNID3*.

   The abbreviation *ca*, for Latin *circa* 'about', is used similarly but more broadly. It comes immediately before a date or age, and signifies only that the date or age is in a general but not a specific range. For example, *ca* is used when an actual composition date is impossible to determine, when a reference is too vague, in ages (as in oral citations, when the collector cannot determine the exact age of the informant), and so on. When any other information about the dating is available, it is supplied in bracketed notes.

5. *Use of bracketed note with "ref. to" in citations*

If a citation explicitly refers to another era, a bracketed note such as "[ref. to WWII]" or "[ref. to 1891]" is often added immediately before the citation. This practice is followed when a word appears to be characteristic of its historical reference rather than the actual date of the cited material, or when the source appears to be particularly trustworthy in depicting an earlier era from firsthand experience. For an earliest citation, it can indicate that a word was probably in use at an earlier date than is directly attested. For example, a term that was current during the Vietnam War may not be discovered in print until later, presumably an accident of the sampling process; this is borne out by the fact that veterans' memoirs are often not published until years after the events described. However, although the fallible evidence of recollection is allowed in the citations, boldface dates are not "backdated" on the basis of such evidence. Bracketed notes are supplied only when the information is notable in some way; no attempt was made to characterize the historical setting of each source when it does not illuminate an aspect of the word's use.

The bracketed note with "ref. to" is occasionally used for geographical or other designations when these are relevant or of special interest: "[ref. to Princeton University]."

Oral citations have not been specifically designated, but it will be clear from the lack of other bibliographical evidence if a citation is oral, as opposed to one taken from television, radio, or print sources. The usual form is **1976** N.Y.C. man, age *ca*38: [citation]. Any citation not personally collected by Jonathan Lighter will give the name of the collector: **1971** Former 1/Lt, U.S. Army (coll. J. Ball): [citation]. The plan of the project has prevented any systematic search for oral citations, and the geographic distribution of informants is necessarily limited to the

editors' personal experience. It is hoped that the wide range of print and broadcast sources used will counterbalance any unequal representation so introduced.

Detailed information about the nature and location of typescript or manuscript works appears in the final volume of this dictionary.

Page references indicate the page on which the word under discussion appears, not where the extract begins. When quoting from alphabetical dictionaries or glossaries, volume and page numbers have usually been omitted. When quoting from an entry for a different word, the style is ***1812** Vaux *Vocab.* s.v. *cadge* (the entry under discussion is *game*). The abbreviation "unp.," for "unpaged," is used for texts that are not paginated. Occasionally chapter references rather than page references are given, especially for books that are easily accessible in differently paginated editions. When quoting drama or poetry (act, scene, and) line numbers are typically given rather than page references.

An author's name has been placed in brackets when a work was published anonymously or pseudonymously but the true name of the author is known. Thus, Thomas C. Haliburton is known to be the author of *The Clockmaker; or, The Sayings and Doings of Samuel Slick of Slickville*, but since this book (published in three series) was attributed to "Sam Slick," Haliburton's name is given in brackets. Authors known primarily by their pseudonyms have these names in quotation marks: "Fab 5 Freddy," "M. Twain," "O. Henry." Authors known exclusively by their pseudonyms or changed names (Woody Allen, Bob Dylan) have these names given without comment. Names of musical groups are also given in quotation marks.

Citations are recorded exactly as they appear in the source with minor exceptions made to conform to modern American standards of punctuation. When quoting from a dictionary, glossary, or other word list, the word or phrase being glossed has been put in italics. When reading through a block of citations, it is easier to recognize a word or phrase with definition when the word is italicized. And on a practical basis, there are so many different conventions adopted by various sources—regular type, italics, boldface, small capitals, and indents and dashes of various sorts—that trying to represent them accurately would be difficult.

Since the main concern has been to represent the meaning of the slang word, a source has often been quoted selectively, as by starting or finishing a quote in the middle of a sentence or by use of ellipses, in order to save space and emphasize the slang use. Although the citation itself has never been altered (except as noted above), some of these practices may change the style or occasionally the meaning of an author's words. In no case should a citation be taken to represent the viewpoint of the quoted author.

Selection

Examples found naturally in running texts have been favored over those that only appear in word lists of dubious origin or reliability. Most words and phrases claimed as "slang" are nonce terms or "oncers," never to be seen or heard of again. Some become true "ghost words," recorded in slang dictionaries for many years but never encountered in actual usage. We have attempted to exclude such expressions from this dictionary. However, in certain cases words only attested in word lists have been included when the editors felt that the lists were an accurate reflection of usage and that additional evidence would be difficult to find due to the nature of the evidence.

The number of citations given does not necessarily correspond to an entry's actual frequency of usage. However, unusually common expressions are often accompanied by multiple citations. The additional citations are included for several reasons: first, to give some suggestion of the commonness of the sense; second, to indicate continuity through its history or intensity in one period of the usage; and third, to illustrate nuances that cannot succinctly be placed in the definition. The editors have tried to supply their own citations from primary sources wherever possible, rather than quoting from secondary sources; the interested reader may thus be able to find additional evidence by consulting the *Oxford English Dictionary*, the *Dictionary of American Regional English*, the *Dictionary of American-*

isms, the journal *American Speech*, and other standard references.

In every case, the earliest citation per sense is the earliest that can be documented from the corpus. With language in general, and especially with slang, words and senses may be used regularly for quite some time before they are recorded in print. On a surprising number of occasions this dictionary has been able to provide antedatings of slang recorded in other historical dictionaries, notably the *Dictionary of American Regional English* and the second edition of the *Oxford English Dictionary*. It has not been possible to provide up-to-the-minute examples of every sense, but many senses lacking recent citational evidence retain currency nevertheless. Indeed, any well-attested entry with citations as late as the 1960's is probably still current.

Phrases

This dictionary organizes phrases under the main word of the phrase, usually the word least subject to variation. The editors feel that the increasingly common practice of locating phrases by the first word of the phrase (placing *have an edge on* under *have*, for example) is confusing and obscures the relationship of different phrases stemming from the same word. Also, slang phrases often have so many variants that the main word may be the only stable one of the phrase. Where there is potential for confusion, cross references have been added.

Phrases, which are always printed in boldface type, may appear in two places in an entry: as a run-on to an existing definition, or in a separate phrase section at the end of the standard definitions.

The phrase is given as a run-on to a definition if the phrase directly results from and is similar to that meaning, and often if the available evidence is insufficient to make it a separate phrasal entry. A run-on phrase also fits in with the development of other senses of the word.

bum *n.*....**3.** *Hobo.* an act of begging; usu. in phr. **put the bum on (someone)** to beg from (someone).
gonger *n.* [orig. unkn.] *Narc.* an opium pipe; in phr. **kick the gonger** to smoke opium.

Phrases appear in a separate section if their meaning is relatively independent of any sense in the definition section, or if the use as a phrase is significantly broader or more common than the use as a word alone. In potentially confusing cases there are cross references from the phrase section to the definitions and vice versa, and the reader is advised to look over the entire entry to be sure of finding a desired construction.

Phrases in the separate section are alphabetized by the first word of the phrase. In this case, no other method was practicable; furthermore, very few entries have so many phrases that finding any one would be difficult. The section itself is introduced by the symbol "¶" followed by "In phrases:". Each phrase is also preceded by the "¶" symbol for clarity.

The phrase section otherwise resembles a small entry in most respects. Sense division conforms to the same criteria as discussed above (see *Definition*): senses are ordered by date of first citation; each sense may have labels; etc. Variants of a phrase are enclosed in square brackets, usually with "or" preceding the next element:

> ¶ **put** [or **tie**] **on the feedbag** to eat a meal.
> ¶ **chew** [**up**] **the scenery** *Theat.* to overact.

It is possible to have an "Also vars." note following a definition in the phrase section. We have not attempted to account for every possible variation in a phrase, for as much as a slang word itself may vary, the phrases in which it may be found may vary even more. As with many other elements in this dictionary, our description of variants is intended to be a general, not an absolute, guide to the possibilities.

Pronunciation Key

Vowels

ɑ	farm
æ	cat
ai	nice
au	shout
ɛ	set
ei	claim
ɛə	fair
ɪ	ship
i	keep
ɪə	hear
ɔ	pause
ɔi	boil
ou	rope
ʊ	good
u	rude
ʊə	poor
ə	about
ʌ	tub

Consonants

b	big
d	dog
ð	then
ʤ	jump
f	fun
g	get
h	hum
j	yes
k	kit
l	love
m	me
n	no
ŋ	ring
p	pot
r	run
s	sip
ʃ	shore
t	tap
ʧ	chip
θ	think
v	violin
w	wish
z	zipper
ʒ	azure

Stress

ˈ primary stress
ˌ secondary stress

These are vertical stress marks that precede the stressed syllable.

LIST OF ABBREVIATIONS

This list does not necessarily include standard abbreviations.

*	(before the date of a citation, used to indicate a non–North American source); (*also*, in etymologies, used to indicate an unattested or reconstructed form)
<	is derived from
>	from which is derived
a	*ante* (before)
abbr.	abbreviation, abbreviated
absol.	absolute(ly) (grammatical sense)
acad.	academy
adap.	adaptation, adapted
adj.	adjective(s), adjectival(ly)
adv.	adverb(s), adverbial(ly); (*also*) advertisement
adver.	advertising
Afr	Africa(n)
alter.	alteration
AmE	American English
Amer.	America(n)
AmSp	American Spanish
anthol.	anthology
aph.	apheretic
app.	apparently
arch.	archaic
art.	article
AS	*American Speech*
assoc.	associated
astron.	astronomy
ATS	Berrey & Van den Bark, *American Thesaurus of Slang*
attrib.	attributive(ly)
Austral.	Australia(n)
av.	aviation
BDNE, BDNE2, BDNE3	Barnhart, Steinmetz, & Barnhart [*Second/Third*] *Barnhart Dictionary of New English*
bib.	bibliography
biog.	biographical, biography
Black E	Black English
BrE	British English
Brit.	British
C.	century
ca	*circa* (about)
Canad.	Canadian, Canadianism
cap.	capital(ized)
CB	citizens band
cf.	*confer* (compare)
ch.	chapter
Chi.	Chicago
coll.	collect(or), collected (by)
collec.	collection
collect.	collective(ly)
colloc.	collocation
colloq.	colloquial(ism), colloquially
comb(s).	combination(s)
comb. form	combining form
comm.	communication(s)
Confed.	Confederate, Confederacy
conj.	conjunction
constr.	construed; (*also*) construction
contr.	contraction
DA	Mathews, *Dictionary of Americanisms*
DAE	Craigie & Hulbert, *Dictionary of American English*
DARE	Cassidy, *Dictionary of American Regional English*
DAS	Wentworth & Flexner, *Dictionary of American Slang*
DAUL	Goldin, O'Leary & Lipsius, *Dictionary of American Underworld Lingo*
def.	define(d), definition(s)
der., deriv.	derived, derivative
devel.	develop(ment)
dial.	dialect(al)
dict.	dictionary
dim.	diminutive
DN	*Dialect Notes*
docu.	document

DOST	Craigie & Aitken, *Dictionary of the Older Scottish Tongue*
DSUE	Partridge, *Dictionary of Slang and Unconventional English*
Du	Dutch
E	English
ed.	edition, editor, edited (by)
EDD	Wright, *English Dialect Dictionary*
elab.	elaborated, elaboration
ellipt.	elliptical(ly)
eques.	equestrian(ism)
erron.	erroneous(ly)
esp.	especially
ety.	etymology, etymological(ly)
euphem.	euphemism, euphemistic(ally)
ex(x).	example(s)
exclam.	exclamation, exclamatory
expl.	explanation
F	French
F & H	Farmer & Henley, *Slang and Its Analogues*
fem.	feminine, female
fig.	figurative(ly)
fr.	from
freq.	frequently; (*also*) frequentative(ly)
G	German
gamb.	gambling
gaz.	gazette
Gk	Greek
Gmc	Germanic
gram.	grammar, grammatical(ly)
Heb	Hebrew
Hiberno-E	Hiberno-English
hist.	history, historical
hndbk.	handbook
homosex.	homosexual(ity)
hosp.	hospital
hum.	humorous(ly)
illus.	illustrate(s), illustrated
imit.	imitative(ly)
imper.	imperative(ly)
Ind	Indian
infl.	influence(d)
interj.	interjection, interjectional(ly)

intrans.	intransitive(ly)
Ir	Irish
It	Italian
IUFA	Indiana University Folklore Archives
JAF	*Journal of American Folklore*
Japn	Japanese
joc.	jocular(ly)
Jour.	Journal (in titles)
journ.	journalism
juve.	juvenile
L	Latin
lang.	language
lit.	literal(ly); (*also*) literature
M	Middle
mag.	magazine
masc.	masculine (grammatical sense)
ME	Middle English
MED	*Middle English Dictionary*
med.	medical, medicine
MexSp	Mexican Spanish
mil.	military
mo.	month(ly)
mod.	modern
ModE	Modern English
MS	manuscript
N	North(ern)
n.	noun
NADS	*Newsletter of the American Dialect Society*
N & Q	*Notes and Queries*
narc.	narcotics
nat.	national
naut.	nautical
NDAS	Chapman, *New Dictionary of American Slang*
N.E.	Northeast
nec.	necessary, necessarily
N.O.	New Orleans
No.	North(ern)
N.Y.(C.)	New York (City)
obj.	object
obs.	obsolete
occ.	occasion, occasional(ly)
OE	Old English

OED	Murray et al., *Oxford English Dictionary*
OED2	Simpson & Weiner, *Oxford English Dictionary*, 2d edition
OEDAS	*Oxford English Dictionary Additions Series*
OEDS	Burchfield, *Oxford English Dictionary Supplement*
OF	Old French
opp.	opposite
orig.	origin, original(ly)
p(p).	page(s)
PADS	*Publication of the American Dialect Society*
pap.	papers (in titles)
pass.	passive
perh.	perhaps
Pg	Portuguese
phr.	phrase(s)
pl.	plural
pol.	politics, political
pop.	popular(ized)
poss.	possessive
ppl.	participle, participial
p.ppl.	past participle
prec.	precede, preceding
prep.	preposition, prepositional(ly)
pres.	present
pris.	prison
prob.	probable, probably
pron.	pronounce, pronunciation; (*also*) pronoun
pros.	prostitution
prov.	proverb, proverbial(ly)
Qly.	Quarterly (in titles)
quot(s).	quotation(s)
RAF	Royal Air Force
redup.	reduplication, reduplicative(ly)
ref.	refer(s), referring
reflex.	reflexive(ly)
repr.	represent(s), representing
resp.	respelling
rev.	revise(d), revision; (*also*) review
RHD	*Random House Dictionary of the English Language*
RHD2	*Random House Dictionary of the English Language*, 2d edition

R.R.	railroad
Russ	Russian
S	South(ern)
sc.	*scilicet* (namely)
S.E.	Standard English
sel.	selected
sing.	singular
Sks.	Sketches (in titles)
sl.	slang
SND	Grant, *Scottish National Dictionary*
So.	South(ern)
Sp	Spanish
specif.	specific(ally)
st.	stanza
stu.	student
suff.	suffix
sugg.	suggest(ed)
supp.	supplement
s.v.	*sub vocem* (under the word)
S.W.	Southwest
Sw	Swedish
syn.	synonym(ous)
theat.	theater, theatrical(ly)
trans.	transitive(ly)
transf.	transfer(red)
TS	typescript
ult.	ultimately
uncap.	uncapitalized
uncert.	uncertain
und.	underworld
univ.	university
unkn.	unknown
unp.	unpaged
USAF	United States Air Force
USCG	United States Coast Guard
USMC	United States Marine Corps
usu.	usually
UTSQ	University of Tennessee Student Questionnaire
v.	verb
var(s).	variant(s)
vaud.	vaudeville, vaudevillian
vet. med.	veterinary medicine
W	West(ern)

W9	*Webster's Ninth New Collegiate Dictionary*	*WNID, WNID2, WNID3*	*Webster's New International Dictionary* [2d, 3d editions]
W10	*Merriam-Webster's Collegiate Dictionary*, 10th edition	WWI	World War I
		WWII	World War II
WDEU	Gilman, *Webster's Dictionary of English Usage*	Yid	Yiddish

Random House
Historical
Dictionary
of
American Slang

A *n.* **1.** [partly euphem.] ASS.—esp. in figurative senses.
1941–42 Gach *In Army Now* 157: In a Pig's A, we're glad! **1951–53** in *AS* XXIX (1954) 95: *Cut A*...To leave. "I'd better cut A for home." **1957** Laurents & Sondheim *West Side Story* 210: You bet your fat A, I am! **1958** Whitcomb *Corregidor* 45 [ref. to WWII]: Do you mean that just because I volunteered to do this work while you guys sit on your fat A's, I'm getting rewarded by having to stay here? **1954–60** *DAS* s.v. *cut: Cut A*...A euphem. for "cut ass" [i.e., to leave]. **1968** "R. Hooker" *MASH* 64: You betcher ever-lovin' A, buddy-boy. **1979** Univ. Ark. student, age 20: I was really busting A. **1991** G. Trudeau *Doonesbury* (synd. cartoon strip) (Apr. 29): Ray! Time to haul A, man! We're moving out in ten minutes!
2. *Narc.* amphetamine; an amphetamine tablet or capsule.
1967 Bronsteen *Hippy's Hndbk.* 12: *A*...Amphetamine. **1968** [A. Hoffman] *System* 28: Amphetamine, usually called A or meth or speed, is also quite dangerous, if you don't know what you are doing. **1969** Postman et al. *Lang. in America* 205: A's are amphetamines.

A and A *n.* [ASS, 3.b. + *a*lcohol] *Mil.* rest and recreation leave; R AND R. Cf. I AND I; B AND B. *Joc.*
1966 J. Lewis *Marines* 9 [ref. to Korean War]: Better we should call it A 'n A...Ass'n Alcohol! **1966** E. Shepard *Doom Pussy* 47: They had put in two months' patrol in the jungle and were due to go...to exotic old Hong Kong for some R & R—or A & A (Ass and Alcohol), as they put it.

aardvark *n.* **1.** a slow-witted person having a coarse or foolish appearance; oaf; fool.
[**1961** J. Heller *Catch-22* 62: You know Captain Aardvark, don't you? He's that nice guy who came up to you and said, "Aardvark's my name, and navigation is my game." He wore a pipe in his face and probably asked you what college you went to.] **1968** S. Ross *Hang-Up* 131: Get in, you aardvarks....Come on, you raunchy paranoics. **1970** *Current Slang* V 3: *Aardvark*...a stupid person. **1977** *Time* (May 30) 5: The title "Hark, Hark, a Quark—Maybe"...was the mark of an aardvark. **1979** Univ. Tenn. student, age 24: He's such an aardvark. We used to say that in junior high in San Diego. That was in 1970.
2. *Av.* an ungainly aircraft; (*cap.*) *USAF.* the General Dynamics F-111 Switchblade fighter-bomber.
1963 E.M. Miller *Exile* 154: All I fly are antediluvian aardvarks like the Goon and the Charlie 45. *a***1973** in Tuso *Vietnam Blues* 97: You can take those goddamn Aardvark jets. **1975** in Higham & Siddall *Combat Aircraft* 101: Those who fly the F-111 know it as the "Aardvark" (no doubt for its long, slender proboscis). **1984** Trotti *Phantom* 244: *F-111.* Aardvark. **1991** Reinberg *In the Field: Aardvark*, nickname for the F-111, General Dynamic's swing-wing attack aircraft.

Ab *n. S.W.* [fr. *abolitionist*] a Union soldier during the Civil War.
1862 in Peticolas *Rebels* 43: The Ab's had gotten in 300 yards of us, and I began to load and shoot as fast as I could at them. *Ibid.* 49: Provisions abandoned by the Abs in their flight. *Ibid.* 141: The Ab captain replied that he would surrender. **1885** G.H. Pettis *Frontier Service* 25: They had assured the native population...that when the "Abs"—meaning the Union troops—arrived they would massacre all the men and abuse all the women.

aba-daba *n.* [perh. alteration of *after*, infl. by "The Aba-Daba Honeymoon," ragtime song (1913) by Arthur Fields and Walter Donovan, where imitative of monkeys' chatter] dessert.
1961 Clausen *Season's Over* 19 [ref. to Ringling Bros. circus, *ca*1945]: "St. Louis on the aba-daba, George." The waiter returned with a second dessert....She explained, "The circus used to play two sections of St. Louis, so St. Louis means doubles. Aba-daba is any dessert in the cook-house." [***1961** Partridge *DSUE* (ed. 5) 975: *Abdabs* was in World War II, used occasionally for "afters" [i.e., "dessert"].]

abbess *n.* a woman who manages a brothel.
1759 in Silber *Songs of Independence* 146: If you please, Madam Abbess, a word with your nuns. ***1782** in *F & H* 4: An old *Abbess*...dresses up a luscious maid [for a customer]. ***1826** "Blackmantle" *Eng. Spy* II 268: We took our chocolate with the lady *abbess* and her *nuns*.

Abbeville Kids *n.pl.* [sugg. by *Dead End Kids, Billy the Kid*, etc.] *Mil. Av.* fighter pilots of the German *Luftwaffe* stationed near Abbeville (Somme), France. Now *hist.*
1944 *N.Y. Times* (Mar. 12) 25: When [Flying] Fortresses raided Stuttgart last Sept. 6 they came up against Hermann Goering's "Abbeville Kids," a particularly nasty bunch of Nazi fighters. **1944** Stiles *Big Bird* 14: Eight months ago...the Abbeville Kids were waiting at the coast for loose formations. **1962** Mahurin *Honest John* 115: One famous *gruppe* [was] stationed in Abbeville, France—and dubbed the Abbeville Kids by our pilots. **1972** Facos *Silver Lady* 108: The Abbeville Kids—the sharpest of Goering's forces.

Abdul *n.* [a stereotypical Arabic male given name] *Mil. in Mid. East.* a Turkish man or Arab.
***1925** Fraser & Gibbons *Soldier & Sailor Wds.* [ref. to WWI]: *Abdul*: The usual name on Eastern Fronts in the war for a Turkish soldier. **1991** Dunnigan & Bay *Shield* 360: Kuwait War Slang...*Abdul*—Generic term for any Arab.

Abe *n.* a coin or currency note bearing the likeness of Abraham Lincoln; (*specif.*) **Brown Abe** a penny; (also **Abe Lincoln**) a five-dollar bill.
1944 Burley *Harlem Jive* 135: Brown Abes and Buffalo heads—Pennies and nickels. **1954–60** *DAS: Brown Abe*...A penny. **1966** R.E. Alter *Carny Kill* 43: One Abe Lincoln it is. **1967** Maurer & Vogel *Narc. & Narc. Ad.* (ed. 3) 339: *Abe*. a five-dollar bill. **1966–73** W. Burroughs *Exterminator!* 20: Get me this letter out, Screw./It's worth an Abe to you.

aber nit *interj.* [Pennsylvania G] never! not!
1896 *DN* I 421: *Nit*: a decided negative, much stronger than *no*...In [Ohio] also *aber nit*. **1903** *Pedagog. Sem.* V 372: I guess aber nit. I don't think. **1918** Mencken *Amer. Lang.* 152: *Aber nit*, once as popular as *camouflage*, is obviously *aber nicht*. **1927** S. Lewis *Elmer Gantry* ch. iii: Prexy Quarles and Juanita! Aber nit! Never get them two together!

Abie *n.* [dim. of *Abraham*, regarded as a typical Jewish male given name] a Jewish man.—used esp. in direct address.—usu. considered offensive.
1914 *DN* IV 158: *Aby*, n. Jew. **1936** Mackenzie *Living Rough* 139: We jerked our guns and Abie kicked loose with the dough. **1944** Burley *Harlem Jive* 133: *Abie*—The tailor. **1965** R. Marks *Letters* 42: My senior drill instructor finally realized I was Jewish and as a result he now calls me "Abey." **1973** R. Roth *Sand in Wind* ch. iv: You're a dead man, Abie....You're gonna be sorry, Jewboy.

Abie Kabibble *n.* [name of featured character in comic strip *Abie the Agent*, created (1914) by Harry Hershfield] a Jewish man.—usu. considered offensive.
1929–30 J.T. Farrell *Young Lonigan* ch. iv: You got to soft soap some of these Abie Kabibbles. **1936** M. Levin *Old Bunch* 80: "Hullo, Pisano!" "Hullo, you Abe [*sic*] Kabibble!"

Able Dog *n.* [former mil. communications alphabet *Able* 'A' + *Dog* 'D', for *AD*] *Mil. Av.* a Douglas AD (later A-1) Skyraider ground-support aircraft.
1961 W.T. Larkins *USMC Aircraft* 147: Douglas AD-4...Able Dog on K-16 airstrip, Korea. **1989** Leib *Fire Dream* 186 [ref. to Vietnam War]: A1-Es...pilots always called them A-Ds, or Able-Dogs,...[as in] the Korean War. **1991** Linnekin *80 Knots* 230: AD Skyraider...Able Dog.

Able Mabel *n.* [former mil. communications alphabet *Able* 'A' + *Mabel*, rhyming, for *AM*] *Naval Av.* a Martin AM-1 Mauler attack aircraft. [These planes equipped some first-line Navy squadrons 1947–50.] Now *hist.*
1953 *ATS* 709: *Able Mabel*, the Martin AM-1 Mauler. **1979** Former WAF A3c, age 49: (heard in reminiscence on Okinawa, 1960–64). **1991** Linnekin *80 Knots* 392: Martin's...airplane should have been called Able Mike instead of its actual nickname, Able Mable [*sic*].

Able Sugar *adj.* [former mil. communications alphabet *Able* 'A' + *Sugar* 'S', for APESHIT] *Mil.* crazy or out of order; haywire.

1955 C. Blair *Beyond Courage* 16: At that precise instant, the rudder pedals became "Able Sugar" (completely useless), and the joy stick could not be budged either fore or aft. **1957** J.L. Barrett *D.I.* (film): Thirty days in the brig and you'll go Able Sugar. [**1961** L. Sanders *4-Yr. Hitch* 23: Commander Ape-Shit...Ol' Able-Sugar.]

aboard *adv.* **1.** Orig. *Naut.* (of food or, esp., drink) in one's stomach. Cf. BOARD.

1833 N. Ames *Old Sailor's Yarns* 68: Old Cuff was ashore on liberty and...likewise had his "beer aboard." **1895** F.P. Dunne, in Schaaf *Dooley* 275: Hogan—th' big slob, he come with a kag of nails aboord. **1917** Empey *Over the Top* ch. i: He had about four "Old Six" ales aboard. **1942** W.L. White *Expendable* 7: I put aboard the thickest charcoal-broiled filet mignon I could buy there. **1945** Colcord *Sea Lang.* 20: He's never ugly, no matter how much he has aboard.

2. *Baseball.* on base. [The 1907 quot. has been erroneously cited by Nichols, "Baseball Terminology," as an occurrence of this term.]

[**1907** *McClure's Mag.* (Apr.) 680: "Git a board!" he now advised sarcastically, while the man on third suggested a "shovel" as probably more effective.] **1939** E.J. Nichols *Base Term.*: Aboard. On base. **1950** P. Cummings *Dict. Base.*: Two men on base: "Two aboard." **1966** *RHD*: A homer with two aboard. **1992** *Olympic Games* (NBC-TV) (July 19): He'll go deep with two men aboard.

¶ In phrases:

¶ **all aboard** ready to take action.

1868 H.I. Williams *Beauty* 13: Getchem was all aboard. How could he cut out her companion?

A-bomb *n.* [after *A-bomb*, informal for *atomic bomb*] **1.** a kind of alcoholic mixed drink.

1945–48 *USMC Marianas Coll.* (unp.): What is your capacity for...Rye Scotch Wine Beer...A Bomb Boiler Maker [etc.]?

2. *Drag Racing.* a converted Model-A Ford capable of exceptionally rapid acceleration.

1951–53 in *AS* XXIX 53: *A-Bomb*...a "hopped up" Model A Ford. **1957** *Life* (Apr. 29) 140: *A-bomb*: Modified Model A Ford.

3. *Narc.* a cigarette containing a mixture of cannabis and an opiate, or of cannabis and cocaine.

1970 Landy *Underground* 21: *A-bomb*...Cigarette made of...marijuana and heroin or opium and hashish. **1972** *Nat. Lampoon* (Oct.) 41: Marijuana and Heroin [cigarette] (A-bomb). **1973** D.E. Smith & Wesson *Uppers* 142: *A-bomb*. Mixture of marijuana and cocaine.

A-bone *n.* [patterned after *T-bone*, a Model T] *Drag Racing.* a Model-A Ford.

1951–53 in *AS* XXIX 53: I hear Jim built up a hot A-bone. **1966** W.G. Parks *Drag Racing* 223: *A-bone*—Model-A Ford. **1990** P. Dickson *Slang!* 23: *A-bone*. Model-A Ford, especially one that has been converted into a...street rod.

abort *n.* *Mil. Av.* a foul-up; mess; snafu; ABORTION, 2.

1978 Former USAF missile crewman, served 1972–73: An *abort* was anything that screwed up—a date, a fishing trip, whatever. **1979** Former WAF A3c: [When I was in Florida in 1958, the air force flight engineers] used to say, "That date was an abort all the way," meaning the girl didn't do what they wanted. The rats.

abortion *n.* [cf. *OED*, def. 3] **1.** an object, esp. a machine, of ludicrous or ungainly appearance; (*also*) an unreliable mechanical device that provokes anger by breaking down.

[***1865** Sala *Diary* II 21: But who will find a rhyme for that most unrhythmical abortion—the policeman's helmet?] **1943** Wakeman *Shore Leave* 31: "I'd like to know the guy who designs these abortions," I said, pointing to the juke box. **1951–53** in *AS* XXIX 53: Get that abortion out of my way. **1957** Kohner *Gidget* 27: An old beaten-up [surfboard] with a lot of notches....."What about this abortion?" **1958** McCulloch *Woods Words*: *Abortion*—A queer piece of machinery....Also a swear word used on any...machine...which breaks down. **1975** N.Y.C. man, age 27: The damn [automobile]'s an abortion and it's not even paid for yet.

2. a hateful or ludicrous undertaking or enterprise; fiasco.

1949 Van Praag *Day Without End* 69: Christ, what an abortion! **1969** *Playboy* (Sept.) 114: I agree that the draft system in the U.S. is an abortion as it stands, but I don't think a lottery system is any solution. **1973** R. Roth *Sand in Wind* 227: Let's get this abortion over with. **1978** *Penthouse* (Apr.) 130: The guy that runs this abortion charges into the TV circle.

3. a very ugly person.

1968 Baker et al. *CUSS* 69: *Abortion*. An ugly person, female. **1972** R. Wilson *Forbidden Words* 13: Who's that abortion at the door? **1979** Univ. Tenn. student, age 30: How can she date that abortion?

about half *adj. & adv.* **1.** *adv.* very, quite, exceptionally.

1962 N.B. Stone *Ride High Country* (film): That old man is about half rough. **1979** Univ. Tenn. student, age 24: She's about half cute.

2. *adj.* feeling well.

1969 *Current Slang* I & II 1: About half...Well, relatively happy...South Dakota.—How are you? I'm about half. **1975** Univ. Tenn. students: "How are you?" "Oh, 'bout half."

abs *n.pl.* *Bodybuilding.* the abdominal muscles.

*a***1984** in *AS* LIX (1984) 198: *Abs n* Abdominal muscles. **1989** *U.* (Spring Break Issue) 26: Got a yearning for bulging biceps, washboard abs and gorgeous glutes? **1992** *Sports Close-Up* (CNN-TV) (July 12): Where are your abs? What happened to your stomach muscles?

absobloodylutely *adv.* absolutely. *Rare* in U.S.

[***1914** *OEDS*: Absoballylutely.] **1923** McAlmon *Companion Vol.* 191: It's the absobloodylutely awful censors. ***1935** in *OEDS*. **1942** *ATS* 25: Absobloodylutely.

absofuckinglutely *adv.* absolutely.—usu. considered vulgar. Cf. FUCKING, *infix*.

*1921 *Notes & Queries* (Nov. 19) 415 [ref. to WWI]: The soldier's actual speech...was absolutely impregnated with one word which (to use it as a basis for alliteration) the fastidious frown at as "filthy"....Words were split up to admit it: "absolutely" became "abso-----lutely." ***1945** S.J. Baker *Austral. Lang.* 258: Transconti-bloody-nental, abso-f-----g-lutely, inde-bloody-pendent. **1970** Major *Afro-Amer. Slang* 19: *Absofuckinglutely*: without doubt. **1973** Huggett *Body Count* ch. viii: That's right, Carlysle, that's abso-fucking-lutely right. **1985** Bodey *F.N.G.* 224: "Like, don't it seem like the time has gone fast now?" "Abso-fuckin'-lutely." **1987** Pedneau *A.P.B.* 228: "Do I detect some anger?" "Abso-fucking-lutely."

absogoddamlutely *adv.* absolutely.

1962 Viertel *Love & Corrupt* 122: This I will absogoddamlutely do.

absorb *v.* to eat or drink.

1874 *Hist. Mulligan Guard* 19: They...absorbed the red-eye themselves. **1885** "Lykkejaeger" *Dane* 90: I absorbed what "hen fruit" and "cow juice" I considered necessary for my health and strength. **1901** W. Irwin *Sonnets* (unp.): Little Willie...helped absorb the grub. **1903** A.H. Lewis *Black Lion* 167: It's as true as that burgundy you're absorbin'. **1928** Carr *Rampant Age* 174: Le's go absorb a few...ha-dogs. **1945** O'Rourke *E Co.* 28: He saw a man...returning from absorbing a lot of PX beer.

absotive *adj.* [prob. back formation fr. ABSOTIVELY] absolute.

1924 in *Amer. Legion Wkly.* (Jan. 2, 1925) 4: Well, at last we got our absotive orders.

absotively *adv.* [*absol*utely + posi*tively*] absolutely and positively. Also (*vulgar*) **absogoddamntively.**

1926 Wood & Goddard *Dict. Amer. Slang*: Absotively. Absolutely and positively. **1936** Levin *Old Bunch* 29: "Positively, Mr. Gallegher?" "Absotively, Mr. Shean!" **1956** "R. Macdonald" *Barbary Coast* 51: I'm absotively delighted to see you again. **1976** Dills *CB* (ed. 3): *Absotively and Posilutely*: definite agreement. **1977** Univ. Fla. student, age 25: I had a friend who had "*Absotively and Posilutely*, Mr. Weevil" painted on his van. **1986** Ciardi *Good Words* 92: My army instructors in WWII were overwhelmingly Southerners...and such flourishes as *absogaddamntively* and *posifuckinglutely* flowed from them constantly. **1993** *Garfield & Friends* (CBS-TV): "Are you certain...?" "Absotively posilutely."

absotootly *adv.* absolutely.

1954 Blackburn *Legend of D. Crockett* (film): There's nothin' so absotootly irresistible as an old-fashioned grin. **1974** N.Y.U. student, age 20: Oh, absotootly.

absquat *v.* [fr. ABSQUATULATE] to abscond, depart.

1868 [H.W. Shaw] *Billings on Ice* 100: Then, if circumstancis made it imperativ, they closed their bissiness by affekting an honorabil compromise, *now*, they "cave in," "squeal," or "absquat."

absquatiate *v.* [pseudo-L, app. < *ab*scond + *squat* + repudi*ate* (or a similar word), but perh. merely a misprint for *absquatilate*, var. ABSQUATULATE] to abscond or depart.

1839 in Marryat *Diary* 263: The editor of the *Philadelphia Gazette* is wrong in calling *absquatiated* a Kentucky *phrase*....It may well prevail there, but its origin was in South Carolina....By the way...*absquatalized* is the true reading.

absquattle *v.* [shortening and alter. of ABSQUATULATE] to abscond or depart.

  1842 Strong *Diary* I 184: So Governor Dorr has run away again—fairly absquattled—sword and all. **1848** W.E. Burton *Waggeries* 17, in *DA*: Let's licker one more round and then absquattle.

absquatulate *v.* [pseudo-L, < *ab*scond + *squat* + *-ulate* (as in spec*ulate*)] **1.** to depart or abscond; flee, run away.

  1830 *Painesville* (Ohio) *Telegraph* (June 15) 1, in *DA*: Obsquatulate—to mosey, to abscond. **1834** [S. Smith] *Jackson* 36: By golly, if you absquotulate, you are ded before you can say Jack Robinson. **1837** Bird *Nick* II 87: Your blooded brown horse has absquatulated. **1842** in Thornton *Amer. Gloss.*: The example of our absquatulating cashier. **1846** McClellan *Mex. War Diary* 13: My quarters in the Camargo…were the *Palace of Don Jesus*, the brother of the Alcalde—he (the Don) having absquatatated [*sic*]. **1855** Burgess *500 Mistakes* 48: "He has absquatulated and taken the specie with him:" *absconded* is a more classical word. **1858** in *DA*: That wouldn't make a dew drop absquatulate from a rose leaf. **1862** in Thornton *Amer. Gloss.*: We'll absquatilate with the horses. **1873** [Perrie] *Buckskin Mose* 18: The vagabond had "absquatulated" with the whole of the joint-stock funds. **1874** Carter *Rollingpin* 17: I give you one hour to raise the wind, so git up and git! Dust! Obsquatulate! *a*1979 *Time*, in *World Book Dictionary*: Anybody who has read a thriller by Ian Fleming is bloody well aware why the Russians have absquatulated with so many of Britain's state secrets. **1989** *Boston Globe* (Jan. 9) 15: Harvard students do not keep fowling pieces in their studies anymore, and the last partridge absquatulated from Somerville shortly after the Civil War.

  2. (facetiously, of things) to separate, fall away.

  1842 in Thornton *Amer. Gloss.*: The shingle had absquatulated from the shutter.

absquatulation *n.* a sudden disappearance or absconding.

  1847 H.N. Moore *Fitzgerald & Hopkins* 164, in *OED*: Artaxerxes and Euphrosyne, after the absquatulation of their pet daughter with the Irish nobleman incog.,…were completely confounded. **1849** *Knickerbocker* (Nov.) 407: I'll risk my pile that his mammy ain't apprised of his absquatilation. **1862** *First Minnesota* (Berryville, Va.) (Mar. 11), in *DA*: Our short residence in Berryville, and the sudden absquatulation of the local editor, is our apology for the meagre variety in the local column. **1884 in *OEDS*. **1942** *ATS* 59: Departure…*Absquatulation*.

absquatulator *n.* [fr. ABSQUATULATE] an absconder.

  1842 in Thornton *Amer. Gloss.*: The career of a foreign absquatulator.

absquatulize *v.* [pseudo-L, < *ab*scond + *squat* + *-ulize*; cf. ABSQUATULATE] **1.** to abscond or depart.

  1829 *Camden* (S.C.) *Jrnl.* (July 3) 3, in *PADS* XXI 19: *Absquatulize*…to top one's broom, to hop the twig, to go on leg-bail. **1839** in Marryat *Diary* 263: *Absquatalized* is the true reading. **1839** in *AS* XXXVII 22: *Absquatalise*, to be off; *absquatalised*, gone—gone, for instance to Texas or—the devil know where.

  2. to drive away, expel.

  1839 *Ky. Observer*, in *DA*: "Yes, you low, vulgar, ill-born, illiterate scamp; I'll absquatalise you in an instant,"…raising his foot to effect his purpose.

Abyssinia *interj.* [pun on *I'll be seeing you*] I'll be seeing you! So long!

  1934 Weseen *Dict. Amer. Sl.* 173: *Abyssinia*—I'll be seeing you. **1935** *AS* (Dec.) 316: The cant word in the last two or three years that has been popular in the United States and lately penetrated here [*sc.* London] is "Abyssinia," which was supposed to be the knowing way of saying, "I'll be seeing you." **1937** in Galewitz *Great Comics* 39: "G'bye now!" "Abyssinia!" **1976** Flexner *Amer. Talking* 179: The cute *Abyssinia*…saw some jive use in the 1930's.

Abyssinian polo *n.* [patterned after AFRICAN GOLF] *Gamb.* the game of craps. *Joc.*

  1942 *ATS* 704: Game of Dice. Abyssinian polo, African dominoes, [etc.]. **1977** Garcia *Crooked Gambling* 264: *Abyssinian Polo*—A dice game.

accident *n.* ¶ In phrase: **have an accident, 1.** *Und.* to be arrested.

  1936 Van Cise *Fighting Underworld* 301: *Accident*—When a crook is arrested. **1941** Brackett & Wilder *Ball of Fire* (film): Benny the Creep had an accident.

  2. Orig. *Und.* to be maimed or killed in retribution.

  1941 Mahin & Grant *Johnny Eager* (film): You know, you're a character

that can always have an accident. **1942–49** Goldin et al. *DAUL* 17: Mister, a lotta ghees…that don't pay off have accidents happen to them. **1960** *Untouchables* (ABC-TV): Last time somebody did that to me they had an accident—for good! **1979** Univ. Tenn. student, age 27: If he doesn't watch his p's and q's he's going to have a little accident.

AC-DC *adj.* [fr. abbr. *AC/DC* for alternating current/direct current] sexually active with or attracted to both males and females; bisexual.

  1954–60 *DAS*: AC-DC…Some jocular use since c1940. **1962** Mandel *Mainside* 230: Maybe I was what they call AC-DC. That's a cute way of putting it, isn't it? **1965** Bryan *P.S. Wilkinson* 243: But Hippolyte was not a true Lesbian, she was AC-DC. **1969** Bartell *Group Sex* 83: "AC-DC" means enjoying homosexual as well as heterosexual relationships. **1982** M. Mann *Elvis* 93: Are you…AC-DC, bisexual? **1993** *English Today* 35 (July) 9: A Gay glossary…*AC-DC* Bisexual.

ace *n.* **I.** Senses in which the idea of preeminence is primary: an outstanding person or thing.

  A. Favorable senses.

  1. the best one; a thing which is held in high esteem; something of merit.

  1840 *Spirit of Times* (Apr. 11) 61: Two of his best "trumps," (leaving out the "Ace," Boston)…have been out of training. **1899** Cullen *Tales* 274: Council Bluffs is all right for the variety show knockabouts to abuse, but it's an ace with me. **1918** *Variety* (Aug. 16) 10: A really funny lyric written by Harry Ruby. It's going to be an "ace" for any number of Hebrew comedians.

  2. an estimable or solidly dependable person; good-hearted individual; "trump."

  1848 in Blair & Meine *Half-Horse* 197: Dick, you're an ace…and the feller what turns you ups got a good hand. **1903** Townsend *Sure* 145: It was up to me to be an ace to two queens, for nobody else…could make it interesting for dose two goils. **1906** *Nat. Police Gaz.* (July 21) 3: If he was half the sport and good fellow you are he'd be an ace. **1906** Green *Actors' Boarding House* 123: Leona, you're an ace. *Ibid.* 183: He was an ace, an' he never whimpered, not once. **1918** Witwer *Baseball to Boches* 46: He's an ace, and we would row our lifeboat from here to Hades if he asked us! **1932** in *AS* IX (1934) 26: *Ace*—A person who can be trusted. **1959** Hecht *Sensualists* 106: You're an ace. **1965** Cassavetes *Faces* 223: Jackson is an ace too. **1979** N.Y.C. man, age 30: She's a real ace. She won't let you down.

  3.a. a person who is outstanding in the possession of a specific quality; an expert, adept, or leading figure.

  1897 in Smith & Smith *Police Gaz.* 208: He had engaged a soubrette who was an ace when it came to looks. **1897** A.H. Lewis *Wolfville* 150: He's a world-beater.…He's shorely four kings an' an ace. **1905** "H. McHugh" *Search Me* 115: You two guys put up your last dollar on me and you didn't know whether I was an ace or a polish. **1910** *N.Y. Eve. Journ.* (Apr. 18) 14: I'm just a deuce and you're the ace. **1919** Darling *Jargon*: *Ace*—One who is a high expert in his work or profession. **1921** Casey & Casey *Gay-Cat* 130: The Seven Soblacoffs. Poland's Premier Aces of the Air [*sc.* acrobats]. **1931** Uhler *Cane Juice* 23: He's…a knock-out ace on the boxing team. **1933** J.T. Farrell *McGinty* 203: We're all aces on the day shift. **1942** *Yank* (Oct. 7) 23: Frank Filchock, ex-Redskin passing ace. **1944** Stiles *Big Bird* 78: And what an ace with the women. It was sensational. **1957** Ness & Fraley *Untouchables* 6: His elder sister married F.B.I. ace Alexander Jamie. **1967** Spillane *Delta* 12: Gavin Woolart, the ace from the State Department, was running the show. **1970** T. Wolfe *Radical Chic* 108: So the young aces from the Mission come trooping in, and they want to see the head man.

  b. Specif. *Baseball.* an outstanding pitcher; (*specif.*) a team's best pitcher.

  1902 in P. Dickson *Baseball Dict.*: McCreedie [a pitcher]…gives promise of being an Ace. **1939–40** Tunis *Tomkinsville* 113: Buzzy Adams, the big Chicago ace, was noted for loosening up the batters. **1942** *Yank* (Sept. 16) 22: Scorer Robs Hank Borowy, Yankee Ace, of No-hitter. **1978** N.Y.C. man, age 29: Guidry's [the N.Y. Yankees'] ace. They gotta win tonight. **1983** Whiteford *Talk Baseball* 75: *Ace*…a team's best pitcher, usually a starting pitcher. **1984** B. James *Abstract 1984* 236: Remember that the [statistical] system is set up to evaluate relief *aces*, not relief *pitchers*. **1989** P. Dickson *Baseball Dict.*: *Ace*…A team's top pitcher.

  4. a prominent individual; BIG SHOT.

  1899 Cullen *Tales* 47: With $420 I could be an ace and get a start in [Chicago]. **1929** M. Gill *Und. Slang* (unp.): *Ace*—Chief or boss. **1947** Goffin *Horn* 225: That guy's a sure 'nuf ace. He packs 'em in at the Vendome.…Louis Armstrong's a big shot.

5. [perh. a direct borrowing of F *as*] *Mil. Av.* a combat airman who has shot down five or more enemy aircraft. Now *S.E.*

1916 McConnell *Flying for France* 108: When a pilot has accounted for five Boches he…is spoken of as an "Ace" which in French aerial slang means a super-pilot. **1918** Chi. *Daily Trib.* (June 1) 3: Lieut. Douglas Campbell of San Jose, Calif., has brought down his fifth German airplane, thereby winning the coveted distinction of "ace." **1934** Weseen *Dict. Slang* 132: *Ace of aces*—an aviator superior to all others. **1943** J.C. Whittaker *Angels* 23: Eddie Rickenbacker, America's No. 1 ace of World War I. **1943** Foss & Simmons *Flying Marine* 154: Nearly every boy in the [flight] wound up an ace. **1978** L. Davis *MiG Alley* 2: Col. Royal "King" Baker makes ace, shooting down his fifth MiG over North Korea, Spring 1953. *Ibid.* 11: Capt. Ralph Parr…became a double ace. **1987** G. Hall *Top Gun* 29: Lt. Randy Cunningham…was…the Navy's first Vietnam ace.

6. [poss. by reanalysis of ACES, *adj.*, 2] close or best friend; (*also*) (one's) hero or idol.

1941 *Pittsburgh Courier* (May 24) 11: Chauncey, Betty's "ace," was still "tops" with the girl. **1942** *Pittsburgh Courier* (Aug. 1) 13: Ace…a good pal. **1946** Boulware *Jive & Slang*: Ace…a good pal. **1954** W.G. Smith *South St.* 267: I'm stickin' my nose in but you're my ace, I got to talk to you. **1962** Gilbert *Jody Calls* 5: Fischle, Fischle, he's my ace;/He's the one with the monkey face. **1967** Mailer *Vietnam* 164: D. J.'s ace, Tex Hyde. **1975** *Black World* (June) 76: A curlin poster of my ace, Muhammad Ali. **1980** Whalen *Takes a Man* 148: Your ace here has about had it. **1988** *Comic Strip* (WKCH-TV): Hey, Bullwinkle! I'm your ace.

B. Ironic, unfavorable senses.

7. [sugg. by **(5)**, above] *Mil. Av.* a pilot or student pilot who has destroyed five or more friendly aircraft.

1918 in Guttersen *Granville* 19: When a fellow smashes five ships he's a "cadet ace." **1924** *Adventure* (Sept. 30) 156: I'm one of the leading German aces now. The only man…who's crashed more American ships than I is Richtofen. **1966** J. Lewis *Marines* 60: He [a U.S. pilot] was a Japanese ace. He crashed six of ours!

8. (used in direct address to a man, usu. implying clumsiness or stupidity).

1925 Faulkner *Soldier's Pay* 46: Whatcher get so drunk for, ace? [**1945** in *AS* XXI 310: *Ace.* A show-off.] **1953** in Russ *Last Parallel* 126: We ain't soldiers, ace. **1961** Terry *Old Liberty* 143: We got a whole fraternity here, ace. **1968** Sackler *Great White Hope* 940: Easy now, ace, let the man preach it. **1976** *Bob Newhart Show* (NBC-TV): You name it, ace—and you got it. **1980** Univ. Tenn. student: Great goin', ace! **1992** *Roc* (Fox-TV): Smooth move, ace.

9. a police officer.

1949 Algren *Golden Arm* 99: The aces shoved old Gold into the wagon with him. **1951** Algren *Chicago* 102: The aces will tell the boy behind the bars, "come on out of there, punk."

II. Senses in which the primary idea is singleness. [fr. the single pip on the playing card]

10. a. a dollar or a dollar's worth.

1898–1900 Cullen *Chances* 106: Just send a few aces along on it….It's 100 to 1. *Ibid.* 108: Get an ace down on Rolling Boer for me. **1907** *Reader* (Sept.) 346: It was a two-ace bet. **1927** in *AS* II 282. **1946** Mezzrow & Wolfe *Blues* 186: Lay an ace [of marijuana] on me so's I can elevate myself. **1952** Brossard *Darkness* 10: Can you lend me an ace? **1966** *RHD.* **1985** *Two Fathers' Justice* (NBC-TV film): Here's an ace. Go treat yourself.

b. *Gamb.* one hundred dollars.

1974 Angelou *Gather Together* 33 [ref. to 1945]: Tag says one ninety dollars….they both yours for an ace fifty. **1981** P. Sann *Trial* 186: A lousy fourteen aces….I slipped seven…new C-notes into each sneaker.

11. *Pris.* a one-year prison term.

1927 *AS* II 282: Ace…one year in jail. **1928** Lawes *Life & Death* 4: Why, an ace is only sleeping time! Don't take your shoes off or you'll miss your train. **1943** *AS* XVII 71: He drew an ace…in the can. **1976** Braly *False Starts* 361: An ace? That's no hill for a stepper.

12. *Narc.* a single item (of several); *esp.* a single cannabis cigarette, a pill, etc.

1938 *New Yorker* (Mar. 12) 40: An ace is a single stick [marijuana cigarette] and sells for 15 cents. **1943** *Time* (July 19) 54: "Gimme an ace" (meaning one reefer), "a deuce" (meaning two), or "a deck" (meaning a large number). **1967** Maurer & Vogel *Narc. & Narc. Add.* (ed. 3) 339: Ace…One of anything. **1980** Folb *Runnin' Lines* 227: Ace…A single barbiturate or amphetamine-filled capsule or pill.

13. a small, usu. round, table designed to seat a single patron. Cf. DEUCE, *n.*, 5.

1961 "T. Williams" *Iguana* 110: Checking in hotels alone, eating alone at tables for one in the corner, the tables waiters call aces. **1979** Minn. woman, age 49 [reportedly heard in nightclubs, early 1950's].

14. *Cinema.* a spotlight that uses a thousand-watt lamp.

1978 Mercer *Film Terms.*

III. Other senses.

15. [for letter *A*; cf. ACE, *v.*, 4] *Stu.* the academic grade A.— usu. constr. with *pull*.

1964 in *Time* (Jan. 1, 1965) 56: Grades need casual names. A's are aces. **1977** Univ. Tenn. grad. student, age 30: I hear he pulled an ace in chemistry. **1979** Former WAF A3c: At the Flight Engineers School at West Palm Beach Air Force Base in 1958 they talked about *pulling an ace* or *getting an ace* or *acing it* on an exam. **1992** *Simpsons* (Fox-TV): Check out this hand [i.e., a report card]—all aces!

16. *Army.* a white serviceman.

1966 in *National Observer* (May 3, 1975) D: The Pentagon likes to emphasize that there is nothing in a serviceman's record jacket, IBM card, or aptitude-test papers that indicates his race. Yet Negroes and whites here [in Vietnam] refer to whites as .001s or "aces" and Negroes as .002s or "deuces."…If you have a unit with 90 deuces and 10 aces, and you get in a firefight, you going to have higher casualties among the deuces.

17. [fr. the acronym, infl. by **(5.)** & **(8.)**, above] a member of an organization identified by the acronym ACE, such as the Army Corps of Engineers.

1975 *Nat. Lampoon Birthday Book* 184: At 0600 hours the next morning, the Aces went in for the big one.

¶ In phrases:

¶ **ace in the hole** [fr. the poker term] an especially effective final resource, esp. if deliberately held in reserve.

1908 Green *Maison de Shine* 86: Eva's acting as if she had a ace in the hole. **1916** Marcin *Cheaters* 100: *Wilson*:…Listen, if you've got anything bigger than a deuce in the hole, I'd like to see it. *Lazarre*:…Well, here's our ace. **1918** in Acker *Thru War* 138: There was always the possibility of the Kaiser having an "ace in the hole." **1936** R. Adams *Cowboy Lingo* 169: The shoulder holster…was often called an "ace in the hole." **1964** Gregory *Nigger* 112: One of the first things I did was borrow $800 from Lilian, my rich ace in the hole.

¶ **ace up (one's) sleeve** [alluding to the presumed practice of cardsharps or prestidigitators] a hidden resource, ploy, or maneuver.

1927 Coe *Gangster* 56: The district attorney had another ace up his sleeve. **1949** Robbins *Dream Merchants* 402: Certificates of equal value would be given for each share of old stock, only there was a…hidden trick. They had an ace up their sleeve. Instead of issuing just two million shares, they would issue four million. **1953** *ATS* (ed. 2) 262: Have an advantage…have an ace *or* card up one's sleeve. **1954–60** *DAS.* **1966** *RHD.* **1967** Spillane *Delta* 103: Any aces I have up my sleeve I keep there or play out to take the pot. **1979** McGivern *Soldiers* 186: There had to be a catch in the deal somewhere, an ace up somebody's sleeve.

¶ **both ways from the ace** from both sides; thoroughly.

1916 S. Lewis *Job* 321: The boss gets it…both ways from the ace. **1927** Raine *Colorado* 226: I'm there both ways from the ace, ma'am.

¶ **hold aces** [or **every ace**] [or **an ace full**] [fr. poker] to effectively control a situation.

1894 C. King *Initial Experience* 111: I think ye hold an ace full, Tonto. **1908** Raine *Wyoming* 241: That sweet relative of yours holds every ace in the deck, and he'll play them, too. **1935** Coburn *Law Rides Range* 100: I'm holdin' all the aces. **1966** Braly *On Yard* 233: That's why he's such a big wheel. He's holding aces.

ace *adj.* **1.** high in esteem.—used predicatively.

1903 Ade *Society* 106: The gabby young Squab who is a ten-strike with the Dolly Grays never stands very Ace with the poker players. *Ibid.* 178: He never could stand Ace with the sure-enough Fellows until he had demonstrated that he was a Good Fellow.

2. expert, "crack"; (*hence*) foremost, outstanding, great.— orig. in prenominal use only.

1930 Gilman *Sob Sister* 27: You know, the *Blade's* ace reporter. **1934** in Brookhouser *Our Years* 449: John Dillinger, ace bad man of the world, got his last night. **1934** Weseen *Dict. Slang* 246: An ace football player, an ace punter, and ace catcher, and ace swimmer, an ace boxer. **1936** Mencken *Amer. Lang.* (ed. 4) 182: I have encountered *ace* lawyers, *ace* radio-crooners, and *ace* gynecologists in headlines. **1952** Grey *Hoods*

14: Mark had gathered together with ace men from every neighborhood on the East Side for this event. It was an all-star gang. *Ibid.* 182: He's the politician's ace strong-arm guy. **1953** Paley *Rumble* 148: Ace men of the waterfront squad knew who controlled every dock. **1970** Landy *Underground* 21: That's really ace! **1977** *'Teen* (Nov.) 17: The British sextet has ace production and a truly lovely sound that makes for good listening. **1980** N.Y.C. woman, age 27: Shelley Duvall is really ace [in the movie *Popeye*]. **1982** *L.A. Times* (Sept. 20) VI 2: Grimes said a lot of the "ace faces," the sharpest guys and girls, were there that night. **1988** *21 Jump St.* (Fox-TV): My new captain thinks I'm real ace, and this is a pretty good gig.

3. Esp. *Black E.* (of a friend) intimate, closest.—used attributively. Cf. ACE BOON COON.

1944 Burley *Hndbk. Jive* 101: Well, Babes, me, your ace stud, was driving it! *Ibid.* 103: My ace lane'll scrape you to the core. *Ibid.* 113: I'm waiting for my ace hen to trilly by. **1954** in Wepman et al. *Life* 39: I thought you were…my ace man. **1964** Rhodes *Chosen Few* 40: This is my ace boy, Blood. **1966** Bullins *Buffalo* 209: What could she gain by messin' round on me with my ace buddy! **1977** Eble *Campus Slang* (Apr.): *Ace buddy*—close friend: Pete is my ace buddy. **1991** *CBS This Morning* (CBS-TV) (Aug. 26): For my ace boy, Harry Smith.

4. satisfactory, O.K.—used predicatively.

1957 Ellison *Web of City* 47: If you wanna bow out, that's ace with me.

5. *Navy.* holding a first-class rating.—used postpositively. Cf. DEUCE.

1974 E. Thompson *Tattoo* 350 [ref. to *ca*1950]: Thirty years in the Navy and *still* only a fireman ace!

ace *v.* **1.** *Und.* to resist (interrogation or cross-examination) tenaciously and successfully.—also used with *it*.

1929 *AS* VI 131. **1942–49** Goldin et al. *DAUL* 17: Mike the burglar is one ghee you can count on to ace it when there's a rumble…on a caper.

2. to maneuver (someone) into (something), esp. through the use of flattery or deceit.—also intrans., to take part uninvited.—constr. with a preposition.

1929 *AS* IV 337: *Ace in*—To place yourself or a friend in the good graces of someone. **1935** Pollock *Underworld* (unp.): *Ace in*, to but-in [*sic*], interfere. **1941** D'Usseau & Collins *Lady Scarface* (film): You're acin' yourself straight for the chair. **1943** *AS* XVIII 71: We aced in…with that mob…by using pressure. **1956** Yordan *Harder They Fall* (film): I could have aced you right into the gutter. **1970** Landy *Underground* 21: I aced in on their conversation. *a*1990 R. Herman, Jr. *Force of Eagles* 9: Both intent on acing the other out in a bid for her attention.

3. to be in charge of; lead.

1953 Paley *Rumble* 93: If you want to go off with Rocky and make him ace the rumble, go ahead.

4. [cf. ACE, *n.*, 15] Orig. *Stu.* to manage (a difficult situation) successfully; *esp.* to score a grade of A on (an examination) or in (a course).—often used with *it*.

1955–57 Felder *College Slang*: *(He) aced it*—He accomplished it with great ease. **1958** J. Davis *College Vocab.*: *Ace*—…to make an A on a test. **1960** Swarthout *Where Boys Are* 19: He aced his courses without buying books. **1963** *AS* XXXVIII 168: To acquit oneself creditably in an examination: *ace it*. **1966** IUFA *Folk Speech*: *Ace a test*…get an A on a test. **1968** Baker et al. *CUSS* 10: *Ace it*. Succeed at the last minute. **1971** N.Y.U. student, age 20: The best thing about it is anybody can ace the final. **1974** Univ. Tenn. student, age 31: I was embarrassed talking to him, but I aced it. **1977** *Atlantic* (Aug.) 30: I developed the conviction that there would always be someone better, someone who aced it every time. **1979** Gutcheon *New Girls* 328: She was going to ace her exams. **1980** Eble *Slang*: *Ace*…used to mean "to make the grade A" but now has generalized to mean "to do well, to get a good grade." **1987** Breathed *Bloom County* (synd. cartoon strip) (Jan. 7): I still feel in control….I think I'm gonna ace this! **1993** *Are You Afraid of Dark?* (Nickelodeon TV): You don't think I can ace a test?

5. to outwit; gain an advantage over.—sometimes constr. with *out*.

1960 Kirkwood *Pony* 122: He started in frowning because I'd aced him on the cat deal. **1961** in *Downbeat* (Jan. 1962) 2: Sis, you've aced me again. **1971** Capon *Peacock* 43: Jesus…aces out the Devil on the Cross and ends up risen…as King of Kings. **1975** Julien *Cogburn* 94: Cogburn? Cogburn aced ya? Let's go.

6. to kill.

1975 R. Parker *Mortal Stakes* 135: If I was Doerr I coulda aced you right there at the curb when we picked you up. **1979** *Howard Duck* (May) 26: You ace Howard, Lester—and the whole world will know

you for what you are! **1981** Ballenger *Terror* 62: It isn't your fault they got aced. **1986** *Larry King Live* (CNN-TV) (Apr. 15): What do you do with a mad dog? You ace him. **1987** *Miami Vice* (NBC-TV): How many more of these dudes we gonna ace?

¶ In phrases:

¶ **ace out, a.** to deprive (someone) of (something), esp. by underhanded or dishonest means.

1933 Ersine *Prison Slang* 14: The gang aced the mark out of his roll. **1939** in W.C. Fields *By Himself* 324: The story of the theatrical mother and the infant prodigy with the inebriate father who is aced out of the family. **1951** West *Flaming Feud* 112: "How come Nick ditched her? She brought plenty business."…"I gotta hunch the Dood aced her out. He and Nick stick closer than two mustard plasters." **1968** Baker et al. *CUSS* 70: *Ace out*. Take someone else's date away. **1977** N.Y.C. bartender, age 30: They were really trying to ace him out of his job. **1982** *L.A. Times* (Feb. 21) VI 1: Earlier at the same hotel, Broger was aced out of a particular suite he'd requested. **1991** D. Anderson *In Corner* 159: Jerry's father and a trainer…were trying to ace me out.

b. to extricate oneself from difficulty by deceit or cleverness.

1951 West *Flaming Feud* 138: If she squawks, we go to the pen. Wallington will ace out of it—he's got pull. **1961** Peacock *Valhalla* 332: Play nuts and you'll ace out of it.

c. see (**5.**), above.

¶ **ace through** to get through safely or easily.

1942–49 Goldin et al. *DAUL* 17. **1983** Univ. Tenn. student: You just aced right through that puzzle.

ace boon *n.* [short for ACE BOON COON] *Black E.* ACE BOON COON.

1971 Dahlskog *Dict. Contemp. Us.*: *Ace boon*…One's very best friend, a buddy.

ace boon coon *n.* [ACE, *adj.*, 3 + BOON COON] *Black E.* closest (black) friend.

1962 Crump *Killer* 200: We're ace-boon-coons, remember? **1963** *Time* (Aug. 2) 14: *Ace boon coon*. Girl friend or buddy. **1965** C. Brown *Manchild* 79 [ref. to *ca*1950]: I knew K.B. about a year before we became ace boon coons. **1966** Reed *Pall-Bearers* 9: Sammy is my ace boon koon so you guys treatum real good. **1967** P. Thomas *Mean Streets* 182: You can share good memories with an ace-boon coon. **1971** H. Roberts *Third Ear*: *Ace boon coon*…good friend. **1984** *TriQuarterly* (Spring) 160: Littleson was my ace boon coon. **1990** *Essence* (Feb.) 54: Lenny Kravitz and Lisa Bonet are a couple. A pair. Friends. Ace boon coons.

ace cool *n. Black E.* closest friend.

1988 Norst *Colors* 189: His main man, his ace cool—Killer Bee.

ace-deuce *n.* [lit., the point 3 in craps; cf. CRAP OUT] a sudden fit of panic or consternation.—constr. with *throw*. Also **acey-deucey.**

1921 *Variety* (July 1) 5: When he climbed thru the ropes I nearly threw ace deuce. He was nearly as big as Mike Gibbons. **1964** *Almanac of Naval Facts*: *Acey-deucey*…a sudden fit or display of temper.

ace-deuce *adj.* first-rate, excellent. Also **acey-deucey.**

1927 *Vanity Fair* (Nov.) 134: "Ace-deuce" is "nothing better." **1954–60** *DAS*: *Acey-deucey*…O.K. **1990** Rukuza *W. Coast Turnaround* 120: The shotgun….For your situation it's acey-deucey.

2. with one side higher than the other; (*specif.*) (of a jockey) riding with one long and one short stirrup. Also as adv. Also **ace-deuce-and-a-half.** [In various card games the ace is the high card and the deuce the low.]

1948 Mencken *Amer. Lang. Supp. II* 768: *Acey-deucy* [*sic*]. A jockey riding with one short stirrup and one long one. **1958** *N.Y. Post* (June 22) 36: Arcaro…explained an acey-deucey rider is one with a high right stirrup and a low left one. This gives a rider more leverage. **1963** Williamson *Hustler* 62: My hat's…sittin' ace-deuce* on my head….*Low and to one side. **1968** Ainslie *Thoroughbred* 463: *Acey-deucy*—riding style in which right stirrup is shorter than left, enabling jockey to balance more easily on turns. **1974** R. Carter *16th Round* 144: Their jailhouse caps were cocked ace-deuce-and-a-half on the sides of their heads. **1979** C. Higgins *Silver Streak* (film): Awright! [Wearing your hat] ace-deuce! That's bad! **1988** Shoemaker & Nagler *Shoemaker* 78: He used to ride acey-deuce all the way, with his left stirrup dropped…low.

ace-flat *adj.* ACE-HIGH; A-ONE.

1941 *AS* XVI 159: *Ace-flat copper*. A decent, fair-minded, considerate policeman.

ace-high *adj.* [in poker, alluding to an *ace-high* straight or a hand with *aces high*] **1.** preeminent; first in favor or esteem; first-rate; faultless; absolute. Also **aces-high.** Cf. DEUCE-HIGH.

[**1885** S.S. Hall *Gold Buttons* 8: Well, Ace-High, what's up now in Hard-Up?] **1896** Ade *Artie* 78: Ain't I told you that anybody I bring stands ace-high? **1902** "J. Flynt" *Little Bro.* 139: Blackie had said't he was goin' to be an aces-high Prushun. **1906** "O. Henry" *Four Million* 51: From the very first dose he was ace-high and everybody else looked like thirty cents to her. **1916** S. Lewis *Job* 194: Sandy's girl thought you was ace-high. **1926** "Max Brand" *Iron Trail* 71: Everything that's known about Larned is ace-high. **1928** Bodenheim *Georgie May* 11: He was supposed to be ace-high with that 36 he totaled. **1928** Dahlberg *Bottom Dogs* 54: A big guy who was aces high [at] fightin' micks. **1960** Stradley *Barbarians* 8: Where we go, we're ace-high and nobody tangles with us. **1964** Redfield *Actor* 159: It is depressing at the start but one goes eventually into an ace-high trance. **1971** Faust *Willy Remembers* 68: A town that will always rate aces-high in my account book. **1972** Jenkins *Semi-Tough* 250: You're aces high with me, Duke.

2. [ref. to games in which the ace is the lowest card] of minimal eminence or value.

1900 S.E. White *Westerners* 113: You wasn't [even] ace-high, Billy.

aceman *n.* [ACE, *adj.*, 2 + *man*] leader (of a street gang).

1953 Paley *Rumble* 50: Pooch was going to help the aceman of the Diggers. *Ibid.* 85: Didn't yuh tell the guys it was just goin' to be a gab between acemen? **1958** Meltzer & Blees *H.S. Confid.* (film): When do I meet the aceman?

ace note *n.* [ACE, *n.*, 10 + *note*] a one-dollar bill.

1929 *AS* IV 337: *Ace note*—A dollar bank note. **1946** Dadswell *Sucker* 96: Ace-note...one dollar. **1967** Maurer & Vogel *Narc. & Narc. Add.* (ed. 3) 339.

ace-one *adj.* A-ONE, best.

1962 in Wepman et al. *Life* 141: If you see another bone from this here gal,/St. Peter will call Satan his ace-one pal. **1989** *Saved by Bell* (NBC-TV): Ace-one!

aces *adj.* **1.** first-rate; quite satisfactory; fine; tops.—usu. used predicatively. Occ. as adv.

1901 "H. McHugh" *John Henry* 11: I tell you boys, it's aces when your lady friend does that after a short clinch. **1903** "H. McHugh" *Coin* 80: Say, you're aces wit' me, Mr. Henry. **1916** Lait *Beef* 189: Everything aces now? **1931** Cressey *Dance Hall* 42: You look aces to me. Come on. **1941** in Grayson *New Stories* 128: He acts like everything's aces. **1968** Westheimer *Sentry* 172: You're aces, Lieutenant....I won't forget it. **1976** *N.Y. Times Bk. Review* (June 13) 1: But no: silent, absent or plain silly, Lardner was aces with them. **1979** *Nat. Lampoon* (Dec.) 59: I hook on with the Tigers and I play aces, man. I hit the ball a fuckin' ton! **1984** W. Allen *Broadway Danny Rose* (film): You're doin' an aces job. **1990** Sydney (CBS-TV): Syd, you're aces! Aces!

2. in a position of friendship and influence.—constr. with *with.*

1932 Berg *Prison Doctor* 210: I know a guy who is aces with—well, never mind who. But he can put the "fix in," don't worry. **1953** *ATS* (ed. 2) 310: In One's Favor; "In Good With."...*in aces with.*

aces and eights *adj.* ACES, 1.

1920 Ade *Hand-Made* 17: "Except for this one peculiarity, you think she's all right?" "Aces and eights."

aces-high see ACE-HIGH.

ace-spot *n.* [ACE, *n.*, 10 + one-*spot*] a one-dollar bill.

1917 *Editor* (Feb. 24) 152: Ace-spot...one dollar.

aces-up *adj.* [lit. (of a poker hand) having aces as the high cards] fine; preeminent; in high favor; ACE-HIGH, 1.

1902 in "O. Henry" *Works* 195: The fasting dodge was aces-up for a while. **1903** "Hugh McHugh" *Coin* 34: Murf,...you're aces-up with me from this moment. **1918** Lardner *Treat 'em Rough* 34: Shorty says that he is a nut that thinks he is aces up with all the mighty. **1932** *AS* VII 328 [at Johns Hopkins Univ.]. **1937** *Life* (June 7) 41 (ad): Camels are aces-up with me.

acey-deucey *adj.* **1.** ACE-DEUCE, *adj.*, 2.

2. [AC-DC, infl. by ACE-DEUCE, *adj.*, 2] sexually active with or attracted to both males and females; bisexual.

1971 Rodgers *Queens' Vernacular* 32: Bisexual...AC-DC, acey-deucey. **1978** Univ. Tenn. student, age 24: Old Fred ain't just queer—he's acey-deucey.

3. (of a friend) closest; ACE, *adj.*, 3.

1977 Bunker *Anim. Factory* 126: Earl described [him] as his "acey-deucey partner"....But you're [like] my son.

Aches and Pains *n.* [facetious folk ety., in allusion to the aches and pains that bathing in the thermal baths there was hoped to cure] *Army.* Aix-les-Bains (Savoie), France, site of a U.S. Army leave area 1917–19. Now *hist.*

1919 [Wilkins] *Co. Fund* 41: I heard one of the fellows say that passes will be open in a few days for Aches and Pains. **1919** Kauffman *Victorious* 351: Aches and Pains. **1926** Boughton *11th Engrs.* 230: Another form of diversion was provided in leaves to Aix-les-Bains, the leave area in the French Alps more familiarly known as "Aches and Pains."

acid *n.* **1.** *Restaurant.* vinegar.

1948 Mencken *Amer. Lang. Supp. II* 751: [Slang of] Food dispensers. *Acid:* Vinegar.

2. [lysergic *acid* diethylamide] the hallucinogen LSD-25; in phr. **acid trip** a TRIP on LSD.

1965 Reeves *Night Action* 24: What'll you have, gin or pot or acid? **1967** *Fact* (May) 32: I kept referring to my use of acid as deepening my religious experience. **1967** Bronsteen *Hippy's Hndbk.* 12: *Acid Rock* n. rock and roll with a psychedelic orientation. **1971** Simon *Fool* 114: My brain began buzzing with the first surges of an acid trip. *Ibid.* 115: I knew this wasn't just another acid high. **1973** Childress *Hero* 99: A breed of junkies and acid trippers. **1979** Univ. Tenn. student, age 20: I think she does acid before every lecture. **1985** B.E. Ellis *Less Than Zero* 83: Heston has some great acid. **1985–87** Bogosian *Talk Radio* 33: Jill was doin' acid, I think. **1992** *Amer. Detective* (ABC-TV): Twenty-five cents a hit for acid. **1993** *New Yorker* (Oct. 11) 101: [Jerry Garcia's] last transcendental acid trip was in the sixties....He developed three-hundred-and-sixty degree vision, died a few thousand times, [etc.].

¶ In phrases:

¶ **put the acid on** to request money of. *Rare* in U.S.

*****1906** in *OED* (Australia). **1912–14** in E. O'Neill *Lost Plays* 144: Probably some fresh "townie" who thinks Jack's indebted to him...and wants to put the acid on him for a dollar or two. *****1935**, *****1938**, *****1945**, *****1947** in *OED* (Australia).

¶ **stand the acid** [ref. to the acid test for the purity of gold] to withstand the severest trial or adversity, "stand the gaff."

1899 A.H. Lewis *Sandburrs* 48: Oh, d' old woman Worden was dead flossy in her day, an' stood d' acid all right, all right, every time.

acid freak *n.* [ACID, 2 + FREAK 'habitual user'] a habitual user of the hallucinogen LSD.

1966 H. Thompson *Hell's Angels* 237: Acid freaks are not given to voluble hospitality. **1969** *ETC.* (June) 173. **1979** Univ. Tenn. student, age 31: That's right from the days of the acid freaks!

acidhead *n.* [ACID, 2 + HEAD 'habitual user'] a habitual user of the hallucinogen LSD.

1966 *Life* (Mar. 25) 28: Los Angeles "acid heads" (LSD users). **1966** Goldstein *One in Seven* 134: The acid-heads (students who use LSD) will raise their sugar cubes in a psychedelic toast. **1967** *Time* (Apr. 28) 11: One would think the demonstrators were almost exclusively New Leftists, acidheads, pacifists, young, and not to be taken seriously. **1967** Yablonsky *Hippie Trip* 131: I know this girl, Lisa, and her three-year-old baby boy is an acid head. She turned him on. **1970** *Playboy* (Apr.) 23: A few acidheads suddenly stopped thinking about their minds. **1988** *L.A. Times* (Mar. 9) VI 1: Aging acid-heads of the 1960s, get ready for the flashback to end all flashbacks! **1993** *New Republic* (May 24) 26: An acid-head ex-Republican-county-chairman.

acid test *n.* [ACID, 2, punning on the *acid test* for the purity of gold] **1.** a hallucinatory experience induced by the taking of LSD and considered as a test of maturity, courage, etc.

1967 Maurer & Vogel *Narc. & Narc. Add.* (ed. 3) 339: A common phrase among [LSD] users is, "Can you pass the acid test?" (meaning, can you take the psychological consequences of using this drug? Have you been initiated to it?) **1979** Former Univ. Ariz. student, age 31: The freaks used to say in the '60s, "Can you pass the acid test?" That meant they wanted you to drop acid. **1992** L. Joplin *Love, Janis* 184 [ref. to 1967]: Leary was trying to form a psychedelic religion. Kesey wanted to hold a "Graduation Test," signaling the next step after the acid test.

2. [app. coined by Ken Kesey's Merry Pranksters group, *ca*1965] a party or public celebration given for the purpose of taking LSD.

1967–68 T. Wolfe *Kool-Aid* 270 [ref. to 1965]: They were pulling off Acid Tests that seemed like they were orchestrated. **1969** Lingeman

Drugs: *Acid test*…parties held in the mid-sixties…the intention being to mimic and enhance the LSD experience. **1992** L. Joplin *Love, Janis* 151 [ref. to 1966]: Organizer Stewart Brand…took over the management of a grand acid test in San Francisco. **1992** *Rolling Stone Album Guide* 288: [The Grateful Dead was the] house band for the famous acid tests that transformed San Francisco into one large freakout.

acid test *v.* to create or enhance an atmosphere suggestive of hallucinations induced by LSD in (a room); make psychedelic.
  1970 Landy *Underground* 22: I'm going to acid test my apartment with strobe lights.

ack-ack *n.* [former British signalmen's pronunciation of *AA* 'antiaircraft'] *Mil.* antiaircraft gun, artillery, or fire.
  1926 Boughton *11th Engrs.* 211 [ref. to 1918]: As soon as one searchlight would find a plane the others would concentrate on the same point, and then all the "ack-acks" [anti-aircraft guns] would turn their fire upon the plane. **1941** *Saturday Evening Post* (Jan. 11) 12C: Marked up on the board to the credit of the Ack-Ack gunners. **1942** *Time* (Feb. 16) 20: His bombers braved uncannily accurate ack-ack fire. **1944** Ramey *In Cavalry* 140: A trail of "ack-ack" was bursting all around the Messerschmitt. **1947** *ATS* (Supp.) 15: *Ack-ack boys*, antiaircraft personnel. *Ibid.* 22: *Ack-ack gun*, an antiaircraft gun. **1955** Sack *Shimbashi* 56: I'm from ack-ack. I'm sort of looking around. **1968** W.C. Anderson *Gooney Bird* 227: They've got ack-ack down there. **1978** in Higham & Williams *Combat Aircraft* 54: Ack-ack fire was still extremely heavy over most targets.

ackamarackus *n.* [pseudo-L] pretentious nonsense, bluff. Also **ackamaracka.**
  1933 D. Runyon, in *Collier's* (Oct. 28) 8: A monocle in one eye…is strictly the old ackamarackuss. **1936** in E. O'Neill *Letters* 456: I…give them both barrels of the old akamarakus! **1950* Tempest *Lag's Lexicon*: "Don't give me any of the old ackamaracka" = don't tell me tall yarns, don't try to bluff me.

ack-emma *n.* [former British signalmen's telephone pronunciation of *AM* for "air mechanic"] *Mil. Av.* an air mechanic. Now *hist.* Also **ak-emma.**
  *1917 Lee *No Parachute* 12: Two ack-emmas ran out when he circled. **1918** [Grider] *War Birds* 164: I have three expert Ak Emmas who do nothing else but look after my bus and do my bidding. **1926** Springs *Nocturne* 260 [ref. to WWI]: An Ak Emma was sucking in gas for me when a mag shorted, and the motor started up and threw him about twenty feet.

ackety-ack *n.* [elaboration of ACK-ACK] *Mil.* ACK-ACK.
  1928 Wharton *Squad* 23 [ref. to 1918]: Overhead, the cadenced beat of the motors is broken by the countless antiaircraft guns—the ackety-acks—that are firing all about.

acknickelous *adj. Rap Music.* marvelous.
  1988 "Three Times Dope" *Greatest Man Alive* (rap song): E.S.T., the acknickelous wonder. **1989** *CBS This Morning* (CBS-TV) (Aug. 30): *Acknickelous* is somethin' that's fresh or really cool.

acorn *n.* **1.** the head.
  1920 Ade *Hand-Made* 45: He got it into the Acorn that each [racetrack] was operated as a Gift Enterprise.
  2. [euphem.] BALLS (in any sense).
  1975 in Holder *Dict. Euphem.* 2: The spray hit him in the acorns. **1989** *Night Court* (NBC-TV): You don't have the *acorns* to reach for the brass ring!

acorn-cracker *n.* [cf. CRACKER] a rustic, a yokel.
  1905 *DN* III 68: Country jakes are sometimes called *acorn-crackers* [in N.W. Ark.].

acro *n.* [shortening of *acrobatics*] *Av.* aerobatic maneuvers.
  1967 H.M. Mason *New Tigers* 105: Acro is fun, and I feel like I can fly that mother out of any attitude and at any speed.

acrobat *n.* usu. *pl. Gamb.* a loaded or unfairly beveled die.
  1924 M. Anderson & Stallings *What Price Glory?* I i: Seven, baby. [*He smiles with satisfaction.*] Look at those acrobats act.

across *adv.* [prob. orig. ellipt. for "across the river, bay, etc.," ref. to specific prisons] to prison.
  1924 G. Henderson *Keys to Crookdom* 416: *Send across.* Send to prison.
  ¶ In phrase:
  ¶ **put** or **toss across** [cf. syn. PUT OVER] to perpetrate (a deception).

1912 *Adventure* (May) 138: So you tossed one across on the Duke. **1913–15** Van Loan *Taking the Count* 86: You ain't going to put anything like that across on me!

act *n.* [all of these senses are likely to be of theat. orig.] **1.** enterprise, undertaking, state of affairs; esp. in phr. of the sort **crab** [or **queer**] **the act** to spoil things; thwart (someone's) plans, to interfere (with someone or something).
  1891 in F. Remington *Sel. Letters* 117: Have got to peg away [earning a living] or the bank act will go to the bow-wows. **1906** H. Green *Actors' Boarding House* 69: If only he would consent to play her act, because…the other pianist would crab it! **1908** McGaffey *Show Girl* 58: A crate of lemons [i.e. idiots] got off to crab the act. **1911** A.H. Lewis *Apaches of N.Y.* 107: Venus shows Hippy how to crab Atalanta's act. **1922** E. Wilson *Twenties* 116: To crab…someone's act. **1931** Stevenson *St. Luke's* 314 [ref. to ca1910]: Insisted he hadn't crabbed the act. **1929–33** Farrell *Young Manhood of Lonigan* 169: When we're sure they can't crab our act, we'll let them know. **1940** O'Hara *Joey* 75: He won't crab our act. **1942** *ATS* 266: Hinder; thwart; balk. Ball up…queer the act. **1945** Hartman & Sharelson *Princess & Pirate* (film): Some middle-aged crooner kept crabbing my act. **1966** H. Thompson *Hell's Angels* 186: All it did was queer the act. **1975** V.B. Miller *Trade-Off* 5: Part of my job is to give [heroin sellers] the hook—pull 'em offstage and cancel their act. **1978** Pilcer *Teen Angel* 118: Coppers were always spoiling their act, making them return the pullovers they stuffed in their bags from Alexander's and telling them to keep moving. **1979** D. Brewer, on WINS radio (June 23): If your youngster is lucky enough to attend a school where junk food is prohibited, don't blow the act at home this summer.
  2.a. customary form of behavior, "routine"; intentions or doings.—constr. with possessive pronoun only.
  1971 H. Roberts *3d Ear* (unp.): *A-C-T* (spelled out) n. activities of greatest interest and immediacy; one's thing. **1974–77** Heinemann *Close Qtrs.* 62: And he'd whip his act on us. "Hey, you troopers! Where's your steel pots? Who is your platoon leader?" **1978** Lieberman & Rhodes *CB* (ed. 2): *Act*—Game; i.e., What is your act? What are you trying to prove? **1978** Truscott *Dress Gray* 429: Christ, man, your act is so full of shit I can hear your asshole puckering. **1980** H. Gould *Ft. Apache* 293: Cool your act, my man. You just get too excited behind this shit. **1984** C. Crowe *Wild Life* (film): I'm sick of your act. You either leave or I'll get someone to throw you out. **1986** Merkin *Zombie Jamboree* 244: I suffer them all to live because snuffing them's not my act.
  b. customary behavior regarded as needing improvement.—esp. in phr. **clean up (one's) act** to begin behaving in a more proper or appropriate fashion, to change (one's) ways for the better.
  1971 *Curr. Slang* (Winter) 3: *Clean up your act!*…To stop swearing, dress nicely, and act like a lady/gentleman. **1974** Univ. Tenn. student, age 23: This place is a mess. I've got to clean up my act. **1975** V.B. Miller *Trade-Off* 88: Like, let's say you spend twenty or so years getting your act cleaned up and you're pretty confident that you can handle almost anything life throws at you. **1977** Sayles *Union* 287: There could be a dozen [who] would look like the kid in the picture, you cut their hair and cleaned up their act a little. **1977** *L.A. Times* (Nov. 6) II 1: "Keep your act straight now, hon," a red-haired, middle-aged guard tells Suzanne. "We don't want to see you back here again." **1979** Univ. Tenn. student, age 26: I've already blown two tests. Time to clean up my act. **1980** *N.Y. Daily News* (Sept. 10) 20: But if what the Liberals are going to do results in the election of Ronald Reagan, all those votes that John Anderson racks up…are not going to help New York, unless…God tells Reagan to change his act. **1990** *World Today* (CNN-TV) (July 27): Northrop has cleaned up its act.
  3. individual, person.—used only with qualifying adj. Cf. *tough act to follow*, below.
  1979 Calif. man, age 33: This Chris sounds like a class act. **1987** *'Teen Mag.* (Jan. 1988) 12: Be a Class Act. **1990** *Cosmopolitan* (Mar.): In this young woman's case, the stealthy acquisition of luxurious trifles only established her as a low-class act.
  ¶ In phrases:
  ¶ **clean up (one's) act** see (**2.b.**), above.
  ¶ **get (one's) act together** to begin to behave more effectively or appropriately; shape up; get started.
  1973 *Zap Comix* 6 (unp.): Get your act together and right on cause I'm going to do a number on the establishment's head! **1976** R. Price *Blood Brothers* 126: You better get your act together, bro. **1978** D. Drysdale, on *ABC Monday Night Baseball* (ABC-TV) (July 24): He's got his act

together and he's pitching very well. **1978** Calif. man, age 33: It's time you got your act together and took it on the road. **1979** *Buck Rogers* (NBC-TV): Why don't we cut out this nonsense till you people get your act together. **1979** *N.Y. Times* (Dec. 16) 7: I'm getting my act together and taking it on the road. **1980** *N.Y. Times* (June 15) IV 4E: The White House reportedly told the Department of Defense "to get its act together." **1989** *New Yorker* (May 9) 6: I could do this if I could get my act together.

¶ **in** [or **into** or **in on**] **the act** involved.—usu. constr. with *get.*

1959–60 Bloch *Dead Beat* 60: Jill got into the act. **1960** J. Miles, in Kennedy *Intro. to Poetry* 46: Then the usher came out and got into the act. **1962** Stephens *Blow Neg.* 165: Now everybody is trying to get into the act. **1966** Elli *Riot* 243: The apple polishers are startin' to get in the act. **1967** Spillane *Delta* 54: "Any heavies in the act?"..."Russo Sabin. He's a hatchet man for Carlos Ortega." **1977** in C. Fuller *UFO Cong.* 346: People hear a story like this and they want to get in on the act. **1979** WINS radio news (Dec. 24): The State Department has hired four New York City law firms to prepare a defense for the hostages [in Iran], but only one firm...is still in the act. **1981** C. Nelson *Picked Bullets Up* 215: Everybody got into the act.

¶ **play** [or **pull**] **the —— act, a.** to involve oneself with (in a manner deducible only from context). Cf. similar use of ROUTINE.

1884 Costello *Police* 475: He...may have done the "baby act" by carrying...an abandoned foundling to the [matron at police headquarters]. **1896** Ade *Artie* 65: I go and get a cigar and do the friendship act. **1904** in *DA*: They did the hospitality act up in great shape. **1972** N.Y.U. student, age 20: I'm still doing my sidewalk act [i.e., walking the sidewalks looking for employment].

b. to behave in the manner of (the specified noun).

1885 in Lummis *Letters* 286: All the time playing the baby act, and whining for help. **1887** *Harper's Mag.* (May) 990: He at once began...to abuse the Negro, accusing him of...doing the dude act in charcoal. **1894** Bridges *Arcady* 56: But I didn't do no cry-baby and holy cherub act when the coppers chased me into the Press Office. **1896** Ade *Artie* 80: She ought to see us doing the slave act there the first of every month. **1903** Ade *Society* 31: It did seem to him that a lot of big, lazy Lummixes were doing the Soldier Act [i.e., "soldiering," loafing]. **1906** "O. Henry" *Four Million* 97: If yer don't know de guy, and he's tryin' to do de Johnny act, say de word, and I'll call a cop in t'ree minutes. **1943** in Kittredge & Krauzer *Great Amer. Detective* 174: Who was the big bald-headed bozo pulling the sneak act?

¶ **tough** [or **hard**] **act to follow** a thing or person hard to surpass or outdo.

1969 N.Y.C. man, age 20: That's a tough act to follow. **1975** in *OEDAS* I: A hard act to follow; after the...surge in GNP, growth is sure to be slower. **1979** Univ. Tenn. student, age 26: "That's a hard act to follow." We used that in high school [in Maryville, Tenn.] in the late '60s. [**1979** Univ. Tenn. Eng. prof., age *ca*50: I'm certain I learned this term in the winter of 1962–63 on my second trip to America [from England]. It struck me as purely American.] **1979** *N.Y. Times Mag.* (Dec. 23) 9: Will the ex-actor he's playing opposite find him a tough act to follow? **1979** *Penthouse* (Dec.) 35: He's a tough act to follow, but you look to me like you can measure up. **1988** *Wkly. World News* (Apr. 12) 38: The Scots are a hard act to follow when it comes to boozing and smoking, according to a new survey in Britain. **1992** *Vanity Fair* (Feb.) 80: Her parents were a hard act to follow, but she has already outdone them.

acting gadget *n. Army.* acting corporal; acting noncommissioned officer.

1944 Kendall *Service Slang: Acting gadget*...acting corporal. **1945** in Shibutani *Co. K* 303: Acting gadgets...Acting NCOs. **1963** J. Ross *Dead Are Mine* 252 [ref. to WWII]: How come you sailed for all those acting gadget details?...Acting Platoon Sergeant, Acting Platoon Guide, Acting First Sergeant.

acting jack *n.* [*acting* + lance *jack* 'lance corporal'] *Army & USMC.* acting corporal or acting sergeant.

1917 *Marines Mag.* (Mar.) 35: Pseudonym—Acting Jack. *Ibid.* (Nov.) 50: Private McAllister was appointed Acting Jack on October 2d, and is performing his new duties like a veteran. **1927** Thomason *Marines & Others* 139: The steam-fitter was an acting-jack—acting corporal, I mean, in no time. **1930** *Our Army* (Feb.) 21: Acting Jack. **1969** Hughes *Under a Flare* 77: Charley had this acting-jack bit on his records when he came in. **1987** Lanning *Only War* 208: These "acting jacks" got nothing for their extra responsibilities except more work.

action *n.* **1.** *Gamb.* **a.** gambling activity.

1887 Francis *Saddle & Moc.* 145: That's my kind [of game]....You get "action" there every turn. No waiting for any durned cards to come up. **1899–1900** Cullen *Tales* 226: Quick action you're giving me for my money, ain't it? **1908** in H.C. Fisher *A. Mutt* 23: Lazell [a racehorse] was scratched yesterday, hence Mutt got no action on his money. **1909** in "O. Henry" *Works* 1520: I've heard of places in this here town where a fellow could have a good game of old sledge or peg a card at keno....Know where a fellow could get action on $9 or $10? **1930** *Sat. Eve. Post* (Apr. 5) 5: There is no real action until a guy is out on a point. **1959** Tevis *Hustler* 99: Somebody told me about a [pool] room called Arthur's where there's action. **1966** Wanderone & Fox *Bank Shot* 63: He was one of the highest rollers and top action men of all time. **1979** R. Foster *Concrete Cowboys* (film): "Poker is my middle name."..."In that back tent there's a lot of action going on."

b. money, profits.—often in phr. **piece of the action** a share in any kind of profit or in any potentially self-serving activity.

1957 Wilbur & Veiller *Monkey on Back* (film): You want a piece of my action, Sam? **1958** Gardner *Piece of Action* 12: A piece of the action on one good retail product and I'll get my own studio and my hours will belong to me. **1963** in H. Ellison *Sex Misspelled* 51: She could go peddle her ass...and raise the action that way. **1968** *Star Trek* (NBC-TV): "What's in it for you?" "A piece of the action." **1971** Di Pippo *Rhetoric* 12: Romeo's got a piece of the action with the whores too. They don't work unless he gets a cut. **1972** Overgard *Hero* 40: And you take a cut off the top of the action? **1974** A. Bergman *Big Kiss-Off* 63: So Uncle Irv figured he'd get some action on...loan-sharking. **1978** *N.Y. Times* (Dec. 15) IV 1: [Peking] is satisfied with a bland assertion that Hong Kong is a part of China—so long as it gets a fair piece of the action that colony's bankers and traders generate. **1979** *Nat. Lampoon* (Dec.) 63: Hell, no. Legalize weed? And have A.J. Reynolds and Salem step all over my action? **1983** R. Salmaggi, on WINS radio (Dec. 31): So director Tobe Hooper will be doing a sequel [to his *Texas Chainsaw Massacre*], but this time he'll be getting a *big* slice of the action.

c. a wager, bet; stakes.

1961 Scarne *Comp. Guide* 68: I was handling about half a million dollars of action a day. **1966** Wanderone & Fox *Bank Shot* 182: The higher the action, the deadlier I shot. **1970–71** Rubinstein *City Police* 376: There is not a single numbers player who...cannot find a writer to take his action. **1980** *Mother Jones* (Aug.) 36: By taking action [i.e., bets] a worker can insure that he will be one of the last workers laid off since the mob will take care of him since he is making money for them.

d. records of wagers and money won and lost.

1970 La Motta et al. *Raging Bull* 13: Slips...Action. Tomorrow's bets....No dough. **1973** Droge *Patrolman* 103: They would ride through the neighborhood in their car and pick up the "action"—gambling records—from the various runners. **1974** Radano *Cop Stories* 171: Pick up whatever action you want....Write it on the sidewalk. Write it on your forehead [for all I care].

2. [prob. sugg. by mil. sense and recent S.E. sense, "excitement"] profitable crime, esp. street crime; brisk criminal activity.

1927 in Hammett *Knockover* 341: "So meet me at Van Ness and Geary before eleven o'clock." "Action?"..."Maybe....Bring your little popgun along." **1935** in R. Nelson *Dishonorable* 295: Sometimes I'm sorry we're [now] respectable. There's no chance for action. **1942–49** Goldin et al. *DAUL* 17: Shape up...tonight, Joe, there's action—a Brooklyn score. **1949** in *Harper's* (Feb. 1950) 73: What kind of action? What's in it? **1963** Braly *Shake Him* 13: It's no burn. There's action in there. You'll find a lot of them holding. **1963** *True* (May) 43: The 18th is a strange precinct: it takes in a piece of almost every kind of action you can find in New York City. The con games are big and slick...the muggings are vicious and quick, [etc.]. **1974** Rose *Storyville* 174: By comparison, the "action" still to be found in the vicinity of the old Negro red-light district...seems almost benign in its honest depravity. **1980** Gould *Ft. Apache* 97: Street action in numbers and drugs had stopped.

3.a. erotic motions of the hips and pelvis; (*hence*) sexual ability.

1929–30 Dos Passos *42d Parallel* 354: "Jeez, baby, you got some action," he said after they'd been dancing a little while. **1953** Paley *Rumble* 72: The guys knew he only went for girls with action. **1961** Russell *Sound* 128: She's a dancer, hell, and she got a lot of action. I mean them Spic women really give you something in the feathers. **1970** G. Walker *Cruising* 46: Lynch saw her hard, round bottom move in tight, rhythmic circles. She had some action there, he thought. **1973**

Hirschfield *Victors* 134: Benny, you're hung like a horse, great action.
b. sexual intercourse; sexual activity. [The example in brackets, although used in a sexual sense, was prob. intended to mean merely "activity."]
[*1609 Shakespeare *Pericles* IV ii 7: They [*sc.* prostitutes] with continual action are even as good as rotten.] **1956** in Algren *Lonesome Monsters* 195: "The hell with all that," the apprentice pimp decided. "How about some action?" **1957** Laurents & Sondheim *West Side Story* 179: How's the action on your mother's mattress, Action? **1963** Braly *Shake Him* 146: I thought he wanted some action himself. **1966** H. Thompson *Hell's Angels* 192: Rape's no fun, anyway…and we get all the action we can handle just standing around. **1971** *N.Y. Times Mag.* (Nov. 28) 92: Only action he get is with his hand. **1976** Univ. Tenn. student, age 24: I wouldn't go out with her if I didn't think there's a chance for some wild action. **1977** *Urban Life* VI 182: A sexual exchange or as it is usually called, "action."
c. interesting or exciting activity; (*esp.*) active, provocative socializing with the opposite sex.
1958 Frees *Beatniks* (film): What's goin' on in there?…Any action? Women? Chicks? **1959** on *Golden Age of TV* (A & E-TV, 1988): Let's check the action in the saloon! **1960** *Mad* (Sept.) 20: This kick is a wild bit you can pull on that cat who's always looking for a party to go to, and who keeps bugging you to clue him in on where the action is. **1966** IUFA *Folk Speech*: Being in on all the action…being at the proper college gang places. **1968** S. Ross *Hang-Up* 21: "Where are you going?"…"The Strip, where else?" "Too early for any action." **1974** *Nat. Lampoon* (Apr.) 52: I go into those singles bars once in a while. I check out the action. I'm only human, y'know. **1976** Rosen *Rim* 70: A supersquare, she decided…screw him, she'd hit the action later. **1989** "Tone Loc" *Funky Cold Medina* (rap song): Cold coolin' at a bar, and I'm lookin' for some action.
4.a. that which is performed or done; manner of doing; doings; (*hence*) situation, state of affairs; concern; in phr. **What's the action?** (used as a greeting).
1943 *Yank* (Jan. 13) 20: Those studs put down some fine action [i.e., play music well]. **1944** Burley *Orig. Hndbk. Jive* 15: I'm down with the action to my own satisfaction. *Ibid.* 133: *Action*: motivating force, issue, situation, proposition. **1955** Stern *Rebel Without a Cause* (film): You understand the action? Sticking but no jabbing [in a fight with switchblades]. **1962** Crump *Killer* 97: There's to be no fighting among ourselves….So cool that action or suffer the penalty. **1962** Serling *New Stories* 10: Sorry I'm late, boss….What's the action? **1965** C. Brown *Manchild* 314: They were bad enough to cut each other's throats, shoot each other…and all that sort of action. **1965** Harvey *Hudasky's Raiders* 176: Hey, Cummings?…What's the action? **1966** Wanderone & Fox *Bank Shot* 198: I'm getting ready to do a television series with…Elizabeth Taylor and Kim Novak and Natalie Wood. You can't hardly beat that kind of action. **1971** Sorrentino *Up from Never* 4: Would he go fa that action? *Ibid.* 186: Maybe he ain't got the guts for this action. **1977** *Kojak* (CBS-TV): This is Lieutenant Kojak. The action is scrubbed. **1978** Univ. Tenn. student, age *ca*20 [calling attention to a newspaper story]: Hey, dig this action! **1981–85** S. King *It* 359: "Piss on this action," Rich muttered frantically to himself.
b. thing, stuff.
1960 *Mad* (Sept.): Cool it—when you stash some action in the refrigerator. Pad—the action you write on. **1968** Heard *Howard St.* 140: That was some boss action [*sc.* narcotics], baby. I mean it swung.
c. preference; interest; desire; way of doing things; business.
1966 Braly *On Yard* 202: When they learn that ain't your action, there's going to be a lot of suckers…hitting hard. **1972** Rodgers *Queens' Vernacular*: *Action*…one's ideology, philosophy of living. "What's his action?" **1976** *S.W.A.T.* (NBC-TV): "What was his action?" "Ritchie had a piece of everything."
d. (used postpositively as an intensifier of an activity, situation, etc.).
1980 L. Birnbach *Offic. Preppy Hbk.* 220: Heavy —— action…Whatever one does a lot. "Heavy tanning action." **1987** Univ. Chicago student, age 19 (coll. J. Sheidlower): You want to go down to the gym for some bench press action? **1989** *CBS This Morning* (CBS-TV) (May 5): This is biscuits and gravy with a little bacon action right here. **1992** N.Y.C. man, age 23 (coll. J. Sheidlower): I think it's time for some serious sleep action.
5. *Und.* a handgun; a weapon.
1969 H. Brown *Die Nigger* 86: I had my action with me, a .38.
¶ In phrases:

¶ **piece of the action** see **(1.b.)**, above.
¶ **tighten (one's) action** [poss. from guitar tuning] to start acting more effectively.
1976 Braly *False Starts* 224: Tough enough, Cherokee, [if] you tighten your action.
¶ **where the action is** [cf. 1960 quot. at **(3.c.)**, above] the scene of greatest activity, interest, opportunity, etc. Now *S.E.*
1966 *Life* (June 24) 76: To live you've got to know where the action is, you've got to know who the phonies are, and you've got to know what risks to take. **1966** *Life* (July 29) 16: Creative literary types who are serious about their calling will have to come to science, where the action is. **1967** *N.Y. Times*, in *BDNE* 31: It is clear today that the early years of a child's life are critically important in the development of learning processes and capacity. "In many ways," he observed, "that's where the action is." **1968** *Harper's* 96: [He]…transferred to the University of Chicago, which was where the action was supposed to be in the 1930s. **1978** Rutgers Univ. physicist, age 30: [The study of] solar neutrinos is where the action is in physics. **1990** *U.S. News & W.R.* (Dec. 31) 14: Combatants are where the action is, but the families are at the mercy of media, rumor and speculation.

actorine *n.* [*actor* + *-ine* (fem. suff.)] actress.
1896 Ade *Artie* 49: She said she was an actorine. **1915** in *DN* V 6: Looking agonized seems to be the chief business of the moving picture actorines. **1936** *AS* XI 28: *Actoreen.*

Ada from Decatur *n.* [pun on *eighter* + *Decatur* (Ala. or—as in 1984 ex.—Tex.) for rhyme] *Craps.* the point eight.
1918 Crowe *Pat Crowe* 87: You probably recall the thrilling adventures of Snake Eyes, Little Joe,…Ada from Decatur, and Box Cars. **1920** in Fitzgerald *Stories* I 212: Ada from Decatur rolled over the table. [**1939** Hart *135th Sq.* 30: Eighter from Decatur, the County seat of Wise.] **1978** Hayakawa *Lang. in Thought & Act.* 174: In craps, the dice-thrower will call for "Little Ada from Decatur," and if he rolls a seven before a eight, he attributes his failure to "the wrong kind of call." **1984** Sample *Racehoss* 30: Ada!! frum Decatur, the county seat a' Wise. *Eight!*

Adam *n.* **1.** [ADAM TYLER] *Und.* accomplice.
*1797 in Partridge *Dict. Und.* 4. **1859** Matsell *Vocabulum* 7: *Adam.* An accomplice; a pal. **1956** *AS* (May) 97: The *sneaker* [narcotics smuggler] needs an *Adam*, or partner, who is an *ace*…that is, a man who can be depended on.
2. (In various facetious phrases ref. to time immemorial).
1839 *Spirit of Times* (Oct. 26) 397: As great races…as have ever been run since Adam was a yearling. **1839–40** [Cobb] *Green Hand* I 37: He spoils his manners by detailing what was stale before Adam was a reefer or Eve out of leading strings. **1896** Hamblen *Many Seas* 65: Some of them…had been on the coast since the year one when Adam was an "oakum" boy in the Brooklyn navy yard. **1936** Partridge *DSUE* 949: When Adam was an oakum boy at Chatham Dockyard. Indefinitely long ago. [in use] ca. 1860–1900. **1945** Colcord *Sea Lang.* 21: Adam was an oakum-boy, since. This phrase comes from the shipyards….It is fairly common alongshore. **1993** *N.Y. Times* (Sept. 17) C1: There has not been a fresher or brighter morning since Adam named the animals.
3. (In facetious variants of colloq. *not know someone from Adam* [*1784, OEDS]).
1894 in *DARE*: He didn't know me from Adam's off-ox. **1908** *DN* III 285: He wouldn't know me from Adam's housecat. **1912** *Ibid.* 570: He wouldn't know (somebody or something) from Adam's off ox. **1941** Roberts & Sanford *Honky-Tonk* (film): I don't know these two dudes from Adam's off ox, but I'm gonna see this is a fair fight. **1965–70** in *DARE* s.v. *Adam's off-ox* [165 informants].
4. MDMA (methylene dioxymethamphetamine), an amphetamine derivative used as a psychotropic drug. Cf. ECSTASY.
1985 *L.A. Times* (Mar. 29), in *OEDAS* II 29: Yet another new drug…MDMA….On the street, its name is "ecstasy" or "Adam." **1985** *Psychology Today* (May) 68: MDMA…a psychedelic drug sold on the street as "Adam" or "Ecstasy." **1989** E. Goode *Drugs in Am. Soc.* (ed. 3) 182: Consider MDMA, called "ecstasy" on the street (and "Adam" by some), is [*sic*] a synthetic derivative of amphetamine. *1990 T. Thorne *Dict. Contemp. Sl.*: *Adam* is an acronym from the initials, used by middle-class Londoners during the vogue for the drug since the mid-1980s.

Adam and Eve *n.* [facetious allusion to Genesis 4:1] an order of two poached or fried eggs.—usu. in phr. **Adam and Eve**

on a raft two eggs on toast.—with *wrecked*, scrambled.
1909 T.A. Dorgan, in Zwilling *TAD Lexicon* 14: Gimme Adam an' Eve on a raft—Wreck em. [Arrow pointing:] Poached eggs on toast. **1916** *Editor* (June 3) 582: Adam and Eve on a slippery raft [i.e., on buttered toast]. *****1921** *N & Q* (Nov. 26) 424 [ref. to Brit. Army, WWI]: *Adam and Eve on a raft.* Poached eggs on toast. **1923** McKnight *Eng. Words* 45: Adam and Eve on a raft, wreck 'em. *****1925** Fraser & Gibbons *Soldier & Sailor Words* 3 [ref. to Brit. Army, WWI]: *Adam and Eve on a Raft*: Eggs on toast. *Adam and Eve Wrecked*: Scrambled eggs. **1930** "D. Stiff" *Milk & Honey* 198: Adam and Eve on a raft....With their eyes open. **1978** MacKillop & Cross *Speaking of Words* 175: Almost everyone who has ever worked in a restaurant...knows a handful of words for standard items on the menu—"Adam and Eve on a raft," etc. **1990** *Mystery Science Theater* (Comedy Central TV): Adam and Eve on a raft!

Adam's ale *n.* drinking water. *Joc.*
*****1643** in *F & H* I (rev.) 16: They have been...allowed only a poore pittance of Adam's ale, and scarce a penny bread a day. *****1698–99** "B.E." *Dict. Canting Crew*: *Adam's-ale*, Water. **1708** in Whiting *Early Amer. Provs.* 2: And was in fact but Adam's ale. **1821** Waln *Hermit in Phila.* 26: And must go home and live on *Adam's Ale* and *Aqua Pumpaginis*. **1837** A. Greene *Glance at N.Y.* 185: The Croton water...will prove highly agreeable to such persons as value themselves on their connoisseurship...of "Adam's ale." **1861** Heartsill *1491 Days* 40: At length we are forced to camp; and that too without any of "Adam's Ale." **1898** Green *Va. Folk Speech* 38. **1923** McKnight *Eng. Words* 45: Chaser of Adam's ale (glass of water). **1938** in *AS* (Apr. 1939) 89: I drink nothin' but Adam's ale. **1949, 1966** in *DARE*. **1982** *N.Y. Times* (Aug. 29) 9: The rhubarb "sass" and Adam's ale (water) are passed. **1988** *Chicago Tribune* (June 9) Food Guide 1: Water becomes *Adam's ale* in over-the-counter argot. *****1991** *Daily Telegraph* (Apr. 8) 25: Tony Bonvoisin bottles and sells water, an increasingly common activity in a country still developing its thirst for Adam's ale.

Adam's arm *n.* a shovel.
1942 *ATS* 77: Shovel; spade. *Adam's arm*. **1965** O'Neill *High Steel* 269: *Adam's arm*: a shovel.

Adam Sourguy *n.* [a cartoon character created by J.A. Murphy in 1909] *Theat.* a sour-tempered pessimist.
1910 *Variety* (June 18) 10: Adam Sowerguy starting his show. **1923** *N.Y. Times* (Oct. 14) VIII 4: *Adam Sourguy*—A backstage pessimist in the music hall.

Adam's whip *n.* penis.
1952 Larson *Barnyard Folklore of Idaho* 81: Penis...prong, dong,...Adam's whip, tally-whacker.

Adam Tyler *n.* [orig. unkn.] *Und.* a confederate of a pickpocket.
*****1665** R. Head *Eng. Rogue* (unp.): Tip the Cole to Adam Tyler...Give what money you pocket-picked to the next party, presently. *****1698–99** "B. E." *Dict. Canting Crew*: *Adam-Tiler*, a Pickpocket's Camerade, who receives Stolen Money or Goods, and scowers off with them. *****1725** *New Canting Dict.*: Tip the Coal to Adam-Tiler, i.e. Give the Money, Watch, Handkerchief, &c., to a Running Companion, that the Pickpocket may have nothing found upon him, when he is apprehended. **1859** Matsell *Vocabulum*: *Adam-Tiler*. A fellow whose business it is to receive the plunder from the "File"—the one who picked the pocket—and get away with it. **1866** *Nat. Police Gaz.* (Nov. 24) 3: It was rare to see a "file," "Adam Tyler" or "bulk" on the cars.

Ada Ross *n. Craps*. ADA FROM DECATUR.
1942 *ATS*: Ada Ross the stable hoss...a throw of eight. **1984** Sample *Raceboss* 30: Got eight for a point...."Oh Ada Ross was a pacin' good hoss!"

addle cove *n.* [addle + COVE 'guy', on pattern of *addlepate*] *Und.* fool, "sucker." [The 1955 quot. is based on the appearance of the term in Matsell and does not reflect independent testimony.]
1859 Matsell *Vocabulum*: *Addle-Cove*. A foolish man. **1955** Kantor *Andersonville* 118: Collins is the name, you addle cove—Willie Collins!

addlings *n.* [prob. add + *-ling* + *-s*] *Naut.* pay. *Rare* in U.S.
*****1846** in *EDD* (Northamptonshire). **1889** *United Service* (Sept.) 279: The best we [American seamen] can wish is an accumulation of "addlings" (pay), plenty of "dibbs" (ready cash), and no "dead horse" (back debt) to work off. *****1961** Burgess *Dict. Sailing*: *Addlings*. Accumulated pay or wages.

adjective-jerker *n.* [*adjective* + JERK 'to dispense' + *-er*, agentive suff.] *Journ.* a hack journalist.
1888 *Globe-Democrat* (St. Louis), in Farmer *Amer.*: Genevieve spent four hours last night in constructing a three-line letter, which she sent to an adjective-jerker on a society weekly, and in which she said she would spend the summer months in the Rocky Mountains.

ad lib *n.* [fr. S.E. verb] Orig. *Theat.* a remark, esp. a sarcastic or provoking remark.
1925 *AS* (Oct.) 36: "Can the ad lib"...means politely, "Will you be good enough to hush?" **1964** Thompson & Rice *Every Diamond* ix: His caustic ad libs singed the ears of many a dissenting fan. **1968** N.Y.C. man, age *ca*40: I'm fed up with him and his cheap ad libs!

admiral *n.* [one in charge of "vessels"] *Mil.* a person who cleans or is responsible for urinals, kitchen equipment, etc. In full, **admiral of the vessels.** Also (*Navy*) **admiral of the head.** *Joc.* Cf. CAPTAIN OF THE HEAD.
1939 *AS* (Oct.) 239: *Admiral*. Maid, "In charge of the vessels." **1941** Horman *Buck Pvts.* (film): "Do they have admirals in the army?" "Sure. We're gonna put you in charge of all the vessels." **1944** *Slanguage Dict.* 47: *Admiral*—army slang denoting a male nurse. **1944–46** in *AS* XXII 54: *Admiral of the vessels*. Kitchen police. **1980** Ciardi *Browser's Dict.*: *Admiral of the head. Naval slang*. The naval equivalent of an army latrine orderly.

admiral's mate *n.* [patterned after *gunner's mate, boatswain's mate*, etc.] *Navy.* a boastful sailor who claims to have special knowledge of the intentions of a ship's officers.
1914 *DN* IV 150: *Admiral's mate*...An egotist. *****1962** Granville *Sailor's Slang*: *Admiral's mate*...one who always knows the ship's movements, when leave will be granted, [etc.].

admiral's watch *n.* [to contrast with *starboard watch* and *port watch;* an admiral or other commanding officer does not belong to a watch] *Navy.* a night spent sleeping in one's quarters instead of standing watch; those men not on a night watch.
1918 Kauffman *Our Navy* 9: Once in the schedule's cycle, a man is in the "Admiral's Watch"—passing an entire night abed—but that luxury is inevitably balanced by the "Admiral's Watch with the Belly Out," which is the watch that runs from midnight to four.

adrift *adj. Naut.* (of objects) misplaced or missing; (of people) missing; unaccounted for.
1841 [Mercier] *Man-of-War* 92: "What's become of all our brooms and our *squilgees?*"..."They're all adrift." *****1919** Downing *Digger Dial.*: *Adrift*...A.W.L. **1942** *Yank* (Nov. 11) 4: Navy [slang]...*Adrift*—Anything that is floating around unattached. As a blonde in a nightclub without an escort. **1961** L. Sanders *4-Yr. Hitch* 35: He never left gear adrift as Forrester...did. *****1962** in Partridge *Concise* 3: If there's anything adrift it will come off your slop chit, nobody else's. *****1977** R. Bassett *Tinfish Run* 249: *Adrift*. Late, particularly when mustering or returning from leave. **1979–88** Noel & Bush *Naval Terms* (ed. 5) 4: Gear that is adrift may find its way into the lucky bag.

advertise *v.* to blatantly call attention to oneself or one's intentions; (*specif.*) (in card games) to throw off a card in the hope of tempting other players to discard a required similar card.
1931 D.W. Maurer, in *AS* (June) 329: Mac gets plastered and tries to advertise in a grab-joint when the cops get him. **1961** Scarne *Comp. Guide to Gamb.* 671: *Advertise*...To discard a card in order to try to lead an opponent into discarding another of same rank or near rank or same suit. **1962** Barron *Prof. Gambler* 136: *Advertise*—in rummy games, throwing off a card hoping to get other players to discard a needed similar card. **1971** Rodgers *Queens' Vernacular* 18: *Advertise*...to dress in a sexually provocative manner. **1975–76** Dills *CB* 12: *Advertising*—a marked police car that has its lights turned on. **1976** Lieberman & Rhodes *CB* 121: You have a smokey heading westbound...who's advertising.

A.E.F. *n.* [reinterpretation of official abbr. of American Expeditionary Forces] *Mil.* (interpreted in various facetious ways; see quots.). Now *hist.* [All quots. ref. to WWI.]
1919 Piesbergen *Aero Sq.* 21: You know what A.E.F. stands for?...After England Failed. **1921** *Amer. Legion Wkly.* (Mar. 18) 9: You're wrong, buddy—it means After England Failed. **1926** Nason *Chevrons* 176: The American Excavationary Forces. **1928** Richardson *Band* 65: Some said that A.E.F. stood for "After England Failed." **1964** in Mason *Men at Arms* 66: A.E.F., where are you?...Gee, dis just can't be de Ass End First! **1968** Myrer *Eagle* 129: We got the best platoon leader in the whole Ass End First. **1973** Laffin *Amer. in Battle* 91: The initials AEF

stood for "Arse End First" according to many American soldiers.

aeroplane var. AIRPLANE.

afloat *adj*. tipsy, drunk. *Joc*. Cf. AWASH.

  1809 P. Freneau *On a Honeybee Drinking from a Glass of Wine and Drowned Therein* 35–36: Go, take your seat in Charon's boat,/We'll tell the hive, you died afloat. **1898** *Survival of Fittest* (unp.): Here's to the good old Patriarch [*sc*. Noah] and his ship and here's to "Antediluvian" [brand of spirits] which helped to keep them both afloat! **1940** in Peters *Wisc. Folk Songs* 264: Said she, "Mr. Pat, I can see you're afloat." **1969** *Amer. History Illus.* (Jan.) 51: When the Navy was really afloat—both at sea and ashore.

afoul ¶ In phrases:

  ¶ **fall afoul of** *Naut*. to meet and attack; set upon.
  1833 in [S. Smith] *Letters of Downing* 107: He fell afoul of him with a great club and knocked him down.

  ¶ **run** [or **come**] **afoul of** Orig. *Naut*. meet, "run into." Now *S.E.*
  1848 [Judson] *Mysteries of N.Y.* 200: You've spotted the right place and run afoul of the right feller. **1850** Melville *Moby Dick* ch. xxix: Coming afoul of that old man. **1885** Siringo *Tex. Cowboy* 62: He was…just fixing to…ship them to Galveston when I ran afoul of him. **1905** in A. Adams *Chisholm Trail* 125: Every time I run afoul of fresh beef…it reminds me of the time I was a prisoner among the Yankees. **1941, 1945, 1970** in *DARE*.

Africa or **African** *n*. [cf. analogous use of *Irish, Dutch*] anger (of a black person).

  1838 *So. Literary Messenger* IV 162: Well, it sort o' raised his Africky, at first. **1880** J.C. Harris *Uncle Remus* 269: Well, you des oughter see me git my Affikin up.

African billiards *n*. [alluding to the supposed popularity of the game among blacks] *Gamb*. the game of craps. *Joc*.—usu. considered offensive.

  1919 [Wilkins] *Co. Fund* 45: Galloping dominoes. African billiards.

African bones *n.pl*. [see AFRICAN BILLIARDS] *Gamb*. dice. *Joc*.—usu. considered offensive.

  1935 Pollock *Und. Speaks: African bones*, dice.

African dominoes *n.pl*. [see AFRICAN BILLIARDS] *Gamb*. dice; the game of craps. *Joc*.—usu. considered offensive.

  1919 Law *2d Army Air Serv*. (unp.): First in popularity is the ancient and honorable game of…"African dominoes." **1920** *Amer. Legion Wkly*. (July 20) 8: Thoughtfully he picked up the African dominoes. **1929** in Segar *Thimble Theatre* 54: Gimme them African dominoes! **1937** Parsons *Lafayette Esc*. 266 [ref. to WWI]: Rarely did we indulge in African dominoes, for it was too difficult to keep score. **1961** Scarne *Comp. Guide to Gamb*. 251: Suppose that Joe Doe, a right bettor, throws the African dominoes 1,980 times. **1966** *RHD*.

African golf *n*. [see AFRICAN BILLIARDS] *Gamb*. the game of craps. *Joc*.—usu. considered offensive.

  1919 Piesbergen *Aero Sq*. 66: Bob was always an important figure at African golf. **1919** A. Kauffman *Lost Sq*. 20: It was the great pastime of African golf. **1921** Witwer *Leather* 27: I got into that African golf tourney because I thought I could grab off enough doubloons to take us into New York *right*. **1922** *Leatherneck* (Apr. 22) 5: African golf: a game of chance played with dice; so called because of its popularity among the sons of Ham. **1932** *AS* VII 328: *African golf*—Gaming with dice. **1952** E. Brown *Trespass* 7: Black-face vaudevillians…demonstrate their…addiction to "African golf."

African golfball *n*. **1.** *pl*. [used in AFRICAN GOLF] *Gamb*. dice. *Joc*.—usu. considered offensive.

  1923 *Amer. Legion Wkly*. (Jan. 19) 23: All the campaigns saw the same brand of African golf balls. **1923** McKnight *Eng. Words* 46: Bones…or *African golf balls* or…*galloping dominoes* for dice. **1974** (quot. at AFRICAN PILLS).

  2. [ref. to stereotype of blacks' fondness for watermelon] *Black E*. a watermelon. *Joc*.—usu. considered offensive.

  1980 Folb *Runnin' Lines* 227: African golf ball…Ironic reference to watermelon.

African pills *n.pl*. [see AFRICAN BILLIARDS] *Gamb*. dice. *Joc*.—usu. considered offensive.

  1975 Former 2d Lt. 42d Div., U.S. Army, served 1917–19: In my outfit they had a lot of guys from the South. They were all the time shooting craps and they called the dice *African pills* or *African golfballs* or *bones*.

African plum *n*. [ref. to stereotype of blacks' fondness for watermelon] *Black E*. a watermelon. *Joc*.—usu. considered offensive.

  1973 Andrews & Owens *Black Lang*. 96: *African plum*—Watermelon.

African pool *n*. [cf. AFRICAN BILLIARDS] *Gamb*. the game of craps. *Joc*.—usu. considered offensive.

  1919 *Camp Knox News* (Oct. 25) 2: Four hours African pool. Six hours with Hoyle.

aft *n*. afternoon.

  1885 *Puck* (Apr. 8) 83: What's on deck this aft? **1907** in H.C. Fisher *A. Mutt* 3: If I only had a live hunch for this aft. **1930** in D.O. Smith *Cradle* 14: Later in the aft. **1942** in *Journ. Gen. Psych*. LXVI (1945) 131: I'll do it this aft', sir.

afterbird *n*. [*after* 'located closer to the stern of a vessel' (ref. to the location of the officers' quarters) + BIRD 'fellow'] *Naut*. a ship's officer.

  1884 Symondson *Abaft the Mast* 280: The "after birds" do not like the apprentices entering the forecastle…[or] accompanying its inmates ashore.

aftergafter *n*. [*after*burner + *gafter*, joc. rhyme] *Mil. Av*. afterburner.

  1957 Wallrich *Air Force Airs* 70: Here's an early jet-era song, one that dates back to the days of tailpipes rather than "aftergafters" and "go-go pipes."

aftsheets *n*. [cf. syn. STERNSHEETS] *Naut*. rump. *Joc*.

  1942 *Life* (May 18) 81: Every time any of those kids got any parental praise, the others ganged up and gave him a few good kicks in the aftsheets.

against *prep*. **1.** [poss. of prizefighting or cockfighting origin, ref. to putting one contender against another; or a literal trans. of G *gegen* 'against, toward'] toward; into; into participation in.

  1878 *Nat. Police Gaz*. (Apr. 27) 6: When a man "is steered against the joint" [directed to a gambling casino] in Chicago, and gets beaten…he hunts up…a special [officer]. **1884** Carleton *Poker Club* 35: Tooter Williams had volunteered to steer [him] against the game. **1894** Gardner *Dr. & Devil* 58: Erving "ran up against" red and black, hazard and roulette. **1920** Ade *Hand-Made* 41: Ranse now began to go against the à la carte. **1929** Booth *Stealing* 283: I didn't know you were going against this racket.…When did you turn out?

  2. *Narc*. using, addicted to, or under the influence of (a drug).—sometimes constr. with *up*.

  1892 Norr *Chinatown* 47: We were all up against the dope, and it was a great crowd that smoked at 4, 11, and 17 Mott street in those days.…Actors and actresses came down to Mott street then to go against the hop. **1899** Kountz *Baxter* 53: I have never been against the pipe, because I'm too young. **1906** Green *Actors' Boarding House* 271: So yer agin the dope?…I used to smoke onct in a while. **1925–26** Black *Can't Win* 60: They'll put her against hop and you'll have a bum on your hands. **1926** *Variety* (Dec. 29) 5: I picked up a three-a-day habit against food.…I'm still an addict. **1934** W. Smith *Bessie Cotter* 236: Getting drunk and going against the coke. **1964** in B. Jackson *Swim Like Me* 133: The trouble with the Frenchman, he was up against the coke.

  3. face to face with; required to deal with.—usu. constr. with *up*. Now *S.E.*; in phr. **put up against** to introduce to, "put next to."

  1896 Ade *Artie* 44: He'd think he was up against the cold outside, and that's where he is, huh? *Ibid*. 57: Well, yesterday he was up against a new proposition. **1902–03** Ade *People* 59: I'm not going to put you up against any Profs. **1942** *ATS* 330: Up against, confronting, encountering. **1979** N.Y.C. man, age 30: I've never been up against this kind of situation. **1990** *U.S. News & W.R.* (Jan. 22) 59: Getting the borough council to place a limited ban on polystyrenes took longer…but, then, the youngsters ran up against a counter-attack from styrofoam suppliers.

  ¶ In phrases:

  ¶ **up against it** in great difficulty, desperate.
  1895 Townsend *Fadden & Others* 166: Me friend Shiner Simpson is up against it, and I wants to help him. **1895** Townsend *Fadden Explains* 208: Joe's been up against it three days, spending the rent Pietro gave him. **1896** Ade *Artie* 7: I saw I was up against it, so I lasted the best way I could. *Ibid*. 46: The first thing you know you're up against it, and you

don't care whether there's any night cars runnin' or not. **1899** *Sat. Eve. Post* (Nov. 18) 396: You's up agin it for fair. **1912** Lowrie *Life in Prison* 125: I was in th' can ag'in, up against it for robbery. **1927** Nicholson *Barker* 76: Lissen, Hap, you gotta help me. I'm up against it. How much *money* you got? **1935** Pollock *Und. Speaks: Up against it*, addicted to dope. **1949** Robbins *Dream Merchants* 245: All they had to do to make money was turn out some pictures and issue some stock. But now…they're up against it. **1970** N.Y.U. prof., age *ca*35: Well, if you're really up against it, I can postpone the exam till next Monday. **1975** *Sing Out* (July) 6: But there's different kinds of being up against it. **1990** *Nat. Review* (Feb. 5) 63: Aw shutup, Tony. You're up against it now.

agate *n.* usu. *pl.* testicle. Hence **agate-cracker** a demanding, racking task; "ball-buster." Cf. syn. STONE.
   1941 *AS* XVI 236: Pig testicles are *agates*. **1968** Baker et al. *CUSS* 70: *Aggit-cracker* [*sic*] Work (study) hard and concentratedly. **1990** Thorne *Dict. Contemp. Slang: Agates* testicles.

¶ In phrase:
¶ **get (one's) agates cracked** (of a man) to engage in sexual intercourse.
   1969 Montana man, age *ca*65: We used to say [in the 1920's], "It's been a long time since I got my agates cracked."

-age *suffix.* [abstracted from word*age*, shrink*age*, etc.] *Stu.* (used to create joc. usu. collect. nominal forms of obvious meaning).
   1965 in Partridge *DSUE* (ed. 7) 978: Dressage…understandage…workage. **1981** Eble *College Slang* (Mar.): I've got mass studyage to do.…"How's the weather?" "Rainage." *a***1989** in Eble *College Slang* 17: Bookage, buckage, fundage, snowage,…foodage. **1989** Munro *UCLA Slang* 15: As we drove by a couple making out…Mark pointed and said, "Ooh, neckage!" **1990** *21 Jump Street* (Fox-TV): We ran into this major babage ["babes," i.e., attractive young women]. **1991** *Houston Chronicle* (Nov. 13) 5D: *Fundage:* Cash.

agent *n.* [shortened fr. ROAD AGENT] *West.* highwayman; stagecoach robber.
   1876 in *DA:* The driver finally succeeded in satisfying the "agent" that no express box was carried by San Andreas. **1880** *Harper's* (July) 195: We…concluded that the "agents," or robbers, had an excellent eye for position. *Ibid.* 196: The "agents" were enjoying social games of chance and skill in the halls of the gay town.

agfay *n.* [Pig Latin form of FAG] a homosexual man, FAG.—used derisively.
   1942 *ATS* 473: Male Homosexual: Agfay. **1965** *Time* (Mar. 26) 23B: Personally, I've always understood that fairy meant homosexual.*…*As do homo, nola, pix, flit, queer, fag, faggot, agfay, fruit, nance, pansy, queen, she-male, mary—and a variety of other, more pungent terms. **1974** *Coq* (Apr.) 44: An agfay smile and the clothes to match.

aggie *n.* [*agricultural college* + *-ie*] *Stu.* a student at an agricultural college; (*pl.*) (a nickname for) the football team or other sports team of an agricultural college. Now *colloq.*
   1902 in *DA:* Swamp Michigan "Aggies." **1906** in *DA.* **1975** Univ. Texas student: Texas A & M is the real home of the Aggies. And U.T.-Austin is the real home of Aggie jokes. **1983** *Nat. Lampoon* (Nov.) 14: The…state aggie college. **1984** *N.Y. Post* (Dec. 12) 78: Vince Washington [of Utah State College] hit a 12-foot jump shot…to lift the Aggies.

aggro *adj.* [Brit. and Austral. slang *aggro* 'aggravation or aggression'] **1.** *Rock Music & Stu.* inclined toward aggressiveness or hostility; belligerent.
   1982 Sculatti *Catalog of Cool* 27: The Rolling Stones and other aggro units. **1989** P. Dickson *Slang!* 212: *Agro.* Mad; pissed off. ***1990** Thorne *Dict. Contemp. Slang:* I guess I was a bit aggro last night.
2. *Stu.* powerful; aggressive; excitingly good.
   1986 *Prime News* (CNN-TV) (Oct. 31): The surf, as they say, is…aggro. And that's good. **1990** Munro *Slang U.* 21: He's such an aggro skater. **1991** *N.Y. Times Mag.* (June 30) 36: *Aggro* (adj.):…Used to describe the in-your-face, barbarians-at-the-wave surfing style of the 80's.

agony *n.* **1.** Orig. *Theat.* melodramatic gestures, histrionics, overacting.—esp. in phr. **pile on** [or **up**] **the agony** to overact; exaggerate; show off.
   1837 Neal *Charcoal Sks.* 124: He must commence the play hawfully, and keep piling on the hagony till the close. *Ibid* 125: Winkins…taught him when and where to come the "hagony;" when and where to cut "terrific mugs" at the pit. **1839** *Amer. Joe Miller* 56: I think, in the last

part of his capers, that he was *piling on the agony a leetle too stiff.* **1839** Marryat *Diary* 267: Well, I don't go much to theatricals, that's a fact; but I do think *he piled the agony up a little too high* in that last scene. **1862** Patrick *Rebel* 62: She sang in opera style and piled on some of the most excruciating agonies, but she sang better than…the others. **1873** *Galaxy* (Feb.) 157: You are piling up the agony a little too high, as the comic men in the newspapers express it. ***1881** in *F & H* I (rev.) 24: Sooner or later that organ will shake the Cathedral to bits…there was a great deal too much noise. You lose effect when you pile up the agony like that. **a***1909** *F & H* I (rev.) 24: *To Pile Up (or On) The Agony*…To exaggerate; to use the tallest terms in lieu of the simplest…as a newspaper when "writing up" murder, divorce, and other sensations. **1943** Chandler *High Window* 441: Skip the agony, toots. **1952** C. Sandburg *Young Strangers* 337 [ref. to 1890]: The slang of the day had it, "she certainly could put on the agony."
2. version.
   1889 "Mark Twain" *Conn. Yankee* 203: What seemed to be the crude first-draft or original agony of the wail known to later centuries as "In the Sweet Bye and Bye."
3. style, fashion, "rage."
   1902–03 Ade *People* 160: He bought a new kind of Writing Paper, said to be the Latest Agony. **1906** *DN* III 124: *Agony*, n. Style, mode, fashion. "It's the latest agony."

agony box *n.* **1.** a piano.—used derisively.
   1902–03 Ade *People* 216: He learned to play all the "Pinafore" music on the Agony Box.
2. a phonograph or radio. *Joc.*
   1929 Gill *Und. Slang* (unp.): *Agony box*—phonograph. **1942** *ATS* 609: Radio. *Agony box.* **1964** Leitner & Lanen *Dict. Fr. & Amer. Slang: Agony box*…la radio.

agony cart *n. Hosp.* a low cart used to bring instruments, bandages, medicines, etc., to a patient's bedside.
   1918 F. Gibbons *They Thought We Wouldn't Fight* 342: In our ward that vehicle was known as the "Agony Cart." **1973** E. Jackson *Fall Out* 350 [ref. to WWI]: Traynor…pushed the "agony cart" and assisted Miss Small with the bandages.

agony column *n. Journ.* a newspaper column devoted to personal advertisements, esp. those seeking assistance. Now *S.E.*
   ***1870** in *F & H* I (rev.) 24: The advertisement of the committee…appeared in the agony column of the *Times.* ***1881** in *F & H:* There were anonymous appeals to runaways in agony columns. ***1890** A.C. Doyle *Sign of Four* ch. ix: I tossed the paper down upon the table, but at that moment my eye caught an advertisement in the agony column. **1932** Biggers *Agony Column* (book title). **1942** *ATS* 499: *Agony column,* the personal-advertisement section of a newspaper. **1969** Kent *Lang. of Journ.: Agony Column,* the classified column for personal messages, as for those trying to contact missing relatives, etc. **1976** Rosten *To Anywhere* 68: The "Agony" columns.

agony pipe *n. Jazz Journ.* clarinet.
   1935 *Vanity Fair* (Nov.) 71: Among these [rare terms] are *agony pipe, wop-stick,* and *licorice-stick* for clarinet. **1940** *New Yorker* (Sept. 14) 19: The driving syncopation and lift of the agony pipes, the noodling of the brass section. **1942** *Yank* (July 1) 21: Artie Shaw…unhooked his agony pipe…and changed to navy blue [i.e., joined the Navy]. **1964** Gold *Jazz Lexicon* 230: *Agony pipe* for clarinet…listed in several glossaries of the 1930's [is], according to jazzmen, specious.

agony shift *n.* a late-night or evening work shift.
   1944 Kendall *Service Slang* 57: *Agony shift*…night work. **1953** *ATS* (ed. 2) 245: *Agony shift*…a shift between the day and "graveyard" shifts, from about 4 P.M. to midnight.

agony wagon *n.* AGONY CART.
   [**1929** Gill *Und. Slang* (unp.): *Agony wagon*—Ambulance.] ***1936** Partridge *DSUE* 6 [ref. to WWI]. **1980** Manchester *Darkness* 130 [ref. to WWII]: A doctor and two nurses made their rounds accompanied by a wheeled cart we called the "agony wagon" because the doctor took various…instruments from it to probe your wounds.

A.H. *n.* [euphem. initialism] ASSHOLE, 1 & 2.—also in phr. **in the pig's a.h.** in great trouble; (*also*) "no indeed," "like hell," "bullshit."—usu. considered vulgar.
   1931 Dos Passos *1919* 31 [ref. to WWI]: Well, you're in the pig's a.h. for fair. **1938–39** Dos Passos *Young Man* 80: In the pig's a.h.…A workin' stiff is lucky to end up in a decent poorhouse when he gets old. **1967** Mailer *Vietnam* 38: A high grade of A.H. [obnoxious person] is

not easily recognized as any kind of A.H.

A-head *n. Narc.* **1.** [A, 2 + HEAD 'habitual user'] a habitual user of amphetamines.

1966 Goldstein *One in Seven* xii: An "A-head" is an amphetamine user. **1967** McNeill *Moving Through* 35: Al, a young but ageless A-head, lives on a 9th Street block. **1975** in L. Bangs *Psychotic Reactions* 178: There's A-heads and there's speedfreaks.

2. [ACID, 2 + HEAD 'habitual user'; infl. by (**1**), above] a habitual user of LSD.

1970 Landy *Underground* 23: *A-head*...one who takes LSD. **1979** Tenn. man, age *ca*24: I was practically an A-head myself. **1982** A. Shaw *Dict. Pop/Rock* 168: [An] "A" head [uses] LSD.

A-hole *n.* [euphem. initialism] ASSHOLE, 1 & 2.—also in phr. **A-hole buddy** ASSHOLE BUDDY.—usu. considered vulgar.

1942 *ATS* 150: Anus...a-hole. *Ibid.* 367: Terms of disparagement...A-hole...big bozo [etc.]. **1956** Chamales *Never So Few* 366: "Fire in the hole."..."Explosion up the a-hole." **1958** Frankel *Band of Bros.* 254: Your A-hole buddy. **1959** Morrill *Dark Sea* 85: Most of us ex-cons carried emergency tools up our a-hole. **1962** Quirk *No Red Ribbons* 90: If he wants me to be his A-hole buddy, he's got a long wait. **1963** Rubin *Sweet Daddy* 22: Imagine—those a-holes thinking they could make a pross happy. **1977** Olsen *Fire Five* 97: Those A-holes are needling you, son. *a***1990** Westcott *Half a Klick* 98: You...A-hole.

-aholic *suffix.* [abstracted and altered from *alcoholic*; later quots. infl. by *workaholic*] a person enthusiastic about, obsessed with, or addicted to (the initial element). Also **-holic, -oholic.**

1964 E. Wilson *Wilson's N.Y.* 180: You'll find New York's magnitude growing on you. You become a New Yorkaholic. **1972** *Time* (July 24) 53: Thousands of men were on it consistently enough to be dubbed "hashaholics" by their buddies. **1976** *Business Week* (Mar. 29) 94: Sheron says he used to be a "chocoholic," but lost 50 lb. in nine months last year. **1976** *L.A. Times* (Sept. 16) IV 6: Swinging at a softball with the intensity of a workaholic who has allotted himself a couple of hours to be a playaholic. **1977** *L.A. Times* (Dec. 8) IV 5: Remember when we first met and I told you I was a foodoholic? **1981** *Psych. Today* (May) 37: One...respondent pinpointed her problem by describing herself as a "chargeaholic." **1982** *L.A. Times* (Oct. 29) V 17: Sugarholics can be just as bad as alcoholics. **1983** *Time* (Dec. 26) 80: Her mother is a danceaholic. **1985** *N.Y. Times* (Jan. 13) 14: She was a "bookaholic." *a***1989** in Eble *College Slang* 17: Bookaholic, Cokeaholic, foodaholic.

aimie var. AMY.

air *n.* **1.** *R.R. & Trucking.* **a.** air brakes.

1897 Hamblen *Gen. Mgr.* 295: Say, did you pull the air on me? **1907** *Amer. Mag.* (Sept.) 580: I gave the "hoot, hoot," put on some air, but the freight backed in time. **1934** in Fenner *Throttle* 53: It was like velvet, the way Danny'd handle air. **1938** *AS* (Dec.) 307: *Grab a handful of air.* Apply the brakes, usually suddenly. *Ibid.* 308: *Reach for some air.* Apply the brakes. **1942** *AS* (Apr.) 103: *Give it the air.* Apply the brakes. **1958** McCulloch *Woods Wds.* 113: *Lose the air*...To lose control of [a] train or truck because airbrakes failed.

b. air horn.

1938 *AS* (Dec.) 308: *Lay on the air.* Usually means excessive use of the loud air horns.

2. a curt or unexpected ousting, jilting (of a lover), snub (of an acquaintance), leaving (of a place), etc.—usu. in phr. **to give** [or **get**] **the air.** [Very freq. in 1920's.]

1900 Ade *More Fables* 134: The Fable of Why Essie's Tall Friend Got the Fresh Air. **1919** *Variety* (Mar. 28) 40: He was sore by that time and gave the place the air. **1919** in De Beck *Google* 22: We've gotta popularize it or we're gonna get the air. **1922** in *DN* V 147: *Given the air.*—When a fellow or girl is thrown down on a date. **1924** Marks *Plastic Age* 199: And now you give the Dramat[ics] Club the air just as if an activity or two wasn't anything in your young life. **1925** Faulkner *Soldiers' Pay* 188: When a uniform showed up he got the air. **1926** in Lardner *Best Stories* 337: But of course they're old friends and I can't give 'em the air. **1928** Hammett *Red Harvest* 39: You're an ex-boy-friend of Dinah's who was given the air. **1928** in Fortune *Fugitives* 52: Saw Scottie and gave him the air. He's a pain in the neck to me. **1929** Kaufman *Cocoanuts* (film): How about you and I givin' this joint the air and indulgin' in some snappy neckin'? **1951** Yordan & Wyler *Detective Story* (film): She gave me the air. **1975** Amer. Cancer Society ad, WINS radio (Dec. 17): I gave the air to smoking when I stopped to smell a rose. **1986** R. Campbell *In La-La Land* 41: Manny Ostrava hinted at it when he gave us the air.

3. [fr. HOT AIR; cf. similar S.E. sense] empty talk, nonsense.

1929 *AS* (June) 337: *Air*—False talk. **1940** Zinberg *Walk Hard* 114: This champ glory is all a lot of air. **1952** Uris *Battle Cry* 114: Come on, jackass, turn off the air and pull.

¶ In phrases:

¶ **catch air, a.** to leave hurriedly; get out.

1924 in Clarke *Amer. Negro Stories* 27: Bes' thing f' you to do is catch air, toot sweet. **1928** Fisher *Jericho* 30: You two,...catch air. *Ibid.* 271: Never seen a man catch air so fast. **1971** Faust *Willy* 129: I told you mister, catch air.

b. to leave the ground. Also **pop air.**

1980 Univ. Tenn. student theme: I felt the truck catch air as I went over the bank. I flipped twice. **1992** Thatcher & Brannon *Thrasher* 10: Popping airs can be extremely dangerous [while skateboarding].

¶ **dance on air** see s.v. DANCE.

¶ **fan the air** [cf. *shoot the breeze* s.v. BREEZE] to chatter; gossip.

1929 Perelman *Ginsbergh* 120: HE NEVER fanned the air with stories about being office manager of the Du Pont de Nemours Company.

¶ **give the air** see (**2.**), above.

¶ **hit the air** to go outside; get out.

1928 O'Connor *B'way Racketeers* 66: I paid for the third bottle...and then we hit the air. **1955** Ellson *Rock* 16: Let's hit the air.

¶ **let the air out of** [in allusion to deflating a balloon] to disappoint; go back on.

1959 Zugsmith *Beat Generation* 25: Jester observed the old rules. He would never let the air out of a friend.

¶ **make the air** *Pris.* to be released from prison.

1952 Mandel *Angry Strangers* 55: Lukey, you bum....When did you make the air?

¶ **put in the air** [prob. ref. to *hold up*] *Und.* to rob (someone).

1911 A.H. Lewis *Apaches of N.Y.* 76: Suppose right now I was to go out an' get put in th' air; do you think I'd squeal? **1935** Pollock *Und. Speaks: Put him up in the air*: a pickpocket successful in robbing his victim.

¶ **split the air** to travel at great speed.

1870 Duval *Wallace* 68: I split the air so fast with my nose that it took the skin off of it.

¶ **take the air** to leave, get out.—esp. in imper.

1918 *Bugler* (Jan. 19) 3: When you hear Sgt. Weber tell any one to "take the air," you know that the formation has been 'smissed. **1921** *Pirate Piece* (Nov.) 3: We don't know who yuh are, buddy, but take the air. **1928** Burnett *Little Caesar* 10: Well, if he don't show up in ten minutes I'll take the air. **1934** Jevne & Purcell *Joe Palooka* (film): You, take the air! **1934** in Ruhm *Detective* 104: Think it over, Rube....And take the air. I hate your guts. **1940** Raine & Niblor *Fighting 69th* (film): All right. Take the air. The party's over.

¶ **throw** [or **toss**] **in the air** to jilt. Cf. *give the air*, at (**2**), above.

1896 Ade *Artie* 29: It's all off with me and the girl....She tossed me in the air. **1897** Ade *Pink Marsh* 134: She'd th'ow me in 'e aih an' staht out to fin' some suckeh to buy one of 'em bloomeh suits.

¶ **try** [or **make a try for**] **(someone's) air** [in allusion to strangulation] *Pris.* to assault or attempt to kill (someone).

1970 L.D. Johnson *Devil's Front Porch* 173: I thought he might try my air* but he turned and walked away....*Fight me. **1971** Hilaire *Thanatos* 62: Some of the cons made a try for his air.

¶ **turn on the air** [prob. sugg. by FAN OUT 'leave in a hurry'] to take to one's heels; rush off.

1970 L.D. Johnson *Devil's Front Porch* 173: He turned on the "air" and zoomed around the way he had come.

¶ **[up] in the air, a.** angry; excited; unnerved.—usu. constr. with *go.* [The related sense "unsettled" is S.E.]

*a***1849** in C. Hill *Scenes* 175: Now I am in the air; I can scarcely keep myself cool. **1902–03** Ade *People* 157: He married a Type-Writer 19 years old...and then [his son] Joel did go up in the air. **1906** *N.Y. Eve. Post* (Jan. 13) 4: Representatives...have "gone up in the air" because they could not "land" their men. **1907** "H. McHugh" *Beat It!* 30: George...stung Uncle Gregory for $5.75, which caused uncle to go up in the air...bouncing between the floor and the ceiling for five minutes. **1908** *Atlantic* (Aug.) 225: It takes character to face a whole dynasty of [batters], one after the other, and not "go up in the air," especially when bayed at by a maniacal public. **1911** Van Loan *Big League* 59: [Women] get a man all up in the air till he can't hit a flock of balloons. **1928** Dahlberg *Bottom Dogs* 149: When his son…heard of it, he went up in the air. **1942** Garcia *Tough Trip* 85: At this the young buck went up in the air in right style. He tried to knife me, but one of the bucks caught his arm and held it.

b. lost, finished; in a bad way.

1899 Cullen *Tales* 172: I thought my $100 was up in the air for a cinch when the bunch went to the post. **1910** Hapgood *City Streets* 52: After de third or fourth [prison term] it's all up in de air wid 'em.

air *v.* **1.** [fr. AIR, *n.*, 2] to jilt, dismiss, or forcibly eject.

1919 *Variety* (Mar. 28) 10: The producer who "cheats" on his show…should be promptly "aired." **1922** J. Conway, in *Variety* (Jan. 6) 7: He aired that Jane who vamped him. **1931** Lorimer *Streetcars* 82: Ting's aired him.…Out on his ear. *ca*1931 in Mencken *Amer. Lang.* (ed. 4) 585: Why don't you air her and do a single [act]? **1939–40** O'Hara *Pal Joey* 16: That personality boy…has aired the femme that got him the job and is now trying to move into society.

2. to leave.

1972 Gaines *Hungry* 219: C'mon, y'all, less air this place.

¶ In phrases:

¶ **air (one's) paunch** [or **belly**] *West.* **a.** to talk noisily, boast, chatter.

1928 Santee *Cowboy* 88: Pretty Dick had been airin' his paunch about Canada an' tellin' what good horses he had rode up there.

b. to vomit.

1936 R. Adams *Cowboy Lingo* 233: "Airin' his paunch" was vomiting. **1942** *AS* (Feb.) 75: To vomit is to *air the paunch.* **1954–60** *DAS: Air (one's) belly* to vomit.

¶ **air (one's) lungs** to talk noisily, complain.

1911 in Fletcher *Up Trail in '79* 7: He aired his lungs by cussing everything from his cow pony to the minister we met in the road. **1936** R. Adams *Cowboy Lingo* 233: "Airin' his lungs" was cussin'.

¶ **air (one's) tonsils** to talk emptily.

1968 Cuomo *Among Thieves* 215: When Orninski opened his mouth, it was because he had something to say. He wasn't just airing his tonsils, like most of the guys you met.

air artist *n.* [AIR, *n.*, 1 + ARTIST] *R.R.* a locomotive engineer who is especially skilled in handling air brakes.

1958 McCulloch *Woods Words: Air artist*—a railroad engineer specially skilled in handling airbrakes when taking heavy trains down severe grades. **1962** *AS* (May) 131: *Air artist.*

airball *n.* **1.** *Basketball.* a missed shot that entirely misses the rim, net, and backboard.

1974 Univ. Wisc. student: An airball is one that doesn't draw iron. **1976** in *Webster's Sports Dict.* **1980** Pearl *Dict. Slang.* **1988** Frazier & Offen *W. Frazier* 185: Dollar shot an airball, not touching even the side of anything.

2. a dull or inconsequential person; (*also*) AIRHEAD.

1984 "W.T. Tyler" *Shadow Cabinet* 11: The man's an airball, a bubblegum airball. **1991** *Married with Children* (Fox-TV): Thank you, my little airball.

air-breather *n. Av.* a jet aircraft; AIR-SUCKER.

1984 Trotti *Phantom* 247: SR-71…Certainly the world's fastest, highest flying air-breather.

air buggy *n. Av.* an aircraft. *Joc.*

1945 J. Bryan *Carrier* 27: The ticker printed, Pilots Man Your Air Buggies.

airchine *n.* [*aircraft* + m*achine*] *Av.* aircraft.

1968 W. Anderson *Gooney Bird* 32: The Convair is a great airchine, and it was at least born in this decade.

air-chopper *n.* [fr. its fancied resemblance in shape to a rounded blade used for dicing or chopping] *Navy.* a naval officer's high cocked hat.

1882 *United Service* (Feb.) 227: Slew your air-choppers fore and aft, or you will never get on shore with this headwind. *Ibid.* 223: Put your air-chopper in your locker.

air-condition *v.* to riddle with holes.—esp. as past ppl. *Joc.*

1938 *AS* XIII 315: *Air Conditioned*…A car with broken windows. **1940** Baldwin *Bro. Orchid* (film): This is the first time that I've seen shoes that are air-conditioned. **1941** *Slanguage Dict.:* Air-conditioned socks. **1943** in Kittredge & Krauzer *Great Amer. Detect.* 176: The first flatfoot that lays a finger on me gets his giblets air-conditioned. **1984** *Fall Guy* (ABC-TV): A .357 Magnum…[can] air-condition an elephant.

air dance *n.* [cf. *dance on air* s.v. DANCE] ¶ In phrase: **do an air dance** to be hanged.

1929–31 in Partridge *Dict. Und.* (ed. 2) 788. **1968** R. Salmaggi, on WINS radio (Aug. 8): No less than half a dozen baddies do an air dance in [the film] *Hang 'Em High.*

airedale *n.* **1.** [cf. syn. MUTT] **a.** *Horse Racing.* a worthless racehorse.

1923 Witwer *Fighting Blood* 215: Knight Errant and Citrus, hey? Blah! A couple of Airedales!

b. a fool; an offensive or worthless individual.

1924 Wilstach *Anec. Erotica* 17: Hey there, you airdale. **1927** Mayer *Us Girls* 38: Don't be an AIREdale, my dear! **1947** *Merrie Melodies* (animated cartoon): T'row dat airedale *out!* **1942–49** Goldin et al. *DAUL* 17: I ain't playin' the fall guy…this rap.…What do I look like, an airedale?

c. an unattractive woman; DOG.

1956 *Private Secretary* (ABC-TV): A very unattractive lady! A dog! An airedale!

d. *Hobo.* a drifter, hobo.

1968 Spradley *Drunk* 77: An airedale [is a tramp who] travels from town to town. **1982** D.A. Harper *Good Company* 86: That One-Eyed *Jack*—that airdale we talked to.…That's what they are. See, they don't want nothin' to do with anyone else no more.

2. a heavily whiskered or long-haired man.

1925 *Amer. Legion Wkly.* (Jan. 16) 20: An extra [in films] with long hair is nicknamed "airedale." **1925** Bailey *Shanghaied* 58: The old Airdale (the skipper wore a stubble beard) must be for'ard, and not in! **1930** in Weaver *Coll. Poems* 252: Pointin' to all us guys that had growed beards, "Ten of them airedales tomorrow, nine o'clock!"

3. one hired to oversee the work of others, as a foreman or a hired guard.

1926 Finerty *Criminalese: Airdale*—a special guard. *ca*1940 in Mencken *Amer. Lang. Supp.* II 766: Airedale, bloodhound, or minute-man. A foreman. **1942** *ATS* 419: *Airedale*…a guard.

4. *Stock Market.* a high-pressure salesman.

1931 in Partridge *Dict. Und.* **1948** Mencken *Amer. Lang. Supp.* II 773: *Airedale.* A successful stock salesman. **1964** Wyckoff *Stock Mark. Terms: Airdale.* Slang expression for a fast-talking, sharply-dressed salesman such as might be associated with a bucket shop.

5. [pun on *air*] **a.** *Navy.* a U.S. Navy aircrewman.

1942 *Yank* (Oct. 14) 14: Referring to those of us in naval aviation as "airdales." **1943** *Amer. Mercury* (Nov.) 555: *Airedale*—naval aviator. **1945** Jensen *Carrier War* 22: The [carrier] pilots are…known affectionately to surface sailors as "Airedales" or "birdmen." **1966** Noel *Naval Terms: Airdale* / Jocular term for a naval aviator. **1969** Searls *Hero Ship* 122: There were tanned airedale gunners whose best friends were the ensigns with whom they flew. **1981** Former Navy yeoman, served in Vietnam, 1970–72: An *airedale* was a naval aviator. **1990** *Newsweek* (Apr. 9) 8: *Airdales:* What sailors call Navy fliers.

b. *Navy.* an airplane handler or member of a naval air division.

1943 *Yank* (Nov. 19) 4: "Airedales" [are] sailors who push planes into position on the flight deck. **1944** Olds *Helldiver Sq.* 90: These deck crewmen, sometimes called "airedales," constantly darted in and around the closely packed planes. **1944** *Reader's Digest* (Sept.) 76: The plane-handlers on an aircraft carrier are referred to as "airedales." **1945** in *AS* (Dec. 1946) 310: *Airedales.* Used in the Navy Air Force to describe the men who service the planes of an aircraft carrier. **1953** Dibner *Deep Six* 63: I'm mustering my airdales and showing them what a great guy they got for a division officer.

c. *Army & USMC.* any aircrewman or member of any air force. [Quots. ref. to Air Force or Army fliers.]

1959 [Sabre & Eiden] *Glory Jumpers* 139 [ref. to WWII]: That Airedale cut the tow at least five miles from our landing field. **1967** W. Crawford *Gresham's War* 184 [ref. to Korean War]: The Pentagon would do *anything* to cut down the Crotch so the houndfaces, deck apes, and airdales looked better. **1974** Former L/Cpl, USMC, age *ca*25: [In Vietnam, 1970] we called Air Force guys or flyers *airedales, flyboys, zoomies.* **1982** R.A. Anderson *Cooks & Bakers* 126: Those airedales have everything, Lieutenant.

air farce *n. Mil.* air force.—used derisively.

1965 Pollini *Glover* 94: The ol Air Farce. *a*1989 R. Herman, Jr. *Warbirds* 45: Goddamn Air Farce!…Too damn late.

air guitar *n.* an imaginary guitar one pretends to play.

1982 *Wash. Post* (June 6) E1: "Heavy Metal!" the chubby one would shout, and begin playing a rough lick on his air guitar in the cramped compartment. **1984** *People* (Apr. 9) 47: When they opened for the Stones in 1981, Mick Jagger was stageside making like any other fan—playing air guitar. **1984** N. Stephenson *Big U.* 137: Dancing around playing the air guitar. **1985** *N.Y. Times Mag.* (Sept. 1) 40: I play air guitar. It probably looks dumb on an outsider, but to the man who plays, it is quite serious. **1986** *Newsweek* (June 9) 75: In a famous scene in "Risky Business," Tom Cruise played air guitar in his underwear to "Old Time Rock & Roll." **1987** *New Yorker* (June 19) 20: He…would stop tapping and start playing the air guitar with a rock-and-roll bump and grind. **1992** *N.Y. Observer* (June 22) 15: They…have been known to play air guitar to *Sympathy for the Devil* on top of the tables.

airhead *n.* [*air* (implying emptiness rather than brains) + *head*, poss. orig. a pun on *airhead* 'area in enemy territory for bringing in supplies by air'; cf. BALLOONHEAD.] an empty-headed person.
  1972 (cited in *W10*). **1974** N.Y. man, age 24: She's an airhead. She's got nothing in her brain. I heard that in 1971 at SUNY at Geneseo. **1979** *Nat. Lampoon* (Apr.) 21: Zip up, airhead, or so help me God…. **1979** Univ. Tenn. student, age 23: *Airhead* is what we used to call real spacey people in high school. That was in 1970 in Millington [Tenn.]. They were all Navy kids there. **1979** Austin Peay State Univ. instructor, age 32: I heard *airhead* at Davidson College, 1964–68. Usually it referred to dates. "She turned out to be a real airhead." **1982** Bonnie Raitt, in *High Fidelity* (June) 73: A lot of my friends thought I had moved to the beach and turned into Gidget. But it's not like I suddenly became an airhead. **1985** *Time* (Jan. 14) 72: To him, as to the Dadaists in Berlin, this was for air heads. **1990** *Cosmopolitan* (Apr.) 176: He thought she was a California airhead. **1992** *Sally Jessy Raphaël* (synd. TV series): I dated airhead girls.

airhog *n. Av.* an overly enthusiastic person who spends an undue amount of time flying.
  1933 Stewart *Speech of Amer. Airman* 43. **1942** Hamann *Air Words: Air hog.* One who likes flying. **1991** Kluger *Yank* 115: But that didn't stop the airhogs from trying.

airhole *n.* [partly euphem.] ASSHOLE, 1 & 2.
  *a*1925 in Fauset *Folklore from N.S.* 134: Mary had a little lamb,/Its face was black as charcoal,/Every time it shook its tail,/He showed his little airhole. **1985** *Webster* (ABC-TV): I wear white socks with black shoes. A lot of people think I'm an airhole.

air-jammer *n. R.R.* a maintenance worker who connects air hoses between railroad cars.
  1934 *AS* (Feb.) 73. **1942** *Amer. Mercury* (June) 740: Air Jammer—carman who connects air hose on freight, and air, signal and steam hoses on passenger cars.

air jockey *n. Mil.* airplane pilot, aircrewman.
  1960 MacCuish *Do Not Go Gentle* 330 [ref. to WWII]: Ah, an Air Corps mascot, eh? I have a deep feelin' for the air jockeys. **1976** Dills *CB '77: Air Jockey:* Pilot. **1978** Former USAF missile crewman, age 27: Major Hamm was one ballsy air jockey. **1981** C. Nelson *Picked Bullets Up* 302: The air jockeys showed the ladies a good time.

air-jumper *n. R.R.* AIR-JAMMER.
  1977 R. Adams *Railroader* 5: *Air jumper:*…air jammer.

air-knocker *n.* **1.** *Army.* aircrewman.
  1975 Former 1/L, 11th Armored Cavalry, age 25: An *airknocker* is an Army pilot—a warrant officer.
  2. *Av.* (see quot.). Now *hist.*
  1978 Gann *Hostage* 199 [ref. to *ca*1940]: Known as an Aeronca C-3, or "Airknocker," it was underpowered and slothful.

airmail *n.* garbage thrown from a high window.
  1952 in Legman *Limerick* 418: Shit…thrown out an upper-story window…[is] called "sending the airmail." **1964** Selby *Last Exit* 245: Throwing garbage out of windows is referred to as AIRMAIL. We do not want any AIRMAIL from this project. **1990** P. Dickson *Slang!* 212: *Air mail.* Garbage thrown out the window.

air monkey *n.* [AIR, 1 + MONKEY 'workman'] *R.R.* an air brake repairman.
  1931 *Writer's Digest* (May) 41: *Air monkey*—Air brake repairman. **1932** *R.R. Stories* (Oct.) 366. **1939** *Sat. Eve. Post* (Apr. 15) 26: The grunt told him the air monkey and the car toad had okayed it with the jambuster.

air patch *n.* [*air*field + cotton *patch*] *USAF.* an air base.
  1951 R.L. Richards *Air Cadet* (film): Here it is, boys, Willy [Williams] Airpatch. **1955** Scott *Eagle* 11: Back at Willy Air Patch he had them refuel the ship. **1963** E.M. Miller *Exile* 123: I…had a nice flight into

Grandview airpatch. **1966** Shepard *Doom Pussy* 127: It was…Bill Bunting on the Tiger line from Clark Airpatch. **1968** W.C. Anderson *Gooney Bird* 24: I want to welcome you to Eglin air force patch. *a*1989 R. Herman, Jr. *Warbirds* 154: At least we've got one warbird on this air patch.

air pig *n. Av.* airship. Now *hist.*
  1933 Stewart *Speech of Amer. Airman* 43: *Air Pig.* A zeppelin or dirigible.

airplane *n.* **1.** [sugg. by syn. PONY] *Stu,* an interlinear or other translation of a foreign-language text.
  1912 *DN* III 570: *Aeroplane,* n. An interlinear translation.
  2. [a method of "getting HIGH"] *Stu.* the burning stub of a cannabis cigarette, the fumes of which are inhaled by sniffing.
  1968–70 *Current Slang* III & IV: *Air plane*…To light a marijuana cigarette stub and breathe the smoke through the nose. **1971** N.Y.U. student, age 21: You light the roach and snort it. It's called an *airplane.* [**1986** *NDAS: Airplane:* A tweezerlike clip for holding a marijuana cigarette stub.]

air pudding *n.* [*air* + *pudding*; cf. Brit. syn. *wind pudding*] nothing to eat; nothing.
  1862 in J.W. Haley *Rebel Yell* 54: While our friends at home suffer through roast turkey…we cram ourselves on air pudding. **1927** in Dundes *Mother Wit* 201: The Brotherhood can't print booklets,…pay organizers…on *air pudding and wind sauce.*

air-sucker *n. Av.* a jet aircraft.
  1964 *AS* XXXIX 118: *Air Sucker*…Slang for a jet aircraft.

air-tight *n.* [packed in *airtight* cans] *West.* canned food.
  1897 A.H. Lewis *Wolfville* 330: Flour, whiskey, tobaccer, air-tights an' sech.…Which you Eastern shorthorns is shore ignorant. Air-tights is can peaches, can tomatters, an sim'lar bluffs. **1923** *Outing* (Mar.) 263: I decided the party had been on airtight (canned meat) long enough. **1936** R. Adams *Cowboy Lingo* 148: "Air-tights" were canned goods.

air-to-mud *adj. Mil. Av.* air-to-ground.
  *1979 in Partridge Concise: Fine for air-to-air, but not so good for *air-to-mud. a*1989 R. Herman, Jr. *Warbirds* 168: We're an air-to-mud attack wing. *a*1991 Kross *Splash One* 36 [ref. to Vietnam War]: The 8th has a multiple mission—air-to-air and air-to-mud. **1991** Dunnigan & Bay *Shield* 360: *Air-to-Mud*…ground-attack missiles.

aisle *n. Theat.* ¶ In phrases:
  ¶ **lay** [or **roll**] **them in the aisles** to delight or dazzle an audience; (*esp.*) to convulse an audience with laughter.
  1925 *AS* I 37: They "lay 'em in the aisles." **1931** in Gelman *Photoplay* 186: The jovial clown…had rolled 'em in the aisles with his elephantine antics. **1939** "E. Queen" *Dragon* 202: The speaker gave a poor performance last night…but he guarantees to lay 'em in the aisles today. **1942** *ATS* 584: Knock 'em dead…roll 'em in the aisles. **1946** Gresham *Nightmare Alley* 126: Well, kid, we laid 'em in the aisles. **1949** Chandler *Little Sister* 176: I amuse myself. I do a brother act that has me rolling in the aisles. **1955** E. O'Connor *Last Hurrah* 120: Leave everything to me.…I'll lay 'em in the aisles. **1979** Univ. Tenn. instructor, age *ca*25: Go to it. Roll 'em in the aisles.
  ¶ **rolling** [or **bleeding**] **in the aisles** (of an audience) delighted, dazzled; (*esp.*) convulsed with laughter.
  1924 Wilstach *Stage S1.* 21: I Hope You Leave Them Bleeding in the Aisles: That is, I hope you are a wham, a wow. **1940 in OEDS:* Rolling in the aisles. **1979** N.Y.C. man, age *ca*30 [leaving movie]: They weren't exactly rolling in the aisles.

A.K. *n.* **1.** [euphem. initialism of E Yid *alter kaker* 'old shitter'] Esp. *Theat.* a crude or obnoxious old man.
  1920 *Variety* (Aug. 27) 7: Thorek Cuts Out Goat Gland Optimism. Theatrical surgeon says, Goat and Monkey N.G. for A.K. **1920** *Variety* (Sept. 3) 5: I'm going to give you a great time, you poor A.K. **1942** *ATS* 572: Veteran actor: A.K. (antediluvian knight). **1943** *AS* (Feb.) 45: A.K.…may refer to any old-fogey or has-been, whether he is an actor, a husband, or a superannuated athlete. **1943** Halper *Inch from Glory* 49: Nah, I'm an A.K. I'm thirty-five. **1944** Hart *Winged Victory* (film): I'll be callin' on you when you're an old A.K. with three grandchildren. **1964** Faust *Steagle* 130: It's all the A.K.s lookin' for a handout like my brother Milton.
  2. [perh. infl. by prec.] ASS-KISSER.
  1939 *AS* (Feb.) 24: *A.K.*, v. To curry favor with a superior. *n.* A cadet who indulges in this practice. **1966** in *DARE: A.K.* (ass-kisser). **1970**

Landy *Und. Dict.: A.K. n.* Ass kisser. **1971** Selby *Room* 28: *Public defender*...My *ass* defender. Couldn't even afford that, the rotten a.k.'s. Afraid to bug the judge.

A.K. *v.* [fr. A.K., *n.,* 2, or independently fr. ASS-KISS] to curry favor (with).

1939 (quot. at A.K., *n.,* 2). **1947** Willingham *End as a Man* 241: "Neatness." "A.K'ing." **1951** Thacher *Captain* 163: The only way to be friends with that guy is to let him A.K. you all over the deck. **1968** Baker et al. *CUSS* 69: *AK*...curry favor with a professor. **1968** *Harper's* (Nov.) 139: One knows something of where they have been: the midnight compromises and the mandatory a.k.-ing, [etc.]. **1971** Faust *Willy* 180: Bernier never even looked over, naturally a.k.'ing Dick Merriwell and Jack Armstrong.

Alabama Kleenex *n.* paper towels or toilet paper. *Joc.*

1966 Shepard *Doom Pussy* 53: Blood spurted from his face, so a pilot went to the bathroom to get some Alabama Kleenex.

Alabama marbles *n.pl. Gamb.* dice.

1920 *Amer. Legion Wkly.* (July 23) 17: Winning all the top kick's jack with the Alabama marbles.

Alabama wool *n.* cotton; cotton clothing. *Joc.*

1942 *ATS* 136: Cotton. Alabama wool. **1958** McCulloch *Woods Words: Alabama wool*—Cotton clothing, especially underwear. **1980** Ala. social worker, age 27: "Alabama wool" is cotton.

alarm clock *n.* **1.** an alarmist; persistent worrier.

1922 Tully *Lawler* 120: Why, Auntie! You awful alarm clock. I never felt better than I have this summer.

2. *Stu.* a chaperon.

1925 *AS* I 33: To the sophisticated young miss of flapperdom...an alarm clock is a chaperon.

Albany beef *n.* [*Albany,* N.Y. + *beef*] *Naut.* sturgeon meat. *Joc.*

1779 in Whiting *Early Amer. Prov.* 6: This fish is a favorite with the Dutch, at Albany, and is on that account by some called Albany beef. **1791** in *DA.* ***1867** Smyth *Sailor's Wd. Bk.: Albany Beef.* A name for the sturgeon of the Hudson River, where it is taken in quantity for commerce. **1880** in *DA.* **1889** *United Service* (Sept.) 279: We shall only wish that the crew...may have an abundance of "soft Tommy"..."spuds"...and no "Albany beef" (tough sturgeon).

alchy var. ALKY.

alcy or **Elsie** *n.* [orig. unkn.] *Mil.* a fine imposed by a court-martial.

1906 M'Govern *Sarjint Larry* 35: Is it a ten dollar alcy yez are afther awantin'? **1942** *ATS* 806: *Elsie,* a fine imposed by court-martial, as "a $10 Elsie."

alderman *n.* [ref. to the supposed stoutness of aldermen] a prominent paunch.

1929–33 Farrell *Manhood* 278: Say, I'll be damned, Studs, if you ain't getting an alderman. ***1961** Partridge *DSUE* (ed. 6) 978: *Alderman.* A prominent belly...ca. 1890–1940.

aleck *n.* [short for SMART ALECK] wiseacre, impudent person, upstart.—constr. with a modifying adj.

1908 in Blackbeard & Williams *Smithsonian Comics* 33: I can whip the fresh alec that made this drawing of me! **1916** *DN* IV 280: That sharp Alec of a man. **1934** W. Smith *B. Cotter* 226: Acting in court like a wise-aleck and pretending to be tough.

¶ In phrase:

¶ **give Aleck** [app. dim. of *Alexander*] to thrash, trounce, "give hell."

1848 *Life in Rochester* 67: I gin him Aleck, you may bet your life.

alfalfa *n.* **1.** whiskers, beard. *Joc.*

1898 Markey *Iowa* 130: Brother Moulton is also out in full "alfalfa." **1924** H.L. Wilson *Prof.* 187: Be sure to let the alfalfa grow once more.

2. the country.—constr. with *the. Joc.* Cf. ALFALFA, *adj.*

1906 *Nat. Police Gaz.* (Dec. 8) 10: Me back to the alfalfa. **1983** Stapleton *30 Yrs.* 155: His family talked him into retiring and moving to New Hampshire, or "out in the alfalfa," as Fatback put it.

3. bed or mattress, "hay."—constr. with *the. Joc.*

1911–12 Ade *Neighbors* 48: He began to prefer to take a 10-Grain Sleeping Powder and fall back in the Alfalfa.

4. money. *Joc.*

1917 in R. Peyton *At Track* 136: I bites...Goldfinger's alfalfa stack fer twenty-one iron men. **1956** *Names* IV 160: *Alfalfa* [= money]. Noted orally within the last decade. **1954–60** *DAS: Alfalfa*...Money; esp. a

small...sum. **1990** Thorne *Dict. Contemp. Slang: Alfalfa.* American...Money.

5. dehydrated vegetables. *Joc.*

1920 Skillman *A.E.F.* 169 [ref. to WWI]: *Alfalfa.* Hydrated vegetables. **1950** *West. Folk.* IX 158: *Alfalfa.* Dried spinach.

6. nonsensical talk. *Joc.*

1937 Odets *Golden Boy* 270: All other remarks are just so much alfalfa. **1940** Ellis & Logan *Star Dust* (film): I don't go for that alfalfa....Hollywood hooey. **1954–60** *DAS: Alfalfa*...baloney. *Not common.*

7. tobacco. *Joc.*

1939 Howsley *Argot: Alfalfa*...smoking tobacco. **1940** *AS* XV 335: Tobacco is...*alfalfa.*

alfalfa *adj.* provincial; rustic and foolish. Cf. ALFALFA, *n.,* 2.

1912 Lowrie *Prison* 140: I'll bet one of them alfalfa judges has handed him a ten-spot. **1913** J. London *Valley of Moon* 168: The second Sharkey, the alfalfa sportin' writers are callin' him. *Ibid.* 172: An' what did the alfalfa judge hand 'm? Fifty years. **1968** R. Adams *Western Wds.* (ed. 2): *Alfalfa desperado.* A cowboy's name for a hay-hand.

alibi *n.* [L *alibi* 'elsewhere', in allusion to the accused's assertion of not being present at the scene of the crime] Orig. *Und.* **1. a.** an excuse of any kind, esp. given to conceal deliberate wrongdoing. Now *S.E.*

1899–1900 Cullen *Tales* 295: You can begin to patch up your alibi when we get there. **1927** in Galewitz *Comics* 7: I'm not in the mood to listen to any alibis. **1929–31** D. Runyon *Guys & Dolls* 129: He probably has a good alibi for the half he does do. **1932** Hawks *Crowd Roars* (film): That's a sucker's alibi. **1956** Kubrick & Thompson *Killing* (film): I was just trying to make an alibi for you. **1978** N.Y.C. man, age 30: You'd better cook up a good alibi.

b. a person or thing that may be relied upon to add credence to someone's alibi.

1944 C. Davis *Leo McGuire* 220: A young lady...told me she was your alibi, that she was with you in a hotel room the afternoon of the robbery. **1968** S. Ross *Hang-Up* 84: She's an alibi, too. She'll swear we were here last night.

2. an alternative plan of action.

1924 Zuppke *Football* 87: A team which always has an alibi is never beaten, while one that hasn't one admits defeat.

3. *Carnival.* [ellipt. for *alibi joint;* see ALIBI, *adj.*] a fraudulent game of skills or chance, as at a fairground.

1961 Scarne *Comp. Guide to Gamb.* 506: I recently visited a carnival in Windsor, North Carolina, which was loaded with two-way joints and alibis. **1979** Crews *Blood & Grits* 162: You work hanky-panks or alibis or flats?

alibi *adj. Carnival.* (of a game) dishonest, rigged. Cf. ALIBI, *n.,* 3.

1961 Scarne *Comp. Guide to Gamb.* 500: When it's an alibi joint he displays inexpensive prizes and makes use of slightly larger hoops. *Ibid.* 458: It's an alibi store, so called because the operator always has an alibi which pretends to explain why the player lost.

alibi *v.* **1.** *intrans.* to offer an alibi.

1909 in *OEDS.* **1936** Duncan *Over Wall* 158: We can alibi as innocently as you sip your coffee. **1945** *Best from Yank* 214: [The signers of the letter] alibi that perhaps they are old-fashioned. **1955** Archibald *Av. Cadet* 145: They are paid to make pilots out of knuckleheads, and they can't alibi either.

2. *trans.* to offer an alibi for (something or someone).

1911 Howard *Enemy to Soc.* 102: Aaw, hell! I can alibi you out of anything for ten dollars. **1928** O'Connor *B'way Racketeers* 73: A drug-store blonde who has...nothing to alibi her presence but a good bank balance. **1929** Burnett *Iron Man* 94: Don't always be alibi-ing her. **1935** Coburn *Rides Range* 74: I'll help alibi you. **1959** Ryan *Longest Day* 35: Many of Rommel's senior officers have stood shoulder to shoulder in an effort to alibi the circumstances surrounding Rommel's absence from the front on...D Day. **1962** "Ed McBain" *Like Love* 41: In effect then, you alibied her, is that right? **1968** K. Cooper *Aerobics* 137: Fat men are most adept at alibiing their condition.

Alibi Ike *n.* [nickname of fictional baseball player in short story "Alibi Ike," by Ring Lardner] a person who habitually makes excuses for his actions.

1915 R. Lardner, in *Sat. Eve. Post:* His right name was Frank X. Farrell...."Alibi Ike" was the name Carey wished on him the first day he reported down South. **1926** Wood & Goddard *Amer. Slang: Alibi Ike.* One who excuses all his faults. **1958** Abbott *Damn Yankees* (film): "I was wrong. He *is* different." "Alibi Ike!" [said to a woman]. **1964** Thompson & Rice *Every Diamond* 139: *Alibi Ike.* Player who has an excuse for every mistake. **1977** *N.Y. Post* (Aug. 6) 26: What should I do?—[signed] Alibi Ike. **1987** D. da Cruz *Boot* 21: He can already spot candidates for failure: the belligerent, the foot-draggers, the Alibi-Ikes.

Alice *n.* **1.** [ref. to policeman's blue uniform; a pun on song title "In My Sweet Little Alice Blue Gown," by Joseph McCarthy & Harry Tierney (1918)] *Homosex.* the police; a policeman. Also **Alice blue gown, Alice blue.** All *Joc.*
1971 Rodgers *Queens' Vernacular: Alice*...common euphemism for the uniformed law. *Ibid.* 125: *Alice Blue Gown; Alice blues.* **1972** *Anthro. Ling.* (Mar.) 98: *Alice*...The police.
2. [poss. ref. to *Alice's Adventures in Wonderland*, by "Lewis Carroll," infl. by initial *a* of ACID; infl. by first two letters of *LSD*] LSD.
[**1967** "Jefferson Airplane" *White Rabbit* (song): One pill makes you larger, and one pill makes you small.... Go ask Alice, when she's ten feet tall.] **1971** Rodgers *Queens' Vernacular* 20: *Alice*...(SF, late '60s) LSD-25, acid.

alive *adj.* carrying money, flush.
1933 Ersine *Prison Slang: Alive,* adj. Having money. "Put the bee on Joe; he's alive."

alkali *n. West.* bitter coffee. *Joc.*
1927 *AS* (June) 389: Other names for coffee are *ink, mud, alkali* and *embalming fluid.*

alki var. ALKY.

alkied *adj.* [ALKY, 1 + *-ed*] drunk.—sometimes constr. with *up.*
1942 *ATS* 122: Drunk...alkied (up). **1954–60** *DAS: Alkied, alkied, alkeyed.* **1970** Rudensky & Riley *Gonif* 88: There must have been a dozen cops getting alkyed.

alky *n.* **1.** [shortening of *alcohol* + *-y*] alcohol; (*specif.*) alcoholic liquor, esp. whiskey.
1844 in *DA.*: After strong devotional homage before the throne of old King Alchy, [he] is in the habit of manifesting his affection for his family by severely beating them. *ca*1850 in G. Jackson *Early Songs* 225: They drink not of Alchy, but from the cool shades. **1858** in W.P.A. *S.F. Songster* 51: "Old Alky" makes their bowels yearn. **1916** in J. London *Short Stories* 691: Druggist's alcohol...is known in tramp-land as "alki." **1927** *Variety* (May 11) 1: Pop, Ginger Ale, "Alky."...1 pint alky 2.50. **1929** *AS* IV 337: Alki—Alcohol. **1930** *Amer. Mercury* (Dec.) 454: He's in the alky racket. **1942–49** Goldin et al. *DAUL* 276: That rubbing alky will knock you off. **1951** Hunt *Judas Hour* 10: Must've drunk alky instead of wine. **1967** Kolb *Getting Straight* 7: The drink was grapefruit juice blended half and half with lab alky, two hundred proof. **1980** *Popular Science* (Jan. 1981) 63: When running 100 percent alky, you do have to watch for dilution, especially in cold weather when the oil is cold.
2. [cf. ALKY STIFF] an alcoholic, drunkard.
1956 P. Moore *Chocolates* 134: I continued to be an alkie. **1968** Spradley *Drunk* 39: May have beatnik or alky offspring who requires sanitorial seclusion. **1977** *Atlantic* (June) 72: Here was an alky offering instead of asking. He took a modest gulp. **1983** *Nat. Lampoon* (Mar.) 69: Yves is a closet alkie. **1989** "Captain X" *Unfriendly Skies 131:* Druggies and alkies and crazy people.

alky cooker *n.* one who is engaged in the illegal distillation of alcohol; (*also*) an illegal still.
1930 Pasley *Capone* 44: They were the combine's alky cookers. **1931** *AS* (Dec.) 104: *Alki cooker*...One who has charge of distilling alcohol. **1933** Ersine *Prison Slang: Alky Cooker.* 1....a still tender, usually one tending an illegal still. 2. An illegal still. **1935** Mackenzie *Been Places* 184: He has thousands of them employed as alky cookers and distillers. **1969** Halper *Chi. Crime Bk.* 47: When Prohibition came, his father became an alki cooker on the North Side.

alky stiff *n.* [ALKY, 1 + STIFF 'fellow'] a habitually drunken tramp or beggar.
1913 J. London *J. Barleycorn* 112: An alki stiff is a tramp who drinks druggist's alcohol. **1918** [Livingston] *Delcassee* 44: *Alkee stiff,* White Line Stiff...Confirmed consumers of alcohol. **1973** Knopf *Emperor of N. Pole* (film): You stew bums and alky stiffs.

all ¶ In phrases:
¶ **all the way** (of a hamburger, etc.) served with lettuce, tomato, pickle, onions, relish, etc.
1957 MacDonald *Death Trap* 76: Spotlights were focused on a huge replica of a hamburger "all the way" that revolved slowly on a pedestal. **1966** IUFA *Folk Speech: Cheeseburger all-the-way*—Cheeseburger with everything on it. **1980** Knoxville, Tenn., short-order cook, age *ca*50: Two hamburgers all the way! Two cheeseburgers!
¶ **go all the way** see s.v. WAY.
¶ **that's all she wrote** *Mil.* "that's all"; "that's the end." Cf. DEAR JOHN.
1948 *AS* XXIII 250 [ref. to WWII]: That's all she wrote. An expression of termination. **1948–50** J. Jones *Eternity* 39 [ref. to 1941]: If she got caught with you, all she'd have to do is to holler rape and it would be Dear John, that's all she wrote. **1961** Peacock *Valhalla* 366: They want a part of your ass....Dear John, that's all she wrote. **1963** Lester & Gordon *Sgt. Ryker* (film): But if they find you guilty a second time, that's it, brother. That's all she wrote. **1969** Spetz *Rat Pack* 53: If Charlie doesn't use that trail, we'll be outflanked, and "That's all she wrote." **1970** Thackrey *Thief* 409: That was all she wrote, baby. **1970** Wakefield *All the Way* 236: I'm shaving the beard and that's all she wrote. **1979** Ark. man, age 51: That's all she wrote, she didn't write no more.

allay *v.* [F *allez!* 'go!'] *Mil.* to go, hurry, run. Also **alley, allez.**
1918 Swan *My Company* 55: We'd better "allez" to a shell-hole. **1921** Dos Passos *Three Soldiers* 79: I got ordered back and had to alley down to this goddam camp. **1928** MacArthur *War Bugs* 57: One member of the gun crew "allayed" to the kitchen for bread and coffee. **1942** in *Americans vs. Germans* 88 [ref. to WWI]: Allez to beat hell. **1945** *Sat. Rev.* (Nov. 3) 7.

allee-samee [pidgin for *all the same*] **1.** *adv.* in the same way; nevertheless.
1856 in C.A. Abbey *Before the Mast* 65: All e same. **1883** in Ware *Passing Eng.* 6: They were not quite married, but...lived together allee-samee. **1885** *Puck* (June 17) 251: He got renominated...allee-samee. **1886** E.L. Wheeler *N.Y. Nell* 9: I twig you allee-samee, as the Chinamen say.
2. *prep.* like; like a. Also **all-same.**
1926 C.M. Russell *Trails* 133: He packs a medicine bag, all-same savage. **1945** Colcord *Sea Lang.* 22: Allee samee hell you will.

allerickstix *interj.* [G *alles richtig*] all right, fine.
1890 *DN* I 60: *Allerickstix* (used in common schools of Cincinnati): all right. E.g. "How did you get through examination?" "Allerickstix." Presumably a corruption of German *alles richtig.* **1980** in *DARE: Allerickstix*—I heard this used in Akron, Ohio, in an English context, about 1922 by a young male, about 14–15 years old.

alley *n.* **1.** *Baseball.* the undefended area between two outfielders, or between an outfielder and a foul line, into which a ball may be hit, usu. for extra bases. Now *S.E.*
1912 *Amer. Mag.* (June) 199: *Alley*—Imaginary lines between right and center and right and left fielders [*sic*] down which hard hit balls go between the fielders, usually for home runs. "Down the Alley" means a home run hit. **1962** Houk & Dexter *Ballplayers* 78: Mickey [Mantle]...races into the alley to turn a potential...triple into a put-out. **1978** Bill White, N.Y. Yankees announcer on WINS radio: Then he hit a shot down the alley in left for a triple.
2. (one's) range of talents or liking.—usu. in phr. **up** [or **down**] **(one's) alley** well suited to (one's) tastes or talents.
1924 in E. O'Neill *Letters* 187: As a production it must be right "up his alley." **1929** in *DA:* Fun's fun, but box-fighting's your trick and anything else is out of your alley. **1930** Gilman *Sob Sister* 65: It's about time a good murder broke anyway, and this one is right up your alley, Jane. **1932** Binyon & Bolton *Million* (film): Baseball is right down my back alley. **1938** Macaulay & Wald *Bro. Rat* (film): Why don't you drive a roller coaster? It'd be more up your alley. **1949** Gardner *Negligent Nymph* 34: When I read what was in the bottle, I realized it was right down my alley. **1977** Univ. Tenn. grad. student, age 28: I can see why *Beowulf's* right up your alley. **1979** *Business Week* (Mar. 5) 56: Tough financial problems are right down our alley. **1992** Hosansky & Sparling *Working Vice* 33: You won't even have to carry a gun. It's right up your alley.
3. *Baseball.* the middle of the strike zone conceived as an imaginary corridor extending directly from the pitcher's mound across the middle of home plate to the catcher's glove.
1929 *N.Y. Times* (June 2) IX 2: "In the alley" or "in the slot" is...a ball that cuts the heart of the plate, and "up his alley," a ball that comes at the speed and in the position that a particular batter finds easiest to hit. **1933** Farrell *McGinty* 287: The ball shot straight down the alley and Buck missed. **1938** Nichols *Baseball Term.* 22: *Down the alley:*...a ball

pitched over the middle of the home plate. **1945** Warner Bros. *Looney Tunes* (animated cartoon): Put it right over the plate. Right down the old alley. **1947** *Redbook* (July) 29: I keep…one eye on the alley between the pitcher's mound and home plate.

¶ In phrases:

¶ **Up an alley!** Go away! Get lost!

1900 Ade *More Fables* 98: Uncle Brewster…thought it his Duty to tell the officer that the Theater Folks were a Pack of Robbers. "Up an Alley," said the Policeman. **1902–03** Ade *People* 74: That will be all from you.…Mosey! Duck! Up an Alley!

¶ **up the wrong alley** mistaken, "barking up the wrong tree."

1952 Sandburg *Strangers* 380 [ref. to 1890's]: You're up the wrong alley, sister. I ain't got but two nickels and they wouldn't do you any good.

alley var. ALLAY.

alley apple *n.* **1.** a rock, stone, or brickbat, as thrown in a street brawl.

1927 *AS* (June) 390: A rock is an *alley apple*. **1930** Irwin *Amer. Tramp & Underworld Sl.* **1946** in *DAS*: A fellow's blonde usually stepped in…and slugged the other gee with an alley apple. **1979** W. Safire, in *N.Y. Times Mag.* (Nov. 11) 15: A loose brick that can be thrown is called an "alley apple" in Washington [D.C.]. **1985** *New Yorker* (Aug. 19) 49: So he…came back with a…pistol…and I saw an alley apple lying there.…A piece of red brick.

2. a piece of horse manure on a city street. Now *Rare.*

1954–60 *DAS: Alley apple*…A piece of horse manure. **1967** in *DARE: Alley apples*—horse droppings. Old fashioned term, used chiefly by males.

alley cat *n.* a person, esp. a woman, who frequents back alleys; *(specif.)* a sexually promiscuous individual.

1926 in *OEDS*: Thinking up a way of insulting that mangy alley cat! **1941** *Time* (June 16) 85: Alley cat (applied to a woman). **1968** Gover *Saves* 108: She's…an alley cat. **1971** Dahlskog *Dict. Contemp. Us.: Alley cat*…a person with loose sexual morals; a tomcat.

alley-cat *v.* to behave in the manner of an ALLEY CAT; *(specif.)* to promiscuously seek sexual partners, as in bars, etc.

1964 Leitner & Lanen *Dict. Fr. & Amer. Slang* 2: *To alley cat around*…courir les femmes. **1978** *Goin' South* (film): No drinkin', no gamblin', no wife-beatin', and no alley-cattin'.

alley-cleaner *n.* a firearm that can be used to disperse a mob.

1957 *AS* (Oct.) 192: *Alley cleaner, n.* A handgun. Originally applied to a riot gun.

alley lily *n.* ALLEY APPLE, 1.

1924 Nason *Three Lights* 16 [ref. to WWI]: A stone sailed toward the liaison detail.…"Hey! Lay off the alley lilies!" he called sleepily.

alley rat *n.* a person who dwells in or frequents slum alleys; a guttersnipe.

1914 Yore *Songs* 18: The Alley Rat. **1929–33** Farrell *Manhood* 229: And what the hell, the kid was just a goddamn alley rat. **1936** Farrell *World I Never Made* 349: "Go on, you alley rats," Margaret yelled at the kids. **1942** *ATS* 424: *Alley rat*…a night prowler [i.e., thief].

alley rifle *n.* ALLEY APPLE, 1.

1969 *N.Y. Post* (Oct. 11) 70 [ref. to Georgia, 1942]: Alley rifles [were rocks].

allez var. ALLAY.

all-fired *adj.* [perh. euph. for *hell-fired*] excessive, extreme; remarkable.

1845 *Knickerbocker Mag.* (Aug.) 182: The doctor'll charge an all-fired price to cure me, I s'pect. **1855** in Thornton *Amer. Gloss.* I 10: Here is the all-firedest fence yet. **1890** Roe *Striking Contrast* 23: What an all-fired heap of money! **1910** G. Rice, in M. Gardner *Casey* 55: What an all-fired battin' average he possessed. **1914** Z. Grey *W. Stars* 130: I don't see any call fer sech all-fired fuss.

all-fired *adv.* excessively, extremely. Also **all-firedly**.

1833 A. Greene *Duckworth* II 176: He was seldom downright drunk; but was often all-firedly sprung. **1837** *Yale Lit. Mag.* II 149: Star's an all-fired good ox. **1850** in Thornton *Amer. Gloss.* I 10: You will get all-firedly licked. **1910** *N.Y. Eve. Journ.* (Feb. 3) 14: He pitched…all-fired great ball. **1952** Vonnegut *Player Piano* 60: He doesn't look so all-fired bright to me. **1955** Abbey *Brave Cowboy* 27: She's so all-fired pig-headed. **1971** Capon *3d Peacock* 17: Why is God so all-fired insistent on

preserving my brother-in-law's freedom to gum up everybody's life?

alligator *n.* **1.** a frontier rowdy, esp. a boatman of the Ohio or Mississippi Valley.

1808 in *DA*: I am an alligator, half man, half horse; can whip any on the Mississippi, by G-d. **1860** in R.B. Browne *Lincoln-Lore* 337: Old Kentuck sent forth a man,/A "horse and alligator." **1861** in *DA*: But the millions of Yankees—from codfish to alligators—…know little of these treasures of theirs. **1945** in *DARE*: I'm the toughest goldarned alligator in the North Woods.

2. a worthless or underhanded individual.

1839 *Spirit of Times* (July 6) 208: Sit down you gray-haired alligator!…You have perjured yourself from the start! **1947–53** Guthrie *Seeds* 251: That ole crazy alligator. What made 'im…pull a stunt like that?

3.a. [punning on *alligator fr. *allegate*] one who makes allegations; proponent. *Joc.*

1839 *Spirit of Times* (June 15) 175: He is emphatically…the "supreme alligator" of anything that savors of *advance*. **1884** Hartranft *Sidesplitter* 41: Them 'ere allegations is false, and that 'ere alligator knows it! ***1914–21** Joyce *Ulysses* 337: —Who made those allegations? says Alf. —I, says Joe, I'm the alligator. **1980** *Harper's* (Sept.) 19: Any recruit "allegator" [*sic*] can cause a reportedly offending drill instructor to be temporarily suspended from training duties only on grounds of reasonable cause. **1993** *N.Y. Times* (Oct. 11) A17: I can only recall the old "Amos 'n Andy" show:…"I denies the allegation and I resents the alligator."

b. a "bigmouth"; chatterbox.

1976 Dills *CB '77* 2: *Alligator:* CBer who talks too much; CBer who has a "big mouth."

4. [shoe resembles mouth of *alligator*; also punning on *alligator* shoes] a shoe whose upper has become detached from the sole at the toe. *Joc.*

1878 Bellew *Tramp* 31: We tramps, when our boots had attained a certain stage of decay, used to call them alligators, from a certain fanciful resemblance they bore to the head of that amiable creature.

5. a native or longtime resident of Florida.

1909 Ware *Passing English* 6: Alligators…People of Florida. **1934** Weseen *Dict. Amer. Slang* 302: *Alligators*—Inhabitants of Florida.

6. *Horse Racing.* an old, slow racehorse.

1935 D. Runyon & H. Lindsay, in R. Nelson *Dishonorable* 272: That old alligator couldn't do a mile in a van. ***1943** in Partridge *DSUE* (ed. 7) 981.

7. [poss. cf. (**2.**) & (**3.**), above; expl. in 1955 and 1957 quots. prob. fanciful] *Jazz.* a devotee of swing music. Now *hist.*

1936 in Gold *Jazz Lex.: Alligator*—a non-playing swing devotee. **1937** *New Yorker* (Apr. 17) 27: *Alligators*—non-performing *swing* devotees—are sometimes permitted to attend. **1938** *N.Y. Post* (Feb. 3) 15: Now then, the alligators, that's the swing fans, get the drift. **1943** *N.Y. Times* (May 9) II 5: Some alligators clocking the action started for the stage. **1946** in Gold *Jazz Lex.*: He talked of "jitterbugs" and "alligators"—more conservatively known as swing music enthusiasts. [**1955** in Shapiro & Hentoff *Hear Me Talkin'* 97 [ref. to N.O., *ca*1920]: Some guys would come in…to learn what you were doing. We'd call them alligators…because they were guys who came up to swallow everything we had to learn.] [**1957** in Rosset *Evergreen Reader* 24 [ref. to N.O., 1919]: We used to call white musicians "alligators." That was the way we'd describe them when they'd come around and we were playing something that we didn't want them to catch on to. We'd say, "Watch out, there's an alligator."] **1966** *RHD*.

8. *Auto.* a kind of cab-over tractor, access to the engine of which must be gained head first through the interior of the cab.

1971 Tak *Truck Talk: Alligator:* an old-time cabover tractor that lacked the tilt-cab mechanism for easy access to the engine.…These cabovers were called alligators because they looked as if they were about to swallow the…garageman.

¶ In phrases:

¶ **make like an** [or **play**] **alligator and drag ass** [extension of *drag ass*, to leave] to leave, clear out. *Joc.*—usu. considered vulgar.

1951–53 in *AS* XXIX 53: Make like an alligator and drag ass, *v. phr.* To leave in a hurry. **1975** Ark. man, age 42: O.K., let's play alligator and drag ass.

¶ **see** [or **dig**] **you later, alligator** [prob. fr. (**7.**), above] (used as a farewell). [The expected response is **in** [or **after**]

a while, crocodile, or **on the Nile, crocodile.**]
1954 in IUFA *Folk Speech*: Saying: Dig you later, alligator. **1956** Bill Haley & His Comets *See You Later, Alligator* [rock song title]. **1966** N.Y.C. high school students, age 17: "See you later, alligator." "In a while, crocodile." **1972** Hannah *Geronimo* 128: See you later, alligator. **1978** Pilcer *Teen Angel* 183: "See you later—alligator!" Dot said. God, was she ever corny. **1979** Univ. Tenn. grad. students: "See you later, alligator." "On the Nile, crocodile." **1984** *Business Week* (Feb. 27) 104: Today, customers say, "Give me the product, give me the price, and see you later, alligator." **1991** D. Anderson *In Corner* 45: The fighter says, "See you later, alligator!"

¶ **up to one's ass** (*vulgar*) [or **ears**] **in alligators** in a dangerous or hopelessly confused situation; (*hence*) confused, agitated.
[**1877** in Hearn *Occid. Gleanings* I 217: Swamps...if you walk right to the end of Canal street beyond the graveyard, and into the swamp, why, you'll be up to your neck in alligators.] [**1959** W.R. Anderson *Nautilus* 216: "Lady alligators [are man's best friends.]...These lady alligators...lay about 1,000 eggs...[and devour] 999!"..."How does that make her man's best friend?" "If that lady alligator didn't eat those 999 eggs, we'd be up to our necks in alligators."] **1964** in Lucas *Dateline: Vietnam* 29: If a man gets in hot water, he's in "deep trouble." If he's in real deep trouble, he's "up to his ears in alligators." [**1972** *N.Y. Times Mag.* (Mar. 12) 106: Secretary of State Richard Stone dismissed the whole thing as "ludicrous....We're right in the middle of the Okefenokee Swamp and hip-deep in alligators."] **1973** W. Crawford *Gunship Cmndr.* 14: Joe, you were...so up to your ass in alligators over returning to Southeast Asia, you failed to read everything in that envelope. *Ibid.* 62: They know they'd be up to their asses in alligators if they removed themselves from flight status...for admitted use of marijuana. **1977** Univ. Tenn. students: "You got much work to do?" "I'm up to my ass in alligators right now." **1980** Knoxville insurance salesman, age 36: When you're up to your ass in alligators, you don't make plans to drain the swamp. **1980** Garrison *Snakedoctor* 145: I'm up to my ass in alligators, and I gotta drain the swamp. **1988** Dietl & Gross *One Tough Cop* 27: He said they were up to their ass in alligators.

¶ (In other prov. expressions).
1972 Wambaugh *Blue Knight* 162: The guy couldn't run no faster than a pregnant alligator. **1975** C.W. Smith *Country Music* 118: [Beer] whose taste Heavy had likened to alligator piss.

alligator bait *n*. *Gulf So.* **1.** a black person, esp. a child or young woman.—usu. considered offensive.—used contemptuously. Also collect.
[**1864** in Glatthaar *March to Sea* 56: Alligators...will pass by a white man to catch a colored man—something very strange.] **1901** Oliver *Roughing It with Regulars* 75: Pickaninnies or as they are most commonly known, "alligator bait," swam around the boat. **1916–22** Cary *Sex. Vocab. I.: Alligator bait*. A negress. *To get a piece of alligator bait*—To have intercourse with a negress. **1942** *ATS* 360: Negro child: Alligator bait. **1944** Burley *Harlem Jive* 133: *Alligator-bait*—A colored man, usually one from Florida. **1947** Goffin *Horn* 96: Get the hell out of here,...alligator bait! **1954–60** *DAS.* **1970** in *DARE*.
2. a worthless individual.
1957 in Algren *Lonesome Monsters* 139: Don't you jump bad with me, you alligator bait, you.
3. liver.
1926 *AS* I 650: *Alligator bait*—fried or stewed liver. **1927** *DN* V 137: *Alligator bait*...stewed or fried liver. This is a staple article of food at construction camps. Bull's liver is kept until rotten to make it tender. **1930** "D. Stiff" *Milk & Honey* 198. **1930** Irwin *Amer. Tramp & Und. Slang.*

alligator horse *n*. [fr. *half horse, half alligator*, describing a rowdy frontiersman] ALLIGATOR, 1. Now *hist.*
[**1809** Irving *History of N.Y.* VI 85 in *DA*: The back-wood-men of Kentucky are styled half man, half horse, and half alligator by the settlers on the Mississippi, and held accordingly in great respect and abhorrence.] **1826** S. Woodworth *Melodies* 221 in *DA*: We'll show him that Kentucky boys are "alligator horses." **1850** in *DA*: "Eh! him, a horse, eh!" said the Judge. "Yes, sir, an alligator horse." **1938** P. Crawford *Hello, Boat!* 7: What would a flatboat man do on a keelboat? I'm no alligator-horse.

alligator mouth *n*. an inclination to boast, bluster, or threaten; (*hence*) a person so inclined.—often contrasted with *hummingbird ass* or similar phr.
[**1922** in S. Smith *Gumps* 22: Publish that, you pen pusher with the

mouth of an alligator and the brain of a minnow.] **1961** Peacock *Valhalla* 21: Don't let your alligator mouth overload your canary ass. **1969** Bouton *Ball Four* 272: And a fellow who talks big but appears to lack courage is said to have an *alligator mouth* and a *hummingbird ass.* **1977** Scholl *Baseball Gloss.: Alligator mouth.* A player who boasts or derides other players but lacks the courage to back up his words. *a*1979 Peers & Bennett *Logical Laws* 6: Don't ever let an alligator mouth overload a hummingbird rear end. *a*1989 C.S. Crawford *Four Deuces* 113: Again I let my alligator mouth overload my hummingbird ass.

all in *adj.* [sense (2) is prob. the original meaning, but no early citations are known] **1.** done for, having reached the point of collapse, failure, etc., "used up"; (now the dominant meaning) exhausted, tired out.—used predicatively.
1868 J. Chisholm *So. Pass* 158: Now I've struck a big thing/And yet...Before another season goes,/It may be all in. **1902** in *DA*: The horse was holding up to his clip, but it could easily be seen that he was "all in." **1904** Ade *True Bills* 46: When you are all in...a new generation comes along and gives you a good swift bump. **1905** *Nat. Police Gaz.* (July 1) 10: He has busted mitts, a diaphanous stomach, and is all in. **1905** *Nat. Police Gaz.* (July 8) 3: I had run him in the mud until my horse was "all in." **1905** "H. McHugh" *Get Next* 97: I cut loose with the observation that men were all in at 40. **1908** in H.C. Fisher *A. Mutt* 24: I fear he will never speak again, madame. He's all in. **1908** Train *Crime Stories* 312: Dodge reached New York a physical wreck....Jesse, too, was, as the expression is, "all in." **1913** A. Palmer *Salvage* 117: The other was nearly "all in" but gasped gamely, "Bill, I'll never quit." **1920** in Woods *Horse-Racing* 299: Man o' War...ran a hard race, but he was not all in at the end. **1926** Dunning & Abbott *Broadway* 30: Gawd, I'm all in. **1939** Dos Passos *Young Man* 25: Hell, my feet are wet and I'm all in. **1953** R. Wright *Outsiders* 94: "You're all in," she commented sympathetically. **1975** Univ. Tenn. student: You go to the show. I'm all in.
2. [ref. to having put *all* of one's money *in* the pot] Esp. *Poker.* out of money, broke.—used predicatively.
1907 in H.C. Fisher *A. Mutt* 14: Sorry, I ain't got [the money]....I'm all in. **1908** McGaffey *Show Girl* 195: The inheritance...was pretty near all in. **1986** Hayano *Poker Faces* 120: Collusive partners in a game will keep raising until a third or fourth unsuspecting player is "all-in" (has no more chips left). *Ibid.* 185: *All-in.* Betting all of one's remaining chips.

all-nighter *n.* an activity which lasts all night; (*esp.*) an entire night spent in study or a party lasting all night.
1964 Trimble *Sex Words: All-Nighter*...Night-long sex session. **1966** in IUFA *Folk Speech*: College Slang: *Pulled an all-nighter:* when one stays up all night. **1968** *Sat. Rev.* (Nov. 30) 27: Ludicrously out of place, like a dowager at a hippy all-nighter. **1968** Baker et al. *CUSS* 70: *All-nighter*, A wild party. **1973** N.Y.U. *Cold Duck* (Jan. 16) 19: One can't very well pull an "all-nighter" without an ample supply of coffee. **1979** Univ. Tenn. grad. student, age 28: It's gonna be another all-nighter tonight. **1982** P. Michaels *Grail* 193: If you plan to make it an all-nighter.... **1992** *L.A. Times Mag.* (Sept. 27) 20: It is in her frilly office at Mozark Productions in Studio City...that she can most often be found, merrily pulling all-nighters.

Allotment Annie *n.* *Mil.* a woman who bigamously marries servicemen in order to unlawfully collect pay allotments as a dependent. Now *hist.*
1970 *N.Y. Times Bk. Review* (Nov. 22) 26 [ref. to WWII]: The enterprising young women known as Allotment Annies...frequented military bases, bigamously married one departing serviceman after another and collected the $50-a-month wife's allotment for each. **1985** Westin *Love & Glory* 121 [ref. to WWII]: Putting on a uniform brings old girl-friends out of the woodwork—Allotment Annies, ya know.

all-over *n.* a careful visual inspection. Cf. ONCE-OVER.
1915–16 Lait *Beef, Iron & Wine* 95: He gives me the all-over like he was gonna buy me or something.

all right *adj.* excellent, great; (of persons) dependable, trustworthy, friendly.—often used as an interj. [Owing to its similarity in meaning to S.E. senses ("correct; satisfactory"), this expression has become colloq. in the 20th C.; but beginning about 1970, it has seen wide use, esp. among teenagers, as an emphatic interjection having exclamatory stress on final syllable.]
*1823 "J. Bee" *Slang* 6: Bang-up—quite in fashion, at the top of the mode. All right. **1862** in McClellan *Civil War Papers* 213: The President is all right—he is my strongest friend. **1872** Burnham *Secret Service* vi:

All-Right: one who may be trusted; sure. **1899** Kountz *Baxter's Ltrs.* 36: Jim, should anyone ever tell you that grand opera is all right...he is not a true friend. *Ibid.* 43: That's a new one on me, and it's all right. **1903** T.W. Jackson *Slow Train* 72: You vas a good fellow, you vas all right. **1913–15** Van Loan *Count* 20: The Doc. is all right....He knows how a feller can keep in shape. **1931** B. Morgan *Five-Star Final* (film): "Whadda you say to a bathing beauty race to Hollywood?" "Do you want them to *swim* there?" "Aw r-i-i-ight!" **1947** Mailer *Naked & Dead* 199: This was *all right*. **1950** Calmer *Strange Land* 207: He's an all right officer. An all right guy. You didn't mind helping him out because you knew he would come through if you needed him. **1959** F.L. Brown *Trumbull Pk.* 419: Harry laughed, "Well, *all* right!" **1968** Lockridge *Hartspring* 46: They're a bunch of swell all-right guys. **1968–71** Cole & Black *Checking* 42: Harry: Awww righttt! **1970** in B. Jackson *Swim Like Me* 59: Some people in audience laugh and clap, one says, "All *right*, all *right*!" **1970–72** in *AS* L 55: *All right*...Agreed! I approve! **1975** V.B. Miller *Trade-Off* 35: The judge [was] an all-right guy.

allrightnik *n.* [E. Ashkenazic E, fr. AmE *all right* + -NIK] a nouveau riche person, esp. a Jew, who is stereotypically philistine and smug.
   1918 Mencken *Amer. Language* 156: Allrightnick means an upstart, an offensive boaster. **1923** Ornitz *Haunch, Paunch & Jowl* 205: The Ghetto called anyone who was well off—one who is *all right in this world*, that is well fixed, an *Allrightnik*. **1936** Levin *Old Bunch* 184: Mr. Klein reminded him...of all the landlords they had ever had: The *allrightniks* to whom rent had to be paid. **1954** *New Yorker* (May 15) 132: There are moments when we feel about Joseph that he is a little what is meant by the Yiddish word *allrightnik*, when we are tempted to sympathize with the brothers in their resentment at his reading of dreams that is always to his own advantage. **1972** Jason Epstein, in *N.Y. Times Mag.* (Mar. 26) 108: It was, to use a term favored by the intellectuals of the fifties, the allrightniks who did the most expensive travelling. **1973** *Atlantic* (May) 96: Soviet allrightniks want to give up everything, to become paupers, if only they can start over in a language they don't know, [etc.].

all-same var. ALLEE-SAMEE, 2.

allsbay *n.* [Pig Latin form of BALLS 'nonsense'] utter nonsense, "baloney."
   *1943 in Partridge *Dict. Und.* 6: "That's allsbay," interrupted Limpy Joe, querulously. ***1957** in Partridge *Dict. Und.* 788. **1972** R.A. Wilson *Forbidden Words* 16: Allsbay...probably the best-known pig latin word in modern American.

all that *adj. Rap Music.* first-rate, perfect. Also **all dat, all o' dat.**
   1991 Nelson & Gonzales *Bring Noise* 211: Overall, *Raising Hell* ain't all that. **1991** *Source* (Oct.) 33: Yo, this album is all that. **1991** in *Rap Pages* (Feb. 1992) 7: All o' dat Jack shows up. **1992** "Fab 5 Freddy" *Fresh Fly Flavor* 63: *You all that*—You look good. **1993** *Real World* (MTV): Don't walk away 'cause you think you all that!

all-the-same *prep.* [cf. ALLEE-SAMEE] quite the same as.
   1908 McGaffey *Show Girl* 15: He thinks of something, and people miles away think of the same thing. All the same wireless.

all-time *adj.* Esp. *Surfing.* memorably good; absolutely first-rate. [The prolepsis in 1945 quot. shows it to be slang, rather than S.E. use.]
   1945 Coming attractions preview for *Billy Rose's Diamond Horseshoe* (film): the latest...all-time hit songs! **1961** Kohner *Gidget Goes Hawaiian* 6: Let's just say [the weather] was *all-time*. Which, in case you're not up-to-date, means the utmost, the greatest. **1968** N.Y.U. student: When I was in California this summer the surfers used to say...*"That surf was all-time!"* All-time great. **1981** Noel *VNR Dict.: All-time.* Surfer's slang for great, fantastic, wonderful. **1983** Wambaugh *Delta Star* 270: Man, that was all-time what I read about you in the paper last January! All-time!

all-timer *n.* [one "for all time"] an outstanding example, an "all-time classic."
   1973 Gent *N. Dallas* 147: "An all-timer," Maxwell groaned [*sc.* a hangover].

all-wool *adj.* first-class.
   1864 in J.W. Haley *Rebel Yell* 155: We gave them an "all wool" yell and tore after them.

-alorum or **-alorium** *suffix.* [pseudo-L; prob. extracted fr. *cockalorum*] (used for humorous emphasis).
   1896 Ade *Artie* 87: Does she? She's a scorchalorum. **1902** "H.

McHugh" *Woods* 46: It looks to me like a cinchalorum. **1939** Appel *Power House* 81: Crap!...Crapalorium.

Alphabet City *n. N.Y.C.* the Lower East Side of New York City in the vicinity of Avenues A, B, C, and D.
   1980 L. Birnbach *Offic. Preppy Hndbk.* 165: There are several Preppunk types who...spend their weekends in alphabet city (Avenues A, B, C, and D) on the Lower East Side of New York wearing oversized hand-painted T-shirts and black sneakers. **1984** Mayor Edward Koch, in *N.Y. Times* (Apr. 27) A27: The neighborhood, known as Alphabet City because of its lettered avenues that run easterly from First Avenue to the river, has for years been occupied by a stubbornly persistent plague of street dealers in narcotics. **1986** Stroud *Close Pursuit* 18: The men who built Alphabet City are all dead now. **1987** D. Silver & H. Keith *Mondo New York* (film): But now I live where it's really tough—I live in Alphabet City. **1988** Ad for *N.Y. Newsday*, on WABC-TV (June 8): People are living in teepees on the lower East Side of New York, in what we call Alphabet City. **1991** Nelson & Gonzales *Bring the Noise* 19: The streets of Alphabet City are...jammed with drug dealers.

also-ran *n.* [orig. a racehorse that *also ran* in a race but failed to win, place, or show] a loser in a race, contest, election, or competition of any kind. Now *colloq.*
   1896 Ade *Artie* 16: They ain't even in the "also rans." **1899** Cullen *Tales* 17: That insidious town always counted me among the also-rans before I had a show to find out where I was at. **1902** K. Harriman *Ann Arbor Tales* 248: The "also-rans"...are just waiting for the end. **1945** in *DA*: Within a few hours some would be glorious in victory...some would be colorless "also rans." **1980** *Time* (Nov. 3) 101: In 98 years, the Quaker City also-rans contrived to reach the World Series just three times. **1983** *Nat. Lampoon* (Nov.) 4: Past years as an also-ran.

altitude-happy *adj.* [*altitude* + -HAPPY] *Av.* giddy from the effects of too much oxygen.
   1955 Scott *Eagle* 66: Hair-brained throttle jockeys..."altitude happy" from too much oxygen.

altogether *n.* complete nakedness.—constr. with *the.* Now *colloq.*
   *1894 (cited in Partridge *DSUE*). **1978** Wharton *Birdy* 199: There I am...in the "altogether."

alum *n.* precisely what is wanted.—constr. with *the.*
   1879 Dacus *Frank & Jesse* 349: "But...the train will stop if I do!" "That's the alum! precisely what we wanted to do, my buck."

aluminum overcast *n. USAF.* any very large multi-engined aircraft. *Joc.*
   1961 Barr & Howard *Missileman* 59: C-124 cargo planes...[were] known throughout the Air Force as the "Aluminum Overcast." **1962** Harvey *Strike Command* 174: The Lockheed F-104—called a "razor blade on a pregnant hatpin"—and the "aluminum overcast"...the C-124. **1968** W.C. Anderson *Gooney Bird* 20: My last assignment was in C-124's at Travis...The Aluminum Overcast. **1971** Drendel *Aircraft* 3: He may call it...an aluminum overcast. **1975** Former B-52 navigator, age 31: We generally called the 52's *BUFs* or *aluminum overcasts*. I've also heard it applied to C-141's and C-130's. **1985** Boyne & Thompson *Wild Blue* 349: I don't think these aluminum overcasts [B-52's] will hold together at four hundred knots on the deck in the mountains.

Aluminum Womb *n. USAF.* the U.S. Air Force Academy. *Joc.*
   1965 *Life* (Feb. 12) 68: The "aluminum womb"—that's what we [cadets] call the academy.

Alvin *n.* [considered to be a typical rustic name; cf. ELMER, HICK, RUBE] *Carnival.* a gullible fellow, esp. a countryman.
   1942–49 Goldin et al. *DAUL:* Yeah, some Alvin beefed on us to the town clown. **1976** Braly *False Starts* 72: I registered the unconscious contempt of the barkers for the Alvins and the Clydes who strolled the midway, fat silly sheep who thought it fun to be fleeced.

amateur *n.* a sexually promiscuous young woman who is not a prostitute.—also in phr. **to lose (one's) amateur standing** to become a prostitute.
   *1851–61 Mayhew *London Labour* IV 221: This class have been called the "amateurs," to contradistinguish them from the professionals, who devote themselves to [prostitution] entirely as a profession. **1929–33** Farrell *Manhood of Lonigan* 227: "She did so well hustling she's in the business for good now." "She sacrificed her amateur standing, huh?" ***1934** Yeates *Winged Victory* 13: Isn't England the paradise of the enthusiastic amateur, who has almost got official recognition as part of

the war? **1935** Wolfe *Time & River* 120: I never knew she was a perfessional. I thought she was an amatoor. **1941** Kendall *Army & Navy Sl.* 19: *Gull*...a girl ashore who has lost her amateur standing. **1942** Wylie *Vipers* 68: Brothers, husbands, and sons...are busy...contracting venereal diseases from millions of whores and amateurs. **1946–50** J. Jones *Here to Eternity* 171: You mean she kept her amateur standing. **1957–64** Selby *Last Exit* 108: The bartender refilled her glass and marked her for an amateur. **1965** Capote *Cold Blood* 250: Hustlers, mostly...but plenty of amateurs, too. Nurses, Secretaries.

amateur night *n.* [ref. to theatrical *amateur nights*, when nonprofessional and typically unskilled entertainers are given an opportunity to perform] a situation marked by, or an example of, glaring ineptitude. Sometimes also **amateur hour.**—sometimes as adj.
1939 M. McCall *Maisie* (film): Hey, what is this? Amateur night? There's a [real] doctor right in there. **1964** Barthelme *Caligari* 26: Child's play, amateur night, with whom do they think they have to deal? **1974** Lahr *Trot* 194: Jenny, I know you're interested in movies....But believe me—this is amateur night. "Underground" is the wrong name for this monkey business. **1977** Dunne *Confessions* 319: Well, she must've done it with pliers and a screwdriver. It was real amateur night. **1977** Avallone *White Knight* 108: You might just as well have just been born. Because you're strictly Amateur-Night. **1978** *U.S. News & W.R.* (Nov. 6) 24: In some races...inexperienced Republican candidates ran inept campaigns. Observed one top GOP official: "We're having some amateur hours." **1979** *Business Week* (Oct. 22) 88: Britain's leaders have been deeply shocked by what they regard as "amateur night" in the Carter White House. **1984** "W.T. Tyler" *Shadow Cabinet* 16: Now it's amateur night in Washington—four years of it.

Amazon *n.* [cf. S.E. sense] **1.** a sexually attractive, statuesque young woman.
[**1943** *Yank* (Aug. 13) 12: Because they're all over 6 feet, Bunny Waters, Helen O'Hara and Dorothy Ford...have been dubbed Glamazons by Hollywood.] *a***1954** in Botkin *Sidewalks* 268: Presenting the sensational and lovely amazon.... **1968** Baker et al. *CUSS* 71: *Amazon.* A sexually attractive person, female. **1974** Univ. Wisconsin student, age 22: Man, she's *really* an Amazon! **1978** De Christoforo *Grease* 102: This Amazon chick...gives me a real sexy smile as she's takin' her bra off. **1983** *Nat. Lampoon* (Feb.) 80: All the fashion models...Amazons. **1989** *Rage* (Knoxville, Tenn.) (Sept.) 24: Wildest Fantasy: To be captured by alien Amazon women.
2. a tall person of either sex.
1969 *Current Slang* I & II: *Amazon*, n. A very tall girl or boy.—[used by] college females, New York State.

ambassador *n.* [ref. to "delivering a message," i.e., semen] penis. *Joc.*
1927 [Fliesler] *Anecdota* 108: He was about to inject the tip of his feebly erect ambassador.

ambidextrous *adj.* bisexual.
1966 Gass *Omensetter's Luck* 205: Certainly not Socrates—with his ambidextrous bat and balls. *****1967** Partridge *DSUE* (ed. 6) 981: *Ambidextrous.* Both hetero- and homosexual: since ca. 1935. **1968** Wells *Taboo Breakers* 17: AC-DC. Bisexual. Other euphemisms include *ambidextrous,* [etc.]. **1971** Rodgers *Queens' Vernacular* 32: Bisexual...AC-DC...ambidextrous. **1982** *Time* (Feb. 22) 70: A teacher named Ed...is confused as to whether he is straight, gay or ambidextrous.

ambisextrous *adj.* [blend of *sex* + *ambidextrous*] bisexual. *Joc.*
1926 in J.M. March *Wild Party* 84: He was ambisextrous. **1962** Cory & LeRoy *Homosexual & Soc.* 261: *Ambisextrous*...Bisexual (rare). **1966** *Time* (Mar. 11) 67: In 1736 she ran off to Venice with a dreamily beautiful but coldly ambisextrous adventurer. **1971** Rodgers *Queens' Vernacular* 23: Bisexual...ambisextrous. **1983** *Time* (June 13) 64: *Fen* is quite unlike *Cloud Nine,* Churchill's wickedly ambisextrous foray into the man-woman relationship in the heyday of Victoria's imperial sway.

ambish /æmˈbɪʃ/ *n.* [by shortening] aggressive ambition or enthusiasm.
1897 *Cosmopolitan* (Mar.) 567: I've never had no ambish to get married. **1908** in Fleming *Unforget. Season* 88: Full of "good old ambish." **1914** *DN* IV 130: He gets ahead because he has so much ambish. **1917** Hunt *Draft* 328: But the old ambish had been awakened. **1920** Weaver *In American* 30: I got to have somep'n to keep up my ambish. **1926–35** Watters & Hopkins *Burlesque* 21: The old woman's ridin' me because I ain't got no ambish.

ambition *n.* [intentional malapropism] ammunition.
1928–29 Nason *Slicker* 10 [ref. to 1918]: We don't want to have to lug gun, tripod, and "ambition."

amble *v.* to leave, get out.
1936 R. Adams *Cowboy Lingo* 221: Other commands to "go" were:..."hit the breeze," "pull yo' freight," "hit the trail,"..."amble,"...or "dust."

ambrotype *n.* ¶ In phrase: **Not on your ambrotype!** [var. of syn. *not on your tintype!*] Not at all! Never!
1895 Wood *Yale Yarns* 161: Not on your ambrotype, old man!

ambulance-chaser *n.* **1.** a lawyer or lawyer's agent who obtains clients by inciting accident victims to sue for damages, or through similar unethical practices; pettifogger.
1897 *Congressional Record* (July 24) 2961, in *DA:* In New York City there is a style of lawyers known to the profession as "ambulance-chasers," because they are on hand whenever there is a railway wreck, or a street-car collision, or a gasoline explosion with...their offers of professional service. **1934** in Ruhm *Detective* 104: A cheap, lousy ambulance chaser. **1936** Duncan *Over Wall* 28: They appointed me a lousy ambulance-chaser who was a scrammer. **1953** *ATS* (ed. 2) 504: Ambulance chaser *or* lawyer...a lawyer who specializes in damage suits for accident victims, hence a second-rate lawyer. **1982** Mamet *Verdict* (film): He's had four cases in the last three years. He's an ambulance chaser.
2. a hack journalist who specializes in sensational accounts of accidents.
1934 Faulkner *Pylon* 67: I'm just a poor bastard of an ambulance-chaser: I aint supposed to know news when I see it at thirty-five bucks a week or I'd be getting more.

Ambush Alley *n. Mil.* a stretch of road made treacherous by enemy fire.
1952 Geer *New Breed* 204: The Marines labeled the road [in Korea] "Ambush Alley." **1965** Donlon *Outpost* 130: Somehow, somebody threw in a 2E ton truck which could be taken to Nam Dong only by driving it thirty miles through "ambush alley." **1965** Marks *Letters* 104: We down here at Chu Lai have "ambush alley"—every time we run a patrol here the V.C. ambush it. **1971** *N.Y. Post* (Mar. 24) 5: The story of "Ambush Alley" is written on the face of this GI slumping wearily against his tank after his unit pulled back to Lang Vei...from North Vietnamese ambushes...along Route 9. **1991** Reinberg *In the Field: Ambush Alley,* part of Highway Route 9 near Khe Sanh nicknamed by U.S. soldiers because of numerous and treacherous Viet Cong ambushes.

Ameche *n.* [actor Don *Ameche* played the inventor of the telephone in the film *The Story of Alexander Graham Bell* (1939)] a telephone; telephone number; telephone call. Also **Don Ameche.** *Joc.* Now *hist.*
1941 Brackett & Wilder *Fall of Fire* (film): "Stick close to the Ameche—" "The *what?*" "The telephone." **1944** Kendall *Service Slang: Don Ameche*...A telephone message. **1948** Hargrove *Got to Give* 82: Give me a buzz on the Ameche and I will make the appointment for you. **1956** Hunter *Second Ending* 138: "Okay, so what's the Ameche?" She gave him the number. **1974** *Coq* (Apr. 44): We...decide to call our buddy Vince Aletti on the Ameche. **1993** *N.Y. Times* (Dec. 8) B8: Mr. Ameche was indelibly linked with the title role in "The Story of Alexander Graham Bell" and for many years after the 1939 film, many Americans referred to their telephones as "the Ameche."

A.M.F. *interj.* [euphem. initialism] "Adios (or aloha), motherfucker"; goodbye; the finish—usu. considered vulgar. *Joc.*
1963 in Tamony *Motherfucker* 7: "A.M.F....adios mother fucker,"..."goodbye friend." [**1966** Braly *On Yard* 120: And that's adios mother fuckers.] **1973** Layne *Murphy* (unp.): A.M.F....Adios mother fahckers. **1974** N.C. man, age 22: A.M.F. Adios, motherfucker! **1980** D. Cragg *Lex. Mil.:* AMF. Adios (or Aloha) Motherfucker.

AM-FM *adj.* AC-DC; bisexual.
1987 *Newsweek* (July 13) 44: Bisexuals...AC/DC. AM/FM. The double-gaited set. The nicknames have always been a little nasty.

amgrunt *n.* [*am*phibious + GRUNT 'U.S. Marine', prob. by analogy with *amtrack* 'amphibious tracked vehicle'] *USMC.* a member of an amphibious Marine Corps unit.
1971 Dibner *Heroes* 45: Incidentally, these amgrunts are handpicked volunteers and very gung-ho.

amidships *adv. Naut.* in the belly.
1886 P.D. Haywood *Cruise* 93: He gave Buster a whack amidships. **1899** C. Robbins *Gam* 73: When the fire crept up amidships [of the

effigy] he blew himself to bits. **1945** Colcord *Sea Lang.* 23: The cow kicked him square amidships and laid him out stiff as a handspike.

amigo *n.* [Sp 'friend'] *Mil.* a Filipino insurrectionist.
  1899 *Harper's Wkly.* (July 8) 684: The little white flags of the "amigos" thrust themselves out. **1910** *Ibid.* (Mar. 5) 16: Krag-Jorgensen rifles were cracking merrily in their users' pursuit of the wily amigo. **1914** *Collier's* (June 6) 23: Sure enough, on the left bank I could see a squad of amigos!

ammo *n.* [*amm*unition + *-o*] *Orig. Mil.* ammunition. Now *colloq.*
  1911 in Tuchman *Stilwell & China* 39: Many had new ammo belts and plenty of cartridges. **1917 No Parachute* 49: It does seem darned silly not to have guns and ammo that work. **1918** in R. Henderson *14th Eng.* 93: Ammo is running very heavy. **1953** White *Down Ridge* 152: Up to this point, they had seemed short of ammo. **1969** Eastlake *Bamboo Bed* 45: When your ammo's gone use your rifle as a club. **1981** C. Black *Ark* 99: Guns, rifles, ammo. **1992** Cornum & Copeland *She Went* 5: We were sitting on ammo boxes.

ammo-humper *n.* [AMMO + HUMP 'carry' + *-er*] *Mil.* an ammunition storage specialist.
  1980 M. Baker *Nam* 74 [ref. to *ca*1970]: I knew according to training that I'd be an ammo humper for a while and then work my way up to assistant [machine] gunner. **1988** Clodfelter *Mad Minutes* 37 [ref. to 1965]: The Ammo "humpers"...had seen V.C. snipers. *a***1989** C.S. Crawford *Four Deuces* 280: My ammo humper is all shot tuh shit in his legs.

ammunition *n.* **1.** food. *Joc.*
  1924 *Papers Mich. Acad. Sci.* 293 [ref. to 1918]: *Ammunition*, pies and pastry as doled out by the Salvation Army. **1942** *ATS* 96: Food...Ammunition.
  2. [cf. FORTY-FIVES, BULLETS] *Mil.* beans.
  1928 *Papers Mich. Acad Arts & Sci.* X 274 [ref. to 1918]: *Ammunition*, beans. **1945** *Sat. Rev.* (Nov. 24) 14: *Ammunition*—beans.

amoeba-brained *adj.* stupid.
  *a***1967** Bombeck *Wit's End* 44: And-so's-your-amoeba-brained-wife. **1972** R. Wilson *Forbidden Times* 21: You motherfucking, amoeba-brained asshole!

amp *n. Hosp.* a surgical amputation; an amputee.
  1942 *ATS* 513: *Amp*, an amputation. **1960** Partridge *DSUE* (ed. 5): *Amp*...an "amputee": Canadian...since *ca*1946. *a***1985** in K. Walker *Piece of My Heart* 407: Are you a double amp? *a***1987** in K. Marshall *Combat Zone* 214: What I see is a typical patient: a double amp.

amped *adj.* [*amp*hetamine or *amp*ule + *-ed* adjectival suffix] under the influence of an amphetamine or other stimulant; (*hence*) very excited, anxious, or eager; frenetically active.—sometimes constr. with *up* or *out.*
  1972 Smith & Gay *Don't Try It* 197: *Amped.* High on stimulants, usually amphetamines. **1974** Hyde *Mind Drugs* 151: *Amped.* "Wired" or spaced out on crystal or methedrine. **1982–84** Chapple *Outlaws in Babylon* 132: The agents were amped out. They were hyped. **1985** "Blowdryer" *Modern Eng.* 4: Someone who is amped is freaky, weird, their volume is too high. The effect can come about naturally or with the help of amphetamines. **1986** *New Gidget* (synd. TV series): Calm me down! I'm so amped up it's incredible! **1989** *48 Hours* (CBS-TV) (May 4): She goes out to use crystal, and that gets her amped out. **1989** *Village Voice* (N.Y.C.) (June 20) 39: It's near midnight...and the hip-hop boutique...is amped. **1990** Munro *Slang U.* 22: *Amped:* high on cocaine or coffee. **1991** *Gabriel's Fire* (ABC-TV): "Psyched?" "Amped!" **1991** *Houston Chronicle* (Nov. 13) 5D: *Amped:* Excited.

ampersand *n.* the rump. *Joc.*
  1838 *Crockett Almanac 1839* 7: Doughboy slipped a ball inter [the bear's] ampersand jest as I struck him. **1936* Partridge *DSUE.*

amputate *v.* [fr. *amputate (one's) mahogany*, slang pun on *cut (one's) stick* s.v. CUT 'to leave, to abscond'] to clear out, abscond.
  1842 *Spirit of Times* (Oct. 29) 410: To Bolt...to mizzle—to evaporate—to amputate. **1889** Farmer *Americanisms: Amputate, to*—thieves slang for decamping; to take flight. Used in the same way as "to cut," "to skip," in English slang.

amscray *v.* [Pig Latin form of SCRAM] to clear out, get out.
  1934 Weseen *Dict. Amer. Slang* 173: *Amscra* [*sic*]—To depart. **1935** Pollock *Und. Speaks*: Scram...beat it...(amscray). **1937** *AS* (Oct.) 199: The word *scram*...has been reported from the dialog of...[the movie]

Born to Dance in distorted form as *amskray.* **1954** Freeman *Francis Joins WACs* (film): Amscray before they find you here. **1974** E. Thompson *Tattoo* 318: Scram! Amscray! **1982** *Square Pegs* (CBS-TV): To use one of your favorite expressions, *amscray!* **1990** G. Trudeau *Doonesbury* (synd. cartoon strip) (Apr. 2): Okay, okay!...You counted us! Now amscray!

amy or **aimie** *n.* **1.** [*amy*l nitrite] a capsule, tablet, or ampule containing amyl nitrite.
  1966 "Petronius" *N.Y. Unexp.* 60: Kids are...popping 12 cc. of amies from Europe. **1969** Tynan *Oh! Calcutta!* 165: Amies, grass, body lotion. **1970** Landy *Und. Dict.: Amy*...Amyl nitrite.
  2. [*am*phetamine + *-ie*] a capsule or tablet containing an amphetamine.
  1969 Geller & Boas *Drug Beat* xv: *Aimies:* The amphetamine group of stimulants including benzedrine, dexedrine, and methedrine.

anarchy *n.* [fr. color red, associated with revolutionary anarchism] iodine.
  1883 Peck *Bad Boy* 90: She puts anarchy on my bruises, and gives me pie.

anchor *n.* **1.** [ref. to the shape] a pick.
  *1863 in T. Taylor *Plays* 209: There'll be room for thee if thou canst swing the old anchor....Why, the pick, to be sure. **1926** *AS* I 650: *Anchor*—tamping pick. **1927** *DN* V 437. **1930** "D. Stiff" *Milk & Honey* 198: *Anchor*—a pick. Companion tool of the shovel or *banjo.*
  2. [Cf. ANCHORMAN, a] *U.S. Nav. Acad.* the midshipman having the lowest academic standing in his class.
  1906 *Army & Navy Life* (Nov.) 498: *Anchor* is the facetious cognomen given a midshipman who has dropped to the bottom of his class.
  3. a brake.—esp. in phr. **throw out the anchor** apply the brake.
  *1936 in *OEDS.* **1941** *Slanguage Dict.: Anchor*...among truck drivers, an emergency brake. **1942** *AS* (Apr.) 105: Throw Out the Anchor. To use the emergency brake. **1969** *Current Slang* I & II: *Anchors*, n. Automobile brakes. **1976** *Nat. Lampoon* (July) 56: D.D. throws out the anchor and brings her rig...to a sudden stop. **1976** Whelton *CB Baby* 99: Running around with worn-down anchors like these.
  4. *R.R.* a caboose.
  1977 R. Adams *Railroader* 6: *Anchor:* A caboose.
  ¶ In phrases:
  ¶ **drag anchor** to move slowly, dawdle; drift mentally.
  1923 Southgate *Rusty Door* 129: His mind's draggin' anchor. **1942** *ATS* 57: Be Slow...drag the anchor. *Ibid.* 632: *Drag anchor*...to do less than one's best. **1944** Halsey *Some of My Friends* 67: I'm the Pride of the Fifth Ward, Jeff. I'm the People's Choice....Don't mind me, I'm dragging my anchor. *a***1950** R. Spence *Gorilla* 106: Come on! You're draggin' your anchor! **1978** *N.Y. Post* (July 12) 31: Don't drag yer anchor, Thinbad. Let's *go!*
  ¶ **drop anchor, a.** *Horse Racing.* (of a jockey) to restrain a running racehorse.
  1945 Colcord *Sea Lang.* 23: Holding in a race horse so as to throw a race is, in track slang, dropping anchor.
  b. *Navy.* to take decisive action against, "lower the boom."
  1971 Murphy & Gentry *Second in Command* 260: When the Court of Inquiry convened, there had to be a "single consistent account" of the events. Otherwise, Bucher claimed, the Navy would drop anchor on all of us. **1993** *TV Guide* (Aug. 7) 41: Readers drop anchor on Larry Hagman.
  ¶ **heave anchor** *Naut.* to die.
  1925 Bailey *Shanghaied* 56 [ref. to 1890's]: He'll heave anchor soon.
  ¶ **swallow the anchor** *Naut.* to give up seafaring life.
  *1909 Ware *Passing English* 237: Swallered the anchor...said of a sailor who comes home, loafs and does not show signs of going to sea again. **1921** E. O'Neill *Anna Christie* 132: You've swallowed the anchor. **1929* Bowen *Sea Slang* 136: *Swallowing the Anchor.* Settling down ashore. **1930** in Botkin *Amer. Folk.* 191: "I heard how he was buried," said the Sailor Who Had Swallowed the Anchor. **1961** Bosworth *Crows* 7: Some swallowed the anchor, as the old saying had it, and returned to Stooping Oak, Tennessee, or Comfort, Texas. **1972** Pearce *Pier Head* 111: That was before he decided to swallow the anchor and got married.

anchor *v.* to remain, stay for a time.
  1906 Burke *Prison Gates* 9: I went to the "timber" (country) and "floated" to Chicago where I anchored. **1966** in B. Jackson *Swim Like Me* 113: I decided to go over to her table and anchor a little while.

anchor-chain liberty *n. Navy.* unauthorized liberty, absence without leave.

    1952 Cope & Dyer *Petty Officer's Guide* 328: *Anchor chain liberty.* (Slang) Unauthorized liberty. Original idea was that a man climbed down the anchor cable, now it covers any form of unauthorized going or coming.

anchor-clanker *n. Navy.* **1.** a deck hand; (*hence*) a sailor.

    1952 Cope & Dyer *Petty Officer's Guide* 328: *Anchor clanker.* (Slang) A deck hand. **1964** Hunt *Ship with Flat Tire* 21: When she heard I'd signed up to be an anchor-clanker, she turned heel and walked away. **1965** Marks *Letters* 127: I'm glad you did have an enjoyable time with those two "anchorclankers" (sailors). **1986** M. Skinner *USN* ix: What the anchor-clankers are up to.

    2. something amusing, HUMDINGER.

    1973 Former U.S. Navy enlisted man, age 25 [ref. to 1968]: Something's really funny, you say, "That's a real anchor-clanker." Or if it's real unfunny, too.

anchorhead *n. Mil.* a sailor—used derisively.

    1968 W. Crawford *Gresham's War* 32 [ref. to 1953]: Like the anchor-head says: "She's four-oh."

anchorman *n.* **a.** [cf. ANCHOR, 2; sugg. by *anchorman* 'last person on a tug-of-war team'] Orig. *U.S. Nav. Acad.* the student having the lowest academic standing in his class.

    1928 *AS* III 452: *Anchor man.* The man lowest in class standing. **1943** Scott *Co-Pilot* 8: For all that, I finally graduated—even if it was just about as the anchor man. **1943–44** *Running Light*: Anchor Man—There, but for the grace of God, walks a civilian. **1966** Noel & Bush *Naval Terms*: *Anchor man*: Last man of a list or group in academic standing. **1969** *Current Slang* I & II [in use at USAF Academy].

    b. the last man in any group or sequence.

    1952 Uris *Battle Cry* 45 [ref. to WWII]: Daily game of trying not to be the last to drink from a pitcher of coffee or milk or you have to take it to be refilled. L.Q. always seems to be anchor man on the milk pitcher. **1960** Kirkwood *Pony* 220: Come on, chicken, we'll have us a gang-bang. You can be anchor man! **1961** Scarne *Comp. Guide to Gamb.* 671: *Anchor Man. Black Jack.* A player who sits to the dealer's extreme right and is the last player to play his hand.

anchor strawberry *n. Naut.* a prune. *Joc.*

    1960 *Midwest Folk.* 76: Prunes were another big favorite [on river steamboats], but...they were [called] "anchor strawberries." **1969** Sorden *Lumberjack Lingo*: *Anchor Brand Strawberries*—Prunes. A term [formerly] used on Great Lakes lumber ships.

and how *interj.* [trans. of G *und wie!*; not fr. Yid, as sometimes thought] emphatically so; yes, indeed. [This phr. suddenly gained wide currency in the 1920's. No citations are known between 1865 and 1926.]

    1865 in *AS* (Dec. 1933) 80: *And how?* as the Germans say; American-ice—you'd better believe it. **1926** *Variety* (Apr. 7) 23: "Kongo" is a melodrama—and how! **1928** McEvoy *Show Girl* 33: Are you mixed up in this?...And how. **1930** Pasley *Capone* 234: Here Ended the Bootleg Battle of the Marne. And how! **1932** Berg *Prison Dr.* 211: Sure, I was soft in those days. And how! **1949** in F. Brown *Honeymoon* 76: "Out of this world?" "And how." **1964** Leitner & Lanen *Dict. Fr. & Amer. Slang: And how!*...et comment!

Andrew Miller *n.* [Wilfred Granville (in Partridge *DSUE* (ed. 7) derives the term from the name of a British "press-gang 'tough,' " but corroboration is lacking] *Navy.* a warship. Now *hist.*

    [***1812** Vaux *Vocab.*: *Andrew Miller's lugger*: A king's ship or vessel.] **1849** Melville *W. Jacket* 28 [ref. to 1843]: And what did you know, you bumpkin! before you came on board this *Andrew Miller*? *Ibid.* 362: I've seen service with Uncle Sam—I've sailed in many *Andrew Millers*. ***1864** Hotten *Slang Dict.*: *Andrew Millar*, a ship of war.—*Sea.* **1980** Valle *Rocks & Shoals* 327 [ref. to *a*1860]: *Andrew Miller*...The seaman's nickname for an American man-of-war. The connotation is one of minute regulation and strictness.

Andy Maginn *n.* [rhyming slang] the chin.

    1934 in Partridge *Dict. Und.* **1935** Pollock *Und. Speaks: Andy Maginn*, the chin. **1954–58** in *West. Folk.* XXXVII 304: *Andy Maginn:* Chin.

angel *n.* **1.** [ref. to the childlike innocence of angels in conventional representations] **a.** a naive or otherwise exploitable person who may be imposed upon for money or other favors; (*specif.*) *Und.* the prospective victim of a swindle; an innocent.

    1882 A.W. Aiken *Joe Buck* 4: Such "angels" as the Californian, willing and able to pay for the liquor, and noble-minded enough not to object to the quantity a man took. **1891** Maitland *Slang Dict.: Angel*...one who possesses the means and inclination to "stand treat." **1904** *Life in Sing Sing* 246: *Angel.* A person easily victimized. **1914** Jackson & Hellyer *Criminal Slang* 24: *Chump*...a victim, an "angel." **1924** G. Henderson *Keys to Crookdom* 396: *Angel.* Person supplying money without getting anything in return. Also called sucker, sap, easy mark, boob, etc. **1935** *AS* (Feb.) 12: *Angel.* The victim or prospective victim of criminals (Obs.). **1941** Kendall *Army & Navy Slang: Angel*...anyone who buys a drink. **1964** Trimble *Sex Words: Angel*...A homosexual who plays a Sugar Daddy role with a passive partner. **1964** in *DARE: An angel*—a greenhorn buyer at an auction, who can be depended upon to buy unsound horses.

    b. [orig. a specialization of (**a.**), but now taken to ref. to the kindness of angels in conventional representations] a person or (*later*) a group providing financial backing for an enterprise; (*specif.*) *Theat.* the financial backer of a theatrical production. Now *S.E.*

    1897 in Smith & Smith *Police Gaz.* 208: The leading lady of the company had a bald-headed angel on the string. **1897** in *Dict. Canad.* (s.v. *grubstake*, v.): By mining law, the "angel" receives one-half of all the grub-staked one discovers. **1902** Mead *Word-Coinage* 183: "An angel" is a man who innocently backs unprofitable or questionable enterprises to profit of the promoters solely. It is a term of contempt. **1903** in Bierce *Letters* 64: Scheff appears not to know who the "angel" in the case is. **1909** *WNID: Angel*...a nonprofessional financier backer of a play or other amusement enterprise. *Slang. a*1904**–11** Phillips *Susan Lenox* II 113: I'm going to start a business...if I can find an angel. **1923** *N.Y. Times* (Sept. 9) VII 2: *Angel:* A person who backs a show. **1928** O'Connor *B'way Racketeers* 76: The chump who tosses his bankroll into any racket involving a theatrical enterprise is...referred to...with the label of "Angel." **1929** Booth *Stealing* 109: They were "resting" until the following week, when rehearsals would begin and the "angel's" purse-strings would be loosened. **1950** *Sat. Eve. Post* (July 22) 53: Among the party's fellow-travelers are a number of financial angels. **1959** Gault *Drag Strip* 24: So they can find an angel, some grownups with more money than sense to finance their club and pay the rent on that garage. **1963** *Wash. Post* (Oct. 24) A21: Its financial angels include some of the best-heeled tycoons in Fairfield County. **1973** Berman *Exploring Cosmos* 64: Some of the older major observatories...were founded by grants from wealthy individuals. The chief financial angel available today is the U.S. government. **1981** *L.A. Times* (Jan. 4) VI 1: If today's soaring home prices and mortgage rates make it impossible for many families to buy a house, one way out is to find an "angel"—a partner with some money to invest in your home.

    c. *Pris. & Police.* a person who will exert influence or do favors on behalf of another.

    1942–49 Goldin et al. *DAUL*: My mess-hall angel just lost his job. **1986** Stroud *Close Pursuit* 224: Speculated...about the identity of Wolfie's "rabbi" or "angel."

    2. *Baseball.* clouds that may silhouette a fly ball, thus making it easier to catch.—usu. constr. in pl.

    1909 in *AS* XXXVI 29: Pitilessly the sun beats down from a sky, broken only by the fleecy white clouds that the players call "angels," because they afford so benevolent a background for the batted ball. **1937** in Nichols *Baseball Term.* **1964** Thompson & Rice *Every Diamond* 139: *Angels....*Clouds in the sky that make it easier to judge fly balls.

    3. *Hobo.* [cf. ANGELINA] a young, effeminate homosexual partner.

    1927 *DN* V 437: *Angel*, n. A type of homosexual pervert. Also "cannibal." **1941** Legman *Lang. of Homosex.* 1157: *Angel.* A pedicant, the passive partner in pedication. (Tramp slang).

    4. *Mil. Av.* [orig. radio communications code] one thousand feet of altitude.

    *1943 in *OEDS.* **1945** J. Bryan *Carrier* 142: It's now 240, 14 miles, angels 30. **1946** G.C. Hall *1000 Destroyed* 381: High winds at angels 30. **1947** *ATS* (Supp.) 40: Heads up, bandit at four angels. **1955** Scott *Eagle* 18: We'll be no lower than Angels Forty-five. **1957** Berkeley *Deadly Mantis* (film): Climb to angels three. Bogey ninety miles. **1966** Cameron *Sgt. Slade* 28: He got rid of that Angels Twenty atmosphere in his head. **1991** Reinberg *In the Field: Angels*, term for altitude in thousands of feet.

    5. *Radar.* a false target propagated on a radar screen by weather conditions, flying birds, or other natural phenomena. Now *colloq.*

1947 in *OEDS*. **1959** *N.Y. Times* (Aug. 30) 26: Some angels are known to be produced by birds; others by sharp temperature or moisture gradients in the atmosphere. **1964** R. Hall *UFO Evid.* 82: The celebrated Washington radar sightings of July 1952 occurred during a period when typical angels were being seen there abundantly. **1968** in Condon *Scientific Study* 788: Depending upon the magnitude of the radar "cross-section" some "angels" can be ascribed to echoes from birds or even insects. **1974** *Pop. Sci.* (Nov.) 10: Three scientists...help investigate "angels"—baffling images that show up on radar screens and confuse air traffic controllers all over the world. **1979** *L.A. Times* (Jan. 3) I 8: The numerous radar echoes...were probably the familiar radar angels that are so prevalent in the Southern Hemisphere at this time of year.

6. *Mil.* a motorized vehicle, esp. a helicopter, used for rescue; a member of a rescue party.—often attrib. See also ANGEL TRACK.

[**1950** *Nat. Geographic* (Sept.) 313: Navy helicopters...During carrier take-offs and landings, they hover like guardian angels.] **1953** Russ *Last Parallel* 311: The area was crowded with loaded stretchers, corpsmen, and "angels" as members of the rescue party were called. **1965** *N.Y. Times* (June 1): Any [pilot] being launched from the carrier is protected by "angels"—helicopters that hover near bow or stern to snatch him from a ditched plane. **1967** Ford *Muc Wa* 120: "They want an Angel at Muc Wa....What the hell's an Angel?" "A helicopter, sir." **1967** Reed *Up Front in Vietnam* 145: A rescue helicopter...called the "Angel Helo"...picked Luker up. **1986** Coonts *Intruder* 11: The duty search-and-rescue helicopter, the Angel, took up a holding pattern.

7. ANGEL DUST.

1984 W. Gibson *Neuromancer* 134: These...terrs [terrorists] put angel in the water. *a***1989** Spears *NTC Dict.*: Angel...sort of numbs you.

¶ (in prov. expressions).

1950 *Nat. Geographic* (Sept.) 294: The...stratojet takes off "like a homesick angel," as airmen say. **1963** W.C. Anderson *Penelope* 214: The airplane...started climbing heavenward like a homesick angel.

angel *v.* [fr. ANGEL, *n.*, 1.b.] Esp. *Theat.* to finance. Now *S.E.*

1929 in *OEDS*. **1936** *AS* (Oct.) 220: Having induced his Maecenas to *angel* the show...our producer starts looking for a cast. **1940** Thompson & Raymond *Gang Rule* 29: For amusement, he angeled the two musical shows, "Strike Me Pink" and "Forward March." **1949** *Newsweek* (May 16) 60: Last week...Aunt Anita agreed to angel a new Manhattan morning tabloid. **1957** *Sat. Eve. Post* (May 25) 96: Though Whitney angeled dramatic plays with success, his experiences with Broadway musicals were horrific. **1974** *Dick Tracy* (synd. cartoon strip) (July 28): I "angel" various commercial ventures. I financed the big brass health rings. **1976** *L.A. Times* (Nov. 7) III 1: And Harry Frazee isn't going to angel a musical with him.

angel buggy *n.* [cf. ANGEL-MAKER] *Trucking.* a truck carrying explosive or highly flammable cargo.

1977 Dills *CB* (ed. 4) 3: *Angel Buggy:* truck hauling dangerous cargo (nitro, etc.).

angel cake *n. Mil.* hardtack. Now *hist.*

1963 Rickey *Beans & Hay* 266 [ref. to late 19th C.]: Ragged, gaunt enlisted men could usually...joke about...a diet of "angel cake" (hardtack) and "Cincinnati chicken" (salt pork).

angel cake and wine *n. Pris.* bread and water as a punishment diet. Also **angel food cake and wine.**

1942 *ATS* 97: Bread and Water. Angel-food cake and wine. **1944** Kendall *Service Slang*: Angel cake and wine...bread and water in confinement. **1967** Colebrook *Cross* 239: Landing in "the can, to live on angel cake and wine."

angel dust *n. Narc.* **1.** phencyclidine (PCP), an animal tranquilizer used as an illicit hallucinogen.

1970 WINS radio news (Nov. 29): A hallucinogenic drug called "angel dust" on the street. **1971** *Nat. Lampoon* (Sept.) 4: Now, packed away in my saddlebags is every narcotic you've ever heard of—smack, snow, red birds, yellow jackets, angel dust, DPT, THC, STP, black gungi—the works! **1972** Smith & Gay *Don't Try It* 197: *Angel Dust.* PCP (Phencyclidine, or "Sernyl," an animal tranquilizer...that is smoked, inhaled, or swallowed in a powdered form.). **1976** *L.A. Times* (Mar. 5) IV 6: Friends say he had been drinking and smoking marijuana and angel dust—a drug believed to cause bizarre behavior—in the weeks before his death. **1978** *Rolling Stone* (Oct. 19) 92: The instruments sound like the Longines Symphony on angel dust. **1982** *L.A. Times* (Mar. 14) VI 2: Distributed as tablets, powder, or crystals under such street names as

angle [*sic*] dust, peace, mist, crystal, and tic, the drug can be snorted, popped or smoked in rolls with mint leaves or marijuana. **1990** Stuck *Adolescent Worlds* 90: Would you use angel dust if a friend offered it to you? **1993** *New Yorker* (Jan.11) 57: She smoked a bag of angel dust—phencyclidine, or PCP.

2. (occ. applied to other narcotic drugs).

[*****1945** S.J. Baker *Australian Lang.* 141: Cocaine is called *angie* or *angel*, apparently as a comment on the effects of that drug.] **1971** Guggenheimer *Narc. & Drug Abuse: Angel dust.* Marijuana. **1971** Woodley *Dealer* 128: There's angel dust—that's parsley dipped in acid (LSD). That's a high. **1973** Newark, N.J., man, age 22: *Angel dust* is two things. Mainly it's that stuff that comes sprinkled on mint leaves; they use it to tranquilize livestock....But I've also heard it to mean cocaine.

angel factory *n.* a Christian school or seminary.—used derisively.

1929 in *AS* V 238: Those theologs attend the angel-factory. **1985** *L.A. Times* (Oct. 24) IX 6: Public school opponents...like to dub Valley Christian the "Angel Factory," which amuses the Crusaders. **1992** *Chicago Trib.* (Feb. 9) Chicagoland 8: "We're not an angel factory," said David Roth, the headmaster [of Wheaton Christian High].

angel food *n.* **1.** [cf. ANGEL CAKE] *Mil.* hardtack. *Joc.*

1899 J. Young *Remin. & Stories* 432: Hardtack by itself is commonly known as "angel food." A soldier who was asked [why]...simply laughed and replied, "Cause it ain't."

2. *Hobo.* religious preaching.—used disparagingly.

1926 *AS* I 650: *Angel food*—mission preaching. **1929** *AS* IV 337: *Angel food*—Mission-house preaching. **1930** "D. Stiff" *Milk & Honey* 199: *Angel food*—Mission preaching about the Bread of Life. **1960** *Tenn. Folk. Soc. Bull.* XXVI 117: The sermons heard in mission halls were [called] *angel food* [by hobos].

angeliferous *adj.* angelic.

1837 Bird *Nick* ch. xvi: Tarnal death to me, but it's anngeliferous madam that helped me out of the halter! **1839** in Blair & Meine *Half Horse* 66: The angeliferous critter stood still as a scarecrow in a cornfield. **1856** in *DA*: One of the most splendiferous, angeliferous...female critters I ever sot my two gooseberry eyes onto.

angelina *n.* [cf. ANGEL, *n.*, 3] an effeminate homosexual youth, esp. a catamite.—used contemptuously.

1930 "D. Stiff" *Milk & Honey* 199: *Angelina*—Punk or road kid acting as a hobo's companion. **1941** Legman *Lang. of Homosex.* 1157: A pedicant...angelina. **1948–51** J. Jones *Here to Eternity* 12: Houston made his angelina First Bugler over me. *Ibid.* 109: If you don't watch yer step, you're gonna find your ass busted back to private and do a little straight duty. Which would probably kill a college angelina like you.

angel juice *n.* rainwater; water. *Joc.*

1944 Kendall *Service Slang: Angel juice*...water.

angel-maker *n.* [alluding to a dead person going to heaven] a device that can inflict death, such as a dangerous vehicle or a gun.

1934 Traven *Death Ship* 247: The *Empress of Madagascar*...Angel-maker and baby-farmer. **1970** Lincke *Jenny* 63: The N-9 was mother to the Navy term "Angel Maker," and many a blue-clad airman is floating around in heaven with the words "here under the auspices of an N-9" stenciled in gold on his halo. **1979** Ky. man, age 42: Al Capone carried a heater, an angel-maker.

angel puss *n.* [angel + PUSS 'face'; var. of colloq. *angelface*] a person, esp. a young woman, having an angelic or pretty face. *Joc.*

1941 *Slanguage Dict.: Angelpuss*...angelface; a slightly ironic term of endearment. **1964** Leitner & Lanen *Dict. Fr. & Amer. Slang: Angel puss*...figure d'ange. **1979** in Fierstein *Torch Song* 169: No offense, Angel-Puss, but you're mistaken.

angel's footstool *n.* [ref. to its height] *Naut.* the highest sail of a full-rigged vessel. *Joc.*

1883 C. Russell *Sailor's Lang.: Angel's footstool.*—An imaginary sail jokingly assumed to be carried by Yankee vessels. It is pretended to be a square sail and to top the sky-sails, moon-sails, cloud-cleaners, etc. *****1961** Burgess *Dict. Sailing: Angel's footstool.* A fancy name given to one of the sky-sails.

angel's seat *n.* [ref. to its height] *R.R.* the cupola of a caboose. *Joc.*

1946 in Botkin & Harlow *R.R. Folklore* 350: The shack was in the angel's seat of the ape wagon.

angel's tit *n.* [cf. ANGEL TEAT] a kind of alcoholic mixed drink (see quot.).
  1984 H. Gould *Cocktail* 158: An angel's tit was originally known as a King Alphonse.…It's made by floating heavy cream on…dark crème de cacao and topping it with a cherry.

angel teat *n.* well-mellowed whiskey. *Joc.*
  1945 Mencken *Amer. Lang. Supp. I* 261: *Angel-teat* is missing [from Bartlett's *Americanisms*]. **1946** *AS* 21 194: *Angel teat* [is] a mellowed whiskey with a rich bouquet.

angel track *n.* [ANGEL + TRACK] *USMC.* an armored personnel carrier used as a field ambulance.
  1971 Glasser *365 Days* 242: *Angel track.* An APC [armored personnel carrier] used as an aid station. *a***1982** Dunstan *Vietnam Tracks* 69: The enemy frequently attacked "angel tracks," paying no heed to the prominent red crosses.

angle *n.* **1.** [poss. sugg. by the importance of *angles* in pocket billiards] a scheme; a workable method of deception or exploitation.
  1920 J. Conway, in *Variety* (Dec. 31) 8: He finally caught the proper angle.…When in Rome do as the Romans do. **1921** J. Conway, in *Variety* (Mar. 18) 5: I thought I was hep to all the angles. **1927** Coe *Gangster* 185: I had to find some angle to git to you. **1938** Baldwin & Schrank *Case of Murder* (film): Don't you get the angle? It must be the bookies' dough. **1950** M. Spillane *Vengeance* 59: I wonder what would happen if I shafted my old buddy Dinky Williams.…Maybe it's an angle. **1967** Michaels *Women of Berets* 80: I'm going to buy a farm and live on the money I get paid not to grow crops. You can't beat that for an angle. **1976** Hoffman & Pecznick *Drop a Dime* 16: In his own terminology, he was a "wise guy," someone who lived by his wits, working at "angles" rather than at an honest job. **1979** Norwood *Survival of Dana* (film): I'm always schemin'. Always lookin' for an angle.
  2. an ulterior motive, hidden purpose.
  1929 in D. Runyon *Guys & Dolls* 65: This is considered most surprising…but people figure the chances are she has some other angle. **1940** Burnett *High Sierra* 12: "I'm paying all expenses and I want service." "What's your angle?" "What do you care?" **1958** Chandler *Playback* 109: Now you tell me something. What's your angle? **1964** Ellson *Nightmare St.* 25: Why is Dallas doing this for you? He must have an angle.
  3. *pl.* exploitable subtleties of a particular subject.
  [**1908** in H.C. Fisher *A. Mutt* 25: A. Mutt Is Not Overlooking Any Angle of the [Racing] Game.] **1938** Bezzerides *Long Haul* 158: You got to know the angles. Every God-damned thing in this world has got angles. **1958** Feiffer *Sick Sick Sick* (unp.): I can practice! Learn all the angles! Maybe take a few evening courses.
  ¶ In phrases:
  ¶ **get an angle on** to discover something useful about, "get a line on."
  1974 Gober *Black Cop* 31: Maybe that's where I can get an angle on them. I'd like to keep a line on what the Harbor Division is coming up with.
  ¶ **shoot an angle** [or **the angles**] to scheme, plot.
  1954 Chessman *Cell 2455* 89: When authority got a hold of you, you out-toughed or out-slicked it. You'd shoot an angle. **1962** Perry *Young Man* 95: He just slinks along, shooting the angles. **1966** Elli *Riot* 19: He's a troublemaker—always shootin' angles.

angle *v.* to scheme.
  1925 in Hammerstein *Kern Song Bk.* 62: When a man begins to angle and a heart he tries to entangle. **1929** *AS* IV 337: *Angle*—To make money or a livelihood by illegitimate means. **1930** *Amer. Mercury* (Dec.) 454: We angle so the monkey takes the fall. **1935** *AS* IX 12: *To Angle*…To be searching for a job that will yield some loot. **1955** *Phil Silvers Show* (CBS-TV): It takes a lot of angling and finagling to be a success in the world today. **1982** *Harper's* (Feb.) 25: This is the kind of story that's pleasant if you like the protagonist…: rich woman angles for job she doesn't need.

angle shooter *n.* a schemer. Hence **angle-shooting**, scheming.
  1947 in Weinberg et al. *Tough Guys* 216: Some angle shooter, some racketeer. **1953** T. Runyon *In for Life* 194: Angle shooters! **1958–59** Lipton *Barbarians* 154: Comparison shopping…is strictly for the "angle shooters." *Ibid.* 155: Sponging, scrounging, borrowing and angle-shooting are too undependable as a regular source of income. **1982** Hayano *Poker Faces* 48: Other angle shooters continually stretch the boundaries of legality and propriety.

angora *n.* ¶ In phrase: **get (one's) angora** [sugg. by syn. *get (one's) goat*] to irk, annoy, anger or exasperate (someone).
  1915 "High Jinks, Jr." *Choice Slang: Angora*, (to get your)…Synonymous with "Get your goat." **1918** Kauffman *Navy at Work* 7: I had some sympathy for the Dutchman before I got on this job, but after coaling ship for the first day, they'd got my angora. **1925** *Amer. Legion Wkly.* (Jan. 16) 21: This business life gets my angora. **1926** Wood & Goddard *Amer. Slang: Angora*, to get one's. To discomfit or rattle one. **1927** Breddan *Under Fire* 86: The bombing planes of the enemy were trying to get our angora.

animal *n.* **1.** [cf. syn. BEAST] *U.S. Mil. Acad.* a newly arrived cadet.
  1871 Wood *West Point* 337: *Animal.*—A name given to new cadets on their arrival. **1894** C. King *Cadet Days* 128: But so big a gathering of the "animals" attracted the instant attention of their natural enemies, the yearlings.
  2. [sugg. by PONY] *Stu.* a translation of a foreign-language text, PONY.
  1900 *DN* II 21: *Animal, n.* A literal translation, pony.
  3.a. a vulgar, brutish, or violent person. Now *colloq.*
  *****1892** in Wilkes *Austral. Colloq.* 4: That animal ran up a great wall in our faces. **1900** *DN* II 21: *Animal*…A very vulgar person. **1915** *DN* IV 231: *Animal*…A girl, usually of doubtful repute. *****1945** S.J. Baker *Austral. Lang.* 156: *Animal.* A term of contempt for a person. **1966** in IUFA *Folk Speech: Animals:* boys who maul girls. **1968** Baker et al. *CUSS* 71: *Animal.* An ugly person, male.…A sexually attractive person, male. A sexually expert male. **1976** G. Kirkham *Signal Zero* 43: I usually try to eat before the animals [street criminals] start coming out. **1980** *N.Y. Post* (July 5) 1 (headline): Mob Stones Ambulance As Man Dies. They're animals, says cop after tragedy.
  b. a passionate sexual partner, esp. a woman.
  1965 C. Brown *Manchild* 301: She is a stone animal, Sonny. She'll mess you mind up. You'll never want to leave there. **1968** (quot. at (3.a.), above). **1971** Rodgers *Queens' Vernacular* 21: That girl's a real animal once she gets goin'! **1973** Hirschfeld *Victors* 130: "On three drinks, I'm an absolute animal."…She *was* an animal, a carnal beast. **1990** *Get a Life* (Fox-TV): Women on the rebound are *animals!*
  4. an athletic or muscular man, esp. a bodyguard or hired thug.
  1921 J. Conway, in *Variety* (Oct. 21) 7: If they make any kind of a fight with my animal [*sc.* a prizefighter] they can cum back in a return match and grab plenty. **1938** (quot. at ANIMAL CAR). **1958** McCulloch *Woods Words: Animal*…A green hand in the woods. **1961** Scarne *Comp. Guide to Gamb.* 392: This is where we find the racketeers, hoodlums, and their *animals* (professional strong-arm men). **1963** *AS* 179: A college athlete:…animal. **1968** Baker et al. *CUSS* 71: *Animal*…a strong, often offensive male.…An athletic person. **1969** R. King *Gambling & Crime* 233: *Muscle Man, Animal*—Bouncer or strong-arm guard in gambling joint. **1974** Cherry *High Steel* 215: *Animal* is standard [construction workers'] argot for a guy whose strength—and use thereof [is considerable].
  ¶ In phrases:
  ¶ **get (one's) animal** [sugg. by syn. *get (one's) goat*] to exasperate or annoy (someone).
  1922 in W.C. Fields *By Himself* 121: This Radio outfit's got my animal; it's going to drive me coo-coo!
  ¶ **go the whole animal** [sugg. by syn. *go the whole hog*] to act without any restraint.
  1832 [M. St.C. Clarke] *Sks. of Crockett* 40: But didn't I go the whole animal? **1889** Farmer *Americanisms: To go the whole animal.*—a variant of "to go the whole hog."
  ¶ **see the big animal** *see the elephant* S.V. ELEPHANT.
  1848 in Oehlschlaeger *Reveille* 221: He thought he had seen the "big animal."

animal *adj.* [reanalysis of S.E. phr. *go animal* 'to start behaving like an animal'] wildly disorderly, rowdy; wild, unrestrained.—esp. in phr. **go animal.**
  1965 in *West. Folk. Qly.* XXXVI 244: He was really animal at the party last Saturday. **1968** Baker et al. *CUSS* 71: *Animal, go.* Go wild. **1979** *High Society* (Aug.) 78: Tracy's tongue was a wild thing.…She went animal in my mouth.

animal car *n.* [fr. ANIMAL, *n.*, 4; the caboose is where the crew normally lives] *R.R.* a caboose.
  1938 *AS* (Feb.): *Animal car.* Wash car or living car [for R.R. linemen].

1977 R. Adams *Railroader* 6: *Animal car.* A caboose.

animal cracker *n.* [arbitrary ref. to National Biscuit Company's "Barnum's Animals," cookies first marketed in 1904] an eccentric or foolish person; KOOK.
    1925 in E. Wilson *Twenties* 212: Well, don't try to high-hat us, you animal-cracker from Pittsburgh! **1928** Marx Brothers *Animal Crackers* (film title). **1928** MacArthur *War Bugs* 242: All the new officers looked like animal crackers. **1929** E. Wilson *Daisy* 133: Get away, you animal cracker! **1972** in *Penthouse* (Jan. 1973) 85: In other words…[she] is an animal cracker. [**1973** *Nat. Lampoon* (Mar.) 31: Sometimes you don't have the sense God gave animal crackers.]

animal crackers *adj.* [fr. the *n.*] crazy; CRACKERS. [Judging from the currency of the noun, this use is almost certainly much earlier than attested.]
    1992 R. Perot, news conference on CNN-TV (June 24): This is animal crackers!

animal farm *n.* [a place for ANIMALS, *n.*, 3 or 4.; sugg. by title of *Animal Farm*, novel (1945) by "George Orwell" (Eric A. Blair), commonly assigned in U.S. colleges since late 1950's] a place, as a dormitory, barracks, etc., occupied by persons who are coarse, stupid, or violent; a place for ANIMALS, *n.*, 3 or 4.
    *a***1961** Boroff *Campus U.S.A.* 33: Football players…are just hulking mercenaries to many students. "Animal farm" was the scornful epithet of one student. **1969** *Current Slang* I & II: *Animal farm, n.* The weight training room in the gym. **1968–70** *Current Slang* III & IV: *Animal farm, n.* Dormitory. **1981** Hathaway *World of Hurt* 68: They send you to the animal farm…you'll be in deeper shit than you know what to do with. **1982** Goff, Sanders & Smith *Bros.* 38 [ref. to 1968]: We'll…have you at the holding barracks, down on a place called Animal Farm. **1990** Clark *Wds. of Vietnam War* 233: Ft. Benning's holding company was nicknamed the Animal Farm.

animule *n.* [*animal* + *mule*] animal. *Joc.* [The date of "1834(?)" assigned to their ex. by *F & H* is implausibly early on several grounds.]
    1862 in J.M. McPherson *Chrons. of Civil War* V 120: Like all *long-eared animules*. **1871** Schele de Vere *Americanisms* 578: *Animules* is, in California and the Southwestern Territories, a favorite substitute for *animals*, with a sly pun upon *mules*. *a***1890** *F & H* I 55: Ten miles to town!…Them animules is too beat to do that.

ankle *n.* [cf. syn. LEG] a young woman.
    1942 *ATS* 770: College Girl…Ankle. **1946** "Evans" *Halo in Blood* 67: She strikes me as an ankle who doesn't yell easily.

ankle *v.* [infl. by *amble* and *angle*] **a.** to walk.
    1926 Maines & Grant *Wise-Crack Dict.*: *Ankled by*—Went by and not riding. **1926** Finerty *Criminalese* 6: *Ankle along*—Be on your way. **1929** Bodenheim *60 Secs.* 260: She ankled over to Central Park. **1932** Lorimer *Streetcars* 120: I asked you three times how about ankling out. **1933** Weller *Not to Eat* 318: Let's ankle down to Willy's. **1958** R. Russell *Perm. Playboy* 65: This kid…ankled over and tapped Spoof on the shoulder. **1964** Leitner & Lanen *Dict. Fr. & Amer. Slang: To ankle it…aller à pied.*
    b. *Theat.* to leave (a performance); to quit (a production).
    1973 *Lang. of Show Biz*: *Ankle a show.* To leave the show, walk out. Voting with your feet. **1977** in *Film Comment* (Jan. 1978) 53: So I "ankled"—to use a Hollywood term—I ankled *White Lightning* and went to *Sugarland Express.* **1984** Blumenthal *Hollywood* 44: I ankled for Fox and my boss went indie.

ankle-biter *n.* **1.** a small child. *Joc.*
    1963 Anderson *Penelope* 65: I once had a patient…who had given birth to fourteen little ankle-biters. **1966** Shepard *Doom Pussy* 36: Mark, one-and-a-half, a little ankle-biter he had never seen. **1976** Dills *CB '77* 2: *Anklebiter:* very young child; unruly child; child. **1981** *Incredible Hulk* (NBC-TV): Five ankle-biters whose only distinction is they were born in volume. **1987** *Werewolf* (Fox-TV): You were gonna move to the country and raise ankle-biters. **1988** Groening *Childhood Is Hell* (unp.): Squirt. Shorty. Runt. Ankle-biter.
    2. a dog. *Joc.*
    1978 Lieberman & Rhodes *CB* (ed. 2) 287: *Ankle-biter*—a child or dog.

ankle express *n.* the legs as a means of locomotion. *Joc.*
    1919 Ashton *F, 63* 52: At six a.m. we started for Limoges, ankle express, heavy marching order. **1917–20** in J.M. Hunter *Trail Drivers* I 244 [ref. to 1865]: From Austin I took the "ankle express" for my home in Llano

County, seventy-five miles away. **1920** J. McKenna *315th Inf.* 229: We left Neuville for Rimacourt via "Ankle Express." **1920** in *DA*: I took the "ankle express" for my home. **1968–70** *Current Slang* III & IV: *Ankle express, n.* Walking.—College students…Kentucky. **1983** Eble *Campus Slang* (Mar.): *Ankle Express*—to walk: How are you getting uptown? Good old ankle express.

ankle satchels *n.pl.* long trousers.
    1966 Wanderone & Fox *Bank Shot* 50: Once I got into those ankle satchels, I was playing pool for cash in rooms all over Washington Heights.

annex *v.* to lay hold of roughly, grab; get; steal.—occ. constr. with *to. Joc.*
    1845 in G.W. Harris *High Times* 51: Jule Sawyer was *thar*, and jist *annexed to her* rite off, and a mity nice fit it was. *a***1889** in Barrère & Leland *Dict. Slang* I 41: The "Prince" said…that he had no intention of "annexing" the spectacles, which he picked up quite by accident. **1902** Cullen *More Tales* 31: I was…wondering how I was going to annex the mazuma to get one of the overcoats. **1907** *McClure's Mag.* (Mar.) 525: I intend to annex your bankroll quick.

Annie *n. Homosex.* AUNT, 2.
    1953 Brossard *Saboteurs* 118: He was described to me…as an "old Annie" who was good for a couple of bucks if you wanted to put out.

Annie Oakley *n.* [ref. to *Annie Oakley* (1860–1926), American sharpshooter; see 1923 quot.]
    1. *Circus & Theat.* a complimentary ticket of admission; free pass; (*occ.*) a meal ticket.
    1916 T.A. Dorgan, in Zwilling *TAD Lexicon* 14: [He] never paid to see a fight in his life…He…got an Annie Oakley from a friend. **1922** in *AS* (Feb. 1923) 76: Miss Oakley explained that Ban Johnson is the man who invented the term "Annie Oakley" for free passes. *Ibid.* 77: The term…originated among hangers-on of circuses and street fairs and was…an opprobrious word.…It has been in the grifter vocabulary for at least twenty years. **1923** *N.Y. Times* (Sept. 9) VIII 2: *Annie Oakley:* A pass to a theatre. Annie Oakley was a famous shot; all passes are punched with holes. **1931** *AS* (June) 329: *Annie Oakley, n.* A meal ticket. **1939** *Hell's Kitchen* (film): Did you get the duckets, Judge? The Annie Oakleys—the tickets. **1959** *Esquire* (Aug.) 28: If you go in a show and I come into town to see you, can you get me a couple of Annie Oakley's?
    2. *Baseball Journ.* a base on balls.
    1940 in *DARE:* Newson's Annie Oakley average last season…was 3.85. **1942** *ATS* 646. **1964** Thompson & Rice *Every Diamond* 139: *Annie Oakley.* Intentional base on balls.
    3. (see quots.).
    1953 McEwen & Lewis *Encyc. Naut. Knowl.* s.v. *sail: Annie Oakley*…a parachute spinnaker characterized by a series of holes down its middle for freeing it of dead cushioning air. **1981** Noel *VNR Dict.* 11: *Annie Oakley* A yacht's spinnaker pierced with small holes for better control.

annihilated *adj.* extremely drunk or high.
    1975 Univ. Tenn. student: Man, I was annihilated. **1978** *UTSQ:* Drunk…polluted, annihilated. **1987** *Soapbox* (PBS-TV): They were so annihilated they don't remember…whether they had a good time or not. **1988** *Sonya Live in L.A.* (CNN-TV) (Dec. 29): If a person is completely annihilated and can't even walk to the car, unfortunately we cannot drive that teenager home.

another ¶ In phrase: **tell me another** "I don't believe you."
    1953 Brossard *Saboteurs* 21: Oh, sure, sure…Tell me another. **1958** Frede *Entry E* 8: *Hah.* Tell me another. C'mon, Bogard, old boy, tell me another.

ant *n.* [fr. *ants in (one's) pants*, below] **1.** *pl.* restlessness.
    1935 E. Anderson *Hungry Men* 17: I sure get ants when I have to stay in a spot long. **1945** Bellah *Ward 20* 73: I'm the nervous type. I got ants.
    2. *pl.* sexual desire; sex appeal.
    1941 Chodorov & Fields *La. Purchase* (film): I need a girl to go after the Senator, a girl with plenty of *ants.* **1960** Steinbeck *Winter* 250: Your glance gives me ants whenever we romance.
    ¶ In phrase:
    ¶ **ants in (one's) pants** [or **britches**] restlessness, irritability; eagerness for action or sexual activity. [1930, 1933 quots. are prob. nonce euphemisms.]
    [**1930** Lait *On Spot* 199: Ants in the Socks…Designating a person of energy and pep.] **1931** in Oliver *Meaning of Blues* 153: I got ants in my pants, baby, for you. [**1933** "J. Spenser" *Limey* 67: C'mon, Batty.…I've got ants in my toes. Let's go.] **1937** Steinbeck *Mice & Men* 57: An' Curley's pants is just crawlin' with ants, but they ain't nothing come of it

yet. **1939** Kaufman & Hart *Man Who Came to Dinner* 334: I'll get the ants out of those moonlit pants. **1942** Davis & Wolsey *Madam* 127: And where the entertainment is bawdy we can figure on a big follow-up [in the brothel]. People just don't go home...with ants in the pants. **1949** Quigley *Corsica* 38: These two buddies of mine had ants in their britches, and they wanted to...go to some other place where there might be some babes. **1955** Blair *Courage* 115: He told Margaret he had "ants in his pants."...It was some sort of indescribable urge to fly, to move around, to seek adventure. **1974** Millard *Thunderbolt* 150: You got ants in your pants or something? **1989** *Boston Globe* (Nov. 19) 49: I see the kid with the ants in his pants, coming back next year, setting his feet, looking downfield and making that play. **1992** *Atlanta Journal* (Feb. 25) A8: The girls sit quietly, the boys have ants in their pants.

¶ (In other prov. expressions).

1938 Steinbeck *Grapes of Wrath* 50: A man didn't get enough crop to plug up an ant's ass. **1980** Gould *Ft. Apache* 15: I got the lowest job in the world. I'm lower than a pregnant ant. **1982** Del Vecchio *13th Valley* 291: You ain't got enough brains to plug up an ant's ass. **1983** Groen & Groen *Huey* 219: The projectile had missed..."by no more than an ant's ass," said the crew chief.

ante *n.* cash on hand, money to be spent.—often in phr. of the type **raise the ante.** [The sense "price" has prob. always been colloq.]

1895 Townsend *Fadden* 103: We'll talk 'bout dat later....We're shy on our ante yet. **1890** *Harper's* (Feb.) 428, in *OED2*: I raised the ante, and sold three hundred papers at ten cents each. **1891** Campbell et al. *Darkness & Daylight* 135: Blokes is allus axin' 'bout dat dere kid, but you is de fust one what ever raised de ante. **1908** in H.C. Fisher *A. Mutt* 60: I...refuse to send A. Mutt an invitation until he kicks in with his ante. **1928** Burnett *Little Caesar* 158: Raised the ante, did they? Last I heared it was five grand. *ca*1930 in Fife & Fife *Ballads of West* 153: An' the devils swiped his ante/When he went to sleep. **1934** Berg *Prison Nurse* 95: Still, the way things are breaking, we will have to boost the ante. **1944** in Gould *Tracy* 6: I want more ante....I want *fifty thousand.* **1952** Felton & Essex *Las Vegas* (film): Rollins wanted him to up the ante on the necklace. **1972** Newman & Benton *Bad Company* (film): We better go out and get us some more ante.

ante *v.* to pay, hand over, contribute; *(hence)* to do one's share.—often constr. with *up.*

1861 in *DA:* You have heard of the difficulty that *The Bulletin* has fallen into. I have had to "ante up" there at the rate of $200. **1873** J. Miller *Modocs* 62: I shall hang up at Cottonwood to-night, and if I don't make the sports *ante,* my name ain't Boston. **1879** *Nat. Police Gaz.* (Sept. 13) 14: They "anteed" up enough to pay a week's rent in advance. **1880** in F. Remington *Sel. Letters* 28: They have but to call me around and ante up one [cigar] and I can judge to their satisfaction. *ca*1880 in *Calif. Folk. Qly.* II (1943) 98: When we strike it [rich] we'll ante. **1903** C. Jackson *3d Degree* 204: I loaned [the knife] to another fellow; he promised to ante up with it the next day, but he didn't. **1922** *Leatherneck* (Apr. 29) 5: Kick In—Pay up, come across, put in your share, ante. **1936** *AS* (Dec.) 368: *Ante.* To work harmoniously with others; as, "His wife would not ante." **1970** Gilroy *Private* 3: Yale....Convinced they take anyone who can ante, we apply. **1989** *U.S. News & W.R.* (Dec. 4) 82: Would-be collectors unable to ante up $40 million for a Picasso can dip into the lucrative fine-arts market by buying drawings. **1990** *U.S. News & W.R.* (Oct. 15) 22: The government has recovered just a fraction of the $500 billion taxpayers may have to ante up to bail out failed S&L's.

antelope *n.* **1.** a hog. *Joc.*

1848 *Ladies' Repository* (Oct.) 315: *Antelope,* A hog. *Antelope lay,* To steal hogs.

2. a mule. *Joc.*

1899 Hamblen *Bucko Mate* 131: See if you can build a fire while I dress this antelope.

antifogmatic *n.* [*anti-* + *fog* + *-matic* (poss. fr. aro*matic*)] a warming alcoholic drink taken to counteract the unhealthful effects of fog or cold. *Joc.*

1789 in *DA* 34: Rum. Its great utility in preserving the effects of the damp and unwholesome air of the morning, has given it the medical name of an Antifogmatick. **1824** in Paulding *Bulls & Jons.* 191: The half pint of whiskey which every man takes up in the morning the first thing he does after getting up, is called an anti-fogmatic. **1833** *Mil & Nav. Mag.* 106: Come, take an antifogmatic then. **1839** in Blair & Meine *Half Horse* 66: We'll now take a flem-cutter, by way of an anti-fogmatic. **1899** H.K. Douglas *Stonewall* 258: I reversed my decision not to take an "antifogmatic" so early in the morning.

antifreeze *n.* [ref. to its warming quality] alcoholic liquor, esp. whiskey.—occ. used opprobriously.

1947–53 Guthrie *Seeds* 89: Smells like a very expensive antifreeze lotion to me....Who poured this whiskey in this radiator in the first place? **1958** McCulloch *Woods Words: Anti freeze*—Any alcoholic drink. **1960** MacCuish *Do Not Go Gentle* 335 [ref. to WWII]: Think he should drink this antifreeze? **1962** W. Robinson *Barbara* 294 [ref. to WWII]: McConnell passed the canteen to Barska. "Anti-freeze" McConnell said. **1965** Bonham *Durango St.* 161: We just took a little antifreeze to loosen up our engines. **1974** Cherry *High Steel* 89: Timmy, despite a body full of antifreeze, complained without pause.

antismash *n. Mil. Av.* collision lights, as on ships or aircraft.

1983–86 G.C. Wilson *Supercarrier* 239: "When my antismash comes on, be on your merry way." The antismash are warning lights designed to avoid midair collisions. **1992** Parsons & Nelson *Fighter Country* 156: *Anti-Smash* Collision warning lights.

ant-killer *n.* **1.** a big shoe or foot. Also **ant-stomper.**

1845 in Harris *High Times* 48: "Bill Jones, quit a smashin' that ar cat's tail!" "Well, let hir keep hir tail clar of my ant killers." **1979** Virginia woman, age 35: Big shoes are *ant-stompers.*

2. *Baseball.* a sharply hit ground ball.

1874 *Chi. Inter-Ocean* (July 7) (cited in Nichols *Baseball Term.*).

antsy *adj.* [fr. *ants in (one's) pants* s.v. ANT above] restless, uneasy, impatient. [1838 quot. is uniquely early; though app. intended in this sense, its spelling and early date make its relationship to current usage problematic.]

1838 in *DARE:* Minard's talking & Peake's scribbling were enough to drive anyone ancey. **1950** in *DARE: Antsy:* ["eager or anxious"]—[used] by teenagers. **1954** *Time* (Aug. 16) 30: I got "antsy." You know, when you've got cancer, every minute counts. **1958** McCulloch *Woods Wds.: Antsy*...having ants in the pants, being overanxious to get going. **1965** *New Yorker* (Apr. 10) 144: Everyone here in town is getting antsy. **1966** Pei *Story of Lang.* (ed. 2) 189: Antsy, agitated, worried. **1970** Grissim *White Man's Blues* 54: An intensely antsy audience. **1972** *Rookies* (ABC-TV): Just don't get antsy on us. **1973** *New York* (Oct. 1) 45: *Mad*men get a little antsy over that kind of philosophical or psychoanalytical crap. **1978** *Rolling Stone* (Sept. 7) 24: The local bands got to warm up an antsy, packed house. **1988** Poyer *Med* 23: The men get antsy cooped up.

A Number One *pron.* [blend A-ONE + *number one* 'oneself'] I, me, myself; himself, herself; yourself. See also A-ONE.

1924 Henderson *Keys* 396: *A No. 1.* Used in place of the personal pronoun I. **1936** J.T. Farrell *World* 397: She just looks out for A-Number-One in every way that she can.

anus *n.* [sugg. by lit. syn. ASSHOLE] ASSHOLE, 2.a.

1973 Wilstach *Stunt-Man* 94: Aw, come on, Lamarr!...We have to put up with that anus? **1979** Ark. English instructor, age 27: The man's an incredible anus.

anvil chorus *n.* [ref. to "The Anvil Chorus," in opera *Il Trovatore,* by Giuseppe Verdi (1853)] carping criticism or critics.

1898 "B. Baxter" *Baxter's Ltrs.* 20: I've heard knockers in my time, but Estelle is the original leader of the anvil chorus. **1906** "H. McHugh" *Skiddoo* 10: You are...still singing second tenor in the Anvil Chorus. **1920** "B. Standish" *Man on First* 127: The anvil chorus is hushed. **1941** *Sat. Eve. Post* (May 17) 18: Fletcher [was] the leader of the anvil chorus. **1972** in Galewitz *Great Comics* 136: A swell example you're setting for Annie—you and your anvil chorus pals. **1972** in Shores *Contemp. Eng.* 179: The substance of this anvil chorus of dispraise was that the new dictionary was unsatisfactory on three counts.

anxious *adj.* delightful.

1944 Burley *Harlem Jive* 78: *Anxious*—wonderful, excellent.

¶ In phrase:

¶ **on the anxious seat** [or **bench**] anxious, restless, eager.

1839 *Spirit of Times* (Dec. 14) 487: We met old daylight thar, and our dogs soon showed symptoms of bein' on the "anxious seat." **1884** Carleton *Poker Club* 43: Dis ain't no prar meetin'—ceptin' Brer Williams seems to be on de anxious seat. **1887** Francis *Saddle & Moc.* 226: Oh, the boys kept him on the "anxious seat" for two or three days, and that cured him. **1888** *Stag Party* (unp.): And I was on the "anxious" seat, Uncertain how to move. **1901** Irwin *Sonnets* (unp.): O goo-goo eye, how glassy glazed thou art To...Keep thy Willie on the anxious seat. **1902** Clapin *Americanisms: Anxious bench*...still common enough in New England, in a figurative sense. **1906** in *DA:* The entire diplomatic corps at Havana is...on the "anxious bench." **1945** *Newsweek* (Mar. 12)

78: After nearly a month on the anxious seat, Frank Sinatra, 26,...learned his draft classification. **1965** Gallery *8 Bells* 224: Then I was really on the anxious seat. There were a number of things Mr. Johnson might do, all of them unpleasant.

any *pron.* [by ellipsis] any sexual intercourse.—used without expressed antecedent.—usu. constr. with *get*.
  *1945 S.J. Baker *Australian Lang.* 124: The jocular greeting between man and man, *gettin' any?* **1950** Bissell *Stretch on River* 53: I didn't know whether she was giving these guys any, and...I didn't even want to think about it. **1958–59** Southern & Hoffenberg *Candy* 215: Gittin' any? Hee-hee. **1954–60** *DAS:* "Getting any" = "How is your sex life?" **1969** N.Y.C. editor, age *ca*40: Had any lately? **1978** Truscott *Dress Gray* 242: The nearly sacrosanct admission he hadn't "gotten any" from his girlfriend. **1980** Kotzwinkle *Jack* 157: Steve gettin' any, you think? **1982** *All Things Considered* (Nat. Pub. Radio) (July 2): Men and boys often talk of sex as, "Did you get any?" "Did you get some?" **1989** *Tracey Ullman Show* (Fox-TV): How's it goin', Jerry? Gettin' any?

anyhoo *adv.* [intentional malapropism] anyhow. *Joc.*
  1946 Burns *Gallery* 345: Anyhoo I'm glad. **1954–60** *DAS:* Anyhoo...a jocular mispronunciation considered sophisticated c1945–c1950. **1973** N.Y.C. man, age 26: Anyhoo, let's go. **1984** in "J.B. Briggs" *Drive-In* 227: But anyhoo, while I was down there.... *a***1988** C. Adams *More Straight Dope* 29: Anyhoo, thanks for the plug on my song.

anymouse *adj.* [intentional malapropism] *Navy.* anonymous. *Joc.*
  1979–88 Noel & Bush *Naval Terms* (ed. 5): *Anymouse* Naval aviation slang for anonymous. Anymouse reports of aircraft accidents are sent in to *Approach Magazine.*

anywhere *adv.* ¶ In phrase: **not be anywhere** to suffer by comparison, be worthless.
  1871 "M. Twain" *Roughing It* 246: And ain't they cool about it, too? Icebergs ain't anywhere.

Anzio Annie *n.* [cf. BIG BERTHA for female given name applied to a large gun] *Mil.* a railroad gun employed by the German army to shell the Allied beachhead at Anzio, Jan.–May 1944. Now *hist.* Also **Anzio Express.**
  [***1944** Mar., in Rock *Field Service* 286: The Germans occasionally would shell the place with a special long-range gun; [British] troops affectionately called this gun "Anzio Archie."] **1944** *Stars & Stripes* (June 17) (Mediterranean ed.) 1: Anzio Annie, the Anzio Express or "the goddam gun in the hills"...is dead now. **1945** *Sat. Review* (Nov. 3) 7: Anzio Annie is a German rail gun that used to drop 10-inch shells into the famous Beachhead. **1963** J. Ross *Dead Are Mine* 133: The "Anzio Express"...fired an eleven-inch projectile...into the vicinity of the harbors of Anzio and Nettuno. **1980** Tenn. actor, age *ca*55: It'd take more than a little pop like that to scare me. I used to listen to Anzio Annie every night.

AO *n.* [mil. initialism *a*rea of *o*perations] *Mil.* immediate vicinity; place of activity.
  1977 Carabatsos *Heroes* 124: Ken held the rifle by his side....Spray the fucking AO. **1987** Pelfrey & Carabatsos *Hamburger Hill* 168: Un-ass my AO. **1989** Leib *Fire Dream* 12: AO meant Area of Operations; to a mud marine, it meant wherever he was. **1992** Dixon *Army Terms* 75: When a soldier wants people to get out of his A.O., he will yell "un-ass my A.O."...Larry first heard this in 1967.

A-OK *adj.* [A-ONE + OK; term introduced by Project Mercury astronauts, disseminated during television coverage of suborbital flight of Cmdr. Alan B. Shepard, May 5, 1961] perfect; excellent; fine. Also as *adv.*
  1959 (cited in *W9*). **1961** May 8, in *AS* XXXVIII 228: "A-okay," as everybody now knows, means all's well, everything [is] functioning perfectly. **1961** *Newsweek* (July 31) 18: As the rocket arched out of sight, there was the feeling that everything would be A-Okay, even routine. **1964** Redfield *Ltrs. fr. Actor* 30: He's...pretending to the world that everything is A-okay. **1965** *N.Y. Times* (Oct. 24) Ghana ad section 13: Ghana's abundant resources...can only spur the nation's...industrial development into an orbit that can only spell AOK. **1965** Marks *Ltrs.* 71: Last night I saw "Charade"...an A-O.K. flick. **1972** Jenkins *Semi-Tough* 84: These boys and your daughter have promised me that their behavior in the future will be A-O.K. **1972–79** T. Wolfe *Right Stuff* 227: "A-Okay"...was a Shorty Powers paraphrase borrowed from NASA engineers who used to say it during radio transmission tests because the sharper sound of *A* cut through the static better than *O*. **1980** *N.Y. Post* (July 31) 7: Ex-President Gerald Ford...[gives] the A-

OK signal...after sinking a birdie putt at his invitational golf tournament. **1982** Junior Achievement radio jingle: We're makin' it, movin' it, doin' it A-OK. **1992** *Mother Goose & Grimm* (CBS-TV): I checked out the basement and everything's A-OK.

A-one or **A number one** *adj.* [from Lloyd's rating of ships, "in first-class condition"] first-class, excellent. Now *S.E.* See also A NUMBER ONE.
  1846 [Codman] *Sailor's Life* 195: Cook,...do you consider yourself "A.1" in your profession? **1859** O.W. Holmes *Prof. at Breakfast Table* 165: John...asked me to try some "old Bourbon," which he said was A1. **1877** E.L. Wheeler *Deadwood Dick* 79: It only remains for you to aim straight and rid your country of an A No. 1 dead-beat swindler! **1877** Walling *N.Y. Chief* 283: Silverware, such as would have been rated "A1 swag." **1899** Robbins *Gam* 152: Coffee, to be A1, must be black as night, strong as death, an' hot as hell! **1903** Merriman *Ltrs. from Son* 74: Such awful rot...may appear to you as A1 inspiration. **1923** in Pound *Ltrs.* 185: Hope the Kittens are A-1. **1928** McKay *Banjo* 127: Why, he's A number one—a sweet potato in the skin. **1953** Harkins *Road Race* 24: It's in A-1 shape inside and out. **1960** Kirkwood *Pony* 254: Tanner...'s got a reputation for being an A-1 bastard. **1964** Leavitt & Sohn *Stop & Write* 206: How could anyone ever have a coat like dat. Gee whiz, dat's A1...wow! **1976** J. Harrison *Farmer* 140: She was an A-1 drunk. **1978** Truscott *Dress Gray* 44: He's Hedges' fuckin' A-number-one hit man.

apcray *n.* [Pig Latin form of *crap*] nonsense; rubbish.
  1937 in Partridge *Dict. Und.* 9: This idea...is a lot of apcray. **1945** J. Bryan *Carrier* 32: And as for a cruiser being sunk...—apcray! **1966–75** Winchell *Exclusive* 283: "That's show biz!" and all-that-other apcray.

ape *n.* **1.** a stupid, violent, or offensively uncouth person; a hired thug.
  1931 Faulkner *Sanctuary* 48: Do you think that ape will? **1935** Lindsay *Loves Me Not* 46: Don't be an ape, Broughton! There's nothing private going on! **1938–40** Clark *Ox-Bow* 46: Sit down you big ape. **1971** Dahlskog *Dict. Contemp. Us.:* Ape...an athlete, esp. a college football player. **1973** Ward *Sting* (film): He's got his apes with him.
  2. *Logging.* a rigging man.
  1930 in *DARE.* **1958** McCulloch *Woods Words:* Ape—A rigging man (often called tame ape).
  3. [sugg. by initials of *A*ir *P*olice] *USAF.* Air Policeman, AP.
  1965 Pollini *Glover* 29: Dumb A.P., that's all, man, dumb ape. **1973** USAF veteran, served in Vietnam 1972–73: The APs are called *apes.* Everybody called them that. **1990** G.R. Clark *Words of Vietnam War:* Air Police...(nicknamed Apes).
  4. *Film.* a motion-picture crewman.
  1970 Southern *Blue Movie* 74: "You gonna put up the actors and the apes in the same hotel?!?" It is classic Hollywood protocol that the actors be quartered separately from the technicians ("apes" or "gorillas" as they are affectionately called).
  ¶ In phrase:
  ¶ **like a stripe** [or **striped**]**-assed ape** headlong, at great speed.—usu. considered vulgar.
  [**1947** in *DA* s.v. *Lizzie:* They would run like a spotted-bottomed ape.] [**1950** *Best Army Stories* 82: And he takes off like a striped ape.] **1952** Randolph & Wilson *Down in Holler* 181: He was runnin' like a stripe-assed ape. **1952** Uris *Battle Cry* 107 [ref. to WWII]: If that son of a bitch gets up, you'd better take off like a stripe-assed ape. **1957** Atwell *Private* 87 [ref. to WWII]: With that he takes off like a great striped-assed ape. **1960** Leckie *Marines* 2 [ref. to WWII]: He would have taken off through the bush like a stripe-assed ape. **1970** Thackrey *Thief* 241: Just run like a striped-ass ape. **1972** Pearce *Pier Head Jump* 113: I'm still runnin' for the door like a striped-ass ape. **1972–76** Durden *No Bugles* 13: I remember Ubanski runnin' like a striped-ass ape.

ape *adj.* **1.** drunk. Also **aped.** [1915 quot. is uniquely early; later use is undoubtedly a specialization of **(2.).**]
  1915 *DN* IV 231: *Aped*...drunk. "He's aped again." **1971** Cole *Rock* 21: The small, select party continues until everyone is pretty well ape. **1981** Univ. Tenn. student: *Ape* or *smashed* means drunk. **1985** Eble *Campus Slang* (Oct.): *Ape*—very drunk. "Carla was ape last night."
  2. [orig. in phr. *to go ape,* lit., "to begin acting like an ape"] crazy with delight or anger; violently emotional.—usu. in phr. **go ape.** See also APESHIT, *adj.*
  1955 *AS* XXX 117 [USAF]: *Go Ape*...React in an irrational manner; go into a frenzy. **1957** Shulman *Rally* 44: I'm here to tell you everybody went ape. **1958** Gilbert *Vice Trap* 113: Remember when Mitch went real ape on just beers! **1960** Swarthout *Where Boys Are* 78: I do not go

ape over jazz. **1960** MacCuish *Do Not Go Gentle* 74 [ref. to WWII]: He's mean. Puts away the booze and goes ape. **1961** *AS* XXXVI 150: (quot. at APESHIT, *adj.*). **1961** Rubin *In Life* 12: I nearly went ape once. Ape, you know: For the nut wagon, crazy, mishuga. **1961** Kohner *Gidget Goes Hawaiian* 69: The audience went ape. **1964** Redfield *Ltrs. from Actor* 192: Clem Fowler goes absolutely ape whenever I appear at his dressing room with a sweater or a club shirt....[He says] "Let the rest of the people wear their crappy sports outfits." **1965** Conot *Rivers of Blood* 230: I'm gonna climb a tree and go ape! **1966** *New Yorker* (June 4) 32: I don't blame you for being ape for her. **1969** Coppel *Laughter* 105 [ref. to WWII]: Christ, it wouldn't take too much more of that to drive him completely ape. **1974** Millard *Thunderbolt* 139: Leary, you've gone completely ape. **1978** Wharton *Birdy* 95: I'm completely ape. **1983** *Time* (Apr. 11) 26: He threw furniture and chased her from their suburban home. "I went ape," he says. **1990** J. Updike *Rabbit at Rest* 69: You'll both go ape in there.

¶ In phrase:

¶ **go ape** to malfunction; to perform unpredictably. See also **(2.),** above.

1965 *Time* (Aug. 27): Missiles sometimes came off the pad and went ape. **1966** Shepard *Doom Pussy* 207: These gah-dam fuel gauges are going ape. **1969** Broughton *Thud Ridge* 81: My...navigational gear...went ape. **1983** *Pop. Sci.* (Apr.) 64: When these systems go ape, there's no place for trial and error or guesswork.

ape hangers *n.pl.* exceptionally sweeping V-shaped handlebars, as on a customized motorcycle. Hence, as attrib., **apehanger.**

1965 *New Yorker* (Dec. 11) 164: The sweeping handlebars known among the motorcycle avant-garde as ape hangers. **1966–71** Karlen *Sex & Homosex.* 318: Tooled-up, apehanger cycles. **1979** *Easyriders* (Dec.) 116: Apehanger Days.

apehead *n.* idiot.

1928 Dahlberg *Bottom Dogs* 145: That apehead.

ape oil *n.* [cf. APE, *n.*, 2] whiskey.

1940 *AS* (Dec.) 446 [Tenn.]: *Ape Oil.* Liquor. "Sallie's man likes his ape oil."

ape out *v.* to go ape s.v. APE, *adv.*

1968 Baker et al. *CUSS* 71: *Ape Out.* Go wild.

apeshit *n.* [fr. APESHIT, *adj.*] a vulgar or crazy person.—usu. considered vulgar.

1960–69 Runkel *Law* 101 These apeshits that go aroun' [molesting] little girls; stuff like that. *a*1990 Westcott *Half a Klick* 33: Stand at attention when I talk to you, ape-shit.

apeshit *adj.* [prob. elaboration of APE, *adj.*; cf. syn. BATSHIT fr. BATS] APE, *adj.*—usu. considered vulgar. See also APE, *adj.*

1951 Sheldon *Troubling of Star* 25: What do I want to fight for? You going apeshit? *ca*1952 in [*41st Fighter Sq. Songbk.*] 17: They'll drive you ape shit, they'll drive you insane. **1961** *AS* XXXVI 150: The exaggerated, unflattering connotation of wild, self-dirtying activity was ascribed to individuals or organizations that had *gone ape* (or *apeshit*) during the Second World War, but this meaning seems to have disappeared. **1961** Plantz *Sweeney Sq.* 193 [ref. to WWII]: If Captain Christiansen goes to base hospital, I'm riding next to this ape-shit bastard. **1967** Mailer *Vietnam* 132: Can you imagine your daddy getting that ape shit? **1972** Pearce *Pier Head Jump* 144: No wonder you guys have gone so apeshit over this thing. **1977** Olsen *Fire Five* 81: Some shifts he drives us apeshit. **1986** Sally Field, in *Playboy* (Mar.) 49: I would stand on the coffee table and scream at him. I would go apeshit. I changed from a sweet, helpless being into Godzilla. **1992** *Billboard* (May 16) 1: It's a natural occurrence for people to hear the music and go apeshit.

ape wagon *n.* R.R. caboose.

1946 in Botkin & Harlow *R.R. Folklore* 350: The shack was in the angel's seat of the ape wagon. **1977** R. Adams *Railroader* 7: *Ape wagon*: a caboose.

apey *adj.* crazy; APE.

1951 Sheldon *Troubling of Star* 165: He always went slightly apey when he drank. **1962** W. Crawford *Give Me Tomorrow*: They'll drive you apey, they'll drive you insane. **1990** *L.A. Times* (June 6) C6: The beautiful beaches and crystal-clear water...I completely went apey.

apple *n.* **1.** [fr. syn. *horse apple*] a horse turd.

*****1800** in G. Ashton *Eng. Satire on Napoleon* 99: Some horse dung being washed by the current from a neighbouring dunghill, espied a number of fair apples swimming up the stream, when, wishing to be thought of consequence, the horse dung would every moment be bawling out,

"Lack-a-day, how we apples swim!" **1924** Anderson & Stallings *What Price Glory?* I ii: He seen Cooper pulling a fag at reveille this morning, What's Cooper doing now? Boy, following the ponies, following the ponies. *He's* out collecting apples.

2.a. [app. sugg. by prov. "one rotten apple spoils the barrel"] fellow, person, "customer."—used chiefly with a preceding adj. [The evidence suggests that *rotten apple* is the orig. form and that others arose by analogy.]

1887 DeVol *Gambler* 181: George, those fellows are rotten apples. **1923** Riesenberg *Under Sail* 18: There's no choosing between them rotten apples aft. **1933–35** D. Lamson *About to Die* 192: Now that's a square apple for you, see? **1938** *AS* XIII 191: *Square Apple* (one who is not a professional criminal)...Restricted to the West Coast. **1942** *ATS* 773: A poor companion on a "date"; a bore...sad apple. **1944** H. Brown *Walk in Sun* 57: Tyne, you're a smart apple. **1947** M. Spillane *I, Jury* 20: Whoever pulled the trigger was a smart apple. **1948** Seward & Ryan *Angel's Alley* (film): I need sharp apples, Mahoney, because I operate big. **1950** Bissell *Stretch on River* 24: I was always getting trapped...by some sad apple who wants information, sympathy, fifty cents, encouragement [etc.]. **1951** H. Robbins *Danny Fisher* 313: Sam was a pretty sharp apple. **1954** J.D. MacDonald *Condemned* 114: You, milady, are a rough apple. You're rough as a cob. **1957** Laurents & Sondheim *West Side Story* 205: O.K., wise apples, down to the station house. **1962** Dougherty *Commissioner* 19: Seen from this angle he looked what, in Bonaro's words he was—"a bad apple." **1962** Viertel *Love & Corrupt* 259: His wife...was a sad apple. **1965** Spillane *Killer* 101: He's a hard apple. He's hard on everybody and he's harder on himself. **1967** Longo *Priest* 94: She was a real tough apple. **1975** R.P. Davis *Pilot* 150: I don't hobnob with those apples. **1981** G. Wolf *Roger Rabbit* 202: I hate wise apples.

b. a foolish, ineffectual person; (*specif.*) Und. the victim or prospective victim of a confidence game, "sucker."

1928 in Perelman *Old Gang* 43: "I can't say," replied the poor apple. **1935** Pollock *Und. Speaks: Apple*, person engaged in a legitimate occupation. **1940** *AS* (Apr.) 120: A victim, or intended victim...apple. *Ibid.* 190: *To feel like an apple.* To feel embarrassed. **1947** *ATS* (Supp.) 2: Unpopular Person; "Drip." Apple...goon...troll [etc.]. **1957** Ellison *Web of City* 35: Where's the apple? **1959** Zugsmith *Beat Generation* 57: These married apples, they want you to punish them for enjoying it. **1966** Braly *Cold Out There* 38: Jesus, would you shake the apples. They'd think they were up against King Kong. **1972** Grogan *Ringolevio* 2: They were always the ones who caught the ball that was hit into the bleachers and were never the apples who got hit in the head. **1973** N.Y.C. pool player, age 24: An *apple* is a sucker who's just waiting to be plucked. Like if you're hustling pool, you wait for an *apple*. *a*1988 D. Smith *Firefighters* 144: He never swore. His biggest thing, if you were a screwup, was to call you an apple.

3. *West.* saddle horn, pommel.

1915 in J.I. White *Dogies* 145: I'm grabbin' the apple and blind as a bat. **1933** *AS* (Feb.) 28 [Tex.]: *Apple.* Saddle horn. **1936** R. Adams *Cowboy Lingo* 44: [The saddle horn] went by such slang names as "nubbin," "apple," "Lizzie," "biscuit," and many others.

4. *Mil.* a grenade; bomb.

1918 *Forum* (Oct.) 408: A Prussian threw a hand grenade....That trench apple sure did scatter a little hell around. **1918** in *Ark. Hist. Qly.* XVIII (1959) 12: In case Fritz does drop us a few apples. **1939** D. Runyon *Take it Easy* 79: To have any airplane come along and drop a few hot apples on them. **1956** Hargrove *Girl He Left* 129: Andy picked up his two grenades....The apples felt strangely heavy in his hands. **1964** *Fugitive* (ABC-TV): Just at the time this apple goes off. **1982** Goff, Sanders & Smith *Bros.* 56 [ref. to 1968]: Some dude would take a hand grenade and...say, and they meant it, man..."I'm gonna stick this mouthful of apple down your throat."

5.a. a baseball—constr. with *old.*

1919 *Amer. Legion Wkly.* (July 11) 15: You hear the bat crack at the "old apple." **1931** *Collier's* (Apr. 25) 8: Jo-jo belts the old apple right through a high window. **1939–40** Tunis *Kid from Tomkinsville* 30: I seen you take a coupla belts at that old apple. **1952** Malamud *Natural* 70: Nice work, Bumpsy, 'at's grabbin' th' old apple. **1974** Perry & Sudyk *Me & Spitter* 12: I tried everything on the old apple.

b. a football.

1974 Blount *3 Bricks Shy* 55: 'Cause you can't score without that *apple.*

c. a basketball.

1980 (quot. at PILL).

6.a. Esp. *Boxing.* the Adam's apple.

1922 J. Conway, in *Variety* (Jan. 13) 7: We never figured that Tomato would have any trouble hittin this guy in the apple but...he aint got no neck. **1974** Radano *Cop Stories* 40: His mouth keeps twitching, his apple keeps moving but he never says a word.

b. [prob. sugg. by CHOKE, *v.*] *Baseball.* (see quots.).

1964 Thompson & Rice *Every Diamond* 142: *The Apple:* What bothers a poor competitor in a crisis. **1989** P. Dickson *Baseball Dict.: Apple comes up, the*...Fails to accomplish a desired result in a key situation. A reference to one's Adam's apple; to choke.

7. a big city; *specif.* (and usu.) **The Apple**, New York City, esp. its jazz and entertainment centers. Cf. syn. BIG APPLE. [Orig. jazz slang.]

1938 Calloway *Hi De Ho* 16: *Apple:* the big town, the main stem, Harlem. **1943** *Yank* (Jan. 13) 20: Lenox Avenue at 125th Street...the core of the Apple. **1944** Burley *Harlem Jive* 18: The average Lane today is from the Apple, or at least from some Apple, whether it's the Big Apple, the Windy Apple, the Tropic Apple, or the Bunker Hill Apple. *Ibid.* 114: This is the Apple....This is New York City. **1961** Russell *Sound* 64: Come on, doll. Next stop is the Apple. **1964** Redfield *Ltrs. from Actor* 214: The economics of the Apple forbid such old-fashioned customs. **1965** Borowik *Lions* 61: Here in the big town, or as the musicians call it The Apple. **1967** Gonzalez *Dues* 18: I had been going to New York but at eighteen I didn't think I was ready to try the "Apple" yet. **1971** Wells & Dance *Night People* 109: *Apple* n. Big City. **1974** V. Smith *Jones Men* 25: It's supposed to be his wedding thing from the Apple, you know. **1979** J.T. Maher, in *Comments on Ety.* (Jan. 1989) 12: I distinctly recall the alto man using a phrase [in 1934] that puzzled me for many years—puzzled me to the point where I was convinced I hadn't heard right. He said that one of the players who hadn't made the trip had "stayed in the apple 'cause he wasn't feelin' just right." **1982** *Business Week* (June 21) 10: In his anxiety to depict another Harlem, though, Anderson himself has trouble remembering what the Apple was all about.

8. *pl.* a woman's breasts.

1942 *ATS* 145: Breasts. *Apples, boobys* [etc.]. **1975** C.W. Smith *Country Music* 256: A peasant blouse that showed the tops of those lovely little apples. **1967–80** Folb *Runnin' Lines* 288: *Apples* Breasts.

9. *Bowling.* a weakly or inaccurately bowled ball.

1966 *RHD.* **1980** Pearl *Pop. Slang: Flat apple* (Bowling) a dead ball. **1982** Considine *Lang. Sport* 83.

10. a style of soft, billed cap with a very prominent over-sized crown.

1966 Braly *On Yard* 129: Red had attempted to block his rainhat into a style currently in vogue with pimps and hustlers called the Apple. **1967–80** Folb *Runnin' Lines* 109: You all dressed up and you have your apple hat on. **1992** *L.A. Times Mag.* (Oct. 18) 6: A bead-wearing, apple-capped, paintbrush-totin', long-haired flower child in the '60s.

11. [sugg. by initials *APL*, official designation] *Mil.* barrack ship.

1971 Glasser *365 Days* 28: The men climbed...up the ladders to the LST's and "apples."

12. *Pol.* a Native American who has adopted the values of white American society. Cf. BANANA; COCONUT; OREO.

1980 *Mother Jones* (Dec.) 31: It is possible for an American Indian to share European values, a European world view. We have a term for these people; we call them "apples"—red on the outside (genetics) and white on the inside (their values). **1981** Eyre & Wadleigh *Wolfen* (film): "He killed an apple." "What?" "A conservative Indian. Red on the outside, white inside." **1982** Least Heat Moon *Blue Hwys.* 189: But I'm no apple Indian—red outside and white underneath.

¶ In phrases:

¶ **apples to ashes** a certainty; unquestionable, *dollars to doughnuts* s.v. DOUGHNUT.

1899 A.H. Lewis *Sandburrs* 26: Youse put a poor sucker in d' dark hole an' be d' end of ten hours it's apples to ashes he ain't onto it whether he's been in a day or a week. **1901** A.H. Lewis *R. Croker* 47: It would have been, in the language of sport, "apples to ashes on the big one." **1911** A.H. Lewis *Apaches of N.Y.* 151: It's apples to ashes he's gunnin' for Goldie.

¶ **bob for apples** *Med.* [cf. **(1)**, above] to digitally examine or disimpact the rectum of a patient.

1972 *Nat. Lampoon* (July) 76: *Bobbing for apples.* The unclogging of the tract of a superconstipated patient with the finger. Traditionally performed by doctor in training. *a***1990** in *Maledicta* X 31: *Bobbing for apples* digital fecal disimpaction.

¶ **for sour apples** even a minimal amount; at all.

1886 F. Whittaker *Pop Hicks* 17: You can't ride for sour apples. **1911–12** J. London *Smoke Bellew* 117: He couldn't have bucked for sour

apples at any other table. **1936** in Paxton *Sport USA* 7: I couldn't hit for sour apples. **1980** Hogan *Lawman's Choice* 134: They don't count for sour apples.

¶ **How do you like them apples?** "What do you think of that, and what do you think you can do about it?"—used with ironic force. Also vars.

[**1926** Dunning & Abbott *Broadway:* How do you like them grapes?] **1928–29** Nason *Slicker* 228 [ref. to WWI]: Well, I'm a sergeant. So how's that for little apples? **1941** in H. Gray *Arf* (unp.): Sissy, eh? How d'yuh like *them* apples? [Delivers punch in nose.] **1957** Townley *Up in Smoke* (film): How do you like them apples? **1964** Webb *Cheyenne Autumn* (film): You callin' me a liar? Take a look at *them* apples. **1962–68** B. Jackson *In Life* 141: How do you like that for apples? **1971** Horan *Messiah* 170: How do you like those apples? **1976** Chinn *Dig Nigger Up* 177: How do you like them apples? **1983** J. Davis *Garfield* (synd. cartoon strip) (Feb. 2): Good! They shot the lion! What do you think of those apples, Garfield? [a cat]

¶ **know (one's) apples** see s.v. KNOW.

¶ **polish apples** to curry favor, as with a teacher. See also APPLE-POLISHER.

[**1901** Bull *Flashes* 41: When I was a lad,...I polished up the apples on the big fruit stand,/I polished up the apples so from day to day,/That now I am the monarch of the Great Midway!] **1927** *AS* (Mar.) 277 [Stanford Univ.]: *Polish apples*...curry favor in conversation. **1961** Boyd *Lighter Than Air* 13: A little late to polish the apple, isn't it? **1963** in R. Atkinson *Long Gray Line* 85: Those who seem to get ahead in aptitude ratings are those who "polish apples." **1964** Berg *Looks at U.S.A.* (unp.): How come a wise guy like *him* keeps getting ahead, while I just stand still! He must have polished a lot of apples! **1984** "W.T. Tyler" *Shadow Cabinet* 184: Polishing the apple with the JCs.

¶ **rotten apples** a minimal amount, "beans."

1952 Mandel *Angry Strangers* 231: I don't care rotten apples about your sister, but I hate FUZZ worse'n poison.

¶ **small apples** of little consequence, unimpressive.

1887 Call *Josh Hayseed* 65: He's pooty small apples with the high and mighty 'mong perlite folks.

¶ **the whole apple** everything.

1884 Beard *Bristling* 13: This glorious victory....Is only a foretaste, a nibble, sahs!...We'll march to Boston...and the whole apple there.

¶ **tough apples!** [euphem. of *tough shit*] "Tough luck!" "I don't care about your misfortune."

1971 Faust *Willy* 89: Tough apples.

apple butter route *n. Hobo. Local.* the rural area along the route of the Norfolk and Western Kentucky Railroad between Portsmouth and Circleville, Ohio.

1917 [Livingston] *Coast to Coast* 121: The portion of the Norfolk and Western which in south-eastern Ohio runs from Portsmouth to Circleville was dubbed the "Apple Butter Route." **1925** Mullin *Scholar Tramp* 137 [ref. to 1912]: The Apple Butter Route in southern Ohio over a division of the N. & W. **1927** *DN* V 437: *Apple butter route,* n. The N. and W. Ky. between Portsmouth and Circleville where hobos are given hand-outs of bread and apple-butter.

applecart *n.* **1.** (one's) body as a receiver of harm, esp. a knock-down blow.—usu. in phr. of the type **upset (one's) apple-cart** to knock violently to the ground.

*****1788** Grose *Vulgar Tongue* (ed. 2): Down with his apple-cart, knock or throw him down. **1834** Caruthers *Kentuckian in N.Y.* I 23: Smash my apple-cart if I can see into it. **1836** *Every Body's Album* I 93: I only want to caution you, or I'll upset your apple-cart. **1841** [Mercier] *Man-of-War* 110: I'll *capsize* your *apple-cart* for you. **1882** *Judge* (Oct. 28): But what some other boy...would try to "smash my apple-cart."

2. the planned or actual good order of things.—usu. in phr. of the type **upset the applecart** to spoil things.—in 19th and 20th C. *Colloq.* or *S.E.*

1788 in Whiting *Early Amer. Prov.* 11: S. Adams had almost overset the apple-cart by intruding an amendment of his own fabrication. **1984** *N.Y. Times* (Apr. 12) B14: The press rewards therefore the squeaky wheel, the solo performer, the guy who tries to upset the applecart one way or another. **1990** *New Republic* (July 9): New theoretical winds...upset a lot of applecarts during the last decade or so.

3. [sugg. by initialism *APc*, official designation] *Navy.* Small Coastal Transport. Now *hist.*

1950 Morison *Naval Ops. in WWII* VI 134 [ref. to 1942]: Two APcs* set forth from Milne Bay on the 29th....*Pronounced "apple-cart," APc is the abbreviation for "Small Coastal Transport." Many of them had been built in Maine like fishing draggers.

applehead *n.* a stupid person, BLOCKHEAD.
> **1951** *N.Y. Times* (Sept. 24) 34: You, sir,...are an applehead. **1962** Mandel *Angry Strangers* 365: A week at least, you applehead freak. **1962** Mandel *Wax Boom* 295: What's good?...This apple-head Spiro? **1971** Wells & Dance *Night People* 117: Apple-head.

applejack *n.* APPLE, 10.
> **1971** in Sanchez *Word Sorcerers* 178: An they wore cocked Apple jacks with red process rags wrapped round they heads. **1971** Woodley *Dealer* 12: Applejacks—dusters—tilted forward over their foreheads covering Afros or slick hairdos.

apple-knocker *n.* [cf. APPLE-SHAKER, 1] **1.** an ignorant rustic; a fool.
> **1919** Kuhn *Co. A.* 8: The "apple-knocker" contingent was mustered into the National Guard of the State of New York on April 16, 1912. **1920** in Randolph *Church House* 71 [Ozarks]: One of these apple-knockers has took me for ten dollars, that's what's the matter. **1924** Tully *Beggars* 108: I'll bum the apple knocker for a buck and give it to you. **1928** Wharton *Squad* 287 [ref. to WWI]: Can it, you apple-knocker! **1933** Ersine *Prison Slang*: Appleknocker...was originally applied only to farmers, but now it is used with reference to any person on whom the speaker looks with contempt. **1939** *New Yorker* (Nov. 4) 26: Them other sailors was apple-knockers. They were so dumb they couldn't find their nose with both hands. **1946** Michener *Tales of S. Pacific* 45: The engineering officer was an appleknocker from upstate New York. **1972** Sherburne *Ft. Pillow* 19: Cheers and huzzas from the Illinois apple-knockers. **1976** *Nat. Lampoon* (July) 59: Beat it, apple-knocker. **1980** *Texas Monthly* (June) 211: The crowd was about...one-third rednecks—I mean real apple-knockers in gimme caps and dingo boots. **1988** *N.Y. Newsday* (Sept. 19) 60: To be an effective leader, Marino would have to represent the interests of all the people in New York State, whether they be upstate apple knockers or inner city children or those middle-class folks in his suburban base.

2. one who picks apples; (*broadly*) fruit picker.
> **1922** N. Anderson *Hobo* 93: An "apple knocker" picks apples and other fruit. **1925** Mullin *Scholar Tramp* 290: I was invited to a long table crowded with jovial apple-knockers, where I ate such a meal as I had not in months. **1930** "D. Stiff" *Milk & Honey* 35: Among the various harvest hands are the "apple knockers" and the "berry glaumers." **1967** Spradley *Drunk* 16: Most apple knockers were drunk from wines, fines, etc. **1982** D.A. Harper *Good Company* 14: The fruit tramp, what we call the apple knocker. **1988** *L.A. Times Mag.* (Jan. 24) 37: Douglas Meador...is a self-styled former "apple knocker" from Washington State.

3. an inexperienced youthful worker; naive newcomer, greenhorn.
> [**1930** Buranelli *Maggie* 14 [ref. to WWI]: The greenest hand aboard the *Maggie* was a New Jersey farmer whom the other gobs called the "Apple Knocker," he was so green.] **1942** Lindsay & Crouse *Strip* 224: Listen, you appleknocker, haven't you ever seen a burlesque show? **1958** McCulloch *Woods Wds.*: *Apple-knocker*—a part time logger, usually not very skilled at woods jobs. **1966** Wanderone & Fox *Bank Shot* 7: As an apple-knocker on a brand-new beat, I asked what I thought was a cautious question.

apple-knocking *adj.* being an APPLE-KNOCKER.
> **1948** in Hemingway *Sel. Letters* 645: Cut out the show boat you apple-knocking son of a bitch.

apple orchard *n.* [APPLE, 2.b.] *Police.* a location where summonses are frequently incurred by traffic-law violators and other minor offenders.
> **1970** Wambaugh *Centurions* 294 [ref. to L.A., 1964]: "Do you know a good spot to sit? Some good spot where we could get a sure ticket?" "An apple orchard, huh? Yeah, drive down Broadway, I'll show you an apple orchard, a stop sign that people hate to stop for. We'll get you six tickets if you want them."

apple-peeler *n.* a knife.
> **1856** *Harper's Mag.* (May) 731: The president and some of his adherents whipped out their apple peelers (pocket-knives), and threatening death to all who approached, heroically stood their ground. **1978** Lieberman & Rhodes *CB* (ed. 2) 287: *Apple peeler*—knife.

apple-picker *n.* a farmer; an ignorant rustic. Cf. APPLE-KNOCKER.
> **1913–15** Van Loan *Count* 297: You biff this apple picker once on the chin, and we cut the money.

apple pie *adj.* [fr. prov. "easy as apple pie"] simple, easily done.
> **1939** Bessie *Men in Battle* 65: This was apple-pie for me, and I felt sort of ashamed to compete. **1972** *Atlantic* (Feb.) 102: His students have...anecdotes about how he caught a wrong fingering in some vertiginously rapid passage, or how he reduced a hard run, riff, or frill to apple-pie ease merely by changing a single upbow to a downward stroke.

apple-polish *v.* [back formation fr. APPLE-POLISHER] to curry favor with; flatter.
> **1951** in *DAS* 7: Are you trying to apple-polish me? **1976** Dyer *Erroneous Zones* 66: Teacher's pet and apple-polishing are clichés for a reason.

apple-polisher *n.* [see *polish apples* s.v. APPLE] a person who attempts to curry favor with a superior, as a pupil with a teacher; flatterer.
> **1927** in *AS* III 128: *Apple-polisher.* One who *hoses* a prof, that is, tries to wheedle him out of a good grade. **1942** *ATS* 380. **1964** B. Kaufman *Down Staircase* 68: Harry Kagan is a politician and apple-polisher. **1966** Elli *Riot* 243: The apple polishers are startin' to get in the act. **1968** Brunvand *Folklore* 333: Ask a college class what word they use to denote a fellow student who curries favor with the teacher....Of students over 45, men and women give "apple-polisher" almost without exception. *a*1988 D. Smith *Firefighters* 123: Guys referred to the aide as a double-dealing, double-clutching, clipboard-carrying apple polisher. **1984–88** Hackworth & Sherman *About Face* 400: To me, he was an apple-polisher and an asskisser.

applesauce *n.* **1.** *Theat.* silly, trite comedy.
> **1918** *Variety* (Apr. 12) (vaudeville sec.) 7: Just to be back slipping on a little grease-paint, stepping forth with some comic to do "apple-sauce." **1923** *N.Y. Times* (Oct. 7) VIII 4: *Apple Sauce*: Hokum that falls soggy like a wet towel. **1924** *Sat. Eve. Post* (July 12) 15: Her routine's just a lotta apple sauce she's copped off other comics.

2. nonsense; flattery; insincerity; lies.—also used as interj.
> **1919** T.A. Dorgan, in Zwilling *TAD Lexicon* 15: They spill a lot of applesauce about big money. **1920** in *Collier's* (Jan. 1, 1921) 18: That's all apple sauce! **1923** Witwer *Fighting Blood* 89: That's all apple sauce to me. **1926** in Lardner *Haircut & Others* 65: Yes, Mr. Jollier, but I wasn't born yesterday and I know apple sauce when I hear it and I bet you've told that to fifty girls. **1926** in Galewitz *Great Comics* 73: You can't hand me none o' that applesauce! **1928** Carr *Rampant Age* 132: It's a buncha applesauce. **1943** Pyle *Brave Men* 137: He said that in his paintings he was trying to take the applesauce out of war, trying to eliminate the heroics with which war is too often presented. **1969–71** Kahn *Boys of Summer* 31: "Applesauce," said Gordon J. Kahn. "Bosh." **1979** International Jewellers Exchange ad (WINS radio) (Dec. 23): And so you can get the finest jewelry at the lowest possible price. And that's no applesauce. **1987** *Wkly. World News* (Sept. 15) 13: Branded the story...as "applesauce."

applesauce *interj.* (used in expressions of surprise or disbelief).
> **1884** Hartranft *Sidesplitter* 161: "Airthquakes and apple-sauce!" exclaimed the schoolmistress, as she fainted. **1889** Cox *Frontier Humor* 448: Apple sass and spinage! I never did see a man so riled.

apple-shaker *n.* **1.** a lubber; ignorant rustic. Cf. APPLE-KNOCKER.
> **1871** Willis *Forecastle* 15: At that the sailors set up a roar, and the officer called me a "hay-maker," "apple-shaker," etc., and ordered me up on the mainyard...until some of the hay seed had blown away from me.

2. a heavy storm.
> **1905** in *AS* XXXVI 251 [Me.]: We're liable to catch a reg'lar old "apple-shaker" most any day now.

apple-shiner *n.* APPLE-POLISHER.
> **1935** in *DAS* 8: Dean J.R. Schulz of Allegheny College states that in his section of Pennsylvania *apple shiner*, not *apple polisher*, is the term invariably used.

apple-squeezer *n.* an ignorant rustic. Cf. APPLE-KNOCKER.
> **1930** Nason *Corporal* 206: G'wan, run away back to your own outfit o' apple-squeezers before someone shakes his fist at yuh an' knocks yuh outta the sector with the breeze from it.

apron *n.* **1.** a woman. Cf. syn. SKIRT.
> **1925** *Flynn's Mag.* (Jan. 3) (cited in Partridge *Dict. Und.* 9).

2. [cf. obs. syn. *aproner*] a bartender.
> **1929** Hostetter & Beasley *Racket* 219: *Apron*—Bartender. **1944** Burley *Harlem Jive* 133: *Apron*—A bartender, bar-keeper. **1946** in *DAS* 8: The nearer of the two aprons unfolded his arms and drifted over. **1949** "J. Evans" *Halo in Brass* 33: I found a place at the bar and one of the aprons

came along and asked my pleasure.

aqua pumpaginis *n.* [pseudo-L, "pump water"] drinking water. *Joc.*

*1785 Grose *Vulgar Tongue*: *Aqua Pumpaginis*, Pump water. (Apothecaries Latin). **1821** Waln *Hermit in Phila.* 26: And must go home and live on *Adam's Ale* and *Aqua Pumpaginis*.

Arab *n.* **1.** *Theat.* a Jew.—used disparagingly.

1927 *Vanity Fair* (Nov.) 67 (attrib. to Jack Conway, ed. of *Variety*): "Arab" (A Jew). **1945** Mencken *Amer. Lang. Supp. I* 645: Under the heading of Verbotens of 1929…*Variety* once printed a list of the words and phrases forbidden to vaudevillians in that year. It included…*Arab* (signifying a Jew).

2. [poss. sugg. by Longfellow, "The Day Is Done" (1845): "…shall fold their tents, like the Arabs,/And as silently steal away"] a workman who habitually contrives to absent himself from difficult tasks.

1958 McCulloch *Woods Wds.*: *Arab*—a workman who wanders around on a job, always managing to be away when there's dirty or heavy work to be done.

arb *n.* *Finance.* an arbitrageur.

1977 *Business Week* (May 16). **1984** *Business Week* (Mar. 26) 116: Some "arbs" have moved out, causing the oil stocks to fall. **1986** *Newsweek* (May 26) 46: The snooping Levine so annoyed an "arb" that the trader threw him out. **1986** W. Safire, in *N.Y. Times Mag.* (June 22) 6: The arbs are usually the natural allies of the takeover crowd. **1989** *Newsweek* (Oct. 30) 67: Investment banks, money managers and even arbs who had lost a bundle on takeover stocks jumped in.

Arbuckle *n.* [ref. to Arbuckle Coffee; see 1933 quot.] *West.* a naive, inexperienced worker.

1932 in *AS* (Feb. 1933) 29 [Tex.]: *Arbuckle.* Tenderfoot. **1933** J.V. Allen *Cowboy Lore* 61: [A green hand is] also called "Arbuckle" on the assumption that the boss sent Arbuckle coffee coupons to pay for…such a green hand.

Archibald *n.* [allegedly sugg. by British popular song "Archibald, Certainly Not!" Cf. ARCHIE] *Mil. Av.* an anti-aircraft gun. Now *hist.*

*1917 *Atlantic* (May) 600: I sit here watching our "Archibalds" *strafing* an empty sky. **1918** W. Bishop *Winged Warfare* 29: "Archie," of course is an anti-aircraft cannon. How the airmen first happened to name him "Archibald" I do not know. **1919** Rickenbacker *Flying Circus* 124: Those blooming Archibalds!

Archie *n.* [cf. ARCHIBALD] *Mil. Av.* **1.a.** antiaircraft artillery or its fire; antiaircraft gun. Now *hist.*

*1915 *OEDS.* *1917 Lee *No Parachute* 13: I've seen Hun archie in action. **1918** [Grider] *War Birds* 127: We didn't hear any bombs explode but Archie kept up a lot of fuss. **1918** McBride *Emma Gees* 28: I…have yet to see one hit by a shell from an Archie. **1919** Kelly *What Outfit?* 160: They're goin' at him with the archies, but might just as well use pea-shooters. **1919** Barth *20th Aero* 54: You don't mind a bunch of Archies/Shooting at you from the ground.

b. an antiaircraft shell. Now *hist.*

*ca1916 in Ward-Jackson *Airman's Songbook*: I don't want an Archie where I sit down,/I don't want my cranium shot away. **1917** Lahm *Diary* 10: A British archie had made a hole about 8" deep in front of hdqts in the morning…; another archie had gone thru the hospital from roof to cellar—failed to explode. **1927** Cushing *Doughboy Ditties* 57: "Onions" and "archies" are hurled through space. **1927** in Asprey *Belleau Wood* 90: Archies were breaking in the sky at different places.

2. an antiaircraft gunner or crewman. Now *hist.*

*1919 *Athenaeum* (May 23) 360 [ref. to WWI]: The humorous "Archie" for a member of the antiaircraft force. **1932** Ward *Parades* 30 [ref. to WWI]: A moment later, the British "archies," as the antiaircraft gunners are called, send their searchlight beams into the sky.

archie *v.* *Mil. Av.* to subject to antiaircraft artillery fire.—usu. constr. in passive. Now *hist.*

*1917 Lee *No Parachute* 16: The only machines I'd seen were the distant ones being archied. **1918** in N. Hall *Balloon Buster* 108: I was archied with white fire. **1918** Biddle *Airman* 137: We got rather heavily "Archied" coming out. **1939** Hart *135th Aero* 148 [ref. to WWI]: We had been archied very heavily.

ardent *n.* [*ardent* spirits] whiskey; liquor.

1849 P. Decker *Diaries* 43: Vulgarity and a too-free use of *ardent.*

area *n.* [euphem.] *Stu.* the female genitals; groin.

1970–72 in *AS* L 55: Cover your area! **1975** Trinity College grad., age 24: "The area" meant your genitals. "She's having trouble in the area," stuff like that. **1993** *Mystery Sci. Theater* (Comedy Central TV): Ow! Right in the area!

area-bird *n.* *U.S. Mil. Acad.* a cadet ordered to walk punishment tours in the barracks area; a cadet who has walked many such tours.

1941 *AS* XVI 163: *Area bird:* cadet walking punishment tours in area of barracks. **1978** Truscott *Dress Gray* 278: There was almost a goddam riot going on.…These two crazy area-birds fucking the area.

arfy-darfy *n.* [fanciful rhyme; ult. orig. unkn.] ¶ In phrase: **on the arfy-darfy** on the roam; tramping, hoboing. [All three quots. are by N. Algren.]

1964 *Sat. Eve. Post* (Sept. 26) 44: A moon on the arfy-darfy. That will never return. **1965** Algren *Boots* (Intro.) 5: Fired, dead, absconded or gone on the arfy-darfy. **1968** Algren *Chicago* 134: Then each man knows where his life has gone.…Gone on the arfy-darfy/Never to return.

argee *n.* ["Poss. a spelling out of r.g. = *rotgut*"—*DA*; cf. R.G.] cheap, inferior whiskey.

*a1861 in *DA*: Some like it…but taint like good old Argee to me. **1861** in *DA*: What a hard lot we were all round, livin' on nothing but argee whiskey.

Argie *n. & adj.* an Argentinian; Argentinian.

*1982 R.M. Hunt, Governor of Falklands, in *Maclean's* (Apr. 19) 32: I'm not surrendering to the bloody Argies! **1982** *N.Y. Post* (May 22) 1: Brits Down 14 Jets As Argies Blitz 5 Warships. **1988** Maloney *Thunder Alley* 127: The Argies never got a word out of me. *1992 Englishman in N.Y.C., age 28 (coll. J. Sheidlower): Those Argie wines are a great bargain.

arithmetic bug *n.* [see 1920 quot.] a louse or other verminous insect. *Joc.*

1920 W. Carter *Devil Dog* 34 [ref. to WWI]: It was here we first made the acquaintance of man's most clinging companions, "cooties," which were…named "Arithmetic Bugs," by the boys, because they added to our troubles, subtracted from our pleasures, divided our attention and multiplied like --ll. **1961** Bosworth *Crows* 104: They [sc. cockroaches] were real arithmetic bugs!…They could multiply—very rapidly. They could add—to our trouble. And they knew how to subtract from our comforts. **1973** Jackson *Fall Out* 404 [ref. to WWI]: "And what are arithmetic bugs?" "Dat's cooties, Sah."

Arizona *n.* [see 1962 quot.] *Restaurant.* an order of buttermilk.

1946 in *AS.* **1954–60** *DAS: Arizona*…Buttermilk. **1962** *N.Y. Times* (Feb. 13) 34: It is said that in other parts of the West, buttermilk is referred to in lunch-counter jargon as "Arizona," the idea being that anyone who orders it ought to be in Arizona for his health.

Arizona cloudburst *n.* *West.* a sandstorm. *Joc.*

1965 in *West. Folklore* XXV 37: *Arizona cloud burst.* A sandstorm.

Arizona nightingale *n.* [cf. MISSOURI NIGHTINGALE] *West.* a burro. *Joc.*

1940 in *DARE*: Because of his extraordinary bray, [the burro] is sometimes called the "Arizona nightingale." **1944** R. Adams *Western Wds.*: *Arizona nightingale.* A prospector's burro. **1962** *N.Y. Times* (Feb. 13) 34: The "Arizona nightingale" is the hardy burro of prospecting days, with a terrifying bray. **1969** in *DARE*: Joking nicknames for mules…*Arizona nightingale.*

Arizona peacock *n.* *West.* a roadrunner. *Joc.*

1956 *AS* (Oct.) 181: *Arizona peacock.* Roadrunner.

Arizona stop *n.* [cf. syn. ST. LOUIS STOP; CALIFORNIA STOP] *West.* the act of slowing down at a stop sign without coming to a full stop. *Joc.*

1962 *AS* (Dec.) 266 (Calif.): *Arizona stop*…slowing down, but not making a full stop at a stop sign.

ark *n.* **1.** a ship or boat; vessel. *Joc.* Cf. early use in *OED.*

*1698–99 "B.E." *Dict. Canting Crew: Ark*…a Boat or Wherry. *1811 *Lexicon Balatron.*: Let us take an ark and winns, let us take a sculler. *Cant.* **1859** Matsell *Vocabulum: Ark.* A ship; a boat; a vessel. **1930** (cited in Partridge *Dict. Und.* 10). *1961 Burgess *Dict. Sailing: Ark*…A derogatory allusion to any particular ship the speaker doesn't like.

2. a low barroom; a dive.

*a1981 in McKee & Chisenhall *Beale* 28: One…night in 1924,…Two-Gun had been located in a South Memphis Negro ark.

Arkansas asphalt *n. Constr.* logs used in road construction. *Joc.*

1965 in *West. Folklore* XXV 37: *Arkansas asphalt.* Logs laid side by side to form a "corduroy" road. [Heard in] Houston, Texas, 1948–49.

Arkansas chicken *n.* salt pork, bacon. *Joc.*

1905 *DN* III 69: We've got plenty of Arkansas chicken.

Arkansas credit card *n. So.* a length of hose or tubing used for the illicit siphoning of gasoline, as from an unattended automobile. *Joc.*

1976 Dills *CB '77* 3: *Arkansas Credit Card:* rubber siphon. **1978** *N.Y. Times Mag.* (Jan. 1) 16: But in Mississippi…they call a plastic tube for siphoning gas from the tanks of unattended automobiles an "Arkansas credit card."

Arkansas flush *n. Poker.* a worthless hand consisting of four cards of a single suit and one indifferent card. *Joc.*

1950 in *AS* (Feb. 1951) 97: *Arkansas Flush.* A hand composed of four cards in one suit and the fifth in an off suit.

Arkansas lizard *n.* a louse. *Joc.*

1918 in *AS* (Oct. 1933) 24 [Ft. Leavenworth, Kans.]: *Arkansas Lizard.* Louse.

Arkansas toothpick *n.* a bowie knife or other long, esp. double-edged, sheath knife used for hunting or as a weapon; (occ.) a jackknife. *Joc.*

1836 *Crockett's Almanack 1837* 46 (caption): An Arkansaw Toothpick. **1853** in Cohen & Dillingham *Humor of S.W.* 332: I had no tools to work with, save an old hatchet and my "Arkansas tooth-pick." **1877** Bartlett *Americanisms* (ed. 3): *Arkansas Toothpick.* A Bowie-knife of a peculiar kind, the blade of which shuts up into the handle. *ca*1890 Stearns Co. *K* 58 [ref. to Civil War]: One of our boys…found an "Arkansas Tooth Pick," a knife about a foot and a half long, with a curved blade. **1962** D. Hamilton *Murderers' Row* 28: Those rugged old timers…opened up a wilderness with their Arkansas toothpicks.

Arkansas wedding cake *n.* corn bread. *Joc.*

1958 McCulloch *Woods Words: Arkansas wedding-cake.* Cornbread.

Arky *n.* a native of Arkansas, esp. a migrant worker.—used contemptuously. Also **Arkie.**

1927 Dobie *Tex. & S.W. Lore* 101: Men who are mentally sluggish…are quickly dubbed "Arkansas" or "Arky"; men from that state seem to be considered defective or lacking in mental powers. **1945** Drake & Cayton *Black Metro.* 88: With thousands of white "Okies" and "Arkies" on the road, it was unfair to single out Negroes for attack. **1959** Gault *Drag Strip* 54: "An Okie or an Arkie?" "What's the difference? They all live on Montenegro Street." **1982** D.A. Harper *Good Company* 24: Had a couple of Arkies I had to live with.

arky *adj.* [fr. Noah's *ark*] outdated, old-fashioned.

1898 Green *Va. Folk-Speech* 45: She had on a very *arky* bonnet.

arkymalarky *n.* [rhyming elaboration of MALARKEY; cf. ACKA-MARACKUS] malarkey, nonsense.

1936 Sandburg *People, Yes* 131: Yuh come to me wid a lot uh arkymalarky.

arm *n.* **1.** penis—usu. considered vulgar.

1975 *DAS* (2nd Supp. Ed.) 672: *Arm*…the penis. **1977** Dillard *Lex. Black Eng.* 33: Other Black terms for the penis include *arm*.

2. ITALIAN SALUTE.—constr. with *the*.

*a*1989 C.S. Crawford *Four Deuces* 95: I had purposely given the gooks the arm.

¶ In phrases:

¶ **deal them off the arm** to wait tables.

1932 D. Runyon, in *Collier's* (June 11) 7: My friend deals them off the arm for the guys in her mamma's boarding house to save her mamma the expense of a waitress. **1934** in *DAS* 143: After she gets through dealing them off the arm all day her feet generally pain her. **1946** Mezzrow & Wolfe *Really Blues* 81: Has to deal 'em off the arm in hashhouse again.

¶ **drop the arm on** see *put the arm on*, below.

¶ **off the arm** impromptu, "off the cuff"; (*hence*) at a price informally agreed upon.

1942 S. Johnston *Q. of Flat-tops* 32: Shonk, it turned out, was an "off-the-arm poet." **1974** N.Y.C. cabdriver, age 25: Carrying a fare off the meter is doing it *off the arm.*

¶ **on the arm** [cf. syn. *on the cuff*] Esp. *Police.* free of charge; (*also*) on credit; on consignment.

1926 Maines & Grant *Wise-Crack Dict.* 11: *On the arm.*—Something for nothing in show business. **1950** *New Yorker* (Nov. 11) 74: We…took a taxi down to the Paradise. We could put it on the arm there. **1951** *N.Y. Herald Tribune* (Mar. 12) 1: Commissioner Murphy said he had got in touch with twelve to fifteen…lawyers to represent a cop when he is in trouble and to do it "on the arm." **1971** WINS radio news (Oct. 31): Apples have traditionally been "on the arm" for policemen. **1973** Maas *Serpico* 60: Meals…completely "on the arm"—free. **1981** Graziano & Corsel *Somebody Down Here* 207: These shots [drinks] are zilch shots, on the arm. **1984** D. Smith *Steely Blue* 144: Somehow the scotch he'd been drinking on the arm at the Holy Name racket seemed out of place [here]. **1991** Hasburgh *NYPD Mounted* (film): I took it on the arm….On consignment.

¶ **put the arm on** *Und.* **a.** to assault from behind by yoking the forearm tightly about the victim's throat; (*hence*) to rob, esp. in this manner.

1928 Panzram *Killer* 60: There I put the arm on him and we dragged him through the fence on the left side of the road. **1933** Ersine *Prison Slang* 15: Take that yap out in the alley and put the arm on him. **1937** Reitman *Bertha* 261: I'd "put the arm on him," holding him tight around his neck while my pals would go to it and rob him. **1958** Horan *Mob's Man* 3: The guys…said you put the arm on the East Side [numbers banks]. **1966** Elli *Riot* 29: Get ready to put the arm on him.

b. to seize or use physical coercion against; (*hence*) to coerce or pressure.

1930 D. Runyon, in *Collier's* (Sept. 13) 7: So you take us to him at once, or the chances are I will have to put the arm on somebody around here. **1950** *Sat. Eve. Post* (July 15) 124: It was a signal for the waiter to…put the arm on the customer who was trying to stiff him. **1981** G. Wolf *Roger Rabbit* 57: How did you…put the arm on Rocco?

c. to apprehend, take into custody, place under arrest. Also **drop the arm on.**

1929–31 D. Runyon *Guys & Dolls* 137: I was going over to your Maw's house to put the arm on you. **1938** Baldwin & Schrank *Case of Murder* (film): We want you to put the arm on Remy Marco. **1939** R. Chandler *Big Sleep* 65: Handcuffed. Marlowe put the arm on him for you. **1943** *Hollywood Detective* (Dec.): I'll either put the arm on the real killer or persuade Sandra Shane it was some other guy she gandered on the stairs. **1953** R. Chandler *Long Goodbye* 39: They can drop the arm on you for shacking up in a hotel in this town. **1961** Kanter & Tugend *Pocketful of Miracles* (film): Mr. Dude, sir, a couple of coppers comin' to put the arm on you. **1965** Bonham *Durango St.* 145: We'll put the arm on him for breaking and entering your house. **1966** Herbert *Fortune & Men's Eyes* 79: I'da give my right eye to 'a seen Queenie's face when they put the arm on her with that load of mink coats and diamonds. **1978** Diehl *Sharky's M.* 191: Puttin' the arm on hookers an' perverts.

d. to ask or demand money of.

1939 *New Yorker* (Mar. 11) 43: One dingo got a dollar and one of the President's best cigars by "putting the arm" on Mrs. Roosevelt at the entrance of her town house. **1939** O'Hara *Files* 107: If you're trying to put the arm on me for dough…you better forget it. **1940** O'Hara *Pal Joey* 193: I had a lot of fun…writing…to my friend Ted without putting the arm on him for a couple of bucks. **1954** Schulberg *Waterfront* (film): Ask any rummy on the dock if I ain't good for a fin when they put the arm on me. **1971** *All in the Family* (CBS-TV): Every time Archie gets a bill he says, "That kraut's puttin' the arm on me." **1976** in Hayano *Poker Faces* 74: When broke they…put the arm on the regulars for a stake. **1980** Santoli *Everything We Had* 55: Look, I'm not trying to put the arm on you or anything, but here's what's happening. **1989** L. Roberts *Full Cleveland* 162: Some dude…puts the arm on me for two hundred bucks.

e. to expose, "put the finger on."

1978 Truscott *Dress Gray* 370: Three cadets and a lady reporter putting the arm on a couple of spooks ["spies"] from God-only-knows-where.

f. *Horse Racing.* (of a jockey) to illicitly restrain a running horse.

1984 W. Murray *Dead Crab* 134: At least twenty thousand losers he's put the arm on coming out of the gate.

armful *n.* ¶ In phrase: **grab an armful of boxcars** *Hobo.* to steal a ride on a freight train.

1918 in *AS* (Oct. 1933) 27: Grab 'N Armful O' Boxcars. Get aboard a freight train. **1932** in Kornbluh *Rebel Voices* 93: I was grabbin' armfuls of box cars lookin' for a job. **1948** Manone *Trumpet* 35: So I grabbed me an armful of boxcars and hoboed my way to New York.

arm-man *n.* [prob. ellipt. for *strong-arm man*] *Und.* a robber who habitually employs violence, esp. one who assaults his victims from behind and restrains them with a headlock.

1914 Jackson & Hellyer *Crim. Slang: Arm Man*...Current amongst "heavyweights." A strong arm man; a holdup; a highway robber. **1935** Pollock *Und. Speaks: Arm man*, a hold-up man...who...does not carry a pistol or other weapon. His victim is straightened out by putting arm around neck and...is struck a powerful blow by accomplice in the pit of the stomach.

armored *adj. Mil.* canned.—used only in combs. *Joc.*

1941 *N.Y. Times* (Sept. 19) 25: Armored cow is canned milk. **1942** *Yank* (Nov. 4) 15: Other Leatherneck shortcuts to the English language are "armored heifer" for canned milk, "red lead" for ketchup. **1945** *Yank* (Dec. 14) 22: "Will you pass the armored cow?" "The what?" **1946** Bowker *Out of Uniform* 124: Most foods had various slang names, such as "armored cow" for condensed milk, but such terms had no real validity or usefulness. **1958** McCulloch *Woods Wds.: Armored tit.*—Canned milk.

armored bikini *n. Mil.* a kind of protective supporter for a man's groin.

1971 Flanagan *Maggot* 138 [ref. to *ca*1960]: The bayonet instructor outfitted them with boxing gloves, football helmets, face-guards, and the tin-cupped jock-straps called "armored bikinis" which were tied on over the recruits' trousers.

armor plate *n.* **1.** *Mil.* hardtack.

1916 in *Editor* (Jan. 13, 1917) 33: Army Vernacular..."Armor plate"—Hardtack.

2. *Navy.* cash, change.

1918 Ruggles *Navy Explained* 102: The sailor men of the navy probably coin more words for money than any other body of men....Sheckles, iron men,...evil metal,...jingles, gilt,...armor plate...and many others.

armpiece *n. Esp. Journ.* an attractive woman escorted to social functions chiefly for the sake of her appearance.

1983 W. Safire, in *N.Y. Times Mag.* (June 12) 20: She would warn him not to *get fresh*...lest she be considered his *doxy*, now armpiece. **1986** *Chicago Tribune* (TempoWoman) (Nov. 23) 4: Gloria Steinem has been his long-time love and armpiece. **1988** N.Y.C. editor: An *armpiece* is a woman who makes an eye-catching appearance on her escort's arm. **1991** *Vanity Fair* (Jan. 1992) 144: First, Dick was dragging his armpiece along with him, and now I'm this femme fatale. I went from being a bimbo to Medusa. **1992** *Newsday* (CNN-TV) (Jan. 17): Women as stars, not as armpieces, not as victims.

armpit *n.* **1.** the vilest location (in a given area); a vile place. Cf. ASSHOLE, 3, and PITS.

1968 Lockridge *Hartspring* 155: This damned armpit of a world. **1968–70** *Current Slang* II & IV: *Armpit of the nation*, n. Las Cruces. **1972** Newman & Benton *Bad Company* (film): This here town's the armpit of America. **1973** C. Browne *Body Shop* 94: Nam is so filthy, crap in the streets, armpit of the world. **1974** Univ. Tenn. student: This place is an armpit. **1972–76** Durden *No Bugles* 113: This goddamn misbegotten armpit of the world. **1982** *Wash. Post* (July 6) A15: Fort Leonard Wood, Mo. [is] lovingly remembered as the armpit of the world by countless thousands of Army trainees. **1989** *TV Guide* (Feb. 4) 33: It was the armpit of the world.

2. an obnoxious individual.

1968 Baker et al. *CUSS* 72: *Armpit*, An obnoxious person.

¶ In phrases:

¶ **my armpit!** Not at all! No indeed!

1976 Woodley *Bears* 24: "He's shy."..."Shy my armpit!"

¶ **up to (one's) armpits** [cf. *up to the ass* s.v. ASS, *n.*] to a great extent; completely; thoroughly; having a large amount of.

1958 Frankel *Band of Bros.* 120: Up to his armpits in debt. **1975** *U.S. News & W.R.* (Aug. 11) 5: Others in his regime were "up to their armpits" in graft. **1977** Olsen *Fire Five* 149: The fix is in, up to the armpits. **1989** Jesse Helms, in *N.Y. Times* (May 20) 10: Henry Kissinger has been up to his armpits in deals with foreign countries. **1992** *N.Y. Times Bk. Review* (Aug. 9) 11: Soon he's up to his armpits in exercise trainers, music arrangers and Paul Stuart tweeds.

armpit sauce *n.* [alluding to its strong odor] *Mil.* a Vietnamese sauce, made from fermented fish (Vietnamese *nuoc mam*).

1966 Mulligan *No Place to Die* 52: Nuoc Mam....The G.I.'s...call it simply "armpit sauce." **1981** Former Navy yeoman, served in Vietnam 1970–72: *Armpit sauce* meant *nuoc mam*. It was a term that was used only

occasionally. **1983** C. Rich *Advisors* 450: Nuoc mam...is not called armpit sauce for nothing. **1991** L. Reinberg *In the Field* 10: *Armpit sauce*, slang for nuoc mam, the prevalent Vietnamese sauce, made from fermented fish.

Armstrong *n.* [pun on proper name] a tool or machine operated or serviced by muscular strength rather than machinery; *(specif.)* a hand-stoked locomotive.

1923 *DN* V 200: *Armstrong*, n. A grain cradle. Applicable to any primitive form of tool used by hand. **1929** in Davidson *Old West* 30: With one man twisting an old "armstrong,"/His work was hard and his hours were long. **1932** *R.R. Stories* (Oct.) 366: *Armstrong*—Engine not equipped with stoker. **1939** *Sat. Eve. Post* (Apr. 15) 26: Well, they rolled the old Armstrong out of the pigpen. **1945** Hubbard *R.R. Avenue* 331: *Armstrong*—Old-style equipment, operated by muscular effort, such as hand-brakes, some turntables, engines without automatic stokers, etc.

Armstrong *adj.* operated by hand; requiring or involving the exertion of muscular strength.

[*1864 in *F & H* II 35: Captain Armstrong is again abroad, muscular and powerful, riding his favorite hobby in the steeple-chase field, preparing thus early in the season for pulling, stopping, and putting the strings on.] [*1889 Barrère & Leland *Dict. Slang* I: *Armstrong, Captain* (turf), a dishonest jockey. "He came *Captain Armstrong*" is equivalent to saying that the rider *pulled* with a strong arm, thus preventing his horse from winning.] **1914** *DN* IV 102: *Armstrong*, adj. Operated by the arm as opposed to machinery;—used jocosely of scythes, sickles or saws, etc. **1920** in *Dict. Canadianisms.* **1926** Maines & Grant *Wise-Crack Dict.: Armstrong Wheeler*—Wheelbarrow when a hobo has to use it. **1932** *AS* (June) 329: *Armstrong heaters*—arms when used to hold a girl. **1942** *AS* (Apr.) 102: *Armstrong starter.* Crank handle [of a truck]. **1950** *West. Folklore* IX 115: *Armstrong plow.* A shovel. **1958** McCulloch *Woods Wds.* 3: *Armstrong method.*—Any work done by hand, not machine. **1971** Tak *Truck Talk: Armstrong starter:* A hand-crank used on early trucks.

Armstrong patent *n. Naut.* any of various heavy devices that must be operated by hand; *(also)* muscular strength used for such work.

1912 *Independent* (Apr. 18) 819: She was fitted alow and aloft...with dummy blocks and "Armstrong" patents. **1977** Hugill *Songs of Sea* 20: All the...ropes are moved by Armstrong's Patent—i.e., men's muscle power.

arm-twister *n.* a vehicle equipped with a manual starter.

1938 *AS* 315: *Arm Twister.* A car which must be hand cranked.

army[1] *n.* [*arm* + *-y*, dimin. suff.] *Hobo.* a person, esp. a beggar, who has lost one or both arms.

1930 "D. Stiff" *Milk & Honey* 36: If he has an arm missing, he may be called "army." **1937** Reitman *Bertha* 301: Army or wingey (armless) [as nicknames].

army[2] *n.* ¶ In phrase: **You and what army?** "I defy you to do as you threaten"; "You can't do this without the help of many others."

1932 *AS* VII 338: *You and what army?*—"You are not able to do it alone." **1932** Mahin *Red Dust* (film): "I ought to slap you out of here." "You and what man's army?" **1962** *Mad* (Nov.) 9: Oh yeah? Him and what army? **1971** Giovanni *Gemini* 17: "I'll beat you up myself!"..."You and what army, 'ho'?" **1980** Lorenz *Guys Like Us* 180: Herman laughed in his face. "You and what army?" **1988** Groening *Childhood Is Hell* [unp.]: You and what army?

Army brat *n.* a child of a member of the regular army, esp. the daughter of a commissioned officer. Cf. BRAT.

1931 in D.O. Smith *Cradle* 205: The latter is an Army brat and his uncle is an Admiral in the Navy. **1934** *Our Army* (Nov.) 5: A highly scandalous service novel, written by an Army "brat." **1941** *AS* (Oct.) 163: *Army Brat.* Son or daughter of Army officer. **1942** Sanders & Blackwell *Forces* 14: *Army Brat*...A son or daughter of an army officer or enlisted man. **1943** Hersey *G.I. Laughs* 171: *Army brat*, officer's daughter. **1964** Pearl *Stockade* 134: Sixteen years old, Canadian Army brat. **1971** *N.Y. Post* (Sept. 15): I was in 16 different grammar schools. Then I'd be whisked away, because my father was in the Army and I was an Army brat. **1990** *N.Y. Times Book Review* (Jan. 21) 21: Mary R. Truscott, a second-generation Army brat, paints a broad picture of how the military shapes its children.

army chicken *n.* frankfurters and beans.

1942 *Sat. Eve. Post* (Nov. 28) 66: Like the soldiers themselves, most cooks deplore the frequent appearance of "army chicken"—beans and frankfurters.

army game *n.* **1.** any ruthlessly played or unfair gambling game, esp. chuck-a-luck, poker, or the shell game.—constr. with *the old.*

1890 Quinn *Fools of Fortune* 275: Chuck-a-luck…is sometimes designated as "the old army game," for the reason that soldiers at the front [during the Civil War] were often wont to beguile the tedium of a bivouac by seeking relief from monotony in its charms. *Ibid.* 390: "Dutch House" was considered as particularly skillful in conducting "the old army game." **1896** Ade *Artie* 9: You didn't think this [poker] game was a game o' muggins.…This was the real old army game. **1906** *Variety* (Jan. 6) 9: Watch the little ball—the old army game, you can't win where you can't lose. **1912** Furlong *Detective* 165: "The old army game" (chuck-a-luck). **1915–17** Lait *Gus* 93: Where'd you get that stuff to take Gus, here, for eighty-five cen's wit' that there old army game, huh? **1925** Halsey *Sally of Sawdust* (film): This is not a game of chance—it's a game of science and skill—the old army game. **1946** in W.C. Fields *By Himself* 9: It's the old army game.…Find the little pea. It's the old army game. A boy can play as well as a man. **1964** Smith & Hoefer *Music* 60: Three-card monte…became known as "the Old Army game."

2. any form of trickery, deception, or evasion; (now *specif.*) the shifting of responsibility to others, "passing the buck."—constr. with *the old.*

1910 *N.Y. Eve. Jour.* (Apr. 23) 10: Possums are too sly to be caught on this old army game. **1919** G.W. Small *47th* 96: Favorite saying/"The Old Army Game." **1928** Sandburg *Good Morning* 20: Never give a sucker an/Even break and the Old Army Game goes—. **1930** Fredenburgh *Soldiers March!* 60: It's the old army game: first, pass the buck; second, never give a sucker an even break. **1930** Nason *Corporal* 138: Why, I thought it was the Old Army game! Button, button, I never heard of it! **1932** Halyburton & Goll *Shoot & Be Damned* 184: It's the old army game—you win or you lose. **1941** Horman *Buck Pvts.* (film): Oh, I get it. The old army game. **1959** Lipton *Barbarians* 56: The breaks…usually go to the cagey ones who know how to play the old army game and the canny ones who know how to stay out of trouble. **1963** Stern *Grapevine* 151: He was giving you the old Army game, honey.

army Latin *n.* foul or profane language. *Joc.*

1864 in J.W. Haley *Rebel Yell* 201: The teamsters.…Their command of "army Latin" is absolutely astounding.

army strawberry *n.* a prune.

1941 *AS* (Oct.) 163: *Army Strawberries.* Prunes.

-aroo see **-EROO**.

around the bend see s.v. **BEND**.

around the horn see s.v. **HORN**.

around the world see s.v. **WORLD**.

arse see s.v. **ASS**.

arsey-turvey *adv.* [fr. **ARSEY-VARSEY**, infl. by *topsy-turvy*] upside down; head-over-heels.

ca*1860** in Hugill *Shanties & Songs* 55: The cholera begins to rage and some have got the scurvy,/chickens dying from old age, steerage arsey-turvey. **1936** Le Clerq *Rabelais* 37: May the drunkard's pip rot your guts if the little lecher wasn't forever groping his nurses upside-down, arsey-turvey.

arsey-varsey *adv.* [fr. *arse*] upside down; backwards-front; reversed; confused. Also vars.

******1539** in *OED:* Ye set the cart before the horse…cleane contrarily, and arsy-versy as they say. ******1577** in *F & H:* The estate of that flourishing towne was turned arsie versie, topside the other waie. ******1607** in *F & H:* Jesu, are wimen so arsy varsy. ******1612–*1725** (All in *F & H*). **1797** in Whiting *Early Amer. Proverbs* 13: Everything seems to be *arsa-varsa* here, the wrong side uppermost. **1934** Brewer *Riders* 70: An abrupt rise…flips plane arsi-versi. **1966** *RHD:* Arsy-varsy. Slang.…Also arsy-versy.

art *n. Circus.* performers (as distinguished from other employees).

1926 Norwood *Other Side* 59: That's the art—I mean the performers.

Arthur Duffy *n.* ¶ In phrase: **take it on the** [or **do an**] **Arthur Duffy** [Arthur F. Duffy held the world record of 9 3/5 seconds for the 100-yard dash from 1902–1905] to run away, escape. Also vars.

1905 in "O. Henry" *Works* 1474: Do an Arthur Duffy to the near-

est…delicatessen store. **1914** T.A. Dorgan, in Zwilling *TAD Lexicon* 15: Get me a repeating gat an' if them greasers don't do an Arthur Duffy I'm willing to be shot at sunrise the next day. **1926** *Writer's Mthly.* (Dec.) 541: *Took it on the Arthur Duffy*—Ran away. **1934** in Partridge *Dict. Und.:* If he wants to escape from prison he will…take it on the Arthur Duffy. **1936** Duncan *Over Wall* 112: As I was climbing from the car, I took it on the Arthur K. Duffy. **1951** Fowler *Schnozzola* 46: He pointed out that the customers were "taking an Arthur Duffy," or running for the door without pausing at the cloakroom for their hats. **1958** *Sat. Eve. Post* (Sept. 20) 86: The little thug took it on the Arthur Duffy, as the boys say, and went home to Los Angeles.

article *n.* person; "customer."—usu. used with a prec. adj. [Before Emancipation, often applied colloquially in the slave trade to slaves offered for sale.]

******1811** *Lexicon Balatron.* A prime article. A handsome girl. ******1820–21** P. Egan *Life in London* 52: Ask the "*Neat Article*" to take a bit. **1840** *Spirit of Times* (Nov. 21) 446: A neat little article, ain't she? **1857** M. Griffith *Female Slave* 175: Wal, as she is a fancy article, I'll jist say twelve hundred dollars. **1859** Matsell *Vocab.: Article.* Man. "You're a pretty article." A term of contempt. **1871** Still *Underground R.R.* 168: These passengers were most "likely-looking articles." *Ibid.* 398: A tough-looking "article." **1902** Hapgood *Thief* 96: Johnny and Patsy, who were what is called in the under world "slick articles," put their heads together and worked out a scheme. *a***1909** Tillotson *Detective* 131: In the vernacular of the police, the writers of begging letters are about the slickest article in the metropolis. *a***1904–11** Phillips *Susan Lenox* II 148: You're a very superior article—you are. **1917** Mills *War Ltrs.* 249: Ginger [the cat] is a pretty slick article. **1929** "E. Queen" *Roman Hat* 73: We knew that he was a slick article. **1945** in *Combat* 72: Really sharp articles who were…dressed…to kill. **1948** Lait & Mortimer *N.Y. Confidential* 219: Hundreds of smart New York articles…thrive because they…know the right people. **1957** J.D. MacDonald *Price of Murder* 86: He's a very smooth article. **1957** Hall *Cloak & Dagger* 139: They were hard-looking articles, and all soldier. **1977** Dunne *Confessions* 47: Never underestimate Des Spellacy.…A very cool article.

artillery *n.* **1.** a handgun or handguns; firearms of any kind; (*broadly*) weapons of any kind.

1821–22 W. Irving *Bracebridge Hall* 236: They now and then get a shot from the artillery of some refractory farmer. **1885** *Puck* (May 13) 164: He must leave all his artillery behind. **1890** Langford *Vigilante* 166: Turn your artillery loose! **1897** A.H. Lewis *Wolfville* 16: As the Lizard makes his bluff, his hand goes to his artillery like a flash. **1903** A. Adams *Cowboy* 198: We were in the livery, surrendering our artillery. **1928** W.R. Burnett *Little Caesar* 175: Small bootleggers who were not equipped with artillery. **1940** Chandler *Farewell* 11: This isn't time to pull the artillery. **1943** Guthrie *Glory* 421: "Here's their artillery."…He dumped a double handful of knives and the necks of three wine bottles. "No guns." **1962** D. Hamilton *Murderers' Row* 27: What's with the crummy artillery?

2. [cf. syn. **GUN**] *Narc.* an actual or makeshift hypodermic syringe or syringes; (*broadly*) one who is addicted to the injection of narcotics. Also **light artillery.**

1915 Howard *God's Man* 39: *Artillery*…hypodermic syringes. **1930** *Amer. Mercury* (Dec.) 456: *Light artillery,* n. A drug addict who uses a hypodermic needle. "Lay away from him; he's light artillery." **1937** Johnston *Prison Life* 101: When regular "artillery" is not available, the hypos improvise with a safety pin and an eyedropper. **1975** Wambaugh *Choirboys* 220: Hepatitis…from a piece of community artillery passed from junkie to junkie.

3. [cf. syn. **BULLETS**] *Mil.* beans. Also **light artillery.**

1916 in *Editor* (Jan. 13, 1917) 33: "Artillery" or "Boston Bullets"— Beans. **1923** McKnight *Eng. Words* 55: *Bullets* or *artillery* for "beans." **1942–44** in *AS* (Feb. 1946) 31: *Artillery,* n. Beans. **1946** *AS* (Apr.) 89: Light artillery (beans).

4. attractive female breasts; shapely female figure. Also **field artillery.**

1929 J.T. Farrell *Calico Shoes* 224: Mira, she could shake her field artillery like the cat's tonsilitis. **1976** Chinn *Dig Nigger Up* 182: Her bra and panties were bright red.…My eyes roamed over her familiar artillery.

artillery bull *n.* [prob. ellipt. for "artillery bull's-eye"] *Army.* failure to hit any part of a target on a rifle range; (*hence*) the red flag used to signal such a failure.

1921 *Sentinel* (May 13) 14: Artillery Bulls [title of joke column]. **1929** *Our Army* (Oct.) 21: *Artillery Bull.* A complete miss on the target range. **1936** *Our Army* (May) 21: The dreaded "Artillery Bull." A miss! **1946** *Amer. Legion Mag.* (May) 26: The red flag on the firing range, in our outfit, was called an "artillery bull."

artist *n.* **1.** *Und.* a skillful pickpocket, sneak thief, confidence man, or other criminal.

1859 Matsell *Vocab.: Artist.* An adroit rogue. ***1886** Davitt *Prison Diary* 36: The possession of one of these lady artists who may be renowned for cleverness, is an object of much desire and professional wooing among her male admirers. **1903** A.H. Lewis *Boss* 168: If anyone who can…raise a row in New York City goes shy his watch or leather, th' artist who gets it can't come here ag'in. **1929** *AS* (June) 337: Artist—a skillful crook.

2. a person notable for the use, employment, or perpetration of something.—usu. used with a preceding attrib. noun.

1903 *Independent* (Nov. 26) 2796: I am a marlin spike artist, instead of an author. **1904** Ade *True Bills* 19: Nellie was the best single-handed Waffle Artist in the business, bar none. **1908** in H.C. Fisher *A. Mutt* 162: I'm on to all you bunk artists. **1911** Van Loan *Big League* 176: Cunningham, the Reds' spitball artist. **1918** Beston *Full Speed* 193: Most of us are balloon observers, though Joe here…is a sea-plane artist. He runs one of the planes. **1918** *Radiator* (June 6) 2: Section 639 tells us about the low-gear artist who used to play the organ in church at home. ***1925** Fraser & Gibbons *Soldier & Sailor Wds.* [ref. to WWI]: *Castor Oil Artist:* A surgeon. A doctor. **1928** Callahan *Justice* 4: He was known as one of the best short-change artists that ever stood behind a bar. **1930** Fiaschetti *Gotta Be Rough* 9: I had plenty of evidence against the little blackmail and bomb artist. **1932** *R.R. Stories* (Oct.) 366: Artist—One who is particularly adept (usually with such prefix as brake, pin, speed, etc.). **1952** Viereck *Beasts* 29: I noticed the check artist. **1964** J.D. Harris *Priest* 136: They're goofball artists, junkies. **1964** Howe *Valley of Fire* 33: Greaves was a shit-artist. **1987** *The Pick-Up Artist* [film title]. **1987** E. White *Beautiful Room* 94: A juicehead and goofball artist.

artsy-fartsy *adj.* [*art* + *fart*, sugg. by *artsy-craftsy*] foolishly or pretentiously artistic. Also **arty-farty.**

1965 Tavel *Lady Godiva* 20: And so stylish too! So arty-farty! **1968** Van Dyke *Strawberries* 41: You've been on your artsy-fartsy Stein kick at least since Christmas. **1977** Patrick *Beyond Law* 20: I would check out the arty-farty showbiz crowd. **1978** Univ. Tenn. instructor, age 28: Isn't that [topic] a little artsy-fartsy for you? **1981** *Maclean's* (June 29) 52: I don't want anything artsy-fartsy—I want them all to cry at the end. **1985** "J. Michaels" *Pvt. Affairs* 185: Santa Fe. Artsy-fartsy place, doesn't have anything to do with the rest of us.

arty *n.* [by shortening; orig. a written abbr. taken over into speech] *Mil.* artillery.

1864 O.W. Holmes, Jr., in M.D. Howe *Shaping Yrs.* 163: Our H.Q. were exposed all day to pretty sharp arty. practice. **1864** in D. Chisholm *Civil War Notebook* 32: Changed places with the 7th N.Y. Heavy Arty. ***1942** in *OEDS.* ***1945** S.J. Baker *Austral. Lang.: Arty.* The artillery. **1956** Heflin *USAF Dict.: Arty*…an authorized abbreviation. **1971** T. Mayer *Falcon* 162: Let's get arty and the gunships then. **1977** Caputo *Rumor of War* 257: Is our own arty firing now? **1982** R.A. Anderson *Cooks & Bakers* 39: He was killed by our arty.

ASAFP *adv.* [initialism] "as soon as fucking possible"; immediately.

1985 J. Hughes *Weird Science* (film): I want you out of here ASAFP! **1990** Munro *Slang U.* 23: A.S.A.F.P. as soon as possible, or sooner.

Asbestos Joe *n.* *Naval Av.* an asbestos-suited firefighter aboard an aircraft carrier.

1943 Mears *Carrier* 41: He falls almost into the arms of two asbestos-suited men, the "Asbestos Joes," who are running to his aid.

ash *n.* ¶ In phrase: **haul** [or **drag**] **(one's) ashes, 1.** (usu. of a man) to engage in sexual intercourse, esp. after a period of abstinence.—usu. constr. in passive.

1906 in Longstreet *Wilder Shore* 317: Come here to jolly the girls. Get our ashes hauled. *ca***1925** in Bechet *Treat It Gentle* 145: Street Department Papa, Mama Wants Her Ashes Hauled Today. **1929** Hemingway *Farewell to Arms* 168: We'll both get drunk and be cheerful. Then we'll go get the ashes dragged. Then we'll feel fine. **1929** in Oliver *Blues Trad.* 120: Now you know by that, babe, I need my ashes hauled. **1938** in A. Lomax *Mr. Jelly Roll* 20 [ref. to N.O., 1890's]: She's going up there to get her ashes hauled. **1942** Hollingshead *Elmtown's Youth* 339: When I want my ashes hauled, I want it now. **1952** Bellow *Augie March* 263: If one of them didn't haul your ashes you might make faster time with the other. **1958** Berger *Crazy in Berlin* 302: Yeah, he held a gun

on her to make her haul his ashes. **1961** Gover *Misunderstanding* 193: Boff us cats gonna haul his ashes. **1966** Brunner *Face of Night* 211: How many times did you get your ashes hauled today? **1967** Dibner *Admiral* 231: We got to get your ashes hauled. **1970** Longstreet *Kimball* 8: A john who had hauled his ashes could…ask me to put it on the slate. **1970** in *Nat. Lampoon* (Jan. 1971) 26: Wanna get your ashes hauled? **1988** *Miami Vice* (NBC-TV): All I had to do was tell him he could get his ashes hauled.

2. [prob. by confusion with HAUL ASS] to leave, to stir, to go.

*ca***1938** in D. Runyon *More Guys* 199: He may decide to haul ashes out of Harlem before anything happens to him. **1964** Redfield *Ltrs. fr. Actor* 188: I shook my head and hauled my ashes. I stumbled soberly as I got up from my chair. **1967** in T.C. Bambara *Gorilla* 71: I usually hauls my ashes over to one of them centers.

ash-and-trash *n.* [cf. ASS-AND-TRASH] *Mil. Av.* cargo flown on military aircraft; (hence) a routine supply flight. [All quots. ref. to Vietnam War.]

1983 Groen & Groen *Huey* 19: His first missions were "ash and trash" flights—flying top brass…or picking up supplies. *Ibid* 63: Are you going on an ash and trash sometime soon? **1984** Holland *Let Soldier Die* 22: Mostly administrative flights and "ash and trash"—resupply and other around-the-park things. *Ibid.* 33: You've been unhappy…flying ash and trash. **1986** "J. Hawkins" *Tunnel Warriors* 329: Ash-'n'-Trash Relay flight. **1983–88** J.T. McLeod *Crew Chief* 312: We called them ash and trash, or milk runs. **1991** C. Holley *Aeroscouts* 244: Ash-and-Trash. Slang, referring to non-combat missions.

ash breeze *n.* [ref. to ash wood oars] propulsion given to a boat by rowing rather than by the wind.

1834 *Visit to Texas* 105: We…took advantage of what is sometimes called the "ash breeze": that is, our oars. **1883** in *DARE*: The guide was giving her an ash breeze for all she was worth. **1957** Beck *Folklore of Me.* 115: The "ash breeze" (oars) replaced worn-out sails.

ashcan *n.* **1.** [fr. the shape] *Navy.* a depth charge; (*occ.*) a naval mine.

1918 Connolly *U-Boat Hunters* 158: One of our destroyers dumped over a 300-pound "ashcan" and got Mr. U-boat. **1918** *Sat. Eve. Post* (Oct. 12): The depth charge is known in the navy as…the "ash can." **1919** in Niles *Singing Soldiers* 167: Droppin' ash-cans, that's our game.…If we hit our own "subs" it's all the same. **1943** Coale *Midway* 32: The ashcan is set for forty-five feet. **1947** Morison *Naval Ops.* I 210: The familiar 300-pound "ash-can" set to fire by hydrostatic (water) pressure down to a depth of 300 feet, was evolved during World War I. **1948** A.M. Taylor *Lang. of WWII: Ashcan Patrol:*…mine layers, units of the U.S. Army. **1966** Noel *Naval Terms.*

2. [fr. the shape] *Army.* **a.** a heavy artillery shell.

1918 Minder *This Man's War* 279: We were in one shell-hole and a great big ash-can exploded about fifteen feet behind us. **1920** Cutler *55th Arty.* 190: When one of these "ash cans" struck and exploded within twenty-five yards of the Bat. E commander's post, it caused one battery to think, for them, *la guerre* was *fini.* **1928** Scanlon *Mercy* 110: The shells they used were the really large caliber—ash cans. **1930** *AS* (June) 382 [ref. to WWI]: *Ashcan.* A large German shell.

b. an aerial bomb.

1919 Law *2nd Army* (unp.): Jerry also obliges with a few air raids, but his ash cans fall out in the open. **1920** [J. Crawford] *306th F.A.* 96: And then…came the uneven brrm-brrm, brrm-brrm, of Boche planes and the whizz and crashing explosion of the falling "ash cans."

3. an obnoxious person.

1929–30 J.T. Farrell *Young Lonigan* 66: She was a sweet kid…and not an old ashcan like Helen Borax. **1939** Appel *Power-House* 217: What fun was it chewing the rag up [at] the club? They were all a pack of ash-cans. Fivo, Murphy, and Chisel and Mike, the whole pack.

4. *Cinema.* a large, powerful arc light enclosed in a cylindrical reflector.

1942 *ATS* 599: *Ash can,* a powerful arc light having the general shape of an ash can. **1966** *RHD: Ashcan*…an arc light of 1000 watts, enclosed in a reflector.

5. a dilapidated, noisy motor vehicle, "crate."

1953 Harkins *Road Race* 40: An old man in an undershirt appeared at a second-story window and shouted, "Get those ash cans out of here!"

6. *Army.* a German *Nebelwerfer* rocket. Now *hist.*

1959 Toland *Battle* 33 [ref. to 1944]: Then came the sounds of ash-cans—"screaming meemies."

ashcan *v.* to throw in an ashcan; discard, get rid of.

1938 *AS* 195: *Ashcanned.* **1971** N.Y.U. professor, age *ca*60: So I just took the paper and ashcanned it. **1981** *Chicago Sun-Times* (Aug. 28) 73: The president of CBS Sports…developed a personal distaste for the Greek, but he still was reluctant to ashcan the bum. **1983** *L.A. Times* (Dec. 28) III 4: The Redskins wasted all last week boning up on Detroit and have had to ashcan those plans.

ashcat *n.* [orig. a person, esp. a small child, who hangs about a fire and idly pokes the ashes; see *EDD*] **1.** a sooty or dirty individual, esp. a child.

1854 in G.W. Harris *Lovingood* 33: I say, you durn'd ash cats, jis' keep yer shuts on, will ye? **1869** "M. Twain" *Innocents Abroad* ch. 25: They sit in the alleys and nurse their cubs. They nurse one ash-cat at a time, and the others scratch their backs against the doorpost and are happy.

2.a. *Naut.* a member of a steamship's engine room gang; (*specif.*) a stoker.

1899 *Century* (Sept.) 660: Two mates, two ash-cats. **1925** *DN* V 335: *Ash cat.* One of the ship's gang which hauls out and dumps ashes. ***1929** Bowen *Sea Slang: Ash Cat.* A Merchant Service fireman.

b. *R.R.* a fireman for a locomotive.

1942 *Sat. Eve. Post* (June 13) 27: The firing is done by the "ash cat," "bakehead," or "tallowpot." **1975** *Railroad* (Mar.) 44: Marty Shut, the ashcat, raked the fire and covered it with great shovelfuls of coal.

ashcat Sam *n.* ASHCAT, 1.

1910 in *DA* 46: He came home at night looking like an ash-cat-Sam.

ash-eater *n.* ASHCAT, 2.b.

1948 Mencken *Amer. Lang. Supp. II* 713: A locomotive…fireman is an *ash-cat, ash-eater,…tallowpot* [etc.].

ash-handle *n.* [the bat is made of ash wood] *Baseball.* a baseball bat.

1981–85 S. King *It* 534: Don't matter how much you choke up on that ash-handle.

ashore *adv.* [by extension of S.E. sense] *Navy & USMC.* on liberty; (*also*) away from a Navy or Marine base.—usu. constr. with *go.*

1924 Anderson & Stallings *What Price Glory?* I i [ref. to USMC near Bois de Belleau, France, 1918]: Say, if the skipper's going ashore [*sc.* to Paris] they'd better get him out of here before he gets too drunk to navigate. **1945** *Best from Yank* 60: Going ashore early tonight, eh, Wilcoxen? **1949** McMillan *Old Breed* 16 [ref. to USMC, 1942]: As many as could began to "go ashore" from the camp into Wellington. **1979** Former Navy supply man [ref. to 1950's]: "To go ashore" meant to go on liberty—even if you were already stationed on shore. Sometimes they'd say, I can hear those voices calling, "Come ashore! Come ashore!" **1980** Manchester *Darkness* 144: In Washington we were told we could go "ashore." **1988** Hynes *Flights of Passage* 150 [ref. to WWII]: Other pilots…married…and moved "ashore."

Asian two-step *n.* *Mil.* a krait or other large poisonous Asian snake.

1966 Mulligan *No Place to Die* 279: The G.I.'s called them "the Asian two-step" because after one bites you, you take two steps and fall over dead. **1991** L. Reinberg *In the Field* 12: *Asian two-step*, slang for a krait (snake) found in the Vietnam jungle.

Asiatic *adj.* [fr. colloq. *n.* *Asiatic* 'member of the armed forces, esp. the U.S. Navy, on a Far Eastern station; member of the U.S. Asiatic Fleet'] *Mil.* crazy or eccentric as a result of overly long service in the Far East; (*broadly*) crazy.

[**1942** *Leatherneck* (Nov.) 141: *Asiatic*—Used to describe a man who has spent many years on Asiatic stations.] **1945** in *AS* (Oct. 1946) 238: *Asiatic.* A soldier whose long tour of duty in the Far East has so affected his nerves that he has become queer. **1946** Heggen *Mr. Roberts* 126: Boy, when you finish up your five years out here, you'll really be Asiatic! You'll really be seeing flying fish then! **1949** McMillan *Old Breed* 230: "Asiatic," prewar parlance to describe the eccentric pattern of behavior characteristic of those who had been too long in Far East stations. **1953** Eyster *Skies* 101: I'm not Asiatic….I'm ready for more. **1959** Cochrell *Beaches* 49: Loosen up, Mac….You'll go Asiatic this way. **1962** W. Robinson *Barbara* 229 [ref. to service in Europe, WWII]: What's the matter with you two? You gone Asiatic? **1967** in Morris & Morris *Word & Phr. Origins* II 112: I first joined the Navy in 1926 and even then a sailor who had stayed with the Asiatic Fleet too long was sure to be *Asiatic* when he returned to the States. Some called it *crazyatic*…he had stayed in the tropics too long. **1968** in B. Edelman *Dear Amer.* 258: He might be a little Asiatic from Vietnamesitis and Overseasitis. **1969** Crumley *Cadence* 34: They were, to a man, crazy. They called it "going Asiatic."

asleep *adj.* ¶ In phrase: **asleep at the switch** [orig. ref. to railroad switches] inattentive; oblivious of responsibility.

1908 McGaffey *Show Girl* 178: Waiter, are you asleep at the switch? **1912** Mathewson *Pitching* 258: The crowd laughs at him…."Bescher [is] asleep at the switch again!" **1915** *DN* IV 219: The net player was asleep at the switch and never saw the return. **1934** *WNID2: Asleep at the switch.* Not alert to a duty or opportunity. *Slang.* **1968** Coppel *Order of Battle* 64 [ref. to WWII]: He…was entitled to wear the American Defense Medal ribbon on his blouse. In the Air Corps, this yellow bit of silk was known as the Asleep-at-the-Switch ribbon. If it had a battle star on it, we said that the wearer could have reached the switch. **1975** V.B. Miller *Passing Grade* 75: The rest of the class, asleep at the switch, is impressed by Caz's work. **1988** Poyer *Med* 243: Everybody aboard…was asleep at the switch!

asparagus *n.* [intentional malapropism] aspersion.—constr. with *cast.* *Joc.*

1916 in Dos Passos *14th Chron.* 43: Don't think that I'm "casting asparagus" at your letter. **1918** T.A. Dorgan, in Zwilling *TAD Lexicon* 92: I won't let anybody cast asparagus at my repertation [*sic*]. **1925** Ranck *Doughboys* 31: Say, look here, are you trying to cast "asparagus" on the courage of our doughboys? **1927** Aiken *Blue Voyage* 84: Are you castin' asparagus on my story?

aspirin *n.* *Baseball.* a fastball that is especially difficult to hit. In full, **aspirin tablet.**

1942 *ATS* 646: Fastball. *Aspirin.* **1959** Brosnan *Long Season* 273: Throwing aspirin tablets. Pitching the ball so swiftly that it looks smaller than it actually is. **1985** *L.A. Times* (Feb. 20) III 3: You find yourself trying to pick up some of the latest inside sports phrases so your writing won't be embarrassingly dated. You know that a fastball pitcher used to be "throwing aspirin tablets," then he was "throwing smoke," then he was "bringing gas." **1992** N.Y.C. man, age *ca*37: If you're hitting aspirin, you're trying to hit a ball that's going so fast it looks like an aspirin tablet.

ass *n.* [orig. dial. var. of ME *ars* < OE *ærs*] Also (in U.S. mainly a written euphem.) **arse.** [Common English from the Old English period; regarded as a vulgarism primarily since the late 17th C. (but see also 1992 quot.). The 1672 quot. below is the earliest clearly slang use. Rarely printed in U.S. before 1930's. Though still generally avoided in polite use, the word has lost some of its offensive character in recent years, esp. in joc. contexts.]

1.a. the rump; the buttocks, rectum, and anus.—in recent use, also collect.—usu. considered vulgar.

1672** *Covent Garden Drollery* 18: Now he that sate here, had much the better place,/He broke not his neck though he wetted his Ar—. **1695** in D. Greenberg *Crime in Colonial N.Y.* 172: The sheriff might Kiss His * *. ***1698** in N. Ward *London Spy* 41: Here's a health to mine A—s and a fart for those that owe no money. ***1699** in N. Ward *London Spy* 66: The wind's in my A—s. **1714** in Meserve & Reardon *Satiric Comedies* 6: Give me leave to run my hot Iron into your Arse. *ca1740** in W.H. Kenney *Laughter in Wilderness* 65: Till from the seat which he'd sat his arse on,/Uprose and thus began the parson. **1752** in Breslaw *Tues. Club* 386: Heads, Shoulders, arses, arms, Elbows and Toes. **1776** in W. Morgan *Amer. Icon* 65: Next see the Hypocritic parson/Who' thay all wish to turn an A—s on. **1778** [Connor] *Songbag* 24: And as he walked up to London to pick up a lass/He showed them how well he could riggle his arse. **1853** in Eliason *Tarheel Talk* 140: I will burn his damd ass off with tar and his Boys too! **1863** in *Journ. Ill. Hist. Soc.* LVI (1963) 325: An English upstart…whose face reminds me forcibly of a baby's spanked a—s. **1863** in Harrocks *Dear Parents* 37: Eyes Backurts, Ass Upparts…*Tention, Grab Tails….*in Double quick time. **1877** in J.M Carroll *Camp Talk* 114: Yes, Glide on yr. arse! ***1888** Elworthy *W. Somerset Wd. Bk.: Ass*…the seat, the buttocks, the back part of the person….Occasionally the anus is so called, but in such cases the context or some qualifying word points the meaning. **1888** in F. Remington *Sel. Letters* 62: Making a frame of their ass and the saddle for a landscape. **1902** in Tomlin *H. Tomlin* 123: G—d— you, the next time you are reported to me I am going to whip your G—d— a— all off of you. **1918** in Carey *Mlle. from Armentieres* I (unp.): We shot the Boche with mustard gas,/And put some blisters on his ass. **1934** "J.M. Hall" *Anecdota* 184: Sodomy or…taking it or giving it in the ass. **1936** J.T. Farrell *World I Never Made* 113: Well, if he wanted to look at her ass moving when she walked, let him. **1943** Guthrie *Glory* 425: What th' hell d'ya want in a war, boy, a soft ass cushion? Ha! Ha! Ha! **1945** J. Bryan *Carrier* 15: Don't ever gamble with him. He'll win your hat, ass, and overcoat! **1970** *Harper's* (Sept.) 59: He don't set [*sic*] on his ass and howl for help just because he's blind. **1990** J. Updike *Rabbit at Rest* 86: Fifty-two years old and she still has a solid ass. ***1992** Oxford Comp. Eng. Lang.* s.v. *censorship:* William Caxton preferred to take the self-censoring route of euphemism, avoiding coarse language, as when he used *buttocks* for *arse* in his edition of Thomas Malory's *Morte Darthur* (1485).

b. [cf. 1902 quot. at **(a)**, above; cf. identical use of BALL] (used emphatically and figuratively with *off* to receive the action of trans. as well as ordinarily intrans. verbs).—usu. considered vulgar. [*to work (one's) ass off* 'to work hard' is prob. the most freq. colloc.]
1915 H.L. Mencken, in Riggio *Dreiser-Mencken Letters* I 205: The war is in its last stage, and the Germans have knocked the ahss off'n 'em. **1924** in Hemingway *Letters* 132: I've been working my ass off. **1934** H. Miller *Trop. Cancer* 53: I'm flattering the ass off you. **1936** Kromer *Waiting* 115 [ref. to ca1915]: You're gonna run your ass off when the whistle blows. **1938** Bezzerides *Long Haul* 135: I tore my ass off getting here. **1949–51** J. Jones *Eternity* 160: Why the hell should I work my ass off here with no cooperation or appreciation? **1952** Uris *Battle Cry* 58: I'll drill their goddamyankee asses off, soon's this rain stops. **1958** Plagemann *Cocoon* 82: I'm going to work your ass off. **1960** Sire *Death-makers* 169: I'm going to sleep my ass off. **1963** J. Ross *Dead Are Mine* 265: Son of a bitch is living his ass off in North Africa. **1966** "Pendleton" *Iron Orchard* 4: Just froze my ass off waitin' for you, is all. **1969** Whittemore *Cop* 44: Minelli here's been coaching you and you suppos-edly studied your ass off. **1972** *Newsweek* (May 1) 27: Nobody wants a candidate who'll bore your ass off. **1991** *CBS This Morning* (CBS-TV) (Nov. 18): I worked my *ass* off!

2. tail end; rear (of an object); esp. the seat of the trousers.—usu. considered vulgar.
***1556** in *OED:* Whypped...at the carttes arse...for vacabondes. ***1721** N. Bailey *Dict.:* Arse, (among sailors) the Arse of a Block or Pulley, through which any Rope runs, is the lower end of it. ***1726** A. Smith *Mems. of J.G. Wild* 38: He...had been whipt at the Cart's Arse. ***1860** in *OED:* The ass of the block is known by the scoring being deeper in that part to receive the splice. **1945** Drake & Cayton *Black Metro.* 191: I could grab one by the ass of the pants and throw him out on the street. **1962** Mandel *Wax Boom* 211: Spoldren hit another Tiger [tank] right in the ass with two bazooka rockets.

3.a. a woman's posterior and vagina; vagina.—usu. considered vulgar.
***ca1684** in R. Thompson *Unfit for Modest Ears* 127: And yet I am informed here's many a lass/Come for to ease the itching of her arse. ***1684** in [Ashbee] *Biblio.* II 328: They'll scrape acquaintance with a standing tarse,/And impudently move it to their arse. ***1686** in *F & H* I (rev.) 69: Her rapacious arse/Is fitter for thy sceptre than your tarse. ***1731** "H. Thrumbo" *Merry-Thought* III 14: I have had a Cl-p/By a sad Mishap....G-d d—n A-se/And that fir'd my T-rse [i.e. *tarse* 'penis']. **1778** Connor *Songbag* 24: And because she denied him a shove on the grass/It's good as his word he got flames to her A—e. ***ca1830** in Holloway & Black *Broadsides* II 233: As through the streets she goes, with her barrow as she'd pass, soliciting her customers to buy her precious Ar—. **1888** *Stag Party* (unp.): He baited his hook with Elizabeth's arse. *ca*1918 in *Immortalia* 108: Eight months rolled by and the ninth did pass,/And a little dutch soldier marched out of her ass. **1942** McAtee *Supp. to Dial. of Grant Co.* 2 [ref. to 1890's]: *Ass*...the word also applied to the female pudendum. **1968** Stahl *Hokey* 104: I've always felt that the quickest way to a woman's heart is up her ass.

b. an act of copulation, esp. as experienced by a man; (*hence*) a person, esp. a woman, considered as a sexual partner.—esp. in phr. **piece of ass.**—also collect.—usu. considered vulgar.
*ca*1910 in Levine *Black Culture* 279: White folks on the sofa,/Niggers on the grass,/White man is talking low/Nigger is getting ass. **1916** Cary *Venery* I 6: *Ass*—Generic for women. **1918** in Carey *Mlle. fr. Armentieres* II (unp.): Oh, Captain, may I have a pass?/For I want to get a piece of ass. **1916–22** Cary *Sex. Vocab.* III: *Good ass.* A competent fuck-stress. **1926** in E. Wilson *Twenties* 255: Want your ass again?—When you jazz last? **1930** in H. Miller *Letters to Emil* 69: A fine gal...the finest little piece of ass in Montparnasse. **1934** H. Miller *Trop. of Cancer* 199: If only she had slipped me a piece of ass once in a while. **1942** McAtee *Supp. to Dial. of Grant Co.* 7 [ref. to 1890's]: Bout of copulation..."a [piece] of ass." **1942** H. Miller *Roofs of Paris* 270: Once [women have] had a piece of ass you can't spank them out of wanting it. **1943** J.T. Far-rell *My Days of Anger* 125: O'Neill, These days the beaches are full of ass you'd give your life to kiss. **1947** Mailer *Naked & Dead* 146: You

think you can give her a better piece of ass than anybody else? **1950** Stuart *Objector* 266: Aldington's got a neat way of getting ass, too. **1958** Gardner *Action* 72: Look at...the one leading the piece of blonde ass into the butterscotch Buick. **1963** Rubin *Sweet Daddy* 8: That was the first time I thought of the bucks in the ass business [prostitution]. **1966** S. Harris *Hellhole* 155: [Men] ain't no good, you know....They worse than rattlesnakes and we women be better off if only we didn't need them so much for ass. **1970** *Harper's* (July) 64: All these guys want...is a quick piece of ass, and I'm the guy with all the phone numbers. **1978** Washburn *Deer Hunter* (film): I get more ass than a toilet seat.

c. anal copulation; (*hence*) a person, esp. a male homosexual, regarded as an object of anal copulation.—sometimes in phr. **piece of ass.**—also collect.—usu. considered vulgar.
1934 "J.M. Hall" *Anecdota* 23: "Me cunt is in no condition for fucking tonight." "How about a piece of ass, then?" **1958** Talsman *Gaudy Image* 18: Cause I'm a fairy, that's why, a queen who falls in love with ass. *Ibid.* 61: I know you had good ass. **1966–67** P. Thomas *Mean Streets* 251: There was always the temptation [in prison] of wanting to cop some ass....If you weren't careful you became a piece of ass. **1977** Sayles *Union Dues* 286: Another old fag....It was probably no picnic to be out cruising for ass, either.

4.a. [cf. identical use of BALL] (one's) body, person, or self—sometimes functions as an intensifier of pronouns (e.g., *your ass* 'you, yourself'; *our asses* 'ourselves').—usu. considered vulgar. [Perh. orig. in imprecations only, as in D'Urfey and Royall quots. below; also cf. *1731 quot. at (3.a.), above, constrs. of which sort must have infl. the devel. of this sense.]
1698–1719** in D'Urfey *Pills* IV 200: A Pox of their A—ses. [1788** Grose *Vulgar Tongue* (ed. 2): Bring your a—e to an anchor, i.e. sit down.] **1817** in Royall *Letters from Ala.* 89: "D—n your *ars* and your *finities*," said the farmer. **1865** in Boyer *Naval Surg.* I 360: The old cap-tain...says that he was a "damn fool" for leaving the service. "Yes!" says he. "I must say that I kicked my — out of the service." **1916** T.S. Eliot, in V. Eliot *Letters* 125: Her taste was...klassic/And as for anything obscene/She said it made her ass sick. [**1919** Emmett *Give Way* 148: A placard arose from our trench in full view of the Germans: "Give your hearts to Jesus: Your tails belong to us."] **1927** *Immortalia* 34: They took him to the jail-house,/And threw his ass in a cell. **1934** Faulkner *Pylon* 43: Here I have been running my ass ragged eight days a week try-ing to find something worth telling. **1935** Algren *Boots* 185: Get your arse downstairs. **1944** in McMillan *Old Breed* 320: I brought my a—outa there, swabbie. That's my souvenir of Peleliu. **1949** Ellson *Tomboy* 268: It'll be just too bad for our asses. **1956** Chamales *Never So Few* 238: Beats my ass, come to think of it. **1959** Leckie *Marines:* Some-body's killed Carson's ass. **1967** Salas *Tattoo* 12: Give your soul to Jesus, dad, because your ass belongs to the man at the institute. **1978** Groom *Better Times* 81: You think the guy's gonna speak up now? They'd kill his ass. **1989** *21 Jump St.* (Fox-TV): Get your ass over to solitary right now! **1992** *New Yorker* (Dec. 28) 150: I told Jimmy Carter, "I am going to keep your skinny ass in the White House." **1993** *Real World* (MTV): I'm gonna sock your ass in those mouth.

b. [cf. identical use of BALL] (one's) life or well-being, "hide," "skin," "neck"; in phr. **to be (one's) ass** to result in punishment, injury, ruin, etc., for (one).—usu. considered vulgar.
1821** *Real Life in Ireland* 144: Major Gram...swore he would not budge an inch to save his ** *. [**1928** Fisher *Jericho* 149: Once they see you slippin', it's yo' hiney from then on.] **1947** Mailer *Naked & Dead* 40: I'm tired of taking the men out and risking their ass. **1949–51** J. Jones *Eternity* 367: If I miss Reveille any more, now, it'll be my ass. **1951** Thacher *Captain* 7: It's my ass if somethin's missin'. **1979** Crews *Blood & Grits* 98: One-handing it through a ninety-degree turn on city streets in a power slide where you were in danger of losing your ass as well as the car. **1988** Barrow & Munder *Joe Louis* 124: When you lose your head, your ass goes with it.

c. an individual; esp. in phr. **every living ass** "every man jack," everybody, "every living soul."—also collect.—usu. considered vulgar.
1946 Mezzrow & Wolfe *Blues* 52: Not a living ass in that band could play a note. **1962** Killens *Thunder* 12 [ref. to WWII]: All right! All right! Every living ass!...Every living ass with a swinging dick! **1965** Himes *Imabelle* 96: They gonna be some ass flyin' every whichway. **1969** Gordone *No Place* 411: I don' ask a livin' ass for nothin'. **1971** Wells & Dance *Night People* 71: Well, man, my theory is every ass for himself! **1974** R. Carter *16th Round* 114: Every living ass on the post

had to be standing tall.

5.a. effrontery; (*also*) good luck (as opposed to skill).—usu. considered vulgar.

*1958 in Wilkes *Austral. Colloq.* 5: See all the snooker balls going into the pockets—he had more arse than a married cow playing snooker, I can tell you. ***1960** in Partridge *DSUE* (ed. 7) 985: A man would need plenty of arse to pinch another man's book. **1962** Sagarin *Dirty Words* 60: In the poolroom, one says of a player who is lucky that...*he's got plenty of ass*...He is lucky....He is not talented. *Ibid.* 61: *Ass* means nerve: "It took a lot of ass to do that."...The implication is "lack of judgment." **1964** Pearl *Stockade* 28: You got a big ass getting reprieved like that. **1964** Brand *Bawdy Sing-Along* (LP): They had the refinement, we had the guts and ass. **1970** A. Joyce *Five Easy Pieces* (film): Where do you get the ass to [criticize] *her?* **1974** Strasburger *Third* 159: Whew, that *really* took balls. Or ass. **1984–87** Ferrandino *Firefight* 152: Pool players who shoot eight ball without calling their shots, sinking impossible combinations on luck, on pure ass.

b. ability and determination; (*specif.*) the actual ability and determination to carry out a promise, threat, etc., as opposed to an empty boast.—usu. in metaphorical provs.— usu. considered vulgar. See also ALLIGATOR MOUTH. Cf. *bring ass to get ass*, below.

1961 Peacock *Valhalla* 21 [ref. to 1953]: Don't let your alligator mouth overload your canary ass. **1962** in Wepman et al. *The Life* 29: You overloaded your ass....Never jump on more than your ass can hold. **1973** Haney *Jock* 47: Cheryl let her mouth overload her ass, is how Mary sums up the situation. **1973** Herbert & Wooten *Soldier* 353: It's the bulldog mouth and the puppydog ass and they're all over the place. **1974** R. Carter *14th Round* 80: You're just about ready to let your mouth write a check your ass can't cash! **1976** Braly *False Starts* 211: I was all mouth and no ass. **1967–80** Folb *Runnin' Lines* 235: *Don't let your mouth overload your ass; don't let your mouth write a check your ass can't cash.* Don't talk too much, in such a belligerent manner, or there's going to be a fight. *a***1986** K.W. Nolan *Into Laos* 224: Keep your mouth shut....Don't let your mouth write a check your ass can't cash.

c. in phr. **fly with (one's) ass** (of an aviator) to fly by relying on luck and (one's) own experience, rather than on charts or instruments; fly "by the seat of (one's) pants."—usu. considered vulgar.

1977 Langone *Life at Bottom* 146: You really have to fly with your ass....There's hardly any landmarks that you can follow with any certainty.

6. [ellipt. for syn. RED ASS] anger, annoyance, irritation.—usu. constr. with *the*.—usu. considered vulgar.

1964 R. Moore *Green Berets* 43: Those boys have a big case of the ass with us. **1967** Duncan *New Legions* 73: It's starting to give me a bad case of the royal ass. **1970** Whitmore *Memphis-Nam* 15: Now that would give my old man the ass. **1973** W. Crawford *Gunship Cmndr.* 29: He's got a big case of the ass at the army for asking him to pay off the debt. **1977** N.Y.C. bartender, age 30: Now she has the ass at me. **1978** W. Brown *Tragic Magic* 112: Hey, don't get the ass at me, Mouth. **1979** N.Y.C. man, age 31: He's got a bad case of ass. **1984–87** Ferrandino *Firefight* 124: The new CO...gave him a royal case of the ass.

7. (used with modifying possessive to express contempt or negation).—usu. considered vulgar. Cf. *my ass*, below.

1972–76 Durden *No Bugles* 1: "Right," he said. "Right's ass," I thought. It's all wrong. *Ibid.* 50: "We got a long walk." Long walk's ass. A long walk was an understatement. **1986** Dye & Stone *Platoon* 69: "I hear he extended his tour." "Extended's ass, man." **1988** Dye *Outrage* 59: "C'mon, Gunny..." "C'mon's ass, boy."

¶ In phrases:

¶ **Ask my ass!** "I will not answer your question"; "I will not comply with your request."—usu. considered vulgar.

*1785 Grose *Vulgar Tongue*: Ask, or Ax my A—e. A common reply to a question; still deemed wit at sea, and formerly at court, under the denomination of selling bargains. **1842** in Leyda *Melville Log* I 145: When I told him to haul down the fore tack, he replied saying "Ask my arse." I then struck him.

¶ **ass-over-appetite** head-over-heels; end-over-end; topsy-turvy; in confusion. Also **-teakettle, -tip, -tit,** and other vars.—usu. considered vulgar.

1938 Steinbeck *Grapes of Wrath* 200: You jus' scrabblin' ass over tit, fear somebody gonna pin some blame on you. **1942** McAtee *Supp. to Grant Co. Dial.* [ref. to 1890's]: *Ass over appetite* (applecart *or* end-ways), adv. phr. Head over heels. [**1946** G.C. Hall *1000 Destroyed* 229: He dis-

played a rump-over-tea-kettle aggressiveness in seeking dog-fights.] **1948** Cozzens *Guard of Honor* 260: I leaned on it and went ass-over-teakettle. **1920–54** Randolph *Bawdy Elements* 90: *Ass over appetite* means...head over heels. [**1954** E. Hunter *Jungle Kids* 144: He went down, butt over teacups.] **1955** E. O'Connor *Last Hurrah* 98: Here's the city goin' over the hill to the poorhouse, arse over teakettle, and that dirty devil runnin' for four more years. **1956** Algren *Wild Side* 207: The king...pitched himself ass over appetite. **1959** Searls *Big X* 250: I still don't know if she can be yawed at this speed without going completely ass over teakettle. **1963** Doulis *Path* 209: He's 'bout to go ass over tin cups. **1967** Kolb *Getting Straight* 34: I went ass over teakettle along the ties for a hundred yards. **1968** Myrer *Eagle* 104: Down I went, ass over appetite. **1970** Thackrey *Thief* 424: And this time, when I belted her, she went ass-over-tincup across the room. **1972** in *Penthouse* (Jan. 1973) 104: Footballers falling ass over elbow. **1972–76** Durden *No Bugles* 20: Shock waves knocked me ass over elbows. **1976** Hayden *Voyage* 230: I got tumbled ass over tip. **1982** R.M. Brown *Southern Discomfort* 28: Bunny was so het up she was ass over tit.

¶ **bite my ass** (used as a derisive retort; also as an interj. of astonishment).—usu. considered vulgar.

1954 in IUFA *Folk Speech*: How'd you like to take a big bite out of my ass? **1957–62** Higginbotham *USMC Folklore* 24: Why don't you jump up and bite my ass. **1966** D. King *Brave & Damned* 86: Well bite my ass. How the goddamn hell you make radioman? **1966** F.C. Elkins *Heart of Man* 73: How'd You Like to Bite My Ass? **1970** W.C. Crawford *Kill. Zone* 35: Jump up and bite my ass. **1971** Ohio Univ. student, age 20: Country boys always say, "Well, bite my ass!" when they hear something funny. **1972** Jenkins *Semi-Tough* 262: Bite my ass, Puddin. **1978** Univ. Tenn. student: How'd you like to bite my ass?

¶ **bring ass to get ass** [app. of boxing origin] to risk one's own well-being in order to defeat someone else. Cf. **(5.b.),** above.—usu. considered vulgar.

1959 F.L. Brown *Trumbull Pk.* 352: If they want to whip ass they'll have to bring ass. **1974** R. Carter *16th Round* 129: He would have to *bring* ass to *get* ass;...he couldn't leave his in the corner when he came to get mine. **1977** Hamill *Flesh & Blood* 51: They gotta bring ass to get ass, and they just ain't gonna *get* us. **1978** W. Brown *Tragic Magic* 153: "The ones who kick ass are the ones who bring the most ass."..."All right everybody, it's time to bring ass."..."You Got To Bring Ass To Get Ass."

¶ **bust** [or **break**] **(one's) ass, 1.** to exert (oneself) to the limit of endurance; to toil, labor, or strive furiously.—usu. considered vulgar.

[**1937** Di Donato *Christ in Concrete* 11: Master Geremio, the Devil himself could not break his tail any harder than we are here.] **1941** in M. Curtis *Letters Home* 81: I intend to come out a corporal or break my ass trying. **1944** in *Amer. Journ. Sociol.* LVII (1952) 436: I'm not going to bust my ass on stuff like this. **1948** Mailer *Naked & Dead* 228 [ref. to WWII]: What's we breakin' our asses for? Let's take it easy. **1948** Cozzens *Guard of Honor* 45: "What'd you have done if I'd yelled: Bail out!"..."Busted my thick ass, General." **1963** J. Ross *Dead Are Mine* 48: I'll make it or bust my homesick ass trying. **1965** Herlihy *Midnight Cowboy* 207: I been figuring the main thing we break our ass here for is to keep warm. **1969** in Bouton *Ball Four* 348: We had to keep busting ass. **1980** Gould *Ft. Apache* 218: We break our asses and he gets all the...credit. **1982** *N.Y. Post* (Aug. 17) 60: These people like to boo [while] we're out there busting our asses. **1988** *21 Jump Street* (Fox-TV): I've busted my ass making letter-perfect cases.

2. *Av.* to be killed in an airplane crash.—usu. considered vulgar.

1945 in *JAF* LXIII (1950) 463: Halfway to China/He busted his ass. **1959** [*41st Ftr. Sq. Songbk.*] 8: On top of old Fuji he busted his ass. **1961** Plantz *Sweeney Sq.* 137 [ref. to WWII]: No turns. You'll bust your ass in this canyon. **1969** Searls *Hero Ship* 151 [ref. to WWII]: O.K....I'll sign it....But I hope you bust your ass. **1985** Boyne & Thompson *Wild Blue* 213: If he busted his own ass in a fighter it was one thing. Taking all these trusting people with him was another. **1991** Linnekin *80 Knots* 77: He can't do that! He's going to bust his ass!

3. to beat (someone) up; to thrash (someone) savagely.— usu. considered vulgar.

1954 Weingarten *Dict. Slang* II: Very common in street language. "Get out of that car or I'll break your ass for you." **1980** Texas man, age *ca*30: Somebody oughta bust his ass.

4. to harass; (*hence*) to annoy.—usu. considered vulgar.

1965 Linakis *In Spring* 32 [ref. to WWII]: Disciplinarians would bust your ass from sunup to sundown. **1983** *Nat. Lampoon* (Aug.) 45: She was always busting my ass. She'd follow me to school, [etc.]. **1987** D. Sherman *Main Force* 99: "Sorry, bro," Zietvogel finally said. "I didn't mean to bust your ass, but it's the truth."

¶ **chew ass** see s.v. CHEW, *v.*, 3.

¶ **creep up (someone's) ass** to demean oneself as a means of currying favor with (someone).—usu. considered vulgar.
*****1698–1706** in D'Urfey *Pills* IV 113: Old Proverbs...I'll not creep in her A— to bake in her Oven. [*****1903** *F & H* I (rev.): *Arse-Hole Creeper* = a parasite.] **1971** N.Y.C. woman, age 83: You've crept up her ass long enough.

¶ **cut ass** see s.v. CUT, *v.*

¶ **from ass to appetite** completely.—usu. considered vulgar.
1952 Clayton *Angels* 28: I'll cut [him] open from ass to appetite.

¶ **get in (someone's) ass** to cause trouble for (someone); act against (someone); to thrash (someone).—usu. considered vulgar.
1966 Braly *On Yard* 133: Now I want my stuff, or I'm going to get in your ass. **1968** Gover *JC Saves* 102: 'Cause if Son still got gettin' up my ass in mind, I sure don't wanna go back there. **1967–80** Folb *Runnin' Lines* 239.

¶ **get it in** [or **up**] **the ass** to be victimized, vanquished, or killed; "get it in the neck."—usu. considered vulgar.
1945 in Shibutani *Co. K* 125: He's dumb and fucks up...and then we get it in the ass. **1955** Puzo *Dark Arena* 162 [ref. to 1940's]: Everybody gets it up the ass. **1961** C. Cooper *Weed* 89: She was getting it right up the ass. **1961** Forbes *Goodbye* 66 [ref. to WWII]: It's all the same to me, if I get it in the ass [on a bombing mission] tonight, then I don't get it in the ass next week. **1967** W. Crawford *Gresham's War* 178 [ref. to Korean War]: You will do as you are told...or get it dead in the ass, sideways! **1970** La Motta et al. *Raging Bull* 5: I was always the kid getting it in the ass. If it wasn't my old man belting me around, it was...a teacher slapping me silly.

¶ **get (one's) ass in an uproar** to become severely agitated or concerned.—used derisively.—usu. considered vulgar.
1952 Lamott *Stockade* 64 [ref. to WWII]: Don't get your ass in an uproar, Lieutenant. **1979–82** Gwin *Overboard* 152: Don't be gittin' your purty little ass in a uproar.

¶ **get (one's) ass up** to become annoyed or angry; "get (one's) back up."—usu. considered vulgar.
1884 in Athearn *Forts of Mo.* 289: I guess he got his a— up because I did not address him as Col. **1972** Wambaugh *Blue Knight* 96: I'm always the first one to get my ass up when the brass tries to restrict my freedom with idiotic rules.

¶ **get (one's) ass on (one's) shoulders** to become unduly haughty, angry, or excited.—usu. considered vulgar.
1954 Killens *Youngblood* 114: All them Harlem Negroes got their ass on their shoulders. Think they better than the colored down here. **1968** Maule *Rub-A-Dub* 122 [ref. to WWII]: Captain's got his ass on his shoulder. [**1973** Andrews & Owens *Black Lang.* 91: When a child lifts a shoulder to tell his parents he'll do what he wants, he'll be told, "Don't be getting your behind up on your shoulder, cause I can get mine just as high as yours."] **1973** W. Crawford *Gunship Cmndr.* 19: You've got your ass clear up over your shoulders and you don't even know why. **1975** in *Tenn. Folk. Soc. Bull.* XLIV 140: "Got your ass on your shoulder."..."You're mad for no good reason (that I know of)." **1978** W. Brown *Tragic Magic* 43: Girls never dug her either. They always thought she had her ass on her shoulders.

¶ **get on (someone's) ass** to get on (someone's) nerves.—usu. considered vulgar.
1953 Eyster *Customary Skies* 73 [ref. to WWII]: Yuh know it gets on Malone's ass.

¶ **hang it in your ass!** (used as a derisive retort); "stick it in your ear!"—usu. considered vulgar.
[**1955** E. Hunter *Jungle Kids* 101: I told Donlevy where he could hang his phony rap.] **1968** Stuard (unp.): Hang it in your ass...meant the same as "go to hell" [in Vietnam, 1965]. **1972–76** Durden *No Bugles* 55: Hang it in your ass, you silly sonofabitch. **1974** Tenn. truckdriver, age 27: [Demonstrating hand gesture—right forefinger hooked over left thumb which forms circle with left forefinger.] This means, "hang it in your ass."

¶ **hang (one's) ass out** to expose (oneself) to danger; "stick (one's) neck out."—usu. considered vulgar.
1947 Schulberg *Harder They Fall* 231: Three months ago your ass was hanging out. *Ibid.* 289: He says he don't want the dough....And six

months ago his ass was hangin' out. **1954** Schulberg *Waterfront* 243: The round-collar bastard leaves me standin' here with my ass hangin' out. [**1966** Shepard *Doom Pussy* 65: You're a mighty snazzy chicken to be hanging your fanny out coverin' this cockeyed hassle.] **1975** De Mille *Smack Man* 55: Your ass is still hanging out so you got a lot more cooperating to do. **1979** N.Y.C. man, age *ca*30: Don't hang your ass out on a long shot.

¶ **hang (someone's) ass** to punish; (*hence*) to defeat thoroughly; trounce.—usu. considered vulgar.
1961 Coon *Meanwhile* 198: We sure hung their ass, didn't we? **1975** S.P. Smith *Amer. Boys* 140: You do one more thing like yesterday and I'm going to hang your ass.

¶ **have (one's) finger up (one's) ass** to stand about idly; be inattentive or slow to act.—usu. considered vulgar. Also vars.
[*****1942** in Partridge *DSUE* (ed. 7) 1453: *Take* (or *pull*) *your finger out!*...addressed "to a person who is slow or lazy."...The semantics: "Stop scratching your backside and get on with the job!"] **1948** Mailer *Naked & Dead* 367: You men better get your finger out of your ass. *Ibid.* 408: Goddam it, you men, stop standing around with your finger in your ass! **1949–51** J. Jones *Eternity* 155: Don't stand there with your finger up your ass. [**1951** Wouk *Mutiny* 215 [ref. to WWII]: Well, what are *you* doing, standing around with your thumb in your bum and your mind in neutral?] **1958** Frankel *Band of Bros.* 110 [ref. to 1950]: What did you want me to do? Sit here with my thumb up my ass waiting for you? **1960** MacCuish *Do Not Go Gentle* 287 [ref. to WWII]: He had gone in without watching the trail, his thumb up his ass, and had messed things up good. **1972** Wurlitzer *Quake* 147: Move it. Move it. Get your thumb out of your ass. **1972** Grogan *Ringolevio* 292: When are you guys gonna take your fingers out of your assholes and—. **1974** Cherry *Steel* 26: I stayed up top with my finger up my ass until 11:45. **1974** Kurtzman *Bobby* 13: The doctor's got his thumb up his asshole. **1978** Truscott *Dress Gray* 219: You gonna call the room to attention, Hand, or you gonna just stand there with your fuckin' thumb up your ass like some kind of dufus fool? **1981–85** S. King *It* 74: Well get your thumb out of your ass and do something about it.

¶ **have (one's) head up** [or **in**] **(one's) ass** to be very stupid or inattentive.—usu. considered vulgar.
[**1941** in Wiener *Flyers* 45: Get your head out. To use your head while flying.] **1924–44** in *AS* XXI 33: *Head Up Your Ass*, adj. Stupid, absentminded. (Sometimes "Head in your ass.") **1949** Van Praag *Day Without End* 162: If they'd get a few line soldiers back there, maybe they'd learn to get their heads out of their asses. **1955** Klaas *Maybe I'm Dead* 257: Get your heads out of your asses! **1962** E. Stephens *Blow Negative* 431: Boy, you have been living with your head up your ass too long, Harry. **1968** Coppel *Order of Battle* 100: If you hadn't been so fucking slow to get your head out of your ass, it would never have happened. **1969** Briley *Traitors* 206: If they believe that crap about American imperialism, it's because they got their heads up their asses! **1986–91** Hamper *Rivethead* 153: Some of these bastards got their heads up their asses.

¶ **have (one's) nose up (someone's) ass** to curry favor with (someone) in a blatant manner. Cf. BROWNNOSE.—usu. considered vulgar.
1971 Selby *Room* 30: Just keep their goddamn noses stuck up the judges ass.

¶ **hold (one's) ass** to be patient, "hold (one's) horses."—usu. considered vulgar.
1961 Granat *Important Thing* 157: Hold your aaaasss! Well, where was I?

¶ **How's your ass?** (used as a greeting).—usu. considered vulgar.
*ca*1960 in IUFA *Folk Speech: How's your ass?* **1966** Fariña *Down So Long* 16: Give me the Victorian for "how's your ass, ace?" **1970** N.Y.U. student, age 19: Hello, Bill. How's your ass? **1979** Gutcheon *New Girls* 334: How's your work, how's your ass, how's your kid, how's your dog?

¶ **in (someone's) ass** nagging or scolding; (*also*) close by.—usu. considered vulgar.
1966 C. Cooper *Farm* 84: She's *always* in yer ass about somethin. **1967** "Iceberg Slim" *Pimp* 141: He don't allow her outta his sight. Any club he plays she hasta be right there stuck in his ass.

¶ **jump through (one's) ass** to go wild with fear or confusion; panic.—usu. considered vulgar.
1969 Spetz *Rat Pack* 71: Your Viet Cong friends have obviously gotten the big brass very worried, and they are now jumping through their asses in one huge flap. **1975** De Mille *Smack Man* 99: The courts...jump through their asses to understand criminals.

¶ **jump up my ass** (used as a derisive retort).—usu. considered vulgar.

[**1972** Jenkins *Semi-Tough* 238: Anybody who don't want to wish me luck can jump up an armadillo's ass.] **1973** Gwaltney *Destiny's Chickens* 43: I'm tempted to tell John Slim to jump up my ass. **1975** Tenn. woman, age 23: You can tell him to jump up my ass.

¶ **jump up (someone's) ass** to attack (someone).—usu. considered vulgar.

1977 Olsen *Fire Five* 93: One more word, I'm gonna jump right up your ass!

¶ **kick ass** see s.v. KICK, *v.*

¶ **kiss** [or **suck**] **my ass, 1.** (used as a derisive retort; also as an expression of amazement).—also with *my* replaced by another pronoun.—sometimes with *ass* prec. by intensifying adj.—usu. considered vulgar. [The appearance of this phr. in a lit. sense in Chaucer's *Milleres Tale, ca*1389, strongly sugg. its existence metaphorically as well in ME.]

[*ca*1389 Chaucer *Milleres Tale* A 3734: But with his mouth he kiste hir naked ers.] *ca*1554–76 in G. Hughes *Swearing* 104: Com kiss myne arse! *1633 in *F & H* I (rev.): Kiss my hand! Kiss my arse, noble ladies. *1693 in Burford *Bawdy Verse* 191: So kiss my Arse, disdainfull sow! **1695** in D. Greenberg *Crime in Colonial N.Y.* 172: The sheriff might Kiss His * *. *a1700 in Berckman *Hidden Navy* 135: And tell him of the danger, he sayes the Navy Officers may (saving yr presence) kisse his Arse, hee will observe noe orders, not hee. *1705 in *N & Q* (Feb. 1971) 46: Without saying so much…as kiss my a—se. *1731 "H. Thrumbo" *Merry-Thought* II 10: And you may kiss my A-se. **1819** [Clopper] *Bawl-fredonia* 47: They swore, tossed up their noses, and bade any one of their lower casts, who would accost them to kiss * * *. **1846** in J.M. McCaffrey *Manifest Destiny* 91: Tell Johnny Wool to kiss our ——. **1846** in *Ark. Hist. Qly.* XII (1953) 305: Tell Johnny Wool to kiss our —. **1862** in J.M. Merrill *Battle Flags* 188: God damned Dutch son-of-a-bitch…kiss my arse. **1863** in Wiley *Billy Yank* 312: Kiss my arse. **1888** *Stag Party* 17: Yez can suck me arse. **1920** T. Dreiser, in Riggio *Dreiser-Mencken Letters* II 390: J. Jefferson J. can kiss my ass. *1914–21 Joyce *Ulysses* 147: He can kiss my royal Irish arse. [**1928** Fisher *Jericho* 55: Well, kiss my assorted peanuts!] **1930** J.T. Farrell *Guillotine* 292: Kiss my ass. **1942** McAtee *Supp. to Grant Co. Dial.* 2 [ref. to 1890's]: *Ass*…anus, as in the elegant retort, "Suck my —." *a1957 McLiam *Pat Muldoon* 14: And you can kiss my royal Irish —. **1962** Sagarin *Dirty Words* 27: Well, for Christ's sake becomes *Well, for kiss my ass!* [**1962** McKenna *Sand Pebbles* 426: All you Polocks can kiss my royal Canadian.] **1969** Green & Peckinpah *Wild Bunch* (film): How'd you like to kiss my sister's black cat's ass? **1978** Shem *House of God* 219: You bastard, you kiss my royal Norwegian ass. **1982–84** Chapple *Outlaws in Babylon* 167: "Suck my ass," says Ace.

2. (also used in extended phr. of (1), above.—usu. considered vulgar.

[**1926** Dunning & Abbott *Broadway* 243: I wouldn't stay and entertain your gang of goofers if you kissed my foot in Macy's window at high noon.] **1949–51** J. Jones *Eternity* 38: Smith no less. I'll kiss your ass in Macy's window at high noon on Sataday if I ever heard of a Smith in Brooklyn. **1953–57** Giovannitti *Combine D* 55 [ref. to WWII]: "If we make it by Christmas I'll kiss your fat ass."…"In Macy's window?" **1962** Killens *Thunder* 36 [ref. to WWII]: Well, kiss my ass in Macy's window—I'll be a rotten mama-jabber! **1966** "T. Pendleton" *Iron Orchard* 187: I'll kiss yer ass in Sanger Brothers' winder if I don't walk right up to that ol' man and say, "Coker, you old sonofabitch." **1971** Faust *Willy* 140: If he's in England I'll kiss Churchill's ass in Macy's window. **1971** Horan *Blue Messiah* 441: In a few months any one of them will kiss your ass in Macy's window.

¶ **kiss** [or **lick** or **suck**] **(someone's) ass** to curry favor with (someone), esp. in a blatant or degrading manner.—usu. considered vulgar.

*1748 Smollett *Roderick Random* ch. vii: A canting scoundrel, who has crept into business by his hypocrisy, and kissing the a—se of everybody. **1864** in T. Jones *Letters* 176: Still water lies very deep, so if Mack stands by the government and prosecutes the war they will cry God speed. They will lick his ass to ease his stomach. **1934** H. Miller *Trop. of Cancer* 78: For the price of a drink he will suck any…ass. [**1934** H. Miller *Trop. of Cancer* 158: I had learned how to kiss the boss's.] **1937** E. Anderson *Thieves* 86: I never was cut out to work for any two or three dollars a day and have to kiss somebody's ass to get that. **1947** in J. Jones *Reach* 113: Ol Eddie was sure sucking his ass. **1966** King *Brave & Damned* 192: "Thank y'all kin'ly, suh," the Runner said, sucking ass. **1973** Karlin, Paquet, & Rottmann *Free Fire* 129: I got tired of lickin' battalion's

ass and salutin' all the time. **1976** Lee *Ninth Man* 76: You're going to have to lick some ass and get us some help. **1966–80** McAleer & Dickson *Unit Pride* 358: You still kissin' my ass, being real friendly like, still hopin' to get me to commit perjury? **1985** "J. Michaels" *Pvt. Affairs* 185: *We* work for a living; you fancy boys…get rich licking tourists' asses.

¶ **lock asses** to fight, brawl, "lock horns."—usu. considered vulgar.

1953 Petry *Narrows* 267: Don't you go lockin' asses with him, Sonny.…He's spoilin' for a fight. **1964** Rhodes *Chosen Few* 25 [ref. to *ca*1950]: If I ever had t' lock asses with Prong, I'd try my damnedest to shoot him before he got a chance t' get his blade out. **1974** Univ. Tenn. student, age 23: If you don't quit that shit me an' you gonna lock asses.

¶ **lose (one's) ass** to lose all (one) has, as in gambling; lose (one's) position; lose everything.—usu. considered vulgar.

[*1788 Grose *Vulgar Tongue* (ed. 2): He would lose his a—se if it was loose, said of a careless person.] [**1933** Martin *International House* (film): "I'm sitting on something." "I lost *mine* in the stock market."] *a1950 P. Wolff *Friend* 32: If he ever wrote…to the inspector general, somebody would lose his ass. **1959** Tevis *Hustler* 97: Once a poker player notorious for his ability to lose, he had recently turned to pool…and invariably lost his ass. **1962** Kesey *Cuckoo's Nest* 102: No wonder I'm losing my ass. **1966** "T. Pendleton" *Iron Orchard* 56: Now boys, you *know* don't *nobody* whistle comin' outa no dice hall if he done lost his ass. He *bound* to won *somethin'*.

¶ **my ass!** (used, esp. postpositively, to express negation or contempt; also as an exclamation of dismay, anger, etc.).—sometimes with *ass* prec. by intensifying adj. Cf. *your ass*, below.—usu. considered vulgar.

[*1601 B. Jonson *Poetaster* IV 4: Valiant? So is mine arse.] [*1694 in *F & H* I (rev.) 69: Your Leominster superfine wool is mine arse to it; mere flock in comparison.] [**1890** in Ownby *Subduing Satan* 140: She said she believed that she had religion. I told her that she did not have no more religion than my "ass."] **1923** in J. O'Hara *Sel. Letters* 7: Oh my ass, a singular lack of enthusiasm. *1932 F. Richards *Old Soldiers* 111 [ref. to WWI]: "We'll have to surrender. They've got around the back of us." "Surrender my bloody arse!" **1934** Binns *Lightship* 233: Captain, me arse!…You're a broken-down old washerwoman! **1941** *Chippie Wagon* 58: My ass he did! **1945** Bowman *Beach Red* 89: Oh, my aching ass! How could we have been so dumb! **1949–51** J. Jones *Eternity* 159: "In the Old Army…an officer was an officer, not a clothes horse."…"Old Army, my bleeding ass." **1955** Goethals *Chains* 150 [ref. to WWII]: "Oh my aching ass—" the G.I. mutters. **1958** Cooley *Run for Home* 130: Cigarettes my achin' ass! No cigarette never hurt nobody! **1962** W. Robinson *Barbara* 23 [ref. to WWII]: "You want I should open it now?" "My royal ass!" *Ibid.* 309: Oh my sainted ass! **1967** H. Bennett *Black Wine* 84: "Now now honey."…"Now now my red ass!" Eloise cried. **1967** Taggart *Reunion* 94: Debt and general dissolution my purple ass! **1967** Brelis *Face of S. Viet.* 26: "My ass you did," argued another Marine. **1976** C.R. Anderson *Grunts* 130: "Relax, that's a rock ape." "My dying ass—that's a gook!" **1977** Sayles *Union Dues* 264: Humphrey my royal Irish ass. **1990** *Capital Gang* (CNN-TV) (Aug. 11): Replacement costs, my ass! **1990** *Murphy Brown* (CBS-TV): "Lucky shot." "Luck, my ass!"

¶ **my ass to** [or **for** or **on**] (used as a curse); "a fig for"; etc.—usu. considered vulgar.

*1698–1720 in D'Urfey *Pills* V 284: Here's a Health to the Tackers, my Boys,/But mine A—se for the Tackers about. **1929–30** Dos Passos *42d Parallel* 89: My ass to habeas corpus. **1936** LeClercq *Rabelais* 120: My arse to your quacks! **1958–65** Alfred *Hogan's Goat* 60: If you come to crow about it,/My ass on you then, kid.

¶ **not know (one's) ass from** —— to be ignorant, stupid, or confused.—usu. considered vulgar. [*a hole in the ground, (one's) elbow,* and *third base* are app. the most freq. colloc.]

1862 in T. Jones *Letters* 69: Colonels and captains so drunk that they did not know a garrison wagon from a house or in other words did not know their ass from a musket. [*1897 Conrad *Nigger of Narcissus* ch. iii: Hadn't savvy enough to know his knee from his elbow.] *a1903 *F & H* I (rev.) 67: *He doesn't know his Arse from his elbow* = (1) He is utterly stupid, and (2) absolutely ignorant. [**1921** *DN* V 158: Can't tell his head from a hole in the ground.] **1936** in M. Crane *Roosevelt* 68: Some bastard off in Washington that doesn't know a milch cow from a steer or his ass from a hole in the ground. [**1936** J.T. Farrell *World I Never Made* 123: Jesus, Dan, you don't know your butt from a hole in the ground, do you?] **1938** Steinbeck *Grapes of Wrath* 67: Don't know his ass from a hole in the ground. **1939** Appel *People Talk* 425: I didn't know my ass from a stalk of bananas. **1939** Bessie *Men in Battle* 91: God *damn* this lousy outfit!…They don't know their ass from a hot rock. **1942** McAtee *Supp. to Grant Co. Dial.* 4 [ref. to 1890's]: "Don't know his ass from a hole in the ground," saying meaning he is stupid. **1947** Willingham *End as Man* 226: The guy probably doesn't know his ass from Mammoth Cave. **1949** Van Praag *Day Without End* 46: Don't know your ass from a hole in the wall! *a***1950** P. Wolff *Friend* 19: Don't know his ass from his elbow. **1955** Goethals *Chains* 71 [ref. to WWII]: You're so screwed up you don't know your ass from third base. **1958** Cooley *Run for Home* 63: A…brand-new deck boy who didn't know his ass from a wind-scoop about ship's work! **1959** Kanin *Blow Up Storm* 121: Rupert…does not know his ass from a hot rock. **1961** J. Jones *Thin Red Line* 60 [ref. to WWII]: He don't know his ass from third base, and he ain't about to, ever. **1962** Viertel *Love & Corrupt* 94: Them guys? They don't know their ass from their armpit! **1963** Tracy *Brass Ring* 379: He's too drunk to know his ass from third base. **1963** Cameron *Black Camp* 27: Those medics don't know their asses from their elbows. **1965** Beech *Make War* 181: Besides, the only one who knew his ass from a hole in the ground was Neeley. **1966** "T. Pendleton" *Iron Orchard* 39: He don't know his ass from his lef' foot. **1969** Searls *Hero Ship* 42: As a pilot, he still didn't know his ass from his aileron. **1970** Wambaugh *Centurions* 328: I never worked this crummy division in my life. I don't know my ass from pork sausage. **1972** Davidson *Cut Off* 142: I kept running into misanthropes like myself who didn't know their ass from a rifle barrel. **1972–76** Durden *No Bugles* 17: I never figured there was many in the Army who knew their ass from the back side of a checker board. *Ibid.* 70: You think ol' Cockatoo knows 'is ass from a jug of apple cider? **1973** Chandler *Capt. Hollister* 11: Doesn't know the ass from up on an M-l. **1983** S. King *Christine* 295: Jimmy didn't know his ass from ice cream. **1985** N. Kazan *At Close Range* (film): He's the only one…who knows his ass from a pitchfork.

¶ **not on your ass!** no indeed, "not on your life."—usu. considered vulgar.

1960 Hoagland *Circle Home* 57: You thinkin' I eat steak?…Not on your ass. I eat the same as you.

¶ **off (someone's) ass** no longer annoying, harassing, vexing, scolding, etc.—usu. considered vulgar.

1969 Lynch *American Soldier* 73 [ref. to 1953]: You should get off his ass, Gerber.

¶ **(one's) ass is dragging** (one) is fatigued, dejected, or beaten.—usu. considered vulgar. Cf. *drag ass* s.v. DRAG. [Freq. euphemized in print.]

[*****1780** in *F & H* (rev.) 70: My arse hangs behind me as heavy as lead.] [**1918** *La Trine Rumor* (Oct.) (unp.): Sgt. Johnston on the hike at the twenty-seventh kilometer, with tailboard dragging.] [**1942** in Legman *Limerick* 23: It's too much.…My backsides are dragging the floor.] **1945** in Shibutani *Co. K* 128: My ass was really draggin' yesterday. **1948** I. Shulman *Cry Tough* 114: And if his pop…hadn't made him three suits, his ass would be dragging. **1954** Killens *Youngblood* 108: Get through, Mr. Charlie's ass be dragging the ground. **1961** J. Jones *Thin Red Line* 42 [ref. to WWII]: Jeez, my ass is draggin.…All this gear. **1961** R. Crane *Born of Battle* 86: I'll run this platoon till their asses drag the ground, sir. **1962** Killens *Thunder* 42 [ref. to WWII]: His ass was dragging the natural ground. **1980** N.Y.C. man, age 30: Workin' all day—God, my ass is draggin'.

¶ **(one's) ass is grass** Esp. *Mil.* (one) is doomed to suffer punishment, danger, death, etc.; (one) is "history."—usu. considered vulgar. Also vars.

1955–56 in *AS* XXXII 262: Your ass is grass and I'm the lawnmower. **1963** Coon *Short End* 133: You just remember one thing, now and always. Your ass is grass and I'm the lawnmower. **1969** *Playboy* (Oct.) 123: If an inspector spots him, his ass is grass. **1970** Thackrey *Thief* 49: And as soon as I seen the both of them, I knew my ass was grass and here come a lawnmower. **1972–76** Durden *No Bugles* 68: Ya ass is grass an' these dudes gonna mow y' down. **1974** Price *Wanderers* 15: The rest of the gang was hustled away and told not to come back or their ass was grass. **1976** Price *Bloodbrothers* 174: I guarantee you, the next time you need a fuckin' cop in here your ass is cream cheese. **1978** W. Brown *Tragic Magic* 154: "Is his ass grass?" "Yeah." **1987** Waldron *Billionaire Boys* (NBC-TV): "If we arrest Joe Hunt without enough evidence to make it stick, Joe's out." "And our ass is grass."

¶ **(one's) ass is in the wind** (one) is exposed to difficulty or danger.—usu. considered vulgar.

1964 Rhodes *Chosen Few* 74 [ref. to 1950]: Looks like her ass is in the wind now.…What's Darly gonna do?

¶ **(one's) ass is mud** "(one's) name is mud"; (one) is in danger.—usu. considered vulgar.

[**1937** E. Anderson *Thieves Like Us* 51: If you're not foxy and don't see that shotgun laying there in the grass, your pratt is mud.] **1961** Gover *Misunderstanding* 42: I so scared my ass gonna be mud. **1961** McMurtry *Horseman* 25: If you drop that coffee your ass is mud. **1962** Tregaskis *Viet. Diary* 264: I was afraid I might hit some of the Arvin troops, and our ass'd be mud. **1976–79** Duncan & Moore *Green Side Out* 259: My ass is mud if I don't…report! *a***1993** Rishell *Black Platoon* 50: Or your ass is mud!

¶ **(one's) ass sucks buttermilk** [or **wind**], **1.** (one) is thoroughly confused or terrified; *(hence)* (one) is talking absolute nonsense.—used derisively.—usu. considered vulgar.

1920–54 Randolph *Bawdy Elements* 84: A loud-mouthed stranger…started telling people what to do. "His ass seems to be sucking wind," said one of our neighbors contemptuously. *ca***1954** in IUFA *Folk Speech*: "Your ass sucks buttermilk!" (i.e., you're crazy, you don't know what you're talking about.) **1961** Forbes *Goodbye* 168 [ref. to WWII]: Your ass is suckin' straight wind, brother! **1964** Howe *Valley of Fire* 102: Shock? Your ass sucks buttermilk in a Kansas windstorm! [**1967** Partridge *DSUE* (ed. 7) 1525: *Your ass-hole's sucking wind.* You don't know what you're talking about.…common in [Canadian] Army of 1939–45.] **1969** N.Y.C. editor, age 40: Your ass is suckin' wind! **1970** N.Y.C. Vietnam veteran, age 23: That ambush—everybody's ass was sucking wind. **1976** Selby *Demon* 14: Aaaahhhh bullshit.…Your ass sucks wind. **1988** Dye *Outrage* 107: Made it!…My ass was sucking buttermilk out there.

2. (a violent threat of imprecise meaning).—usu. constr. in future.—usu. considered vulgar.

1964 Rhodes *Chosen Few* 65 [ref. to 1950]: We don't tolerate no fuckoffs here. Your ass will suck wind before this day is over. *Ibid.* 204: Sergeant Moreau's ass is gonna suck wind payday. **1967** *Playboy* (July) 170: Your ass'll be suckin' wind. **1987** Kubrick et al. *Full Metal Jacket* (film): I will PT you till your ass is sucking buttermilk!

¶ **on (one's) ass** in financial or other ruin; "on (one's) beam ends," helpless.—usu. considered vulgar.

*****ca***1917** in O'Canainn *Songs of Cork* 61: He puts us in the family way/ And leaves us on our ass. **1928** in J. O'Hara *Sel. Letters* 37: If it hadn't been for The New Yorker I'd be on my ass good and proper. **1935** in Hemingway *Sel. Letters* 413: He is on his ass in Havana. **1946** Steinbeck *Wayward Bus* 97: In less than a week he'd be out on his ass. **1952** Kerouac *Cody* 177: He's completely broke and on his ass. **1961** J.A. Williams *Night Song* 15: Look, man. You're on your ass. What, you too proud to work for me? **1974** E. Thompson *Tattoo* 410: The company was really on its ass. **1979** Crews *Blood & Grits* 72: I started yelling and screaming that you just didn't tattoo somebody when he was out on his ass [i.e., unconscious]. **1985** Boyne & Thompson *Wild Blue* 267: We're in real trouble. This place is on its ass. *a***1989** in Kisseloff *Must Remember This* 304: Times really got tough for her in the '30's. She was really on the balls of her ass then.

¶ **on (someone's) ass** harassing, vexing, scolding, pursuing (someone).—usu. considered vulgar.

1948 Shulman *Cry Tough!* 128: Those lousy contractors can't do anything right and I gotta be on their ass all the time. **1950** Stuart *Objector* 19 [ref. to WWII]: They're on your ass, aren't they? **1955** Goethals *Chains* 143 [ref. to WWII]: Shane's gonna have the whole goddam German Army on his ass the way he's running around out there. **1957** Herber *Tomorrow* 12 [ref. to WWII]: Do something else, and I'll be on your ass like a short raincoat. **1963** J.A. Williams *Sissie* 28: He was on my ass like white on rice. **1967** Welles *Babyhip* 13: They were always on her ass, always beseeching her to do this or that boring, hopeless, stupid thing like visit her grandmother, or go to classes. **1987** Slogan on T-shirt (N.Y.C.): Bosses are like diapers—on your ass all day long. **1991** D. Anderson *In Corner* 89: If Leon stays on Ali's ass, Leon can win this fight.

¶ **out of (one's) ass** crazy, "out of (one's) mind."—usu. considered vulgar.

1970 Zindel *Never Loved Your Mind* 92: And when I told him I wanted earphones for my last birthday, he said, "You're out of your ass." **1973** R. Roth *Sand in Wind* 81: The Private's out of his ass. **1978** R. Price *Ladies' Man* 186: He wouldn't have known I was talking out of my ass.

¶ **out the ass,** *a.* in excessive quantity; to an excessive degree; blatantly; *(also)* no good, reprehensible.—usu. considered vulgar.

1969 Rabe *Hummel* 26: You [are] lyin' outa your ass. **1972** Haldeman *War Year* 42: Nah. We got clerks out the ass in this company. **1975** Larsen *Runner* 289: Jesus, we got stew coming out the ass. **1976** Univ.

Tenn. student, age 23: She was crazy out the ass. **1976** Univ. Tenn. student, age 22: That stuff is really out the ass. **1979** *Easyriders* (Dec.) 6: They know you're paying out your ass for insurance.

b. emphatically well; to a great degree.—usu. considered vulgar.

1971 Nashville, Tenn., racecar driver: That guy can drive out the ass. **1979** Ark. State Univ. student: Write? I can write. I can write out the ass! **1987** Zeybel *Gunship* 112 [ref. to Vietnam War]: Cost-effective out the ass! **1988** *Lame Monkey* (Univ. Tenn.) (Mar. 21) 8: He sucks out the ass! Can't teach worth a shit!

¶ **pain in the ass** see s.v. PAIN.

¶ **piece of ass** see **(3.b., c.)**, above.

¶ **piece of (someone's) ass** vengeance against (someone), esp. in the form of a brutal beating.—usu. considered vulgar.

1959 "D. Stagg" *Glory Jumpers* 20 [ref. to WWII]: When you come for a piece of my ass, you won't be getting no virgin. **1966** Fariña *Down So Long* 206: I don't like people getting too close. Especially maniacs who want a piece of my ass for something. **1978** Truscott *Dress Gray* 138: God dammit, Terry, I want a piece of Grimshaw's ass! That stupid son of a bitch!

¶ **pull (something) out of (one's) ass** to invent or produce (something) seemingly from nowhere; to succeed narrowly.—usu. considered vulgar.

1974 Univ. Wisc. student, age 23: Tennessee just pulled it [a football game] out of their ass. **1978** Truscott *Dress Gray* 332: They pulled names out of their asses and threw them around trying to describe the undescribable. **1979** Hiler *Monkey Mt.* 230: Two weeks restriction, for leaving the barracks when I was supposed to be on bed rest....Shit, he just pulled that outta his ass.

¶ **scratch a beggar's ass** to be impoverished.—usu. considered vulgar.

1767 "A. Barton" *Disappointment* 79: He'd soon make my owners scratch a beggar's arse.

¶ **shake (one's) ass** to hurry up, stir, "shake a leg."—usu. considered vulgar.

1927 *Immortalia* 10: He didn't wake/His ass to shake/But slept on as he oughter. **1950** Stuart *Objector* 263: How about shaking your ass? **1953** Paley *Rumble* 106: C'mon, shake your ass. We got a date. **1964** Abrahams *Jungle* 235: Go on, son, shake ass, son, shake ass. **1971** Faust *Willy* 107: Proving once and for all that he could do the job if he would only shake his ass.

¶ **shut your ass!** shut up!—usu. considered vulgar.

1951 W. Williams *Enemy* 214 [ref. to WWII]: Oh, shut your ass and give me the dope. **1962** Killens *Thunder* 379 [ref. to WWII]: Shut your fat ass, you dirty-mouth peckerwood mother-fucker! **1966–67** Stevens *Gunner* 75 [ref. to WWII]: You can shut your ass, Vic. **1967** Michaels *Berets* 103: Shut up!...Shut your ass. **1970** Quammen *Walk the Line* 143: Just shut your ass up and hear it! **1971–72** Giovannitti *Medal* 33: Shut your ass. **1977** Torres *Q & A* 54: "Shut yo' ass!" Texidor hissed.

¶ **stack asses** to thrash opponents, as in a brawl; to employ violence.—usu. considered vulgar.

1972 Jenkins *Semi-Tough* 252: Let the other side know you've come to stack asses.

¶ **stick** [or **shove**, etc.] **it up (someone's) ass** to brutally manhandle, victimize, or betray (someone).—usu. considered vulgar.

1971 Horan *Blue Messiah* 184: Servin' under Blackjack on the Border, chasin' Villa and his goddamn greasers, then shovin' it up the Kaiser's ass. **1966–80** McAleer & Dickson *Unit Pride* 176: Don't let us catch you again. Or we'll really tuck it up your ass. *Ibid.* 365: Miller really tried to stick it up your ass but good. **1986** R. Campbell *In La-La Land* 53: I learn that the world ignores you when it ain't stickin' it up your ass.

¶ **stick** [or **shove**, etc.] **it up** [or **in**] **your ass** [or **asshole**] (used as a derisive retort).—usu. considered vulgar.

[**1813** in *N.Y. Hist. Soc. Proc.* XXIV 160: Lieut. Wise said to the prisoner his bayonet was now of no service, to which Jackson replied he would stick it in their arse.] **1864** in Wiley *Billy Yank* 201: Shove it up your arse. **1884** in Miller & Snell *West Was Wild* 613: I'll take the pistol from you and shove it up —. **1888** *Stag Party* (unp.): I told 'em to stick it in their arse. **1926** in Fitzgerald *Corres.* 194: He can stick it up his ass for all I give a Gd Dm for his "criticism." **1927** [Fliesler] *Anecdota* 85: Take this steak back to the chef and tell him to stick it up his arse. **1929** in Hemingway *Poems* 28: If you do not like them.../Stick them up your

—. **1936** J.T. Farrell *World I Never Made* 255: She would tell him to stick his tainted money up his ass-hole! **1939** Trumbo *Johnny* 44: Another guy said to just walk in politely and tell Jody Simmons to shove the job up his ass. **1964** Kesey *Great Notion* 191: You can take the...whole business and shove it up your ass. **1964** *AS* XXXIX 117: Cram...it up your ass. **1973** Karlin, Paquet & Rottman *Free Fire Zone* 29: Hart can run it up his ass. **1983** Wouk *Winds of War* (ABC-TV): You can tell Reichsmarschal Goering to take his Swiss bank accounts and stick them up his fat ass.

¶ **suck my ass** see *kiss my ass*, above.

¶ **suck (someone's) ass** see *kiss (someone's) ass*, above.

¶ **take it in the ass** to be brutally manhandled, victimized, or betrayed.—usu. considered vulgar. See also 1934 quot. at **(1. a.)**, above.

1980 J. Webb *Sense of Honor* 47: The Woops...were taking it in the ass just as bad, poor bastards.

¶ **talk like a man with a paper ass** [or **asshole**] to talk nonsense.—usu. considered vulgar.

1953 *ATS* (ed. 2) 165: *Talk Nonsense*...Talk like a man with a paper ass-hole. **1955** E. Hunter *Jungle Kids* 110: You're talking like a man with a paper.... **1957** Atwell *Private* 125 [ref. to WWII]: Listen to him; he talks like a man with a paper ass. **1958** Camerer *Wear Wings* 96 [ref. to WWII]: Don't talk like a man with a cardboard ass. **1961** Peacock *Valhalla* 26: You're talking like a man with a paper ass-hole. **1980** Folb *Runnin' Lines* 246.

¶ **tear (one's) ass** [or **asshole**] to injure (oneself); get into trouble; be overwhelmed and defeated; **tear (someone's) ass** to trounce, punish, kill (someone).—usu. considered vulgar. Cf. *tear (someone) a new asshole* s.v. ASSHOLE, *n.*, 6.

*****1750** *Exmoor Scolding* 15: Why, thare's Odds betwe' Sh—ng and Tearing Won's Yess. [**1900** *DN* II 67: Tore, adj. Worsted; defeated.] [**1932** Lorimer *Streetcars* 166: I'll say you sure tore your pants with this town....What do you think you are?] **1961** C. Cooper *Weed* 66: You're gonna get your asshole tore right out, treatin' me like this. **1961** Killens *Thunder* 61 [ref. to WWII]: You didn't let me go back into that cracker town and tear my royal ass again. **1964** Rhodes *Chosen Few* 129 [ref. to *ca*1950]: All right, providing mine don' tear their asses either. **1966** Braly *On Yard* 136: If you got your ass torn up every time you shot craps, after a while you'd put craps down. *Ibid.* 229: I think you tore your ass this time. **1970** Cain *Blueschild* 125: You done really tore your ass. **1979** Crews *Blood & Grits* 117: Some of his pictures have just torn my ass with boredom.

¶ **tear (someone) a new ass** to ruin or destroy (someone).—usu. considered vulgar.

1973 Layne *Murphy* (unp.): He'll Tear You A New Ass. **1991** *Current Affair* (synd. TV series): You can't come in here to the Cleveland area [to interview me] and think you're goin' to tear me a new ass.

¶ **think the sun sets** [or **shines**] **in ([some]one's) ass** to worship stupidly (someone or oneself); idolize (someone) in a self-degrading manner.—usu. considered vulgar.

[**1914** in Cray *Erotic Muse* 193: The sun could set in the crack of my ass/and never singe a hair.] [**1935** J. Conroy *World to Win* 340: You must think the sun rises and sets in his hind end.] [**1946** Nason *Mercury* 19: You'd think the sun set in the crack of the Second Armored's neck, to hear him talk about it.] *****1966** G.M. Williams *Camp* 85: You'd think the krauts got the sun shining out of their...arses. **1969** Gordone *No Place* 429: I worshiped the groun' you walked on. I thought the sun rose an' set in yo' ass. *****1979** *Monty Python's Life of Brian* (film): They must think the sun shines out of your arse! **1980** *Oui* (Aug.) 71: O'Rourke is a better man....The sun shines out of his asshole. **1987** E. Spencer *Macho Man* 4: I was one of those kids who thought that the sun shone out of his ass.

¶ **up (someone's) ass** immediately behind; (*hence*) hounding, annoying, or bothering (someone).—usu. considered vulgar.

1971–72 Giovannitti *Medal* 18: Corporal Thomas, with a pack bigger than mine and the weight of the field radio to boot, stayed right up the sergeant's ass. **1974** *Nat. Lampoon* (Aug.) 76: Haig's really up my ass for a statement. **1975** Betuel *Dogfighter* 30: What's up your ass anyway? **1989** L. Roberts *Full Cleveland* 49: It's bad enough having your man up my ass all day.

¶ **up the ass** in excess; in great number or amount.—usu. considered vulgar.

[**1951** [VMF-323] *Old Ballads* 20: Now we don't mind the hardships, we've faced 'em in the past/But we wonder if our congressmen have had

40's [i.e., antiaircraft guns] up the ass.] **1963** Rechy *City* 138: Then he shows me this collection he's got—all kinda weird costumes. An boots!—boots an costumes up the ass. **1968** *Rolling Stone Interviews* 52: I could play almost every song, man, I know country music up the ass on the guitar. **1969** Sidney *Love of Dying* 53: There ain't no beer in Korea for enlisted men. Only ice cream. Ice cream up the ass. **1972** Bunker *Beast* 46: Got book learnin' up the ass, but doesn't know a fuckin' thing about life or people. **1980** Manchester *Darkness* 23 [ref. to WWII]: Wounded Marines had had macho acts, in a phrase of the day, up their asses to their armpits. **1985** M. Baker *Cops* 119: There's one hundred FBI agents, two hundred uniform troopers there when I walk in. Law enforcement up the ass.

¶ **up to the ass** [or **asshole**] overwhelmed (by), surrounded (by), in the midst (of), surfeited (with), "up to (one's) neck."—usu. considered vulgar.

1864 in Patrick *Reluctant Rebel* 234: Where was General Jackson at the battle of Waterloo? Up to his — in blood and hair and — God almighty damn. [**1893** Hampton *Maj. in Washington* 36: Mr. Smith was like a grave-digger, up to his hips in business.] *a**1903** *F & H* (rev.) 67: *Up to the arse* = deeply engaged. **1921** H.L. Mencken, in Riggio *Dreiser-Mencken Letters* II 426: I am up to my arse in the revision of "The American Language." **1970** Longstreet *Kimball* 79: Come fifty years and the country would be up to its ass in darkies. **1980** L.N. Smith *Venus Belt* 13: Denver's up to its asshole in [snow]. **1980** Univ. Tenn. student, age 22: I'm already up to my ass in work. **1983** S. Wright *Meditations* 154: Up to our asshole in impedimenta.

¶ **your ass!** *my ass*, above.

[**1928** Fisher *Jericho* 33: "Start out as my agent." "Agent yo' hiney."] [**1928** McKay *Banjo* 221: "Boody Lane."…"Boody Lane in your seat."] [**1936** *Our Army* (Apr.) 26: Seventy-fives, your foot!] **1944–48** A. Lyon *Unknown Station* 257: "I thought the shower was a favor." "Favor your ass! It's an order." **1952** Mandel *Strangers* 47: "But don't—" "*Don't*, your hairy ass!" **1962** Killens *Thunder* 263 [ref. to WWII]: Salty sea, your ass. **1966** Little *Bold & Lonely* 75: Easy? Your ass! I've had it rough, boy. I mean rough. **1970** Ponicsan *Last Detail* 151: With two dollars in change? Your aunt's ass. **1971** Flanagan *Maggot* 9: Your old lady's ass it is! Didn't your drill instructor just tell you your name is shit?

¶ (In provs. and phrs. of infreq. occurrence, explained in context. In vulgar speech the word *ass* may be substituted freely for other parts of the body alluded to in provs. or idioms. For additional phrs., see above, under the most important word of the phr. The inventory of expressions cited below should be regarded as representative rather than exhaustive.).—all usu. considered vulgar.

*1722** [T. Sheridan] *Wonderful Wonder* 20: This relates to the Proverb, You rose with your A—se foremost, you are so lucky to-day. *Ibid.* 21: Another—*You have Wrinkle in your A—se more than you had before.* [*a**1893** *F & H* III 70: To take French leave…English Synonyms: To retire up (one's) fundament.] **1916–22** Cary *Sex. Vocab.* I: *Ass like the back of a hack*—Broad bottomed. *No more ass than a soda cracker*—said of a woman with flat buttocks. **1928** in Read *Lex. Evidence* 46: Like a pole-cat's ass thou smellest bad. [**1936** in D. Runyon *More Guys* 161: Lou…cannot really find his hip pocket with both hands.] [**1936** Kingsley *Dead End* 685: Angel: Hey, Gimpty, got a match?…T.B. (*murmurs*): My pratt and your face. Dat's a good match!] *ca**1944** in Kaplan & Smith *One Last Look* 82: Colder than a polar bear's ass. **1945** Bowman *Beach Red* 39: With his face as red as a spanked baby's ass. [**1946** H.A. Smith *Rhubarb* 162: A bunch of crazy baseball players who couldn't find their behinds if their britches was on fire, that ain't won a pennant in seventeen years!] *a**1950** P. Wolff *Friend* 148: I think your brains are in your ass. **1951** Willingham *Gates of Hell* 86: A gub-gub bird is simply a bird that flies around and around in a circle so fast and so perpetually that eventually he flies up his own ass. **1956** I. Shulman *Good Deeds* 57: But you can thank your sweet ass, *paisan*, that you're not a Jew. **1956** Algren *Wild Side* 143: Talk to my ass…my head is hard. **1957** Herber *Tomorrow* 48: My ass bleeds for you, Petersen. [**1958** Gilbert *Vice Trap* 57: You'll be throwing that old thirty-two heat around, with your butt cutting plenty of washers [i.e., working feverishly].] **1958** Davis *Spearhead* 19: He couldn't find his ass with both hands. **1960** Hoagland *Circle Home* 206: "My ass bleeds," he said (in mock sympathy). **1960** Granat *Important Thing* 157: We were all expectin' to get our ass handed to us on a sling any minute now. **1961** Peacock *Valhalla* ch. iv: Floyd couldn't hit his ass with both hands in broad daylight. He was a lousy shot. **1961** Garrett *Which Ones?* 17: Well, keep your ass clean [i.e., stay out of trouble] and if you've got to loaf, loaf gracefully. **1962** W. Crawford *Tomorrow* 36: "Give my hat and ass for a hot bath." "Who wants 'em? Both got holes." **1962** Killens *Thunder* 73: When he came into the

Army he didn't have nothing but his hat and his ass. **1963** Boyle *Yanks* 85: That's your ass talking now, Sarge. Your head knows better. **1963–64** Kesey *Great Notion* 196: Next time I run across Hank Stamper I aim to kick his ass till his nose bleeds. **1964** Pearl *Stockade* 92: Watch yourself, boy, or you'll be cooling your ass [i.e., "cooling your heels"] on one of those iron cots in solitary. **1965** Conot *Rivers* 359: I'd a told that white motherfucker to fly up his own ass! **1966** "T. Pendleton" *Iron Orchard* 9: That Bruner'll have yo' ass workin' buttonholes [i.e., working feverishly] 'fore sundown t'morra. Run you off inside a week. **1966** Neugeboren *Big Man* 60: You be lucky you don't get your ass handed to you by some young sharpie. **1966** Brunner *Face of Night* 59: Five cops and the captain in on it…and you ain't satisfied. My ass bleeds for you. **1966** Cameron *Sgt. Slade* 35: Eisenhower's coming…sure as your ass, Ferris. **1969** Gordone *Somebody* 433: You jus' don't b'lieve a hard head makes a sof' ass. **1969** Jessup *Sailor* 449: I found her ass-high and balls-deep into a guy, and that ripped it. **1970** Ponicsan *Last Detail* 31: I just wanted to crawl up my own ass and disappear. **1970** Woods *Killing Zone* 22: "You people would all be a lot happier if you knew where you were." "Up your ass looking for papaya." **1972** Bunker *No Beast* 72: Better learn how to talk to people or you'll get your ass brought to you, Jack. **1972** Jenkins *Semi-Tough* 72: It can also get colder than a nun's ass. **1972** S. Peckinpah, in *Playboy* (Aug.) 66: She's a feisty little gal and I enjoy drinking with her…but here she's cracking walnuts in her ass [i.e., behaving stupidly]. **1974** Blount *3 Bricks Shy* 134: I remember when he couldn't hit his ass with both hands. **1974** Strasburger *Rounding Third* 5: Everyone smirks…for days afterwards, like someone's stuck a feather half way up their ass. **1974** R. Carter *16th Round* 56: Just come on down here and put your ass where your mouth is. **1975** Univ. Tenn. students: "Got a match?" "Your face and my ass." **1975** U.C.L.A. student: When I was a kid they'd say, "What time is it?" And you'd say, "Half past a monkey's ass. And a quarter to his balls." **1972–76** Durden *No Bugles* 41: Don' make no more sense'n whistlin' up a pig's ass. *Ibid.* 127: Who says you can't make a silk purse from a sow's ass? **1977** Schrader *Blue Collar* 108: He'll make us pay through the ass forever [i.e., "through the nose"]. **1978** E. Thompson *Devil to Pay* 330: Man, you know about religion the way my ass chews gum. **1979** N.C. man, age 28: "He was so scared his ass was cutting buttonholes." I've known that since I was a kid, fifteen or twenty years. **1982** R. Sutton *Don't Get Taken* 111: Car people say…"There's an ass for every seat." [i.e., any car can ultimately be sold.] **1982** Cox & Frazier *Buck* 1: Anybody got an extra can of C-rations? I could eat the ass out of a skunk. **1983** Beckwith & Fox *Delta Force* 58: I didn't sleep a damn wink. You couldn't have drilled a flax seed up my ass with a sledgehammer. I was scared. **1983** S. King *Christine* 48: And…they moved like their feet was on fire and their asses were catching. **1984** Bane *Willie* 209: We really have a lot of sayings in Abbott [Tex.] where I grew up, like "A hard head makes for a sore ass." **1990** *Nat. Lampoon* (Apr.) 106: He's talking through his ass!

ass *v.* ¶ In phrases:

¶ **ass around** [in BrE, orig. 'to behave like an ass [fool]'; but in U.S. always considered as an arbitrary application of ASS, *n.*, 1.a.] to fool about, act irresponsibly, trifle.—usu. considered vulgar. [1664 quot. prob. does not illustrate this sense.] [*1664** in *F & H* I (rev.) 69: Then (at his Ease) Arsing about.] *1914–21** Joyce *Ulysses* 312: Arsing around from one pub to another. **1942** *ATS* 262: Idle; Loaf; Loiter…*ass…around.* **1953** Paley *Rumble* 134: She goes assing around telling everybody my business. **1962** Killens *Thunder* 213: We don't have that much time to ass around. **1969** "Iceberg Slim" *Mama Black Widow* 223: Stop assing around, Jack. **1982** Goff, Sanders & Smith *Bros.* 64: You ass around too God damn much.

¶ **ass up** to botch, spoil (something).—usu. considered vulgar.

1932 *AS* VII 329: *Assed-up*—mixed up.

-ass or **-assed** *comb. form.* **1.** [fr. ASS, *n.*, 4.a.] (a derogatory intensive suffix used to form nouns). See BLANKET-ASS, DUMB-ASS, JERK-ASS, JIVE-ASS, SHIT-ASS, SMART-ASS, and WISE-ASS.—usu. considered vulgar. [Chiefly restricted to above items; not used as freely as adj.]

2.a. [orig. -*assed*, prob. generalized from lit. or quasi-lit. collocations] (a derogatory intensive suffix freely affixed in vulgar speech to form adjs. from adjs. and attrib. nouns). See also BIG-ASS.—usu. considered vulgar.

[*a**1903** *F & H* I (rev.) 66: *Hardarsed* = niggardly.] **1919–20** in R. Cochran *V. Randolph* 61: [I lost my temper when] a silly ass barber shaved my neck. *1922** in Lawrence *Mint* 127: Look at me, look me in the face, you short-arsed little fuck-pig. **1923** *Poems, Ballads, & Parodies* 19: When along came one of those city chaps,/One of those oily-assed fiends. **1929** in Longstreet *Falcons* 269 [ref. to WWI]: The people…spoke a strange tongue that was nearly related to what we had been taught. "Lousy broad-ass a's," said John. **1930** Farrell *Calico* 274: She's a fat-ass cousin of mine. **1934** Appel *Brain Guy* 43: Betting his life on…a dumb-ass crack. *ca***1944** in Valant *Aircraft Nose Art* 295: Wild Ass Ride. **1944** Caldwell *Tragic Ground* 88: She gets to look worse every day. I reckon it's my own fault, though, because she was scrawny-assed before I married her. **1949** Algren *Golden Arm*: I spent thirty-four months havin' green-ass corporals chew me up. **1951** D.P. Wilson *6 Convicts* 46: Last time I filled in some papers a smart-ass D.A. tries to have me shipped back to Italy. **1953** W. Fisher *Waiters* 31: Poor-ass Southern crackers. *Ibid.* 74: Just another broke-ass waiter. **1956** Chamales *So Few* 235: Something to brag to your snobby-ass society friends about. *Ibid.* 430: The dirty sneaky-ass little shit. **1956** Gold *With It* 257: Well then you're nothing but another dumb-ass mark. **1956** Holiday & Dufty *Lady Sings Blues* 61: So I had to be darkened down so the show could go on in dynamic-assed Detroit. **1959** Farris *Harrison High* 174: Now, they got a rough-ass line. **1961** McMurtry *Horseman* 10: The wildest of the thousand wild-ass cowboys in the Texas cattle country. **1962** Schultz *Custom* 191: Mrs. Prissy-assed bitch. **1962** Leckie *Strong Men* 188: Sharp-assed stones. **1964** Rhodes *Chosen Few* 14: Crazy-ass guys. **1965** Bryan *Wilkinson* 380: Because it looks good on some silly-assed record. **1965** W. Crawford *Bronc Rider* 110: Get some air in this sad-assed place. **1967** Dubus *Lieut.* 146: We'll first off get roaring-ass drunk. **1967** Brelis *S. Vietnam* 57: He had some kind of whoreass powder or talcum like lilacs and he stank of that. **1968** Tauber *Sunshine Soldiers* 68: You've got to let him know that you're a mad-assed motherfucker. **1969** C. Brown *Mr. Jiveass* 25: He was the laziest ass dog in the county. **1969** Lynch *Soldier* 289: Man, I'm not some green ass replacement. *Ibid.* 29: You climbed the barbed wire fence and you got you some wild ass gook pussy. **1969** Gardner *Fat City* 132: You rotten-assed bastard! **1969** Pharr *Numbers* 245: That stupid-assed judge was on the level. **1970** *N.Y. Post* (May 9) 2: And America wasn't made to have these pansy-assed creeps running around wild. **1971** Wells & Dance *Night People* 107: He'll be here soon telling some of his sad-ass jokes. **1971** Simon *Sign of Fool* 84: Cold, hungry and dog-ass tired. **1974** *College English* (Sept.) 109: Above the giant-ass auditorium…here comes a monkey. **1975** Univ. Kans. student: He was such a piss-ass poor teacher, nobody could follow him. **1978** Truscott *Dress Gray* 110: It was a sorry-ass state of affairs. **1980** Univ. Tenn. student: He wrote on some weird-ass topic.

b. (used as (**2.a.**), above, but used to form adverbs).—usu. considered vulgar. [This usage appears to be much less common.]
1947–53 Guthrie *Seeds* 4: Eddie jest tears cold-ass away from every one we've set in his track. **1969** Gardner *Fat City* 119: I'll flat-ass leave her. **1971** Simon *Sign of Fool* 84: We were too cold, hungry, and dog-ass tired to say anything. **1976** Hayden *Voyage* 230: It was flat-ass ca'm. **1982** Del Vecchio *13th Valley* 255: He best ass gonna abide by the consequences. **1987** E. Spencer *Macho Man* 104: We have just got to get out of this hostile motherfucker right-ass now! *a***1991** J.R. Wilson *Landing Zones* 197: That 106 round hit dead ass on top of the gooks.

3. [poss. by inexact analogy with HAUL ASS; also cf. BARREL-ASS, CUT ASS, DRAG ASS, SHAG-ASS, TEAR-ASS] (used as a quasi-obj. suffix after usu. intrans. verbs implying exertion or rapid movement; also as infix).—usu. considered vulgar.
1942 *ATS* 55: *Tear-ass around*, to hasten or rush around. *Ibid.* 56: *Run…tear-ass along.* **1951** W. Williams *Enemy* 124 [ref. to WWII]: You'd think they'd get tired up there.…Whistling ass in circles just looking at water, all cramped up in that little cockpit four hours at a time. **1960** MacCuish *Do Not Go Gentle* 140 [ref. to WWII]: Hop ass on to that thing with pogo sticks. **1961** Gover *Misunderstanding* 36: Madam gonna send for the firetruck we don' git ass back downstairs. **1963** in H. Ellison *Sex Misspelled* 52: He went sprawl-assing out of the car. **1965** Hersey *Too Far* 183: Up, up, heave ass, you phonies. **1966** Garfield *Last Bridge* 43: Quit jaw-assing over this telephone. **1966–69** Woiwode *Going to Do* 72: You mean you were cattin-ass around New York. **1969** Eastlake *Bamboo Bed* 56: You can get full power and bounce ass off. *Ibid.* 157: Let's fly ass out of here. *Ibid.* 224: I'd like to clear ass out of this exposed fucker. **1970** Thackray *Thief* 215: I…barreled ass down the road. **1970** Quammen *Walk Line* 53: And then when the honkey fuzz moves in to bust it up, get ass out of there just soon enough. **1974** E. Thompson *Tattoo* 486: Get-ass-out-of-there! **1976** Calloway & Rollins *Moocher & Me* 154 [ref. to 1930's]: Andy, if you don't have an arrangement of "St. Louis Blues" by tomorrow morning, you can pack

ass. **1984–88** Hackworth & Sherman *About Face* 50: We were able to scoot ass with no friendly casualties. *a***1988** D. Smith *Firefighters* 141: He doesn't want the other guy to turn ass and run.

ass-and-trash *n.* [cf. ASH-AND-TRASH] *Mil. Av.* personnel and equipment flown by military aircraft.—usu. considered vulgar. [All quots. ref. to Vietnam War.]
1983 R.C. Mason *Chickenhawk* 144: Fly ass-and-trash (people and equipment) around the division. *Ibid.* 146: An ass-and-trash mission along Route 19. **1990** G.R. Clark *Words of Vietnam War* 37: *Ass-and-Trash Runs*…Pilot slang for routine helicopter missions, such as ferrying supplies, passengers [etc.]. **1991** Mains *Dear Mom* 249: *Ass-and-Trash Mission* The carrying of men and equipment.

ass-backwards *adv. & adj.* backwards-front; mixed up; confused. Also **ass-backward**.—usu. considered vulgar.
[****1896** in *EDD*: That's an assurd-backuds form o' diggin' taters.] **1942** McAtee *Supp. to Grant Co. Dial.* 2 [ref. to 1890's]: *Ass-backwards*, adv.…backwards. **1947–52** R. Ellison *Invisible Man* 137: We're an ass-backward people. **1956** Chamales *So Few* 498: Down here everything is ass backwards. **1957** Gutwillig *Long Silence* 185: I think you're going at this ass-backwards. **1958** Cooley *Run for Home* 121: He's probably give it to you all ass-backward. **1960** Sire *Deathmakers* 194: He spends the rest of his life running around ass-backwards. **1968** Myrer *Eagle* 393: Of all the zany, ass-backward strategies. **1968** Huss & Silverstein *Film* 130: Hardy initiates a sight gag…to indicate that rich people like everything "ass backwards." **1970** N.Y.U. geology prof., age *ca*36: But when they got to the surface of the moon, it was all ass backwards. **1977** Univ. Tenn. history prof., age 30: Verdun was a strange, ass-backwards plan that didn't work.

ass bandit *n.* **1.** an eager seducer of young women.—usu. considered vulgar.
1954 Ellson *Owen Harding* 158: Owen Harding…the old reliable ass bandit. **1970** Grissim *Country Music* 268: Most of the great country entertainers who have thrilled millions have been notorious ass bandits.
2. an aggressive homosexual anal sodomist.—usu. considered vulgar.
****1961** Partridge *DSUE* (ed. 5) 983: *Arse bandit*…A notorious sodomite. ****1966** G.M. Williams *Camp* 126: A lot of poncey old arse-bandits. **1979** in *Maledicta* III 231: *Ass-bandit* has a limited circulation [in the sense "anal sodomist"]. **1981–85** S. King *It* 20: I ought to make you *eat* that hat, you fucking ass-bandit!

ass-belly *n.* a grossly fat person.—usu. considered vulgar.
1972 DeLillo *End Zone* 117: That ass-belly sixty-two got his fist in.

ass bite *n.* a worthless, despised individual, ASSHOLE.—usu. considered vulgar.
1973 *Zap Comix* no. 6 (unp.): Ass Bite Mother Fucker.

ass-bite *v.* to harass (an employee or the like).—usu. considered vulgar.
1976 *N.Y. Folklore* II 231: The good officer "brown-noses" his superiors and "ass-bites" those beneath his rank.

ass-blow *v.* [ASS, *n.*, 1.a. + BLOW 'to fellate'] to engage in active oral stimulation of the anus. Also as *n.*—usu. considered vulgar.
1941 Legman *Lang. of Homosex.* 1157: *Ass-blow* To anilingue; usually used as a past participle, e.g. *to get ass-blowed.* **1971** Rodgers *Queens' Vernacular* 172: To lick or suck anus…*ass-blow.* **1972** R.A. Wilson *Forbidden Words*: *Ass Blow*, Anilingus.

assbone *n.* ["coccyx" may be the orig. meaning] the rump.—usu. considered vulgar.
1972 Pearce *Pier Head* 32: Before some other idiot breaks his goddamn ass bone. **1972** Kaufman *Northfield Raid* (film): Damn, my ass-bone's gone to sleep already.

ass-breaker *n.* BALL-BREAKER, 1, 2, & 3.—usu. considered vulgar.
1961 J. Jones *Thin Red Line* 38 [ref. to WWII]: Well, here's a real ass-breaker. I sure can collect them. **1962–63** in Giallombardo *Soc. of Women* 200: *Ass breaker.* A bitter disappointment; a slave-driver; a strict disciplinarian.

ass-bucket *n.* a contemptible or inconsequential fellow.—usu. considered vulgar.
1953 W. Fisher *Waiters* 218: Who the hell is this jerk? Just another ass-bucket. **1954** Killens *Youngblood* 108: Donchall ass-buckets know Mr. Charlie ain't gon stand for no millionaire Negroes?

ass burglar *n.* ASS BANDIT, 2.—usu. considered vulgar.

    1979 in *Maledicta* III 231: *Ass burglar* or *ass bandit* [as synonyms for "pederast"].

ass-buster *n.* a remarkable fellow.—usu. considered vulgar.

    1973 Ace *Stand on It* 93: Cousin Ned was right. Yer going to grow up to be a real ass-buster.

ass-busting *adj.* exhausting.—usu. considered vulgar.

    1973 Roth *Sand in Wind* 42: And we had these ass-busting working parties *every fucking day.* **1979** Hurling *Boomers* 31: A day of heads-down, ass-busting work.

ass-chewing *n.* [fr. phr. *chew (someone's) ass;* see s.v. CHEW] *Mil.* a harsh, prolonged scolding and reprimand, as from a superior officer.—usu. considered vulgar.

    1954 F.I. Gwaltney *Heaven & Hell* 232 [ref. to WWII]: Grimes…gave the new frigup an ass-chewing. **1963–64** Kesey *Great Notion* 179: I can hear myself sounding just exactly like old Henry doing some first-rate ass-chewing. **1965** MacMahon *Post-Bellum* 61 [ref. to WWII]: I'll be damned if I'm gonna take an ass-chewing every morning. **1966** J. Lewis *Marines* 159: Half expecting the ass-chewing he knew he rated. **1967** *Playboy* (Sept.) 224: This was no ordinary ass-chewing session. **1969** Crumley *Cadence* 231: He expected push-ups and an ass-chewing. **1972** West *Village* 205: Don't let Dang's ass-chewing get to you. **1973** Herbert & Wooten *Soldier* 149: I'll take the gig and the ass-chewing. **1986** R. Walker *AF Wives* 123: Was he in for one of the general's notorious ass chewings? **1986–91** Hamper *Rivethead* 193: A major ass-chewing was in order.

ass-deep *adj. & adv.* **1.** of a depth sufficient to reach one's rump.—usu. considered vulgar.

    1950 in Leckie *March to Glory* 29: The snow is ass-deep to a man in a jeep. **1974** Widener *N.U.K.E.E.* 153: Drake was now floundering around the Alaskan wilderness in snow ass-deep to a tall moose. **1982** Cox & Frazier *Buck* 64: Let the snow fall. Let it get ass-deep to an elephant.

    2. deeply involved with; having a superabundance of.—constr. with *in.*—usu. considered vulgar.

    1958 Gilbert *Vice Trap* 75: She used to be ass deep in codeine and bennies. **1961** Coon *Meanwhile* 34 [ref. to Korean War]: I'm going to be ass-deep in rolling heads before I'm through…by God! **1972** Jenkins *Semi-Tough* 236: Old Billy Clyde…is gonna get himself ass-deep in…Scotch. **1973** Herbert & Wooten *Soldier* 346: Even if I'd been ass-deep in scopes. **1981** R.B. Parker *Savage Pl.* 54: I'm ass-deep in file memos from Mary Jane.

ass-eating *n.* [fr. phr. *eat (someone's) ass out;* see s.v. EAT OUT] *Mil.* ASS-CHEWING.—usu. considered vulgar.

    1949 J. Jones, in *Harper's* (June) 96 [ref. to WWII]: There may be some bad effects. I may even get an ass-eating. **1949–51** J. Jones *Eternity* 38 [ref. to 1941]: "The Warden" and "Dynamite" is just givin' Willard a ass eatin, thats all. **1953** Bissell *Pajama* 141: You come up here to give *me* an ass-eatin because Mr. O'Hara gave *you* an ass-eatin. **1966** "T. Pendleton" *Iron Orchard* 38: Cap Bruner would make no mention of the error other than giving Picketts a private "ass-eating."

-assed see -ASS.

ass-end *n.* **1.** tail end, rear.—usu. considered vulgar.

    1930 J.T. Farrell *Calico* 295: You're old and fat, and your can looks like the ass-end of a motor truck. **1933** Stewart *Speech of Airman* 45: *Ass End.* The rear portion of a plane. **1952** Uris *Battle Cry* 42: You should be at the ass end of the line, like I am. **1953–57** Giovannitti *Combine D* 127: Here comes the ass end. **1958** Frankel *Band of Bros.* 179: I'm so hungry I could eat the ass-end out of a skunk. **1966** S. Stevens *Go Down Dead* 30: I…dive for ass end of car park by corner.

    2. the least desirable portion or share; bad treatment.—usu. considered vulgar.

    1945 in Shibutani *Co. K* 133: You always get the ass-end of the deal. **1944–46** in *AS* XXII 54: *Ass-End.* A raw deal, the worst part of anything. **1957** Brown *Locust Fire* 100: We catch the ass end of every deal.

    3. the most remote or hateful place or position.—usu. considered vulgar.

    1960 MacCuish *Do Not Go Gentle* 265 [ref. to WWII]: In plenty of ways Ajo is the ass end of the world. **1963** Coon *Short End* 13: It's the infantry….The ass end of the infantry at that. **1964** Newhafer *Tallyho* 93: We have to fight this war from the ass end. **1969** Hamill *Doc* 43: This is the ass end of the West, Doc, it ain't even got a name. **1971** Horan *Blue Messiah* 234: I spent a lot of weary months up in the ass end of the Bronx because of you two guys. **1972–76** Durden *No Bugles* 190: This

is the ass-end of creation.

    4. (in various phrs. adequately explained in quots.). Cf. A.E.F.—usu. considered vulgar.

    1942 McAtee *Supp. to Grant Co. Dial.* 2 [ref. to 1890's]: *Ass end foremost,* adv. phr., backwards….*Ass end to,* adv. phr., with the breech advanced; backwards. **1963** Parks *Learning Tree* 162: Them two [boys] are the ass-ends of nothing. **1973** Ace *Stand on It* 2: Go into the goddam turn frontwards instead of ass-end-to.

Ass-End Charlie *n. Mil. Av.* the trailing aircraft in a formation; the last individual in a line.—usu. considered vulgar. Also quasi-adv. [All quots. ref. to WWII.]

    *1942 in *OEDS: Arse-end Charlie.* **1943** in M.W. Bowman *Castles* 75: *Ascend* [sic] *Charlie* [B-17 of 88th Bomb Group, USAAF]. **1944** Liebling *Back to Paris* 246: In this gang, we have no ass-end Charlies. **1948** Cozzens *Guard of Honor* 522: Watch the low flight, left! Ass-end Charlie's gone to sleep. **1947** Wolfert *Act of Love* 434: There has to be two flying wing on each other and an Ass-End Charlie. **1961** Plantz *Sweeney* 202: Put me in another flight. I'll fly ass-end Charlie. **1964** Newhafer *Tallyho* 140: Winston has the second section and Stepik flies ass-end Charlie.

Ass-End First see A.E.F.

ass-fuck *n.* **1.** an act of anal copulation.—usu. considered vulgar.

    1940 Del Torto: Make date for assfuck. **1941** G. Legman, in Henry *Sex Variants* II 1157: *Ass-fuck*…An act of pedication. **1974** "L. Lovelace" *Diary* 66: He gave me the best ass-fuck I've ever had.

    2. an instance of cruel victimization.—usu. considered vulgar.

    1977 Schrader *Blue Collar* 14: No way he was gonna take this ass-fuck forever.

ass-fuck *v.* to engage in active or passive anal copulation (with).—usu. considered vulgar.

    1940 Del Torto: Want to be assfucked. **1941** G. Legman, in Henry *Sex Variants* II 1157: *Ass-fuck*…To pedicate. **1971** Rader *Govt. Inspected* 105: Get ass-fucked like a bender by a butching lover. **1974–77** Heinemann *Close Quarters* 184: She would…ass-fuck. **1984** Ehrhart *Marking Time* 66: Pam, that old boyfriend of yours—you…even ass-fuck the guy! **1992** Madonna *Sex* (unp.): That's what ass-fucking is all about. It's the most pleasurable way to get fucked.

ass-grabbing *adj.* annoying, vexatious.—usu. considered vulgar.

    1965 Bryan *Wilkinson* 82: You'll be finished, FINISHED! Don't you see? You'll never even get a cent of your precious ass-grabbing pension!

ass hammer *n.* [ref. to the effect of engine vibrations on the buttocks] a motorcycle.—usu. considered vulgar.

    1970–72 in *AS* 55: *Ass hammer n.* Motorcycle.

asshead *n.* [cf. BUTTHEAD] idiot.—usu. considered vulgar.

    1965 Lurie *Nowhere* 37: You know what I want, ass-head. **1967** Mailer *Vietnam* 208: So, ass-head America contemplate your butt.

asshole *n.* [ME *arce-hoole*] Also (*Rare* in U.S.) **arsehole.**—usu. considered vulgar. [See note at ASS, *n.,* which is usually considered to be less offensive. Additional phrases in which these words appear interchangeably may be found at ASS.]

    1. the anus or rectum.

    *a1500 in R. Yeager *15th C. Studies* 141: Ars hole. ***ca1558** in *F & H* I (rev.) 68: As white as midnight's arse-hole or virgin pitch. ***1680** in J. Thorpe *Rochester's Poems* 37: Till slimey Cunt, to grimey A-se hole turn. ***ca1703** in *F & H* I (rev.) 69: May…Fistulas thy arse-hole seize by Dozens. **1865** (quot. at (3.), below). **1888** *Stag Party* (unp.): And there's yer ass hole. **1889** Barrère & Leland *Dict. Slang* I 347: "No more *eyes* nor arseholes," said of a one-eyed man. [**1916** L. Stillwell *Common Soldier* 214 [ref. to Civil War]: He hasn't got sense enough…to doctor an old dominecker hen that is sick with a sore (anus) [sic].] **1916–22** Cary *Sex. Vocab.* III s.v. *human body:* The Anus…ass hole. **1924** E. Pound, in *Antaeus* (no. 21) (1976) 38: One of the worst fahrts nature ever let loose from her…arse-hole. **1938** Steinbeck *Grapes of Wrath* 226: Fat, sof' fella with little mean eyes an' a mouth like a ass-hole. **1952** in Randolph *Pissing* 23: The doctor fastened a big plaster over his ass-hole. **1969** Pharr *Numbers* 148: If you take one more step inta this room I am gonna kick your asshole through your teeth! **1987** D. Sherman *Main Force* 183: When I tell you to do something, I expect to hear your asshole pop, do you understand me?

    2.a. a foolish or despicable person.—usu. considered vulgar. [1784 quot. is uniquely early, but an alternative meaning of this ex. is unclear.]

*ca1784 in W. Blake *Complete Poetry & Prose* 451: If I have not presented you with every character in the piece call me Arse— **1933** in Randolph *Pissing* 106: It looks to me like the Almighty just throwed all them ass-holes together, and made the Easton family. **1941** in A. Hopkins *Front & Rear* 113: We're a bunch of bastards…assholes of the earth and the universe. **1945** in Shibutani *Co. K* 222: He's a combat man, and I'm just a…chairborne asshole. **1947** Mailer *Naked & Dead* 188: Lieutenant (SG) Dove, USNR. A Cornell man, a Deke, a perfect asshole. *a*1950 P. Wolff *Friend* 189: I was an asshole. **1950** Stuart *Objector* 21: This country will go far with ass holes like you. *Ibid.* 263: So I shot him with his own gun, the stupid ass hole. **1952** Uris *Battle Cry* 141: How do you like that Bryce, what an asshole. **1954** Ellson *Owen Harding* 102: You stupid ass-hole. **1961** Sullivan *Shortest Years* 179: So whaddid you do yasself, you great, virtuous asshole? **1962** G. Ross *Campaign* 419: What an asshole.…And there's thousands of him. **1963** Rubin *Sweet Daddy* 8: You know, me and all the ass-holes—you know—all us neighborhood guys. **1972** Jenkins *Semi-Tough* 10: So far as I can tell, we've got a real good bunch of assholes around here. **1973** Whitlatch *Stunt Man* 99: Jay, you're a loud-mouthed asshole! **1977** M. Franklin *Last of Cowboys* 93: In the book of assholes, Charlie, they're gonna give you a whole chapter. **1978** S. King *The Stand* 419: And behold, the Wicked Witch of the West, or some Pentagon assholes, visited the country with a great plague. **1992** *Early Prime* (CNN-TV) (Aug. 5): The [French-Canadian] paper singles out…[an] "Asshole of the Week."

b. ASS, *n.*, 4.a. or b.—usu. considered vulgar.

1973 Overgard *Hero* 236: Get over here and shape up your asshole, buddy. **1977** J. Wylie *Homestead Grays* 100: Patton's genius was being used to guard Montgomery's asshole. **1986** Heinemann *Paco's Story* 38: An' ya'll better make me look good in front of the commandant or it'll be your assholes.

3. the most detestable spot (in a given area); a detestable place. Cf. ARMPIT, 1.—usu. considered vulgar.

[**1859** O.W. Holmes *Prof. at Breakfast Table* 24: My lively friend has had his straw at the bung-hole of the Universe!] **1865** in Horrocks *Dear Parents* 152: Captain Brooks…says that if the world was a bull this would be the "ass hole." **1918** in E. Wilson *Prelude* 274: The ass-hole of the Army. **1926** in Mencken *New Ltrs.* 205: [Los Angeles] is the one and true arse-hole of creation. **1927** *Immortalia* 64: It's the asshole of the land. **1928** Dahlberg *Bottom Dogs* 195: The freight was tied up in that union pacific asshole of a place. **1934** H. Miller *Trop. Cancer* 24: And not one man…has been crazy enough to put a bomb up the asshole of creation and set it off. ***1950** Dylan Thomas, in *OEDS*: This arse-hole of the universe. **1959** Lipton *Barbarians* 276 [ref. to 1920's]: In every small town I hit during those days there was always someone to assure me that it was "the ass-hole of the world." **1962** Killens *Thunder* 67 [ref. to WWII]: Georgia is a helluva state,/…The asshole of the forty-eight. **1967** Smart *Long Watch* 33 [ref. to WWII]: Norfolk…in the view of all sailors, the Ass-Hole of the Universe. **1969** Foley & Burnett *Best Stories '70* 289: I ain't got all night to spend in this asshole. **1971** Polner *No Parades* 51: "Shit, take a look at this ass hole."…His eyes swept over the dusty airfield, the quonset huts, the barbed wire. **1973** N.Y.U. prof. emeritus, age *ca*75: In 1917 we called Camp Wadsworth, S.C., "the asshole of the world." **1976** Braly *False Starts* 91: California's the asshole of the universe. **1989** S. King, in Thorne *Dict. Contemp. Sl.*: A bleak, snow-swept hillside in Hernon, Maine…the asshole of the universe. **1993** *New Yorker* (July 12) 46: There is no truth here. There is no justice. This is the asshole of the world.

4. *Construction.* a loop or kink in a line or cable.—usu. considered vulgar.

1959 *AS* (Feb.) 76: *Asshole, n.* A kink in a line. **1968** R. Adams *West. Words* (ed. 2): *Asshole.* In logging, a kink in the logging cable.

5. ASS, *n.*, 3.c.—usu. considered vulgar.

1964 in Wepman et al. *The Life* 128: You can get some cunt, asshole, or head. **1962–68** in B. Jackson *In Life* 400: I have had a little feminine asshole since. **1990** Costello & Wallace *Signifying Rappers* 78: He seen you sellin asshole/Door to door.

6. Esp. *Mil.* a bullet wound; a serious wound; (*fig.*) a violent rebuke.—usu. in phrs. of the sort **tear (someone) a new asshole** to injure or rebuke (someone).—usu. considered vulgar.

1968 Heard *Howard St.* 243: Keep comin' so I can blow you a new ass-hole! **1969** Hamill *Doc* 37: You'll end up with two assholes. One of them will be in your head. **1970** Woods *Killing Zone* 89: Sir, what if he makes a run for it?…Twelve extra assholes. **1971** in R.L. Baker *Hoosier Legends* 161: Old Dillinger had him 16 inches, and he used to just rip

that bitch a new asshole every night. **1972** U.S. Marine recruit, age 19: At Quantico the D.I.'s 'll say, "Go ahead, swing on me, slime, and I'll cut you a new asshole. I'll tear you a new asshole." **1973** Layne *Murphy* (unp.): Kaboom!…I Just Blew You A New Asshole. **1976** Former U.S. Marine, age 24, served 1970–72: They cut him a new ass-hole and kicked him out of school. **1976** Former member 11th Armored Cavalry Regt., served 1973–76: The colonel went over to tear him a new asshole. **1978** Truscott *Dress Gray* 340: If I hear that you have anything more to do on this Hand thing, Slaight, I'll rip you a new asshole. **1980** J. Webb *Sense of Honor* 37: He tore my company a new asshole this morning. **1979–82** Gwin *Overboard* 56: I teach her dat deck, she be tearin' dem deckhan's a new asshole, her. *Ibid.* 125: She sho cut dem han's a new asshole, her. [**1983** *T.J. Hooker* (CBS-TV): "At the time I would have reamed him a new—" "Spare me the details."] **1984** H. Gould *Cocktail* 188: He got the thirty-eight out.…"I like givin' people extra assholes." **1986** Paoli *From Beyond* (film): The DA's gonna chew me a new asshole for what you've done!

¶ In phrases:

¶ **break out into assholes** to become thoroughly terrified.—used derisively.—usu. considered vulgar.

[**1978** W. Brown *Tragic Magic* 142: But if we catch you again you better not run the same shit on us, cause if you do, we'll make both your faces break out into assholes.] **1979** Homer *Jargon* 215: Was he scared? Man, he broke out into assholes and shit himself to death. **1982** A. Shaw *Dict. Pop/Rock* 54: *Breaking out into assholes.* Rock jargon for being real scared, real terrified.

¶ **cut** [or **tear**, etc.] **(someone) a new asshole** see **(6)**, above.

¶ **[from] asshole to appetite** from end to end; thoroughly; totally.—usu. considered vulgar.

[***1899** in S.J. Baker *Austral. Lang.* 85: Another sheep [is] described as…wrinkled from *breech** to breakfast time*, or from *afternoon to appetite*, meaning in sailor's parlance from stem to stern, but the Australian bushman generally puts his saying stern first.…**[note by Baker, 1945] A euphemism for a more authentic use.] **1952** Uris *Battle Cry* 112 [ref. to WWII]: I tell you men, if I ever get my meathooks on that bastard I'll rip him open from asshole to appetite. **1920–54** Randolph *Bawdy Elements* 90: A man…announced that, he was "going to stump the county from *ass-hole to appetite*." **1967** Mailer *Vietnam* 50: D.J. knows them asshole to appetite.

¶ **have a paper asshole** to lack toughness.—usu. considered vulgar.

1945 Bowman *Beach Red* 92: You sound like a man with a paper asshole. Don't you think I'd like to shoot my way out of this if I thought it could be done? **1952** Mandel *Angry Strangers* 168: "I get mad at people, but I wind up hating myself for it."…"You got a paper asshole is all."

¶ **jump through (one's) asshole** to throw a tantrum.—usu. considered vulgar.

1972 Pearce *Pier Head* 53: He ain't gonna *say* nothin'. Old bears like that bastard? They just scream and howl and jump through their asshole.

¶ **keep a tight asshole** [prob. ref. to avoiding diarrhea, which is associated with panic] *Mil.* to avoid panicking; keep cool.—usu. considered vulgar.

[**1918** in *Immortalia* 109: Eyes right! Assholes tight!] **1947** Mailer *Naked & Dead* 17 [ref. to WWII]: Maybe you think I wasn't keeping a tight asshole when those Jap AA batteries opened up. **1970** Whitmore *Memphis-Nam* 57: I want all you men to keep a cool head and a tight asshole. **1979** Cassidy *Delta* 68: "Well, keep a tight asshole!" "Same to you." **1980** Manchester *Darkness* 437 [ref. to WWII]: One of the last orders before going into action was, "keep your assholes tight," but often that wasn't possible.

¶ **lock** [or **cross**] **assholes** *lock asses* s.v. LOCK.—usu. considered vulgar.

1975 De Mille *Smack Man* 166: I'm tired of crossing assholes with you over this case. **1984** Caunitz *Police Plaza* 195: I wouldn't wanna have to lock assholes with either one of them.

¶ **my asshole!** *my ass!* s.v. ASS, *n.*—usu. considered vulgar.

1973 Gwaltney *Destiny's Chickens* 41: "Now Effie, don't you be unkind to me." "Unkind my goddam asshole!"

¶ **out the asshole** *out the ass* s.v. ASS, *n.*—usu. considered vulgar.

1970 Rudensky & Riley *Gonif* 47: They can have guns coming out their ass holes, but nobody's going to use White for a duck! **1970** *Southern Blue Movie* 28: We'll give 'em so much fuckin' human interest, it'll be comin' out their ass-hole!

¶ **snap assholes** [or **asses**] to brawl.—usu. considered vulgar.

1952 Uris *Battle Cry* 208 [ref. to WWII]: No sass, Yankee, or you and me is going to the deck....We'll snap assholes for fair. *Ibid.* 311: We got enough hard times without two guys in the squad snapping asses all the time. **1970** Thackrey *Thief* 395: You want to snap assholes—you do it out in the alley.

¶ **tangle assholes** to brawl, tangle.—usu. considered vulgar.

[**1924** Anderson & Stallings *What Price Glory* 74 [ref. to WWI]: But say, the skip and this top soldier are going to tangle pantlegs over another little matter before they have been together one day.] [**1929–33** Farrell *Manhood of Lonigan* 194 [ref. to 1918]: I just tangled holes with some...wiseacre down at Sixty-third and the Grove.] **1957** in W.S. Burroughs *Letters* 354: A man can only come off second best, he tangle ass holes with a gash. **1960** MacCuish *Do Not Go Gentle* 139 [ref. to WWII]: We tangle assholes with the Japs, we're gonna shout 'em to death. **1967** Ford *Muc Wa* 130: Ain't he the guy we tangled ass holes with at the airport? **1974** N.C. man, age 24: You don't quit that shit you an' me gonna tangle assholes. I'm gonna stroke your head.

¶ **tear (someone) a new asshole** see (6), above.

¶ (In other phrs. adequately explained by context).—all usu. considered vulgar.

1931 J.T. Farrell *McGinty* 340: Shure I could drive [a truck] up a goose's a—hole without touching the feathers. **1940–46** McPeak [ref. to U.S. Navy, WWII]: Get going fast, all I want to see is heels and assholes. **1949** Robbins *Dream Merchants* 334: He don't know the front end of a camera from his asshole. **1966–67** P. Thomas *Mean Streets* 90: Her and her clique think they got gold-plated assholes. **1969** Pharr *Numbers* 148: If you take one more step inta this room I am gonna kick your asshole through your teeth! **1973** Gent *N. Dallas* 96: If you guys ain't ready they'll run right down yer throats and out yer assholes. **1975** Oliver Springs, Tenn., man, age 27: You ask a guy, "Were you an ass-hole baby?" That's a real nice insult. I first heard that about 1973. **1976** Price *Bloodbrothers* 147: That neighborhood'll be black as a coalminer's asshole at midnight. **1977** J. Wylie *Homestead Grays* 27: Look at 'em, bunched up tighter than a donkey's asshole. **1966–80** McAleer & Dickson *Unit Pride* 26: She's uglier than a bagful of assholes. **1985** Petit *Peacekeepers* 7 "Excuses are like assholes," our drill instructors were fond of telling us. "Everyone has one, and they all stink." **1986** Dye & Stone *Platoon* 63 [ref. to Vietnam War]: Assholes are like assholes, Taylor. Everybody's got one. **1991** in *Rap Pages* (Feb. 92) 12: And opinions are just like assholes, right? [**1992** *Donahue* (NBC-TV): You need him like you need another—you-know-what.] **1993** O. Stone, in *New Yorker* (May 17) 47: Clinton is talking through his asshole.

asshole *adj.* stupid; contemptible; damned.—usu. considered vulgar.

1935 in J. O'Hara *Sel. Letters* 106: He thinks it's the ass-hole job of the world. **1956** Chamales *So Few* 387 [ref. to WWII]: You're an asshole moralist. **1964** Pearl *Stockade* 54: Well, it's an asshole regulation. **1965** Lurie *Nowhere* 287: What an ass-hole idea! **1966–67** W. Stevens *Gunner* 14 [ref. to WWII]: We got to go to asshole Regensburg. **1969** Searls *Hero Ship* 276: I'd be facing some *real* charges instead of these ass-hole things. **1971** S. Stevens *Way Uptown* 220: The more I listened to his crazy idea, the more asshole it got. **1972** Pearce *Pier Head* 160: Asshole luck. **1972** Giovannitti *Medal* 18: He's got sixteen months in this asshole war. **1975** in Cheever *Letters* 309: The globe on the State House is brilliant but most of it is asshole. **1975** J. Jones *WWII* 130: At least in my outfit, we got blind asshole drunk every chance we got. **1977** Schrader *Blue Collar* 22: This bastard thinks I'm gonna hand out my asshole pamphlets on my day off.

asshole *v.* **1.** to grovel, truckle.—usu. considered vulgar.

1940 J.T. Farrell *Father & Son* 311: He noticed, too, how poor relations looked up to these men, even ass-holed before them.

2. *Mil. Av.* (of a guided missile) to strike (a jet aircraft) squarely from behind.

1986 Coonts *Intruder* 187 [ref. to Vietnam War]: We're gonna be assholed by a SAM! *a***1989** R. Herman, Jr. *Warbirds* 250: One of their own SAMs assholed the lead son of a bitch.

¶ In phrase:

¶ **asshole around** to loaf; trifle.

[**1920–54** Randolph *Bawdy Elements* 88: *To assle around* is to loaf, or to wander idly about.] **1968** Baker et al. *CUSS* 72: *Asshole around.* Waste time, not study.

asshole bandit *n.* [cf. ASS BANDIT] Esp. *Pris.* an anal sodomist; a homosexual rapist.—usu. considered vulgar.

***1970** Partridge *DSUE* (ed. 7) 985: *Arse-hole bandit.* A variant of *arse bandit.* **1970** S. Ross *Fortune Machine* 217: It'll keep...the asshole bandits away. **1974** Andrews & Dickens *Over Wall* 20: Luther was an expert con man, mugger, drunk roller...and...an asshole bandit. **1976** Chinn *Dig Nigger Up* 52: He was an expert...asshole bandit. **1982** Cox & Frazier *Buck* 189 [ref. to Korean War]: He got real nice. Seems he too is an asshole bandit.

asshole buddy *n.* **1.** [this sense prob. developed fr. **(2)**, below, but early evidence is lacking] best friend, close friend (with no imputation of homosexuality).—usu. considered vulgar.

1942–45 in *AS* (Oct. 1948): *Asshole Buddy.* Comrade in arms. *a***1949** D. Levin *Mask of Glory* 103: Who is Kostaikis's asshole buddy? **1954** Killens *Youngblood* 103: He my ass-hole buddy, ain't he? **1958** T. Berger *Crazy in Berlin* 105: Get your ass-hole buddy out of here. **1960** Sire *Deathmakers* 262: We're your asshole buddies. **1966** Bogner *7th Ave.* 361: Hey, pal, asshole buddy, you gotta stop worrying about things like that. **1967** Mailer *Vietnam* 71: He and Big Grizzler were not rushing to be asshole buddies. **1970** Sorrentino *Steelwork* 14: They banded together. Comrades in arms, ass-hole buddies. **1975** *Nat. Lampoon* (Oct.) 28: This is supposed to make me his asshole buddy, his lifelong friend.

2. a partner in, esp. reciprocal, anal intercourse.—used derisively.—usu. considered vulgar.

1953 Del Torto: Why didn't you and your ass-hole buddy & that sentry try a threesome? **1958** Cooley *Run for Home* 118 [ref. to Merchant Marine, 1920's]: What's the matter, Kid? Don't you want to be ass-hole buddies? *Ibid.* 278: I think you and your ass-hole buddy, Ioway, are corn-holin' together. **1959** Burroughs *Naked Lunch* 92: Me and my ass-hole buddy, Lu. **1969** Lynch *Amer. Soldier* 218: You got yourself a new asshole buddy? **1975** Memphis, Tenn., man, age 28: I bet those two guys are asshole buddies. **1976** Hayden *Voyage* 420: They was kind of asshole buddies, I guess you could say.

asshole-deep *adj.* ASS-DEEP.—usu. considered vulgar.

1963 in Wepman et al. *Life* 82: Snow and sleet...asshole-deep. **1969** Searls *Hero Ship* 185 [ref. to WWII]: My God, Barney, the lab's asshole-deep in strike pictures! **1973** Collins *Carrying Fire* 220: Here I am asshole deep in a 131-step EVA checklist and they want to talk about baseball! *a***1989** C.S. Crawford *Four Deuces* 54: Standin' asshole-deep in high-explosive rounds.

asshole malaria *n.* malaria with dysentery.—usu. considered vulgar.

1961 J. Jones *Thin Red Line* 81 [ref. to WWII]: Maybe they'll get asshole malaria so bad they'll get themselves shipped out.

asshole-sucker *n.* (used as a violent term of abuse).—usu. considered vulgar.

1934 "J.M. Hall" *Anecdota* 168: Calling him an ass hole sucker and cunt lapper for interfering. **1972** Grogan *Ringolevio* 349: That group of psychedelic asshole suckers who decided to pay to have him [killed]. **1974** Kurtzman *Bobby* 38: Hell if I'm goin to tell you. Dirty asshole sucker!

assholingest *adj.* [irreg. superlative of ASSHOLE, *adj.*] most idiotic.—usu. considered vulgar.

1972 Ponicsan *Cinderella* 76: That's about the assholingest excuse I ever heard.

asshound *n.* [ASS, *n.*, 3.b. + HOUND 'eager enthusiast'] a man who obsessively seeks opportunities for sexual intercourse.—usu. considered vulgar.

1952 Lamott *Stockade* 50 [ref. to WII]: That asshound Fischer won't make any trouble. **1962** Mandel *Mainside* 52: They think they'll find all sorts of evidence confirming their dark suspicion, which is that officers are all either queer or ass-hounds.

assig *n.* [by shortening] assignation, meeting, rendezvous.

***1698–99** "B.E." *Dict. Canting Crew*: *Assig*, now us'd for Assignation, an Appointment or meeting. ***1796** Grose *Vulgar Tongue* (ed. 3): *Assig*, an assignation. **1821** Waln *Hermit in Phila.* 26: Had an *assig* with a *Quicunque Vult*—a snug little *cinder-gabbler*.

ass-in-the-grass *adj. Mil.* engaged in combat, under fire.—usu. considered vulgar.

[**1973** Herbert & Wooten *Soldier* 131: The "grunt," the guy whose ass was in the grass in the field.] *Ibid.* 145: I was spending about twenty nights a month with ass-in-the-grass troops. **1985** Tate *Bravo Burning* 209: Lowly ass-in-the-grass realities. **1986** Stinson & Carabatsos

Heartbreak Ridge 3: Your basic ass-in-the-grass [rifleman]. **1990** G.R. Clark *Words of Vietnam War* 37: *Ass-in-the-Grass Test.* A form of military "field audit" to roughly evaluate the number of soldiers a unit had patrolling in the field compared to the actual number…available to the unit.

ass-kick *n.* an exceedingly hard task.—usu. considered vulgar.
   1973 Karlin, Paquet & Rottmann *Free Fire* 5 [ref. to Vietnam War, 1969]: Ass kick, ain't it, Cruit?

ass-kicker *n.* **1.** a person who habitually employs physical violence as a form of coercion; tough disciplinarian; bully.
   1967 "Iceberg Slim" *Pimp* 45: His infamy as the top ass-kicker of the nineteen-twenties. **1967–68** T. Wolfe *Kool-Aid* 74: If somebody is an ass-kicker, then that is what he's going to do on this trip, kick asses.
   2. an exceedingly difficult task or opponent.—usu. considered vulgar.
   1973 Karlin, Paquet & Rottmann *Free Fire* 4: "Fuckin ass kicker, ain't it?" grinned Larson as he poured the salt tablets. **1982** Goff, Sanders & Smith *Bros.* 129: The elements were bad and the enemy was an ass-kicker. **1983** Univ. Tenn. student: That last [math problem]'s an ass-kicker, ain't it? **1986** Dye & Stone *Platoon* 16: This fuckin' terrain is an ass-kicker.
   3. a person or thing considered to be remarkably exciting, amusing, successful, etc.—usu. considered vulgar.
   1971 Woodley *Dealer* 107: My pops was an educated hustler, worked his way through college being a hustler. He was an ass-kicker, my mother said.…He had been…everything. **1971** N.Y.U. student: That was an ass-kicker of a flick. **1990** *Car & Driver* (Nov.) 159: Three times NASCAR champion, he runs true as the sport's infamous ass-kicker. And loves it.

ass-kicking *n.* **1.** a beating; defeat.—usu. considered vulgar.
   [**1937** E. Anderson *Thieves* 68: You going to see a guy get the damnedest behind-kicking a man ever got.] **1943** in M. Curtiss *Letters Home* 234: Better a little ass-kicking now than…later. **1954** Chessman *Cell* 84: You looking for another ass-kicking, maybe? **1972** Bunker *No Beast* 67: It was a pretty fair ass-kicking. **1984** Nettles & Golenbock *Balls* 112: It was just a couple of old-fashioned ass-kickings we got. **1983–86** Zausner *Streets* 30: I got one ass kicking out of another.
   2. (in prov. expressions of the sort **one-legged man at an ass-kicking contest**).
   1966 "T. Pendleton" *Iron Orchard* 112: Around work he was…"helpless as a one-legged man at a ass-kickin'." **1972** Davidson *Cut Off* 30 [ref. to WWII]: She was as useless to me as a one-legged man at an ass-kickin'. **1972** Jenkins *Semi-Tough* 210: No chance, I said.…Did a one-legged man ever win an ass-kickin' contest? **1987** Robbins *Ravens* 11: Putting in a strike meant that you were busier than a one-legged man at an ass-kicking contest, the pilots said.

ass-kicking *adj.* terribly exciting; sensational.—usu. considered vulgar. Cf. KICKY.
   1977 *Nat. Lampoon* (Aug.) 35: Tight, ass-kickin', ass-lickin' rock 'n' roll from this new band. **1979** *Easyriders* (Dec.) 111 (ad): Ass-kickin' light switches.…Bitchin' nickel finish over solid metal. **1983** K. Miller *Lurp Dog* 131: That was some full-blown asskickin' bitch of a party. **1984** Algeo *Stud Buds & Dorks*: Very good…ass-kicking.

ass-kiss *v.* [back formation from ASS-KISSER] to curry favor (with) in a self-degrading manner. —usu. considered vulgar.
   1961 J. Jones *Thin Red Line* 414 [ref. to WWII]: Don't asskiss me, you cheap fuck. **1978** Strieber *Wolfen* 38: He [did] not try to ass-kiss.

ass-kisser *n.* one who abjectly curries favor; toady.—usu. considered vulgar.
   1766 J. Adams *Diary & Autobiog.* I 300: Made him in Thatchers Phrase a shoe licker and an A—se kisser of Elisha Hutchinson. [**1928** Bodenheim *Georgie May* 128: You bin gawging youahself with the grub—you and youah back-kissahs.] **1953–57** Giovannitti *Combine D* 161: Asskisser. **1960** Krueger *St. Patrick's* 28: Perkle was the Adam of all the bootlickers and ass-kissers of the human race. **1965** Lurie *Nowhere* 37: Ass-kissers and creeps. **1970** E. Thompson *Garden* 70: We don't have to cater to such a lot of ass kissers. **1982** D. Williams *Hit Hard* 47: I know what this little ass-kisser does around here. **1988** Norst *Colors* 10: "Right!" some lone ass-kisser chimed in.

ass-kissing *n.* the currying of favor.—usu. considered vulgar.
   1942 in M. Curtiss *Letters Home* 85: I was disgusted with all the ass kissing…that goes on. **1953–57** Giovannitti *Combine D* 117 [ref. to WWII]: Ass-kissing doesn't do any good around here. **1978** *New West*

(July 31) 81: The number of times Robinson mentioned KSAN-FM, which was broadcasting the show…verged on ass-kissing. **1988** *Newsweek* (June 13) 30: "There's too much ass-kissing going on," said the campaign manager of one of Bush's Republican rivals.

ass-kissing *adj.* obsequious, sycophantic.—usu. considered vulgar.
   1952 Malamud *Natural* 40: A greedy, penetrating, ass-kissing voice. **1963** J. Ross *Dead Are Mine* 174 [ref. to WWII]: And you bitched about the ass-kissing assistant section chiefs. **1966** Elli *Riot* 85: I'm not ruining my reputation by taking that ass-kissing petition out front! **1977** Dunne *Confessions* 26: An ass-kissing clerk, Fuqua. **1986** *New Republic* (Mar. 3) 10: Why do you think you can go around acting like us right-wing pundits are a bunch of ass-kissing, money-grubbing, know-nothing jerks?

assle *v.* [poss. fr. *hassle* infl. by ASSHOLE] ¶ In phrase: **assle around** to fidget; to trifle.—usu. considered vulgar.
   [*a**1903** *F & H* I (rev.) 66: To arsle = (1) To move backwards, and (2) to fidget.] **1920–54** Randolph *Bawdy Elements* 88: To assle around is to loaf, or to wander idly about. **1975** Ark. man, age 24: Quit asslin' around—quit screwin' around.

ass-lick *n.* ASS-KISSER.—usu. considered vulgar.
   [*a**1500** in R. Yeager *15th C. Studies* 142: Ars lyke.] **1977** Olsen *Fire Five* 146: He's Steicher's biggest ass-lick, but not a bad guy when you can get him alone.

ass-lick *v.* [back formation fr. ASS-LICKER] to curry favor in a self-degrading manner.—usu. considered vulgar.
   1968 Baker et al. *CUSS* 72: Ass lick. Curry favor with a professor.

ass-licker *n.* **1. a.** [cf. G *Arschlecker*; Yid *tokhes-leker*, and Du *gatlikker*] ASS-KISSER.—usu. considered vulgar.
   1938 H. Miller *Trop. Capricorn* 16: Besides, I wasn't a good ass-licker. **1967** Ford *Muc Wa* 19: He…marched toward the dispatch office, followed by a wedge of majors and captains and all-purpose ass-lickers. **1969** Girodias *New Olympia* 753: I don't play ass-licker for nobody! **1971–72** Giovannitti *Medal* 98: So that's it.…You're his ass-licker. **1992** G. Hays & K. Moloney *Policewoman One* 12: The department is chockfull of asslickers already.
   b. (used as a vulgar term of abuse).
   1972 Carr *Bad* 107: You ass-lickers are gonna have to come in and get us!
   2. a homosexual anilingue.—usu. considered vulgar.
   1966 Fry TS.: Call…for Cock Sucker Ass Licker Toe Sucker.

ass-licking *n.* abject and degrading flattery. —usu. considered vulgar.
   ***1912** D.H. Lawrence, in *OEDS*: Arse-licking. **1946** in T. Williams *Letters* 182: I wish I had taken down some of her remarks, such as, about Hollywood, "Between the ass-licking and the throat-cutting there is never a dull moment!" **1992** *Toronto Star* (Apr. 18) K1: Being an actor has nothing to do with talent. It's all politics and image and ass-licking.

ass-licking *adj.* obsequious, sycophantic; (*hence*) despicable, goddamned.—usu. considered vulgar.
   [**1921** K. Burke, in Jay *Burke-Cowley Corres.* 86: That bastard buttock-licking *Dial*.] **1939** M. Levin *Citizens* 104: You asslicking…sonofabitch, what do you want? **1942** H. Miller *Roofs of Paris* 278: You're a dirty ass-licking whore! **1963–64** Kesey *Great Notion* 135: He…runs again through the string of names he's been calling Hank Stamper "…cocksuckin', asslickin', fartknockin', shiteatin'…." **1968** P. Roth *Portnoy* 53: That ass-licking little boy…in search of…his mother's approbation. **1972** Wurlitzer *Quake* 94: Give me one ass licking chance and I'll take care of that problem.

assload *n.* a great deal; too many or too much; SHITLOAD.—usu. considered vulgar.
   1957 in J. Blake *Joint* 161: My gear is still at the hotel…containing an assload of barbiturates, amphetamines, T.O., PG…and assorted shit. **1966** Braly *On Yard* 19: They got an assload a time out in that cou'troom. **1970** Thomas *Total Beast* 106: It's an assload, ain't it?

ass man *n.* **1.** [ASS, *n.*, 3.b.] a man who engages in frequent sexual intercourse with many women.—usu. considered vulgar.
   1954–60 *DAS* 10: *Ass man*…A youth or man who devotes much time to coitus…a youth or man whose obsession or hobby is sex. **1963** Rubin *Sweet Daddy* 32: So I'm an ass man—so that means I got a diploma in straightening out queers or something? *Ibid.* 152: *Ass Man*—a man who devotes much time to the sexual conquest of women. **1971** Dahlskog

Dict.Contemp. Us.: They say he's a big *ass man.* **1978** C. Miller *Animal House* 11: Good old Otter—the assman's assman.

2. a man who is particularly aroused by a woman's buttocks.—usu. considered vulgar.

1968 Bullins *Wine Time* 388: But Lou, Baby, you are married to an "A" number one ass man…and *yours* is one of the…greats. **1970** Thackrey *Thief* 186: Take it from me, baby—I been an ass man all my life. **1970** A. Lewis *Carnival* 267: Disproportionately large nates, a display of which drew salvos of applause from the ass-men. **1973** Hirschfeld *Victors* 147: You an ass man or a thigh man?

ass pack *n.* FANNY PACK. —usu. considered vulgar.

1952 Uris *Battle Cry* 118 [ref. to WWII]: The ass pack…is rigged so it hangs…level with a man's backside, thus leaving room on his back for the radio. *a*1987 Bunch & Cole *Reckoning* 135: Carry it behind you on top of your asspack.

ass paper *n.* toilet tissue.—usu. considered vulgar.

1939 Bessie *Men in Battle* 264: Poor quality stock…Good ass paper. **1980** Univ. Tenn. student, age 23: They're out of ass paper in the john.

ass-peddler *n.* a prostitute.—used contemptuously.—usu. considered vulgar.

1942 *ATS* 471: Prostitute…*ass peddler.* **1981** P. Sann *Trial* 129: An ass-peddler…who had a book ghosted on her…life.

ass-scratcher *n.* an idler.—usu. considered vulgar.

1934 Faulkner *Pylon* 66: And you can thank whatever tutelary ass-scratcher you consider presides over the fate…of that office.

ass-sucker *n.* ASS-KISSER.—usu. considered vulgar.

1942 McAtee *Supp. Grant Co. Dial.* 2 [ref. to 1890's]: *Ass-sucker,* n. bootlicker, toady. **1968** Stahl *Hokey* 80: The ass-suckers and louses commonly known as adults. **1975** McKennon *Trail* 220: Only people that call me Mister are ass suckers and stool pigeons.

ass-tickler *n.* something amusing.—usu. considered vulgar. Cf. RIB-TICKLER.

1972 Jenkins *Semi-Tough* 14: Old Billy Clyde's salary is up there in big figures now, and if you lump three years together, it's a real ass-tickler.

ass-tight *adj.* very tight; (of friends) very close.—usu. considered vulgar.

1960 C.L. Cooper *Scene* 252: Yeah, I know the Feds are doing an ass-tight job, holding the stuff down, but what I can't stand is them hogging the credit! **1966–67** P. Thomas *Mean Streets* 123: Many a tooth has been lost between fine, ass-tight *amigos.*

ass-waxing *n.* [ASS, *n.*, 1 + WAX 'thrash' + *-ing*] a thrashing, trouncing.—usu. considered vulgar.

1967 W. Crawford *Gresham War* 178: You men knock off this cheap shit or get ready for an absolute ass-waxing.

assways *adv.* backwards; askew.—usu. considered vulgar.

1934 H. Miller *Trop. Cancer* 93: He stands there with…his hat on assways. **1989** *Dream Street* (NBC-TV): The world is assways, upside-down.

ass-whipped *adj.* physically exhausted.—usu. considered vulgar.

1974–77 Heinemann *Close Quarters* 219: But the next morning the three of them would stumble out of the woods…soaked to the skin and ass-whipped.

ass-whipping *n.* a beating.—usu. considered vulgar.

1954 McGraw *Riots* 68: I got an ass-whipping I'll never forget.

ass wipe *n.* **1.** a worthless, contemptible person, esp. if also obsequious.—usu. considered vulgar.

1952 Bellow *Augie March* 173: You little asswipe hoodlum! **1956** Chamales *So Few* 475 [ref. to WWII]: Forget whether Joe Asswipe likes you or not. **1969** Mitchell *Thumb Tripping* 117: And turn your lights on, asswipe! *Ibid.* 119: Watch your goddamn language, asswipe. **1974** Price *Wanderers* 194: At least he would be away from these two asswipes. **1980** Ark. man, age 28: That obnoxious little asswipe!

2.a. material for wiping the anus; toilet tissue.—usu. considered vulgar.

1958 T. Berger *Crazy in Berlin* 60 [ref. to WWII]: Course I coulda let him take this stuff for ass-wipe. **1961** H. Ellison *Memos* 118: Sell them ass-wipe on television. **1970** Wambaugh *Centurions* 191: Well, the old thief's got enough asswipe stashed to last a week. **1971** Dahlskog *Dict. Contemp. Us.:* Ass-wipe…Toilet paper. **1981** C. Nelson *Picked Bullets Up* 289: I ain't going to write an order on asswipe.

b. *Mil.* invasion currency; MPC.—usu. considered vulgar.

1942–51 in Mich. State Univ. Folk. Archs. *Army: Jargon* 29: *Ass-wipe*— Invasion money.

ass-wiper *n.* **1.** ASS-KISSER.—usu. considered vulgar.

1950 Partridge *DSUE* (ed. 3) 981: *Arse-wiper.* A workman that toadies to the boss; a servant to the mistress. **1968 Baker et al. *CUSS* 72: *Ass-wiper.* One who does organization's dirty work so as to advance.

2. something overpoweringly difficult to deal with.—usu. considered vulgar.

1966 Braly *On Yard* 32: You look like you kicked an ass wiper [*sc.* a heroin addiction]. **1976** Univ. Tenn. student, age 18: This job's gonna be an ass-wiper.

astonisher *n. Journ.* an exclamation point.

1888 Nye & Riley *Railway* 64: What in three dashes, two hyphens and an astonisher do you want here! **1927** *AS* II (Feb.) 239: But few outside the trade know that parentheses are "finger nails" or that exclamation points are "screamers," "astonishers," or "shouts."

A.T.C. *adj.* [official initialism of *A*ir *T*ransport *C*ommand] *Mil.* allergic to combat.—used facetiously.

1944 *New Yorker* (May 27) 24: That's what I was doing when I transferred from A.T.C.…Maybe I'd listened to that allergic-to-combat gag once too often. **1947** *ATS* (Supp.) 32: ATC, Allergic to Combat.

atmosphere *n.* [pun on syn. *give the air* s.v. AIR, 2] ¶ In phrase: **give the atmosphere** to reject.

1938 in Gelman *Photoplay* 209: Women…are the bunk.…The boys and me decided to give 'em the atmosphere. We play poker and pal around, you know, just the boys.

atomic cocktail *n.* [sugg. by *atomic bomb*] *Med.* a liquid oral medication containing a radioactive isotope.

1949 in *AS* XXIX 71: A…girl drank her second "atomic cocktail" Wednesday hoping to cure a rare glandular ailment.…A glass of radio-active phosphorous. **1953** in *Ibid.*

attaboy *n.* [fr. colloq. *attaboy!*] *Mil. & Police.* a commendation.

1975 Wambaugh *Choirboys* 288: There's lots a vice sergeants in this town that'd…write you an attaboy. **1976–79** Duncan & Moore *Green Side Out* 188: This guy was anxious to get an "attaboy." **1980** W.C. Anderson *BAT-21* 161: He landed back at the base, expecting at least one atta-boy for a job well done. **1983** Beckwith & Knox *Delta Force* 62: I wasn't interested in…getting into a firefight, then returning to a big "attaboy" for ten VC killed. **1986** "J. Cain" *Suicide Sq.* 169: That might get you an attaboy in Germany but won't do you any good over here. *a*1987 Coyle *Team Yankee* 114: Your people done good. Give 'em an atta boy.

attic *n.* mind, memory, head.

1823 (cited in Partridge *DSUE*, quot. not given). **1859 Hotten *Slang Dict.:* Attic, the head; "Queer in the attic," intoxicated. **1870 in *OED.* **1908 Univ. Tenn. *Volunteer* (unp.): You lack in gray stuff in the attic. **1930** J.T. Farrell *Calico* 26: They all know you're vacant in the attic. **1933** J.T. Farrell *McGinty* 37: He had some machinery jammed out of whack in his attic. **1967** *Lit Dict.* 10: When you are reading this book, you are copping some knowledge and storing it in your attic. **1978** Diehl *Sharky's M.* 272: He's just, uh…a little loose in the attic.

attitude *n.* [prob. fr. phrs. such as "You'd better change your attitude," "I don't like your attitude," etc.] a hostile or haughty attitude; assertive spirit; (*hence*) a cold reception, hostility, etc.—in phr. **cop an attitude** to become arrogant or insolent.

1962 Maurer & Vogel *Narc. & Narc. Add.* (ed. 2) 289: *Attitude.* Hostile or aloof and uncooperative. **1962–63** in Giallombardo *Society of Women* 202: *Cop an Attitude.* To become angry. **1969** *New York* (Sept. 22) 25: You trying to get an attitude with me?…You *have* got an attitude. **1971** *N.Y. Times Mag.* (June 20): *Attitude:* An angry, fighting style. Someone who "catches a quick attitude" is easily agitated and ready to fight. **1972** *Penthouse* (Aug.) 70: He chickened out. Afraid of getting an attitude from the other end. **1972** Smith & Gay *Don't Try It* 200: *Cop an Attitude.* Be obnoxious, have a chip on one's shoulder. **1973** N.Y.C. man, age 26: That bitch has got an attitude. **1975** Sepe & Telano *Cop Team* 118: The face…was…cloaked with an "attitude." **1978** W. Brown *Tragic Magic* 30: Chilly came to my bunk with an attitude. **1980** *N.Y. Daily News* (Manhattan ed.) (Aug. 20) 3: I know people who…complain that "the cashiers give you attitude." **1987** Fischer & Jeremias *Lost Boys* (film): All you do is give attitude lately. **1988** CBS-TV spot ad for *Cagney & Lacey:* And guess who cops an attitude! **1989** G. Trudeau *Doonesbury* (synd. cartoon strip) (Oct. 3): If you don't cop an attitude, they don't *respect* you! **1990** *Time* (Aug. 13) 73: He has the moves, the wardrobe and the attitude too. **1992** *Royal Family* (CBS-TV): Well, that's enough attitude for one day.

auctioneer *n.* [pun on *knock down* 'to sell at auction'] *Boxing.* a knockdown blow.

1863 in *F & H* I: And who in return for a craven blow, can deliver the auctioneer well over the face and eyes. **1870** *Putnam's Mag.* (Mar.) 301: If our glorious Benicia had administered an auctioneer on my knowl-edge-box I couldn't have been more completely grassed.

auger *n.* penis. *Joc.*

ca1910 in Logsdon *Whorehouse Bells* 40: And to my sad misfortune, his auger wouldn't bore.

auger *v.* [pun on *bore*, prob. infl. by dial. pronun. of *argue*] *West.* to talk to (someone) at length.

1928 Santee *Cowboy* 101: So I laid in camp an' augered the cook, an' he let me play the coffee-pot. **1938** Lomax & Lomax *Cowboy Songs* 120: We started for the ranch next day,/Brown augered me most all the way./He said that cow-punching was nothing but play. **1940** F. Hunt *Trail fr. Tex.* 111 [ref. to 1870's]: Maybe you kin auger yerself into a job.

¶ In phrase:

¶ **auger in** [orig. joc., implying a boring into the earth] *Mil. Av.* (of an aircraft) to dive and crash in a tailspin; crash-land.

1944 in Wallrich *A.F. Airs* 34: Now I lost my wingman over the field/ And the rest augered into the sea. **1955** *AS* XXX 116: *Auger In*...Crash; make a crash landing (usually not fatal). **1955** Scott *Look of Eagle* 25: At five point five Gees you'd have augered in. **1956** Heflin *USAF Dict.* 60: *To auger in*, to crash in a tail spin. *Slang.* **1958** *AS* XXXIII 181: (of a parachutist): *Auger In*—To hit the ground in such a manner as to result in injury. **1958** Whitcomb *Corregidor* 276 [ref. to 1942]: When a plane was hit at minimum altitude, it simply "augured" in. That was the expression they used. **1982** *All Things Considered* (Nat. Pub. Radio) (Aug. 8): The engine stalled and she just augered in. She was killed.

August ham *n.* *Black E.* watermelon.—usu. considered offensive. *Joc.*

1925 Van Vechten *Nigger Heaven* 239: Ah sighs fo' August ham. *Ibid.* 285: *August ham*—water-melon.

aunt or **auntie** *n.* **1.** [orig. euphem.; cf. Yid *mume* 'procuress, madam of a brothel' (lit. 'aunt')] a prostitute or procuress, esp. the madam of a brothel or bawdy-house.—constr. esp. with a pronoun.

***1606** in R.G. Lawrence *Comedies* 19: I need not say "bawds," for everyone knows what "aunt" stands for in the last translation. ***1611** Shakespeare *Winter's Tale* IV ii: Summer songs for me and my aunts,/ While we lie tumbling in the hay. ***1698–99** "B.E." *Dict. Canting Crew*: *Aunt*, a Bawd, as *one of my Aunts*, one of the same order. ***1785** Grose *Vulgar Tongue*: *Aunt*, mine aunt; a bawd or procuress. **1849** *Nat. Police Gaz.* (Sept. 29) 3: He said we will go and see our aunt first, won't we?...I had never been in such a house before....I knew what kind of a house it was by his saying "my aunt's;" and whenever "my aunt's" was spoken of, I knew he meant this kind of a house. **1908** Sullivan *Crim. Slang:* Auntie—the keeper of a house where young girls (who live with their parents) are hired to ruin. **1929** M. Gill *Und. Slang* [unp.]: *Auntie*—landlady in a house of vice. **1935** *AS* (Feb.) 12 [ref. to period before 1910]: *Auntie*. The *madame*...in a brothel. **1964** Trimble *Sex Words* 20: *Aunt* or *Auntie*...a female prostitute up in years.

2. [prob. infl. by **(1)**, above] *Homosex.* a middle-aged or elderly effeminate male homosexual.—used disparagingly.

1930 "D. Stiff" *Milk & Honey* 199: *Auntie*—*Angelina* grown older. **1931–34** in Clemmer *Pris. Community* 330: *Auntie*, n. An elderly, male homosexual. **1940** Del Torto *Gallery* 151: What started as a seduction at twelve goes on till we're senile old aunties. **1949** *Gay Girl's Guide* 3: *Auntie:* Homosexual past 40, desperate, shameless and abject, generally pursues extreme youth. **1942–49** Goldin et al. *DAUL* 20: Them fags...learned the boosting grift...from their aunt. **1969** S. Harris *Puritan Jungle* 152: I mean, that he could think I was a fruit like him and would end up an auntie. Man, I was in an absolute depression. **1972** *Anthro. Ling.* (Mar.) 98: *Auntie*...An elderly homosexual who is often prissy and solicitous.

¶ In phrases:

¶ **ask my aunt!** [prob. euphem. for *ask my ass* s.v. ASS, *n.*] "I will not answer your question."

1898–1900 Cullen *Chances* 75: D'je play that one?" inquired Red Beak Jim...."Ask my aunt," growled the main guy.

¶ **my aunt!** [prob. euphem. for *my ass!* s.v. ASS] no indeed! not at all! I don't believe it!

1942 *ATS* 190: I Don't Believe It! Applesauce! baloney!...my aunt! my eye! [etc.].

¶ **so's your Aunt Tillie!** emphatically not! Also vars.

1930 Franklyn *Knights* 147: Awh so's your Aunt Emma! **1931** Hellinger *Moon* 222: Is that romance? So's your Aunt Tilly. **1942** *AS* 300: So's your...Aunt Susie! [*1945 in Partridge *DSUE* (ed. 7) 987: She's got no more idea how to run this house than my Aunt Fanny.] **1971** Sorrentino *Up fr. Never* 28: "Told ya ya stink."..."Up your Aunt Tilly's." **1973** *Playboy* (Mar.) 50: How To Talk 1920's...So's Your Aunt Tillie—"You're full of hot air." **1979** Univ. Tenn. student, age 27: I've heard "So's Your Aunt Fanny!" on TV.

¶ **your** [or **my**] **Aunt Fanny!** [perh. orig. euphem. for syn. *your ass!* s.v. ASS, *n.*] (used esp. postpositively to express disbelief or derision). Also vars.

1928 *AS* (Feb.) 259: And in our grandmother's day a favorite expression of derision was "Your Aunt Mitty," but our boys say, "So's your old man." **1953** W. Fisher *Waiters* 9: "The horse, of course." "Horse your Aunt Minnie." **1963** Cameron *Black Camp* 18: "Jesus, that's tough." "Tough my Aunt Fanny." **1992** N. Cohn *Heart of World* 277: Artistry my Aunt Fanny.

¶ (In other prov. expressions). [For 1969 and 1989 quots., cf. BALLS.]

1932 Berg *Prison Dr.* 126: Oh Yeah? Sure. If my aunt had wheels she'd be a trolley car! **1955** Klaas *Maybe I'm Dead* 329: Oh, my aunt-furkin' uncle! Here they come again! **1969** N.Y.C. man, age *ca*40: [ref. to 1930's]: We had an expression—if another kid said, "Balls!" we'd say, "If your aunt had 'em, she'd be your uncle!" **1989** Leib *Fire Dream* 14: "If we had shovels, we could dig in a bit...." "If my aunt had balls, she'd be my uncle."

Aunt Flo [pun on menstrual *flow*] the menses.

1954 *AS* (Oct.) 298: Aunt Flo has come. **1989** Munro *U.C.L.A. Slang* 16: Aunt Flo dropped in unexpectedly. **1992** *UTSQ*: She's having a visit from Aunt Flo (menstrual period).

Aunt Jane *n.* **1.** [folk ety. of *Tijuana* as *tía Juana*, Sp 'Aunt Jane'] Tijuana, Mexico.

1928 Sharpe *Chicago May* 288: *Aunt Jane*—Tia Juana, Mexico.

2. [sugg. by UNCLE TOM] a black woman who is subservient to whites.

1963 *Time* (Aug. 2) 14: *Aunt Jane*. A female Tom. **1967** (quot. at AUNT JEMIMA, 2).

Aunt Jemima *n.* **1.** *Gamb.* (in craps) a particular point, perhaps three.

1909 M'Govern *Krag* 155: "Now comes Little Joe!" "There sure am Aunt Jemima!" "Come seven; come eleven!" "Little Phoebe needs a new dress!" "Ninety days!" "CRAPS!"

2. [fr. a trademark of General Foods, Inc.; by analogy with UNCLE TOM] a black woman who is subservient to whites.

1967 *DAS* (Supp.) 672: *Aunt Jemima* = Aunt Jane. **1969** H.R. Brown *Die* 67: If you don't begin to tell your own story, you will always be Aunt Jemima. **1989** Chafets *Devil's Night* 190: He attacked the Reagan administration and called the members of its civil rights commission "Uncle Toms and Aunt Jemimahs."

Aunt Mary *n.* [sugg. by UNCLE TOM] AUNT JANE, 2.

1974 R. Carter *16th Round* 13: There were no such people in our young lives as Mister Charlie and the Devil—meaning white people—or Aunt Mary and Boy—meaning our mothers and fathers.

Aunt Sally *n.* [sugg. by UNCLE TOM] AUNT JANE, 2.

1968–70 *Current Slang* III & IV: *Aunt Sally, n.* Female equivalent of an Uncle Tom. Used in a derogatory sense by younger Blacks to describe a member of the older generation.—Watts [section of L.A.].

Aunt Thomasina *n.* [sugg. by UNCLE TOM] AUNT JANE, 2.

1963 *Time* (Aug. 2) 14: *Aunt Tomasina*...A female Tom. **1970** *N.Y. Times* (Nov. 29) II 19: And the biggest Uncle Tom or Aunt Thomasina in the world wants to be free as the biggest, baddest Black Panther you'll ever find.

Aunt Tillies *n.pl.* [*aunt* + *Tillie*, regarded as an old-fashioned feminine name] a woman's nightgown.

1943 Wray & Geraghty *Falcon & Co-Eds* (film): I *would* have to have on these Aunt Tillies!

au reservoir *interj.* [intentional malapropism of F *au revoir*] "Goodbye." *Joc.*

1889 Farmer *Americanisms: Au Reservoir.—Au revoir.* A mere play upon sounds. Common and now often heard in England. **1906** *DN* III

125: *Au reservoir…Au revoir.* Facetious. **1918** *Sat. Eve. Post* (Jan. 19) 16: Au reservoir, old timer. **1918** *Sat. Eve. Post* (Nov. 9) 85: Au reservoir! **1955** O'Connor *Last Hurrah* 321: Not all ready to say au reservoir so soon, Tansy?

Aussie *n. & adj.* [dim. of *Australian*] Australian. Now *colloq.*
　　*1917 in *OEDS*. **1918** in Hall & Niles *One Man's War* 301: An Aussie flyer named McCormick. **1919** Wilson *364th Inf.* 93: British soldiers, and particularly "Aussies" with their turned-up hats, were everywhere in evidence. **1942** S. Johnston *Flat-tops* 133: The Aussies came out with tools but virtually no materials. **1945** G. Frank et al. *Seawolf* 61: More likely he was an Aussie. **1961** T. Williams *Night of Iguana* 227: The Aussie salesman asked me out in a sampan with him. **1962** Bonham *War Beneath the Sea* 90 [ref. to WWII]: "Wait'll you eat Aussie steak!" "What's wrong with it?" "It's mutton…old enough to have a driver's license." **1968** Phillips *Small World* 83: A charming Aussie girl.

autodog *n. Navy.* (see quots.).
　　1983 LaBarge & Holt *Sweetwater Gunslinger* 226: You want to buy the sliders and autodogs? *Ibid.* 279: *Auto-dog*—Soft ice cream which comes out of machines. **1986** M. Skinner *USN* ix: *Autodog*—Navy slang for soft ice-cream.

autogetem *n.* [*auto* 'automatic' + *get 'em* 'kill them'] *Mil.* the setting on a rifle for fully automatic fire.
　　1972 Casey *Obscenities* 42: Ack had his M-sixteen/On autogetem…. [Note] autogetem: automatic. **1980** DiFusco et al. *Tracers* 34 [ref. to Vietnam War]: Baby San, you know where to find "autogetem" on your M-16? **1991** L. Reinberg *In the Field* 13: *Auto-getem*, slang for automatic weapons fire.

autograph hound *n.* a collector of autographs, esp. an offensive person who clamors for the autographs of celebrities. Now *colloq.*
　　1933 in Ruhm *Detective* 72: He was an autograph hound….He collected autographs. Autographs of all the stars….He had five hundred of 'em. **1981** *Nat. Lampoon* (Oct.) 57: I can't stand these goddamn autograph hounds, Richard!

automobubble *n.* [intentional malapropism based on *automobile* + *bubble*] an automobile. *Joc.* See also BUBBLE.
　　1902 in Blackbeard & Williams *Smithsonian Comics* 23: John also "springs" for an "automobubble ride." **1968** Swarthout *Loveland* 103: Do we go for spins in their big automobubbles?

avalanche *n.* [intentional malapropism] ambulance. *Joc.*
　　1871 Schele de Vere *Amer.* 580: Avalanche, a corruption of ambulance, was already before the late Civil War much used in Texas and the outlying territories. **1903** R. Stiles *4 Years* 63 [ref. to Civil War]: You 'listed ter git killed and I 'listed ter drive a avalanche.

ave *n.* [spoken use of written abbrev.] avenue.
　　1985 "Run-D.M.C." *My Adidas* (rap song): I bought 'em off the ave with the black Lee denim. **1986** "Beastie Boys" in B. Adler *Rap!* 45: King of the Ave. **1987** *Village Voice* (N.Y.C.) (July 14) 26: The IROC-Z is premier on The Ave.

aviator *n.* [pun on *flier*] **1.** speeding driver.
　　1971 Tak *Truck Talk*: Aviator: a speeding driver. **1973** *AS* XLIV 202: *Aviator.* Speeding driver. **1976** Dills *CB '77* 3: That aviator is looking to feed the bears.
　　2. *Police.* (see quot.).
　　1972 J. Mills *Report* 13: *Aviator.* A police superior with no steady assignment who "flies" from job to job filling in for others of his rank who are ill or on vacation.

avocados *n.pl.* a woman's breasts.
　　1932 Nicholson & Robinson *Sailor* 7: How's that for a shape? Looka them avocados!

awash *adj.* drunk. *Joc.* Cf. AFLOAT.
　　1942 *ATS* 122: *Drunk…awash.* **1970** *Harper's* (Oct. 1) 72: She was already a trifle awash.

awesome *adj.* Esp. *Sports & Stu.* exceptionally good; wonderful. [This term is discussed in *WDEU*, p. 154, which also supplies an ambiguous 1925 quot. in a sporting context.]
　　1975 R. Hill *O.J. Simpson* 56: His first-year statistics were awesome. **1976** Univ. Tenn. student: There's no doubt about it, she's awesome. **1978** Shefski *Football Lang.* 94: A…ball carrier with awesome speed. **1980** L. Birnbach *Offic. Preppy Hndbk.* 218: *Awesome…*Terrific, great. "The saxophone player is awesome." **1988** *N.Y. Times Mag.* (Dec. 11) 24: In the old days we [college students] used to say "awesome" to express an approving wonderment….*Far out* was another common

term of 20 years ago that seems to have completely disappeared.

awful *adj.* **a.** frightful, offensive, exceedingly bad or inferior; unpleasant; terrible. Now *colloq.*
　　ca**1786** in S. Rodman *Amer. Poems* 44: Adam's wife destroyed his life/In manner that is awful. **1809** in *DAE*: I fear our…nation/Is in an awful situation. **1810** in Bartlett *Amer.* (ed. 2): The country people of the New England States make use of many quaint expressions….Every thing that creates surprise is *awful*…."What an *awful* wind! *awful* hole! *awful* hill! *awful* mouth! *awful* nose!" etc. **1815** in *DARE*: *Awful*, ugly. **1816** Pickering *Vocab.*: *Awful*, Disagreeable, ugly. *New England.* In New England many people would call a disagreeable medicine, *awful*; an ugly woman, an awful-looking woman….This word, however, is never used except in conversation, and is far from being so common in the Seaports now, as it was some years ago. *1834 C. Lamb, in *F & H* I 83: She is indeed, as the Americans would express it, something awful. **1847** Field *Pokerville* 103: Madison is an "awful place for revivals." **1864** in Cate *Two Soldiers* 249: Have an awful time. **1864** in Jackman *Diary* 145: Our fare was "awful." *a**1880** in *F & H* I 83: In an awful fix. **1905** *DN* III 2: *Awful*…ugly, disagreeable. **1908** McGaffey *Show Girl* 90: You've made an awful good showing. **1909** *WNID*: *Awful*…Frightful, exceedingly bad; monstrous; as, an *awful* bonnet. *Slang.* **1918** H.L. Mencken *Amer. Lang.* 306: "*Awful* children," "*awful* weather," and an "*awful* job" have entirely sound support, and no one save a pedant would hesitate to use them.
　　b. great or remarkable in degree, quality, duration, number, etc. Now *colloq.*
　　[*1794 Hester Lynch Piozzi, in *WDEU*: The word *awful* should however be used with caution, and a due sense of its importance; I have heard even well-bred ladies now and then attribute that term too lightly in their common conversation, connecting it with substances beneath its dignity.] *1818 J. Keats, in *OEDS*: It is an awful while since you have heard from me. **1843** in Bartlett *Amer.*: Pot-pie is the favorite dish, and woodsmen…are *awful* eaters. **1847** Field *Pokerville* 103: We have an "awful" curiosity to do so. **1871** Schele de Vere *Amer.* 437: An *awful* swell. **1956** in *DARE*: His gran'daddy was an awful hunter; he hunted bear a lot. **1958** N.Y.C. man, age ca70: He was always an awful kidder, that guy. **1962** M.M. Bryant *Current Amer. Usage* 35: "An *awful* lot of them" or "an *awful* bore."

awful *adv.* exceedingly. Now *colloq.* [The form *awfully* has always been colloq. in U.S.]
　　1818 in *DA*: [It is] awful hot. *1832 in *OED2*: An awful bad sermon. **1837** in N. Hawthorne *Centenary Ed.* IX 209: Awful hot! Dreadful dusty! **1848** Bartlett *Amer.*: An awful cold day. **1846–51** in Bartlett *Amer.* (ed. 2): I never thought she was so awful handsome as some folks does. **1861** in Norton *Army Letters* 15: He was awful mad. **1861** in *Register of Ky. Hist. Soc.* LXVII (1969) 137: Was "*awful*" glad. **1864** in Jackman *Diary* 136: Looks "awful" dark. **1867** in S. Hale *Letters* 31: Sherbet [is] awful good! **1871** Schele de Vere *Amer.* 437: He gets awful mad. *1883 in *F & H* I 83: I'm awful glad you two have made acquaintance. **1918** H.L. Mencken *Amer. Lang.* 306: "*Awful* sweet"…still [sounds] slangy and school-girlish. **1921** in *DAE*: Looks awful good to me. **1952** *Collier's* (Nov. 29) 32: I was awful scared.

AWOL *abbr.* [from standard mil. abbr., "*absent without leave*"] *Mil.* (facetiously interpreted as "A Wolf on the Loose" or "After Women or Liquor").
　　1942 Sanders & Blackwell *Forces* 17: A.W.O.L.:…A wolf on the loose. **1944** Kendall *Service Slang*: A.W.O.L….A Wolf On the Loose. After Women or Liquor. **1947** *AS* (Apr.) 109: A.W.O.L.—also pronounced disyllabically as A-WOL has come to signify "after women and liquor" and "a wolf on the loose."

AWOL bag *n.* [(jocularly) a bag to be used when going absent without leave] *Mil.* overnight bag. *Joc.*
　　1956 Hargrove *Girl He Left* 108: He had providently purchased a bottle and stowed it in his A-wol bag. **1967** Ford *Muc Wa* 26: Ski charged across the room…swinging his Awol bag to clear a path. **1969** *Esquire* (Sept.) 118: He picked up his duffel and small A.W.O.L. bag and started for the airstrip. **1971** Cole *Rook* 327: He pointed at my AWOL bag. **1978** Groom *Better Times* 464: The crew chief…took his AWOL bag for him. **1991** L. Reinberg *In the Field*: *AWOL Bag*, slang for an overnight bag.

A.W.O. Loose *adj. Mil.* absent without leave. [Early quots. ref. to WWI.]
　　1920 [Simmons] *20th Engrs.* (unp.): But that was not being done in those days in Paris with men A.W.O. Loose. **1925** Nason *Three Lights* 197: If we turn up *minus* one G.I. ambulance and A.W.O. Loose for two

or three days, you know where we go. **1927** *Amer. Legion Mo.* (June) 73: I been nursin' him half way across France so's I wouldn't get slapped in the mill for bein' AWO loose! **1929** Springs *Carol Banks* 112: I'm going A.W.O. Loose. **1931** Tomlinson *Best Stories of War* 357: You been busted?…Huh? Drunk? A.W.O. Loose? **1944** Tregaskis *Invasion* 215: They would desert and go back to their outfits at the front, go "A.W.O. Loose," rather than put up with the delay and inactivity at the Repple Depples. **1965** Linakis *In Spring* 25: Before everybody started going A.W.O. Loose, nobody expected a firing squad.

awse *adj.* awesome.
1989 Bynum & Thompson *Juv. Delinquency* 270: "Hip,"…"neat," "cool,"…"awse" (short for awesome).

ax or **axe** *n.* **1.** a finishing action, such as a dismissal from a position, defeat in a game, expulsion from school, rejection of a lover, etc.—esp. in phr. **get** [or **give**] **the ax.**
1883 in *DA*: The *axe*, or rather the guillotine, is made to represent the dismissal of Government officials upon the coming of a new President or in case of some grave complications. **1897** *Volunteer* 140 (football cheer): Gibem the ax, the ax, the ax!/Gibem the ax, the ax, the ax!/Where, O where?/In the neck, the neck, the neck!/In the neck, the neck, the neck!/There, O there! **1919** in Horowitz *Campus Life* 122: Therefore study constantly and avoid the axe. **1924** *Adventure* (Sept. 30) 148: Failure on both subjects meant the axe. **1936** Levin *Old Bunch* 163: I'll try and hold up [delay] the ax. **1942** *ATS* 28: Eliminate; Discard; Get Rid Of…give the axe. *Ibid.* 67: Discharge; "Fire"…give the axe. *Ibid.* 68: Be Discharged or "Fired"…get or feel the axe. *Ibid.* 135: Kill; Murder…give the ax. *Ibid.* 136: Be Killed…get the ax. *Ibid.* 236: "Shut Up"…give yourself the axe. *Ibid.* 338: Jilting.—The air,…the axe,…the brush-off. **1951** in *DAS* 11: They give guys the ax quite frequently at Pencey. It has a very good academic rating. **1953** Brossard *Saboteurs* 184: The old lady gets the axe. **1959** Morrill *Dark Sea* 91: The Old Man was one of them holy-christers that put the axe on real sailoring. **1968** Hoffman *Revolution* 65: She agreed to go along and of course got the ax from the administration. **1968** Baker et al. *CUSS* 73: *Ax, get the.* Treated unfairly on an exam. **1968** Hudson *Need* 159: The pharmacist nearly got the ax. **1978** Univ. Tenn. student, age 18: Bill's girlfriend just gave him the ax. **1990** *Ebony* (Dec.) 52: Joan Rivers got the ax and he got the milestone gig of his life hosting Fox's doomed *Late Night Show.*
2. a straight razor or knife.
1896 in A. Charters *Ragtime Songbk.* 43: I'm goin' down the street with my ax in my hand.…/I'll take 'long my razor, I'm goin' to carve him deep. **1929** *Sat. Eve. Post* (Apr. 13) 51: A knife or a razor is a chev, an ax, a blade, or steel. **1969** Gordone *No Place* 449: What's ya, crazy, Pops? Put that ax away. **1972** Claerbaut *Black Jargon* 57: *Ax*…a knife, usually serving as a weapon.
3. the penis.—usu. considered vulgar.
1915 in Randolph & Legman *Roll Me in Your Arms* 161: When I was young and in my prime,/ Sunk my axe deep 'most every time. **1967** "Iceberg Slim" *Pimp* 50: His…axe cast a cruel shadow.
4. [sense development unkn.; perh. orig. sugg. by *sax*; perh. infl. by *swing*] *Jazz.* a musical instrument, esp. one on which jazz or rock music is played, as a saxophone, trumpet, or guitar.
1955 in *Tenn. Folk. Soc. Bull.* XXI (1956) 22: *Ax*—saxophone. **1956** Hunter *Second Ending* 132: I picked up my ax and almost brained the son-of-a-bitch. **1956** in Gold *Jazz Lexicon*: You wanta make it with me

tonight? Bring your ax. **1956** Blake *Joint* 143: He bring his axe into the club often…and we gas one another. **1958–59** Lipton *Barbarians* 85: Any jazz instrument is an "ax"—in Phil's case, the bass. **1961** J. Williams *Night Song* 44: Eagle, the last year, had been sounding plaintive, almost whiny on his ax. **1968** *Rolling Stone Interviews* 140: His axe was trombone. **1971** Wells & Dance *Night People* 72: I dig you man, but it's funny how my old lady would rather me starve than put my axe down. **1980** N.C. man, age 29: My guitar is my ax, man.

ax or **axe** *v.* to dismiss or discharge; drop, cancel, reject, etc.
*1922 in *OEDS*. **1942** *ATS* 67. *Ibid.* 275. **1950** *Time* (Oct. 30) 47: So far this year, CBS has axed…its summer symphony broadcasts. **1979** *N.Y. Post* (Dec. 10) 6: Doorman axed for aiding celeb-tenant. **1980** *N.Y. Daily News* (Dec. 24) 14: Haig axes policy team for news leaks to media. **1982** Univ. Tenn. *Daily Beacon* (June 25) 3: Parton, Osmonds Ax Concert. **1982** *N.Y. Post* (Aug. 27) 93: The trade had been made.…Oscar axed it. **1990** *U.S. News & W.R.* (Nov. 19) 79: Inappropriate domestic spending is not axed, nor is our military budget reorganized.

ax-holder *n.* a hand. *Joc.*
ca1885 in Botkin *Sidewalks* 44: "I like your face monstrous well. Give me your axholder!" Trap gave him his hand.

axle *n.* [euphem. for ASS, *n.*, 1] ASS, *n.*, 1.
1934 H. Roth *Sleep* 315 Aaa, kiss my axle. **1958** *Time* (June 9) 94: Man, you're draggin' your rear axle in waltztime.
¶ In phrase:
¶ **get one's axle greased** (of a man) to engage in sexual intercourse, esp. after a period of abstinence.—usu. considered vulgar.
1962 Killens *Thunder* 194 [ref. to WWII]: God dammit, why in the hell don't you two studs get off your dead asses and go into town sometimes and get your axles greased?

axle grease *n.* **1.** Esp. *Mil.* oleomargarine or butter.
1883 Peck *Bad Boy* 222: Pa says that last oleomargarine I got here is nothing but axle grease. **1906** H. Green *Boarding House* 58: Pass the axle grease! **1919** *Lit. Digest* (Feb. 8) 90: Two kinds of butter [in the Army]—"salve and axle grease." **1919** Darling *Jargon Bk.*: *Axel* [sic] *Grease*—Butter. **1922** *Leatherneck* (Apr. 22) 5: *Axle Grease:* Butter named because of the similarity in appearance, consistency and, sometimes, taste. **1936** *AS* (Feb.) 42: *Axle Grease.* Butter. **1942** *Yank* (Nov. 11) 4: Navy [slang]…*Axle-grease*—Butter. **1956** *AS* (Oct.) 192: *Axle grease* is butter [in USMC].
2. bribe money.
1891 Maitland *Slang Dict.* 20: *Axle-grease*, money; esp. that used for purposes of bribery.

axman *n.* a man who uses an AX, 2; (*specif.*) a barber.
1929 *Sat. Eve. Post* (Apr. 13) 50: [The convict] is skinned by the axman or the barber. **1942–49** Goldin et al. *DAUL* 20: *Axeman.*…A prison barber.…[Also] One who uses a knife when fighting.

Aztec two-step *n.* diarrhea or dysentery contracted in Mexico by a foreign tourist. Cf. MONTEZUMA'S REVENGE.
1953 Sherman *The Aztec Two-Step* (title). **1958** Ferlinghetti *Coney I.* 18: A couple of Papist cats/is doing an Aztec two-step. **1962** Shepard *Press Passes* 6: There was kaopectate, seconal, jolly pills, nose drops, tablets to discourage the Aztec two-step. **1968** WINS radio news (Aug. 24): The Aztec two-step. **1987** *Tour of Duty* (CBS-TV): There's nothing funny about the Aztec two-step.

B.A. *n.* **1.** [*b*usted *a*ristocrat; facetiously alluding to *B*achelor of *A*rts] *Army.* an officer, esp. a cadet officer, who has been reduced in rank.

1900 *Howitzer* (U.S. Mil. Acad.) 117: *B.A.*—"Busted Aristocrat," one who has once worn chevrons but has been relieved of them. **1938** in *AS* XIV 32: *B.A.*—"Busted Aristocrat," cadet officer reduced to the ranks. **1976** Berry *Kaiser* 170 [ref. to WWI]: Three of Pershing's generals...were knocked way down in rank when they hit the dock back home—they used to call these men BA's for "Busted Aristocrats."

2. *Naut.* Buenos Aires, Argentina.

1925 Dos Passos *Manhattan* 294: Ze best joint I've been in since B.A. **1929–30** Dos Passos *42d Parallel* 149: I deserted in B.A., see, and shipped out East on a limey. **1940** *Life* (Oct. 28) 67: All the dancin' stars of the tango bars/Will escort you about B.A. **1947** Schulberg *Harder They Fall* 68: We're still down in B.A. **1973** Haston *High Places* 98: B.A. is a pleasant city; reminds me a lot of Paris.

3. [*b*are *a*ss] *Stu.* an act of exposing one's buttocks, esp. from the window of an automobile, as an obscene prank.—sometimes constr. with *hang.* Cf. MOON. Cf. PRESSED HAM.

1970 *Current Slang* V 20: Hang a B.A., v. To exhibit one's naked posterior. Known [also] as "mooning" or "hanging moons." **1973** Lucas, Katz & Huyck *Amer. Graffiti* 24: A guy...is pushing his bare buttocks against the side window—a classic BA...with pressed ham. **1976** *West. Folklore* XXXV 270: The [surfers]...would do "BA's" ("bare-assing") out car windows or next to passenger trains. **1981** *Nat. Lampoon* (July) 53: Both me and Barney [were] hanging our asses out the windows and yelling "B.A." as loud as we could....We ran thirty-five red lights in a row with continuous B.A.'s on both sides of the car. **1990** Munro *Slang U.* 25: That guy just hung a B.A. in front of my mom!

B.A. *adj.* [*b*are-*a*ss(ed)] naked, nude.

1933 Farrell *Guillotine Party* 70: How'd you like to come in on one of our B.A. parties? **1971** Faust *Willy* 35: There we were b.a. as the East River and it is the start of a real bare-ass war.

babbler *n. Hunting.* a hound that bays or barks inopportunely.

***1732** in *OED.* **1949** Cummings *Dict. Sports: Babbler*...A foxhound that bays when not on the line. **1979** Cuddon *Dict. Sports & Games* 69: A babbler is a hound that gives tongue too freely. A serious shortcoming.

babe *n.* **1.** *U.S. Mil. Acad.* the youngest member of a class of cadets.

1871 Wood *W. Point Scrapbook* 337: Babe—Name given to the youngest man in the class. **1889** Farmer *Americanisms*: Babe...A term of little wit or point applied to the youngest member of a class at the West Point...Military Academy. **1900** *Howitzer* (U.S. Mil. Acad.) 117: *Babe*—The youngest member of a class.

2. a man, fellow, esp. one who is somehow remarkable—now used only in direct address. Cf. BABY, 1.a. and c.

[**1859** Bartlett *Americanisms* (ed. 2) 17: *Babes.* The name of a set of Baltimore rowdies.] **1898–1900** Cullen *Chances* 52: He's uh babe, yo' heah me! **1901** Irwin *Sonnets* (unp.): There are foxier, warmer babes than I. **1906** H. Green *Actors' Boarding House* 61: "How's that, babe?" he asked coolly. **1921–25** J. Gleason & Taber *Is Zat So* 50 [man to man]: Leave it to me, babe. **1929** Perelman *Ginsbergh* 144: We're both lucky fellows, babe. **1933** Ford & Tyler *Young & Evil* 207: Relax babe...I don't hold nothin against youse guys. **1961** Brosnan *Pennant Race* 14: "Who you rootin' for tonight, Gab?"..."I'm with you, babe." **1962** Carr & Cassavetes *Too Late Blues* (film): Later, babe. **1966** Neugeboren *Big Man* 4 [a man speaking to a man]: How's it going, babe? **1964–66** R. Stone *Hall of Mirrors* 243: After this we're national, babe. **1980** N.Y.C. man, age 30: Talk to you later, babe. **1987** *Night Court* (NBC-TV): Look, babe, cut me some slack here. **1992** G. Trudeau *Doonesbury* (synd. cartoon strip) (Sept. 30): How long you been a Chip, babe?

3.a. sweetheart (used as an endearment to either sex). Also **babes.** Cf. BABY, 1.b.

1890 in Dobie *Rainbow* 162: But I like my Houston babe. **1893** in Dobie *Rainbow* 165: I'll lay my Gatlin' at my head, Babe. **1903** Ade *Society* 106: It makes him Hop-Eyed to see some 90-pound Rabbit...chase up to the Goddess and give her the kitchy-kitchy Business under the

Chin and call her "Babe." **1911** *JAF* (July) 278: I love my babe and wouldn't put her out of doors. **1915** in Handy *Blues Treasury* 94: Sweet Babe, I'm goin' to leave you, and the time ain't long. **1921** in Kimball & Bolcolm *Sissle & Blake* 102: First you take your babe and gently hold her. **1926** in Handy *Blues Treasury* 120: Ain't had no lovin' since my babe's been gone./...When he gets lonesome he will think of me. **1944** Burley *Harlem Jive* 13: Listen Babes, you're mellow, understand? **1952** E. Brown *Trespass* 110: "Really, babe," she said, "really, I'm sorry." **1953** W. Fisher *Waiters* 162: Pay 'em no mind, babes. **1967–69** Foster & Stoddard *Pops* 34: She'd say, "Oh babe, I didn't do so good." **1990** *Cosmopolitan* (Sept.) 84: Try Workin' Your Way Back to Me, Babe!

b. a woman, esp. if attractive.—sometimes considered offensive. Cf. BABY, 1.d.

1905 Brainerd *Belinda* 75: It isn't likely that any of those babes are in the game with Liz. **1915** *DN* IV 231 [W. Reserve Univ.]: *Babe, n.* A pretty girl. "She's some babe." **1920** Bissell *63rd Inf.* 148: Some time in May there came...rumors of a lot of "babes." **1922** S. Lewis *Babbitt* 172: The bonniest bevy of beauteous bathing babes in burlesque. **1933** *Leatherneck* (May) 37: Fellows who call girls "Babes." **1937** *Review of Revs.* (June) 43: *A babe*—Any female between 18 and 80. **1940** Goodrich *Delilah* 447: Come on, babe, let's take a walk. **1941** H.A. Smith *Low Man* 64: These girls are hard, tough-talking babes. **1941** Boardman, Perrin & Grant *Keep 'Em Flying* (film): Look, I got special plans for that babe. **1946** Michener *S. Pacific* 341: I looked across the aisle and there was this babe. **1957** Leckie *Helmet* 94: Think of all them babes lining the street. **1964** "Doctor X" *Intern* 224: Look, let's get this babe home before she kills somebody. **1961–64** Barthelme *Caligari* 3: The old babe is on a kick tonight. **1973** Lucas, Katz & Huyck *Amer. Graffiti* 56: What a bitchin' babe....And...she's all mine. **1977** *N.Y. Post* (July 23) 2: The people start coming out to see it—especially the babes. **1990** *Cosmopolitan* (Nov.) 124: I'll bet the snake is even seeing some babe behind the bimbo's back right now.

c. *Stu.* (among young women) an attractive young man.

1973 *TULIPQ* (coll. B.K. Dumas): He's a real *babe*....Mr. *America!* **1982** Pond *Valley Girl's Gd.* 43: I mean, he was *kind* of a babe. **1983** *L.A. Times* (Aug. 23) VI 1: He is such a babe. He is definitely cuter than Rick Springfield. **1983** Glass *Deprogram Valley Girl* 28: *Babe:* attractive member of either sex. *Ibid.* 57: Bobby is a bitchen babe. **1985** B.E. Ellis *Less Than Zero* 23: She's going out with the biggest babe. *Ibid.* 132: "He's gorgeous."..."Total babe." **1987** Univ. Tenn. student theme: A "babe" is a good-looking or very charming person of the opposite sex.

4. *Stu.* a freshman.

1927 *AS* II 275: *Babes*—freshmen [at Stanford Univ. and elsewhere on Pacific Coast].

babelicious /ˌbeibəˈlɪʃəs/ *adj.* [BABE, 3 + de*licious*] (of a person of the opposite sex, esp. a woman) stunningly attractive. [Introduced on the sketch "Wayne's World" on *Saturday Night Live* (NBC-TV) and popularized in the movie *Wayne's World* (1992).]

1992 *N.Y. Times* (Mar. 8) II 15: *Babelicious* (adj.)...A tasty babe [*sic*]. **1993** *Beavis & Butt-Head* (MTV): She's babelicious. **1993** *TV Guide* (Sept. 25) 22: Kelly...isn't just a babe. She's a megababe. She's babelicious.

baboon *n.* a person regarded as resembling a baboon in ugliness, stupidity, or primitive behavior.

***1614** B. Jonson *Bartholomew Fair* II i: Are you underpeering, you baboon? ***1677** in D'Urfey *Two Comedies* 184: A stallion in his youth,...a baboon in his age. **1835** in Paulding *Bulls & Jons.* 18: Old Lewis Baboon [Louis XVI]...was killed by his tenants in a drunken frolic. **1848** Thompson *House Breaker* 6: I'll split that baboon skull of yours as I would a cocoa-nut! **1865** in *DA* s.v. *Illinois:* [The Appeal] was noticeably free from vituperation, calling the President "Mr. Lincoln," instead of the "Illinois Baboon." **1925** Riesenberg *Under Sail* 294: Fred, take that baboon and loose the fore upper tops'l. **1970** N.Y.U. students: "See you later, alligator." "Not too soon, you big baboon." **1981** *Nat. Lampoon* (Nov.) 73: Big baboon!

baboon-faced *adj.* having a face like that of a baboon; very ugly.

1942 Burnett & Butler *Wake Island* (film): Why, you baboon-faced, no good—

baboon jacket *n.* [cf. MONKEY JACKET] *Naut.* a short work jacket.

1839 Olmsted *W. Voyage* 104: The overcoats worn by sailors, are known by rather whimsical names. There are two kinds, the *baboon jacket*, a short coat without any skirts, and the *monkey jacket*, differing from the other in having a kind of ruffle around the lower edge answering to skirts.

baby *n.* **1.a.** (used as a familiar term of address between persons of the same sex, esp. between men). [Esp. in vogue in the 1960's.]

1835 in Paulding *Bulls & Jons.* 138: Well, corporal,…well, my fine fellow, have you dished that rebellious rogue, my son Jonathan—hey, baby?…Out with it, my hearty! **1921** *Variety* (Dec. 30) 4: "Hello, baby, what's new?" said the 47th Street regular as he inhaled his morning Java. "New York, New Haven, New London," responded his actor-pal. **1928–30** Fiaschetti *Gotta Be Rough* 13: "Say, boy, you're a gonner." "Listen, baby, you're going to croak." **1933** Mizner & Holmes *20,000 Yrs. in Sing Sing* (film): OK, baby, it's all right with me. **1934** Wohlforth *Tin Soldiers* 17: The hell we can fix it up, baby. This is a barracks. They want it like this. **1939** "E. Queen" *Dragon's Teeth* 118: I'm with you, baby. **1944** Stiles *Big Bird* 146: You're okay…baby…your wing is okay. No smoke…no flame…stay in there, baby. **1949** Gresham *Limbo Tower* 65: It's oke by me, baby. **1951** Lampell & Buchman *Saturday's Hero* (film): Joey, have a wonderful time in college, baby. **1952** "E. Box" *Fifth Position* 93: Hi, Baby.…long time no see!…Louis [had] absorbed a great deal of Nineteen twenty slang which sounds very funny coming from him. **1962** Carr & Cassavetes *Too Late Blues* (film): Not now, baby, I'm busy. **1963** in H. Ellison *Sex Misspelled* 41: "Hey, baby, what's shakin'?" "Howya doin', man?" **1965** C. Brown *Manchild* 171: The first time I heard the expression "baby" used by one cat to address another was up at Warwick in 1951.

b. darling, sweetheart.—used esp. in direct address.—occ. as interj., "wow!" "man!" etc. Now *colloq.*

1869 Stowe *Oldtown* 184: Yes, Tina, I *am* glad…but, baby, we can't stop to say so much because we must…get…way off before day-light. *Ibid.:* Don't let's talk any more, baby. **1889** Harte *Dedlow Marsh* 9: "Lean on me, baby," he returned, passing his arm around her waist. **1890** in Dobie *Rainbow* 162: Well, Baby, your house rent's due. **1891** Maitland *Amer. Slang:* Baby, a prostitute's lover, or "fancy man." **1892** in Dobie *Rainbow* 162: My baby likes whiskey straight. **1897** *A Hot Time in the Old Town Tonight* (pop. song): There'll be a hot time in the old town tonight, my baby. **1911** *JAF* (July) 281: If my baby ask for me/ Tell her I boun' to go. **1914** in Handy *Blues Treasury* 72: Cause my baby he done lef dis town. **1923** McKnight *Eng. Words* 59: Oh, baby! **1924** *DN* V 262: *Oh baby* [exclam. of]…joy. **1925** in Handy *Treasury of Blues* 49: Late last night when my baby came home/I heard a mighty knocking on my door/…Told him baby don't you knock no more. **1938** in A. Lomax *Mr. Jelly Roll* 121 [ref. to *ca*1905]: One of them good looking girls told me, "Baby, come on and leave this town." **1944** Quillan & Bennett *Show Business* (film) [a woman speaking to a man]: OK, baby, but you promised me last night. **1948** J. Stevens *Jim Turner* 119 [ref. to *ca*1910]: "First time, baby?" I heard the woman say. **1960** Oster *Country Blues* 81: My baby she don't love me, and I can't see why. **1968** "The Box Tops" *The Letter* (song): My baby just wrote me a letter. **1970** D.L. Lee *We Walk* 21: We wore 24 hr. sunglasses & called our woman *baby*. **1990** "Iggy Pop" *My Baby Wants to Rock and Roll* (song title).

c. a person, fellow, "customer." [Most common *ca*1895–1930.]

1880 in Davidson *Old West* 25: For punishing booze, he can beat any baby;/They say that for women, Old Tom is hell bent. **1896** in Crane *NYC Sketches* 182: Dat dar Kent…he was a hard baby—'deed he was. **1897** Ade *Pink* 165: 'Ey's only one hot baby, misteh, an' 'at's Misteh Peteh Jackson. **1900** *DN* II 42: He is a hot-baby in Greek. **1900** Cullen *Chances* 53: It's a cake-walk fo' dat baby [a racehorse]. **1903** A.H. Lewis *Boss* 186: Keep your peepers on them babies. **1911** A.H. Lewis *Apaches of N.Y.* 77: All the same, I'll lay for them babies. **1914** Lardner *Al* 148: Say, I wish I could of heard what they said to that baby on the bench. **1918** Witwer *Baseball* 191: They are hard-lookin' babies, Joe. **1924** T. Boyd *Pts. of Honor* 120: "That's the baby," affirmed the colonel in his grotesque, out-of-date slang. **1930** Farrell *Calico Shoes* 192: "That's the ticket," Swede! "That's the babee!" **1932** L. Berg *Prison Doctor* 217 [a woman speaking]: And I'm the baby that's going to see to that! **1939–40** Tunis *Kid from Tomkinsville* 63: When he's good that baby is sure good. **1953** Freeman *Destination Gobi* (film): That mean-lookin' baby

in the fur hat…looks like trouble. **1953** R. Wright *Outsider* 143: And you got a fat chance of collecting 'cause that baby's where you can't get at 'im. **1957** Murtagh & Harris *Cast Stone* 303: Baby. A prostitute's customer.—*a hundred-dollar baby.* A man willing to pay $100 for a girl. **1967–69** Foster & Stoddard *Pops Foster* 41: They were rough babies who drank a lot and really romped. **1989** *Dream St.* (NBC-TV): You better back these babies off.

d. an attractive young woman. [*OEDS* 1839 quot., not cited here, only dubiously illustrates this sense; those for 1870–1918 are prob. better regarded as exx. of **(b)**, above.]

1897 Ade *Pink* 171: If I evah land at baby…I jus' got to have one of em wahm lettehs. **1900** *DN* II 21: *Baby, n.* A pretty girl. **1906** H. Green *Boarding House* 30: Swell Fift' Avenoo babies they is, too. **1920** *Hicoxy's Army* 118: At St. Malo, all the "babies" called him father. **1922** *Pirate Piece* (Sept.) 3: Delegates were checked in by one swell "baby." **1923** Ornitz *Haunch* 40: The gang had its female followers, who were admiringly called "tough babies." **1927** McKay *Harlem* 78: Oh, I got a sweet baby way up yonder the other side of the hill. **1931** Hellinger *Moon* 203: Some guys are just born dumb. And it takes a baby like me to find out where the pickings are best. **1944–49** Allardice *At War* 43: You couldn't even rate a smile from the baby I'm seein'.

2. a bottle or glass of liquor.—occ. in phr. **kiss the baby** to drink from a bottle of liquor.

*****1853** in *OEDS:* A stone bottle of ardent spirits called baby for shortness and secrecy. *Ibid.:* He has nabbed a "baby!" **1865** Sala *Diary* I 119: In Vermont…when you have the "office" given you, and enter the "right place," you ask how the "baby is?" *ca*1875 in Aswell *Humor* 341: "Kiss baby, gents," said the man from Buffalo Wallow.…Then all was silence except for a brief community gurgling. *a*1903–09 *F & H* I (rev.) 88: *To kiss the baby*…(American).—To take a drink. **1936** Washburn *Parlor* 83 [ref. to 1890's]: In Clark Street was the Workingman's Exchange, a saloon in which "babies" (16-ounce glasses of beer) could be had for a nickel. **1956** Neider *Hendry Jones* 103: He lifted a whisky bottle to his mouth,…said "Kiss me baby" and passed the bottle around. **1965** Wallace *Skid Row* 202: Baby is born—the bottle gang has enough money for the bottle.

3.a. a thing of excellence. [Now merged with **(b)**, below.]

1898–1900 Cullen *Chances* 29: It's a baby. It's a looloo. It's a cachuca. **1900** *DN* II 21 [at Tufts College]: *Baby*…Anything nice. **1902** Cullen *More Tales* 95: It's a baby of a maxim for prophetic truthfulness.

b. an item, thing, esp. if large or formidable.—often applied to weapons and motor vehicles.

1907 *Army & Navy Life* (Oct.) 429: A man wearin' all them fierce lookin' cartridges and them two big baby guns attached. **1908** in McCay *Little Nemo* 157: See up there? Watch this baby [an automobile] climb up there! Watch! **1918** Lindner *Letters* (Sept. 5): The French "75" is some baby of a gun, a bitch dog for a fight. **1922** *Sat. Eve. Post* (July 29) 13: Watch the next baby [fast ball]! **1944** H. Brown *Walk in Sun* 108: I don't know how much armor those babies carry. **1957** E. Brown *Locust Fire* 27: Around fifty of those babies will demolish the runway. **1959** Groninger *Run from Mt.* 21: The big baby is the Headquarters Building. **1960** Archibald *Jet Flier* 33: Who's flying this baby? **1967–69** G.M. Foster & Stoddard *Pops Foster* 2: You've got to grip those babies [bass strings] to get a tone. **1977** Langone *Life at Bottom* 76: Tryin' to grab a pair of pliers in them babies is worse than tryin' to take a piss in hockey mitts. **1981** *Mr. Merlin* (CBS-TV): You're just cranking these babies [i.e., counterfeit bills] out!

4. (one's) special project, interest, or responsibility.—constr. with possessive pronoun. [1890 quot. in *OEDS* does not illustrate the slang use of this word.]

1929 A.C. Doyle *Maricot* ch. 1: "What in thunder is it?"…"That's my baby, sir.…Yes, Mr. Headley, that's what I am here for." **1936** M. Davis *Lost Generation* 56: They have no sense either of responsibility or obligation to the country or society.…It's not their baby. **1948** Hargrove *Got to Give* 95: From the opening commercial to the closing, it's your baby. **1949** Grayson & Andrews *I Married a Communist* (film): It's your baby. **1951** *New Yorker* (Feb. 17) 22: It's my baby to sell. **1970** Boatright & Owens *Derrick Floor* 53: If you don't want to clear them up now, why it'll be your baby to clear them up later.

5. [cf. BABY SHIT] *U.S. Mil. Acad.* mustard.

1935 in IUFA *Folk Speech:* Baby…mustard. **1941** *AS* (Oct.) 163: *Baby* s.v.: Mustard. **1942–44** in *AS* (Feb. 1946) 31: *Baby, n.* Mustard.

6. *USAF.* an extra fuel tank that extends the range of a fighter aircraft until the tank is jettisoned.

1946 G.C. Hall, Jr. *1000 Destroyed* 34: Pilots called these extra fuel tanks "babies," and doubtless the literal-minded Krauts were rather confused the first time they heard a U.S. pilot shout to another, "Drop your baby!" **1956** Heflin *USAF Dict.* 67: *Baby, n.* An extra fuel tank on an airplane, which may be jettisoned. *Slang.*

7. *Pris.* a ball and chain.

1954 Gaddis *Birdman* 25 [ref. to Leavenworth Federal Penitentiary, *ca*1912]: "Carrying the Baby" was a common form of punishment. Offenders were chained for months to a twenty-five pound iron ball. In order to walk, they had to carry the ball.

8. (see quot.).

1978 Time-Life eds. *Gamblers* 61: Three-card monte was played with a couple of insignificant cards…and a face card or an ace, which was called the "baby."

9. *Wrestling.* a wrestler who adopts a heroic persona in professional matches.

1980 *AS* (Summer) 144: [A "heroic" wrestler] is called…a *baby,* short for *babyface.*…Thus, a match between good guys and bad guys would be a work of babies and heels.

¶ In phrases:

¶ **baby needs a pair of shoes** [sugg. that one has expenses to meet] (a traditional exclamation of crapshooters).

1918 Witwer *Baseball* 293: Joe, the air is full of "Baby needs shoes!"—"Come on, little fever!"—"Ha, Big Dick from Boston!" **1919** *Amer. Legion Wkly.* (July 25) 18: "Little Joe." "Baby needs a pair of shoes." "Roll you bones." **1947** Motley *Any Door* 94: Come on seven, come on seven, baby needs shoes.

¶ **have a baby** to experience fright, shock, or anger; (*also*) to fret.

*1950 Partridge *DSUE* (ed. 3) 985: *Baby, have a.* To be much shocked or non-plussed or flabbergasted: middle-class: since ca. 1930. **1965** Linakis *In Spring* 224: I thought they were going to have a baby when they saw me. **1965** Horan *Seat of Power* 105: For Christ's sake! Stop havin' a baby! **1972** in *Playboy* (Feb. '73) 181: They go extra innings, I'm gonna have a baby or something.

¶ **play baby** [or **the baby act**] to act in an infantile manner; to whine or complain; to feign innocence.

1872 Burnham *Secret Service* vii: *Play Baby,* to whine; "squawk," or assume innocence. *Ibid.* 203: He didn't "squeal" on his assaulters, or "play baby." **1900** Willard & Hodler *Powers That Prey* 183: Any one 'ud think that that copper had hit you with a baseball bat the way you play the baby act. **1947** *Chi. Tribune* (June 28) 8: In 1935, when the atrocious Wagner law went into effect, did employers and stockholders play the baby act and go on strike?

¶ **plead the baby act** [from a legal idiom; see *OEDS* s.v. *baby* B2] to attempt to excuse one's actions by pleading youth or inexperience.

1868 *Putnam's Mag.* II 570, in *DA:* Don't plead the baby act, Chinny! **1888** in *OEDS:* [Mr. S.S. Cox] admits…authorship…but pleads the baby act, and says he was a boy when he wrote it. **1891** Maitland *Amer. Slang Dict.* 21: *Baby act,* "to plead the". to plead infancy as a defense to a suit at law. Otherwise to beg off on the ground of youth or inexperience; to weaken.

¶ **spank the baby** (see quot.).

1970 *Playboy* (Apr.) 104: At times he [Furry Lewis, blues guitarist] slapped the guitar box with two fingers or the heel of his hand as, in the same motion, he brushed the strings. "Call that spank the baby," he said.

¶ (In prov. comparisons).

1935 S. Lewis *Can't Happen* 8: His red face was smooth as a baby's bottom. **1939** "E. Queen" *Dragon's Teeth* 23: No, son, the set-up is as smooth as a baby's —. **1953** Eyster *Customary Skies* 10: White as a baby's ass, ain't it? **1960** Barber *Minsky's* 235: She mighta been bald as a baby's ass for all I know. **1964** Newhafer *Tallyho* 146: He wanted his plane shining like a baby's ass. **1965** Beech *Make War* 53: A senior officer with a baby's-ass shave. **1969** Stern *Eagles* 69: Slick as a baby's ass.…I'll agree with you there. **1979** Crews *Blood & Grits* 103: His head is shaved as slick as a baby's ass.

baby *adj.* small.—used prenominally. Now *colloq.*

1891 Clurman *Nick Carter* 40: He's a baby terror, he is. **1896** Ade *Artie* 10: I'll try it, an' if it don't go, it's a baby risk. **1945** in *Calif. Folk. Qly.* V 378: The *zoomies* are being briefed in the ready room of a…*baby flat top.*

baby blues *n.pl.* [S.E. cliché, *baby-blue eyes*] blue eyes.

1972 Wambaugh *Blue Knight* 23: Lemme see them baby blues. **1977** Cormier *Cheese* 55: I see the possibility of laughter in your baby blues. **1981** "J. Geils Band" *Centerfold* (song): I was shakin' in my shoes/

Whenever she flashed those baby blues. **1985** B. Griffith *Having Fun Yet* 54: Behind those baby blues. **1987** *Wkly. World News* (Oct. 13) 5: Up to his baby blues in rubber balls.

baby bond *n. Finance.* a bond having a face value of about one hundred dollars or less.

1978 J. Rosenberg *Dict. Business* 37.

babycakes *n.* darling, sweetie.—usu. in direct address.

1967 *Lit Dict.:* Baby cakes—A name for someone you truly dig, but mostly your main chick or girl. You can shorten it to Cakes or Cakie. **1969** *Current Slang* I & II 5: *Baby cakes,* n. An attractive boy or girl. [Used by] college females, New York State. **1978** J. Webb *Fields of Fire* 238: Baby Cakes seemed impressed. **1978** Maupin *Tales* 62: Don't mention it, Babycakes. **1979** Gutcheon *New Girls* 292: Fat chance, baby-cakes. **1993** *N.Y. Times* (Mar. 5) A 18: I still try to irritate [Congresswoman] Pat Schroeder by calling her Babycakes.

baby carriage *n. Mil.* a machine-gun cart.

1939 H. Allen *Like This* 84 [ref. to WWI]: They dragged the bodies back into the undergrowth and went on, taking the machine gun on the "baby carriage" along with them. **1941** Kendall *Army & Navy Slang* 1: *The baby carriage.*…machine gun cart.

baby-doll *n.* an attractive young woman; (in direct address) darling, sweetie.

1908 in H.C. Fisher *A. Mutt* 128: And a swell little broiler will call this big cheese baby doll. **1911** A.H. Lewis *Apaches of N.Y.* 147: For th' price of a beer, I'd have snatched one of them baby-dolls bald-headed. **1912** in S. Smith *Gumps* xii: Baby doll! Oh kiddo! **1915** "High Jinks, Jr." *Choice Slang* 42: *Baby-doll*—A pretty, demure girl. "A queen." **1935** Marion, Hanemann & Loos *Riffraff* (film): Dutch is no good for a swell baby-doll like you. **1943** J. Mitchell *McSorley's* 220: What in the world is the matter, baby doll? **1946** "T. Williams" *27 Wagons* 11: I fell in love with this baby-doll. **1950** Bissell *Stretch on the River* 125: Boy, I sure fixed you up when I innerduced you to that baby doll, I sure did. **1982** *U.S. News & W.R.* (July 26) 30: Representative John Hutchinson…fired two female aids because…his wife protested hiring "any baby dolls," meaning young, single, attractive women. **1991** Nelson & Gonzales *Bring Noise* 175: The adolescent babydoll doesn't remember…Aretha Franklin.

baby food *n. Mil.* cereal served at mess.

1941 Kendall *Army & Navy Slang* 1: *Baby food.*…cereal. **1945** *Sat. Review* (Nov. 24) 14: *Baby food,* cereal.

baby-herder *n. West.* a nursemaid.

*ca*1888 Newspaper clipping in N.Y.P.L. copy of Matsell *Vocabulum:* For many things cowboys use names which would be puzzling to anyone East of the Mississippi Valley. A nurse girl he calls a baby herder and a valise is termed a go-easter.

Baby Huey *n.* [elaboration of earlier syn. Huey, after *Baby Huey,* a cartoon character in the form of an overgrown duckling] *Mil.* a Bell UH-1 helicopter.

1969 in Tuso *Vietnam Blues* 50: We took some "Baby Hueys." **1987** S. King *Misery* 41: Give me a Baby Huey and a load of napalm!

baby-kicker *n. Show Bus.* a small key light.

1984 J. Green *Newspeak* 15.

baby-lifter *n. R.R.* a brakeman on a passenger train. *Joc.*

1931 *Writer's Dig.* (May) 41: *Baby-Lifter*—Passenger brakeman. **1977** R. Adams *Lang. of R.R.* 9: *Baby-lifter:* A passenger-train brakeman.

baby pro *n. Police & Prost.* **1.** an underage prostitute.

1961 R.E.L. Masters *Forbidden* 383: The "Lolitas" of American whoredom, or "baby pros" as they are known in the profession. **1980** Algren *Dev. Stocking* 124: He knew a baby pro when he saw one. **1981** A.K. Shulman *On Stroll* 151: Maybe Sweet Rudy is right about baby-pros.
2. child prostitution.

1981 A.K. Shulman *On Stroll* 112: That was why he risked the dangers of baby-pro.

baby rape *n.* statutory rape.

1975 T. Berger *Sneaky People* 202: Baby rape will land you in the hoosegow.

baby-raper *n. Esp. Pris.* a person who commits statutory rape; (*broadly*) a despicable man. Hence **baby-raping,** *n., adj.*

1961 Peacock *Valhalla* 45: The baby-raper cost me two months at the brig in Pendleton. **1966** Elli *Riot* 47: We'll get the finks and baby-rapers to dig it! **1971** Curtis *Banjo* 161: No more, baby-raper. **1971** Hilaire *Thanatos* 116: You know what the baby-rapers…are saying? **1973** Overgard *Hero* 143: NO GOOD BABYRAPIN', FATHER-EFFIN, SISTER SHAG-

GIN', MOTHER MOLESTIN', BROTHERBOFFIN.... **1990** Rukuza *W. Coast Turnaround* 42: You...graverobbin' baby raper.

baby-san *n.* [*baby* + Japn honorific *-san*; cf. *mamma-san, papa-san, boy-san, girl-san*] *Mil.* **1.** an East Asian baby or child; an East Asian young woman.—esp. in direct address.

1954 in *AS* XXX 45: For example, servicemen in Japan have their *boysans*—usually grown men—to clean barracks, *papasans* to drive and do janitorial work, *mamasans* to tend bar, and sometimes *babysans*—meaning a woman rather than a child—for inspiration. **1962** Tregaskis *Vietnam Diary* 37: Then Razor began a kidding attack on Pappy's "baby-san," the "baby-sans" being the Vietnamese women who clean up the barracks, do the laundry, and so forth. **1964** Peacock *Drill & Die* 234: Your daughter—baby-san? **1969** Former member, 101st Airborne Div., served in Vietnam 1967–68: We'd say, "Hey, baby-san, let's get groovin'." **1973** Karlin, Paquet & Rottman *Free Fire Zone* 161: GI like baby-san to give massage? **1975** S.P. Smith *Amer. Boys* 414: Come on up, Baby-san. You still got work to do. **1978** Groom *Better Times* 344: Ol' Papa-san and Mamma-san and Baby-san all got a rifle or grenade buried somewhere. **1980** M. Baker *Nam* 210: It was a baby-san and a papa-san. I guess she was a teenager, maybe about fifteen or sixteen. **1982** Del Vecchio *13th Valley* 28: Baby-san plays a mean flamenco guitar.

2. (see quot.).

1990 G.R. Clark *Words of Vietnam War* 44: GIs also referred to other GIs who were sexual virgins as "baby-sans" and "cherries."

baby shit *n.* [cf. BABY, *n.*, 5] *Mil.* mustard.—usu. considered vulgar.

1973 Col. A.F. Moe (letter to J.E.L.) [ref. to WWI]: *Baby shit,* mustard. *a***1982** Berry *Semper Fi* 209 [ref. to WWII]: He vividly remembers his first supper on [Parris] Island...."Hey, buddy," he was told, "pass me the baby shit." **1983** Cragg et al. *Soldier Talk* 16: Baby Shit...World War II...Mustard. **1988** Fussell *Wartime* 91 [ref. to WWII]: In the U.S. Marine Corps, mustard becomes *babyshit.* **1991** L. Reinberg *In the Field* 15 [ref. to Vietnam War]: Baby shit slang for mustard.

¶ In phrase:

¶ **yellow as baby shit** very cowardly.

1974 E. Thompson *Tattoo* 200: You're yellow as baby shit, Andersen.

baby-sit *v.* **1.** to monitor (the workings of a machine), esp. in circumstances where a malfunction is thought unlikely.

1976 *Popular Science* (Apr.) 146: Most of us don't have the time to babysit manual vents. **1977** L.I., N.Y., man, age *ca*30: We'll need somebody to babysit the equipment. **1980** *St. Louis Post-Dispatch* (Jan. 13) 11: He went to every radio station in town before being hired by one of them to "babysit" a machine that played news and commercials. **1981** *Business Week* (Aug. 3) 62: Yet it will also displace workers and require others to take jobs whose primary human function is to baby-sit equipment. **1983** Nelkin & Brown *Workers* 14: We...just mostly babysit the machines.

2. to oversee the progress or development of.

1977 *L.A. Times* (Jan. 15) I 20: She was babysitting paper work that had been in preparation for months. **1982** *Maclean's* (Dec. 27) 23: We literally babysat the development of a new policy.

baby-skull *n.* [cf. Brit. *baby's head* 'meat pudding'] an apple dumpling.

1900 *DN* II 21 [Univ. Conn.]: *Baby-skull, n.* Apple dumpling.

baby-snatcher *n.* **1.** [cf. BABY-LIFTER] *R.R.* a brakeman on a passenger train.

1920 McKenna *315th Inf.* 152: "Bill" Groark, the ex-Baby Snatcher.

2. *Med.* an obstetrician.

1925 S. Lewis *Arrowsmith* ch. x: He was going to be an obstetrician—or, as the medical students called it technically, a "baby-snatcher."

baby split *n. Bowling.* a 2–7 or 3–10 split.

1949 Cummings *Dict. Sports* 12. **1979** Cuddon *Dict. Sports & Games* 69.

baccy *n.* tobacco. Also **bacca.** [Slang when not dial.]

1821 J.F. Cooper *Spy* 26. **1847** Ruxton *Life in Far West* 10: Any 'bacca in your bag, Bill? **1848** in Borden *Dear Sarah* 153: Jasus, ye any baccy on board? **1850** Garrard *Wah-To-Yah* 166: A little bacca, if it's a new plug. **1851** Webber *Hunter-Naturalist* 76: Sundry presents of "baccar" pipes. **1862** in Boyer *Nav. Surgeon* I 23: I would order them to the sick bay and stop their "baccy" (tobacco). **1887** Francis *Saddle & Moccasin* 191: My business ain't sitting under a stoop chewing other people's baccy. **1948** Kaese *Braves* 140: And when you have that, you've got a little extra 'baccy in your 'baccy pouch. **1982** Heat Moon *Blue Hwys.* 46: Took thirteen months a year to grow 'bacca. **1983** Univ. Tenn.

Daily Beacon (Apr. 29) 9: Bit of 'baccy. **1985** *Time* (Feb. 18) 27: Tobacco may be an evil weed to some, but to the farmers who grow it, "bacca" has long been manna.

baccy stick *n.* a leg.

1885 *Uncle Daniel's Story* 67: Massa...you see dese heah "backer sticks" (meaning his legs) "dey go, dey go if dey shoot." *Ibid.* 77: Dick...has not been seen since his "backer sticks" ran off with him.

bach var. BATCH.

b-ache *n.* [fr. the v.] Esp. *U.S. Mil. Acad.* a complaint. [1969 def. is prob. inaccurate.]

1938 in *AS* XIV 32: B-Ache—Complaint. **1941** *AS* XVI 163: B-Ache. Complaint. **1961** Ford *Black, Gray and Gold* 132: I should have written my B-ache. **1969** *Current Slang* I & II 5: B-Ache, n. A minor excuse.—Air Force Academy cadets.

b-ache *v.* [for BELLYACHE] Esp. *U.S. Mil. Acad.* to complain, whine.

1900 *Howitzer* (U.S. Mil. Acad.) 117: B-Ache—Talk, to tell one's troubles to the policeman. **1907** *Army & Navy Life* (Nov.) 559: We went to chow and met some more officers and came home and B-ached again. **1909** Moss *Officers' Man.* (ed. 2) 283: B-ache.—to complain. **1941** *AS* XVI 163: B-Ache....to complain. **1969** *Current Slang* I & II 5: B-Ache, v. To complain...[used by] Air Force Academy cadets.

bachelor's hall *n.* the home of a bachelor.—usu. in phr. **keep bachelor's hall** to set up housekeeping as a bachelor; live without a wife and away from women.

1746 in Whiting *Early Amer. Proverbs* 16: I shall...keep Biahalors [*sic*] Hall one year Longer. **1763** in Franklin & Mecom *Letters* 76: I have half a mind to keep House that is, Bachelor's Hall, in that which was Sister Douse's. **1781** in *DA*: Fixt the things in the house to keepe Bachelders Hall. **1828** in Hill *Voyages* 3: I'm still keeping bachelor hall. What fine fun it is to have no one to trouble you!—no wife to scold, no children to bawl, and to go home when I like, etc., etc. **1864** in Brobst *Civil War Lttrs.* 54: I will be already to keep a bachelor's hall when I get home. **1878** in Bunner *Letters* 46: Branisly...is keeping bachelor's hall in 34th St. **1899** B.F. Sands *Reefer* 55: My uncle...was keeping bachelor's hall on F street.

b-acher *n.* Esp. *U.S. Mil. Acad.* a chronic complainer.

1905 *Howitzer* (U.S. Mil. Acad.) 292: B-acher—One who b-aches.

back¹ *n.* ¶ In phrases:

¶ **have (one's) back up** [see *1785 quot.] to be angry or offended.

1783 in Whiting *Early Amer. Proverbs* 17: Other wise their backs had certainly been up on account of his disdainful speech. *1785** Grose *Vulgar Tongue: His back is up,* i.e. he is offended or angry; an expression or idea taken from a cat. **1849** Mackay *Western World* 44: Didn't our Prez'dent's message put the old Lion's back up? **1877** *Puck* (May) 7: The cat...gets its back up when mad, just like many other mad people. **1968–71** Cole & Black *Checking* 140: You shouldn't get your back up against the wall when you speak to an officer. **1975** J.I. White *Git Along Dogies* 55: He most likely would have gotten his back up had anyone called him [a poet]. **1980** Houp & Pearsall *Reporting Tech. Info.* 271: The second letter will surely put the reader's back up. Do people really write foolish, rude letters like this one?

¶ **my [aching] back** (an exclam. of dismay, disbelief, or the like). [Esp. common in the armed forces in WWII.]

1928 Nason *Sgt. Eadie* 260 [ref. to WWI]: Oh, my back!...Lookut the bridge! **1945** *Yank* (Mar. 2) 6: American slang goes over big with Russian GIs....The most popular expression among the Russian girl KPs...is "Oh, my aching back!" **1944–46** in *AS* XXI 242: *Oh my aching back* (often contracted to *Oh my back,* or simply *My back*). This is used in a variety of situations; *e.g.,* upon the receipt of bad news...; to express general discontent...; to express sardonic amusement. **1946** J.H. Burns *Gallery* 4: O my back! Sure you don't want to buy my cigarettes too? **1947** *AS* XXII 214: Oh, my aching back! must have originated in the hard work and fatigue duty associated with basic training and one's following assignments. **1948** *AS* XXIII 249: Oh, my achin' back. A mild expression of disgust. **1963** W.C. Anderson *Penelope* 124: Oh, my bloody, achin' back! **1980** Manchester *Darkness* 166 [ref. to WWII]: We groaned, "My aching back," or simply, "My back." **1981** Univ. Tenn. instructor: "There aren't any more copies left." "Oh, my aching back."

¶ **on (one's) back** harassing or annoying (one).—usu. in phr. **get off (one's) back** to stop harassing or annoying (one). Often as imper. [*OED2* cites *on (one's) back* as S.E.

(Get) off (one's) back seems to have gained wide U.S. currency only during WWII.]
[*1880 in *OEDS*: I'm never off his back.] [*ca*1920 in Kornbluh *Rebel Voices* 26: Then dump the bosses off your back.] 1947 Schulberg *Harder They Fall* 172: 'Fi c'd jus' get this town off my back.... 1950 Stuart *Objector* 9 [ref. to WWII]: "Climb off my back, soldier," the sergeant answered harshly. 1955 Ruppelt *Report on UFOs* 222: But somehow out of this chaotic situation came exactly the result that was intended—the press got off our backs. 1957 Atwell *Private* 136 [ref. to WWII]: Hey, how's about gettin' off my back, hey? 1957 Thornton *Teenage Werewolf* (film): Aw, get off my back, will ya? 1959 Brosnan *Long Season* 198: Get off my back, Willard....I was unavoidably detained in Chicago. 1964 Peacock *Drill & Die* 16: Now I'll have two officers on my back instead of one. 1972–75 W. Allen *Feathers* 167: Hey, man, get off my back. 1976 Haseltine & Yaw *Woman Doctor* 58: Come on, Mom, get off my back. 1977 R.S. Parker *Effective Decisions* 43: Get off my back. 1981 D.D. Burns *Feeling Good* 132: That stupid SOB is on my back again! 1982 P. Michaels *Grail* 136: I'm sorry Bob, I didn't mean to get on your back.

¶ **up (one's) back** harassing or annoying (one).
1987 *Stingray* (NBC-TV): We got Bondy up our backs with this lawsuit!

back[2] *n.* [prob. fr. *greenbacks*] money.—constr. in pl.
1966 Braly *On Yard* 27: Tight as he is I don't think I get any backs at all, but he comes up with a twenny.

back *adj.* (of a drink) as a chaser.—used postnominally.
1982 Basel *Pak Six* 90: Beer with Cuddy back. 1983 Flaherty *Tin Wife* 247: I'd rather a good shot of Fleischmann's with a beer back. 1985 *Golden Girls* (NBC-TV): How about a shot of gin with a beer back? 1987 *Nat. Lampoon* (Dec.) 12: I thought a shot of sour mash and a frosty mug back.

back *adv. Black E.* to an extreme degree; completely.—used postpositively.
1942 *Pittsburgh Courier* (Jan. 3) 7: "Home" was sharp back...and a perfect gentleman. 1962 in Wepman et al. *Life* 28: He was stashed [i.e., supplied with money] 'way back,/Wore a diamond on each toe. 1967 in T.C. Bambara *Gorilla* 73: I likes to grit....I grit back, I won't lie. 1968 Gover *JC Saves* 127: He was t' be really mellow back. 1970 *Current Slang* V 5: *Back*, adv. Really; very (used as an intensifier). He is z-ing-*back!* 1970 A. Young *Snakes* 65: "Would you say that dude was stoned?"..."Stoned *back!*"

¶ In phrases:
¶ **put back** [cf. syn. *knock back* s.v. KNOCK] to consume (food or drink) heartily.
1974 Cherry *High Steel* 45: How much vodka have you put back today, Timmy?

¶ **set back** to cost. Also vars.
1896 *DN* I 422: How much did it put you back? 1902 Dunne *Observ. by Dooley* 177: On th' conthr'y, Hinnissy, it sets him back a large fortune. 1907 "O. Henry" *Complete Stories* 1416: This suit set me back sixty-five. 1909 *DN* III 402: "How much did that put you back?" "Six dollars." 1932 D. Runyon, in *Collier's* (Jan. 30) 8: A chinchilla flogger that moves Israel back thirty G's. 1937 Steinbeck *Mice & Men* 57: What's it set you back? 1957 Denker *Time Limit* (film): This must've set you back plenty. 1981 N.Y.C. man, age *ca*40: It'll set you back plenty, but that kind of a trip would be worth it. 1990 *U.S. News & W.R.* (Aug. 13) 68: With a reservation 72 hours in advance, a $185 room in Geneva will set you back only $122.

back *v.* ¶ In phrase: **back off the boards** [or **earth**] to surpass thoroughly.
1898 Kountz *Baxter's Letters* 17: I had the Rothschilds backed clear off the boards. 1918 in *Wisc. Mag. of History* LXII 234: I thought the Czechs were a fine bunch of soldiers, but I am now convinced that our own "doughboys" have everything backed off the earth. 1921 *DN* V 155: *Backed off the boards.* v. phr. To be beaten, to be surpassed. "This radiator's got the one in my apartment backed off the boards." 1929–32 J.T. Farrell, in *AS* XXXVI 227: As a Romeo, he's got Studs backed off the boards.

backasswards or **backassward** *adj. & adv.* [intentional metathesis of ASS-BACKWARD; cf. BASSACKWARDS] *adj.* confused, muddled; (*adv.*) backwards.
1947–51 Salinger *Catcher* 35: You always do everything backasswards. No wonder you're flunking out of here. 1971 *Playboy* (May) 42: The title role...is based on several back-assward assumptions about comedy. 1976 *Rolling Stone* (Oct. 7) 8: *Rolling Stone* stapled!...No more worries

about friends turning pages upside down and backasswards. *a*1989 R. Herman, Jr. *Warbirds* 293: I also think you got it back-asswards.

backbone *n. Publishing.* the spine of a book.
1982 T.D. Connors *Dict. Mass Media* 20.
¶ In phrase:
¶ **from backbone to breakfast time** through and through. Cf. *[from] asshole to appetite* s.v. ASSHOLE.
1907 *Independent* (May 23) 1186: Aleck Jackson, our negro cook, a thoro sailor from backbone to breakfast time.

back burner *n.* a condition or position of low priority.—usu. constr. with *on the.* Also attrib. Cf. FRONT BURNER.
1963 in *OED2*. 1965 *N.Y. Times* (June 13) 4 E 3: How does anything else get done? Who looks after the backburner problems...? 1968 *U.S. News & W.R.* (Feb. 5) 23: Truce talks, once more, have been temporarily pushed to the back burner. 1976 *Atlantic* (Feb.) 4: When Reagan left office in January, 1975, Lake started a political consulting firm and kept himself on the back burner in Washington. 1982 *Time* (Nov. 8) 19: Hot Issues on the Back Burner: After the election, Reagan and Congress will have lots to confront. 1990 *U.S. News & W.R.* (Nov. 19) 52: Their pleas have gone largely unheard in India, where Kashmir has been consigned to the back burner.

backcap *n.* an act of ruining by defamation.
1872–73 "M. Twain" *Life on Miss.* 294: Now i didn't fear no one giving me a back cap (*exposing his past life*) and running me off the job.

backcap *v.* [orig. unkn.] to attempt to thwart or ruin by defaming (someone); to disparage or criticize meanly.
1887 DeVol *Gambler* 91: I was surprised to see you back-capping my game. 1889 *Century Dict.*: *Backcap*...To depreciate or disparage (U.S. slang). 1891 Maitland *Amer. Slang Dict.* 21: *Backcap*...to do one an ill-turn by speaking evil of him or carrying tales, or otherwise to "spoil his game." 1892 Moore *Own Story* 656: If I had a chance offered me...do you think you wouldn't say something that would back-cap me? 1895 *Harper's* (May) 917: Say, Kit, what makes you want to be tancin' all ter time, wit' all ter people backcappin' you ant sayin' yer gittin' to be a de't spider? 1896 Ade *Artie* 57: She's a nice girl, though. I don't want to back-cap her. 1901 Ade *Modern Fables* 40: All the influential Moguls of the Party signed his Petition. Then they sat down and wrote Private Letters to Back-Cap him. 1913 Jocknick *Early Days* 145 [ref. to 1870's]: So I back-capped him, same's I did Jack.

back-chat *n.* backtalk. *Rare* in U.S.
*1901 in *OEDS*. 1935 S. Lewis *Can't Happen* 22: 'Nother words, have a doctor who won't take any back-chat, but really boss the patient and make him get well whether he likes it or not!

backclap *v.* to disparage; BACKCAP.
1896 Ade *Artie* 7: Mrs. Morton got me a good seat and then back-clapped the show a little before it opened up so I didn't expect to be pulled out of my chair—and I wasn't.

back-door *n.* **1.** the rectum and anus. Also in phr. **back-door work** anal intercourse.—usu. considered vulgar.
*1694 in *F & H* I (rev.) 94: Joan's back-door was filthily puffing and roaring. *1785 Grose *Vulgar Tongue* s.v. *back: Back gammon player*, a sodomite. *Usher*, or *gentleman of the back door*, the same. *1810 in W. Wheeler *Letters* 39: Three ounces and a half of the bitter gall Epsom salts, and two hours knapsack drill in double quick time would open my back door. *1880 *Pearl* (Dec.) 634: I expect he thought I was doing a bit of backdoor work and as he may be a particular old boy he must not know me again. 1916 Cary *Venery* I 8: Back Door—The anus....*Back Door Work*—Sodomy. 1942 H. Miller *Roofs of Paris* 34: I set John Thursday knocking at her back door. 1970 Landy *Und. Dict.* 27: He fucked her in the back door. 1985 "Blowdryer" *Mod. Eng.* 70: Anal Orifice...*Back door.*
2. the position directly to the rear of a moving vehicle or flying aircraft; (*hence*) another vehicle or aircraft occupying this position.
1975–76 Dills *CB* 13: *Backdoor*—last CB vehicle in a group of two or more. *Backdoor Closed*—rear covered for police. *Backdoor Sealed Up*—rear CBer will notify if police are on the move from behind. 1976 Whelton *CB Baby* 14: So you give me a shout on your back door if you need another steer. 1985 Heywood *Taxi Dancer* 11 [ref. to 1966]: Bogeys at your back door. 1988 *Supercarrier* (ABC-TV): Forgot to check your back door, amigo!

back-door *v. Mil.* to obtain without authorization.
*a*1989 R. Herman, Jr. *Warbirds* 221: My first sergeant back-doored copies of the reports from the typists.

back-door action *n.* adultery.
> **1978** Rascoe & Stone *Who'll Stop Rain?* (film): A little back-door action.

back-door furlough *n. Mil.* an absence without leave; a desertion.
> **1927** *Amer. Legion Mo.* (May) 62 [ref. to WWI]: Whenever any of the gang grabs a back-door furlough the odds are…he's having a vacation at the Front and the least we can do is protect him at this end.

back-dooring *n.* adultery.
> **1981** Hathaway *World of Hurt* 230: He thought of the other two women, the bored back-dooring.

back-door man *n.* **1.** *Med.* a proctologist.
> **1962** Killens *Thunder* 201: No, no, soldier, I'm not the dentist. I'm strictly a back-door man.

2. an adulterous male lover.
> **1969 Led Zeppelin *Whole Lotta Love* (song): Shake for me girl, I want to be your back-door man. **1970** Major *Afro-Amer. Slang*: Back-door man: a married woman's lover, who is, incidentally, a legendary figure in blues numbers. **1972** *Nat. Lampoon* (July) 49: Last week, my aunt's normally sedate St. Bernard held me in a corner, snarling and baring her teeth, until I consented to be her back-door man. **1982** A. Shaw *Dict. Pop/Rock:* "Backdoor man." Blues jargon for the lover of a married woman, generalized to mean someone who finds a way to skirt the rules.

3. an anal sodomist.
> **1972** *Nat. Lampoon* (Oct.) 81: I'm a backdoor man. **1992** N.Y.C. man, age 26: I always thought "back-door man" in [the Led Zeppelin song] "Whole Lotta Love" meant ass-fucker.

back-door parole var. BACK-GATE PAROLE.

back-door trots *n.* diarrhea.
> **1801 in *OEDS*. **1898** Green *Va. Folk-Speech* 47: Back-door-trots, n.pl. The diarrhoea. **1912** *DN* III 570 [Ind.]: Back-door trots, n. phr. Diarrhea. **1958** Bard & Spring *Horse Wrangler* 82 [ref. to 1890's]: We had what was called "the back door trots," only there wasn't any back door.

back down *v.* ¶ In phrase: **back 'em [on] down** *Trucking.* to reduce one's speed.
> **1975** Dills *CB Slanguage: Back 'em on down*…slow down. **1977** *Sci. Mech. CB Guide* 156: Back 'em down at the interchange for construction.

backdrop *n.* ¶ In phrase: **hold up the backdrop** *Theat.* to play a nonspeaking role, esp. as part of a group of bystanders.
> **1929** *Bookman* (Apr.) 150: A girl who does nothing more than come on to fill up a scene is said to "hold up the backdrop."

back-gate parole *n. Pris.* death in prison, esp. by suicide. Also vars.
> **1929** *Sat. Eve. Post* (Apr. 13) 50: If he dies in prison, he takes a back-gate parole. If he escapes, he takes a bush parole. **1935** Pollock *Und. Speaks: Back-door parole*, to die in prison. **1942–49** Goldin et al. *DAUL* 21: A back-gate commute. **1969** Gordone *No Place* 428: You lookin' to take some kinda back gate commute? Suicide? **1972** P. Thomas *Savior* 159: Or guilty with a way out, the back-door parole, eh, Tato?

back-lip *v.* [fr. LIP] to speak insolently to; to backtalk.
> **1955** Ellson *Rock* 29: Broke a chair on a wise cat's head for back-lipping me.

back number *n.* a person having out-of-date interests or ideas; an old, old-fashioned, or unsophisticated person.— occ. as adj., out of date, old and useless.
> **1882** Peck *Sunshine* 153: There is always some old back number of a girl who has no fellow. **1883** Peck *Bad Boy* 133: It was just like a old back number funeral. **1887** Peck *Pvt. Peck* 233: A lot of colored men were leading about forty old back-number horses and mules. **1890** C.C. King *Portia* 195: Since their coming into the Society of Fort Ryan, she had become "a decided back number." **1902** Townsend *Fadden & Paul* 279: You has been a back number so long you is not next to de ways of fashionable society. **1908** in Fleming *Unforgettable Season* 9: Tenney [is] a back number; Bridwell, a poor hitter. **1925** Dos Passos *Manhattan* 209: I may be a back number but I can still tell a goldbrick with my eyes closed. **1958** J. King *Pro Football* 10: One who withdraws from the NFL for a year or two "tends to become a back number," because the game progresses so rapidly.

back rations *n.* [pun] *Naut.* a flogging.
> **1830** N. Ames *Mariner's Sks.* 201: Wearing a Scotch bonnet…or a checked red flannel shirt, would in our service, subject the wearer to

"drinking with the ducks" or getting "his *back* rations" in the gangway.

back-scratcher *n.* a sycophant.
> **1942** *ATS* 380: Flatterer…*back-scratcher.* **1990** *Simpsons* (Fox-TV): Back-scratcher! Bootlicker! Egg-sucker!

backscuttle *v.* to have anal intercourse with; (*also*) to copulate with (a woman) from behind.—usu. considered vulgar. Occ. **backscull.** Also as *n.* an act of anal intercourse; an act of intercourse from behind.
> **1888** *Stag Party* 95: Common, old fashioned f—k $1.00. Rear fashion $1.50. Back-scuttle fashion $1.75. **a1903 *F & H* I (rev.) 96: *To have* (or *do*) *a back-scuttle*…To possess a woman dog-fashion. **1927** [Fliesler] *Anecdota* 42: Three nude men were practicing a spinctrian posture, that is to say, in vulgar language, back-scuttling each other. Speaking of back-scuttling…. *Ibid.* 141: He was…about to backscuttle her. **1938** H. Miller *Capricorn* 213: Finally I decided to make an end of it by turning her over and back-scuttling her. **1975** Legman *No Laughing Matter* 262: "Back-scuttle"…specifically refers in American slang (as also "back-scull") to rectal intercourse.

backshoot *v. West.* to shoot (a person) in the back.
> **1956** Evarts *Ambush Riders* 79: I want another look at the skunk who backshot my Ed. **1982** Braun *Judas Tree* 92: He tried to backshoot me! **1982** "J.R. Roberts" *One-Handed Gun* 92: Suppose somebody back-shoots me to get to him?

backside *n.* (occ. used as a euphem. for ASS in fig. senses). [The literal sense, "buttocks," has always been colloq. or S.E.; see *OED*.]
> **1792** Brackenridge *Mod. Chiv.* 136: Do not many…prefer kissing a great man's backside, to being independent? **1989** "Captain X" & Dodson *Unfriendly Skies* 60: He's just trying to save his backside up there.

back slack *n.* [fr. SLACK] backtalk.
> **1908** Kelley *Oregon Pen.* 77: No back slack or I'll fix you every chance I get. **1908** *Independent* (Feb. 20) Mister Swindel ventured no reply to this outspoken piece of "back slack."

backslide *n. Esp. CB.* a return trip, as in a truck.
> **1976** *Sci. Mech. CB Guide* 156: We'll catch you on the back slide.

backstop *n.* **1.** *Baseball.* a catcher.
> **1887** Chi. *Inter-Ocean* (cited in Nichols *Baseball Terminology* 3). **1938** (quot. at (2.), below). **1956** Topps Chewing Gum Baseball Card No. 92: A clever backstop, he knows how to handle pitchers. **1987** *N.Y. Times* (Aug. 25) 25: Other players included…Jeffrey Dujon, a "wicket keeper" (catcher) whose defensive skills have been compared with those of the top backstops in the Major Leagues. **1992** *Sports Illustrated* (July 6): In a pickup game you would choose her as your catcher over, say, Tom Berenger, the backstop in *Major League.*

2. (see quot.).
> **1938** "Justinian" *Amer. Sexualis* 11: *Back stop.* n. pessary; diaphragm; a mechanical contraceptive usually composed of rubber and metal, and employed by the female. A post-war American neologism derived from the function of the catcher or "backstop" in baseball parlance.

backwash *n.* **1.** [*back*talk + hog*wash*] insolent or nonsensical talk; backtalk.
> **1906** *Independent* (Jan. 4) 28: But he never took anybody's backwash and he never starved for want of a mouth. **1926** Nason *3 Lights* 143: You're full o' backwash! **1938** T. Wolfe *Web & Rock* 44: I'm not takin' any backwash from him.

2. *Stu.* saliva, as mixed with the remnants of a drink.
> **1992** Fla. man, age 26 (coll. J. Sheidlower): "Backwash" is incredibly common. That's what you call the last bit of soda in a bottle, when it's all full of spit. **1992** Riverside, Calif., woman, age *ca*31 (coll. J. Sheidlower): *Backwash* is the stuff you get in the bottom of a bottle. I first heard that in junior high school, in the early 1970's.

bacon *n.* **1.** the penis.—usu. considered vulgar.
> **1916–21** Cary *Sex. Vocab.* I: *Bacon.* The penis. **1928** in Oliver *Meaning of Blues* 149: He boiled my first cabbage and he made it awful hot,/Then he put in the bacon and it over-flowed the pot.

2. [sugg. by PIG] a policeman; police.—used derisively.
> **1974** Univ. Tenn. student theme: Today cops are called *fuzz, pigs,* or *bacon.* **1975** H. Ellison *Deadly Streets* 11: When the local bacon finally arrived, the guys had split. **1975** (cited in Spears *Drugs & Drink* 19). **1977** Hamill *Flesh & Blood* 19: Cops, man. That's why he's here. He banged out some bacon. **1980** Univ. Tenn. student: That's the local bacon watching the strip for dealers. **1981** Romero *Knightriders* (film):

I smell bacon [as police car approaches]. **1992** *Simpsons* (Fox-TV): I smell bacon! See if he's wearing a wire!

3. [extracted fr. *bring home the bacon,* below] money.
1986 N.Y. State Lottery TV ad: Some people think a million in the Lotto jackpot is not a lot of bacon. But if you win, you'll be in hog heaven!

¶ In phrases:

¶ **bring home the bacon** to earn wages, esp. as the head of a household; to make a profit; *(broadly)* to succeed in an endeavor.
1909 T.A. Dorgan, in Zwilling *TAD Lexicon* 15: He'll bring home the bacon as sure as you're wearing a hat. *****1924** P.G. Wodehouse, in *OEDS:* It may be that my bit will turn out to be just the trifle that brings home the bacon. **1926** Siringo *Riata & Spurs* 130: Many [hunters]…have "brought home the bacon" in larger amounts [than I]. *Ibid.* 132: These…cowboys…sometimes "brought home the bacon" by killing their opponents. **1942** *ATS* 273: Succeed…bring home the bacon. *Ibid.* 532: Earn; make profits…*bring home the bacon.* **1945** in Truman *Dear Bess* 520: I'm sick of the whole business—but we'll bring home the bacon. **1971** Sheehan *Arnheiter* 89: The officers must…be "imaginative and audacious" and always…"bring home the bacon." **1981** Fiskin *Cutter and Bone* (film): It's my main squeeze bringin' home the bacon. **1981** Enjoli perfume ad (WBIR-TV, Knoxville, Tenn.): I can bring home the bacon,/Fry it up in the pan,/And never ever let you forget you're a man!/'Cause I'm a woman!

¶ **cook** [or **fry**] **(someone's) bacon** to ruin, "cook (one's) goose."
1868 Woodruff *Trotting Horse* 120: In the early part of the seventh mile he was beaten. The rating for six miles…had "cooked his bacon," to use a common expression. **1986** R. Zumbro *Tank Sgt.* 206: We'll fry his bacon on the way out.

¶ **make bacon** to copulate. *Joc.*
1973 T-shirt seen in N.Y.C. with cartoon of copulating pigs and caption, "Makin' Bacon." **1978** Univ. Tenn. student: Forget about small talk, I want to make bacon. **1992** *Simpsons* (Fox-TV): She liked makin' bacon on the beach.

¶ **save (one's) bacon** to save (one's) life; to rescue (one) (from any kind of threat or danger).
*****1654** in *OEDS.* **1666** G. Alsop, in W.H. Kenney *Laughter* 77: I resolve…to plead *Non compos mentis,* to save my Bacon. **1666** in Whiting *Early Amer. Provs.* 17. **1698–99** "B.E." *Dict. Canting Crew: He sav'd his bacon,* he has escaped with a whole skin. *****1709** in D'Urfey *Pills* I 161: I'll make Peace, and save my Bacon. **1707, 1731,** etc., in Whiting *Early Amer. Proverbs* 17. **1779** in Moore *Songs & Ballads of Revolution* 276: We…were glad to save our bacon,/Rather than be killed or taken. *****1785** Grose *Vulgar Tongue: He has saved his bacon,* he has escaped. **1816** Weems *Hymen's Sgt.* 1: 'Tis *population alone* that can save our Bacon. **1838** *Crockett Almanac* (1839) 25: We laid our yards aback as that was the only way to save our bacon. **1847** Robb *Squatter Life* 155: I thought you had jined meetin' and saved your bacon. **1848** Bartlett *Amer.: Save one's bacon.* A vulgar expression, meaning to save one's *flesh* from injury, to preserve one's *flesh* from harm or punishment. **1878** Willis *Our Cruise* 25: A whole shipload of Chaplins won't save yur bacon. **1897** Hamblen *General Manager* 20: Ye have ter jump ter save yer own bacon. **1939–40** Tunis *Kid from Tomkinsville* 59: The Kid squeezed his arm as they slipped into the dugout. "Boy, you sure saved my bacon that time." **1954** Kibbee & Webb *Vera Cruz* (film): Hey, you saved my bacon back there. **1974** *Kojak* (CBS-TV): You were the one who hollered for help and I saved your bacon. **1984** McNamara *First Directive* 196: I hear the broad saved your bacon. **1992** G. Wolff *Day at Beach* 15: I wasn't sacked after all. Ben Bradlee saved my bacon.

¶ **string of bacon** *Mil.* campaign ribbons.
1976 Former U.S. Marine, age 24: He had so many campaign ribbons—a *long* string of bacon.

bacon-faced *adj.* having a fat or jowly face. Hence **bacon-face,** *n.*
*****1785** Grose *Vulgar Tongue: Bacon faced,* full faced. **1821** Waln *Hermit in Phila.* 28: Bacon-faced—Bran-faced…—Cribbage-faced. **1858** in Harris *High Times* 128: Each pot-bellied,…bacon-faced son ove a gun ove 'em is ready to swar that he's made money by the swap. **1990** *Married with Children* (Fox-TV): We'll just have to get by on our good looks. See you on skid row, bacon-face.

bad *adj.* **1.a.** Esp. *Black E.* (of persons) very tough; pugnacious; formidable; *(hence)* formidably skilled. [The familiar and now S.E. (Western) *bad man* undoubtedly represents this,

rather than the broader S.E. sense.]
1855 in *DA:* The "bad man" was floored by the weight of a walking stick that the quaker had been known to carry. [**1877** in F. Remington *Sel. Letters* 14: I can spoil [eat] an immense amount of good grub at any time in the day. I am almost as bad as Wilder, who is acknowledged to be the "baddest" man in school in that line.] **1877** Flipper *Colored Cadet* 262: A darkey would approach the young man, cautiously, feel of his buttons and clothes, and enthusiastically remark: "Bad man wid de gub'ment strops on!" **1884** Peck *Boss Book* 42: Freddy is a bold, bad man, and we would bet on it. **1888** in *OED2:* The "bad men", or professional fighters, and man-killers, are of a different stamp, quite a number of them being, according to their light, perfectly honest. **1889** in *Iowa Jour. Hist.* LVII (1959) 204: He was "bad" on eye teeth, yanked out cuspids and bicuspids, snatched out grinders…without pain or delay. **1894** in A. Charters *Ragtime Songbk.* 50: In came a big guy looking for a fight.…"I'm so bad I'm afraid of myself.…Nobody knows how bad I am." **1897** Ade *Pink* 194: Belle walk jus' like she 'uz takin' last chance at 'e cake, an' had a bad lady to beat out. **1911** *JAF* (July) 268: He can boast of his achievements as "a bad man" with his "box" [guitar]. **1921** Z. Grey *Mysterious Rider* 45: He could do anythin' under the sun better'n any one else. Bad with guns!…He never hunted trouble, but trouble follered him. **1938** in A. Lomax *Mr. Jelly Roll* 54 [ref. to 1890's]: Sheep Eye's here and I'm the baddest sonofabitch that ever moved. **1942** *Pittsburgh Courier* (Mar. 14) 7: Admit you're…one of the "baddest" guys in the regiment. **1955** Ellson *Rock* 58: He beat three of their baddest cats one time. **1960** R. Reisner *Jazz Titans* 150: *Bad:* good. Example: A bad man on flute. **1973** *New Yorker* (June 16) 52: Bullins is a bad dude. There's no better playwright in the American theatre. **1980** Wielgus & Wolff *Basketball* 72: Don't tell me you're looking for some badder dude [in a basketball game]! **1984–88** Hackworth & Sherman *About Face* 103: Neil tried to get bad, but my guys and I went back to staring at our fire. **1992** *Donahue* (NBC-TV): I have a college education. *That's* what makes me bad.

b. (of liquor or drugs) strong, potent.
1955–57 Kerouac *On Road* 151: Then we got hold of some bad green, as it's called in the trade…and smoked too much of it. **1970** A. Young *Snakes* 60: You talk about some baaaaad reefer! **1976** Calloway & Rollins *Moocher & Me* 11: They sold that *baaad* bourbon…in tin cans for a dollar.

2. Esp. *Black E.* wonderful; deeply satisfying; stunningly attractive or stylish; sexy.
1897 Ade *Pink* 224: She sutny fix up a pohk chop 'at's bad to eat. **1927** in Charters & Kunstadt *Jazz* 219: In Duke Ellington's dance band Harlem has reclaimed its own.…Ellington's jazzique is just too bad. **1928** Fisher *Jericho* 306: Too Bad…Marvelous. **1929–32** in *AS* (Dec. 1934) 289: *Too-Bad.* Excellent, as in "That was a too-bad game." **1960** in T.C. Bambara *Gorilla* 56: I'm gonna pack my…bad suspenders and my green hat. **1961** J.A. Williams *Night Song* 128: That was a bad short [car]. **1965** Linakis *In Spring* 117: Say, mac,…how about taking these bad chicks over to Henrietta's pad? **1965** in Sanchez *Word Sorcerers* 194: We gon move on. Keep on being badDDD togetha. **1967** Colebrook *Cross* 243: Don't you think it's a *bad* color? **1970** A. Young *Snakes* 50: I don't care how good somethin be soundin on a record it's always badder when you catch it in person. **1971** Wells & Dance *Night People* 66: "Just what is it you're saying under your bad breath when you see a real bad chick?" "I say, 'Dear Lord, I see what I want, but I'll be thankful for anything I can git. Amen.'" **1972** *Tuesday Mag.* (May) 11: We were cookin' [playing music] so much, oh man that was bad. The people couldn't believe it. That was really bad. **1976** Rosen *Above Rim* 68: You the baddest looking fox in sight. **1978** Price *Ladies' Man* 86: I…came out, dressed to kill…and I looked most bad, most bad. **1980** N.Y.C. man, age *ca*19: She a bad-lookin' freak [a sexy-looking girl]. **1989** S. Robinson & D. Ritz *Smokey* 50: The Four Tops was the baddest [musical] group around. **1989** *Rude Dog & Dweebs* (CBS-TV): Hey, you're lookin' bad, Tweek.

¶ In phrases:

¶ **get (one's) head bad** *Black E.* to get drunk or high.
1964 H. Rhodes *Chosen Few* 218: He's…too damn young t'know better than t'git his head bad on 'at one per cent brew over at th' slopchute. **1970** A. Young *Snakes* 128: Let's get our heads bad and get down with these mucky-mucks. **1974** Angelou *Gather Together* 143 [ref. to *ca*1950]: 'Hos get their heads bad and forget about tending to business.

¶ **in bad** in trouble or disfavor.
1907 in H.C. Fisher *A. Mutt* 7: I certainly got in bad. **1908** in H.C. Fisher *A. Mutt* 21: Old Mutt is "in bad" again at home. **1908** in Fleming *Unforgettable Season* 237: Manager Jawn got in bad with the…umpires. **1909** Irwin *Con Man* 40: Hayden is in bad just

now....He's under indictment and heavy bail. **1910** *N.Y. Eve. Jour.* (May 21) 8: Billy Papke Is "In Bad" With Frisco Fight Fans. **1911** Van Loan *Big League* 221: I'm in bad as it stands, and it won't do no harm to look at this wonder. **1911** A.H. Lewis *Apaches of N.Y.* 83: I just leaves a namesake of yours, an' say, he's in bad! **1912** *Hampton's Mag.* (Jan.) 842: I won't be definite because I don't want to get anyone in bad. **1917** in Truman *Dear Bess* 233: I am sure in bad with you I guess. **1919** *Century* (Nov.) 3: Once she got me in bad by bringing a homesick country guy a book to read. **1934** in Fenner *Throttle* 61: McCreedy realized he'd get in bad if he hedged even a little. **1955** Graziano & Barber *Somebody Up There* 113: You're in bad enough already. **1963** D. Tracy *Brass Ring* 32: Kelly had to keep Hobey from putting himself...in bad with The Serpent. **1970** Boatright & Owens *Derrick* 139: Some of these damn guys are going to get in bad. **1970** in P. Heller *In This Corner* 44: And that's where I got in bad. They hollered bloody murder about that decision.

¶ **to the bad** in bad condition, in a bad way; showing a financial loss.

1902–03 Ade *People You Know* 114: A bug-eyed Maniac with his collar to the bad was found wandering hither and thither with $90 in his Left Hand. **1907** in H.C. Fisher *A. Mutt* 3: $22.00 to the bad in two days.

bad actor *n.* **1.** a troublemaker; a habitual brawler; a dangerous individual.

1901 Irwin *Sonnets* (unp.): And that bad actor, Murphy, by her side. **1908** Raine *Wyoming* 139: I ain't half such a bad actor as some of the boys. **1913** Light *Hobo* 76: All yeggmen were bad actors and...thieves. **1915** *Thru the Mill* 18: He was of vicious temperament and a "bad actor." **1917** E.R. Burroughs *Oakdale Affair* 58: The Oskaloosa Kid's a bad actor....The little shrimp tried to croak me. **1918** *N.Y. Eve. Jour.* (Aug. 23) 13: The wife is having me watched. She's got a crazy notion that I'm a bad actor. **1924–27** Nason *3 Lights* 104: Bad actors, those Boche, and they wanted that town badly. **1930** C. Shaw *Jack-Roller* 59: I was told that I was becoming a "habitual runaway" and a "bad actor." **1950** A. Lomax *Mr. Jelly Roll* 133: He was a bad, bad actor—killed his brother-in-law, and then beat the rap. **1958** J. Ward *Buchanan* 69: Pretty bad actor is he? **1977** *N.Y. Times Mag.* (Aug. 28) 29: [He] was a bad actor; he had a lot of enemies.

2. a vicious or unbroken horse.

1915 H.L. Wilson *Ruggles* 64: He's a bad actor. Look at his eye! **1922** Rollins *Cowboy* 286 [ref. to 1890's]: Every rider of a "bad actor," a horse that acted viciously, was on the look-out for kicks and bites. *a***1940** in Lanning & Lanning *Texas Cowboys* 163: I was always picking out bad actors on the home ranch. **1968** Ainslie *Thoroughbred* 463: *Bad actor*— Fractious horse. **1971** Dahlskog *Dict.*: That horse is a *bad actor*.

3. a dangerous substance.

1976 *N.Y. Times* (July 9) A 9: The sludge contains some "bad actors"— heavy metals like chromium and nickel that could accumulate to levels toxic to plants, and elements like arsenic, mercury and cadmium that are potentially toxic to man and animals.

bad apple see s.v. APPLE.

bad-ass *n.* **1.** a dangerous, browbeating individual; bully.— usu. considered vulgar.

1956 *AS* XXXI 191: A marine who postures toughness is sarcastically labeled a *badass*. **1961** Peacock *Valhalla* 345 [ref. to Korean War]: They's a lot of bad asses at South Camp, ain't they? **1970** Ponicsan *Last Detail* 7: Bad-Ass...in navy parlance means a very tough customer. **1973** Lucas, Katz & Huyck *Amer. Graffiti* 142: The first bad-ass...grabs Terry by the shirt. **1977** Caputo *Rumor of War* 245 [ref. to 1966]: I've got a platoon full of the baddest badasses in the Nam. We're bad, baaaad fuckin' killers. **1978** De Christoforo *Grease* 169: Feeling like a mean, lean bad ass. **1989** *48 Hours* (CBS-TV) (Mar. 30): Maybe you're real bad-asses with the .45s and .357s.

2. *Mil.* BAD GUY, 2.

1988 Dye *Outrage* 189: Makin' a guess, I'd say the bad-asses saw her.

bad-ass or **bad-assed** *adj.* bad (in any common sense, esp. in slang senses).—usu. considered vulgar. Also semi-adv.

1955 in J. Blake *Joint* 110: Wanted to be a hard-nose badass type. **1958** Stack A Lee 2: There was this bad ass Indian they call Geronimo....Over in the corner sit old bad ass Stack. **1959** in Abrahams *Deep Down* 138: Before I throw open my bad-ass cashmere and pull my bad-ass gun....I had that old bad-ass Benny Long in my thirty-eight years. **1971** *Playboy* (Aug.) 32: Bo Diddley has been typed and hyped as..."the most outrageous, bad-assed guitar man alive," as the liner notes on his most recent disc have it. **1972** Sapir & Murphy *Death Therapy* 53: Oh, you come down real badass, man....Ah kill a honkey as soon as ah look at him. **1973** Childress *Hero* 23: Also I don't wanta get caught off guard

in this bad-ass wilderness. **1974** V. Smith *Jones Men* 11: She was dressed in all white with a bad-ass mink round her shoulders. **1974** E. Thompson *Tattoo* 522: I come from poor people, you would say "bad" people. I've been pretty badass myself. **1974–77** Heinemann *Close Quarters* 22: There would stand one of those barrel-chested, bad-ass-looking NCOs. **1979** Hiler *Monkey Mt.* 155: They don't give a bad-ass fuck about King, man. **1980** Kotzwinkle *Jack* 207: He's one bad-ass mother. **1982** Braun *Judas Tree* 95: He had put himself crosswise of Virginia City's bad-ass sheriff. **1983** *Nat. Lampoon* (Aug.) 46: Danger: Badass Thermos-Nuclear Device. **1989** Munro *U.C.L.A. Slang* 17: *Badass*...very good, incredible, *awesome*.

bad-ass *v.* to bully; to behave like a bully.—usu. considered vulgar.

1974–77 Heinemann *Close Quarters* 96: "Listen," he said again, trying to bad-ass me. "When I tell you to slow down, that's exactly what I mean." *Ibid.* 150: We'd load the guns and bring up ammo...on the fly, bad-assing up to the gate and blowing through town quick as horses.

bad boy *n.* any effective or impressive object or device.

1984 *Miami Vice* (NBC-TV): Now that bad boy'll knock a tree down. **1987** G. Hall *Top Gun* 96: *Hummer* Any ingenious machine...whose actual name can't be recalled. Also "puppy," "bad boy." **1990** *In Living Color* (Fox-TV): All you gotta do is hook this bad boy up in your home. **1993** *Donahue* (NBC-TV): When you pump that bad boy up is there any guarantee that you'll be able to get it down?

bad crowd *n.* BAD ACTOR, 1.

1883 Sweet & Knox *Through Texas* 13: They said that he "always went heeled, toted a derringer, and was a bad crowd generally."

baddy or **baddie** *n.* a villain in a motion picture, novel, or other literary or dramatic work; (hence, usu. *Joc.*) a scoundrel, villain, etc.

1937 in *AS* (Apr. 1938) 107: One of the screen's consistent baddies, Bruce Cabot, feels the effect of the regime of vigorous villains. **1946** *Amer. N & Q* (Dec.) 119: Baddies [are] movie villains. *****1958** in *OEDS*: The Communists are goodies and John L. Lewis is a baddy. **1963** in S. Lee *Son of Origins* 35: Wonder who the mutant baddie is. **1966** *Time* (Apr. 29) 53: A suspect is scared witless by a "bad guy" detective and is then saved by a "good guy" who coaxes him to shame the baddy by talking freely. **1968** Spooner *War in Gen.* 88: Everyone on the block gets turns at being Ho Chi Minh or one of the baddies. **1975** *Harper's* (May) 103: While the old familiars have been going legit, a big, new baddy has blown into town. **1980** S.E. Martin *Breaking & Entering* 67: My cousin on the department told me police don't have to act like "baddies" and that the department was looking for new talent. **1982** *New Yorker* (Sept. 6) 98: Miller...cues us to exult along with the good guys whenever one of them kills a baddie. **1990** *Cosmopolitan* (June) 88: [He has played] a loathsome bad guy plugged by Kevin Costner in *Silverado*, and a depraved baddie done in by Anthony Perkins in *Psycho III*.

bad egg see s.v. EGG.

bad eye *n.* **1.** strong, vile liquor.

1875 J. Miller *First Fam'lies* 126: Old Bad Eye...made from...bad rum, worse tobacco, and first-class cayenne pepper.

2. a hard or determined look about the eyes.

1896 Ade *Artie* 67: "He has a bad eye," said Miller. "Yes, and as the guy says on a stage, I don't like his other one very well, neither." **1948** McIlwaine *Memphis* 200: A black with a bad eye who was celebrated in the ballad, "Stack-o-Lee." **1949** W.R. Burnett *Asphalt Jungle* 82: Brannom [was] a big, tough-looking boy with a bad eye on him.

bad-eye *v.* to glare at.

1964–66 R. Stone *Hall of Mirrors* 53: He got up to...bad-eye the Dutchmen.

badge *n.* a police officer or detective.

1925 *Collier's* (Aug. 8) 30: Police authorities are "badges." **1956** H. Ellison *Deadly Streets* 42: We're dyin' to see you cool a badge. **1957** Lacy *Room to Swing* 155: That's...the end of my being a badge. **1960** Stadley *Barbarians* 72: The badges here got hostile and told us to beat it. **1966** in B. Jackson *Swim Like Me* 80: Along come two badges patrolling their beat. **1967** in H. Ellison *Sex Misspelled* 137: We worked like a pair of good homicide badges. **1970** Rudensky & Riley *Gonif* 93: It was a nice feeling...when the badges or Feds were closing in. **1990** *Hull High* (NBC-TV): The last thing we need is a badge scamming our friends.

badge *v. Police.* to identify oneself as a police officer by showing (someone) one's badge.

1975 Wambaugh *Choirboys* 263: You get a broad in the car, you get your offer like a told you, then badge her and bring her back here quick.

badge-heavy *adj.* (of a police officer) overbearing; ready to exert pressure.

1972 Wambaugh *Blue Knight* 52: I always was as badge heavy and obnoxious as I could be when I was in there. **1984** H. Searls *Blood Song* 115: Take orders. Hope we don't get made by some badge-heavy asshole that thinks he can shoot. **1992** Hosansky & Sparling *Working Vice* 212: He started to appreciate her. She wasn't badge-heavy.

badger *n.* **1.** a Wisconsinite.—usu. cap. Now *colloq.*

1833 in Hoffman *Winter in West* I 210: There was…a keen-eyed, leather-belted "badger" from the mines of Ouisconsin. **1855** Whitman *Leaves of Grass* 40: A boatman over the lakes or bays or along coasts…a Hoosier, a Badger, a Buckeye. **1862** in *Ark. Hist. Qly.* (1959) XVIII 58: We gave them three cheers as good ones as ever greeted a set of Badger boys. **1948** in *DA:* A survey of sentiment in 10 counties disclosed Badger citizens in rural and urban areas are increasingly concerned over the spread of communism.

2. *Und.* **a.** a panel thief.

1858 *Spirit of Times* (Feb. 27) 412: He was the "badger" at Moll Hodge's famous "panel" establishment in West Broadway and was sent up for 4 years and 8 months. **1859** Matsell *Vocabulum* 9: *Badger.* A panel thief; a fellow who robs a man's pocket after he has been enticed into bed with a woman. *Ibid.* 27: The badger got under the doss, and frisked the bloke's poke of two centuries and a half, and then bounced the flat till he mizzled. **1872** Crapsey *Nether Side N.Y.* 139: The stranger has been lured to the lair of a "badger" and is about to undergo…the panel game.…One room was prepared with a secret door…which…gave easy access to the "badger" as the male confederate of the prostitute is called. **1873** Loning *N.Y. Life* 339: The requisites for a "panel-house"…are, a crafty, cunning street walker; a…sturdy…"Badger"— and a room prepared specially for the purpose. **1928** (quot. at PAY-OFF).
b. the hoodlum who plays the role of the threatening husband or brother in a BADGER GAME, b. Cf. BADGER MAN.

1873 Loning *N.Y. Life* 340: The "badger" acts only the role of the jealous husband.
c. the woman who acts as decoy in a BADGER GAME, **2.**

1879 *Snares of N.Y.* 80: The "badger" must be an attractive woman, and the…"badger puller," a man of some nerve and good appearance. **1896** in *DA:* A female badger and her lover may be poor and unable to rent a house. **1902** R.A. Woods *Amer. in Process* 216: Some of these street-walkers are "badgers," or women whose business it is to entice men to rooms where they may be robbed by accomplices. **1928** M. Sharpe *Chi. May* 282: Women, mostly with male assistants, are the badgers. **1929** Hotstetter & Beesley *Racket* 219: *Badger*—Person, usually a woman, who lures victim of a conspiracy into a compromising or incriminating situation.

3. [cf. quots. at BADGER WORKER, BADGER HOUSE] *Und.* BADGER GAME.

1904 Hapgood *Autobiog. Thief:* The molls won't steal now.…They are ignorant. All they know how to do is the badger. **1966** Braly *On Yard* 27: That's badger.…Any fool with a broad can work that.

4. a man wearing whiskers.

1909 *Century Dict.* (Supp.): [*Badger*]…7. A soldier who wears short whiskers [Colloq., U.S.].

¶ In phrase:

¶ **let the badger loose** [cf. syn. *cut the wolf loose* s.v. WOLF] *West.* to celebrate wildly, cut loose.

1975 Swarthout *Shootist* 19: At this rate, El Paso would soon be as citified as Denver, far too highfalutin for a man who liked to let the badger loose now and then.

badger *v.* (see quot.).

1909 *WNID: Badger*…To extort money from, by the badger game. *Cant.* **1925** (cited in Partridge *Dict. Und.* 17).

badger game *n.* [cf. BADGER, *n.*, 2.a.; cf. BADGER HOUSE] *Und. & Police.* **1.** a form of theft in which a prostitute's accomplice emerges from a hidden door or panel and robs the prostitute's customer while he is engaged with her or drunk or asleep; panel game.

1879 *Snares of N.Y.* 80: The "badger game" is an improvement, or a modification, of the "panel game."
2. a blackmail stratagem in which a man is lured by a woman into a sexually compromising position and is then confronted by her male accomplice, who plays the role of the woman's husband or relative.

1909 *Century Dict.* (Supp.): *Badger game*, a blackmailing scheme in which a man of means is enticed by a woman into a compromising relation, and is then pounced upon by her alleged husband and forced to pay smart-money. **1924** Henderson *Crookdom* 228: I know of one case where a man alone worked a variation of the badger game on women. **1930** Lavine *3d Degree* 155: Any man who accompanies a…dance-hall hostess to her apartment…runs a risk of being…subjected to the well-known badger game. **1960** R. Brooks *Elmer Gantry* (film): The old badger game, huh? **1979** Weverka *By Decree* 90: I was well aware of the so-called badger games wherein a man is enticed into a compromising position and then is confronted by the woman's confederate.

badger hole *n. Army.* a deep hole dug by a soldier for protection; foxhole.

1865 C. Barney *Field Service* 194: Smoking them (the rebs) out of their badger holes.

badger house *n.* an establishment where the BADGER GAME is frequently perpetrated. Also **badger crib.**

1859 Matsell *Vocabulum* 63: Panel-cribs are sometimes called badger-cribs, shakedowns, touch-cribs. **1879** *Snares of N.Y.* 80: We have spoken specially of "panel" and "badger houses." **1881** [Trumble] *Man Traps of N.Y.* 17: One or two cribs, as these places are called, though they also enjoy the euphonious appellation of "badger houses"—are quite notorious. a**1909** *F & H* (rev.) I 103: *Badger*…(American thieves').—A panel-thief…hence, *badger-crib.*

badger man *n.* BADGER, 2.b.

1916 Scott *17 Yrs.* 62: Another type…is the badger man—a sort of blackmailer, whose work is helped to its consummation by a woman companion.

badger moll *n. Und. & Police.* BADGER, 2.c.

1905 *Nat. Police Gaz.* (Nov. 25) 3: To be a Badger Moll a woman had to have nerve, assurance, a fair amount of good looks, [etc.].

badger worker *n.* BADGER, 2.

1894 Gardner *Doctor & Devil* 52: Old-time "panel games," "badger workers," "confidence games." **1910** *New England Mag.* (July) 587: A woman who decoys men and then her accomplice (alleged husband) blackmails them is called a "badger worker." **1948** Lait & Mortimer *New York* 113: But cases of "badger" workers are everyday occurrences.

badge-toter *n. West.* a law officer.

1969 M. McCoy *Guns of Greed* 5: He's all that dangerous, just one badge-toter? **1980** Hogan *Lawman's Choice* 30: Things've been running pretty smooth without no badge-toter.

bad guy *n.* [infl. by *badman*] **1.** a villain, as in a Western movie or other melodrama. [This expression prob. dates to the early days of motion pictures, at least among children.]

1944 *Partisan Rev.* XI 491: Then, as always, it will be the good guys vs. the bad guys. **1954–60** (Common among N.Y.C. schoolchildren). **1962** Serling *New Stories* 52: The two "bad guys" stood at the bar and watched fearfully as he approached them. **1971** Edmonson *Lore* 5: All American children know that "good guys" and "bad guys" wear different colored stetsons. **1971** Capon *3d Peacock* 41: In the first place, the story does not cast the Devil simply in the role of the bad guy. **1971** D. Long *Black Love* 7: When i was young/I used to be thinking cowboys/ All the time.…/I shot bad-guys from behind/Parked cars. **1975** in Story *Guardians* 9: Nowhere else but in comic books can you still recapture the fairy tale fun of finding characters bigger than life, plots wider than any movie, and good guys battling bad guys with the fate of entire galaxies hanging on the outcome. **1990** (quot. at BADDY). **1990** *Nation* (Dec. 31) 830: Unless it can be set up as a simple good guy/bad guy issue.

2. an enemy; *(Mil.)* an enemy soldier (widely used during the Vietnam War).—usu. constr. in pl.

1961 Barr & Howard *Missileman* 69: America and its free-world allies were the "good guys." The Russians and the Communist block were the "bad guys." **1966** Shepard *Doom Pussy* 143: Naturally they'd rather be in a fighter plane. But somebody has to scout around looking for the bad guys. **1966** *Sat. Review* (Nov. 19) 34: Our nation is always the good guy; whichever nation happens to be our contemporary enemy is the bad guy. **1968** W.C. Anderson *Gooney Bird* 75: Then we gotta choose between hitting civilians or letting the bad guys escape. **1971** Mayer *Falcon* 21: The bad guys used Yards or anybody else who happened to be handy as porters or to help build fortifications. **1971** *N.Y. Post* (Jan. 6) 50: No sign of bad guys. **1971** *Newsweek* (Sept. 13) 41: "Bad guys…bad guys!" Men frantically grabbed weapons and scrambled into the jungle. **1980** Santoli *Everything* 134: The bad guys never came out until it was bad weather. **1982** *GI Joe* (Dec.) (unp.): I definitely want this hunk o' armor 'tween me and the bad guys the next time out. **1991** *War in the Gulf* (CNN-TV) (Feb. 2): We had a ground FAC controlling us saying, "Yes, these are the bad guys."

3. *Police.* a malefactor, esp. a violent criminal.

1965 in J. Mills *On the Edge* 2: I've been up against the bad guys. **1973** D. Barnes *See Woman* 36: The bad guy ran into the crowd. **1974** Radano *Cop Stories* 37: "He's a bank guard." "No trouble there telling the good guys from the bad guys." **1988** Dietl & Gross *One Tough Cop* 259: The three bad guys nailed him before he could go for his gun. **1990** C.P. McDonald *Blue Truth* 26: The three bad guys jumped into the Torino.

bad hat *n.* [sense development obscure] BAD ACTOR, 1.

1914 *DN* IV 211: *Bad egg, — hat, lot, penny,* a rascal. **1935** Algren *Boots* 29: Stubby had come to be known throughout the county as a "bad hat."

Badian /'beɪdʒən/ *n.* a native of Barbados.

1959 P. Marshall *Brown Girl* 23 [ref. to 1930's]: That's a Bajan for you. **1971** Giovanni *Gemini* 76: The faces—the beautiful Bajans.

Bad Lands *n.* **1.** a dangerous slum section of a city, esp. Chicago.

1892 *Scribner's* (July) 8: "The Bad Lands" is...the abode of vice and crime [in Chicago]. **1906** *Nat. Police Gaz.* (June 9) 6: For years Ollie Roberts was known in St. Louis as the "Queen of the Bad Lands." **1922** F.L. Packard *Doors of Night* 12: The world of the Bad Lands—with its own language, its own customs and its own haunts. **1947** *Chicago Tribune*, in *DA*: I remember a Christmas eve...when I toured the west side bad lands, tough saloons and brothels. **1979** *Toronto Star* (Sept. 22) B1 [ref. to Belfast]: The Ardoyne [is] a grim treeless district of grimy row housing surrounded by Protestant "badlands" and guarded by wire-caged army outposts and soldiers.

2. any dangerous area.

1990 G.R. Clark *Words of Vietnam War* 45: Badlands was...used in a general sense to describe a particularly hostile enemy area.

badman *n. Ice Hockey.* a rough player who is frequently sent to the penalty box.

1949 Cummings *Dict. Sports* 17.

bad medicine *n.* [perh. a translation of a Native American expression] *West.* a dangerous, unfortunate, or objectionable person or thing; BAD NEWS.

1844 Carleton *Logbooks* 50: I can't tell nothing, *no how.* Bad medicine—heap—booh! ugh! *bad medicine.* **1860–61** R.F. Burton *City of Saints* 213: He...had redeemed his vow by reappearing *in cuerpo,* with gestures so maniacal that the sulky Indians all fled, declaring him to be "bad medicine." **1871** Crofutt *Tourist's Guide* 75: The Sioux were so badly whipped that from that time forward they called the Utes "Bad Medicine." *Ibid.* 126: The Indians...call him "bad medicine" and keep out of his way most of the time. **1874** McCoy *Cattle Trade* 106: It was, as a year's transaction, "bad medicine" [i.e., unprofitable]. **1891** Maitland *Slang Dict.: Bad medicine.* Said of one who is objectionable for any reason. **1931** Z. Grey *Sunset Pass* 30: Ask Preston! Bad medicine! And he's her brother! *ca***1936** in Moriarty *True Confessions* 65: "Nick's bad medicine," she said, shaking her head. **1940** Baldwin *Brother Orchid* (film): Say nothing to them, Clarence. They're bad medicine. **1958** Compton's *Pictured Encyc.* III 65: If your hands are soft, pieces of adhesive tape should be put in advance on places where blisters might form. Blisters are "bad medicine." **1962** in *Dict. Canadianisms* 24: "Bad medicine," "chaffy"...and "pizen," are applied to anything worthless on the Eastern slope of the Rockies. **1970** La Motta et al. *Raging Bull* 108: Take it easy. Those guys are real bad medicine. **1987** *Outlaws* (CBS-TV): This place is bad medicine.

bad mouth *n.* [cf. earlier dial. sense in *DARE*] **1.** disparaging remarks, maligning.—usu. in phr. **put the bad mouth on** to disparage or malign.

1960 C.L. Cooper *Scene* 6: Rudy wondered how the bad mouth about him had started. *Ibid.* 198: It wouldn't have happened if that evil bad mouth hadn't gone out against him. **1968** Heard *Howard St.* 38: Who you puttin' bad mouth on—. **1972** Jenkins *Semi-Tough* 104: Like if she would change in any way and start putting a lot of bad-mouth on a man for some reason. **1975** S.P. Smith *Amer. Boys* 246: I don't want to put the bad mouth on my man now, but almost every day...you find him...face buried in a [pornographic] book. **1980** Conroy *Lords of Discipline* 220: No one puts the bad mouth on my girl.

2. one who badmouths. Also **badmouther.**

1967 *L.A. Times* (Mar. 12) West 55: This is the year of the bad-mouths....Pyne and Burke have been escalating their ratings...by fill-

ing the night with the kind of belligerent banter you used to get only from drunks. **1967–68** T. Wolfe *Electric Kool-Aid* 41: The intellectual badmouthers of America's tailfin civilization. **1968** Gover *JC Saves* 154: You sound like that streetcorner badmouth. **1978** *L.A. Times* (Feb. 12) VIII 22: Sure there are poor losers, bad mouthers, unstable personalities. **1982** *Working Woman* (Jan. 1983) 26: "Why are you giving up your job?" Beware of badmouthers.

badmouth *v.* [of African orig.; see *DARE*] **1.** to malign, disparage. Also absol. [Esp. common since the late 1960's.]

1941 J. Thurber, in Paxton *Sport* 296: He bad-mouthed everybody on the ball club and he bad-mouthed everybody offa the ball club, includin' the Wright brothers....He was...sulkin' and bad-mouthin' and whinin'. **1958** Gilbert *Vice Trap* 110: I'd real bad-mouth him, because I wanted to hurt him back. **1960** MacDonald *Slam the Big Door* 120: But you keep on bad-mouthing her every chance you get. **1966–67** F. Harvey *Air War* 100: Don't badmouth Uncle Ho. He's the boy who threw out the French. **1967** J. Kramer *Instant Replay* 203: You learn...never to bad-mouth an opponent. *a***1968** in Haines & Taggart *Ft. Lauderdale* 76: They were all the time bad-mouthing. **1969** *Harper's* (July) 72: Then the spurned client goes around bad-mouthing lawyer Burnett. **1971** Curtis *Banjo* 253: Maybe somebody'll bad-mouth me for killin' some folks. **1973** *Business Week* (Aug. 4) 42: We've got to stop bad mouthing. **1977** Caron *Go-Boy* 71: On the ground...was Tomato Face, badmouthing and urging everybody on to a more concerted effort. *Ibid.* 262: *Badmouthing*—threatening verbal attack. **1978** Kopp *Innocence* 107: Some cat...bad-mouthed his best buddy's chick.

2. to utter obscenities.

1972 Carr *Bad* 20: We can't have that badmouthing around the ring....You're off the playground for a week!

badmouther *n.* see s.v. BADMOUTH, *n.,* 2.

bad news *n.* **1.** [cf. earlier syn. DAMAGE] the amount charged for service, esp. as stated on a bill or restaurant check.

1910 T.A. Dorgan, in *N.Y. Eve. Jour.* (May 14) 12: Waiter—what's the bad news? **1923** Ornitz *Haunch* 190: Wait till you see the bad news for all that champin' you slewed. **1926** Maines & Grant *Wise-Crack Dict.: Bad news*—Piece of pasteboard handed by the waiter after a meal. **1941** *Slanguage Dict.: Bad news*...a bill. **1970** N.Y.C. man in restaurant: Now let's take a look at the bad news.

2. a dangerous or disastrous person, thing, situation, etc.—(in recent use) also attrib.

1917 Imbrie *Ambulance* 115: New men were apt to be confused by the talk, for the squad possessed a vocabulary and language all its own. Everything was either "good news" or "bad news," depending on how it struck the Squad. **1928** MacArthur *War Bugs* 71: That first shell was bad news, but the second was worse. *Ibid.* 167: Big buckets of high explosive hammered the hollow. Some of them were bad news. *****1946** in Partridge *Forces' Slang* 8: You fellows want to watch your step with these French weemen. Sure they're bad news. **1956** Fleming *Diamonds* 120: They're supposed to be from Detroit. Strictly bad news. They do the strong-arm work. **1965** Hersey *Too Far to Walk* 88: Was he bad news! **1975** *Welfare* (TV documentary): They are really bad-news people. **1972–76** Durden *No Bugles* 164: He...takes care of any bad-news bastards. **1976** Conroy *Santini* 452: It's bad news to piss off Apache Bill. **1980** M. Baker *Nam* 36: I came down with a couple of guys who were Puerto Rican street gang material from the big city and thought they were bad news. **1983** S. King *Christine* 493: We're going on the theory that they picked up a bad-news hitch-hiker who escaped after the accident and before the troopers arrived. **1993** *Oprah* (syndic. TV series): If I was bad news, you would be history.

bad paper *n. Mil.* any discharge other than an honorable discharge.

1971 *Seattle Times* (July 25) A24: The Concerned Veterans of Vietnam announced that it has helped nine veterans with less-than-honorable discharges win reversals of this "bad paper." **1972** *Harper's* (Aug.) 18: The black veteran suffers from special difficulties in reintegrating with society, frequently as a result of unjust "bad paper" (less than honorable) discharges. **1979** *L.A. Times* (Feb. 17) I 1: The 3 million men and women from all eras who carry "bad paper"—military slang for an administrative discharge under less than honorable conditions. **1985** *L.A. Times B. Rev.* (Mar. 17) 9: This knowledge makes Reston particularly sympathetic toward those veterans with "bad paper" discharges.

bad-rap *v.* [*bad* + RAP, *v.*] to criticize unjustly; malign; BUM-RAP.

1967 Yablonsky *Hippie Trip* 190: So...I'd rant and rave and scream...and shout and bad-rap people. **1969** in *Rolling Stone Interviews* 177: Did you ever get bad-rapped for playing some of your sexy songs in small towns? **1976** H. Ellison *Sex Misspelled* 21: People...badrap the same attempts to discover the answers to interpersonal relationships. **1978** Selby *Requiem* 245: Ah aint bad rappin ya. Ah just want to set you straight. **1979** *St. Louis Post-Dispatch* (Oct. 14) 8b: Givens said that he never "bad-raps other unions."

bafflegab *n. Pol. & Journ.* confusing or unintelligible jargon; doublespeak.

1952 in *AS* XXVIII 208: Milton Smith, the assistant general counsel of the U.S. Chamber of Commerce, has coined a new word "bafflegab" designed solely for Washington bureaucrats. **1953** in *Ibid.*: Even I— and I've been exposed for an awfully long time to financial bafflegab— squirmed uncomfortably. **1967** *Wall Street Journal* (Mar. 14): For collectors of bafflegab, the art of impressing an audience with verbal bushwa, the meeting of personnel officials was a gold mine....As the parade to the rostrum continued, the bafflegab glossary expanded: Narrowing parameters, functions of situational variables, diagnostic-planning activity, [etc.]. **1968** *Everett* (Wash.) *Herald* (May 31) 4: Proposals to overhaul our welfare system will be among the key issues...of the 1968 Presidential campaign....The following Q & A is a guide through the bafflegab. **1980** J. Ciardi, in *Atlantic* (Aug.) 36: Double-talk, a form of rapid, smoothly articulated, and well-modulated baffle gab with a normal syntax but with meaningless key words, has long been a popular specialty of comedians. **1983** *L.A. Times* (June 16) V 18: The automobile insurance business can be considered complex only by someone who has never delved into the health-insurance field, where bafflegab is the norm. **1990** *Maclean's* (June 11) 68: He is so blunt as to shock the locals so accustomed to obfuscation and bafflegab.

bag *n.* **1.** womb; (*hence*) vagina; scrotum.—usu. considered vulgar. [Slang when not dial.]
***1886** in *EDD*: *Bag.*...The womb of any domestic animal. ***a1903–09** *F & H I* (rev.) 104: *Bag*...(old). The womb. **1916–22** Cary *Sex. Vocab.* I: *Bag.* The female privities. **1938** "Justinian" *Americana Sexualis* 12: *Bag.* n. Of the female, the vaginal orifice; of the male, the scrotum. **1939** Appel *Power-House* 401: All your dumb mothers wasted time carrying you mutts around in their bags.

2.a. a sexually promiscuous woman, slut; a prostitute. [Perh. 1893 quot. could as easily belong under **(b)**, below, but the usage reflected in **(1)** sugg. that this is the earlier sense.]
1893 in *Independent* (Dec. 19, 1901) 3012: I have seen several women on the tramp, but generally very low down creatures. The boys call them Bags, old Bags. A man along with a Bag don't stand very high in Haut-Beau [hobo] society. **1922** Paul *Impromptu* 121: A hard-looking bunch of bags. Do you think it's safe to take a chance? **1924** P. Marks *Plastic Age* 155: I'm out with bags all the time....My sex instincts don't need sublimating. *Ibid.* 202: I don't get potted regularly or chase around with filthy bags or flunk my courses or crib my way through. **1926** Dunning & Abbot *B'way* 237: You don't want to be pegged with them bags, do you? **1939–40** O'Hara *Pal Joey* 28: You got to be a bag to know some of the things she called me. *Ibid.* 60: The highest paid bag in Chi. **1947** Motley *Any Door* 256: He looked around for a broad, any old bag at all. **1963** D. Tracy *Brass Ring* 158: You never even met Mary and as soon as I tell you her name you make a bag out of her. [**1964** in *Fact* (Jan. 1965) 25: *Bag n.* A fellow (male) homosexual. *Derogatory.*]

b. a woman who is unattractive, obnoxious, or otherwise unpleasant.
1922 J. Conway, in *Variety* (Jan. 27) 11: He picks out a bag with a lame brain. **1926–27** in *AS* III 218: *Bag*, n.—A girl—usually a rather unattractive girl. "Say Cress, who was that bag I saw you with yesterday?" **1927** Mayer *Between Us Girls* 105: There were simply heaps of poisonous old bags on board who did nothing but sort of sit around and criticize you mercilessly for simply everything you perpetrated. **1933** "W. March" *Co. K* 128: What the hell is the old bag making a speech about? **1946** Michener *So. Pacific* 149: Half of them called her "that bag" and the other half wanted to know who the movie star was. **1952** E. Brown *Trespass* 130: I'm just an old bag. **1955–57** Kerouac *On Road* 105: Oh, shut up, you old bag! **1960** Swarthout *Where Boys Are* 43: As far as I'm concerned, Marjorie Morningstar was as much a bag as [Richardson's] Pamela. **1963** J. Ross *Dead Are Mine* 106: They're after a place called Femina Morte. "Dead Woman." Hell of a name for a crossroad. Maybe some bag was killed there. **1964** Brewer *Worser Days* 85: So that's the old bag he's been chasin'. **1969** Moynahan *Pairing Off* 73: That old bag was always in the way of saying, "Now children, children." **1979** Gutcheon *New Girls* 170: *Write*, you illiterate bag. **1981** C. Nelson *Picked Bullets Up* 13: Another dumb old bag who'll kill herself taking care of him.

3. the scrotum; *pl.* the testicles.—usu. considered vulgar. [Also dial.]

1921 *John's Gun* 1: Your hard, stony bag knocks at my ass hole. **1927** *AS* II 359: That driver doesn't know B from bull's bag about loading his wagon. **1928** *DN* VI 60: A paper bag is always a *sack* or a *poke*, since *bag* means scrotum in [the Ozarks]. **1942** McAtee *Supp. to Grant Co. Dial.* 2 [ref. to 1890's]: *Bag*, n. scrotum. **1942** in Legman *Limerick* 44: The bag fans your bum on the ride. **1946** *PADS* (No. 6) 5: *Bag: n.* The scrotum. **1956** E. Hunter *Second Ending* 227: I was hooked clean through the bag and back again. **1954–60** *DAS*: *Bags*...The testicles. *Not common.* **1974** (quot. at *bite the bag*, below).

4. a condom.
1922 *Erotic Appliances* 20: A young man...at last got a "nice young lady" to consent to the act of connection, only, that he would use one of those rubber bags she had heard of. **1965** Trimble *Sex Words* 21: BAG...A rubber Prophylactic worn over the Penis. **1971** N.Y.U. student [telling a joke]: So when the farmer sees all the eggs are empty he runs into the chicken house with his shotgun and he says to the roosters, "Who's the sonofabitch that's been using the bag?" **1974** Price *Wanderers* 92: I don't got no bags but I'll pull out before I come. **1978** Pilcer *Teen Angel* 17: A scumbag....Rubber....Stringbean Palovsky wants a bag.

5. *Pris.* a straitjacket.—constr. with *the.* Now *hist.*
1925–26 Black *You Can't Win* 363 [ref. to *ca*1900]: The jacket is no longer in use and no purpose would be served by living over those three days in the "bag." *Ibid.* 365: He held up the "bag" in front of me.

6.a. *Av.* an observation balloon, blimp, dirigible, etc.
1928 Maitland *Knights of Air* 209 [ref. to WWI]: Luke flew directly toward the "bags," while Wehner climbed high above Luke to protect him against enemy air attack. **1933** Stewart *Sp. of Amer. Airman* 46: *Bag.* Any dirigible, balloon, or kite balloon. **1945** Hamann *Air Words*: *Bag.* A balloon or gas-filled aerostat. **1952** Cope & Dyer *Petty Off. Hndbk.* 420: *Bag* (Slang) An airship, blimp. **1955** *Science Digest* (Dec.) 74: And it's a nice way to go to sea—in the bags.

b. *Circus.* a toy balloon.
1931 *Nat. Geo.* (Oct.) 514: The *bag guy* is the balloon seller. **1945** Coplan & Kelley *Pink Lemonade* (unp.) (caption): There's always time for a young lady to conduct business with the "bag guy," as circus slang has dubbed him.

7. usu. *pl.* a woman's breast.
1938 "Justinian" *Amer. Sexualis* 12: *Bag*, n....pl. Female breasts. **1962** Sagarin *Dirty Wds.* 79: *Bags* (breasts). **1970** E.W. Johnson *Sex* 86: Breasts, *bags*, boobies, tits. **1971** *AS* XLVI 82: Breasts:...balloons...boobs...bags.

8.a. *Police & Fire Dept.* a uniform.—constr. with *the.*
1944 *Amer. N & Q* (Apr.) 4: *Bag*: Fun-poking name for a fireman's uniform. *Ibid.* (Sept.) 85: *Bag.* New York City Police Department slang for *uniform*; especially common among detectives. **1958** *N.Y. Times Mag.* (Mar. 16) 87: *Bag*—[Policeman's] Uniform. **1963** *True* (May) 100: "Sometimes I think I oughta go back into the bag."...In cop's argot, the bag is the blue uniform, and working in the bag means...walking a post or cruising in a radio car. **1973** Droge *Patrolman* 191: If you failed to meet the quota consistently you would "get flopped back into the bag (uniform)." **1974** Milius & Cimino *Magnum Force* (film): The only reason I don't bust you into the bag this minute is because you were his friend. **1974** Charyn *Blue Eyes* 48: I wore the bag once, Isobel. At the academy. Grays instead of blues. I wouldn't mind giving up my detective shield. I can survive in a bag.

b. a man's suit of clothes.
1968 in Andrews & Dickens *Big House* 13: He was sharp in his silk bag. **1972** in Andrews & Dickens *Big House* 29: That's a mean bag....Botany?

9. *Stu.* an obnoxious individual. Cf. **(2.b.)**, above.
1944 *Life* (May 15) 65: They now understand that a drip is a "bag." **1970** *AS* XLV 301: Twice in response to questions about *lunch guy*, the informants [at Princeton Univ. in 1965] offered, "He's a bag," which they explained as "the kind of guy who brings his lunch in a bag."

10. *Narc.* a small packet, typically an envelope or folded paper, containing heroin, marijuana, or the like.
1952 Ellson *Golden Spike* 43: Suppose I give you a bag? **1957** Gelber *Connection* 51: Like what happened to the dollar cap, to the three dollar bag? And that was some good shit, too. **1959** Trocchi *Cain* 174: I'll get a bag and we'll split it. **1963** in *Maclean's* (Jan. 4, 1964): A *bag* is a two-for-a-nickel matchbox filled even with pot and poured into a payroll envelope. **1963** *Sat. Eve. Post* 76: A "$12 bag" contains enough heroin for two or three users. **1965** Nat Hentoff, in *New Yorker* (June 26) 33: A bag is a glassine envelope containing a mixture of heroin and milk sugar, with some baby powder and perhaps a little quinine added. **1976** Haseltine & Yaw *Woman Doctor* 115: Can't fool you, can I? I had five bags. **1980** Gould *Ft. Apache* 165: There's a guy in a phone booth sell-

ing bags. I see him almost every day.

11. Orig. *Black E.* **a.** Esp. *Jazz.* category.

1960 in Cerulli *Jazz Word* 188: Lack of acceptance is a drag....Man, that's really in another bag. **1961** *Downbeat* (Feb. 2) 30: Soul is...melodically a bit doubtful as to what jazz bag it belongs in. **1962** H. Simmons *On Eggshells* 223: An original dip into the nut bag. **1964** Rhodes *Chosen Few* 28: This cat is in another bag, baby....You'll hafta watch yourself t'keep from laughin'. *Ibid.* 40: "How's poor Prong these days?" "He's still in his own bag." *Ibid.* 44: He had gone through his usual mental game of trying to put everyone new he met into a particular bag. **1971** E. Tidyman & J. Black *Shaft* (film): What you think and what you can prove are two different bags, man. **1971** *Playboy* (June) 46: Their aim is to plunder the entire pop-music bag and demonstrate the versatility...of their...talents. **1972** Rossner *Any Minute* 116: I'd put his aunt in this bag and...I labeled the bag *nuts.* **1973–76** J. Allen *Assault* 36: The white-collar crime is an altogether different bag.

b. one's style or customary way of doing things; pattern of behavior.

1962 *Jazz Jrnl.* (Mar.) 30: "Bag" is a current piece of trade jargon for hip musicians, and means something between a personal style and a body of work. **1962** *N.Y. Times Mag.* (May 20) 45: *Bag:* a point of view or pattern of behavior. That chick comes out of a very intellectual "bag." **1963** in H. Ellison *Sex Misspelled* 58: This...is how we fool ourselves into thinking we're honorable men....There isn't one of us who isn't in that bag. **1963** J.A. Williams *Sissie* 71: What bag you working out of, baby? **1965** Hentoff *Jazz Country* 59: He had his own "bag"—you know, style—but it didn't fit with anyone else's. **1965** C. Brown *Manchild* 196: She was good and sewed up in that religious bag. **1966** IUFA *Folk Speech*: *What's the bag*—this phrase is used for what are you doing. **1970** Gattzden *Black Vendetta* 62: They gotta take flash shots—prints—...the whole bag. **1971** *N.Y. Times Mag.* (Nov. 28) 91: We ain't into the kill thing. Anybody on that junk is workin' out of a fruit and nuts bag. **1974** Beacham & Garrett *Intro 5* 65: I'd never play outa that kinda bag, no matter what. **1973–76** J. Allen *Assault* 9: I asked about him going to the church, 'cause I was really curious...."Man, like what happened? What made you get out of this bag?"..."I can't steal, so I turned to the Lord." **1977** Caron *Go-Boy* 159: "Are you threatening me?" "No, that ain't my bag." **1977** *L.A. Times* (Dec. 4) Calendar 91: If the Four Seasons can have an album that does 400,000 here and is the biggest album they've ever had in Europe, why change that bag? **1981** *Nat. Lampoon* (Nov.) 14: We're getting into the conservative bag, but geez!

c. strong, esp. temporary, interest; area of expertise or interest; preference; mood.

[**1963** *Time* (Aug. 2) 14: Some Negro terms are virtually untranslatable into ordinary English; *bag* means (among other things) to pursue one's own pleasures.] **1964** in *Time* (Jan. 1, 1965) 57: *I am in a pizza bag* means "I want pizza." **1965** *Harper's Bazaar* (Apr.) 143: *Bag:* What you're hung up on. I'm in a Bogart bag. **1966** I. Reed *Pall-Bearers* 72: "Sometimes I meditate over these issues on long walks." "You're still in dat bag, huh Bukka?" **1970** *Harper's* (Apr.) 6: Black Studies is not my bag. **1971** *Playboy* (June) 44: She's into the pop-rock-folk bag with a vengeance. **1973** Holliday & Kearney *Night of Lepus* (film): Rabbits aren't exactly Roy's bag. **1973** Childress *Hero* 26: He's forever ready to jump into a new bag if it's what he calls "a promisin-lookin thing." **1977** R.S. Parker *Effective Decisions* 14: We have already referred to a passive hoping-for-the-best...attitude. If this is your bag,...be careful it doesn't get over your head. **1978** *Rolling Stone* (Feb. 9) 40: Most of them really weren't into an antiwar bag. **1981** C. Nelson *Picked Bullets Up* 22: Although that is hardly my bag, I can get into it. **1985** M. Baker *Cops* 220: He thought it was great, this was his bag.

d. position; situation.

1964–66 R. Stone *Hall of Mirrors* 222: It's the dracula syndrome. It's the drink blood or die bag. **1964–67** Speicher *Baby Paradise* 66: Must be harder for a guy like you...or you wouldn't be in this bag. **1969** Marine *Black Panthers* 108: Being, as he said, "in a bad bag,"...Cleaver gave in. **1969** *Daredevil* (Dec.) 8: This is one bag even you can't know anything about. **1970** J. Dickey, in *Atlantic* (Feb.) 98: God damn phraseology....We're in another bag now, baby. **1970** R.N. Williams *Exiles* 139: There isn't the freedom that there was in basic [training]. You get into AIT and it's a whole different bag. **1974** Gober *Black Cop* 107: But that don't give you no reason to put me in such a bad bag....Baby, you'll be killing me dead.

12. bed, SACK—constr. with *the.*—esp. in phr. **hit the bag** to go to bed; take a rest.

1961 L.G. Richards *TAC* 45: Most "sacked out" or "hit the bag," still the most popular indoor sport in the Air Force. **1968** Baker et al. *CUSS* 75: *Bag*...bed. **1970** *Current Slang* V 14: *Bag*,...n. A bed.—Where's

Jack? Where he usually is, in the bag. **1981** Univ. Tenn. student: "He's still in the bag" means he's still in bed. **1984** Trotti *Phantom* 6: It was after three-thirty when I rolled into the bag.

¶ In phrases:

¶ **bite the bag** Orig. *Juve.* to be very unsatisfactory; SUCK; *(hence)* (used to express contempt and rejection).

[**1952** in W. Savage *Comic Books* 61: Why don't he go bite on a big juicy duffel bag?] **1968** Baker et al. *CUSS* 75: *Bite the bag*: expletive of disapproval or contempt. **1974** Detroit man, age *ca*30: In the early '60's I heard a series of expressions referring to the testicles, which was called one's *bag.* The first was *Bite the bag!* which meant go 'way, to hell with you. And the other was *bag-biter* which meant a low individual. **1974** in L. Bangs *Psychotic Reactions* 144: Well, bite the bag, peons! **1983** Naiman *Computer Dict.* 18: Their new [computer] terminal really bites the bag.

¶ **chase the bag** [fr. **(10)**, above] *Narc.* to seek heroin for purchase; *(hence)* to be addicted to heroin.

1972 Smith & Gay *Don't Try It* 199: *Chasing the bag.* Trying to get dope. **1976** Chinn *Dig Nigger Up* 185: After "chasing the bag" for three months...it dawned on me. **1988** *N.Y. Newsday* (Jan. 25) 41: [An addict's] whole day is what they call "chasing the bag," trying to get his next fix.

¶ **come out of a bag** *Black E.* to behave in an objectionable manner.

1983 Sturz *Wid. Circles* 39: That's the real deal, Marvin. This is no time to come out of a bag, Marvin.

¶ **give the bag, a.** to leave (a person) suddenly.

*****1592** in *F & H* I 97: If he mean to give her the bagge, he selleth whatsoever he can, and so leaves hir spoild both of hir wealth and honestie. *****1592** in *OED:* To giue your masters the bagge. *****1607** in *OED:* I fear our oares haue giuen us the bag. *****1647** in *OED:* He being sometime an Apprentice on London bridge...gave his Master the bag. **1666** G. Alsop *Maryland* 92: Troubles and confusion...the best way to give them the bag, is to go out of the World and leave them. **1788** in *OEDS:* He must give us the bag,/Adhere to Old England, and sail with her flag. **1787–89** R. Tyler *Contrast* 55: General Shays has sneaked off and given us the bag to hold. *****1796** Grose *Vulgar Tongue* (ed. 3): *He gave them the bag,* i.e. left them. *****1823** "J. Bee" *Slang* 5: To give the *Bag* to any one; to leave him suddenly. *****1888** in Barrère & Leland *Dict. Slang & Cant* I 65: When of oof they had bereft him, his own tart had promptly left him...She had given him, quite cheerfully, the bag.

b. to jilt, reject (a suitor).

1798 in Whiting *Early Amer. Provs.* 18: Should you give me the bag...I'll hang my "nown self" with a bridle. *ca***1800** in Whiting *Early Amer. Provs.* 18: On his promise to marry me I gave all my other sweethearts the bag. **1806** in *OEDS:* "To give the bag" is an expression common with the lower classes in New England, and indicates that Miss Delia will not honour Mr. Damon with her company in a tete-a-tete conversation. **1825** in *OEDS:* Sent away, with a flea in your ear; some girl has given you the bag. **1825** in *JAF* LXXVI (1963) 278: So now let Betty Webster give me the bag agin, I guess she wont have a chance very quick. **1828** in Whiting *Early Amer. Provs.* 18: I never was courted but once in my life, and then I gave the bag.

¶ **have a bag on** to be drunk.

1947 Mailer *Naked & Dead* 211: Watch out for your old man when he's got a bag on. **1956** Ferrer & Morgan *The Great Man* (film): She showed up with half a bag on. **1972** Grogan *Ringolevio* 100: By eleven thirty he had half a bag on.

¶ **hold the bag** to be left in the lurch. Now *colloq.*

1760 in Whiting *Amer. Prov. Phrs.* 19: The Enemy once fixed here would be, the English term it, given [*sic*] us the Bag to hold. **1791** G. Washington, in Whiting *Amer. Prov. Phrs.:* He will leave you the bag to hold. **1793** T. Jefferson, in *OED:* She will leave Spain the bag to hold. **1871** Still *Underground R.R.* 435: He concluded that he would leave him the "bag to hold alone." **1875** Sheppard *Love Afloat* 394: 'E's afeard 'e might take the schooner and go hoff some time, and forget to come back hany more...and leave 'is old brother to 'old the bag. **1931** *Amer. Merc.* (Dec.) 416: The guy left holdin' the bag pays for five drinks. **1932** R. Fisher *Conjure-Man* 273: I'm holdin' the well-known bag. *ca***1935** in R.E. Howard *Iron Man* 129: Dutchy had pulled out for good while the fight was going on, leaving us suckers holding the bag. **1938** Bellem *Blue Murder* 51: That's why she lammed away and left me holding the bag. **1955** Graziano & Barber *Somebody Up There* 355: I hated to leave Irving and Jack holding the bag. **1971** Cameron *First Blood* 148: He ran off and left Koblinsky and me holding the bag! **1982** Rucker *57th Kafka* 63: You ain't gonna sneak off and leave *me* holding the bag.

¶ **in the bag, 1.** *Mil.* taken as a prisoner of war.
*1919 in *OEDS:* Unless I went out to the Front again and got put in the bag and sent to the same Boche prison. ***1943** in P. Jordan *Tunis Diary* 149: It looks as though a whole French division is in the bag. **1948** I. Shaw *Young Lions* 424: I'm afraid if we just sat here and waited, we'd all end up in the bag. **1955** L. Shapiro *6th of June* 196: John apparently was hit so there's a chance he's in the bag. **1968** Westheimer *Sentry* 218 [ref. to WWII]: I ain't been in the bag that long. **1969** *N.Y. Post* (Nov. 22) 30: As British and American soldiers used the term, "in the bag" defined the whereabouts of former compatriots taken prisoner.

2. secured, completed; as good as won; a certainty; (*specif.*) *Und.* made amenable by bribery.
1921 J. Conway, in *Variety* (July 1) 5: They think I had the fight in the bag. **1929** in Mencken *Amer. Lang. Supp. I* 442: It's *in the bag.* **1930** *Variety* (Jan. 8) 123: But he's got to know that the game is fixed....The gilly outfits that travel a merry-go-round, a cooch show and 8 joints have the town constabulary in the bag weeks before they play the burg. **1934** Jevne & Purcell *Joe Palooka* (film): The fight is in the bag! **1934** in Fenner *Throttle* 72: The run was almost as good as in the bag. **1936** Steel *College* 309: It's in the bag....I can pin that killing down. **1937** in H. Gray *Arf* (unp.): It's in th' bag—we can't miss. **1938** "E. Queen" *4 Hearts* 22: They'll fall all over themselves grabbin' for the contracts. It's in the bag. **1946** Gresham *Nightmare Alley* 106: It's in the bag. **1955** R.L. Scott *Look of the Eagle* 84: He took a careful fix on the radio compass and grinned in smug satisfaction that they had Elmendorf "in the bag." **1957** Fuchs & Levine *Jeanne Eagels* (film): Now will you stop worrying? It's in the bag. **1966** in T.C. Bambara *Gorilla* 39: And there I was, smiling, you dig, cause it was in the bag. **1983** *USA Today* (Dec. 16) 1: Strong '84 Economy Is "In the Bag."

3. (of a prizefight, horse race, or similar sporting event) illicitly prearranged by the paying of bribes or other trickery; fixed; (of a person) bribed; (*hence*) in phr. **go in the bag** (of a competitor) to lose deliberately; (*Und.*) to accept a bribe.
1926 Maines & Grant *Wise-Crack Dict.* 9: *In the bag*—Prearranged result in a contest. **1927** C.F. Coe, in Paxton *Sport* 150: For every crooked fight, for every match that is in the bag, there are a thousand that are clean and hard fought. **1942** *ATS* 633: Play According to Prearrangement. *Go in the bag*, lay down and roll over. **1947** Schulberg *Harder They Fall* 251: But Gus has always been on the level....Gus never went into the bag for anybody in his life. **1956** Yordan *Harder They Fall* (film): Dundee never went in the bag [deliberately lost a prizefight] for anyone. **1970** in P. Heller *In This Corner* 40: It was in the bag for Jeffries to win. **1980** Pearl *Slang Dict.*: *Bag, go in the v.* (*crime*) to accept a bribe. **1988** Sayles *Eight Men Out* (film) [ref. to 1919]: We played like a bunch of bushers today, but nobody's in the bag.

4. in debt.
1928 O'Connor *B'way Racketeers* 75: They had me in the bag for nearly ten G's before I pulled the string and let the joint go blooey. **1929** McEvoy *Hollywood Girl* 202: The company was in the bag for half a million dollars already on the picture. **1957** MacDonald *Price of Murder* 68: Hell, if you're really in the bag, why not screw Catton, take all that's left and do like I'm going to do?

5. drunk.
1940 Zinberg *Walk Hard* 126: Never pick up a broad when you're in the bag. **1958** in C. Beaumont *Best* 207: The Cap thinks I'm in the bag....I suppose that's what you think too. **1959** *AS* XXXIV 156: *Potted, stoned, smashed, clobbered, in the bag* [all in use at Univ. Fla.]. **1968** Baker et al. *CUSS: Bag, in the.* Drunk. **1972** Mills *Report* 153: He sounds like he's been at a party, half in the bag, not very pleasant. **1972–76** Durden *No Bugles* 141: Why don't we go out 'n' sit in some comfortable bar, get half in the bag, then wander back. **1985** E. Leonard *Glitz* 207: He's in the fucking bag half the time. **1986–91** Hamper *Rivethead* 180: The old man was already in the bag.

6. in trouble, "in a hole."
1968 Baker et al. *CUSS* 75: *In a bag*: in an undesirable situation.

¶ In phrases:

¶ **punch the bag** to complain; to talk at length, gossip, chat, etc. Hence **bag-puncher, bag-punching,** *n.*
1901 Ade *Modern Fables* 27: He was out every Night with a lot of Bag-Punchers who showed him how to convert his Ready Money into Popularity. **1903** Merriman *Letters from Son* 159: I'll give you an exhibition of bag-punching that will make your head swim. **1926** in Hemingway *Sel. Letters* 188: Too much bag punching at the start of the review of McAlmon's Distinguished Air. **1926** Maines & Grant *Wise-Crack Dict.* 12: *Punching the bag*—incessant talking. **1927** *N.Y. Sun* (July 18): In the

American League a player who is given to talking a great deal is called a "barber," while in the National League he is called a "bag-puncher." The significance of the former is unmistakable, but for the latter there is no explanation. **1928** Ruth *Baseball* 20: The boys were sitting around the club house punching the bag and "barbering" a little about what we might expect in the series.

¶ **put on the bag** [cf. *put on the feedbag* s.v. FEEDBAG] to dine.
1924 Wilstach *Stage Slang* 21: Putting on the Bag: Eating.

bag *v.* **1.a.** to catch (a wrongdoer); (*hence*) to arrest; to jail.
*1824 Byron *Don Juan* XVI: The constable...Had bagg'd this poacher upon Nature's manor. **1859** Matsell *Vocabulum: Bagged.* Imprisoned. **1861** in H.L. Abbott *Fallen Leaves* 84: I came very near bagging the little one's father on a suspicion of selling rum to the soldiers. **1881** [Trumble] *Man Traps* 30: Cribbed it you know, 'fraid I'll be bagged if I hock it. **1887** Flinn *Chicago Police* 156: The police justices are kept busy in "bagging" mechanics who have degenerated into vagrants and the justices are giving them "time" to leave town. **1952** J.B. Martin *Life in Crime* 105: If the coppers...picked up guys and bagged 'em that they knew were starting out on the rackets,...it would cut down 80 per cent of what happens. **1965** C. Brown *Manchild* 16: They were both bagged a week later for smoking pot. **1968** Radano *Beat* 69: I remember when I was in plainclothes. I was looking to bag this hooker. **1973** D. Barnes *See Woman* 35: They bagged him...got him cuffed and in the rear of the car. **1982** *N.Y. Post* (Aug. 20) 103: Cops Bag Holdup Gang.

b. *Mil.* to take prisoner, to capture.
1861 in [N. Bartlett] *Soldier's Story* 51: News was...transmitted...that "Old Fuss and Feathers" had been bagged at last. **1863** Connolly *Army of Cumberland* 60: I determined to "bag" him. **1864** Berkeley *Confed. Arty.* 73: About 1 p.m. our boys brought out an entire Yankee regiment they had bagged. **1865** Cooke *Wearing Gray* 76: Sir Percy had publicly announced his intention to "bag Ashby." **1883** Parker *Naval Officer* 246: Lee was about to bag McClellan's entire army. **1896** S. Crane *Comp. Stories* 269: That's some satisfaction, any how, even if you did bag me. **1918** Beston *Full Speed* 92: Bagged him, boat and all. **1919** T. Kelly *What Outfit?* 180: "Those guys sure bagged some Boches," and the guard picked up a faster step with his prisoners.

c. to gain, achieve, secure, or win for oneself, esp. after repeated attempts.
1911 O. Johnson *Stover at Yale* 139: By George, if that bodysnatcher of a Miss Sparkes hasn't bagged Stover—well, I never! **1934** Weseen *Dict. Slang* 247: *Bag a title*—To win a championship. *Bag a win*—To win a game or a contest. **1951** *AS* XXVI 230: Iowa State bags tie with Mississippi. **1981** Univ. Tenn. student: I somehow managed to bag a real winner—now if he'll only propose!

d. to get (something that is not material, esp. sleep); in phr. **bag Z's** to sleep.
1968 Baker et al. *CUSS* 75: *Bag Z's* [sleep]...bag bennies [benefits]. **1980** Birnbach *Preppy Hndbk.* 218: *Bagging Z's*...taking a nap. **1984** Univ. Tenn. student: I gotta bag some sleep. **1983** Eble *Campus Slang* (Mar.) 1: *Bag Some Rays*—sun bathe. Also *catch some rays.* **1989** *CBS This Morning* (CBS-TV) (Apr. 25): It might be a good day to go out and bag some of that sunshine.

2.a. to shoot; to kill (an enemy).
*1844 in *F & H* I (rev.) 106: To bag a dozen head of game without missing. **1871** *Overland Mo.* (Nov.) 459: We bagged fifteen Apaches, all told, that day—real fighting men, no boys or squaws. **1971–72** Giovannitti *Medal* 19: He doesn't want to get bagged in the back.

b. *Mil.* to destroy (an enemy aircraft or other target) in combat; shoot down.
1919 Hubbell *Co. C* 112: Allied Flyer Bags Boche...the machine burst into flames and the German aviator, to avoid being burned alive, jumped from the plane in mid air, falling to his death while thousands of Americans cheered. **1961** Foster *Hell in Heavens* 26: Don Aldrich has been doing all right, too; he's bagged five Zeros and Spears has got four. **1966** F. Elkins *Heart of Man* 47: There was the bridge....I bagged it, first time. **1969** Broughton *Thud Ridge* 60: "Dutch got bagged," he announced with deflating certainty. **1986** Coonts *Intruder* 98: We have to keep going regardless of who gets bagged. **1993** *Beavis & Butt-Head* (MTV): You bagged a jumbo jet!

3. to steal.
*1857 in *OED:* The idea of being led up to the Doctor...for bagging fowl. ***1862** in *F & H* 98: They would not call it stealing, but *bagging* a thing or, at the worst, cribbing it— concealing the villainy under a new name. ***1870** *N & Q* (4th Series) VI 517: He bags another fellow's cap when he has lost his own. **1892** *DN* I 216: *Bag it* = steal it. **1902** Clapin *Americanisms* 34: Slang "to bag," meaning to steal. **1975** M. Thomas *Heavy Number* 43: I bagged some clippers. **1987** *Ohara* (ABC-

TV): The kid bagged my new car!

4.a. *Juve.* to fail to attend (school or a class); in phr. **bag it** to play truant. [Mainly restricted to Philadelphia area.]

1892 *DN* I 216: In Camden, N.J., the boys "*bag it.*" **1917** *DN* IV 337: I *bagged* my arithmetic class today. **1938** O'Hara *Hope of Heaven* 36: I used to be able to sign my old man's name to excuses when I bagged school. **1950** *New Yorker* (Nov. 11) 60: I took to baggin' school.

b. to disregard, abandon, or be done with; quit.—also constr. with *up*; in phr. **bag it!** "shut up!" "go away!" etc.

1962 Quirk *No Red Ribbons* 280: He's going to close the shop and tell the union to bag it. **1968** Baker et al. *CUSS* 75: *Bag...*To discontinue or give up doing something, as "bag an exam," "bag studying;" *Bag it:* (1) Shut up, be quiet; (2) Forget it. **1969** *Current Slang* I & II 6: *Bag it,* v. Forget it; skip it.—High school and college students, both sexes, Michigan.—You can tell her I said to bag it. **1968–70** *Current Slang* III & IV 6: *Bag it...*Shut up (command). New Mexico State.—It's noisy here. Bag it! **1971** Dahlskog *Dict.: Bag...*To forget or skip, as: Tell him to *bag* it. **1971** in Robinson *Comics* 213: Say, Molly, our relationship's getting stale, so I've decided to bag it, O.K.? **1974** Blount *3 Bricks Shy* 39: "You know, like...bag it." In other words, I guess, "give up on it." **1976** *N.Y. Post* (Dec. 23) 28: If I were you, I'd ask my husband to bag the deal. And on the double. **1975–78** T. O'Brien *Cacciato* 53: Screw [the] mission....I vote we bag it up. It's nuts. **1978** J. Webb *Fields of Fire* 158: He was offering his body as a sacrifice in the name of not bagging a superior's order. **1980** *Newsweek* (Feb. 4) 35: I wish Dad would bag the eleventh commandment, take the gloves off and come out fighting. **1982** in *Nat. Lampoon* (Feb. 1983) (front cover): Bag it, Kimberly—I disagree to the max! **1983** *Verbatim* IX (No. 4) 1: *Bag the za* (meaning "cancel the pizza"). **1986** Bozzone *Buck Fever* 43: Let's bag this job....I'm serious.

c. *Mil.* **bag it** to loaf, malinger, or evade one's duty.

1978 J. Webb *Fields of Fire* 95 [ref. to Vietnam War, 1969]: You stupid shit. What the hell you doing? You shoulda loaded those before. Hurry up. Quit bagging it, Senator. *Ibid.* 210: Let her boyfriend get drafted and come over here to take my place. Except he's probably found a way to bag it. **1980** J. Webb *Sense of Honor* 141: Quit *bagging* it.

d. *Stu.* to fail to meet with (someone); stand up.

1989 *Life* (July) 27: One time he told her to meet him at a café, but he *bagged* her.

5. to classify.

1967 Maurer & Vogel *Narc. & Narc. Add.* 340: *Bag.* To put in a classification as convict, thief, con man, etc.

6. to botch. Cf. **(4.b.)**, above.

1968 Baker et al. *CUSS* 75: *Bag...*To do poorly on something, to fail, as "bag an exam."

7.a. [cf. BAG, *n.*, 12] *Stu.* to go to bed; to sleep. Also **bag it.**

1968 Baker et al. *CUSS* 75: *Bag...*(sometimes intransitive, sometimes with "it")...to sleep, to go to bed. **1970** *Current Slang* V 14: I'm going to bag for a while. **1968–70** *Current Slang* III & IV 6: *Bag it,* v. To sleep—college students, both sexes, South Dakota.

b. Esp. *Stu.* to take (a person) to bed; to copulate with.

1976 "S. Jones" *CB Joke Bk.* (unp.): A trucker was bagging a farm girl in the hayloft. **1984** J. Hughes *16 Candles* (film): It would devastate my reputation as a dude...I've never bagged a babe. **1989** G.C. Wilson *Mud Soldiers* 198: My sister has five dates set up for when I get home....I'm going to bag every one of them. **1992** *Herman's Head* (Fox-TV): "Didja bag her?" "Jay, I don't 'bag' women." "Didja nail her then?"

8.a. to bring one's lunch in a paper bag.—constr. with *it*.

[***ca1895** in *EDD* I 129: *Bag...out:* to dine away from home....Used of farm servants [in Yorkshire] taking their food away in the fields.] **1971** Jacobs & Casey *Grease* 9: You think they'd spend a dime on their lunch? They're baggin' it.

b. *Narc.* to inhale fumes from glue placed in a bag.—constr. with *it*.

1965 Conot *Rivers* 91: "Man, I'm starting to float! I'm floatin' like I was a bird on a cloud!" a 13-year-old, who was bagging it over in one corner, exulted. He was holding a bag, a tube of glue inside, and, as he sniffed it, the bag moved in and out like a bellows.

9. to wear, to sport.

1972 Andrews & Dickens *Big House* 29: He was bagging a pure white doublebreasted suit.

10. *Basketball.* to score a basket.

1979 *Texas Monthly* (Sept.) 150: When any shooter "bags" successfully, it is like jumping through the hoop himself.

¶ In phrases:

¶ **bag onto** to grab; (*hence*) to pay attention to.

1942–49 Goldin et al. *DAUL* 21: *Bag onto,* v. 1. To lay hands upon; to seize; to steal. *Ibid.:* Bag onto that ghee's spiel....There's a hipster.

¶ **bag (one's) head** [or **face**] to cover (one's) head with a bag; (*hence*) (*imper.*) shut up; go away.

1863 in J.H. Gooding *Altar of Freedom* 15: Rise up...else—go and bag your heads. **1877** in J.M. Carroll *Camp Talk* 115: The bright sun evidently made a mistake—as now he is bagging his head. **1896** Hamblen *Many Seas* 149: "Oh," said I, "go and bag your head." **1914** *DN* IV 73: *Go bag yer head!* Angry, scornful, or sarcastic advice [Maine]. **1968** in Rowan & MacDonald *Friendship* 33: I could have told them to bag their ass. **1984** *TriQuarterly* (Spring) 313: Maggie...suggests that he go bag his face.

bagaga *n.* [orig. unkn.] penis; (*hence*, as v.) to copulate with.

1963 Rubin *Sweet Daddy* 50: I feel with my...bagaga. *Ibid.* 80: I ought to...tell you to bagaga yourself up your own ass. *Ibid.* 152: *Bagaga:* penis. **1971** Rodgers *Queens' Vernacular* 48: Cock...bagaga.

bagbiter *n.* [fr. *bite the bag* s.v. BAG, *n.*] *Computers.* a person or thing that is infuriatingly objectionable, second-rate, or the like.

1982 *Time* (Nov. 8) 92: *Bagbiter* (equipment or a program that fails, usually intermittently). **1983** Naiman *Computer Dict.* 31: What a bagbiter! **1991** E. Raymond *New Hacker's Dict.* 46: [*Bagbiter* is] Something, such as a program or a computer, that fails to work, or works in a remarkably clumsy manner....A person who has caused you some trouble...typically by failing to program the computer properly.

bag-biting *adj. Computers.* infuriatingly objectionable or second-rate; LOUSY—used attrib.

1983 Naiman *Computer Dict.* 18: The bagbiting system is wedged again. **1991** E. Raymond *New Hacker's Dict.* 46: This bagbiting system won't let me compute the factorial of a negative number.

bagel *n.* **1.** a Jew.—used disparagingly.—usu. considered offensive. Also **bagel baby.**

1955 Salter *Hunters* 35: I'm a wop...incidentally there's a little bagel in me too. **1969** U.S. Marine: The D.I.'s at Parris Island call Jewish guys "Bagel." **1971** Jeffers & Levitan *See Parris* 38: Tell me, Bagel boy, are you an old-fashioned Jew? Don't just stand there, Bagel. Are you an old-fashioned Jew? **1974** Charyn *Blue Eyes* 78: Coen ran around with bohemians and bagel babies from the High School of Music and Art. **1977** Dunne *True Confessions* 32: We'll get the bagel to take a few pictures.

2. [fr. the shape of a bagel] *Sports.* a zero; loss; shutout; (*specif.*) *Tennis.* a score of 6–0 in a set; a match in which all sets have been won 6–0. Also **bagel job.** Also as v.

1976 *AS* LI 292: *Bagel job.* Win of a set 6:0 or of a match with all sets 6:0. **1978** Pici *Tennis Hustler* 14: I want to blitz Captain Hank, do a bagel job on him. *Ibid.* 17: Without your bagels, I'm losing weight already. *Ibid.* 172: He got bageled 6–0. **1984** N.Y.C. man, age 36: A good reliever knows how to rack up bagels. **1984** *Wash. Post* (May 15) D2: The Milwaukee Bucks swept the Boston Celtics, 4-0....Four straight. Quadruple bagels. **1986** *Chicago Tribune* (July 6) Sports 2: *Bagel Job:* A shutout game, 6-0....A double bagel or triple bagel could be a shutout match. Also used as a verb: to bagel, or shut out. The term was coined in 1973 by Eddie Dibbs, a leading American player. **1987** *Wash. Post* (Sept. 2) B1: Lendl became only the fourth man in 20 years of Open tennis to pull off a triple-bagel. **1993** *New Yorker* (Oct. 4) 177: Gabriela [Sabatini] used to be seeded to meet Steffi [Graf] in the final, having bageled her way through the draw.

bagel-bender *n.* a Jew.—usu. considered offensive.—used disparagingly.

1977 Dunne *True Confessions* 32: Show me a job you run into a bad person sometime, I'll show you a bagel bender doesn't want it. **1990** Thorne *Dict. Contemp. Slang: Bagel-bender...*a Jew....Used principally in the USA.

bagel job *n.* see BAGEL, 2.

baggage *n.* ¶ In phrase: **get away with the baggage** to escape detection in or to avoid the consequences of mischief or wrongdoing.

1873 Beadle *Undeveloped West* 672: How the swindlers "got away with the baggage," is it not all recorded?

baggage-bouncer *n.* BAGGAGE-SMASHER.

1885 "Lykkejaeger" *Dane* 93: My...strength of back stood me in good stead as the big baggage bouncer and wrestler with the heavy freight generally.

baggage room *n.* the stomach.

1858 in Harris *High Times* 132: Arter I got my baggage-room full, I sot down ag'in.

baggage-smasher *n.* **1.** one who handles luggage as an occupation; porter.

1851 in *DA: Baggage Smashers*....a party of French emigrants having just arrived, the cartmen on the wharf seized their baggage and began packing it off in the most approved New York style. **1871** Schele de Vere *Americanisms* 358: The *baggage-smasher;* as the porter is commonly called. **1882** Sala *America Revisited* I 26: The porters...are so traditionally reckless that they are popularly known as "baggage-smashers." **1905** *DN* 3: *Baggage smasher,* n. One who handles baggage. *Slang.* **1931** Farrell *McGinty* 256: He...sat in the North Depot, watching the people come in with baggage smashers lugging their grips. **1945** Hamann *Air Words: Baggage smasher.* Flight clerk. **1968** *AS* XLIII 285: *Baggage Smasher.* A trainman assigned to the baggage car on a passenger train. Also, the man assigned to load baggage at a station stop.

2. a baggage thief.

1856 "P. Doesticks" *Plu-ri-bus-tah* 86: You shall there be met by swindlers,/shoulder-hitters, baggage-smashers/And all kinds of shameless rascals. **1861** in *AS* XXV 171: Gamblers, ticket-swindlers, emigrant-robbers, baggage-smashers, & all the worst classes of the city. **1866** [Williams] *Gay Life in N.Y.* 11: Charlie had read the newspapers. He had heard of "baggage smashers" who made away with countrymen's trunks and left the owners shirtless in a strange city. *Ibid.* 14: It seems that honest boy of yours...is a notorious baggage smasher, as such thieves are called.

bagged *adj.* **1.a.** *Gamb.* prearranged, "in the bag."

1942 *ATS* 254: Prearranged. *Bagged...in the bag...all sewed or sewn up.* **1970** in P. Heller *In This Corner* 41: He thought it was bagged. Johnson knocked him out in the fifteenth round. **1980** Pearl *Dict. Slang: Bagged,* adj. *(crime)* with predetermined results, of a race or game of chance.

b. *Und.* having been made amenable by a bribe.

1974 Teresa & Renner *Vinnie* 140: They weren't like the...cops who were bagged. They used to crack down.

2. drunk.

1953 Paley *Rumble* 41: Is he bagged? **1961** Kanter & Tugend *Pocketful of Miracles* (film): Sounds like she's bagged again. **1964** in J. Blake *Joint* 366: Take it easy up there, chum, the guy's bagged. **1971** *Evening News* (CBS-TV) (Dec. 28): Soused, bagged, looped, smashed, bombed—call it what you will. The pigs are drunk.

3. fatigued, exhausted.

1968 Baker et al. *CUSS* 76: *Bagged....*Very tired. **1980** M. Baker *Nam* 155: Between the heat and what you had to look at on the ward every day, you were bagged.

-bagger *suffix.* [sugg. by use in baseball to classify base hits] *Firefighting.* a fire (classified by the specified number of alarms).

1983 Stapleton *30 Yrs.* 216: We usually had eight or ten five-baggers a year. *Ibid.* 216: Which fire division the nine-bagger occurred in.

baggie *n.* **1.** *pl.* Orig. *Surfing.* baggy shorts or trousers.

1963 *Time* (Aug. 9) 42: "Baggies" are the loose-legged boxer swim trunks worn by the boys. **1964** *Look* (June 30) 55: *Baggies:* loose-fitting trunks. **1968** *Pop. Science* (July) 68: So, outfitted in a $30 rubber wet suit...and a pair of garish, knee-length semipantaloons called "baggies," I was ready to groove. **1977** *L.A. Times* (July 24) IV 3 [ref. to 1960]: He wanted a baggie design similar to what Hawaiian surfers were using....The "baggies," as they were known to surfers, soon became popular. *a*1981 in S. King *Bachman* 630: A man in bell-bottomed baggies. **1985** Schwendinger & Schwendinger *Adolescent Sub.* 98: Surfer's "baggies" (blousy male surfer underpants with gaudy decorations).

2. [fr. *Baggies,* a trademark for plastic sandwich bags] a large plastic bag or a plastic bag–like object; *(specif.)* **a.** *Mil.* a body bag, **b.** a condom.

1971 *AS* XLVI 83: Trojans, raincoats,...baggies, balloons. **1973** D. Chandler *Hollister* 172: Some of us may wind up in a big green baggie and others in jail. **1984** Ehrhart *Marking Time* 46: Just so long as it isn't their kids coming home in Baggies anymore. **1984** J.R. Reeves *Mekong* 90 [ref. to 1970]: They're gonna send you home in a baggie! **1991** LaBarge *Desert Voices* 51: Blown off arms and blown off legs...the Iraqis...put them in baggies and sent them home along with [the] patients.

baggywrinkle *n.* (see 1961 and 1979–88 quots.). Also vars.

1908 in J.H. Williams *Blow Man Down* 144: A bristling mustache which stuck to his upper lip like a bunch of "bag o' wrinkle" tacked onto an outrigger. **1961** Burgess *Dict. Sailing* 18: *Baggywrinkle.* Fat bunches of yarns, sennet, or other padding, that are specially made and placed to prevent chafing. **1979–88** Noel & Beach *Naval Terms* (ed. 5) 23: *Baggywrinkle* Old pieces of line wrapped around stays and shrouds to prevent sail chafing.

bag job *n.* [cf. syn. BLACK-BAG JOB] Esp. *FBI.* an illegal and clandestine entry by intelligence or counterintelligence agents to gather information.

1971 *Time* (Oct. 25) 31: A companion tactic, the "bag job," in which [F.B.I.] agents enter a home or office and examine or copy documents, personal papers or notebooks. **1973** *Harper's* (Nov.) 75: Illegal entry, known as a "bag job," became one of the intelligence megamachine's accepted data acquisition methods. **1974** *Atlantic* (Apr.) 89: That is not to say that there were no FBI bag jobs after 1966, but the manpower trained to perform them dwindled. **1981** Ehrlichman *Witness* 140: Hoover regaled us with stories of late-night entries and FBI bag jobs at other embassies. **1984** Wallace & Gates *Close Encounters* 174 [ref. to 1973]: The culprits in the Ellsberg "bag job" (as Liddy called it).

bag lady *n.* **1.** Orig. *N.Y.C.* a homeless woman who carries her belongings in bags, typically paper shopping bags. Now *colloq.*

1972 (cited in *Oxf. Dict. Mod. Slang*). **1975** in *BDNE3.* **1977** *Natural History* (Nov.) 78: She is what New Yorkers call a "bag lady," although not all such people are women and not all carry everything they own in bags. **1978** N.Y.C. man, age 34: You see bag ladies hanging out on the benches outside Central Park. It's pathetic. **1980** *Atlantic* (Mar.) 74: The Manhattan district attorney's office has attempted to prosecute fully a local bag lady who...lives in the subways. **1982** *Nebr. History* LXIII 260: Destitute women akin to the pathetic "bag ladies" often seen on city streets today. **1984** Univ. Tenn. instructor: The neighborhood bag lady passes by our dumpster every morning.

2. *Und.* BAG WOMAN.

1977 S. Gaines *Discotheque* 28: [She] was the bag lady for bingo games in churches. **1982** (quot. at BAG WOMAN).

bagman *n.* **1.** *Und.* a man who delivers or, esp., collects illicit payments.

1935 Pollock *Underworld Sp.: Bagman,* a bill collector. **1937–40** in Whyte *Street Corner Soc.* 242: The ward politician pays the "bag man," who turns the money over to the "big shot." **1944** Burley *Hndbk. Harlem Jive* 21: Jack, you can dig the bagman's play. **1945** *Collier's* (Sept. 29) 33: A side-money collector, also known as a "bagman" because he carries the cash in a suitcase, was...picking up payments from retailers and wholesalers en route. **1955** Deutsch *Cops* 44: The captain's man, or his equivalent, is found in many metropolitan police forces, and is known elsewhere as the "bagman" or the "ice man"—ice being a euphemism for graft. **1962** Perry *Young Man* 112: After the schlumping, Fish comes running around to my bagman with his face all swollen. **1970** Longstreet *Nell Kimball* 67: Everyone [was] on the take, the boodle being paid to bagmen, who handled the graft. **1970–71** Rubinstein *City Police* 375: The "fixer" and the "bagman" became established fixtures. **1971** Waters *Smugglers* 127: A few days later he would make shoreside contact with a "bagman" from the rummy syndicate authorized to make the pay-off. **1976** Adcock *Not Truckers Only* 36: He, too, kept in touch with his "bag men" via mobile CB radio. **1982** P. Michaels *Grail* 98: A considerable number of IRA supporters and bagmen. **1983** *ABC Network News* (Sept. 9): He acted as the bagman who delivered more than $200,000 to Watergate burglars. **1993** *Nation* (Mar. 22) 367: Israeli police had arrested three Arab-Americans, accusing them of being organizers and bag men for [an Islamic fundamentalist group].

2. *Narc.* a man who sells narcotics, esp. heroin.

1965 in W. King *Black Anthol.* 308: 'Cause when a cat gives a bagman dough, he loses everything if the bagman gets copped. **1966** Samuels *People vs. Baby* 105: Half-Pint bought directly from the..."bag man." **1966** Brunner *Face of Night* 211: Any chance of getting the big bagman would be gone. *Ibid.* 231: Bag-man—a peddler of narcotics. **1971** Rader *Govt. Inspected* 28: Thelma...hated the bag man, the pusher, killing slowly. **1978** J. Webb *Fields of Fire* 15: Addicts in their twos and threes...scratching and sniffing, searching for the bag man.

bag of guts *n.* a fat or worthless person.—used contemptuously.

1894 *DN* I 328: *Bag o' guts:* a useless individual; a "bum"....Also implies a big man with little brains. **1908** *DN* III 288: *Bag o(f) guts, n. phr.* A useless, lazy person. **1912** *DN* III 566: *Bag of guts, n. phr.* A worthless, clumsy fellow, fat and lazy. **1942** Wilder *Flamingo Rd.* 52: Titus, you old bag of guts you. **1977** Bredes *Hard Feelings* 86: He's fat, all right, but not a bag of guts.

bag of nails *n.* [cf. CAN OF WORMS] a confused thing or state of affairs.
> **1859** Matsell *Vocabulum* 9: Bag Of Nails. Every thing in confusion. **1889** Farmer *Americanisms: Bag of nails* (Cant)—A state of confusion or topsy-turvydom. **1944 AS* XIX 191: *Bag Of Nails.* Anything confusing. (Given by an informant as rhyming argot, but the rhyme cannot be found.) Recorded in Australia, 1895.

bag of wind *n.* a person who talks or boasts to no purpose, WINDBAG.
> **1891** Maitland *Slang Dict.*: *Bag of wind*, a boastful fellow.

bagpipes *n.pl.* lungs.
> **1834** Caruthers *Kentuckian* I 20: He's the chap what plumped a bullet right into old Tecumseh's bagpipes. **1858* A. Mahew *Paved with Gold* 285: Keep them bag-pipes o' your'n quiet.

bag rat *n. Golf.* a caddy.
> **1937** *AS* (Apr.) 155: *Bag rats,* a caddy's term of affection for one another.

bag-slinger *n.* a streetwalker.
> **1938** *Bedside Esquire* 86: I can understand such stories where an old *madame* essays "Little Eva" or "Peter Pan" or "The White Sister," but Sally was going to play the bag-slinger in "Rain" and it wouldn't have hurt to let the public know she had plenty of what it takes. [**1965* S.J. Baker *Australian Lang.* (ed. 2) 145: *Bag-swingers* who solicit custom from sailors are said to *cover the waterfront.*]

bagwoman *n. Und.* [cf. BAGMAN] a woman who delivers or, esp., collects illicit payments.
> **1966** *RHD*: *Bagwoman. Slang.* A female bagman. **1977** L. Jordan *Hype* 263: Louise had played bagwoman, dropping off a goodwill check at the local precinct house. **1982** W. Safire, in *N.Y. Times Mag.* (Jan. 2, 1983) 6: A bag lady, or bagwoman, is one who transmits illegal payoffs.

bahli-bahli *interj.* [Korean] *Mil. in E. Asia.* "Hurry up!"
> **1963** *Sat. Eve. Post* (July 27) 25: More leisure and better educational opportunities have failed to increase the tiny store of Korean words in the GI's vocabulary; *bahli-bahli* (hurry), *idi-wa* (come here) are about all that he can manage. **1980** D. Cragg (letter to J.E.L., Aug. 10) 1: I've been familiar with [this expression] for over twenty years. "C'mon, move your asses balli-balli!"

Bahnhof queen *n.* [G *Bahnhof* 'train station' + QUEEN] *Mil.* a German streetwalker.
> **1980** D. Cragg *Lexicon* 25: *Bahnhof Queen.* A streetwalker. From the years of the German Occupation when prostitutes regularly strolled about the railroad stations in Germany. **1980** D. Cragg (letter to J.E.L., Aug. 10) 1: First heard in Germany [1959–61]. "Jones picked up a Bahnhof Queen and got a dose of the clap."

bail *v.* [fr. *bail out*] to leave; go; (*hence*) to run out on, renege on (someone).
> **1977** Filosa *Surf. Almanac* 181: *Bail*...To leave, depart, exit. **1982** *Time* (Nov. 8) 9: *Time to book* means time to leave, which can also be *time to bail.* **1983** Pond *Valley Girl's Guide* 51: Or when you leave a party, you go, "Let's bail." **1983** Glass *Deprogram Valley Girl* 27: *Bail:* To leave. **1990** Munro *Slang U.* 26: *Bail*...to leave. **1990** *Bill & Ted's Adven.* (CBS-TV): Let us bail! **1992** *Middle Ages* (CBS-TV): You think you're the first guy to bail on me?

bail out *v.* to become insane.
> **1970** Knight *Black Voices* 78: You know me baby...I am your ace man. You must have bailed out—else you just been crazy all the time.

bait *n.* **1.** intended prey or victim.
> **1872** Beidler *Delegate* 27: I felt all happy, singing Yankee Doodle, until one of those fellows they call in the north police, said, "You're my bait." **1879** *Snares of N.Y.* 80: He it is he [*sic*] who has first to find the "*bait*" (victim) for the badger to work on.

2. [cf. JAILBAIT] an individual likely to attract some specified form of undesirable attention.—usu. used in comb.
> **1942** Sanders & Blackwell *Forces* 121: *Draft-Bait.* A selectee; one awaiting to be drafted into the armed service. **1945** in *Calif. Folk. Qly.* V 383: Recruits are *boots* and *barber bait.* **1954** Crockett *Mag. Bastards* 11: "Officer bait," the GI's called the Red Cross women. **1965** Trimble *Sex Words* 21: *Bait*...an effeminate who receives unwanted attention from male homosexuals. **1968** Spooner *War* 61: He had often been told that he was prime "queer bait," being fair and smooth skinned. **1970** Qua-

mmen *Walk Line* 128: The old man was a booze-eyed whore bait. **1986** Graffito, Univ. Tenn.: Queer Bait! **1988** Univ. Tenn. student theme: A young girl in a bar...who still attends high school...is called *bait* or *jail bait.*

¶ In phrase:

¶ **get (one's) bait back** to succeed in fathering a son.
> **1927** [Fliesler] *Anecdota* 100: "What'd he weigh?"..."Four pounds."..."Hell, you hardly got your bait back!" **1958** Plagemann *Steel Cocoon* 186: A damn good man...to make a son on your first try. You sure got your bait back, didn't you, boy?

bake *v.* to arrest.
> **1899** Young *Remin. & Stories* 432: Should a soldier inform a civilian that his bunkie was "baked by a bull for jumpin' a gump"...his meaning would be that his tent mate had been arrested by the provost guard for stealing a chicken.

bakebrain *n.* idiot.
> **1949** Algren *Golden Arm* 28: The oney place you're big is in the belly, bakebrain. *Ibid.*: Ever try mindin' your own business, you moldy-lookin' sandlot spigot-headed bakebrain?

baked *adj. Stu.* drunk or high.
> **1975** *UTSQ*: Drunk...bombed...baked. **1978** *Adolescence* XIII 501: A person who was "high" on marihuana was referred to as "baked," "wasted," [etc.]. **1990** Munro *Slang U.* 27: *Baked*...high on marijuana.

baked wind *n.* [pun on HOT AIR] empty talk. *Joc.*
> **1901** Irwin *Sonnets* (unp.): A baked-wind expert, jolly with my clack. **1923** McKnight *English Wds.* 65: *Hot air* becomes *baked wind.*

bakehead *n. R.R.* a fireman on a steam locomotive.
> **1929** *Bookman* (July) 524: I'm surprised to find a student tallow-pot up in the cab takin' orders from the bakehead. **1931** *Writer's Digest* (May) 41: *Bakehead*—Locomotive fireman. **1942** *Sat. Eve. Post* (June 13) 27.

Baker Sierra *n.* [radio code *Baker* 'B' + *Sierra* 'S' for B.S. 'bullshit'] *Mil.* nonsense.
> **1986** "J. Cain" *Suicide Squad* 170: Got some baker-sierra for your pocket notebooks, so I wanna see everyone's pen scribblin'.

Baker Two-Bits *n.* [radio code *Baker* 'B' + *two bits* '25¢', for *25*] *USAF.* the North American B-25 Mitchell medium bomber. Now *hist.*
> **1975** in Higham & Siddall *Combat Aircraft* 3: The "Baker Two Bits," as she was affectionately known, served as the backbone of the Air Force's multiengine pilot training program.

Baker Two-Dozen *n.* [radio code *Baker* 'B' + *two dozen* '24'] *USAF.* the consolidated B-24 Liberator heavy bomber. Now *hist.*
> **1957** Wallrich *AF Airs* 22: The "Baker two-dozen." **1978** B. Smith, Jr. *Chick's Crew* 115: We were very scornful of the Baker Two Dozens (B-24's) as we derisively called them [in 1944].

bald *adj.* ¶ In phrase: **snatch bald** to *snatch baldheaded* s.v. BALDHEADED, *adv.*
> **1962** T. Berger *Reinhart* 405: I'll put my knife in him and that's no lie....I'll snatch him bald...I'll rip out his gizzard [etc.].

baldface *n.* [prob. short for *bald-faced whiskey*, but 1834 form *boldface* may be the true origin] raw or inferior whiskey. Occ. **ballface.**
> **1834** *Mil. & Nav. Mag. of U.S.* (June) 248 [ref. to Ill., 1831]: But stranger, let's have a horn of your *bold-face*, if you've got the article aboard. [**1836** *Spirit of Times* (Feb. 27) 15: He has refused to keep anything to drink but ball-faced whiskey.] **1839** *Spirit of Times* (Dec. 28) 511: In a most sovereign manner did he feast and quaff "ball-face." **1840** in Thornton *Amer. Gloss.* I: He called lustily for a horn of bald face and molasses. **1843** *Spirit of Times* (Mar. 4) 7: Trot out a half pint of *Old Bald Face!* **1843** in Harris *High Times* 28: Treating temperance men to watermelons and topers to *Old Bald-face.* **1845** Hooper *Suggs* 85: The Captain and "Lewtenant Snipes" sat down, with a bottle of bald-face between them, to a social game. **1845** in Porter *Quarter Race* 85: Who-oo-whoop! Whar's the crock of bald-face and that gourd of honey? **1847** in Oehlschlaeger *Reveille* 45: A "passel" of the "baldface." **1847** in H.C. Lewis *Works* 113: Music, "bald face," and cigars. **1848** *Knickerbocker* XXXII 402: What is classically denominated "bald-face," or old brown whiskey. **1851** Burke *Peablossom* 149: Mat Cain, the blacksmith, drunk up my last bottle of "ballface," an' when I 'tacked him 'bout it, sed he thought it was milk. **1867** Harris *Lovingood* 57: A black bottil ove bald-face smashed agin a tree furnist me. **1870** *Coon Hunt* 13: Evidently a liberal patron of "old bald face." **1884** Hartranft *Side-*

splitter 188: He was *refreshing* himself with a glass of "bald face."

baldfaced shirt *n.* a white dress shirt. *Joc.*

1889 Farmer *Americanisms: Bald-faced shirt.*—The name by which a Western cowboy knows a white shirt. It is thought to come from the fact of Hereford cattle having white faces. **1922** Rollins *Cowboy* 108: The shirt…always was collarless and starchless (not "boiled," "biled," or "bald-faced").

baldhead *n. Auto. Repair.* a bald tire.

1937–41 in Mencken *Amer. Lang. Supp. II* 724.

baldheaded *adj.* **1.** hairless, bare; (*hence*) shining white.

1880 in Trachtenberg *Vistas* 176: For when you are wed they will bang till you're dead/With the bald-headed end of a broom. **1900** Wister *Jimmyjohn Boss* 38: Bashful of Sam's napkins, boys?…Or is it the bald-headed china? **1917** *DN* IV 312: *Bald-headed end of a broom, n. phr.* The handle. Slang. **1958** McCulloch *Woods Wds.* 6: *Bald-headed*…Tires worn smooth…Anything bare. **1970** Former infantryman, served in Korea 1965–66: A lot of the gook whores had baldheaded pussies. They shaved 'em that way.

2. completely unprepared. Cf. *snatch baldheaded* s.v. BALDHEADED.

*ca*1895 in Dolph *Sound Off* 9: We went to Arizona for to fight the Indians there;/We were nearly caught baldheaded but they didn't get our hair.

3. *Naut.* (see 1929 quot.). Also **baldhead.**

1929 Bowen *Sea Slang* 6 [ref. to 19th C.]: *Bald-headed.* In square rig, a ship with nothing over her top-gallants. A schooner without top-masts. **1953** McEwen & Lewis *Encyc. Naut. Knowl.* s.v. schooner: Baldhead s[chooner], any s[chooner] having no topmasts. **1984** *Write Course* (PBS-TV): It's a gaff-rigged baldheaded yawl. Anybody knows that.

4. narrow, bare.

1931 McConn *Studies* 43: It is his ambition to make D in all courses which is a bald headed pass.

baldheaded *adv.* **1.** without forethought or preparation, recklessly; headlong, all-out.

1847 in Lowell *Poetical Wks.* 201: I scent which one pays the best an'/Go into it baldheaded. **1871** Schele de Vere *Amer.* 581: *Bald-headed*, to go it, is a very peculiar but not unfrequent phrase in New England, suggestive of the eagerness with which men rush to do a thing without taking time to cover their head. "Whenever he had made up his mind to do a thing he went at it *bald-headed*" (*Our Young Folks*, 1869). **1875** Minstrel *Gags* 136: Dat barkeeper…went for Tambo bald-headed. **1888** in *F & H* I (rev.) 119: The Chicago Republicans…have gone baldheaded for protection. **1893** in F. Harris *Conklin* 173: He went bald-headed for me. **1922** Rollins *Cowboy* 183: If you had used sense, and not gone at it bald-headed…we'd have gotten them this time sure. **1958** McCulloch *Woods Wds.* 6: *Bald-headed*…(adv.) To go at a job by main strength and ignorance, having no real savvy of how to do it. **1980** Syatt *Country Talk* 24: I'll slap you baldheaded if I hear of you doin' that again.

2. to the point of frustration or exhaustion.

1889 "M. Twain" *Conn. Yankee* 353: I prophesied myself bald-headed trying to supply the demand.

¶ In phrase:

¶ **snatch** [or **grab** or **jerk**] **baldheaded** to defeat thoroughly, thrash, beat up, etc.; (*hence*) to stun, amaze.

1866 in "M. Twain" *Letters from Hi.* 13: The next lurch of the ship would "snatch him bald-headed," as Mr. Brown expressed it. **1868** in G.W. Harris *High Times* 193: Don't you b'lieve the durn'd ole raskil dident threaten tu snatch me bald-headed for duin' hit apupus, to break his han' saw. **1869** *Overland Mo.* (Feb.) 190: None but a wild and savage animal, of course, would "snatch a gentleman bald-headed," as the old man expressed it. **1871** in *F & H* I (rev.) 119: The crowd then gave a specimen of calumny broke loose, And said I'd snatched him bald-headed, and likewise cooked his goose. **1877** Wheeler *Deadwood Dick* 78: If more than one of em don't get their fingers burned when they snatch Deadwood Dick bald-headed, why I'm a Spring creek sucker. **1885** Harte *Shore & Sedge* 53: I used to be the organist and tenor in our church in the States. I used to snatch the sinners bald-headed with that. **1886** Nye *Remarks* 343: It takes a youth 15 years of age to arraign Congress and jerk the administration bald-headed. **1891** Garland *Main-Travelled Roads* 8: She'd snatch 'im bald-headed, that's what she'd do. **1891** [Landon] *Eli Perkins* 296: I can snatch a man bald-headed while he waits. **1918** *Sat. Eve. Post* (Aug. 17) 47: She would come down here and grab me bald-headed because I had wrote to you. **1938** Lomax & Lomax *Cowboy Songs* (ed. 3) 136: Snatched him bald-headed and spit on the place where the hair come off. **1941** Roberts & Sanford *Honky-*

Tonk (film): Right now I'd give twenty bucks to snatch you baldheaded. **1945** in *DA* 64: Just let me get hold of 'em, I'll jerk 'em bald-headed! **1953** Peterson *Giant Step* 65: And he'll either cough up that ten bucks or I'll snatch him bald-headed. **1962** Pamplin *Scamps of Bucksnort* 41: You come over here again and I'll snatch you baldheaded!

baldheaded hermit *n.* the penis.—usu. considered vulgar. In phr. **throw the baldheaded champ** to perform fellatio. Also —— **champ,** —— **sailor,** —— **friar.** All *Joc.*

*1698–1706 in D'Urfey *Pills* IV 72: *A Riddle*…'Tis a Fryer with a Bald-Head,…a Gun that shoots point-blank, [etc.]. ***a1890** *F & H: Bald-headed-hermit*…The penis. **1916** Cary *Venery* I 9: Baldheaded Hermit— The penis. **1929–33** J.T. Farrell *Young Manhood* 289: I was talking about the bald-headed sailor. **1962–68** B. Jackson *In the Life* 182: [When] you try to throw the bald-headed champ (perform fellatio), boy, you have reached rock bottom in my opinion.

baldheaded row *n. Theat.* the front row of seats at a stage performance, esp. a burlesque, presumably occupied by old men. Also **baldhead row.**

1887 in *DA* 64: The arts and wiles of the occupant of the bald-head row were of no avail, the proud Italian girl treating them with scorn. **1889** Farmer *Americanisms* 34: *Bald-headed Row*—The first row of stalls at theatres, especially those which make a feature of ballets [burlesques]. The term is a cynical allusion to the fact that these seats are generally occupied by men of mature age; the innuendo is obvious. **1889** Barrère & Leland *Dict. Slang* I 70: *Bald-headed row* (American), the front seats in the pit of a theatre. It is an old joke in the United States, that whenever there is a great "leg-piece," or a "frog-salad" (*i.e.,* a ballet with unusual opportunities for studying anatomy), the front seats are always filled with veteran roués, or "Uncle Neds." **1929–33** J. Lowell *Gal Reporter* 277: She was not half so attractive to the "bald-headed row." **1943** in *DA* 64: One night I went to a USO show given in a rest area and was put in the bald-headed row. **1952** Sandburg *Young Strangers* 273: It was supposed to be filled with gay old "birds" when a burlesque or leg show came, and people called it the "bald-headed row." **1978** Gann *Hostage* 204: A highly developed paradise for the patrons of "bald-headed row." **1992** G. Wolff *Day at Beach* 102: Hootchy-Kootchy, carnival style…get…right down there in the baldheaded row.

baldy *n.* **1.** a bald or partly bald person or (*occ.*) thing. [In 1863 quot., applied to a mountain.]

1849 Melville *White Jacket* 189 [ref. to 1843]: He was a fine little Scot, who, from the premature loss of the hair on the top his head, always went by the name of *Baldy.* **1856** in E. McGowan *Narrative* 161: Dear "Old Baldy." **1863** in *DA* 64: Within the perlieus [*sic*] of the Rio Chiquito and "Old Baldy." **1873** in Ownby *Subduing Satan* 85: Hurry up, baldy. **1881** in *DA*: Baldy is 12,000 feet above the sea, 5,000 feet above its eastern base. **1899** "Flynt" *Tramps* 384: The baldy 'e comes himself 'n' asted what I wanted. *Ibid.* 392: *Baldy:* An old man. **1927** *DN* V 437: *Baldy* n. An old man. (Not necessarily baldheaded.) **1930** "D. Stiff" *Milk & Honey* 199: *Baldy*—generally an old man "with a high forehead." **1944** C.B. Davis *Leo McGuire* 176: You didn't split with the little baldy at all. **1953** "L. Padgett" *Mutant* 11: No ordinary man could guard his mind against a Baldy. **1967** *DAS* (ed. 2) 672: *Baldy*…A worn automobile tire having little or no tread left. **1974** A. Bergman *Big Kiss-Off* 174: Husband, a fat baldie of about fifty. **1976** Dyer *Erroneous Zones* 49: Funny-face, Shorty, Fatty, or Baldy. **1983** *Newsweek* (Feb. 28) 11: Hollywood continues to stereotype one minority too embarrassed to raise a fuss: the baldies.

2. a haircut, typically given to military recruits, in which the hair is clipped as short as possible; a shaved or bald head.

1941 *Sat. Review* (Oct. 4) 9: *Baldie.* Army haircut. **1952** Malamud *Natural* 89: Pop scratched his baldy. **1952** Ellson *Golden Spike* 192: Hey, you see the guy with the baldy? **1972** P. Thomas *Savior* 54: I can even remember the look on your face when you saw me with a stone baldy. **1980** Univ. Tenn. student: Why don't you get yourself a baldy like the guy in [the film] *Taxi Driver? a*1989 in Kisseloff *Must Remember This* 561 [ref. to 1920's]: In the summertime, everybody'd insult the barbers by sayin', "We want a baldy."…Any jackass can give a baldy.

baled hay *n. Army.* dehydrated vegetables.

1916 L. Stillwell *Common Soldier* 266 [ref. to Civil War]: The Germans in the regiment would make big dishes of soup out of this "baled hay," as we called it.

bale of straw *n.* a blonde person. Also **bale of hay.**

*ca*1928 in Wilstach *Stage Slang* (unp.): Toting a "bale of straw" is going out with a blonde. **1933–34** Lorimer & Lorimer *Stag Line* 157: I'm gonna belch to the main guy for a pitch next that bale of straw peddling the slum. **1947** in *Look* (Jan. 6, 1948) (cited in Partridge *Dict. Und.* (ed. 3) 790): Bale of hay.

ball[1] *n.* **I.** Senses that refer, literally or figuratively, to the testicles.

1.a. a testicle.—usu. considered vulgar.

*a**1325**, *1456 in *MED* II 621. *ca**1500–12** W. Dunbar, in *DOST* 175: Thy bawis hingis throw thy breik. *a**1585** in *DOST*: Whether thow wilt let belt thy bawes. *1629 in *DOST*: He would show him a buck that would let him take him by the baaes. *1757 in J. Atkins *Sex in Lit.* III 218: Why, what's become of those two Balls? *a**1790** in Farmer *Merry Songs* V 223: He plac'd his Jacob whare she did piss,/An' his balls whare the wind did blaw. *1882 *Boudoir* 161: Balls and all. **1889** *Century Dict.* I 430: *Ball*...A testicle: generally in the plural. (Vulgar.) *a**1904–09** *F & H* (rev.) 120: *Ball*...(vulgar).—See *Ballocks*. **1918** in Carey *Mlle. from Armentières* II (unp.): His dick stood up and his balls hung down. **1922** E. Pound, in V. Eliot *Letters* 505: The ball-encumbered phallus. **1936** Farrell *World I Never Made* 47: There's more to him in his little finger than your precious son has in both of his balls. **1941** W.C. Williams, in Witemeyer *Williams-Laughlin* 66: You've got...to kick a jackass in the balls sometimes to make him move. **1942** H. Miller *Roofs of Paris* 237: I'd give my left ball. **1942** McAtee *Supp. to Grant Co. Dial.* 2 [ref. to 1890's]: *Balls*, n., testicles. *Ibid.* 3: Cold enough to freeze the balls off a brass monkey. **1965** Karp *Doobie Doo* 111: You bet your balls you would have. **1981–85** S. King *It* 887: She hiked one...foot...into his balls.

b. *pl.* [cf. identical use of ASS] (used emphatically and figuratively esp. with *off* to receive the action of trans. as well as ordinarily intrans. verbs). [Used only of men.]

1934 H. Miller *Tropic of Cancer* 97: I'm grinding my balls off on that job. **1935** Algren *Boots* 41: That's the idee—sweat the bastards' balls off. **1938** H. Miller *Capricorn* 70: Working my balls off and not even a clean shirt to wear. **1944** Tobin *Invasion Jrnl.* 82: Froze balls off. **1951** W. Williams *Enemy* 80: You can count on plenty of waiting on this duty. You can wait your balls off. **1953** Brossard *Saboteurs* 30: Every morning up at four and that mountain air freezin' your balls off. **1958** Cooley *Run for Home* 26: They wanted me to sit out [on] one of those bobbin' booby hatches and freeze my balls off all winter. **1967** Wolf *Love Generation* 16: Thus we find that the whole twentieth century has been dancing its balls off. **1969** Searls *Hero Ship* 145: They build the cockpits too small and you freeze your balls off before you get to ten thousand feet. **1969** Whittemore *Cop!* 13: Yeah, I'll laugh my balls off.

2. *pl.* **a.** [cf. **(5)**, below; for 1934 quot. and others, see ety. at **(5)**, below] utter nonsense; rubbish.—usu. considered vulgar.—Usu. as interj.

[*a**1680** in J. Thorpe *Rochester's Poems* 112: Ballocks, cry'd *Newport*, I hate that dull *Rogue*.] **1857** in *Calif. Hist. Soc. Qly.* VI (1927) 11: [An editorial] by an individual by the name of Ball, or two brothers of that name. We can only say to this "pair of Balls" that we read the [slurring] article in question about ourself [etc.]. *1861 in W.H. Russell *Russell's Civil War* 122: The...story all balls & Pip himself a disgusting and foolish creature. *1889 Barrère & Leland *Dict. Slang* I 71: *Balls, all* (popular), all rubbish. *a**1890** *F & H*: *Ballocks!* (or *all balls!*)—a derisive retort (cf. *¡cojones!*—a Spanish oath). **1901** Wister *Philosophy* 18 [ref. to ca1882]: "If I were to stop thinking about you, you'd evaporate." "Which is balls," observed the second boy...in the slang of his period. **1915** E. Pound, in Joyce *Letters* II 364: I am so damn sick of energetic stupidity. The "strong" work...balls! **1917** M. Cowley, in Jay *Burke-Cowley Corres.* 46: All this talk about temperance at the front—balls. Aviators are drunk half the time. *1914–21 Joyce *Ulysses* 135: All balls! Bulldosing the public! **1925** McAlmon *Silk Stockings* 54: You're talking plain balls, Foster. **1929** Seabrook *Magic Island* 241: "Balls," said Dr. Wilson. "If your sprained ankle bothers you, phone me." **1934** H. Roth *Call It Sleep* 340: "I don't know 'em—de odder one." "Aw, balls!...You ain' game fer nutt'n." **1948** Wolfert *Act of Love* 480: I got respect for rank and all that, but Mangan's a lot of balls. **1957** Gutwillig *Long Silence* 121: Oh balls, you've got plenty of money. **1963** Packer *Alone at Night* 31: Balls, Jen! **1977** *Rolling Stone* (Oct. 20) 57: The notion that a newspaperman doesn't have a duty to his country is perfect balls. **1990** *New Yorker* (Aug. 27) 84: The wrong tactic is to stand up and say "Balls" when a European idea is surfaced....Instead, one should stand up and say, "What a good idea."

b. *pl. interj.* (used as an expression of disappointment, disgust, or resignation).—usu. considered vulgar.

1923 McAlmon *Companion Vol.* 5: Balls! But there's nothing to do until that contract is drawn up. **1928** Dahlberg *Bottom Dogs* 209: Balls, could that soused Swede have followed him. **1935** Cobb *Paths of Glory* 130: Oh, balls! This isn't a cinema. **1961** Boyd *Lighter Than Air* 61: He searched his mind for something strong enough to describe his out-

rage. "Balls!" **1966** Shepard *Doom Pussy* 118: "Oh, balls," growled Crunch as his jaw dropped slack. "The bastard took the last copy of *Playboy*."

c. *pl. interj.* [cf. *nuts to* s.v. NUTS] In phrase: **balls to** [or **on**] a curse; to hell with.—usu. considered vulgar.

1936 Kingsley *Dead End* 702: Balls to yew, faw eyes! **1937** Hemingway *Have & Have Not* 91: "Balls to you," said the lawyer. **1940** *Tale of a Twist* 11: Balls on this....I'm going in on the couch and get some sleep. **1962** W. Robinson *Barbara* 103: Balls on Exit-3!

3. *pl.* [cf. syn. BALLS-UP] a botch; muddle.—usu. considered vulgar. *Rare* in U.S.

*1889 Barrère & Leland *Dict. Slang* I 71: "To make balls of it," to make a mistake, to get into trouble. **1933** Hemingway *Take Nothing* 72: Knowing that it was all a bloody balls.

4.a. *pl.* virile courage; guts; strength of character.—usu. considered vulgar.

*a**1890–93** *F & H* III 237: *More guts* (also *more balls*) *than brains* = a fool. **1926** in Hemingway *Sel. Letters* 211: Mike when drunk and wanting to insult the bullfighter keeps saying—tell him bulls have no balls. *1928 D.H. Lawrence *Lady Chatterley* XIV 236: You say a man's got no brain, when he's a fool....And when he's got none of that spunky wild bit of a man in him, you say he's got no balls. When he's sort of tame. **1941** Schulberg *Sammy* 242: Listen, Sammy, I watched you a long time. You got balls. You're O.K. with me. **1952** Mandel *Angry Strangers* 23: You got to have ba-a-alls to paint right, man. **1958** Arrowsmith *Satyricon* 52: If we had any balls...he'd be laughing out of the other side of his face. **1965** Hersey *Too Far to Walk* 184: He's got a pair of balls like they're stainless steel. **1966** Braly *On Yard* 252: I got more balls than a pool hall. **1968** Radano *Walking Beat* 147: Nothing bothers him: my partner. His balls are so big it's a wonder he ain't ruptured. **1970** M. Thomas *Total Beast* 61: Bunch of cowards! Ain't got the balls of a hummingbird! **1971** Cameron *First Blood* 100: I think he's got the balls of a butterfly. **1974** Cherry *High Steel* 40: Angie...had big brass balls and a club foot. **1982** *Harper's* (Nov.) 29: Marines...show that they have balls by their devotion to the squad, platoon, or company. **1990** *Current Affair* (synd. TV series): You gotta give me credit—I got balls. **1992** *Donahue* (NBC-TV): [You] say your mother-in-law has brass balls.

b. *pl.* energy; spirit; appeal.—usu. considered vulgar. [The sense of "ornamentation," present in 1890 quot., may have infl. orig. application.]

1890 in F. Remington *Sel. Letters* 97: The last letter had balls and fringe on it—you are a word painter. **1958** in *DAS* 17: That copy is too weak. Rewrite it and put balls on it! **1963–64** Kesey *Great Notion* 265: That [music]...hasn't got any more balls than it does beat. I like somethin' with a little more *balls* on it. **1965** in H. Ellison *Sex Misspelled* 342: He tapped the book with a fingernail. "This has guts, Andy. Real balls." **1971** Dahlskog *Dict.*: *Balls, give (something) some*...To impart strength, power, or zip to something; to beef something up. **1972** R. Wilson *Playboy's Forbidden Words* 25: "She has balls," said of an actress...mean[s]...she has the power to turn the audience on. **1979** *Rolling Stone* (Feb. 8) 23: Leo's got a lot of balls. He's not just playin' it for the paycheck. He likes the music. **1987** D.O. Smith *Cradle* 15 [ref. to 1930]: The yearlings found out that John Lawlor had a loud, well-timbred voice (they called it "balls") and had him mimic the adjutant.

c. *pl.* effrontery; audacity.—usu. considered vulgar.

1964 Gelber *On Ice* 104: What nerve! What balls! The bitch didn't leave one cigarette around! **1971** Horan *Blue Messiah* 441: And above all, they respect people with iron balls. **1978** *Rolling Stone* (Dec. 28) 6: It takes a lot of balls to peddle such a low-quality product at outrageously inflated prices. **1981** *Nat. Lampoon* (Feb.) 59: Ya know, you guys gotta have big balls to come over here in twos.

5. *pl.* [cf. **(2.a.)**, above; this sense and some quots. at **(2.a.)**, above, may be influenced by E Yid *bobkes* 'absolutely nothing', lit. 'sheep dung', i.e., pellets ("balls") of worthless matter] absolutely nothing.—usu. considered vulgar.

1934 H. Roth *Call It Sleep* 271: Balls you'll ged. **1939** M. Levin *Citizens* 37: What can they do to me?...Balls they can do to me. **1949** Mende *Spit & Stars* 76: But what does the customer give him for a tip? Balls.

6. *pl.* [cf. identical use of ASS] one's body, person, or self—sometimes functions as an intensifier of pronouns; one's life or well-being, "hide," "skin," "neck."—usu. considered vulgar. [Used only of men.]

1960 Roeburt *Mobster* 78: Is that what's got your balls in a sweat? **1964** Newhafer *Tallyho* 91 [ref. to WWII]: I'll have their balls for this. **1967** P. Roth *When She Was Good* 46: He had every intention...of working his balls into the ground. **1967** Colebrook *Cross* 323: He is being asked…"to put his balls on the line." **1968** Tiede *Coward* 337: If you interrupt me once more I'll bust [demote] your balls so low you'll be able to chin yourself on a dime. **1970** Appleman *12th Year* 9: I know you fall into either one of those places, Mac, you get your balls clipped. **1972** Ponicsan *Cinderella Liberty* 128: If you're not back here by 2400…you can give your heart to Jesus cause your balls'll be on my key chain. **1966–80** McAleer & Dickson *Unit Pride* 132: You know that artillery that's been knockin' our balls off lately?

7. *pl. Mil.* the double-zero radio frequency.

1983 M. Skinner *USAFE* 41: A popular squadron [radio frequency] being "balls"—double zeroes, called "double nuts" in the Navy. **1992** Cornum & Copeland *She Went* 6: "Bengal one-five"…was Garvey's call sign. Mine was "Bengal zero-zero," commonly known…as "Bengal balls."

II. Other senses.

8. [cf. SHOT] a glass of whiskey or other liquor.

[***1821** in *OEDS: Ball of fire*, glass of brandy.] **1866** in Hilleary *Webfoot* 154: The [officers] are having a ball in the Hospital in honor of their baby's birth day. Something new to keep the whiskey running. **1882** *Puck* (Nov. 8) 156: It is quite a well known fact among purists that "ball" is a synonym for "drink." **1888** Bangs *Katharine* 38: And while we're out we'll "ketch a ball." **1893** S. Crane, in Baym et al. *Norton Antho.* II 716: Th' on'y thing I really needs is a ball. Me t'roat feels like a fryin' pan. **1893** in F. Remington *Sel. Letters* 168: We had a "ball" and I said "Here is to Mrs. Clark." **1898** Norris *Moran* 73: Stand by a bit an' we'll have a ball. **1921** O'Neill *Hairy Ape* 227: Say, ain't dere a back room around dis dump? Let's go shoot a ball. **1925** Nason *Top Kick* 8: How'd yuh like to go out and have a ball of *vin rooge*? **1932** C. McKay *Gingertown* 57: You throw me a good ball a whisky, sistah. **1938** Ward *Fog* 285: What're you doing, Uncle Percy—having a ball all by yourself?…Just trying to give my aching head a break—Have a—er, some ginger ale? **1938** Connolly *Navy Men* 141: I'd a slipped him another ball o' brandy. **1955** O'Hara *N. Frederick* 347: Do you feel like a snort?…Do you want a ball? **1959** in Cannon *Nobody Asked* 147: But if they would find him and sit him down on his stool, loosen him up with a few balls, I'm sure he'd reach back and handle Archie Moore's case with a song. **1974** Radano *Cop Stories* 164: Sure it's cold. I know what it is to want a ball. I put gallons away myself. **1980** Whalen *Takes a Man* 81: Give me a beer and a ball will ya, Moose? **1984** D. Smith *Steely Blue* 144: It had been years since he'd had a beer and a ball….A boilermaker.

9. *Narc.* a small package of morphine or another narcotic, as used by an addict.

1912 Lowrie *Prison* 79: Guys what I never suspicioned o' usin' dope went around beggin' friends f'r a ball right out in th' open.

10. a dollar, esp. a dollar coin.

1895 *Harper's* (Oct.) 780: I'll give ye five balls fer 'im. **1899** "J. Flynt" *Tramping* 392: *Ball:* a silver dollar. **1927** *DN* V 437: *Ball*…A silver dollar.

11. a woman's breast.

1951 Elgart *Over Sexteen* 124: "She has dice for earrings and eight-balls for a bra—"…"My God—eight?" **1963** Rubin *Sweet Daddy* 35: Wow, could I use her now. Biggest balls you ever saw…great big ones that stick out in points.

12. *pl.* [cf. syn. NUTS] a person or thing that is regarded as extraordinarily good or bad.—used predicatively only.—constr. with *the*.—usu. considered vulgar.

1938 Bellem *Blue Murder* 186: All dames are the balls.…Yeah, including you. **1968** Baker et al. *CUSS* 76: *Balls, the* = nuts, the. *Ibid.* 164: *The nuts*…A socially adept person. Extraordinary, unusual, hard to believe.

13. a thing for which one is expected to take the responsibility of completing, performing, etc.—constr. with possessive pron.

1973 Herbert & Wooten *Soldier* 253: From that point on, it was my ball.

¶ In phrases:

¶ **balls and all** completely.—usu. considered vulgar.

1952 H. Grey *Hoods* 89: He fell for it, balls and all. **1980** Ciardi *Browser's Dict.* 16: *Balls and all.* Entirely (Testicles and penis. The whole man.)

¶ **break** [or **bust**] **(one's) balls** [cf. *break (one's) ass* s.v. ASS; cf. BALLBREAKER] **a.** to exert (oneself) to the limit of endurance; to work or try (one's) hardest.—usu. considered vulgar.

1944 in Atwell *Private* 53: In camp we bust our b—s learning how to climb over a mountain so they can't see you. **1955** Graziano & Barber

Somebody Up There 51: Here I'm busting my balls to be a wise guy. **1966–67** W. Stevens *Gunner* 85 [ref. to WWII]: We're breaking our balls to get out of here. **1968** L.J. Davis *All Had Fled* 189: Listen to that, just busting my balls to be let out.

b. to punish severely; to thrash.—usu. considered vulgar.

1952 Ellson *Golden Spike* 76: I'm going to bust your balls for you. **1955** Graziano & Barber *Somebody Up There* 98: Bust this guy's balls, tell off this cop, rob that joint,…shoot pool, [etc.]. *Ibid.* 134: What parole officer [he] is going to break the balls of when he gets out. *Ibid.* 186: You going to bust his balls, huh Rocky? **1974** in H.S. Thompson *Shark Hunt* 363: Those dirty bastards!…We'll break their balls! **1979** McGivern *Soldiers of '44* 94 [ref. to WWII]: "Was he drinking?" "Shit, yes. I told him Haskell would bust his balls." **1980** Garrison *Snakedoctor* 163: You fuck this up, and I'll personally break your balls.

c. to provoke anger; (*hence*) make oneself a pest, as by complaining or scolding; to harass, hector, nag, etc.—usu. considered vulgar.

1955 Puzo *Dark Arena* 181 [ref. to 1940's]: You used to break my balls about it when we were GIs. **1960** H. Selby, Jr., in *Provincetown Rev.* III 73: Some of the girls bugged her and she broke their balls. **1961** *New Directions* 17 220: Go tell ya troubles ta jesus and stop breakin my balls. **1962** in Bruce *Essential Lenny* 40: Why do you keep breaking our balls for this crime? **1963** J. Ross *Dead Are Mine* 272 [ref. to WWII]: But it was the "PBs Only" signs that broke your balls. Peninsular Base Section Troops Only.…If you wore the ODs of the combat troops you were dead. **1967** P. Roth *When She Was Good* 280: You busted his balls, and you were starting in on little Eddie's. **1970** Whitmore *Memphis* 156: Terry's been shot up and won some medals. What the hell are you breaking balls about? **1971** Faust *Willy* 37: Did he ever break balls! Champion…whiner of all time. **1974** A. Bergman *Big Kiss-Off* 60: Hey, Jack, don't break my balls. Things are bad enough. **1966–80** McAleer & Dickson *Unit Pride* 370: Miller's sendin' us to run up and down hills to bust balls. **1980** Whalen *Takes a Man* 19: Ah, I've had my balls busted by professionals, McClusky. **1991** D. Anderson *In Corner* 26: Butch was just trying to break balls, to upset Mike.

d. [cf. *bust (one's) ass*, 2, s.v. ASS] to meet with disaster.—usu. considered vulgar.

1957 E. Brown *Locust Fire* 106 [ref. to WWII]: Or, let's not bust our balls on the mountains, men. It costs the government ten thousand dollars to turn a mammal into a bird.

¶ **by the balls** at one's mercy; in one's control.—usu. considered vulgar.

1918 in Kimball & Bolcolm *Sissle & Blake* 69: Jim and I have P— by the balls in a bigger way than anyone you know. **1924** in Mencken *New Ltrs.* 182: Altogether, God has me by the balls. ***1929** Manning *Fortune* 151: Once we're in the army, they've got us by the balls. **1934** H. Miller *Tropic of Cancer* 155: Paris…grabs you by the balls. **1938** Bezzerides *Long Haul* 27: You always talk like you had the world by the balls. **1941** Schulberg *Sammy* 152: Then they've got you by the balls, but good. **1947** A. Petry, in Chambers & Moon *Right On!* 130: White folks got us by the balls. **1961** Garrett *Which Ones* 25: They have got a grip on you. They've got you by the balls. ***1971** I. Anderson *Locomotive Breath* (song): And the all-time winnner/Has got him by the balls. **1975** Kangas & Solomon *Psych. of Strength* 56: Her sick headaches have her husband by the balls. **1977** J. Olsen *Fire Five* 233: The lawyer says I got her by the balls. **1982** Del Vecchio *13th Valley* 88: The NVA had I Corps by the balls. **1991** *Vanity Fair* (Jan. 1992) 108: [She is a] young woman who has taken her career by the balls.

¶ **carry the ball** [adopted from S.E. football usage] to assume or successfully bear responsibility.

1939 Fessier *Wings of Navy* (film): Looks like you'll be carrying the ball from now on. **1963** in S. Lee *Son of Origins* 38: Now let's prove we can carry the ball. **1963** D. Tracy *Brass Ring* 357: You just lay back and count up your leave time, kid. Old Hobey will carry the ball. **1966** *RHD* 114: You can always count on him to carry the ball in an emergency. **1977** R.S. Parker *Effective Decisions* 44: It might be that you were led to believe that somebody else would carry the ball for you.

¶ **drop the ball** to blunder at a critical moment.

1940 Goodrich *Delilah* 55: The Captain never interfered with his three officers, never failed to give them the chance to go through with it, unless, as Ensign Snell phrased it, they were "about to drop the ball." **1943** in M. Curtiss *Letters Home* 136: Our job is obvious. *Don't drop the ball.* **1945** in *Calif. Folk. Qly.* V 380: The diametric opposite of this is *to drop the ball* or the more popular *flub the dub.* **1957** Gutwillig *Silence* 252: Boy, that was a clumsy question. You sure dropped the ball. **1959** Searls *Big X* 94: "Mitch, I'm sorry I was so nasty. I really am." "Forget it, honey. I dropped the ball." **1961** Crane *Born of Battle* 52: The big man dropped the ball, didn't he? **1983** *Green Arrow* (July) 17: Now it's up to me…and I won't drop the ball!

¶ **full balls** *Mil. Av.* at full throttle; full speed; all out.—usu. considered vulgar.

1964 Newhafer *Tallyho* 352 [ref. to WWII]: "Full balls," Marriner called as he shoved his throttle forward. *Ibid.* 391: I want them on full balls, and I want to see them light this place up like Coney Island. **1973** W. Crawford *Gunship Cmndr.* 67: Christ, I hope you guys are coming fullballs.

¶ **get (one's) balls in an uproar** [cf. syn. *get one's bowels in an uproar*, presumably the earlier form] to become unduly angry, excited, frightened, etc.—usu. considered vulgar. [1947–60 quots. all ref. to WWII.]

1947 Mailer *Naked & Dead* 479: Well, hold on, Jackson, let's take a breat'.…You don' wanta be gettin' your balls in an uproar. **1949** Van Praag *Day Without End* 39: "Don't get your balls in an uproar, shorty," Motoya taunted. **1958** T. Berger *Crazy* 427: Don't get your balls in an uproar. I'm looking out for you. **1960** Sire *Deathmakers* 158: Now look, Grandpa,…don't get your balls in an uproar. **1961** Partridge *DSUE* (ed. 5) 988: *Balls in an uproar, get one's.* To become unduly excited: Canadian Army: 1914–18. **1962** T. Berger *Reinhart* 399: No, first you pull him off the street with his balls in a uproar, *then* tell him to go jerk hisself off. **1966** Bogner *Seventh Ave.* 159: Sure, have one, your balls are in an uproar. **1967** Ragni & Rado *Hair* 86: Don't get your balls in an uproar, Sheila.

¶ **get (one's) balls off** (of a man) to achieve orgasm; (*hence*) to experience a thrill of perverse pleasure.—usu. considered vulgar.

1964 R. Kendall *Black School* 86: You wanta get your balls off with one of my broads? **1971** *Nightsounds* (Jan. 8) 5: If you want to get your balls off.… **1978** Diehl *Sharky's Machine* 217: You get your balls off thinking about all the people you control.

¶ **have (one's) balls under (one's) chin** to be terrified.—usu. considered vulgar.

1937 Hemingway *Have & Have Not* 170: Quit stalling, he said to himself.…Where're your balls now? Under my chin, I guess, he thought. **1965** Linakis *In Spring* 29: He had his balls under his chin, and it took nerve for him to cross a room.

¶ **have something on the ball, 1.** *Baseball.* to throw a pitch with unusual speed or an unusually deceptive motion. Hence ——. Now *S.E.*

1911 Van Loan *Big League* 131: Joe Mulford…"put something on the ball" for the new man. **1912** *Collier's* (Apr. 13) 19: He's got nothing on the ball—nothing at all. **1914** *Collier's* (Aug. 1) 7: Swede didn't have a thing on the ball but the maker's name. **1914** Lardner *You Know Me* 141: He had good control but who would not when they put nothing on the ball? [**1978** N.Y. Yankees vs. Detroit Tigers (WINS radio): Guidry had something on that last pitch.]

2. to be especially capable, alert, efficient, etc.—often used allusively.

1936 in H. Gray *Arf* (unp.): What's he got on the ball that makes *him* so dog-goned *good*? **1936** in C. Sandburg *Letters* 340: Both of them constantly warn their publics that I have nothing on the ball and my writings should be eschewed as being too mushy to chew. **1936** Farrell *World I Never Made* 69: They got as much stuff on the ball in the game of life as old Three-fingered Brown has when he toes the mound. **1938** Bellem *Blue Murder* 14: She had plenty on the ball. **1939** Wald et al. *Roaring Twenties* (film): She's got a lot of stuff on the ball. **1946** Dadswell *Hey, Sucker* 71: Any form of entertainment that pulls so many millions of customers a year must have "something on the ball." **1955** L. Shapiro *6th of June* 210: I figured you the only officer I had with real stuff on the ball. **1967** Yablonsky *Hippie Trip* 284: Now a great teacher who they all think seemed to have it on the ball said, "Judge not, that ye be not judged." **1990** Vachss *Blossom* 111: This one detective, Sherwood, he's got a lot on the ball.

¶ **hit the ball** to work hard and effectively; to perform satisfactorily or well.

1919 Yarwood *Overseas* 72: We've wanted to "duck," but we staid on the job/Yes, we all hit the ball for Corporal Schwab. **1921** *Sentinel* (Feb. 4) 8: He said he was hittin the ball strong over in that Recruit Center. **1926** *Amer. Legion Mo.* (Aug.) 64: Only a sample of what the gang can get away with when they hit the ball. **1928** Callahan *Man's Grim Justice* 266: I made them hit the ball all the same. **1934** Peters & Sklar *Stevedore* 59: We've got to hit the ball on this Thompson business right away. **1938** Smitter *Detroit* 161: "Bucking the line, is he?"…"Just not hitting the ball, that's all." **1939** Attaway *Breathe Thunder* 234: I was the

only man she ever took up with that could really hit the ball…and almost every time. **1945** Hubbard *R.R. Ave.* 347: "Hit the ball"…means "Get busy—no more fooling." **1983** Rovin *Pryor* 119: [A hit] assures you another turn at bat, and as long as you keep hitting the ball you're a moviemaker.

¶ **holy balls!** (an exclam. of surprise, shock, etc.).—usu. considered vulgar.

1943 Mears *Carrier* 145: The chief who was with us kept repeating three expressions involuntarily. They were "Hell's fire," "Holy balls," and "A red-ass mule." **1969** *New Amer. Review* (Aug.) 96: Holy balls.…What kind of a room do you call that? **1974** Millard *Thunderbolt* 28: Holy balls! Fifty bucks! **1977** N.Y.C. man, age *ca*50: Holy balls!

¶ **keep (one's) eye on the ball** to be on the alert, be careful.

1907 in *DA* 66: We were forever being told "Keep your eye on the ball." **1908** in C.H. Burton *Letters* 73: You certainly have to "keep your eye on the ball" to understand that gentleman.

¶ **my balls!** not at all!—used postpositively.—usu. considered vulgar.

1935 T. Wolfe *Time & River* 73: —Damn fool! Go to bed!—Go to bed, my balls! I'll go to bed when I'm God-damn good and ready! **1947** Willingham *End as a Man* 165: Laurie my balls!

¶ **no skin** [or **sweat**] **off** [**of**] **(one's) balls** of absolutely no consequence to (one); **not give the sweat off** [**of**] **(one's) balls** to be unwilling to give anything.—usu. considered vulgar.

[**1928** Dahlberg *Bottom Dogs* 130: You're keepin' up the old homestead by the sweat of your groins.] **1936** Farrell *World I Never Made* 185: He ain't any sweat off my balls. **1949** Bezzerides *Thieves' Market* 126: He wouldn't give you the sweat off his balls. **1959** Groninger *Run from Mtn.* 24: No sweat off my balls. **1973** Overgard *Hero* 151: You can do as you damn please, it's no skin off my balls. **1975** T. Berger *Sneaky People* 99: My old man don't give me the sweat off his balls. **1980** McAleer & Dickson *Unit Pride* 82: He wouldn't give us the sweat off his balls.

¶ **on the ball** alert, capable, or efficient; acting effectively; accurate.

1939 W.C. Williams, in Witemeyer *Williams-Laughlin* 48: The novella by Quevedo…[is] right on the ball. **1941** Kendall *Army & Navy Slang* 6: *Get on the ball*…concentrate, get going. **1941** Boardman, Perrin & Grant *Keep 'Em Flying* (film): Get on the ball, Jackpot. **1942** in *Best from Yank* 138: Let's get on the ball out there, Pvt. Durkee. **1944** Stiles *Big Bird* 4: Sam…told us we'd have to be on the ball from here on in. **1944** H. Brown *Walk in Sun* 124: If you aren't on the ball, you haven't got a chance.…You got to be smart these days. **1945** Wolfert *Guerrilla* 49: Let's get on the ball there.…Let's give it the old college try. **1944–48** A. Lyon *Unknown Station* 132: Hope this rumor is on the ball. **1948** Wolfert *Act of Love* 133: Keep the native runners on the ball. **1958** Camerer *Damned Wear Wings* 183: New crew—doing its job, on the ball. **1960** Matheson *Warriors* 111: I ain't saying that just because a guy is older, he's automatically on the ball. I'm just saying he's had more time to get on the ball. **1964** "Doctor X" *Intern* 53: Maybe he'll be back on the ball by Monday. **1966** *RHD*: Her typing is on the ball. **1966–67** Harvey *Air War* 23: Cool, tough, on-the-ball comportment on that…flightdeck. **1972–75** W. Allen *Feathers* 99: You guys better get on the ball.

¶ **play ball** [fr. the umpire's opening call in a baseball game] **1.** to begin; to get going, esp. as one of a group.

1891 Maitland *Slang Dict.* 206: *Play ball* (Am.), go on with what you are about. **1897** *Critic* (Sept. 13) 153: Again, the injunction "play ball" is gentle, and seemly, in comparison with the brusque "get a move on." **1902** Townsend *Fadden & Mr. Paul* 45: But he was a chappy alongside de countess when she started playing ball. **1926** Wood & Goddard *Slang* 4: *Ball, to play.* Go ahead.

2. to cooperate.

1902 Townsend *Fadden & Mr. Paul* 278: He'll give him de time of his life if he'll sign up to play ball wit him whenever he's wanted. **1918** Kyne *Valley of Giants* 281: He always played ball with the absent Thatcher. **1930** Cozzens *San Pedro* 59: You don't lose your ship every day, now I come to think of it, but he's playing ball. **1935** D. Clarke *Regards to B'way* 100: I'll always play ball with my friends, too. **1940** R. Chandler *My Lovely* 63: Both of you figured that you were dealing with an organized gang and that they would play ball within the limits of their trade. **1947** in Bradbury *Golden Apples* 134: Quit putting things back together and I'll play ball with you. **1950** Felsen *Hot Rod* 68: There won't be anything against your record for six months…if you play ball. **1968** *N.Y.P.D.* (ABC-TV): If you don't play ball, I'm gonna hold you, Martin. **1968** M. Brooks *Producers* (film): I'm bribing you. Just play ball and there's a lot more where that came from. **1970** Segal *Love Story* 48: I certainly wish you would play ball now and then, Oliver.

¶ **that's the way the ball bounces** "that's the way things are and there's nothing one can do about it." Cf. *that's the way the cookie crumbles* s.v. COOKIE.

1952 Mandel *Angry Strangers* 204: I was born in a fix, Joe. That's the way the ball bounces. **1954** K. Beech *Tokyo* 207 [ref. to 1952]: "That's the way the ball bounces." The phrase is an old one in American football. But in Korea…it was used by the GI to describe events beyond his control. **1954** Ellson *Owen Harding* 13: Forget about it. That's the way the ball bounces. **1955** McGovern *Fräulein* 119: Hell, that's the way the little ball bounces, sometimes. **1956** Hargrove *Girl He Left* 20: He just wasn't a timorous type. Well, that's the way the ball bounces. **1958** Salisbury *Shook-Up* 3: That's the way the little ball bounces. **1958** C. Beaumont *Best* 66: Says I, that's how the cards fall! That's how the big ball bounces!

¶ **to the balls** completely.—usu. considered vulgar.

1935 O'Hara *Butterfield 8* 281: Most of my friends, my *men* friends, they say, "I was stewed to the balls last night." **1963** D. Tracy *Brass Ring* 378: You can't ask me to take the troops out…with me plastered to the balls. **1965** Eastlake *Castle Keep* 164: We're fed up to the balls with spies. **1974** Radano *Cop Stories* 43: He follows him around until he catches Mack stewed to the balls.

¶ (In other prov. expressions whose meaning is adequately explained by context).—all with ref. to (1), above.—usu. considered vulgar.

1938 "Justinian" *Americana Sexualis* 12: Balls…It is used, also, to jibe at a foolish or highly wishful remark, e.g. "Balls!" said the Queen, "If I had them I'd be King!" **1955** Klaas *Maybe I'm Dead* 395: He's madder than a bull with its balls in a wringer. **1953–57** Giovannitti *Combine D* 368: And if my grandmother had balls she'd be my grandfather. **1963** Gant *Queen St.* 43: Have it your way.…It's no hair off my balls. **1967** Braly *On Yard* 93: I'd say that was as plain as the balls on a tall dog. **1971** N.Y.C. supply clerk, age *ca*50: There's a saying we used to have in high school. "*Balls*," said the Queen. "*If I had 'em I'd be King.*"…That was in 1940 or '41. **1972** Sherburne *Ft. Pillow* 70: You'll probably have an hour, and you better spend some of it digging those trenches deeper. The way they are now, they ain't up to the balls on a midget. **1977** Langone *Life at Bottom* 54: We stop at last, jolted by what one of the passengers exclaims is as out of place as balls on a whale. **1966–80** McAleer & Dickson *Unit Pride* 391: "That's right neighborly of you."…"Balls," said the queen. "If I had them I'd be the king," he replied. **1985** Tate *Bravo Burning* 185: Any guy that won't fight for his country is lower than a snake's balls. **1986–89** Norse *Memoirs* 134 [ref. to 1940's]: I stood up. "If my grandmother had balls she'd be my grandfather," I said, reverting to Brooklyn surrealism.

ball² *n.* **1.a.** Esp. *Black E.* a party or celebration.

1929–32 in *AS* (Dec. 1934) 287 [ref. to Lincoln Univ.]: *Ball.* Any riotous or hilarious party or prearranged gathering. **1945** Drake & Cayton *Black Metro.* 609: Informal groups of friends and acquaintances are always ready to "have a ball" on a moment's notice—sometimes a game of cards, occasionally a real "boogie woogie." **1952** Ellson *Golden Spike* 144: I'll pitch a ball at my house. **1969** Horman & Fox *Drug Awareness* 463: *Ball*—a party.

b. a riotously good time; (*hence*) that which provides a riotously good time.—usu. constr. with *have* or (esp. *Black E.*) *pitch*.

1929–32 in *AS* (Dec. 1934) 289 [ref. to Lincoln Univ.]: *Pitch a Ball.* To have a riotous time at any social gathering. **1938** Calloway *Hi De Ho* 16: *Have a ball*—to enjoy yourself, stage a celebration. **1939** "Jimmy Johnson and His Orchestra" *Havin' a Ball* [song title]. **1940** in Handy *Blues Treasury* 170: When he plays it's a ball,/He's the daddy of them all. **1944** Bontemps & Cullen *St. Louis Woman* 19: "Ain't this the life, Lil Augie?"…"Oh gal, I'se havin' a ball." **1945** Himes *If He Hollers* 18: I bet y'all had a ball down on Central Avenue. **1946** Boulware *Jive & Slang* 6: *Pitch A Ball*…Have a good time. **1948** Manone & Vandervoort *Trumpet* 61: There were always plenty of chicks and liquor to be had, and we pitched a ball every night. **1952** E. Brown *Trespass* 20: These two fools told me you was having some kind of special ball here. **1956** Holiday & Dufty *Lady Sings* 45: There'll be blue lights and red lights and we'll pitch a ball. **1956** Ross *Hustlers* 11: When he was high, he was a ball, and everybody liked him. **1956** P. Moore *Chocolates* 2: I really had a ball this spring. **1955–57** Kerouac *On Road* 165: A ball, you know, I'm just looking for a ball. **1957** MacDonald *Price of Murder* 17: Danny's wedding gift of five…hundred dollar bills, wrapped in a sheet

of hotel stationery on which he had scrawled, Have a ball, kids. **1957–58** Lipton *Barbarians* 315: Ball—As a noun, a good time; as a verb, sexual intercourse. **1964** in A. Sexton *Letters* 249: In a bar he is a ball! **1972** Kopp *Buddha* 144: By the time [a patient] was telling about instances of explicit cruelty, she was having a ball. **1981** *Time* (Dec. 21) 14: I'm having a ball at my ball. **1983** Univ. Tenn. freshman theme (Apr. 8): The fun never stops. It is a ball a minute!

2. an act of copulation; (*hence*) a person regarded as a sexual partner.

1952 Mandel *Angry Strangers* 435: Don't you want me to go with you for the ball?…Don't you want to make it with me, Buster? **1972** R. Wilson *Playboy's Forbidden Words* 24: She was a good ball.

¶ In phrase:

¶ **open the ball** to be the first to act; to start things going; (*often*) to start a fight.

[***1812** in *OED*: Waltz and the battle of Austerlitz are…said to have opened the ball together.] **1854** "Youngster" *Swell Life* 230: I'll open the ball [i.e., start the fight]; now lie close in. **1862** in C.W. Wills *Army Life* 93: One black-eyed vixen opened the ball with "I don't see how you can look people in the face, engaged in the cause you are." **1863** in *Jour. Ill. Hist. Soc.* XXX (1938) 466: It is said that the ball opens in the morning. **1863** in Glazier *Fed. Cav.* 169: The enemy "opened the ball" this morning by shelling the cavalry pickets. **1870** *Putnam's Mag.* (Mar.) 301: Pearce opened the ball for the Atlantics. **1881** in A.E. Turner *Earps Talk* 45: As soon as those damned Earps make their appearance on the street today, the ball will open. **1891** Maitland *Slang Dict.* 195: *Open the ball*, to commence anything, from a fight to a picnic. **1962** L'Amour *Killoe* 25: You boys can open the ball any time you like. **1967** L'Amour *Matagorda* 53: This may be it, but let me open the ball.

ball *v.* **1.** [cf. *ball it off* and *ball the jack*, below; also cf. HIGHBALL] to travel or drive at high speed.

1939 Attaway *Breathe Thunder* 228: He was being dragged to the open door of the "balling" car. **1951** *AS* XXVI 307: *Balling*…Driving fast. Reported as formerly in use. **1952** J.C. Holmes *Go* 105: But come on, let's ball up there and take a look. **1955–57** Kerouac *On Road* 15: And he balled that thing clear to Iowa City. *Ibid.* 20: The Rock Island [train] balled by. **1957** Hall *Cloak & Dagger* 139: The way that Patton's balling across France, we'd better hurry. **1970** Gaffney *World of Good* 279: Better let Whitey ball on through.

2. Orig. *Black E.* to have a riotously good time; celebrate; have fun.

1942 Z.N. Hurston, in *Amer. Mercury* 93: *Balling*—having fun. **1946** Mezzrow & Wolfe *Really Blues* 37: Joe…felt like balling…cause he beat Big Izzy for ten grand in the crap game. **1952** E. Brown *Trespass* 109: And then for a while he'd go balling with Apres. **1954** W.G. Smith *South St.* 99: All I can do is look what's being put down, mind the play and ball the best I can. **1958** Russell *Permanent Playboy* 356: "Let's ball, dig," by which she means, Let's try a new far-out sound on the hi-fi. **1959** L. Hughes *Simply Heavenly* 159: Ball, ball, let's ball awhile! **1966** S. Harris *Hellhole* 221: In the meanwhile, Chuck and I had money all the time. Baby, we were balling. **1967** P. Welles *Babyhip* 23: But I dig brown people, they're cool. They know how to ball. **1970** *Harper's* (Jan. 1971) 86: He envied some of his less talented but more openly manic Village friends their concentration on "living," on public "balling." **1970** *Rolling Stone Interviews* 388: At the time balling meant dancing, at the time it didn't mean sex. **1992** *Jerry Springer Show* (synd. TV series): And Nancy, too, likes to ball.

3. to copulate or (*trans.*) copulate with.—usu. considered vulgar. [Used of either sex.]

*ca*1953 Hughes *Fantastic Lodge* 70: He kept wanting to ball me. *Ibid.* 80: We were sitting on the bed after balling. **1956** Ginsberg *Howl* 12: Who balled in the morning in the evenings in rose gardens and the/grass of public parks. **1958** Gilbert *Vice Trap* 112: She'd balled like she invented it. **1961** R. Russell *Sound* 16: You just want to eat good food, listen to good music, ball a beautiful chick, take things at your ease. **1961** T.I. Rubin *In Life* 76: He'd call every day to find out, and then we'd have this here week of balling and eating. **1966** Susann *Valley of Dolls* 149: You're nothing now—just another broad who's been balled by Lyon Burke. **1968** *Playboy* (Aug.) 112: Why can't we just stay here and ball each other? **1972** Kellogg *Lion's Tooth* 107: Probably balling somebody else. **1973** *Harper's* (Sept.) 36: The typical West Side woman…swings. That last means she'll ball you if she's so inclined. **1977** Harnack *Under Wings* 42: She balled you—really? **1982** *Harper's* (July) 72: She'd ball half the dudes in town for a snort of junk. **1990** Munro *Slang U.* 27: Mark balled Kathy. Kathy balled Mark.

¶ In phrases:

¶ **ball it off** to travel at a fast rate.

1847 Downey *Cruise* 36: In the course of 24 hours we got a fair wind and were soon balling it off at the rate of 12 knots on our course for Valparaiso.

¶ **ball it up** to celebrate riotously.

*ca*1953 Hughes *Fantastic Lodge* 35. *1962 in *OEDS:* A so-called friend invites you…to a coloured joint—to ball it up for a night. **1964** Smith & Hoefer *Music* 30: All the kitchen mechanics and pot wrestlers were balling it up on their afternoon off.

¶ **ball the jack, 1.** to go fast (said esp. of a railroad train), make haste; *(hence)* to run away. [1913 quot., from a well-known ragtime song, gave the phrase wide currency and ref. specif. to the performance of a dance step presumably introduced by the song; whether the phrase itself was coined at the same time is uncertain.]

1913 Jim Burris & Chris Smith *Ballin' the Jack* (song) 4: Now that's what I call "Ballin' the Jack." **1914** in Handy *Blues Treasury* 74: Said a black headed gal make a freight train jump the track/But a long tall gal makes a preacher ball the jack. **1918** in Niles *Singing Soldiers* 25: I come to France to make de Kaiser ball de Jack. **1929** in N. Cohen *Long Steel Rail* 457: For the Four-twenty-seven was sure ballin' the jack. **1932** Pagano *Bluejackets* 72: It was not long before we were "balling the jack" across the plains of Leon. **1940** Byron Parker & Mountaineers *Peanut Special:* That thing's pickin' up. She's ballin' the jack. **1945** Hubbard *R.R. Ave.* 346: Verb *highball* or phrase *ball the jack* means to make a fast run. **1952** Clayton *Angels* 167: I ain't ballin' the jack out of here till I pump that well dry. **1974** Bernstein & Woodward *President's Men* 57: Maury came through here like a goddamned train…he was really ballin' the jack.

2. to work hard and efficiently. [The accuracy of the def. given in 1927 quot. is suspect.]

1918 *Camp Pike Carry-On* (Nov. 14) 7: Familiar Expressions…*Ball the jack.* **1919** in White *Amer. Negro Songs* 276: The nigger is happy,/His load off his back./But when the policeman comes snoopin',/He's gotta ball the jack. [**1927** *AS* II 348: *Ball the jack*—to risk everything on one attempt. "The team balled the jack on that play."] **1948–51** J. Jones *Eternity* ch. v.: Tell me, how's that outfit of yours getting along? Still balling the jack?

ball and chain *n.* **1.** one's wife, esp. if domineering. Usu. *Joc.* Hence **ball-and-chained,** *adj.* married.

1921 *Collier's* (June 25) 24: He deliberately attempted to commit suicide by askin' me "How's the ball and chain?" meanin' my wife. **1925** Kearney *Man's Man* 24: Well, Mel, congratulations to you and your "ball and chain." **1926** Maines & Grant *Wise-Crack Dict.* 5: Ball and chain—The wife. **1929** Springs *Carol Banks* 160: Your wife won't let you? That's right. You boys with the ball and chain have to check in every afternoon. **1933** Clifford *Boats* 58: That ball-and-chain of mine out there? **1943** Farrell *Days of Anger* 68: Lillian, Marty's ball-and-chain. **1950** in F. Brown *Honeymoon* 12: And all of them are married except me. Why not send a man who's already got a ball and chain? **1964** *Dick Van Dyke Show* (CBS-TV): The old "ball and chain's" fine. **1972** W.C. Anderson *Hurricane* 22: They've proved they can get along…without being ball-and-chained.

2. one's domineering girlfriend. *Joc.* [Much less freq. than **(1.).**]

1932 Farrell *Guillotine Party* 182: She's his ball-and-chain, all right. **1937** *AS* (Feb.) 74: *Ball-and-chain*—girl friend.

ballast *n.* **1.** (one's) good sense.—only in phr. **lose (one's) ballast.**

*1889 Barrère & Leland *Dict. Slang* I 71: A man is said to "lose his *ballast,*" when his judgment fails him, or when he becomes top-heavy with conceit. **1954** Felton *20,000 Leagues* (film): The professor's losin' his ballast.

2. *R.R.* (see quot.)

1945 Hubbard *R.R. Ave.* 332: Ballast—Turkey or chicken dressing.

ballbag *n.* a jockstrap. Also **ballbasket.**—usu. considered vulgar. *Joc.*

1968 W. Crawford *Gresham* 45: Hey! Black belt! I just struck a man without warning. Do I lose my gook ballbasket? **1971** Hilaire *Thanatos* 230: So go gum a ball-bag or something.

ball-bearing *adj.* [lit., bearing BALLS, 1.a.; pun on *ball bearing*] Esp. *Mil.* (of a man) performing duties typically performed by (a woman).—used derisively.—usu. considered vulgar.

*a*1945 in Fussell *Wartime* 252: MACs, MACs,/Ball-bearing WACs.

[**1946** Plagemann *All for Best* 69: After Waves were admitted to the Navy the [hospital] corpsmen were sometimes called "fur bearing Waves."] **1976–79** Duncan & Moore *Green Side Out* xv: *Ball-bearing BAM*—[USMC] Clerk (Male). *Ibid.* xxxvi: Yeoman…ball-bearing WAVE. Clerk. **1980** McDowell *Our Honor* 81 [ref. to *ca*1952]: He usually referred to sailors as "ball-bearing WAVES." **1983** Elting et al. *Soldier Talk* 17: Ball-bearing WAC…A male soldier performing what had come to be regarded as women's work, typing…clerking…etc. **1986** *NDAS: Ball-bearing hostess*…A male cabin attendant on an aircraft. **1989** "Captain X" & Dodson *Unfriendly Skies* 158: These guys have had to take a lot of ribbing…"ball-bearing stewardesses"….The insults are many.

ballbreaker or **ballbuster** *n.* [cf. *break (one's) balls* s.v. BALL, *n.*]**1.a.** that which is bitterly trying or unpleasant; esp. an agonizing or arduous task, experience, etc.—usu. considered vulgar.

[**1934** *WNID2: Ball breaker.* A skull cracker [i.e., a wrecking ball].] **1942–49** Goldin et al. *DAUL* 22: *Ballbreaker*…A bitter disappointment; the cause of a bitter disappointment. **1954** Weingarten *Dict. of Slang* 15: *Ball-breaker, -buster* (n.) 1) A person who repeatedly annoys one or assigns difficult tasks. 2) A task that is difficult or annoying. Both 1) and 2) are common in the language of the streets. 1950 or earlier. **1973** Haring *Stranger* 135: You can't believe what I've been through. And then today, a real ball-breaker. **1974** A. Bergman *Big Kiss-Off* 85: This bewildering ball-breaker of a case was becoming comprehensible. **1975** Univ. Tenn. student: This [job] is going to be ballbuster. **1981** *Nat. Lampoon* (Sept.) 44: The first week was a ballbuster. **1984–87** Ferrandino *Firefight* 16: It's a real ballbuster. If you think you're tired now, wait till we get ready to set up. **1991** Ganz & Mandel *City Slickers* (film): It's *the* big friggin' ballbuster of a job!

b. a demanding, contentious, harassing, or otherwise vexatious individual; *(specif.)* a cruel taskmaster or a nagging or domineering woman.—usu. considered vulgar.

*ca*1944 in Valant *Aircraft Nose Art* 295: Bugs' (Ball) Busters. **1942–49** Goldin et al. *DAUL* 22: *Ball-breaker*…A strict disciplinarian; a slave-driver; one who plagues others with requests for favors. **1950** Stuart *Objector* 16 [ref. to WWII]: Jesus Christ…I got a ball breaker on my hands. **1954** (quot. at **(a.),** above). **1962** Riccio & Slocum *All the Way Down* 36: We…figured you as a real ball-breaker and just another bullshit social-worker creep. **1963** Morgan *Six-Eleven* 57: She's a working nympho…a real ball-breaker….A ball-goddamned-breaker. **1964** Faust *Steagle* 208: I won't take any shit from you or any other ball breakers. **1965** Karp *Doobie Doo* 10: The Telephone company and the Police. Authoritarian ballbreakers. **1966** Susann *Valley of Dolls* 74: Ed is a ballbreaker—the writers are ready to quit and he's thrown out the producer. **1971** D. Smith *Engine Co.* 89: He yells a lot, and he's a ball breaker, but he'll never hurt ya. **1972** Rossner *Any Minute* 83: You think any woman with guts is a ballbuster. **1973** Droge *Patrolman* 70: "Well, you're late and when you're assigned here again see to it that you're on time. Is that clear?" Now I knew he was a ball-breaker. **1975** Kangas & Solomon *Psych. of Strength* 56: She is also competitive with the man and is a "ball breaker." **1977** Schrader *Blue Collar* 6: I mean, he was a real ballbuster when he came up, but that was thirty years ago. **1980** Kotzwinkle *Jack* 178: They're all from Gina's gang….A bunch of ballbreakers. **1981** *Nat. Lampoon* (Feb.) 52: That bitch. What a ballbuster. Good thing I didn't fall in love with her. **1982** Levinson *Diner* (film): At least she's not a ballbreaker. If she was a ballbreaker there'd be just no way. **1990** Kathleen Turner, on *Siskel & Ebert Special* (CBS-TV) (May 21): He said she was a ballbreaker and horrid.

2. an extraordinary person, thing, event, etc. (in a positive sense).—usu. considered vulgar. [Orig. an ironic application of above senses.]

[**1952** Randolph & Wilson *In Holler* 103: *Cod* still means scrotum or testicles in the Ozarks….A young man in Springfield, Missouri, described a certain sorority dance as a "regular cod-buster."] **1969** Jessup *Sailor* 258: Cadiz, you're a ball breaker. **1970** Seelye *Finn* 56: The cannon let off such a reglar old ball-buster right before me that it made me deef with the noise and nearly blind with the smoke. **1974** *Nat. Lampoon* (Nov.) 16: Bob just grins. "Okay, but I'm telling you it's a ball-buster. Just wait and see." **1978** *Rolling Stone* (July 27) 45: He comes out with a ball-buster of a bankroll, a cold $35,000 in cash, and throws it on the table. **1985** Sawislak *Dwarf* 122: I've got a ball-buster story and I may need you to dictate while I write. **1976–87** G.A. Fine *With the Boys* 106: Boys desire to have girlfriends who are "cute" or "sexy" or "ballbreakers."

3. *Mil.* a kind of antipersonnel mine, BOUNCING BETTY.—

usu. considered vulgar.

1971 T. Mayer *Falcon* 13: He and some of his boys had lined a trailside with ball-breakers, antipersonnel mines that pop up to the right height and spit out steel pellets.

ballbreaking or **ball-busting** *n.* harassment.—usu. considered vulgar.

1948 J.H. Burns *Lucifer* 168: My God! Is there no finale to this ball-breaking? **1980** Whalen *Takes a Man* 97: Save your ball-busting for the firehouse, Williams. **1988** Maloney *Thunder Alley* 367: All the ballbusting at Top Gun. **1991** *New Republic* (Mar. 4) 15: I fear tomorrow's right-winger may be slicker, more aggressive, and more detached from the consequences of geopolitical ballbusting.

ballbreaking or **ball-busting** *adj.* being a BALLBREAKER (in any sense).—usu. considered vulgar.

1944 (cited in Weingarten *Slang Dict.*): Ball-busting. **1959** Kerouac *Dr. Sax* 39: Jey-sas Crise gawd damn ball-breaking sonofabitch if I ain't an old piece of shit. **1964** Faust *Steagle* 63: You can keep your ball-bustin American broads. **1973** Birkby & Harris *Amazon* 46: Don't be a ball-breaking bitch! **1975** Sepe & Telano *Cop Team* 171: You must have a ball-breaking dry-cleaning bill. **1979** *Easyriders* (Dec.) 55: Keep your eyes peeled for a "ball-bustin' bargain." **1980** Santoli *Everything* 93: That was really a ball-breaking hump. We had no water and no food.

ball-clanker *n.* a man who boasts of his courage or sexual prowess.—usu. considered vulgar.

1960 Kirkwood *Pony* 17: The only men you're ever exposed to are such big-mouthed ball-clankers that you automatically don't want to be like them. *Ibid.* 27: We talked about ball-clankers, too.

ball-crusher *n.* BALLBREAKER, 1.—usu. considered vulgar.

1970 S. Ross *Fortune Machine* 51: A small voice said she was a ball-crusher. **1977** Langone *Life at Bottom* 75: "It's a real ball crusher," says a First Class Utiliesman they call Haulaway Joe, who was there in 1971 when they started the construction with surveying and laying the foundation. "Fuckin' tools get brittle and break, you know."

ball-cutter *n.* a demanding, nagging, or domineering woman.—usu. considered vulgar.

1962 Kesey *Cuckoo's Nest* 57: No, that nurse ain't some kind of monster chicken, buddy. What she is is a ball-cutter. **1964–66** R. Stone *Hall of Mirrors* 295: I shall kick her in the snatch....Talk about ball-cutters, for Christ sake. **1979** Hiler *Monkey Mt.* 179: These college girls are all ball-cutters....Just a bunch of stuck up cunts!

ballface *n.* **1.** see BALDFACE.

2. (see 1870 quot.).

*a***1849** in C. Hill *Scenes* 170: You up country looking ball face. *a***1870** in *DAE: Ballface*, contemptuous epithet applied by negroes to white persons.—Salem, Mass., 1810–20.

ballgame *n.* a challenging or competitive situation; *(hence)* state of affairs; in phr. **that's** [or **there goes**] **the ballgame** "that is the end," esp. of one's chances; "that finishes it."

1930 Bodenheim *Roller Skates* 127: Ain' no double plays coming off in this ballgame, chicken. **1945** Dos Passos *Tour* 13: Cleaning up after the ballgame....Even now we can't dig a new latrine without turning up a dead Jap or two. **1946** Steinbeck *Wayward Bus* 164: There's a backwash cutting in under the piles above the bridge, and if it cuts a channel in back, there goes your ball game. **1948** Wolfert *Act of Love* 453 [ref. to WWII]: "That's all, only the bulldozer [destroyed]?"..."That's quite an only. That's the ball game." **1954** Freeman *Francis Joins WACs* (film): You know how much it means to me to win this ballgame. **1957** Atwell *Private* 465: Well, boys,...there goes the ballgame. **1961** Baar & Howard *Missileman* 194: Once on station we're in good shape...It's getting to the ballgame that you get knocked off. **1961** Coon *At Front* 282: This was the ballgame. **1968** A. Hoffman *Revolution* 66: You know, months of delay before it comes out. By then it's a whole new ballgame. **1970** *Sat. Review* (Oct. 10) 55: When it comes to covering the news in any kind of detailed way, we are just almost not in the ball game. **1971** *New Yorker* (Mar. 13) 30: If an invasion took place...some official of our government would no doubt announce that we were in a whole new "ballgame." **1975** *Business Week* (June 30) 89: We're not getting the cash flow, and that's what the ball game is all about. *ca***1979** in J.L. Gwaltney *Drylongso* 60: I will take ten [blows] from them to give them one because I know that will be the ball game. **1982** P. Michaels *Grail* 127: By Christmas we should have a whole new ball game. **1990** *U.S. News & W.R.* (June 25) 51: The opportunity for the Democrats is to try to get the middle class back in the ballgame.

ballgusted *adj.* [of fanciful orig.] "darned." *Joc.*

1834 Caruthers *Kentuckian in N.Y.* II 216: I wish I may be tetotally ballgusted, if here ain't another pretty piece of business.

ball hawk *n. Sports.* a player, esp. a baseball fielder, who is skilled in catching or gaining possession of the ball. Also as v.

1920 *N.Y. Times* (Oct. 10) (cited in Nichols *Baseball Term.*). **1921** J. Conway, in *Variety* (May 20) 7: Watch my pair of ball hawks. **1923** Wilce *Football* 84: Ends...Types—blocker...; tall pass receiver;..."ball-hawk." **1942** *ATS* 661: *Ball hawk*, a player who is in on every play or recovers a great many fumbles. **1949** Leahy *Notre Dame* 201: Instruct your tacklers to be "ballhawks." We want them to know where the ball is for every minute of the game. *Ibid.* 151: The Chicago Cardinals use their outstanding end, Mal Kutner as a defensive halfback because of his "ball-hawking" ability. **1950** Cummings *Dict. Baseball* 3: *Ball hawk*...a fielder who gets a quick start toward a batted ball, notably an excellent outfielder. **1958** Fuoss *Quarterback* 102: Some teams are strong pass defenders and excellent "ball hawks." **1964** Thompson & Rice *Every Diamond* 30: He was a better-than-average ball hawk and an excellent base runner. **1978** Wharton *Birdy* 304: Birdy's mother, the left-center field ball hawk. **1990** *Wash. Post* (Nov. 15) D6: He's getting to be a ball hawk...He's playing the ball well, reacting to the ball in the air and flying for it.

ball hooter *n.* [orig. unkn.] *Logging.* a logger who rolls logs down hillsides that are too steep for wagon teams. Now *hist.*

1942 in *ATS.* **1956** Sorden & Ebert *Logger's Wds.* 1 [ref. to *a*1925]: *Ball-hooter*, One who rolls logs down a hillside.

balling *adj.* [fr. BALL, *v.*, 2] excitingly active, wonderfully alive.

1952 Mandel *Angry Strangers* 230: Along come three Vipers and some balling chick with them. **1961** H. Ellison *Gentleman Junkie* 150: You dated...balling chicks with nice smooth shins above their bobby socks. **1963** Bruce *Essential Lenny* 143: A woman—firm, with fantastic measurements: 96, 4, 53; 112 pounds; two feet tall! Grotesque? But a balling chick.

ballistic *adj.* ¶ In phrase: **go ballistic, 1.** (orig. of a guided missile) to go out of control; *(occ.)* reach great heights; *(hence)* to become angry or irrational; go haywire. [Very common in late 1980's.]

1971 Windchy *Tonkin* 237 [ref. to 1964]: One Phantom launched a heat-seeking Sidewinder at a burning boat; the missile "went ballistic" and strayed—possibly the boat was just making smoke. **1985** Dye *Between Raindrops* 326 [ref. to Vietnam War]: You're the second guy this morning that went ballistic over that headline. **1985** *Misfits of Science* (NBC-TV): I've got three senior citizens who are gonna go ballistic out there! **1987** Lt. Col. O.L. North, testimony before congressional committee (CNN-TV) (July 7): To coin a phrase, I think the Iranians went ballistic when they saw what they got. **1988** Vice-Pres. G. Bush, on CNN-TV (Dec. 16): In fact I saw a story yesterday, and I went a little ballistic. **1989** *New Republic* (Nov. 6) 128: He would go ballistic over the idea of reopening the capital gains tax break for real estate. **1990** *Wash. Post* (Sept. 19) A23: I deem his attack on Pat Buchanan to be an example of Rosenthal gone ballistic.

2. to become astonishing.

1990 *New Yorker* (May 7) 38: When I heard her yesterday, I thought, Shakespeare goes *ballistic*....It isn't fair to have somebody that good in this competition. **1991** *Village Voice* (N.Y.) (Sept. 10) 43: The birds come banging their beaks on your second-story window, pleading to get in behind the glass before the ozone level goes ballistic.

ballistics *n.pl. Rap Music.* vivid, forcefully delivered rap lyrics.

1991 Nelson & Gonzales *Bring the Noise* 96: Street corner ballistics. **1991** *Source* (Oct.) 58: Base Poet kicks simple ballistics about a subject you probably might think sounds corny. **1991** in *RapPages* (Feb. 1992) 3: Time to...kick the ballistics on real Hip-Hop gettin' faded at the board room.

ball-less *adj.* lacking nerve, GUTLESS.—usu. considered vulgar.

1958 A. King *Mine Enemy* 20: An altogether ball-less wonder. **1966** D. King *Brave & Damned* 82: All right, you bunch of ballless recruits! **1967** Dubus *Lieutenant* 161: They tell 'em to change the recommendation of a board and sign it and these ball-less wonders change the recommendation because I know that will be the ball game. **1987** D. Barnes *Deadly Justice* 55: Bullshit forced on him by a ball-less captain and a chicken-shit deputy chief.

ballock *n.* usu. *pl.* [OE] a testicle.—usu. considered vulgar. Now *rare* in U.S. Also vars. [Early exx. are in *OED, MED.*]

***1763** in J. Atkins *Sex in Lit.* IV 155: Prick, cunt and bollocks. **1863** in

Horrocks *Dear Parents* 33: John Brown's Bollucks lies a dangling in the air. **1888** *Stag Party* 42: Jupiter...grabbed hold of the cuss by the neck and the ballachs. *Ibid.* 222: The tarantula lies in wait for a bite at the unsuspecting bollicks of the traveler. **1899** B.W. Green *Va. Folk-Speech* 50: *Bollocks, n.pl.* Testicles. Bollocks. **1927** *Immortalia* 32: It kept his massive bollocks busy. **1928** in Read *Lexical Evidence* 34: The man...should have/His ballicks smashed. **1942** McAtee *Supp. to Grant Co. Dial.* 2 [ref. to 1890's]: *Ballocks*...meant scrotum and testicles together, not the latter alone. **1947–53** Guthrie *Seeds* 7: I'll frizzle my damn ballicks off sa dern bad I'll not be able to top that new gal wifey of mine.

ballock *v.* (see quot.).
   1730–82 in Read *Lexical Evidence* 34: In their combats [in Virginia] unless specially precluded, they are admitted (to use their own term) "to bite, b-ll-ck, and goudge," which operations, when the first onset with fists is over, consists in fastening on the nose or ears of their adversaries with their teeth, seizing him by the genitals, and dexterously scooping out an eye.

ballocks up see BOLLIX UP.

ballocky naked *adj.* completely naked. Also **ballocky bare-assed.**
   1966–80 McAleer & Dickson *Unit Pride* 71: There were the three prisoners...ballocky naked. **1980** in *N.E. Folklore* XXVIII (1988) 20: Stripped me right down ballocky-bare-assed. *Ibid.* 97: Stripped ballocky-ball-assed.

ball of dirt *n.* the earth.
   1898 Norris *Moran* 47: There ain't no manner of place on the ball of dirt where you're likely to run up afoul of so many...unexpected things—as at sea.

ball off *v.* [fr. BALL¹, *n.*, 8] to buy a drink for; to treat.
   1894 Gardner *Doctor & Devil* 26: "Hey, whiskers," said she to Dr. Parkhurst, "going to ball me off?"..."Have something on me." **1895** *DN* I 412: *Ball off*—to treat. "He balled off his customers." N.Y.

ball of fire *n.* **1.** a person exhibiting unusual energy, ability, or drive.
   1900 *DN* II 35: *Fire, ball of*...Brilliant student, usually with the added idea of great energy [at Yale Univ.]. **1931** Stevenson *St. Luke's* 26: I just saw Tony....No ball of fire. **1942** *Flying Tigers* (film): You're going to have a little trouble with that ball of fire. **1947** Overholser *Buckaroo's Code* 6: You ain't no ball of fire between the ears, neither. **1963** Ross *Dead Are Mine* 93: What about Miles? I remember he used to be quite a ball of fire back at Fort Lewis. **1981** G. Wolf *Roger Rabbit* 83: A regular ball of fire as a cook and housekeeper.
   2. a fast vehicle.
   1940 *R.R. Mag.* (Apr.) 51: Redball, Ball of Fire—Fast freight train. **1959** Gault *Drag Strip* 15: Any sensible father would take that ball of fire away from you.
   ¶ In phrase:
   ¶ **great balls of fire!** (an exclamation of amazement, impatience, etc.).
   1906 *DN* III 139: *Great balls of fire, interj. phr.* A student's exclamation [at Univ. Ark.]. **1944** C.B. Davis *Leo McGuire* 180: "Great balls of fire," he said in a hushed voice. **1963** W.C. Anderson *Penelope* 87: "Great balls of fire!" exclaimed Callaghan, his eyes extending a good inch from his head.

ball of wax *n.* situation, state of affairs; in phr. **the whole ball of wax** everything.
   1953 in *W9.* **1966** *RHD* 114: He went out to Chicago and in no time came back with the contract for the whole ball of wax. **1968** Hawley *Hurricane Yrs.* 179: It's all pretty much the same ball of wax. **1969** Everett (Wash.) *Herald* (Apr. 18) 12D: I figure we're entitled to pensions, vacations...the whole ball of wax. **1972** Burkhart *Women in Pris.* 211: That's a whole different ball of wax altogether. **1976** *U.S. News & W.R.* (Nov. 1) 32: A solution to the economic situations, crime, inflation, the whole ball of wax. **1978** Truscott *Dress Gray* 19: He'll have the whole ball of wax wrapped up for us. **1982** Braun *Judas Tree* 135: Stimson's a different ball of wax. **1984** "W.T. Tyler" *Shadow Cabinet* 169: CBS, NBC, ABC, the whole ball of wax. **1986** R. Walker *AF Wives* 279: Being a wing commander is a whole different ball of wax.

ball of yarn *n.* the female genitalia.—esp. in phr. **wind (someone's) ball of yarn** (of a man) to copulate with (someone). *Joc.* [The traditional Anglo-Irish bawdy song that employs this metaphor seems to have arisen in the 19th C. See Cray

1969 for a discussion.]
   1941 in Peters *Wisc. Folk Songs* 266: And he wound up my little ball of yarn....Keep...both hands on your little ball of yarn. **1942** in Randolph & Legman *Roll Me in Your Arms* 97 [song learned in 1890's]: I wound up her little ball of yarn. **1942** Algren *Morning* 96: I guess you know what you get fer windin' up that little ball of statutory yarn. ***1964** Healy *Ballads from Pubs* 94: Sure I spied a pretty miss/And I kindly asked her this/May I wind up your little ball of yarn./...I...won't meddle with your little ball of yarn. **1969** Cray *Erotic Muse* 32: She let me wind her little ball of yarn.

balloon *n.* **1.** a security certificate issued by the Confederation.
   1787 in *DAE* I 125: Continental certificates (or what some term balloons)...are those not adopted by any particular state.
   2. a long-winded person, BLOWHARD, GAS BAG.
   1864 F.C. Adams *Story of Trooper* 228: He called me a balloon, yes sir, a balloon...a wind bag. **1892** Garland *Prairie Folks* 134: Go it, you old balloon!
   3. a canvas pack or bedroll.
   1929 *AS* IV 337: *Balloon*—canvas pack or bed-roll. **1929** Milburn *Hobo* 72: But my troubles pale when I hit the trail/A-packing my old balloon! **1930** "D. Stiff" *Milk & Honey* 199: *Balloon*—A roll of bedding carried on the back; a bindle. **1948** J. Stevens *Jim Turner* 127 [ref. to *ca*1910]: I was ready to shoulder my roped balloon of tarp, blankets and duds. **1958** McCulloch *Woods Words* 7: *Balloon*—...An old time logger's pack sack.
   4. *Sports.* a ball hit, kicked, or thrown high in the air.
   1942 *ATS* 663: *Balloon*, a lofty kick. **1978** Pici *Tennis Hustler* 70: You ain't gonna get too many aces with that balloon, boy.
   5. *USAF.* a lieutenant.—usu. constr. with *first* or *second.*
   1951 R. Richards *Air Cadet* (film): I wonder what it'll feel like to kiss a second balloon. **1955** B.J. Friedman, in *Antioch Rev.* XV 377: What are you? A first or second balloon?...You're quite a balloon. That's all I can say. **1956** *AS* XXI 227: A *second balloon*...a second lieutenant. **1959** Scott *Tiger in Sky* 45: I guess it was simply more of the character of the new "second balloons" getting their heart in their work. **1963** E.M. Miller *Exile to Stars* 122: He was not a new "second balloon." **1984–88** Hackworth & Sherman *About Face* 114 [ref. to Korean War]: One day some second balloon...might come in and take over your platoon.
   6. *pl.* a woman's breasts, esp. if large.
   1962 Sagarin *Dirty Words* 79: Balloons,...lemons,...melons, [etc.]. **1971** Rhinehart *Dice Man* 200: I was staring at Arlene's balloons undulating in the light of the chandelier. **1979** M. Brooks *High Anxiety* (film): It's as valid as if a man envied a woman's balloons.
   7. a condom.
   1966 Fariña *Down So Long* 58: How many unborn children flushed in rubber balloons. **1971** Jacobs & Casey *Grease* 31: Those ain't leaves. They're used balloons. **1973** *Penthouse* (Apr.) 106: I blew into it, realizing how it got its nickname, balloon.
   8. *Narc.* a toy balloon, condom, or other small parcel of any material used to contain heroin or a similar drug.
   1967 Maurer & Vogel *Narc. & Narc. Add.* (ed. 3) 340: *Balloon.* A quantity of drugs packaged in small paper, cellophane or rubber parcels. **1970** Horman & Fox *Drug Awareness* 463: *Balloon*—a small packet of narcotics. **1972** Smith & Gay *Don't Try It* 13: She is...hustling for enough bread to cop a balloon.
   9.a. a dollar.
   1973 Boyd & Harris *Baseball Card* 252: The Red Sox shelled out 90,000 balloons for...a...third baseman. **1974** *Nat. Lampoon* (Oct.) 84: You owe us two thousand balloons. **1983** Stapleton *30 Yrs.* 220: Yahoo, two-hundred-eighty-eight balloons.
   b. *Gamb.* one hundred dollars.
   1971 Sorrentino *Up from Never* 190: I got anudder balloon in the bank....That'll give us a hundred and twen'y-eight bucks, right?
   10. *pl.* [sugg. by BALL¹, *n.*, 4] audacity; courage; nerve. *Joc.*
   1974 Radano *Cop Stories* 200: "Officer, I want that man arrested for assault. You saw him hit me." This guy had some pair of balloons!
   11. *Post Office.* a large sack of mail.
   1978 J. Rosenberg *Dict. Business* 40: *Balloon:* a huge sack or pouch of mail.
   12. *Journ.* (see quot.).
   1989 *Newsweek* (Sept. 4) 8: *Balloon:* A story promoted on page one over the name of the paper.
   ¶ In phrases:
   ¶ **go up in a balloon** to be ruined; come to nothing; meet with disaster.

1872 Burnham *Secret Service* viii: *Up in a balloon.*—gone hopelessly into thin air! A fiasco. **1874** Alger *Julius* 50: All at once his rags took fire, and he went up in a balloon. **1875** Daly *Pique* 291: Where's our fifty thousand dollars gone to? Up in a balloon, I suppose. **1880** Pinkerton *Prof. Thieves & Detective* 159: Damnation! I'm up in a balloon this time! It's all over. The damned thing's gone.

¶ **when the balloon goes up** when the great excitement or undertaking begins; (esp.) *Mil.* when the awaited attack is launched.

*1924 in *OEDS*: "When's the magistrate's court?"..."The balloon, I believe, goes up at 10 A.M." **1925* Fraser & Gibbons *Soldier & Sailor Wds.* 15 [ref. to WWI]: *The balloon*, a colloquial term used of any event, e.g. "What time does the balloon go up?" the speaker meaning, "What time is the parade?" **1955** L. Shapiro *Sixth of June* 252 [ref. to 1944]: We don't talk about when the balloon goes up. We're real happy slobs. **1962** T. Berger *Reinhart in Love* 128: There you are!...The balloon is going up! **1976** Atlee *Domino* 102: Park had his alert on, and everybody was afraid the balloon might go up. **1983** P. Theroux, in *L.A. Times* (Nov. 18) V 32: Belfast is a sort of filthy version of Bel-Air. It's Bel-Air after the balloon has gone up. *a1987* Coyle *Team Yankee* 20: If the balloon goes up in the next couple of days. **1987** J. Thompson *Gumshoe* 276: This won't do you much good...if the balloon goes up. **1990** *Time* (Nov. 5) 39: If the balloon goes up, winning will require more men and equipment than previously acknowledged.

balloon *v.* **1.** [sugg. by syn. *go up in one's lines* or *go up in the air*] (of an actor) to forget one's lines during a performance; (of an athlete) to lose one's composure, become rattled.

1913 in M. Gardner *Casey* 89: But was the Frogtown slabster sent balloonin', terrified? **1923** *N.Y. Times* (Sept. 9) VIII 2: *Balloon:* to go up in one's lines.

2. [fr. BALLOON, *n.*, 3] to pack one's bedroll and take to the road.—constr. with *it*.

1958 McCulloch *Woods Words* 7: *Balloon it*—To pack up and leave camp.

3. [fr. BALLOON, *n.*, 8] *Narc.* to package (heroin) in a toy balloon, condom, etc., for sale to an addict.

1968–70 *Current Slang* III & IV 6: *Balloon*, v. To package heroin for sale. (Drug users' jargon).

balloonatic *n.* [blend *balloon* + *lunatic*] **1.** a balloonist; a member of a balloon crew; (*hence*) *Mil.* a member of a balloon corps. Usu. *Joc.*

*1865 in *F & H* (rev.) I 122: That Nadar, the balloonatic, has sold his balloon. **1874** Rudge & Raven *IOGB* 6: It was conceived and brought forth under the auspices of two aerial heroes, or transatlantic balloonatics, as they were often called. **1917** in Rossano *Price of Honor* 35: The fifteen...balloonatics have to stand watch. **1917* in A. Lee *No Parachute* 73: I'd hate to be a balloonatic, dangling on a parachute with that enormous blazing mass just above me, though they seem to get away with it every time. **1918** [Grider] *War Birds* 103: The Guardian Angel parachute that all the balloonatics use. **1919** *Camp Knox News* (July 19) 4: One facetious balloonatic...took a lantern. **1920** Haslett *Luck on Wing* 100: However, he had the Prussian idea of discipline and he took it out on the balloonatics whenever he felt they needed it. **1925** *Amer. Legion Wkly.* (Mar. 20) 24: A National Guard infantryman by choice and balloonatic by accident. **1929* Bowen *Sea Slang* 6: *Balloonatics.* The men handling the naval kite balloons during the War. **1975** *L.A. Times* (Nov. 9) I 7: Balloonists, he said, are "dedicated people with a flair for the unusual. Balloonatics, we are sometimes called."

2. *Mil.* an airplane pilot who strafes enemy observation balloons. *Joc.* Hence **balloonatical**, *adj.*

1918 J.N. Hall *High Adventure* 139: The orders have just come...and I decided that the first men I met after leaving the bureau would be balloonatics....Now, if you can make fire come out of a Boche sausage, you will have done all that is required. **1919** Rickenbacker *Flying Circus* 140: I think, Reed,...we are the rottenest lot of balloonatical fakers that ever got up at two-thirty in the morning.

balloonbrain *n.* BALLOON-HEAD.

1949 R. Smith *Big Wheel* (film): Where's that balloonbrain? That's what I want to know. **1958–65** Alfred *Hogan's Goat* 21: Corner-boy Boyle and Bessie the balloon brain.

balloon-head *n.* [cf. AIRHEAD] a silly, empty-headed person; dolt. Hence **balloon-headed** empty-headed.

1931 Farrell *McGinty* 316: You balloon head, you got yours comin'. **1937** Weidman *Wholesale* 43: Listen, you balloon-headed schmuck. **1940** Farrell *Father & Son* 585: Listen, you balloon head, I'm a Repub-

lican, and proud of it. **1957** Margulies *Punks* 45: You can't jump better than that, balloon-head? **1971** *Playboy* (June) 217: If the film bombs,...McQueen will be one more balloon-head movie star who meddled with directing. **1978** Pilcer *Teen Angel* 33: Hey, balloon-head!

balloon-hound *n. Mil.* a member of the crew of an observation balloon.

1918 Beston *Full Speed* 194: The balloon hounds are the whole show here.

balloon juice *n.* **1.** [pun on HOT AIR] empty or nonsensical talk.

1900 *DN* II 22: *Balloon-juice, n.* Empty, noisy talk [at Yale Univ.]. **1901** Irwin *Sonnets* (unp.): Murphy's handy spiel/Is cheap balloon juice of a Blarney brew. **1926** Maines & Grant *Wise-Crack Dict.* 5: *Balloon-juice*—Hot air. **1947** A. Reynolds *Home Sweet Homicide* 94: You're full of balloon juice. **1990** G. Keillor, in *New Yorker* (Oct. 20) 36: "That's a lot of balloon juice," said Zeus.

2. helium.

1943 *N.Y. Times Mag.* (Nov. 21) 39.

balloon soup *n.* [cf. BALLOON JUICE] nonsense, empty talk.

1928 Springs *Blue Sky* 258: I know you will say that I'm an Anglophile and that I bow down before the British and all that old balloon soup. **1930** *AS* VI 203: *Balloon soup:* term for an endeavor to fool someone.

ball out var. BAWL OUT.

ballpark *n.* **1.** an acceptable, expected, or approximate range.—constr. in phr. of the sort **in the ballpark.**

1957 in *AS* LI (1976) 121: I thought I would start with a figure that we could plus or minus a billion or so and be within the ball park. **1965** *S.F. Examiner Book Week* (Mar. 28) 6: NAL guaranteed Whalen an advance of $100,000, which is not bad for a first book. "The other bids were in the same ballpark," Whalen said. **1968** in *AS* LI (1976) 120: However, the figures I have indicate this pay-out "is in the ball park." **1969** *Current Slang* I & II 54: *In the ball park*, adj. Approximate but not exact.—Air Force Academy cadets. **1973** *Business Week* (Jan. 13) 88: Other experts regard [the figure] as high but not completely out of the ballpark. **1978** *L.A. Times* (Nov. 11) III 1: McDonald's first offer made on Monday was $1 million for two years, which kept the Mets in the bidding ballpark. **1990** *U.S. News & W.R.* (Mar. 5) 28: The $10–$20 billion range is the ballpark you have to work in.

2. one's home territory, regarded as giving an advantage over an opponent; (*hence*) field of expertise or knowledge; category.

1963 *S.F. Call-Bulletin* (Nov. 6) 51: Otherwise, they might find pockets of overbuilding in their own "ball park." **1971–72** Giovannitti *Medal* 41: We were in VC territory—in the enemy ball park. **1974** J. Robinson *Bed/Time/Story* 124: Well. Production crews—that's out of my ball park. **1975** in *AS* LI (1976) 120: We have no expertise; we should stay in our own ballpark. **1976** *Atlantic* (Jan. 1977) 79: The 707 is the plane with which British officials are happiest to see Concorde compared; Concorde, they argue, is in the same ball park. **1978** Univ. Tenn. grad. student: I'm afraid that's more your ballpark than mine. **1978** *Popular Science* (Sept.) 114: Saw quality is a whole different ball park from special features.

ballpark *adj.* [fr. BALLPARK, *n.*, 1] (of numbers, estimates, etc.) approximate. [Not used predicatively; see *AS* LI (1976), 118–22.]

1967 *Wall St. Journal* (June 7) 4: I think they accepted it as a guess. I thought it was a ball-park figure. **1973** *Time* (Nov. 3) 50: His uniform's cost? "Two thousand," said Elton. "But that's just a ballpark figure." **1976** Joan Didion, in *Harper's* (Oct.) 49: She goes up to her room and she's up there alone maybe three, four hours, ball-park figure, you aren't sure which. **1978** *Rolling Stone* (Dec. 28) 100: How much brains does it really take to be the brains behind Kiss? Less than Einstein, more than sweet potatoes would be my ballpark answer. **1984** Kagan & Summers *Mute Evidence* 397: We did it kind of wildlike. I'd be the first to say it's a ballpark number.

ballplayer *n.* [cf. *play ball* 'to cooperate' s.v. BALL[1], *n.*] *Und.* a person willing to cooperate with criminals for the sake of a bribe, business advantage, or the like.

1942–49 Goldin et al. *DAUL* 22: The D.A....was a ballplayer so the beef...was quashed. **1953** Manchester *City of Anger* 150: With a ballplayer, every step mattered. But...I'm no ballplayer. This a different racket. **1962–63** in Giallombardo *Soc. of Women* 200: *Ballplayer.* Anyone capable of being bribed or influenced into criminal activity.

balls *adj.* BALLSY; daring, audacious.—usu. considered vulgar.

Cf. syn. GUTS.

1984 M. Skinner *Red Flag* 93: The wall of Eagles is a scare tactic, a balls maneuver.

balls-ass *adj.* **1.** see BALLS-NAKED.—usu. considered vulgar. **2.** BALLSY. —usu. considered vulgar.

1967 Mailer *Vietnam* 99: The...hills...rang with ball's ass shooting.

balls-naked *adj.* (of a man) completely naked.—usu. considered vulgar. Also vars.

[*1915–22 Joyce *Ulysses* 610: See them there stark ballock-naked.] **1955** Graziano & Barber *Somebody Up There* 226: I'm on the scales, balls naked. **1958** Cooley *Run for Home* 153 [ref. to 1920's]: I see this miserable shit, ball-ass naked, hanging by his hands from the overhead beam. **1969** Linn & Pearl *Masque* 64: Dave reminded him that the first time they'd met he'd been balls naked. **1977** Berry *Kaiser* 106 [ref. to WWI]: We weren't the slightest bit self-conscious about sitting around balls-ass naked and drinking. **1978** Hamill *Dirty Laundry* 60: I said there is a pervert right outside your station house, Nolan. Balls-ass naked. *a*1989 in Kisseloff *Must Remember This* 437 [ref. to *ca*1918]: We just went balls naked...not a stitch on.

balls-out *adj.* [prob. from BALL[1], *n.*, 1; cf. *full balls* s.v. BALL[1], *n.*] **1.** all-out; at full speed.—usu. considered vulgar. Also as *adv.*

1942–45 in Campbell & Campbell *War Paint* 92: Balls Out. **1959** Searls *Big X* 167: Those guys were heroes, Zeke. They went balls-out. Nowadays we nibble at the fringes of danger...and draw back before anybody gets hurt. *Ibid.* 82: He'd be an idiot to go balls-out on his next hop. **1967–68** T. Wolfe *Kool-Aid* 88: A risk-all balls-out plunge into the unknown. **1973** Ace *Stand On It* 7: But just to qualify—just to get into the race—you got to wheel four laps around that old track, balls-out, in a tricked-up, fragile-ass racecar that weighs maybe fifteen hundred pounds or so. **1974** Blount *3 Bricks Shy* 117: You go balls-out. **1978** Diehl *Sharky's Machine* 79: After that, it's a balls-out race. **1980** W.C. Anderson *BAT-21* 161: This is a balls-out invasion....They ain't kidding around. **1983** A.J. Foyt, in *AutoWeek* (Sept. 5) 6: I'm used to balls-out running and wheel-to-wheel competition. **1993** *New Yorker* (Mar. 29) 62: Time was limited. And that's why they went balls out on the nuclear program.

2. *Mil.* BALLSY; tough and aggressive.—usu. considered vulgar.

1969 Broughton *Thud Ridge* 86: The true fighter pilot must have that balls-out attitude that immediately makes him someone suspect to his superiors. **1982** *Atlantic* (May) 66: Richard V. Allen...recalls hearing Haldeman describe Howard Hunt that summer as a "balls-out" CIA operative. **1985** Bodey *F.N.G.* 239: He tells us Prophet was balls-out when he first came, that he really does deserve the Silver Star. **1990** Niemann *Boomer* 131: Just balls-out, roaring, fighting drunks.

balls-to-the-wall *adj.* Esp. *Mil.* all-out, unrestrained, with maximum effort; at top speed.—usu. considered vulgar.

1966–67 Harvey *Air War* 144: You know what happened on that first Doomsday Mission (as the boys call a big balls-to-the-wall raid) against Hanoi oil. *Ibid.* 150: You're in good hands with Gen. Disosway as long as you go in on those targets balls to the wall. **1969** *Current Slang* I & II 6: *Balls to the wall*, adj. Putting out maximum effort.—Air Force Academy cadets. **1979** Former USAF aircrewman, age 45: *Balls-to-the-wall* flying is full throttle. I've always thought that it referred to the ball-topped throttle in a piston-engined plane being pushed all the way forward till it nearly touches the firewall. **1980** Santoli *Everything* 224: The Vietnamese Marines got together a huge armored force...and went balls to the wall up the Cua Viet River to cut the NVA off. **1983** Groen & Groen *Huey* 32: Arata took off—balls to the wall. **1985** *Campus Voice* (Apr.) 23: It was raw, balls-to-the-wall energy. **1992** *Nation* (Apr. 27) 567: [The songs feel] curiously static, reassuringly timeless, almost ahistorical....The contrast with the sheer balls-to-the-wall dynamics of the performance is enormous.

balls-to-the-walls *adj.* [cf. S.E. *(one's) back to the wall*] desperate.—usu. considered vulgar.

*a*1989 C.S. Crawford *Four Deuces* 64 [ref. to Korean War]: The captain and the Funny Gunny have been balls to the walls ever since our last cryptographer left. *Ibid.* 106: We were in a balls-to-the-walls situation. **1989** Eble *College Slang* 34: *Balls to the walls* A tense...situation which requires the ability to fight back. "From now until the end of the month, it's balls to the walls."

balls-to-the-wind *adv.* at top speed.—usu. considered vulgar.

1983 "J. Cain" *Dinky-Dau* 139: Drop it and fly balls-to-the-wind to his assistance.

balls-up *n.* [prob. from *ball up*, *v.* infl. by BALL[1], *n.*, 1] Esp. *Mil.* a botch, a fiasco.—usu. considered vulgar. Cf. BALL-UP.

1934 Yeates *Winged Victory* 220 [ref. to 1918]: A fairly easy shot...which I...made a bawls-up of. **1939 Hemingway *Sel. Letters* 498: I think the biggest balls up in history would have resulted from his gigantic tank offensive projected for 1919. **1977** in L. Bangs *Psychotic Reactions* 231: I...commenced my second misinformed balls-up of the evening. *a*1979 in S. King *Bachman* 380: Abraham, how did you get into a balls-up like this? **1983** Elting et al. *Soldier Talk* 17: *Balls-up*...Total, pointless confusion.

ballsy *adj.* [BALL[1], *n.*, 4 + *-y*] **1.** audacious; spirited; spunky.—usu. considered vulgar.

1935 Algren *Boots* 183: I don't keep nobody, ballsy. **1966** Braly *On Yard* 179: Six years ago I was still pretty ballsy. **1970** *Playboy* (Nov.) 262: A ballsy girl with whom he's having a relationship. **1971** A. Goldman, in *Atlantic* (Feb.) 106: Jazz was "loose," "groovy," "hip," "ballsy," "funky," "soulful," dwn to the "nitty-gritty" long before the current generation was born. **1977** Coover *Public Burning* 7: That ballsy Greek girl of long ago. **1981** *Maclean's* (Mar. 30) 62: Gray's ballsy verses are not only signs of our times—they're the only way to play this game.

2. virile and aggressive; brave in a manly way.—usu. considered vulgar.

1966 Manus *Mott the Hoople* 70: At least you're men, there's something ballsy about you. **1967** Dibner *Admiral* 227: Not a salty swashbuckling ballsy pirate like Hardtack Harry Paige. **1973** Vincent Price, in *N.Y. Post* (May 5) 15: Revenge is one of these great ballsy things.... "You killed my wife and now I'm going to kill you." **1980** Santoli *Everything* 96: This one guy, Clare—...Ballsiest motherfucker I had ever seen.

ballum rancum *n.* [pseudo-L, 'rank ball'] an orgiastic dance, as engaged in by prostitutes and their customers at a brothel. [The **1788 quot. is a note added by Grose to the second edition of his book.]

1677–78 in J. Dryden *Dramatic Works* IV 339: We'll divide the Estate betwixt us, and have fresh Wenches, and *Ballum Rankum* every night. **1684 T. Otway *Atheist* III: A bawdy Dancing-School: some better Whores than ordinary designing a private *Ballum rancum*. **1785 Grose *Vulgar Tongue*: *Ballum Rancum*, a hop or dance, where the women are all prostitutes, a dance at a brothel. **1788 Grose *Vulgar Tongue* (ed. 2): *Ballum Rancum*...N.B. The company dance in their birth-day suits. **1822 Waln *Hermit in Phila.* 30: *Ripe for fun—hot water conventions* or *Ballum-Rancums!*

ball-up *n.* [fr. the *v.*] a confused or muddled situation. Cf. BALLS-UP.

1900 *DN* II 17: Nouns derived from verbs and modifying adverbs, as *ball-up*. **1927** J. Stevens *Mattock* 92: There was a ball-up as a lot of us started forward with the first squad instead of going squads right. *Ibid.* 186: What the hell's all this ball-up in the replacements' service records, sergeant? **1952** in *DAS*: The ball-up abroad has been supervised by Harry's advisers.

ball up *v.* [semantic devel. obscure] **1.** *Intrans.* to become confused or muddled.

1856 B.H. Hall *College Wds.* 19: *Ball up.* At Middlebury College, to fail at recitation or examination. **1900** *DN* II 22: *Ball-up*, *v.i.* To become confused [reported from 66 different colleges]. **1961** *WNID3*: *Ball up...vi* to get balled up: become badly muddled or confused.

2. *Trans.* to confuse or muddle badly, esp. mentally; to mix up; to entangle oneself (with).—esp. as *ppl. adj.* **balled up** confused; (*hence*) mentally unbalanced.

1884 in Lummis *Letters* 53: That knapsack balls me all up. **1885** "M. Twain," in *Letters* II 465: I heard a canvasser say, yesterday, that while delivering eleven books he took 7 new subscriptions. But we shall be in a hell of a fix if that goes on—it will "ball up" the binderies again. **1887** *Harper's Mag.* (Sept.) 605: "You seem balled up about something."..."Balled up!...I'm done for." **1895** Gore *Stu. Slang* 12: He tried to explain the problem but he got all balled up. **1896** Ade *Artie* 57: She had him balled up till he couldn't say a word. **1900** *DN* II 22: *Ball-up*, *v.t.* To confuse [reported from 40 different colleges]. **1901** Ade *Modern Fables* 181: He wears out a pencil or two and gets all Balled Up. **1907** Siler *Pugilism* 24: The average referee, however, gets "balled up" to the extent he either crowds eight seconds into ten, or stretches his ten count into twelve or more seconds. **1908** in "O. Henry" *Comp. Stories* 1495: Pardon me,...but you got balled up in the shuffle, didn't you? **1915** Lardner *Gullible* 29: They got it all balled up the night I seen it....The actors forgot their lines and a man couldn't make heads or tails of it. **1918** Mencken *Amer. Lang.* 142: *Balled up* and its verb, to *ball* *up*, were originally somewhat improper, no doubt on account of the slang significance of *ball*, but of late they have made steady progress toward polite acceptance. **1920** Fitzgerald *Paradise* 133: He's got me all balled up. I've misjudged him. **1931** Dos Passos *1919* 279: Bud…had gotten balled up with a girl in Galveston who was trying to blackmail him. **1933** E. Caldwell *God's Acre* 141: Too many men talking will get you all balled up, and you won't know which way is straight up and which is straight down. **1934** in Fenner *Throttle* 67: There wasn't even a chance of getting another engine out to take that special, see? It might ball things up worse than ever if they tried. **1936** Dos Passos *Big Money* 40: He got all balled up…and ended by telling her he'd come. **1939** *New Directions* 139: You're all balled up, dicky bird. **1942** R. Casey *Torpedo Junction* 17: Plane traffic was…balled up. **1947** Overholser *Buckaroo's Code* 161: We was all balled up in our thinking. **1952** Randolph & Wilson *Dawn in Holler* 103: *Balled-up*…is still in bad taste in the Ozarks (because of a presumed sexual origin). **1953–57** Giovannitti *Combine D* 117: He's all balled up, just like me, but about different things. **1957** Fuchs & Levine *Jeanne Eagels* (film): Sometimes I wonder. I get all balled up. How's it gonna be? **1957** *Father Knows Best* (CBS-TV): She's selling the house, and got it all balled up, and going up there to straighten things out. **1959** Bechet *Treat It Gentle* 132 [ref. to 1921]: "Your Honour, I'm all balled up." That's what I said.…But my God, you should have seen the judge. Later, it was explained to me: in England, *all balled up*, that's a bad expression, it's a hell of a thing to say, you just don't use it.

3. *Trans.* to botch, spoil, ruin, or impair.
   1915 T.A. Dorgan, in *N.Y. Eve. Jour.* (Aug. 3) 10: You balled me up with that dame. **1918** "M. Brand" *Harrigan* 111: Are you going to let one stranger ball up our game? **1925** Mullin *Scholar Tramp* 123: His childhood was tragically "balled up" by circumstances which had branded him with…passionate bitterness. **1927** *AS* II 348: If he goes to town this evening he will ball everything up. **1930** "D. Stiff" *Milk & Honey* 66: The hobo went to the doctor man,/"I'm all balled up," said he,/"Give me some pills, and to wash them down,/Some Three-Star Hennessy." **1934** Cain *Postman* 44: It was those tests for being drunk. If they gave me the gas first, that would ball up the breath test, the most important one. **1975** Univ. Tenn. student: The rain really balled up our vacation.

bally *n.* [by shortening] **1.** *Circus & Carnival.* BALLYHOO².
   1929 *Sat. Eve. Post* (Oct. 12) 29: *Bally*. Ballyhoo, or anything to draw a crowd. **1934** Weseen *Dict. Slang* 135: *Bally*—Ballyhoo; advertising. **1942** *ATS* 622: *Bally, ballyhoo*, a talk or demonstration outside a show to attract a crowd. **1946** Dadswell *Hey, Sucker* 129: To classify her as "The Outdoor Show Girl" would be as far from reality as to say that any one bally-girl or line-girl or fan-dancer, is a composite of this whole fascinating scene. **1951** Mannix *Sword-Swallower* 5: Why, you'll be giving another bally in a week. **1953** Gresham *Midway* 4: *Bally:* a sample performance of a show given on a platform in front of the tent. The platform itself; the people in the sample performance. **1961** Clausen *Season's Over* 27 [ref. to ca1945]: Bally broads were the girls who did the "ballyhoo" out front to bring the townspeople in.

2. *Circus & Carnival.* a stand or platform from which a barker advertises a show and on which a sample performance of the show may be given. In full, **bally stand**. [It is possible that *bally* here orig. represents a dial. pronun. of *ballet*.]
   1921 Casey & Casey *Gay-Cat* (glossary): *Spiel*—the talk made on the bally stand. **1931** *Amer. Mercury* (Nov.) 351: *Bally, n.:* The platform in front of the sideshow. **1942** *ATS* 617: *Bally, bally stand*, the platform in front of a show on which a "ballyhoo" lecture or free exhibition is given. *a*1953 in *AS* XXVIII 114: *Bally cloth, n.* Canvas or cloth used to cover the lower portion of a stand. **1972** *Playboy* (Feb.) 76: A big woman…mounted a bally and began barking: "…See the Human Pincushion!"

¶ In phrase:

¶ **tip the bally** *Circus & Carnival.* to upset one's plans, to "upset the applecart."
   1956 H. Gold *Not With It* 257: I know you now, Bud. She really tipped the bally on you. You want to be Joy's good little husband.

bally *adj. & adv.* [app. BALL¹, *n.*, 2 + *-y*, of arbitrary application] "darned".—used as a euphem. for BLOODY.
   *1885 in OEDS 193. **1889* Barrère & Leland *Dict. Slang* I 71: *Bally* (society), a word in use among the young men of the present day to emphasise a speech. Coined by the *Sporting Times*, from the Irish word "bally-hooly." It is mostly used as a euphemism for "bloody." **1899** F. Norris *Blix* 225: Billy…clum up in that bally pulpit. *Ibid.* 289: Our Mug

an' Billy get a schooner that's so bally small. **1900** [Willard & Hodler] *Powers* 183: I'm gettin' bally tired o' hearin' you whine. **1908** Paine *Stroke Oar* 180: You have walked into his affections…with your bally scratch crew of Dutchmen. **1920** Kemp *Chanteys* 27: I hate the bally Bo'sun, and all the bally crew.

bally *v.* [fr. BALLYHOO²] *Circus & Carnival.* to ballyhoo; to lure (a crowd) by ballyhooing.
   1927 Nicholson *Barker* 102: Bally—To drum up a crowd. **1931** *Amer. Mercury* (Nov.) 351: *Bally*…v. to spiel in front of a show. **1970** A. Lewis *Carnival* 12: But I can't distinguish a single word even though I know he's ballying William Durks.

ballyhack *n.* ruin, destruction. Also vars. [Taken to be a euphem. for *hell*.]
   1843 [W.T. Thompson] *Scenes in Ga.* 77: To blow all [his] cherished notions to Ballyhack. *ca*1845 W.T. Thompson *Chron. Pineville* 77, in *DAE:* It was just the easiest thing…to blow…all…notions to Ballyhack. **1845** Judd *Margaret* 55, in *DAE:* "Obed is here too." "Let Obed go to Ballyhack. Come along out." **1848** Bartlett *Americanisms: Ballyhack.* "Go to Ballyhack!" A common expression in New England. I know not its origin. It savors in sound, however, of the Emerald Isle. **1895** *DN* I 396: He knocked the plate all to ballyhack. **1905** *DN* III 3: *Ballyhack* or *ballywack, n.* to go to Ballyhack is to go to hell. **1908** *DN* III 288: I wish he was in *Ballyhack*…."Go to Ballyhack!" **1929–30** Dos Passos *42d Parallel* 147: Everything was well on its way to ballyhack. **1934** *WNID2: Ballyhack…ballywack…ballywrack…n.* Ruin; destruction; perdition. *Slang.*

ballyhoo¹ *n.* [app. < Sp *balahú* 'schooner'] *Naut.* an unseaworthy or slovenly ship. Also **ballyhoo of blazes**. Also vars.
   1836 *Knickerbocker* (Aug.) 203: Jack Marlinspike, who had been first dickey of an Indiaman, couldn't get a situation afore the mast of a Ballyhoo coasting brig. **1847** Melville, in *AS* XX 184: Be off wid ye, thin, darlints, and steer clear of the likes of this ballyhoo of blazes as long as ye live. **1849** Melville *White Jacket* 28: On board your greasy ballyhoo of blazes? **1867** G.E. Clark *Sailor's Life* 224: We lay here…with half steam up, watching the old ballyhoos behind the fort. **1885** H.H. Clark *Boy Life in USN* 131: Isn't this a good deal better than to be shut up all day in an old ballyhoo? **1893* Wawn *South Sea Islanders* 310: The *Lizzie* was the worst old "ballahoe" for sailing that I ever put my foot on board of. **1897** Kipling *Capts. Courageous* 89: This bally-hoo's not the *Ohio*. *Ibid.* 270: Instid of this bally-hoo o' blazes. **1899** Robbins *Gam* 88: The old ballahoo settled away.

ballyhoo² *n.* [orig. unkn.; see note] *Circus & Carnival.* **1.** a flamboyant free performance given outside a circus or carnival attraction, in an attempt to lure customers to buy tickets for the show inside. [Although the idea of "sham" seems to be present in the 1880 quot. below, the quotation's actual relevance to other appearances of the word is unclear. No connection has been demonstrated between this word and the nautical BALLYHOO¹, or the Irish village of Ballyhooly; for inconclusive discussions, see *AS* X (1935), 289–91; XX (1945), 184–86; XL (1965), 32–39; and cf. Partridge *DSUE* s.v. *ballyhooly*.]
   [**1880** *Harper's* (July) 217: He fired, and brought down a clever composition of wood and pasteboard. Subsequent references to the "ballyhoo bird" were never relished by the victim of the practical joke.] **1901** *World's Work* (Aug.) 1100: First there is the ballyhoo—any sort of a performance outside the show, from the coon songs of the pickaninnies in front of the Old Plantation, to the tinkling tamborines of the dancers on the stage of "Around the World." **1910** *Variety* (Aug. 20) 12: The act of "The Maid of Mystery" is performed in the street.…But New York…is too big for a "ballyhoo" of this sort. **1915** in *DN* IV 204: Some famous bonehead plays have been pulled in this city [Lincoln, Nebr.], but no council ever equalled the record of the present commissioners in turning loose a crowd of tent show freaks and ballyhoo artists and pop corn sellers on the principal street, only a short distance from the retail business center, and inviting them to do their worst. **1926** *AS* I 282: *Ballyhoo*—The free exhibition of a few attractions in front of the kid show [i.e., sideshow] to draw patronage. *Bally stand*—The platform upon which they appear. **1934** *Billboard* (Dec. 29) 178: And it was at [the Columbian Exposition of 1893 at] Chicago that a number of words long since in use were formed and given meanings. The word "ballyhoo" being the keynote of the carnival business was one of the first to be used on the midway. **1946** Dadswell *Hey, Sucker* 26: I…firmly believe that the midway with its giddy rides and bedlam of noisy ballyhoo is an institution in this country.

2. a barker's noisy advertising pitch promoting a circus or carnival attraction; (*hence*) noisy, flamboyant, or vulgar publicity or advertising of any kind; self-praise; insincere talk. Now *S.E.*

1901 Bull *Flashes* 42: My ballyhoo will draw the crowd. **1908** *Sat. Eve. Post* (Nov. 21) 25: It is the practice of almost every statesman to prepare the country for his performance by beating the drum and blatting a few lines of ballyhoo. **1910** *Variety* (Aug. 20) 12: The "ballyhoo" is not for vaudeville. **1917** *Editor* (Feb. 24) 154: *Spiel*, or *Ballyhoo*—a talk. **1918** Mencken *Amer. Lang.* 92: Again, there is the very characteristic American word *ballyhoo*, signifying the harangue of a *ballyhoo-man*, or *spieler* (that is, barker) before a cheap show, or, by metaphor, any noisy speech. It is (presumably) from Ballyhooly, the name of a village in Cork, once notorious for its brawls. **1930** in R.E. Howard *Iron Man* 20: You could help me better than anyone else—you know the ballyhoo. **1934** Weseen *Dict. Slang* 229: *Ballyhoo*—Publicity in advance of a prizefight. *Ibid.* 305: *Ballyhoo*—Advertising harangue, either oral or printed. Extravagant praise of an article in an effort to sell it. Any speech that is regarded as insincere or motivated by selfish interest. **1936** Washburn *Parlor* 87: That was first-rate ballyhoo, later copied by the cinema to herald rube pictures and stunt stuff. **1938** "E. Queen" *4 Hearts* 47: And to the tune of the loudest ballyhoo you've ever blasted out of this studio. **1939** in Moriarty *True Confessions* 85: Our show…is just what the ballyhoo says. **1942** Liebling *Telephone* 11: The volcano was visible from all parts of the midway, a great ballyhoo for the village. **1952** J.B. Martin *Life in Crime* 20: It was right after the war and during the war there'd been a lot of ballyhoo about the uniforms and everything else, that probably had something to do with [my enlisting in the navy]. **1956** in Loosbrock & Skinner *Wild Blue* 114: But I am not thinking of the "ballyhoo era" from mid-1927 on. **1984** *N.Y. Times Bk. Review* (Jan. 1) 20: In Detroit he put the old Hollywood ballyhoo on four wheels.

3. a barker at a circus or carnival.

1915 *Variety* (June 4) 5: Dick Martin [is] the raucous ballyhoo. **1922** Fitzgerald *Beautiful & Damned* 96: At eighteen he was a side show ballyhoo; later, the manager of the side show. **1922–24** McIntyre *White Light Nights* 232: It is the ballyhoo's job to fill the lumbering vehicles.

ballyhoo[3] *n.* [orig. unkn.] BALLYHACK.

1883–84 Whittaker *L. Locke* 196: 'Tis the thafe! Give him ballyhoo, b'ys!

ballyhoo *v.* [fr. the n.] **1.** *Circus & Carnival.* to perform ballyhoo; to perform an act in the open air. Hence **ballyhooer**, *n.*

1901 in *DA:* Last of the professions on the Midway are those of the "barker," "ballyhooer" and "spieler." **1910** *Variety* (Aug. 13) 4: [Playing to a street audience] is called "ballyhooing." **1912** in Mencken *New Ltrs.* 38: Wright will do some bally-hooing out on the coast. **1922** N. Anderson *Hobo:* These organizations are generally financed by solicitations. Men and women are employed to canvass places of business; to "drum" on the streets and to make house-to-house calls. This practice of "drumming" on the streets is known as "ballyhooing."

2. to advertise boisterously and flamboyantly; to praise extravagantly, as with ballyhoo. Now *S.E.*

1922 *Collier's* (Mar. 4) 7: I don't like to ballyhoo myself, Mickey, but here's a picture which will make you and Mr. D. Griffith bite your nails. **1929–31** Runyon *Guys & Dolls* 134: I figure it is some kind of advertising dodge put on…to ballyhoo the circus. **1935** Coburn *Law Rides Range* 78: That gyp-artist he's ballyhooing for District Attorney. **1980** Manchester *Darkness* 64: Signs ballyhoo…Male-Female Sexantics!

balmy *n.* a drunk.

1857 (quot. at CUT, *adj.*).

baloney *n.* [pop. pronun. of *bologna*] **1.** an oafish, stupid, or clumsy person; idiot; worthless individual; (*occ.*) a slut. Also vars.

1920 *Collier's* (June 5) 10: Kane Halliday, alias Kid Roberts, had won his first professional fight by knocking out a boloney with the *nom du ring* of Young Du Fresne. **1920–21** Witwer *Leather Pushers* 41: That's for you to know some boloney at this fight club here. *Ibid.* 67: Rocky Martin and Sailor McGann, them two boloneys of his. **1925** *Collier's* (Jan. 24) 23: You rich boloneys think you own the ocean. **1926** Dunning & Abbott *Broadway* 247: The big baloney never had anything to do with it. **1928** in Blackbeard & Williams *Smithsonian Comics* 154: There's that overstuffed boloney back here again. **1930** Bodenheim *Roller Skates* 256: Keep out of this, you boloney. **1929–31** J.T. Farrell *Young Lonigan* 90: All Studs had to do to get the place, for himself and

Lucy, was to clean up on a couple of big boloneys, that owned it. **1931** Uhler *Cane Juice* 325: He's the big boloney of the outfit. **1932** Nicholson & Robinson *Sailor Beware* 120: Say, pipe down, you baloneys. **1935** Odets *Waiting for Lefty:* You gutless piece of baloney. **1944** *AS* XIX 104: A woman who is neither your sister nor your mother is a *dingbat*, a *baloney*, or a *split-tail.* **1992** *Simpsons* (Fox-TV): I don't know where it is, ya baloney!

2. [poss. infl. by *blarney*] humbug, pretentious nonsense; foolishness.

1922 *Variety* (June 30) 6: The local papers are full of baloney about the pennant. **1926** Dunning & Abbott *Broadway* 218: You know what I mean, dazzled—and then suddenly they get wise to themselves that the whole works is a lot of boloney and they realize where the real guys in this world is at—. **1926** Maines & Grant *Wise-Crack Dict.* 10: *Lots of bologna*—Gross exaggeration. **1927** in Robinson *Comics* 67: That's a lotta boloney! An' no matter how you slice it it's still boloney! **1927** *Amer. Legion Mo.* (Apr.) 38: The first slice of bolony. **1929** Cruze *Great Gabbo* (film): Bowing down, clicking his heels, and all of that imported baloney. **1929** Brecht *Downfall* 172: Boloney, Maggie. *Ibid.* 215: No matter how thin you cut it, it's still boloney. **1930** Bodenheim *Roller Skates* 31: See what kind of boloney he pulls. **1930** Rogers & Adler *Chump at Oxford* (film): That's a lot of baloney. **1933** "W. March" *Co. K* 145: I believed all the baloney you're talking now. **1936** Sandburg *People, Yes* 160: No matter how thick or how thin you slice it, it's still baloney. **1954** G. Kersh, in Pohl *Star of Stars* 24: Baloney! What you say might go for philosophers, and all that. **1964** *Dick Van Dyke Show* (CBS-TV): Aw, hereditary! Baloney! **1966** J. Mills *Needle Park* 124: A bunch of boloney. **1969** Eastlake *Bamboo* 260: Christians believe in the brotherhood of man and all that baloney. Just baloney. Words that mean nothing. **1971** Faust *Willy* 73: She took my hand right away, with no phony boloney. **1983** *Rolling Stone* (Feb. 3) 10: There's a big mystique about computers, but it's a lot of baloney. **1990** *U.S. News & W.R.* (May 28) 26: One of my best things is baloney.…I'm a good liar.

3. a penis; in phr. **hide the baloney** to copulate.—usu. considered vulgar. *Joc.* Cf. MEAT.

1928 in Oliver *Blues Tradition* 178: His boloney's certainly worth a try,/ Never fails to satisfy. **1934** H. Roth *Call It Sleep* 357: Tell 'er wut I wuz doin', kid.…We wuz hidin' de balonee! **1941** in Legman *Limerick* 121: "What's it got,/My dear, that I've not?"/Sighed she, "Just a yard-long bologna." **1983** Flaherty *Tin Wife* 238: It was never love but "hide the bologna time." **1983** J. Hughes *Nat. Lampoon's Vacation* (film): You ever bop your baloney? **1986–89** Norse *Memoirs* 421: You and your big bologna.

4. an automobile tire.

1930 *Amer. Mercury* (Dec.) 454: *Baloney, n.:* An automobile tire. "Go glom me two baloneys for me boat." **1942** *AS* (Apr.) 102: *Bolognas.* Tires. **1971** Tak *Truck Talk* 7: *Baloneys:* truck tires. **1976** *Nat. Lampoon* (July) 93: I just ran by a basket case with just his *baloneys* left.

5. *Construction.* a very heavy cable of any kind.

1944 *AS* XIX 230: *Baloney.* Electric cable for traveling cranes. **1958** McCulloch *Woods Words* 7: *Baloney*—a. Very fat electric cable…[or] a very big skyline. **1959** *AS* XXXIV 76: *Baloney, n.* The large wire rope used in logging.

¶ In phrase: **hide the baloney** see **(3),** above.

baloney-bender *n.* one who habitually flatters or talks nonsense.

1926 Maines & Grant *Wise-Crack Dict.* 5: *Bologna bender*—Thrower of so-called bull. **1937** Weidman *Wholesale* 54: To a baloney bender this is what's known as making a virtue out of a necessity. To me it's just using your head for something else besides a brace to keep your ears apart. **1971** Berg *Sick World* 74: Oh, oh, here comes that old baloney bender.…All he does is flatter. **1980** N.Y.C. man, age *ca*50: That guy's such a baloney-bender.

balonus *n.* [*balon*ey + -*us*, pseudo-L suffix] nonsense, BALONEY, 2. *Joc.*

1929 in Runyon *Guys & Dolls* 67: Of course this message is nothing but the phonus bolonus. **1941** Phillips *Pvt. Purkey* 58: Washington says the report is strictly balonus. **1972** *Nat. Lampoon* (Apr.) 20: Extra Added Balonus!

Baltimore beefsteak *n.* *U.S. Nav. Acad.* calf's liver. *Joc.*

1941 *Guide to U.S. Nav. Acad.* 149: *Baltimore Beefsteak*—Calves liver, so to speak.

Baltimore chop *n.* *Baseball.* a sharply batted ball that strikes the ground at or in front of home plate and bounces high in the air.

1910 *Baseball Mag.* (Apr.) 61 (cited in Nichols *Baseball Term.*). **1942** *ATS* 655: *Baltimore chop,* a bounder that strikes the plate and bounces high in the air. **1950** Cleveland *Great Mgrs.* 22: The Orioles also developed a neat bit of baseball known as the "Baltimore chop." **1976** in *Webster's Sports Dict.* **1993** N.Y.C. man, age *ca*40: A *Baltimore chop* is when the batter tops [the ball] and it goes way up in the air after a bounce.

Baltimore Whore *n.* [the planes were designed by the Martin Aircraft Corp. of Baltimore, Md.] *USAF.* the Martin B-26 Marauder medium bomber. Now *hist.*

1970 Model aircraft hobbyist, N.Y.C.: The B-26 was called the Baltimore Whore because it was a very hard airplane to fly. **1983** Elting, Cragg & Deal *Soldier Talk* 17: *Baltimore Whore* (World War II)…The B-26 medium bomber.

Balto *n.* [by shortening; orig. a written abbr. taken over into speech] Baltimore, Md.

1864 in C.H. Moulton *Ft. Lyon* 169: I shall go to Washington or Balto. tomorrow. **1914** H.L. Mencken, in Riggio *Dreiser-Mencken Letters* I 136: Publisher of the Balto. Sun. **1926** (quot. at LEGIT). **1936** *Esquire* (Sept.) 165: Balto correspondent. **1943** in P. McGuire *Jim Crow Army* 19: I were the first Balto. boy to be drafted into the Army. **1976** Adcock *Not Truckers Only* 45: A Tale of Two Cottonpickers…Stepping Out to Balto.

BAM *n.* [*b*road-*a*ssed *m*arine] a woman in the U.S. Marine Corps.—usu. considered offensive.

1948 Taylor *Language of WWII* 29: *Bams:* The almost universal term used by GI's to refer to women marines. The derivation is not printable! **1954** Crockett *Bastards* 107 [ref. to WWII]: "I knew a Bam from Baltimore." Her eyebrows went up. "Bam?" "Broad-assed—…Skip it." **1959** Cochrell *Beaches* 251 [ref. to WWII]: He had been drunk the night he told her why women marines were called BAMs. **1972** Meade & Rutledge *Belle* 122: We might even ask the Marines…for a detachment of BAMS. **1980** McDowell *Our Honor* 81: Women Marines—known throughout the Corps as BAMS, an unflattering acronym for Broad-Assed Marines. **1986** Merkin *Zombie Jamboree* 259: Art, did you know any BAMs? **1991** Dunnigan & Bay *From Shield to Storm* 360: Kuwait War Slang…*BAM*—Big-Assed Marine (female Marine).

Bam *n.* Alabama. Cf. BAMA.

1907 in Sampson *Ghost Walks* 391: The Man from Bam. **1914** in Handy *Blues Treasury* 76: Letters come from down in "Bam." **1942** *Amer. Mercury* (July) 34: *Bam,* and *down in Bam*—down South.

bam[1] *n.* [orig. unkn.; cf. BAMBOOZLE] an imposture, "put-on." *Rare* in U.S.

*1725 *New Canting Dict.*: A Bam, a Sham or Cheat; a knavish Contrivance to amuse or deceive. ***1728** in *OED:* He called the Profession of a Doctorship, in Physic, a *Bamm,* upon the world, which is a *Bite,* in modern language. ***1762** in *OED* I 645: He is all upon his fun; he lecture! Why, 'tis all but a bam. ***1815** Walter Scott *Guy Mannering,* in *OED:* Humble efforts at jocularity chiefly confined to what were then called bites and bams, since denominated hoaxes and quizzes. ***1821–26** Stewart *Man-of-War's-Man* I 147: Some stout hearts there were, indeed, who seemed to think the story all a bamm, and even volunteered to go and sit in the top until the ghost made its appearance. **1838** [Haliburton] *Clockmaker* (Ser. 2) 80: I thought I should have snorted right out to hear the little critter run on with such a regular bam. ***1874** in *F & H* I (rev.) 124: That tale of Gordon Frere was all a bam.

bam[2] *n.* [orig. unkn.] *Narc.* **1.** a cigarette made from low-grade marijuana. Also **bammy.**

1952 Weston *Narcotics U.S.A.* 275: *Bams.* Weak marijuana cigarettes. **1953** W. Brown *Monkey on My Back* 83: But the effects of the bammies they were smoking were largely psychological. **1956** E. Hunter *Second Ending* 252: "From cheap bammies you can pick up at about three for a quarter—" "Bammies?" "Low-grade marijuana." **1959** Murtagh & Harris *In Shadow* 93: One dollar for three "Bams," weak marijuana cigarettes.

2. a pill, such as a diet pill, containing an amphetamine.

1970 Landy *Underground Dict.* 28: *Bam*…Amphetamine. **1972** Mills *Report* 96: *Bams* are glass ampules of an amphetamine junkies like to mix with heroin. **1975** De Mille *Smack Man* 117: *Bam*…an amphetamine capsule. **1981** *Wash. Post* (July 26) A14: He prefers "bam," the street name for Preludin—a prescription diet pill that some persons use as a heroin booster or substitute. **1981** *U.S. News & W.R.* (Nov. 23) 42: Officers pose as peddlers of "bam," the slang term for a diet pill used to intensify heroin jags. **1982** *Harper's* (Apr.) 86: Billy shared with the jury his terrible drug problem, and admitted that he got into that stranger's

car to buy BAM (phenmetrazine).

bam *v.* [cf. BAMBOOZLE] to hoax or impose upon. Also absol.

*1707 Cibber *Double Gallants* 71: *Saun*….I never mind Accounts; I don't understand 'em. *Sir Sol.* Pray, Sir, what is't you do understand? *Saun.* Bite, Bam, and the best of the Lay, old Boy. ***1738** J. Swift *Polite Con.* III: Bam for Bamboozle, and Bamboozle for God knows what. ***1760** in *F & H* I 112: We shall certainly bam the old gentleman. *ca*1777 in Silber *Songs of Independence* 165: Brave sailors are wiser than thus to be bambed. ***1830** Marryat, in *F & H* I 112: Now, you're bamming me—don't attempt to put such stories off on your old granny. **1838** [Haliburton] *Clockmaker* (Ser. 2) 159: How the critters were bammed by that hoax. *Ibid.* 173: Oh, Mr. Slick,…how you bam!

Bama *n.* Alabama; the University of Alabama. Cf. BAM. Also dial.

1941 *Pittsburgh Courier* (Apr. 19) 17: 'Bama's Team Rated Threat. **1944** *Yank* (Jan. 28) 14: Well, who…won the game? Yea 'Bama! **1944** in Himes *Black on Black* 200: I done picked all over. From 'Bama to Maine. **1956** in Rowan *Go South* 165: Keep 'Bama white. **1968** Lockridge *Hartspring* 57: You 'Bama cutie. **1979** Charyn *7th Babe* 288: The caravan drove to a spot near the 'Bama state line. **1985** Boyne & Thompson *Wild Blue* 209: A set of two granddaddy Bama thunderstorms.

bambi *n.* [fr. *Bambi,* deer protagonist of Walt Disney's film *Bambi* (1942)] *Adver.* a trained animal, esp. a house pet, used in a television commercial.

1979 Homer *Jargon* 85: Perhaps the most famous *bambi* was Nine-Lives' Morris the Cat.

bamboo *n.* **1.** *Narc.* a bamboo pipe used for the smoking of opium.

1899 Ade *Chicago Stories* 249: Me settin' around on my shoulder-blades lookin' like one o' these bamboo boys full o' the hop. **1915** (quot. at SLEIGHRIDING). **1926** *N.Y. Times* (Oct. 10) VIII 20: They idle in "sucking the bamboo" (smoking opium). **1936** Dai *Opium* 196: *Bamboo.* Opium pipe.

2. [sugg. by GRAPEVINE; cf. BAMBOO TELEGRAPH] *Mil. in Far East.* a rumor, as spread by word-of-mouth through a jungle. Also semi-adj.; (also) BAMBOO TELEGRAPH.

1899 Markey *Iowa to Phils.* 244: Dinner over, the shacks are again filled and the "bamboo reports" and arguments begin afresh. *Ibid.* 253: Aguinaldo, so the "bamboo" stated, had declared…he would establish his headquarters and sleep in San Fernando. *Ibid.* 264: The good news was immediately communicated to the officers and men, the former assembling at regimental headquarters in order to handle the precious documents and assure themselves that it was not "bamboo." **1982** F. Hailey *Soldier Talk* 3: *Bamboo.* Latrine rumor ("I heard it on the 'Bamboo'")…Bamboo wireless.

bamboo *adj. Mil. in East Asia.* **1.** (see quot.).

1913 *Review of Reviews* (Aug.) 201: With the soldier, anything that belonged peculiarly to the Philippines was described as "bamboo":…the "bamboo government" is the Philippine civil government in distinction from the U.S. military.

2. (of a Westerner) having become completely acclimated to Eastern Asia and given up Western ways.

1931 *Our Army* (Oct.) 35: What do they care for the Service I knew/ Late Issue troopers who call me "Bamboo." **1931** *Our Army* (Nov.) 13: Of course, Jasper came to be known as Brown, the "bamboo" barber, because he lived with a native woman. **1941** in Thomason *Stories* 437: You'd better be some kind of bamboo American, drifting around, making a survey or something. **1942** White *Expendable* 71: There was, for instance, a bamboo American—some man who'd married a Filipino wife and gone native—who managed a big pineapple plantation. **1963** Keats *Fought Alone* 63: It would…prevent them all from degenerating into so many bamboo Americans to whom life consisted of a native woman and a brood of half-castes playing in the mud.

3. ASIATIC, 2.

1957 E. Brown *Locust Fire* 14 [ref. to WWII]: "I don't see no crow," said McQuinn. "You must be going bamboo." **1961** Peacock *Valhalla* 226: Wondering if he was going bamboo obviously! **1959–65** Algren *Sea Diary* 35: "Man, do you think I'm going bamboo?" is all I've heard from Concannon for days….He's keeping *me* from going bamboo. **1987** Robbins *Ravens* 125: Somewhere along the way, CIA colleagues say, Tony Poe went "bamboo"…"a little mad."

bamboo *v.* [by shortening] to bamboozle.

*a*1870 in *DAE:* [*Bamboo*]: To cheat; to bamboozle.—Conn., but probably imported from the Southern States.

Bamboo Bomber *n. Mil. Av.* a Cessna AT-17 Bobcat advanced training aircraft.

1954 Le Vier & Guenther *Pilot* 173 [ref. to 1944]: Our twin-engine Cessna, the Bamboo Bomber. **1984** J. Dailey *Silver Wings* 161 [ref. to WWII]: AT-17s..."The good old 'Bamboo Bomber,' " Eden joked dryly, referring to the plywood construction of the airplane. **1991** Linnekin *80 Knots* 346: Cessna...[produced] the twin-engine bomber and navigation trainer known affectionately and derisively as the "Bamboo Bomber"—lots of plywood in that one.

bamboo fleet *n. Navy.* the Asian or South Pacific Fleet.

1913 *Review of Reviews* (Aug.) 201: The "bamboo fleet" is the [U.S.] fleet assigned to Philippine waters. **1919** *Our Navy* (July) 22: Admitting that we are a tin can cruiser of the bamboo fleet variety, still we must be given credit for winning the South American baseball championship. **1942** *Yank* (July 8) 9: They were the "Bamboo Fleet" [in Philippine waters].

bamboo juice *n. Mil. in East Asia.* any East Asian liquor. Also **bamboo gin.**

1945 in *AS* XXI 47: Our liquor is about like the Stateside stuff, except when we run out and have to fall back on the native stuff....We call it Bamboo Juice and one straight will put you in never-never land! **1984** Ark. man, age *ca*35: I remember a character in an old war movie saying, "He's been hittin' the bamboo juice again." I can't place it exactly, but I've known the term for a long time. **1986** Willeford *About a Soldier* 94 [ref. to 1940]: Bamboo gin was homemade [in the Philippines] and bottled in miscellaneous bottles.

bamboo telegraph *n.* [cf. BAMBOO, *n.*, 2] oral communication between isolated individuals or groups in a jungle; GRAPE-VINE. Also **bamboo wireless.**

1929 Wise *Marines* 136 [ref. to 1915]: It was now I got my first experience in the bamboo wireless of the Haitian jungle. They could spread news over the wireless almost as fast as the telegraph wire. **1945** Wolfert *Amer. Guerrilla* 78: Bamboo telegraph usually brought word to one American [in the Philippines jungle] of the existence of another. **1963** Keats *Fought Alone* 76: Every scrap of gossip and unsubstantiated rumor that the bamboo telegraph spread ultimately became common property. **1991** L. Reinberg *In the Field* 16 [ref. to Vietnam War]: *Bamboo telegraph,* slang for word-of-mouth communication. This term was applied to both friendly and enemy sides, especially in rural regions.

bamboozle *v.* [orig. unkn.] **1.** to fool or swindle; to confuse. Occ. absol. Now *S.E.*

***1703** in *OED:* The old Rogue...knows how to bamboozle. *Ibid.:* Sham Proofs that they proposed to bamboozle me with. **1781** in Mencken *Amer. Language Supp. I* 11: *Bamboozle*...is first, a cant phrase; secondly, a vulgarism; thirdly, an idiom of the language. ***1811** *Lexicon Balatron.: To Bamboozle.* To make a fool of any one, to humbug or impose on him. **1838** [Haliburton] *Clockmaker* (Ser. 2) 32: I'll bambousle him, I'll befogify his brain. **1849** Melville *White Jacket* 218: He bamboozled you, Jack. **1855** Brougham *Chips* 322: 'Sposin that a chap cheats and bamboozles during his life. **1902** "J. Flynt" *Little Bro.* 176: Robert Jemmison's that bamboozled he won't even let his old mother say what she thinks. **1928** Bodenheim *Georgie May* 72: Wuhk lak a mule, oah panhandle, oah steal, oah bamboozle. **1936** in R.E. Howard *Iron Man* 219: They bamboozled me into haulin' their ammernishun for 'em. **1975** T. Berger *Sneaky People* 29: If you think I'd try to bamboozle a family man, you're wrong. **1981** Hofstadter & Dennett *Mind's I* 71: The man, however, is doing his best to bamboozle the interrogator by responding as he thinks a woman might.

2. to treat roughly *or* hustle (someone) about.

1833 [S. Smith] *Maj. Downing* 130, in *DAE:* The President [was]...bamboozled about from four o'clock in the morning till midnight...and then...jammed into Funnel Hall two hours.

bamboozled *adj.* **1.** "darned."

1834 Caruthers *Kentuckian* II 206: But I'm tetotally bamboozled if I ain't tellin you of the killed and wounded, before I've told you who fout. **1924** *DN* V 271: I'll...be bamboozled....be blowed...be damned.

2. befuddled; tipsy.

*a***1856** Hall *College Wds.* 461: The various words and phrases in use, at one time or another, to signify some stage of inebriation [are]:...shot in the neck, bamboozled, weak-jointed. **1984** Algeo *Stud Buds & Dorks:* To be drunk...*bamboozled.*

bamfoozle *v.* BAMBOOZLE. [Mostly dial.]

1851 M. Reid *Scalp-Hunters* 113: So as to bamfoozle any Injuns thar is in these parts. **1884** Baldwin *Yankee School-Teacher* 167: Does yer 'spec

dat de matter of dem few miles am gwine ter bamfoozle *hit?* **1917** *DN* IV 340: *Bamfoozle,* v.t. = bamboozle, which is not heard [in southeastern Ohio]. **1950** in *DARE:* Sayward might be bamfoozled a little but not beat out.

bammy *n.* see BAM[2].

bamsquabbled var. BUMSQUABBLED.

banana *n.* **1.** penis. Usu. *Joc.* See also *get (one's) banana peeled,* below.

1916 Cary *Venery* I 8: *Banana*—The penis. **1928** Read *Lexical Evidence* 36: I have a girl in Indiana/She like to play with my banana. **1941** in Legman *Limerick* 277: He...electrified his banana. **1948** J.H. Burns *Lucifer* 123: This babe named Fay writes to me today....I'm slippin the green banana to three at once. Bro-ther. **1976** Conroy *Santini* 296: If I'd known she was giving it away for free, I'd have played hide the banana with her myself. *Ibid.* 296: One thing led to another and before you knew it my big hairy banana was whistlin' Dixie when it struck gold in them thar hills. **1983** *Glimpse* (Mar.) 2: A woman...wanted to put her nickname, Banana, on her plates. But she was told that's not acceptable. "It denotes a male organ."

2. [cf. BANANAHEAD] a stupid or worthless person, *(esp.)* a silly or crazy individual.

1919 *Amer. Legion Wkly.* (July 18) 20: Does that mean anything to you, you poor benighted banana, still over there in the land of the Frenchies? **1923** Witwer *Fighting Blood* 296: Shut up, you ingrateful banana! **1926** Dunning & Abbott *Broadway* 219: I wonder if that banana gave me a phoney name. **1959** E. Hunter *Conviction* 78: Besides, everybody knows about you and Alice. Even that banana she's got for a husband. **1962** Carr & Cassavetes *Too Late Blues* (film): What a bunch of bananas. **1966** "Petronius" *N.Y. Unexp.* 41: Devastating hodgepodge of West Side bananas...changes nightly. **1976** *N.Y. Times Bk. Review* (Aug. 8) 8: That can save a stroller-pushing mother from turning into a banana. **1976** *S.W.A.T.* (NBC-TV): Ever since this banana got me into S.W.A.T. training I haven't had time to brush my teeth. **1980** Gould *Ft. Apache* 264: That fuckin' banana. Who does he think he's playin' with? **1983** *Nat. Lampoon* (Mar.) 96: Holy Moley, what a lucky banana! **1988** Maloney *Thunder Alley* 354: He's up against someone better than those bananas.

3. *pl.* [cf. BANANA OIL] nonsense, BALONEY.

1929 Hemingway *Sel. Letters* 318: Aren't all the magazines of culture now defunct? It all sounds like ballroom bananas to me. **1971** *Playboy* (May) 204: What a *crock* of shit....What a load of bananas.

4. *Auto. Industry.* a bumper guard on an automobile.

1941 in *AS* XVI 240: *Banana.* Bumper guard.

5. *Black E.* an attractive young light-skinned black woman.

1944 Burley *Harlem Jive* 12: That fine banana, understand, is as mellow as a cello, as fine as red wine. *Ibid.* 133: *Banana*—yellow girl. Mulatto, young, pretty.

6. *Football.* (see 1978 quot.).

1949 Leahy *Notre Dame* 109: Whenever we call a "banana" pass, it is not called to either one of the ends specifically. *Ibid.* 110: This play will work...better if you have the opposite end running a "banana." **1958** J. King *Football* 201: With the Rams we once had a "banana" pass, which was simply a case of one of our halfbacks charting his running course as a bend. **1978** Shefski *Football Lang.* 14: *Banana.* A bending pass route used by pass receivers in an effort to split two defensive players.

7. *Vaud.* a slapstick comedian.—usu. as **top banana** a starring comedian; and **second banana** a supporting comedian, esp. a straight man. See also TOP BANANA.

1953 in *DAS* 18: So they made me into a comedian..."third banana." **1953** in *AS* XXXI 63: In television and radio, Mr. Carney has played second banana to many great comedy performers. **1955** *Newsweek* (Mar. 28) 53: Known to the trade as "supporting comedians" or "second bananas," they get their laughs and paychecks...with a carefree regularity. **1974** M.J. Smith *When I Say No* 203: She asked me if I would role-play the manipulative parts in her demonstration of the assertive verbal skills—if I would be her "second banana"...and be manipulative upon her cue. **1979** *Portrait of Stripper* (CBS-TV movie): There's not too many calls for a top banana—or a second banana. **1981** G. Wolf *Roger Rabbit* 3: Instead, they made me a second banana to...Baby Herman.

8. *Mil. Av.* FLYING BANANA.

1962 in J.C. Pratt *Viet. Voices* 122: The Army is still flying the obsolete twin-rotor bananas. **1964** J. Lucas *Dateline* 90: The lumbering Banana lost its balance and fell into a nearby canal. **1968** Cameron *Warriors* 17: Our banana lost its forward rotor coming into the l.z. [landing zone].

9. usu. *pl.* a dollar.

1970 Ponicsan *Last Detail* 182: Eight years for [stealing] a lousy forty fucking bananas. **1972** *All in the Family* (CBS-TV): A year in the can and five hundred bananas. **1974** Sann *Dead Heat* 34: Your...tickets would bring back three and a half million bananas. **1980** Univ. Tenn. professor, age *ca*38: Six hundred bananas is a lot of bread. **1992** *Garfield & Friends* (CBS-TV): Jon's been brainwashed out of 200 bananas and we've got to get his money back.

10. an Asian who has adopted the values of white American society.—usu. used derisively. Cf. APPLE, COCONUT, OREO.

1970 *Seattle Times Magazine* (July 5) 9: These Filipinos may not be "oreos" or "bananas," as blacks and other Asians depict their colleagues having dark skins outside and a white mentality inside. **1979** D. Thoreau *City at Bay* 125: Called Banana Boy because of his preference for white girls, "yellow on the outside, white on the inside." **1982** *L.A. Times* (Apr. 19) II 4: The Sansei inappropriately labeled the Nisei "bananas"—yellow on the outside, but white on the inside.

¶ In phrases:

¶ **bust (one's) bananas** to exert (oneself) to the limit.
1971 Faust *Willy* 112: I bust my bananas and what do I get?

¶ **flip (one's) bananas** to become suddenly insane.
1972 *WCBS-TV News* (Jan. 28): Well, sometimes a man just—to use a phrase that's become a cliché nowadays—flips his bananas.

¶ **get (one's) banana peeled** (of a man) to engage in copulation.—usu. considered vulgar. *Joc.*
*ca*1889 Field *Bangin'* st. x: And thus the tawdry hussy his ripe banana peeled. **1971** *Nat. Lampoon* (Oct.) 65: Wanna get your bananas peeled?

¶ (In joc. proverbs):
1965 N.Y.C. high school student: He's got one foot in the grave and the other on a banana peel. **1984** Hindle *Dragon Fall* 30: Let's just say the old biddy has got one foot in the grave and the other one on a banana peel.

banana ball *n. Sports.* a thrown or hit ball having, or appearing to have, a sharply curved trajectory. Cf. BANANA, 6.
1962 in Davies *Golf. Terms* 19: So he had this banana-ball slice that sometimes sailed over two fairways. **1970** Scharff *Encyc. of Golf* 415: *Banana ball.* A flagrantly bad slice, curving to the right in the shape of a banana. **1973** Boyd & Harris *Baseball Card* 107: Stu Miller threw the ultimate banana ball. You had time for a Coke and a sandwich while waiting for his fast ball to arrive. **1981** Univ. Tenn. student: A *banana ball* is a long slice [in golf]. **1984** *N.Y. Times* (Apr. 10) A 18: The family quickly learned a great deal about golf, especially the dread banana balls as they came curving in from the nearby ninth tee and crashed through the windows.

banana belt *n.* the warmer parts of a typically cold region.
1898 in *DARE:* The glittering prospectuses that used to invite the world to come to the "banana belt" of the Dakotas. **1959** in *DARE: Banana belt:* Words used to describe the "tropical" areas of Alaska, notably the warmer southeastern region with its lush forests, heavy undergrowth, rapid-growing vegetation, and moist climate. **1963** in *BDNE2.* **1977** in *BDNE2:* Southern Catskill Mountain country [is] often joshingly referred to as "The Banana Belt."

banana cake *n.* a crazy or eccentric person; FRUITCAKE.
1975 *Barney Miller* (ABC-TV) (July 24): They've got some banana cake on top of a building with home-made wings. **1977** *Switch* (CBS-TV) (Mar. 27): You didn't tell me she was a banana cake. **1989** *Night Court* (NBC-TV): What—let a banana cake loose on the streets of New York?

banana fleet *n. Navy.* the Caribbean fleet of the U.S. Navy. Now *hist.* Cf. BAMBOO FLEET.
1971 in P. Heller *In This Corner* 153 [ref. to 1920]: Our duty was down in the Caribbean, what they called the "banana fleet."...Called it the "banana fleet" because it was in the banana territory.

bananahead *n.* a fool; idiot.
1949 W.R. Burnett *Asphalt Jungle* 205: You...big...bananahead! **1963** E.M. Miller *Exile to Stars* 220: But I'll be damned if I'll have that banana-head Blair Winsted in here. **1975** Stanley *WWIII* 224: Where does that leave the rest of those bananaheads? **1990* Anderson & Trudgill *Bad Lang.* 88: "Stupid Person"...*bananahead.*

banana-nose *n.* a long or hooked nose; (*hence*) a person having such a nose. [1936 quot. illustrates a well-known humorous insult.]
1920 McKenna *315th Inf.* 152 [ref. to 1917]: Jack Fields, better known as "Old Eagle Beak" and "Banana Nose." [*1936 Our Army* (Sept.) 22: Schnozzle, is that your nose or are you eating a banana?] **1946** *News-*

week (Mar. 4) 74: The epithet—"Banana Nose"—was pretty mild. **1968** Radano *Beat* 36: Now if you don't start back to that pier I'll change your banana nose into a cherry smash! **1971** Sorrentino *Up from Never* 34: Keep him out there, banana nose.

banana oil *n.* [app. an elaboration of earlier *oil* 'flattering or unctuous talk', on semantic model of APPLESAUCE and similar terms; S.E. sense not attested until 1926] flattering nonsense; idle talk.
1924 B. Conners *Applesauce* 11: *Pa.*...He's full of applesauce....*Ma.* Full of applesauce! (*Amazed.*) What do you mean by that? *Pa.* Banana oil! Soft soap! Applesauce! **1921–25** J. Gleason & R. Taber *Is Zat So?* 53: That same bottle of banana oil. **1926** Maines & Grant *Wise-Crack Dict.* 6: Banana oil—Yes, he has some. **1927** *AS* II 275: *Banana oil*—senseless talk. **1928** McEvoy *Show Girl* 5: I got to...pour a lot of banana oil into Miss Schwartz's ear. **1951** Longstreet *Pedlocks* 417: "Suppose I didn't love you, Harry?" "Banana erl, baby." **1956** in Russell *Perm. Playboy* 81: Beatrice...was drinking it all in, the booze and banana oil. **1966** Cameron *Sgt. Slade* 171: And now they were spreading the old banana oil to keep him happy. **1971** Faust *Willy* 124: I am not falling for that banana oil. **1980** *Nat. Lampoon* (Oct.) 18: Nothing mean, mind, but to him I say banana oil.

banana race *n.* [orig. unkn.] *Gamb.* (see quot.).
1980 Pearl *Slang Dict.: Banana race n.*...a racing competition with an illicitly predetermined outcome.

bananas *adj.* **1.** *Und.* homosexual.—used predicatively.
1933 Ersine *Prison Slang* 15: *Bananas., adj.* Homosexual, *queer.* **1935** Pollock *Underworld Speaks: He's bananas,* he's sexually perverted; a degenerate.

2. [perh. related to *go ape* s.v. APE] crazy, NUTS.—used predicatively. [This sense became rather faddish during the late 1960's.]
1957 A. Capp, in *S.F. News* (Mar. 30) 11: They say you're bananas!! **1966** "Petronius" *N.Y. Unexp.* 210: If You're Bananas Enough to Land in Jail.... **1967** P. Welles *Babyhip* 11: Dad...you're always bugging me, driving me bananas. Why don't you just stop bugging me and leave me alone. **1970** Calley & Sack *Lieut. Calley* 16: Believe me, I *would* be bananas then if I didn't cease to be "Calley" those days. **1975** Ebon *Bermuda Triangle* 101: The magnetic compass had gone completely bananas. **1978** *Rolling Stone* (Mar. 23) 49: The raiders are consumerism at its extreme and they just storm in there and go bananas. **1983** *All Things Considered* (Nat. Public Radio) (Apr. 13): When you mention the word "nuclear," people start to go bananas. **1990** *National Review* (Nov. 5) 20: President Freedman chose to go bananas.

¶ In phrase:

¶ **rough bananas** something extremely difficult.
1957 Ellison *Web of the City* 29: I gotta stand with Candle. Gonna be rough bananas, though.

bandage factory *n.* a hospital.
1941 Macaulay & Wald *Manpower* (film): You're not gonna stay cooped up in this bandage factory.

Band-Aid *n.* [fr. *Band-Aid,* trademark used for an adhesive bandage] *Mil.* a medical corpsman.
1980 D. Cragg *Lexicon* 26: *Band-Aid.* A medical corpsman. **1982** Del Vecchio *13th Valley* 591 [ref. to Vietnam War]: *Band-aid:* A medic. **1985** T. Wells *444 Days* 46: You're on your own, Band-Aid.

B and B *n.* [for *booze* (or *beer*) and *broads*] *Mil.* rest and recreation, R & R. *Joc.* Cf. A AND A; I AND I.
1963 *Sat. Eve. Post* (July 27) 73: "I'm a B and B man," Daddy liked to boast. "Booze and broads." **1966** Shepard *Doom Pussy* 151: Then on to Bangkok for four days R & R (B & B?) the day after. **1967** Michaels *Women of Green Berets* 130: Instead of the usual R and R, a leave ought to be called B and B. But a name like that one would be honest; and who the hell wants to be honest about liquor and sex? **1979** Former USAF mechanic: In Vietnam we sometimes called R and R *B and B,* standing for "beer and broads."

bandbox *n. Navy.* a wooden gunboat.
1862 in Walke *Naval Scenes* 84: *Vive la* bandboxes!

bandbox *adj. Army.* showy, adept at performing drills and marching in parade.—used prenominally.
1862 in C.H. Moulton *Ft. Lyon* 67: Col. Wells is very proud of his Regiment and...I should judge it is his intention to make it a "band-box" organization.

B and D *n.* [*bondage and discipline*] sexual acts involving sadomasochistic and fetishistic play, typically the tying up of one of the partners, spanking, the wearing of exotic leather costumes, etc. Cf. S AND M.

1969 Bartell *Group Sex* 82: "B and D" refers to bondage (various forms of restraint) and discipline (spanking, whipping, etc.). **1974** Lahr *Trot* 80: "B and D?" "Bondage and Discipline. I need it." *a*1989 Goodwin *More Man* 27: Men who enjoy B & D—bondage and discipline.

B and E *n.* [breaking *and* entering; orig. technical police abbr.] *Police.* the crime of breaking and entering; burglary. Often attrib.

*1961 Partridge *Dict. Und.* 788: *B. and e.*…Breaking and entering, as a criminal offence. **1965** *Acronyms & Initialisms Dict.* (ed. 2) 123: *B & E*…Breaking & Entering. **1976** Schroeder *Shaking It* 66: "B and E, sir." "Handy with the old crowbar, eh?" **1979** *Nat. Lampoon* (Sept.) 46: The B & E Artist, Cheap Thrills. **1982** *Harper's* (Aug.) 77: Charlie One, I think there's a B and E going on! **1987** *Newsweek* (Mar. 23) 61: By 15 he was a skilled B & E man, plundering the shopping center.

bandhouse *n. Pris.* a local workhouse, house of correction, detention home, etc. [Restricted largely to Chicago and surrounding area; 1926 quot. seems to refer to the 1890's.]

1914 Healy *Delinquent* 335: They are all in states prison or the reformatory now. One got three years in the band house. **1915–16** Lait *Beef, Iron & Wine* 38: He'll do a petty sneak turn an' he'll get a year in the bandhouse. **1926** Clark & Eubank *Lockstep* 173: *Band house*—House of Correction. **1930** [Conwell] *Pro. Thief* 76: A person who is in the bandhouse (work house) for beating an A. & P. store with a four-dollar check would refer to himself as a "paper-hanger"; a thief would refer to him as a clown. **1930** Shaw *Jack-Roller* 100: I thought if I was to go back to the "bandhouse" I'd rather have some new scenery. **1936** Dai *Opium* 196: *Bandhouse.* The workhouse.

bandit *n.* **1.a.** *Mil. Av.* a flying aircraft identified as hostile; in phr. **bandit train** a group of such aircraft in formation. Cf. BOGEY. [An official term in radio communications.]

1942 in C.R. Bond & T. Anderson *Flying T. Diary* 86: The RAF…radar at Rangoon…passed information that "bandits" were in the…area. **1942** in *OEDS.* **1943** Bayler & Carnes *Last Man Off Wake* 1: Bandits—south of the field—about four miles off—flying high! *1948 Partridge *Forces' Slang* 10: *Bandit.* To an Ack-Ack gunner, enemy aircraft. In the R.A.F., it was the official term. **1951** Morison *Naval Ops.* VII xxxv: Bogey is an unidentified plane; bandit, a plane identified as enemy. **1962** Mahurin *Honest John* 40: Since the early days of World War II enemy aircraft have always been referred to as Bandits. **1966** Cameron *Sgt. Slade* 15: They were FW-190's—"bandits," not "bogies," as they'd originally thought. **1972** *N.Y. Times Mag.* (Mar. 19) 11: As an F-4 navigator, Commander Souder's job is to keep an eye on the radar for "Bandits"—MIG's. **1978** L. Davis *MiG Alley* 24 [ref. to 1951]: "Bandit Trains" of around 75 MiGs would cross the Yalu at…40,000 feet. **1981** "K. Rollins" *Fighter Pilots* 32 [ref. to Korean War]: It's a bandit train…multiple flights [of MiGs] in trail formation. **1984** Cunningham & Ethell *Fox Two* 145: *Bandit.* An aircraft identified as hostile.

b. *USAF Acad.* a nearby person who is to be avoided or challenged. *Joc.*

1969 *Current Slang* I & II 7: *Bandit,* n. Enemy aircraft; sometimes said of instructors, colonels, and such.—Air Force Academy cadets.

2. *Gamb.* ONE-ARMED BANDIT.

1963 in J.H. Clarke *Harlem* 173: But who…wants to be bothered with li'l ol' women and their damned nickles [*sic*] and dimes playin' the bandits. **1980** *L.A. Times* (June 29) VII 4: In a year "the bandits" can net enough to pay a club's entire overhead. **1982** Heat Moon *Blue Hwys.* 202: Bandits wouldn't turn a dime if they didn't rattle and roll.

¶ In phrase:

¶ **like a bandit** at an uncontrollable rate; with great success.

1974 *Playboy* (Feb.) 204: A week at home and I was eating like a bandit. **1975** Mostert *Supership* 88: They had been "making out like bandits," to quote a phrase used to me in…1973 by one American broker. **1976** *Happy Days* (ABC-TV): Look at my feet! They're movin' like bandits. **1980** J. Webb *Sense of Honor* 296: This plebe made out like a bandit. **1985** G. Trudeau *Doonesbury* (synd. cartoon strip) (Apr. 2): Unlike our farm belt cousins, California farmers have been makin' out like bandits! **1990** *New Republic* (Jan. 29) 23: Many…have made out like bandits in Washington real estate. **1992** *This Week* (ABC-TV) (Apr. 19): And I'll make out like a bandit.

bandowzer *n.* [orig. unkn.] a heavy blow.

1833 in *DA* 70: We expected to see the man get a bounce on the nose,

a dough bat, or a bandowzer.

B and W *n.* [orig. a semi-official abbr.] Esp. *Navy.* bread and water as a punishment diet. Now *hist.*

1864 in *Civil War History* 23 (1977) 78: Theodore Jarvis, Boy, was confined in D[ouble] Irons in brig B + W for theiving [*sic*] by Com'dr. **1869** in Boyer *Nav. Surgeon* II 251: Sentence—solitary confinement…on b and w. **1914** *DN* IV 150 [ref. to U.S. Navy]: *B. and W.* for *bread and water.* **1926** Thomason *Marines* 174: Slip 'em a deck court or a few days B and W, just to show 'em that you disapprove. **1933** *Leatherneck* (Apr.) 21: Five days "B and W." **1947** *AS* XXII 111 [ref. to WWII]: A bread-and-water diet may be called *B. and W.,* though in the Navy and Marine Corps the more usual signification is the alliterative *piss and punk.* **1968** Cuomo *Thieves* 325: They put you in a very small cell up there without a mattress and put you on B and W—which is bread and water. **1977** Heinl *Marine Off. Guide* (ed. 4) 591: *B & W* (n): Solitary confinement on bread and water, now only authorized on board ship. **1982** T.C. Mason *Battleship* 133 [ref. to 1941]: Three days solitary on B & W.

bang *n.* **1.** a pelvic thrust during copulation; (*hence*) an act of copulation; a person regarded as a sex partner.

*1691 in Adlard *Forbidden Tree* 29: There could not have been more claps and more bangs,/For he made her old buttocks rattle. *ca1785 in Barke & Smith *Merry Muses* 175: She pay't him twice for every bang. **1931–34** in Clemmer *Pris. Community* 330: *Bang,* n. A copulation. *1936 Partridge *DSUE* 31: *Bang*…5. A piece of sexual intercourse.…*have a bang, be a good bang:* low: c.20. **1938** "Justinian" *Americana Sexualis* 12: *Bang.* n. A single act of coition.…"I gave her a quick bang." U.S., C.20. **1953** Strickland & Wortsman *Phenix City* 34: Jeez, Corp,…why don't you give her a bang. **1965** Trimble *Sex Words* 22: *Bang*…n.…A particular person as a Sex Object. **1966** Susann *Valley of Dolls* 149: All you have left is maybe a few more bangs from Lyon Burke before he gets bored with you. **1970** Zindel *Your Mind* 70: Realistically I was after one thing.…A bang. **1970** in *Playboy* (Jan. 1971) 76: The guy's a terrific bang. I wouldn't say he's exactly a sex maniac, but he'll do until one comes along. **1971** *Blushes & Bellylaffs* 32: How to have a good day? Start off with a bang! **1966–80** McAleer & Dickson *Unit Pride* 71: Let's throw a bang into her anyway.

2. *Narc.* an injection or inhalation of cocaine, morphine, or heroin; (in 1953 quot.) a draw on a cannabis cigarette.

1922 Murphy *Black Candle* 49: I have heard it is a common expression amongst people whom you would hardly suspect, to jocularly ask another if they could give them a "bhang" which is a slang expression for a snuff of cocaine. *Ibid.* 61: He resorts to a "shot" of morphine or a "bhang" of cocaine. **1927** *Immortalia* 36: An itchy-nosed pimp…/ Pulled out a bindle and took a bang. **1929** Tully *Shadows* 201: I took six or seven bangs of coke an' floated away to Chicago, China, an' the North Pole. **1929** *Sat. Eve. Post* (Apr. 13) 54: An addict…is a gangster, and a bang is a load, a charge, or a hyp of the drug he uses. **1934** in *Jour. Abnormal & Soc. Psych.* XXX 361: *Bang*—an injection of a drug. **1952** J.B. Martin *Life in Crime* 35: Well, a bang of that [morphine] in the morning and she hasn't got any troubles. **1953** W. Brown *Monkey on My Back* 31: A couple of the older boys "caught wise" to what he was doing and wanted to try "a bang." **1955** D.W. Maurer, in *PADS* (No. 24) 193: Narcotic addicts…have a prearranged time to *fix* or *take a bang.* **1973** W. Burroughs, Jr. *Ky. Ham* 27: My father took three bangs of H a day.

3. a thrill of enjoyment—esp. in phr. **get a bang out of.**

1929 in Runyon *Guys & Dolls* 72: He seems to be getting a great bang out of the doings. **1941** Riskin *Meet John Doe* (film): We heard your broadcast and we got a big bang out of it. **1945** in Hodes & Hansen *Sel. from Gutter* 19: Man, I sure got a bang out of it. **1952** Bellow *Augie March* 268: I don't think I gave her much of a bang. **1953** Brossard *Saboteurs* 115: I get a real bang out of thinking of all those…scholars. **1958** A. King *Mine Enemy* 21: The marks get a bang out of all that ice.

4. *Printing & Computers.* an exclamation point.

1931 B. Morgan *Five-Star Final* (film): Put a five-column box around it with a double bang. **1967** *Time* (July 21) 38: "Bang" is printer's slang for an exclamation point. **1983** Naiman *Computer Dict.* 18: Quote take your hand off my knee bang endquote shrieked the duchess period. **1990** *Discover* (July) 32: An exclamation point—a *bang* in typesetters' slang. **1991** E. Raymond *New Hacker's Dict.* 48: If one wanted to specify the exact characters "foo!" one would speak "Eff oh oh bang."

5. a try, a CRACK.

1940 Burnett *High Sierra* 149: I'm going to take a trip down to the Islands and take a bang at some of them sealskin babes.

6. *Und.* a criminal charge, RAP.

1951 *Sat. Eve. Post* (Mar. 24) 78: "Hell, what they got you locked up for?"…"Ah, Sargeant Dooley got me. It's a bum bang; he's got us for robbery. Some guy accuses us, but he didn't identify us."

7. a period of time served in the armed forces or in prison; HITCH.

*a*1977 in S. King *Bachman* 54: Sullen young men who had to choose between a bang in the Navy and a bang in South Portland Training and Correction.

8. *Stu.* a grade of B.

1979 *Univ. Tenn.* grad. student: When I was in college [1964–68] an A was an *ace*, a B was a *bang*, a C was a *cat* or a *hook*, a D was a *dog*, and an F was a *frog*. B+ was a *bang and a half*. C+ was a *hook and a half*.

9. *Und.* a murder.

1988 H. Gould *Double Bang* 209: Tell me how to do this chick without making it look like a street bang.

¶ In phrase:

¶ **bang for the buck** [fr. military spending; "bang" in sense of "firepower"] value for one's money.

1968 Safire *New Lang. of Pol.* 34: John Foster Dulles laid down the policy of "massive retaliation"…in 1954 and told the Council on Foreign Relations [that]…"it is now possible to get, and share, more basic security at less cost." Defense Secretary Charles E. Wilson promptly dubbed the policy the "New Look"…and said it would provide a "bigger bang for a buck." **1981** *Business Week* (Sept. 7) 86: By 1986 the bang for the buck will be something like $3 or $4 of additional savings for each $1 that the Treasury loses in tax revenue. **1984** *L.A. Times* (June 14) I 16: An obsessive desire to get an ever-greater bang out of the PAC's political bucks. **1990** *U.S. News & W.R.* (June 4) 34: His efforts "provided a lot of bang for the buck"; 3 of 4 inmates who took part stayed off drugs during their parole. **1992** Hosansky & Sparling *Working Vice* 137: He couldn't see how the city would get "our bang for our buck" pursuing that issue.

bang *v.* **1.** to copulate; to copulate with.—usu. considered vulgar.

1698–1720 in D'Urfey *Pills* V 89: He…kist her bonny Mow, Sir;/…And bang'd her side Weam too, Sir. *ca*1775 in Barke & Smith *Merry Muses* 131: But an I had kend, what I ken now,/I wad a bang'd her belly fu'. *ca*1790 in Barke & Smith *Merry Muses* 95: A sodger wi' his bandileers/Has bang'd my belly fu'. *Ibid.* 106: The mair she bangs the less she squeels,/An' hey for houghmagandie. *Ibid.* 161: The lads ne'er think it is amiss/To bang the holes whereout they piss. **1802 *Frisky Songster* 14: And the blue bells of Ireland, go well boys, well,/And the clapper strikes every side bang her a-se well. *ca*1889 E. Field *Bangin' on Rhine* st. iii: Full many a chippy had he banged, and many a whore, 'tis said. **1916 Cary *Venery* I 8: *Bang*—To bang a woman—To fuck her. **1927** *Immortalia* 104: Bang away, my Lulu. **1931–34** in Clemmer *Pris. Community* 330: *Bang*…To copulate. **1946** J.H. Burns *Gallery* 196: Didja bang yaself silly all las night? **1953** Brossard *Saboteurs* 144: She did not suspect that I was banging Lucille. **1955–57** Kerouac *On Road* 37: Marylou…insists on banging in the interim. **1959** Morrill *Dark Sea* 186: You don't bang her often enough. **1962** Hecht *Gaily* 22: Doc entered his office and found Mr. Bolger, head of the composing room, banging a naked lady on his couch. **1966 *Playboy* (Oct.) 189: You're a stupid fat fool and couldn't bang a shotgun with a hair trigger. **1967** Taggart *Reunion* 138: They's some guys ain't never banged a broad, ever hear of a guy never had hisself a frail, Leowen? **1972** McGregor *Bawdy Ballads* 58: She bangs like a shithouse door/ Swings back for more and more. **1979** Hiler *Monkey Mt.* 36: Says they're all clean and they bang like beavers. **1992** G. Wolff *Day at Beach* 107: To "get in," to get "it,"…to "bang" it had been my preoccupation [in adolescence].

2. to surpass, to beat. Also **bang Banagher** to surpass everything.

1817 in *DARE*: We were not prepared for this—to use a sheer Yankee phrase, "it bangs everything." *a*1825 in Shay *Sea Songs* 138: We make the boasting Frenchman fly/And bang the haughty Dons, sir. **1829** in Blair & Meine *Half Horse* 59: He soon became famous as "the best shot in the country," and was called bang-all, and on that account was frequently excluded from participating in matches for beef. **1836** *Spirit of Times* (Oct. 8) 269: Her trainers and jockies "bang Banagher, and Banagher bangs the Devil." **1848** Bartlett *Amer.*: To beat, i.e. excel, to surpass. "This bangs all things."—*Ohio.* **1850** in Strong *Diary* II 8: Could arrange a choral symphony for it that should bang Beethoven's. **1871** "M. Twain" *Roughing It* 246: Well, for clean, cool, out-and-out cheek, if this don't bang anything that ever I saw, I'm an Injun! **1876** J. Miller *First Fam'lies* 180: Well, that bangs me all hollow! **1882** "M. Twain" *Life on Miss.* 304: Don't it just bang anything you ever heard of? **1889 Barrère & Leland *Dict. Slang* I 77: "Bangs

Banagher," beats the world.

3. *Und.* to steal (a watch or the like) by breaking it off from a chain; (*broadly*) to steal.

1902 Hapgood *Autobiog. of Thief* 45 [ref. to 1883]: I received my first lesson in the art of "banging a super," that is, stealing a watch by breaking the ring with the thumb and forefinger, and thus detaching it from the chain. **1904** *Life in Sing Sing* 258: *Banging supers at the red wagon.* Stealing watches at the ticket wagon. **1955** D.W. Maurer, in *PADS* (No. 24) 50: It takes…skill to bang a *prop* or *souper*. **1992** *Likely Suspects* (Fox-TV): We got a…dancer who's bangin' jewels.

4. *Narc.* to inject or inhale a narcotic drug; (*occ.*) to smoke (a marijuana cigarette).—occ. constr. with *up.*—used also intrans. Hence **banged up** under the influence of a narcotic drug.

1925–26 J. Black *You Can't Win* 159: You're in with what "gow" I've got. Let's bang it up. **1930** *Amer. Mercury* (Apr.) 320: The mutts bang up on foolish powder. **1933** Ersine *Prison Slang* 16: *Bang, v.* To take a shot of dope, usually by injecting it into the arm or leg. **1938 in Partridge *Dict. Und.* 19: I liked smoking, but wanted a connexion for morphia, as I preferred to "bang." **1942–49** Goldin et al. *DAUL* 22: I'm gonna…bang a few reefers. **1953** Anslinger & Tompkins *Narc.* 305: *Bang a reefer.* To smoke a marijuana cigarette. **1953** Gresham *Midway* 15: You see that he gets his…deck of "M" so he can bang himself night and morning and keep the horrors away. **1956** Resko *Reprieve* 237 [ref. to 1940's]: A reefer…is…banged…—never smoked. **1962** Riccio & Slocum *All the Way Down* 54: Every night we'll all bang up. **1965** Himes *Imabelle* 34: He banged himself in the arm while the mixture was still warm. **1980** M. Baker *Nam* 26: Half of them was banged up high as kites. **1986** *L.A. Times* (Mar. 11) V 5: I had a boyfriend…who bangs up cocaine, crank, and once in a while, heroin.

5. *Esp. Und.* to shoot, esp. to shoot dead.—also constr. with *out*, *off*, or *over*.

1927 *DN* V 438: *Bang, v.* To kill by shooting. **1927–28** in R. Nelson *Dishonorable* 181: Because they banged my old man. *Ibid.* 182: Afraid the witness'd get banged, uh? **1930** Lait *On the Spot* 199: *Bang off*…To shoot. **1934** in O'Brien *Best Stories 1935* 3: If I had my gun we could bang some lizards. **1934** Appel *Brain Guy* 155: Alla you guys stay put or I'll bang your guts. **1942–49** Goldin et al. *DAUL* 23: *Bang out*…To shoot and kill. **1980** Gould *Ft. Apache* 80: And who ever heard of a wino banging out two cops with a gun? **1983** *Univ. Tenn.* student: A horse breaks its leg, you gotta bang him. **1988** H. Gould *Double Bang* 33: Just for the fun of banging out a guy. **1989** *Dream St.* (NBC-TV): You better back these babies off or they gonna bang you over.

6. *Und.* to arrest.

1933 Ersine *Prison Slang* 16: *Bang, v.*…To arrest.…*Banged, adj.* Arrested.

7.a. to impress, "bowl over."—constr. with *over.*

1940 O'Hara *Pal Joey* 79: It is good news that you are banging them right over every where you go.

b. to thrill.

1962 Perry *Young Man* 154: It don't bang me to sit around listening to a lot of guys trying to out-holler each other.

8. *Boxing.* to throw punches.

1947 Schulberg *Harder They Fall* 256: He just can't bang.…And when a heavyweight can be reached and he can't bang.… **1991** D. Anderson *In Corner* 47: Marvin went out and banged with Hearns right away.

9. to make or execute (a turn, as in driving an automobile).

1968–70 *Current Slang* III & IV 7: *Bang a U-ey, v.* To make a U-turn.— Young male construction worker, Massachusetts.—First you bang a U-ey. **1975–76** Dills *CB* 14: *Bang a Uey*: make a U turn. **1976** *Science & Mech. Guide to CB* 156: Take a left then bang a uey.

10. to inflict, "hit with."

1974 Sann *Dead Heat* 40: All sixty tellers were to be banged simultaneously with the big tickets. **1988** *N.Y. Newsday* (July 15) 37: All they wind up getting is the $150 fine they bang you for selling [beer].

11. *Und. & Police.* to take part in gang fights as a *gangbanger* s.v. GANGBANG, *v.*, 2.

1988 Norst *Colors* 85: I banged twelve fucking years, baby. **1990** Bing *Do or Die* 20: Do your mama get on you about bangin'?**…*gangbanging*—being in a gang.

¶ In phrases:

¶ **bang (someone's) ear** see EAR, *n.*

¶ **bang the bush** to surpass everything.

1838 [Haliburton] *Clockmaker* (Ser. 2) 130: Well, says I,…if that don't bang the bush.

bang-bang *n.* **1.** gunfire; (*Mil.*) enemy fire; shooting, shelling; armed combat.

1942 *AS* XVII 91: *City of Bang Bang*. Chicago....an obvious reference to the gangster wars. **1944** in Rock *Field Service* 277: The ferry...was under fire. [Even] without the bang-bang it was a shaky affair. **1971** *Newsweek* (Sept. 13) 40: We haven't seen any bang-bang for so long we're getting damn lax. **1982** Woodruff & Maxa *At White House* 206: The only time they could get a story on the air was when it included videotape footage of "bang bang" (gunfire). **1983** *Afternoon Contact* (WKGN radio) (Sept. 25): Hot wars are called *bang-bang* in the trade [of journalism]. **1990** *Newsweek* (Aug. 27) 29: For TV, the real problem with the gulf story is that the pictures stink. A little "bang bang," to use the industry vernacular, would change that in a hurry.

2. *Mil.* a firearm. *Joc.*

1954–60 *DAS* 19: *Bang-bang*...A gun. **1980** Cragg *Lexicon* 26: *Bang-Bang*. Any firearm, but usually the infantryman's rifle or individual weapon. **1992** Mowry *Way Past Cool* 55: Leastways we score ourselfs a new bang-bang.

3. [pidgin; cf. BOOM-BOOM, POM-POM] *Mil.* copulation.

1980 Cragg *Lexicon* 26: *Bang-Bang*...Pidgin English for the act of fornication.

bang-bang *adj.* **1.** characterized by gunfire or armed combat.

1948 in Galewitz *Great Comics* 280: Spray gets to go State-side...and we get a job flying in a bang-bang zone. **1973** Hirschfeld *Victors* 76: You don't think he's so dumb to stick around when it's bang-bang time....He's got brains. **1982** *Dial* (July) 44: Hodding Carter had two...shows to demonstrate the tendency of the media to feature blood and thunder, what is now called bang-bang journalism.

2. rapid and exciting.

1988 *N.Y. Post* (June 7) 70: Wade Boggs made the throw and nipped...Ward on a bang-bang play.

Bangclap *n.* [*Bang*kok + CLAP, alluding to the high rate of venereal diseases in the city's many brothels] *Mil.* Bangkok, Thailand.—usu. considered vulgar. *Joc.* [Quots. ref. to Vietnam War.]

1978 J. Webb *Fields of Fire* 121: Hey. How was it in Bang-clap? *Ibid.* 122: I'm taking R & R in Bang-clap. **1980** D. Cragg (letter to J.E.L., Aug. 10) 1: I first heard this during my second Vietnam tour, [beginning] May 1965. "I'm gonna take my R & R in old Bangclap." **1984** Former Spec. 4, U.S. Army: Most everybody in the Far East knew that *Bangclap* meant *Bangkok*. The idea was that they had an especially resistant VD strain there. **1991** L. Reinberg *In the Field*.

banger *n.* **1.a.** something that is usually large or great in degree; whopper; (*specif.*) a big lie.

[*1657** in *OEDS* 198 (sense not obvious).] *1814** in *OED*: A Sportsman entire—who says nay, tells a banger. *1846** in *EDD*. *1854** in *EDD*. **1889** *Century Dict.* I 440: *Banger*...something very large; especially, a lie (Slang). *a1890** *F & H* I 118: *Banger*. (common)—A lie. That's a banger! That is a whopper! **1898** B.W. Green *Va. Folk-Speech* 50: *Banger, n.* A large person. A great falsehood. *1899** Whiting *John St.* viii: They earn half-pence by well-told bangers. They are sent out to lie.

b. a thing of excellence.

1864 in R.G. Carter *4 Bros.* 452: Tell father to thank Mr. Davis for his gift; the hat is a *banger*, a *peeler.*

2. *Stu.* (esp. at Yale Univ.) a heavy clublike cane carried by a student. Now *hist.*

1846 *The Yale Banger* [title of literary magazine]. **1854** *Yale Lit. Mag.* 20: 75: The Freshman reluctantly turned the key,/Expecting a Sophomore gang to see,/Who, with faces masked and bangers stout,/Had come resolved to smoke him out. **1871** Bagg *Yale* 43: *Banger*, a heavy club-cane, mostly carried by Sophomores. **1871** *Yale Naught-Ical Almanac* 7: He waxes bold. Contemplates going out with a "banger." **1906** in *DAE*: Secretary Taft...has rescued from some museum...his old "banger" of student days. **1913** *Century Dict.* I (Supp.): *Banger-rush...n.*, a cane-rush, common in colleges, in which two sides struggle for the possession of a cane or banger. **1992** *Yale Alumni Mag.* (Feb.) 16: In the 19th century, sophomores continued to cherish their few rights over the freshmen, especially those of sporting tophats and "bangers," the clublike canes used for noisemaking and protection, as well as for bashing high hats.

3. [cf. SMACKER] a dollar.

1934 Weseen *Dict. Slang* 294: *Banger*—A dollar; a silver dollar. **1942** *Time* (Jan. 12) 70: A dollar, no longer a buck, had become a "banger."

4. a noisy, poorly maintained motor vehicle.

*1967** in *BDNE* 55. **1970** *New Yorker* (Mar. 14) 33: At ease astride his ancient Harley two-stroke banger. **1970** Partridge *DSUE* (ed. 7) 994: *Banger*...A motor-car that "bangs" (is noisy): motorists': since ca. 1930.

5.a. cylinder.—usu. as the second element in compounds.

1970 Thompson *Garden of Sand* 155: The car barked with the beat of its little four-banger heart.

b. an automotive engine.

1979 Frommer *Sports Lingo* 155: *Big Banger*. A big engine.

6. *Boxing.* an aggressive boxer.

1977 Hamill *Flesh & Blood* 48: "He's a banger."..."Banger? He's a goddam killer."

7. [sugg. by *Bang's disease* 'brucellosis'] *Vet. Med.* an animal afflicted with brucellosis.

1978 Univ. Tenn. student: A cow that's developed brucellosis is called a *banger*. Don't ask me why.

8. *Police & Und.* a member of a street gang; *gangbanger* s.v. GANGBANG, *v.*, 2.

1985 "Blowdryer" *Mod. Eng.* 57: *Banger*...Someone who indulges in gang activity. **1988** *Newsweek* (Mar. 28) 23: If he passes the test, the peewee then becomes a "banger" or "gang banger" and is entitled to share in the gang's fortunes. **1989** *21 Jump St.* (Fox-TV): Just makin' sure these bangers keep their noses clean. **1990** Costello & Wallace *Signifying Rappers* 41: Bangers keep showing up...demanding certain "requests."

9. a gun.

1988 *Knightwatch* (ABC-TV): You never know what's gonna happen, Babs—a blade, a banger....

bang house *n.* a brothel.

1984 Former Spec. 4, U.S. Army: "You know that hotel ain't nothin' but a damned bang house." "Don't go to no bang houses." I heard those phrases a lot at Ft. Jackson, S.C., in 1971–72.

banging shop *n.* [cf. KNOCKING SHOP] a brothel.

1970 Longstreet *Nell Kimball* 85: A banging shop life is...dull...most of the time.

bang-on *adj.* exact; precisely accurate.

1981 G. Wolf *Roger Rabbit* 216: A bang-on duplicate of himself.

bangster *n.* *Narc.* an addict who takes a narcotic drug by injection.

1929 *Sat. Eve. Post* (Apr. 13) 54: An addict is a *bangster*, and a *bang* is a...charge...of the drug he uses.

bang-stick *n.* **1.** a rifle or other firearm. *Joc.*

*1961** Partridge *DSUE* (ed. 5) 989: *Bang-stick*. A rifle: partly marksmen's, partly Services': since ca. 1925. **1972** Morris *Strawberry Soldier* 138: A pistol is not a magic bang stick. **1985** Dye *Between Raindrops* 177: Subcaliber fucking bang-sticks and a couple of measly-assed hand grenades.

2. *Sports.* a device used by divers to shoot sharks or other fish underwater.

1973 P. Benchley *Jaws* 280: Some people call it a bang stick....Anyway, it's basically an underwater gun. **1983** *N.Y. Times* (Sept. 27) A 18: Hunters use "bangsticks," poles with .44-caliber bullets on the end, which were designed to protect scuba divers.

bangtail *n.* a racehorse; a horse of any kind.

[*1870** in *OED*: A good mare with a bang tail.] **1921** *Collier's* (Aug. 27) 20, in *DA*: If by some miracle the bangtail wins—beat it! That was Dopey's graft. **1933** Ersine *Prison Slang* 16: *Bangtail, n.* A race horse. **1939** C.R. Cooper *Scarlet* 178: Still working the bang-tails? **1944** R. Adams *West. Words*: *Bangtail*. A mustang or wild horse. **1947** *Sat. Post* (June 14) 12, in *DA*: For centuries, bangtails have been drugged on occasion to make them run faster. **1958** *AS* XXXIII 268: Ranching Terms From Eastern Washington...*Bangtail*. See Horse.

bangtail *v.* [cf. HIGHTAIL] to hurry, race.

1941 *Chippie Wagon* 55: You didn't bangtail out here to talk over old times.

bang-up *n.* **1.** a young sport, a dandy.

*1811** *Lexicon Balatron.* vi: We trust, therefore, that the whole tribe of second-rate Bang ups, will feel grateful for our endeavour to render this part of the work as complete as possible. **1821** Waln *Hermit in Phila.* 23: "I warrant the *bang-ups* have *crooked their elbows*," quoth Tom, as we Chestnut Street [*sic*], about eight o'clock in the evening. *Ibid.* 27: Another of the *Bang-ups*...left the room. *1882** *Punch*, in *F & H* I (rev.) 129: These then are the *dandies*, the *fops*, the *goes* and the *bang-ups*, these the *Corinthians* of to-day.

2. a heavy overcoat.

[**1810** in *OEDS* 198: One article was…a *bang-up* great coat.] **1835** in *OEDS* 198: Dames in *bang-ups,*/Shawls swath'd round men. **1842** in Thornton *Amer. Gloss.* II 37: A gentleman dressed in a dark colored fashionable *bang-up*, with tight-bodied coat, neck-cloth, breast pin, hair and whiskers to match. **1842** in *Ibid.*: That gentlemanly looking man in the snuff-colored *bang-up*, that's Mayor Scott. **1853** Lippard *New York* 51: A man in a coarse, brown *bang-up* addressed the crowd. **1871** Schele de Vere *Americanisms* 439: *Bang-up*, the old word for a heavy overcoat.…"He was clothed in an old *bang-up*, black vest, grey pants, and straw hat." (Philadelphia *Ledger*, June 11, 1853). **1902** Clapin *Americanisms* 36: *Bang up.* An old word for a heavy overcoat, still surviving in some parts of the Union.

bang-up *adj.* **1.a.** intensely fashionable; stylish.

***1810** in *OEDS*: "Bang-up" seems the watch-word to be/From one tip-top driver to t'other. ***1819** [T. Moore] *Tom Crib's Mem.* 13: That bedizen'd old Georgy's *bang-up tog* and kicks! ***1821** *Real Life in Ireland*: Four-dozen *bang-up* ladies. **1873** in Thompson *Youth's Companion* 687: "'Ave a shine?" asked the boy. "They don't look bang up, they don't!" He pointed to Jack's shoes. **1885** Harte *Shore & Sedge* 106: It's more bang-up style.

b. excellent. [Now colloq. and no longer used predicatively; *bang-up job* is the most freq. collocation.]

***1821** *Real Life in Ireland*: 204: [The] whiskey punch…was prime, bang up. **1882** *Judge* (Nov. 11) 10: "How are you?"…"Bang up. Wanter go to a dog fight?" **1910** *DN* III 452: The dinner was *bang-up*. **1931** Dos Passos *1919* 333: Let's go and have a bangup supper. **1949** Maier *Pleasure I.* 105: Take in some dances and shows—have a bang-up time. **1952** "E. Box" *Fifth Position* 143: *And* you did a bang-up job. **1975** J.I. White *Git Along Dogies* 111: It's a bang-up male quartet arrangement. **1975** McCaig *Danger Trail* 28: Some bang-up proposition that will get your ledgers well up on the profit side. **1981** Univ. Tenn. student, age 18: I'll do a bang-up job. **1990** *Nation* (June 11) 835: Given the exigencies of their budget…they did a bang-up job.

2. drunk.

1821** *Real Life in London* I 290: Well *prim'd* with *snuff*…and bang-up with *gin* and *bitters*. **1825** Paulding *J. Bull* 116: The driver being at length "prime bang up," that is to say, as drunk as a lord. [1889** Barrère & Leland *Dict. Slang* I 75: *Banged* up to the eyes is drunk.]

3. without money; penniless; broke.

1854 in *DAE*: The other person, who to use his own classic expression, was "bang up," and wanted to borrow fifty dollars.…I am "bang up." I have got a note of four hundred to pay.

4. finished.

1861 M.A. Denison *Ruth Margerie* 81: "Witness will stop."…"I'm bang-up your Honor."

bang-up *adv.* completely, very; directly, squarely.

1929 "E. Queen" *Roman Hat* v 67: I'm brought bang-up against my profession. **1970** Longstreet *Nell Kimball* 3: I was…bang-up proud of the place. **1990** *Cosmopolitan* (July) 188: Judith Krantz knows how to tell a bang-up good story.

bang wagon *n.* an ambulance.

1962 Crump *Killer* 159: Maybe we'd better call the bang wagon.

banjax *v.* [orig. uncert.; app. fr. Hiberno-E dial.] to batter; break; beat.

***1939** in *OED2*. **1972** *New Yorker* (Oct. 28) 40: So she ups and banjaxed the old man one night with a broken spade handle. **1978** Shem *House of God* 395: Not with Finton's banjaxed leg.

banjo *n.* **1.** [fr. the shape] a frying pan.

***1900–10** in Wilkes *Dict. Austr. Colloq.* 15: *Banjo*: a bush name for a frying pan. **1973** Mathers *Riding Rails* 118: The hobo carried…a "banjo" (a small frying pan).

2. [fr. the shape] a shovel, esp. a short-handled shovel. Also in phr. **banjo and anchor** a shovel and pick.

***1918** in *OEDS*: We are still wielding the old "Banjo" in good style. ***1919** Downing *Digger Dial.* 10 [ref. to A.I.F., WWI]: *Banjo*—A shovel. *Swing the Banjo*—Dig. **1920** *Hist. 26th Engrs.* 128 [ref. to WWI]: Many were chosen to wield the muck-stick and the banjo. **1921** *Variety* (Dec. 30) 4: I wouldn't go out of New York again if I [had to] take the old banjo out of hock and go diggin' sewers. **1926** Maines & Grant *Wise-Crack Dict.* 6: *Pick and banjo*—Pick and shovel to a hobo. **1926** *AS* I 650: *Banjo*—short handled shovel. **1928** Wharton *Squad* 41 [ref. to WWI]: Th' banjo an' anchor boys ain't used to this kinda place. **1930** "D. Stiff" *Milk & Honey* 199: *Banjo*—A short-handled shovel. **1940** in *AS* XVIII 162: *Banjo*. [R.R.] Fireman's shovel. **1941** *AS* (Oct.)

163: *Army banjo*. Shovel. **1942** *AS* (Dec.) 279: [Phila. Navy Yard]. *Banjo*. A shovel. **1946** Mezzrow & Wolfe *Really Blues* 39: You're gonna get a pick and banjo. **1976** Hayden *Voyage* 29: Banging his banjo on the lower lip of boiler number seven.

3. [fr. BANJO-EYED] an eye.

1921 J. Conway, in *Variety* (Aug. 26) 7: He was so cock-eyed that one of his banjos was trained on Kelly every time he went up to hit.

4. a machine gun.

1942 Sanders & Blackwell *Forces* 80: *Chicago Banjo*:…A machine-gun. **1971** Curtis *Banjo* 115: Thompson submachine gun.…Call 'em Tommys or Banjos for short.

5. *Baseball.* BANJO HIT.

1943 *AS* XVIII 104: The *Texas Leaguer* [is called a]…*banjo* [in the International League]. **1971** (quot. at JAPANESE LINER).

6. (see quot.).

1971 Tak *Truck Talk* 8: *Banjo*: The differential housing on a drive axle.

7. *Naval Av.* (*cap.*) a McDonnell F2H Banshee shipboard jet fighter. Now *hist.*

*a***1986** Hallion *Nav. Air War* [ref. to Korean War]: The "Banjo" had nearly a 45-foot wingspread. **1991** Linnekin *80 Knots* 315 [ref. to 1950's]: The "Banjo" had an impressively long service life. **1992** Parsons & Nelson *Fighter Country* 135: The squadron turned in the "Banjo" for the F4D Skyray.

8. *Baseball.* BANJO HITTER.

1990 *Simpsons* (Fox-TV): Those banjos couldn't carry Pie Traynor's glove.

banjo eyes *n.* [alluding to the round white drumhead of a banjo] a person having large, wide-open eyes. Hence **banjo-eyed**, *adj.*

1926 Norwood *Other Side of Circus* 58: How about…the Banjo-eyed Kid? **1928** in Blackbeard & Williams *Smithsonian Comics* 155: Bye Bye Banjo Eyes. **1929** Connelly *Green Pastures* 203: Say, listen to me, Banjo Eyes. What right you got to stop a lady enjoyin' herself? **1929** in Galewitz *Great Comics* 111: Nice work, banjoeyes! *Ibid.* 115: I was talkin' about that banjoeyed nephew of his. **1932** *Time* (July 4) 6: Mr. Albert Hillard of Nevada questions the reference to my husband as "banjo-eyed" Norman Klein. **1937** Thompson *Take Her Down* 114: A banjo-eyed bellboy hurriedly departed in search of a bucket. **1939** Bessie *Men in Battle* 170: Wasn't Mr. Chamberlain interested in concluding an agreement with Banjo-Eyes? [i.e. Francisco Franco]. **1954** DeWitt & Salkow *Sitting Bull* (film): I'm sure gettin' banjo-eyed watchin' that moon, Cap'n. **1970** Longstreet *Nell Kimball* 46: I'd cling to Charlie's arm in the street, wide-eyed, banjo-eyed when we walked.

banjo hit *n. Baseball.* a weakly hit ball that falls between the infield and the outfield.

1937 *Pittsburgh Press* (Jan. 11) (cited in Nichols *Baseball Term.*). **1946** *N.Y. Times Mag.* (July 14) 18: *Texas leaguer*: hit between infield and outfield; also *banjo hit*, humpback liner, looper, pooper, sinker, stinker. **1964** Thompson & Rice *Every Diamond* 139: *Banjo hit*: A ball hit on end of the bat for a hit. **1984–88** in Berry *Where Ya Been?* 260: He's the guy whose banjo hit had ended up costing us the pennant in '49.

banjo hitter *n. Baseball.* a batter who habitually makes BANJO HITS.

1942 *ATS* 647: *Banjo hitter*…one expert at knocking "Texas leaguers." **1959** Brosnan *Long Season* 20: Servants to a bunch of banjo hitters! **1973** Boyd & Harris *Baseball Card* 210: My favorite banjo hitters of the fifties were Pete Runnels…Dan Mueller…and Bob Dillinger. **1980** Lorenz *Guys Like Us* 72: C'mon, you banjo hitter, give it here.

bank *n.* ¶ In phrase: **take to** [or **put in**] **the bank** [pop. by the eponymous hero of the TV series *Baretta*; cf. S.E. *bankable* 'prestigious enough to ensure profitability', current since late 1950's] to be absolutely assured of (something); to bank on.

1977 A. Patrick *Beyond Law* 59: If I catch you on my turf again, I'm gonna push your pretty face in! And you can take *dat* to de bank! **1979** Crews *Blood & Grits* 142: I *ain't* gonna get stuck in this thing, an you can take dat to the bank. *Ibid.* 143: Put it in the bank, I *will* be out of *Baretta*. **1980** *N.Y. Post* (June 20) 78: I will remain the champion. Take that to the bank. **1980** in *Nat. Lampoon* (Jan. 1981) 8: I'll tell you what's wrong with this great country of ours, and this is something you can take to the bank. **1990** *Wkly. World News* (Jan. 30) 17: I was right about the 80s and I'm right about the 90s. You can take that to the bank. **1991** *CBS This Morning* (CBS-TV) (Jan. 28): When we tell you we've done something, you can take it to the bank.

bank-burster *n. Und.* a bank burglar. [Presumably pronounced "-buster."]
　　1880 Pinkerton *Prof. Thieves & Detectives* 59: He associated with a gang of "bank bursters" in one section.

banker *n. Und.* a bank robber.
　　1933 Ersine *Prison Slang* 16: *Banker*...3. A *jugrooter.* "Three bankers came in today with the book."

bankie *n.* [*bank* + -IE] *Und.* a bank robber.
　　1887 Walling *N.Y. Chief of Police* 539: The cells of the three "bankies" were at once thoroughly examined.

bank-snatcher *n. Und.* a bank robber.
　　1890 *Harper's Mag.* (Feb.) 472: One of the most daring bank snatchers in the city effected two robberies in the course of a single day. *1920 in Partridge *Dict. Und.* 20: The most reasonable theory was that the theft...had been accomplished by a gang of Americans, who make a specialty of this class of crime, and are known as "bank snatchers."

bank sneak *n.* [*bank* + SNEAK] *Und.* one of a gang of thieves who rob banks by stealth during business hours.
　　1872 Crapsey *Nether Side* 15: Bank-sneaks of the first class do not number over fifty persons. **1880** Pinkerton *Prof. Thieves & Detectives* 70: A "bank-sneak" is one who, with confederates, makes an excuse of transacting some sort of business at a bank during a time when few of the employees are within. The attention of the cashier...is wholly absorbed by the principal "sneak." **1888** *Chicago Daily Inter-Ocean* (Feb. 16) cited in Farmer *Amer.*: Buffalo officers to-day picked out...Jones, the notorious bank sneak and burglar known professionally in every city of the United States. **1889** Farmer *Amer.*: *Bank-sneak*...A bank thief. **1910** in *DA*: The bank sneak is simply a bank robber.

banneger *n.* [sugg. by *to bang Banagher* s.v. BANG, *v.*, 2.] a heavy blow with the fist.
　　1951 Algren *Chicago* 66: The Cap...raps him a smashing banneger in the teeth.

banner *n.* **1.** [poss. sugg. by *carry the banner*, below] *Hobo.* a bed or bedroll.
　　1925 *Writer's Mo.* (June) 485: *Banner*—A bed. **1933** Ersine *Prison Slang* 16: *Banner, n.* A bed, *flop, kip, balloon.* "Spread your *banner* in that empty reefer."
2. *Circus.* (see quot.).
　　1926 Norwood *Other Side of Circus* 272: A necktie—a *banner.*
¶ In phrase:
¶ **carry** [or **pack**] **the banner** [poss. orig. an allusion to Longfellow's poem "Excelsior" (1841), in which a youth, bearing "a banner with a strange device," freezes to death during the night] (among itinerants) to be a tramp; to spend a night without lodging.
　　1878 A. Pinkerton *Strikers, Communists* 53: Watch any printing office in America for a month....Every day or two a new face appears, and one that has become familiar disappears. They have gone to "carry the banner."..."Carrying the banner" is a slang phrase among printers, denoting that the ensign-bearer is living without work, upon his wits, which are usually equal to any emergency. **1891** in Partridge *Dict. Und.* 107: He "carried the banner," i.e., was in the habit of sleeping out of doors at night. **1899** *Sat. Eve. Post* (Nov. 18) 397: "I was carryin' de banner all night," said the prisoner. **1903** Kildare *Mamie Rose* 50 [ref. to *ca*1875]: Those who had "carried the banner"* in the Frankfort street hallway... *To spend the night without a bed. **1903** *Independent* (Dec. 31) 3105: In this dilemma there was nothing left for us to do but to "carry the banner" till morning, which we decided to do. **1904** *Life in Sing Sing* (gloss.): *Carrying the banner.* Walking the streets. **1907** London *Road* 43: I have made some tough camps in my time, "carried the banner," in infernal metropolises, bedded in pools of water, slept in snow. **1914** Jackson & Hellyer *Crim. Slang* 16: *Carrying the banner*, meaning to walk the streets all night or otherwise endure the hardship of loss of sleep. **1929** Milburn *Hornbook* 229: T'ree nights he's packed the banner. **1935** E. Anderson *Hungry Men* 42: I'll be carrying the banner myself in another week. **1961** Bendiner *Bowery Man* 22: Many then desert the flophouses and prefer to "carry the banner"—a bit of Bowery poetry for spending an unpoetic night on a pier or a park bench, or in the doorway of a warehouse. **1968** Spradley *Drunk* 114: A tramp who is not able to score for any flop money may have to walk the streets all night or "carry the banner."

banshee *n.* ¶ In phrase: **like a banshee** (used broadly as an emphatic comparative).
　　1976 *Urban Life* V 302: Try to talk to her and she comes on like a ban-

shee. Who needs that? **1983** *N.Y. Daily News* (Mar. 25): Teentalk Glossary...*party like a banshee*—to have a good time. *a*1984 in Safire *Stand Corrected* 24: I worked like a banshee all day. *Ibid.* 25: Running like a banshee.

banzai *n.* **1.** [short for *banzai charge*] *Mil.* an assault by Japanese infantry. Now *hist.*
　　1945 Huie *Omaha to Oki.* 27: Before the Japs pulled their last big "banzai" on Iwo Jima. **1946** Hough *Island War* 243: What Saito planned [on Saipan] was, in short, a Banzai in the grand manner. It was to be frankly suicidal. **1960** Bonham *Burma Rifles* 127: They made six attacks that day—every one of them a real banzai. **1968** J. Kelly *Unexpected Peace* 50: With the help of the rain, they would probably pull a banzai. One final all-out banzai. *a*1982 in Berry *Semper Fi* 230: Then came the banzai....We might have been overrun.
2. Esp. *Drag Racing.* an all-out effort, as in an automobile race.
　　1976 *Webster's Sports Dict.* 28.

banzai *v. Mil.* (of infantry) to charge with fanatic enthusiasm.
　　1972–74 Hawes & Asher *Raise Up* 64 [ref. to Korean War]: The motherfuckers came out of their foxholes and banzaied back so fast the Chinese dropped their guns and ran.

banzai *interj.* [Japn] (used to express excitement or enthusiasm).
　　1980 Novak *High Culture* 37: I started running down the hill toward the school, yelling "Banzai!" **1980** *Time* (Sept. 6) 86: NBC will have a jump on the other two networks, which just might cause NBC President Fred Silverman to yell "Banzai!" **1980** W.C. Anderson *BAT-21* 30 [ref. to Vietnam War]: A direct hit—"Banzai" he muttered. *Ibid.* 112: Banzai!...I saw them. **1983** De Lello *Bad Boys* (film): I get some privileges too. Banzai!

baptize *v.* **1.** to dilute (an alcoholic beverage) with water, esp. as a means of defrauding the purchaser.
　　*1636 in *OED*: He wil give his best friends his baptised wine. *1811 *Lexicon Balatron.*: *Baptized*, or *Christened.* Rum, brandy, or any other spirits that have been lowered with water. **1859** Matsell *Vocabulum* 10: *Baptized.* Liquor that has been watered. **1942** *ATS* 114: *Baptized booze, —stuff,* & c., diluted liquor.
2. to pour cold water upon.
　　[*1823 "J. Bee" *Slang Dict.*: *Baptist.*—A pickpocket caught and ducked.] **1864** in H. Johnson *Talking Wire* 171: One of the boys got a little too much "how come you so" and the capt. thought it necessary that he should be baptized. **1889** Meriwether *Tramp at Home* 222: "Baptize him!" ordered the mate....A bucket of water brought me back to life and agony.

barb[1] *n.* [shortening of *barbarian* '(among ancient Greeks) a non-Greek'] *Stu.* a student who is not a member of a Greek letter society.
　　1900 *DN* II 22: *Barb, n.* A nonfraternity man. **1918** *DN* V 22: *Barb,* adj. Characteristic of a "barb," i.e., a non-fraternity man or woman. "He has *barb* manners." **1925** S. Lewis *Arrowsmith* ch. ii: In college Martin had been "barb"—he had not belonged to a Greek Letter secret society. **1927** *AS* II 275: *Barb*—a non-fraternity student. **1942** A.C. Johnston *Courtship of A. Hardy* (film): She's sort of a sad apple, a barb. **1943** Shulman *Barefoot Boy* 36: And you know how bad off a fellow is who don't join no fraternity at all. Damn barb. **1946** W.A. White *Autobiog.* 169 [ref. to 1888]: The Phi Delts allied themselves politically with the Barbs (the nonfraternity men). **1987** Horowitz *Campus Life* 66 [ref. to Univ. Nebr., 1890's]: As a "Barb," his primary recreation was the literary society.

barb[2] *n.* a barbiturate pill. Also **barbie.**
　　1966 Goldstein *One in Seven* 55: The price of "bombitas" and "barbs" on the streets has already skyrocketed. **1966** Young & Hixson *LSD* 138: "Bennies" and "barbs." **1970** Cortina *Warrior* 72 [ref. to 1950's]: I usta fool around with other things too...barbies...barbiturates. **1973** *Drug Forum* II 283: He appears intoxicated (reportedly on barbs and/or white port). **1977** *Rolling Stone* (Oct. 20) 8: What I wrote was "booze and barbs," as in barbiturates. **1980** Luceno *Head Hunters* 50: In high school they had leagued together dealing sopers and barbs from their lockers.

barb *v.* to barber.
　　1865 Sala *Diary* II 155: You can be shaved, or "barbed," as the locution is.

Barbary Coast *n.* [sugg. by the *Barbary Coast* of N. Afr., formerly notorious for its pirates] the criminal and red-light district of San Francisco. Now *S.E.*

1867 in B. Harte *Harte's Calif.* 125: [The] "Barbary coast"—as the back slums of Pacific street are called. **1869** *Overland Mo.* (Oct.) 298: Bearing on his face and person the marks of the "Barbary Coast," bad liquor, an empty pocket, and a prolonged spree. **1871** Crofutt *Tourist's Guide* 206: The BARBARY COAST, a noted resort for thieves, cut-throats, and the vilest of the vile, is situated on Pacific St., between Kearny and Dupont Sts. We give the precise locality so that our readers may *keep away*. Give it a "*wide berth*," as you value your life. **1880** in *DA*: On the Barbary Coast...the patrolmen are above suspicion. **1914** Ellis *Billy Sunday* 18: Go to the lowest dive in New York's "Tenderloin" or in San Francisco's "Barbary Coast." **1928** Dahlberg *Bottom Dogs* 205: Toward midnite, he happened into barbary coast. **1966** Hugill *Sailortown* 210: About the middle sixties the name "Barbary Coast" came into common use for the district, and its old appellation of Sydney Town died....Several boundaries of the area are given by different writers, but the most popular limits seem to be Broadway on the north, Clay and Commercial on the south, Grant Avenue and Chinatown on the west and the Waterfront and East Street on the east. In later times Barbary Coast came to mean the Pacific Street area only—a quarter known to sailors as "Terrific Street." **1977** *Barbary Coast* [title of ABC-TV series set in San Francisco, 1880's]. **1990** *New Republic* (Aug. 13) 23: With her manners and wealth, she was not exactly the saloon queen of the Tenderloin, the majorette of Castro Street, the toast of the Barbary Coast.

barbecue *n.* **1.** [prob. sugg. by *chicken* or *chick*] Esp. *Black E.* an attractive young woman.

1938 Louis Armstrong and His Orchestra *Struttin' with Some Barbecue* [Decca phono. record Dec 1636, recorded Jan. 12]. **1944** Burley *Harlem Jive* 133: *Barbecue*—A very attractive girl. **1948** Manone & Vandervoort *Trumpet* 145: I am your solid barbecue. I ain't signifying....Do you dig?

2. *Mil.* a napalm attack.

1968 *Newsweek* (Mar. 18) 37: "Captain Gunn wants a barbecue."...Napalm splashed in on the NVA positions.

barbed wire or **barbwire** *n.* strong whiskey or brandy.

1891 Devere *Tramp Poems* 7: Walt Fletcher...at best done nothing wuss than punish barb-wire whisky. **1912** in Service *Coll. Poems* 208. **1919** *Hist. 307th F.A.* 185: Not all of the "barbed wire" was consumed within the battalion. **1928** Nason *Eadie* 121: Wow!...Who ordered this extract of barbed wire?

barbed-wire city *n. Mil.* a prison stockade.

[**1947** *ATS* (Supp.) 20: Guardhouse...*wire city*.] **1964** Peacock *Drill & Die* 8: Trudo here...spent two months in Barbwire City for calling Bizal a son of a bitch. **1966** Parks *G.I. Diary* (Jan. 11): They caught two AWOL's today. It's barbed-wire city for them for six weeks. **1971** U.S. Army veteran, age 29, served 1961–62: "Barbed-Wire City" meant the stockade.

barber *n.* [fr. the proverbial talkativeness of barbers] Esp. *Sports.* a tediously loquacious person.

1927 *N.Y. Sun* (July 18): In the American League a player who is given to talking a great deal is called a "barber."...The significance...is unmistakable. **1929** *N.Y. Times* (June 2) IX 2: A talkative ballplayer is termed a "barber," while one who "rides" opposing players is called a "jockey." Leo Durocher, the young shortstop of the Yankees, has won considerable fame in both of these rôles. **1931** Farrell *McGinty* 44: There's the door, you goddamn barber. **1970** Scharff *Encyc. of Golf* 415: *Barber.* A talkative player.

¶ In phrase:

¶ **like a barber's cat** (see quots.).

[***1873** Hotten *Slang Dict.* (ed. 4) 78: *Barber's Cat*, a half-starved sickly-looking person. Term used in connexion with an expression too coarse to print.] ***1948** Partridge *DSUE* (ed. 3) 984: *Like a barber's cat*, all wind and piss: late C.19–20. **1952** H. Grey *Hoods* 202: You're-full-of-wind-and-piss—like-a-barber's-cat.

barber *v.* to talk tediously and at length; to gossip idly.

1928 Ruth *Baseball* 20: The boys were sitting around the club house..."barbering" a little about what we might expect in the series. **1929** in Hammett *Knockover* 57: What the hell am I doing barbering with a lousy dick? **1929–31** Farrell *Young Lonigan* 111: We gets to barbering about one ting an' anoder. **1931** Farrell *McGinty* 45: Mike Mulroney roared to Billy to quit barbering and get going. **1944** Paxton *Murder, My Sweet* (film): I shouldn't oughta sit here and barber with you.

barber chair *n. Logging.* a stump to which an upright slab of the felled tree remains attached. Also as *v.* (see 1974 quot.).

1938–41 in Mencken *Amer. Lang. Supp. II* 758. **1956** Sorden & Ebert

Logger's 1 [ref. to *a*1925]: *Barber-chair.* A stump with part of the tree still on it due to the tree splitting when falling. **1958** McCulloch *Woods Words* 7: *Barber chair*—a. A tree which is split up the trunk in falling, leaving the split portion on the stump, instead of breaking through cleanly to the undercut. b. The act of making a tree into a barber chair. **1959** *AS* (Feb.) 76: *Barber chair. n.*...a stump on which a slab is left standing that splintered off the tree as it fell. **1968** R. Adams *West. Wds.* (ed. 2) 12. **1974** *Pop. Science* (Nov.) 137: Proceeding in the normal undercut/backcut fashion might force the tree to "slab" (or, as the loggers say, "barber-chair," or split vertically fr. the stump). **1979** *Harper's* (Oct.) 37: An improperly undercut tree has...barberchaired (split because of a heavy lean and insufficient undercut) and wiped out the man felling it. **1979** Toelken *Dynamics of Folklore* 54: *Barber chair*, a tree that starts to split and fall before the cut is finished.

barber pole *n.* [ref. to the spiral stripes of a barber pole] *Logging.* (see quot.).

1958 McCulloch *Woods Words* 7: *Barber pole*—A tree which has grown with an extreme twist.

barber's clerk *n. Naut.* an irresponsible sailor who is overparticular about his appearance.

*1835 C. Dickens *Sks. by "Boz"* 155: Barber's clerk!...Throw him o-ver! **1844** J.F. Cooper *Afloat & Ashore* 44: The parson's son was likely to turn out a regular "barber's clerk" to the captain. **1849** Melville *Redburn* ch. vi: A sailor!...a barber's clerk, you mean. ***1929** Bowen *Sea Slang* 7: *Barber's clerk.* A dainty, well-groomed seaman who is poor at his job. ***1962** W. Granville *Dict. Sailors' Sl.*: *Barber's clerk.* One who thinks more of his personal appearance than of his work; a skulker who always wants to be "watch ashore."

barbie *n.* [orig. Austral. E] a barbecue.

1976 in *BDNE3*. **1984** *L.A. Times* (July 31) IV 14: In recent months, the slogan "Gooday—Put a shrimp on the barby" has become known in Southern California households as a result of an aggressive tourism promotion of Australia [featuring actor Paul Hogan]. **1986** *N.Y. Times* (Dec. 1) 6: The whole congregation...was invited to the giant "barbie." **1990** *U.S. News & W.R.* (July 9) 57: Watch yer billy boil, waltz with Matilda,...and throw a shrimp on the barbie. **1991** *Tiny Toon Adventures* (synd. TV series): It's time to throw another shrimp on the barbie.

bar-dog *n. West.* a bartender. Hence **bar-dogging** tending bar.

1944 R. Adams *West. Words: Bar-dog.* A bar tender. **1967** Gries *Will Penny* (film): Maybe I'll get a job bar-doggin'.

bare *adj.* ¶ In phrase: **go bare** *Insurance.* to carry no insurance coverage.

1976 in *BDNE2*. **1977** *Dallas Times Herald* (May 1) 40A: A TMA survey last year showed that more doctors were "going bare" (doing without insurance). **1985** *L.A. Times* (Apr. 14) IV 2: Doctors were caught in the hysteria and some threatened to "go bare"—practice without insurance—while others threatened to quit. **1986** WINS radio news (Mar. 31): "Goin' bare" means to do business without carrying liability insurance.

bare-assed or **bare-ass** *adj. & adv.* with unclothed buttocks, (*usu.*) naked; (*hence*) utterly unprotected; bare; (*also*) barefaced, blatant.—usu. considered vulgar.

*1562 in *F & H* I (rev.) 68: To beg a breeche of a bare arst man. **1744** A. Hamilton *Gentleman's Progress* 161: Would have been obliged to strutt about bare-arsed. *ca*1888 *Stag Party* 190: Slim was embarrassed [*sic*]....He was em-bare-arsed, too. ***1928** D.H. Lawrence, in *OEDS*. **1935** Farrell *Guillotine Party* 70: We'll have another of our famous bare-ass parties. **1936** Kingsley *Dead End* 687: Well, go in bareass. **1939** Appel *People Talk* 269: I come into this world bare-ass and I'll leave it bare-ass. **1946** Heggen *Mr. Roberts* 97: Holy Christ! She's bare-assed! **1955** T. Anderson *Your Own Beloved Sons* 63: You going on that bare-ass patrol, up that valley?...Up that valley in two bare-ass jeeps? **1960** Barber *Minsky's* 254: There you sit bare-ass readin' a book without a stitch on. **1962** T. Berger *Reinhart* 122: I ain't got a brown, bare-ass penny I can call my own. **1962** E. Stephens *Blow Negative* 292: Right in the broad bare-ass daylight. **1971** Dahlskog *Dict.* 5: *Bare-assed*...Naked; without hair on the rump; blatant; undisguised; bare-faced. **1980** Manchester *Darkness* 209: The troops ashore were left bare-assed.

bareback *adv. & adj.* **1.** (of a tractor truck) without an attached trailer.

1942 *AS* (Apr.) 102: *Bareback.* Tractor without a trailer. Also *Bob Tail.* **1971** Tak *Truck Talk* 8: *Bareback*: said of a tractor less its semi-trailer. **1978** Lieberman & Rhodes *CB* (ed. 2) 288: *Bareback*—Truck without trailer.

2. without the use of a condom.—usu. considered vulgar.

1954–60 *DAS* 20: *Bareback…adj. & adv.* Without a contraceptive; said of the male only, in ref. to the act of coitus. *****1961** Partridge *DSUE* (ed. 5) 990: *Bareback riding…*Coition without contraceptive: male: C.20. **1963** Rubin *Sweet Daddy* 110: Some of them use rubbers. But most guys want bareback. **1968–70** *Current Slang* III & IV 7: We took a chance and did it bareback. **1971** Horan *Blue Messiah* 268: Did you go in bareback? **1980** M. Baker *Nam* 207: I never got the clap and I always went in bareback.

bare-balls *adj.* completely naked.—usu. considered vulgar.

*a***1965** Shirota *Lucky Come Hawaii* 172: He had been planning to swim bare-balls.

barefoot or **barefooted** *adj. & adv.* **1.** [cf. syn. BARELEGGED] (of an alcoholic drink) undiluted; (of coffee or tea) without cream or sugar; straight.

*ca***1845** in *DA* 76: I thought even a Yankee knew that "stone fence barefooted" is the polite English for whiskey uncontaminated—pure, sir! **1866** Lowell *Biglow Papers* "I take my tea barfoot," said a backwoodsman when asked if he would have cream and sugar. **1878** Beadle *West. Wilds* 183: It was…corn [whiskey] bare-footed. **1888** Whitman *November Boughs* 406: "Barefoot Whiskey" is the Tennessee name for the undiluted stimulant. **1918** Ross *With 351st* 40: At some meals we have coffee without a grain of sugar—barefoot coffee—and some meals, no coffee at all. **1980** *N.Y. Times Mag.* (Jan. 27) 8: Coffee is serious stuff, but jocular types may call it *barefoot* (black) and *with socks on* (white).

2. *R.R.* (of a car or locomotive) lacking brakes or the ability to brake.

1940 *Railroad Mag.* (Apr.) 37: *Barefoot*—Car or engine without brakes.

3. (of a motor vehicle) lacking one or more tires.

1937–41 in Mencken *Amer. Lang. Supp.* II 724. **1971** Tak *Truck Talk* 8: *Barefoot*: refers to a tractor or trailer that lacks one or more tires.

4. without the use of a condom; BAREBACK, 2.

1963 D. Tracy *Brass Ring* 248 [ref. to 1930's]: You could go barefoot here with no risk at all if you wanted to. **1970** Ahlstrom & Havighurst *400 Losers* 177: See, my Dad, he gave me a box of rubbers, and he tells me not to go barefoot again.

5. *CB.* without a linear amplifier.

1975–76 Dills *CB* 14: Hey, good buddy, are you sure you're running barefoot in that mobile? You're blowing my windows out. **1976** *Sci. Mech. CB Gde.* 156: *Barefoot.* Transmitter with legal power output. *This rig is running barefoot.* **1977** Corder *Citizens Band* 76: Attention to all CB operators. I'm no longer running barefoot.

6. *CB.* without a license to operate.

1976 Adcock *Not Truckers Only* 33: A friend of mine in Montana is one such "barefoot" (unlicensed) CBer.

barefoot pilgrim *n.* (see quot.).

1980 *AS* (Winter) 310: Car salesmen in north Georgia employ [an intriguing] term…a gullible or uninformed customer is a *barefoot pilgrim*.

barelegged *adj.* [cf. BAREFOOT, 1] (of an alcoholic drink) undiluted, straight.

1704 in *DA* 76: But the pumpkin and Indian mixt bred had such an aspect, and the bare-legg'd punch so awkerd or rather awfull a sound, that we left both.

bare poles *n.* ¶ In phrase: **under bare poles** *Naut.* scantily clad; unclothed.

1823 J.F. Cooper *Pilot* 299: A man does look like the devil…scudding about a ship's decks in that fashion, under bare poles! **1849** Melville *White Jacket* 17: For no idea had I of scudding round Cape Horn in my shirt; for *that* would have been almost scudding under bare poles indeed. **1917** *DN* IV 335 [Nantucket]: *Scud under bare poles…*To be scantily clad. **1945** Colcord *Sea Lang.* 29: *Bare poles, under.* With all sails furled, while at sea, due to stress of weather. In coastal dialect it is facetiously used to mean naked, stripped.

bares *n.pl.* one's bare hands.

1969 *Current Slang* I & II 7: *Bares,* n. Hands, as in "paws."—Air Force Academy cadets.— I had it in my *bares.* **1971** Dahlskog *Dict.* 5: *Bares, n.* The bare hands.

barf *n.* [fr. the v.] **1.** vomit; (*hence*) repulsive food; in phr. **barf on a board** creamed chipped beef on toast.

1962 in *AS* (Oct. 1963) 174: *Barf* "beef stew." **1966** Bob Dylan *Tarantula* 33: The barf &/Gook in the book/Of his cook. **1968** Brunvand *Study Amer. Folklore* 299: "Tuna Wiggle," "Barf on a Board," and other traditional names for institutional cooking. **1969** *Current Slang* I & II

7: *Barbequed barf,* n. Dormitory or dining hall food.—College males, Texas. **1971** Jacobs & Casey *Grease* 11 [ref. to 1950's]: Wait'll you have the chipped beef. Better known as "Barf on a Bun." **1973** N.Y.C. telephone switchman, age 21: I've heard Marines in Vietnam call "shit-on-a-shingle" *barf-on-a-board.* **1974** Lahr *Trot* 206: He didn't have to wipe up your barf. **1976** Woodley *Bears* 141: Let's see YOU make this team, barf-breath! **1980** Kotzwinkle *Jack* 170: He woke in a puddle of barf. **1984** N. Stephenson *Big U.* 129: All that barf on the floors. **1986** Watterson *Calvin* 10: This smells like bat barf. **1988** *Night Court* (NBC-TV): Wake up and smell the rubber barf.

2. a repulsive or despicable person.

1964 *Time* (Jan. 1, 1965) 56: A *zilch* is a [person who is] a total loss, and so is a *wimp,…gink, barf,* [etc.]. **1968** Baker et al. *CUSS* 76: *Barf.* An ugly person, female.

barf *v.* [orig. unkn.; not fr. Yid *varfn* or G *werfen* 'to throw'; no corresp. sense of "vomit" exists in these languages] to vomit. [This and derived terms esp. common among college students.]

1947 (implied at BARFER). **1956** P. Moore *Chocolates* 95: I turned around and barfed. **1958** J. Davis *College Vocab.* 14: *Barf*—Regurgitate. **1958** Frede *Entry E* 120: I'm barfing. **1960** MacCuish *Gentle* 199 [ref. to 1940's]: Gettin' so every time I barf—I bleat. **1960** Swarthout *Where Boys Are* 89: I'd barf. **1961** H. Ellison *Gentleman Junkie* 173: Otherwise you'll barf right then. Your stomach can't hold it down for very long. **1966** Fariña *Down So Long* 15: Got her drunk on grasshoppers and she barfed all over the back seat of the car. **1970** Dunn *Attic* 65: She stiffened as though I'd barfed on him. **1971** Rowe *5 Yrs.* 256: For nearly two hours, his stomach turned inside out, racking him with dry heaves when there was nothing left to barf. **1974** *Harper's* (Nov.) 89: They are barfing on the floor, they are moaning. **1979** Gutcheon *New Girls* 118: You barf all over my sister, and you say you're *sorry?* **1988** Univ. Tenn. psychology prof., age 58: I started college at the University of Chicago in September 1948, and my first roommate in the dormitory frequently used the word *barf* to mean throwing up after drinking too much. I had never heard the word before, and it made something of an impression on me.

¶ In phrase:

¶ **barf [me] out!** *Stu.* "how disgusting!" See also BARF OUT.

1982 S. Black *Totally Awesome* 19: It's like *barf out!* **1982** A. Land & W. Crawford *Valley Girl* (film): Barf me out!

barf *interj.* "I am disgusted!" Also **barfaroo.**

1970–72 in *AS* 50 (1975) 56: *Barf…interj.* A term of disapproval or disgust. **1976** Conroy *Santini* 301: "Oh barf," Mary Anne said. "The birth of the golden Apollo." **1980** Univ. Tenn. student: Oh, barf! You're not going into that again. **1982** in *Nat. Lampoon* (Feb. 1983) 14: These doughnuts are rubbery. Barf-a-roo. **1988** Groening *Childhood Is Hell* (unp.): Oh, *barf.*

barfbag *n.* **1.** a paper bag routinely provided to airline passengers for use in case of vomiting as a result of severe motion sickness.

1966 E. Shepard *Doom Pussy* 92: Jones was there in a flash with a small brown envelope containing a plastic barf bag, then distributed more to the others. **1968** Moura & Sutherland *Tender Loving Care* 193: She headed for another barf bag and went at it again. **1972** W.C. Anderson *Hurricane* 139: We'll have barf bags aboard. **1980** N.Y.C. man, age *ca*30: The price of the food is figured into your ticket. And the price of the barfbag too. **1984** Heath *A-Team* 180: Do they have barf bags on this plane? **1990** R. Dorr *Desert Shield* 13: Although the flying was rough, no one…needed a barf bag.

2. a disgusting, worthless person. Cf. SCUMBAG.

1972 Wambaugh *Blue Knight* 67: You can't be a varsity letterman when you deal with these barf-bags. *Ibid.* 219: Get out of my park, you barf-bags. **1976** Univ. Tenn. student: That cock-sucking barfbag. **1978** S. King *Stand* 124: Would you like to try for two teeth, barfbag? **1982** "J. Cain" *Commandos* 352: I've had plenty of handcuffed barfbags fight me…all the way to the slammer. **1990** *Tenn. Ling.* X (Winter) 38: Insults…"Scum,"…"Trash,"…"Barf bag."

barfer *n.* [fr. BARF, *v.*] a disgusting, worthless person.

1947 A. Reynolds *Home Sweet Homicide* 14: "My Pete."…"That barfer!"…"You shush-up about Pete!" *Ibid.* 33: You barfer!

barfly *n.* **1.** a drunkard, derelict, or other person who hangs about bars, esp. in order to cadge drinks.

1906 A.H. Lewis *Confessions* 211: Three dull-witted bar-flies—thick, beer-soaked toughs, such as hang about the East Side bar-rooms, had done the job. **1910** in *DA* 75: Then, after having confessed to so much money, he hastened out, for he wud not be stung by bar-flies. **1918** Tibbals *Sgt. Jim* 26: The cities were filled with poolroom loafers and bar-flies. **1919** Darling *Jargon Bk.* 4: *Bar Fly*—One who hangs around bar rooms. **1929** E. Wilson *Daisy* 115: I've fought fleas and rats and bedbugs in my time—and Greenwich Village bar-flies—so I guess I could cope with a tarantula! **1956** in Asimov et al. *Sci. Fi. Short Shorts* 175: You old bar fly. **1966** "Petronius" *N.Y. Unexp.* 193: He became a permanent barfly and tramp. **1975** McCaig *Danger Trail* 8: Now the barflies…gathered around the keg, for it was not every day that free beer was available at Fort Benton. **1987** C. Bukowski *Barfly* (film title).

2. *Specif.*, B-GIRL, 1.

1985 T. Wells *444 Days* 23: A barfly came slinking up and wanted me to buy her a Coke. It was just like in Saigon, where the bar girls sit on your lap and want you to buy them a drink. **1993** *Newsweek* (Jan. 11) 12: A smokey is a CB term for people I learned to…bribe with a barfly when I tended bar at 16.

barf out *v.* to disgust, revolt, GROSS OUT. Hence **barfed out** *adj.* disgusting.

1982 in *Nat. Lampoon* (Feb. 1983) (front cover): Like, the government's nuclear evacuation plans are totally barfed out, unworkable, and mega-stupid. **1984** Univ. Tenn. instructor: That barfs me out.

barfulous *adj.* [BARF + -*ulous* (sugg. by incred*ulous*)] *Stu.* disgusting or terrible; repulsive. Also vars.

1983 Naiman *Computer Dict.* 18: CP/M documentation is absolutely barfulous. *Ibid.* 23: *Barfulous* (can [also] be used of something which works OK but is ugly or clumsy). **1985** Univ. Tenn. student theme: "Barfous"…describes a horrible-looking person.

barfy *adj.* **1.** *Esp. Stu.* nauseating; repulsive.

1957 Kohner *Gidget* 9: My English comp teacher…that barfy looking character. **1960** Swarthout *Where Boys Are* 154: So barfy to look at they can never get dates on their own. **1978** Skolnik *Fads* i: Poodle Skirts and Barfy Bermuda Shorts. **1981** Wambaugh *Glitter Dome* 174: Nobody would pick up anybody as barfy-looking as you. **1988** *Mama's Family* (NBC-TV): Marriage is barfy. **1988** Groening *Childhood Is Hell* (unp.): Yucky food. Barfy beets.

2. *Stu.* nauseated.

1968 Baker et al. *CUSS* 77: *Barfy*. Have a minor illness, feel sick.

barge *n.* *Surfing.* a very large surfboard.

1977 Filosa *Surf. Almanac* 181. **1979** Cuddon *Dict. Sports & Games* 85.

bar-hog *n.* **1.** a heavy drinker who hangs about the bar in a saloon.

1932 Riesenberg *Log of Sea* 143 [ref. to 1904]: The stevies from the other hatches began to pile in behind the bar hogs.

2. B-GIRL, 1.—used contemptuously.

1966 in B. Edelman *Dear Amer.* 107: This is the usual approach of a bar-hog!…A girl will be sitting next to you and she'll begin with "Hello. What is your name?"

barhop *n.* [cf. BELLHOP] a bartender.

1908 McGaffey *Show Girl* 121: Tell the barhop to mix me up a life preserver in a rose glass. **1930** Bodenheim *Roller Skates* 140: Slapped that barhop groggy down in Laredo, 'cause the 'hop was flipping his mouth about the bones being loaded.

barhound *n.* [*bar* + HOUND] BARFLY.

1923 McAlmon *Companion Volume* 193: What are you, a lady or a barhound? **1986–91** Hamper *Rivethead* 186: A bar hound like you will never beat the clock.

bark *n.* the human skin; (*also*) one's scalp.—sometimes in phr. **take the bark off** to give a hiding to; thrash.

***ca*1758** in *OED*: And dang the bark/Aff's shin. **1845** Hooper *S. Suggs* 10: Oh, never mind the money, Bill; the old man's going to take the bark off both of us. **1848** in *AS* XVI 181: Bark…a scalp. ***1858** A. Mayhew *Paved with Gold* 190: He…returned the [blow] on Jack's cheek, "peeling the bark." ***1876** in *OED*: With the "bark" all off his shins from a stone whack on a hockey stick. **1883** Hay *Bread-Winners* 214: "Is anybody hurt?" "I've got a little bark knocked off." **1884** Beard *Bristling with Thorns* 334: Drat ef I don't take the bark off that niggah myself. **1944** Burley *Harlem Jive* 133: Bark—Skin.

¶ In phrase:

¶ **with the bark on, 1.** (of a statement) with no attempt to improve, mitigate, soften, etc.; plain; unvarnished.

1839 *Spirit of Times* (Dec. 28) 511: I see Long has "spoke the word with the bark on." **1872** "M. Twain" *Roughing It* ch. xv: That is the word with the bark on it. **1884** Beard *Bristling with Thorns* 358: Dat's de word wid de bark on. **1885** in *DAE*: "I don't like her,…and that is the truth,

dear."…"With the bark on. No more do I." **1903** in *DA*: Your Westerner with the bark on is fond of…picturesque figures of speech.

2. (see quot.).

1925 *AS* I 137: Chase us some of them spuds with the bark on (unpeeled potatoes)….Pie with the bark on [i.e., with a crust].

bark *v.* **1.** [back formation fr. BARKER, 1.a.] to advertise a store, carnival, theatrical performance, etc., by standing at the entrance and calling out to passersby; to be a BARKER. Now *colloq.* or *S.E.*

***1821** *Real Life in London* I 365: Ladies' dresses also used to be *barked* in Cranbourn Alley. **1904** Hobart *Jim Hickey* 84: We could make sandwich money in front of a hootchy-kooch palace, barking at the Rubes. *a*1904–11 Phillips *Susan Lenox* I 224: Pat, ready to take tickets, was "barking" vigorously in the direction of the shore, addressing a crowd. **1948** *Time* (July 19) 90: Another triumph for Liberty's brand of mass production plus carnival barking.

2. *Und.* to fire a gun.

1859 Matsell *Vocabulum* 10: *Barking*. Shooting. **1904** *Life in Sing Sing* 263: What does that greaser do but flash his rod and bark away….What does the fellow do but draw his pistol and shoot.

3. to boast, crow.

***a*1898** in *EDD*: Jimmy'd done a deal o' barkin' 'cos he'd licked all he'd fo'tten. **1967** *Lit Dict.* 3: Barking—When one is *barking*, he's bragging, blowing his horn, chest-beating about his greatness.

4. [sugg. by DOG, *n.*] (of the feet) to ache.

1938 in *AS* (Apr. 1939) 89: *Barking Dogs*. Aching feet. "My dogs are barking." **1947** Helseth *Martin Rome* 118: "Listen at them dogs bark," she invited. **1950** Riesenberg *Waterfront* 184: My dogs sure are barking! **1990** Ruggero *38 N. Yankee* 22: My dogs are barking here, Dale.

bark-eater *n.* (see quot.).

1958 McCulloch *Woods Words* 7: *Bark eater*—a. a logger. b. a sawmill hand.

barkeep *n.* barkeeper, bartender. Also as *v.* Now *colloq.* or *S.E.*

1846 *Spirit of Times* (July 4) 218: We embarked…in company with…a *barkeep* to mix the l—q—rs. **1856** in Dwyer & Lingenfelter *Songs of Gold Rush* 120: The "bar keep" tells him. **1895** F.P. Dunne, in Schaaf *Dooley* 92: "We havn't anny," says th' barkeep. **1947** Overholser *Buckaroo's Code* 31: He turned to the barkeep. **1975** Hinton *Rumble Fish* 8: You could paint, write, barkeep, or bum around. I tried barkeeping once. **1979** F. Thomas *Golden Bird* 110: He asked the barkeep.

barker *n.* **1.a.** a person who offers merchandise by standing near a shop entrance and calling out loudly to passersby to praise what is for sale there; (*specif.*) (in modern use) an employee of a carnival or other show who solicits patronage in this manner. Now *S.E.*

***1698–99** "B.E." *Dict. Canting Crew*: *Barker*, a Salesman's Servant that walks before the Shop, and cries, Cloaks, Coats, or Gowns, what d'ye lack, Sir? ***1725** *New Canting Dict.*: The Cove has bilk'd the *Barker*; i.e. The Rogue has cheated the Salesman's Man. ***1785** Grose *Vulgar Tongue*: *Barker*, the shopman of a dealer in second hand clothes, particularly about Monmouth-street, who walks before his shop, and deafens every passenger with his cries of clothes, coats, or gowns, what d'ye want *gemmen*, what d'ye buy? ***1821** *Real Life in London* I 105: To stand at the door like a *barker* at a broker's shop. ***1822** in *OED* I 673: As shopmen and barkers tease you to buy goods. ***1823** "J. Bee" *Slang* 6: *Barkers*.—Fellows placed at the door of Mock Auctions to invite soft people to get *shaved*; also bidders and pretended buyers planted within to trap the unwary—of both genders. *Barkers* also invite vehemently passengers to buy household goods in Moorfields, and dresses in Cranbourn-alley. **1859** Matsell *Vocabulum* 10: *Barker*. One who patrols the streets for customers in front of his employer's shop; vide Chatham Street. **1871** Schele de Vere *Americanisms* 319: He was one of the most accomplished *strikers*, or barkers, as they are called, in the employ of the hells. (*The Country Merchant*, p. 317.) **1888** in *F & H* (rev.) 140: I am a barker by profession. The pedestrian agility required to pace up and down before the "Half-Dime Museum of Anatomy and Natural History," soliciting passers-by to enter is of itself enormous. **1897** *Harper's Wkly.* (Jan. 9) 44: As many as fifty shops in a row, with all the "barkers" and "pullers-in" and quaint signs in Yiddish, German, and English that once made Baxter street a street to be avoided by all but athletes and artists. **1904** *Life in Sing Sing* 246: *Barker*…a person who solicits attendance in a loud voice. **1921** Conklin & Root *Circus* 156: Spaf was a sleight-of-hand performer and voluble "barker." **1930** in R.E. Howard *Iron Man* 8: I sat in the "athletic tent" of a carnival…grinning at the antics of the barker. **1942** Liebling *Telephone Booth* 4: No carnie says "barker." The man…is the "outside talker," his oration is…"the open-ing." **1951** Mannix *Sword-Swallower* 35: The…talker…was what I would have called the show's barker, but I afterward learned that the term "barker" is never used in a carnival. **1963** Horwitz *Candlelight* 92: He looked over the crowd like a barker at a state fair.

b. an auctioneer.

1904 *Life in Sing Sing* 246: *Barker.* An auctioneer. **1917–20** Dreiser *Newspaper Days* 92 [ref. to 1892]: The noisy "barkers," as they were called,…"knocked down" [cheap jewelry] to…yokels.

2.a. a pistol or revolver; gun.

1814 in *DAE*: Travellers would do well to keep a pair of barkers in their retinue, and otherwise be prepared against highwaymen. ***1815** W. Scott *Guy Mannering* ch. xxxiii: "Had he no arms?"…"Ay, ay, they are never without barkers and slashers." **1855** Brougham *Chips* 177: Have you got the barkers? **1867** Clark *Sailor's Life* 60: If you have got a barker, Ned, that can pick us off, you are…lucky. **1872** Thomes *Slaver* 99: It ain't time for the barkers. *ca***1875** Williams *Binnacle Jack* 93: You are over fast wi' your barker, methinks. **1878** Beadle *W. Wilds* 41: More'n once the robbers would tackle some gritty man that was handy with his "barkers." **1902** Raine *Raasay* 66: I flung him from me and covered him with my barker. **1915** in C.M. Russell *Paper Talk* 117: This often caused him to pull his barker an…his cartriges were never blanks. **1919** in C.M. Russell *Paper Talk* 141: If your as handy with a barker as you ar with a reaitta your a scalp getter. **1927** McKay *Harlem* 150: I'se got a A number one little barker I'll give to you. **1969** Sanders *Anderson Tapes* 140: You knew you'd have to carry a barker on this job?

b. [cf. syn. BULLDOG] *Mil.* a big gun or artillery piece.

1842 J.F. Cooper *Wing & Wing* I 75: Four more carronades, with two barkers for'ard. **1863** in J.H. Gooding *Altar of Freedom* 65: Their attention being directed to James Island's "barkers," and Fort Moultrie. **1870** Greey *Blue Jackets* 91: If I had a few barkers I'd darn soon show you who I was you cussed fool. **1886** in *DAE*: The glittering brass "barkers" ran swiftly after, impelled by dozens of sturdy arms. **1941** *AS* (Oct.) 163: *Barker.* Heavy artillery gun.

3. *pl.* [sugg. by DOG, *n.*] a shoe.

1929 *Sat. Eve. Post* (Apr. 13) 54: Shoes are [called] pinchers or barkers [by crooks]. **1944** Burley *Harlem Jive* 133: *Barkers*—shoes.

4. *Journ.* a word or phrase set in larger type than the head-line that appears below it.

1982 T.D. Connors *Dict. Mass Media* 23.

barking iron *n.* a pistol. Now *hist.*

*1785 Grose *Vulgar Tongue*: *Barking irons*, pistols, from their explosion resembling the bow-wow or barking of a dog. (*Irish*). ***1812** Vaux *Vocab. Flash Lang.*: *Barking-Irons*: pistols; an obsolete term. **1825** Paulding *J. Bull in Amer.* 56: Seeing the barking iron [he] shrunk back. ***1847** in *F & H* (rev.) 141: Put up your barking iron, and no more noise. **1955** Kantor *Andersonville* 117: It's a little more than a fortnight since the Union cavalry, bless their barking irons, tried to capture Richmond.

bark-machine *n.* a worthless horse given to chewing bark from trees. Also **bark-mill.**

1845 in G.W. Harris *High Times* 48: I hitched my bark-machine up to a saplin that warnt skinned, so he'd git a craw-full of good fresh bark afore mornin. *Ibid.* 52: I…could have got away if my bark-mill hadn't *ground* off the saplin.

barky *n.* [*bark* + -*y*] *Naut.* a sailing vessel.—used affectionately. [The early quotes given by the *OEDS* seem to be S.E.]

*1703 in *OEDS*. **1791** [W. Smith] *Confess. T. Mount* 19: A vessel, a *bar-key.* ***1805** in *OEDS*. ***1831** B. Hall *Voyages* II 15: Before he turned over a totally new leaf on board the "old barky." **1839** Briggs *Harry Franco* I 155: She was "a good wholesome lump of a barkey." **1893** Hill *20 Yrs. at Sea* 130: The old barkey won't stand many more hours of this hammering. *a***1899** B.F. Sands *Reefer* 159 [ref. to *ca*1843]: The most of us…concluded to remain with our old "barkie," no matter when she was ordered. **1899** Robbins *Gam* 87: She's the *Ganges*, shipmates, the *Ganges*, poor barky! **1899** Boyd *Shellback* 131: One would think your old barky was full up. **1931** Lubbock *Bully Hayes* 60: The old barkey was for Davy Jones' locker.

barkwell and holdfast *n.* [cf. proverb "Brag's a good dog, but Holdfast is better"] one who will back up his words with tenacious action; a formidable fighter.

1834 Caruthers *Kentuckian* 189: He [the preacher]'s a bark-well and hold-fast too; he doesn't honey it up to em and mince his words.…He knocks down and drags out.

barley *n.* beer. Also **barley pop, barley water.**

*1821 *Real Life in London* II 207: *A boulter of barley*—A drink—or a pot of porter. **1884** in Lummis *Letters* 71: Dealer in Barley Water and Bad Cigars. **1942** *ATS* 113: Beer:…*barley water.* **1969** *Current Slang* I & II 7: *Barley water*, n. Beer.—College males, South Dakota. **1970** in P. Heller *In This Corner* 182: The blood and the barley don't mix. **1972** Claerbaut *Black Jargon* 57: *Barley* n. beer: He's got some barley. **1975–76** Dills *CB* 14: *Barley pop*: Beer. **1985** Univ. Tenn. student theme: "Barley pop," "grog" and "brew" can all be used in reference to beer.

barley wagon *n.* a beer truck.

1980 Pearl *Slang Dict.*: *Barley wagon* n. (Truckers' CB) a truck carrying beer.

barmaid *n. Bowling.* a pin hidden behind another pin in a leave.

1976 *Webster's Sports Dict.* 29. **1980** Pearl *Slang Dict.*: *Barmaid* n. (Bowling) a pin that remains standing behind another after the first ball of the frame has been played.

barn *n.* **1.** *Naut.* a large ungraceful sailing ship.

1830 Ames *Mariner's Sks.* 5: My *debut* as a bluejacket took place in 1815, on board an "old barn of a hooker," that was built during the war down east, where every one knows that they build ships by the mile and saw them off in length to accomodate [*sic*] purchasers.

2. [cf. BARN DOOR] the fly of the trousers. *Joc.*

1938 "Justinian" *Americana Sexualis* 12: *Barn.* n. The trouser fly. Whimsical derivation from the "horse" concealed beneath the fly. U.S., C.20. **1942** Algren *Morning* 17: Button yer barn at least.

3.a. *Navy.* a dock; a submarine pen. [Early quots. ref. to WWII.]

1951 Wouk *Caine Mutiny* 188: Let's head for the barn. **1958** Grider *War Fish* 108: Let's head for the barn, boys. **1959** Sterling *Wahoo* 52: She was heading for the "barn" with determination. **1963** W.C. Ander-son *Penelope* 196: Let's head for the barn.

b. *Mil.* a barracks.

1971 Jeffers & Levitan *See Parris* 2: DI's refer to recruits as animals also, and the term has led, naturally, to a nickname for the barracks, which are known as "barns." **1971** *Winter Soldier* (film): They called where we lived "the barn."

c. [shortening of *carbarn*] a garage or hangar.

1973 N.Y.C. bus driver, age *ca*50: Let's take her back to the barn. **1980** W.C. Anderson *BAT-21* 203: Picked up a hit. Headin' for the barn. **1982** *N.Y. Times* (Sept. 14) C 3: A fleet of wooden Roman war-ships…has found a temporary port of call in an empty trolley barn in Mainz, West Germany.

¶ In phrase:

¶ **in the barn** (of a traveling show) having closed opera-tions, either for the season or permanently.

1946 Dadswell *Hey, Sucker* 31: Others, to be sure, will "go in the barn" with real profit. *Ibid.* 34: Royal American…went "in the barn" and the tri-partnership broke up. *Ibid.* 59: In the winter…shows are "in the barn."

¶ (In prov. phr. describing poor marksmanship).

1862 in Upson *With Sherman* 28: I don't believe one could hit the broad side of a barn with them. **1880** C. King *With Crook* 120: They couldn't hit a flock of barns at that distance, much less an Indian skip-ping about like a flea. **1929** Parker *Old Army* 351: Even in firing at a target the Filipinos were so excited that they "couldn't hit a flock of barns." **1983** *N.Y. Times* (July 31) Sec. 11 21: At first they could not hit the proverbial broadside of a barn, not to mention the shower curtain they strung up as a target. **1990** *New Republic* (Feb. 19) 42: Their mis-siles couldn't hit the broad side of a barn.

barnacle[1] *n.pl.* [ref. to "an instrument consisting of two branches joined by a hinge, placed on the nose of a horse, if he has to be coerced into quietness when being shoed or surgically operated upon"—*OED*] spectacles.

*1571 in *OED*: These spectacles put on. *Grim*, They be gay barnacles, yet I never see the better. ***1593** in *OED*: Eye glasses, otherwise called Bernacles. ***1693** in *OED*. ***1785** Grose *Vulgar Tongue*: *Barnacles*…a nick name for spectacles. ***1820–21** P. Egan *Life in London* 230: The gentleman in the *green barnacles*. ***1823** in *OED*. **1849** Melville *White Jacket* 127: Portentous round spectacles which he called his *barnacles*. **1924** Garahan *Stiffs* 43: I'll be damned if I will sail with a bos'un that wears barnacles.

barnacle[2] *n. Naut.* a veteran seaman.

1908 *Independent* (Apr. 23) 905: It only required one glance at his weatherbeaten face…to proclaim him a case-hardened old barnacle; a genuine "sailor of the sail." **1942** *ATS* 735: Seasoned Seaman. *Barnacle…Billy Barnacle, old salt.* ***1961** Burgess *Dict. Sailing* 20: Barnacle…An old salt.

barnacleback *n.* [cf. SHELLBACK] *Naut.* a veteran seaman.

1846 *Spirit of Times* (June 6) 177: The monotony of this place has been relieved…by the drilling of Uncle Sam's "web-feet" or "barnacle backs" that came here from the squadron. **1878** McElroy *Andersonville* 176 [ref. to Civil War]: This old "barnacle-back" was as surly a growler as ever went aloft. **1893** Hill *20 Yrs. at Sea* vii: License…must be allowed any old barnacle-back when he starts out to spin a yarn. **1895** Sinclair *Alabama* 76 [ref. to Civil War]: Kell was standing near, and observing an old "barnacle-back" among the prisoners. **1896** Hamblen *Many Seas* 47: The old "barnacle backs" in the forecastle were hatching up a scheme. **1967** Lockwood *Subs* 79: We…had—as the barnaclebacks called it—"come up through the hawse-pipe."

barnacle tub *n. Naut.* an old, unseaworthy vessel.

1900 Hammond *Whaler* 137: "A reg'lar ol' barnacle tub," Jim pronounced her.

barnburner *n.* **1.** *Pol.* a radical member of the Democratic party of New York State. Now *hist.*

1841, 1845 in *DA.* **1877** Bartlett *Amer.* (ed. 4) [ref. to *ca*1810]: This school of Democrats was termed *Barnburners,* in allusion to the story of an old Dutchman, who relieved himself of rats by burning down the barns which they infested,—just like exterminating all banks and corporations, to root out the abuses connected therewith. **1977** Coover *Public Burning* 60: I had to cool the barnburners, soften up the hardshells, keep the hunkers and cowboys in line.

2. an exciting or excellent thing, person, or time; a HUMDINGER; (*specif.*) a strong hand in the game of bridge.

1934 *AS* (Oct.) 237: A *barn-burner* is an exceptionally good hand [in bridge]. **1945** J. Bryan *Carrier* 154: The cards loved us; we held one barn-burner after the other and were 2800 points in front. **1951** Wouk *Caine Mutiny* 22: She's no barn-burner. **1957** M. Shulman *Rally* 185: A barn-burner! **1967–68** T. Wolfe *Kool-Aid* 307: Kesey's Pals in LSD Party in L.A.—a barnburner [of an article] about the Watts Test. **1971** *Business Week* (Feb. 13) 88: [He] questions whether multipurpose checking can be made into a profitable business for his bank. "It doesn't look like a barn burner." **1976** Berry *Kaiser* 168: It was hilarious, unbelievable! I can't remember everything that happened, but it was a real barn-burner. **1979** Cuddon *Dict. Sports & Games* 85: *Barnburner.* An exceptionally close and exciting contest. **1981** D. Winfield, on WINS news (Aug. 4): The last half of the season is going to be a barnburner, in my estimation. **1983** *U.S. News & W.R.* (Apr. 18): We had a real barn burner in March, with sales up 13 percent from a year ago. **1983–86** G.C. Wilson *Supercarrier* 51: You're an intelligent, capable man. You could be a barn burner. **1990** *CBS This Morning* (CBS-TV) (Jan. 4): The Noriega trial promises to be a barnburner.

barn door *n.* **1.** (see 1896 quot.).

1865 in *DA:* Skirts were trodden on, and came out at the gathers; and there was more than one "barn-door" vent. **1896** *DN* I 383: *Winklehawk,* triangular tear in cloth.…*Barndoor* is reported from Massachusetts in the same sense. **1967–69** in *DARE.*

2. [cf. BARN-DOOR BRITCHES] the fly of the trousers.

1950 in *DARE.* **1958** T. Berger *Crazy in Berlin* 187 [ref. to 1940's]: I noticed my top fly button was loose and I fastened it. And then I thought…with your ass about to be blown off…you button the barn door. **1968** in Bronner *Children's Folk.* 41: Close your barn door before the horses get out. **1975** T. Berger *Sneaky People* 35: Better close the barn door before the horse gets out. **1976** Knapp & Knapp *One Potato* 89: Barn door's open./The cock is running wild. **1985** Bodey *F.N.G.* 101: The buttons of my barn-door have popped off.

3. *pl. Theat. & Film.* metal flaps, doors, etc., hung in front of a spotlight to control the light beam.

1942 *ATS* 600: Light shield…*barn door.* **1982** T.D. Connors *Dict. Mass Media* 23.

4. *Av.* a large, slow-moving airplane.

1945 Hamann *Air Words: Flying barndoor.* Any no-good airplane. **1961** Plantz *Sweeney Sq.* 144: The fighter planes of both squadrons were kept busy flying cover for the slow-moving "barn doors."

barn-door britches *n.* (see 1939 quot.). Now *hist.* Also **barn-door trousers.**

1884 G.W. Cable *Dr. Sevier* ch. xxxix: His high waisted, barn-door trowsers. **1939** in *AS* XXII 72: Their trousers, too, are of a special style: instead of being buttoned up the front, they are buttoned on the sides much like sailors' trousers. Often they are referred to as "barn-door

britches," but the technical name is "front-fall trousers." At an earlier date these trousers were common in other groups and were not uniquely Amish. **1947** in *AS* XXII 72: The term "barn-door britches" was in common use in my home community in the southern part of Johnson County, Iowa, where the population is predominantly Pennsylvania Dutch in origin.

barney[1] *n. & v.* [orig. unkn.] (see quot.).

1851 B.H. Hall *College Wds.* 15: *Barney.* At Harvard College, about the year 1810, this word was used to designate a bad recitation. To *barney* was to recite badly.

barney[2] *n.* [evidently related to E dial. *barney* 'humbug, cheating', itself of unknown orig.; see *OED*] *Sports.* a fraudulent sporting event, (*specif.*) a fixed prizefight or race.

1859 Matsell *Vocabulum* 125: *Barney.* A fight that is sold. **1880** *N.Y. Clipper Almanac* 44: *Barney*—A race in which there has been a "cross" or "sell-out." ***1882** in *OED:* Blackguardly barneys called Boxing Competitions. ***1885** in *OEDS:* Few genuine matches have taken place this season,…though exhibitions and barney contests have been plentiful. ***1889** Barrère & Leland *Dict. Slang* I 82: (Racing) the person who prevents a horse winning a race, is described as "doing a *barney.*" The same phrase is applied to the horse itself. (Running), humbug, rubbish; in racing, when a man does not try to win. ***1897** in *F & H* I (rev.) 145: The morning the Derby was run for, the barney was well understood/ Old Feet gave the jockey the cough drop, which I'd fated for the animal's good. **1906** *Nat. Police Gaz.* (Oct. 6) 6: Some alleged fights of the "barney" order gave the thieves plenty of opportunity to work. **1938** in *DAS:* [The fight] looked like a barney—as if there were some collusion. **1946** in *DAS:* Not too much [drug could be given to the dogs] for fear the contest might look like the barney it was.

barney[3] *n.* a cloddish fellow.

1929 in Perelman *Don't Tread* 3: A flock of dumber barnies than the clerks at the Sub-Treasury I never met. **1989** P. Munro *U.C.L.A. Slang* 16: *Barney* person who's not with it…ugly guy. My blind date turned out to be a total barney.

barn rat *n.* a horse that is reluctant to leave its barn or stall.

1949 Cummings *Dict. Sports* 23: *Barn rat…*A horse reluctant to leave its stable or barn. **1979** Burn *Horseless Rider* 103: Is the horse a "barn rat"—reluctant to leave the barn alone and determined to race back to it the moment he is turned in the direction of home?

barnstorm *v.* [back formation from *barnstormer*] to travel as a BARNSTORMER. Now *S.E.*

1888 Pierson *Slave of Circumstances* 43: I'm not much on shows. Don't you go and get the barn-storming fever on you.…They do say that when a girl gets the stage fever on her that it's more deadly than the Yellow Jack. **1896** in *DA:* The last I heard of him [*sc.* a cabinet official], [he] was barnstorming down in Georgia in favor of a gold monometalism. **1908** in Fleming *Unforgettable Season* 14: He…went through Pennsylvania with them on their barnstorming trip. **1920** E. Hemingway, in *N.Y. Times Mag.* (Aug. 18, 1985) 19: Stanley Ketchell came to Boyne City once, barn storming with a burlesque show. **1927** Lindbergh *We* 28: As a result we barnstormed most of the Nebraska towns southeast of Lincoln together, and it is to him that I owe my first practical experience in cross-country flying.…"Barnstorming" is the aviator's term for flying about from one town to another and taking any one who is sufficiently "airminded" for a short flight over the country. **1928** in *OEDS* I 206: He gave exhibitions at county fairs, or barnstormed as the pilots say. **1933** in *OEDS:* I had an old army plane, and as a gypsy flyer I barnstormed thirty-seven states. **1943** Arnold & Eaker *Flying Game* 148: By purchasing these planes, hundreds of pilots who had received their discharges were enabled to "barnstorm" the country, make exhibition flights at small towns, [etc.]. **1945** J. Bryan *Carrier* 86: A bunch of barn-storming youngsters. **1947** in *DA:* Barnstorming Presidential Candidate Harold Stassen whirled through Belgium in one day. **1958** Camerer *Damned Wear Wings* 70: Never knew you'd barnstormed. **1964** Thompson & Rice *Every Diamond* 119: Two of our outfielders…didn't make our 1956 barnstorming trip to Japan.

barnstormer *n.* Orig. *Theat.* one who tours small rural towns to give performances; (*hence*) a politician making a rapid tour delivering campaign speeches, typically in rural areas; (*later*) an itinerant aviator giving exhibitions of stunt flying, etc., at county fairs. All senses now *S.E.*

***1859** Hotten *Slang Dict.* 3: *Barn stormers,* theatrical performers who travel the country and act in barns, selecting short and frantic pieces to suit the rustic taste. **1884** in *DAE:* A St. Louis writer…said that the advent of Mr. Irving had ended the career of the "barn-stormers," who, with their companies of "sticks,"…were bidden to vanish for evermore. I should be…sorry to call Mr. Booth a "barn-stormer." *1884 in *F & H* I 129: If this be barn-storming, Betterton and Garrick were barn-stormers. 1885 *Nat. Police Gaz.* (Oct. 24) 14: "Barn-stormer!" cried the comedian. "Did I understand you, miss, to say barn-stormer, and to me?…You haven't any right to address an old gentleman in such language." *1889 Barrère & Leland *Dict. Slang* 82: *Barn stormer* (familiar), a term formerly applied to itinerant actors who acted in barns, like the troupe of Scarron's Roman Comique, and that of Gautier's Capitaine Fracasse. 1926 *AS* (Apr.) 369: [Baseball players] are "yannigans" on the spring training trip and "barnstormers" when they play outside their own leagues. *1928 in *OEDS*: *Barnstormers*, itinerant flyers, appearing at fairs and race tracks, like Lindbergh in his earlier years.

Barnyard *n. Stu.* Barnard College. *Joc.*
    1966 Goldstein *1 in 7* 78: "Smithies," "Cliffies," and "Barnyard" girls are common appendages at pot parties at Yale, Harvard and Columbia. **1992** Columbia Univ. alumnus, class of 1982: In the politically incorrect days, we used to call Barnard *Barnyard*. It was spelled *Barñard*.

barnyard golf *n.* the game of pitching horseshoes.
    1930 in *DA*: There were an even score of contestants who participated in the barnyard golf or horseshoe pitching contests. **1948** Mencken *Amer. Lang. Supp. II* 755: Golf…has also engendered…*barnyard golf*, horseshoe-pitching. **1949** Cummings *Dict. Sports* 23.

barnyard savage *n.* a loutish farm dweller.—used contemptuously.
    1903 A. Adams *Log of a Cowboy* 81: I reckon the girl was all right, but the family were these razor-backed, barnyard savages. [*a1909 *F & H* I (rev.) 145: *Barndoor-savage.* A country yokel; farm-labourer; clodhopper.] **1958** *AS* XXXIII 265: *Barnyard savage* [reported in use in upper Midwest].

bar-prop *n.* BARFLY.
    1980 Kotzwinkle *Jack* 163: The bar-prop waved a floppy arm and swiveled on his stool.

barracks bag *n. Army.* **1.** a heavy artillery shell. [Though common in WWI, the term seems not to have regained currency in WWII; cf. SEA-BAG.]
    1919 *Lit. Digest* (Mar. 15) 78: Fritz opened up with some barrack bags. **1919** McGrath *354th Inf.* 230: Suddenly every battery on the other side of the line turned loose, and he was convinced he'd bring back several "Barracks Bags" and "GI" cans in addition to his regular load. **1919** T. Kelly *What Outfit?* 80: That two-twenty—we call 'em barracks bags, they're so damn big—landed 'bout thirty feet from our last latrine. **1921** Dienst *353d Inf.* 66: Fritz had spotted the kitchen. He immediately got busy and sent over one of his "barrack bags."
    2. a bomb dropped from an airplane.
    1919 Hubbell *Co. C* 132: Jerry spotted the target, rode the night sky, shoved half a dozen "barracks bags" over the side of his bombing plane and flew away in the dark dome of night.
    ¶ In phrase:
    ¶ **blow it out your barracks bag!** *Army.* see S.V. BLOW OUT.

barracks breeze *n.* [cf. *shoot the breeze* S.V. BREEZE] *Army.* gossip among enlisted men; rumor.
    1980 D. Cragg (letter to J.E.L., Aug. 10) 1: I can't remember when I first heard this used. "That's just a rumor…barracks breeze."

barracks fatigue *n. Army.* sleeping or loafing in barracks, BUNK FATIGUE.
    1941 Kendall *Army & Navy Slang* 1: *Barracks fatigue*.…loafing in quarters.

barracks lawyer *n.* [var. of GUARDHOUSE LAWYER] *Army.* a contentious enlisted soldier who pretends to knowledge of military regulations; a chronic complainer. Also **barracks-room lawyer.** [Early quots. ref. to WWII.]
    *1948 Partridge et al. *Forces' Slang* 11: *Barrack-room lawyer.* 1955 Shapiro *6th of June* 71: He missed his calling. He's a real barracks-room lawyer. 1964 R. Allen *High Forest* 258: The best little barracks-room lawyer this side of the glass house. 1970 Just *Military Men* 62: Barracks lawyers came later. 1978 Truscott *Dress Gray* 380: Now don't you try playing barracks lawyer with me, Slaight. 1980 H. Gould *Ft. Apache* 161: This son of a bitch was a barracks lawyer, a troublemaker.

barracks rat *n. Army.* a soldier who lives in or prefers to remain in a barracks.
    1980 D. Cragg (letter to J.E.L., Aug. 10) 1: Barracks rat…I first heard this [1959–61] in Germany. **1980** D. Cragg *Lexicon Mil.* 27: *Barracks*

Rat. One who lives in the barracks. **1984** Former Spec. 4, U.S. Army: In the early 1970's a *barracks rat* was a guy who'd hang around the barracks when he had a chance to go out and do something else.

barracks 13 *n. Army.* a guardhouse.
    1941 *Army Ordnance* (July) 79: *Barracks 13*…Guardhouse. **1943** *Yank* (Jan. 13) 15: For fatigue duty around Barracks 13. **1984** U.S. Army veteran, age *ca*35 [ref. to 1973]: I got guard duty on this guy at Christmas time for drug possession, and I asked, "Where do I take him?" and the desk sergeant in the PMO's office said, "Barracks 13." I asked him, "What's that?" and he said, "The guardhouse."

barracuda *n.* **1.** a violent or aggressive person, esp. a criminal.
    1935 Marion, Hanemann & Loos *Riffraff* (film): That barracuda ain't gonna give you any money. **1950** Hecht *Where Sidewalk Ends* (film): Morrison. Big barracuda. **1968** M.H. Albert & J. Guss *Lady in Cement* (film): First the shark…then the barracuda. **1975** *Kojak* (CBS-TV): I don't like barracudas who shake down public officials and then kill them when they come clean. **1978** Diehl *Sharky's Machine* 81: A barracuda. A competitor with big needs, big hungers.
    2. a domineering or quarrelsome person.
    1957 *Phil Silvers Show* (CBS-TV): "Is that the Mildred that—?" "Yeah. The barracuda!" **1966** Susann *Valley of Dolls* 387: She smiled. "The barracuda." **1976** *Kojak* (CBS-TV): "Who's the barracuda with McNeil?" "The head of the Organized Crime Bureau." **1978** Selby *Requiem* 133: Your mother isn't a barracuda like mine. *1979 "J. Gash" *Grail Tree* 28: The honest old public—a right swarm of barracudas.
    3. a passionate sex partner, esp. a woman.
    1972 Jenkins *Semi-Tough* 99: [She] had a bad complexion…but was hung and could turn into some kind of barracuda in the rack. **1973** U.S. Navy veteran, age 25: A *barracuda*—that's somebody who'll eat [in sexual sense] anything. **1983** R. Salmaggi, on WINS radio news (Sept. 1): In addition there's a barracuda of a suburban vamp who's after Keaton.
    ¶ In phrase:
    ¶ **put the barracuda on** to treat roughly.
    1981 Hathaway *World of Hurt* 258 [ref. to 1960's]: Hope you put the barracuda on her. We gotta uphold the team reputation.

barrage *n. Mil.* a large number, amount, or supply (of). [Quots. ref. to WWI.]
    1926 Nason *Chevrons* 175: There's a barrage of military police in back of you that a rat couldn't get through. **1928** Nason *Top Kick* 208: Lay off the gas barrage [loquacity] an' let's do somethin'. **1930** *AS* (June): Sending over cocoa barrages. *1936 Partridge *DSUE* 35: *Barrage.* An excessive number or quantity: military: 1917; ob.

barrel *n.* **1.** a slush fund provided by or for a political candidate. Cf. PORK BARREL.
    1876 in *DA*: The "barrel" is empty, the canvass ahead, And still they are crying for more. **1884** in *F & H* I (rev.) 147: We are accustomed to barrel-campaigns here.…The Democrats depend upon carrying it with the money. **1909** *WNID* 186: *Barrel campaign.* A political campaign in which money is freely used. *Slang, U.S.* **1913** in *DA*: The nominations of the party will not be the result of "compromise" or impulse, or evil design—"the barrel" and the machine.
    2. a huge amount (of money); a fortune.
    1887 Field *Garland* 21: Mr. Heron-Allen…is making a barrel of money in Chicago. **1890** Quinn *Fools of Fortune* 357: The mysterious…friend has a "barrel of money." **1891** Garland *Main-Travelled Roads* 98: I've kept looking ahead to making a big hit and getting a barrel of money. **1892** Norr *China Town* 51: The gang spent a barrel, but it was money thrown away. **1909** "Clivette" *Cafe Cackle* 69: He had a chance to make a barrel of coin if he could get a little backing. **1911** Van Loan *Big League* 175: Cost the Pinks a barrel of money. **1913–15** Van Loan *Taking the Count* 322: He's got some proposition about making a barrel of dough. **1969** *N.Y. Post* (May 17) 53: He made his first barrel with "The Immoral Mr. Teas."
    ¶ In phrases:
    ¶ **blow (one's) barrel** *blow (one's) top* S.V. TOP.
    1947 Carter *Devils* 245: "Arab," laughed Finkelstein, "you're blowing your barrel. No man'll step out to be killed."
    ¶ **give both barrels** [alludes to the firing of both barrels of a double-barreled shotgun] to act with the greatest force or vigor against.
    1955 in C. Beaumont *Best* 124: I let him have both barrels. "I saw Ruth this afternoon." **1958** S.H. Adams *Tenderloin* 166: Give him both barrels, upper case.
    ¶ **have (one's) barrel full** to be drunk.
    1889 "M. Twain" *Conn. Yankee* 46: That same old weary tale…he *will*

tell till he dieth, every time he hath gotten his barrel full and feeleth his exaggeration-mill a-working.

¶ **in the barrel, 1.** in debt; out of money.

1935 in Paxton *Sport* 206: Dizzy was in and out of the barrel a dozen times during that training period. Rickey had tired of making good all the pieces of paper that Dizzy had signed, and the young man was on a dollar-a-day basis. **1942** Z.N. Hurston, in *Amer. Mercury* (July) 86: Cold in hand, hunh?...A red hot pimp like you *say* you is, ain't got no business in the barrel. **1942–49** Goldin et al. *DAUL* 277: I'm in the barrel for plenty.

2. in danger, trouble, or difficulty. [Sugg. by the prov. phrase *shooting fish in a barrel* and by the punch line of a bawdy joke (given by Legman, *No Laughing Matter*, 166).]

[**1938** in Legman *No Laughing Matter* 166: Wednesday is your day in the barrel.] **1973** *Saturday Rev.*: Society (Mar.) 10: The first guy who blows the assignment is said to be "in the barrel." **1982** R.A. Anderson *Cooks & Bakers* III: Looks like it's our turn to spend a month in the barrel....Con Thien. **1983** E. Dodge *Dau* 60: He had to—it's your turn in the barrel. **1985** Heywood *Taxi Dancer* 159: They were really going to catch it. He was damn glad that he was where he was. He'd already had his turn in the barrel. *a***1989** R. Herman, Jr. *Warbirds* vii: Barrel, the: Slang for alert duty, being on alert, or the alert facility. *Ibid.* 9: Normally, two pilots and their backseaters would only stay on alert for twenty-four hours before someone else would replace them and go into the "Barrel."

¶ **over a barrel** in a helpless position.

1938 Chandler *Big Sleep* ch. xxx: We keep a file on unidentified bullets nowadays. Some day you might use that gun again. Then you'd be over a barrel. **1941** Mahin & Grant *Johnny Eager* (film): You're the boss. You've got everybody over a barrel. **1945** in *OEDS*: You sure have me over a barrel. You caught me red-handed. **1963** D. Tracy *Brass Ring* 310: That old bastard had your uncle over a barrel. **1970** Conaway *Big Easy* 43: Novak's got us over a barrel....But we ain't moving. **1974** A. Bergman *Big Kiss-Off* 121: The way I figure it, you don't have me over any kind of a barrel. **1981** D. Burns *Feeling Good* 136: Being overcharged by a repairman who has you over a barrel.

barrel *v.* to drive, fly, or travel very fast. Now *colloq.* Also (*vulgar*) **barrel-ass.**

1930 *AS* V 4: *Barrel*—Make haste or hurry, or cause to make haste. Used especially of vehicles. "They went barreling up the hill for dinner." "He sure does barrel that Ford of his." **1942** *AS* (Apr.) 102: *Barreling.* Running with the throttle wide open. Also *Floorboarding; Highballing.* **1949** *PADS* (No. 11) 17: *Barrel along*...To go fast. **1951-53** in *AS* XXIX 93: *Barrel ass, v. phr.* To drive fast. **1956** Heflin *USAF Dict.* 73: *Barrel, v.intr.* With *along, around, down, through,* etc.: To move rapidly, esp. in an aircraft. *Slang.* **1959** Toland *Battle* 254 [ref. to WWII]: Barrel-ass out of here. **1963** Morgan *Six-Eleven* 293: If it's green we go barrel-assing on. **1972** R. Barrett *Lovomaniacs* 201: He'd have to split...and barrel-ass out to the coast. **1976** *Harper's* (Feb.) 41: His way of barrel-assing through the streets in a Datsun 240-Z, scattering peasants in his way. **1982** *L.A. Times* (Sept. 11) I 25: [He] is accused of driving his van in a reckless fashion when he barreled through an intersection last weekend and smashed into a taxi. **1990** *U.S. News & W.R.* (May 14) 72: Try telling a helmeted canoeist barreling down the Chattooga...that canoeing is for Fred Rogers types only.

barrel-ass *n.* a fat person.—usu. considered vulgar.

1949 Mende *Spit & Stars* 160: That barrel-ass Johnson is making us memorize about a million of them speeches.

barreled *adj.* drunk.

1914 *DN* IV 68: *Barreled up, adj.* Intoxicated. **1965** *Playboy* (Nov.) 178: *Barreled* [in list of synonyms for *drunk*].

barrel fever *n.* illness caused by excessive drinking, (*specif.*) delirium tremens.

***1796** Grose *Vulgar Tongue* (ed. 3): *He died of the barrel fever;* he killed himself by drinking. **1821** Waln *Hermit in Phila.* 26: Must look out for a *barrel fever;* winter *caterwauling* cursed unhealthy. **1927** *DN* V 438: *Barrel fever,* n. The delirium tremens. ***1943** S.J. Baker *Australian Slang* (ed. 3).

barrelhead *n.* an oaf.

1928 MacArthur *War Bugs* 67: Well, you big barrel head, why don't you salute?

barrelhouse *n.* **1.** (see 1922 quot.). Now *hist.*

1883 Peck *Bad Boy* 81: After I had put a few things in his brandy he concluded it was cheaper to buy it, and he is now patronizing a barrel house. **1896** Ade *Artie* 32: I see barrelhouse boys goin' around for

hand-outs that was more on the level than you are. **1907** *McClure's* (Apr.) 587: Nights, the ten-cent lodging house. Days, and the long evenings, the "barrel house"—that curious dive so strangely like the thieves' den of the Middle Ages. **1914** V. Lindsay *The Congo* st. 1: Fat black bucks in a wine-barrel room/Barrel-house kings with feet unstable. **1918** Chi. *Sun. Trib.* (Mar. 24) V (unp.): Joe [was] raised in alleys, reform schools, and "barr'l houses." **1918** E. O'Neill *Straw* 58: Put that bottle away, damn it! And don't shout. You're not in a barrel-house. **1922** N. Anderson *Hobo* 27: The barrel-house was a rooming house, saloon, and house of prostitution, all in one. Men with money usually spent it in the barrel-houses....Not infrequently the barrel-house added to its other attractions the opportunity for gambling. **1931** Harlow *Old Bowery* 500: It was almost one continuous row of "barrel houses," dives and lodging houses catering to mendicants. **1948** J. Stevens *Jim Turner* 138 [ref. to *ca*1910]: It's a sound that makes the old barrelhouse stiffs remember the beer. **1948** Chaplin *Wobbly* 86: In dull times or in winter, seasonal workers made way for "barrel-house stiffs" and human derelicts who constituted the backbone of the "skid road's" population. ***1966** Hugill *Sailortown* 324: In Valencia they hung around a barrel-house called Mare Nostrum. **1977** *Wash. Post* (Nov. 4) Weekend 7: The atmosphere's more West Coast singles' bar than barrelhouse.

2. *Jazz.* [orig. quasi-adj. or -adv.] a markedly rhythmic style of jazz once associated with barrelhouses.

[**1924** in Dixon & Godrich *Blues & Gospel* 44: Barrel House Blues.] **1926** in *OEDS*: Trumpets and trombones...in that semi-muffled voice aptly described by the term "barrel-house tone." **1935** *Vanity Fair* (Nov.) 71: Additional synonyms for hot music are...barrel-house (slang for "cheap saloon"). **1937** *AS* XII 182: The barrelhouse style is very African. **1939** Goodman & Kolodin *Swing* 41: They jammed everything they played and went in for a lot of barrelhouse stuff. **1944** Burley *Harlem Jive* 133: Barrel house—free and easy, low down music, lowdown performance, in the vernacular. **1958** in *OEDS*: Barrel-house retains a close allegiance with ragtime. **1982** *Newsweek* (Sept. 13) 96: Maniacally percussive, they resemble...either barrelhouse raised to the nth degree or Bartok fissioned by an atom smasher. **1992** *Rolling Stone* (Apr. 30) 28: The Grey Ghost, a legendary local bluesman...prefaced the keynote proceedings with some vintage barrelhouse piano.

barrelhouse *v.* **1.** to frequent barrelhouses.

1913 in R.S. Gold *Jazz Talk* 11: I don't care what Mister Crump don't 'low/I'se gonna bar'l-house anyhow. **1942** Davis & Wolsey *Call House Madam* 135: He's barrelhousing around....Out f—ing again.

2. to drive at top speed, **BARREL.**

1959 O'Connor *Talked to Stranger* 106: "Did you barrel-house the cars?" "Oh, we did a lot of hot-rodding on some of them. Races and things."

barrel shirt *n. Army.* a barrel that a soldier is made to wear as a form of punishment. Also **barrel jacket.**

1858 Vielé *Following Drum* 222: One...was sentenced to wear a "barrel jacket" every day...an old flour barrel with a hole cut for his head...and a pair of holes for his arms. **1865** Dennett *South as It Is* 107: They'd put a barrel-shirt on him.

barrel shop *n.* a low drinking saloon.

1904 *N.Y. Tribune* (Oct. 12) 1: A poisonous substitute for whiskey sold in the low "barrel shops" along Tenth Avenue.

bar-room *n. Logging.* a bunkhouse.

1938 Holbrook *Mackinaw* 254: *Barroom.* That part of a New England camp where the loggers sleep. **1956** Sorden & Ebert *Logger's* 2 [ref. to *a*1925]: *Bar-room,* That part of a camp where the loggers slept. Term used occasionally in the lake states, more often a New England term.

barry *n. Music.* baritone.

1923 Ornitz *Haunch* 75: Hymie is comedy barry (baritone). **1951** Sheldon *Troubling* 164: Hey, Frank—you can sing barry, can't you?

barslave *n. West.* bartender.

1926 C.M. Russell *Trails* 6: I remember him tellin' the barslave not to take my money.

barstool jockey *n.* **BARFLY.**

1980 Ciardi *Browser's Dict.* 212: *Barstool jockey* A barfly.

bar toad *n. West.* **BARFLY.**

1958 McCulloch *Woods Words* 7: *Bar toad*—Same as bar fly.

base *n. Narc.* freebase cocaine.

1982 F. Robbins & D. Ragan R. Pryor 109: I used to smoke base but that stuff will kill you. **1983** "Grandmaster Melle Mel" in L.A. Stanley *Rap* 154: Rock! Bass [*sic*]! Blow!...free base. **1988** "Public Enemy" *Liv-*

ing Baseheads (rap song): He stripped the Jeep to fill his pipe...where they rocked to a different kind of base.

¶ In phrases:

¶ **change (one's) base** [Gen. G.B. McClellan's widely reported dispatch in 1862 that his retreat from the Peninsula campaign against Richmond was merely a "change of base" prompted this derisive use of the phrase] to retreat, esp. hurriedly; to flee.

1863 in *DA:* Judge Baird's defeat...caused him to change his "base" to California. **1865** *Harper's* (May) 691: He...made tracks for Frisco. He changed his base—*he did.* **1868** J.R. Browne *Apache Country* 462: Pop had his turkey-buster well in hand; and Chiv changed his base. **1906** Buffum *Bear City* 21: You old rendezvous of a starvation outpost, you ought to change your base.

¶ **get to first base** [alluding to the game of baseball] to meet with initial or preliminary success or approval, often in romantic contexts; (*specif.*) to engage in lovemaking that goes no further than kissing.—usu. used in negative contexts.

[**1908** in H.C. Fisher *A. Mutt* 104: Funny I can't get past this first base.] **1928** in Farrell *Guillotine Party* 22: He...wanted to stroke her silky hair, and he hadn't gotten to first base. **1929** Cruze *Great Gabbo* (film): You'll never get to first base. You got to have class. **1930** Lait *On Spot* 112: They won't get to first base. **1929–31** Farrell *Young Lonigan* 156: He liked Cabby Devlin, but he couldn't get to first base with her. **1936** Connell & Adler *Our Relations* (film): We can't go in the street dressed like this. Why, we wouldn't get to first base. **1937** Wexley & Duff *Angels* (film): That preacher won't get to first base. **1938** Smitter *Detroit* 8: I had tried to make a date with her once but never got to first base. **1938** in F.S. Fitzgerald *Letters* 31: I thought I'd read Italian to read Dante and didn't get to first base. I should have known...that I had no gift for languages. **1944** Micheaux *Mrs. Wingate* 174: That silly attempt at love didn't get to first base with her. **1948** A. Lyon *Unknown Station* 16: He told me about his wife, with whom he hadn't been able "to get to first base" before they were married. **1953–57** Giovannitti *Combine D* 286: It didn't get him to first base with the Kommandant. **1957** Gurney & Martin *Invasion of Saucer Men* (film): I wonder if you could tell me how to get to first base with you. **1963** Holzer *Ghost Hunter* 7: Still, that was one more potential case I lost before even getting to first base. **1969** *Hell-fighters* (film): Fellow as ugly as you are couldn't get to first base without a fire. **1981** *N.Y. Times* (July 1) B 7: I couldn't get to first base with her.

¶ **get to second base** [alluding to the sexual sense of *get to first base,* above] to engage in lovemaking that goes no further than fondling the woman's breasts.

1977 in G.A. Fine *With Boys* 109: Dan got to first base and was "halfway to second" [with Annie]. **1986** R. Walker *AF Wives* 467: Well, she's real...you know, uptight. I haven't even gotten past second base yet. **1987** G.A. Fine *With Boys* 177: *Getting to second base with a girl* (i.e., fondling her breasts). **1988** *Wonder Years* (ABC-TV) [ref. to 1960's]: I bet the guys who wrote this [sex education textbook] have never been to second base.

¶ **get to third base** [alluding to the sexual sense of *get to first base,* above] to achieve a level of sexual intimacy short of intercourse; (*usu.*) an act of "below-the-waist" petting.

1947 Mailer *Naked & Dead* 428: I got to third base last night, I'll make her yet. **1977** in G.A. Fine *With Boys* 109: The following day Stew said Dan "almost got to third" [with Annie]. **1981** *Nat. Lampoon* (July) 10: I made it to third base with Sheryl Burrito in the backseat when the car was new.

¶ **off (one's) base** or **off base, 1.** infirm; in a bad way; muddled; confused.

1882 in *DA:* The Boston lady held up her hands in holy horror, and was going to explain...how she was off her base. **1883** Peck *Bad Boy* 28: The boy knew the failing, and made up his mind to demonstrate to the old man that he was rapidly getting off his base. **1885** *Puck* (May 13) 165: The gintleman's pint is off its base. **1894** *Harper's* (Dec.) 107: I'm a sure loser whenever I try to [talk] to a lady like you. I get way off my base. **1958** Drury *Advise & Consent* 397: Is his poor health knocking him off base mentally?

2. insane; (*hence*) very much mistaken. [Now used without possessive.]

1887 *N.O. Lantern* (Apr. 9) 2: Has been off his base ever since. **1893** James *Mavrick* 59: If he expected to bring wild animals into camp and not have them killed he was simply off his base. **1895** C. King *Capt.*

Dreams 31: See here, Johnny...you're as far off your base as any skate I've struck for a year. **1904** *Munsey's Mag.* (Oct.) 90: To be off one's base is to be off one's head. **1906** *McClure's* (Dec.) 150: The woman's dying...and Bill's off his base. **1908** *DN* III 290: *Off one's base*...out of one's mind. **1913** *Lit. Digest* (Sept. 6) 379: He is "quite off his base in knocking the use of slang." **1933** Clifford *Boats* 226: Because I carry that bright little fella...they think I'm a bit off my base. **1953** *I Love Lucy* (CBS-TV): If you're thinking what I think you're thinking, you're way off base. **1954** Gaddis *Birdman* 33: Doc, isn't Stroud a bit off his base? **1957** Shulman *Rally* 99: No, he was way off base. All the woman wanted was...a little booze and sympathy. **1958** S.H. Adams *Tenderloin* 147 [ref. to 1890's]: "It's Dr. Farr." "You're off your base." **1959** Gault *Drag Strip* 45: You're off base, Juan....This Board of Supervisors has the reputation of thinking only of the county, the *whole* county. **1963** D. Tracy *Brass Ring* 136: A North End girl agreed with her date even when he was three feet off base. **1982** *New Directions* (Nat. Public Radio) (July 2): When did you first get the idea that our currently accepted views of life and nature were more or less off base? **1982** *Science Digest* (Sept.) 8: Dr. Erwin is way off base. **1990** *Nation* (Sept. 10) 223: When President Bush says that our boys in Saudi Arabia are defending "our way of life," he's not so far off base.

3. taking undue liberties, "out of line." [Currently the most freq. sense and used invariably without the possessive.]

1943 in Ruhm *Detective* 363: I see I've got a little off base. **1947** *Time* (Oct. 20) 11: Your Latin American department was off base in its comparison of the Portillo Hotel in Chile with our famous Sun Valley. **1969** Crumley *Cadence* 75: Sir, I know I'm off base, but the events of this morning seem to call for unusual actions. **1980** Univ. Tenn. *Daily Beacon* (Apr. 16) 2: In questioning the loyalty of the cheerleaders...he was totally off base. **1978–86** J.L. Burke *Lost Get-Back Boogie* 26: You're really off base, Iry.

base v. *Narc.* to smoke (freebase cocaine). Also intrans. Hence **based out** under the influence of freebase cocaine.

1987 *Larry King Live* (CNN-TV) (Jan. 7) [ref. to 1983]: I started basing cocaine. *a*1990 E. Currie *Dope and Trouble* 20: They gone be all based out. **1990** *New Yorker* (Sept. 17) 63: "But then some of our guys started basing"—smoking cocaine—"so they were perceived as weak."

Baseball Annie n. *Baseball.* (see quots.). Also **Baseball Sadie.**

1964 Thompson & Rice *Every Diamond* 139: *Baseball Sadie:* Gal whose weakness is ballplayers. **1969** Bouton *Ball Four* 218: A [stewardess] can come under the heading of class stuff...in comparison with some of the other creatures who are camp-followers or celebrity-fuckers, called Baseball Annies. It is permissible...to promise a Baseball Annie dinner and a show in return for certain quick services for a pair of roommates. And it is just as permissible...to refuse to pay off. **1973** *Wall Street Journ.* (Aug. 30) 8: The "baseball Annies" of Phoenix, a breed of minor league groupies, are a fairly comely lot and a number of players have dallied with them from time to time. **1979** Cuddon *Dict. Sports & Games* 91. **1981** C. Nelson *Picked Bullets Up* 179: Did I have a Baseball Annie waiting for me in whatever city I played? **1988** *Eyewitness News* (WABC-TV) (June 15): Susan Sarandon...[plays] a Baseball Annie—what ballplayers call groupies. **1992** *Newsweek* (Apr. 20) 64: Ballplayers were still hitting the bars of the Florida coast, and the baseball "annies," as they're known, were still out looking for them.

baseburner n. buttocks.

1883 Peck *Bad Boy* 178: Come out here and bring in that kindling wood, or I will start a fire on your base-burner with this strap.

base-camp commando n. *Mil.* a soldier stationed at a rear-echelon base camp.—used derisively. [Quots. ref. to Vietnam War.]

1986 R. Zumbro *Tank Sgt.* 128: So I decided to see if a "base-camp commando" could arrange for a few casualties. **1987** Pelfrey & Carabatsos *Hamburger Hill* 48: The guy was a base camp commando, an REMF—rear-echelon motherfucker.

basehead n. *Narc.* a habitual user of freebase cocaine.

1983–86 Zausner *Streets* 21: *Base head:* Someone who loves freebasing cocaine on a regular basis. **1988** "Public Enemy" *Nation of Millions* (LP): Night of the Living Baseheads [song title]. **1990** *New Yorker* (Sept. 10) 66: Terry and co-workers called their customers "baseheads" and thoroughly despised them.

base wallah n. [orig. Brit. mil. slang, *base + wallah* 'fellow' (< Hindi)] *Army & Journ.* a rear-echelon soldier serving at a base establishment. *Rare* in U.S.

1925 in Fraser & Gibbons *Soldier & Sailor Wds.* 18 [ref. to WWI]: *Base wallah.* Anyone employed at a Base, or having a job behind the front

lines. *1934 Yeates *Winged Victory* 370 [ref. to WWI]: Some base-wal-lahs. **1953** H. Carter *Main Street* 162 [ref. to WWII]: The Americans [in Egypt] were mainly base-wallahs and fliers.

bash *n.* **1.** a heavy or crushing blow, as with the fist or a blunt instrument. Now *colloq.*

*1805 in *OED*: An' gae her a desperate bash on The chafts. *ca1817 in *OEDS*: Then, giving two or three bashes on the face, he left me. *a1889 in Barrère & Leland *Dict. Slang* I 84: "Upper-cuts," "exchanges," "bashes," "knock-downers," "body-punches," [etc.].

2.a. a celebration or feast, esp. a boisterous party. [The term seems to have entered U.S. usage via the armed forces during WWII.]

*1901 in *OEDS*: Let us go out and do a bash! [*1919 in *OEDS*: Ye ken what a man's like when he's been on the bash.] [*1924 in *OEDS*: The village tailor…had an unfortunate weakness for getting terribly "on the bash" perhaps twice a year.] **1944** E.H. Hunt *Limit* 123: Quite a bash, wasn't it? **1944** *AS* XIX 310: Lieutenant Joe Klass, a young American Spitfire pilot, wrote…late in May of the new colloquial vocabulary of American prisoners of war in German camps, [including] *bash*, banquet. **1947** *Tomorrow* (Aug.) 29: Jive terms that seem to be persisting…a *bash*, for "a party" or "good time." **1948** *AS* XXIII 219: One could store or *stash* food for a big *bash*. This involved eating two or three days' rations at one time for the novel sensation of a full stomach. **1948** Manone & Vandervoort *Trumpet* 124: This bash started at nine o'clock at night and lasted until early A.M. **1955** Klaas *Maybe I'm Dead* 394 [ref. to WWII]: I'm throwing a big bash tonight. You're invited. *Ibid.* 479: *Bash*. A mixture of various foodstuffs. **1953–57** Giovannitti *Combine D* 69 [ref. to WWII]: Why not let's have a real bash and see what happens tomorrow. **1961** Brosnan *Pennant Race* 114: Let's dig that bash with Buddy Morrow's band tonight. **1970** N.Y.U. student: Who's giving the next bash? **1981** *N.Y. Times Mag.* (July 26) 61: The Queen permitted Prince Andrew…to stage a bash at Windsor Castle complete with a rock band and dozens of stunning young women. **1983** Breathed *Bloom Co.* 146: Yet another Bloom County New Year's Eve community bash. **1985** MacLaine *Dancing* 3: The slight headache…was from the prebirthday bash the night before. **1990** *Nation* (July 9) 39: We want to invite you to the party….The bash is presented by a group of Bay Area independent booksellers, [etc.].

b. a thrill of enjoyment; BANG, *n.*, 3; BOOT.

1969 Girodias *New Olympia Rdr.* 771: It was pretty wild, and you might get a bash out of it.

3. a try, an attempt.

*1948 Partridge et al. *Dict. Forces' Slang* 11 [ref. to WWII]: *Have a bash at*, to make an attempt. *1950 in *OEDS*: He's decided to have a bash at tightening up the discipline. **1969** *Current Slang* I & II 7: *Bash*, n. Try, attempt.—College students, both sexes, California.

bash *v.* [orig. unkn.; see note] **1.a.** to smash or crush with a blow; (*hence*) to punch or beat; (in recent use esp.) to assault; beat up. Hence **basher**. [Orig. northern English dial., now S.E., *bash* first appears in the U.S. in glossaries of underworld slang; it seems not to have gained wide currency in the U.S. before the 1930's.]

*1790 in *OED*: Fir'd wi' indignance I turn'd round,/And basht wi' mony a fung/The Pack, that day. *1812 Vaux *Vocab. Flash Lang.*: Bash, to beat any person by way of correction, as the woman you live with, &c. *1834 in *OED*: The callant has…bashed my neb as saft as pap. **1851** in R.H. Dillon *Shanghaiing Days* 234: They awake on board ship, broke and with bashed heads. *1882 in *OED*: A proposition to "smash" or "bash" in the tall hats aforesaid. *a1889 in Barrère & Leland *Dict. Slang* I 84: My mother goes in and bashes him over the head with a poker. **1904** *Life in Sing Sing* 246: *Bash*. To break; to assault. *1923 H.L. Foster *Beachcomber* 221: Some one threatened to "bash 'is bleedin' fyce in!" **1924** G. Henderson *Keys to Crookdom* 397: *Bash*. To break. To "bash in" a skull. **1933** Ersine *Prison Slang* 16: *Bash*, v. To hit, crush. "Bash him in the nose." **1938** Bellem *Blue Murder* 64: He bashed it square against my jaw. **1939** Saroyan *Time of Your Life* II: Bashed his head with a brass cuspidor. **1963** W.C. Anderson *Penelope* 73: That doesn't mean I'm not going to bash him in the breadbasket. **1963** D. Tracy *Brass Ring* 316: You just try it…and see whose kisser gets bashed. **1975** S.E. Hinton *Rumble Fish* 83: He clobbered them….Bashed one of them really good. **1981** C. Nelson *Picked Bullets Up* 8: I'll bash your brains in. **1987** *Daily Beacon* (Univ. Tenn.) (Nov. 12) 4: "Skinhead" groups…who proudly sport neo-Nazi and fascist insignia, having taken to bashing blacks, Jews, and other minority-group members. **1989** *New Republic* (June 12) 6: Anti-discrimination legislation gives victims of gay-bashing a means of obtaining…protection…, and helps make it a little more likely that

murderers of gay people will not be dismissed as "troubled youths."

b. to disparage or condemn; speak abusively of. [This use, chiefly as a combining form *-bashing*, became voguish in the late 1980's, esp. in political contexts.]

*1963 in *Barnhart Dict. Comp.* I (1982) 35. **1979** *Maclean's* (June 18) 38: Erasmus—who had exonerated Vorster…only months before…this time bashed him so badly that he was forced to resign. **1982** S. Black *Totally Awesome* 32: You can get your parents to stop bashing you around for smashing up the car again. **1984** *L.A. Times* (Jan. 29) IV 5: Administration and congressional leaders—known in some circles as the "Japan-bashers"—who view Tokyo as the chief culprit behind current U.S. economic problems are out for revenge. *ca1984 in *Safire Look It Up* 27: French Gaullist leader Jacques Chirac was tagged [by *The Economist*] in 1975 as an "articulate Commie-basher." **1986** *Newsweek* (June 9) 12: America-bashing has replaced soccer as a world sport. **1987** *Big Story* (CNN-TV) (Apr. 11): The President has avoided Soviet-bashing in this affair. **1988** *N.Y. Times* (July 31) E 2: Britain is a rare Western European state where politicians can score points by hefty Brussels-bashing. **1989** *Campus USA* (Spring) 17: Critics bashed it. Kids loved it. **1990** *Donahue* (NBC-TV): They were bashing—but with words—gay people. **1992** *N.Y. Times* (Jan. 24) A 29: I am hardly a Japan-basher, usually the contrary.

2. *Mil.* (of POW's in Germany) to eat hungrily. Now *hist.* [Quots. ref. to WWII.]

1945 *N.Y. Times Mag.* (Nov. 4) 12: "Bash" meant eating the better part of a food package without thought of the morrow. **1955** Klaas *Maybe I'm Dead* 42: What you got to bash, Major? *Ibid.* 389: Two loaves of bread. Three cans of meat. A pound of marge. Two chocolate bars and two pounds of dried fruit. Boy, am I going to bash tonight! *Ibid.* 468: He's inside bashing some of the chow Junior liberated. **1953–57** Giovannitti *Combine D* 69: Let's bake it and bash it. *Ibid.* 452: That's what you get for bashing everything the first day.

3. Esp. *Skiing.* to travel quickly and often out of control. See also BASHER, 1.

1965 *Ski* (Dec.) 72: He was the kind of skier who bashed down the mountain without knowing when he was over his head. **1984** *L.A. Times* (June 24) VI 20: A quick, tight clutch…spelled potential trouble. But no matter, we would bash on, regardless.

4. to produce with little effort; knock out.

1968–70 *Current Slang* III & IV 7: *Bash out*, v. To write out without much thought about content or organization.—High school and college students, both sexes, South Dakota.

5. *Communications.* to relay (a radio or TV signal).

*a1989 R. Herman, Jr. *Warbirds* 71: When I downlinked, we bashed the message the long way around, away from Soviet monitoring activity.

bashed *adj.* intoxicated. Cf. SMASHED.

1982 Eble *Campus Slang* (Nov.) 1: *Bashed*—drunk. Synonym: trashed.

basher *n.* **1.** *Skiing.* a poor skier who often loses control of his run; (*hence*) a fast skier. Cf. BASH, *v.*, 3.

1949 Cummings *Dict. Sports* 88. **1963** *AS* XXXVIII 204: *Basher*, n. A fast skier. Occasionally, a reckless skier or a fast skier who loses control.

2. *Film & Theat.* a scoop light.

1982 T.D. Connors *Dict. Mass Media* 25.

basket *n.* **1.** the belly; stomach; BREADBASKET.

*1889 Barrère & Leland *Dict. Slang* I 85: (Old cant)…"a kid in the *basket*" said of a woman in the family way. *1895 in *EDD* I 177: I'd sooner have fifty, than one in the basket. **1929** in *DAS* 21: [A blow] flush to the basket. **1942** Algren *Morning* 262: "In the kitchen, Tucker!" "In the basket!" **1944** Burley *Harlem Jive* 133: *Basket*—The stomach.

2. *Naut.* an unseaworthy vessel.

1903 in *AS* XXVII 251: Why…don't you folks turn out and condemn the tormented ole basket? *1940 in Bradford *Mighty Hood* 18: These one-funneled baskets are no mucking good.

3. Esp. *Homosex.* the scrotum and penis, esp. as outlined by the trousers.

1941 G. Legman, in G. Henry *Sex Variants* II 1157: *Basket*. The scrotum, or, rather, the size of the testicles and scrotum as seen or felt through the trousers….Also…the penis and testicles together, or their size. **1949** *Gay Girl's Guide* 3: *Basket*: Male genitals as outlined against thin or tight clothing, generally used in connection with sailor pants, Levis or swimming trunks. **1949** Monteleone *Crim. Slang* 17: *Basket*…testicles. **1958** Motley *Epitaph* 246: A young fellow in a very tight-fitting pair of faded blue jeans. Eyes follow him. "Oh my God! What a basket!" a young man shrills in feminine-like voice. **1966** "Petronius" *N.Y. Unexp.* 97: Lisping, swishing, excessive "basket" stuffing are all passé. **1972** R. Wilson *Playboy's Forbidden Words* 28: *Basket shopping* means looking over the passing men as heterosexuals look over the ladies. **1974** E. Thompson *Tattoo* 110: He rubbed his blue-jeaned basket vigorously. **1986** *Village Voice* (N.Y.) (June 10) 10 (cartoon): Wow, what a basket! [ref. to a bull]. **1987** E. White *Beautiful Room* 79: I can't tell if you pack a big basket or not.

4. prison.—constr. with *the*.

1978 Diehl *Sharky's Machine* 55: I dumped eighteen goddamn pushers...and fourteen got the basket.

basketball *n. Mil.* (see quots.).

1973 Huggett *Body Count* 301 [ref. to Vietnam War, *ca*1968]: Puff the Magic Dragon. A plane like an old two-engine DC-3 but equipped to throw the big flares, called basketballs. **1991** L. Reinberg *In the Field* 17: *Basketball*, refers to illumination-dropping aircraft mission.

basket case *n.* Orig. *Mil.* **1.** a quadruple amputee.

1919 in C.A. Smith *New Words:* The Surgeon General of the Army, Maj. Gen. Merritte W. Ireland, denies emphatically that there is any foundation for stories that have been circulated in all parts of our country of the existence of "basket cases" in our hospitals. A basket case is a soldier who has lost both legs and both arms and therefore cannot be carried on a stretcher. [**1937** Binns *Laurels* 157 [ref. to WWI]: The lieutenant he told them about, sent home in a basket; a blind, wriggling worm, without arms or legs.] **1946** Bowker *Uniform* 39: On the gruesome side, there was the hardy perennial about "basket cases" who had lost all four limbs. In almost every section of the country, one could hear whispers that a certain near-by hospital was the secret repository for hundreds of helpless heads-and-torsos....However, [the rumor] did not happen to be true. **1946** J.H. Burns *Gallery* 29: Did you pour coffee for your basket cases at the airport last night?

2.a. a person who has been made helpless by stress or emotional illness.

1952 Bellow *Augie March* 74: If *he* went wrong he was a total loss, nowise justified, a dead account, a basket case, an encumbrance, zero. **1956** I. Shulman *Good Deeds* 13: There wasn't any appreciable difference between a basket case and me. **1958** Drury *Advise & Consent* 300: Good Christ,...this guy's a mental basket-case. **1962** in Algren *Lonesome Monsters* 23: I've been married to this basket case for almost a month now. He refuses to see his shrink any more. **1969** *N.Y. Times* (Mar. 9) II 13: Why aren't you a basket case after 25 years of [acting]? **1973** O'Neill & O'Neill *Shifting Gears* 121: In the long run we would have had three basket cases instead of just one. **1974** Millard *Thunderbolt* 44: My God, he's a mental basket-case. **1977** *L.A. Times* (May 1) IX 19: Coming home was a time of anxiety. As one said, "I was a basket case when I started closing out my apartment in Rome." **1990** *Cosmopolitan* (Nov.) 282: Sometimes, Phil stops calling altogether. When this happens, Laura becomes a basket case.

b. anything, as a country, whose functioning is impaired.

*1973 in *OED2:* The real basket cases of European agriculture are the Italians and the Bavarians. **1976** *Dallas Times-Herald* (Dec. 26) H1: Two years ago the DSO was a basket case, tired and broke, a sad thing to be clucked over and pointed to as an object of pity. **1978** *Business Week* (July 3) 34: The program addresses itself to the crises in transport and agriculture that have reduced Zaire to an economic basket case. **1981** *Time* (Aug. 24) 46: The suburbs, Rouse argues, "sucked the blood out of the central cities and left behind some of the urban basket cases we see today." **1990** *U.S. News & W.R.* (Feb. 26) 13: Yet, even with drug money, much of the region is an economic basket case.

c. a person who behaves in a wildly eccentric manner.

1977 *Harper's* (May) 96: Alekhine...exhibited enough irrational behavior at his matches for even Archie Bunker to finger him as a basket case....At one tournament, he urinated on the chessboard. **1982** S.P. Smith *Officer & Gentleman* 94: You guys are a couple of basket cases. **1993** Ephron et al. *Sleepless in Seattle* (film): You're a basket case!

3. a vehicle or piece of machinery that has been abandoned and stripped of many of its parts.

1971 Tak *Truck Talk* 9: *Basket case:* an abandoned tractor that has had most of its original equipment stripped off or stolen. **1978** *Tico Times* (San Jose, Costa Rica) (Oct. 13) 12: Mechanical basket cases, especially trucks, will probably disappear from the roads until they can be presented with all their body parts in place. **1979** *Easyriders* (Dec.) 126: Wanted: Knucklehead or shovelhead engine and tranny. Basket case okay. **1986** Oddo *Street Rod Hndbk.* 28: A...*basket case*...is a disassembled car.

basket days *n. Homosex.* (see 1972 quot.).

1971 Rader *Govt. Inspected* 134: Basket Days. **1972** *Anthro. Linguistics* 98: *Basket Days* (n.): A period of mild weather that permits persons to

wear clothing that reveals the contour of their genitals or "baskets."

basketeer *n.* [BASKET, 3] *Homosex.* a male homosexual who seeks sex partners by observing the outline of their genitals through the trousers. Also as *v.*

1941 G. Legman, in Henry *Sex Variants* II 1157: *Basketeer.* To go about the streets...on foot or in an automobile, looking over the genitals of the men as they show through their trousers. **1970** *Evergreen Rev.* XIV 77: Sally used to cruise the quads like it was Greenwich Avenue, selecting her boys like a basketeer on the milk run. **1971** Rader *Govt. Inspected* 40: I learned to mark the basketeer on Sixth Avenue in the afternoon.

basket man *n. Und.* BAGMAN, 1.

1935 Pollock *Und. Speaks: Basket man*, graft collector for the crooked underworld bosses and politicians.

bassackwards or **bassackward** *adj. & adv.* [euphem. metathesis of ASS-BACKWARDS; cf. BACK-ASSWARDS] backwards; reversed; *(hence)* mixed up; foolish; not right.

1932 R. Fisher *Conjure-Man* 25: This...sounds all bass-ackwards to me. **1938** Steinbeck *Grapes of Wrath* 413: You're lookin' at it bass-ackwards. **1942** McAtee *Supp. to Grant Co. Dial.* [ref. to Ind., 1890's] 3: *Basackwards* [*sic*]...euphemism for ass-backwards, meaning merely backwards. "You're doin' that jes —." **1954** E. Hunter *Jungle Kids* 54: If they spotted me with my leg all bassackwards, they'd call the cops. **1964** H. Rhodes *Chosen Few* 84: Another case of man's almighty faculty for making bassackwards decisions. **1966** Cameron *Sgt. Slade* 19: A prop trying to windmill bassackwards would slow us down something fierce. **1968** Swarthout *Loveland* 153: To write home for money, besides being bassackwards, would have gone against the grain of our independence. **1974** Millard *Thunderbolt* 16: Hell, Reverend, I didn't see your bassackward collar before. **1979** *Mother Jones* (Dec.) 4: Anybody that can sell you and the voters bass-ackwards billions math is...an extraordinary politician.

bass fiddle *n.* a deep voice.

1864 "E. Kirke" *Down in Tenn.* 125: Dey greab as ef dey wus his chillen,/An' I haff suspec' dey ar';/For dey's his nose, his big base fiddle,/An' his reddish wooly ha'r.

bastard *n.* **1.a.** a contemptible individual (usu. a man); a cruel or selfish person. [Long considered to be one of the strongest abusive terms in English, *bastard* has lost some of its force to more overtly sexual insults.]

*1598 B. Jonson *Everyman in Humour* II iii: Can it call whore? Cry bastard? Oh, then kiss it,/ A witty child. ***1599** Shakespeare *Henry V* III ii: Ish a villain, and a bastard, and a knave, and a rascal. ***1675** in Duffett *Burlesque Plays* 104: Out thou stinking, sneaking bastard. ***1698** Ward *London-Spy* 42: You White-liver'd Son of a Fleetstreet Bumsitter....*You* Bastard. **1744** A. Hamilton *Gentleman's Progress* 24: The servant...was a Scotsman; the names he gave his master were...little bastard, and shitten elf. **1759** in Silber *Songs of Independence* 146: So at you, ye bastards, here's give you Hot Stuff. ***1774** in R. Palmer *Sound of History* 77: Such a spunging old ba—d sure never was known. ***1830** in *OEDS: Bastard*, a term of reproach for a mischievous or worthless boy. **1834** in A. Cook *Armies of Streets* 24: Down with the Englishman! down with the British b——! **1866** in H. Johnson *Talking Wire* 317: The prisoner said—"we want to clean out the bastard." **1872** Burnham *Secret Service* 415: And if I miss anythin, I will make you squeel, you dam ignorant dum bastard. **1878** McElroy *Andersonville* 344 [ref. to Civil War]: Bad luck to the blatherin' bastards that yez are, and to the mothers that bore ye. **1887** M. Roberts *W. Avernus* 239: I wish I'd killed the bastard anyhow. **1877–88** in J.W. Crawford *Plays* 131: *Jack:* (Drawing pistol) What! You old bastard. ***1892** in Wilkes *Austral. Colloq.* 20: Here's the bleedin' push, me covey—here's a bastard from the bush! **1902** Wister *Virginian* 216: Not a bastard one but's laying for his chance to do for you. **1902** in Steinbach *Long March* 184: Your d—n b——d of a husband. **1917** in Pound *Pound/Joyce* 290: Suspicion is a damned good thing, but I get so much of it from rich bastards that I don't like to see it in a man I want to think well of. **1921** *N & Q* (Nov. 19) 418: There was one word pretty well banned [not much used] in the British Army, which profusely decorated the speech of overseas men and Americans, and that was "bastard." **1922** Tully *Emmett Lawler* 175: Men run this world that us kids live in, the selfish bastards. **1929** Brecht *Downfall* 152: That bastard...don't like me, but maybe I'll fool her, too. **1933** in Inman *Diary* 555: She's the bastard with the...varicose veins. **1933** Hammett *Maltese Falcon* 209: She's probably a little bastard, but she's in a tough spot. **1934** H. Roth *Call It Sleep* 252: Hol' it, yuh dumb bassid. **1940** in T. Williams *Letters* 12: You must think me an awful bastard not having written sooner or sent money. **1942** Garcia *Tough Trip* 304 [ref. to 1880's]: Don't do it...you hairy-faced whore's bastard. **1949** Mende *Spit & Stars* 118: But she, she was a bastard from bastards. A heart like stone. **1952** E. Brown *Trespass* 82: What bastard would pull off a stunt like that? **1968** Duay *Fruit Salad* 127: We must keep killing these giant bastard insects. **1971** Capaldi *Art of Deception* 142: After all, he is trying to be nice and you are being a bastard. **1977** *Nat. Lampoon* (July) 46: If you print that, you bastard's ghost, it'll cost you the first amendment. **1991** D'Souza *Illiberal Educ.* 202: [Male] chauvinist goddamn bastard.

b. a fellow; a person suffering hardship or ill luck.—constr. with *poor* or similar adj.—usu. considered vulgar.

1861 in J.M. Merrill *Battle Flags* 58: The poor damn bastards ought'a have a plan. [*ca***1882** in Wilkes *Austral. Colloq.* 21: Now then, Harry, you old—, what the — is it going to be?] [*****1903** in Wilkes *Austral. Colloq.* 21: Seen better days, poor (fellow).] **1918** in Hall & Niles *One Man's War* 325: Imagine those poor bastards, going to church with the long-range guns giving them hell all day. **1925** in Hemingway *Sel. Letters* 181: He lives altogether in his imagination. The poor old bastard. **1927** in T. Wolfe *Letters* 118: Joe, you old bastard, how the hell are you? *****1929** Manning *Fortune* 21: The poor bastard's dead, sir. **1932** Nelson *Prison Days & Nights* 87: Get it, long as you don't have to take it from some poor bastard that can't afford to lose it. **1933** N. West *Miss Lonelyhearts* 81: I'm a humanity-lover. All the broken bastards. **1934** H. Miller *Tropic of Cancer* 123: The poor bastard...he's better off dead than alive. **1936** *New Directions* 158: A turtle is...a tough old bastard. *****1945** S.J. Baker *Australian Lang.* 256: *Bastard* and *bugger* are frequently used as terms of genial or even affectionate address between men. **1949** Robbins *Dream Merchants* 202: The poor bastard jumped. **1955** Reynolds *HQ* 296: The poor bastards are sick is the way I see it.

2.a. a vexatious or physically taxing job; a cruel place, situation, or state of affairs; an unpleasant surprise, etc.

*****1915** in Wilkes *Austral. Colloq.* 21: Of all the bastards of places, this is the greatest bastard in the world. **1924** P. Marks *Plastic Age* 9: Rest yourself after climbing that goddamn hill....It's a bastard, that hill is. **1934** Appel *Brain Guy* 44: What a damn bastard of a life. No job. Nothing. **1938** "Justinian" *Americana Sexualis* 12: *Bastard.* n....a difficult problem or situation. **1941** in Hemingway *Sel. Letters* 525: That bastard of a trip will be added on top of all the book earned and three quarters of it confiscated by taxes. **1949** Van Praag *Day Without End* 160: This'll be a bastard! **1951** Leveridge *Walk on Water* 43: Life's a Christ's bastard. **1961** in Hemingway *Sel. Letters* 917: It is a bastard to be here without my library, reference, etc. **1962** Hecht *Gaily* 48: But you're better for this blizzard. It's a real bastard. **1963** *AS* XXXVIII 167: A difficult college course...*bastard.* **1966–80** McAleer & Dickson *Unit Pride* 101: The old man says we've got to attack that hill again today....Ain't that a bastard?

b. an annoying object or thing; *(occ.)* something delightful (as in 1928, 1935 quots.).

1921 Dos Passos *3 Soldiers* 42 [ref. to WWI]: One of those bastard U-boats. **1927** *Immortalia* 59: I rustled and I tussled 'til I got the bastard home. **1928** Carr *Rampant Age* 112: That sandwich is a bastard—don't miss it. **1932** in Hemingway *Sel. Letters* 354: That is the only thing could ruin the bastard from being a great piece of literature. **1934** in Inman *Diary* 556: Bet this year will be another...bastard. *****1934** Yeates *Winged Victory* 329 [ref. to 1918]: That'll get the bastard crashed. **1935** Wolfe *Time & River* 71: Why, God help this lovely bastard of a train! **1938** Steinbeck *Grapes of Wrath* 363: Harsh ol' bastard, ain't she. **1939** Appel *People Talk* 290: The truck's two top logs roll off...."You bastards!" The boom man jumps out of the way. **1990** Poyer *Gulf* 382: We got to get that bastard out of there, John.

¶ In phrase:

¶ **as** [or **like**] **a bastard** (used as a strong comparative).

1923 Ornitz *Haunch* 68: He grew up and was smart, smart as a bastard, just as the saying goes. **1928** in Hemingway *Sel. Letters* 282: Am lonely as a bastard. **1929** Brecht *Downfall* 302: [She] started to yell like a bastard and I stuck my hand over her mouth. **1932** Hecht & Fowler *Great Magoo* 97: Hot as a bastard, ain't it? *a***1938** Adamic *My America* 54: He's a writer and...he writes like a bastard, no kiddin'. *Ibid.* 55: He thought this "funny as a bastard." **1938** Bezzerides *Long Haul* 54: You made him work like a bastard til he was nuts for sleep. **1941** Schulberg *Sammy* 243: Salica must be gettin' richer 'n a bastard. **1943** in *Best from Yank* 21: I was still scared as a bastard. *****1945** S.J. Baker *Australian Lang.* 166: Drunk as a bastard. **1947** Schulberg *Harder They Fall* 36: Them kids, that's what makes you want to work like a bastard. **1948** Manone & Vandervoort *Trumpet* 123: I...ran out of there like a bastard. **1947–51** Salinger *Catcher in Rye* 102: My voice was shaking like a bastard. *Ibid.*

212: It began to rain like a bastard. **1953** M. Harris *Southpaw* 92: I would of run like a bastard. **1961** Granat *Important Thing* 133: She was mad as a bastard. **1963** Hayden *Wanderer* 32: Cold as a bastard on deck. **1966–80** McAleer & Dickson *Unit Pride* 53: These watches cost like a bastard, too. **1980** in *N.E. Folklore* XXVIII (1988) 89: It's paining me like a bastard.

bastardly *adj.* despicable; hateful.—sometimes considered vulgar. [S.E. senses in *OED* (1552–1785) are marked *obsolete*.]

1918 in Dos Passos *14th Chronicle* 127: Those bastardly dastards of mechanics. **1928** *Our Army* (Dec.) 8: The bastardly recruiters. **1928** Bodenheim *Georgie May* 7: She was becoming more low-down and bastardly every day. **1929–30** Dos Passos *42d Parallel* 351: The bastardly...war. **1933** "W. March" *Co. K* 127: I haven't had enough to eat since I joined this bastardly outfit! **1934** H. Miller *Tropic of Cancer* 119: I hate these bastardly cunts. **1941** Guthrie *Born to Win* 150: Get that bastardly son of a bitch! **1943** in Hemingway *Sel. Letters* 544: I...promise not to be self-righteous, no-good and bastardly. **1943** Bayler & Carnes *Wake I.* 264: Why the bastardly thing's got a wake. **1964–66** R. Stone *Hall of Mirrors* 70: The whole bastardly house shakes. **1971** Contini *Beast* 6: But the depravity and bastardly acts that go on in prison are something else again.

bastard-well *adv.* BLOODY-WELL.—usu. considered vulgar.

*****1922** T.E. Lawrence *Mint* 62: Cunt shouldn't bastard-well drink if he can't carry it. **1951** Leveridge *Walk on Water* 11: I'm bastard well fed-up, and if I weren't a bastard I don't know how the bastard hell I could bastard well take it.

baste *v.* [cf. PASTE, *v.*] **1.** to strike hard; beat. [Orig. colloq. or S.E.: *OED* 1533–1847.]

1805 *Port Folio* (Aug. 24) 261: To make my donkey nimbly go,/I baste him with my stick first. *****1859** Hotten *Slang Dict.*: Baste, to beat. *a***1910** Bierce *Shapes of Clay* 226: My old 'oman...has frequent basted me. **1937** *Esquire* (Nov.) 171: Broderick did not have to baste a single one of them, either.

2. *Und.* to kill.

1900 "J. Flynt" & Hodler *Powers* 170: He was a copper, and we fly cops have got to send some bloke to the chair for bastin' him. **1902** "J. Flynt" *Little Bro.* 142: Oh, he'll show up somewhere, and then you can baste him—you'll be a grown-up by that time.

basuco var. BAZUKO.

bat[1] *n.* **1.** a low prostitute, esp. one who walks the streets at night to solicit customers; *(hence)* a dissolute or sexually promiscuous woman. [1612 quot.—by far the earliest—occurs in the context of poetic S.E.]

*****1612** J. Sylvester *Lachrimae Lachrimarum* (unp.): All Epicures, Witt-Wantons, Atheists/Mach-Aretines, Momes, Tap To-Bacchonists,/ Bats, Harpies, Sirens, Centaurs, Bib all nights,/Sice-sinck ap Asses, Hags Hermaphrodites/...Have pull'd this Waight of Wrath. *****1811** *Lexicon Balatron.*: Bat. A low whore: so called from moving out like bats in the dusk of the evening. **1859** Matsell *Vocabulum* 10: Bat. A prostitute who walks the streets only at night. *Ibid.*: You lie, you bat—I couple with no cove but my own. **1900** *DN* II 22 [at various colleges]: Bat, n. 1. a loose woman. **1915** *DN* IV 231 [at Harvard & Western Reserve Univ.]: Bat...A prostitute. **1918** in [O'Brien] *Wine, Women, War* 85: Battle of bats a mand men. **1923** *DN* V 201 [Ozarks]: Bat, n. A disreputable woman. **1925** in *AS* II 348 [W. Va.]: Bat, an old...a woman of ill fame. "I wouldn't be running around with that old bat." **1930** *Amer. Mercury* (Dec.) 454: Bat, n. A prostitute. "The bat's copper-hearted." **1932** *AS* (June) 329 [at Johns Hopkins Univ.]: Bat—a street walker. **1934** Appel *Brain Guy* 161: Damn it, he should be glad someone, even a little bat like Madge, cared for him. **1937** Reitman *Box-Car Bertha* 197: "Bats"...These are aged or worn-out prostitutes...sought by bums and odd types. **1946** *PADS* (No. 6) 5 [Va.]: Bat: n. A woman of ill repute. **1951** *Time* (Oct. 29) 50: The [television] code specifically bans a number of words and phrases [from television broadcasting], among them: *nut* (applied to a woman); *nuts* (except when meaning crazy), [etc.]. **1966** S. Harris *Hellhole* 161: Molly still designates [criminals] by the names with which she first learned to identify them [before 1910]: "cats" or "gooks"—the small-time madams she presently meets in the House of Detention; "bats" or "owls"—streetwalkers who work at night.

2.a. a foolish or worthless person.

1894 in S. Crane *Complete Stories* 194: Go ahead, you old bat. **1900** Wister *Jimmyjohn* 24: "Why, you're an old bat!" said the boy to his foreman and clapped him farewell on the shoulder. [**1905** *DN* III 76:

"She says he's crazy as a bat." Common.] [**1908** *DN* 302 [Ala.]: Crazy as a bat...Very crazy.] **1914** *DN* IV 103: *Bat, n.* A disorderly or dissolute person. **1915** *DN* IV 197: Crazy bat! Can't you understand? Now listen. **1928** Carr *Rampant Age* 132: They're mostly just dizzy bats that have regular contests seein' who can stay drunk the longest. **1962–68** B. Jackson *In Life* 171: In order to survive in the life of crime, it's just like anything else. A bat can't go it. *Bat? You mean a dingbat?* Yeah. **1979** Selmier & Kram *Blow Away* 101: That bat [*sc.* Charles de Gaulle] in the palace down the way is senile.

b. a quarrelsome woman; BATTLE-AX.

1906 H. Green *Actors' House* 81: She's an old bat, ain't she?....Been hearing about her since I was a kid. **1928** in O'Brien *Best Stories of '28* 58: Now keep out of this, do you hear, you old bat. **1944** Burley *Harlem Jive* 133: *Bats*—Creaking old cronies [*sic*] chasing young men. **1970** Harington *Lightning Bug* 149: That ain't your son, you old bat! That's my man Willy. **1992** *Young Ind. Jones* (ABC-TV): Some old bat who's too senile to remember what doughnut she ordered.

c. an unattractive woman or man.

1929–32 in *AS* (Dec. 1934) 287: *Bat.* Any unattractive girl. **1933** Ersine *Prison Slang* 16: *Bat*...an ugly old man. **1947** *PADS* (No. 8) 21: *An old bat,* meaning an unpleasant person. **1971** *Essence* (Sept.) 74: Brother [i.e., black] language for an ugly "chick": *bat.*

3. a dollar.

1895 J.L. Williams *Princeton* 34: I lost twenty-five bats on it. **1900** *DN* II 23 [At Princeton Univ.]: *Bat, n.* Dollar.

4. *pl.* horrific hallucinations sometimes imagined by alcoholics; delirium tremens; (*hence*) insanity.

1904 *Life in Sing Sing* 246: *Bats.* Delirium tremens. **1927* in *OEDS*: Have you taken the "bats" or what? **1935** D.W. Maurer, in *AS* (Feb.) 12: *Bats.* 1. Temporary insanity resulting from solitary confinement. (Obs.) 2. Delirium tremens. **1967** [Beck] *Pimp* 156: A stud would have to be slick as grease to plant bats in the skull of a bitch that was sane.

¶ In phrases:

¶ **have bats in the belfry** to be insane. See also BATS and BELFRY.

1899 "B. Baxter" *Baxter's Letters* 39: The leader...acted generally as though he had bats in his belfry. **1899** A.H. Lewis *Sandburrs* 10: Mary don't last in d' Chink swim more'n a year before there's bats in her belfry for fair; any old stiff wit' lamps could see it. *Ibid.* 26: Mollie's...got bats in his steeple half d' time. **1902** Mead *Word Coinage* 185: She has a bat in her belfry. **1911** A.H. Lewis *Apaches of N.Y.* 113: I always figgered Louie had bats in his belfry. **1916** S. Lewis *Job* 145: He's got bats in his belfry. **1925** Dos Passos *Manhattan Transfer*: Cookoo, bats in the belfry, that's what he's saying to himself. **1927** *AS* II 348: That's all one could expect from a man who has bats in his belfry. **1938** Smitter *Detroit* 294: You got a slight case of bats in the belfry. **1952** C. Sandburg *Young Strangers* 169: It wasn't an insult among us kids [in Illinois, *ca*1890] to say..."Say, your head wasn't screwed on wrong, was it?" or "You've got bats in your belfry." **1980** *N.Y. Times* (Oct. 4) 26: No one can say that Harry Hoover...has bats in his belfry, not after the deal he got for the sale of his cave.

¶ **like a bat out of hell** at tremendous speed.

1909 *DN* III 399 [Ark.]: *Like a bat out of hell, adv. phr.* Very quickly. **1912** *DN* III 577: When I saw him he was going like a bat through hell. **1918** in Mills *War Letters* 353: He turned tail and headed for Germany like a bat out of hell. **1948** Manone & Vandervoort *Trumpet* 156: I came wingin' in like a bat out of hell. **1948** Webb *Four Steps* 22: He came back in here like a bat out of hell. **1970** Terkel *Hard Times* 33: We make an orange freight....It goes like a bat out of hell, a rough ride. **1977** "Meat Loaf" *Bat out of Hell* (song): Like a bat out of hell, I'll be gone when the morning comes.

¶ **on the bat** *Und.* practicing prostitution.

[**1860* Hotten *Slang Dict.* (ed. 2) s.v. *batter:* "On the batter," "on the streets," "on the town,"...given up to roystering and debauchery.] **1933** Ersine *Prison Slang* 16: *Bat, n.*...Practicing prostitution. "She's on the bat."

bat² *n.* [perh. fr. dial. E *bat* 'rate of stroke or speed, pace'] a drinking spree; binge; (*hence*) (with prec. adj.) a spree of any kind; JAG.

1846 Durivage & Burnham *Stray Subjects* 102: Zenas had been "on a bat" during the night previous, and had squandered full half-a-dollar on himself, in white-eye and sweetening. **1889** Field *Western Verse* 100: He borrerd all the stuff he could and started on a bat. **1896** Ade *Artie* 45: Worse'n any poker party. A bat—real old bat. **1896** Walker *Amherst Olio* 169: The noble freshmen returned to crown/The events of their wild debauch and "bat." **1898** "B. Baxter" *Baxter's Letters* 18: I

always cry some during a bat. **1905** *Lippincott's Mag.* (Nov.) 590: A drink!...That means a bat and he's only just through the reg'lar monthly one. **1908** *Atlantic Mo.* (Aug.) 190: [Automobiles] carry our daughters on their shopping bouts and their calling "bats." **1914** S. Lewis *Mr. Wrenn* 147: Your bat's over, ain't it, old man? **1929** W.R. Burnett *Little Caesar* 177: He's been on a bat with some Chicago guys. **1940** Zinberg *Walk Hard* 93: A good bat will do me good, take the edge off me. **1943** in Ruhm *Detective* 360: He's working himself onto a singing bat. **1953** R. Wright *Outsider* 49: A brown-skinned girl...encouraged him to continue his "bat" as long as he had money to spend. **1972** Grogan *Ringolevio* 128: It was a bat, a lengthy run of pure debauchment.

bat³ *n.* **1.** [orig. dial. E; *OED* gives quotations from *ca*1400 to 1864; extensive evidence in *EDD*] a sharp blow; knock.

1909 *WNID: Bat*...5. A stroke; a sharp blow. *Colloq. or Slang.* **1938** W. Sherman & V. Sherman *Crime School* (film): You'll be more than scared if I give ya a bat in the mouth. **1972** in *Playboy* (Jan. 1973) 146: Shut your fuckin' mouth, I give you a bat in the head.

2. *R.R.* a throttle.

1897 Hamblen *General Mgr.* 86: All right then; get hold o' this bat, an' let's see ye shape yerself.

3. *Horse Racing.* a jockey's whip.

1925 Faulkner *N.O. Sketches* 97: We was neck and neck at the half; at the three quarters the other horse drawed ahead a little. The stands was whooping fit to kill, and the other jock went to the bat. **1942** *ATS* 78: *Bat, dick,* a riding whip. **1951** D.W. Maurer, in *PADS* (No. 16) 32: *Go to bat*...Of a jockey: to use his whip, especially in the stretch.

4. a complaint or other provoking remark; an uttered word.

1929–33 J.T. Farrell *Manhood* 281: One more bat out of you while I'm shooting, and it'll be curtains for you, punk. **1955** N.Y.C. woman, age *ca*60: I don't want to hear another bat out of you.

5. the penis.

1942 *ATS* 147: Male Pudendum...*balls and bat.* **1966** Gass *Omensetter's Luck* 205: Certainly not Socrates—with his ambidextrous bat and balls. **1971** Reisner *Graffiti* 108: Slang words for penis....horn, peg, hose, joint, bat, pistol, ad infinitum. *Ibid.:* Men with short bats stand close to the plate.

¶ In phrases:

¶ **at bat** [fr. baseball] taking one's turn, esp. before a judge.

[**1884** Nye *Baled Hay* 52: Common decency ought to govern conversation without its being necessary to hire an umpire to announce who is at bat and who is on deck.] **1902** Hobart *Up to You* 38: Clara J. was at the bat. **1908** in H.C. Fisher *A. Mutt* 104: For two years now you've been at bat. And you're just where you started at. **1920** Ade *Hand-Made Fables* 17: The other Portion of the Sketch advanced to Bat (before the judge) and began his Recital. **1966** Braly *On Yard* 21: You're first at bat Henry. Take off your cap and come along.

¶ **go** [or **come**] **to bat** to take one's turn; (*specif.*) *Und.* to appear before a judge to stand trial, testify, or receive sentencing.

1899 A.H. Lewis *Sandburrs* 176: D' priest is goin' to bat an' says "Is there any duck here to give d' bride away?" **1902** Townsend *Fadden & Mr. Paul* 23: De foist mug to come to de bat...was Charlie Wu Lung, minister plenty-potation from China. **1926** in *AS* (Mar. 1927) 281: *Go to bat*—To get one's sentence. **1927** in Hammett *Knockover* 275: Dan Morey and I had nailed her, but none of her victims would go to bat against her, so she had been turned loose. **1927** Coe *Me—Gangster* 59: The old man...demanded an immediate trial...and we were ready to go to the bat. **1928** O'Connor *B'way Racketeers* 43: The racketeer knows he has two strikes on him every time he goes to bat in a Federal Court. **1933** D. Runyon, in *Collier's* (Dec. 23) 8: The judge throws the book at him when he finally goes to bat. **1963** Williamson *Hustler!* 141: I went up to bat on the sale first. *Ibid.* 146: Next day we went to bat and got four days apiece. **1966** Brunner *Face of Night* 193: Jim-Jim was there but I don't know what he got, he was just going to bat when I left. Brozek got two-ten. **1971** Horan *Blue Messiah* 158: Do you want to go to bat?...Do you, Howell? I'll defend you. **1985** M. Baker *Cops* 255: If...the [victim]...has gotten all our subpoenas and makes all his appearances, then you might go to bat....The case load is incredible.

¶ **go to bat for** to take the part of, support wholeheartedly.

1916 P.B. Kyne *Cappy Ricks* 344: I'll go to bat for you. **1936** in Ruhm *Detective* 189: But I like her, even if she is funny. And I'm going to bat for her. **1951** Sheldon *Troubling Star* 160: I guess Major Ronsdale must have gone to bat for you. **1955** Deutsch *Cops* 98: A virtual "protector" who will "go to bat" for him in time of trouble. **1982** Mutual Radio News broadcast (Oct. 12): The Justice Department is going to bat for private schools with discriminatory policies.

¶ **right** [or **hot**] **off the bat** at once, immediately. Now *colloq.*

1907 in Butterfield *Post Treasury* 79: "So, boys, so…and you want to begin now?" "Right off the bat." **1910** Raine *Bucky O'Connor* 65: Turn loose your yarn at me hot off the bat. **1916** in *DA* 86: It would have been hard to name so many correctly right off the bat. **1947** Overholser *Buckaroo's Code* 91: I had a hunch right off the bat he wasn't no Eastern dude. **1957** in C. Beaumont *Best* 147: We ought to get one thing die-straight right off the bat here. **1963** D. Tracy *Brass Ring* 309: Right off the bat I guess he put the pressure on them. **1977* T. Jones *Ice* 57: Off the bat I'd say yes.

bat[4] var. BATT.

bat *v.* **1.** [as "to cudgel," dial. E; cites in *OED, ca*1440–1859, and *EDD*] to strike.—sometimes constr. with *around*.

1877 in *DAE:* When the book was not wanted…those lounging about the saloon were in the habit of…"batting" each other over the head with it. **1907** S.E. White *Arizona* ch. xi: Men got batted over the head often enough in those days. *a*1909 *F & H* I (rev.) 153: *To bat one on the head* (American).—To strike one on the head. **1949** Gordon & Kanin *Adam's Rib* 22: He started battin' me around. **1962** Ragen & Finston *Toughest Prison* 31: Some dick bats you on the ear, an' right away you wish you'd never left home.

2. to wander, move aimlessly, kick around.—usu. constr. with *around*.

1896 S. Crane *George's Mother* 139: I can't fin' me feet in dis bloomin' joint. I been battin' round heh fer a half hour. **1897** Work *Waifs of Press* 191: He went West and batted around there for several years, and then came back to Kentucky. **1935** D. Clarke *Regards to B'way* 144: I give you all the money you want to play bridge and bat around with the right people and I never say a word, do I? **1935** Coburn *Law Rides Range* 68: I've batted around this old world since I was knee-high to a burro.

3. to complain, chatter, utter a word.

1925 *Collier's* (Sept. 19) 7: I didn't mean to bat out of turn. **1939** "E. Queen" *Dragon's Teeth* 131: So what are you battin' about? **1945** Kanin *Born Yesterday* 226: What the hell are you two battin' about? **1980** N.Y.C. woman, age 65: She's always battin' about something.

4. to dissipate.—usu. constr. with *around*.

1915 *DN* IV 231: *Bat…v.i.* To go on a "spree," to carouse. **1926* in *OEDS: Bat round,* have a good time, go from place to place (in quest of pleasure). "We've been batting round all evening." **1938** Bellem *Blue Murder* 71: He bats around with other dames. **1944** E. Caldwell *Tragic Ground* 51: But men with young daughters are out batting around with other men's young daughters.

5. *Und.* to arrest.—constr. with *out*.—usu. constr. in passive.

1933 Ersine *Prison Slang* 16: *Batted,* adj. 1. Arrested. **1955** D.W. Maurer, in *PADS* (No. 24) 198: If a tool gets *batted out* or *nailed* in the act, he is in jail. **1971** Guggenheimer *Narc. & Drug Abuse* 5: *Batted out.* arrested.

6. to substitute.

1934 in Fenner *Throttle* 56: He'd been batting as roundhouse foreman while old man Swanson was sick.

7. *Stu.* to earn (a specific grade).

1935 F.H. Lea *Anchor Man* 5: Midshipmen…able to bat a two-five in…calculus.

¶ **In phrases:**

¶ **bat a thousand** to have a perfect record of success; **bat zero** to be completely and chronically unsuccessful; **bat five hundred** to be halfway successful. [All fr. baseball.]

1920 Ade *Hand-Made Fables* 142: In the matter of correct Pronunciation, he batted 1,000. **1929** "M. Brand" *Beacon Creek* 124: I've had my ups and downs. I've just batted over five hundred; that's all. **1943** *AS* XVIII 110: *You're batting a thousand* (you're absolutely right). **1954** MacDonald *Condemned* 20: She batted zero with me. **1958** Abbott *Damn Yankees* (film): When your luck is battin' zero, get your chin up off the floor. **1981** G. Wolf *Roger Rabbit* 7: Yeah, maybe Rip Kirby bats a thousand.

¶ **bat them out** [ref. to baseball practice of batting out fly balls] to gossip, chat.

1928 *Our Army* (Oct.) 17: We were batting 'em out, talking over things in general.

¶ **bat (oneself) out** to work oneself to exhaustion.

1947 *N.Y. Folklore Qly.* 295: It was a rugged trip, weather bad and the crew really batted themselves out.

¶ **bat the breeze** see s.v. BREEZE.

bat-ass *v.* to go at top speed.—usu. considered vulgar.

1985 Tate *Bravo Burning* 110: We saw him bat-assing across a paddy dike.

batbrain *n.* BIRDBRAIN.

1948 A. Murphy *Hell & Back* 25: Nuts! They're all a bunch of batbrains. **1967** Schaefer *Mavericks* 135: And I'm too blamed busy chasing juvenile bat-brains in sporty cars.

bat-brained *adj.* stupid.

1972–79 T. Wolfe *Right Stuff* 80: They regarded the military psychiatrist as…[a] bat-brained version of the chaplain. **1989** Zumbro & Walker *Jungletracks* 176: Their own bat-brained preconceptions.

bat carrier *n. Und.* (see 1931 quot.).

1931 *AS* VI 437: *Bat carrier*—A police informer. **1956** *AS* XXXI 100: [Narcotics] Agents frequently secure information from clues furnished by *bat carriers* or *belchers* (informers).

batch or **bach** *n.* a bachelor.

1855 in *DA:* You will soon be…a "dried up" old bach., and in fact, "good for nix." **1855** *Knickerbocker Mag.* 45 158: The President was an "old bach." of some sixty-five summers. **1862** in Norton *Army Lttrs.* 127: I got in with J.H., a bilious, crotchety, quarrelsome old bach. **1874** J. McCoy *Cattle Trade* 14: Although young, Peryman is what the ladies term an "Old Bach." **1932** L. Berg *Prison Doctor* 128: Me, I'm a "bach" for keeps. I ain't wasting my dough on any of these stir ladies [i.e., prison homosexuals]! **1936** R. Adams *Cowboy Lingo* 198: A "batch" was an unmarried man, usually one living alone. **1947** in *DA:* No, I'm no old bach but a middle-aged father of two kids.

¶ **In phrases:**

¶ **keep bach hall** to keep house as a bachelor. Also **keep bach.** See also BACHELOR'S HALL.

1878 in *OEDS:* A cabin…where two brothers and "a hired man" were "keeping bach." **1883** in *DAE:* Don't you know any house, or any place, where we could keep "bach" together? **1904** in *DA:* Ye've kept bach hall since seventy-three!

¶ **on the batch** living or keeping house as a bachelor.

1902 in F. Remington *Sel. Letters* 301: My "injun" and I…[are] on the batch.

batch or **bach** *v.* to camp, keep house, or live as a bachelor (*occ.,* as a spinster).—often constr. with *it*.

1862 in S. Clemens *Twain's Letters* I 216: It costs me $8 or $10 per week to "batch" in this d—d place. **1864** in Brobst *Civil War Lttrs.* 78: When I get back you can come and see me when I am batching. **1888** *Century Mag.* (Jan.) 412: He had always "bached it" (lived as a bachelor). **1896** in Cather *Short Fiction* 503: No wonder he wants to get married.…Batchin's pretty hard on a man. **1906** London *Moon-Face* 61: She climbed the three flights of stairs to the rooms where she and her sister "bach'ed." **1926** C.M. Russell *Trails* 63: Me an' Murphy's batchin' together. **1928** C.T. Harris *Mem. Manhattan* 111: The old gentleman had a room in a printing loft on Beekman Street, where he "bached" it. **1931** Adamic *Laughing* 92: Bob had two rooms and a kitchen; he "batched." **1937** E. Anderson *Thieves Like Us* 124: He got him a hot plate…and he's just batching fine. **1952** Bonham *Snaketrack* 76: Ridge "bached" in a room off the jail. **1954** Matheson *Born of Man & Woman* 199: You and I bached while Mary and Glad went to see the fashion show. **1968** Johnson & Johnson *Count Me Gone* 9: Doug and me would batch around—goof off and not shave and drink some beer and leave the dishes in the sink. **1979** *U.S. News & W.R.* (Feb. 19) 19 (adv.): My wife is in the hospital. So for a week I've been batching it.

batch out var. PATCH OUT.

batch up *v.* to live together as man and wife though unmarried.

1959 Oliver *Meaning of Blues* 123: Unions may be casually made with couples "batching up" with little ceremony.

Bates *n. Und.* a middle-aged man, esp. a real or intended victim of pickpockets or swindlers. Also **Mr. Bates, John Bates**, etc.

1908 Sullivan *Criminal Slang* 13: *John Bates*—A sucker. *a*1909 Tillotson *Detective* 93: *Mr. Bates*—a mark. **1924** G. Henderson *Keys to Crookdom* 409: *Johnny Bates.* Victim, sucker, sap. **1947** D.W. Maurer, in *AS* XXII 168: *Mr. Bates.* A sucker or mark [in a three-shell game]. **1955** D.W. Maurer, in *PADS* (No. 24) 55: I…topped a leather in Mr. Bates' left prat when I blowed I was getting a jacket from these two honest bulls.…This bates, he was tall, lots taller than I am. *Ibid.* 105: A *bates* is a man over forty. *Ibid.* 120: Kid, case that Bates and come back. **1983** *N.Y. Times* (Sept. 6) B 6: A "bates" is a male over 40, and is regarded as an ideal mark because he can be expected to carry more money, wear looser clothes, [etc.].

batfest *n. Baseball Journ.* a baseball game in which many runs are scored.

1908 *Atlantic* (Aug.) 224: The red-blooded look not kindly upon...the "batfest." **1929** in *AS* XXVI 29: For some reason, his teammates were beginning to hit Merriwell, and Needham wanted his share in the batfest.

bath *n.* ¶ In phrases:

¶ **go to the baths** [sugg. by *take a bath*, below] to sustain a damaging financial loss.

1981 *N.Y. Times Mag.* (June 21) 24: "You must be excited about the Sinatra album." Wexler said, "Would you like to go to the baths with me on it?" "The baths?...I keep hearing it'll sell a half-million records." "The Messiah will have to come before we'll sell 50,000," Wexler said.

¶ **take a bath** Orig. *Gamb.* **1.** to go bankrupt; to sustain a damaging financial loss.

1936 *Esquire* (Sept.) 159: A producer going into bankruptcy "takes a bath," from whence is derived "he's in the tub." **1945** in D.W. Maurer *Lang. Underworld* 192: *To take a bath:* To lose heavily or to go broke. **1969** *Woodstock* (film): These people [the promoters] are gonna take a bath....But there are some things worth more than a dollar. **1972** in *Playboy* (Jan. 1973) 146: "I need eighteen thousand dollars and I need it right away."..."You guys did take a bath out there, didn't you?" **1975** *Business Week* (Oct. 27) 110: Our profits won't make up for the bath we took last fall and winter. **1980** Sec. Agriculture B. Bergland, on *Face the Nation* (CBS-TV) (Jan. 13): Some of the shipping industries are going to take a bath on this grain situation. **1984** *Time* (Feb. 13) 34: He saw no reason why the state should bail Lilco out of its losses. "Let them take a bath...they're a private corporation." **1990** *U.S.A. Today* (Aug. 28) 2B: There were a lot of people doing business in Kuwait who were sure they had no exposure....They are going to take a bath.

2. to fail miserably; to flop; to be completely outdone.

1974 *U.S. News & W.R.* (May 20) 22: There is already a strong prospect that Republican congressional candidates will...take a bath in next November's elections. **1974** *Business Week* (Dec. 21) 158: Big-ticket Impressionist and Modern paintings...have been taking a bath. **1974** Lahr *Trot* 15: I took a bath on the College Boards. Five hundred in English. Five-fifty in math. **1980** J. Webb *Sense of Honor* 295: "So how did service selection go?" "The marines took a bath. Too much TV coverage of the war." **1982** Univ. Tenn. *Daily Beacon* (Nov. 4) 2: As...Sen. Robert Dole, R-Kan., put it, the GOP "took a bath" in elections for the U.S. House.

bat hide *n.* (see quot.).

1929 *AS* IV 357: Will Rogers, in a recent magazine article used, in addition to do-re-mi...the term *bat hides*, meaning money.

bathouse *n.* [cf. BUGHOUSE] a hospital for the insane.

1902 "H. McHugh" *Back to Woods* 38: I could see myself in the giggle-giggle ward in a bat house. **1929** Barr *Let Tomorrow Come* 267: An insane asylum [is] a bughouse or bathouse. **1931** (cited in Partridge *Dict. Und.*).

Bathroom Charlie *n.* (see quots.). Also vars.

1939 *AS* XIV 239: *Bathroom Charlie.* Guest who ducks into the bathroom to avoid tipping the bell-boy. **1954** "Collans" & Sterling *House Detect.* 219: *Bathroom Bertha.* Female guest who ducks into the bathroom to avoid tipping bellman; male equiv., *Bathroom Benny.*

bathtub *n. Av.* (see quots.). Now *hist.*

1944 *Official Guide to AAF* 368: *Bathtub:*—ball turret. **1945** Hamann *Air Words:* Bathtub...Originally referred to the stationary belly turret of pre-power turret days on B-17's. The turret was shaped somewhat like a bathtub and the gunner had to lie face down in it. **1956** Heflin *USAF Dict.* 76: *Bathtub, n.* A popular term applied to any tub-like protuberance on the underside of an aircraft, as the lower engine cowling on a P-40 airplane. **1965** *Air Officer's Guide* 436: *Bathtub*—ball turret.

bathtub sailor *n. Navy.* [fr. suggestion that the sailor's only nautical experience has been playing with toy boats in a bathtub] a coast guardsman or land-based sailor.

1944 Kendall *Service Slang* 35: *Bathtub sailors....*gobs on special duty who have never been on water. **1973** U.S. Navy veteran, age 25: Coast Guardsmen were *fresh-water sailors* or *bathtub sailors.*

bathtub weather *n. Naut.* unusually fine or calm sailing weather.

1894 Henderson *Sea Yarns* 60: We had bath-tub weather all the time.

bats *adj.* [fr. *bats in the belfry* s.v. BAT[1]] crazy; NUTS. Also **bats in the belfry.**

[**ca1801–05* in W. Blake *Poetry & Designs* 209: The Bat that flits at Close of Eve/Has left the Brain that won't Believe.] **1919** Hurst *Humoresque* 314: "Are you bats?" she said. **1926** Hormel *Co-Ed* 161: I'm bats about it. **1940** K. Fearing *Collected Poems:* I will agree that your lady friend...is not crazy, bats, nutty as they come. **1947** Helseth *Martin Rome* 125: You're crazy!...Yeah, you're bats. **1950** Kemp *Skiers' Song Book* 44: I'm bats in the belfry, but I love her anyhow. **1964** "H. Green" *Rose Garden* ch. xiv: "What is bats?" "It means bats-in-the-belfry. It means that up in your head, where the bells ring, it's night and the bats are flying around, black and flapping and random and without direction." **1979** Gutcheon *New Girls* 33: "Don't your parents just drive you *crazy?*"..."Absolutely bats." **1983** Flaherty *Tin Wife* 266: The guys will...think I'm bats. **1990** *Bill & Ted's Adven.* (CBS-TV): Ring, ring, ring! It's driving me bats!

bat's balls *n.* CAT'S MEOW.—usu. considered vulgar.

1966 J. Lewis *Marines* 9: "This here R 'n R's the bat's balls," one of the officers at the nearby table roared.

bat sense *n.* a modicum of intelligence.

1974 Univ. Tenn. student: He's the only one on the show who's got bat-sense.

batshit *n.* [sugg. by BATS, BULLSHIT, etc.] **1.** lies, nonsense, rubbish. Also **bat crap.** [1944–53 quot. might just as easily illustrate (2).]

1944–53 *MSU Folklore* GF2-1: (Army: Jargon) 29: G.I. Language. *Bat shit.* Blew his stack. Brownie points...Eagle shits. [**1963** Southern & Kubrick *Dr. Strangelove* (film): Major Batguano.] **1964** H. Rhodes *Chosen Few* 137: "Maybe a good licking will help keep em in their place." BATSHIT!!! **1968** N.Y.C. man, age *ca*50: Don't give me that bat crap! [**1969** *Playboy* (Sept.) 92: To contend that violence is the only tactic open to students seeking change is pure bat droppings.] **1969** Pharr *Bk. of Numbers* 92 [ref. to 1930's]: Now she's so bored and rich, she's got to go slumming with a black-assed Little Caesar to get her kicks....How do you like that batshit? **1970** *Current Slang* V 19: *Batshit, n.* Anything untrue or unimportant. [*a***1987** Bunch & Cole *Reckoning for Kings* 341: The idea...was total bat guano.] *a***1987** Bunch & Cole *Reckoning for Kings* 241: What batshit the Five O'Clock Follies is.

2. a crazy person.

1982 Del Vecchio *13th Valley* 310: You fucken bat shit.

batshit *adj.* crazy.

1970 Calley & Sack *Lieut. Calley* 104: Most of America's males were in Korea or World War II or I. They killed, and they aren't all going batshit. They escaped it. **1972** Grogan *Ringolevio* 227: He...wanted to know whether the private...was trying to punk out of that war, or was truly bat-shit. **1973** R. Roth *Sand in Wind* 19: You'd go batshit in some of the other squads just looking for someone to talk to. **1975** Univ. Tenn. instructor, age 33: He must be batshit!

batshit *v.* to BULLSHIT.

1970 *Current Slang* V 19: *Bat-shit,...v.* To chat, b.s.

batso *adj.* [BATS + *-o*, poss. infl. by It *pazzo*] crazy.

1978 *Penthouse* (Apr.) 128: Look, I'm totally batso.

batt *n.* [by shortening; orig. a written abbr. taken over into speech] *Mil.* battalion, (*specif.*) a battalion headquarters. Also **bat.**

1862 Edmondston *Jour.* 145: Under...appointment to Raise a Bat he...concluded to go to Head Quarters. *ca***1890** Stearns *Co. K* 48 [ref. to 1861]: That was a home thrust for the "Fourth Batts," and it was a long time before they heard the last of it. *Ibid.* 49: Perhaps he had the "Fourth Batt. fever." **1948** A. Murphy *Hell & Back* 169: I'll telephone batt to hold up our mortar fire. **1958** Frankel *Band of Bros.* 116: Pluto's friends had two bats of sloggers. **1980** Manchester *Darkness* 275: The First Bat's down there. **1988** Poyer *Med* 370: Overrun by a batt of...regulars.

batted *adj.* [fr. BAT[2], *n.*] drunk.

1933 Ersine *Prison Slang* 16: *Batted...*Drunk.

batter[1] *n.* [orig. unkn.; cf. BAT[2], *n.*] a drinking spree; a binge.

*1839 in *OEDS:* My hat was smash'd...Ae night when on the batter. **1845** Corcoran *Pickings* 66: 'Twas plain they'd on the batter been,/So batter'd was their every feature. **1856** *Knickerbocker Mag.* 48 502: Ellis...had just returned from a prolonged batter in Paris. ***1865** in *OEDS:* It was among working-men that I first heard "on the batter" employed as an equivalent for going "on the spree." **1928** Santee *Cowboy* 12: It was here I pulled a batter an' come near to spillin' all the beans. ***1957** in *OEDS*: Have you been on the batter, you old gubbins? **1982** *Lift Up Your Heart* (WKGN radio) (May 22): Some alcoholics have an especially difficult time recovering from a drinking batter.

batter² *n.* [sugg. by DOUGH] money.
> **1899–1900** Cullen *Tales* 351: This is too much of the batter for you to have on you all at one and the same time, Tommy.

batter³ *n.* Hobo. (see quot.).
> **1942–49** Goldin et al. *DAUL* 24: *Batter, on the*. Operating as a panhandler; by panhandling technique.

batter *v.* [fr. the act of knocking at a door] *Hobo*. to beg or beg from (a person, residence, etc.) or on (a thoroughfare); (*specif.*) to beg by knocking at the door of a private house or place of business.
> **1891** *Contemporary Rev.* (Aug.) 255: Begging is called "battering for chewing." **1893** *Century* (Nov.) 105: They have "battered" in this community for years. **1895** (quot. at TENNER). **1899** "J. Flynt" *Tramping* 107: Standing in front of shops and "battering" the ladies as they passed in and out. *Ibid.* 385: "Battering" (begging) [comes] from knocking at back doors. **1907** London *Road* 17 [ref. to 1892]: The kids began "battering" the "mainstem" for "light pieces." **1914** *Sat. Eve. Post* (Apr. 4) 11: You'll have to batter for handouts this mornin'. **1917** [Livingston] *Coast to Coast* 21: Everywhere we "battered" we were tartly sent on our way. **1925** Mullin *Scholar Tramp* 13: If he winds up at your back door and asks for something to eat, he is slamming a gate or battering a private (to distinguish from battering a restaurant). **1935** J. Conroy *World to Win* 57: I mooched the stem, and Dude there battered the privates.

battering ram *n.* BATTLE-AX.
> **1930** in J.T. Farrell *Grandeur* 202: I always felt that old lady of yours was a goddamn battering ram and that you've always been too good for her.

battery *n.* *West.* a handgun.
> **1870** Duval *Big-Foot* 165: Didn't I send 'em to the right-about though, when I unmasked my "battery" on them? **1871** B. Harte *Works* (1910) XII 139 in DA: A man would pull out his battery for anything—maybe the price of whisky. **1877** in Miller & Snell *Why West Was Wild* 295: Shaw turned his battery upon the officer and let him have it in the right breast. **1906** "M. Twain," in *DA* 88: There's no telling how much he does weigh when he is out on the war-path and has his batteries belted on.

¶ In phrase:

¶ **get (one's) batteries charged** (of a man) to engage in copulation.
> **1935** J. Conroy *World to Win* 253: Why, you cheap sport....You can't get your batteries charged for nothing. **1936** in Oliver *Blues Tradition* 189: You gotta have these batteries charged. **1944–46** in *AS* XXII 56: *To get your battery charged*. To visit a whorehouse. [**1966** Elli *Riot* 177: His reading connection...supplied him with sexy, under-the-shelf novels, called battery chargers.] **1992** G. Wolff *Day at Beach* 105: Charge your battery.

battery acid *n.* [fr. the unpleasantly acidic taste] Esp. *Mil.* **1.** bad coffee.
> **1941** *AS* (Oct.) 163: *Battery Acid*. Coffee. **1942** Kahn *Army Life* 136: One group of selectees from the North stationed at a Southern camp, where the coffee was generously laced with chicory and other odd-tasting substances, almost immediately coined the term "battery acid" for this dubious nectar and continued to describe their coffee that way even after they had been shipped back North and were breakfasting more palatably. **1945** *Yank* (Dec. 14) 22: Coffee, sarge—you know, battery acid. **1970** C. Howard *Doomsday Sq.* 189: On one condition....We pour out this battery acid you call coffee and let me make some. **1970** Thackrey *Thief* 191: "Coffee," she said....There was still some battery acid left from the night before. I dumped a little of it into a pot and put that on the stove.

2. lemonade or grapefruit juice. [Quots. ref. to WWII.]
> **1945** in *Calif. Folk. Qly.* V 381: *Battery acid*...synthetic lemonade; so called from its acrid taste, in spite of sweetening. **1946** *Amer. Legion Mag.* (Apr.) 71: *Battery juice, battery acid*: Powdered lemonade or grapefruit juice. **1949** Maier *Pleasure I.* 42: The nauseating beverage which the Gunner had called "rotgut and battery acid."...The "battery acid" [was] a canned mixture of orange and grapefruit juices. **1949** McMillan *Old Breed* 235: For drink there was "battery acid," a pale, bitter, synthetic lemon drink. **1942–51** *MSU Folklore* GF2-1 (Army: Jargon) 29: *Battery Acid*—Lemonade; sometimes coffee or tea. **1961** R. Davis *Marine at War* 40: It was hard cheese, dust-dry crackers, and lemonade which we mixed in our canteens from little packets of powder. The

Marines called it "battery acid," and it tasted like it. **1978** Gann *Hostage* 276: We...went to the mess hall for a breakfast of "battery acid" (canned grapefruit juice), lukewarm "shit on a shingle"...and Force Ten coffee.

battle *n.* *Black E.* BATTLE-AX.
> **1944** Burley *Harlem Jive* 133: *Battle*—A very unattractive girl. **1948** Manone & Vandervoort *Trumpet* 145: I ain't no battle from the kerosene circuit....I'm a dicty chick from the Big Apple.

battle-ax *n.* a quarrelsome, unattractive, old, or domineering person; (*specif.*) a combative, domineering old woman. [Although applied to men in 1919, 1938, 1964 quots. below, such usage of this well-known expression is now rare.]
> **1896** Ade *Artie* 49: Say, there was a battle-ax if you ever see one. She had a face on her that'd fade flowers. **1903** *Cincinnati Enquirer* (May 9) 13: *Battle-ax*—An old-timer, especially a woman. **1906** H. Green *Actors' House* 12: Them big battleaxes has had their day. **1916** S. Lewis *Job* 192: Home's the place for a woman, except maybe some hatchet-faced old battle-axe like the cashier at our shop. **1919** *DN* V 64: The old *battle-axe*, what became of him? **1930** Graham & Graham *Queer People* 80: That old battle-axe can't make pictures, can she? **1932** *AS* VII 329: *Battle-ax*—a stout female. **1937** Osborn *Borrowed Time* 317: You see this old battle-ax here—her name is Demetria Riffle. **1937** Thompson *Take Her Down* 170: Go on, you old battle-axe. **1938** "E. Queen" *4 Hearts* 24: Oh, these old female battle-axes don't faze me. **1938** *AS* (Feb.) 5: *Battle-axe*, n. A strong man. This expression is in frequent use around Pine Bluff, Arkansas. **1953** Gresham *Midway* 92: Instead of a gorgeous babe in sequined shorts and bra I would use a battle-ax. **1956** J. Brown *Kings* 106: She's got to tell the old battle-ax first. **1963** Stallings *Doughboys* 60. **1967** Terry *Gloaming* 223: Sit down, you old battle-ax. **1972–75** W. Allen *Feathers* 51: Anna, an old battle-ax, enters with candle. **1975** T. Berger *Sneaky People* 231: The old battleax smirked silently. **1977** Hassler *Staggerford* 66: Now, what right has that old battle-ax of a secretary got making the superintendent's decisions?

battle-happy *adj.* *Mil.* eccentric, neurotic, or psychotic as a result of exposure to combat.
> **1944** *Life* (Oct. 9) 60: Next morning two thoroughly frightened battle-happy guys go down to the beaches to try to find our ship. **1944** Mauldin *Up Front* 101. **1948** A. Murphy *Hell & Back* 181: You battle-happy son-of-a-bitch! *Ibid.* 188: What's wrong with that joe? Battle-happy? **1952** Uris *Battle Cry* 223: The battle-happy Seymour turned and left. **1962** W. Crawford *Tomorrow* 48: First off Lootinit Zoller asked Dodge if he was battle-happy. Dodge said no, he wasn't shook, and he wasn't asiatic either. He was just plenty browned off. **1968** J. Kelly *Unexpected Peace* 73: You fellas are so battle happy that fightin's become second nature to you. **1984** *Playboy* (Feb. 1985) 24: He attacks everything from pacifism to feminism to environmentalism like a battle-happy machine gunner with an endless belt of verbal ammunition.

battle juice *n.* *Mil.* liquor.
> **1922** *Pirate Piece* (June) 3: He gets brimmed up even though they was a law against handing out Battle Juice to the Uniform.

battle rat *n.* *Mil.* a combat soldier.
> **1965** Hardman *Chaplains' Raid* 141: If I don't get to Ella, all I'll ever be is a brig and battle rat.

battle rattle *n.* *Mil.* combat neurosis. Also pl.
> **1953** *ATS* (ed. 2) 815: *Battle rattle, bat fag, G.I. fever*, combat fatigue. **1955** Blair *Beyond Courage* 154 [ref. to Korean War]: *Shadduck's Special Cure All*. Take for any disease including "Battle Rattle," the Common Cold, or Sore Feet. **1957** Anders *Price of Courage* 158: You got the battle-rattles from bein' up here...or somethin'.

battle-rattled *adj.* *Mil.* suffering from combat neurosis.
> **1984–88** Hackworth & Sherman *About Face* 758: The word was I was a little "battle-rattled."

battleship *n.* **1.** a large clumsy shoe or boot; a clumsy foot; GUNBOAT.
> **1919** *DN* V 64: *Battle-ships*, a term applied to the feet. "Get your *battle-ships* out of the way so I can sit down." New Mexico. **1940** *AS* (Apr.) 211: The G.I. overshoes are called *gun boats* or *battleships*.

2. *R.R.* a heavy locomotive or railroad car.
> **1925** in *AS* I 250: *Battleship*—The heaviest type of engine. **1931** *Writer's Digest* (May) 41: *Battle-ship*—Usually referred to the superheater type or any large locomotive. **1933** O'Hara *Samarra* 131. **1940** in *AS* XVIII 162: *Battleship*. A large locomotive or large interurban car.

3. *Black E.* BATTLE-AX.

1931 Bontemps *Sends Sunday* 189: Tisha an' them ole battleships round yonder by de swamp.

4. a very shapely young woman.

[**1949** *Set-Up* (film): You oughta see the mouse I got waiting outside. Built like a brick battleship.] **1973** N.Y.U. student: Wow! She's a battleship! Looking for a bust in the mouth?

¶ In phrase:

¶ **enough to float a battleship** see s.v. FLOAT.

battlewagon *n.* **1.** *Navy.* a battleship. Now *colloq.*

1918 Paine *Fleets* 294: The old battle-wagons sure do roll up mileage in a month. **1919** *Our Navy* (July) 23: The finest battle-wagon a-sailing the sea. **1922** *Leatherneck* (Apr. 22) 5: Battle Wagon: A battle ship. **1925** Thomason *Fix Bayonets* 172: Minds me of once I was on a battle-wagon in the China Sea. **1926** *Adventure* (Jan. 20) 176: We dropped the battle-wagon and picked up the destroyers. **1928** *AS* III 452: Battle wagon—War-ship. **1932** Nicholson & Robinson *Sailor Beware!* 4: He wasn't on that battlewagon two days 'fore he had her blowin' smoke rings. **1943** in Sherrod *Tarawa* 56: Those battlewagons will open up…and rock that island. **1952** Uris *Battle Cry* 1: I've sailed the Cape and the Horn aboard a battlewagon with a sea so choppy the bow was awash half the time under thirty foot waves. **1958** Cope & Dyer *Bluejackets' Man.*: Battle-wagon. Slang for battleship. **1959** in Loosbrock & Skinner *Wild Blue* 136: The two old battlewagons sank beneath the waves. **1967** Dibner *Admiral* 181: He could be skippering a brand new battle wagon and be close to home until she's ready. **1968** *Newsweek* (Apr. 8) 45: The battlewagon's big rifles can fire…23 miles. **1980** J. Webb *Sense of Honor* 61: Admiral Donald Kraft was of the battle-wagon breed.

2. *R.R.* (see quots.).

1926 *AS* I 650: Battle wagon—an iron coal car. **1927** *DN* V 438: Battlewagon, n. (1) A heavy, iron coal car. **1960** *Tenn. Folk. Soc. Bull.* XXVI 117: A locomotive was a *hog* [to hobos during the Depression]; a tender a *battlewagon.*

3. a police patrol wagon; an armed or armored vehicle.

1927 *DN* V 438: Battlewagon…The police patrol wagon. *1949 in OEDS: The "battle- wagon"…was a new, cut-down Ford station wag-gon…It was fitted with mountings for two machine guns in front and two behind. **1985** WINS radio news (Aug. 5): They parked their battlewagon in a pig-sty behind a pub. **1989** Zumbro & Walker *Jungle-tracks* 61: Franklin had already mounted up on his battlewagon.

4. BATTLE-AX.

1943 Halper *Inch from Glory* 15: The old battle-wagon,…she's got my number all right. **1952** Larson *Barnyard Folklore* 76: Feminist…suffrag-ette…battle axe, battle wagon.

battle-whacky *adj.* BATTLE-HAPPY.

1948 A. Murphy *Hell & Back* 28 [ref. to WWII]: You're dreaming things, Mike. You're battle whacky.

bat turn *n. Mil. Av.* (see quots.).

1983 M. Skinner *USAFE* 50: Bat turn: A very tight, fast change of heading….A reference to the rapid 180-degree Batmobile maneuver of the old Batman TV series. *Ibid.* 68: Press on with a bat turn. **1987** G. Hall *Top Gun* 28: A skyful of six-G bat turns. *Ibid.* 49: Another God-awful bat turn. *Ibid.* 92: Bat-Turn A tight, high-G change of heading. A reference to the 180-degree Batmobile maneuver in the old "Batman" television series. **1988** Maloney *Thunder Alley* 82: Putting the F-14 into a long, wide-out bat-turn.

batty *adj.* [fr. *bats in the belfry* s.v. BAT[1]] insane; crazy.

1903 *Cincinnati Enquirer* (May 9) 13: Batty—Foolish or luny. **1903** Kleberg *Slang Fables* 23: She…acted so queer…that he decided she was Batty. **1905** *DN* III 60 [Nebr.]: She is *batty. Ibid.* 69 [Ark.]: He's *batty.* Slang. **1910** *DN* IV 10 [Minn.]: That boy is *batty* about her. **1915** *DN* IV 224 [Tex.]: "He is perfectly *batty.*" "I'm *batty* about her." **1919** Darling *Jargon Book* 4: Batty—Without good sense. **1928** McEvoy *Show Girl* 67: He's batty about some night club girl. **1929** *AS* IV 338: Batty—Crazy. **1929–31** J.T. Farrell *Young Lonigan* 109: The batty old half-blind Jew. **1943** J. Mitchell *McSorley's* 83: I was afraid they'd think I was batty when I asked for permission to measure their noggins. *1950 C.S. Lewis *Wardrobe* 21: "Batty," said Edmund, tapping his head. "Quite batty." **1950** in F. Brown *Honeymoon* 67: I think you *can* drive yourself batty if you let yourself think about it, Howard. **1970** R.N. Williams *New Exiles* 280: I was going batty. **1990** *U.S. News & W.R.* (Oct. 15) 92: The man would have gone batty had he not written.

batwing *n.* [ref. to the shape] **1.** a swinging door, as in a saloon.—constr. in pl.

1947 Overholser *Buckaroo's Code* 95: Cotton swung toward the batwings.

2. a bowtie.

[**1961** *WNID3*: A black batwing tie for evening wear.] **1982–84** in Safire *Take My Word* 38: I pulled out my *boiled shirt,*…tied my white pique *batwing*; and climbed into my *monkey suit.*

3. *So.* a convex flask for whiskey holding approximately one pint.

1977 Wilder *You All* (ed. 3) (unp.): Bat wing—A short pint—14 ounces—of whiskey.

baum *v.* [var. of *balm*] (see quot.).

1851 B.H. Hall *College Wds.* 16: Baum. At Hamilton College, to fawn upon; to flatter; to court the favor of any one.

bawl *v.* BAWL OUT, 2.

1915 in Lardner *Haircut & Others* 165: That spoiled whatever chance we had o' gettin' the jump on 'em; but the boys didn't bawl me for it.

bawling iron *n. Naut.* a speaking trumpet.

1857 Willcox *Faca* 31: "Captain, where's your bawling-iron?" "My what?" "Your bawling-iron, boy! or speaking trumpet, or whatever ye call it?"

bawling out *n.* a scolding or reprimand. Also **bawling, balling [out].** [1911 quot. seems specif. to mean a police lineup.]

[**1911** A.H. Lewis *Apaches of N.Y.* 89: The Central Office never once had the pleasure of mugging and measuring and parading him at the morning bawling out.] **1915** *DN* IV 231: Ball-out…n., a scolding. Also *balling-out.* **1918** in Wallgren *A.E.F.* (unp.): He was just gettin' a bal-lin.' **1925** Weaver *Coll. Poems* 161: She gave me the biggest bawlin'-out! **1962** Riccio & Slocum *All the Way Down* 70: What a balling out that inferior priest gave Tommy Hanlon. **1977** Lieb *Baseball* 18: The bawling out came in a game…in 1921.

bawl-out *n.* [fr. the v.] a scolding or reprimand. Also **ball-out.**

1915 *DN* IV 231: Ball-out…n., a scolding. **1918** in [Casey] *Cannoneers* 228: The whole battery heard the bawl-out and they looked a little grumpy when the French officer…arrived to put us through the jumps. **1951** in *DAS* 23: The general bawl-out.

bawl out *v.* **1.** to announce, make known.

1901 Irwin *Sonnets* (unp.): Mame bawled herself out as Murphy's fin-ansay. **1908** *New Broadway Mag.* (Aug.) 140: All we can do is "mug" him, thumb-print him, and "bawl him out" to the force. **1927** *AS* II 275 [at Stanford Univ.]: Bawl…In noun usage the directory of addresses of faculty and students. It "bawls out," i.e., publishes, each student's grades.

2. to scold or reprimand. Also **ball out.**

1899 Bowe *13th Minn.* 168: The boys turned loose…and bawled the officers out to their faces. **1900** Mabey *Utah Batt.* 30: But as soon as he made such an attempt he was immediately "bawled out." **1907** Bush *Enlisted Man* 8: The way he "bawled me out" made me feel like hitting him in the jaw. **1907** in *DA.* **1915** *DN* IV 231: Ball out, v.t. To scold; ridicule. **1918** Rowse *Doughboy Dope* 33: A man we know says his former C.O. claimed he was once balled out by General Pershing. **1925–26** in *AS* II 348: The minister bawled us out for talking in church. **1929** Brooks *Psych. of Adolescence* 460: Suppose…the boss "bawls you out" because you haven't done as much as he thinks you should? **1930** Lavine *3d Degree* 175: The captain would bawl him out for looking for trouble. **1937** Odets *Golden Boy* 290: Who's bawling you out? **1938** "E. Queen" *4 Hearts* 126: Got to bawl out a producer. **1952** M. Chase *McThing* 94: Be firm with her. Bawl her out. **1954** in Yates *Loneliness* 18: She bawl ya out, or what? **1975** Karon *Black Scars* 126: The boss is bawling him out. **1989** *Changing Times* (Jan. 1990) 73: With the October "bail 'em and bawl 'em out" session still branded in your memory, now is the time to mend the battle wounds.

bay *n.* ¶ In phrase: **over the bay** drunk.

1787 in Whiting *Early Amer. Proverbs* 21: Two or three of the gentlemen got rather over the bay. **1830** Martin *Narrative* 145: Soon after entering the hut, I observed one who was to appearance, "pretty well over the bay." **1833** in *DA.* **1842** in Jackson *Early Songs of Uncle Sam* 234: You're getting quite frequently "over the bay." **1865** in J. Miller *Va. City*: Had a *carousing* time generally and most of us got two-thirds "Over the bay." **1867** Clark *Sailor's Life* 221: "You were pretty drunk when you came aboard…." "Yes sir, we were a little over the bay." **1895** *DN* I 398: Over the bay: drunk. Minn., N.Y. He was a little *over the bay.*

bay horse *n.* (see quots.).

1957 *Social Problems* V 314: Dehorns…are habitual drinkers of…bay rum ("bay horse") and canned heat. A man on bay rum is referred to as a "bay horse jockey." **1965** Wallace *Skid Row* 203: Bay horse—bay rum.

Bay horse jockey—one who drinks bay rum.

bayonet course *n. Army.* medical treatment for venereal disease, specif. for syphilis, involving frequent regular hypodermic injections.
1948 *AS* XXIII 31 [ref. to WWII]: Army slang *bayonet course* for venereal treatment. **1981** *Maledicta* V 227: *Taking the bayonet course:* Bismuth subcarbonate and neoarsphenamine were administered weekly [for the treatment of syphilis before the advent of antibiotics] over a period of years....the bismuth...was injected into the *arse* muscles.

bay window *n.* a potbelly.
1889 Farmer *Americanisms: Bay window.*—A slang phrase applied to women when pregnant or to men who, in English slang, have "corporations." **1890** Kerbey *War Path* 183: He...protruded his bay-window belly. **1919** Johnson *Heaven, Hell, or Hoboken* 23: The proverbial Santa Claus "bay window," too. **1920** in De Beck *Google* 97: Say—watcha drinkin these days to give you a bay winder like that? **1925** *Sat. Eve. Post* (Oct. 3) 54: Spud's worked some of his bay window off. **1929–30** Dos Passos *42d Parallel* 210: A brighteyed man with a hawk nose and a respectable bay window. **1950** L. Brown *Iron City* 32: You'll lose that bay window sure.

bazongas *n.pl.* [prob. joc. alter. of BAZOOKA, 2] a woman's breasts. Also **bazoongas, bazonkas.**
1972 *Nat. Lampoon* (July) 52: See if the chick with the big bazongas is in Foto Funnies again. **1973** *Nat. Lampoon* (Aug.) 45: Willya look at the bazoongas on that belly-dancer! **1973** *TULIPQ* (coll. B.K. Dumas): Breasts: *tits, bozongas.* **1972–76** Durden *No Bugles* 158: Her fuckin' bazongas are bigger'n anything I seen in the last three months. **1987** *UTSQ:* Breasts...*boobs, tits, bazonkas.* **1990** Dickson *Slang!* 196: *Bazongas.* Breasts.

bazonkas *adj.* [infl. by BERSERK, BONKERS, BANANAS, and BAZONGAS] crazy.
1975 *Nat. Lampoon Comical Funnies* (unp.): They'll go bazonkas for this. **1978** Maggin *Superman* 60: Jimmy called up from Princeton and everybody went bazonkas.

bazoo *n.* [prob. fr. *bassoon*] **1.** one's voice or mouth; esp. in phr. **blow [off]** or **shoot off (one's) bazoo** to boast, talk loudly or out of turn, complain, etc. Also **bazoon.**
1877 Bartlett *Amer.* (ed. 4) 49: Blowin' his Bazoo. Gasconade; braggadocio. Tennessee. **1880** Nye *Boomerang* 130: You doubtless hear the gentle murmur of my bazoo. **1881** Nye *Forty Liars* 205: Just uncoil your ear and absorb about two and one-half gallons of my bazzoo. **1885** *Puck* (Sept. 23) 50: I hail you with the sound of my bazoo. **1890** Kirkland *Co. K* 74 [ref. to 1861]: I'd...jine the brass band and blow [my brains] out through me bazoo. **1897** A.H. Lewis *Wolfville* 31: It ain't been usual to blow my own bazoo to any extent. **1901** Irwin *Sonnets* (unp.): To just one girl I've tuned my sad bazoo,/Stringing my pipe-dream off as it occurred. **1902** in *DA:* You are jest my sort of a Christian—better'n me, a sight, fer you don't shoot off yore bazoo on one side or t'other. **1903** *DN* II 306: "He blows his own bazoo," meaning that he is boastful and obtrusive. **1906** *DN* III 126 [Ark.]: *Bazoo, n.* Mouth, talk. "Shut up your *bazoo.*" **"**We've had enough of your *bazoo.*" **1912** Lowrie *Prison* 176: "What's the matter with your *bazoo?*" "Oh, I've got a cold." *Ibid.* 282: There was a phony note in his bazoo that I couldn't get away from. **1918** *N.Y. Eve. Jour.* (Aug. 17) 7: Don't you hear old Ban's bazoo? **1929** Tully *Shadows* 247: You're all the time sayin' things...a-shootin' off your bazoo like I was a murderer or somethin'. **1929–31** J.T. Farrell *Young Lonigan* 27: She's always blowing off her bazoo. **1930** Sage *Last Rustler* 169: If some...don't keep their bazoos closed, there'll be some strange faces in hell for breakfast one of these mornings. **1934** W. Smith *Bessie Cotter* 262: Shooting off his bazoo like he owned the dump. **1939** E. O'Neill *Iceman* 125: If dis big tramp's goin' to marry me, he ought to do it, not just shoot off his old bazoo about it. **1945** Seaton *Junior Miss* (film): I don't like to blow my own bazoo, but I bowl a sweet 385. **1959** Morrill *Dark Sea* 108: That big bazoo of yours is griping all the time. **1966** Terkel *Div. Street* 43: He couldn't keep his big bazoo shut. **1986** Kubicki *Breaker Boys* 148: Now shut yer bazoo an' git to work!

2. GAZOOK. Also [prob. infl. by *business*] **bazoonus.**
1903 Townsend *Sure* 43: You'll hear wise bazoonuses pass it along dat dere is so much trouble in de world you'll get more dan you can take care of. **1929** Hotstetter & Beesley *It's a Racket* 219: Bazoo—An easy victim.

3. *Army.* bazooka.
1950 *Life* (Sept. 4) 38: He had one of those new big "bazoos" with him, and lay there in a hole watching.

4. WAZOO; ASS.
1990 J. Updike *Rabbit at Rest* 38: You have to be good enough to lick their bazoo.

bazooka *n.* **1.** [sugg. by *bazooka,* a comic "musical instrument" created by U.S. comedian Bob Burns in the late 1930's] *Mil.* a tube-shaped, portable rocket launcher that fires an armor-piercing rocket. Now *S.E.*
1943 Bayler & Carnes *Wake* I. 247: Jeeps, peeps, bogeys and bazookas have dropped their quotation marks. **1943** *Time* (Apr. 5) 74: Major General Levin H. Campbell, Jr....last week stripped some of the mystery from one secret U.S. weapon, the rocket-firing anti-tank gun which soldiers have dubbed the bazooka. **1943** *Yank* (May 7) 11: Recently made known to the public was...the Bazooka. A rocket gun. **1944–48** A. Lyon *Unknown Station* 71: And you don't have to carry the bazooka and the bazooka round. **1972** Haldeman *War Year* 80: Sounds like a bazooka....Does Charlie have bazookas? **1976** W. Johnston *Super Sweathogs* 8: With bazookas the police can wipe out the entire kid population. **1985** Dye *Between Raindrops* 128: A bazooka to carry on guard...would have been better.

2. usu. *pl.* a woman's breast, esp. if large.
***1963** in Partridge *DSUE* (ed. 7) 1196: The bird (girl) might be high (high principled) in which case he would get no dice or merely "a bit of bazooka" (petting). **1968** Stahl *Hokey* 167: Her loaded bazookas smacked me in the eyes. **1973** *TULIPQ* (coll. B.K. Dumas): Breasts: boobs, bazookas. **1978** T. Sanchez *Zoot-Suit* 106: What a pair of bazookas that dame's packing. **1978** Pilcer *Teen Angel* 6: Humboldt's most colossal bazookies. **1984** in "J.B. Briggs" *Drive-In* 279: Those bazookas might of got out of control and...people could...of been boobed to death.

bazookas *adj.* [fr. *berserk* infl. by *bazooka*] crazy.
1973 *Evening News* (WCBS-TV) (May 18): He just goes crazy. When "Sgt. Pepper" came out, he went bazookas.

bazoom *n.* [joc. alter. of *bosom*] bosom; *pl.* breasts.
1928 Hecht & MacArthur *Front Page* 456: McCue....I wouldn't mind a nice big blonde. *Murphy (outlining a voluptuous bust)* With a bozoom! **1931** Stevenson *St. Luke's* 235: Baring his snow-white buzzoom to yon naked sward. **1936** Levin *Old Bunch* 579: She hauls something out of her buzzoom. **1936** Boothe *Women* 432: I don't think there's another girl our age who has bazooms like mine. **1951** Sheldon *Troubling* 72: Magnificent bazooms. And passionate. *Very* passionate. **1961** Rosten *Capt. Newman* 124: A tomato with a big bazoom. **1969** Gordone *No Place* 420: Yo' buzzooms will blow up like gas balloons. **1971** Sonzski *Punch* 135: The waitress with the buzooms was clearing it.

bazoombas *n.pl.* BAZOOM.
1989 *Night Court* (NBC-TV): Individuality, personality, and the best bazoombas. **1989** Chapple & Talbot *Burning Desires* 257: Bazoombas.

bazuko *n.* [< Colombian Sp *bazuco*] *Narc.* a cocaine derivative consisting of coca paste mixed with other ingredients. Also **basuco.**
1984 *Business Week* (Aug. 27) 50: Addiction to *bazuko*—a brain-destroying mixture of cocaine, marijuana, and sometimes even brick dust—is reaching epidemic proportions among Colombia's youth. **1988** *Time* (Mar. 21) 46: *Basuco,* a crude, habit-forming derivative of coca paste, was introduced into the local market by the cartel in 1984. **1989** *48 Hours* (CBS-TV): They're comin' out with a cheaper version [of crack] now; they call it *bazuko*—a dollar, two dollars. Kids eight years old smoke it. **1989** Radford & Crowley *Drug Agent* 82: Next week it's crack, or bazuko. **1992** *Vanity Fair* (July) 100: The cheap drug of choice is not crack but bazuko, a by-product of cocaine manufacturing, the color of dried plantains.

BB *n.* **1.** a bedbug.
1917 *DN* III 357: *B.b.* Bedbug. **1940** in Cheever *Letters* 57: The bbs turned out to be too damned much and I ended up...trying to sleep in the bath-tub.

2. [sugg. by *BB,* a kind of small shot fired from an air rifle] *Mil. Av.* **a.** a bullet or high-explosive round.
1945, 1955 (quots. at BB-STACKER). **1980** *Air Classics: Air War over Korea* 47: Lt. Peter Carmichael, a fighter jockey...sucked a Mig down into his own backyard and hosed it with 20 mm BBs. **1984** Cunningham & Ethell *Fox Two* 76 [ref. to Vietnam War]: The MiG's 23mm BBs were falling short. *Ibid.* 78: That 37mm puts out a BB the size of a grapefruit.

b. in phr. **golden BB** an unlucky hit from a shell or missile that brings down an aircraft.

1975 in Higham & Siddall *Combat Aircraft* 107: One of the Nellis crews, who was hit by a "golden BB" in December [1968], told of the Communist prison guard who…said, "You F-111…Whoosh!"

3. [cf. ASPIRIN] *Baseball.* an unhittable fastball.

1961 Brosnan *Pennant Race* 15: He had just one minor league season, but he could "throw BB's," as all young men should. **1978** F. Healey, on N.Y. Yankees vs. Detroit Tigers (Sept. 13) (WINS radio): You can hear the pop from the catcher's glove. Gossage is throwing some BB's down there. **1993** *Sports Close-Up* (CNN-TV) (Sept. 25): Juan Guzman, throwin' BB's.

4. *Business.* an unusually effective or efficient person, esp. a business executive.

1979 Homer *Jargon* 18: BB's. Barn Burners: people who are unusually skilled at getting their work done.

B-ball *n.* the game of basketball; *(also)* a basketball. Also vars.

1967 Sack *M* 29: "Well, weren't you this cold playing b-ball?" "What, sir?" "Playing basketball." **1976** Whelton *CB Baby* 119: Nothing like a little B-ball. **1983** Univ. Tenn. graffito: Check out the B Ball arena. **1985** Univ. Tenn. instructor, age 36: Who's got the B-ball? **1986** E. Weiner *Howard Duck* 10: All I wanted was to have a brew and watch some B-ball. **1980–89** Chesire *Home Boy* 181: Off to play a little b-ball.

BB-brained *adj.* stupid.

1968 Swarthout *Loveland* 150: And the least I will do is insure he isn't two-timed by any BB-brained…whippersnapper.

b-boy *n.* [break dance + boy; modeled on B-GIRL] a male break dancer or *(broadly* and now *usu.)* aficionado of rap music. Also **B-boy.**

1984 Toop *Rap Attack* 12: Three b boys are working their pitch near Times Square. *Ibid.* 15: In 1979 the b boys and b girls (as they had come to be known) were in for a shock. **1984** S. Hager *Hip Hop* 32: There was no such thing as b-boys when we arrived, but Herc gave us that tag [in 1973–74]. He called his dancers the b-boys. **1988** *Playboy* (July) 12: The hardcore B-boy look starts out with a Kangol hat and Bally shoes. **1989** *Village Voice* (N.Y.) (June 20) 39: The now standard B-boy look—sideways baseball cap, rope chains, sweat suit, and laceless name-brand sneakers. **1992** *Rolling Stone* (Feb. 6) 77: In hip-hop culture B-boys use the term *juice* to describe their street-level power and prowess.

BB-stacker *n. Mil. Av.* **1.** an armament technician.

1945 in *Calif. Folk. Qly.* V 378: Bee-bee stackers…Armorers who load machine-gun belts with bullets and ready them in the plane. **1955** *AS* XXX 116: Bee-Bee Stacker, *n.* An armament technician, part of whose job it is to load bullets into belts for machine guns. **1987** D. Brown *Flight of Old Dog* i: To all the bomber pukes,…knuckle-busters, and BB stackers of the Strategic Air Command.

2. a BB-BRAINED person.

1960 Swarthout *Where Boys Are* 10: I want *serious* readers, not a bunch of BB-stackers. **1961** Kohner *Gidget Goes Hawaiian* 22: She's…[a] real B.B. stacker.

B drink *n.* (see quot.).

1960 *Tenn. Folk. Soc. Bull.* XXVI 117 [ref. to 1930's]: A "B" drink…a strong brew of tea that looks like whiskey, and is served to the girls whose escort pays for whiskey.

B-drinker *n.* a woman employed by a bar to entice men into buying drinks; B-GIRL.

1935 Pollock *Und. Speaks*: Bee drinker, female entertainers [*sic*] in night clubs who drink cold tea camouflaged as liquor, for which customers pay the full price. **1981** O'Day & Eells *High Times* 48 [ref. to 1930's]: I told Blondie I wasn't born to be a B-drinker.

B.E. *v.* [cf. B AND E] *Police.* to burglarize.

1971 Goines *Dopefiend* 144: What we goin' take off, Snake? We goin' B-E a joint this morning?

beach *n.* **1.** *Naut.* dry land; the landsman's world.

1892 in Evans *Sailor's Log* 370: Yesterday afternoon I "struck the beach" and had a delightful hour in the ruins of Netley Abbey, certainly one of the most beautiful spots I have ever seen. [**1900** McManus *Soldier Life* 105: He's got a soft, easy, "beached job" as the navy lads say.…He runs the custom house.] *1925 in *OEDS*: Hitherto he had been accustomed to view "the Beach" as an incident in his normal life, an environment that asked nothing of him and gave nothing in return. *1929 Bowen *Sea Slang* 9: Beach, On the. Ashore, whether for an afternoon's leave or from having left the sea altogether. **1933** in R.E. Howard *Iron Man* 103: "To think of goin' on the beach at my age!" screamed the Old Man. **1943** Chase *Destroyer* (film): You've been on the beach too long. **1951** W. Williams *Enemy* 25: You think you'd be

shacked in Norfolk if you was on the beach? **1953** Dibner *Deep Six* 12: Ensign King'll handle the division while I'm on the beach. **1964** Newhafer *Tallyho* 266: You raise a little hell on the beach? **1966** Noel & Bush *Naval Terms* 62: Beach:…Slang, the shore. **1967** Dubus *Lieut.* 165: Let's hit the beach [go ashore on liberty]. **1972** *N.Y. Times Mag.* (Mar. 19) 18: They go over code names…of the radio relays that guide them from the carrier to "the beach" (any sailor's word for solid land) and westward to the target zone. **1981** Ballenger *Terror* 90: You son of a bitch, someday I'm going to meet you on the beach.

2. *Golf.* a sand trap.

1970 Scharff *Encyc. of Golf* 415: Beach. Any sand hazard on the golf course. **1992** L.I. (N.Y.) man, age 56: When you're in the sand trap you're on the beach. When you chip to the green, you can say you're on the dance floor.

3. a desert.

1991 *N.Y. Times* (nat. ed.) (Jan. 23) A 6: Instead of "boondocks," privates and sergeants tramp hereabouts across "beaches" (or deserts) and wadis (dry river beds).

¶ In phrases:

¶ **hit the beach** *Naut.* to go ashore, esp. on liberty.

[**1892** in F. Remington *Sel. Letters* 147: Glad to see you when you "strike the beach" here.] **1911–12** J. London *Smoke Bellew* 36: When they hit the beach at Dyea freight was seventy cents. **1914** *DN* IV 150: Hit the beach…to go ashore on leave. **1961** Burgess *Dict. Sailing*: Hit the beach…Go ashore, e.g. on leave. **1968** Blackford *Torp. Sailor* 11: About a score of us would "hold the ship down"…while the rest of the crew "hit the beach." **1975** in Meconis *Clumsy Grace* 14: You knew who was flying this plane—this was some guy that you used to hit the beach with.

¶ **on the beach** *Orig. Naut.* discharged from naval service, esp. if still out of work; being a beachcomber; *(hence,* in general use) out of work; destitute.

1899 Wildman *Malayan Coast* 234: I had seen hundreds of them "on the beach" in Singapore…"Loafer" was written all over him. **1903** London *People of Abyss* 127: England is always crowded with sailormen on the beach. **1905** *Lippincott's Mag.* (Oct.) 386: Having been lately…cashiered for sundry abhorrent practices.…Cyrus Akerson was now "on the beach," in the vernacular of the Pacific. *1923 in *OEDS*: Hundreds of the trawlermen to-day find themselves "on the beach," owing to the distressed condition of the fishing industry. *1925 Fraser & Gibbons *Soldier & Sailor Wds.* 20 [ref. to WWI]: Beach, On The: Discharged. Set aside. **1927** *DN* V 457: On the beach, *adj.* Down and out. **1931** Dos Passos *1919* 8: Haven't got any dunnage. I've been on the beach. **1933** Stewart *Speech of Airman* 68: Put on the beach [to suspend (a Naval aviator) from flying]. **1935** in *OEDS*: You on the beach, kid?…On the bum?…What I mean to say, kid—have you got any money? **1950** *Time* (Nov. 27) 19: In 1947, at the age of 52, he was on the beach again, this time apparently for good. But he refused to believe he was through. **1956** Holiday & Dufty *Lady Sings* 147: When I was really on the beach, without a police card, friends of mine tried to help me. **1970** Della Femina *Wonderful Folks* 97: In most other lines of work, usually you…don't tell your neighbors you're on the beach. **1975** in Mack *Real Life* (unp.): How long you been on the beach?…I mean out of a job. **1989** L. Roberts *Full Cleveland* 21: He left them…and he was on the beach. **1990** *CBS This Morning* (CBS-TV) (May 3): The expression we used to use in radio [in the 1970's] was to be *on the beach,* to be fired.

beach *v. Naut.* to discharge or, *(esp.)* to dismiss summarily, from nautical service; *(hence)* to fire (a person); *(refl.)* to resign from nautical service.

1906 Beyer *American Battleship* 163: When a person of this character is "beached" (man o' war lingo) he is discharged for ineptitude, which, in plain English, means worthless. *1925 Fraser & Gibbons *Soldier & Sailor Wds.* 20 [ref. to WWI]: To be beached. To be turned adrift. Put out of employment. (Navy). **1979** WINS radio (June 15): Drinking on the job [aboard a N.Y.C. ferryboat] occasionally results in someone being "beached" or fired. **1980** *Magnum P.I.* (CBS-TV): Haven't seen you since you beached yourself, what—four, five months ago? **1985** *N.Y. Times Book Rev.* (Dec. 22) 6: In the 1930's, the Navy "beached" the young Heinlein, then a gunnery officer on the U.S.S. Roper, when he became ill.

beach bunny *n.* [cf. SKI BUNNY, SNOW BUNNY] *Surfing.* (see 1966 quot.).

1965 *N.Y. Times* (Aug. 22) 6 72: He drank excessively, smoked pot, littered the beaches, was a hazard to swimmers, frolicked with beach bunnies and earnestly avoided all forms of work. **1966** in Versand *Polyglot*

126: *Beach bunny*....A bikini-wearing girl who frequents a beach but does not engage in surfing or swimming. **1968** Kirk & Hanle *Surfer's Hndbk.* 136: *Beach bunny*: girl beginner; girl non-surfer who follows surfing crowd; also, beach chick. **1985** *Campus Voice* (Apr.) 41: A bare-busted beach bunny strutting her spectacular stuff. **1992** *Freshman Dorm* (CBS-TV): Just to see how many beach bunnies he can attract.

beachcomber *n. Naut.* a loafer, drifter, or petty criminal who lives on or near the shore, esp. a non-native in a South Pacific port. [S.E. after *ca*1880.]

    1836 *Naval Magazine* (Nov.) 520: He is not one of your envious "beach-combers" who...if a poor devil was launching from bad to worse, would "slush down his ways" that he might go faster. **1840** R.H. Dana *2 Yrs. Before Mast* ch. xix: In the twinkling of an eye I was trans-formed from a sailor into a "beach-comber" and a hide-curer. **1847** Melville *Omoo* ch. xxi: I'm nothing more nor a bloody *beach-comber.**...*This is a word much in vogue among sailors in the Pacific. It is applied to certain roving characters, who, without attaching them-selves permanently to any vessel, ship now and then for a short cruise in a whaler; but on condition only of being honorably discharged the very next time the anchor takes hold of the bottom, no matter where they are. ***1880** in *OED*: The white scamps who, as "Beachcombers," have polluted these Edens and debauched their inhabitants. **1927** *DN* V 438: *Beachcomber*, n. A sailor tramp.

beachie *n.* [beach + -IE] *Naut.* a beachcomber.

    1966 Hugill *Sailortown* 314: Some of the "beachies" got jobs coolie-driving over at the Howra Graving Dock. **1969** Jessup *Sailor* 141: I had cashed and I just played it like a beachie who keeps hanging around after his money has run out.

beach-pounder *n. Naut.* a coast guard or shore patrolman.

    [***1889** Barrère & Leland *Dict. Cant* I 90: *Beach-tramper* (nautical), coast guard.] **1944** *Slanguage Dictionary* 47: *Beach-pounder*—member of Coast Guard; one who patrols or "pounds" the beach.

bead *n.* ¶ In phrase: **draw a bead on** to look at; see.

    1851 M. Reid *Scalp Hunters* 30: Draw a bead on them eyes, if yer kin; and jest squint down at them ankles. *ca*1885 in Botkin *Sidewalks* 45: I reckon I never drew a bead on quite so many handsome gals since Moses.

bead-jiggler *n.* [ref. to rosary *beads*] a Roman Catholic. Also **bead-mumbler.**—used contemptuously.

    1966 IUFA *Folk Speech*: Bead mumbler—A term given to anyone of the Catholic religion. **1968** "R. Hooker" *MASH* 25: Y'all seem to be a mighty effective bead-jiggler, Dago...but how do I know one of my boys couldn't do as well?

beady *n.pl.* [beady eye] an eye.

    1978 Truscott *Dress Gray* 250: She was downstairs in some room cry-ing her little beadies out.

beagle *n.* **1.** [presumably from the popularity of fox hunting in the state] a Virginian.

    1845 in *DA*: The inhabitants of...Virginia [are called] Beagles. **1886** in *DA*: Virginia is the Old Dominion...but its people are Beagles.

    2. *Horse Racing.* an inferior racehorse, DOG.

    1923 Witwer *Fighting Blood* 214: 'At beagle's a sprinter, and a mile and a eighth's too much race for him. **1951** D.W. Maurer, in *PADS* (No. 16) 12: *Beagle*...A derogatory term for a racehorse.

    3. a nose.

    1926 Wood & Goddard *Amer. Slang* 5: Beak, beagle. Nose. **1933** Ersine *Prison Slang* 16: *Beagle*, n. A man's nose.

    4. a sausage, esp. a hot dog.

    1927 *DN* V 438: *Beagles*, n. Sausages; an obvious attempt to invent an original synonym for "dogs." **1941** *Slanguage Dict.* 6: *Beagle*—a sausage.

    5. an unattractive young woman, a DOG (in 1951 quot., uniquely applied to a pretty girl); a gloomy or unpleasant person of either sex. [*EDD* I 203 adduces roughly similar, but prob. coincidental, usage in British dialects since the 17th C.]

    1946 J.H. Burns *Gallery* 121 [ref. to WWII]: Y'are all right, lootenant. But who's that ole beagle with ya? Shoulda left him home. **1951** Thacher *Captain* 107 [ref. to WWII]: Know where that beagle was pointed? Waste no time, man. **1953** *Abbott & Costello Go to Mars* (film): They don't sound no worse than some of them beagles I seen you goin' around with. **1959** Zugsmith *Beat Generation* 134: And what about those beakels [*sic*] downstairs?...They'd fink on their own mother.

beak[1] *n.* **1.** a nose (regardless of size or shape).

***1715** E. Ward *Vademecum for Malt Worms* 23 (cited by W. Matthews, *N & Q* June 22, 1935, p. 441). **1750–51** in Breslaw *Tues. Club* 271: [His] honorable nose was of the first rate magnitude...a prominent beak. ***1815** in *EDD*: To the beak o' the second aw held up me fist. **1822** in A.F. Moe (letter to J.E.L., Aug. 18, 1974): You could put your beak deep enough into a pint pot when you were a younker. **1859** Matsell *Vocabulum* 125: Technical words...in General Use by Pugilists....*Beak*. The nose. **1907** in H.C. Fisher *A. Mutt* 20: Tom Corbett's beak. **1910** T.A. Dorgan, in *N.Y. Eve. Jour.* (Apr. 21) 19: Select some part of the anatomy such as the beak or the bread basket. **1911** Van Loan *Big League* 137: Looks to me like you broke his beak. **1912** Field *Watch Yourself Go By* 446: He has a beak like Dan Rice and feet like Dr. Thayer. **1921** *DN* V 156: *Beak*, n. Nose. General. **1933** Witherspoon *Jarge* (unp.): Well, the skipper's an old feller named Meatrose Thomp-son, with a big red beak. **1951** D.W. Maurer, in *PADS* (No. 16) 12: *Beak*...a horse's nose...."Give me two tickets right on the beak." Also, "Playmay won by a beak." **1982–84** Chapple *Outlaws in Babylon* 79: Mozambique, two in the stomach, one in the beak. **1990** J. Simon, in *National Review* (Dec. 3) 55: Watching de Medeiros's deconstructed-Kewpie doll face—over-sized and deliquescent saucer eyes, nasty little pointy chin, nastier huge pointy beak—exude mimosaceousness all over the place is exquisite torture.

    2. the face or mouth.

    1899 in Davidson *Old West* 150: He was a vulture of the plains with whiskers on his beak. **1912** *Pedagogical Seminary* (Mar.) 96: "Shut your beak,"..."choke it,"..."cut out the ruff,"..."drown it,"..."off," "souse it,"..."button your lip." **1929–31** J.T. Farrell *Young Lonigan* 29: Close your beak.

    ¶ In phrase:

    ¶ **dip (one's) beak** to take a drink, esp. of liquor.

    1855 Brougham *Chips* 393: You must dip your beak in the hot tea, eh! **1910** in Wilstach *Stage Slang* 47: Will you dip your beak in a scuttle of suds? **1932** M. Anderson *Rain* (film): Well, boys, let's dip the beak. **1941** *Birth of Blues* (film): You wouldn't like to dip your beak with me, would you? **1966** Brunner *Face of Night* 151: I sure miss the old days....Going out at night, and girls, and dipping my beak in a glass of beer.

beak[2] *n.* **1.** [earlier English criminal slang *beck*, of uncert. orig.] *Und.* a magistrate; a judge.

***1749** in Farmer *Musa Pedestris* 50: Never snitch to bum or beak. ***1753** J. Poulter *Discoveries*: A rum Beak; a good Justice. A *quare beak*; a bad Justice. **1791** [W. Smith] *Confess. T. Mount* 19: A judge, a *beeks* [*sic*]. ***1796** Grose *Vulgar Tongue* (ed. 3): *Beak*. A justice of peace, or magis-trate. ***1810** *Rambler's Mag.* II 66: Not being at the office yesterday, took a stroll there—found the *beaks* and *titlarks* reading the papers and taking snuff. *Ibid.* 68: *Beaks*—magistrates. ***1811** *Lexicon Balatron.*: *Beak*, a justice of peace, or magistrate. Also a judge or chairman who presides in court. I clapp'd my peepers full of tears, and so the old beak set me free; I began to weep and the judge set me free. ***1812** Vaux *Vocab.*: *Beak*, a magistrate; the late Sir John Fielding, of police memory, was known among [criminals] by the title of the blind *beak*. **1848** *Ladies' Repository* (Oct.) 315: *Beak*, a mayor, or magistrate. **1852** *Harper's Mo.* (Dec.) 90: They...takes me afore the beak. **1866** *Nat. Police Gaz.* (Apr. 21) 3/3: Next day they were brought before the "beak"; enough evi-dence having been produced, they were "sent up" for trial at the assizes. **1868** *Detective's Manual* 181: I'm all O.K. with the "beak." ***1870** in Davitt *Prison Diary* I 151: The beek only giv me 14 days, and her got 21 for hitten me fust and been fuddled. **1871** [Banka] *Prison Life* 493: Judge,...Head Beak. ***1896** in *EDD*: P'raps if I didn't I shouldn't have been dragged up before the beak so many times for a disturbing of the public peace. **1920** in E. Pound *Letters* 160: If I was as ornery in my clear verse as you are in yourn, I'd be up before the beak. **1944** *Papers of Mich. Acad.* XXX 590: The beak threw me a finif....The judge sen-tenced me to five years. **1942–49** Goldin et al. *DAUL* 24: *Beak*. (Cen-tral and Mid-Atlantic States; rare) A Criminal Courts judge.

    2. a police officer; an officer of the law.

***1799** in *OEDS*: Took a gentle walk to the [police] office...paid my respects to Sir William, and the rest of the beaks. ***1820–21** P. Egan *Life in London* 228: The *beaks* were out on the *nose*. ***1829** W. Maginn *Memoirs of Vidocq* (cited in Partridge *Dict. Und.* 27). **1845** *Nat. Police Gaz.* (Oct. 11) 58: If we follow your plan, the beaks will know there are others into it, and then perhaps suspicion will fall upon us. **1845** *Nat. Police Gaz.* (Oct. 16) 55: The panel thief...is called upon to divide with the law, and instead of being arraigned by a judge, disgorges to a "beak."

beak[3] *n. Mil. in Philippines.* a Filipino.—used disparagingly.—usu. considered offensive.

1991 Beason *Strike Eagle* 120: The Beaks use it as a sewer....Beaks, flips, Filipinos. Just another name.

beaked *adj.* [perh. alter. of *piqued*] annoyed; irritated; angry.
1989 *N.Y. Times Bk. Review* (Dec. 31) 22: I got it! Let's do a thing about a wife who gets beaked at her old man and kills the kids!

beam *n.* ¶ In phrases:

¶ **broad in the beam** Orig. *Naut.* having wide hips. Now *S.E.*
1836 *Spirit of Times* (Feb. 20) 7: Ned Curtis had a wife; a strapping craft, broad in the beam, with a high stern, and very bluff in the bows.

¶ **off the beam** mistaken; *(hence)* thinking or behaving eccentrically or crazily; no good; (of an action) uncalled for; improper. [See note at *on the beam*, below.]
1941 *AS* (Oct.) 167: *Off the Beam.* Incorrect. (Air Corps). **1941** Kendall *Army & Navy Sl.* 10: *Off the beam....*acting wild. **1943** D. Hertz *Pilot #5* (film): I think we're all way off the beam. **1944** *Slanguage Dict.* 59: Dracula's daughter—an off the beam chick. **1945** *AS* (Apr.) 83: This doesn't mean that the person under discussion was off the beam or suffering from any mental aberration. **1945** in F. Brown *Angels & Spaceships* 88: Wait a minute, Pete, you're off the beam. **1945** T. Williams *Glass Menagerie* 35: I shouldn't have done that—That was way off the beam. **1946** J.H. Burns *Gallery* 73: You're slightly off the beam, but I like you. **1957** MacDonald *Price of Murder* 125: You guys are nuts....You guys are way off the beam. ***1961** Burgess *Dict. Sailing* 16: *Away Off the Beam.* To be a long way out in any surmise or prophecy. **1982** Heat Moon *Blue Hwys.* 88: Here nobody asks "What happened to you? You off the beam again?"

¶ **on the beam** Orig. *Av.* exactly right; thinking correctly; "on the ball." [The *beam* referred to in both these expressions is evidently the radio beam used to guide aviators through conditions of poor visibility; both phrases became widely familiar during WWII.]
[**1936** *Pop. Sci. Mo.* (Mar.) 32: "When you're in the beam, check with your compass."...Scotty's first lesson on the beam.] **1941** in *OEDS*. **1942** *Pittsburgh Courier* (Jan. 17) 7: Stay on the beam—Don't make mistakes. **1942** in Gould *PruneFace* (unp.): "Right, Tracy?" "You're on the beam, kid!" **1943** *Word Study* (Feb.) 5: He gives them a brief lecture, the essence of which is that they must keep *on the beam.* **1943** *AS* (Apr.) 155: You're on the BEAM. Terms denoting satisfaction and agreement. **1944** Hart *Winged Victory* (film): Gotta keep him on the beam till Tuesday. **1944** in Galewitz *Great Comics* 49: Now you're on th' beam, baby. **1944** *Official Guide to AAF* 369: *On the beam*—acting effectively or satisfactorily. **1946** J. Adams *Gags* 109: Entertaining all those G.I.'s, you had to be on the beam or they really let you have it. **1946** J.H. Burns *Gallery* 292: Ya ain't been on the beam since ya quit ya shackin. **1948** *Neurotica* (Summer) 38: This girl was all on the beam and really kicking off. **1952** Chase *McThing* 96: Boy, was I ever tough with her! She'll get on the beam now. **1970** Landy *Underground Dict.* 141: *On the beam*...Feeling fine. **1982** Rucker *57th Kafka* 66: "It's too dangerous. I don't think we should risk it." He was right on the beam.

beam-end *n.* ¶ In phrase: **on (one's) beam-ends** Orig. *Naut.* knocked into a sitting or lying position; *(hence)* at a serious disadvantage; ill; destitute; helpless. Now *colloq.*
1801 in Whiting *Early Amer. Provs.* 21: But here I am on my beam ends. **1815** Brackenridge *Mod. Chiv.* 650: A stroke that, in the sailor's phrase, brought him on his beam ends. ***1835** Marryat *Midshipman Easy* 60: I'm glad to see you up again, youngster....You've been on your beam ends longer than usual, but those who are strongest suffer most. **1841** [Mercier] *Man-of-War* 188: He was on his *beam-ends*/Without a stiver in his purse. **1853** [Ballantine] *Autobiog.* 13: If...you should ever see a messmate on his beam ends, give him a lift. **1868** Macy *There She Blows!* 250: Down they went on their beam-ends right into the mud or wherever they chanced to be. **1875** Sheppard *Love Afloat* 90: First he took a rank sheer to port...then he fairly grounded and went on his beam-ends. **1887** M. Roberts *W. Avernus* 37: Now I and my partner were truly on our "beam ends," and 20 cents alone stood between us and absolute bankruptcy. **1904** in Paxton *Sport U.S.A.* 13: He saw the scrub full-back thrown on his beam-ends, the ball in his arm.

beamer see BEEMER.

beam up *v.* [fr. *beam* 'teleport', on the NBC-TV show *Star Trek* (1966–69); "Scotty" was the nickname of the ship's engineer, who operated the equipment] *Narc.* to take or become high on crack or another drug.—usu. constr. with *[to] Scotty.* Also in phr. **beam me up, Scotty** give me

cocaine or crack.
1986 *Newsday* (N.Y.) (Oct. 6): Phrases that refer to getting high on crack include....*beam me up, Scotty.* **1988** "EPMD" *Strictly Business* (rap song): You sniff blow?...M.C.'s look me in my face/Then their eyes get weak/Pulse rate descends/Heart rate increases/Like "beam me up, Scotty"/I control your body. **1988** *Spin* (Oct.) 47: *Beam me up, Scotty...*give me crack. **1990** *New York* (May 28) 27: Drug-related expressions are well documented. "Beaming up" means a crack high. **1992** *N.Y. Review of Books* (July 16) 23: "Beam me up, Scotty." This phrase was first applied to the act of getting high. **1992** Gelman *Crime Scene* 104: Being despiteful meant beaming up to Scotty with a sweet drag on a glass pipe. **1993** *Donahue* (NBC-TV): She's about to beam up, or get high. A lot of the language comes from *Star Trek.*

beamy *adj.* [fr. *off the beam* s.v. BEAM + *-y*] eccentric; crazy.
1962 G. Ross *Last Campaign* 38 [ref. to U.S. Army, 1950]: Well, don't take it too hard....That old bastard's a little beamy. What the hell? After thirty-five years in this sonovabitch, who wouldn't be?

bean *n.* **1.a.** a coin or piece of money; *(specif.)* a small gold coin; a dollar; *pl.* money. [Despite the dates, phr. *not have a bean* is prob. the source of the specif. applications; *not worth a bean* was already proverbial in 13th C. (see *OED*).]
*1799 in Partridge *Dict. Und.* 317: A few queer *half beans* [half guineas] and a few *whites.* *1811 *Lexicon Balatron.*: *Bean*, a guinea. **1859** Matsell *Vocabulum* 10: *Beans.* Five-dollar gold-pieces. *1885 in *OEDS*: "Here's some of the beans," he continued figuratively, as he drew five sovereigns from the same pocket. *1889 Barrère & Leland *Dict. Slang* I 92: The term *beans* is also used for money; a "haddock of *beans*," a purse of money. **1893** Friend *Thousand Liars* 68: Lives nowhere and sleeps anywhere; sometimes got a sack, sometimes ain't got a bean. **1902** Townsend *Fadden & Mr. Paul* 68: A Willie who has bet his last bean on a sure ting hoss dat "also ran." **1906** M'Govern *Bolo & Krag* 39: They was betting fifty beans on a lousy bob-tailed flush. **1907** in H.C. Fisher *A. Mutt* 17: Bet every bean on Flying Onion. **1908** in Fleming *Unforgettable Season* 54: Four bits (a slang expression signifying half a bean). **1910** *N.Y. Eve. Jour.* (Apr. 22) 20: A hundred beans a week! That's th' job for you, Sap. **1911** *Hampton's Mag.* (Feb.) 192: Why don't you sing a little song about having a few beans for yourself in the cut-up. **1911** T.A. Dorgan, in *N.Y. Eve. Jour.* (Jan. 12) 16: And those poor boobs pay five beans per. **1920** Ade *Hand-Made Fables* 84: He will shoot every Bean in the old Tin Box and die poor. **1923** *N.Y. Times* (Sept. 9) VIII 2: *Beans:* Money. *1928 in *OEDS*: None of the Fentimans ever had a bean, as I believe one says nowadays. **1952** Mandel *Angry Strangers* 251: Tell 'im I want four hundred beans. **1953** Chandler *Goodbye* 12: The guy was down and out, starving, dirty, without a bean. **1960–61** Steinbeck *Discontent* 53: You haven't got a bean, Eth. **1961** Ellison *Gentleman Junkie* 142: He was into me for about seventy beans. **1968–70** *Current Slang* III & IV 8: *Beans*, n. Money.—College students, both sexes, Kansas. **1978** De Christoforo *Grease* 86: They must be worth two beans apiece, easy.

b. one hundred dollars.
1967 in T.C. Bambara *Gorilla* 70: So for four beans you can move right in, and everything's yours.

2. *pl.* [cf. *know beans*, below] anything at all.—esp. in phr. **not know** [or **care**] **beans** and extended vars.
1833 A. Greene *Duckworth* II 66: He don't know beans. **1841** [Mercier] *Man-of-War* 245: They couldn't do old *goose-rump*, beans. **1855** in Thornton *Amer. Gloss.* I 50: Whatever he knows of Euclid and Greek,/ In Latin he don't know beans. **1857** in Thornton *Amer. Gloss.* I 50: Well then...I don't care beans for the railroad, not a single old red-eyed bean, nor a string-bean. **1907** *DN* III 246: *Know beans when the bag's untied*...To be sophisticated. **1912** *DN* III 571: He never said *beans* to me about it. **1965–70** in *DARE*: He doesn't know beans from apple butter. **1982** Knoxville, Tenn., woman, age *ca*40: Most of those people don't give beans about our country. **1983** W. Safire, in *N.Y. Times Mag.* (Aug. 7) 6: He doesn't know...beans,...*beans from barley, beans from baloney, beans from buttons, beans from bats, beans from applebutter* and *beans from bullfrogs.* **1990** *Cosmopolitan* (Aug.) 188: You don't know beans, but I see your potential and can teach you how to succeed.

3. a poker chip. [In 1866 quot., actual beans.]
[**1866** in Hilleary *Webfoot* 154: The most popular game is "poker," fifteen beans for a plug [of tobacco].] **1871** *Overland Mo.* (Aug.) 125: The game chosen was..."freeze-out," each taking one hundred beans. **1882** Steele *Frontier Army* 220: Many a game of "poker" had been played there, and the small box of "beans" still sat upon the cloth. **1904** Ade *True Bills* 4: She pulled in a white bean and her Husband told her she ought to go back to Jack-Straws. **1928** Santee *Cowboy* 71: Mebbe stud-

poker at ten cents a bean. **1951** *AS* XXVI 97: *Beans*. [Poker] chips.

4. a bullet or piece of shot.

1898 Bellamy *Blindman's World* 268: Give 'em a lesson with a good load of beans from the old shotgun. **1928** *Papers of Mich. Acad.* 277 [ref. to WWI]: *Beans*...ammunition. **1936** R. Adams *Cowboy Lingo* 168: No cartridges in the cylinder was "no beans in the wheel." **1943** W. Simmons *Joe Foss* 65: It is no fun playing with these boys when you do not even have a bean in your guns.

5. a foolish notion or complaint.

1897 F. Norris *Vandover* 321: "Ah, Dolly, you've got a bean," muttered Ellis. **1899** F. Norris *McTeague* 45: You got a bean about somethun, hey? Spit ut out.

6. the head; in phr. **off (one's) bean** crazy; mistaken; in phr. **flip (one's) bean** [infl. by *flip (one's) lid* s.v. LID] to go crazy.

1905 C. Dryden *Champ. Athletics* 16: While pitching, Mr. Bender places much reliance on the *bean* ball. **1908** in H.C. Fisher *A. Mutt* 82: The [phrenologist] took one peep at Pickels' bean. **1908** H. Green *Maison* 130: Pop swung on a guy an' come near knockin' his bean offa him. **1910** *N.Y. Eve. Jour.* (Mar. 16) 15: James Austin...pegged one eight feet over Captain Chase's bean. **1910** in *AS* XXVI 29: A "bean," you ask? Why, *bean* is baseball language for head. **1912** *DN* III 571: *Bean*, n. The head. **1913** *Sat. Eve. Post* (Mar. 15) 8: Keep that in your bean, young man. **1915** in Paxton *Sport USA* 83: Forget it....I got a bad bean on me tonight. Forget it. **1919** I. Cobb *Life of Party* 22: I gotta right to belt you one across the bean. **1922** *DN* V 156: I'll knock your bean off. **1924** P. Marks *Plastic Age* 23: You certainly used the old bean. **1926** in Lardner *Haircut & Others* 16: He wanted Julie Gregg and worked his head off tryin' to land her. Only he'd of said bean instead of head. **1928** *AS* III 409: Other expressions which one sometimes hears or sees in popular speech or popular literature are..."solid ivory"...and "loose in the bean." **1941** Hargrove *Pvt. Hargrove* 71: If you're insinuating that I don't have to work, you're off your bean, sonny. **1960** N.Y.C. man, age *ca*50: That's using the old bean. **1966** Neugeboren *Big Man* 92: Next thing I know he's flipped his bean, dancing around me. **1982** Washington, D.C., man (WKGN radio) (Aug. 8): That was one of those profound questions that we all have to rattle around in our beans now and then.

7. a baseball.

1910 *N.Y. Eve. Jour.* (Mar. 15) 12: "Hack" lost a pound or two of blubber chasing the bean.

8. [cf. *old bean*, below] a foolish or obnoxious person; SQUIRT.

1919 *DN* V 70: *Poor bean*, an awkward, stupid fellow. "You *poor bean!* Why don't you ask some girl?" New Mexico. **1940** Simonsen *Soldier Bill* 40: If a bean like this fellow went to heaven, Bill was satisfied to go to the other place. **1978** Truscott *Dress Gray* 209: This little bean thinks he speaks rather clearly. *Ibid.* 230: In any squad, it would be three or four good beans, three or four take-'em-or-leave-'em beans, and a couple of dead-head fuck-ups.

9. *Narc.* a capsule or tablet of a drug, *esp.* (in recent use) Benzedrine.

1929 *Chi. Tribune* (Oct. 11) 14: A package of drug wrapped in paper is called a "deck"....If it is in a capsule it is called a "berry," a "bean" or a "cap." **1967** Maurer & Vogel *Narc. Add.* (ed. 3) 341: *Bean*. A Benzedrine tablet or capsule. *bean trip.* Intoxication from ingesting Benzedrine. **1970** Horman & Fox *Drug Awareness* 463: Bean—capsule. **1970** Cole *Street Kids* 9: After school go home. Grab a bean and cut out. **1971** Rodgers *Queens' Vernacular* 134: Going *up* on beans is like coming *down* on acid. **1978** Lieberman & Rhodes *CB* (ed. 2) 289: *Bean popper*—Pill popper.

10. *pl.* food; mealtime. Also in extended use.

1942 *ATS* 106: Meal...beans...eats...mess. *Ibid.* 107: Mealtime. Bean—, chow time. **1945** Hubbard *R.R. Ave.* 332: Beans...lunch period. **1970** *Current Slang* V 3: Beans, n. Food. *Ibid.* 4: *Bean time*, n. Mealtime; lunch break. **1971** in *AS* XLIV 247: Even if no meal is actually involved, [railroad] crews *go to beans* when they take a break.

11. (see quot.).—usu. considered vulgar.

1942–49 Goldin et al. *DAUL* 24: Bean. (Irish-American, especially in New York State) The hymen. "To cop a bean"—To have sexual intercourse with a virgin.

12. *S.W.* a Mexican.—used contemptuously.—usu. considered offensive.

1949 Monteleone *Crim. Slang* 18: Bean...A Mexican peon. **1965** Bonham *Durango St.* 92: Them beans think they got off clean shootin' out Whitey's tire that time! **1966** *Life* (Mar. 4) 24: His father was a "bean" (local slang [in Tucson] for a Mexican). **1967** Salas *Tattoo* 52: Are you

the little guy who got cornered by the beans from Santa Clara about a year ago and fought so hard losing they gave you a free pass? **1987** D. Barnes *Deadly Justice* 63: We find out the bean ain't even a citizen.

¶ In phrases:

¶ **beans!** (used to indicate surprise, annoyance, disbelief, etc.).

1911 O. Johnson *Stover at Yale* 15: Oh, beans! **1924** *DN* V 263: Oh beans.

¶ **for beans** with the slightest degree of skill or success.

1959 N.Y.C. woman, age *ca*35: He can't sing for beans. **1978** in Lyle & Golenbock *Bronx Zoo* 189: A record of 8 and 2 doesn't look too shabby, but I still have only seven saves, and I'm still pitching for beans.

¶ **full of beans, 1.** spirited, lively, full of life.

*1854 in *OEDS*: 'Ounds, 'osses, and men, all in a glorious state of excitement! Full o' beans and benevolence! **1927** Finger *Frontier Ballads* 61: On the mornin' of my marriage I hitched him to the carriage and thought the old horse was full of beans. **1947** Schulberg *Harder They Fall* 16: They were full of bounce and beans. **1968** Hawley *Hurricane Yrs.* 110: Promising you'd send him back to his job...full of beans. **1980** J. Carroll *Land of Laughs* 33: He looked strong enough and still full of beans. **1992** *CBS This Morning* (CBS-TV) (Mar. 10): These kids were more fun, more full of beans.

2. full of nonsense, full of BULL.

[**1932** *AS* VI 332: *Full of bean soup*—expression of disbelief or contempt.] **1942** *ATS* 179: Foolish; nonsensical; ridiculous...*full of beans*. **1954–60** *DAS* s.v. *full*. **1975** Harington *Ark. Ozarks* 118: Where do you get that stuff? You're full of beans. **1981** Wolf *Roger Rabbit* 212: I think you're full of beans. **1983** Ad for *Nat. Enquirer* (ABC-TV) (June 2): Why are many "facts" about caffeine full of beans?

¶ **give (someone) beans** to thrash, trounce, give hell.

1835 in *AS* XL 127: I pose you heard ob de battle New Orleans,/ Whare Ole General Jackson gib de British beans. **1847** in Dolph *Sound Off* 405: Little Texas when quite in her 'teens/Did give 'em a dose of lead and beans. *1899 Whiteing *John St.* 271: Go it, Tom Thumb! give 'im beans. I'll old yer coat! **1919** Fox *Boys Over There* 110: All I could do was yell to the boys to give them "beans," for I was knocked down. *1946 in *OEDS*: He wanted to give me beans, but Florence wouldn't let him. She said "Father you are not to touch him. It was a pure misunderstanding."

¶ **hill** [or **row**] **of beans** (used as a symbol of worthlessness).

1863 in *OEDS* I 224: I...karn't take Preston's note—'tain't wuth a hill o' beans. **1904** in "O. Henry" *Complete Stories* 640: Well, he wasn't a hill of beans to her. **1929** *AS* V 119: They "don't amount to a hill of beans." **1942** Epstein et al. *Casablanca* (film): The problems of three little people don't amount to a hill of beans in this crazy world. **1957** Bannon *Odd Girl* 155: And he'll never amount to a row of beans. **1990** *Cosmopolitan* (June) 212: Her domineering father [taunted] her ambition by saying, "you'll never amount to a hill of beans."

¶ **know beans** [cf. later syn. phrs. like *know (one's) onions*, etc., and **(2.)**, above] to be very knowledgeable.

*ca*1849 in Jackson *Early Songs of Uncle Sam* 58: When dancing I know beans, And I widgion ping the greens,/At heel and toe, oh I'm one of the boys! **1856** *Knickerbocker* XLVIII 315: We never saw, and our metropolitan friends, (country-born, and "knowing beans," tomatoes etc.,) say they never saw, such a sight. **1888** in Farmer *Americanisms*: A dainty Boston girl who, of course, knows beans. *Ibid.* One has to know beans to be successful in the latest Washington novelty for entertainment at luncheons. **1917** *DN* IV 395: The full phrase in the '80's was, *He don't know beans when the bag's untied.*

¶ **old bean** old fellow, old friend (used as a friendly term of direct address). [Common in U.S. in the early 1920's; now regarded as an affected Briticism and no longer in freq. use.]

*1917 in *OEDS*: Chorus—"Good night, old bean." **1920** in Hemingway *Sel. Letters* 38: Sorry as hell old bean that I haven't written you before. **1923** McKnight *Eng. Words* 59: There has...been undue commotion over the child of two and a half years who addressed his parent as "Old bean." **1926** in Gelman *Photoplay* 94: Take a sleeping potion, old bean. *1934 Yeates *Winged Victory* 16 [ref. to 1918]: Robinson...called everybody "old bean" or "old tin of fruit," these phrases being brand new.

¶ **some beans** quite something.

1850 in Blair & Meine *Half Horse* 218: By golly, you're some beans in a bar-fight.

¶ **spill the beans** see s.v. SPILL, *v.*

¶ **tough beans!** "your misfortune means nothing to me!" "tough luck!"

1963 *N.Y. Times Mag.* (Nov. 24) 52: Too bad for you…"Tough beans." **1966** *Get Smart* (NBC-TV): Tough beans, Charlie! **1980** *Univ. Tenn. Daily Beacon* (Apr. 16) 2: Road Ends—Tough beans! **1981** *Nat. Lampoon* (Oct.) 67: But you know what they told me? They told me, "Tough beans!" **1991** *Darkwing Duck* (synd. TV series): Tough beans, Whiffle kid!

bean *v.* to hit on the head; (*specif.*) *Baseball.* to hit on the head with a pitched, thrown, or batted ball.

 1910 in *DA:* He is in extreme danger of being "beaned," which, in baseball, means hit in the head. **1914** Lardner *You Know Me Al* 60: Jennings says He won't never hurt my boys by beaning them. **1915** *N.Y. Eve. Jour.* (Aug. 7) 6: The players must not bean the umps.…If a bottle of pop is bounced from the bean of an umpire, the club must pay for whatever damage is done to aforesaid bean. **1918–19** MacArthur *Bug's-Eye View* 17: Thrills were provided when Mr. Daugherty was beaned with a mess utensil. **1925** in Hammett *Big Knockover* 226: I'll put this one you beaned in the cooler. **1925–26** in *AS* II 348: John has never played ball since the pitcher beaned him last summer. **1953** Morris *Deep Sleep* 57: The Grandmother…thrust her battered cane into the bird box, and came within an ace of beaning the lady cardinal. **1991** *Roseanne* (ABC-TV): She beaned him on the neck. **1992** *N.Y. Observer* (Apr. 13) 2: A group of black youths…beaned a Hasidic man with a bottle.

beanbag *n.* [cf. BEAN, *n.*, 12; BEAN BANDIT, BEAN EATER, 2; BEANER, 3] a Mexican.—used contemptuously.—usu. considered offensive.

 1971 Barnes *Pawns* 63: He is called "shithead," "turd," "maggot," "punk," "fatso," "Private Nigger," or "beanbag" (an epithet for Chicano) depending on the DI's vocabulary and the recruit's physical or racial characteristics.

bean ball *n. Baseball.* a ball pitched deliberately at a batter's head to force him away from home plate.

 1905 C. Dryden *Champ. Athletics* 16: While pitching, Mr. Bender places much reliance on the *bean ball.* **1912** in *DA* 92: *Bean ball*—A fast ball pitched at or near the head of a player who is standing too close to the plate with intent to drive him back. **1912** Mathewson *Pitching* 42: He's got a mean "bean" ball, and he hasn't any influence over it. **1914** Lardner *You Know Me Al* 147: I guess this is where I shoot one of them bean balls. **1955** *AS* XXX 153: A *bean ball* is a ball that beans (or at least threatens to bean) the batter. **1967** *U.S. News & W.R.* (Jan. 1, 1968) 12: De Gaulle keeps throwing fast pitches at the head of the U.S. batter. The difference is that, in baseball, the umpire throws the beanball pitcher out of the game. **1981** *N.Y. Times* (Mar. 26) D18: Beanballs Trigger Fights in Pirates-Tigers Game.…After Pittsburgh's John Candelaria had knocked down John Wockenfuss with a pitch…Howard Bailey hit Bill Robinson in the face with his first pitch in the bottom of the inning. **1987** *People* (Aug. 24) 89: Let there be basebrawl. Let there be beanballs, knockdowns, brushbacks and retaliatory bench-clearing melees.

bean bandit *n.* [cf. BEAN, *n.*, 12; BEAN EATER, 2; BEANER, 3] a Mexican or other Latin-American.—usu. considered offensive. *Joc.*

 1959 Brosnan *Long Season* 230: Come on, Orlando, you bean bandit…get 'em out one more time. **1968–70** *Current Slang* III & IV 7: *Bean bandit*, n. A Mexican or Mexican-American (derogatory).—New Mexico State. **1971** Polner *No Victory Parades* 12: Guys would call Mexicans "bean bandits" and nobody would be offended. **1976** C.R. Anderson *Grunts* 165 [ref. to 1969]: They withdrew to the time and place in which Whites, Blacks and other ethnic group members could call each other "chuck dudes," "splibs," "bean bandits," or "wops" without a trace of racism intended or detected.

bean belly *n.* a potbelly. [*1854 quot. appears as a disparaging nickname, prob. ref. to the contents rather than the size of the bellies.]

 [*1854 in *EDD:* Leicestershire bean-bellies.] **1960** (quot. at BEANIE, 1). **1968** Radano *Walking Beat* 16: I take a good look at this guy. A monkey! He has a bean belly, a head shaped like a football, and he's so small if you spit on him you drown him!

beanbrain *n.* a simpleton. Hence **beanbrained.**

 1952 Bellow *Augie March* 48: You'll see how beanbrained she is. **1976** Woodley *Bears* 90: Come on, bean-brain. **1981** *Taxi* (ABC-TV): Suck rope, beanbrain! **1989** *21 Jump Street* (Fox-TV): Tie it yourself, bean-brain.

bean can *n.* (see quot.).

 1958 McCulloch *Woods Words* 8: *Bean can*—a lunch bucket.

bean-counter *n.* a person concerned with small financial details; (*specif.*) an accountant.

 1975 *Forbes* (Nov. 15) 20: Watkins [was] a smart, tightfisted and austere "bean-counter" accountant from rural Kentucky. **1980** *Newsday* (N.Y.) (Mar. 8): Kurt Vonnegut and I found ourselves talking instead about the trashing of Pantheon Books by bean counters at Random House…obedient to the bottom line of the masters at Advance Publications. **1982** Abodaher *Iacocca* 297: Riccardo had come to Chrysler from an accounting firm and thus was a penny-pincher—a "bean-counter," as a finance-oriented individual is referred to in business. **1983** *Business Week* (Dec. 19) 4: Marketing involves fundamentally unquantifiable ideas and people, thus making the return-on-investment guarantees demanded by the "bean counters" impossible to provide. **1987** *Night Court* (NBC-TV): Those bean-counters in accounting have finally seen fit to give me some assistance. **1987** Weiser & Stone *Wall St.* (film): A group of heavy-set, well-dressed bean-counters. **1989** Apple Computer ad (ABC-TV): Greg's the creative guy. Clancy's just a bean-counter. **1990** *Time* (Sept. 17) 29: For years these vessels have figured in Western bean counters' assessments of the Red Menace.

bean-eater *n.* **1.** a Bostonian.

 1867 Clark *Sailor's Life* 252: Take that, you beaneater. **1881** in *DA.* **1891** Maitland *Amer. Slang Dict.* 28: *Bean-eaters*, natives of Boston, Mass. **1892** L. Moore *Own Story* 34: Then he would call the Boston bean-eater's attention to the fact that he was not dealing a check game. **1908** Fleming *Unforgettable Season* 8: Tenney…has been a Beaneater ever since. **1911** Spalding *Base Ball* 97 [ref. to 1873]: A few weeks later we were playing the Athletics…with the local [Phila.] crowd very bitter against the "Bean Eaters" because of the intense rivalry between these…clubs. **1926** Wood & Goddard *Amer. Slang* 5: *Bean-eater.* Bostonian. **1948** Kaese *Braves* 49: Kelly helped make the name popular [in 1887] by calling himself a "beaneater." *Ibid.* 50: Clarkson won thirty-three games for the Beaneaters in 1888.

2. [cf. BEAN BANDIT, BEANER, 3] a Mexican.—used contemptuously.—usu. considered offensive.

 1919 *DN* V 63: *Bean-eater*, a name given to the low class Mexican. That row of adobes is filled with *bean-eaters.* New Mexico. **1936** R. Adams *Cowboy Lingo* 198: To the cowboy a Mexican was a "greaser," "oiler," "shuck," "chili," "chili-eater," or "bean-eater." **1974** A.C. Clark *Revenge* 65: You and that…Mexican bean-eater done fucked me up! **1990** *L.A. Times* (Apr. 5) J1: Fuentes said the allusion to Latinos as beaners, or bean-eaters, is as offensive as labeling a black person as someone who likes watermelon and chicken.

bean-eating *adj.* Bostonian.—used contemptuously.

 1892 L. Moore *Own Story* 133: You miserable, bean-eating cheat! **1897** Hamblen *General Mgr.* 231: The h-ll you will, you bean-eatin', psalm-singin' son of a down-east Jew.

beaned up *adj. Trucking.* under the influence of Benzedrine tablets.

 1971 Tak *Truck Talk* 9: *Beaned up*: bennied up. **1976** *Nat. Lampoon* (July) 93: You beaned-up mother, this is a 10-17.

beaner *n.* **1.** something excellent, knockout.

 1911 *DN* III 540: *Beaner*, n. Term of appreciation, or compliment; equivalent to fine or excellent. "That new dress is a beaner," "That story is a beaner." **1913** *DN* IV 16: "The show at the Lyric is a *beaner.*" **1923** *Chi. Daily Trib.* (Oct. 9) 22: Let's see diary—what shall we call her? I have it—my S.P.—that's a beaner. **1940** in Galewitz *Great Comics* 45: "Boy, oh boy!" "Have I got a secret 'at's a beaner." "I have no time to listen to secrets even if they are beaners."

2. *Baseball.* a bean ball.

 1912 Mathewson *Pitching* 42: Bing! Up comes another "beaner."

3. [cf. BEAN BANDIT, BEAN EATER, 2] a Mexican.—used contemptuously.—usu. considered offensive.

 *ca*1965 in Schwendinger & Schwendinger *Adolescent Subcult.* 208: *Beaners* (Mexican-Americans). **1968–70** *Current Slang* III & IV 8: *Beaner*, n. A Mexican or a Mexican-American (derogatory).—New Mexico State. **1983** R. Thomas *Missionary* 147: You know how the beaners are when it comes to time. **1983** *L.A. Times* (Aug. 7) I 22: They were calling me a "beaner" at (mostly white) Alhambra High School. **1985** Univ. Tenn. student theme: The terms "Chicano," "Latino," "Hispano," …"beaner," "bean-eater," and "greaser" are [applied to Hispanics]. **1990** *Nation* (July 16) 86: [Some] skinheads…claim they're white power but yet they'll screw a beaner chick or a half-breed gook.

beanery *n.* a cheap restaurant where beans are frequently served; (*Joc.*) a restaurant of any sort; (*obs.*) a boarding house.

1887 in *OEDS:* Go to, illustrious reader; get thee to a beanery. **1889** in Duis *Saloon* 90: It is cheaper to live at the barroom than at the poor beaneries. **1899–1900** Cullen *Tales* 364: Every piker and beanery worker in San Francisco. **1902–03** Ade *People You Know* 99: Once there was a home-like Beanery where one could tell the Day of the Week by what was on the Table. **1904** *Life in Sing Sing* 246: *Beanery.* Restaurant. **1920** Ade *Hand-Made Fables* 38: A refined joint that was a cross between a salon and a beanery. **1931** *Writer's Digest* (May) 41: *Beanery Queen*—Waitress. **1962** *Time* (Dec. 21) 44: Empty tables at the royal beanery. **1968** Simoun *Madigan* (film): When I was grabbin' a bite at a beanery, he was having sandwiches at the Stork Club. **1974** E. Thompson *Tattoo* 42: All sorts of guys they met at one or another pool hall or beanery.

bean flag *n. Navy.* ¶ In phrase: **fly the bean flag** [cf. BEAN RAG] to be menstruating.
1954 *AS* XXIX 298: The Vernacular of Menstruation....Explicit or implicit reference to the color red:...*fly the bean flag* or *the red flag* (M[asculine expression], navy).

bean foundry *n.* BEANERY.
1902 *Independent* (Nov. 6) 2635: Soup kitchens and bean foundries were opened at various points in the poorer quarters of the city.

bean gun *n. Army.* a rolling field kitchen.
1941 *AS* (Oct.) 163: *Bean Gun.* Rolling kitchen. **1942** Colby *Army Talk* 222: *Bean Gun.* Sometimes heard for "slum cannon"—never popular and going out of use.

bean hauler *n. Trucking.* (see quots.).
1971 in *AS* XLIV 202: *Bean hauler.* Driver who transports fruits and vegetables. **1971** Tak *Truck Talk* 9: *Bean hauler:* a trucker who transports dry food products.

beanhead *n.* BEANBRAIN.
1919 *DN* V 61: *Bean-head,* a dull, stupid person. "John is such a *beanhead.*" New Mexico. **1970** Quammen *Walk the Line* 7: I'm supposed to be on your side, you little beanheads. **1982** Univ. Tenn. instructor, age 41: That bunch of beanheads don't know whether they're coming or going. **1989** *Night Court* (NBC-TV): You've acted...like a world-class beanhead.

Bean Hotel *n. Army in West.* cookhouse. *Joc.*
1864 in H. Johnson *Talking Wire* 179: I have just returned from the Bean Hotel as we call our cookhouse.

bean house *n.* BEANERY.
1978 Lieberman & Rhodes *CB* (ed. 2) 289: *Bean house bull*—Tall tales.

beanie *n.* **1.** BEAN BELLY.
[**1873** Sutton *N.Y. Tombs* 479: John Kane, *alias* "Beeny"...is...about 5 feet 6½ inches in height, and weighs nearly 160 pounds.] **1960** N.Y.C. woman, age 72: The kids [at the turn of the century] used to call a fat belly a *beanie.* "That's some beanie you've got." "You're getting a regular beanie." It's short for *bean belly.*
2. a small, esp. brimless, cap; an overseas cap or skullcap; (*rarely*) a person wearing a beanie; (*occ., Joc.*) a hat.
1918 *Scribner's* (Dec.) 759: The comfortable overseas service cap, familiarly known as the "beanie," adorning their heads. **1943** in *OEDS.* **1954–60** *DAS* 24: During the late 1940s a children's fad was wearing elaborately ornamented beanies. **1961** Sullivan *Shortest, Gladdest* 38: We had to restrain Anson from goosing two girls, both accompanied by burly beanies. **1977** Harnack *Under Wings* 48: We dutifully wore our freshman beanie caps. **1980** H. Gould *Ft. Apache* 38: Sergeant Applebaum. He's an orthodox Jew....Plus he refuses to take the beanie off, even though it's not Police Department issue. **1983** *Nat. Lampoon* (Apr.) 5: Hold on to your beanie. **1983** Helprin *Winter's Tale* 71: He wore a crenellated beanie...over his waxed crew cut. **1990** *Cosmopolitan* (May) 142: My life spills out into one messy pile of letters and cards, a freshman beanie, photographs and newspaper clippings, [etc.]. **1991** Dunnigan & Bay *From Shield to Storm* 371: Green Berets or "beanies."
3. a blackjack.
1952 M. Chase *McThing* 27: He's been breaking windows with a rubber beanie. **1953** W. Brown *Monkey on My Back* 90: There'd be a shank in my ribs or a beanie laid over my skull.
¶ In phrase:
¶ **flip (one's) beanie** to *flip (one's) lid* s.v. LID.
1964 Hill *Casualties* 164: Have you flipped your beanie, Clay? *Six watermelons!*

bean jockey *n. Mil.* a person who waits on tables.

1937 *AS* (Feb.) 74: *Bean-jockey*—tablewaiter. **1966** Noel & Bush *Naval Terms* 218: Messman...Slang: *bean jockey.*

beanpole *n.* a lanky person.
1837 in Strong *Diary* I 59: One of Frederic Anthon's bean-pole sisters. **1928** Dahlberg *Bottom Dogs* 51: The teacher was a tall, thin, straight-up-and-down sort of dry beanpole.

bean rag *n. Navy.* (see 1971 quot.).
1939 O'Brien *One-Way Ticket* 10 [ref. to ca1925]: At seven o'clock a signalman hoisted the bean rag. **1944** Kendall *Service Slang* 19: *Bean rag*...pennant flown at mess time. **1971** Noel & Bush *Naval Terms* (ed. 3) 32: *Bean rag:* Slang for flag flown in port to indicate that the crew is at mess and that other than routine honors should not be expected.

Beans *n. Mil.* (used as a nickname; see quot.).
1907 J. Moss *Officers' Manual* 243: Beans—the commissary sergeant.

beans and motherfuckers *n.pl.* (see quots.).
1990 G.R. Clark *Words of Vietnam War* 52: Beans-and-Motherfuckers (Ham and Lima Beans). **1991** Reinberg *In Field:* Beans and motherfuckers, slang for unpopular C-ration lima beans and ham.

bean sheet *n. Labor.* (see quots.).
1942 *ATS* 504: *Bean sheet,* a union card used as a means of getting food or lodging. **1965** R. O'Neill *High Steel: Bean Sheet:* a union card used to get food or lodging.

bean-shooter *n.* [cf. BISCUIT-SHOOTER] *Army.* (see quots.).
1909 J. Moss *Officers' Manual* (ed. 2) 283: *Bean-Shooter*—a commissary officer. **1944** Kendall *Service Slang* 2: *Bean shooter*...civilian dietician at post.

bean-slinger *n.* a cook.
1907 *Army & Navy Life* (Oct.) 430: Caan't a feller look around fer somethin' tew eat without all you damned bean-slingers follerin' him up?

bean stripe *n.* HASHMARK.
1944 Kendall *Service Slang* 36: Hashmark....often called bean stripes.

Beantown *n.* Boston, Mass.
1901 "J. Flynt" *World of Graft:* Throughout the Under World, Chicago is known by its nickname, "Chi."...Other cities have similar nicknames....Boston, "Bean-Town." **1904** T.A. Dorgan, in Zwilling *TAD Lexicon* 17: The talented gent...fears that the culture of the Bean Town might get to him. **1918** *Stars & Stripes* (Feb. 8) 3. **1964** Faust *Steagle* 25: Go back to Beantown, ingrate. **1970** *Playboy* (Dec.) 289: It's not as ridiculous as it sounds, if you've ever spent a winter in Beantown. **1976** Lieberman & Rhodes *CB Handbook* 122: *Beantown*—Boston. **1984** *Good Night, Beantown* [CBS-TV series]. **1989** Radford & Crowley *Drug Agent* 134: I wasn't due back in Beantown until the following day. **1990** *U.S. News & W.R.* (Oct. 29) 80: Even diversified Beantown is feeling the chill wind of a regional recession.

bean wagon *n.* a cheap restaurant; (*specif.*) one made from a converted railroad dining car.
1947 Willingham *End as a Man* 101: In one of the bean wagons downtown. **1954–60** *DAS* 64.

beany *adj.* crazy.
1914 *DN* IV 103: *Beany, adj.* Mentally defective, whether feeble-minded or insane. **1919** *DN* V 71: *Beany,* crazy. She's gone *beany* about him! New Mexico.

bear *n.* **1.a.** a Russian. [First two quots. represent literary, not slang, use.]
*****1794** in *OEDS:* Those Russian Bears after having devoured the Unhappy Poles are...to direct their fell tusks against France. *****1804** in *OEDS:* Take the two Nations...and trust me the Bears would triumph. *****1813** in J. Ashton *Eng. Satires on Napoleon* 342: D—d John Bull—d—d Russian bears. **1863** in Lyman *Meade's H.Q.* 62: General Meade at once orders the 6th Corps to parade, and gets hold of all the ambulances of the staff, which are forthwith sent to the depot, after the serene Bears. **1922** Dean *Flying Cloud* 4: Oh, I can whale a Yankee, a Saxon bull or bear,/And in honor of old Paddy's land I'll still those laurels wear. **1927** Finger *Frontier Ballads* 45: For I can whip a Yankee, a Finn or Russian bear. **1992** *N.Y. Newsday* (Sept. 2) 50: The Russian bear, an enigma himself and once a formidable chess gladiator, could again rise up to do ferocious battle.
b. (*cap.*) the Soviet Union.—constr. with *the.*
*ca*1974 in J.L. Gwaltney *Drylongso* 20: Everybody is bugging the Bear to let these Jews leave there.
2. *Naut.* a makeshift device used for scrubbing decks.
1889 *Century Dict.* I. **1923** Riesenberg *Under Sail* 48 [ref. to 1897]: The

bear consisted of a heavy box, a thick thrum mat lashed on the bottom of it, and the inside loaded with broken holy stones and charged with wet sand. Four stout rope lanyards were rigged to the corners and served to haul the thing back and forth while the sand filtered down through the mat, providing the necessary scouring agent. **1925** Bailey *Shanghaied* 22 [ref. to 1898]: Ben's and my first task at sea comprised helping two other men in "pulling the monkey's tail" or, as it is sometimes termed, "pulling the bear." The…process consists in four…men dragging about the main deck a cumbersome wooden box heavily laden, to whose bottom a layer of glass or sandpaper is fixed. By this process the decks are kept scrupulously clean. ***1929** Bowen *Sea Slang* 9: *Bear*…A matted stone or shot, or a coir mat filled with sand, dragged over the deck to clean it after the fashion of a holystone.

3. an exciting or otherwise excellent example (of something); a superior individual, (*specif.*) an unusually attractive young woman *or* a person who is notably adept or expert. [All nuances common *ca*1910–40; increasingly rare since.]
1908 in H.C. Fisher *A. Mutt* 161: I'm a bear at this stuff. **1910** T.A. Dorgan, in *N.Y. Eve. Jour.* (Jan. 19) 12: It will be a bear of a fight. **1910** T.A. Dorgan, in *N.Y. Eve. Jour.* (Mar. 3) 16: That's the funniest [joke] I ever heard.…That's a bear. *a***1904–11** Phillips *Susan Lenox* II 316: Oh, he's a playsmith—and a bear at it. **1911** Van Loan *Big League* 213: He was a bear for givin' 'em the hip. **1912** in *DN* IV 26: *Bear*, n. A general term of approbation. It's a *bear*—it's all right, first-rate. She's a *bear*—she's "classy," or a good "ragger." **1913** *Sat. Eve. Post* (May 31) 12: I'll bet he's a bear among the women. **1912–14** in E. O'Neill *Lost Plays* 174: You ought to have seen the bear I lamped this afternoon. Some queen, take it from me. **1913–15** Van Loan *Taking the Count* 24: You're a bear when it comes to fixing up bad hands. **1915** *N.Y. Eve. Jour.* (Aug. 12) 10: "Wheezer" was a bear in the opening inning. **1915–16** Lait *Beef, Iron & Wine* 96: "You're a bear," she said with feeling. **1918** in [Grider] *War Birds* 225: They say that his latest stunt was a bear. **1919** Farrell *1st U.S. Engrs.* 121: There's a "Y" there that's a bear. **1923** in Truman *Dear Bess* 313: I used to be a bear at it but I doubt my ability now. **1923** in Lardner *Best Stories* 291: No…she ain't no bear for looks. **1929** Burnett *Iron Man* 129: She's a bear for looks.…I wish I had a wife like that. **1929–30** J.T. Farrell *Young Lonigan* 74: It had been a bear of a fight. **1948** Wolfert *Act of Love* 514: He's a bear on running the ball. **1980** *N.Y. Daily News* (Dec. 18) 41: Even his severest critics agree that Haig has an excellent mind, is a bear for work and is a disciplined and organized leader of men. **1989** *New Yorker* (May 9) 49: Why don't you tell those two about that game? That sounded like a *bear*.

4. a formidable task or taskmaster; something or someone that is hard to deal with.
1915 *DN* IV 231: *Bear, n.*…A professor who "overworks" his students. **1958** P. O'Connor *At Le Mans* 36: But be careful. This track is a bear. **1962** in *AS* XXXVIII 167: A difficult college course: *bear…bitch…bastard.* **1968** Baker et al. *CUSS* 77: *Bear*…Difficult course. Difficult exam. **1974** Univ. Tenn. student: A difficult examination, or anything hard, is called a bear. **1980** WINS radio (Dec. 21): At this time of year, toy-shopping can be a bear. **1984** M. Skinner *Red Flag* 97: It's going to be a real bear to do your job and stay alive. **1993** *Guiding Light* (CBS-TV): It's really been a bear meeting people with the same interests.

5. Esp. *Black E.* an unattractive woman.
1954 L. Armstrong *Satchmo* 88 [ref. to *ca*1915]: After I discovered my chick was just as tough as Mary Jack the Bear, I was afraid of her. **1957** *N.Y. Times Mag.* (Aug. 18) 26: *Bear*—An unattractive girl. **1966** *Dayton* (Ohio) *News* (June 7): Homely persons (mostly girls) are scrounge, scab, toredown, *bear*, ax, mule, tack, nail and scamp. **1971** Torres *Sting Like a Bee* 142 [ref. to 1964]: You are too ugly. You are a bear. **1982** A. Shaw *Dict. Pop/Rock* 30: "*Bear.*" In black jargon, a very homely woman, as in the '49 R & B hit by Little Esther, "Double Crossing Blues."

6. the vulva.
[**1928** in Oliver *Blues Tradition* 187: She got somethin' round an' it looks just like a bear,/Sometimes I wonder what in the hell is there.] **1961** Peacock *Valhalla* 180: I woke up with my nose down there one night and woulda sworn to God I was staring that old grinnin' bear right in the face.…I always maintain that he who eats the hole will eat the pole.

7. (used, esp. in Black E., as a symbol of hardship or worthlessness; see esp. 1969, 1985 quots.).
1942 *Pittsburgh Courier* (Feb. 7) 13: You're like the bear.…You ain't nowhere. **1942** *Amer. Mercury* (July) 85: Oh, just like de bear—I ain't nowhere. Like de bear's brother, I ain't no further. Like de bear's daughter—ain't got a quarter. *Ibid.* 96: *The bear*—confession of poverty. **1948** Manone & Vandervoort *Trumpet* 171: And those gags about his nags are just nowhere like the bear. [**1950** *PADS* (No. 14) 13 [S.C.]:

"The *bear* got him," he was overcome by the heat, had a sunstroke.] **1956** N. Algren *Walk on Wild Side* 69: "I had thirty-two days wrestling with the bear so I worked on myself to keep from getting even crazier."…"What's wrestling with the bear?" "Solitary [confinement]." **1969** *Current Slang* I & II 8: *The Bear*, n. Misfortune; an unfortunate event.—College males, New York.—Sometimes you get *the bear*; sometimes *the bear* gets you. **1983** Proffitt *Gardens of Stone* 98: Some days you eat the bear, some days the bear eats you. **1985** M. Brennan *War* 52 [ref. to 1967]: There's a saying that goes, "Some days you get the bear, and some days the bear gets you."

8. *Jazz.* [fr. arbitrary rhymed phr. *square as a bear*] a SQUARE.
1951 *Amer. Journ. Sociol.* XXXVII 140: Well, you could have a sexy little bitch to stand up in front and sing and shake her ass at the bears.*…*Synonym for "squares."

9. *N.W.* (see quot.).
1958 McCulloch *Woods Words* 191: *The big bear walks*—a. Time to eat. b. Time for something to happen.

10. *Mil. Av.* a large jet aircraft.
1966 Newhafer *Bugles* 78: We've got to run those bears in for an hour, Joe. Might as well head up along the Parallel. **1967** H.M. Mason *New Tigers* 14: "Okay, you've got the airplane…" the magic words that mean I can fly this "bear." **1990** Tuso *Vietnam Blues* 245: *Bear.* An affectionate name for an aircraft.

11. *USAF.* the backseat pilot, radar navigator, or electronic warfare officer in a combat aircraft.
1966–67 in Tuso *Vietnam Blues* 76: It shakes up the pilots; it shakes up the bears. **1979** D.K. Schneider *AF Heroes* 22: The pilot and bear had constantly to scan the horizon in all directions. **1984** Doleman *Tools of War* 116: While his pilot cruised enemy territory, the Bear would search…for any of the enemy's…radars…used to spot targets for the SAMs. **1984** Sweetman *Phantom* 38: The back-seat EWOs became known as "bears."

12. usu. *pl.* [sugg. by the SMOKEY-THE-BEAR HAT used by many highway patrol officers] a highway patrol officer or state trooper.
1975 Dills *CB Language*: *Bears*: Police of any kind. **1975** *Atlantic* (May) 42: Might be a bear wants to give us some green stamps. **1976** Lieberman & Rhodes *CB Handbook* 122: *Bear*—Policeman.…*Bear in the Air*—Police patrolling in helicopters.…*Bear Report*—Where are the police? For example…"Westbounder, what's the bear report?" *Ibid.* 127: *Don't Feed the Bears*—Don't get a ticket. **1979–82** Gwin *Overboard* 152: We call them state troopers bears.

¶ In phrases:

¶ **does a bear shit in the woods?** "emphatically yes."— usu. considered vulgar. *Joc.* Also vars.
[**1928** Ruth *Baseball* 10: "How about it young man…do you want to play baseball?"…Did I want to play baseball? Does a fish like to swim or a squirrel climb trees?] **1966** in IUFA *Folk Speech*: Does a wild bear shit in the woods? **1966** Braly *Cold* 38: "You telling me you're rooting?" "Does a bear crap in the woods?" **1971** Rowe *Five Yrs.* 451: "Can you hang on for that extra day?" I was definitely grinning when I answered, "Does a bear crap in the woods?" **1972** Bunker *No Beast* 163: "That good, huh?" "Does a bear shit in the woods?" **1978** Maupin *Tales* 3: "Connie…you're single?"…"A bear shit in the woods?" **1981** Rod Serling's *TZ Mag.* (June) 23: "Is that pencil in the museum too?" "Does a bear shit in the woods?" **1984** W.M. Henderson *Elvis* 123: "Will you talk to Byron here?" "Does a bear shit black?"

¶ **hear the bear growl** to expose oneself to danger; go into battle.
1862 in W.C. Davis *Orphan Brig.* 106: [Disappointed at not] hearing the bear growl.

¶ **loaded for bear** see s.v. LOADED.

¶ **the average bear** [sugg. by the signature line "Smarter than the average bear," associated with the animated cartoon character Yogi Bear, featured on the syndicated TV series of that name, first broadcast in 1958] the average person.
1982 *Sports Illustrated* (Oct. 4) 75: Pitt linebacker Yogi Jones, who is stronger than the average bear, had 14 tackles. **1983** Beckwith & Knox *Delta Force* 81: I ain't the average bear, and I didn't come here to pack it in. **1988** *Newsmaker Saturday* (CNN-TV) (Feb. 20): He needs to work on pushing his message in a way that the average bear down here [in S.C.] can understand.

¶ **turn (one's) bear loose** *West.* to take violent action.
1923 J.L. Hill *Cattle Trail* 78 [ref. to 1883]: If you don't like it just turn

your pet bear loose.

¶ **walk in and see the bear dance** [ref. to once-popular exhibitions of dancing bears] to come and see the fun.
1821 Waln *Hermit in Phila.* 25: Walk in and see the bear dance!

bearcat *n.* BEAR, 3. [Esp. common *ca*1910–35.]
1909 T.A. Dorgan, in Zwilling *TAD Lexicon* 17: Oh mommer!! There's a bearcat [*sc.* a golf swing]. **1910** T.A. Dorgan, in *N.Y. Eve. Jour.* (Jan. 4) 12: This Hayes person is no bearcat with the mittens, having lost twice to Freddy Welch. **1910** T.A. Dorgan, in *N.Y. Eve. Jour.* (Feb. 4) 14: Johnson's Right-Hand Uppercut a Real Bear-Cat. **1913** in J. Reed *Young Man* 28: I could see straight up about a million miles in the sky. The stars are bear-cats down there. **1915** R. Lardner *Gullible's Tr.* 29: *Carmen's* a bear cat.…If they was all as good as *Carmen*, I'd go every night. **1915** R. Lardner, in Butterfield *Post Treasury* 142: But why should a man pull an alibi for bein' engaged to such a bearcat as she was? **1915–16** Lait *Beef, Iron & Wine* 15: And the director said he had "discovered" a bearcat; and engaged Alec at once, for famous compensation. **1917** F. Hunt *Draft* 137: Honest, that guy is the whitest guy that you ever saw around this old camp. He's a bearcat. **1919** [Cober] *Btty. D* 63: He was quiet and unassuming, but when it came to shooting two bits he was a "bear-cat." **1928** A. York *Sgt. York* 63: But even if we-uns in the Cumberlands ain't been bothered to death with feuds, we've got to admit that we've had our share of bushwhackers. What a lot of baar-cats they were! **1928** W.R. Burnett *Little Caesar* 77: Ain't she a bearcat! **1929–31** Farrell *Young Lonigan* 154: George was a bearcat at forging handwriting. **1938** in McArdle *Collier's* 351: Regan's a bear cat on the draw. **1951** Styron *Lie Down* 197: Isn't that a bearcat of a name? **1958** "Traver" *Murder* 113: In fact, I used to be quite a little bearcat at the business. **1960** Carpenter *Youngest Harlot* 56: He's the old bearcat on the harmonica. **1971** Dahlskog *Dict.* 6: *Bearcat, n.* Something powerful or potent, as: a car that's a *bearcat* on hills; an aggressive or vigorous person; a beautiful and passionate girl.

beard *n.* **1.** a woman's pubic hair.—usu. considered vulgar.
*****1726** A. Smith *Mems. of J. Wild* 118: He was lugging out his Dagger, to whip her through the Beard. *****a1890–93** F & H III 19: The female pubic hair…beard. **1927** (quot. at BEARD-JAMMER). **1982** (quot. AT BEARD RIDE).

2.a. a bearded man, *esp.* (1950's to present) a bearded beatnik, hippie, or avant-garde intellectual.—usu. used derisively. Also extended vars.
1927 *AS* 367: "Beards" or "brush-peddlers" ("extras" with natural whiskers). **1957** *N.Y. Times Mag.* (Aug. 18): *Beard*—An avant-garde type; also a hipster. **1965** *Sat. Eve. Post* (July 3) 36: All the beardos and weirdos came out from the university…and screamed about how wrong it was to put a cross on public property. **1967** *L.A. Times* (Jan. 13) West 13: I am not ignoring the shaggy beardniks of Telegraph Avenue, nor forgetting that outside agitators use Berkeley students to promote alien causes. **1968** *Time* (May 3) 21: Housewives, hippies, businessmen and beards marched. **1973** Breslin *World Without End* 237: All the beards and fags showed up to picket.

b. *N.Y.C. Police.* a man who is a Hasidic Jew.
1967 G. Green *To Brooklyn* 248: Otzenberger'll be on our backs forever we lose one of dem beards. **1973** Droge *Patrolman* 31: The precinct is one-third Blacks, one-third Puerto Ricans, and one-third "Beards.".…The "Beards" the sergeant had referred to were the Hasidic Jews. **1984** Caunitz *Police Plaza* 98: He has two beards with him.

3. [alluding to the use of a beard as a disguise] **a.** Orig. *Gamb.* a go-between who places bets for another in order to protect his identity; (*broadly*) an unacknowledged agent. Also as *v.*
1956 "T. Betts" *Across the Board* 15 [ref. to *ca*1920]: I played horses, using them as betting commissioners, or "beards," as they were called at the race track. *Ibid.* 171: He needed a beard on this coup; he never could have bought it on his own. **1963** *Sat. Eve. Post* (Apr. 27) 37: "The fixers usually have guys 'bearding' for them"—placing their bets for them—"but the smart bookmaker knows who the beards are." **1968** M.B. Scott *Racing Game* 50: He sometimes employs a "beard" or front man. In the days before parimutuel betting, the beard was an essential accomplice of the [odds] manipulator. *Ibid.* 75: Such an owner…is usually a "beard" for a gambler. **1970** in Cannon *Nobody Asked* 146: They were getting real good information [on horseraces] and they had a "beard" who was spreading it around for them. The copper…hears the guys in Chicago giving their information to the beard [who]…starts in getting action from the cop. No tremendous bets. A fifty here, a hundred there. **1974** Sann *Dead Heat* 20: You just come up with an army of beards to cash the win tickets Wednesday. **1982** Sculatti *Cat. of Cool* 212: Dean and

Ehrlichman were Tricky Dick's beards at Watergate.

b. *Homosex.* an escort or companion of the opposite sex whose presence is intended to conceal a person's homosexuality. Also as *v.*
1971 B. Rodgers *Queens' Vernacular* 30: *Beard* ([known in] Las Vegas, mid 60's…) a woman who dates homosexual men to help them socially. [Also] to date a woman to prevent suspicion of being homosexual. "Are you bearding tonight or is that your lesbian mommy?" **1982** *Maledicta* VI 128: Well, maybe some [lesbians] will marry a *gay* as a *beard* (a male front). **1982** *Harper's* (Oct.) 43: The same friends who had covered for him in the security investigation came through with a mixture of unwitting dates and willing "beards." **1984** W. Allen *Broadway Danny Rose* (film): Who ya beardin' for, ya little cheese-eater? **1988** *21 Jump St.* (Fox-TV): You're gonna like her. She's nice. You're just gonna be the beard. **1992** *N.Y. Times Bk. Review* (July 26) 5: Humiliated, shamed and still a closeted homosexual,…he maintained determined liaisons…with women who "bearded" him. **1993** *New Republic* (Aug. 16) 25: The male pair have to rearrange their lives…A young Chinese woman is brought in as a "beard."

bearded clam *n.* the vulva.—usu. considered vulgar. *Joc.* Also **bearded oyster, bearded lady.** Cf. CLAM, *n.*, 1.a.
1916–22 Cary *Sexual Vocab.* I: *Bearded oyster.* A woman's pudendum. **1965** Trimble *Sex Words* 23: *Bearded Clam*…the Vaginal area as highlighted by the Pubes. *Bearded Lady*…Bearded Clam. **1974** Univ. Tenn. student: Know what a *bearded clam* is? Same as a *furburger*. **1975** Wambaugh *Choirboys* 22: He gobbles one beaver and gets promoted. I've are close to three hundred bearded clams in my time and never even got a commendation. **1988** Billy Crystal, in *Playboy* (Mar.) 47: They [women] can't talk about their balls or how they farted last night. Can't talk about the great piece of ass they saw. Can't talk about beavers and bearded clams. **1988** Hynes *Flights of Passage* 35 [ref. to WWII]: The female organ was "the bearded clam" or "the mossy doughnut."

beard-jammer *n.* (see quot.).
1927 *DN* V 438: *Beard-Jammer. n.* A whore-master.

beardman *n.* BEARD, 3.a.
1956 "T. Betts" *Across the Board* 85 [ref. to *ca*1920]: The Speed Boys worked with beardmen in the business world who moved big bets for them away from the track.

beard ride *n.* an act of cunnilingus.
1982 *Nat. Lampoon* (Sept.) 93: Wild Beard Rides 50¢.

beard splitter *n.* (see quot.).
1785 Grose *Vulgar Tongue: Beard Splitter*, a man much given to wenching.

bearfight *n.* a violent fistfight.
*a*1940 in Lanning & Lanning *Texas Cowboys* 63 [ref. to *ca*1900]: I saw some shootings and many bear fights.

bearfuck *n.* *Mil.* a confused or chaotic undertaking.—usu. considered vulgar.
1983 K. Miller *Lurp Dog* 92 [ref. to Vietnam War]: The mission turned out to be another disappointing bearfuck.

bear hat *n.* SMOKEY-THE-BEAR HAT.
1978 Lieberman & Rhodes *CB* (ed. 2) 289: *Bear Hat*—Police hat.

bear hug *n.* *Business.* an aggressive or decisive takeover offer, usu. a follow-up to one previously rejected.
1978 J. Rosenberg *Dict. Business* 45: *Bear hug:* an unnegotiated corporate takeover proposal, made privately or publicly to directors. **1980–82** in *Barnhart Dict. Comp.* III (1984) 37: A week later came the "bear hug": another letter with an informal offer of $21 a share…, $4 a share more than the stock was selling for on Wall Street. **1988** Odean *High Steppers* 110: The *bear hug*…became a common method of attack. **1990** *Changing Times* (May) 20: The Street was bullish on Aardvark Industries when a raider swooped in with a bear hug but cooled off after the company made it to a safe harbor.…Such was the takeover talk of pushy brokers.…But…the takeover slang of the 1980s is already passé.

bear meat *n.* an easy target.
1972 Bunker *No Beast* 163: It [a bank to be robbed]'s bear meat. If we brought the cannons we'd get him right now.

bear's ass *n.* BEAR, 4.
1990 Cher, on *Inside Edition* (synd. TV series): I'm a tough person to work with. I mean I can be a bear's ass.

bear sign *n.* **1.** *West.* a doughnut.
1903 A. Adams *Log of a Cowboy* 280: She asked me to make the bear sign—doughnuts, she called them.…Making bear sign is my long suit.

1969 L'Amour *Conagher* 49: "Are you the lady that bakes the bear sign?" "Bear sign?...Do you mean doughnuts?"
2. berry jam.
1942 *ATS* 483: *Bear sign*, berry jam. **1958** McCulloch *Woods Words* 9: *Bear sign*—Blackberry jam, particularly if very seedy.

beast *n.* **1.** *U.S. Mil. Acad., USAF Acad.* a newly arrived first-year cadet. Also (in recent use) short for BEAST BARRACKS.
1871 O. Wood *West Point Scrapbook* 337: *Animal.*—A name given to new cadets on their arrival. *Beast.*—A name also applied to new cadets. **1900** *Howitzer* (No. 1) 117: *Beast*—A new cadet. **1934** Wohlforth *Tin Soldiers* 19: Stand UP!! you Beasts! **1938** in *AS* XIV 32: *Beast*—New cadet. **1965** Donlon *Outpost* 56 [ref. to 1955]: And no matter what a "plebe" does, he is not going to win approval from his cadet captain, whom we called "the king of the beasts." **1976** *N.Y. Times Mag.* (Sept. 5) 11: The cadets were in the midst of Basic Cadet Training (popularly known as "Beast"). **1978** Truscott *Dress Gray* 39: You remember that plebe from Beast last year? **1981** Stiehm *Bring Men & Women* 52: *Beast*...Basic Cadet Training (BCT). **1986** R. Walker *AF Wives* 233: Believe me, I'm going to be kind to the poor beasts that take our place next year.
2.a. a very unattractive or slovenly woman, esp. if sexually passionate or promiscuous; *(occ.)* *Stu.* a homely or unpopular person of either sex.
[**1934** Weseen *Dict. Slang* 306: *Beastess*—A coarse or degraded woman; a girl or a woman disliked.] **1946** J.H. Burns *Gallery* 23: I knew a Polish beast once. She loved it. **1948** *AS* XXIII 248: *Beast*. Distasteful female. **1951** W. Williams *Enemy* 37 [ref. to WWII]: I had something fine night before last. A beast, strictly a beast, you understand, but it was sure fine. Why is it you always line up these fine beasts just before you get underway? **1955** *AS* XXX 302: *Beast*...Woman of loose morals. **1955–57** Felder *Collegiate Slang* 1: *Beast*—a most unattractive girl. **1958** in *AS* XXXIV 154: Unpopular girls (and on rare occasions unpopular men), with no reference whatsoever to looks, are *roaches*, *beasts*, and *pigs*. **1959** Maier *College Terms* 4: *A real beasty*—bad date. **1963** E. Hunter *Ten Plus One* 103: This was a beautiful girl. Though who knows, she may have grown up to be a beast, huh? **1972** *Nat. Lampoon* (Apr.) 34: Then you got your ordinary pig or beast. Really foul, but they'll fuck a duck. **1975** T. Berger *Sneaky People* 61: She was there with another girl,...a beast who had pimples and wore glasses.
b. a sexually attractive woman; one's girlfriend.
1946 Heggen *Mr. Roberts* 59: The last time I was there, that was a year ago, man, I found a fine little beast. Cutest little doll you ever saw, blonde, a beautiful figure, really a beautiful girl. **1956** Longstreet *Real Jazz* 150: A girl is [called] a *beast*. **1957** H. Simmons *Corner Boy* 28: That beast of yours doesn't think so. *Ibid.* 49: Man, dig that crazy [rump] on the big beast in the plaid skirt! **1957** MacDonald *Death Trap* 78: Hey, Rook! Where'd your beast go?
3.a. a large powerful vehicle or device, esp. a hot rod, airplane, or guided missile; *(specif.)* **the Beast** [or **Beastie**] *Naval Av.* the Curtiss SB2C Helldiver dive bomber.
1944 Olds *Helldiver Squadron* 81: Training got underway with the plane which later won from other young pilots the awe-inspiring nickname "The Beast." **1951–53** in *AS* XXIX 93: "Hot Rod" Terms...*Beast*, *n.* A car. **1955** R.L. Scott *Look of Eagle* 67: They wanted to get the beasts fired up. **1957** *Life* (Apr. 29) 140: *Beast*...Exceptionally fast car. **1958** Gilbert *Vice Trap* 71: Your jalopy's no real beast, O.K. *Ibid* 5: *Beast*, *Bomb*—hotrod. **1959** *Sat. Eve. Post* (May 16) 115: Atlas, known as the "Beast" among the missilemen is designed to fly 7500 miles with a warhead of somewhat over one and a half megatons....But just how beastly do the Beasts look through Mr. Khrushchev's eyes? **1959** Searls *Big X* 125: We were actually going to fly those little beasts up the Ginza strafing and dropping firebombs. *Ibid.* 219: I was the only guy left that could fly this beast. **1959** Heflin *Aerospace Gloss.*: *Beast*, *n.* A familiar term for a large rocket. **1959** Farris *Harrison High* 140: Look at the beast, will you? **1960** *Twilight Zone* (CBS-TV): This beast gulps fuel. We know that only too well. **1961** L.G. Richards *TAC* 234: It is their job to tame the new beast and break it for squadron pilots. **1962** Quirk *Red Ribbons* 61 [ref. to 1940's]: A Beastie pulled out of formation in a gentle spiral...the Helldiver skimmed in beautifully. **1963** Dwiggins *S.O.Bees* 114: I'd say that beast isn't fit to go aboard a flattop. **1966** J. Lewis *Marines* 84: The old beast quit on me right at the end of the runway. **1973** M. Collins *Carrying the Fire* 67: But the Saturn V was truly a new beast, far heavier and more powerful than any flying machine the world had ever seen. **1974** Stevens *More There I Was* 87: Sarge,...help me *hold* this beast [airplane]. **1975** in Higham & Siddall *Combat Aircraft* 71: It was hard to believe I was in the same ground-loving beast that had to be pried into the air for takeoff. **1976** Schroeder

Shaking It 121: Those beasts cost about twenty dollars a mile to run; even a flat tire on them costs about forty-five dollars to fix. **1978** Wharton *Birdy* 112: I had to wash and simonize the beast once a week. **1978** Lieberman & Rhodes *CB* (ed. 2) 289: *Beast*—Very powerful CB station. **1987** D. Brown *Flight of Old Dog* 246: Two available airfields to set this beast down on. **1990** G.R. Clark *Words of Vietnam War* 42: B-52 Bomber...Beast. **1991** Linnekin *80 Knots* 233: The SB2C...soon earned the nickname The Beast; I never, ever, heard anyone call it Helldiver out loud.
b. a clumsy tool or device.
1974 Cherry *High Steel* 45: What're ya usin' a beast like t'at for? Get somet'in' smaller.
4. *Narc.* a heroin addiction, MONKEY.
1958 in Wepman et al. *The Life* 98: Not as long as Mable his whore was able/To satisfy his beast.
5. *Black E.* a white person or white persons in power regarded as enemies and oppressors of blacks.—used contemptuously.—usu. considered offensive.
1968 *U.S. News & W.R.* (Oct. 28) 71: "I realize, myself, that the beast was our enemy."..."Where do you get this word 'beast'? Is that just the latest thing for honkie?" **1969** *Time* (Sept. 19) 22: "I don't want any stringy-haired beast* broad on my wall."..."*Beast," a term that originated with the Black Panthers, is rapidly replacing "Chuck" as the black soldier's standard epithet for the white man. **1968–70** *Current Slang* III & IV 8: *Beast*, *n.* Caucasian—Watts. **1971** *N.Y. Post* (June 3) 58: You say you're going to take that to a white man's court?...You know what the beast is going to do with that?

beast barracks *n.* [BEAST, 1] *U.S. Mil. Acad., USAF Acad.* (see 1970 quot.).
1900 *Howitzer* (No. 1) 117: *Beast Barracks*—The home of the Beasts, from the time they report until they go into camp. **1911** *Howitzer* (No. 11) 214: I succeed in looking like a plebe on the second day of Beast Barracks. **1934** Wohlforth *Tin Soldiers* 74: Thank God Beast Barracks is over. **1970** *N.Y. Times Mag.* (July 5) 20: [Plebes of 1969] were the first newcomers in over 100 years who have not had to endure the eight-week introduction to the academy known as "Beast Barracks"*...*The name does not refer to a specific place but is a general term referring to the period in which the new plebes are initiated into the rigors of academy life and learn its customs and details. **1985** J. McDonough *Platoon Leader* 9: But West Point was exciting—from the very first days of "Beast Barracks" (the equivalent of basic training) there was talk of "the war in the jungles."

beasty *adj.* *Stu.* disgusting.
1982 S. Black *Totally Awesome* 68: Take time to laugh about the beasty hairdo on the saleswoman in the dress shop. **1985** *Knoxville* (Tenn.) *Journal* (Apr. 27) A2: "Grody"...[and] "beasty"...mean disgusting or undesirable. **1990** T. Thorne *Dict. Contemp. Slang: Beastie*...American...disgusting, coarse, or disreputable.

beat *n.* **1.** territory that one has claimed as one's own, orig. for criminal purposes.
1836 in *OED*: A highwayman could never get more than the value of his beat. **1865** (cited in Partridge *Dict. Und.* 27). **1933** Ersine *Prison Sl.* 17: *Beat*...a district reserved to its own use by a bootleg or *stickup* gang. "Stay out of our *beat*, or you get a one-way ride." **1935** in Oliver *Blues Tradition* 154: Take a tip from me, stay off Joe Louis's beat. **1942** *Amer. Mercury* (July) 84: You got to get out on the beat and collar yourself a hot.
2. *Journ.* SCOOP, *n.*
1857 in Fornell *Galveston Era* 31: [Scoring] news beats [on competitors]. **1873** *Harper's* (July) 231: One of these "enterprising" individuals secured his first "beat" by riding in from the first Bull Run defeat on a horse not his own, and taking news of the disaster to Philadelphia by rail, before an injunction was laid down on the transmission of the truth. **1890** Munroe *Orders* 87: He afterward obtained a number of just such "beats" from the same source. **1902** Clapin *Americanisms* 44: *Beat*....In newspaper parlance, an exclusive story, or important news which a reporter has obtained for his own paper in advance of others. When the story is exceedingly important, it is called a *king beat*. **1910** Hapgood *Types* 105: The editor perhaps likes the most intelligent work of the reporter, but he likes to have a large reserve of "copy" on hand, and, above all, he likes a "beat." **1925** L. Thomas *World Flight* 116: In those two minutes I had scored a world news beat. **1926** Wood & Goddard *Amer. Slang* 5: *Beat*. In journalism, precedence in news; a scoop. **1930** Gilman *Sob Sister* 44: It was your first big beat, wasn't it? Did that make the gang sore! **1958** S.H. Adams *Tenderloin* 18: The *Police Gazette* had a resounding beat on the John L. Sullivan story. **1963** E.M. Miller

Exile to Stars 48: You couldn't give me a beat on who the next wing commander will be, can you?

3.a. *Mil.* a shirker or malingerer.

1863 in Wightman *To Ft. Fisher* 99: A "beat" is one who plays sick, shirks guard duty, drills, roll call, etc., and is always missing in a fight. **1878** Willis *Our Cruise* 69: One morning [the bear] suddenly appeared in the sick-bay, and for once the "beats" were fully exposed. **1887** Billings *Hard Tack* 95 [ref. to Civil War]: The original idea of a *beat* was that of a lazy man or a shirk who would by hook or by crook get rid of all military or fatigue duty that he could; but the term grew to have a broader signification. *Ibid.* 101: It was a sad fate to befall a good duty soldier, to get on a detail to procure wood, where every second or third man was a shirk or a *beat*. **1890** *United Service* (Aug.) 201: Battle-scarred veteran or…hospital "beat." **1899** F.E. Daniel *Rebel Surgeon* 154: The "beats" were not all conscripts and privates.

b. a person who will not pay debts or meet obligations; one who habitually sponges on others; DEADBEAT; FREELOADER. See also FAREBEAT.

1865 in *DA*: Before "this cruel war" broke out, he was what's termed a "beat." **1869** Logan *Foot Lights* 371: The circus actors are frequently short of funds and are sometimes broke…The landlord…must sift the "beats" from their more worthy brethren.…With the former class he deals sternly, showing them no mercy. **1872** McCabe *N.Y. Life* 218: "Slouches," "bums," and "beats," the names given to those gentlemen whose principal object in this world is to sponge upon poor humanity to as great an extent as the latter will permit. **1879** *Puck* (Sept. 27) 455: Drummer [salesman].—A man who often strikes "beats." **1890** *Puck* (Feb. 19) 434: That Hokeson's getting to be a regular beat.…Wants me to lend him the twenty dollars I borrowed off him yesterday, until tomorrow. **1939** *AS* (Oct.) 239: *Beat.* Guest who leaves without paying his bill; guest who fails to tip.

c. a no-account individual; loafer.—usu. used contemptuously.

1868 [Williams] *Black-Eyed Beauty* 23: I'll go out and hunt that young beat's name up in the D'rectory and if we can't rake his pile, I'm only fit for kindling. *Ibid.* 42: The beat turns red and walks over to her and gives her a roll. **1888** *Outing* (Apr.) 41: Just don't feel too sure ye've busted them beats. **1936** in F. Brown *N.C. Folklore* III 429: Walking on the railroad/Looking like a beat,/Sleeping out under a water tank/ Without anything to eat.

d. a swindler.

1882 D.J. Cook *Hands Up* 192: On the contrary, he was considered as a loafer and beat, and was frequently arrested for crimes of greater or less magnitude. **1882** Campbell *White Slave* 200: Count Strain, *a beat*. **1884** "M. Twain" *Huck. Finn* ch. xxviii: I could swear they was beats and bummers, that's all. **1888** Bidwell *Chains* 30: A New Orleans boarding house and hotel "beat" ingratiated himself into my father's confidence and soon became his right-hand man. It was not long before my father was again moneyless and out of business. **1909** Irwin *Con Man* 154: You're a lot of professional beats, and you ought to be arrested.

4. a policeman who walks a beat.

1874 (quot. at STAKE).

5. a swindle.

1875 Lloyd *Lights and Shades in S.F.* 101: He is not much sought after by the crimps, unless it be for the opportunity of avenging some "beat" that he has perpetrated upon them. **1933** Ersine *Prison Sl.* 17: *Beat, n.* 1. a swindle, con job. **1971** Simon *Sign of Fool* 12: It's a beat. Those motherfuckers burned me.

6. one that surpasses all competitors; outstanding specimen.—constr. with *the*.

1883 Hay *Bread-Winners* 128: Of all Andylusian jacks, you're the beat.

7. a defeat.

1884 Carleton *Poker Club* 48: I doan mine losen my substance, an' I doan mine a squar' beat.

8. an act of escaping or deserting, esp. a jailbreak.

1856 in C.A. Abbey *Before the Mast* 81: The 2d mate…told the mate…that some of the men had made a "*moonlight beat*" (I.E.) [*sic*] cleared out. **1902** Hapgood *Autobiog. of Thief* 326 [ref. to 1898]: There's going to be a beat tonight. **1942–49** Goldin et al. *DAUL* 298: There's a beat (escape) so we gotta lock in. **1956** Resko *Reprieve* 149 [ref. to 1940's]: Escape. Making a beat. That was all I thought of.

9. the customary pattern of events.

1991 K. Thompson *Angels & Aliens* 244: Thus the beat goes on.

¶ In phrases:

¶ **get a beat on** to gain a clear advantage over.

1872 Burnham *Secret Service* 25. **1889** Farmer *Amer.* 46: As used by thieves and their associates, *to get a beat on one*…implies that the point has been scored by underhand, secret, or unlawful means.

¶ **on the beat, 1.** engaged in sponging or swindling.

1876 W. Wright *Big Bonanza* 359: The saloon-keepers…have some…amiable gentlemen to deal with occasionally, but more frequently such as are "on the beat."

2. *Hobo.* by beating one's way.

1909 Munro *N.Y. Tombs* 69: The longest ride I ever knew anyone to make "on the beat" on a passenger train.

beat *adj.* **1.** worn to exhaustion, as weary as can be.—often (esp. before 20th C.) constr. with *out*.

[**1746** in *DA*: I…ordered him to put on faster. He told me his horse was about to beat out.] **1820–21* P. Egan *Life in London* 78: And never stood still till he was *dead beat!**…*"Dead beat"* or *"beat to a standstill!"* Common phrases in the Sporting World, when a man or a horse is…completely exhausted from over-exertion, or the constitution breaking down, as to give up the object in view. **1830** J. Martin *Narrative* 288: I have often been so beat out with long and tedious marching that I have fallen asleep while walking the road. **1845** Durivage & Burnham *Stray Subjects* 78: The steer crashed his head against the barn-door, and rolled over, dead beat, in a snow heap. **1859* in *F & H* I 157: The lad was getting beat, and couldn't a'gone much further. **1866** Dallas *Grinder Papers* 46: I meant to go to Barnum's, but I begin to feel beat out. **1868* C. Dickens, in *OEDS*: I was again dead beat at the end. **1869** "Thankfulla" *Du Le Telle* 9: As Aunt Stebbins said, we were "clean beat out." **1869** Stowe *Oldtown* 128: Well, she does look beat out. **1870** Duval *Big-Foot* 79: The boys…were…pretty well "beat out." **1884** "M. Twain" *Huck. Finn* ch. xli: So we cruised along upshore till we got kind of beat out. **1896** in S. Crane *Complete Stories* 260: Bill's little mar—she was plum beat when she come in with Crawford's crowd. **1907** S.E. White *Arizona Nights* 119: I'm not going to tell you how dead beat we got. **1936** *Amer. Mercury* (May) X: *My Chops is Beat*—when a brass man's lips give out. **1939** Goodman & Kolodin *Swing* 227: We were so beat with the jobs we had been playing and disgusted with what had happened. **1940** Zinberg *Walk Hard* 172: Man, you really are beat to your socks. **1945** Himes *If He Hollers* 137: You look beat. **1947** Hart *Gentleman's Agreement* (film): You look kind of beat. I'm worried about you. **1950** in F. Brown *Honeymoon* 9: Just I'm a little beat, Bob. **1952** Uris *Battle Cry* 233: Too beat out to think, even about home. **1960** Carpenter *Youngest Harlot* 119: I can't take it no more, Mom. I'm just clean beat out. **1966** Farrar *N.Y. Times Crosswords* XIV 37: Exhausted: slang…*dead beat*. **1985** N.Y.C. man, age 36: I'm totally beat.

2. [cf. *beats me* s.v. BEAT, *v.*] abashed; astonished; (*hence, occ.*) at a loss, helpless.

1835 Longstreet *Ga. Scenes* 212: Well, the law me, I'm clear beat! **1877** Bartlett *Amer.* (ed. 4) 35: We sometimes hear, especially from the mouths of old people, such expressions as, "I felt *beat*," "I was quite *beat*," i.e. utterly astonished. **1881** in *DA*: When the feller…got the light on the [railroad] pass…he was the wust beat feller you ever see. **1924** F.P. Adams *Velvet* 83: When you ain't here, I'm off the world…I'm beat. **1933–35** Lamson *We About to Die* 194: Boy, I'll bet that kid was very beat. I wonder what his old man had to say to him after that. What a hero that made of him! *Ibid.* 210: I listened to that old dude praying for me for two or three hours—and I was very beat.

3. without money; broke. Also (*emphatically*) **beat to the socks.** [In 1912 quot., sense seems to be "without paying a fare."]

[**1912** Ade *Babel* 108: Doc, have I got any of them boys travellin' beat in my system?] **1935** W. Winchell, in Tamony *Americanisms* (No. 24) 9: "Beat to the socks" (broke). "Stud is beat" (the chump hasn't a dime). **1940** in Oliver *Meaning of Blues* 319: Baby, I'm beat to the socks, do you dig just what I mean?/I've got a terrible financial embarrassment and I'm sticking with Jim Clean. **1942** *Yank* (Dec. 23) 19: A Negro outfit at Camp Claiborne, La.…"beat to my socks" indicates a lack of money.

4. desperate (for something); (*specif.*) *Narc.* suffering from withdrawal sickness, in need of heroin.

1939 in R.S. Gold *Jazz Talk* 13: *Beat:* tired, lacking anything, low in spirit. **1952** Ellson *Golden Spike* 21: Are you beat?…No, I had me a fix. **1954** in Wepman et al. *The Life* 39: You must be beat for conversation. **1961** Parkhurst *Undertow* xx: They're beat: they're beat for companionship, beat for company an' beat for understandin'.

5. Orig. *Jazz* or *Black E.* **a.** battered; worn-out; shabby; old; unattractive.

1938 *AS* XIII 314: "He looks *beat*." "He is *solid beat*." *Ibid.* 317: Beat means bedraggled, fagged out. **1939** in R.S. Gold *Jazz Talk* 13: He came from the beat side of town. **1942** *Pittsburgh Courier* (Jan. 17) 13: Hello, beat chicks! **1942** Z.N. Hurston, in *Amer. Mercury* (July) 86: Didn't I see you last night with dat beat chick scoffing a hot dog? Dat chick you had was beat to de heels....I said you was with a beat broad. **1952** "M. Roscoe" *Black Ball* 12: My car...*was* a little beat around the edges....A black '49 Merc that looked like it had seen a lot of miles, coming and going. **1955–57** Kerouac *On Road* 17: He wore a beat sweater and baggy pants. **1964** in Wepman et al. *The Life* 89: His vine [suit] was beat.

b. worthless; inferior; no good.—(in recent esp. *Stu.* use) used predicatively.

1944 Burley *Hndbk. Harlem Jive:* You're picking up nickels and laying down dimes, but your jive is beat and sour as limes. **1952** Ellson *Golden Spike* 244: *Beat stuff*—heroin of poor quality. **1953** W. Brown *Monkey on My Back* 38: They bought some junk from a cat in the park, but it was the real beat stuff (highly adulterated) and they couldn't even get a charge. **1956** Ross *Hustlers* 81: It was a real beat story, nothing much happened. *a***1968** in Haines & Taggart *Ft. Lauderdale* 102: I got into a beat Ford with two of my buddies. **1983** *N.Y. Daily News* (Mar. 25): Teentalk glossary...*beat*—out of style, worthless. **1984** *N.Y. Times* (June 1) B 4: In street parlance, a diluted drug is a "beat drug." **1989** *U.S. News & W.R.* (Apr. 10) 29: Some of them chase me away....Ain't that beat? **1989** Eble *Campus Slang* (Fall) 1: *Beat*—boring, unexciting: "Last night we went to a party but left after ten minutes because it was beat."

6. disillusioned; sad; world-weary. [In 1953 quot., as n.]

1947 in W.S. Burroughs *Letters* 11: What they want is some beat clerk who believes...other people don't like him. **1952** J.C. Holmes *Go* 122: I hooked up with this real beat hipster who'd been on benny since the army, see. **1953** W. Fisher *Waiters* 36: The "beat," the defiled, those besmeared by...life. **1956** Ross *Hustlers* 82: I didn't dig it at all. I left that movie beat. **1955–57** Kerouac *On Road* 73: The beat countermen and dishgirls...made no bones about their beatness. **1958** in C. Beaumont *Best* 110: So he and Bud...found a beat doll who thought the whole thing would be fun.

beat *v.* **1.** to cheat; swindle; bilk; trick.

1849 in Huntington *Songs Whalemen Sang* 48: Our noble commander [is] contriving some plan...for to beat/From us everything...fit for to eat. **1862** in Wightman *To Ft. Fisher* 65: Somebody-else's overcoat and all, by golly! "I never was so beat in all my life." **1872** in *Calif. Folk. Qly.* V (1946) 209: It "beat" many of the unsuspecting. **1873** in *OEDS:* Johnson...left...for the east after having beat several creditors. **1874** [Pember] *Metropolis* 60: That sucker...has been beat out of his money, and hasn't found it yet. **1875** Burnham *Counterfeits* 30: This is another branch of the deceit...of those who are ready to venture upon "*any* thing to beat" the U.S. collectors of revenue which justly accrues to the credit of the Government. **1883** Gerrish & Hutchinson *Blue and Gray* 214: No one thought it wrong to "beat" the sutler whenever chance permitted. **1883** Peck *Bad Boy* 213: Ma says she believes Pa was in partnership with the man to beat her out of her thousand dollars. **1887** M. Roberts *W. Avernus* 18: I was then...somewhat green...in the methods of "beating the road," or, more literally, cheating the [railway] company. **1900** Johnston *Hus'ling* 43: Who wants to beat you out of your sheep, you chump? I can pay for all I buy. **1930** [Conwell] *Thief* 11: A professional thief must not squawk on another thief even when he has been beat by the other. **1946** Dadswell *Hey, Sucker* 38: The concessionaires, with police protection, were given full privilege to "beat the suckers for everything you can get." **1970** Wexler *Joe* (film): I got beat last week. **1978** Kopp *Innocence* 36: They had taken me in by beating me out of my cigarettes. **1981** N.Y.C. street peddler: You don't get beat when you buy on the street! Check it out, check it out!

2. to succeed in robbing; to rob; *(hence)* to avoid paying (a debt, bill, fare, etc.).

1859 Matsell *Vocabulum* 10: "Beat the flat," rob the man. **1872** Crapsey *Nether Side of N.Y.* 60: There is a big watch movement factory here...and I have beat it already for a little but I'm waiting for some good pal to help me clean it out. **1882** Pinkerton *Bank-Robbers* 91: We heard [the bank] was "beat" last spring, and we thought we'd come on and see if it was easy to "do." **1892** L. Moore *Own Story* 168: I had been told if a person could "beat" this safe he would never want for money again. *Ibid.* 173: Dan said, "I have never beaten a strong-box." **1921** (quot. at PINCHER). **1932** V. Nelson *Prison Days & Nights* 26: I'd like to see you get clipped for something....There's nobody that can holler as loud as a thief who's been beat for something. **1946** J. Adams *Gags* 32: Whatcha tryin' to do, beat de cab bill? **1955** Q. Reynolds *HQ* 239: They grabbed the three just as they were about to "beat" a victim. **1963**

Williamson *Hustler!* 36: We had beat a milkman for a lot of butter.

3. [cf. *beat (one's) way,* below] *Hobo.* to steal a ride on (a train).—also constr. with *it.* Also absol.

1885 in Lummis *Letters* 240: He had "beat" the train from Manuelito, having imposed upon the conductor by some pitiful tale or other. **1891** in *OEDS:* To beat one's way, or to beat the conductor or the railroad, are equivalent phrases for travelling in the cars without paying any fare. **1894** in G. Shirley *W. of Hell's Fringe* 209: [He] claimed to be a bum trying to beat a ride. **1899** *Century* (June) 262 (caption): Beating a Passenger-Train. **1907** Peele *Without a Ticket* 66: You'd better be careful if you intend to beat to Pensacola. **1925–26** J. Black *Can't Win* 75: "Traveling?" he asked...."Beating it."

4. to avoid or evade (punishment or conviction).

1912 Lowrie *Prison* 159: We get ten or twelve men for "the rope" in a year, but most of 'em beat it on appeal. **1915–16** Lait *Beef, Iron & Wine* 173: I don't guess they was a guy in the town could a' beat that [charge] for me excep' you. **1916** Scott *17 Yrs.* 83: I...stood trial in two of the cases and "beat" (was acquitted in) both. **1926** Clark & Eubank *Lockstep* 42 [ref. to 1894]: I told him the only way for his brother to beat the "rap" was to get all the money he could and furnish bond and beat it. **1929** Hostetter & Beesley *It's a Racket* 219: Beat the rap—To escape punishment on a criminal charge. **1930** Lavine *3d Degree* 146: She was convicted on the larceny charge, but she "beat" the murder indictment. **1933–35** Lamson *About to Die* 195: There ain't no beef too tough to beat. **1972** Carr *Bad* 145: He beat the beef, and the authorities were mad.

5.a. to escape from (prison).

1902 Hapgood *Autobiog. of Thief* 43 [ref. to 1880's]: He had just escaped from the Catholic Protectory....I grew bolder, for if Jack could "beat" the "Proteck" in three months, I argued I could do it in twenty-four hours. **1912** Lowrie *Prison* 33: "Why is he wearing a red shirt?"..."Fer tryin' to beat the place." **1927** Finger *Frontier Ballads* 26: We can beat this old fort clean. **1927** Murphy *Gray Walls* 38: It was my intention to try and "beat the dump" (escape). **1928** Callahan *Man's Grim Justice* 115: If I can only make a friend out of that mutt...I'll be able to beat this joint. **1929** Booth *Stealing* 308: Say, Dan an' another guy beat the joint up above, yesterday. **1932** in *AS* (Feb. 1934) 26: *Beat a stir.* To escape from prison. **1967** [Beck] *Pimp* 259: "Shorty," what if I told you I could beat this joint?

b. [cf. *beat it,* below] to leave (a place) quickly.

1959 N.Y.C. teenager: Man alive, let's beat this dive.

6. *Mil.* to evade or avoid (duty), by or as by malingering.

1921 *Sentinel—15th Inf.* (Jan. 7) 8: My resolutions are—...That I'll beat no more duty.

¶ In phrases:

¶ **beat ass** to rush; *beat feet.*—usu. considered vulgar.

1974 L.D. Miller *Valiant* 21 [ref. to WWII]: Then he whirled around and beat ass back for the nearest fallen tree. **1985** M. Baker *Cops* 39: I couldn't wait to beat my ass down there to tell the other guy.

¶ **beat feet** to leave; clear out; *(hence)* to hurry.

1944 *Life* (May 15) 65: To "beat feet" means time to leave. **1967** Talbot *Chatty Jones* 100: Now beat feet, buster, and I mean fast. **1972** Casey *Obscenities* 42: This dink just/Got hit by a truck/...That beat feet after hitting him. **1974** Kingry *Monk & the Marine* 101: That way we could beat feet in case we had to. **1976** Conroy *Santini* 378: Vamoose, Sayonara, Adios, Au Revoir, and beat feet it out of here. **1982** "J. Cain" *Commandos* 353: Hit the red lights and beat feet. **1990** Poyer *Gulf* 384: If we don't make it back,...beat feet for the pickup.

¶ **beat hollow** to surpass, to outdo. Now *colloq.* or *S.E.*

*****1771** in *F & H* I (rev.) 171: Of town-tops taken in...beat hollow, etc. *****ca1800** R. Southey, in *OED:* This Scotch phenomenon, I trow, Beats Alexander hollow. *****1803** in J. Ashton *Eng. Satires on Napoleon* 223: Oh,...this beats the Egyptian Poisoning hollow! **1833** [S. Smith] *Pres. Tour* 15: The Bostonians beat every thing I've seen yet all holler. **1854** in McCauley *With Perry* 114: They are the neatest and prettiest I have ever seen—beats Niphon, China and Singapore all hollow. **1868** *Galaxy* (Mar.) 329: "This beats me hollow" said bright Apollo. *****1889** in *F & H* I 170: Germans beat the English hollow at drinking beer.

¶ **beat it** to go away, clear out (esp. *imper.*); to go or travel (now rare); to go in a hurry. [The assertion, occ. repeated, that Shakespeare employed this phrase in a modern slang sense in *Comedy of Errors* II i 74 and *2 Henry VI* III i 211 stems from a misreading of these lines.]

[*****1665** R. Head *Eng. Rogue* 37: Beating the hoof we overtook a cart.][*****1691** in *OED:* They all beated it on the hoof...to London.] [*****1698–99** "B.E." *Dict. Canting Crew: Hoof it,* or *beat it on the hoof,* to walk on Foot.] **1878** Mulford *Fighting Indians* 39: Most of the pack whirled about and speeded for the tepees, others stood irresolute and bewildered. The Gatling guns sang rapidly for a few seconds, and how those reds, so boastful at their war dance the night before, did "beat it!" **1904** *Life in Sing Sing* 261: *As I had plenty of the darb I blew away and beat it back to Chic.*...As I had plenty of money, I parted from them and returned to Chicago. **1906** H. Green *Actors' House* 8: We better beat it to the table, or it'll be wait in the hall for ours! **1907** *Army & Navy Life* (Dec.) 744: You won't do, beat it. **1907** in H.C. Fisher *A. Mutt* 19: Now when I give you the winner, beat it for the pool room. **1908** *Hampton's Mag.* 457: "Say, you got a drum in your ear, ain' you?"..."Sure."..."Then beat it," returns the Infant Prodigy gleefully. "Ma-a-a-a!" he bleats exultantly, "who's the goat?" **1909** in "O. Henry" *Complete Works* 1630: You better put an egg in your shoe and beat it. **1910** *Everybody's Mag.* (Jan.) 118: I'm going to beat it home. **1919** Z. Grey *Wheat* 169: We've got to beat it out of here. **1921** Casey & Casey *Gay-Cat* 159: I'd beat it while the beatin' was good. **1926** Tully *Jarnegan* 67: I've beat it six hundred miles on one meal. **1927** C. McKay *Harlem* 8: Sure, daddy. Let's beat it. **1957** Mayfield *Hit* 16: I think you'd better beat it, buddy. **1970** Boatright & Owens *Derrick Floor* 41: He...jumped in his old buckboard and beat it for Spindletop. **1992** Mamet *Glengarry Glen Ross* (film): Hit the bricks, pal, and beat it!

¶ **beat (one's) time, 1.** to confound (one).
1869 "M. Twain" *Innocents Abroad* ch. lvii: Well, you take it along—but I swear it beats my time, though. **1870** Ludlow *Heart of Cont.* 280: But d—d if you ain't a queer 'un? You beat my time, anyhow. **1871** "M. Twain" *Roughing It* 269: Great Neptune, *ain't* he guilty? This beats my time.

2. to steal (someone's) sweetheart.
1932 *AS* VII 329: *To beat one's time*—to "cut out" a rival by a more elaborate display of attention, presents or entertainment. **1949** Daves *Task Force* (film): I said give me time, not *beat* my time.

¶ **beat (one's) way** to get along by sponging, cheating, or swindling; (*specif.*) to make (one's) way by stealing rides on railroad trains, usu. in freight cars.
1873 *Harper's Mo.* (Dec.) 12: "Beatin' yourn way down?"..."No, Sir! Can't beat the people in this locality much." **1878** Mulford *Fighting Indians* 24: It is not very often that one can beat his way on the Western [rail]roads. **1883** Peck *Bad Boy* 288: [The prodigal son] started home, beating his way on trains, and he didn't know whether the old man would receive him with open arms or pointed boots. **1885** Siringo *Texas Cowboy* 25: I would have spent the dime for something to eat, and then beat my way across the river. **1891** Powell *Amer. Siberia* 77: Ha! ha! ha!...a man that can't beat his way in prison ought to be fried in oil! **1891** *Contemporary Rev.* (Aug.) 256: In the States almost all proficient roadsters "beat their way" on the railways. **1897** *Cosmopolitan* (Mar.) 568: There was a good many tramps a-beatin' their way through on the freight trains all the time. **1915** Braley *Workaday World* 101: But though I have to beat my way I'm game to make the trip.

¶ **beats me** [perh. fr. poker: "that hand beats mine"; also cf. BEAT, *adj.,* 2] "it baffles or puzzles me."
1864 in C.W. Wills *Army Life* 266: But...pitching tents under the noses of Rebel 32-pounders beats *me* and I guess it beats *them.* ***1882** in *OED:* "This beats me altogether," mused the lawyer. **1883** Hay *Bread-Winners* 123: Well, that beats me....I never seen anything yet that favored a hospital. **1911** Van Loan *Big League* 80: Beats me where he gets 'em all. **1913** *Sat. Eve. Post* (Mar. 15) 8: Those whiskers, that's what beats me! **1960** Sire *Deathmakers* 116: Beats the shit out of me. **1972** Pearce *Pier Head* 167: Beats the shit outta me. I think he's blown his stack.

¶ **beat the books** *Stu.* (see quot.).
1944 *Slanguage Dict.* 59: *Beating the books*—studying hard.

¶ **beat the breeze** [or **bull**] *bat the breeze* s.v. BREEZE.
1944 in Butterfield *Post Treasury* 434: Okay, I'll go back and beat the breeze. **1974** Miami Univ. student: We were just beating the bull.

¶ **beat the Dutch** to be amazing.—often used in negative conditional constructions.—in some vars. considered offensive. Also vars. Cf. *to beat the band,* below.
1775 in Whiting *Early Amer. Provs.* 124: Our cargoes of meat, drink and clothes beat the Dutch. *ca***1833** in Barrère & Leland *Dict. Slang* I 95: Well, if this don't beat the bugs! **1836** *Davy Crockett's Almanack* I (No. 3) 40: I can take the rag off...astonish the natives—and beat the Dutch all to smash. **1840** in Thornton *Amer. Glossary* I 51: Of all the goings on that I ever *did* hear of, this *beats the Dutch.* **1840** *Spirit of Times* (Nov. 21) 447: Well, if that don't cap all!...that beats the bugs. **1843** in Thornton *Amer. Glossary* I 51: [On seeing Niagara,] she exclaimed, "I declare, it *beats the bugs!*"—I fainted. **1845** N.J.T. Dana

Monterrey 15: The married officers for writing beat the Jews. **1871** Schele de Vere *Americanisms* 83: That *beats the Dutch*...to this day...is used whenever a peculiarly astonishing fact is announced. **1877** Bartlett *Americanisms* 35: There is a common expression, "That *beats Buck,*" synonymous with the Irish, "That bangs Banagher." **1883** *Harper's Mag.* (Nov.) 970: Well, ef that don't beat the Jews! **1905** in Opper *H. Hooligan* 105: It beats the Dutch. **1909** *DN* III 392: Be surprising. "That does *beat the cats.*" **1912** Field *Watch Yourself* 23: Well ef that don't beat the bugs. **1925–26** in *AS* II 348: An expression of surprise. "That beats the band." **1939** *AS* XIV 267: If it is startling news, it "beats the Jews" or "beats the Dutch." **1968** J.P. Miller *Race for Home* 243: Well...well, now, if that don't beat the Jews. Whupped to an inch of his life, and still worrying 'bout their dadgum battery.

¶ **beat the pup** (of a male) to masturbate.
1956 Resko *Reprieve* 70 [ref. to *ca*1940]: Louieeeee! Stop beatin ya pup!

¶ **beat the sheets** to sleep soundly.
1954 *I Love Lucy* (CBS-TV): I can see I ain't the only one that's been a-beatin' the sheets.

¶ **beat the sidewalk** to walk a police beat.
1917–20 Dreiser *Newspaper Days* 268 [ref. to 1893]: Before that he had "beat the sidewalk," as he said, traveled a beat.

¶ **beat [up] (one's) gums** [or **chops**] Orig. *Jazz* or *Black E.* to talk loudly or to no purpose; to chatter; to complain. See also *bump (one's) gums* s.v. GUM[1].
1935 W. Winchell, in Tamony *Americanisms* (No. 24) 9: "Beating up his gums off time" (talking out of turn). **1942** Z.N. Hurston, in *Amer. Mercury* (July) 85: Last night when I left you, you was beating up your gums and broadcasting about how hot you was....I was just beating up my gums when I said I was broke. **1942** *Harper's Mag.* (July 9): Stop beating your gums, brother. **1943** *AS* (Apr.) 155: *You Ain't Just Beatin' Your Gums.* Terms denoting satisfaction and agreement. **1944** *AS* XX 147 [Army]: *Beat Your Gums.* Talk a lot about something. **1946** Mezzrow & Wolfe *Really Blues* 86: Frankie...used to drop in on Mike to beat up his chops a while. **1954** Ellson *Owen Harding* 16: He gave me a long, weird look and then began beating his gums with Pooch. **1956** Longstreet *Real Jazz* 150: *To beat your chops* is to talk. **1963** Rubin *Sweet Daddy* 58: No use beating your chops. **1967** in Parks *G.I. Diary*. **1980** Manchester *Darkness* 343: We kept beating our gums by candlelight, hour after hour. **1982** *Sports Talk* (WKGN radio) (July 16): You don't want to hear me beating my gums all night.

¶ **can you beat it** [or **that**]? "isn't that extraordinary?" Now *colloq.* or *S.E.*
1917 in *OEDS:* They pay me money for that. Can you beat it? **1919** S. Lewis *Free Air* 97: In the soft, tree-dimmed dooryard among dry, blazing plains it seemed indecent to go on growling "Gee," and "Can you beat it?" **1924** Howard *What They Wanted* 147: Can you beat it? He ain't even got the nerve to speak to her.

¶ **to beat the band** to an unsurpassable degree. Also vars. Cf. *beat the Dutch,* above.
1887 Francis *Saddle & Moccasin* 124: The Apaches were out to beat hell. **1897** Norris *Vandover* 321: Ida was rigged up to beat the band. **1906** in McCay *Little Nemo* 70: Work your strange power on the little pest to beat the band. **1972–75** W. Allen *Feathers* 208: Looking "spiffy" then, is quite a compliment, and one who does is liable to be dressed to "beat the band." **1982** E. Johnson, on *Atlanta Braves Baseball* (WKGN radio) (June 28): It's still raining to beat the band here....Boy, we have never seen it rain so hard.

beat artist *n. Police.* a swindler.
1971–73 Sheehy *Hustling* 68: That beat artist? He's got himself a home in Westchester. **1976** *N.Y. Post* (Sept. 10) 3: On Tuesday two white guys got beat for a dollar....They bought a joint from a known beat artist. **1965–78** J. Carroll *B. Diaries* 83: Lots of beat artists, but two P.R.s...are trustworthy enough.

beater *n.pl. Und.* (see quot.).
1859 Matsell *Vocabulum* 10: *Beaters* Boots.

beatnik *n.* [*Beat* Generation + -NIK, infl. by Russ. *Sputnik;* coined by San Francisco columnist Herb Caen early in 1958; see R. Rex, "The Origin of *Beatnik,*" *AS* L (1975), pp. 329–30] a member of the Beat Generation; (*broadly*) a bohemian. Now *S.E.*
1958 in *OEDS:* [San Francisco] is the home and the haunt of America's Beat generation and these are the Beatniks—or new barbarians. **1959** in Parkinson *Casebook on Beat* 194: Beatniks and Tradition. **1966** *English Studies* XLVII 54: The typical Bohemian has become the beatnik poet or pseudo-philosopher. **1971** B. Cook *Beat Generation* 91:

Beatniks and Hipsters. **1973** Lucas, Katz & Huyck *Amer. Graffiti* 68: Yeah, beatniks are losers. **1979** D. Thoreau *City at Bay* 22: The patrol car drove slowly along upper Grant Avenue, passing the famous haunts of the beatnik era. *a***1988** C. Adams *More Straight Dope* 155: Probably…you are some kind of hippie beatnik who would rather live in the forest eating roots and berries than hold down a job like a man.

beat-nuts *n.* [*beat* + NUT 'testicle'] *So.* a chronic masturbator.—usu. considered vulgar.

1975 C.W. Smith *Country Music* 93: "He become a beat-nuts or something?"…"Well…He seems a lot…simpler, anyway."

beat-off *n.* **1.** an act or instance of masturbation.—usu. considered vulgar.

1972 Jenkins *Semi-Tough* 170: They had a beat-off contest. **1977** *Nat. Lampoon* (Aug.) 36: Mass public beat-offs are shaking up *St. Paul, Minn.* **2.** *Stu.* (see quot.).

1970–72 in *AS* L 56: *Beat-off, n.* Unattractive, repulsive person, one who is so unappealing sexually that it is thought he or she must resort to masturbation as the only available sexual activity.

beat off *v.* (of a man) to masturbate; (*hence*) to loaf, waste one's time. Also *refl.*—usu. considered vulgar.

1962 Mandel *Mainside* 357: Not beat off in your sack or cut classes. **1968** P. Roth *Portnoy* 18: I…beat off standing up into a urinal. **1968** Baker et al. *CUSS* 78: *Beat off.* Waste time, not study. **1970** Segal *Love Story* 12: What does it look like I'm doing, Felt, beating off? **1970** Calley & Sack *Lieut. Calley* 66: It beats beating off—no, I wouldn't even say so. **1972** in Bernstein & Woodward *President's Men* 229: Quit beating yourself off, kid,…and get some information.

beat-up *n. Mil. Av.* an instance of stunting low; (*hence*) a strafing attack.

*****1940** in *OEDS:* Comes back over the 'drome, above the heads…twenty feet off the ground.…The boys call this a "beat-up." **1946** G.C. Hall, Jr. *1000 Destroyed* 269: Here is the way the London *Daily Express* viewed the beat-ups. *Ibid* 270: The beat-ups were interspersed with escort missions.

beat-up *adj.* **1.** tired out; exhausted. Cf. BEAT, BEAT OUT.

1863 *Blackwood's Mag.* XC 766: [I'm] bate up wid foitin. *****1914** in *OEDS:* We were all beat up after four days of the hardest soldiering you ever dreamt of. **1944** Stiles *Big Bird* 40: I felt as beat up as if we'd gone all the way. **1944** *Slanguage Dict.* 59: *Beat up*—tired out; exhausted. **1951** in *DAS:* Finally beat up as were, we…decided to return to camp.

2. battered, as if having been beaten up; (*hence*) shabby, worn-out, dilapidated, old.

1930–35 Lamson *About to Die* 187: When his wife sees him all beat up that way she lets out an awful screech I guess. **1939** Goodman & Kolodin *Swing* 73: Over on one side was an old beat-up piano. **1944** Kendall *Service Slang* 57: *Beat up*…In a condition for salvage. **1944** in Himes *Black on Black* 240: Why go to hell, you beat-up biddy! **1946** *AS* XXI 251: *Beat up.* An adjectival phrase of all work meaning damaged, worn-out, or of unimpressive appearance. **1955** Abbey *Brave Cowboy* 34: Where's that old beat-up Dodge of yours? **1960** Bannon *Journey* 39: She Likes to laze around in nothing but an old beat-up bathrobe. **1960–61** Steinbeck *Discontent* 51: A beat-up tarot deck of fortune-telling cards. **1963** Horwitz *Candlelight* 35: Like the head on a beat-up Roman coin I bought. **1967** Shepard *Red Cross* 88: A beat-up leather bag. **1977** Harnack *Under Wings* 20: Their car was a beat-up 1939 Chevrolet. **1980** W.C. Anderson *BAT-21* 184: A beat-up old geezer twice my age.

beat up *v. Mil. Av.* **1.** to fly low over, esp. in order to create consternation.

*****1940** in *AS* XVI 76 [ref. to RAF]: *To Beat Up.* To dive on a friendly flying field as practice, a gesture of triumph or sheer joie-de-vivre. **1944** Liebling *Back to Paris* 141: They sometimes drop low and "beat up" gun positions, airdromes, [etc.]. **1964** Caidin *Everything But Flak* 31: To Crewdson this meant beating up farms with crop-dusting planes, and the thrill of brushing his landing gear through trees. **1984** Trotti *Phantom* 250: The 101st Airborne had a bunch of these [observation helicopters], which they used for beating up the elephant grass.

2. to strafe. [Early quots. ref. to WWII.]

1946 G.C. Hall, Jr. *1000 Destroyed* 267: I was beating up this drome when I saw building and some sort of pole by it. **1961** G. Forbes *Goodbye to Some* 13 [ref. to WWII]: Here and there are little bomb bursts to show where we have beaten up something on the ground. **1963** E.M. Miller *Exile* 45: The Guard dogfaces were flying vintage prop-jobs down the valleys beating up the trains and the flak installations.

beat up on *v. Journ.* to attack verbally.

1980 in Safire *Good Word* 286: I was shook up at the usage of a *New York Times* editorialist who denounced the mayor for "beating up on judges." **1990** *New Republic* (Nov. 19) 20: [They] might well wonder, whether, to borrow the catch phrase most favored by U.S. politicians beating up on Japanese business practices, the playing field was level.

beau *n.* **1.** a beautiful woman.

1833 in Jackson *Early Songs of Uncle Sam* 70: O what a beau my granny was.

2. var. of BO.

beau-catcher *n.* a loose curl in a woman's hair.

*****1818** in *OEDS:* A girl…twisting her hair into rings, which they term "beau-catchers." *ca***1884** Campbell *My Partner* 78: An' one freckle-faced thing, with big beau-catchers, turned up her nose like that.…I flew at them beau-catchers, and tore some of them out by the roots. *****1909** Ware *Passing English* 23: *Beau-catcher*…a flat hook-shaped curl, after the Spanish manner gummed on each temple, and made of the short temple hair, spelt sometimes *bow-catcher*.…Now obsolete on this side of the Pyrenees.

beaucoup *n.* [< F] a large number or amount; plenty.—usu. constr. with *of.* Also vars.

1918 Swan *My Co.* 47: Have a good look boys; it's the last femme you'll see for beaucoup de weeks. **1925** Bailey *Shanghaied* 168 [ref. to 1899]: "Beaucoup of time," he returned gruffly. "I ken fetch shore, fog or no." **1967** Beck *Pimp* 95: I'll have "boo-koos" in a month. **1962–68** in B. Jackson *In the Life* 190: I've had a beaucoup of them. **1974** *Univ. Tenn.* student: "I've seen bookoos of those things."…"I've known that expression since at least 1960. **1993** *Unsolved Mysteries* (NBC-TV): He had beaucoups of money.

beaucoup *adj.* Esp. *Mil.* **1.** very much or very many. Also vars. [1862 quot. sugg. early use in Amerindian English pidgin.]

1862 in T. Jones *Letters* 34 [Ark.]: The first thing they seen was the Indians. They were coming yelping like mad devils saying, "Bookkoo shoot Wagons [field pieces] kill everybody." **1918** *Sat. Eve. Post* (Nov. 9) 90: We've been spendin' *beaucoup* francs lately for Uncle Sam. **1918** in Day *Camion Cartoons* 58: All the time we were there it was "beaucoup" work. **1919** Glock *316th Inf.* 91: There was "bow-koo" this and that—especially that. **1920** *Hicoxy's Army* 98: Oatmeal with bo-coo milk. **1928** Wharton *Squad* 281: For them we'd had billets and buckcoo frauleins. **1944** in *Best from Yank* 20: Take *beaucoup* grenades. **1944** Kapelner *Lonely Boy* 51: I've had beaucoup ensigns and captains. **1945** *Sat. Rev. of Lit.* (Nov. 3) 7: Man, I really drank beaucoup vino last night! **1949** Quigley *Corsica* 55: "Lots of flak on the target?" "Beaucoup." **1958** Berger *Crazy in Berlin* 426: I bet you beaucoup marks that's what we got to ride. **1970** Whitmore *Memphis–Nam* 67: Con Thien meant beaucoup pain to any grunt. **1979** *Business Week* (July 16) 82: I think there are just *beaucoup* opportunities [in energy]. **1994** *N.Y. Times* (Jan. 12) D 5: The…commercials eschew the traditional trappings.…There is, however, beaucoup sex.

2. big, long, significant; very much of a. Also vars. [Early quots. ref. to WWI.]

1919 Fiske *350th Inf.* 110 [ref. to 1918]: So on the night of October 29th we polished our hobnails on a "beaucoup" hike to Rougegoutte. **1920** Riggs & Platt *Battery F* 23 [ref. to 1918]: Arriving here at noon we ate our lunch and prepared for a "Bokoo" inspection by General Fleming and Colonel Morse. **1974–77** Heinemann *Close Quarters* 27: You boo-coo VC, you lyin'…dink. **1992** Ad on WBIR-TV (Knoxville, Tenn.) (Sept. 28): This fall there's a "Boo" "Coo" [*sic*] balloon bonus!

3. excellent; first-rate.

1920–21 Witwer *Leather Pushers* 55: She's a *beaucoup* looker all right. **1929** Milburn *Hobo* 220: To string with me you gotta be a moocher that's boo coo. **1929** *Our Army* (Aug.) 42: "Fort McPherson is a beaucoup place to soldier in," declared a doughboy of the Twenty-second Infantry.

beaucoup *adv.* very much; (*usu.*) very. Also vars. [Early quots. ref. to WWI.]

1921 *Amer. Legion Wkly.* (May 20) 10: I like that beaucoup. **1927** *Amer. Leg. Mo.* (May) 23: You'll be bokoo sorry when I'm gone. **1965** *N.Y. Times* (Nov. 3) 2: South Vietnam's French colonial heritage is represented in the vocabularies of most American soldiers by two words—"Finis" and "Beaucoup." The latter is sometimes used in such exotic locutions as "It's beaucoup hot out here." **1966–67** P. Thomas *Mean Streets* 105: You was in there a beaucoup long-ass time. **1973** S. Roth *Sand in the Wind* 55: It wasn't "bucoo" cold, but it was a lot colder than what he'd been drinking. *Ibid.* 169: We'd have to be bucoo careful.

beaut *n.* **1.** a beautiful person or thing. Also vars.

1866 in *DA*: Hopeful is not a beauty, and he knows it; and though some of the rustic wits call him "Beaut," he is well aware that they intend it for irony. **1895** Wood *Yale Yarns* 231: A Miss Standish,—a beaut. **1896** Ade *Artie* 7: One on each arm, see?…They was beauts too. **1898** Kountz *Baxter's Letters* 3: I…bought a hunting-knife with a nickel-plated handle. It was a beaut, and stood me three fifty. **1899** *Memoirs of Dolly Morton* 78: There'll be a mouthful for you, my bronze beaut. **1906–07** Ade *Slim Princess* 50: You'll never break a woman's heart by telling her that she is a beaut. **1918** *Chi. Sun Trib.* (Feb. 17) V (unp.): Lots o' men get a slant at a beaut an' what happens in their insides they mistake for love. **1950** Bissell *Stretch on the River* 24: She really had an excellent pair of beauts [i.e., breasts]…and very thrilling legs. **1955** L. Shapiro *Sixth of June* 157: There's one that's a beaut. What's her name, baby? **1955–57** Kerouac *On Road* 182: A brand-new convertible. "This one is a beaut!" **1968** D.L. Phillips *Small World* 83: A charming…girl.…"She's a real beaut…and a great morale-booster." **1992** *Simpsons* (Fox-TV): Miss Montana—a beaut from Butte!

2. that which is a splendid example (of its kind), *esp.*, an adept person; an impressive or powerful thing, such as a blow.

1899 Gunter *M.S. Bradford* 73: It's…a beaut. **1899** A.H. Lewis *Sandburrs* 1: I'll show you a bute. **1901** J. London *God of His Fathers* 122: Ain't it a beaute? **1903** T.W. Jackson *Slow Train* 49: She had a kind of a Montana voice. It was a Beaut. **1903** A.H. Lewis *Boss* 272: I know that gang of card sharps…an' they're a bunch of butes at that. **1904** in "O. Henry" *Complete Works* 1437: Ain't it [a black eye] a beaut? **1905* in Wilkes *Austral. Colloq.* 25: He's a bute.…Quick as a flash; his nerves are all on ball-bearings. **1907** in McCay *Little Nemo* 86: We are going to have a storm, and it's going to be a beaut. **1910** *N.Y. Eve. Jour.* (Apr. 1) 19: McGraw…stung a beaut to centre that enabled Murray to hike over the pan. **1918** *DN* V 22: *Beaut, n.* a thing of beauty; anything which excels in own quality. "A beaut of a snow-storm." **1930** in J.T. Farrell *Calico Shoes* 190: That right had been a beaut. **1953** Eyster *Customary Skies* 165: I got me a beaut of a blister. **1960** MacDonald *Slam the Big Door* 37: He busted Mueller a beaut right in the eye. **1963** D. Tracy *Brass Ring* 466: I hope you'll think it's a beaut but you may scream. **1975** McCaig *Danger Trail* 31: That's a beaut of a shiner you're wearing. **1978** Kopp *Innocence* 35: Don't forget your cigarette case.…It's really a beaut. **1982** W. Safire, in *N.Y. Times Mag.* (Jan. 2, 1983) 6: *Skell* is a beaut of a bit of slang.

3. (used in ref. to **(1)** and **(2)**, above, but in a strongly ironic sense).

1866 (quot. at **(1)** above). **1895** Gore *Stu. Slang* 6: Five flunks…that's a beaut of a record. **1895** Townsend *Fadden* 14: 'Is face was all blood from where 'is nut was cracked…an' holy gee 'e was a bute! **1897** in Hoppenstand *Dime N. Detective* 81: You've got a beaut of an eye, Dick. **1903** Harriman *Homebuilders* 68: "Say, he'd be a beaut at a dance, wouldn't he?"…"Don't make fun of him, Jake." **1905** W.S. Kelly *Lariats* 239: Ain't he a bute, gals? **1930** Graham & Graham *Queer People* 95: Our glorious press. Aren't they beauts? **1977** *Sports Illustrated* (July 4) 62: He would try to turn guys' stomachs. He had no scruples. He was a beaut.

beautiful *adj.* clever or shrewd; wonderful; (*also*) pleasing or admirable. [In recent usage assoc. esp. with the entertainment industry.]

*1863 in T. Taylor *Plays* 168: Oh, beautiful, beautiful!…It would be a sin to drop such a beautiful milch cow [source of profit]. **1903** *DN* II 306: *Beautiful, adj.* Excellent. **1967–68** von Hoffman *Parents Warned Us* 46: He came out of that trip a beautiful human who only sells good shit now. **1978** Strieber *Wolfen* 153: Oh, Morty was beautiful too. Smarter than Dick Neff. **1985** B. Griffith *Having Fun Yet* 33: Doc, you're a beautiful dude. **1991** Hasburgh *NYPD Mounted* (film): "Are you OK?" "I'm beautiful."

beauty *n.* **1.** a remarkable person.

1832 [M. St.C. Clarke] *Sks. of Crockett* 144: Stranger, you are a beauty.…I'd vote for you.

2. *Narc.* BLACK BEAUTY.

1967 Colebrook *Cross* 42: Their acceptance of trying pot, stuff, coke, greenies, acid, or beauties.

beauty-mark *n.* one's face or appearance. Also **beauty spot**.

1864 in Stanard *Letters* 41: One…fell…and *almost broke her* nose. Poor girl, I guess it will *spoil* her *beauty spot* and…teach her a lesson. **1921** Casey *Gay-Cat* 60: I'd know your beauty-mark a block away.

beaver *n.* **1.** *West.* a fellow, a geezer.

1833 J. Hall *Harpe's Head* 135: You are the *severest old beaver* to *tote* wood that I've seen for many a long day. **1847** Ruxton *Life in Far West*

10: Any 'bacca in your bag, Bill? This beaver feels like chawing. **1850** Garrard *Wah-to-Yah* 207: Do'ee hyar, this beaver went down to Taos without bringin' a pint of "baldface." *Ibid.* 216: Why, the old beaver says as he was in hell once. **1866** in *DA*: The soldiers called each others "gophers" and "beavers." **1872** G. Gleason *Specter Riders* 16: This beaver never did, that's sartin. **1896** Brown *Parson* 12: I'll bet you a penny he'll be a mixed sort of a beaver! **1958** Traver *Anatomy of Murder* 216: If this talky old beaver wants to prolong the agony old Smoky ain't going to spoil his fun.

2. [fr. the use of beaver pelts, in lieu of money, in barter] *Fur Trapping.* money. Now *hist.*

1847 Ruxton *Life in Far West* 54: Ho, boys, hyar's a deck, and hyar's the beaver (rattling the coin). **1949** Guthrie *Way West* 35: He would saw open the big log where he had cached his beaver, banks being what they were.

3. a beard; (*hence*) a bearded man; (*occ.*, as in *a*1991 quot.) a mustache. [A game called "Beaver," in which points are scored for sighting bearded men, arose about 1922 in Great Britain; see *OEDS*.]

1871 in N. Cohen *Long Steel Rail* 52: Out into the daylight darts the Pullman train,/Student's beaver [is] ruffled the merest grain. **1910** *Variety* (Aug. 20) 13: I was…glancing at the beautiful beaver he carried. It was some pad. **1910** in *OEDS*: He provided a list of celebrated clean-shaven men and also of celebrated beavers, as bearded men are technically termed. **1934** Weseen *Dict. Slang* 136: *Beaver*—A man with a luxuriant natural beard; the beard itself. **1936** Levin *Old Bunch* 477: "Beaver!" Lou claimed, spotting J. Hamilton Lewis. **1942** H. Miller *Roofs of Paris* 196: Johnny…would look ever without his beaver. **1943** J. Mitchell *McSorley's* 90: "By God, it's the bearded lady!" He followed her to the elevator, shouting, "Beaver! Beaver!" **1947** *Merrie Melodies* (animated cartoon): What's up, beaver puss? **1958** Hailey & Castle *Runway* 20: Dun was…fingering his great bush of a mustache.…The little man [asked], "What do they call you—Beaver?" **1960** *Perry Mason* (CBS-TV): "Ever try a beaver?" "A beard? I'm not the type." **1968** E.M. Parsons *Fargo* 31: Didn't recognize you without all that beaver. **1980** Ciardi *Browser's Dict.* 21: *Beaver*…A cry in the group play of children, the first one to see a fully whiskered man crying "Beaver!" *a*1991 Kross *Splash One* 60: Roscoe, is that you behind that beaver?

4. a hat (of any sort). [Cf. *OED*.]

1885 Byrn *Greenhorn* 6: I grabbed my beaver (made of straw, though). **1894** Bridges *Arcady* 22: His plug, dicer, beaver, tile—don't you know your mother tongue?

5.a. a woman's pubic hair; (*hence*) the vulva.—usu. considered vulgar.

1927 *Immortalia* 167: She took off her clothes/From her head to her toes,/And a voice at the keyhole yelled, "Beaver!" **1965** Reuss *Field Collection* 185: "Beaver" (female genitalia or pubic hair). **1966** Rimmer *Harrad Exper.* 241: Only in nudist magazines do they have a beaver. **1969** in Bouton *Ball Four* 38: While "The Star-Spangled Banner" was played you could run under the stands and look up at all kinds of beaver. **1970** *N.Y. Times* (Apr. 19) II 11: "Persons Under 17 Not Admitted"…—why? because of all those naked boobs and beavers? **1970** Southern *Blue Movie* 135: The assistant makeup man adroitly and selectively thinned the beaver. **1972** R. Wilson *Forbidden Words* 32: *Beaver*. The female pubic hair. A *beaver shot* is a photograph showing the pubic hair, and a *split beaver* is a photo in which the lips of the vulva are open and visible. **1973** *TULIPQ* (coll. B.K. Dumas): Female sexual organs: *beaver*. **1974** Lahr *Trot* 63: My left leg is kneeing beaver. **1976** Atlee *Domino* 119: The beaver split.…The gaping vagina, kid. **1976–77** Kernochan *Dry Hustle* 36: Hey, you know Roxanne with the red beaver? **1978** Fisher & Rubin *Special Teachers* 27: A tiny plastic woman with…[a] wide-open beaver. **1983** Ehrhart *VN-Perkasie* 178: Wall-to-wall beavers. Two-piece bikinis with little hairs stickin' out around the crotch.

b. an erotic film, magazine, or the like, that features female nudity; (*specif.*) a film featuring female nudity but not explicit scenes of sexual intercourse.—usu. attrib. See also BEAVER SHOT.

1967 *Playboy* (Nov.) 178: Beaver films [are] girlie flicks of completely nude females without any sexual activity. **1970** Southern *Blue Movie* 26: A [cinematic] view of the pubic region—the "beaver shot" it was called—occurred only as a brief glimpse. **1970** *Nat. Lampoon* (Apr.) 58: Let's stem the tide of French postcards, Tijuana bibles, lewd photos, beaver books and rubber novelties. **1971** *N.Y. Times* (Jan. 3) 23: She began turning out the sort of nudie movies called beavers; then…she graduated...to pure porn. **1971** *Playboy* (July) 182: She...appears to have few hangups about sex, discussing how she has strolled nude on beaches and appeared in early "beavers." **1972** Wambaugh *Blue Knight* 25: She [a stripteaser] was back down on Main Street competing with beaver movies between reels. **1974** Stone *Dog Soldiers* 3: I'm back at the theater...for a brand new beaver special which is the most depressing flick this place has put on yet. **1976** H. Ellison *Sex Misspelled* 29: But he has a stack of beaver magazines hidden away in his work bench. **1978** *New West* (Mar. 27) 18: Nor did the TV audience get to see the pink, or beaver, shots so delightedly being shown by the prosecutor to the five-woman, one-man jury.

c. a young woman or young women.

1968 *Harper's* (June) 72: This left plenty of time to scan the stands for "beaver"—the team's euphemism for buxom Southern belles....The coach would usually send a bat boy up to ask the beaver for a date. **1968–70** *Current Slang* III & IV 8: *Beaver,* n. A girl.—College males, Kansas. **1975** Dills *CB Slanguage* 16: *Beaver:* woman or girl. **1976** Whelton *CB Baby* 15: The prettiest little beaver you ever eyeballed is sitting in the driver's seat. **1976–79** Duncan & Moore *Green Side Out* 106: There's a beaver in the control tower. **1981** Cody & Perry *Iron Eyes* 166 [ref. to *ca*1940]: Another such ready-for-action beauty was among the "bevy of beavers," as [Errol] Flynn called them, at the fund-raising party for Bibs Brave. **1979–82** Gwin *Overboard* 152: Got a beaver, thass a roger. Seen her hitcherhikin'...for the Intercoastal. **1985** Knoxville, Tenn., man, age 36: That's one tough-lookin' little beaver. **1992** *Geraldo* (synd. TV series): Are there any commercial beavers [i.e., prostitutes] out there?

6. EAGER BEAVER.

1952 MacDonald *Damned* 136: He was a real beaver, and then all of a sudden he goes flat.

¶ In phrases:

¶ **make beaver** *Fur Trapping.* to hurry, "make tracks."

1850 Garrard *Wah-to-Yah* 114: With the skins under my arm, I bowed myself out, and "made beaver" for Mr. Bent's lodge, on the way passing through a bottom in hopes of finding deer.

¶ **shoot a beaver, 1.** (of a man) to look surreptitiously under a woman's skirt; to seek a glimpse of a woman's pubic area.

1969 in Bouton *Ball Four* 37: I better explain about beaver-shooting. A beaver-shooter is, at bottom, a Peeping Tom. It can be anything from peering over the top of the dugout to looking up dresses to hanging from the fire escape on the twentieth floor to look in a window. *Ibid.* 38: Now some people might look down on this sort of activity. But in baseball if you shoot a particularly good beaver you are...a folk hero of sorts. **1969** *Current Slang* I & II 29: *Shoot a beaver* v. To catch a glimpse of a girl's thigh or undergarments.—College males, South Dakota. **1980** Gould *Ft. Apache* 192: N.G. on those revolutionaries we got....The only thing they shoot is beaver.

2. (of a woman) to expose to view the vulva and pubic area; (*broadly*) to sit with the legs outspread to attract attention.

1974 Kingry *Monk & Marines* 100: She had just finished with one marine and looked over at me and shot me a beaver and gave it a pat and smiled. **1976** New Brunswick, N.J., woman, age 24: She was sitting there with her skirt hiked up, shooting beavers all over the office. **1976** Knapp & Knapp *One Potato* 79: Shoots beavers at all the boys! **1980** *Penthouse* (Dec.) 50: Whenever she had the chance, she would...shoot me a beaver.

¶ **split beaver** the vulva with the labia spread; an erotic photograph of this.

1969 Bartell *Group Sex* 66: Some magazines feature a fad called "split beaver"—closeups of females, wearing garter belts and stockings or nothing at all, pictured seated, sprawling, or kneeling, front or rear view, with legs spread. **1970** Landy *Underground Dict.* 175: *Split beaver*...A photograph of a woman with her legs spread, showing the vagina and pubic area. **1970** *Playboy* (Nov.) 223: Pubic hair was also being exhibited, and this led promptly to the "split beaver," in which the camera was trained almost exclusively on the vaginal lips. **1972** *Nat. Lampoon* (July) 50: At home scrutinizing split-beaver magazines. **1990** L. Nieman *Boomer* 42: Hard-core porn. We were talking split beaver here.

¶ (in prov. phrase):

1969 Jessup *Sailor* 382: It's going to blow cold as a beaver's ass.

beaver *v.* [app. sugg. by phr. to *chew up*] *USAF.* (see 1956 quot.).

1956 Heflin *USAF Dict.* 78: *Beaver,* v. tr. To shoot holes in an *aircraft. Slang.* **1989** T. Blackburn *Jolly Rogers* 115 [ref. to WWII]: It

took...four...Corsairs...4,200...rounds to beaver the Betty out of the sky.

beaver dream *n. Fur Trapping.* a delusion.

1904 J. London *Faith* 20: It took me two months to do it, but I did it. And that's no beaver dream.

beaver patrol *n.* **1.** the act of girl watching; (*hence*) a group of young men seeking women.

1969 *Current Slang* I & II 8: *Beaver Patrol,* n. Girl watching.—College males, Washington State. **1971** Dahlskog *Dict.* 6: *Beaver patrol, on*...cruising around on the lookout for a sex partner; girl watching with a view toward more interesting developments. **1973** *Playboy* (Sept.) 58: The Beaver Patrol. A 15-year-old girl posing in the nude and a 19-year-old college student photographing her were arrested...in Santa Clara County, California. **1974** Lahr *Trot* 223: Back to the Beaver Patrol. **1976** Lieberman & Rhodes *CB Handbook* 123: *Beaver*—A girl. *Beaver Hunt*—Looking for girls. *Beaver Patrol*—Looking for girls. **1978** Caption on T-shirt seen in N.Y.C.: Beaver Patrol.

2. [sugg. by EAGER BEAVER] a team of enthusiastic workers. *Joc.*

1974 Bernstein & Woodward *President's Men* 178: Both had been members of the "Beaver Patrol," composed of bright, fiercely loyal young men brought to the White House from the advertising and marketing worlds by Haldeman.

beaver scout *n.* [joc. allusion to Boy Scout rank *eagle scout*] EAGER BEAVER. *Joc.*

1955 Archibald *Aviation Cadet* 63: Now he's getting eager....A beaver scout.

beaver shot *n.* a glimpse or view of a woman's pubic area, esp. the unclothed pudenda. See also BEAVER, *n.*, 5.b.

1970 *Current Slang* V 19: *Beaver Shooting,* n. (also *shooting beaver*) a practice popular among undergraduates that involves contriving unobtrusively to look up the skirt of a female. Clear views are known as (good) *beaver shots.* **1980** Conroy *Lords of Discipline* 460: Beaver shot. Ten o'clock. Yellow dress. **1986** "J. Cain" *Suicide Squad* 22: Did they treat you to any beaver shots?

beavertail *n.* [sugg. by shape and surface texture] a blackjack.

1972 Wambaugh *Blue Knight* 242: I put my gun in my holster, reached for my beavertail, and sapped him across the left collarbone. **1983** Helprin *Winter's Tale* 521: Brass knuckles,...spiked beaver tails, blackjacks.

beazle *n.* [origin unkn.] *Stu.* a worthless fellow.

1931 Lorimer *Streetcars* 224: "He—he said the same thing to you," she gasped. "The beazle!" **1933–34** Lorimer *Stag Line* 46: Terrible beazle....Who would want him?

be-back *n. Retail Sales.* a potential customer who tells a salesperson that he or she may return at a later time to actually make a purchase.

1982 R. Sutton *Don't Get Taken* 101: These "be-backs" are the bane of car salesmen....Nine out of ten times a "be-back" won't ever be back.

bebop *v.* [fr. S.E. *bebop,* infl. by BOP] **1.** to brawl, esp. as a member of a teenage street gang.

1965 C. Brown *Manchild* 108 [ref. to 1950's]: They said that bebopping was...out of style. *Ibid.* 141: Gus had lost one of his arms bebopping in Brooklyn.

2. to walk in a jaunty or cocky manner; (*broadly*) to go or come.

1977 *Dallas Times Herald* (June 26) 2I: I would have gone bebopping in there...without really knowing much about it. **1978** Selby *Requiem* 8: Tyrone bebopped his way down the subway steps. **1979** D. Milne *Second Chance* 15: Cool. Let's bebop over right now. **1984** *Time* (Nov. 5) 15: This old boy just bebopped up to me and said, "Good morning." **1990** *Cops* (Fox-TV): Why'd you turn around and bebop the other way when you saw us?

bebopper *n. Pris.* a juvenile delinquent.

1966 Elli *Riot* 173: A tough-talking bebopper...[with] a cheap reputation.

becack *v.* [*be-* + *cack* 'excrement'] to foul with excrement.—usu. considered vulgar.

1666 G. Alsop *Maryland* 72: Like so many *Don Diegos* that becackt *Pauls.*

becket *n. Naut.* a trouser or jacket pocket.

***1805** J. Davis *Post-Captain* 66: Your husband is now walking up and down the gun-room with his hands in his beckets. **1836** *Naval Mag.*

(Nov.) 557: I never poked my hands in my beckets, sir, and never hauled on the list unless I was actual sick. **1855** Wise *Tales for Marines* 121: That's all the pleasure I has, when I gets a little chink in my becket. ***1929** Bowen *Sea Slang* 9: *Beckets, Hands out of.* The old order for a youngster to take his hands out of his pockets. **1975** Gould *Maine Lingo* 10: Amblin' along with his hands in his beckets.

bed *n.* ¶ In phrases:

¶ **in bed with** allied with; working together, esp. for some questionable purpose.

1974 Weisman & Boyer *Heroin Triple Cross* 137: What takes time is to learn…who they're in bed with. **1980** Univ. Tenn. grad. student: This Zia in Pakistan—he's just another dictator who's going to be kicked out like the Shah. He's trouble. We shouldn't get into bed with this guy. **1982** *Nat. Lampoon* (Sept.) 18: I'm sure we can get into bed on this one. **1987** *Crossfire* (CNN-TV) (Sept. 3): How do you feel about being in bed with the Marxist-Leninist rulers of Nicaragua? **1990** *Nation* (Nov. 19) 618: Arizona's two U.S. Senators…were caught in bed with Keating. **1992** *Time* (Mar. 9) 26: Bush had to get in bed with the pro-lifers to get the '88 nomination.

¶ **put to bed, 1.** Esp. in extended phr. **put to bed with a shovel** to bury (someone); kill (someone).

***1785** Grose *Vulgar Tongue: Put to bed with a mattock and tucked up with a spade,* saying of one that is dead and buried. **1859** Matsell *Vocabulum*: With shovels they were put to bed/A hundred stretches since. **1906** A.H. Lewis *Confessions* 202: Put me to bed with a shovel, but that sucker was lushy. **1911** A.H. Lewis *Apaches of N.Y.* 123: An' once a guy's been put to bed wit' a shovel, if youse can't speak well of him youse had better can gabbin' about him altogether. **1938** E.J. Mayer et al. *Buccaneer* (film): I'll put you to bed with a shovel. **1988** Dietl & Gross *One Tough Cop* 170: If…a guy's coming at me with a gun or a knife, I'm gonna put him to bed.

2. to wind up; finish; (*specif.*) *Journ. & Publishing.* to ready (a book or an edition, as of a newspaper) for the press.

1921 U. Sinclair *K. Coal* 210: Last edition put to bed yet? **1982** *Business Week* (June 21) 40: With modest changes, "the monetary issue can be put to bed." **1983** Helprin *Winter's Tale* 304: We just put *The Whale* to bed.

bed athlete *n.* a sexually promiscuous person. Also **bedroom athlete.**

1947 Spillane *Jury* 120: "A bed athlete," she said. **1972** *Pub. Weekly* (Apr. 3) 20: Chester Himes, ex-convict, jewel thief, bedroom athlete, busboy, [etc.].

bedbug *n.* **1.** [fr. phr. *crazy as a bedbug*] an eccentric or crazy person.

1832 in [S. Smith] *Letters of Downing* 104: Nabby ran about from house to house like a crazy bed-bug. **1838** [Haliburton] *Clockmaker* (Ser. 2) 191: She…carried on like a ravin' distracted bed-bug. [**1907** *DN* III 206: When the snake struck at her, she went *crazy as a bedbug.*] **1940** Zinberg *Walk Hard* 170: His manager was a card, a bedbug if there ever was one. **1959** in Partridge *Dict. Und.* (ed. 3) 792: I knew her son, a real bedbug who had gone nuts one day and later was sent to the bughouse across the road. **1981** Graziano & Corsel *Somebody Down Here* 122: What's with this bedbug next to me?

2. a person who enjoys staying in bed.

1903 T.W. Jackson *Slow Train* 87: I suppose you would call yourself a big bed bug.

3. *R.R.* (see quot.).

1940 in *AS* XVIII 162: *Bedbug.* Pullman Porter.

bedbug-hauler *n.* *Trucking.* a moving van or a furniture van; (*hence*) the driver of such a van. Also **bedbugger.**

1971 Tak *Truck Talk* 9: *Bedbug hauler:* a trucker who drives a moving van. **1972** *N.Y. Times Mag.* (Nov. 12) 74: 45 or 50…moving vans (known in the trade as "bedbug haulers"). **1976** Lieberman & Rhodes *CB Handbook* 123: *Bedbug Hauler*—Moving van. **1977** Avallone *White Knight* 50: This one was wheeling a bedbug hauler. A cargo of Cedar Rapids furniture. **1990** Rukuza *W. Coast Turnaround* 36: Between a Dollar truck and a bedbugger. *Ibid.*: Bedbuggers always had women.

Bedcheck Charlie *n.* *Mil.* (a nickname given to a lone raiding plane making regular evening or night attacks). Now *hist.*

1945 *Yank* (Mar. 16) 17: *Bed Check Charlie,* the Jerry plane that flies over…every night at midnight. **1945** T. Anderson *Come Out Fighting* 23: The *Luftwaffe* was in the air, and "Bedcheck Charlie" was operating on his regular schedule. **1946** Howard & Whitley *One Damned Island* 225: To add to the misery…were the Jap nuisance bombers—"Bed Check Charlies"—which zoomed in to drop antipersonnel bombs. **1963** Ross *Dead Are Mine* 189: Bedcheck Charlie put in his first appear-

ance of the evening.…All the antiaircraft guns in Nettuno and Anzio opened up on him. **1969** R.E. Turner *Big Friend* 110 [ref. to June 1944]: "Bedcheck Charlie" [was] a particularly irritating [Me-]109. **1978** L. Davis *MiG Alley* 21 [ref. to 1951]: [Chinese] Po-2s, "Bedcheck Charlies,"…slipped in under the radar. **1980** S. Fuller *Big Red* 79 [ref. to WWII]: Perhaps Bedcheck Charlie was right behind.

bed down *v.* *West.* (see quot.).

1936 R. Adams *Cowboy Lingo* 171: When one killed another, he "bedded him down."

bedlam *n.* *Army.* bachelor officers' quarters. Now *hist.*

1889 C. King *Laramie* 15: Even "Bedlam," the ramshackle, two-story frame rookery, once sacred to the bachelor element, had now two families quartered therein. **1924** Ostrander *Army Boy* 101 [ref. to 1866]: "Bedlam," the quarters of the unmarried officers at Fort Laramie. **1956** Boatner *Mil. Customs* 124: *Bedlam* Bachelor Officer's quarters (BOQ) (*obs.*).

bedoozle *v.* to confuse or bewilder. *Joc.*

1863 in Wightman *To Ft. Fisher* 105: Fred says you are so far bedoozled as to suspect me. *a***1890** *F & H* I 160: *Bedoozle*…(American).—To confuse; to bewilder. Probably a corrupt form of…"bedazzle."

bedoozling *adj.* amazing; extraordinary, marvelous. *Joc.*

1862 in Wightman *To Ft. Fisher* 49: The orderly…says in a bedoozling sort of way, "Front." **1864** in Wightman *To Ft. Fisher* 177: We…took a bedoozling smoke and chatted and laughed. *Ibid.* 180: A memento of the "bedoozling" occasion.

bedpan alley *n.* [sugg. by TIN-PAN ALLEY] (see quot.).

1944 Kendall *Service Slang* 49: Bed pan alley.…the hospital.

bedpan commando *n.* [*bedpan* + COMMANDO] *Mil.* a hospital orderly; (*hence*) a medical corpsman. Also **bedpan jockey, bedpan mechanic.** Now *hist.*

1944 in *AS* XX 147: *Bedpan commando.* Medical corpsman. **1968** "R. Hooker" *MASH* 43 [ref. to Korean War]: He was given the job of third assistant bedpan jockey in the postop ward. **1971** N.Y.C. draftsman, age *ca*47 [ref. to WWII]: A *bedpan commando* was what we called the man in the hospital who did work like the nurses. **1979** Former U.S. Navy mechanic, age 48 [ref. to 1950's]: A *bedpan mechanic* was a hospital corpsman or a male nurse. We had one guy—a corpsman—who was always giving advice about airplane engines. And one day the crew chief turned and looked at him and said, "A qualified bedpan mechanic can do just about anything." **1988** Fussell *Wartime* 257: [The] hapless medical orderly [of WWII was]…demeaned…into a *bedpan commando.*

bedpost *n.* usu. *pl.* *Bowling.* a 7–10 split.

1949 Cummings *Dict. Sports* 31. **1979** Cuddon *Dict. Sports & Games* 79. **1980** Pearl *Slang Dict.*: *Bedpost n.* (Bowling) a split leaving the two rear corner pins—the 7 and 10—standing.

bedrock *n.* **1.a.** bottom, "rock-bottom"; the essentials.—esp. in phr. **down to bedrock** down to essentials (in any sense); (*hence*) thoroughly, through and through. All now *S.E.* [All the *bedrock* phrases seem to have orig. as miners' slang in the Rocky Mountains.]

1869 in *DA*: We came down to "bed-rock," as the miners say, i.e. an extra flannel shirt and a pocket-comb. **1873** J. Miller *Modocs* 71: But I have thought it all out, clean down to the bed-rock. **1887** *Lippincott's Mag.* (Jan.) 105: Thar will be found the prints of a woman's feet…and your poet has brought the matter down to bed-rock. **1945** in *DA*: The number now available is down to bedrock and even grandpap had to go back to the pits to make up that number. **1966** *RHD*: Let's strip away the cant and get down to bedrock.

b. broke, barely surviving; desperate.—constr. with a prep.

1871 Crofutt *Tourist's Guide* 204: To be out of money, is [among Western miners]…on the "*bed rock.*" **1883** Hay *Bread-Winners* 100: He is in the penitentiary now, and the family is about down to bedrock. **1887** Francis *Saddle & Moccasin* 143: I was mighty hard up at the time—right down on the bed rock—and it is just possible that I may have been monkeying with the cards a little. **1942** Davis & Wolsey *Call House Madam* 81: They've come to me hungry. Lean like a starved rabbit. Nice looking little fools at bedrock. **1979** G. Wolff *Duke of Deception* 87: We were at absolute bedrock, ground zero. Duke sold the car, and then he hocked his watch.

2. (also semi-adj.) *West.* a thing of outstanding excellence.

1902 Wister *Virginian* 249: That play is bed-rock, ma'am! Have you got something like that? *Ibid.* 252: That's a bed-rock piece, ma'am!

¶ In phrase:

¶ **from bedrock** from the start, through and through.

1889 *United Service* (July) 62: She was born in the regiment and a daisy from bedrock.

bedrock *v. West.* (see quot.).

1968 R. Adams *West. Words* (ed. 2): *Bedrock 'im* An expression used in the mountain range country to mean *ride a horse down* or *break his heart.*

bedsteader *n. Trucking.* (see 1971 quot.).

1942 *AS* (Apr.) 102: *Bedsteader*, Sleepy driver. **1971** Tak *Truck Talk* 10: *Bedsteader:* a sleepy driver who cannot be depended to stay awake on night runs.

bee[1] *n.* **1.** an ambitious desire.

1902 *N.Y. Eve. Jour.* (Dec. 8) 1: Ohioan Calls "Rot" Report Indicating that He Has the Presidential Bee. **1922** S. Lewis *Babbitt* 12: Far as I can figure out, Ted's new bee is he'd like to be a movie actor.

2. *Navy.* a member of the Seabees.

1945 *Yank* (May 25) 19: The 'bees got partial credit for destroying a pillbox. **1977** Langone *Life at Bottom* 76: On a good day, says Haulaway, the Bees can work outside for a half-hour before going back into the shacks to warm up for a half-hour.

3. *Narc.* an addiction to heroin.

1960 C.L. Cooper *Scene* 10: Look, I can use ten things a week and not get another bee. **1967** Maurer & Vogel *Narc. & Narc. Add.* (ed. 3) 341: *Bee that stings* A drug habit, especially one coming on; *a monkey on my back.*

¶ In phrases:

¶ **bee in someone's bonnet** a ludicrous idea; whim.

1891 Maitland *Amer. Slang Dict.* 29: Politicians occasionally get a Presidential "bee in their bonnet." **1983** Helprin *Winter's Tale* 411: Craig Binky...got a bee in his bonnet...and took off...without saying where he was going.

¶ **put the bee on** [perh. sugg. by STING, *v.*] **1.** to spoil, ruin, or put an end to; defeat.

1908 McGaffey *Show Girl* 165: These reformers are trying to put the bee on our pleasures. **1942** *ATS* 9: Impair: put out of order, spoil...*put the bee on.* **1943** Cave *Long Nights* 44: He'd...lob a couple of shells in the general direction of Henderson Field...and then duck down again under cover before anyone could put the bee on him.

2. to ask for money or other assistance from (someone).

1914 in W.C. Fields *By Himself* 51: You are constantly kicking about the difficulty of making both ends meet and want to put the bee on me for a few extra dollars. **1914** Jackson & Hellyer *Vocab.* 84: He tried to put the B. on me for the third touch this week. **1918** T.A. Dorgan, in *N.Y. Eve. Jour.* (Aug. 3) 7: I'll put the bee on the old man.—I'll tell him that I'm on the bum and need 10 bucks. **1929** Barr *Let Tomorrow Come* 40: I go in a dump an' put the B on the boss. *Ibid.* 267: *Put the B on*— To beg. **1938** "E. Queen" *4 Hearts* 126: If you let this pirate put the bee on you, you're a bigger sap than you pretend to be. **1947** Motley *Any Door* 328: I gotta put the bee on you for the night....I can't sleep out in this! **1954** "Collans" & Sterling *House Detect.* 50: Gettin' me up here, then puttin' the B on me! Twenty bucks! **1959** Zugsmith *Beat Generation* 85: Skid Row boozers putting the bee on them. **1978** *Mary Worth* (synd. cartoon strip) (Aug. 9): Now I can put the bee on you! Like how about donating that new faculty lounge you've said for years that we needed?

3. to swindle, fool, victimize, get the better of; (*occ.*) to outdo.

1920 Witwer *Kid Scanlan* 304: "Somebody put the bee on us!" howls Honest Dan. **1921** *Variety* (Feb. 4) 3: The rate of tax is set in these terms....(...to pin the bee on New York City and no other town.) **1923** in *OEDS*: I've heard a heap of fairy tales in my time...but this puts the bee on the lot. **1932** Lorimer *Streetcars* 146: You must of put the bee on Davy....How'd you work it? **1934** Faulkner *Pylon* 279: One Florentine falls in love with another Florentine's wife and he spends three acts fixing it up to put the bee on the second Florentine! **1934** L. Hughes *White Folks* 60: And she really put the bee on Mr. Lloyd. **1933–35** Lamson *About to Die* 206: If you try to put the bee on guys like that, the bee will turn around and bite you, an' serve you right for havin' larceny in your heart. **1938** *AS* XIII (Feb.) 5 [Ark.]: *I'll put the bee on him.* That is, I'll plague him.

4. to put pressure on; to charge with responsibility.

1934 in Fenner *Throttle* 59: Blake...pulled his prize boner and tried to save his skin by putting the bee on Danny...."Special at five o'clock for the Old Man. Hell poppin' at the other end, and you're to get him there." **1971** Dahlskog *Dict.* 6: *Bee on (someone), put the,*...to light a fire under, as *Put the bee on him* to get that order shipped.

bee[2] *n.* [clipping of *Frisbee*, trademark name of a brand of fly-

ing disk] *Stu.* a plastic flying disk.

1980 *N.Y. Times Mag.* (Sept. 7) 130: Playing V-ball, tossing a bee around or going on a za run were possibilities that crossed our minds.

Beeb *n.* [abbr. of acronym *BBC*] *Communications.* the British Broadcasting Corporation. *Rare* in U.S.

*1967 in *OED2*: *Beeb.* My daughter, who works in the B.B.C., always calls it so. **1975** *DAS* (ed. 2) 676: *Beeb*...The...British Broadcasting Corporation. Chiefly Brit. use. ***a1980** in Partridge *DSUE* (ed. 8): *Beeb, the.* The BBC...since late 1920s. **1991** T. Anderson, on *NBC-TV Special Report* (Dec. 6): I heard it on the Beeb.

beef *n.* **1.a.** human flesh; (*hence*) weight.

*1785 Grose *Vulgar Tongue*: *To be in a man's beef,* to wound him with a sword. ***1811** *Lexicon Balatron.*: Say you bought your beef of me; a jocular request from a butcher to a fat man, implying that he credits the butcher who serves him. **1846** [Codman] *Sailors' Life* 131: I lent a hand to capsize some of the beef off o' Miss Carroll. ***1862** in *OEDS*: Chelmsford stood higher in the leg, and showed less beef about him. **1900** *DN* II 22: *Beef, n.*...Weight, as of an athlete. **1908** in H.C. Fisher *A. Mutt* 89: But he isn't fat enough....We must name a candidate with enough beef. **1938** "Justinian" *Americana Sexualis* 12: *Beef. n.* The lower lumbar regions of the female. **1983** *N.Y. Post* (Sept. 2) 70: Benson needs more beef, they say,...Umphrey needs more strength,...Ard...needs more experience.

b. muscles; (*hence*) strength; power.

1849 Melville *White Jacket* 217 [ref. to 1843]: I'll teach you to be grinning over a rope that way, without lending your pound of beef to it. **1851** Melville *Moby-Dick* ch. xxxix: Oh, *do* pile on the beef...Oh! my lads, *do* spring. **1883** Russell *Sailors' Lang.* XIV: "More beef!" is a cry often raised when men hauling on a rope find they want help. **1899** Robbins *Gam* 81: Help—quick—more beef! **1906** Ford *Shorty McCabe* 153: I didn't have beef enough to stop a hundred-an'-eighty pound swing without feelin' the jar. **1910** *N.Y. Eve. Jour.* (Apr. 9) 8: There was a lot of beef behind the wallop. **1923** Riesenberg *Under Sail* 206: His "beef" on a rope was negligible. **1925** Farmer *Shellback* 111: Put some beef into it. **1933** in R.E. Howard *Iron Man* 126: I...crashed my left to his jaw, with all my beef behind it. **1948** Wolfert *Act of Love* 468: Come on, come on, get beef into it. **1956** Heflin *USAF Dict.* 78: *Beef,*...Strength or power, as in "the airplane has plenty of beef." *Slang.* **1958** J. King *Pro Football* 123: The offense...counters the defense with beef of its own. **1965** Bonham *Durango St.* 27: He was surprised to find the shirt much too tight for him through the shoulders. I really put on some beef up there, he realized. **1966** Olsen *Hard Men* 43: Garth is all beef and cussedness. **1968** Gomberg *Breakout* (film): Get some beef into it, you guys.

2.a. the vagina; (*hence*) a woman or women regarded as a source of sexual gratification.—usu. considered vulgar.

*1788 Grose *Vulgar Tongue* (ed. 2): *To be in a woman's beef;* to have carnal knowledge of her. ***1823** "J. Bee" *Slang* 8: "In her *beef,*" in a woman's secrets. **1941** Roberts & Sanford *Honky-Tonk* (film): The judge is right. This place does have the best beef. And I'm gonna get me a honey. **1971** Dahlskog *Dict.* 6: *Beef, n.*....A girl; a chick. **1974** R. Carter *16th Round* 123: The price of beef went up to forty and fifty marks for the very same quickie.

b. the penis; (*hence*) copulation as experienced by a woman? See also *hot beef injection*, below.—usu. considered vulgar.

*1889 Barrère & Leland *Dict. Slang* I 100: *Beef...*(Popular), the penis. **1973** Goines *Players* 47: Maybe her old man ain't givin' her enough beef at night.

3. *Und. & Police.* **a.** a complaint of wrongdoing, as made to a police department; an oral or written report of a crime.

1899 [Willard] *Tramping* 388: It'll be his last beef if I ever find him. **1927–28** Tasker *Grimhaven* 180: The [cops] had the beef by that time. **1929** Booth *Stealing* 149 [ref. to ca1916]: Most of the beefs from the residence section give a description that tallies with you to a T. **1977** Olsen *Fire Five* 143: He wants to cool the beef, whatever it is, and get out of here. **1984** *U.S. News & W.R.* (Jan. 30) 51: If I brought in two suspects looking that bad, there would be brutality beefs flying all over.

b. a criminal charge, esp. one for which a person has been tried and convicted; RAP; sentence of imprisonment.

1928 *Amer. Mercury* (May): "I'm ditched for fifteen flat—an' on a bum beef!" A *bum beef,* in the patois of the profession, means that the gentleman was innocent. **1933–35** Lamson *About to Die* 140: You talk to much about your beef....The other boys, they all got beefs. Some of 'em got beefs just as bum as your beef. **1976** Schroeder *Shaking It* 66: "Now then, what's your beef?" "B and E, sir." **1977** Caron *Go-Boy* 103: You can pretty well tell a guy's beef from the [length of] time he's shaking.

c. *Police.* a crime, CAPER.

1968 "H. King" *Box-Man* 4: I got into another beef and was sent to Monroe. **1974** *Kojak* (CBS-TV police series): We got a big beef comin' down…right now—and two suspects are talkin' about it on a police phone!

4. complaint; complaining; objection, protest, grounds for complaint.

1899 Ade *Fables* 35: He made a Horrible Beef because he couldn't get Loaf Sugar for his Coffee. **1898–1900** Cullen *Chances* 22: The plunger made a terrific beef. **1902** in F. Remington *Sel. Letters* 300: I don't want to make a "beef" but…why don't you come and see [us]. **1905** [Hobart] *Search Me* 16: I told you not to cut a beef about the has-happened. **1906** H. Green *Actors' House* 59: He puts up a beef about the elbows shakin' him down ag'in. **1919** in E. O'Neill *Letters* 92: I hope you won't think my "beef" about the picture the result of…any…conceit. **1931** D. Runyon *Guys & Dolls* ch. iv: In case of a beef from her over keeping the baby out in the night air. **1952** Mandel *Angry Strangers* 351: Don't let him give you any beef. **1952** Chase *McThing* 79: What's the beef? He's not hurt. **1968** *Star Trek* (NBC-TV): In the language of the planet, what's your beef? **1976** G.V. Higgins *Deke Hunter* 153: I agree with you….So where's the beef? **1983** *Green Arrow* (July) 22: Queen's safe, so what's your beef? **1991** W. Chamberlain *View from Above* 97: My beef was that all the sentiments…were…contrived.

5. an argument; dispute; altercation; commotion, etc.

1899 Cullen *Tales* 48: The…sport made the beginning of a beef about the thing being a job. **1933–35** D. Lamson *About to Die* 107: Frame him…get him in a beef with the captain or the lieutenant. **1945** Hartman & Shavelson *Wonder Man* (film): Now be a good joe and slip her a kiss and square the beef so she'll know you're on the up and up. **1952** Uris *Battle Cry* 100: You looking for a beef, Marine? **1954** Sherdeman *Them* (film): So what's all the beef? **1962** G. Olson *Roaring Road* 62: Pa'll have a fit!…Then there'll be a big beef. **1972–75** W. Allen *Feathers* 207: Incidentally, if the two players disagreed on the rules, we might say they "got into a beef."

6. a mistake, a blunder.

1895 Gore *Stu. Slang* 4: *Beef*…An error; an awkward blunder. **1900** *DN* II 22: *Beef, n*….a mistake. [Reported from four separate universities.] **1915** [Swartwood] *Choice Slang* 54: *Make a beef*…To make a mistake or error.

7.a. a line of talk designed to attract patrons; sales pitch.

1921 J. Conway, in *Variety* (Apr. 1) 7: I make my usual beef and we draw the usual assortment of bohunks and set-ups who think they can fight after readin' the sportin' page.

b. chatter; idle talk.

1935 D.W. Maurer, in *AS* (Feb.) 12 [ref. to period before 1910]: *Beef.* Meaningless chatter; gossip. **1942–49** Goldin et al. *DAUL* 25: *Beef, n*….Gossip; small talk.

8. a bill or charge for services.

1939 *AS* (Oct.) 239: *Beef.* Bill for the [hotel] guest's account.

9. (see quot.).

1950 *New Directions* 312: Shelves of liquescent "beef"*…*hard liquor.*

10. *Skateboarding.* a fall from a skateboard. Also as v.

1987 J. Thompson *Gumshoe* 157 [ref. to 1978]: I heard the race of skateboard wheels and laughter…."You really beefed that time!" **1990** P. Dickson *Slang!* 213: *Beef.* A butt fall in skateboarding. **1992** Thatcher & Brannon *Thrasher* 64: *Beef.* Any fall where blood is shed, scabs are formed, and bones are bruised.

¶ In phrases:

¶ beef to the heels *N.E.* (of persons) stocky or stalwart. Also in extended phrs.

*ca1880 in *F & H* I 163: Dolly was…not beef to the heels, by any means. *a1890 *F & H* I 163: *Beef to the heels like a Mullingar heifer* (Irish).—A stalwart man or a fine woman. **1928** J.M. March *Set-Up* 21: They aint so hot./Beef to the heels! **1958** in *DARE*: Built like a Mullingar heifer, *beef to the heels.* **1967** in *DARE*: *Beef to the heel.*

¶ cry [or **give**] **beef** *Und.* to shout for help from police; to raise a hue and cry after. *Rare* in U.S.

*1698–99 "B.E." *Dict. Canting Crew* s.v. *whiddle*: Whiddle, c. to tell, or discover. He *whiddles*, c. he Peaches….They Whiddle beef, *and we must brush*, c. they cry out thieves, we are Pursued, and must Fly. *1725 *New Canting Dict.*: To cry Beef upon us; they have discover'd us, and are in pursuit of us. *1811 *Lexicon Balatron.*: *To cry beef*; to give the alarm. They have cried beef on us. *Cant.* **1867** *Nat. Police Gaz.* (Jan. 26) 3: Johnny "gave beef" most lustily, which brought the "coppers" to the spot. *Ibid.* (Oct. 19) 4: I heard the cry of "beef" three times, once from a bloke, who said he lost a "real super" valued at "centuries." *1879

Macmillan's Mag. (Oct.): He followed, giving me hot beef (calling "Stop thief"). *1889 in Barrère & Leland *Dict. Slang* I 100: I guyed, but the reeler gave me hot beef/And a scuff came about me and hollered.

¶ hot beef injection *Stu.* an act of sexual intercourse.—usu. considered vulgar. *Joc.*

1983 D. Greenburg & S. O'Malley *Private School* (film): Maybe I should have said "givin' her a hot beef injection!" **1985** J. Hughes *Breakfast Club* (film): Do you slip her the hot beef injection? **1991** Munro *Slang U.* 174: He asked me if my boyfriend has ever slipped me the hot beef injection.

¶ ride the beef *Und.* to take blame, as for a crime; take the rap.

1936 Twist *We About to Die* (film): The way to get along in a place like this is to ride your own beef. **1954** Chessman *Cell 2455* 88 [ref. to 1930's]: I heard you rode the beef for a lot of other people when your partner squealed. **1966** Elli *Riot* 162: They're doin' it now because they know we'll ride the beef. **1974** Goines *Eldorado* 37: I'll ride the beef out first, before I'd let everybody fall on the same…charge. **1992** *Amer. Detective* (ABC-TV): So you're gonna ride the beef yourself.

¶ Where's the beef? [sugg. by the catch phrase of a TV advertising campaign for Wendy's, Inc., in 1984] Esp. *Pol.* "Where is the real content or substance?"

1984 *L.A. Times* (Mar. 25) IV 1: Hart's critics say that he claims to offer "new ideas" but has so far failed to campaign on the issues. "Where's the beef?" Mondale taunts. **1984** *Newsweek* (July 23) 40: Mondale seized on that hamburger homily, "where's the beef?" **1985** *N.Y. Times Higher Ed. Supp.* (Mar. 3): *Where's the beef?* A question asked when something is believed to be missing, as in a sandwich or a conversation seriously lacking content. **1990** Cmiel *Demo. Eloquence* 11: If "the dreaded 'L' word" ["liberal"] was central to the [presidential] campaign of 1988, "Where's the beef?" served in its place four years before. **1992** *CBS This Morning* (CBS-TV) (Apr. 6): Charges like this have been bombarding us for weeks now. Where is the beef? Or is there any?

beef *v.* **1.a.** *Und.* to cry out; (*hence*) to say; to talk.—also (*obs.*) constr. with *it.*

[*1812 Vaux *Vocab. Flash Lang.*: *Beef*: stop thief! to *beef* a person is to raise a hue and cry after him, in order to get him stopped.] **1866** *Nat. Police Gaz.* (Nov. 24) 3: Lizzie "beefed" to her pal, "Let's namese"; there's Billy [a policeman], and he'll be sure to run us in. *1879 *Macmillan's Mag.* (Oct.): To *beef* it, or to give hot *beef*, is to give chase, pursue, raise a halloo and cry. **1931** Wilstach *Under Cover Man* 23: Smiley beefed to his girl that he was going to turn rat. **1940** *Current Hist. & Forum* (Nov. 7) 22: Even the well-educated inmate learns…not [to] *beef above anyone's knowledge* (not talk highbrow). **1944** Calloway *Hepster's Dict.*: *Beef* (v.): to say, to state. Ex., "He beefed to me that, etc."

b. to talk loudly or to no purpose; (*specif.*) (and now exclusively) to complain.

1866 *Nat. Police Gaz.* (Nov. 3) 2: Why don't you "cheese" it;…they will "tumble" to our "lay" if you "beef" out like you are now doing. **1888** in Farmer *Americanisms*: He'll beef an' kick like a steer an' let on he won't never wear 'em. **1889** in *DA*: He will be coming down town again soon on crutches, "beefing" about cancer of the stomach. **1894** in Ade *Chicago Stories* 32: Now he wants to beef. **1896** Ade *Artie* 9: Everybody keepin' books and beefin' about the way the hands was runnin'. **1900** *DN* II 22: *Beef*…To object….To talk without saying anything. **1898–1900** Cullen *Chances* 21: The plunger…beefed about the $500. **1904** *Life in Sing Sing* (gloss.): *Beefer.* A loquacious person. **1908** in Fleming *Unforgettable Season* 273: But the game is lost, so what's the use of beefing? **1912–14** in E. O'Neill *Lost Plays* 49: Shut up! I ain't got time to listen to your beefin'. **1916** *Railroad Man's Mag.* (Aug.) 707: After some beefin', Pauline…produces the finn. **1918** Swan *My Co.* 130: Many boys feel that they are not soldiers until they begin to "beef." **1921** Casey & Casey *Gay-Cat* 98: What yer beefin' about, anyway? **1929** Cruze *Great Gabbo* (film): That guy's beefin' ever since he opened here. **1929** "E. Queen" *Roman Hat* 33: While you stand beefing about a little thing like being detained an hour or so, a person who has committed murder may be in this very audience. **1942** Liebling *Telephone* 92: He is always beefing. **1956** Algren *Wild Side* 130: Opportunity is knocking the door down and you're beefing about a little rain. **1975** McCaig *Danger Trail* 2: A lot of beefing because the river is too low for the big packets to reach Benton.

c. to argue.

1950 Riesenberg *Reporter* 22: I saw you beefing with him last week at the office.

2.a. *Und.* to inform (on an associate) to a police department or similar authority.

[***1785** Grose *Vulgar Tongue: To cry beef, (cant)* to give the alarm. They have cried beef on us.] **1899** "J. Flynt" *Tramping* 388: When a man denounces to the police a beggar who has accosted him in the street, the latter...says that the bloke "beefed" on him (gave him away)....My pal, he "beefed" (turned state's evidence). **1900** [Willard] & Hodler *Powers That Prey* 40: I never yet beefed on a pal an' I'm not goin' to begin. **1906** Burke *Prison Gates* 8 [ref. to 1880's]: All of the coin and coppers in the world could not have induced me to "beef." **1931** Hellinger *Moon* 53: If he don't get it, he'll beef on the whole bunch of us. **1976** "N. Ross" *Policeman's Bible* 161: You'll be asked to turn stool pigeon and beef on a few other coppers.

b. *Pris. & Police.* to bring disciplinary charges or file a complaint against.

1942–49 Goldin et al. *DAUL* 25: *Beef*...To submit a formal written report of a convict's misconduct. **1966** Braly *On Yard* 64: He would beef you because he didn't like your looks. **1970** Wambaugh *Centurions* 54: Some bitch in Newton Division beefed a policeman last week. Says he [attacked her]. **1974** *Police Woman* (NBC-TV): She beefed me to Internal Affairs. **1987** Norst & Black *Lethal Weapon* 100: You afraid he'll beef us to the deputy chief?

3. to drive (a boat or the like) forward by muscle power.

1860 *Yale Lit. Mag.* 26 83: The first boat in is the winner of the race, so they turn, and "beef her" for the home stretch.

4. *West.* to kill (a person).

1899 A.H. Lewis *Sandburrs* 116: I don't say this Cheyenne is held for beefin' the Chinaman sole an' alone. **1903** A.H. Lewis *Black Lion* 165: He...beefs five an' creases another; an' all to the same one gun. **1934** in *OEDS:* "Yo' kills niggers?" "Like flies," Charley assured me. "You want to beef a few for you?" **1939** "L. Short" *Rimrock* 121: Three jaspers tried to beef me tonight....I killed two. **1947** Overholser *Buckaroo's Code* 45: I don't know why Harriman or Donahue...would want you beefed, but...they do. **1951** West *Flaming Feud* 10: "Beef any of our boys?"..."They pegged Pecos, that's all."

5. (see quots.).

1900 *DN* II 22: *Beef, v.t.*...To loaf; waste time...To make a mistake...To find fault with. **1918** *DN* V 18: *Beef.* Act the bully. *Slang.*

6. to knock down, to hit hard.

1902 Remington *John Ermine* 174: I beefed him under the ear, and we took his guns away, sir. **1926** J. Black *Can't Win* 185: When one of them got peeved...some hard-fisted miner beefed him like an ox. **1958** *AS* XXXIII 268: *Beef*...Metaphorically, to knock (a man) down.

beef boat *n. Navy.* a supply or cargo ship. Also **beef box.**

*ca***1863** in M. Turner *Navy Gray* 119: Raise the beef boat. **1907** Mahan *Sail to Steam* 187 [ref. to Civil War]: Transportation being given me on one of the "beef boats," as the supply vessels were familiarly known. **1918** Connolly *U-Boat* 225: "Beef boats" travel with all fleets. **1918** *Everybody's* (Nov.) 19: Pease, an ensign four years graduated, would go into the great war on a beef-box! **1936** Denlinger & Gary *War in Pacific* 87: The storeships are the "beef boats" of a navy. **1966** Noel & Bush *Naval Terms* 63: *Beef boat:* Slang: supply ship.

beefcake *n.* [sugg. by CHEESECAKE] **1.** photographs or motion pictures of partially clad muscular men.

1949 in *AS* XXIX 282: Alan Ladd has a beef—about "beefcake," the new Hollywood trend toward exposing the male chest. **1967** Schmidt *Lexicon of Sex* 18: *Beefcake*...A picture or photograph depicting a muscular Adonis, in his splendor. **1972** R. Wilson *Playboy's Forbidden Words* 33: *Beefcake* Homosexual slang for male pin ups. **1978** Maupin *Tales* 31: A collage of *Playgirl* beefcake photos. **1980** *Time* (Jan. 28) 52: Beefcake has sold as well, including...NBC's heart-throb Highway Cop Erik Estrada. **1984** *Time* (Jan. 23) 66: *The Six Million Dollar Man* was simply state-of-the-art beefcake.

2. a muscular, sexually attractive man.

1982 *L.A. Times* (Apr. 15) VI 4: Had things worked out, Marinaro might have become just another Hollywood beefcake. **1983** in "J.B. Briggs" *Drive-In* 174: *Yor* is about this curly-headed blond beefcake with oil all over his skin. **1985** Eble *Campus Slang* (Oct.) 1: *Beefcake*—a male with a fantastic body and good looks, better than a hunk. "I drooled in awe as twelve beefcakes walked past." **1985** Finkleman *Head Office* (film): I'm probably just a cheap pickup to you. Just another great-looking piece of beefcake.

beefer *n.* **1.** a grumbler.

1896 Ade *Artie* 33: I ain't one o' them beefers that's got it in for people just because they've got the coin and make a front with it. **1930** (quot. at **(2)**, below). **1967** *L.A. Times* (Mar. 12) West 57: A chance for ordinary axe-grinders...to air their gripes....A large percentage of these beefers seem to a casual viewer to be suffering from social disturbances.

2. *Und.* an informer.

1899 "J. Flynt" *Tramping* 392: *Beefer*—one who "squeals" on, or gives away, a tramp or criminal. **1926** *AS* I 650: *Beefer*—informer (to "beef" is to inform). **1930** "D. Stiff" *Milk & Honey* 199: *Beefer*—one who whines. Sometimes an informer.

beefhead *n.* **1.** a Texan.—used derisively.

1872 *Harper's Mag.* (Jan.) 318: Texas, Beef-Heads; Vermont, Green Mountain Boys. **1886** in *DA*: Texas is the Lone-Star state,...its people are Beef-Heads for some unknown reason. **1967** Edson *Fast Gun* 60: Hey, beefhead!...Where'd you get that horse?

2. a blockhead; MEATHEAD.

1992 N. Cohn *Heart of World* 119: He had been frog-marched off to court between two Irish beefheads.

beefsteak *v.* to rub raw.

1922 Rollins *Cowboy* 125 [ref. to 1890's]: These men..."gimletted" or "beefsteaked" far more horses' backs and tired far more ponies.

beef trust *n.* a grossly fat person or people; *(specif.)* fat women exhibited in a carnival sideshow; (in 1928 quot.) the heavyweight division of boxing.

1928 T.A. Dorgan, in Zwilling *TAD Lexicon* 93: The New York Boxing Commission...will allow Tommy to mingle with the beef trust. **1931** J.T. Farrell *McGinty* 190: What about that beef trust you got for a wife? **1940** *AS* (Apr.) 211: Fat boys belong to the *beef trust.* **1946** Mezzrow & Wolfe *Really Blues* 85: The beef trust was out in full force—These landladies were all shaped up like barrels. **1946** Dadswell *Hey, Sucker* 23: Nearby are the fat girls of the "Beef Trust." **1991** R.C. Allen *Horrible Prettiness* 176: In 1899 W.B. (Billy) Watson built...Billy Watson's Beef Trust around the size of his female performers, some of which weighed as much as two hundred pounds.

beef up *v.* to strengthen or build up. Occ. intrans. Now *colloq.*

[***1889** Barrère & Leland *Dict. Slang* I 100: (Common), "*beef up!*" or "put your *beef* to it!" An ejaculation...to use one's strength, to use one's muscles to good account.] **1944** *Time* (Jan. 24) 22: This time the Eighth proved that it had beefed up its reserves. **1945** *Time* (Mar. 12) 30: For four weeks the Germans had nervously watched as Marshal Georgi K. Zhukov beefed up a tremendous force for the assault aimed at Berlin. **1945** J. Bryan *Carrier* 150: It may be a special, beefed-up, high-octane kind. **1955** in Loosbrock & Skinner *Wild Blue* 38: The Spad 13 [was] beefed-up to take a new 235-hp Hisso. **1956** Heflin *USAF Dict.* 78: *Beef, v. tr.* With *up:* to strengthen, improve, or better the performance of an *organization* or a *mechanism*, as of an airplane or one of its parts. *Slang.* **1967** in H. Ellison *Sex Misspelled* 134: Have him do a rewrite on the part of Angela. Beef it up. **1973** Ace *Stand on It* 143: He went out and bought an old Packard and beefed that son of a bitch right up to where he could have driven it smack through a Brontosaurus. **1978** B. Johnson *What's Happenin'?* 8: Burleson had beefed up 18 pounds from the end of the previous season to 256. **1983** *Mutual Radio News* (Mar. 13): President Reagan said not enough students are taking math and science courses. He said that schools need to beef up the basic skills. **1989** Weber *Defcon One* 34: Beef up security at the gates.

bee-gum hat *n.* [So. *bee gum* 'a hollow tree or log serving as a beehive'] *So.* a man's high hat.

1880 J.C. Harris *Uncle Remus* 230: Wid a bee-gum hat an' a brass watch. **1915–18** *Coll. Kans. State Hist. Soc.* XIV 304 [ref. to Civil War]: This man had his "beegum" hat filled with sugar. **1929** Dobie *Vaquero* 185 [ref. to 1890's]: Attire of the latest fashion, including a bee-gum hat. **1939** in *DARE:* In this section [of N.C.] any high hat is called...in derision, a "bee gum."

bee-juice *n.* honey.

1885 "Lykkejaeger" *Dane* 52: Artificial honey, the substitute for the "bee-juice," being composed of genuine honey, wax and sugar.

beeline *n.* a quick and direct route. Now *S.E.*

1845 Hooper *Simon Suggs* 143: I maid a brake on a bee line for Urwinton. **1851** Webber *Hunter-Naturalist* 208: "Well, what would you advise, Charlie?" "Why, that we both make a bee-line for home, right off." **1903** *DN* II 306: He made a bee-line for home. **1909** in McCay *Little Nemo* 204: Striking out on a bee-line towards the forty-seventh parallel. **1931** *PMLA* XLVI 1305: He made a bee-line (went directly) fer home. **1940** Stout *Where There's a Will* 44: She would make a bee-line for the office door. **1979** Weverka *By Decree* 13: He made a bee-line for the cabs awaiting us outside. **1991** C. Fletcher *Pure Cop* 280: He makes a beeline upstairs.

Beemer *n.* [BMW + *-er*] a BMW automobile. Also **Beamer.**

1982 S. Black *Totally Awesome* 83: BMW ("Beemer"). **1985** *L.A. Times* (Apr. 13) V 4: I'd much rather drive my Beemer than a truck. **1989** L.

Roberts *Full Cleveland* 39: Baby boomers...in...late-model Beemers. **1990** *Hull High* (NBC-TV): You should see my dad's new Beemer. **1991** *Cathy* (synd. cartoon strip) (Apr. 21): Sheila...[ground] multigrain snack chips crumbs into the back seat of my brand-new Beamer! **1992** *Time* (May 18) 84: Its residents tend to drive pickups or subcompacts, not Beemers and Rollses.

beenie *n.* [BN + -ie] *Naval Av.* bombardier navigator.
1986 Coonts *Intruder* 61 [ref. to 1972]: Marty Greve was the best goddamn "beenie" who ever strapped an A-6 to his ass.

Beep *n.* [cf. VEEP] *N.Y.C. Pol.* a borough president.
1980 *N.Y. Daily News* (Tonight) (Manhattan) (Aug. 23) 5: Still, the Queens Beep...concedes he's heard the Cabinet rumors, too. **1985** *Our Town* (N.Y.C.) (Aug. 23) 1: David Dinkins' Third Bid for Beep. **1992** *Midtown Resident* (N.Y.C.) (Oct. 5) 5: Borough President Ruth Messenger's mayoral aspirations are well known....Several house parties have been held already for the Beep.

beep *n.* [cf. syn. PEEP] *Mil.* a 4 x 4 command car; jeep.
1942 *Sat. Eve. Post* (May 23) 24: A beep driven by the captain...picked its way through...civilian traffic.

beep *v. Radio & TV.* **1.** [prob. sugg. by the "beep-beep" sound made by the fast-moving Roadrunner, a character in the *Looney Tunes* series of animated cartoons produced by Warner Bros.] (see quot.).
1970 Zindel *Your Mind* 111: I...didn't have a cent so I started beeping the Chinks—you know, skip out on the bill—that's how I met Bob—he was beeping the Chinks too.
2. to delete (an offensive word) from a broadcast or recording by replacing it with a beeping sound.
1972 W.C. Anderson *Hurricane* 142: We're going to have to beep a few four-letter words.

beeper *n.* [because operated by a remote electronic signal] *Mil. Av.* a drone aircraft.
1946 in *OEDS*: Radio operators of the drone-controlled planes or "beepers," were Capt. John Evans [etc.].

beer *v.* to give a beer to.
1983 L. Frank *Hardball* 55: Beer me! **1993** N.Y.C. man, age 24 (coll. J. Sheidlower): Hey, can you beer me?

beer barrel *n.* **1.** a beer drinker's paunch.
1939 Appel *Power Talk* 386: Hit him in the beer barrel! **1942** *ATS* 144: Drunkard's paunch...*beer barrel*.
2. a beer drunkard.
1942 *ATS* 110: Drunkard...*beer barrel*. **1986** Ciardi *Good Words* 31: *Beer barrel*...A beer sot.

beer bust *n.* see BUST.

beer-buzzer *n.* one who cadges beer, as in a saloon.
1890 Howells *Hazard* 391: Why, confound the old Dutch beer-buzzer!

beer call *n. Mil.* BEER MUSTER.
1972–79 T. Wolfe *Right Stuff* 139 [ref. to *ca*1960]: It was beer-call time, as they said in the Air Force.

Beer City *n.* BEER TOWN.
1976 *Sci. Mech. CB Gde.* 154: I'm going to lay over in Beer City.

beered up *adj.* drunk from beer.
1930 F. Pasley *Capone* 130: Joey...used to get beered up. **1976** in H.S. Thompson *Shark Hunt* 542: He's all beered up and wants to come up there for breakfast. **1982** Univ. Tenn. grad. student: My mother always used to talk about the town drunk being thrown back in jail for being all beered up. **1985** Sawislak *Dwarf* 52: The kids got beered up on a Saturday night.

beer goggles *n.pl. Stu.* a beer-induced lack of judgment, esp. in flirting with or associating with someone of the opposite sex.
1987 Univ. Tenn. student theme: Sometimes people have too much to drink and [hug and kiss] with someone that they ordinarily would not have if they were completely sober....A common excuse is "My *beer goggles* were on." **1987** Eble *Campus Slang* (Oct.) 1: *Beer goggles*—so overindulgent in beer that members of the opposite sex start to look better: "He must have on beer goggles." **1990** P. Munro *Slang U.* 34: Arnold had beer goggles and suddenly every girl at the bar was looking good. **1993** *Simpsons* (Fox-TV): Beer Goggles. See the world through the eyes of a drunk.

beerhead *n.* a beer drunkard; (*joc.*) a German.

1944 D. Runyon, in *Collier's* (Feb. 12) 70: Kindly do not refer to our people as Krauts....beer-heads, Heinies, Boches [etc.]. **1974** Loken *Come Monday Mornin'* 27: Those young beerheads come roarin' through.

beer jerk *n.* [cf. SODA JERK] BEER-JERKER.
1986 Ciardi *Good Words* 31: *Beer jerk*. A bartender....Now rare and prob. obs.

beer-jerker *n.* **1.** one who draws beer in a saloon. Also **beer-yanker**.
*ca*1867 in M.S. Goldman *Gold Diggers* (caption): Julia ——, hurdy and beer jerker. **1873** T.W. Knox *Underground* 636: The attendants or waiters are denominated "beer-jerkers." **1875** in *DA*. **1881** Nye *Forty Liars* 7: The division bartender and most noble beer yanker. **1886** Nye *Remarks* 430: The beerjerker was never too proud to speak to the most humble. **1889** Barrère & Leland *Dict. Slang* I 102: Beer-slinger...*beerjerker*.
2. (see quot.).
1970 Boatright & Owens *Derrick* 90 [ref. to *ca*1910]: The girls were what they called beer jerkers. They'd get a fellow up in a little booth...and bleed him for all they could.

beer mill *n.* a saloon where beer is sold.
1879 in "M. Twain" *Letters* I 367: We went to a beer mill to meet some twenty Chicago journalists.

beer muscle *n.* a beer drinker's paunch. *Joc.*
1933 in E. O'Neill *Letters* 413: Beer muscles? Well, look out and be sure it's muscle! **1942** *ATS* 144: Drunkard's paunch...*beer muscle*.

beer muster *n. Navy.* a beer party.
1962 Mandel *Mainside* 12: But that new squadron's giving a party. Big beer muster. **1966** Noel & Bush *Naval Terms* 63: *Beer muster*: Slang: beer party ashore.

beer racket *n.* see RACKET.

beer-slinger *n.* a bartender or waiter in a beer saloon.
1889 Barrère & Leland *Dict. Slang* I 102: *Beerslinger* (American), a term for a barman in a lager-beer "saloon" or tavern. It originated in Philadelphia in 1848–49, about which time lager-beer was first brewed in America. **1903** Kildare *Mamie Rose* 71 [ref. to *ca*1885]: Others...officiated as waiters—"beer slingers!" **1907** *Army & Navy Life* (Dec.) 744: "What is your occupation?" "Beer slinger." **1939** Howsley *Argot* 6: Beer Slinger.—A bartender.

Beer Town *n.* [Milwaukee is the home of several nationally known breweries] Milwaukee, Wisc.
1961 Brosnan *Pennant Race* 160: Our arrival in Milwaukee failed to excite the good burghers of Beer-Town. **1978** B. Johnson *What's Happenin'* 58: Around Beer Town. **1980** WINS radio (July 31): In sports the Yankees bop into Beer Town.

bees [fr. BEES AND HONEY] money.
1929 in Hammett *Knockover* 51: You know her father had the bees. That's what Joe was after. She didn't mean anything to him but an in to the old man's pockets.

bees and honey *n.* [rhyming slang] money. *Rare in U.S.*
***1892** in *OEDS*: "Bees and honey"...for "money." **1919** T.A. Dorgan, in Zwilling *TAD Lexicon* 17: How about the bees and honey brother—Could you slip me a little change? **1928** Sharpe *Chicago May* 288: Bees and honey—money. ***1960** in *OEDS*.

bee's knees *n.* [cf. CAT'S PAJAMAS, etc.] an extraordinary person, thing, idea, etc.; the ultimate; something of great excellence. Also (*vulgar*) **bee's nuts**.—constr. with *the*.
1923 Witwer *Fighting Blood* 101: You're the bee's knees for a fact! [**1924** *DN* V 263: Exclamations in American English...*bee's knees* (surp[rise]).] **1926** Maines & Grant *Wise-Crack Dict.* 5: Bee's knees—Bee—Utiful. **1957** in R. Russell *Perm. Playboy* 140: "Was it ever an evening!"..."The bee's knees!" **1970** in H.S. Thompson *Shark Hunt* 483: Up until that time we'd all thought the .357 Magnum was just about the bee's knees. **1973** *Oui* (Feb.) 86: It's a yogurt shake and it's the bee's knees. **1977** Sayles *Union Dues* 145: Okay, so he thinks Pancho Villa is the bee's knees, right? **1977** Bredes *Hard Feelings* 136: You're the bee's knees, Joanna. **1986** Rosman *Time Flyer* (film): the bee's knees. You can't beat warm buttermilk. **1992** Eble *Campus Slang* (Spring) 1: *The bee's knees*—the best; the greatest.

beeswax *n.* **1.** fellow.—constr. with *old. Joc.*
1855 in Meserve & Reardon *Satiric Comedies* 127: Old beeswax, come rosin your bow.
2. [intentional malapropism] (one's own) business. *Joc.*

1934 H. Roth *Call It Sleep* 313: Mind yuh own beeswax! **1936** Kingsley *Dead End* 728: None a yuh beeswax! **1972** *All in the Family* (CBS-TV) (Nov. 25): Why don't you mind your own beeswax, hanh? **1973** Yount *Trapper's Last Shot* 53: Ain't none a his beeswax. **1976** Knapp & Knapp *One Potato* 60: None of your beeswax! **1978** *M.A.S.H.* (CBS-TV): None of your beeswax! **1986** Ciardi *Good Words* 33 [ref. to 1920's]: None of your beeswax.

beetle *n.* **1.** [sugg. by BUG] a crazy, eccentric, or foolish individual; a buff.

1911–12 Ade *Knocking the Neighbors* 200: She is a raving Beetle. **1920** Ade *Hand-Made Fables* 53: He was a Beetle on the kind of music that put Joe to sleep. **1920** *Amer. Leg. Wkly.* (June 25) 7: Many a mademoiselle has chosen a beetle with a green ribbon over his chest from a flock of clean-cut doughboys. *Ibid.* (July 30) 8: Those beetles could never have made the welkin ring. **1963** Westlake *Getaway Face* 51: I've got to hold onto this beetle for two weeks.

2. *Horse Racing.* an inferior racehorse.

1913–15 Van Loan *Taking the Count* 336: Them dinky-legged beetles go good in the slop. **1932** Berg *Doctor* 12: Well, de weather man says rain and dat beetle ain't no mudder. **1950** *Collier's* (Dec. 9) 17: He's taken to betting the beetles—two here, two there. Even had a four-horse parlay going yesterday. **1968** M.B. Scott *Racing Game* 13: [Inferior horses] are "pigs," "dogs," "beetles," or "goats."

3. a young woman.

1931 J.T. Farrell *Guillotine Party* 87: Hennessey entertained them with an anatomical description of the last beetle he had picked up. "The nearer the bone, the sweeter the meat." **1941** Kendall *Army & Navy Slang* 1: A beetle…a girl to Alaska soldiers. **1953** Paxton *Wild One* (film): The beetles missed ya! All the beetles missed ya!

4. [Japanese *beetle*] *Mil.* a Japanese.—used contemptuously.—usu. considered offensive.

1957 E. Brown *Locust Fire* 25 [ref. to 1944]: I thought them little beetles would be crawling over the joint. *Ibid.* 117: By God, he would love to see those bowlegged beetles rolled back.

beetle-crusher *n.* **1.** a large or clumsy boot or shoe.

*1860 Hotten *Slang Dict.* (ed. 2) 94: *Beetle-crushers*, or *squashers*, large flat feet. ***1869** in *OEDS*: The infliction which the beetle-crusher of a recent arrival had just inflicted on his pet corn. ***1929** Bowen *Sea Slang* 10: *Beetle Crushers.* The bluejacket's name for a Marine's boots, never his own. **1966** E. Shepard *Doom* 118: I slipped into my Charlie Chaplin beetle-crushers.

2. *Mil.* an infantry soldier. Also **beetle-cruncher.**

[*1871 in *OEDS*: The possibility…of exchange into a sedate, beetle-crushing corps.] ***1889** Barrère & Leland *Dict. Slang* I 103: An infantry soldier is derisively termed "beetle-crusher" by the cavalry. ***1977** T. Jones *Ice* 16: He turned to the red-capped beetle-crusher. **1980** S. Fuller *Big Red* 43 [ref. to WWII]: Every infantryman felt that he and a small group of beetle-crushers did all the fighting in every battle. **1989** Berent *Rolling Thunder* 145: Spears, you beetle cruncher. You're just jealous.

beetle-headed *adj.* stupid. Hence **beetlehead** a stupid person.

*1785 Grose *Vulgar Tongue*: *Beetle headed*, dull, stupid. **1821** Waln *Hermit in Phila.* 28: *Beetle-headed*…and *Chuckle-headed!!!* **1943** Perrin & Mahoney *Whistling in Brooklyn* (film): Come on, beetlehead. **1959** Duffy & Lane *Warden's Wife* 142 [ref. to 1920's]: Where did you get the idea that prisoners are beetleheads?

Beetle Juice *n.* *Astron.* the star Betelgeuse. *Joc.*

*1943 (cited in Partridge *DSUE* (ed. 7) 1001.). **1950** F. Brown *Space* 85: "We were fleeing a Betelgeuse fleet when we warped into your space."…"What's the beetle juice got to do with it?" **1954** Coleman *Relativity* 94: Beetlejuice or Bust! **1960** N.Y.C. high school science teacher, age *ca*30: The brightest star in Orion is Betelgeuse—or Beetle Juice, as some people call it.

beetle-stomper *n.* *Army.* BEETLE-CRUSHER, 2.

1982 Goff, Sanders & Smith *Brothers* 125 [ref. to Vietnam War]: Guys in the rear called us boonie rats, beetle stompers, bush beetles, funky grunts. **1990** G.R. Clark *Words of Vietnam War* 54: *Beetle Stompers*…Infantry soldier[s].

Beezer *n.* [pron. of initials *BSA*] a vehicle manufactured by British Small Arms, Ltd.

1966 H.S. Thompson *Hell's Angels* 132: When the Angels went out on a run he joined them on his old Beezer. ***1970** Partridge *DSUE* (ed. 7) 1001: [Since *ca*1920, esp. at Cambridge.]

beezer *n.* [perh. < Sp *cabeza* 'head'] **1.** the head.

1915 Howard *God's Man* 206: I'd bend a paving stone over his beezer. **1917** F. Hunt *Draft* 311: Eight privates, three corporals and the top sergeant was sittin' on [the goat's] beezer and pullin' of his whiskers. **1927–28** Tasker *Grimhaven* 110: If the hogs ate your beezer with all the phony ideas you've got in it, they'd croak! **1941** *Slanguage Dict.* 6: *Beezer*.…sometimes the head. **1969** in *DARE*: Head…*beezer*.

2. the nose.

1908 T.A. Dorgan, in Zwilling *TAD Lexicon* 17: Pipe the beezer on him—he looks like a pelican. **1910** T.A. Dorgan, in *N.Y. Eve. Jour.* (Apr. 2) 8: Yes, but watch this one on your beezer. **1913** T.M. Osborne *Pris. Walls* 311: Charley Murphy is wiping his beezer on the bar towel. **1913–15** Van Loan *Taking the Count* 183: Now don't be turnin' up that busted beezer of yours so proud an' haughty. **1915** in Grayson *New Stories* 550: In the patois of the [boxing] profession…the nose becomes a beezer, the eye a lamp. **1920** Ade *Hand-Made Fables* 12: A Beezer that never could have been colored by the use of Malted Milk. **1926** *Amer. Legion Mo.* (July) 81: I'll give you a slam in the beezer as soon as it gets light. **1931** Stevenson *St. Luke's* 285: I'll sock *him* in the beezer *first.* **1934** H. Roth *Call It Sleep* 271: Yea, an' a bust onna beezer! **1943** *Newsweek* (Oct. 4) 94: A baseball comedian with a Bergerac beezer, Schacht had been a minor-league pitcher. **1957** Townley *Up in Smoke* (film): All right, Beezer, Tony wants to see ya. **1985** Dye *Between Raindrops* 68: Fucking piece of rock must have gotten you right on the Goddamn beezer.

befoozled *adj.* befooled, befuddled.

*a***1867** Harris *Lovingood* 199: I swar he wer the wust befoozled man I ever saw. He rub'd his eyes wif his fis', an' batted em a few times.

behind *n.* **1.** the rump. [1786 quot. designates the back part of a woman's gown.]

[*1786 in *OED*: Two young Ladies…with new Hats on their heads, new Bosoms, and new Behinds in a band-box.] ******a***1830** George IV, in *OED*: Go and do my bidding—tell him he lies, and kick his behind in my name! **1840** *Spirit of Times* (May 2) 99: I got a kick in the behind. **1840** *Crockett's Comic Almanac* (unp.): I'll be blowed if you ain't blunting all his rails with your behind! ***1926** D.H. Lawrence *Letters* (Jan. 19) 647: Lucky I'm not a professional behind-kicker. **1936** Kingsley *Men in White* 418: If this happens again, Pete, you get your behind kicked in. **1960** in T.C. Bambara *Gorilla* 53: Froze his behind off one winter in Chicago. **1981** D. Burns *Feeling Good* 75: Get off your behind. **1992** *Crier & Co.* (CNN-TV) (Aug. 6): They refused to let her be anything but bust and behind—can I say that on [TV]?

2. ASS, *n.*, 3.b.

1968 Standish *Non-Stand. Terms* 6: Q. Do you know why the ice man was late on the 2nd floor? A. He got a little behind on the first floor. **1977** *Nat. Lampoon* (Aug.) 64: Maybe ya got a li'l behind in mind! Check it out.

3. ASS, *n.*, 4.

1981 in *West. Folklore* XLIV (1985) 9: The police out to get your behind. **1985** Sawislak *Dwarf* 35: The governor really fried Jimmy McGrath's behind. *a***1988** D. Smith *Firefighters* 153: He then set the fire to cover his behind.

behind *prep.* Esp. *Black E.* **1.** after.

1908 in Fleming *Unforget. Season* 273: Moreover, the gents who did not score behind or in front of Lobert's swat went on and touched the next base. **1962** H. Simmons *On Eggshells* 12: But they didn't go home behind that, hell no. **1963** Williamson *Hustler!* 74: We could…snort it.…Then guys would smoke refers behind it. **1965** C. Brown *Manchild* 176: Shit, if you let somebody stick you up and go on living behind it, you didn't have any business dealing drugs.

2.a. over; about; for.

1955 in *Tenn. Folk. Soc. Bull.* XXII (1956) 22: *Wig behind* [something]— to really go for something. **1965** C. Brown *Manchild* 308: [Just] be cool behind it. **1973** Wideman *Lynchers* 42: And Childress didn't make a big deal behind knowing the cat. **1991** *Donahue* (NBC-TV): The mens here are so weak in Dallas behind a pretty woman.

b. because of; from; as a result of, etc.

1957 H. Simmons *Corner Boy* 38: I'd get mad behind anybody goofing over you. **1958–59** Lipton *Barbarians* 28: I get my kicks behind those problems, Larry. I enjoy them. **1962** M. Braly *Shake Him* 174: I might have to go to jail for a while behind that roust. **1962** H. Simmons *On Eggshells* 156: They thought…you could get a habit behind it. **1965** C. Brown *Manchild* 194: That's selling two-dollar pussy.…The whores would look down on her behind this sort of thing. **1966–67** P. Thomas *Mean Streets* 79: We almost blew the jewels behind your copping that. **1972** Wambaugh *Blue Knight* 33: Went to Q behind armed robbery.

1973–76 J. Allen *Assault* 60: My next beef with the law came when I was seventeen, and it was behind my woman Ann. **1992** *Crier & Co.* (CNN-TV) (Aug. 14): I have seen hundreds…of [patients] die behind AIDS.

3. while under the influence of; using (a drug).

1962 H. Simmons *On Eggshells* 156: You couldn't perform…worth a damn behind no reefer. **1963** M. Braly *Shake Him* 139: I've seen so many good heads, strung-out and ragged behind smack. **1967** Fiddle *Shooting Gallery* 140: In 1963 I got hit by a car behind goofballs. **1969** Mitchell *Thumb Tripping* 23: He found Sol…shivering and wasted behind Methedrine. **1971** Simon *Sign of Fool* 57: She was as stoned on acid as anyone and working behind it, to boot! **1979** D.G. Glasgow *Black Underclass* 29: To relax behind some scotch in his air-conditioned crib.

4. in or into full understanding or knowledge of; HIP to.—often constr. with *it*.

1967 Yablonsky *Hippie Trip* 191: But that's cool and if he leaves for that reason he should leave because he's not behind it enough to stay. **1970** Landy *Underground Dict.* 31: *Behind it*…Aware of; understanding. **1977** Sayles *Union Dues* 277: Jim, this is *war*. You get behind what I'm sayin?

5. besides, on top of.

1970 Landy *Underground Dict.* 31: *Behind*…in addition to.

6. engrossed or excited by, INTO.

1970 Landy *Underground Dict.* 31: *Behind it*…Involved with; engrossed in…*He was really behind it.* Ibid. 87: *Get behind it*…Enjoy a high that is induced by a drug. **1975** Harrell & Bishop *Orderly House* 79: One girl…used to get behind it so much that I had to turn the radio up…every time she had a climax.

¶ In phrases:

¶ **get behind** to begin to smoke or drink (something). Also vars.

1874 Carter *Rollingpin* 15: Dennis soon found himself stationed behind ten cents' worth of a two-bit Havana. **1970** *Playboy* (Feb.) 29: Get behind an A & C Grenadier [cigar]. **1971** Pepsi-Cola ad. (NBC-TV) (Sept. 10): Put yourself behind a Pepsi.

¶ **groove behind** to enjoy greatly. Cf. GROOVE.

1966 Fariña *Down So Long* 60: Try to groove behind the daytime cosmos and you get a faceful of whipped cream. **1967** Wolf *Love Generation* 5: I started to groove behind my trip. **1971** E. Sanders *Family* 205: The Count Dracula Society, a society of well-known filmmen and writers who groove behind old vampire movies.

beige *adj.* bland; uninteresting; unimaginative; boring.

1982 *N.Y. Times* (Sept.) C 10: *Beige*: Boring, fer sure. **1984** Mason & Rheingold *Slanguage*: Pink plastic flamingo's [*sic*] in one's front yard are beige. **1988** N. Stone *Tricks of Trade* (film): Maybe that's what was wrong with your marriage—too beige. **1991** P. Munro *Slang U.* 34: What a beige personality!

bejabbers *n.* [fr. Hiberno-E dial. *bejapers, bejabbers,* euphem. for *by Jesus*] BEJESUS.

1959 E. Hunter *Killer's Wedge* 67: Jesus, it scared the living — bejabbers out of me. **1972** W.C. Anderson *Hurricane* 189: Twirling the beejeebers out of a sling psychometer. **1980** *U.S. News & W.R.* (Nov. 17) 31: Democrats who are still around have had the bejabbers scared out of them. **1982** R. Baker, in *N.Y. Times Mag.* (Aug. 8) 12: An extraterrestrial creature beat the bejabbers out of Little Orphan Annie at the box office. **1985** WINS radio news (Dec. 21): She proceeds to shoot the bejabbers out of the hotel.

bejeepers *n.* BEJABBERS.

1977 *U.S. News & W.R.* (Sept. 5) 30: That "scares the beejeepers out of people." **1981** R.B. Parker *Savage Place* 3: Someone was hugging the bejeepers out of something.

bejesus *n.* [fr. *by Jesus*] **1.** (used as an emphatic expletive); DAYLIGHTS; stuffing. Also vars.

[**1861** Wilkie *Iowa First* 103: Be Jasus, I'll kill any man's sheep that bites me.] [**1908** *DN* III 290: Faith and bejazus!] **1934** W. Smith *Bessie Cotter* 23: He'll beat the be-jesus out of her. **1936** Kingsley *Dead End* 734: Lemme ketch you doin' this again and I'll beat the b'jesus out a you! **1939** M. Levin *Citizens* 280: Al…was running the bejesus out of that old furnace. **1952** B. Malamud *Natural* 48: He fell flat on his stomach, the living bejesus knocked out of him. **1954** R. Lindner *50-Min. Hour* 127: They scare the bejesus out of me. **1958** A. King *Mine Enemy* 61: The little woman bawled the bejeezus out of us. **1960** Krueger *St. Patrick's Batt.* 29: They had a way of waiting, after he'd given them an order, not long enough to bawl the bejesus out of them, but just enough to see if this Michael Fitzgerald was going to obey. **1963** D. Tracy *Brass Ring* 300: The kid had just come back from having the bejesus shot out

of him. **1973** *Oui* (Apr.) 28: Sings the bejeezus out of the old standards. **1975–78** O'Brien *Cacciato* 59: I don't want to scare the bejasus out of you. **1983** *Newsweek* (Feb. 28) 50: Fella oughta kick the bejesus out of a liberal now and then just to stay in shape. **1985** MacLaine *Dancing* 38: Scared the bejesus out of him. **1989** "Captain X" & Dodson *Unfriendly Skies* 73: A Seven-Four's wake can still knock the bejeezus out of you.

2. (used as an intensive or comparative expletive); HELL.

1943 Wolfert *Tucker's People* 409: Let them be bright as bejesus. **1955** Abbey *Brave Cowboy* 184: Who the be-jesus told you that? **1973** W. Burroughs, Jr. *Ky. Ham* 8: I couldn't understand why he hadn't gotten the Bejeezis out of there. **1978** Strieber *Wolfen* 229: Cops scared to bejesus of something that looks like a dog. **1990** Updike *Rabbit at Rest* 238: Perky as bejesus.

bejesus *adj.* (used as an emphatic expletive); (*also*) entirely self-assured.—used prenominally. Also vars.

1884 in Lummis *Letters* 4: A youthful looking Plug Ugly…with a "be-Jesus" swagger. **1930** Lait *On the Spot* 199: Begeezes…High and mighty. (A gangster might speak of a "begeezes copper.") **1971** *Go Ask Alice* 98: That's the only beJesus thing that keeps me from croaking.

belay *v. Naut.* to cease; stop.—usu. imper.

1796** in *OED*: My timbers! what lingo he'd coil and belay. ***1805** J. Davis *Post-Captain* 55: Belay there!…You may tell that to the marines. **1867** Smyth *Sailor's Wd. Bk.* 94: *Belay there.*—Stop! that is enough! *Belay that yarn.*—We have had enough of it! *a1933** in *DARE*: "Belay there a minute." Used by a sailor. **1945** Colcord *Sea Lang.* 33: "Belay your jaw!" means "Shut up!" **1990** P. Dickson *Slang!* 153: *Belay that.* Stop that.

belaying-pin soup *n. Naut.* a beating with a belaying pin. Now *hist.*

1873 Jewell *Among Our Sailors* 178: He then ordered us to keep walking, or next time he would give us some belaying-pin soup, meaning that he would beat us with a belaying-pin. **1887** Davis *Sea-Wanderer* 81 [ref. to 1831]: Stand by to wake 'em up with a little belaying-pin soup. *ca***1910** in W.M. Camp *S.F.* 257: There is too much belaying-pin soup…too much bullyragging and knocking down. **1924** Colcord *Roll & Go* 8: Belaying-pin soup and monkey's liver. **1938** E.J. Mayer *Buccaneer* (film): You shut your trap or I give you belaying-pin soup till you slip your cable! **1976** Hayden *Voyage* 174: More brutality. More of what Monk refers to as "belaying-pin soup."

belch *n.* **1.** a loud complaint.

1899–1900 Cullen *Tales* 332: I'll take care of the cockney, if he makes any belch. **1908** in Fleming *Unforget. Season* 178: After the game Ganzel acknowledged the decision was right, but he made an awful belch at the time. **1911** Van Loan *Big League* 175: You remember what an awful belch there was…when they said the Pinks laid down to let the Grays win? **1922** *Variety* (July 14) 5: To the layman they had a belch comin', but I know I have a real ball club. **1928** O'Connor *B'way Racketeers* 185: That was the cue for the suckers to come around and make their belch. **1928** in E. Wilson *Twenties* 468: I've got a hell of a big belch, Frank. **1946** Evans *Halo in Blood* 9: What's the belch, friend? **1947** *New Yorker* (May 31) 31: What the *Times* calls a *reproof* or a *remonstrance,* the *News* calls a *belch* or a *beef.*

2. a drunken derelict.

1935 E. Anderson *Hungry Men* 64: Those old smoke belches from the Bowery are gumming it up. **1937** E. Anderson *Thieves Like Us* 44: Unlatch that pump, you nosy old belch.

belch *v.* to complain, cry out, or speak out of turn; to blab or gab; (*Und.*) to inform. Hence **belcher** a complainer or informer.

1901 "J. Flynt" *World of Graft* 219: *Beef, Belch.* To "squeal" or "split" on a pal. **1902** Hapgood *Autobiog. Thief* 190 [ref. to *ca*1890]: He certainly preferred to go to stir rather than have the name of being a belcher. **1904** *Life in Sing Sing* 246: *Belched.* spoke; turned informer. **1908** McGaffey *Show Girl* 237: He…lets them know that if he ain't in on the frame-up he'll belch. **1912** Lowrie *Prison* 216: He belched everything he knew. **1914** Jackson & Hellyer *Vocab.* 16: "He cannot stand the gaff without belching."…Also used to denote the giving of information. **1919** *Variety* (May 9) 9: He didn't come from the stock that belches. **1922** *Variety* (July 28) 5: One of them belched…that it was too bad that some men married women old enough to be their mothers and was tied down for life. **1929** Hammett *Maltese Falcon* 71: You belched for help and got to take it. **1949** Mende *Spit & Stars* 116: College guys, big professors…they all keep on belching one thing—the mind. **1971** Sorrentino *Up from Never* 84: Oh, you're always belchin' about something.

belfry *n.* the head, regarded as the seat of sanity or intelligence. See also *bats in the belfry* s.v. BAT[1].

1906 Ford *Shorty McCabe* 216: There might have been a few cobwebs in the belfry. **1908** in H.C. Fisher *A. Mutt* 40: There is no doubt that the defendant had a few screws loose in his belfry even in childhood. **1911** H.S. Harrison *Queed* 84: Something loose in his belfry, as ye might have surmised. **1913** *Chi. Daily Trib.* (May 1) 15: The hit…was converted into a play by a bit of speed on foot and in the belfry. **1925** McAlmon *Silk Stockings* 14: She must be batty in her belfry. **1930** Farrell *Grandeur* 215: Bill…was…a little off in de belfry. **1933** Halper *Union Square* 210: No man can keep that up…without going batty in the belfry. **1948** Wolfert *Act of Love* 433: Buster, you've had it. The bats are playing ping-pong with the bells in your belfry.

Belgie *n.* [E *Belg*ium + -*ie*, infl. by Du *België* 'Belgium'] Esp. *Mil.* a Belgian.

1919 Johnson *Heaven, Hell or Hoboken* 151: Guess the Frogs and Belgies thought we were pro-German. **1928** MacArthur *War Bugs* 248 [ref. to WWI]: The Belgies now insisted that we sleep in their feather beds. **1976** Simon *Murder by Death* [film]: I'm not a Frenchie, I'm a Belgie.

Belgique *n.* [< F 'Belgium'] *Mil.* a Belgian; Belgium.

1925 Fraser & Gibbons *Soldier & Sailor Wds.* 21 [ref. to WWI]: *Belgeek.* Belgium: a Belgian. **1965** Linakis *In Spring* 10 [ref. to 1945]: You hear this Belgique mouthing off about us to the old man?

believer *n.* ¶ In phrase: **make a believer out of** to convince. Cf. *make a Christian out of* s.v. CHRISTIAN.

1966 "Minnesota Fats" *Bank Shot* 86: So they sent a couple of real huskies around to make a believer out of Cokes, and old Hubert whacked them out with his bare fists. **1968–73** in Elting et al. *Soldier Talk* 342: Willy Peter/Make you a buh-liever.

bell *n.* **1.** usu. *pl.* [sugg. by the naut. custom of striking the bell to indicate periods within each watch] o'clock.

1908 in H.C. Fisher *A. Mutt* 113: I'll…set the alarm for 3 bells. The early bird catches the shrimp. **1915** R. Lardner, in Butterfield *Post Treasury* 140: I can't go…unless they leave me come home at eight bells. **1919** O. Wilkins *Co. Fund* 41: I'll be able to "kooshay" till eleven bells Sunday morning. **1919** *Blackhawk Howitzer* 51: What time is it? Good God, only nine bells! **1924** in Lardner *Haircut* 75: I got a date for eight bells. **1928** Bodenheim *Georgie May* 10: What's the time, Mistah? Christ, only five bells. **1933** in Galewitz *Great Comics* 37: Quittin' time for dates is 10 bells. **1959** in Cox *Delinquent, Hipster, Square* 32: Sounds real crazy, Daddy-O, I'm with it. Ten bells? **1987** N.Y.C. woman, age 71: So you'll call me Monday at eleven bells. **1992** Eble *Campus Slang* (Spring) 1: *Bells*—o'clock. "I have my Chem exam at eight bells tomorrow."

2. *pl.* bell-bottomed trousers.

*1945** (cited in Partridge *DSUE* (ed. 7) 1003). **1970** *New Yorker* (Mar. 21) 39: A pair of red velvet bells. **1970** M. Brennan *Drugs* 57: Bells: bell-bottom pants. **1971** Woodley *Dealer* 146: "Bells, man," he said, pulling his bell-bottom pants leg down over the holster. "Sometimes I wear bells." **1978** Fisher & Rubin *Special Teachers* 9: Red and silver platform shoes, fourteen-inch custom-made bells. **1980–84** in P. Eckert *Jocks & Burnouts* 91: Um, they smoked. They wore Levi big bells.

3. BELLHOP.

1972 in *Playboy* (Jan. 1973) 242: "Hotel?"…"Three K, promo, free drinks and that stuff, tips for the bells."

¶ In phrases:

¶ **from the bell** from the very beginning.

1973 Goines *Players* 26: I'd like to ask you a few very personal questions, Vickie, but from the bell, I want you to know that I don't want any lies.

¶ **four bells and a jingle** [ringing four bells is the traditional signal to a ship's engine room to increase speed] *Naut.* (at) top speed. Occ. **four bells.**

1907 *Army & Navy Life* (Sept.) 310: Our battleships are headed this way three bells and a jingle. **1926** *AS* (Oct.): They alone make the ship go four bells and a jingle. **1937** Thompson *Take Her Down* 247: "Give her four bells and a jingle," (meaning emergency full speed). **1938** Connolly *Navy Men* 194: The practice of our destroyers after a torpedo attack was to give the ship the old four bells and a jingle-full speed toward where a periscope had been seen. **1956** Moran & Reid *Tugboat* 316: All hands are going four bells. **1956** Wier & Hickey *Naval Social Customs* 102: Off he went at four bells and a jingle. **1967** Lockwood *Subs* 46: Reaching for the engine bell pull, Metcalf rang up four bells and a jingle, which called for everything the engineer could give her.

¶ **hop bells** to work as a bellhop.

1942 *ATS* 259: *Hop bells,* (work) as a bell hop. **1954** L. Armstrong *Satchmo* 133: I kind of liked hopping bells because it gave me a chance to go into the houses and see what was going on. **1958** Cooley *Run for Home* 33: I hop bells up the street. **1967** Wepman et al. *The Life* 114: I'd…Hopped bells in the hotels of Chi.

¶ **knock seven bells out of** *Naut.* to beat vigorously; "knock hell out of."

1849–50 in Glanz *Jew in Folklore* 180: Hands off…or I'll knock seven bells out of ye. **1887** M. Roberts *W. Avernus* 191: Get up, or I'll knock seven bells out of you! **1906** *Independent* (Jan. 4) 31: I saw Captain Larruper…in his usually morning pastime of knocking seven bells out of the cabin boy with a rope's end. **1924** Garahan *Stiffs* 61: You wait, I'll knock seven bells out of the…old stiff one of these days. **1939** Willoughby *Sondra* 128: That light cruiser needs some guy to knock seven bells out of [him]. *1977** T. Jones *Incredible Voyage* 213: The Celts had the habit of knocking seven bells of shit out of one another when they found who had been sleeping with whom the night before.

¶ **ring (someone's) bell** Orig. *Sports.* to hit (someone) very hard, esp. on the head. Also vars.

1969 in Bouton *Ball Four* 35: The cups are metal inserts that fit inside the jock strap, and when a baseball hits one it's called ringing the bell. **1972** G. Shaw *Meat on Hoof* 48 [ref. to 1963]: He could hardly wait to get at it—he would "ring some bells." **1981** Yates *Cannonball Run* (film): I think he's just had his bell rung. **1983** Ehrhart *VN-Perkasie* 352: The corpsman had been trying to find out if I'd had my bell rung too badly to continue fighting. **1985** Univ. Tenn. instructor, age 36: To *ring somebody's bell* is to hit them on the head. It's a football expression. **1984–88** in Berry *Where Ya Been?* 208: He really had his bell rung!

¶ **ring the bell, 1.** to induce an orgasm.

1918 in Carey *Mlle. from Armentieres* II (unp.): Many a shot that rang the bell/Was just a dud to this Mademoiselle. **1974** E. Thompson *Tattoo* 162: "Don't think I can't ring your bell, buddy," she added aggressively.…"I'll show you what this sex stuff is all about."

2. to be especially successful or impressive. Now *S.E.*

1928 in *OEDS*: This [book], liberally illustrated, with a great jacket, rings the bell. **1951** Hunt *Judas Hour* 125: Your country…doesn't happen to ring any bells with me. **1966** *RHD*: This new book rings the bell with teenagers.

3. to impregnate a woman.

1935 J. Conroy *World to Win* 42: Hade Pollard…had rung the bell nine times to get six boys and three girls. **1962** McMurtry *Cheyenne* 178: I done rung the bell a time or two before, in my life.

4. see *ring (someone's) bell,* above.

¶ **with bells [on], 1.** eager and ready to enjoy oneself.

1899 Cullen *Tales* 89: I had enough to get back here with bells on inside of a couple of months. **1907** Hobart *Beat It!* 96: We'll meet you at the pier with bells on. **1907** in H.C. Fisher *A. Mutt* 14: Mutt will be there with bells to-morrow. **1911** A.H. Lewis *Apaches of N.Y.* 268: Mark Antony is there with bells on. **1914** Paine *Wall Between* 251: He'll be there with bells on. **1919** Barth *20th Aero Sq.* 43: The next morning we were there with bells on. **1922** F.S. Fitzgerald *Beautiful & Damned* 187: All-ll-ll righty. I'll be there with bells on. **1936** M. Levin *Old Bunch* 221: I'll be there with bells on. **1966** *RHD*: I'll come to your party with bells on. **1992** Seattle woman, age 25 (coll. J. Sheidlower): I suspect we'll all be there for dinner with bells on.

2. (used as an intensifier).

1906 H. Green *Actors' Boarding House* 28: We're gettin' back with bells on. **1930** Bodenheim *Roller Skates* 156: You can have it…with bells on. **1960** R. Leckie *Marines* 3: The same to you with bells on.

belle *n. Homosex.* a male homosexual who habitually imitates feminine behavior.

1940 in T. Williams *Letters* 6: The "crowd" here is dominated by a platinum blond Hollywood belle named Doug and a bull-dike named Wanda. **1944** in T. Williams *Letters* 135: Lots of the belles are showing up with wives this season. **1949** *Gay Girl's Guide* 3: *Belle:* Used with various connotations such as 1) any homosexual; 2) a young, flashy and possibly beautiful homosexual. Often used interchangeably with *queen*. **1952** "E. Box" *Fifth Position* 126: One for the belle, I said to myself. **1956** *Social Problems* III 258: Raymond…gave me a letter of introduction to one of the local belles. **1972** *Anthro. Linguistics* (Mar.) 99: *Belle* (n.): A male homosexual who is noticeably effeminate and usually fairly young and attractive. *a1990** Bérubé *Coming Out* 25: Here was this man who was a screaming belle…a queen if ever I saw one!

bellhop *n.* **1.** a bellboy or bellman, as in a hotel. Now *colloq.*

1902 Dunne *Obser. Mr. Dooley* 15: Kings an' imprors duck about their jooties like bell-hops. **1907** *McClure's* (Mar.) 554: You've got to be the "bell hop." **1910** Ade *Knew Him When* 14: He is not a bell hop—the boys used to dress like that. **1920** *Variety* (Sept. 10) 5: He...gives the old ones to the bell hop. **1925** Loos *Gent. Prefer Blondes* 40: So I sent out a bell hop friend of Dorothy. **1946** J. Adams *Gags* 85: "What are you, a big shot?" said the bellhop. **1950** A. Lomax *Mr. Jelly Roll* 205: A bellhop will do almost anything for twenty dollars. **1959–60** Bloch *Dead Beat* 116: He'd been a bellhop. **1971** J. Campbell *Myths to Live By* 165: Into this single chamber three permanent guests are to be introduced by the bellhop, one by one. **1979** C. Freeman *Portraits* 337: Bellhops know everything if you slip them a few dollars.

2. *Mil.* a U.S. Marine.—used derisively. In full, **sea-going bellhop.**

1928 *Our Army* (Oct.) 11: [U.S. Marines have been] called..."Seagoing Bellhops," but "Leatherneck" meets with...official approval. **1929** *Our Army* (Feb.) 46: Marines have been good humorously dubbed "Bellhops." **1943** *Amer. Mercury* (Nov.) 552: Marines are *bellhops* and *girenes* to the bluejackets. **1958** Frankel *Band of Bros.* 46: With bellhops, they can smell a brew ten miles away. **1960** Leckie *Marines!* 144: So, now you sea-going bell hops...get t' hell over the side and start chipping them plates. **1962** Quirk *Red Ribbons* 50: I accept the compliment on behalf of all sea-going bellhops. **1967** Dubus *Lieut.* 167: Just a minute, bellhop. **1980** Manchester *Darkness* 419: A supercilious pair of junior army officers who were reconnoitering the front, addressing us as "bellhops." **1982** T.C. Mason *Battleship* 8: While [the Marines] looked resplendent at inspections in their "seagoing bellhop" dress uniforms, they were still cops. **a1990** Westcott *Half a Klick* 196: I don't take orders from bellhops.

3. *Mil. Av.* (see quot.).

1969 Cagle *Naval Av. Guide* 389: *Bellhop* A specially equipped airplane serving as a radar relay.

bellhop *v.* to work as a bellhop.

1926 Hormel *Co-Ed* 192: Bell-hopped for two months at a Cape Cod hotel. **1928** Dahlberg *Bottom Dogs* 255: I was bellhopping at the plaza. **1954** "Collans" & Sterling *House Detect.* 13: Bellhopping in a big resort hotel was the best possible training for a young man who was going to spend most of his life as a house detective. **1954** Bissell *High Water* 41: Brother Tim [is] bellhoppin' over to the hotel. **1965** *Time* (Mar. 19) 55: After that it was bellhopping in Nashville...for a dime a week and tips.

bellhopper *n.* BELLHOP, 1.

1900 Ade *More Fables* 98: The Bell-Hopper told him to Turn In and get a Good Night's Rest.

bellows *n.pl.* the lungs.

*1821 *Real Life in London* II 57: *Bellows*—A cant term for the lungs. **1821–26* [Stewart] *Man-of-War's-Man* I 129: Pray, what is't to me after my bellows have ceased, and my toplights doused, what you makes on me? **1842** *Spirit of Times* (Oct. 29) 416: Bellows to mend [i.e., weak lungs] is no treat to me. **1846** in Lowell *Poetical Wks.* 185: *His* bellowses is sound enough. **1884** Blanding *Sailor Boy* 41: "Go in, Bill." "Inflate your bellows." **1900** *Volunteer* (Univ. Tenn.) 173: I wished she had punctured his bellows or put a crimp in his safety-valve. **1910** T.A. Dorgan, in *N.Y. Eve. Jour.* (Jan. 4) 12: Jake's stomach and bellows are not what they used to be. **1922** in S. Smith *Gumps* 22: It's my own bellowing and comes from my own bellows. **1926** *Sat. Eve. Post* (Nov. 6) 136: Let's hope it missed my bellows!

bell ox *n.* *Logging.* a crew foreman.

1956 Sorden & Ebert *Logger's* 3 [ref. to *a*1920]: *Bell-ox*, Foreman.

bell-ringer *n.* **1.** an outstanding success.

1940 *AS* (Apr.) 204: *Bell-ringer.* A decided success. **1968** Hawley *Hurricane Yrs.* 73: He'll come up with an idea. I don't say it'll always be a bell-ringer.

2. *Horse Racing.* (see quot.).

1968 M.B. Scott *Racing Game* 101: The bellringer is someone who seeks to make a wager *after* the horses have left the starting gate.

bellrope *n.* penis.

1969 Green & Peckinpah *Wild Bunch* (film): Me and Tector was gettin' our bellrope pulled by two—two!—Honda whores! **1970** Landy *Underground Dict.* 31: *Bell rope*...Penis.

bells and whistles *n.pl.* inessential but engaging features; gimmicks.

1969 (cited in *W10*). **1982** *Atlantic* (Oct.) 31: "Bells and whistles" is Pentagon slang for extravagant frills. **1983** Naiman *Computer Dict.* 19: The program's basically written; all we're doing now is adding some bells and whistles. **1984** *Business Week* (Sept. 10) 48: Eighty percent of our customers don't want the bells and whistles. They just want a play-

back unit. **1989** *CBS This Morning* (CBS-TV) (Dec. 28): This is for your person who really likes bells and whistles [on an exercise bicycle]. **1991** *New Yorker* (Sept. 2) 58: Eggers' design had indeed sprouted a number of bells and whistles, among them inflatable rubber ailerons at the back of its fuselage.

belly *n.* **1.** *Entertainment Industry.* a belly laugh.

1928 J. Conway, in *Variety* (Sept. 19) 47: Stanley also gets a few bellies. **1932** Hecht & Fowler *Great Magoo* 34: "Lots of jokes?"..."Full of bellies."

2. nerve; determination; "guts."

1949 in *Harper's* (Feb. 1950) 72: He has plenty of belly, or courage. **1966** Olsen *Hard Men* 46: Maybe that would give you some belly.

belly *v.* to consume, put into the belly.

1947 R. Carter *Baggy Pants* 275: Let's belly the rest of that bottle and be off!

bellyache *n.* [fr. the *v.*] a complaint, esp. if unjustified; complaining.

1929 Burnett *Iron Man* 10: Now start your bellyache. **1938** Bellem *Blue Murder* 13: I was just about to put up some more belly ache when I heard a noise.

bellyache *v.* [cf. syn. GRIPE] to whine or complain. Hence **bellyacher,** *n.*

*a*1881 in F & H I (rev.): *Bellyache, to.*—A coined word, meaning "to grumble without good cause." Employees *bellyache* at being overworked or when they fancy themselves underfed. A vulgarism. **1898* (cited from Dorset in *EDD* I 237). **1900** Willard & Hodler *Powers That Prey* 183: You've been belly-aching around these joints for the last two months. **1903** in C.M. Russell *Paper Talk* 50: Well I kept bellyaking saying my turn an the big kid saying youl get yours. **1909** J. Moss *Officer's Manual* (ed. 2) 283: *Bellyache.*—to complain. **1927** McKay *Harlem* 12: Was always bellyaching for a chance over the top. **1928** Dobie *Vaquero* 104: If in the midst of such gruelling and desperate work there was plenty of "belly-aching," there was plenty of cheer. **1928** Scanlon *Have Mercy* 5: But we didn't belly-ache very much. **1927–30** Rollins *Jinglebob* 31 [ref. to 1880's]: He won't have no real ground for belly-achin'. **1930** in *DA*: These voluble doubters were commonly called old croakers, backbiters, "bellyachers." **1933** E. Caldwell *Little Acre* 8: I reckon there's enough to complain about these days if a fellow wants to bellyache some. **1943** J. Mitchell *McSorley's* 118: I put the bite on him real often, and he never bellyached. **1945** Dos Passos *Tour* 45: Bellyachin' about strikes an' the loads of stupids we've got in Congress. **1955** S. Wilson *Gray Flannel Suit* 65: You took an easy job, and we both bellyached all the time because you didn't get more money. **1969** Gardner *Fat City* 10: I'm sick of your bellyaching. **1983** *Fall Guy* (ABC-TV): Wonder what he's bellyachin' about this time. **1983** *Agronsky & Co.* (radio news show) (Mar. 6): I hear them bellyachin' about a miserable little sixty-million-dollar apportionment. **1990** *Car & Driver* (Oct.) 92: We might have whined and bellyached about that, too.

belly-bomber *n.* a greasy hamburger. Cf. syn. GUT BOMB.

1985 WINS radio news (Mar. 23): There are even discount hamburgers. ...You can order up 100 belly bombers delivered to your door for $82.

belly-burglar *n.* BELLY-ROBBER.

1919 Warren *Ninth Co.* 34: The Engineer's Dictionary. Cooks—*Belly-burglars.* **1927** *AS* (June) 391: A sheriff who puts his guests on meager rations is cursed as a *belly burglar.* **1929** *Frontier* (Jan.) 95 [ref. to *ca*1908]: The boss of the [loggers] cookhouse in those days was invariably referred to as "the belly-burglar." **1948** J. Stevens *Jim Turner* 117 [ref. to *ca*1910]: The belly burglar, as the crew called the cook, got up at four.

bellybutton *n.* **1.** the navel. Now *colloq.* or *S.E.*

1877 Bartlett *Amer.* (ed. 4) 39: *Belly button.* The navel. **1945** Bowman *Beach Red* 31: You can stand in mud up to your bellybutton. **1962** R.E. Pike *Spiked Boots* 41: Ice water up to your belly-button. **1970** Della Femina *Wonderful Folks* 188: But no belly buttons on the air....Forget that every kid has a belly button. **1976–77** C. McFadden *Serial* 18: By wearing his shirts unbuttoned to the belly button.

2. *Mil. Av.* a ball turret. Now *hist.*

1958 Camerer *Damned Wear Wings* 24 [ref. to WWII]: Saw it all from my ringside seat...curled up in that bubble of a belly button.

belly-cheater *n.* *West.* BELLY-ROBBER. Now *hist.*

1911 Fletcher *Up the Trail* 9 [ref. to 1879]: Mr. Snyder discharged our cook, who was a worthless scamp and a belly cheater. *a*1940 in Lanning & Lanning *Texas Cowboys* 61 [ref. to 1890's]: John Held...was the belly-cheater when we were out with the chuck wagon. **1972** Bercovici & Prentiss *Culpepper Cattle Co.* (film): Hey, you old belly-cheaters.

belly cut *n. Med.* a surgical operation on the abdomen.
  1980 *AS* (Spring) 47.

belly fiddle *n. Jazz.* a guitar or string bass.
  1939 Calloway *Swingformation Bureau*: A git-box or a belly fiddle is a…guitar. **1940** *New Yorker* (Sept. 14) 19: Like a bass-man picks at a belly fiddle.

belly grease *n.* hard liquor.
  1931 Hellinger *Moon* 234: Slip me another shot of belly grease and we'll all have laughs.

belly gun *n.* a short-barreled handgun carried at one's waist *or* pressed into a victim's waist.
  1926 Finerty *Criminalese* 10: Belly gun—Snubnosed weapon carried on abdomen. **1929–31** in Partridge *Dict. Und.* 31: *Belly gun*…a short-barrelled .32–.20 gun: squat, ugly type of weapon for cramming against the stomach of a victim and firing with deadly results. **1935** Pollock *Underworld Speaks*: *Belly gun*, a short-barreled pistol usually jammed against the stomach of a victim. **1943** Chandler *High Window* 366: I had a…Colt .32, same caliber as that, but a belly gun. A revolver, not an automatic. **1972** *N.Y. Times* (Aug. 13) 4 3: The so-called "Saturday night specials," "belly guns" and "man stoppers." **1978** Time-Life *Gamblers* 144: The barrel was sawed off this…revolver…to convert it into a belly gun, which a gambler could hide by tucking it into the waistband of his trousers.

belly guts *n.* molasses candy.
  1849 in *DA*: *Belly Guts*, a Pennsylvania word, now becoming obsolete, being supplanted by the more elegant, though perhaps not quite correct, name of molasses candy. **1870** *Nation* (July 28) 56: Molasses candy…"Belly guts" was the name it bore [in E. Penna., ca1825]. **1871** Schele de Vere *Amer.* 441: *Belly-guts* is the unaesthetic name given in Pennsylvania to molasses candy.

belly queen *n. Homosex.* (see 1965, a1972 quots.).
  1965 Trimble *Sex Words* 24: *Belly Queen*…A male homosexual preferring face-to-face intercourse. *a*1972 Rodgers *Queens' Vernacular* 30: *Belly queen* 1. homosexual attracted to lean, trim stomachs. 2. one who rubs his penis on his partner's stomach until ejaculation. **1988** *Nat. Lampoon* (Apr.) 28: Where there are belly-queens, there is disease.

belly-robber *n. Esp. Mil.* **1.** an individual in charge of administering provisions; (*specif.*) a cook.
  1914 *DN* 150: Belly-robber…commissary steward. **1916** *Rio Grande Rattler* (Sept. 13) 1: All cooks are familiarly known…as "belly robbers." **1917** *Editor* (Jan. 13) 33: "Belly robber"—Mess sergeant. **1919** W. Duffy *GPF* 349: Mess Sgt.— you can't be called a belly-robber, you always gave us lots of fodder. **1920** *Amer. Legion Wkly.* (Oct. 8) 13: They ate steak with the belly robbers, while the rest of the company got slum or goldfish or gravelly beans. **1929** *Sat. Eve. Post* (Apr. 13) 50: Of course, the kitchen officer [in a prison] is the belly robber. **1940** *AS* (Dec.) 450: *Belly Robber.* A phrase usually applied to the steward or the cook on a ship which feeds badly. **1942** *Leatherneck* (Nov.) 141: Belly Robber—Cook or baker. **1946–51** J. Jones *Here to Eternity* 168: I was acting bellyrobber on one stripe. **1961** Kerchove *Intern. Maritime Dict.* (ed. 2): *Belly-robber.* (U.S.) Slang term for chief steward. **1963** Ross *Dead Are Mine* 130: I wouldn't have minded if he hadn't pulled it in front of those belly-robbers and jeep jockeys. **1963** G. Coon *Short End* 117: I had decided to…catch some food, or whatever it was our belly-robbers would be passing off as food. **1971** Curtis *Banjo* 167: An enormous mess-hall where thousands of men carrying tinware went past the lines of cursing belly-robbers. **1974** Vietnam veteran, age *ca*26: The *belly robber* is the cook or the mess sergeant. We had one guy at Ft. Polk who was always talking about "hanging out with the belly-robbers." *a*1989 C.S. Crawford *Four Deuces* 132: His regular duty being an assistant belly robber.
  2. an officer or other person in authority who administers provisions in a niggardly manner; (*hence*) anyone who takes more than a fair share of available provisions. Hence **belly-robbing**, *adj.* [Prob. the orig. sense.]
  1918 Ruggles *Navy* 21: A commissary steward or paymaster who the crew thinks is grafting off them and not giving them their full allowance is known as a "belly-robber." Used in the old days before Uncle Sam saw to the buying himself. **1929** Barr *Let Tomorrow Come* 118: We'll go hungry anyway, you belly-robbin' bastard. **1930** "D. Stiff" *Milk & Honey* 199: *Belly robber*—a boarding boss who tries to save money on food. **1935** C. Odets *Paradise* 191: The bellyrobbers have taken clothes from our backs. **1936** Duncan *Over the Wall* 135: I'm going to tell you all you damned belly robbers what I think of you before I leave. **1937** Johnston *Prison Life* 34: I bet the warden would make a

great hit with the cons if he'd can that belly-robber in the commissary. **1938** Noble *Jugheads* 101: The mess sergeant was a stingy belly-robber. **1959** Sterling *Wahoo* 101: Bunch of belly-robbers. **1960** R. Leckie *Marines* 3: A couple of chowhounds had already gotten in line for seconds….I shoved right in front of them…."Deadbeat, hell, you belly-robber," I said. **1966** D. Gallery *Start Engines* 156: They're still belly-robbers in my book.

belly-rub *n. Esp. So.* a dancing party.
  1928 Fisher *Jericho* 88: She's right hyeh at d'belly-rub to-night. **1937** *AS* (Feb.) 74: *Belly-rub, crab-exchange*—dance of low-grade nature. **1941** *AS* (Feb.) 21: *Belly-rub*, A dance. **1943** *AS* (Feb.) 66: *Belly-rub* (a dance). S.C., N.C., Tenn. **1944** *PADS* (No. 2) 53: *Belly-rub*, n. Almost any dance. N.w. Ark….Nashville, Tenn.; Durham, N.C.; Charleston, S.C. **1965** Schmitt *All Hands Aloft* 253 [ref. to WWI]: "All cadets hev' half day off to go achore for de big belly rub, t'night!"…I had forgotten about the dance to be given by the American ladies.

belly-rub *v.* to dance very close to one's partner.
  1971 T.C. Bambara *Gorilla* 8: You want me to belly rub with the Raven, that it?

belly timber *n.* food; provisions.
  *1607 in *OED*: We had some belly-timber at your table. **1625, *1663* in *OED. ca1740* in W.H. Kenney *Laughter in Wilderness* 64: Now order store of belly-timber. **1753, *1820* in *OED*. **1830** J. Martin *Narr. Rev. Soldier* 83: After we had got regulated again, we began to contrive how we were to behave in our present circumstances, as it regarded belly timber. **1833** J. Neal *Down-Easters* I 71: As if he hated the very knives and forks for interfering with a more summary method of getting into what he called the "belly-timber." **1847** Downey *Cruise of Portsmouth* 216: Matelo's…[were] loaded to the bends with what they called Belly Timber. **1858* A. Mayhew *Paved with Gold* 269: He helps to bring in the "belly timber" (food). **1898** Green *Va. Folk-Speech* 56: *Belly-timber, n.* Food; that which supplies the belly. **1979** in *AS* (Summer 1981) 157: He could really put away the belly-timber.

belly-up *adj.* dead; (*hence*) finished; in or into failure or bankruptcy.—usu. constr. with *go*.
  [**1878** Hart *Sazerac* 43: Pretty soon would the fish would come belly-on the water.] **1920** in Dos Passos *Chronicle*: Labor's belly up completely—The only hope is the I.W.W. **1929–30** Dos Passos *42d Parallel* 358: He wanted to get in on it before the whole thing went bellyup. **1970** in H.S. Thompson *Shark Hunt* 26: That's the time to strike. They'll go belly up every time. **1972** *New Yorker* (Nov. 11) 80: It had already crossed Liebergot's mind that the astronauts could be what they called "belly up" in a matter of hours. **1973** *Nat. Lampoon* (Sept.) 49: The Boondogglers almost went belly-up in 1970. **1980** *Mork & Mindy* (ABC-TV): Well, no. She hasn't gone belly up. **1983** *Minding Your Business* (WKGN radio) (May 25): If a [pension] plan should go belly-up, in steps the PBGC. **1990** *New Republic* (Nov. 19) 7: We're trying to encourage capital investment and joint ventures that will keep the economy from going belly-up.

belly up *v.* to approach and stand with one's stomach against (a bar or table); (*hence*) to approach boldly.
  1907 S.E. White *Arizona* 80: The Irishman bellied up to the bar again, and pounded on it with his fist. **1933** Witherspoon *Liverpool Jarge* (unp.): We…bellied up to the long bar. **1938** Holbrook *Holy Old Mackinaw* 17: Champagne was poured from original bottles into washtubs, and all invited to belly-around and drink hearty. **1951** West *Flaming Feud* 44: Together they bellied up to the bar. **1958** Bard & Spring *Horse Wrangler* 119: They were bellied up to the bar and havin' a drink. **1958** McCulloch *Woods Words* 10: *Belly up*…an invitation to shove up to a table, in other words, "come and get it." **1969** *Atlantic* (Aug.) 95: The Atlanta Arts Alliance did belly up to the bar quite admirably. **1974** *Time* (Jan. 14) 45: The time is upon us, gentlemen, to belly up to the buzz saw and do something about this. **1978** L'Amour *Proving Trail* 3: I bellied up to a table in the Bon Ton and ordered. **1992** M. Gelman *Crime Scene* 96: I couldn't…belly-up to the bar with them like some other cop reporters.
  2. to die; (*hence*) to fail or go bankrupt.
  1975 *L.A. Times* (Nov. 4) 1 1: [The fruit flies] swarmed for a few moments, and then 4 million of them bellied up. **1979** D. Thoreau *City at Bay* 27: The old farts are gonna belly up. **1980** R.L. Morris *Wait until Dark* 121: Payoffs and bribes to police and other officials caused the majority [of speakeasies] to belly-up. **1986** Heinemann *Paco's Story* 130: Plenty good Marines bellied up because of cocksuckers like him.

bellywash *n.* **1.** a soft or weak drink, esp. as contrasted to strong beer or hard liquor.
  1889 *Century Dict.*: Belly-wash…Any kind of drink of poor quality.

(Vulgar.). **1900** *DN* II 22: *Bellywash.* Any soft drink. **1903** *Independent* (Nov. 26) 2795: Jungle fever and dysentery soon became epidemic throughout the ship. In vain the port sawbones dosed us with various kinds of "belly wash." **1926** Wood & Goddard *Amer. Slang* 5: *Belly-wash.* Soft drink, soda water, etc. **1926** E. Springs *Nocturne* 151: You'll have to wait until you get back to town or go in and bum some synthetic belly-wash. **1927** *AS* (Oct.) 25: All soda water, coca cola, and near beer are called "belly wash." **1928** Santee *Cowboy* 82: Tex drunk straight whisky…an' I took belly-wash (soft drink). **1928** MacArthur *War Bugs* 252: A belly wash of grenadine and plain water cost another fifty cents. **1929** Botkin *Folk-Say* I 108: They had a spot of bellywash—their quaint characterization for…coffee. **1932** *AS* (June) 329: *Belly-wash*—bad liquor. **1933** Clifford *Boats* 162: He drank half of the glass of champagne. "I'll probably get tight on this bellywash." **1966–67** Stevens *Gunner* 173: This stuff here ain't nothin but bellywash. **1979** E. West *Saloon* 110: A few outraged observers claimed to have paid up to two dollars for a shot of bellywash. **1988** *N.Y. Daily News* (June 9) 45: *Bellywash* (Pepsi).

2. thin, unappetizing soup.

1934 Kromer *Waiting* 65: How much of this belly-wash can you eat? **1954–60** *DAS.*

belly wax *n. Juve.* (see quot.).

1893 *DN* I 328: *Bellywax*, n. molasses candy.

belt *n.* **1.** a heavy blow, as with the fist.

1864 in R.L. Wright *Irish Emigrant Ballads* 517: An' I gav' a big "Yankee" a belt in the gob. **1864** in J.W. Haley *Rebel Yell* 210: A belt in the gob. **1886** Nye *Remarks* 89: Williams snatched off the belt of your little Norfolk jacket, and then gave you one in the eye. **1892** *DN* I 235: Hit him a belt. *1899 in OEDS: Will I give him [sc. a horse] a couple o' belts, your Honour? **1907** Hobart *Beat It!* 35: The foregoing thought hit me a belt in the thinker. **1909** *DN* III 408: *Belt, n.* A blow. **1912** Ade *Babel* 112: An awful belt across the head. **1923** in W.F. Nolan *Black Mask Boys* 61: One belt on the head.

2. a swallow, as of strong liquor. Cf. SLUG.

1922 *DN* V 326: *Belt, n.*…Drink. **1943** H.A. Smith *Putty Knife* 124: He…handed me the bottle and I took a belt at it. **1957** Lacy *Room to Swing* 53: I'd like a few more belts. **1971** B.B. Johnson *Blues for Sister* 87: I'd go out looking for a belt…and I don't drink!

3. a surge of excitement; a thrill, as from liquor or drugs; KICK.

1932 D. Runyon, in *Collier's* (Dec. 3) 7: He always seems to be getting a great belt out of life. **1936** Dai *Opium Add.* 196: *Belt.* The sensation derived from the use of drugs. Also called *kick, boot, drive.* **1948** Lait & Mortimer *New York* 119: White women learned where they could get a "belt," a "jolt," or a "gow." Reefer-smokers are called "gowsters." **1979** *L.A. Times* (Apr. 8) VIII 3: I really got a belt out of it….It seemed like more of a game sometimes than a business.

4. an attempt; crack.

1953 in C. Beaumont *Best* 49: Science, mathematics, and chemistry—with an occasional belt at electronics.

5. an act of copulation.

1961 Forbes *Goodbye to Some* 76 [ref. to WWII]: They caught some nurse peddlin' her ass….She was gettin' five hundred a belt.

¶ In phrases:

¶ **pull (one's) belt** *Army.* to place (one) on report.

1919 *Twelfth U.S. Infantry* 116: Just to save some "Buddie" from going to the "mill" or having his "belt pulled."

¶ **under (one's) belt** within (one's) belly; *(hence)* to (one's) credit.

1839 *Spirit of Times* (Dec. 21) 498: Away we went, each bearing, under his belt, his full share of the antifogmatical…compound. **1870** Duval *Big-Foot* 219: I secured at least a gallon "under my belt." **1896** Ade *Artie* 34: He loved me that night. Mebbe that's because he had a few under his belt. **1908** in H.C. Fisher *A. Mutt* 32: I could run forever with that hunch under my belt. **1920** in Hemingway *Sel. Letters* 39: Dempsey…has never had a real fight yet, Geo. has a pile of them under his belt. **1925–26** Black *You Can't Win* 220: Those hop fiends….Everything is…rosy to them when they get a few pills under their belts. **1929** in R.E. Howard *Book* 62: I had no great amount of liquor under my belt. **1990** *U.S. News & W.R.* (Mar. 5) 59: An entrepreneur with two successful start-ups under his belt.

¶ **wear the belt** [from the custom of awarding a bejeweled belt to boxing champions] to be recognized as surpassing all others in a certain field. Also vars.

1865 [Browne] *Ward: Travels* 43: As a slap-jackist, she has no ekal. She wears the Belt. **1868** Macy *There She Blows!* 56: It ain't no use to talk

any after dat story….We's heard enough. I guess Cooper can take de belt. [**1889** *Century Dict.* I 519: *To hold the belt*, to hold the championship in pugilism or some other athletic exercise.]

belt *v.* **1.a.** to flog with or as with a belt; strike hard.

*1818 in *EDD* I 238 [Scotland]: I wish he had belbit your shoulders as aft as has done mine. *1854 in *OEDS*: He got a good belting. **1866** (quot. at SNOUT). **1866** in Hilleary *Webfoot* 189: Noticed the belting of men over the head and shoulders with a musket if they did not keep just to the mark. **1876** "M. Twain" *Tom Sawyer* 26 [ref. to ca1845]: Hold on, now, what 'er you belting *me* for? **1878** McElroy *Andersonville* 361: Belting other fellows over the head with a capstan bar. **1883** "M. Twain" *Huck. Finn* ch. ii: They don't think nothing of…belting a Sunday-School superintendent over the head. **1892** Garland *Prairie Folks* 247: I was just a-goin' to when Bill belted you one. **1899** F.P. Dunne, in Schaaf *Dooley* 105: An' lavin' him belt a steer over th' head with a sledge-hammer. **1932** V. Fisher *Tragic Life* 121: I'll belt you in your eye. **1937** Hellman & Kingsley *Dead End* (film): Go on home or I'll belt ya one. **1971** Cameron *First Blood* 21: Why'd you belt Palmer here?

b. to defeat soundly, as in a brawl; to trounce.

1837 Neal *Charcoal Sks.* 46: He intends to belt me, does he? **1898** Green *Va. Folk-Speech* 56: *Belt*, v. To beat; to whip.

c. *Baseball.* to score runs against (a pitcher).

1939–40 Tunis *Kid from Tomkinsville* 50: Well, it's not the first time you been belted, I guess. **1992** Strawberry & Rust *Darryl* 178: HoJo had belted Danny Cox out of the park. *Ibid.* 184: I've seen this guy belted so bad he didn't know where he was.

2. to guzzle (whiskey or other liquor); hence in phr. **belt the bottle** to drink habitually or excessively.

1845 in Harris *High Times* 46: He can belt six shillins worth of corn-juice at still-house rates and travel. **1850** in Blair & McDavid *Mirth* 105: "That's the best red eye I've swallowed in a coon's age," said the speaker, after belting a caulker. **1857** *Spirit of Times* (Dec. 26) 544: A gallon pitcher, about half full (the other half his Honor had belted) of "red-eye." **1922** *DN* V 326: *Belt*…v. Drink. **1930** D. Runyon, in *Collier's* (Feb. 1) 8: Then I get to belting that old black bottle around. **1930** D. Runyon, in *Collier's* (Mar. 22) 21: Handsome Jack takes to belting the old grape right freely to get his zing back. **1960** in *OEDS*: He is given to belting the bottle. **1965** Linakis *In Spring* 16: I belted a few armagnacs. **1966** "Minnesota Fats" *Bank Shot* 48: The…Volstead Act…said any sucker found belting the booze was a public enemy. **1979** McGivern *Soldiers of '44* 190: The way he's belting that booze, he could be passed out somewhere. **1981** P. Sann *Trial* 115: You're not goin' to start beltin' the sauce again?

3. to hurry, rush.

1894 *Outing* 24:57: I belted along as fast as the waders and treacherous footing would allow. **1953** J. Crosby, in *N.Y. Herald Tribune* (Mar. 11) 25: As for the propriety of Godfrey's belting around in Air Force planes, I see nothing wrong in it. **1965** *Sat. Eve. Post* (Feb. 13) 70: An old Jaguar belted through into the straight and passed him.

4. to copulate with (a woman).

1961 G. Forbes *Goodbye to Some* 129 [ref. to WWII]: Did you belt any of those nurses?

¶ In phrase:

¶ **belt it** (of a man) to masturbate.

1977 Dunne *Confessions* 82: He was belting it, I bet. And saying ooohhh and ahhhhhh on the telephone.

belted *adj.* (see quot.).

1971 Guggenheimer *Narc. & Drug Abuse* 5: *Belted.* Under the influence of drugs or alcohol.

belt out *v.* **1.** to knock unconscious; *(hence)* to beat up; *(hence, in 1966 quot.)* to defeat soundly, trounce.

1942 *ATS* 674: *Knock out.* Belt out,…cold-cock,…cream,…kayo [etc.]. **1947** Schulberg *Harder They Fall* 94: Chased around the ring, caught flat-footed,…finally belted out. **1955** Graziano & Barber *Somebody Up There* 363: That was why I got belted out by Tony Zale in Newark four years ago. **1966** "Minnesota Fats" *Bank Shot* 104: I might be in Cleveland one day belting out Oklahoma Whitey, who hung at a [pool] room called the Bucket of Blood. **1973** Breslin *World Without End* 25: You fuckin' near belted him out. **1977** Hamill *Flesh & Blood* 39: I hear you belted out a couple of cops before you got here.

2. *Music.* to sing (a song) in a loud or forceful manner. Now *colloq.*

1953 *Sat. Review* (Dec. 12) 55: Standing there…belting out…Porter's "Get Out of Town." **1959** in Steinbeck *Once Was a War*: One of the finest jazz combos I ever heard was belting out pure ecstasy. **1975** Boatner & Gates *Dict. Amer. Idioms* 25: She belted out ballads and hillbilly songs one after another all evening.

3. to kill; murder.

1966 "Minnesota Fats" *Bank Shot* 36: My God, Evaline….Jack Kennedy's been belted out in Dallas. He's gone.…He's dead. **1970** R. Sylvester *Guilty Bystander* 242: I belted them both out.…I found one and then I tracked down the other. **1980** J. Breslin, in *N.Y. Daily News* (Dec. 12) 6: Mark David Chapman belted out John Lennon with four [bullets] in the chest.

4. to eat or drink greedily.

1966 "Minnesota Fats" *Bank Shot* 56: So every day we would sit around belting out the marinated herring and smoked tongue and corned beef. *Ibid.* 57: I…just stood around belting out the hot dogs and eyeballing the dolls.

belt song *n. Music.* (see quot.).

1980 Pearl *Slang Dict.: Belt song n.*….A song requiring a dynamic singing style.

Beltway bandit *n. Journ. & Pol.* an avaricious government contractor or consultant.

1978 *Wash. Post* (Jan. 25) (quoted in Safire, 1984): Some "Beltway bandit" ought to be hired to put one team of computer experts to work designing crime-proof defenses. **1978** *Harper's* (June) 48: There are also the consultants—the "beltway bandits," as they are sometimes called. These are the people who do government work for a fee. **1984** W. Safire, in *N.Y. Times Mag.* (Feb. 20): The coinage of *Beltway bandits* should not be derogated as a nonce phrase, because it fills a need. **1989** Kanter & Mirvis *Cynical Amer.* 4: Duplicity…by politicians…and…larceny and greed by brokers and "Beltway bandits." **1991** Dunnigan & Bay *From Shield to Storm* 463: Most were defense consultants or scholars ("beltway bandits" is the Washington terminology).

BEM *n.* "Bug-Eyed Monster," of the type common in pulp science-fiction adventures.

1950 F. Brown *Space* 83: Already it's beginning to look like a science-fiction send-off. Good old bug-eyed monsters. Bems to you. **1954** Lindner *50-Min. Hr.* 197: My passage from BEM's through Burroughs to Wells, Heard and Stapledon was swift. **1958** in *OEDS.* **1982** *Time* (May 31) 60: At first startled glance…you could call him [E.T., an extraterrestrial in the film of the same name] a BEM.

Ben *n. Und.* a vest. See also BENNY.

1866 *Nat. Police Gaz.* (Nov. 3) 2: With one end of his "slang" hanging from his "ben." **1930** "D. Stiff" *Milk & Honey* 199: *Benny*—An overcoat. A vest used to be called a *ben.*

bench *v. Sports.* to confine to the bench as a substitute player; to remove or exclude from a game. Now *S.E.*

1917 in *DA:* Some of you stuffed sausages will be benched mighty quick if you don't wake up. **1978** B. Johnson *What's Happenin'* 192: He committed seven…turnovers before being benched. **1983** *Time* (Dec. 26) 78: Plunkett was benched for a while again this season (in favor of Marc Wilson, who promptly broke his shoulder).

¶ In phrase:

¶ **ride** [or **warm**] **the bench** *Sports.* to be a substitute player. Now *S.E.*

1911 Van Loan *Big League* 201: Bush warmed the bench. **1958** J. King *Pro Football* 113: Shaw was unfortunate enough to be hurt, or I might still be riding the bench. **1973** in H.S. Thompson *Shark Hunt* 79: Despite Kiick's obvious unhappiness at the prospect of riding the bench again next year behind all-pro running back Mercury Morris. **1984** WINS radio news (Sept. 4): The decision was, after five years of riding the bench, to start Gary Hogeboom.

bench jockey *n.* [elaboration of earlier syn. JOCKEY] *Baseball.* a player who loudly derides members of an opposing team during a game.

1939 in P. Dickson *Baseball Dict.* 50: All the bench jockeys on the circuit were quickly counting ten on every pitch Lefty made. **1960** Meany *Yankee Story* 47: Most of the acrimony can be traced to the riding the Yankee bench jockeys gave the Cubs for giving Mark Koenig only a half-share. **1961** Brosnan *Pennant Race* 188: Elio Chacon had joined the chorus of bench jockeys. Elio's accent and choice of epithets were better for laughs than agitation. **1969–71** Kahn *Boys of Summer* xv: Opposing bench jockeys forever shouted "black bastard," "nigger lover" and "monkey-fucker" [at Jackie Robinson]. **1973** *Penthouse* (Mar.) 38: Jim Messina (erstwhile bench jockey and then starter for the Buffalo Springfield, one of the greatest teams of all time).

bench jockeying *n. Esp. Baseball.* loud derision of members of an opposing team by players on the bench in the dugout

during a game.

1958 *N.Y. Times Mag.* (Mar. 30) 17: Leo (the Lip) Durocher…was a maestro of bench jockeying. **1971** Coffin *Old Ball Game* 65: "Bench Jockeying" is one way in which baseball has developed its own sounding. **1972** Robinson & Duckett *Never Had It Made* 74: His office warned the Phils to keep racial baiting out of the dugout bench jockeying. **1992** *Newsweek* (Dec. 21) 60: Trash-talking…Once upon a time this was just old-fashioned bench jockeying.

bench-warmer *n.* **1.** an unemployed individual who lounges on a bench, as in a public park.

1903 *Independent* (Mar. 19) 667: At the very first of my consorting with the "bench-warmers" I noticed the lack of fellowship among them. **1927** *DN* V 438: *Bench warmer, n.* A weary hobo whose home is a park bench.

2. *Sports.* a substitute player who is not taking part, or who rarely takes part, in a game. Now *S.E.*

1905 *Sporting Life* (Sept. 9) 16 (cited in Nichols *Hist. Dict. Baseball*). **1941** *Sat. Eve. Post* (May 17) 87: The bench warmers do most of the yelling.

bend *n.* **1.a.** a spree, BENDER, 1.

***1879** in *OEDS:* "Going on the spree" or "having a bend." **1887** Francis *Saddle & Moccasin* 84: They do say as he was 'customed to go on a scoop—on a bend, occasionally, as it were. ***1891** R. Kipling, in *OEDS:* I went on the bend with an intimate friend. **1933** Guest *Limey* 159: Dora…"made" an old farmer that'd come from Iowa for a "bend" (razzle). **1975** Kennedy *Train Robbers* (film): Now I go on a bend…and I get the blind staggers.

b. a hallucinogenic experience induced by a drug.

1967 in Lingeman *Drugs* 30: This is not the way for an STP user to mend a bum bend.

2. *Baseball.* a curve ball.

1908 *N.Y. Eve. Jour.* (Feb. 10) (cited in Nichols *Hist. Dict. Baseball*).

3. *Theat.* a bow taken by a performer.

1920 J. Conway, in *Variety* (Dec. 24) 5: He has been draggin her out for bows all week and she has taken so many bends she's getting humpbacked. **1923** *N.Y. Times* (Sept. 9) VIII 2: *Bends:* Bows. **1925** *AS* (Oct.) 37: They "take three bends and an encore."…"Then you take your bends."

¶ In phrases:

¶ **around** [or **round**] **the bend** crazy.

***1929** Bowen *Sea Slang* 114: *Round the bend,* an old naval term for anybody who is mad. **1955** Klaas *Maybe I'm Dead* 13 [ref. to WWII]: Take it easy, Jim. Don't go round the bend now. **1953–57** Giovannitti *Combine D* 11 [ref. to WWII]: Day-dreaming. You'll be going around the bend if you keep it up. *Ibid.* 18: He told Popeye I was around the bend. **1968** J. Kirkwood *Good Times* 152: Oh, I must be headed round the bend. **1968** D. Westheimer *Young Sentry* 224 [ref. to WWII]: You must be around the bend. **1969** Maitland *Only War* 188: He's nuts. Gone right around the bend. **1975** *Barbary Coast* (ABC-TV): I gotta tell you, you're goin' around the bend. **1975** V. Miller *Trade-Off* 92: The word has gotten out on the grapevine that Lieutenant Kojak is around the bend. **1976** Fuller *Ghost of Flt. 401* 237: We went ahead—being careful to close the curtains so that a caller or a passerby wouldn't think we had gone round the bend. **1978** I.M. Marks *Fear* 13: Am I normal, Doctor? Am I going round the bend? **1983** Helprin *Winter's Tale* 28: You think I've gone around the bend.

¶ **get a bend on** to become intoxicated.

1927 Steele *Meat* 199: I'm a heller when I get a bend on.

¶ **on the bend** *Und.* by dishonest or crooked means; (hence, as adj.) practicing theft or other crime; crooked.

***1863** in *OEDS:* I'll order my executor to buy my coffin off the square. He shall get it on the bend, somehow or other. **1928** Coe *Swag* 171: You say she wouldn't believe you when you told her Bill was on the bend?…You told this frail that Bill was a crook an' she wouldn't believe you. **1931** (cited in Partridge *Dict. Und.* 31). **1942** *ATS* 456: Engaged in theft: *On the bend.*

bend *v.* **1.** *Naut.* to don (clothing); in phr. **bend sail** to dress.

***1805** J. Davis *Post-Captain* 150: I will send…for a tailor: I will bend a new suit of [clothes]. *Ibid.* 161: How nicely she bends her sails!*…*Dresses. **1823** J.F. Cooper *Pilot* 298: You were a little apt to bend your duds wrong for the first month, or so. **1841** [Mercier] *Man-of-War* 182: When I get my long togs bent, I'm *there.* **1867** *Galaxy* (Apr. 1) 728: His ablutions ended, he shaves, "bends" a clean shirt and finishes his efforts at self-ornamentation. **1932** Bone *Capstan Bars* 152: *Bend, To*…to don in the manner of clothing. **1961** Hugill *Shanties* 592 [ref. to 1920's]: Paddy Griffiths told me that in his young days it was customary for Merchant Johns to "bend" shore-going shoes which possessed rather higher heels than those worn by landsmen. **1975** J. Gould *Maine Lingo* 12: To *bend* a necktie is to get all rigged out sartorially.

2. *Baseball.* to pitch (a curve ball).

1910 *N.Y. Eve. Jour.* (Mar. 4) 16: That is the fellow who bended 'em to us yesterday. **1911** Van Loan *Big League* 65: Any pitcher would be a fool to try and "bend one" under the circumstances.

3. *Und.* to steal. Also intrans.

1930 *Amer. Mercury* (Dec.) 454: *Bend, v.* To steal. We bend a boat to hist the hooch. **1938** D. Castle, in Partridge *Dict. Und.* 31: They line up punks and kids for their rackets. Teach them the ropes; how to bend, cop a heel, case a lay [etc.].

4. to engage in passive homosexual anal copulation. Also **bend over.**—used intrans.

1966 M. Braly *On Yard* 246: Maybe you think I bend over for...anything with a prick. **1972** R. Wilson *Playboy's Forbidden Words* 33: "He sucks for the luck." "He bends for his friends." **1982** Del Vecchio *13th Valley* 198: Cherry ain't going ta bend over for ya.

5. *Av.* to bank (an aircraft).

*ca*1964 K. Cook *Other Capri* 8 [ref. to WWII]: When I bend that sonovabitch off the target, I don't want to look back and see you going forty fuckin directions. **1966–67** Harvey *Air War* 12: But a fellow usually bends his bird around rather smartly when he sees one coming up. **1984** Trotti *Phantom* 72 [ref. to Vietnam War]: Come on, airplane, bend...turn, you mother!

¶ In phrases:

¶ **bend an ear** see s.v. EAR.

¶ **bend on** [or **onto**] *Naut.* to get; find; acquire for oneself.

1942–48 in *So. Folk. Qly.* XIII (1949) 204: A Warrant Carpenter of about twenty years' service...referring to a well-known movie star...remarked, "I would like to bend her on like an old...boot." **1959** Morrill *Dark Sea* II [ref. to WWII]: If you need to dip your wick, bend onto a legitimate hustler. **1964** *Almanac of Naval Facts* (gloss.): *Bend on*...to acquire, e.g. "bend on a hangover."

¶ **bend out of shape** to shock, to astonish; (*also*) to anger or annoy.—usu. in adj. phr. *bent out of shape* s.v. BENT, 5.

1974 C.W. Smith *Country Music* 259: It came to me in a flash the perfect way to bend that entire Bible-thumping crew completely out of shape! **1977** Olsen *Fire Five* 97: Don't let 'em bend you outa shape. That's what they're looking for.

¶ **bend over!** [an allusion to anal copulation] "shut up!" "get out!" etc.—used contemptuously.—usu. considered vulgar.

1990 Munro *Slang U.* 35: *Bend over!*...You're bothering me! You suck! Get a life! **1992** *Donahue* (NBC-TV): Who asked you? Bend over!

¶ **bend (someone's) ear** see s.v. EAR.

¶ **bend the throttle** Esp. *Av.* to fly or drive at great speed.

1941 *Army Ordnance* (July) 79: *Bend the throttle*....To fly above normal cruising speed. **1941** *AS* (Oct.) 163: *Bend the throttle.* To fly a plane or drive a vehicle above normal speed.

bender *n.* **1.a.** [poss. from Scots dial. *bend* 'to drink, esp. to drink hard or greedily...a draught of liquor', and *bender* 'a drinker'; see *EDD* I 241] a carousal; a spree.—usu. in phr. **on a bender.**

1845 Corcoran *Pickings* 62: I was on an almighty big bender last night. **1846** in Lowell *Poetical Wks.* 176: "I won't agree to no such bender," Sez Isrel. **1847** in Dolph *Sound Off* 392: At Buena Vista I was sure/That Yankee troops surrender,/And bade my men hurrah, for you're/All going on a bender. **1848** Judson *Mysteries* 43: We left three individuals in the street, who were bent upon having, what our fashionable bucks call "*a real bender.*" *Ibid.* 526: "Bender." To go upon a spree, get drunk, and raise a muss, is to go on a bender. **1855** Thomson *Doesticks' Lttrs.* 169: Crew all "on a bender" in the engine room, firemen all drunk on the boiler deck. **1857** S.C. Smith *Chili* 271: The old man had been some days on a "bender," and his skin was pretty well filled with whisky. **1862** in Patrick *Rebel* 48: I promised mother that I would not drink any more....The last time I got on a bender, I lost all my money. **1865** in Woodruff *Union Soldier* 42: I met some old chums and we got on a regular Bender-run, the first time *I've been on it*, in a long time. **1891** Maitland *Amer. Slang Dict.* 30: "On a bender," on a drunk. **1934** H. Miller *Tropic of Cancer* 46: He's been on a bender...for the last five days. **1935** Coburn *Law Rides Range* 53: How long have you been on this bender, Pete? **1935** O'Hara *Dr.'s Son* 95: Yes, Casey was a swell guy and would be good company on a bender. **1936** "E. Queen" *Halfway*

House 150: I'm the old-fashioned girl on a sudden bender. **1941** in Fenner *Throttle* 172: If he takes that ten-spot, chief,...he'll spend it on a bender, and you'll never see him again. **1961** Kanter & Tugend *Pocketful of Miracles* (film): She'll be all right. She's on a bender, that's all. **1977** Sayles *Union Dues* 113: It used to be...it was wives after their husbands gone off on a bender. **1978** Strieber *Wolfen* 4: Secretly all four men hoped that the two AWOL officers were off on a bender or something. **1990** *Nation* (June 4) 785: After the binge (history on a bender): delirium tremens.

b. a rampage.

1862 "Barritt" *East & West* 50: If the Missouri *should* get on a "bender" as Charley says, I hope I may see it.

c. a drinking party.

1889 Barrère & Leland *Dict. Slang* 106: Hans Breitmann joined de Turners,/November in de Fall,/Und dey gived a boorsten bender/All in de Turner Hall.

2. a HUMDINGER; CORKER.

*1842 in *OEDS*: Ma vice [fist] es wat I kal a bender. **1854** in Barrère & Leland *Dict. Slang* I 106: I led her through the festal hall,/Her glance was soft and tender;/She whispered gently in my ear,/"Say, Mose, ain't this a bender?" *1895 R. Kipling, in *OEDS*: By Jove, it's a bender of a night. **1919** Darling *Jargon Book* 4: Bender—a very bad storm, game, or man.

3. usu. *pl.* a leg; a knee.

1849 H.W. Longfellow, in *DA*: Young ladies are not allowed to cross their benders in school. **1925** in *OEDS*: They say family prayers there with the servants every night, all down on their benders. **1942** *Yank* (Dec. 23) 18: He fell to his benders and opened his sack. **1944** Burley *Hndbk. Harlem Jive* 26: And his boots came up over his fat benders two. **1946** Boulware *Jive & Slang* 3: Deuce of Benders...knees. **1958** Bontemps & Hughes *Negro Folklore* 481: *Benders:* knees.

4. *Circus.* a contortionist; an acrobat.

*1873 T. Frost *Circus Life* 154: You know Willio, the bender? Well, he is dead. **1902–03** Ade *People You Know* 84: I never see any Benders that could get away with a Talking Act.

5. *Baseball.* a curve ball.

1901 Patten *Frank Merriwell's Marvel* 73 (cited in Nichols *Dict. Baseball Term.*). **1908** in Fleming *Unforgettable Season* 44: They had swung their floating ribs out of shape trying to hit his benders on the snoot. **1914** [Patten] *Lefty o' the Bush* 26: He's got a few good benders, not to mention some speed. **1923** *Chi. Daily Trib.* (Oct. 12) 25: Irish Meusel stepped into one of Mr. Pennock's benders and poled it into the same stand. **1950** Cummings *Dict. Baseball* 8: *Bender*...a curve ball. A term not often used in modern times. **1978** F. Messer, on *N.Y. Yankees vs. Minn. Twins* (WINS radio) (July 21): Looking for the fastball, he got the bender.

6. [sugg. by BENT, 3.b.] *Und.* a stolen car.

1937 Hoover *Persons in Hiding* 246: This car's a bender. One of your gang probably stole it. **1937–41** in Mencken *Amer. Lang. Supp. II* 724.

7. *Homosex.* a male homosexual who habitually assumes the passive role in anal copulation.

1971 Rader *Gov't Inspected* 105: Get ass-fucked like a bender by a butching lover. *a*1972 B. Rodgers *Queens' Vernacular* 148: The homosexual who prefers the passive role in [copulation]...*bender.* **1987** Eble *Campus Slang* (Oct.) 1: Ankle grabber—homosexual....Also *Bender.*

Bengal Tiger *n. Naut.* a sudden storm common in the Bay of Bengal. [1893 def. may be in error.]

[**1893** Wawn *South Sea Islanders* 71 [ref. to 1875]: We were becalmed out in the open sea, miles away from the land, broiling under the "Bengal Tiger" (the sun) and drifting slowly westward.] **1912** J.H. Williams, in *Independent* (Apr. 18) 820: Then we knew that one of those appalling bay squalls, known as the "Bengal Tiger," was about to envelop us.

Benjamin *n.* an overcoat. Also **upper Benjamin.** See also BENNY, 1.

*1810 in *OEDS*: One article was an *upper benjamin*, eight guineas. *1812 Vaux *Memoirs* 277: Upper-Ben, Upper-Benjamin...A great-coat. **1859** Matsell *Vocab.* 10: *Benjamin.* A coat. **1866** *Nat. Police Gaz.* (Apr. 21) 3: The two wear "benjamins" with voluminous capes on them, which are sufficient to conceal a small-sized "doss" without anyone "tumbling" to what they had there. **1871** [Banka] *Prison Life* 493: Overcoat,...*Benjamin.* **1878** *S.F. Trade Herald* (Aug.) 2: To soak...yer upper benjamin. **1889** Barrère & Leland *Dict. Slang* I 108: *Benjamin* or *benjie* (common), a waistcoat or coat....Dr. C. Mackay says it was so named from a celebrated advertising tailor in London. **1904** *Life in Sing Sing* 246: *Benjamin.* An overcoat. **1923** *N.Y. Times* (Sept. 9) VIII 2: *Benjamin:* a coat. **1924** Henderson *Keys to Crookdom* 397: *Benjamin.* An overcoat.

1944 D. Burley *Harlem Jive* 134: *Benjamin or Benny*—An overcoat.

Benjie *n.* [alluding to portrait of Benjamin Franklin] a one-hundred-dollar bill. See also BENNY, 2.

1985 *Kids' World Almanac* 148: $100—benji, C-note.

Benning School for Boys *n.* [located at Ft. Benning, Ga.] *Army.* the Army Infantry Officer Candidate School.

1942 *Yank* (Oct. 21) 4: "Benning School for Boys"…the officer candidate school at the Infantry School. **1970** Calley & Sack *Lieut. Calley* 25: And in March, 1967, I went to Fort Benning, Georgia, to Fort Benning School for Boys. That's what we called the officer candidate school there. **1984–88** Hackworth & Sherman *About Face* 212: Our earliest days at Benning School for Boys.

benny *n.* **1.** an overcoat; (see also 1914 quot.). Also **Ben, upper Ben.** See also BENJAMIN.

*1812 Vaux *Memoirs* 277: *Upper-Ben,*…a great-coat. ***1876** in *F & H* I (rev.) 200: In offering these Bens, the plan was to put them on to show how well they fitted. **1902** Cullen *More Tales* 32: That 'ud enable me to yank one of the bennies out of the eaves. **1903** McCardell *Chorus Girl* 29: He had one of them dust-proof Bennys that delegates to Granger conventions wear. **1910** T.A. Dorgan, in *N.Y. Eve. Jour.* (Jan. 11) 12: "Yep, saw them all," said Ferdinand, peeling off the fur benny. **1914** Jackson & Hellyer *Vocab.* 16: *Ben,*…An overcoat. *Benny*…A sack coat. **1915–17** Lait *Gus* 237: He…wore…a long, green benny. **1917** *Wadsworth Gas Attack* (Dec. 8) 8: Baa-baa bennies, i.e. coats lined with sheep skin. **1919** I. Cobb *Life of Party* 22: "Dat ain't such a bum benny you're sportin'."…"Oh, please don't take my overcoat." **1922** N. Anderson *Hobo* 54: They usually make it a point to get on hand at the beginning of winter a large supply of overcoats, or "bennies." **1924** G. Henderson *Keys* 397: An overcoat. Also called a binny. **1926** Norwood *Other Side of Circus* 272: An overcoat—a Bennie. **1929** Tully *Shadows* 105: "Take off his bennie," commanded Nitro Dugan. **1952** C. Sandburg *Young Strangers* 392 [ref. to 1890's]: Along next October you'll need a "benny," I heard in one jungle, and learned that a "benny" is an overcoat. **1956** *N.Y. Times* (Nov. 18) 59: The academy has requested additional design work on a reefer, benny or a short overcoat for routing wear. **1962** in Wepman et al. *The Life* 31: A raglan benny with slits in the back. **1966–80** Folb *Runnin' Lines* 229: *Benny*…coat.

2. a straw hat; a hat. Earlier **Benjy.**

*1867 Smyth *Sailor's Wd. Bk.*: *Benjy.* A low-crowned straw hat with a very broad brim. ***1883** Russell *Sailors' Lang.* 14: *Benjie.*—The name of a straw hat worn by sailors. ***1886** in *EDD*. ***1891** in *EDD:* Any kind of a straw hat in Wilsden is called "a streea ben" or "benjy." **1922** S. Lewis *Babbitt* 121: I tip my benny to him. **1930** Biggers *Chan Carries On* 43: Now, if you'll just take off the benny—the hat, you know—the light isn't so good. **1941** *Slanguage Dict.* 6: *Benny*…sometimes, a hat.

3. a fellow; chap; character.

1926 E.W. Springs *Nocturne* 133: It's the rich Bennie on the avenue that has to keep nets under his windows. **1926** *Pirate Piece* (Apr.) 2: I guess some of these bennies don't know they was an armistice. **1928** E.W. Springs *Blue Sky* 38: These bennies who can't keep their minds off the skirts ought to be exempted for…pathological incapacity. **1929** Perelman *Ginsbergh* 186: You'll curse yourself for letting a smooth benny like me slip through your fingers. **1929** E.W. Springs *Carol Banks* 106: All the other Bennies had ladies festooned about them. **1944** Kendall *Service Slang* 2: *Benny*….also a sloppy soldier. **1972** *Anthro. Linguistics* (Mar.) 108: *Steam Bath Bennie (n):* A male homosexual who frequents public steam baths.

4. Benzedrine or a similar amphetamine; a tablet or capsule of an amphetamine; a Benzedrine inhaler.

1949 *Time* (Oct. 10), in Berg *New Words* 40: A few girls secretly resort to "bennies." **1952** J.C. Holmes *Go* 47: Oh, I've been trying benny but it speeds everything up. **1952** Kerouac *Cody* 126: We had to…go into Houston and get a gross of benny. *Ibid.* 106: Fifteen dexies, five bennies. *ca*1953 Hughes *Fantastic Lodge* 64: He was on bennies. **1956** Hunter *Second Ending* 112: Everybody takes bennies now and then. *Ibid.* 262: "What the hell's a benny?" "Benzedrine inhaler." **1955–57** Kerouac *On Road* 123: She took tea, goofballs, benny, liquor. **1957–58** Lipton *Barbarians* 315: *Bennies*—Affectionate diminutive for Benzedrine pills. **1966** Elli *Riot* 12: Benny inhalers were expensive. **1975** Hinton *Rumble Fish* 24: Some cat who's been washing down bennies with sneaky pete. **1982** *L.A. Times* (July 17) III 11: The drugs of preference in pro football were pep pills and alcohol. "Bennies were not that unusual when I came into the league."

5. benzine.

1961–68 in *AS* XLIV (1969) 10: Painter Jargon…*Benny,* n. Benzine.

6. *pl.* [sugg. by *beneficial rays*] *Stu.* tanning rays of the sun.

1968 Baker et al. *CUSS* 79: *Bennies, bag the* (beneficial rays of the sun) Sunbathe. *Bennies, catch the* Sunbathe. *Bennies, soak up the* Sunbathe. **1971** N.Y.U. student: At Rhode Island if you're going to sit out in the sun and get a tan, you'd say you were going to "soak up bennies"—beneficial rays.

7. usu. *pl.* [fr. *benefit*] *Mil.* a benefit or good thing of any sort; goodie. [The relation, if any, of 1941 quot. to this sense is uncertain.]

[**1941** Kendall *Army & Navy Slang* 1: A *benny*….a break in formation during which a soldier can rest or smoke.] **1970** Ponicsan *Last Detail* 33: There sure are the benies if you don't have an education. *Ibid.* 51: "Maybe he's up late working on some big deal." "Like more benies for us." *Ibid.* 65: Let's go get some benies in the club car. **1972** Casey *Obscenities* 31: It's just another one/Of the many bennies/In today's action army….bennies: benefits. **1972** O'Brien *Combat Zone* 53 [ref. to 1968]: What's the problem? Mess hall not dishing out the bennies? **1974** Former 1Lt, 25th Div., served in Vietnam 1970–71: *Bennies* are benefits. You look for a job with lots of *bennies.* Or it can mean any good things—"There were lots of *bennies* at Brennan's wedding." **1976** C.R. Anderson *Grunts* xiv: Life in the *bush* was only rarely broken by the *bennies,* benefits like warm beers and letters from…the United States. *Ibid.* 58: A bare dirt path with no jungle to cut through was usually regarded as a benny. **1991** L. Reinberg *In the Field: Bennies,* slang for benefits. In the field, that meant a warm shower, hot food, and a cot.

8. a roasted potato; MICKEY.

1974 N.Y.C. biologist, age 27: On Long Island in the '50's they called a roast potato a *benny.* I've never heard them called *mickeys.* It wasn't a *benny* till it was cooked.

Benny boy *n. Mil.* a young male Filipino transvestite.

1966–67 Harvey *Air War* 18: The "Benny Boys"…cater…to the homo trade. **1986** Willeford *About a Soldier* 99 [ref. to 1940]: Many were boys dressed as women, and they were called binny boys, the P.I. term for homosexuals.

bennyhead *n.* [BENNY, 4 + HEAD] *Narc.* a habitual user of Benzedrine or other amphetamine.

1958 Talsman *Gaudy Image* 216: She had the quick temper of a bennyhead, all right. **1966** Elli *Riot* 45: C'mon, you Benny-heads, hold it down.

bent *adj.* **1.** intoxicated by liquor or drugs. Also (in recent use) **bent out of shape.**

1833 A. Greene *Adv. of Duckworth* II 176: He was seldom downright drunk; but was often…confoundedly bent. **1927** *New Republic* (Mar. 9) 71: [synonyms for *drunk*] Half seas over, fried, stewed, boiled, bent, sprung [etc.]. **1933** Weseen *Dict. Amer. Slang* 272: *Bent*—intoxicated. **1968** Heard *Howard St.* 161: He was, barely able, it seemed, to keep his head up. **1969** Lingeman *Drugs* 22: *Bent*…High or intoxicated from an hallucinogen or narcotic. **1969** *Current Slang* I & II 8: *Bent out of shape,* adj. Drunk.—College males, Minnesota; Air Force Academy cadets. **1970** Horman & Fox *Drug Awareness* 463: *Bent out of shape*—under the influence of LSD. **1972** Bunker *No Beast* 273: We were both bent, full of weed and pills. **1975** *Nat. Lampoon* (Aug.) 18: Hey, everybody, let's all get bent, piss ourselves, and send our shorts to China. **1980** Birnbach et al. *Preppy Hndbk.* 108: Drunk…*Bent out of shape.* **1984** Univ. Tenn. student (list of slang): Drunk: *wasted, blown, bent, polluted, stoned.* **1984** Mason & Rheingold *Slanguage: Get bent*—To get high, or drunk.

2. [sugg. by BROKE] nearly broke; almost penniless.

1909 in C.S. Mills *War Letters* 150: "What's the matter, old man?…Broke?" "Not yet, friend…but I'm—well, bent." **1918** Gibbons *Songs from Trenches* 52: Some wuz shofers out o' jobs/And them not broke wuz bent. **1921** *Variety* (Feb. 11) 11: He may be a little bent now and want to borrow, but he's got coin. **1926** Maines & Grant *Wise-Crack Dict.* 5: *Badly bent*—almost broke. **1929** T. Gordon *Born to Be* 31: By the end of the week, he was pretty badly bent again and his horse was still sick and couldn't travel. **1970** S. Booker, on WINS radio news (Oct. 13): Broke, or, as they say in the ghetto, *bent.*

3. *Und.* **a.** dishonest; corrupt; crooked.

1914 Jackson & Hellyer *Vocab.* 17: *Bent*…crooked; larcenous…"His kisser shows that he's bent." **1927** *DN* V 438: *Bent,* adj. dishonest; an attempt to invent an original synonym for "crooked." **1927** Coe *Me—Gangster* 263: They don't need a bent mug to do it for them. ***1948** in Partridge *Dict. Und.* (ed. 2) 793: A "bent screw"…a crooked warden who prepared to traffic with a prisoner. ***1977** T. Jones *Ice* 57: He had probably taken his share of the "bent" booze. **1978** Strieber *Wolfen* 42: Maybe the two dead cops were bent…maybe that's why they were dead. *Ibid.* 45: We've got a bent cop's wife right here.

b. stolen.

1930 E.H. Lavine *3d Degree* 39: A member of the Auto Squad arrested a city fireman…for having sold a stolen or *bent* car to a complainant. **1937** Hoover *Persons in Hiding* 245: Could it be possible that you suspect me of being in a stolen car?…You'll never find *me* in a bent job.

4. perverse; sexually deviant or unconventional; KINKY.

***1959** in *OEDS*. **1969** L. Sanders *Anderson Tapes* 118: I…found out he was, bent, sex-wise. **1970** Landy *Underground Dict.* 32: *Bent*…Gay, homosexual. **1973** *Penthouse* (Mar.) 43: If it's *bent* we've got it. **1984** Mason & Rheingold *Slanguage: Bent*…homosexual. **1989** R. Miller *Profane Men* 152: Bent gents who give it the Greek way. **1990** *Current Affair* (synd. TV series): Human beings have this kind of bent thing—they like to see people get creamed.

5. angry or excited; (in a weakened sense) out of sorts, not well.—usu. in phr. **bent out [of shape].** See also *bend out of shape* s.v. BEND.

[**1965** *N.Y. Times* (Dec. 27) 20: Exams…might leave one "all beat [*sic*] out of shape."] **1966** M. Braly *On Yard* 234: If he gets bent out of shape there's no way to predict what he might do. **1968** D.L. Phillips *Small World* 131: I'm afraid Jack may be a bit bent out of shape in the morning….But still Jack was able to take us to Melbourne. **1968** Stuard *Folklore Coll.* (unp.): The big word for mad over there [in Vietnam] is "bent." **1969** *Current Slang* I & II 8: *Bent,*…adj. Angry or extremely displeased—*bent out of shape, torqued.*—Air Force Academy cadets. **1968–70** *Current Slang* III & IV 9: *Bent,* adj. Annoyed, angry, "put out."—Air Force personnel, Viet Nam. *Ibid.* 54: *Get bent,* v….To act upset.—college males, New Hampshire. **1970** Quammen *Walk Line* 88: Got bent out of shape and kept asking me who I was. *Ibid.* 92: Ain't all them honkies gon' be a little bent out when they see [me]? **1971** Rodgers *Queens' Vernacular* 31: He was really bent when he found out that his professional guest split with all the grass. **1974** WINS Radio (July 29): You're feelin' a little bit down and bent out of shape. **1978** Maupin *Tales* 19: Anyway, I was really bent out of shape at that point. **1979** Hiler *Monkey Mt.* 141: Look…don't get bent outta shape, you two….Just get rid of that bottle before someone else sees it, okay? **1981** *Nat. Lampoon* (Nov.) 14: Don't get bent out of shape if I sleep in one of your T-shirts. **1982** Braun *Judas Tree* 100: Don't get bent out of shape!…No harm done! **1982** Castoire & Posner *Gold Shield* 94: Don't get bent about it. I won't ask you again. **1992** *Bev. Hills 90210* (Fox-TV): Everybody's getting so bent out of shape over this wedding.

6. *Naut.* affected by the bends.

1971 Noel & Beach *Naval Terms* 33: *Bent*…slang for a victim of the bends. **1993** N.Y.C. man, age 25 (coll. J. Sheidlower): When someone has the bends, you say he's *bent*. It's very common among scuba divers.

7. Esp. *Black E.* old or old-fashioned.

1981 in Safire *Good Word* 79.

8. demented; crazy.

1989 Munro *U.C.L.A. Slang* 20: You are so bent. I can't believe that you partied all night, even though you have a midterm today. **1993** *Are You Afraid of the Dark?* (Nickelodeon TV): "Let's go to Miss Clove's house." "Are you *bent*? After last night?"

¶ In phrases:

¶ **bent out of shape** see **(1)** and **(5)**, above. See also *bend out of shape* s.v. BEND.

¶ **bent up** infatuated, in love; MASHED.

1892 Garland *Spoil of Office* 40: "That's Miss Graham," whispered Shepard; "she's all bent up on Radbourne." **1899** Garland *Eagle's Heart* 274: I never saw her worse bent up over a man. I believe she'd marry you, Mose, I do. **1979** Gram *Foxes* 220: God, you're really bent up.

¶ **get bent!** Esp. *Stu.* "go to hell!"

1969 J. Bouton *Ball Four* 389: In high school [*ca*1955]…"Get bent"…was used to put a guy down. **1968–70** *Current Slang* III & IV 54: *Get bent*, v. Leave, "go to hell." (command)—college males, South Dakota. **1970** W.C. Woods *Killing Zone* 136: Get bent. You might of done it yourself. **1970** in *Playboy* (Jan. 1971) 248: "Get bent," I said. **1971** Jacobs & Casey *Grease* 24: Hey, get bent, LaTierri! **1973** J.E. Martin *95 File* 147: Tell him to get bent and hang up. **1973** Lucas, Katz & Huyck *Amer. Graffiti* 98: Yeah, well, get bent, turkey. **1974** Strasburger *Rounding Third* 61: No. Get bent, Phillips. **1983** *Nat. Lampoon* (Mar.) 12: Get bent, Elephant. **1990** *Simpsons* (Fox-TV): "Hi, Bart!" "Get bent!"

bent-nail syndrome *n. Med.* (see quot.).

1969 Ruben *Everything About Sex* 7: A rare condition (fortunately) known as Peyronies Disease; the medical nickname is "bent-nail syndrome." In this malady the penis is literally bent out of shape.

bentwing *n. Mil. Av.* an airplane having a gull-shaped or swept-back wing design, esp. the F4U, F-84, or F-86. [The novelty of such designs—particularly the swept-back wing required by high-speed flying—has long disappeared, making this term rare.]

1951 [VMF-323] *Old Ballads* 13: But when it comes to fightin' Migs, those bent-wings just don't ra[te]. **1956** W.A. Heflin *USAF Dict.* 79: *Bentwing, n.* An airplane with sweptback wing, esp. an F-84 or F-86. *Slang.* **1978** in Higham & Williams *Combat Aircraft* 12: There was a softer lateral feel to the aircraft while taxiing than other "bent wings" I had flown. **1991** Linnekin *80 Knots* 130 [ref. to *ca*1950]: The Corsair…"Bent-wing Bird."

Benz or **Benzie** *n. Narc.* Benzedrine.

1948 Webb *Four Steps* 19: Four dozen benzies. **1970** Landy *Underground Dict.* 32: *Benz*…World War II slang for Benzedrine.

benzine *n.* inferior whiskey. Hence in phr. **hit the benzine can** to drink whiskey to excess, hit the bottle.

1862 in R.G. Carter *4 Bros.* 77: Two of us…extracted the "benzine" from his pocket. **1868** Harris *High Times* 294: "Hoss" Lovingood openly avows his willingness…to "maul the benzine" out of Grant, *pere*. **1872** Crapsey *Nether Side* 129: They have…the sickening stench of the vile liquor…which the slums…have called benzine. **1882** S. Watkins *Co. Aytch* 200: But the benzine and other fluids became a little promiscuous and the libations of the boys a little too heavy. **1883** Peck *Bad Boy* 288: He spent his money in riotous living, and saw everything that was going on, and got full of benzine, and struck all the gangs of toughs, both male and female. *ca***1900** *Buffalo Bill* 173: He lived on a ranch near Virginia City, Mont., and every few days came into town and filled up on "benzine," and took the place by shooting along the streets and riding into saloons. **1901** [Hobart] *John Henry* 11: Papa drops in with his usual bundle of benzine, and an A-flat hiccough on the side. **1902** in *DA* 108: If a student has "hit the benzine can" too hard the night before, he is anxious to get "on the water wagon."

benzine *v.* [ref. to the spot-removing properties of benzine; cf. BENZINE BOARD and more recently WASH OUT] *Army.* to remove (a commissioned officer) from command, esp. for incompetence; to dismiss (an officer cadet) from training.—usu. passive.

1918 in Truman *Dear Bess* 240: Now we've got to stay in this magnificent training camp and in all probability get benzined and sent home. **1920** *Amer. Legion Wkly.* (Jan. 30) 6 [ref. to WWI]: When a bird was blooeyed, it was the same as saying he was benzined, or vice versa. **1926** [O'Brien] *Wine, Women & War* 316 [ref. to WWI]: *Benzined*, said of an officer brought before a Board of Inquiry and retired, reduced in rank, or transferred to innocuous desuetude. **1927** [R.J. Casey] *Cannoneers* XI [ref. to WWI]: The Battery's "boss"…attended the first officers' training camp at Fort Sheridan and was "benzined" on graduation day. **1931** R.G. Carter *Border with MacKenzie* 334 [ref. to 1870's]: The army officers who had been "mustered out" or "benzined" from the service for various causes upon the reduction and consolidation a few years previous, were a motley aggregation.

benzine board *n. Army.* a board of officers appointed to determine another's fitness to retain command or responsible for the dismissal of cadets from officers' training. [The term seems to have been coined *ca*1870 to characterize the boards that were appointed in 1869 to reduce the number of officers commissioned or promoted during the Civil War.]

1882 C. King *Col.'s Daughter* 81 [ref. to *ca*1875]: The "Benzine Board" speedily made more vacancies in the cavalry than in the rest of the arms of the service combined. **1890** Crook *Autobiog.* 159: I was assigned [in 1871] as a member of a retiring and "Benzine Board" in San Francisco. **1918** in Truman *Dear Bess* 240: We'd all figured that we'd beaten the benzine board by a nose when we were ordered abroad. **1920** *Amer. Legion Wkly.* (Jan. 30) 6 [ref. to 1918]: Benzine board was army for reclassification board, which sat at Blois. **1920** *Infantry Jrnl.* (Mar.) 743: He will never be found out until he falls low enough in something else to be called before a "Benzine Board." **1920** [Fletcher] *113th F.A.* 27: They needed no "benzine board," as the well-known military efficiency board is called in the army, to suggest resignations. **1921** Dienst *353d Inf.* 5: The new officers…crammed for special examinations…under threat of summons before the "benzine board." **1927** C.A. Lindbergh *We* 113: After failing his final check flight a cadet was ordered to appear before…the "Benzine Board." **1935** Archibald *Heaven High* 10 [ref. to 1918]: The "Benzine Board"…was to judge each student as to his personal qualifications to become an officer. **1937** Nye *Carbine & Lance* 121: [In 1871] the commissioned personnel of the army was reduced by the operation of a "benzine board."

benzine buggy *n.* a motor vehicle. Also **benzine cart.**

1901 [Hobart] *Down the Line* 77: John Henry and the Benzine Buggy. **1903** [Hobart] *Out for the Coin* 56: I promised Tom faithfully I wouldn't buy a benzine buggy until he invents the dingus. **1906** Ford *Shorty McCabe* 297: You can sit just as close on the back seat of one of them big benzine carts. **1907** Hobart *Beat It!* 74: A crazy Benzine Buggy. **1918** *Camp Meade Herald* (Nov. 8) 1: He fell for it like a Ziegfield chorus girl would fall for a…benzine buggy. **1925** S. Lewis *Arrowsmith* ch. ix: Mr. Babbitt has just adorned his thirty-fourth birthday by buying his first benzine buggy from yours truly. **1925** *Amer. Legion Wkly.* (June 5) 18: Can you even lift that benzine buggy [*sc.* an airplane] off the water? **1926** Wood & Goddard *Amer. Slang* 5: *Benzine buggy.* Automobile.

benzinery *n.* a drinking saloon. *Joc.*

1884 Sweet & Knox *Mustang* 624: The fellow had been sent, for a flask of mescal, to the Mustang Spring—the name of the benzinery, probably.

Benzo *n.* a Mercedes-Benz automobile.

1986 *Morning Call* (Allentown, Pa.) (Aug. 18): Slang recently recorded by court reporters:…*Benzo:* Mercedes-Benz. **1991** *Yo! MTV Raps* (MTV): Ridin' around in their Jeeps and Benzos. **1992** "Fab 5 Freddy" *Fresh Fly Flavor* 8: *Benzo*—A Mercedes Benz. **1992** *Martin* (Fox-TV): If you want a ride in the Benzo.

Berdoo *n. W. Coast.* San Bernardino, Calif.; **SAN BERDOO.**

1914 Knibbs *Songs of Outlands* 21: The dry old plain from Needles to Berdoo. **1942** *ATS* 46: *Berdoo,* San Bernardino, California. **1966** Thompson *Hell's Angels* 3: Frisco, Hollywood, Berdoo and East Oakland.

berk *n.* [Brit. rhyming sl. *Berkeley Hunt* 'cunt'; in U.S. infl. by *jerk*] a stupid or offensive person. *Rare* in U.S.

*****1936** in *OEDS: The berk.* *****1938, *****1954, *****1959, *****1960, *****1963 in *OEDS.* **1971** Dahlskog *Dict.* 7: *Birk, n.* A dull-witted, obtuse person; a clod. *****1980** Leland *Kiwi-Yank Dict.* 13: That berk then tried to change lanes right in front of me. **1983** Helprin *Winter's Tale* 480: Those saps, tools, berks, and ocuses.

berry *n.* **1.** an easy opponent; something easily done; a cinch. **1887** in *DA:* Harkins started to pitch…for the Brooklyns, but he proved to be a berry for the local sluggers. **1900** *DN* II 22: *Berry, n.* 1. Anything easy or "soft." 2. A good thing.

2.a. a gemstone, **ROCK.**

1916 in E. Wilson *Prelude* 165: *Berry* (jewel).

b. a testicle.

1920–54 (quot. at **WEIGHTS**). **1978** in *Maledicta* VI (1982) 23: Testicles…*berries.*

3.a. a dollar; *pl.* money.

1916 T.A. Dorgan, in Zwilling *TAD Lexicon* 17: I got another berry—I just put the bee on the stenog for an ace. **1918** H.C. Witwer *Baseball to Boches* 147: When…I go back to baseball, I can drag down six thousand berries a year pitchin'. **1918** Rowse *Doughboy Dope* 69: Find the guy in the 8th Company who had the two berries coming from Buck-Eye. **1920** *Variety* (Dec. 31) 8: That suit had set him back 14 berries. **1925** Dos Passos *Manhattan Trans.* 367: Oh about fifty berries and six dollars off me. **1930** J.V. Weaver *Coll. Poems* 247: Two hundred berries a week for the first year. **1935** Clarke *Regards to B'way* 165: I mean it. One thousand berries a week. **1935** Coburn *Law Rides Range* 48: I was strapped and needed a hundred berries. **1936** *New Directions* 67: I wouldn't work here for a thousand berries a week. **1941** Halliday *Tickets* 12: Spread the berries out in front of me. **1957** C. Willingham *Strange One* (film): You have a Cadillac car and two hundred berries a month.

b. *Pris.* a month or year of a prison term.

1928 Bodenheim *Georgie May* 118: "What'd they plastah you?" "Six berries. Poah Dopey got five yeahs in the state-pen."

4. (see quot.).

1929 *Chicago Tribune* (Oct. 11) 14: A package of drug [*sc.* narcotics] wrapped in paper is called a "deck," a "check," or a "bindle." If it is in a capsule it is called a "berry," a "bean," or a "cap."

5. [cf. **HUCKLEBERRY**] a fellow.

1931 Dos Passos *1919* 146: Another berry horned in ahead of me and got it.

¶ In phrases:

¶ **pick a berry** Hobo. (see quot.).

1918 in *AS* (Oct. 1933) 30: *Pick a Berry.* To steal from a clothesline.

¶ **the berries, 1.a.** that which is attractive or pleasing; the height of excellence. Earlier, **all to the berries.** [A fashionable expression *ca*1920–30.]

1908 McGaffey *Show Girl* 28: Say, that [girl]…is all to the berries, ain't she? **1917** in Rendinell *One's Man War* 33: I growed a moustache aboard boat and I thought it was the berries till we landed in France. **1921** *Amer. Legion Wkly.* (July 29) 14: It's the berries/When I'm at a talkfest with you. **1923** *Bomb* (Iowa State College) 422: This bird Hooper is wearing a white collar now and seems to be quite the berries. **1925** in W. Faulkner *N.O. Sketches* 40: You know—thinking I was the berries all the time. **1929** L. Thomas *Woodfill* 294: That lad Buhnke was the berries. **1931** Hellinger *Moon* 312: Their meals were always the berries. **1952** Bissell *Monongahela* 9: Ain't it the berries? **1960–61** Steinbeck *Discontent* 76: Great! That's the berries. **1968** Baker et al. *CUSS* 79: *Berries, the:* nuts, the. **1972** *N.Y. Times* (Dec. 17) II 26: Movie "Gigi" (1958)…Gorgeous. The berries. **1980** Lorenz *Guys Like Us* 107: "Tell me if this isn't the berries." "Yeah.…Some fun." **1982** Ad for strawberry coconetta wine, WINS radio (Aug. 12): It's the berries, the absolute berries! Creamy, dreamy, pink and luscious!

b. something very unpleasant or exasperating; the last straw.

1942 *ATS* 32: Something poor, mean, contemptible…*the berries* (ironically). **1960** in *DARE: Berries, the.* The extreme, whether of good or of bad; the limit. **1966–70** in *DARE:* Ain't that the berries. **1974** V.B. Miller *Girl in River* 129: Ain't that the berries? **1983** Eilert *Self & Country* 221: Yuk…that's the berries. I'd rather be shot.

2. exactly what a situation calls for; the truth.

1920 "B.L. Standish" *Man on First* 127: It don't take the shine off your little performance. You were there with the berries. **1926** Hormel *Co-Ed* 161: It's the ripe red berries on the modern girl, all right.

3. RAZZBERRY.—occ. sing.

1926 Tully *Jarnegan* 249: Now, damn her, she can read in all the papers about the guy she slipped the berries to. **1927** in Brookhouser *Our Years* 172: And don't I give them the berries quick?…Soon as I see they're heading for a dumb time I say "razzberry." **1929** Perelman *Ginsbergh* 182: I wanted to fold up my tents a long time ago and give this barracks the berry. **1936** in Robinson *Comics* 182: "What was that??" "Oh somebody givin' a fighter th' berries."

Berserkly *n.* Berkeley, Calif.; the University of California at Berkeley. *Joc.*

1976 Former Univ. Calif. student: But that's how it was at Berserkly [in 1972]. **1988** Lewin & Lewin *Thes. of Slang* 40: Berkeley, California *Berzerkely.* **1991** *Mac & Mutley* (Discovery Channel TV): You'll find out why they call Berkeley "Berserkly."

berserko *n.* [*beserk* + -*o*] a rash or volatile person. Also as *adj.*

1982 Hayano *Poker Faces* 47: Extremely loose, action-provoking players [are] called *berserkos* or *desperados.* **1985–90** R. Kane *Veteran's Day* 30: Here comes this kid. Berserko. Hysterical.

Bertha *n.* **1.** *Mil.* **BIG BERTHA, 1.a., b.** Now *hist.*

1918 Murrin *In France* 338: Within shell range of the German Berthas or Minnies. **1919** Streeter *Same Old Bill* 24: The Fritzes might want to park a few Berthas right where we were. **1922** Herzog *Yanks* 98: Gee! that sure is some Bertha [a U.S. weapon].

2. **BIG BERTHA, 2.**

1984 Mason & Rheingold *Slanguage: Bertha, n.* A very fat woman. **1990** P. Munro *Slang U.* 35: *Bertha* overweight girl.

beshit *v.* to foul with excrement.—*usu.* considered vulgar.

1714 in Meserve & Reardon *Satiric Comedies* 6: The Body's Beshit. *Ibid.* 7: A Turd…may beshit a Vestment. **1746** in Micklus *Comic Genius* 119: His whole Talk and especially his Comparisons turn upon *B-sh-tt-ng* and being *B-sh-t.* **1776** in W. Morgan *Amer. Icon* 65: They'r ready to Be S—t their Breech's.

best hold *n.* [prob. of wrestling orig.] (one's) chief talent or specialty.

1862 in C.W. Wills *Army Life* 93: I found that eating was my best "holt." **1866** in *Iowa Jour. of Hist.* LVII (1959) 202: A carpenter of teeth was he,/ A den-tist…teeth were his "best hold." *a*1881 G.C. Harding *Misc. Writings* 170: "Ring's" best hold was rabbit hunting. **1887** E. Custer *Tenting* 146 [ref. to 1866]: [The cook] said his "best holt" was on meats.

bet *v.* ¶ In phrase: **you bet[cha]** without any doubt; "yes indeed"; "you may rest assured."—often in extended phr. of the sort **you bet your (life, ass, boots, bottom dollar,** etc.).

1852 in *DA*: He's around when there's money in the pipe—bet your life on t-h-a-t. **1856** *Spirit of Times* (Sept. 6) 3: You may bet your old boots on that. **1857** in *OEDS*: I saw all the "boys" and distributed to them the papers and "you bet," they were in great demand. **1864** "Kirke" *Down in Tenn.* 50: Ye kin bet high on thet; he haint nothin' else. **1865** in *DA*: You bet your sweet life we fellows stand by Clagett. **1868** in *OEDS*: "You bet" or "You bet yer life," or "You bet yer bones," while to "bet your boots" is confirmation strong as holy writ—in the mines, at least. **1872** Holmes *Poet* 71: You bet! Give me a stick and see if I don't. **1879** Grant *Tin Gods* 6: You bet your hat on it! **1879** Campbell *Partner* 54: GRACE...Will I Joe? JOE. You bet your boots. **1885** in Lummis *Letters* 243: You can bet your shirt-tail he will treat you right. **1887** J.W. Nichols *Hear My Horn* 10: You can bet high that I did not do it. **1887** Francis *Saddle & Moccasin* 145: You bet your buttons! **1889** in F. Remington *Own West* 23: You can bet your neck, she was a funeral. **1892** Garland *Spoil of Office* 40: An' I have it, too, betyerneck. **1893** in F. Remington *Sel. Letters* 166: One publisher won't do any *charity* to another you can bet your pants. **1903** *Pedagog. Sem.* X 374: You bet your neck....You bet your life. **1914** J. London *Jacket* 74: But you bet your sweet life you'll have to go some to smile ten days from now. **1917** U. Sinclair *King Coal* 116: You bet you! **1918** in MacArthur *War Bugs* 194: Now for the dirty part:...But when danger's hovering around/You bet your elbow [*sic*] they're never found. **1928** Wharton *Squad* 131 [ref. to WWI]: It's gonna be a big drive an' we're gonna be sold front row seats—you c'n bet your ass on that. **1928** W.C. Williams *Pagany* 50: See you later. You bet, she said, laughingly. **1928** Dahlberg *Bottom Dogs* 26: You bet your boots, mother. **1935** Wolfe *Time & River* 10: But you can bet your bottom dollar that he never got it from his father. **1936** in *OEDS*: "You're homesick, what?" "You betcher!" **1951** Thacher *Captain* 89: You can bet your ass on that. **1956** Shulman *Good Deeds* 111: And you can bet your sweet [*sic*] I'm not taking his section next semester. **1958** Taradash *Bell, Book & Candle* (film): You bet your boots it is. **1960** H. Selby, Jr., in *Provincetown Rev.* III 80: You bet yasweetass no. **1961** *Newsweek* (July 31) 27: You can bet your boots the figure is over 1000. **1975** McCaig *Danger Trail* 18: You can bet your whole stack on that. **1975** S.P. Smith *Amer. Boys* 152: You bet your booty. **1979** Gutcheon *New Girls* 136: You bet your ass it would. **1980** McDowell *Our Honor* 20: Or you can bet your sweet katookus you'll know why. **1981** *Rod Serling's Mag.* (July) 34: You bet your buns I do! **1983** *Nat. Lampoon* (Feb.) 88: "Do you have pie today?" "You bet." **1990** *Tracey Ullman* (Fox-TV): You bet your ass that's not a dress. **1992** R. Perot, in *TV Guide* (June 20) 9: Bet your hat you can!

Betsy *n.* [prob. var. of *Brown Bess*, a musket] a musket or rifle, esp. one's own; (in later use) a pistol or handgun—often constr. with *old*. [During the Davy Crockett craze of 1955, millions of Americans learned that Crockett referred to his rifle as *Old Betsy*.]
1832 [M. St.C. Clarke] *Sks. of Crockett* 66: With no companion save his favourite *Betsy*, (his rifle). **1847** in Blair & Meine *Half Horse* 88: He could "'jest shoot whar he'd a mind to with his *Betsy*," as he familiarly termed his "shooting iron" [*sc.* a rifle]. **1856** in *DA*: Jest let them raise that check agin me, an if I don't shoot, why old Betsy won't blizzard. **1869** in *DA*: Mr. Fredericks proceeded immediately on the horse, loaded "Betsey," (his shotgun). **1887** DeVol *Gambler* 92: He went back for his gun, but I had old Betsy out and up to his head before he could say Jack Robinson. **1936** Washburn *Parlor* 93: "Drop that cane or I'll kill you," said the gambler, whipping out a Betsy from his pocket. **1958** J.B. West *Eye* 13: I'd have never let her get that close to Betsy. **1965** in *OEDS*: "You notice I'm toting a Betsy." "Betsy?" "Equalizer, rod, gat, iron." **1978** Diehl *Sharky's Machine* 127: Me and Betsy here is all the protection I need. **1983** *Los Angeles* (Oct.) 356: The food at the Betsy (considering the neighborhood, I wonder if anyone told Serna that the name is a 1930s American slang term for a gun) is 99 per cent pure French.

Betty *n.* **1.** [cf. BLACK BETTY] *So.* a cowhide whip.
1858 E.A. Pollard *Black Diamonds* 24: Caesar had caught it...from Betty—an allegorical coquette in the shape of a red cowhide.
2. *Mil.* BOUNCING BETTY.
1972 O'Brien *Combat Zone* 151 [ref. to 1960's]: What about the Bouncing Betties, damn it? One of my men hits a Betty and he's dead. **1981** *Rod Serling's Mag.* (Sept.) 41: While they're dragging him off the trail, Barrio gets himself fucked up on a betty mine. **1981** C. Nelson *Picked Bullets Up* 318 [ref. to Vietnam War]: Herndon...had tripped a Betty attached to the gate.
3. *Stu.* an attractive young woman.
1989 Eble *Campus Slang* (Fall) 3: *Fly Betty*—a girl who dresses fashionably and with flair. **1989** P. Munro *U.C.L.A. Slang* 20: *Betty* pretty girl

(used by males). The girl in Abnormal Psychology is a definite betty. *a*1990 P. Dickson *Slang!* 213: Betty. A hot girl. *1991 Thorne *Dict. Contemp. Slang* 36: Betty n....a girl...A mildly derogatory usage among some teenagers. **1992** *Middle Ages* (CBS-TV): My buddy and I went lookin' for...Betties....That's surfer talk.

Betty Coed *n.* [popularized by pop. song "Betty Co-Ed," by J. Paul Fogarty and Rudy Vallee (1930), and motion picture *Betty Co-Ed* (1947)] a typical middle-class college girl, esp. a member of a campus sorority. Also adj.
1961 Kohner *G. Goes Hawaiian* 20: You look so— so—Betty Coed. **1978** Pici *Tennis Hustler* 85: A pair of Betty Co-eds from Savannah.

Betty Crocker *n.* [a trademark of General Foods, Inc., for cake mixes, etc.] *Army.* a rear-echelon soldier.—used derisively. [Quots. ref. to Vietnam War.]
1969 in Lanning *Only War* 66: Some of the Betty Crocker assignments over here are easier than stateside jobs. **1987** in Lanning *Only War* 68: The grunt term "Betty Crocker" seemed most appropriate for the Saigon warriors. They would have looked...at home...in aprons. **1991** L. Reinberg *In Field* 20.

Betty Martin *n.* [orig. unkn.] a drubbing; beating.
1815 in Whiting *Early Amer. Provs.* 30: We'll give 'em "Betty Martin."

bezabor *n.* [orig. unkn.; perh. cf. syn. GAZEBO] a peculiar or unintelligent fellow.
1930 *AS* VI 97 [ref. to 1830's]: *Bezabor*—a peculiar character. "He's a queer old bezabor." **1935** *Bedside Esquire* 218: Here's what happened. Leo, the old bezabor, thought it out. **1940** *Sat. Eve. Post* (Feb. 10) 88: Lay down, you big bezabor.

bezark *n.* [orig. unkn.] an odd or contemptible man or woman.
*ca*1925 in D. Runyon *Poems for Men* 15: This bezark...was once so quiet that we called him Silent Sam. **1929** in R.E. Howard *Book* 64: At this moment some bezark came barging up to our table and...leaned over and leered engagingly at my girl. *Ibid.* 78: Add to this the fact that he frequently shoved me against the wall, and you can get an idea what kind of a bezark I was fighting. **1932** *AS* (June) 329: *Bezark*—a person [at Johns Hopkins Univ.]. **1942–49** Goldin et al. *DAUL* 259: Don't crack to that bezark (girl) of yours about touches (robberies).

bezazz var. BIZAZZ.

B.F. *n.* **1.** [cf. syn. D.F.] a "bloody fool."
1894 in J.M. Carroll *Benteen-Goldin Letters* 223: He was a "B.F." of [the] first water. *1918 in Fraser & Gibbons *Soldier & Sailor Wds.* 12: He's an out and out B.F.!
2. boyfriend.
1926 Lardner *Haircut* 59: A G.F., that's a girlfriend, and a B.F. is a boy friend. I thought everybody knew that. **1932** *AS* (June) 329: B.F.—boy friend. **1971** Rodgers *Queens' Vernacular* 31: BF (les[bian] sl[ang], mid '60s, acronym for boy friend) the lesbian who assumes the male role in a partnership romance.

BFD *interj.* [big fucking [or fat] deal] "so what?" "who cares?"
1971 Dahlskog *Dict.* 7: BFD, big fat deal, an ironic comment meaning "What's so great about that?" **1982** Mich. man, age 35: Yeah, well, BFD. **1988** J. Brown & C. Coffey *Earth Girls* (film): "There's a UFO in my pool. A UFO." "BFD." **1988** P. Fonda, on *Unauthorized Bio.* (Fox-TV): He was very angry that I had destroyed his honeymoon—BFD! **1992** Mowry *Way Past Cool* 12: "I the first, 'member?" "BFD!"

BFE *n.* [BUMFUCK (or BUMBLEFUCK), EGYPT] *Mil. & Stu.* a remote place.—usu. considered vulgar.
1989 P. Munro *U.C.L.A. Slang* 20: Troy...lives out in B.F.E....*Bum Fuck, Egypt*. **1991** UTSQ: BFE—out in the middle of nowhere...Bumblefuck, Egypt.

B flat *n.* [pun on *bee*] a bedbug. *Joc.*
*1836 in *F & H* I (rev.) 210: The author's greatest suffering arose from...those insects known in polite life by the delicate name of *B flats*. **1868** Brewer *Dict. Phrase & Fable*: B-flats.—Bugs. The pun is "B" (the initial letter), and "flat," from the flatness of the obnoxious insect. **1900** *DN* II 22: B-flat,...bedbug.

BFWS *n.* [big fat wide shot] *TV & Film.* an extremely wide camera shot.
1982 T.D. Connors *Dict. Mass Media* 27.

B-girl *n.* **1.** [see note] a woman employed by a bar, nightclub, or the like, to act as a companion to male customers and to induce them to buy drinks, and usually paid a percentage of what the customers spend. Now *S.E.* [Peter Tamony dis-

cusses the origin and development of this term in *Americanisms* (No. 6) (1965); he derives the initial ultimately from *beading-oil*, ref. to in 1911 quot. As 1935 quot. suggests, however, the idea of *putting the bee* on customers in a *bar* has also contributed to the term's evolution.]
[**1911** *Social Evil in Chicago* 194: The mixed drinks brought to the prostitute are counterfeit. For instance the girl orders a "B" ginger ale highball. This is colored water made in imitation of this drink.] [**1935** Pollock *Underworld Speaks: Bee drinker*, female entertainers in night clubs, who drink cold tea camouflaged as liquor, for which customers pay the full price.] **1936** in Tamony *Americanisms* (No. 6) 7: No B Girls buzzing around you here to sip tea you think is a highball. No hostesses. **1938** *True Story* (Dec.) (cover): I Was a California "B" Girl. **1939** C.R. Cooper *Scarlet* 58: The B girl hangouts of Nevada and California. *Ibid.* 68: The B girl gets no salary, but a percentage of the drinks she sells....She is served "specials," which usually are nothing but caramel-colored water. **1941** B. Schulberg *Sammy* 140: I seem to meet nothing but B-girls out here. **1951** MacDonald *Murder for Bride* 38: For a B-girl, she was very, very nice. **1959** W. Williams *Ada Dallas* 18: A B-girl...has drinks with customers, except of course there is no alcohol in hers, and she sees that the customer has a great many drinks and spends all his money. **1962** Quirk *No Red Ribbons* 77: Whores and B girls in bistros. **1963** D. Tracy *Brass Ring* 271: A covey of B-girls battened on the...crowds. **1976** B.A. Floyd *Long War Dead* 23: Stay clear of the B-girls in Mama San Portia's in Da Nang. **1981** Wolf *Roger Rabbit* 128: Any ordinary B-girl in any ordinary juke joint.

2. [cf. B-BOY] a young woman who is a performer or devotee of rap music.
1988 *N.Y. Times* (Aug. 29) C 15: B-boy, b-girl n....a devotee of rap music. **1991** in *RapPages* (Feb. 1992) 22: I was a straight "B" girl, Adidas and all of that.

B-head *n.* [cf. A-HEAD] *Narc.* (see quots.).
1979 Homer *Jargon* 191: The *B-head* takes barbiturates. **1982** A. Shaw *Dict. Pop/Rock* 168: [A] "B" head [uses] barbiturates.

b'hoy *n.* [prob. orig. intended to represent /bʰɔi/, a Hiberno-E pron. of *boy*; later presumably also as spelling pron. /bəˈhɔi/] Esp. *Journ.* a rowdy lower-class young man, esp. of Irish descent and associated with the Bowery in New York. Also vars. Now *hist.* [R.M. Dorson, *America in Legend* (1973), 99–108, discusses the stereotype.]
1834 in Sante *Low Life* 79: Beulah Spa, or Two of the B'hoys. **1846** *Knickerbocker* XXVII 467: A smile on his lips peculiar to one of the bo-hoys. **1847** in Bartlett *Amer.* 31: Such a Mayor as the *b'hoys* would force upon the city [of New York]! **1847** in Oehlschlaeger *Reveille* 45: A *sans ceremonie* peculiar to the "b'hoys" of the frontier. **1849** P. Decker *Diaries* 81: Met Capt. Goodhue one of the "Bohoys" of long hair...a "Mountain Man." **1850** in *Mo. Hist. Soc. Bull.* VI (1949) 11: All clever fine b'hoys. **1853** *Harper's Mag.* VII 472: A New York "bhoy," one of that class who...wear wide trowsers, and low-crowned hats, eschew the use of coats, and are nowise particular as to the purity of their linen. **1868** in Schele de Vere *Amer.* 583: The *b'hoy* is fast disappearing...and the day is not far off, we apprehend, when the Bowery will know him no more. **1941** in Dorson *Amer. in Legend* 106: Old Mose, or Big Mose, the legendary hero of the Bowery b'hoys. **1973** Dorson *Amer. in Legend* 99: "B'hoy" signified to New Yorkers...from 1846 to 1866 a gay rowdy of the town...a loafer-dandy. **1991** Sante *Low Life* 77: The...Bowery...B'hoy, the essence of the proletariat, of the "soap-locks, butt-enders, and subterraneans."

bi *adj. & n.* bisexual.
1956 J.M. Reinhardt *Sex Perversions* 47: Bi—noun or adjective. Bisexual. **1972** J.W. Wells *Come Fly* 65: I never had any bi experiences while I was a stew. **1972** *Anthro. Linguistics* (Mar.) 99: Bi (adj.): Abbreviated form of bisexual. **1978** Maupin *Tales* 111: A lot of guys who come here are gay...or at least bi. **1982** Univ. Tenn. grad. student: Everybody nowadays just takes it for granted that Whitman was either gay or a bi guy. **1985** B.E. Ellis *Less Than Zero* 29: He's bi....I think. **1992** *Sonya Live* (CNN-TV) (Mar. 25): Discriminatory against gay, lesbian, and bi kids.

bib[1] *n.* *Stu.* a bible student.
1900 *DN* II 22: Bib...a student at the biblical institute. [Reported from Yale and Northwestern Univs.]

bib[2] *n.* ¶ In phrases:
¶ **put on the bib** to eat.
1938 Bezzerides *Long Haul* 53: Here come the eats; let's put on the bib.

¶ **slop a bib full** to say a great deal, say a MOUTHFUL.
1925 L. Thomas *World Flight* 321: We had listened to orators from coast to coast slopping whole bib-fulls of "blah" about our heroism.

bible *n.* **1.** *Naut.* a holystone. Now *hist.*
1821–26 Stewart *Man-of-War's-Man* I 45: Small hand-stones...have long been known by the cant name of *Bibles*. **1841** [Mercier] *Man-of-War* 92: Give us the *bibles*, do. **1867** Smyth *Sailor's Wd. Bk.* 98: Bible...a squared piece of freestone to grind the deck with sand in cleaning it; a small holy-stone, so called from seamen using them kneeling. *1883** Russell *Sailors' Lang.* 14: *Bibles*. Small holystones...also termed "prayerbooks." *1906** in *OEDS*: Holystones for polishing decks...are commonly known to sailors as "Bibles." **1923** F. Riesenberg *Under Sail* 155: In holystoning we used two sizes of stones, the larger ones called "bibles" and the small pieces, useful for getting into the corners and along the edges of paint work, known as "prayerbooks." **1980** Mack & Connell *Naval Trads.* (ed. 5) 260: Larger [holystones] were called "Bibles."

2. a book of regulations pertaining to one's specific field of endeavor, *esp.* military regulations; an authoritative standard reference text or similar compilation; a professional or occupational handbook.
1893 Putnam *Blue Uniform* 48: Major, this regiment has but one guide for conduct—and the book Regulations is its Bible! **1898** Doubleday *Gunner Aboard "Yankee"* 67: The reading of the ship's bible will take up most of the morning....The ship's bible is the book of rules and regulations of the United States Navy. It is read once a month to the officers and crew of every ship in the navy. **1962** *AS* XXXVII 267: Bible, n. The California Vehicle Code. **1965** Twist & Susaki *None But Brave* (film) [ref. to WWII]: It seems you haven't read your bible as well as you claim. **1971** Tak *Truck Talk* 11: Bible: 1. The Interstate Commerce Commission's regulations book on trucking, driver and equipment standards. 2. a book of road maps, an atlas. **1982** R. Sutton *Don't Get Taken* 119: We got another sucker with a Bible [book of used-car prices and information].

3. *West.* a book of cigarette papers.
1944 R. Adams *Western Wds.*: Bible The cowboy's name for his book of cigarette papers.

4. a cheaply printed pornographic booklet; TIJUANA BIBLE.
1968 Lockridge *Hartspring* 130: My classmate whispered vulgar words or opened eight-page Bibles.

bibleback *n.* a sanctimonious individual; (*also*) a Christian clergyman or missionary.
1858 Viele *Following Drum* 162: The postmaster...was...the only man in the settlement who owned a Bible, in consequence of which he had acquired the familiar cognomen of "Bible-back," a name that he stoutly resented! **1918** Ruggles *Navy* 130: The navy man generally calls a very religious person a bible pounder or bible back. **1922** Colton & Randolph *Rain* 73: You Bible-backs don't fool me. **1932** Nelson *Prison Days & Nights* 211: But what does [the chaplain] know? Only what them goddam bibleback cons tell him over in his office. **1938** in Partridge *Dict. Und.* 35: The "Bible-backs" [religious prison workers]. **1949** Montelleone *Crim. Slang* 21: Bible-back. A religious hypocrite.

bible-pounder *n.* a Christian clergyman or revivalist; (*also*) a sanctimonious Christian. Also vars.
1885 *Century Mag.* (Mar.) 678: He kin preach all round any o' yer Meth'dist bible-bangers 'at ever I see. *1889** Barrère & Leland *Dict. Slang* I 111: *Bible-pounder* (popular), a parson. *a1890** *F & H* I 186: *Bible-pounder* (common).—A clergyman. **1891** Maitland *Slang Dict.* 85: *Bible-banger* (Eng.), a clergyman. **1918** Ruggles *Navy Explained* 130: The navy generally calls a very religious person a bible pounder or bible back. *1923** in *OEDS*: Bible-thumper. **1929** Gill *Und. Slang*: Bible pounders—Preachers. *1929** Bowen *Sea Slang* 11: *Bible Thumper*. A pious seaman. *1932** F. Richards *Old Soldiers* 80 [ref. to WWI]: He looked at me in disgust and told me I was fast developing into a bloody Bible-puncher. Any man who was a bit religious was known as a "Bible-puncher." **1940** Fougera *Custer's Cavalry* 123: Hey, Bible Thumper,...do me a favor, will you? **1942** Wilder *Flamingo Rd.* 216: There ain't a bible slapper in the state but what is gettin' his tail warmed up for the governor's chair. *1942** in *OEDS*: We don't want any damned Bible bangers around here! **1959** Morrill *Dark Sea* 203 [ref. to WWII]: I guess I'm no phonier than half the other Bible-punchers around here. **1965** Hardman *Chaplains Raid* 64: She fell for that crap about you consorting with the Bible bangers. **1968** Spradley *Drunk* 39: Now I'm a Bible-thumper—I don't succeed though. **1969** Stern *Brood of Eagles* 107: Man sounds like a Bible-banger, don't he?...Hit the glory road. **1970** E. Thompson *Garden of Sand* 10: The

Bible-banger pulls the plug on the last electric Christian guitar. **1971** Flanagan *Maggot* 249: The big Bible-pounder, goddam Holy Joe. **1975** Clark & Coleman *Unidentified* 77: It seems oddly out of character for a young lady so passionate and irreverent to become such an ostentatious Bible beater. **1975** Julien *Cogburn* 126: Funny—I didn't take you for a Bible thumper! **1979** Decker *Holdouts* 161: A bunch of Bible pounders stirred up a fuss. **1982** R.M. Brown *So. Discomfort* 79: Looks like Linton's coming this way with an army of Bible-thumpers.

bic *v.* [< Vietnamese *biet*] *Mil. in Vietnam.* to understand. Now *hist.*

  1980 D. Cragg (letter to J.E.L., Aug. 10): Bic [To understand] A post–May 1965 Vietnam War expression [taken from Vietnamese]. **1989** W.E. Merritt *Where Rivers Run Backward* 114: Just be careful he don't climb your ass. You bick? *Ibid.* 182: Next time…I'll have a round in the chamber. You bick, you bastard? **1991** L. Reinberg *In the Field*: Bic, used by GIs meaning to comprehend.

bicho *n.* [Sp slang] *Hispanic.* penis.

  1967 *DAS* (Supp.): Bicho…The penis. *From the Sp.* **1985** E. Leonard *Glitz* 27: This little girl, she's leading you around by your *bicho*.

bicycle *n.* **1.** *Stu.* a published translation of a foreign-language work; PONY.

  1900 *DN* II 22: Bicycle, *n.* A translation used to assist in getting a lesson, or in class.

  2. a motorcycle, BIKE, 2.

  1937 *Rev. of Reviews* (June) 43: Bicycle—Motorcycle. **1941** *Slanguage Dict.* 6: Bicycle, *n.* among truck drivers, a motorcycle.

  3. (see quot.).

  1982 A. Shaw *Dict. Pop/Rock* 35: "Bicycle." Singles-bar jargon for "bisexual." Only those in the know understood the reference in the 1978 Top 10 hit recording by Queen, "I Want to Ride My Bicycle." **1990** P. Dickson *Slang!* 196: Bicycle. Bisexual.

¶ In phrases:

¶ **get on (one's) bicycle** to get going; get busy.

  1964 *Fugitive* (ABC-TV): Scully, get on your bicycle.

¶ **on (one's) bicycle** *Boxing.* going backward in the ring to avoid an opponent.

  1936 S.I. Miller *Battling Bellhop* (film): Stay on that bicycle and keep moving. **1949** Cummings *Dict. Sports* 288: On the bicycle…Boxing, going backward ("back-pedaling") in order to avoid the opponent. **1966** in M.H. Greenberg *In Ring* 169: Stay on your bicycle. Dance him around in there. **1967** Lipsyte *Contender* 102: Off ya bicycle, go and fight!

bicycle *v.* [sugg. by *back-pedal*] *Boxing.* to jog backward from an opponent in the ring.

  1949 Cummings *Dict. Sports* 33.

bid *n.* **1.** a request or invitation. Now *colloq.*

  1908 McGaffey *Show Girl* 145: So she put in a bid for a divorce and got it. **1909** *WNID*: Bid…An invitation; as, a *bid* to a wedding. Slang, U.S.

  2. *Und.* a prison term, BIT, 4.

  1965 C. Brown *Manchild* 305: Man, I just got out of Sing Sing. I did three years on a one-to-five bid. *Ibid.* 411: You're facing an armed robbery bid. **1967** in Wepman et al. *The Life* 163: Just do your bid and go home. **1992** "Fab 5 Freddy" *Fresh Fly Flavor* 9: Bid—A jail sentence.

biddy *n.* [Hiberno-E dimin. of *Bridget*] **a.** Orig. *Hiberno-E.* a woman, esp. a young woman. [Now mostly Black E.]

  *1785 Grose *Vulgar Tongue*: Biddy, or *chick-a-biddy*, a chicken, and figuratively a young wench. **1866** in Hilleary *Webfoot* 188: One of the "Biddies" stripped herself to the waist and armed [herself] with a "sprig of shilalah." **1868** O.W. Holmes, in *F & H* I (rev.) 213: The biddies are all alike, and they're all as stupid as owls.…A pack of priest-ridden fools. **1875** A. Pinkerton *C. Melnotte* 42: The shirts were stolen by one of these d—d Irish biddies to give to her beau. **1877** Bartlett *Amer.* (ed. 4) 41: Biddy. An Irish servant girl. *1887 in *F & H* I (rev.) 213: How he gave to one old biddy "five guineas to buy a jack," and to another substantial help towards her boy's schooling. *1947 in *OEDS*: Few of our chaps have a biddy [sc. an Italian girl] up the alley here. **1952** E. Brown *Trespass* 94: A shoddy ditty 'bout a shady biddy. *1958 in *OEDS*: He is already installed as the local delinquent, using his considerable charm on the local biddys. **1967** Schmidt *Lexicon of Sex* 19: Biddy…A female—esp. a young girl. **1967** Riessman & Dawkins *Play It Cool* 52: Bitty *n.* young girl. Where's that sharp little bitty from Newark? **1981** in Safire *Good Word* 84: The brothers be bad and the "biddies" be brickhouses. **1984** Toop *Rap Attack* 158: Bitty: female.…"Are there going to be a lot of bitties at the party?" **1989** *Village Voice* (N.Y.) (May 9) 39: He's describing at length the blow job this biddy gave him.

b. a fussy or quarrelsome old woman.—usu. constr. with *old.* [Now colloq. and the dominant sense in U.S. speech, it is presumably much older than the dates below suggest.]

  1938 Bellem *Blue Murder* 214: Did you see that old biddy on the porch? **1955** *AS* (Dec.) 302: Biddy, *n.* Mean woman. **1962** T. Berger *Reinhart* 291: Christ, have you ever smelled the hair of some old biddy under the dryer? **1976** Wren *Bury Me Not* 53: The ol' biddies 'round here gossip 'bout anybody. **1966–80** McAleer & Dickson *Unit Pride* 204: But these same old biddies were getting slammed by their husbands every night. **1985** MacLaine *Dancing* 145: I'd hear you and the old biddies talking about their CD's or their investments in the stock market. **1986** Gilmour *Pretty in Pink* 51: She was such a sour-faced biddy.

biff¹ *n.* **1.** [earlier Scots dial. *baff, beff*] **a.** a whack; a hard punch or blow. Also as interj.

  [*1768 in *OED*: With beffs and flegs, Bumbaz'd and dizzie.] **1847** Robb *Squatter Life* 137: I hit him, *biff*, alongside of his smeller. **1887** Peck *Pvt. Peck* 170: I was to haul off and give him one "biff" in the nose. **1890** *DN* I 72: To give one a biff in the ear. **1904** F. Lynde *Grafters* 368: Hawk's next biff was more to the purpose. **1907** Siler *Pugilism* 191: "Biffs"—Are blows delivered. (see also "Wallups," "Smashes," "Soaks," "Jabs," "Pokes," "Stabs.") **1918–19** MacArthur *Bug's-Eye View* 126: They were greeted with many a lusty biff on the bean. **1923** J.L. Hill *Cattle Trail* 66: He…gave him a biff. **1980** Lorenz *Guys Like Us* 206: Laughing, they exchanged biffs to the shoulder.

  b. *Baseball.* a base hit.

  1908 in Fleming *Unforgettable Season* 126: That romantic biff came in the fifth.

  2. zest; liveliness; zip.

  1918 in Gelman *Photoplay* 45: Just dragging yourself through your daily tasks, with no bif or pep or get-up-and-go about you.

  3. see BIFFY.

biff² *n.* [prob. var. of BIFFER] *Stu.* (see 1989 quot.).

  1929–32 (quot. at BIFFER). **1989** P. Munro *UCLA Slang* 20: Biff…dumb, dunce-like girl.…That girl is such a biff, and she isn't even in a sorority.

biff *v.* **1.** to whack; to hit hard.

  *1888 in *OEDS*: He playfully biffed him with a brick. **1890** *Nat. Police Gaz.* (Sept. 27) 1: The Girls Biffed Each Other. **1897** *Cosmopolitan* (Dec.) 218: He Biffed the Cop! **1902** Fox *Christmas Eve* 20: Captain Wells descended with no little majesty and "biffed" him. **1903** Clapin *Amer.* 50: He biffed him on the ear. **1930** Dos Passos *42d Parallel* 14: Hey, Milly, I'll biff you one if you don't stop crying. *ca*1935 in R.E. Howard *Iron Man* 128: He biffed me…hard on the jaw. **1938** Bellem *Blue Murder* 17: "Your husband biff you, Nelià?" "Yes. He's always beating me." **1968** I. Reed *Yellow Back Radio* 56: Biffing the man on the head with his cane. **1975** Goldman *Robin & Marian* 8: At the end of this mindless biffing around, Robin's pate would be sorely split. **1991** *Big Story* (CNN-TV) (Nov. 23): One time they gave me a bit of a biffing.

  2. *U.S. Nav. Acad.* (see quots.).

  1894 *Lucky Bag* (No. 1) 66: Biff…to do a thing well. **1900** *DN* II 22: Biff, *v*….to do anything well. *Ibid.*: Biff, *v.* to study hard.

  3. (see quot.).

  1895 Gore *Stu. Slang* 3: Biff…*v.* To refuse; to repulse; to slight [at Univ. of Michigan].

  4. [cf. BIFF², *n.*] *Stu.* to fail.

  1989 P. Munro *U.C.L.A. Slang* 20: My chemistry midterm was impossible. I totally biffed it.

biffed *adj.* [fr. BIFF, *v.*, 1] drunk.

  1925 L. Thomas *World Flight* 123: One of their chief religious ceremonies consists of getting absolutely "blotto," as our British friends say. And the more hilariously "biffed" they become the holier they are.

biffer *n.* [orig. unkn.] Esp. *Black E.* an offensive, unattractive, or promiscuous woman.

  1929–32 in *AS* (Dec. 1934) 288 [Lincoln Univ.]: Biffer (sometimes shortened to *biff*). A girl not considered good-looking, a girl of low character. **1959–60** R. Reisner *Jazz Titans* 150: Biffer: an ugly girl. Example: I was out with a biffer last night, which proves I dig distortion. **1970** Winick & Kinsie *Lively Commerce* 41: "Biffer," "prossie,"…"pig-meat" are some other slang designations [of prostitutes]. **1979** J.L. Gwaltney *Drylongso* 232: They start callin' 'em biffas an' whores just for doin' what they begged 'em to do!

biffy *n.* [prob. orig. a childish pronun. of *bathroom*] a lavatory. Also **biff.**

1942 *ATS* 87: Toilet…*biffy*. **1952** S. Bellow *Augie March* 303: I had to go to the biffy to take a leak. **1956** Reinhardt *Perversions* 47: *Bif* [*sic*]…Restroom. **1964** Hunt *Ship* 88: Ain't seen this much biffy paper since they sent the destroyer to Lebanon. **1968** G. Swarthout *Loveland* 91: I'd been twelve years old, I recalled, before I apprehended that girls used biffys for the same purposes as boys. **1968** *CUSS* 79: *Biff*, Washroom…*Biffy*, Washroom. **1970** Lincke *Jenny* 100: They were heading for the biffy. **1971** Rodgers *Queens' Vernacular* 194: I left the window open in the bif. **1976** J.G. Fuller *Ghost of Flt. 401* 165: She went immediately to the biffy—the airline term for washroom. **1985** Heywood *Taxi Dancer* 89: Like a five-year-old too busy to head for the biffy. **1989** P. Munro *UCLA Slang* 21: *Biffy* portable toilet. **1991** *Mystery Sci. Theatre* (Comedy Central TV): Last one out of the biff's a rotten egg.

big *n.* **1.** BIG SHOT.

1948 Lait & Mortimer *New York* 121: [Street gang] war counsellors [are] known as "bigs." **1972** *N.Y. Daily News* (July 20) 14: Mob Big Denies Tie to Sinatra. **1980** *N.Y. Post* (July 2) 4: 44 GOP bigs call for ERA in plank. **1983** *Nat. Lampoon* (Mar.) 57: Lydia…is the ten-year-old daughter of a Politburo big. **1988** *Forbes* (Nov. 14) 16: Long before Joyce Jillson became famous as a White House astrologer, she had been telling Hollywood bigs what their stars held for them.

2. usu. *pl.* [fr. BIG LEAGUE] a major sports league.

1973 Boyd & Harris *Baseball Card* 104: Big Steve tore apart the Piedmont League but he couldn't get arrested in the bigs. **1979** *Maclean's* (Dec. 3) 47: Only changes in government had as much impact on…café society was the elevation of the Quebec Nordiques to the "bigs." **1983** *All Things Considered* (Nat. Public Radio) (Mar. 2): What's it like in the bigs? **1990** *Cosmopolitan* (Apr.) 237: They figure [the pension] on how many days you been in the bigs.

big *adj.* **1.** (of money) in large amounts. Now *colloq.*

1887 DeVol *40 Yrs. a Gambler* 28: We had won some big money, and were about to quit. **1905** U. Sinclair *Jungle* 236: It was explained to him what "big money" he…could make. **1908** in H.C. Fisher *A. Mutt* 52: Why don't you bet big money. **1930** *Bookman* (Dec.) 397: Swamis cut in heavy on the big dough. **1936** Dos Passos *The Big Money* [title]. **1955** in Wepman et al. *The Life* 77: The bigger the bucks the better. **1962** in Wepman et al. *The Life* 50: Those big bucks would soon be here. **1990** *U.S. News & W.R.* (July 23) 46: Measures that would raise big bucks would affect broad segments of the elderly.

2. excellent and impressive.

1893 in Matthews *Manhattan* 107: It reminds me of an Eyetalian gal I saw dance once in Cheyenne. She was a daisy, too; but this is bigger.…This is a heap bigger.

3. well-known, as by word of mouth.

1970 La Motta et al. *Raging Bull* 168: First, it's very big all around town that you're gettin' a hundred thousand bucks to dump this fight.

¶ In phrases:

¶ **be big on** to enjoy very much; to be enthusiastic about.

1867 in W.H. Jackson *Diaries* 138: All of 'em big on the Injin story and bored us until late. **1877** in J.M. Carroll *Camp Talk* 100: "Morpheus" is the fellow big on sleep. **1973** *Business Week* (Sept. 15) 98: We're very big on setting goals around here. **1983** Breathed *Bloom Co.* 33: Yes. Penguins are big on fresh raw herring.

¶ **in a big way** conspicuously; to a great extent; (*hence*) passionately.—often constr. with *go for.*

1897 in F. Remington *Sel. Letters* 288: You are the thing in a very big way. **1931** Rouverol *Dance, Fools, Dance* (film): You've got me going, sister—in a big way. **1929–33** J. Lowell *Gal Reporter* 184: I could go for you in a big way, baby. **1939** Fessier *Wings of Navy* (film): I could go for Yvonne in a big way. **1949** in *DAS*: He said the soldiers went for pinups "in a big way." **1990** *National Review* (Sept. 17) 15: The large oil companies will not step up domestic exploration in a big way. **1990** *Car & Driver* (Sept.) 23: My trusty BMW 2002's header pipe rusted through in a big way.

big *adv.* conspicuously; notably; (*also*) with great success; to a great extent.

1865 in M. Lane *"Dear Mother"* 343: Both [were] big drunk. **1893** in F. Harris *Conklin* 206: He must win, and win "big," by a large margin. **1897** Paramore *Klondike* 13: Unless it paid big. **1908** McGaffey *Show Girl* 150: The show went big that night. **1912** in J. London *Letters* 363: That the book should sell big, I have all the confidence in the world. **1913** *Sat. Eve. Post* (Mar. 15) 6: Her act always "went big." **1920** Ade *Hand-Made Fables* 12: He had been going big because he improved his [golfing] stance. **1923** in J. O'Hara *Sel. Letters* 7: He made a crack to me that didn't get by so big. **1928** in Galewitz *Great Comics* 143: Any

guy that goes big with dogs an' kids is all right, b'lieve me. **1929–30** Dos Passos *42d Parallel* 114: The speech went big when Perez translated it. **1937** *Esquire* (Feb.) 63: She'll get places. And big. **1950** Spillane *Vengeance* 31: Your acid witticisms. They'll put me over big with the gang. **1954** N. Johnson *Night People* (film): I used to think that guy was a little crazy. But I've changed my mind. He's *big* crazy. **1958** J. King *Pro Football* 125: Conerly waited until his ninth season to make it "big." **1961** Scarne *Guide to Gambling* 59: They…make use of stooges who pretend to have won big on the tout's tips. **1962** T. Berger *Reinhart* 42: That'll go over big! **1963** D. Tracy *Brass Ring* 300: Kelly was bound to hit big anywhere else he turned his head. **1973** Layne *Murphy* (unp.): First time he comes to bat he strikes out big/As shit. **1973** J.E. Martin *95 File* 104: Things are breaking big. **1981** C. Nelson *Picked Bullets Up* 137: The story goes over big out here in the jungle. **1986** Univ. Tenn. English instructor: If you make that mistake, you'll be marked off big for it. **1993** *As World Turns* (CBS-TV): I miss you big.

¶ In phrase:

¶ **take it big** to react very emotionally; be dismayed.

1932 in *OEDS*: I see now why you took it so big when I mentioned that Soup Slattery was in town. **1933** Makin & Furthman *Bombshell* (film): She's takin' it big.

Big A *n.* a city or other named entity that bears the initial *A.*—usu. constr. with *the.* [Nonce coinages of the type (*Big* + initial) are freq. created; the fashion seems to have arisen during the 1940's. This dictionary lists only a sampling.] *Specif.:*

1. (see quot.).

1955 *AS* XXX 302: *Big A*…A local term referring to the Alcove Bar, a cocktail lounge near the Wayne [Univ.] campus.

2. *USAF.* an Atlas ICBM. Now *hist.*

1959 W.A. Heflin *Aerospace Gloss.*: *Big A.* The Atlas.

3. Atlanta, Ga.

1976 Lieberman & Rhodes *CB Handbook* 123: *Big A*—Atlanta. **1985** Univ. Tenn. instructor: You heading down to the Big A again this weekend?

4. [fr. BIG APPLE] New York City.

1980 Algren *Devil's Stocking* 79: That's how it goes in the Big A, girls. **1985** *The Equalizer* (CBS-TV): This the Big A. If you go out into those streets, you'll find out what guerrilla warfare really is. **1988** Lewin & Lewin *Thesaurus Sl.* 255: New York City. *Big A, Big Apple.*

5. the disease AIDS.

*****1986** in Partridge *Concise* 31: The big A. **1987** *Wkly. World News* (June 9) 12: AIDS. The big A has scared the living daylights out of the producers of the latest spy epic. **1992** *Donahue* (NBC-TV): We're all worried about this deadly virus that's goin' around.…The Big A.

6. Australia.

1987 R. Miller *Slob* 201: Man, soon's I can get me another two grand we're goin' to fuckin' Big A, man.…Fuckin' *Australia*, man.

Big Apple *n.* [the development and dissemination of(**1.a.**) and (**1.b.**) are traced in meticulous detail by G. Cohen et al. in *Comments on Ety.* (Jan. 1989 *et seqq.*); cf. APPLE]

1.a. Broadway and the jazz and entertainment centers of New York City; (*hence*) (now the usu. sense) New York City itself.—constr. with *the.*

[An internationally known nickname since the early 1970's (see 1989 quot.). Various factors—the absence of capitalization or quotation marks around what would have been considered an unusual term, the large gap between the first and second citations, and the evident novelty of the term in the 1920's—make it probable that the 1909 quot. represents a metaphorical or perhaps proverbial usage, rather than a concrete example of the later slang term; its appearance in a book of essays about New York City may have influenced journalistic use in the 1920's.]

1909 Martin *Wayfarer*, in *Comments on Ety.* (Oct. 1989) 4: It [the Midwest] inclines to think that the big apple [New York City] gets a disproportionate share of the national sap. **1927** W. Winchell, in *Bookman* (Dec.) 378: To the lonely and aspiring hoofer, the fannie-falling comedian, Broadway is the Big Apple, the Main Stem, the goal of all ambition. **1928** *N.Y. Times* VIII 6: Motion picture slang…*The Big Apple*—New York City. **1935** McIntyre *Big Town* 42: On nights out McGraw was…one of the liveliest spenders on the Big Apple. **1936** Duncan *Over the Wall* 194: Suppose you were ordered to go to New York and planned to take in the big apple. **1946** Mezzrow & Wolfe *Really Blue:*

149: As soon as we hit The Big Apple...New York. **1948** Manone & Vandervoort *Trumpet* 145: I'm a dicty chick from the Big Apple. **1954** in Wepman et al. *The Life* 39: You wait till I get back to the Big Apple. **1955** Tarry *Third Door* 292: A native of Brooklyn, he was thrilled to meet someone from "The Big Apple." **1957** Lacy *Room to Swing* 61: This is the Big Apple, buster. **1967** Taggart *Reunion* 288: The Big Apple, New York, New York. **1966–72** Winchell *Exclusive* 2: Texas Guinan's, the most popular and prosperous sip-and-sup spot along The Big Apple. **1986** Pietsch *NYC Cab Driver* 13: I think this money is New York money. This dough is earmarked for the Big Apple. **1989** *Comments on Ety.* (Oct.) 32: But until 1971 when Mr. [Charles] Gillett [president of the New York Convention and Visitors Bureau] started The Big Apple campaign the term was known only in the jazz world.

b. *Horse Racing*. the New York metropolitan racing circuit, including the major Long Island tracks; the racing "big time."—constr. with *the*.

1921 in *Comments on Ety.* (Oct. 1989) 4: The L.T. Bauer String, is scheduled to start for "the big apple" tomorrow. **1922** in *Comments on Ety.* (Oct. 1989) 5: It looks like a big year on "the big apple." **1926** in *Comments on Ety.* (May 1992) 4: The elderly son of Ultimus is a stake runner in the going, as he has shown often around "the big apple." *Ibid.* Around "the big apple" you hear little of this horsemen's organization. *Ibid.* When racing at the [New Orleans] Fair Grounds [in 1920]..."Why, we ain't no bull-ring stable; we's goin' to 'the big apple.'" **1927** in *Comments on Ety.* (Jan. 1989) 2: Beau Belmont can not recall a big apple racing period that left the barrier to a better start. **1928** in *Comments on Ety.* (Jan. 1989): Jamaica, New York, April 23. Racing came back to the Big Apple yesterday and...there was a throng of 10,000 at the Jamaica course to greet the thoroughbreds. **1928** in *Ibid.*: On the big apple. Activities at Ancient Aqueduct. **1952** Holmes *Boots Malone* (film): What makes you think you're a jockey? Just because you won some two-bit heat down in the toolies? This is the big apple! **1956** "T. Betts" *Across the Board* 61: Jamaica and Aqueduct, on a circut once known as the Big Apple. **1968** Ainslie *Thoroughbred Racing* 463: *Big Apple*—a major racing circuit.

c. Orig. *Jazz*. a big city.

1944 Burley *Hndbk. Harlem Jive* 144: *Big Apple*...any big town. **1981** Raban *Old Glory* 86: Wabasha had once, at least, intended to be a really big apple.

d. a jazz dance popular in the late 1930's.—constr. with *the*. Now *S.E.*

1937 in *OEDS*: The rage of the winter is the Big Apple and its related steps. **1938** "E. Queen" *4 Hearts* 176: It was an earthquake, a temblor. California was doing the Big Apple! **1938** Smitter *Detroit* 9: I'll show you how to do the Big Apple. **1958** *PADS* XXX 48: That defunct dance, the Big Apple.

2. the highest prize.

1971 Vaughan & Lynch *Brandywine* 36: He's going in for the big apple. The Medal of Honor.

big ass *n.* BIG SHOT.—used derisively.—usu. considered vulgar.

1963–64 Kesey *Great Notion* 332: This goddam bigcity bigass in his suntan and slacks. *Ibid.* 356: There's just a few Big-Asses; they own the world an' all the corn.

big-ass or **big-assed** *adj.* big.—usu. considered vulgar. See also -ASS, 2.a.

1945 (quot. at *like a big-assed bird*, below). **1952** Mandel *Angry Strangers* 63: We were big-assed birds for the Promised Land. **1955** T. Anderson *Own Beloved Sons* 14: We ain't enough, in case of a big-ass attack. **1961–65** Selby *Last Exit* 266: Abraham opened the door of his big-ass Cadillac. **1970** *N.Y. Post* (July 1) 3: Tom, you know Tom, that big-ass colored guy, man, that guy is just wild. **1971** T. Mayer *Weary Falcon* 27: She's under that big ass tree over there. **1974** Blount *3 Bricks Shy* 187: He has a big ass head. **1974–77** Heinemann *Close Quarters* 151: So he ups and walks to the ridgeline by this big-ass tree. **1977** Langone *Life at Bottom* 34: He'll sit there in this big-ass office downtown in Manila. **1978** B. Johnson *What's Happenin'* 156: Cops see nigger drivin' big-ass car and he wants to *tawk to you*. **1966–80** McAleer & Dickson *Unit Pride* 218: Just like a big-assed prize. **1991** *Wash. Post Mag.* (Apr. 28) 23: There were some big-ass close-outs, some whopper deals.

¶ In phrase:

¶ **like** [or **free as**] **a big-assed bird** swiftly.—usu. considered vulgar. Cf. BIG-ASS BIRD.

1945 *Yank* (July 13) 17: The [Infantry Field Manual] says they [second lieutenants] should be out in front like a big-assed bird. **1944–46** in *AS* XXII 56: *To take off like a big-ass bird*. To leave in a hurry. **1954** Ellson *Owen Harding* 2: If you see one, take off like a big-ass bird. **1955** Goethals *Chains* 104: Tell me, why'd you grab those bars and take off like a big-assed bird? **1958** T. Berger *Crazy* 59 [ref. to WWII]: Take off like a big-ass bird, Jack. **1970** Gaffney *World of Good* 284: I was free as a "big-assed bird." **1980** McDowell *Our Honor* 128: They wear tennis shoes even in the dead of winter, and they sneak up like big-assed birds and run you through with a bayonet. **1984–88** in Berry *Where Ya Been?* 182: This guy took out after Will like a big-ass bird!

big-ass *v. S.W.* to make a fool of.—usu. considered vulgar.

1984 Sample *Raceboss* 209 [ref. to 1960's]: I'm gon' bleeve ya'll tryin to big-ass me. *Ibid.* 262: Them nigguhs o' yourn is jes flat out big-assin you.

big-ass bird or **big-assed bird** *n. Av.* a usu. multiengine airplane having very large tail surfaces; (*esp.*) the Boeing B-17 Flying Fortress.—usu. considered vulgar. Now *hist.* Cf. *like a big-assed bird* s.v. BIG-ASS, *adj.*

[**1944** in Gurney *War in Air* 70: Der Grossarschvogel [name of B-17 aircraft].] **1961** in *JAF* LXXVIII (1965) 54: Airborne, airborne, have you heard?/We're gonna jump from the big-ass bird. **1965** Jablonski *Flying Fortress* 37 [ref. to WWII]: Possibly the most commonly used name for the B-17 was the [*sic*] affectionate recognition of the increased size of the empennage..."Big Assed Bird." **1967** Burgett *Currahee!* 77 [ref. to 1944]: The [C-47] rose heavily. "Flap your wings, you big-assed bird," I yelled. **1978** B. Smith, Jr. *Chick's Crew* 115: B-17's....We also called them Big Ass Birds [in WWII].

big auger *n. West.* an important person; BIG SHOT; boss.

1868 *Galaxy* (July) 114: "A most agreeable summer resort," begins Big-auger....No people outside State's prison are hated more cordially and justly than the Bigaugers. **1903** A. Adams *Log of a Cowboy* 125: I can't quite make out this other duck, but I reckon he's some big auger—a senator or governor, maybe. *Ibid.* 135: It's the easiest thing in the world for some big auger to sit in a hotel somewhere and direct the management of a herd. **1905** in A. Adams *Chisholm Trail* 130: The big augers of the outfit lived in Wichita, Kansas. *a*1940 in Lanning & Lanning *Texas Cowboys* 5 [ref. to *ca*1880]: "Big auger," "bull moose," and similar terms were used when referring to the ranch owner. **1940** F. Hunt *Trail from Tex.* 183 [ref. to 1870's]: The big auger'd send this herd over Niagara Falls if it was in his way. **1967** Gries *Will Penny* (film): Well, that's the story he gave the big auger.

Big B *n.* a city or other named entity that bears the initial *B*.—usu. constr. with *the*. [See note at BIG A.] *Specif.*:

1. *USAF*. Berlin, Germany.—also constr. with *the*.

1944 in *Best from Yank* 87: But it was for Berlin, the "Big B," to be hit in daylight. **1944** Stiles *Big Bird* 76: Maybe back to Big B. **1945** Hamann *Air Words*: *Big B.* Berlin. **1946** G.C. Hall, Jr. *1000 Destroyed* 155: Pappy saw what the show was—Berlin or big "B." **1957** Goldberg *Air Force* 66: Next, the Eighth went after "Big B"—Berlin itself. **1963** Horwitz *Candlelight* 73: We were briefed for Big B. Berlin. **1978** Ardery *Bomber Pilot* 167: Calls came for the B-24s to take the trip over The Big B. *a*1984 in M.W. Bowman *Castles* 120 [ref. to 1944]: Each day we would walk into the briefing session wondering if the tape on the wall map would stretch to "Big-B" that morning.

2. Baltimore, Md.

1974 Strasburger *Rounding Third* 151: The ride back from Philly to Big B.

big banana *n.* **1.** the top prize or recognition; the focus of interest or attention.—constr. with *the*.

1980 Lorenz *Guys Like Us* 229: You're playing for the big banana, and your left fielder develops a tummyache. **1988** *Crossfire* (CNN-TV) (June 24): The big banana...is the vice-presidency.

2. BIG SHOT.

1984 *L.A. Times* (Oct. 10) VI 1: Palmer...is also a big banana in ABC's broadcast booth.

Big Ben *n. Craps*. the point ten. [More commonly called BIG DICK.]

1962 Crump *Killer* 183: Crow tossed the dice, their roll stopped on ten. "Big Ben, I've got it made then!" **1984** Sample *Raceboss* 30: Gets ten for a point...."Oh *Big Ben!*"

big bench *n. Journ.* the United States Supreme Court.—constr. with *the*.

1929 Hotstetter & Beesley *It's a Racket* 219: *Big Bench*—The Supreme Court.

Big Bertha *n.* **1.** *Mil.* **a.** a German long-range gun of the heaviest caliber; (*broadly*) a heavy artillery piece. Now *hist.* [All quots. ref. to WWI; cf. BERTHA, BUSY BERTHA.]

*1914 in *OEDS.* **1918** Battey *Sub. Destroyer* (Mar. 13): Heard Panther men on Paris leave lost clothing when "Big Bertha" shell burst in apartment house. **1918** Straub *Diary* 153: I saw the base of "Big Bertha," the gun that was used to bombard Paris. **1918** in Paine *Yale* II 142: "Big Bertha" discharged a shell into Dunkirk every seven minutes. **1919** McKenna *Btty. A* 109: German big Berthas dropping over some ten or twelve 210 mm. shells. **1928** Scanlon *Have Mercy* 238: Some big gun, perhaps a Big Bertha. **1932** Halyburton & Goll *Shoot & Be Damned* 28: The Big Berthas continued to drop their shells far behind us.

b. a heavy artillery shell fired by a Big Bertha. Now *hist.* [Quot. ref. to WWI.]

1915–18 Hall & Niles *One Man's War* 48: The big [German] shells [were] called "Big Berthas" at that time.

2. an overweight woman.—often used as a derisive nickname.

1921 *Pirate Piece* (May) 4 [ref. to WWI]: Big "Boitha" (who has just taken her first lesson in English from F Battery "slickers")—Ahh! You pip' down, greazeball. **1941** Kendall *Army & Navy Slang* 2: *Big Berthas*...hefty dames.

3. something unusually large or impressive.

1931 *Writer's Digest* (May) 40: *Big Bertha*—A 30-passenger Fokker plane. **1951** Mannix *Sword-Swallower* 99: I had a special attachment on the machine that stepped up the amperage. I called it my "Big Bertha." **1962** Houk & Charles *Ballplayers* 141: One homer...was a Big Bertha, over the left field terrace, over the fence, over Brooklyn Avenue.

Big Blink *n.* [sugg. by BIG SLEEP] death.—constr. with *the. Joc.*
1983 Goldman & Fuller *Charlie Co.* 331: I thought, "This is it, the Big Blink."

Big Blue *n.* **1.** [orig. the nickname of the IBM model 360 mainframe computer, the casing of which was blue] *Business.* IBM corporation.
1984 *U.S. News & W.R.* (June 18) 61: Even AT&T, with all its resources, won't find it easy to muscle in on Big Blue. **1984** *USA Today* (Sept. 28) 1: IBM jolts industry...Big Blue reaches out. **1986** WINS Radio News (Mar. 26): Big Blue—IBM—down three-eighths. **1991** *N.Y. Times* (Oct. 20) Business F 2: Big Blue also said it had trimmed sales, administrative and research expenses.

2. *Stu.* the University of Michigan; (*specif.*) (and *usu.*) a sports team, esp. the football team, of the University of Michigan.
1987 Univ. Mich. graduate: University of Michigan. Yeah, I went to Big Blue. **1992** Car bumper sticker: Go Big Blue!

Big Board *n. Business.* any major stock exchange; (*specif.* and *usu.*) the New York Stock Exchange, Inc.—constr. with *the.*
1934 in *WNID2.* **1973** *Business Week* (Aug. 18) 69: We're the broker for nearly 20% of all the shares traded on Tokyo's Big Board. **1978** J. Rosenberg *Dict. Business* 47. **1984** *Knoxville* [Tenn.] *Journal* (Oct. 6) B6: Advances held an 8–7 edge on declines at the Big Board. **1990** *U.S. News & W.R.* (Aug. 13) 66: Meanwhile, at the Big Board, all program trades involving the sale of baskets of stocks...were diverted to a "sidecar," or special file.

big boot *n.* a powerful person; BIG SHOT.
1969 *Cimarron Strip* (CBS-TV): Buchman's a man with a big boot. We hired out to the big boots—the Buchmans and the like.

big bopper *n.* [the professional pseudonym of Jape "J.P." Richardson (1930–59), disk jockey and rock singer] a person holding paramount authority.
1966–80 McAleer & Dickson *Unit Pride* 77: So far as authority went...Coggins was the big bopper now. **1978–86** J.L. Burke *Lost Get-Back Boogie* 10: Tell them the big bopper from Bogalusa is primed and ready. **1989** *Saved by the Bell* (NBC-TV): I'm the big bopper around here.

Big Boss *n.* God.—constr. with *the.*
1926 Nichols & Tully *Twenty Below* 85: 'Bove churches, 'bove everything, to the Big Boss in the clouds.

big boy *n.* **1.** something that is a large, heavy, or impressive example of its kind; (*esp.*) *Mil.* a heavy artillery piece, shell, bomber, tank, etc.
1917 in Bryan *Ambulance* 64: Three big "boys" had fallen near him as he passed through Montzeville. **1918** *Stars & Stripes* (Feb. 8) 3: The "big boys" are here....They have more machinery attached to them

than the average small factory. **1918** in Peat *Legion Airs* 117: Limber up the big boys, and make the Boches dance. **1924** Barker *Along Road* 18: Five "big boys" roared over our heads like elevated trains, to burst in the valley below. **1925** Fraser & Gibbons *Soldier & Sailor Wds.* 22 [ref. to WWI]: *Big Boys*, large guns, "Heavies." **1928** Nason *Eadie* 170: Wham! Wham! Wham! Big boys, eight-inch [shells] at the least. **1943** Wolfert *Tucker's People* 68: Leo saved the $100 bill for last...."I can't use a big boy like this, boss. Scare the bartender to death if I flash this one on him." **1945** Hubbard *R.R. Ave.* 332: *Big Boys*—Special trains for officials. **1962** W. Robinson *Barbara* 222: The big boys, the bombers, drummed an appearance long before they could see...them. **1965** Capote *In Cold Blood* 377: The United States Supreme Court—the Big Boy, as many litigating prisoners refer to it. **1970** Flood *Innocents* 193: We had some self-propelled 155-millimeter "Big Boys"...in addition to the usual...105-millimeter guns. **1971** Glasser *365 Days* 113: I want the two big boys leading the first and third platoons. *Ibid.* 242: *Big Boys* slang for tanks.

2.a. (used as a semi-humorous term of address to a man).
1918 R. Lardner *Treat 'Em Rough* 124: Au revoir for this time, Big Boy. **1918** in *OEDS*: "Hold on, Big Boy," he called. **1924** in Clarke *Amer. Negro Stories* 23: Where y' want to go, big boy? **1927** *Amer. Legion Mo.* (May) 25: How do you get that way yourself, big boy? **1931** Cressey *Taxi-Dance Hall* 36: Say, listen Big Boy, there ain't no Santa Claus! **1935** Coburn *Law Rides Range* 57: Go button your mouth, big boy. **1967–69** Foster & Stoddard *Pops* 49: Come on and drink, big boy. **1985** Sawislak *Dwarf* 53: It's focused on you, big boy.

b. an important or influential man; BIG SHOT.
1924 in R. Lardner *Haircut* 175: So it looks like all I have to do is wait for the big boys to get back and then play my numbers for them and I will be all set. **1928** W.R. Burnett *Little Caesar* ch. 1: The Big Boy can't fix murder. He can fix anything but murder. **1929** Hostetter & Beesley *It's a Racket* 219: *Big Boy*—Federal judge. **1931** Grant *Gangdom's Doom* 36: There's bad feeling between Larrigan and Varona, and the big boy doesn't like it. **1936** M. Davis *Lost Generation* 32: The politicians run everything....An' the big boys run the politicians. **1942** *N.Y. Times Mag.* (Jan. 25) 30: *Big boy*—A judge of a high court. **1950** Calmer *Strange Land* 186: It's up to the big boys to figure it out. Like Roosevelt, like Churchill and Stalin. **1958** S.H. Adams *Tenderloin* 311: "We ain't askin' you to do anything," the Big Boy said persuasively. *Ibid.* 348: That's Police Commissioner Brophy. One of the Big Boys. **1961** L.G. Richards *TAC* 163: Even the big boys wouldn't have given the map a second glance. **1979** in Terkel *Amer. Dreams* 370: Any individual can buck the big boys without help from others? **1983** Ad for *Charlie's Angels* (synd. TV series): This week—the Angels hit Las Vegas for a game with the big boys. And the penalty for losing is—death!

c. God.—constr. with *the.*
1962 T. Berger *Reinhart* 99: In the eyes of the Big Boy upstairs we are all even as children. **1965** Conot *Rivers of Blood* 258: One...pressed a...pistol to the back of Harold Myers's neck declaring, "Man, you are going up to meet the Big Boy."

big-bug *n.* a wealthy, influential, or celebrated person; BIG SHOT. Also attrib. [A ubiquitous term in the 19th C.]
1817 in Royall *Letters from Ala.* 117: Being asked by one of the big bugs to rub down his horse. **1827** in *Jour. Amer. Folk.* LXXVI (1963) 291: Awl darn big buggs [are] putty much awl humbuggs. **1827** *Harvard Register* (Oct.) 247: He...desires to be a big-Bug, rattling in a natty gig. **1834** *Mil. & Nav. Mag.* (May) 173 [ref. to 1813]: The "Big Bugs" were at a loss what next to do. This *nom de guerre*, as expressive of officers above the rank of Colonel, came into vogue about these times of leisure. *Ibid.* 175: *Big Bug*, as synonymous with General...went at once into vogue. **1836** *Spirit of Times* (Feb. 27) 16: It's a heb-a-bominable, as the big bugs calls the weekly papers. **1848** Judson *Mysteries* 13: I mauled some o' the bigbug swells a bit ago. **1849** *Nat. Police Gaz.* (Jan. 20) 3: The press...I am sorry to say, take part with the *big bugs*; but as you are above such considerations I ask you to...say a word for the poor and oppressed of the human family. **1852** Hazen *Five Years* 29: We can safely say, that for once in our lives, we have slept in a big-bug bed! **1857** in Olmsted *Papers* II 307: He told me the land in the vicinity was owned by "big-bugs."...He himself is an overseer for "one of the biggest kind of bugs." **1868** [Williams] *Black-Eyed Beauty* 50: Did you know Crockford's mother—the big bug that kept the hell? **1876** Miller *First Fam'lies* 189: Washington, Caesar, Horace Greeley, all sich big-bugs. **1876** in *Buffalo Bill* 207: You see a lot of big-bugs an' officers came out/One time to hunt the buffler an' fish fer speckled trout. **1884** "M. Twain" *Huck. Finn* ch. v: You think you're a good deal of a big-bug, *don't* you? **1885** *Puck* (Apr. 29) 138: Jones was the biggest bug we had in Deadman's Gulch, and he was solid with the boys. **1893** Coes *Blunders* 3: Well, did you hear of all de big bugs dat was to be at the con-

vention? **1900** Fisher *Job* 6: The whole town came out regularly to meet the stage…and gambled on the probability that a telegram from 'Frisco had held it for a special train of "bigbugs." **1905** *DN* III 60: The *biggest bug* of the crowd. **1908** *Hampton's Mag.* (Sept.) 310: Himself conversed with very "tony" callers, big-bugs. **1911** Howard *Enemy to Society* 5: Some big bug [is] sick, I reckon. **1922** in O'Brien *Best Stories of '22* 24: And me trying to pass myself off as a bigbug and a swell. *ca***1938** in Rawick *Amer. Slave* II (Pt. 1) 52: Miss Nina…live 'mong de big bugs in Winnsboro. **1958** S.H. Adams *Tenderloin* 39: There is also a Tammany bigbug in the picture. **1962** L'Engle *Wrinkle in Time* 30: Calvin O'Keefe….He's a big bug.

big bullet *n. Mil. Av.* an air-launched guided missile.
1985 Boyne & Thompson *Wild Blue* 519 [ref. to Vietnam War]: The MiG was in a position to be hit by the…Sparrow missile, the huge "big bullet" of a rocket that the Phantom fought with.

Big Burg *n.* a big city; (*specif.*) New York City.—constr. with *the.*
1918 Stringer *House of Intrigue* 28: He usually fought clear of the Big Burg. **1933** Guest *Limey* 5: I…boarded the train for New York…I had no plans beyond looking around the "big burg." **1948** Lait & Mortimer *New York* x: This is a commentary on and compendium of the Big Burg from the inside out.

big-butt *n.* BIG-BUG.—used derisively.
1912–43 *Frank Brown Collection* I 522: *Big-butt: n.* An aristocrat, a "big-wig," "bigbug."

Big BX *n.* [jargon *BX* 'base exchange'] *USAF.* BIG PX.
*ca***1968** in Tuso *Vietnam Blues* 189: And go back home to the Big BX. **1980** W.C. Anderson *BAT-21* 37 [ref. to 1972]: Back to the land of the big BX.

Big C *n.* a city or other named entity that bears the initial *C.*—usu. constr. with *the.* [See note at BIG A.] *Specif.:*
1. *Narc.* cocaine.
1959 Schmidt *Narc. Lingo.* **1968** D.B. Louria *Drug Scene* 207: *Big c.* cocaine. **1983** *Time* (Apr. 11): He and his girlfriend…come into this mostly Hispanic neighborhood every Sunday to buy cocaine ("Big C") and heroin ("Big D," for dope).
2. cancer.
1964 N.Y.C. high school student: John Wayne says he licked the Big C. **1967** W. Murray *Sweet Ride* 84: "He's had a lung removed." "The Big C?" "Yes." **1970** L. Gould *Friends* 18: Always knew it would be Big C for me, kid; no heart attacks in bed for old Richie. **1971** J. Updike *Rabbit Redux* 17: The side effects may be worse. You know: the big C. **1977** WINS radio report (Aug. 13): Littler…beat Big C. **1980** in *Penthouse* (Jan. 1981) 32: The Big C…thousands of cancer patients may be dying annually simply because new treatments are deliberately being withheld or excluded from necessary funding. **1983** *Rolling Stone* (Feb. 3) 55: I've got the big C now. I'm gonna die. **1984** Amer. Heart Assoc. ad (WUTK Radio) (July 14): Yeah, the Big C—cancer. **1986** Cash & Epps *Legal Eagles* (film): He got the Big C the year he was released from prison. **1988** Norst *Colors* 13: He'd forestalled the Big C.
3. Chicago, Ill.
1976 Lieberman & Rhodes *CB Hndbk.* (1977 ed.) 305: *Big C*—Chicago. **1977** *Amer. Dict. CB* 97: Chicago, Illinois—*Big C.*

big casino *n.* **1.a.** the most important or influential person (in a given sphere, place, etc.); a big person.
1893 F.P. Dunne, in Schaaf *Dooley* 54: Did ye niver read "Thadjus iv Warsaw" Jawn?…Well, sir, there's my idale iv a good smashin' book. There's nobody in there lower than th' big casino. **1903** Hobart *Out for Coin* 30: A Kaintucky hossman info'med yo' uncle that yo' all was big casino on the Eastern tracks, suh! **1908** in H.C. Fisher *A. Mutt* 128: A human hummingbird invariably grabs a female Taft and looks like big and little casino. **1951** West *Flaming Feud* 82: First you had to prove you were the Big Casino. How? By curling up Rock. **1958** McCulloch *Woods Words* 11: *Big casino—*The head man; foreman. **1987** *Crossfire* (CNN-TV) (Apr. 28): I know you're after him. He's the big casino. You want to knock him down.
b. that which ruins or finishes, esp. a fatal illness.
1951 Fowler *Schnozzola* 213: He feared he had cancer, a disease referred to by Broadwayites as "Big Casino." *Ibid.* A strong man simply can't take a draw with Big Casino. The odds are too long. **1956** "T. Betts" *Across the Board* 129: Cassidy…was hit in the stomach with big casino. **1968** Longstreet *Wilder Shore* 24: Aches and pains were plentiful, followed by epidemics of small-pox, yellow jack, big casino (syphilis), and other uncontrolled and strange diseases abounded. *Ibid.* 216: Seldom, before the age of penicillin, was a sailor…left uninfected by

Big Casino or Little Casino, the major and minor diseases of Venus. **1981** Sann *Trial* 20: The Big Casino which had taken her mother and two sisters. **1986** *Crossfire* (CNN-TV) (May 25): When did you first get the feeling that [the Watergate scandal] was big casino for your career and reputation?
c. the most or best that can be attained; something of the greatest importance.
1983 Wambaugh *Delta Star* 123: "What's big casino?" "What else? The Nobel Prize. That's what he called it." **1988** McLaughlin Group (TV series) (Sept. 4): California is the big casino [in the presidential election]. **1992** *Wash. Post* (Nov. 30) A3: Only the top quark remains unsighted, making it the Big Casino for researchers in particle physics.
2. one's best resource or asset.
1922 Rollins *Cowboy* 80: Whatever idea or physical asset was expected when ultimately put in use to bring success was one's "big casino." **1927** Rollins *Jinglebob* 229 [ref. to 1880's]: The bronco…prepared, as cowboys said, to "play his big casino." **1936** R. Adams *Cowboy Lingo* 229: Whatever idea or physical asset was expected to bring success was one's "big casino." If expectation miscarried, the disappointed person ruefully asserted that his "big casino" had been trumped.

Big Charley *n.* [mil. communications alphabet *Charley* 'c'] **1.** *Mil.* a Chinook helicopter.
1966 Baxter *Search & Destroy* 36: The crew chief of a "Big Charley" chopper is almost always cold because of the draft from his open window.
2. *CB.* the Federal Communications Commission.
1977 Perkowski & Stral *Joy of CB* 166: *Big Charlie*…The Federal Communications Commission. Originally a ham term.

big cheese *n.* the most important or influential person; boss; BIG SHOT.—often used derisively. See also CHEESE, *n.*
1914 in R. Lardner *Haircut* 144: They was one big innin' every day and Parker was the big cheese in it. **1921** S.V. Benét *Wisdom* 233: The other guy's the big cheese. **1924** *DN* V 289: *The big cheese, n.phr.* An important person. **1928** Treadwell *Machinal* 500: You and the big chief.…You and the big cheese. **1929** "E. Queen" *Roman Hat* ch. viii: Are you the big cheese around here? **1929–30** J.T. Farrell *Young Lonigan* 102: He had licked Weary Reilley and become…a big cheese around Indiana. **1931** Dos Passos *1919* 257: He started to say something sarcastic about the big cheese, as he called him. **1934** H. Miller *Tropic of Cancer* 20: Elsa is the maid and I am the guest. And Boris is the big cheese. **1952** Bissell *Monongahela* 209: You're the big cheese, it's all up to you. **1953** A. Kahn *Brownstone* 121: What's the sixty-four dollar word for today from the big cheese? **1956** G. Green *Last Angry Man* 239: You're not such a big cheese. **1970** Zindel *Your Mind* 2: Mr. Donaldson…was the big cheese in the inhalation-therapy department. **1975** Keel *Mothman* 136: Ashtar is a big cheese in the Intergalactic Federation. **1975** Hynek & Vallee *Edge of Reality* 197: The guy who was in charge there at that time, the big cheese in charge of the whole area there, had been a real big shot in Japan.

Big Chill *n.* [app. sugg. by *The Big Chill,* title of popular 1983 motion picture] an unfortunate or depressing state of affairs; (*specif.*) death.
1984 *Mother Jones* (May) 10: The controversy stirred up within Apple's top echelons indicates that a Big Chill may be setting in at the company. **1987** *Campus Voice* (Spring) 48: Stunt men…and sky divers routinely flirt with death, and increasing numbers of people claim to have come closer to the Big Chill than any daredevil has.

big-cock *adj.* big; huge.—usu. considered vulgar.
1965 W. Eastlake *Castle Keep* 233: When I asked in bigcock surprise how with all that education she got into this bed racket, she said…"By luck, mister. Sheer luck!" **1971** S. Stevens *Way Uptown* 120: They'd ride around in their plastic wagons dressed in their plastic suits and that big cock gun strapped to their plastic belts.

big cough *n. Und.* a bomb.
1929 Hotstetter & Beesley *It's a Racket* 219: *Big Cough*—Bomb containing a heavy charge of explosive. **1930** in Adamic *Dynamite* 353: The technique of detonating a "big cough" to do deliberate murder. **1936** Mackenzie *Living Rough* 139: And sometimes we had to let off a "big cough" and wreck his joint.

big curtain *n.* [cf. CURTAINS] *Theat.* death.
1904 Hobart *Jim Hickey* 100: Jim, that big curtain worries me.

Big D *n.* a named entity that bears the initial *D.*—sometimes constr. with *the.* [See note at BIG A.] *Specif.:*
1. Dallas, Texas.

1930 in Fortune *Fugitives* 73: I'll jump right up and start towards Big D. **1942–44** in *AS* (Feb. 1946) 31: *Big D*, n. Dallas. **1950** in W.A. Owens *Texas Folk Songs* 183 [ref. to *ca*1940]: Negroes on the chain gang in Lamar County talked…a great deal about Dallas, "Big D." **1961** Terry *Old Liberty* 118: We took 67 straight in to Big D Dallas. **1967** Mailer *Vietnam* 13: Dallas. Big D. **1969** Angelou *Caged Bird* 208 [ref. to 1940's]: They had known or claimed to have known the bright lights of Big D (Dallas) or T Town (Tulsa, Oklahoma). **1971** *Newsweek* (May 3) 32: Only once in the last twenty years had a mayoral candidate bucked Big D's big-business leadership and won a popular election. **1978** *Atlantic* (Dec.) 68: The *Times Herald* gave the test to about twenty students…in North Dallas….It was a big F for the big D. **1984** *L.A. Times* (Aug. 19) VII 2: David G. Fox, a legend in Dallas…is serving as chairman of the welcoming committee whose job it will be to make visiting Republicans happy during their days and nights in the Big D. **1992** *CBS This Morning* (CBS-TV) (Sept. 28): Scott Pelley is standing by in Big D with the latest.
2. Detroit, Mich.
1961 C. Cooper *Weed* 46: He finally got back to big D. **1970** A. Young *Snakes* 102: I can gig…here in Big D.
3. Denver, Colo.
1969 *Current Slang* I & II 9: *Big D*, n. Denver.—Air Force Academy cadets. **1986** De Sola *Abbr. Dict.* (ed. 7) 129: *Big-D of the West* Denver, Colorado.
4. death.
1977 Caputo *Rumor of War* 258: Death is a pleasure. The Big D is the world's most powerful narcotic, the ultimate anesthetic. **1982** *California* (Aug.) 120: It gives death a whole new dimension, in a way. It domesticates it, lending the Big D a casual, round-the-house feel. **1989** G. Trudeau *Doonesbury* (synd. cartoon strip) (Oct. 27): This could be *the death thing*, the Big "D"! *1992 English Today* (Apr.) 58: The little death rather than the *Big D*.
5. *Sports.* defense.
1979 Cuddon *Dict. Sports & Games* 276: D…short for "Defence"; often referred to as "the big D." **1987** *Daywatch* (CNN-TV): Most upsets begin with the big D.

big dad *n.* BIG DADDY.
1987 D. da Cruz *Boot* 296: *Big Dad* Senior Drill Instructor [USMC].

big daddy *n.* **1.a.** a man in a position of influence and authority; BIG SHOT.
1948 Kaese *Braves* 137: His [sc. George Stallings's] players [ca1912] called him "George," "Chief," or "Big Daddy." **1961** T.I. Rubin *In Life* 155: *Big Daddy*…a synonym for…"Big Shot" or "Boss." **1963** *Twilight Zone* (CBS-TV): Big Daddy wants to know what's so funny. **1966** Elli *Riot* 84: Wait'll Big Daddy [sc. a prison warden] gets back….He'll have that clown countin' our dirty socks for the next five years. **1967** Riessman & Dawkins *Play It Cool* 52: Eddie struts like he thinks he's a big daddy. **1969** *Current Slang* I & II 9: *Big daddy*, n. A leader.—College females, New York. **1970** Quammen *Walk Line* 31: Ain't that one of those…big-daddy schools out east for rich dudes or smart dudes whose…old men are ambassadors? **1975** Hynek & Vallee *Edge of Reality* 81: What you're saying…is very much in agreement with what some of the big daddies have said about cancer research. **1986** R. Campbell *In La-La Land* 9: As long as you let him be big daddy, he'd make your life sweeter. **1991** Nelson & Gonzales *Bring Noise* 166: The big daddies at the FBI.
b. Esp. *Black E.* grandfather.
1955 T. Williams *Cat Tin Roof* 2: Big Daddy…threw down his fork. **1965–70** in *DARE.* **1974** *TULIPQ* (coll. B.K. Dumas): Grandmother *Big mama*. Grandfather *Big daddy*. **1982** A. Walker *Color Purple* 227: Something was funny bout his mama…cause she and big daddy was so old and strict and set in they ways.
c. a big man.—often used as a nickname.
1972 USAF Sgt., age 19: Here comes big daddy! **1978** T. Jones *Wayward Sailor* 252: Big Daddy had flown the coop.
2.a. a male sweetheart or friend.—often used as a term of address.
1959 *Many Loves of D. Gillis* (CBS-TV): Hey, big daddy, what're you doin'? **1961** T.I. Rubin *In Life* 155: *Big Daddy*…also…a sweetheart. **1968** Heard *Howard Street* 11: What's the matter, big daddy, didn't you dig it? **1971** J. Brown & A. Groff *Monkey* 38: I kept telling myself, "O.K., Big Daddy, you've got to settle down."
b. *Prost.* a pimp.
1961 T.I. Rubin *In Life* 155: *Big Daddy* pimp or procurer; kept man. **1963** T.I. Rubin *Sweet Daddy* 64: My bust [was] strictly for being a big daddy.

3. a large or important thing; the largest or most prominent specimen (of a given kind).
1965 *Time* (Nov. 5) 62: How Uncle Sam turned into Big Daddy is delineated in *The Encyclopedia of U.S. Government Benefits*. **1968** Zerwick & Brown *Cassiopeia* 14: And finally "Big Daddy," the king of all radio-telescopes, was constructed. **1969** A. Schlesinger, Jr., in *Atlantic* (Jan. 1970) 86: One is permitted to doubt whether even a conservative Administration in Washington would find it possible in the decade ahead to…become again the Big Daddy of the hemisphere. **1971** Dahlskog *Dict.* 7: That fish is the *big daddy* of them all. **1973** *Business Week* (Oct. 6) 93: The Big Daddy of them all, a government data bank that will list absolutely everyone. **1977** Filosa *Surf. Almanac* 182: *Big daddy*—A giant breaker. **1978** B. Johnson *What's Happenin'* 92: Houston….It'll be the monster by the year 2000. It'll be the big daddy, maybe. **1982** Sculatti *Catalog of Cool* 47: The absolute Big Daddy of anthropomorphic auto-horror movies.

big deal *n.* **1.** that which is of great interest or importance; (*hence,* as an ironic interj.) "so what?" "who cares?"
1943 *School & Society* LVIII 169: *Big deal*: an uncalled-for action. **1944–48** A. Lyon *Unknown Station* 21: "How was town?"…"Big deal…GIs staggering all over the place." **1948** Kingsley *Detective Story* 344: She's afraid this might crimp her chances to be the next Mrs. Forbes….Big deal! **1950** Stuart *Objector* 163: Big deal, Heath thought. **1946–51** J.D. Salinger *Catcher* ch. i: The game with Saxon Hall was supposed to be a very big deal around Pencey. **1952** MacDonald *Damned* 136: Well, the world is full of cheap guys who think perfume from J.C. Penney is a big deal. **1952** "M. Roscoe" *Black Ball* 51: The sun came up. Big deal. Daylight was here again. **1952** in Yates *Loneliness* 33: Some weekend. Big, big deal. **1955** H. Robbins *79 Park Ave* 253: What's such a big deal? People get married all the time. **1957** H. Danforth & Horan *D.A.'s Man* 230 [ref. to 1942]: Several high ranking police officials were summoned…to discuss…"a big deal raid." **1961** Dillon *Judi* 8: I thought going to a Prom was a big deal. **1968** Wojciechowska *Tuned Out* 13: I've never made a big-deal secret out of it. **1968** J. Kramer *Instant Replay* 225: Big deal. Who cares? **1971** in L. Bangs *Psychotic Reactions* 6: What's so big deal about playing buzzsaw fiddle? **1971** Simon *Sign of Fool* 140: Richie bailed my ass out of jail. Big deal. **1976** Whelton *CB Baby* 127: Right. What's the big deal? **1977** Newman & Berkowitz *Take Charge* 23: But no one seems to appreciate it. Nobody thinks it's a big deal. **1983** *Good Morning America* (ABC-TV) (Feb. 4): Performing in Carnegie Hall. Is that a big deal for you? **1990** *Garfield & Friends* (CBS-TV): Big fat hairy deal! I want my lasagna back.
2. a person who is the object of interest and attention; a celebrated or important individual. Occ. as adj.
1944–46 in *AS* XXIII 54: *Big Deal*. A BTO, a big shot. **1952** in Yates *Loneliness* 45: What the hell's he think,…he's some kind of a big deal now, just because he's a hotshot with that stupid bayonet? **1956** Ross *Hustlers* 112: I'd be a big deal after…I'd walk down the streets. Everybody'd make way….I'd be a big shot. **1959** Sabre & Eiden *Glory Jumpers* 169: I'm supposed to feel like a big deal, now, is that it? **1961** Pollini *Night* 51: He's a big deal, ya know. **1964** Leavitt & Sohn *Stop, Look & Write* 188: They looked as though they thought they were very big deal. **1971** Freeman *Catcher* (film): I'm not underestimating you. I know you're a big deal. **1972** Jenkins *Semi-Tough* 40: You're all wise guys, is that it? Big football deals. **1983** *Nat. Lampoon* (Nov.) 12: A big-deal Regional Sales Supervisor with a la-di-da M.B.A. degree.

big-deal *v.* **1.** to obtain by clever trading or negotiating.
1945 Lindner *Stone Walls & Men* 46: When you sell a stock now, no sales-talk, no promotion, no big-dealing. **1949** McMillan *Old Breed* 241: Often one man or combination of men in the tent had Big Dealed the components of coffee.
2. to magnify the importance of.
1963 Rubin *Sweet Daddy* 136: Doc this here call-girl stuff [is] mostly big-dealed up by the newspapers.

Big Deuce *n. Mil.* BIG Two.
1982 Sculatti *Catalog of Cool* 213: (The) *Big Deuce*…World War II.

Big Dick *n.* **1.** *Craps.* the point ten.—usu. in phr. **Big Dick from Boston**; occ. in other vars. [The reason for the application of this name is not now traceable.]
1890 Quinn *Fools of Fortune* 540: The quaint expressions of "come seven, come eleven," "where's my point," "little Joe," "big Dick from Boston," and the like, are now frequently heard from the lips of the high-toned white gamblers. **1911** *Howitzer* (U.S. Mil. Acad.) 177: Big Dick from Boston—eighty miles from home. **1918** Witwer *Baseball* 293: Ha, Big Dick from Boston! **1920** in Hemingway *Dateline: Toronto* 34: Beeg Deeck from Bawston! **1949** in Clark *Dict. Gamb. & Gam.*

1987 Clark *Dict. Gamb. & Gam.*: *Big dick from (Battle Creek, Boston, etc.)…same as big dick.*

2. BIG SHOT. Also as *v.* (*constr.* with *it*) to act the bigshot.—usu. considered vulgar.

1974 *Univ. Tenn.* grad. student: That's where the big dick of the KKK used to live. *Ibid.*: That's some damn big-dick school. **1988** Clodfelter *Mad Minutes* 94 [ref. to 1965]: I dig the idea of big dicking it around town with those paratrooper wings on my chest.

Big Ditch *n.* **1.** a canal; (*specif.*) **a.** the Erie Canal.—usu. constr. with *the.* Cf. syn. DITCH.

1825 in *AS* XXI 305: The project…was called by its friends "the great canal," and by its opponents by the "big ditch." **1872** *Harper's Mag.* (May) 841: Tammany used the "big ditch" scheme as one of the most effective weapons against him. **1880** in *DA*: The head of water in the Big Ditch is pretty fair and so are the clean-ups.

b. the Panama Canal.—usu. constr. with *the.*

1915 Poole *Harbor* 163: For within a few years the Big Ditch would open across Panama. **1922** Hisey *Sea Grist* 43: We were actually about to enter the "big ditch" twenty-six hundred miles from home! **1928** *Collier's* (Aug. 25) 15: Panama City, the Big Ditch with its marvelous locks…Balboa, Colon, [etc.]. **1928** in O'Brien *Best Stories of '28* 132: She's the hardest drinker on the Big Ditch. **1948** *Sat. Eve. Post* (Oct. 9) 15: Our vaunted Big Ditch is vulnerable to planes, submarines—and saboteurs. **1982** F. Hailey *Soldier Talk* 18: *Ditch, the big.* The Panama Canal.

2. the Atlantic Ocean.—constr. with *the.*

1909 in *DA*: I'm the biggest fool this side o' the big ditch. **1915** Howard *God's Man* 211: It's due tomorrow night—a blow-off one girl's giving who's going across the big ditch—Europe.

3. *USMC.* Guadalcanal.—constr. with *the.* Now *hist.*

1960 MacCuish *Gentle* 345: "What outfit you with on the Canal?" "Raiders. You on the Big Ditch?"

Big Divide *n.* the line between life and death.—constr. with *the.*

1902 Cullen *More Tales* 32: It's a sure thing that I'm going to weigh out and make my little stretch-run over the Big Divide at least five years earlier than nature…intended.

big dog *n.* **1.** BIG-BUG, BIG SHOT.—sometimes constr. with intensifying prep. phr. based on *tanyard, meathouse,* etc. [Relevance of 1833 quot. is prob. indirect.]

[**1833** in *DA*: For the rale genuine grammar larnin' I am a six-horse team and a big dog under the wagon.] **1843** Field *Pokerville* 84: Mr. Jake Bagly…was a "big dog" as well as the doctor, and could do as he 'd—d' pleased, any how! **1845** J.J. Hooper *Suggs* 126: The reverend gentleman…was the "big dog of the tanyard." **1847** in Eliason *Tarheel Talk* 260: Dick…pretends to be the biggest dogg in the meat house. **1847** in *DA*: At any rate, he belonged to "one of the first families in Virginia,"…and [was], altogether, the "big dog" at Pokerville. **1859** Bartlett *Amer.* (ed. 2) 31: In some parts of the country the principal man of a place or an undertaking is called the "big dog with a brass collar." **1871** Schele de Vere *Amer.* 583: *Big Dog of the Tanyard* is the name often given to an overbearing person who will allow no one else to speak or to differ from his views. The bold figure of speech is derived from the fact that tanyards are generally guarded by fierce bulldogs. **1877** Pinkerton *Maguires* 90: Lawler is the big dog in these parts now. **1882** "Dum John" *Autobituary* 71: In Washington you'll have a hard row,…"Unless you're either a *Big Dog* yourself,/ Or have a *Big Dog* for a friend." **1887** Francis *Saddle & Moccasin* 199: He was in the German army—servant to some big dog on the staff. ***1889** Barrère & Leland *Dict. Slang* I 112: *Big dog with a brass collar, the,* the principal or head of a concern, or the biggest "wig" of a place. **1939** Appel *People Talk* 281: Marcus Daley…[gave] Rogers an interest in his mines. He thought he'd be the big dog. **1944** Stiles *Big Bird* 6: We used to eat at the big dogs' mess hall…with the colonels and the majors. **1945** in Daley *Sports of Times* 21: Sam Crawford then was the big dog in the meat-house and I was just a brash kid. **1955** Archibald *Aviation Cadet* 154: *Big dog:* big shot. **1955** Graziano & Barber *Somebody Up There* 259: My gas tank had to run dry tonight, and I couldn't be a big dog and even drive her two blocks to the station. **1964–67** Speicher *Baby Paradise* 172: Risking trouble with the big dogs of the Diocese. **1970** Benteen *Apache Raiders* 43: All right, Sergeant, if he's the big dog of your company, I'll go in with you. **1976** Atlee *Domino* 68: General Waldo…was a big dog in this tightening situation. **1978** Ardery *Bomber Pilot* 21 [ref. to WWII]: Chet Tucker became the "big dog"…or [cadet] battalion commander. **1980** Grizzard *Billy Bob Bailey* 210: I don't care what the big-dog police commissioners say. **1987** Weiser & Stone *Wall St.* (film): You want to be

pissing in the tall weeds with the big dogs. **1992** *This Wk. with D. Brinkley* (Aug. 23) (ABC-TV): [Pres. Bush] said this week, "If you can't run with the big dogs, stay under the porch!"

2. a bus operated by Greyhound Bus Lines, Inc.

1976 *Sci. Mech. CB Gde.* 154: I have a Big Dog in the grass over here.

big dollar *n. Gamb.* one thousand dollars.

1961 Scarne *Guide to Gambling* 115.

big drink *n.* [cf. DRINK] **1.** the Mississippi River.—constr. with *the.*

1844 in *DA*: There never would have been any Atlantic ocean if it hadn't been for the Mississippi, nor never will be after we've turned the waters of that big drink into the Mammoth Cave. **1850** *Spirit of Times* (June 8) 234: Dodge…tells a little joke of his adventures on the "big drink" some years ago. **1860–61** R.F. Burton *City of Saints* 19: The pellucid waters of the "Big Drink!"*…*A "Drink" is any river: the Big Drink is the Mississippi. **1864** "Kirke" *Down in Tenn.* 108: I's bin on the Big Drink (Mississippi) an' seed how they does it. **1867** in *DA* 113: The states lying east of the Mississippi [are divided from] the states and territories lying west of the Big Drink. **1871** Schele de Vere *Amer.* 600: The Mississippi appears quite frequently as the Big *Drink*. **1926** Wood & Goddard *Slang* 5: *Big drink.* The Mississippi.

2. the ocean, esp. the Atlantic Ocean.—constr. with *the.*

1883 Keane *Blue-Water* 189: If this thing carries me across the big drink without trouble, that's about all it will do. **1884** in *DA*: Many of the Transatlantics will doubtless take a journey across what they call the "big drink" to hear her. **1899** F.P. Dunne *Countrymen* 160: 'Tis th' prisint intintion iv mesilf to hire a good big tug an' put a hook into Ireland, an' tow it over th' big dhrink. **1926** Wood & Goddard *Amer. Slang* 6: *Big drink*…any ocean. **1964** Caidin *Everything but Flak* 38: I had always wanted to fly across the big drink. **1976** Simon *Murder by Death* (film): Both sides of the big drink.

big duke *n.* BIG MITT.

Big E *n.* a named entity that bears the initial *E.*—usu. constr. with *the.* [See note at BIG A.] *Specif.: Navy.* the aircraft carrier USS *Enterprise.*

1943 Mears *Carrier* 89: The "Big E," the carrier *Enterprise,* was part of a task force consisting of a large new battleship and accompanying cruisers and destroyers. **1945** J. Bryan *Carrier* 81: They've already hit the Big E again. **1948** S.E. Morison *Naval Ops.* III 235: It had to be "Sara" rather than "Lady Lex" or the "Big E." **1958** Camerer *Damned Wear Wings* 44 [ref. to WWII]: Wearin' more armor plate than the Big E. **1981** Mersky & Polmar *Nav. Air War in Viet.* 61: Huge banners welcoming home the "Big E" were in abundance. **1991** M. Dunn *Sidewinder* 331: "Big E"—Nickname for the USS *Enterprise.*

Big Easy *n.* New Orleans, La.—constr. with *the.* [App. coined by Conaway as the title of his 1970 novel; the name became popular after the release of the 1986 film based on the book.]

1970 Conaway *Big Easy* 43: The building he sought was on the edge of Storyville, spawning ground of Dixieland and voodoo and other amenities of the Big Easy. *Ibid.* 134: Most everyplace has had it—Atlanta, even Memphis. The Big Easy's just ten years behind. **1987** *Frank's Place* (CBS-TV): My first Christmas in the Big Easy. **1987** *World News Saturday* (Dec. 12) (ABC-TV): To appreciate the joy in the town called the Big Easy, you have to realize that nothing was easy for the Saints. **1988** *Time* (Aug. 29) 26: A Big Time in the Big Easy.

big enchilada *n.* a head man; most important person or thing.—usu. constr. with *the.*

1973 in *Submission of Pres. Conversations* (Mar. 27) 347: [Haldeman:] He is as high up as they've got. [Ehrlichman:] He's the big enchilada. **1974** *N.Y. Post* (May 11) 21: He was in that instance the willing handmaiden of John N. Mitchell, "the big enchilada" of the transcripts. **1978** Safire *Pol. Dict.* (ed. 2) 48: *Big Enchilada* the top man, or main target.…"I coined the phrase [in 1973]," former White House aide John Ehrlichman informed the author from his incarceration in 1977. "I've cooked my own enchiladas for years." **1985** Dye *Between Raindrops* 165: Kill the fucker.…Get at the Big Enchilada and get it over with. **1988** *TV Guide* (Aug. 13) 36: Meanwhile, the Big Enchilada had his own game plan for bringing Pam into further prominence.

big eye *n.* **1.** a curious or intent look.—constr. with *the.*

1958 J. Thompson *Getaway* 57: These little inland villages…where every stranger gets the big-eye.

2. television.—constr. with *the.*

1964 "Dr. X" *Intern* 218: I…read a couple of murder mysteries and watched the Big Eye. **1974** Fishwick *Parameters* 34: Everything is visible with the Big Eye.

3. *USAF.* a radar picket plane.

1966–67 Harvey *Air War* 106: Lockheed Connie C-121 radar-picket planes called Big Eyes. **1991** L. Reinberg *In the Field*: Big Eye, USAF airborne EC-121 early warning radar aircraft used from April 1965 to March 1967.

4. *pl. Mil.* binoculars; (*specif.*) large, post-mounted night-vision binoculars.

1971 Murphy & Gentry *Second in Command* 114 [ref. to 1968]: With the "Big Eyes," or 22-inch binoculars, you could see the smoke from the factory chimneys. **1984** Hammel *Root* 22: A pair of stanchion-mounted "big-eyes" binoculars. **1991** J.T. Ward *Dear Mom* 77 [ref. to 1969]: "Big Eyes" (large 50,000 dollar Starlite scope) for night observation.

5. *Theat.* a ten-thousand-watt Luminaire.

1982 T.D. Connors *Dict. Mass Media* 27.

big-eye *v.* to stare or watch; ogle.

1937 E. Anderson *Thieves Like Us* 26: Them Square Johns…are always big-eyeing this way. **1937** in Partridge *Dict. Und.* 36: He had opened an account in a bank just to big-eye it good. **1958** Gilbert *Vice Trap* 122: The people in it big-eyed us.

big ferry *n.* the Atlantic Ocean.—constr. with *the*.

1855 Brougham *Chips* 301: It is [impossible] for a fellow as has made himself somebody on the other side of the big ferry…to think that he can sneak through this here land of liberty as if he was nobody.

big fifty *n. USAF.* (see quot.). Now *hist.*

1943 *Amer. N & Q* (Dec.) 133: Big Fifty: referring to a bomber pilot's fifty missions from an Allied bomber station in Italy, at the completion of which he has the choice of staying on to begin another fifty, changing to another kind of plane, requesting duty as a ground officer, or going home.

big fish *n.* **1.** a powerful or influential person; a ringleader. Cf. BIG-BUG.

1836 in *DA*: He is a big fish—anything he says will be believed. **1846** J.F. Cooper *Redskins* 277: Why, who do you think would trouble himself about my 'arnin's. It is the big fish, only, that folks…care about, in such matters. **1847** *Nat. Police Gaz.* (Feb. 6) 170: There's a "*big fish*" whom Stewart thinks one of his best friends, that ought to help me. **1848** in R.L. Wright *Irish Emigrant Ballads* 521: Oh, den de big fish 'gin to fear,/Dey thought the burnin' was too near. **1884** Triplett *American Crimes* 106: A man who was a "*big fish*" and very intimate with Stewart was waiting until he was killed. **1889** Reynolds *Kansas Hell* 211: Let the prison net be strong enough to hold the big fish as well as the little ones. **1931** Wilstach *Under Cover Man* 2: A general raid on [the underworld]….The result had been a lot of minnows, not a big fish in the collection. **1953** W. Fisher *Waiters* 60: The expression "big fish"—the waiters' nickname for Monroe—had stuck in his mind. **1965** Spillane *Killer Mine* 82: The guy's a cop who's supposed to run down a big fish, only when he catches him he takes a pay-off instead. **1973** *Sub. of Pres. Convers.* 288: Sure if you get the big fish out there in front of the television cameras I think you fellows would be tough. **1985** *Morning Edition* (Nat. Pub. Radio) (June 12): Then the Government can move on to try what prosecutors call the "big fish" in this case.

2. an important matter or undertaking.

1864 in Hay *Lincoln* 198: I wish you to be there when they meet. It is a big fish. Mr. Chase has resigned. **1957** Lacy *Room to Swing* 38: I was downtown on a case. A big fish, honey.

bigfoot *n.* [see 1985 quot.; alluding to legendary humanoid of the Pacific Northwest] *Journ.* a prominent political journalist or news analyst.

1980 in Safire *Good Word* 25: Among the boys on the bus, "Big Foot" is a jocular term for a columnist, editor, or journalism celebrity who deigns to mingle with the working stiffs. **1985** in Safire *Look It Up* 4: The origin of *Big Foot*; when Hedrick Smith of the *New York Times*, with his foot in a cast, joined the press plane in the 1980 campaign, his *Times* colleague…Drummond Ayres, good-humoredly dubbed him that. **1989** *TV Guide* (Aug. 26) 36: Edged out of his job…by the growing number of "Bigfeet" in the network's news division. **1990** *New Republic* (Apr. 16) 43: He's used his Big Foot status to get himself invited to sessions that a mere sportswriter wouldn't have been allowed near. **1990** *New York* (Sept. 3) 10: News stars who play Bigfoot, descending from the skies in times of crisis and crowding out lesser correspondents.

bigfoot *v. Journ.* to preempt or otherwise exercise one's privi-

lege over as a BIGFOOT.

[**1982** J. Breslin, in *L.A. Times* (Aug. 25) II 7: In the city now we have Mayor Koch, voice braying, big-footing about the state in search of coronation.] **1986** *New York* (Dec. 15) 15: [Dan Rather] arrived just before the president went on the air, but Bob Schieffer was in place and [Rather] decided not to bigfoot him. **1992** *N.Y. Observer* (Oct. 26) 19: Dworkin Bigfoots Abortion Book….Andrea Dworkin stopped the presses on a new book about women's reproductive health recently.

big four *n. Bowling.* a 4-6-7-10 split.

1949 Cummings *Dict. Sports* 33. **1976** *Webster's Sports Dict.* 38.

big friend *n.* usu. *pl. USAF.* a friendly bomber, as when escorted by fighters. Cf. LITTLE FRIEND.

1944 *Official Guide to AAF* 368: Big friends—Friendly bombers. **1945** in *AS* (Dec. 1946) 310: Big friend. A bomber. See *little friend*, below. **1948** Miller & Rackin *Fighter Sq.* (film): Bring the big friends home. **1956** Heflin *USAF Dict.* 79: Big friend. A friendly bomber. *Slang*, esp. among fighter pilots. **1957** *Sat. Eve. Post* (Aug. 10) 41: So it had to be a Big Friend from…Strategic Air Command. **1958** Johnson & Caiden *Thunderbolt* 108: The "Big Friends" flew a staggered box formation. **1965** *Air Officer's Guide* 436: Big friends—friendly bombers.

Big G *n. R.R.* a named entity that bears the initial *G.*—usu. constr. with *the*. [See note at BIG A.] *Specif.*: the Great Northern Railroad.

1982 D.A. Harper *Good Company* 29: It's only lately…that the Big G comes through here.

biggie *n.* **1.** BIG SHOT.

1926 Finerty *Criminalese* 9: Biggie—Personage of importance; a celebrity. **1928** Fisher *Jericho* 26: Ain't you my boy, Biggy? *Ibid.* 297: *Biggy* Sarcastic abbreviation of *big boy*. **1931** in *OEDS*: *Biggie*, important person, celebrity. **1937** *Hollywood* (Jan.) 10: Bob Burns…is the easiest of the biggies to sign for a benefit and he's always on tap when some charity outfit needs a hand. **1941** *Pittsburgh Courier* (Oct. 25) 8: "Biggies" In Woman's World At Conference. **1947** Schulberg *Harder They Fall* 200: The place the Hollywood biggies go when they want food. **1956** G. Green *Angry Man* 109: Last week's test run convinced Whitechapel biggies that the comic's half hour won't suit their purposes. **1965–70** J. Carroll, in *Paris Rev.* (No. 50) 103: A biggie at the U.N. **1972** *New Yorker* (Jan. 8) 31: I'm a biggie in the world of finance. **1982** P. Michaels *Grail* 188: A foreign national is involved. A biggie at that. **1983** *N.Y. Post* (Aug. 17) 13: Navy Biggie Faces Kickback Charges.

2. something of importance; that which is decisive; BIG DEAL; in phr. **no biggie** no difficulty, no cause for concern.

1970 N.Y.U. student: That exam's gonna be a biggie. **1972** Jenkins *Semi-Tough* 196: We've won a biggie. **1973** M. Richler, in *Harper's* (Aug.) 36: He, and he alone, has the biggie going into production. **1978** B. Johnson *What's Happenin'* 218: This was the biggie….The Sonics [lost] by twelve [points]. **1978** J. Webb *Fields of Fire* 153: Break a pane of glass. Shimmy a loose door. Ain't no biggy. **1982** Pond *Valley Girl's Gd.* 60: No biggie—Like, don't worry about it. **1985** *Teenage Mutant Ninja Turtles* (CBS-TV): If we don't find a certain subway tunnel, the world's gonna end at midnight. No biggie! *a*1989 R. Herman, Jr. *Warbirds* 26: Career counseling, no biggy.

3. *pl.* major baseball leagues, BIGS.

1973 Hirschfield *Victors* 100: First you play Class D, the minors…maybe…one day you make it to the biggies.

4. a dollar.

1977 *Kojak* (CBS-TV): It's gonna cost you double—one hundred thousand biggies.

Big Green *n.* **1.** Dartmouth College; (*specif.* and *usu.*) a sports team, esp. the football team, of Dartmouth College. [The colors of the college are green and white.]

1931 in J. O'Hara *Sel. Letters* 55: I now pick…Cornell to knock off that big Green team the following week. **1951** in Young, Becker, & Pike *Rhetoric* 32: He announced to the world that the Big Green had been out to extinguish the Princeton star. **1980** L. Birnbach *Preppy Hndbk.* 218: *Big Green n.* Dartmouth College. **1984** *N.Y. Post* (Dec. 12) 78: The [Harvard] Crimson outscored the Big Green 35–6 from the foul line.

2. (see quot.).

1990 *Today* (NBC-TV) (Mar. 22): The Big Green—to give its official name, the [California] Environmental Protection Act of 1990.

big gun *n.* **1.** a prominent, powerful, or influential person; leading individual; BIG SHOT. See also GUN, *n.*

1834 in *DAE*: The big guns of the nation are there [in Washington]. **1845** Smith *Vernon* 35: Horatio Sharp, the "big gun" of the profession,

has been seen walking by my office this afternoon, two or three times. **1862** "E. Kirke" *Among Pines* 248: That big gun—Daniel Webster [made] mince-meat of Hayne. **1863** in T. Whitman *Dear Walt* 60: He would go and see Storrs and some other of the big guns of those societies. **1865** in C.H. Moulton *Ft. Lyon* 240: He might just as well have taken [the surrendered sword] and made a "big gun" of himself. **1866** "M. Twain" *Letters from Hawaii* (Apr.). **1872** Burnham *Secret Service* iv: *Big gun*, a prominent man, a noted person, or leader. ***1889** Barrère & Leland *Dict. Slang* I 113: The other evening he was invited to meet the Prince of Wales, and had the honour of supping with Albert the Jolly, and a host of other big guns. **1891** *Munsey's Mag.* 235: One ob dem is a big gun, I'm suah, kase all de res' looks up ter him an' pays him much respects. **1900** Ade *More Fables* 189: He was Dragged away…to meet all the Big Guns of one of these Towns that call a Lecture a Show. **1899–1901** *Railroad* 19: We've got a big gun aboard and I want to show him that a little thing like this don't flustrate *us* any. *Ibid.* 31: The "big gun"…[was] the president of the…Railway. **1907** Siler *Pugilism* 139: After you trim that dub Mayo you'll be in line for some of the big guns. **1911–12** Ade *Knocking the Neighbors* 72: Getting an audience with a Big Gun was just as easy as Opening a Time-Lock with a Hat Pin. **1919** *DN* V 64: All the *big guns* went to the national convention. **1934** *WNID2*: *Big gun*…An important or influential person. *Slang*. **1970** G. Walker *Cruising* 189: Lynch pictured him telling all the big guns at headquarters how he'd figured it all out. **1983** *N.Y. Post* (Sept. 2) 56: Tennis' big guns go on display.
2. *Surfing.* a long, heavy surfboard.
***1966** Baker *Austral. Lang.* (ed. 2) 253: *Big gun*, a surfboard about 10 ft. long and weighing more than 40 lb. for use in a big surf. **1976** *Webster's Sports Dict.*

big guy *n.* **1.** (*cap.*) God.—constr. with *the.*
1926 Nichols & Tully *Twenty Below* 54: Let him sleep—the Big Guy's yellin' for him. He'll be sleepin' longer this time to-morrow, I guess. **1927** *DN* V 438: *Big guy, the, n.* God. **1927** Tully *Circus Parade* 10: I never worry about dying.…When the Big Guy yells my name I'll go. **1943** in Fussell *Wartime* 165: The Big Guy is on our side. **1982** in "J.B. Briggs" *Drive-In* 12: Don't mess around with the Big Guy. **1988** *Atlantic* (Apr.) 14: It's times like now, when…you're maybe thinking about the Big Guy.
2. (used as a semi-humorous or affectionate term of address to a man); BIG BOY, 2.a.
1980 *Mork & Mindy* (ABC-TV): Lighten up, big guy! It's eating you up! **1984** McInerney *Bright Lights* 87: I know all *about* wet, big guy. **1985** Univ. Tenn. student: Whatcha want to watch next, big guy? **1986** Univ. Tenn. instructor, age 37: How's it goin', big guy?

Big H *n.* a named entity that bears the initial *H*.—usu. constr. with *the*. [See note at BIG A.] *Specif.*:
1. *Narc.* heroin.
1954–60 in *DAS*. **1965** J. Hersey *Too Far to Walk* 164: Not curare, peyote, morning-glory; not big H nor booze nor marijuana nor model airplane glue. ***1967** (cited in Partridge *DSUE* (ed. 8) 75). **1969** *N.Y. Post* (Mar. 12) 53: Heroin—the big H, horse, junk. **1985** Dye *Between Raindrops* 294: Heroin, man.…The Big H, man.
2. a heart attack.—constr. with *the*.
1983 "B. Knott" *Tasteless Jokes II* 19: "And what did you die of, may I ask?" "The Big H," says the fellow, a florid, overweight type.

big hair *n.* long hair worn teased and sprayed. *Joc.*
1988 Univ. Tenn. student theme: *Big-hair:* Whorlish hair—processed (hairspray, mousse, gel, etc.). **1989** *Rage* (Knoxville, Tenn.) (Sept.) 24: I Hate: Girls with big hair, guys with big hair, animals with big hair. **1989** *CBS This Morning* (CBS-TV) (Dec. 7): He's up there on stage with big hair and Spandex pants. **1990** P. Munro *Slang U.* 36: *Big hair*…teased hair. **1992** *N.Y. Times* (Mar. 4) C 6: For every mall-going teenager reveling in the big-hair look, there is a hairdresser dying to beat it back with a shovel.

big hat *n.* **1.** BIGWIG.
1952 Mandel *Angry Strangers* 303: Northern big hats throttling the South he tells me, Yankee business.…It's Yankee big hats and not Yankees he hates so well. **1967** in *DARE*: He'd like to be the big hat around here. [**1991** *N.Y. Times* (Apr. 28) F 4: He told a Silicon Valley newspaper that his new competition still had a long way to go: "Big hat. No cattle."]
2. [see 1969 quot.] a state trooper.
1967 in *DARE*: Big-hat man. **1969** *AS* XLIV 202: *Big hat*—State trooper, state patrolman, or state policeman, especially one whose uniform includes a big hat. **1971** Tak *Truck Talk* 12: *Big hat*: a state trooper. **1979** *Nat. Lampoon* (Sept.) 47: Wait 'til you see yer reflection

in the big hat's *mirrored shades*.

big hole *n.* **1.** *R.R.* the emergency position of an air brake valve; (*hence*) an emergency application of air brakes.
1931 *Writer's Digest* (May) 41: *Big Hole*—emergency position of the air brake valve; the act of applying brakes abruptly to the full reduction. *Ibid.* 40: He threw the old teakettle into the big hole. **1937** *AS* (Apr.) 154: BIG HOLE. Emergency application of brakes.
2. *Trucking.* the lowest gear position.
1942 *AS* (Apr.) 102: Big Hole. Low gear. Also *Company Notch; Creeper; Grandma Hole; Growler; Number One; Ought Hole; Supreme Low.* **1959** *AS* (Feb.) 76: *Big hole, n.* The "lowest" gear in a logging truck.

big-hole *v. R.R.* to bring (a locomotive) to an emergency stop.
1916 *Editor* (Mar. 25) 343: *Big-hole*—To bring a locomotive to a sudden stop. **1945** Hubbard *R.R. Ave.* 100: His engineer "big-holed her"—railroadese for making an emergency application of the air brake. **1970** *Current Slang* V 4: *Bighole, v.* to release all the air from the airline of a train, thereby applying the brakes fully.—We were about to hit a car, so the engineer *bigholed* the train.

big hook *n. Constr.* a wrecking crane.
1929 *Bookman* (July) 525: A swell two-weeks job for every big hook in the country. **1931** *Writer's Digest* (May) 41: *Big Hook*—Wrecking crane.

big house *n. Und.* a prison or penitentiary. [In Brit. slang of *ca*1850 and after, the term has meant "the workhouse." See *OEDS* and Partridge *Dict. Und.*]
1913 *Sat. Eve. Post* (Apr. 19) 12: There ain't nothing in it but cops…and the Big House at the end. **1916** *Lit. Digest* (Aug. 19) 424: The malefactor is sent away to the "big house." **1926** in Ruhm *Detective* 67: That's plenty to send you back to the big house. **1927** in Hammett *Knockover* 276: I saw him in the Folsom big house yesterday. **1929** J. Tully *Shadows* 33: I jist do a little burglin', an', hot damn, de cops git me! An' now dey takes dis heah niggah back home to de Big House agin. **1934** in North *New Masses* 93: Trail along with the gang and wind up in the big house. **1944** C.B. Davis *Leo McGuire* 86: You're just taking out a long-term lease on a Big House cell. **1952** Himes *First Stone* 32: We're just a couple of old cousins in the big house. **1961** C. Cooper *Weed* 133: I got that woman…to help me send him off to the big house. **1967** J. Colebrook *Lassitude* 189: Sandra and Pat are both in the "big house"—Pascagoula, the State Reformatory for Women. **1976** Chinn *Dig the Nigger Up* 118: I was in the "big house." **1991** D. Anderson *In Corner* 17: The Big House. That's what they call the maximum-security prisons in New York.

bight *n. Naut.* a predicament; jam.
1932 Nicholson & Robinson *Sailor Beware!* 28: Pop left things in a hell of a bight. **1957** Campbell *Cry for Happy* 9: Yendo is in a bight. **1971** Gallery *Boarders* 182: You've sure put my ass in a bight.

Big I *n.* a named entity that bears the initial *I*. [See note at BIG A.] *Specif.: Navy.* the aircraft carrier USS *Independence.*
1966 Mulligan *No Place* 184: Now he sat…on the bridge of the *Independence*—or "Big Eye" [*sic*]—sipping his ninth cup of coffee.

big idea *n.* purpose, intention.
1917 Lardner *Gullible's Travels* ch. iii: Then we done a little spoonin' and then I ast her what was the big idea. **1919** Darling *Jargon Bk.* 50: *What's the Big Idea*—what is your idea or meaning in doing, saying, or trying to do this thing. **1920** Witwer *Kid Scanlan* 303: What's the—what's the big idea? **1922** E. Rice *Adding Machine* 120: Go on! What was the big idea? **1938** "E. Queen" *4 Hearts* 45: Wham goes the big idea. **1939** Saroyan *Time of Your Life* I: Yeah, but what's the big idea? You can't push me around. **1939** *Hell's Kitchen* (film): "Maybe he's gonna get mad." "That's the big idea." **1950** Felsen *Hot Rod* 93: What was the big idea? **1961** S. Baker *Practical Stylist* 3: What's the big idea, Mac? **1990** *U.S. News & W.R.* (June 9) 31: NATO needs a big idea.

big Ike *n. So.* an important or self-important man.
1902 in *DA* 113: He's a big Ike in some church in Atlanta. **1908** *DN* III 291: *Big Ike*…a person of much importance, especially in his own opinion. *ca*1938 in Rawick *Amer. Slave* II (Pt. 1) 77: They strutted 'round, big Ike fashion,…talkin' free…and familiar. **1954–70** in *DARE*.

big Injun see s.v. INDIAN.

Big J *n.* a named entity that bears the initial *J*. [See note at BIG A.] *Specif.*:
1. *Mil.* Japan.
1961 Peacock *Valhalla* 17 [ref. to Korean War]: You ever been in Big J before? *Ibid.* 118: Since we been here in Big J.

2. *S.W.* Juárez, Mexico.

1968–70 *Current Slang* III & IV 9: *Big-J, n.* Juarez, Mexico.

3. *Navy.* the battleship USS *New Jersey.*

1967 De Sola *Abbr. Dict.* (ed. 3) 49: *Big-J:* battleship USS *New Jersey.* **1985** Petit *Peacekeepers* 148: The *New Jersey* arrived off the shore of Beirut....The "Big J" was formidable.

Big John *n. Navy.* (see quots.).

1983 La Barge & Holt *Sweetwater Gunslinger* 55: The crash crew and P-16 fire-fighting equipment were in position....Big John, a forklift with a bucket, was fired up too. **1986** M. Skinner *USN* ix: *Big John*— The fixed crane on an aircraft carrier.

big joint *n.* [cf. JOINT] *Und.* a prison.

1927 in Partridge *Dict. Und.* 36: I can't go back to the big joint without putting up a fight.

big jump *n.* death.—constr. with *the.*

1942 *ATS* 143: Death...*the big jump.* **1968** R. Adams *West. Wds.* (ed. 2): When a person died, he was said to have taken the *big jump.*

Big K *n.* a named entity that bears the initial *K.* [See note at BIG A.] *Specif.:* Korea.

1976–79 Duncan & Moore *Green Side Out* 160: During the Big "K" police action.

big kahuna see KAHUNA.

Big L *n.* a named entity that bears the initial *L.* [See note at BIG A.] *Specif.:*

1. *USAF.* London, England.

1945 Hamann *Air Words: Big L.* London.

2. love.

1987 *Night Court* (NBC-TV): You don't suppose it could be the Big L?

big league *n.* usu. *pl.* [alluding to the major professional baseball leagues] the sphere of the most intense competition and professional activity in business, politics, research, etc.

1974 A. Bergman *Big Kiss-Off* 47: This guy plays in the big leagues and...you and me are pretty small potatoes to him. **1975** *Business Week* (June 2) 73: When it comes to photography today, this is the big league—coming from nowhere...to take the professional and advanced amateur markets away from all other types of camera. **1983** *Green Arrow* (July) 13: I know when I'm beaten, honey! I can't play in the big leagues. **1990** *U.S. News & W.R.* (Apr. 2) 39: Stars and directors in such films....catapult into the big leagues before the smaller companies have a chance to capitalize on their fame.

big-league *adj.* BIG-TIME; high-class. Also as *adv.*

1919 Witwer *Alex the Great* 35: Can you tell me why them big league dames fall for these guys like Alex? **1922** in Cornebise *Amaroc News* 163: A couple years ago the big-league style babies all said that a figure should ought to resemble the letter "I". **1922** J. Conway, in *Variety* (Jan. 27) 11: She sees a chance to grab off a big league meal ticket and throw away the grease paint for life. **1942** in Galewitz *Great Comics* 267: However, when the chips were down, this kid proved herself big league all the way. **1947** Greene & Macauley *Born to Kill* (film): Sure it's big-league. **1952** "E. Box" *Fifth Position* 64: Elmer is big league, bald and ulcerous. **1961** R.L. Scott *Boring Holes* 178: In the nation's capital it was strictly "big league." **1970** *Business Week* (Apr. 18) 62: He...is a big-league philanthropist and patron of the arts. **1980** *U.S. News & W.R.* (July 28) 34: So far, Reagan has not been subjected to big-league scrutiny. **1991** *Morning Report* (CNN-TV) (June 21): This guy went absolutely big-league bonkers.

Big M *n.* a named entity that bears the initial *M.* [See note at BIG A.] *Specif.:*

1. *Narc.* morphine.

1959 Schmidt *Narc. Lingo.* **1963** Gant *Queen St.* 107: Heroin, morphine—snow, *big M.*

2. marriage.

1969 *Current Slang* I & II 9: *The Big "M" n.* Marriage.—College students, both sexes, Minnesota.

3. Memphis, Tenn.

1975 Dills *CB Slanguage* (1976 ed.) 17: *Big M:* Memphis, Tenn. **1976** Bibb et al. *CB Bible* 87. **1977** Lieberman & Rhodes *CB Hndbk.* 305.

Big MAC *n.* [alluding to the trademark name of a type of McDonald's hamburger] the Municipal Assistance Corporation or a bond issued by it.

1975 *WCBS-TV Evening News* (June 9): The proposed Municipal Assistance Corporation, or "Big MAC." **1977** *New West* (Jan. 31) 8:

Kudlow is especially bearish about the near-term prospects of Municipal Assistance Corporation bonds (called Big MACs).

big mama *n.* **1.** Esp. *Black E.* grandmother.

1946 C. McCullers, in *DARE:* When Berenice said *we,* she meant Honey and Big Mama. **1954** Killens *Youngblood* 6: She sat on the back porch listening to her Mama and her Big Mama talk. **1965–71** in *DARE.*

2. something that is very large.

1976 Lieberman & Rhodes *CB Hndbk.* 123: *Big Mama*—9-foot whip antenna. **1977** in Curry *River's in My Blood* 71: The steamer *Sprague.* Everybody used to call it the "Big Mama" on the river. **1991** *N.Y. Times* (Aug. 28) C 8: *Big Mama:* The ocean.

Big Man *n.* **1.** *Und.* the Pinkerton Detective Agency.—constr. with *the.*

1901 "J. Flynt" *Graft* 201: There was nobody I hated worse to have on my track, exceptin' the Big Man, than a Secret Service guy. *Ibid.* 219: *Big Man,* the Pinkerton Detective Agency. **1927** *DN* V 438: *Big man, n.* The Pinkerton Detective Agency.

2. God.—constr. with *the.*

1981 Ballenger *Terror* 165: Once you go into that coma you're on your way to the Big Man's House in the Sky.

big medicine *n. Orig. West.* a powerful or influential individual; *(hence)* an important thing.

1898 Brooks *Strong Hearts* 47: He's big medicine, you know, and we folks don't any of us dare to sarse back, or he'll work a charm on us that'll wind us all up. **1985** Sawislak *Dwarf* 101: Nuclear power and arms control were emerging as big medicine in the national campaign.

big mitt *n. Gamb.* a method of swindling at cards. Also **big duke.**

1902 in *McClure's Mag.* (Jan. 1903) 1: Fac-Simile of the First Page of "The Big Mitt Ledger." **1949** Gresham *Limbo Tower* 111: He would not itch to teach the rotter a lesson and thus be drawn into the "big duke" wherein the cold deck performs its time-honored function.

Big Mo *n.* **1.a.** *Navy.* the battleship USS *Missouri.*

1945 *Yank* (Sept. 28) 4: When we pulled alongside the "Big Moe" she looked like the Yankee Stadium. **1947–53** *ATS* (ed. 2) 825: *Big* or *Mighty Mo,* the battleship Missouri. **1986** *CNN News* (May 10): Big Mo Rides Again....The battleship *USS Missouri.* **1991** *N.Y. Times* (nat. ed.) (Feb. 5) A 5: "Big Mo" Goes to War, Again.

b. the University of Missouri; *(also)* the state of Missouri.

1964 *AS* (May) 119: *Big Mo* is a not uncommon term for the University of Missouri. **1992** *Time* (Sept. 28) 33: *Big One* [*sc.* a catastrophic earthquake] for Big Mo?

2. *Pol.* beneficial momentum, as in a political campaign.

1980 in Safire *Good Word* 123: George Bush...had a brief and passionate attachment to "Big Mo" (momentum) after [the Iowa primary]. **1985** Tate *Bravo Burning* 149: Big Mo was on our side. **1988** *Morning Edition* (Feb. 19) (Nat. Pub. Radio): We've been hearing a lot in politics recently about *big mo*...momentum. **1989** *Life Goes On* (ABC-TV): We'll get a jump on him and start building the big mo. **1992** *Today Show* (NBC-TV) (Feb. 18): Tsongas...has the big mo.

big moment *n.* a person with whom one is infatuated or in love.

1929 *Sat. Eve. Post* (Oct. 5) 21: The minute I slapped the old eyes on Eddie I realized that he was my big moment. **1929** in E. Wilson *Twenties* 523: She wanted me to go to Child's, so that they could see Marty, Ethel's "big moment." **1930** Creelman *Half Shot* (film): I had a lot of trouble with *my* big moment. He's A.W.O.L. **1937** Hoover *Persons in Hiding* 136: This outlaw was the "big moment" of Piquett's life. **1941** *Slanguage Dict.: Big moment*...a person with whom one is preoccupied, infatuated or in love.

bigmouth *n.* a loud, talkative person, esp. if lacking discretion.

1889 Barrère & Leland *Dict. Slang* I 113: During his trial for murder, the wretched Guiteau often interrupted the judge by crying out, "Shut up, big mouth." **1895** Foote *Coeur D'Alene* 68: And all the bigmouths was talkin'. **1919** *DN* V 62: *Big-mouth,* a loud noisy person. "I can hear *big-mouth* coming." California. **1938** Rawlings *Yearling* 288: Now mister impudent bigmouth. **1963** *Twilight Zone* (CBS-TV): A dull, argumentative big-mouth who sets back the art of conversation a thousand years. **1978** *'Teen* (Mar.) 86: Some bigmouth from school is bound to see us and say something.

bigmouth *v.* to brag or ballyhoo.

1967 N.Y.C. man, age 21: He's always bigmouthing about something. **1981** W. Safire, in *N.Y. Times Mag.* (Sept. 13) 16: Reporter Curt

Suplee used *big-mouthing* in The Washington Post last month to mean "to promote loudly."

Big Muddy *n. West.* **1.** the Missouri River.—usu. constr. with *the.* [S.E. or colloq. during 19th C.]

1825 in *DA.* **1859** Greeley *Overland Journey* 49: "Big Muddy"...rushes by Leavenworth...turbid as ever. **1913** Brown *Broke* 119: The policeman glanced significantly towards the "Big Muddy." **1923** J.L. Hill *Cattle Trial* 14: The vast...unsettled grazing lands across the Big Muddy. **1942** *ATS* 71. **1948** *Newsweek* (Aug. 30) 21: We're going clear to the Missouri River and smash this stuff back across the Big Muddy. **1982** Heat Moon *Blue Hwys.* 127: The Big Muddy is nearly twenty times as long. **1984** Sample *Racehoss* 109: Crossing the Mississippi River and the Old Big Muddy at least a dozen times.

2. the Mississippi River.—constr. with *the.*

1846 *Crockett's Almanac* (unp.): Down the Mississippi...Ben and me went to take passage down the Big Muddy. **1956** M. Wolff *Big Nick.* 5: Here's to that crazy big muddy river....It's the Mississippi we're talking about, man. **1992** Hall & Wood *Big Muddy: Down the Mississippi through America's Heartland* [book title].

big nickel *n. Gamb.* the sum of five hundred dollars or five thousand dollars.

[**1929–31** cited in Partridge *Dict. Und.* 37 as "a large sum of money."] **1961** Scarne *Comp. Guide to Gambling* 115: A "big nickel" is $500...[or] could mean $5,000. **1981** D.E. Miller *Jargon* 292: Big nickel....$500.

big noise *n.* **1.** uproar, trouble.

1863 in McKee *Throb of Drums* 93: There is nothing of importance going on here...but there may be a big noise here before long. **1956** in *DAS* 35: Big Noise from Moscow, Mumbled Words from Washington. **1961** Ellison *Memos* 95: That was one cat less for your team when the big noise came.

2. a celebrated or important person; BIG SHOT; person in charge.

1906 H. Green *Boarding House* 255: Who's your friend, the big noise? **1910** T.A. Dorgan in *N.Y. Eve. Jour.* (Jan. 13) 16: Paul Moore, the Philadelphia bantam, is the big noise right now in New York. **1910** *N.Y. Eve. Jour.* (Apr. 21) 14: Maybe he figured that some have to "stand beneath," while the big noises reach the top. **1922** Jordan *Btty. B* 186: [He] was the "big noise" in the Battery Rendering Co. **1922** E. Rice *Adding Machine* 106: Maybe the boss kept you late tonight. Tellin' you what a big noise you are and how the store couldn't 'a' got along [without you]. **1926** Nichols & Tully *Twenty Below* 33: Is he the Big Noise? **1941** *Great Guns* (film): I'm the big noise around here, and you guys do the listenin', see? **1956** Heflin *USAF Dict.* 79: Big noise...An important official. **1970** Martin *Kelly's Heroes* (film): The colonel's a big noise in German intelligence.

3. (see quot.).

1956 Heflin *USAF Dict.* 79: Big noise. Slang....a large bomb.

big-nose *n.* [app. a translation of one or more Chinese expressions] an Occidental.

1942 *Time* (Apr. 6) 84: An assortment of the people whom the Chinese call Big Noses—foreign missionaries, doctors, teachers and their families. **1961** R. Crane *Born of Battle* 107: Like some Koreans say we are *kho-jang-ee*—big noses. **1966** Derrig *Pride* 110: Yet even though we give you the planes and equipment, you still have to call us "big noses" in to help. **1968** W. Corson *Betrayal* 140: Sometimes the appeal is based on an imagined or real injustice done to the potential Vietcong by...a "big-nose" foreigner.

big number *n.* a person of importance.

1942 Davis & Wolsey *Call House Madam* 20: A lot of big numbers who'd made the steep grade and landed in the top brackets. **1954–60** *DAS* 35: Big number = big man.

Big O *n.* a named entity that bears the initial *O.* [See note at BIG A.] *Specif.:*

1. *R.R.* a railroad conductor belonging to the Order of Railroad Conductors.

1930 Irwin *Tramp & Und. Slang: Big O.*—A railroad conductor; from the Labour Union, The Order of Railroad Conductors, or "Big O." **1942** *Sat. Eve. Post* (June 13) 27: The big O is applied to a conductor, since the emblem of the Order of Railroad Conductors centers around a large O. **1945** Hubbard *R.R. Ave.* 189: Then the Big O—member of the Order of Railway Conductors—came up. **1946** in Botkin & Harlow *R.R. Folklore* 350: The shack was...blowing smoke to the Big-O.

2. *Narc.* opium.

1954–60 *DAS* 35: Big O...Opium used for smoking. **1985** J.M.G.

Brown *Rice Paddy Grunt* 235: I lit up a..."Big O" joint from Lai Khe.

3. an orgasm.—constr. with *the.*

1968 Vidal *Breckinridge* 257: I was about to reach the big O, shrieking with pleasure. **1972** R. Wilson *Forbidden Words* 35: The Big O. Orgasm. **1973** *Nat. Lampoon* (Aug.) 71: The hunt for the big O becomes ever more frantic. **1983** Univ. Tenn. instructor: There sure are a lot of books out showing women how to hit the big O. *1992 English Today* (Apr.) 58: Pre-orgasmic women contemplate the *Big O.* **1993** *Married with Children* (Fox-TV): Suppose we create the perfect simultaneous big O.

4. *Mil.* Okinawa.—constr. with *the.*

1972 U.S. Army S/Sgt., age *ca*22: I stuck for eighteen months on the Big O. **1985** Former SP4, U.S. Army: The *Big O* was in such frequent use [in the Far East, early 1970's] that nobody had to ask what it meant.

5. Omaha, Nebr.

1975 *Atlantic* (May) 41: This is that, ah, Toby Trucker eastbound for that big O town.

big —— oh *n.* a birthday (of the specified age, the "oh" representing zero) *or* (a specified age, the "oh" representing zero).—constr. with *the.*

1980 Lorenz *Guys Like Us* 7: I'm thirty, Jo. The big three-oh. Some say you're through then. **1984** *N.Y. Daily News* (Aug. 10) 10: Sherry Lansing, who has two pictures in preproduction at Columbia, hit the big Four-Oh on Tuesday and celebrated all over L.A. **1985** Malcolm *Final Harvest* 3: Rudy...had already passed what they called "The Big Four Oh." **1986** *Night Court* (NBC-TV): You're forty years old? The *big four-oh?* **1987** *Nat. Lampoon* (June) 73: Because this birthday was different. This one was the big Four-Oh. **1988** *Channel 6 Eyewitness News* (Mar. 31): Senator Albert Gore...says that hitting the big four-oh will improve his chances for the White House. **1988** *Time* (Mar. 14) (cover): But dealing with the Big Five-Oh could be my greatest challenge! **1990** Updike *Rabbit at Rest* 238: I hit the big six-oh last October. **1991** *N.Y. Times* (June 2) 2 29: With a title like "Thirtysomething," the end was fate. At some point the characters would have to hit the big Four-Oh and the ABC series would have to end or be renamed. **1991** *Modern Maturity* (Dec. 1991–Jan. 1992) 23: 1991 was a red-letter year. The year they were all turning the big "five-o." **1991** *Street Justice* (Fox-TV): "What is this, twenty-nine?" "Uh-*uh.* The big three-oh."

big one *n.* **1.a.** a banknote of large denomination; (*specif.* and *usu.*) one thousand dollars.

1863 in T. Taylor *Plays* 173: Now to plant the big 'un. **1908** McGaffey *Show Girl* 237: Wilbur's got the wise guys so leary...they naturally slip him a big one every time they get a chance. **1935** Pollock *Underworld Speaks: Big 'un*, a $1000.00 bill. **1955** Q. Reynolds *HQ* 283: A half kilo of pure H would be worth at least fifteen big ones. **1956** "T. Betts" *Across the Board* 312: Big One $1,000. **1958** Meltzer & Blees *H.S. Confidential* (film): I've got four big ones....Four G's. **1961** Scarne *Guide to Gambling* 115: One big one: $1,000....Other bookies may use these code words differently. A "big one" might mean $100. **1970** Della Femina *Wonderful Folks* 94: Big money. Maybe ninety big ones a year. **1972** *Banyon* (NBC-TV): Fourteen big ones...two $7000 insurance policies. **1973** Boyd & Harris *Baseball Card* A: A hundred big ones for the Brooklyn Bazooka Baron. **1977** T. Berger *Villanova* 45: We asked ten thousand, "ten big ones" in his parlance. **1982** *Steve Roper* (synd. cartoon strip) (Apr. 27): Whattaya think of that, joker? A check for five big ones!

b. one million dollars.

1967 Spillane *Delta* 18: If you guarantee I can keep the forty big ones. **1970** T. Southern *Blue Movie* 52: Three big ones, baby!..."Three million!" **1980** R. Salmaggi, on WINS radio (June 18): Christopher Reed will be getting three big ones for the role. I mean millions of dollars, dear heart.

c. *usu. pl.* a dollar.

1971 Faust *Willy* 40: He made eighty thousand big ones his top year. **1973** *Sanford & Son* (NBC- TV): "We got $20 for that." "That's right—20 big ones. Two-oh!" **1975** V.B. Miller *Trade-Off* 35: The judge...set Maurie's bail at one hundred thousand big ones. **1976** Conroy *Santini* 67: Sell her for about two hundred thousand big ones. **1980** in *Penthouse* (Jan. 1981) 164: Miss Bramazerro gave me a bank book which said I had a hundred big ones in the vault. **1982** Del Vecchio *13th Valley* 75: Ten grand...Ten thousand big ones. **1989** J. Connolly & D. Loucka *Dream Team* (film): We gotta come up with 165 big ones.

2. *Pris.* one year of a prison sentence.

1928 Bodenheim *Georgie May* 130: Poah gal, still got three big ones to go. **1966** Braly *On Yard* 177: Two years...two big ones in this jailhouse.

3.a. *Mil.* World War II.—constr. with *the.*

1960 Bluestone *Cully* [ref. to ca1955]: Back in the Big One. **1980** Santoli *Everything* 102: He was a sergeant in the big one. **1983** Eilert *Self & Country* 182: I had one of those people tell me that the wounds were much worse in the big one. Can you believe it? **1984** N. Stephenson *Big U.* 24: Most…had been recruited out of Korea or the Big One. **1988** Clodfelter *Mad Minutes* 70: In 1965 and 1966 most U.S. soldiers were as patriotic as our fathers in the "Big One." **1990** G. Trudeau *Doonesbury* (synd. cartoon strip) (Feb. 14) 7: He was a decorated naval aviator during the big one.

b. a major disaster, such as a nuclear war or a major earthquake.

1989 Weber *Defcon One* 100: If the "Big One" [a global thermonuclear war] ever happened. **1990** *People* (Oct. 22) 32: The earthquake of Oct. 17, 1989, was not the Big One that Californians have been told to expect, but it was big enough. **1992** *Time* (Sept. 28) 33: Big One [*sc.* a catastrophic earthquake] for Big Mo? **1994** *N.Y. Times* (Jan. 21) A 18: The "maximum credible earthquake"—a magnitude of 8.5 on the Richter scale, more commonly known as "The Big One."

4. *Mil.* the congressional Medal of Honor.—constr. with *the.*

1962 Quirk *Red Ribbons* 29 [ref. to WWII]: "You going to buy your own medal factory when you get back?"…"There's still the Big One to get." **1985** Tate *Bravo Burning* 175: I've put you up for the Big One, kid. **1984–88** Hackworth & Sherman *About Face* 91 [ref. to Korean War]: Aguda was a good man. He deserves the big one. *Ibid.* 119: The Man got the big one the hard way.

5. [cf. *bite the big one,* below] penis.—constr. with *the.*

1991 *43d Annual Emmy Awards* (Fox-TV) (Aug. 25): I'd like to thank my husband, Parker, the man who has given me the big one for the last eight years. [Gasps from audience.]

6. *Baseball.* a home run.

1992 *Sports Close-up* (CNN-TV) (June 26): [He's] second on the team in big ones, batting average, and runs batted in.

¶ In phrases:

¶ **bite the big one** see s.v. BITE.

¶ **get the big one** to be killed.

1929 Hammett *Maltese Falcon* 36: Pull a chair around. So Miles got the big one last night?

¶ **have the big one** to die of a heart attack. [Introduced on the NBC-TV comedy series *Sanford and Son,* 1972.]

1972 *Sanford & Son* (NBC-TV): This is it! I'm havin' the big one! Ohhh! I'm comin' to meet you, darlin'! **1978** in Lyle & Golenbock *Bronx Zoo* 101: My mother almost had the big one when she saw me do that.

¶ **hit a big one** to blunder into trouble.

1958 Johnson & Caidin *Thunderbolt* 40 [ref. to WWII]: You hit a big one, Mister! Shaddup!

¶ **make little ones out of big ones** to break rocks, lay roads, or dig ditches, esp. as a prisoner under guard.

[**1907** Peele *N.C. to S. Calif.* 68: You're likely to get a job making "little rocks out of big rocks."] **1915** Howard *God's Man* 189: It's lucky you had friends with a pull or you'd be on the inside looking out—making little ones out of big ones, old sport. **1918** Crowe *Aviator* 50: He didn't seem to mind making little ones out of big ones for the next couple of years. **1919** Laird *12th Engrs.* 35: Locomotive engineers, firemen, conductors, etc., "make little ones out of big ones." **1931** Tomlinson *Best Stories* 16: Tell that…no-account orderly that he'll be making little ones out of big ones if I see him chewing tobacco again. **1939** E. O'Brien *Ticket* 142: You'll be down there with Mac makin' little ones out of big ones. **1940** Simonsen *Soldier Bill* 37: "Making little ones out of big ones"…meant…crushing rock in the guardhouse. **1948** R. Chaplin *Wobbly* 264: Too bad "making little ones out of big ones" isn't a recognized trade on the outside. **1962** Killens *Thunder* 279: I'm going to have your dead ass put in the stockade and you'll be making little ones outa big ones.

Big Orange *n.* **1.** any university having orange as a school color, as Syracuse University or the University of Tennessee; (*specif.* and *usu.*) a sports team, esp. the football team, of these universities.—usu. constr. with *the.*

1973 Bebb *The Big Orange* [title]. **1974** Knoxville, Tenn., poster: Welcome to Big Orange Country. **1985** Univ. Tenn. football fans: Go Big Orange! **1991** *CBS This Morning* (CBS-TV) (Apr. 3): Syracuse—the home of the Big Orange.

2. [sugg. by BIG APPLE] Los Angeles, Calif.—constr. with *the. Joc.*

1982 Sculatti *Catalog of Cool* 75: Los Angeles…a no-nonsense, non-snob appraisal of the Big Orange. **1984** Blumenthal *Hollywood* 163: Nicknames for "The Coast"…La-La Land…The Big Orange. **1986** De Sola *Abbr. Dict.* (ed. 7) 129: *Big Orange*: Los Angeles. ***1992** *English Today* (Apr.) 58: New York is the *Big Apple,* Los Angeles is the *Big Orange.*

Big P *n.* a named entity that bears the initial *P.*—usu. constr. with *the.* [See note at BIG A.] *Specif.:*

1. *USAF.* Ploesti, Romania. Now *hist.*

1966–67 Stevens *Gunner* 231 [ref. to WWII]: Frank really sweated the big P, didn't he?

2. *Mil.* the Pentagon Building.

*a***1989** R. Herman, Jr. *Warbirds* 79: Rumor at the Big P has it that Waters had a bad briefing with Sundown.

big parade *n.* a world war, esp. World War I.—constr. with *the.* [The name was evidently first applied as the metonymic title of the 1925 motion picture *The Big Parade,* directed by King Vidor, screenplay by Laurence Stallings; the term is not used in the film to designate the war directly.]

[**1925** Stallings *The Big Parade* [film title].] **1927** *Amer. Leg. Mo.* (Nov.) 54: Witt Mullins…during the Big Parade wore the blue on U.S.S. *Arkansas.* **1934** Traven *Sierra Madre* 249: Didn't I kill quite a number of Heinies in the big parade?…Hell, how they jumped. **1942** *ATS* 807: *The Big Parade,* the World War. **1952** Himes *First Stone* 275: Goddamn, that looks like the Big Parade.

Big Pecker *n.* [*big* + PECKER 'penis'; so called for the side-looking radar pod projecting beneath the belly of the aircraft] *Mil. Av.* the Grumman OV-1B Mohawk radar observation plane.—usu. considered vulgar.

1987 Chinnery *Life on Line* 43 [ref. to 1965]: Going to fly your big pecker around on autopilot all night, Walt?

big place *n. Pris.* a prison.—constr. with *the.*

1970 in *DARE:* A county or city jail…*Big place.* **1978** Cleaver *Soul on Fire* 101: None of them had been in the Big Place.

big pond *n.* the Atlantic Ocean.—constr. with *the.*

1833 J.K. Paulding *Lion of West* 34: He tells me you have come among us to take a squint at things in general on this here side of the big pond. *Mrs. Wollope.* The big pond! Oh, the Atlantic. **1840** [Haliburton] *Clockmaker* 18: He is…the best live one that ever cut dirt this side of the big pond. **1844** J.F. Cooper *Afloat & Ashore* 159: Then you will learn that all hands of us, on the other side of the Big Pond, understood Latin. **1853** C. Hill *Scenes* 52: But the features of the play were from the other side of the "big pond." **1879** Sala *America Revisited* I 73: I was many times inclined to forget that I had crossed the "big pond." **1902** *Outing* (June) 345: Irish and Gordon setters…have hardly sustained their reputation on either side of the big pond. **1992** *Geraldo!* (synd. TV series): As they say on this side of the big pond.

big potato *n.* **1.** *pl.* an important or powerful person.—usu. used predicatively.

1884 *Life* (Jan. 24) 48: His honored father was one of the biggest potatoes—as the phrase is—in [Boston]. **1893** in F. Harris *Conklin* 241: It isn't that the big potatoes want pertic'lar to come to the top; it is that the little potatoes are *determined* to get to the bottom. **1935** C.J. Daly *Murder* 19: I thought this lad was big potatoes. **1936** in H. Gray *Arf* (unp.): Live in a city and yuh can think yer pretty big potatoes. **1978** Diehl *Sharky's Machine* 348: I mean, this guy's big potatoes. He's powerful.

2. (*cap.*) [sugg. by BIG APPLE, BIG ORANGE] *Diplomatic Service & Journ.* Moscow, Russia. *Joc.*

1988 *Prime News* (CNN-TV) (June 7): It's summer in the Big Potato, as Moscow is affectionately known by its foreign residents. **1992** *News Hour* (CNN-TV) (June 10): It might be a little early to expect sex shops on every corner here in the Big Potato.

big puddle *n.* [cf. syn PUDDLE] an ocean; (*specif.*) the Atlantic Ocean.

1926 C. Wood & Goddard *American Slang* 6: Big pond or puddle. The Atlantic Ocean. **1942** *ATS* 71: Ocean…big drink, big pond…or –puddle. **1983** Univ. Tenn. grad. student: You're never going to get me in a plane over the Big Puddle.

big push *n.* [elaboration of syn. PUSH] a boss.

1918 in Rossano *Price of Honor* 79: Say, are you the big push in this outfit?

Big PX *n. Mil.* the United States of America as a place of civilized conveniences and consumer goods. Also **Land of the Big PX.**

1955 McGovern *Fräulein* 238: America, the land of opportunity! America, the land of the big PX! **1962** Harvey *Strike Command* 100: Just the same old stuff as home—the Big PX. **1966** R. Marks *Letters* 180: We will discuss it upon my return to the land of the big PX (the states for those of you who don't know military jargon). **1966** E. Shepard *Doom Pussy* 72: To the men stationed out in the boonies, the United States is the Land of the Big PX and the All-Night Generator. **1968** W.C. Anderson *Gooney Bird* 208: We'll have a tall one back in the land of the big PX. **1968** Myrer *Eagle* 768: The perpetual freeload at the Big PX. **1969** Spetz *Rat Pack* 19: The Land of the Big PX and Round-Eyed women. **1971** Sloan *War Games* 15: A trip to the Big PX, as America was called, was the working girl's dream. **1973** Jong *Flying* 65: German clocks brought fortunes in the "land of the Big PX." **1976** C.R. Anderson *Grunts* 26 [ref. to 1969]: The Big PX, the *World*, Man—Stateside! **1974–77** Heinemann *Close Quarters* 262: Home...the land of the big PX and the twenty-four-hour generator. **1988** Dye *Outrage* 127: Trading intelligence for a ticket to the Big PX.

Big Q *n.* [cf. syn. Q] a named entity that bears the initial *Q.* [See note at Big A.] *Specif.*: *Und.* San Quentin prison.

1961 Ellison *Memos* 90: From Dannemora to big Q, Joliet to Alcatraz. **1975** Princeton Univ. student, age 24: You'll wind up in Big Q. **1981** P. Sann *Trial* 200: All ready to whisk him off to the big Q.

Big R *n. Army.* the rotation of a soldier from overseas duty back to the United States.—constr. with *the.*

1960 *AS* (May) 121 [ref. to Korean War]: *R & R* was also called the *little r* to distinguish it from the *big r*, or rotation to the States. **1961** Crane *Born of Battle* 148 [ref. to 1951]: But August left something with the division: the unbelievable fact of the "Big R." Rotation was now more than a wistful rumor. **1963** T. Fehrenbach *This Kind of War* 537 [ref. to 1952]: But R & R...was only a stopgap. Soon there rose talk of Big R—rotation to the United States. **1971** Cole *Rook* 198: One eye on Panmunjon and the other on the Big R.

big rag *n. Circus.* the main tent; *(hence)* the circus itself.

1937 *Lit. Digest* (Apr. 3) 22: The Big Rag—the main circus tent—the "Big Top." *Ibid.* 21: Say, Mac! Is Jimmy Whalen still on the big rag? **1942** *ATS* 618: Big rag...the main circus tent. **1961** Clausen *Season's Over* 183 [ref. to *ca*1945]: They've got the brains and the know-how to keep this Big Rag moving every day.

Big Red *n.* **1.** any university having red as a school color, as Cornell, University of Indiana, University of Wisconsin, and University of Oklahoma; *(specif. and usu.)* a sports team, esp. the football team, of these universities.

1942 *Yank* (Oct. 7) 23: *Cornell*—Unless the Big Red brushes up on defense, their potent offense may prove inadequate. **1964** *AS* (May) 119: At the University of Oklahoma, the football team is often called the *Big Red*. **1980** Birnbach *Preppy Hbk.* 218: *Big Red*, n. Cornell University. **1984** Automobile bumper sticker: Indiana University. Go "Big Red"! **1988** W.E. Roberts *Viewpoints* 49: Because the word Hoosier is so well known in athletic circles, I am a bit surprised to learn that the term "Big Red" seems to have been used more and more in the last couple of years....[and] the slogan "Go Big Red" has gained prominence. **1990** *CBS This Morning* (CBS-TV) (Sept. 24): The University of Wisconsin....Go Big Red!

2. *Army.* the First Infantry Division. [The official nickname of the division is "The Big Red One," sugg. by the red numeral one featured on its shoulder patch.]

1970 Southern *Blue Movie* 214: I was a *medic* with the *Big Red* in Normandy.

Big Red Machine *n.* **1.** *Baseball.* the Cincinnati Reds baseball team.

1989 P. Dickson *Baseball Dict.* 54: *Big Red Machine*...Nickname for the Cincinnati Reds...when the team is playing well, such as when the Reds won back-to-back World Series in 1975–76. **1990** *CBS This Morning* (CBS-TV) (Oct. 18): Today the surging Big Red Machine moves into Oakland two games ahead.

2. *Mil.* military forces of the Soviet Union and the Warsaw Pact. Now *hist.*

1983 M. Skinner *USAFE* 11: The Big Red Machine [is] just twenty minutes away.

Big Richard *n. Craps.* Big Dick, 1.

1918 in Sherwood *Diary* 145: Hathaway, Baumeister, Fink and Fisher are having a "cut-throat" crap game...and it will be a wonder if I don't

get "Big Richard," "Phoeba," "snake eyes," "box cars," and like terms mixed into the writing of this diary.

big rod *n.* a person in charge; boss; Big Wheel.

1929 Hotstetter & Beesley *It's a Racket* 219: Big Rod—The head of a "mob." **1970** D. Wakefield *All the Way* 26: What a fool he'd been to imagine a Big Rod like that would really want to hang around with a nobody. **1971** Jacobs & Casey *Grease* 40: The big rod of the Burger Palace Boys? I didn't even know he saw me here.

bigs see s.v. Big, *n.*

big savage *n.* [cf. *big Indian* s.v. Indian] *Logging.* a labor foreman.

1942 *ATS* 480: Foreman...*big savage.*

big school *n. Pris.* Big House.

1921 (cited in Partridge *Dict. Und.*). **1926** *AS* (Sept.) 650: *Big school*—penitentiary. **1930** "D. Stiff" *Milk & Honey* 199: *Big school* or *house*—The state penitentiary.

big screech *n.* Big Noise, 2.

1911 A.H. Lewis *Apaches of N.Y.* 267: All this time Caesar is the big screech.

big shit *n.* **1.** a person or persons of importance or *(usu.)* self-importance.—usu. considered vulgar.

1934 H. Miller *Tropic of Cancer* 125: They'd make him out to be a *big* shit if they could. But...there was little they could invent about him. **1953** in Clarke *Amer. Negro Stories* 218: He called himself mister-some-big-shit-on-a-stick. **1965** Conot *Rivers of Blood* 319: Now all of a sudden they get the Guard in, and they're big shit! **1968** P. Roth *Portnoy* 159: You hypocrite and phony! Big shit to a bunch of stupid spics. **1971** Dahlskog *Dict.* 7: Big shit...a big shot; an important person who is disliked. **1978** Wharton *Birdy* 101: He's enjoying being the big shit. **1971** Wells & Dance *Night People* 102: Okay cats,...let's make it I'm the big s--- till the bigger s--- comes along.

2. Big Deal, 1.—usu. considered vulgar.

1960 N.Y.C. high school student, age 13: Well, *big shit!* Who the fuck cares? **1968–71** Cole & Black *Checking* 125: "Trees make the air better?" "Right." "Big Shit!" **1977** Bredes *Hard Feelings* 58: "I'm truly sorry."..."Big shit." **1978** Pilcer *Teen Angel* 80: Big shit....Let's get going already. **1980** J. Webb *Sense of Honor* 226: All right, so you hate it. Big shit....Who loves it? **1992** Hosansky & Sparling *Working Vice* 125: This flatbacker's only gonna cut me five hundred to one thousand. Big shit.

bigshit *adj.* self-important; undeserving of expected interest, prominence, etc.—usu. considered vulgar.

1968 P. Roth *Portnoy* 158: All your big words and big shit holy ideals. **1969** Pharr *Numbers* 291: And yet he is a bigshit M.D.

big shot *n.* [cf. Big Gun] an influential, important, or celebrated person or *(occ.)* thing; *(specif.)* person in charge; boss. Cf. Big Gun. [This previously unrecorded term enjoyed a sudden and tremendous vogue *ca*1928–32, esp. as applied to criminal gang leaders.]

1927 in Perelman *Old Gang* 25: They are big shots but too well-known to shake a loose ankle with the gals. **1928** *New Yorker* (Dec. 8) 23: We don't go around among the gamblers much, but a chap who has watched the big shots at their play has told us a little about McManus. **1928** Panzram *Killer* 158: A big shot is a leading light of crookdom. **1929** in Gelman *Photoplay* 125: That talkie will be one of the Big Shots of the talkie year. *Ibid.* 127: Old-timers come back...and the big shots go boom. **1929** in *AS* (Feb. 1930) 238: Jack is the big-shot of his fraternity. **1929** Burnett *Iron Man* 107: Gate-crashers, bunco men, small time and big shot gamblers. **1929** "C. Woolrich" *Times Sq.* 250: They'll think you're a big shot *there*, alright, in that dress. **1930** Graham & Graham *Queer People* 37: He evidently thinks I'm a big shot, and I don't see why I shouldn't let him think so. **1931** Uhler *Cane Juice* 48: But rules are for the rabble. We big shots don't worry about them. **1932** in Adamic *My America* 69: I am a reporter on the Detroit *Times*. The big shot likes my stories. **1933** Milburn *No More Trumpets* 71: He can't kick out all the biggest shots in the University, can he? **1935** Clarke *Regards to B'way* 117: Joe Loeb is a big shot with Continental Pictures. **1939** Goodman & Kolodin *Swing* 39: "Bix" was already a big shot. **1941** Nixon *Possum Trot* 81: The Possum Trot people are chiefly workers, tenant farmers, and other small farmers, not capitalists or "big shots." **1943** Crowley & Sachs *Follow the Leader* (film): But who's the bigshot? **1945** Lindner *Stone Walls & Men* 171: Summer I was 16...Learned to drive a car and was a *Big Shot.* **1954** G. Kersh, in Pohl *Star of Stars* 31: He'd been a big shot in Basle....He was...Paracelsus.

1963 D. Tracy *Brass Ring* 4: All this time you've been saying how you were going to be the big shot at North Breton High. **1965** Bonham *Durango St.* 140: He's a big-shot player, the biggest. **1967** J. Kramer *Instant Replay* 46: The Washington coach took me to practice and made me feel like a big shot. **1973** Lucas, Katz & Huyck *Amer. Graffiti* 14: "He ain't even worth racin'!" "The big shot!" **1978** B. Joel *Big Shot* (song): You had to be a big shot, didn't you? You had to prove it to the crowd....All your friends were so knocked out. **1990** *National Review* (Sept. 17) 16 (headline): [ref. to Donald Trump] He Used to Be a Big Shot.

big-shot *v.* to behave like a BIG SHOT; (*specif.*) to treat someone to food or drink.
     1958 Motley *Epitaph* 203: Louie big-shot for the beer. **1962–68** B. Jackson *In Life* 225: He wanted to go to bed with the girl and was big-shotting. **1978** Univ. Tenn. prof., age *ca*50: The main reason people go to these conferences is to bigshot around.

big show *n.* **1.a.** *Mil.* a war, esp. a world war.
     1883 Watkins *Co. Aytch—A Side Show of the Big Show* [title] [ref. to Civil War]. **1918** in Hall & Nordhoff *Flying Corps II* 142: The Big Show is over now. **1918** Penner *120th Field Arty.* 54: Us for the big show. **1938** Pratt *Navy* 381: The Big Show [*sc.* World War I]. **1939** Callaway *Packs & Rifles* 20 [ref. to 1918]: With less than a month's training I was on my way across to the big show. **1945** Bowman *Beach Red* 64: People come from all over and they call it the Big Show. **1977** Moskin *U.S. Marine Corps* 443: World War I was the Marine Corps' first Big Show.
     b. *Mil.* a battlefront; battle.—constr. with *the.*
     1917 Appleton *With Colors* 17: Stickin' for the Big Show! Will it ever start? **1918** *Inf. Jrnl.* (Nov.) 434: The big show at Chateau Thierry has been on all this week. **1918** in Acker *Thru the War* 68: By the time you receive this we will have made another trip—up to the big show. **1918** in Janis *Big Show* 139: And there they were...going up to take their places in the Big Show. **1919** Rickenbacker *Flying Circus* 183: At dinner that night...word came to us that the Big Show was to start at five o'clock the following morning. **1934** Brewer *Riders of the Sky* 101 [ref. to 1918]: It was a quiet sector; the "Big Show"/At Chateau-Thierry claimed the Kaiser's aces.
     2. the BIG TIME, 2; (*specif.*) major-league baseball.
     1908 in Fleming *Unforgettable Season* 232: The big show would be much better off [without the spitball]. **1912** Mathewson *Pitching* 1: Few realize that during his first two years in the big show Joe Tinker looked like a cripple at the plate. **1914** R. Lardner *You Know Me, Al* 22: Well, Al, it will seem funny to be up there in the big show when I never was really in a big city before. **1921** *Variety* (Aug. 19) 4: He...had just come up to the big show from Fort Worth in the Texas League.

big sleep *n.* death.—constr. with *the.* [Raymond Chandler gave currency to this term in *The Big Sleep* (1938) and is usually credited with coining it.]
     1938 Chandler *Big Sleep* 139: And in a little while he too, like Rusty Regan, would be sleeping the big sleep. **1948** McHenry & Myers *Home Is Sailor* 26: If Jesus couldn't keep me from being a whore, I don't see how he could keep me from going into the big sleep. **1973** Gent *N. Dallas* 23: Subsequent headlong rushes to the big sleep had involved less deadly implements. **1975** *Harper's* (Feb.) 125: This book discusses the philosophical significance of the Big Sleep, the biological obligation of every animal to die. **1981** P. Sann *Trial* 57: You're now in the land of the Big Sleep.

Big Smoke *n.* **1.** *West.* BIG SHOT.
     1909 in Sampson *Ghost Walks* 487: Enter right now, Big Smoak, Big Noise, [etc.]. **1936** in *DA*: He had charge of all the round-ups and arranged dates upon which to hold them, and was considered a big smoke.
     2. Pittsburgh, Pa.—constr. with *the.* Also **Big Smoky.**
     1930 Irwin *Tramp & Und. Slang*: Big Smoke...Pittsburgh, Pa. **1939** *Chi. Tribune* (graphic section) (Jan. 22) 9: Big Smoke—Pittsburgh. **1942** *ATS* 48: Pittsburgh. Big Smoke, Big Smoky. **1973** *Nat. Lampoon Encyc. of Humor* 45: Well, we've still got thirty-two hours to make it to the Big Smoke.

big snag *n.* BIG SHOT.
     1842 *Ben Hardin's Crockett* (unp.): He sometimes took the name of...Big Snag of the Desert.

big spit *n.* an act of vomiting. *Rare* in U.S.
     *1959 in *Austral. Nat. Dict.* ***1967** in Partridge *DSUE* (ed. 8): [Australian] euphemisms for vomit...include...the big spit. **1971** H.S. Thompson *Las Vegas* 121: My attorney was doing the Big Spit, again in the

bathroom. *Ibid.* 153: Suddenly he was doing the Big Spit again, leaning over the side. ***1990** Thorne *Dict. Contemp. Sl.* 38: *The big spit* an act of vomiting.

big squeeze *n.* BIG WHEEL. Also **big squash.**
     1910 Ade *I Knew Him When* 61: The Big Squash...sat in the Mahogany Office and pushed the Buttons. **1912** J. London *Bellew* 13: He's the editor and proprietor and all-around big squeeze of *The Billow.* **1925** *Sentinel—15th Inf.* (Jan. 9) 6: He was the real big squeeze around the dump and was always popping off about something. **1967–68** in *DARE.* **1969** *Everett* [Wash.] *Herald* (Aug. 9) 20H: The big squeeze of this company is an able man, but he came up through the law department.

Big Stem *n.* [cf. MAIN STEM] Esp. *Theat.* the entertainment area of Broadway, New York; (*broadly*) New York City.—constr. with *the.*
     1934 Appel *Brain Guy* 8: Whose fault was it if he was nuts about money? It was the fault of the Big Stem, fault of the Big Stink. You simply had to have dough. **1939** Appel *Power-House* 19: The kid should've stayed home and never come to the Big Stem. **1946** in Inman *Diary* 1334: She...enjoyed "show business" for itself and being "on the road" more than "on the big stem."

big stick *n.* **1.** a boss; BIG SHOT.
     1908 in "O. Henry" *Works* 726: In fact, I'm the Big Stick. **1918** Wagar *Spotter* 30: We have gathered here...for the purpose of flim-flamming the big stick in the office, who demands too much of us. **1929** T. Gordon *Born to Be* 189: The Big Sticks were ushered into the front room. You have never seen so much bowing and scraping in all your life. **1936** in Kromer *Waiting* 215: Show the Big Sticks and High Muckity-Mucks what they looked like. **1968** in *DARE*: Thinks he's a big stick.
     2. *Baseball.* a heavy hitter.
     1970 *STRATCOM Relay* (USACC-Taiwan) (Aug.) 6: Big sticks for the game were Ron Freeman and "Shorty" Keating. **1987** *CNN Sports* (CNN-TV) (Apr. 4): Cleveland's expecting big things from the Tribe's big sticks.

big sticks *n.pl. Logging.* the forest.—constr. with *the.*
     1933 Weseen *Dict. Slang* 77: Big Sticks—The woods. **1942** *ATS* 482: Woods: *The big sticks.* **1954–60** *DAS*: Big Sticks A forest...logger use. *a***1986** Sorden & Vallier *Lumberjack Lingo* 13: Big Sticks. The woods.

big stuff *n.* a large or important or influential person.—used predicatively or in direct address only.
     1911 *N.Y. Eve. Jour.* (Jan. 5) 22: Say you, big stuff—what do you mean by stacking us up against that steam roller? **1927** in *OEDS*: "Bagler's big stuff." I got his slang. Big stuff meant that Bagler was a crook who conducted extensive deals. **1937** in Galewitz *Great Comics* 220: If I make it, I'll be "big stuff." **1946** Gresham *Nightmare Alley* 47: I remember that guy when he was big stuff. **1958** Coleman *Adolescent Society* 35: She really thinks she's big stuff. **1985** Bodey *F.N.G.* 234: Go ahead, bigstuff. **1987** B. Ford & Chase *Awakening* 29: We . . . thought we were such big stuff.

Big Stunt *n.* a world war; (*specif.*) World War I.—constr. with *the.*
     1919 *Lit. Digest* (Jan. 18) 56: James P. McKinney...was wounded in the right arm by shrapnel in the "Big Stunt."

big swing *n. Pris.* the gallows.—constr. with *the.*
     1965 Capote *In Cold Blood* 295: He intended taking every step possible to avoid "a ride on the Big Swing."

Big T *n.* a named entity that bears the initial *T.*—usu. constr. with *the.* [See note at BIG A.] *Specif.:*
     1. *Aerospace.* a Titan rocket.
     1959 W. Heflin *Aerospace Glossary: Big T.* The Titan.
     2. Tucson, Ariz.
     1975 Dills *CB Slanguage* (1976 ed.) 17.
     3. Tampa, Fla.
     1976 Lieberman & Rhodes *CB Hndbk.* 305. **1977** *Amer. Dict. CB* 94.

big-talk *v.* to talk big; to impress by boasting.
     1950 Bissell *Stretch on the River* 14: Don't try and big talk the other deckhands.

big thing *n.* **1.** a cause for wonder or excitement; something quite extraordinary.
     1846 *Lives of the Felons* 15: Harry White...a "stool pigeon"...had informed him...that a "big thing" was coming off shortly in that city. **1856** in C.A. Abbey *Before the Mast* 73: Sam said that we could have...all our meals on board the boat. Thinking this a "big thing" we told him to provide for us at once. **1861** in C.W. Wills *Army Life* 44:

The man that captures him will do a big thing. **1862** in Wightman *To Ft. Fisher* 42: Big thing! Within my dog house [tent] *by candle light!* **1862** in Clemens *Twain's Letters* I 56: Our tunnel…bids fair to become a "big thing" by the time the ledge is reached—sufficient to supply a mill. **1863** in T. Whitman *Dear Walt* 35: I think it would be a "big thing" for George to get them as they [shirts] would be very useful. **1864** in H. Johnson *Talking Wire* 119: There are only six of us but we consider ourselves a *big thing.* **1865** in S.C. Wilson *Column South* 323: We will be mustered out on Wednesday and will probably start home Thursday. Big thing. **1866** in H. Johnson *Talking Wire* 326: They think it is a "big thing" to be a commissioned officer. **1876** in *N. Dak. Hist.* XVII (1950) 170: Man rattlesnake bitten yesterday all right. Says whiskey is a "big thing." **1884** Nye *Baled Hay* 65: It would be a big thing for humanity.

2. a successful jest.

1864 *Tales of Picket-Guard* 32: "A big thing on the judge," interrupted Charlie.

big-ticket *adj.* high-priced; expensive.—used prenominally.

1945 (cited in *W9*). [**1954–60** in *DAS*: *Big ticket* A sale of an expensive item; a big sale to one customer.] **1961** *WNID3*: Buying of big-ticket items like refrigerators is on the increase. **1974** *Business Week* (Feb. 2) 59: The technique could be used for almost any big-ticket project, including mass transit. **1984** *Time* (Feb. 13) 13: High on the Pentagon's shopping list were two controversial big-ticket items. **1990** *New Republic* (Nov. 5) 13: Congress…left untouched the big-ticket items—more than $700 million annually.

big time *n.* **1.** an exciting or enjoyable time.

1863 in Norton *Army Letters* 183: The brigade was flying round, getting into line, drums beating and a big time generally. **1864** in D. Chisholm *Civil War Notebook* 7: Then for a last big time, I went to the Theatre. **1866** in H. Johnson *Talking Wire* 329: Mr. Crow…caught a mouse…and had a big time with it. **1914** Ellis *Billy Sunday* 275: The children will have a big time with him. **1931** Lorimer *Streetcars* 22: It don't give me any big time muzzling some girl. **1942** in *DA*: They had a big time at Smith's when he came home drunk. **1956** in Loosbrock & Skinner *Wild Blue* 99: The country…set out to have a big time.

2. the highest level of attainment or prestige in any given area; *(specif.* and *orig.)* the most prestigious theaters or the major leagues of sports.—constr. with *the.* Now *colloq.* or *S.E.*

1910 *Variety* (Aug. 20) 12: The "ballyhoo" is not for vaudeville, present day vaudeville, "big" or "little time." **1910** in *OEDS*: The "big time," as such theatres as Percy Williams' and William Morris' are termed. **1912** Mathewson *Pitching* 208: Hand springs that made him look more like a contortionist rehearsing for an act which he was going to take out for the "big time" than a ball player getting ready for the season. **1913** *Sat. Eve. Post* (Mar. 29) 8: The "big time"—comprising the finest theaters in the largest cities. **1920–21** Witwer *Leather Pushers* 127: This one [trick] had been staged dozens of times out in the bushes, but very rarely on the Big Time. **1921** *Collier's* (June 25) 3: Like as not I will have to go back pitchin' baseball in some bush league on the account I am too old for the Big Time. **1923** Revell *Off the Chest* 205: You certainly have put St. Vincent's Hospital on the "big time." **1926** Dunning & Abbott *Broadway* 218: As soon as I get Billie ready, we're all set for a lot of nice booking on the big time. **1929** Hostetter & Beesley *It's a Racket* 219: *Big Time*—The city; any metropolitan district. **1946** J. Adams *Gags* 26: I always connected [the Waldorf-Astoria] with the "big time." **1963** M. Shulman *Victors* 142: Chase blamed his scrappy education…for his own failure to make the big-time. **1965** C. Brown *Manchild* 212: He'd gotten back on the street and made the big time right away. He had brothers in numbers. **1973** Haney *Jock* 81: Barbara Jo was the first female jockey to hit the big time.

3. *Pris.* a long prison sentence or a sentence to be served specif. in a state or federal corrections facility.

1939 Howsley *Argot* 16: *Doing Big Time*—up for life. **1961** Braly *Felony Tank* 22: He didn't really trust anyone who hadn't served big time. **1965** Ward & Kassebaum *Women's Pris.* 64: "Big time" (reformatory or penitentiary time). **1966** Braly *Cold Out There* 38: What else could you be? Much big time as you pulled? **1993** *N.Y. Times* (Mar. 23) B 1: The people doing the big time in the system really aren't the people you want doing the big time.

4. a person or persons of consequence or accomplishment.—often used ironically.

1967 Spillane *Delta* 74: Morgan the Raider. Damn.…I'm talking to "big time." **1967** *Lit Dict.* 4: *Big time*—a put down name for a cat who thinks he is boss, cool and hip but he is really a seed. **1967** Hinton *Out-*

siders 112: What's up with the big-times?

big-time *adj.* being or involved with the BIG TIME, *n.,* 2.; *(hence)* prominent, prestigious; highly skilled; popular; significant, important.

1914 in *AS* XXXII (1957) 209: They buy and sell for all "big time" acts and all "big time" theaters. **1918** in Lindner *Letters* 90: The American soldier is "Big Time." **1920–21** Witwer *Leather Pushers* 86: A real, Big Time manager of pugs. **1928** Fisher *Jericho* 195: He's a big-time dickty. **1929** Barr *Let Tomorrow Come* 8: The rap is the label that shows you big-time or a tanker. **1931** Dos Passos *1919* 330: "Bigtime stuff," said Ripley, looking around at the decorations on the uniforms and the jewels on the women. **1935** Lindsay *She Loves Me Not* 17: They'll be watching for me everywhere. This is a big-time murder. **1935** in *OEDS*: Of the big-time news-hawks who had gathered in Keedora, only Matter remained. **1944** Stiles *Big Bird* 87: Six-plane formations is lazy-man's stuff after big-time 60-ship wing formations. **1945** Dos Passos *Tour* 253: Von This and Von That, bigtime Nazis every one. **1948** in P.C. Berg *New Words* 40: In 1943, Aspen, Colo., was discovered by big-time skiers. **1950** in *DAS* 36: Korea begins the big-time use of jet planes in battle. **1952** Ellson *Golden Spike* 73: Yeah, club fighting was big-time once. Now it ain't crap. **1954** Dodd *On Football* 10: Those playing in so-called "big-time" schedules. **1956** Ross *Hustlers* 68: She posed down them stone stairs like she was a big-time model. **1967** J. Kramer *Instant Replay* 225: At least I've been a big-time movie star. **1969** Layden & Snyder *Diff. Game* 66: I was also able to book a big-time game for my team…with Washington and Jefferson. **1972** T.C. Bambara *Gorilla* 87: The junk man…went about his business like he was some big-time president. **1974** N.Y.U. student: It's time to make some big-time decisions. **1978** B. Johnson *What's Happenin'* 57: I first got involved in the big-time sports world twenty years ago. **1990** *Joan Rivers Show* (TV series): Dieters who lost and then gained it all back—I mean big-time weight.

big-time *adv.* in a significant or obvious way; on a large scale; indeed.

1957 Lacy *Room to Swing* 85: The New York City police are good, big-time. **1981** Eble *Campus Slang* (Mar.) 1: I've got to study big time for this test. **1981** *Easyriders* (Oct.) 106: I think that all the Nam vets are getting fucked big time and that ain't right. **1983** Knoxville, Tenn., lawyer, age 29: These girls were giving him the eye big-time. **1984** Hammel *Root* 131: They drew five "big time" from the waiting militia fighters. **1989** *21 Jump St.* (Fox-TV): We have got to party big-time. **1990** *New Yorker* (Nov. 5) 39: Schwarzkopf said that if Iraq makes any use of chemical weapons "they will pay for it big time." **1992** *N.Y. Times* (Feb. 2) D 17: The President made clear what we suspected: that he is clueless, big time.

big-time *v.* to show off a sense of one's own importance.—sometimes constr. with *it.*

1943 *Amer. Jour. Sociol.* XLVIII 567: Sporting Life (Big-timing or High Life). **1946** J.H. Burns *Gallery* 23: We kept on our MP brassards and big-timed it through Casablanca in our leggins. **1953** W. Fisher *Waiters* 212: This is what his big timing's done for me. **1962** H. Simmons *On Eggshells* 151: The colored folks big-timed in the bars around town. **1965** Himes *Imabelle* 63: That was the way jokers in Harlem carried their money when they wanted to big-time.

big-timer *n.* a person involved in the BIG TIME, *n.,* 2; a prominent or accomplished individual.

1920 Witwer *Kid Scanlan* 126: The girl that was with the troupe was…a big-timer. **1928** Carr *Rampant* 155: The football captain, or some other…big timer. **1929** T. Gordon *Born to Be* 138: The shop was full of big-timers from the Clef Club. **1931** Hellinger *Moon* 234: I used to be around with Theda Bara and June Caprice and all the other big timers of the day. ****1932** in *OEDS*: Only the big timers—I'll interpret that, gentlemen: it means the more important armies—would be employed. **1934** L. Hughes *White Folks* 56: He used to bring some awfully cheap women there sometimes—big timers, but cheap inside. They didn't know how to treat a servant. **1937** Hoover *Persons in Hiding* 25: They spent some time at Herb Farmer's, where they met the "big-timers." **1978** *L.A. Times* (Oct. 9) I 23: Big-timers often hire friends—$5 an hour and all the cocaine you want is standard pay. **1972–79** T. Wolfe *Right Stuff* 212: Reporters and cameramen and other Big-Timers.

big toad *n.* a person of real or *(usu.)* fancied importance.

1846 in Oehlschlaeger *Reveille* 132: He was (to use a provincialism of [Arkansas]) "a big toad in that puddle." **1862** in Dunkelman & Winey *Hardtack Regt.* 41: I think if it weren't for the big toads we and the rebs I mean reb souldiers would not quarrel or fight much. **1877** Bartlett *Amer.* (ed. 4) 42: *Biggest toad in the puddle.* A western expression for a head-man; a leader of a political party, or of a crowd. **1902** Clapin *Americanisms* 50: *Big bug.* A disrespectful but common mode of allusion to persons of wealth, distinction or social importance...Other forms are *big dog, big toad.* **1903** Ralph *Journalist* 125: Those of us who never aspire to be more than a "big toad in a little puddle." **1966** Reynolds & McClure *Freewheelin Frank* 20: And the big toad...nigger is still down there...throwing bottles through the air. **1968** N.Y.C. editor, age 40: You got to decide whether you want to be a big toad in a little puddle or a little toad in a big puddle.

big top *n.* **1.** *Circus.* the main tent of a circus. Now *S.E.*
  1846 in Harris *High Times* 61: He...had on petticoats of the proportions of a circus tent, with a huge big-top on for a night-cap. **1895** in *OEDS*: Having settled where the "big top" will stand, the location of the other eleven tents is determined with mathematical precision. **1909** Irwin *Con Man* 87: My assistant...would keep them entertained about the big top until supper-time. **1910** *Variety* (June 11) 13: The old "Big Top" was used in the Boston week, pending arrival of the new one. **1920** Conklin & Root *Circus* 148: Childers announced to the crowd in the "big top" that there was an opportunity for one or two to connect themselves with the show if they cared to. *1938** Streatfield *Circus Shoes* 42: The first thing to come off the train will be the big top. That's the circus tent.
  2. *Pris.* a maximum-security prison.
  1955 Graziano & Barber *Somebody Up There* 80 [ref. to 1930's]: He went straight to the big top, Rikers Island. **1971** J. Brown & A. Groff *Monkey* 40 [ref. to 1930's]: Heading for "The Big Top" [Leavenworth] via Kansas City.

Big Town *n.* New York City; (*occ.*) Chicago.—usu. constr. with *the.*
  1902 Cullen *More Tales* 78: You've got the [notion] that you'll be able to work me for the ride to the big town. **1915** Howard *God's Man* 189: Anybody'd think you'd just come to the Big Town the way you take it, Sonny. **1922** Tully *Emmett Lawler* 201: Just hit the Big Town, kid? **1929** Perelman *Ginsbergh* 184: I'm going down to the Big Town to start a little three-card-monte racket. **1933** Ersine *Pris. Slang* 18: *Big Town.* 1. In the East, New York City. 2. In the West, Chicago. **1943** *Yank* (Oct. 15) 16: Miss Roche...drops in from Big Town. *ca*1943 in L'Amour *Over Solomons* 34: I'd feel better if I was in Chicago, or Memphis, or the Big Town. **1944** Stiles *Big Bird* 120: Martin...came from the big town and was a student at N.Y.U. before the war. **1961** Brosnan *Pennant Race* 47: Fresh, young appetites, not yet jaded by Big Town exposure, *can* be satisfied by night life as lived in Pittsburgh and Philadelphia. **1971** Tak *Truck Talk* 13: *Big Town:* New York City.

Big Two *n.* *Mil.* World War II.—often constr. with *the.*
  1961 Peacock *Valhalla* 55 [ref. to Korean War]: He was a prisoner of war during Big Two. **1978** T. Suddick *Good Men* 139: They found Japanese soldiers on the islands in the Pacific up to twenty-nine years after the Big Two ended. **1980** McAleer & Dickson *Unit Pride* 37: A Commie POW camp probably was like the Jap camps during the Big Two. **1985** Dye *Between Raindrops* 92: Poor old Pop [was] a veteran of The Big Two. **1986** Merkin *Zombie Jamboree* 48: Tell me more about Big Two.

Big Ugly *n.* *Mil. Av.* (a nickname for) any large aircraft having an ungainly or non-aerodynamic appearance.
  1982 W.R. Dunn *Fighter Pilot* 115: The P-47 received its share of nicknames [during WWII]:...T-Bolt, Big Ugly, [etc.]. *a*1989 R. Herman, Jr. *Warbirds* 174: The Phantom was a hulking sixteen-ton monster that deserved its moniker Big Ugly.

Big V *n.* a named entity that bears the initial *V.*—usu. constr. with *the.* [See note at Big A.] *Specif.:*
  1. *Mil.* Vietnam.—constr. with *the.*
  1972 Pelfrey *Big V* 2: That's the way it is in the Big V.
  2. Las Vegas, Nev.
  1977 Stone *Blizzard* 144: Got better things to do—like workin' the Strip in Big V.

big vegetable *n.* BIG SHOT. Cf. BIG POTATO, BIG SQUASH.
  1977 Monaghan *Schoolboy, Cowboy* 20 [ref. to 1908]: The big vegetable in these parts...is Tom Isles.

big water *n.* *Mil.* an ocean.—constr. with *the.*
  1961 L.G. Richards *TAC* 207: Why did Daddy have to go across the Big Water...[to] Italy?

big wazoo *n.* [cf. WAZOO] BIG WHEEL.—used derisively.
  1978 Truscott *Dress Gray* 246: He figured any minute the Big Wazoo was gonna come down and call his number.

big wheel *n.* **1.** [cf. syn. WHEEL] an important or influential person; BIG SHOT.
  [**1927** *AS* (Mar.) 277: How's your big wheel?—mode of greeting.] **1942** *ATS* 363: Person of importance or self-importance...*big cog* or *wheel*. *Ibid.* 423: Underworld or Gang Leader...*big wheel*. **1944** Stiles *Big Bird* 6: A few big wheels...came through the cadet schools to give us the lowdown. **1944** in Inks *Eight Bailed Out* 35: Also we want to see the big wheel and find out when we're going home. **1946** W. Haines *Command Decision* 66: The joint's full of big wheels today. **1947** Spillane *I, Jury* 104: Heretofore I thought Kalecki was the big wheel behind the syndicate. **1948** J.H. Burns *Lucifer* 212: Mr. Grimes was especially assiduous in paying court to undergraduate Big Wheels, like the President of the Student Council. **1948** Ellson *Tomboy* 42: Happy was playing a record about being a big wheel in the Harps. **1948** Lay & Bartlett *12 o'Clock High* 16: And yet his old man was a big wheel in the German-American Bund. **1950** C.W. Gordon *High School* 63: Of course everyone likes to be thought of as a "big wheel" *Ibid.* 67: Girls were "big wheels" too. **1957** Bannon *Odd Girl* 155: He's a big wheel on campus—talented, everybody knows him. **1985** N.Y.C. man, age *ca*35: What makes him think he's such a big wheel?
  2. *Mil.* the general staff.—constr. with *the.*
  1948 Wolfert *Act of Love* 431 [ref. to WWII]: He was going to show the brass on the big wheel that war had changed. *Ibid.* 464: Well, everything else is nailed down now for the big wheel.

big whoop *interj.* "so what?" "who cares?"
  1981 Hartwell & Bentley *Open to Lang.* 311: At the high school...*bogue* and *groovy*...and *big whoop*. **1987** S. Strak *Wrestling Season* 54: Big whoop. So's Underdonk.

bigwig *n.* an important person or official; BIG GUN, 1.
  *1703 in *F & H* I (rev.) 217: Dun or don—nob or big wig—so may you never want a bumper of bishop. *1792 in *OED*: Though those big-wigs have really nothing in them, they look very formidable. *1815 in *OED*: As poet-translator, no big wig ranks stouter. *1821 *Real Life in Ireland* 152: A full day at the bar...amongst the *big wigs*. *1825 "Blackmantle" *Eng. Spy* I 121: As soon as you have made your bow to the *big wig*. *a*1848 in Bartlett *Amer.* 31: What great things they did to the bigwigs to home. **1855** Brougham *Chips* 327: We've been spendin' a werry fashionable hour among them ar' big wigs. *1858 A. Mayhew *Paved with Gold* 270: When the big wigs chooses [*sic*] to have a row, they alwers tries to get us...to do the fighting. **1867** Smyth *Sailor's Wd. Bk.*: *Big-wigs.* A cant term for the higher officers. **1884** Hartranft *Sidesplitter* 147: Every blessed drop of licker he swallows there is a taxed to pay the salary of some of them ere great bigwigs. **1935** Sayre & Twist *Annie Oakley* (film): What will the President and the rest of the big wigs say? **1968** R. Adams *West. Words* (ed. 2): *Bigwig.* A logger's name for foreman or boss. **1971** LeGuin *Lathe of Heaven* 16: No wonder the Med School bigwigs had sent this one here. **1973** Overgard *Hero* 89: Now and then we get a Cuban big-wig Perez wants to show off for. **1986** M. Skinner *USN* 21: But even the bigwigs envy the ship's captain.

Big Wind or **Big Windy** *n.* WINDY CITY.—constr. with *the.*
  1944 Burley *Orig. Hndbk. Harlem Jive* 16: Pops, I just fell in from the Big Wind. **1977** Lieberman & Rhodes *CB Hndbk.* 305: Big Windy—Chicago.

bike *n.* **1.** a bicycle. Now *S.E.*
  1882 in *DAE*: Much I should like/To know why you.../Take such a header/From off your "bike." **1895** in F. Remington *Sel. Letters* 267: Every living human being in America rides "bike." Did you see my...article...on "bikes"? **1895** Remington *Pony Tracks* 147: Old man, show 'em what bikes are good for. **1895** in *DAE*: Mrs. Tony Pastor...can be seen on her favorite "bike" daily. **1899** Ade *Fables* 78: He wore an old Pair of Bike Shoes. **1909** *WNID*: *Bike n. + v.* Slang for bicycle.
  2. a motorcycle.
  [**1913** *Sat. Eve. Post* (June 7) 27: Gas-Bike Possibilities.] *1913 G.B. Shaw, in *OEDS*: In the morning I brave the bike at last. **1918** *Ladies' Home Jour.* (Oct.) 7: Suppose his..."bike" is put entirely out of commission. **1919** Dreer *Immed. Jewel* 208: We were all discussing it when we heard your "bike." **1924** Stallings & Anderson *What Price Glory?* 61: Bike working? Sidecar trimmed? *1924 T.E. Lawrence, in *OEDS*: The bike was raw & new, a man-killer. **1957** Shulman *Rally* 173: How's the bike runnin', Grady? **1980** Kotzwinkle *Jack* 185: Where's my bike?
  3. *Police.* a motorcycle patrolman.
  1958 *N.Y. Times Mag.* (Mar. 16) 87: *Bike*—Motorcycle cop.
  4. [because freq. "ridden"] *Stu.* a promiscuous young woman.
  1984 Hindle *Dragon Fall* 20: A word that would properly

describe…[her]. *Promiscuous, lewd, risqué,* and/or *bike* never seemed to fit.

bike *v.* to ride a bicycle. Hence **biker,** *n.* Now *S.E.*

1883 in *DAE*: Three poor, miserable "bikers." **1895** in *DAE*: Frank Weston and his wife…are to be seen "biking" it nearly every evening. **1895** *Harper's* (Nov.) 961: Bob and Jack are coming to-night to give me my first lesson in biking. *Ibid.* 962: You go down on the "L." I'll bike.

biker *n.* a motorcyclist; (*specif.*) a member of a motorcycle gang.

1968 McNeill *Moving Through Here* 166: It is true that they are bikers. **1968** *Harper's* (Nov.) 96: Hippies, ex–Hippies, diggers, bikers, dropouts from college. **1970** *Nat. Lampoon* (Aug.) 45: Right wing bikers called "Hitler's Heroes"…attacked everyone…with chains, tire irons and zip guns. **1970** *Playboy* (Dec.) 190: The bikers were lined up in full formation. **1980** Kotzwinkle *Jack* 195: He adjusted one of his zippers, a biker's scowl on his face as he spoke to Gina. **1983** *Fall Guy* (ABC-TV): We're goin' back with the meanest, baddest biker bunch ever.

bikie *n. Police.* a motorcycle patrolman.

1976 *N.Y. Times Mag.* (Sept. 12) 112: We did it to get the bikies.

Bikini State *n. CB.* Florida.—constr. with *the.*

1975 Dills *CB Slanguage* (1976 ed.) 17. **1976** Bibb et al. *CB Bible* 64: Down in the Bikini State, you'll hear…Bob Cole of WWOK, Miami.

bilge *n.* nonsense; BILGEWATER. Now *S.E.*

*****1908** in *OEDS*: Let's go….This is awful bilge. **1920** in E. Pound *Letters* 157: Which is bilge, just sloppy inaccurate bilge. **1926** E. Hemingway *Sun Also Rises* 55: Let's not talk. Talking's all bilge. **1931** Adamic *Laughing* 211: I was inclined to agree with Mencken that idealism was "bilge." **1932** Berg *Prison Doctor* 51: The kind of bilge they pull every time they want to get the public worked up. **1938** Wolfe *Web & Rock* 477: Oh, stop talking bilge! **1984** *Agronsky & Co.* (Mutual Radio Net.) (July 22): That speech was terrible—just bilge, and you know it.

bilge *v. U.S. Nav. Acad. & (obs.) U.S. Mil. Acad.* **1.** (of a cadet) to be forced to resign for academic or other deficiency; (*hence*) to flunk.—often constr. with *out.* Also trans., to compel to resign. See also BILGER.

1869 *Overland Mo.* (Feb.) 183: Next day the water and whipping tests were repeated and continued until one-half of the remainder of the "class" "bilged." **1877** Lee *Fag-Ends* 27: For they intended, if they "bilged,"/That sneaking man to maul. *Ibid.* 68: He'll be frigidly bilged in May. *Ibid.* 32: They're bilging upper classmen here/For hazing plebes so green. **1877** Flipper *Colored Cadet* 313 [ref. to U.S. Mil. Acad., 1870]: But wiser counsels prevailed, and the cadets consented to tolerate Jimmy Smith and not drown or kill him for four weeks, when it was thought the examiners would "bilge" him. **1888** in M.L. Bartlett *Lejeune* 21: Exams they are a comin'….We'll…bilge upon the semi-an. **1894** *Lucky Bag* (U.S. Nav. Acad.) (No. 1) 66: *Bilge*…to be dismissed or dropped. **1898** Allen *Navy Blue* 154: A number of members of the class were almost certain to drop, or "bilge" at the end of the term. **1906** *Army & Navy Life* (Nov.) 498: *Bilge* is to be dropped, dismissed, or be obliged to resign. **1919** Fiske *Midshipman* 11 [ref. to 1870's]: The semiannual examination resulted in "bilging" more than half the class. **1927** *AS* (Aug.) 452: *Bilge, bilge out*—To fail in classes; equivalent of "flunk," which involves expulsion from the Naval Academy. **1941** *Guide to U.S. Nav. Acad.* 149: *Bilge.* To…flunk. **1946** Sawyer *Gunboats* 17: It seemed to us the primary purpose of the academic staff was to "bilge" all hands if possible. **1951** in *DAS* 36: We ought to have you bilged out of the Academy. **1967** Lockwood *Down to Sea* 14 [ref. to 1912]: But in the first two years I lost two roommates by "bilging"—resignation due to unsatisfactory marks.

2. *Navy.* to ruin or destroy.

1914 Paine *Wall Between* 266: The tip was out that unless we came frolicking right along in a hurry your outfit of marines was bilged entirely. **1918** *Lit. Digest* (Sept. 28) 50: A man gets bilged, you know, if he sticks around on a ditch all the time. **1959** *Sat. Eve. Post* (May 9) 80: They'll pass me over [for promotion] sure….Maybe a second time too. Then I'm bilged.

bilger *n. U.S. Nav. Acad. & U.S. Mil. Acad.* a cadet who has been forced to resign for academic or other deficiency; a dropout.

1846 in N.C. Delaney *J.M. Kell* 42: Bilgers. **1855** Wise *Tales for Marines* 97: He had been a "bilger" at his examinations for the second time. **1877** Lee *Fag-Ends* 23: The "Entrance Exam" is over and gone,/ The bilgers have fled evermore. **1894** *Lucky Bag* (U.S. Nav. Acad.) (No. 1) 66: *Bilger*…Cadet dropped from the rolls. **1906** *Army & Navy Life* (Nov.) 498: *Bilger* is a dismissed cadet, or one who has been required to resign. *ca***1909** in Warren & Warren *Everybody Works* 108: Should you

fail you are a "bilger." **1928** *AS* (Aug.) 452: *Bilger*—One who has bilged out. **1933** Butler & Thomas *Gimlet Eye* 146: The boys were "bilgers"—failures—from West Point. **1935** F.H. Lea *Anchor Man* 297: He's a bilger from my class.

bilge rat *n. Naut.* **1.** a wretch; LOWLIFE.

1929 in Sagendorf *Popeye* 23: Aw, shut up, you bilge rat! **1946** *2 Yrs. Before Mast* (film): You bilgerats!

2. a member of a ship's engine crew; SNIPE. Also vars.

1942 Sanders & Blackwell *Forces* 39: Bilge Rats:…members of the engineers' crew. (U.S.N.). **1940–46** McPeak (U.S. Navy): A man who worked below deck…was called a "snipe" or a "bilge rat." **1959** Morrill *Dark Sea* 149: In the argument, White called them "bilge rats that don't belong above decks." *Ibid.* 34: This bilge-lizard is trying to lower my price. *Ibid.* 133: These bilge-woppers from the Engine Department like to come up on the Captain's deck in good weather. **1972** Sapir & Murphy *Death Therapy* 145: You bilge rats produce some power. This is the Navy, man, not an excursion boat.

bilgewater *n.* **1.** nonsense; drivel.

[**1876** "M. Twain" *1601* 1: The Duchess of Bilge-water.] *****1878** G.M. Hopkins, in *OEDS*: Write no bilgewater about it. *****1945** S.J. Baker *Australian Lang.* 128: *Bilgewater*…misleading chatter. **1957** Kohner *Gidget* 9: He is dishing out a lot of bilge water if you ask me. **1965** McKenna *Sand Pebbles* 168. **1973** Saletan & Cox *Songs & Sounds of the Sea* 11: The fo'c'sle tales weren't all bilge water. **1979** F. Thomas *Golden Bird* 113: They do say he hied off at times, lookin' for antiques, but that's bilgewater. **1982** R.M. Brown *So. Discomfort* 177: Balderdash and bilgewater!

2. *Naut.* a vile or weak beverage, soup, etc.

1940 *Life* (Oct. 28) 99: *Bilgewater* (soup), *collision mats* (pancakes), *Joe* (coffee). **1942** *ATS* III: Inferior beer…*bilgewater.* **1945** Yates & Mankiewicz *Spanish Main* (film): "What kind of bilgewater is this?" "Canary wine!"

¶ In phrase:

¶ **stir up** [or **sweeten**] **(one's) bilgewater** *Naut.* to brighten (one's) spirits.

1852 Hazen *Five Years* 261: Always like to shake hands with an old friend—stirs up one's bilge water, don't it? **1871** "M. Twain" *Roughing It* 333: He took a level tumblerful of whiskey every morning before he put his clothes on—"to sweeten his bilgewater," he said.

bilk *n.* **1.** a swindler; cheat; fraud; crook; (*also*) a sponger. Orig. *S.E.*

*****1790** in *OED*: Johnny W–lks, Johnny W–lks, Thou greatest of bilks. *****1821** *Real Life in London* I 361: The *bilk* is in a hurry. *****1836** F. Marryat, in *OED*: The wagoner drove off, cursing him for a bilk. **1865** Harte *Sk. of Sixties* 69: He…hissed after the retreating form of the Baronet, the single word: "Bilk!" **1867** in McClure *Rocky Mtns.* 211: The most degrading epithet that one can apply to another is to call him "a bilk."…The term was entirely novel to me, and…the landlord explained…that a "bilk" is a man who never misses a meal and never pays a cent. **1867** A.D. Richardson *Beyond Miss.* 445: A "bilk" is an impostor. **1869** *Overland Mo.* (Mar.) 278: He's one o' them bilks as parts his har onto the middle on his head, and talks like a preacher. *****1873** Hotten *Slang Dict.* (ed. 4): *Bilk,* a cheat, or a swindler. Formerly in general use, now confined to the streets, where it is common and mostly used in reference to prostitutes. **1880** in Rosa *Wild Bill* 304: He is a dead beet and a bilk and I can prove it. **1883** Peck *Bad Boy* 191: You are a high-toned…sort of a bilk. *ca***1900** in S.Z. Starr *Jennison's Jayhawkers* 66: [He was a] bilk of the first water. *a***1904–11** Phillips *Susan Lenox* II 160: You damned old bilk.

2. a swindle.

1867 in A.K. McClure *Rocky Mtns.* 370: He denounced the whole affair as a stupendous "bilk,"—a mere swindle to get winter's grub. **1868** J. Chisholm *So. Pass* 41: I think there is no chance for this country to prove a "bilk." *a***1889** in Barrère & Leland *Dict. Slang* I 115: Strong drink, he said, was (hic) a bilk. **1896** in Rose *Storyville* 129: People are wondering how Miss Alice Schwartz liked the bilk Nettie Griffin gave her.

bilk *v.* to swindle or cheat. Hence **bilker,** *n.* Now *S.E.*

*****1675** in Duffett *Burlesque Plays* 82: I won't…bilk you, as your Bullies do. *****1677** Wycherley *Plain Dealer* V iii: Ay, a great lawyer…bilked me too. *****1698–99** "B.E." *Dict. Canting Crew*: *Bilk*…to cheat. *Bilk the Ratling-cove,* to sharp the Coach-man of his hire. *Bilk'd,*…defeated, disappointed. *****1717** in *OEDS*: *Bilker.* *****1748** in *F & H* I 194: *Bilk*…to cheat…deceive, gull…; also to go out of a publick-house or tavern without paying the reckoning. **1749** in Breslaw *Tues. Club* 162: They Storm bawdy houses, kick poor whores, bilk hackney coachmen, and break windows. **1781** in M. Mathews *Beginnings of Amer. Eng.* 27: It is often said...a man is *bilked*, he is *bit*. ***1785** Grose *Vulgar Tongue:* Bilking a coachman, a box keeper, or a poor whore, was formerly among men of the town thought a gallant action. ***1825** "Blackmantle" *Eng. Spy* I 166: That *covey* wants to *bilk* the gate. ***1858** A. Mayhew *Paved with Gold* 255: We've "bilked" (swindled) my nabs. **1866** *Nat. Police Gaz.* (Nov. 17) 2: How a Buxom Widow Was "Bilked." *a*1909 Tillotson *Detective* 90: *Bilked*—Fooled. **1978** Time-Life *Gamblers* 56: Two cardsharps...were busily bilking a young traveler out of a considerable sum.

Bill *n.* [perh. sugg. by *billy goat;* cf. syn. WILLY] *Mil.* corned beef hash.—usu. constr. with *canned* or *corned.* Also **bill.** Now *hist.*

1909 *Man-o-Warsman* (Feb.) 221: We are still living on canned "Bill" January 8th, and are just moving along slowly. **1917** *Wadsworth Gas Attack* (Nov. 27) 23: One slice of canned Bill's easy. **1917** in Niles *Singing Soldiers* 11: Now from the cook shack Jonah took a mess pail full of bill. **1918** *Stars & Stripes* (Mar. 1) 7: Corned bill. **1918** in [Casey] *Cannoneers* 259: And we haven't eaten anything but tinned Bill. **1918** Ruggles *Navy* 33: Canned Willie. Also known as canned bill. **1918** in Dolph *Sound Off* 152: And let me eat my fill/Of old corn Bill. **1918** Kauffman *Navy at Work* 6: "Mulligan," shredded Bill and onions. **1925** Thomason *Fix Bayonets* 227: The cooks issued corn-bill hash. **1926** Nason *Chevrons* 288: Ain't they anything to eat here but canned bill?

bill[1] *n.* the nose; in phr. **dip the bill** to take a drink of liquor.

1834 Caruthers *Kentuckian* II 208: I've been poppen my bill into it, and out of it again, like a kingfisher in a mill-dam. **1867** Harris *Lovingood* 146: He'd lick his lips...es ef he'd been dippin his bill into a crock ove chicken gray [*sic*]. **1938** Chandler *Big Sleep* 186: Let's dip the bill. Got a glass? **1950** in *DAS:* There is a shortage of fighters. The GI Bill of Rights allowed a lot of impoverished [ex-soldiers] to get educated instead of getting their bills busted.

bill[2] *n.* **1.** one dollar.

[*ca*1895 in *Independent* (Feb. 6, 1902) 334: He tells of a street fakir...who besides making him a Present of a $5.00 Bill for my kindness...told me that he had Blowed fifty Bills last night—denomination not stated.] **1915** in White *Amer. Negro Folksongs* 205: A hundred bills to anyone/Who'd in that mansion stay. **1956** Hunter *Second Ending* 121: Fifteen bills will buy a fairly decent alligator belt. **1965** Yordan & Sperling *Battle of Bulge* (film): That's gonna bring me thirty bills a bottle where we're going. **1966** Terry *Tightly Closed* 171: He paid me to do it. A lousy two thousand bills. **1970** Conaway *Big Easy* 186: Let's see three bills fifty. **1971** N.Y.U. student: If it was me, I'd go down and collect for the other forty-six bills.

2. one hundred dollars.

1929 Hotstetter & Beesley *It's a Racket* 219: *Bill*—One hundred dollar banknote. **1948** Seward & Ryan *Angel's Alley* (film): We oughta get at least two bills from Tony for this hack. **1955** Salter *Hunters* 45: "Four bills, that's all." "Four hundred dollars?" **1960** J.A. Williams *Angry Ones* 69: Minimum. A bill a week. **1961** Brosnan *Pennant Race* 194: In this series, it might cost you a bill. **1965** C. Brown *Manchild* 163: So I gave him half a bill, fifty dollars. **1969** Crumley *One to Count Cadence* 205: Raise your fee from what, fifty, to one bill for sure. **1982** Del Vecchio *13th Valley* 121: Maybe six bills a month.

Bill Daly *n.* ¶ In phrase: **on the Bill Daly** *Horse Racing.* (of a racehorse) gaining a lead at the start of a race and maintaining it till the finish line is crossed. Occ. **Bill Bailey.**

1941 in *DAS* 37: She [a racehorse] beat a flock of platers here last year. She might go out on the Bill Daley and hang on. **1942** *ATS* 694: Be on the Bill Daly...to get away from the barrier in the lead. **1968** Ainslie *Thoroughbred Racing* 463: Bill Daly—Rider who takes lead as soon as possible is "on the Bill Daly." Famous trainer, "Father Bill" Daly, used to tell jockeys, "Get on top right away and improve your position." **1979** Racing fan at Churchill Downs, Ky.: [of a horse] He'll be on the Bill Bailey all the way. **1981** WINS radio (July 9): There's a well-known racetrack expression, *on the Bill Daly,* which refers to horses that go to the lead at the start of a race and stay there all the way.

bill-poster *n. Und.* a forger.

1936 Mencken *Amer. Language* (ed. 4) 579: The Western crooks sometimes call a forger a *bill-poster.* **1941** *Slanguage Dict.* 7: *Bill-poster*...a forger.

billies *n.pl.* [BILL[2] + *-ie* (dim. suff.) + *-s*] banknotes; cash.

1982 *Time* (Sept. 27) 56: One conspicuous difference: the amount of billies a true Val pours into clothes, sunglasses, tanning oil, [etc.]. **1982** Pond *Valley Girls' Guide* 52: *Billies*—Like money. **1985** "Blowdryer"

Modern Eng. 6: *Billys*...Cash, money.

Billy *n.* BILL.

1918 in Rendinell *One Man's War* 112: There was bread, hardtack, canned Billy scattered everywhere.

billy *n.* **1.** a short crowbar, as used by burglars; (*hence*) a bludgeon, club, or blackjack; (*specif.*) (now *S.E.*) a police officer's nightstick.

1848 [Judson] *Mysteries* 490: [He] broke down her guard with a short iron crow-bar, or "billy," as the burglars term it. **1850** "N. Buntline" *G'hals of N.Y.* 67: A good wipe over the head with a *billy.* **1851** [G. Thompson] *Bristol Bill* 21: "Billies" and "jimmies," "jacks," "braces" and "bits"...have for...twenty year formed the paraphernalia of a burglar's outfit. *a*1859 in Bartlett *Amer.* (ed. 2) 33: A poor German was taken to prison, and, on examining him, it was discovered that he was a victim to the *billy.* ***1873** Hotten *Slang Dict.* (ed. 4): *Billy,* a policeman's staff. **1893** in Dreiser *Jour.* I 206: It is said that Wallace always carried a "billy" [blackjack]. **1928** Callahan *Man's Grim Justice* 32: He suddenly whipped a "billy" out of his pocket and banged me over the head. **1938** Bellem *Blue Murder* 68: Then somebody whaled me over the head with a billy.

2. a countryman, hillbilly.—used derisively.

1940 in Welsch *Got Yourself a Horse* 57 [ref. to 1890's]: That "billy" turned to the woman and said "Jezibel, you-all get the young-uns out here." *Ibid.* 59: One old scrawny "billy" said he had come five "mounting" miles...over the hog backs.

Billy Bad-Ass *n.* BAD-ASS.—usu. considered vulgar.

1970 Ponicsan *Last Detail* 7: Bad-Ass...in navy parlance means a very tough customer....The term is always used with the name Billy to achieve the effect of the alliterative trochee. *Ibid.* 176: Well, we picked us up a helluva billy bad-ass here. **1974** Memphis, Tenn., student: "He's trying to be a real Billy-Joe Bad-Ass." That means he thinks he's bad or tough. **1992** G. Wolff *Day at Beach* 115: Here are the hard guys, Billy Bad-Ass and his gang.

billy-be-damned *n.* [cf. BILLY HELL; conceivably both terms orig. as euphems. for the devil] (used as an emphatic standard of comparison; "hell," "Sam Hill"). Also as *adj.*

1849 in Windeler *Gold Rush Diary* 28: Theodor looked as big as billy be damned. **1850** in Blair & McDavid *Mirth* 102: I pledged my word he was dead as Billy-be-damned! **1886** in *JAF* (Apr. 1946) 110: Ev'rybody call me Sam, but I don't know gilly-be-dam [*sic*]. **1898** Dunne *Dooley in Peace & War* 61: It's hotter down here thin Billy-be-dam'd. **1898** Norris *Moran* 65: Lord, it's as plain as Billy-b'damn. **1902** in "O. Henry" *Works* 1640: Them billy-by-dam yaller-back novils. **1914** Paine *Wall Between* 148: And you ran and jumped into a boat and pulled like billy-be-damned. **1924** Tully *Beggars of Life* 28: She's colder'n Billy-be-damned outside. **1928** Scanlon *God Have Mercy* 77: The woods were blacker than Billy-be-damned. **1942** McAtee *Supp. to Grant Co. Dial. in '90's* 3: *Billy-be-damned,* n. phr., a standard of unpleasant comparison, as in "hotter than —"; used with a great variety of adjectives, as colder, tighter, onrier. **1964** "Dr. X" *Intern* 249: It immediately began bleeding like Billy-be-damned.

billy goat *n.* **1.** a lecherous man.

1859 in Eliason *Tarheel Talk* 71: Do you still attract the "sparks"? "*Johnny horses*," "*Billy goats*" and *Tom* boys?...she has given up all hopes of her *Tom boy* and her *Billy goat hasn't bleated* yet. **1938** "E. Queen" *4 Hearts* 104: He was a man, that billy-goat!

2. a rambunctious or cantankerous man.

1921 U. Sinclair *K. Coal* 124: Get the hell off that tipple, you old billy-goat!

3.a. a starter for a diesel engine; (*also*) a diesel engine.

1958 McCulloch *Woods Words* 11: *Billy goat*—A small starting motor used on a big diesel engine. **1962** *AS* (May) 132. **1971** Tak *Truck Talk* 13: *Billy goat:* The 318hp Detroit diesel engine.

b. (see quot.).

1958 McCulloch *Woods Words* 11: *Billy goat*...A gas burner with coils used to get up enough steam to pump cold oil for starting fire in an oil-burning donkey; a kind of oil superheater.

billy-goat *v.* to philander; TOMCAT.

1938 Steinbeck *Grapes of Wrath* 89: He's a billy-goatin' aroun' the country. Tom-cattin' hisself to death. **1967** Schmidt *Lexicon of Sex* 20: *Billy-goat*...Of a male, to engage in extra-cardiac love affairs, via the pudendal route.

billy hell *n.* (used as an emphatic standard of comparison; also as "hell," "stuffing," etc., and as expletive constr. with *the*).

1897 Fox *Hell Fer Sartain* 78: Thar'd 'a' been billy-hell to pay right thar! **1903** Adams *Log of a Cowboy* 64: The man...said if he owned hell and Texas, he'd rent Texas and live in hell, for if this isn't Billy hell, I'd like to know what you call it. **1915** Braley *Workaday World* 34: Yes, he takes a heap o' chances, and he works like Billy Hell. **1921** Carter *Marine, Sir* 112: I'll get billy-blue-hell if I'm late tonight. **1933** J. Conroy *Disinherited* 273: This will hurt like billy hell. **1936** Duncan *Over the Wall* 77: Farrell...whipped billy-hell out of him. **1939** O'Brien *One-Way Ticket* 140: She's salty as billy hell. **1940** W. Guthrie, on *Broadsides* (WUOT radio) (June 29, 1984): You got to raise old billy hell till you get your farm back. **1970** Terkel *Hard Times* 438: So why in the billy hell has this happening taken the limelight for me over all the others? **1988** Poyer *Med* 255: Word is this weather's going to turn Billy Hell.

billy-o *n.* (used as an emphatic standard of comparison).
*1885 in *OEDS*: Shure it'll rain like billy-oh! **1915** Howard *God's Man* 164: You'd get on like billy-o. **1939–49** O. Nash *Versus* 136: I woo nymphs like billy-o/With my well-known punctilio.

Billy Rumor *n. Army.* rumor.
1863 in O.J. Hopkins *Under the Flag* 86: Old Billy Rumor reports a large body of Rebel cavalry a short distance from here.

bim *n.* **1.a.** BIMBO², 2.
1925 *Lit. Digest* (Mar. 14) 65: I got played for fish by some bim. **1925** *English Journal* (Nov.) 704: To call the girl you expect to marry your "bim" is to make a light thing of marriage. **1931** C. Ford *Coconut Oil* 149: You know what I think o' bims aroun' my camp when dere's training to be done. **1932** *AS* (June) 329: *Bim; bimbo*—a girl. **1938** O'Hara *Hope of Heaven* 109: That bim I was with last night. Charlotte. **1944** C.B. Davis *Leo McGuire* 253: So the kid...immediately becomes the most popular bim in the neighborhood. **1948** Lait & Mortimer *New York* 196: Whose bim is dat one? **1952** S. Bellow *Augie March* 231: Only a year ago he would not have given a second glance at such bims. **1953** R. Chandler *Goodbye* 289: Seems like the bim was one of his sleepy-time gals. **1956** Levin *Compulsion* 106: They had scouted the train looking for a couple of bims, but all the time Judd had felt sure they wouldn't really find any. **1959** Lederer *Never Steal Anything Small* (film): Gentlewomen, no bims. **1964** in Jackson *Swim Like Me* 116: A bim that won't bolt while you doin' a little jolt/Is just one out of a thousand, my friend. **1974** *Gunsmoke* (CBS-TV): Two fancy-headed bim! **1986** Bozzone *Buck Fever* 9: Where's the "bims"? **1989** *Dream Street* (NBC-TV): I'd find him...with his hand up some old bim's dress. **1992** *Middle Ages* (CBS-TV): "My buddy and I went lookin' for bims." "Bims?" "Betties....That's surfer talk."
b. BIMBO², 1.
1925 *Sat. Eve. Post* (Oct. 3) 20: I started with you bims as a heavyweight.
2. *Black E.* a policeman.
1957 H. Simmons *Corner Boy* 45: This was the risky part...if the bims should happen along right now. **1962** H. Simmons *On Eggshells* 213: Man, the bims around this mammy-tapping town is something, ain't they? **1970** Landy *Underground Dict.* 33: *Bim*...Policeman—e.g. The bims went bam and took me to the slams.

bimbette *n.* [BIMB(O)², 2 + -*ette* (fem. dim. suff.)] BIMBO², 2. *Joc.*
1982 (cited in *Oxf. Dict. Mod. Slang*). **1985** *Los Angeles* (Apr.) 141: Written by Juanita Bartlett, it marks the first TV use, to my knowledge, of the word *bimbette*. a**1986** in *NDAS*: Itching to play something more demanding than bimbettes and stand-by wives. **1987** Weiser & Stone *Wall St.* (film): I know this eighteen-year-old bimbette that will just love you. **1989** L. Roberts *Full Cleveland* 134: Brenda or some other bimbette. **1990** *Oprah* (ABC-TV): And in comes my husband with this bimbette, you know. **1992** *Vanity Fair* (July) 48: Although [Benny] Hill is a peeper and a chaser in his sketches, his pursuit of bimbettes wasn't propelled by a satyr's charging penis.

bimbo¹ *n.* BUMBO.
1837 in Thornton *Amer. Gloss.* I: *Bimbo* is a rascally compound of brandy and sugar, flavored with lemon peal [*sic*]. An invention of the devil to make drunkards. **1840** *Spirit of Times* (Dec. 12) 487: Presenting us with a cask of "bimbo." **1853** Derby *Phoenixiana* 173: My morning glass of bimbo. [Facetious recipe then given.]

bimbo² *n.* [prob. < It *bimbo* 'baby' as calque of U.S. slang senses of BABY] **1.** a stupid, inconsequential, or contemptible fellow; BOZO; (*broadly*) fellow.
1918 in Rossano *Price of Honor* 99: She flop! An' il bimbo he break da boni. **1919** *American Mag.* (Nov.) 69: Nothing but the most heroic measures will save the poor bimbo. **1920–21** Witwer *Leather Pushers*

10: *You* know, one of them bimbos which flings a wicked spear and hurls a mean hammer. **1924** H.L. Wilson *Professor* 83: I am a pretty fast baby and a handy bimbo with firearms. **1924** Anderson & Stallings *What Price Glory?* 117: I hung a shanty on the bimbo's eye. **1927** *AS* (Mar.) 275: *Bimbo*—person. **1953** R. Chandler *Goodbye* 142: Big Willie Magoon...a vice squad bimbo. **1972** Wurlitzer *Quake* 62: I'm not exactly sure who you are. John Hodiak or Michael Rennie....Some forties bimbo. **1974** *Odd Couple* (ABC-TV): I caught this bimbo stealing a TV set. **1978** Schrader *Hardcore* 110: Look at the bimbo! He's wearing an Army coat with Navy pants! **1979** in Terkel *Amer. Dreams* 371: Fuzzy-headed liberal bimbos. **1982** R. Sutton *Don't Get Taken* 96: The bimbos in Detroit rode home in limousines while their plants continued to pursue...flashy styling. **1983** Calif. man, age *ca*40: You gotta be some kind of bimbo to believe that. **1986** in *Smithsonian* (Jan. 1987) 43: An alligator is no mental marvel, but it's not a total bimbo either. **1989** Ramis & Aykroyd *Ghostbusters II* (film): Yeah, you! The bimbo with the baby. **1990** *Donahue* (NBC-TV): I think [Vice-President] Quayle is the stereotypical bimbo. **1992** *Middle Ages* (CBS-TV): You *are* a bimbo, Duane!

2. a young woman, esp. one who is promiscuous or unintelligent; FLOOZIE.
1920 in Zeidman *Burlesque* 126: This Dix bimbo is a dangerous woman...a sassy girl with...more than a figure—a physique. **1921** *Variety* (Feb. 18) 11: He scarcely met this bimbo, when he wants to know if there are any more like her. **1925** *Literary Digest* (Mar. 14) 65: A girl is almost universally called a "woman" [by college students] or, in humorous disrespect, a "bimbo." **1927** *Vanity Fair* (Nov.) 67: Among some of [Jack] Conway's more famous expressions are: "Bimbo" (for a dumb girl). **1928** Delmar *Bad Girl* 8: A bimbo....Picked her up on Seventh Avenue. She wanted to go for a sail so I took her. **1929** *Our Army* (Mar.) 6: My Bimbo is waiting/And she's sure good dating. **1929** Perelman *Ginsbergh* 119: There was once a certain Moorish bimbo...by the name of Etta Falcovsky. **1938** H. Miller *Capricorn* 96: He calmly glanced about the room and decided which bimbo was the least sottishlooking. **1942** Lindsay & Crouse *Strip for Action* 10: Say, these burlesque bimbos ought to be live ammunition. **1949** Maier *Pleasure* I. 108: I guess those two Navy guys are out in the bushes somewhere with those French bimbos. **1965** Cassavetes *Faces* 217: We had a couple of bimbos with us that knew more dirty limericks than you could shake a stick at. **1968** "R. Hooker" *MASH* 73: The bimboes are on a real Christian kick. **1972–75** W. Allen *Feathers* 33: Sure, a guy can meet all the bimbos he wants. But the really brainy women—they're not so easy to find on short notice. **1977–80** F.M. Stewart *Century* 84: They caught me with a bimbo in my room. **1986** *Cheers* (NBC-TV): Who's the bimbo *du jour*? **1987** *CBS This Morning* (Dec. 31): *Bimbo* as it's used now is kind of an attractive airhead. **1990** *Cosmopolitan* (Nov.) 124: I began wondering if this turn of events also puts me into the bimbo category. Was I too flirtatious?...What about all that sexy lingerie I used to wear for him?

Bimmer *n.* BEEMER.
1986 Eble *Campus Slang* (Mar.) 1: *Bimmer*—a BMW car: "John got a new bimmer for Christmas." **1990** P. Dickson *Slang!* 23: *Bimmer.* A BMW.

Bimmy *n.* [earlier *Bim* 'a Barbadian'; see *OEDS*] a West Indian black.
[**1852** in *OEDS*: *Bim.*] **1976** R. Price *Blood Brothers* 115: West Indians...I hate the fuckin' Bimis with a passion.

bin *n.* LOONY BIN.
*1938 E. Waugh, in *OEDS*: To my certain knowledge she's driven three men into the bin. **1971** *New Yorker* (July 3) 25: They put me in the bin because I...talked non-stop one day for twenty-three hours. **1973** Jong *Flying* 91: There was...a French actress who'd "spent time in a bin." **1979** G. Mehta, in *Harper's* (Aug.) 47: Sent her round the bend. Completely schiz....I think she's in a bin somewhere in the Midwest now. a**1988** M. Atwood *Cat's Eye* 190: She's crazy....She should be in a bin.

bin *v.* to commit to a LOONY BIN.
1967 Rosenthal *Sheeper* 236: Only a question of time before we're all binned or hated.

binder *n.* usu. *pl.* a wheel brake.
*1942 in *OEDS* [ref. to RAF]: *To jump on the binders,* to apply the brakes. **1945** Hubbard *R.R. Ave.* 333: *Binders*—Hand brakes. **1953** in Botkin & Harlow *R.R. Folklore* 326: He told this student to set a binder (hand-brake) on the first car in. **1956** Heflin *USAF Dict.* 81: *Binder, n.* The wheel brake of an airplane. *Slang.* **1962** G. Olson *Roaring Road* 55: Maybe you went a little deeper...before hitting the binders, that's all.

1962 *AS* XXXVII 267: *Binders*, brakes. Most often used in referring to emergency stops. "Hit the binders!" **1972** Wambaugh *Blue Knight* 12: Just then a wino lurched across Main Street…and a Lincoln jammed on the binders almost creaming him. **1979** Frommer *Sports Lingo* 165: *Grab the binders*. To brake a motorcycle.

bindle *n.* [prob. < G *Büntel* 'package'; discussed in *Comments on Ety.* XII, 9–10 (Feb. 1983), pp. 34–5]
1. *Hobo.* a pack or bedroll; bundle of one's belongings.
1897 (quot. at BINDLE STIFF). **1900** "J. Flynt" *Policeman* 262: Among the "Bindle Men," "Mush Fakers," and "Turn-pikers" of the middle West, the East, and Canada, there exists a crude system of marking "good" houses. **1907** (quot. at BINDLE STIFF). **1916** *Lit. Digest* (Aug. 19) 425: A package is a "bindle," derived from "bundle." **1921** Casey *Gay-Cat* 111: He carried in one arm a roll of clothing, the "bindle" tied compactly with a bit of hay-rope. **1929** *AS* (June) 338: *Bindle*—A bed-roll or pack. **1930** "D. Stiff" *Milk & Honey* 199: *Bindle*—Bedding roll slung on the back. **1937** Steinbeck *Mice & Men* 17: Bring your bindle over here by the fire. *Ibid.* 20: Lennie put his bindle on the neighboring bunk and sat down. **1942** *AS* 219: *Bindle*. A blanket roll. **1981** N. Cohen *Long Steel Rail* 383: A canvas bag or a hobo's bindle, for carrying one's personal belongings.
2. *Narc.* a small envelope or paper of morphine, heroin, cocaine, etc.
1921 in E. Murphy *Black Candle* 214: We would call these "decks," but some people would call them "bindles." **1926** in Partridge *Dict. Underworld* 39: I didn't know he was in the bindle graft. **1927** *Immortalia* 36: Pulled out a bindle and took a bang. **1935** Pollock *Underworld Speaks*: *Bindle*, a small package (two or three grains) of morphine, cocaine or heroin, sold to addicts by street peddlers. **1950** Riesenberg *Reporter* 171: A couple of bindles of the H are missing. **1970** L.D. Johnson *Devil's Front Porch* 104: These bindles*…sold ordinarily for $1.50.…*Small packets of dope. **1975** Wambaugh *Choirboys* 220: Harold stripped a paper bindle from the inside of the hype's belt where it had been taped. **1982** *L.A. Times* (Mar. 15) II 3: His assignment is to buy two "dime" ($10) bindles of marijuana.

bindle stiff *n.* **1.** a migratory laborer who carries his belongings in a blanket roll or other bundle; a tramp. Also **bindle bum, bindle bo.**
1897 in J. London *Reports* 314 [ref. to 1892]: Because of his predilection to carrying his bed with him, he is known in trampland as the "bindle stiff." **1907** J. London *The Road* 25: A bindle-stiff is a working tramp. He takes his name from the roll of blankets he carries, which is known as a "bindle." **1921** Casey & Casey *Gay-Cat* 41: He's none o' yer bindle stiffs or backdoor moochers. **1922** Tully *Emmett Lawler* 153: The "bindle stiff"…seldom rides…but is contented usually to walk from town to town. **1924** Henderson *Keys to Crookdom* 397: *Bindle*. A bundle. *Bindle stiff* is a bundle stiff, tramp. **1930** "D. Stiff" *Milk & Honey* 19: In those days the hobo carried his bed for which he was known as the "bundle stiff" or "bindle bo." **1934** Berg *Prison Nurse* 15: They called themselves "bindlestiffs." **1937** Steinbeck *Mice & Men* 86: You bindle bums think you're so damn good. **1946–51** J. Jones *Eternity* ch. xlii: They were workstiffs and bindlebums like you and me. **1975** T. Berger *Sneaky People* 46: Many ruined millionaires were alleged to have become bindlestiffs. **1982** Heat Moon *Blue Hwys.* 8: The man took me for a bindlestiff. **1982** D.A. Harper *Good Company* 58: We don't call nobody bindle stiffs—that's old-time talk. Bindle stiff is a guy that carries a whole bunch of little packages—gunny sacks…pots and pans, everything they need.
2. a man of little influence or ability.
1929 A.C. Doyle *Maricot* ch. iii: Look it here, you Bindlestiff. Keep your hands off my coat. **1962** Barron *Pro. Gambler* 136: *Bindle-stiff*—an amateur.

bine *n. Mil.* carbine.
1953 in Russ *Last Parallel* 67: When operating properly, the 'bine is perfect for night action, when rapid fire at short range is needed.

bing[1] *n. Med.* an injection, shot.
1918 *Stars & Stripes* (Feb. 8) 3: Bing spot. *Ibid.* (Mar. 8) 4: An antityphoid bing in your left arm. **1929** *AS* (June) 338: *Bing room*—A room wherein drug addicts meet to "cook up" their drugs. **1936** Dai *Opium Add.* 196: Bing, Bingo, Bang. A shot of drugs.
¶ In phrases:
¶ **go bing** go BLOOEY, 1.
1924 in Dos Passos *14th Chronicle* 357: If your job goes bing for any reason…walk down Florida with me.
¶ **put the bing on** *Hobo.* to beg money from.

1935 E. Anderson *Hungry Men* 21: "A good bum," Acel thought, "would approach the fellow and put the bing on him."

bing[2] *n.* [orig. unkn.] *Pris.* an isolation cell; solitary confinement.
1932 Berg *Prison Doctor* 109: They might as well throw you in the bing and lose the key! **1946** Mezzrow & Wolfe *Really Blues* 303: *Bing*: jail cell for solitary confinement. **1955** Graziano & Barber *Somebody Up There* 176: Down in the Bing, the prisoners' name for the Hole. **1967** S. Fiddle *Portraits* 199: Were you ever in the "bing" in jail? **1970** T. Seligson, in *Evergreen Rev.* (Apr.) 46: Boys sent to the bing (the solitary confinement cell). **1971** *Inter. Jour. Addictions* 6:10: All them years [in prison] I have never been in the bing,…never been in keeper lock, nothing. **1972** Burkhart *Women in Prison* 443: *Bing* solitary confinement. **1974** Piñero *Short Eyes* 104: I'm going to…slam you in the bing. **1975** *N.Y. Post* (July 22) 16: Solitary confinement, which…prisoners call "the bing."

bing *v.* to hit or punch.
1909 in P. Dickson *Baseball Dict.* 55: Bing one, Cap! **1942** *ATS* 671. **1970** in P. Heller *In This Corner* 105: Every now and then he'd bing me with that right hand.

binge *n.* [fr. dial. E *binge* 'to soak', ult. orig. unkn.] an extended period of indulgence, esp. in alcohol; a spree. Now *S.E.*
*1854 in *OEDS*: A man goes to the alehouse to get a good binge, or to binge himself. *1889 Barrère & Leland *Dict. Slang* I 118: *Binge* (Oxford), a big drinking bout. **1933** Weseen *Dict. Amer. Slang* 273: *Binge*—A spree. **1938** Bellem *Blue Murder* 82: Well, Joe didn't come home all night. He was on a binge. **1941** *AS* (Feb.) 70: On a bat, *on a binge*, on a drunk. **1948** *Neurotica* (Summer) 43: As final as the last beer on an all-night binge. **1955** L. Shapiro *Sixth of June* 134: The men…began chortling about the biggest binge in history. **1956** P. Moore *Chocolates* 71: You're on the verge of another binge, a real bender. *1958 Heuvelmans *Unknown Animals* 257: Mark Twain wrote a humorous article about [giant footprints] in which they were the result of a memorable binge. **1966** "Petronius" *N.Y. Unexp.* 15: Generally hard-core drinkers,…men and women on binges. **1970** Sugarman & Freeman *Serenity* 87: She responded to this blow to her self-esteem by going on a movie binge. **1966–80** McAleer & Dickson *Unit Pride* 153: Afterward [we'll] go on a binge. **1990** *U.S. News & W.R.* (Dec. 17) 71: For corporate managers…it signified perhaps another predatory binge that could bring new bosses, new stresses and uncertain futures.

binge *v.* to engage in a binge. Hence **binger.** Now *S.E.*
*1881 in *EDD*: A doyed a-bingein. *1910 H. Belloc, in *OEDS*: It is plainly evident that they know how to binge. **1967** *L.A. Times* (Jan. 29) West 5: The mesmerized "binger" may experience a temporary euphoria only to find himself in a worse plight upon the inevitable awakening. **1974** *Seattle Times Mag.* (Dec. 1) 10: Like the alcoholic, I binged, but on food not liquor. **1980** *Harper's* (Oct.) 91: Some writers, alas, cannot be binged on because they have written too little. **1983** *Hour Magazine* (ABC-TV) (May 5): I used to binge on sweets. **1990** *Cosmopolitan* (Apr.) 216: There are people who get depressed by dieting, which may cause them to binge and deviate from the program.

binged *adj.* drunk.—often constr. with *up.*
1916 in Hall & Niles *One Man's War* 130: Jim was "binjed up" so he wasn't altogether accountable. **1935** Pollock *Underworld Speaks*: *Binged*, apparently feeling trim on account of having imbibed a few drinks (not intoxicated). **1941** (quot. at GOOFED, 1.a.). **1942** Davis & Wolsey *Call House Madam* 20: Directors' wives and executives' sweethearts…were binged to the hairline.

bingle *n.* [poss. blend *bing* + *single*] *Baseball.* a base hit; (*specif.*) a single.
1902 *Sporting Life* (Sept. 6) 4: He is not a good ground coverer, loses bingle after bingle near second base, and is a light hitter. **1908** *Atlantic* (Aug.) 229: Sharky poked a bingle. **1910** *N.Y. Eve. Jour.* (Mar. 15) 12: New York fairly slaughtered Summers, something like thirteen or fourteen bingles, and yet lost out by ivory base running. **1914** *S.F. Call* (May 8) 9: The fans are quick to forget when the timely bingle is delivered. **1916** *Chicago Defender* (July 15) 7: "Knucks" James…[got] two bingles. **1920** [Patten] *Man on First* 15: He won that game…with a neat two-cushion bingle in the eighth. **1952** B. Malamud *Natural* 141: Here a lucky bingle, there a lucky error. **1969–71** Kahn *Boys of Summer* 38: Come on, Goody, get a hit, get a little *bingle*, next time up. **1972** *WCBS-TV News* (Sept. 15): "Why do they call it a *bingle*?" "A *bingle* is a word used to describe a base hit sometimes."

bingle *v.* **1.** *Baseball.* to hit safely; single.
1908 *Baseball Mag.* (Dec.) 35 (cited in Nichols, *Dict. Baseball Term.*).

1914 [Patten] *Lefty o' the Bush* 105: We bingled out a couple of merit marks for ourselves.

2. *USAF.* to drop (a bomb) from an aircraft, PICKLE.

1972 *N.Y. Times Mag.* (Oct. 28) 100: He could drop his ordnance within any 5-, 10- or 15-second period, and the chances were that…it wouldn't make much difference, so he just…bingled it off.

bingo[1] *n.* [orig. unkn.; cf. BIMBO[1]] any hard liquor.

*1698–99** "B.E." *Dict. Canting Crew*: Bingo, c. Brandy. *Bingo-boy*, c. a great Drinker or Lover thereof. *Bingo-club*, c. a set of Rakes, Lovers of that Liquor. *1725** *New Canting Dict.*: Bingo, Brandy or Geneva. **1750** Carew *Life* 337: Bingo-Mort, a female drunkard, a she brandy drinker. *1823** "J. Bee" *Slang Dict.*: Bingo—A dram of any sort. *1839** in *OEDS*: From morn to night we'll booze a ken, And we'll pass the bingo round. **1859** Matsell *Vocabulum* 11: Bingo. Liquor. **1872** Burnham *Secret Service* iv: Bingo, whiskey, brandy, or other strong drink. *Ibid.* Half a tumbler full of the bingo. **1966** Herbert *Fortune & Men's Eyes* 80: It was probably better than selling bingo to winehounds.

bingo[2] *n.* a hard blow. [1902 quot. is possibly syn. with—or a misprint for—BINGLE.]

1902 *Sporting News* (Nov. 15) 2: "Truck" Egan is…playing a swell short and getting his timely bingoes of yore. **1920** Ade *Hand-Made Fables* 30: Business had taken a Bingo on the head and dropped lifeless.

bingo[3] *n.* *USAF.* an empty fuel tank; the condition of having just enough fuel to return to base. Also as adj., interj.

1956 Heflin *USAF Dict.* 81: Bingo, *interj.* "Running low on fuel." Used as a radio code word among jet pilots. **1961** L.G. Richards *TAC* 63: "Bingo fuel" is the minimum pounds necessary to reach your alternate for a safe landing. Our tankers had a "bingo" too. **1962** Harvey *Strike Command* 10: "They were all down to the edge of bingo time"…"You are a few seconds from bingo." **1966** *Time* (Aug. 19) 37: When Kasler's fuel gauge hit "bingo" (minimum remaining to get home)…he elected to refuel from an orbiting KC-135 tanker and return to his downed buddy. **1969** Broughton *Thud Ridge* 78: I was bingo myself and then some, and I knew that there was no time to waste in getting us to that tanker. **1975** in Higham & Siddall *Combat Aircraft* 75: The wingman called, "Bingo fuel." **1991** L. Reinberg *In the Field*: Bingo, pilot term for out of gas or almost empty fuel tank.

bingo *v.* [fr. BINGO[3]] *USAF.* to divert (an aircraft) for refueling.

1966–67 Harvey *Air War* 5: He can bingo some of the incoming planes to nearby Danang. **1984** Trotti *Phantom* 132 [ref. to 1960's]: This…allows Pri-Fly to keep track of your fuel weight to determine whether to strike you below deck for fuel rather than chance having to bingo you back to the beach.

bingo *interj.* **1.** (used to express excitement, surprise, etc., or the sound of a blow).

*1927** in *OEDS*: I just laid my hands on him when—bingo! I was on the ground with four inches of good knife in me. **1937** in Paxton *Sport* 252: Bingo! That was what we were waiting for. **1982** *U.S. News & W.R.* (Apr. 5) 15: In 1976, the U.S. thought it had licked inflation….But by '79, bingo: Up to double digits again.

2. see BINGO[3], *n.*

bink *n.* [cf. BING[2]] *Und.* a jail.—constr. with *the*.

1943 Wendt & Kogan *Bosses* 101 [ref. to 1890's]: I didn't ever t'ink you'd do a t'ing like dat, tell on a guy what got t'rowed in th' bink. *Ibid.* 147: We'll put Billy Skakel an' his push in th' bink.

binocs *n.pl.* binoculars.

1943 Loosbrock & Skinner *Wild Blue* 210: These binocs don't help worth a damn in this light. **1978** Truscott *Dress Gray* 146: Old Hedges probably got a fix on his nuts with his binocs. **1980** S. Fuller *Big Red* 14: Looked…through the binocs. **1987** J. Thompson *Gumshoe* 295: Maybe watching through binocs.

bio *n.* a biography.

1947 (cited in *W10*). **1961** in *WNID3*. **1965** in A. Sexton *Letters* 272: Please send me a copy of the bio if you can. **1966** *Time* (Feb. 11) 55: In 1956 Hollywood slapped together a screen bio entitled *The Buster Keaton Story*. **1970** *N.Y. Times* (Mar. 22) II 24: Those bios say I was born in 1924. Well, that's wrong. **1971** W. Murray *Dream Girls* 132: Would you like to see my bio? **1983** *Newsweek on Campus* (May) 32: The editorial assistant…decided to change my bio line on that piece.

biog *n.* a biography.

1942 *ATS*: Biography: biog, close-up. **1972** R. Barrett *Lovomaniacs* 109: The guy really is a lot older than those studio biogs claim.

bip *v.* *Und.* (see quots.). Hence **bipper,** *n.*

1966 *Houston Chronicle* (July 31): Bipper or hotel bipper is a person, usually a woman, who looks for unlocked doors in a hotel, motel or apartment house….If the room is empty, she helps herself to valuables. **1962–68** in B. Jackson *In the Life* 88: Me and a friend was going to go up through Oklahoma bipping—scallybipping (burglarizing a house when they saw the wife out back hanging clothes). *Ibid.* 128: You go in there and ransack their house and get their money,…[the burglars are] known as "bippers," "scallybippers."

bipe *n.* a person who is bisexual.

1983 Univ. Tenn. instructor, age *ca*35: I'll never forget I was at a party in New Orleans in '68 or '69 and this huge guy started feeling my friend's ass. This girl said to me, "Watch out for him; he's a bipe." I said, "A bipe! What the hell is that?" She said, "A bisexual."

bippy *n.* [discussed by Peter Tamony, Sol Steinmetz, and David L. Gold in *Comments on Ety.*, Jan. 1982 *et seq.*] (used as a joc. euphem. for ASS, esp. in phr. **you bet your [sweet] bippy**). [The word and phr. were introduced and popularized by *Rowan & Martin's Laugh-In*, an NBC-TV comedy series.]

1967 *Rowan & Martin's Laugh-In* (NBC-TV) (Jan.): You bet your sweet bippy! **1969** in Bouton *Ball Four* 105: A lot of guys would have told the trainer to shove the tea up his bippy. **1970** *Playboy* (Feb.) 38: You can bet your sweet bippy he's not going to appreciate your telling him. **1976** *Atlantic* (Mar.) 103: Surprised, guys?—you can bet your bippy I was! **1983** *Happy Days* (ABC-TV): You bet your bippy! **1990** *Current Affair* (synd. TV series): Uh-huh. You bet your bippy.

bird *n.* **I.** Senses referring especially to people.

1.a. a remarkable person or thing; HUMDINGER.—often used ironically, occ. *attrib.*

1839 *Spirit of Times* (Dec. 21) 498: If you jist could see one man what the Gineral Government sent out with an office to these parts,—he is a bird! **1840** *Spirit of Times* (June 27) 199: Kendall [a racehorse] has made a good beginning, and *Sufferer* may yet prove a "*bird.*" **1846** Neal *Ploddy* 138: Had Hammer lived in earlier times, he would have been the very flower of chivalry—at present he only rejoices in the distinction of being a "bird." **1849** in *DA*: Mr. E.P.S. was the next witness called, a perfect "bird" in his way, and who can't be beat. **1856** in Thornton *Amer. Gloss.* I 64: A sleigh, drawn by a "perfect bird" of a three-mile bay mare. **1856** in *Ibid.*: Isn't Mrs. Partington a "perfect bird"? **1889** "M. Twain" *Conn. Yankee* ch. vii: Raphael was a bird. We had several of his chromos. **1890** Quinn *Fools of Fortune* 394: The [gambling] place was expensively furnished, and was conducted on a scale of prodigal extravagance. The "sporting" fraternity knew it as a "bird house." **1896** Ade *Artie* 56: That wedding was a bird. **1899** Ade *Fables* 84: She's a Bird. Do you know her well? **1899** Norris *McTeague* 44: That's the dog….Ain't he a bird? Say, ain't he a bird? **1902** Townsend *Fadden & Mr. Paul* 4: "And besides," says she, "it is bourgeoisie"—dat's a boid of a woid; get it spelt right. **1904** in Opper *H. Hooligan* 51: England is a boid of a country. **1904** Hobart *Jim Hickey* 11: Isn't this a bird of a place for a show to get stranded? **1909** in McCay *Little Nemo* 164: Isn't that [pitch] a bird? *a*1904–11 Phillips *Susan Lenox* II 313: She was a bird—she was. She handed me a line of grand talk. **1922** E. Paul *Impromptu* 10: Them Egyptian undertakers were birds….Some of the stiffs keep a couple of thousand years. **1922** C. Sandburg *Letters* 213: That was a bird of a letter you sent on six weeks ago. **1928** C. McKay *Harlem* 7: But the best of all was the boid uvva time I had in San Francisco. **1938** Wolfe *Web & Rock* 168: Damned if you ain't a bird! **1970** Cortina *Slain Warrior* 9: He really was a bird. He was a rich kid. **1971** *Blushes & Bellylaffs* 29: Boy! that must be a bird! **1972** Sherburne *Ft. Pillow* 192: Yes, he's a bird, all right.

b. *Specif.*, a dissolute or profligate person; HIGHFLYER.

1852 in Thornton *Amer. Gloss.* I 63: The same reason…kept Mr. Simpson, and other "birds" of his set, out of the exclusive society. **1853** in Thornton *Amer. Gloss.* 64: The *Perfect Bird* has no wings, yet he is considered "fly" upon all sporting matters. The *Perfect Bird* carries a brick in his hat, and a stone in his boot. In the language of his class, the *Perfect Bird* generally turns out to be a bad egg. **1867** in *Iowa Journ. of Hist.* LVII (1959) 219: The *Transcript* says they are to have an aviary full of wild birds. Our city has a knave-iary full of wild "birds" already. **1887** in *DAE*: There are men in every college, of whom Yale has its full number, denominated in student slang as "birds." The "birds" are firm believers in the old Epicurean theory that everything in life is subservient to pleasure.

c. *Stu.* ODDBALL.

1920 Fitzgerald *Paradise* 56: If only that St. Paul's crowd at the next table would not mistake *him* for a bird, too. **1958** J. Davis *College Vocab.* 6: Bird—A nervous-type, odd, undesirable person. **1961** Terry *Old Lib-*

erty 24: Michael Spicer…was a real bird, even if he was Bo's cousin. *Ibid.* 69: Spooks and birds…participated in the Spring Retreat, even if they hadn't seen a girl all year.

2. a young woman. Occ. **birdie.** Hence **bird-watcher, -watching.** [A development independent of ME *bird, burd,* etc.]

1838 Glascock *Land Sharks* I 22: Waddy waited until the widow with the wherewithal had taken her seat; when, to further his purpose, he instantly, as sailors say, "brought his person to an anchor abreast of his bird." **1848 [Judson] *Mysteries* 45: Sixteen, pure, *green,* he means. I must see the bird. *Ibid.* 357: What bird do you mean? Not Charley's sister? **1886** Harbaugh *Coldgrip in N.Y.* 5: Have you got the bird, Foxy?…Blindfold her and fetch her up. **1894** in *Amer. Heritage* (Oct. 1960) 110: Mr. Willie Rawlings Does Chicago With a Couple of Gay Birds. **1900** *DN* II 23: *Bird, n.* A girl [at Yale, Vassar, and several other colleges]. *a*1904–11 Phillips *Susan Lenox* I 395: Don't look so scared, birdies. **1915 in *OEDS:* There's another bird there—and cawfee. **1922** *Bomb* (Iowa State College) 395: If you are game, you must look up the Tri Delta poultry farm. They have a wonderful collection of birds, guaranteed to be young, unsophisticated, and uppish. **1925 Fraser & Gibbons *Soldier & Sailor Wds.* 23 [ref. to WWI]: *Bird:* Sweetheart. Any girl; *e.g.,* to walk out with a Bird. **1926** Wood & Goddard *Amer. Slang* 6: *Bird.* A young girl. **1934** Benchley *Chips* 175: I have always been interested in birds, but never can seem to get them interested in me. Most of my friends are men. **1962** Carr & Cassavetes *Too Late Blues* (film): Who's the bird? **1967** Gonzales *Paid My Dues* 120: Jim enjoyed these young birds but…he wasn't about to get married. **1970** *Playboy* (Sept.) 56: Booze and birds are the chosen weapons against the all-too-familiar boredom of Army life. **1972** *Penthouse* (Aug.) 116: Bird-watching…not the only summer activity. Summer brings out the best in man, beast and bird-watchers…whether the birds be of the feathered or the bikinied variety. **1984** McNamara *First Directive* 171: Some of these corporations deal in birds [prostitutes] by the dozen.

3. an individual; fellow; person; (*occ.,* as in 1975 quot.) an object. [Perh. sugg. by S.E. prov. quoted by Marryat and Stowe, 1829 and 1852.]

[**1829 Marryat *F. Mildmay* 193: I am too old a bird to be caught with such chaff.] **1843** [W.T. Thompson] *Scenes in Ga.* 81: A pretty pair of birds, really,…to circumlocutin' about the country in this way. [**1852** Stowe *Uncle Tom's Cabin* 38: Haley, notwithstanding that he was a very old bird, and naturally inclined to be suspicious of chaff, was rather brought up by this view of the case.] **1853 in *OEDS:* I suppose the old bird was your governor. **1855** Brougham *Chips* 314: When the pop'lar voice calls a man—as it wulgarly does at times—"a bird," they haint so far wrong. **1862** O.W. Holmes, Jr., in M.D. Howe *Shaping Years* 122: I was told by cheerful birds like Tremlett & Co. that we *must* surrender or be cut to pieces in 36 hours. **1863** in J.W. Haley *Rebel Yell* 74: A braver or better looking officer it has not been our pleasure to look upon. He is a gamey looking bird. **1870** in Hay *Lincoln* 318: My Dear Jim—Take care of him. He is a brick. Yrs. muchly, Tom. **1872** Burnham *Secret Service* 81: He's too chary a bird for that! **1877** *Puck* 1 (Mar.) 13: You may…be as knowin' as the old bird that laid the Atlantic cable. **1882** "M. Twain" *Life on Miss.* 127: You've had no *orders!* My, what a fine bird we are! We must have orders! **1891** Maitland *Slang Dict.* 136: A "cool hand," a person with plenty of assurance. Sometimes a "cool bird." **1895** *Harper's* (Nov.) 846: I'll tell you about Congress.…You can divide them birds in two lots. Those who know better and those who don't. **1896** Crane *George's Mother* 139: Say, me frien', where d' d' Johnson birds live in heh? **1896** Brown *Parson* 125: The Texas bird was very fond of a good horse. **1899** Norris *McTeague* 19: Ain't she a queer bird? **1899** Thomas *Arizona* 82: That last batch of recruits had one or two gay birds in 'em. **1910** T.A. Dorgan, in *N.Y. Eve. Jour.* (Apr. 21) 19: Jack is the bird with the striped sweater. **1911** Van Loan *Big League* 36: If this bird hits anything on me…it'll be a curve. **1911** T.A. Dorgan, in *N.Y. Eve. Jour.* (Jan. 3) 14: That bird doesn't belong in the prize ring. **1919** Sandburg *Race Riot* 3: Does it seem to you that you get more tough birds from out around the stockyards than anywhere else in Chicago? **1920** E. O'Neill *Diff'rent* 230: You forgot I was in France—and after the dames over there these birds here look some punk. **1926** [Wright] *Benson Case* 327: I know that bird. **1932** Binyon & Binyon *If I Had a Million* (film): I thought you birds was writin' and dressin'. **1965** Elder *Dark Old Men* 117: The trouble with this bird is that he…became a thinker. **1970** Boatright & Owens *Derrick* 97: As near as I can tell, them's the birds. **1972** Pearce *Pierhead Jump* 13: He's a regular Kildare, this bird. **1975** Univ. Tenn. student: I've done some long papers. I've done some *long* birds.

4. *Slave Trade.* a black slave; BLACKBIRD, 1.

1887 Davis *Sea-Wanderer* 179 [ref. to 1836]: We soon negotiated for about 1,100 "birds" (black birds) of whom two-thirds were stout adults, the remainder consisting of women and full-grown boys.

II. Senses referring to physical representations of birds or to the ability of flight.

5. [cf. YELLOW BIRD] a gold dollar.

1857 in *DA:* Bill…put in her…hand the "bird" he had received from Morley. **1891** King *By Land & Sea* 123: Tell him it's two eagles a quart, a bird an' a bit a pint, an' six-bits a half-pint.

6.a. *Navy.* the eagle insignia denoting the rank of petty officer.

1905 *Bluejacket* (Feb.) 157: You come along with a stripe and a "bird." **1918** (quot. at CROW). **1928** *AS* III 452: *Bird, buzzard*—Gold eagle insignia, denoting rank of Midshipman Petty Officers.

b. *Mil.* BIRD COLONEL; (*hence*) promotion to the rank of colonel.—often in phr. of the sort **make bird.**

1959 Searls *Big X* 186: I'm just a light colonel, but I'd like to make bird some day. **1962** Tregaskis *Vietnam Diary* 52: He'd been selected for bird (full) colonel. Next day he was shot down. So we made a bird, lost a bird, in 24 hours. **1970** *Atlantic* (Oct.) 93: And checking over the career to see what it was that had gotten bird for him. **1973** *Harper's* (Apr.) 43: Officers were required to put in an average of only 4.2 months, just long enough to have combat command on their records and win their birds. **1984** Riggan *Free Fire* 109 [ref. to Vietnam War]: All the birds and generals and secret service men in the President's entourage. **1985** Heywood *Taxi Dancer* 241 [ref. to Vietnam War]: You've got a good shot at your full bird this time. **1984–88** Hackworth & Sherman *About Face* 757: I was glad I was going to make bird.

7. any artificial object that travels through the air or space. *Specif.:*

a. *Mil.* an artillery shell in flight.

1910 Stirling *In Philippines* 13 [ref. to 1900]: A few brace of hot ten-inch birds, exploding near them from our coffee kettle of a monitor soon made 'em change their minds. **1918** in Gow *Soldier Letters* 326: A point where a "Jack Johnson" or some similar bird might land at any minute.

b. *Mil. & Av.* an airplane.

1918 Roberts *Flying Ftr.* 339: *Wassin Bird.* A French flying machine of the Voisin type. **1918** in Clark *Soldier Letters* 155: The watch sighted a "bird." We were told to sit down, and keep quiet. **1918** [Penner] *120th F.A.* 272: Echelon at Berry much excited by presence of Boche birds over-head. **1918–19** MacArthur *Bug's-Eye View* 28: This bird had been shot down five minutes earlier and…there was a dead man in the cockpit. **1919** Kelly *What Outfit?* 124: Where the hell is the American birds? **1920** Bingham *Explorer* 134: It was not uncommon for several of these queer-looking birds to be flat on their backs at the same time. **1938** *Test Pilot* (film): It's a shame to bust up a pretty bird like this. **1944** Ind *Bataan* 154: They put several holes here and there in the old bird. **1944** Stiles *Big Bird* 10: I overcontrolled the throttles…trying to fly that big bird close. **1953** in Loosbrock & Skinner *Wild Blue* 456: The speed hits 120, and the bird lifts off. **1958** Mayes *Hunters* (film): The rest of our birds came back on a wing and a curse. **1959** *Sat. Eve. Post* (May 2) 67: They tell me the C-133 is a miraculous bird. **1961** Plantz *Sweeney Sq.* 185: You'd better protect your birds. Have fun, flyboys. **1978** B. Johnson *What's Happenin'?* 19: So Hop and I got on the bird and came to Seattle.

c. Esp. *USAF.* a guided missile.

1948 *Ga. Review* II 205: Guided missiles.…These birds had their flaws—the main one being the difficulty of predicting the point of impact. **1951** *Time* (May 21) 34: These "birds" (so the missilemen call them) are the heirs presumptive of war. **1957** *Time* (Apr. 1) 16: Soon more than 300 scientists, engineers and technicians were primping and pampering "the Bird." **1958** in Harvey *Air Force* 118: The three-stage bird began to rise slowly. **1959** P. Frank *Babylon* 70: An ensign from *Saratoga*…sighted the bogy and…fired a bird. **1959** Scott *Tiger in Sky* 125: It was obviously of a class called "guided missiles."…They have lived with this "bird" for almost a year. **1959** W. Heflin *Aerospace Gloss.: Bird, n.*….This term, used as early as 1918 in reference to the Liberty Eagle (experimental pilotless biplane), is common among technicians who handle missiles. **1962** [Astronauts] *We Seven* 88: The Redstone was already a well-proven bird when it was first considered for use in Project Mercury. **1962** *Newsweek* (Nov. 5) 29: Large tank trailers carry fuel for the Soviet "birds." **1963** in S. Lee *Son of Origins* 31: There can be only *one* explanation—the bird was tampered with! **1964** *USS Long Beach* 23: This "bird" is fired aloft by the largest piece of ordnance handling equipment in the Navy. **1983** *Time* (Feb. 21) 18: The MX missile, the intercontinental bird that only its parent Air Force seems truly to love. *a***1984** T. Clancy *Red Oct.* 87: He could fire his birds in both directions and start World War III.

d. *Aerospace.* an artificial satellite or space probe.

1955 Reifer *New Words* 30: Bird…a proposed earth satellite. **1959** W. Heflin *Aerospace Gloss.*: *Bird, n.*…a missile, earth satellite, or other inanimate object that flies. **1981** *Christianity Today* (Nov. 6) 84: NCN president Ray Kassis said his company hoped to invade space on Satcom III, a descendant of the first "bird" (industry insiders' name for the satellites). **1983** *Good Morning America* (ABC-TV) (June 2): The Western weather satellite—the brand-new bird, taxpayers, is sending back pictures for you. **1989** *CBS This Morning* (CBS-TV) (July 6): We lost our bird….We had trouble talking to Paris this morning.

e. [cf. WHIRLY-BIRD] Esp. *Army.* a helicopter.

1962 Tregaskis *Vietnam Diary* 21: I had a flight of three birds. **1962** *Nat. Geo.* (Nov.) 732: All but two of the birds…were off on a sweep. **1964** Hunt *Flat Tire* 157: Call me a helicopter. Flash my ship and get me a bird at once. **1964** J. Lucas *Dateline* 31: There's something about riding one of those old birds into Viet Cong country that borders on the nonsensical. **1972** Pelfrey *Big V* 49: The chow bird came in half an hour after our return. **1973** Herbert & Wooten *Soldier* 274: Take them back to the LZ and get them on the first birds along with the wounded. **1982** Del Vecchio *13th Valley* 43: You and I are going to catch a bird to Evans. **1984** J.R. Reeves *Mekong* 165: I thought I was going to have to deck him before we could get him on the bird.

8. *pl.* (*cap.*) *Baseball.* the Baltimore Orioles baseball team.

1983 WINS radio news (Sept. 1): The Birds' win streak was ended at eight.

III. Other senses.

9. disapproval or derision; *specif.*:

a. Orig. *Theat.* the booing or hissing of a player or performance.—usu. constr. with *the*. [Now often indistinguishable from (**b**) and (**c**), below.]

*****1825** in *OEDS*: And the end of their folly marked by the attacks of the big birds (*geese*) driving them off the stage. *****1864** Hotten *Slang Dict.* s.v. *big*: *Big-Bird, to get the, i.e.,* to be hissed, as actors occasionally are by the "gods." *Big-bird* is simply a metaphor for goose.—*Theat. Slang.* *****1884** in Ware *Passing English*: Professor Grant, Q.C., had both the "bird" and the "needle" at the Royal on Monday. *****1886** in *F & H* I (rev.) 214: *To be goosed,* or as it is sometimes phrased, to *get the big bird*, is occasionally a compliment to the actor's power of representing villainy, but more often is disagreeably suggestive of a failure to please. *****1889** Barrère & Leland *Dict. Slang* 112: *Big-bird* (theatrical), "to get the big bird," to be hissed. The *bird* is supposed to be, and is very often, a goose. *****1895** in *OEDS*: Three or four of the most prominent artistes…have been…threatened with…the "bird," that is, hissing. **1923** *N.Y. Times* (Oct. 7) VIII 4: *Getting the Bird*—Having dislike made audible in various forms by the audience. **1939–40** Tunis *Kid from Tomkinsville* 239: Just hear those Dodger fans…giving him the bird.

b. BRONX CHEER.—constr. with *the*.

1921 E. O'Neill *Hairy Ape* 241: Democracy, hell! Give him the boid, fellers—the raspberry! (*They do.*). **1923** *N.Y. Times* (Sept. 9) VIII 2: *Get the bird* = same as get the raspberry. **1926** Donahue *What Price Glory?* (film): Find out who's givin' me th' bird and I'll slip you twenty bucks. **1930** *AS* (Feb.) 238: *Bird:* A noise made with the lips to indicate dissatisfaction with something. "The students gave that speaker the bird." **1930** Benchley *Chips* 24: One rubber mouth appliance, for making the sound commonly known as "the bird." **1932** Berg *Prison Doctor* 134: That goddam spade just floated by and gave me the bird. **1943** *Looney Tunes* (animated cartoon): "Give me the bird! Give me the bird!" "If the Hayes office would only let me, I'd give him the bird!" **1955** Reifer *New Words* 30: *Bird*…A jeering sound expressing disapproval.

c. ridicule, mockery, or rejection in any form.

*****1925** Fraser & Gibbons *Soldier & Sailor Wds.* 23 [ref. to WWI]: *Bird, To Get The:* To fail in a request. To be "shut up"; *e.g.*, I went and asked for leave, and got the bird properly. **1926** Maines & Grant *Wise-Crack Dict.* 15: The *bird*—ridicule in English. **1927** H. Liggett *A.E.F.* 19: In the language of the A.E.F., he was giving the enemy "the birdy." **1928** MacArthur *War Bugs* 235: Behind us boomed the guns, giving Mr. Smith the bird (as the English have it). **1929** Perelman *Ginsbergh* 121: Their neighbors gave them the bird and called them tight. **1929** in E. Wilson *Twenties* 514: *Slang*…to give'm th' bird. **1934** Wohlforth *Tin Soldiers* 223: She's just trying to give Emil the bird. **1937** Lay *I Wanted Wings* 114: Getting left twenty feet behind on the take-off was a certain method of getting the "bird" from the rest of the boys. **1961** R. Russell *Sound* 119: It was Red's way of giving them the bird. **1968** Smart *Long*

Watch 21: Them titties…was all rubber! He didn't have no more titties than you or me. Boy, did we give *him* the bird! **1990** *Capital Gang* (CNN-TV) (Mar. 31): [He's] getting his kicks…giving Gorbachev the bird.

d. the FINGER, 4.

1966 F.C. Elkins *Heart of Man* 17: The Russian tail-gunner…[gave] one of our F-8 pilots the international one-finger salute, the bird. **1968** Baker et al. *CUSS* 80: *Chuck a bird…flash the bird…flick the bird…flip a bird…fly a bird…give the bird* To gesture with the middle finger….[Also] *pop the bird…shoot a bird…shoot the bird…throw the bird.* **1970** *N.Y. Times Mag.* (Nov. 22) 113: Then this guy [*sc.* a Russian bomber pilot] wanted a shot of my underside—the missiles and stuff….I shook my head and didn't move….Then he shot me a bird—flipped me the old one-fingered international salute. He was annoyed. **1971** Dahlskog *Dict.* 24: *Flash* (*flip*) (*fly*) *the bird*, to give the finger to someone. **1971** Vaughan & Lynch *Brandywine* 60: A fist with the middle finger raised in the traditional "bird" salute. **1973** Lucas, Katz & Huyck *Amer. Graffiti* 34: They flip him the bird, and he lets them pass. **1974** Huggett *Body Count* 213: "Fuck you" was yelled in clear English. Another one shot the truck a bird. **1978** in Lyle & Golenbock *Bronx Zoo* 100: I gave him the double bird. Both middle fingers. *Ibid.* 101: She'll never forget seeing her son flipping the bird in front of 40,000 people. **1980** Luceno *Head Hunters* 5: She caught his…grimace…in the rearview and gave him a thirty-second bird out the open top before…turning at the Collins' intersection. **1983** Univ. Tenn., prof., age 47: When I was growing up in Dallas, I am almost certain, the *bird* referred to this [finger] gesture and nothing else. Maybe they just had more gestures up north to choose from! **1980–89** Cheshire *Home Boy* 40: I'd just fired the bird at this kid.

10.a. the penis. Also **birdie.** In phrs. **jerk** [or **beat**] **(one's) bird** to masturbate, (*hence*) to pull (one's) leg or cater to; **get (one's) bird in a splint** to get into a predicament.

*****1902** *F & H* V 288: Penis…*bird.* **1927** *Immortalia* 95: He painted the tip of his birdie's head. **1938** "Justinian" *Americana Sexualis* 38: *Swallow The Bird.* phr. See Cocksucker. **1964** in Gover *Trilogy* 271: Sticks his…bird back in his pants. **1964** Hill *Casualties* 227: Maybe *you* got our bird in a splint, you dumbskull. **1966** E. Kazan *Arrangement* 26: All the Bird knows is I WANT! **1968** J.P. Miller *Race for Home* 156 [ref. to 1930's]: Bet that boy don't beat his bird like all them other no-'count boys I know. **1970** Sorrentino *Steelwork* 141: Hear ya been in Hollywood, Cooky. Gotta eat the bird up there to get up high out there, right? **1976** Price *Bloodbrothers* 46: He hangs aroun' gettin' laid an' jerkin' his bird. *Ibid.* So he jerks his old man's bird for a few weeks, then he does what he wants. **1976** Selby *Demon* 44: She started to gobble his bird. **1978** in *Maledicta* VI (1982) 23: Penis…*birdie.* **1989** R. Miller *Profane Men* 117: That old throbbing in my bird whenever I think about you.

b. the vulva or vagina.

1960 Barber *Minsky's* 200: That phony LoLo coming out for a curtain call and doing a back bend instead of a bow and opening up her grass skirt and showing them a big red rose in her bird. **1964** Rhodes *Chosen Few* 49: You din' git that bird? *Ibid.* 159: Sounds like she didn't give you that bird yet. **1969** K. Tynan *Oh! Calcutta!* 124: There's a girl with a two-toned bird! **1972** *Anthro. Linguistics* (Mar.) 99: *Bird* (n.): The penis or vulva. *Bird washing* (n.): Mutual cunnilingus. **1975** Wambaugh *Choirboys* 319: I kneel there and look right at her bird and up it goes.

c. ASS; in phr. **not on your bird!** "no indeed!" *Joc.*

1966 Allen *Tiger Lily* (film): Never! Not on your bird! **1968** Cameron *Warriors* 18: You bet your bird I gottem. **1972** N.Y.U. student: In case of nuclear attack, place your head between your legs and kiss your bird goodbye. **1980** Kawasaki snowmobile ad, WINS radio (Sept. 12): [Old Man Winter says] I'll freeze your bird! **1987** Bombeck *Family* 149: "Is this an ultimatum?" "You bet your sweet bird it is!"

d. in phr. **how's your bird?** "how are you?" *Joc.*

1964 N.Y.C. high school student, age 16: Hey man, how's your bird? **1972** *Rowan & Martin's Laugh-In* (NBC-TV): How's your bird, baby? **1978** *West. Folklore* XXXVII 99: "Bird" also means a phallus (as in the popular catchphrase, "How's your bird?").

11. BIRDMAN. Also **birdie.**

1918 Roberts *Flying Ftr.* [opp. 328]: A pair of Birds, Author and Machine. **1918** *N.Y. Eve. Jour.* (Aug. 21) 13: Ty Cobb has also announced his intention of becoming a navy "bird." **1919** Janis *Big Show* 64: We went over to the 94th Squadron Headquarters and met all our American "birds." **1947** Harrison *Red Cross* [ref. to WWI]: The officers and men of a combat division had a pet abomination, the aviators, whom in picturesque slang they dubbed "fur-lined birds"; their great coats with heavy fur collars suggested the quip. The "birds" were a pampered class. **1981** C. Nelson *Picked Bullets Up* 29 [ref. to 1966]: A grunt is a marine, as a soldier is a doggie, an airman a birdie, and a sailor a squid.

12. *Industry.* an unwanted or unexplained squeaking noise made by machinery. Also **birdie**.

1962 E.M. Miller *Exile to Stars* 257: The car needed a grease job; something squeaked. He had a "bird" up in front somewhere. **1972** Ponicsan *Cinderella Liberty* 100: A used Rambler, which had a number of birdies in it we were all used to. **1982** T.D. Connors *Dict. Mass Media* 28.

13. *(cap.)* a Ford Thunderbird automobile; Thunderbird brand wine.

1961 J. Flynn *Action Man* 45: The Merc sedan, two down from your Bird. **1964–67** Speicher *Baby Paradise* 130: Bromley's bird?…He drives it around with a sign says it's our prize. **1970–71** Higgins *Coyle* 84: The Kraut spotted Danny Theos the other day in a big maroon Bird. **1975** Dill *CB Slanguage* (1976 ed.) 17: *Bird*: Ford Thunderbird.

14. *Golf.* a birdie.

1976 in *Webster's Sports Dict.* **1983** *N.Y. Post* (Sept. 5) 39: Morgan…combined seven birds with three bogeys for a closing 67–272. **1984** *N.Y. Post* (Sept. 3) 34: Clutch birds lift Levi in B.C. open.

¶ In phrases:

¶ **dirty bird** a dirty or underhanded individual. Hence **I'll be a dirty bird!** (used as an exclam. of surprise). *Joc.* [Popularized in 1954 by comedian George Gobel; the television show on which it first appeared debuted on Oct. 2 of that year.]

1954 *TV Guide* (Dec. 4) 6: The public…paid [George Gobel] the final accolade of writing one of his *bon mots* into the language. "I'll be," everybody is now telling everybody else, "a dirty bird." **1958** N.Y.C. grade school pupil: Well, I'll be a dirty bird! **1972** M. Rodgers *Freaky Fri.* 39: "I'd guess you have a rawndyvooo with a secret lover, right?" she said.…The dirty bird! **1973** Lucas, Katz & Huyck *Amer. Graffiti* 52: I was a dirty bird. Carol's not grungy.

¶ **for the birds** to be regarded with contempt or scorn; not to be taken seriously; no good. Also *(vulgar)* **shit for the birds.**

1944 Olds *Helldiver Squadron* 98: That's something strictly for the birds. **1944** in *AS* XX 148: *That's For The Birds.* It's meaningless.…*Shit For The Birds.* Nonsense, drivel, irrelevant matter. **1945** in Shibutani *Co. K* 350: Boy, if that ain't shit for the birds. **1948** J.H. Burns *Lucifer* 362: Saluting and parading.…Shit for the birds. **1951** Salinger *Catcher in Rye* ch. i: Strictly for the birds. **1953** Peterson *Giant Step* 63: This kid stuff is for the birds. **1956** Chamales *Never So Few* 380: That's real shit for the birds how we're going to punish them guys when it's over. **1957** *AS* XXXII 240: In 1942, when I entered the U.S. Army, the disparaging term *that's for the birds* was in common use among officers and enlisted men.…The metaphor alludes to birds eating droppings from horses and cattle. **1957** S. Harris & J. Murtagh *First Stone* 30: Bertha said kissing and holding hands was a big deal for the birds, not for her. **1958** Feiffer *Sick Sick Sick* (unp.): This party is for the birds. Let's cut out. **1960** Kirkwood *Pony* 159: An actor's life is for the birds. **1961** Peacock *Valhalla* 181: This peacetime is for the goonie birds. **1968** Smart *Long Watch* 98: God damn it, this transfer of four key men is a crock of shit for the birds. **1969** Bullock *Watts* 60: Most people view the community as a "drag" and that all the publicity given Watts is "for the birds." **1970** Grissim *Country Music* 161: Now ah don't drink. To me drinkin' is for the birds. **1971** Faust *Willy Remembers* 100: Now that was shit for the birds and no kid of mine was going to sit there and take it. **1980** Peck & Young *Little Darlings* (film): This nature stuff's for the birds though, man. **1992** *All Things Considered* (Nat. Pub. Radio) (Oct. 5): This idea that everyone can go to college and pay for it by public service is for the birds.

¶ **have a bird** to have a fit of temper.

1981–85 S. King *It* 11: Put all this stuff back, too. Or Mom'll have a b-bird.

¶ **hear the birdies sing** *Boxing.* to be knocked unconscious; to be unconscious. Also vars.

1922 Tully *Emmett Lawler* 286: "He's got a jaw like concrete.…" "But you made him listen to birds singin' once, Emmett." **1942** *ATS* 674: Be knocked out…hear the birdies. **1944** *Collier's* (Sept. 16) 64: Mac…heard the birdies sing.

¶ **join the birds** [or **bird gang**], **1.** Esp. *R.R.* to leap to safety, as from a moving train.

1916 *Editor* (Mar. 25) 343: *Join the bird gang*—jump from a moving train when it is in danger of leaving the track or other danger. **1929**

Bookman (July) 525: The tallow-pot sees what's comin' and joins the birds. **1930** in Botkin & Harlow *R.R. Folklore* 325: I started to join the bird gang, and he grabbed me by the arm. **1958** McCulloch *Woods Wds.* 99: *Join the birds*—To unload or jump off in great haste from any moving equipment in danger of accident. **1975** *Railroad* (Mar.) 43: He'd joined the birds just prior to the collision and his resultant injuries still pained him.

2. *West.* to jump or be thrown from a bucking horse.

1930 Sage *Last Rustler* 162: The old horse…sunfished in the air and Whisky Tom joined the birds.

3. to run away or desert.

*a***1969** J. Kimbrough *Defender of Angels* 62 [ref. to 1920's]: For a time I thought Papasita would join the bird gang and take to flying high. **1969** Bosworth *Love Affair* 80: An officer's log said, "Dubose has, I believe, made his Entire Elopement." Or, as the Navy used to say later, Dubose had "joined the birds."

¶ **like a big-assed bird** see s.v. BIG-ASS, *adj.*

¶ **make (one's) bird** *Mil.* to run away; escape.

1978 J. Webb *Fields of Fire* 152: Knock on the door and hide. If somebody answers wait until the door is shut and make your bird.…If a neighbor comes to a window, wait until they go away, then make your bird. **1983** Eilert *Self & Country* 221 [ref. to 1968]: We got hit with rockets. Everyone made their bird. While I was running I fell in a mantrap. **1985** Dye *Between Raindrops* 299 [ref. to Vietnam War]: Thought you'd be dead by now. Or at least made your bird back to the Press Center. **1985** Petit *Peacekeepers* 141: The jeeps raced back to the C.P.…"The Generals made their bird," Cav announced.

¶ **out of (one's) bird** insane. Also **lose (one's) bird** to go insane.

1970 *N.Y.U* student, age 20: I think this guy is out of his bird, that's what. **1971** *Jean Shepherd's America* (WGBH-TV) (Apr. 18): I was happy. I'm tellin' you, I was out of my bird. **1972** *Playboy* (Apr.) 80: Totally freaked out of his bird. **1972** TV commercial (Nov. 1): Have you lost your *bird?* **1973** Schiano & Burton *Solo* 84: When I get back to Clancy at the precinct, he's out of his bird. **1973** Chandler *Hollister* 140: I ordered you when I was out of my bird? **1982** in M.M. Hunt *Story of Psych.* 628: Anybody who tells you that jury research is designed to pick a fair jury is out of his bird.

¶ **to throw at the birds** in excess; in great amounts.

1878 Hart *Sazerac* 181: Why, consarn it, I've got appertite to throw at the birds. **1896** Ade *Artie* 20: I could tell from the dress and the talk and all that she'd never had any diamonds to throw at the birds. **1899** Ade *Fables* 70: These superficial Johnnies who played golf all the Time had Money to Throw at the birds.

bird *v.* ¶ In phrase: **not just a-birding** [euphem. for BIRD TURD] not just talking nonsense.

1947 *ATS* (Supp.) 5. **1948** A. Murphy *Hell & Back* 204 [ref. to WWII]: And you ain't just a-birdin', son. **1953** Felsen *Street Rod* 82: You're not just a-birding, Dad. **1965** W. Hoffman *Yancey's War* 21: "They deserve recognition." "You ain't birding."

birdbath *n.* **1.** *Navy.* a maintop. Now *hist.*

1982 T.C. Mason *Battleship* 171 [ref. to 1941]: I raced…up a series of steep ladders inside the cage mast to the exposed "bird bath" at the very top.

2. *Mil.* a facility for the spray-washing of vehicles.

1980 D. Cragg (letter to J.E.L., Aug. 10): If anyone wants me, I'll be down at the birdbath. **1990** in *Texas Mo.* (Jan. 1991) 94: In the "birdbath"…National Guard troops…wash dozens of personnel carriers with high-pressure water cannons.

bird boat *n. Navy.* **1.** [cf. BIRD FARM] (see quot.).

1944 Kendall *Service Slang* 20: *Bird boat*…. aircraft carrier.

2. (see quot.).

1969 Bosworth *Love Affair* 110: Minecraft and [other navy ships] named after birds, are popularly called the "bird boats," although they are ships with names of their own.

birdboy *n.* BIRDMAN.

1942 Sanders & Blackwell *Forces* 40: Bird-Boy:…An aviator. **1952** Sperling & Sherdeman *Retreat, Hell!* (film): Wow, here come our bird-boys!

birdbrain *n.* a person of small intelligence; scatterbrain. Hence **birdbrained**, *adj.*

[***1785** Grose *Vulgar Tongue*: Bird witted, inconsiderate, thoughtless, easily imposed on.] **1933** A. Woollcott, in Wallgren *AEF Cartoons* ii: When Bruce Bairnsfather started drawing his famous Old Bill sketches for the London weeklies, some bird-brain in the House of Commons got up and demanded that he be disciplined for insulting the heroes of the nation by his grotesque drawings. **1941** Boardman, Perrin & Grant *Keep 'Em Flying* (film): Listen, you bird-brained baboon—. **1943** Perrin & Mahoney *Whistling in Brooklyn* (film): Beat it, birdbrain! **1948** A. Murphy *Hell & Back* 74: The bird-brain owes me ten bucks. **1950** *Life* (Aug. 14) 65: A bosomy bird-brain whose lunatic laugh and immense goodwill are somehow never adequate to keep herself and her associates out of a world of trouble. **1960** Leckie *Marines* 32: Hey, birdbrain.... Ain't you got no better sense'n to wash downstream? **1967** *Love on a Rooftop* (ABC-TV): My daughter has been living with that bird-brained Bluebeard for eight months! **1992** *Crier & Co.* (CNN-TV) (May 18): Only a birdbrain would protect an owl at the expense of loggers' jobs.

birdcage *n.* **1.a.** a prison or prison cell.
1891 Maitland *Amer. Slang Dict.* 56: *Cage*, a prison. Often *bird-cage*. **1934** *Jour. Abn. & Soc. Psych.* 360: As soon as I got out of the bird cage (cell) this morning, I went to the mess hall. **1941** Macaulay & Wald *Manpower* (film): After a year in that birdcage I don't feel like wisecracking about it. **1954** Chessman *Cell 2455* 7: In this way...they walk Henry to the bird cage. **1959** Duffy & Lane *Warden's Wife* 92: The "birdcages" were enclosed within walls instead of opening out onto...porches.

b. a sleeping space in a flophouse that is separated by chicken wire from adjoining spaces.
1949 *Collier's* (Aug. 27) 60: "Bird cages" are six feet by four feet and contain a bed and a locker. **1967** Maurer & Vogel *Narc. & Narc. Add.* (ed. 3) 342: A *bird cage joint* or flophouse where the cots are separated by chicken wire.

2. *Stu.* (see quot.).
1900 *DN* II 23: *Bird-cage, n* Dormitory for women students.

3. *Sports.* any of various types of face masks.
1906 (cited in P. Dickson *Baseball Dict.* 55). **1942** *ATS* 649: Catcher's mask. *Bird-cage.* **1976** *Webster's Sports Dict.* 42.

4. (see quot.).
1929 Gill *Und. Slang:* Bird Cage—House of vice.

5. *Photography.* a camera.
1933 Mahin & Furthman *Bombshell* (film): You got enough plates in that birdcage of yours? **1942** *ATS* 554: Camera. *Birdcage.*

6. an elevator having a sliding metal gate.
1934 Halper *Foundry* 101: He picked out of a mass of...boys who rode up in the "bird cage," all after that ten-dollar-a-week job. **1942** *ATS* 83. **1988** DeLillo *Libra* 394: They ran to the birdcage elevators.

7. *Med.* the rib cage.
1939 Fearing *Hospital* 146: He...dissected more skin and muscle from the bird-cage.

8. *R.R.* a lantern.
1945 Hubbard *R.R. Ave.* 333: *Bird Cage*—Brakeman's or switchman's lantern.

9. *Av.* (see 1956 quot.).
1955 Scott *Look of Eagle* 7: A quick, last minute check for leaks, the bird-cage was closed, and he accepted the down locks and the red-flagged escape seat pin from the man on the ground. **1956** Heflin *USAF Dict.* 80: *Bird cage*....The place in a jet plane where several converging lines (fuel, oil, hydraulic) suggest a "bird cage."

10. *Av.* (see quot.).
1956 Heflin *USAF Dict.* 81: *Bird cage. Slang.*...A directional gyroscope.

11. *Logging.* (see quots.). Also as *v.*
1958 McCulloch *Woods Words* 12: *Bird cage*—a. A screened shelter to keep meat cool. b. A spark arrester. c. To misuse a wire rope, kinking it so the strands open out giving a bird cage effect. **1959** *AS* (Feb.) 76: *Bird cage, n.* The frayed or ragged strands of wire rope or rope that resemble a cage.

12. *Av.* an air control tower; (*hence*) the controlled airspace around an airport.
1963 Dwiggins *S.O. Bees* 122 [ref. to WWII]: He shot past the birdcage on the carrier's island. **1966** Noel & Bush *Naval Terms* 66: *Bird cage:* Air Control Officer's station on the island of a carrier. **1981** *Time* (Aug. 17) 18: Starting pay at one of the busy "birdcages" near New York, Chicago and Los Angeles is $37,000. **1987** *Atlantic* (July) 104: *Bird-cage*...controlled air space in the vicinity of an airport: "An Aeroméxico DC-9 and a private Piper aircraft collided in the congested *birdcage*...around Los Angeles International Airport."

birdcage hype *n.* [prob. BIRDCAGE, 1.b. + HYPE 'drug addict'] *Narc.* a homeless and destitute drug addict.
1936 Dai *Opium Add.* 196: *Bird-cage hype.* The poorer class of addict. **1959** Murtagh & Harris *Who Live in Shadow* 8: He is what is known

around Junktown as a birdcage hype,...a lame, lazy, crazy cat.

bird colonel *n.* [ref. to the eagle insigne of rank] *Mil.* a full colonel.
1944–46 in *AS* XXII 54: *Bird Colonel.* A full colonel. **1951** Sheldon *Troubling Star* 237: You're a great big important bird colonel now, aren't you, Straker? **1955** Doud *Hell & Back* (film): If I have to, I can prove I'm a bird colonel from intelligence in disguise. **1957** M. Shulman *Rally* 119: Thorwald...[fixed] Guido with a bird-colonel's glare. **1961** *Time* (Oct. 13) 22: From bird colonel to buck private. **1962** G. Ross *Campaign* 18: You won't be able to roll over without some bird colonel stepping on you! **1969** Hughes *Under a Flare* 23: Somebody whispered he was a full bird colonel. Made sense, he had an eagle on his collar. **1969** Eastlake *Bamboo Bed* 234: You don't say no to a full bird colonel. **1977** *L.A. Times* (Feb. 13) Calendar 38: Burt Lancaster [is] the American bird colonel who will stop at nothing...to keep the disease from escaping the train.

bird corporal *n.* [sugg. by the eagle that is part of the insigne] *Army.* a Specialist Fourth-Class.
1980 D. Cragg (letter to J.E.L., Aug. 10): Who's he tryin' to pull rank on, that fuckin' bird corporal? **1988** Clodfelter *Mad Minutes* 42 [ref. to 1965]: The privates and bird corporals (Specialist 4s) were immediately put to work.

birdcrap *n.* BIRDSHIT.
1973 Hirschfeld *Victors* 35: "This is the best-trained, best-equipped army—" "Birdcrap."

Bird Day *n.* Thanksgiving Day.
1969 Hughes *Under a Flare* 223: Thanksgiving was a fantastic day in Vietnam. Bird Day 1966 was my very first away from home.

bird dog *n.* **1.** [sugg. by BIRDMAN] *Mil. Av.* an aviation cadet officer.
1918 *MacArthur Carry-On* (Dec. 27) 1: By a hangar down in Texas, looking lazy at the sky,/Lay a bird dog sadly dreaming, and I heard him softly sigh..../Then the bird dog snapped to attention and his hand came up to salute/For going by with his head held high was a shavetail 2nd Loot. **1945** in Rea *Wings of Gold* 249: Led by our chief junior bird-dog (cadet officer).

2.a. one who seeks, scouts, or spies for another, esp. a carrier of tales; one who runs errands or performs similar tasks; one paid to direct potential customers to a business.
1929 (cited in Partridge *Dict. Und.* 40). **1934** Weseen *Dict. Slang* 308: *Bird-dog*—A stock broker's agent who scouts for prospects. **1939** in Partridge *Dict. Und.* (ed. 2) 794: *Bird dog*...a scout, a lookout, a preliminary information seeker; a prospect contacter in lot rackets; an important person in a kidnapping. **1942** Hollingshead *Elmtown's Youth* 190: They were hated...because they were known to carry tales to the principal. A number of students referred to Mr. White as "Bird Dog," and Mr. Gardner as "Pussy Foot." **1949** *AS* (Feb.) 36: Originally...*bird dog* referred to a geologist, because he "smelled out" oil. Now it includes the geologist, the scout who secures information concerning oil activities of other companies, the local informer who points out likely prospects to leasemen. **1961** Considine *Ripley* 55: Ripley...set up a sort of global bird-dog posse to hunt down...oddities. **1968** F. Wallace *Poker* 210: *Bird Dog*—One who gets players for a [poker] game. **1971** Tak *Truck Talk* 13: *Bird dog:* The chaser car of a two-car radar team, the trouper who "retrieves" a speeding trucker. **1972–76** Durden *No Bugles* 39: Other day I saw y' standin' outside the Captain's hooch while Major Early was inside. Hangin' round listenin'. You Poe's birddog? You an' him figurin' t' make trouble for us? **1973–77** in *AS* (Winter 1980) 309: *Bird dog.* Person who sends customers to a [used-car] salesman, usually for a fee. **1978** J. Rosenberg *Dict. Business* 50: *Bird dog*...An individual paid to obtain business for a high-powered salesman. **1982** R. Sutton *Don't Get Taken* 5: Jerry is...one of the best bird-dogs [for a car dealership]. **1983** *A-Team* (NBC-TV): If he's a bird dog for the military he ain't got no backup.

b. *Army.* a tactical officer.
1945 in Litoff et al. *Miss You* 265: I had to move in with a tactical (bird dog) officer.

c. *Specif.*, a talent scout, *esp.* a part-time talent scout for a sports team.
1950 (cited in P. Dickson *Baseball Dict.* 56). **1959** de Roo *Young Wolves* 110: I'm on the athletic scholarship committee, a bird dog for State. **1960** Garagiola *Funny Game* 2: Today's scouting is so organized that even the scouts have scouts, known as "bird dogs." **1962** Houk & Dexter *Ballplayers* 28: I'm going down to the clubhouse to sign that catcher....You stand at that gate and don't let any of those other bird

dogs get away till I get Houk's autograph. **1964** Thompson & Rice *Every Diamond* 61: He must have gone as a bird dog for his father. *Ibid.* 83: "Bird dogs" flush up the good talent which the regular scout might never see. **1977** in Lyle & Golenbock *Bronx Zoo* 7: A bird dog from Pittsburgh, Socco McCarrey, wanted to sign me.

d. (see quot.).

1978 J. Rosenberg *Dict. Business* 50: Bird dog...business law. An individual paid to spread fraudulent charges.

3. *Stu.* an unattached young man who attempts to ingratiate himself with and lure away other men's dates, as at a dance.

1942 *Randolph Field* 129: Bird dog—A cadet who persistently cuts in on another cadet's girl at a dance. "I wish that bird dog would get a girl of his own." **1942–44** in *AS* (Feb. 1946) 31: Bird Dog, n. One who accompanies a couple and is therefore superfluous. The third party of "Three's a crowd." **1955** Archibald *Aviation Cadet* 35: An aviation cadet, however, did not cut in on another's girl. That was being a bird dog. **1956** Hess *Battle Hymn* 79 [ref. to 1950]: The way he told it, every Korean girl between the ages of six and sixty used to trail him around like his shadow....Our theory was that...Red was the pursuer, not the pursued. This resulted in this salty old member of our outfit becoming known as "Birddog" Varner. **1958** Everly Bros. *Bird Dog* (song): Hey, bird dog, get away from my chick! **1961** Terry *Old Liberty* 69: The bird dogs had a glorious time, when the guys passed out on their dates. **1985** N. Black *Mischief* (film): You no-good bird dog!

4. a tenacious individual, esp. one who tenaciously pursues a particular task.

1949 *AS* (Feb.) 36: Bird dog...the worker who stays with a difficult task until it is completed.

5.a. *Av.* a radio direction finder, automatic direction finder.

1955 Scott *Look of Eagle* 8: So he moved the toggle for...the radio compass he called the "bird-dog." *Ibid.* 32: I have Elmira on my bird-dog and we'll pass south. **1956** Heflin *USAF Dict.* 80: Bird dog. A radio direction-finder. *Slang.* **1961** L.G. Richards *TAC* 167: Bird dog (ADF, automatic direction-finding radio). **1963** E.M. Miller *Exile to Stars* 127: Never quite sure that the bird-dog needles were telling him the absolute truth. **1964** *AS* XXXIX 18: Bird Dog...Slang for a navigational instrument which points in the direction of any radio station tuned into it. **1969** Cagle *Naval Av. Guide* 389: Bird Dog. Radio direction finder equipment.

b. an automatic tracking transmitter.

1989 Radford & Crowley *Drug Agent* 192: The bird dog continued sending its steady beep from the cardboard box.

c. *Av.* (see quot.).

1990 Tuso *Vietnam Blues* 245: Bird dog. A small airborne compass.

bird-dog *v.* **1.** *Stu.* to attempt to ingratiate oneself with and lure away (a young woman who is someone else's date). Also intrans.

1941 *AS* (Oct.) 163: Bird Dogging. Lower classman dancing with upper classman's girl. (Flying Cadets). **1942–44** in *AS* (Feb. 1946) 31: Bird Dog...v. To be a bird dog. **1944** E. Caldwell *Tragic Ground* 106: To hell with Chet!...Chet can go somewhere else to do his bird-dogging! **1956** P. Moore *Chocolates* 150: Stop bird-dogging my date. **1958** J. Davis *College Vocab.* 14: Bird dog—Flirt with someone else's date. **1958** Frede *Entry E* 15: Maybe I can bird-dog someone. **1961** Terry *Old Liberty* 70: Everybody had a date....Except old Bo didn't have a date...so he would just bird-dog a bit. **1970** *Nat. Lampoon* (Nov.) 30: Any drip who tries to bird dog your baby will have a real blast from your homemade zip gun.

2.a. to scout around; (*trans.*) to search for and bring back; scout for.

1948 Wolfert *Act of Love* 456: I worry about you bird-dogging around up front. **1949** *AS* (Feb.) 36: To bird dog pertains to the activity of any bird dog. **1967** Beck *Pimp* 98: Old Preston was back out there bird-dogging suckers. **1972** Haslam *Oil Fields* 93: Bird Dog, v. To search for a given item with great intensity. **1986** *TV Guide* (July 26) 15: When you're bird-dogging young pitchers...you want to begin your assessment with something basic.

b. [cf. S.E. *dog* in similar sense] to follow after (a person) closely, tail; pursue; (*specif.*) to watch or flirt with (a young woman).

1949 *AS* (Feb.) 36: Bird dog...also means *to follow closely*. **1955** Reifer *New Words* 30: Bird-dogging. *Slang.* Following someone closely or persistently; bothering someone repeatedly. **1962** Kesey *Cuckoo's Nest* 167: You oughta be out running around in a convertible, bird-dogging girls. **1965** Bonham *Durango St.* 27: Haven't you kids got anything better to do than bird-dog your brother? **1972** *Banyon* (NBC-TV police series): Jim Rawlins sent me out to birddog ya. **1978** Wheeler & Kerby *Steel*

Cowboy (film): They're gonna think we're bird-doggin' 'em. **1983** Helprin *Winter's Tale* 411: Praeger de Pinto came in...with Martin bird-dogging him all over the place. **1984** J.R. Reeves *Mekong* 190: I didn't know we was goin' to have to bird-dog the damn women all over hell an' creation! **1989** Berent *Rolling Thunder* 23: He concentrated on the stewardess he had been birddogging during the...flight.

3. to oversee or examine (actions, machinery, etc.) closely and persistently; to pursue (a matter) to its conclusion.

1956 Heflin *USAF Dict.* 80: Bird-dog, v. tr. To pursue a *matter* persistently. *Slang.* **1959** *Sat. Eve. Post* (May 2) 26: He sure was a demon when it came to checking out an airplane. From the way he bird-dogged that big C-133 you'd think it was going to crash in flames if the center of gravity was off by a quarter of an inch. **1964** Redfield *Letters from Actor* 87: Stage managers...bird-dog a play in production as well as conduct understudy rehearsals twice a week. **1972** *Business Week* (Oct. 14) 42: We had to keep birddogging the FAA and the manufacturers, but we finally got the changes made. **1973** E. Sevareid, on *5 Presidents on the Presidency* (CBS-TV): It is the assigned constitutional duty of the press to bird-dog the presidency. **1976** *U.S. News & W.R.* (Oct. 11) 60: We really bird-dog them for their first three months on the job. **1983** *Sunset* (Mar.) 114: Monitoring and recording, [an] electronic system in each house will bird-dog energy use through September.

bird farm *n. Navy.* a naval air station or (*later*) an aircraft carrier.

1942 Sanders & Blackwell *Forces* 40: Bird-Farm:...An air station. (U.S.N.A.). **1965** *N.Y. Times* (June 1): The days are gone when a carrier was called a flattop. The craft is now a "birdfarm." **1966** in IUFA *Folk Speech*: Bird farm—Any aircraft carrier. **1967** Dubus *Lieutenant* 32 [ref. to 1950's]: Well, Freeman, there's a chance...that we can get you off this bird farm and fly you back to the States. **1982** T.C. Mason *Battleship* 10 [ref. to WWII]: The sailors on these outlandish "bird-farms" were the "brown-shoe navy" and were considered little better than landlubbers. **1983** LaBarge & Holt *Sweetwater Gunslinger* 120: He's headed for the Bird Farm! **1985** Dye *Between Raindrops* 218: Low on fuel; back to the floating bird-farms. **1988** Poyer *Med* 198: TF-60...America....The big birdfarm herself.

birdhouse *n.* a jail.

1942 *ATS* 433: Jail...birdhouse. **1970** Gattzden *Black Vendetta* 13: Don't try to con an old birdhouse man.

birdie *n.* **1.** see BIRD, 10.a.

2. see BIRD, 11.

3. an effeminate male; sissy. *Joc.*

1921–25 J. Gleason & R. Taber *Is Zat So?* 89: Chickee, old dear....Happee, old boy....Say, where de 'ell does he get this...stuff? What does he take us for—a couple of boidies? **1932** *AS* (June) 329: Birdie—an effeminate man; a pervert. **1971** *All in the Family* (CBS-TV): We don't need any strange little birdies flyin' in and out here.

4. see BIRD, 12.

birdman *n. Av.* a man who is an aviator; FLYBOY. [Though used as S.E. in early aviation journalism, the term soon became jocular or derisive.]

1910 in Butterfield *Post Treasury* 118: The First Birdman, by J.W. Mitchell [title]. **1918** McBride *Emma Gees* 145: Being unable to return the fire, he tried every trick known to the birdman to escape, but without avail. **1927** in D. Parker *Portable Parker* 456: But the lady seems to have even more self-assurance than has the argumentative birdman. **1946** Michener *So. Pacific* 66: "And for you birdmen," the voice continued. "Four flights have set out for your territory." **1959** Chambliss *Silent Service* 51: If that birdman can't do better than that, we're okay for a while. **1967** Stevens *Gunner* 92: He feels that he has nothing more than a weary birdman on his hands. **1973** Herbert & Wooten *Soldier* 287: The bird-men may have been commanders in the technical sense of the word, but they weren't leaders, and the grunts knew it. **1976–79** Duncan & Moore *Green Side Out* 65: With all twelve Marines cheering wildly, the second birdman...knocked the first birdman clear off his mess bench!

birdseed *n.* **1.** [cf. *for the birds* s.v. BIRD] nonsensical talk.

1909 "O. Henry" *Strictly Business* 1587: "Oh, canary-bird seed!" exclaimed Annette. **1954** B. Schulberg *Waterfront* 111: O.K., O.K. Without the bird seed. Whaddya want? **1961** Brosnan *Pennant Race* 113: "Regulars first, Professor!" "Bird seed! You've been on this table more than you've been on base lately." **1983** *N.Y. Times Bk. Review* (Jan. 1, 1984) 10: Are you really able to distinguish this birdseed from the stuff you peek at in the National Enquirer? **1984** "W.T. Tyler"

Shadow Cabinet 192: You talk to her and that's all you get—birdseed.

2. breakfast cereal that resembles birdseed.

1919 Witt *Riding to War* 158: Submarine chicken. Birdseed. Corned Willy. Slum. Goldfish. **1930** *AS* VI 203: *Bird-seed*: dry breakfast cereals. **1936** *AS* (Feb.) 42: *Bird Seed*. Cereal. **1968** Spradley *Drunk* 31: Had bowl of "birdseed" cracked wheat mush, powdered milk, two slices of bread/oleo, ersatz coffee.

birdshit *n.* BIRDSEED, 1.—usu. considered vulgar. Also **bird turd.**

1958–60 Freeman *Out of Burning* 146: That's bird turd. **1972** Rossner *Any Minute* 36: For this she had left Roger. The same old birdshit dropped from a different tree. **1977** Carabatsos *Heroes* 5: Don't pump me with your hero bird shit.

bird's nest *n. Angling.* a snarl on the line on the spool of a casting reel; a backlash.

1949 Cummings *Dict. Sports* 35: *Bird's nest. Angling.* Slang for backlash. **1976** *Webster's Sports Dict.* 42.

bird turd *n.* **1.** an insignificant amount, nothing; *(hence)* a contemptibly insignificant person.—usu. considered vulgar.

1959 [Sabre & Eiden] *Glory Jumpers* 78: Shut up, Bird-turd. **1970** Zindel *Your Mind* 31: I don't think you give a bird turd about politics.

2. see BIRDSHIT.

bird-turd *v.* to speak emptily (to).—used in negative contexts.—sometimes constr. with *a-*.—usu. considered vulgar. [Earliest quots. ref. to WWII.]

1947 Mailer *Naked & Dead* 285: You ain't just a bird-turding, Jack. **1955** Klaas *Maybe I'm Dead* 117: I ain't just a bird-turdin' when I say I got it the hard way. **1958** T. Berger *Crazy in Berlin* 17: You don't mean to bird-turd me? **1959** Brosnan *Long Season* 96: Strange? Odd behavior? You're not just bird-turding there, man! **1963** Ross *Dead Are Mine* 252: You're not just a-birdturdin', Buster....Man, these last few weeks have been rough, real rough. **1966** King *Brave & Damned* 146: I ain't bird turding. **1973** Gwaltney *Destiny's Chickens* 9: You jist ain't bird-turding, boy. **1973** Huggett *Body Count* 313: Are you bird-turdin' me, baby? **1966–80** McAleer & Dickson *Unit Pride* 230: You ain't just a-birdturdin'.

bird-watcher *n.* **1.** *Pol.* an environmentalist.—used derisively.

1979 Homer *Jargon* 34.

2. an airplane enthusiast.

1983 M. Skinner *USAFE* 132: Birdwatcher's Guide to USAFE. *a*1989 R. Herman, Jr. *Warbirds* 155: The birdwatcher leveled his long...lens on the tripod and sighted it down the runway.

birdwood *n.* [poss. from a fancied resemblance to a bird's perch] a cigarette.

1944 Burley *Hndbk. Jive* 134: *Birdwood*—Something to smoke, reefers. **1956** Hargrove *Girl He Left* 26: May I have a birdwood?...I seem to be clean.

birdworks *n.* (see quot.).

1969 *Word Study* (Apr.) 8: A *birdworks* is an aerospace corporation.

birdyback *adv. Transport.* (see quot.).

1971 Tak *Truck Talk* 13: *Birdyback:* The practice of shipping loaded trailers on airplanes.

birthday suit *n.* [the "suit" worn on the day of one's birth] the bare skin; complete nakedness. Now *colloq.*

*1753 T. Smollett, in *N & Q* CCXI (1966) 464: He made an apology for receiving the count in his birth-day suit. **1785–88* Grose *Vulgar Tongue*: *Ballum Rancum*, a hop or dance, where the women are all prostitutes, a dance at a brothel....N.B. The company dance in their birthday suits. **1811* *Lexicon Balatron.*: He was in his birth-day suit, stark naked. **1898** [Tisdale] *Behind the Guns* 215: The climate invited the wearing of "birthday suits." **1927* Lowe-Porter, tr. *Magic Mt.* 501: Before Him we are all in our birthday suits. **1957** McGivern *Against Tomorrow* 105: You won't get far in your birthday suit. **1962** T. Berger *Reinhart* 32: A big blonde wearing glassine panties and otherwise her birthday suit. **1963** W.C. Anderson *Penelope* 174: In their birthday suits? **1964** in Gover *Trilogy* 298: I go paradin around in my birfday suit. **1982** M. Mann *Elvis* 51: He doesn't like anyone to see him in his birthday suit. **1984** Jackson & Lupica *Reggie* 75: I was standing there in my birthday suit with nothing on but shower thongs. **1989** *Cosmopolitan* (Jan. 1990) 180: Star linebacker Lawrence Taylor strips down to his birthday suit and pulls on sky blue briefs. **1992** TV ad for *Hard Copy* (synd. TV series) (Sept. 1): A psychologist who's getting into trouble for working in a suit. His birthday suit!

biscuit *n.* **1.** a young woman.

1855 Brougham *Chips* 327: The *biscuit* had a little anchovy paste about it...but they soon diskivered that...it was only a Boston cracker. **1926** Finerty *Criminalese* 9: *Biscuit*—A flapper who pets. **1932** Nicholson & Robinson *Sailor Beware!* 22: Women don't take me serious. Not the swell biscuits like Chet gets. **1933–34** Lorimer & Lorimer *Stag Line* 48: Don't be funny, biscuit. **1959** Oliver *Meaning of Blues* 147: A desirable young girl is...called a "biscuit," whilst the good lover is a "biscuit-roller." **1980** Birnbach *Preppy Hndbk.* 222: *Reel in the biscuit v.* Lure a girl to bed.

2. a watch.

1905 *DN* III 70: *Biscuit, n.* A watch. "My *biscuit* is too slow." Common slang.

3. *West.* a saddle horn.

1922 Rollins *Cowboy* 290 [ref. to 1890's]: Less accomplished men...might be willing to "choke the horn" or "choke" or "squeeze," the "biscuit," as a hand hold upon the saddle horn was more specifically designated. **1936** R. Adams *Cowboy Lingo* 44: [The saddle horn] went by such slang names as..."biscuit."

4. the face or head; *(hence)* in phr. **out of one's biscuit** insane.

1934 Weseen *Dict. Amer. Slang* 230: *Biscuit*—The face. **1944** Burley *Hndbk. Jive* 134: *Biscuit*—the head. **1969** Gordone *No Place* 424: Way we was raised, husslin' an' usin' yo' biscuit to pull quickies was the only way we could feel like men. **1973** *Roll Out!* (CBS-TV): Oh man, you got to be outa your biscuit.

5. *Und.* **a.** a bomb.

1935 Pollock *Underworld Sp.*: *Biscuit*, a bomb.

b. a pistol.

1948 (cited in Partridge *Dict. Und.* (ed. 2) 794). **1972** Bunker *No Beast* 83: Get a biscuit and rip something off—a bank, anything! *Ibid.* 184: "Take this biscuit"—I handed him the .38.

6. *pl. Black E.* the buttocks.

1936 in Dixon & Godrich *Blues & Gospel* 152: Your Biscuits Are Big Enough For Me. **1965** E. Franklin *Cold in Pongo-ni* 37 [ref. to 1953]: Come on, knock you on your biscuits, Jarvinen.

7. *Narc.* a white tablet, as of methadone.

1972 *N.Y. Post* (Nov. 1) 34: The street price for the 40 mg. tablets [of methadone] or "biscuits" as the addicts call them has stabilized at $5. **1973** *N.Y. Post.* (Jan. 8) 33: This morning I...took a biscuit (methadone pill), went uptown and scored some more coke and a little scag.

¶ In phrases:

¶ **catch with a biscuit** *Und.* to catch with incriminating evidence.

1929 Hotstetter & Beesley *It's a Racket* 221: *Caught with a biscuit*—Caught with incriminating evidence. **1930** in Partridge *Dict. Und.* 41: They had to be caught with the goods or, as the racketeering slang went, found with a biscuit.

¶ **hot in the biscuit** overeager; excited.

1964 Faust *Steagle* 46: I can't do it justice if I'm all hot in the biscuit. **1978** Selby *Requiem* 227: You're the one who was all hot in the fuckin biscuit to get off again last night.

¶ **take the biscuit** to "take the cake." Now *colloq.* and *rare* in U.S.

1897 Siler & Houseman *Fight of the Century* 45: The winner will be entitled to the belt, the biscuit and the whole works. **1901** (quot. at *take the bun* s.v. BUN). **1907* G.B. Shaw, in *OEDS*: You take the biscuit at that, you do. **1961* in *OEDS* I 271: For the sheerest idiocy, it's the comparative "as contemporary as..." that takes the biscuit. **1981* *Business Week* (Apr. 20) 20 (ad): What a nice surprise! Or, as they say in England, "That takes the biscuit!"

biscuit bitch *n.* [sugg. by *Donut Dolly*, the official American Red Cross designation] *Mil.* a female volunteer worker with the American Red Cross.—usu. considered vulgar. Now *hist.* [Quots. ref. to Vietnam War.]

1983 Elting, Cragg, & Deal *Soldier Talk* 87: Donut Dollies...Also called *biscuit bitches*. **1987** Lanning *Only War* 239: The unbecoming name of "Biscuit Bitches" [was] often substituted for Donut Dollies.

biscuit bomber *n. USAF.* a cargo plane used for the air-dropping of rations and other supplies.

1944 *Yank* (Jan. 7) 18: Even jeeps can't travel the trail [in New Guinea], so "biscuit bombers" drop...supplies...daily. **1989** *Wings* (Discovery Channel TV) [ref. to 1942]: Then the "biscuit bombers," as the troops called them, would set off escorted by fighters.

biscuit gun *n. Mil. Av.* **1.** an imaginary device used to shoot food to aviators. *Joc.*

1941 Hargrove *Pvt. Hargrove* 83: Here, a new and gullible man is sent for the *cannon report*, or for the *biscuit gun*, the *flagpole key*, or the *rubber flag* which is used on rainy days. **1944** *Off. Gde. to AAF* 368: *Biscuit gun*—imaginary appliance for shooting food to pilots who are having difficulty in landing. **1956** (quot. at (2), below).

2. a flare pistol or air traffic control projector indicating clearance or no clearance to land to an approaching pilot.

1952 Cope & Dyer *Petty Off. Gd.* 422: *Biscuit gun.* (Slang). Flare pistol. **1955** Archibald *Aviation Cadet* 60: Watch the tower for a clearance, the man with the biscuit gun. **1956** Heflin *USAF Dict.* 80: *Biscuit gun.* A traffic-control projector. *Slang.* It has been suggested that this application arose from the humorous notion that a "biscuit gun" was used to shoot food up to hungry pilots circling for a landing. **1966** E. Shepard *Doom Pussy* 220: Without radio contact you have to rely on "biscuit guns" beamed from the tower. Green light gives clearance to land and red light indicates…"take it around and reenter the traffic pattern." **1975** Stevens *Flat on My Back* 142: I'm turning on the downwind leg, I see your biscuit gun. **1978** Ardery *Bomber Pilot* 20 [ref. to 1940]: The "biscuit gun" [was] a signal spotlight used to give directions from the tower when radio communications fail[ed].

biscuit-headed *adj.* stupid.

1845 Hooper *Simon Suggs* 170: D—n you!…d—n you for a biscuit-headed nullifier!

biscuit hook *n.* a hand.

1932 *AS* VII 329: *Biscuit-hooks.* Hands.

biscuit-roller *n. Black E.* one's female (*occ.* male) lover.

1937 in Oliver *Blues Tradition* 120: I woke up this mornin', my biscuit-roller gone. **1948** in Oliver *Meaning of Blues* 147: Don't your home look lonesome, biscuit roller gone?

biscuit-shooter *n.* **1.** a waitress or (*occ.*) a waiter.

1893 *Harper's* (Dec.) 52: She had performed the duties of…a biscuit-shooter.…When the trains halted for a twenty-minute meal, it was her function to…recite the bill of fare…subsequently bringing the various refreshments [that had been ordered]. *Ibid.* 57: His help meet in her night-gown and the biscuit-shooter each seized a broom. **1895** *Harper's* (Jan.) 288: His biscuit-shooter, with the lust of purchase on her, was brilliantly dressed. **1902** Wister *Virginian* 4: That corn-fed biscuit-shooter at Rawlins yu' gave the canary—. **1904** in *DAE*: The "hash-slinger" (if a gentleman) or "biscuit-shooter" (if a lady) repeated a list of the grub as piled. **1906** M'Govern *Sgt. Larry* (glossary): *Biscuit-Shooter:*— Female servant in officer's family. **1908** in H.C. Fisher *A. Mutt* 59: Olaf Sweetbreads [is a] biscuit shooter in Coffee John's cafe. **1910** *Everybody's Mag.* (Jan.) 110: It's a case of marry…ain't it…To the blonde biscuit-shooter up on First Avenue? **1913** *DN* IV 2: *Biscuit shooter,* n. A waiter in a logging camp. **1916** *Editor* (Mar. 11) 297: *Biscuit-shooter*—waitress. **1927** *AS* II 275: *Biscuit shooter*—waiter at table. **1927** J. Stevens *Mattock* 132: She got herself a job as a biscuit-shooter in a Main Street chophouse. **1927** Rollins *Jinglebob* 106 [ref. to 1880's]: A girl, a biscuit shooter down at Laramie.

2. a cook, as on a cattle drive or in a lumber camp, who also serves food, as on a mess line.

1912 *DN* III 550: *Biscuit shooter,* cook, at camp, ranches, etc. **1920** in *DAE*: *Biscuit shooter,* name for cook in cow camp. **1926** *AS* I 650: *Biscuit-shooter*—short order cook. **1933** *AS* (Feb.) 26: *Biscuit Shooter.* A cook. Biscuit shootin' is the first requirement of a ranch cook.

bishop *n.* the penis; (*hence*) in phr. **beat** [or **flog**] **the bishop** (of the male) to masturbate; **shoot the bishop** to ejaculate semen during sleep.

[***1785** Grose *Vulgar Tongue*: To box the Jesuit, and get cockroaches, (*sea term*) for masturbation. A crime it is said much practiced by the reverend fathers of that society.] **1916** Cary *Venery* II 112: *Shooting a Bishop*—To have a wet dream. **1964** Pearl *Stockade* 50: He sits up in that tower beating the bishop and drooling over that broad. **1968** Baker et al. *CUSS* 80: *Bishop* Male sex organ. **1969** Tynan *Oh! Calcutta!* 39: Five more minutes of this and I'll have to start beatin' the bishop! **1972** R. Wilson *Playboy's Forbidden Words* 12: Masturbation among New York schoolboys is *beating the bishop.* **1973** Flaherty *Fogarty* 132: Tell him…that you flogged the bishop. **1980** Manchester *Darkness* 127 [ref. to WWII]: Knock off beating the bishop, guys.

bishop's nose *n.* the tail of a cooked chicken.—constr. with *the.* Cf. POPE'S NOSE.

1968 J.P. Miller *Race for Home* 148 [ref. to 1930's]: Otto and Caroline now fought over the bishop's nose, which was Otto's favorite piece.

bit *n.* **1.** Orig *Und.* money; cash. *Rare* in U.S.

*1607 in *OED*: The bung and the bit…your purse and the money. ***1781** G. Parker *View of Soc.* II 125: Somebody *naps the bit,* and tells him that such a Coachman had done it. **1791** [W. Smith] *Confess. T. Mount* 18: Money of any kind, bit. *Ibid.* 21: Wedge and bit our sacks did fill. ***1805** J. Davis *Post-Captain* 176: I reckon…she has plenty of bit. ***1812** Vaux *Vocab.*: Bit. Money in general.

2.a. the sum of twelve and a half cents.—used esp. in *two bits, four bits, six bits, eight bits.* [Orig. S.E.; see *DAE.*]

1821 Wetmore *Pedlar* 27: A bit…Twelve and a half cents. **1842** J.L. Scott *Missionary* 84: They had but "six bits" (seventy-five cents) to carry them to Iowa. **1845** in Robb *Squatter Life* 115: But I hev got first rate butter, at two bitts a pound. **1857** in *DAE*: For turkey he asked four-bits. **1861** Berkeley *Sportsman* 350: If you hit the card I will give you a "bit," but if you hit the penknife you shall have a dollar. **1882** Baillie-Grohman *Rockies* 62: I would donate you them 'ar four bits (fifty cents). **1887** W.P. Lane *Adventures* 6: With about *six bits* in my pocket. **1899** Cullen *Tales* 89: They let me have 'em for one dollar (eight bits, they call it out there) apiece, and I conned people into buying 'em for from two dollars to four dollars each. **1908** in H.C. Fisher *A. Mutt* 60: The plunger comes through with the six bits. **1921** in Kornbluh *Rebel Voices* 86: At least seven dollars and six-bits. **1929** "E. Queen" *Roman Hat* 40: He'd only promised me four bits. **1966–69** Woiwode *Going to Do* 121: I just got six bits is all. **1975** T. Berger *Sneaky People* 19: I figure you're ready to bite me for four bits.

b. *Gamb.* the sum of twelve and a half dollars.—used esp. in *two bits, four bits,* etc.

1929 Sullivan *Look at Chicago* 111: "Two bits" in these opulent days meaning twenty-five dollars. **1933** Ersine *Prison Slang* 77: *Two Bits.* Twenty-five cents or dollars. **1967** [Beck] *Pimp* 208: She had put only six bits in my pocket. **1976** "N. Ross" *Policeman* 23: "This is worth two bits, and you know it."…He can't offer you a sawbuck because you already mentioned twenty-five dollars.

c. in phr. **long bit** fifteen cents or (*Gamb.*) dollars.

1859 in Thornton *Amer. Gloss.* I 65: I'd give a long bit myself to see 'em pull hair. **1933** Ersine *Prison Slang* 51: *Long Bit*…fifteen cents or dollars.

d. in phr. **short bit** ten cents.

1854 in Thornton *Amer. Gloss.* I 65: The will that cuts off an expectant heir with a "short bit."

3. a share in profits, esp. the spoils of a crime; CUT.

1889 S.A. Bailey *Crook's Life* 22 [ref. to 1871]: My "bit," as the portion which fell to each member of the gang was called, was proportionatley larger than any of the rest on account of the danger. **1892** Norr *China Town* 40: The flatty wanted $1,000 for his bit. **1896** Ade *Artie* 46: I've heard he gets his bit on nearly every good thing that comes along. **1905** White *Boniface to Burglar* 309 [ref. to late 1860's]: The small-fry thief was…paying his "bit" to the coppers on post. **1907** in H.C. Fisher *A. Mutt* 19: Here he comes with the dough. Now for our "bit." **1914** Jackson & Hellyer *Vocab.* 17: *Bit*…A portion; a division; a share or a part of anything, as profits or proceeds of a transaction.

4. *Pris.* a prison sentence.—occ. in combination with number indicating length.

1866 *Nat. Police Gaz.* (Nov. 10) 3: After doing his "bit" up the river. ***1871** in *OEDS*: Bill, how do they know of your bit in Dover? ***1881–84** Davitt *Prison Diary* I 152: I did a snatch near St. Paul's…and got this bit of seven stretch. *Ibid.* I 200: I was constantly being interrogated as to…where I had done my "last bit." **1902** "J. Flynt" *Little Bro.* 128: Thus began Benny's first "bit" in jail. **1908** in H.C. Fisher *A. Mutt* 82: The General…is now doing a "bit" in the Odessa cooler. **1911** Howard *Enemy to Society* 37: There ain't nothin'…that's worth doin' a "bit" for. **1912** Berkman *Prison* 168 [ref. to 1893]: Now he's doin a five-bit down in Kansas. **1914** Jackson & Hellyer *Vocab.* 17: He did a bit in Joliet. **1917** *New Republic* (Jan. 13) 294: Ferrati, whose "bit" was three to seven years. **1932** Lawes *20,000 Yrs.* 176: The other is doing his first "bit." **1938** *N.Y. Sunday News* (Sept. 4) 41: Chester Yates, handcuffed to a deputy sheriff, was asked: "How long is your bit?" **1967** C. Cooper *Farm* 113: "Are you doing a bit?" "5 years for Sale of Narcotics." **1982** *Maclean's* (June 6) 22: Even at the end of his minimum two-year "bit," his movements and communication are rigidly circumscribed.

5.a. *Theat.* a one-person performance; (*later*) a skit.

*1899 Whiteing *John St.* 35: He does a bit at night in the streets with 'is telescope, showin' the stars—astrolyger by trade. **1921** in Kimball & Bolcolm *Sissle & Blake* 98: There was a young grocery store bit, that suggested the old afterpiece idea.

b. [cf. literal syn. SHTIK] manner of behavior, speaking, etc.;

action or actions.—occ. in phr. **the whole bit** everything; **what's the bit?** "what's going on?"

1958 in *OEDS*: What's the Mister Musician bit? **1960** Warner Bros. *Rabbit's Feat* (animated cartoon): What's up, Doc? What's the bit? What's cookin'? **1960** *Mad* (Sept.): This kick is a wild bit you can pull on that cat who's always looking for a party to go to, and who keeps bugging you to clue him in on where the action is. **1961** *Hollywood* (Calif.) *Citizen-News* (Apr. 17): Instead of using the correct word to describe an idea, many people, merely say, "Bit," and I don't like it. **1961** Kanter & Tugend *Pocketful of Miracles* (film): I want a little town in Maryland where I can play the wife-and-mother bit! **1963** in Wepman et al. *The Life* 86: I blew my health in a bid for wealth/So you could play your bit. **1966** *Time* (May 6) 26: Why, she's doing the whole screaming bit! **1970** Landy *Underground Dict.* 33: Bit...Activity—eg. What's your bit = What are you doing?...My bit is drugs. **1972** R. Barrett *Lovomaniacs* 145: Hey, Vanni, what's the bit? **1979** *Harper's* (Aug.) 65: Are we doing the whole Sunday lunch bit on Saturday? Potatoes?

bitch *n.* **1.a.** a malicious, spiteful, promiscuous, or otherwise despicable woman; (in early use, often *specif.*) a prostitute. Now *colloq.*

*****1400** in *F & H* I (rev.) 231: Whom calleste thou queine skabde biche? *****1699** Ward *London-Spy* 131: The one call'd the other *Adulterous Bitch*, and charg'd her with lying with her Husband. **1710** in D. Greenberg *Crime in Colonial N.Y.* 110: Called her all the ould Whores and Bitches Imagineable. *****1726** A. Smith *Mems. of J. Wild* 133: You cheating B--ch, have you chous'd me so? *****1734** in J. Atkins *Sex in Lit.* 87: Where the Devil do all the B-ches come from? being a common Fleet-street phrase. **1744** A. Hamilton *Gentleman's Progress* 41: You a damn black bitch. **1777** Collins *Brief Narr.* 17: One of them swore that if the Dam'd Rebel Bitch said a word more he would run his bayonet threw her heart. *****1785** Grose *Vulgar Tongue*: Bitch, a she dog, or dogess; the most offensive appellation that can be given to an English woman, even more provoking than that of whore, as may be gathered from the regular Billingsgate or St. Giles's answer, "I may be a whore, but can't be a bitch." **1816** Torrey *Slavery* 48: Choak the d—d b—h. **1845** Clarke & Clarke *Sufferings* 106: She is a d—d deceitful bitch. **1852** B.R. Hall *Barbershop* 81: You black b—! **1863** in T. Whitman *Dear Walt* 32: To day the bitch could do nothing better than spend an hour or two in getting the lid of the cistern up. **1919** Anderson *Winesburg, Ohio* 122: First of all, he hated women. "Bitches," he called them. **1923** Toomer *Cane* 160: Got you now, you she-bitch. **1941** B. Schulberg *Sammy* 139: A cold-hearted bitch. **1956** Hunter *Second Ending* 319: Go to hell, you fat bitch! **1990** *Night Court* (NBC-TV): I say we take the bitch *down*.

b. a woman, esp. a sexually provocative or desirable young woman; BROAD.—usu. considered vulgar.

*****1713** J. Swift *Jour. to Stella* 465: As I...just received your letter, I said aloud—Agreeable B-tch. *****1785** Grose *Vulgar Tongue*: To stand bitch, to make tea, or do the honours of the tea table, or performing a female part. Bitch there standing for woman, species for genus. *ca***1898** in A. Lomax *Mr. Jelly Roll* 48: Every month, the changing of the moon....The blood comes rushing from the bitch's womb. **1927** *Immortalia* 77: Other poor bitches/Stayed pure and got never a thing. **1928** Carr *Rampant Age* 108: Gee, she's a nifty little bitch. **1934** H. Miller *Tropic of Cancer* 263: She's a big, healthy bitch. *ca***1936** in Atkinson *Dirty Comics* 49: I been follerin' that sweet bitch all day. **1941** Attaway *Blood on the Forge* 78: Melody an' me goin' out to git some bitches. **1945** Peeples *Swing Low* 21: Some wonderful bitches in Chattanooga, too. Wonderful bitches. **1951** Sheldon *Troubling a Star* 58: Do you know what that sweet bitch said? **1965** C. Brown *Manchild* 108: I wanted to...see what this beautiful black bitch by the name of Linda looked like. **1967** in T. Kochman *Black & White Styles* 77: Hey, all y'all pretty bitches. **1969** *Playboy* (Dec.) 301: You're going to want a little car of your own to ride around in with the bitches. **1973** J.R. Coleman *Blue-Collar* 62: "Motherfucker" here is often just a synonym for man, no more and no less...."I told the motherfucker we'd pick up him and his bitch at eight." **1978** Strieber *Wolfen* 130: The bitch was beautiful...so beautiful. **1967–80** in Folb *Runnin' Lines* 134: Like you have a young lady. She's your main bitch. **1988** "N.W.A." *Straight Outta Compton* (rap music album): I say life ain't nothin' but bitches and money.

c. Esp. *Pris.* a male homosexual who plays the female role in copulation.

1923 McAlmon *Companion Vol.* 214: All the queer men...are friends of mine—the bitches all love me. **1925** McAlmon *Silk Stockings* 19: He has three automobiles, and all the bitches in Berlin try to keep in with him. **1930** "D. Stiff" *Milk & Honey* 199: Bitch—...more recently a *lamb* or *preshun*. **1952** Himes *Stone* 15: You ain't nothing but a goddamn punk

yourself....You're one of those swap-up bitches. **1967** Schmidt *Lexicon of Sex* 25: Boy used in act of pederasty...*Bitch*.

d. *Homosex.* an ill-tempered, malicious homosexual man.

1933 Ford & Tyler *Young & Evil* 144: Don't be a bitch. **1940** in T. Williams *Letters* 8: He is so apparently less accessible than me—an unmistakable bitch. **1987** C. Joyner *Prison* (film): What the fuck you smilin' at, bitch? **1992** *Simpsons* (Fox-TV): He's such a bitch!

e. *Av.* a recorded female voice that is part of a cockpit voice-warning system.—constr. with *the*.

1991 Linnekin *80 Knots* 331: Harrier pilots call it, simply, "The Bitch."

2. a despicable man. Now *rare* except in homosexual use.

*a***1500** in *OED*: He is a schrewed byche. *****1677** in D'Urfey *Two Comedies* 197: He's a son of a whore, a dog, a bitch. *****1749** H. Fielding *Tom Jones* VI ii: Allworthy is a queer b—ch. *****1818** J. Keats, in *AS* XL (1965) 243: He calls himself a "curious old Bitch"—but he is a flat old dog. *****1904–14** Joyce *Portrait of the Artist* ch. v: Is your lazy bitch of a brother gone out yet? **1921** E. Pound, in V. Eliot *Letters* 498: You bitch. **1923** T. Boyd *Through Wheat* 39: By God, Pugh, you were right, you uncanny bitch. **1925** Riesenberg *Under Sail* 240: Whatever the bloody bitch has up his sleeve is a new one. **1926** Tully *Jarnegan* 244: God-damn his double-crossing soul—the dirty bitch! **1929–30** Farrell *Young Lonigan* 104: Pitch it right, you little bitch. **1934** Appel *Brain Guy* 109: You got your bastard money. Why'd you do it, you damn bitch? **1972** Cleaves *Sea Fever* 27 [ref. to 1920's]: Come on, you poor bitch, I don't wanta see ya drown. **1992** *Newsweek* (Dec. 21) 60: As the opposition scrambled back, yelling, "D-up," meaning "tighten up the defense," Payton fired a perfect pass, producing...his comment "D-up *that*, bitch."

3. (used as an emphatic standard of comparison). See also *fiddler's bitch*, below.

*****1674** in Duffett *Burlesque Plays* 30: Drunk as a Bitch he left me there. [*****1815** in Wetherell *Adventures* 327: We had a fine Ship—sailed like a witch.] **1937** Di Donato *Christ in Concrete* 158: "Cold's a bitch!" he cried when his head bobbed up out of the water. **1937** Steinbeck *Mice & Men* 37: It's brighter'n a bitch outside. **1943** J. Mitchell *McSorley's* 72: I was hungry as a bitch wolf. **1943** Guthrie *Glory* 149: Wowie! Boy! Howdy! Hotter'n a bitch! **1944** Busch *Dream of Home* 285: I was sore as a brindle bitch. **1945** Laurents *Home of Brave* 591: These O.D.'s itch like a bitch. **1951** *Erotic Verse to 1955* 52: Out of the night that was black as a bitch. **1952** H. Ellson *Golden Spike* 72: That's the way I want to die—...stoned as a bitch! **1947–53** Guthrie *Seeds* 107: Feel that wind....Colder'n a bitch. **1957** Atwell *Private* 245: Colder'n a bitch out there. **1961** Granat *Important Thing* 141: It's cold as a bitch tonight. **1965** Pollini *Glover* 262: Go like a bitch. **1966** L. Armstrong *Self-Portrait* 12: Breathing like a bitch, man. **1967** J. Kramer *Instant Replay* 87: My neck keeps aching like a bitch. **1968** L.J. Davis *Whence All Had Fled* 252: It was snowing like a bitch. **1973** Breslin *World Without End* 43: He had rooted like a bitch against Dallas.

4.a. something large or unmanageable, esp. a ship or other vehicle; an infuriating object of any kind.

*****1723** *Comical Pilgrim* 63: G— d— my Soul,/How cursedly the rotten Bitch do's rowl! **1900** in Greenway *Folksongs of Protest* 233: We'll sing, oh, may we never be/On a hungry bitch the like of she. *****1915** in H.M. Tomlinson *Waiting* 4: "Where's that old 'bus come from?"..."Ah! the poor old bitch, sir." **1927** Thomason *Marines* 208: She was a good bus....Not like that bitch of a Two-Eight-O-Nine that I was ridin' last week. *****1931** in T.E. Lawrence *Letters* 722: "She," says the incarnate sailor, stroking the gangway of the *Iron Duke*, "can be a perfect bitch in a cross-sea." **1932** Bone *Capstan Bars* 66: Roll, ye bitch, roll. **1937** Hemingway *To Have & Have Not* 174: If the bitch wouldn't only roll. **1946** S. Wilson *Voyage* 43: When I get this around the bitch [*sc.* an oil drum], take up the slack! **1954** Bissell *High Water* 113: I'll take this bitch clear to Hudson's Bay on double watch. **1961** Hugill *Shanties* 322 [ref. to 1920's]: I felt that I should skip an' join another,/'Twas plain that I had joined a lousy bitch. **1972** Cleaves *Sea Fever* 148: Goodbye, you old bitch...you old hell ship. **1983** S. King *Christine* 120: Come off a there, you bitch.

b. something that is especially hateful, disagreeable, unpleasant, or difficult; (in mod. use *esp.*) a difficult task. [1814 and prob. 1904 quots. are fig. S.E.]

[*****1814** Byron, in *OEDS*: It is well that *one* of us is of such fame, since there is a sad deficit in the *morale* of that article upon my part,—all owing to my "bitch of a star," as Captain Tranchemont says of his planet.] [*****1904** R. Kipling, in *OEDS*: After eight years, my father, cheated by your bitch of a country, found out who was the upper dog in South Africa.] **1928** *AS* (Feb.) 218: Jensen certainly gave us a bitch of an exam. **1929–30** Dos Passos *42d Parallel* 9: Middletown's a terrible bitch of a dump if you ask me. **1932** *AS* (June) 329: *Bitch*—n.—anything difficult, unpleasant, or disagreeable. **1937** Reitman *Box-Car Bertha* 33: The S.P. is the best road to take…but she's a bitch, sister. The shacks are hostile. **1940** M. LeSueur *Salute to Spring* 99: "Oh, she worked so hard," she said…."She wanted above everything to be a success." "It's a bitch," Marilyn said. **1942** in J. Stilwell *Papers* 60: This job is a bitch. *Ibid.* 158: This week has been a bitch. **1943** Guthrie *Glory* 262: Tucson's a bitch, boys, Tucson's a bitch. **1944** Pyle *Brave Men* 192: It's going to be a bitch of a thing to move. The ground is slick and you can't see your hand in front of you. **1945** *Yank* (Aug. 31) 10: I'm glad we didn't have to invade Japan. That would've been a bitch. **1949** "J. Evans" *Halo in Brass* 88: That wind's sure a bitch. **1959** A. Anderson *Lover Man* 67: Life is a bitch, ain't it? **1964** Redfield *Ltrs. from Actor* 21: Yet Hamlet…is a bitch of a part. **1965** in H. Ellison *Sex Misspelled* 343: It has real honesty in it, a bitchofuh lot of depth. **1965** Herlihy *Midnight Cowboy* 79: I…went thoo one bitch of a commotion here for you tonight. **1968** L.J. Davis *Where All Had Fled* 18: He was beginning on a bitch of a headache. **1985** B. Simpson, in H. Cannon *Cowboy Poetry* 171: He said, "Son, life's a bitch,/And then you just die." **1989** R. Miller *Profane Men* 88: The heat is going to…become a palpable essence…before this bitch is finished.

c. an annoying or problematical circumstance; rub; devil.

1971 *Go Ask Alice* 57: The bitch is that none of us ever seem to have enough money. **1980** *Easyriders* (May) 10: The bitch of the whole thing is…I don't get my mag back for about 45 minutes. **1980** Univ. Tenn. grad. student, age 32: The bitch of it was that I was totally unprepared then….*Bitch* means about the same as Hamlet's *rub*. The sense of irony is strong. I've known and used the word in that way for at least fifteen years. **1981** Hathaway *World of Hurt* 23: No, that's the bitch of it. All they can do is pass him on to somebody else. **1985** D. Steel *Secrets* 115: That was the bitch of it. She had never told anyone.

5. a queen in cards; (*esp.*) the queen of spades.

*1873 Hotten *Slang Dict.* (ed. 4) 105: When card-playing in public houses was common, the kings were called butchers, the queens bitches, and the knaves jacks. **1900** *DN* II 23: *Bitch, n.* Queen, at cards. **1960** Loomis *Heroic Love* 165: He wants to know where the Bitch is, and nobody'll tell him. **1969** Crumley *One to Count Cadence* 162: I dropped the queen of spades and thirteen bad points…."Guess ya caught the old bitch again, har har."

6. *West.* a makeshift lamp made from hardened grease.

1904 in *DA*: "I'll light a piece of fat pine," shouted the Boy…."Where's your bitch?" said Dillon. **1926** C.M. Russell *Trails* 159: Sometimes they were forced to use a "bitch"—which was a tin cup filled with bacon grease and a twisted rag wick. It didn't only give light—it gave its owners a smell like a New England dinner. **1930** "D. Stiff" *Milk & Honey* 199: *Bitch*—A tin-can lamp with a shirt-tail wick. **1936** R. Adams *Cowboy Lingo* 13: He invented a light by filling a tin cup with bacon grease into which was placed a twisted-rag wick. This he called a "bitch."

7.a. something or someone that is remarkable or surprising or otherwise extraordinary.

1943 Horan & Frank *Boondocks* 40: That's a bitch, isn't it? **1947–52** Ellison *Invisible Man* 427: Ain't *that* a bitch? *Ibid.* 470: He's a bitch, ain't he? **1952** in Clarke *Amer. Negro Stories* 207: Boy, I'm telling you, these peoples is a bitch on wheels. **1954** W.G. Smith *South St.* 105: Ain't that a bitch? Feelings! Ain't that a bitch! **1960** R. Reisner *Jazz Titans* 150: *Bitch:* something very good. Example: That tune is a bitch. **1964** Gregory *Nigger* 34: Wouldn't that be a bitch, to have a turkey like that in the house and no way to cook it? **1966–67** Harvey *Air War* 93: I realized why a lot of soldiers say the M-79 is such a bitch of a weapon….If there were any VC in that treeline without protection, Mike was certainly killing them. **1969** Hannerz *Soulside* 31: "Ain't that a bitch," said Freddy, and they all chuckled. **1971** Contini *Beast Within* 86: The old bastard kicked off three days later in the hospital. Ain't that a bitch?

b. a person, esp. a man, having remarkable skills.

1946 Mezzrow & Wolfe *Really Blues* 21: That boy was really a bitch, even though he was never taught to play music. **1952** H. Grey *Hoods* 60: He was what we called a "bitch at the wheel." He could do tricks with that car a Hollywood stunt driver would never dream of done. **1961** R. Russell *Sound* 74: Bernie's a bitch with the chords….I mean, he really feeds me good. **1967** Salas *Tattoo* 189: Carmen Cavallero is a bitch on the piano, Aaron….You oughtta hear him on Polonaise. Man!

8. [sugg. by *habitual*] *Pris.* a maximum sentence given under a habitual criminal law.—constr. with *the*.—often constr. with *big*.

1944 *Papers Mich. Acad.* XXX 596: "Bitch," a phonetic clipping, from "habitual" sentence. **1957** in Blake *Joint* 161: They tell me it's possible the judge may hit me with the bitch (habitual criminal) because my

record will have a possible four strikes when I go up for trial. **1966** Elli *Riot* 62: A middle-aged burglar serving life on the Big Bitch, the state's Habitual Criminal Law. **1966** M. Braly *On Yard* 38: If Chilly wasn't doing the big bitch…he'd own half this state. *Ibid.* 200: The judge…hit him with the bitch to run consecutively with his term for robbery. **1970** E.S. Gardner *Cops* 120: I'm going to pick a state which hasn't big bitch (criminal jargon for the law providing that third felony conviction brings an automatic life sentence) and start opening boxes (cracking safes). **1973** Norris & Springer *Men in Exile* 173: I'm doing it all, the bitch.

9. [fr. the v.] a complaint.

1945 *Yank* (Apr. 6) 17: He'd listen to any guy's bitches. **1945** Dos Passos *Tour* 104: Who wouldn't have a bitch…a goddam serious bitch? **1953** Harris *Southpaw* 165: That was the way it was, hardly a gripe or a bitch. **1955** Reifer *New Words* 31: *Bitch. n. Slang.* A complaint. **1957** McGivern *Against Tomorrow* 16: It turned into a gripe list after all; a bunch of bitches for the chaplain. **1958** Frankel *Band of Bros.* 57: You want to know what's behind anybody, you got to figure out what his bitch is. **1963** Ross *Dead Are Mine* 48: I could…put in a bitch to Powers but that would be sneaky. **1979** in Terkel *Amer. Dreams* 315: Hey, what's your bitch? The American Dream has treated you beautifully. **1966–80** McAleer & Dickson *Unit Pride* 248: Why don't you see the chaplain and have him put up a bitch and you won't hafta go back? **1980** S. Fuller *Big Red* 248: What the hell did you expect me to do? Desert with you four bitch artists? **1982** in Thom *Letters to Ms.* 175: I am writing to you with this "bitch," as my friends and relatives deem it, because I want to share it with someone who cares.

10. a clamp used to secure work to a lathe.

ca**1940** in Mencken *Amer. Lang. Supp. II* 760.

11. (see quot.).

1958 McCulloch *Woods Wds.* 108: *Loading bitch*—A loading machine, usually a small donkey [engine].

¶ In phrases:

¶ **blow a bitch** *Naut.* to blow a gale.

1979 T. Jones *Wayward Sailor* 47: It's blowing a bitch.

¶ **fiddler's bitch** (used as a standard of comparison for drunkenness).

1826 in *JAF* LXXVI (1963) 286: Az drunk as a *fiddler's bitch*. **1927** in Bruns *Kts. of Road* 130: I got drunker than a fiddler's bitch. **1931** *PMLA* XLVI 1304: He wuz ez drunk as a biled owl, er a fiddler's bitch. **1935** J. Conroy *World to Win* 265: She was drunk as a fiddler's bitch. **1976** G.V. Higgins *Deke Hunter* 103: Lively enough to steal a car and get himself drunk as a fiddler's bitch.

¶ **pitch a bitch** *Esp. Black E.* to create a disturbance; fly into a rage.

1946 G.W. Henderson *Jule* 132: I'm going to get drunk!…I'm going to pitch me a bitch! **1948** Webb *Four Steps* 58: But wait'll I tell Saint Jesus how many costumes….He'll pitch a bitch. **1970** E. Knight *Black Voices* 112: Man,…that Icewater is pitching a bitch over there. The way he's acting they're going to throw the book at him. **1983** Rovin *Pryor* 26: Pryor says he wouldn't be so bitter today if his parents…had gone to school to "pitch a bitch, just for their child, just scream and yell, 'There is no *nigger* in my family!'" **1989** S. Robinson & D. Ritz *Smokey* 168: Man,…you really pitched a bitch! This jam's a monster!

bitch *adj. Stu.* BITCHING, 2.

1971 Dahlskog *Dict.* 7: *Bitch, bitching, a.* Striking; admirable, as: a real *bitch* (*bitching*) car.

bitch *v.* **1.** to womanize; TOMCAT.

*1675 in *OED*: Jove, thou now art going a Bitching. **1953** Eyster *Customary Skies* 291: When I go bitchin', I hang out a sign. **1967** Schmidt *Lexicon of Sex* 21: *Bitch*…go out whoremongering. **1984** C. Crowe *Wild Life* (film): You're gonna wind up in El Salvador or Nicaragua—and you won't be watchin' Hueys or goin' bitchin'.

2.a. to spoil, ruin, botch, thwart, etc.—often constr. with *up*. [A "1756" ex. cited without documentation in Lederer's *Colonial Amer. Eng.*, p. 31, seems unlikely to belong to this sense.]

*1823 "J. Bee" *Slang Dict.* 10: To *bitch* a business, to spoil it, by awkwardness, fear, or want of strength. ***1856** in *OEDS*: You will bitch my schemes and lose your fifty pounds. ***1877** in *EDD* I 277: He was that stoopid he bitched the whole thing. **1919** Dos Passos *Initiation* 150: That probably bitched car No. 4 for evermore. **1919** in Pound *Pound/Joyce* 157: A…reporter long since assured me that Ulysses had bitched the American market which had begun to take "Portrait" seriously. **1925** Hemingway *In Our Time* 56: Once a man's married he's absolutely bitched. **1928** MacArthur & Hecht *Front Page* 483: You've just bitched up my whole life! That's what you've done! **1928** Wharton *Squad* 132: By God, I'll bitch 'em if I have to put my hand up an' catch a bullet. *Ibid.* 145: I'll bitch 'em all, th' Sergeant, th' Captain, th' whole dam' Army. **1934** in Pound *Letters* 248: That bitches it. **1934** in Hemingway *Sel. Letters* 408: We are all bitched from the start. **1936** M. Levin *Old Bunch* 402: Aw...I bitched up everything. **1939** Kaufman & Hart *Man Who Came to Dinner* 348: It's simply enchanting, and bitches Sherry and Lorraine at the same time. **1941** B. Schulberg *Sammy* 204: You had to stick your neck out like a giraffe. Now you really bitched yourself up. But good. **1943** J. Mitchell *McSorley's* 34: The world is all bitched up....Always was, always will be. **1948** Lait & Mortimer *New York* 18: She bitched up no lines in the next act. **1952** Michener *Bridges* 35: Sometimes I'm so bitter I could bitch up the works on purpose. **1947–53** Guthrie *Seeds* 254: Well, I've mortally bitched up the works. **1958** Camerer *Damned Wear Wings* 207: The world politicians—they'll bitch it up. **1959** Cochrell *Beaches* 296: I'd say you bitched up the case pretty thoroughly. **1972** R. Wilson *Forbidden Wds.* 38: I read the contract and it left me bitched, buggered, and bewildered. **1978** T. Sanchez *Zoot-Suit* 10: Don't bitch it up! *Ibid.* 62: Don't bitch up your life, Cruz. *a***1986** Hallion *Nav. Air War* 30 [ref. to *ca*1948]: General...Armstrong called the Corps "a small bitched-up Army."

b. to swindle; trick.

1924 in Hemingway *Sel. Letters* 119: Having been bitched financially and in a literary way by my friends I take...pleasure in the immediate triumphs of the bull ring. **1940** in Hemingway *Sel. Letters* 505: What a degenerate people the English are....They gave us the worst bitching anybody did in Spain where we fought both Hitler and Mussolini for them for nothing and could have kept them tied up there indefinitely...if they had only given any aid at all—any at all. **1941** B. Schulberg *Sammy* 295: I know you're regular, Al. You never tried to bitch me out of anything. **1965** Harvey *Hudasky's Raiders* 238: Wasted, tricked, bitched, buggered and bewildered.

3.a. to complain.—used intrans. [The sense in **1709 and **1720 quots. is 'to call someone a bitch', which is perh. the origin of this sense.]

[**1709* in *OED*: In wonderful Rage went to Cursing and Bitching.] [**1720* D'Urfey *Pills* VI 287: There was Fighting and Scratching,/And Rogueing and Bitching.] **1918** in Dos Passos *14th Chronicle* 196: My bitching, my twilight, my soucis proceed. **1930** *AS* (Feb.) 238: He bitched about the course. **1934** Appel *Brain Guy* 198: I ain't bitchin'. **1941** B. Schulberg *Sammy* 127: Jesus Christ, what the hell have you got to bitch about when I'm putting the money in your pocket? **1946** Shulman *Amboy Dukes* 20: This way...he won't bitch so much. **1948** Lay & Bartlett *12 O'Clock High* 62: Aw, why don't you bastards quit bitching. **1954** Yablonsky *Violent Gang* 78: I hang in my hallway janitor yells, I go on the stoop neighbors bitch. **1958** A. King *Mine Enemy* 10: So what am I bitching about? **1961** McMurtry *Horseman* 12: I didn't dress up to sit out here an' listen to Ma bitch. **1963** Morgan *Six-Eleven* 11: They still bitching about the holdup at Runsted for the Southbound? **1965** Schmitt *All Hands* 86: I hear there's been some bitching about the grub. **1967** C. Cooper *Farm* 87: I'm sittin here in this filth, but I'm not bitchin about anything. **1968** Baker et al. *CUSS* 81: Bitch and moan. Constantly complaining and irritable. **1978** Matthiessen *Snow Leopard* 165: The B'on-pos...come up bitching from the birth wood where they spent the night. **1990** Updike *Rabbit at Rest* 71: All he did was bitch. **1992** *New Yorker* (Oct. 19) 18: "Where *are* they? I can never find anyone in this place," he bitched.

b. to complain about, disparage.

1952 Brossard *Darkness* 3: Porter was occasionally quite talkative about his wife. Mostly he bitched her, but not vehemently. He laughed about...her ignorance of cultural matters. **1953** Brossard *Saboteurs* 69: All the women thereabouts were jealous of her looks and they consecrated a part of each day to gossiping about her and generally bitching her. **1967** Crowley *Boys in Band* 860: I can't keep up with you two...I thought you were mad at him—now he's bitchin' you. What gives?

c. to scold or upbraid (someone).—constr. with *out*; (*intrans.*) to scold or nag.—constr. with *at*.

1953 Peterson *Giant Step* 51: Yeh! Yeh! I know. I caught their sympathy when Miss Crowley was bitching me out. **1955** Ellson *Rock* 99: She bitches him out forty different ways. **1970** in J. Flaherty *Chez Joey* 17: Meanwhile, the regular Joe's wife was bitching at him for acting so common. **1974** Univ. Wis. student: This old codger was bitching us out for cutting through his yard. **1984** McInerney *Bright Lights* 21: When she's bitching you out, you have wanted to say, [etc.]. **1988** *Rage* (Knoxville, Tenn.) (Mar. 30) 14: Q. How many sorority girls does it take to screw in a lightbulb? A. Four. Three to bitch at it and one to call her boyfriend.

4. to anger.—constr. with *off*.

1959 Himes *Crazy Kill* 44: Reverend Short thinks Dulcy needs saving and she just takes every chance to bitch him off.

5. [fr. BITCH, *n.*, 8] *Pris.* to sentence under a habitual criminal statute.

1976 M. Braly *False Starts* 127: One more bust and they'll bitch me.

bitch bath *n.* the application of perfume or the like to mask body odor.

1953 *AS* (May) 145: A *bitch bath* requires talcum powder, deodorant, and perfume.

bitch box *n.* **1.** Esp. *Mil.* the loudspeaker of a public address or intercommunication system; a radiotelephone amplifier.

1945 in Shibutani *Co. K* 258: [The] bitch box. **1944–46** in *AS* XXII 54: *Bitch-Box.* Public address system. **1948** *New York Folklore* (Spring) 24: *Bitch box*—loudspeaker of public address system. **1956** Hargrove *Girl He Left* 76: You want to answer that bitch box, or you want me...to answer it for you? **1966** M. Braly *On Yard* 169: The Karp got on the bitch box to all the towers on the perimeter. **1971** *PADS* (No. 52) 28: *Bitch box*, n. An intercommunication system in a fire house. "Use the bitch box to get the captain." **1978** Downs *Killing Zone* 29 [ref. to 1967]: Delta Six had a "bitch box" on the back of the CP's radio to amplify any incoming calls, which allowed us to listen. **1990** G.R. Clark *Words of Viet. War* 58: *Bitch Box* Radio amplifier...used to amplify incoming radio traffic.

2. a small box, typically wall-mounted, for the filing of written complaints and suggestions.

1963 Coon *Short End* 202: I'll put a bitch box up in the rec hall. Then when you don't like the way the Jumper is running things, you can complain about it.

bitched *adj.* angry.—also constr. with *up*.

1969 Linn & Pearl *Masque* 176: She's all bitched up about her and Lester not being on the platform with the mayor at City Hall tomorrow. **1970** Zindel *Your Mind* 112: I'm *really* bitched. **1971** *Go Ask Alice* 101: I feel really bitched and pissed off at everybody.

bitching *adj.* **1.** SONOFABITCHING, damned; (*also*) WHOPPING. Also as adv. and infix.

1928 Dahlberg *Bottom Dogs* 148: Now, bitchin' fool, pay fer me! *Ibid.* 224: It was a bitchin' raw deal. *Ibid.* 271: Max...let out a bitchin' oath. **1939** M. Levin *Citizens* 38: That bitchn crane don't operate itself. **1951** Robbins *Danny Fisher* 193: I wanna put my mark on the bitchin' double-crosser. **1956* in Partridge *DSUE* (ed. 7) 1009: Wouldn't that be a bitchin' joke? **1961** Barbeau *Ikon* 161: Just my bitchin' luck to have 'em clobber this place for a week. **1965** Daniels *Moments of Glory* 196: Can you imagine what big news is this month? Her bitching dog has a cold. **1966** Manus *Mott the Hoople* 215: Turn that bitching thing off! **1967** Rechy *Numbers* 184: Mother-bitching-fucker! **1971** in L. Bangs *Psychotic Reactions* 53: A gang that was so bitchin' *bad*. **1972** P. Thomas *Savior* 78: He sure got himself a bitchin' big blade in that one hand. **1976** C.R. Anderson *Grunts* 78: That's the way it's been happening after a bitching hump ever since I been here—just watch. **1978** Wharton *Birdy* 138: It's really a bitchin' cold day. **1980** Eble *College Slang* 1: "That was a *bitchin'* test" means "That was a difficult test." **1980** Garrison *Snakedoctor* 7: Why didn't she keep up with it if the bitching insurance was so bitching important? **1981** Ballenger *Terror* 149: It's a bitchin' thing, leaving those guys. **1981** *Nat. Lampoon* (Oct.) 46: It was bitchin' gnarly, having to watch children with third-degree burns over 95 percent of their bodies do improvisational dance. **1984–88** Hackworth & Sherman *About Face* 198: We drove...in a bitching snowstorm.

2. *Stu.* excellent, wonderful; exceptionally attractive. Also **bitchen.**

1957 Kohner *Gidget* 10: It was a bitchen day too. The sun was out...in Southern California. **1962** *English Jrnl.* (May) 323: Bitchin'...equivalent to *neat* or *swell*. **1963–64** Kesey *Great Notion* 507: Bitchin' weather, don't you say? **1964** in *AS* XL (1965) 193: Bitchin'...can serve both as an interjection (*bitchin'*, man! = "Great") and as an adjective. Anything good can be *bitchin'*....Employed in our observation between 1956 and 1960. **1964** in *Time* (Jan. 1, 1965) 56: No greater praise can be bestowed on a person, place or thing in California than to be *bitchin'*. **1965** *AS* (Oct.) 193: Anything good can be "*bitchin*"—a car, a ball game, a record, a hand of bridge. Employed in our observation between 1956 and 1960. **1966** Tornabene *Teenager* 92: He was really bitchin. I know he's in college but he looks almost twenty-four....*Bitchin:* A short-lived, college freshman word for great, gorgeous, terrific. **1969** *Current Slang* I & II 10: *Bitching*,...adj. Very good looking.—College females, New York. **1969** in Bouton *Ball Four* 28: I add 20 points to my average if I know I look bitchin' out there. **1974** Lahr *Trot* 16: Helen Popkin. She's my cousin. Bitchin', huh? **1976–77** Kernochan *Dry Hustle* 208: Had a car like mine. A bitchin little Spitfire. **1982** S. Black *Awesome Val Guide* 10: Encino…is…totally bitchen. **1985** J. Dillinger *Adrenaline* 196: I feel bitchin'. **1992** *Middle Ages* (CBS-TV): Bitchin'! **1993** *L.A. Times* (Sept. 16) E3: Longboarder's photography and graphics are bitchin'.

bitch kitty *n.* something extraordinary, esp. something extraordinarily difficult; BITCH, *n.*, 4.b.
   1944 *New Yorker* (May 27) 28: She's flying right along. Bitch kitty of an airplane. **1957** Shulman *Rally* 54: We've had some tough town meetings before, but tonight's is going to be a bitch-kitty. **1964** Howe *Valley of Fire* 203: It was a lot better than the county jail….But it was still a bitch-kitty. **1968** W.C. Anderson *Gooney Bird* 60: Ain't that a bitch-kitty? **1985** Dye *Between Raindrops* 221: Crossing the open ground…would be a bitch-kitty. **1989** R. Miller *Profane Men* 127: Secondary depression…[is] a bitch kitty.

bitch session *n.* Esp. *Mil.* an informal airing of complaints. Also **bitching session.**
   1944–46 in *AS* XXII 54: *Bitch Session.* A bull session, gripe session. **1948** Lay & Bartlett *12 O'Clock High* 96: Next time I want there to be plenty of squawks. A real bitching session. **1952** Uris *Battle Cry* 110: I moved over to the bitching session. **1973** Herbert & Wooten *Soldier* 371: I recalled a bitch session I had had with a young lieutenant. **1975** Larsen *Runner* 35: In the midst of their bitch session came welcome news.

bitch water *n.* cologne.
   1949 De Forrest *Gay Year* 189: He looked over the colognes in the medicine cabinet…."Bitch water!"

bitchy *adj.* **1.a.** like a bitch; (*esp.*) spiteful or sarcastic.
   1925 McAlmon *Silk Stockings* 66: An habitual bitchy gaiety. **1942** Davis & Wolsey *Call House Madam* 119: What type does he like? I said rather cruelly looking at her, and felt bitchy after I'd said it. **1946** in Botkin *Sidewalks* 191: A perverse, bitchy girl. **1952** Himes *Stone* 179: [A homosexual] smelling as bitchy as a doll on the make. **1956** P. Moore *Chocolates* 75: They're real bitchy, these fags. **1959** in A. Sexton *Letters* 49: I am very bitchy acting in class….I act like a bitch with these sarcastic remarks. **1990** "Suzy," in *Cosmopolitan* (Mar.) 224: Bitchy…writing is the easiest kind of writing in the world, and if I wanted to do it, nobody could do it better.
   b. (of a woman) having a sexually provocative appearance or behavior; (of objects) provocative; attractive.
   1930 J.T. Farrell *Calico Shoes* 39: He spotted a pearl gray Stutz; bitchey roadster, all right. **1942** H. Miller *Roofs of Paris* 119: Toots…is as bawdy and bitchy as though she were…drunk. **1943** F. Wakeman *Shore Leave* 162: I like bitchy women….You don't have any responsibilities when you're dealing with bitchy women. **1955** L. Shapiro *6th of June* 26: Some chorus gal….Terrific….Didn't dream I'd marry someone even bitchier. **1957** Lacy *Room to Swing* 136: I ought to get into a bitchy dress—something real seductive. **1967** M. Howard *Call Me Brick* 116: I had always been…physically attractive….After my face, my legs were my bitchiest feature. **1982** Del Vecchio *13th Valley* 19: In Sydney, with a bitchy little Sydneysider, he had discovered moments when the Nam was forgotten.
   2. difficult.
   1944 Brooks *Brick Foxhole* 93: I have such a bitchy life….I don't think anybody in the world loves me. **1960** Hoagland *Circle Home* 103: It was a bitchy style to deal with. **1973** *TULIPQ* (coll. B.K. Dumas): If a course is known to be very hard it might be called…"bitchy." **1975** R.P. Davis *Pilot* 126: It was a particularly bitchy trip.
   3. full of complaints; complaining.
   1977 Langone *Life at Bottom* 157: In a couple of months you become very very conscious of the chow, and you start getting bitchy if it doesn't come to specs.

bite *n.* **1.a.** a swindler, cheat, hoaxer, impostor, or the like.
   *1698–99 "B.E." *Dict. Canting Crew*: Bite, c. A Rogue, Sharper or Cheat. ***1726** A. Smith *Mems. of J. Wild* 133: Your Wife's a Bite I see, but…now I have Bit the Biter. ***ca1730** *Country Spy* 36: The ridicule of every *Bite* that frequents that Place. ***1742** in *F & H* I (rev.) 233: Is this wench an idiot, or a bite? Marry me, with a pox! ***1751** T. Smollett *Peregrine Pickle* ch. xcviii: It was conjectured that Peregrine was a bite from the beginning, who had found credit on account of his effrontery and appearance, and imposed himself upon the town as a young gentleman of fortune. **1755** in *DAE*: I'm told horse dealers here are great *Bites*. ***1785** Grose *Vulgar Tongue*: A bite, (cant) a cheat. **1841** in M.W. Brown *Dan Rice* 61: If you have no cash, he'll swear you're a bite. **1904**

in "O. Henry" *Works* 912: Mickey, the Bowery Bite.
   b. an imposture; swindle; hoax; (*also*) a substitute intended to deceive, "ringer."
   *1707 Cibber *Double Gallant* 84: That bite won't do. ***1711** in *F & H* I (rev.) 232: It was a common bite with him, to lay Suspicions that he was favoured by a Lady's Enemy. ***1721** in *F & H* I (rev.) 284: Sharpers would not frequent gaming-tables, if the men of fortune knew the bite. **1723** in *DAE*: After the Proclamation was readd at the Corner of School-Street, a Negro, who stood to hear it, cry'd out, "A Bite, a Bite": Upon which he was immediately seized. **1792** Brackenridge *Modern Chiv.* 7: The jockeys were of the opinion…that the horse was what they call a bite, and that under the appearance of stiffness, there was concealed some hidden quality of swiftness. **1807** in Tyler *Verse* 161: Ah, what a bite,/This comes from loving at first sight. **1840** *Spirit of Times* (Sept. 12) 330: The "sharps"…brought the bay filly as a "bite" on purpose to beat the chesnut, who won the race. **1853** *Knickerbocker* XLII 434: The plaintiff's attorney, on perusing the plea, saw that it was meant for a "bite," and…demurred to it!
   2.a. a share of profits; CUT.
   1926 T.A. Dorgan, in Zwilling *TAD Lexicon* 94: I got two bites in your sawbuck—right, ain't it? **1955–57** A. Miller *View from Bridge* 18: Captain gets a piece,…Tony here'll get a little bite. **1957** Ness & Fraley *Untouchables* 168: He's okay. His bite is fifty bucks. **1965** Spillane *Killer Mine* 59: He always looking for his bite, that bum. **1967** Spillane *Delta* 60: Either way, I tipped the dealers a big bite.
   b. cost; price.
   1958 S.H. Adams *Tenderloin* 291: "What's the bite?" "Fifty-fifty." **1959–60** Bloch *Dead Beat* 74: He had to fight his way up to the ticket window and the damned bite was three bucks, too. **1967** Spillane *Delta* 97: "You have to look no further, senor. I can make all arrangements"…"What's the bite?" **1974** Sann *Dead Heat* 53: Then there's conspiracy, and you can't even begin to figure that bite.
   3. *Baseball.* a hard swing at a pitched ball.
   1914 [Patten] *Lefty o' the Bush* 66: "That's a nibble; take a bite," shouted a coacher.
   4. an unpleasant, esp. surprising, experience. Also (*vulgar*) **bite in the ass.**
   1956 Hargrove *Girl He Left* 37: Time I get out of the Army…why, I'll be almost old enough to vote….Ain't that a bite? **1971** Dahlskog *Dict.* 7: *Bite…n.*….Figuratively, a bite in the ass; hence, an unpleasant experience or happening, as: Getting that traffic ticket was a *bite*. **1973** *TULIPQ* (coll. B.K. Dumas): That exam was a real bite in the ass. **1973** Eble *Campus Slang* (Nov.) 3: *A real bite*—something bad: You mean ten of twelve flunked the test? That's a real bite. **1985** J. Hughes *Breakfast Club* (film): Wouldn't it be a bite missing a wrestling meet! **1989** R. Miller *Profane Men* 245: Ain't that a bite.
   ¶ In phrase:
   ¶ **put the bite on, 1.** to request or demand money (or, *occ.* a favor, etc.) from; to extort money from.
   *1919 Downing *Digger Dialects* 31: *Bite* (n. or v.) (1) A borrowing, to borrow, (2) an attempt to borrow. **1932** D. Runyon, in *Collier's* (Mar. 26) 7: This guy is called Sorrowful because this is the way he always is…especially about the way things are…when anybody tries to put the bite on him. **1938** Chandler *Big Sleep* 55: Why did you put the bite on Mrs. Regan instead of the old man? **1940** Zinberg *Walk Hard* 118: Don't you know that every bum puts bite on a pug? **1940** Burnett *High Sierra* 144: I'm not trying to put the bite on you, Mac….I need the dough, that's all. **1949** W.R. Burnett *Asphalt Jungle* 77: The D.A. had insisted on prosecuting him for putting the bite on the bingo parlors in the river slums south. **1949** Chandler *Little Sister* 180: What's Steelgrave doing all the time we're putting the bite on Weld? **1951** G. Fowler *Schnozzola* 127: We knew we had your confidence, or you would not of gone for the bite. **1952** Felton & Essex *Las Vegas Story* (film): If you're here to put the bite on me for flowers, you ought to tell me who it is. **1953** *I Love Lucy* (CBS-TV): I haven't got a cent. I was going to put the bite on you. **1955** Childress *Trouble in Mind* 156: You know who I had to put the bite on for an extra ten thousand? My ex-wife's present boyfriend. **1956** in Woods *Horse-Racing* 50: There's a tout who puts the bite on everyone he knows and he doesn't pay. **1965** Bonham *Durango St.* 155: Goldie says if I put the bite on him again, it'll be the last thing I ever does. **1966** "Minnesota Fats" *Bank Shot* 11: The Bite. A so-called loan which is usually uncollectable. **1963–78** J. Carroll *B. Diaries* 7: We…put the bite on him for some burgers.
   2. to place blame on.
   1963 Fehrenback *This Kind of War* 608: His own subordinates…get killed or wounded and someone thousands of miles back puts the bite on him, as if he were callous about it!

bite *v.* **1.a.** to swindle or cheat; trick; victimize; (*occ.*) to rob.

*1673 R. Head *Canting Acad.* 35: *Bite* To cheat or cozen. As *bite the Cully*...put the cheat on such a fellow. Or *The Cove was Bit*, The Man was cheated. **1676* in Partridge *Dict. Underworld* 42: *Bite*, c. To cheat. **1698–99* "B.E." *Dict. Canting Crew: Bite the Biter*, c. To Rob the Rogue, Sharp the Sharper, or Cheat the Cheater. *Bite the Cully*, c. to put the Cheat on the silly Fellow. **1707* (quot. at **BAM**, *v.*). **ca1730 Country Spy* 38: May be easily *bit* by these...two-legged Monsters. *1781* in M. Mathews *Beginnings of Amer. Eng.* 27: It is often said, a man is *taken in*, he is *bilked*, he is *bit*. *1783* in Freneau *Poems* 319: You thought, by *resolving*, to terrify Britain—/Indeed, if you did, you were damnably *bitten*. *1792* Brackenridge *Mod. Chiv.* 7: The most knowing...were bit by the bet. *1807* W. Irving *Salmagundi* 211: If the people be such fools, whose fault is it...if they get *bit*? *1821 Real Life in London* I 191: They meet to bite one another's heads off. *1848* Bartlett *Amer.* 32: *Bit*...Cheated, taken in. *1859* Matsell *Vocabulum* 11: *Bit*. Out-witted, "The cove was bit," "The cove has bit the flat, and pinched his cole," outwitted and robbed him....*Bite*. to steal; to rob. *1874* Pinkerton *Expressman* 17 [ref. to 1858]: I have got "bit" once more!

b. to ask money from, often with little likelihood of repayment.

1963 in Cannon *Nobody Asked* 110: The moochers bit him with stories he knew were lies. *1966* "Minnesota Fats" *Bank Shot* 215: Mainliner comes up...and tries to bite me for ten [dollars]. *1982* Leonard *Cat Chaser* 178: You think I come here to bite you for money.

2. to bother, annoy, make irritable. Also (*vulgar*) **bite (one's) ass, bite (one's) britches.**

1898 Norris *Moran* 53: What's biting 'em now? *1899* Norris *McTeague* 45: Well, somethun's bit-un you, anyhow. *1907* S.E. White *Arizona* 153: What's biting the locoed stranger? *1908* Hampton's Mag. (Dec.) 762: First off, what's biting you? *1926* Upson *Me & Henry* 143: What's biting you now? *1927* "M. Brand" *Pleasant Jim* 125: What's wrong? *1929* Brecht *Downfall* 296: What the hell's biting your old man? *1935* Clarke *Regards to B'way* 3: Hello, Sam. What's biting you? *1936* Jones *Trail of Lonesome Pine* (film): He's the laughin'est man I ever seen. Nothin' bites him. *1952* Uris *Battle Cry* 129: What's biting his ass? *1967* Taggart *Reunion* 56: Whut's bitin' *your* ass? *1970* R.N. Williams *Exiles* 132: So, it bit my ass. *1982* in *Nat. Lampoon* (Feb. 1983) 14: Something's been biting her britches for awhiles.

3. to be exceptionally hateful, disappointing, unfair, etc.; **SUCK.**—also constr. with *it*, or followed by various phrases sugg. fellatio (for which see *bite the big one*, below) or coprophilia.

1971 Dahlskog *Dict.* 7: *Bite*, *v*....Figuratively, to bite (eat) shit; hence to fail miserably or humiliatingly. *1975* in G.A. Fine *With the Boys* 169: You bite. *1975 Nat. Lampoon* (Sept.) 53: The activities on campus really bite. *1978* Price *Ladies' Man* 7: Door-to-door really bit on a cold day. Fuck the job. *1978* C. Miller *Animal House* 86: This really bites it. *1981 Hill St. Blues* (NBC-TV): Aw come on, man, this really bites brown air! Let's get out of here. *1986* Merkin *Zombie Jamboree* 279: That's the way I see it, sir, and I think it bites. *1990 Hull High* (NBC-TV): The food in the cafeteria, man. It bites.

4. to steal (usu. an idea, style, etc.); copy or imitate; crib. [This is evidently a new usage rather than a survival from 17th–18th C. cant; cf. Partridge *Dict. Und.*]

[**1673* R. Head *Canting Acad.* 35: *Bite the Roger*. Steal the Portmanteau.] [**1698–99* "B.E." *Dict. Canting Crew: Bite the Wiper*...to Steal the Hand-kerchief.] *1979* "Sugar Hill Gang" in L.A. Stanley *Rap* 325: The sucker M.C.s can bite all night. *1984* S. Hager *Hip Hop* 108: *Bite*—to steal someone else's style. Used by graffiti writers, break dancers, and rappers. *1988 Spin* (Oct.) 47: *Bite*, *vt* steal. *1989 Harper's* (Mar.) 23: In New York City slang,...that word is *bite*. It means to copy, duplicate,...imitate....Well, there's been a whole lot of biting going on. *1989* P. Munro *UCLA Slang* 21: Why did you bite my outfit? Now we look like twins. *1991* Nelson & Gonzales *Bring Noise* 159: English rappers always seem to be biting the style of their American counterparts.

¶ In phrases:

¶ **bite it!, 1.** "go to hell!" "fuck you!"—usu. considered vulgar. Also vars.

1948 Cozzens *Guard of Honor* 427 [ref. to WWII]: "Bite it!" Sergeant Pellerino said amiably. *1949* "R. MacDonald" *Moving Target* 54: I didn't like her...."Why don't you take a bite of me?"...I said. *1957* Kohner *Gidget* 22: "Bite the rag, you guys," he snorted. *Ibid.* 110: "Bite it," I said—and headed for the surfline. *1958* Johnson & Caidin *Thunderbolt* 194 [ref. to WWII]: Tell the rest to bite my butt. *1963* J. Ross *Dead Are Mine* 134 [ref. to WWII]: Bite me in the ass, Stein. *1971 Nat.*

Lampoon (June) 25: Oh, yeah! Then take a bite of this, buddy [indicating penis]! *1973* Detroit man, age *ca*35: When I was a boy in Detroit, we had a saying, *Bite the bag!* It meant, essentially, "Fuck you!" *Bag* referred to the scrotum. *1978* Univ. Tenn. student questionnaire: *Bite the dick, turkey*...Get the fuck out. *1986* Zeybel *First Ace* 152: Bite it. *1992 Married with Children* (Fox-TV): "Drop dead." "Bite me!"

2. to be killed, bite the dust; fail totally.

1968–77 Herr *Dispatches* 56: "He who bites it this day is safe from the next," and that was exactly what nobody wanted to hear. *1979* N. Young, in *Rolling Stone* (Feb. 8) 42: A lot of them are biting it this year. People are not going to come back to see the same thing over and over again. *1989* R. Miller *Profane Men* 186: Here are some of the 482 ways I do not...want to bite it.

¶ **bite [it] off** to stop talking; shut up.

1843 in *DA:* I had to bite it short, for a chap came on board the sloop with Captain Doolittle. *1911* in *DA:* "Ah, bite that off!" Rhode interrupted impatiently. *a1904–11* Phillips *Susan Lenox* I 251: "Oh, bite it off, hamfat,"...had greeted his impressive lectures on the magic lantern pictures.

¶ **bite [on] the bullet** to force oneself to perform a painful, difficult task or to endure an unpleasant situation. Now *S.E.*

*1891 R. Kipling, in *OEDS:* Bite on the bullet, old man, and don't let them think you're afraid. **1923* P.G. Wodehouse, in *OEDS:* Brace up and bite the bullet. I'm afraid I've bad news for you. *1923* Revell *Off the Chest* 195: Keep up the fight, Pardner. Don't let them make you bite the dust, just bite the bullets. *1974* Hejinian *Extreme Remedies* 257: We've got to bite the bullet on that one. *1983 People's Court* (Feb. 18) (ABC-TV): So you'll have to bite the bullet, so to speak.

¶ **bite on the nail** *bite [on] the bullet.*

1943 in Hemingway *Sel. Letters* 550: There are going to be three or four times when everybody is going to have to bite on the old nail in this case.

¶ **bite the big one** Esp. *Juve.* to be very offensive, unpleasant, inferior, etc.; **SUCK;** (*also*) to come to harm; die. Also vars., all with the penis as referent.

1977 Bredes *Hard Feelings* 248: To put it in common language, it bites the bone. *1977 Saturday Night Live* (NBC-TV): Marvelously, marvelously bad. Really bites the big one. *1978* Univ. Tenn. student: That really bites the big one. *1979 Mork & Mindy* (ABC-TV): You promise to love, honor and obey me till one of us bites the big one? *1980* Eble *Campus Slang* (Oct.) 1: Bite the big one—get injured or lose. *1983* Leeson *Survivors* (film): Society is gonna bite the big one...The smart money's gonna head for the hills. *1983* S. King *Christine* 79: That place bites the root anyway. *1984* Hindle *Dragon Fall* 62: This little company really tried, y' know,...but I guess they're presently biting the big one. *1984* J. McCorkle *Cheer Leader* 37: Eat shit....Bite the big one. *1985 Teenage Mutant Ninja Turtles* (CBS-TV): You don't suppose he bit the big one, do you? *1986* J. Hughes *Ferris Bueller* (film): Bite the big one, Junior. *1986* Merkin *Zombie Jamboree* 11: A place that bites the hairy wazoo. *Ibid.* 15: That should bite the big one. *1987 21 Jump St.* (Fox-TV): Weintraub bites the big one! *1988* McDowell & Skaaren *Beetle Juice* (film): You just bit the big one [died] two months ago. *1991 N.Y. Times* (nat. ed.) (Jan. 24) A 7: You think about how you will be remembered if you bite the big one.

¶ **bite the dust** see s.v. **DUST,** *n.*

biter *n.* a contemptible or despicable fellow.

1984 A. Davis et al. *Beat Street* (film): You just like all the biters—you just take a bite and leave the rest. *Ibid.* Yo, biters. All you homeboys are biters.

Bitter Biscuit Line *n. Hobo.* (see 1917 quot.).

1917 Livingston *Coast to Coast* 122: The "Bitter Biscuit Line" is the nickname of the Piedmont divisions of the Southern Railway. *1947* (cited in Partridge *Dict. Und.* (ed. 2) 794).

Bitter Creek *n.* ¶ In phrase: **from Bitter Creek** *West.* tough; ferocious. [The actual Bitter Creek is in Wyoming and Utah.]

1871 Crofutt *Tourist's Guide* 77: The freighter...would swear that he was a "tough cuss on wheels, from Bitter Creek." *1880* Nye *Boomerang* 121: You're a fine haired snoozer from Bitter Creek; ain't ye? *1880* in Rosa *Gunfighter* 41: Give me room and I'll whip an army. I'm a blizzard from Bitter Creek. *1885* in Lummis *Letters* 235: Evidently deeming me a fighter from Bitter Creek. *1885* Siringo *Texas Cowboy* 44: I spent two or three months' wages for an outfit, spurs, etc., trying to make myself look like a thoroughbred Cow Boy from Bitter Creek. *1900 Harper's* (May) 891: I'm wild, and woolly, and full of fleas;/I'm hard to curry above the knees;/I'm a she-wolf from Bitter Creek and /It's my night to ho-o-wl.

bitters *n.pl.* (one's) just deserts or punishment.
　1812 in *DA:* You might get your bitters in Baltimore Town. **1824** in Paulding *Bulls & Jons.* 355: D—n him but I'll do his business; I'll give him his bitters. *a***1846** in *DAE:* The seal soon got his bitters, and the captin cut a big hunk off the tail eend.

bitty *n.* var. BIDDY.

bivvy *n.* Esp. *Mil.* a bivouac; (*specif.*) a bivouac tent or protective dugout.
　1919 Sanborn *131st Inf.* 185: The following morning moving back from the river a short distance we established ourselves in "bivies." This was our position until October 8th. **1919** *318th Regt.* 72: This march was made without interruption and early in the afternoon the men had their "bivies" up. **1920** Herr *Co. F* 37: The next day bivies were dug in the sides of the trenches. **1921** Floyd *Co. F* 30: One afternoon Major Knight…rode his horse over a bivvy which had very little earth overhead. The occupants came tumbling out in great disorder. **1922** Colonna *Co. B* 48: Just as I got back to our bivvies at the tail of B Co., two ash cans—whoppers—arrived…right in the midst of A Co. **1950** Leland *Shell Hole* 242 [ref. to 1918]: Lieutenant Darriell, Sergeant Garey and I sat huddled together in one bivvy while the storm raged. **1979** *Popular Science* (Mar.) 96: Tuck a bivvy sack into your pack and you can travel tentless and still weather a storm. *a***1987** Bunch & Cole *Reckoning for Kings* 345: The bivvy site…would be about twenty meters away from a stream.

biz *n.* business (in any sense); in phr. **that's show biz!** (orig. *Theat.*) "that's the way life is and you ought to resign yourself to it."
　1861 O.W. Holmes, Jr., in M.D. Howe *Shaping Yrs.* 92: This…week…has been the first that really looked like biz. **1862** in Davidson *Old West* 16: And always made it his exclusive "biz"/To mingle in a crowd and "let 'er whiz." **1862** Browne *Artemus Ward* 222: I must forth to my Biz. **1863** in Wightman *To Ft. Fisher* 97: Our officers…"understand their biz." *****1864** Hotten *Slang Dict.* (ed. 3) 90: *Bus,* business (of which it is a contraction) or action, on the stage. **1865** in J. Miller *Va. City:* Mr. Miller's two daughters…carried on that branch of the biz. **1865–67** De Forest *Miss Ravenel* 178: They profoundly respected him because, as they said, "he knew his biz." **1868** Williams *Black-Eyed Beauty* 7: Work-girls in the umbrella and artificial-flower "biz." **1871** Banka *Prison Life* 79: He's an old hand at the biz. **1872** Burnham *Secret Service* iv: *Biz*—Business; occupation; object; trade; calling. **1874** Carter *Rollingpin* 18: Thy tears and supplications have done the biz. **1885** *Puck* (Apr. 29) 138: Biz came in the moment I started. **1889** Barrère & Leland *Dict. Slang* I 207: *Bus*…(Theatrical), contraction of "business." Pronounced *biz.* **1890** Langford *Vigilante Days* 27: That's not my way of doing biz. **1891** Bourke *On Border* 70: I'm gittin' kind o' tired'n' must git th' whole bizz off me mind. **1891** Kirkland *Co. K* 84: Might have staid to hum and tended to our little biz. **1905** *Variety* (Dec. 16) 9: Ain't you in the biz? **1909** *Sat. Eve. Post* (July 3) 6: *They* paid to work, to learn the biz. **1912** Z. Grey *Purple Sage* 67: But I reckon that white flare will do the biz. **1972** in Asimov et al. *Sci. Fi. Short Shorts* 164: Constant interest is an important part of the god biz. **1974** *Playboy* (Feb.) 62: How did you happen to go into showbiz? Had you wanted to be an actor since childhood? **1975** V.B. Miller *Trade-Off* 35: Crooks are always back on the streets before the arresting officers….That's show biz, I guess. **1980** *N.Y. Times* (July 27) II 27: Tom Snyder, who worked…as a national anchor for NBC on the weekends, takes a skeptical view of the anchor's role: "The only thing phonier than show biz is the news biz." **1982** Ad on (WKGN radio) (June 2): Lynn's is the best there is in the cleaning biz. **1990** *U.S. News & W.R.* (Oct. 15) 81: Why does a disciplined, no-nonsense nation like Japan want to get into show biz?

bizarro *n.* [partially sugg. by the character *Bizzaro,* introduced in *Superman* comics in 1957–58] a bizarre person.
　1980 W. Sherman *Times Sq.* 13: Joe thought about arresting the *bizarro.* **1985** Univ. Tenn. prof., age *ca*32: These people are real bizaros.

bizarro *adj.* bizarre; (*also*) crazy.
　1971 *Current Slang* 5: *Go bizarro*…To lose one's composure; to be driven insane. **1973** in L. Bangs *Psychotic Reactions* 122: The bizarro lushed-up Irish scrubwoman Kitty McShane. **1979** *New West* (Sept. 24) 88: His more recent drug-laden, bizarro epistolaries. **1982** Sculatti *Catalog of Cool* 49: Bizarro TV yarn starts with acid flashback. **1986** E. Weiner *Howard the Duck* 47: Whatever bizarro drug someone had slipped her.

bizzaz var. PIZZAZ.
　1970 in *BDNE* 64. **1984** WINS radio news (Aug. 23): The delegates

staged a demonstration with bands, balloons and bizzaz. **1992** *CBS This Morning* (CBS-TV) (Jan. 22): That needed bizzaz too.

bizazzy *adj.* having BIZZAZ.
　1984–88 Safire *Lang. Maven* 149: To establish a bezazzy…tone.

B.J. *n.* **1.** [BLOW JOB] *Pros. & Homosex.* an act of fellatio. Also as v.
　1949 *Gay Girl's Guide* 3: B–J: Abbreviation for Blow-Job. **1969** Ruben *Everything About Sex* 204: Masochistic males…like to be tied up and B.J.'d. **1976** *Urban Life* V 277: Mary decided to stick to just BJ's. **1981–85** S. King *It* 65: One of ya fag friends gonna give you a bee jay? **1988** *Nat. Lampoon* (Apr.) 114: Don't call me up with offers of sex and B.J.s.
　2. *Gamb.* the game of blackjack.
　1957 Gutwillig *Long Silence* 128: The rain stopped…just in time for the "Bee-Jay" party. The last blackjack game had been played May 15.

B.J. *adj.* [see 1981–89 quot.] *U.S. Mil. Acad.* (of a plebe) impertinent.
　1930 in D.O. Smith *Cradle* 50: I was on a starvation diet every meal at this table for having acted smart or "B.J." **1961** Ford *Black, Gray & Gold* 10: Soon gained the reputation of being a B.J. plebe…the expression means "fresh" or impertinent. **1981–89** R. Atkinson *Long Gray Line* 39: The protest was audacious—B.J., in cadet parlance, meaning "bold before June," when plebes were officially recognized by the upperclassmen.

B-joint *n.* a saloon that employs B-GIRLS.
　1967 Dibner *Admiral* 233 [ref. to WWII]: He swears she's working this B-joint, The Oriole. **1975–78** O'Brien *Cacciato* 164: I remember he takes me to this—you know, to this B joint. Half hour later I'm drunk like a skunk.

blabberguts *n.* BLABBERMOUTH.
　1977 Monaghan *Schoolboy, Cowboy* 136 [ref. to 1913]: Hark that no'count blabber-guts.

blabbermouth *n.* Esp. *Juve.* one who talks too much or betrays secrets.
　1936 Steinbeck *Dubious Battle* 249: One minute he's a blabbermouth kid. **1946** J. Adams *Gags* 106: To a blabbermouth— "The last time I saw a mouth like yours there was a fish hook in it." **1950** Solt *Lonely Place* (film): That blabbermouth Junior filed a complaint. **1961** *Car 54* (NBC-TV): You're a big windbag, a blabbermouth and a bore. *****1979** "J. Gash" *Grail Tree* 29: Friend?…Good old blabbermouth.

black *n.* **1.** a blacksmith.
　1776 in T.P. Coffin *Uncertain Glory* 104: A blacksmith by his trade.…As great a black as e'er was seen.
　2. *Narc.* opium.
　[**1924** G.C. Henderson *Keys to Crookdom:* Yen-shee, called "black stuff," is the ashes of smoked opium.] **1949** Monteleone *Crim. Slang* 24: *Black*…Opium. **1964** Anslinger & Gregory *Protectors* 228: Black— Opium. **1979** Pepper & Pepper *Straight Life* 139: He had been shooting "black" (opium).
　3. *Coast Guard.* a vessel engaged in rumrunning. Now *hist.*
　1970 W.I. Norton *Eagle Ventures* 28 [ref. to 1920's]: *Firelight,* a rum ship, or "black," as such ships were popularly called, was already known to the Coast Guard.…The *Eagle* took over trailing the "black" from a destroyer also stationed at Base Four.
　4. a black asphalt highway.
　1972 Buell *Shrewsdale* 93: "Where was this?" "Can't say—on the black somewhere."
　5. *Mil.* black market.—constr. with *the.* See also BLACK, *adj.*
　1983 T. Page *Nam* 42 [ref. to Vietnam War]: On the black you get a hot chopper, a can of Cs or a PBR that fell off the back of a truck.
　6. *Black E.* a fellow black man; black friend.—usu. used in direct address.
　1989 *Rolling Stone* (Oct. 19) 54: Yo, black…I like your suit. **1991** in *Rap Masters* (Jan. 1992) 19: You, Q-Tip, what's this fluff stuff, Black?
　¶ In phrase:
　¶ **in the black, 1.** [ref. to the black ink used to record profits or assets] *Finance.* showing a profit. Now *S.E.* Cf. *in the red* s.v. RED.
　1928 *N.Y. Times* (Mar. 11) VIII 6: *In The Black*—Showing a profit. **1984** Hindle *Dragon Fall* 60: Yes, Out of the red and into black. Deep into black.
　2. *Mil.* (see quot.). Cf. BLACK, *adj.*
　1982 *Atlantic* (Dec.) 58: There were at least two top-secret NSA facilities operating "in the black"—that is, under cover—in Chile. **1987**

Robbins *Ravens* 41 [ref. to 1960's]: Americans "in the black"—that is, on a clandestine posting—from the USAF and Lockheed Aircraft Systems...guided American bombers in northern Laos. *Ibid.* 78: Frank Shaw, a twenty-year-old Air Force enlisted man in the "black."

black *adj.* Esp. *Mil.* secret, clandestine, covert; (*specif.*) not financially accountable to the government *or* not accountable to Congress or the public.

1965 *N.Y. Times* (July 25) 1 30: Black money is that not reported to the government for income tax purposes. **1967** *Time* (Feb. 24) 17: The group...examines in great detail every single "black" (covert) operation proposed. **1974** *Harper's* (Dec.) 56: Caulfield was convinced that Intertel was engaged in "black" operations. **1983** *U.S. News & W.R.* (Apr. 18) 33: There are also the "black," or "illegal," operatives who have blended into American communities as immigrants or even assumed the identity of U.S. citizens. **1983** *L.A. Times* (Aug. 7) I 14: There is no significant movement in Congress to lift the "black" designation from the Stealth cruise missile. **1984** *Atlantic* (Jan. 1985) 27: This was "black" labor: no taxes are paid, no social regulations or minimum wages are honored. **1985** Boyne & Thompson *Wild Blue* 229: A black assignment is beyond Top Secret; it's done in complete secrecy with a budget that is not revealed to the public. The chief briefs the heads of the Armed Services committees, and they are sworn to secrecy. **1987** Averill *Mustang* 288: One of MAAG-16's squadrons had been moved to...Thailand in April 1961 for "black" operations across the Mekong in support of Special Forces teams and...Lao units. **1987** Robbins *Ravens* 397 [ref. to 1960's]: *Black.* Clandestine, in the sense of "black money." **1988** *Newsweek* (May 16) 21: The Pentagon begins a secret, "black" program to develop new armor, using extremely dense depleted-uranium.

black acid *n.* strong black coffee; BATTERY ACID.

1945 *Yank* (Apr. 13) 14: A cup of "black acid" at the Service Club counter.

black-and-tan *n.* **1.** a person of mixed white and black ancestry.

1868 in H. Nathan *D. Emmett* 299: My lubs a brack and tan. **1875** *Minstrel Gags* 131: Oh, we are the happiest black-and-tans/To be found within the land. **1889** Barrère & Leland *Dict. Slang* I 124: *Black-and-tan*...(American)...A mulatto, a mixture of mulattoes and blacks. **1891** in *DA*: "Well, this ain't no duck quackin', Mister Hubbard," said the black-and-tan.

2. a dance hall or saloon frequented by blacks and whites. Also **black-and-tan joint** and other vars.

1887 Walling *N.Y. Chief of Police* 486: It would not be difficult to say where the Black-and-Tan got its name. It is the resort of black men as well as white, but the girls are all white! The mixture of races is all the more revolting. **1891** Riis *Other Half Lives* 18: Another ward...honors with political leadership the proprietor of one of the most disreputable Black-and-Tan dives and dancing-hells to be found anywhere. **1891** Campbell, Knox & Byrnes *Darkness & Daylight* 470: There was a curious resort on Baxter Street...known among white men as "The Black and Tan." **1916** Miner *Prost.* 84: The most dangerous clubs in New York have been the "black and tan joints." **1923** Ornitz *Haunch, Paunch, & Jowl* 40: A black and tan joint in Hell's Kitchen. **1927** Thrasher *Gang* 262: A group of twelve or fifteen colored boys had been hanging around the back room of a notorious black-and-tan café and cabaret in the Black Belt. **1929–33** J.T. Farrell *Manhood* 320: Arnold and I got pie-eyed in a black-and-tan joint. **1963** in H. Ellison *Sex Misspelled* 41: Some college kid had met a hipster in a downtown black-and-tan club. **1988** Barrow & Munder *Joe Louis* 57 [ref. to 1920's]: A "black and tan" (interracial) club in downtown Detroit.

black-and-white *n.* **1.** *pl. Music.* a piano keyboard; piano.

1918 *Chi. Sun. Trib.* (June) V (unp.): I know you're a bearcat at ticklin' the black an' whites. **1937** (quot. at TINKLEBOX).

2.a. Orig. *Police. n.* a black-and-white police patrol car.

1958 Gilbert *Vice Trap* 20: Those black and white birds weren't after me, though. [**1962** *AS* XXXVII 267: *Black and white taxi, n.* A traffic police automobile with white doors, as required by law.] **1965** Calif. policewoman, age *ca*40: We call the squad cars *black-and-whites*. **1976** *S.W.A.T.* (NBC-TV): Keep him ringed with black-and-whites but don't move in on him. **1977** A. Patrick *Beyond Law* 130: Now get a mess of black-and-whites down there on the double! **1981** Univ. Tenn. *Daily Beacon* (Nov. 6) 2: The whole parking lot is *lousy* with black and white! That damn guard must have called them. **1982** P. Michaels *Grail* 180: The area was sealed off by black-and-whites. **1983** *Good Morning America* (ABC-TV) (June 1): The [Los Angeles] police cars are called *black-and-whites*.

b. a police officer; police.

1965 in D. Glasgow *Black Underclass* 110: Then the buses of "black and white" came. **1975** Wambaugh *Choirboys* ch. xi: He pays off all the black and whites and all the vice in this district.

2. *Narc.* a black-and-white capsule containing a drug, esp. Biphetamine.

1970 Landy *Underground Dict.* 34: *Black and white n.*...Biphetamine. Comes from dual color of capsule. **1979** Pepper & Pepper *Straight Life* 283 [ref. to 1961]: "Black-and-whites," Dilantin and Phenobarbital. **1981** (cited in Spears *Drugs & Drink* 47).

Black Annie *n.* [cf. BLACK BETTY, 2] *Pris.* a whip used to flog recalcitrant prisoners.

[**1935** Pollock *Underworld Sp.*: Black aunty, a whip (prison).] **1963** *Newsweek* (Mar. 18) 33: Black Annie. **1969** Hopper *Sex in Prison* 34: Inmates and staff members alike refer to the strap as "Black Annie" or "Bull Hide."

black ass *n.* despondency or disgust.—usu. considered vulgar. Hence **black-assed,** *adj.*

1945 in Hemingway *Sel. Letters* 579: Certainly have the Black Ass today, Miss Mary so much it makes me sick....Am being black assed and temperamental. **1955** in J. Blake *Joint* 110: I had a long spell of black-ass, but it's lighter now, I can cut it. **1961** Hemingway *Islands in Stream* 366: What the hell have you got so much black ass about today, Willie?

black-bag *adj.* Orig. *Espionage.* involving usu. extrajudicial entry and search by a law-enforcement or intelligence agency.—used prenominally.

1966 in "H.S.A. Becket" *Dict. Espionage* 23: "Black bag jobs"...represent an invaluable technique in combating subversive activities of a clandestine nature. **1973** in *Submission of Pres. Convers.* 175: All...involved black bag operations, kidnapping, providing prostitutes to weaken the opposition, [etc.]. **1976** *Atlantic* (Apr.) 42: The danger is not so much the assassin or the black bag job as the Orwellian electronic capacity. **1980** Pearl *Slang Dict.*: *Black-bag job n.* (Politics) illegal entry by the FBI into a foreign embassy, etc., to gather intelligence. **1981** D.E. Miller *Jargon* 214: *Black bag job:* illegal breaking and entering...by an intelligence agency. **1982** ABC-TV *Evening News* (Nov. 22): For years...[he] was an expert in court-ordered "black bag jobs"—break-ins, burglaries, and safe-crackings against foreign agents in the U.S. **1984** Caunitz *Police Plaza* 90: Black-bag stuff? In this day and age? *Ibid.* 214: The scrapings had been obtained by black-bag methods and could not be used in court. **1984** "W.T. Tyler" *Shadow Cabinet* 14: We're not thinking about any black bag job, if that's what you're worried about. *Ibid.* 109: I figure that means black-bag operations...without a court order.

black beauty *n. Narc.* BLACK BOMBER.

1969 *N.Y. Post* (Nov. 19) 5: I had to buy a black beauty (a strong barbiturate) for a dollar. **1969** Lingemann *Drugs A to Z* 24: *Black beauties*...Biphetamine capsules. **1973** in *Playboy* (Jan. 1974) 48: I am a 25-year-old graduate student and I use amphetamines (black beauties and crossroads) quite frequently. **1974** J. Robinson *Bed/Time/Story* 216: Won't be any black beauties for a while now....A guy got picked up with ten thousand of them the other day. **1976** Arble *Long Tunnel* 192: I took a black beauty and I don't know what I got off on. **1980** *Nat. Lampoon* (June) 81: Truckers who've spaced too many black beauties between the Black Labels and Lone Stars. **1990** *New Yorker* (Sept. 10) 56: We...took acid and black beauties—some kind of speed pill.

blackberry *n.* a black person.—used contemptuously.

1859 Tayleure *Boy Martyrs* 10: Don't budge, blackberry! **1981–85** S. King *It* 654: Calling him...nightfighter, Ubangi, spade, blackberry, junglebunny.

Black Betty *n.* **1.** a liquor bottle made of dark glass; (*hence*) liquor; in phr. **kiss Black Betty** to take a drink of liquor from such a bottle. Also **Black Betts.**

1737 *Pennsylvania Gaz.* (Jan. 6) 1: The Drinker's Dictionary...He's kissed black Betty. **1821** in *DA*: He that got first to the bride's house, got black betty....The company stopt and every boy and girl, old and young,...must kiss black betty; that is to take a good slug of dram. **1824** in *DAE*: If any wanted to help himself to a dram,...he would call out "Where's black Betty?" **1833** N. Ames *Old Sailor's Yarns* 277: If you've got any white-eye in that black betty that you're rousing out of your pea-coat pocket, I don't much care if I take a drop. **1845** in *DA*: There I was loaded...with plenty of what some call "Black Betts," or "O be joyful." **1860** W.H. Milburn *Pioneer Preacher* 48: The foremost of the horsemen clutches "black Betty,"...applies her mouth to his mouth, imbibing the consequences. **1880** in *DA*: They didn't forget to pass the old "black betty," filled with good old peach brandy, among the old pioneers. **1956, 1957** in *DARE* [both hist. refs.].

2. [cf. BLACK ANNIE] (see quot.).

1934 Lomax & Lomax *Amer. Ballads* 60: Black Betty is…the whip that was and is used in some Southern prisons.…Oh, Lawd, Black Betty,/…Black Betty, where'd you come from?

3. *Texas.* BLACK MARIA, 1.a.

1965 in Jackson *Swim Like Me* 155: She…rode Black Betty (prison transfer bus) to her new pad. **1984** Sample *Racehoss* 141 [ref. to 1956]: The transfer truck, "Black Betty," slowly backed inside the gates.

blackbird *n.* **1.** a black person; (*specif.*) (*obs.*) a Melanesian.— usu. used contemptuously.

1832 in Wade *Slavery in Cities* 30: With so many blackbirds around it. **1865** Smyth *Sailor's Wd. Bk.*: *Blackbird-catching.* The slave trade. *Black-birds.* A slang term on the coast of Africa for a cargo of slaves. **1869** *Overland Mo.* (Apr.) 355: How would you like to go a blackbird ketchin'…goin' to the Guinea coast for niggers. **1872** Thomes *Slaver* 54: I was within two days' sail of…Cuba, with five hundred blackbirds on board. **1873** Revere *Keel & Saddle* 10 [ref. to *ca*1830]: We were…calculating the handsome profits we should reap from our cargo of blackbirds. **1897** Ade *Pink* 194: She's got mo' feathehs 'an any otheh blackbuhd 'at eveh flew 'long Deahbohn Street. **1903** Adams *Log of a Cowboy* 355: There were about a dozen entries and only one blackbird in the covey. **1969** Angelou *Caged Bird* 106: It was a dangerous practice to call a Negro anything that could be loosely construed as insulting because of the centuries of their having been called niggers, jigs, dinges, blackbirds, crows, boots, and spooks. **1971** Faust *Willy* 52: The blackbirds have an extra inch in their Achilles tendon giving them a terrific advantage.

2. *USAF.* a black airplane, (*specif.*) a night fighter or a high-altitude reconnaissance plane. [In later use, the Lockheed SR-71 reconnaissance plane.]

*ca*1952 in Wallrich *A.F. Airs* 111: We won't take off till the sun goes down,/We fly blackbirds. **1962** Harvey *Strike Command* 203: Francis Powers had taken off in his "black bird" on his last flight over Russia.

3. *Narc.* BLACK BOMBER.

1974 J. Robinson *Bed/Time/Story* 216: Black birds. Black bombers. One of the few truly great pills. Sleek Biphetamine 30's. Pure black capsules. **1975** (cited in Spears *Drugs & Drink*). **1980** Whalen *Takes a Man* 112: Two "blackbirds," or amphetamines.

4. *Labor.* an itinerant or migratory worker.

1980 Bruns *Kts. of Road* 24: The floaters and blackbirds were not as indispensable and not as much in evidence as they once had been.

blackbird *v.* to deal in the capturing and selling of black slaves. Hence **blackbirder,** *n.*

*1873 Hotten *Slang Dict.* (ed. 4) 84: *Blackbirding,* slave-catching. Term most applied nowadays to the Polynesian coolie traffic. **1883* in *OEDS: Blackbirders,* the kidnappers labour purposes on the islands of the Pacific. **1887** Davis *Sea Wanderer* 148: Tom Thorn…had made many voyages to the West Coast of Africa…"black birding" as we strongly suspected. **1897** Kelley *Ship's Company* 140: As cruel a set of swashbuckling brutes as ever "black-birded" on any coast or sea. **1931** Rynning *Gun Notches* 17: My uncle…had been a blackbirder in his day. **1933** in R.E. Howard *Iron Man* 121: The toughest A.B. that ever shipped aboard of a blackbirder.

blackbird-catcher *n.* a slaver or a slaving ship.

1869 *Overland Mo.* (Apr.) 353: I…follered all kinds of business from a regular trader to a "blackbird catcher," and from that to a pirate. **1883** Keane *Blue-Water* 85: He had been in West Coast slavers and Pacific black-bird catchers.

black boat *n. Navy.* a destroyer.

1918 in Battey *70,000 Miles* 303: Destroyers are the "black boats." They were painted black in peace times. **1940** M. Goodrich *Delilah* 413 [ref. to WWI]: The condition that is the most obvious characteristic of a man-of-war, even of a "black boat": a clean tidiness.

black bomber *n. Narc.* a black or black-and-white capsule containing a drug; (*specif.*) a black Biphetamine capsule.

*1963 in *OEDS:* Police who raided the house found…100 methydrine tablets and 99 "Black Bomber" pills. **1972** *Nat. Lampoon* (Oct.) 41: *Biphetamine* 20 mg. (black bomber). **1974** J. Robinson *Bed/Time/Story* 216: Black birds. Black bombers. One of the few truly great pills. Sleek Biphetamine 30's. Pure black capsules.

black bottle *n.* (esp. among hobos) a bottle of poison.

1917 A. Epstein *Negro Migrant* 58: The Negro…feels an aversion to

the hospital, where he thinks the knife and the "black bottle" are frequently used. **1930** "D. Stiff" *Milk & Honey* 199: *Black bottle*—Poison, allegedly given hobos in hospitals. Many hobos believe this bottle exists.

black box *n.* **1.** *Und.* a lawyer.

*1811 *Lexicon Balatron.: Black Box.* A lawyer. *Cant.* **1845** *Nat. Police Gaz.* (Oct. 11) 58: We'll send this to Redmond's "*black-box*" (lawyer).

2. *Orig. Mil. Av.* any compact experimental or secret high-technology electronics equipment, orig. radar equipment; (now *specif.*) a flight recorder.

1945 Hamann *Air Words: Black box.* Radar. **1945* Partridge *R.A.F. Slang* 16: *Black box* or *gen box,* instrument that enables bombers to see through clouds or in the dark. **1947* in *OEDS:* These British night fighters were crammed with "black boxes" all of which had to be operated by the pilot or his navigator. **1948* in *OEDS:* The usual claim was that by means of a ray emanating from a secret device (known to us in the Air Ministry as a Black Box) the inventor had killed rabbits at a short distance. **1956** in Loosbrock & Skinner *Wild Blue* 186: The National Advisory Committee for Aeronautics chose Ocker's black box from more than 4,000 designs. **1956** Heflin *USAF Dict.* 81: *Black box.* Any unit, as a bombsight, robot pilot, or piece of electronic equipment, that may be put into, or removed from, a radar set, an aircraft, or the like, as a single package. *Colloq.* **1959** Chambliss *Silent Service* 130: Wires fed from whatever was in the "black box" to the PPI scope in the conning tower. *Ibid.* 136: Tell sonar to activate the "black box." **1962** E. Stephens *Blow Negative* 271: The military man's famous little black box. **1966–67** Harvey *Air War* 2: Her newest job had made it necessary to bring an army of trained technicians to keep the electronics equipment, or black boxes, peaked out. **1978** in Higham & Williams *Combat Aircraft* 119: Unfortunately some of the "mirrors and magic black boxes" are located in out-of-the-way places [in the F-4 Phantom]. **1982** Del Vecchio *13th Valley* 62: These guys with their little black boxes. **1983** *Good Morning America* (ABC-TV) (Sept. 16): U.S. naval vessels stepped up the search for the black box, or flight recorder, of the doomed Korean airliner.

3. a television set.

1961 in J. O'Hara *Sel. Letters* 371: Books have started to strike back at the black box.

black Cadillac *n. Narc.* BLACK BOMBER.

1974 Univ. Wis. student: They called [Biphetamine capsules] *black Cadillacs* in Milwaukee. **1980** (cited in Spears *Drugs & Drink* 48).

black cat *n.* **1.** *Mil. Av.* a military aircraft painted black for night operations.

1943 *Yank* (May 21) 6: Nightflying Catalina Flying Boats have gained fame as the *Black Cats*. **1961** Forbes *Goodbye to Some* 38 [ref. to WWII]: The real black cats don't use [landing lights] for take-off.

2. *Journ.* (see quot.).

1971 Tuchman *Stilwell* 213 [ref. to 1941]: In a "black cat" or off-the-record talk to the San Francisco Press Club…Stilwell said that war with the Japanese was certain.

black cloud *n.* a black person or group of black people.—used derisively.

1938 in *AS* (Apr. 1939) 89: *Black Cloud,* a crowd of negroes. "The *black cloud* lives in bush town." **1912–43** *Frank Brown Collection* I 521: *Black cloud: n.* A crowd of Negroes.—Central and east [N.C.]. **1943** (quot. at GOLDEN SHOWER)

black coat *n.* a clergyman.

1654 in *DAE:* I'le bring you to a Woman that Preaches better Gospell than any of your black-coates that have been at the Ninneversity. **1701** in *DAE:* We shall bring the Black Coats or Priests. **1828** in *DAE:* She is the only woman of accomplishments, I have met with, who favor [sic] those black coats.

black cow *n.* a serving of chocolate milk.

1918 *DN* V 18: *Black cow,* a chocolate milk. Student slang. **1942–44** in *AS* (Feb. 1946) 31: *Black cow,* n. Chocolate milk. **1992** Brooklyn, N.Y., man, age 56 (coll. J. Sheidlower): When I was a soda jerk [in the early 1950's], I never called chocolate milk *black cow.* Some people did, though.

black diamond *n.* **1.** *pl.* lumps of coal. Now *S.E.*

*1812 Vaux *Vocab.: Black diamonds:* Coals. **1842** in *DAE:* A fleet of boats laden with the black diamonds of the Alleghany. **1849* in *F & H* I (rev.) 242: Were he even trusted with the favourite horse and gig to fetch a sack of black diamonds from the Wharf. **1877** Bartlett *Amer.* 776: *Black Diamonds.* Lumps, small or large, of anthracite coal. **1888** *Scribner's Mag.* (Nov.) 548: The fireman's prosaic labors are lightened

by being poetically mentioned as the handling of black diamonds. **1921** in Kornbluh *Rebel Voices* 315: I…ought to be jugglin' the black diamonds myself.

2. *Slave Trade.* a black slave.

1860 in Farnell *Galveston Era* 247: [The Texas islands afford] an inscrutable hiding place for the "black diamonds."

black dog *n. Mining.* (see quot.). Now *hist.*

1939 in A. Banks *First-Person* 87 [ref. to *ca*1915]: We was burning black dogs—kerosene drilling lamps that look something like bombs.

black duck *n.* an American Indian.—used contemptuously.

1767 in *DA*: A common expression among English soldiers and sometimes English hunters, who, when they have killed an Indian, make their boast of having killed a black duck. **1889** O'Reilly & Nelson *Fifty Years on Trail* 256: I laid on the ground with my glass, watching for "black ducks."

black eye *n.* an injury to one's reputation or performance. Now *colloq.*

1891 Maitland *Amer. Slang Dict.* 34: *Black-eye,* "to give a," is to inflict harm or damage in any scheme. *ca*1940 in Botkin *Treas. Amer. Folk.* 535: It was giving the road a black eye, all right.

black gang *n. Naut.* the members of the engineer's division of a ship. Now *S.E.*

1895 Tisdale *Behind Guns* 50: The black-gang…dug into the coal. **1899–1900** (quot. at JIMMY LEGS). **1906** Beyer *Amer. Battleship* 81: "Black gang"—all men belonging to the engineer's department. **1918** Ruggles *Navy* 24: *Black Gang.* The engineer's division.…Men of the firerooms, engine rooms, evaporators, and every man in the department, are members of the gang. **1946** S. Wilson *Voyage* 236: I was a chief machinist's mate then and the black gang were always fighting with the deck force. **1950** Wouk *Caine Mutiny* 531: The search party were all of the black gang. **1958** Cooley *Run for Home* 25: Off this were the living quarters and the mess-rooms for the deck gang and the engineering crew, known as the "black gang."

black gown *n.* a clergyman.

1731 *Penna. Gaz.* (No. 134) (June 10) 1: No Sea Hens nor Black Gowns will be admitted [on board] on any Terms.…I knew that *Black Gowns* in that Place Signified the Clergy of the Church of England.

black hat *n.* a villain, as in a Western melodrama.

1971 *Playboy* (June) 216: The big shoot-out with the black-hats from CBS produces a numbing series of conferences but no…canceling of the film. **1973** W. Burroughs, Jr. *Ky. Ham* 3: Maybe…some black hat…will just jam the machine completely. **1974** N.Y.C. barmaid, age 22: The *black hats* are the bad guys, like the cops. It comes from cowboy movies. **1980** W.C. Anderson *BAT-21* 161 [ref. to 1972]: Well, from where this peace monger sits, I'd say the black hats are succeeding. **1984** (quot. at WHITE HAT, 2).

blackjack *n.* **1.** *Mining.* sphalerite (zinc sulfide). Now *S.E.*

*1747 in *OED2*: It is most commonly found in hard Veins and Pipes, some do call it Black-Jack. **1819** in *DAE*: Accompanying the lead ores of several mines in Washington county…is found a sulphuret of zinc, which is the "black jack" or "mock lead" of miners. **1889** *Century Dict.* I 573: *Black jack*…3. A Cornish miners' term for the common ferruginous zinc sulphid, of which the mineralogical name is *sphalerite*, and the common name *blende*. Also called *false galena*. **1941** *Missouri Guide* 237 [ref. to 1870's]: The potential value of zinc had been pointed out before the Civil War, but its extraction was difficult. Miners consequently discarded "black jack" as worthless.

2. rum sweetened with molasses.

1863 in *DA*: A mug of "black jack" helps him amazingly. **1877** Bartlett *Americanisms* (ed. 3) 45: *Black-Jack,*…rum sweetened with molasses. **1880** *Scribner's* (June) 293: [His] sole object in life was to vie with his neighbors in the consumption of "black jack" and corn whisky. **1889** Barrère & Leland *Dict. Slang* I 128: *Black jack* (American), rum and molasses, with or without water. A New England drink.

3. a short, leather-covered club, consisting of a heavy head on a flexible handle, used as a weapon. Now *S.E.*

1889 *Century Dict.* I 573: *Blackjack*…A kind of hand-weapon consisting of a short elastic shaft having at one end a heavy metal head cased in netting, leather, etc. **1895** in *DA*: During the scuffle, Miss Alderfer…saw the "black jack" up his sleeve,…and as a result, swore out the concealed weapons charge.

4. [cf. **(2.),** above] black coffee, esp. if sweetened with molasses.

1898 Norris *Moran* 33: A liquid that bore a distant resemblance to cof-

fee was served. Wilbur learned afterward to know the stuff as Black Jack, and to be aware that it was made from bud barley and was sweetened with molasses. **1934** Weseen *Dict. Slang* 77: Loggers' and Miners' Slang…*Blackjack*—Coffee. **1968** R. Adams *West. Words* (ed. 2): *Blackjack.* In logging, coffee.

5. a thug.

1928 Levin *Reporter* 169: Rewrite men are rowdies, blackjacks, pencil-swipers, milk-soppers, and subjects for the priesthood to practice upon.

6. *R.R.* a black coal car.

1945 Hubbard *R.R. Ave.* 333: *Blackjacks*—Fifty-ton Santa Fe coal cars painted black.

7. [cf. YELLOW JACK] ? cholera.

1955 Post *Little War* 6 [ref. to 1898]: Belly-bands…were the intended protection against all the tropical ills: blackwater fever, yellow jack, black jack, Chagres fever and a dozen other names of increasing horrendousness.

8. (see quot.).

1965 Vermes *Helping Youth* 119: Benzedrine drugs…are also known as…"blackjacks."

blackjack *v.* **1.** to hang on a blackjack oak.

1865 Duganne *Camps & Pris.* 404: Prisoner, Jim Reed, what have you got to say why you oughtn't to be black-jacked?

2. to hit with a blackjack. Now *S.E.*

1905 in *DAE*: I got a partner there…blackjacked a man.

blackleg *n.* **1.** a professional gambler or swindler, esp. a race-track swindler.

*1771 in *F & H* I (rev.) 246: The frequenters of the Turf, and numberless words of theirs are exotics everywhere else;…*blacklegs,*…*towntops*…taken in…beat hollow, etc. ***1773** H. Kelly *School for Wives* 57: The dirtiest black legs in town can wear [a sword]. ***1785** Grose *Vulgar Tongue: Black legs,* a gambler or sharper on the turf or in the cock pit; so called perhaps from their appearing generally in boots, or else from game cocks, who[se] legs are always black. **1786** in *DAE*: We lodged where there were a set of gamblers.…We left these blacklegs early next morning. **1821** Martin & Waldo *Lightfoot* 115: I was in company with a number of high fellows, some of whom were *black legs*. **1834** Caruthers *Kentuckian in N.Y.* I 64: I rather suspicion that he's a blackleg. **1844** in U.S. Grant *Papers* I 24: A number of them being what are usually called Black Legs or Gamblers. **1849** Melville *White Jacket* 184: In short…he was a charming blackleg. **1849** W. Irving, in Botkin *Treas. Amer. Folk.* 737: The old black-legs played shy. **1850** G.G. Foster *Gas-Light* 20: Besides, he don't play well enough for a blackleg. **1851** in Chittick *Roarers* 186: Killed in a fight with the blacklegs at "Natchez-under-the-Hill." **1864** in Norton *Army Letters* 223: The process of transportation affords excellent opportunities for taking photographs of "black-legs," etc., for the Rogues' Gallery. **1878** in *Seal & Salmon Fisheries* IV 61: Let an officer arrest a blackleg…and be sued in civil damages by the card sharp, [etc.]. **1884** Sweet & Knox *Through Texas* 339: He takes steps toward future distinction as a blackleg by gambling with marbles. **1895** Coup *Sawdust* 55: The camp-followers…hang on the heels of a circus for the purpose of swindling the public by every variety of device known to the "blackleg fraternity." **1898** Green *Va. Folk-Speech* 60: *Blackleg, n.* A gambler. **1914** Ellis *Billy Sunday* 208: A dirty, cussing, swearing gang of blacklegs on the street.

2. *Naut.* a cockroach.

1839 Olmsted *Whaling Voyage* 15: Huge cock-roaches…swarm in every direction. I found one of these erratic *black-legs* the other day, up in the main-top, wandering about very much at his leisure.

3. *Labor.* a scab worker or strikebreaker.

*1865 in *F & H* I (rev.) 246: If the timber merchants persist in putting on black-legs, a serious disturbance will ensue. **1878** *Nat. Police Gaz.* (May 4) 3: "Blacklegs," in miner's parlance, are those who do not belong to the Miners' Union. ***1889** in *OEDS*. **1902** E.M. Steel *Mother Jones* 28: Stopped P.R from Importing any more Black Legs. **1902** *Independent* (Nov. 6) 2634: He always counseled us to confine our arguments among the "black legs" to moral suasion, and we always did, tho sometimes with the assistance of a hardwood club. **1912** Berkman *Prison* 26: Don't let the soldiers come, I tell you. First *they'll* come; then the blacklegs. **1986** Kubicki *Breaker Boys* 319 [ref. to 1900]: You see 'da pain 'dis blackleg bring us? **1990** Palladino *Civil War* 134 [ref. to 1860's]: Coal miners threatened "blacklegs"…and bosses with pistols.

blackleg *v. Labor.* to work as a strikebreaking laborer; to refuse to participate in a strike.—constr. with *it.*

1888 in Farmer *Americanisms* 58: Knights of Labor…had determined to blackleg it, regardless of the jeers and threats of their companions.

Black Maria *n.* **1.a.** a police or prison van for the transportation of arrested individuals or convicts.
1843 J.C. Neal, in *AS* LXVIII 442: The Prison Van; or, The Black Maria.*...* In Philadelphia...the popular voice applies the name of "Black Maria" to each of these melancholy vehicles. **1847** J.C. Neal *Charcoal Sks.* (Ser. 2) 9: Justice's peculiar stand, where "Black Marias" most do congregate. *Ibid.* 166: Now did you ever see a burglarious sheep in the Black Maria, or a thieving chicken...? **1847** in *DA*: A new Black Maria...a new wagon for the conveyance of prisoners to and from the courts of justice [in Boston]. **1866** Dallas *Grinder Papers* 47: "It's the Black Maria," says he. **1872** McCabe *N.Y. Life* 242: This is known as "Black Maria," and may be daily seen rumbling through the city on its way from the Police Courts to the ferry to Blackwell's Island. **1874** Carter *Rollingpin* 14: At 12 m. the Black Maria leaves the Four Courts for the rock pile. **1884** Costello *Police Protectors* 508: Vehicles known as "Black Marias" are used in bringing prisoners from local places of detention...to the jails to which they have been sentenced. **1892** L. Moore *Own Story* 39: We were handcuffed together and carried to jail in the "Black Maria." **1926** Odum & Johnson *Negro Work. Songs* 75: Good God a'-mighty!/What's a fellow gonna do,/When ol' black mariah*/Come a-sailin' after you?...*Black Mariah* is frequently encountered in Negro songs. It refers to the patrol wagon. **1948** R. Chaplin *Wobbly* 45: Once or twice the "Black Maria" clattered up, and the shamefaced kids were dragged off to the precinct lockup. **1948** Manone & Vandervoort *Trumpet* 65: But we didn't stop playing once in the ride to jail in the Black Maria. **1954** L. Armstrong *Satchmo* 12: New Orleans had fine big horses to pull the patrol wagons and the Black Maria. *1959 Behan *Borstal Boy* 22: About two o'clock I heard the Black Maria back into the yard. **1977–80** F.M. Stewart *Century* 113: A police whistle shrilled and two black Marias roared around the corner.
b. a hearse.
1954–60 *DAS* 41: *Black Maria*...A hearse. **1977** Caron *Go-Boy* 1: Because it resembled an oversized hearse, the reformatory bus with its armed guards and barred windows was called the Black Maria. **1986** Kubicki *Breaker Boys* 161 [ref. to Pa., 1900]: Then...they waited for the dreaded Black Maria—the death wagon—to roll to their doors.
2. *Mil.* (see 1921 quot.). Now *hist.* [Quots. ref. to WWI.]
*1914 in *OEDS* I 281: The 16-inch "Black Maria" shells of the heaviest German artillery. *1921 *N & Q* (Oct. 29) 344: *Black Maria.* Heavy high-explosive German shell—so called on account of thick black smoke emitted when bursting. **1931** Dos Passos *1919* 307: His gang had been wiped out by a black maria.

Black Mike *n. Logging.* stew.
1925 *AS* (Dec.) 137: Stew is "Black Mike." **1968** R. Adams *West. Words* (ed. 2): *Black Mike.* A logger's term for stew.

black molly *n. Narc.* a black capsule containing an amphetamine.
1970 M. Brennan *Drugs* 58: *Black Mollies*: strong amphetamines. **1977** (cited in Spears *Drugs & Drink* 49). **1979** Gram *Foxes* 50: A little blotter acid once or twice and Black Mollys.

blackneck *n.* [*black* + (RED)NECK] *So. Pol.* a rural black Southerner who is opposed to various politically liberal programs. [All quots. ref. to Miss.]
1978 *L.A. Times* (Sept. 23) I 1: There are a weak Democratic candidate, an independent black candidacy and a fragmenting of the "blackneck-redneck" coalition that has seen blacks and rural whites join to preserve Democratic control. **1979** Hattiesburg (Miss.) *American* (July 19) 7: "Redneck-blackneck" coalition. **1980** *AS* (Winter) 294: A term that has been a significant part of the last three gubernatorial races in Mississippi is *blackneck*...a rural black Southerner whose desires and political views may be essentially the same as those of his white (redneck) counterpart.

blackout *n.* black coffee.
1941 Kendall *Army & Navy Slang* 2: *Pass the black-out*...general issue coffee. **1941** Macaulay & Wald *Manpower* (film): One blackout! And blitz it! **1943** *Amer. Mercury* (Nov.) 553: Coffee is known variously as *battery acid, paint remover, Joe, blanko water, blackout, ink, bootleg* or *mud.* *1946 (in Cape Town; cited in Partridge *DSUE* (ed. 7) 1010).

Black Rock *n.* [sugg. by the title of the 1953 film *A Bad Day at Black Rock*; the building is black] *Radio & TV.* the CBS Building at 53rd Street and the Avenue of the Americas, N.Y.C.; CBS headquarters; the CBS network itself.
1974 Lahr *Trot* 59: ABC 1330 Avenue of the Americas New York City 10019....In the trade it's called Hard Rock. There's 30 Rock (NBC), Black Rock (CBS), and Hard Rock. **1978** *N.Y. Post* (July 6) 30: It was

those people at Black Rock (the industry nickname for CBS corporate headquarters on 53d St.). **1988** *N.Y. Post* (June 22) 66: Black Rock finishes first in the weekly ratings race.

black rose *n. Mil.* a putative virulent and incurable form of venereal disease said to be prevalent in Vietnam and Southeast Asia. Also **Vietnam rose.**
1974 Univ. Tenn. student, served in Vietnam 1972: They said all the bar girls had "Vietnam rose." That was some kind of VD that if you got it you wound up on some leper-colony-type island and never went home. They'd tell your family you were KIA. **1991** J.T. Ward *Dear Mom* 48 [ref. to 1969]: The myth of the dreaded "Black Rose" started there (a strain of VD that we could only get from Vietnamese prostitutes).

black rot *n.* extreme boredom.—constr. with *the.*
1864 in *Ohio Arch. & Hist. Qly.* LII (1943) 162: We have enough to do here to keep us from dying with the black rot. I will give you a synopsis of our duties.

blackshoe *n.* [see 1952 quot. for allusion; cf. BROWNSHOE] *Navy.* a U.S. naval officer who is not an aviator or a submariner.
1950 *N.Y. Times* (Feb. 5) 19: The "black shoe Navy" is the sea-going, non-flying Navy. **1952** Cope & Dyer *Petty Off. Gd.* 422: *Black shoe* (Slang). A line officer who is not an aviator; formerly surface officers wore black shoes with khaki uniforms. **1962** Quirk *No Red Ribbons* 14 [ref. to 1940's]: You fellows Black Shoes?...He don't like nobody that can't fly and's got rank. *Ibid.* 15: He expected another Trade School Black Shoe with too much rank and not enough flying ability. **1965** *N.Y. Times* (June 1): The "blackshoes"...sail and service the carrier. **1965** D.V. Gallery *8 Bells* 94: Until [WWII] broke out there was strong rivalry and jealousy between the surface sailors and the aviators, known respectively as the "black shoes" and the "brown shoes." **1966** Noel & Bush *Naval Terms* 66: *Black shoe:* Slang: line officer who is not an aviator. **1970** in Tamony *Americanisms* (No. 26) 11 (U.S. naval officer speaking): It is unusual for a black shoe to get a medal from the brown shoes. **1971** Sheehan *Arnheiter* 27: The "black-shoe" surface-ship sailors and the "brown-shoe" Navy aviators. **1978** in Higham & Williams *Combat Aircraft* 139: The naval service...[was] beset with internal feuding between "black shoes" (nonaviators) and "brown shoes" (aviators). **1980** J. Webb *Sense of Honor* 13: Becoming pilots and marines and submariners and "blackshoe" line officers. **1990** Poyer *Gulf* 49: You know, blackshoes just ain't like us, Buck.

black-shoe *adj. Stu.* (see quot.).
1959 in Cox *Delinquent, Hipster, Square* 19: Barbados is black shoe....Tourists and creeps....*Black shoe* is formal and sober.

blacksmith *n.* **1.** a clumsy or slipshod worker; (*specif.*) an inept journalist.
[**1878** in *DA*: We had a regular "blacksmith" at work in the office, and he beat Keever out of a week's board, and Mrs. Korb ditto, and today he lit out after taking an old pepperbox revolver belonging to somebody else.] **1882** Field *Tribune Primer* 101: If you are a Printer, Do not Be a Blacksmith or you will get Fired. **1887** in *DA*: Shiftless newspaper reporter or journalist [is called] a blacksmith. **1894** Crane *Red Badge* 67: I know I'm a blacksmith at takin' keer 'a sick folks. **1969** Kent *Lang. Journalism*: *Blacksmith.* An inferior reporter; one who merely "pounds out" news stories.
2. *Und.* a safecracker.
1925–26 Black *You Can't Win* 330: A more careful and experienced "blacksmith" would have taken measures to prevent that big safe from falling on its face and burying the money beyond reach. **1949** Monteleone *Crim. Slang* 25: *Blacksmith*...One who does the actual work of opening a safe.

black snake *n. R.R.* a coal train.
1938 Beebe *High Iron* 219: *Black Snake:* Solid train of coal-cars.

black spy *n. Und.* a police informer.
1846 *Lives of the Felons* 57: You'd *"peach"* and turn *"black spy,"* I s'pose? *1858 A. Mayhew *Paved with Gold* 266: You black spy.

blackstick *n. Music.* a clarinet.
1937 *AS* (Oct.) 181: *Blackstick.* Clarinet. **1938** *Blackstick* [song title] [rec. by Sidney Bechet with Noble Sissle's Swingsters, Decca 2129].

blackstrap *n.* **1.** [cf. BLACKJACK, 2] gin or rum mixed with molasses. Now *hist.*
1817 in *DA*: It was afterwards observed by an English sailor that instead of making switchel of the molasses the Yankees had converted it into blackstrap. *1825 "Blackmantle" *Eng. Spy* I 250: We'll...drink

all the *black strap* in your cellar. *a*1848 in Bartlett *Amer.* 33: No *black-strap* to-night, switchel or ginger pop. *a*1881 G.C. Harding *Misc. Writings* 58: It is more infamous than hard cider or "black-strap." **1893** Earle *Old New England* 179: "Black-strap" was a mixture of rum and molasses. **1944** in *DA*.

2. [cf. BLACKJACK, 4] *Army.* black or strong coffee.

1909 Moss *Officer's Gde.* 283: *Black Strap.* Liquid coffee. **1919** Witt *Riding to War* 159: Black strap....Sand. Oleo. [etc.].

3. *West.* (see quot.).

1931 R.G. Carter *On Border* 297 [ref. to 1870's]: On the march they [*sc.* Indians] would live for days on sun-dried or jerked buffalo meat called by the Texans "black strap," and by the Mexicans "callops."

black syph *n.* [fr. *syphilis*] *Mil.* BLACK ROSE. Also vars.

[**1929** M. Gold *Jews Without Money* 268 [ref. to *ca*1905]: Lily died...of what the East Side called "the black syphilis."] **1973** Karlin et al. *Free Fire Zone* 138: Rest up my dingaling 'til I go out and cover it with black syph and glory. **1982** "J. Cain" *Commandos* 91: The ol' Black Syph has finally affected Mikey-boy's excuse for a brain! **1983** S. Wright *Meditations* 114 [ref. to Vietnam War]: All carried The Black Syph for which there was no known cure except...confinement...on Okinawa until a treatment could be found. **1983** Eilert *Self & Country* 180 [ref. to 1968]: "What have you got, terminal clap?"..."The Black Syph." **1986** Merkin *Zombie Jamboree* 104 [ref. to *ca*1970]: The most dreadful of all the army rumors...was the tale of the Black Syph, the Black Clap. **1987** Pelfrey & Carabatsos *Hamburger Hill* 20: They'll keep you in the Philippines with the black VD and you'll never go home.

black tar *n. Narc.* a form of heroin originating in Mexico.

1986 *N.Y. Times* (Mar. 28) A 1: Unlike the powdered heroin that has been sold in the United States for many years, black tar is difficult for dealers to dilute because it is almost solid. **1988** *Newsweek* (Mar. 28) 27: Mexican heroin...[is called] Black Tar. **1989** *Geraldo* (synd. TV series) (May 16): I did a story on black tar heroin.

black water *n. West.* black coffee, esp. if weak.

1850 Garrard *Wah-to-Yah* 128: The "black water" is offered with genuine free-heartedness, and the last plug of tobacco subjected to the rapacious knife of the guest as though it were plenty as the rocks around. **1925** Mullin *Scholar Tramp* 305: They was there to get hot Java and rolls, but what they got wuz stale biscuits...and black water. **1968** R. Adams *West. Words* (ed. 2): *Black water.* A freighter's term for weak coffee.

blacky *n.* **1.** a black person.—used contemptuously.

1816 Paulding *Letters from So.* I 122: I...sold many a poor d—l of a blacky. **1822** in Wade *Slavery in Cities* 126: And equally no doubt to the buck blacky. **1833** J. Neal *Down-Easters* I 95: What'll you have *now* sir, said another blackey. **1838** [Haliburton] *Clockmaker* (Ser. 2) 64: Him don't look like blue nose, said blacky. **1846** Crockett's *Almanac* (unp.): The Malgamation party...go in for Annexation with the blackies. **1968** Guare *Cop-Out* 30: You got the blackies all riled up. **1987** J. Waters *Hairspray* (film): Special Ed?...But that's for retards and the blackies you try to hold back.

2. blacksmith, esp. as a nickname.

1906 Beyer *Amer. Battleship* 82: "Blacky"—the blacksmith. **1918** Ruggles *Navy Explained* 26: Every ship carries one or more blacksmiths. They are always called "blackey."

3. a blackjack.

1953 W. Brown *Monkey on My Back* 198: But he'd never used the gun, only the blackie.

bladder *n.* [prob. < G *Blätter* 'sheets (of paper)'] a newspaper. Cf. BLAT.

1842 C. Mathews *Puffer Hopkins* 228: Busts called Flabby a hoary reprobate, in Monday's Bladder. **1924** T.A. Dorgan, in Zwilling *TAD Lexicon* 18: Best sportin' editor this bladder ever had. **1932** D. Runyon, in *Collier's* (Mar. 26) 8: The Lost and Found columns of the morning bladders. **1936** in D. Runyon *More Guys* 143: Reporters and photographers from the afternoon bladders.

bladder bird *n. Mil.* a tanker helicopter.

1991 Dunnigan & Bay *From Shield to Storm* 259: One [Iraqi missile] hit the CH-47 tanker helicopter ("bladder bird").

blade *n.* **1.** a knife or straight-edged razor used as a weapon; (*esp.*) a switchblade knife.

1896 in A. Charters *Ragtime Songbk.* 43: Took along my trusty blade to carve that fella's bones. **1918** Lardner *Treat 'Em Rough* 28: They call him Nick the Blade on acct. of always haveing a knife on him. **1929** in *AS* VI 131: *Blade.* Knife or razor. **1931** Bontemps *Sends Sunday* 35: Jes' keep yo' blade in yo' pocket, if you please. **1946** in Himes *Black on Black*

257: I didn't like the stud...but I didn't have my blade. **1954** Yablonsky *Violent Gang* 68: We figured he had a blade on him, too. **1958** in Rosset *Evergreen Reader* 158: Man, if you ever come around, I'll get you with my blade, and, man, don't think I can't use it! **1959** E. Hunter *Killer's Wedge* 53: She probably saw him looking at another girl, and so she put the blade to him. **1961** Parkhurst *Undertow* 53: I'm here an' so's my blade. **1967** Hinton *Outsiders* 28: Does Dally have a blade? **1975** Hinton *Rumble Fish* 25: Anybody lend me a blade?

2. *Med.* a surgeon.

1974 Hejinian *Extreme Remedies* 44: But the brain blades got ahead of you. **1981** in Safire *Good Word* 153. *a*1982 Medved *Hospital* 76: [Surgeons] have nicknames around here....we call them blades, or butchers.

blah *n. & interj.* **1.** empty talk, drivel. Also **blah-blah[-blah].**

1918 in O'Brien *Wine, Women, War* 136: Pulled old "blah" about "service," "doing one's bit," etc. **1920** in C. Sandburg *Letters* 186: But he's...always springing important copy book...TRUTHS about making the world better, the hire life, blaa blaa. **1920–21** Witwer *Leather Pushers* 190: That's all blah! **1925** in Hemingway *Sel. Letters* 175: What a lot of Blah Blah that N. Republic review was, still I'm always glad to read them. **1928** C. McKay *Banjo* 182: Quit you' bellyaching blah and get along from here. **1928** Carr *Rampant Age* 171: Us young fellows are gittin' too smart to swallow such blah! **1929** A.C. Doyle *Maricot* ch. iv: Then it was Blah Blah Blah as long as his breath would hold. **1931** Dos Passos *1919* 82: It was all a lot of blah anyway. **1954** L. Armstrong *Satchmo* 210: "I saw him first" and "He's my man" and a lot of blah like that. **1979** Cassidy *Delta* 324: And it's not just the blah-blah that usually comes in these messages. **1991** *Harper's* (July) 74: You get the same blah, blah, blah if you visit Colonial Williamsburg.

2. *pl.* a blasé condition resulting from boredom, minor illness, etc.—constr. with *the.* [Popularized and perhaps coined in an Alka-Seltzer advertising campaign, *ca*1967.]

1968 *Seattle Times* (Dec. 20) I 22 (caption): One-woman capsule to relieve early morning "blahs." **1968** Baker et al. *CUSS* 81: *Blahs, have the* Have a minor illness, feel sick. **1971** Barnes *Pawns* 98: Then came the slow, miserable days as he waits for his time to run out, when he suffers through what one soldier calls the "post-Vietnam blahs." **1971** Dahlskog *Dict.* 8: *Blahs, the*...A tired, bored, depressed feeling; as, to have the Monday *blahs.* **1973** Freese *Headaches* 149: It's fine for what advertisers have dubbed the "blahs." **1975** Delaney *Ultra-Psychonics* 106: Try them when you feel ill at ease...or when you have what some people call the "blahs." **1979** Kiev *Courage to Live* 9: When The Blahs Become the Blues. **1985** Jenkins & Jenkins *Road Unseen* xi: Your concern lifts us over the bumps and blahs of life. *a*1990 R. Herman, Jr. *Force of Eagles* 131: The middle age blahs were getting to me.

blah *adj.* disappointing; unsatisfactory; dull; insipid; lifeless.

1922 *Variety* (Sept. 1) 5: I can drive like an old timer but my direction is very blah. **1922** in *DN* V 146: Started perfectly blaah, though. **1926** *Variety* (Dec. 22) 9: Pre-Holiday Blah Feeling Gets Into Amusement Stocks. **1926** in Lardner *Haircut & Others* 67: She was just blah, but the B.F. [boyfriend] wasn't so bad. **1932** Lorimer *Streetcars* 172: The blah face gave a gloating look. **1964** *AS* XXXIX 119: A *blah* party can be said to be somewhat worse. *ca*1974 in J.L. Gwaltney *Drylongso* 16: My daughter says that white people are just "blah." She means that they don't have no twang to them. **1980** *N.Y. Post* (Mar. 14) 14: Erin Goes Blah for City Jail Boss...The correction officers' Emerald Society has "uninvited" New York prison boss Benjamin Ward from participating in Monday's St. Patrick's Day festivities. **1989** Martorano & Kildahl *Neg. Thinking* 97: Is your life largely blah?

blah *v.* to gossip, talk idly.

1928 Dahlberg *Bottom Dogs* 250: He could blah with a newsie.

blank *n.* ¶ In phrase: **fire a blank** (of a man) to engage in sexual intercourse while physiologically unable to impregnate a woman.

1954–60 *DAS* 183. **1968** Legman *Rationale* 628: *Fire a blank:* emit no semen at orgasm, the seminal vesicles being empty. **1981** C. Nelson *Picked Bullets Up* 123: He'll always fire blanks; no [children of his] will ever exist.

blanket *n.* **1.** a banknote.

1851 in *DA*: I have money enough to singe a cane-brake. Yes sir, enough of Uncle Sam's thousand dollar blankets (meaning one thousand dollar notes) to make a carpet for a steamboat!

2. *Army.* a period of enlistment.

1888 McConnell *5 Yrs. Cavalryman* 120 [ref. to 1866]: If [a soldier] alludes to his chances of re-enlistment he will be heard to say: "I guess I'll take another blanket when this one is run out, one with five pockets in it," alluding to the length of the term, five years. **1896** in J.M. Carroll *Benteen-Goldin Lets.* 259: A five-year blanket. **1909** Moss *Officer's Manual* 284: *Blanket, take another*—same as "Take on" (viz.) "to re-enlist before the expiration of three months after discharge."

3.a. *pl.* pancakes.

1899 Bolton *Second Regt.* 396: "Pancakes" received the name of "ponchos" or "blankets." **1927** *DN* V 439: *Blankets, n.* griddle cakes. **1941** Hargrove *Pvt. Hargrove* 83: Hot cakes become "blankets." **1943** *Amer. Mercury* (Nov.) 553: *Blankets* or *collision mats* for pancakes. **1942–44** in *AS* (Feb. 1946) 31: *Blankets, n.* Hot cakes. **1956** Sorden & Elbert *Logger's* 3 [ref. to *a*1925]: *Blankets*, Pancakes.

b. a pastry crust.

1918 Ruggles *Navy* 127: If the stew is covered over with a crust, as is usually the case, they call it...stew with the blanket on; stew that's afraid to show its face.

4. usu. *pl.* a cigarette paper.

1925 Mullin *Scholar Tramp*: "Got the tumblin's and a blanket on ye?"...I supplied him with tobacco and papers. He made his cigarette. **1930** Irwin *Amer. Tramp & Und. Slang: Tumblings and Blankets.* Tobacco and papers for cigarettes. **1942** *Leatherneck* (Nov.) 143: *Blanket And Freckles*—Paper and tobacco for rolling cigarettes.

5. *Hobo.* an overcoat.

1925 (cited in Partridge *Dict. Und.* 46). **1929** T. Gordon *Born to Be* 225: I parked my blanket and skypiece on the bed. **1933** Ersine *Prison Slang* 18: *Blanket*...An overcoat.

¶ In phrases:

¶ **close to the blanket** *West.* nearly without money.

1942 Sonnichsen *Billy King* 62 [ref. to *a*1900]: A small time gambler...was getting "close to the blanket" and decided to do something to beat the strangers' game.

¶ **split the blanket** to separate; divorce.

1903 *DN* II 331: They *split the blanket* after living together ten years. (Facetious). **1952** Sandburg *Young Strangers* 164 [ref. to 1880's]: A newly married couple "got hitched" and if they separated they "split the blanket." **1973** *Atlantic* (July) 40: These financial moves were made without the assistance of his lifelong business partner....."The judge and I have split the blanket."

¶ **stretch the blanket** to exaggerate.

1870 Duval *Big-Foot* 128: Big-Foot "stretched his blanket" considerably here. **1911** in Truman *Dear Bess* 28: That's saying as much...as is possible without stretching the blanket. **1927** *AS* (May) 348: That man stretched the blanket when he told about Florida. **1975** Julien *Cogburn* 103: I think you are stretching the blanket a bit. **1992** Wittliff *Ned Blessing* (film): I give 'em the straight stuff, too, not stretching the blanket in any direction.

blanket-ass *n.* an American Indian.—used contemptuously.—usu. considered vulgar.

1973 W. Crawford *Stryker* 18: Go on with it, Blanketass. **1974** in Davis *Hearts and Minds* (film): They'd call me *blanket-ass* and chief. **1979** Hurling *Boomers* 96: Johnny was...a half-blooded Sioux....His nickname [was] Blanket Ass. **1981** Cody & Perry *Iron Eyes* 239 [ref. to 1930's]: The...stuntman...got outright nasty and kept calling me "Blanket Ass." *a*1984 in Terry *Bloods* 5: And I had an Indian for a platoon commander who hated Indians. He used to call Indians blanket ass.

Blanket Bay *n. Naut.* bed. Also **blanket harbor.**

1775 in Whiting *Early Amer. Proverbs* 34: Upon which I steered my course for Blanket Bay within School Cape. **1821 Real Life in Ireland* 143: Shaughnessy...finding Gramachree half seas over, had taken the liberty of bringing him to an anchor in Blanket Bay. **1835** *Knickerbocker* (Mar.) 202: Here I am now, moored "head and starn" in *Blanket-Bay.* **1841** Mercier *Man o'War* 223: So let's...make a finish of the little drop of stuff I have left, and then bear away for *blanket bay* and tomorrow we'll be...fresh. **1870** [W.D. Phelps] *Fore & Aft* 341: She was still moored in "blanket harbor."

blanket drill *n. Mil.* sleep; (in 1922 quot.) masturbation.

*1922 in Lawrence *Mint* 224: You know blanket-drill, and what that feels like? **1931* Brophy & Partridge *Songs & Slang* 283 [ref. to WWI]: *Blanket Drill.*—The afternoon siesta, beloved of "old" soldiers. **1941** Hargrove *Pvt. Hargrove* 83: *Blanket drill*—sleep.

blankethead *n.* an American Indian.—used contemptuously.

1956 Nugent *Searchers* (film): Come on, blankethead! **1970** Fenady *Chisum* (film): You heard me, blankethead. Let's go.

blanket party *n. Mil.* a form of retribution in which a soldier is surprised, covered with a blanket, and beaten.

*ca*1969 Rabe *Hummel* 44: *Pavlo:* I got a blanket party. *Pierce:* You're in

my squad and other guys in my squad beat you up. **1974** Former L/Cpl, 5th MarDiv, Vietnam 1967–69: A *blanket party* was when a bunch of guys would sneak up on somebody they didn't like and throw a blanket over him so he couldn't see who they were and beat him up. **1985** Boyne & Thompson *Wild Blue* 59: They would lead...the flight tonight on a blanket party, to try to bring Clay and Beatty in line. **1991** J.T. Ward *Dear Mom* 16: A blanket party is no party. A GI blanket is thrown over a man's head so he can't identify his attackers, and he is beaten, sometimes to death.

blanket stiff *n. Hobo & West.* BINDLE STIFF, 1.

[**1891** *Contemporary Rev.* (Aug.) 255: In the Western States, there is a class of rovers called Blanket Tramps...because they invariably carry blankets with them, sleeping where night overtakes them.] **1893** *Century* (Nov.) 106: Vagabondage in this part of the country is composed principally of blanket stiffs. **1897** *Harper's Wkly.* (Jan. 23) 86: Even the Blanket Stiff in the far West, who almost never sees the inside of a railway car, will wax patriotic on this subject. **1899** "J. Flynt" *Tramping* 392: *Blanket-Stiff:* a Western tramp; he generally carries a blanket with him in his travels. **1902** "J. Flynt" *Little Bro.* 97: Among these was an old "Blanket Stiff" from the West. **1910** in Kornbluh *Rebel Voices* 75: Casting out blanket stiffs for his job's sake. **1930** "D. Stiff" *Milk & Honey* 200: *Blanket stiff*—Western type of hobo who carries his bed. He [is] also called a *bindle bum.* **1936** Mackenzie *Living Rough* 118: Hank told me all about his wanderings as a blanket-stiff around California. **1955** Post *Little War* 20: He unhesitatingly announced that he was a hobo printer—a blanket stiff—who wanted to travel. **1979** (quot. at JUNGLEHOUND).

blap *v.* [of expressive origin; cf. ZAP, BOP, etc.] *Mil.* to kill or destroy, ZAP.

1971 Mayer *Weary Falcon* 27: All we'd done was blapped a couple of Yards.

blarney *n.* [alluding to the *Blarney* Stone, in Blarney Castle near Cork, Ireland; said to impart skill in flattery to those who kiss it]

a. flattery; nonsense. Now *S.E.* [The v. has always been *S.E.*]

*1796 in *OEDS*: I hold it (so to speak) to be all *Blarney.* **1839** *Spirit of Times* (Aug. 24) 294: I would rather have her as a sweepstake chance than any foal in the Union, and no *blarney* in it either. **1839* in *F & H* I (rev.) 253: They were as cunning as foxes, and could tell blarney from good sense. **1902–03** Ade *People You Know* 92: The speech was known to be cut-and-dried Blarney.

b. a flatterer.

1797 in Tyler *Verse* 64: I fear my dear blarneys you are after to flatter me.

blast *n.* **1.** a drink of liquor. [Despite 1866 quot.—ref. to 1862—this sense was uncommon before the mid-20th C.]

1866 in "M. Twain" *Letters from Hawaii* (Apr.): In Washoe, when you are requested to "put in a blast" or invited to take "your regular pison," etiquette admonishes you to touch glasses and say, "Here's hoping you'll strike it rich in the lower level." **1953** in *DAS* 42: Maybe it's a little early in the day for that first blast. **1963** Hayden *Wanderer* 251: Take a blast. **1963** D. Tracy *Brass Ring* 398: Let me have a blast before we go?

2. *Narc.* a draw on a marijuana cigarette or an injection of a narcotic drug.

1952 Mandel *Angry Strangers* 360: I want a blast, I want it quick....I want it mainline for one blast. *Ibid.* 390: Where'd you take a blast, doll, where? **1956** Ross *Hustlers* 25: Pancho broke out a stick and we got a few blasts.

3.a. a pleasurable thrill; fun; an uproariously good time; a funny thing.

*a*1950 P. Wolff *Friend* 77: That's a blast, ain't it? **1952** in *DAS* 42: You get a blast takin' care of me, givin' me presents. **1960** Stadley *Barbarians* 29: Let's let the chick show us a real blast. **1966** (cited in *BDNE2*). **1972** Kellogg *Lion's Tooth* 107: They didn't catch him until Madeline was eight years old. Ain't that a blast? **1977** Langone *Life at Bottom* 151: Those Kiwis are a blast to visit. They like parties. **1983** Univ. Tenn. student: That should be a blast.

b. a wild party.

*1959 in *OEDS*. **1960** in H. Ellison *Sex Misspelled* 288: I decided to throw a small blast. **1961** L.G. Richards *TAC* 139: There was a big blast at the officers' club that night. **1983** *Newsweek on Campus* (Dec.) 21: We throw in...a free beer blast.

c. *Music.* an exciting popular song.

1965, 1973 (quots. at *blast from the past*, below). **1983** *Judge Dredd* (comic book) (Nov.) 4: Right now plug into the number one blast, "Who Put the Boop?"

4. a telephone call.

1955 Reifer *New Words* 31: *Blast*…A telephone call, as in the expression: "Give me a blast." **1966** "Petronius" *N.Y. Unexp.* 58: If you're looking for qualified gents from the right neighborhood, give them a blast. **1970** S. Ross *Fortune Machine* 103: Anything you want, kid, just give me a blast.

5. *Army.* a parachute jump.

1988 Clodfelter *Mad Minutes* 52 [ref. to 1965]: This was to be my thirteenth "blast." **1991** Reinberg *In Field*: *Blast*, slang for a parachute jump.

¶ In phrases:

¶ **blast from the past** Orig. *Music.* a formerly popular recording that remains enjoyable; (*hence*) anything from the past that is now striking or impressive.

1965 *Esquire* (July) 44: Murray the K…has blasts from the past. **1973** N.Y.C. disc jockey: Man, here comes another blast from the past. **1980** Gould *Ft. Apache* 209: "He's an old-fashioned book cop." "A blast from the past."

¶ **put the blast on, 1.** to scold or criticize harshly or vociferously.

1929 in D. Runyon *Guys & Dolls* 66: Miss Missouri Martin…puts the blast on her plenty for chasing…Dave the Dude out of the joint. **1931** in D. Runyon *More Guys & Dolls* 41: Other dolls…are always putting the blast on her behind her back. **1944** *Yank* (Feb. 4) 23: Critics Put the Blast on Navy Big Leaguers. **1949** in *DAS* 42: He…went back to his paper and put the blast on the Federals. **1971** Dahlskog *Dict.* 8: *Blast*…a dressing-down, as: to put (lay) the *blast* on someone. **1981** P. Sann *Trial* 55: Mr. Lyons had the bad habit of putting the blast on me with the owner.

2. to shoot with a gun, esp. to shoot dead.

1940 Burnett *High Sierra* 265: It's all your own fault letting a small-timer like that put the blast on you. **1946** Veiller *Killers* (film): Two professional killers show up in a small town and put the blast on a filling-station attendant…why? **1953** Chandler *Goodbye* 141: Next time…I sure as hell put the blast on you.

blast *v.* **1.** to damn; curse.—used optatively. See also BLASTED, 1. [Orig. S.E.; in 20th C. increasingly euphem.]

*a1634 in *OED2*: Blast you all. ***1762** in *OED2*: Blast me!…if that be all, there is no need of paying for that. ***1780** in J. Farmer *Musa Pedestris* 58: Blast you, you scoundrel! *Ibid.* 59: Blast me! ***1805** J. Davis *Post-Captain* 159: Blast the money! **1811** in W. Dunlap *Diary* 440: God blast them! God blast me if ever I play for them again. ***1825** in *F & H* I 223: No, blast him. **1827** in *JAF* LXXVI (1963) 290: Blast iz ize. **1864** *Battle-Fields of So.* 430: Well, you can now bury the old hag—God b—t her! ***1931** J. Hanley *Boy* 74: God blast you mate.

2.a. to shoot; (*hence*, *trans.*) to fire a bullet into; to shoot dead.

1927 Coe *Gangster* 195: Fifteen hundred shots a minute when you want to blast your way out, kid. **1929** Barr *Let Tomorrow Come* 41: I don't know yet whether I blasted on purpose or if I was just rummier from that whiteline than I thought I was. **1930** *Sat. Eve. Post* (Apr. 5) 5: The coppers are not likely to start any blasting. **1931** Rynning *Gun Notches* 5: He'd get his belt full of shells and go back and blast a lot of tin-horn gamblers all the way to Boot Hill. **1932** in Weinberg et al. *Tough Guys* 47: He'll probably blast me on sight. **1935** Lamson *We About to Die* 197: He'll get blasted pullin' a job, or else he'll get put away for plenty years. **1938** Chandler *Big Sleep* 71: I wasn't told to blast anybody. **1940** Burnett *High Sierra* 192: Just as I was picking it up, this monkey started blasting at me. *Ibid.* 258: If he asks for it, I blast him through the blanket and that's that. **1941** Halliday *Tickets* 82: You blasted two of the local yokels. **1946** Veiller *Killers* (film): "He pulled a fast one and walked away with the take." "No wonder he got blasted." **1952** Bellow *Augie March* 118: In the end they get blasted. **1952** Chase *McThing* 99: But we go out there and blast anyway. *Ibid.* 104: He said he was gonna blast with rods. **1970** *Playboy* (Feb.) 55: They might have come roaring out in an alcoholic rage, looked for the guy they were sore at and really blasted him. **1972** *Banyon* (NBC-TV): Last night your husband got blasted.

b. to defeat soundly (in a game or contest).

1968–77 F. Wallace *Poker* 48: You're getting blasted again.…Must be losing a grand.

c. *Weight Lifting.* to concentrate on developing (muscles), as through lifting weights. Cf. BOMB.

1981 D.E. Miller *Jargon* 230: *Bomb.* Also *blitz, blast.*…I really bombed my quads this morning.

3. [cf. BLAST OFF, 1] to leave.

1933 D. Runyon, in *Collier's* (Feb. 11) 8: I will have to blast.…I will have no part of him.

4.a. to complain.

1942 *ATS* 298: *Complain.*…bellyache, bitch, blast. **1969** N.Y.C. woman, age *ca*80: When I was a girl we would say "Stop blasting" or "What's she blasting about?" I don't think we ever used *gripe*.

b. to scold or criticize severely or vociferously.

1957 Margulies *Punks* 48: The old lady…blasts me for laying on the bed in my clothes. **1973** Chandler *Capt. Hollister* 112: Did the Old Man ever blast you?

5. *Narc.* to smoke (a marijuana cigarette); (*rarely*) to consume (psychotropic drugs or alcohol).—also used intrans.

1943 *Time* (July 19) 54: The viper may then quietly "blast the weed" (smoke). **1952** in W.S. Burroughs *Letters* 127: A good % of the NAR agents blast. **1952** Kerouac *Cody* 125: Really blasting it [*sc.* liquor], huh? **1953** W. Brown *Monkey on My Back* 31: Dave would sneak into the woods "to blast." **1955–57** Kerouac *On Road* 232: The strangeness of Americans and Mexicans blasting together on the desert. **1959** Burroughs *Naked Lunch* 12: I blasted my last stick of Tangier tea. **1972** *Penthouse* (Jan. 1973) 133: Three young hippies…were blasting away on hand-rolled cigarettes of dark brown paper. **1976** J.W. Thomas *Heavy Number* 1: Shannon had started blasting regularly two years ago.

6. *Horse Racing.* to tout a racehorse while misrepresenting oneself as having inside information.

1956 "T. Betts" *Across the Board* 240: Touts were allowed to advertise winners they did not have. This was called "blasting," "dynamiting," or "bulldogging."

blasted *adj.* **1.** damned. Also *adv.*

*1750 in *F & H* I (rev.) 254: Colonel Chartres…who was, I believe, the most notorious blasted rascal in the world. **1817** Fearon *Sketches of America* 240: I always serve my b—d *niggars* that way. **1834** Caruthers *Kentuckian in N.Y.* I 20: I was afraid the blasted tories would sell me to the British. **1843** Field *Pokerville* 101: There wasn't a mite of water in the blasted thing! **1850** in *Calif. Hist. Soc. Qly.* VIII (1929) 19: I'm glad to be out of that Blasted slough. **a1868** N.H. Bishop *Across So. Amer.* 28: Such blasted nonsense. **1902** Harriman *Ann Arbor* 78: It's so blasted cold. **1938** "E. Queen" *4 Hearts* 27: I haven't accomplished a blasted thing. **1948** Wouk *City Boy* 205: Why is this camp so blasted quiet tonight, anyhow? **1972** Cleaves *Sea Fever* 17: It'll break your blasted heart. **1983** *Firestorm* (Apr.) 4: Get away frum me, ya blasted spook!

2. very drunk or high.

1928 in *AS* (Dec. 1931) 88: Blasted. Boiled. Boozed. Bunned. **1934** Weseen *Dict. Amer. Slang* 273: *Blasted*—intoxicated. **1942** *ATS* 122: Drunk…blasted. **1961** Coon *At the Front* 199: When these men come off the lines every one of them…ought to be handed a pint of booze and told to get blasted. **1969** S. Harris *Puritan Jungle* 151: Hustlers can be bug-eyed on alcohol or blasted on narcotics so they are not themselves. **1970** A. Young *Snakes* 63: Let's get blasted! **1971** Cole *Rook* 87: Really drunk, blasted. **1971** *Rowan & Martin's Laugh-In* (NBC-TV): He must really have been blasted. **1978** Truscott *Dress Gray* 392: All of them were blasted out of their skulls. **1993** *Jerry Springer Show* (synd. TV series): You were spendin' forty dollars on weed and gettin' blasted.

blaster *n.* **1.** one that blasts (in any sense), such as a gun, a gunman, a jet plane, or a heavy wave.

1935 Pollock *Und. Speaks*: *Blaster*, a gun-man. **1955** Archibald *Aviation Cadet* 69: What business outfit or airline will use pursuits? Three years in the blasters and you get punch drunk. **1966** N.Y.C. man, age *ca*25: A gun could be called a *gat* or a *blaster*. **1968** Kirk & Hanle *Surfer's Hndbk.* 136: *Blaster*: very hard-breaking wave. **1982** Univ. Tenn. instructor, age *ca*40: I know a lot of shooting enthusiasts and they frequently refer to their pistols as *blasters*.

2. (see 1984 quot.). Cf. GHETTO BLASTER.

1984 S. Hager *Hip Hop* 108: Box or *blaster*—portable tape player and/or radio. **1988** Coonts *Final Flight* 148: Don't you have earphones for that blaster?

blast-off *n.* **1.** [cf. BLAST OFF, *v.*, 3] a sexual orgasm. *Joc.*

1965 Trimble *Sex Words* 238: *Blast-off*…Orgasm. **1960–69** Runkel *Law* 238: She'd brought him right up to blast-off.

2. an exciting time; BLAST, *n.*, 3.a., b.

1969 *Jonathan Winters Show* (TV series): It's going to be a real blast-off. **1987** *TV Guide* (Nov. 7) 40: She confesses that every now and then she likes a "real blast-off," a party with plenty of food and drink.

blast off *v.* **1.** to clear out; leave.
1954 Bruce & Henley *Rocket Man* (film): The first chance I get I'm blasting off. **1955** Reifer *New Words* 31: *Blast off. v.*....To depart; take one's leave. **1957** Gutwillig *Silence* 230: I blasted off down Madison Avenue. **1961** Coon *At Front* 71: Now blast off. I've had a hard day. **1963** Coon *Short End* 74: If she was an old broad or something ugly I'd have told her to blast off. **1969** *Esquire* (Aug.) 71: Blast off....Don't bug me. **1973** N.Y.U. prof., age *ca*40: One more thing before you blast off. **1981** Wolf *Roger Rabbit* 153: They blast off in a hurry. **1986** Gilmour *Pretty in Pink* 86: Shall we blast off?
2. [cf. BLAST PARTY] to become elated or excited, as by the use of drugs.
1961 Ellison *Gentleman Junkie* 172: The *peyote* cactus....I used to blast off on it when I was in Hollywood.
3. [cf. BLAST-OFF, *n.*, 1.] to experience sexual orgasm.
1969 Ruben *Everything Abt. Sex* 91: After I blast-off myself, what do I need a girl friend for?

blast party *n.* [cf. BLAST OFF, *v.*, 2] (see quot.).
1958 *N.Y. Times Mag.* (May 16) 87: *Blast party*—Get-together of marijuana smokers.

blat *n.* [< G *Blatt* 'newspaper', lit. 'sheet'] a newspaper. Cf. BLADDER.
1937 in D. Runyon *More Guys* 214: A high-toned wedding such as you see in pictures in the Sunday blats. **1944** D. Runyon, in *Collier's* (Mar. 18) 11: His racket is to witness all the new plays and write what he thinks about them in a morning blat. **1966** in Perelman *Don't Tread* 233: [As] I read in some blat recently. **1966–72** Winchell *Exclusive* 41: His first big-burg blatt had been the New York *Mail*. **1978** Univ. Tenn. student theme: A rather intriguing version of last night's hoorah seems to be plastered all over the front page of the Charlotte Amalie morning blat.

blat *v.* to talk at length, YAK.
1884 "M. Twain" *Huckleberry Finn* ch. xxv: He blatted along, and managed to inquire about pretty much everybody. **1888** in Farmer *Amer.*: One of these insects of an hour rears up and blatts. **1901** Ade *Modern Fables* 19: For a whole Evening you Blat about your own Affairs. **1925** S. Lewis *Arrowsmith* ch. xviii: He's a fine one, he is, to go around blatting that we'd ought to have more health precautions!

blatherskite *n.* [of Scots origin; see *OED2* s.v. *bletherskite*] **a.** a blustering or offensively loquacious person; blowhard. Now *colloq.*
1791 in *DAE*: A Blatherskite Irishman...kept constantly jawing to & teasing the girl all the way. **1841** in *DAE*: That intense *blatherskite*, "Mr. George Jones, of Stratford-on-Avon and the Virginia Theatres." **1848** Bartlett *Amer.* 34: *Blatherskite.* A blustering, noisy, talkative fellow.—*Western.* **1859** *Spirit of Times* (July 23) 288: The inexperienced legal "*Blatherskite.*" **1866** G.A. Townsend *Non-Combatant* 106: The Confederate major was of the class referred to in polite American parlance as a "blatherskite." **1889** "M. Twain" *Conn. Yankee* 147: She was a perfect blatherskite. **1908** J. London *M. Eden* 325: Yappers and blatherskites! **1977** Coover *Public Burning* 520: You old blatherskite.
b. blustering or empty talk.
1861 in *DAE*: Proving, not by verbal blatherskyte, but by facts. **1864** J.R. Browne *Apache Country* 161: A favorite crochet of his was that all this talk about Apaches was "blatherskite."

blaxploitation *n.* [cf. SEXPLOITATION] the exploitation of blacks, esp. in films featuring black actors and themes presumed to be of interest to blacks.—used attributively.
1972 in *OED2*: This blaxploitation picture's about a pre-Civil War slave. **1976** H.L. Gates, Jr., in *Harper's* (June) 25: We must come to understand that all the "violence" in the "blaxploitation" films only serves to create another form of escapism. **1979** *Mother Jones* (Jan. 1980) 36: Black people had given America almost everything in it that I loved—blues, jazz, gospel, jitterbug dancing, red beans and rice, hot barbeque, blaxploitation movies, most of the good slang, [etc.]. **1984** *L.A. Times* (Aug. 30) VI 1: It led to...what became known as the blaxploitation pictures, violent and plainspoken, reflecting a mix of street reality and fantasies of antihero glory. **1990** L. Horne, in *Ebony* (Nov.) 88: A whole new range of Black stereotypes: the pimp, hustler, addict, rogue cop, hooker. Thus during the '70s we had a decade of so-called "blaxploitation" films.

blaze *v. Stu.* to leave.
1983 *N.Y. Daily News* (Mar. 25): Teentalk glossary...let's leave:...*let's blaze, let's blow this firetrap.* **1982–84** Safire *Take My Word* 109: Gotta

go...*Gotta blaze* (auto usage). **1989** *Newsweek* (Sept. 25) 6: How teenagers talk in...Chicago:...*Blaze*: To leave...."I'm blazin'."

blazer *n.* **1.** HUMDINGER.
1845 in *DA*: T'other gal is likely enough, but the mother's a blazer! ***1892** in *OEDS*: You must prove that you're a blazer—you must prove that you have grit.
2. a trick; hoax; lie.—usu. constr. with *run*.
1906 in *DA*: The Kaiser's telegram...recalled some of his blazers in the past. **1907** S.E. White *Ariz. Nights*: It was just a cold, raw blazer. **1910** in *DA*: The rustlers planned to run a blazer on us. **1934** Cunningham *Triggernometry* 298: He tried to run a blazer on this...cowman.

blazing *adv. & adj.* **1.** (used as an intensive).
1855 in Meserve & Reardon *Satiric Comedies* 127: You chap with the blazing big fiddle. **1857** in *DAE*: The brave official had become what is sometimes called "blazing drunk." **1891** "E. Perkins" *30 Yrs. of Wit* 296: I'm the blazing bloody blizzard of the States.
2. Esp. *Black E.* exceedingly well; exceedingly good.
1864 *Battle-Fields of So.* 285: Tell her...dat I'se gettin' on blazing. *a*1982 in Hartwell & Bentley *Open to Lang.* 60: All you gotta do is snuggle up to the *blazin'* new *April* issue of *16 Magazine*. **1990** *New Yorker* (Sept. 17) 90: She nice, and she got a *blazin'* job. **1993** *N.Y. Times* (Apr. 13) B 6: I'd...get six blazing girls with dope bodies.

blazing iron *n.* [cf. syn. SHOOTING IRON] a gun or musket.
1778 in R.M. Lederer, Jr. *Colonial Amer. Eng.* 32: A New Englander riding in the woods with his blazing iron (the term they give to a musket or a gun).

blazing star *n. West.* (see 1889 quot.).
1889 *Century Dict.* I 582: *Blazing star*...3. A stampede of pack-mules or other animals from a central point. [Western U.S. slang.]. **1901** *Munsey's Mag.* XXV 403: The herd...burst like a bomb-shell into that most disastrous of all plains mishaps—a "blazing star."

bleach *v. Stu.* to absent oneself from a class or other meeting.
1836 *Harvardiana* III 123: 'Tis sweet Commencement parts to reach,/ But oh! 'tis doubly sweet to *Bleach*. **1851** B.H. Hall *College Wds.* 20: At Harvard College, he was formerly said to *bleach* who preferred to be *spiritually* rather than *bodily* present at morning prayers.

bleached baloney *n.* Esp. *Mil.* boneless turkey.
1974 1st Lieut., Army National Guard, age 25: And the bleached baloney made you puke. **1974** Vietnam veteran, age *ca*24: In the army we called the turkey roll *bleached baloney.*

bleak *adj. Und.* attractive.
1859 Matsell *Vocab.* 12: *Bleak-Mort.* A pretty girl. *Bleak.* Handsome; "The Moll is bleak," the girl is handsome. **1866** *Nat. Police Gaz.* (Nov. 24) 3: Curly, who is a "bleak mort," has a certain "bloke" doing business on Broadway "on a string," and the way she "pinches" his "sugar" is "rough."

bleat *v.* to complain in a whining manner.
1869 *Overland Mo.* (Aug.) 121: There is no fear of a man who bleats. **1930** Lait *On Spot* 23: Well, what you bleatin' about? **1946** G.C. Hall, Jr. *1000 Destroyed* 31: The pilots...bleated, "If they had to change, why couldn't they have given us Mustangs instead of these things?"

bleed *n.* ¶ In phrase: **put the bleed on** to extort money from; to blackmail.
1969 Gordone *No Place* 448: Takes a lotta balls to try to put the bleed on Pete Zerroni.

bleeder *n.* **1.** a knife used as a weapon.
*1848 (cited in Partridge *Dict. Und.* 47). **1866** *Night Side of N.Y.* 44: The queer, unclassified sailors belonging to ships in the port—be they Lascars, or what not—are ever expert with their "bleeders."
2. *Baseball.* a very slow ground ball.
1934 Weseen *Dict. Slang* 205: *Bleeder*—A lucky hit. **1937** *Pittsburgh Press* (Jan. 11) (cited in Nichols *Dict. Baseball Term.*). **1949** Cummings *Dict. Sports* 37. **1962** Houk & Dexter *Ballplayers* 176: Mickey got two "bleeders" as we call 'em, squibs that he beat out. **1964** Thompson & Rice *Every Diamond* 140: *Bleeder:* A lucky or fluke base hit. **1969–71** Kahn *Boys of Summer* 141: Sometimes I hit a bleeder first time up and I have to break from the plate in a hurry. **1988** (quot. at ROPE, *n.*).

bleeding *adj. & adv.* BLOODY. [Common in Great Britain and Australia, but rare in U.S.]
*1858 in *OEDS*: Costermongers have lately substituted the participle "bleeding" for the adjective ["bloody"]. "My bleeding barrow" is the latest phrase in vogue. ***1877** in *F & H* (rev.) 258: You make no bleeding error. **1879** *Puck* (Sept. 27) 451: Cornell's a bleedin' low-down

Republican. **1926** Nichols & Tully *Twenty Below* 42: Fetch the bleedin' cop while you're about it. *Ibid.* 61: I'm a bleedin' fool, I am. **1962** Kesey *Cuckoo's Nest* 64: The only thing to do is blow the whole business off the face of the whole bleeding earth. **1963–64** Kesey *Great Notion* 151: What the bleedin' hell you *talkin'* about? **1973** Collins *Carrying the Fire* 37: I tried to figure out just what the bleeding hell we were doing there. **1980** D. Hamill *Stomping Ground* 139: It's nothing short of bleedin' brilliant.

bleep *n.* (used for any expletive that might be regarded as offensive). *Joc.* Also vars.

> **1971** Michelson *Very Simple Game* 200: Or that I should beat the bleep out of so and so. **1975** *L.A. Times* (Oct. 26) III 12: We don't take no bleep from nobody! **1976** (quot. at BLEEP, *v.*, 1). **1981** *N.Y. Daily News* (July 21) 77: What the bleep is going on here?…ABC obviously doesn't give a bleep. **1981** *TV Guide* (Aug. 8) 15: Who gives a bleep about the cost of living? **1988** Robinson & Stainback *Extra Innings* 61: Listen, you little bleep. **1992** *Oprah* (ABC-TV): Or get the bleep out of my house!

bleep *v.* **1.** *Radio & TV.* to delete (an offensive word) from a broadcast or recording by electronic means, replacing it with a beeping sound; delete as offensive. Also vars.

> **1966** *L.A. Times* (Feb. 7) IV 20: ABC attorneys…ultimately ordered certain words and phrases "blooped" out of the tape on ground they might be defamatory. **1966** *Time* (July 1) 57: Jagger's diction is so slurred that many stations unwittingly played the record; others bleeped out the offending phrase. **1975** *L.A. Times* (Dec. 25) IV 48: She gets many a salty visitor to the show, but the one guest who was bleeped most often was Lucy. **1976** *L.A. Times* (Feb. 24) IV 13: Words are blipped out. Harry Morgan as Col. Potter says the war is a pain in the blip. **1981** Gilliland *Rosinante* 6: Why didn't the state-wide TV bleep that…statement?

2. (used to replace any verb that may be regarded as offensive). *Joc.*

> **1971** Klein *Street Gangs* 196: She's been bleeped up with public assistance funds for so long that she has no more initiative. **1978** *L.A. Times Bk. Review* (Mar. 12) 2: J.F.K. could have done so much for his country when so much was needed if he hadn't spent so much time bleeping in the bedrooms of the White House. **1982** *California* (Oct.) 12: I couldn't have gotten a better break if I lived in Hollywood and (bleeped) a million producers.

bleeping *adj.* (used as an intensifier). *Joc.* Also vars.

> **1970** *TV Guide* (Nov. 14) 19: But a bleeping censor…walked in to tell us our little wreck was too horrible. **1976** *L.A. Times* (Oct. 9) II 5: He might consider your question a challenge to his masculinity, an irrational interruption of his blipping reverie. **1978** *Houston Chronicle* Zest (Mar. 19) 9: Cut out the (bleepin') spittin'! **1984** *N.Y. Post* (Aug. 15) 76: He's always bouncing that slider in the bleeping dirt.

blenker *v.* [after Brig. Gen. Louis *Blenker* (1812–63); in a notorious incident, "insufficient rations prompted his starving troops to raid farms" near Warrenton, Va., in April 1862 (P.L. Faust, ed., *Historical Times Illus. Encyc. of the Civil War*, p. 67)] *Army.* to steal (civilian property).

> **1862** in *DA*: He'd "Blenker'd" those dainties….(Note. "Blenkered,"…a term quite common, just now, in the army for anything stolen, which came into use soon after General Blenker's division passed down the Shenandoah Valley.). **1890** *Nation* (Oct. 9) 291: The verb *blenker*, used during the Civil War in the sense of "to plunder"…originated in the plundering habits ascribed, justly or unjustly, to a body of troops in the Northern Army commanded by Gen. Blenker.

blewey var. BLOOEY.

Blighty *n.* [< Hindi *bilāyatī* 'foreign', 'European'; see *OED2*] **1.a.** Orig. *Mil.* Britain; England. [The only sense now current.]

> **1915* in *OEDS*: The only thing they looked forward to was getting back to "Blighty" again. **1919** U.S. Army 114th MG Bn. *With the 114th* 133: "Blighty."—Originating with the Tommies—England, a wound. **1951** Cowley *Exile's Return* 49: We were like soldiers with a few more days to spend in Blighty. **1980** *Air Classics: Air War Over Korea* 47: Back in Blighty the Sea Fury held its own until Sea Hawks began entering service. **1992** Jernigan *Tin Can Man* 53: U-boats…were causing critical shortages in Blighty.

b. *Mil.* home; the United States. [Adapted fr. British Army usage.]

> **1918** in Rossano *Price of Honor* 188: Well, cherish that little acquain-

tance till…[we] get to "blighty," will you? **1918** *Camp Pike Carry-On* (Dec. 19) 6: Neill left Brest and sailed for "Blighty." **1919** in *St. Lawrence U. in the War* 46: He…really continued to improve and talk about going to Blighty.

2. a desirable wound requiring a wounded man's evacuation from combat, esp. to England or to the United States. [All quots. except 1939 ref. to WWI.]

> **1916* in *OEDS* I 289: So-and-so stopped some shrapnel and is back at the base in hospital,…he wasn't lucky enough to get a blighty. **1918** *Yank Talk* 6: Where'd you all get dat blighty, man? **1919** Kuhn *Narr. Co. A* 37: It seemed as though it were only a question of time when each of us would get a "blighty," and then the chief consideration was whether it would be a severe or a slight wound. **1925** Thomason *Fix Bayonets* 164: Lookit fellers! Got a bon blighty—We'll give 'em your regards in Paris! **1928** Wharton *Squad* 132: If I could only get a blighty—a soft wound through the hand, or the calf, or the foot. **1928** Havlin *History Co. A* 143: Pleased with his "blighty,"…he got up…and amid buzzing bullets, walked about two hundred yards, without injury, to a trench in the rear. **1939** Bessie *Men in Battle* 236 [ref. to Spanish Civil War]: I've been waiting to get a nice little blighty for some time.

3. a vacation leave.

> **1933** *Leatherneck* (July) 17: We now have four men enjoying a twenty-day "blighty."

Blimey *n.* [Cockney oath *blimey!*, contr. and reduction of *God blind me!*, infl. by LIMEY] an English person, esp. a Cockney.

> **1918** *Lit. Digest* (July 6) 62: I overheard two "blimeys" fanning buckwheat while they hunted a shellhole. **1924** *Amer. Legion Wkly.* (Dec. 20): The frogs and the blimies. **1932** in H. Miller *Letters to Emil* 114: Tipping the waiter…, tipping the Blimeys right and left. **1939** Howsley *Argot* 8: *Blimey*—an English cockney.

blimp *n.* **1.** a small nonrigid dirigible; (*also*) a kite balloon or (in WWII) a barrage balloon. Now *S.E.*

> **1916* in *OEDS*: Visited the Blimps…this afternoon at Capel. **1917** in Lahm *Diary* 10: A blimp was cruising along the British coast. **1918** *Wadsworth Gas Attack* (Jan. 26) 26: One of the smaller non-rigid dirigibles they call "blimps." **1918** Paine *Fighting Fleets* 286: It was a shocking scandal to besmirch our pure young blimp station in this manner. **1919** *Amer. Legion Wkly.* (July 4) 25: The C-5 Naval dirigible, called a "Blimp," was 192 feet long, forty-five feet wide, forty-six feet high and contained 180,000 cubic feet of hydrogen. **1919** *Our Navy* (Sept.) 36: It made you happy as a blimp. **1919** McCarthy *Hist. Co. D* 35: Men of the Company saw…the escape of the observer from the basket of the "blimp" in a parachute. **1924** Barber *Along Road* 56: Previous to this time, whenever a blimp was shot down, the observer escaped. **1926** Wood & Goddard *Amer. Slang* 6: Blimp. Any non-rigid balloon. **1940* in *OEDS*: The [barrage] balloons, so suitably called blimps, became a major symbol in the first three months of the war. **1956** in Loosbrock & Skinner *Wild Blue* 115: Also a Navy blimp, C-5. **1985** *N.Y. Times* (Aug. 6) C 3: Navy and Coast Guard Show Renewed Interest in Blimps.

2.a. (used as a vague term of contempt); *specif.*, one who is loquacious or full of "hot air."

> **1929** Botkin *Folk Say* I 111: *Blimp* and *junk* are words for disreputable cabs with which it is difficult to attract business. **1936** Levin *Old Bunch* 99: Oh, don't be a blimp. Why, Rose, you can talk better than any of us. **1943** A. Scott *So Proudly We Hail* (film): You big blimp.

b. a promiscuous young woman.

> **1932** *AS* VII 329: *Blimp*—a girl of doubtful morals. **1940** *Life* (Oct. 28) 99: Girls on the beach are referred to [by sailors] as *blimps* or *blisters*. **1941** *Slanguage Dict.* 7: *Blimp*…a girl of questionable character. **1942** Algren *Morning* 41: Widow, divorcees, old maids, blimps cheatin' on their husbands 'n boy friends. **1965** *AS* XL 77: Freshmen in a composition course [at U. Nebr.] defined…*blimp* [as "a woman of loose morals"]. **1970* De Witt *Barrack-Room Ballads* 101: Oh, I wish I was a pimp/For I'd give the boys a crimp/With all my whorey blimps.

3. a grossly obese person.

> **1932–34** Minehan *Boy & Girl Tramps* 15: Here, you, Blimp,…take these tins down to the river. **1941** Kendall *Army & Navy Slang* 2: *A baby blimp*…a jolly fat girl. **1943** *Corvette K-225* (film): Shuddup, ya big blimp! **1950** Rackin *Enforcer* (film): A blimp like you ain't got a girlfriend. **1966** Susann *Valley of Dolls* 404: We forget, our blimp is still a human being. **1972** *Sanford & Son* (NBC-TV): I guess the blimp hasn't been down yet. **1976** Woodley *Bears* 46: That's what the blimp said. **1982** Rucker *57th Kafka* 104: Get out of here, you pompous *blimp!* **1983** *N.Y. Post* (Sept. 2) 46: There's been a major change in her eating habits and…she's beginning to look like a blimp.

4. *Film.* a soundproof covering for a motion picture camera.

1934 Weseen *Dict. Amer. Slang* 136: *Blimp*—A soundproof box that muffles the noise of a camera. **1936** in *OEDS*: A "blimp" in studio jargon is…a soundproof covering for the camera.

5. *Trucking.* (see quots.).

1942 *AS* (Apr.) 102: *Blimp.* Short trailer, high on tractor. **1971** Tak *Truck Talk* 14: *Blimp:* a short, high trailer.

blimp *v.* [imit.] *Av.* to open and close (a throttle) quickly.

1933 Stewart *Speech Amer. Airman* 48: In order to be certain that the engine will pick up readily if he should need it after throttling down for a landing, the pilot "blimps" his engine, or puts it on short bursts when coming in. **1961** Foster *Hell in Heavens* 70: Then he located a rescue boat and flew low over it blimping his engine, and flew off in Craig's direction. **1970** Lincke *Jenny* 98: Ever since, student pilots and other girl-impressers have been blimping their throttle, trying to sound like World War I aces.

blimp jockey *n. Navy.* a blimp pilot.

1955 *Science Digest* (Dec.) 70: The "blimp jockeys" were men apart—in the Navy, but not of it.

blimpo *n.* [BLIMP + -O] BLIMP, *n.*, 3.

1933 Mahin & Furthman *Bombshell* (film): That's just Blimpo [a big dog]. **1982** Trudeau *Dressed for Failure* (unp.): Meanwhile, I'm turning into this misshapen blimpo.

blimp out *v. Stu.* to become overweight rapidly. Also **blimp up.**

1979 Eble *Campus Slang* (Mar.) 1: *Blimp-out*—to eat a lot: Let's go blimp-out. **1980** in Safire *Good Word* 213: "To blimp out" is the result of too much pigging out. **1985** Eble *Campus Slang* (Apr.) 1: *Blimp out*—to gain weight. **1985** Univ. Tenn. *Daily Beacon* (May 29) 7: These pants have just gotten *too small*….Well, people always blimp up in college.

blind *n.* **1.** *Baseball.* a shutout.

1867 in *DA.* **1872** Chadwick *Dime Base-Ball* 29: *Blind.*—This is a provincial term for a blank score.

2.a. *Army.* a fine or forfeiture of pay imposed by court-martial. [The development of this sense is obscure; cf. poker term illustrated by 1890 quot.]

1888 McConnell *Cavalryman* 197 [ref. to late 1860's]: [He] perhaps has a "blind" of ten dollars imposed out of his pay. **1889** C.C. King *Marion's Faith* [ref. to ca1875]: Tin dollars blind an' sivin days…in the gyard-house. [**1890** Quinn *Fools of Fortune* 218: *Blind.*—The ante deposited by the age [player to the left of the dealer] previous to the deal.] **1893** Putnam *Blue Uniform* 58: I shall miss reveille…; then the court will soak me for a two-dollar blind. **1900** McManus *Soldier Life* 104: They expected a severe raking over, and felt that even their belts might be "pulled," with a "blind" and the "jug" as a fine, as guardhouse sentences are called. **1901** Oliver *Roughing It* 45: If he does become intoxicated the chances [are] that a sojourn in the guard house and a "blind" is the result. **1907** *Army & Navy Life* (Aug.) 190: An' six hours shine for a ten plunk blin' aint what it's cracked up to be. **1910** J. Lomax *Cowboy Songs* 250: The proceedings we find Were a ten dollar blind. **1918** G. Griffin *Ballads* 46: Equipment, inspection and "blinds." **1926** *Sat. Eve. Post* (May 1) 126: I hope you get a blind that keeps you poor the rest of your life.

b. *Hobo.* an eviction order.

1897 in J. London *Reports* 320: Got a t'ree hour blin'….The judge gave me three hours in which to leave town.

3. *Hobo.* a blind baggage car. Now *hist.*

1893 in *OEDS*: In hobo language, "beating the blinds" means to steal a ride on the mail car next to the engine. **1895** *DN* I 390: *Jump the blind,* to steal a ride on platform of baggage car. **1910** in N. Cohen *Long Steel Rail* 419: Carries fourteen coaches, got no blinds at all. **1926** *Amer. Mercury* (July) 334: I hit the blinds for the hobo's paradise of the North, New York City.

4. *Stu.* a blind date.—constr. with *drag.*

1921 *DN* V 111: *To drag a blind,* vb. ph. To take (or go with) to a dance a girl (or man) one has never seen. **1926** S. Young *Encaustics* 2: I had to drag a blind and all that.

blind *adj.* **1.** extremely intoxicated.

*****1630** in *OEDS*: For though he be as drunke as any Rat, He hath but catcht a Foxe, or Whipt the Cat. Or some say hee's bewitcht, or scratcht, or blinde, Which are the fittest tearmes that I can finde. *****1845** in *OEDS*: They'll be all *blind* by the time they get home from G.F.'s wedding. **1884** Hartranft *Sidesplitter* 159: The patient who was "blind (drunk)," was deprived of his whiskey. **1893** McCloskey *Across Continent* 75: She gets blind drunk, too. **1927** *New Republic* (Mar. 9) 71: [Synonyms for *drunk*:] polluted,…stinko, blind. *****1930** Brophy & Partridge

Songs & Slang 101: *Blind.*—Adjective: helplessly drunk. **1952** Ellson *Golden Spike* 153: I'm a no-good greedy son-of-a-bitch and I want to be blind. **1958–59** Lipton *Barbarians* 186: And he hits up the whole thing and he gets blind and he starts nodding….And this other guy…gets blind. **1961** Coon *At Front* 170: You really went out and got blind, didn't you, Poole? **1974** E. Thompson *Tattoo* 202: You're all half blind.

2. (of an egg) fried on both sides.

1891 Maitland *Amer. Slang Dict.* 36: *Blind in both eyes* (Am.), eggs fried on both sides.

3. *Homosex.* (of the penis) uncircumcised.

1925 McAlmon *Stockings* 66: You know how I hate—well, you know—blind meat—you know what I mean. **1941** G. Legman, in Henry *Sex Variants* 1150: *Blind…*Uncircumcised; said of the penis. **1956** Reinhardt *Perversions* 47: *Blind…*Uncircumcised.

¶ In phrase:

¶ **strike me blind!** (used as an oath or exclamation).

1898 Norris *Moran* 39: Strike me blind, I'll cut you open.

blind *adv.* ¶ In phrase: **rob blind** to rob completely and without restraint.

1955 in C. Beaumont *Best* 31: He's robbed us blind!

blind *v.* **1.** [alluding to *dazzle*] *Stu.* to impress (an instructor) by answering all questions asked.

1900 *DN* II 23: *Blind,* v.t.…To answer all the questions put by an instructor….To make a false impression of having prepared a lesson by reciting well. [Widespread use reported.]. **1947** *Amer. N & Q* (May) 30: The old expression [ca1902] "blinded," which was what a student giving a perfect answer [in recitation] did to a professor.

2. *Hobo.* to steal a ride on a blind baggage car of (a railway train).

*a***1915** in *JAF* XXVIII (1915) 293: Let me step over yonder and blind the Cannon Ball. **1948** McHenry & Myers *Home Is Sailor* 38 [ref. to 1930's]: Younger 'bos…rode only the faster passenger trains, "blinding the baggage."

blind alley *n. Naut.* mush.

1925 Bailey *Shanghaied* 30 [ref. to 1898]: We received pea-soup on Wednesdays and Saturdays, with "blind alley" on Sundays, the latter often without currants.

blind Charley *n.* a lamppost.

1848 (quot. at STUMP GLIM).

blind gaskets *n.pl.* pancakes.

1919 Warren *20th Engrs.* 34: The Engineer's Dictionary…*Blind gaskets*—Hot cakes. **1945** Hubbard *R.R. Ave.* 345: Hotcakes are *blind gaskets.*

blind pig *n.* **1.** an establishment where alcoholic beverages are sold illegally; a speakeasy.

1886 Nye *Remarks* 303: Mysterious beverages…from a blind pig in Iowa. **1898** Bowe *13th Minn.* 9: The boys raided the "blind pig" at the end of the street car line last night. **1901** *DN* II 136: *Blind pig, n.* A speak-easy; saloon without a license. **1922** N. Anderson *Hobo* 67: In Chicago today bootleggers and blind pigs in the vicinity of the "stem" thrive upon the homeless man's love of liquor. **1925** S. Lewis *Arrowsmith* ch. vi: "Barney's" was a poolroom, a tobacco shop and, since Mohalis was dry by local option, an admirable blind-pig. **1931** J.T. Farrell *McGinty* 218: Hardtack had some moonshine he'd bought at Scotty's blind pig. **1946** Gresham *Nightmare Alley* 31: I'll bet that joint is a blind pig. **1948** Lait & Mortimer *N.Y. Confidential* 43: Of the 50-odd blind pigs only two remained. **1956** Holiday & Dufty *Lady Sings Blues* 36: Prohibition was on its last legs then. And so were the blind pigs, cribs and clubs and after-hours joints that Prohibition set up in business. **1967** *Time* (Aug. 4) 13: A "blind pig" (afterhours club) opened…on a sleazy strip of pawnshops and bars, rats and pimps, junkies and gamblers. **1988** T. Logan *Harder They Fall* 8: Crack houses and after-hours bars known as blind pigs.

2. *Army.* a trench mortar projectile.

1920 *Atlantic Mo.* (Apr.) 516 [ref. to WWI]: It was Beethoven and the other Boches of his sort [whose] tunes…made the whizz-bangs and the blind pigs and the bombs and bullets sound much less dismaying.

3. (see quot.).

1946 Bill *Beleaguered City* 14 [ref. to ca1858]: The [Richmond, Va.] Public Guard wore "P.G." on their hats and went by the name of Blind Pigs in the local slang. For P.G. is "pig" without the *i,* and a pig without an eye must be a blind pig. Q.E.D.

4. a kind of alcoholic mixed drink.

1971 *The Interns* (CBS-TV): How 'bout a wallbanger or a blind pig?

blind-pigger *n.* the proprietor of a BLIND PIG, 1.

1894 in *DA*: Headed by one of the blind-piggers who was under arrest, Rev. Macnamara was severely beaten. **1930** Paisley *Capone* 82: Peter as a saloon-keeper; James as a blind-pigger. **1967** in *DARE*.

blind robin *n.* a smoked herring.

1865 in S.C. Wilson *Column South* 323: Blind Robins and new milk for supper last night. **1887** Hinman *Si Klegg* 243 [ref. to Civil War]: He was sitting on the sugar barrel in the corner grocery, gnawing on a "blind robin." **1889** in *DA*: A reputed banquet whose menu's range confined itself to herrings, or "blind robins," dried beef, and cheese. **1922** *Amer. Legion Wkly.* (July 28) 9: No salt horse and blind robin on this cruise. **1926** *AS* I 616: Smoked herring. "We call them blind robins." **1961** in IUFA *Folk Speech*: Smoked herring are called *blind robins* in Joliet, Ill.

blindside *v.* Orig. *Football.* to strike, hit, tackle, etc., on one's blind side; (*hence*) to take by surprise; attack where one is vulnerable.

1968 (cited in *BDNE3*). **1974** Blount *3 Bricks Shy* 106: When we opened against the Bears in '67, our receiver caught a pass and I went flying downfield and blindsided Butkus. **1975** *N.Y. Times* (Jan. 17) 29: There was a feeling that Hays had been blind-sided by the power structure. **1977** *Atlantic* (Nov.) 30: I find my way not blocked by the known enemy but blind-sided by liberal economists. **1981** Wambaugh *Glitter Dome* 193: She had blindsided him with that kiss. **1983** K. Miller *Lurp Dog* 22: If I die with a weapon in my hand, I won't blindside you when I get to Heaven! **1990** *New Republic* (Feb. 12) 43: Gorbachev said he hadn't been blindsided by his country's humongous problems when he took over.

blind tiger *n.* **a.** *So.* illicit whiskey.

1904 H.N. Brown *Necromancer* 100: And blind tig[er] stands around/ To poison men before the[ir] time. **1968** in *DARE*.

b. an establishment where alcoholic beverages are sold illegally; speakeasy.

1909 *N.Y. Evening Post* (Jan. 28): A "blind tiger" is a private residence, a shed, a tent, or an office room in a building, occupied temporarily, and stocked with beer and whiskey for sale to friends of the proprietor. **1910** W. Archer *Afro-Amer.* 147: They enlarged on the evils of the "blind tiger," or illicit saloon. **1921** Floyd *Co. F* 92: They ran a "blind tiger" with no stock. **1928** Wylie *Heavy Laden* 18: The banished red-light district reappeared in the wake of his "blind tigers." **1928** York *Sgt. York* 71: Another time he went out with the sheriff of another county to raid a "blind tiger" and there was a lot of shooting. *Ibid.* 129: There were drinking shacks, "blind tigers," we used to call them, most every few miles. **1936** Dos Passos *Big Money* 73: Then he went to a blindtiger he knew. **1938** Wolfe *Web & Rock* 57: They were…the runners of blind tigers, the brothel guardians. **1960** Brooks *Elmer Gantry* (film): It's been eight days since I've given you the names of eleven blind tigers. **1971** Curtis *Banjo* 72: You know, it's a blind tiger—a speakeasy. **1980** in *Penthouse* (Jan. 1981) 148: There are still "blind tigers," where a man can buy a gallon of white lightning.

c. the proprietor of a speakeasy.

1924 White *Fire in Flint* 157: Every blamed bootlegger and blind tiger and whoremaster in town rushed into the Klan 'cause they know'd that it was the only way they could keep from getting called up on the carpet!

Blind Tom *n.* ["Quite likely…from Old Blind Tom, a popular black musical prodigy of the period just after the Civil War."—P. Dickson, *Baseball Dict.*, p. 61] *Baseball.* an umpire.—used derisively.

[**1912** in P. Dickson *Baseball Dict.* 61: A spiel printed in letters that Blind Tom could read.] **1942** *ATS* 648: Umpire…*Blind Tom.* **1953** Sher *Kid from Left Field* (film): "What can you expect from a guy who used to be a Blind Tom?" "…An umpire?" "How do you think he got so stupid?" **1955** in P. Dickson *Baseball Dict.* 61: His fourth season as a National League umpire and his twentieth as a blind tom.

blinger *n.* CORKER.

1902 Mead *Word-Coinage* 169: "Blinger," said of anything cruelly effective, as "his reply was a blinger." **1949** *Reader's Digest* (Dec.) 18: 179 of them developed real blingers going through to the phase of secondary infections.

blink *n.* **1.** a look; a glance.

1898 Norris *Moran* 57: Take a blink at her, son.

2. an eye.

1902 Cullen *More Tales* 81: The old chap with the kindly blinks. ***1935**

(cited in Partridge *DSUE* (ed. 7) 1013).

3. a blind person.

1920 *Amer. Legion Wkly.* (May 21) 5: A Man Blinded in the Service Proves That a "Blink" Can See a Joke as Well as Anybody. **1992** Univ. Tenn. psychology prof.: In the late '70's I had a colleague [in San Antonio, Tex.] who was involved in providing group psychotherapy for blind persons. And he was nonplussed when he found out that his patients referred to each other as *blinks.* It was very much an in-group expression.

¶ In phrases:

¶ **on the blink** in a bad way, esp. infirm or malfunctioning; (*earlier*) no good. [Sense of **1838 quot. is (literally) "blinking"; perh. the slang sense was first generalized from electric lighting.]

[***1838** Glascock *Land Sharks* II 40: The General's "top-lights" [eyes]…were already on the blink [from fatigue].] **1899** A.H. Lewis *Sandburrs* 173: She has him on d'blink from d'jump. **1901** Hobart *John Henry* 83: A stranglehold line of business that will put Looey Harrison on the blink. **1904** "O. Henry" *Cabbages* ch. iii: This café looks on the blink, but I guess it can set out something wet. **1906** H. Green *Actors' House* 66: I agreed…not to get put on the blink. **1907** Hobart *Beat It!* 96: Peaches gave an onion saengerfest…and I've been on the blink even sense. **1910** *N.Y. Eve. Jour.* (Apr. 22) 20: This…will soon put our bank roll on the blink. **1914** Knibbs *Songs* 56: But when you put him on the job, he's there and there to stay,/If the fever doesn't put him on the blink. **1914** [Patten] *Lefty o' the Bush* 12: Deever's arm went on the blink in the seventh. **1915** Braley *Workaday World* 153: They put Peter on the blink. **1916** in Truman *Dear Bess* 202: This P.O. is on the blink. **1919** *DN* V 72: *On the blink,* a wretched condition. "My, but I feel *on the blink.*" New Mexico. **1928** Sharpe *Chicago May* 44: Business went on the blink after the World's Fair. **1929** Milburn *Hobo's Hornbk.* 136: 'Scuse me, pard, for hornin' in, but I'm upon the blink./Ain't got a jitney in me kick, and dyin' for a drink. **1931** in E. Pound *Letters* 233: Bourgeois liter-choor is pretty well on the blink. **1934** Appel *Brain Guy* 36: Me? I'm on the blink. A man can't earn an honest living any more. **1948** *Reader's Digest* (Sept.) 82: If the radio goes on the blink it is foolish to worry about the tubes or transmitter. **1951** Sheldon *Troubling Star* 43: That radio compass is on the blink. **1960** Wohl *Cold Wind* 10: She twisted the switch on and off, turned the dials. On the blink. Damn thing never was any good. **1978** Asimov et al. *Sci. Fi. Short Shorts* 96: Oh, well, even my typewriter goes on the blink now and then.

¶ **put the blink on** to put in a bad way.

1917 in T. Lewis *H. Crane's Letters* 59: The war seems to put the blink on ever[y]thing in the confectionary line.

¶ **under the blinks** asleep.

*ca*1880 in E. West *Saloon* 95: "Went under the blinks" (slept).

blink *v.* to see.

1869 *Galaxy* (Feb.) 211: Didn't throw away nothin' after I blinked him, 'cept it was his shooter. **1928** Dahlberg *Bottom Dogs* 105: He made him…ask for a pair of specs so that he could blink straight.

blinker *n.* **1.** an eye.

*1809 in *F & H* I (rev.) 264: The master appeared in person; which stretched the old fellow's blinkers into a stare. ***1816** in *F & H*: A patent pair of goggle winkers, Conceal'd from public view his blinkers. **1839–40** Cobb *Green Hand* I 262: Darken my blinkers, Gust, but your jaw-tackle is too kinkified for me to overhand with my shot wad of a noddle. *Ibid.* 268: I did not take my blinkers off her face. *ca*1840 Hawthorne *Yankee Privateer* 40: Jack will roll his tobacco over in his mouth, give a knowing wink with one of his blinkers, sing out, "Aye, aye, sir;" and laugh in his sleeve. **1878** in Miller & Snell *Why West Was Wild* 299: The one-armed slugger received a slight scratch under his left blinker. ***1889** Barrère & Leland *Dict. Slang* I 136: *Blinkers* (pugilistic), the eyes. **1895** in Ade *Chicago Stories* 133: I sheers off, brings up me right an' lams 'im in his blinkers. a**1904–11** Phillips *Susan Lenox* II 160: Do you want me to push in your blinkers, you damned old bilk, you? **1926** C.M. Russell *Trails* 125: Nature's give him a couple of beady blinkers that ain't wore none by readin'. **1928** Dahlberg *Bottom Dogs* 147: As though shading his blinkers from the sun. **1943** Crowley & Sachs *Follow the Leader* (film): Bad blinkers; I mean bad eyesight, sir. **1944** Burley *Hndbk. Jive* 134: *Blinkers*—Eyes. **1946** Michener *So. Pacific* 181: Any time Dorothy Lamour wants to wobble them blinkers at me, OK. I ain't kicking. **1954** Matheson *Born of Man & Woman* 62: Who regales yo poor blinkers wif giddy persiflage?

2. an eye blackened by a blow.

1848 Baker *Glance at N.Y.* 19: *George.* [*Show eye.*] Look here. *Mose.* That's a blinker—you wasn't quick enough. ***1860** Hotten *Slang Dict.*

(ed. 2): *Blinker*, a blackened eye.—*Norwich*. **1930** Lait *On the Spot* 96: Would it be too personal, Chief, to inquire how you got that blinker?

3. *pl.* eyeglasses. [In earlier S.E., a particular kind of spectacles; see *OEDS*.]

*1860 Hotten *Slang Dict.* (ed. 2): *Blinkers*, spectacles. **1889** Barrère & Leland *Dict. Slang* I 136: *Blinkers*…(Common), spectacles. ***1897** H.G. Wells *Invisible Man* ch. iv: I'm hanged if that bandaged knob of his, and those blinkers, aren't enough to unnerve anyone. **1936** Monks & Finklehoffe *Brother Rat* 177: Why don't you leave…off…[the] blinkers.

4. *Hunting.* a gun dog that refuses to point.

1949 Cummings *Dict. Sports* 38.

5. *Hosp.* a quadriplegic.

1980 M. Baker *Nam* 312: You got fucked, but *there's* a guy who's a blinker—the quadriplegic— and he got worse than you. **1990** G.R. Clark *Words of Viet. War* 63: *Blinker*…Callous GI hospital slang for a quadriplegic.

6. *Film.* a talent scout.

1982 T.D. Connors *Dict. Mass Media* 30.

blinko *adj.* BLOTTO, 1.

1959 J.H. Griffin *Black Like Me*: Let's us go get just roaring blinko drunk and forget all this damned prejudice stuff.

blinky *n.* a blind or nearly blind person.

[***1861** in *OED*: One's eyes became quite blinky watching for the flash.] **1922** N. Anderson *Hobo* 102: Blinky is a man with one or both eyes defected. **1930** "D. Stiff" *Milk & Honey* 200: *Blinkey*—a blind hobo, or one who is "practically blind." **1937** Reitman *Box-Car Bertha* 139: Some were actually blind (blinkies), some deaf (deafies), some dumb (dummies). **1939** *New Yorker* (Mar. 11) 37: There are many beggars known as "blinkies," who have good vision but pretend to be blind. **1945** Yordan *Dillinger* (film): Who's gonna make me? You, blinky? **1972** Wambaugh *Blue Knight* 309: Finally the blind man said something to the meddler and made his own way. "That's telling him, Blinky," I said under my breath.

blip *n.* **1.** [imit.] a blow, as with the fist.

[**1880** J.C. Harris *Uncle Remus* 9: Brer Rabbit draw back wid his fis', he did, en blip he tuck 'er 'side er de head.] **1898** *Volunteer* (Univ. Tenn.) 159: I reckon one blip apiece will do fur the kid, if he'll promise to help on the other "fish." **1893–1903** in *JAF* (Apr. 1945) 129: He up with his fist and gave him a blip. **1977** *Atlantic* (July) 41: Receives a blip on the noodle.

2. *Black E.* a nickel or a penny.

1935 L. Hughes *Little Ham* 71 [ref. to 1920's]: I bet two blips, if you was him, you'd be dead! **1944** in Himes *Black on Black* 207: Ain't got one white quarter not even a blip. **1946** Boulware *Jive & Slang* 2: *Blip*…Nickel. **1946** Mezzrow & Wolfe *Really Blues* 29: I never had a blip in my poke. *Ibid.* 303: *Blip*: nickel.

3. *Black E.* a cause for surprise or comment, esp. something unpleasant; a remarkable person or thing; an individual; a thing.

1947–52 Ellison *Invisible Man* 287: You young Negroes is a blip!…I hope they…put your ass under the jail! **1954** W.G. Smith *South St.* 98: Young cats staring like they want to shoot me. It's a *blip*, man! *Ibid.* 99: Ain't that a blip? **1958** Hughes & Bontemps *Negro Folklore* 481: *Blip*: Very good or very bad. *Man, this beer's a blip!* **1964** in *Time* (Jan. 1, 1965) 56: If a boy is a *blip*, he is said to be *whipped by an ugly stick.* **1966–67** P. Thomas *Mean Streets* 69: Damn, that whole scene was a blip. *Ibid.* 118: She was really a good looking blip. *Ibid.* 241: "Orientation" became a "blip of the past." **1969** Beck *Mama Black Widow* 150: Ain't yu uh blip, Mama dahlin? **1971** in Sanchez *Word Sorcerers* 120: Boy them jealous chumps is a blip! **1978** W. Brown *Tragic Magic* 8: Wasn't that a blip? Here I was feeling I'd done too little on her behalf and she was holding back for fear she'd do too much. *a*1982 Hartwell & Bentley *Open to Language* 322: You say wow! We say ain't that a blip. **1990** *In Living Color* (Fox-TV): Ain't that a blip? Ain't that somethin'?

4. var. BLEEP.

blip *v.* **1.** to switch (an engine) rapidly on and off; rev (a throttle); etc. [Earliest quots. ref. to WWI.]

*1925 Fraser & Gibbons *Soldier & Sailor Wds.* 26 [ref. to WWI]: *Blip, To:* To switch an aeroplane engine on and off. **1931** Tomlinson *Best War Stories* 614: He blipped his motor with his thumb. **1937** Parsons *Lafayette Escadrille* 44: It had a triangular-shaped grip on top, with a contact button on one side so that the motor could be blipped on and off. **1962** G. Olson *Roaring Road* 71: Dave blipped the throttle a few times. **1979** *Popular Science* (Aug.) 120: An input from an astronaut, say, blipping a thruster, takes just !/25 of a second to enter the computers.

1987 J. Thompson *Gumshoe* 3: I blipped the throttle [of the motorcycle] and slid in beside him.

2.a. to hit hard.

*1924 A.A. Milne, in *OEDS*: They…blipped him on the head. **1966** Cameron *Sgt. Slade* 73: A bullet meant for his back was liable to slam right in there and blip some Kraut in the doorway.

b. to shoot (someone).—also constr. with *off.*

1927 in Hammett *Knockover* 285: I don't know him, but if [he] blipped Beno off for talking to me last night, he knows me. **1929** Hammett *Maltese Falcon* 64: You could have blipped them both.

3. var. BLEEP.

blip-chaser *n. Mil. Av.* a radar observer.

1958 in Loosbrock & Skinner *Wild Blue* 534: The pilots good-naturedly nickname [the radar man]…"blip-chaser."

bliss out *v.* to achieve a state or feeling of bliss. Hence **blissed out** feeling blissful. [These terms seem to have been introduced in 1972 by followers of Maharaj Ji, a young Hindu religious leader.]

1973 in *BDNE3*: Initiates learn to see a dazzling white light, hear celestial music, feel ecstatic vibrations….The process is called "blissing out." **1974** *Oui* (May) 91: Maybe there *was* something to this Maharaj Ji. Maybe he did have a way of bringing peace to those who wanted it. "Blissing out" was not my trip, but that didn't make it wrong for the kids. *Ibid.* 100: Rennie Davis…was…blissed out for…three days. **1980** Luceno *Head Hunters* 11: A blissed-out Lady Madonna smile on his face. *Ibid.* 57: Fortunately, everyone was too blissed out to take proper notice. **1980** *N.Y. Times Bk. Review* (Dec. 28) 10: A mad soprano is "no blissed-out canary." **1983** *Superman* (Apr.) 11: If Euphor keeps doing his thing much longer, the entire population of Metropolis will end up as "blissed out" mental vegetables. **1983** *Newsweek on Campus* (Dec.) 5: Film roles as different as a blissed-out surfer…and a street-tough convict. **1986** *Portrait of America* (TBS-TV): I like just blissing out with this stuff. **1989** *Tracey Ullman Show* (Fox-TV): I'm *so* blissed out!

blister *n.* a quarrelsome or annoying person, esp. a woman; (*hence*) an ugly or promiscuous woman, BAG.

*1806 in *OEDS*: A perpetual blister;—alias, a sociable next-door-neighbour, who has taken a violent affection for *you.* **1854** *Yale Lit. Mag.* XX 20: Here's Mrs. Grind now,—rooms to let,—good rooms, but the dowager's a blister. ***1880** in *OEDS*: *Blister*, an annoying person. **1884** "M. Twain" *Huck. Finn* ch. xxix: Well, I never see anything like that old blister for clean out-and-out cheek. **1905** *DN* III 70: *Blister*…an immoral woman. **1917–20** Dreiser *Newspaper Days* 385 [ref. to 1893]: Dubbing her, according to some amazing patois which he had picked up in that brash underworld…a "tart" and a "blister." **1925** Mullin *Scholar Tramp* 98: Draw in yer teeth, ye meddlesome old blister. **1930** P.G. Wodehouse, in *OEDS*: Women are a wash-out….Blisters, all of them. **1940** *Life* (Oct. 28) 99: Girls on the beach are referred to variously as *blimps* or *blisters* (after a battleship's waterline bulge), native girls as *Geechies* (from Geishas). **1967** Terry *Gloaming* 223: Sit down, you old blister. **1967** in Ellison *Dangerous Visions* I 85: I was too old for young girls to be attracted to me for anything but money. And I was too much a poet, a lover of beauty, to take on the wrinkled blisters of my generation. **1968** Radano *Walking Beat* 15: When we arrive there's this blister and her husband. *Ibid.* 16: His wife is jealous. Smells his clothes when he comes home to see if he's been with another blister. **1969** *Current Slang* I & II: *Blister*, n. An annoying person.—College females, New York State.

blister bandit *n. USMC.* (see quot.).

1987 D. da Cruz *Boot* 217: The corpsman issue sick bay chits to the dozen "blister bandits." They will be spared heavy marching duties until their wounds of battle heal. *Ibid.* 296: *Blister bandits* recruits whose blisters exempt them from heavy duties. **1991** Reinberg *In the Field* [ref. to Vietnam War].

blitz *n.* [clipping of G *Blitzkrieg* 'lightning war'] **1.a.** *Journ. & Mil.* an all-out attack or invasion; (*specif.*) an air attack.

*1940 in *OEDS*: Blitz bombing of London goes on all night. **1941** *Pittsburgh Courier* (Oct. 25) 5: Civilians Teach "Blitz" Troops at Camp Claiborne. **1943** *Newsweek* (Oct. 4) 22: In all the blitzes we'd been on (blitz is the Navy synonym for invasion) no officer aboard her had been wounded until the Heinies got an ensign on the morning of D-day. **1965** Daniels *Moments of Glory* 202: But our blitz ran out of gas, literally. **1991** *Sally Jessy Raphaël Show* (synd. TV show): I remember the day right after the blitz [against Pearl Harbor].

b. any vigorous attack or defeat; an utter defeat.

1958 J. King *Pro Football* 34: Halas led the most devastating blitz in football history December 8, 1940,...when the Bears won the NFL title by 73–0 over the Redskins. **1961** Scarne *Guide to Gambling* 673: *Blitz Gin Rummy:* When a player wins a game and his opponent has failed to score any points. **1979** *L.A. Times* (Jan. 23) III 1: And in 3E minutes, U.C.L.A. [basketball team] runs off an 11–2 blitz. **1982** *U.S. News & W.R.* (Jan. 18) 6: Entire small communities along...[the] California coast near San Francisco were wiped out when a freakish blitz of rain...triggered flooding and massive mud slides.

c. *Football.* a defensive rush on the passer.

1963 Huff & Smith *Defensive Football* 99: Sometimes the blitz works. Linemen are bowled over, [etc.]. **1967** J. Kramer *Instant Replay* 41: We held a blitz drill this morning. **1969** *Playboy* (Dec.) 118: They used a lot of various safety blitzes. **1970** Sample *Dirty Ballplayer* 122: If a clenched fist was held up the defense was to be a blitz; two fingers meant a zone defense to the weak side; three meant a regular zone. **1976** *Harper's* (Jan. 1977) 67: I had become much more proficient in the art of picking up [i.e., becoming aware of] blitzes. **1979** *Atlantic* (Dec.) 56: I liked the position, especially when a blitz was on.

2. an extensive advertising or publicity campaign.

1948 *Time* (July 5), in Berg *New Words* 43: The Dewey blitz has been stopped. **1966** H.S. Thompson *Hell's Angels* 240: The Angels' publicity blitz was in high gear. **1968** Safire *New Lang. Politics* 120: A follow-up to...a doorbell-ringing campaign is a telephone blitz. **1970** in H.S. Thompson *Shark Hunt* 99: So now we have a DeLorean-style blitz for Chevrolet, and it's doing beautifully. **1980** Millett *Semper Fidelis* 498: The pro-Corps media blitz. **1991** Lott & Lieber *Total Impact* 34: The football recruiting blitz began.

blitz *v.* **1.a.** *Journ. & Mil.* to attack decisively, esp. fr. the air; to destroy, esp. by bombing.

1939 in *AS* XV (1940) 110: Formal committee chairmen must have known how the poor Poles felt when the German blitzkrieg started "blitzing" around their ears yesterday noon. **1940* in *OEDS*: We "blitz" hun planes in weekend raids. **1942** *Yank* (June 24) 2: The crew use a "blitzed" building for shelter. **1944** in M.W. Bowman *Castles* 114: *Blitzin' Betsy* [nickname of B-17 of 388th Bomb Group, USAAF]. **1944** *Slanguage Dictionary* 48: *Blitz*—to destroy in combat. **1953** G. Webber *Far Shore* 24: Against the blitzed buildings along the shore. **1982** *N.Y. Post* (May 22) 1: Argies Blitz 5 [British] Warships. **1989** *N.Y. Times Bk. Review* (Dec. 31) 11: Hitler decided...to...concentrate on blitzing London to its knees.

b. to defeat quickly or decisively; vanquish, as in a game, fistfight, etc.; to act decisively against.

1940 in *AS* (Apr. 1941) 145: Let's blitz 'em, gals! **1948** Cozzens *Guard of Honor* 223: You'd have to blitz the guy right then and there. *Ibid.* 224: Well, I guess you'll agree I'd better blitz those two lieutenants. Pop thinks the Eleventh Air Force might be a good place for them. **1955** Shapiro *Sixth of June* 13: You didn't know I blitzed you, did you? **1965** Hardman *Chaplains Raid* 94: I say to Brody let's go another hand, ready to blitz hell out of him. **1971** Sorrentino *Up from Never* 100: Only Richie, the Lord High Terror of the neighborhood, tried to take him on, and he got blitzed. **1973** *N.Y. Times* (Sept. 16) II 21: Will Billie Blitz Bobby? **1975** *N.Y. Times* (June 22) V 1: Pat Dobson...was "blitzed" by...the team trainer, in a stakeless gin-rummy game in the club house. **1980** *New Yorker* (July 28) 64: [He] is forced to take over the controls of a big jet when the real crew is blitzed by food poisoning. **1983** *Business Week* (June 13) 66: Three years of worldwide recession blitzed that plan. **1985** Ferraro & Francke *Ferraro* 240: Fritz had blitzed Reagan in the first...debate.

c. to attack; overwhelm; set on vigorously; etc.

1948 Cozzens *Guard of Honor* 223: You'd have to blitz the guy right then and there. *Ibid.* 224: Well, I guess you'll agree I'd better blitz those two lieutenants. Pop thinks the Eleventh Air Force might be a good place for them. **1966** *Time* (Dec. 16) 100: Paperbacks, too, are blitzing the populace. They are spinning off the presses at the rate of a million a day. **1967** *Harper's* (Nov.) 64: We blitzed another midnight snack of sardines and supporting establishments. **1967** *Everett* [Wash.] *Herald* (Nov. 16) 3a: Teams of vandals...blitz the refreshment stands. **1968** S. Ross *Hang-Up* 16: "Hey, Scotty, how'd you do?" "I blitzed them [i.e., an audience]." **1976** *L.A. Times* (July 1) I 1: A covey of...C-130 planes...joined regular air tankers in blitzing the flames with fire-retardant chemicals. **1982** *Southern Living* (May) 128: People in Greenville blitz The Spare Rib...to pick up a couple of pounds of brisket and be back home before the third quarter begins. **1984** *Business Week* (Mar. 12) 23: It is but one of 44 complaints that have hit Commerce Dept. desks...meant to blitz the administration into accepting across-the-board steel quotas.

d. *Football.* to rush or cause to rush (a passer or other

player). Also intrans. Hence **blitzer**, *n.*

1963 Huff & Smith *Defensive Football* 99: Defensive blitzing keeps pressure on the offense. **1965** *Time* (Jan. 8) 34: The idea was to force Parker into a head-to-head duel with Kanicki, thereby clearing the way for other Cleveland blitzers to harass Unitas. **1967** J. Kramer *Instant Replay* 76: The Bears like to blitz...so we had a long blitz drill. **1975** *Atlantic* (Oct.) 71: [He] has the same impulses and instincts as an all-conference linebacker blitzing a quarterback.

2. to go or bring in a hurry; to dash in or clear out.

1941 Macaulay & Wald *Manpower* (film): One [cup of coffee]! And blitz it! **1943** *School & Soc.* LVIII 169: *Let's blitz:* let's leave. **1944** Kendall *Service Slang* 47: *Let's blitz....*leave. **1962** W. Robinson *Barbara* 238: Holbright suggested that one tank company give direct fire support while another blitzed in with tank-riding doughs again. **1963** Huff & Smith *Defensive Football* 15: Leaving me just enough room to blitz through on his outside. *a*1984 T. Clancy *Red Oct.* 144: They blitzed right past those.

3. to inundate with publicity or advertising.

1966 H.S. Thompson *Hell's Angels* 78: The group...managed to blitz the national press in 1965. **1976** *U.S. News & W.R.* (July 26) 75: In 1968, COPE could "blitz" the country with tens of millions of pamphlets favorable to Humphrey. **1983** *Atlanta Constitution* (Mar. 9) 1: Democrat Candidates Blitz Ga.

4. *Stu.* to pass (an examination) easily.

1972 Mills *Report* 105: And then he blitzed the captain's test and they sent him to the Narcotics Bureau. **1983** Univ. Tenn. student: I was sure I'd blitzed the final.

5. *Journ.* to SCOOP (a publication).

1973 in H.S. Thompson *Shark Hunt* 290: The New York Times, badly blitzed on the story at first, called in hotrods from its bureaus all over the country to overcome the Post's early lead.

6. *Weight Lifting.* BLAST, *v.*, 1. c.

1981 D.E. Miller *Jargon* 230: Bomb. Also *blitz*, *blast....*I really bombed my quads this morning.

blitz britches *n.* *Mil.* (see quot.).

1944 Kendall *Service Slang* 57: *Blitz britches....*rayon O.D. panties for wear with skirts.

blitz buggy *n.* *Mil.* a military vehicle or aircraft. Also **blitz wagon.**

1941 *AS* (Oct.) 163: *Blitz Wagon* or *Buggy.* Staff car. **1941** *AS* (Dec.) 203: Newsmen spotted Army Blitz-buggies everywhere. **1945** Hamann *Air Words:* Blitz buggy. Flying fortress; bomber; battle plane....*Blitz wagon.* Bomber; battle plane; staff car. **1955** Reifer *New Words* 32: *Blitz buggy n. Mil. Slang.* A Jeep or a half-ton truck. **1970* Partridge *DSUE* (ed. 7) 1013: *Blitz buggy....*By 1944 its "ambulance" sense was, in the R.A.F., almost official. **1978** Lieberman & Rhodes *CB* (ed. 2) 290: *Bliss* [sic] *buggy*—Army vehicle.

blitz can *n.* *Mil.* (see quot.).

1956 Heflin *USAF Dict.* 83: *Blitz can.* A jerry can. *Slang.*

blitzed *adj.* **1.** very drunk or high.—occ. constr. with *up.*

1966 "Petronius" *N.Y. Unexp.* 168: Fun and cheap no matter how blitzed or broke your crowd is. **1968** Baker et al. *CUSS* 82: *Blitzed* Drunk. **1971** *Current Slang* V 8: *Blitzed,* adj. Intoxicated. **1972** N.Y.U. student: *Blitzed* means drunk or it also means *stoned.* **1974** Kingry *Monk* 37: He was blitzed most of the time, walking as if he was stepping off an invisible porch all the time, the way you do when you are stoned on grass. **1980** Whalen *Takes a Man* 219: I'm gonna watch the late show and get blitzed. **1982** P. Michaels *Grail* 67: He arrives blitzed...and drops off into oblivion. **1983** *N.Y. Daily News* (Mar. 25): Teentalk Glossary...Drunk...bombed, blitzed,...wasted. **1992** *N.Y. Times* (Oct. 21) B 9: More constructive ways to release tension and pressure than getting blitzed, bombed or wasted.

2. tired out; physically or emotionally exhausted.

1971 N.Y.U. student: I am *blitzed.* Whenever I get out of that class I feel ready to collapse. **1972** N.Y.U. student: *Blitzed* is fagged out.

blitzkrieged *adj.* BLITZED, 1.

1974 Eble *Campus Slang* (Oct.) 1: *Blitzkrieged*—adj., having become drunk quickly: After his third glass, he was blitzkrieged. **1979** Univ. Tenn. student: *Blitzed* or *blitzkrieged* is drunk.

blivit or **blivet** *n.* [orig. unkn.] **1.** a bag filled with excrement; (hence) nonsense. Often *Joc.*

1945 Hamann *Air Words:* Blivit bag. A cloth or paper sack in which flyers dispose of human excrement and which they toss overboard. Sometimes used as auxiliary bombs....The expression arose among American flyers in New Guinea and is of Australian origin. **1947** *Tomorrow* (Aug.)

29: What was once known as a *blivet*. **1952** in Legman *Limerick* 418: *A blivet:* two pounds of shit in a one-pound bag...*a trivet:* a pound of shit stuffed in the toe of an old sock, and used as a blackjack; and *a trivet:* a mashed potato turd stuffed down a sink. **1969** Jessup *Sailor* 349: "A thing that's impossible....Like a blivit." "Vas is a blivit?" "Six pounds of sheep-shit in a five-pound bag." **1972** D. Pearce *Pierhead Jump* 176: Anybody that can carry a crate of blivets from point A to point B cheaper than the next guy. **1973** Beck *Folklore & the Sea* 68: Sometimes it is a blivit! which is being constructed, and further inquiry reveals it is "ten pounds of shit in a five-pound paper bag." **1973** W. Crawford *Gunship Commander* 27: The weekly "news" magazines would come down on his neck like...a blivit bursting on stone. **1980** Ciardi *Browser's Dict.* 27: "A blivet...five pounds of shit in a three-pound bag." I have never seen this form in print. It was common in street talk by 1932. **1982** W.E.B. Griffin *Lieuts.* 172: It was a compliment....And a blivet, which is defined as five pounds of horseshit in a one-pound bag.

2.a. a fat or offensive person or thing; an unpleasant task or situation.

1949 Mende *Spit & Stars* 109: He's a beautiful blivit. And a blivit is— ten pounds of shit in a five pound bag. **1954** Brooklyn college student: She looks like a blivit in that outfit. **1960** *Time* (July 11) 107: *Blivit* (a term of personal description usually defined as "10 lbs. of ---- in a 5-lb. bag"). **1967** Crawford *Gresham's War* 181 [ref. to *ca*1952]: Even our junior officers wondered aloud just what it was the Mar/Div did *this* time to anger EUSAK so much to hand us this blivit. **1969** *Current Slang* I & II 11: *Blivit*, n. A really unpleasant situation.—Air Force Academy cadets. **1971** Dahlskog *Dict.* 8: *Blivit*, n. An extremely annoying or confused situation; anything unnecessary or unpleasant. **1978** Fisher & Rubin *Special Teachers* 23: Blimpie didn't add up to quite the blivet his nickname implied. **1978** *Black Sheep Squad.* (CBS-TV): Strategically—this is a blivet, fellas. **1980** Ciardi *Browser's Dict.* 27: To get hit with a blivet = to be up shit creek and overboard. **1980** Conroy *Lords of Discipline* 227: How can you guys stand to look at that fat blivet?...He weighs three hundred pounds.

b. *Mil.* a reprimand or the like.

1980 Cragg *L. Militaris* 39: *Blivit*...a piece of correspondence from higher authority, generally directive in nature, as in "blivit from the front office." *a*1989 R. Herman, Jr. *Warbirds* 202: They...got a blivit from Sundown.

3. *Mil.* a plastic or nylon bag for carrying water or other liquids, esp. a large bladder-like container for airdropping fuel. [Quots. ref. to Vietnam War.]

1982 Del Vecchio *13th Valley* 155: 500-gallon blivets of water and fuel oil. *Ibid.* 358: A five-quart water blivet...a double-layered plastic bladder enclosed in a strong nylon bag, the three bags joined at the top with a canteen neck and screw cap. **1983** Beckwith & Knox *Delta Force* 225: The fuel would be loaded in huge 500-pound rubber blivets and parachuted in. **1985** Bodey *F.N.G.* 56: I am sitting alone on top of an empty water blivet. **1989** Zumbro & Walker *Jungletracks* 220: A five-hundred gallon "Blivit" of diesel fuel was slung underneath.

blizzard *n.* [prob. < dial. E *blizzer* 'a heavy blow'] **1.a.** a violent blow.

1829 *Va. Lit. Museum* (Dec. 15) 418: *Blizzard.* "A violent blow," perhaps from *Blitz*, lightning. *Kentucky*. **1856** in Thornton *Amer. Glossary* I: When some true archer, from the upper tier, Gave him a "blizzard" on the nearest ear. **1872** Schele de Vere *Amer.* 443: *Blizzard*...means in the West a stunning blow or an overwhelming argument. **1881** *Nation* (Apr. 14) 260: In 1836 I first heard the word "blizzard" among the young men at Illinois College, Jacksonville. If one struck a ball a severe blow in playing town-ball it would be said "That's a blizzard." **1889** Farmer *Amer.* 64: He "gave him a *blizzard* on the nose," "on the jaw," "between the eyes," etc.

b. a stinging final remark; a crushing or finishing argument.

1835 Crockett *Tour Down East* 16: The parson...called on me for a toast. Not knowing whether he intended to...have some fun at my expense, I concluded to...give him and his likes a blizzard. **1846** in Harris *High Times* 66: I resolved to give him a parting "blizzard." **1889** Farmer *Amer.* 63: If a man's wife scolded him, she gave him a *blizzard*. **1891** *N.Y. Tribune* (July 19) 14: A blizzard meant a knock-down blow from an argument, not a knock-down blow from a snow-blast.

c. *Specif.*, a heavy or violent snowstorm. Now *S.E.*

1859 in *DA*: A blizzard had come upon us about midnight...shot 7 horses that were so chilled could not get up. **1861** in *DA*. **1862** in Stuart *Forty Yrs. on Frontier* 193: Snowed in the forenoon. Very cold in afternoon. Raw east wind. Everybody went to grand ball given by John Grant at Grantsville and a severe blizzard blew up and raged all night. We danced all night, no outside storm could dampen the festivities. **1870** in

AS III 201: Campbell has had too much experience with northwestern "blizards" [*sic*] to be caught in such a trap. **1880** in *Century Dict.* 590: Whew! how the wind howls; there must be a terrible blizzard west of us, and how ill-prepared are most frontier homes for such severe cold. **1881** *Nation* (Apr. 14) 260: *Blizzard*...a sudden or unexpected storm. This use was in existence as early as 1836 in this part of the state [*sc.* Perry Co., Pa.] Charcoal-burners, watching their pits, would fear a *blizzard*. [But this sense] has died out for many years. **1884** Rowbotham *Prairie-Land* 179: "Blizzards"...are...windstorms accompanied by driving snow.

d. a violent storm of wind, rain, snow, etc. [1934 quot. ref. to wind rather than snow.]

*1888 N & Q 7 (Ser. V) 17 (Mar.) 217: The word *blizzard* is well known through the [English] Midlands....I have known the word and its kin fully thirty years....One who has had to face a severe storm of snow, hail, rain, dust, or wind, would say on reaching shelter that he has "faced a blizzer," or that the storm was "a regular blizzard." **1934** Appel *Brain Guy* 52: Bill said the Greek's had been warm, but this weather was a blizzard.

2. a shot; a series or volley of shots.

1834 Crockett *Life* 152: I saw two more bucks....I took a blizzard at one of them and up he tumbled. **1834** *Davy Crockett's Almanack for '35* 2: I will take them out on a *coon hunt*, show 'em how to tree a catamount, and take a blizzard at a bear. **1835** in Meine & Owens *Crockett Alms.* 44: He...gets hold on the painter's tail with one hand, and with the other he got a blizzard with his pistol. *ca*1836 in Barrère & Leland *Dict. Slang* I 136: The elder boys when they went to school carried their rifles to get a *blizzard* at anything they might meet on the road. **1846** *Spirit of Times* (June 6) 177: We turned one of our 18 pounders to bear on the mass and gave them a "blizzard" to help them along. **1866** in *Century Dict.* I 590: He had ridden right in on top of the 6th Conn. regiment, and our boys had given him what we called "a blizzard." **1887** *N.Y. Evening Post* (Mar. 24), in *Century Dict.* I 590: Along the Atlantic coast, among [bird hunters], the word *blizzard* means a general discharge of all the guns...a rattling volley....This use of the word is familiar to every 'longshore man from Sandy Hook to Currituck, and goes back at least forty years, as my own memory attests.

3. a great fire.

1843 [W.T. Thompson] *Scenes in Ga.* 153: The devil will make a blizzard of my soul for it.

4. a bracing drink of strong liquor.

1881 *Nation* (Mar. 31) 220: There has been an extensive use of the word in Pennsylvania for many years, as [for example] a drink of any intoxicant, generally applied to whiskey...."Let's take a blizzard."

5. *Bridge.* a worthless hand.

1979 Cuddon *Dict. Sports & Games* 146.

blizzard *v.* to fire a volley or series of shots.

1856 in *DA*: Jest let them raise that check agin me, an if I don't shoot, why old Betsy won't blizzard.

blizzard-dodger *n.* a vagabond who travels south in the winter to avoid severe weather.

[**1906** Ford *Shorty McCabe* 37: Just going to dodge a few blizzards [in Palm Beach] and watch the mob.] **1935** Algren *Boots* 17: Big bull-whip he carries makes them blizzard-dodgers hump.

bloat *n.* a worthless individual, esp. one bloated with conceit or drink.

1855 in Dwyer & Lingenfelter *Songs of Gold Rush* 25: We've got the smartest old whisky bloats. *Ibid.* 142: Drink with the bloats. **1860** in *AS* XXII 299: I considered such an old bloat not worth minding. *ca*1861 in *DA* 134: When I think what a mean bloat I was, going to the stub-tail dogs with my hat over my eyes. **1862** in Norton *Army Letters* 89: The fellow...is the veriest bloat and bully in the company. **1863** Hollister *Colo. Vols.* 23: Let's pull the old bloat off his horse. **1869** in R.C. Allen *Horrible Prettiness* 17: Shut up, old bloat! **1871** *Congressional Globe* (Feb.) App. 129: Wife whippers, penitentiary birds, street vagabonds, beastly bloats, and convicted felons. **1872** "M. Twain" *Roughing It* ch. lxxi: The red sun looked...like a blooming whisky bloat through the bars of a city prison. **1883–84** Whittaker *L. Locke* 186: We'll see who hollers first, you darned bloat. **1908** Whittles *Lumberjack* 77: The clerk is...the "bloat that makes the stroke." **1915** in Botkin *Treas. Amer. Folk.* 471: This bloat at bat is liable to spike you. **1975** *Inter. Jour. Addictions* X 430: There ain't no more about this big bloat/Cause you know like I do, that's all she wrote.

block *n.* **1.** the head. [In recent use, almost exclusively in phr. *knock (one's) block off*; no quots. are known between 1635 and 1842.]

*1635 in *OED*: Buy a beaver For thy own block. **1842** *Ben Hardin's Crockett* (unp.): I took...my pike to nok him over the block. ***1862** in *OEDS*: I cleaned a groom's boots on Toosday, and he punched my block because I blacked the tops. ***1873** Hotten *Slang Dict.* (ed. 4): *Block*, the head. **1902** K. Harriman *Ann Arbor Tales* 252: Adjured to make himself scarce or git his block knocked off. **1903** A.H. Lewis *Boss* 183: I'll knock their blocks off quick. **1907** in H.C. Fisher *A. Mutt* 20: Moran will knock his block off. **1908** in Blackbeard & Williams *Smithsonian Comics* 58: After taking a peep at the prisoner's block I am convinced that he has a vacuum in his brain case. **1912** Lowrie *Prison* 370: One guy threatened to knock my block off. **1912** Ade *Babel* 110: I'd get up and try to cool the block with a wet towel. **1914** Ellis *Billy Sunday* 252: David drew his sword and chopped off [Goliath's] block. **1918** in [K. Morse] *Letters* 150: If you want to see the next block, keep yours inside. **1927** S. Lewis *E. Gantry* ch. i: You get somebody to pick on you, and I'll come along and knock his block off. **1929** "M. Brand" *Beacon Creek* 195: Stand away or I'll knock your block off. **1929** in Blackbeard & Williams *Smithsonian Comics* 105: I'm gonna put some sense into dat thick block o' yourn. **1929–30** Dos Passos *42d Parallel* 306: It's all for the experience, as the feller said when they blew his block off. **1931** Uhler *Cane Juice* 26: Me, I gonta knock he goddam block off. **1933** E. Caldwell *God's Little Acre* 148: I'll come down in here with a singletree and knock your blocks clear off your shoulders. **1948** Manone & Vandervoort *Trumpet* 194: He...walks to the guillotine and chops his own block off.

2. Esp. *Und.* a pocket watch; in phr. **block and tackle** a watch and chain.

*1899 in *Austral. Nat. Dict.*: One...had his "block and tackle" (watch and chain) taken from him. **1914** Jackson & Hellyer *Vocab.* 17: *Block*, Noun General usage. **1916** *Lit. Digest* (Aug. 19) 53: A watch may be a "super" in one locality and in another it may be called a "block," or a "turnip," or a "kettle." **1918** [Livingston] *Delcassee* 104: Lots of phoney "blocks" (watches), "hoops" (rings), "stickers" (scarf pins), and many other articles. **1928** Sharpe *Chicago May* 288: *Block and tackle*—Watch and chain. **1929** Hostetter & Beesley *It's a Racket* 220: *Block and Tackle*—Watch and chain. **1947** Mencken *Amer. Lang. Supp. II* 686: [Among sidewalk pitchmen] watches are *blocks*. **1962–68** B. Jackson *In the Life* 303: He had an old dollar block (watch).

3. Esp. *Mil.* one's own neighborhood; home.—constr. with *the.* Cf. **on the block,** below.

*ca***1969** Rabe *Hummel* 62: You back on the block an' you goin' out struttin'. **1968–71** Cole & Black *Checking* 251: I won't fuck you up. I won't tell no one on the block. **1973** Karlin, Paquet & Rottmann *Free Fire Zone* 86: These are guys, man, just off the block. And now they're...dead. **1974–77** Heinemann *Close Quarters* 42: Fucken-A, back on the block he's known as Deadeye Dosier, ain't that right, Deadeye? **1975–78** O'Brien *Cacciato* 70: War's over....Translated it means this: Back on the block. **1978** Hasford *Short-Timers* 95 [ref. to Vietnam War]: Back to the block, back to the Lone Star State, back to the land of the big PX. **1984** J. Fuller *Fragments* 15: Save it for the ladies back on the block. **1990** *New Yorker* (Sept. 10) 84: We get up and go straight out to the block in the morning.

¶ In phrases:

¶ **have been around the block** to have had worldly experience.

1942 Horman & Corley *Capts. of the Clouds* (film): You were gonna put Johnny behind the eight-ball. But you couldn't do that to me. I've been round the block. **1981** Wolf *Roger Rabbit* 101: The man had gone round the block with gum-shoes. **1984** *Post N.Y. Post Parody* 16: These two had shacked up for over two years, and...even before that the bride had been around the block a few times, if you know what I mean. **1985** Ponicsan *Vision Quest* (film): This is a girl who's been around the block a few times. **1985** McDonald's, Inc. ad (ABC-TV): Somebody's gonna have to show her the ropes. Somebody's who's been around the block a few times. **1989** L. Roberts *Full Cleveland* 20: I've been around the block a few times—I have a master's degree in journalism.

¶ **on the block, 1.** *Prost.* being a streetwalker.

1941 *Pittsburgh Courier* (May 3) 7: He was the kind of a guy who put women on the spot if he couldn't put 'em on the block. **1958** Motley *Epitaph* 154: Why don't you go pull on your mother like that? I bet she's on the block right now. **1973** I. Reed *La. Red* 96: Player...at the height of his career had twenty-five hos on the block. **1977** Sayles *Union Dues* 183: Have all the players and working girls...lapping up the news that Inez been put out on the block again...gone back in *harness.*

2. *Sports.* (of an athlete) being offered for trading to another team.

1961 Brosnan *Pennant Race* 94: Hutchinson sent Marshall Bridges to

the bullpen "just in case."..."Guess ah ain't on the block yet, 'Fess. Didn't think he'd evah trust me no more."

¶ **put** [or **slip**] **the blocks to, 1.** to copulate with (a woman) vigorously.

*ca***1888** *Stag Party* 219: The old man puts the blocks to her sister. **1921** McAlmon *Hasty Bunch* 148: Don't blarney me. I'll bet you let Bill O'Brien put the blocks to you. **1924** in Randolph *Pissing in Snow* 133: Then he put the blocks to her again, and both of them went to sleep. **1929–30** Farrell *Young Lonigan* 70: Screwy McGlynn...had put the blocks to nearly every K.M. in the neighborhood. **1930** *Lyra Ebriosa* 12: But I was over in the corner/Putting the blocks to the Winnipeg Whore. **1959** Zugsmith *Beat Generation* 43: Never before had he put the blocks to a fuzz's hotsy. **1962** Dougherty *Report to Comm.* 221: Charley Kane...stood lookout while he put a quick block to that nice little thing in Chelsea. **1967** Dibner *Admiral* 67: He jumped ship...just to put the blocks to a gook broad. **1974** Loken *Come Monday Mornin'* 61: When he first started puttin' the blocks to 'er.

2. to victimize or treat maliciously; do for.

1936 in Partridge *Dict. Und.* 50: We put the blocks to him tomorrow. **1964** Howe *Valley of Fire* 168: Do you really think I was the one who slipped the blocks to you? **1973** W. Crawford *Gunship Cmndr.* 147: Why the hell couldn't you have come to me if you thought March and Bedwell were putting the blocks to you? **1979** McGivern *Soldiers of '44* 101: And that had to be one of Korbick's worst moments,...watching a man whose guts he hated, a man he'd put the blocks to for months marching off the post as smart as a fucking West Point cadet.

¶ **run the block** [fr. *run the blockade* s.v. BLOCKADE] *Confed. Army.* to go absent without leave.

1885 Cannon *Men Only* 104: I have never seen any account in print of a performance familiarly known among [C.S.A.] soldiers as "Running the Block," (blockade). **1886** in *Contrib. to Hist. of Richmond How. Bn.* (No. 4) 29: Nevertheless, like all good soldiers, we some times "ran the block." **1895** W.N. Wood *Big I* 16 [ref. to Civil War]: We were occupied in...drilling and "running the block" to Richmond, much extra duty resulting from the last mentioned. **1936** Monks & Finkelhoff *Bro. Rat* 65: I've been...financing your block-running expeditions for four years. *Ibid.* 94: You don't think I'd take the chance of running the block for anybody else?

blockade *n.* [earlier S. colloq. *blockade whiskey*] whiskey that is illicitly distilled or sold.

1867 in Thornton *Amer. Gloss.* I 72: The guard got drunk on "blockade." **1867** in Thompson *Youth's Companion* 737: You haven't got no *blockade*, (whiskey,) have you? I'd like another swig. **1867** in *DA*: The parson had taken about half a pint of "blockade." **1913** in *DA*: For corn supplies as well that important beverage...known as "blockade." **1929** (quot. at MOON, *n.*).

¶ In phrase:

¶ **run the blockade** *Confed. Army.* to go absent without leave.

1863 in W. White *Diary of War* 165: Concluded to try my hand at "running the blockade" and get to Richmond, if possible. **1864** in Stanard *Letters* 61: I have **run** the *blockade* and come in to take tea with Cary Taylor. **1891** [Daniel] *Richmond How.* 59: Hence, whenever the battery fetched up anywhere in the proximity of Richmond, there was no little "running of the blockade"...and some of the more eager...found it convenient to run into it nightly. **1893** Casler *Stonewall* 99: I told my Captain how I had run the blockade for a canteen of whiskey.

block-and-block *adj.* drunk.

1737 *Pennsylvania Gaz.* (Jan. 6) 1: The Drinker's Dictionary...He is Addled...He's...*Block and Block. Boozy...*Drunk as a *Wheel-Barrow.*

block and tackle *n.* **1.** see BLOCK, 2.

2. a powerful alcoholic drink. *Joc.*

1974 *Sanford & Son* (NBC-TV): This reminds me of a drink we had in the service. We called it a block and tackle: you'd drink one, **walk a block,** and you'd **tackle** anybody.

3. (see quot.). Cf. BALL AND CHAIN.

1980 Pearl *Slang Dict: Block and tackle n.* (Sports) one's superior or anyone who limits one's activities. From football terminology.

blockbust *v. Real Estate.* to subject to BLOCK-BUSTING; to practice BLOCKBUSTING.

1952 Lait & Mortimer *USA* 61: They are kept out...with the same kind of coercion and violence that whites show when their neighborhoods are block-busted. **1966** in *BDNE*: They've started to blockbust some buildings here. **1974** *Business Week* (May 18) 12: Some [real estate agents] blockbust, frightening white families into sacrificing their homes to escape the oncoming black invasion. **1979** *L.A. Times* (Nov. 11) Home 32: Our neighborhood....had been black and Puerto Rican and then it was blockbusted by whites.

blockbuster *n.* **1.** *Journ. & Mil.* a very large aerial bomb with a high explosive charge. Now *colloq.* or *S.E.*
1942 *Time* (Sept. 14) 29: Inside a sturdy observation tower a mile from the exploding block busters which the Army is now testing. **1942** *Twist Bombardier* (film): Come on, Carter boy, drop those blockbusters on 'em. **1951** in Loosbrock & Skinner *Wild Blue* 440: The 2,000 pound blockbusters let go automatically. **1953–57** Giovannitti *Combine D* 128: Listen to that....It sounds like blockbusters. **1966** Lucas *Dateline* 280: The Navy pilot unloads his blockbusters. **1982** D.J. Williams *Hit Hard* 252: B-17 bombers...will drop blockbusters as you move in. **1985** Dye *Between Raindrops* 219: Can't say I've ever seen one of these block-busters dropped. **1991** J.T. Ward *Dear Mom* 109: The skipper...ordered a blockbuster (fifteen-thousand-pound aerial bomb).
2. [punning on idea of laxative] a prune. *Joc.*
1945 *Sat. Review* (Nov. 24): *Blockbusters*—prunes.
3. anything exceptionally large or important. Also quasi-adj.
1946 J.H. Burns *Gallery* 48: The largest woman in captivity....We called her Blockbuster. **1957** in *OEDS*: A blockbuster of an idea for a musical play. **1971** *Seattle Times* (Jan. 17) E1: This is called "in-depth reporting" by academicians. It's a "block-buster" in newsroom parlance. **1974** A. Bergman *Big Kiss-Off* 85: "A hot one, eh Mr. LeVine?"..."A blockbuster." **1983** WINS news report (Sept. 5): Observers have been cautioned not to expect any blockbuster sanctions against the Soviet Union. **1984** Kagan & Summers *Mute Evidence* 114: Senator Schmitt's office had unearthed some blockbuster information. **1990** *Nation* (Dec. 10) 720: The book had stimulated strong objections at Simon & Schuster....Nevertheless, it looked like a blockbuster, and the decision was made to publish it.
4. a real estate agent who practices BLOCKBUSTING. Now *colloq.*
1953 Manchester *City of Anger* 127: We got a blockbuster after our block and somebody wants to sell. **1963** in J.H. Clarke *Harlem* 20: Present-day realtors call them "blockbusters." **1967** in *BDNE.* **1979** in Terkel *Amer. Dreams* 243: It's a nice, strong neighborhood. They're not the people that run at the least provocation by the blockbusters.
5. a powerful blow, as with the fist.
1960 Hoagland *Circle Home* 136: So what to do, stand and trade block-busters with the guy? **1966** H.S. Thompson *Hell's Angels* 244: Terry's off-the-floor blockbuster caught him in the left eye.

blockbusting *n.* *Real Estate.* the practice of inducing home-owners to sell their property at a low price, esp. by exploiting racial fears that minority families will be moving into the neighborhood.
*****1959** in *OEDS*: Once a single negro moves into a block...the houses on both sides of the street from corner to corner are bound to become...Negro....Such "block-busting" [etc.]. **1966** in *BDNE.* **1971** in *BDNE*: Several communities initiated "we-will-not-sell" campaigns to maintain "racial stability" by keeping white families from "panic selling" their houses because of "fear-tactics" by "block-busting" landlords. **1982** *L.A. Times* (May 26) V 1: They contend the college purposely did not make repairs in order to depress the surrounding property values so it could purchase houses more cheaply. This practice is known as blockbusting.

blocked *adj.* drunk or high.
1956 in J. Blake *Joint* 126: I knew he was getting blocked in a very methodical fashion. *****1964** (cited in Partridge *Dict. Und.* (ed. 2) 795). **1970** Landy *Underground Dict.* 35: *Blocked*...Under the influence of a drug, alcohol, or both.

bloke *n.* [orig. unkn.; perh. var. of earlier Brit. und. slang *gloak* 'a man']
1. a man; a fellow. [Though now regarded as an exclusively British term, this word was common in AmE in the late 19th C.]
*****1829** in Partridge *Dict. Und.* 50: The *bloke* come, I *spelld* away. *****1839** Brandon *Poverty, Mendicity, & Crime* (gloss.): *Bloak*—a gentleman.—*Fancy Bloak*—a fancy man. *****1851** H. Mayhew *London Labour & Poor* III 397: If we met an old bloke we propped him. **1859** Matsell *Vocab.* 12: *Bloke.* A man. **1865** *Harper's Mo.* XXX 606: A bloke is a cove and a cove is a man. **1866** *Nat. Police Gaz.* (Nov. 3) 3: Some well-meaning "bloke" putting him "fly" to the whole thing. **1868** [Williams] *Black-Eyed Beauty* 14: The bloke with the thimble, whispered he to her pal. **1868**

Detective's Manual 146: How does the "bloke" feel? **1871** [Banka] *Prison Life* 117: I'll send for the "bloke" after breakfast and ask his pardon. *Ibid.* 493: Man...Bloke. **1872** in "M. Twain" *Life on Miss.* 292: I made up my mind to be a square bloke. **1880** in M. Lewis *Mining Frontier* 127: You kin break me right here if I thought there was a bloke in the mines that didn't know Bill. **1888** *Stag Party* 44: I'm danged if you ain't the freshest bloke that ever crawled out of a corn crib. **1891** Booth *N.Y. Inferno* 54: What do yer want to steal the bloke's coffee for? **1891** Campbell, Knox, & Byrnes *Darkness & Daylight* 135: Blokes is allus axin' 'bout dat ere kid. **1894** Bridges *Arcady* 56: I got onto the bloke wid only tree fingers to his hand. **1896** F.H. Smith *Tom Grogan* 75: Look at da bloke a-jollying Jinnie. **1897** *Harper's Wkly.* 90: In the tenement districts of this city [N.Y.]...every person...who is not known by name is called a "bloke" or a "mug." **1900** [Willard & Hodler] *Powers That Prey* 15: I've been easy on some o' you blokes 'cause I know 't you've got families here. **1907** in H.C. Fisher *A. Mutt* 3: I know a guy wat knows a bloke who knows a friend of a fellow wot used to [etc.]. **1918** *N.Y. Eve. Jour.* (Aug. 4) 10: How could this bloke help but love her? **1920** De Beck *Google* 98: I got more of a wallop in my left than any bloke here. **1922** Tully *Emmett Lawler* 268: Hey, Bloke, you can't put that over on us. **1927** Tully *Circus Parade* 85: Some bloke rolled me for all the dough I had. **1927** *Immortalia* 8: No bloke ever made the trial. **1928** Bodenheim *Georgie May* 43: It's 'bout time them big blokes up north stopped running this country anyways. **1930** Bodenheim *Roller Skates* 29: Aw, I seen a bloke in Boston with that outfit once. **1931** Cab Calloway *Minnie the Moocher* (song): She messed around wid a bloke named Smokey. **1933** D. Runyon, in *Collier's* (May 13) 7: Waldo is a most eccentric old bloke. **1936** Gaddis *Courtesan* 114: And then I go off my nut about a good-looking bloke with biceps and a lot of sex appeal. **1940** *New Directions* 163: Who's tha[t] bloke? **1983** *Morning Line* (WKGN radio) (Apr. 11): I checked you out on television, my man, and you're a good-lookin' bloke.
2. a foolish or worthless person.
1887 *N.O. Lantern* (Oct. 29) 3: Louis Sass, the bloke, thought he was flip. **1887** DeVol *Gambler* 37: He...did not know much about beating a sucker....I had to teach him how to handle the blokes. **1889** S. Bailey *Ups & Downs* 58: It is a shame....for such a nice young fellow as you to get the collar on account of that bloke Mickey Cobey giving you away! **1893** *Life* (Feb. 2) 70: De angels ain't no blokes, an' dey'll be on to yer little game ev'ry time. **1903** A.H. Lewis *Boss* 263: Dat's d' number two d'gree, says d' bloke of a Captain to me mudder. **1929–30** Farrell *Young Lonigan* 82: Once he was fighting some big bloke, and he suddenly...told the big ham his shoelaces were untied. **1932** *AS* VII 329: *Bloke*—a stupid or disagreeable person. **1972** *N.Y. Times Mag.* (Feb. 13) 24: Would you want your daughter to throw away her $15,000 education in order to marry some bloke and become a domestic and a drudge—like your wife? **1968–77** F. Wallace *Poker* 124: Smart thinking is illegal in this game...gives wise guys too much advantage over us blokes.
3. Esp. *Mil.* an English person. Also attrib. [Not nec. ref. to a man.]
1922 Hisey *Sea Grist* 124: The lower class of "Blokes" or "Lime Juicers" have little respect for the American. **1965** Pollini *Glover* 3: Whaddaya like best—Bloke or American stuff? *Ibid.* 4: One thing the Blokes are good for. *Ibid.* 9: Man, these Bloke gals. They sure make them. **1968** J.D. Houston *Between Battles* 62: We all get along pretty well over here, the blokes and the Yanks. **1975** Longmate *G.I.'s* 168: Only one word, "bloke," was constantly misinterpreted. Many GIs [in England during WWII] wrongly assumed that it had a derogatory ring and either used it as an alternative to Limey or to describe an objectionable Englishman. **1985** Westin *Love & Glory* 191 [ref. to WWII]: We've been bivouacked next to the "blokes" for the past few days, and they're first rate in my book.

blokie *n.* BLOKE, 1.
1892 Crane *Maggie* 5: "Ah, we blokies kin lick deh hull damn Row," said a child, swaggering. **1894** *Century* (Feb.) 518: Well, so long, blokie. **1896** Ade *Artie* 26: When any o' you blokies try to push into a game where I am...you're on a dead one. **1900** McManus *Soldier Life* 105: Say, "Bull," who's the little blokie with the whiskers and the silver eagles on his shoulders...that just wheeled by? **1906** Green *Actors' Boarding House* 30: What does them blokies talk about? **1920** Ade *Hand-Made Fables* 88: The famous Wall Street Blokie, Jimmy Hooper.

blonde and sweet *adj.* (of coffee) served with cream and sugar.
1945 in *AS* (Feb. 1948) 37: *Blonde and Sweet*...used to designate coffee with cream and sugar. **1959** Sterling *Wahoo* 48 [ref. to U.S. Navy, WWII]: Make it blonde and sweet. **1978** Lieberman & Rhodes *CB* (ed.

2) 290: *Blond and sweet*—cream and sugar.

blondie *n.* a blond person; (*specif.*) a blond girl.

1905 *Nat. Police Gaz.* (Nov. 18) 3: Come on, Blondie. **1907** in H.C. Fisher *A. Mutt* 3: "Blondy" is a pipe. *a*1904–11 Phillips *Susan Lenox* I 395: So long, blondie. Nother time. *1936 Partridge *DSUE* 66: *Blondie* or *-y*. A blonde girl....from ca1925. **1983** *Nat. Lampoon* (Aug.) 72: That's nice, blondie.

blood *n.* **1.** (used in various obs. oaths, exclamations, and imprecations).

*a*1541 in *OED*: God's blood, the King set me in the Tower. *ca*1590 C. Marlowe, in *OED*: Blood, he speaks terribly. *1707 Cibber *Double Gallant* 159: Blood! Sir—don't think Sir. **1714** in Meserve & Reardon *Satiric Comedies* 36: Blud and 'Owns. **1730** *Penna. Gaz.* CIV (Nov. 12) [2]: Sometimes...*Blood*, and sometimes *Wounds*, and sometimes in a Hurry they blunder out *Blood and Wounds*...the Commander...never applied to any other *Deity* so much as to *Blood and Wounds*. **1751** in Breslaw *Tues. Club* 303: Damn your blood, you old Curmudgeon....Damn your old blood!...I'll blow your brains out! *1762 Sterne *Tristram Shandy*: Blood an 'ounds, shouted the corporal. **1787–89** Tyler *Contrast* 104: I can't laugh for the blood and nowns of me. **1794** in [Alsop] *Echo* 206: Bring back my towel,...d—n your blood! *1803 in Wetherell *Adventures* 50: Damn your blood, you son of a whore. **1836** *Spirit of Times* O! blud an' oons, boys, if here isn't Mr. Power! *1839 in *F & H* I 239: But, blood-an'-'ouns! man, if ould Nick himself were to hit me a blow, I'd be afther givin' him another. **1864** Hill *Our Boys* 41: Blood and tobacker! Oh! Ouch!

2. a young man, usu. wealthy, given to riotous behavior. Orig. (and after *ca*1840 again) *S.E.* Now *hist.*

*1562 in *OED*: A lustie blood, or a pleasaunte brave young roister. *1749 H. Walpole, in *OED*: Anecdotes of the doctor's drinking, who, as the man told us, had been a blood. *1785 Grose *Vulgar Tongue*: *Blood.* A riotous disorderly fellow. **1797** (quot. at BLOODEE). **1803** *Medley; or Mo. Misc.* (Aug.) 142: If our Bloods are determined to persevere/In their swearing in public,/I would recommend the proposition of Roderick Thunderbolt of New York, which follows. **1804** *Monthly Anthology* (Boston) I 154: With some rakes from Boston and a few college *bloods*, I got very drunk. **1823** *Yale Crayon* 15: Indulgent Gods! exclaimed our *bloods*. **1834** Caruthers *Kentuckian* I 17: The "bloods" looked fierce, and exchanged pugnacious looks. **1851** Hall *College Wds.* 178: At Washington College, Penn., students of a religious character are called *lap-ears* or *donkeys*. The opposite class are known by the common name of *bloods*.

3. *Stu.* a perfect recitation.

1851 Hall *College Wds.* 20: At some of the Western colleges....A student who recites well is said to *make a blood*. **1900** *DN* II 23: *Blood, n.* A perfect recitation. [Reported from Harvard and Western Reserve Univ.].

4. ketchup; (*occ.*) tomato juice.

1936 *AS* (Feb.) 42: *Blood.* Ketchup. **1941** Hargrove *Pvt. Hargrove* 42: Ketchup is *blood* [at Ft. Bragg]. **1941** Kendall *Army & Navy Slang* 2: *Blood*...ketchup. **1942–44** in *AS* (Feb. 1946) 31: *Blood, n.* Catsup. **1944** *Reader's Dig.* 76: The hospital orderlies say cheerfully to the wounded, "Will you have mud or blood?"—meaning, "Will you have cocoa or tomato juice?" **1945** *Sat. Review* (Nov. 24) 14: *Blood*—catsup. **1985** (quot. at SORORITY SAUCE).

5. *Black E.* red wine.

1959 F.L. Brown *Trumbull Pk.* 371: He was drinking "blood" like water...down on 58th Street under the El. **1959–60** R. Reisner *Jazz Titans* 151: *Blood:* wine. **1964** in Jackson *Swim Like Me* 89: It wasn't shit for me to drink two or three fifths a some real good blood. **1974** C.M. Rodgers *Ovah* 31: Drop pills, guzzle/Cheap blood/Smoke gold dust.

6. [cf. YOUNGBLOOD] **a.** *Black E.* a black person, (*specif.*) a young black man.—sometimes used collectively.

1965 Conot *Rivers* 117: They take the blood to jail so he can't get a job, so he's got to hustle to make a living. **1965** Bonham *Durango St.* 105: Why should we do that for a bunch of nig—.... Esscuse me, brothers. I meant bloods. **1966** Bullins *Goin'a Buffalo* 180: He looks okay to me. A blood. **1967** *Look* (Nov. 14) 117: One of his most enjoyable evenings in Kansas City brought "all the bloods," the Chief's Negro players, to Pete Carter's steak house. **1969** Bullock *Watts* 278: *Blood:* Same as *Brother* or *Sister*. **1970** Conaway *Big Easy* 119: You mean your great big ole lily-white liberal heart was just a-flopping over with *concern* for us bloods. **1968–71** Cole & Black *Checking* 218: I'm leading this band with these dumb Mexicans, Filipinos and bloods. **1971** Roberts *Black Gloss.*: *Blood n.* a fellow black; friend. **1974** Stone *Dog Soldiers* 83: The bloods at the table were broadcasting cocaine vibrations. **1979** D. Tho-

reau *City at Bay* 48: They can kill as many honkies as they want but if they try to mess with the blood they gonna be sorry. **1987** *Newsweek* (Mar. 23) 74: He would be...required to prove to a new generation of bloods that he was not to be F'd with.

b. [poss. sugg. by *blood brother*] Orig. *Black E.* a close male friend.—often used in direct address.

1965 in Cohen & Murphy *Burn* 109: Turn your inside lights on, Blood, so we can see who it is. **1971** *Black Scholar* (Sept.) 41: What'd you want me to do, blood? **1980** Eble *Campus Slang* (Oct.) 1: *Blood*—Friend (used most often in greetings): "Yo, blood, what's happening?" **1981** in Safire *Good Word* 83: We be tight and you be my blood. **1984** *Diff'rent Strokes* (ABC-TV): Hang in there, blood! **1985** Former U.S. Army SP4, age 35: when I went into the service in 1971, *blood* was already well established. "What's up, blood?" Blacks used it to blacks, and whites used it to whites *and* blacks, but blacks didn't use it to whites. One black guy got highly insulted when a white guy called him *blood*. He threatened to bite off the white guy's nose. **1989** P.H.C. Mason *Recovering* 82: Seawright was as close as a brother to me. He was blood.

blood *adj.* (see quot.).

1851 Hall *College Wds.* 20: *Blood.* at some of the Western colleges this word signifies excellent; as a *blood* recitation.

Blood and Guts *n. Naut.* the Red Ensign of the British Royal Navy. Also vars.

1882 Symondson *Abaft the Mast* 288: Why she stopped there we hardly knew, unless it were to admire our "blood and entrails" (the British ensign), as our Yankee shipmate remarked. **1889** Barrère & Leland *Dict. Slang* I 138: *Blood and entrails* (nautical). This is a slang name given to the British ensign by Yankee sailors. **1896** Hamblen *Many Seas* 59: The "blood and innards" of Old England went to the *Bellerophon's* peak. **1927** *Marine Corps Mag.* (June) 77: The Quartermaster says you must watch the Blood an' Guts, for if you don't give him dip for dip, the brass-bound British skipper will write a letter to the Port Authorities. **1961** Hugill *Shanties* 591: *Blood 'n' Guts.* Deep-water term for the Red Ensign of the [British] Merchant Service.

bloodbath *n.* Esp. *Business.* a disastrous reversal, esp. an instance of great or widespread financial loss.

1967 in Perelman *Don't Tread* 238: The Griffin show was...a blood bath. **1972** M. Rodgers *Freaky Fri.* 121: "How *was* that meeting?"..."It was a bloodbath." **1978** J. Rosenberg *Dict. Business* 52: *Blood bath:* a horrendous loss suffered by investors when the stock market declines sharply. **1983** *Time* (Mar. 21) 50: From that year through 1981, the company lost nearly $3.5 billion, easily the biggest bloodbath by any American company in history. **1987** *Prime News* (CNN-TV) (Oct. 19): Details about today's bloodbath on Wall Street. **1987** *USA Today* (Oct. 20) 2A: I already took the bloodbath. Why sell now?

blood boat *n. Naut.* a ship commanded by brutal officers. Also vars.

*1889 F. Bullen *Sea-Waif* 230: Half the crew...looked as if all the ways of "Western Ocean blood-boats" were familiar to them. **1908** in J.H. Williams *Blow the Man Down!* 48 [ref. to 1880's]: A floating torture-house, a "blood packet." *1929 Bowen *Sea Slang* 14: *Blood Boat.* A particularly hard sailing ship with a brutal afterguard. **1929–33** J. Lowell *Gal Reporter* 154: The packet *Arthur James* was a blood ship. **1933** *USN Inst. Proc.* 336: Our new captain had never served on a "blood tub." **1961** Hugill *Shanties from 7 Seas* 593: *Bloodboat*—A hardcase sailing ship, usually Yank or Nova Scotian, from which crews would desert and fresh ones be supplied by...shanghaiing. **1967** Raskin *True Course* 1: But in truth the graceful white-winged ships were named "blood boats" by seamen in every port of the world. **1967** Dibner *Admiral* 229: He skippered a blood boat, didn't he?...He don't give a shit who he kills. *1969 Hugill *Shanties & Songs* 170: On a Yankee bloodboat round Cape Horn,/Me boots 'n' clothes wuz all in pawn. **1976** Hayden *Voyage* 155: And here I sit shanghaied into the fo'c'sle of a Down East blood boat.

blood box *n.* a bloodmobile or ambulance.

1976 Lieberman & Rhodes *CB Handbook* 123: *Blood Box*—Ambulance. **1980** Pearl *Slang Dict.: Blood box n.* an ambulance.

blood bucket *n.* BUCKET OF BLOOD.

1966 "Petronius" *N.Y. Unexp.* 144: Some good blood buckets [are] below 14th on Third Avenue....The waterfront bars are as rough as ever. **1984** Bane *Willie* 56: Those...'tonks...had names like Blood Bucket and The County Dump.

blood chit *n. Mil. Av.* a notice, typically printed on silk or plastic, supplied to an aviator identifying his nationality and authorizing payment of a reward for his safe return if he is brought down in unsecured territory. Now *S.E.* Also **blood chip.**

1941 in C.R. Bond & T. Anderson *Flying T. Diary* 67: We were issued our Chinese "blood chit" emblems to sew on the back of our jackets today. **1943* in Partridge *DSUE* (ed. 7) 1014: *Blood chit...*A ransom note supplied to pilots flying over possibly hostile territory in the East. **1944** *Life* (July10) 81: They also carried blood chips, notices offering Chinese peasants a reward for return of downed airmen. **1966** E. Shepard *Doom Pussy* 235: He showed me a plastic case, called a Blood Chit, which contained a map of the area...silver, and the Blood Chit itself—a numbered piece of silk cloth worth five hundred dollars to any person who would safely guide a downed American airman out of enemy territory. **1987** Robbins *Ravens* 27 [ref. to Vietnam War]: They were...issued...blood-chits.

bloodee *n.* (see quot.).

1797 Walpole, N.H. *Farmer's Wkly. Museum*, in Hall *College Wds.* 1851 p. 20: Seniors about to take degrees,/Not by their wits, but by bloodees...[Note] A kind of cudgel worn, or rather borne, by the bloods of a certain college in New England, 2 feet 5 inches in length, and 1&/8 inch in diameter, with a huge piece of lead at one end, emblematical of its owner. A pretty prop for clumsy travellers on Parnassus.

bloodhound *n.* **1.** one who pursues escaped prisoners or other wrongdoers; (*hence*) a determined investigator. Now *S.E.*

*1818 W. Scott *Heart Midlothian* ch. xxxiii: The blood-hounds of the law were so close after me. **1866** *Beadle's No.* (Feb.) 145: None of us will see Red River or the Union lines, until the end of the war, unless we "skedaddle," and baffle the "bloodhounds." **1936** "E. Queen" *Halfway House* 53: Nothing on earth will stop those bloodhounds from hunting up the marriage dates.

2. a butcher.

1835 *Mil. & Nav. Mag.* (Jan.) 356: "Austin!" sung out Gordon, "go in the steerage there, you bloodhound," (he was once a butcher).

blood jug *n. Boxing.* the nose.

1849 *Crockett's Almanac* (unp.): He tried several times to taste o' my external blood jug.

blood money *n. Mil.* bonus pay offered for reenlistment.

1900 McManus *Soldier Life* 67: The full-travel pay...which had been cut off in January was...offered as a bait to those who would "take on again," but we indignantly spurned the "blood-money," as it was commonly called.

blood pit *n. Police.* a saloon or other establishment that is a frequent scene of violence; BUCKET OF BLOOD.

1970–71 J. Rubinstein *City Police* 141: When a patrolman refers to a certain corner as being bad, he often means the bar on it, which may be a weekend "blood pit."

blood sheet *n.* [cf. BLOOD CHIT] *Journ.* (see quot.).

1940 Q. Reynolds *London Diary* 24: When we [war correspondents] go on what might be dangerous trips we...have to sign a release absolving the British government from all liability. This release is the "blood sheet."

bloodskin *n.* [sugg. by *redskin*] *Army in West.* an American Indian.—used contemptuously.

1865 in H. Johnson *Talking Wire* 224: We had another fight with the "blood skins."

blood stripe *n.* **1.** *Army.* a chevron of enlisted grade awarded in a combat unit after the death or wounding of the soldier who held the grade previously; a promotion given under such circumstances.

1975 Former 1LT, U.S. Army, age *ca*25: A *blood stripe* is a stripe you get after somebody in your outfit has been killed and you take over his job. **1983** K. Miller *Lurp Dog* 119 [ref. to Vietnam War]: A lot of guys getting killed, a lot of blood stripes coming down the Lurp platoon. **1987** Blankenship *Blood Stripe* 76: Every stripe on his arm was a "blood stripe"—a promotion resulting from the death of the noncom just above him.

2. *Mil.* an enlisted-grade chevron stripped from one person and awarded to another; an enlisted promotion at someone else's expense.

1983 Elting et al. *Dict. Sold. Talk* 29: *Blood stripe...*A promotion at the expense of another. *a*1985 in K. Walker *Piece of My Heart* 307 [ref. to 1950's]: These were what they called blood stripes [at Ft. Monmouth]. In other words, if somebody did something wrong and they lost their stripe, somebody else could get it if you were highly recommended.

1981–89 R. Atkinson *Long Gray Line* 372: George...had the power of "blood stripes": an errant sergeant or corporal would be marched to the battalion sergeant major, who ripped off the soldier's rank chevrons and taped them to the sleeve of a more deserving man.

3. *USMC.* the wide red stripe worn by commissioned and noncommissioned officers on the outer seam of dress trousers.

1985 Petit *Peacekeepers* 46 [ref. to 1983]: They also used their knees to smack me in the thigh, pinning on my "blood stripes."...I had earned the right to wear [corporal's chevrons as well as] the blood-red stripe on my dress uniform trousers.

bloodsucker *n.* **1.** *Naut.* a malingerer or shirker.

1867 Smyth *Sailor's Wd. Bk.*: Bloodsuckers. Lazy fellows, who, by skulking, throw their proportion of the labor on the shoulders of their shipmates. **1875** Sheppard *Love Afloat* 183: Nothin' would do these young bloodsuckers but a fight right off. **1929* Bowen *Sea Slang* 14: *Blood Suckers.* Lazy seamen who put their work on their mess-mates' shoulders.

2. *Hosp.* an individual who performs medical blood tests; hematologist.

1934 Hargan *Pris. Lang.* 361: *Blood sucker*—the doctor who takes the Wassermann test. **1944** Kendall *Service Slang* 49: *Blood sucker...*a person who applies Wasserman tests. **1952** Viereck *Men into Beasts* 42: I won't let them bloodsuckers bleed me to death. **1971** N.Y.C. draftsman, age *ca*50: In the medical corps in World War II we called the hematologists *bloodsuckers.*

blood tub *n.* **1.** *pl.* (*cap.*) a powerful gang of rowdies and criminals in Baltimore, Md.; (*hence*) (*sing.*) a desperate criminal; desperado.

1861 in F. Moore *Rebellion Rec.* I 73: "Blood Tubs" and "Plug Uglies," and others galore,/Are sick for a thrashing in sweet Baltimore. **1868** in S.Z. Starr *Jennison's Jayhawkers* 384: The blood tubs, the blacklegs, the shoulder-hitters and the pimps to whom Jennison is mainly indebted for his election. **1882** A.W. Aiken *Joe Buck* 3: I'm Johnny Skinner, the Cowboy, and I'm a blood-tub on wheels when I strike the war-path. *a*1890 *F & H* I 240: The Blood-Tubs are reported to have been mostly butchers, and to have gotten their epithet from having...dipped an obnoxious German's head in a tub of warm blood, and then driven him running through the town [of Baltimore].

2. see BLOOD BOAT.

blood wings *n. Army.* (see quot.).

1984–88 Hackworth & Sherman *About Face* 449 [ref. to 1960's]: Blood wings were the first set of parachute wings a paratrooper received upon qualification at the levels of novice, senior, and master rating.

Bloody *n.* a Bloody Mary.

1978 Strieber *Wolfen* 155: Hiya, Frenchie...gimme a Bloody. **1980** Birnbach et al. *Preppy Hndbk.* 167: The whole reason to go to brunch is to drink Bloodies. **1981** *Time* (Nov. 30) 79: Sprawling on the sidelines, students and alumni sip beer, bloodies and bourbon. **1985** E. Leonard *Glitz* 162: You like my Bloodies?

bloody *adj., adv., & infix.* **1.** despicable; (*hence*) damned; goddamned. [**1689* quot. reflects early S.E. sense "bloody-minded; cruel," undoubtedly the orig. of the present usage. In 20th C. U.S. usage, considered uncommon and widely regarded as a typical Briticism.]

a. (as *adj.*).

*1681 in Otway *Works* II 137: He has been a bloody Cuckold-making Scoundrel in his time. [**1689* Shadwell *Bury-Fair* IV: A Pox on him....Bloody Rogue!] **1726* A. Smith *Memoirs of J. Wild* 132: Oh! you bloody B--is this all the money you have about you? **1785* in *OEDS*: The prisoner Fennell swore an oath, if he had a knife he would cut his bloody fingers off. **1791** [W. Smith] *Confess. T. Mount* 20: Or else a leaden bullet/Shall pierce your bloody brains. **1800** *Amorous Songster* 60: To school [he] must pack...And for bloody Monday weeps. **1824** in Paulding *Bulls & Jons.* 309: Why, d—me if I don't believe you're [one] of our bloody aristocrats! **1830** Martin *Narr. Rev. Soldier* 136 [ref. to 1778]: "The bloody Yankee," or "the d—d Yankee," was the mildest epithets that they would bestow upon me at such times. **1833** *Mil. & Nav. Mag. of U.S.* (Dec.) 219: Jack, these bloody niggers is only useless ballast. **1840** R.H. Dana *2 Yrs. Before Mast* ch. xx: They've got a man for a mate of that ship, and not a bloody sheep about decks! **1844** J.F. Cooper *Afloat & Ashore* 67: One never knows where a bloody current will carry him in the dark. **1847** Downey *Portsmouth* 15: Then they curse the bloody dirty ship and say, "Twant so last cruise." **1848** in

Blair & Meine *Half Horse* 202: Whar's Camilla—the bloody coward? **1849** Mackay *Western World* I 154: He'll know his place better the next time, the b—y mongrel! **1856** *Ballou's Dollar Mo. Mag.* (Oct.) 323: I see you, Joe Grummer, you bloody rascal!...I'll set up your rigging for ye, my lad, with a taut lanyard. *Ibid.* 326: Hold your tongue, you bloody fool, can't ye? **1856** in F.M. Smith *S.F. Vigilance Comm.* 79: What the bloody h—l is the use of keeping me here, just waiting for you? **1857** S.C. Smith *Chili* 308: I'm darned ef I didn't take ye for a bloody Mexekin. **1863** in S. Boyer *Nav. Surgeon* I 222: A messmate before a shipmate; a shipmate before a stranger; a stranger before a dog; and a dog before a bloody soldier. **1865** in Woodruff *Union Soldier* 79: The Pvt. told the Maj. he would whip him & followed him towards camp, telling the damned Bloody Hoosiers, to "hunt their holes." **1869** Woods *Woman in Prison* 68: That bloody Smith snores so that we can't sleep! **1871** "M. Twain" *Roughing It* 268: I don't understand such bloody foolishness as that. **1885** *Puck* (June 17) 252: We had every bloody check but one. **1895** *Harper's* (July) 240: Been drivin' a bloody lot o' burros for thirty years. **1896** Hamblen *Many Seas* 65: Cursing the *Tanjore* as being the worst "bloody hooker" they ever saw on the "bloody" coast. **1900** Dreiser *Sister Carrie* 307: Ah, you bloody coward! **1911** O. Johnson *Stover at Yale* 14: Come on and get the bloody freshmen! **1914** London *Jacket* 28: They'll take us out and give us bloody hell. **1934** H. Miller *Tropic of Cancer* 251: It was like a bloody, fucking nightmare that you can't throw off. **1935** T. Wolfe *Time & River* 73: Pray for yourself, y' bloody little Deke. **1936** Dos Passos *Big Money* 309: Oh, hell, it's a bloody chore. **1947** Willingham *End as a Man* 177: Pull your bloody neck back! **1958** Rose *Man of the West* (film): I remembered every bloody minute of it. **1962** Crump *Killer* 300: Give me the bloody flower, pops. **1968** W.C. Anderson *Gooney Bird* 23: Furthermore, we're going to be the best goddamned crew in the bloody Air Force. **1971** Murphy & Gentry *Second in Command* 212: Not bloody likely, I thought. **1973** M. Collins *Carrying the Fire* 32: Or maybe...would never ever qualify to be an astronaut, but it was worth a bloody go anyway. **1977** Kleinberg *Live with Computer* 53: Nothing is labeled, nothing is in order. What a bloody mess! **1985** *Lady Blue* (ABC-TV): Give 'em bloody hell. **1989** "Captain X" & Dodson *Unfriendly Skies* 8: Just what the bloody fuck did you think you were doing back there?

b. (as adv., esp. in phr. **bloody well**).

*1676 in *F & H* I 241: He will promise to be bloody drunk. *1684 in *F & H*: The doughty bullies enter bloody drunk. *1693 in *OED*: She took it bloody ill of him. *1706 in *F & H*: Thou art a bloody impudent fellow. *1711 in *F & H*: It was bloody hot walking today. *1753 S. Foote *Eng. in Paris* 29: She's a bloody fine Girl; and I should be glad to —. *1771 T. Bridges *Bank-Note* IV 78: John found himself bloody thirsty. *1801 in *OEDS* I 297: Sir Philip writes a *bloody* bad hand. **1807** W. Irving *Salmagundi* 60: Tells bloody long stories. **1839–40** [Cobb] *Green Hand* I 262: He's going to get out of this bloody bad fix. *1847 in Wilkes *Austral. Colloq.* 35: The word bloody is a favorite oath in that country. One man will tell you that he married a bloody young wife, another, a bloody old one. **1848** [Judson] *Mysteries* 76: And a bloody good blow-out we'll have uv it. **1868** [Williams] *Black-Eyed Beauty* 42: Matty's bloody proud of them. **1869** *Mysteries of Crime* 323: How did you get on today?..."Bloody bad." **1874** *Chicago Inter-Ocean* (Sept. 8), in Krause & Olson *Prelude to Glory* 144: A fellow...admiring the way a pack mule is laden, will call it a bloody good outfit. **1905** in A. Adams *Chisholm Trail* 112: The next day was...*bloody* cold. **1948** Hargrove *Got to Give* 90: It looks like you're bloody well on the block now. **1964** Redfield *Let. from Actor* 90: They'd bloody well better talk to their young friend. **1979** J. Norris *War Story* 186: Which the Viets knew bloody well. **1991** Marcinko & Weisberg *Rogue Warrior* 80: He could bloody well get you court-martialed.

c. (as infix). See also ABSOBLOODYLUTELY.

[**1883** Keane *Blue-Water* 24: He spread gratings, coils of rope, man at the wheel, second mate, and everything not built into the ship, around in a complete "hoo-jolly-rah!"] **1895** *JAF* (July) 227: [*Bloody* is] interlarded by every Cockney into every remark, suitably or unsuitably, and even, as I have heard it, interpolated for the sake of definite and precise emphasis, between two syllables of a word, or used as a term of partially humorous endearment by a shawl-enshrouded mother to an East End child....'Them's the — fellers wot's got all the — power in this — country. If I 'ad my — way, I'd put every — mother's son of 'em under this — river for a — half 'our, and next I'd put every — foreigner in the — country after 'em, and that 'ud give a — Englishman a chance." **1918** E. Pound, in Joyce *Letters* II 424: Et bloody cetera. *1945 S.J. Baker *Austral. Lang.* 258: Transconti-bloody-nental, abso-f-----glutely, inde-bloody-pendent.

2. [cf. BLOOD, *n.*, 1] rowdy, impudent, etc.

1819 A. Pierce *Rebelliad* 44: Arriving at Lord Bilbo's study,/They thought they'd be a little bloody;/So, with a bold, presumptuous look,/ An honest pinch of snuff they took. *Ibid.* 76: They roar'd and bawl'd and were so bloody./As to besiege Lord Bilbo's study. **1856** Hall *College Wds.* 29: *Bloody.* Formerly a college term for daring, rowdy, impudent.

Bloody Asshole *n. Army.* the red and white double quatrefoil insigne of the U.S. Ninth Infantry Division; *pl.* the division itself.—usu. considered vulgar.

1985 J.M.G. Brown *Rice Paddy Grunt* 252 [ref. to Vietnam War]: The "Bloody Asshole" patch of the 9th Division on one shoulder. **1990** G.R. Clark *Words of Vietnam War* 584: 9th Infantry Division...Old Reliables...Bloody Assholes.

bloodyback *n.* a British soldier; redcoat. Now *hist.*

1770 in *DA*: Come, you Rascals, you bloody Backs, you Lobster Scoundrels; fire if you dare. *1785 Grose *Vulgar Tongue*: *Bloody back*, a jeering appellation for a soldier, alluding to his scarlet coat. **1836** *Naval Mag.* (July) 370: But, we know, there are many riflemen and sharpshooters in Sterling's division, by whom...many a "bloody back"...and many a Hessian were laid low. **1984** Fielder & Boothe *G. Washington* (NBC-TV): The bloodybacks have dug a trench parallel to our works.

Bloody Bucket *n.* **1.** *Army.* the red keystone insigne of the U.S. Twenty-eighth Infantry Division; (*hence*) the division itself. [Quots. ref. to WWII.]

1954 Huie *Pvt. Slovik* 4: 28th Division—the old Keystone or "Bloody Bucket"—National Guard outfit from Pennsylvania. **1983** Elting et al. *Soldier Talk* 29: *Bloody Bucket*...The US 28th Infantry Division...its division insignia was a red keystone. **1984–88** Hackworth & Sherman *About Face* 39: The 28th (Bloody Bucket) Division in WW II.

2. BUCKET OF BLOOD.

1956 S. Harris *Skid Row* 25: The low-down bars on Skid Row called "bloody buckets."

Bloody Mary *n.* **1.** *Navy.* (see quot.).

1944 Wakeman *Shore Leave* 20: "Do you know what Bloody Mary is?" Crewson asked, and the boy grinned and said yes, sir, it was tomato stew.

2. a mixed drink made chiefly with tomato juice and vodka. Now *S.E.*

*1956 in *OEDS*: Those two are eating raw steaks and drinking Bloody Marys. **1956** *New Yorker* (Oct. 6) 34: Fighting off acrophobia with a Bloody Mary sixty-five stories above skating-rink level. **1957** *Harper's* (June) 32: The citizen drinks an infusion of tomato juice and vodka called a Bloody Mary. **1971** in Asimov et al. *Sci. Fi. Short Shorts* 120: I was in a bar...having a Bloody Mary. **1985** *USA Today* (Dec. 10) 1D: The Bloody Mary made its national debut in an ad that appeared in late December 1955. In it, George Jessel declared that he invented the drink at 5 one morning.

3. a menstrual period.

1968 Baker et al. *CUSS* 82: *Bloody Mary.* Be menstruating. **1973** *AS* XLVI 82. **1978** Pilcer *Teen Angel* 179: Her period. The curse. Her red letter day. Her bloody Mary. IT!

blooey 1. *interj.* [imit.] (used to represent the sound of an explosion: bang! boom! pow! etc.); esp. in phr. **go blooey** to explode; (*hence*) to break down, malfunction; go awry; come suddenly to ruin; go crazy; disappear, etc. Also vars.

1910 T.A. Dorgan, in Zwilling *TAD Lexicon* 18: [Picture of chicks emerging from their shells] Blooey, blooey. **1915** in Lardner *Haircut* 159: Blooie! Down the left field foul line where he always hits! **1918** *Sat. Eve. Post* (Jan. 19) 17: Blewey!...a shell...blowed everything sky-high. **1918** Swan *My Co.* 223: There's a bomb underneath which explodes when one steps on the disc, and, as the men say, one goes "Bluey, Bluey." **1919** S. Lewis *Free Air* 108: You make one move to stop, and I steer her over—Blooie! Down the bank! **1923** *Our Navy* (June 15) 2: It sounds like a radio gone blooey. **1925** Dos Passos *Manhat. Transfer* 123: Look here, kid, you're goin blooy if you keep up like this. **1926** Nason *Chevrons* 72: He jumped on his horse and went blooey. **1926** Dunning & Abbott *B'way* 247: He hates to see it go blooey just because a big stiff that's rancid with coin comes along and cops his partner. **1929** Milburn *Hobo's Hornbk.* 50: And then things all went blooey and they throwed me in the can. **1935** K. Fearing, in J.P. Hunter *Norton Intro. Poetry* (ed. 2) 177: Going whop to the office and blooie home to sleep and biff got married and bam had children and oof got fired. **1950** R. Angell, in *New Yorker* (July 8) 25: I'd start pressing and getting sore and of course my game would go blooey. **1961** Updike *Rabbit Run* 142: A clear image suddenly in the water wavering like a blooey television set. **1963** Zahn *Amer. Contemp.* 24: Yup. I lit a match to see if I got him. Blooey! **1965** *My 3 Sons* (CBS-TV): I told her my name and blooey! my date's over before it starts. **1972** W.C. Anderson *Hurricane* 115: If anything should happen to him—blooie! **1978** Barry *Ultimate Encounter* 159: His father said that Allen just seemed to have gone blooey after that *thing* happened in the woods.

2. *n.* (*cap.*) *Army.* Blois (Loire-et-Cher), France, site during 1918 of an efficiency board that transferred, demoted, or retired incompetent commissioned officers. Now *hist.*

1920 *Amer. Leg. Wkly.* (Jan. 30) 6: Blooey was A.E.F. for Blois, a placid little town on the Loire, about forty-five kilometers from Tours. **1927** Liggett *A.E.F.* 256: An adverse report would bring an officer of the Inspector General's Department. If he confirmed the report, the officer went before an efficiency board and was sent to Blois, which was pronounced "Blooey" in the A.E.F. **1930** *Amer. Leg. Mo.* (May) 32: "Boys de Cornwilly," for, perhaps, Bois de Cornieville....Manois...known as "Manure." Then there was "Soup-town" for Bouillonville and "Blooey" for Blois. **1931** Bullard *Amer. Soldiers* 28: Officers found incompetent...were sent to Blois—and in Yankee-French that became "Bloo-ey." **1936** Reilly *Amers. All* 602: Blois, or "Bluey" as the soldiers call it. **1968** Myrer *Once an Eagle* 185: Told him if he tried to palm that lousy goldfish off on them one more time he was going to retire him to Blooie.

3. *n.* HOOEY.

1926 Hormel *Co-Ed.* 62: I never realized the old boy wrote anything but highbrow stuff like...the kinda blooey the school-marms are always spouting. **1942** *ATS* 177: Nonsense...blah,...blooey, bluey.

blooey *v.* [fr. BLOOEY, *n.*, 2; for semantic parallel, cf. F *limoger* 'to retire (an army officer)'; 'to fire' < *Limoges*, city in France, and S Afr E *Stellenbosch* 'to relegate (an incompetent officer) to a post where he is unable to do harm'] *Army.* to order (a commissioned officer) to Blois for reassignment, demotion, or retirement; to transfer (an enlisted man) as undesirable. Now *hist.* —usu. passive.

1920 *Amer. Leg. Wkly.* (Jan. 30) 6: He hasn't been on leave and he isn't coming back. He's been *blooeyed!*...Captain Smith has been blooeyed—the benzine board for his. **1927** *Amer. Leg. Mo.* (May) 33: Suppose that old fungus takes a notion to blooey you to Remount? **1934** Weseen *Dict. Slang* 113: *Blued* [*sic*]—Reassigned for duty elsewhere.

blooker *n.* *Mil.* [imit.; cf. syn. BLOOPER] **1.** a grenade launcher.

1973 Roth *Sand in Wind* 257: Tony's only concern was having to give up his blooker. It was a grenade launcher that looked like a single-barreled, sawed-off shotgun. **1978** Groom *Better Times* 6: You'll be runnin' around handin' out fuckin' tangerines ta people steda shooting ya blooker. **1981–83** N. Proffitt *Gardens of Stone* 148: Harmon...fired the blooker.

2. a soldier armed with a grenade launcher.

1973 Roth *Sand in Wind* 259: This Phantom Blooker was merely a mythical Viet Cong...who prowled the Arizona with captured American grenade launchers.

bloomer *n.* **1.** a fine fellow.

1882 *Frank James on the Trail* 36: You'll never cross such a fine piece of stuff as that again, my bloomer.

2.a. a blunder, a mistake.

*1889 Barrère & Leland *Dict. Slang* I 140: *Bloomer* (Australian), prison slang for a mistake. Abbreviated from the expression "a blooming error." **1906** *Nat. Police Gaz.* (Oct. 20) 10: But Jim Jeffries made a bloomer when he essayed to stop two men in one night. **1908** in H.C. Fisher *A. Mutt* 30: Mutt made a bloomer yesterday when he sunk his entire bank roll on a bum skate. ***1911** O'Brien & Stephens *Austral. Slang* 18: *Bloomer*: slang—a blunder or mistake. ? Yiddish, I think. **1923** *Nashville Banner* (Jan. 3) 6: It would...be strange if at times [the referee] didn't pull a "bloomer." **1924** Hecht & Bodenheim *Cutie* 14: Her man thought...bloomers was a slang term which meant a series of mistakes. **1924** H.L. Wilson *Professor* 141: You certainly pulled a bloomer. **1926** Maines & Grant *Wise-Crack Dict.* 5: *Bloomer*—A total failure. **1928** O'Connor *B'way Racketeers* 249: *Bloomer*—A mistake, failure. **1931** Wilstach *Under Cover Man* 135: You wouldn't pull a bloomer in sight of a cop.

b. a complete failure, FLOP; (*specif.*) an unprofitable venture; *Circus.* an unprofitable engagement.

1904 *Life in Sing Sing* 246: *Bloomer.* An empty safe. **1910** T.A. Dorgan, in *N.Y. Eve. Jour.* (Apr. 6) 14: Stanley Ketchel tried out his left wing on a punching bag yesterday...and the thing was a bloomer. Steve hurt it in his fight with Klaus. **1914** Jackson & Hellyer *Vocab.* 18: We...scored a bloomer. **1918** Wagar *Spotter* 32: This line...had been a..."bloomer" as far as profits were concerned. **1920** Ade *Hand-Made Fables* 8: The

Party looked like a Bloomer. **1923** *N.Y. Times* (Sept. 9) VIII 2: *Bloomer:* See flop. **1927** in Truman *Lttrs. Home* 79: Even if we did pull a bloomer at Topeka. **1927** Coe *Me—Gangster* 201: Wait till I git back from this Gander joint an' see if you've picked a bloomer. **1927** Nicholson *Barker* 103: *Bloomer*—bad business. **1931** D.W. Maurer, in *AS* (June) 329: Marion, Indiana, is always a bloomer for me. **1932** Hecht & Fowler *Great Magoo* 94: The world's series is a bloomer. Nobody's paying any attention. **1951** Mannix *Sword-Swallower* 54: This is a bloomer if I ever seen one.

3. a fraud, fake.

1911–12 Ade *Knocking the Neighbors* 130: A Promissory Note that was a Bloomer to begin with. **1918** Stringer *House of Intrigue* 29: My stall could nearly always work, and the hen–flock would...start me off in a taxi...to some bloomer address in the outskirts.

4. a joke.

1919 Darling *Jargon Book* 27: *Pulled a Bloomer*—a joke.

5. *Navy.* (see 1966 quot.).

1919 *Our Navy* (Oct.) 32: [The USS *New Mexico*] has four sets of bloomers, and she uses an awful amount of powder. **1953** McEwen & Lewis *Encyc. Naut. Knowl.* Bloomers. Canvas cover for a large gun. **1966** Noel & Bush *Naval Terms* 75: *Buckler:* Flexible cover attached externally to a turret's front armor plate so that...water cannot enter the Gunport. Slang term is *Bloomer.* Ibid. 67: *Bloomer*...Also used loosely for any canvas cover topside.

6. *Sports.* an athlete who only temporarily appears promising.

1920 (quot. at MORNING GLORY).

7. *Sailing.* a furled sail that has come unsecured.

1970 W.I. Norton *Eagle Ventures* 116: A sudden "bloomer" aloft can throw off even the hardiest of sail handlers.

bloomer cricket *n.* CROTCH CRICKET. *Joc.*

1974 Univ. Tenn. grad. student, age 22: *Bloomer crickets* are damn crabs. I heard an old boy from the mountains use that in western North Carolina, 1973.

bloomer pudding *n.* *S.W.* copulation with a woman. *Joc.*

1968 San Antonio, Tex., high school student (coll. M. Crafton): Sure would like some of her bloomer pudding.

blooming *adj. & adv.* damned. *Rare* in U.S.

*1879 in *F & H* (rev.) I 278: Seasonable slang. For Spring.—You be *blowed!* For Summer.—I'll *warm* yer! For Autumn.—Not so *blooming* green! **1882** in *OED*: Oh, you blooming idiot! **1883** *Life* (Feb. 8) 80: The Dea-con said he'd Go a bloom-ing Dollar. **1885** "Lykkejaeger" *Dane* 118: What a bloomin' fool you must be. **1886** in *Nye West. Humor* 183: We have more...sciatica and one bloomin' thing and another. **1892** in F. Remington *Sel. Letters* 132: It's "bloomin" lucky. **1893** S. Crane, in Baym et al. *Norton Antho.* II 719: I'll be hully, bloomin' blowed. **1894** Henderson *Sea Yarns* 56: I might 'a' knowed better 'n to talk to a bloomin' landlubber. **1896** Crane *George's Mother* 139: I can't fin' me feet in dis bloomin' joint. I been battin' round heh fer a half hour. **1902** Harriman *Ann Arbor* 78: Don't you think it's a bloomin' long way to take him, Billy? **1911** O. Johnson *Stover at Yale* 30: Go right up and sit on the steps of the bloomin' old thing and eat a bag of cream puffs. **1915** Braley *Workaday World* 17: Use your bloomin' head. **1918** in Loosbrock & Skinner *Wild Blue* 54: When the blooming things get too close they rock your ship [like] an Oklahoma cyclone. **1937** in Truman *Dear Bess* 394: Every bloomin' one of 'em will want a ticket. **1974** *N.Y. Times* II (Feb. 10) 11: It will not be so bloomin' offbeat that they'll ban it in Georgia. **1980** W.C. Anderson *BAT-21* 186: "What's not a bad outfit?" "The blooming Air Force." **1992** Sen. E. Hollings (D–S.C.), on *Election 92* (CNN-TV) (Nov. 3): I don't have to get elected to a bloomin' thing.

bloop *n.* **1.** a blunder; BLOOPER, 3.

1966 Gowdy & Hirshberg *Cowboy at Mike* 32: No mention of my bloop was ever again mentioned in anger. **1977** *L.A. Times* (Feb. 21) IV 1: That bloop you pulled in today's column has to be the bloop to end all bloops. **1984** T. Wicker, in *N.Y. Times* (Dec. 30) E 3: So atonement is in order for bloops and clinkers recorded in this space during 1984.

2. var. BLEEP.

3. *Baseball.* BLOOPER, 1.a.—usu. as adj.

1973 N.Y.C. man, age 25: It was just a little bloop single. **1978** *Harper's* (Feb.) 81: There would be an error or a walk or a bloop single. **1982** Considine *Lang. Sport* 10: Bloop single. **1984** *N.Y. Post* (Aug. 13) 28: Another [single] was a bloop. **1984** *N.Y. Post* (Aug. 2) 77: Carlton Fisk got his 1500th career hit, a bloop single, in the first.

bloop *v.* **1.** Esp. *Baseball.* to hit lightly into the air.

1950 *N.Y. Daily News* (Oct. 1): Waitkus blooped another bingle into short center. **1960** Garagiola *Funny Game* 38: The two previous hitters had blooped hits. **1966** *N.Y. Times* (Jan. 30) V 2S: Johnson blooped a double for the lone hit off Hendley. **1975** *L.A. Times* (Dec. 4) IV 1: He blooped a 35-yard field goal…that barely trickled into the end zone. **1982** WINS radio news report (Aug. 28): Willie Upshaw blooped an RBI single. **1984** WKGN radio news (May 29): The Charlotte right-fielder blooped a third-inning single.

2. var. BLEEP.

blooper *n. Baseball.* **1.a.** a weakly batted fly ball that carries just beyond the infield. Now *colloq.* or *S.E.*

1937 *N.Y. Times* (Oct. 8) 29: A "blooper" is a soggy fly [ball]. **1952** Malamud *Natural* 48: The leadoffer hit a blooper to short.

b. a slow pitch thrown in a high arc to the plate.

1946 *N.Y. Times* (July 10) 26: Nothing whatever seemed to puzzle [Williams], least of all Rip Sewell's renowned "blooper" pitch which Ted the Terrible walloped into the bleachers with two abroad [*sic*] to climax a four-run eighth inning. **1982** Considine *Lang. Sport* 10: Originated in 1941 by Pittsburgh Pirates pitcher Rip Sewell (the "ephus pitch"), the blooper was revived in the mid to late 1960s by New York Yankees relief pitcher Steve Hamilton…and the 1980s by Yankees reliever Dave LaRoche.

2. a swinging blow.

1940 (quot. at HINGE).

3. an embarrassing mistake, esp. in a radio or television broadcast.

1947 *Partisan Rev.* XIV 550: Why does Farrell write so badly? Why in his latest book such bloopers as "Art…presents *imaginary images* of life." **1954** "Collans" & Sterling *House Detect.* 92: He demanded to know why Arny had pulled a blooper like that. **1956** *AS* XXXI 252: In radio and television broadcasting…lapses are known as *bloopers, fluffs, slips,* and *boners.* **1958** J. King *Pro Football* 189: The slightest blooper would be picked up in a frightening number of living rooms. **1960–61** Steinbeck *Discontent* 141: I pulled a blooper. **1965** Gallery *8 Bells* 31: But he was intensely loyal to his subordinates and inspired confidence in them. This can often cancel out bloopers in global strategy. **1968** Safire *New Lang. Politics* 43: Blooper is…radio announcers' slang for a Spoonerism or slip of the tongue. **1978** E.L. Young *Afoot* 51: In reprisal, I taunted Jim with a blooper of his. **1985** P. Donahue *Human Animal* 74: Is Bethlehem, Pennsylvania…a "blooper" of cultural evolution?

4. *Mil.* **a.** BLOOKER, 1.

1978 J. Webb. *Fields of Fire* 411: *Blooper:* Nickname for the M-79 grenade launcher, a 40-millimeter, shotgun-like weapon that shoots spin-armed "balls," or small grenades. **1980** Millett *Semper Fidelis* 552: The M-79 or "blooper" fired 40-mm. shells from a shotgun-like grenade launcher. **1983** E. Dodge *Dau* 118: Heavy automatics, AKs, RPGs. They even had some bloopers.

b. BLOOKER, 2.

1985 Dye *Between Raindrops* 259: Blooper, pop a few rounds up the street. Let's go.

c. a grenade fired by a blooper.

1991 J.T. Ward *Dear Mom* 87 [ref. to Vietnam War]: The first two bloopers (grenades) hit the roof of the hootch.

bloop gun *n. Mil.* an M-79 grenade launcher; BLOOPER, 4.a. Also **blooper gun.**

1971 *Everett* [Wash.] *Herald* (Nov. 18) 5F: The track commander climbed onto the top of armored personnel carrier (APC) 21 and sat behind a grenade-firing "blooper gun." **1973** Huggett *Body Count* 40: Bob's got the Bloop gun so he can't be on point. *Bloop* gun? You know, an M-79 grenade launcher….Makes a "bloop" when it fires.

bloopy bag *n. Navy.* a blimp.

1955 *Science Digest* (Dec.) 70: The "bloopy bags" were once in bad repute. **1958** Cope & Dyer *Petty Off. Gd.* (ed. 2) 332: *Bloopy bag.* (slang). Airship, blimp.

blossom-top *n.* a redheaded or red-faced person.—used derisively.

1867 in A.K. McClure *Rocky Mtns.* 292: Dry up, old (hic) blossom-top.

blotto *adj.* **1.** [orig. unkn.] very drunk.

***1917** *Living Age* (Nov. 10) 379: Synonyms for drunkenness…"jingled," "well oiled," "tanked to the wide," "well sprung," "up the pole," "blotto." **1923** Bellah *Sketchbook* 100: Some A.P.M. must have seen you blotteaux. ***1925** Fraser & Gibbons *Soldier & Sailor Wds.* 28 [ref. to WWI]: *Blotto:* Drunk. **1929** L. Thomas *Woodfill* 57: He was always getting what the British call "blotto." **1929** in *AS* (Feb. 1930) 238: *Blotto:*

in a continued state of intoxication. "Jim is gone blotto all the time." **1945** Himes *If He Hollers* 91: You can sit up and drink with me until I go blotto. **1946** in W.C. Fields *By Himself* 18: Take a little wine for thy stomach's sake, but don't get blotto. **1948** Cozzens *Guard of Honor* 109: The policeman, weaving back and forth—my men say he was absolutely blotto. **1948** in Himes *Black on Black* 267: He had been blotto for the past hour but no one knew it. **1959** E. Hunter *Conviction* 20: Stinko, blotto, blind drunk. **1968** Baker et al. *CUSS* 82: *Blottoed,* Drunk and passed out. **1973** Lucas, Katz & Huyck *Amer. Graffiti* 46: Got drunk as hell the night before….Blotto. **1983** Breathed *Bloom Co.* 18: Pickled. Tanked. Blotto. Yes. **1988** P. Beck & P. Massman *Rich Men, Single Women* 73: Completely blotto by now, she tripped over one of the champagne bottles.

2. tired out; dazed; crazy; (of machines) out of order.

1929 in *Americans vs. Germans* 75: I was…blotto from not having no sleep. **1930** *Bookman* (Dec.) 396: But he who is not acquainted with the language of *Variety* is certain…to be baffled—or, to speak more accurately, to go blotto. **1966** Manus *Mott the Hoople* 32: They devoured five helpings…like a squirrel gone blotto. **1973** Blum & Blum *Beyond Earth* 125: Turns out no one who doesn't have cable TV could get a picture that night….Our set went blotto. **1985** Univ. Tenn. prof., age 37: I'm still blotto from painting the house all weekend. **1992** *Newsweek* (Mar. 30) 53: Remember, kids, it was Yeats who wrote, "All things fall and are built again, and those that build them again are blotto."

3. entirely forgotten.

1938 H. Miller *Capricorn* 196: I am thinking of one woman and the rest is blotto.

blow *n.* **1.a.** a spree, party, or celebration; a blowout.

1827 *Harvard Register* (Aug.) 172: My fellow-students had been engaged at a "blow" till the stage horn had summoned them to depart. *Ibid.* 235: And, if no coming *blow* his thoughts engage,/Lights candle and cigar. **1856** Hall *College Wds.* 29: *Blow.* A merry frolic with drinking; a spree….This word was formerly used by students to designate their frolics and social gatherings; at present it is not much heard, being supplanted by the more common words *spree, tight,* etc. **1859** in Hafen & Hafen *Reports from Colo.* 208: They are going to give a grand "free blow" in the shape of a legislative Ball. **1940** *AS* (Oct.) 335 [ref. to Univ. Nebr.]: *Give her a blow.* Refers to a party or gifts to one who is leaving the place where he or she is working.

b. *Stu.* a reveler.

1856 Hall *College Wds.* 30: The person who engages in a blow [spree] is also called a *blow.* "I could see in the long vista of the past, the many hardened blows who had rioted here around the festive board— *Collegian,* p. 231."

2.a. a divulgence or exposure of information to authorities, an act of informing.

1848 *Life in Rochester* 87: This 'ere lady is a going to the Police, to give us a blow on't.

b. *Und.* a sudden discovery of a criminal in the act of committing a crime.

1902 Hapgood *Autobiog. of Thief* 58: [ref. to ca1885]: It was a "blow" of course and she got nailed. *Ibid.* 168: These latter would tell the keepers that he was buggy [insane]; and, if there was not a blow, he might be sent to the hospital. **1904** *Life in Sing Sing* 263: Everything was on the good, when we got a blow…We were discovered.

c. *Und.* a sign of recognition.

1936 in D. Runyon *More Guys* 167: So I do not give him a blow, because the way I look at it, the fewer people you know in this world, the better you are off.

3. ? a complaint.

1852 Stowe *Uncle Tom's Cab.* 42: "I'm in a devil of a hobble and you must help me out."…"A body may be pretty sure of that, when *you're* glad to see 'em; something to be made off 'em. What's the blow now?"

4.a. a brief rest after vigorous or laborious activity; a breather.

***1855** in *DAE:* I seized her bridle, and brought the whole party to a stand. I determined that the horses should now have a good "blow,"…and resolutely held on. **1922** L. Hisey *Sea Grist* 26: I was unaccustomed to the heat and would take a good-sized "blow" at every opportunity. ***1929** Brophy *Soldier's War* 264 [ref. to WWI]: *Blow:* rest, pause. **1939** R.A. Winston *Dive Bomber* 21: Let's take a blow. **1944** *Am. N & Q* (Apr.) 8: *Take a Blow.* Get out and get some air or take a rest. **1944** Kendall *Service Slang* 33: *Take a blow*…a fireman leaves his duties for a breath of fresh air. **1945** in *Calif. Folklore* (1946) 387: To take a few minutes off to rest during a watch period is to *take a blow.* **1948** J. Stevens *Jim Turner* 130 [ref. to ca1910]: As we slogged along in the mud and stopped for blows they told me their stories. **1953** Dodson *All Boats* 440: I've got to have a blow from this endless surgery. **1958** Davis *Spearhead* 61: Go on, take a blow. **1964** McKenna *Sons of Martha* 124: Let's take a blow and have some coffee. **1977** Sayles *Union Dues* 240: It's almost lunchtime, you take a blow. **1980** Whalen *Takes a Man* 64: We're going out and take a blow for awhile.

b. a release from work.

1974 Dubinsky & Standora *Decoy Cop* 88: His foreman gave him an early blow and he arrived at his flat almost an hour early.

5. a pistol.

1928 Hecht & MacArthur *Front Page* 484: Say, with that alky rap and the bank job and the big blow on my hip! I should stick around asking questions from a lot of cops! **1929** *Sat. Eve. Post* (Apr. 13) 54: A pistol may be [called] a heat, a rod, a gat, or a blow, or the big blow. **1935** Algren *Boots* 178: Wait'll ah get me mah big blow.

6. an act of fellatio or cunnilingus; BLOW JOB.—usu. considered vulgar. [1946 quot., in verse, is quasi-verbal.]

1946 in Legman *Limerick* 82: Who knew the very fine art of Blow. **1959** in Kinsey Inst. *Graffiti*: Show hard for blow. **1965** in Fry *Graffiti* (unp.): If you want a blow 869—[etc.]. *a***1968** in Haines & Taggart *Ft. Lauderdale* 104: She gave me the…[best] blows. **1971** *Go Ask Alice* 102: If I don't give Big Ass a blow, he'll cut off my [drug] supply. **1974** Loken *Come Monday Mornin'* 49: I get me…two–three blows a day.

7.a. an inhalation of cocaine, heroin, or a similar drug.

1953 (cited in Spears *Drugs & Drink*). **1961** C. Cooper *Weed* 121: He figured she had just copped a blow somewhere and could not help nodding under the powerful press of heroin. **1963** in Wepman et al. *The Life* 80: Where addicts prowl with a tigerish scowl/In search of that lethal blow. **1979** (quot. at TOOT).

b. cocaine (*occ.* heroin), esp. in crystalline form for inhalation.

1971 Woodley *Dealer* 31: He took from his robe pocket a little aluminum-foil packet of coke…"That's good blow." **1971** Goines *Dopefiend* 105: Did you bring that blow for me? **1974** V.E. Smith *Jones Men* 132: I just copped some nice blow. **1976** Rosen *Above Rim* 240: You got what you require, brother? A chick? Some blow? Some reefer? **1976–77** Kernochan *Dry Hustle* 19: Murphy…bought a pound of blow to sell in New York City. **1977** A. Patrick *Beyond Law* 20: Acquaintances of mine…are connoisseurs of the blow. **1987** Tine *Beverly Hills Cop II* 9: How much blow you think he moved to pay for that car? **1990** Updike *Rabbit at Rest* 159: My body and blow get along fine.

8. *Bowling.* a failure to make a spare.

1976 *Webster's Sports Dict.* 46: *Blow*…A failure to make a spare when there is no split; error. **1979** Frommer *Sports Lingo* 59: *Blow.* Inability to make a spare.

¶ In phrase:

¶ **strike a blow for liberty** (during Prohibition) to take a drink of liquor. *Joc.*

1940 Wald & Macauley *They Drive by Night* (film): Well, you and I'll strike a blow for liberty.

blow *v.* **1.a.** to boast. Orig. *S.E.* Also constr. with *off.*

***ca1390** in *MED* II 997: þe ffrensche men cunne boþe boste & blowe. ***ca1422**, ***ca1450** in *MED*. [For later SE quots., see *OED*.] **1859** Bartlett *Amer.* (ed. 2): *To blow.* To boast, brag, "talk big." **1868** Macy *There She Blows!* 17: You can blow for a short time, but you'll be travelling the same road soon. **1871** Schele de Vere *Amer.* 584: You need not *blow* so, my friend. **1882** Field *Tribune Primer* 83: He is Blowing about the Circulation of the Paper. **1889** "M. Twain" *Conn. Yankee* 401: Why, sometimes when he forgets himself and gets to blowing off, you'd think he was one of the swells of the earth. **1937** Milne & Cobb *San Quentin* (film): Kennedy started blowin' off about the bigshots he knows. **1941** Hargrove *Pvt. Hargrove* 107: I thought I'd let him blow off about his stripe, so I asked him, "Say, what does that stripe stand for?" **1942** Garcia *Tough Trip* 69: He blew about what a good cook he was. **1950** Bissell *Stretch on the River* 17: Of course I had to blow off about papa and Jimmy Rodgers. **1950** Felsen *Hot Rod* 16: He'd blow to everybody that Bud had lost his nerve.

b. *Black E.* to talk (nonsense); spout; talk.

1968 in Cade *Black Woman* 45: Don't pay no mind to that cat. He always trying to blow some shit. **1979** D. Glasgow *Black Underclass* 142: The members…discuss, debate, and "blow on" all questions. **1967–80** Folb *Runnin' Lines* 229: *Blow* 1. Talk forcefully and energetically. 2. Talk seductively to a member of the opposite sex.

2.a. *trans.* to inform on, expose, discover, or reveal (a wrongdoer, a secret, a plot, a secret agent or the agent's identity, etc.). Orig. *S.E.*

***1575** in *F & H* I (rev.) 274: Was all well agreed? did nobody blow ye? ***1721** D. Defoe, in *F & H* I (rev.) 274: I must not be seen anywhere among my old acquaintances, for I am blown, and they will all betray me. ***1745** in C.H. Wilkinson *King of Beggars* 49: Instead of detecting, or (in their language) blowing him, rather encouraged…them. **1767** "A. Barton" *Disappointment* 81: Curse your contrivance! Now I'm blown! ***1788** in Partridge *Dict. Und.* 51: D—n your eyes, make haste along, you are both blown. **1807** W. Irving *Salmagundi* 146: Get the start of her…and blow the whole affair. ***1824** W. Scott, in *EDD* I 308: I will blow her ladyship's conduct in the business. ***1828** in Partridge *Dict. Und.* 51: I say, you won't *blow* me? **1828** Bird *Looking Glass* 9: The poor thing never knew, till I blowed them all, what an infamous old hag she had for a mother. *Ibid.* 90: You will be blown before tomorrow. Decamp's the word. *Ibid.* 119: Who's that you'll blow? What's that you'll tell? *Ibid.* 122: But you'd better confess. I've blown all, all. **1838** [Haliburton] *Clockmaker* (Ser. 2) 23: I told you I wouldn't blow you. **1843** in Barnum *Letters* 17: That brute of a Snelling *blowed* her yesterday. His informant is *Bennett*. **1848** [Thompson] *House Breaker* 44: Boys, what ought to be done to a *snitch*, who *blows* his *pals* to get himself out of quay? **1864** in James *Civil War Diary* 88: A tunnel out of the new stockade was "blown" today. The "blower" was discovered & roughly handled. ***1953** Fleming *Casino Royale* 27: He was completely blown and under really professional surveillance. *Ibid.* 143: The covers which must have been blown over the years, the codes which the enemy must have broken. **1960–61** Steinbeck *Discontent* 142: Don't blow my dirty suspicions to Marullo, will you? **1965** Abel *Missile Crisis* 10: Among them were hundreds of CIA agents now (in the technical term of the spying craft) "blown." **1968** *New Yorker* (Apr. 6) 38: A combination tobacconist's shop and foreign-agents'"drop" which was "blown" when a quisling agent found himself smoking a chart of harbor defenses. **1974** Radano *Cop Stories* 120: So I apologize to Wogs and promise we won't blow his joint to the plainclothesmen. **1980** Kopp *Mirror, Mask* 69: The neurotic fear[s] loss of control that would blow his cover. **1982** Braun *Judas Tree* 129: His cover was blown. **1984** Kagan & Summers *Mute Evidence* 362: He had just blown the cover on an attempted deception. **1987** *Miami Vice* (NBC-TV): So we're blown. We've never been blown before.

b. *intrans.* to inform or confess (to police or other authorities).

1844 *Spirit of Times* (Jan. 20) 557: Go! Get off; I'll not blow on you. **1847** Furber *12 Mos. Vol.* 348: The guard returned, and the bottle was passed around among a few whom they knew would not "blow." **1847** *Nat. Police Gaz.* (June 26) 333: The thief does not like the business of "blowing" on one of the fraternity. **1848** *Life in Rochester* 86: P'raps you'll go to the police office and blow on us. **1848** [Judson] *Mysteries* 252: They'd blow me for some of my work, and I'd be sent up! **1859** Matsell *Vocab.* 12: *Blow.* To inform. **1864** in Bensill *Quiet on Yamhill* 121: He "blowed" on several others, equally guilty. **1864** in James *Civil War Diary* 74: A "tunnel" was "blowed on" today & some of those who dug it…were flogged. **1880** Martin *Sam Bass* 143: They…were afraid he would blow on them. **1884** "M. Twain" *Huck. Finn* 174: I says to myself, shall I go to that doctor, private, and blow on these frauds? **1889** Meriwether *Tramp at Home* 95: "He'll blow on us if we let him loose." "Let him blow!" **1889** Grannan *Criminals* 10: Matches began to squeal and "blowed" about several crimes. **1956** H. Ellison *Deadly Streets* 81: The squeek would blow to the bulls and some of us would get put away.

c. *Und.* to realize, to become aware (of wrongdoing). Also absol.

1902 Hapgood *Autobiog. Thief* 43: The girl did not "blow" (take alarm) and I got hold of the leather easily. *Ibid.* 86: It took the Dutchman about ten minutes after he had returned to his seat to blow that his super was gone. **1930** [Conwell] *Pro. Thief* 46: In case the victim blows (meaning feels his loss). **1940** D.W. Maurer, in *AS* 116: *Blow*…tr. To realize. "The mark never blowed it was a gaff."

d. to become.—esp. in phr. **blow wise.**

1915–16 Lait *Beef, Iron & Wine* 214: He had married me—yes. But it had blown blue. **1930** *Amer. Mercury* (Dec.) 454: Blow wise to what I'm spieling. **1956** N. Algren *Wild Side* 243: Blow wise to this, friend. **1967** Spradley *Drunk* 18: I swung out—blew cool—ready for a drunk. **1969** [Beck] *Black Widow* 219: He blew whoreless.

3.a. to puff upon (a pipe); to smoke (in mod. use esp. marijuana).

***1773** in *SND* I 163: Sit down and blow your pipe. ***1825** "Blackmantle" *English Spy* I 335: Blowing his *steamer*, and drinking *blue ruin*. ***1848** in *OEDS*: I could sit down and *blow* my 'bacco. ***1867** in *EDD* I 308: His bacca he did blah. ***1879** *Jamieson's Scot. Dict.* I 217: To *Blaw*

Tobacco, to smoke tobacco. ***1898** in *EDD* I 308: We'll blow a bit o 'bacca, lads. **1929** Milburn *Hobo's Hornbk.* 152: And we blowed a toy of white stuff, that knocked the willies cold. **1946** Mezzrow & Wolfe *Really Blues* 303: *Blow*: smoke marihuàna. **1949** N. Algren, in *Harper's* (Aug.) 91: You don't *blow* that stuff, do you? **1952** E. Brown *Trespass* 106: They could keep all the gauge you could blow in a lifetime. **1953** W. Brown *Monkey on My Back* 89: He "blew tea" but never touched heroin. **1956** Resko *Reprieve* 237 [ref. to 1940's]: A reefer is…blown—never smoked. **1958** Motley *Epitaph* 100: I bet they're blowing tea right now. **1959** Trocchi *Cain's Bk.* 150: Let's blow some pot, Joe. **1961** J.A. Williams *Night Song* 99: Me, I'm sittin' over in a corner, blowin' a Chesterfield. **1961** R. Russell *Sound* 133: Blowing pot and joy popping all over the place. **1970** N.Y.U. student: I blew two pipes of hash this morning. **1978** *Texas Monthly* (July 28) 169: Another dozen young people…were laughing and drinking and blowing grass. **1982** Del Vecchio *13th Valley* 23: We don't blow no weed.

b. *Narc.* to take (cocaine, heroin, or the like) by inhalation. Also *intrans.*

1915 in Courtwright *Dk. Paradise* 92: The first dose of heroin…is a minute quantity…"blown" up the nose at the suggestion of an agreeable companion. **1917** in Ireland *Med. Dept.* X 69: Heroin takers are often young men from the cities….They…will talk much more freely about their habit if the examiner…uses such words as "deck," "quill," "package," "an eighth," "blowers," "cokie," etc. **1924** Henderson *Keys to Crookdom* 397: *Blowing coke:* Sniffing cocaine into nostrils. **1928** Callahan *Man's Grim Justice* 25: The "coke blowers" I learned were the boys who sniffed cocaine. **1929** Barr *Let Tomorrow Come* 82: Den us kin snatch ouah women an' blow ouah snow. **1963** in Wepman et al. *The Life* 84: I…stopped blowing and started to hit. **1970** Landy *Underground Dict.* 36: Blow snow…Inhale cocaine. **1993** *Seinfeld* (NBC-TV): What kind of snow blower did you set us up with?

4. to curse, damn; "to hell with."—usu. used optatively.—esp. (in early use) in such phr. as **blow me tight, blow me down, I'll be blowed** (used as oaths). [In recent use believed to derive obscenely from **(9.a.),** below; also cf. BLOW IT, below.]

***1781** G. Parker *View of Soc.* I 48: Blow me up…if I have had such a fellow…cross my company. *Ibid.* 105: Blow him up…this is all Hebrew to me. ***1819** T. Moore *Tom Crib* 46: There's nothing like a Bull: And *blow me tight*.—Bill Gibbons ne'er In all his days was known to swear. ***1825** (cited in Partridge *DSUE* (ed. 7) 1015). ***1827** in *OEDS: Blow me* if I do! ***1835** in *F & H* I (rev.) 278: You be blowed! **1836** *Spirit of Times* (Feb. 27) 16: Blow me tight, if I'd a been in his trowsers for biggest jug of rum in all creation. **1837** *Spirit of Times* (June 17) 143: Well, I'm blowed, but I wish I was young again. **1837** Neal *Charcoal Sks.* 161: I ain't potatoes to be put into a bag—blow the bag! **1845** Durivage & Burnham *Stray Subjects* 104: I'm blowed ef you *do*, though. ***1849** in *F & H* I (rev.) 274: Well, if you won't stand a pot…I will, that's all, and blow temperance. ***1856** in *OEDS:* Smoke a *pipe* of *baccer*…blow your yard of *tripe* or *nosey-me-knacker*. ***1859** Dickens *Tale Two Cities* Bk. I ch. ii: One blowed thing after another. **1867** Clark *Seven Years of a Sailor's Life* 162: Hallo, Charley; blowed if I saw you before. **1870** in "M. Twain" *Comp. Stories* 69: Oh, that be blowed! ***1888** Burnett *Editha's Burglar* 41: Well, I'm blowed…if this ain't a rummy go! **1891** *Outing* (Oct.) 72: Oh, blow it all, let's go home! **1891** Campbell, Knox & Byrnes *Darkness & Daylight* 254: Wal, I'm blowed. **1898** *Sat. Eve. Post* (June 18) 7: Wal, I'm blowed. **1898** Stevenson *Cape Horn* 147: Oh, blow that…it goes in one ear and out the other. **1909** *Bluejacket* (Dec. 15) 18: Why blow me tight! **1911** in Mager *Sherlocko* 68: Well, I'll be blowed! **1928** in Segar *Thimble Theat.* 41: Well blow me down, Cap'n, you've touched me soft spot! **1940** *Batman* 1 (unp.): Well blow me down. **1947** Motley *Knock on Any Door* 105: "Aw, blow it!" Nick yelled. **1948** J.H. Burns *Lucifer* 369: Her husband's budget be blowed! **1951** "W. Williams" *Enemy* 168: Well, blow me. **1953** W. Fisher *Waiters* 124: "Well, blow me down," she said. **1960** Leckie *Marines* 17: Aw, blow it, Stacy…you know what I mean. **1965** Spillane *Killer Mine* 14: "That's the general idea, Joe." "Then go blow it. I won't play." **1967** Schaefer *Mavericks* 127: "I'll be blowed," muttered Old Jake. **1970** Cortina *Slain Warrior* 87: Blow the cab, Professor. You come with Rosa-Rosey. **1972** in *Playboy* (Feb. 1973) 181: I don't want to take a shower, it's too much goddamned trouble…even if I do smell like a wet horse….Blow the shower.

5.a. to squander (money); to waste (time).

1874** Hotten *Slang Dict.* (ed. 4): Blew, or *Blow*…to lose or spend money. ***1889** Barrère & Leland *Dict. Slang* I 135: "I blew a bob (I wasted a shilling)," said a costermonger, "when I went to an exhibition of pictures." *ca1895** in *Independent* (Feb. 6, 1902) 334: He had Blowed

fifty bills last night…said if he made one thousand dollars per day he would Blow it. **1896** Ade *Artie* 101: No more chasin' around at nights, no blowin' my stuff against a lot o' dubs. **1899** Ade *Fables* 66: Mae bought an automobile and blew her Allowance against Beauty Doctors. **1902–03** Ade *People You Know* 156: In order to prove that I am in my right Senses, I will Blow mine [*sc.* money]. **1908** Beach *Barrier* 143: I've certainly blowed a lot of money on my friends. **1918** *Sat. Eve. Post* (Nov. 2) 5: Where'll we go blow…that ten cents? **1929** Ferber *Cimarron* 346: Blowing it on houses and travel and diamonds and high-priced cars. ***1932** in *SND* I 164: An' ye daur blaw yer maister's time swappin' drivel wi' yon cat. **1937** Steinbeck *Mice & Men* 15: They go inta town and blow their stake, and the first thing you know they're poundin' their tail on some other ranch. **1939** *New Directions* 137: Why do I write? It's as good a way to blow time as any. **1955** in Wepman et al. *The Life* 77: He tried to blow the rest of his dough. **1957** H. Smith *Religions of Man* 278: Jesus…told…of a young man who blew his entire inheritance on one huge binge and then found himself cadging scraps from the pigs. **1965** C. Brown *Manchild* 306: I got about another fifteen minutes to blow. **1983** *Comedy Store* (WKGN radio) (Mar. 5): So we blew two-and-a-half weeks in *that* village.

b. to treat (someone) as to a drink, meal, etc.; (*rarely*) to buy (drinks) for the purpose of treating.

1896 Ade *Artie* 87: I'm goin' to do the sucker act and blow myself. **1896** *DN* I 412: "*To blow oneself*," to spend money freely. **1896** in S. Crane *N.Y.C. Sks.* 163: Always somebody blowing champagne for the house. **1904** "O. Henry" *4 Million* 40: Sure, Mike,…if you'll blow me to a pail of suds. **1905** *Nat. Police Gaz.* (Nov. 11) 3: Come on, let me blow the crowd; what are you going to have, boys? **1905** *Independent* (Mar. 2) 494: Then we took our fellow clinkers up to Tchoupitoulas Street and "blowed" ourselves, after the time honored custom of seafaring men. **1911** O. Johnson *Stover at Yale* 131: I blew myself to a few glad rags. **1927** S. Lewis *E. Gantry* 19: Say, you girls change your shirts and come on out and we'll blow you to dinner, and maybe we'll dance a little. **1946** Wead & Sheekman *Blaze of Noon* (film): I'll blow you all to dinner. **1968** Wojciechowska *Tuned Out* 80: I'm going to blow mom and dad to a matinee and dinner in town this Saturday. **1978** R. Price *Ladies' Man* 118: C'mon, I'll blow you guys to Tabs.

6.a. to go about or associate.—constr. with *with*.

1895 J.L. Williams *Princeton* 122: You know the crowd you'll blow with and the clubs you'll be in.

b. *intrans.* to go or come.—used with following adv. or prep. construction; (*esp.*) to leave, esp. in a hurry; clear out (occ. constr. with *it*).—also *imper.* **go blow!** "go away!" [1866 quot. prob. reflects a colloq. or S.E. sense, "to go like the wind." Cf. BLOW IN, 2.]

[**1866** *Galaxy* (Nov. 1) 409: Smith lays his forefinger by the side of his long nose, and informs them that…Mosby has burned up White's Ford and blown up the Shenandoah Valley.] **1897** Ade *Horne* 172: If you've finished, Gertie, you might as well blow. **1902–03** Ade *People You Know* 99: A good many Improper Characters came around and sized up the Lay-Out and then blew. **1903** *Cincinnati Enquirer* (May 9) 13: *Blow*—To leave. **1908** in H.C. Fisher *A. Mutt* 73: You ought to be over at the track…Blow! **1910** T.A. Dorgan, in *N.Y. Eve. Jour.* (May 30) 7: Tad Just Blew to Frisco. **1910** *Variety* (Aug. 20) 13: We then blew over to New York. **1912** Lowrie *Prison* 281: With that he blew and left me alone. **1914** Lardner *You Know Me, Al* 131: So I got up and blowed away from the table. **1915** Lardner *Gullible's Travels* 27: I blowed down to Andy's. **1918** Witwer *Baseball to Boches* 175: Well, he blowed, Joe, and there was Jeanne and me alone for the first time. **1919** Kelly *What Outfit* 38: The manager…blew out on stage between acts. **1921** in Cray *Erotic Muse* 194: Frankie blew down to the corner. **1940** M. LeSueur *Salute to Spring* 73: We're only about a half-hour from the bridge where I blow. **1946** Petry *Street* 343: Blow it….Scram, kid. **1947** Motley *Knock on Any Door* 214: I'm going to blow. Thanks a lot. **1948** I. Shulman *Cry Tough!* 84: Blow….We don't pay off hustlers. **1950** M. Shulman *Sleep Till Noon* 74: Take the money out of the till, and blow. **1952** H. Grey *Hoods* 34: Why don't you go blow, before the sergeant catches you in here? **1957** Townley *Up in Smoke* (film): I'm sorry, now will you blow? **1965** in IUFA *Folk Speech*: To leave, given as a command: Insulting: To go blow. **1965** Himes *Imabelle* 36: They take you for your money and they blow. **1967** Colebrook *Cross of Lassitude* 237: "Go ahead…Blow it…Get going!" she orders. **1973** Haring *Stranger* 82: "Go blow, Howard," says Claudine. **1978** Barry *Ultimate Encounter* 62: Something's not right here. Let's blow. **1982** Pond *Valley Girl's Gd.* 59: Like, let's blow. **1989** "Captain X" & Dodson *Unfriendly Skies* 26: You can't just blow in and go blowing back out again.

c. *trans.* to leave (a place or (*rarely*) a person); (in recent stu.

use) in phr. of the type **blow this pop stand** leave this place.
1898 Kountz *Baxter's Letters* 19: I blew the bunch and started up the street. **1902** *Billy Burgundy's Lttrs.* 50. Then we had another and blew the joint. **1906** H. Green *Actors' Boarding House* 210: We'd better blow this burg for a while. **1908** in H.C. Fisher *A. Mutt* 21: The Mrs. blew him this morning and it looks like curtains for the home cooking. **1915** T.A. Dorgan, in *N.Y. Eve. Jour.* (Aug. 16) 10: I'll blow the court at 2 and meet you at the beach. **1915–16** Lait *Beef, Iron & Wine* 186: We blows the place. **1918** *Chi. Sun. Trib.* (Mar. 24) V (unp.): They blew…the premises. **1926** Dunning & Abbott *Broadway* 231: The surest way…would be to blow town. **1929** *Bookman* (Apr.) 150: "Blowing the show" [means] running away from an engagement. **1932** Binyon & Binyon *If I Had a Million* (film): I gotta blow town and I'm in a terrible spot. **1938** in Brookhouser *Our Years* 386: I'll tell you how to save yourself.…Blow your job…I'll blow my job too. **1957** T. Jones *Some Came Running* 137: Let's you and me blow this place. **1959** in Oster *Country Blues* 77: Oh Lord, I got to stop drinkin', Lord, I got to blow this town. **1959** Maier *College Terms* 3: Blow this hole—to leave the place you are in. **1969** *Playboy* (Dec.) 228: Say, you wanna blow the joint now? **1972** *N.Y. Post* (Nov. 17) 85: Mick wanted to hear some music so we blew the hotel and headed downtown. **1974** Univ. Tenn. student: Let's blow this pop stand. **1980** *Mork & Mindy* (ABC-TV): How about you and me blow this Popsicle stand? **1983** *Nat. Lampoon* (Feb.) 16: Let's blow this popcorn stand. **1982–84** Safire *Take My Word* 112: Let's blow this popstand.…Let's blow this popsicle stand. **1984** Algeo *Stud Buds & Dorks*: Blow this…joint/popcorn stand/popsicle stand/taco stand. **1980–89** Chesire *Home Boy* 191 [ref. to 1960's]: Let's blow this Popsicle stand. **1990** *Tiny Toon Adventures* (synd. TV series): If I didn't have tenure I'd blow this pop stand.

d. to get rid of, dismiss (an employee); jilt.
1922 *Variety* (Aug. 18) 5: She had blowed one guy who got all battered up in France. **1960** C. Cooper *Scene* 179: If I didn't think you had the makings of a damn good Narco man, I'd have blown you a good while back.

7.a. to spoil or ruin.
1899 Kountz *Baxter's Letters* 78: You're getting so lately you turn them tears on every night.…You've blowed half our make-up as it is. **1923** *N.Y. Times* (Sept. 9) VIII 2: Blow the Scene: The effect of a scene being messed up through an actor changing the business. **1939** Howsley *Argot* 8: Blowed the Works—made a failure of an undertaking; divulged information. **1964** "Dr. X" *Intern* 144: Well, that blew it. **1968** *N.Y.P.D.* (ABC-TV): That blows his alibi. **1970** in *Rolling Stone Interviews* 408: I do want to blow this political system. **1982** *N.Y. Times* (June 30) A 20: Playing a record backwards will blow your turntable.

b. to botch; bungle; (*specif.*) to lose (a game, a race, an opportunity, money, etc.), esp. through bungling.— often constr. with *it*. Also absol.
1907 in H.C. Fisher *A. Mutt* 3: He blew 10 on "Serenity" [a racehorse]. **1921** J. Conway, in *Variety* (June 17) 7: We blew two ball games to Toronto…because Cuthbert and Algy refused to slide after about a half an hours rain. **1923** in Brookhouser *Our Years* 288: Maybe he means if we pitch to Ruth we'll blow the game. **1928** Coe *Swag* 179: I didn't want to blow that chance. **1928** Sharpe *Chicago May* 67: The sucker…reached into his pocket, and found that his money had been blown. **1930** D. Runyon, in *Collier's* (Jan. 20) 12: I know how it annoys him to blow easy shots. **1930** [Conwell] *Prof. Thief* 28: But when grifting he never criticized the action of any member of his mob; if they blew a score (failed in an attempted theft), it was just blowed. **1932** D. Runyon, in *Collier's* (Mar. 26) 9: You owe me a two-dollar marker for the bet you blow on Cold Cuts. **1933** J.V. Allen *Cowboy Lore* 59: Blowing A Stirrup, Losing a stirrup, which disqualifies a rider. **1933** D. Runyon, in *Collier's* (Feb. 11): Herbie bets the eleven C's…on another good thing in the next race, and this good thing blows. **1934** Weseen *Dict. Slang* 205: Blow a game—to lose a game as the result of errors. **1936** Dai *Opium Add.* 196: Blow a shot. To lose a shot. **1936** Miller *Battling Bellhop* (film): You ain't gonna break your hands on a punk like that on a title shot? **1940** Burnett *High Sierra* 74: He'd taken a chance on blowing the biggest opportunity he'd ever had in his life. **1942** Nichols *Air Force* (film): You blew it. **1943** in Mahurin *Honest John* 130: In fact, I've blown some darned good chances by just that sort of an attack. **1950** Cleveland *Great Mgrs.* 190: Then at Brooklyn they held a 5-to-0 lead with one out in the ninth, and blew the game 6 to 5. **1952** Holmes *Boots Malone* (film): You'll be forced to whip left-handed or blow the race. **1954** in Wepman et al. *The Life* 41: She shrugged and sat 'cause she knew she had blew. **1957** Mulvihill *Five Mission* 16: You were more afraid of blowing an inspection than anything else. **1958** Mayes *Hunters*

(film): Take it easy and don't blow it. **1959** Morrill *Dark Sea* 168: Sir, the Old Man's blown his marbles. He's spraying the Jap sub with gasoline. **1969** *Current Slang* I & II 11: Blow,…v. To miss an opportunity.—College students, both sexes, South Dakota. **1972** T.C. Bambara *Gorilla* 140: And you realize you blew, but too late. **1976** Rosen *Above Rim* 236: And Collins blows the shot! The ball dinked off the front rim! *Ibid.* 4: You blew the call! You choke bastard! **1981** Wolf *Roger Rabbit* 104: He was about to blow his biggest sale of the decade. *a*1991 Dennis Quaid, in B. Greene *Midwestern Boy* 257: I remember meeting Marlon Brando, who was my idol, and totally blowing it.

c. to fail; come to nothing.
1917 in Truman *Dear Bess* 213: If this venture blows, I'll know I'm hoodooed.

d. to miss (a train, an appointment, or the like); (*also*) to pass through (a traffic signal) unlawfully.
1918 T.A. Dorgan, in *N.Y. Eve. Jour.* (Aug. 8) 14: I'll blow my rattler sure—it leaves at 2:46. **1972** Wambaugh *Blue Knight* 49: I…told her about the guy I stopped for blowing a red light at Second and San Pedro. *Ibid.*: 183 This guy blew the stop sign and I chased him. **1976** "N. Ross" *Policeman* 147: He claimed the cops had stopped him…for blowing a red light. **1990** *Cops* (Fox-TV): She blew the stoplight at Alessandro.

8. to lose one's composure under pressure; crack; (*specif.*) (of an actor) to forget one's lines. [Recent use has been influenced by *blow (one's) top* s.v. TOP, and similar phrs. and by **(7.b.),** above.]
1907 *N.Y. Eve. Jour.* (Apr. 25) (cited in Nichols *Baseball Term.*). **1944** W. Duff *Marine Raiders* (film): I blew for a moment. What about it? **1952** Himes *First Stone* 172: And then he blew. He went off like a V-Two Rocket. **1956** Ross *Hustlers* 99: That's when I blew…"What do you mean, *you* got it all set?" **1959** Searls *Big X* 213: Don't blow.…You've taken it up to now.…It's only two more days. **1963** Hayden *Wanderer* 51: Even then, with a script to read, I blew. **1966** "Minnesota Fats" *Bank Shot* 82: Now, Bojangles was the easiest-going fellow you ever met, but if he got the idea some mooch was giving him the filage, he would really blow high. **1969** in *New American Review* 7 (Aug.) 207: Everyone was waiting for me to fold, to blow sky high. **1968–71** Cole & Black *Checking* 233: "Victor's fighting Nuny." "Holy shit, Victor finally blew. He'll kill him." **1971** Glasser *365 Days* 13: No one blew. If we'd panicked, I'd be dead. **1972** Burkhart *Women in Prison* 23: She went in and saw the broad hanging there and just blew it. She really flipped out. **1973–76** J. Allen *Assault* 152: He tried to make JoJo blow, but JoJo hung in there. **1989** *Donahue* (NBC-TV): "Did you blow?" "I cried.…I went into therapy."

9.a. to fellate or (much less freq.) to perform cunnilingus upon.—usu. considered vulgar.
*ca*1930 in K. White *First Sex. Revolution* 95: "Ever run up against a fag?" "Plenty." "What do they do? Blow you?"…"That is all." **1934** "J.M. Hall" *Anecdota* 76: Have you been blue while I was gone?" "Blown, dear, blown!" **1936** in Oliver *Blues Tradition* 174: I can blow your hole till the auger-man comes. **1938** "Justinian" *Americana Sexualis* 13: Blow. v.…*penis in ora*. **1940** *Tale of a Twist* 17: Maybe he thought I should be paid by the hour for blowing him. **1952** Kerouac *Cody* 183: That night was the first night that Elly blew me. **1955** Caprio *Vars. in Sex. Behavior* 109: When we were finished f—g…I asked her to "blow me." **1957** Yablonsky *Violent Gang* 200: After this queer bastard blew us (*laughs*), we beat the hell out of him—but good. **1960** Updike *Rabbit, Run* 185: You were a real hooer?…Did you blow guys? **1961** J. Baldwin *Another Country* 64: I just want to get laid—blowed—loved—one more time. **1969** Sidney *Love of Dying* 84: I want to get blowed. **1971** Contini *Beast Within* 43: Why, I'd love to blow your cock. **1973** Huggett *Body Count* 182: I always said it's not what ya know or who ya know but who ya blow. **1974** E. Thompson *Tattoo* 292: "It ain't who you know, it's who you blow," they consoled themselves. **1977** in Cheever *Letters* 336: Women.…You can blow them, fuck them, [etc.].

b. in phr. **blow yourself!** "go to hell!" Cf. **(4),** above, and *blow it,* below.
1957 Kohner *Gidget* 25: Ah—blow yourself. **1986** J. Hughes *Ferris Bueller* (film): Are you serious?…Blow yourself!

c. to be hateful, contemptible, inferior, etc. SUCK.—usu. considered vulgar.
1960 Reuss & Legman *Songs Mother Never Taught Me* (unp.): Hell Week really blows! **1976** Univ. Tenn. student: The situation really blows. **1986** Gilmour *Pretty in Pink* 81: That won't change the fact that this school blows. **1988** Dye *Outrage* 78: The whole position is like a jet engine: It sucks and blows!

d. to curry favor with; BROWNNOSE.—usu. considered vulgar.

1968 Baker et al. *CUSS* 82: *Blow*…Curry favor with a professor. **1975** Univ. Tenn. instructor, age *ca*30: One of my students tried to blow me at the beginning of class today. **1984** "W.T. Tyler" *Shadow Cabinet* 9: He's blowing every right-winger in town with that spiel, blowing 'em big, right on the tube.

10. *Jazz.* **a.** [generalized from specialized S.E. senses, 'to play (a trumpet or other wind instrument)', 'to play (music) on a wind instrument'] to play (music or any variety of musical instrument); to perform (music or other material); to perform in (an engagement). Also intrans.

1949 in *OEDS.* **1951** *Amer. Jour. Sociol.* XXXVII 140: There aren't any jobs where you can blow jazz. You have to play rumbas and pops and everything. You can't get anywhere blowing jazz….It sure is a drag blowing commercial. **1951** Kerouac *Cody* 38: We blew two hours, me on bop-chords piano. **1950–52** Ulanov *Hist. Jazz* 350: *Blow*: verb used to describe playing of the brass and reeds; in modern jazz parlance, used of all the jazz instruments ("he blows fine piano"). **1953** Russ *Parallel* 330: A jumping Nipponese combo was blowing a strange kind of jazz. *ca*1953 Hughes *Fantastic Lodge* 69: He was always blowing gigs with this square band. And they would play these gigs…for teen-agers. *Ibid.* 113: I'm not going to ever blow again. **1954** W.G. Smith *South St.* 99: You Paddy-talk, you can't blow with Caldonia. **1956** E. Hunter *Second Ending* 137: You blow accordion. **1955–57** Kerouac *On Road* 14: The fellows at the Loop blew but, with a tired air, because bop was somewhere between Charlie Parker…and Miles Davis. *Ibid.* 147: Everybody in Frisco blew. **1958** Ferlinghetti *Coney I.* 11: As if he is *the* king cat/ Who's got to blow/Or they can't quite make it. **1958–59** Lipton *Barbarians* 22: What was it about *any* art except to just cut in and blow, man, just *blow.* *Ibid.* 26: Are we gonna blow some poetry. **1959** A. Anderson *Lover Man* 152: "You blow?"…"Blow?" "Yeah. You play anything?…I blow box [piano]." **1959** *Swinging Syllables: Blow*—To play any musical instrument, often one which is not actually blown as bass or drums. **1961** H. Ellison *Gentleman Junkie* 204: You blow piano that's more than piano. **1961** R. Russell *Sound* 74: You blew piano with Jimmy Vann, huh? **1962** H. Simmons *On Eggshells* 155: Johnny blew [drums] for Charlie. **1963** Braly *Shake Him* 55: The Cambodian prince…blew bongos. **1964** Barthelme *Dr. Caligari* 145: Do you blow good, man? Where's your axe? **1967** Kolb *Getting Straight* 2: At night, he blew fair piano in a jazz group. **1983** *N.Y. Daily News* (Mar. 25): Teentalk glossary…*blow*—sing.

b. to create, whip up.

1957 in *DAS* 45: "He blows great conversation." "She blows scrambled eggs from endville." **1959–60** Reisner *Jazz Titans* 151: He blows fine poetry. **1965** Lurie *Nowhere City* 86: How about if I blow us some eggs, and you can call it an omelette?

11. to vomit, esp. from overindulgence in alcohol.—usu. constr. with a specific or general food item having rhetorical rather than literal meaning, of the type *blow lunch, blow beets.*

1950 Bissell *Stretch on the River* 52: Neither did she get drunk and blow lunch. **1962** Mandel *Mainside* 358: I blow my lunch…because the boys go drinking and I want to be one of the boys. **1968** Baker et al. *CUSS* 82: *Blow beads.* Vomit. *Blow beets.* Vomit. *Ibid.* 83: *Blow dinner…blow lunch.* Vomit. **1969** *Current Slang* I & II 11: *Blow lunch*, v. Regurgitate.—Air Force Academy cadets. **1971** *Playboy* (Jan.) 182: The sour expression of a man who's blown lunch and missed the bowl. **1971** *Current Slang* V 8: *Blow beets*, v. To vomit. **1971** Dahlskog *Dict.* 8: *Blow lunch*, v. To vomit. **1972** *Nat. Lampoon* (Feb.) 6: [He] just *blows lunch right in the guy's face!!!* **1973** *TULIPQ* (coll. B.K. Dumas): *Blow beets.* **1978** Eble *Campus Slang* (Nov.) 1: *Blow groceries*—vomit. **1978** Univ. Tenn. student questionnaire: *Blow beans*—throw up. **1979** Gutcheon *New Girls* 253: She's gonna blow lunch. **1981** Eble *Campus Slang* (Oct.) 1: *Blow grits*—vomit: He drank too much and blew grits. **1983** Huntsville, Ala., teenager: Her old man was blowin' chow in every direction. **1984** Algeo *Stud Buds & Dorks*: To vomit…*blow beets, …chow, …chunks, …cookies, …doughnuts, …grits, …groceries, …lunch, …oats, …tacos.* **1986** *Newsweek* (June 9) 73: So sick that he blew a meal all over [a] fellow actor. **1987** Univ. Tenn. student theme: Some of them get sick and blow a few groceries. **1989** P. Munro *UCLA Slang* 22: If you're going to blow cookies, get out of the car.

12. to pitch (a ball) hard.

1952 in *DAS* 45: Joe Black…[was] blowing his fast one past Yankee bats for a 4-2 win. **1962** Houk & Dexter *Ballplayers* 114: Jim Coates…reminds me of the tall, hardy hillbilly pitchers who used to blow speed and curves over the plate before the war. **1969–71** Kahn *Boys of Summer* 276: That young feller found out right then, you didn't

just blow one by Ole Preach. **1973** C. Gowdy, on *World Series Baseball* (Oct. 16) He blew that one by him.

13. *Mil.* to spring (an ambush).

1984 Riggan *Free Fire* 20 [ref. to Vietnam War]: Him and four of his ARVNs blew an ambush on them.

14. [fr. BLOW AWAY, 3.b., or *blow (one's) mind*, below] to astound.

1986 *Miami Vice* (NBC-TV): That poem you read the other night. It blew everybody.

¶ In phrases:

¶ **blow a cloud** to smoke, esp. a pipe.

***1819** [Moore] *Tom Crib's Mem.* 39: A civiller *Swell*/I'd never wish to *blow* a *cloud** with!…*To smoke a pipe. **1843** Strong *Diary* I 211: It's a Paixhan among pipes—fit to solace the leisure moments of…"cloud-blowing" Jupiter Nicotianus. **1849** [G. Thompson] *Venus in Boston* 26: In this room…they could "ply the lush," and "blow a cloud." **1859** Matsell *Vocab.* 12: *Blow a cloud.* Smoke a segar or pipe. ***1882** in *SND* I 163: He filled his cutty, drank his gill, and tried a cloud to blaw. **1882** *Frank James on the Trail* 42: Two of the mounted force were also engaged in the arduous duty of "blowing a cloud."

¶ **blow a fuse** to go crazy or, (*esp.*) become furiously angry.

1938 Haines *Tension* 187: And instead of blowing a fuse so quick, just think it over. **1940** in Goodstone *Pulps* 117: Spill your story to the nice apoplectic detective before he blows a fuse. **1941** Macaulay & Wald *Manpower* (film): Forget about it or you'll blow a fuse. **1942** *ATS* 869: *Blow a fuse* [go insane]. **1950** Maddow & Huston *Asphalt Jungle* 19: Can you beat that? Where does he come off…blowing a fuse—. **1956** Hargrove *Girl He Left* 143: What's with you, Sheaffer? You blown a fuse or something? **1958** Hughes & Bontemps *Negro Folklore* 481: *Blow your fuse.* To get angry. *That landlady made me blow my fuse.* **1963** Rubin *Sweet Daddy* 86: This joint stinks.…Still, not going to blow a fuse over it. **1966** Jarrett *Pvt. Affair* 77: Maryanne really blew her fuse when she learned that Jack had become involved with…Zelda.

¶ **blow a gasket** see s.v. GASKET.

¶ **blow a valve** [or tube] *blow a fuse,* above.

1954 "Collans" & Sterling *House Detect.* 211: Don't worry about ol' Doc blowing his valve. He'll forget all about it, by mornin'. **1971** Sorrentino *Up from Never* 107: Whadda ya blowin' ya tube fa? So I got fired from that crummy sweatshop that bleeds ya fa a buck an hour.

¶ **blow a vein** to suffer an apoplectic stroke from a fit of rage.

1989 *Dream Street* (NBC-TV): Don't blow a vein, Pop.

¶ **blow blood** *Whaling.* to have a nosebleed.

1833 N. Ames *Old Sailor's Yarns* 234: One of the sailors, feeling somewhat restive under the tight grasp that the corporal laid upon his collar, had [given him] a slap in the face, that caused him, in the Nantucket dialect, to "blow blood."

¶ **blow foam** to drink beer.

*ca*1895 in Dolph *Sound Off*: It was ten dollars less to blow foam.

¶ **blow it** (used as an insulting retort). Cf. **(4)**, **(9.b.)**, above, and *blow it out* s.v. BLOW OUT, *v.*

1879 Dacus *Frank & Jesse* 128: "What's up, strangers, anyhow?" "You blow it! Don't you know that the Corydon bank, up in Iowa, was robbed yesterday?" **1943** *Yank* (Oct. 22) 14: "Get those lights out, second platoon."…"Blow it!" **1944** in Butterfield *Post Treasury* 436: And if the boss got too cranky, he could tell him to go blow it. **1946** J.H. Burns *Gallery* 99: Ah, blow it. **1950** Stuart *Objector* 132: You tell him to blow it. **1951** "W. Williams" *Enemy* 22: Well, you can blow it. You can blow it straight out. **1958** Frankel *Band of Bros.* 84: Can it! Stow it! Blow it! **1959** Cochrell *Barren Beaches* 30: Blow it, Jack.

¶ **blow (one's) cool** see s.v. COOL, *n.*

¶ **blow (one's) cork** see s.v. CORK.

¶ **blow (one's) head** [or skull] *blow (one's) mind,* below.

1953 Hunter *Jungle Kids* 27: Here, man.…Blow your skull. **1968** S. Ross *Hang Up* 84: I'll blow my skull if anybody asks me any questions. **1971** N.Y.U. student: It'll really blow his head. **1971** N.Y.C. bus rider, age *ca*30: Man, I'm gonna blow my head around here! **1980** M. Baker *Nam* 77: What blew my head was what they did to calm me down.

¶ **blow (one's)** [or the] **lid** to go crazy, *flip (one's) lid* s.v. FLIP, *v.*

1935 Lamson *About to Die* 187: An' when she finds out about his money bein' gone she blows the lid for fair. **1944** in Himes *Black on Black* 202: Then it come to me all of a sudden I must be blowin' my lid. **1972** Carpenter *Flight One* 268: Mr. Moeller kind of blew his lid a little, that's all.

¶ **blow (one's) mind, 1.** to lose (one's) mind, go crazy;

(hence) to begin to act without restraint.

1965 John Sebastian *Do You Believe in Magic* (song) (Faithful Virtue Music Co., Inc.): Your feet start tappin' and you can't seem to find/ How you got there so just blow your mind! **1966** in *OEDS*: The Barry Goldberg Blues Band...does an LP called "Blowin' My Mind." **1966** Reynolds & McClure *Freewheelin Frank* 153: Your husband blew his mind and went to that eastern mental ward. **1968** S. Ross *Hang Up* 27: She couldn't stand it. Something had to happen. She'd blow her mind if it didn't. **1968** O.H. Hampton *Young Runaways* (film): You're blowin' your mind. **1987** Averill *Mustang* 304: There was even a resident psychiatrist if you had blown your mind.

2. to alter (one's) perceptions through the use of hallucinogenic drugs, esp. LSD; to become elated or ecstatic through the use of such drugs.

1965 in H. Thompson *Hell's Angels* 255: Blowing our minds and theirs—/softening them, enlarging their consciousness. **1966** *N.Y. Times* (Mar. 21) 1: He regularly turned on with marijuana or blew his mind with LSD. **1966** Goldstein *1 in 7* 189: They are after fun, and every night as they suck upon their treated sugar cubes, they wig-out, they blow their minds. **1967** Bronsteen *Hippy's Hndbk.* 12: *Blow your mind*...to be totally overwhelmed by a new perception on or off drugs.

3. to make insane; to destroy (one's) power of reason.

1966 Reynolds & McClure *Freewheelin Frank* 52: They wanted to blow my mind. **1966** H. Thompson *Hell's Angels* 192: She came to the party...with a big St. Bernard dog, and what an *act* she put on! I tell you it damn near blew my mind. **1970** Cole *Street Kids* 57: He ate with derelict patients, most with their minds blown on rotgut or other exotic Bowery libations. **1971** S. Stevens *Way Uptown* 76: When they ganged him, it blew his mind. **1974** Cherry *High Steel* 99: What does anybody know about what it takes to blow a man's mind?

4. to shock, surprise, stun, dazzle, or amaze (someone); to frighten or panic (someone).

1966 H. Thompson *Hell's Angels* 13: We really blew their minds this time. **1967** *Time* (July 7) 20: Blow the mind of every straight person you can reach. Turn them on, if not to drugs, then to beauty, love, honesty, fun. **1967** Rechy *Numbers* 136: Beautiful....You blew my mind baby. **1967** Yablonsky *Hippie Trip* 25: We all went out on the porch and SANG to them! It just blew their minds, man. **1968** A. Hoffman *Revolution* 66: I enjoy blowing people's minds. You know, walking up to somebody and saying, "Would you hold this dollar for me while I...steal something?" The crazier the better. **1975** *Wond. World of Disney* (NBC-TV): When I tell the guys I flew in a real biplane, it'll blow their minds! **1983** *Rolling Stone* (Feb. 3) 14: It blew his mind that a twenty-nine-year-old was operating on his wife and saving his baby. **1985** B.E. Ellis *Less Than Zero* 188: I've got something at my place that will blow your mind. **1988** *N.Y. Daily News* (June 18) 29: Every once in a while I love to blow their minds like that. **1992** *Freshman Dorm* (CBS-TV): We have an obligation to...seek new ways to blow people's minds.

¶ **blow (one's) nose** *Whaling.* (of a whale) to spout.

1849 Mackay *Western World* I 9: To what exclamations did he not give rise from old and young, as he "blew his nose" as the Alabamian termed blowing a column of water high into the air.

¶ **blow (one's) roof** to go crazy.

1958 Camerer *Damned Wear Wings* 181: So I'm blowing my roof....Is that queer?

¶ **blow (one's) stack** to lose (one's) composure under pressure; (*esp.*) to fly into a rage; go crazy.—occ. used causatively.

1941 Kendall *Army & Navy Slang* 2: He blew his stack...got excited and made a series of mistakes. **1954** Schulberg *Waterfront* 95: Well, gee whiz, ya don't hafta blow ya stack about it! **1957** Gutwillig *Silence* 180: Anyone would blow his stack sooner or later in a mess like this. **1958** Cooley *Run for Home* 267: Is that why you blew your stack? **1959** Southern and Hoffenberg *Candy* 89: Perhaps it would be wiser if Miss Christian didn't see you first thing when she regains consciousness....She might blow her stack. **1960** Leckie *Marines* 14: I probably blew my stack clean through the roof, because I don't remember anything...except charging out...roaring like a bull. **1963** D. Tracy *Brass Ring* 327: Go back to duty?...What did they want him to do, blow his stack completely? **1966** S. Harris *Hellhole* 87: That made me blow my stack...and I packed my clothes and everything and walked out. **1967** N.Y.C. man, age *ca*50: That just blew my stack. **1969** Bullock *Watts* 116: And I just blew my stack, and I got so mad until I cursed her out, and then I cursed the fat woman out, too. **1972** *Odd Couple* (ABC-TV): No wonder Gloria blew her stack! **1980** *N.Y. Post* (Mar. 13) 1: Sen. Edward Kennedy last night blew his stack for the first time at his Chappaquiddick critics. **1981** D. Burns *Feeling Good* 130: Isn't it *human* just

to get angry and blow your stack? **1991** Lott & Lieber *Total Impact* 203: Glanville was irate. He blew his stack.

¶ **blow (one's) top** see s.v. TOP.

¶ **blow sky-high** to rebuke; BLOW UP, 1.

1848 in Barnum *Letters* 39: Her father...blowed her sky-high. **1856** in C.A. Abbey *Before the Mast* 47: The captain blew the mate Sky-high for it but he didn't care.

¶ **blow smoke** see s.v. SMOKE.

¶ **blow steam** to talk emptily.

1955–57 A. Miller *View from Bridge* 17: You think I'm blowin' steam here?

¶ **blow the doors off** see s.v. DOOR.

¶ **blow the gaff** see s.v. GAFF, *n.*

¶ **blow the pipe** to perform fellatio.—usu. considered vulgar.

1917–20 Dreiser *Newspaper Days* 590 [ref. to 1894]: They go down on you—blow the pipe—play the flute. Aren't you on?

¶ **blow the show** [or **scene**] to ruin the entire situation; fail; miss out.

1967 Moorse *Duck* 138: You mean they're going to blow the show, Doc? **1967** Weiss & Lawrence *Easy Come* (film): Yoga....You're either with it all the way, or you've blown the scene. **1989** *48 Hours* (CBS-TV): He's really been blowin' the show this nine weeks.

¶ **blow the whistle** see s.v. WHISTLE.

¶ **blow this pop** [or **popcorn**, etc.] **stand** see (**6. c.**), above.

¶ **blow Z's** to sleep, esp. soundly.

1968 Baker et al. *CUSS* 83: *Blow Z's, ready to.* Very tired. **1975** S.P. Smith *Amer. Boys* 158: Maybe he'd just stay in his tent and blow Z's for a few days.

blow away *v.* **1.** [orig. So. dial., given wide currency during the Vietnam War] **a.** to shoot dead; to kill, as by gunfire or explosion; to destroy, as by explosion.

1913 in Cox *Folk-Songs* 179: John Hardy drew his pistol from his pocket/And threw it down on the tray,/Saying, "The man that uses my yellow girl's money,/I'm going to blow him away, away,/I'm going to blow him away." **1923** in Cox *Folk-Songs* 183: John Hardy will blow him away. **1939** in A. Banks *First-Person* 251: A bunch of them wops showed up in a car n tried to blow him away. **1962** Crump *Killer* 194: But hell, he nearly blowed me away. **1968** *Evening News* (CBS-TV) (Feb. 28): We had to blow the village away. **1969** Whittemore *Cop* 103: My partner blew away one of them burglars today. **1969** *Esquire* (Sept.) 118: His oldest friend had been blown away in January. **1970** *N.Y. Times Mag.* (Feb. 8) 31: We blew their —— away. *Ibid.* 95: If he moves, blow the sonofabitch away. **1970** R.N. Williams *New Exiles* 276: He just reached down for his weapon and blew her away. **1972** *N.Y. Times Mag.* (Dec. 17) 50: Yeah, I blew 'em away like they're f— nothing. **1972–76** Durden *No Bugles* 103: If you ever come anywhere near me I'm gonna blow you away like a big wind. **1982** Del Vecchio *13th Valley* 34: A sniper would blow one of them away. **1983** *Judge Dredd* (comics) (Nov.) (6): Rapid fire! Blow his bones away! **1986** *Time* (Mar. 17) 63: The drivers almost always keep their mouths shut, since they have been told that their wives and kids will be blown away otherwise.

b. *Mil.* to wound seriously by explosion.

1967 in Briscoe *Short-Timer* 30: I was loading an ammo truck and I got blowed away. **1973** Browne *Body Shop* 103: I'd like to talk to guys who are going to Nam....There's no one better than someone who got blowed away to tell you.

2. to defeat decisively; pass (an examination) easily; deal with (a difficulty) handily; ruin; overcome.

1962–63 in Giallombardo *Soc. of Women* 201: *Blow Away.* To silence by forceful argument. **1974** Univ. Tenn. student: I just blew that test away. **1975** *JAF* LXXXVIII 171: Gawain and his men blew away the Danish contingent facing them. **1977** *Nat. Lampoon* (Jan.) 91: The Venturi concept blew away traditional approaches to loudspeaker design. **1977** *Baa Baa Black Sheep* (NBC-TV): I could take you just like your exec and blow you away [in a fistfight]. **1983** *Business Week* (Oct. 10) 102: We'll blow away the low-cost competitors. *a***1989** in Kisseloff *Must Remember This* 325: Benny Goodman...had a band contest with Chick Webb, and he got blown away.

3.a. to make drunk or high.—esp. as ppl. adj. **blown** [or **blowed**] **away.**

1968–70 *Current Slang* III & IV 12: *Blowed away*, adj. Drunk.—General young adults, both sexes, Ohio. **1973** Univ. Mich. student: *Wasted, wrecked, blown away.* They all mean stoned. **1978** *Nat. Lampoon* (Oct.) 4: Blown away, you know, stoned, high, smashed, blotto, wigged...shitfaced. **1979** Hiler *Monkey Mt.* 105: Steve and I got blown away at the club. I insisted on buying. **1979** J. Morris *War Story* 198: He was fairly blown away by then. **1975–82** (Forms *blown away, blowed away*, (rarely) *blew away* heard regularly from Univ. Tenn. students). **1968–90** Linderer *Eyes of Eagle* 217: We spent the evening drinking and getting totally blown away.

b. to surprise, delight, shock, thrill, stun, etc., completely; to overwhelm.

1975 Univ. Tenn. *Daily Beacon* (May 26) 2: Days like this just blow me away—seems like all the world's at peace with itself. **1978** Maupin *Tales* 154: You blow me away sometimes. **1980** Birnbach *Preppy Hndbk.* 218: *Blow away v.* To impress, overwhelm. Also, *blow me away:* "I'm impressed." **1982** S. Black *Awesome Val Guide* 4: They did! It blew me away. **1990** *CBS This Morning* (CBS-TV) (Mar. 20): We were just talking about how blown away we were by Joshua Bell. **1992** *TV Guide* (Sept. 5) 10: He was totally blown away that I'd actually do this.

blowback *n.* repercussions.

1981 D.E. Miller *Jargon* 215: *Blow-back.* Adverse repercussions from an [intelligence] agency operation. **1968–90** Linderer *Eyes of Eagle* 112: Because of some of the blowback from the…incident.

blow back *v.* to return; (*Trans.*) return (money); esp. KICK BACK.

1908 Kelley *Oregon Pen.* 13: He had to blow back $10 to Patsy. **1925–26** Black *You Can't Win* 200: She…orders me to blow back the jane's nine bucks. **1927–28** Tasker *Grimhaven* 139: Come on, you fellows—blow back with the glasses! ***1939** in Partridge *DSUE* (ed. 7) 1015: He was a man who "blew money back to the course" and saved bookmakers from heavy losses. **1981** Graziano & Corsel *Somebody Down Here* 188: He always blows back with the swag.

blowboy *n.* a fellator; (*hence*) a sycophantic fellow.—used contemptuously.—usu. considered vulgar.

1935 (cited in Partridge *Dict. Und.* 52). **1988–90** M. Hunter *Abused Boys* 273 [ref. to *ca*1975]: They would call me names like "the little blow-boy," "kiss-ass," and others, all basically saying the same thing. **1992** Mowry *Way Past Cool* 134: Sellin yourself…Like a blow boy.

blow down *v.* **1.** [orig. dial.] to shoot down; shoot dead.

1871 Still *Underground R.R.* 433: Jim had a…pistol and counted on "blowing a man down if anyone touched" him. **1875** Nowlin *Bark Covered House* 24 [ref. to 1833]: John have the pistols ready….Be ready now and blow them down the moment they burst open the door. **1924** in Cox *Folk-Songs* 187: The very first man that wins my money/I sure will blow him down. **1926** Odum & Johnson *Negro Wk. Songs* 70: Shot my pistol/In the heart o' town./Lawd, the big chief hollered,/"Doncha blow me down." **1933** in Emrich *Folk Poetry* 728: Late last night I was a-making my rounds,/Met my woman and I blowed her down. **1937** Herndon *Let Me Live* 328: Shotguns and pistols/All around me/To blow me down/O Lawd, to blow me down. **1938** Chandler *Big Sleep* 80: Don't send me any more gun punks with orders. I might get hysterical and blow one down. **1940** Lomax & Lomax *Singing Country* 343: Blowed him down….Well, he shot bad Laz'us, partner. **1944** Wheeler *Steamboatin'* 110: Overtook my woman an' I blowed her down….The verdict, murder in the first degree. **1949** "R. MacDonald" *Moving Target* 151: You blow Eddie down when he ain't even heeled. **1963** Charters *Poetry of Blues* 89: I met this joker one morning….I had to talk and plead to keep him from blowing me down. **1971** Polner *Victory Parades* 37: The gook who already has a round in his chamber could blow down a point man, radio man, platoon leader [etc.]. **1975** Wambaugh *Choirboys* 53: You'd like to blow 'em down, wouldn't you? **1986** *Mystery of Capone's Vaults* (WGN-TV): If it was up to me I'd take those two thousand bums, put 'em in Soldier's Field in Chicago, get me another Jack McGurn and blow 'em down.

2. *Naut.* to knock down, send sprawling.

1886 in *JAF* (Apr. 1946) 110: Blow the man down in the hold below. **1912** in R.C. Murphy *Logbook* 103: Give me some time to blow the man down. **1927** Finger *Frontier Ballads* 158: They gave me three months in old Waltontown jail/For booting and kicking and blowing him down. **1961** Hugill *Shanties* 322 [ref. to 1920's]: An' he blowed me down an' kicked me hard a-stern-O.

3. to defeat thoroughly, trounce.

1962 Houk & Dexter *Ballplayers* 118: He'd been the hero of the '58 series, hurling two beautiful games to blow the Braves down.

4. to pass at great speed.

1984 W. Murray *Dead Crab* 211: Charlie's gonna blow him down in the stretch.

blowed see BLOWN.

blowed-in-the-glass var. BLOWN-IN-THE-GLASS.

blowen *n.* [orig. unkn.] *Und.* a woman or girl, esp. if promiscuous; BROAD. Also **blower, blowing.**

*1673 R. Head *Canting Academy* 35: *Blower* One man's particular wench. ***1688** Shadwell *Squire of Alsatia* (gloss.): *Blowing*…a Mistress, or rather a Whore. *Ibid.* II i: My pretty *Blowing* let me kiss thee. ***1788** Grose *Vulgar Tongue* (ed. 2) 52: *Blower* or *Blowen.* A mistress or whore of a gentleman of the scamp. ***1789** G. Parker *Life's Painter* 134: His *blowen*, a female ballad-singer, now joins him. *Ibid.* 151: *Blowen.* A woman. **1791** [W. Smith] *Confess. T. Mount* 18: A woman, a *blowen*….A lady, a *fine blowen.* ***1805** J. Davis *Post-Captain* 76: I have done with blowings, sir….I am spliced. *Ibid.* 165: I can strut up to a blowing…but [not] a modest woman. **1805** *Port Folio* (Aug. 24) 261: No kiddy…sports a finer blowing. **1807** Tufts *Narrative* 293 [ref. to 1794]: *To do him of his blowen*…to rob him of his wife. ***1812** Vaux *Vocab.*: *Blowen.* A prostitute: a woman who cohabits with a man without marriage. ***1821** *Real Life in Ireland* 48: Many a *blood*, and many a *blowen* remember her. ***1839** H. Brandon *Poverty* (gloss.): *Blower*—a girl; a contemptuous name in opposition to jomer. **1848** *Ladies' Repository* (Oct.) 315: *Blowen*, A "strange woman." **1848** [Thompson] *House Breaker* 42: "The Captain is *cutting it fat*, living in this *flash crib*, and having that pretty little girl for a *blowen.*"…"I was going to **** that same little *blowen*, in Boy Jack's *crib*, after I had bought her of her father." *Ibid.* 44: *Blowen* signifies a sweetheart. **1851** [G. Thompson] *Jack Harold* 60: Here's a health to each fair *blowen.**…**Blowen*, a thief's mistress.

blower *n.* **1.** *Circus.* a barker.

1873 T. Frost *Circus Life* 220: The side show commences, with the "blower" taking his position at the door of the entrance, and in a stentorian voice expatiating at large upon what is to be seen within for the small sum of ten cents. **1975** McKennon *Horse Dung Trail* 26: You can relieve the "blower" on the side show once in a while.

2. a telephone or similar voice communications system.

*1926 in *OEDS*: I heard it on the telephone….They got that price from the blower round at the Arts Club. **1946** G.C. Hall, Jr. *1000 Destroyed* 154: The order came over the public address system, or "blower." *Ibid.* 420 *Blower*…telephone, Tanoy, or radio. ***1956** Heflin *USAF Dict.* 84: *Blower*…A radio. British slang. **1972** *All in the Family* (CBS-TV): You get on the blower and tell her "April Fool!" **1975** Mostert *Supership* 136: Picking up the blower, he gravely pronounced to the ship's company, "Twelve hundred. *Twelve* hundred." **1982** W.R. Dunn *Fighter Pilot* 67: Someone would get on the blower (telephone). **1987** E. White *Beautiful Room* 94: I talked to the old fright on the blower.

blower and striker *n. Naut.* second or third mate of a sailing vessel.

1899 Hamblen *Bucko Mate* 34: He did not relax in the slightest degree the performance of his duties as "blower and striker." ***1929** Bowen *Sea Slang* 15: *Blower and Striker, A.* A hard officer, particularly a bucko mate.

blowgun *n.* BLOWHARD.

1869 in E. Wallace *Howling of Coyotes* 105: Hamilton, "the blow-gun," being as usual drunk.

blowhard *n.* **1.** an obnoxiously boastful or garrulous person; windbag. Now *colloq.* or *S.E.*

1823 J.F. Cooper *Pilot* 278: That old Blow-hard has found the days too short for his business, and so he has landed a party to get hold of night. **1834** *Mil. & Naval Mag.* (May) 174 [ref. to 1813]: By his constant exercise, he had, in his old age, become the most accomplished swearer of christian or profane times, and was much better known under the appellation of "old Blowhard." **1850** Garrard *Wah-to-Yah* 171: F.P. Blair, Jr., prosecuting attorney, assisted by—Wharton, a great blowhard. **1857** in *OEDS*: He is a fine old grey-headed blow-hard of fifty-odd. **1865** [Browne] *Ward: Travels* 16: Why don't you go yourself, you old blowhard? **1883** Sweet & Knox *Mustang* 19: Tell that blowhard that he has been fooling with Phil Parker. **1928** in Tuthill *Bungle Family* 13: They were no different than the rest of your father's blow-hard relatives.

2. *Naut.* a heavy gale; a hurricane.

1845 in Robb *Squatter Life* 84: Old "blowhard" tossed the lake wave…top-mast high. **1890** Erskine *Twenty Years* 222 [ref. to 1840's]: I've seen it blowing like blue blazes, but this is a regular old blow-hard, hard enough to blow Yankee Doodle on a frying pan. **1972** W.C. Anderson *Hurricane* 165: My anemometer…registered one hundred and forty-two miles per hour, you big blowhard.

blowhole *n.* **1.** the anus.—usu. considered vulgar.

1947 *AS* XXII 305 [ref. to WWII]: Any suspected malingering or hypochondria is instantly diagnosed as "a bad case of conjunctivitis of the blowhole." **1952** Grey *Hoods* 115: The bum looks like he's got thrombosis of the blowhole. **1960** MacCuish *Do Not Go Gentle* 324 [ref. to WWII]: General, it makes the old blow hole pucker up, an' I'm no good for nothin'. **1971** S. Stevens *Way Uptown* 177: Get...down the street, man, 'fore I shove my [billy] club up your blow hole. **1990** *Tracey Ullman Show* (Fox-TV): I'm *fraught* with sensitivity! I have sensitivity coming out of the blowhole!

2. the mouth.—used contemptuously.

1949 Ellson *Tomboy* 85: "You shut your blowhole," Tomboy said.

3. a blusterer, BLOWHARD.

1959 Morrill *Dark Sea* 32 [ref. to 1940's]: He put up with that other blow-hole, Army Lieutenant Drupp, too, when the whole ship felt like tossing both of them overboard.

blow in *v.* **1.** to spend freely or squander (money), esp. in celebrating; to lose (money) at gambling. Also absol.

1880 Nye *Boomerang* 91: You could...blow in a good many scads that way. **1885** Siringo *Texas Cowboy* 4: Mr. Potts...was an old stove-up New York preacher, who had made a raise of several hundred thousand dollars and was over in Paris blowing it in. **1886** N.O. *Lantern* (Oct. 20) 2: When Davis has a dollar he's dead bent on blowing it all in. **1886** Nye *Remarks* 494: The boys, say, are willing to do the fair thing, say, blow in fifteen per cent. to the central committee. **1887** Francis *Saddle & Moccasin* 144: "He went off on a bend." "To blow in?" *...*Spend his money. **1889** Meriwether *Tramp at Home* 157: They pay up old debts, then do what is called "blow in" the rest of their year's income at poker. **1891** Maitland *Amer. Slang Dict.* 36: "*Blewed it all in*," spent all one's money. *Ibid* 38: Jones blew in all his dust against the game. **1903** A.H. Lewis *Boss* 119: How much stuff do you feel like blowin' in? **1919** Tarkington *Clarence* 10: Blow in all your pay? **1930** Huston *Frankie & Johnny* 69: You're a-blowin' in your woman's money.

2. to arrive—used intrans. Now *colloq.* or *S.E.*

1882 Miller & Harlow *9'-51"* 267: When did the rummy looking Cads blow in? **1889** Field *Western Verse* 97: And Cooper, too, wuz roughin' round fer enterprise 'nd brains,/Whenever them commodities blew in across the plains. **1890** Heskett *Wonderful Telephone* 5: Came up to dis house and de door was open, so I just blowed in. **1895** Remington *Pony Tracks* 67: We were all very busy when William "blew in" with a great sputtering and said, "Is yous ready for dinner, gemman?" **1900** Ade *More Fables* 163: In blew a Country Customer. **1903** Merriman *Letters from Son* 88: A fellow with some sort of monkey togs blew in. **1905** [Hobart] *Get Next!* 70: After breakfast...Jack Gibson blew in. **1906** Ford *Shorty McCabe* 173: Where'd you blow in from? **1908** Paine *Stroke Oar* 19: I forget her name—the tall, dark one that blew into chapel with Bill Henderson's sister. *a*1904–11 Phillips *Susan Lenox* I 23: I just blew in—haven't seen Lottie or father yet.

blow job *n.* **1.a.** Orig. *Prost.* an act of fellatio or (*occ.*) cunnilingus.

1942 in Legman *No Laughing Matter* 385: A man [was] getting a blow-job in a whorehouse. **1945** in Del Torto *Graffiti* (unp.): I'll give you the best blow job. **1949** *Gay Girl's Guide* 3: *B-J:* Abbreviation for Blow-Job. **1954–60** *DAS* 46. *a*1960 Federoff *Side of Angels* 136: One poor queen had given him a blow job in the last row of a movie house. **1961** J. Baldwin *Another Country* 62: She ever give you a blow job? **1965** Fry *Graffiti*: My wife is out side....We both want a blow job. **1965** Conot *Rivers of Blood* 231: She even gave me a blow job for six bits! **1975** Wambaugh *Choirboys* 22: A free blowjob.

b. one who gives a blow job.

1969 Tynan *Oh! Calcutta!* 187: He knows that he is a soldier and a revolutionary first and a great blow job second. **1973–77** J. Jones *Whistle* 167: She's a great blow job.

c. a painfully unpleasant experience or turn of events.

1971 N.Y.U. student: Something's a *blow job*. In that sense, it's the same as a drag or a bummer, only worse.

2. *Mil. Av.* a jet plane.

1945 Hamann *Air Words*: *Blow-job.* A rocket plane or jet-propelled plane. **1955** Scott *Look of Eagle* 16: He [had]...been commander of the jet fighter school at Willy Air Patch where everybody had to transition for the blow jobs. **1975** in Higham & Siddall *Combat Aircraft* 61: It was late 1944....Somebody bellowed, "Hey, Daily Lead. We got one of them blow-jobs at two o'clock low!"...I had my first glimpse of a jet aircraft. **1982** W.R. Dunn *Fighter Pilot* 220: Occasionally...[they] would ride their "blow jobs" in our direction and buzz our airfield. **1985** Yeager & Janos *Yeager* 60: "Blow jobs," the bomber crews called them, but no one was eager to be on the receiving end of the twin-engine German jet fighters.

3. a task requiring the use of explosives.

1957 T.H. White *Mtn. Road* 22: But there's not one of them in Kunming ever seen what goes on in these blow jobs. **1959** [Hunter] *Killer's Wedge* 31: But even safecrackers don't use [nitroglycerin] on blow jobs any more.

blown or **blowed** *adj.* **1.** out of breath; tired to exhaustion.—often (esp. since 1970's) constr. with *out.* [S.E. when used of horses.]

1844 Porter *Big Bear of Ark.* 50: Bullet drove on so fast, that when we came up to where the old 'uns were, I was so all-fired blowed that I hadn't wind enough to laugh. **1887** Hinman *Si Klegg* 323: There was much tugging and lifting, and the men became thoroughly "blown." **1968** Baker et al. *CUSS* 83: *Blown*...Very tired. **1978** R. Price *Ladies' Man* 115: We trailed behind, slightly blown out like soldiers returning home from a three-day gig at Gettysburg. **1980** Birnbach *Preppy Hndbk.* 218: *Blown out adj.* Wasted, tired, hung over.

2. very drunk or high.—now usu. constr. with *out.*

1851 Hall *College Wds.* 21: A person intoxicated is said to be *blown.* **1968** Baker et al. *CUSS* 83: *Blown* Drunk. **1974** N.Y.C. man, age 25: *Blown-out*—it means drunk or stoned—usually drunk—buckling at the knees. **1977** Langone *Life at Bottom* 196: He's really blowed out of his mind on them vodka freezes. *a*1979 in Feldman et al. *Angel Dust* 148: You get so blown on the shit that people can spot you from a mile away. **1980** Novak *High Culture* 172: Smoking from pound bags of herb...totally blown out with other GIs. **1984** Univ. Tenn. student (memo): *Smashed, real happy, blown, blitzed* [all syns. for *drunk*].

blown away *adj.* see s.v. BLOW AWAY, 3.a.

blown-in-the-glass *adj. Hobo.* genuine; authentic; (*occ.*) absolutely trustworthy. Also **blowed** ——. Also —— **bottle.**

[**1880** Bonner *Letters* 65: It has not [Heinrich] Heine's trademark blown in the glass.] **1895** *Harper's* (Oct.) 778: You wants me to be a blowed-in-the-glass stiff. **1899** "J. Flynt" *Tramping* 392: *Blowed-in-the-Glass Stiff:* a trustworthy "pal," a professional. **1900** Cullen *Taking Chances* 5: The genuine, dyed-in-the-wool, blown-in-the-bottle pokerist rarely acknowledges that he is ahead of the game. **1902** Cullen *More Tales* 56: This is the real, dyed-in-the-wool, blown-in-the-bottle— **1907** London *The Road* 25 [ref. to 1892]: I acquired the unmistakable air of the blowed-in-the-glass profesh. **1914** *Sat. Eve. Post* (Apr. 4) 13: Three years I've spent a-trainin' of him to be a blowed-in-the-glass stiff. **1916** *Editor* (May 6) 487: [A] blowed-in-the-bottle stiff. **1916** [Livingston] *Snare* 12: One of the profesh? A reg'lar blown-in-the-glass stiff? **1918** McNutt *Yanks Are Coming* 173: However, most of the blown-in-the-glass cowboys are soon assigned to the special service for which they are fit. **1925** Mullin *Scholar Tramp* 4: Frisco was a hobo of mature experience—a blowed-in-the-glass stiff. **1938** Holbrook *Mackinaw* 124: More blown-in-the-bottle logger ballads seem to stem from Michigan and Wisconsin than elsewhere. **1943** in Steinbeck *Once There Was a War*: Bugs regarded the mess sadly, but then the great philosophy of the "blowed in the glass" souvenir-hunter took possession of him. **1953** Gresham *Midway* 16: Clem Faraday was the first blown-in-the-glass carny I ever knew. **1962** Perry *Young Man Drowning* 210: He's blowed in the glass, kid. **1980** Bruns *Kts. of Road* 40: The veteran blowed-in-the-glass stiff was most often well prepared for battle.

blown out *adj.* **1.** see BLOWN, 1.

2. see BLOWN, 2.

3. crazy, wild.

1982 Univ. Tenn. *Daily Beacon* (Feb. 5) 2: When I get there she's blasted, bombed, and wasted/It's such a blown out scene.

blow-off *n.* **1.** an outburst; a sudden eruption of strife; a fight or argument.

1863 O.W. Holmes, Jr., in M.D. Howe *Shaping Years* 150: I had my blowoff in one of my last [letters] and now let bygones be bygones. **1898* in *OEDS*: a blow-off in this wise [i.e., swearing at golf] does one good now and then. **1907** D. Runyon, in *Lippincott's Mag.* (Oct.) 500: We was in barracks in Manila, before the gugu blow-off. **1931** Bontemps *Sends Sunday* 85: The hour was a bit early for a blow-off; there were too many people about. **1948** Shulman *Cry Tough!* 59: Steve couldn't afford a blow-off with Mitch. **1952** in *DAS* 46. **1952** Bonham *Snaketrack* 15: If you've come back for a blow-off...you don't have to hunt all over New Mexico for it. **1953** Wicker *Kingpin* 242: The first day I thought there'd be a big blowoff. They couldn't seem to find one pleasant word to say to each other.

2. *Und.* a kind of swindle.

1890 Quinn *Fools of Fortune* 350: Another method of inducing "suckers" to wager their money at this [shell] game is known...as the blow-off…the confederate lifts the shell and removes the ball, at the moment when the operator averts his eyes. (The "sucker" bets the ball is gone, but operator shows "it" to be under another shell.)

3. a celebration, as a farewell party.

1899 Cullen *Tales* 91: I'd had it all plotted out…to give my old boyhood home a blow-off for a week or so, and make 'em…sorry that they hadn't pulled…into the great, wide, open world when I did. **1915** Howard *God's Man* 211: It's due tomorrow night—a blow-off one girl's giving who's going across the big ditch—Europe. **1915–16** Lait *Beef, Iron & Wine* 163: His mother died an' he told me it was a swell blowoff, wit' a church an' weepin' neighbors an' everything. **1938** *Test Pilot* (film): Just you and I on a little blow-off. **1944** *Life* (Aug. 28) 13: Chicagoans are already making reservations in night clubs for the big blow-off for "when it's all over." **1976** S.C. Lawrence *Northern Saga* 138: Some were having a final blow-off before they got under way.

4.a. a decisive conclusion; finale; finishing climax; end.

1907 Siler *Pugilism* 135: Then would come the "blow off." The Biffer would then straighten up his pupil with a straight left and follow it up with a knockout. **1910** T.A. Dorgan, in *N.Y. Eve. Jour.* (Apr. 25) 19: The big blow-off comes Wednesday night in Philly, when Langford hooks up with Ketchel. **1911** Howard *Enemy to Society* 294: They'd publish the whole story in th' papers less'n they let Steve take a walk and let that be the blow-off! **1911–12** Ade *Knocking the Neighbors* 6: The Blow-Off came on the Trip to the City. That was the Big Entertainment. **1921** J. Conway, in *Variety* (Feb. 25) 23: I sprung the piece de resistance or some other wrestling term they have for the blow-off. **1922** J. Conway, in *Variety* (May 5) 13: "Ladies and gentlemen, step this way and see the only original hairy ape." That's the blow off. **1923** in Lardner *Best Stories* 286: He was hittin' 'way over five hundred when the blowoff come, along about the last o' May. **1928** Callahan *Man's Grim Justice* 197: This is the blow-off…I'll never see her again. **1930** [Conwell] *Prof. Thief* 235: *Blowoff,* n.—The final act in the operation of a confidence game. **1940** in H. Gray *Arf* (unp.): It is all arranged. The plans of years at last reach their fruition. "Yeah? Maybe—but just *what* day is this big blow-off *due?*" **1943** Halliday *Mummer's Mask* 155: The blow-off is set for seven o'clock tonight.…You don't deserve a preview. **1951** in Cannon *Nobody Asked* 26: It wasn't difficult to anticipate the blowoff. The hatcheck girl ran off and married the kid Fat was sending to college. **1985** Univ. Tenn. *Heartbeat* (Feb. 11) 5: The big blow-off, the cold shoulder.

b. *Specif.* the conclusion of a performance or an engagement, as of a carnival or circus; a show presented after the main show.

1913 *Sat. Eve. Post* (June 21) 17: Just string a few laughs together…and wind up with a blow-off of some sort. **1913** *Sat. Eve. Post* (July 5) 5: For the blowoff Myrtle's lion-taming stunt goes wrong…and you tear in and save the lady. **1922** *Variety* (Aug. 18) 8: An after-show or "blow-off" is added to the regular performance [of dancing girls]. **1931** *Nat. Geo.* (Oct.) 514: The *blow-off* [is] the final night performance in the side-show tent. **1931** G. Milburn, in *Amer. Mercury* (Nov.) 351: Circus Words…*Blow-Off,* n. The end of a show. **1951** Mannix *Sword-Swallower* 33: The blow-off is the extra feature attraction in a side-show, m'boy.…A good blow-off attraction like that fat lady will carry the running expenses of the entire show. **1953** Gresham *Midway* 143: When enough of the tip in the main tent has crowded into the curtained-off section for the blowoff the snake man picks up a seven-foot rattler. **1973** *WCBS-TV News* (Apr. 6): The punch-line—what the clowns call "the blow-off." **1975** McKennon *Horse Dung Trail* 156: On the "blow off" from the big top, after the afternoon performance.…the…circus goers were given an extra show as they passed through the menagerie.

c. the last in a number of events that finally destroys one's patience; the last straw.

1915–16 Lait *Beef, Iron & Wine* 272: Well, that's the blow-off. Here's curtains for you, Gene the Greek. **1931** Grant *Gangdom's Doom* 40: Heeny was killed in the restaurant. But the real blow-off was in the gambling joint. Schultz and Spivak tried to stick up the place. **1939** Goodman & Kolodin *Swing* 98: It was here that the blow-off came.…The incident…seemed to bring matters to a head. **1943** Wolfert *Tucker's People* 27: Now he thought it was funny a five-dollar bet with Shortie should come to be the blowoff when there had been so many other more important things. **1959** Burroughs *Naked Lunch* 31: Well, this rumble in the operating room…was the blow off.

d. [sugg. by **(b),** above] *Carnival.* in a sideshow tent, a curtained-off area where the featured attraction is presented.

1951 Mannix *Sword-Swallower* 170: So we decided it would be best for me to sit inside the blow-off and listen through the thin curtains.

5. a loud, contentious individual.

1964 Thompson & Rice *Every Diamond* 223: He isn't a blowoff, but he won't be pushed off his doorstep. **1987** *RHD2.*

6. a simple task; BREEZE.

1973 *TULIPQ* (coll. B.K. Dumas): If a course is known to be very easy, it might be called a *blow-off.* **1981** Univ. Tenn. student: An easy course is a *whiz course,* or a *blow-off* or a *dump course.* **1982** Pond *Valley Girl's Gd.* 52: Study hall is a blow-off, real easy. **1983** *N.Y. Daily News* (Mar. 25): Teentalk glossary…*blow-off*—an easy task or chore.

7. *Stu.* a procrastinator; loafer.

1987 *Rage* (Knoxville, Tenn.) I (No. 2) 27: Do what you want, when you want. Be a blow-off.

blow off *v.* **1.** to cease.

1845 in *DA:* When we blowed off, I judge he had the wust of it; he looked like he had any how.

2. to treat (someone); BLOW, *v.,* 5.b.—constr. with *to.*

1889 Barrère & Leland *Dict. Slang* I 142: *To blow off,* to treat to drinks. **1892** Bunner *Runaway Browns* 28: I'll blow you all off to the finest breakfast you ever had in your lives. **1894** Bangs *3 Wks. in Politics* 38: I've got all I can do blowing off the ward in my own interest without doing it for Mr. Perkins. **1895** Townsend *Fadden & Others* 180: If he took into his nut t' blow me off at de swellest rest'rant in town he'd do me proud. *a***1904–11** Phillips *Susan Lenox* 41: Nothing pleases me better than to take a nice girl…out and blow her off to a crackerjack dinner.

3. to release pent-up emotions as by scolding, complaining, speaking in an insulting manner, celebrating, etc.; to get angry.—occ. constr. with *it.* Cf. *blow off steam* s.v. STEAM.

1906 Beyer *Amer. Battleship* 84: "Blow off at low pressure"—refers to a talkative person. **1910** *Everybody's Mag.* (Feb.) 254: The old man was just blowin' off a little. **1918** Ruggles *Navy* 27: Some very talkative individual, who is always shooting off. The sailor would say, "He's blowing off at high pressure," or "He's poppin' off." **1937** [Glidden] *Brand of Empire* 137: Let me blow off. It's not every day a man loses a fight like that. **1944** in Hodes & Hanson *Sel. from Gutter* 31: Anyway, the leader blew off, and demanded respect. **1951** C. Palmer *Sellout* (film): "Sorry I blew off, kids."…"We all have to blow off sometime." **1953–57** Giovannitti *Combine D* 139: I asked him what he called me and he blew off again, so I hit him. **1966** Susann *Valley of Dolls* 33: Henry only blew off because he's fond of you. **1968** Baker et al. *CUSS* 83: *Blow it off,* Go wild.

4. (of events) to develop dramatically.

1912 Beach *Net* 156: He's my best dago detective, and I sent him here tonight in case anything blew off.

5. to kill by gunfire or explosion.

1928 Wharton *Squad* 52: I never knowed a fellow could get blowed off like dat nowhere near de enemy. **1980** M. Baker *Nam* 130: Your fucking friend got blown off.

6.a. *Orig. Und.* to dismiss or get rid of (a person), esp. the victim of a swindle or pickpocketing.

1940 D.W. Maurer, in *AS.* **1947** Schulberg *Harder They Fall* 253: I was just thinking like a moon-struck freshman when I was…deciding to blow Nick off. **1958** Gilbert *Vice Trap* 13: If I blew him off he would send the work to the Shell across the street. **1985** *Heartbeat* (Univ. Tenn.) (Feb. 5): Now, when the male gets happy and calls you because you looked at him—blow him off big time. **1985** *Newsweek* (Dec. 23) 52: They just blew us off like a couple of crackpots. **1987** Univ. Tenn. student theme: To be "blown off" is to be rejected [by a member of the opposite sex]. **1990** *Guiding Light* (CBS-TV) (Mar. 21): He put me on hold for ten minutes then blew me off.

b. to disregard or ignore; slough off.

1965 Spillane *Killer Mine* 14: I'm a cop, plain and simple. But I'm just cop enough to blow off a job I don't want to get fixed into. **1962–68** B. Jackson *In Life* 76: Then they'd blow it off. There wasn't nothing ever thought about it. **1968** Baker et al. *CUSS* 83: *Blow it off.* Waste time, not study. **1970** M. Brennan *Drugs* 58: *Blow it off:* Forget it. **1976** "N. Ross" *Policeman* 2: By this time, his system is proven. He knows the bullshit; he can blow off a job. **1980** in *Penthouse* (Jan. 1981) 214: What I saw in front of me was enough to let me blow off my studying for the night. **1983** *N.Y. Daily News* (Mar. 25): Teentalk glossary…*bag*—abandon previous plans (also: *blow off*). **1992** *60 Minutes* (CBS-TV) (Oct. 25): [The hazard] is common knowledge. You just blow it off.

7. *Sports.* to overcome; defeat easily. Also in phr. **blow (someone) off the (court, field, ice,** etc.**).**

*a***1958** in D. McKay *Wild Wheels* 19: Think you'll blow off all the competition tomorrow, Doc? **1954–60** *DAS* 46: *Blow-off…*v.t. To defeat an opponent or opposing team, esp. with ease. **1976** *Webster's Sports Dict.* 46. **1979** Cuddon *Dict. Sports & Games* 116.

blowout *n.* **1.** a large quantity of food or drink (*obs.*); a feast; (*hence*) a hearty celebration.

1815 in B. Palmer *Diary* (Jan. 1): My Rum has just come...I shall now turn and have a Clear blow out. **1821** Waln *Hermit in Phila.* 24: [I've] been out to dine;—a little *blue*—regular *blow-out*;—headache in the morning. ****1821** *Real Life in London* II 57: A dose of *daffy*, or a *blow out of black strap.* ***1823** "J. Bee" *Slang* 12: You may get a famous *blow-out* at the Slambang-shops for ten-pence. ***1821–26** [Stewart] *Man-of-War's-Man* I 185: A gude blow-out o' Mr. Swipey's mess-grog. *Ibid.* II 45: What a blow-out we should have! **1830** N. Ames *Mariner's Sks.* 227: They were going to have a grand *blow out* on board the brig. **1839** *Crockett's Comic Alm.* (unp.): I've been promising my sweetheart...to bring her to Pease establishment for a real blow out. **1840** R.H. Dana *2 Yrs. Before Mast* ch. xx: We...had, besides, what the sailors call "a blow-out on sleep"; not turning out in the morning until breakfast was ready. **1871** Bagg *Yale* 43: *Blow-out,* a supper, spread, convivial entertainment, especially a society celebration. **1871** "M. Twain" *Roughing It* 246: This is a free blowout. **1889** "M. Twain" *Conn. Yankee* 416: All of a sudden comes along a man who slashes out nearly four dollars on a single blow-out. **1896** Crane *George's Mother* 141: Bleecker's goin' t' give a blow-out t'morrah night. **1897** Hamblen *General Mgr.* 245: Two tramps that are having a blow-out of boiled hen. **1904** *Independent* (June 23) 1430: He had come up to treat me to a little "blow out"; to show his appreciation. **1915** in Kornbluh *Rebel Voices* 150: You can talk about your dances, picnics, and blow outs. **1933** Halper *Union Sq.* 26: I'm on my way to a little blow-out down on Bleeker Street. **1958** in Loosbrock & Skinner *Wild Blue* 234: We also had one hell of a blowout in Calcutta. **1974** A. Marx *Everybody* 157: This is a black-tie blowout. **1979** Hiler *Monkey Mt.* 231: He and I and Dave had gotten drunk and stoned as a final blow-out before I went overseas. **1983** *N.Y. Post* (Sept. 2) 31: All play & no work: the 3-day blowout to end 'em all.

2. a quarrel; row; brawl.

1825 J.K. Paulding *Bull in Amer.* 137: We had a *blow out* here last Sunday, and half a dozen troublesome fellows...were done for by the brave *rowdies.* **1842** *Spirit of Times* (Feb. 15): I've had five breezes, seven blowouts, nine shindies, and a dozen ructions on this $1 Relief note. **1858** C.A. Abbey *Before the Mast* 141: The Greaser & his watch had a blow out which came near being a fight. **1929–31** Farrell *Manhood of Lonigan* 200: His father and mother were having a big blow-out. **1975** R.E. Davis *Pilot* 204: It got to me. Our first blowout. **1992** *CBS This Morning* (CBS-TV) (May 26): What if they have their first big blowout right there on the set?

3. a failure (of any sort); a washout.

1938 "Justinian" *Americana Sexualis* 13: *Blow-Out. n.* A premature ejaculation...U.S., c. 20, derived from motoring slang. **1939** Howsley *Argot* 8: *Blow Out*...a job that failed. **1977** R. Bassett *Tinfish Run* 146: It was a damn fool idea in the beginning, but now it's a blow-out. **1984** *U.S. News & W.R.* (June 25) 69: Indianapolis was a total blowout....I feel cellular will be viable only in a handful of large markets.

4. *Sports.* an utter defeat.

1982 WKGN radio news (Oct. 20): A World Series that has featured exciting contests and yawn-inducing blowouts both. **1983** *Mutual Radio Network Sports* (WKGN) (Mar. 12): Last night's blowout was the second straight for the Cavaliers. **1987** Headline News network (Dec. 21): With a 110–71 blowout of Washington. **1991** Lott & Lieber *Total Impact* 213: Our 55–10 blowout of the Denver Broncos.

blow out *v.* **1.** to eat and drink voraciously (*obs.*); celebrate.—constr. with *it.*

1852 in Windeler *Gold Rush Diary* 138: Mond. 14, my Birthsday. Here I am 30 years & not married yet, got 2 bottles portwine & one of brandy, also some cakes & blowed it out. **1990** C.P. McDonald *Blue Truth* 170: Blow it out, have some fun, get away...for a while.

2.a. to kill.

1865 in Hilleary *Webfoot* 45: God damn you blow that light out or I'll blow you out. **1896** F.P. Dunne, in Schaaf *Dooley* 242: But that don't stop people fr'm killin' thimselves f'r fear he'll be ilicted....'Tis a sign iv th' nuttiness iv th' campaign that a man should thry to blow himself out with hard times. **1927** C.J. Daly *Snarl of Beast* 40: A lad might...plant himself in the hall and blow me out, coming down. **1968** R. Adams *Western Wds.* (ed. 2): *Blow out.* A cowboy's expression meaning *to kill.*

b. to die.

1966 Brunner *Face of Night* 13: How is it my fault Jenny blew out? *Ibid.* 231: *Blow out*—to die.

3. to squander, BLOW IN.

1901 *DN* II 136: *Blow out, v. phr. tr.* Like blow in, to spend freely. **1923** Southgate *Rusty Door* 109: You blew out yer last wage and share buyin'

an Encyclopedy Brittainikey 'stead o' new jack boots.

4. to destroy; to spoil; to quash, etc. Cf. **(2.a.)**, above.

1968 S. Ross *Hang-Up* 95: By the time we got there, the tide'd change and the whole thing'd be blown out. **1972–76** Durden *No Bugles* 240: Or when we blow out them bastards up North. **1977** Walton *Walton Experience* 94: "We're going to blow this story out today!" he declared to newspaper reporters.

5. to astound.

1971 in L. Bangs *Psychotic Reactions* 80: *Well*, that just blows her out entirely! **1974** N.Y.C barmaid, age 22: It blows me out that he was here. **1975** Thomas *Heavy Number* 11: His mock disdain blew Shannon out. **1972–76** Durden *No Bugles* 77: That blew me out, too. Some dude sittin' there sayin' things most people never admit, even to themselves. **1976** Price *Bloodbrothers* 62: Stony was blown out by the lowlife.

6. [cf. *blow out of the water,* below] *Sports.* to defeat decisively.

1976 *AS* LI 293: *Blow him out of the court.* Defeat an opponent [in tennis] with overpowering shots. **1976** Univ. Tenn. student: Atlanta just blew them out. They just ate their shit up. **1978** *Wash. Post* (June 11) D6: Before the injuries, we were getting to a point where we felt we could blow out anyone. **1982** WKGN Radio Sports (Oct. 10): They were blown out 7 to 0.

7. to give out.

1984 Nettles & Golenbock *Balls* 106: His back blew out on him.

¶ In phrases:

¶ **blow it out [your ass (*vulgar*)]** (used as an insulting retort). Also (*Mil.*) **blow it out your barracks bag.** Also vars.

1943 *Yank* (Oct. 15) 17 (photo caption): No kidding. He's really blowing it out his barracks bag. **1944** in Huebner *Long Walk* 24: Blow it out your homesick ass! **1944** *Stars & Stripes* (Rome) (July 13): And would Miss DeBoni please explain what the GI boy friend meant when he told the horn-happy driver to "blow it out your barracks bag." **1944** Kendall *Service Slang* 2: *Blow it out of your bag*...refrain from talking, if you will be so good! **1944** in *AS* XX 147: *Blow It Out Your Barracks Bag!* Shut up! Go to hell! **1945** in Dundes & Pagter *Urban Folklore* 107: Do NOT say "Blow it out your —!" **1947** Willingham *End as a Man* 255: Oh, blow it out, bu-low it out. **1950** Calmer *Strange Land* 127: Blow it out, Selig. **1953** Harris *Southpaw* 117: Bob Castetter told Lindon he could blow it out his ass. **1958** T. Berger *Crazy in Berlin* 26: Blow it out your barracks bag. **1960** Carpenter *Harlot* 74: Aw, go blow it outa your duffelbag, goon. **1963** Blechman *Camp Omongo* 11: He told them...go blow it out their asshole. **1963** Gant *Queen St.* 9: Go blow it out of your stacking swivel! **1966** Cameron *Sgt. Slade* 43: Aw, blow it out your barracks bag! **1969** Whiting *St.-Vith* 173: Blow it out, you German son of a bitch! **1972** Meade & Rutledge *Belle* 200: Ahh, blow it out! **1972** Sapir & Murphy *Death Therapy* 25: Blow it out your ears. **1975** C.W. Smith *Country Music* 24: Oh, blow it out your ass, Barker! **1976** Woodley *Bears* 106: Blow it out your tailpipe, buster! **1984** Sample *Racehoss* 146: Blow it outcha soul. **1985** *Golden Girls* (NBC-TV): Just blow it out your ditty bag.

¶ **blow (one) out of the water** [or **tub**] to defeat decisively; ruin. [The bracketed quots. are literal.]

[**1860** Shipley *Privateer's Cruise* 22: Why that craft can blow us out of the water in a couple of broadsides.] [**1866** in J.M. Merrill *Battle Flags* 164: Surrender you damn fool or I'll blow you out of the water!] **1958** S.H. Adams *Tenderloin* 330: If I can find a way I'll blow the whole damned investigation right out of the water. **1963** in Chipman *Hardening Rock* 49: When the light turns green/She blows 'em outta the water like you've never seen. **1966** "Minnesota Fats" *Bank Shot* 255: Extreme English is a many-splendored thing, but if the execution isn't just right, you'll blow yourself out of the tub. **1970** La Motta, Carter & Savage *Raging Bull* 168: Too much more of this publicity can blow us all out of the water. **1975** Cohen *Monsters, Giants* 180: It would blow archaeology, paleontology and a lot of other sciences right out of the water. **1979** Cassidy *Delta* 68: You do everything by the book, or...I'll blow you right out of the water!

blowout patch *n.* **1.** a pancake.

1947 Carter *Devils in Baggy Pants* 169 [ref. to WWII]: Some of us had just returned to our houses for a breakfast of "blowout patches" (pancakes), steak...and coffee.

2. a bandage.

1983 Stapleton *30 Yrs.* 147: He always seemed to be working with a burn that was healing or with a "blow out" patch covering a few stitches.

blowpipe *n.* **1.** BLOWHARD.

1865 in Hilleary *Webfoot* 80: Corpl. Billy is quite a blow pipe, if I know anything about such things. **2.** (see quot.).

1921 *DN* V 111: *Blow-pipe, n.* A rifle.

3. *Av.* (see quot.).

1956 Heflin *USAF Dict.* 84: *Blow pipe.* A jet airplane. *Slang.*

blowser *n.* a coarse, immoral, or offensive woman.

[*1785 Grose *Vulgar Tongue* s.v. *blowse: A blowse,* or *blowsabella,* a woman whose hair is dishevelled and hanging about her face, a slattern.] **1923** Wilstach *Stage Slang* 16: *Blowser* A coarse Jane. **1930** in H. Miller *Letters to Emil* 57: I...see the old blowser standing in her nightshirt. **1931** in Partridge *Dict. Und.* 54: *Blowser.* A prostitute, especially an elderly, or a dirty, dishevelled one. **1973** N.Y.C. woman, age *ca*75: In the 20's we'd call a girl a *blowser* if she was completely, hopelessly immoral. A *blowser* was hardly more than a slut even if she pretended she was. **1983** Flaherty *Tin Wife* 10: They would be hurt if they knew Eddie had called every old blowser in a bar.

blowtop *n.* [sugg. by *blow (one's) top* s.v. TOP] a crazy or excitable person.

1940 in R.S. Gold *Jazz Talk* 22. **1946** Mezzrow & Wolfe *Really Blues* 160: Sure, I was surrounded by...a hundred million blowtops. **1948** Schwartz *Blowtop* 57: A routine homicide without any motive....Some blowtop pulled this, all right. And the Village is full of blowtops. **1952** Mandel *Angry Strangers* 438: Nobody like these blowtop hoodlum kids to push charge for me. **1958** Hughes & Bontemps *Negro Folklore* 481: *Blowtop:* Excitable, erratic. *Minnie's a blowtop.* **1959** Murtagh & Harris *Live in Shadow* 53: You should've seen them blowtops laughing. **1977** Torres *Q & A* 55: You gonna listen to this blowtop, Texidor? **1980** S. Fuller *Big Red* 39: The doctor...[was] pleased with the way he had cured this blowtop so easily. **1980** *Mother Jones* (Jan. 1981) 22: The entire image of Pryor as an insane, dope-addicted, violent blow-top is the creation of the media.

blowtorch *n.* **1.a.** *Av.* a jet airplane; in phr. **blowtorch jockey** (USAF) a jet pilot.

1950 *Nat. Geographic* (Sept.) 311: Some pilots call their jets "blowtorches," "firecans," or just "cans." **1950** *Nat. Geographic* (Nov.) 654: Twin turbines drive McDonnell FH-1 Phantoms, the Navy's first carrier-based "blow torches," at better than 500 miles an hour. **1954** *N.Y. Times Mag.* (Mar. 7) 20: *Blowtorch*—any jet plane. **1955** *AS* XXX 117: *Flying Blowtorch*...Jet aircraft. **1966** Gallery *Start Engines* 13: Curly was, of course, an ace blowtorch jockey. **1968** W.C. Anderson *Gooney Bird* 225: Smart-assed blowtorch jockeys. **1980** W.C. Anderson *BAT-21* 4: An antiquated EB-66 blowtorch. *Ibid.* 29: F-4 pilots...blowtorch jockeys. *a*1986 Hallion *Nav. Air War* 161: Given the fuel consumption characteristics of the early "blowtorches."

b. *Mil. Av.* a pilot or navigator of a jet fighter.

1974 Pratt *Laotian Fragments* 151: The jet jocks...frown. Bad day for the blowtorches.

2. *Av.* a jet engine.

1955 Reifer *New Words* 33: *Blowtorch*...An aircraft jet. **1956** Heflin *USAF Dict.* 84: *Blowtorch, n.* A jet engine or an airplane using a jet engine as its propulsive force. *Slang.*

blowup *n.* **1.** a sudden brawl (*obs.*) or quarrel; a sudden conflict of any sort. Now *colloq.* or *S.E.*

*1809 in OEDS. *1821 *Real Life in London* II 253: Vhen that there man comes home, my eyes vhat a blow up! **1837** Neal *Charcoal Sks.* 165: He has a prompt alacrity at a "blow-out" and has been skyed in a "blow-up," two varieties of the blow-up which frequently follow each other so closely as to be taken for cause and effect. **1838** in *DAE*: Of all stations commend me to that of a *Magazine* editor, provided he can get along smoothly—without any blow-ups. **1845** in Robb *Squatter Life* 69: Why, captain,...I like your boat vastly...but there might be a "blow up" if I stayed on board much longer....That lady...has taken me for the *Mormon* Smith. *1849 Leeves *Diary* 4: Had a regular blow up with Favenza, who has behaved most abominably. **1866** in W.H. Jackson *Diaries* 51: We had a grand "blow up," & Parish and I resigned our position. **1950** in *DAS*: In case of an international blow-up. **1980** Whalen *Takes a Man* 253: She had a big blow-up with Barbara.

2. a business failure; financial collapse.

1820 in *DA*. **1821** in *DAE*: Bank of Missouri. We have the particulars of the blow up of this institution. **1837** Marryat *Diary in America* 60: If any one will look back upon the commercial history of these last fifty years, he will perceive that the system of credit is always attended with a periodical *blow-up*; in England, perhaps once in twenty years; in America, once in from seven to ten. **1895** in *DA.*

3. a scolding; a bawling out.

1835 in *DAE*. **1840** R. Dana *2 Yrs. Before Mast* ch. iv: The Captain...gave him a grand blow-up, in true nautical style. **1871** Schele de Vere *Amer.* 584: A *blow–up* [is] a severe scolding.

blow up *v.* **1.a.** to ruin; (*hence*) to thrash soundly.

*1610 Jonson *Alchemist* I ii: He'll win up all the money i' the town....And blow up gamester after gamester. *1635 J. Shirley *Lady of Pleasure* IV ii: All the gamesters/Blown up? *1660 in *OED*: It blew up this Parliament totally. *1707 Cibber *Double Gallant* 58: If she suspects your Design, you're blown up, depend on't. *1820–21 P. Egan *Life in London* 131: He lives in good style; owing to the great success he has had in repeatedly *blowing up* both young and old. **1832** *Spirit of Times* (Feb. 4) 1: Blow him up, Jack! **1937** E. Anderson *Thieves Like Us* 80: Yessir, that sure blows me up on going back to Alky. **1939** "E. Queen" *Dragon's Teeth* 194: Anyway, when I got back to the yacht, Cole blew up my whole scheme himself without realizing it.

b. to impregnate.

1803 in Eliason *Tarheel Talk* 260: There has Been A talk that Betsey...was Blowed up.

2. to scold vociferously; berate; CHEW OUT.

*1710 in *OEDS*: This plainly showed that the cabal had been blowing her up, but that she could not, however, contradict her own order. **1798** in Long *Nothing Too Daring* 7: As for the first lieutenant's blowing you up every day, why, sir, 'tis because he...would not have you grow up a conceited young coxcomb. *1823 "J. Bee" *Slang* 13: *Blow-up*...to give one a scolding in loud and forcible terms. **1833** in [S. Smith] *Letters of Downing* 131: The most rascally set of fellers...I ever heard of, and I wish you would blow 'em up! **1835** *Mil. & Nav. Mag. of U.S.* (Dec.) 295: I likes a story that when you're telling it again, you can say, "I'm hanged if it ain't as true as the bible!" Then the people can't shake no heads at ye, or if they do you may blow 'em up for it with good conscience. **1835** in Meine & Owen *Crockett* 73: I began to blow him up for staying so long. **1844** *Working a Passage* 94: I saw him sometimes shed tears when the mate "blew him up," as he called his abuse. **1847** McClellan *Mex. War Diary* 30: Patt...gave the Colonel a blowing up for allowing his men to leave the column. **1847** Neal *Charcoal Sks. 2d* 95: Why don't she blow me up like an affectionate woman and a loving wife, instead of standing there in that ghostified fashion? **1848** [Judson] *Mysteries* 367: I just saw young Fitz-Lawrence...blowing up Sam Selden for introducing you. **1848** Bartlett *Amer.:* Blow Up. To scold, to abuse, either in speaking or writing. A vulgar expression borrowed from sailor's language. **1852** Stowe *Uncle Tom's Cabin* 66: I tell you, I blew 'em up well, all of 'em, at home! **1865** J. Pike *Scout & Ranger* 208: "Old Starry" (our pet name for General Mitchell), "blowed me up" that morning for being slow. **1867** Smyth *Sailor's Wd.-Bk.:* Blow Up. To abuse angrily. **1873** in Bunner *Letters* 18: So don't blow me up for not yet joining in fervent adoration where the Ruskinian banners float. **1882** *United Service* (Feb.) 221: Mr. Barnacle was evidently very much out of humor with a person he was blowing up sky-high, and who it appears was the boatswain. **1892** Cox *5 Yrs. in Army* 62: The sergeant bounces into the guard room and "blows up" the corporal in fine style. **1893** [Small] *Comic History* 47: He blowed him up, used cuss words, called him a dough-head, and threatened to have him suspended. **1897** Norris *Vandover* 359: You ought to have heard the blowing up I gave my tailor! I let him have it right straight. **1922** in Ruhm *Detective* 11: And she...blew the widow up every chance she got. **1936** Steel *College* 20: Good night, Howard. Sorry I blew you up. We're all jumpy tonight.

3.a. to collapse (esp. in business); to come to nothing; fail.

1864 in H. Johnson *Talking Wire* 130: The Bannock expedition has blown up. **1903** Ade *Society* 98: I may as well warn you that 95 per cent. of those who go into Business eventually blow up. **1908** in Fleming *Unforgettable Season* 128: In the eighth Wiltse gave up two more runs and in the ninth he blew up completely. **1919** T. Kelly *What Outfit, Buddy?* 185: Since Austria blew up we ought to get behind the Boches and push 'em right in the Rhine. **1928** Dahlberg *Bottom Dogs* 216: She had made one of those war-time marriages, which blew up after the parades were over. **1928** Santee *Cowboy* 152: This outfit's blowed up...if we don't get rain pretty soon. **1968** Poe *Riot* (film): Yeah, I guess it was luck that first plan blew up, man.

b. *Theat.* to forget one's lines during a performance; *Sports.* to lose one's stamina or composure during a contest.

1908 *Atlantic* (Aug.) 229: Stivetts [a baseball pitcher] blew up, because Schreck had his kidding clothes on. **1908** in H.C. Fisher *A. Mutt* 111: [of a boxer] He'll blow up in a minute. **1910** T.A. Dorgan, in *N.Y. Eve. Jour.* (Jan. 11) 12: He blew up after a round or two. **1914** [Patten] *Lefty o' the Bush* 41: Didn't he stop Fryeburg arter Deever blew up? **1913–15** Van Loan *Taking the Count* 23: He fights like an apple woman....Two fast rounds and he blows up. **1930** in R.E. Howard *Iron Man* 26: Many a slugger…blew up and fell before his aimless but merciless attack. **1944** *Reader's Digest* (Apr.) 122: Barrymore "blew up" in his lines at almost the same place in the scene before. **1952** Malamud *Natural* 35: My best pitcher and he blows up every time I put him against a first place team. **1957** N. Frye *Anatomy Crit.* 178: An epilogue in Plautus informs us that the slave-actor who has blown up in his lines will now be flogged. **1966** Susann *Valley of Dolls* 305: I'm a star now—if I look bad or blow up I'm through. **1977** *Golf Mag.* (Aug.) 73: There are lots of players on the Tour who…come down to the wire and blow up.

c. *Computers.* (of a computer or computer software) to malfunction or break down.
1985 Knoxville, Tenn., computer programmer, age 38: When the computer goes down, we say it's *bombed* or it *blew up.* **1989** Freedman *Computer Glossary* (ed. 4): *Blow up*, same as *crash, bomb*, or *abend.* **1991** Raymond *Hacker's Dict.*: *Blow up*…Of software, to fail spectacularly.

4. to lose one's temper; to get furiously angry. Now *colloq.*
1871 "M. Twain," in *Letters* I 189: Redpath tells me to blow up. Here goes! **1931** *Writer's Digest* (May) 41: *Blow Up*—To quit a job suddenly. **1939** E.S. Gardner *D.A. Draws* 184: He blew up. He cursed and raved around a while. **1950** Vidal *Thirsty Evil* 193: He blows up too easily and he doesn't work out on a team.

5. to shoot (someone).
1929 Barr *Let Tomorrow Come* 140: If I had a gun I'd blow you up—for fun. **1970** Conaway *Big Easy* 47: More than one pusher had been blown up in the last six months. **1972** Wambaugh *Blue Knight* 24: More good arrests come from phony traffic stops than anything else. More policemen get blown up that way, too. **1974** *Kojak* (CBS-TV): Who'd you ever blow up? **1977** Torres *Q & A* 28: This Curtis was blowin' people up all over the neighborhood. **1985** M. Baker *Cops* 171: So the guy blew him up. He shot him.

6. *Rap Music.* to achieve great popularity; become successful.
1993 *Source* (July) 40: You blew up around the same time as Rakim and KRS-One.

blowze *n.* [of dial. E orig.] a slovenly or sexually immoral woman.
*1674 in Duffett *Burlesque Plays* 19: Sweet blouz you make us all look sadly. *1701 T. D'Urfey, in Lonsdale *New Oxford 18th C. Verse* 5: Keeps a blowze and beats his spouse. 1726 in *William & Mary Qly.* (Ser. 3) XXXVIII (1981) 276: The marry'd Blowze will rob her Spouse,/To feed her Cuckold-maker. *1750 *Exmoor Scolding* 3: Ya gurt…rousling Blowze.

blubber *n.* corpulence; fat.
1786 in W. Dunlap *Diary* 5: This Falstaff in petticoats striking her fists in her Blubber sides & observing us top to toe. *1811 *Lexicon Balatron.*: *To sport Blubber.* Said of a large coarse woman, who exposes her bosom. *Ibid. Blubber Cheeks.* Large, flaccid cheeks, hanging like the fat or blubber of a whale. *1823 "J. Bee" *Slang* 13: A fat deep-chested woman is said to "sport the blubber," when she makes an exhibition of her bosom. **1877** in J.M. Carroll *Camp Talk* 89: All he lost in weight was blubber, which could well have been spared. *a1890 *F & H* I: *Blubber and guts*…Obesity; a low term. *Blubber-belly*…A fat person. **1942** Maltz & Burnett *This Gun for Hire* (film): I'd whittle off a little of that blubber. **1956** Evarts *Ambush Riders* 135: You're goin' to ride some blubber off tonight.

2. *Whaling.* (see quot.).
1866 "M. Twain" *Letters from Hawaii* (Mar. 18): It is necessary to explain that those ancient, incomprehensible old whalers always called worthless, odd-suit cards "blubber."

¶ In phrase:

¶ **make blubber of** *Whaling.* to beat savagely, "make mincemeat of."
1871 Thomes *Whaleman* 124: Drop him, I tell you, or I'll make blubber of you fellers.

blubber-boiler *n.* *Naut.* a whaling ship or whaling man.—used derisively. Now *hist.*
1849 Melville *Redburn* ch. xxi: Merchant seamen generally affect a certain superiority to "blubber-boilers," as they contemptuously style those who hunt the leviathan. **1850** Melville *Moby Dick* xi: They…repeat gamesome stuff about "spouters" and "blubber-boilers." **1883** Russell *Sailors' Lang.* 16: *Blubber-boiler*—A name for a whaleman. **1938** in Botkin *Treas. Amer. Folk.* 194: When the victim came to, he was lying on the deck of some outbound blubber-boiler.

blubberbutt *n.* a grossly fat person.—used derisively. Also

(vulgar) **blubberass.**
1952 Uris *Battle Cry* 52 [ref. to WWII]: What's the matter, blubber butt? **1968** Westheimer *Young Sentry* 11: Even the enlisted men called him…"Blubberbutt" behind his back. **1971** *Newsweek* (Nov. 29) 20: "Take your homesick eyes off a me, blubberass," the Marine drill instructor bayed at a plump young recruit. **1981** C. Nelson *Picked Bullets Up* 163: Flayed by appropriate nicknames like "Crater Face," "Leper Breath," and "Blubber Butt." **1983** *Cheers* (NBC-TV): It's not for the Andersons. It's for the Blubberbutts.

blubbergut *n.* a grossly fat person.—used derisively. Also **blubberguts.**
1942 *ATS* 386: Fat Person…*blimp…blubber-guts.* **1948** J. Stevens *Jim Turner* 104 [ref. to ca1910]: The unweaned blubber-gut bawled and took on about how I'd broken a rib for him. **1966** "T. Pendleton" *Iron Orchard* 120: Looked like he was about to unload on ol' blubber-gut, then he jest walked off.

blubberhead *n.* FATHEAD. Also **blubber-headed,** *adj.*
*1823 "J. Bee" *Slang* 13: *Blubber-headed*—thick meaty nob. *1821–26 [Stewart] *Man-of-War's-Man* I 175: That huge blubber-headed sea-calf of a countryman of yours. **1876** Cody & Arlington *Life on Border* 34: He is a complete blubberhead. **1928** McKay *Banjo* 7: Why, sure it's better, you…blubberhead. **1931** Farrell *McGinty* 187: Gwan, blubberhead, and do your work. **1932** Nelson *Prison Days & Nights* 58: He was known as…"Old Blubberhead" by the inmates. **1937** Wexley & Duff *Angels* (film): Out of the way, blubberhead. **1945** Fay *Be Poor* 135: You blubberhead. **1947–52** Ellison *Invisible Man* 175: Damn those laboratory blubberheads to hell!

blubber-hunter *n.* *Naut.* **1.** a whaling man.—used derisively.
1830 N. Ames *Mariner's Sks.* 143: Towards the middle of February [sea elephants] were very large and called by the English "blubber hunters" "brown cows." **1840** Olmsted *Whaling Voyage* 327: The merchantman…disdains the dirty "blubber hunter," as he invidiously denominates his rival. **1871** Thomes *Whaleman* 18: Avast there, you blubberhunter. **1878** Shippen *30 Yrs.* 267: I thought you were some infernal rag-picker or blubber-hunter sent to be licked into shape. **1887** Davis *Sea-Wanderer* 90: Ranking themselves in the same category as "blubber hunters" (whale-men). **1894** J. Slocum *Liberdade* 93: "Aye, aye, sir," said the old "blubberhunter." **1899** Robbins *Gam* 14: Just the same rogue as before he turned blubber-hunter.

2. a whaling ship.—used derisively.
1842 J.R. Browne *Whaling Cruise* ch. ii: Better they never was weaned, than go driftin' round the world in a blubber hunter. **1859** *Spirit of Times* (July 30) 291: Falling in with a brother blubber hunter "boiling out." **1887** Davis *Sea-Wanderer* 81: The drunken swabs are not fit to scrape the decks of a blubber-hunter. **1896** Hamblen *Many Seas* 5: The old sea song which I have since heard in many an old "blubber hunter's" forecastle. **1908** J.H. Williams, in *Independent* (Aug. 27) 470: I heartily wished myself back…in that round-bellied, slab-sided, old blubber hunter which I had left at Honolulu. **1912** in R.C. Murphy *Logbook* 80: Britons have a continuing maritime tradition, and the master of a ship—even of a humble wind-jammer and blubber-hunter—symbolizes a relatively lordly estate in their system. *1929 Bowen *Sea Slang* 15: *Blubber Hunter.* A term used for the old whaling ships, not by way of a compliment.

blubbermouth *n.* a person having heavy jowls.—used derisively.
1941 Epstein *Bride Came C.O.D.* (film): Five years ago before I struck oil you thought highly enough of me to call me "blubbermouth."

bludget *n.* [perh. infl. by *bludgeon; -et* app. repr. fem. n. suff. *-ette*] *Und.* (see 1859 quot.).
1859 Matsell *Vocab.* 12: *Bludget.* A female thief who decoys her victims into alley-ways, or other dark places, for the purpose of robbing them. **1866** *Nat. Police Gaz.* (Nov. 3) 2: I "piped" issuing from the side door those two notorious "bludgets," Poll Sullivan and Hattie Clark.

blue *n.* **1.** *pl.* [earlier S.E. *blue devils*] a feeling of sadness, despondency, or melancholy.—usu. constr. with *the.* Now *S.E.*
*1741 in *OEDS.* **1770** in Whiting *Early Amer. Proverbs* 37: Gamble has been long indisposed with the Blues. **1807** Irving *Salmagundi* xv: I saw he was still under the influence of a whole legion of the blues. **1818** in Royall *Letters from Ala.* 119: Have you got the blues again? **1823** [J. Neal] *Errata* I 31: He was inclined to the blues. **1839** Marryat *Diary* 264: I have the blues, the worst kind, no mistake. **1842** in Eliason *Tarheel Talk* 260: I had the blues terribly yesterday evening owing to my disappointment in not hearing [from you]. **1846** in U.S. Grant *Papers* I

114: I came back to my tent and to drive away, what you call the Blues, I took up some of your old letters. **1847** in Peskin *Vols.* 114: The merriest and most healthy man here gets the Blues. **1847** in *Calif. Hist. Qly.* (Jan. 1923) 237: Got the blues very bad indeed in consequence of Isadora having jilted me. **1865** in Springer *Sioux Country* 67: I have the blues like hell. **1908** in H.C. Fisher *A. Mutt* 124: I got the blues already. **1956** M. Wolff *Big Nick.* 10: You just got the blues today, that's all.

2. *Naut.* a bluejacket.

1830 Ames *Mariner's Sks.* 100: One of these…thought proper to arrest our washerwoman as she was coming to the ship with a boat load of clean clothes for us "blues."

3. *Stu.* a strict and strait-laced student; a prude.

1842 *The Dartmouth* IV 117: The students here are divided into two parties,…the *Rowes* and the *Blues*. The Rowes are very liberal in their notions; the *Blues* more strict. *Ibid.* 118: Lucian called him a blue, and fell back in his chair in a pouting fit. **1849** *Yale Tomahawk* (Nov.): None ever knew a sober "blue,"/In this "blood crowd" of ours. **1850** *Yale Lit. Mag.* XV 81: I wouldn't carry a novel into chapel to read…because some of the blues might see you. **1851** Union College *Parthenon* 6: To acquire popularity…he must lose his money at bluff and euchre without a sigh, and damn up hill and down the sober church-going man, as an out-and-out *blue*. **1851** Hall *College Wds.* 21: In several American colleges, a student who is very strict in observing the laws, and conscientious in performing his duties, is styled a *blue*.

4.a. a police officer in a blue uniform.—usu. pl.

*****1844** in *OEDS*: Whether this here mobbing…will grow to such a riot that the Oxford Blues must quell it. **1867** [Williams] *Brierly* 20: The crushers are getting to know too much. I believe the best of our trade join the blues. **1868** [Williams] *Black-Eyed Beauty* 7: In the streets, which the "blues" had cleared of the stages and carts [were] a double set of contrary streams of people. **1869** *Overland Mo.* (Aug.) 114: The "Blues," as Donahue sarcastically termed all policemen. *****1889** Barrère & Leland *Dict. Slang* I 147: The police force is sometimes spoken of as the "blues." **1935** Pollock *Underworld Sp.*: *Blue,* a uniformed policeman. **1967** deCoy *Nigger Bible* 234: I just missed getting locked up myself, or maybe shot by a "blue." **1974** *N.Y. Post* (Aug. 24) 21: Mayor Beame had made a campaign promise to put more blues on the streets. **1976** "N. Ross" *Policeman* 17: The Blacks and the blues refused to fight in the wet, so the wagon men just picked up the losers. **1983** Helprin *Winter's Tale* 13: He…turned the horse around, intending to charge through…the blues. **1983** *Hill Street Blues* (NBC-TV police series) (title). **1989** *Booker* (Fox-TV): Ask those two blues what's goin' on.

b. a U.S. soldier in a blue uniform.

1848 in R.L. Wright *Irish Emigrant Ballads* 522: Dey killed two blues ob Germantown,…/To shoot 'em back de soldiers rally. **1866** in Hilleary *Webfoot* 179: The insult given to the "Blues" of this post. *Ibid.* 197: The swallows…never…cry at the blues. **1905** "W. Hale" *Cowboy & Ranchman* 121 [ref. to 1870's]: When you mentioned the blues in the war they got on the prod.

5. *Angling.* a bluefish.

1897 *Outing* (Sept.) 546: The blues are here!…an' they're bitin' like savages! **1943** P. Harkins *Coast Guard* 57: Well, plenty of blues and tuna out there. **1982** WINS news report: There'll be great fishing for blues this weekend.

6. *Narc.* any of various blue capsules or tablets.

1970 Landy *Underground Dict.* 36: *Blue*…Pill of the amphetamine type. **1972** Nat. Lampoon (Oct.) 41: Dexamyl 15 mg. (blue). **1973** *Seattle Times* (June 3) 3: When a woman is under the influence of "reds" and "blues" both, it must have been a terrifying thing….We have strict rules about drugs.

7. *Mil.* [orig. in ref. to the blue river lines on terrain maps; cf. BLUE FEATURE and BLUE LINE] a river or stream.

1971 *Newsweek* (Sept. 13) 40: Hump up the mountain…hump down the mountain…wade the "blue" (river). **1986** Thacker *Pawn* 15 [ref. to Vietnam War]: Bear's at the blue. Says the water is pretty deep. *Ibid.* 33: The rest got wet when we crossed that blue. **1987** R. Miller *Slob* 131: He knew Charlie loved to dig down next to blue and make a slanting escape tunnel that would exit out below the water table. **1984–88** Hackworth & Sherman *About Face* 672: Especially careful not to fire "across the blue" (as the troops in the Delta called any canal, stream or river) into friendlies.

8. *pl.* blue eyes.

1979 *Easyriders* (Dec.) 5: From outta nowhere a Frisbee came sailin' down the street, catchin' 'im between the blues.

9. *Baseball.* the umpires.—used collect.

1983 L. Frank *Hardball* 68: The umpires (or "Blue," as they are often referred to, in reference to their uniform color) are often the target of

the players' frustrations.

¶ In phrase:

¶ **sing the blues** to complain, esp. in a whining fashion. Also vars.

1918 Straub *Diary* (May 5) 76: It has been rainy and very miserable all day long…and everybody seems to be singing the blues. **1939–40** O'Hara *Pal Joey* 51: A year ago you were the one crying the blues. **1942** White *Expendable* 22: The doctors were all reservists, going around with long faces, singing the blues about the way the war was going. **1943** in W.C. Fields *By Himself* 487: I have many beefs, but no one…is interested in the singing of the blues. **1949** De Forrest *Gay Year* 38: He had helped some who had come to him to "sing the blues." **1962** Carr & Cassavetes *Too Late Blues* (film): It's just a little too late to be crying the blues, isn't it? **1963** Coon *Short End* 222: I think you're belting down beer and singing the blues. **1973** Childress *Hero* 10: Some cats moanin the blues, cryin bout how whitey does. **1973** Crawford *Gunship Cmmdr.* 97: All the enlisted men are whining the blues because their club's still closed. **1977** Olsen *Fire Five* 126: So don't go singing the blues about…the lady fireman. **1978** in Lyle & Golenbock *Bronx Zoo* 78: Thurman was so pissed. He was moaning….He was singing the blues. **1983** P. Dexter *God's Pocket* 35: He didn't cry the blues when he lost. **1988** *N.Y. Post* (June 21) 80: I don't sing the blues when I lose and I keep the same grin when I win.

blue *adj.* **1.a.** disappointed; sad; despondent; melancholy. Now S.E.

*****1788** Grose *Vulgar Tongue* (ed. 2): *Blue, to look blue,* to be…disappointed. *****1821** *Real Life in London* I 401: Martin's friends began to look *blue,* but still expected, the fight being young, there was yet much to be done. *****1825** "Blackmantle" *Eng. Spy* I 369: Looking as *blue* as Megrim, and feeling…*fretful.* **1831** in [S. Smith] *Letters of Downing* 72: I felt kind of blue, and I guess I blushed a little. **1844** Strong *Diary* I 224: Last night I found myself growing blue again. **1846** in Harlow *Old Bowery* 191: I felt almighty blue. **1859** Chamberlain *My Confession* 130: These sounds made me shiver and I felt blue enough. **1862** in Jackman *Diary* 41: We saw the field officers riding about looking "blue"; but we were too near worn out to pay any attention to impending danger. **1863** in Whitman *Correspondence* I 92: We feel disappointed here about Charleston—I felt as blue about it as anybody. **1866** C.H. Smith *Bill Arp* 136: I very often feel *blue.* **1909** in McCay *Little Nemo* 203: I feel awful blue about the whole thing. **1977** R.S. Parker *Effective Decisions* 40: Depression…is the feeling of being melancholy or "blue."

b. unpromising or discouraging.—usu. constr. with *look.*

1864 in Huckaby & Simpson *Tulip* 44: Things looked "quite blue" out there, so you know Pa was despondent. **1870** Medbery *Wall St.* 173: The outlook was of the bluest. **1879** Cody *Life* 94: The situation,…to say the least, looked pretty blue. **1882** F.W. Dawson *Confed. Service* 28: Things looked rather blue.

2. *Und.* counterfeit.

1791 [W. Smith] *Confess. T. Mount* 18: Bad money, *blue bit.*

3. drunk.

1813–18 Weems *Drunk. Look. Glass* 72: For coming home one night, *quite blue,* from a grog shop, he got his neck snapped short by a fall into his own *saw pit.* **1821** Waln *Hermit in Phila.* 23: *Blue as razors,* no doubt; — *drunk as wheel-barrows,* — *fuddled,* — *and corned.* **1838, 1844** in *DAE.* **1847** Robb *Squatter Life* 154: By his frequent libations he not only got *blue,* but everything he looked at was multiplying. **1848** Bartlett *Amer.*: *Blue*…A synonym in the tippler's vocabulary for *drunk.* **1851** *Polly Peablossom* 105: The blue tickets he sold out to some uppercountry flat-boatmen who were pretty *blue.* **1864** [Armstrong] *Red-Tape* 276: Tin cups, canteens, cap-covers, anything that would hold the article were made use of, and they are a blue old crowd, from the General down. **1866** C.H. Smith *Bill Arp* 136: About twice in a while I go to the doggery and get *blue.* **1919** *Century* (Dec.) 293: Did you take notice to those old birds about the tents…blue with dynamite rum and ready to drool for a hand-out. *****1945** S.J. Baker *Austral. Lang.* 166: A man who is drunk is said to be *blue.*

4. (used as an intensive).—occ. quasi-adv.

1821 Waln *Hermit in Phila.* 27: A blue greenhorn. **1856** Hall *College Wds.* 203: At Princeton College, the word *blue* is used with *fizzle,* to render it intensive; as, he made a *blue fizzle,* he *fizzled blue.* **1862** in Berkeley *Confed. Arty.* 10: One old gentleman tried to keep up his umbrella; but the crowd forced him to put it down by hollering at him, "Put down that umbrella, put down that *blue* umbrella." a**1870** *Coon-Hunt* 21: I cussed him blue! **1928** Dahlberg *Bottom Dogs* 58: Larry was scared blue. **1929** "E. Queen" *Roman Hat* ch. viii: She was scared blue but she was kind of plucky, too. **1933** in R.E. Howard *Iron Man* 107: Glory had rushed out of the building after me, screaming blue murder.

1964 N.Y.C. teenager: He gives me any more trouble, I'm gonna carve his blue ass with my switchblade. **1967** Dibner *Admiral* 26: She was screaming blue murder. **1977** Univ. Tenn. student: He's got a blue million of 'em. **1981–85** S. King *It* 78: What the blue *hell?*

5. *Stu.* overly conscientious in one's studies. Cf. BLUE, *n.*, 3.

1851 Hall *College Wds.* 21: "Our real delvers, midnight students," says a correspondent from Williams College, "are called *blue.*"

6. *Confed. Army.* in federal military service.

1864 *Battle-Fields of So.* 283: Send all de blue ornary cusses to [hell]. **1905** "W. Hale" *Cowboy & Ranchman* 119 [ref. to 1870's]: I have killed a whole herd of you blue scoundrels during the war.

7. Esp. *Theat.* (of material in a performance, or the performance itself) indecent, risqué; *(hence)* pornographic.

[***1824** in *OEDS*: *Thread o' Blue,* any little smutty touch in song-singing, chatting, or piece of writing.] ***1864** Hotten *Slang Dict.* (ed. 3) 78: *Blue,* said of talk that is smutty or indecent. **1921** *Variety* (Jan. 28) 6: Albee Admonishes House Mgrs. to Suppress "Blueness" Warns Circuit Men to Guard Against Extremes or Spicy Comedy, Bare-Leg Display, Etc.…Nothing of a vulgar nature is to be permitted on any Keith stage. **1921** *Variety* (Nov. 18) 10: It's composed of…generous slathers of hoke, not a little vulgarity, a line or bit of business approaching the blue here and there. **1924** *Sat. Eve. Post* (July 12) 15: *Blue*—off-color lines or business. **1925** G.M. Cohan *Broadway* 59: You're playing to a lady audience in this house. No rough stuff, no blue jokes or anything else like that. **1940** *Time* (Mar. 25) 48: Such "blue" songs are naturally not allowed on the radio networks. **1946** J. Adams *Gags* 24: Something blue? Well, we've got to keep the women amused, too. **1949** C. Gorham *Mr. Dolan* 66: How would you like to come up to my place and see a blue movie? **1952** *Collier's* (Apr. 26) 77: They tell me he never cracked a blue joke in his life. **1970** T. Southern *Blue Movie* (title). **1971** Brower *Late Creature* 59: A few blue movies. **1981** Raban *Old Glory* 40: Posters for the blue-movie houses showed nipples and pudenda. **1991** *Time* (Oct. 21) 79: Redd Foxx…a nightclub comic specializing in blue humor.

8. *Restaurant.* (of beef) very rare.

1972 A.K. Shulman *Ex-Prom Queen* 95: All the beefs were roasted very rare, or, as we called it, "blue."

9. *Und.* being an undercover police officer.—used predicatively.

1985 *CNN News* (CNN-TV) (Oct. 14): Are you blue?…You better not be blue, guy!

¶ In phrases:

¶ **get the blue envelope** to be fired from one's job.

1902–03 Ade *People You Know* 85: We was so strong that we killed the rest of the Bill, so we got the Blue Envelope.

¶ **make a blue fist of** to make a botch of.

1834 Caruthers *Kentuckian in N.Y.* 25: A chap would make a blue fist of takin a dead aim…with the butt end of a psalm in his guzzle.

¶ **till all is blue** to the very end; to an extreme.

1806 in Thornton *Amer. Gloss.* I: The land we till is all our own;…Therefore we'll fight till all is blue. **1827** in *JAF* LXXVI (1963) 294: I'le stikk tu himm til all's blu. ***1831** J.L. Gardner *Military Sketch-Bk.* II 28. ***1837** in *F & H* (rev.) 285: I'll drink till all's blue. **1859, 1862, 1888** in *DAE*. ***1901** in *F & H* (rev.) 285: And argue in a didactic, not to say opinionated manner, till all was blue.

¶ **turn blue!** (used as a sarcastic retort).

1953 Chandler *Goodbye* 247: Beat it. Turn blue. **1955** *Phil Silvers Show* (CBS-TV): Why don't you turn blue? **1960** Thom *Subterraneans* (film): Turn blue! Travel! Go! **1963** Cameron *Black Camp* 12: "Turn blue, medic," growled a surly voice.

blue-and-white *n. Police.* a blue-and-white patrol car. Cf. BLACK-AND-WHITE.

1974 V.E. Smith *Jones Men* 164: And make sure none of them goddamn blue-and-whites move before they're supposed to. **1978** Diehl *Sharky's Machine* 51: Sharky was assigned to a blue-and-white. **1980** Garrison *Snakedoctor* 91: I'll call in for a blue-and-white. **1985** M. Baker *Cops* 247: Two or three o'clock in the morning, it's quiet. A blue and white sails down the street. **1988** Kienzle *Marked for Murder* 77: Several blue-and-whites as well as unmarked police cars were double parked.

blue angel *n. Narc.* a blue capsule; BLUEBIRD, 4.

1967 Maurer & Vogel *Narc. & Narc. Add.* 104: Blue angels. **1970** Landy *Underground Dict.* 36: *Blue angel*…Amytal. **1972** C.T. Rowan, in *Seattle Times* (May 7) 12A: On the street, these drugs…are called "downers" or "goofballs." Most popular are the "red devils" (seconal), "yellow jackets" (nembutal), "blue angels" (amytal) and "Christmas

trees" (tuinal). **1972** *Nat. Lampoon* (Oct.) 38: Amytal (blue angel).

blue balls *n.pl.* **1.** venereal buboes.

[***1788** Grose *Vulgar Tongue* (ed. 2): *Blue Boar.* A venereal bubo.] **1912** in R.C. Murphy *Logbook* 128: "Blue-balls" (meaning buboes or swellings in the groin), went on Mr. Almeida.…The Old Man's visage screwed up into the expression we dread to see. "Bring him up," he roared; "blue-balls, clap, pox, strangury, good God, what next?" **1930** Waldron *Old Sgt.* 27: These complications may produce an infection of the glands in the groin which produces "blue balls." **1936** in Kromer *Waiting* 226: Terrible diseases…hard and soft chancres…last, but not least, blueballs. **1950** *New Directions* 383: We're gonna get the syph, the clap and blueballs, all for free! **1951** UMF-323 *Old Ballads* 12: He had the syph and the seven-year itch…the clap and the blue balls too. **1956** in Oliver *Blues Tradition* 240: Now your mammy got the blue-ball, your sister got the pox. **1982** D. Williams *Hit Hard* 59: Some positive suggestions to cut down on these cases of syphilis, gonorrhea, and blue balls.

2. testicular discomfort caused by sexual stimulation without ejaculation.

1916–22 Cary *Sex. Vocab.* II: *Blue balls.* Orchitis, or swelling of the testicles. **1938** H. Miller *Capricorn* 196: Little Nemo walks around with a seven-day hard-on and a wonderful pair of blue balls bequeathed by Lady Bountiful. **1968** *Playboy* (May) 78: "Blue balls" or "lover's nuts," in which the male complains of severe pain in the testicles if stimulated without reaching orgasm. **1973** Hirschfeld *Victors* 78: All she ever did was give him blue balls. Swap spit and dry hump for a while, that was as far as she'd go. **1977** Butler & Shryack *Gauntlet* 184: He hurt. He was suffering from what they called "blue balls." **1978** Pilcer *Teen Angel* 85: Does D.B. give you anything besides a case of blue balls?

3. gonorrhea.

1938 "Justinian" *Americana Sexualis* 13: *Blue Balls.* n. Gonorrhea. Derived from the swelling and discoloration of the scrotum when the gonnococcus attacks the testicles. U.S. C. 20. Low coll. **1952** Larson *Barnyard Folklore* 84: Gonorrhea: dose, clap, blue balls. **1954–60** *DAS*: *Blue balls*…gonorrhea. **1988** Dye *Outrage* 62: A case of the blue-ball clap.

blue-bellied *adj.* despicable. [Applied esp. to Northerners and Unionists during the Civil War.]

1752–56 A. Hamilton *Tuesday Club* I 98: Nasty, blewbellied, blanket ars'd…Son of a whore. **1852** *So. Lit. Messenger* XVIII 681: A dratted, blue-bellied federal whig! **1865** in *DA*: The mackerel-eating, blue-bellied, psalm-singing Abolitionist. **1878** McElroy *Andersonville* 271: Them blue-bellied New England Yankees. **1882** Sweet *Sketches* 172: The…idea was to chase the blue-bellied Yankee around the room. **1888** in *War Papers* I 37 [ref. to Civil War]: You d—d blue-bellied Yankee, —comer here! **1888** Hawes *Cahaba* 85: D—n the white-livered, blue-bellied devil! **1911** L.B. Giles *Tex. R.* 44 [ref. to Civil War]: Give up them pistols, you — — blue-bellied — —. **1931** in Botkin *Treas. Amer. Folk.* 350: You blue-bellied rascal!

bluebelly *n.* **1.** a New Englander; *(hence)* any Northerner.—used contemptuously.

1827 in Pickering *Inquiries* 92: The inhabitants are chiefly Americans.…In short "blue bellies" of all sorts and condition. **1857** T. Gladstone *Englishman in Kans.* 43: No highfalutin airs here, you know. Keep that for them Blue-bellies down East. **1867** in Rosa *Wild Bill* 60: If you'd heard me swear and cuss the blue-bellies, you'd a-thought me one of the wickedest of the whole crew. **1939** Appel *People Talk* 211: Old Bob LaFollette…said to some of those Republican bluebelly farmers:…"You're going to be devoured in twenty years." **1945** in *DA*: The Southern cowman refers to a Yankee as a "blue belly." **1968** in *DARE.*

2. a U.S. soldier; *(specif.)* a Union soldier during the Civil War.—used contemptuously. Now *hist.*

1863 in E.Z. Starr *Jennison's Jayhawkers* 260: Coming down here with…whites, niggers, Red Legs, Blue Legs and Blue Bellies, with orders to sack, burn, destroy, tear to pieces, &c., &c. **1863** in *DA*: A Provost Marshal's pass…must be presented to a pair of drunken blue-bellies, who are stationed at each church door. **1864** H.S. White *Pris. Life* 36: "There go the Yanks," "O, see the blue bellies." **1865** [Williams] *Joaquin* 12: He had one finger cut off in a skirmish of guerrillas, who had been a little mistaken in an idea which they had had of catching a detachment of Uncle Sam's blue-bellies napping. **1865** Sala *Diary* I 355: The men were exceedingly clean, and well set up—qualities which the "blue-bellies" or volunteers on active service, and enlisted men, have not the time to acquire. **1889** Barrère & Leland *Dict. Slang* I 147: "Blue bellies" was a term applied by the Confederate soldiery during the Civil War to the Federals, on account of their blue gaber-

dines. **1898** C. King *Warrior Gap* 232: The...cutthroats...had galloped in strong force...to murder Dean and his whole party of the hated "blue bellies." **1908** Fletcher *Rebel Pvt.* 6: One Southerner with his superior marksmanship could shoot down the d— Bluebellies as fast as they would come in sight. **1964** Landon & Huffaker *Rio Conchos* (film): You bluebellies got a law against killin' Apaches? **1977** Watts *Dict. Old West* 37: *Blue belly*. A soldier, on account of his blue uniform.
3. a police officer in a blue uniform.—used contemptuously.
****1909** Ware *Passing English* 130: "I gave the blue belly a fill"—would mean that you sent the policeman on the wrong scent. **1949** Monteleone *Crim. Slang* 28: *Bluebelly*...A policeman.

bluebird *n.* **1.** *Confed. Army.* a U.S. soldier.
1861 in *DA*: How are you, my blue-bird; and what do you think of this brilliant assemblage? **1867** Cooke *Wearing Gray* 176: The startled "blue birds," as we used to call our Northern friends, did not wait; the squadron on picket...hastily got to horse. **1867** Crawford *Mosby* 129: John Munson and Walter Whaley brought in two bluebirds, one walking and the other riding. **1870** F.M. Myers *Comanches* 296: The next thing was to toll the "blue birds" into his trap.
2. a police officer.
1918 Stringer *House of Intrigue* 72: That con-man had caught sight of either a bluebird or a singed cat—which latter is simply an officer in plain clothes. **1963** *Time* (Aug. 2) 14: Busters,...blue boys, bluebirds....Policemen.
3. *Mil.* a member of the WAVES.
1944 Kendall *Service Slang* 52: *Blue bird*...what a girl Marine calls a WAVE.
4. *Narc.* a blue capsule, esp. one containing sodium amytal. Also **bluejay.**
1953 Chandler *Goodbye* 219: Bluejays are sodium amytal. Redbirds are seconal. **1967** Maurer & Vogel *Narc. & Narc. Add.* (ed. 3) 343: *Bluebirds.* Sodium Amytal in capsules. **1969** N.Y.C. man, age *ca*40: You don't mix gin and bluebirds! **1972** *Nat. Lampoon* (Oct.) 41: Amytal (blue bird).
5. *Police.* a blue squad car.
1976 G.V. Higgins *Deke Hunter* 37: Six years in a bluebird...grabbing guys for driving...drunk.

bluebird weather *n. Av.* clear, ideal flying weather. Also **bluebird sky.**
1958 Camerer *Damned Wear Wings* 49 [ref. to WWII]: We're at 21,000 feet. Except for...blobs of...cumulus at 10,000 feet, maybe, it's bluebird weather. *Ibid.* 118: Bad enough to go over that place in bluebird weather. **1985** Heywood *Taxi Dancer* 25 [ref. to Vietnam War]: Just a bluebird sky and clumps of rime ice on the windscreen.

blue-blasted *adj.* damned.
1864 "Kirke" *Down in Tenn.* 123: Them blue-blasted nigger-tradin' Secesh.

blue blazer *n. Baseball.* a hard-pitched fastball.
1973 M. Moore, on *World Series* (NBC-TV) (Oct. 14): And there's the blue blazer!

blue blazes *n.* hell (in any informal sense).
1813–18 Weems *Drunk. Look. Glass* 117: Ye blue blazes of damnation! ****1832** B. Hall *Voyages* (Ser. 2) II 191: What the blue blazes shall I do next? **1882** Watkins *Co. Aytch* 133: The weather was cold as blue blazes. **1889** Barrère & Leland *Dict. Slang* I 147: *Blue-blazes* (common) hell. **1930** in Botkin & Harlow *R.R. Folklore* 325: Where the blue blankety blazes you going? **1941** in Botkin *Treas. Amer. Folk.* 126: Stack [was] mad as blue blazes because he had lost the magic hat. **1961** *You Bet Your Life* (NBC-TV): What in the blue blazes are you talking about?

blueboy *n.* **1.** a policeman.
****1883** in *OEDS*: The instrumental "blue boys" belonging to several metropolitan divisions. **1908** in Fleming *Unforgettable Season* 227: He will send a couple of hundred blue-boys to...make themselves useful should they be needed. **1958** Rumaker *Stories* 119: Take your clammy claw off me, blueboy. **1963** *Time* (Aug. 2) 14: Busters,...blue boys....Policemen. **1967** Hoffman *Revolution* 53: I think he is a rightwing heckler, and we're having a fist fight when the blue boys arrive. **1970** Gattzden *Black Vendetta* 44: The blueboys...start asking...questions. *a*1976 Roebuck & Frese *Rendezvous* 178: Those are the blue boys you have to watch out for. **1983** *Green Arrow* (July) 4: Blue Boys, He's all yours. Love, G.A.
2. (see quot.).
1919 Darling *Jargon Bk.* 5: *Blue Boy*—A blue steel automatic gun.

3. *Narc.* a blue capsule, esp. amytal. Cf. BLUEBIRD, 4.
1952 Himes *First Stone* 247: The Sodium amytal capsules...were blue so we called them blue boys.

blue bullet *n. Narc.* a blue capsule containing a barbiturate, esp. amytal. Cf. BLUEBIRD, 4.
1970, 1971, 1980 (cited in Spears *Drugs & Drink* 57).

blue cheer *n.* [sugg. by *Blue Cheer*, a trademark for laundry detergent] *Narc.* a blue pill or pills containing LSD and Methedrine.
1970 Landy *Underground Dict.* 37: *Blue cheer*...Type of LSD usually mixed with Methedrine. **1971** *N.Y. Post* (Sept. 16) 35: Giebelstadt, freakout from "Blue Cheer."

bluecoat *n.* **1.** a blue-uniformed U.S. soldier. Now *hist.* [In earlier use, as in cited *DAE* quot., S.E. or colloq. for any blue-uniformed individual.]
1676, 1686, 1687, 1723 in *DAE*. **1833** in *DAE*. **1862** in Heartsill *1491 Days* 67: And as for the "Blue Coats," they had as well register in Heaven at once. **1863** in Mohr *Cormany Diaries* 326: I was the first "blue coat" they had seen. **1864** in J.H. Wilson *Gen. Alexander* 54: It was grand to see these long lines of blue coats...move up the hillside as if on parade, without firing a shot. **1865** in Hilleary *Webfoot* 62: Some blue coat...killed a cow last night. **1866** *Beadle's Mo.* (May) 397: Two or three blue-coats sit on the porch of a pleasantly shaded house. **1873** [Perrie] *Buckskin Mose* 122: I'll be hanged if I haven't half a mind to ride after the blue-coats. **1879** [Tourgée] *Fool's Errand* 153: Just wait until the Blue Coats are gone. **1881** in Botkin *Treas. Amer. Folk.* 99: If we can't whip any company of "blue coats," why then I'll change my name and herd sheep in the States. **1896** King *Garrison Tangle* 45: The horse seemed to recognize his master as the foremost of the familiar bluecoats. **1964** *Gunsmoke* (CBS-TV): The sight of a bluecoat understandably riles him. **1980** M. Marshall *Gato* 88: Two of the blue coats are dead.
2. a blue-uniformed police officer.
****1852** in *OEDS*. **1875, 1878** (in *DAE*.). **1883** *Judge* (Jan. 13) 4: Chosen for the extirpation of all blue-coats in creation. **1890** Roe *Police* 223: The blue-coats ran after them. **1910** *N.Y. Eve. Jour.* (Feb. 3) 14: A score of bluecoats tried to break up the show. *a*1904–11 Phillips *Susan Lenox* I 284: She no longer saw the bluecoat for the intervening crowds. **1929** "E. Queen" *Roman Hat* ch. i 21: A group of bluecoats were hustling their way inside, their night sticks ready. **1955** Q. Reynolds *HQ* 36: Mayor Jimmy Walker...reviewed the new batch of bluecoats. **1966** J. Mills *Needle Park* 115: Some lousy bluecoat...busted him...for just *being* there. **1974** Univ. Tenn. student: Watch out for the bluecoat. **1987** Santiago *Undercover* 84: The point is we're bluecoats, and we can't do our own narcotics investigation.

blue dart *n.* **1.** *Baseball.* an especially hard-hit line drive. Also **blue darter.**
1942 *ATS* 655: *Blue dart*...a batted ball that travels in a straight line not far from the ground. **1950** Cummings *Dict. Baseball* 8: *Blue darter*....A sharply hit ball, through or over the infield. Not a long drive. **1964** Thompson & Rice *Every Diamond* 140: *Blue-darter:* Line drive hit. **1977** (quot. at SCREAMING MEEMIE). **1988** Mays & Sahadi *Say Hey* 49: I smacked a lot of blue darts, a lot of line drives.
2. *U.S. Mil. Acad.* (see quot.).
1978 Truscott *Dress Gray* 172: Slaight caught a glimpse of a "Blue Dart" or two in there—the light blue forms with which one cadet could pillory another by writing a special report....The Blue Dart needn't be signed by the cadet writing it.

blue devil *n.* **1.** *Confed. Army.* a federal soldier.
1864 in L.J. Daniel *Soldiering* 157: I can see some of the Blue Devils from where I sit.
2. *Narc.* BLUEBIRD, 4.
1968–69 McWhirter *Dunlop Encyc.* 523: Phenobarbitone (luminal)...slang names: barbs, *blue devils* or blue heavens. **1970** Horman & Fox *Drug Awareness* 464: Blue devils—"Amytal" (brand of amobarbital, Eli Lilly and Company). **1971** Dahlskog *Dict.* 8: *Blue devils*...Blue capsules containing a barbiturate. **1974** *TULIPQ* (coll. B.K. Dumas): Drugs...grass, herbs, blue devils, coke.

blue-eyed *adj.* **1.** drunk.
1856 Hall *College Wds.* (ed. 2) 461: Some stage of inebriation...*fogmatic, blue-eyed*, a passenger in the Cape Ann stage.
2. (used in oaths and curses); "darned."
[**1902** A.H. Lewis *Wolfville Days* 273: I'm the bloo-eyed lynx of Whiskey Crossin', an' I weighs four thousand pounds.] **1938** Holbrook

Mackinaw 7 [ref. to *ca*1910]: Vulgar and shopworn phrases like "blue-eyed, bandy-legged, jumped-up ol' whistlin' Jesus H. Mackinaw Christ." **1959** on *Golden Age of Television* (A&E-TV, 1988): What in the blue-eyed world are you talkin' about? **1970** Grissim *White Man's Blues* 193: This'll baffle the blue-eyed world! **1972** R. Barrett *Lovomaniacs* 402: Not that there was a thing in the ever-lovin', blue-eyed world I could do about it.

blue feature *n.* [from cartographic jargon; cf. BLUE, *n.*, 7 and BLUE LINE] *Mil.* a body of water. *Joc.*
  1982 Del Vecchio *13th Valley* 477 [ref. to Vietnam War]: Rope's gonna drown Little Brother in the blue feature.

blue flu *n.* an organized protest action by police officers (*occ.* other municipal employees) in which individuals claim that influenza or some other illness prevents them from reporting to work.
  1967 Hersey *Algiers Motel* 152: I had one day out on blue flu. **1971** Horan *Blue Messiah* 580: There was a possibility that some department could be hit with what he called "blue flu, a newly discovered strain of influenza." **1971** *N.Y. Post* (Nov. 20) 3: Acting Fire Commissioner Vincent Canty has pledged that the city will receive full fire protection despite a new epidemic of "blue flu" among uniformed firemen. **1976** WINS news broadcast (Sept. 6): Yesterday about a hundred [police] officers [in New Orleans] were home with what is being called the "blue flu." **1976** *N.Y. Times Mag.* (Sept. 12) 111: As the second year of busing began, the Police Patrolmen's Association [of Boston] called a "blue flu" sickout in a dispute over assignments and overtime. **1981** WHEL radio news (Knoxville, Tenn.) (Apr. 23): There's a case of blue flu going around, and we don't have any policemen on duty this morning. **1983** *AP Network News* (WKGN radio): The police sick-out in Columbus, Ohio....Now, more on the blue flu. **1989** *TV Guide* (Jan. 28) 99: When the police union decides to strike, the Jump Street cops come down with a bad case of blue flu. **1992** Hosansky & Sparling *Working Vice* 114: A "Blue Flu" sick-out lasted two days.

bluegrass *v.* [alluding to Kentucky, the *Bluegrass* State] *Narc.* to commit (a drug addict) to Lexington Federal Narcotics Hospital (Lexington, Ky.) for treatment.
  1953 W. Brown *Monkey on My Back* 116: Upon his arrival in Lexington, he would be "blue-grassed," legally declared a drug addict under the laws of Kentucky. **1958** A. King *Mine Enemy* 178 [ref. to *ca*1950]: Go down and blue-grass yourself, why don't you? **1961** R. Russell *Sound* 104: They blue-grassed me to Lex, and all that shit.

bluehead *n.* cheap, powerful whiskey.
  1856 in *DAE* I 256: I thought I would ask you if you wouldn't swallow a "slug" of Carthage blue-head. **1857** *Spirit of Times* (Dec. 26) 544: Judge Lister—with a gallon of "blue-head" under his shirt.

blue heaven *n. Narc.* BLUEBIRD, 4.
  1954 Maurer & Vogel *Narc. & Narc. Add.* 292: Blue heaven. Sodium amytal (in capsules). **1964** Harris *Junkie Priest* 47: Junkie talk for barbiturates floated through his mind: *goofballs, nembies...redbirds, blue heavens.* **1966** Goldstein *One in Seven* 202: Sodium Amytal capsules become "blue heavens." **1968** *Adam-12* (NBC-TV): He's sellin' blue heavens.

bluejacket *n.* **1.** *Naut.* a naval seaman, usu. below the rating of petty officer. Now *S.E.*
  *1805 J. Davis *Post-Captain* 136: The blue jackets stand no chance. **1808** in Nevins & Weitenkampf *Cartoons* 25: Oh! poor Sailors!—poor blue Jackets! **1814** in B. Palmer *Diary* (Jan. 28): I guess he wants a few Blue Jackets to man those fir built Frigates of ours. ***1830** F. Marryat, in *OED*: Every "blue jacket" would walk over. **1839–40** Cobb *Green Hand* I 74: My duty lay with the blue jackets. **1841** [Mercier] *Man-of-War* 139: He'll do something for the blue jackets when he becomes President.
  2.a. a blue-uniformed U.S. soldier.
  1862 in S.C. Wilson *Column South* 16: Mrs. S. almost shedding tears to see the "blue Jackets" again. **1862** in M. Lane *Dear Mother* 124: The Texans...commenced the fun by picking off the blue jackets whenever they showed themselves. **1863** in Swinfen *Ruggles' Regt.* 90: I've seen blue-jackets run under similar circumstances. **1863** E.H. Rhodes *All for the Union* 125: A Rebel officer under a guard of blue jackets went past. **1870** F.M. Meyers *Comanches* 44: To which the blue jacket replied, he "guessed he would."
  b. a blue-uniformed police officer.
  1862 [W.G. Stevenson] *In Rebel Army* 35: A "blue jacket," the sobriquet of the [Confederate] military policemen that then guarded the city [of Memphis], stepped up.

bluejackets *n.pl. Logging.* lice; GRAYBACKS.
  1956 Sorden & Ebert *Logger's* 10 [ref. to *a*1925]: *Crumbs,* Lice. Same as *blue-jackets.*

bluejay *n.* **1.** *Logging.* a member of a road-repair crew.
  1942 *ATS*: Blue jay...a road repairman. **1956** Sorden & Ebert *Logger's* 28 [ref. to *a*1925]: Road monkey,...Same as *blue-jay.*
  2. see BLUEBIRD, 4.

blue jeans *n.pl. CB.* a blue-uniformed police officer or officers.
  1976 (quot. at NIGHTCRAWLER).

blue johnny *n.* a U.S. soldier.
  1866 in Hilleary *Webfoot* 203: The boat landed but "nary" "Blue Johnny" stepped ashore to receive the kiss of his patient wife or pining sweetheart.

blue-light *n.* **1.** *Pol.* a New England Federalist opposed to the War of 1812. [See *DA* for allusion.]
  1814, 1815 in *DA.* **1833** J. Neal *Down-Easters* I 47: Calling one another blue-lights, jacobins, tories, democrats and enemies to the country. **1847** in *DA.*
  2.a. *Orig. Naut.* a pious or sanctimonious person. Also attrib.
  *1826 (cited in Partridge *DSUE* (ed. 6) 1013). **1849** Melville *White Jacket* 58: One of them was a blue-light Calvinist. **1872** *Myself* 38: One of the spectators...was denounced as a "blue-light!" ***1929** Bowen *Sea Slang.* **1959** E.J. Warner *Gens. in Gray* 151: Thomas Jonathan "Stonewall" Jackson, "Old Jack," "Old Blue-Light," was born in Clarksburg (West) Virginia, on January 21, 1824.
  b. *Stu.* a student who informs on his fellows.
  1856 Hall *College Wds.* (ed. 2) 30: *Blue-Light.* At the University of Vermont this term is used, writes a correspondent, to designate "a boy who sneaks about college, and reports to the Faculty the short-comings of his fellow students. A *blue-light* is occasionally found watching the door of a room where a party of jolly ones are roasting a [stolen] turkey,...that he may go to the Faculty with the story, and tell them who the boys are." **1900** *DN* II 23: *Blue-light* n. A student who seeks to ingratiate himself with the faculty by informing.

blue lightning *n. West.* a pistol.
  1869 *Overland Mo.* (Aug.) 126: Among names of revolvers I remember the following: Meat in the Pot, Blue Lightning, Peacemaker, Mr. Speaker, Black-eyed Susan, Pill-box, My Unconverted Friend. **1922** Rollins *Cowboy* 148 [ref. to 1890's]: The affronted citizen would be justified, if he "dug for" his own "blue lightning."

blue line *n.* [from cartographic jargon; cf. BLUE, *n.*, 7, and BLUE FEATURE] *Mil.* a river or stream.
  1976 C.R. Anderson *Grunts* 47 [ref. to 1969]: [The marines] inched...down toward the flat grassy plain with its refreshing wet "blue line" in the middle...."This is Six! Tell your people they can stop at this here blue line, but to fill only two canteens." *Ibid.* 48: He says he sees too many people bunched up down around that blue line. **1989** Zumbro & Walker *Jungletracks* 108: We found a blue line with a hard bottom.

blue machine *n.* [sugg. by GREEN MACHINE] the U.S. Navy.—constr. with *the.*
  1978 Lieberman & Rhodes *CB* (ed. 2) 291: *Blue machine*—Navy base. **1983** Univ. Tenn. student: The Navy is *the* big blue machine.

Blue Max *n.* [see 1963 quot.; U.S. currency is founded on J.D. Hunter's novel *The Blue Max* and esp. on the 1966 film based on it] *Mil.* the congressional Medal of Honor.
  [**1963** J.D. Hunter *Blue Max* 168: The *Ordre Pour le Mérite*...The Blue Max: Germany's highest award for an individual act of gallantry.] **1984–88** Hackworth & Sherman *About Face* 91: A Silver Star is a damned high decoration, but it's not the Blue Max, it's not even a Distinguished Service Cross. *Ibid.* 841: *Blue Max.* Slang for the Medal of Honor. **1990** P. Dickson *Slang!* 233: *Blue max.* The Medal of Honor, from its blue field.

blue meanie *n.* [sugg. by the *Blue Meanies,* fantastic cartoon ogres in the film *The Yellow Submarine* (1968)] a mean person; (*specif.*) (*pl.*) police officers.
  1969 in J.C. Pratt *Vietnam Voices* 392: The "Blue Meanies" broke their heads. **1970** *Time* (May 18) 8: With [U.C.L.A.] students advancing on and retreating from the police—the "blue meanies." **1970** Letter to ed., in *N.Y. Post* (June 8): [refers to police and right-wing blue-collar workers as "blue meanies"]. **1975** Wambaugh *Choirboys* 266: Oh, you're so

cute when you're all mad! You blue meanie! **1978** Maupin *Tales* 54: Has the Blue Meanie gone to lunch yet? **1988** *Daily Beacon* (Univ. Tenn.) (Apr. 18) 7: Friday night: The Blue Meanies invade the Strip. "Hold it, kids! Let's see some I.D.!"

bluenose *n.* **1.a.** a native of Nova Scotia or (in later extended use) Newfoundland, New Brunswick, or Prince Edward Island; (*broadly*, and now *obs.*) a Canadian. Also **bluenosers**. [The earliest quot. is couched in Scots and is app. a contemptuous name for a Scots Presbyterian.]

[***1698–1706** in D'Urfey *Pills* V 43: Forsaking aw other Loons, lubberloons, black Lips, blue Nases, an aw Swigbell'd caves?] **1785** in *Dict. Canadianisms* 59: The Blue-noses, to use a vulgar appellation, who had address sufficient to divide the Loyalists, exerted themselves to the utmost of their power and cunning. **1825** in *Dict. Canadianisms* 59: During the course of the past week I had employed…a long blue nose to do the odd jobs. **1837** in Hawthorne *Amer. Notebooks* 45: Personages at the tavern—the Governor, somewhat stared after…; Councillors…; the Adjutant General of the state; two young Blue-Noses from Canada or the provinces. **1845** in *Dict. Canadianisms* 59: Of the other original settlers [in New Brunswick], or as they are particularly termed, "blue noses," they are composed of the refugees and their descendants. **1869** *Galaxy* (Aug.) 180: The "Blue Nose" from Nova Scotia was sitting side by side with the "Boer" from the Cape of Good Hope. **1877** *Puck* (Apr.) 2: The Nova Scotians are beginning to kick against the name of "Blue Noses." *Ibid.* (June) 11: Spring rises…and girds up her loins preparatory to fleeing over the border to the land of the blue-noses. **1883** Russell *Sailors' Lang.* 16: Blue nose.—A name given to a Nova Scotian. **1886** Leman *Old Actor* 24: I'm a blue Nose…born in Halifax, N.S. **1891** Maitland *Amer. Slang Dict.*: Blue noses…natives of Nova Scotia. **1903** *Our Nav. Apprentice* (July) 51: He had become accustomed to hearing himself styled "blue-nose" on account of his suspected Nova Scotian origin. **1907** *DN* III 182: *Bluenose, n.* A native of Nova Scotia, New Brunswick, or Prince Edward's Island who is not of French extraction. **1927** Finger *Frontier Ballads* 33: "Blue-nose," we called him in affection, because he came from Nova Scotia. **1934** Weseen *Dict. Slang* 310: *Blue nose*—A Canadian. **1978** *Toronto Star* Canadian Sec. 2 [ref. to Nova Scotia]: It's hot here in town but we bluenosers know it's always a lot colder on the shore.

b. a Northerner, (*specif.*) a New Englander. Cf. BLUE-NOSED, 1.

1830 in Thornton *Amer. Gloss.* I: A real *"blue-nose,"* fresh from the land of steady habits. **1886** P.D. Haywood *Cruise* 35: A "blue-nose captain" and Yankee-Irish mates.

c. *Naut.* a Nova Scotian oceangoing vessel.

1883 Keane *Blue-Water* 203: Eavesdropping and vigilant spying are brought to a wonderful degree of perfection among the officers under the "blue-nose" system [aboard Nova Scotian vessels]. **1889** *Century Dict.* I 600: *Blue-nose*…A Nova Scotian vessel. **1907** J.H. Williams, in *Independent* (May 23) 1184: I was in the ship "Restitution"…a Blue-nose clipper, hailing from St. Johns. **1925** Farmer *Shellback* 8: The *Katardin* was a "bluenose," making the run across the Atlantic.

d. *Naut.* a person who has crossed the Arctic Circle.

*1948 (cited in Partridge *DSUE* (ed. 7) 1016 [ref. to WWII]). **1958** Cope & Dyer *Petty Off. Gd.* (ed. 2) 332: *Blue Nose.* One who has crossed the Arctic Circle.

2. [cf. BLUE-NOSED, 2] an excessively puritanical person; prude.

1927 in *OEDS*. [**1928** *Amer. Mercury* (Aug.) 436: The very year that the Blue-Nozzle Curse fell on us.] **1930** Graham & Graham *Queer People* 238: I don't like the looks of some of those blue-noses on the jury. **1936** in Pyle *Ernie's America* 327: But what about [prohibitionists]?…What about the professional bluenoses? **1939** in W.C. Fields *By Himself* 333: It'll keep these blue noses around here from wagging their tongues out of shape. **1941** Klein & MacKenzie *Died with Boots On* (film): Listen, men. I'm not doing this to be a bluenose. I know how tough it is not to be able to take a drink. **1952** Lait & Mortimer *USA* 19: Blue-noses are temporarily in power. **1958** S.H. Adams *Tenderloin* 167: Shock the blue noses and stimulate trade. **1962** T. Berger *Reinhart* 262: Bluenose Reinhart…slept very late…in his chaste bed. **1983** Univ. Tenn. instructor, age 36: When I think of a *bluenose*, I think of somebody who bans books in Boston. **1992** *N.Y. Observer* 21: In the screening room are…the head censor…and Tyler, an apprentice blue-nose.

blue-nosed *adj.* **1.** being or pertaining to a BLUENOSE 1.a., 1.b. Also **bluenose.**

1809 Irving *Knickerbocker*: A goodly, blue-nosed, skim'd milk, New-England cheese. **1866** C.H. Smith *Bill Arp* 87: General Johnston was

retreating and the blue-nosed Yankees were to pollute our sacred soil. **1869** in *Dict. Canadianisms* 60. **1893** Hampton *Major in Washington* 6: Some of Sherman's blue-nosed Hessian cavalry came through our country in 1865 and ripped up my place. *Ibid.* 106: The few dilapedated blue-nosed Yankees that had the gall to come into the hotel. **1943** J. Mitchell *McSorley's* 59: I'm a bluenosed Yankee, fed on codfish and cranberries. **1948** in *DA:* I'll say what I got to say standin' up, you danged blue-nose Yankee!

2. sternly moralistic; (*hence*) excessively puritanical.

1890 *Amer. N & Q* V 6: Can you tell me why Presbyterians are sometimes called "blue-nosed"? **1929** *Variety* (Apr. 3) 11: This picture may aggravate bluenose censors. **1946** Gresham *Nightmare Alley* 43: We don't want to start no trouble in this burg….This is bluenose. **1948** *Atlantic Mo.* (Mar.) 25: Hypercritical bluenosed censorship.

bluenoser *n.* **1.a.** BLUENOSE, 1.a.

1863 in *Dict. Canad.* 60: I also felt a sort of quivering curiosity to see a New Brunswick "Blue Noser," as very probably he might differ in some respects from our Canadian "Rouges." **1908** J.H. Williams, in *Independent* (Aug. 20) [ref. to 1880's]: The second mate…was a tall, lanky, loose-jointed, squint-eyed "Bluenoser" from the wilds of Nova Scotia. **1938** Holbrook *Holy Old Mackinaw* 19: The Blue Nosers [Newfoundlanders] cut them loose under cover of darkness.

b. BLUENOSE, 1.c.

1883 Keane *Blue-Water* 178: No sailor would think of joining a "bluenoser" (as a Nova-Scotian ship is called) until reduced to the last degree of destitution.

2. BLUENOSE, 2.

1971–73 Sheehy *Hustling* 42: A blue-noser's battle against sexual liberation.

Blue Peter *n. Naut.* a blue flag flown by a vessel as a signal that it is about to leave port. Now *S.E.*

*1802 in B. Hall *Voyages* I 61: We have now got up a Blue Peter at the fore-top, which is a signal for immediate sailing. **1821–26** Stewart *Man-of-War's-Man* I 45: A gun was fired, and blue Peter hoisted—the usual signal for a Man-of-War. ***1831** Trelawny *Adv. Younger Son* ch. vii: Then I hoist the blue Peter. **1849** Melville *White Jacket* 366: Blue Peters and sailing signals. **1903** J.H. Williams, in *Independent* (Nov. 26) 2791: "Blue Peter" was now lowered from the fore truck to the cap, to indicate immediate sailing.

blue pigeon *n.* **1.** lead.

*1732 in *OEDS*: We could find no better business than stealing lead—we call it the *Blue Pigeon*, or the *Buff-Lay*. ***1781**, ***1789** in *OEDS*. **1859** Matsell *Vocab.* 12: *Blue-Pigeon-Flying.* Stealing lead off the tops of houses. ***1887** in *OEDS*.

2. *Naut.* a sounding lead.

1856 *Harper's Mag.* 589: The speed [of the vessel] was slackened, and the "blue pigeon" kept constantly moving. **1857** C. Nordhoff *Merchant Vessel* ch. viii. **1857** [Willcox] *Faca* 66: "No observation of the sun today…we have to steer by the blue pigeon." "Pray what's that, captain?"…"The lead and line, sir." **1889** Barrère & Leland *Dict. Slang* I 148: *Blue pigeon*…a nickname for the sounding lead. **1961** Burgess *Dict. Sailing* 29: *Blue Pigeon.* The sounding lead.

blue pill *n.* a bullet, or piece of shot.

1834 J. Downing *Jackson* 111: They saw no hopes from fitin, they wern't fond of blue pills. **1840** *Spirit of Times* (Dec. 19) 499: And didn't the blue pills fly through the chinks of my cabin, right smart! **1849** Melville *White Jacket* 74: Whereas I was altogether unaccustomed to having blue pills playing round my head. **1861** Wilkie *Iowa First* 61: Suppose some fellow…should give me a dose of those indigestible blue pills? Who'd care for my amiable widow? **1861** in Bartlett *Amer.* (ed. 4) 53. **1862** in C.H. Moulton *Ft. Lyon* 51: We could treat them to a few doses of blue pills, both large and small ones. *ca***1880** Bellard *Gone for a Soldier* 96: With that dose of blue pills, the game left. **1883** Keane *Blue-Water* 135: Another blue-pill took him about a foot behind the shoulder. **1893** Hampton *Maj. in Washington* 128: He let him have a blue pill in the elbow.

blue pipe *n. Med.* a vein.

1981 in Safire *Good Word* 154.

blue plum *n.* BLUE PILL.

*ca***1840** in *Ala. Review* XI (1958) 133: A supper of Blue plums [from a shotgun]. **1889** Farmer *Amer.* 69: A bullet…*blue plum.*

blue ruin *n.* cheap, powerful liquor, esp. gin or corn whiskey. Now *hist.*

*1811 *Lexicon Balatron.*: Blue Ruin. Gin. ***1819** [Moore] *Tom Crib's Mem.* 39: The Hero…sits there,/*Swigging Blue Ruin**, in that chair....*Gin. **1821** Waln *Hermit in Phila.* 31: A *stuffing night* [*sic*] *of the trencher* who would rather eat *Welch-Rabbit* than *swig blue ruin.* **1833** A. Greene *Duckworth* I 181: They...were thinking in their hearts only of the spirit of blue ruin. **1837** *Every Body's Album* II 125: Just tip the blunt to the dealer in *heavy wet* and *blue ruin* and you'll be as intimate as if you had been acquainted for years. **1841** [Mercier] *Man-of-War* 237: Empty space was all that remained where he so anxiously anticipated to find his beloved *blue ruin.* **1864** "Kirke" *Down in Tenn.* 88: Mug after mug of clear "blue ruin" had gone down his throat. **1866** Brockett *Camp, Battle Field, & Hospital* 170: Only pursuin' a jug o' blue ruin I'se out thar hid under a log. **1867** [Williams] *Brierly* 10: Boys of tender age...were drinking "blue ruin" in the company of remorseless men. **1872** Burnham *Secret Service* vi: *Jersey Lightning*, a peculiar New Jersey drink; "blue ruin." *Ibid.* 401: Eyes blinded by the "blue ruin" of those depraved districts. **1890** *Overland Mo.* (Feb.) 141: Under the mellowing influence of "blue ruin," as he termed the liquor, he kept everyone in a roar of laughter. *a*1923 in J.M. Hunter *Trail Drivers* II 821: Whiskey and every other kind of "blue ruin" flowed freely. **1981** T.C. Boyle *Water Music* 5: He has been drinking gin—a.k.a. Strip-Me-Naked, Blue Ruin, the Curse.

blues see s.v. BLUE, *n.*

blueshirt *n.* **1.** *Naut.* BLUEJACKET, 1.
1901 King *Dog-Watches* 218: During my ramble around the sailor district I formed the acquaintance of one of "Uncle Sam's blue shirts." *ca*1910–19 J.H. Smith *War with Mex.* II 34 [ref. to 1847]: The "blue-shirts," as the seamen were called.
2. a blue-shirted firefighter.
1944 *Amer. N & Q* (Apr.) 4: *Blueshirt.* A fireman, so-called because of the blue shirt he wears; thereby distinguished from an officer, who wears a white one.
3. a blue-uniformed police officer.
1976 "N. Ross" *Policeman* 17: In less than two minutes...there were blue shirts all over the street.

blueskin *n.* **1.** "an ardent supporter of the American Revolution" (*DAE*).
1782, 1783 in *DAE.*
2. an excessively solemn or moralistic person; (*hence, derisively*) a Presbyterian. Cf. BLUENOSE, 2. Now *hist.*
1783 in R.M. Lederer, Jr. *Colonial Eng.* 32: James Rivington, printer of late to the king,/But now a republican. Let him stand where he is/And he'll turn a true Blue-Skin. **1787–89** Tyler *Contrast* 58: It is no shame, my dear Blueskin, for a man to amuse himself. **1823** *Yale Crayon* 22: I, with my little colleague here,/Forth issued from my cell,/To see if we could overhear,/Or make some blue-skin tell. **1848** Bartlett *Amer.*: *Blue-skins.* A nickname applied to the Presbyterians, from their alleged grave deportment. **1856** Hall *College Wds.* (ed. 2) 31: *Blue-Skin*, this word was formerly in use at some American colleges with the meaning now given to the word *Blue.* **1987** Horowitz *Campus Life* 59: Yale undergraduates [*ca*1825] called anyone reporting to the faculty on fellow students a "Blue Skin."
3. a black person or person of mixed black and white descent.—used contemptuously.
***1788** Grose *Vulgar Tongue* (ed. 2): *Blue skin*, a person begotten of a black woman by a white man. **1821** J.F. Cooper *Spy* 83: "You seem very careful of that beautiful person of yours, Mr. Blueskin." "A bullet hurt a colored man as much as a white," muttered the black, surlily. **1835** *Knickerbocker Mag.* VI 22: "I say, blue-skin," squeaked little Martin, as the negro was about to raise his gun. *ca*1835 in Spaeth *Read 'Em* 18: O it's old Suky Blueskin, she in lub wid me. **1841** [Mercier] *Man-of-War* 144: But come, blue-skin. **1845** in Robb *Squatter Life* 111: "What, Missus dar, *too*!" shouted the nigger...and off the cussed blueskin started fur the house. **1919** Sanborn *131st Inf.* 204: Where you all goin', blue skin?
4. BLUEBELLY, 1, 2.
1863 J.L. Fisk *Exped. to Rocky Mtns.* 31: I went to the [Mormon] tabernacle and heard Bishop Woolley incite the flock to sneer at the "blue skins," (meaning our soldiers stationed there). **1864** *Battle-Fields of So.* 178: Darn the blue-skins any how; who's scared of the blue-bellies? [that is, Eastern men].

blue sky *n. Narc.* heroin.
1986 Stroud *Close Pursuit* 49: A minor in blue sky and toot. **1990** P. Dickson *Slang!* 113: *Blue Sky.* Heroin.

blue-sky *adj. Finance.* financially unsound; consisting of or pertaining to fraudulent investment.
1906 in *OED:* They were what I would term "blue sky and hot air"

securities. **1912** in *DA:* The "Blue Sky" law of Kansas prohibits the sale...of stocks or bonds of any company chartered outside the state. **1916** in Truman *Dear Bess* 191: I can sell mine by the blue-sky route. **1972** R. Barrett *Lovomaniacs* 421: It bugs him to have blue-sky paper out. **1982** *Random House Coll. Dict.:* Blue-sky law...a law regulating the sale of securities, esp. one designed to prevent the promotion of fraudulent stocks. **1983** R. Thomas *Missionary* 104: Some blue-sky shares.

blue-sky *v.* to speculate freely; (also, *trans.*) to discuss in a freely speculative manner. Hence **blue-skyer**, *n.*
1957 M. Shulman *Rally* 184: You guys...blue-sky it...and wrap it up. **1963** Coon *Short End* 181: "How do you know about this, Captain?" I asked. It seemed to me he was blue-skying to beat hell. **1975** Hynek & Vallee *Edge of Reality* 165: We could do a little blue-skying, as to what we think might happen. **1982** *L.A. Times* (Sept. 15) VI 1: The blue-skyers of cable who envision 80 channels or more are talking nonsense.

blue-sky artist *n.* a person who habitually makes grandiose plans or promises that he or she cannot carry out or fulfill.
1979 G. Wolff *Duke of Deception* 245: "He was a blue-sky artist," Mother says of Father.

Blue-Star Commando *n.* [sugg. by the blue star insigne of the Services of Supply] *Army.* a member of the U.S. Army Services of Supply. Now *hist.* [Quots. ref. to WWII].
1944 in Standifer *Not in Vain* 107: He's a Blue Star Commando in the Service of Supply. **1944** in Litoff et al. *Miss You* 202: Blue star commandos [are rear-echelon troops]. **1945** *Yank* (Mar. 2) 5: There's much talk and laughter about "Blue Star Commandos" (SOS and rear-area troops) wearing...paratrooper boots and combat jackets. **1947** C. Mac-Donald *Co. Commander* 64: Blue Star Commandos. **1963** Cameron *Black Camp* 34: You won't find no Blue Star Commandos here.

blue-steel *n.* a blue-steel pistol.
1941 in Botkin *Treas. Amer. Folk.* 129: He comes...with a blue steel in his hand. **1964** Brewer *Worser Days* 58: "Forty-five blue steel," said the colored fellow, pointing the gun in the sheriff's face.

blue streak *n.* a streak of light like a lightning flash, supposedly produced by a fast-moving object (*obs.*); (*hence*) in phr. **talk** [or **curse**, etc.] **a blue streak** to talk, etc., vigorously and without restraint. Now *colloq.*
1830 in *DA:* To pass Mr. Rowan with such rapidity as not even to leave a "blue streak" behind him. **1906** *Independent* (Nov. 29) 1259: Shorty Mason had the ball, and up comes Zollicoffer like a blue streak. **1914** in *DA:* To talk a blue streak. **1961** L.G. Richards *TAC* 50: Talking a blue streak and unable to sleep. **1962** Farago *10th Fleet* 156: The crew talked a blue streak. **1972** Indiana man, age *ca*19: Man, I'm gonna toke up a blue streak! **1978** Mullen *Old Fisherman* 32: He could cuss a blue streak.

bluesuit *n.* **1.** a blue-uniformed police officer.
1970 Wambaugh *New Centurions* 73: Man, when the bluesuits stops me, I always gets nervous. **1975** Wambaugh *Choirboys* 265: Pete Zoony, who generally worked dayside vice, was not known by many bluesuits on the nightwatch. **1988** Norst *Colors* 15: A pair of blue suits emerging from a...Pontiac.
2. BLUESUITER.
1974 Pratt *Laotian Fragments* 135: There's a definite blue suit flavor in all but a few. **1984** J. Green *Newspeak* 27: *Blue suits*...the military personnel on an air base, as opposed to...civilian contractor's employees.

bluesuiter *n. USAF.* a member of the U.S. Air Force.
1963 W.C. Anderson *Penelope* 104: He's...tired of NASA copping all the glory for the work our bluesuiters have been doing on those space launchings. **1974** Pratt *Laotian Fragments* 165: He's more liable to listen to...a blue-suiter. **1984** Trotti *Phantom* 94 [ref. to Vietnam War]: In Da Nang, even the blue suiters became believers. **1985** Yeager & Janos *Yeager* 158: As a blue suiter I wasn't going to get a dime out of the deal. **1987** Lanning *Only War* 220 [ref. to 1969]: They told the REMF "blue suiters" to back off.

blue whistler *n.* a large pellet of buckshot; a bullet. Now *hist.*
1845 in H.C. Lewis *Works* 93: I determined to go this time for the "antlered monarch" by loading one barrel with fifteen "blue whistlers," reserving the other for small game. **1885** S.S. Hall *Gold Buttons* 3: Who mought send a few blue whistlers s'archin' fer [us]. **1888** in *F & H* I (rev.) 294: His thirteen blue whistlers tore the brute's liver into shreds and made a great hole in his side....I lifted my double-barreled shotgun and let drive a volley of blue whistlers straight at bruin's yawning jaws. **1893** Hampton *Maj. in Washington* 140: When I got an order to go to the front, you bet it meant there was to be blue whistlers in the air.

1922 Rollins *Cowboy* 76 [ref. to 1890's]: Thus a "blue whistler," because of the pistol's blue frame, denoted a bullet. **1934** Cunningham *Trigger-nometry* 7: Six-shooter ain't like a sawed-off ten-gauge loaded with Blue Whistlers. **1951** West *Flaming Feud* 11: Thar he was, pinned down like a hog-tied calf, with the Blue Whistlers a-singing like canaries. **1970** Benteen *Apache Raiders* 90: You break bad, I'll give you a dose of your own blue whistlers.
2. *West.* a prairie gale accompanied by rapidly falling temperatures; norther.
1928 Dobie *Vaquero* 278 [ref. to 1890's]: Then about twelve o'clock one night a "blue whistler" snorted down upon us. **1932** in *AS* VIII (1933) 80: The blue whistler that came up Friday night sure came from the North Pole Saturday and Sunday.
3. *Petroleum Industry.* a natural gas well.
1944 Boatright & Day *Hell to Breakfast* 141: A gas well is a "blue whistler." **1972** Haslam *Oil Fields* 94: *Blue Whistler*, n. A high pressure gas well that blows in due to its own pressure. The escaping gas emits a whistling sound.

bluff *n.* **1.** [cf. S.E. senses] an insincere excuse; a pretense or deception of any sort; a fraud.
***1861** H. Mayhew *London Labour* I 231: *Bluff*, an excuse. **1879** B. Harte, in Barrère & Leland *Dict. Slang* I 150: There is a strong suspicion that the...performance is a bluff of the "messenger" to keep from the public the real motives of the murders. **1884** in *F & H* I (rev.) 295: The offer was only a bluff. **1887** Francis *Saddle & Moccasin* 130: "You got the stock, though?" "Oh, yes, I run a bluff on 'em." **1893** W.K. Post *Harvard* 72: You can't give me no such bluff as that. **1896** Ade *Artie* 50: I don't know how I'll ever keep up the bluff o' workin' today. *Ibid.* 104: Any singin' I ever done was a horrible bluff. **1907** S.E. White *Arizona Nights* 140: Say, this yere bluff about roosters bein' gallant is all wrong. **1913** in Truman *Dear Bess* 147: I'll have to put up some strong bluff anyway. **1979** Kienzle *Rosary Murders* 69: Convinced them...just a good bluff.
2. one who bluffs; imposter; deceiver; FOURFLUSHER.
1899 Ade *Fables* 54: Once there was a Bluff whose Long Suit was Glittering Generalities. **1900** *N.Y. Eve. Post* (Dec. 10) 2: Aw, you don't know who's a game of bluff and who ain't in dis town. **1904** S.E. White *Blazed Trail* 27: "You're a bluff!" said he, insultingly. **1917** in Truman *Ltrs. Home* 31: They know he's a bluff and would steal from his grandma. **1917–20** Dreiser *Newspaper Days* 663: Ye dye yer hair, ye fat bluff! **1927** in Galewitz *Great Comics* 7: He said my father was a big bag of wind and nothing but a bluff and that everyone knew he was only a false alarm. **1932** "Max Grand" *Jackson Trail* 45: You're a bluff, eh? You think you can put over easy ones like that on us, eh? **1934** Duff & Sauber *20 Million Sweethearts* (film): I admit Rush is a bluff and a blowhard.

bluff *v.* [prob. < Du *bluffen* 'to brag, boast'] **1.** to frighten, intimidate, discourage.—often constr. with *off.*
1839 in *DA*: Whom no rain, mud or doubt could bluff off. **1839** in *DAE*: I've stood three pluck one too often to be bluffed off even if there was forty against me. **1845** in Blair & McDavid *Mirth* 82: Our man [was] sorta thinkin' he'd bluffed the dog. **1846** Field *Pokerville* 87: Can't bluff you, old hoss. **1847** in J.M. McCaffrey *Manifest Destiny* 58: We were too thirsty to be bluffed off in that way. **1848** *Ladies' Repository* (Oct.) 315: The Flash Language...*Bluff*, to attempt to frighten by talking or showing weapons. **1848** Bartlett *Amer.* 39: *To bluff off.* To put off a troublesome questioner, or dun, &c. **1852** in *DAE*: In a recent murder-trial...where the usual course of intimidating or "bluffing" the adverse witnesses was resorted to. **1863** in H.L. Abbott *Fallen Leaves* 220: We have suddenly...struck up a great tooting of drums & horns...to bluff the rebels. **1866** [H.W. Shaw] *J. Billings* 111: I don't think that ought tew bluff yu oph. **1877** Bartlett *Amer.* (ed. 4) 53: *To bluff off...*to frighten a person in any way, in order to deter him from accomplishing his ends. **1888** in *DAE*: Does he think he can bluff me? He'd better try it! **1903** Adams *Log of a Cowboy* 95: You haven't got near enough men to bluff me. **1917–20** Dreiser *Newspaper Days* 608: In the language of a subsequent decade [1900's], "they had me bluffed." **1926** C.M. Russell *Trails* 88: It's the first hoss I ever see that I'm plumb scared of....He's got me pretty near bluffed. **1943** W. Simmons *Joe Foss* 138: Yet they bluffed the Zeros for miles by having the two wingmen turn menacingly toward the enemy whenever a Zero tried to make a turn.
2. [orig. a technical term in the game of poker, which itself is also called *bluff*] to mislead or deter by a mere show of confidence or assurance.—also *(obs.)* constr. with *off.* Now S.E.

1845 in *DA*: Inasmuch as I believe you are only trying to bluff me off, I go two hundred. **1854** in *DA*: I thought I would bluff back on him. *a***1859** in Bartlett *Amer.* (ed. 2): You ain't a-goin' to bluff dis child. **1859** Matsell *Vocab.* 13: *Bluff.* To bluster; look big. **1877** Bartlett *Amer.* (ed. 4) 54: *To bluff on Poker* is to bet on a worthless hand as if it were a good hand. **1944** in *DA*: With five guns frozen up and inoperative, the gunners successfully bluffed the Germans. **1990** *National Review* (Nov. 5) 20: The Shamirites have grown...accustomed to thinking of the Palestinian problem as one that can be bluffed away.

blunderbox *n.* [folk ety. fr. *blunderbuss*] an old or clumsy firearm.
1851 M. Reid *Scalp Hunters* 73: D'yur think 'ee kud hit a spread blanket wi' that beetle-shaped blunderbox?

blunderbuss *n.* **1.** a clumsy or blundering person.
***1692** in *OED*: Not such a hair-brain'd blunderbuss as you. ***1698–99** "B.E." *Dict. Canting Crew: Blunderbuss*, a Dunce, an ungainly fellow. ***1768** in *OED*: He must be a numskull, not to say a beetle, nor yet a blunderbuss. **1966** Kenney *Caste* 53: He must have had all he could take of blunderbusses. **1968** Baker et al. *CUSS* 84: *Blunder bust.* [sic] A person who always does the wrong thing.
2. [lit., "a bus that blunders," punning on S.E. meaning] a large motor vehicle that handles poorly.
1941 K. Burke, in Jay *Burke-Cowley Corres.* 245: The old Blunder Bus...the Cadillac. **1974** Scalzo *Stand on Gas* 112: The big blunderbusses aren't fast enough compared to today's highly modified Chevys. **1984** *N.Y. Times Mag.* (Sept. 1) 28: My dad's got me and one of my friends in the back seat of our old family blunderbuss.

blunt *n.* **1.** money, cash, esp. coins.
***1708** *Mem. of John Hall* (ed. 4) 11: *Blunt*, money. ***1717** *History of the Press-Yard*: The cull looks as if he had the *Blunt*, and I must come in for a share of it. ***1788** Grose *Vulgar Tongue* (ed. 2): *Blunt*, money (cant.). ***1819** [Moore] *Tom Crib's Mem.* 36: At morning meet, and,—*honour bright,*—/Agree to share the *blunt*. ***1821** W.T. Moncrieff *Tom & Jerry* 3: I always takes the *blunt* with von hand, and gives the pot with t'other. **1836** *Spirit of Times* (July 16) 170: Every body is on the *qui vive*—some to look after the *blunt*—others to "*drop it*," as the sporting folks say. **1837** *Every Body's Album* II 125: Just tip the *blunt* to the dealer in *heavy wet* and *blue ruin.* ***1838** Dickens *Oliver Twist* ch. xxxix: I must have some blunt from you tonight. **1842** *Ben Hardin's Crockett* (unp.): They don't keer whose feelings they hurt if they only gits the blunt. **1845** Smith *Vernon* 35: The "stars" always have to fork over "the blunt," or else they know what to depend upon. **1846** *Nat. Police Gaz.* (Jan. 17) 170: Instead of "*dummies*" (pocket books) with several thousands in "*flimsies*" inside of them, we shall not be able to get a "*skin*" (purse) with more than $100 in "*blunt.*" **1848** *Ladies' Repository* (Oct.) 315: *Blunt*, Money in general. ***1850** Leeves *Diary* 53: The fun is expensive, & yet there is no grudging the blunt to such roaring folks say. **1853** G. Thompson *Garter* 39: He had plenty of *blunt* about him. **1854** "Youngster" *Swell Life at Sea* 229: Give me the blunt. **1868** [Williams] *Black-Eyed Beauty* 97: Here's the pretty lady what give us the blunt tother day! ***ca1870** in R. Palmer *Touch on Times* 250: To see if I had got such stuff/ As blunt or grub, tobacco, snuff. **1899** A.H. Lewis *Sandburrs* 231: I've got d' blunt.
2. [fr. Phillies *Blunt*, trademark for a brand of inexpensive cigar] *Narc.* a cigar stuffed with marijuana.
1988 "Big Daddy Kane" *R.A.W.* (rap song): I'll smoke ya up like a blunt. **1992** "Fab Five Freddie" *Fresh Fly Flavor* 9: *Blunt*—Marijuana wrapped in an emptied-out cigar wrapper. **1993** *Village Voice* (N.Y.C.) (June 22) 34: Now they're puffing on their own macho blunts....The turn to blunts was definitely influenced by rasta and reggae. **1993** *Source* (July) 14: In rap music, "pass the blunt"...[is] the cliche of the week. **1993** *Time* (July 26) 56: To create a "blunt," teenagers slice open a cigar and mix the tobacco with marijuana.

BM *n.* **1.** a bowel movement.
1962 Killens *Thunder* 12: It would take time for him to get used to having a B.M. in the chorus of six or seven other men. **1965** Friedman *Totempole* 12: Bad b.m. **1966** Kenney *Caste* 18: When did you have your last BM? **1968** Cuomo *Thieves* 119: Jimmy made B.M. in the potty. **1974** Terkel *Working* 475: Then they'll have a B.M. **1975** in Thom *Letters to Ms.* 43: Her baby dropped a large BM on the carpet.
2. [beautiful *m*usic] *Music Industry.* (see quot.). *Joc.*
1981 D.E. Miller *Jargon* 125: *BM*...usually Top-40 tunes that have been rearranged...for play in shopping malls, elevators, etc....Music to wait by.

BMO *n. Mil. in Mid. East.* (see quots.). *Joc.*
1991 *Newsweek* (Jan. 21) 8: *BMOs:* Black Moving Objects, meaning

Saudi women in traditional black dress. **1991** Dunnigan & Bay *From Shield to Storm* 360: BMO—Black moving object (Arab woman wearing traditional veil and black dress). **1992** Cornum & Copeland *She Went* 25: Saudi...women...in...black robes. The soldiers called them BMOs—Black Moving Objects.

B.M.O.C. *n.* [*big man on campus*] *Stu.* a socially prominent and influential male undergraduate.
   1934 Weseen *Dict. Slang* 175: B.M.O.C.—A big man on the campus, that is, a student who is prominent in activities. **1943** Shulman *Barefoot Boy* 43: "We have one of the biggest B.M.O.C.'s in Alpha Cholera."..."What's a B.M.O.C.?"..."A Big Man on Campus." **1947–48** Burns *Lucifer* 72: He would be a BMOC simply by virtue of his exquisite sadism. **1964** *AS* XXXIX 119: The familiar *B.M.O.C.* "big man on campus." **1970** D. Wakefield *All the Way* 125: "B.M.O.C.," the girl said with a grin. **1971** *Playboy* (Aug.) 32: Tepper takes over as the contemporary B.M.O.C. who fools around with a faculty wife. **1972** *Washington Sq. Jrnl.* (Nov. 1) 2: Nothing quenches a B.M.O.C.'s* man-sized thirst like Akadema Red!...*Big Man on Campus. **1979** Norwood *Survival of Dana* (film): "What's a B.M.O.C.?" "Big Man On Campus, in my generation."

BNG *n.* FNG. [Quots. ref. to Vietnam War.]
   1991 C. Roberts *Combat Medic* 147: The BNG (Brand New Guy)...stared. **1992** Lehrach *No Shining Armor* 381: BNG. Brand-new guy or new arrival to Vietnam.

B.O. *n.* **1.** offensive body odor. [Vigorously popularized in advertising by Lifebuoy soap *ca*1930.]
   1931 *Amer. Merc.* (Dec.) 432: Halitosis and B.O. acquire a new baby brother. **1932** *Our Army* (Feb.) 46: [Ad for Lifebuoy soap]. **1933** in *OEDS*. **1945** Dos Passos *Tour* 22: A lot of those girls...are very clean. Not in a sanitary way, but no B.O. and all that. **1960** Hoagland *Circle Home* 158: He was so scared of having B.O. his actions made her afraid she had it. **1964** D. Berg *Looks at U.S.A.* (unp.): And I'll bet he's got B.O. or something even worse. **1973** Haring *Stranger* 117: Connie refers to her as B.O. Bradshaw behind her back, because she doesn't use a deodorant. **1973** R.M. Brown *Rubyfruit* 166: Do you think B.O. will do the trick? **1978** Pilcer *Teen Angel* 10: And she had unbelievable BO. **1966–80** McAleer & Dickson *Unit Pride* 155: At least it'd help kill the BO. **1980** Manchester *Darkness* 236: What was then called B.O. **1984** J. McCorkle *Cheer Leader* 42: Makes me smell...gardenias, roses, liquor, B.O.
   2. *Entertainment Industry.* box-office appeal.
   1936 *Esquire* (Sept.) 64: *Variety*...see beaucoup b.o. behind Corio's strip 'n' tease.

bo¹ *n.* [of dial. E orig.] **1.** a fellow.—used in direct address. Also (*obs.*) **beau.**
   *ca***1729** in Lonsdale *New Oxford 18th C. Verse* 217: Their common tune is *Get her Bo,*/The weary lass cries, "Music so." *1825 Glascock *Nav. Sk. Bk.* I 148: Small helm bo—steady—ey-a. *1829 Glascock *Sailors & Sts.* I 210: "You may say that, bo," said a third. *Ibid.* 183: "Never mind that, bo," cried Cheerly, the captain's coxswain. **1855** Brougham *Chips* 330: What would you say to 'em, bo? *1874 in *OEDS*: Half a gallon a day, bo, and no more. **1884** Kingston *Frolic* 306: What, don't you know, Bo? *Ibid.* 307: You are right there again, and no mistake, Bo. *1886 P.D. Haywood *Cruise* 77 [ref. to Civil War]: That's right, Bo, that's the name on it. **1899** Boyd *Shellback* 30: Hould on to me tight, bo, till I shplit the bafe wid the axe. **1902** Wister *Virginian* 28: "This way, Pard."..."This way, Beau."..."This way, Budd." **1909** "O. Henry" *Strictly Business* 1577: Say, 'Bo,...where did you cop out dat doll? **1910** *Variety* (Aug. 20) 13: Say, beau, I'm there with that dancing too. **1915** Braley *Workaday World* 104: All right, let's licker, bo! **1915** H.L. Wilson *Ruggles* 59: Say, Bo,...have I got my fingers crossed or not? **1919** S. Lewis *Free Air* 57: Yea, bo, I'm feelin' good! **1920** in Fitzgerald *Stories* I 182: Hello, Bo! **1927** C. McKay *Home to Harlem* (*passim*). **1930** Cozzens *San Pedro* 18: Never mind that, Bo! **1940** Chandler *Farewell, My Lovely* 11: What you got down there, bo? **1945** Himes *If He Hollers* 27: You said it, bo. **1951** Thacher *Captain* 81: Take it easy, beau, don't get excited. **1952** Sandburg *Young Strangers* 170 [ref. to 1890's]: How are they comin' fer yuh, Bo? **1952** Kahn *Able One Four* 27: Yeah, bo. Hungry, you take her. **1955–57** Kerouac *On Road* 55: Say, bo, what was all the noise around here last night? **1958** Meltzer & Blees *H.S. Confidential* (film): You sure got the bread, bo. **1975** Greer *Slammer* 77: More than that, bo. **1981** *Nat. Lampoon* (Feb.) 48: Make you think twice next time, Bo. **1988** Dietl & Gross *One Tough Cop* 99: I couldn't remember all their names....So, I just said..."How you doing, Bo?"
   2. a hobo; in phr. **on the bo** traveling as a hobo.
   1899 "J. Flynt" *Tramping* 388 [ref. to *ca*1890]: He cautioned me not to

say anything to the "boes" (hoboes). **1904** *Life in Sing Sing* 246: Bo. Tramp or hobo. **1907** London *Road* 31 [ref. to 1894]: "Which way, Bo?" was our greeting, and "Bound east" was the answer each of us gave. **1908** in Kornbluh *Rebel Voices* 42: The bad "shack"...packs a big gun and makes the "boes" get. **1914** Knibbs *Songs* 18: And though he was a Bo like me, he'd been a gent, once, I could see. **1922** Tully *Emmett Lawler* 169: Been on the 'bo yourself, ain't you, Lad? **1927** Shaw *Jack-Roller* 80: The brotherhood was made up of ordinary "bos," pickpockets, panhandlers, petty thieves [etc.]. **1948** Ives *Wayfaring Stranger* 133: I said, "I'm a bo." **1981–85** S. King *It* 296: The 'bo was gone. **1989** in *Harper's* (June) 52: Today, most of the boes...are old-timers.

bo² *n. Stu.* BOHO.
   1958 J. Davis *College Vocab.* 5: Bo or Boho—Bohemian—A nonconformist, usually an Art or Speech and Theater major.

bo³ *n. Narc.* marijuana; BOO³.
   1975, 1984 (cited in Spears *Drugs & Drink* 60). **1988** Norst *Colors* 17: "You got any Bo...?" "Man, I don't smoke that shit."

bo *v.* to be a hobo.
   1918 *Chi. Sunday Trib.* V (Oct. 27) 2: When I was "boin' " round...I met up with a lot o' 'bos in the northern woods. **1928** Dahlberg *Bottom Dogs* 189: That's what one gets ridin' the blinds, boeing about.

board *n.* a leg.
   1972 Jenkins *Semi-Tough* 276: I got to have good boards on this one.
   ¶ In phrase:
   ¶ **on board** (of whiskey) within one's stomach; ABOARD.
   *1821 *Real Life in London* I 28: Till he gets his *grog on board*. **1904** in A. Adams *Chisholm Trail* 83: But with just the right amount [of whiskey] on board, he was a hail fellow well met.

board *v.* **1.** *Naut.* to attack or assault; (*hence*) to consume voraciously. Also in phr. **board in the smoke** to attack by surprise. Orig. *S.E.*
   *a1547, *1580, *1596, *1600, *a1726 in *OED*. *1805 J. Davis *Post-Captain* 25: Come, Hurricane, let us board the beef in the smoke. **1840** Crockett *Almanac 1841* 10: She jumped back, and thort he war going to board her in the smoke. **1867** Smyth *Sailor's Wd.-Bk.*: Board Him. A colloquialism for I'll ask, or accost him....To make acquaintance with, fasten on. *Board Him in the Smoke*. To take a person by surprise, as by firing a broadside, and boarding in the smoke. **1933** Witherspoon *Jarge* (unp.): I see he was makin' ready to board this swab and work him over without no more argument. *1949 Granville *Sea Slang of 20th C.* 39: *Board in the smoke* To take someone by surprise.
   2. *Naut.* to mount and copulate with.
   *1676 in D'Urfey *Two Comedies* 57: I'le teach thee the most new and dextrous way of picking wenches up. Then thou shalt know their tempers,...whether they are i' th' boat or may be boarded. *ca*1708 in D'Urfey *Pills* III 313: Here's one spend all his Pay [in] boarding a Whore. **1778** in [Connor] *Songbag* 128: I boarded her the truth I'll tell. **1927** [Fliesler] *Anecdota* 44: He attempted to board his still virginal spouse. **1967** Dibner *Admiral* 26: He was...naked and in the act of boarding her and she was screaming blue murder.
   3. *Naut.* **a.** to make advances to; make acquaintance with; accost. [Orig. *S.E.*; *OED* gives S.E. quots. from *a*1546 to *a*1726.]
   *1805 J. Davis *Post-Captain* 144: Board her with sugar-plum phrases. *1821 *Real Life in Ireland* 14: There he was boarded by a lawyer. **1867** (quot. at (**1.**), above).
   b. to ask money of.
   1867 (quot. at (**1**), above). **1899** Fell *Merchant Seamen* 53: So long as they get the money in cash, they go and "board the tailor," and thus get a few dollars with which to enjoy themselves.

boardinghouse reach *n.* (see 1992 quot.).
   1947 in Botkin *Sidewalks* 241 [ref. to *ca*1900]: The "boardinghouse reach" at the dining room table was supposed, in the popular idea of humor, to be necessary to overcome restrictions as to food in boardinghouses. **1960** N.Y.C. woman, age *ca*70: He's got a boardinghouse reach. **1992** N.Y.C. woman, age *ca*60: My family used *boardinghouse reach* in the 1930's. It meant when you reach rudely across the table to take something instead of requesting someone politely to pass it. They'd say, "Look at that boardinghouse reach."

boar pussy *n. Pris.* homosexual anal copulation.—usu. considered vulgar.
   1984 Sample *Racehoss* 163 [ref. to 1950's]: You...ack lak you ain' never had no boar pussy before.

boar's nest *n. So. & West.* a men's bunkhouse or dormitory.—constr. with *the.*

1893 in Wister *Out West* 152: One of the hands has christened [the bunkhouse] "The Boar's Nest" because inhabited by bachelors exclusively. **1931–34** in Clemmer *Pris. Comm.* 242: In the old dormitory, or the "Bore's Nest," as it was known among the convicts, much of the gambling was done. **1936** *AS* (Oct.) 279: *Boar's nest.* The men's dormitory. Name also applied to one's room in the men's dormitory [at S. Dak. State Univ.]. **1944** *Slanguage Dictionary* 48: *Boar's nest*—untidy bunk and bunk area. [**1964** Thompson & Rice *Every Diamond* 140: *Bear's Nest:* A poor hotel.] **1965** O'Neill *High Steel* 269: *Boar's nest:* a bunkhouse on a construction job. **1968** S.O. Barker *Rawhide Rhymes* 16: He's done forsook the Boar's Nest, with a grin upon his face. **1970** Grissim *White Man's Blues* 46: It was unofficially referred to as the Boar's Nest.

boast *n.* ¶ In phrase: **make the boast** *Pris.* to be released on parole.

1904 *Life in Sing Sing* 256: *Making the Boast.*—Being released by order of the parole board. **1926** *N.Y. Times* (Oct. 10) VIII 20: "Making the boast" (getting by the Pardon Board).

boat *n.* **1.** [cf. GUNBOAT] a large shoe or boot; (*also*) a large foot.

[**1869** Stowe *Oldtown* 186: And his feet,—why, one of his shoes would make a good boat for me!] **1956** Hargrove *Girl He Left* 142: What have you got on those boats? Oil of chromium? **1958** J. Davis *College Vocab.* 12: *Boats*—Shoes. **1973** *Oui* (Mar.) 69: On your feet you've got those stacked-heel, two-toned, perforated leather...*boats.* **1987** *Time* (Aug. 17) 10: George Raft (tiny feet). Gregory Hines (boats).

2. an automobile, esp. if large.

[**1908** in McCay *Little Nemo* 157: Rides like a boat, doesn't it?] **1914** T.A. Dorgan, in Zwilling *TAD Lexicon* 19: This boat of mine has gone 65,000 miles. **1913–15** Van Loan *Taking the Count* 48: I'm going to step on this old boat and find out if she can still do sixty miles an hour. **1917** in Gelman *Photoplay* 23: Let's take a spin in the little old boat—got ninety out of her yesterday out in the country. **1918** *Chi. Sun. Trib.* (Feb. 3) (comics): You'll never find another car that'll give you the satisfaction that old boat gave you. **1919** S. Lewis *Free Air* 108: I can drive this boat's well as you can. **1919** Darling *Jargon Bk.* 4: *Big Boat*—A large automobile. **1921** in McArdle *Collier's* 235: Nah! Boat. Automobile. Do you get me? **1931** Barry *Animal Kingdom* 341: Say, the old boat is frozen stiff. **1959** *Lucille Ball–Desi Arnaz Show* (CBS-TV): That's some boat you got there. What kind of mileage do you get? **1959** Russell *Perm. Playboy* 307: Hank, how badly do you want this boat, anyway? **1963** Rubin *Sweet Daddy* 133: You and me driving along in this great big boat. **1972** Claerbaut *Black Jargon* 58: *Boat, n.* a car; automobile. **1974** A. Bergman *Big Kiss-Off* 173: You double park these boats all over town. **1977** Sayles *Union Dues* 204: We're gonna...put this boat on cruisomatic...onto the Nawtheast Expressway.

3. *Av.* an airplane.

1918 *Stars & Stripes* (Feb. 8) 8: The engine of my boat died on me just over Rombach. **1919** *N.Y. Times Mag.* (Mar. 30) 4: An airplane was rarely called by its rightful name; it was usually a boat, ship, bus, or taxi. **1938** *Test Pilot* (film): He's kidding you. It's a good boat.

4. *Pris.* a busload of new prisoners; (*Navy.*) a newly arrived group of naval trainees.

1956 Resko *Reprieve* 109 [ref. to ca1940]: Just come in on the Sing Sing boat? **1966** IUFA *Folk Speech*: *Boat*—a new recruit of sailors. **1978** Sopher & McGregor *Up from Walking Dead* 46: The new boat just arrived.

5. *pl. Navy.* the submarine service.—constr. with *the.* [*Boat* is a technical S.E. syn. for *submarine.*]

1962 E. Stephens *Blow Negative* 15: You been in [the Navy] before, I bet....In the boats?" "In the what?" "Submarines." *Ibid.* 31: Only surface ships carry a real live supply officer....In the boats it's a line officer's job.

6. *Poker.* a full house. Also **full boat.**

*ca*1969 Rabe *Hummel* 57: Full boat. Jacks and threes. **1978** Univ. Tenn. student theme: "A boat"...is a full house. **1983** *Hardcastle & McCormick* (ABC-TV): "What'd you have?" "A boat. Nines over threes." **1987** Clark *Dict. Gamb. & Gaming: Full boat*...Same as a full house. Rare.

7. *Stu.* an easy academic course. Cf. BOAT RIDE.

1980 *AS* (Winter) 277 [in use at Gettysburg College].

¶ In phrases:

¶ **eyes in the boat** *Navy & USMC.* looking straight ahead.—usu. as imper. [The literal use is a common command in rowing.]

1988 Hynes *Flights of Passage* 26 [ref. to WWII]: "Eyes in the boat!" he would shout as we marched past the C.O....a salty way of telling us not to gawk around. *a*1990 Westcott *Half a Klick* 30: Slater wisely locked his eyes "in-the-boat."

¶ **missed too many boats** *Navy & USMC.* to have become demented from lengthy service on an overseas station.

1913 *Review of Reviews* (Aug.) 200: "He has missed too many boats"...means that the person mentioned has stayed so long in the islands that his ability is impaired. **1930** in Grayson *Stories for Men* 140: They were...the nuts who "had missed too many boats." **1936** S.I. Miller *Leathernecks Have Landed* (film): "Why haven't you gone home?" "I've missed too many boats." **1958** Cope & Dyer *Petty Officer's Guide* (ed. 2) 357: *Missed Too Many Transports* (or *Boats*). Said of a person who has gone asiatic, island-happy—that is, queer in the head from being too long overseas. **1980** Manchester *Darkness* 422 [ref. to WWII]: He was Asiatic, had..."missed too many boats."

¶ **miss the boat, 1.** to miss one's opportunity.

***1929** Bowen *Sea Slang* 90: *Miss the Boat, To.* To be late for anything. **1935** E. Pound, in Ahearn *Pound/Zukofsky* 163: Most americans miss the boat/But it is more irritatin' to see 'em catch it; and then step off. **1971** *Nat. Lampoon* (June) 30: That's how Marx missed the boat. **1984** Kagan & Summers *Mute Evidence* 285: And I missed the boat on something very important.

2. to fail to menstruate.

1960 Swarthout *Where Boys Are* 235: Incidentally, I was preg....I'd been sure for five days. I had missed the boat by that much.

¶ **rock the boat** to create difficulty for one's superiors or associates. Now *colloq.*

1915 "High Jinks, Jr." *Choice Slang* 67: Sit down, your rocking the boat—You're causing a disturbance. **1961** in H. Ellison *Sex Misspelled* 312: He tried to rock the boat, and see what he's like? **1965** Horan *Seat of Power* 66: I don't know if De Lorenzo is so honest he would rock the boat in his own office. **1972** Singer *Boundaries* 194: Their outward demeanor is harmonious and inconspicuous; they would never rock the boat. **1979** in Terkel *Amer. Dreams* 316: Don't rock the boat. Keep a low profile. Get in line. **1984** Kagan & Summers *Mute Evidence* 290: The people there had nice government jobs, they didn't want to rock the boat by coming out in support of anything controversial. **1986** F. Walton *Once Were Eagles* 121: But when a guy is nearing retirement age, he doesn't want to rock the boat.

boat-jumper *n.* a newly arrived or unassimilated immigrant.

1984 Caunitz *Police Plaza* 111: She's a real boat jumper, brogue and all.

boat plug *n. Naut.* a short person.

1849 Melville *White Jacket* 213 [ref. to 1843]: From his diminutiveness he went by the name of *Boat Plug* among the seamen.

boat race *n.* **1.** *Horse Racing.* a fraudulent race in which the winner has been illicitly predetermined.

1917 in R. Peyton *At Track* 150: There were rumors that "a boat race" was being contemplated. **1934** D. Runyon, in *Collier's* (Feb. 3) 7: The fifth race...is nothing but a boat race, and everything in it is as stiff as a plank, except this certain horse. **1942** Liebling *Telephone* 82: The count spent a couple of weeks promoting a bookmaker known as Boatrace Harry. **1956** "T. Betts" *Across the Board* 150: For a "boat race" Mahoney ruled seven steeplechase jockeys, and a trainer off for life. **1968** Ainslie *Thoroughbred* 463: *Boat race*—A fixed race. **1970** Thackeray & Burk *Thief* 183: It was a boat race. Fixed. And everybody knew it except me. **1973** Haney *Jock* 175: *Boat race:* a race wherein participants collaborate illegally to determine winner beforehand.

2. any dishonestly arranged sporting competition.

1968–70 *Current Slang* III & IV 12: *Boat race, n.* An event arranged only for show. A "fixed fight."...That football game was a real *boat race.*

boat ride *n.* a pleasant, leisurely task; an easy task.

1963 D. Tracy *Brass Ring* 379: This is a boat ride, f'crissake. There ain't a kraut within half a mile.

Boats *n. Naut.* boatswain or boatswain's mate.—usu. used in direct address. Occ. **Boatsie.**

[***1803** in Wetherell *Adventures* 33: The Boats. Mate of the deck also came up.] **1920** *Atlantic Mo.* (Feb.) 220: Boats, who cleans the ship's bell? **1944** in *Combat* 104: Come on, Boats. **1948** Wolfert *Act of Love* 134: Take off there, Boatsie. Take off. **1958** Cooley *Run for Home* 11: He had heard about "Boats," as the crew called him. **1968** Maule *Rub-A-Dub* 32: We better check in with Boats. **1977** Brennan *Prej. Man* 99: Hey, Boats, let's go! **1990** Poyer *Gulf* 364: Boats, is Mr. Charaler down there? *Ibid.* 368: Report to the chief boats.

Boat School *n. Navy.* the U.S. Naval Academy at Annapolis, Md.—constr. with *the.*

1983–86 G.C. Wilson *Supercarrier* 101: He's a 1978 graduate of the "Boat School," the U.S. Naval Academy. **1988** Poyer *Med* 390: It was like an all-nighter back at the Boat School.

bob[1] *n. Mil.* BOBTAIL, *n.,* 1.a.

1906 Beyer *Amer. Battleship* 82: "Six months and a bob"—refers to one who has been court-martialed and sentenced to six months in prison and eventually given a dishonorable discharge. **1915** Garrett *Army Ballads* 25: He's bound to get Ten and a Bob for sure. *Ibid.* 269 [ref. to 1898]: Ten and a Bob—A prisoner's sentence of ten years and a dishonorable discharge from the Army.

bob[2] *n.* [adopted from Brit. slang *bob* 'shilling'] a dollar.—*pl.* usu. *bob.*

1930 D. Runyon, in *Collier's* (Jan. 20) 12: It is very difficult to get any Peggy Joyces for twenty-five bobs per week. **1934** D. Runyon, in *Collier's* 7: He has fifty bobs...to bet. **1957** M. Shulman *Rally* 210: If you want to pick up a few bob, keep your eye peeled. **1963** G.L. Coon *Short End* 139: They usually had some way to pick up a few bob elsewhere. **1989** *Larry King* (CNN-TV) (Aug. 30): Mickey Rooney, who has "bet a bob or two," as they say.

bob *adj.* safe.

***1785** Grose *Vulgar Tongue*: All is bob, all is safe. **1846** *Lives of the Felons* 57: All is *bob* (safe) now.

bob *v. Mil.* to BOBTAIL, *v.,* 1.a.

1918 Ruggles *Navy Explained* 86: Any man given an undesirable or bad conduct discharge is a kicked man. He is always spoken of with scorn as a man "who was kicked or bobbed out of the service."

bob *interj.* [orig. euphem. for *God*] (used for emphasis in interj. phrs.): **so help me bob!** "indeed I am telling the truth"; **no** [or **yes**] **sirree bob!** "no (or yes) indeed!"

***1820–21** P. Egan *Life in London* 182: So help me bob, you have forgot poor Neddy. ***1823** "J. Bee" *Slang* 13: So help me bob. **1856** in *DA*: He can't get me with his big words, nosiree bob. **1859** in *DA*: A witness...replied "Yes, siree, Bob!" **1882** A.W. Aiken *Joe Buck* 5: So help me Bob! he'd kill you, fer sure! **1909** *DN* III 362: No, siree, Bob! **1979** *Nat. Lampoon* (Dec.) 4: I'm tops...yessirree Bob. **1989** "Capt. X" & Dodson *Unfriendly Skies* 72: Nosirreebob! Fella, this is America!

bobbery *n.* [Anglo-Indian < Hindi *bāp re* 'O father!'] *Naut.* a noisy disturbance; commotion.—usu. constr. with *kick* [*up*].

1800 in Whiting *Early Amer. Proverbs* 38: The Russians having kicked a baubery with the Chinese....They will...pull hair and kick up too much baubery. ***1803** in *F & H* I 269: If I don't go back and kick up such a bobbery—. ***1833** Marryat *Peter Simple* ch. ii: I'll bet a wager there'll be a bobbery in the pigsty before long, for they are ripe for mischief. **1836** Cather *Voyage* 12: She...got hold of the liquor... and..."kicked up the bobbery." **1867** Smyth *Sailor's Wd.-Bk.*: Bobbery. A disturbance, row, or squabble; a term much used in the East Indies and China.

bobble *n.* a botch; (*Sports.*) an error or fumbling of a ball.—also used figuratively.

1901 in P. Dickson *Baseball Dict.* 63: I'm mighty afeerd you'll make a bobble of it. **1916** L. Stillwell *Common Soldier* 85 [ref. to Civil War]: Well, sometimes he would be badly stumped, and ludicrous "bobbles" would be the result. **1918** in Truman *Dear Bess* 246: If you get those seven things off without a bobble, the Battery shoots...at two-second intervals. **1927** *AS* (Mar.) 275: Bobble—mistake.

bobble *v. Sports.* to fumble (a ball) momentarily. Now *colloq.*

1942 *ATS* 659: Fumble; miss...*bobble, boot.*

bobby *n.* [fr. *Bobby,* hypocoristic form of *Robert,* after Sir Robert Peel, founder (1828) of the Metropolitan Police system of London] a policeman. *Rare* in U.S.

***1844** in *OEDS*. **1866** *Nat. Police Gaz.* (Nov. 24) 3 [N.Y.C.]: Dodger began to think...that there was such a thing as an incorruptible "bobby" that could not be "greased." **1904** in "O. Henry" *Works* 1401: I'd like to be one of those bobbies on horseback. **1908** McGaffey *Show Girl* 186: Cheese, there's a bike cop. Can you lose him? Goodby, Bobby.

bobbysoxer *n.* [resp. of *bobby socks* (popularly worn by teenage girls *ca*1940) + *-er*] a teenage girl usu. regarded as naively immature and an enthusiastic follower of youthful fads in music, fashion, etc. Now *hist.*

1944 in *OEDS*: About 6,000 bobby soxers attended the concert. **1946** J.H. Burns *Gallery* 19: I heard their laughter, stylized like a sound track for bobby-soxers. **1958** Althea Gibson, in *Sat. Eve. Post* (Sept. 6) 77: In my second match, I beat Christine Truman, the bobby-soxer I'd played at Wimbledon. **1976** *Newsweek* (Aug. 2) 45: It was the kind of cheering, stomping ovation that only former bobby-soxers could achieve. **1986** *L.A. Times Bk. Review* (Oct. 22) 1: [Frank Sinatra] launched a career that made him the idol of what were then called bobby-soxers. **1990** *New Republic* (Dec. 17) 33: She was never a bobbysoxer, for example, nor one of those girls fighting against going all the way.

bobo *n.* **1.** *Baseball.* a protégé or favorite.

1959 Brosnan *Long Season* 82: So we finally all got together—Solly Hemus's bullpen—critics, bo-bos, and just plain pitchers. *Ibid.* 269: Bo-Bo. A ballplayer who is considered by his teammates to be the particular pet or favorite of the manager, the front office, the newspapers, the broadcasters. **1980** *N.Y. Post* (June 30) 76: Thirty years ago, [Billy Martin] walked on the field for the first time at Yankee Stadium, a scrappy kid second baseman from Berkeley, already Casey Stengel's pet from his days with the Oakland Oaks, and Joe DiMaggio's bobo.

2. *Black E.* a white person, perceived as an authority figure.

1990 *In Living Color* (Fox-TV): You know—the Man. Mr. Charlie. Bobo.

bobstay *n. Naut.* the frenum of the penis; (*hence*) the penis itself. Cf. BOWSPRIT, 2.

***1788** Grose *Vulgar Tongue* (ed. 2): Bobstay. The frenum of a man's yard. ***ca*1875** on *Martin Carthy—2d Album* (Topic LP 12TS341, A6): But I fear a little fire-bucket burnt me bobstay through;/That saucy little trim-rigged doxy! **1967** Schmidt *Lexicon of Sex* 23: Bobstay...Frenulum of the prepuce, connecting the prepuce with the lower surface of the glans penis. **1976** N.Y.C. folk singer, age *ca*40: She grabbed me by the bobstay. ***1984** T. Jones *Heart of Oak* 98 [ref. to WWII]: There I was to learn to keep my bobstay and shit-kickers clean. *Ibid.* 276: Bobstay: foreskin membrane.

bobtail *n.* **1.** [so called because the "character" clause was cut off] *Mil.* **a.** a dishonorable discharge or a discharge without honor.

1878 Mulford *Fighting Indians* 38: A *bobtail discharge* is one with the character clause torn off, and is considered the most disgraceful one a soldier can receive. **1888** McConnell *5 Yrs. Cavalryman* 120 [ref. to 1866]: In case...that the man has been...one to whom the officer cannot consistently give a good character, the lines or "character" are cut off, and a mutilated discharge of this kind is universally known in Army parlance as a "bob-tail" discharge. **1890** C. King *Army Portia* 272: Served with him at Fort Wayne until he got a "bobtail" discharge. **1900** McManus *Soldier Life* 101: Most of the prisoners received sentences of dishonorable discharge or "bobtails," as they are commonly called in the army. **1907** *Reader* (Sept.) 345: They was laying for me with a general court to give me a bobtail and a dash at Alcatraz. **1909** Moss *Officers' Man.* 283: Bob-tail—a dishonorable discharge, or a discharge without honor. **1918** *Wadsworth Gas Attack* (Jan. 12) 15: No More "Bob-Tails" For Slackers. **1921** *Sentinel* (Jan. 14) 15: His bob-tail's coming back by mail. **1937** *AS* (Feb.) 75: *Bobtail*—(yellow-colored) dishonorable discharge.

b. a former military serviceman who has been discharged dishonorably or without honor.

1890 King *Army Portia* 152: Sergeant Wren openly accused him of having been in service somewhere before, and, as he had no papers to show, he must be either a deserter or a "bobtail."*...*A soldier whose discharge paper has had the "Character" cut off. **1918** *Everybody's* (Jan.) 23: Men of many wars, deserters, bobtails, but fighters all.

2. *Poker.* BOBTAIL FLUSH.

1884 Carleton *Poker Club* 21: The calmness of one who expects to fill a bobtail.

3.a. a small horse-drawn car having no rear platform. In full, **bobtail car.**

1875 in *DA*. **1886** Nye *Remarks* 24: He...tried to board a Fifteenth street bob-tail car. **1889** Farmer *Amer.* 71: *Bobtail car.*—The popular name for a small tram-car horsed by a single animal, and on which the only official is a driver.

b. *R.R.* (see quot.).

1945 Hubbard *R.R. Ave.* 333: *Bobtail*—Switch engine.

4. *Trucking.* a truck tractor when not equipped with a semitrailer; (*hence*) a motor truck that is not a truck tractor, esp. a delivery truck.

1944 Boatright & Day *Hell to Breakfast* 148: A short-bed four-wheel truck is a "bob tail." **1958** McCulloch *Woods Words* 14: *Bobtail*—A six-wheel truck used for hauling logs without a trailer. **1978** J. Rosenberg *Dict. Business* 53: *Bobtail*: a small truck used for deliveries, or a trailerless tractor.

bobtail *adv. Trucking.* without a trailer.
1971 Tak *Truck Talk* 15: *Bobtail*: said of a trucker when he drives a tractor without its semi-trailer, as in "runs bobtail."

bobtail *v.* **1.** *Mil.* **a.** to discharge from military service with a BOBTAIL.
1906 M'Govern *Sarjint Larry* 34: After his tenth glass he confided to me that his real name was "McCann," but that having been "bobtailed" in a former enlistment, to get into the army again he had to adopt a new name. **1909** Moss *Officers' Man.* 283: To be "bob-tailed"—to be dishonorably discharged or to be given a discharge without honor. **1914** *Collier's* (June 6) 8: Ye'll be bobtailed out av the service. **1918** Griffin *Ballads of Regt.* 64: 'Tis the whiskey...has "bob-tailed" some thousands, I hear. **1918** in Truman *Ltrs. Home* 60: If the censor opens this letter,...I'll be jugged or jimmied or bobtailed, to say the least. **1936** *Our Army* (June) 23: I didn't retire—I was bobtailed!
b. to fine.
1918 *Stars & Stripes* (May 5) 5: I had a summary [court-martial] a long time ago, but when they pulled me up the court officer didn't turn up, so I wasn't bobtailed no pay for that.
2. *Poker.* to try to fill a straight or a flush.
1948 J. Stevens *Jim Turner* 122 [ref. to *ca*1910]: He might be...bobtailing or fourflushing. I could only imagine.
3. *Trucking.* to drive without a trailer.
1972 *N.Y. Times Mag.* (Nov. 12) 97: We..."bobtail" to the truck stop where he had parked the trailer for two nights while the tractor was undergoing...repairs.

bobtail flush *n. Poker.* a worthless hand consisting of an incomplete flush.
1881 Field *Tribune Verse* 221: It is the old time bob-tail flush. **1881** Nye *Forty Liars* 70: Tomorrow it will be but a bob-tail flush. **1883** Field *Sharps & Flats* I 61: While other rash Shoshones groaned/O'er various bobtail flushes. **1883** Peck *Bad Boy* 186: A contrite heart beats a bobtail flush. **1886** Nye *Remarks* 214: Lawyers...knew more of the habits of a bob-tail flush. **1907** "O. Henry" *Heart of West* 149: I was sure Solly would be tickled to death with these [poker] hands, after the bob-tail flushes he'd been getting on the ranch. **1968** R. Adams *Western Words* (ed. 2): *Bobtail flush.* In five-card poker, a worthless three-card flush.

bo-chaser *n. R.R.* (see quot.).
1945 Hubbard *R.R. Ave.* 333: *Bo chaser* is freight brakeman or railroad policeman.

Boche *n.* [< F *Boche*, either aph. form of *alboche* = *al*lemand 'German' + c*aboche* 'blockhead' or shortening of *tête de caboche*] *Mil.* **1.** a German soldier; German troops. Now *hist.*
1914 in E. Pound *Letters* 45: He has killed two "boches." **1918** *Stars & Stripes* (Feb. 8) 5: Boche Tries to Bean Him With Bombs. **1918** in Straub *Diary* (Apr. 24): We immediately drew our guns as there was danger of Boche being hidden in the O.P. **1918** in Ross *With 351st* 29: "Old Boche" is ever on the alert, scouting in his elusive little airplanes. **1919** Sweeney *Negro in World War* 227: I was climbin' over some barbed wire tryin' to get to those d—n Boches, and they shot me. **1925** in Thomason *Stories* 430: We goes in camions two-three days to Verdun, where it 'pears like ole Boche is breakin' thoo de w'ite sogers. **1942** in Truman *Dear Bess* 483: I...got to France, fired some three-inch bullets at the Boche, went home [etc.]. **1980** Millett *Semper Fidelis* 294 [ref. to WWI]: Get a Boche!
2. the German language.
1924 *Adventure* (June 20) 164 [ref. to WWI]: How can I tell whether a fellar's speakin' French er Canuck er Boche er Greek?

bod *n.* **1.a.** the human body; (*specif.*) the figure or physique; in phr. **how's your bod?** "how are you?"
***1933** in *OED2*: The Red, the White and the Blue...covers the dead bod. **1962** in IUFA *College Songs: Parodies: Sacrilegious:* He said my name is Jesus and I've come to save your bod. **1966** IUFA *Folk Speech: Bod*—Refers to a girl's body. **1967** *Lit Dict.* 5: *bod*—Hip, shortened form of the word "body." She's got a groovy *bod*. **1968** Swarthout *Loveland* 20: High sassiety and babes with fine bods. **1972** in *Penthouse* (Jan. 1973) 119: I...have average looks and a thin bod. Several chicks have told me to forget it because I'm not built well enough for them. **1973** Lucas et al. *Amer. Graffiti* 79: Hi cousin, how's your bod? **1973** Roth *Sand in the Wind* 93: You signed your putrid bods over to Uncle Sam. **1977** Herr *Dispatches* 202: Collins, get your bod up here. **1983**

Breathed *Bloom Co.* 44: You gave us bods like bottles. **1983** *USA Today* (Aug. 2) 2D: John Travolta plans to share his tips on building a beautiful bod in a health and fitness book. **1990** *Cosmopolitan* (Aug.) 32: Arnold Schwarzenegger is in complete command of his bod, from the most mountainous bicep to the most minuscule corpuscle.
b. *Stu.* a person of the opposite sex who has a sexually attractive physique.
*a***1961** Boroff *Campus U.S.A.* 46: "Let's go check the bods in the fishbowl"...means, "Let's go to the glass-enclosed reference room in Honnold Library and look over the girls." **1968** Baker et al. *CUSS* 84: *Bod.* A sexually attractive person, male...[or] female. **1969** *Current Slang* I & II 12: *Bod*,...n. A girl with sex appeal.—College students, both sexes, Texas.—I took out a real *bod* last night.
c. copulation.
1971 Sanders *Family* 25: Accused of sending...Candy and...Elizabeth to Needles, California in order to deal out bod.
2. [perh. ult. of Scots orig.; see *OED2*] *Mil. Av.* a person. *Joc.*
1945 *N.Y. Times Mag.* (Nov. 4) 12: "Bod" meaning fellow. ***1953** in *OED2*: The rest go to the camp with the R.A.A.F. bods. **1986** Zeybel *First Ace* 107: Once a bod...swooped over the North, nothing was limited.
3. a dead body.
[**1933** (quot. at **(1.a.)**, above).] **1971** T. Mayer *Weary Falcon* 22: Check the bods out first....Check for weapons.

bodacious *adj.* [perh. *bold* + au*dacious*] *So. & Midland.* **1.** enormous; formidable; strong; excessive; big. Also *adv.*
1843 [W.T. Thompson] *Scenes in Ga.* 167: Take that, you bowdacious fool. **1845** in *OED2*: She's so bowdacious unreasonable when she's riled. **1925** (quot. at SCRONCH). **1970** Whitmore *Memphis-Nam-Sweden* 170: He had the biggest, most "bodacious" hands I'd ever seen. Real bone-crackers. **1977** Corder *Citizens Band* 89: He must be pumping some bodacious power. **1977** Coover *Public Burning* 415: A evil hour of darkness and adversity and bodacious peril. **1982** S.P. Smith *Officer & Gentleman* 44: That's one bodacious pair of ta-tas on that blonde. **1983** *Nat. Lampoon* (Aug.) 46: Turn up the radio...until the frequency is truly bodacious. **1987** D. Sherman *Main Force* 25: Looks like someone was expecting to get into one bodacious fire fight. **1989** D. Sherman *There I Was* 53: It can get bodacious hot.
2. impudent, insolent; (*also*) daring.
1967 Colebrook *Lassitude* 49: Well, don't you be bodacious! **1969** B. Beckham *Main Mother* 101: Tom was bodacious enough even to strut around school with Carolyn. **1973** I. Reed *La. Red* 49: Since Minnie is heading it up, them gals be around her has become bodacious. Them girls talk to a man any way they want to talk to him. **1974** Carr *Bad* 212: He thought it hysterical that this hick should turn bodacious and rip off...the Champ. **1985** N.O. woman, age 35: That's a bodacious lie!
3.a. very exciting or impressive. Also *adv.*
1976 Whelton *CB Baby* 168: A couple of days and you'll be doing a bodacious job again, for sure. **1977** Univ. Tenn. student: You can have a *bodacious* shirt, a *bodacious* noise. Or a movie that's really enjoyable could be *bodacious*. It's about the same as outrageous—striking, forceful. **1985** Ark. man, age 35: I remember a headline in the *Arkansas Gazette* a few years ago: Bo Derek is *Bodacious!* **1981–85** S. King *It* 439: They played bodacious.
b. Esp. *Stu.* very appealing, esp. sexually attractive; (*often*, of young women) having large breasts. Cf. 1982 quot. at **(1)**, above.
1985 Graham & Hamdan *Flyers* ch. xxviii: *Bodacious*—adj. used...to describe females with massive chests. **1991** P. Munro *Slang U.* 40: *Bodacious* very cool, appealing. **1991** *Saved by the Bell* (NBC-TV): Let's sculpt bodacious bikini babes. **1992** *TV Guide* (July 18) 1: Top Turn-Ons. TV, TV on the wall, who's the most bodacious of all?

bodaciously *adv. So. & Midland.* **1.** in an impressive manner; outright; entirely.
1832 J. Hall *Legends of W.* 38: It's a mercy...that the...*varments* hadn't used you up, body-aciously. [*sic*] **1840** in *DA* s.v. *exflunct*: The Administration is bodaciously used up. **1847** in *Indiana Mag. History* 429: This night it seemed as if we were to be taken "bodeaciously," if I may use a Kentuckism. **1880** J.C. Harris *Uncle Remus* 265: You'll be slippin' round arter hours some time er nudder, an' you'll slip bodaciously inter de calaboose. **1965** Ark. teenager: Man, she was cryin' bodaciously.
2. extremely; very.
1934 in Botkin *Treas. Amer. Folk.* 430: I can't say so bodaciously much for it. **1977** Coover *Public Burning* 92: I'd do it tonight, if I wasn't so

bodaciously whacked. **1984** Holland *Better Off Dead* (film): Greendale is a bodaciously small town. **1985** Ark. man, age 35: He's bodaciously rich.

bodaggle *n.* BULLDAGGER.
1976 Arble *Long Tunnel* 213: "Like, some of the other women miners were bodaggles." I asked what bodaggles were. "Lesbians. Male dikes. You know, butches."

bodice-ripper *n.* a fast-paced romantic novel, set typically in England in the 18th or 19th C., that includes scenes of sexual passion and usu. a female first-person narrator.
1982 *N.Y. Times* (Jan. 28) C 20. **1986** *Time* (Nov. 3) 84: It would be hard to call this book a bodice ripper because nobody is wearing enough bodice to rip. *a*1989 in Safire *Coming to Terms* 104: The term "bodice-ripper" refers specifically to *historical* romance novels, books featuring a great deal of historical costume description and sex tinged with a degree of violence.

bodini *n.* [< It *bodino, budino* 'blood sausage'] the penis. *Joc.*
1960 Reuss & Legman *Songs Mother Never Taught Me* (unp.): If all them young ladies wore a tiny bikini/I'd walk around with a three foot bodini. **1980** McDowell *Our Honor* 81: Till I unzipped my fly/When she saw my budini/I thought she would die.

body *n.* women as objects of copulation; (*hence*) copulation. Cf. BOOTY, 2.
1916 Cary *Venery* I 20: *Body*—Generic for women. **1965** C. Brown *Manchild* 183: I learned that you just can't go and try to get some body from every chick that looks nice.

body bag *n.* an undershirt. *Joc.*
1813–18 Weems *Drunk. Look. Glass* 65: "And naked came we too!" replied they, and snatching off their *body bags*, committed them to the flames. **1848* (cited in Partridge *DSUE* (ed. 7) 1019).

body companion *n.* a louse. *Joc.*
1848 *High Private* 42: Many a poor *body-companion* was sent into the mighty deep that morning.

body condom *n.* a rubberized waterproof antiexposure suit.
1968 Yglesias *Orderly Life* 98: Come on, put on your body condom….The plane's coming in now.

body count *n.* a count of persons who are actually present.
1971 Dahlskog *Dict.* 8: *Body count, n.* A count of persons; a head count; nose count. **1983** Univ. Tenn. instructor: What kind of body count did you have in that class?

body exchange *n.* a place to meet a sexual partner; (*specif.*) a singles bar or a party.
1962–65 Cavan *Liquor License* 177: They heard it [a bar] was a "body exchange." **1971** (quot. at MEAT MARKET).

body guard *n.* a louse. *Joc.*
1863 in C.H. Moulton *Ft. Lyon* 127: Plenty of "body guards"…come voluntarily at their own will.

body shop *n.* **1.** a singles bar or other establishment where sexual partners may be picked up.
1971 Meggyesy *Out of League* 104: On the West Coast [singles bars] are known as "body shops" with a male-female ratio on Saturday night of about 6 to 1. **1974** N.Y.C. man, age 27: I've seen places all over the country called *The Body Shop*. They're bars or strip joints. **1978** Maupin *Tales* 202: Off to the body shops? **1980** R.L. Morris *Wait Until Dark* 53: Today countless pubs and "body shops" attract a riot of color and nationality.
2. a mortuary or morgue.
1972–76 Durden *No Bugles* 147: Dags had Longfeather drive us to the body shop. The place where they try to fix up dudes who've been had. They plug up the holes with cotton, I think. **1980** D. Cragg (letter to J.E.L., Aug. 10) 2: I first heard this…after I returned from Vietnam, post September 1969. "Too many guys from that company wind up in the body shop."
3. *Hosp.* a ward where paraplegic patients are treated; a place where prosthetic devices are fitted, etc.
1973 Browne *Body Shop* (title).

body-snatcher *n.* **1.** *Und.* a police officer.
[**1821* *Real Life in London* I 166: A Bailiff or his follower—they are also called Body-snatchers.] **1858* A. Mayhew *Paved with Gold* 254: We should have the "body-snatchers" (police officers) after us. **1918** T.A. Dorgan, in Zwilling *TAD Lexicon* 19: Here's one of those cops that ain't made a pinch in a month—a body snatcher—you know, Jim. **1932** L.

Berg *Prison Doctor* 212: And the boy friend was an undercover man for them! A body snatcher! *Ibid.* 214: But the city was lousy with stools for the body snatchers.
2. an undertaker.
1887 Peck *Pvt. Peck* 202 [ref. to Civil War]: Mr. Body-snatcher, you can postpone the funeral. **a1890* F & H: *Body-Snatcher…*(common.)—An undertaker. **1933** *Leatherneck* (Feb.) 23: A friend of mine was laid off after working twenty-five years for the same firm of body-snatchers [undertakers]. **1947** in Hecht *From Bohemia* 58: He hammered down the body-snatchers from four grand to $500. **1970** Thackrey & Burk *Thief* 210: So that's where I headed…wondering how long it would take the body-snatcher to holler copper.
3. a woman who is sexually forward; (*specif.*) a streetwalker.
1894 *Harper's* (Sept.) 581: No doubt these are not the nice girls; they are body-snatchers, mostly….You know what I mean—girls who can't let a man go by without reaching out for him. **1911** O. Johnson *Stover at Yale* 139: By George, if that body snatcher of a Miss Sparkes hasn't bagged Stover—well, I never. **1935** Pollock *Underworld Speaks*: *Body-snatcher,* a prostitute.
4.a. *Mil.* a stretcher-bearer.
1918 *Stars & Stripes* (Feb. 8) 6: He was one of the best bets on the Border where he served in the Body-Snatchers. **1919* *Athenaeum* (Aug. 8) 729: "Body-snatchers," stretcher-bearers. [**1948** A. Murphy *Hell & Back* 3: Then why didn't you get hooked up with a body-snatching outfit? You look like a natural for the buzzard detail.] [**1953** Russ *Last Parallel* 183: A body-snatching team would be working near our outpost within an hour….They loaded the Chinese bodies on the stretchers.]
b. *Army.* a member of a patrol that seeks to capture enemy personnel for interrogation.
1983 Groen & Groen *Huey* 26 [ref. to Vietnam War]: Special forces body-snatchers or LRRP snipers went in. *Ibid.* 58: John admired the body-snatchers.
5. (see quot.).
1927 *DN* V 439: *Body-snatcher, n.* A contractor who entices, by higher wages, better living conditions, etc., hoboes who have been transported, often long distances, at the expense of other contractors.

boff[1] *n.* [fr. the *v.*] **1.** a heavy blow; BOP, *n.*, 1.a.
1921 J. Conway, in *Variety* (Apr. 8) 7: Tomato socked Pepper on the button with a boff that you could hear all over the buildin. **1944** D. Runyon, in *Collier's* (Jan. 15) 53: I quietly gave Girondel a boff over his pimple with a blackjack.
2. copulation; an act of copulation.
1956 Longstreet *Real Jazz* 62: So no more legal boff and soon, no more legal booze. **1961** Heller *Catch-22* 394: I thought I might as well give the stupid broad another boff just for old times' sake. **1968** Spooner *Three Cheers* 130: Beauregard had been administered…an "exceptionally good boff" before breakfast. **1973** Hirschfeld *Victors* 237: Bet she's a great boff. **1977** Hamill *Flesh & Blood* 216: You wanna ball me, boy?…Hell, I'd like to give you a boff, boy. **1985** Heywood *Taxi Dancer* 20: A boff in the sack with his old lady.

boff[2] *n.* [prob. fr. BOFFO, 3] *Theat.* a hearty laugh.
1945 in *DAS*: Always trying for a boff…a laugh. **1947** *ATS* (Supp.): *Boff,* laughter. **1959** in Marx *Groucho Letters* 268: I love…hearing the boffs. **1981** Univ. Tenn. student: That party wasn't exactly big boffs.

boff *v.* [orig. dial. E; var. of S.E. *buff*] **1.a.** to hit hard, esp. over the head.
[**1776* D. Herd *Ancient & Mod. Scot. Songs* II ("Fare Ye Weel, My Auld Wife"): Fare ye weel, my pyke-staff,/Wi' you nae mair my wife I'll baff.] **1929–31** D. Runyon *Guys & Dolls* 130: Trying to boff Big Jule with his blackjack. **1950** in *DAS*: LaGuardia bade his cops to muss them up and boff them around on sight. **1964–67** Speicher *Baby Paradise* 41: One…might…boff you with [a] picket sign.
b. to kill.
1974 Strasburger *Rounding Third* 20: Virgin Boy Boffed in Car Crash…Dies Unfulfilled.
2. to copulate with. Also absol.
1937 Weidman *I Can Get It Wholesale* 6: Five minutes ago you were in such a hurry that you wouldn't even let me take time out to get boffed. **1952** in Legman *Limerick* 259: With bologna you know you've been boffed. **1958** [E. Hunter] *Killer's Choice* 6: They boffed, they drank, they belched, they fought, they swore—but they stood erect. **1968** Vidal *Breckinridge* 129: Letitia…who I used to boff in the old days. **1968** P. Roth *Portnoy* 116: It is her pleasure while being boffed. **1969** Tynan *Oh! Calcutta!* 19: After I boff you, my time is my own. **1974** Strasburger *Rounding Third* 7: I always *hear*…about beauties getting boffed in the back seat of cars. **1981** *Nat. Lampoon* (Aug.) 14: I used to

boff this woman named Tirza. **1992** *Herman's Head* (Fox-TV): We spent the night boffing one of New York's most powerful broads.

boffo *n.* **1.** a dollar.

1922 in *DN* V 147: *Boffos*—dollars, otherwise known as rocks, chips, seeds, berries, and jack. **1928** *N.Y. Times* (Mar. 11) VIII 6: *Boffos*—Dollars. **1931** *Amer. Merc.* (Dec.) 416: You got a jernt that's woith a million boffos. **1981** *Natural History* (July) 89 (adv): That's right, [a map of] the entire country is yours for just a buck—a solitary simoleon, greenback, smacker, boffo, bean, eight-bits, frogskin, lettuce leaf, shinplaster.

2. *Pris.* a year in prison.

1930 *AS* VI 437: *Boffo.* A year. "He was handed ten boffos." **1934** *Jour. Abnormal & Soc. Psych.* 361: *Boffoes*—years.

3. a hilarious joke; a laugh; BOFF.

1969 in H.S. Thompson *Shark Hunt* 209: Nixon's reaction to this boffo was not reported in the press. **1985** Frede *Nurses* 332: The biggest current jokes, I mean real boffos. **1992** *New Republic* (July 6) 26: A performer...out only for boffos wouldn't have mentioned the suicide.

4. *Theat.* a tremendous success.

1981 *N.Y. Times Mag.* (June 21) 16: The Duke Ellington songbook is lavishly made into "Sophisticated Ladies," and it's instant boffo.

boffo *adj.* [prob. alter. of theat. *buffo*] **1.** *Theat.* tremendously entertaining or successful; (*esp.*) hilarious in a slapstick manner; (*hence*) very impressive or effective.

[**1906** Ford *Shorty McCabe* 215: Now look at the buffo combination I've been up against.] **1949** in *DAS*: Red-blooded boffo entertainment for both sexes. **1968** Kirkwood *Good/Bad Times* 150: Talk about acting! He staged a boffo production at his house in Laurel Canyon. **1968** *For Love of Ivy* (film): You know what that B stands for? "Boffo!" **1973** *Oui* (May) 40: Even with training, Mark's performance on the Crosby show was less than boffo. **1981** in Cross *Mediaspeak* 203: Reagan Gives a Boffo Performance in His First Appearance in the Capital. **1982** Zicree *Twi. Zone Comp.* 143: In an effort to achieve out-and-out boffo comedy. **1983** S. Kelly, in *Nat. Lampoon* (Aug.) 37: Our ludicrous leader and his supporting cast of boffo zanies. **1987** *Ampersand's Entertainment Gde.* (Summer) 12: Box office biz was...boffo in '86. **1992** *Crier & Co.* (CNN-TV) (Aug. 21): That was a boffo speech.

2. *Theat.* (of a critical review) enthusiastic.

1945 *Pageant* (Apr.) 71: A "boffo" *Variety* review means money in the bank. **1992** *N.Y. Times* (July 7) B 5: They floated away on the fragrance of the boffo...review.

boffo *interj.* "pow!" WHAMMO!

1945 Fay *Be Poor* 132: But the kid—boffo!—he's a goner.

boffola *n.* [BOFF + -OLA] **1.** Theat. BOFF², *n.*

1955 O'Connor *Last Hurrah* 190: One solid boffola from beginning to end...guaranteed to make you split your sides with good clean laughter. **1970** H.A. Smith *Rude Jokes* 111: Boffolas That'll Break Up a Laredo Daisy Chain. **1980** Ciardi *Browser's Dict.* 45: *Boffola*, a joke or comic turn that elicits a striking (knock-'em-dead) response.

2. *Theat.* noisy promotion; hoopla.

1980 Wylie *Bigfoot* 172: More Buffs and Some Boffola: An Abominable Snow Job?

bog *n. Mil.* a bow gunner in an armored vehicle.

1962 W. Robinson *Barbara* 12 [ref. to WWII]: They've got their bog riding out of uniform—no crash helmet.

Bogart *adj.* [see BOGART, *v.*] rough, hostile, aggressive; in phr. **jump bogart** to become aggressive.

1966 Braly *On Yard* 201: This is the first time they've jumped bogart and just snatched them. **1976** Rosen *Above Rim* 55: There's no call for all that Bogart stuff.

bogart *v.* [fr. Humphrey *Bogart*, U.S. actor who often played cigarette-smoking tough guys in motion pictures] **1.** Esp. *Black E.* to force or coerce; bully; intimidate. Also **Bogart.**

[**1951** *West. Folk.* X 172: *To pull a Bogart* To act tough.] [**1952** Mandel *Angry Strangers* 337: You just try to stop being like Bogart.] **1966** Braly *On Yard* 166: Cool Breeze jus' bogart his way in. **1969** *Current Slang* I & II 12: *Bogart*, v. To injure or hurt; to protect at the cost of violence.—High school males, Negro, Washington, D.C.—Them 'bama chukkers better not bogart us no more. **1971** Dahlskog *Dict.* 8: *Bogart*...To fight or injure (someone) by violence. **1974** R. Carter *16th Round* 208: I had to bogart my way into Charlie Scott's dressing room. **1978** W. Brown *Tragic Magic* 35: When he walked he was a V.I.P. brougham limousine Bogarting its way into two lanes. **1978** *Wash. Post* (May 4) D1: Bullet Coach Dick Motta said the 76ers "were trying to come out and 'bogart' us. They were trying to be intimidating." **1980** Wielgus & Wolff *Bas-*

ketball 39: *Bogart* (v.) To make a strong move on [another player] inside. **1988** "Ice-T" *I'm Your Pulsar* (rap song): I don't ask, the Ice just bogarts.

2. to hog (esp. a marijuana cigarette).

1969 Fonda, Hopper & Southern *Easy Rider* (film): Don't bogart that joint...pass it over to me. **1971** N.Y.U. student: "Don't bogart that joint" means don't hog it. Because Bogart always used to hold his cigarette for a long time and puff on it. **1972** Smith & Gay *Don't Try It* 198: *Bogart.* Monopolize, not pass, a joint. **1982** *Nat. Lampoon* (Sept.) 16: Swilling coffee...and bogarting them Gauloises. **1985** *Nat. Lampoon* (July) 71: Chet, man, don't bogart that...joint. **1993** *Mystery Sci. Theater* (Comedy Central TV): Quit bogarting that joint, Floyd!

bogey *n.* **1.** BOOGIE¹, *n.*, 2.

1940 Zinberg *Walk Hard* 261: That dirty coon pimp!...The bogey bastard! **1955** in *AS* (Feb. 1956) 98: Negro...bogey.

2.a. *Mil.* an unidentified aerial target on radar; an unidentified and presumably hostile flying aircraft. Now *S.E.* Cf. BANDIT.

1943 in Loosbrock & Skinner *Wild Blue* 209: Bogies coming. Direction southeast. **1944** *Off. Gd. to AAF* 368: *Bogie*—unidentified aircraft. **1945** J. Bryan *Carrier* 67: A bandit is an enemy plane, whereas a bogey is merely...unidentified....However, "bogey" has now been extended to include both terms. **1945** Dos Passos *Tour* 90: A bogey. A bogey. We have the bogey. Two-engined plane flying low over water. It's a [Japanese] Jill....Torpedo plane. **1951** Sheldon *Troubling of Star* 134: Bogie—ten o'clock low! **1953** Eyster *Customary Skies* 79: Bogie still around? **1956** W. Taylor *Roll Back Sky* 108: Sure is a good idea, never doing any work on the shelter until the bogies come over. **1961** L.G. Richards *TAC* 59: Bogeys at twelve o'clock level. **1968** Broughton *Thud Ridge* 50: I've got four bogies, ten o'clock low. **1969** W. Sullivan, in Sagan & Page *UFOs* 261: I was associated with radar in its early days, and watched "bogies" do the most incredible things. **1983** *Time* (Sept. 12) 14: An unidentified aircraft—a "bogey" in military slang.

b. *USAF.* an unfamiliar young woman. *Joc.*

1963 E.M. Miller *Exile* 134: It was a big night, with lots of color and clatter, and what the Air Defense people called "unidentified long-legged bogies." **1969** *Current Slang* I & II 12: *Bogey*, n....girl.—Air Force Academy cadets.

bogey *v.* [fr. *Bogey*, nickname of Humphrey Bogart] *Narc.* BOGART, *v.*, 2.

1985 Briskin *Too Much* 237: Why is it fine for him to bogey a joint and not me?

bogey hat *n.* [BOGEY, *n.*] *Navy.* a combat helmet worn during an enemy air attack.

1944 Olds *Helldiver Squadron* 55: On the bridge there was a scurry for steel helmets, "bogie hats."

bog-pocket *n.* a skinflint. *Joc.*

1941 *AS* (Oct.) 163: *Bog-Pocket.* Tightwad. **1945** Hamann *Air Words*: Bog-pocket. Tightwad.

BOGSAT *n.* [acronym of *a b*unch *o*f *g*uys *s*itting *a*round a *t*able] *Pol.* policy or decision making by a small group of associates. *Joc.*

1984 *N.Y. Times* (Feb. 9) 29: Dan Fenn, special assistant to President John F. Kennedy, [asserted] that each President was reduced to choosing his team by a process he calls "BOGSAT"—"a bunch of guys sitting around a table." **1986** *N.Y. Times* (June 11) 14: He concluded that it really was no more than BOGSATT...."Bunch of guys sitting around the table," said [Congressman Les] Aspin, an old Pentagon hand with a penchant for acronyms.

bog-trotter *n.* [in earliest use, a bumpkin dwelling in boggy country; see *EDD*] a rural Irishman; (*broadly*) an Irish person.—used derisively. Now usu. *hist.*

***1682** in *OED*: An idle flam of shabby Irish Bogtrotters. *ca**1708** in D'Urfey *Pills* I 244: You seemple Bogtrotter. *a*1733, *1753, *1773 in *OED*. **1792** Brackenridge *Mod. Chiv.* 15: This servant of mine is but a bog-trotter. **1798** in *DAE* s.v. *desperado*: Except imported desperadoes, Bog-trotters noted for bravadoes. **1821** [Martin & Waldo] *Lightfoot* 43: We fell in with a number of bog-trotters, who gave us some provisions. **1848** Bartlett *Amer.*: *Bog-trotter.* A derisive epithet applied to Irishmen. **1864** Lyman *Meade's HQ* 208: Send bog-trotters, if you please, for Paddy will fight—no one is braver. **1865** in Commager *Blue & Gray* II 390: Stand aside, you useless bog-trotter! **1906** Ford *Shorty McCabe* 217: Dennis, you low-county bog-trotter. **1928–29** Nason *White Slicker* 53: You benighted bog-trotter! **1940** E. O'Neill *Long Day's Journey* II i: With your Irish bog-trotter idea that consumption is fatal.

*a*1957 McLiam *Pat Muldoon* 32: Dirty little bog-trotter...peat stuck between his toes. **1975** McCaig *Danger Trail* 21: Those bogtrotters talk big. **1981** Wambaugh *Glitter Dome* 238: He felt like his old man must have felt as a bogtrotter at Ellis Island.

bogue *n.* [fr. the adj.] **1.** *Narc.* withdrawal symptoms or sickness.

1969 Lingeman *Drugs* 26: *Bogue.* 1. sickness from withdrawal of drugs. 2. the first stages of withdrawal symptoms, as in "I've got the *bogue.*"

2. *Und.* a stupid or contemptible person.

1970 Gattzden *Black Vendetta* 40: The bogue...thought he was in a hotel room.

bogue *adj.* [fr. BOGUS¹] **1.a.** counterfeit, fake.

1957 *N.Y. Times Mag.* (Aug. 18) 26: *Bogue*—Fake, phony, false, bogus. **1954–60** *DAS: Bogue*...Bogus; false; fake.

b. contemptible; no good; offensive.

1960 C. Cooper *Scene* 52: I can't understand why your stuff is bogue; Marsha Lee's and Leslie's is okay. **1965** in W. King *Black Anthol.* 302: Grunting now and then, as though in reply to Gloria's bogue chatter. **1967** Rosevear *Pot* 157: *Bogue:* Meaning bad, very bad. **1970** A. Young *Snakes* 44: Don't be layin no bogue needles on my choice jams, man! *Ibid.* 143: Bogue nigger, must dont know who he messin with. **1986** Eble *Campus Slang* (Oct. 1): *Bogue*—unappealing, overly graphic, disgusting: "The ax scene in *Friday the 13th* was so bogue."

2. *Narc.* suffering withdrawal symptoms.

1960 C.L. Cooper *Scene* 8: I'm bogue, but I ain't gonna indulge. I'm tryin' to kick. *Ibid.* 267: Don't pay no attention if I get bogue again. *Ibid.* 307: *Bogue:* sick from lack of heroin. **1971** Dahlskog *Dict.* 9: *Bogue, a.* Craving narcotics; in need of a fix. **1971** Guggenheimer *Narc. & Drug Abuse* 55: *You are boog* [sic]. You are sick. **1971** *Newsweek* (July 5) 27: But we tell 'em we have the flu when we get bogue.

bogus¹ *n.* [orig. unkn.] **1.** Orig. *Und.* counterfeit coins; counterfeit money.

*ca*1798 in Greene *Band of Bros.* 113: *Coney* means Counterfeit paper money....*Bogus* means spurious coin, &c. **1838** in *DA:* Oliver Cowdery and David Whitmer's bogus-money business. **1847** *Nat. Police Gaz.* (Jan. 9) 137: "Bogus," is base coin; "Queer," is counterfeit banknotes. **1848** [Thompson] *House Breaker* 16: [He] deposited his *bogus* in a large pocket-book. **1855** Brougham *Basket of Chips* 144: The bogus-filled, deceitful wallet. **1859** Matsell *Vocabulum* 13: *Bogus.* Bad coin. **1970–71** Higgins *Coyle* 75: There's a hell of a lot of bogus flying around in tens and twenties.

2. a machine for coining counterfeit money.

1827 in *DA:* He never procured the casting of a Bogus at one of our furnaces. *Ibid.:* The eight or ten boguses which have been for some time in operation. **1846** *Nat. Police Gaz.* (Jan. 24) 177/4: They could transfer themselves and their "*bogus*" machinery from one country to another.

3. a fraudulent imitation.

1857 *Knickerbocker Mag.* XLIX 278: Don't run your bogus on me. **1906** *Nat. Police Gaz.* (Aug. 11) 6: He'd had a bogus of the genuine pin made before the job was pulled off. **1944** in *DA:* The broadcast...was officially described in London as "obviously an enemy propaganda story" and "a complete bogus." **1972** in *Nat. Lampoon* (Jan. 1973) 23: Hey man, you really got strung out. Someone handed you a bogus.

bogus² *n.* [fr. CALIBOGUS] a liquor made of rum and beer or rum and molasses.

1848 Bartlett *Amer.* 40: *Bogus,* a liquor made of rum and molasses. **1893** Earle *Old New England* 179: "Calibogus," or "bogus," was rum and beer unsweetened.

bogus *adj.* [fr. the n.] **1.a.** counterfeit; fraudulent; PHONY. Now *S.E.*

1847–49 Bonney *Banditti* 100: I have a little bogus gold but have been dealing mostly in horses. **1853** in S. Clemens *Twain's Letters* 21: I despise the infernal bogus brick columns. **1859** Matsell *Vocabulum* 13: *Bogus*....false. **1866** *Night Side of N.Y.* 63: Watch out for bogus fives representing issues of the Wamsutta Bank, Fall River. **1887** Walling *N.Y. Chief of Police* 133: The "bogus" piano-tuner smiles serenely. **1933** in S. Smith *Gumps* 85: She had the low-down on that bogus Count. **1935** Hurston *Mules & Men* 56. **1974** N.Y.C. woman: But the letter turned out to be bogus.

b. *Stu.* pretentious.

1982 Pond *Valley Girls' Gd.* 53: *Bogus*...mega-phony....A totally bogus chick.

2. contemptible; worthless; no good; malfunctioning.

1876 W. Wright *Big Bonanza* 48: [The miners] thought that, after all, what they had might be some sort of "bogus stuff"—base metal

of some new and strange kind. **1940** *Current Hist. & Forum* (Nov. 7) 22: You may forever remain *boagish* (a person who tries to use the proper slang but doesn't quite know how). **1963** M. Braly *Shake Him* 50: "You sound kinda bogus." "Bogus?...What's bogus about not wanting to get busted?" **1974** Terkel *Working* 438: This [job] is bogus, it's bullshit, it's not worthy. **1983** Naiman *Computer Dict.* 22: *Bogus*...useless; stupid. **1983** *N.Y. Daily News* (Mar. 25): Teen Talk Glossary...*bogus*—no good. **1987** *Daily Beacon* (Univ. Tenn.) (Jan. 21) 7: Get real. It's a bogus assignment and I really can't get into it. **1989** Weber *Defcon One* 8: Our radar is bogus.

bogus boy *n. Finance.* (see quot.).

1902 Clapin *Americanisms* 64: *Bogus boys.* A broker's term designating the swindlers and frauds who are the pests of Wall Street and other commercial districts.

bohawk *n.* [prob. alter. of BOHUNK, 1] a person having bohemian interests.

1952 Mandel *Angry Strangers* 237: She's oney a bohawk anyway....Like—one of them screwy artiss. *Ibid.* 309: In violet light the bohawks argued about the meaning of art, the art of meaning.

boho *n.* [fr. the adj.] Orig. *Stu.* a person of unconventional, esp. artistic, interests or habits; bohemian.

1958 J. Davis *College Vocab.* 5: *Boho*...A nonconformist, usually an Art or Speech and Theater major. **1967–68** Wolfe *Kool-Aid* 22: What a curious bunch of bohos. *Ibid.* 30: Something out of late North Beach, the boho with the thousand-dollar wardrobe. **1984** H. Gould *Cocktail* 33: He was a Boho; he had shed his past like a molting bird. **1991** Nelson & Gonzales *Bring Noise* 261: New-jack bohos like Digital Underground.

boho *adj.* Orig. *Stu.* bohemian; unconventional.

1958 J. Davis *College Vocab.* 5: *Boho*—Bohemian. **1970** Segal *Love Story* 3: Her costume...was a bit too Boho for my taste. I especially loathed that Indian thing she carried for a handbag. **1970** *Nat. Lampoon* (Dec.) 67: She was plain as oatmeal and twice as lumpy. I rated her C+ overall. Even if she was kind of boho. **1971** Dahlskog *Dict.* 9: *Boho*...Of Bohemian or hippie appearance; as, *boho* clothing. **1980** Birnbach et al. *Preppy Hndbk.* 87: Sarah Lawrence College. Boho city. There are no grades. **1987** *Nat. Lampoon* (Oct.) 40: So I like your clothes and haircut....What're you supposed to be—boho? **1991** Nelson & Gonzales *Bring Noise* 1: What dreadlocks are to the Black boho chic of the mid-'80s/present.

bohunk *n.* [prob. *Bohemian* + *hunky*] **1.** a person of Central or Eastern European descent.—used contemptuously. Also attrib.

1903 in *DA: Bohunk*—A Bohemian; foreigner. **1913** in Truman *Ltrs. Home* 21: I bet there'll be more bohunks and Rooshans up there than white men. **1915** Lardner *Gullible's Travels* 13: A Bohunk Sokol Verein picnic. **1919** C. Sandburg *Smoke & Steel* 4: A nigger, a wop, a bohunk changes. **1926** in Thompson *Youth's Companion* 42: Simi Hussinecz...was called a "bohunk" in America. **1926** *AS* (Nov.) 88: Any [non-English]...foreigner in the northern [coal] camps is termed a *Bohunk,* although the nickname applies [strictly] only to Austrian miners. **1927** Hemingway *Men Without Women* 155: I don't want this bohunk to stop me. **1930** "D. Stiff" *Milk & Honey* 38: The various brands of Slavs are known as "bohunks" or "hunkies." *Ibid.* 200: *Bohunk*—A Polish or other Slavic laborer. **1947** Davenport *East Side, West Side* 84: In those days nobody called 'em Czechs. They were "Austrians," or maybe Bohemians, politely, or else just Bohunks. **1963** D. Tracy *Brass Ring* 11: These kids are no different from North End bohunks. **1971** *All in the Family* (CBS-TV): Ain't she turnin' into a happy little bohunk. **1976** Hayden *Voyage* 464: You...no-good Bohunk. **1984** J. Hughes *16 Candles* (film): He already asked me if Rudy was the oily variety bohunk.

2. a Slavic or Eastern European language.—used contemptuously.

1936 Mackenzie *Living Rough* 117: His songs are sung in every language, in Bohunk, in Wop, in Chink, in Spick, in every language.

3. a bumpkin; an ignorant lout.—used contemptuously. Also attrib.

1919 *Camp Pike Carry-On* (Jan. 9) 3: Petronius was a Bohunk from Iowa. **1921** J. Conway, in *Variety* (Apr. 1) 7: We draw the usual assortment of bohunks and set-ups. **1925** Gross *Nize Baby* 196: Swell gang of bohunks y' bunk up agenst—orders stuff an' den don't wanna come troo. **1928** Bodenheim *Georgie May* 30: Ah know what youah up to, you lousy bohunk! **1932** *AS* (June) 329: *Bohunk*—a clumsy or stupid person; used to signify disapproval. **1933** McGuire & Kalmar *Kid from Spain* (film): Aah, ya bohunk—you're yellow. **1936** *Mr. Deeds Goes to Town* (film): A corn-fed bohunk like that falling into a fortune is hot copy.

bohunkus *n.* [pseudo-L, poss. sugg. by BOHUNK and by dial. *hunkers* 'haunches'] *So.* the rump; (*hence*) the self, one's person. Cf. ASS.

1941 E. Welty, in Baym et al. *Norton Anthol.* (ed. 2) II 1764: They can just rest back on their little bohunkus. **1959** L. Hughes *Simply Heavenly* 132: But I was the *only* one that got throwed out on my—bohunkus. **1973** *TULIPQ* (coll. B.K. Dumas): Butt, bohunkus, behind. **1976** *N.Y. Folklore* II 239: The posterior anatomy is called…the *rear, rump,* or *bohankas.* **1980** Grizzard *Billy Bob Bailey* 21: Kiss your bohunkus goodbye. **1989** *Golden Girls* (NBC-TV): Get your bohunkus back here and listen to me!

boil *v.* **1.** to rush headlong.—used intrans.

1858 in Harris *Lovingood* 226: Arter that feller fell in the river, I jist biled, tuck down the lane. **1932** Harvey *Me and Bad Eye* 16: The First Sargent comes boiling out and says, "Shut your damn mouths."

2. to infuriate.—used trans.

1958 Talsman *Gaudy Image* 173: That boiled him 'cause he went right on talkin' low like he hadn't heard, but he was red-necked mad.

boiled *adj.* **1.** drunk.

1884 in Lummis *Letters* 180: One would have to be pretty industrious…to get "biled" on this native wine. **1886** J.A. Porter *Sketches of Yale Life* 156: There is a balm for a headache caused by last night's debauch to have it said you were "slightly cheered" or "slewed" or "boiled." **1905** in Paxton *Sport USA* 24: Why, I had to put him in a cab and send him home; boiled as an owl he was. **1912–14** in E. O'Neill *Lost Plays* 176: You know what I mean—he's soused, pickled, stewed, boiled. **1918** in [O'Brien] *Wine, Women & War* 11: Most of gang solemnized occasion by getting boiled. **1923** in J. O'Hara *Sel. Letters* 9: I don't get as much kick out of deciding to get boiled and *then* going to a saloon. **1928** MacArthur *War Bugs* 21: Slightly boiled, we visited people's houses. **1929** L. Thomas *Woodfill* 239: Well, I let 'em get boiled a few times without saying much. **1931** Dos Passos *1919* 182: They…got to Bordeaux boiled as owls. **1937** E. Anderson *Thieves Like Us* 34: If he wants to get boiled, he'll go clear up to Muskogee. **1951** Styron *Lie Down in Darkness* 205: What prompted you to come out and get boiled to the eyes like this? **1955** Shapiro *6th of June* 134: All right, men….Go and get boiled if you like. **1959** Zugsmith *Beat Generation* 12: Their old man's boiled. **1971** *Playboy* (Nov.) 177: Jack staggered out the door…biled as an owl. **1972–79** T. Wolfe *Right Stuff* 17: While otherwise blissfully boiled, in an expense-account restaurant in Manhattan. **1991** *Reflections of Silver Screen* (AMC-TV): He had a photographer with him that was quite boiled.

2. infuriated.—also constr. with *up.*

1929 E. Booth *Stealing* 261: This solitary pacing earned me the reputation of being constantly "boiled up." **1948** in Bradbury *Illus. Man* 47: You, you're boiled because someone stole your act, got here ahead and made you unimportant. **1949** Mende *Spit & Stars* 34: Sometimes you get me so boiled up, that I could…. **1955** Graziano & Barber *Somebody Up There* 169: I would sit down there in the dark getting boiled up all over again at everybody I hated. **1974** A. Bergman *Big Kiss-Off* 116: So I got a little boiled about that.

¶ In phrase:

¶ **drunk as a boiled owl** see s.v. OWL.

boiler *n.* **1.** *Army.* a heavy artillery shell; an exploding aerial bomb. [Quots. ref. to WWI.]

1918 *Literary Digest* (Sept. 7) 55: Shell shock…is caused by a "boiler" bursting very near to a man. **1919** Streeter *Same Old Bill* 44: We heard one of those high powered wash boilers go off. **1919** *307th Field Arty.* 150: Occasionally some awful "boilers" exploded here. **1923** LaBranch *Btty. in France* 76: The men were told not to smoke, lest the planes would surely see the glare of the cigarettes, and drop a few "tin boilers" on them. **1927** Blumenstein *Whiz Bang* 18: Whang, over came one of those big German boilers, striking about ten feet from the nest. **1928** MacArthur *War Bugs* 187: The first boiler full of death habitually took a final turn with a squeal that unbuttoned every vertebra on the front.

2. a dilapidated motor vehicle or (*occ.*) airplane; (*rarely*) any motor vehicle.

1915 T.A. Dorgan, in Zwilling *TAD Lexicon* 19: You can't fool anybody by covering that old boiler with a blanket. Everyone knows it's a flivver. **1919** Witwer *Alex the Great* 87: Sure, old top, we'll give you a spin!…That's if this boiler will roll. **1929** in Hammett *Knockover* 56: I had picked up a boiler and parked it over on Turk Street. **1938** in H. Gray *Arf* (unp.): Hey, fellers! Lookit th' fancy boiler a-comin'! **1947**

Spillane *I, the Jury* 107: I got the boiler rolling and turned across town to get on Broadway. **1956** Heflin *USAF Dict.* 85: *Boiler, n.* A worn-out or obsolete airplane or airplane engine. *Slang.*

3. the stomach.

1922 Rollins *Cowboy* 129: Occasionally, in the desert, water was…so alkalinely saturated as hopelessly to "rust the boiler" of whoever drank it. **1925** (cited in Partridge *Dict. Und.* 59). [**1958** McCulloch *Woods Words* 15: *Boiler compound*—any medicine taken inside.] **1964** Thompson & Rice *Every Diamond* 140: *Boiler:* Stomach. **1969** in Bouton *Ball Four* 271: *Boiler,* as in "he's got the bad boiler," or upset stomach.

4. *R.R.* a steam locomotive.

1929 (quot. at SWELLHEAD). **1952** in *DAS.*

¶ In phrase:

¶ **bust (one's) boiler, 1.** to come to grief; to injure (oneself) by overexertion. Also **bust my boiler!** *interj.*

1826 Flint *10 Yrs.* 78 [ref. to 1816]: To encounter any disaster, or meet with a great catastrophe, is to "burst the boiler." **1834** *Davy Crockett's Almanack* (1835) 4: I…hid…until the old gentleman passed by, puffing and blowing as though his steam was high enough to burst his boiler. **1847** Robb *Squatter Life* 142: A fellar that's yearnin' arter matrimony is mity likely to git his fires dampened, or bust his biler. **1850** in Blair & McDavid *Mirth* 102: I…commenced laughin…If I didn't think I'd a-bust my boiler, I wish I may never see Christmas! **1854** [Avery] *Laughing Gas* 117: Bust my biler! 'Zekiel, but of all mortal critters you're the biggest. **1879** *Puck* (Oct. 22) 522: The gawddess of Freedom is on the eedge of bustin' her biler! **1882** S. Watkins *Co. Aytch* 96: But we had jumped him and were determined to catch him, or "burst a boiler." **1912** Field *Watch Yourself* 248: Ef hit wus a show with hosses an' gals ur singin' niggurs he'd bust a biler to go.

2. to become furiously angry.

1834 Caruthers *Kentuckian in N.Y.* I 218: I['ll] give them a touch of Kentuck pipes [i.e., yelling] that'll make them think somebody's busted thar biler. **1837** (quot. at HOOSIER).

boiler acid *n.* strong, bad-tasting coffee. Also **boiler compound.**

1943 Bayler & Carnes *Last Man* 72: Our volunteer pot-walloper heated up the remainder of last night's coffee, or "boiler compound," as it was more commonly known. **1966** "T. Pendleton" *Iron Orchard* 50: Let's go to the fire and take on a little more of Charley's boiler acid.

boiler-buster *n. Naut.* a stoker.

1878 Willis *Our Cruise* 27: One of them…served as seaman, gunner, diver, and boiler-burster in Admiral Rowley's fleet.

boilerhouse *v. Petroleum Industry.* (see quot.).

1944 Boatright & Day *Hell to Breakfast* 141: Any kind of faked or altered reports are "boiler housed," referring to the alleged practice of pumpers "gauging their tanks in the boiler house."

boilermaker *n.* **1.** *Und.* (see quots.).

1908 Sullivan *Criminal Slang* 4: *Boilermaker*—A [prostitute's] lover. **1931–34** in Clemmer *Pris. Community* 330: *Boilermaker, n.* A prostitute's lover.

2. usu. *pl. Mil.* a member of a brass band.

1918 *Literary Digest* (Oct. 19) 60: The woodpeckers gave way to a trained quartet of lady boiler-makers and the band to a troupe of Swiss bell-ringers. **1919** Roth *Co. E.* 190: On the dock the 303d Engineer band (popularly known as the "Boiler Makers") vied with a French band in blare of bugles and roll of drums. **1932** *Our Army* (July) 44: And the band is out in the middle of the parade ground and rite along site of the boiler-makers is fifteen (15) chairs lined up. **1933** *Leatherneck* (Dec.) 29: First Sergeant Knowles, band maestro, and his Boiler Makers, deserve a great deal of credit. **1942** *Yank* (July 29) 20: A courageous Army tuba player and his fellow "boilermakers."

3.a. a drink of whiskey followed by a drink of beer. Now *S.E.*

[**1934** Weseen *Dict. Slang* 273: *Boilermaker's delight*—Poor whiskey, moonshine]. **1941–42** Gach *In Army Now* 154: I…had a boiler-maker sent over to Wocky. **1951** Pryor *The Big Play* 25 [ref. to 1920's]: "Sissy drink," denounced Brock and ordered a boilermaker. **1953** *ATS* (ed. 2) 109: *Boilermaker*…a whisky with a beer "chaser." **1955** Q. Reynolds *HQ* 136: A few boilermakers (rye with beer chasers). **1974** *Police Woman* (NBC-TV): I thought a boilermaker or two might help.

b. a drink of beer and whiskey combined.

1957 (cited in Spears *Drugs & Drink* 61).

boilerplate *n.* **1.** *Journ.* **a.** ready-to-print copy provided by a news agency.

1893, 1905 in *OED2.* **1936** A.P. Hudson *Humor of Old So.* 13: The introduction of [newspaper] "boiler plate," the stereotyping which is the curse of everything else in the United States. **1938** Alter *Utah Journalism* 172: There were two pages of "boiler plate" out of four pages, 6 columns. **1960** in H.S. Truman *Confid.* 168: The country press, weeklies and some small dailies, except where they are controlled by "boiler plate," are still free.

b. writing or speech that is heavily clichéd; platitudes.

1909 in "O. Henry" *Works* 780: Plato is boiler-plate…Æsop has been copyrighted by Indiana; Solomon is too solemn. **1975** *Atlantic* (Nov.) 10: The President's talk, from staff-prepared notes, was full of boilerplate and hyperbole. **1982** *Harper's* (Apr.) 96: They also favor impersonal constructions, words like "large" and "good," boilerplate like "having-to-do-with." **1987** *Larry King Live!* (CNN-TV) (May 5): This is the sort of boilerplate you hear from journalists when they're accused of wrongdoing.

2. *Law.* (see 1981 quot.)

1974 *Business Week* (Nov. 23) 38: The only satisfactory solution to the immense number of contractual problems that a shortage economy brings is to discard "boilerplate" contracts. **1975** *L.A. Times* (Sept. 20) I 5: Pentagon officials have explained that this escape clause is "boiler plate" in all letter-of-offer agreements to sell weapons abroad. **1981** D.E. Miller *Jargon* 28: *Boilerplate*: Standardized provisions of certain legal documents…which are reproduced verbatim without any specific material included. **1982** Goldin & Sky *Being a Writer* 57: Each publisher has what is called a "boilerplate" contract, the basic agreement.

3. *Skiing.* snow that is frozen and crusty.

1976 *Webster's Sports Dict.* 48.

boiler room *n.* a room full of noisy activity. *Specif.:*

a. a room or office used by stock swindlers, confidence men, illegal bookmakers, telemarketers, etc.

1931 (cited in Partridge *Dict. Und.* 59). **1933** Ersine *Prison Slang* 19: *Boiler Room.* The office of a bucket shop, or any room full of excited and noisy people. **1950** Maddow & Huston *Asphalt Jungle* 50: Full Shot. Cobby's "Boiler Room." **1957** *N.Y. Post* (Mar. 26) 18: Boiler Room or Bucket Shop—Can You Tell the Difference? **1970** Della Femina *Wonderful Folks* 52: A couple of guys who run a boiler room who claim they're going to take his agency public and make everybody a bundle. **1974** *Police Woman* (NBC-TV): I've located what I think is the boiler room on the building scam. **1978** Bequai *White-Collar Crime* 26: *Boiler-room operators* are also common in the securities industry. A number of manipulators will, through hard-sell tactics and a barrage of false or misleading information, induce members of the uninformed public to invest in unknown companies whose stock may be worth little, if anything. **1986** Heinemann *Paco's Story* 92: She solicits over the phone, selling kitchen hardware, magazine subscriptions, and insurance deals.…There's a six-phone boiler room at the back.

b. *Pol.* a political campaign headquarters.

1968 Safire *New Lang. Politics* 120: A telephone blitz—calls made from a "boiler room" to remind favorably inclined voters to turn out on election day. **1972** in Bernstein & Woodward *President's Men* 171: McGovern headquarters in California was used as a boiler room to rally hardcore anti-war militants to confront the President.

boiling *adj.* drunk.

1882 Field *Tribune Primer* 103: He can get Bilin' slower on More Liquor than any Government official.

boilo *n.* (see quots.).

1934 J. O'Hara *Appt. in Samarra* ch. iii: Boilo is hot moonshine. **1935** J. O'Hara *Dr.'s Son* 49: I could imagine Doctor Myers drinking boilo, which is hot moonshine.

boing *interj.* [imit.; see note] (used to indicate sudden amazement, realization, or great interest, esp. at the appearance of an attractive person of the opposite sex). [The sound is understood to imitate that of a tightly wound spring suddenly unwinding.]

[**1944** *Life* (May 15) 65: Kay Kayser's imitation of a twanging spring is the new wolf cry.] **1948** Miller & Rackin *Fighter Sq.* (film): Boing! The old lady hasn't talked to me since. **1964** Berg *Looks at U.S.A.* (unp.): Whatcha got, Hal? [looking at men's magazine gatefold] Boinng!! **1965** *Dick Van Dyke Show* (CBS-TV): I still go boing when I think of him. I'm improving. I used to go *boi-oing!* **1993** McDonald's restaurant TV ad: Then I get this idea. Boing!

boinger *n.* a rear shock absorber on a motorcycle.

1979 Frommer *Sports Lingo* 164.

boink *v.* to have sexual intercourse (with).

1987 Eble *Campus Slang* (Apr.) 1: *Boink*—have sex. X: "Look at that chick!" Y: "I sure would like to boink her."…Popularized by the TV show "Moonlighting." *a***1988** C. Adams *More Straight Dope* 208: I'm 35 and don't seem to want to boink anywhere near as much as I used to. **1989** P. Munro *U.C.L.A. Slang* 23: *Boink*…to have sex…to have sex with. **1989** *Murphy Brown* (CBS-TV): Mr. Kinsella, I boinked your wife. **1992** *Mystery Sci. Theater* (Comedy Central TV): You know all that oinkin' and boinkin' we did on the island? It don't mean a thing.

boke or **boko** *n.* [orig. unkn.] the nose. [Esp. common in England, *ca*1870–90.]

1859 Matsell *Vocabulum* 13: *Boke*, the nose. *Ibid.* 125: Technical Words…In General Use by Pugilists.…*Boko.* The nose. **1866** *Nat. Police Gaz.* (Nov. 24) 3: Very few "guns" showed their "bokes" at all. ***1874** Hotten *Slang Dict.* (ed. 4) 91: *Boko*, the nose. Originally pugilistic slang, but now general. **1889** Barrère & Leland *Dict. Slang.* I 156: *Boko* (common), a nose.…Originally a large nose.

boksok *adj. Mil. in Philippines.* crazy.

1942 *Leatherneck* (Nov.) 143: *Boksok*—Crazy or amok. From "Tagalog," native Philippine dialect.

bollicking *adj.* BLOOMING; BLOODY.

1927 Barry *Paris Bound* 272: What about this bollicking ballet? Do you really want to help me get it down?

bollix *v.* [shift of BALLOCKS, infl. by BALL UP] to mix up, spoil, ruin, or botch; impair; injure.—usu. constr. with *up.* Also vars.

1937 Weidman *Wholesale*: You're getting your cues all bollixed up. **1939** in J. O'Hara *Sel. Letters* 153: If I bollixed up the intent of your note, just put in a Life with Father or a Mr. North and vamp till ready. **1942** McAtee *Supp. to Grant Co. Dial.* [ref. to 1890's]: *All bolluxed up* meant thoroughly messed, mishandled, spoiled. **1947** in Perelman *Don't Tread* 72: Some bright boy…had bollixed up the cargo completely. **1953** "L. Padgett" *Mutant* 14: A hereditary bollixed mind. **1953** A. Kahn *Brownstone* 180: Maybe they'll get bolixed up in Army snafu and forget about me. **1956** Waldhorn *Concise Dict.* 8: *Ballocks up, to* See *ball up, to.* **1957** Herber *Tomorrow* 277: Everything's all bollixed up. **1958** Cooley *Run for Home* 248: You came along and bollixed up all my fine plans. **1960** Simak *Worlds* 23: I had been uptown to attend to some banking difficulties that Helen and Marge had gotten all bollixed up. **1961** *N.Y. Post* (July 14) 58: "If there's another home run," a defeated-looking Chicago man commented, "we're bolluxed." **1963** D. Tracy *Brass Ring* 21: He'd bolluxed up the whole thing so it couldn't be fixed at all. **1966** E. Shepard *Doom Pussy* 212: She's bollixed it up good now. **1978** Matthiessen *Snow Leopard* 168: It looks like this day has really been bollixed up. **1985** *Our Town* (N.Y.C.) (Aug. 11) 2: The present boss says it was all bollixed before he took over.

boll weevil *n.* **1.** Esp. *Petroleum Industry & R.R.* a raw or clumsy worker, as on an oil drilling crew.

1925 Dobie *Hunting Ground* 64: The "boll weevil" is supposed to be a greenhorn about his business, and the name is often used derisively by "roughnecks" to characterize fellow workmen who show unfamiliarity with their work. **1928** Dobie *Drinkin' Gou'd* 46: I was learning the game as a "boll-weevil." **1929** J.M. Saunders *Single Lady* 246: Boll weevils and plumber's helpers. **1944** Boatright & Day *Hell to Breakfast* 140: One of the most universally used terms is "boll weevil," which means an inexperienced man. "Boll weevil tongs" are chain tongs that even a boll weevil cannot put on the pipe wrong. **1951** in Botkin & Harlow *R.R. Folklore* 326: He had the misfortune to catch a "boll weevil" (raw recruit) with only two weeks' experience. **1966** "T. Pendleton" *Iron Orchard* 36: Take that boll-weevil an' git to piss-antin' them joints over here. **1970** Boatright & Owens *Derrick* 154: We called them boll weevils because they didn't know anything when they come…in off the farm.

2. *Pol.* a conservative Southern Democrat.

1981 *N.Y. Times* (June 14) IV 4: The 47 or so Southern conservatives in the House, known informally as the boll weevils, have moved to center stage.…The boll weevils have been lumped together in the public mind, but in fact they are quite distinctive individuals. **1981** in *Newsweek* (Jan. 4, 1982) 32: The "boll weevil" Democrats in the House illustrate the point: Democrat Phil Gramm of Texas was working for the [Republican] Administration's budget cuts almost from the beginning. **1987** *Newsday* (CNN-TV) (Oct. 6): A crucial vote among the so-called "boll weevils" of the judiciary committee. **1991** *CBS This Morning* (CBS-TV) (Mar. 15): You've already told us about your boll-weevil Democrat credentials.

bolo[1] *n.* [*Bol*shevik + -o] *Mil.* a Bolshevik. Now *hist.*

1919 *Amer. Leg. Wkly.* (July 11) 6: When the Allied ships had reached Archangel several weeks previously the Bolsheviki, or, as the Americans call them, the "Bolo" had fled from the city. *Ibid.* 24: I asked a "Bolo" officer. **1923** *York Co. A* 123: At nine a.m. the Bolo artillery opened up from Yevievskaya and bombarded steadily until three in the afternoon. *Ibid.* 133: The village of Vistofka was taken by the Bolos and retaken by Lieut. McPhail. **1925** in Hemingway *Sel. Letters* 149: But when a male's had the luck Bill's had to take for years it's a wonder he isn't a Bolo. **1931** in Thomason *Stories* 328: Just about that time, we were right excited over the Bolos—all hands were solemnly warned against Red propaganda. **1931** Dos Passos *1919* 261: John Bull's putting his hands on all the world's future supplies of oil...just to keep it from the bolos.

bolo² *n.* [poss. fr. BOLO¹; poss. alluding to a *bolo* knife; poss. after *Bolo* Pascha, German agent in France in WWI] **1.a.** *Army.* a poor marksman who fails to make the minimum score on a firing range; (*hence*) any clumsy or unproficient enlisted man.

1929 *Our Army* (Nov.) 41: The bolo squad. **1936** *AS* (Feb.) 61: A rifleman whose skill at marksmanship is notoriously poor is a *bolo*...and one company...used to present its low score man each year, in derision, a specially procured bolo [knife]. **1941** Kendall *Army & Navy Slang* 2: *Bolo*....Soldier who fails on firing range. **1952** *Combat Forces Journal* (Sept.) 8: The average bolo does not wear L target centers on his baggy blouse. **1956** Boatner *Mil. Customs & Trads.* 112: A "bolo" is a man who fails to...get the minimum score on the range with his weapon. Since this is the ultimate disgrace..."bolo" also means an "eight-ball." **1974** U.S. Army officer, age *ca*30: A guy who fails a proficiency is called a *bolo*. In fact, anybody who's a real klutz could be called a *bolo*. **1975** U.S. Army officer, age *ca*27: If you *bolo* an examination you are [called] a *bolo*.
b. *Army.* a failure to demonstrate proficiency, as on a firing range.

1974 U.S. Army officer, age *ca*30: A *bolo* is essentially a zero. It's a failure to demonstrate proficiency with a weapon, such as a rifle or a machine gun. **1974** Levinson *Slovik* (film): Another bolo, Slovik.
2. [after the curved blade of the *bolo* knife] *Boxing.* a swinging uppercut.

1950 in *OEDS.* **1959** Ellison *Gentleman Junkie* 216: I took him out with one solid bolo to the mouth. **1970** in P. Heller *In This Corner* 216 [ref. to 1930's]: He was afraid to throw his bolo because I had a counter for it.

bolo³ *n.* [< Cuban Sp *bolo*, a now obsolete coin] *Cuban E.* a dollar.

1972 P. Thomas *Savior* 8: Them mothers take his watch, his gold chain, and about eighteeen or twenty bolos.

bolo⁴ *n.* [see 1990 quot.] *Police.* a vehicle that is being sought by police.

1985 *Miami Vice* (NBC-TV): The bolo I was followin' was a cop car. **1990** P. Dickson *Slang!* 102: Bolo. Police shorthand for "be on the lookout for."

bolo *v.* [fr. BOLO², *n.*, 1.] **1.** *Army.* to fail to demonstrate proficiency, as on a firing range; to fail an examination. Also trans.

1944 "E. Palmer" *GI Songs*: All I ever did was bolo/When they tried to make a tanker out of me. **1952** *Combat Forces Journal* (Sept.) 8: Or else issue shotguns to all who bolo. **1967** Sack *M* 54: But though a boy could purposely "bolo" his written test...he would just be surrendering himself to...fate. **1975** U.S. Army officer, age 27: To *bolo* is to be a complete flunk-out, like on the rifle range. Or it can be used more generally, "You boloed on the examination," or "You boloed the exam." **1978** Groom *Better Times* 6: You bolo on the rifle range and I help you get a rating and you make fun of that too. **1981** Hathaway *World of Hurt* 12: If you shitbirds think you're going to bolo that test and give Mike Company a bad name, well, you just think again.
2. *Mil. in Gulf War.* to destroy or kill in battle.

1991 Dunnigan & Bay *From Shield to Storm* 360: Kuwait War Slang...*Boloed*—Destroyed, as in a Hummer crash or from an enemy bullet in the head.

bolo badge *n. Army.* a qualification badge; (*also*) any nonregulation or unofficial badge or insigne.

1968 J. Kelly *Unexpected Peace* 105 [ref. to WWII]: Then his gaze moved down to the bolo badges. *Ibid.* 106: But those bolo badges!...Made him look plum stupid. **1974** Former U.S. Army EM, served 1968–70: A *bolo badge* is one of those imitation medals or nonregulation badges they sell at the PX.

bolo man *n.* **1.** *Navy.* a warrant officer. [1901 quot. reflects the original S.E. sense, 'a Filipino insurrectionist armed with a bolo knife'.]

[1901 in Dolph *Sound Off*: In the land of dopey dreams, Peaceful, happy Philippines,/Where the bolo-man is hiking night and day.] **1918** in Battey *Sub. Destroyer* 302: A warrant officer is known as a "bolo man." This, I understand, dates back to the Spanish-American War, for on state occasions the said officer used to carry a cutlass and that...was called a bolo as soon as the sailors found out what a bolo was. **1926** (quot. at UNDERGROUND SAVAGE).
2. *Army.* BOLO², *n.*, 1.a.

1936 *AS* (Feb.) 61: A rifleman whose skill at marksmanship is notoriously poor is a...*bolo man.* **1936** *Our Army* (May) 21: These were the weak sisters. The flinchers, the "Nervous Nells," the perennial "bolomen."

Bolshie *n.* a Bolshevik.

1919 in C. Sandburg *Letters* (Apr. 14) 157: He considers the bolshies "economically impossible and morally wrong in social theory." **1919** *Our Navy* (Aug.) 68: The Bolshies got to them. **1931** *Amer. Merc.* (Dec.) 407: Dem damn big-mouth Bolsheys. **1939** in J. O'Hara *Sel. Letters* 150: Now that the n. y-er is running Mencken, of course, we can't have any bolshy propaganda. **1947** in Truman *Dear Bess* 545: I'd like very much to explode on the Bolshies. **1951** Cowley *Exile's Return* 52: Americans were fighting the Bolshies in Siberia. **1962** Viertel *Love & Corrupt* 256: You think you'll be able to handle our Bolshy allies? **1987** *N.Y. Times* (July 6) 31: But who except knee-jerk Bolshie-bashers believed then...?

bolt *n.* *Pris.* [**1.** an escape. [Not attested in U.S., but related to other slang senses.]

*****1811** Vaux *Memoirs*: A sudden escape of one or more prisoners from a place of confinement is called a *bolt*.]
2. *Stu.* a refusal of students to attend, or remain in, a class meeting; (*hence*) a cancellation of a class meeting.

1851 Hall *College Wds.* 22: *Bolt.* An omission of a recitation or lecture. **1856** Hall *College Wds.* (ed. 2) 32: In [Union College]...we would call a "class meeting" to consider upon the propriety of asking Professor — — for a *bolt. Ibid.*: One writer defines a *bolt* [as] the promiscuous stampede of a class collectively. Caused generally by a few seconds' tardiness of the Professor. **1900** *DN* II 24: *Bolt, n.* Refusal of a class to attend college exercises for the purpose of coercing the faculty [Reported in use at a large number of colleges]. **1955** *AS* (Dec.) 302 [Wayne State Univ.]: *Bolt, n.* A class out by a professor.
3. *Pol.* a refusal to support a candidate, platform, or policy of one's political party. Now *S.E.*

1852 in Eliason *Tarheel Talk* 261: The worst feature...is the *bolt*...from the regular nomination! **1858** in Thornton *Amer. Gloss.* I: It is known that there would have been some such bolt from the nominations, had the nominations been made. **1903** A.H. Lewis *Boss* 116: We...are goin' to make a bolt for better government.
4. (*cap.*) *Mil. Av.* the Republic P-47 Thunderbolt fighter-bomber. Now *hist.* [Quots. ref. to WWII.]

1946 G.C. Hall, Jr. *1000 Destroyed* 33: So the 'Bolts roared up and down France without German opposition. **1958** Johnson & Caidin *Thunderbolt* 139: The rugged old 'bolt,...she'll bring me home.
5. a pimple or boil.

1969 in Bouton *Ball Four* 272: A pimple or boil is called *a bolt*, as in "get a wrench for that bolt."
6. *Narc.* (see quot.).

1986 *Special Assignment* (CNN-TV) (May 10): PCP is referred to on the street as "lovely," "angel dust," "killer weed," and "bolt."
7. *Stu.* (see quot.).

1990 in *Texas Mo.* (Jan. 1991) 158: The kind of fellow who, because of his good looks, is known as a bolt (fraternity parlance for "handsome").
¶ In phrases:

¶ **ride the bolt** *Pris.* to be executed by electrocution. Cf. syn. *ride the lightning.*

1957 in J. Blake *Joint* 166: One of the...lads here is scheduled to ride the bolt for group-rape.

¶ **work the bolt** *Mil.* to try to further one's interests, esp. in an obnoxious or manipulative way.

1929 *Our Army* (Oct.) 41: "Working the bolt" means making great efforts without shooting, without results....A man who "shoots off his mouth" too much is said to be "working the bolt." **1948** DeMond & Foote *King of Gamblers* (film): That's workin' the bolt clear across the country. **1980** Manchester *Darkness* 146 [ref. to WWII]: Manipulating people was called *working one's bolt.* **1988** Dye *Outrage* 191: If I can work my bolt, they'll send him all the way back to Stateside.

bolt *v.* **1.** [cf. current S.E. senses] **a.** to flee; *Mil.* to desert; *Stu.* to absent oneself from a class meeting; to cut class.

*1811 Vaux *Memoirs: Bolt:* to run away from or leave any place suddenly is called *bolting,* or *making a bolt:* a thief observing an alarm while attempting a robbery, will exclaim to his accomplice, *Bolt,* there's a *down.* *1811 *Lexicon Balatron.: To Bolt.* To run suddenly out of one's house, or hiding place, through fear; a term borrowed from a rabbit warren, where the rabbits are meant to bolt, by sending ferrets into their burrows: we set the house on fire, and made him bolt. *Ibid.* s.v. *pig:* Floor the pig and bolt: knock down the officer and run away. *1821 *Real Life in London* 85: Or else what should he *bolt* for?...*Bolt*—Run away; try to make an escape. **1842** *Spirit of Times* (Oct. 29) 410: To Bolt...to mizzle—to evaporate—to amputate—to levant. **1856** Hall *College Wds.* 33: *Bolt.* At Union College, to be absent from a recitation....At Williams College....A correspondent writes: "We sometimes *bolt* from a recitation before the Professor arrives, and the term most strikingly suggests the derivation....a thunder-*bolt.*" **1855** Brougham *Chips* 348: The Cap'n was for boltin'. **1864** *Battle-Fields* 85: They..."bolted" at the first fire. **1870** Greey *Blue Jackets* 72: "Harry Tomlin!" "Bolted at Singapore." *1899 Whiteing *John St.* 169: They say he is a first-rater,—college professor in his own country,—but had to bolt because they wanted to send him to Siberia.

b. to leave.

1845 *Vade Mecum* (Phila.) (May 23) 4: After any player has *bragged,* the rest must either *go it,*...or *bolt.* **1866** *Night Side of N.Y.* 74: "William, where is my Sarah Jane?"..."She's bolted." **1973** Eble *Campus Slang* (Nov.) 1: *Bolt*—to leave, with an implication of suddenness or immediacy: You ready to bolt? **1977** *NBC's Saturday Night* (NBC-TV): OK, let's bolt. **1980** Birnbach *Preppy Hndbk.* 223: Let's bolt. **1987** *Magical World of Disney* (NBC-TV): Well,...I gotta bolt.

2. *Pol.* to refuse to support one's political party; *(trans.)* to refuse to support (a candidate, policy, etc.); to leave (a political convention) in protest. Now *S.E.*

1814 in *DA:* When a member wishes to "bolt," he "totes" himself out of the house before the ayes and noes are called. **1833** in *DA:* Does the Doctor apprehend that the editor is about to "bolt"? **1852** in Eliason *Tarheel Talk* 261: This lawyer has been a "free-soiler," having "*bolted*" our party. **1871** Schele de Vere *Amer.* 585: Carl Schurz has *bolted* from the Republican party. **1892** Garland *Spoil of Office* 88: They're going to bolt the convention and there'll be fun in the air.

bolter *n.* a person who flees an obligation.

*1821 *Real Life in London* II 36: A *bolter*...is one...who...*brushes off,* and leaves his bondsmen to pay his debt. *a*1899 B.F. Sands *Reefer* 78 [ref. to 1833]: The...scholars reported for examination on the day named,...being in number seventy-eight, exclusive of the "bolters" who could not stand the fire.

bolus *n.* [metonymical use of *bolus* 'round mass of medicinal material'] a physician, pharmacist, or other person who administers pills.—used esp. as a nickname.

*1788 Grose *Vulgar Tongue* (ed. 2) 47: *Bolus,* a nickname for an apothecary. *1838 Glascock *Land Sharks* II 94: You, Billy! You, Bolus! D'ye hear, ye lubberly...blister-spreadin'-pill-rollin'-platter-faced pyeaw. 1848 *Ladies' Repository* (Oct.) 315: *Bolus* A physician. **1865** Harte *Sk. of Sixties* 70: Dr. Bolus says his lungs are entirely gone. *1878 in *F & H* I 279: The doctor...."Good for old Bolus....I believe him." *a*1881 G.C. Harding *Misc. Writings* 156: She sent fur old Bolus, an' he perscribed fur her nerves.

bomb *n.* **1.a.** any unexpected statement or development having a sudden sensational effect. Now *colloq.*

1918 *Chi. Daily Tribune* (Oct. 16) 3: Paris Sees U.S. Reply As Bomb For Autocracy..."A straight blow," is the caption of an article...[in] the Temps today, dealing with President Wilson's latest reply to Germany. **1958** Gardner *Piece of the Action* 85: Louis, I got a bomb to drop....Some damn good news. **1969** *Current Slang* I & II 13: *Bomb,* n. An unexpected, unpleasant situation—Air Force Academy cadets. **1981** *N.Y. Post* (July 14) 22: A bomb dropped in our lap recently when we learned that our next door neighbors are homosexuals.

b. something excellent or unusually successful; DYNAMITE; a SMASH.

1974 V. Smith *Jones Men* 23: Nice....This is a bomb, baby. **1974** *Odd Couple* (ABC-TV): With the right person playing Scrooge it could be a bomb. **1989** S. Robinson & D. Ritz *Smokey* 218: I had all the tunes done, except I knew the real bomb was still on Marv's demo tape.

2.a. an old or dilapidated vehicle; JALOPY.

*1950 in Wilkes *Austral. Colloq.* 43: Bomb,...A dud—usually refers to second-hand motor vehicles in poor mechanical shape. *1953 in *OEDS.* **1969** *Current Slang* I & II 13: Bomb,...n. An old, rattly car.—College females, New York State. **1971** Sorrentino *Up from Never* 3: When are ya gonna make ya old man get some seat covers in this bomb? **1972** *Playboy* (Sept.) 110: He worked the stick through about five speeds to get the bomb up to 25. **1973** Schiano & Burton *Solo* 184: A 1944 Plymouth...a real old bomb they got for about $25. **1984** D. Smith *Steely Blue* 144: Between the seats of the geriatric...bomb he was driving.

b. a fast car. Cf. A-BOMB.

1953 Felsen *Street Rod* 45: That was the ticket all right. Work quietly and make a real bomb out of the coupe. **1955–57** Felder *Collegiate Slang* 1: *Bomb*—an exceptionally nice car. **1958** Gilbert *Vice Trap* 69: We got to have a bomb, for one thing. Because you run for the border after the play. **1959** *Swinging Syllables: Bomb*—Souped up automobile (3 or more carborators). **1959** Gault *Drag Strip* 117: Juan was paired off against Flip Donovan's new bomb. **1960** Hoagland *Circle Home* 206: You wanna go fast?...When I drive, I drive, and this is a bomb. **1960** Swarthout *Where Boys Are* 16: I was going anyway so I bought a car, a year-old Porsche, a real bomb. **1972** N.Y.U. student, age *ca*20: He drives a bomb. **1988** Dietl & Gross *One Tough Cop* 95: The car I always wanted was a Corvette. A bomb.

3. *Narc.* **a.** a large or potent marijuana cigarette.

1951 Kerouac *Cody* 24: In fall 1950 when I was so much on weed, three bombs a day. **1964** Larner & Tefferteller *Add. in Street* 33: I paid 75 cents a stick, or a dollar for a bomb. **1964** in Jackson *Swim Like Me* 133: We smoked around five bombs a day. **1967** Rosevear *Pot* 157: *Bomb:* A fat, or thick, marihuana cigarette. Also...[one] with fast-acting qualities.

b. unusually pure heroin.

1960 C.L. Cooper *Scene* 8: I got a bomb to knock your nuts out...the choicest to come along my way for a long time. **1969** Lingeman *Drugs* 26: *Bomb*...high-potency, relatively undiluted heroin. **1971** Goines *Dopefiend* 93: Lee here says he knows where to cop the bomb at. We can get a half a piece of stuff for one hundred.

c. a capsule containing a strong stimulating or sleep-inducing drug.

1966 in J.C. Pratt *Vietnam Voices* 239: Our "red bomb" sleeping pills. **1968** J. Hudson *Case of Need* 185: Bombs....Speed. Lifts. Jets. Bennies. **1984** D. Jenkins *Life Its Ownself* 122: Dexatrim and Vivarin, the caffeine bombs. **1991** *Donahue* (NBC-TV): Time for my blue bomb—meaning Halcion.

4. *Esp. Publishing & Entertainment Industry.* a complete failure; FLOP; fiasco.

1952 "E. Box" *Fifth Position* 64: It looks like a bomb from where I sit. **1956** P. Moore *Chocolates* 36: Those last two pictures were really bombs. **1959** *Life* (Nov. 23) 45: *Bomb*—a terrible [phonograph] record. **1960** Kirkwood *Pony* 196: But as far as I was concerned the barbecue had turned out to be a bomb. **1961** *New Yorker* (Oct. 28) 43: What had once been called a failure became a "bomb." **1965** Hersey *Too Far to Walk* 124: I had Jejune['s class] last year. What a bomb.

5.a. a strikingly sexy woman; BOMBSHELL.

1956 Margulies *Punks* 110: She's a bomb....a great, big wonderful bomb.

b. *pl.* a woman's breasts, esp. if large.

1968 Baker et al. *CUSS* 85: *Bombs* The female breasts. **1973** J. Torres et al. *Scream Blacula* (film): Here, come on, come on, let me get a good feel of those bombs. **1974** E. Thompson *Tattoo* 112: But look at them bombs on her!...Bigger than your head!

6.a. a hard blow, as with the fist.

1970 Quammen *Walk the Line* 146: But usually he just wants to prove that he can punch out—drop his "bombs" on them as, he puts it—absolutely anybody in the world. **1981** Graziano & Corsel *Somebody Down Here* 41: I hit him with one of my bombs in the first round and I save him the trouble of going the other five.

b. *Jazz.* a heavy drumstroke.

1953–58 J.C. Holmes *Horn* 39: Lecturing another [drummer] on "them bombs you always dropping on the bridge." **1961** R. Russell *Sound* 73: "How about this kid Tiny he had on drums?"..."He dropped too many bombs. Red was dragged real bad after the first week."

c. *Baseball.* a hard-hit ball, esp. a home run.

1962 Houk & Dexter *Ballplayers* 225: It was a happy bomb by a great bomber.

d. *Surfing.* a big wave; BOMBER, 5.

1968 S. Ross *Hang-Up* 94: They're tubing out like big bombs today.

e. *Meteorology* (see quot.).

1986 *Science News* (May 17) 314: It started out as a relatively innocuous storm system off the Carolina coast on Feb. 18, 1979. By late that evening it had mushroomed into what some meteorologists call a bomb—a cyclonic fury, hundreds of kilometers wide, that develops in less than a day.

7.a. *Football.* a long forward pass.

[**1939** L.R. Meyer, in Paxton *Sport* 320: For in our system only two things are necessary to unlimber the bombers. *Ibid.* 324: I can hardly recall a game in which the enemy didn't propose to stop our passing game with rushing. I can't think of a better way to handcuff a bombing attack.] [**1940** Buckner *Rockne* (film): Notre Dame Bombs Army With Forward Pass.] **1960** in *OEDAS:* Ralph Gugliemi...threw four TD bombs in '59. **1966** *WNID3* (Add.). **1973** in H.S. Thompson *Shark Hunt* 75: Without the ever-present likelihood of a game-breaking "bomb" at any moment, they could focus down much tighter on stopping Miami's brutal running game. **1983** Mutual Radio Network news (Apr. 12): The big throw was a 98-yard bomb in the fourth quarter. **1992** Pro Nerf TV ad: They said you'd never throw the bomb.

b. *Basketball.* a long shot at the basket.

1966 Neugeboren *Big Man* 179: This guy lets go a long bomb from the outside and I got Morgan boxed out. **1976** *Webster's Sports Dict.* 48. **1980** Wielgus & Wolff *Basketball* 25: Dribble along the periphery and pull the trigger on bombs. If you happen to be off target, long rebounds...may come your way. **1984** *N.Y. Post* (Dec. 12) 78: Two drives and a three-point bomb in a 1:02 span. **1988** *Daily Beacon* (Univ. Tenn.) (Jan. 7) 8: Bell canned two three-point bombs to give the Vols a slight lead.

¶ In phrases:

¶ **lay a bomb** *Publishing & Entertainment Industry.* to fail miserably; *lay an egg* s.v. EGG.

1955 in Derr *Frontiersman* 29: Davy was the biggest thing since Marilyn Monroe, but he...laid a bomb. **1964** *Dick Van Dyke Show* (CBS-TV): Oh, Buddy, it didn't lay such a big bomb.

¶ **like a bomb** very fast.

1954 *AS* XXIX 99: *Like a bomb,...*very fast. **1966** *New Yorker* (Dec. 31) 30: I went like a bomb through the studio wall. **1980** Univ. Tenn. instructor, age 32: He went through here like a bomb.

bomb *v.* **I.** Senses having to do with failure, harm, or physical damage.

1.a. *Orig. Publishing & Entertainment Industry.* to fail miserably; FLOP.—since *ca*1968, occ. constr. with *out.*

1953–58 J.C. Holmes *Horn* 131: The...band...[will] bomb because it's too far out for the average ginmill owner. **1963** Morgan *Six-Eleven* 254: I was hedging my bet a little in case the whole set-up bombed with you. **1966** Susann *Valley of Dolls* 49: Maybe I'll come live with you if *Hit the Sky* bombs. **1968** in *Rolling Stone Interviews* 65: You know, if we'd gone on first, we would have bombed. **1970** Della Femina *Wonderful Folks* 135: So the campaign bombed out. **1970** Corrington *Bombardier* 59: I think this whole crazy deal is going to bomb out. **1975** Zezza *Love Potion* 225: Well, I'd thought of selling shoes if the Tingle test bombs. **1984** *Chicago Sun-Times* (June 15) 3: An effort by Vrdolyak to undercut Washington by attracting blacks to the last county party fund-raiser bombed.

b. *Stu.* to fail an examination.—often constr. with *out.*—also used trans.

1962 in *AS* XXXVIII (Oct. 1963) 168: To fail to pass an examination: flunk...flag...*bomb.* **1968** Baker et al. *CUSS* 84: *Bomb* Do poorly on an exam. *Bomb out.* Do poorly on something. **1972** N.Y.U. student, age *ca*19: If you *bomb out* on an exam, it means you really failed badly. **1989** P. Munro *U.C.L.A. Slang* 23: My chemistry final was so hard that I totally bombed it.

2.a. *Baseball.* to hit hard, esp. for a home run; (*also*) to score numerous hits or runs against (a pitcher).

1959 Brosnan *Long Season* 33: I wouldn't be surprised if all four [pitchers] got bombed four days in a row. **1968** *N.Y. Times* (Mar. 19) 57: Hal McRae...bombed the first pitch...to left field for a two-run homer. **1969** in Bouton *Ball Four* 118: Anyway, I guess Gary didn't pitch around enough...hitters because they bombed him out in the first inning with three runs. **1969** *N.Y. Daily News* (Sept. 24): Donn Clendenon...bombed a tremendous home run over the centerfield fence....Ed Charles, the oldest Met, bombed his third homer over the right-center fence.

b. *Sports.* to defeat soundly.

1961 Brosnan *Pennant Race* 123: But we're gonna play a ball club I *see* bombing us the way the Cubs did. **1982** WKGN radio news (June

28): The Orioles bombed Detroit 13–1.

3. to punch hard or repeatedly; to beat up.

1960 Hoagland *Circle Home* 65: He got in too close for Four to bomb him. **1961** Ellison *Memos* 41: Join—or get bombed. **1966** Elli *Riot* 76: First guy that gives me a bad time gets bombed. **1970** La Motta, Carter & Savage *Raging Bull* 203: You got no zing. Why are you lettin' these sparring partners bomb you around the way they do? **1971** Rader *Govt. Inspected* 48: They jumped too soon too often. Once they bombed a teacher, once an off-duty Anglican priest.

4. to criticize harshly.

1970 Della Femina *Wonderful Folks* 175: He can't bomb it directly, like saying, "You're crazy," or he'll lose his job. **1971** N.Y.U. English professor, age *ca*40: Melville's critics really bombed him. **1973** *Penthouse* (May) 64: I read two reviews of *Rage* in the trade papers and they bombed the shit out of it.

5. to thwart in a calculated or underhanded manner.

1970 Della Femina *Wonderful Folks* 202: Somebody bombed the agency. Who knows why?

6. *Surfing.* **a.** to be thrown from a surfboard; WIPE OUT.—also constr. with *out.*

1968 Kirk & Hanle *Surfer's Hndbk.* 136: *Bomb:* spill; wipe out; fail. *Bombed-out:* lost board by falling, being knocked down, or washed or blown off board by collapsing wave; wiped out. **1977** Filosa *Surf. Almanac* 183: *Bombed out....*Knocked off a board by a wave.

b. (of a heavy breaker) to overtake and fall upon (a surfer).

1977 Filosa *Surf. Almanac* 186: *Get bombed.* To be avalanched by a big wave.

7. (of equipment or machinery) to break down.—constr. with *out.*

1973 Collins *Carrying the Fire* 334 [ref. to 1969]: Rarely could the problem be carried all the way through without some component "bombing out," as we called it.

8. *Finance.* to reduce the price of (a stock) dramatically, as by selling large numbers of shares.

1981 "Adam Smith," on *Larry King Show* (WHEL radio) (Apr. 1): They were starting for the phones to bomb the stock.

9. *Computers.* (of a computer program) to fail spectacularly.

1981 *AS* (Spring) 64: *Bomb out vi* Terminate abnormally, especially because of programmer error. **1991** Raymond *New Hacker's Dict.*: *Bomb...*general synonym for *crash.*

II. Other senses.

10.a. to drive or go fast; to drive.—occ. constr. with *it.*

1960 Hoagland *Circle Home* 173: Cars bombed and barrelled by. **1966** Neugeboren *Big Man* 169: The fuzz bombs through all the time, checking. **1967** Moorse *Duck* 43: And the girls come and we bomb off into the night. **1969** *Current Slang* I & II 13: *Bomb,...*v. To go somewhere quickly.—College students, both sexes, Minnesota.—I'll *bomb* over to the post office to see if I got any letters. *Bomb around,* v. To move quickly from place to place. **1972** Wambaugh *Blue Knight* 222: I was...slicing through the heavy traffic and then bombing it down Vermont. **1976** C. Keane *Hunter* 89: Better than us bombing through the door, no?

b. to drive or wander about idly.—constr. with *around.*

1973 Lucas, Katz & Huyck *Amer. Graffiti* 20: Hey, Curt, let's bomb around, I wanna try out my new wheels! **1974** Eble *Campus Slang* (Nov.) 1: *Bomb*—to go joyriding in an automobile: We had nothing to do, so we bombed around the country until night fell. **1978** Price *Ladies' Man* 239: We haven't hung out and bombed around in a dog's age. **1985** Wells *444 Days* 169: Then they put...us in a van, and we went bombing around Tehran for what seemed like hours. **1992** *New Yorker* (Sept. 14) 26: My girlfriend...and I would bomb around in her jeep.

11. *Bodybuilding.* to train intensely; (*trans.*) to work to develop (muscles). Cf. BLAST.

1972 C. Gaines *Stay Hungry* 27: The Mr. Southeast [contest]....He was second last year...so he's...bombing for it already. He's got to get his arms up and spread his delts some. *Ibid.* 52: Yeah, he's here but he's bombing and he don't need to be bothered. **1981** D.E. Miller *Jargon* 230: I really bombed my quads this week. *a*1984 in *AS* LIX 198: *Bomb v.* Train muscles intensely with a combination of heavy weights for "bulk" and light weights for "definition."

12. *Skydiving.* to dive headlong from an aircraft in a jump.

1979 Cuddon *Dict. Sports & Games* 119.

13. to spray-paint graffiti on. Also absol.

1984 S. Hager *Hip-Hop* 108: *Bomb*—to write a large amount of graffiti at one time is to "bomb." *1988** in Thorne *Dict. Contemp. Slang*: Welcome to a freshly-bombed station. **1993** *Donahue* (NBC-TV): Spray-painting....In New York we called it *bombing*.

14. to fumigate.

1985 Frede *Nurses* 99: He can bomb a room...Fumigation only.

bombed *adj.* **1.** *Esp. Stu.* **a.** drunk.—since *ca*1967, often constr. with *out*.

1956 P. Moore *Chocolates* 8: Daddy was a little bombed. **1957** Bannon *Odd Girl* 42: Laura, our roommate is bombed. **1958** J. Davis *College Vocab.* 10: *Bombed*—Drunk. **1961** Terry *Old Liberty* 39: There's pictures of guys partying obviously bombed. **1963** *N.Y. Times Mag.* (Nov. 24) 52: The effects of drink. "I'm...bombed out of my mind." **1965** Herlihy *Midnight Cowboy* 198: He's just bombed, that's all. **1968** Kirkwood *Good Times/Bad Times* 217: A man of about fifty, bombed out of his mind, staggered over. **1969** *Playboy* (Sept.) 193: Boozy, bombed-out party school. **1972** Wambaugh *Blue Knight* 130: Cruz was pretty well bombed out, and...he decided not to have another beer.

b. high on a drug.—also constr. with *out*.

1965 Vermes *Helping Youth* 134: It's the addicts, you're the squares. I'm the hepcat because when you're bombed out, I'm digging the scene. **1969** Lingeman *Drugs* 26: *Bombed out.* High or intoxicated on a drug. **1969** Maitland *Only War* 28: I always think I'm the only one bombed when I'm bombed. **1969** Geller & Boas *Drug Beat* XVI: *Bombed out:* High on marijuana or any other drug.

c. extremely fatigued.—constr. with *out*.

*a***1984** in Terry *Bloods* 9: At that time you had worked so hard during the day you were just bombed out.

2. *Gamb.* (of dice) loaded.

1961 H. Ellison *Gentleman Junkie* 144: He used bombed ivories, loaded down with every kind of b.b. shot.

bomber *n.* **1.** *Boxing.* an unusually aggressive and hard-hitting boxer; (*hence*) any unusually aggressive person.

1937 in *AS* (Feb. 1938) 33: A name which recalls the *Brown Bomber*. **1970** La Motta, Carter & Savage *Raging Bull* 84: Wait till the real bombers get through with us, there won't be a high-class doll east of the Hudson who'll look at us twice. **1976** Pileggi *Blye* 88: His lawyer, a matrimonial "bomber" for whom Blye often worked. *Ibid.* 192: You don't need Clarence Darrow...in these cases. What you need is an animal. You need a bomber. The kind of guy who will get you as much as there is and maybe more.

2. *pl.* (*cap.*) *Baseball.* BRONX BOMBERS.

1946 *N.Y. Times* (July 14) V 1: Bombers Drop...Behind Leading Red Sox. **1960** *N.Y.C.* grade school student, age 12: The *Bombers* are the Yankees. **1984** *N.Y. Post* (Aug. 3) 72: And a win tonight over the Indians...would push the Bombers over .500 for the first time this season.

3. *Narc.* a large or potent marijuana cigarette.

1952 J.C. Holmes *Go* 141: Look, I'll make a bomber, a big thick one just for you. **1955–57** Kerouac *On Road* 232: Victor proceeded to roll the biggest bomber anybody ever saw. **1961** C. Cooper *Weed* 14: He rolled the joint for action, nothing huge, no bomber. **1972** *Playboy* (Mar.) 189: Zonked-out and glassy-eyed, waving hash bombers at the camera. **1977** L. Jordan *Hype* 49: That's a fucking bomber, man.

4. *Narc.* a capsule containing a strong depressant or stimulant.

1950 (cited in Partridge *Dict. Und.* (ed. 2) 825). **1961** Brosnan *Pennant Race* 130: Jimmy swallowed his "bomber," a Dexedrine pill, and declared himself ready. *Ibid.:* The trainer gave me a "bomber" to keep me awake for the bridge game on the long plane trip to Chicago and San Francisco. **1962** in *OEDS:* Barbiturates....Kids...call them goofballs and bombers. **1965** Herlihy *Midnight Cowboy* 188: She opened a fist and showed him a big brown capsule...."It's a bomber—good for about four hours." **1969** Lingeman *Drugs* 26: *Bomber.* 1. (since around 1944) a barbiturate. *Obsolete.* **1979** Alibrandi *Custody* 212: "Musta been a fuckin' bomber," she smiled, referring to the lude. **1992** *Biography* (A&E-TV) [ref. to 1975]: Blue bombers—doses of Valium to help him sleep.

5. *Surfing.* (see quot.).

1968 Kirk & Hanle *Surfer's Hndbk.* 136: *Bomber:* very hard-breaking wave.

6. *pl.* a woman's breasts.

1979 Alibrandi *Custody* 38: Her...blouse hid her bombers about like a parachute draped over two ICBMs.

6. *Juve.* a loud breaking of wind.

1980 *Nat. Lampoon* (Aug.) 79: You always blow bombers on the school bus, Tubby! **1981** *Nat. Lampoon* (Aug.) 76: I've got it! Let's light bombers! [illustration].

bomb farm *n. Mil. Av.* a stockpile of bombs for the arming of aircraft.

1966 Noel & Bush *Naval Terms* 70: *Bomb farm:* Topside stockpile of bombs used for rearming carrier aircraft.

bomb-happy *adj. Mil.* suffering from combat neurosis.

1942 in Rock *Field Service* 88: The fellow was completely bomb-happy (army slang for shock and in no way derogatory). **1943** *S.F. Chronicle* (Dec. 1) 2: A barrage so incessant...that many troops of the crack 65th Nazi Division were rendered "bomb happy," and fell easy prisoners. **1944** Ind *Bataan* 120: "Bomb-happy," was the explanation I heard from one of these hide-outs. **1944 *1945* (cited in Partridge *DSUE* (ed. 7) 1020).

bombo var. BUMBO¹, BUMBO².

bomb-proof *n. Mil.* **a.** a military, civilian, or governmental position that protects its holder from hardship or battle.—also used attrib.

1865 Cooke *Wearing of Gray* 42: Those secret enemies might originate the falsehoods aimed at him from their safe refuge in some newspaper office, or behind some other "bomb-proof" shelter—*he* would *fight.* **1918** [O'Brien] *Wine, Women & War* 92: Kindly folks at home evidently getting after lads in Washington bomb-proofs. **1918** *N.Y. Times* (Sept. 8) III 8: Here are the facts about the so-called "swivel chair" and "bomb-proof" commissions.

b. a soldier or other person whose safe situation enables him to avoid battle and hardship.—also used attrib. Now *hist.*

1867 *Harper's Wkly.* (Apr. 6) 211 [ref. to Civil War]: The "bomb-proof" editors will probably continue to repeat the heroics of the war. **1869** *Overland Mo.* 128 [ref. to Civil War]: In the cis-Mississippi States [those who avoided danger] were generally dubbed "bomb-proofs." **1871** Schele de Vere *Americanisms* 281: Officials, who were not expected to expose themselves to the fire of the enemy, like quartermasters, commissaries, etc., were nicknamed *bombproofs.* **1876** in *DA:* While the war lasted, it was the delight of some of the stoutly built fellows to go home for a few days, and kick and cuff and tongue-lash the able-bodied bomb-proofs. **1886** P.D. Haywood *Cruise of Alabama* 7: Of course the worst...were the bomb-proof heroes that demolished Yankee armies...at dinner-tables. **1894** Maury *Recolls.* 149 [ref. to Civil War]: The bomb-proofs and the newspapers complain of his retreats. **1927** S.V. Bénet *John Brown's Body* 155 [ref. to Civil War]: "Bomb-proof" officers, veterans back on leave.

bombproof *adj.* invincible; tough; battle-hardened.

1864 in Wightman *To Ft. Fisher* 202: "Bombproof Jack"...was sitting nearby. **1917** in Truman *Dear Bess* 232: We'll be hard-boiled and bomb-proof when we get to Berlin. **1939** Howsley *Argot* 10: *Bomb Proof*—impervious to surprise, shock; hardened; one without any nervous reaction. **1944** Pennell *Rome Hanks* 64: Those sonsuhbitches thought they were bombproof.

bombshell *n.* a strikingly sexy woman.

1933 Mahin & Furthman *Bombshell* (film): I see Lola Burns, the bombshell herself. **1942** *ATS* 194: *Blonde Bombshell*...Jean Harlow, motion-picture actress. **1971** Jacobs & Casey *Grease* 33: I hear she's a real bombshell. **1980** Manchester *Darkness* 176: She had lined up a bombshell for him..."She puts out...and she's classy." **1990** *New Republic* (Aug. 20) 25: If other decades possessed their blond bombshell superstars, is it not fitting that the present era should have one of its own?

bomb squad *n. Football.* members of a football team who are frequently chosen for hazardous plays.

1971 Meggyesy *Out of My League* 109: Bomb squads are usually composed of those players...the coaches don't mind risking for use on punts and kickoffs. The chance for serious injury is...high on these plays. **1980** Pearl *Slang Dict.:* Bomb squad *n.* (Sports) the group of football players on a team used in the most dangerous plays.

bomfog *n.* [acronym for *b*rotherhood *o*f *m*an under the *f*atherhood *o*f *G*od, closing line of a radio speech by John D. Rockefeller, Jr., on July 8, 1941; later used as a slogan by Nelson Rockefeller; see 1978 quot.] *Pol.* platitudinous political rhetoric or obfuscation. Also as *v.*

1965 *Lompoc* (Calif.) *Record* (May 19) 10B: A good recent candidate, however, is BOMFOG....Taken from Brotherhood of Man and Fatherhood of God, it describes platitudinous political piety. **1978** Safire *Pol. Dict.* 67: Bomfog was originated by Hy Sheffer who was at one time [Gov. Nelson Rockefeller]'s stenotypist. Hy...started using it in the late 1959–60 national effort. Since the Governor used the phrase "the brotherhood of man under the fatherhood of God," so often, Hy began to simplify it on the stenotype machine. **1978** *Newsweek* (Feb. 6) 30: How to master the glut of data and improve the bomfogging reports that make up the "product" of the U.S. intelligence community. **1979** Homer *Jargon* 35: *Bomfog.* Any speech heavy on bombastic rhetoric and light on true substance. **1987** W. Safire, in *N.Y. Times* (Feb. 2) 21: Admiral Poindexter…pumped out some bomfog about having to check his files, never admitting…authorship.

bon *adj.* [< F] *Mil. in France.* good.—esp. in phr. **no bon** no good. Now *hist.*

　　1918 *N.Y. Eve. Jour.* (Aug. 17) 2: Company on the right got in? Bon—bon—that's fine! **1919** Sweeney *Negro in World War* 274: "Some chow, hey Buddy?"…"Pretty bon….I'd like to have beaucoup more of their chicken." **1919** *Amer. Legion Wkly.* (Aug. 8) 26: It was no bon, I thought. ***1919** *Athenaeum* (Aug. 8) 729: "Bon" and "no bon"…terms of approval or the reverse. *ca*1930–73 E. Mackin *Suddenly Didn't Want to Die* 119 [ref. to 1918]: Red, you've got one *bonne* sector there!

bonaroo var. BONNEROO.

bone[1] *n.* **1.** usu. *pl.* **a.** a die. [Colloq. or literary in early use.]

　　***1386–1400** Chaucer *Pardoner's Tale* I. 368: This fruyt cometh of the bicche bones two. **ca*1460 in *OED*: I was falsly begylyd with thyse byched bones. **a*1529 J. Skelton, in *OED*: On the borde he whyrled a payre of bones. ***1624**, ***1724** in *OED*. **a*1780 Woty *Poems* 88: But hark! the box and rattling bones* I hear….*A term for Dice. *Ibid.* 97: At cards, or *bones.* ***1823** "J. Bee" *Slang* 14: The *Bones,* dice. **1849** Melville *Redburn* ch. xlvi: Gambling? red and white, you mean?—cards?—dice?—the bones?—Ha, ha! **1856** *Spirit of Times* (Mar. 1) 28: We might as well exercise the "bones" for an hour or so…the dice. ***1874** Hotten *Slang Dict.* (ed. 4) 90: *To rattle the bones,* to play at dice. **1891** McCann & Jarrold *Odds & Ends* 83: Here's the leather and here's the bones. **1891** Maitland *Amer. Slang Dict.* 41: *Bones*…dice. **1897** Ade *Pink* 157: I see Clay Walkeh an' some mo' boys rollin' 'e bones. **1900** *DN* II 24: *Bones, n.*….Dice. **1912** J.W. Johnson *Ex-Coloured Man* 93: Gimme the bones. **1912** Stringer *Shadow* 164: He would sit…stolidly "rolling the bones" as he talked. **1913** in Tyler *Crime* 377: At any rate, the Negro gambler, coming up from the South with his "bones," has taught it to the whole country.…Children of four or five are taught to "roll the bones" for their older brothers. **1918** T.A. Dorgan, in *N.Y. Eve. Jour.* (Aug. 3) 7: Well, the bones are still warm.…Hurry up with the jack. **1918–19** MacArthur *Bug's-Eye View* 67: The bones rattled merrily and far into the night. **1928** Dahlberg *Bottom Dogs* 35: Lady, what's the matter with these bones, are they loaded? **1929** Segar *Thimble Th.* 53: Come on ol' bones! Get hot! And stay hot! **1936** M. Davis *Lost Generation* 32: An' I kin pick up ten dollars a month shootin' the bones. **1948** McIlwaine *Memphis* 338: Dope, booze, and bones always helped to bring on woman trouble. **1953** Eyster *Customary Skies* 253: Stop polishing them bones and throw. **1978** Time-Life *Gamblers* 76: Down amid the cargo, the roll of the bones. **1984** J. Fuller *Fragments* 14: It's the same every time you pick up the bones. **1992** *Down the Shore* (Fox-TV): Eddie, roll them bones!

　　b. *Gamb.* a loaded die.

　　1965 C. Brown *Manchild* 151: And I'd take some loaded craps down there, some bones, and I would beat the paddy boys out of all their money. They were the only ones dumb enough to shoot craps with bones.

　　c. a domino.

　　1978 *N.Y. Times Mag.* (Mar. 26) 22: Willie Nelson plays in a "bones" (domino) tournament, a popular Texas pastime.

2.a. a gambling chip.

　　1866 *Night Side of N.Y.* 58: At his side sat the cashier, very busy in converting greenbacks into "bones."

　　b. a dollar; (*pl.*) money. [The meaning of 1839 quot. is suspect; it seems to mean "money," but it is not certain, and the fifty-year gap between it and the next quot. make a definitive conclusion difficult.]

　　1839 in R.B. Hayes *Diary* I 30: I am about to…write an answer to your…"bone" letter; "bone" 'cause it had forty dollars in it. **1889** S. Bailey *Ups & Downs* 26: On the strength of this, Mickey struck me for the loan of a hundred "bones," and I had to tell him that he was too fresh. **1896** Ade *Artie* 9: I guess I saw as much as two bones change hands. **1899** Dunne *Dooley in Hearts* 58: Well, sir, Hogan was that tickled he give th' good man five bones out iv th' taypot. **1910** *N.Y. Eve. Jour.* (Feb. 2) 18: The balcony's the best I got left boss—here's two fer 10 bones. **1910** in Roe *Prodigal Dtr.* 84: He would pay me twenty-one bones (dollars) a week. **1911** *Hampton's Mag.* (Oct.) 434: Ten bones'd get the whole outfit. **1914** *Sat. Eve. Post* (Apr. 4) 10: Not fur five bones

would I sell him. **1919** S. Lewis *Free Air* 105: Could yuh loosen up and slip me just a couple bones? **1922** in E. Pound *Letters* 177: Thanks fer 5 bones recd. **1928** Dahlberg *Bottom Dogs* 249: Doing extra work in mob scenes at three bones per day in Hollywood. **1934** Lomax & Lomax *Amer. Ballads* 131: Oh, pass me half a million bones or mo'. **1955–57** Felder *Collegiate Slang* 1: *Bones*—money. **1965** Himes *Imabelle* 97: I've got five bones says the black dog wins by a knockout. **1973** Andrews & Owens *Black Lang.* 111: *Bone*—Dollar. **1983** *N.Y. Daily News* (Mar. 25): Teentalk Glossary…*bones*—money, cash. *a*1987 Bunch & Cole *Reckoning for Kings* 281: An' you owe me seventy-five bones.

3.a. an erection of the penis. Also **bone-on.**

　　1916 Cary *Venery* I 21: *Bone*—An erect penis. A man with an erect penis is said to have a bone. From a raccoon, the male of which has an osseous structure in its organ of generation. **1927** *Immortalia* 121: He was always there with a bone on. **1928** in Read *Lexical Evidence* 38: All wishing to be sucked off get a bone on and wait. **1930** *Lyra Ebriosa* 5: His sceptre was his Royal Bone/With which he used to brown the Bastard King of England! **1934** H. Miller *Tropic of Cancer* 2: Think of the human race walking around with a bone on. **1941** in Legman *Limerick* 57: There was an old man of Cajon/Who never could get a good bone. **1959** Farris *Harrison High* 85: Personally, I get just as much bone with a tongue as with a titty. **1970** Southern *Blue Movie* 232: I never got such a terrific bone-on in my life. **1975** T. Berger *Sneaky People* 219: She could feel his bone-on. **1978** Truscott *Dress Gray* 303: The cadet had a bone. He was turned on.

　　b. a gesture of contempt made by raising the middle finger; FINGER.

　　1957 Kohner *Gidget* 53: All Jeff did was flip the bone at his old man, which is a very dirty way of telling somebody where to get lost. **1968** Baker et al. CUSS 85: *Bone, flag the…Bone, flip a…Bone, give the…Bone, shoot a.* To gesture with the middle finger. **1970** Thackrey *Thief* 174: As I went by, I flipped him the bone. **1972** Wambaugh *Blue Knight* 83: One asshole…flipped me the bone and then scowled into the camera. **1982** Univ. Tenn. grad. student, age 29: When I was growing up in Arkansas, the kids used to say, "to shoot the bone at somebody." It meant to give them the finger. This was no later than 1967.

4.a. BONEHEAD, 1.

　　1912–14 in E. O'Neill *Lost Plays* 184: Kill it, kill it, you bone!

　　b. a blunder; BONEHEAD PLAY.—usu. in phr. **pull a bone** to make a blunder, GOOF.

　　1913 *Sat. Eve. Post* (May 31) 28: A man ought to be fined for "pulling a bone" like that. **1917** in E. Wilson *Prelude* 166: Pulled a bone. **1918** *Independent* (Jan. 26): In his hurry he had pulled a bone. **1918** *N.Y. Eve. Jour.* (Aug. 1) 12: Holke…"pulled a bone" when he jumped his club the day before. **1918** *Sat. Eve. Post* (Aug. 3) 5: If I'd pulled that bone I'd have got a court instead of a medal. **1919** Cavanaugh *Football* 242: The most expert of players will pull an occasional "bone." **1919** Witwer *Alex the Great* 29: When you claim it's a simple matter to make good here, you have gone and pulled a bone. **1919** Kauffman *Lost Squadron* 42: I don't know that you have pulled such an awful bone. **1919** Resbergen *Overseas* 73: Pulled my first civilian "bone" today. **1919** [Wilkins] *Co. Fund* 29: Everybody tries to outdo everybody, even at pulling bones. **1931** Hellinger *Moon* 32: Something tells me that you're gonna pull an awful bone. **1967** in Wepman, Newman & Binderman *The Life* 163: You must do time/Whenever you pull a bone.

5. a marijuana cigarette.

　　1978 *Adolescence* XII 500: Marihuana cigarettes were called "joints," "j's" or "bones." **1980** Birnbach *Preppy Hndbk.* 278: *Bones n.* Marijuana cigarettes. **1988** *N.Y. Times* (June 4) 36: Joint…roach…bone.

6. *U.S. Nav. Acad.* hard study.

　　1877 Lee *Fag-Ends* 50: 'Twas while a mid, on furlough brief,/From "bone" and drill am I.

7. *Stu.* an overdiligent student; GRIND. [The spelling *Bohn* has been influenced by "Bohn's Classical Library." See BONE, *v.*, 4.a.]

　　1895 Gore *Stu. Slang* 4: *Bohn,* or *boner*….A hard student. **1900** *DN* II 24: *Bohn, n.* 1. A close student. [Sense reported from 13 colleges.]

8. [fr. colloq. *bone in (one's) throat*] an annoyance.

　　1944 Olds *Helldiver Squadron* 69: In the rear seat…was Sam (Gunner) Kelly…for whom the patrol had been, as he told Dale, "one hell of a bone."

9. [cf. S.E. *throw (someone) a bone*] a bribe.

　　1877 Bartlett *Amer.* (ed. 4) 58: *Bone.* A term well understood in New York, and perhaps in other large commercial cities; it means a fee paid by passengers to custom-house officers for permission to pass their baggage with a slight examination. If the *bone* is large, the trunks may not be opened at all.

¶ In phrases:

¶ **bite the bone** [allusion is to **(3.a.)** above] *Juve.* to be disgusting, inferior, etc.

1977 Bredes *Hard Feelings* 248: To put it in common language, it bites the bone.

¶ **bone in her teeth** [or **mouth**] *Naut.* foam and spray trailing from the bow (of a fast-moving vessel).

1627 in J. Smith *Complete Works* III 64: If the Bow be too broad, she will seldome carry a Bone in her mouth or cut a feather, that is, to make a fome before her. **1827** J.F. Cooper *Red Rover* 71: Leaving the "bone in her mouth" under her stern as a light-house for all that come after! ***1829** in Partridge *DSUE* (ed. 7) 1021: Bless you, Ma'am, she has only got the bone in her mouth—she is spanking away like a young whale, at nine or ten knots an hour. **1835** [Ingraham] *South-West* I 59: Carrying even in so light a breeze, a "bone in her teeth." **1894** J. Slocum *Liberdade* 13: She went flying before the tempest…with a large "bone in her mouth." **1925** in Thomason *Stories* 484: And now her veteran engines again dug up extra knots…and [she] held on with a white bone in her teeth across the blue sea. ***1929** Bowen *Sea Slang* 17: *Bone in her teeth.* The bow-wave of a ship. **1958** Grider *War Fish* 46: The periscope…picked up the escort, a small destroyer, with a bone in his teeth, headed right at us.

¶ **jump [on] (someone's) bones, 1.** to copulate with. [1952 quot. appears in a folk song of 19th-C. origin, recorded in Belfast.]

*1952 in Lomax *Folksongs of Britain* V: The Bold English Navvy…Sure, he'll jump on your bones with his navvy boots on. **1965** *Esquire* (July) 45: When you slept with a girl you *got into her panties* while the prosperous teen-ager *jumped on her bones.* **1968** *Playboy* (June) 80: I want to stay alive in order to get you home and jump on your bones. **1973** *Penthouse* (June) 136: I'd…pick me up on some gold, grab my fox, an' jump on her bones! **1974** *Tonight Show* (NBC-TV): No one jumped on anyone's bones. **1977** Butler & Shryack *Gauntlet* 125: Have *I* tried to jump on your bones? **1983** Van Devanter & Morgan *Before Morning* 54: You must jump his bones….Have him jump your bones…and make him think it's all his idea. **1990** *Sonya Live in L.A.* (CNN-TV) (Apr. 25): She's ready to jump his bones right there.

2. to attack (someone) physically or verbally.

1989 *Donahue* (NBC-TV): I tell ya—you got a *lot* of old people jumpin' on *your* bones. **1991** *Donahue* (NBC-TV): The big geek is in the closet waiting to jump on the guy's bones.

¶ **lay bones** *Juve.* to stand lookout for the approach of an adult.

1882 *Puck* (Nov. 22) 181: Cast your optic on his junior brother "laying bones" athwart the fence hard by. Aha! Anon he steadfastly turns his troubled gaze along the well-worn path that leadeth unto the farmer's domicile. **1898** (quot. at CHEESE, *v.*).

¶ **roll (one's) bones** to stir (oneself); to run. See also **(1),** above.

1836 in J.Q. Anderson *With Bark On* 259: Roll your bones—go it, you cripples! **1889** "Scribe" *Sport Among Rockies* 32: When Charlie, the cook, in stentorian tones cried out, "Roll your bones," the writer opened his eyes.

¶ **to the bone** [extracted fr. such phrs. as *soaked* or *chilled to the bone*] Esp. *Black E.* to an extreme; thoroughly; "to the limit."

1932 C. McKay *Gingertown* 12: The men…were all chocolate-to-the-bone. **1955** Graziano & Barber *Somebody Up There* 321: You're beat to the bone and only want to go to sleep. **1967** *Lit Dict.* 37: The cat was dressed in his glad rags…and conked to the bone. **1971** Dahlskog *Dict.* 36: *Laid to the bone,* wearing one's best clothes; all dressed up. **1974** *TULIPQ* (coll. B.K. Dumas): Drunk…*stoned to the bone.* **1982** G. Thorogood *Bad to the Bone* (song). **1988** *U.S. News & W.R.* (Jan. 18) 34: And he'd get silked down to the bone. **1992** Majors & Billson *Cool Pose* 81: He wearing the very popular silk mohair wool worsted—continental to the bone. **1993** *Oprah* (ABC-TV): Men will lie to the *bone!*

bone[2] *n. Music.* a trombone.

1918 *DN* V 23: *Bone, n.* Trombone. (Heard only twice from traveling, second-rate bandmen.). **1942** in R.S. Gold *Jazz Talk* 24. **1963** M. Braly *Shake Him* 87: Furg's 'bone was a brass bowl hooked in his nervous system. **1971** Wells & Dance *Night People* 90: I like the sound of the bones and organ together. *Ibid.* 117: *Bone, n.* Trombone.

bone *adv.* [sugg. by *to the bone* s.v. BONE, *n.* and S.E. *bone-weary*] *Black E.* thoroughly.

1983 Sturz *Wid. Circles* 62: I'm not bone mean like some of those entrenched criminals.

bone *v.* **1.a.** to steal.

*1698–99 "B.E." *Dict. Canting Crew: I have bon'd her Dudds, Fagg'd, and Brush'd,…I have took away my Misstress Cloathes, Beat her, and am Troop'd off.* ***ca1800** in Holloway & Black *English Broadsides* 46: But the cash that she bon'd for a Bucket of Water. **1837** J.C. Neal *Charcoal Sks.* 182: If I tries little speckilations such as boning things, I'm sartin to be cotch. **1846** in H.L. Gates, Jr. *Sig. Monkey* 93: When you bone [them], den ob course you secure em, and git a bone-us for youself. **1859** Matsell *Vocabulum* 13: *Bone.* To take; to steal. ***1881–84** Davitt *Prison Diary* I 122: He will beg from house to house in town or country and "Bone" anything of value which he may find unwatched or otherwise unprotected in his way….The thief-cadger will help himself to whatever is worth "boning" and of easy removal.

b. to apprehend and place under arrest.

*1698–99 "B.E." *Dict. Canting Crew: Bone,…to Apprehend, Seize, Take, or Arrest. I'll Bone ye,…I'll cause you to be Arrested.* ***1788** Grose *Vulgar Tongue* (ed. 2): *Boned,* Seized, apprehended, taken up by a constable. ***1812** Vaux *Memoirs: Boned:* taken in custody, apprehended; *Tell us how you was boned,* tell us the story of your apprehension; a common request among fellow prisoners in a jail. ***1821** *Real Life in London* I 86: And sure enough you're *boned.* **1850** in *Calif. Hist. Soc. Qly.* VIII (1929) 272: A police man [*sic*] Boned the lad…& brought him to the station house. **1859** Matsell *Vocabulum* 13: *Boned.* Arrested; taken; carried off.

2.a. to beg or demand money from; to make a request of; to charge.

1856 in C.A. Abbey *Before the Mast* 74: He must needs "bone" Sam about it. **1859** Matsell *Vocabulum* 13: *Bone…*to ask him for it. **1892** Garland *Prairie Folks* 53: I'd bone him f'r pay f'r that shote. **1896** in Cather *Short Fiction* 557: I'll bone him for some of his free-lunch stuff. **1896** Ade *Artie* 34: Now, you know you can't go up and bone a stranger for stuff, can you? **1900** *DN* II 24: *Bone…*To ask for, dun…to charge with. [Reported from numerous colleges.]. **1903** Ade *Society* 149: If you jolly him up…you might get a nice Photograph of him, and then he will Bone you for one in Return and nail it up in his Den and tell all the other Johnnies that you are crazy about him. **1918** E. Pound, in J. Joyce *Letters* II 424: I will try to bone a few quid more out of someone. **1918** *Chi. Sun.-Trib.* V (Mar. 24): A square citizen if a beggar boned him an' he had no money wouldn't cuss at the panhandler an' wouldn' kid him neither. **1949** W.R. Burnett *Asphalt Jungle* 64: If I never welched, why bone me—and in front of a stranger!

b. to seek and obtain.—constr. with *up.*

1900 *Howitzer* (U.S. Mil. Acad.) (No. 1) 117: *Bone…*also to seek and find, as to bone up a skag.

3. to work hard; to strive.—also constr. with *in, through, down,* etc.

1841 in *DA:* Webb wants to be Postmaster….He has been round boring every big-bug in the State to bone for him. *a***1861** in *DA:* We was about sick of putty-heads and sneaks that…didn't dare to make us stand round and bone in. **1864** in W. Wilkinson *Mother* 223: I…bone right down to sterne every day war & blood letting. **1883** *Century Mag.* (June) 273: I'm going to bone right down to it. *a***1903** *F & H* I (rev.) 316: *To bone into it…*to apply oneself closely; to study hard. **1903** Ade *Society* 86: So he tucked back his cuffs and took a fresh Grip on the World of Trade and boned like a Turk, making payments on the house. **1951** *AS* XXVI 238: He boned his way through the difficulty. **1959** Scott *Tiger in Sky* 105: He's reached that age when he should have been boning for general long ago, if he's ever going to be one.

4.a. *Stu.* to study (a subject) intently.—also (esp. in 20th C.) constr. with *up.*—Also intrans. Hence **boning, boner,** *n.*

1859 in O.E. Wood *West Point Scrapbook* 88: Much study,…you call it boning, is quite weary to the flesh. **1862** in *DA:* Not unfrequently I took the liberty to suggest to him that if he did not leave poetry and bone math more than he was doing we should be deprived ere long of his excellent society. **1887** E. Custer *Tenting* 181 [ref. to 1860's]: I have known the General to "bone up," as his West Point phrase expressed, on the smallest details of some question at issue. **1894** *Lucky Bag* (U.S. Nav. Acad.) (No. 1) 66: *Bone…*to study. **1897** Norris *Vandover* 293: He at last became content to settle down to work under a tutor, "boning up" for the examinations. **1897** Kelley *Ship's Company* 73: He ought to be "boning" for the examination near at hand. **1898** Allen *Navy Blue* 132: He had boned (studied) hard the night before. **1900** in C. Sandburg *Letters* 4: I have a mental photograph of you boning physics in the atmosphere of the past week. **1909** Moss *Officers' Man.* 283: *Bone,* to study. **1911** O. Johnson *Stover at Yale* 120: Boning out the Greek?…Don't you use a trot? *Ibid.* 128: Get out, Dopey, we're boning! **1918** *DN* V 23: *To bone, vb.t.,* and *intr.* to study hard; to prepare a lesson with great effort. "He's *boning.*" "I *boned up* my math." **1918** McNutt *Yanks* 51: Some of them are studying French....I'm boning hard trying to recall what I once knew about surveying. **1926** Nason *Chevrons* 49: "It isn't really necessary to bone the map," said the lieutenant. **1927** *AS* II 275: *Bone*—study hard....*boner*—a student. **1927–30** Rollins *Jinglebob* 38: So I started to bone reasonably hard. **1948** *Time* (Sept. 6), in Berg *New Words* 45: L.B. is assigned to bone up on rockets and jets. **1956** Vidal *Thirsty Evil* 212: Start boning up on Latin again. **1958** Chandler *Playback* 98: This is a rich town, friend....I've studied it. I've boned up on it. **1963** *AS* XXXVIII 167: To study extremely diligently for an examination:...*bone up.* **1970** G. Walker *Cruising* 81: Wander over to the French Club for some conversational *français* to bone up for the language requirement? **1992** G. Wolff *Day at Beach* 16: I boned up on Haiti.

b. *U.S. Mil. Acad.* (used in numerous ephemeral idioms in the general sense of **(a)**, above).

1871 in O.E. Wood *West Point* 337: *Boning Adjutant*—Being excessively military. *Boning Muscle*—Exercising in the Gymnasium. *Bone Corporal*—A plebe afraid of being reported. *Boning Demerit*—Keeping from being reported. **1900** *Howitzer* (U.S. Mil. Acad.) (No. 1) 117: *Bone Gallery*—To make superhuman efforts in the gym or riding hall to excite the admiration of the fair spectators. *Boning Toast*—Playing on one of the scrub football teams for the food of the training table. **1905** *Howitzer* (U.S. Mil. Acad.) (No. 6) 292: *Bone Gallery*—To play to the grandstand in order to make the ladies say "Ah!" *Bone Chevrons*—To seek the approbation of the [Tactical Dept.]. *Bone Toast*—To obtain a place on an athletic team for the purpose of appeasing hunger. **1909** Moss *Officers' Man.* 283: *Bone*—to study; to try; to cultivate. *Bone bootlick on*—to cultivate the favor of. **1929** E. Colby, in *Our Army* (Nov.) 26: A person who always extends the glad hand...is said to "bone popularity." To "bone bootlick" is to make fancy efforts to please a superior officer....To "bone tenths" is the army way of saying a man tries excessively for [academic] marks alone....The man who "bones tenths" does not think of acquiring knowledge. **1939** *AS* XIV 32: *Bone*...*check book*—practice economy; *dis*—observe strict discipline; *file*—try for high class standing; *muck*—try to put on muscle in gymnasium; *reverse*—regarded with disfavor. **1956** Boatner *Mil. Customs* 113: "Bone a reverse" is West Point slang for getting on somebody's "black list." **1961** Ford *Black, Gray & Gold* 40: He managed to curry favor with the Upperclassmen, or "bone suck" as the cadets would say.

c. to annoy; to irritate. [Meaning in 1858 quot. is ambiguous; there it may mean 'punch or hit' (otherwise unrecorded).]

1858 *Harper's Mag.* (Mar.) 566: You had better go to the head-waiter, and he will give you some....And if he don't give you some, *bone* him! **1900** *DN* II 24: *Bone v.t.*...to bore...To worry. [Reported from a few colleges.].

5.a. to betray by informing.

1868 [Williams] *Black-Eyed Beauty* 10: He got...waylaid and whaled after school because he had a way of "boning on fellers—(more plainly, tale-telling)" and currying favor with the master.

b. to report for misbehavior.

1936 Monks & Finklehoffe *Brother Rat* 151: The O.D.'ll be out here and bone the three of us. *Ibid.* 156: Keep that up and I'll bone you.

6.a. [cf. BONE, *n.*, 3.a. and *jump (someone's) bones* s.v. BONE, *n.*] to copulate with.

1971 Hilaire *Thanatos* 180: Any chance me bonin' that gal? **1978** W.R. Campbell *Dead Man Walking* 5: *Boned.* The prison term for sexual intercourse. It is synonymous with...balled. **1980** *Nat. Lampoon* (Dec.) 14: In general behave like mad Sir Lancelot taxed with the boning of Queen Guinevere. **1985** Eble *Campus Slang* (Apr.) 2: *Bone*—to engage in sexual intercourse. **1988** S. Lee *School Daze* (film): You bonin' my own frat brother.

b. to victimize.

1983 *N.Y. Daily News* (Mar. 25): Teentalk Glossary...*boned*—given a bad grade.

bone box *n.* **1.** the mouth.

*1785 Grose *Vulgar Tongue: "Shut your bone box,"* shut your mouth. **1821* *Real Life in Ireland* 16: Fair in your *bone-box!* You foul *galoosh!* **1858* A. Mayhew *Paved with Gold* 190: Jack jerked his drumsticks against Ned's "bonebox," with a force that must have loosened every tooth. **1859** Matsell *Vocabulum* 13: *Bonebox.* The mouth. *Ibid.* 100: Oh! button your bone-box, Peg.

2. an ambulance.

1976 Lieberman & Rhodes *CB Handbook* 124: *Bone Box*—Ambulance

or hearse. **1976** *Sci. Mech. CB Gde.* 155: We need a bone box at Exit 34. **1977** Avalone *White Knight* 5: Nobody had been sent in the bonebox, luckily.

bone carpenter *n.* a surgeon. Also **bone chiseler, bone bender, bone butcher.**

1882 Baillie-Grohman *Rockies* 47: That thar boss bone-carpenter. **1919** Emmett *Give, 'Way to Right* 269: I'll mark your record so the "bone-chiselers" will keep off you. **1929** *Bookman* (July) 525: I...see the shacks and the hogger carryin' the kid over to the bone bender's. **1958** McCulloch *Woods Words* 15: Bone butcher—The company doctor.

bone cart *n.* the body or back. *Joc.*

1865 in M. Lane *Dear Mother* 343: Wheeled my luggage to the other train on my *bone cart.*

bone dance *n.* ¶ In phrase: **do the bone dance** *Stu.* to have sexual intercourse.

1989 P. Munro *U.C.L.A. Slang* 34: My parents walked in while I was doing the bone dance. **1989** Eble *College Slang* 101: Intercourse: Bone Dance, Bop, [etc.].

bonehead *n.* **1.** a blockhead.—often used attrib.

1908 in Fleming *Unforgettable Season* 253: The epithets hurled at Chance [included]..."bone head." **1908** *Chicago Daily Tribune* (Sept. 24) 12: Then came the bonehead finish which left the bugs puzzled and wondering. **1911** T.A. Dorgan, in *N.Y. Eve. Jour.* (Jan. 10) 14: Don't pull any bonehead stuff because this gal thinks you're a mountain of wisdom. **1911** Howard *Enemy to Society* 102: Don't go gettin' the idea that we're a lot of boneheads. **1912** *Adventure* (May) 49: He calls me a bonehead. **1912** Mathewson *Pitching* 302: That's the "gink" who has been calling me a "bone head." **1914** *Smart Set* (Oct.) (front cover): One Civilized Reader Is Worth a Thousand Boneheads. **1919** McGrath *354th Inf.* 172: Too much credit cannot be given Lieut. Sanborn who toiled and labored patiently with many a seemingly impossible bonehead. **1921** *Ohio Doughboys* 84: Mr. Edison says, "Most men are boneheads." **1927** S. Lewis *Elmer Gantry* 19: You don't think I'm just a bonehead, do you? **1930** in R.E. Howard *Iron Man* 14: If he was a bonehead, I'd understand it. But he's brainy in other ways. **1952** Bellow *Augie March* 209: Why, you're a lousy bonehead! **1967** Lockwood *Down in Subs* 55: This bonehead...put lubricating oil in the pump instead of olive oil. **1981** *N.Y. Times Mag.* (Sept. 13) 18: That would simply imply that *flaunt* has more than just a bonehead relationship with *flout.*

2. BONEHEAD PLAY.

1918 *DN* V 23: *Bonehead* n. A stupid error. Often with the vb. *to pull.* "He pulled a *bonehead* all right." **1928** Harlow *Sailor* 48: Having pulled off a "bonehead" with the jibs I took it gracefully. **1928** Sharpe *Chicago May* 34: Many of the criminals betray themselves by talking too much, or pulling boneheads, or leaving trails that anybody can see and understand. **1963** E.M. Miller *Exile to Stars* 38: No more boneheads, Turk. From now on this would be a game of chess.

boneheaded *adj.* stupid.

1903 in *DA:* You talk like a bone-headed fool. **1915** in Grayson *New Stories* 552: If these boneheaded boys can learn to box, so can I.

bonehead English *n.* *Stu.* a remedial course in elementary composition.

1927 *AS* II 275: *Bonehead English*—English for insufficiently prepared freshmen. **1974** *CBS News* (CBS-TV) (Dec. 19): U.S.C. calls it "Subject A." The students call it "bonehead English." **1976–77** C. McFadden *Serial* 73: Jason...was currently teaching night classes in bonehead English. **1984** *Rendezvous* (Fall) 72: This method of trying to get us "bonehead English" candidates to eliminate the "comma fault" was an arrogant use of her power. **1989** *CampusUSA* (Spring) 13: Since the late 1950s, almost all entering freshman have had to take Freshman English, or what used to be called "Bonehead English."

bonehead play *n.* a foolish and obvious blunder.

1911 A.H. Lewis *Apaches of N.Y.* 107: I don't know as I'd call it a vice so much as a bonehead play. **1928** MacArthur *War Bugs* 104: Shelter halves were oozing with mud, another result of the bonehead play. **1940** E. O'Neill *Long Day's Journey* I: A very bonehead play! **1951** Bowers *Mob* (film): It sounds like a bonehead play, but the badge he flashed was the McCoy. **1957** Shulman *Rally* 184: She was much too smart for such a bonehead play. **1962** Perry *Young Man* 121: That was a bonehead play. **1973** *N.Y. Post* (Mar. 23) 89: The individual made a bonehead play, in my judgment.

bone-on *n.* see BONE, *n.*, 3.a.

bone orchard *n.* a graveyard. Cf. MARBLE ORCHARD.

1872 Burnham *Secret Service* iv: *Bone-orchard*,—a cemetery; a grave-yard; burial place. *Ibid.* 415: You're makin' good time towards the bone-orchard—*you* ar. **1901** Irwin *Sonnets* (unp.): Into the old bone orchard I am blowing. **1912** Ade *Babel* 110: I figured that I was booked for the crazy-house or the bone-orchard, I couldn't tell which. **1917** *Living Age* (Nov. 10) 379: The American who called a cemetery a "bone orchard" seems to us to have been something of an artist in a low way. **1957** T. Williams *Orpheus* 32: Cypress Hill...is the local bone orchard. ***1967** in MacColl & Seeger *Freeborn Man* 71: But a finer bone-orchard will never be found. **1968** I. Reed *Yellow Back Radio* 48: But what would happen if I popped off like the rest of the swells what's pushing up dai-sies out in the bone orchard? **1976** *Nat. Lampoon* (July) 44: Not a plot of ground such as you might find in a bone orchard. **1980** in McCauley *Dark Forces* 134: But I reckon you're just not ready for the bone orchard yet. **1986** Philbin *Under Cover* 166: [A] fast...way to the bone orchard.

bone-polisher *n.* **1.a.** [so called because one of the duties of a boatswain's mate on board a man-of-war prior to 1850 was to administer floggings] *Navy.* a boatswain's mate; (*also*) an officer who commonly metes out floggings.
1841 [Mercier] *Man-of-War* 211: In my opinion, old bone-polisher, I think you'd sooner run a mile than fight a minute any time. *Ibid.* 279: From the orderly at the cabin-door to the *bone-polishers* in the ward-room, steerage, and cockpit. **1849** Melville *White Jacket* 198 [ref. to 1843]: "*Jacket!*" cried a dandy *bone-polisher* of the gun-room. **1857** in *OED*: He became body servant and bone-polisher to No. 2.
b. *Navy.* a cat-o'-nine-tails.
*a***1848** in *OED*: Master at arms, brush up the bone-polishers. *a***1909** *F & H* I (rev.) 319: *Bone-polisher*...(common). The cat-o'-nine-tails.
2. *Hobo.* a watchdog.
1937 *Lit. Digest* (Apr. 10) 12: *Bone polisher.* Vicious dog.

boner *n.* **1.** BONEHEAD PLAY.
1912 *American Mag.* (June) 200: *Boner*—a stupid play; a blunder in the science of the game. **1915–17** Lait *Gus* 178: He found out before he got back to Piccadilly that he pulled a boner. **1918** *Chi. Sun-Tribune* (Mar. 24) II 1: A pair of boots and a boner let in the tying tallies. **1920** Ade *Hand-Made Fables* 119: Before he had a Chance to pull a Boner and sug-gest the prehistoric Euchre, all the Card Tables were whisked away. **1927** "M. Brand" *Pleasant Jim* 61: You've been put in hell because of a boner that I pulled. **1947–53** Guthrie *Seeds* 199: I've pulled just about the worst boner of this whole trip so far, guys. **1955** Q. Reynolds *HQ* 127: He'd give you a tongue-lashing you'd never forget if you pulled a boner. **1981** Wolf *Roger Rabbit* 43: I had made a colossal boner.
2. an erection of the penis.
1966 Fariña *Down So Long* 283: She caught me with a boner, dammit, bound to stick in her memory, get her all screwed up. **1968** P. Roth *Portnoy* 200: Such grave thoughts will cause my "boner" to recede. **1970** Standish *Non-Stand. Terms* 6: *Bone.* (n.) An erect penis....During the Fifties, a common variant of this term was "Boner." **1980** in *Nat. Lampoon* (Jan. 1981): The more you rub, the bigger a boner that weirdo gets. **1985** J. Schumacher & C. Kurlander *St. Elmo's Fire* (film): Come on, I'm gettin' a boner now. **1992** N.Y. linguist, age *ca*45 (coll. J. Sheidlower): I remember *boner* from New York City before 1962. I'm certain of that date, for I left the city in that year.
3. a stupid or objectionable person.
1986 Stinson & Carabatsos *Heartbreak* 89: This crazy boner'll tap you by Tuesday. **1993** *Mystery Sci. Theater* (Comedy Central TV): Dad's such a boner!

bonerack *n.* an emaciated horse.
1968 E.M. Parsons *Fargo* 10: I'm tired and cold and don't need no pounding on this damned bonerack.

Bones *n. Mil.* a surgeon or hospital steward.—used in direct address.
1892 Frye *From HQ* 10: "No, that's a contribution from the colonel," replied Sawin, *alias* "Bones." **1893** Frye *Field & Staff* 14: Bones, our surgeon—Dr. Sawin, outside the service—broke into the room. **1898** *Sat. Eve. Post* (Oct. 1) 215 [ref. to Civil War]: A shout of "Bones! Bones!" rang along our lines. It was the hospital steward, sure enough. **1957** O'Connor *Co. Q* 88: The regimental surgeon was usually known as "Mr. Bones." **1966** *Star Trek* (NBC-TV): What do you make of it, Bones?

bone-setter *n.* a surprise.
1821 Waln *Hermit in Phila.* 30: D—d near losing *in hockley*,—gave the cards a *flirt* and a *cut*....Broke the bank...and marched off with a *cool* six hundred....Wasn't that a *bone-setter*...my boy?

bone-shaker *n.* an early model of bicycle without rubber tires;

velocipede. Now *hist.*
1871 in Somers *Sports in N.O.* 220. ***1874** in *F & H* I (rev.) 321: In 1870 and 1871, the low, long bone-shaker began to fall in public esteem. ***1884, *1885, *1901** in *F & H.*

bone-softener *n.* a bludgeon; a club.
1896 Hamblen *Many Seas* 398: If any of them are fractious, I'll just give them a rub on their sore heads with my bone-softener.

bonetop *n.* BONEHEAD, 1.
1913 *Sat. Eve. Post* (Mar. 15) 37: Get it straight, you bonetop! **1919** *DN* V 62: *Bone-top*...a dull fellow; one who makes blunders. "The old *bone-top* forgot to close the windows of the chapel last night." California.

boneyard *n.* **1.a.** a cemetery.
1866 "M. Twain" *Lttrs. fr. Hawaii* 277: It's one of them infernal old ancient graveyards....I suppose you didn't know that boneyard was there. **1865–67** De Forest *Miss Ravenel* 277: Can't save him....Bone-yard tomorrow. *a***1867** Harris *Lovingood* 164: They went tu start tu the bone-yard, but durn me ef he staid thar hissef till funeral time. **1871** "M. Twain" *Roughing It* 252: Some roughs jumped the Catholic bone-yard. **1880** [Pilgrim] *Old Nick's Camp-Meetin'* 42: Big Bill went to the boneyard feet foremost with an ounce of lead through his lights. **1899** *Sat. Eve. Post* (Aug. 12) 98: Well, take your choice: the bed or the bone-yard. **1908** *DN* III 292: *Boneyard*...a cemetery. **1921** E. O'Neill *Hairy Ape* 233: Yuh look like stiffs laid out for de boneyard. **1930** "D. Stiff" *Milk & Honey* 200: *Boneyard*—Any graveyard. Also refers to a hospital, or to a medical college where they practice on the bodies of departed hobos. **1969** Moynahan *Pairing Off* 115: Or suddenly *you* will be ready for the boneyard. **1980** D. Hamill *Stomping Ground* 54: He took a last look at the boneyard and made a left turn.
b. a place for the collection and often disposal of old vessels, machinery, or the like, often used as a source of spare parts.
1913 J. London *J. Barleycorn* 57 [ref. to 1890's]: A sugar barque towed from the "boneyard" to sea. **1931–34** Adamic *Dynamite* 389: The *Osk-awa* was...put in the "boneyard"...[with] hundreds of other ships in no better condition. **1935** E. Anderson *Hungry Men* 96: Ships are coming out of the boneyards. **1938** Smitter *Detroit* 106: In a couple days you'll see it standin' out there in the boneyard. *Ibid.* 141: We passed the bone-yard....ten acres of...scrapped machinery. **1943** Steinbeck *Once There Was a War* (Sept. 5): It is a giant bone yard, where wrecked tanks and trucks and artillery are brought and parked, ready for overhauling. **1945** Hubbard *R.R. Ave.* 127: For a time she rusted on the rip track, and now there she goes to the boneyard. **1948** Cozzens *Guard of Honor* 409: Well, hundreds of planes ended like this—right here at Ocanara in the bone yard they had what could be collected of a couple of dozen. **1956** Heflin *USAF Dict.* 88: *Boneyard*...Any place, usually in the open, where wrecked or worn-out parts and equipment are gathered. *Slang.* **1967** Raskin *True Course* 68: Soon the "boneyards" at Tompkins Cove and the James River had more than twice as many vessels as were in ser-vice flying the American flag. **1968** R. Adams *West. Words* (ed. 2): *Bone-yard.* In river boating, any location where worn-out steamboats were moored while being scrapped or awaiting disposition.
2. an emaciated horse.
1905 *DN* II 70: *Boneyard*, n. An emaciated horse. "That old boneyard ought to be killed." Common [in Arkansas]. **1918** in *Dict. Canadianisms* 65.

bong *n. Stu.* (see quots.). Also as *v.*
1990 Munro *Slang U.* s.v. *beer bong*: Beer bong, device consisting of a funnel attached to a tube for drinking beer quickly. **1992** *Newsweek* (Mar. 30) 53: His friends from the University of Massachusetts fun-nel—"bong"—a quart of foaming Budweiser into his mouth.

bong *v.* [cf. BOING and BOINK; also cf. syn. Brit. slang *bonk*, cur-rent since mid-1970's] to copulate with.
1985 *Golden Girls* (NBC-TV): Elliot has bonged every female member of the country club....Elliot is bongin' every woman at your country club.

bong *interj.* (used to suggest the sound of a blow).
1970 Terkel *Hard Times* 33: He lashes out at the girl's head, bong! Jeez, I think he's killed her.

bongo *n.* **1.** *Skateboarding.* a bruise or other injury.
1979 Frommer *Sports Lingo* 192. **1979** Cuddon *Dict. Sports & Games* 119.
2. *pl.* a woman's breasts.
1986 *Playboy* (Apr.) 20: Breasts...bongos. **1991** *Simpsons* (Fox-TV): A nice pair of bongos.

bongo *adj.* [cf. BONKERS] crazy.

1959 Zugsmith *Beat Generation* 59: There Arthur Garretts will drive the finks bongo. **1972** Chevrolet ad on WINS radio (Apr. 20): Man, you're a little bongo in the drums! **1974** N.Y.C. high school student: He's ready to go bongo!

bonk *n.* **1.** a blow, esp. on the top of the head.
   1970 N.Y.U. student: It's like a bonk on the head. **1981** *Maclean's* (Jan. 12): The "coco-bonk" still produces snickers for NHL fans who remember the night when…Shack delivered an odious blow with his head. **1984** Univ. Tenn. instructor, age 32: He got a bad bonk. **1991** *MacGyver* (ABC-TV): You got a pretty good bonk on the head.
   2. *Cycling.* see BONK, *v.*, 2.

bonk *v.* **1.** to hit on the head; to hit (the head).
   [*1936* Partridge *DSUE* 78: *Bonk*, v. To shell: military 1915–18. Gen. in passive.] *1961* Partridge *DSUE* (ed. 5) 1008: *Bonk*…to hit (v.t.) resoundingly: mostly Public Schools': from 1919. **1966** *Star Trek* (NBC-TV) [children chanting]: Bonk, bonk, on the head. **1969** *Playboy* (Aug.) 208: I bonked him with the [bottle of] Black & White. **1972** *Playboy* (Feb.) 22: A British judge jailed a man for bonking his wife with a hammer. **1975** Goldman *Robin & Marian* 10: He bonked stout fellows on the head, getting bonked in return. **1976** Price *Bloodbrothers* 135: They ain't just gonna sit there waitin' to be bonked. **1978** J. Webb *Fields of Fire* 153: If they move, bonk 'em one.
   2. *Cycling.* to reach a state of exhaustion; "run out of gas." Also as *n.*
   1979 Cuddon *Dict. Sports & Games* 119: *Bonk*…A state of extreme fatigue caused by overexertion and lack of blood sugar. **1990** *Bicycling* (July) 75: You can refuel the muscles by ingesting more carbohydrate, or suffer the pain and possible humiliation of bonking. **1991** *On the Menu* (CNN-TV) (July 13): If you feel yourself, as we [cyclists] say, "bonking" or "hitting that wall," a drink of water is a very good idea.

bonkers *adj.* crazy. [In somewhat earlier British slang, the term meant 'drunk'.]
   1957 in *OEDS*. *1967* in *BDNE*. **1970** *Harper's* (June) 37: Pretender, perhaps, to a Balkan throne, but perhaps just bonkers. **1971** *Playboy* (Mar.) 212: I think you're absolutely bonkers. **1971** Dahlskog *Dict.* 9: He went *bonkers* and they locked him up. **1976–77** Kernochan *Dry Hustle* 183: He must still be completely bonkers about you. **1977** WNBC *Newscenter 4* (NBC-TV) (Aug. 20): And I had a cold, too. My ears were going bonkers. **1978** Jastrow *God & Astronomers* 11: When an astronomer writes about God, his colleagues assume he is either over the hill or going bonkers. **1983** Breathed *Bloom Co.* 78: I think she's bonkers over me. **1993** Burger King TV ad: Burger King is going bonkers!

bonneroo *adj.* [orig. unkn.] *Pris.* especially good; excellent; best; (*hence,* of a convict) enjoying privileges. Also vars.
   1926 *Writer's Mo.* (Dec.) 541: *Bonnie Rue*—Anything that is better than the ordinary, like a Bonnie Rue job, or Bonnie Rue food. **1933** [Guest] *Limey* 265: We were "boneroo" men from the start, wearing neat, made-to-measure "boneroo" uniforms. We could buy all the extras we wanted. *Ibid.* 269: I think the word "boneroo" has a Mexican origin. At San Quentin it means, among many other things, "privileged." A "boneroo guy" is a man with enough influence and money to wear boneroo clothes and have a boneroo job and mix with a boneroo bunch. **1935** Pollock *Und. Speaks*: Bonarue, above the average, as a good job, cell, clothing, food. **1935** Lamson *We About to Die* 108: Altogether [life] is very bonny-roo, or would be if it weren't in the Hole. *Ibid.* 113: Bonny-roo clothes and a necktie to wear on Sundays. **1950** Duffy *S. Quentin* 98: "Bonaru"…is used in other penitentiary; it means good or excellent—i.e., a bonaru job—but even the unofficial prison historians know nothing of its origin. **1966** Braly *On Yard* 121: These are boneroo free-world shoes. **1972** Carr *Bad* 72: He had bonneroo rolls and cookies.

bonneroos *n.pl. Pris.* BONNEROO items; (*specif.*) a cleaned and pressed prison uniform. Also vars.
   1961 *Social Problems* X 148: In California [prisons], special items of clothing, and clothing that is neatly laundered, are called "bonaroos." **1967** Salas *Wicked Cross* 138 [ref. to early 1950's]: Get those nasty duds off and put on your bonerues. **1978** Nolan & Mann *Jericho Mile* (film): You got my bonneroos?

bonnet *n.* **1.** *Gamb.* a SHILL; CAPPER.
   1851 W. Kelly *Ex. to Calif.* II 248: Every table is attended by a set of accomplices, or "bonnets," who stake their money on the right cards.
   2. a hat.
   1859 Matsell *Vocab.* 13: Bonnet. Hat. **1896** Ade *Artie* 56: Since he's started to that dancin' school I think he hears funny noises under his

bonnet. **1899** Kountz *Baxter's Letters* 87: I have something to tell you, and…it's strictly under your bonnet. **1910** T.A. Dorgan, in *N.Y. Eve. Jour.* (Jan. 14) 18: Here's yer bonnet, Harry. So long. **1922** S. Lewis *Babbitt* 36: Not merely a place where you hang up the old bonnet but a love-nest for the wife and kiddies. **1955** Archibald *Aviation Cadet* 73: Hold on to your bonnet, Mister! **1976** Hayden *Voyage* 125: Fetch this young gent's bonnet from the floor yonder.
   3. the head; the mind.—used esp. in fig. contexts.
   1902 Townsend *Fadden & Mr. Paul* 87: "Your bonnet is full of 'lectric fans," I says. **1966** Jarrett *Private Affair* 116: And if Mayor Daley and ex.-Professor Orlando Wilson think they are going to change it, they have rocks in their bonnets. **1967** Talbot *Chatty Jones* 177: In love with Octavia! You've blown your bonnet. **1978** *N.Y. Times* (July 2) V 3: That always stuck in my bonnet. **1966–80** McAleer & Dickson *Unit Pride* 414: Daigle and Murphy have orders to put one right into his bonnet if he bugs out on us. *a*1982 in Berry *Semper Fi* 396: I thought he was off his bonnet.
   ¶ In phrase:
   ¶ **under (one's) bonnet** in strict confidence; "under (one's) hat."
   1896 (quot. at **(2)**, above)

bonnet *v.* to crush the hat of (a person) over his eyes.
   1833 J. Neal *Down-Easters* II 120: Bravo! handsomely done! handsomely bonnetted, by the Lord Harry! *1835* C. Dickens *Sketches by "Boz"* 229: Two young men, who, now and then, varied their amusements by bonneting the proprietor of this itinerant coffee-house. **1859** Matsell *Vocab.* 13: "Bonnet him," knock his hat down over his eyes. **1879** Rooney *Quaint Conundrums* 38: A giant fist descends from the ceiling and "bonnets" him. *1882* in *F & H* I 287: The students hustled and "bonneted" a new professor.

bonny lay *n.* [*bonny* + LAY; cf. BONNY THROW] *Und.* the practice of highway robbery.
   1807 Tufts *Autobiog.* 293 [ref. to 1794]: To go upon the bonny lay…to undertake highway robbery.

bonny throw *n. Und.* a highway.
   1791 [W. Smith] *Confess. T. Mount* 19: The highway, *bonny-throw*. *Ibid.* 20: Go out on the bonny throw.

bonus baby *n.* [cf. earlier *bonus player*, as in 1950 quot.] Esp. *Baseball.* a promising young player who is paid a substantial bonus for signing his first professional contract. Also in transferred senses.
   [**1950** *Sat. Eve. Post* (July 8) 93: A bonus player—meaning a boy who received more than specified minimums for signing—can be kept only one year in the minors.] **1957** N.Y.C. man, age *ca*30: Johnny Antonelli was the Giants' first bonus baby. **1962** *N.Y. Times* (Sept. 16) V 53: Ed Kranepool, the Mets' 17-year-old bonus baby, completed his first official game in a Met uniform Friday. **1967** in J. Flaherty *Chez Joey* 49: Exceptions…are paid directly by the parent club and include some bonus babies. **1973** Wagenheim *Clemente!* 38: This [1954] was the era of the "bonus baby," and untested…high-school stars were commanding six-figure amounts. **1976** *Webster's Sports Dict.* **1983** Whiteford & Jones *Talk Baseball* 83: *Bonus baby* A young player…paid a huge sum to induce him to sign his first professional contract. The term was common in the 50s and early 60s. **1983** *Ebony* (Oct.) 40: Paramount reportedly gave Murphy a whopping $4 million cash bonus, making him the movie industry's first "bonus baby." **1992** Strawberry & Rust *Darryl* 108: I was just another bonus baby.

bonzo *adj.* [cf. *Bonzo*, the name of a British cartoon puppy fr. 1920's, and the 1951 film comedy *Bedtime for Bonzo*, featuring a chimpanzee; "Bonzo" was also the nickname of Led Zeppelin's drummer John Bonham] crazy.
   [*1970* The Bonzo Dog Band (rock band).] **1979** Univ. Tenn. student: People are going bonzo here tonight. **1981** Wambaugh *Glitter Dome* 80: Someone was trying to drive Captain Woofer bonzo. **1983** Eilert *Self & Country* 230: We don't want to be the only two…to go bonzo.

boo[1] *n.* [fr. BOODLE[1], *n.*, 2.b.] money, loot.
   1884 in Lummis *Letters* 181: I kept my watch and scanty "boo" carefully out of sight.

boo[2] *n.* BOOGER[2], *n.*
   1900 *DN* II 136: *Boo*, n. Usually in pl. Mucus in nose. St. Lawrence Co., N.Y. "There are boos in your nose." Also…in sing. "There's a big boo."

boo[3] *n.* [orig. unkn.; cf. BOOJIE] *Narc.* **1.** marijuana.

1959 in R.S. Gold *Jazz Talk* 24. **1959–60** Reisner *Jazz Titans* 151: *Boo*: Marijuanana [*sic*]. **1961** C. Cooper *Weed* 12: He still felt a nice buzz from the Boo. **1964** R.S. Gold *Jazz Lex.* 29: *Boo*…shortened form of *jabooby*, etym. of which is unknown; some currency since c. 1935.…marijuana. **1965** *Harper's* (Aug.) 49: The story…[sounds] as if it originated with somebody full of Mexican boo smoke. **1966** Fariña *Down So Long* 67: You know my manic thing with boo. **1967** P. Welles *Babyhip* 135: Marijuana, grass, the weed, Maryjane, Boo. **1970** A. Young *Snakes* 40: That's what keep me goin, brew, boo, and bobbycue. **1976** Price *Bloodbrothers* 151: She lays this dynamite boo on me. **1978** Rascoe & Stone *Who'll Stop Rain?* (film): Just a little boo, *mon colonel*. Want to try some? **1985** "Blowdryer" *Mod. Eng.* 80: Marijuana…*Boo*.

2. *Narc.* cocaine.

1983 *All Things Considered* (Nat. Public Radio) (Sept. 18): Cocaine…*boo*, a precious white substance that deviates the septum. …This is a novel…about the bar business and the *boo* business.

boo⁴ *n.* [fr. interj. *boo!*, humorously assoc. with ghosts] *Journ.* a ghostwriter.

1979 Homer *Jargon* 102: Some of the most renowned journalists …have…earned money (but no credit) as *boos*.

boob¹ *n.* [fr. *booby* and BOOBY HATCH] **1.** BOOBY HATCH, 1.

1908 Sullivan *Crim. Slang* 4: *Boob*—The lockup, station house, or city prison. **1911** Howard *Enemy to Society* 159: Rats…was…suspected of stooling for the coppers and swearing many a right guy into the boob. **1922** *Variety* (June 30) 6: They…were lucky to get out of town without gettin' hoosed in the local boob. **1936** Dai *Opium Add.* 196: *Boob*. The jail. Also called *the can* or *the bucket*. **1952** B. Wilder & E. Blum *Stalag 17* (film): Anybody caught throwin' rocks at low-flying German airplanes will be thrown in the boob.

2.a. a fool; SUCKER; CHUMP.

1907 in H.C. Fisher *A. Mutt* 19: He looks like a boob.…Wonder if he has a bank roll. *Ibid.* 20: I've been an awful boob. *a***1904–11** Phillips *Susan Lenox* II 71: Miss Tuohy's a boob. **1911** A.H. Lewis *Apaches of N.Y.* 17: Not until can he empty every pocket…is he fit to go out into the world and look for boobs. **1911** *Hampton's Mag.* (June) 740: I wouldn't have a fat-headed boob like that around me. **1919** T. Kelly *What Outfit?* 81: Put your [gas] mask on, you boob, ain't you got any sense? **1925** Paine *First Yale* I 48: I didn't solo that summer, neither did Alphy and Earl, my hated rivals in the boob flier class. **1928** C. McKay *Banjo* 96: Why, it's splendid, you boob! **1930** R. Benchley *Chips* 10: There'll be an awful lot of boobs who didn't. **1933** G. Milburn *No More Trumpets* 187: I told the big boob to watch out for them loose boards! **1934** H. Miller *Trop. of Cancer* 102: They think it's sinful here—the poor boobs! **1940** Stout *Where There's a Will* 119: You're a damn bullheaded boob. **1968** Cuomo *Thieves* 87: A man in my position pressured by a boob like Frank Kale? **1980** *N.Y. Daily News* (Tonight) (Aug. 23) 3: Bayh Bobs Up As Billy Boober. Who would ever call Billy Carter a boob? Why, Sen. Birch Bayh, of course. **1984** Kagan & Summers *Mute Evidence* 297: Unsophisticated, back-country boobs.

b. an inmate of an insane asylum; lunatic.—often attrib.

1908 in Blackbeard & Williams *Smithsonian Comics* 58: Old Mutt is in the booby hatch. He got a great welcome from the boobs. **1932** in Partridge *Dict. Und.* 80: We'll have the Marquis bugged.…Settled in the boob house, the nut foundry. **1944** Busch *Dream of Home* 104: Ask that, and people would decide that you were ready for a boob-academy.

boob² *n.* usu. *pl.* [var. pronun. of syn. BUB] a woman's breast.

1929–31 Farrell *Young Lonigan* 89 [ref. to *ca*1916]: Studs didn't usually pay attention to how girls looked, except…to notice their boobs, if they were big enough to bounce. **1929–33** Farrell *Manhood of Lonigan* 266: When Arnold went at her, her boobs had almost fallen out. If they only let the boobs really fall out in scenes like that. **1948** J.H. Burns *Lucifer* 377: Betsy Wagner's got one helluva pair of boobs. **1958** J. Davis *College Vocab.* 13: *Boob*—Breast. **1960** Barber *Minsky's* 142: Then see how many slummers come down to see your flat-boob soubrettes. **1960** Wohl *Cold Wind* 34: Would she open up her shirt so he could see her boobs? **1962** Kesey *Cuckoo's Nest* 48: The too-red lipstick and the too-big boobs. **1967** W. Murray *Sweet Ride* 66: They hire me for my boobs. **1968** Baker et al. *CUSS* 85: *Boob sling*. A brassiere. **1969** R. Welch, in *Playboy* (Jan. 1970) 77: But just mention Brigitte Bardot to most men and the first thing that pops into their heads is boobs. Marilyn Monroe and boobs. Raquel Welch and boobs. It's just ridiculous. **1970** Byrne *Memories* 19: Now it may be asked how I knew what Gretchen Schwartz's boobs looked like. **1980** *Mother Jones* (Sept./Oct.) 2: They all have big boobs. **1990** *National Review* (Aug. 6) 55: Ilona Staller won her seat by a landslide after baring her boobs at election rallies.

boob *v.* **1.** to bungle; botch.—also constr. with *up*. Also absol.

1919 T.A. Dorgan, in Zwilling *TAD Lexicon* 111: The Judge Boobed Another. *****1935** in *OEDS*: The camera seems wholly in place as journalism: but when it tries to re-create it boobs. *****1941** *AS* XVI 76: Slang of the R.A.F.…*He boobed it*, he made a mess of it. **1945** Hamann *Air Words*: He boobed it. **1958** Davis *Spearhead* 144 [ref. to WWII]: I really boobed things up yesterday, sir. **1989** T. Blackburn *Jolly Rogers* 140: The old pro had really boobed it.

2. to hoodwink.

1944 C.B. Davis *Leo McGuire* 174: They'd rather let the bet ride than admit they'd been boobed.

boo-birds *n.pl. Sports.* spectators at a sporting event who boo loudly.

1977 (cited in *Barnhart Dict. Comp.* V (1986) 6). **1984** Nettles & Golenbock *Balls* 229: I'm trying to get the boo birds off Roy. **1986** *Morning Edition* (Nat. Public Radio) (July 22): Even the notorious boobirds on the rail who had cursed Cordero [later cheered him]. **1986** *Eyewitness News* (WABC-TV) (Sept. 10): And Orosco becomes the new but temporary target of the boo birds. **1991** Lott & Lieber *Total Impact* 163: That brought out the boo-birds in droves.

boob job *n.* a surgical operation for breast enlargement.

1989 E. Goodman (synd. column) (Sept. 19): Susan Akin, the 1986 Miss America, has said: "I'll admit to a boob job." **1991** W. Chamberlain *View from Above* 3: Young ladies don't have to get a "boob job" for me, though. **1992** *Jerry Springer Show* (synd. TV series): If I get the boob job, I get more work and more money.

Boob McNutt *n.* [protagonist of eponymous comic strip (1915–34) created by cartoonist Rube Goldberg] a foolish or crazy person.—used derisively.

1945 Hecht *Spellbound* (film): You'd wind up in the arms of some Boob McNutt with spiked hair. **1960** Barber *Minsky's* 320: You think *you* caught a Boob McNutt? Listen to this one.

boo-boo *n.* [orig. unkn.] **1.a.** a joke.

1901 [Hobart] *Down Line* 93: Swift had an idea that when it came to cracking merry booboos he could pull Lew Dockstader off the horse.

b. a dollar.

1905 Hobart *Search Me* 116: I have a hundred thousand booboos in the kick. **1924** *Adventure* (July 10) 162: Where's the five thousand smacks comin' from?…The five thousand booboos!

c. *pl.* the testicles.

1951 T. Capote *Grass Harp* 67: Catherine said, "In the booboos; Collin, kick his old booboos." So I did. Big Eddie's face curdled.

2. an embarrassing blunder; mistake.

1954 MacDonald *Condemned* 140: I nearly made a terrible booboo when a man came hurrying out. **1955** *Phil Silvers Show* (CBS-TV): For the sharpest operator on the post, you sure have pulled a boo-boo. **1958** J. Davis *College Vocab.* 15: *Pull a boo boo*—Make a mistake. **1958** J. King *Pro Football* 190: This booboo is most likely to happen when a referee indicates a timeout. **1959** Hersey *War Lover* 129: The Bubu Factory. **1959** Lederer *Never Steal Anything Small* (film): Hermie makes a giant booboo and drops the entire crate in the drink. **1959** *Sat. Eve. Post* (May 9) 82: It isn't often you'll catch Lieutenant Harding in a navigational boo-boo. **1959** Goodman *Wheeler Dealers* 16: That'll be the day I pull a real booboo. **1969** D.H. Menzel, in Sagan & Page *UFO's* 126: UFOlogists have warned about the danger of repeating the historic boo-boo of the French Academy about 1800 in failing to recognize that stones could fall from the sky. **1970** Calley & Sack *Lieut. Calley* 17: I have pride in America.…Sure, it has many flaws. It has made booboos, if you would call them that. **1973** M. Collins *Carrying the Fire* 220: One little boo-boo at this stage of the game and all the oxygen will depart my suit and I will die. **1980** *N.Y. Daily News* (Dec. 20) 29: It appears to me that Steinbrenner has made another boo-boo. **1988** Shoemaker & Nagler *Shoemaker* 73: I had made a big, big booboo.

3. a minor bruise, injury, or blemish.

1954–60 *DAS*: *Boo-boo*…A minor flesh wound. *Limited to children's use.* **1968** Baker et al. *CUSS* 85: *Boo-boo*. A pimple. **1983** *N.Y. Post* (Sept. 2) 72: Jerry Butler missed preseason with nagging booboos. **1970** La Motta, Carter & Savage *Raging Bull* 228: Well, now…whaddaya know. Champ Pimp got himself another boo-boo. *a***1984** in Safire *Stand Corrected* 258: At least as early as 1950, California high school students referred to a facial blemish—pimple, acne, or whatever—as a "booboo."

boo-boo *v.* to blunder.

1961 L. Sanders *4-Yr. Hitch* 70: Waiting for one to booboo and move. **1978** *Rolling Stone* (Jan. 26) 7: Boy, oh, boy, did Chet Flippo boo-boo. *****a***1981** *Macquarie Dict.*: *Boo-boo*…*v.i.* to make an error.

boob trap *n.* an establishment that cheats or overcharges its patrons; CLIP JOINT.

1925 S. Lewis *Arrowsmith* ch. xxiv: I suppose this Rouncefield Clinic is nothing but a gilded boob-trap—scare the poor millionaire into having all the…treatments the traffic will bear. **1937** in Galewitz *Great Comics* 121: So this is the boob trap Lord Plushbottom paid $30,000$^{\underline{00}}$ for. **1941** in Galewitz *Great Comics* 123: To let me…take you out to these boob traps and the races and ever'thing. **1954–60** *DAS: Boob trap.* A nightclub.

boob tube *n.* television; a television set.

1963 W.C. Anderson *Penelope* 110: Ah…can find out a lot about you humans by watchin' yo' boob tube. **1965** Hersey *Too Far to Walk* 188: It had never been remotely like this on the boob tube. **1966** Mission Control (Houston) to Gemini 12 spacecraft (Nov.): Smile! You're on the boob tube! **1969** *Playboy* (Mar.) 30: A brief but effective satire on the visual chewing gum that's telecast on the boob tube. **1970** Abigail Van Buren *Dear Abby* (synd. column) (May 16): "Drop ins" are persons whom we never invite because almost anything the boob tube has to offer is preferable to their company. **1992** *N.Y. Times* (June 24) A 20: As if the boob tube were some satanic fruit…in our Eden of clear thinking.

booby[1] *n.* usu. *pl.* [var. of syn. BUBBY] a woman's breast.

1916 in Wentworth *ADD* 79. **1934** H. Miller *Trop. Cancer* 111: At ten o'clock she was lying on the divan with her boobies in her hands. **1938** "Justinian" *Americana Sexualis* 13: *Booby. n.* Teat. Generally used in the plural, "boobies." C. 19-20 euphemism for the vulgarism "tit." **1956** Holiday & Dufty *Lady Sings Blues* 95: You can be up to your boobies in white satin. **1961** T.I. Rubin *In Life* 26: Okay looking, but not great: big boobies, though, a good walk. **1961** in Barthelme *Caligari* 3: The new girl's boobies are like my secretary's knees, very prominent and irritating. **1963** Horwitz *Candlelight* 171: Her boobies are the most magnificent teats in Britain. **1969** Marsh & Liston *Centerfold* 4: Female breasts or, as the parlance goes, boobies. **1974** E. Thompson *Tattoo* 228: Dolores…would sometimes let them play with her boobies. **1992** *L.A. Law* (NBC-TV): I'm glad you like smart girls. *I* like big boobies.

booby[2] *n.* **1.** [fr. BOOBY HATCH, 1] a jail; a lockup.—also used attrib.

1919 Darling *Jargon Bk.* 5: *Booby Hack*—A police wagon. **1924** Hecht & Bodenheim *Cutie* 46: They had you stretched out on the curbing waiting for the booby wagon. **1929** G. Milburn *Hobo's Hornbk.* 150: Judge Grimes…called the constable,/Who tossed us in the booby, and took away our mule. **1938 in OEDS: Booby or Booby Hutch,* the cells.

2. *Army.* an explosive booby trap.

1975 S.P. Smith *Amer. Boys* 160 [ref. to Vietnam War]: Punjis and boobies. Pretty slow.

booby *v. Mil.* to equip with an explosive booby trap.

1943 *Yank* (Sept. 17) 3: They…inched their hands underneath to see if it was "boobied"—that is, if it would explode when they lifted it up. **1977** Natkin & Furie *Boys in Co. C* (film): It could be mined! The whole place could be boobied!

booby hatch *n.* **1.** a police station or jail.

1859 Matsell *Vocabulum* 13: *Booby-Hatch.* Station-house; watch-house. **1866** *Nat. Police Gaz.* (Nov. 17) 3: The Dutchman went to the "booby hatch." **1894** F.P. Dunne, in Schaaf *Dooley* 158: They have him put away in th' booby hatch fr assault with intint to dhrive a pickax into Sarsfield Casey's back. **1897** Ade *Pink Marsh* 114: She'd tell somebody else an' they'd have him in the booby-hatch in about two hours. **1905** *Nat. Police Gaz.* (Dec. 23) 3: The one that's pinched and in the booby hatch now. **1912** *Hampton's Mag.* (Jan.) 842: I'd been in this booby hatch a couple of days. **1919** Darling *Jargon Bk.* 5: *Booby Hatch*—A police station. **1925** G. Mullin *Scholar Tramp* 130: While we was goin' to the booby-hatch together, I gave him such spiel that he…turned me loose. **1938** "R. Hallas" *You Play the Black* 204: And don't come back…[or] you'll be sent up to the booby hatch for a rest cure. **1968–70** in *DARE.*

2. an insane asylum or psychiatric hospital.

1896 F.P. Dunne, in Schaaf *Dooley* 242: They're crazy, plumb daffy, Jawnny. In this whole City iv Chicago there ain't wan hundhred silver men that cuddent give post-graduate insthructions to th' inmates iv th' booby hatch out at Dunning. **1907** in H.C. Fisher *A. Mutt* 6: Hither, dippy one, to the booby hatch. **1908** in Blackbeard & Williams *Smithsonian Comics* 58: The state paid all expenses in the booby hatch and…the boobs were fed regularly. **1917** in S. Lewis *Selected Short Stories* 225: That's a private booby hatch. Maybe they got swell rooms, but I don't want to be stowed away with a bunch of nuts. **1918** *N.Y. Eve.*

Jour. (Aug. 7) 16: "This here sugar shortage is gonna make me a millionaire!" "Booby-hatch next stop." **1923** *Time* (Mar. 10) 15: Liane['s]…specialty is driving lover after lover to ruin, death, or the booby-hatch. **1930** Bodenheim *Roller Skates* 184: Let's both stay in the booby-hatch. Which padded cell are you gonna have? **1937** Steinbeck *Mice & Men* 79: They'll take ya to the booby hatch. They'll tie ya up with a collar, like a dog. **1942** in F. Brown *Angels & Spaceships* 49: Tell anybody? And get locked in a booby hatch? Not me. **1978** Clark & Coleman *Creatures of the Outer Edge* 21: These things…are not supposed to exist, and to say that one has seen them…is to identify oneself as ripe for the booby hatch. **1980** J. Carroll *Land of Laughs* 106: Fletcher was in the booby hatch for three years. **1981** C. Nelson *Picked Bullets Up* 74: A hoochmate who supervises the booby hatch has offered me an apprenticeship there.

booby house *n.* **1.** BOOBY HATCH, 2.

1899 A.H. Lewis *Sandburrs* 26: If it wasn't for d' hop I shoots into him wit' a dandy little hypodermic gun me Rag's got, he'd be in d' booby house. **1911** A.H. Lewis *Apaches of N.Y.* 206: I for one shall retire to th' booby house an' devote th' remainder of an ill-spent life to cuttin' paper dolls.

2. BOOBY HATCH, 1.

1968 in *DARE.*

booby hutch *n.* BOOBY HATCH.

1889 Barrère & Leland *Dict. Slang* I 161: *Booby-hutch* (thieves), the police-station. **1926** Nichols & Tully *Twenty Below* 10: I never saw such a dam booby hutch. **1938* in *OEDS: Booby-hutch,* the cells.

booby wagon *n.* PADDY WAGON.

1967 in *DARE.*

boocoodles var. BOOKOODLES.

Boochie *n. Japanese E.* a Japanese.

1945 in Shibutani *Co. K* 104: It's tough enough to be a Boochie. *Ibid.* 288: I figured the Boochies wouldn't like the Nisei.

boodle[1] *n.* [< Du *boedel* 'estate; property'; def. **(1)** reflects a direct application of the Dutch word]

1. the effects (of a deceased person).

1699 in R.M. Lederer *Colonial Amer. Eng.* 34: Elisabeth had the Boedel of Jan Verbeck, desceased [sic], in hands.

2.a. a crowd or pack (of individual persons or things).—usu. constr. with *whole.*

1827 in *JAF* LXXVI (1963) 289: He…turnd out the hol boodle ov um. **1833** in [S. Smith] *Letters of Downing* 108: He'd fight the whole boodle of 'em. **1858** Holmes *Autocrat Breakfast Table* 139: He would like to have the whole *boodle* of them (I remonstrated against this word, but the professor said it was a diabolical good word…) with their wives and children shipwrecked on a remote island. **1884** in *F & H* I 288: At eleven o'clock the "whole *boodle* of them," as Uncle Nahum called the caravan…had to boot and spur for church. **1929** *N.Y. Sunday News* (Nov. 3): *Boodle* means a lot of anything. **1961** G. Forbes *Goodbye to Some* 184: A whole boodle of them!

b. *Und.* booty; loot.

1848 [G. Thompson] *House Breaker* 6: Let us have a room…where we can *ogle the boodle* and *reg up.**…***Let us have a room…where we can examine the booty, and divide the spoils. **1851** [G. Thompson] *Jack Harold* 60: I…began to rob and steal,/And when I made the boodle,* oh! how proud I used to feel!…**Boodle,* booty. **1886** *Chi. Trib.* (Mar. 2) 10: As long as I got the boodle I didn't care what they wanted to run the sharp in for. **1887** (cited in Partridge *Dict. Und.* 62). **1921** A. Jennings *Through Shadows* 50: I had an idea it would take two men to carry the boodle.

c. the contents of a cache.

1961 Ellison *Gentleman Junkie* 40: He was convinced that if she had a boodle somewhere—He would never find it. **1984** Univ. Tenn. student: A *boodle* is a stash.

d. Esp. *Stu.* a parcel of snack foods and the like, or the contents of such a parcel; sweets.

1900 *Howitzer* (U.S. Mil. Acad.) I 117: *Boodle*—Contraband articles which satiate the appetite; as, tobacco, confectionery, etc. **1904** *Howitzer* (U.S. Mil. Acad.) V 220: Boodle—Contraband and unauthorized eatables and drinkables. **1934** Wohlforth *Tin Soldiers* 61: Lay off candy and cigarettes and other boodle. **1936** *Nat. Geographic* 778: Cake, candy, ice cream, and other illicit eatables are "boodle." **1955** Graziano & Barber *Somebody Up There* 39: Their families would…bring them "boodles"—packages with candy, a cake, salami, or maybe a sweater or some low shoes. **1961** A.J. Roth *Shame of Wounds* 60: "The visitors come at one with boodles." "What's a boodle?" "Stuff from home, like candy and bananas and stuff. Some kids even get butts." **1978** Truscott *Dress Gray* 123: "Boodle"...was cadet slang for candy.

3. *Und.* **a.** a parcel or quantity of counterfeit banknotes.

1845 *Nat. Police Gaz.* (Dec. 6) 125: This is among the first issue of a new budget or "boodle," and the public will do well to be on their guard against the above bills. **1846** *Nat. Police Gaz.* (Feb. 21) 209: A large "boodle" of spurious notes. **1859** Matsell *Vocab.* 13: *Boodle.* A quantity of bad money. **1892** L. Moore *Own Story* 57: I always kept a boodle in stock, ready to put on the market at a moment's notice. *Ibid.* 60: He had printed a large boodle in the Prescott Bank.

b. counterfeit banknotes.

1858 *Harper's Wkly.* (Apr. 3) 222: "Boodle" is a flash term used by counterfeiters....The leaders were the manufacturers and bankers of the "boodle." **1872** Burnham *Secret Service* iv: *Boodle*, counterfeit notes, placed in bundles or parcels....*Boodle-carriers*, the bearers and sellers of "boodle" funds. **1889** Barrère & Leland *Dict. Slang* I 161: *Boodle* This word in the United States is applied among thieves only to counterfeit or bad money.

c. a roll of banknotes; BUNDLE.

1884 in *DAE*: *Boodle*...has come to mean a large roll of bills such as political managers are supposed to divide among their retainers. *a*1890 *F & H* I 289: *Fake-boodle* (American thieves).—A roll of paper, over which, after folding, a dollar bill is pasted, and another bill being wrapped round this it looks as if the whole roll is made of...bills. *ca*1894 McCloskey *Across Continent* 81: There was a young fellow coming in the opposite direction with a big boodle of money....How big? A boodle? A New York boodle? No—bigger than that. Almost as big as a Chicago boodle. **1894** *Harper's* (Dec.) 104: I've got a chance to make a big boodle. **1940** D.W. Maurer, in *AS* (Apr.) 116: *Boodle.* A bank-roll made up to resemble the *mark's* money. **1956** Gold *Not With It* 194: He had lost the swell primping and posings of the carnie with a boodle in his pocket. **1965–70** in *DARE*.

4. money or profits; (*specif.*) money used for or obtained through graft. Also attrib.

1884 in *OED*: "Sinews of war," and "living issues," "soap," and other synonyms for campaign boodle are familiar. **1885** *Puck* (Apr. 29) 138: I hit 'em heavy, and after getting the boodle, went East to have a hurrah. **1887** DeVol *Gambler* 55: We divided the boodle that he had brought with him. **1888** in *F & H* I 289: Go in hot for making money....Don' you do noding vot's grooked...Aber rake right in dot boodle. **1888** *Phila. Bulletin* (Feb. 24): The best man in the world cannot make an honest living by being a City Councilman. The office is an unsalaried one, and any money that is made out of it is boodle. This is the new term for plunder, fraud, and every form of stealing that can be practised by office-holders. **1889** S.A. Bailey *Ups & Downs* 11 [ref. to 1871]: I called to see Mickey, and put him in the way of raising some boodle, but he is out. *Ibid.* 42: I asked him...how he was fixed in regard to boodle. As I supposed, he said he was strapped, and I loaned him $5. *a*1890 *F & H* I 289: Some elections cannot be conducted without *boodle* first and last....*Boodle* is money used for purposes of bribery and corruption; and the same word is used to indicate the money that comes as spoils, the result of some secret deal, the profits of which are silently divided. The term is likewise used to cover the ill-gotten gains of the bank-robber, or the absconding cashier. **1891** McCann & Jarrold *Odds & Ends* 35: He never spent any of his boodle. **1891** in Smith & Smith *Police Gazette* 127: Champion Tonsorialists Clipping for Boodle and Glory. **1894** *Century* (Feb.) 518: Don't ye want boodle, booze, togs, and a good livin'? **1895** Townsend *Chimmie Fadden* 19: Say, me name's Dennis, an' not Chimmie Fadden; if dem folks up dere ain't got boodle ter burn a wet dog wid. **1898** Atherton *Californians* 33: I've a pocket full of boodle; papa gave me my allowance today. **1906** Buffum *Bear City* 244: Boodle is more convincing than evidence. *a*1904–11 Phillips *Susan Lenox* I 289: The boys with the boodle'll flock in. **1939** "E. Queen" *Dragon's Teeth* 94: Giving up the old boodle for lo-o-ove. **1942** in *DA*: *Boodle, n.* ordinary money with no implication of graft. **1946** Gresham *Nightmare Alley* 218: The convincer boodle did the trick, babe. **1958** "Traver" *Anat. of Murder* 208: The Lord knows what his slice of the boodle will be. **1966** King *Brave & Damned* 266: Working stiffs who had bundles of boodle in their mitts and a great dryness in their throat. **1970** *Playboy* (Apr.) 174: It's the greedy guy who wants to get his hands on your boodle who's the easiest target for a hustle. **1973** *Playboy* (June) 24: For a long time Serpico was reluctant to blow the whistle on his boodle-chasing colleagues. **1985** *N.Y. Post* (Mar. 20) 68: They see the NCAA cleaning up from TV boodle. **1992** N. Cohn *Heart of World* 308: Jimmy Walker was mayor, and boodle was in bloom.

boodle[2] *n.* [alter. of BOOTY] the vagina.

1980 *Nat. Lampoon* (Dec.) 33: I mean their pimps are always abusing them and pouring toilet-bowl cleaner in their boodles.

boodle *adj. Und.* being a jail where the jailers are amenable to bribes.—used prenominally.

1910 Livingston *Life:* The county jail is a "boodle proposition."...They have these boodle jails all over the United States....They fine you thirty dollars and thirty days; you can't pay the thirty dollars but the judge gets one dollar a day for every day you are supposed to be locked up. **1930** "D. Stiff" *Milk & Honey* 200: *Boodle jail*—A jail that may be worked for a good winter's lodging. **1980** Bruns *Kts. of Road* 52: American boodle jails, the stiffs called them.

boodle *v.* **1.** to engage in graft. Cf. BOODLER, 2.

1890 in *DA.* **1892** Garland *Spoil of Office* 258: If the voter is a boodler, he will countenance boodling. **1904** in *DA*: If you're going to boodle, you've got to do it on a party basis.

2. *Stu.* to neck.

1947 *ATS* (Supp.) 8: "Necking"...boodling. **1975** *DAS* (ed. 3): *Boodle*...[to] neck....Collegiate use c1915.

boodle bag *n.* [cf. BOODLE, *n.*, 2.d.] a small pouch for money, worn esp. around the neck.

1927 W. Winchell, in *Vanity Fair* (Nov.) 134: "The Grouch bag," or "boodle bag" is the purse that actors wear pinned to the underclothing. **1935** Watters & Hopkins *Burlesque* 36: I'm always goin' to keep this boodle bag. **1950** in *DARE*.

boodle fight *n.* [cf. BOODLE, *n.*, 2.d.] *U.S. Mil. Acad.* a small party at which unauthorized snacks are consumed.

1928 Dolph *Sound Off* 579: Gone were the good old days when drills ceased at noon and a cadet could lounge in his tent or attend a "boodle fight" on contraband sweets.

boodler *n.* **1.** a counterfeiter; a passer of counterfeit money.

1872 Burnham *Secret Service* 346: Numbers of men...had been approached by these "boodlers." *a*1890 *F & H* I 290: *Boodlers* and shovers are the men who issue false money.

2. *Pol.* a person, esp. a politician, who seeks or accepts bribes; grafter.

1887 *Chi. Tribune* (May 3) 160: The boodlers met in the lower corridor. **1888** in *F & H* I 290: "We have elections and campaigns, and political parties, and bosses, and ringsters, and boodlers, and—" "Boodlers?...Well, well! Why, you are freemen just like us." **1896** Ade *Artie* 63: He turned out to be a boodler, eh? **1898** Norris *Moran* 227: We're rich—rich as boodlers, you and I! **1902** *N.Y. Eve. Jour.* (Dec. 6) 12: The Alderman who shall then refuse to vote for the franchise will stamp himself a "boodler." **1908** in H.C. Fisher *A. Mutt* 49: Tobasco surprises a brace of boodlers, who have been paid to be surprised. **1957** O'Connor *Co. Q* 92: Boodlers, thieves, cowards, troublemakers, or whatever. **1984** P.J. Buchanan, in *N.Y. Post* (Aug. 31) 33: But whether or not these boodlers are given "input" into spending $30 billion in social programs is our business.

boody var. BOOTY.

booful *adj.* [intentional malapropism, as in baby talk] beautiful. *Joc.*

1905 in J. London *Short Stories* 207: It's just booful. **1910** in J. London *Letters* 311: Your two boo'ful letters! *Ibid.* 313: Another booful letter from you. **1942** *ATS* 38.

boog *n.* (fr. BOOGIE[1], 2] a black person.—used contemptuously.

1937 *Esquire* (July) 80: That boog would never of got me if I hadn't been sick. **1948** J.H. Burns *Lucifer* 146: I've been noticing you're bunghole buddies with the boog in this dump. **1960** Hoagland *Circle Home* 69: Good to see a white man fix a boogie for a change. Nobody's fightin' now but boogs. **1970** Southern *Blue Movie* 205: Those...boogs may turn *cannibal* any minute! **1977** Sayles *Union Dues* 22: Everybody is doing okay, Irish, Poles, the ghinnies even, paddling along, all except the boogs.

boog *v.* **1.** [fr. BUG] *Black E.* to annoy.

1934 in Dixon & Godrich *Blues & Gospel* 100: My Man Is Boogan Me.

2. to BOOGIE.

1936–40 McDonogh *Fla. Negro* 47: I Wonder who is Booging my Woogie Now. **1941** *Life* (Jan. 27) 78: To go booging. **1945** in Bechet *Treat It Gentle* 228: Boogin' with Big Sid Catlett. **1968** A. Myrer *Once an Eagle* 435: Head like a 'gator, Nose like a yam, But when she wants to boog-it, ooh! ooh! hot damn! **1973** Andrews & Owens *Black Lang.* 81: To *boog* is to party.

boogaloo *n.* [elaboration of BOOGIE; see note at v.] a black person.—used contemptuously.

1974 Miami Univ. student: A *boogaloo* is a nigger. **1974** Univ. Tenn. student: A coon is also a *boogaloo*. **1981** *Nat. Lampoon* (Sept.) 51: No boogaloos is an instant thing you notice in Switzerland.

¶ In phrase:

¶ **put the boogaloo on** (see quot.).

1972 Casey *Obscenities* 14: We gotta put the boogaloo/On headquarters-one-five…[footnote] *put the boogaloo on:* hassle, give trouble to.

boogaloo *v.* (see quots.). [This and the other uses of the word have all been influenced—and in this case inspired—by the dance of this name, popular in the mid-1960's.]

1971 Dahlskog *Dict.* 9: *Boogaloo, v.* To fool around. **1983** *Reader's Digest Success with Words* 84: Black English…boogaloo = (1) "to dance" (2) "to fool around."

booger[1] *n.* [orig., regional Brit. pronun. of BUGGER] **1.** BUGGER; BASTARD (in all senses). See also BUGGER, *n.*

*__1708__ in D'Urfey *Pills* I 59: From ev'ry Trench the bougers fly. *__1709__ in D'Urfey *Pills* I 161: But these Bougers…riot on each small Occasion. **1770** in R.M. Lederer, Jr. *Colonial Eng.* 34: Where were the boogers, where were the cowards? **1811** in Howay *New Hazard* 37: He…called us thieves, country boogars, infernal scoundrels. **1813** in Howay *New Hazard* 121: Knock the boogar stiff with a…hammer. **1850** in *Mo. Hist. Soc. Bull.* VI (1949) 14: And then an old "booger"…will only give them tolerable good marks…to try to stimulate them still more. **1932** in Randolph *Pissing in Snow* 14: The little booger put the bucket on my head. **1934** Weseen *Dict. Slang* 311: *Boogers*—Mischievous children; lice. **1936** in Ruhm *Detective* 173: You're sure a tall booger. **1939** Thompson *Body, Boots & Britches* 69: Out, you black booger! **1912–43** *Frank Brown Collection* I 521: *Booger*…A friendly term applied to some object previously named. "I ran back and climbed that *booger* [a flagpole]." **1954** Arnow *Dollmaker* 151: Don't you go fallen off my lap, yo little ol booger, you. **1956** in *DARE*. **1978** Univ. Tenn. student: That paper's gonna be a booger. **1983** in Kaplan & Smith *One Last Look* 27: The air force physical exam was supposed to be a real booger and I doubted I could pass it.

2. *So.* copulation with a woman; PUSSY.

1959 Groninger *Run from Mtn.* 13: If you ain't married and need a little bugger, you go down to Macon Ridge, where there's a cathouse. **1983** K. Weaver *Texas Crude* 71: In Texas there are three gradations of Sexual Woman. Number one is Cock….Number two is Booger….Number three is Pussy.

booger[2] *n.* [prob. fr. *bogey* infl. by BUGGER] a particle of nasal mucus.

1891 *DN* I 214. **1908** *DN* III 292: *Booger*…A dried flake of mucus from the nose: used of children. **1968** L.J. Davis *Whence All Had Fled* 169: Complete strangers looked at him like he had a disgusting booger hanging from his nose. **1972** Kellogg *Lion's Tooth* 8: Clearing a booger out of his nose. **1974** Carter *16th Round* 36: He picked a booger out of his nose. **1980** *Nat. Lampoon* (Oct.) 48: Then I'd leave a big booger on the mouthpiece of the phone and go to bed. **1984** *TriQuarterly* (Spring) 307: Pushed closed one nostril and snotted out a gob of boogers on your seat.

booger[1] *v.* to shy or panic (as a horse or cow). Also **bugger**. Hence **boogered**, *adj.* frightened.

1893 in *DARE*. **1896** *DN* I 413. **1902** Clapin *Americanisms* 67: *Booger.* In parts of New York, to shy, be frightened. That horse *boogers* a little at dogs. **1905** *DN* 71: "He *boogers.*" Used of a skittish horse [in Arkansas]. **1928** Dobie *Vaquero* 253 [ref. to 1880's]: Amos' horses …"boogered" at every chance sight or sound. **1936** in Botkin *West. Folk.* 486: This herd had been buggering and running from everything. **1942** *ATS* 841: *Boogered,* afraid, buffaloed. **1962** McMurtry *Cheyenne* 120: My horse buggered at a damn skunk and off I went. **1968** S.O. Barker *Rawhide Rhymes* 126: But if a horse is fit to ride, it don't make no sense to booger him. **1970** in *DARE*: Boogered. **1970** Longstreet *Nell Kimball* 48: I'd wander around the town, getting over being scare-boogered. **1977** Watts *Dict. Old West* 40: *Booger.* To scare; sometimes to be scared.

booger[2] *v.* to BUGGER (in all senses). See also BOOGER OFF, ——— UP.

1908 *DN* III 292: *Booger*…Occasionally used in the sense of *bugger.* **1942** McAtee *Supp. to Grant Co. Dial. in '90's* 3: *Bugger* (rhyming with sugar), v., copulate *per ano.* **1951** [VMF-323] *Old Ballads* 6: The bung of the hedgehog, the hedgehog/Can scarcely be boogered at all. **1965** W. Crawford *Bronc Rider* 98: "Really bugged, huh?" "So goddamned boogered I can't even think straight."

boogering *adj.* damned; FRIGGING.

1963–64 Kesey *Great Notion* 37: Son of a gun, *look* at the boogerin' stuff! *Ibid.* 100: That damned menagerie in the goddam boogering cat cage.

booger off *v.* [var. pronun. BUGGER OFF; cf. BOOGER[1], *v.*] Esp. *USAF.* to flee.

1946 G.C. Hall, Jr. *1000 Destroyed* 151: They boogar off and don't protect the bombers like we do. **1955** *AS* XXX 116: *Bug Out; Booger Off; Leap Off*…Leave suddenly and rapidly. [USAF]. **1956** Heflin *USAF Dict.: Booger off.* To bug out.

booger up *v.* to BUGGER UP.

1930 in *AS* (Feb. 1931) 230: *Boogered up.* Battered, spoiled, damaged. After the accident we found that the car was all boogered up. **1968** R. Adams *West. Words* (ed. 2): *Boogered up.* A cowboy's expression meaning *crippled.*

boogery *adj.* *West.* jumpy.

1947 Overholser *Buckaroo's Code* 157: I was kind o' boogery there for a minute. **1952** Overholser *Fab. Gunman* 67: So boogery you couldn't think straight.

boogie[1] *n.* [var. pronun. of *bogey*] **1.** a particle of nasal mucus.

1890 *DN* I 18: *Boogie*…ball of mucus in the nose. **1902** Clapin *Americanisms* 67: *Boogie.* Ball of mucus in the nose. A term mostly restricted to school children. **1970** N.Y.U. student: A piece of snot is called a *boogie,* not a *booger.* Everybody knows that.

2. a black person.—used contemptuously.

1923 in *OEDS*. **1926** *AS* (Sept.) 650: *Boogie*—A negro. **1928** Fisher *Jericho* 13: This boogy…thinks he's bad. **1929** Hammett *Dain Curse* 212: Minnie was ripe for it—poor boogie. **1937** E. Hemingway *To Have & Have Not* 209: One morning I seen that big boogie there mopping it up with a bucket. **1945** Drake & Cayton *Black Metro.* 144: You know, that thing called love is great. But I don't think I could ever marry a boogie (Negro). **1968** P. Roth *Portnoy* 197: She was with some boogey. **1969** R. Pharr *Bk. of Numbers* 165: There's more crackers get invited to the White House than boogies, see what I mean?

3. [cf. BOOGIE HOUSE] **a.** *Black E.* a sexually promiscuous woman.

1957 Traill & Lascelles *Just Jazz* 13: A "boogie," of course, is a "bad girl."

b. the vagina.

1969 *Zap Comix 4* (unp.): When I start sneezin' my boogie starts to ooze. **1971** S.C. Wilson *Bent* (unp.): That filthy slut has slivers in 'er boogie. **1986** Merkin *Zombie Jamboree* 105: Viet Cong whores put razor blades up their boogies.

4. *Black E.* energy; animation.

1980 "Treacherous Three" in L.A. Stanley *Rap* 356: Put the Boogie in Your Body. **1981** J. Spicer, in L.A. Stanley *Rap* 301: Money puts the boogie in the stock exchange.

boogie[2] *n.* [prob. fr. POGEY] *Pris.* a prison hospital.

1926 Tully *Jarnegan* 31: The "big house" was the penitentiary itself. The hospital was the "boogie." A "screw" was a guard. The "big screw" was the deputy warden. **1927** *DN* V 439: *Boogie, n.* (1) The prison hospital.

boogie[3] *n.* see BOOGIE-WOOGIE, *n.*

1929 in Dixon & Godrich *Blues & Gospel* 213: Pitchin' Boogie. *Ibid.* 280: Guitar Boogie.

boogie *v.* **1.** to dance (to swing, rock 'n' roll, etc.); to celebrate, as at a wild party.—since *ca*1976, also constr. with *down.*

1947 *ATS* (Supp.) 8: *Boog, boogie, jive, jump*…To "cut a rug." **1955** in Gold *Jazz Lex.* 30: Oh let's boogie, children. **1955–57** Kerouac *On the Road* 72: We'll hitch-hike to New York….Come on man, let's do it. "If you can't boogie I know I'll show you how." That last part was a song of hers she kept singing. **1973** *Oui* (Apr.) 67: Throngs of young ritzies pay to boogie sedately on the stainless-steel floor. **1980** Univ. Tenn. student: Mondays are a bitch when you been out boogyin' all weekend. **1980** in Safire *Good Word* 216: "Boogie down" is used to say, "Hey, let's dance!" **1981** *Nat. Lampoon* (Nov.) 78: Tomorrow I'll bring over my Don Ho albums and we'll all boogie down.

2. to copulate. Also *trans.*

1960 in Oster *Country Blues* 298: Yeah, I got the blues, baby, feel like boogyin' all the time./I got a good-lookin' gal, but she don't pay me no mind. *__1979__ (cited in Partridge *DSUE* (ed. 8) 116). **1982** *Nat. Lampoon* (Sept.) 16: Would Ronnie be averse to being boogied…during his…speech?…It would assure Ronnie the gay vote. **1992** Randolph & Legman *Blow Candle Out* 682: *Boogie,* to fuck, probably from "booger," bugger.

3. [pop. by John Hartford's song "Baby, Let's Boogie" (1974)] to get going, get busy; to get to work, do business; to go, esp. in a hurry.

1972 B. Rodgers *Queens' Vernacular* 35: *Boogie*…to work hard, to slave. **1974** Univ. Tenn. student: Let's get out of here. Let's boogie. **1976** J.W. Thomas *Heavy Number* 107: It ain't going to take long for that jet to boogy out here. **1978** Maupin *Tales* 222: We'll just boogie on down to The Palms. **1980** *N.Y. Times* (Aug. 10) 36: There are a lot of people who've never been through a hurricane.…The word is—boogie on out. **1980** G.F. Will, in *N.Y. Daily News* (Sept. 10) 19: When a Communist deepthinker is really ready to get down and boogie, out comes the key concept: dialectics. **1980** Wielgus & Wolff *Basketball* 39: *Boogie* (v.) To drive [on a basketball court]. **1982** "J. Cain" *Commandos* 256: Well, he boogies off into the blizzard. **1983** Breathed *Bloom Co.* 119: Prepare my transportation! Let's boogie! **1985** *Miami Vice* (NBC-TV): Make it fifty and we boogie. **1990** C.P. McDonald *Blue Truth* 44: It was day shift…and…[we] were ready to boogie.

boogie house *n.* [prob. fr. BOOGIE[1], *n.*, 3.a., even though this is not attested until much later] *Black E.* a whorehouse. Also **boogie joint**.

1930 Huston *Frankie & Johnny* 106: Boogie-joints and bucket-shops opened up on Twelfth, Carr, Targee, and Pine Streets [in St. Louis]. **1931** Bontemps *Sends Sunday* [40: In the boogie places where he sometimes went with his cronies he slapped the teeth out of the strumpets who disgusted him.] *Ibid.* 50: Tha's a ole boogie-house song. **1957** Traill & Lascelles *Just Jazz* 13: Brothels were called "boogie houses" in many parts of the old South. *a*1973 in Bontemps *Old South* 49: You ain't got no cause to be hanging around saloons, much less trying to hear boogie house music.

boogie-joogie *n.* **1.** *Black E.* boogie-woogie music.
1957 Simmons *Corner Boy* 143: Kenny liked boogie-joogie.
2. *Black E.* trickery; nonsense.
*ca*1974 in J.L. Gwaltney *Drylongso* xv: Boogie-joogie—nonsense, trickery. *Ibid.* 19: I get tired of that one-nation-under-God boogie-joogie.

boogie-woogie *n.* [cf. BOOGIE[3]] *Black E.* (see 1942, 1958 quots.). [The relationship between these senses and the S.E. sense 'a style of jazz music' remains problematical.]
1935 in Dixon & Godrich *Blues & Gospel* 216: Let's Pitch A Boogie Woogie. **1936–40** McDonogh *Fla. Negro* 47: Just what the meaning of "Boogie-Woogie" is must be left untold; no one could be found who knew the exact meaning of the words, but for several years songs using them in their titles have been popular. **1942** Z.N. Hurston, in *Amer. Mercury* (July) 94: *Boogie-woogie.…*For years in the South, it meant secondary syphilis. **1946** Mezzrow & Wolfe *Really Blues* 60: Al pitched a boogie-woogie over Mitzi's romance. **1958** Hughes & Bontemps *Negro Folklore* 486: *Pitch a Boogie-Woogie*: Raise sand; fuss; quarrel violently. His wife pitched a boogie-woogie when he wasn't home for dinner.

boogie-woogie *v. Jazz.* (see quot.).
1938 *AS* (Apr.) 151: *Boogy-woogy.* To enjoy oneself to the limit.

booging *adj.* BOOGERING.
1963–64 Kesey *Great Notion* 88: He don't need good ears to know where to draw the boogin' line. *Ibid.* 152: What the boogin' devil you *talkin'*?

boojie *n.* [orig. unkn.; cf. BOO[3], 1] *Narc.* a marijuana cigarette.
1939 C.R. Cooper *Scarlet* 147: Houston, Texas, [is] another center for "muggles," "reefers," "Indian hay," "Boojies," or "Mary Anns," as marihuana cigarettes are known.

boojie or **boojy** /'buʒi/ *adj.* [fr. *bourgeois*] *Black E.* bourgeois; offensively middle-class; elitist. Also as *n.*
1970 Major *Dict. Afro-Am. Sl.* 30: *Boojy:* bourgeois. **1977** Smitherman *Talkin & Testifyin* 251: *Boojy*, an adjective, derived from *bourgeoisie*, referring to elitist blacks whose money and position make them think they're white. **1967–80** Folb *Runnin' Lines* 230: *Boojie*…Bourgeois black person. *a*1986 R. Price, in *NDAS*: Exaggerating the slumminess of the tenements and playing down the boojy trappings of our apartment. **1992** *AS* LXVII 351: African-American terms (*bougies, homies*, [etc.]). **1993** *Martin* (Fox-TV): Stop tryin' to turn me into a boojie snob like your father. *Ibid.:* Instead of going to some boojie museum.

book *n.* **1.** *Gamb.* a pack of playing cards. Also pl.
1706 in F & H (rev.) 327: Clean cards here.…Burn this book, 't has an unlucky air. Bring some more books. **1811 *Lexicon Balatron.*: Books, Cards to play with. *To plant the books;* to place the cards in the pack in an unfair manner. **1853 W.G. Simms *Sword & Distaff* 241: "Hev you

any *books*?" Books meant cards in the vernacular of the forest. **1889** Barrère & Leland *Dict. Slang* I 162: *Books* (card players), a pack of cards. **a*1909 *F & H* I (rev.) 327: *Books*…A pack of cards: used mainly by professional card-players.
2.a. BOOKIE.
1898–1900 Cullen *Chances* 16: The books give them the cold-storage countenance and say, "Nix, no more." **1907** in H.C. Fisher *A. Mutt* 3: I wanta get this [bet] on before the books get wise. **1931** Wilstach *Under Cover Man* 81: A thick-set, white-haired "book" noticed Brownie's entrance. **1939** C.R. Cooper *Scarlet* 132: Joe the Book—he was the guy who shot that fellow last year. **1965** Yurick *Warriors* 79: Why don't they patronize Your Neighborhood Book? **1972** Wambaugh *Blue Knight* 69: What's a guy get for bookmaking?…You ever see a book get joint time?
b. a bookmaker's business.
1911–12 Ade *Knocking the Neighbors* 180: The down-town Books were being raided. **1949** W.R. Burnett *Asphalt Jungle* 140: You've always been a good boy—except for running a book. **1954** Chessman *Cell 2455* 291: I had been associated with an individual engaged in closing down the "books" (places where illegal wagering is done on horse races) of a competitor.
3. Orig. *Pris. & Police.* **a.** the maximum sentence for wrongdoing; (*hence*) all charges that can possibly be lodged.—esp. in such phr. as **throw the book at.**
1908 Hopper & Bechdolt *9009* 7: "You'll wish they'd handed you the book and you'd been hung," he snarled; "Ye'll wish that more'n once before ye've croaked in this mill." **1927** *DN* V 448: *Give one the book, v.* To give a convicted person the maximum penalty. **1933** D. Runyon, in *Collier's* (Dec. 23) 8: The judge throws the book at him when he finally goes to bat. **1940** in H. Gray *Arf* (unp.): What? Bribery, gambling, harboring criminals—the whole book, eh? Are you certain you have enough proof? **1941** in Fenner *Throttle* 183: A very good performance…but they'll throw the book at you for it. **1944** C.B. Davis *Leo McGuire* 208: I was out on parole there and they'd throw the book at me. **1946** Gardner *Backward Mule* 180: They'll throw the book at you even if you could fight free on the other charge. **1948** Webb *Four Steps* 49: He's here for ninety-nine years.…The judge…gave Pete the book. **1948** A. Murphy *Hell & Back* 67: "I'll report you," he screams. "You'll get the book." **1954** Davis & Lay *Strategic Air Command* (film): You know, I ought to throw the book at you. **1955** Q. Reynolds *HQ* 153: So we have to throw the book at you. You might have got away with a five-to-ten. **1982** D.J. Williams *Hit Hard* 112: Move one inch outside this barracks until authorized and I will hit you with the…book. **1986** R. Campbell *In La-La Land* 20: Five'll get you twenty they'll drop the book on you.
b. *Specif.*, a sentence of life imprisonment.—constr. with *the.*
1920 Murphy *Gray Walls* 15 [ref. to Idaho State Pen., 1915]: The Judge gave you the "book" (meaning life term) didn't he? **1926** *Writer's Mo.* (Dec.) 541: *Doing the Book*—Life imprisonment. **1927–28** Tasker *Grimhaven* 11: Well, I'm doing one life jolt, and two one-fiftys, and one twenty-to-forty—yes sir, doing the book and twenty-two to a hundred and forty on top of it. **1932** Berg *Prison Doctor* 48: "How much time have you got?"…"A three spot. But I'm a three time loser. Next time it might be the book." **1934** Cunningham *Triggernometry* 348: "Doing the book" in Santa Fé. **1936** Duncan *Over the Wall* 203: Scores of prison-simple men doing the book. **1938** Lawes *Invisible Stripes* 19: I hear they give you the book. **1940** Burnett *High Sierra* 49: I was doing the book, myself.…Life.
4.a. conventional or customary methods; esp. in phr. **throw the book away** to ignore conventional rules, theories, etc.—constr. with *the.* Now *colloq.*
1941 in Fenner *Throttle* 181: Ninety-two's engineer should by the rules have brought his train under control immediately. But they'd thrown the book away on the West End. **1950** Hemingway *Across River* 293: Now we throw away the book and chase for keeps. **1971** Torres *Sting Like a Bee* 38: Ali moves away by walking backward instead of moving to the sides or ducking, which the "book" would call for. **1982** Goff, Sanders & Smith *Brothers* 59: Lotta times the shit hit so fast, the book didn't help. **1988** Mays & Sahadi *Say Hey* 90: But that went against the "book"—the unwritten set of rules which…[said] that you never intentionally put the winning run on first.
b. Esp. *Sports.* accumulated knowledge or experience, esp. about a player's or a team's abilities, performance, etc.; (*hence*) judgment based on experienced observation.
1955 Graziano & Barber *Somebody Up There* 120: Back in the Tombs,

they gave me the book on this joint, Coxackie. **1964** Thompson & Rice *Every Diamond* 142: *The Book:* Information on the strength and weaknesses of other clubs. **1973** Boyd & Harris *Baseball Card* 160: He remained one of the top pitchers in the American League, with one of the most complete books ever seen on the batters he faced. **1983** N.Y.C. man: What's the book on Guidry against left-handed hitters? **1985** E. Leonard *Glitz* 55: You could always deal with guys at the top. But little guys…there was no book on guys like that. **1990** P. Dickson *Slang!* 202: *Book* (basic jock talk)…Data on an opponent.

¶ In phrases:

¶ **everything in the book** [or **books**] everything known or available.

1955–57 Kerouac *On Road* ch. vi: That night Marylou took everything in the books. **1960* in *OEDS:* They'll soak me for defamation of character and everything else in the book.

¶ **for the book** [or **books**] Orig. *Sports.* (of an event) memorable; (*hence*, in wider use) extraordinary.—esp. in phr. **one for the book.**

[**1910** *N.Y. Eve. Jour.* (Apr. 1) 19: It is certainly chronicled in the book—that on the last day of March, 1910, a club of the American League gave a club of the National League one of the worst beatings ever recorded in the annals of Southern training.] **1923** Witwer *Fighting Blood* 170: Gents, this [prizefight] was one for the book! **1934** Berg *Prison Nurse* 115: And you was the mugg that was sticking up for the skirts, too! If that ain't one for the book. **1940** Wexley *City for Conquest* (film): This is really a night for the books. **1942** Epstein & Epstein *Male Animal* (film): What a play that was! The old statue-of-liberty play! That's one for the books! **1949** Pirosh *Battleground* (film): They say the fight they put up was one for the *book.* **1977* T. Jones *Incredible Voyage* 262: Jesus Christ, this was a turn up for the books!

¶ **for the end book** [*end book* the least experienced bookmaker at a racetrack; see D.W. Maurer in *AS* XXI (1946), p. 69]. *Gamb.* (see quot.).

1935 Pollock *Und. Speaks: That's one for the end book*, a statement which is not given credence. **1946** *AS* XXI 69: *That's* one for the end book.

¶ **in my book** "to my way of thinking."

1964 in *OEDS:* In my book, you're still a *putz.* **1978** Maggin *Superman* 25: Listen, pal, anyone who goes out on a limb like that for a perfect stranger is all right in my book. **1980** W.C. Anderson *BAT-21* 187: In my book, Colonel, that's a…hero.

¶ **make book** [**on**] *Gamb.* to be absolutely assured (of something); count on. Also vars.

1949 W.R. Burnett *Asphalt Jungle* 63: Gus knew hundreds of men, but there were only three he'd make book on. **1952** Holmes *Boots Malone* (film): "It's been a long time since you've been in here, Malone." "I'll make book it seems longer to me." **1971** Sorrentino *Up from Never* 3: "Ya think she'll be there now?" "I'd take book on it." **1974** Lahr *Trot* 55: You can lay book on it. I give off a sense of responsibility.

¶ **pull a book** *Stu.* to study intently.

1968 Baker et al. *CUSS* 86: *Book, pull a big.* Work (study) hard and concentratedly.

¶ **throw the book at** see (**3. b.**), above.

¶ **wrote the book** is an expert practitioner. [1906–07 quot. is an unmistakable allusion to this phrase.]

[**1906–07** Ade *Slim Princess* 52: "You have traveled a great deal?"…"Me and Baedeker and Cook wrote it."] **1915** Howard *God's Man* 128: Jealousy? She wrote the book. **1975** Univ. Tenn. instructor: He wrote the book when it comes to dirty tricks.

book *v. Gamb.* **1.** to be a bookmaker; to take bets on.

1956 "T. Betts" *Across the Board* 124: Dollar John booked in the style of Ferrone. **1981** Graziano & Corsel *Somebody Down Here* 29: He's booking horses on the corner. *a*1989 in Kisseloff *Must Remember This* 193 [ref. to 1920's]: Georgie was bookin' in a poolroom right off a bar.

2.a. *Stu.* to study intently.—also constr. with *it.* Hence **booking**, *n.*

1962 in *AS* XXXVIII 167: To study extremely diligently for an examination…*book it.* **1966** in *IUFA Folk Speech: Bookin' it:* studying. **1968** Baker et al. *CUSS* 85: *Book.* Work (study) hard and concentratedly [also]…*Book it.* **1975** S.P. Smith *Amer. Boys* 139: He was sick of booking and Susie had gone to study with a friend. **1980** in Safire *Good Word* 304: I've got to go book for my Govy final.

b. *Stu.* to look at; examine.

1968–70 *Current Slang* III & IV 13: *Book*…To look at. **1982** Pond *Valley Girls' Gd.* 53: *Book the joint*—Check it out.

3. [infl. by BOOG, BOOGIE, *v.*] to leave.; to go fast; move

along.—also constr. with *it, up.*

1974 U.C.L.A. student: "Time to book this joint." I heard that in L.A. in 1972. **1974** Univ. Tenn. student: *Let's book, let's book it up,* let's split. **1974** Blount *3 Bricks Shy* 31: *Keep on Bookin'*….Like keep on truckin'. **1978** J. Webb *Fields of Fire* 197 [ref. to 1969]: Bagger, you book on out o' here, man. I gotta rap with a brother, hear? **1979** *S.F. Examiner & Chronicle* (Apr. 1) 12: *Book,* v. To drive one's wheels (automobile) with effectiveness, as in *booking down the road.* **1982** Pond *Valley Girls' Gd.* 53: O.K., if you're in a hurry you go, "Wo, like a gotta book it." **1983** *N.Y. Daily News* (Mar. 25): Teentalk Glossary…*book*—move quickly. **1983** K. Miller *Lurp Dog* 226: Mopar was flat bookin'! *a*1984 in Terry *Bloods* 2: That little short snake…bites you and you're through bookin'.

booked *adj.* Orig. *Sports.* fated; destined.

*1823 "J. Bee" *Slang* 15: *Booked;* ring mostly, for any event being already settled beforehand, as so certain 'tis already set down in the *book* of history. **1849** in *Calif. Hist. Soc. Qly.* XXII (1943) 242: Three different times we thought ourselves booked for "Davy Jones' Locker." *ca*1895 G.B. Sanford *Rebels & Redskins* 169 [ref. to Civil War]: Our comrades had about concluded we were "booked for the Libby"—in other words, all taken prisoners. **1912** Ade *Babel* 110: I figured that I was booked for the crazy-house or the bone-orchard, I couldn't tell which. **1964** in Wepman, Newman & Binderman *The Life* 125: A game all bad motherfuckers were booked to lose.

bookie *n. Gamb.* a bookmaker. Now *S.E.*

*1885 in *F & H* I 291: No rowdy ring, but a few quiet and well-known bookies who were ready enough to lay the odds to a modest fiver. **1891** Maitland *Amer. Slang Dict.* 42: *Bookie,* a bookmaker, one who makes book on a race. **1892** *Outing* (Aug.) 356: Almost as much more was still to arrive from the Western "bookies" with whom he had backed Hartland during the past winter. **1902** *N.Y. Eve. Jour.* (Dec. 5) 16: In consequence, there was more work laid out for the "bookies." **1907** in H.C. Fisher *A. Mutt* 3: I hope the bookies don't get wise and bar me. **1942** Liebling *Telephone* 77: The bookie peeled several hundred-dollar bills off his bankroll. **1945* S.J. Baker *Australian Lang.* 173: *Bookie* is to be found [in Australia] in 1884, a year earlier than the "Oxford Dictionary's" first textual record. **1953** in Pohl *Star of Stars* 52: The bookie…counted out fifteen thousand dollars. **1961** in Zicree *Twi. Zone Comp.* 141: An unregistered bookie, whose entire life is any sporting event with two sides and a set of odds. **1964** in A. Sexton *Letters* 249: He looks like a bookie but he thinks like a whiz. **1972–75** W. Allen *Feathers* 36: Like those bookie joints that have barbershops outside for show.

bookoo var. BEAUCOUP.

bookoodles *n.* [blend BOOKOO + OODLES] lots; OODLES.

1965–68 in *DARE: Boocoodles.* **1969** *Current Slang* I & II 13: *Boo-koodles* n. A plethora.—College students, both sexes, Kansas.

book rat *n.* BOOKWORM.

1872 *Scribner's Mo.* (Nov.) 79: The Book Rat, as we got to calling him…was the scholar of our crew, and was forever writing in a notebook. **1882** Harbaugh *Bravo Bill* 4: This is an onhealthy locality for book-rats, an' boys! *Ibid.* 10: Whar's ther boy—ther book-rat?

book-sharp *n. West.* an author; an intellectual.

1880 in M. Lewis *Mining Frontier* 103: Er some o' them long-toed roosters what the book-sharps talk about.

bookworm *n.* Esp. *Stu.* an introverted person who spends much time studying and reading books. Now *S.E.*

1929 "E. Queen" *Roman Hat* ch. vi 75: Forget it, you bookworm. **1957** Bannon *Odd Girl* 86: I'm supposed to be a real bookworm, you know. **1980** McDowell *Our Honor* 98: Oh, you're the bookworm, right?

boom *n.* **1.** an enthusiastic endorsement or surge of interest.

1899 in J. London *Letters* 19: He would…inaugurate a boom to put my name before the public. *Ibid.* 34: Markham received a somewhat similar boom about the time he brought out "The Man with the Hoe." **1905** *Variety* (Dec. 16) 2: Vaudeville has robbed me of too many happy hours in the variety theaters to ever expect a boom from me.

2. *Narc.* BOO³, 2.

*1946 *Cape* (Union of S. Africa) *Times* (May 22) (cited in Partridge *Dict. Und.* 63). **1953** W. Brown *Monkey on My Back* 187: Unless you can sneak in some boom. Man, I haven't had a blast since I been in this f— place.

3. *Naut.* the erect penis. Cf. JIB-BOOM.

1958 Cooley *Run for Home* 39 [ref. to 1920's]: Okay, kid. Stand by to hoist your boom! Here come the playmates! *Ibid.* 350: She's got his boom topped! You should see the salami that kid's got stuck on him! **1976** Haseltine & Yaw *Woman Doctor* 111: Did any of the nurses ever…strip, just to see if he'd raise the boom in salute?

¶In phrases:

¶ **lower** [or **drop**] **the boom** to deliver a heavy blow; to take a final decisive action against.

1935 Pollock *Und. Speaks: Lowered the boom*, sought by the police [*sic*]. **1939** *AS* (Oct.) 239 [L.A.]: *To Drop The Boom.* To refuse further credit. **1940** Dempsey & Stearns *Round by Round* 124 [ref. to 1916]: As a sailor, the story ran, he had knocked men overboard with a single punch, when he "lowered the boom" on them. **1941** *AS* (Oct.) 167: *Lower the Boom.* To deliver a knockout punch. **1946** G.C. Hall, Jr. *1000 Destroyed* 28: Then one day the boom was lowered…"We're going to fly Thunderbolts." **1951** Morris *China Station* 44: Once more in here and we lower the boom. You got that? **1952** Grant & Taylor *Big Jim McLain* (film): Thanks, mister, for lowering the boom on that character. **1953** J.M. Cain *Galatea* 225: Firpo lowered the boom, and Jack all but went out before he climbed back in the ring. **1956** Holiday & Dufty *Lady Sings* 128: Then the judge lowered the boom. **1958** McCulloch *Woods Wds.* 113: *Lower the boom*…b. To fire a man. c. To take severe action of some kind against a man. **1964** Rhodes *Chosen Few* 12: BAM! They drop the boom. **1967** Dibner *Admiral* 229: I was there when the skipper lowered the boom on him. **1983** WKGN radio news (Apr. 6): The First Tennessee Bank has lowered the boom on eighty-six employees….The eighty-six were given their pink slips as expendable.

¶ **rig in (one's) booms** *Navy.* to draw in (one's) elbows.

1906 Beyer *Amer. Battleship* 85: "*Rig in your booms*"—pull in your elbows. **1918** *Scribner's* (July) 17: Even so difficult a thing as table manners is taught by the upper classmen to those who need instruction. The ears of the backward one will be dinned with the cry, "Man overboard!" when he leaves his spoon in his cup, or "Boat your oars!" when his knife and fork are leaning against his plate, or "Rig in your booms, mister!" if his elbows tend to a horizontal position. **1942** in *Yank* (Jan. 6, 1943) 18: Rig in your starboard boom. **1969** Bosworth *Love Affair* 39: At chow, a shipmate's elbow is in his ribs, and the cry of "Rig in your boom" is frequent.

¶ **top (one's) boom** *Naut.* get going; depart.

*1818 A. Burton *Adventures of Johnny Newcome* (cited in Partridge *DSUE* (ed. 7) 1022). *1838 Glascock *Land Sharks* II 20: Suppose you now top your boom and join the jollies, and the rest of the fine-weather fry, in a jaw on the poop. *Ibid.* 41: No talk. Top your boom. Discipline of the ship's going to the very devil! **1838** Crockett *Almanac* (1839) 2: You may just top your boom, and make a General clear out. **1841** [Mercier] *Man-of-War* 143: Who told you 'twas your turn next? Top your boom now in short order. **1849** Melville *White Jacket* 293 [ref. to 1843]: Top your boom and sail large, now. If I see you again, I'll have you up to the mast….Top your boom, I say, and be off. **1852** Hazen *Five Years* 352: Top your boom, and hunt us a coach. *1871 G. Meredith, in *F & H* I 294: And now top your boom and to bed here. **1886** P.D. Haywood *Cruise* 133: When you hear a man "topping his boom"…and "splicing the main-brace," he has more likely been steering a clam wagon than going…to sea. **1891** Maitland *Amer. Slang Dict.* 43: *Boom* (sea term) "To top one's boom," to start off.

boom *adv. & interj.* suddenly. Also **boom-boom**.

1951 in Mailer *Ad. for Myself* 113: But, boom-boom, the war had ended. **1953** G. Webber *Far Shore* 34: Then, boom, we have to sail across the ocean for this super-special job. **1970** S. Ross *Fortune Machine* 19: Boom, the cocktail waitress…pranced up to them. **1991** LaBarge *Desert Voices* 185: So we're there, boom, ready to go.

boom *v.* **1.** to hurry.

1837 J.C. Neal *Charcoal Sks.* 96: You're right in the way, and if you don't boom along, why Ben and me will have to play hysence, clearance, puddin's out with you afore you've time to chalk your knuckles.

2. to drub (someone).

1890 Goss *Recollections* 244 [ref. to Civil War]: "I tell you," said one of the Maine men, who had come from the lumber district, "we boomed 'em good."

3. to promote (a candidate, product, locale, etc.) enthusiastically. Now *S.E.*

1883 *Moose Jaw News*, in Avis *Dict. Canad.* 67: Their town is all the better for not having been "boomed" to any considerable extent. **1888** in *F & H* I (rev.) 329: The city of Paris is said to be diminishing instead of increasing in population. They don't know how to *boom* a town over there. *1891 in *OEDS*: Messrs. J.S. Fry…are booming their manufacturers in a novel way. **1904** in Bierce *Letters* 98: Your decision to "boom" me almost frightens me. **1906** *Nat. Police Gaz.* (Feb. 3) 3: What you want is a manager—someone to boom you. **1966** in *OEDS*: One minor political figure in Alabama, a certain Shorty Price, decided to

boom his own wife for governor.

4. to travel as a BOOMER, 3. b.; to work itinerantly.

1906 in A. Adams *Chisholm Trail* 182: Well, boom if you want. **1974** Cherry *High Steel* 30: I'm gettin' too old to boom around all t'e time. **1990** L. Nieman *Boomer* 48: Come booming. The streets are paved with gold.

boom-boom[1] *n.* **1.** *Boxing.* a one-two punch.

1949 Cummings *Dict. Sports* 43.

2. a firearm. *Joc.*

1983 Eilert *Self & Country* 35: The script says no bad guys in the area and no boom-booms to hurt Mr. C. Stunning.

boom-boom[2] *n.* [pidgin] *Mil. in Far East.* copulation.—often used attrib. Also as v.

1964 Faust *Steagle* 11: No boom boom with Lowella, aah please? **1970** Southern *Blue Movie* 246: Feral no try *boom-boom.* **1975** S.P. Smith *Amer. Boys* 5: Papa-san, you take me back to laundry for boom-boom. *Ibid.* 408: Hey girl, for how many p. you boom-boom my friend? **1982** Goff, Sanders & Smith *Brothers* 126 [ref. to Vietnam War]: We'd want some boom-boom, a piece of tail. **1989** D. Sherman *There I Was* 281: After I boom-booma a whole shitload of geishas.

boom-boom girl *n. Mil. in Far East.* a native woman who is a prostitute.

1966 *Sat. Eve. Post* (July 16) 38: Troopers drink beer and wait their turn to pass through a second door, beyond which lie the quarters of the "boom-boom" girls. **1970** *Esquire* (Nov.) 119: At twilight two of the boomboom girls came by. **1971** Barnes *Pawns* 126: They'll…make out with the boom-boom girls. **1976** C.R. Anderson *Grunts* 38: There had been the boom-boom girls from Cua Viet Village hanging around the perimeter wire, but if any one ever touched one it was a guaranteed case of the clap. **1988** C. Roberts & C. Sassar *Walking Dead* 150 [ref. to ca1966]: Numbah one Hong Kong boom-boom girls.

boom-boom house *n. Mil. in Far East.* a brothel. Also vars.

1966 *Time* (May 6) 29: A 25-acre sprawl of "*boum-boum* parlors." **1974** Kingry *Monk & Marines* 19: Seventy five percent of the men got venereal disease on R&R (in boom-boom parlors over which you had no control). **1977** Caputo *Rumor of War* 102 [ref. to 1965]: Whorehouses….Boom-boom houses, they are called in the local slang. **1988** Clodfelter *Mad Minutes* 44 [ref. to 1965]: Bars and "boom-boom houses."

boom box *n.* a large portable stereo radio and tape player.

1981 WINS radio news (Aug. 8): On the street they be known as "boom-boxes." **1985** *Time* (May 27) 77: Madonna comes onstage with a big portable stereo boom box. **1987** *Campus Voice* (Spring) 33: First we just recorded on a boom box that had a dual cassette. **1993** *New Yorker* (Sept. 6) 22: Digable Planets, whose début album…ought to be on every hipster's boom box this summer.

boom bucket *n. Mil. Av.* (see quots.). *Joc.*

1956 *Britannica Book of the Year* 750: *Boom bucket n.* The ejection seat of a jet aeroplane. **1967** H.M. Mason *New Tigers* 218: *Boom bucket*: The MA-15 ejection-seat trainer. **1968–70** *Current Slang* III & IV 13: *Boom bucket*, n. Ejection seat of a military aircraft.—Air Force personnel, Viet Nam.

boomer *n.* **1.** *So.* a mountaineer.—usu. constr. with *mountain*.

1859 [Taliaferro] *Fisher's R. Sketches* 33: A mountain "Boomer," dressed in a linsey hunting-shirt down to his knees. **1884** Triplett *American Crimes* 460: Clayton's militia (composed of "mountain Boomers," thieves and thugs, under the command of officers no more honorable than themselves). **1922** H. Kephart *S. Highlanders* 280: They call themselves mountain people or…sometimes humorously mountain boomers.

2.a. something extremely large.

*1885 in *OEDS*: When the shades of evening come, I choose a boomer of a gun. [Australia]. **1889** Barrère & Leland *Dict. Slang* I 163: *Boomer* (American), a very big specimen…A very great lie; a very long hit at cricket would be described as a *boomer*…(used by "slangy" Australians).

b. something extremely exciting and successful.

1887 in *DAE*: This sale will be a boomer for the very finest soft or stiff hat goes for $1.98. **1966** H.S. Thompson *Hell's Angels* 106: I'd never been on a holiday run, and…this one had the makings of a real boomer. **1976** *Business Week* (Jan. 26) 28: With inventories down and order books already fat, the outlook for the first quarter is a boomer.

c. a boom town.

1889 in *DA*: If the Custer mill starts again this fall…old Custer with her numerous mines and high-grade ores will be a "boomer."

3.a. *West.* a participant in a land boom; a settler in an area that has been opened up by a land rush. Now *hist.* and *S.E.*
1884 *Chi. Tribune* (May 13) 5: The boomers report a large number of people...now in the Indian Territory. **1884** in *No. Dak. Hist.* XVII (1950) 56: Comstock, another boomer,...is Senator. **1885** in *Real West* (July 1979) 21: The "boomers" have been driven from Oklahoma by Federal troops, and many of them are said to be in distress. **1906** Mac-Fadden *Rambles* 7: These "boomers" succeeded far beyond their...expectations. **1941** *Nat. Geographic* (Mar.) 269: Again and again as "boomers," "sooners" and squatters, whites invaded the country.
b. *Esp. West.* a person, usu. a drifter, who makes a living in areas of sudden business prosperity, esp. an itinerant railroad worker or logger.—often used attrib.
1893 in Avis *Dict. Canad.* 67: "Boomers" of every description were seen coming down the hills and up the valleys. **1901** in N. Cohen *Long Steel Rail* 391: A boomer...travels the road because he likes to travel and there is not much work in it. **1906** in A. Adams *Chisholm Trail* 182: I passed up that country, and here I am a "boomer." **1909** Warner *Lifer* 26 [ref. to 1880's]: I became a "boomer" brakeman. That is a man who will not work in any one place more than a few months, and who spends the greater portion of the year knocking about from one railroad town to another. **1916** *Editor* (Mar. 25) 343: *Boomer*—Wandering railroader. **1917** *Editor* (Feb. 24) 152: *Boomer*—a hobo who solicits subscriptions to magazines, or engages in clerical work or anything high-toned while he is on the bo. **1924** G. Henderson *Crookdom*: *Boomer*. A high-class travelling criminal. **1924** Tully *Beggars of Life* 92: He proved to be, in the parlance of the road, a "boomer," a sort of hobo, or migratory railroad worker. **1926** *AS* (Jan.) 251: *Boomer*—a migratory worker, such as a telegraph operator, electrician, or brakeman. **1929** G. Milburn *Hobo's Hornbk.* 63: Eastbound Jack was a boomer shark. **1930** "D. Stiff" *Milk & Honey* 200: *Boomer*—A hobo who is always on the go. He has a *travel itch.* **1933** Ersine *Pris. Slang* 20: *Boomer, n.* A thief who works one district for a short time and then moves to another, leaving the local thieves to stand the *heat.* **1941** *AS* (Oct.) 232 [logging]: *Boomer.* An itinerant worker who works but a few days. **1951** Pryor *The Big Play* 37: Dixon Street...was the stronghold of the boomers (those parasites who followed oil booms to trade on the excitement and easy money). **1951** J. Wilson *Dark & Damp* 148: Men who sink shafts and remain in the mine a few months after coal is struck are called "boomers." **1952** Bissell *Monongahela* 224: Them short-order cooks is worse between roamers than steamboaters. **1961** Kalisher *R.R. Men* 26: I knew an old time boomer that travelled the country....He was a boomer switchman. **1970** Boatright & Owens *Derrick* 156: Boomers...were gamblers and highjackers and all such stuff as that—that's what we called the boomers. **1979** Terkel *Amer. Dreams* xviii: The guests were boomer firemen, journeymen carpenters, and ex-Wobblies.
4. *Surfing.* a heavy breaker, esp. if unridable.
1957 Kohner *Gidget* 11: I've seen those boomers in a movie. **1961** Kohner *G. Goes Hawaiian* 8: Boomers ten feet high. **1968** Kirk & Hanle *Surfer's Hndbk.* 136: *Boomer*: wave that crashes suddenly, violently with a roar. **1977** Filosa *Surf. Almanac* 182: *Boomer* A gigantic, unridable wave.
5. a thundercloud or thunderstorm.
1970 in *DARE.* *a*1979 in S. King *Bachman* 329: It's gonna be a boomer!" Parker yelled gleefully. **1983** *Good Morning America* (ABC-TV) (June 24): And there are some boomers moving through the Southeast. **1987** *Eyewitness News* (ABC-TV) (July 3): There is a possibility of a shower, maybe a boomer. **1990** *CBS This Morning* (CBS-TV) (Aug. 22): Thunderstorm activity—boomers, as they call them on the radio.
6. *Navy.* a nuclear-powered submarine that carries strategic missiles; (*also*) a crewman on such a submarine.
1976 *Dict. Amer. Hist.* (rev.) 302: The "boomers" of the nuclear-powered navy use a new technical language. **1983** Elting et al. *Dict. Soldier Talk* 351: *Boomers*...Officers and men of the new nuclear-powered elements of the U.S. Navy. *a*1984 T. Clancy *Red Oct.* 42: We deploy our boomers a lot further forward than they do. **1979–88** Noel & Bush *Naval Terms* (ed. 5) 41: *Boomer* Slang: a submarine that carries large ballistic missiles.
7. *Journ.* a member of the post-WWII "baby boom" generation.
1982 *Lompoc* (Calif.) *Record* Family Weekly (May 23) 4: In the 1960's, the first wave of boomers hit adolescence and gave us the youth society: Rock 'n' roll, demonstrations, blue jeans, [etc.]. **1984** *U.S. News & W.R.* (Nov. 5) 68: As consumers, boomers reshape the marketplace as they go from blue jeans and backpacks to buying houses and cars. **1985** Makower *Boom!* 11: Where the Boomers Are. **1986** R. Stone, in

Harper's (Dec.) 50: I began to think that I was seeing stoned cops, stoned grocery shoppers and stoned boomers. **1987** *Daily Beacon* (Univ. Tenn.) (Apr. 27) 4: Many "boomers" led the fight to raise the drinking age. **1991** R.F. Laird *The Boomer Bible* (title).

booming *adj.* grand.
1884 "M. Twain" *Huck. Finn* ch. xvii: We can just have booming times—they have no school now. *1889** Barrère & Leland *Dict. Slang* I 163: Look at that booming guana! He has been feeding sumptuously on the carrion.

booming *adv.* tremendously.
1884 "M. Twain" *Huck. Finn* ch. xxiv: They was booming mad. **1893** "Palmer" *Question of Honour* 101: It'll be such a boomin' surprise to Dely!

boom jockey *n.* a boom operator, esp. a sound technician who operates a boom microphone.
1947 Mencken *Amer. Lang. Supp.* II 698: *Boom jockey.* A sound man who follows the action with a microphone.

boom rat *n. Logging.* (see quots.). Also (*West.*) **boom poke, boom cat.**
1911 *Century Dict.* (*rev. ed.*) II (Supp.): *Boom-rat*...In *lumbering,* one who works on a boom. (Slang.). **1956** Sorden & Ebert *Logger's* 4 [ref. to *a*1925]: *Boom-rat,* One who works on a boom. **1957** in Avis *Dict. Canad.* 67: Working in the logging camps as a boomcat while in his teens. **1958** McCulloch *Woods Wds.* 15: *Boom cat*—a boom man, particularly one who is very catty on logs. *Ibid.* 16: *Boom poke*—A man who works on a boom or raft.

boom wagon *n. Trucking.* a truck that carries nitroglycerin or other explosives.
1942 *AS* (Apr.) 102: *Boom Wagon.* Nitroglycerin truck. **1971** Tak *Truck Talk* 16: *Boom wagon:* a truck carrying explosives. **1976** Lieberman & Rhodes *CB Handbook* 124: *Boom Wagon*—Truck carrying dangerous cargo.

boom[1] *n.* [prob. fr. syn. BONE, 2.b.] *Black E.* a dollar.
1957 Simmons *Corner Boy* 14: Fifty dollars, Sweet Jesus, fifty boons you'll never see again!

boon[2] *n.* [orig. obscure; perh. infl. slightly by *boon companion;* cf. BOON COON]
1. *Black E.* a very close friend; best friend.
1962 Killens *Then We Heard* 175 [ref. to WWII]: All we can do now, my bosom boon, is wait till the shit hits the fan. **1962** Crump *Killer* 87: Hi, sexy boon. **1971** Dahlskog *Dict.* 9: *Boon*...A good friend. **1973** Childress *Hero* 22: You see me, you see him. He was my boon!
2. a black person.—usu. contemptuous in white use.
1967–68 in *DARE.* **1974** N.Y.C. man, age *ca*25: Yeah, niggers. They call 'em *coons* and *boons* and *spades.* **1976** Whelton *CB Baby* 81: Did you see that son of a bitch of a boon! **1977** Bredes *Hard Feelings* 289: It's like I'm inviting some gang of crazed boons to carve...[me] into fishbait. **1979** in L. Bangs *Psychotic Reactions* 272: "All the boons just sat there laughing at me."..."What's boons?" "Black guys...From 'baboons,' I guess." **1982** Del Vecchio *13th Valley* 86: "If it aint Bro Boon."..."Is that Bro Boon like in Bro Coon," Jax intoned with mock arrogant disgust.

boon coon *n.* [orig. unkn.; cf. BOON[2], 1; poss. infl. by BOOKOO] *Black E.* a very close friend; a best friend. See also ACE BOON COON.
1958 A. Gibson *Be Somebody* 13 [ref. to 1930's]: We were what we called boon-coons, which in Harlem means block [*sic*] buddies, good friends. **1958** Hughes & Bontemps *Negro Folklore*: Stacy's my boon-coon. **1971** Wells & Dance *Night People* 71: Say, now you're my boon-koon, I'll tell you something I couldn't tell you when I first joined the band.

boondock *n.* usu. *pl.* [< Tagalog *bundoc, bondoc* 'a mountain'] **1.** Orig. *Mil.,* esp. *USMC, in Philippines.* mountains or jungle; (*hence*) wilds of any sort; a remote area.—usu. constr. with *the.* [Became widely known during the 1960's.]
[**1905** MacKinlay *Tagalog Hndbk.* 44: The mountain: *Ang bundok.*] **1909** *WNID: Bun-doc* n., Also, *bondoc* [Tag.] A mountain. Also, in colloq. English (usually *pl.,* pronounced bŭn´-dŏŏks), the hills and woods in general; the wilds; any place at a distance from a center of population. *Phil. I.* **1930** in *Leatherneck* (Jan. 1931) 16: Our company commander...conceived the idea of taking off with half the members of the compound to make Hey! Hey! in the boondocks [in Haiti]. **1931** *Leatherneck* (Oct.) 20: Our leading contender...is...Sergeant "Pop" Dahms,

who is famous for...breaking all the new trails in the "boondocks" around here [Lakehurst, N.J.]. [**1931** *Our Army* (Dec.) 5: Old Mount Aryat still looms up from the plain as it did when you first saw it through a cloud of red dust and battle smoke. Some scrap taking that old "bondoc"—a colored regiment did it.] **1942** Tregaskis *Guadalcanal Diary* (Sept. 10): The general has moved into the "boon-docks," as the marines call the jungles. **1944** Brooks *Brick Foxhole* 21: An' the...brick buildin's wid the steam heat? An' the boondocks wid little dirt paths arunnin' through 'em? **1955** Scott *Look of Eagle* 184: We'll be...far away from the operations tower, down in the "boondocks" like they park jets on all fields. **1955** Abbey *Brave Cowboy* 190: Two squaws jumped out of the back and started running across the boondock. **1956** Hargrove *Girl He Left* 127: Then you crawled off through a lot of boondock. **1957** Leckie *Helmet for Pillow* 14: At New River [N.C., 1942] there were no dress blues, no girls, no dance bands; there was only beer and that marshland called the boondocks. **1958** McCulloch *Woods Words* 94: *In the boondocks*—Away back in the woods. **1969** Hughes *Under a Flare* 10: I would for sure lose my relatively safe position as a clerk and wind up building bridges in the boondocks. **1971** Sorrentino *Up from Never* 253: The boondocks, as they called the swamps, were a maze of growth, quicksand, and water moccasins. **1973** Karlin, Paquet & Rottmann *Free Fire Zone* 23: They bounced over a rotting railroad bridge and into the boondocks beyond. **1976** *N.Y. Times* (Sept. 8) 63: He comes from a Georgia boondock called Plains. **1980** W.C. Anderson *BAT-21* 22: And in the boondocks of Nam they got insects you wouldn't believe.

2. *Mil. Av.* the rough ground that surrounds a runway; *(hence)* any unfinished area used as a landing field.

1941 in C.R. Bond & T. Anderson *Flying T. Diary* 58: His engine cut out about halfway down the runway and he went off into the boondocks and tore off his landing gear. **1967** H.M. Mason *New Tigers* 219: *Boon-docks*...To pilots, any field, meadow, or pasture, as opposed to a standard runway.

boondock *v.* **1.** Orig. *USMC & Navy.* to go into or through boondocks; to march through boondocks as punishment or training; *(also, trans.* to send into boondocks).

1947 in *Calif. Folk.* VI 160 [ref. to WWII]: *Boondocker....*On Guam we applied it to men who liked to go out into the jungle, that is, who liked to *go boondocking.* **1952** Uris *Battle Cry* 43 [ref. to 1942]: "Phew," Jones sighed, "I thought he was going to boondock us for sure." *Ibid.* 47: At least you'll go boondocking with us if this head isn't finished. **1965** E. Franklin *Cold in Pongo-ni* 132 [ref. to Korean War]: You lose that weapon I'll have you boondockin' three weeks with a pack full of sand.

2. *Specif. Stu.* to go with a date into a wooded or isolated area for the purpose of love-making.

1950 *Word Study* (May) 8: *Boondocks*...in Tennessee college circles has been made into a verb, as an equivalent for "to park" and "to neck." **1968–70** *Current Slang* III & IV 14: *Boondock, v.* To take beer, broad, and blanket to the woods.—College students, both sexes, Kentucky. **1971** Dahlskog *Dict.* 9: *Boondock, v.* To neck, esp. in a car parked in an isolated area.

3. *Specif. Trucking.* to travel on back roads.

1971 Tak *Truck Talk* 16: *Boondockin':* the trucker's practice of avoiding all major roads, of traveling on less frequented ones, when running illegally. **1976** Lieberman & Rhodes *CB Handbook* 124: *Boondocking*—Running back roads at night to avoid weigh stations. **1976** *Nat. Lampoon* (July) 59: D.D. takes the "Moonlight Express"—boondockin' down the back roads dodgin' chicken coops an' smokies, with her gear-shift in pay-hole and her foot to the wood.

boondocker *n.* **1.** usu. *pl. USMC.* a combat boot; field shoe.

1942 *Leatherneck* (Nov.) 143: *Boon Dockers*—Not to be confused with Wedgies. They are field shoes weighing roughly 9,000,000 pounds (after a long march). **1943** *Sat. Eve. Post* (Mar. 20) 86: Field shoes, or boon dockers, weigh upwards of two pounds apiece. **1943** in Sherrod *Tarawa* 97: Two dead Japs...have been discovered wearing Marine helmets, jungle dungarees and boondockers. **1945** Monks *Ribbon & Star* 63: He tapped the noses of the rounds in the clip against the sole of one of his boondockers. **1952** Uris *Battle Cry* 32: The seabags became crowded with a barrage of skivvies, socks, overcoats, belts, boondockers, high-top dress shoes, field scarfs, and the rest of the wardrobe of a Marine. **1958** Frankel *Band of Bros.* 6: As good a Marine as ever took a dump between a pair of boondockers. **1959** Cochrell *Barren Beaches* 182: Another pair of boondockers shot to hell. **1960** Leckie *Marines* 31: He just stared at George...like he was something stuck to the soles of his boondockers. **1966** Heinl *Marine Officer's Gd.* 591: *Boondockers:* Field shoes or boots. **1972** Wambaugh *Blue Knight* 52: I'd land on that Dragon with both boondockers. **1976** *L.A. Times* (Sept. 15) IV 1: He

was probably expecting you to any moment drop your rifle on the toe of your right boondocker. **1990** Poyer *Gulf* 220: His boondockers slipped, the leather soles losing the treads.

2. *USMC.* a serviceman, esp. a combat infantryman, who is or has been in the boondocks; *(also)* a serviceman from a remote area.

1945 in *Calif. Folklore* V (1946) 385: A *boondocker* is a person who lives in the *boondocks,* or jungle. **1947** in *Calif. Folklore* VI 160: *Boondocker...*On Guam we applied it to men who liked to go out into the jungle, that is, who liked to *go boondocking.* **1957** Myrer *Big War* 169: Well, old boondocker...that's the end of the carnival. **1968** Myrer *Once an Eagle* 611: Just a rugged boondocker, a driver, thinking in terms of units, percentages, risks. **1972–79** T. Wolfe *Right Stuff* 37: He was the boondocker, the boy from the back country.

3. *Stu.* a picnic held in the woods esp. for the purpose of drinking beer, necking, etc.

1966 *Life* (Mar. 4) 80C [ref. to 1964]: The fests were called "boondockers"...kids' drinking parties. **1969** *Current Slang* I & II 14: *Boon-docker,* n. Beer party in the country.—College students, both sexes, California.—There was a *boon-docker* last week. **1981–83** N. Proffitt *Gardens of Stone* 174: And they had their *boondockers,* taking their keg of beer, their old blankets, and their dates to some dry desert river bed.

boondoggle *n.* [claimed to have been coined as a name for an ornamental leather cord] Esp. *Pol.* an extravagant and useless project. Now *colloq.* [The specificity and uniqueness of the first quot., in which the term means "gadget," suggest that this sense was never very common and perhaps not very old. The remainder of the quots. illustrate the usual meaning, which came to prominence in 1935 and which the first quot. attempts to explain.]

[**1935** *N.Y. Times* (Apr. 4) 2: "Boon doggles" is simply a term applied back in the pioneer days to what we call gadgets today.] **1935** S. Lewis *Can't Happen* 198: The Universal Electric Corporation....They don't mind Jews there as long as they sing at their work and find boondoggles worth a million a year to the company. **1947** in *OEDS:* The cost of this boondoggle has been estimated at perhaps 50 million dollars. **1978** J. Webb *Fields of Fire* 106: Tim Forbes will confess his boondoggle, and we will admire his honesty. **1982** *N.Y. Post* (Aug. 13) 34: And The Boondoggles Go On. **1983** *Morning Contact* (WKGN radio) (May 27): That little boondoggle agency has just got itself in deeper and deeper. **1985** *Our Town* (N.Y.C.) (Aug. 11) 2: Now let his savvy explain the 63rd Street subway boondoggle. **1985** Wells *444 Days* 198: They had my passport, so they knew that I had been to all of these countries, and they wanted to know why I said, "I was on a boondoggle." Then it took me nearly an hour to explain what "boondoggle" meant. **1992** *L.A. Times Mag.* (May 31) 12: *Boondoggle* n. Business trip whose location is chosen for travel/vacation motives.

boondoggle *v.* **1.** (see quot.).

1935 *Chi. Tribune* (Oct. 4), in *DA:* To the cowboy it meant the making of saddle trappings out of odds and ends of leather, and they boondoggled when there was nothing else to do on the ranch.

2. Esp. *Pol.* to engage in a boondoggle. Hence **boondoggler**, *n.*

1935 in Gelman *Photoplay* 181: I told her I thought it was a government "boon doggler" in Milwaukee who unearthed the marriage registration of a Mae West and a Frank Wallace. **1936** in Butterfield *Post Treasury* 358: The word "boondoggling" alarmed some New Dealers. **1937** *AS* (Feb.) 6: *Boondoggling* became the current term [during the 1936 elections] for describing the waste assertedly evident in...government agencies and bureaus. Administrators of relief became *boondogglers* to the Republican press and orators. **1939** Appel *People Talk* 12: It's a nice park they're building....And they're not boondoggling. **1942** in *DA:* Boondogglers or social experimenters. **1950** *Sat. Eve. Post* (Mar. 25) 12: The product of these projects...is likely to be just more boondoggling. **1963** Hecht *Gaily* 59: I lay claim to similar ownership of years passed, and the right to boondoggle while recounting them. **1965** Hardman *Chaplains Raid* 184: Goodnight, you lousy boon-doggling creep. **1970** Terkel *Hard Times* 8: A WPA boondoggler leaning on his shovel. **1973** *AS* XLVI 82. **1979** Ennes *Liberty* 179: Cumshaw experts and boondogglers. **1985** Boyne & Thompson *Wild Blue* 468: He accused Brown of wanting to boondoggle to Bangkok while a war was going on.

boonie[1] *n.* an outdoor privy.

1944 in *DARE:* "Boonie" is widely used in Tidewater, Virginia for privy. **1969** in *DARE* [Calif.].

boonie[2] *n.* **1.** usu. *pl.* Orig. *USMC & Navy.* BOONDOCK, *n.* 1.

[The "1942" quot. is uniquely early and is likely to be an editorial intrusion from the 1960's or later.]

[**1942** in C.R. Bond & T. Anderson *Flying T. Diary* 122: Bob and I talked over the situation…and I brought him up to date on what had transpired while he was in the boonies.] **1956** D. Howard, in *AS* (Oct.) 190: U.S. Marine Corps Slang…The whole platoon may get a forced march through the *boonies* (woods, jungles, etc.). **1961** Peacock *Valhalla* 62 [ref. to 1953]: Tent Camp Two out in the boonies. **1965** *N.Y. Times* (Nov. 3) 2: The "boonies," short for boondocks, are the hills or, loosely, any area outside a city or an American compound. **1966** Shepard *Doom Pussy* 61: Boondocks or "boonies," military slang for just about as far from civilization as you can get. **1968** Schell *Military Half* 69: I ask you, if we can't win the allegiance of a captive audience in these camps, how are we going to win their hearts and minds out in a hamlet way off in the boonies somewhere? **1971** Polner *No Victory Parades* 29: For every guy who resists the draft one of us gotta go, and he gets sent out into the boonies to get his backside shot at. **1972** Pelfrey *Big V* 124: Second lieutenant and can't [even] hump the boonies. **1977** Langone *Life at Bottom* 203: Take a Eskimo. He gets his ass lost stumblin' around in the boonies. **1980** Manchester *Darkness* 323: "Boonie-stomping"—prowling the bush in search of relics of the battle—is a popular sport among Americans on the isle [of Okinawa]. **1982** Del Vecchio *13th Valley* 44: 105 days in the boonies, up the Sông Bo and Rao Trang rivers, on the hills…and in the swamps. **1990** Ruggero *38 N. Yankee* 93: We've been humping around the boonies.

2. BOONDOCKER, 1.

1969 *Current Slang* I & II 14: *Boonies*, n. An isolated place (boondocks); unusual boots (boon-dockers).—Air Force Academy cadets. **1982** S.P. Smith *Officer & Gentleman* 57: Good shine on those boonies, Seeger. **1990** Poyer *Gulf* 310: He slipped into his boonies.

3. *Stu.* BOONDOCKER, 3.

1969 *Current Slang* I & II 14: *Boonie*, n. Beer, blanket, and boy party.—College females, New York State. **1974** N.Y.C. man, age *ca*27: *Go on a boonie* is to go on a picnic with sex. I heard that upstate in 1968–69.

boonie[3] *n.* BOON[2], *n.*, 2.—used contemptuously. Also **booner.**

1970 in Estren *Underground Comics* 6: This one we got at a Black Panther meeting just recently…I bet those booners just loved her. **1971** Sorrentino *Up from Never* 236: Then you better move, fat boy, or this boonie here is gonna make your rear-end have a jet stream. **1976** Price *Bloodbrothers* 197: They take some boonie after he works all day at Nedick's and they make him take a bath.

boonie *adj. Mil.* ASIATIC.

1983 *Weird War Tales* (Feb.) 3: Maybe I *am* gettin' booney like the Skipper says.

boonie cap *n. Mil.* a fatigue cap; (*occ.*) a baseball-style cap. Also **boonie hat.**

1972 Pelfrey *Big V* 125: There were four, with AK-47s and cloth boony hats. *Ibid.* 133: Popeye wore a boony cap with a CIB in front. **1982** "J. Cain" *Commandos* 137: Just another off-duty soldier with a floppy boonie-hat hiding his face. **1983** Van Devanter & Morgan *Before Morning* 230: Wearing my fatigue shirt and boonie hat. **1985** Former U.S. Army Spec. 4, age 35 [ref. to 1970's]: The *boonie cap* was a baseball cap, especially when it was worn turned around with the bill in the back.

boonie rat *n. Army.* a combat soldier serving in jungles, hills, or swamps.

1967 D. Reed *Up Front* 3: His father in World War II and Korea was the GI or Dogface. In Vietnam, he goes by an assortment of names—the Grunt, Boonie Rat, Line Dog, Ground Pounder, Hill Humper, or Jarhead. **1970** in Del Vecchio *13th Valley* 75: Boonie Rats, Boonie Rats,/Scared but not alone. **1980** Santoli *Everything* 167: Not just my guys, but Boonie Rat out there with a commissioned unit. **1982** Goff, Sanders & Smith *Bros.* 48 [ref. to 1968]: These guys were boonie rats and damn near all of them wore CIBs. **1986** Thacker *Pawn* 62 [ref. to 1970]: Then, by God, I'll have every one of you boonie rats on Article Fifteen charges. **1984–87** Ferrandino *Firefight* 110: Boonyrat eleven bravos.

booshwah var. BUSHWA.

boost *n. Und.* an act of "boosting"; a theft.

1928 *New Yorker* (Dec. 8) 58: I see a nice-looking Dodge just waiting for a boost.

boost *v.* Orig. *Und.* **1.a.** to shoplift; (*hence*) to steal (usu. small items).

*a***1909** Tillotson *Detective* 90: *Boost*—To shoplift. **1914** Healy *Delinquent* 548: You come on, I know a place where we can boost. **1928** Cal-

lahan *Man's Grim Justice* 33: He broke me in, taught me how to smoke [opium], how to boost (steal). **1956** Gold *Not With It* 84: I ate what I boosted in small cans from the A&P. **1958** A. King *Mine Enemy* 33: They'd boost (steal) more than they'd pack. **1962** Kesey *Cuckoo's Nest* 88: I'm afraid some thief in the night boosted my clothes whilst I slept. **1973** "J. Godey" *Pelham* 205: I'm sorry we didn't boost a few packages. **1981** *Hill St. Blues* (NBC-TV): For all we know, he went down to his car and somebody boosted his battery. **1989** *Tracey Ullman Show* (Fox-TV): What kind of fool's gonna boost a thirty-pound bag of Beefy Bites? **1993** *New Yorker* (Jan. 11) 65: Florence…concealed the clothes she selected to "boost"…under her coat.

b. *Specif.*, to steal (an automobile).

1928 *New Yorker* (Dec. 8) 58: Every time you boost a bus you're in a tight jam. **1961** H. Ellison *Memos* 184: Prostitution, gambling, auto theft (in this case known as "boosting"). **1977** Sayles *Union Dues* 205: So what you do, you live in Chollistown and you want to move, is you boost a car….We never boosted a luxury car before. **1982** *Hardcastle & McCormick* (ABC-TV): They were tryin' to boost a Mercedes and the cops nailed 'em dirty. **1988** *N.Y. Post* (June 6) 31: When they were kids growing up in the barrio, Apache and…Speedy would occasionally boost a car.

2. to rob.

1966 J. Mills *Needle Park* 22: But Bob boosted cabs….That was the lowest of the low. Nothing was easier or simpler, required less nerve and produced smaller profits than boosting cabs. *Ibid.* 105: He boosted a vet's office. **1966** Samuels *People vs. Baby* 69: He preferred to boost cars. **1969** Lingeman *Drugs* 27: I *boosted* supermarkets for meat and sold it. **1988** *Highwayman* (NBC-TV): There are certain individuals in here who think I did boost that armored car.

booster *n. Gamb.* **1.** SHILL; CAPPER.

1906 Wooldridge *Hands Up* 110: This motion is seen by the countryman and the "booster." **1908** Train *Crime Stories* 112: "Old Stone wins!" cried the "booster" at the [ticker]tape in a voice husky with excitement. *Ibid.* 118: In the train of the "wire-tappers" thronged the "flimflammer," "confidence man," "booster," "capper" and every sort of affiliated crook. **1909** Irwin *Con Man* 35: He was working as a booster in a Chicago poker club. **1915** Howard *God's Man* 196: "Song—song," shouted the "boosters"…posing as simple melody-loving private citizens. **1922** Murphy *Black Candle* 188: He fell victim to a drug "booster" till, ultimately, he became a ragged wreck living in the noisome alleys of Chinatown. **1931** G. Milburn, in *Amer. Mercury* (Nov.) 351: Circus Words…*Booster*, n. A schill; a come-on man. **1939** C.R. Cooper *Scarlet* 98: Equally, there are more percentage girls, "boosters," drink-forcers and female bar hangers-on in one of the largest of Eastern cities than could be found in all of the Atlantic Coast during the speakeasy period.

2. *Und. & Police.* a shoplifter or petty thief.

1908 Sullivan *Criminal Slang* 2: *A swell booster*—a successful female shoplifter. **1911** A.H. Lewis *Apaches of N.Y.* 39: A gifted booster….the quickest hand…of all the gon-molls between the two oceans. **1914** Healy *Delinquent* 548: Mike heard the boys call me a "dollar booster," because I stole a dollar once. **1914** Jackson & Hellyer *Crim. Slang* 18: *Booster*….A shoplifter. **1928** Sharpe *Chicago May* 161: I had an experience with a dope-fiend booster (shop-lifter) in Philadelphia. **1942** Liebling *Telephone* 66: Paddy the Booster…sells neckties he steals from haberdashers. **1956** Holiday & Dufty *Lady Sings Blues* 146: If I had been a booster or a petty thief I'd have the parole board helping me to get a job. **1974** Angelou *Gather Together* 32: Boosters and thieves wove their paths among the night people,…making contacts and taking orders. **1981** Graziano & Corsel *Somebody Down Here* 7: I musta become the biggest coal booster in the neighborhood. **1983–86** Zausner *Street* 21: *Booster*: A shoplifter.

boot *n.* **1.** expulsion; ejection; defeat; sudden and callous rejection, etc.—constr. with *the.*

1881 C.M. Chase *Editor's Run* 23: I got the boot, with an invitation to "Go to H—l!" **1888* H. Rider Haggard *Col. Quaritch* xii: There'll be the money to take over the Moat Farm and give that varmint Janter the boot. **1904* in *OEDS*: His vivacious accounts of "padding the hoof," "getting the boot," [etc.]. **1906** *Nat. Police Gaz.* (Aug. 18) 6: A fellow who gets the boots at a fair and square game. **1929–33** J. Lowell *Gal Reporter* 74: The boss was sore so I got the boot. **1940** O'Hara *Pal Joey* 70: I would give the boot to that rum-pot. **1955** O'Connor *Last Hurrah* 373: It's the kind of thing that helped Churchill get the boot right after the war. **1972** Hannah *Geronimo Rex* 248: Nobody ever told me how the old man took the news when I got the boot from med school. **1977** T. Berger *Villanova* 43: Her roommate…got the boot from a boyfriend's bed in the middle of the night. **1982** A.P. radio network news

(July 6): There are indications that...an active Republican feminist will also be given the boot. **1984** Jackson & Lupica *Reggie* 168: However, if Billy got the boot, who do you think the public was going to believe?

2. *Sports.* a fielding error.

1913 *Chi. Daily Trib.* (May 1) 15: All but one of the Tiger boots proved costly. **1915** in Lardner *Haircut & Others* 160: They'd got their two [runs] on boots and we'd hit ourn in. **1926** *AS* (Apr.) 370: An error is a "boot." **1929** *N.Y. Times* (June 2) IX 2: The professionals call an error or a wild throw a "boot."

3.a. *Orig. Navy & USMC.* a recruit in basic training; (*hence*) an ignorant or inexperienced enlisted man or (in more recent use, as in 1953 quot.) junior officer. Also *attrib.*

1911 *Fleet Review* (July) 32: "Fear not dear boots," the steward said,/ "Stew to you at supper will be fed." **1911** *Fleet Review* (Oct.) 53: It seems so very funny,/When a "boot" is short of money. **1918** Ruggles *Navy Explained* 25: *Boot.* A young sailor who has recently enlisted in the Navy; a man who is exceedingly wooden in the performance of his duties and who is always uncouth in his habits. **1919** Cowing *Folks at Home* 3: In his "boot" days...this United States Marine underwent the recruit training which fitted him for overseas service. **1925** Thomason *Fix Bayonets* 39 [ref. to WWI]: Pipe down, you Boot. **1927** J. Stevens *Mattock* 51: It'd take a year to make my mob of boots into regular soldiers. **1931** *Our Army* (Oct.) 15: [The sergeant] swears at me and calls me "Boot." **1939** O'Brien *One-Way Ticket* 75: I'm just a big boot, Kelly. I know that, all right. **1940** *Life* (Oct. 28) 89: He will emerge in uniform and canvas puttees, a full fledged "boot." **1942** *Leatherneck* (Nov.) 143: *Boot*—Marine recruit. **1951** J. Wilson *Dark & Damp* 204: Double time that boot to the brig, and throw the goddam key away. **1953** Dibner *Deep Six* 135 [ref. to WWII]: You nuts, boot? Ever hear of radio silence?...Trade-school boots! **1964** in R. Marks *Letters* 10: Being a "boot" is murder. **1968** Maule *Rub-A-Dub* 32: Probably all boots on the other watches. **1974** E. Thompson *Tattoo* 195: I'm home on boot leave. **1987** *21 Jump St.* (Fox-TV): Even a boot like you should know that.

b. *Navy & USMC.* basic training in a boot camp.

1944 A. Scott et al. *Here Come WAVES* (film): They really put him through boot over there. **1945** Huie *Omaha to Oki.* 153: Aisenberry "forgot all that judo I learned in boot and started swinging." **1957–62** Higginbotham *Folklore of USMC* 6: *Boot*—bootcamp or a trainee. **1963** J.A. Williams *Sissie* 26: After boot he hung around for a while. **1964** Rhodes *Chosen Few* 11: I took boot here. **1964** Howe *Valley of Fire* 57: Man, you ought to go through Marine Corps boot. **1970** A. Lewis *Carnival* 287: If he was suspicious he didn't say nothin' and a few days later I'm in Paris Island doin' my boot. **1978** Suddick *Good Men* 43: You'll pray you were back in boot after you been [in prison] a week.

4. a surge of pleasure or amusement; KICK. Also (*vulgar*) **boot in the ass.**

1929 in *AS* (Aug.) 456: *Boot.* A satisfactory sensation. "It gave me a boot." **1942** *Yank* (July 8) 5: His Boston accent...gives me a hell of a boot, it sounds so English. **1949** W.R. Burnett *Asphalt Jungle* 53: What a gag! And there'd been a time when he'd got a terrific boot out of it. **1951** Robbins *Danny Fisher* 224: Maxie'll get a big boot outta that. **1954** MacDonald *Condemned* 73: It's like he gets some kind of a big boot out of that. **1956** E. Hunter *Second Ending* 45: I mean you still get a boot, but not like in the beginning. **1963** D. Tracy *Brass Ring* 264: Something that will give them a boot when they read it. **1969** *Daredevil* (Dec.) 11: Yeah! He'll get a boot out of that! **1973** P. Benchley *Jaws* 238: Or...something that'll give you a boot in the ass to catch, like a mako.

5. BOOTLEGGER, 1.

1921 J. Conway, in *Variety* (Aug. 12) 4: They...go good until they get acquainted with the bootleggers, then their leanin' up against lamp posts and picking up pebbles to alibi the boots all summer. **1942** Pegler *Spelvin* 135: Why don't you take me and her down to the boots and buy her a bag of beer? **1947** Schulberg *Harder They Fall* 206: Drake was an ex-chauffeur for Nick back in his boot days.

6. *Esp. Black E.* a black person.—sometimes used contemptuously.

1954 W.G. Smith *South St.* 98: Boy, if them officers on the ship that brought Suzette over had known that she was coming to marry a *boot*, they'd have thrown her overboard! *Ibid.* 99: The jive put down by Claude and me is strictly boot stuff, got to be. **1957** H. Simmons *Corner Boy* 101: Never seen a boot neighborhood yet wasn't a mess. **1962** in LeRoi Jones *Home* 74: Recently, a young Negro novelist writing in *Esquire*...mentioned that...boots have neither a language of their own nor a characteristic cuisine. **1962** H. Simmons *On Eggshells* 162: A lot of paddy studs still didn't know that boots were human. **1962** Crump *Killer* 360: The last hired was the first fired, particularly if they

happened to be boots. **1970** A. Young *Snakes* 42: They don't even be makin sense to one another much less to other boots. **1980** Gould *Ft. Apache* 33: He'd run through his whole repertoire on the "boots" and the "pineapples," the current precinct names for blacks and Puerto Ricans. **1983** Rovin *Pryor* 115: *Boot* was a ghetto term used to describe shoeshine boys and generally included all black men who were low on the profession totem. **1992** Fla. Nat. Guardsman, on *Daywatch* (CNN-TV) (Aug. 25): You're not goin' anywhere, boot. You're goin' to jail.

7. a condom.

1971 Dahlskog *Dict.* 9: *Boot*...A condom. **1972** in *Playboy* (Jan. 1973) 250: What difference it make? My husband don't like the rubber boots, you take the pill you're liable to grow a tail or something.

8. a tire for a motor vehicle.

1951–53 in *AS* XXIX (1954) 94: *Boots*, n. Tires. **1969** *Current Slang* I & II 14: *Boots*, n. Tires.—High school males, California.—He made a pit stop to change *boots*. **1971** Dahlskog *Dict.* 9: *Boot*...*n.pl.* Automobile tires. **1981* in Partridge *DSUE* (ed. 8) 118.

9. [sugg. by BOOTLICK] *Stu.* a subservient action meant to curry favor; a state of ingratiation (with a professor). Cf. BOOTER, 2.

1908 *DN*: He tried to get in a boot on the professor, but it wouldn't work. **1912** in *PADS* VI 7: He had a boot on the professor.

¶ In phrases:

¶ **bet (one's) boots** see s.v. BET.

¶ **die in (one's) boots** [or **with (one's) boots on**] to die, usu. shamefully, by violence, as by hanging or gunfire. [The evolution of the sense in current S.E., 'to die bravely in a Western gunfight', 'to die while still vigorously engaged in one's work', along with the positive connotations, is a recent development.]

1865–67 De Forest *Miss Ravenel* 5: An excellent place for a dissecting class....So many negroes are whipped to death, so many white gentlemen die in their boots, as the saying is, that we rarely lack for subjects. **1871** Crofutt *Tourist's Guide* 63: Slade's...wife...had ridden...30 miles for the avowed purpose of shooting Slade, to save the disgrace of having him hung, and she arrived...with revolver in hand, only a few minutes too late to execute her scheme—the desperado was dead, and he died "with his boots on." **1871** "M. Twain" *Roughing It* 259: They killed each other on slight provocation, and hoped and expected to be killed themselves—for they held it almost shame to die otherwise than "with their boots on," as they expressed it. **1873** Beadle *Undeveloped West* 435: It will be said in Western dialect, "They died in their Boots." **1873** Miller *Modocs* 95: Dying with the boots on means a great deal in the mines. It is the poetical way of expressing the result of a bar-room or street-battle. **1874** McCoy *Cattle Trade* 292: As many as eleven persons were shot down on a single evening, and many graves were filled with subjects who had "died with their boots on." **1889** O'Reilly & Nelson *Fifty Years on Trail* 136: If you don't mend your ways you'll die with your boots on, for the men won't stand your abuse any longer. *Ibid.* 274: The number who had died with their boots on, that is, had been either shot or hanged, was very great. **1904** in Asbury *Gem of Prairie* 139: Here Lies the Red Crook, Harvey Van Dine, aged 21. Died With His Boots on Mar. 1st, 1904. **1911** in C.M. Russell *Paper Talk* 85: Some cashed in with their boots on.

¶ **give the boots** put the boots to, below.

1899–1900 Cullen *Tales* 297: Well, if they ain't ringers for each other you can give me the boots. **1917** *Editor* (Feb. 24) 153: *Give a Man the Boots*—To kick and stamp a man. **1952** Mandel *Angry Strangers* 355: I fixed Wengel's ass good. I'm giving him the boots.

¶ **go it, boots!** (used as a cry of encouragement).

1839 *Spirit of Times* (Mar. 23) 30: Wooden legs are cheap. Go it, Boots, with a perfect looseness. **1843** in *DA*. **1845** Durivage & Burnham *Stray Subjects* 58: "Go it, Boots!" shouted the crowd. **1865** Byrn *Fudge Fumble* 26: I...said, "go it boots, your Daddy's rich." **1889** Barrère & Leland *Dict. Slang* I 416: *Go it, boots!* cr[y] of encouragement to a man on foot or on horseback, "doing time." **1912** Field *Watch Yourself* 268: Go it boots, you'll win in a walk.

¶ **have one in the boot** *Horse Racing.* (see quot.).

1968 Ainslie *Racing Guide* 469: *Have one in the boot*—To ride a horse whose owner or trainer has made bets, including one for the rider.

¶ **have (one's) boots on** [or **laced**] *Esp. Black E.* to be ready and alert; to be HIP. Also vars. [1872 quots. prob. do not illustrate this usage, which is typical of jazz circles of the 1940's.]

[**1872** Burnham *Secret Service* vi: *High-heeled boots*, triumphant, confident appendages! *Ibid.* 86: Their chums and pals were then upon their "high-heeled boots," and did a flourishing business.] **1940** *Current Hist. & Forum* (Nov. 7) 22: The...inmate learns to *get his boots on* (be wise). **1941** *Pittsburgh Courier* (Apr. 19) 24: *Put on your boots*—Get wise to yourself. **1942** *Yank* (Dec. 23) 18: Their boots were laced, they were really in there. **1946** Boulware *Jive & Slang* 2: *Are Your Boots Laced?*...Do you understand? **1948** Manone & Vandervoort *Trumpet* 172: Well, what do you mean when you say, "He's got his boots on?" "Why, he solid understands the situation." **1967** Maurer & Vogel *Narc. & Narc. Add.* 344: In the know, informed...have (one's) *boots on, keep (one's) boots on,* etc. "Tell Joe to put his boots on, to wise up."

¶ **lick boots** to curry favor in a servile manner. See also BOOTLICK, *v.*
1929–30 Farrell *Young Lonigan* 21: He had been made ward committeeman because he had licked everybody's boots. **1958** J. Ward *Buchanan* 53: It'll come sooner'n you expect, you don't quit lickin' Hallett's boots. **1977** N. Hancock *Greyfax* 246: No more licking boots for my living. I'll be my own master for a change.

¶ **out of (one's) boots** thoroughly and in a finishing manner.
1864 *Battle Fields of So.* 251: I believe if the enemy were "whipped out of their boots" they would still shout "victory." **1886** Abbot *Blue Jackets* 187 [ref. to Civil War]: If I'd only have had one old cannon aboard, we'd have licked ye out of yer butes! **1892** F. Harper *Iola Leroy* 9: Secesh routed. Yankees whipped 'em out of their boots. **1898** Cahan *Bridegroom* 52: I beat him clean out of his boots by a stripling. *Ibid.* 102: You have been cheated out of your boots by a stripling.

¶ **put** [or **throw**] **the boots to, 1.** to kick and trample in a savage beating; stomp.
1894 in Ade *Chicago Stories* 30: I ain't a goin' to do a t'ing but trun de boots into dat skinny guy. **1904** Hobart *Jim Hickey* 43: The...ex-pugilist...put the boots to me. **1913–15** Van Loan *Taking the Count* 125: Down he goes for de count, an' T-bone comes out from behin' and puts de boots to him proper. **1918** Ruggles *Navy Explained* 86: If you don't get this deck clean I'll put th' boots to ya! **1920** Ade *Hand-Made Fables* 73: A chance to throw the Boots into the Gink who had driven them out into the Desert. **1921** E. O'Neill *Hairy Ape* 251: No gat, no knife. Shall we give him what's what and put the boots to him? **1925** G. Mullin *Scholar Tramp* 285: De dinge slowed 'im wid a pair o' brass knucks, and den put de boots to 'im. **1966** Elli *Riot* 240: You're damn lucky the whole crew didn't put the boots to you when you were floppin' around on the floor. **1970** Thackrey *Thief* 393: And then I just purely whipped his ass...and put the boots to him, and told him to forget my name.
2. to victimize thoroughly and deliberately; (*hence*) to vanquish.
1896 Ade *Artie* 33: He threw the boots into me the worst I ever got 'em. Ooh! He made me feel like a tramp. **1902** [Hobart] *Back to Woods* 109: I put the boots to you. I gave you the gaff for $6,000...and...I'm sorry. **1910** *N.Y. Eve. Jour.* (Mar. 16) 14: The Colts...put the boots to the Hoosiers yesterday 11 to 3. **1948** J.H. Burns *Lucifer* 365: But Ben could only think of how the boots had been put to himself.
3. [sugg. by *mount* and *ride*] to copulate with vigorously.
1933 West *Miss Lonelyhearts* 83: They got her into the back room...and put the boots to her. They didn't let her out for three days. **1934** H. Miller *Tropic of Cancer* 107: He takes it for granted that Carl put the boots to her. **1945** in Legman *No Laughing Matter* 335: An ignorant lad is advised by a friend to go ahead boldly and "put the boots" to his bride. **1948** J.H. Burns *Lucifer* 365: According to them, the boots would be put to Helen, to Marietta, to Skippy, to Martha, and to Connie. **1969** Cameron *Tunnel War* 20: She probably...read that stuff some Austrian doctor kept writing about snakes and cigars and wanting to throw the boots to your mother. **1980** McDowell *Our Honor* 37: You mean to say you haven't got a hard-on?...Did you beat it down? Did you do the wash by hand? Or did you already put the boots to someone? **1985** *Nat. Lampoon* (Sept.) 42: They want to meet a fox/And put the boots to her.

boot *adj.* Navy & USMC. [BOOT, *n.,* 3.a.] (of a junior officer) raw; inexperienced. Also (*vulgar*) **boot-assed.**
1944 in Rea *Wings of Gold* 200: Boot ensigns are being made ground instructors. **1961** G. Forbes *Goodbye to Some* 66 [ref. to WWII]: Mr. Prime says he don't want two boot ensigns. **1964** Newhafer *Last Tallyho* 37 [ref. to WWII]: A boot ensign and he wants to know who do I think I'm talking to. *Ibid.* 138: It is damned rare when a boot-assed ensign becomes a division leader. **1973** Roth *Sand in Wind* 11: He wondered whether this had been the same speech all the boot lieutenants received. **1980** M. Baker *Nam* 63: I'm a boot lieutenant and that's the lowest thing in the Marine Corps. **1982** Downey *Losing the War* 32 [ref.

to WWII]: All right, you boot-ass bastards. Let's go! **1987** D. Sherman *Main Force* 44 [ref. to 1966]: Willie, you're so boot, I ain't even given you a nickname yet.

boot *v.* **1.** to eject, expel, dismiss, spurn, etc.—often constr. with *out.*
1848 in Eliason *Tarheel Talk* 261: I have been pecked,...alias booted, alias slippered. **1868** Harris *Lovingood* 304: So many hollered for him that the ringmaster wer feard to boot him out. **1880** *Harper's Mag.* (Dec.) 160: He angrily bade the bore to leave...and never show his face there again; if he did, he would be booted out. **1930** Graham & Graham *Queer People* 204: He'll use his drag to get you booted out of the studio. **1935** *AS* (Feb.) X 27 [ref. to *ca*1910–20]: For "dismissed" [from school] even in a fairly mild usage, *booted* or *lofted* were preferred.
2.a. to walk or run; run away.—constr. with *it* or (*vulgar*) *ass.*
1905 in *DARE:* Boot it. **1907** *DN* III 241: *Boot,* v.i. Go afoot. "I booted down in a hurry." *boot it*...To walk. "I booted it to town." **1962** in Cray *Erotic Muse* 256: I'm booting ass tomorrow.
b. to go quickly; (*hence*) accelerate.—usu. constr. with *it.*
1945 *Yank* (Mar. 23) 7: I wanta get behind the wheel of a big ol' GMC and really boot it. **1988** Maloney *Thunder Alley* 66: "Boot it, Ghost!" Woody yelled as the F-14 streaked down the asphalt strip. *Ibid.* 286: Ryder heard the Skyhawk pilots boot their engines.
3. to botch or bungle; (*specif.*) *Sports.* to make an error in play by kicking or dropping (the ball).
1908 in Fleming *Unforgettable Season* 239: Bridwell...booted the ball, and Overall scored. **1915** T.A. Dorgan, in *N.Y. Eve. Jour.* (Aug. 5) 12: He'll spoil all in a minute—he'll boot it sure. **1915** in Lardner *Haircut & Others* 157: Then Collins boots one on Murray and they've got a run. **1940** W.R. Burnett *High Sierra:* We sure been a long time on this caper and we don't want to boot it now. **1961** Brosnan *Pennant Race* 66: They might boot three or four and we'll tie it up. **1962** Houk & Dexter *Ballplayers* 135: Frankly, I don't know how he [the umpire] could have booted that decision. **1976** G.V. Higgins *Deke Hunter* 86: I booted one that should've been a double play. *a***1988** C. Adams *More Straight Dope* 142: You raise three issues, and have managed to boot all of them.
4. *Stu.* to BOOTLICK.
1912 in *PADS* VI 7: He booted the professor.
5. to BOOTLEG.
1933 D. Runyon, in *Collier's* (Dec. 23) 7: There is no money in booting any more.
6. *Jazz & Black E.* to make aware; to HIP. Cf. *have (one's) boots on* s.v. BOOT, *n.*
1944 Burley *Harlem Jive* 15: Let me boot you to my play. **1958** Hughes & Bontemps *Negro Folklore* 481: *Boot:* To explain, to describe, inform authoritatively. *That chick booted me about love.*
7. *Narc.* (see 1953 quot.).
1953 W. Brown *Monkey on My Back* 37: Jerry had shown him how to boot (to draw blood into a syringe in such a way as to mix it with heroin, and then to shoot it back into the vein). **1956** E. Hunter *Second Ending* 242: I'll boot that mother-loving White God until it comes out of my ears. **1965** *Reader's Digest* (June) 230: The technique, known as "booting," is believed to prolong the drug's initial effect. **1971** *Inter. Jour. Addictions* VI 10: When you were shooting junk, did you boot? **1983** *Time* (Apr. 11) 31: [He] is injecting heroin into his arm, each time drawing a little blood back into the syringe. This pumping technique, known as booting, prolongs the rush. **1988** *N.Y. Times* (Feb. 5) B 5: One of the drug users...began to "boot" his mixture of cocaine, inserting it into the vein, withdrawing the mixture with blood back into the syringe several times to repeat the initial high. **1991** "Magic" Johnson *Avoid AIDS* 20: Some drug users "boot" the drug, meaning they mainline it and then pull blood up into the syringe two or three times to...get every bit of high out of the injection.
8. *Stu.* to vomit.
1971 *Current Slang* V 8: *Boot,* v. To vomit. **1977** Sayles *Union Dues* 57: Booted his insides all over my God damn shoes. **1978** C. Miller *Animal House* 101: You're a...hero! Nobody ever booted on Dean Wormer before. **1980** Birnbach *Preppy Hndbk.* 113: Vomiting...[to] Barf...Blow lunch...Boot...Upchuck. **1983** *Nat. Lampoon* (Apr.) 32: The objective being to eat all eight pieces without booting. **1989** *U.* (Apr.) 19: I feel so awful I might wind up booting. **1989** P. Munro *U.C.L.A. Slang* 23: I only drank ten beers before I booted.
9. *Entertainment Industry.* to promote the sale of; plug.
1981 *N.Y. Times Mag.* (June 21) 28: The major companies..."booted" the albums with singles, which are necessary billboards, and these singles went to the radio stations and juke boxes.

boot-ass *n.* [BOOT + -ASS] *Navy & USMC.* an ignorant or inexperienced enlisted person or officer.—usu. considered vulgar. Also attrib.
1973 Huggett *Body Count* 16: Goddamn, if the boot-ass wanted to be stubborn, he'd show him. Maybe the lieutenant didn't think serving two tours in Nam meant anything.

boot camp *n.* Orig. *Navy & USMC.* a basic training center for recruits in one of the armed services. Now *colloq.* or *S.E.*
1916 *Marines Mag.* (Jan.) 30: Eighteen men from Paris Island (Boot Camp)…nothing so bad as the recruit led to believe in the boot camp. **1919** *Marine Corps Gaz.* (Mar.) 17: If military discipline be rigidly enforced, the recruit, after his preliminary service in the "boot" camp, may perform any reasonable kind of organized labor. **1919** Catlin *A Few Marines* 277: Boot camp. **1928** Scanlon *Have Mercy* 4: Aw, pipe down on that bootcamp stuff! **1936** S.I. Miller *Leathernecks Have Landed* (film): You're out of boot camp now. **1958** Cope & Dyer *Petty Off. Gd.* (ed. 2): Boot camp. Slang for naval recruit training center. **1966** Heinl *Marine Off. Gd.* 591: Boot camp. Recruit depot.

booter *n.* **1.** BOOTLEGGER.
1944 D. Runyon, in *Collier's* (Jan. 15) 52: I hear the Vasserkopf is an old booter and he may remember the trick.
2. *Stu.* [cf. BOOT, *n.*, 9] a sycophant.
1947 *Amer. N & Q* (May) 30: "Booter" used to be [*ca*1902] the word for one who tried to curry favor with a member of the faculty or worm his way into some secret society.
3. *Sports Journ.* a soccer player.
1976 *Webster's Sports Dict.* 50.

Boot Hill *n.* [alluding to *die with (one's) boots on* s.v. BOOT] *West.* a cemetery for those who have died by violence, as by hanging or in gunfights.—often used as proper name. Also (*rarely*) **Boots Hill.** Now *hist.*
1877 in R.M. Wright *Dodge City* 144: Dodge boasts of two burying spots, one for the tainted…who have generally died with their boots on. "Boot Hill" is…[its] title. **1877** in Miller & Snell *Why the West Was Wild* 7: "Boot-Hill" is the somewhat singular title applied to the burial place of the class just mentioned [in Dodge City]. **1882** Dodge *Wild Indians* 627: Julesburg was celebrated for its desperadoes. No twenty-four hours passed without its contribution to Boots Hill (the cemetery whose every occupant was buried in his boots). **1901** in *DA.* **1916** in *Calif. Folk. Qly.* I (1942) 270: There's a new grave up on Boot Hill. **1930** E. Ferber *Cimarron* 160: The body, unclaimed, was interred in Boot Hill, with only the prowling jackals to mourn him, their own kin. **1947** Overholser *Buckaroo's Code* 45: Now he's ready for boot hill.

bootie *n.* BOOTLEGGER, 1.
1929 *Sat. Eve. Post* (Apr. 13) 76: That new bootie…carries a powerful line of hooch. **1933** D. Runyon, in *Collier's* (Dec. 23) 7: I am a bootie for a long time.

bootleg *n.* **1.** illicit liquor, esp. whiskey. Also attrib.
1898 in *Amer. Heritage* (Aug. 1980) 57: That Never Failing Nerve Restorer, commissary boot leg. **1924** Henderson *Keys to Crookdom* 398: Bootleg. Contraband whisky. *Bootlegger.* One who sells bootleg. **1928** in H. Crane *Letters* 315: Gradually I'm becoming acquainted with all the brands of bootleg that the Westcoast offers. **1931** Rouverol *Dance, Fools, Dance* (film): You don't think I'd drink bootleg, do you? **1937** Reitman *Box-Car Bertha* 65: There were several tea shops and bootleg joints on the near north side of Chicago that catered to lesbians. **1969–71** Kahn *Boys of Summer* 274: A sheriff would catch some old guy making bootleg and get him in the pen a year. **1971** *Playboy* (May) 90: You've long been known for your robust drinking habits, whether it's rotgut bootleg or imported Scotch. **1975** W. *Day of Locust* (film): I've drank bootleg better than this. **1982** Heat Moon *Blue Hwys.* 26: Shine's paid for a lot of college education in these hills,…but don't try to tell me that about bootleg.
2. [see also BOOTLEG, *adj.*, 2] imitation or adulterated (orig. with chicory) coffee; (*hence, broadly*) bad coffee.
1904 Hoffman *Blasted Hopes* 35 [ref. to 1888]: I…was refreshed by the steaming beverage called coffee but which my fellows called bootleg. **1904** *Life in Sing Sing* 20: A large piece of bread and a cup of the mixture locally honored by the title of "bootleg," but appearing on the dietary scale as coffee. *Ibid.* 8: [Bootleg] is made for the most part from charred crusts of bread, with a small addition of ground coffee-beans or peas. **1912** in J.H. Williams *Blow the Man Down* 71 [ref. to 1887]: Next morning after we had disposed of our early refreshment of bootleg and hardtack. **1912** Lowrie *Prison* 20: I had been in jail several weeks without a drink—save water and "bootleg." **1917** *Editor* (Jan. 13) 33: Army

Vernacular…"Bootleg"—Coffee. **1927** *Liberty* (Aug. 10): Bootleg in the morning, bootleg at night,/Beans on Sunday and them out of sight. **1928** Tilton *Cap'n George Fred* 52 [ref. to 1870's]: The coffee was called "bootleg"—I suppose it was made from old boots parched and ground.
3. *Black E.* BOOTLEGGER, 1.
1927 Hughes *Fine Clothes* 18: Go to de bootleg's/Git some gin to make you laugh.
4. any bootleg item, as a recording.
*1951 in *OEDAS:* Victor presses bootlegs! **1979** in L. Bangs *Psychotic Reactions* 276: The 1974 recorded-live bootleg *Metallic K.O.* **1990** in Groening *How to Go to Hell* (unp.): We will prosecute bootleggers of our bootlegs.

bootleg *adj.* **1.** illicitly transported or produced; (*hence*) unauthorized; unsanctioned; unregulated. Now *colloq.*
1889 in Barrère & Leland *Dict. Slang* I: There is as much whisky consumed in Iowa now…on the boot-leg plan. **1920** *Collier's* (Mar. 6) 9: They call it bootleg licker. **1929** *Variety* (Apr. 10) 1: A market for bootleg disk records. **1941** *Harper's Mag.* (Oct.) 541: Massachusetts hams recently engaged a bootleg station in lengthy conversations. **1955** Graziano & Barber *Somebody Up There* 148: These bootleg fights aren't exactly amateur, according to the rules. **1956** Heflin *USAF Dict.* 89: *Bootleg, a.* Of an activity: Unauthorized or unscheduled, as "bootleg flying time." **1964** E. Wilson *Wilson's N.Y.* 36: A "gypsy" or "bootleg hack"…is not medallioned…and therefore not supervised…by police. **1970** in P. Heller *In This Corner* 180: I started in 1929 in bootleg shows [i.e., boxing matches]—five, ten dollars, fifteen dollars a fight. **1971** Sorrentino *Up from Never* 125: His name is Johnny Mandello. He was a bootleg fighter. **1983** R. Thomas *Missionary* 23: It was a special bootleg copy, fresh off the Xerox machine.
2. imitation.
1893 MacDonald *Prison Secrets* 116: His honor's "boot-leg" beverage, by courtesy termed coffee. **1895** in *DA:* The menu at the meal stations along through Texas and Arizona consists of whit-leather steak, overdue eggs, bad-smelling butter, corn dodgers, and "boot-leg" coffee. *ca*1900 in Millett *Semper Fidelis* 155: I'm tired of bootleg coffee and the commissary bean. **1901** King *Dog-Watches* 81: The "boot-leg" coffee served us. **1903** J.H. Williams, in *Independent* (Nov. 26) 2794: For breakfast we were invariably presented with boot leg coffee and a pan of rotten potatoes.

bootleg *adv.* in an unsanctioned manner, esp. in the form of a bootleg recording.
1985 B.E. Ellis *Less Than Zero* 34: I got *Temple of Doom* bootleg.

bootleg *v.* [app. first applied to contraband that could be concealed in one's boot] **1.** to smuggle or smuggle through; to sell illicitly.
1898 Kerlin *Camp Life* 29: The cases, since pay-day especially, have been frequent, "two-step moonshine" having been boot-legged into camp. **1903** in *DA:* In the Pulpit Was a Minister When Arrested for "Boot-Legging." **1906** in *DN* III 127: William Castell, charged with bootlegging whiskey, was tried before Mayor Eason this morning. **1912** in Truman *Dear Bess* 77: I'd say give 'em booze all they want, because they bootleg anyway. **1928** in *OEDS:* She "bootlegged" a baby into her home and…pretended to her husband that it was hers. **1928** in Dobie *Drinkin' Gou'd* 224: They bootlegged them out to the plains. I knew one guy that got rich bootlegging them. He had a patented jack that would…lift a well right out of the ground. **1930** *AS* VI 156: I bootlegged this paper from my dad's office. I bootlegged these cigs from the girl-friend. **1938** Haines *Tension* 205: Margrave wasn't going to wait around here burning copper to bootleg to junk yards. **1938** *AS* (Apr.) 156: *Bootleg 'em.* To rush a special order through outside of regular channels. **1969** Layden & Snyder *Different Game* 3: These stories moved over the telegraph wires, and if some maverick student tried to bootleg a story behind the publicity man's back, Rock…[could] shut him off at the telegraph key. **1982** "W.T. Tyler" *Rogue's March* 185: Did Lutete ask for material or did Miles just bootleg what he thought would be useful?
2. to manufacture or transport liquor illicitly. Now *S.E.*
1922 in Ruhm *Detective* 9: He had been mixed up in a shady deal—bootlegging or something. **1943** in Loosbrock & Skinner *Wild Blue* 330: Angels don't gamble or bootleg. **1970** Terkel *Hard Times* 203: Everybody bootlegged.

bootlegger *n.* **1.** one who smuggles or sells illicit liquor; (*later*) one who produces liquor illicitly. Now *S.E.*
1890 in *OEDS:* The "boot-legger" is…a man who wears boots in whose tops are concealed a flask or two of liquor. **1907** in Shirley *Hell's*

Fringe 453: An alleged "bootlegger." **1920** in V. Randolph *Church House* 70: And pretty soon there was nobody left in Polk county, only the bootleggers, and they had to make their living by selling whiskey to each other. **1922** in Ruhm *Detective* 9: I guess I could shoot as good as any bootlegger. **1992** Hosansky & Sparling *Working Vice* 66: The captain...protected the bootleggers during prohibition.
2. *R.R.* (see quot.).
1940 *R.R. Mag.* (Apr.) 38: *Bootlegger*—Train that runs over more than one railroad.

bootlegger turn *n.* a 180-degree turn in an automobile accomplished by a sudden application of the brake. Also vars.
1955 in *AS* (Feb. 1956) 98: He will return to his side of the border in a *bootlegger turn*. **1967** in *DARE*: Bootlegger's turn. **1978** E. Thompson *Devil to Pay* 113: He threw the Ford into a bootlegger's turn. **1980** in *Penthouse* (Jan. 1981) 148: The Dodge whipped around the other way as neatly as in the movies—better perhaps, because it was the moonshiners who *invented* the maneuver. It's called a "bootleg turn," in fact. **1991** Marcinko & Weisman *Rogue Warrior* 248: Every trick from bootlegger's turns to head-on crashes.

bootleg play *n. Football.* a hidden-ball play.
1946 L.H. Baker *Football* 97: What is a bootleg play? **1958** J. King *Pro Football* 55 [ref. to 1945]: The Giants were amazed by Waterfield when he scored on a bootleg play....He held the ball lengthwise against the brown of his pants. **1976** *Webster's Sports Dict.*

bootlick *n.* BOOTLICKER.
1834 *Mil. & Naval Mag.* (Nov.) 204: You boot-lick! **1849** *Yale Banger* (Nov.) 6: Bootlick hypocrites upraised their might. **1850** *Yale Battery* (Feb. 14): Then he arose, and offered himself as a "*bootlick*" to the Faculty. **1877** Bartlett *Amer.* (ed. 4) 59: *Boot-Lick*. A lickspittle; a toady. **1882** C. King *Col.'s Daughter* 83: He hated Bucketts and called him a "bootlick" behind his back. **1894** *Lucky Bag* (U.S. Nav. Acad.) 66: *Boot lick* (n.)...A sycophant. **1915** Poole *Harbor* 47: "Bootlick, bootlick," I heard murmurs all over the hall. I had answered better than I had to. Hence I had licked the professor's boots. I did not offend in this way again.

bootlick *v.* to curry favor [with] in a servile manner. Now *colloq.*
1845 J. Hooper *Simon Suggs* 54: "Gracious heavens! General, I wouldn't stake so much on a single card," said a young man who was inclined to boot-lick any body suspected of having money. **1849** *Yale Gallinipper* (Dec.): Crouching, fawning, bootlicking hypocrites. **1850** in Eliason *Tarheel Talk* 261: One little fool...suspected...I was bootlicking. **1856** Hall *College Wds.* (ed. 2) 34: *Bootlick*. To fawn upon; to court favor. **1869** *Carmina Princetonia* 43: I "boot-licked" fellows for election. **1891** *Outing* (July) 316: Oh, I'm sure of passing in everything. Don't bootlick anyone for me, Uncle Dick. **1894** *Lucky Bag* [U.S. Nav. Acad.] 66: *Bootlick* (v.)...To toady. **1909** J. Moss *Officers' Man.* (ed. 2) 283: *Bootlick*—to flatter. **1929–30** J.T. Farrell *Young Lonigan* 53: He bootlicked around until he became a ward committeeman. **1935** T. Wolfe *Time & River* 74: To hell with you, you damn little bootlicking—. **1951** Cowley *Exile's Return* 54: These he accused of slander, dullness, theft, bootlicking, ingratitude. **1953** *Combat Forces Journal* (June) 8: It couldn't be worse than "bootlicking" superiors.

bootlicker *n.* [cf. earlier S.E. *foot-licker*] a servile individual who attempts to curry favor with those in authority; toady. Now *colloq.*
1848 *Yale Banger* (Oct.) 23: Three or four bootlickers rise. **1856** Hall *College Wds.* (ed. 2) 34: *Bootlicker*. A student who seeks or gains favor from a teacher by flattery or officious civilities; one who curries favor. **1965** in Cleaver *Soul on Ice* 66: The bootlickers, Uncle Toms, lackeys, and stooges for the white power structure have done their best to denigrate Malcolm. **1969** H.R. Brown *Die Nigger* 53: I looked around and the bootlickers were getting scared. **1986** R. Walker *AF Wives* 241: There's always a few bootlickers and finks.

boots *n.* **1.** a bootblack.
1845 Corcoran *Pickings* 69: If a gemman...calls "boots"—dats me. **1869** Logan *Foot Lights* 199: Is this gentleman a "Boots" that he is tintinabulated at thus ruthlessly? **1871** *Galaxy* (May) 759: The hostler...is generally both landlord and "boots." **1877** *Puck* (July 25) 6: The fellow who makes out the bills wears them; the "boots" wears them. **1893** Coes *Black Blunders* 8: I'se de boots of dis house. **1906** MacFadden *Rambles* 154: Valets, maids, barbers, bellboys, and "boots" are all on the alert. **1983** (quot. at BOOT, *n.*, 6).
2. *Black E.* BOOT, *n.*, 6.

1967 Riessman & Dawkins *Play It Cool* 54: Boots n. (always with plural -s)...a Negro...*There's a boots playing quarterback on the Mustangs.*

bootstrap *v.* [fr. colloq. *pull (oneself) up by (one's) bootstraps*] to help or improve (oneself) without outside assistance. Also absol.
[**1949** *N.Y. Times* (June 19) VII 10: Dale Carnegie's classic bootstrapper, "How to Win Friends and Influence People."] **1951** *Time* (Aug. 27) 91: For its bootstrapping job, the [petroleum] industry is earning its merited reward. **1958** in *OED2*. **1968** *Business Week* (Nov. 2) 103: Sullivan's idea of Negroes bootstrapping themselves has solidified his business support. **1974** *Everett* (Wash.) *Herald* (Sept. 27) 5b: The tribe has been "bootstrapping" itself for the past 40 years as it struggled to develop the land of the reservation. **1983** Beckwith & Knox *Delta Force* 90: The Army gave me the year to bootstrap. I found I loved school and I graduated with a 3.5 grade average.

boot topping *n. Naut.* a Plimsoll line. Also **boot top.**
1953 McEwen & Lewis *Encyc. Naut. Knowl.: Boot-topping.*...That portion of a vessel's plating between light and load water lines. **1961** Burgess *Dict. Sailing* 33: *Boot top.* Ship's side-plating between light and load water lines. **1968** Blackford *Torp. Sailor* 40 [ref. to 1916]: Within inches of the water we...cut in the black boot-topping. **1975** Mostert *Super-ship* 228: Every ship has its Plimsoll line....the familiar red "boot topping" that covers the vessel's bottom as far as her waterline.

boot up *v.* to get high or intoxicated, esp. on heroin. Also as *n.*
1953 Kramer & Karr *Teen-Age Gangs* 62: How about a boot-up?...I'd go for a bang. *Ibid.* 63: I'll get the deck and we'll boot up. **1958** *Life* (Apr. 14) 141 [ref. to ca1950]: He had pushed narcotics to boot us up for the clash. **1960** Freeman *Out of Burning* 158: We booted up on [wine].

booty or **boody** *n.* **1.** Esp. *Black E.* the buttocks; rump. Also fig. [1838 quot. means simply 'body'.]
[**1838** [Haliburton] *Clockmaker* (Ser. 2) 65: De dear little lily, de sweet little booty, de little missy baby. Oh, how I do lub 'em all!] **1928** in Oliver *Meaning of Blues* 216: I can strut my boody, make my sweet pigmeat. **1959** F.L. Brown *Trumbull Pk.* 363: Getting kicked in the booty would be mighty discouraging too. **1962** Crump *Killer* 42: Will ya dig de bootie on dis beauty! **1966** "T. Pendleton" *Iron Orchard* 6: I know this oil patch like my old lady's boody, son. **1975** S.P. Smith *Amer. Boys* 167: He work his booty off up there. **1987** in *Black Teen* (Jan. 1988) 11: I didn't do the nude scenes....I was a prude. I just looked at the "booties." **1992** *In Living Color* (Fox-TV): Her booty...hangs so low it sweeps up after itself.
2. *Black E.* the vulva and vagina; (*hence*) copulation; (in homosexual use) anal copulation. Cf. parallel sense development of ASS, BUTT, etc.
1925 Van Vechten *Nig. Heaven* 215: Now...that you've gone white, do you really want...pinks for boody? **1926** in Handy *Treasury of Blues* 51: I love you papa, pretty papa but your game's too strong/I had a lot of bootie but the panic's on. **1928** Bodenheim *Georgie May* 9: 'Member the black skunk that called me "cheap white booty." *Ibid.*: How's booty to-night? *Ibid.* 101: Wanna try mah booty? **1935** Z.N. Hurston *Mules & Men* 192: If you want good boody/Oh, go to Ella Wall. **1952** J.K. Larson *Barnyard Folklore of Idaho* 75: Copulation—n., booty,...ass, tail, pussy, [etc.]. **1952** in Wepman, Newman & Binderman *The Life* 148: Booty-grinder, sweetspot-finder. **1968** Oliver *Blues Tradition* 204: Before 1908, James P. Johnson had learned similar tunes in Jersey City...like...*She Got Good Booty.* **1973** I. Reed *La. Red* 73: Now Give Me Some That Booty, Bitch!! **1976** Wepman, Newman & Binderman *The Life* 178 [ref. to 1960's]: *Booty n.* See round-eye. **1978** W. Brown *Tragic Magic* 104: I'm givin' up neither money or bootie! *a*1973–87 F.M. Davis *Livin' the Blues* 36 [ref. to Kansas, ca1920]: A woman had a "pussy"...or "booty" (in school we giggled when the teacher told how Romans burned...conquered cities after gathering all the booty).

booty bandit *n. Pris.* an aggressive homosexual anal sodomist; homosexual rapist.
1962 Crump *Killer* 293: I lost 'em fightin' a booty bandit in a black cell. **1970** *Evergreen Rev.* (Apr.) 79: The aggressive [homosexuals in prison] were called "Booty Bandits." **1972** Carr *Bad* 60: They started calling us the "Booty Bandits"; all the other cons knew about us and were afraid. **1990** Vachss *Blossom* 107: This booty bandit got your name on his list.

booty-struck *adj. Black E.* lecherous; CUNT-STRUCK.
1964 Abrahams *Down in Jungle* 168: I'm booty-struck and got to fuck/ And I got grinding on my mind.

booze *n.* [fr. the *v.*] **1.a.** alcoholic liquor of any kind, esp. whiskey or beer. Also vars.

*ca*1325 in *MED* II 1099: Drynke to hym deorly of fol god bous. *ca*1500 in *MED*: Not synke in watur but swymme in boos. *1536 in Partridge *Dict. Und.* 63: Bouse. *1632 in *OED*: No bouse, nor no tobacco? *ca*1635 in Partridge *Dict. Und.* 63: To pay for my booze of all things I am willing. *1641 R. Brome, in R.G. Lawrence *Comedies* 194: This bowse is better than rum booze. *1665 R. Head *Eng. Rogue* 23: All their cry now was for Rum-booz [i.e. good liquor]. *Ibid.* 24: They tipped to each other a gage of booz. *1714 *Memoirs of John Hall* (ed. 4) 11: Booze. *1732 in *OED*: We…had a profusion of "peck & booz" (terms for meat and drink). *1785 Grose *Vulgar Tongue: Boose,* or *Bouse*. Drink. *1821 Moncrieff *Tom & Jerry* II vi: Have you ordered the peck and booze for the evening? 1859 Matsell *Vocab.* 14: Booze. Intoxicating drink. 1895 in J.I. White *Git Along Dogies* 66: Booze—girls and booze! *1895 in Ware *Passing Eng.* 43: "I heard some men shout that they wanted some more booze." *Mr. Justice Wright:* "What?" *Mr. Willis:* "Booze, my lord, drink." *Mr. Justice Wright:* "Ah." 1899 Kountz *Baxter's Letters* 69: He sopped up all kinds of booze except wine. 1905 *Independent* (Mar. 2) 490: You can have your meals and as much booze as you can drink until you go aboard tomorrow, but that's all. *ca*1905 in McCay *Little Nemo* 9: The booze that he has put away would float a ship. 1907 in C.M. Russell *Paper Talk* 55: One drink of this boose [*sc.* mescal] will make a jack rabbit spit in a rattel snakes eye. 1914 *Amer. Lumberman* (Apr. 25) 33: We didn't have no booze around. 1929 "E. Queen" *Roman Hat* 40: I could smell the booze on his breath. 1932 L. Lawes *20,000 Yrs.* 199: The case is diagnosed as "booze." 1956 Longstreet *Real Jazz* 71: Dave went on the booze. 1958 in A. Sexton *Letters* 45: The man left two bottles of booze. 1960 Bannon *Journey* 54: I think he was out somewhere swilling booze this afternoon. 1973 Zuckerman *Merriwell* 130: If you were out of booze, you were out of luck. 1975 Zezza *Love Potion* 337: Call me Ben.…I sell booze.

b. (used attrib.).

1867 *Nat. Police Gaz.* (Apr. 6) 2: He now keeps one of the best fitted up "booze cribs" in Brooklyn. 1879 in Miller & Snell *Why West Was Wild* 157: We…were…"getting to the booze joint." 1896 Ade *Artie* 64: He…dug up the long green and he's puttin' it out at the booze joints. 1907 *American Mag.* (Sept.) 463: God may call me into a booze mill to save a soul and I'll go. 1914 Ellis *Billy Sunday* 333: He would never head you into a booze joint. 1926 C.M. Russell *Trails* 31: Me and my friend drops into a booze parlor on the Canadian line. 1936 R. Adams *Cowboy Lingo* 237: Pat took a booze joint and, after smokin' the place up and runnin' everybody out…fell asleep.

2. a drinking spree.

*1786 R. Burns, in *OED*: An' if we dinna hae a bouze, I'se ne'er drink mair. *1850 in *OEDS*: The sawyers who were to have got the board out of the bush, had been on the booze. *1864 in *OEDS*: An occasional hard booze, and its consequent headache. 1867 *Nat. Police Gaz.* (Oct. 26) 4: He met him on a "booze." 1879 *Puck* (Sept. 27) 451: I was jes' on a quiet, gentlemanly booze wid Maginnis an' some of de b'yes. 1894 *Century* (Feb.) 518: It's jes filled with a blasted lot of gay-cats (men who will work) who've been on a booze.

booze v. [dial. var. of earlier *bouse* < Middle Du *busen* 'to drink heavily'] **1.** to drink booze, esp. so as to get drunk.—in mod. use also constr. with *it [up]*. Also trans. Now *S.E.* Hence **boozing,** n.

*ca*1325 in *MED* II 1100: Hail, ye holi monkes…Late and rathe ifillid of ale and wine! Depe cun ye bouse. *1566–67 Harman *Caveat:* They bowle and bowse one to another. *1648 R. Herrick, in *OED*: Still I be bousing. *1665 R. Head *Eng. Rogue* 23: Most part of the night we spent in boozing. *1823 in Byron *Works* 920: Who…like Tom could…/Booze in the ken? 1836 Cather *Voyage* 24: They are continually boozing. 1848 Bartlett *Amer.* 43: To Boose. To tipple. 1849 Melville *White Jacket* 46: On shore, at least, Jack might *bouse away* as much as he pleased. *1853 Thackeray *Barry Lyndon* ch. xiii: Gambling and boozing with low Irish black-legs! 1894 *Century* (Feb.) 518: I've boozed around this town…off and on for the last seven years. 1896 Ade *Artie* 101: No more boozin'. 1901 in Bierce *Letters* 51: You'd not regret going to Santa Cruz and boozing with him. 1908 J. London *M. Eden* 141: I got to booze up. 1914 S.H. Adams *Clarion* 40: College-bred and all that. Boozes, though.

2. to squander on booze.—now usu. constr. with *away*.

*1566–67 Harman *Caveat:* Why, hast thou any lowre [money] in thy bonge [purse] to bouse? *1936 Partridge *DSUE* 81: Booze…V.t. To spend or dissipate in liquor: mid-C 19–20. Often *booze away* (e.g. a fortune). 1969 N.Y.C. man, age *ca*40: He's out boozing his rent money.

3. to entertain by furnishing booze to.

1959 Goodman *Wheeler Dealers* 57: We…booze 'em at one-fifty a crack.

booze clerk n. a bartender. *Joc.*

1898 Kountz *Baxter's Letters* 17: Ordinarily I call the booze clerk by his first name. 1903 *Enquirer* (Cincinnati) (May 9) 13: *Booze clerk*—A bartender. 1918 in *Wisc. Mag. of History* LXII 227: Hornbeck and I were among those who acted as booze-clerks and my arms have not yet got the soreness out of them on account of pulling corks. 1920 Ade *Hand-Made Fables* 268: The Booze-Clerk was Pythias to every Damon who came in for a pick-me-up.

boozed adj. drunk.—in recent use occ. constr. with *up*. Also (*obs.*) **bowzed.**

1737 *Penn. Gazette* (Jan. 6) 1: The Drinker's Dictionary…He's …Boozy, Bowz'd, [etc.]. *1850 in *F & H* I 297: Boozed in their tavern dens,/The scurril press drove all their dirty pens. 1879 in Miller & Snell *Why West Was Wild* 405: Means was pretty well "boozed," as the saying is. 1886 *N.O. Lantern* (Sept. 22) 3: This fortune teller gets boozed up. *1891 cited in Partridge *DSUE* (ed. 7) 1023 [Australia]: Boozed up. 1918 *Chi. Sun.-Trib.* V (Mar. 24) (unp.): Some half boozed bum what's got a sad soak on. 1923 Ornitz *Haunch, Paunch, Jowl* 41: Begrimed, frowsy, boozed up. 1928 Dahlberg *Bottom Dogs* 128: On election nite…everyone got all boozed up. 1958 J. Davis *College Vocab.* 9: *Boozed*—Drunk. 1963 Horwitz *Candlelight* 151: I can only walk up these stairs when I'm boozed.

boozefest n. [BOOZE + *fest*] a carouse.

1923 in *AS* (Dec. 1931) 87: At a booze-fest. 1942 *ATS* 119: *Boozefest*…a spree or drinking party. 1967 Talbot *Chatty Jones* 17: The booze fest might last all night. 1968 Baker et al. *CUSS* 87: *Booze fest.* A drinking party.

booze fighter n. a person who drinks frequently and excessively; a sot. Hence **booze fighting** excessive and frequent drinking. Also as adj.

1903 in *DA: Booze fighter*—One who drinks whisky to excess. 1906 in *McClure's* (Jan. 1907) 335: He's too strong a booze fighter to run fast. 1911 O. Johnson *Stover at Yale* 21: Keep out of the crowd that is out booze-fighting. 1914 Ellis *Billy Sunday* 50: You look as though you were a booze-fighter. 1913–15 Van Loan *Taking the Count* 33: A cigarette-smoking, booze-fighting ball of butter. 1918 McNutt *Yanks* 223: I know lots of habitual booze fighters out there who are beginning to realize that total abstinence is a pretty good bet. 1919 *DN* V 63: *Booze-fighter*, a drunkard. "It will be hard on the *booze-fighter* if the saloons close." New Mexico. 1924 H.L. Wilson *Professor* 112: No booze fighter ever won a decision. 1927 Richardson *Mountain Songs* 94: Come all ye booze fighters ef you want to hear/'Bout the kind of booze that they sell 'round here. 1933 in R.E. Howard *Iron Man* 46: You took to booze-fighting. Went to the gutter. Went broke. 1942 Garcia *Tough Trip* 136: Beaver Tom was only a booze fighter.

boozehead n. [BOOZE + HEAD] BOOZEHOUND.

1969 in *Playboy* (Feb. 1970) 55: This particular generation gap might almost be called chemical warfare—the potheads versus the boozeheads. 1972 B. Harrison *Hospital* 212: If you want me to tell some boozehead the evils of drinking, you're out of luck.

booze-hoister n. a heavy drinker of booze.

1914 Ellis *Billy Sunday* 118: The greater part of them are booze-hoisters. 1922 N. Anderson *Hobo* 67: They are prone to go to town occasionally to indulge in a cocaine spree much as a "booze hoister" indulges in a liquor spree. 1925 S. Lewis *Arrowsmith* ch. i: And don't be a booze-hoister like me, either.

boozehound n. [BOOZE + HOUND] a heavy drinker of booze; alcoholic.

1911 Van Loan *Big League* 73: Why, I'd rather deal with three booze hounds than one fellow full of that love dope! 1923 *Bomb* (Iowa State College) 412: I had with me two booze hounds, a fotografer, and a Whizz Bang. 1926 "M. Brand" *Iron Trail* 103: The worst booze-hound that I ever knew. 1929 Sturges *Strictly Dishonorable* 617: I suppose I should have let that old booze-hound get away with that stuff. 1942 Garcia *Tough Trip* 58: Most of them were booze hounds who blowed in their money by gambling. 1945 Drake & Cayton *Black Metro.* 567: Wid a hophead daddy and a booze houn' mammy. How he ever gonna be any doctah? 1946 A. Petry *Street* 181: You knew what would happen when you brought that old booze hound here to live. 1960 MacCuish *Do Not Go Gentle* 16: Hey, looka the booze hound! 1967 Hinton *Outsiders* 113: Bob was a boozehound. 1989 "Captain X" & Dodson *Unfriendly Skies* 160: They've been regular booze-hounds.

boozer n. [dial. pronun. of earlier *bouser, bowser*] **1.** a heavy drinker of booze. Now *colloq.*

*1606 in Partridge *Dict. Und.* 64: Boucer…bowser. *1611 in *F & H* I

297: A tipler, *bowser.* *1657 in *OED:* These common Bowsers and daily Drunkards. *1789 G. Parker *Life's Painter* 138: And sneaking Snip, the boozer. **1812** in Howay *New Hazard* 102: Jack said he was neither son of [a] bitch nor boozer. **1814** in B. Palmer *Diary* (Mar. 18): Propper old grog buiser just fit for a New York porter house. **1851** [G.A. Worth] *Recoll.* 38: This landlord was a boozer stout. **1899** *Tip Top Wkly.* (Apr. 22) 5: What do you take us for?…Do you think we are a lot of boozers? **1904** *Life in Sing Sing* 246: Booser. A drunkard. **1913** A. Palmer *Salvage* 77: There goes the boozer's girl. **1974** Radano *Cop Stories* 113: One cop said he thought Frank was a boozer. **1977–80** F.M. Stewart *Century* 394: Is she a big boozer?

2. Esp. *Irish-Amer.* a drinking saloon. [A common term in Ireland, Britain, and Australia; not common in U.S.]

*1895 in *EDD* I: I pops around at the Bowzer. **1969** Moynahan *Pairing Off* 151: Look, I run a boozer. For years she took half my late night business. **1982** L. Block *Eight Million Ways* 267: If I went to Durkin's boozer I'd drink. **1987** *Day Watch* (CNN-TV) (June 26): Britons and tourists alike are tossed out of the boozer until 5 p.m.

boozery *n.* a drinking saloon. *Joc.*

1916 in *DN* V 10: Their husbands loafed and lushed in the boozeries. **1956** G. Green *Last Angry Man* 310: Bayard had decided to open his own, as he put it, "boozery."

booze up *v.* to make drunk.

1962 in A. Sexton *Letters* 151: She held my hand and boozed me up and took me over to the T.V. station.

booze-up *n.* a drinking bout. [A common term in Britain and Australia; rare in U.S.]

*1897 in *OEDS:* We…had a *booze-up* together. **1962** Killens *Heard the Thunder* 385 [ref. to WWII]: And the party was a booze-up. **1963** E.B. Holland *Gay as a Grig* 98: After a good booze-up…and still a bit tiddly. **1969** Maitland *Only War* 16: Schlitz had been roaring that evening during a gin-sodden pre-mission booze-up in the N.C.O.'s mess. **1977** Coover *Public Burning* 461: Cowboy shootouts and…Sunday booze-ups.

boozing ken *n.* [BOOZE, *v.* + KEN] Orig. *Und.* a drinking den; a saloon. Now *hist.*

*1566 Harman *Caveat:* A *bousing-ken,* a ale house. *1641 R. Brome, in R.G. Lawrence *Comedies* 193: When they at bowsing ken do swill. *1665 R. Head *Eng. Rogue* 35: We straight betook ourselves to the "boozing ken." *1698 Ward *London-Spy* 40: We e'en turn'd our selves into the Smoaky *Boozing-Ken* amongst them. *1714 *Memoirs of John Hall* (ed. 4) 11: *Boozing Ken,* an Ale-house. *1785 Grose *Vulgar Tongue: Bowsing ken,* an alehouse or ginshop. *1834 in *F & H* I 298: The hovel which they termed their *boozing-ken.* **1848** *Ladies' Repository* (Oct.) 315: *Boozing ken,* A coffee-house. **1849** [G. Thompson] *Venus in Boston* 32: I paid a visit to a noted "*boozing ken.*" **1872** Burnham *Secret Service* iv: *Boozing-ken,* a low drinking-house for thieves or counterfeiters. *Ibid.* 99: He too was a constant frequenter of the tap-room and the "boozing-ken." **1883** Hay *Bread-Winners* 187: We keep men to loaf with the tramps and sleep in the boozing kens. **1899** A.H. Lewis *Sandburrs* 28: An' then I'll bring him over to this boozin' ken of ours, an' cop youse a knock-down to him. **1903** A.H. Lewis *Boss* 13: The house he's talkin' about…ain't no tavern. It's a boozin' ken for crimps and thieves. **1913** J. London *J. Barleycorn* 109: A boozing ken in sailor-town. **1927–29** W.N. Burns *Tombstone* 30: The saloons were not the boozing kens of old frontier tradition. **1992** Randolph & Legman *Blow Candle Out* 842: Fashionable inns and boozing kens.

boozy *adj.* [dial. pronun. of earlier *bousy, bowsy,* etc.] drunk; tipsy. Now *S.E.*

*1536 in Partridge *Dict. Und.* 63: Bousy cove. *1592 in *F & H* I 298: To marke the bowsie drunkard to dye of the dropsy. *1688 Shadwell *Squire of Alsatia* I i: You know we were Bowsy last night. *1719 D'Urfey *Pills to Purge Melancholy* II 297: All flustered and boozy, the drunken Old Sot. **1722** B. Franklin, in *AS* (Feb. 1940) 103: *Boozy, cogey, tipsey, fox'd,* [etc.]. **1736–37** (quot. at BUZZY). *1785 Grose *Vulgar Tongue: Boosey,* drunk. **1797** in Tyler *Verse* 61: 'Tis stammering, staggering, boozy Joe. **1813–18** Weems *Drunkard's Looking Glass* 60: The patient goes by a variety of nick-names…such as *boozy—groggy—blue—damp* [etc.]. **1823** Cooper *Pioneers* 183: Poor fellow! he was quite boozy last night and hardly seems to be over it yet. **1862** in Mohr *Cormany Diaries* 247: Many of the boys got a little boozy. **1872** Crapsey *Nether Side of N.Y.* 36: They…fleece boozy sailors. **1905** *DN* III 4: *Boozy,* adj. Slang, drunk. **1911** *JAF* (July) 275: Sometimes my baby gets boozy. **1956** in Asimov, Greenberg & Olander *Sci. Fi. Short Shorts* 175: I came to, still boozy. **1976** Rosten *To Anywhere* 22: I got my hands under the boozy lady's arms.

bop *n.* [fr. the *v.*] **1.a.** a punch; a blow.

1932 *AS* (June) 329: Bop…n.—a blow. **1942** *ATS* 609: Blow—n.…bang…bop…chop, clip, [etc.]. **1970** La Motta, Carter & Savage *Raging Bull* 8: One bop [with a lead pipe], I figured, and Harry would go down. **1980** J. Carroll *Land of Laughs* 92: I gave him a bop on the head and he lay down.

b. vigor; punch.

1976 Calloway & Rollins *Moocher & Me* 160: Listen, let's liven this music up a little, let's get some bop in this thing, let's cut loose.

2. (see quot.).

1948 in Botkin *Sidewalks* 405: The bebops, or bops as they are known in the jazz mills, call themselves progressive musicians.

3.a. a street fight between teenage gangs.

1954 *Harper's Mag.* (Nov.) 38: As I found out, once a bop really starts even the most even tempered of your boys will shove you aside. **1955** Yablonsky *Violent Gang* 46: Third is a bop. That can be a small group, five, ten, twenty guys from one team, having it out with the same number from a different team.…It's just one of the clashes. **1958–60** Freeman *Out of Burning* 104: This was the first…bop I had taken part in. **1965** in H. Ellison *Sex Misspelled* 319: It was a bop, and they felt the sting of participation.

b. a member of a teenage gang.

1958 *Life* (Apr. 14) 126: I was…a little smarter than most of the other bops, or gang members. *Ibid.* 127: Lenny…had been a bop in a street club as a kid. **1964** K. Clark *Dark Ghetto* 49: But the alienation of the Negro poor is such that the "hustler" or "bop" or unwed ADC mother, the members of the "deviant subculture," [etc.].

4. *Narc.* a dose; HIT.

1971 Dahlskog *Dict.* 9: Bop, *n.* A drug in pill or tablet form; as, to take (drop) a *bop.* **1980** Pearl *Slang Dict.: Bop, n.*…(*drug culture*) a pill.

5. *Black E.* nonsense; JAZZ.

1973 Andrews & Owens *Black Lang.* 12: Little white kids don't really believe that bop but…they get caught in the go along. **1974** Gober *Black Cop* 104: Yeah, you talk all that off the wall bop.

bop *v.* [see *EDD;* cf. *OED* bob 'punch', from ME; also cf. syn. POP] **1.a.** to punch; to strike; (*hence, intrans.*) to thump or thud.

1928 in Segar *Thimble Th.* 28: I bopped him hard enough to knock over an elephant. **1929** in Runyon *Guys & Dolls* 65: Dave…bops One-Eyed Solly right in the mouth. **1932** in J. O'Hara *Sel. Letters* 64: I bopped her on the snout and let it go at that. **1938** Bellem *Blue Murder* 46: I…bopped him in the kisser. **1945** C. Himes *If He Hollers* 41: One would carry his whiteness like a loaded stick, ready to bop everybody else…with it. **1946** H.A. Smith *Rhubarb* 137: She called me a Republican…and tried to bop me with a shoe. **1956** M. Levin *Compulsion* 71: But *this* time—the look on the kid's face when he was bopped! **1970** A. Young *Snakes* 85: I'll…pick up this tablespoon and bop you right in your devilish mouth! **1973** Childress *Hero* 68: My heart went to boppin fast and my head drew tight. **1984** Univ. Tenn. *Daily Beacon* (Oct. 16) 8: I'm going to bop you a good one.

b. to kill; to murder.—also constr. with *off.*

1934 Appel *Brain Guy* 198: Yesterday'n today I bops two guys. Me. I kilt two guys. *Ibid.* 222: How easy to bop a man off. **1938** Chandler *Big Sleep* 50: It's kind of goddamned lucky for you I *didn't* bop Gieger. **1939** "E. Queen" *Dragon's Teeth* 123: You sure she didn't bop Marg herself? **1941** "G.R. Lee" *G-String* 153: Was business so bad…that you had to bop off LaVerne for publicity? **1968** J. Kelly *Unexpected Peace* 55 [ref. to WWII]: Ol' Vic just bopped off three of 'em. **1987** *Sable* (ABC-TV): He's already bopped Farina and Carr.

c. *Sports.* to defeat.

1984 *N.Y. Post* (Aug. 14) 73: Tigers bop Braves.

3. to assault with weapons; (*hence*) to engage in gang fighting.

1953 Paley *Rumble* 92: He wants no bopping on our side. *Ibid.* 94: Don't futz around if we start getting bopped. **1954** *Harper's Mag.* (Nov.) 38: The white and Puerto Rican gangs call them "rumbles." The American Negroes of Brooklyn and Central Harlem speak of "bopping." **1957** Yablonsky *Violent Gang* 15: In the old Dragons, you know, we used to bop…and talk later. **1957** *New Yorker* (Sept. 21) 127: You start bopping, they'll throw you right out of here. **1959** E. Hunter *Matter of Conviction* 17: "His bopping hat," Gunnison explained. "A high-crowned narrow brimmed fedora." **1962** Riccio & Slocum *All the Way Down* 30: They were always bopping and rumbling. **1966** Samuels *People vs. Baby* 38: The younger Vikings weren't bopping. **1970** E. Knight *Black Voices* 30: Our specialty was bopping the whiteys that came to the colored sections of town looking for women. **1973** Schiano & Burton

Solo 42: We had a bopping gang, the Italian Dukes.

4.a. to dance to bop music. Now *S.E.*

1956 in Safire *Stand Corrected* 59: Crazy legs, bopping all over the floor. **1957** *Sing Out!* (Winter) 35: From Calypso to blues to bop to. **1958** Jimmie Thomas *Rockin' Robin* (song): He bops through the treetops all day long. **1965** Hersey *Too Far to Walk* 87: Ginny was bopping with some frightful jerk. **1972** Chipman *Hardening Rock* xiii: We have become what we listened to and bopped to.

b. to walk in a rhythmic or swaggering manner; to amble; to go; to leave; *(hence)* to move rhythmically.—also constr. with *off*.

1959 *AS* (May) 156: With all plans made clear, it's time to *bop out, bop off*, or *ease on*. **1963** in Chipman *Hardening Rock* 78: He bopped on off down the sidewalk. **1966** N.J. high school student: Hey, man, here we *bop* to class. Like this. **1967** *Zap Comix* (Oct.) 16: Bopped over to the East Side with a dealer name of "Teenage Ric." **1969** *New American Rev.* (Apr.) 215: Bop over to the One-Eyed Indian Bar. **1970** in Wertheim & Gonzalez *Talkin' About Us* 128: So...Priam got up and bopped. **1970** A. Young *Snakes* 30: Bopping around the neighborhood or downtown. **1971** Jacobs & Casey *Grease* 41: And some lucky guy and gal is gonna go boppin' home with a stack of terrific prizes. **1975** Hinton *Rumble Fish* 102: Let's go boppin' around again tonight. **1980** T. Jones *Adrift* 126: I'm boppin' along, man. **1983** Sturz *Wid. Circles* 60: Bopping (dipping) as she walked, dressed in sneakers, jeans and scarves. **1988** Dietl & Gross *One Tough Cop* 43: No limp....He bops...you know the way they do. **1991** in *Rap Masters* (Jan. 1992) 58: We're suppose [*sic*] to...bop our heads to the beat.

c. to be exciting.

1982 Goff, Sanders & Smith *Brothers* 187: We had only been there for an hour, and things were really getting bopping.

5. *Mil. Av.* to destroy in a strafing attack.

1957 Morison *Naval Ops. in WWII* VI 208 [ref. to 1943]: Not until the Bougainville campaign did "barge-bopping" become a fine art.

6. to copulate with. Cf. BOFF, 2.

1974 Strasburger *Rounding Third* 52: Initial strategy was to bop her one right at the door. **1986** Merkin *Zombie Jamboree* 27: He wasn't bopping her. They were just hanging out. **1989** Eble *Campus Slang* (Spring) 1: *Bop*—have sex.

bopper *n.* **1.** a gang fighter.

1962 Riccio & Slocum *All the Way Down* 30: Just as his clothes were typical of a "bopper," so was his background. **1966** Samuels *People vs. Baby* 38: The Dragons uptown were boppers. **1966–67** P. Thomas *Mean Streets* 269: If I joined up with the boppers. **1967** Hinton *Outsiders* 122: He a pretty good bopper? **1968** I. Reed *Yellow Back Radio* 44: Well boss we took care of them hard boppers.

2. TEENYBOPPER.

1968 in L. Williams *City of Angels* 40: The antique clothes shop where the freaky boppers...squeal. **1971** L. Bangs *Psychotic Reactions* 10: A crowd of blooming boppers, presumably cordoned off from their idols. **1978** S. King *Stand* 42: The junior high boppers will collect your records. **1984** N. Stephenson *Big U.* 33: Some bopper who would suffer an emotional crisis every week.

3. a hard blow; *(hence)* *Baseball.* a hard-hit ball.

1970 in *DARE*. **1984** *N.Y. Post* (Aug. 13) 36: Four times, Sandy [Koufax]...came away with a no-hitter. Not a big bopper, blooper or bingle sullied his efforts on those occasions.

4. a hitter; slugger.

1977 L. Nelson, on N.Y. Mets baseball (WOR-TV) (Aug. 20): The big bopper in the batting order of the Cincinnati Reds—George Foster.

boppy *adj.* energetic; happy; cheerful; "jazzy."

*a***1984** Safire *Stand Corrected* 55: Now we need a boppy ending. **1991** *Mac & Muttley* (TDC-TV): Now she's feeling boppy.

borax *n.* [fr. the furniture formerly given as premiums by manufacturers of borax soap; discussed by D. Shulman, "Borax Reconsidered," *AS* LX (1985), pp. 283–85] *Manufacturing.* shoddy manufactured goods, esp. furniture.

1929 in Mencken *Amer. Lang.* (ed. 4) 218: How the Borax House came by its name is a question that the learned have not yet dealt with. **1936** in *AS* LX (1985) 284: *Borax*...now denotes through the furniture trade (and also in the architectural magazines) the flimsy, flashy sort of furniture that consists largely of molded ornaments stuck on veneered furniture. **1942** Chandler *High Window* ch. xxv: A...lamp from...some borax emporium. **1961** Partridge *DSUE* (ed. 5) 1010: *Borax*...cheap furniture: Canadian: C. 20. **1978** J. Rosenberg *Dict. Business* 53: *Borax*. Inexpensive items (e.g., furniture) that are usually poorly designed and

constructed. **1985** D. Shulman, in *AS* LX 283: *Borax* was usually applied in a derogatory sense to cheap furniture as well as other merchandise sold in a discount store or on an installment plan.

Bordens *n.pl.* [sugg. by *Borden's*, a trademark for milk and dairy products] a woman's breasts. *Joc.*

1941 "G.R. Lee" *G-String* 85: Get a load of those Bordens. **1970** in *DARE*: [*Breasts:*] Borden's and Elsie's [*sic*].

bore *n.* **1.** an annoyance, nuisance; a tiresome or dull person, activity, etc. Now *S.E.*

***1778** in *OED*: Advice is well enough—reproof's a bore. **1788** in W. Dunlap *Diary* 21: That damn'd *bore*....Society [is] the greatest bore in natshure...to me. **1797** in Tyler *Verse* 67: The house...might prove...a cursed bore. **1788–1806** W. Dunlap *Father of Only Child* 31: He is an unsufferable bore. ***1820–21** P. Egan *Life in London* 15: The worst of *bores* and the most tiresome of companions. **1848** Bartlett *Amer.* 43: *Bore.* A tiresome person or unwelcome visitor, who makes himself obnoxious by his disagreeable manners, or by a repetition of visits. **1849** P. Decker *Diaries* 142: I washed...socks...which is a "grand bore." **1858** O.W. Holmes *Autocrat* 9: All men are bores, except when we want them. **1911** E. Howe *Sayings* 40: If...people did not express their disgust, where would the bores stop?

2. a hoax.

1800 in *DA*: A Federal bore. **1811** in Thornton *Amer. Gloss.* I: A hoax, a quiz, a bore.

¶ In phrases:

¶ **clean out (one's) bore** *Mil.* to treat or be treated for venereal disease.

1945–48 *U.S.M.C. Marianas Coll.* (unp.): He's going to the states, yeh, to clean out his bore.

¶ **full bore** Esp. *USAF.* full speed, full blast.

***1943** in Partridge *DSUE* (ed. 8) 435: I went after him full bore. **1956** Heflin *USAF Dict.* 224: *Full bore.* Top speed. Also used adverbially, as in "he climbed full bore." British slang. **1963** Dwiggins *S.O.Bees* 153 [ref. to WWII]: Blackburn saw a lone P-40 going full bore. **1973** Gwaltney *Destiny's Chickens* 94: Full bore, by God, all the way. **1976** Hayden *Voyage* 124: Gus Skeantlebury's Parlor was going full bore.

bore *v.* **1.** to annoy.

1788 in W. Dunlap *Diary* 22: What a curst boring fellow...that is. **1848** in Peskin *Vols.* 291: Irish Jimmy...so bored him that he released him from confinement. **1858** O.W. Holmes *Autocrat* 9: Do not dull people bore you?

2. to ridicule, scold, or humiliate.

1800 in *DAE*: A mere sportive hoax, to bore some of the laziness of the district. **1816** in Waterhouse *Young Man of Mass.* 88: About this time there came on board of us a recruiting sergeant, to try to enlist some of our men....He met with no success. Some of the men "*bored*" him pretty well. We had a very good will to throw [him] overboard. **1813–18** Weems *Drunk. Look. Glass* 66: The young red-faced blockhead would still *spout* and *bore* the company.

3. to shoot a hole in; DRILL.

1865 [Williams] *Joaquin* 38: Gay row at McNamara's! Two bored—I'm after the doctor! **1878** Pinkerton *Reminiscences* 150: Why *don't* you shoot?...Give the "pop" to me, I'll bore him! **1885** in Westerheimer *Cowboy* 79: That old duffer in the wig is too snide. Watch us bore him. **1889** S. Bailey *Ups & Downs* 29: He advised me to get a gun, as the crooks always call a pistol, and if Jim attempted any more of his funny business, to pull the gun and give him a bluff, or, if necessary, to "bore" him in the leg once. **1934** Kromer *Waiting* 118: I will bore the first bastard that lays a hand on me. **1943** in *Best from Yank* 8: I could see just about six inches of his rump sticking out and I bored him. **1958** Bickham *Gunman's Gamble* 6: Man,...I thought you was gonna bore me.

¶ In phrases:

¶ **bore a hole in** to shoot (a person); DRILL.

***1838** Glascock *Land Sharks* I 195: I've just as good a chance o' gettin' a hole bored in my cannister. **1846** in Harris *High Times* 66: I'll bore a hole in *you*, when I get to ye. **1883** Sweet & Knox *Mustang* 18: I'll bore holes in him till he can't hold water.

¶ **bore holes in the sky** *Mil. Av.* to fly about aimlessly. Also vars.

1950 *Time* (Sept. 4) 18: Kenney's bombers spent much of their time making easy training flights, "just boring holes in the air," as one of them recalls it. **1955** *AS* XXX 121: *Bore holes*, v. phr. Make a local flight with no specific mission. **1956** *AS* XXXI 227: *Bore four holes in the blue*, v. phr. Used to describe a worthless mission or purposeless flight....The "four holes" refer to the four engines of a large aircraft.

1968 W.C. Anderson *Gooney Bird* 103: Sometimes, especially during a moonlit night, we do nothing but sit up here and bore holes in the sky. **1987** Zeybel *Gunship* 57: We bored holes until it was time to RTB.

¶ **bore (someone) a new one** to victimize; REAM.

1954 in *DARE*: They bored 'im a new one in that hog tradin'.

¶ **bore (someone's) ear** to weary with talking or scolding.

*****1785** Grose *Vulgar Tongue*: Bore, a tedious troublesome man or woman, one who bores the ears of his hearers with an uninteresting talk, a term much in fashion about the years 1780, and 1781. **1890** Bunner *Short Sixes* 13: Well, I got to step, or the Sooprintendent'll be borin' my ear.

¶ **not know whether (one)** [or **(one's) asshole**] **is bored or punched** to be very dull-witted or confused. [The vulgar form is the original.]

*****1961** Partridge *DSUE* (ed. 5) 983: *He doesn't know if his arse-hole is bored or punched. He's a complete fool...since ca*1910. **1975** J. Gould *Maine Lingo* 20: *Bored or punched* A measurement of ignorance. Not to know if a hole is *bored or punched* is to be uninformed. **1983** W. Safire, in *N.Y. Times Mag.* (Aug. 7) 6: He doesn't know...*whether he's bored or punched.*

boress *n.* [orig. unkn.] *Stu.* a prank. Also **borass**. Also as *v.*

1958 J. Davis *College Vocab.* 14: *Boress*—To waste time, to do nothing in general, to slough off. As a noun: a prank or trick pulled on someone else. **1965** in IUFA *Folk Speech*: The word "borass" means a joke or trick played on someone, such as moving someone's furniture out of his room and hiding it. **1966** in IUFA *Folk Speech*: *Boress*: a joke. **1970** *Current Slang* V 4: *Boress,...v.* To make a practical joke—High school students, both sexes, California....*Boress,* n. A practical joke. **1970** Wakefield *All the Way* 217: It was some kind of borass Gunner was pulling, a stunt to shake people up or something.

bork *v.* [after Judge Robert H. *Bork,* whose appointment to the Supreme Court was blocked in 1987 after an extensive media campaign by his opponents] *Pol.* to attack (a candidate or the like) systematically, esp. in the media. Also as *n.*

1988 *Chicago Tribune* (Nov. 30) 20: Honest disagreement is one thing; "borking" is something else. **1989** Sen. M. Wallop (R.-Wyo.), on *CBS This Morning* (CBS-TV) (Feb. 9): I feel strongly...that...he [*sc.* John Tower] is being borked....The charges that have been leveled against him...have all proved groundless, baseless. **1990** *National Review* (Apr. 30) 54: *Borking:* perhaps the most galling domestic injustice of the Eighties was the deceptive campaign by which the Left denied Robert Bork a seat on the Supreme Court. **1991** *CBS This Morning* (CBS-TV) (July 9): An opponent of Judge Clarence Thomas said yesterday, "We're going to bork him." **1992** *L.A. Times* (Aug. 23) M6: Perhaps...Hillary Clinton is being "borked"—attacked in the same orchestrated, systematic manner which ultimately undermined the U.S. Supreme Court nomination of Judge Robert H. Bork. **1993** *New Republic* (May 17) 20: More than sixty right-leaning national and state organizations will close ranks to coordinate a huge preemptive bork. *Ibid.* The strategies used to bork Zoe Baird and gays in the military.

Borneo *n.* ¶ In phrase: **go Borneo** [sugg. by "The Wild Man of Borneo," a sideshow staple] *Stu.* to become drunk; go crazy; act wild.

1980 Birnbach et al. *Preppy Hndbk.* 108: Drunk...Gone Borneo. *Ibid.* 217: Let's...go Borneo. **1983** *N.Y. Daily News* (Mar. 25): Teentalk Glossary...crazy (*go borneo, wigged out*).

borrow *v.* to steal. *Joc.*

1821 [Martin & Waldo] *Lightfoot* 70: He had been in the city lately, and had *borrowed* a purse from a nobleman, at the theatre, three nights before. **1848** [Judson] *Mysteries* 36: I...borried two cloaks for my uncle from "the Astor." **1876** Dixon *White Conquest* I 218: So Manuel and the younger men went out into the White settlements and "borrowed" about thirty horses and as many cows. **1922** Rollins *Cowboy* 305: Such men...were assumed...not to feel the pinch if any of their stock were "borrowed" by acquisitive persons.

Borscht Belt *n.* Orig. *Entertainment Industry.* a group of resorts in the Catskill Mountains of New York and Pennsylvania that cater primarily to a middle-class Jewish clientele. Also (*obs.*) **Borscht Circuit.**

1936 *Esquire* (Sept.) 160: On the "Borscht circuit" (Catskill Mt. dialectery summer hotels). **1940** S. Lewis *Bethel Merriday* 165: I've been out on the Borscht circuit all summer. **1941** H.A. Smith *Low Man* 144: Torch singers, restaurant owners, booking agents...borscht circuit social directors...and burlesque queens. **1942** Liebling *Telephone* 61:

All you got is floor shows, fraternal entertainments, and in the summer the borsch circuit. **1946** J. Adams *Gags* 29: Years of "social directoring" on the borscht circuit*....*Borscht circuit* or *borscht belt*. Borscht is a Russian beet soup that is served almost daily in Jewish summer resorts. **1958** Gardner *Piece of the Action* 178: We get a little club work, borscht circuit. **1969** Gordone *No Place* 419: Got this job playin' the Borsh-Belt. **1970** *Playboy* (Nov.) 92: Has the area changed much since you worked the Borscht Belt as an entertainer? **1977** Lyon *Tenderness* 225: Grossinger's Hotel, the queen of all the resort hotels in New York's Catskill Mountain "borscht belt." **1984** D. Smith *Steely Blue* 158: The Borscht Belt Bugler, he called him.

bosco *n.* [poss. < It or fr. BOSKY] a foolish or insignificant person.

1925 *Amer. Legion Wkly.* (June 5) 7: Any Broadway bosco will tell you. **1973** *TULIPQ* (coll. B.K. Dumas): A naive person:...*dumbo, boscoe.*

bosh *n.* [Turkish *boş* 'empty, worthless'; "the word became current in Eng. from its frequent occurrence in Morier's novel *Ayesha* (1834), which was extremely popular."—*OED*] utter nonsense or foolishness, rubbish. Now *S.E.*

*****1834** J. Morier *Ayesha,* in *OED*: The [other] parts...are spurious. They are *bosh*—nothing. *****1852** Dickens *Bleak House* ch. xxi: Bosh! It's all correct. **1856** in C.A. Abbey *Before the Mast* 82: There is some talk of our going to San Francisco but I guess it is all "bosh." **1863** in J.H. Gooding *Altar of Freedom* 27: The yarns...is all bosh. **1864** in C.W. Wills *Army Life* 296: Mrs. Lee Henty's grand plantations...are principally "bosh," at least as far as northern Georgia is concerned. *****1880** in *F & H* I 299: I have heard that bosh before. **1889** Field *Western Verse* 36: This talk about the journalists that run the East is bosh. **1939** A.C. Johnson et al. *Hardys Ride High* (film): You don't take that bosh seriously, do you, old man? **1954–60** *DAS*: *Bosh*...Nonsense, blah. *Colloq.*

bosky *adj.* intoxicated; tipsy.

*****1730–36** N. Bailey *Dict.*: *Bosky,* half or quite fuddled. **1736–37** in *AS* (Apr. 1937): He is Addled...Boozy...Buskey. *****1825** "Blackmantle" *English Spy* I 324: Then will we get *bosky* together. *****1843** in *OED*: Became, to use a colloquial expression, uncommonly bosky.

Bosox *n. Baseball Journ.* the Boston Red Sox.

*a***1953** *ATS* (ed. 2) 642: Red Sox, Bosox, the Sox. **1992** Strawberry & Rust *Darryl* 214: We had to play the Bosox.

boss *n.* **1.** the leader of a criminal gang; (*hence*) the leader of a political machine. Both now *S.E.*

1845 *Nat. Police Gaz.* (Oct. 11) 58: I agree with the Boss. *****1859** in *F & H* I (rev.) 337: "So, boss," began the ruffian, not looking at him, "we ain't fit company for the likes of that kinchin, eh?" **1861** in *DA*: Abe...was sent for by "boss" Seward. **1899** Dunne *Dooley in Hearts* 67: There was wanst a boss in th' Sixth War-rd, an' his name was Flannagan. **1943** Mitchell *McSorley's* 13: The anarchist...thought no man was as foul as a Tammany boss.

2.a. (one's) father.

1855 (quot. at GOVERNOR, 1).

b. God.—also constr. with *the.*

1912 in Mencken *New Ltrs.* 37: But if the practical joking of our humorous Boss ever gives me the chance to write about you in the past tense.... **1979** in J.L. Gwaltney *Drylongso* 232: The Boss hurled [Satan's] ass down to low stones!

3. the best (of many); the champion example; the finest.—constr. with *the.*

1878 Willis *Lights & Shadows* 76: The *Tennessee*....She's the boss of the navy—she'll be Queen of the China Seas! **1879** Rooney *Quaint Conundrums* 51: "How did you like the opera, pet?"..."It's the boss!" **1881** Nye *Forty Liars* 205: There is no question about its being the supreme boss of the hotel gang in this country. **1881** in Peck *Peck's Sunshine* 84: Our girl...that takes this [prize], must be "the boss." She must be jolly and good-natured...healthy...well-formed, [etc.].

boss *adj.* **1.** chief, leading, best, dominant, etc.

1836 in *DA*: I am a boss shoemaker. **1840** in *DAE*: Charley Moggs, long known as the boss loafer of Bickerbray. **1867** in *DAE*: If all are fed together the "boss" cattle fill themselves. **1877** Bartlett *Amer.* (ed. 4) 60: Veteran Hatch caught the *boss* string of trout. **1877** Burdette *Mustache* 245: Oh, Gog's blakey, but he wur the boss ghosht. **1881** in Nye *West. Humor* 51: He finds in his boss editorial that God is spelled with a little g. **1881** Ingraham *Buffalo Bill from Boyhood* 95: You is the boss boy I ever see. **1882** D.J. Cook *Hands Up* 248: "See here," said Bemis, "I've got the boss hand but I don't want to win your money." **1887** Hinman *Cpl. Si Klegg* 22: She's goin' ter be the boss comp'ny, too! **1895** Townsend *Chimmie Fadden* 81: She's de boss jollier you ever seed. **1899**

A.H. Lewis *Sandburrs* 243: It's d' boss hard luck story, an' that ain't no vision. **1902** Townsend *Fadden & Mr. Paul* 281: Dat was de boss song of all. **1918** Witwer *Baseball to Boches* 95: The French doughboy...drags down the sensational sum of a nickel a day for fightin', and it ain't no wonder they're such boss scrappers. **1963** *Time* (Aug. 2) 14: *Mello, phat, stone, boss.* General adjectives of approval. **1963** Charters *Poetry of Blues* 51: I'm the Black Ace, I'm the boss card in your hand. But I'll play for you, mama, if you please let me be your man. **1967** Kolb *Getting Straight* 39: In Ward A, man. That's for the boss nuts, the real experts. **1968** in E. Knight *Belly Song* 15: That lil cat is the Boss Black Poet. **1985** *Miami Vice* (NBC-TV): Does DEA have any idea how long this guy's been a boss importer? **1992** G. Wolff *Day at Beach* 107: To get "it"...had been my boss preoccupation.

2. first-rate, splendid, attractive, fashionable, impressive, etc.

1873 *Harper's Mo.* (Dec.) 8: This is boss ile, double-distilled. **1880** *Harper's Mag.* (Mar.) 522: He returned, and said that he "had a boss time." **1880** in Eliason *Tarheel Talk* 261: If a coast man wants to express the superlative degree he says "That is a 'Boss' log or a 'Boss' suit.' " **1883** Peck *Bad Boy* 248: I told Pa of a boss scheme to fool them. **1883** Sweet & Knox *Mustang* 102: It was a boss sight to see how mad that old mudcat was. **1888** *Bklyn. Daily Eagle* (Mar. 18): Take it all together, with scarcity of food and little sleep, we had a boss time. **1890** *Puck* (Feb. 19) 437: She wrote me that she got [the song] McGinty the first day, and it was boss! **1890** Janvier *Aztec Treasure House* 170: It's a boss invention. **1892** Garland *Spoil of Office* 30: Yes, we have Friday exercises and there are two debating clubs. They're boss for practice. *Ibid.* 93: It's boss fun. *Ibid.* 96: Ain't this boss? This is what I call doin' a thing up brown. **1895** Clurman *Nick Carter* 70: Isn't that a boss counterfeit?...See what a perfect imitation of silk-fiber paper. **1898** Kountz *Baxter's Letters* 21: He was nobby and boss. He was dropping his r's like a Southerner. **1907** *Army & Navy Life* (Nov.) 644: Bill Stickles was considered a boss scrapper. **1910** Lomax *Cowboy Songs* 249: He had lots of pluck, on himself he was stuck,/In his Government straights he looked boss. **1943** Holmes & Scott *Mr. Lucky* (film): You see, I'm a boss gambler. That's my business. **1954** in Wepman, Newman & Binderman *The Life* 40: I go for you, Sam, I think you're boss. **1955** in Wepman, Newman & Binderman *The Life* 73: His socks were boss, and, man, did they cost! **1960** *Esquire* (June) 129: That aspirin is a boss kick. **1962** L. Hughes *Tambourines* 218: Stacked, solid—neat, all-reet—boss, baby! That means—attractive. **1964** Larner & Teffertteller *Addict* 137: You wait and see. Because it's good, baby; you'll have a boss time. **1965** C. Brown *Manchild* 112: He said he had a real boss feeling. **1966** in T.C. Bambara *Gorilla* 43: Me and Violet was in this very boss fashion show at the center. **1967** Gonzales *Paid My Dues* 94: She ushered him into a chauffeur driven limosine and to a boss pad in the East Seventies. **1968** Kirk & Hanle *Surfer's Hndbk.* 136: *Boss:* great. **1973** Lucas, Katz & Huyck *Amer. Graffiti* 29: He's so boss. **1978** *Rhoda* (ABC-TV): This is an incredibly boss deal. **1984** Holland *Better Off Dead* (film): Of course I'm going to go out with him. He's so *boss!* **1992** *Mystery Science Theater* (Comedy Central TV): It's boss! Neat!

boss *adv.* splendidly.

1980 *Bosom Buddies* (ABC-TV): Works boss, Mike, man. Take it up.

boss *v.* to dominate or domineer.—often constr. with *around* or *it.* Now *colloq.* or *S.E.*

1856 in *F & H* I 301: The little fellow that bosses it over the crowd. **1874** Pember *Metropolis* 111: I'd better boss the talkin'. I'm more used to it like. **1883* in *F & H* I 301: The Irish are [are] easily bossed or bribed on the one hand. **1887** Peck *Pvt. Peck* 76: If I have got to be bossed around by a Yankee...I guess I will tie to him. **1887** M. Roberts *Avernus* 214: An uneducated Yorkshireman who was "bossed" by his wife. **1888** *Texas Siftings* (July): Lovely woman hires a servant/And bosses her around all day. **1906** Ford *Shorty McCabe* 171: The way she bossed Felix around...was a caution.

boss *interj.* mister.—used only in direct address, as to a stranger. Also **bossy.**

1839 Briggs *Harry Franco* I 31: "Why don't you get in, boss?" said one of the men on the dock. *Ibid.* II 51: I suppose, bossy, you mean to pay for that ere? **1847** in Dorson *Long Bow* 71: She goes pooty, don't she Bos? **1859** Bartlett *Amer.* (ed. 2) 44: *Boss.*...The blacks often employ it in addressing white men in the Northern States, as they do *massa* (master) in the Southern States. **1862** [C.F. Browne] *Artemus Ward* 199: Yes, boss,...an' I wish 'em honorable graves. **1878** [P.S. Warne] *Hard Crowd* 2: Hold on there, boss! I've got the drop on you. **1879** *Snares of N.Y.* 81: Say, boss, can I doss here to-night? **1880** "M. Twain" *Tramp Abroad* ch. xiii: Why, boss, he's ben the pizenest kind of a Free-will Baptis' for forty year. **1883** Peck *Bad Boy* 268: I tell you, boss, it has

struck in me too deep for pills. **1888** Pinkerton *Scaffold* 39: Say, boss,...can't you do something for a poor cove, wot has no place to sleep? **1904** in Opper *Hooligan* 2: "Hurry up with my coffee and soup." "In a minute, boss." **1919** S. Lewis *Free Air* 107: All right, boss. No bad feelin's!

Boston dollar *n.* (see quots.). *Joc.* Also **Boston quarter.**

1902 in *DA*: It was revolutionary to see the newcomer carefully hand him a "Boston dollar."...Cowboy satire for a copper [penny]. **1942** *ATS* 733: Railroad [slang]...*Boston quarter*, a nickel or dime tip.

Boston strawberries *n.pl.* [Boston is famous for beans; cf. BEANTOWN; also cf. ARMY STRAWBERRIES, MINER'S STRAWBERRIES] baked beans. *Joc.*

1884 in *AS* (Feb. 1945) 71: "Give me a plate of beans," he said to the waiter. "One plate of Boston strawberries," yelled that functionary.

bosun's share *n. Naut.* (see quot.).

1925 Bailey *Shanghaied* 111 [ref. to 1899]: I get up for my share [of the coffee] and receive the "bo'sun's share" (all grounds).

bot *n.* a bottle of liquor.

1881 in Aswell *Humor* 370: "Set 'em up agin," or "open another bot." **1884** Dougherty *Stump Speaker* 6: McGinty bet a bot/His pup could battle McGonigle's dog. **1892** S. Crane *Maggie* 8: You'd better let up on the bot', ol' woman, or you'll git done. **1895** Townsend *Chimmie Fadden* 13: "It's yuse, an' yer stealin' champagne," 'e says, holdin' up de bot I'd swiped. **1895** Wood *Yale Yarns* 17: We all went out and had a "bot."

botch *n.* gonorrhea.—constr. with *the.*

1962 E. Stephens *Blow Negative* 177: Boy, if some guy who knows I got the botch sees me coming out of here he will never come in again.

bottle *n.* [fr. BOTTLE AND STOPPER] *Und.* a police officer.

1966 Braly *Cold Out There* 69: A class neighborhood, the bottles bust you on sight.

¶ In phrases:

¶ **hit the bottle** see s.v. HIT, *v.*

¶ **rattle** [or **pop**] **the bottle** (of males) to masturbate.

1952 (quot. at MARBLE, *n.*). **1977** List of slang from Univ. Tenn. instructor: Family jewels..."poppin' the bottle"...walnuts.

bottle *v.* to stop at once (*esp.* talking).—often constr. with *it.* Cf. syn. CAN.

1885 *Puck* (Apr. 22) 115: Bottle that and listen to me. **1924** in Clarke *Amer. Negro Stories* 27: King Solomon sought words of thanks. "Bottle it," said Uggam. **1925** Van Vechten *Nig. Heaven* 13: Bottle et. *Ibid.* 285: *Bottle it....*equivalent to the colloquial English *shut up.* **1930** Lait *On the Spot* 24: Aw, bottle it. *Ibid.* 200: Bottle it!...Shut up! **1964** Smith & Hoefer *Music* 195: We learned in Harlem to "bottle it," an expression that means the same as today's "cool it." Both mean shut up.

bottle and stopper *n.* [rhyming slang] a police officer; COPPER.

1919 T.A. Dorgan, in Zwilling *TAD Lexicon* 19: Bottles an' stoppers those are coppers. **1927–28** Tasker *Grimhaven* 180: We moped because the bottles and stoppers had the beef by that time. **1928** Sharpe *Chicago May* 288: *Bottles and stoppers*—coppers. **1929** *AS* (June) 338: The vocabulary of Bums...*Bottle and stopper.* A policeman. **1943** Holmes & Scott *Mr. Lucky* (film): Shall I call a bottle and stopper? **1944** *Papers Mich. Acad.* XXX 590: Now all the bottles and stoppers are wise. **1978** *West. Folklore* XXXVII 304.

bottle-assed *adj.* having wide hips and buttocks; (*hence*) *Printing.* (used figuratively of clogged type).

1770 in *OEDS*: [The type] drives out, or gets in, either at the head, or the foot, and is, as Printers call it, *Bottle-arsed.* **1890* *F & H* I 302: *Bottle-arsed, adj. phr.* (printers)—Type thicker at one end than the other—the result of wear and tear. **1909* *F & H* I (rev.) 339: *Bottle-arsed—*broad in the beam; full-buttocked. **1968** W.C. Anderson *Gooney Bird* 29: Bottle-assed wet-behind-the-ears blowtorch jockeys. **1970** G. Sorrentino *Steelwork* 105: Choke, you bottle-assed basted.

bottle baby *n.* a drunk, esp. a drunken derelict.

1925 in Armitage *Held* 23: You needn't worry about Clarabelle, the bottle baby. **1943** Fetridge *2d Navy Reader* 107: I might say that most of my chronic shirkers, officer haters, over-leavers and bottle babies are all petty officers today. **1946** Mezzrow & Wolfe *Really Blues* 86: The musicians...were bottle babies, always hitting the jug. **1953** Paley *Rumble* 80: That's that bottle baby we just passed an hour ago. **1954** Schulberg *Waterfront* 29: "Get lost," Terry mumbled as he watched the one-armed bottle-baby drift off into the morning mist. **1958** *N.Y. Times*

Mag. (Mar. 16) 87: *Bottle baby*—a derelict, a Bowery bum. **1963** Hayes *Carpetbaggers* (film): Rina Marlowe—a lush, a bottle baby, arrested five times for drunken driving. **1968** Cuomo *Thieves* 180: He's a bottle baby, Flash. **1989** L. Roberts *Full Cleveland* 167: You can always spot the bottle babies.

bottled *adj.* drunk.—in recent use, also constr. with *out.*

1927 N.Y. Times (Jan. 9): British pilot tells police, "If you say I am bottled, I will agree." **1964** in Bruce *Essential Lenny* 99: Ah, he's bottled out. **1965** Longstreet *Sportin' House* 183: But Kate, who was usually bottled, would take on anyone.

bottled sunlight *n.* whiskey or beer. *Joc.* Also **bottled sunshine.**

1893 in F. Remington *Sel. Letters* 168: The jug…contained the "bottled sun-light" of 40 summers hence. **1894** in F. Remington *Wister* 112: The two kinds of discussion differing in the degrees of "bottled sunlight" which occupies the center while we sit around. *1943 in Partridge *DSUE* (ed. 5) 1011: *Bottled sunshine.* Scottish service (esp. Army) name for beer.

bottle fatigue [pun on *battle fatigue*] *Mil.* (see quot.).

1956 Heflin *USAF Dict.* 89: *Bottle fatigue.* Fatigue resulting from heavy drinking. *Jocular.*

bottle-scarred *adj.* [pun on *battle-scarred*] made slow-witted by alcoholism. *Joc.*

1894 *Confed. War Jour.* (Mar.) 192: The next day's paper spoke of General Pillow as a "bottle-scarred hero." **1899** Skinner *14th Illinois* 447: The "bottle" scarred veterans and heroes of two hundred and fifty dress parades. **1945** House *Texas* 75: He used the phrase, "the battle-scarred veteran," but it came out in the paper, "the bottle-scarred veteran."

bottle up *v.* to quit; (*hence*) call it quits.

1881 A.A. Hays *New Colo.* 70: If I had to live here, I'd just *bottle up and die!* *1909* Ware *Pass. English* 44: *Bottle up*…To refrain; restrain oneself. **1946** Boulware *Jive & Slang* 2: *Bottle Up And Go,* Scram…Leave.

bottle-washer *n.* person in charge.—constr. with *head,* etc. Cf. chief cook and bottle-washer.

1856 [Sleeper] *Tales* 193: The head bottle-washer, or Rajah, as they call him.

bottom *n.* Orig. *Boxing & Horse Racing.* stamina and determination; energy. Now usu. *hist.* or horse-racing jargon. Also semi-adj.

1747 in *F & H* I 303: I have mentioned strength and art as the two ingredients of a boxer. But there is another, which is vastly necessary; that is, what we call a *bottom.*…There are two things required to make this *bottom,* that is, wind and spirit, or heart, or wherever you can fix the residence of courage. **1792** Brackenridge *Mod. Chiv.* 7: Horses of…speed and bottom. *1796* Grose *Vulgar Tongue* (ed. 3): *Bottom*…in the sporting sense, strength and spirits to support fatigue; as a bottomed horse. Among bruisers it is used to express a hearty fellow who will bear a good beating. **1824** in Nevins & Weitenkampf *Cartoons* 33: The foremost fellow shows fine *bottom.* **1835** *Spirit of Times* (Dec. 12) 2: Their…candidate had just finished a stump speech…."He's a screamer."…"He's bottom."…"He's grit to the back bone." **1835** in Paulding *Bulls & Jons.* 10: This caused people to say he had no *bottom*; but whoever said so lied, as they found to their cost whenever they put Jonathan in a passion….A capital boxer, of most excellent bottom. **1843** Field *Pokerville* 109: Mal Boeuf, also boasted some astonishing feats of "bottom." **1866** in Hilleary *Webfoot* 157: The…boys…put in the time galloping up and down the road…trying their horses in regard to bottom. **1962** Peewee Russell, in *New Yorker* (Aug. 11) 38: Something's always going. There's a lot of bottom in the group. **1962** A.J. Liebling, in *New Yorker* (Nov. 10) 211: A "bottom" fighter was one who won simply by wearing out his opponents. **1963** G. Frazier, in *Boston Herald* (Mar. 13) 8: In our own day, "bottom" goes by many names— "grace under pressure" and all the rest.

bottom *adj.* **1.** Orig. *Gamb.* (of a dollar) being the last in one's possession.—used prenominally.

1857 in *DA:* To use his own expressive phraseology, he "slips up for his bottom dollar." **1868** in *DA:* You bet your bottom dollar. **1875** Strong *Yellowstone* 6: He was…shot in the back by a cowardly s— of a b— while goin' his bottom dollar on a squar' game of "draw." **1985** N.O. woman, age 34: You can bet your bottom dollar I'll be at that [football] game.

2. Orig. *Prost.* (of a woman) most reliable; favorite.—used prenominally.

1967 [R. Beck] *Pimp* 215: There ain't more than three or four good bottom women promised to a pimp in his lifetime….He's gotta keep

his game tighter on his bottom bitch than on any bitch in the stable. **1971–73** Sheehy *Hustling* 56: Redpants thus earned a position as Sugarman's new "bottom woman." **1976** *Kojak* (CBS-TV): I took her into my stable, made her my bottom girl. **1981** A.K. Shulman *Stroll* 133: At twenty-eight, she was the bottom lady of Sweet Rudy, and an old hand in the life. **1983** K. Miller *Lurp Dog* 48: My bottom lady always did say I was too flamboyant to wear gray. *a1984* Sereny *Invisible Children* 62: The girlfriend she rang was Slim's "bottom-lady," Gina. **1983–86** Zausner *Streets* 113: I got along with all of them real well except his bottom hoe.

bottom-line *v. Business.* to state succinctly; to sum up.

1984 *Scientific Amer.* (Sept.) 114: I wanted to bottom line what's going to make Zapata! the hottest selling all-sport shoe in our line. **1989** *CBS This Morning* (CBS-TV) (Aug. 5): And let me bottom-line this for you, Kathleen.

botts *adj.* [< It *pazzo*] crazy.

1975 Sepe & Telano *Cop Team* 116: What are you going, botts?

boulder-holder *n.* a brassiere.—usu. in phr. **over-the-shoulder boulder-holder.** *Joc.*

1970 Partridge *DSUE* (ed. 7) 1025. **1971** *Nat. Lampoon* (Mar.) 47: Doltic over-shoulder-boulder-holder. **1975** Univ. Tenn. *Daily Beacon* (Feb. 6) 2: It was about an over-the-shoulder boulder-holder that some buxom lass had just let fly. **1976** Knapp & Knapp *One Potato* 83: All girls wearing an over-the-shoulder boulder-holder are said to be using falsies. **1978** Pilcer *Teen Angel* 85: She had an over-shoulder boulderholder. **1982** *World Acc. to Garp* (film): "What's the definition of a brassiere?" "An over-the-shoulder boulder-holder."

bounce *n.* **1.** a trip.

1879 *Snares of N.Y.* 81: Take a bounce on the Hudson Road to Spuyten Duyvil Creek. **1980** Pearl *Slang Dict.: Bounce n.*…(Truckers' CB) the return drive.

2.a. a discharge or dismissal; expulsion, rejection, jilting, etc.—usu. constr. with *grand.*

1877 Bartlett *Americanisms* (ed. 4) 777: To get the *grand bounce* is to be dismissed from service; particularly from an office under government. **1882** Field *Tribune Primer* 93: His Sweet Heart…has Given him the Grand Bounce. **1889** Reynolds *Kansas Hell* 138: Gus immediately got the "bounce." He was informed by his employer that he did not want to make his home a harbor for horse thieves. *Ibid.* 206: That evening…the prisoner got the "grand bounce." **1890** Howells *Hazard* 533: Well, I guess she's given him the grand bounce at last. **1900** *DN* II 24: "Get the grand *bounce*," to be expelled [from school]. *a1904–11* Phillips *Susan Lenox* I 330: As soon as I ketch a gal livin' beyond her wages I give her the bounce. **1953** Brossard *Saboteurs* 76: Her ambition was to give her pooped husband the bounce and then go off with some high-speed character. **1971** Dahlskog *Dict.* 9: She gave him the bounce.

b. a forcible ejection.—constr. with *grand.*

1880 Nye *Boomerang* 192: On yester morn I did give him the grand bounce, and now he hath joined a hold-up outfit on the overland stage route. **1882** *Judge* (Oct. 28) 7: The Yaller Dog he gut [*sic*] the grand bounce. **1883–84** Whittaker *L. Locke* 163: I'm the only son, and he gave me the grand bounce. **1895** Townsend *Chimmie Fadden* 11: Say, if I didn't come near gittin' de gran' bounce, de straight turn out, me name's not Chimmie Fadden.

c. a reprimand or punishment.—constr. with *grand.*

1892 Frye *From Headquarters* 158: Who'll get the grand bounce for running the guard last Thursday night?

3. *Mil. Av.* an aerial attack (on a flying aircraft).

1943 in Mahurin *Honest John* 130: If I have got things pretty well figured out before I make a bounce, I stand a much better chance of bagging that guy I'm going down after. **1956** Hess *Battle Hymn* 87: I made the bounce and let the YAK-9 start after me. **1958** Johnson & Caidin *Thunderbolt* 109: Ours was the most vulnerable position, the perfect spot to receive a bounce from the Germans. **1978** Ardery *Bomber Pilot* 138 [ref. to WWII]: They must be waiting for the perfect moment to make the "bounce." *a1991* Kross *Splash One* 108: Alert for a "bounce" by either F-4s or Sabres.

4. *Pris.* a prison sentence.

1957 in Blake *Joint* 161: Hopefully I look for a 3 to 5 bounce. **1977** Dunne *Confessions* 85: A 207….That's a gas-chamber bounce.

bounce *v.* **1.a.** to bully; to intimidate.

1811 *Lexicon Balatron.: Bounce.*…To bully a man out of anything. *The kiddey bounced the swell of the blowen;* the lad bullied the gentleman out of the girl. *1812* Vaux *Memoirs: Bounce:* To bully, threaten, talk loud, or affect great consequences; to *bounce* a person out of anything, is to use threatening or high words, in order to intimidate him. **1846** Melville *Typee* 52: But you don't bounce me out of my liberty, for all your yarns. **1859** Matsell *Vocab.* 125: *Bounced.* Frightened with stories of another's prowess. **1892** in F. Harris *Conklin* 157: The boys don't like a man to bounce....No one can bounce the crowd here in Garotte. They're the worse crowd you ever struck in your life....No one can bounce this camp. **1986** Stroud *Close Pursuit* 95: Wolfie, you gonna bounce every nigger in town? Your attitude sucks, buddy.

b. *Hunting.* to hunt; to scare up; flush.

1838 *Crockett Almanac* (1839) 34: I'd been bouncing deer on Tantivy prairie. **1839** *Crockett Almanac* (1840) 11: The rest of the time he spent in...bouncing deer. **1841** *Spirit of Times* (July 3) 211: I reckon we bounced a little the biggest old he [bear] that ever was rustled up in these parts. **1968–70** in *DARE.*

c. to assault; to attack from ambush.—formerly constr. with *into.*

1848 "Pry" *Life in Baltimore* 81: You're one of the party of Rackers what bounced into four or five of our fellers as we was bringing our real home from...Canton. **1876** in Bruns *Kts. of Road* 48: Yesterday a west-bound train on the Toledo, Wabash Western Railway was bounced at Chapin Station by about 100 of these gentry. **1878** Hart *Sazerac* 88: The fleas used to swim off to shore...and wait for that dog to come out, and then they'd bounce him ag'in. **1975** Larsen *Runner* 294: [German soldiers] could bounce us any time. **1988** Maloney *Thunder Alley* 233: It's the Green Army column...they're getting bounced.

d. to cajole; JOLLY.

1867 *Nat. Police Gaz.* (Jan. 5) 3: She wears a long fur cloak, and when caught in the act, Billy comes up, and if he cannot "bounce" the woman, he plays the detective and arrests his [own] woman. **1927** in *AS* (Feb. 1928) 218: *Bounce.* To influence by cajolery or flattery. To *bounce the prof* is to talk him out of a keen grade.

e. to kill.

1878 [P.S. Warne] *Hard Crowd* 8: Better take a fool's advice an' git while yeou kin! You'll git bounced, sure!

f. *Mil. Av.* to attack (an aircraft) in flight.

1943 in Liebling *Back to Paris* 5: About twenty Stukas came over, and a dozen P-40's bounced them and shot down eight. **1946** G.C. Hall, Jr. *1000 Destroyed* 228 [ref. to WWII]: It meant that you could bounce a Jerry before he got set and that you got to him ahead of competing pilots. **1948** Cozzens *Guard of Honor* 260: I was just bouncing a Wop, and I heard this goddamn firing in the air. **1955** Blair *Beyond Courage* 15: Confident that no MIG could "bounce" them while in such a fast dive, Schinz momentarily took his eyes off the MIG's below. **1956** Heflin *USAF Dict.* 89: *Bounce*...To attack an enemy *airplane* from the air, usually from a higher altitude, taking the enemy unaware. **1958** Johnson & Caidin *Thunderbolt* 92: If you get bounced by those people, don't play the hero. **1958** Mayes *Hunters* (film): He'll bounce you for simulated combat. **1990** Poyer *Gulf* 154: How about those F-14s that bounced us?

2.a. to dismiss; discharge; expel; fire; reject; spurn, etc., esp. summarily.

1873 Small *Kts. of Pythias* 4: I guess I won't join the Knights of Pythias....I've been bounced enough in my time. **1876** in *DAE:* Where are the soldiers of the Union army...? Nearly all gone, a clean sweep; to use a phrase that I never heard before, although I am told that it is common in some sections of the country, they are "bounced." **1878** Willis *Our Cruise* 15: I got bounced, but they'll be glad to get the likes o' me afore long. **1881** Nye *Forty Liars* 88: When the railroad king heard of it, he bounced the entire outfit. **1888** McConnell *5 Yrs. Cavalryman* 100: Of course there were now and then officers...who enthusiastically followed a trail until it became too warm, and then went into camp, but they were exceptions and always were "bounced" when their "peculiarities" became known at headquarters. **1889** Alger *Snobden's Office Boy* 116: I hear you've been bounced. **1893** Bangs *Coffee & Repartee* 69: He was bounced, of course, without a cent of pay. **1900** *DN* II 24: *Bounced: adj.* Excused indefinitely [from school]; suspended. **1909** in Ware *Pass. English* 45: He did not feel greatly injured by being bounced from a club which numbered only seven lame old men and two dogs. **1949** Bezzerides *Thieves' Highway* (film): I got a hunch they're gonna bounce me after they find out where the apples are. **1956** Metalious *Peyton Place* 246: I got bounced [from school], Dad. **1958** Drury *Advise & Consent* 52: I'm always afraid they're going to bounce me out of the club any day for being so casual about it all. **1962** E. Shepard *Press Passes* 198: Students had...bounced him from office and out of the country a few weeks earlier. **1982** WKGN radio news (June 2): Injuries bounced him out of the top spot [in the L.A. Rams lineup]. **1991** *TV Guide* (Apr. 20) 34: Then she became pregnant...and she was "bounced."

b. to eject forcibly.—often constr. with *out.*

1874 *Nat. Police Gaz.* (Dec. 5) 2: Nym Crinkle runs that shebang and he'd bounce both of us. **1877** "Wonder" *Drummer* 16: We have got to vacate this town suddenly or we'll be bounced out. **1877** Bartlett *Americanisms* (ed. 4) 62: I daresn't go in there; the bar-tender's drunk, and I might get bounced. **1880** Sala *America Revisited* II 112: He is "bounced" out of the car without the employment of much physical force. **1883** *Life* (July 19) 36: Red Handed Bill was thus bounced by a cop. **1895** Wood *Yale Yarns* 87: Shall we bounce him, sir? **1925** Cobb *Many Laughs* 97: You'd 'a' seen a job of bouncing that would 'a' made you open your eyes. **1932** in Ruhm *Hard-Boiled Detective* xi: Got a couple of drunks?...Why don't you bounce 'em? **1939–40** O'Hara *Pal Joey* 42: She heard her old man threaten to get me bounced out of town.

c. *Pris.* to be discharged from prison.

1963 Rubin *Sweet Daddy* 91: Comes D-Day, I bounce, Doc.

3. *Poker.* to raise (an opponent).

1883 *Life* (Feb. 8) 80: He bounced the Dea-con an-oth-er Hun-dred.

4.a. to knock to the ground; to knock out.

1918 Witwer *Baseball* 161: But the guy Windy bounces comes to and bends a gun over his head. **1920** Witwer *Kid Scanlan* 42: The kid bounces the other with a short left. *Ibid.* 103: If I don't bounce that tramp in two rounds, I'll give my end to them starvin' Armenians! **1942** Chandler *High Window* 367: You don't have any boys that can bounce me hard enough to make me tell it different. **1970** *N.Y. Times Mag.* (June 28) 24: I don't like to see anybody get bounced. I saw some of these [demonstrating] kids go down and I didn't think they were gonna get up.

b. *Sports. Journ.* to defeat.

1974 WINS radio (Aug. 11): Oakland bounced Boston 5–3. **1982** WKGN radio news (June 1): Baltimore bounced the Rangers 8–7. **1983** *Morning Report* (WKGN radio) (Mar. 7): The Bulls bounced the Pacers 106–98.

5.a. (of a check) to be returned unpaid for lack of funds; to fail of payment. Now *S.E.*

1931 Hellinger *Moon* 284: The check...bounced back in beautiful fashion. **1931** Wilstach *Under Cover Man* 166: "You boys take checks?" "Long as they don't bounce back in our faces." **1939** Goodman & Kolodin *Swing* 81: The promoter gave Pollack a check that bounced. **1951** W. Styron *Lie Down in Darkness* 357: And the check bounced higher than a kite.

b. to issue (a check) backed by insufficient funds.—used trans.

1936 Monks & Finklehoffe *Brother Rat* 30: If you bounce any checks in the Commandant's face you'll *never* pitch. **1985** Univ. Tenn. instructor, age 34: I guess I'll just have to bounce another check.

c. *Publishing.* (of a manuscript or the like) to be returned as unacceptable.

1954 Matheson *Born of Man & Woman* 193: Everything is all right...except for my latest story which won't get started [and]...my novel which has bounced five times.

6.a. to stand treat; to pay; SPRING.—used intrans.

1939 *AS* (Oct.) 239: *To Bounce.* To pay a bill; to ask for payment. **1951** in *DAS:* Knowin' you gals have to bounce for this sure improves the flavor! **1972** Wambaugh *Blue Knight* 19: I never make anyone bounce for two things in one day.

b. to agree (to).—constr. with *for.*

1948 Seward & Ryan *Angel's Alley* (film): Slip wouldn't bounce for it, that's why.

7. to rob.

1942 Algren *Morning* 48: You never wanted to help out wagon-bouncing 'r coppin' by the five-'n-dime.

8. to copulate with.

1952 MacDonald *Damned* 158: I've...bounced more hundreds of women than I want to think about. **1976** Univ. Tenn. instructor, age 32: Then he takes her home and bounces her. **1981** Ballenger *Terror* 74: Here's to the women we're going to bounce when we get home.

9. to socialize or carouse, as in a bar.

1973 Droge *Patrolman* 165: We would go "bouncing" many a night and drink until our stomachs burst. **1980** W. Sherman *Times Sq.* 12: He...joined...some of the other cops when they went "bouncing."

10. to work as a bouncer.

1986 *Larry King Live* (CNN-TV) (Apr. 17): I worked for a while bouncing at bars.

bounce around *v.* **1.** to beat up, esp. as a means of coercion.

1942 Liebling *Telephone* 32: I bounced him around [in the prize ring], but I didn't know enough to finish him. **1962** Perry *Young Man* 126: Let me bounce this son of a bitch around first, Chief. I know how to soften these young punks up. **1972** Bunker *No Beast* 67: Two goons caught me in a parking lot and bounced me around. **1985** *Miami Vice* (NBC-TV): A trick bounced her around good.

2. to treat roughly or unfairly.

1973 Breslin *World Without End* 23: Well, don't fuckin' bounce me around. **1984** "W.T. Tyler" *Shadow Cabinet* 11: I still think someone ought to bounce that meatball around....Just the way he's dumping on those bureaucrats.

bounceback *n. Hosp.* a patient who repeatedly returns to a hospital for treatment.

1981 in Safire *Good Word* 152.

bounce field *n. Naval Av.* (see quot.).

1958 Cope & Dyer *Petty Off. Gde.* 333: *Bounce field.* (Slang). A simulated carrier deck ashore.

bounce off *v.* **1.a.** to kill.

1916 in Hall & Niles *One Man's War* 149: Hope I'm not bounced off before I get a chance to spend it. **1927** Niles *Singing Soldiers* 131: Why, I'm going to be bounced off in a few days—what's the use of wasting money on French barbers? **1929** Niles, Moore & Wallgren *Songs* 77: Artillery—slow as the seven year itch! Horses always gettin' bounced off.

b. to die.

1918 in Niles, Moore & Wallgren *Songs* 196: The brave young lad was bouncing off.

2. to leave; to abscond.

1938 Chandler *Big Sleep* 70: He liked Regan and was hurt the way he bounced off without telling me the old man good-bye.

3. to submit (an idea) to (someone) for an informal opinion.

1983 *Mutual Radio Network News* (Apr. 11): They've done well to bounce this off several Congressmen before submitting it to the President.

bounce-out *n.* a spree, celebration, BLOWOUT.

1841 [Mercier] *Man-of-War* 250: I know your coppers are hot since that *bounce-out* you had ashore at market yesterday.

bouncer *n.* **1.** a large specimen.

*1596 in Partridge *DSUE* 85: My book will grow such a bouncer, that those which buy it must be faine to hire a porter to carry it after them in a basket. *1811 *Lexicon Balatron.: Bouncer.* A large man or woman. **1898** Green *Va. Folk-Speech* 65: *Bouncer,* n. A large, strong, vigorous person. **1967–69** in *DARE.*

2.a. a bully; thug.

*1698–99 "B.E." *Dict. Canting Crew: Bouncer,* a Bully. *1748 in *F & H* I 306: *Bouncer*...A bully or hectoring bravado. *1851–61 H. Mayhew, in *F & H* I 305: Those who cheat the Public...Bouncers...defrauding, by...swaggering or using threats. **1865** *Nat. Police Gaz.* (Apr. 29) 4: Old Moyamensing is almost as famous for its lawless gangs of boys and young men, as it was in the days of the "killers" and "bouncers."

b. a great lie; whopper; (*hence*) a liar.

*1811 *Lexicon Balatron.: Bouncer.* A great lie. **1823** Cooper *Pioneers* 46: I will let Marmaduke tell a few bouncers about it before I come out upon him. **1833** *Mil. & Naval Mag.* (Aug.) 380: Such a *bouncer.*...I mean that he's the greatest liar that ever walked a deck. *1858 A. Mayhew *Paved with Gold* 291: "That's a bouncer!" exclaimed Phil, laughing. **1898** Green *Va. Folk-Speech* 65: *Bouncer*...A bareface lie. **1901** F.P. Dunne *Mr. Dooley's Opinions* 87: Th' bouncer,...th' con, th' bunk, th'...lie.

c. a man employed to eject rowdy patrons from a saloon, restaurant, etc. Now *S.E.*

1883 in Rosa & Koop *Rowdy Joe* 127: Simmons, a sort of "bouncer" for a dance hall. **1885** *Puck* (July 15) 316: She...ejected him as deftly as a professional "bouncer." **1887** Walling *N.Y. Chief of Police* 483: Occasionally his duties as money-changer are interrupted by those of the "bouncer." **1891** Maitland *Amer. Slang Dict.* 44: *Bouncer,*...one hired in a saloon, dive, or low theatre or other place of entertainment for the purpose of throwing out objectionable visitors. **1897** Norris *Vandover* 330: The bouncer and three other waiters charged into them. **1898** Westcott *David Harum* 41: Billy...is...the "bouncer" at the Altman House, an ex-prize-fighter...employed to keep order and...thrust out the riotous. **1902** S.E. White *Blazed Trail* 18: He was seized by the collar and trousers in the grip known to "bouncers" everywhere. **1903** A. Adams *Log of Cowboy* 204: The bouncer of the dance hall...had his eye on our crowd. **1924** Hecht & Bodenheim *Cutie* 46: The bouncers step in. **1942** Liebling *Telephone* 56: McGuire...is a bouncer in Jollity

Danceland. **1982** *New Dimensions* (Nat. Public Radio) (June 11): They don't call them bouncers because they dribble tennis balls. They call them bouncers because they throw people around and out.

3. *Finance.* a worthless check that is returned for lack of funds; (*occ.*) the writer of such a check.

1927 *New Republic* (Jan. 26) 277: "Bouncer"...may be either (1) a rubber check returned by the bank as no good or (2) the person who passes ("bounces") the rubber check. **1930** *Amer. Mercury* (Dec.) 454: *Bouncer, n.* A worthless check. "I think he's regular and he slips me a bouncer." **1962–63** in Giallombardo *Soc. of Women* 201: *Bouncer.* A bad check.

4. *R.R.* a caboose.

1940 *Railroad Mag.* (Apr.) 38: *Bouncer*—caboose. **1947** in *DA.*

bouncing baby *n. Mil.* BOUNCING BETTY.

1943 in Liebling *Back to Paris* 288: The Italians...had mined the roads and shoulders of the roads...with what the engineers called "bouncing babies." The babies were metal containers that were blown into the air by a charge of black powder when a soldier stepped on a hidden trip wire. They were packed with high explosives and steel ball bearings, and were timed to explode about chest high in the air. **1943** *Yank* (July 16) 13: Bouncing Baby...is the American name for...dreaded Nazi..."S" mine...in Tunisia...Exploding waist high, each spews 350 steel balls.

Bouncing Betty *n. Mil.* a kind of land mine that, when tripped, shoots from the ground to explode at about chest height.

1943 G. Biddle *Artist at War* 109: We found a Bouncing Betty on the edge of a swimming hole. **1944** Ramey *In Cavalry* 102: Alongside the road and in the fields were the so-called "Bouncing Betty." **1966–67** Harvey *Air War* 109: The Arvins had abandoned 1,500 of our "Bouncing Betty" mines on Marble Mountain. **1968** W. Crawford *Gresham's War* 65 [ref. to Korean War]: One of their officers was killed accidentally tripping a Bouncing-Betty. **1970** Whitmore *Memphis-Nam-Sweden* 54: These particular mines were Bouncin' Betties. When someone steps on a Betty, it bounces up to stomach level, explodes and cuts a person in half. **1971** Polner *No Victory Parades* 25: One of them...was killed on patrol by a "Bouncing Betty" mine. He stepped on it and it almost cut him in half. **1991** *N.Y. Times* (nat. ed.) (Jan. 29) A 4: "Bouncing Betty" bomblets pop up into the air before exploding.

bounty hunter *n. Police.* an officer who seeks to make a large number of arrests.

1975 Sepe & Telano *Cop Team* 41: A "bounty-hunter," a cop who'd arrest his own mother. **1985** M. Baker *Cops* 237: I started being a bounty hunter, which is a guy who gets a lot of arrests. The system being what it is, you can get overtime if you make the arrest.

bow[1] *n.* usu. *pl. Naut.* bosom.

*1805 J. Davis *Post-Captain* 27: Yes sir, she is nice and bluff about the bows. **1836** *Spirit of Times* (Feb. 20) 7: Ned Curtis had a wife...broad in the beam, with a high starn, and very bluff in the bows. **1844** Ingraham *Midshipman* 20: She rounds in the bows like a duck. *a*1900 in J. Colcord *Songs of Sailormen* 54: She was round in the counter and bluff in the bow.

bow[2] *n.* [fr. el*bow*] *Basketball.* the elbow.

1980 Wielgus & Wolff *Basketball* 40: Bow (n.) Elbow. Bows are thrown to settle scores and get position. **1989** Chafets *Devil's Night* 9 [ref. to *ca*1961]: Man, you gotta use your 'bows. **1990** P. Dickson *Slang!* 202: *Bow.* (Basketball) elbow.

bow and arrow *n. West.* an American Indian.—used disparagingly.

1842 *Ben Hardin's Crockett* (unp.): Was said to have a cross of the Indian blood in his veins, or, to use our backwoods phrase, "had a little of the bow and arrow in his bones." **1930** in *DARE.*

bow-and-arrow squad *n. Police.* a police assignment consisting of officers who have been relieved of armed duty.—usu. constr. with *the. Joc.*

1973 Breslin *World Without End* 13: They relieve him of all armaments and assign him to units known, in police jargon, as Bow and Arrow Squads. **1983** Flaherty *Tin Wife* 238: She had often heard stories of various cops relegated to the "bow & arrow" squad for ventilating some saloon's ceiling. **1986** *NDAS.*

bowels *n.pl.* ¶ In phrase: **get (one's) bowels in an uproar** to become unnecessarily excited, angry, agitated, etc.

[**1900** Remington *With Bark On* 109: His bowels were in tremolo. His heart lost three beats.] **1932** Harvey *Me and Bad Eye* 162 [ref. to WWI]: What are you getting your bowels in such a uproar about? **1933** "W.

March" *Co. K* 73 [ref. to WWI]: Now, Cookie, don't get your bowels in an uproar. **1941** Schulberg *Sammy* 15: If he matters that little, why in hell are you getting your bowels in an uproar? **1942** Wilder *Flamingo Rd.* 228: I don't know why I should get my bowels in an uproar over the rest of the world. **1958** Traver *Anat. Murder* 99: Don't get your bowels in an uproar. **1971** *Blushes & Bellylaffs* 6: I'm going to be an unwed father, but you don't see me gettin' my bowels in an uproar! **1978** Maupin *Tales* 69: I'm leaving. Don't get your bowels in an uproar. **1987** W. Allen *Radio Days* (film): All right, all right! Don't get your bowels in an uproar.

bower *n*. Orig. *Gamb*. close friend; assistant; accomplice, etc.—usu. constr. with *right*, occ. with *left*. [The *right* and *left bowers* are the two highest cards in the game of euchre.]
1847 in Blair & Meine *Half Horse* 99: Jabe Knuckles was there, too, one of Mike's "bowers," but Jabe, unaccountably had *softened down* his character, considerably. **1863** [Fitch] *Annals of Army* 501: Smith…would furnish him with a letter of introduction to his "right bower" in Nashville. **1905** Phillips *Plum Tree* 212: The most I could do then was to supply my local "left-bower," Silliman, with funds and set him to work for a candidate. **1926** Finerty *Criminalese* 9: Bower—A friend. **1929** Dobie *Vaquero* 60: Cortina's "right bower" was Alberto Garza. **1936** Washburn *Parlor* 146: Harris [was] the "right bower" of Alderman Hinky Dink Kenna of the First Ward. **1962** Quirk *Red Ribbons* 171: He settled for making Three his unofficial right bower. **1964** Marshall *World War I* 45: Joffre's right bower was…General Belin.

bowhead *n. Stu*. a silly coed who typically wears bows in her hair; a shallow sorority girl.
1989 P. Munro *U.C.L.A. Slang* 24: The bowheads were in an uproar. **1990** P. Dickson *Slang!* 213: Bowhead…a bouncy cheerleader type who ignores her intelligence, is superficial, and wears bows in her hair. **1991** Univ. Tenn. student paper: Bowheads—Sorority girls. Very pejorative!

bowl *n. Narc*. **1.** a pipeful of marijuana or the like.
1972 N.Y.U. student: I did three bowls of hash this morning and I'm, like, wasted. **1982** Del Vecchio *13th Valley* 109: After they torch up a bowl be powerful mellow. **1985** B.E. Ellis *Less Than Zero* 130: Jeff and I smoked a couple of bowls. **1985** Bodey *F.N.G.* 36: When I come up they quit talking, and I see they're smoking a bowl. **1991** *N.Y. Times* (Feb. 5) B 1: A man…admitted to having "smoked a bowl" before venturing out…for pizza.
2. a pipe for smoking marijuana or the like.
1974 *New Times* (Sept. 20) 38: That is a bowl….They call it a bowl. It's what they smoke marijuana out of. **1977** in Rice *Adolescent* 273: Bowl—pot pipe. **1985** J.M.G. Brown *Rice Paddy Grunt* 98: We'd pass a few bowls around listening to the night sounds.

bowlegs *n. Army*. a cavalryman or cavalrymen.
1907 J. Moss *Officer's Gde*. 243: Bow-legs—cavalrymen. **1929** E. Colby, in *Our Army* (Nov.) 26: Because constant riding of horses usually bows his legs, the cavalryman is called Bow Legs.

bowline *n*. ¶ In phrase: **slip (one's) bowline** *Naut*. to die. Cf. syn. *slip (one's) cable* s.v. CABLE.
1848 in Blair & Meine *Half Horse* 186: I don't much like to string a feller up in cold blood, and that's what I'd had to done…ef he hadn't slipped his bow-line.

bowling alley *n. R.R.* (see quot.).
1940 *Railroad Mag.* (Apr.) 38: Bowling Alley—Hand-fired coal-burning locomotive.

bowl out *v*. [extended fr. the cricket term] to overcome, get the better of; *(hence) Mil*. to kill, knock out of action.
*1805** in *OEDS*: He wished me to be made acquainted with it, that in the event of his being "bowl'd out" I might know how to conduct the ship. *1821** *Real Life in London* II 340: He *bowls them out* by harassing expenses. *1829** Marryat *F. Mildmay* 44: "I hope plenty of the lieutenants are bowled out!" said another; "we shall stand some chance then of a little promotion!" **1863** in H.L. Abbott *Fallen Leaves* 201: I think I shall get to a majority…if I don't get bowled out of course. **1864** in Abbott *Fallen Leaves* 241: Probably 250…of the 400 which go in, will get bowled out.

bow port *n. Naut*. the mouth.
1835 *Mil. & Naval Mag.* (Dec.) 295: I was at Falmouth, and I was in a public house, with a pipe in my bow port, and a pot of beer afore me.

bowser *n*. [a bowser once commonly given to dogs] **1.** a dog; POOCH.
1965, 1980 (implied by BOWSER BAG). **1986** *USA Today* (July 28) 2D: But lest you begin thinking that everybody…loves cats, listen to…Duke Ostendorf…proud owner of two huge bowsers, Rocco and Slim. "I hate cats….Dogs are loyal."
2. *Stu*. a very unattractive member of the opposite sex, esp. a young woman; DOG.
1978 *UTSO*: [Unattractive] Male…dog, bowser. Ibid. [another student]: [Unattractive] Female…dog, gorilla, witch, pup, bowser. **1980** Eble *Campus Slang* (Oct.) 2: Bowser—physically unattractive female: "Martha's sister is a bowser." "Sue has a bowser face." **1981** Spears *Slang & Euphem.* 44: Bowser…bowzer,…an ugly young woman. **1988** *TV Guide* (Oct. 22) 23: A college fraternity threw a "Bowser Ball," to which only the ugliest coeds were invited. **1992** *Herman's Head* (Fox-TV): It'd be different if you were a real bowser.

bowser bag *n*. [cf. DOGGIE BAG] a paper bag provided by a restaurant for patrons who wish to take uneaten portions home, as for feeding to a pet dog.
1965 *L.A. Times* (July 5) V 8: Because of the size of their in-bone prime ribs, they must have the most bulging bowser bags in town….They figure about 160 lbs. of prime beef and bones go to the dogs every day. **1980** Abigail Van Buren *Dear Abby* (synd. column) (Sept. 16): How do you feel about "bowser bags" at mealtime in a private home?

bowsprit *n. Naut*. **1.** the nose. Also *(obs.)* BOLTSPRIT.
*1698–99** "B.E." *Dict. Canting Crew*: He has broke his Boltsprit, he has lost his Nose with the Pox. *1785** Grose *Vulgar Tongue*: Bowsprit, the nose, from its being the most projecting part of the human face, as the bowsprit is of a ship. *1794** in Holloway & Black *Broadside Ballads* 30: A splinter knocked my nose off,/My bowsprit's gone, I cries. *1820–21** P. Egan *Life in London* 23: Sall Walker shows her bowsprit nose. **1835** *Mil. & Naval Mag.* (Dec.) 297: Well, the people beginned to look funny, and Joe's partner told him to let down his bowsprit, and not say no more. **1935** Marion et al. *Riffraff* (film): How would you like a good…sock right on the point of your bowsprit, son?
2. the penis. Cf. BOBSTAY.
*1741** in J. Atkins *Sex in Lit.* IV 98: His Grace…used to penetrate with his bowsprit even into the…palace. *1889** (cited in Partridge *DSUE* (ed. 8) 126). **1967** Schmidt *Lexicon of Sex* 25: Bowsprit…The genital beak of the male. **1969** *Playboy* (Dec.) 157: [Syns. for penis:]…bowsprit.
3. a cigar.
1906 in *McClure's* (Jan. 1907) 332: The mild-Key West-two-for-a-dollar bow-sprit in my mouth turned flat an' tasteless.

bow-wow *n*. [sugg. by DOG] **1.** a sausage.
1900 *DN* II 24: Bow-wow, n. Sausage [in use at several colleges]. **1906** M'Govern *Sjt. Larry* (gloss.): Bow-Wow: Vienna Sausage. **1909** M'Govern *Krag* 101: The beef stew is always "slum;" the sausage invariably "dog" or "bow-wow." **1934** Weseen *Dict. Slang* 288: Bow-wow—Sausage.
2. a very unattractive or unsatisfactory person or thing; DOG. *Joc*.
1935 *AS* X 270: Bowwow. A stunted, aged steer, unsuited for beef or fattening. **1942** in *DARE*: In cracker cow-jargon, a bowwow is a runty steer. **1977** Schrader *Blue Collar* 66: Shit, you think every chick's a fox. That bitch is a bow-wow. She eats Gainesburgers. **1987** Weiser & Stone *Wall St.* (film): Those [were] bow-wow stocks you mentioned. **1988** *Wkly. World News* (Apr. 5) 13: Funny guy calls pretty princess a bow-wow!
¶ In phrase:
¶ **go to the bow-wows** to "go to the dogs."
*1839** C. Dickens *N. Nickleby* ch. lxiv: He has gone to the demnition bow-wows. **1867** A.D. Richardson *Beyond Miss.* 207: Deserted buildings…and a general tendency to "the demnition bow wows." **1891** in F. Remington *Sel. Letters* 117: Or the bank act will go to the bow-wows. **1893** W.K. Post *Harvard* 118: Everything was going to the bow-wows. **1904** Ade *True Bills* 113: All was going to the Bow-Wows. **1948** W.C. Williams, in Witemeyer *Williams-Laughlin* 148: After which Papa will be freer (poorer) to go to the…bow wows. **1968** in *DARE*: That man is headed straight for the damnation bow-wows.

box *n*. **1.a.** the vulva or vagina.
*ca1605** Shakespeare *All's Well* II iii 275: Too'th warrs my boy, too'th warres/He weares his honor in a boxe vnseene,/That hugges his kickie wickie heare at home,/Spending his manlie marrow in her armes. *1631** B. Jonson *Bartholomew Fair* I i 293: Good Lord, how long your little wife stays! Pray God, Solomon, your clerk, be not looking i' the wrong box, Master Proctor. *a1640** in Pinto & Rodway *Common Muse* 379: [Papists] make an Idoll of the Masse,/Hee [the Puritan] idolatizeth with a Lasse;/They kisse and cringe vnto the Pax,/Hee to his Mistres bawdy Boxe. *1699** Ward *London-Spy* 140: Does she not deserve it, Sir,

for trusting her Money in a box that has neither lid nor bottom to it? **1916** Cary *Venery* I 22: Box—The vagina. This is a gambler's expression, from the deal box, used in the game of faro, an instrument by which he makes his living. **1918** in Carey *Mlle. from Armentières* II (unp.): Mademoiselle from Bully-Grenay/With hair on her box like a bale of hay. **1927** *Immortalia* 97: She wore no pants and her box was bare. **1930** *Lyra Ebriosa* 18: She…filled up her box with sand. **1934** H. Roth *Call It Sleep* 412: No splinters in dese boxes, dough….Real clean—. **1938** "Justinian" *Americana Sexualis* 14: Box. n. The female pudend. Coll., of possible nautical derivation. C. 19-20. Obsolescent. **1941** in Legman *Limerick* 44: There was a young girl of Pawtucket/ Whose box was as big as a bucket. **1942** McAtee *Supp. to Grant Co. Dial. in '90's* 3: Box, n. female pudendum. **1960** in IUFA *Folk Speech*: Anyone who won't eat box won't fight for his country; and I'm a fightin' son-of-a-bitch. **1987** *Penthouse Letters* (Oct.) 53: I never thought I'd get my whole cock into her box.

b. a young woman.

1955–57 Kerouac *On Road* 152: Sal, I ran to Marylou with some of that tea. And do you know that the same thing happened to that dumb little box?—the same visions, the same logic. **1967** in M.W. Klein *Juve. Gangs* 98: Words like Punk, Chump, Box, Pigeon, and Fag emerge and represent the standardization of the typical moral relations with the victim as perceived [by the victimizer]. **1974** N.Y.C. man, age *ca*30: A good-lookin' chick is a *box* or a *hammer*. **1985** Schwendinger & Schwendinger *Adolescent Sub.* 137: The sexual victim, for instance, is a Piece of Ass, Box, or Cunt, and nothing more. **1991** Eble *Campus Slang* (Fall) 1: *Box*…female.

c. copulation.

1963 T.I. Rubin *Sweet Daddy* 35: No chicks, no box. **1967** Baraka *Tales* 10: Me and Chris had these D.C. babes at their cribs….Oooooo, that was some good box.

d. *Homosex.* the scrotum and penis; BASKET.

1965 Trimble *Sex Words* 29: Box…The Penis or male Genitalia, particularly in Homosexual usage. **1972** *Anthro. Linguistics* (Mar.) 99: Box (n.): The genitalia; also referred to as the "basket." **1984** Mason & Rheingold *Slanguage*: Box…The bulge in the male body that appears through tight jeans.

e. *Black E.* the buttocks.

1965 in W. King *Black Anthol.* 305: You sho got a niaz box, baby….See how she shakes that thang?

2. a coffin.

1864 in J.W. Haley *Rebel Yell* 169: How the old man's bones would rattle in his box if he could see how fast old Virginia is going to the "Demnition Bow Wows." **1878** [P.S. Warne] *Hard Crowd* 8: Sam an' Joe, yeou knock a box together. **1892** F.P. Dunne, in Schaaf *Dooley* 45: He has a fine box and a mausolyum. **1898** Green *Va. Folk-Speech* 66: Box, n….A coffin. **1914** *Collier's* (May 9) 22: I have never heard the regular army man given a…kindly word until by whole battalions he began to come home in boxes. **1928** Bodenheim *Georgie May* 36: She'd hit the snow…until it poked her into the old box. **1932** Parker *30 Yrs. in Army* 32: I'll either get you there on your feet or you'll go in a box. **1935** C. Odets *Paradise Lost* 202: Then sticking him dead in the box. **1943** J. Mitchell *McSorley's* 66: I give myself three more years and they'll have me in a box. **1969** P. Hamill *Doc* 94: If I see you in this town again, you'll go out of it in boxes. **1976** *Kojak* (CBS-TV): If he put Azure in a box, why not say so?

3. *Naut.* a ship, esp. if unseaworthy.

1851 Ely *Wanderings* 161: You don't want to go in an old box that will take two or three days in getting there. **1896** Hamblen *Many Seas* 67: The English sailors had christened our ship the *Boston Box*. **1914** Paine *Wall Between* 205: I was aboard the *Paducah* gunboat last night—a comical lookin' little box she is. **1923** Southgate *Rusty Door* 109: Yeah, she's a tight little box, this *Colleen Bess*. **1934** Traven *Death Ship* xxviii: You never shipped on a box like this one.

4. a prison cell; a lockup; (*hence*) a jail, prison, or stockade.

***1834** in *F & H* I 312: In a box of the stone-jug I was born. **1882** in Sonnichsen *Billy King* 59: I…stayed in the "box" until this morning. **1897** Ade *Pink Marsh* 123: Misteh Johnson, he's a coppeh. He come in on a small game o' craps, an' 'at's what 'at cullud fellow's singin' to him at 'e box. **1932** L. Berg *Prison Doctor* 128: Anything goes in this box if you can lay it on the line. **1955** Q. Reynolds *HQ* 84: Now and then we'll…make a good collar and have the satisfaction of seeing the bums go into the box for a long stay. **1972** Casey *Obscenities* 18: An they went with me/To the box all right/An the prisoners were all out….*box:* stockade barracks for maximum security prisoners.

5. *Und.* a safe. Hence **box man** a safecracker.

1902 in "O. Henry" *Works* 974: The "box man," as the ingenious safe

burglar now denominates himself. **1902** Hapgood *Autobiog. Thief* 120 [ref. to 1880's]: He was one of the most successful box-men (safe-blowers) in the city. **1908** "O. Henry" *Voice of City* 1353: Pickpocket, supper man, second-story man, yeggman, boxman, all-round burglar. **1909** Fletcher *Up the Trail* 98 [ref. to 1889]: Open your box! **1912** Stringer *Shadow* 87: Loony Ryan [was] an old time "box man." **1913** *Sat. Eve. Post* (Mar. 15) 10: He was carryin' de keester full of kale which he blowed out of de box in Winnepeg. **1920** Murphy *Gray Walls* 25: This is my third jolt for a box (blowing a safe). **1949** in *Harper's* (Feb. 1950) 69: The decline of the box-busting racket is a case in point. **1950** Maddow & Huston *Asphalt Jungle* 28: A box man—him we pay most—maybe twenty-five thousand dollars. **1966** R.E. Alter *Carny Kill* 115: I'm no box man. **1962–68** B. Jackson *In the Life* 72: The old box-men…they was not dope fiends. *ca***1978** *Rockford Files* (NBC-TV): Uncle Charlie used to be a top box man. He could easily show her how to crack a safe.

6. a piano; esp. in phr. **beat** [or **bang**] **the box** to play dance music on a piano.

1908 *Hampton's Mag.* (Oct.) 457: He's a good boy on the box, though. **1915** Howard *God's Man* 194: The rapid staccato rag-time that the Cagey Kid began to "beat outa the box," as he phrased it. **1918** *Stars & Stripes* (Mar. 29) 7: A ham piano artist bangs the box to beat the band. **1918** in E. Janis *Big Show* 142: So I said, "Can anyone beat the box?" Loud shouts of "Can they?!" **1920** S. Lewis *Main St.* 210: She was "all het up pounding the box"—which may be translated as "eagerly playing the piano." **1936** *Harper's* (Mar.) 447: Skill on the piano [was] not confined to "beating the box." **1941** Perrin & Grant *Keep 'Em Flying* (film): And when he plays on that box,/The joint rocks. **1959** A. Anderson *Lover Man* 152: I blow box….Piano. **1965** C. Brown *Manchild* 229: This gave me a stronger urge to blow piano, or blow a box, as they used to say. **1970** Corrington *Bombardier* 17: "I don't feel so lonely up behind the box," Fats said slowly.

7.a. a fiddle.

[**1845** in Harris *High Times* 48: That pot-gutted pine box of a fiddle.] **1911** *JAF* 258: The old-time negro with his "box" (a fiddle or guitar).

b. a guitar; (*also*) a banjo.

1911 (quot. at (a), above). **1925** Odum & Johnson *Negro & His Songs* 157: In general, however, the…songs…are accompanied by the "box" or fiddle when large or small groups are gathered together for gayety. **1929** Barr *Let Tomorrow Come* 110: "Get down the old box and give us a song."…Tom takes the guitar off the shelf. **1935** Z.N. Hurston *Mules & Men* 33: Man, you know I don't go nowhere unless Ah take my box with me. **1936** Benton & Ballou *Where Do I Go?* 103 [ref. to *ca*1910]: Several of the Negro convicts had "boxes," that is banjos. **1938** Steinbeck *Grapes of Wrath* 363: This was my father's box. Wasn't no bigger'n a bug first time he give me a C chord. **1941** Attaway *Blood on the Forge* 41: Reckon I wants a new E string for my box. **1943** Guthrie *Bound for Glory* 384: So I flipped a few strings to see if the box was in tune. **1944** Wheeler *Steamboatin'* 86: Bless the Lawd, honey, he don't nevuh mind singin' an' he jes' loves to play on the box. **1959–60** R. Reisner *Jazz Titans* 151: *Box:* phonograph, or piano, or guitar.

c. an accordion or concertina.

1980 Kotzwinkle *Jack* 165: "Give us a tune on the box, Leo." Leo…opened the straps of his accordion.

8.a. a phonograph, radio, or tape recorder; (in recent use *esp.*) a portable stereo radio and cassette player.

***1924** in *OEDS*: I…play Beethoven & Mozart to myself on the box. **1930** Gilman *Sob Sister* 49: "And now ladies and gentlemen," shouted the angry box. **1943** *AS* (Apr.) 154: *Jive on the box.* Music on the radio. **1945** C. Himes *If He Hollers* 64: The box was blaring Erskine Hawkins' "Don't Cry, Baby." **1958–59** Lipton *Barbarians* 38: I've got a guarantee on this box. **1962** H. Simmons *On Eggshells* 68: He started selecting some records for the box. **1969** Bullock *Watts* 19: Many of the youngsters carry their most prized possession—a "box" (radio)—from which "soul" sounds blare incessantly. **1970** E. Thompson *Garden of Sand* 222: Turn up the friggin' box so we can *all* hear! **1983** Sturz *Wid. Circles* 79: The young man had his "box" suspended from his shoulder by a leather strap—a fifty-five pound radio in flashing silver tones. **1984** Hindle *Dragon Fall* 68: Turning to his "big box," he switched from *Radio* to *Tape*. **1986** Merkin *Zombie Jamboree* 278: I got five words off the box from Lieutenant DerHammer.

b. a jukebox.

1971 S. Stevens *Way Uptown* 131: James Brown was on the box but you couldn't' hardly hear him for the noise. **1985** N. Black *Mischief* (film): Don't they have any Elvis on this box?

c. an intercom; SQUAWK BOX.

1948 Cozzens *Guard of Honor* 50 [ref. to WWII]: Probably as soon as

I left he was on the box to the general. **1951** [VMF-323] *Old Ballads* 2: The call is coming over the box, it's pilots man your planes. **1966** F.C. Elkins *Heart of Man* 73: It was only Norris using our ready room box.

d. a television set.—usu. constr. with *the.*

1950 in Marx *Groucho Letters* 168: I have solved the television problem by having a remote control installed on the ugly box. **1957** Gutwillig *Long Silence* 241: Any new clues for the box? **1970** *Playboy* (Dec.) 122: They go home and watch the box with the wife and kids. **1972** *N.Y. Times* (Oct. 28) II 15: What I play on the box is a rosy-cheeked young kook. **1978** R. Price *Ladies' Man* 6: It made me feel like an invalid to have the box on.

9. *Photography.* a camera.

1918 *Outlook* (June 26) 346: I'd always have such a big head in the morning I couldn't shoot the box.

10. an automobile trailer.

1942 *AS* (Apr.) 103: *Box.* Trailer. Also *Tag Along.*

11. an elevator.

1974 A. Bergman *Big Kiss-Off* 135: Can you get Vito to run this box for about a half-hour?

12. [fr. ice*box*] a refrigerator.

1978 R. Price *Ladies' Man* 152: Raid the box, hole up with Bogey, you know? **1981** *Easyriders* (Oct.) 17: So I liberated a cold one from his box and kicked my tired ass back.

13. *Mil.* a defensive pillbox.

1961 Pirosh & Carr *Hell Is for Heroes* (film): That box has got us nailed down tight.

14. the mouth.

1930 Huston *Frankie & Johnny* 69: Close your box. **1951** *New Yorker* (May 12) 32: First crack outa Don's box is "What is with you, Sonny?"

15. the head.

1903 (quot. at *out of (one's) box,* below). **1966–70** in *DARE.*

¶ In phrases:

¶ **knock out of the box** [alluding to baseball jargon *box* 'batter's position'] to defeat and eliminate; *(hence)* to kill.

1891 in Leitner *Diamond in Rough* 155: We'll just get onto the devil's curves/And knock him out of the box. **1970** Terkel *Hard Times* 354: Successful businessmen—the stock market just knocked 'em right out of the box. **1972** E. Grogan *Ringolevio* 327: They can taste what it'll be like when those few who own everything are knocked out of the box. **1988** "N.W.A." *Straight Outta Compton* (rap song): I'm knockin' niggers out the box daily.

¶ **out of** [earlier **off**] **(one's) box** insane.

1903 *DN* II 322: *Offen his box* or *off his box*...Mistaken. If he thinks he can fool me he is *offen his box*. **1908** *DN* III 290: *Off one's box*...out of one's mind. **1966** Neugeboren *Big Man* 54: You're out of your box, girl. **1967** P. Welles *Babyhip* 48: He had blown his wig, was totally out of his box. **1971** N.Y.U. professor: You're out of your box.

box *v.* **1.** [fr. BOX, *n.,* 2] *Hosp.* to die.

1972 *Nat. Lampoon* (July) 76: *Box* To die. **1974** *N.Y. Times Bk. Review* (Aug. 4) 5: Even death is evaded in the private slang of the interns and residents: "gorks" just "box." **1978** Shem *House of God* 153: Yeah, and then she boxed. **1981** in Safire *Good Word* 154: She boxed just after...rounds.

2. *Pris.* to imprison.

1979 Homer *Jargon* 76.

box-beater *n.* a piano player.

1915 Howard *God's Man* 190: She fell for a honkatonk box-beater at Billy's. **1940** Ottley & Weatherby *Negro in N.Y.* 249: A piano at which a "box-beater" extracted weird...harmonies.

boxcars *n.pl.* **1.** *Craps.* a throw of twelve on the dice.

1909 T.A. Dorgan, in Zwilling *TAD Lexicon* 19: Coffroth poured out a pair of sixes (box cars). **1918** (quot. at SNAKE EYES). **1923** McKnight *English Words* 46: *Box cars* for two sixes. **1929** Nordhoff & Hall *Falcons* 28: Fever in the south! Big Dick from Boston! String of box cars! Fade you! Let her ride! **1955** Graziano & Barber *Somebody Up There* 47: The fat kid throws boxcars. **1961** in Himes *Black on Black* 104: Boxcars! Craps! Twelve! The loser! **1968** R. Adams *West. Words* (ed. 2): *Boxcars.* In dice, the roll of twelve. **1982** in *Nat. Lampoon* (Feb. 1983) 35: You're a free man once you throw a million dice in the air and they all come up boxcars.

2. big feet or shoes.

1950, **1965–70** in *DARE.*

box city *adj.* [BOX, *n.,* 2 + CITY] dead.—sometimes as n., constr. with *in.*

1981 *Sha-Na-Na* (CBS-TV): I hate to say this, but you've passed away. You're box city. **1989** *ALF* (NBC-TV): You could have developed pneumonia—ended up in box city.

boxed *adj.* **1.** Esp. *So.* drunk; *(also)* drugged, high.—also constr. with *out.*

1947 T. Williams *Streetcar* 84: Are you boxed out of your mind? **1958**, **1959** in R.S. Gold *Jazz Talk* 30. **1967** Rosevear *Pot* 158: *Boxed*: High or intoxicated. **1968** in *DARE: Thoroughly drunk*...Boxed out. **1969** Lingeman *Drugs* 28: *Boxed.* High or intoxicated on a drug. **1970** Southern *Blue Movie* 173: I was just too boxed to notice. *Ibid.* 196: She's *boxed,* for Chrissake....Wonder what she's *on?* **1975** Stanley *WWIII* 163: Some of the boys got boxed out on 3.2 beer.

2. [fr. BOX, *n.,* 2] dead.

1966 Braly *Cold Out There* 156: Either way you end up boxed and tagged. **1972** *Nat. Lampoon* (July) 76: This one was boxed when I found him this morning.

box fighter *n.* *Boxing.* a boxer.

1926 Dunning & Abbott *Broadway* 222: I cleaned spittoons in my time, fella, and I'm proud of it—that's when Porky tried to make a box fighter of me. **1960** Glemser *Fly Girls* 141: He is a box fighter.

boxhead *n.* a Scandinavian.—used contemptuously. Cf. SQUARE-HEAD.

1943 J. Mitchell *McSorley's* 133: You remember the night you fought Boxhead Tommy Hansen at the Pelican A.C.? **1984** Elting, Cragg & Deal *Soldier Talk* 352: *Boxhead* (1920–30; Navy)...A Swede or Norwegian.

box-headed *adj.* thickheaded.

1918 in Truman *Ltrs. Home* 53: They had a box-headed censor over there and I am morally certain he destroyed that [letter].

box lunch *n.* cunnilingus; *(rarely)* fellatio. *Joc.*

1965 Trimble *Sex Words* 29: *Box Lunch* or *Box Lunch at the Y*...1. Cunnilingus. 2. Fellatio. **1970** Southern *Blue Movie* 31: Anyone for *box lunch?* **1971** *Coming Dear!* 26: Confucious say: Workman usually pick hair from teeth after box lunch. **1972** R. Wilson *Playboy's Forbidden Words* 48: *He goes down for a box lunch* means he performs cunnilingus. **1976** Selby *Demon* 45: The next time he wanted a box lunch, hahahaha.

box man *n.* **1.** see BOX, *n.,* 5.

2. *Baseball.* a pitcher.

1908 in Fleming *Unforgettable Season* 45: Soon [he] had the rival box-men guessing.

box office *n.* *Entertainment Industry.* that which is or is likely to be extremely profitable and popular with audiences. Now *colloq.*

1932 Murfin & Markson *What Price Hollywood?* (film): I'm box office! I got "box office" stickin' out all over me! **1935** in *OEDS:* Exactly the touch the treatment needed to make it box-office. **1945** *House on 92d St.* (film): "That...would take a remarkable memory." "Sure, but it ain't box office." **1948** Robinson & Smith *J. Robinson* 75: He was "box office" in Montreal and everyone knew it. **1968** Vidal *Breckinridge* 22: Well I was better box office. **1984** Univ. Tenn. instructor, age 31: It's a good idea but it's just not box office.

box of glue *n.* [rhyming slang] a Jewish person.—usu. considered offensive.

1927–28 Tasker *Grimhaven* 180: We took it on the heel and toe down to the old box of glue on the corner, and got a fin for the lay-out. **1935** Pollock *Und. Speaks: Box of glue,* a Jew.

box rustler *n.* *West.* (see 1941 quot.).

1939 Abbott & Smith *Pointed Them N.* 95 [ref. to 1880's]: In that kind of theaters they used to have curtained boxes running all around inside, and box rustlers was what they called the girls that worked them. **1941** in *DARE* [ref. to 1870's]: The women did their song and dance on the stage and then, in costumes that...were considered the extreme of indecency, mingled with the customers in the boxes, encouraging the sale of liquors. The women became known as box-rustlers and box-rustling theaters sprang up all over the west.

box score *n.* *Mil.* the number of dead, wounded, missing, etc.

1951 Sheldon *Troubling Star* 259: Count the Chinks you get. They'll want the box score. **1962** Gurney *War in Air* 165: Box Score: Losses U.S. B-17's 43, U.S. P-51's 14, [etc.].

box slugger *n.* [fr. BOX, *n.,* 5] *Und.* a safecracker.

1970 Rudensky & Riley *Gonif* 49: Two major outfits on the outside were in dire need of a box slugger and would collaborate to break me out.

boy *n.* **1.a.** *pl.* criminals, rowdies, thugs, etc.; (*esp.* in 19th C.) corrupt politicians or their hangers-on.—constr. with *the*.

*ca***1815** *The Night Before Larry Was Stretched* (Dublin broadside ballad): De night before Larry was stretched,/De boys dey all paid him a visit. **1834** *Knickerbocker Mag.* III 34: The landlord after telling me not to mind the *boys*, went about his business. **1847–49** Bonney *Banditti* 91: I know all the boys south and west, as well as those about the lead mines. I can give you four hundred names if you want them. **1876** J. Miller *First Fam'lies* 7: The "boys" didn't want a man above them who knew too much. **1878** Bardeen *Hume* 245: A good-natured fellow, with fair education, a good deal of energy, and tact enough to keep on the right side of "the boys." **1884** in *Mag. Amer. Hist.* (Jan. 1885) 98: *Boys.*—This word is often used nowadays to designate the political hangers-on of a candidate or party. **1885** *Uncle Daniel's Story* 109: You could go to Congress after you had been [in Chicago] a week, if you only knew how to handle the "boys." **1892** L. Moore *Own Story* 389: The Warden and his boys got "rattled." **1927** C.J. Daley *Snarl of Beast* 13: It may be one of the boys…[stalking] along…[intending to commit a] murder. **1933** G. Fowler *Timber Line* 385: Delaney knew all the sinister "boys." **1981** Graziano & Corsel *Somebody Down Here* 103: The guys running the casino were "The Boys."

b. the police.—constr. with *the*.

1867 (quot. at SOAP, *n.*).

2. a hump on a man's back.—used derisively.

****1873** Hotten *Slang Dict.* (ed. 4): Boy, a hump on a man's back. In low circles it is usual to speak of a humpbacked man as two persons—him and his *boy*. **1933** Hammett *Thin Man* 303: "Hey, garsong—you with the boy on your back!" The somewhat hunchbacked waiter…pushed through people [etc.].

3. a coin or banknote.

****1780** in Partridge *Dict. Und.* 68: When the money was produced, the next day, she said *there was no more of the boys but two shillings.* **1899** Cullen *Tales* 82: The lowest I've got here is one of the five-hundred dollar boys. **1902** Cullen *More Tales* 108: He peeled me off seven of the one-hundred boys. **1961** Gover *$100 Misunderstanding* 18: No bread? No bones, no berries, no boys? *Ibid.* 21: I might jes's well git me three lil boys fer myself.

4. *Narc.* heroin. Cf. GIRL.

*ca***1953** Hughes *Lodge* 108: I'd been hooked for some time and knew practically all there is to know about boy. **1960** C.L. Cooper *Scene* 58: Boy is the junkie's term for heroin. **1974** Goines *Eldorado* 69: Dig, my man, how about dropping off two spoons of boy, and a hundred dollar bag of girl? **1986** *Miami Vice* (NBC-TV): Some of that heavy-duty boy that Luther had. **1989** R. Miller *Profane Men* 115: I got yellow jackets,…girl, boy, [etc.].

boy *interj.* "wow!" "gosh!" "man!" etc.

1894 in Ade *Chicago Stories* 24: S-s-t! Boy! Same as the last time. **1900** *Nation* (Sept. 6) 194: These biskits are light as a feather, but, boy, they'd be heavier 'n lead/If I thought that my hosses was shiv'rin'. **1917** in *OEDS*. **1976** in Dundes *Interp. Folklore* 161: Among the other evidence of male chauvinism in American folk speech, one finds exclamations such as "Oh boy!" "Oh brother!" or "Man!" with no analogues of "Oh girl!" "Oh sister!" or "Woman!"

boychik *n.* [E *boy* + E Yid. dim. suff. *-tshik*] a boy; fellow.—usu. used affectionately.

1965 in *BDNE3*. **1972** *Time*, in *BDNE3*: The [Woody] Allen persona—the urban boychik as social misfit—is, of course, an act. **1982** P. Michaels *Grail* 147: He's not through yet, boychik. **1991** Marcinko & Weisman *Rogue Warrior* 207: Listen, boychik.

boyfriend *n.* a male friend of a man.—used disparagingly.

1930 in W.F. Nolan *Black Mask Boys* 164: That's why your boyfriends tried to get you. You were holding out on them. **1935** R. Graves *Speed Limited* (film): Here's your boyfriend, Smitty.

boy-girl *n.* **1.** Esp. *Pris.* a male homosexual who plays a feminine role; GIRL-BOY.

1952 Viereck *Men into Beasts* 133: Jack managed to spend whole nights in the cell of his boy-girl. **1974** R. Carter *16th Round* 76: Each of my associates mounted the boy-girl's back.

2. (see quot.).

1981 *Time* (July 6) 59: A few…mix their C with heroin in a process called "speedballing" or "boy-girl."

boy in the boat *n.* the clitoris. Cf. MAN IN THE BOAT.

1916 Cary *Venery* I 22: *Boy in the Boat*—The clitoris. *ca***1930** in Tamony *Americanisms* (No. 31) 14: He loved to dive and also to fish…/Face is all wrinkled and his breath smells like smoke—/Talking about

that boy in the boat. ****1961** Partridge *DSUE* (ed. 5) 1012: *Boy in the boat.* Clitoris: low; late C. 19–20. **1968** Oliver *Blues Tradition* 203: In September 1936, Georgia White recorded *The Boy in the Boat* with the subtitle *BD's Dream*…an abbreviation of "Bull-Dyker's Dream." **1984** Univ. Tenn. instructor, age 36: The *boy in the boat* is the clitoris. *a***1973–87** F.M. Davis *Livin' the Blues* 36 [ref. to *ca*1920]: At an early age we talked about a "purr-tongue" or a "boy-in-the-boat."

boyo *n.* [*boy* + *-o*, perh. sugg. by BUCKO] *Irish-Amer.* boy; fellow.

****1870** G.M. Hopkins, in *OEDS*. **1932** Hecht & Fowler *Great Magoo* 20: A very jaunty boyo. **1951** in *DAS*: And we can't afford to wait much longer, me boyo. **1955** L. Shapiro *Sixth of June* 114: It's the boyo in command I'm thinking of. **1974** E. Thompson *Tattoo* 286: A boy with boyo's [*sic*], he was eager in their interests and skilful in their sport. **1982** P. Michaels *Grail* 147: Relax, boyo. **1994** *New York* (Jan. 17) 54: He's the sort of boyo who snickers when his father tells him that "honest money goes further."

boy-san *n.* [*boy* + *-san*, Japn honorific] *Mil. in Far East.* boy; young man.

1971 Sloan *War Games* 49: Boysan, you will wear your headgear at all times when out of doors. **1980** DiFusco et al. *Tracers* 10 [ref. to Vietnam War]: Girlsan. Boysan. Mamasan. Papasan. Babysan. **1984** Riggan *Free Fire* 316 [ref. to Vietnam War]: Hey, boysan.

boys and girls *n.pl.* folks; gentlemen.—used in direct address. *Joc.*

1920–21 Witwer *Leather Pushers* 253: Yes, boys and girls, Nada was a pulse-quickener of the first water. **1930** Graham & Graham *Queer People* 18: "Boys and girls," Vance called, waving his arms like a prize-fight announcer, "want you to meet my old friend, Mr. White, from the *Examiner*." **1941** Huston *Maltese Falcon* (film): Well, boys and girls, we put it over nicely. **1942** Freeman & Gilbert *Larceny, Inc.* (film): Nine hundred fifty dollars, boys and girls, and that ain't steamheat [said to three men]. **1942** Chandler *High Window* 365: Was sapped with something hard before being shot. Likely with a gun butt. All that mean anything to you boys and girls?

boys' town *n.* [fr. *Boys' Town*, the name of an orphanage for boys in Nebraska] *Navy.* the junior officers' quarters on shipboard.

1979–88 Noel & Bush *Naval Terms* (ed. 5) 43: *Boys' town* Slang: junior officer's living space. **1983–86** G.C. Wilson *Supercarrier* 27: Officers lived in rooms…Junior Officers lived in Boys Town—rooms crammed with up to eight people.

bozack *n.* [orig. unkn.] *Black E.* the penis.

1987 "EPMD" in B. Adler *Rap!* 67: I like to let my rhymes flow.…/ Grab my bozack. **1990–91** *Street Talk!* 1: Bozack male genitals, penis "Get off my bozak [*sic*]!" "Stop bothering me!"

bozo *n.* [perh. < Sp *bozal* 'simple, stupid'; perh. < It *bozzo* 'cuckold; bastard'; perh. elab. of BO¹ in "carny lingo" or "carnese"—for which see *DAS* 608; the term is discussed by G. Cohen in *Comments on Etymology*, Nov. 1992 pp. 9ff.] a clumsy, clownish, or foolish fellow; oaf; a rude or annoying person.

1916 in Hall & Niles *One Man's War* 159: That you, Bertie, you old bozo! **1918** in Rendinell *One Man's War* 123: One bozo says, "Joe, the last guy who cut my hair got bumped off." **1919** Duffy *G.P.F. Bk.* 127: That's right bozo, come up here and crab de whole works. **1921** *Variety* (July 8) 5: He had bet half a grand that Bozo would stay with Tomato. **1924** H.L. Wilson *Professor* 61: Boss, this bozo, he's pretty fast company. **1929** in *AS* (Feb. 1930) 238: *Bozo.*—a large crude individual. "Is that bozo from your school?" **1931** Perelman & Johnstone *Monkey Business* (film): Say, I can help you bozos? **1947** Motley *Knock* 179: Read it and weep, bozo—I'm the law. **1949** Inge *Little Sheba* 255: A big brawny bozo like Turk, he probably forces her to kiss him. **1966** Brunner *Face of Night* 23: Don't talk like that, don't be a bozo. **1972** *Nat. Lampoon* (Nov.) 9: You weren't counting the stops, were you, you daydreaming bozos! **1978** Pilcer *Teen Angel* 11: You wouldn't believe some of the bozos in my class. **1982** *Chicago Sun-Times* (Nov. 22) 10: Everybody knows a bozo—the Porsche owner who hogs two spaces in a crowded parking lot;…the grocery shopper with too many items in the express lane. **1992** Pres. G.H.W. Bush, campaign appearance in Mich. (Oct. 30): My dog Millie knows more about foreign affairs than those two bozos!

bozo *adj.* crazy.

1983 Eilert *Self & Country* 164: If someone tells me how lucky I am to be alive once more I'll go bozo. **1989** P.H.C. Mason *Recovery* 180: I was full-goose-bozo…yelling, screaming, totally incoherent, foaming at the mouth.

BP *n.* BABY PRO.
   1971 *Go Ask Alice* 160: In fact at twelve she was already a BP*….*Baby prostitute. *Ibid.* 161: She began living as a high class BP.

B.R. *n.* [initialism of b*ankroll*] a bankroll; (*hence*) money.
   1915 T.A. Dorgan, in Zwilling *TAD Lexicon* 19: Ain't cha—take the rubber off the old b.r. and buy? **1928** *N.Y. Times* (Mar. 11) VIII 6: *B.R.*—Bank roll. Big money; the financing of pictures. **1931** G. Milburn, in *Amer. Mercury* (Nov.) 351: Circus Words…*B.R. n.* A roll of currency; a bank roll. **1942** Davis & Wolsey *Call House Madam* 41: If…she didn't have the b.r., Sherman advanced the money for her wardrobe. **1951** Mannix *Sword-Swallower* 136: That's where I really make my b.r. **1970** Landy *Underground Dict.* 39: *B.R.*…money, from the first two letters of the word bread, which means money.

bra *n. Parachuting.* (see quot.).
   1982 Goff, Sanders & Smith *Bros.* 44 [ref. to 1968]: A bra…was where the strings were mistied. They would cut right through the center of the chute and cause it to double fold so the canopy wouldn't support you.

brace *n.* **1.** *Gamb.* BRACE GAME; swindle.
   1879 (quot. at SKIN). **1890** Quinn *Fools of Fortune* 365: I was in a "brace" at another man's game.
   2. a bracing drink; bracer.
   1899–1900 Cullen *Tales* 197: I took a brace and went back and opened up the merry-go-round again.

brace *adj.* [sugg. by BRACE GAME] *Gamb.* dishonest; crooked; rigged.
   1890 Quinn *Fools of Fortune* 188: Public gaming resorts are ordinarily classified under two general headings—"square" and "brace."…In a "brace" house…"luck" is dependent solely upon the will of the dealer.…There exists a popular misapprehension as to the relative proportion of "square" and "brace" resorts.…all the fraudulent contrivances so dear to the heart of the "brace" dealer. **1904** [Limerick] *Villagers* 75: They had to run a brace game of hearts and deal from the bottom. **1908** in *OEDS: Brace box* [used in faro]. **1911** in C.M. Russell *Paper Talk* 85: Here's to the crooked gambler/Who dealt from a box that was brace.

brace *adv.* with a rigged deck; with manipulated cards; dishonestly.
   1942 Sonnichsen *Billy King* 60 [ref. to a1900]: They dealt…with crooked boxes or with cards manipulated so that the dealer was sure to win. This was known as "dealing brace" or "the real thing."

brace *v.* **1.** *Gamb.* **a.** to cheat in a BRACE GAME.
   1878 Pinkerton *Criminal Reminiscences* 198: George Deval was…"braced" and beaten out of his own…funds.
   b. to manipulate (a gambling game) fraudulently; to rig.
   1931 in *DA*: Although not easily done, faro is sometimes "braced." Tiny holes are punched in the cards.
   2. to accost; to ask (someone for or about something); to solicit (someone) for immoral purposes.
   1889 Farmer *Americanisms: Brace, To* (Cant). to get credit by swagger. **1891** in G. Shirley *W. of Hell's Fringe* 119: I came near…shooting me a newspaperman. By God, the next one that braces me *will* be shot! **1901** Irwin *Sonnets* (unp.): Why am I minus when it's up to me/To brace my Paris Pansy for a glide? **1901** "J. Flynt" *World of Graft* 63: Four or five tramp friends…said that they were glad to see me and immediately "braced" me for a loan. **1904** *Life in Sing Sing* 246: *Brace.* To ask. *a*1904–11 Phillips *Susan Lenox* II 157: We can go right up and brace men with the cops looking on. **1926** Tully *Jarnegan* 66: I'm gonna brace the first guy that passes.…I don't give a good God-damn if it's a policeman—there ain't no law when you're hungry. **1934** W. Smith *B. Cotter* 121: I always said…that no guy would brace a dame in the street if the dame don't give him some encouragement. **1945** Fay *Be Poor* 152: I had a fellow "brace" me on the Avenue the other day for some money. **1952** *Time* (Mar. 3) 22: Two patrolmen had spotted Willie. When braced, Willie had naturally denied his identity. **1958** S.H. Adams *Tenderloin* 106: They look kinda snooty. I'd never have the nerve to brace 'em. **1959** *Alfred Hitchcock Presents* (CBS-TV): I'm gonna walk down and brace him. **1969** L. Sanders *Anderson Tapes* 51: He…braces the doorman, and shows his ID. **1977** Monaghan *Schoolboy, Cowboy* 42 [ref. to 1908]: They're three ways to brace a Jane—an' two of 'em is wrong.…Let 'em know you're as smart as they be.

brace and bits *n.pl.* [rhyming slang for *tits*] a woman's breasts.

1928 Sharpe *Chicago May* 287: *Brace and bits*—breasts. **1935** Pollock *Und. Speaks: Brace and bits*, a woman's breast [*sic*].

brace game *n. Gamb.* a fraudulent game, esp. of faro; (*hence*) a swindle; SKIN GAME.
   1875 in *DAE*: The brace game flourishes for no other purpose than to cheat the gambling fraternity. **1880** in M. Lewis *Mining Frontier* 129: The book don't state what he went broke on, but I reckon he got steered up agin some brace game. **1882** Peck *Peck's Sunshine* 38: Some deacon is playing a brace game on him on the hereafter. **1897** A.H. Lewis *Wolfville* 15: I now announces that this yere game is a skin an' a brace. Tharfore I returns for my money; an' to be frank, I returns a-shootin'. **1903** Clapin *Americanisms: Brace game* A swindling operation. **1906** Buffum *Bear City* 25: When not a proprietor where brace games were dealt, the associate of desperate ruffians. **1938** Asbury *Sucker's Progress* 317: As a matter of fact, there were hundreds of brace games throughout the town. **1978** Time-Life *Gamblers* 89: There were hundreds of brace games throughout the town.

bracelets *n.pl. Pris. & Police.* iron arm-fetters; handcuffs.
   1661 (cited in *F & H* I 315). **1671 in *F & H* I 315: Fetters confined my legs from stragling, and bracelets were clapt upon my arms. **1848 [Judson] *Mysteries* 262: Not if ye call carryin' the bracelets workin' in iron, Bill! **1866** "E. Kirke" *Guerillas* 43: Bracelets! bracelets here for this young hyena! **1870** Duval *Big-Foot* 236: Our hand-cuffs or "bracelets," as we termed them. **1872** Burnham *Secret Service* iv: *Bracelets*, a figurative expression for iron hand cuffs. *Ibid.* 204: The officer …clapped the "bracelets" upon his wrists. **1883** Hay *Bread-Winners* 265: Lend me a hand with these bracelets. **1891** Clurman *Nick Carter* 61: Take off these bracelets. **1891** Powell *Amer. Siberia* 253: I'll trouble you to slip on these bracelets. **1895** Townsend *Chimmie Fadden* 144: De Sergeant started t' put de bracelets on de mug. **1900** Greenough & Kittredge *Words & Ways* 69: Handcuffs are *bracelets*. **1930** Biggers *Chan Carries On* 183: I thought for a minute it was going to end in a pair of bracelets for some bimbo. **1944** C.B. Davis *Leo McGuire* 168: It's against regulations to take off them bracelets. **1952** Chase *McThing* 124: Shut up and hold out your wrists for the bracelets. **1954** Bissell *High Water* 123: I was hauled away with the bracelets on by a dick in a derby hat. **1967** J. Colebrook *Cross of Lassitude* 298: Gee, thank the Lord, I never had those bracelets on yet. **1977** Butler & Shryack *Gauntlet* 35: But if you mess around, I'll put the bracelets on.

bracket-faced *adj.* (see 1785 quot.).
   1698–99 "B.E." *Dict. Canting Crew: Bracket-faced*, Ugly, Homely, Ill-favor'd. **1785 Grose *Vulgar Tongue: Bracket faced*, ugly, hard featured. **1821 Waln *Hermit in Phila.* 27: A hanger-on to bracket-faced, carrotty-pated, gravy-eyed ape-leaders!

brad *n.* a coin; (*hence*) (*pl.*) cash; money.
   1810 in Holloway & Black *Broadsides* II 251: His friends, all Yankees, they did meet,/To stump the brads for the look'd for feat. **1812 Vaux *Memoirs: Brads*, halfpence; also money in general. **1821 Moncrieff *Tom & Jerry* I iv: Tip the brads—and down with the dust. **1839 *Spirit of Times* (Nov. 16) 439: The friends of the Yankee colt now began to offer their "brads" 2 to 1 that Independence would win the money. **1840** *New Yorker* (Mar. 21) 7: O the coach—went to see the old un—raise the wind—get some brads—flare up, have a lark, eh? **1856** "H. Hazel" *Jack Waid* 10: Vithout [*sic*] a brad in my pocket. **1872** Burnham *Secret Service* iv: *Brads*,—money—dollars and cents—"dust," "chink," etc. *Ibid.* 86: Bill saw his chance, he had the "brads" and he "went in." **1884** *Life* (Oct. 16) 215: I ain't got de "brads" now, but I—I'll pay you Monday mornin' shuah.

brag *adj. So.* worthy of bragging about; (*hence*) best.
   1836 in *OEDS*. **1838** in *DA*: The Moselle was a new *brag* boat and had recently made several exceedingly quick trips. **1843** Field *Pokerville* 174: Out for a "brag trip" with a rival boat behind. **1847** in Peskin *Vols.* 164: Lt. Hagner made some brag shots. **1865** J.K. Hosmer *Bayonet* 263: He…said he was "his massa's brag man." **1904** Hough *Law of Land* 114: He's got that brag dog of his along.

brag sheet *n.* a list of accomplishments.
   1972 *Nat. Lampoon* (Aug.) 60: Let's face it, you could be congressman from the Black Lagoon and you'd still be better off if old John Q. is eyeballing your mug and not your brag sheet.

braid *n.* [fr. GOLD BRAID] Esp. *Navy.* high-ranking officers.— occ. in sing.
   1945 in *Calif. Folklore* (1946) 386: High-ranking [naval] officers are the braid, brass, big brass, or brass hats. **1959** Morrill *Dark Sea* 179 [ref. to WWII]: Meantime, I'll see if I can ram a hot poker up some of the braids. **1959** Mahin & Rackin *Horse Soldiers* (film): The big braid's been

sittin' under that tree all morning.

brain *n.* **1.** *pl.* a person who acts as a planner or guiding intelligence for a group, gang, organization, etc.; (*Mil.*) an intelligence officer; (*R.R.*) a conductor.

1865 in C.W. Wills *Army Life* 380: "Old Brains" (Halleck) issued the proclamation. **1880** Pinkerton *Prof. Thieves & Detective* 583: Sheridan...took a step higher in the profession, becoming the "brains" and leader of "bank-sneaks." **1906–07** Ade *Slim Princess* 79: I found out who was the real brains of that outfit up at the palace. **1912** Field *Watch Yourself Go By* 395: This fellow...was the brains of the gang. **1918** *Scribner's* (May) 559: Here, Brains [intelligence officer], something for you. **1922** *Leatherneck* (Apr. 22) 5: *Company Brains:* The Company clerk. So called because he is the general source of all information, correct and otherwise. **1923** McKnight *English Wds.* 44: To the vocabulary of railroad men belong such words as...*gold buttons* or *brains* for "conductor." **1923** Wilce *Football* 84: The quarter-back should be the "brains" of the team. **1924** in *Flynn's Mag.* (Jan. 3, 1925) 693: *Brains*, the one who works out plans for a robbery. **1927** in Hammett *Knockover* 322: He was the brains behind Bluepoint Vance's bond tricks. **1928** McCartney *Additions* 281 [ref. to WWI]: *Brains*, the intelligence officer. **1929–30** Dos Passos *42d Parallel* 137: He was the brains of the firm. **1938** Haines *Tension* 142: Go straight to our designing office and give this to the head brains. His name is Setterquist; he's square and, for a designer, smart. **1940** *Railroad Mag.* (Apr.) 38: *Brains* or *The Brains*—Conductor. **1944** Boatright & Day *Hell to Breakfast* 142: The Engineers are called...the "Brains Department" or just "Brains."

2. an intellectually brilliant person; (*hence*) an obnoxious intelligent person.

*1914 W. Owen, in *OEDS*: This gentleman is....what the French call "a Brain." **1923* E. Wallace, in *OEDS*: I felt like a fourth form boy listening to a "brain," and found myself being respectful. **1951–52** Frank *Hold Back Night* 39: They were selected for the job because they were, in Army slang, "brains." **1963** *True* (May) 100: Except for specialized units such as Narcotics, Homicide, and Safe and Loft, most of these "brains" (as they are called by uniformed force) work out of the precincts. **1963** D. Tracy *Brass Ring* 266: What do the brains down at Yale say about it? **1966** in *Amer. Jour. Sociol.* LXXII 460: Very negative connotations are associated with the status of a "brain"—a person who devotes all his energies to getting high marks. **1967** Lockwood *Down to Sea* 15: Our number one brain, Harold E. Saunders, always stood at the top of the class. **1972** A.K. Shulman *Ex-Prom Queen* 138: You have to be a Brain to get into those Eastern colleges. **1979** Gutcheon *New Girls* 36: She was thought of at school as a "brain," a mixed blessing in any children's popularity contest. **1984** Univ. Tenn. student: I really don't want to be a brain.

brain *v.* to hit (someone) hard on the head.

1938 H. Miller *Trop. Capricorn* 38: He said he would brain her if she didn't stay off that roof. **1958** J. Jones *Pistol* 44: Don't come near me...or I'll brain you with it. **1958** P. O'Connor *At Le Mans* 49: If some eager beaver climbs the snow fence to help you push, brain him with anything that's handy.

brain bag *n. Transport.* a bag, briefcase, etc., that holds maps, manuals, charts, instructions, or the like.

1963 E.M. Miller *Exile* 74: Pete...picked up his topcoat and brainbag, the black kit in which the airline pilot keeps his flight manuals and charts. **1971** Tak *Truck Talk* 17: *Brain bag:* any briefcase, portfolio or attaché case in which a trucker carries trip reports, company papers, bills of lading, state permits, [etc]. **1972** Carpentier *Flight One* 48: He went into the house carrying his brainbag.

brain box *n.* **1.** the head; skull; mind.

*1823 (cited in Partridge *DSUE* (ed. 8) 128). **1841** [Mercier] *Man-of-War* 154: I thought I poked *savey* enough into that fellow's brain-box to sing out when he should chance to make a *slippery bend* of it. **1855** Brougham *Chips* 356: He has stowed away all he kin carry in...his brain-box. **1881** [Small] *Farming for Fun* 31: He was completely dumb-founded, and tapped his brain-box several times, as if to assure himself that he was awake. **1885** S.S. Hall *Gold Buttons* 3: I've gut thar forty-graphs all in my brain-box. **1915** Howard *God's Man* 140: Just plain anarchy of the brain-box. **1921** Marquis *Carter* 123: That bar was right over the old man's brain-box. **1960** Hoagland *Circle Home* 157: Hit him in the brainbox! **1961** L.G. Richards *TAC* 64: Weight of the brain bucket resting on the brain box cuts off circulation. **1971* Moorcock *Warlord of Air* 86: I mean, well—the old brain-box and all that—a trifle shaky, um? **1976** in *DARE*: Been goin' around with 'is hat off too long. Froze 'is brain box.

2. a crash helmet.

1954 *N.Y. Times Mag.* (Mar. 7) 20: *Brain box*—helmet.

3. *Naut.* a pilothouse; (*hence*) a shack occupied by a clerk or foreman of a longshoremen's crew.

1952 Bissell *Monongahela* 217: You drop her against the pilings...and while the deckhand is tying off you jump down out of the brain box and knock the face wires loose. **1979** K. Fox, in R. Carson *Waterfront Writers* 13: Clerk's Shack (Pier 9). Sitting in a barren brain box/Built with two-by-fours.

4.a. *Industry.* a box that holds records, specifications, manuals, maps, etc. Cf. BRAIN BAG.

1942 *ATS* 753: *Brain box*, the place in which linemen's specifications are kept.

b. any sort of mechanical or electronic device that functions as a controlling mechanism.

1942 *ATS* 246: *Brain box*, the combination of a safe. **1956** Heflin *USAF Dict.* 90: *Brain box.* A device, esp. an electronic device, used to control a mechanism. *Slang.*

brain bucket *n.* **1.** the skull; the head.

1856 *Ballou's Dollar Mo. Mag.* (Oct.) 324: Grabbing a short capstan bar, he fetched me such a clip on top of my brain-bucket as to drive all my senses clear down to my boots.

2. Orig. *USAF.* a crash helmet.

1955 *AS* XXX 116: *Brain Bucket*; Hard Hat...Plastic crash helmet worn by pilots. **1955** Reifer *New Words* 35: *Brain bucket.* Air Force Slang. A helmet to be worn by crew members in case of an airplane crash. **1959** Scott *Tiger in Sky* 42: Now, my head had to be encased in a plastic thing called a "brain-bucket." This hard hat...actually hid the whole human head. **1961** L.G. Richards *TAC* 64: Weight of the brain bucket resting on the brain box cuts off circulation. **1963** E.M. Miller *Exile* 234: Keep it under your brain-bucket. **1969** *Current Slang* I & II 15: *Brain-bucket*, n. A motorcycle helmet; a crash helmet.—College males, Texas; Air Force Academy cadets. **1980** W.C. Anderson *BAT-21* 4: He had been cramming his cranium into a brain bucket helmet. **1992** K. Thatcher & B. Bannon *Thrasher* 52: There is no such thing as an inexpensive helmet that will sufficiently protect your head....In other words, spend the bucks for a top-quality brain bucket.

brain cage *n. R.R.* a caboose.

1945 Beebe *Highball* 219: The modern stream-lined brain cages of the Lehigh Valley are in reality small mobile apartments with electric iceboxes and sponge rubber mattresses on their berths.

brain capsule *n.* a cigarette. Cf. BRAIN TABLET.

1904 Hughie Cannon *Little Gertie Murphy* (N.Y.: Howley-Dresser Co., 1904) (sheet music): I can't even smoke a brain capsule,/When I'm out wid dis little dame.

brainchild *n.* a very intelligent person.

1969 Rev. J. Jackson, on *Mike Douglas Show* (CBS-TV) (Feb. 11): Let's face it, Lester Maddox is no brainchild.

brain college *n.* an insane asylum. Cf. NUT COLLEGE.

1898 Dunne *Dooley in Peace & War* 194: In this counthry, whin a man begins f'r to see sthrange things, an' hitch up cockroaches, an' think he's Vanderbilt drivin' a four-in-hand, we sind him to what me ol' frind Sleepy Burk calls th' brain college.

brain-dead *adj.* exceedingly stupid; (*also*) mentally fatigued.

1984 Mason & Rheingold *Slanguage*: Brain dead...zoned out. **1987** Weiser & Stone *Wall St.* (film): This guy is totally brain-dead. **1989** P. Munro *U.C.L.A. Slang* 24: *Braindead* stupid, unable to think. **1992** *Larry King Live* (CNN-TV) (July 8): Oh, that's brain-dead politics.

brain fart *n.* a nonsensical idea; (*also*) a sudden lapse in logic or memory.—usu. considered vulgar.

1983 LaBarge & Holt *Sweetwater Gunslinger* 90: Oh, oh. Another brain fart. **1989** P. Munro *U.C.L.A. Slang* 24: *Brainfart!* (exclamation used about a sudden loss of memory or train of thought, or a sudden inability to think logically) **1991** *UTSQ*: I normally remember my social security number but I had a brain fart.

brainiac *n.* [sugg. by *Brainiac*, a villainous superintelligent alien appearing in *Superman* comics since the late 1950's] a know-it-all or very intelligent person.—used derisively.

1986 Sliwa & Greenberg *Attitude* 51: It's time for the brainiacs to stop inventing new excuses for criminal behavior! **1987** M. Groening *School Is Hell* (unp.): The 81 Types of High School Students...Superjock, Prom Queen,...Cheerleader,...Brainiac. **1990** *Teenage Mutant Ninja Turtles* (CBS-TV): I really miss that brainiac. **1990** *Simpsons* (Fox-TV): Why don't you go build a rocket ship, brainiac? **1992** Majors & Billson *Cool Pose* 47: To strive for academic success may result in being labeled a "brainiac."

brainless wonder *n.* a scatterbrained person; dolt.
  1926 Springs *Nocturne* 234: "Take a tip from me," she went on, "and steer Tim away from that brainless wonder." **1945** Hubbard *R.R. Ave.* 334: *Brainless wonder,* a term…applied to any train or engineman or official who does things his fellows consider queer.

brain locker *n. Naut.* the skull; the head. Cf. SHOT LOCKER, SNOT LOCKER.
  1904 *Our Naval Apprentice* (Oct.) 53: Like many of the other veterans of the Home his "brain locker" is filled with recollections of the past.

braino *n.* a very intelligent person.—used derisively.
  1982–84 Safire *Take My Word* 242: A term of opprobrium for intellectuals is *braino.* **1986** R. Walker *AF Wives* 164: They were grinds—what they called "brainos" at the academy.

brain oven *n. Mil.* a combat helmet.—used contemptuously.
  1984 J.R. Reeves *Mekong* 276 [ref. to 1970]: The hard hats were also called "brain ovens."

brain pan *n.* the head; the mind. [The sense 'skull' is archaic S.E.]
  1851 in W. Morgan *Amer. Icon* 133: Wake him up dead, wid a bullet in his brain pan. **1889** Barrère & Leland *Dict. Slang* I 175: *Brain-pan*…(Common), the head. **1907** *Lippincott's Mag.* (Apr.) 549: Your brain-pan is sure sad with a hang-over, Didsey. **1907** *Lippincott's Mag.* (May): Does that filter through your boiler-iron-plated brain-pan? **1977** *N.Y. Post* (July 22) 65: Owens…prefers not to think of himself as a disc jockey. He calls himself a josh dickey. That's the way his brainpan works. **1993** *N.Y. Times* (Feb. 5) B 7 [ref. to boxing]: Men…punch each other in the brain pan.

brain plate *n. R.R.* (see quot.).
  1940 *Railroad Mag.* (Apr.) 38: *Brain Plate*—Trainman's cap or hat badge.

brainstem *n. Stu.* a crazy or eccentric person.
  1984 Hindle *Dragon Fall* 41: Some total brainstem tossed some kinda bomb onto your side of the floor.

brainstorm *n.* a sudden idea.—often used sarcastically. Now S.E.
  1925 in *OEDS:* He had a brainstorm. **1932** *AS* (June) 329: *Brainstorm*—a sudden and usually fortunate thought. **1941** Schulberg *Sammy* 136: Then I had the brainstorm of getting an English star like Howard to play the part. **1946** Mezzrow & Wolfe *Really Blues* 17: Then I got a brainstorm. **1965** *Time* (Mar. 19) 86: They were…builders and draftsmen to turn the Smith brainstorms into blueprints. **1979** Kunstler *Wampanaki Tales* 23: Sure, it was your brainstorm. **1993** *CBS This Morning* (CBS-TV) (June 7): Then, one of the guys working here had a brainstorm.

brain tablet *n.* BRAIN CAPSULE.
  1933 *AS* (Feb.) 31: *Brain tablet.* Cigarette. **1936** R. Adams *Cowboy Lingo* 206: The cigarette itself was referred to as a "brain tablet."

brain trust *n.* a group or staff of planners or advisers; *(Mil.)* general staff or headquarters staff.—also applied jocularly to an individual. [Popularized as S.E. in 1933 as a designation for advisers of Pres. F.D. Roosevelt.]
  1910 (cited by M.M. Mathews, in *AS* XXXII (Feb. 1957) 57 in sense "college faculty"). **1918** *Sat. Eve. Post* (Aug. 3) 7: Of course, you'd be way back, cookin' up fancy dishes for the Brain Trust, while I'd be up front can-openin' for a bunch of roughnecks. **1918** Palmer *Amer. in France* 88: Through the Chief of Staff and through the Commander-in-Chief, this "brain trust," as the line called it, had its policies executed when they were approved. **1920** [Coburn] *26th M.P.'s* 55: is an important member of the outfit, as his suggestions are valued very highly by the "brain trust." **1920** *Howitzer* 178: The "Brain Trust" of the Signal Corps is located at Fort Monmouth, N.J. **1928** McCartney *Additions* 281 [ref. to WWI]: *Brain Trust* (Am.), the General Staff. **1937** Odets *Golden Boy* 254: He writes he's a regular "brain trust." **1940** *AS* (Feb.) 29: "Brain Trust" was originally used by the line of the Army as a sort of sour grapes crack at the first American general staff established by Elihu Root in 1901…that's where the phrase came from…[Signed, General] Hugh S. Johnson. **1942** in Stilwell *Papers* (Dec. 8): Just had such a billet-doux from the Brain Trust. **1958** Frankel *Band of Bros.* 181: You're part of this brain trust. **1959** E. Hunter *Conviction* 153: The brain trust at my sweatshop decided they ought to send me to Syracuse for the weekend. **1972** Jenkins *Semi-Tough* 110: Regardless of…what Big Ed the Brain Trust thinks. **1980** S. Fuller *Big Red* 288: The brain-trust boys in London…had accumulated a mountain of OSS information. **1983** *N.Y. Post* (Aug. 17) 6: Brain Trust…Francis Coppola…has

enlisted the aid of author William Kennedy as a "period consultant"…on the 1930's. **1991** *Newsweek* (Dec. 23) 24: Even after the putsch, he has not created a brain trust for himself.

brain truster *n.* a member of a BRAIN TRUST; BRAIN, 1.
  1933 in *OEDS:* The Roosevelt "brain trusters." **1959** Fuller *Marines* 64: "That's the Board of Directors," Maxwellington said sourly. "The battalion brain-trusters." **1964** McKenna *Sons of Martha* 119: Them braintrusters down in the ice plant. **1980** W.C. Anderson *BAT-21* 121: Maybe some of the brain trusters…[in the Pentagon] can come up with some ideas.

brain wave *n.* a sudden idea.—usu. used sarcastically.
  1890 *Harper's Mag.* (Apr.) 744: Lucilla, with what she was fond of terming a brain wave, comprehended the situation. **1927** Aiken *Blue Voyage* 104: Well…what's this brainwave? **1931** Lubbock *Bully Hayes* 53: Someone at last had a brain-wave. **1955** Reifer *New Words* 35: *Brainwave*…a sudden inspiration. **1958** J. King *Pro Football* 13: The spectators see everything but the brainwave. **1964** Rhodes *Chosen Few* 90: When did you get this brainwave? **1969** Maitland *Only War* 128: Both men chewed it over for a while, and then Pinkermann had a brain-wave.

brakie *n. R.R.* a brakeman.
  1887 M. Roberts *W. Avernus* 237: No, it won't be all right, brakie. *Ibid.* 238: The brakie came down a step and made a kick at him. **1891** *Contemporary Rev.* (Aug.) 255: Railway brakemen [are called] "brakies." **1897** Hamblen *General Manager's Story* 16: You don't see but mighty few brakeys as old as we be. **1899** Cullen *Tales* 41: The brakie came along and prodded me and yelled "Chicago!" **1926** C.M. Russell *Trails* 149: The brakie pilots me to a little joint across the tracks. **1926** "M. Brand" *Iron Trail* 23: The brakie reached a hand for the lantern. **1952** in Fenner *Throttle* 14: But you'll still be a third-rate brakie busting couplings on slow freights and fouling up the main line. **1973** Mathers *Ridin' the Rails* 12: A brakey come back and he said say if I was you people I'd get outa here.

branch *n. Riverboating.* a pilot's license.
  1896 Hamblen *Many Seas* 122: If you are a pilot, where is your "branch"? (The pilot's license.)

brand artist *n. West.* a rustler who alters the brands on horses or cattle. Now *hist.*
  1922 Rollins *Cowboy* 243 [ref. to 1890's]: "Brand artists,"…gentlemen who, with…a piece of hot metal, added marks to those already on a beast and made the final result identical with the "artist's" registered brand.

bran-faced *adj.* freckle-faced.
  1788 Grose *Vulgar Tongue* (ed. 2): *Bran-faced,* freckled. **1821 (quot. at CRIBBAGE-FACED).

brannigan *n.* [fr. the Irish family name *Brannigan*; reason for adoption unkn.] **1.** a state of intoxication; *(also)* a drunken spree.
  1892 Norr *China Town* 31: The boxer was carrying…what in Pell street parlance is termed a "brannigan," a condition produced by two gallons of mixed ale to one quart of whiskey. **1902–03** Ade *People You Know* 210: He had accumulated a very neat Brannigan, and was paying a lot of Attention to a wonderful Piece of Work sitting opposite. **1911–12** Ade *Knocking the Neighbors* 49: The Reveler finds his bright crimson Brannigan slowly dissolving itself into a Bust Head. **1927** *New Republic* (Mar. 9) 72: People going on *sprees, toots, tears, jags, bats, brannigans,* or *benders.* *a*1940 in Fitzgerald *Notebooks* 276: Slang. Branegan (party). **1976** Berry *Kaiser* 312: You'd really tie a package on. Oh but we had a Branigan that night!
  2. a brawl; wrangle; dispute.
  1940 Sturges *McGinty* (film): I could beat him to the punch. Boy, we had some brannigan. **1941** *AS* XVI 70: *Brannigan*…a fight. **1949** Grayson & Andrews *I Married a Communist* (film): These brannigans where nobody wins and everybody loses. **1965** N. Daniels *Moments of Glory* 107: Now if anybody isn't awake after this brannigan, get 'em up.
  1967–70 in *DARE.*
  3. a fiasco.
  1970 Lincke *Jenny* 82: In this brannigan, Dargue with Foulois as his observer…took off from San Geronimo for Chihuahua City.

brary *n. Stu.* a library.
  1968–70 *Current Slang* III & IV 15: *Brary* n. Library. **1981** Eble *Campus Slang* (Oct.) 2: *Brary*—library. **1988** Eble *Campus Slang* (Fall) 2: I'm heading to the brary to study.

brass *n.* **1.** money; cash. [In earliest S.E. use, ref. solely to bronze or copper coins; the denotation broadened in the latter part of the 18th C.]

*1597–98 in *OED*: Shame that the muses should be bought and sold for every peasant's brass. *1794 R. Burns, in *OED*: His auld brass will buy me a new pan. *1796 in *F & H* I (rev.) 357: He expects to finger the *brass*, does he? *1811 Byron, in *OED*: Who ne'er despises books that bring him brass. 1815 Brackenridge *Mod. Chiv.* 625: They themselves would pay the brass. 1836 *Spirit of Times* (July 9) 165: There is a third defaulter who, I think, will "fork out the brass." 1859 Matsell *Vocab.* 14: *Brass*. Money. 1889 in Barrère & Leland *Dict. Slang* I 176: But my *brass* all went to/Old Nick, and the rent too. 1898 Green *Va. Folk.-Speech* 67: *Brass, n.* Money. 1955 Kantor *Andersonville* 119 [ref. to Civil War].

2. effrontery; impudence. [Orig. S.E., increasingly slangy in U.S. throughout 19th C.; now colloq. or S.E.; cf. S.E. *brazen*.]

*1682 J. Dryden, in *OED*: And like the Sweed is very Rich in Brass. *1773 Goldsmith *She Stoops to Conquer* III: To me he appears the most impudent piece of brass that ever spoke with a tongue. 1836 in Strong *Diary* I 28: I'm surprised he could raise brass enough to read it [aloud]. 1841 in M.W. Brown *Dan Rice* 62: You always can tell him by the brass in his face. 1856 *Ballou's Dollar Mo. Mag.* (Mar.) 219: Perseverance and impudence, or rather "brass," to use a very expressive term. 1862 C.F. Browne *Artemus Ward* 117: Thay aint over stockt with branes, but they hav brass enuff. 1928 C. McKay *Banjo* 148: His partner hands them the raw colonial brass. 1948 L. Allen *Reds* 208: He had more brass than a second-hand junk dealer. 1956 Algren *Wild Side* 131: I wouldn't have the common brass to knock on no lady's door and show her one of them unnatural-lookin' things. 1965 Borowik *Lions* 38: I don't know where I got the brass to even think about becoming an actress. 1975 Julien *Cogburn* 48: You have a lot of brass, Marshal Cogburn. 1975 V.B. Miller *Deadly Game* 28: You got real brass, Kojak. 1977 *N.Y. Times Bk. Review* (Dec. 25) 22: Who has the time or brass to insist that charity solicitors show their licenses? 1986 *Stingray* (NBC-TV): You got a lot of brass for a white man.

3.a. [in mod. use sugg. by BRASS HAT] *Mil.* high-ranking officers; commissioned officers.—usu. constr. with sing. v., referred to with pl. pronoun, also with sing. reference. [Early quots. seem to be chance occurrences; general currency began during WWII.]

ca1864 in Allan *Lone Star Ballads* 59: The Brass-Mounted Army…*They* issue Standing Orders to keep us all in line,/For if *we* had a showing the *brass* would fail to shine.…At every big plantation or negro-holder's yard,/Just to save the property, the General puts a guard;/The sentry's then instructed to let no Private pass—/The rich man's house and table are fix'd to suit the "brass." 1899 in *DA*: It was not a big brass general that came;/But a man in khaki kit. *1934 Yeates *Winged Victory* 39 [ref. to 1918]: This must surely put the wind up.…[the] brass.…He had shown those brass-hats plainly…and so ministered to the prejudice against brass that all right-minded people had. 1941 Hargrove *Pvt. Hargrove* 84: Higher *brass*—the higher ranks of officers. 1944–48 A. Lyon *Unknown Station* 40: We…displayed all our equipment for some well-dressed…brass so that he could check the number of tent pins we had. 1950 Calmer *Strange Land* 15: The officers disappear through a door behind the map, leading into the cloistered world of the big brass. 1951 in F. Brown *Honeymoon* 47: The high brass wouldn't believe my theories. 1951 D.P. Wilson *Six Convicts* 10: To Connie I was just some more dumb Brass. 1952 Uris *Battle Cry* 15: The noise you hear in the background is the public address system paging Admiral Parks. They've been paging several top brass during this second period. 1955 Sack *Shimbashi* 47: I spoke mostly to officers, thinking the brass would know more about these matters than the enlisted men. 1962 *Newsweek* (Nov. 12) 23: In Havana, Mikoyan was greeted by top Cuban brass. 1965 Adler *Letters from Viet.* 97: Hell, we've only got a toehold on this part of the country, and the brass is acting as if they already owned it. 1969 Linn & Pearl *Masque* 140: Enlisted men like to gripe that the brass get all the gravy, but the brass know that it's the sergeants who run the Army. 1971 N.Y.C. man, age 73: I was in the Navy from June 1918 to February of the next year, and I can tell you we called the officers "the brass" at that time. I don't think we ever used the term "brass hats" or anything else. 1982 D.J. Williams *Hit Hard* 287: Jesus, the big brass got no heart. 1984 Kagan & Summers *Mute Evidence* 332: So I think the brass maybe covered it up.

b. officials or executives (*rarely*, as in 1983 quot., with sing. reference); administrators, managers, etc.

1945 *Yank* (Dec. 7) 14: My company "brass" insist that all employees wear a coat and tie to the office. 1948 Kingsley *Detective* 338: If this man's hurt, the big brass'll be down here throwin' questions at me.

1952 in Fenner *Throttle* 24: Then, his suit grimy and rumpled, his face sweating and smudged, he went back to join the brass in the lurching cars. 1952 Viereck *Men into Beasts* 47: I know a thing or two about one of the top brass here. 1953 Roman *Vice Squad* (film): I know all about your influence with the political brass in this town. 1958 King *Pro Football* 32: NFL owners…are much closer to their game as a sport than is the custom with top brass. 1964 Fielder *R.R.s of the Black Hills* 86: Conductor—The Brains, the Brass.…(Brass Hat being an official). 1964 *Flintstones* (NBC-TV): We'll be rubbin' elbows with the company brass. 1965 Conot *Rivers* 183: The brass were confused and astonished. 1968 Simoun *Madigan* (film): Suppose somebody sees you? Like some of the top brass for instance? 1971 *Playboy* (June) 211: The CBS money brass is due in town tomorrow. 1975 Hynek & Vallee *Edge of Reality* 189: The top scientific brass said there was nothing to it and the military brass themselves didn't understand it. 1977 Olsen *Fire Five* 11: The brass keep threatening to tear down the station and transfer us. 1983 N.Y.C. store mgr., age ca50: Look busy at 11 o'clock. There's a brass coming—Mr. Kline. Don't be drinking coffee. 1990 C.P. McDonald *Blue Truth* 7: Cool it, the brass!

¶ In phrase:

¶ **double in brass** (orig., in a circus) to play in a brass band besides doing other work; (hence, in general) to play two roles. Now *colloq.* or *S.E.*

1912 Field *Watch Yourself* 348 [ref. to 19th C.]: I do not double in brass or anything else. I'm a minstrel, not a contortionist. 1923 *N.Y. Times* (Sept. 9) VIII 2: *Doubling in Brass*—To play two parts; originally to play in the band and a part in the play. 1936 Ferber & Kaufman *Stage Door* 835: Young lady, willing, talented, not very beautiful, finds herself at liberty. Will double in brass, will polish brass, will *eat* brass before very long. 1949 Chandler *Little Sister* 194: We're just a small town police force. We got to double in brass once in a while. 1982 T.C. Mason *Battleship* 130: In those days, radiomen were expected to "double in brass" as rifle squads.

brass ankle *n.* Esp. *S.C.* a person of mixed white and black ancestry.

1930 *DN* VI 79: Brass ankle…A person who passes for white, but who is suspected of having "a streak down his back." 1940 *AS* (Dec.) 446 [Tenn.]: *Brass Ankle.* Mulatto. "The hotel cook is a brass ankle." 1943 *AS* (Apr.) 152: [In South Carolina] *Brass ankle,* for "mulatto," is very often used by the older generation, though less often by younger speakers. 1947 *So. Folklore* (Sept.) 190: Barty, the "brass ankle,"…says, "If you can't gid a horse, ride a cow." 1967 in *DARE*.

brass-ass *n. Mil. & Pris.* a commissioned officer; an official.—usu. considered vulgar.

1952 Himes *First Stone* 186: I just don't want this thing to get out of hand and get the brass-ass down on me. 1963 Parks *Learning Tree* 78: "What son-of-a-bitch said that?" "Me, you stupid brass-ass!" 1970 E. Thompson *Garden of Sand* 419: Fuckin' brass-asses.

brass-ass or **brass-assed** *adj.* insolent.—usu. considered vulgar.

1974 Millard *Thunderbolt* 6: There can't be any more brass-assed nerve left in the country. That bastard's got a corner on it all. 1987 in *N.O. Review* (Spring 1988) 51: You're going to stand up in my face like a brass-ass monkey and try to belittle me?

brass balls *n.* [BRASS, 2 + BALLS] effrontery; (*also*) tremendous courage.—usu. considered vulgar. Cf. BRASS GUTS.

1968 Baker et al. *CUSS* 88: *Brass Courage. Brass balls* Courage. 1975 Univ. Tenn. student: You need brass balls to eat this stuff. 1972–76 Durden *No Bugles* 68: I mean this guy's got brass balls like the size of cantaloupes. 1976 Conroy *Santini* 222: I want to know which one of you worthless nits had the brass balls to cough when I was talking.

brass buggy *n. Army.* a staff car.

1976 Berry *Kaiser* 210 [ref. to 1918—107th U.S. Inf.]: A group of us were sitting by the roadside in July or August when this staff car drove up. We hated those "brass buggies"—they never meant anything good.

brass button *n.* **1.** a soldier, esp. a commissioned officer. [1866 quot. appears to mean "regular soldiers," but it may actually mean "military discipline."]

ca1863 in Allan *Lone Star Ballads* 116: Swelling round with gold lace plenty,/See the gay "brass button" gentry. [1866 in Hilleary *Webfoot* 166: Part of the volunteer company, "with no brass buttons in it," returned because their horses gave out.] 1871 *Galaxy* (Apr.) 539: You army fellers run me pootty close.…I don't want to fight brass buttons. 1887 in *DA:* Many wealthy civilians were anxious to get into the giddy whirl, but they were barred out by the brass-button brigade. **1936** Levin *Old Bunch* 169: He might have known that brass button would have no sense of humor.

2. a police officer.

1905 *McClure's Mag.* (Sept.) 466: I don't want to see a brass-button on this block until I give the word.

3. *R.R.* a passenger conductor.

1940 *Railroad Mag.* (Apr.) 39: Brass Buttons—Passenger conductor on railroad or streetcar line. **1942** *ATS* 723: Conductor…*brass buttons.*

brass-chaser *n.* (see quot.).

1928 Bodenheim *Georgie May* 122: Women in various stages of disarray…stood behind the bars at the front of their cage and called out to the turnkeys, hoping to ogle specks of favors out of them—brass-chasahs the other women called them.

brass collar *n.* Esp. *R.R. & Pris.* an official.

1916 *Editor* (Mar. 25) 343: Some Railroad Slang…*Brass collars*, high officials. **1931–34** in Clemmer *Pris. Comm.* 187: I must tell you about some "brass-collars" (wardens and their deputies) who have cost the American people many dollars. **1934** *AS* (Feb.) 73: *Brass collar.* Official, corresponding to the army term *brass hat.* **1934** Cunningham *Trigger-nometry* 198: Rewards and notoriety…might keep memory of him green among the Brass Collars at Austin. **1942** *American Mercury* (June) 741: *Brass collars*—higher-up officials. **1945** Hubbard *R.R. Ave.* 179: Strikers…had been too active to please the brass collars.

¶ In phrase:

¶ **big dog** [or **bull** or **man**] **with the brass collar** a person of importance; BIG SHOT. Cf. also BIG DOG.

1859 Bartlett *Amer.* (ed. 2) 31: In some parts of the country the principal man of a place or undertaking is called the "big dog with a brass collar." **1921** Conklin & Root *Circus* 304 [ref. to 1880's]: Some of the canvasmen called [the circus owner] "the man with the brass collar." **1925** *Adventure* (Dec. 20) 29: Maybe you can tell me who's the bull with the brass collar around here.

brass guts *n.pl.* effrontery; (*also*) tremendous courage.—also constr. in sing. Cf. BRASS BALLS.

1942 *ATS* 372: Brave or reckless person…*brass guts.* **1946–51** J. Jones *Here to Eternity* ch. xvii: That takes a lot of guts. Brass guts….But he had to have a brass gut to even ask you a thing like that.

brass hat *n.* **1.** [sugg. by the gilt ornamentation on the caps of officers in the British Army; the term gained U.S. currency during WWI] *Mil.* a senior military or naval officer; a commissioned officer.

*1893 R. Kipling *In the Rukh*: If I only talk to my boys like a Dutch uncle…dey do better. But if my fat-head glerk…say dot Muller der Inspector-General…is much annoyed…dot does no goot….I tell you der big brass-hat pizness does not make der trees grow. ***1916** in C.H. Burton *Letters* 221: I am also rather glad that I won [a commission] rather than having it given me by some "brass hat" I met at dinner. **1917** *Wadsworth Gas Attack* (Dec. 15) 21: *Brass Hat*—A staff officer. **1918** [Grider] *War Birds* 146: We had a bunch of Brass Hats from the War Office down at Hounslow today. **1919** Emmett *Give 'Way* 109: Look out…Big Brass Hat! *Ibid.* 181: A hard-boiled "brass-hat" came upon this lad, swearing, "You damn coward….Let us pass." Without emotion the soldier replied, "Lieutenant, I am no coward." **1919** Kauffman *Victorious* 306: The damn-fool brass hats. **1930** Fredenburgh *Soldiers March* 187: Goddam brass hats. **1937** Parsons *Lafayette Esc.* 61: It got so prevalent that the brass hats began to regard even the legitimate breakdowns with a fishy eye. **1943** Scott *God Is My Co-Pilot* 187: I'd just shot up a transport-load of "brass hats." **1945** Bryan *Carrier* 15: Half the brass hats in the Fifth Fleet came aboard to see it. **1946** S. Wilson *Voyage* 14: If I got on a nice, smooth-running ship I might think that some of the brass hats knew what they were doing. **1947** Carter *Baggy Pants* 10: So we rolled along,…cussing the brass hats that had got us in such a dam' mess. **1948** Lay & Bartlett *12 O'Clock High* 76: Damn generals…brass hats who cancel leaves. **1963** Lester & Gordon *Sgt. Ryker* (film): And when the little guys were gone, the fat-mouthed brass hats took over. **1971** J. Anderson, in *N.Y. Post* (Feb. 16) 38: These brass hats want a hard-fisted crackdown on any enlisted man who opens his yap too wide, wears his hair long or fails to salute with the proper snap.

2. an official or executive.

1937 *Rev. of Reviews* (July) 30: *Brass hat*…Now used to describe an *administrator* or *executive*, especially in business. Synon: big shot; tycoon; the old man; the boss. **1938** Haines *Tension* 239: The reporters and brass hats riding private cars full of speeches and champagne and fancy sandwiches would come later. **1939** *Railroad Mag.* (Dec.) 32: Nat-

urally the Santa Fe "brass hats" frowned on engine failures. **1941** Macaulay & Wald *Manpower* (film): Wait till I get down there and tell those brass hats. **1941** in Fenner *Throttle* 170: Now that a new set of officials rode the swivel chairs, they wanted no intruder on the line who might throw in with the brass hats. **1977** Olsen *Fire Five* 4: Me, I can't imagine a fire station with women. I don't think the brass hats can, either. **1987** C. Newman *Sixth Precinct* 161: With the brass hats downtown.

brasshead *n.* **1.** dolt; blockhead.

1959 Russell *Perm. Playboy* 472: Even the dumbest brass-head you ever knew thinks.

2. *Army.* BRASS HAT, 1.

1980 S. Fuller *Big Red* 288: At least one brass head must have been helped by the local French underground.

brass monkey *n.* (used in various prov. phrases, some vulgar).

1857 in C.A. Abbey *Before the Mast* 108: It would freeze the tail off of a brass monkey. [**1865** Cooke *Wearing Gray* 399: His comparison of distance was, "As far as a blue-winged pigeon could fly in six months;" his measure of cold was, "Cold enough to freeze the brass ears on a tin monkey!"] **1866** Dimsdale *Vigilantes* 128: It was cold enough to freeze the tail of a brass monkey. **1868** Aldrich *Bad Boy* 134: To quote from Charley Marden, it was "cold enough to freeze the tail off a brass monkey." **1870** Duval *Big-Foot* 148: It is hot enough to scald the throat out of a brass monkey. **1872** Burnham *Secret Service:* Talk the leg off a brass monkey. **1879** in *DA:* Would singe the hair on a brass monkey. **1907** *Army & Navy Life* (Nov.) 559: I'se most frozen—stiffer than a brass monkey. **1920** in Sandburg *Letters* 175: He came from a climate that would freeze the nose off a brass monkey. **1926** Nichols & Tully *Twenty Below* 10: What a night! It'd freeze the tail off a brass monkey. **1927** Sandburg *Good Morning* 208: It would freeze the whiskers off a brass monkey. **1935** Wolfe *Time & River* 67: That old pukey stuff! Why, it'd rot the guts of a brass monkey! **1943** Horan & Frank *Boondocks* 88: We must have looked bad enough to scare the pants off a brass monkey. **1959** Cochrell *Barren Beaches* 4: This weather'd freeze the rigs on a brass monkey. **1960** Bluestone *Cully* 16: Man, I'm so hungry I could eat the balls off a brass monkey. **1963** Ross *Dead Are Mine* 80: I do know you've got a two-star general hot enough to melt the balls off a brass monkey. **1965** Bryan *Wilkinson* 377: Jesus, colder than a brass monkey! **1969** Pharr *Numbers* 185: You got more nerve than a brass monkey. **1970** Thompson *Garden of Sand* 424: She and me been in scrapes that would scare the nuts off a brass monkey. ***1979** T. Jones *Wayward Sailor* 6: A cold fit to freeze the balls off a brass monkey. **1980** Garrison *Snakedoctor* 102: That guy could talk the balls off a brass monkey. **1993** *Newsweek* (Jan. 18) 55: A…mud bath "cold enough to freeze the balls off a brass monkey."

brass-mounted *adj.* **1.** wearing brass military insignia; (*hence*) given to strict military discipline.

1863 in Connolly *Army of Cumberland* 147: When I get home I shall appreciate plain bread and butter more than I ever did before I was "brass-mounted." *ca*1864 in Allan *Lone Star Ballads* 58: The Brass-Mounted Army…O how d'ye like the army,/The brass-mounted army,/The high-faluting army,/Where eagle buttons rule? **1866** in Hilleary *Webfoot* 179: Getzler said that he could…wipe out every "brass mounted son of a bitch in the Garrison." **1890** Langford *Vigilante Days* 20: Dry up there, you brass-mounted hirelings, or I'll snatch you bald-headed.

2. (used as an intensive).

1880 Nye *Boomerang* 198: The…world…don't care a brass-mounted continental one way or the other. **1883** "M. Twain" *Life on Miss.* 26: I'm the old original iron-jawed, brass-mounted, copper-bellied corpse-maker from the wilds of Arkansaw!

brassneck *n. Army.* BRASS HAT, 1. [Quots. ref. to WWI.]

1926 *Amer. Legion Mo.* (Aug.) 16: Maybe when the smoke clears away the brass-necks will have you hog-tied in the guardhouse. **1927** *Amer. Legion Mo.* (May) 62: Well, if the brassneck wanted to have a fit that was his business. **1927** *Amer. Legion Mo.* (Dec.) 11: Seventeen tracers have been fired back and forth between my outfit and the army brassnecks.

brass off *v.* [adopted from British armed forces during WWII; cf. BROWNED OFF, CHEESED OFF, PISSED OFF] Esp. *USAF.* to anger or disgruntle.—constr. esp. in p.ppl.

[**1925** Fraser & Gibbons *Soldier & Sailor Wds.* 35 [ref. to WWI]: *Brass Off, To:* To grumble.] ***1941** *Sat. Review* (Oct. 4) 11: *Brassed off.* To be very much fed up with boredom. ***1941** in Wiener *Flyers* 45: *Brassed off.* Fed up. **1944** Liebling *Back to Paris* 223: I have a lot of men with itchy trigger-fingers here and your people are pretty lucky they didn't get brassed off. **1954** Morison *Naval Ops.* IX 351: Brassed off a bunch of

Krauts! **1955** *AS* (May) 120: *Teed Off; Brassed Off; Browned Off; Pissed Off*....Angry; indignant. **1956** Heflin *USAF Dict.* 91: *Brassed off*, a. Of a person: Angered, disgusted, dejected. *Slang.*

brass-pounder *n.* Esp. *R.R.* a telegrapher.
   1916 *Editor* (Mar. 25) 343: Some Railroad Slang...*brass-pounder*—telegrapher. **1918** *Grindstone* (Baldwin-Wallace College) 64: His hobby is telegraphing and for several summers he has served as brass pounder for the Wheeling and Lake Erie R.R. **1929** *AS* (Oct.) 48: *Brass-pounder*—telegrapher. **1931** *Writer's Digest* (May) 41: *Brass Pounder*—A telegraph operator. **1941** in Fenner *Throttle* 169: Ain't that the brass-pounder what caused us this grief? **1941** *AS* (Oct.) 164: *Brass Pounder*. Radio telegrapher. **1962** Morris & Morris *Word & Phr. Origs.* 321 [ref. to 1904]: One "brass pounder" in Peoria played checkers nightly by wire with another.

brass tacks *n.* the basics; fundamental issues; "nuts and bolts." Now *colloq.*
   1895 in F. Remington *Sel. Letters* 277: How little I know...when you get down to brass-tacks. **1949** *Sat. Eve. Post* (Jan. 29) 70: He was ignoring...a good opening, if it was brass tacks he wanted to get down to. **1963** B. Garfield *Apache Canyon* 126: With Inyo I want to get right down to brass tacks.

brass up *v.* to pay up; to pay off. *Rare* in U.S.
   *__1898__ in *OEDS*: Now...p'raps you'll pay the man. Go on—brass up!...Along comes Mister Internashonal, an' brasses up every stiver o' that twenty-eight quid. **1908** Sullivan *Criminal Slang* 4: *Brass up*—Divide the spoils. *__1909__ Ware *Pass. English* 46: Now then, brass up, or we'll shove you through it.

brass wig *n. Black E.* BRASS HAT, 1.
   1946 Boulware *Jive & Slang* 2: Brass Wigs...Army officers.

brat *n.* **1.** a child, esp. a daughter, of a professional military officer.—usu. constr. with *army, navy*, etc. See also ARMY BRAT.
   1963 W.C. Anderson *Penelope* 47: I was brought up as a typical service brat. **1976** Conroy *Santini* 49: I met some Air Force brats in Atlanta. **1978** Kopp *Innocence* 53: It is not unusual for a service brat to have lived in several countries. **1980** Univ. Tenn. student: I was a navy brat. **1982** S.P. Smith *Officer & Gentleman* 37: I'm a service brat, pal. Same as you. **1984** *N.Y. Post* (Aug. 2) 32: My husband and I are "military brats." We both...grew up on [Army] posts. **1990** *N.Y. Times Bk. Review* (Jan. 21) 21: *Brats* [title of book]....As a Navy brat, I thought the chapters...to be overdrawn....An intense curiosity about other military brats.
   2. *Pris.* a catamite.
   1929 (quot. at HOOK). **1932** Berg *Prison Doctor* 75: His brat. **1953** T. Runyon *Life* 99: Carrying sacks of canteen stuff for their boys—also known as...gunsels,...brats, and, mostly, punks.

brat pack *n.* [modeled on RAT PACK; app. coined in the 1985 *New York* magazine article] any loosely affiliated group of young, up-and-coming members of a usu. creative or artistic profession. Hence **brat packer**.
   1985 *New York* (June 10) 42, in *Oxf. Dict. New Words*: The Brat Packers act together whenever possible. **1986** Gilmour *Pretty in Pink* 19: The arrogant leader of the Lakefront brat pack. **1988** in *N.Y. Times Mag.* (Jan. 24) 14: *Brat pack*...applies mainly to young authors who write what is called *hip lit.* **1989** *CampusUSA* (Spring) 17: "Young Guns"...The brat pack western. **1990** *Newsweek* (Nov. 26) 85: Brat-pack novelist Bret Easton Ellis. **1991** *Newsweek* (Apr. 29) 54: Very few star designers have emerged in the last decade....That's why the New York brat pack's clothes are so appealing.

brave *n.* ¶ In phrase: **on a brave** suddenly and temporarily courageous.
   1877 in *Contrib. to Hist. Soc. of Montana* II 270: The Indians got on a "big brave" and said we could clean out the Nez Perces without Howard's help.

bravo *n. Army.* (see quot.).
   1980 Cragg *L. Militaris* 349: Bravos. Infantrymen. From the letter "B"...suffixed to the digits of the MOS code for an infantryman, i.e., 11B.
   ¶ In phrase:
   ¶ **fly Bravo** [the signal flag for the letter B (*Bravo* in mil. communications) is red] *Navy.* to be menstruating.
   1972 R. Wilson *Forbidden Words* 107: A menstruating woman is said to be flying bravo.

brawl *n.* a wild party or celebration.

1927 in *AS* (Feb. 1928) 218: *Brawl*—A rough party, particularly a drunken party. **1930** Graham & Graham *Queer People* 8: Joe Greet, directing a comedy at Culver City, heard of the budding brawl in some mysterious fashion. **1931** Lorimer & Lorimer *Like Streetcars* 56: I just came around, Maudie,...to see if you'd go on this New Year's Eve brawl my family's throwing. **1936** Kingsley *Dead End* 729: What a brawl that's turning into! **1942** "D. Ormsbee" *Sound of American* 31: It was a bigger brawl than I had planned. **1948** J.H. Burns *Lucifer* 300: I'm glad you're dressed sensibly for my brawl. **1951** Sheldon *Troubling of Star* 114: Ordinarily I stay away from brawls like the Wing-Ding last night! **1956** Vidal *Thirsty Evil* 218: After Steven's I went to a real brawl in the Village. **1959** R. Russell *Permanent Playboy* 103: He has a lot of liquor so we always come to his brawls.

Brazzie *n.* a Brazilian.
   1945 Mencken *Amer. Lang. Supp. I* 610: In Brazil many Americans call the natives *Brazzies.*

bread *n.* **1.** Esp. *Black E.* the vulva or vagina.
   1954–60 *DAS*: Bread...The vagina. *Never common.* **1965** Trimble *Sex Words* 30: Bread...The Vagina as an object of Cunnilingus. **1967–69** Foster & Stoddard *Pops* 56 [ref. to N.O., ca1915]: "Gee, I know she's got good bread." It meant she's got good pussy.
   2. [sugg. by DOUGH] Orig. *Und.* money. [The term became universally known during the 1960's.]
   1935 Pollock *Underworld Speaks*: The man is out of bread, he has no money. **1952** Ellson *Golden Spike* 192: "How much bread have you got?" "A dime." **1953** W. Brown *Monkey on My Back* 38: Jerry thought he just needed a fix and was out of bread (money). *ca*1953 Hughes *Fantastic Lodge*: He's got a lot of bread. He stays at the Plaza. **1955** in Yablonsky *Violent Gang* 58: We just needed some bread (money). **1957–58** Lipton *Barbarians* 315: Could you lay some bread on me? **1958** Motley *Epitaph* 119: He showed Juan the bread—a roll of bills carried in his trouser pocket. **1958** in Rosset *Evergreen Reader* 156: We'll take it and break the bread in three. **1959** Zugsmith *Beat Generation* 121: I'll still give you all the bread you need. **1959–60** R. Reisner *Jazz Titans* 151: Bread: money. **1961** J.A. Williams *Night Song* 26: Hey, you cats, lay some bread on me and I'll play your sides. **1961** Kanter & Tugend *Pocketful of Miracles* (film): Look, Queenie, the Dude has gotta make some bread! **1962** Perry *Young Man* 175: You need any bread? I can let you have a couple of bucks if you want. **1964** E. Wilson *Wilson's N.Y.* 26: New York...Dictionary....Bread—Dough. **1975** Thomas *Heavy Number* 6: It had to cost some real bread. **1978** De Christoforo *Grease* 145: I knew he was sliding him some bread, just to cover the evening. **1984** *Miami Vice* (NBC-TV): So here's your film. Let's see some bread. **1988** *Newsweek* (May 16) 27: If you are nice to him, he will put a great deal of bread in your pocket.
   ¶ In phrase:
   ¶ **the greatest thing since sliced bread** the greatest thing ever.
   1966 N.Y.C. high school student: This is the greatest thing since sliced bread. **1987** *Sports Close-Up* (CNN-TV) (June 27): If somebody could break the .400 barrier it would be the greatest thing since sliced bread.

bread bag *n.* the stomach; belly.
   *__1834__ (cited in Partridge *DSUE* (ed. 7) 1028). **1847** Downey *Portsmouth* 156: He was also most awfully subject to the cholic and when he had crammed his bread bag to the utmost tension he would be seized with sudden pains. **1859** Matsell *Vocab.* 14: *Bread-bag.* The stomach.

bread barge *n.* a tub or box for hardtack for the crew's mess on shipboard.
   1840 Dana *Two Yrs. Before Mast* ch. xxxii: The bread barge and beef kid were overhauled. **1852** Hazen *Five Years* 61: Drawing a biscuit and a piece of old meat from the bread barge, he proceeded to dispatch them in quite a summary manner. **1883** Russell *Sailors' Lang.* 21: *Bread-barge.*—A tray for holding ship's biscuit for immediate consumption. **1887** Davis *Sea-Wanderer* 290: A bread-barge [is] a small box, say two feet long by fifteen inches in breadth and depth, with a hole near one end of a side large enough to admit a hand and take out [a biscuit]....When the barge is empty, some one calls out to the youngest of the watch, "There's a southerly wind in the bread barge." **1923** in O'Brien *Best Stories of '23* 11: Give us a bit o' hard tack out o' the bread barge. **1931** Lubbock *Bully Hayes* 76: Pass me the bread-barge.

breadbasket *n.* orig. *Boxing.* the belly; stomach.
   *__1785__ Grose *Vulgar Tongue*: Bread basket, the stomach; a term used by boxers. *I took him a punch in his bread basket*; i.e. I gave him a blow in the stomach. *__1819__ [Moore] *Tom Crib's Mem.* 18: *Home hits* in the *bread-basket, clicks* in the *gob.* **1821** Waln *Hermit in Phila.* 31: He was declared to be a *cow-hearted flincher* who would rather provide for his *bread-basket*

than risk his *noddle* in a *row!* **1834** Caruthers *Kentuckian in N.Y.* I 20: Old Hickory's the boy to *sculp* the bloody creters; he's the boy to walk into their bread-baskets. **1850** *Spirit of Times* (Oct. 26) 522: He would…deposit whatever it might be in his *breadbasket.* **1850** Garrard *Wah-to-Yah* 217: Thinks I—you saint-forsaken, infernal hell-chief, how I'd like to stick my knife in your withered old breadbasket. **1855** Wise *Marines* 61: I whirled quickly round, and planted a blow full into the old skipper's breadbasket. **1859** Holmes *Prof.* 280: He…struck the young man's other fist a severe blow with…his…*epigastrium* [or] *bread-basket.* **1862** C.F. Browne *Artemus Ward* 183: Be a little more keerful how you make my bread basket a depot in the futer. **1867** in Somers *Sports in N.O.* 161: [Turner delivered] a small one in the breadbasket. **1892** in McArdle *Collier's* 12: Corbett…lands left twice on John's breadbasket. **1925** Cobb *Many Laughs* 98: I socked him with my right in the bread-basket and he doubled up like one of these here carpenter's rules. **1968** Cuomo *Thieves* 9: What'samatter? The old breadbasket getting empty? **1971** Wells & Dance *Night People* 93: The waiter would be…digging me, holding his bread-basket (stomach) and frowning, because I was eating curry so early.

breadbox *n.* BREADBASKET.
    1919 *Twelfth Inf.* 115: Many a recruit has hitched his belt and squared his shoulders…only to come out needing another hitch in the region of the bread-box and a chest-developer to hold his shoulders back.

breadhooks *n.pl.* fingers; hands.
    1912 Lowrie *Prison* 141: Let's see y'r breadhooks, kid. **1913** Light *Hobo* 71: My "bread-hooks" were on one of those pails. **1925** *Adventure* (Dec. 20) 9: After you've had your breadhooks on it I wouldn't feed a pig out of it. **1926** Nason *Top Kick* 142: Not while my bread hooks are workin' and there's a place to hang on to. **1966–68** in *DARE.*

bread locker *Naut.* BREADBASKET.
    1869 *Overland Mo.* (Apr.) 354: Many's the time I'd a gone to bed without a shot in my bread-locker but for the old woman.

bread pill *n.* a cannonball.
    1845 J.H. Barnum *Life* 17 [ref. to *ca*1805]: We gave them so many bread pills from our stern guns that it made them sick at the stomach.

bread room *n. Naut.* the stomach; belly.
    *1760–61** T. Smollett, in *F & H* I 322: He ordered the waiter…to…bring along-side a short allowance of brandy or grog, that he might cant a slug into his bread-room.…The waiter…returned with a quartern of brandy, which Crowe, snatching eagerly, started into his bread-room at one cant. **1842** [Mogridge] *Soldiers & Sailors* 25: A sailor came up to us, and said that "Poor Jack" was in shallow water, and that, having nothing in his "bread-room," he would let us have a real India silk handkerchief for little or nothing.

bread-snapper *n.* a young child.
    *1935** (cited in Partridge *DSUE* (ed. 8) 131). **1959** M. Harris *Wake Up* 36: You have got to pay the rent every day and feed the breadsnappers.

bread-snatchers *n.pl.* the hands.
    1966–68 in *DARE.*

bread trap *n.* the mouth.
    1879 Burt *Prof. Smith* 151: I hope you will now be satisfied and close your bread trap for five minutes. **1914** Giles *Rags & Hope* 99 [ref. to Civil War]: Oh, close your bread-trap and give us a rest.

break *n.* **1.** an escape, esp. a forcible escape, as from prison. Now *S.E.*
    1846 in Oehlschlaeger *Reveille* 132: I made a break for home. **1864** in *Civil War Hist.* VIII (1962) 123: The Rebs are trying to pull the wool over our eyes…to keep the Boys from making a break. **1865** Duganne *Camps & Pris.* 346: Six officers were in the party, but this number grew to fifteen before the "break" was made. **1880** Pinkerton *Prof. Thieves & Detectives* 577: Boyle…returned the cheering intelligence that they would be over to Kalamazoo on a certain night, and give them "a break," that is, liberate them. **1884** in Lummis *Letters* 86: Another second…and we'd 'a had a break here for the hills. **1908** Kelley *Oregon Pen.* 99: Many convicts wanted him to lead a break. **1912** Lowrie *Prison* 147: The mess hall guards imagined that some kind of a riot or "break" was in progress in the yard. **1929** "E. Queen" *Roman Hat* ch. v 58: So they got you after all, you sap! I told you not to try to make a break for it! **1930** in Grayson *Stories for Men* 138: The break Tip engineered is classic in the annals of escape. **1937** Johnston *Prison Life* 24: Several big breaks had occurred and many were attempted.

2. a blunder.
    1880 in M. Lewis *Mining Frontier* 128: You all know that I'm just learnin' the game an' of course I may be expected to make wild breaks. **1884** in Miller & Snell *Why West Was Wild* 515: Their first break was

to "drop their wad" on the wrong horses. **1884** Nye *Baled Hay* 200: Possibly science may be wrong. We have known science to make bad little breaks. **1890** Roe *Police* 368: After threatening the officer's life if he made any "breaks," the thief again started off. **1891** Maitland *Amer. Slang Dict.* 47: "A bad break," a mistake. **1892** Norr *China Town* 19: Tut! Tut! me boy…don't make no bad breaks. **1894** *Harper's* (Dec.) 104: I hope I haven't made no break. **1896** Ade *Artie* 85: They'd all stand around and kid me when I made bad breaks. *ca*1900 *Buffalo Bill* 100: I forgot all about it and dined elsewhere. This was a "bad break." **1903** Ade *Society* 68: Mr. Quinsy knew a Druggist who took a Daily Paper, and so, the first thing every Morning, he went to the Drug Store to find out what a Fool Break had been made by Congress. **1914** S. Lewis *Our Mr. Wrenn* 11: I made one little break in my accounts. **1922** Colton & Randolph *Rain* 86: I'm here to watch that Sadie don't make a fool break. **1935** Coburn *Law Rides Range* 6: And they was hopin I'd make a break so they could kill me. **1966–69** in *DARE.*

3.a. a chance turn of events.—in later usage, often pl.
    1865 (quot. at KICK, *v.*). **1880** in Martin *Sam Bass* 143: This is a bad break, boys. I believe there is something wrong. **1890** Langford *Vigilante Days* 307: This is a pretty break, isn't it? **1923** *N.Y. Times* (Oct. 7) II 1: The breaks of the game, plus good pitching, will decide the series. **1924** Hecht & Bodenheim *Cutie* 11: This was a mean break. **1926** Tully *Jarnegan* 65: A lucky break. *Ibid.* 228: A tough break—eh, Jimmy? **1931** Hellinger *Moon* 181: It's the breaks that count in football. **1931** Uhler *Cane Juice* 123: It would be a tough break for him. **1932** Berg *Prison Doctor* 60: But you got to take the breaks the way they come. **1932** Nelson *Prison Days & Nights* 121: From the gangsters' point of view, this was merely "the breaks of the game." **1933** Deleon & Martin *Tillie & Gus* (film): The breaks are against me. **1936** Miller *Battling Bellhop* (film): It's just the breaks and you can't do anything about it. **1981** *Rod Serling's Mag.* (Sept.) 19: There's such a thing as the breaks.

b. a stroke of good luck.
    1912 Mathewson *Pitching* 71: Very few of the fans who saw this first game of the 1911 world's series realize that the "break" in this contest came in the fifth inning. **1922** Tully *Emmett Lawler* 254: Give two guys like Lee and Jackson, the breaks, the army, and guns, and grub, and they'd have kept Napoleon and Hannibal busy. **1926** Dunning & Abbott *Broadway* 219: No…it's just the breaks.… Jack got the breaks and mine ain't here yet. **1927** in E. Wilson *Twenties* 354: To get a break—a good break. **1929** *Sat. Eve. Post* (Oct. 5) 24: A break…[is] just slang.…It means that when things go right for you, that's a break. If they go wrong, it's a bad break. **1930** J.V. Weaver *Poems* 251: The way one guy is born to be a king,/And others never get no breaks. **1934** H. Miller *Tropic of Cancer* 177: He deserved a break—at least once in a lifetime. **1939** Rossen *Dust Be My Destiny* (film): I can't get over it. Me, a nobody, gettin' a break!

4.a. special consideration or treatment.
    1902 Cullen *More Tales* 65: Hadn't the burg of Chicago given me a bum break previously, anyhow? **1932** Nelson *Prison Days & Nights* 27: The warden and the screws fall all over themselves giving them all the good jobs and all the best breaks. **1935** Lindsay *Loves Me Not* 17: You boys get a pretty good break. It's nice here. **1943** in W.C. Fields *By Himself* 198: They had all upped the price from three smackers up to five bucks and at that you're getting a break.

b. fair treatment, simple kindness; relief.
    [**1884** in Miller & Snell *Why West Was Wild* 613: If I had ever a break with you I would take the pistol from you and shove it—.] **1929** Burnett *Iron Man* 251: It's raining cats and dogs out there. Give the guy a break. **1931** J.T. Farrell *McGinty* 99: Aw, Mame, give a guy a break. **1950** Stuart *Objector* 163: Look, give me a break, Dad. **1968** L.J. Davis *Whence All Had Fled* 15: Maybe…they were giving him a break.

¶ In phrase:
¶ **even break** a fair and equal chance or (*obs.*) match; a fifty-fifty chance.
    1896 Ade *Artie* 49: I think it'd be about an even-money break that she's seven times seven. **1904** A.H. Lewis *President* 73: These yere shotguns ain't no even break for them rifles the Yanks are shootin'! **1907** Siler *Pugilism* 28: To avoid dispute and to give each man an even break…count the seconds loudly as they elapse. **1908** *Atlantic* (Aug.) 224: [Baseball fans] desire that skill shall match skill in "an even break." **1911** in *OEDS:* Now he wanted an "even break," where once he would have called all his wits into play to avoid it. **1920** Ade *Hand-Made Fables* 48: She was getting no worse than an Even Break. **1931** Ripley *Believe It or Not! 2d* 1: The pirates are gone, but the spirit still lives.…Just try to get an even break from a Moor in a bargain.

break *v.* **1.** to dash suddenly; (*hence*) to leave.—also (*obs.*) constr. with *away.*

1843 Field *Pokerville* 107: He "broke" for the boat. **1847** Robb *Squatter Life* 36: He must "break for the tall timber." **1896** Ade *Artie* 53: Break away! I'm tryin' to forget all about that. **1973** Andrews & Owens *Black Lang.* 88: *Break*—Leave.

2. (of events) to develop; go.

1905 in Paxton *Sport USA* 24: He knows that things are liable to "break wrong" for him some time and that then he will be the object of criticism. *Ibid.* 26: Things broke bad, didn't they? **1907** in H.C. Fisher *A. Mutt* 7: Showing here how tough things broke for A. Mutt yesterday. **1910** *N.Y. Eve. Jour.* (Apr. 15) 20: Things did not break the Giants' way in other cases. **1912** Mathewson *Pitching* 243: Luck seems to be breaking against them. **1914** *Sat. Eve. Post* (Aug. 15) 8: They say my homer was lucky…but, believe me, it was time things broke for me. They been breakin' for *him* all his life. **1919** Witwer *Alex the Great* 41: Well, how are they breakin', Buck? **1928–30** Fiaschetti *Gotta Be Rough* 90: Things weren't breaking right, and he was broke. **1930** Graham & Graham *Queer People* 115: Everything broke lucky for her. **1934** Faulkner *Pylon* 126: If things break right today, tonight I'll get you a bottle. **1939** Rossen *Dust Be My Destiny* (film): Things looked like they were going to break right for us. **1939–40** O'Hara *Pal Joey* 10: I figured things would begin to break a little better around August. **1941** in W.C. Fields *By Himself* 410: I'm sorry things are not breaking so well for you in New York. **1947** Schulberg *Harder They Fall* 131: We'll have to see how things break. **1958** Gardner *Piece of the Action* 90: Well, things haven't been breaking for me too well, Nina. **1982** M. Mann *Elvis* 67: When things are breaking wrong for you,/ This is the thing that you should do. **1988** Shoemaker & Nagler *Shoemaker* 30: My career was breaking good.

3. *Entertainment Industry.* (of a property) to become suddenly and increasingly popular or successful; to introduce (a property) successfully.

1959 *Life* (Nov. 23) 45: *Breaking*—a record moving up on the charts. **1977** S. Gaines *Discotheque* 119: I can't guarantee I'll break a record. You know, out of every dozen records I take on, I only manage to break one.

¶ In phrases:

¶ **break bad** *Black E.* to become aggressive or angry.

1972 in W. King *Black Anthol.* 142: He ain' do nothin', though, did he….Long as he ain' *break bad* and do nothin', it don't even count. *ca*1974 in J.L. Gwaltney *Drylongso* 20: Those paddies…told [the Czechs] to break bad with the Bear to begin with. *ca*1979 in J.L. Gwaltney *Drylongso* 146: She would break real bad with her daddy and stomp her foot and just get all out of hand. **1992** *N.Y. Times* (Sept. 30) E 7: I don't want to make eye contact with this sucker because he may break bad on me.

¶ **break in two, 1.** to break the bones of (someone) in a fight.

1904 in Paxton *Sport USA* 14: We're going to break you in two, young fellow. **1929** Barr *Let Tomorrow Come* 53: Yeah, you'll bust him. He'll break you in two. **1956** Neider *Hendry Jones* 19: Why you runt. You aiming to get broke in two?

2. (of a horse) to start to buck wildly.

1926 W. James *Smoky* 112: Without warning Smoky "broke in two." **1926** C.M. Russell *Trails* 7: This cayuse…breaks in two and unloads. **1927** Rollins *Jinglebob* 90 [ref. to 1880's]: Woof…stifled an impulse to "come apart," "break in two"…and "hop for mama."

¶ **break starch** *Army.* to separate stuck-together portions of stiffly starched clothing; to put on a fresh and stiffly starched uniform.

1980 Cragg *Lex. Milit.* **1983** K. Miller *Lurp Dog* 33 [ref. to Vietnam War]: Sure, they didn't care too much about shaving and breaking starch, but they were good field troops. **1985** Former SP4, U.S. Army: When you send your clothes to the Quartermaster laundry in the service, they come back so heavily starched they'll stand up by themselves. You literally have to break the trouser legs apart, break open the pockets. Doing that, or putting on a freshly starched uniform, was always called *breaking starch*, at least back in 1971.

break-ass *adv.* at breakneck speed.—usu. considered vulgar.

1966–67 W. Stevens *Gunner* 56: Them mechanics're working breakass down on the line.

break down *v.* **1.** Esp. *Black E.* to explain; (*hence*) to tell.

1965 in Cleaver *Soul on Ice* 37: Man…what they doing out there? Break it down for me, Baby. **1966** in B. Jackson *Swim Like Me* 126: I tell her to break it on down and tell me what she mean. **1974** Piñero *Short Eyes* 74: Break it down, Juan. **1986** *Miami Vice* (NBC-TV): Let's take a ride and I'll break it down for you. **1989** *Tracey Ullman Show* (Fox-TV): You're a big drag. I guess you want me to break that down. **1993** *Source*

(July) 43: I asked her how she came to do the show, and…she began to break it down.

2. *Trucking.* to decelerate (a truck).

1977 *Sci. Mech. CB Gde* 158: Better break 'er down unless you have a surplus of green stamps.

breakfast *n.* ¶ In phrase: **have (someone) for breakfast** *West.* to discover the body of (someone who had been murdered during the night). *Joc.*

1863 in *Contrib. Hist. Soc. of Mont.* I 224: They still have a "man for breakfast" occasionally.*…* A western phrase, meaning some one was killed in a row during the night. **1866** [Browne] *Ward: Travels* 148: A few years since they used to have a dead man for breakfast every morning. **1871** Crofutt *Tourist's Guide* 37: The roughs congregated there, and a day seldom past but what they "had a man for breakfast." **1880** *Harper's* (July) 195: They spoke in cheerful local parlance at Las Vegas of having "had a man for breakfast" (euphemism for a murder during the previous night). **1890** Langford *Vigilante Days* 377: "We've got a woman for breakfast this time, and a Chinawoman at that," said X. Beidler…. (The expression "a man for breakfast," signifies, in mining parlance, that a man has been murdered during the night).

breakfast pipe *n.* the gullet.

1858 in Harris *High Times* 152: Hit started up agin an felt like ontu a terbacker wum a crawlin up my breakfus pipe.

break off *v.* ¶ In phrase: **break it off in** to punish or victimize severely and deliberately.

1893 in Wister *Out West* 158: *Texas Vocabulary….To break it off in a person* to get the better, to outdo, to spring and bind. **1903** [Hobart] *Out for the Coin* 23: Why, for four years the Bookies broke it off in me till I looked like a porcupine in distress. **1906** *DN* III 128: *Break it off in, v. phr.* To rebuke sternly. "Bud won't do it any more; the old man *broke it off in* him." **1947–51** Motley *We Fished* 254: They really put it in you and broke it off. **1953** Taradash *Here to Eternity* (film): How long are you guys gonna keep breaking it off in that kid Prewitt? **1969** H.A. Smith *Buskin'* 61: Let that dirty son of a bidge miss just *one* alimony payment and by God I break it off in him, the no-good cheap bassard! *a*1987 Bunch & Cole *Reckoning for Kings* 24: Shit, Lieutenant. I thought you'd gone and broke it off in me!

break out *v.* **1.** to appear; to make one's appearance. *Joc.*

1861 Wilkie *Iowa First* 45: A swelling under his blanket "broke out" under mine. **1899** Willard *Tramping* 387: The man who has "just broken out" is…one who has newly joined the [tramp] fraternity.

2. *Rap Music.* to leave.

1984 Toop *Rap Attack* 158: Fellas I'm gonna break out because I have to meet my woman. **1984** Hager *Hip Hop* 108: Break out—depart.

break up *v.* **1.a.** to upset severely; to make nervously ill; (now *esp.*) to cause to weep. Now *colloq.*

1825 in *OEDS:* She says, her sister is going to be married—& that she fears it will break her up. **1883** Peck *Bad Boy* 117: I didn't want to play no joke on Ma, cause the cats nearly broke her up. *Ibid.* 228: This affair breaks me all up. **1884** *Life* (Sept. 18) 165: Coming on at this time it bhreaks me all up. **1885** Siringo *Texas Cowboy* 164: To use a western phrase, she broke me all up on the first round. **1902** "J. Flynt" *Little Bro.* 174: Miss Myrtaugh wuz so broke up she'd hed to run out o' the meetin'. **1907** *Reader* (Sept.) 348: It like to broke these guys that'd been so friendly to him all up. **1932** Hecht & Fowler *Great Magoo* 163: Breaks me up. I never seen you cry before.

b. to convulse with laughter (now *colloq.*); (*hence*) *Show Bus.* to delight (an audience).

1895 "M. Twain," in *N. Amer. Rev.* (Jan.) 61: Well, humour is the great thing, the saving thing,…so, when M. Bourget said that bright thing about our grandfathers, I broke all up. **1895** *Harper's Mag.* (Sept.) 845: A most pathetic stream of arguments and blasphemy, which broke Joan all up, and made her laugh as she had not laughed since she played in the Domremy pastures. **1929** E. Wilson *Thought of Daisy* 96: Well, when he read that aloud in the office just after he'd written it the other day, he almost broke up the shop! **1941** in W.C. Fields *By Himself* 396: He is laughing and "breaking himself up" as he continues. **1950–52** Ulanov *Hist. Jazz* 350: *Break it up:* to "stop the show," "Kill 'em," "fracture 'em," to achieve the major success in a sequence of performances. **1956** M. Wolff *Big Nick.* 66: It…breaks me up, I can't help but laugh. **1957** Gelber *Connection* 42: He breaks me up….I like him.

2. to display strong emotion; weep or laugh.

1959 Brosnan *Long Season* 77: I glanced at the stewardess to see if she could take any more without breaking up. **1960** *Mad* (Sept.): All of the hipsters always break up when I make the scene. They keep laughing at me, and I don't know why.

breastworks *n.pl.* a woman's breasts.

*1826 "Blackmantle" *Eng. Spy* II 316: The frigate yonder with the brown breastworks. **1864** in *Civil War Times Illus.* (Jan. 1973) XI 27: "Storming the Enemy's Breastworks." This is decidedly one of the best pictures we have ever seen of the kind. It represents an amorous Union soldier while playing with a Secesh maiden, making a very indelicate assault....we must conclude that the Breastworks unconditionally surrendered. *a*1889 F. Kirkland *Anec. of Rebellion* 236: Madam, your breastworks seem to have been iron clad. **1930** *Lyra Ebriosa* 6: O, Mrs. Jones, she had no breastworks./She had nothing beneath her blouse. **1929–31** J.T. Farrell *Young Lonigan* 61: He had...a pair of breastworks like a woman. *Ibid.* 114: Kenny commented on the large breastworks she had. **1934** Halper *Foundry* 392: An expert on brandies, summer roads, fillies, and female breastworks. **1940** Zinberg *Walk Hard* 91: Ruth must have some breastworks. I'd like to undress her. **1946** in Inman *Diary* 1325: I've gained all this plumpness in the breastworks since my operation. **1958** Camerer *Damned Wear Wings* 149: Slim hips, a small waist, and generous breastworks. **1961** Coon *At Front* 201: Her waist...[was] completely overshadowed by breastworks of such magnitude and design as to stagger credulity.

breath ¶ In phrase: **change (one's) breath** to take a drink of liquor. Now *hist.*

1865 Sala *Diary* II 307: The orators "change their breath" before they speak, and sup afterwards. **1891** Maitland *Amer. Slang Dict.* 62: *Change your breath*, take a drink. **1987** J.I. Roberson *Blue & Gray* 90 [ref. to Civil War]: Asking a compatriot to have a drink was an offer to "change his breath."

breathe *v.* to allow (a horse) to rest.

1927 Rollins *Jinglebob* 45 [ref. to 1880's]: Hour after hour the expedition moved indolently onward, stopping occasionally to "breathe" the horses, and a moment later resuming its torpid course.

breather *n.* **1.** a lung.

1911 A.H. Lewis *Apaches of N.Y.* 87: She'd have put him hep to that bullet in his breather, mebby.

2. a humdinger; SNORTER.

1866 Marcy *Army Life* 370: This yere hill o' yourn *am* a breather; ef it ain't, d—n me.

breeched *adj.* having money in one's pockets.

*1811 *Lexicon Balatron.*: *Breeched*. Money in the pocket: *the swell is well breeched, let's draw him*; the gentleman has plenty of money in his pocket, let us rob him. *1812 Vaux *Vocab.*: *Breech'd:* flush of money. **1836** (quot. at GOLDFINCH, 2).

breech-loader *n.* a passive anal sodomist.

1914 T.S. Eliot, in V. Eliot *Letters* 42: In burst King Bolo's big black queen/That famous old breech loader.

breed *n.* [fr. half-*breed*] *West.* a person who is half Indian and half white.—now considered offensive.

1870 in Avis *Dict. Canad.* 76: The "breeds" in their ire said on him they'd fire. **1899** in J. London *Short Stories* 41: When the "breeds" rose...the full-bloods kept the peace. **1908** Beach *Barrier* 13: A few "breeds" like these little fellows. **1925–26** Black *You Can't Win* 229: I soon mastered Chinook, practicing on the two "breed" boys. **1935** Coburn *Law Rides Range* 5: Every white man, breed and Injun in this section of Montana knows what Shotgun does to me. **1958** Bickham *Gunman's Gamble* 40: He's tall, heavy-set, dark. Maybe a breed or a greaser. **1974** in *Atlantic* (Jan. 1975) 60: They'll tell you he's a Feejee Indian from Africa. They'll call him a breed.

breeder *n. Homosex.* a heterosexual person.—usu. used contemptuously. [The definition in the 1981 quot. is probably erroneous.]

1981 Eble *Campus Slang* (Mar.) 2: *Breeder*—one who is currently dating (applied to males and females)..."He's a breeder." **1982** *Time* (Nov. 8) 91: Homosexuals possess a decadently rich special vocabulary that is on the whole inaccessible to *breeders*. **1984** *N.Y. Times* (July 16) A 16: To local homosexuals, those who aren't are simply "breeders." **1985** "Blowdryer" *Mod. Eng.* 71: *Breeder*...A heterosexual. **1981–89** J. Goodwin *More Man* 18: Gays have adopted the word *breeders* (often..."filthy breeders") to refer contemptuously to straights. **1989** P. Munro *U.C.L.A. Slang* 24: She has pretty good taste for a breeder. **1991** C. Paglia, in *New Republic* (Dec. 2) 26: The scornful term "breeders," used by some urban gays about heterosexual couples with children.

breeze *n.* **1.** a disturbance; a quarrel.—usu. constr. with *raise* or *kick up*.

1772 in Whiting *Early Amer. Proverbs* 45: The Tories give out...that they expect what they call a Breese before long. **1775** in Whiting *Early Amer. Proverbs*: They would take that Occasion to beat up a Breeze. **1778** in Whiting *Early Amer. Proverbs*: A Faction in the Army...endeavoring to blow up a breeze & get Gen. Wash. superseded by G. Gates. *1785 Grose *Vulgar Tongue*: *To kick up a breeze*; to breed a disturbance. *1819 [T. Moore] *Crib's Memorial* 5: Something may happen to kick up a *breeze*. **1821** Waln *Hermit in Phila.* 30: Who'll *raise a breeze? kick up a dust?* and *play the d—l?* **1837** J.C. Neal *Charcoal Sks.* 156: When Auster chooses to kick up a breeze, he is very nearly as good at a practical joke as Boreas. **1840** in Eliason *Tarheel Talk* 144: The servants...are very worthless. One, always drunk...another sick....I think she would raise a breeze. **1843** in Eliason *Tarheel Talk* 290: The young *Bucks* tried to raise a breese but could not make [it]. **1855** Brougham *Chips* 311: Some of the manufacturers...tries to persuade themselves that they are kickin' up a jolly breeze. **1867** Smyth *Sailor's Wd. Bk.*: *Breeze, To kick up a.* To excite disturbance, and promote a quarrelsome row. **1898** Green *Va. Folk-Speech* 68: *Breeze,* n. A noisy quarrel; a disturbance; a row.

2.a. empty or inflated talk Cf. *shoot the breeze*, below.

1914 Jackson & Hellyer *Vocab. Slang* 19: *Breeze,* Noun General Usage. Loquacity; guile; "hot air"; "bull con." **1943** Coale *Midway* 173: Your attention, gentlemen, please knock off the breeze.

b. gossip; rumor.

1959 Duffy & Lane *Warden's Wife* 21 [ref. to 1906]: Since no one knew any of the dull, factual details concerning this latest "breeze," there was plenty of...conjecture about a mass escape.

3. something easily accomplished; a snap.

1928 Ruth *Babe Ruth's Book* 299: *Breeze,* an easy chance. **1937** Wexley & Duff *Angels* (film): Forget it, it's a breeze. **1944** H. Brown *Walk in Sun* 146: What the hell....It might be a breeze. *1945 S.J. Baker *Australian Lang.* 271: *It's a breeze*, it is easy. **1958** J. King *Inside Football* 199: Sounds like the quarterback has a breeze, doesn't it? **1985** Univ. Tenn. instructor: The course is a breeze if you come to class.

4. air, as used in air brakes or tires.

1939 (quot. at DONICKER). **1945** Hubbard *R.R. Ave.* 335: *Breeze*—Service air.

¶ In phrases:

¶ **bat the breeze** to gossip, chat. [Less freq. than syn. *shoot the breeze*, below.]

1941 Hargrove *Pvt. Hargrove* 43: Batting the breeze is the military equivalent of "bull-shooting." **1944** M. Hart *Winged Victory* (film): Sit down and bat the breeze awhile. **1944** *Slanguage Dict.* 47: *Batting the breeze*—talking; shooting the bull. *1945 S.J. Baker *Australian Lang.* 154: *To bat the breeze*, to gossip or talk. **1946** Nason *Contact Mercury* 42: Meanwhile, some so-and-so is sawing the chain off my jeep...while I stand here batting the breeze! **1951** Leveridge *Walk on the Water* 170: Come on inside....Let's bat the breeze. **1958** Cooley *Run for Home* 126: I've been batting the breeze long enough. **1974** Radano *Cop Stories* 99: They're batting the breeze, walking out to their assignments.

¶ **bust** [or **burn** or **fan**] **the breeze** *split the breeze*, below.

1894 in J.I. White *Git Along Dogies* 92: With my silvered spurs...I'll fan the breeze. **1926** C.M. Russell *Trails* 127: They crawl their ponies an' bust the breeze. **1930** Sage *Last Rustler* 10: I wanted to ride good horses [and] fan the free breeze. **1933** *AS* (Feb.) 28: *Burnin' the breeze.* Going at full speed. **1951** West *Flaming Feud* 152: Saddle your bronc and bust the breeze. **1952** Hopson *High Saddle* 125: They took the whole outfit and burned the breeze for Mexico. **1973** Yount *Last Shot* 67: Boy, he wuz burnin the breeze....Goin off that bridge woulda kilt a sober man.

¶ **give the breeze** *give the air* s.v. AIR.

1930 in Blackbeard & Williams *Smithsonian Comics* 161: So you gave old Senator Schnopps the breeze, huh? **1929–31** Runyon *Guys & Dolls* 84: If she thinks I am the same way the chances are she will give me the breeze.

¶ **hit the breeze** Orig. *West.* to clear out; take off.

1883 *Cheyenne Wkly. Leader* (Aug. 23): And he "hits the breeze," and rides at ease. **1891** Ryan *Told in Hills* 191: Let us "move our freight," "hit the breeze," or any other term of the woolly West that means action. **1894** O. Wister, in Remington *Wister* 92: To the several phrases of going known to the pioneer as vamose, skip, light out, dust, and git, the cowboy adds, burn the earth, hit, hit the breeze, pull your freight, jog, amble, move, pack, rattle your hocks, brindle, and more. **1904** in "O. Henry" *Works* 1176: Stop your funnin'....We got to be hittin' the breeze. **1914** D.W. Roberts *Rangers* 71: They began to "hit the breeze" in different directions. **1918** Griffin *Ballads* 36: Hit the breeze! Get down and nip! **1926** C.M. Russell *Trails* 126: So he hits the breeze, not runnin' straight, but sidewindin', duckin', an' dodgin' like a grouse-hen tollin' [*sic*] ye from her nest. **1971** E. Sanders *Family* 44: Manson....hit the breeze, off to the Mojave Desert.

¶ **on** [or **in**] **the breeze** happening; of current interest. [Quots. ref. to Vietnam War.]

1985 Bodey *F.N.G.* 192: What's on the breeze, brother? **1986** Dye & Stone *Platoon* 71: Mah man! What's in the breeze, Taylor?

¶ **punch the breeze, 1.** *hit the breeze*, above.

1891 Bourke *On Border* 155: He. . . made up his mind to skip the hull outfit 'n punch the breeze fur Maz'tlan. **1951** T. West *Flaming Feud* 31: Aw, punch the breeze!

2. to talk at length; to chat idly.

1918 Wagar *Spotter* 12 [ref. to 1911]: "Punching the breeze," was a phrase used to denote that the poor conductor talked too long with a passenger.

¶ **shoot the breeze** to talk or converse; to talk emptily.

1919 *Co. D, 314th Engineers* 58: The next comes the corporals, a wise lot they are,/They're sociable clucks, but, by gosh, nothing more./For work they are useless, and not worth a hang./Breeze shooting's their specialty, not dodging whiz bangs. **1933** *Leatherneck* (Feb.) 37: Starting with a membership of five reservists who got together to absorb coffee and doughnuts and "shoot the breeze." **1935** *Our Army* (May) 47: Langley Laffs. Shooting the Breeze in the Air Corps. **1942** W.L. White *Expendable* 26: Texas was pretty sick, so...I shot the breeze with the Ohio boy. **1942** Tregaskis *Guadalcanal Diary* (July 26): They were occupied in this day of rest principally with "shooting the breeze." **1955** Stern *Rebel Without a Cause* (film): If you just want to talk, come in and shoot the breeze. **1961** Rosten *Capt. Newman* 155: Why not take a load off your feet and shoot the breeze with Doc. **1962** E. Shepard *Press Passes* 25: I sat up till all hours listening to Martin Agronsky, Walter Kiernan and their colleagues shooting the breeze. **1965** Cleaver *Soul on Ice* 21: A large group of Negroes was on the prison yard shooting the breeze. **1983** N.Y.C. man, age 35: Just sittin' around shootin' the breeze. **1992** *Seinfeld* (NBC-TV): I just came by to chat, you know—shoot the breeze.

¶ **split the breeze** to go at great speed; to clear out.

1899 in Davidson *Old West* 77: Go! Pull your freight and vanish!/Get out and split the breeze. **1937** E. Anderson *Thieves Like Us* 117: We'll get...an extra can or two of gasoline and we'll split the breeze. *****1959** Opie & Opie *Lore & Lang. Schoolchildren* 193: Expressions inviting a person's departure...*split the breeze*, [etc.]. **1968** S.O. Barker *Rawhide Rhymes* 27: A bear can split the breeze.

¶ **take the breeze** to leave.

1931 D. Runyon, in *Collier's* (May 16) 13: With this she takes the breeze. **1946** Gresham *Nightmare Alley* 255: Come on, crumb, take the breeze.

¶ **up a breeze** Esp. *Black E.* in a most impressive or notable way. Cf. *up a storm* s.v. STORM.

1929–32 in *AS* (Dec. 1934) 290: Up a Breeze. In a wonderful manner. **1935** Z.N. Hurston *Mules & Men* 215: Lyin' up a breeze. **1945** Himes *If He Hollers* 103: You was talking up a breeze a while ago. **1946** Mezzrow & Wolfe *Really Blues* 20: Yellow was blowing up a breeze on the cornet. **1948** Manone & Vandervoort *Trumpet* 20: Man, I can still see those bands blowing up a breeze. **1954** B. Schulberg *Waterfront* 10: He can talk up a breeze like *That matter to which you have reference to which* and stuff like that. **1956** Holiday & Dufty *Lady Sings Blues* 54: All alone in a room upstairs, snoring up a breeze.

breeze *v.* **1.a.** to leave, clear out; abscond, escape, etc.

[**1907** in *OED2*: He breezed through the Louvre at such a pace that he broke all the rapid sight-seeing records.] **1913** in J. Reed *Young Man* 29: When's the next boat?...I'm going to breeze. **1914** Jackson & Hellyer *Vocab. Slang* 19: Breeze, Verb...to move on, to leave. **1917** Depew *Gunner* 97: He said that the German must have tried an advance and that as soon as the Forts got into action, the Germans breezed. **1918** *Stars & Stripes* (Feb. 8) 6: Divvy up among yourselves and then breeze!—beat it!—allez! **1928** Fisher *Jericho* 155: When I reach for Pat, he's breezed. **1949** H. Ellson *Tomboy* 6: Let's breeze. I'm getting stiff laying here. **1957** Margulies *Punks* 50: Let's breeze, man. **1958** *Life* (Apr. 28) 70: If I didn't get out legally...I would breeze. **1965** C. Brown *Manchild* 143: If I was to breeze and they came after me, one of us would get hurt.

b. to get away from.

1970 Cortina *Slain Warrior* 14: You got to learn to beat people out of things, you got to learn to breeze the cop.

2. to go ahead successfully with little effort; to succeed easily.

1906 *Nat. Police Gaz.* (July 21) 6: Why, look at that Tommy Foster 'way out in front and only breezing—only romping—look at him! **1959**

Brosnan *Long Season* 165: In both games I had breezed for seven [innings], then blown my victory.

3. *Baseball.* to strike out.

1910 *Baseball Mag.* (Sept.) 83 (cited in Nichols *Baseball Term.*). **1914** [Patten] *Lefty o' the Bush* 36: Git th' fust one, boy!...Breeze him!

4. to discuss informally.

1956 Chamales *Never So Few* 195 [ref. to WWII]: After that we...will get together and bolt a few and breeze this operation.

Breeze *interj.* [fr. COOL-BREEZE] Esp. *Black E.* buddy; man.—used in direct address.

1969 *Current Slang* I & II 15: Breeze, n. Casual term of greeting.—High school males, New York.—Hello, *breeze*, what's happening? **1975** S.P. Smith *Amer. Boys* 97: Sure thing, breeze. I wouldn't want to have no unfair advantage. **1982** Del Vecchio *13th Valley* 1: Breeze, when you get this far up-country aint nobody here ee-ven kin figure what them numbers mean.

breeze in *v.* **1.** *Horse Racing.* to win a race easily.

1902–03 Ade *People You Know* 116: He said that Rinkaboo would breeze in, that he would win on the Bit, doing Buck and Wing steps. **1907** in H.C. Fisher *A. Mutt* 4: Show me the guy who scratched "Redwood." He would 'ave breezed in and I was down strong. **1908** T.A. Dorgan, in Zwilling *TAD Lexicon* 20: Jeff was faster, cleverer, and a harder hitter...and would have "breezed in," as they say at the track.

2. to arrive, esp. in a carefree manner. Now *colloq.* or *S.E.*

1908 in H.C. Fisher *A. Mutt* 22: I knew you were the goods as soon as you breezed in. **1910** *Variety* (June 18) 7: Harry Robinson...breezed into New York this week from Chicago. **1913** *Sat. Eve. Post* (Mar. 1) 18: She was goin' over Romeo in the Byzantine Room, an' me an' Nolan breezed in. **1915** Lardner *Gullible's Travels* 122: Well, the Hatches breezed in Monday night. **1918** Witwer *Baseball* 23: I breezed in.

breeze-puncher *n.* an excessive talker.

1918 Wagar *Spotter* 95: He is also a "breeze puncher."

breezer *n.* (see quot.).

1929 *AS* IV 236: *Breezer*—an open car; a touring car.

breeze session *n.* BULL SESSION.

1956 Brinkley *Don't Go Near the Water* 10 [ref. to WWII]: A breeze session.

breeze up *v.* to become angry or agitated.

1875 Sheppard *Love Afloat* 44: Well, you needn't breeze up about it. Heave ahead with the baptizin'.

breezing *n.* a scolding or upbraiding.

1836 *Spirit of Times* (July 2) 159: So I gin Hannah a reglar breezin' for actin' so like a raven distracted bed bug.

breezy *adj.* rowdy; short-tempered.

1837 *Every Body's Album* II 175: Now, as Tom had *three sheets in the wind*, no wonder the audience got *breezy*. *****1931** (cited in Partridge *DSUE* (ed. 5) 92).

brevet *n.* (see 1972 quot.). Now *hist.*

1844 Strong *Diary* I 224: She...will probably try to make herself a dowager by brevet. *a***1899** B.F. Sands *Reefer* 68 [ref. to *ca*1833]: His housekeeper or "brevet-wife," a pretty quadroon. **1972** S.Z. Starr *Jayhawkers* 26: He had not provided himself with a wife pro tem, or a "wife by brevet," as such ladies were called during the Civil War.

brew *n.* **1.** beer; a serving of beer.

1907 T.A. Dorgan, in Zwilling *TAD Lexicon* 20: I never hung around saloons hiding the brew. **1910** T.A. Dorgan, in *N.Y. Eve. Jour.* (Mar. 2) 16: They say that Owen tore into the brew like a sailor on the other side. **1918** Griffin *Ballads* 20: They opened up the "brew" and ["mountain"] "dew." **1943** O'Sheel & Cook *Semper Fidelis* 75: Yeah, stateside brew at Peleliu. **1944** in *Best from Yank* 35: Where is a better place to have a brew? **1947** Guthrie *Born to Win* 195: That...bar where we gang around and guzzle the brews. **1947–51** Motley *We Fished* 168: Let's have a couple of brews. **1951** in Elliott *Among the Dangs* 159: You got it, man....Two of the brew. **1952** Uris *Battle Cry* 1: A gang of beardless youths...who'd get pickled on two bottles of brew. **1955–57** Kerouac *On Road* 78: They gabble and brawl over brews. **1957** J. Jones *Some Came Running* 29: Hope you men haven't drunk up all the brew today. I'm sure ready for my brews today. **1959** E. Hunter *Conviction* 130: I'd like a brew. **1963** Boyle *Yanks Don't Cry* 226: Come on, you guys, how about a cold brew? *****1980** Leland *Kiwi-Yank. Dict.* 18: (A) brew: a glass of beer.

2. coffee; a serving of coffee.

1917 Burroughs *Oakdale Affair* 74: A hunk of bread, a little mug of brew. **1952** Geer *New Breed* 3: In the coffee mess, extra pots of "brew" were set going. **1955** Klaas *Maybe I'm Dead* 437: You got any coffee left? I'll be over for a brew in a few minutes. **1973** Herbert & Wooten *Soldier* 39: Of course, jumping isn't everybody's cup of brew.

Brew Crew *n. Baseball.* the Milwaukee Brewers baseball team.—constr. with *the.*
> **1987** *Sports Update* (CNN-TV) (Apr. 19): Yesterday the Brew Crew won its eleventh straight game. **1989** P. Dickson *Baseball Dict.* 71.

brewhaha *n.* [pun on *brouhaha*] a serving of beer. Also **brewha.**
> **1989** P. Munro *U.C.L.A. Slang* 24: *Brewhaha, brewha*…can of beer, drink of beer. **1991** *Houston Chronicle* (Nov. 13) 5D: *Brew-ha:* Beer.

brewski *n.* (BREW + *-ski*) *Stu.* beer; a serving of beer.
> **1978** *NBC's Saturday Night* (NBC-TV): Here you go. A couple of brewskis. **1980** Eble *Campus Slang* (Mar. 1) *Brewski*—beer: Let's go to Trolls and have a few brewskis. **1985** "Blowdryer" *Mod. Eng.* 7: Got any brewski? Thanks, champ! **1986** *Twilight Zone* (CBS-TV): I'm very thirsty. I think I'll have a brewski. **1991** G. Trudeau *Doonesbury* (synd. cartoon strip) (Apr. 22): A six-pack of ice-cold brewskis.

briar *n.* **1.** *Und.* a saw.
> **1807** Tufts *Autobiog.* 292 [ref. to 1794]: *Briar*…a saw.

2. *Midland.* BRIAR-HOPPER.
> **1972** E. Wilson, in *N.Y. Post* (Mar. 17) 49: "No," contended a lady reader, "It's the Kentuckians who are 'briars.' "

briar-breaker *n. S.W.* BRIAR-HOPPER.
> **1934** Cunningham *Triggernometry* 189: The worst old "briar-breaker" in Kimble County.

briar-hopper *n. Midland.* a rustic; bumpkin.
> **1940** *AS* (Dec.) 447: *Briar Hopper.* Dirt farmer. "Tilman's jist a plain briar hopper." **1962** T. Berger *Reinhart* 400: A specimen of what was called locally a "Briarhopper," a person with Kentuckian antecedents. **1972** E. Wilson, in *N.Y. Post* (Mar. 17) 49: "We switch some Polish jokes around and put them on to the 'briar-hoppers' in West Virginia."…" 'Briar-hoppers' are from Indiana." "No…It's the Kentuckians….West Virginians are hillbillies, Kentuckians have always been briar-hoppers and ridge-hoppers and always will be."

brick *n.* **1.** a solidly reliable, generous, or otherwise admirable person.
> *ca*1822 in Foner *Labor Songs* 15: I think you're a brick to do that, Johnny Green. *1840 in OED:* Father Dick…was a Regular Brick. **1856** Wilkins *Young N.Y.* 22: Au revoir, Rose—You're a brick. **1856** Hall *College Wds.* 38: *Brick.* A gay, wild, thoughtless fellow, but not so *hard* as the word itself might seem to imply. **1862** in R.G. Carter *4 Bros.* 88: Our colonel is a "brick." **1867** Clark *Sailor's Life* 33: Ned, you are a brick; you did just right. **1867** in "M. Twain" *Sketches & Tales* 82: She was a brick. **1871** Small *Free Masonry* 19: Brother,…you are a brick. Allow me to congratulate you. **1876** "M. Twain" *Sawyer* 161: Well, he must 'a' been a brick. **1889** Pierson *Vagabond's Honor* 157: I allus said you was a brick in the old days. **1897** Hamblen *General Mgr.* 104: Bully for the old man! he's a brick. **1934** H. Miller *Tropic of Cancer* 65: Serge is a brick, there's no doubt about that. **1936** "E. Queen" *Halfway House* 139: Thanks just the same. You're a brick. **1950** M. Shulman *Sleep Till Noon* 127: In those movies the parents weren't unkind or cruel. They were perfect bricks to their children. **1985** Boyne & Thompson *Wild Blue* 41: Best to Joan. She's a brick.

2. *Esp. U.S. Naval Acad.* an unpleasant or uninteresting young woman.
> *ca*1909 in Warren & Warren *Everybody Works* 109: The occasional few girls…who prove stupid are ungallantly but confidentially termed "bricks." **1962** in *Harper's* (Jan. 1963) 50: Cutting in is encouraged so that no one is stuck with a "brick."

3. *Gamb.* (see 1961 quot.).
> **1961** Scarne *Complete Guide to Gambling* 674: *Brick.* A crooked die that has been cut so that it is not a true cube. **1969** King *Gambling & Org. Crime* 230: *Brick*—a crooked die.

4. *pl. Auto. Racing.* a track for automobile racing.
> **1934** Weseen *Dict. Slang* 248: *Bricks*—An automobile race track.

5. a blunder; (*specif.*) *Basketball.* a very poor shot.
> **1959** Goffman *Presentation of Self* 209: We may speak of "bricks" or of…having "put his foot in it." **1980** Eble *Campus Slang* (Oct.) 2: *Brick*—Badly missed basketball shot: "Dudley Bradley just shot another brick." **1990** P. Munro *Slang U.* 45: *Brick*…mess; failure….That shot didn't even hit the rim—it was a real brick.

6. a bricklike package made by binding a blocklike object or

objects tightly in cellophane.
> **1983** T. Page *Nam* 42: A brick of Ektachrome. **1985** Ark. man, age 35: I heard a Navy photographer talk about a *brick* of film in the summer of 1973.

7. *Mil.* a walkie-talkie.
> **1983** M. Skinner *USAFE* 100: For a full colonel,…a brick is an absolute necessity. *a*1989 R. Herman, Jr. *Warbirds* vii: *Brick:* a walkie-talkie. *Ibid.* 355: He…keyed his brick. *a*1991 Kross *Splash One* 161: Adams could hear his handheld brick chirping.

¶ In phrases:

¶ **a few bricks shy of a load** eccentric or simple-minded. Also vars.
> **1969** in H.A. Smith *Rude Jokes* 165: He's a few bricks shy of a load. **1974** Blount *3 Bricks Shy* 3: I recall the afternoon of November 11, 1973…Craig Hanneman, a reserve defensive end from Oregon…cried: "You picked the right team! Oh, a great bunch of guys! And a bunch of crazy fuckers!…We're all about three bricks shy of a load!" **1978** Katz *Folklore* 28: Have you ever known anyone "two bricks shy of a load?" **1979** Hurling *Boomers* 102: Anyone who'd want to live…in the city is jest about a dime short and two bricks shy of a load. **1983** R. Thomas *Missionary* 133: Velveeta's sort of pretty and halfway smart, even if she is six bricks short of a load. *a*1989 in Logsdon *Whorehouse Bells* 277: They think I'm one brick shy of a load.

¶ **beat** [or **press**] **the bricks** to walk the street, esp. if searching for employment.
> **1928** Burnett *Little Caesar* 102: Go press the bricks….This ain't your funeral. **1972** Ponicsan *Cinderella Liberty* 145: Really comfortable on your feet when you're beatin' the bricks.

¶ **built like a brick shithouse, 1.** (of persons, usu. men) having a solid or powerful build.—usu. considered vulgar. Also vars. and euphemisms.
> [**1903** A.H. Lewis *Boss* 183: That'll be enough to give us th' Tammany bunch as solid as a brick switch shanty.] **1922** Tully *Emmett Lawler* 286: He's built like a brick schoolhouse. **1925** in Hemingway *Sel. Letters* 151: The Blonde Bastard is built like a brick slaughterhouse and hits like a middle weight. **1928** in Hemingway *Sel. Letters* 287: Pat has doubled his weight in three months…built like a brick shithouse. **1929–31** Farrell *Young Lonigan* 122: They said she was built like a brick outhouse. [**1936** Tully *Bruiser* 58: "He's built like a brick barn."…"You mean a tiger."] **1938** "Justinian" *Americana Sexualis* 35: Built like a brick *shithouse*, referring to a heavy, cloddish, sexually unappetizing female. **1939** Shaw *Sailor off Bremen* 22: "He's built like a brick privy," Flora remarked. **1942** McAtee *Supp. to Grant Co. Dial.* 3 [ref. to 1890's]: "Built like a brick shithouse," description, especially of a hefty woman built solidly and close to the ground. **1942** Algren *Morning* 119: The boy…was built like a brick backhouse. **1966** Neugeboren *Big Man* 179: This white guy, played for St. Francis, built like a brick shithouse. **1976** Price *Bloodbrothers* 201: Jesus Christ, he was built like a brick shithouse, like a fuckin' *rock.*

2. (of women) having prominent breasts and slim hips.—usu. considered vulgar. Also vars. and euphemisms.
> **1933** J. Conroy *Disinherited* 91 [ref. to *ca*1918]: Wilma's a baby doll, build like a brick outhouse. **1936** Monks & Finklehoffe *Brother Rat* 24: The doll was…stacked up like a brick…(Jenny *appears in doorway*) Hello, there, Jenny. **1944** Busch *Dream of Home* 144: She's put up like a brick outhouse. **1947** Willingham *End as a Man.* 74: She's…stacked up like a goddamn brick sh—. **1956** G. Metalious *Peyton Pl.* 158: It was the consensus of town opinion that Constance MacKenzie was built like a brick shit house. **1959** Ogburn *Marauders* 72: Boy, was she stacked! You've heard of the well-known brick…. **1960–61** Steinbeck *Discontent* 194: Built like a brick outhouse…soft and smooth and strong and good. **1961** Bosworth *Crows* 11: I've got a chick…stacked like a brick benjo in a Sumida river fog. **1964** Mirvish *There You Are* 222: The Sicilian babe….Small, stacked like a brick shithouse. **1970** Appleman *12th Yr.* 20: She was well formed: "Stacked like a brick shithouse" was the customary compliment.

¶ **have a brick in (one's) hat** to be very drunk.
> **1845** Durivage & Burnham *Stray Subjects* 61: He wore a "brick" within his hat—the change was all complete. **1847** in *DA:* A youth who came home one night…having "a brick in his hat." **1853** Downey *Filings* 64: Judging from the size of the heads of the male portion of the populace…there had been lots of "bricks" toted about in the course of the preceding night. **1859** Avery *Comical Stories* 57: A fast young man, with a large pressed brick in his hat. **1866** *Galaxy* (Sept. 1) 35: Instead of distinctly asserting that a man is drunk…it is the custom to say that he is "tight," or "boozy," or "slewed," or "tipsy," or "corned," or "obfis-

cated," or "jolly," or "muddled," or "fuddled," or "discomfuddled," or "swipesy," or "set up," or a little "upset," or a little "so-so," or "pretty well how-come-you-so," or "high," or "elevated," or "pot-valiant," or "half seas over," or "slightly mixed," or a little "top-heavy," or that he has a "brick in his hat," or a "drop in his eye," or "two sheets in the wind, and the other shivering," or "three sheets in the wind," or he has his "perceptive faculties somewhat disturbed," or he has had a "drop too much," or is on a "lark," or on a "spree," or on a "bum," or on a "bat," or "over the bay," or "tightly slight." **1884** *Life* (Sept. 4) 133: I am afraid, Gulliver, you had a "brick in your hat." **1889** *Bat & Ball* 8: Bringing home a bit of a brick in his hat. **1892** King *Soldier's Secret* 29: The tepee of Two-Bricks-in-his-Hat. **1921** *DN* V 157: *Brick in his hat*, n. phr. Applied to an intoxicated person, meaning "he is top heavy." "He's got a brick in his hat."

¶ **hit the bricks, 1.** *Pris.* to be released from prison or other confinement.

1931 *AS* VI (Aug.) 439: *Hit the bricks:* To be released from prison. **1933** [Guest] *Limey* 10: Well, what would it be worth to you to "hit the bricks"? (be turned loose). **1931–34** in Clemmer *Pris. Comm.* 237: I'll drop religion when I hit the bricks. **1935** Lamson *About to Die* 202: Well, all the guy has to do is find somebody higher up that will take [a bribe]…and the guy hits the bricks. **1954** McGraw & McGraw *Riots* 268: *Hit the streets* or *Hit the bricks:* Be released. **1954** Chessman *Cell 2455* 95: When I hit the bricks this time I'm going to get me a stable of high class bitches. **1968** Cuomo *Thieves* 62: Because when you hit the bricks, you know, you gotta work, you gotta find a job. **1970** Cain *Blueschild Baby* 9: I hit the bricks Monday.

2. *Police.* to go out on patrol.

1970–71 J. Rubinstein *City Police* 41: He will tell them to "hit the bricks." **1972** Wambaugh *Blue Knight* 142: As soon as I hit the bricks and started cruising I began thinking about the case I had this afternoon. **1975** Wambaugh *Choirboys* 53: Come on, goddamnit, let's hit the bricks.…We ain't through yet.

3. to clear out; get going.

1971 Sanders *Family* 40: The group spent about ten days in the…area, then hit the bricks. **1982** Braun *Judas Tree* 208: Hit the bricks, and be damn quick about it. **1985** Resnick *Maxie* (film): Scram! Hit the bricks! Take a powder! **1986** *Cheers* (NBC-TV): Go on! Hit the bricks!

4. beat the bricks, above.

1980 Pearl *Pop. Slang* 71: *Hit the bricks v.* to walk, often in search of employment.

5. *Labor.* to go out on strike.

1947 Boyer *Dark Ship* 153: Old-timers are constantly talking about "hitting the bricks"…indicating strikes. **1948** McHenry & Myers *Home Is Sailor* 191: When are we going to hit the bricks? Who'll run the ships for Wall Street if we tell them to go to hell? **1958** Appel *Raw Edge* 213: They might be hittin' the bricks, too. **1967** Raskin *True Course* 10: The ISU called a strike on all coasts. The seamen hit the bricks. **1983** WINS radio news (Aug. 7): 700,000 AT&T workers hit the bricks. **1992** *Newsweek* (Dec. 14) 68: The district has already cut salaries by 12 percent…and the teachers are ready to hit the bricks.

6. *Naut.* to run aground.

1973 Beck *Folklore & the Sea* 66: In England, when a vessel runs aground inadvertently, the captain will note he "got on the putty," while in the United States the ship "hit the bricks."

¶ **like a ton of bricks** [cf. earlier colloq. *like a thousand of brick*] heavily; vigorously. Now *colloq.*

1916 H.L. Mencken, in Riggio *Dreiser-Mencken Letters* I 260: Hay fever has fallen on me like a ton of bricks. **1958** S.H. Adams *Tenderloin* 172: We're on to him like a ton of bricks. **1978** Wharton *Birdy* 12: Boy, you really fell like a ton of bricks for that…map. **1983** Nelkin & Brown *Workers* 71: He was fine one day and then went down like a ton of bricks.

¶ **on the bricks** *Pris.* on the street and out of prison; *(Police.)* on the street as a patrolman; *(also)* walking the streets looking for work, etc.

1933 Ersine *Pris. Slang* 21: A grand will put you on the bricks [out of jail]. **1944** *Papers Mich. Acad.* XXX 90: After I pulled a deuce and a half…I'm on the bricks. **1957** in J. Blake *Joint* 171: Too tough for you on the bricks, old partner? **1967** in H.S. Thompson *Shark Hunt* 111: The article naturally bombed, and Lionel was back on the bricks where he'd spent the last half of his forty-odd years. **1962–68** B. Jackson *In the Life* 183: He's back on the bricks (out in the free world). **1970** Rudensky & Riley *Gonif* 178: I hadn't been on the bricks long enough to earn a real big bundle. **1977** Butler & Shryack *Gauntlet* (film) 12: Shockley and Maynard Josephson had, in police jargon, been "on the bricks" together for fifteen years. They'd been uniformed patrolmen

together, then plainclothes, then detectives. *Ibid.* 22: Quit bellyaching. You're off the bricks. Enjoy it.

¶ **throw a brick** *Und.* to commit a minor felony.

1967 Fiddle *Portraits* 347: Throw a brick. Commit an illegal act. **1974** Piñero *Short Eyes* 62: And all you can do [outside of prison] is throw a brick.

¶ **to the bricks** *Black E.* thoroughly; through and through.

1928 in Oliver *Blues Tradition* 59: Hey, whip that thing down to the bricks, boys. **1938** *AS* (Apr.) 152: *On down to the bricks.* As excellently as possible. **1948** Manone & Vandervoort *Trumpet* 9: The bad times had us beat down to the bricks. **1957** Bannon *Odd Girl* 32: I'm beat to the bricks, as my friend Bud would say. **1961** R. Russell *Sound* 146: I mean all the studs in fancy duds and foxy chicks togged to the bricks is gonna be there. **1968** Algren *Chicago* 137: He's stoned to the bricks.

brick agent n. [sugg. by *on the bricks* s.v. BRICK] *FBI.* a field agent.

1977 Villano & Astor *Brick Agent* (title).

brick house n. [sugg. by *built like a brick shithouse* s.v. BRICK] a woman having a sexually attractive figure.

[**1962** S. Smith *Escape from Hell* 24: She cooks like a demon and she's built like a brick house.] **1977** W. King, Jr., et al. *Brick House* (song title). **1979** Eble *Campus Slang* (Mar.) 2: Brick house—a good-looking girl (used by males). **1980** Univ. Tenn. student: She's a brickhouse, man! **1981** in Safire *Good Word* 84: The Commodores, a soul group, created the term "brickhouse" and composed a song of the same name. **1989** P. Munro *U.C.L.A. Slang* 24: Dolly Parton is a brickhouse.

brickie n. *Constr.* a bricklayer.

*1880 in *OEDS*: "Navvy" and "bricky" seem to them amusing specimens of wit. **1937** Di Donato *Christ in Concrete* 219: An American bricklayer, "Hicky Nicky the floatin' bricky." **1962** Viertel *Love & Corrupt* 95: All the trades are goin' to hell—plumbers, steam-fitters, not just the brickies. **1976** Price *Bloodbrothers* 233: A brickie on the twenty-fourth floor…tossed it over the side. **1987** *N.Y. Times Bk. Review* (June 21) 13: Us brickies on the kiln bottom held our breath.

bricklayer n. an inept seaman.

[*1883 Russell *Sailor's Lang.* 21: *Bricklayer's clerk.*—One of the hundred names given to a lubberly sailor.] **1893** in J. London *Short Stories* 5: Our green hand, the "bricklayer." **1913–14** London *Elsinore* 193: They were not exactly sailors—Mr. Mellaire sneeringly called them the "bricklayers."

bricktop n. a head of red hair; (*hence*) a red-headed person.

1856 [M. Thompson & E. Underhill] *Elephant Club* 163: A head of hair which the youth of America are accustomed to designate as a "bricktop." **1884** Beard *Thorns* 21: Dad fetched ef he's fool nuff ter want that brick-top! **1947** Motley *Knock on Any Door* 39: Hi, Bricktop, hello, Bricktop, whatcha say, Bricktop?

brickwall v. *Journ.* STONEWALL.

1981 J. Bushinski, on WINS radio (Sept. 14): The same Prime Minister Begin began brickwalling the Palestinian autonomy negotiations.

bricky adj. [fr. *have a brick in (one's) hat* s.v. BRICK] tipsy.

1852 in *DA*: Peter Smith was taken up for being a bit "bricky."

Brickyard n. [short for HOGAN'S BRICKYARD] *Auto. Racing.* the Indianapolis Motor Speedway.—constr. with *the*.

1986 *CNN Sports News* (CNN-TV) (May 10): An amazing day today out at the Brickyard.

bride and groom n. an order of two eggs, as at a short-order restaurant. Cf. ADAM AND EVE.

1934 Weseen *Dict. Slang* 288: *Bride and groom*—Two eggs. "On a raft" adds the toast. **1953** *ATS* (ed. 2) 759: *Bride and groom on the rocks*…scrambled eggs.

bridge-jumper n. *Gamb.* (see quots.).

1968 M.B. Scott *Racing Game* 98: The bridge jumper is the no-risk, ultra-conservative player who makes large bets on hot favorites for show.…The expression…refers to a race track belief that if a player has had many no-risk successes, he will put an end to it all at the first setback. **1968** Ainslie *Thoroughbred Racing* 464: *Bridge-jumper*—Bettor who specializes in large show bets on odds-on favorites. **1984** W. Murray *Dead Crab* 145: I don't play the Pick Six.…It's for bridge-jumpers and other crazies.

bridge snake n. *Constr.* a structural ironworker.

1980 Bruns *Kts. of Road* 8: Itinerant miners, loggers, bridge snakes, skinners, muckers, tunnel workers, [etc.]. *Ibid.* 200: *Bridge snake.* Structural iron worker who usually carried hand tools for work on bridges, culverts, fences, etc.

brig[1] *n.* **1.** *Navy.* a makeshift place of confinement on shipboard; (*hence,* now exclusively) a shipboard jail. Now *S.E.*
***1803** in Wetherell *Adventures* 40: His doom is in the Brig (the irons), another makes too much noise, go in the Brig. **1832** Wines *Two Yrs. & Half in Navy* I 65 [ref. to 1829]: Another mode of punishment is confinement—the "brig"—the ship's prison—which is nothing more than the space between the two forward guns on the starboard side of the gun deck. **1836** *Every Body's Album* I 222: Them previously put in the *brig* were set at liberty. **1847** Downey *Portsmouth* 113: Legs and the Corporal of the Guard were ordered to convey him to the Brig. **1849** Melville *White Jacket* 64: They were ordered into the "brig," a jailhouse between two guns on the main-deck, where prisoners are kept. *Ibid.* ch. xxxiii: The same evening these four found themselves prisoners in the "brig" with a sentry standing over them. **1886** P.D. Haywood *Cruise* 48 [ref. to Civil War]: He…was placed in the brig (ship's jail). **1947** Boyer *Dark Ship* 268: I hit him and they…put me in the brig. **1966** *Voyage to Bottom of Sea* (ABC-TV): Put him in the brig under close guard.
2. *Mil.* a guardhouse or prison stockade; a military prison.
1899 Bowe *13th Minn.* 173: The officers kept trying to make the discharged soldiers from the regular army…drill and do fatigue duty, and they absolutely refused and nearly every day some of them were marched to the Brig (calaboose). **1919** T. Kelly *What Outfit?* 55: When we got to the brig we found practically the whole outfit lined up there. **1920** *Amer. Legion Wkly.* (Aug. 7) 7: Ah's outer de brig, Ah's delivuh'd an' free. **1920** *Amer. Legion Wkly.* (June 11) 12: I was…wondering if he were in the brig for being out after taps again. **1942** *Leatherneck* (Nov.) 143: *Brig*—Prison. **1944** Kendall *Service Slang* 21: *Brigtimer*…a prisoner.

brig[2] *n. Mil.* a brigadier general.
1899 King *Found in Phils.* 12: He and the "brig" rode over to the Presidio an hour ago. **1924** Anderson & Stallings *What Price Glory?* II: The Brig. wants a prisoner, and he also wants that nest wiped out. **1977** *Baa Baa Black Sheep* (NBC-TV): That Colonel Lard's a real comer. Should be getting his brig's star soon.

brig *v.* **1.** *Navy,* later also *Mil.* to loaf or shirk.
1901 *Our Nav. Apprentice* (Sept.) 14: The captain questioned him daily how so much drunkenness and "brigging" was possible on a ship so well policed. **1974** Former 2LT, 42d Div., AEF, 1917–18 [ref. to WWI]: If a man was just standing on his shovel instead of digging, if he was just loafing, the sergeant or the looie would come and say, "Are you briggin'? Get to work! No briggin' on the job."…You call it *goldbrickin'*, but we called it *briggin'*.
2. *Navy,* later also *Mil.* to confine in a brig.
1920 *Amer. Legion Wkly.* (Aug. 20) 13 [ref. to WWI]: Don't you know [the M.P.'s] motto? "Brig 'em young!" **1930** Irwin *Tramp & Und. Slang* 37: *Brig*…To imprison or confine. **1957** Leckie *Helmet for Pillow* 121 [ref. to WWII]: "Brig 'em!" **1957** Herber *Tomorrow to Live* 70 [ref. to WWII]: They walk the straight line or…they get brigged.

bright *n. Black E.* morning.—usu. constr. with *early.*
1941 D. Raye & H. Prince *Boogie Woogie Bugle Boy of Co. B* (pop. song): He wakes 'em up in the early bright. **1942** *Yank* (Sept. 23) 14: It was three a.m. in the early bright. **1944** Burley *Hndbk. Jive* 137: *Early bright*—Morning. **1950** L. Brown *Iron City* 108: Well along about five in the bright.…I had forgot all about this guy. **1961** R. Russell *Sound* 16: Like, when I get up in the early bright I turn on, then just keep an edge going all day. **1967** Lit *Dictionary* 13: *Early bright*—Early morning: if you are up in the early bright, your kite will fly right. **1971** Dahlskog *Dict.* 10: *Bright, n.* The daytime; early morning, as: I'll see you in the *bright.*

bright boy *n.* a know-it-all.
1927–28 in R. Nelson *Dishonorable* 153: *Pratt:* Why did you come then? *Miller:* Well, bright boy, because you did? **1936** Twist *We About to Die* (film): You're gonna keep that date, bright boy.

bright-eyed and bushy-tailed *adj.* alert and eager.
1942 Casey *Torpedo Junction* 319: Mr. Casey's been asleep but…he's now bright-eyed and bushy-tailed. **1944–48** A. Lyon *Unknown Station* 265: He appeared to be as bright-eyed and bush-tailed…as ever. **1961** L.G. Richards *TAC* 51: After the 600-calorie breakfast of steak and eggs…we were all bright-eyed and bushy-tailed. **1976** W. Johnson *Super Sweathogs* 72: I want to see the students bright-eyed and bush-tailed! **1983** Sturz *Wid. Circles* 9: The kids come in…bright-eyed and bushy-tailed, thinking about the exciting things going on.

brig rat *n. Navy & USMC.* a prisoner who is confined to a brig; a troublemaker who has often been imprisoned in a brig.
[***1821** W. Scott *Kenilworth* ch. iii: Thou gallows-bird—thou jail-rat.] **1942** *Leatherneck* (Nov.) 143: *Brig-Rat*—Prisoner. **1944** Kendall *Service Slang* 35: *Brig-rat*…a prisoner. **1957** Myrer *Big War* 145: Stand at attention when I talk to you or you'll be one sorry little brig-rat. **1959** Sabre & Eiden *Glory Jumpers* 14: Give me a regiment of brig-rats. **1964** Howe *Valley of Fire* 273: Brig rats. Rubbydubs but they know the score. **1966** Braly *On Yard* 179: He could imagine Red in the Navy, a brig rat of course,…shipping over until the sailors' home claimed him. **1971** Jeffers & Levitan *See Parris* 126: The Brig Rats. **1989** Leib *Fire Dream* 143: How's your brig rat?

brim *n. Black E.* a man's hat, esp. a fedora; STINGY-BRIM.
1965 *Esquire* (July) 44: Hats…are called *brims* [by teenagers]. **1969** B. Beckham *Main Mother* 139: Cats…adjusted their brims by checking the reflections in store windows. **1972** Claerbaut *Black Jargon* 59: Let me take your brim, mellow. **1967–80** Folb *Runnin' Lines* 231: *Brim* Hat. **1990** "Above the Law," in L.A. Stanley *Rap* 1: With my brim cold bent to the side. **1990** "Boo-Yaa" *New Funky Nation* (rap song): I…grab my brim and tilt it back.

bring *v. Pris.* to be sentenced to (a term of imprisonment); to serve out (a prison sentence).
1912 Lowrie *Prison* 31 [ref. to 1890's]: Wadger bring?…I mean…how long'd yer get? **1920** Murphy *Gray Walls* 20: "What 'id you bring?" he asked (meaning the term of sentence). **1925–26** Black *You Can't Win* 355 [ref. to 1890's]: "How long do you bring?" "Ten years." **1971** Keith *Long Line Rider* 120: "How much did you bring?" "Twenty-one years." **1978** W. Brown *Tragic Magic* 101: When I went up before the [parole] board, they told me to bring it all.
¶ In phrase:
¶ **bring it** *Baseball.* to pitch hard.
1975 in Eastman et al. *Norton Reader* (ed. 4) 22: Aren't you the guy from Davenport? The one who could really bring it? **1987** *Time* (July 13) 72: A lot of today's starters aren't very quick, and it seems the relievers can't bring it at all. **1989** *CBS This Morning* (CBS-TV) (Mar. 30): And he's a very good pitcher on top of it. He really brings it, as they say.

bringdown *n.* Esp. *Black E.* something that is depressing, dispiriting, or tedious.
1939 in A. Banks *First Person* 255: Man, a poor white man is a bringdown. **1944** Burley *Jive* 135: *Bring down*—Not up to par, depressing. **1944** La Guardia Comm. *Marihuana* 129: The test questions were frequently called a "bring down" in that they forced the subject to face reality and abandon his pleasurable feelings. **1946** Mezzrow & Wolfe *Really Blues* 26: That was a bringdown. **1948** Manone & Vandervoort *Trumpet* 187: It's just a bring-down. **1959** Burroughs *Naked Lunch* 36: Get this stiff outa here. It's a bring down for my live patients. **1966** Kornbluth *New Underground* 51: We sophisticate our tastes in order to…shove the poignancy of "bring downs" into impersonal shadows. **1987** *Nat. Lampoon* (June) 84: Moran felt disappointed.…What a bringdown!

bring down *v.* Esp. *Black E.* to sadden or depress; to dispirit; to spoil (someone's) enjoyment.
1935 in Gold *Jazz Talk* 33: That brings me down. **1941** D. Raye & H. Prince *Boogie Woogie Bugle Boy of Co. B* (pop. song): It brought him down because he couldn't jam. **1948** Manone & Vandervoort *Trumpet* 145: I'll cop me a hitch on the main line and bring you down. **1952** Holmes *Go* 139: Aw, come on.…Why do you want to bring me down, man? **1952** Mandel *Angry Strangers* 390: Don't bring me down, Dinch, cut it out. **1958** R. Russell *Perm. Playboy* 65: It was break-time and Spoof was brought down about Honker, about how bad we were sounding. **1966** Fariña *Been Down So Long* 224: It brought me down, baby. Do I look down? **1993** *Mystery Sci. Theater* (Comedy Central TV): You're bringing me down, man!

bring-'em-near *n. Naut.* a telescope. Also **bring-'em-close glasses** binoculars.
1836 *Every Body's Album* 193: So he ups with his bring-'em-near (that's what the sailors call a spy-glass, Sir) and looks out. **1867** Smyth *Sailor's Wd.-Bk.:* Bring 'Em Near. The day-and-night telescope. **1926** C.M. Russell *Trails* 125: There's no tellin' what butte holds a red sentinel.…He don't need no bring-'em-close glasses.

briny *n.* **1.** [fr. *S.E.* cliché *the briny ocean*] the ocean. *Joc.*
*1831 in *OEDS:* What is he to do without a sharp 'un to chaffer with the Parleys across the briney? ***1856** in *F & H* I 330: The luckless plight in which a stout gentleman found himself, by the temporary loss of his apparel, while he was disporting in the *briny.* **1886** Abbot *Blue Jackets*

of '61 270: Halloo, Jack….how do you like playing mud-turtle? Better stick to the briny. **1894** J. Slocum *Liberdade* 32: If ever "old briny" was welcomed, it was on that Christmas day. **1908** McGaffey *Show Girl* 105: But if the briny mingles with my marcel wave—good night, nurse! **1918** in Hemingway *Sel. Letters* 8: We are plowing the briny Wednesday. **1964** *AS* (Oct.) 280: *Briny, n.*…an ocean. **1991** M. Brooks & R. DiLuca *Life Stinks* (film): Sailor wanted his ashes sprinkled in the old briny.

2. tears. *Joc.*

1879 in Davidson *Old West* 124: I ain't no hand to blubber,/And the briny ain't run for years. **1939** Howsley *Argot* 9: *Briney*—Tears.

brisket *n.* the chest.

*1785 Grose *Vulgar Tongue*: *Brisket-Beater.* A Roman Catholic. *1789, *1790 in *OED.* *1823 in *OED* s.v. *gam*: I…clutched him by shoulder and brisket. *1823 "J. Bee" *Slang*: *Brisket-cut* [A punch to the breast or collar-bone.]. **1860** [Shipley] *Privateer's Cruise* 81: No quarter to the knaves. Hew them to the brisket. **1896** in A.E. Turner *Earps Talk* 3: Holliday…jerked a knife…and…caught Bailey just below the brisket. **1926** C.M. Russell *Trails* 161: In winter a girl wears a fox skin, but her brisket is bared to the weather and there ain't nothin' on her that's warmer than a straw hat. **1934** H. Roth *Call It Sleep* 103: And he's afther kickin' me in the brisket till I'm blue as me own coat! **1935** Coburn *Law Rides Range* 10: A man had always ought to shoot for the brisket. **1939** S. Herzig *They Made Me a Criminal* (film): In the brisket! In the brisket! **1947** Overholser *Buckaroo's Code* 19: If you showed up with a slug in your brisket, Keno and his whole bunch got fired. **1968** R. Adams *Western Wds.* xii: A heart in his brisket as big as a saddle blanket.

Brit *n.* a British or English person. [Rare in U.S. before 1970's.]

*1901 in *OEDS:* The Brit is at his old game. **1932** E. Pound, in *Pound/Lewis* 178: You are the only Brit' (or half-brit) artist I shd. think mentioning seriously. **1940** E. Pound, in *Pound/Lewis* 219: Extracting 7/6 a shot from the Brits. **1964** *Time* (Dec. 18) 27: "Yankee go Home"…"Bugger off, Brit!" **1975** *Nat. Lampoon Comical Funnies* (unp.): Those Brits and Frogs had called us over there to bail them out of a mess. **1978** *Bk. of Numbers* 234: With free medical treatment, Brits have grown accustomed to dash off to their doctor. **1980** *N.Y. Times* (Aug. 31) II 1: That was more than 40 years ago. Today there are sufficient English around (or "Brits," as they are now called to meet the nationalistic feelings of the Welsh, the Scots and the Northern Irish) to form 100 cricket teams. **1982** Knoxville, Tenn., man, age *ca*37: The sun never sets on the British Empire because God doesn't trust the Brits in the dark. **1983** *Good Morning America* (ABC-TV) (May 23): Small, cheap ships are a false economy, as the Brits learned the hard way. **1991** LaBarge *Desert Voices* 103: The Brits were great to work with.

britches *n.* ¶ In phrase: **caught with (one's) britches down** to be caught completely unprepared.

1843 in Barnum *Letters* 21: All open next Monday—and of course catch me with my breeches down. **1936–37** Kroll *Share-Cropper* 42: You think you caught me with my britches down and can drive a hard bargain. **1992** G. Wolff *Day at Beach* 78: I had caught the USIA with its britches down.

bro *n.* **1.a.** brother.

*a1666 in *OEDS:* I accompanyd my Eldest Bro (who then quitted Oxford) into the Country. **1776** in *S.C. Hist. Mag.* LVIII (1957) 68: Your Sincerely Affectte Bro. **1849** P. Decker *Diaries* 164: One to my Bro Charles. **1864** in D. Chisholm *Civil War Notebook* 37: Bro Ed…and Sam Johnson was over from the 85th. *ca*1910 in Womack *Mighty Men* 398 [ref. to Civil War]: It was…at dawn…when my Bro breathed his last. *1936 Partridge *DSUE* 94: *Bro.* Brother: Charterhouse: C. 20. **1943** in J. O'Hara *Sel. Letters* 175: Okay by me, bro. **1966–67** P. Thomas *Mean Streets* 133: Ain't yuh-all gonna eat, bro?

b. a friend; buddy.

[**1839** in *Mo. Hist. Rev.* XVII (1923) [opp. p. 168]: "How do you do, pro" (meaning brother) said one [Indian].] **1957** H. Simmons *Corner Boy* 132: "Thanks, bro," the driver said. **1962** H. Simmons *On Eggshells* 52: Bro,…now's as good a time as any to start. **1963** Williamson *Hustler!* 163: He called me "little bro" and I called him the same thing. *ca*1969 Rabe *Hummel* 80: You understand me, Bro? **1970** J. Freedman *Old News* 126: Tell 'em, bro. **1974** Blount *3 Bricks Shy* 91: I'm going to dinner, Bro. **1978** Hasford *Short-Timers* 51 [ref. to 1968]: Joker's my bro, sir. We enlisted personnel are tight, you know? **1991** *Beverly Hills 90210* (Fox-TV): Go for it, bro.

c. a fellow.

1981 *Easyriders* (Oct.) 22: Some bros have a putt for every occasion

that's likely to crop up. **1986** Philbin *Under Cover* 121: Do you know Slim?…Tall, skinny bro?

2. [cf. syn. BROTHER] Esp. *Black E.* a man.

1970 Ifetayo *Black Woman* 14: Rap/To the bro, get him together. **1971** H. Roberts *3d Ear* (unp.): Bro' n. A black male. **1988** *Rage* (Univ. Tenn.) I (No. 11) 39: Very light-skinned and is snubbed by team "bros."

broad *n.* **1.a.** *Gamb.* a playing card, esp. in three-card monte.

*1781 G. Parker *View of Society* II 168: *Black-Legs*, who live by the *Broads** and the *Turf*….*Cant for cards. *1789 in *F & H* I 332: Who are continually looking out for flats, in order to do them upon the *Broads*, that is *cards.* **1791** [W. Smith] *Confess. T. Mount* 19: Cards, *broads* or *flats*. *1812 Vaux *Memoirs*: *Broads*: cards; a person expert at which is said to be a good *broad-player.* *1823 "J. Bee" *Slang* 17: *Broads*—Cards. **1859** Matsell *Vocab.* 14: *Broad Pitching.* The game of three-card monte. *Broads.* cards. *1877 in *F & H* I 332: He…became one of a gang who practised with the *broads* card-sharping and the "confidence trick." **1897** F.P. Dunne, in Schaaf *Dooley* 148: Fr'm a priffssor of political economy to a boy that hurls th' *broads.* **1898** Dunne *Dooley in Peace & War* 1: Talk about th' County Dimocracy picnic, where a three-ca-ard man goes in debt ivry time he hurls th' *broads.* **1906** Wooldridge *Hands Up* 95: These gangs [were] also known as "broad" gangs. *Ibid.* 96: The stranger was then conducted to the "broad" joint.…Two other confidence men began discussing a game played with four cards, three of which have stars printed on them and one of which bears a picture of a girl kicking a hat. The stranger is induced to make bets that he can pick out the fourth card. **1909** Irwin *Con Man* 120: "The broads"…is the grafter's name for three-card monte. **1921** Conklin & Root *Circus* 168 [ref. to *ca*1880]: Along with them went the three-card monte men to "spread the brods," as they called their game. **1930** *Variety* (Jan. 8) 123: Some racketeers…ride trains to "play broads" (3-card Monte). **1967** Rose *Flim Flam Man* (film): They call it three-card monte. Up in St. Louis they call it "tossin' the broads." **1978** Time-Life *Gamblers* 63: Cards were often known as "broads."

b. *Circus.* a ticket of admission, transportation, etc.

1912 Field *Watch Yourself* 393 [ref. to 1880's]: "Fix the olly! I gave him broads to the show! He's right as a guinea! Fix him! Have this cheap Green County bilk pinched. I'll land him in the quay!" All of this…meant that the boss wanted the winner of the capital prize arrested and thrown into jail. **1914** Jackson & Hellyer *Vocab. Crim. Slang* 20: "Beating the broads" is corrupting the conductor or other collecting functionaire of a transportation line.

2.a. a sexually promiscuous woman; a prostitute; slut. [Especially common in early use and prob. the orig. sense; now subsumed by **(b).**]

1914 Jackson & Hellyer *Vocab. Crim. Slang* 19: *Broad,* Noun Current amongst genteel grafters chiefly. A female confederate; a female companion, a woman of loose morals. Broad is derived from the far-fetched metaphor of "meal ticket," signifying a female provider for a pimp, from the fanciful correspondence of a meal ticket to a railroad or other ticket. **1926** *Amer. Mercury* (Mar.) 369: *Broad* is usually applied by New Yorkers to women who, it is hoped or believed, are of uncertain morals. **1926** *Amer. Legion Mo.* (July) 47: I got my eye on a dame, too. She ain't no broad, even if I did meet her in camp. **1927** *AS* II 275: *Broad*—loose girl. **1928** C. McKay *Banjo* 7: They likened their ship to an easy woman by calling it the "broad." **1931** Cressey *Taxi-Dance Hall* 14: Guess they got in a fight over one of these "broads." **1943** in *DAS:* I *read* that book. Only had one dame in it and she was a broad. **1968** Algren *Chicago* 137: Keyboard or callbroad, cruiser or tout/…Straightbroad, boothbroad, headbroad or plain whore. **1971** N.Y.C. woman, age *ca*80: They first started using the word *broad* in the '20's, and then it meant "prostitute" more than anything else.

b. a woman.—often used contemptuously.

1911 *Hampton's Mag.* (Sept.) 172: Pretty soon what is technically known as a "broad"—"broad" being the latest New Yorkese—hove into sight. **1913** T.A. Dorgan, in Zwilling *TAD Lexicon* 20: She was some broad too. **1915** Howard *God's Man* 135: Listen, you poor imbecile broad. **1918** *Everybody's* (Aug.) 108: Say, it was the homeliest bunch of broads I ever set eyes on. **1918** Ruggles *Navy Explained* 82: The best girl is the Jane, widder, skirt, calico, the old lady, weezel, broad, judy, [etc.]. **1924** Hecht & Bodenheim *Cutie* 31: Her Nibs was a regal looking broad. **1924** Anderson & Stallings *What Price Glory?* 55: What became of them two broads? *Kiper:* My wives? *Lipinsky:* Yeah. **1927** C. McKay *Home to Harlem* 32: Sure, let's go and look the crazy old broad over. **1929** G. Milburn *Hobo's Hornbk.* 91: In the Sweet Potato Mountains/All the broads are plump and fair. **1930** "D. Stiff" *Milk & Honey* 201: *Broad* or *brod*—A woman, generally young. **1930** Dos Passos *42d*

Parallel 62: I've heard tell there's swell broads in Seattle. **1942** Liebling *Telephone* 11: She must have seen plenty other broads jump into them volcanos at home. **1961** *Bullwinkle* (NBC-TV): All I did was hit some dumb broad with a bucket. **1969** *Playboy* (Dec.) 108: I don't like going out on a date unless I know a little bit about the broad beforehand. By the way, broad to me is not a detrimental term for women; it's simply another word for female. **1968–73** Agar *Ripping & Running* 157: *Broad*, meaning "woman," is likely to be known by most speakers of…American English. **1982** Castoire & Posner *Gold Shield* 181: A broad with big jugs. **1989** *Murphy Brown* (CBS-TV): Afraid the old broad will call you?

c. *Pris.* a male homosexual who plays the feminine role.
1966 Braly *On Yard* 200: He was a broad in Tracy….A…drag queen. **1977** Bunker *Animal Factory* 50: "Is that kid Ron a broad?"…"You trying to turn him out?"

broadbrim *n.* a Quaker.
*1749 H. Fielding, in *OEDS:* This the Quaker had observed, and this…inspired honest *Broadbrim* with Conceit. **1776** in Meserve & Reardon *Satiric Comedies* 93: I hope you wont leave one broad-brim on the continent. **1860** H.L. Hosmer *Adela* 117: Hist, broadbrim,…you are talking treason.

broadie *n.* BROAD, 2.
1932 Nelson *Prison Days & Nights* 35: These visits, especially from the broadies, are a pain in the whatsis. **1952** Mandel *Angry Strangers* 99: It's the broadie I seen you wit this mornin. **1960** Bluestone *Cully* 89: Madon', that broadie's really stacked. **1966** E. Shepard *Doom Pussy* 172: I'm probably just getting you heated up and sending you into the arms of some broadie over there. **1987** *Growing Pains* (ABC-TV): So who are these two good-lookin' broadies, eh?

broad-pitcher *n.* BROAD-TOSSER.
*1870 (cited in Partridge *DSUE* (ed. 8) 138). **1968** R. Adams *Western Wds.* (ed. 2) 35: Broad pitcher. In three-card monte, a dealer. **1978** Time-Life *Gamblers* 63: The three-card monte dealer was commonly called…a "broad pitcher."

broad-spieler *n.* [BROAD, 1.a. + SPIELER] *Gamb.* a professional cardplayer, esp. a practitioner of three-card monte.
1909 Irwin *Con Man* 38: I was still only a small cheater, and he was the best "broad-spieler" on the road. *Ibid.* 124: I was the "broad spieler," which means that I did the actual work of manipulation. **1914** Jackson & Hellyer *Vocab. Crim. Slang* 20: A "three-card monte man" is a *broad spieler.*

broad-tosser *n.* *Gamb.* a practitioner of three-card monte.
1926 Maines & Grant *Wise-Crack Dict.* 6: Broad-tosser—Three-card skin game artist. **1970** A. Lewis *Carnival* 30: One of the gentlemen is an ex-three-card-monte man, or "broad-tosser," forced to leave that vocation when arthritis impaired his manual dexterity. **1984** W. Murray *Dead Crab* 105: A maneuver only a broad-tosser as skillful as I am can get away with.

Brodie *n.* **1.a.** a dive, leap, tumble, or fall.—usu. constr. with *do.* [On July 23, 1886, Steve Brodie claimed to have leaped from the Brooklyn Bridge; his claim, which could not be verified, elicited great public interest in N.Y.C.]
1899 Kountz *Baxter's Letters* 76: K.C.…did a Brodie out of his chair and lit on his eye. **1900** Ade *More Fables* 160: She would…resolve to do a Steve Brodie out of the Window if she saw his Hand slipping over toward hers. **1910** T.A. Dorgan, in *N.Y. Eve. Jour.* (Mar. 30) 12: Bob Murphy was just caught as he tried to do a "Brodie" from the third floor of the hotel. **1920** *Variety* (Dec. 31) 12: [At] Steve Brodie's…they shake hands with the bridge jumper whose jumping feats have originated the expression "doing a Brodie." **1926** *Writer's Digest* (Dec.) 541: *Throwing a Brodie*—Committing suicide. **1928** Callahan *Man's Grim Justice* 39: He was scared to death. I thought he was going to do a Brodie. **1928** Nason *Eadie* 65: They busted [the lifeboat] gettin' over the side, so I did the Steve Brodie. **1934** D. Runyon, in *Collier's* (Mar. 3) 7: King cannot drive them through Central Park without doing a Brodie off the seat. **1936** Duncan *Over the Wall* 339: How did you like that Steve Brodie I took off the cat-walk? **1953** "J. Cain" *Galatea* 151: Instead of doing a Brodie he went down like a limp dishrag. **1974** Blount *3 Bricks Shy* 241: A Black Angus bull…causing himself and his cage to go end over end— "doing a brodie." **1976** Berry *Kaiser* 38: Then all of a sudden, wham, I took a Brodie, right on my face.

b. *Boxing.* a pretended knockdown.
1911 T.A. Dorgan, in *N.Y. Eve. Jour.* (Jan. 13) 16: He fixed up five or six sparring partners to do a Brodie with Keefe, and the latter fell for it hook, line, and sinker.

c. *Entertainment Industry.* an utter failure; FLOP.
1917 *N.Y. Times* (Dec. 23) IV 6: They "did a Brodie up at the Royal." **1923** *N.Y. Times* (Oct. 14) VIII 4: *Brodie*—A complete and unmitigated flop—a débâcle. **1925** *AS* (Oct.) 37: When an act fails to get applause, the performers have "flopped." They have "taken a Brodie" or "died standing up" or "passed out." **1973** *Lang. of Show Biz* 29: *Brodie*. The term is widely used by all show business to label a show that takes a dive or a "bath"; a flop.

d. *Orig. Calif.* a spin made by a skidding vehicle. Also as v.
1953 Paxton *Wild One* (film): Somethin' hit my cycle or somethin', I did a big brodie and went out. **1962** *AS* XXXVIII 267: *Brodie marks.*…An extensive pattern of spinning skid marks on pavement. **1966** in *DARE*. **1977** in Rice *Adolescent* 272: *Brodie*—spin a car 360, also called a donut. **1992** D. Burke *Street Talk* I 119: *Brodey (to do a)*…to spin a car 180 degrees.

2. a long chance.
[**1912** Mathewson *Pitching* 197: It was rapidly and unanimously decided to imitate "Steve" Brodie and take a chance.] **1918** Hall *High Adventure* 33: Look here, Pete…tell him I know it was my fault. Tell him I "took a Steve Brody."…I wondered if he translated that literally. Steve took a chance, but it is hardly to be expected that a Frenchman would know of that. **1926** Maines & Grant *Wise-Crack Dict.* 7: *Do a Steve Brodie*—Take a chance. **1936** in W. Burnett *Best* 1057: The air injections had helped—a little. Enough so the surgeon had said, yes, he'd take a Brodie,…this fellow just might stand a thoracoplasty. **1953** Gresham *Midway* 122: "I took a Brody on it." (Mind reader's term for taking a chance—Steve Brody took a chance when he jumped off the Brooklyn Bridge). **1967** Maurer & Vogel *Narc. & Narc. Add.* (ed. 3) 345: An awful Brody he took, but he made a clean get.

Brodie *v. Entertainment Industry.* to fail utterly; FLOP.
1926 J. Conway, in *Variety* (Dec. 29) 5: "Brodied"…"failed." **1927** *Vanity Fair* (Nov.) 67: He trusts that he doesn't "flop" or "brody," meaning that he hopes he will not fail. **1934** Weseen *Dict. Slang* 137: *Brodie*—To fail. **1936** *Esquire* (Sept.) 162: An act…flopped, brodied. **1940** in Marx *Groucho Letters* 26: I may motor east…if the radio deal brodies. **1959** Ellison *Gentleman Junkie* 216: Those are the kind that brodie when the gaff gets too thick.

broiler *n.* [sugg. by syn. CHICKEN] a young woman, *(esp.)* *Theat.* a small chorus girl.
1904 in "O. Henry" *Works* 1334: She had ascended…[from] "broiler"…[in] the famous "Dickey-Bird" octette, in the successful musical comedy, "Fudge and Fellows." **1906** Ford *Shorty McCabe* 46: She was a regular Casino broiler. **1908** in H.C. Fisher *A. Mutt* 128: And a swell little broiler will call this big cheese "baby doll." **1909** C. Chrysler *White Slavery* 97: He wants…"broilers," chorus girls or show girls. **1910** *Variety* (Sept. 24) 14: A dozen charming looking "broilers" as Italian boys or girls. **1913** in *AS* XXXIV (1959) 20: We would like to know upon whom we place the blame for designating [young women]…as "ponies," "squabs," and "broilers."

broke *n.* Esp. *Gamb.* one who has been financially ruined; a person who is broke.
1966 "Minnesota Fats" *Bank Shot* 12: A Broke. A mooch without a quarter. *Ibid.* 94: I was always picking up old brokes and taking them to Washington Heights for a good meal. **1968** Blackford *Torp. Sailor* 32: Leaving a handful of brokes, nondrinkers, and the draft of boots who were afraid to leave the station.

broke *adj.* [with *broken*, formerly the S.E. p.ppl. of *break* 'to bankrupt']
1. bankrupted; *(hence)* without money. Now *S.E.*
*1661 in *F & H* VII 118: The Mermaid Tavern is lately broke, and our Christ Church men bear the blame of it, our ticks…amounting to 1500 £. ***1669** Pepys *Diary* (Mar. 12): Being newly broke by running in debt. ***1716** in *OEDS:* Alexr. Mackpherson…is much in arear and quit broke. **1821** in *OEDS:* I have been broke now twelve months…yet I move on in the old way. **1837** *Spirit of Times* (June 10) 132: I saw right on the last paper where most everybody in Orleans was broke. **1842** *Spirit of Times* (Apr. 2) 58: Barrett, poor fellow, is dead broke. **1844** *Spirit of Times* (Feb. 10) 580: Jim Wills was in Pittsburgh in that situation so common to play actors, viz., flat broke. **1847** in Blair & Meine *Half Horse* 129: He was "flat broke." **1848** "Pry" *Life in Baltimore* 80: As soon as I got back to Baltimore I was dead broke. **1848** [Judson] *Mysteries* 238: I am broke, flat broke! I haven't a dollar left! **1863** in Connolly *Army of Cumberland* 129: The usual salutation in Chattanooga now is: "How much money have you got," the universal answer being "Pretty well broke." **1866** *Night Side of N.Y.* 37: He declares himself "dead broke" and swears…hain't a cent of it left. **1869** in Spotts *With Custer* 104: We

are half fed and "dead broke." **1893** in J.I. White *Git Along Dogies* 94: But there's none more anxious to see spring/Than a cowboy who is broke….Cash gone, I'm a broke cowboy. **1898** in J. London *Letters* 10: They always go broke. **1908** in H.C. Fisher *A. Mutt* 27: I'm certainly up against it now. Dead broke! **1925** Mullin *Scholar Tramp* 67: I'm as broke as the ten commandments. **1931** Dos Passos *1919* 177: Joe hung around Boston broke for a couple of weeks. **1948** McHenry & Myers *Home Is Sailor* 163: If the company goes broke,…the ships won't sail at all. *a***1960** Fedoroff *Side of Angels* 241: "Where you live?" "No place, sir. I'm flat broke. I had to move out."

2. *Gamb.* without chips.

1848 [G.G. Foster] *N.Y. in Slices* 27: When one of the players is "broke," he passes a V or an X up to the dealer, and receives its equivalent in buttons.

¶ In phrase:

¶ **go for broke** [app. orig. Nisei or Hawaiian E; publicized during WWII as the motto of the Army's 442d Regimental Combat Team, recruited from Japanese Americans] to risk everything, esp. in a single, final attempt; (*hence*) to go all out.

1943 in Meyer *Stars & Stripes Story of WWII* 228: Our main slogan, though, is "Go for broke." That means the same thing as "Shoot the works" in American slang. The fellows first started to use the expression in a crap game. **1945** *New Yorker* (Mar. 31) 50: "I want to see everybody have a good time and get drunk. Let's go for broke." "Go for broke" is a Hawaiian pidgin expression conveying the idea of all-out endeavor. **1945** *Reader's Digest* (July) 66: The 442nd has a regimental motto…a picturesque Hawaiian idiom of the crap game, "Go for Broke"—meaning "shoot the works." **1964** Faust *Steagle* 177: Screw bomb plots, go for broke. **1966** Ward *Day of Absence* 25: Race members are urged to go for broke, yet cautioned not to ham it up too broadly. **1980** W.C. Anderson *BAT-21* 118: I'm sure they have urged their Viet buddies to go for broke to get hold of this…Colonel of ours. **1992** Strawberry & Rust *Darryl* 156: That was the kind of "go for broke" baseball that I enjoyed.

broke-dick *adj.* worthless.—usu. considered vulgar. Also **broken-dick**.

1967 Salas *Tattoo Wicked Cross* 208 [ref. to 1950's]: Beat on the punk, knock him around,…make him bawl like a broke-dick dog. **1980** DiFusco et al. *Tracers* 43 [ref. to Vietnam War]: You are one big broken-dick motherfucker, man. **1987** J. Thomas *Predator* (film): I wouldn't wish that on a broke-dick dog. **1990** Ruggero *38 N. Yankee* 241: The fuckers give us a broke-dick helicopter.

broken arrow *n.* [ref. to the penis] an inability to father children.

1963 Boyle *Yanks Don't Cry* 95 [ref. to WWII]: I'll make out like a burglar when I hit the States and tell all the gals…I've got a broken arrow. **1965** Leckie *Challenge* 195 [ref. to WWII]: You think I want a broken arrow?

broken-dick var. BROKE-DICK.

broken striper *n. Navy.* a chief warrant officer.

1914 *DN* : *Broken-striper*…A chief warrant officer. **1934** Weseen *Dict. Slang* 125: *Broken striper*—A chief warrant officer.

broker *n.* [BROKE + -(e)*r*] **1.** Orig. *Gamb.* a person who is broke.

1937 in D. Runyon *More Guys* 99: If there is anything that is a drug on the market around the tracks, it is the story of a broker. *a***1959** W.L. Warner *Living & Dead* 210: The "boomer" of yesterday and the "broker" of today. **1967** Maurer & Vogel *Narc. & Narc. Add.* (ed. 3) 345: *Broker.* A down and out addict.

2. *Commercial Fishing.* a commercial fishing trip that fails to meet expenses.

1942 *American Neptune* (July) 232 [ref. to 1915]: When the gross profits failed to equal the expenses, the trip was called a "broker." **1966** in *DARE*. **1977** Bartlett *Finest Kind* 111: Years ago there was a superstition among the fishermen that any boat going out on a Friday was certain to return to port with a broker; a busted trip on which no one would make any money.

broley *n.* [orig. unkn.] *Penna.* (see quots.).

1931 in J. OHara *Sel. Letters* 55: People like the half breed and so on…can be made to fit in with the brolies and the Irish and dirty black Protestant Welsh of Sch. Co…. **1934** J. O'Hara *Samarra* ch. iii: The hunkeys, the schwackies, the roundheaders, the broleys—regional names for non-Latin foreigners.

bromide *n.* **1.** [coined by the humorist Gelett Burgess, in ref.

to the sedative effect of medicinal bromide] an uninteresting or tiresomely conventional person.

1906 G. Burgess *Are You a Bromide?* (title). **1909** Irwin *Con Man* 126: We'll say that the sucker is about an average-minded man—What they're calling a "bromide" nowadays.

2. a platitude or cliché. Now *S.E.*

1920 Ade *Hand-Made Fables* 12: [He] pulled the dear old Bromide that he could drink it or leave it alone. **1923** Revell *Off the Chest* 44: George Kaufman and Marc Connelly can't get enough bromides into a three-act comedy to put a healthy audience to sleep. **1957** Kohner *Gidget* 81: "It's normal to be curious, Paul." "Save the bromide, Doctor." **1965** *Bonanza* (NBC-TV): You don't believe that old bromide, do you?

bronc *n. West.* a bronco. Now *S.E.*

1893 T. Roosevelt *Wilderness Hunter* 418: I saddled up the bronc' and lit out for home. **1897** *Cosmopolitan* (Mar.) 556: We was jes' about thro' breakin' our first batch of bronks. **1907** *McClure's* (Feb.) 435: So you just straddle your bronk, an' you an' me'll light out. **1911** in C.M. Russell *Paper Talk* 85: Here's to the driver that sat on the coach…[to] herd his bronk team with his whip. **1922** Rollins *Cowboy* 28: "Bronco"…was often contracted into "bronc" or "bronk," and also was interchangeable…with "mustang" and…"cayuse". **1947** Overholser *Buckaroo's Code* 148: It's Cotton's bronc….I gave him my black.

bronc *v. Med.* to examine by means of bronchoscopy.

1981 in Safire *Good Word* 152: The patient was bronked.

bronc-buster *n. West.* BRONCO-BUSTER. Now *colloq* or *S.E.*

1942 *ATS* 823. **1976** Wren *Bury Me Not* 63: We could use a good bronc buster.

bronc-fighter *n. West.* BRONCO-BUSTER.

1910 in C.M. Russell *Paper Talk* 79: I was sum suprised when you started filling me up what a bronk fighter you was. **1915** in J.I. White *Git Along Dogies* 144: Yore uh bronc fighter by the looks o' yer clothes. **1926** C.M. Russell *Trails* 165: The modern bronc fighter saddles an' steps across the bronc in a narrer chute. **1930** Sage *Last Rustler* 136: A bronc fighter on that outfit by the name of Bill.

bronco *n. Esp. West.* a rowdy.

1928 Callahan *Man's Grim Justice* 139: Play [women] once in a while, broncho, but don't tie up with 'em. **1944** Huie *Can Do!* 25: The…toughest and…most efficient bunch of hairy-chested broncos who ever went to war under the Stars and Stripes. **1953** E. Leonard *Bounty Hunters* 70: And a broncho chief doesn't get to be as old as he is on his good looks. **1971** Curtis *Banjo* 158: And I'll do my best to keep them broncos off'n you, if you'll just level with me.

bronco *adj.* [< Sp] *West.* wild; unrestrained; rowdy; (*hence*) thoroughgoing.

1866 in *OEDS*: The Territory did not keep fast horses and other things, and go to bronco bailes, and play whiskey poker. **1887** Francis *Saddle & Moccasin* 146: Sam's too broncho*; he gets all-fired mean sometimes when he's full….*Wild. **1898** in F. Remington *Sel. Letters* 224: You have been *broncho* so long. **1936** Duncan *Over the Wall* 213: Gee, Oregon, but you're sure gowed-up….You'll go broncho whiffing so much of that damned merry. **1942** Garcia *Tough Trip* 252: Those Injuns and the Pend d'Oreilles were bronco Catholics and prayed every time they ate. **1967–70** in *DARE*. **1970** Benteen *Apache Raiders* 63: Said he'd swear he saw a bunch of bronco Chirichauas, maybe thirty.

bronco-buster *n.* [bronco + BUST + -*er*] *West.* a horse-breaker. Now *S.E.*

1887 in Farmer *Amer.* 89: An Eastern or English horse-breaker and Western *broncho-buster* have so little in common with each other. **1888** T. Roosevelt, in *Century* (Feb.) 507: The flash riders, or horse-breakers, always called "bronco busters," can perform really marvelous feats. **1889** *Outing* (Feb.) 394: The life of one of these "broncho busters," as they are called, requires much nerve and daring. **1899** Garland *Eagle's Heart* 88: That's what a broncho buster would do. **1905** W.S. Kelly *Lariats* 260: Yer claim to be a broncho buster. **1922** Rollins *Cowboy* 39: To these various legitimate titles, conscious slang added "bronco peeler," "bronco twister," and "bronco buster."

bronc-peeler *n. West.* BRONCO-BUSTER. Also **bronco-peeler**.

1904 Bower *Lonesome* 197: But Pink was not known all over Northern Montana as a "bronco-peeler" for nothing. **1914** in *DA*: He used to brag he was the boss Bronc-peeler at this ridin' game. **1922** Evarts *Settling of Sage* 35: They're bronc peelers that can ride 'em before they're broke. **1925** W. James *Drifting Cowboy* 27: The bronc peeler would be picking a bunch of green colts from the stock horses and start in breaking. **1926** W. James *Smoky* 126: Jeff recognized that man as his "bronc peeler" Clint. **1938** in Botkin *Treas. Amer. Folk.* 193: It was the way of the ranch-hand, the mustanger, the bronc-peeler.

bronc-stomper *n. West.* BRONCO-BUSTER.

1935 Coburn *Law Rides Range* 7: Almanac Jones bet that bronc stomper from the Long-X a bottle of whiskey. **1936** McCarthy *Mosshorn* (unp.): *Bronc Buster*…also called a bronc-stomper, bronc-peeler, and bronc-fighter. **1979** Decker *Holdouts* 92: Used to be a helluva bronc stomper, but he got his back hurt and had to take to bartending. **1992** J. Garry *This Ol' Drought* 89: The cowboy, quite a bronc stomper, was steering him…by hitting him on the side of the head with his hat.

bronc-twister *n. West.* BRONCO-BUSTER. Also **bronco-twister.**

1912 *DN* III 550: *Broncho twister*, same meaning as "broncho buster." **1916** in *DA:* You'd have made a fine bronc twister. **1922** (quot. at BRONCO-BUSTER). **1926** W. James *Smoky* 81: Clint [was] the bronc twister of the "Rocking R" outfit. **1927** Rollins *Jinglebob* [ref. to 1880's]: Things has to look fairly skedaddlesome afore a bronc twister begins…to worry.

Bronx Bombers *n.pl.* [Yankee Stadium is situated in the Bronx, N.Y.] *Baseball Journ.* the New York Yankees.

1937 in *AS* (Feb. 1938) 33: *Bronx Bombers* (Yankees)…is apt because of the heavy hitting of the team. **1990** *U.S. News & W.R.* (Aug. 6) 48: [Yankees owner Steinbrenner] declared that the Bronx Bombers of yore were too devoted to home runs.

Bronx cheer *n.* a loud spluttering noise made with the tongue protruding from the lips to show contempt or disgust; RASPBERRY. Now *colloq.* or *S.E.*

1927 T.A. Dorgan, in Zwilling *TAD Lexicon* 20: The old Bronx cheer ringing in his ear. **1929** in *OEDS:* Maxim gave him a Bronx cheer. **1936** C. Sandburg *People, Yes* 238: Bronx cheers, the razzberry, the bum's rush. **1942** *Life* (Nov. 2) 46: Bronx cheer (razz) punctuates Wallace's rendition of *Der Fuehrer's Face.* **1944** Kapelner *Lonely Boy* 58: Skinny stuck his tongue between his lips and produced a Bronx Cheer. **1948** in Asimov, Greenberg & Olander *Sci. Fi. Short Shorts* 32: He….blew a low outrageous note like the sound of a Bronx cheer. **1952** in Yates *Loneliness* 45: Our response would have been a long and unanimous Bronx cheer. **1955** Nabokov *Lolita* 48: When angry Lo with a Bronx cheer had gone, I stayed on from sheer inertia. **1969** Moynahan *Pairing Off* 95: The sound of a muted bronx cheer wafted through the wire. **1970** Corrington *Bombardier* 49: As he reached the door, Krepinski gave him a Bronx cheer. **1990** *CBS This Morning* (CBS-TV) (Jan. 2): Zsa Zsa…got a round of Bronx cheers from spectators. **1993** *New Yorker* (June 7) 8: They listened…contemptuously and then gave him a big Bronx cheer.

Bronx Indian *n. N.Y.C.* BROOKLYN INDIAN.

1942 *ATS.*

Bronze John *n.* [play on YELLOWJACK] yellow fever.

1862 in A.K. Davis *Boy Col.* 143: N.O.…has fallen…not without the consoling reflection that the Yankees will have to encounter "Bronze John" or "Yaller Jack." This…is the year for…yellow fever. **1869** *Overland Mo.* (Aug.) 130: As for diseases, "Bronze John" is pretty well known for yellow fever. **1955** in *DARE.*

Brooklyn *n. Bowling.* (see 1979 quot.).

1949 Cummings *Dict. Sports* 51. **1979** Cuddon *Dict. Sports & Games* 165: *Brooklyn*…A hit made on the side of the headpin opposite to the hand delivering the ball.

Brooklyn Indian *n. N.Y.C.* a Jew.—used disparagingly. *Joc.* Cf. BRONX INDIAN.

1967 *West. Folklore* XXVI 189: *Brooklyn Indians*—Jews…heard in service during World War II.

Brooks *n.pl. Baseball.* the Brooklyn Dodgers. Now *hist.*

1946 *N.Y. Times* (July 14) V 2: MacPhail bought him for the Brooks…in mid-season of 1939. **1950** Cleveland *Great Mgrs.* 222: But in 1949 the best the Brooks could do was to win a single game.

broom *v.* to hasten, esp. away; to leave.—usu. constr. with *off.*

*1821 Moncrieff *Tom & Jerry* 6: That will do—now then Dicky, mizzle!—be scarce!—broom! **1932** in *AS* (Feb. 1934) 26: *Broom.* To flee from danger; to leave. **1944** Kendall *Service Slang* 46: *Brooming*….rapid speed. **1944** Burley *Hndbk. Jive* 135: *Broom* (verb)—To walk, run, flee, move hurriedly away. **1946** Mezzrow & Wolfe *Really Blues* 144: All our buddies broomed off to Tin-Pan-Alley-land **1956** Hargrove *Girl He Left* 16: He would have taken one look at her….and broomed off quickly, leaving no forwarding address. **1958** Gilbert *Vice Trap* 79: Man, broom off. Can't you see I'm pre-occupied? **1958** Russell *Perm. Playboy* 66: Broom off, son….Broom 'way off. **1961** R. Russell *Sound*

22: He broomed in from the Apple. **1967** Talbot *Chatty Jones* 152: Afterward I'm brooming off. **1973** in R.S. Gold *Jazz Talk* 34: Lenny would take off for a couple of days and broom down to L.A.

broom handle *n. Naut.* (see quot.).

1835 *Mil. & Nav. Mag. of U.S.* (Sept.) 46: We had as well send down them there broom handles (*i.e.,* royal yards,) and take two reefs in the pudding bags (topsails).

broomie *n. West.* a range mare; broomtail.

1922 Rollins *Cowboy* 28 [ref. to 1890's]: Both South and North might betake themselves to slang and talk of "fuzzies" (Range horses) and "broomies" or "broom tails" (Range mares). **1945** in *DARE.* **1967** Schaefer *Mavericks* 118: He was usin' that thing to spot lil ol' broomies back in the canyons.

brother *n.* **1.** (used in direct address to a man, esp. one whose name is not known).

1912 *DN* III 572: Say, brother, can you tell me how far it is to Veedersburg? **1915** Poole *Harbor* 156: I'm in a hole, brother, a hell of a hole. **1921** J. Conway, in *Variety* (Feb. 25) 23: And believe me, brother, I did. **1926** Tully *Jarnegan* 65: It's on me, brother. **1928** Fisher *Jericho* 297: *Brother.* A form of address, usually ironic. A bystander, witnessing the arrest of some offender, may observe, "It's too bad now, brother." **1940** Busch & Swerling *Westerner* (film): You're loco, brother.

2. *Black E.* a black man; SOUL BROTHER.

1910 T.A. Dorgan, in *N.Y. Eve. Jour.* (Feb. 3) 14: If Johnson hooks that right up, those meerschaum-colored brothers in the South will be wearing diamond rings and plug hats. **1919–21** Chicago Comm. *Race Relations Negro in Chi.* 563: The poor proprietor of the place, if he or she is one of the "brothers" or "sisters," is almost helpless in the matter. **1946** Boulware *Jive & Slang* 2: *Brother in Black*….Negro. **1962** H. Simmons *On Eggshells* 226: Brothers and sisters, you dig that? **1963** *Time* (Aug. 2) 14: *Brother*….Fellow Negro. **1975** Wambaugh *Choirboys* 32: You don't just hate brothers. You hate *everyone.* **1979** Hiler *Monkey Mt.* 126: I wonder where all the brothers are? **1988** *Right On!* (June) 24: It's the first hour show on the air with a brother in the lead. **1987–91** D. Gaines *Teenage Wasteland* 135: In teen jail like the baddest of the bad—the brothers (blacks).

3. *Black E.* fellow; comrade in arms.

*a***1984** in Terry *Bloods* 91: Then this white brother said, "say, hey. I'm from D.C." **1990** *Kid 'n' Play* (NBC-TV): Play, you're a cool brother….You're a lucky brother. **1992** *Mystery Sci. Theater* (Comedy Central-TV): Ohh! The brother's got his own horn section! **1994** *New Yorker* (Jan. 17) 39: He greeted me as "brother"…he smiled and hailed numerous "brothers" and "sisters," black and white, who greeted him.

¶ In phrase:

¶ **everybody and his brother** absolutely everybody.

1928 Fisher *Jericho* 182: Then every son-of-a-gun and his brother unhitches a hell of a whoop. **1983** Univ. Tenn. instructor: Everybody and his brother's got one of those Walkmans now.

brother-in-law *v.* to surreptitiously court the wife or girlfriend of (another man).

1924 in D. Hammett *Continental Op* 64: "Where's Kewpie?" I asked. "Brother-in-lawing Ed?" a big Swede girl leered at me.

brought down *adj.* [fr. BRING DOWN, *v.*] *Black E.* sad; dispirited; downcast.

1946 Mezzrow & Wolfe *Really Blues* 22: When he's brought down he gets ugly. **1948** Manone & Vandervoort *Trumpet* 98: Whenever I am sad or brought down, if I can just get back to New Orleans for a little while I feel fine again.

brown *n.* **1.** a copper cent.

1857 in Thornton *Amer. Gloss.* II 971: All the "browns" his uncle lent him.

2.a. anal copulation.—usu. considered vulgar.

ca*1888–94** in Karlen *Sex. & Homosex.* 173: Are you fond of a bit of brown?…We [homosexuals] always say a bit of brown among ourselves, and a cunt's a bit of red. **1934** "J.M. Hall" *Anecdota* 16: Lots of brown, lots of brown,…In fairy town. ***1961** Partridge *DSUE* (ed. 5) 1016: *A bit of brown,* an act of sodomy: ?mid-C.19–20. **1967** J. Hersey *Algiers Motel* 101: No, your honor, this is what they call it. They usually refer to it as either a fuck or a brown.

b. the anus; ASS; in phr. **up your brown!** (used as a vulgar retort).—usu. considered vulgar.

1916 Cary *Venery* I 24: *Brown*—The fundament. *Up one's brown*—To commit sodomy. **1927** *Immortalia* 87: He knocked her down upon her brown. **1929–30** J.T. Farrell *Young Lonigan* 71: Up your brown!

sneered Weary. **1931** J.T. Farrell *McGinty* 180: Jesus, every one of us gets it rammed up our brown before we're through. **1938** "Justinian" *Americana Sexualis* 14: Up your brown! **1948** Wolfert *Act of Love* 420: I'll give him…a bulldozer…right up his brown till it's stuck there. **1965** Linakis *In Spring* 209: "It seemed that the president of the court was a friend of the colonel's." "No wonder they stuck it up your brown." **1967** Schmidt *Lexicon of Sex* 21: Bite the brown…To lick…the anus. **1983** *Nat. Lampoon* (Feb.) 61: Better you get bombed in the brown than him, hey?

3. BROWN-NOSE.

1943 *School & Soc.* LVIII 169: *Brown*: one who flatters a teacher to improve marks. **1965–70** in *DARE* I 395. **1987–91** D. Gaines *Teenage Wasteland* 91: Browns…were busy sucking up to teachers.

4. *Black E.* a young brown-skinned black person, esp. one's sweetheart.

1914 in Handy *Treasury of Blues* 71: You ought to see dat stovepipe brown of mine/Lak he owns de Dimon Joseph line. **1927** in N. Cohen *Long Steel Rail* 406: Just want to talk to that brown of mine. **1929** T. Gordon *Born to Be* 224: All the pretty browns in town'll be there. **1954** Killens *Youngblood* 112: I likes me one of them teasing browns.

¶ In phrase:

¶ **in the brown** currying favor with a superior.

1938 R. McDavid, in *AS* (Feb. 1939) 27: *Get In The Brown (With)*, v. To win favorable recognition (of superiors). **1964** Faust *Steagle* 55: Get out of the brown…Cut the goddam sir. I was only a corporal.

brown *adj. & adv.* ¶ In phrase: **do [up] brown, 1.** to swindle, victimize, trounce, or defeat (someone) thoroughly.

*1824 in Partridge *DSUE* (ed. 5) 1016: He is then said to be "cooked," or "done brown" and "dished." **1842** *Spirit of Times* (June 4) 162: No less than $1500 were picked up by one party in…Georgetown…Of course in Washington many were "done brown." **1846** Durivage & Burnham *Stray Subjects* 94: *Ham* was a sort of "Jethro"—the butt of his two brothers—who had done him "brown" so many times that they called him "burnt." **1847** in J.R. Lowell *Poetical Wks.* 195: Fer the matter o' thet, it's notorious in town/Thet her own representatives du her quite brown. **1847** in *Indiana Mag. of Hist.* (1961) 35: Old Zack has done it up brown. **1851** Melville *Moby-Dick* ch. iii: I rayther guess you'll be done *brown* if that ere harpooner hears you a-slanderin' his head. **1854** St. Clair *Metropolis* 93: Taken in and done for…Done brown, too, at that. ***1861** in *F & H* I 338: If we wallops him well, we will do him up brown. **1895** Townsend *Fadden & Others* 5: Dem's 'er very words. No, not "done 'im brown"; dat's wot dey meaned—say, "trashed 'im well." Dat's right. **1897** Hamblen *General Mgr.'s Story* 84: The old man had him just where he had wanted to get him for years, and he did him up brown. **1932** V. Fisher *Tragic Life* 214: This is where I do you up brown.

2. to do (something) thoroughly, excellently, or perfectly.

1843 in G.W. Harris *High Times* 29: Those are places where things are done up brown! **1867** Clark *Sailor's Life* 37: We…rambled about the town until we had "done it brown." **1873** *Slang & Vulgar Forms* 11: *Done up brown*, for *handsomely, thoroughly, effectually,* or *adroitly done*.…A very low phrase. **1908** Paine *Stroke Oar* 132: You did your duty, Mr. Hansen, and you did it up brown. **1914** Z. Grey *West. Stars* 134: You're so hell-bent on doin' it up brown. **1930** in D.O. Smith *Cradle* 137: We could have done things brown with 10 more percent. **1961** Sullivan *Shortest, Gladdest Years* 148: I'd like to see you do it up brown, too. **1971** Horan *Blue Messiah* 168: Let's do it up brown.

brown *v.* **1.** to darn; curse.—used optatively.

1927 C. McKay *Home to Harlem* 34: Well, I'll be browned! **1928** C. McKay *Banjo* 33: But brown me ef I'm a telling-it-too-much kind a darky.

2. to have active anal copulation with.—usu. considered vulgar.

1929–33 Farrell *Manhood of Lonigan* 188: "We'll brown the Kaiser," shouted Kenny. **1933** Ford & Tyler *Young & Evil* 163: He wanted to brown I mean bugger me. **1934** "J.M. Hall" *Anecdota* 16: "Where did you get that simply divine new overcoat?" "Browning King's, dear." "I didn't ask you how, I asked you where." **1949** *Gay Girl's Guide* 4: *Brown*: To have anal intercourse, with reference to active partner. **1953–55** Kantor *Andersonville* 260: They talked of corn-holing, browning and other mysteries unknown to Floral Tebbs. **1971** *Blushes & Bellylaffs* 85: "Which do you like the best, Browning or Kipling?"…"I wouldn't know…I've never been kippled." **1987** E. White *Beautiful Room* 40: Being screwed—we call that being browned.…Continental gentlemen like to brown each other. **1986–89** Norse *Memoirs* 89: "Born to be browned," he crooned airily.

3. *Stu.* BROWN-NOSE, *v.* Also **brown up to.**

1961 *AS* XXXVI 150: *To brown*…a teacher. **1965** W. Hoffman *Yancey's War* 23: "It's your business if you want to brown the cooks.…You've been buying the cooks beer." "Now, Charley, brown's a pretty strong word." **1965–70** in *DARE*: Brown. *Ibid.* Brown up to. **1974** Kingry *Monk & Marines* 170: He had browned up to Father Peter enough and sold us each out.

brown-bag *v.* **1.** (in areas where the sale of liquor is prohibited) to carry liquor in a public place or restaurant concealed in a brown paper bag; to drink liquor so concealed.—also constr. with *it*. Hence **brown-bagger.**

1966 in *OEDAS*: "Brown-bagging"—buying the bottle at a state liquor shop and carrying it in a plain brown wrapper to restaurants. **1967–68** von Hoffman *Parents Warned Us* 190: He listened, brown-bagging booze. *Ibid.* 190: The only brown-baggers left on the street were people who enjoyed it, real juiceheads. **1972** *Business Week* (Dec. 23) 102: It has no liquor license, but don't be surprised to see the likes of Onassis and Stavros brown-bagging their wine—it often happens. **1979** W. Cross *Kids & Booze* 100: I was brown-bagging it all over. **1979** in Raban *Old Glory* 303: Brown-bagging is *legal*. What's *illegal* is carrying around your bottle without your bag.

2. to take one's lunch to work.—also constr. with *it*. Hence **brown-bagger.**

1968 *U.S. News & W.R.* (Sept. 16) 73: I'm a "brown-bagger"—carry my own lunch to work. **1973** Wambaugh *Onion Field* 70: Few policemen brownbagged on a Saturday night. It was the night to eat as well as they could afford. **1982** *U.S. News & W.R.* (Apr. 19) 49: It's the difference between brown-bagging it and going out to lunch or affording a concert ticket every now and then. **1987** J. Thompson *Gumshoe* 206: He'd just been there—"brown-bagging" it at lunchtime—when Morris's call came in.

brown-bagger *n.* **1.** *Stu.* an overly diligent student.

1950 in Safire *Language Maven* 17: The deskbound undergraduate has been…damned as…a *brown bagger*. **1984–88** in *Ibid.* 18: When I was a student at MIT [*ca*1954], excessively studious students were called brown-baggers because they always carried their books with them, often in a shapeless brown bag.

2. *Mil.* a married man in military service.

1947 *ATS* (Supp.) 13: *Brown bagger,* a married serviceman. **1956** *AS* XXXI 227: *Brown-bagger, n.* Originally, a married person [in the U.S. Air Force] who brought his lunch in a brown paper bag. Today, a common term for any married man. **1958** Frankel *Band of Bros.* 180 [ref. to 1950]: Bet you…that guy in the second plane's a second looie, and no brown-bagger. **1961** L. Sanders *4-Yr. Hitch* 148: Brownbaggers…had wives and family ashore in the area.

3. see BROWN-BAG, *v.*

brownbar *n.* [cf. BUTTERBAR; infl. by BROWN-NOSE] *Mil.* a second lieutenant. [Quots. all ref. to Vietnam War.]

1977 Caputo *Rumor of War* 31: I was alliteratively known as the "boot brown-bar," slang for a second lieutenant. **1978** Former USAF missile crewman: We called second lieutenants *brownbars* or *second johns* in 1973. **1978** Former USAF B-52 navigator: A second lieutenant was a *brownbar*. That was a common expression in 1968. **1978** *Nat. Lampoon* (July) 67: *Brown bar*…Second Lieutenant. **1978** J. Webb *Fields of Fire* 87: Snake measured his new Brown Bar carefully, not yet accepting him. **1980** Baker *Nam* 121: They were all with colonels and didn't want to know no brown bar out of the bush. **1985** Dye *Between Raindrops* 252: How many chances does a brown-bar get to command a company in combat?

Brown Bess *n.* Esp. *Mil.* a musket. Also **Brown Betty, Brown Betsy.** Now *hist.*

*1785 Grose *Vulgar Tongue*: *Brown Bess*, a soldier's firelock. *To hug brown bess,* to carry a firelock, or serve as a private soldier. **1833** J. Hall *Soldier's Bride* 241: "Brown Bess,"—for so he called his rifle. **1842** *Ben Hardin's Crockett* (unp.): I klapped the breech of brown Betty to my shoulders. **1849** *Spirit of Times* (Nov. 10) 452: I took "Brown Betsy," my old two shooter [double-barreled gun]. **1857** *Spirit of Times* (Dec. 19) 531: Theories coeval with "old Brown Bess" and her advocates. **1864** *Battle-Fields of So.* 312: Many old wiseheads still seem to prefer the smooth-bore musket—brown Bess as it is called. **1941** Craige *Marines* 69: Most numerous were tower muskets, the celebrated British "Brown Bess," captured from the enemy. **1944** Pennell *Rome Hanks* 44: Two Shawnees…had killed his father with an old Brown Betsy.

Brown Bet *n.* a brown bottle containing liquor. Cf. BLACK BETTY.

1807 J.R. Shaw *Autobiog.* 116: Tipping me a little out of brown Bet, which contained some double fortified stimulus [*sic*].

brown bomber *n. Army.* a laxative pill.

1941 Kendall *Army & Navy Slang* 2: *Brown bombers*...CC pills, the army laxative. **1957** Atwell *Private* 92 [ref. to 1944]: Bout the only thing Ah got here's a brown bomber....Unless you're powerful constipated, don't think Ah'd advise it. **1984** Elting et al. *Soldier Talk.*

brown bottle *n.* a brown beer bottle.

1976 *Sci. & Mech. CB Gde.* 158: How're you fixed for brown bottles?

browned off *adj. Esp. Mil. Av.* downcast, disgusted, or fed up; (*hence*, most commonly) angry. [Adopted esp. from RAF, 1941–42; see Partridge *DSUE* (ed. 5) 1016 for discussion.]

***1936** Partridge *DSUE* 97: *Browned-off.* Depressed; disgusted; having given up hope: Royal Air Force: from *ca*1920; slightly ob[solescent]. ***1938** in *OEDS*: What the hell had he got to be so browned off about? He ought to be feeling proper chirpy. **1940** in *AS* XVI 76 (RAF): *To Be Properly Browned Off.* To be fed up. **1941** *Sat. Eve. Post* (Oct. 4) 11: *Browned off.* To be fed up with boredom. **1945** J. Bryan *Carrier* 106: The Admiral's going to be plenty browned off when we get back. **1946** G.C. Hall, Jr. *1000 Destroyed* 244: The other pilots were browned off...they were vexed and disappointed because no Huns had come up to meet them. **1946** Bowker *Out of Uniform* 35: Most of them were browned off at the theorists, considering such stuff libelous, no matter how well-intentioned. **1946** Dos Passos *Tour* 262: And are we browned off?...Oh, my aching back! **1957** E. Brown *Locust Fire* 157: "And the next morning the prices were tripled on everything." "There must have been some browned-off G.I.'s out there. **1962** W. Crawford *Give Me Tomorrow* 48: First off Lootinit Zoller asked Dodge if he was battle-happy. Dodge said no he wasn't shook and he wasn't asiatic either. He was just plenty browned off. **1965** Borowik *Lions* 70: And also she's just plain browned off. **1967** D. Reed *Up Front in Viet.* 104: Delta Six is browned off. They won't let him go in after wounded. **1968** Coppel *Order of Battle* 98: Porta's really browned off, Dev. **1970** Woods *Killing Zone* 98: Is he browned off?

browneye *n.* **1.** *pl.* [ref. to the color of the nipple and areola] a woman's breasts.

1932 *AS* (June) 329: *Big brown eyes*—breasts. **1968** Baker et al. *CUSS* 89: *Brown eyes.* The female breasts. **1990** P. Dickson *Slang!* 196: *Big brown eyes.* Nipples and areolas.

2. the anus; (*hence*) anal copulation.

1954 Wepman et al. *The Life* 111: Her cunt opened like a gash,/And her brown-eye lost all its feeling. **1967** Maurer & Vogel *Narc. & Narc. Add.* (ed. 3) 345: *Browneye.* Coitus *per anum.* **1971** Hilaire *Thanatos* 278: They can't see nothing except a brown eye looking back. **1976** *Nat. Lampoon* (July) 72: My personal physician, Dr. Sawyer Browneye, warned me. **1983** K. Weaver *Texas Crude* 77: *The winking brown eye.* The anus. **1986–89** Norse *Memoirs* 95 [ref. to WWII]: We waited in line and watched "short-arm" and "brown-eye" inspection.

brownie *n.* **1.** a copper coin; (*specif.*) a U.S. cent.

***1823** "J. Bee" *Slang: Brownie*, a copper coin. **1924** in D. Hammett *Continental Op* 65: He's going to need every brownie he can scrape up. **1928** Peterkin *Sister Mary* 295: Me an' my chillen don' want not a brownie you got. **1944** Burley *Hndbk. Jive* 135: *Brownie.* Cent. **1950** *PADS* XIV 17: *Brownie*...A cent piece. **1958** Bontemps & Hughes *Negro Folklore* 481: *Brownie*: Cent, a penny. **1981** in *DARE* I 395.

2.a. a brown-skinned Asian person.—usu. used contemptuously.

1876 Miller *First Fam'lies* 85: Washee-Washee will lie...but he steals no more—do you, little brownie? **1899** Bonsal *Golden Horseshoe* 313: We wanted to push the brownies over the Zapote and bag Imus which has been [Aguinaldo's] principal powwow place for a long time. **1966** Wilson *LBJ Brigade* 70: We ain't here ta defend or capture anythin', we're here ta kill the brownies.

b. *Angling.* a brown trout.

1949 Cummings *Dict. Sports* 52.

c. *Black E.* **BROWN**, *n.*, 4.

1945 Saxon *Gumbo* 13: When them ships come in, that's when I made money. All them sailors wanted a brownie. **1960** Oliver *Convers. with Blues* 36: My brownie done quit me—God knows, she had it all.

3. *R.R.* a demerit.

1910 in Botkin & Harlow *R.R. Folklore* 313: You are supposed to take the "Brownies" without talking back. **1929** *Bookman* (July) 525: I thought the most I'd get would be thirty days or thirty brownies but darned if he didn't fire me off the road. **1931** *Writer's Digest* (May) 41: *Brownies*—Demerit marks placed against an employee's service record.

1941 in Fenner *Throttle* 175: Billy Lomax, the fireman...got the blame and ten brownies. **1942** *Sat. Eve. Post* (June 13) 27: Joe Smith just got hit with sixty brownies. **1945** Hubbard *R.R. Ave.* 335: *Brownies*—Demerits. This system is traced back to George R. Brown, general superintendent of the Fall Brook Railway (now part of the New York Central) in 1885.

4. a male homosexual anal sodomist; catamite.

1916 in J. Katz *Gay/Lesbian Almanac* 367: In New York they are known as "fairies."...In Philadelphia they are known as "Brownies." **1921** Lind *Impersonators* 89: Androgynes [are] known as "fairies," "fags," or "brownies." ***1931** Hanley *Boy* 140: In any ship excepting this...he'd be used as a Brownie. **1968** Gover *JC* 121: Hell, he don't gotta hit on teenage boys. Plenty brownies hangin out. **1972** *Anthro. Linguistics* (Mar.) 99: *Brownie* (n.): A homosexual who prefers anal intercourse.

5.a. the anus.

1927 [Fliesler] *Anecdota* 186: "What have you...a large Brownie or..."..."Ah didn't come here to be insulted." **1950** Del Torto [caption under drawing of toilet paper]: Film for your brownie. **1985** "Blow-dryer" *Mod. Eng.* 70: Anal Orifice...Brownie.

b. the buttocks; (*hence*) the female genitalia.

1977 Stallone *Paradise Alley* 55: C'mon, Doll, whatta savin' ya brownie for, the worms? *Ibid.* 75: She was one of the hookers hawkin' their brownies over at the Sunset Hotel.

6. *Stu.* **BROWN-NOSE**.

1944 in *AS* XX 147: *Brownie.* A person who is always asking and answering questions in class to impress the instructor. Also a person who stays after class to try to insinuate himself into the teacher's good graces. **1966** in *IUFA Folk Speech*: *Brownie*—Someone who tries to butter up a teacher or influencial [*sic*] person. **1968** in Brunvand *Study Amer. Folklore* 333: Ask a college class what word they use to denote a fellow student who curries favor with the teacher: students under 30 years of age will usually answer "brown-nose" or "brownie," the boys' etymology relating the term to a particularly offensive anatomical contact, the girls' to the practice of Brownie scouts of working for merit points. **1969** Zindel *Hamburger* 3: "Now I'll turn the meeting over to the class president, Pierre Jefferson"..."A big brownie." **1965–70** in *DARE*. **1978** Wheeler & Kerby *Steel Cowboy* (film): The company brownies get all the good jobs. **1992** L. Johnson *My Posse* 66: Every...student refused to speak to me. Even the "brownies."

7. *pl. cap. Baseball.* the St. Louis Browns. Now *hist.*

1974 A. Bergman *Kiss Off* 126: To me they looked like the same old Brownies.

brownie *v. Stu.* **BROWN-NOSE**, *v.*

1965–70 in *DARE*.

brownie point *n.* [from the point system used for advancement by the Brownies of the Girl Scouts of America; but strongly reinforced by **BROWN-NOSE**] a credit toward advancement or good standing, esp. when gained by servility, opportunism, or the like.

1944–53 in *MSU Folklore* GF2.1: Army Jargon 29: Blew his stack. Brownie points. **1958** J. Davis *College Vocab.* 12: *Brownie Points*—Apple polishing marks. **1962** in *AS* (Oct. 1963) 169: To curry favor with a professor...*get brownie points.* **1966** Jarrett *Pvt. Affair* 30: At the time he was piling up Brownie points with vice raids and needed a new sitting duck. **1975** Hynek & Vallee *Edge of Reality* 197: [Project] Blue Book was always looking to make brownie points for the Pentagon. **1976** Conroy *Santini* 15: You rack up brownie points with Mom and maintain the image of the perfect son? **1987** Horowitz *Campus Life* 191: Students also seek to better their marks by getting "brownie points."

brownie queen *n. Homosex.* a male homosexual who performs the passive role in anal copulation.

1962–68 B. Jackson *In the Life* 418: Supposed to be when you get fucked in the back....We call that a brownie queen. **1972** *Anthro. Linguistics* (Mar.) 99: *Brownie Queen* (n.): A homosexual who receives anal intercourse (the insertee). **1987** E. White *Beautiful Room* 40: Being browned, and the person is a brownie queen.

browning queen *n. Homosex.* **BROWNIE QUEEN**.

1949 *Gay Girl's Guide* 4: *Browning Queen (B-Q)*: A homosexual whose principal interest is anal. Properly used with reference to passive partner, loosely used for active one, too (for which, rarely, *Browning-King*). **1971** Rader *Gov't. Inspect.* 40: The browning queens made their nightly circuits.

brown job *n.* **1.** an instance of insincere flattery or brown-nosing.

1964 Allen *High White Forest* 347 [ref. to WWII]: You don't need a brown job from me. But…you're a better soldier than Lemmering ever was.

2. *Homosex.* an act of anilingus.

1970 Landy *Underground Dict.* 40: *Brown Job n.* Oral copulation of the anus. **1976** Men's room graffito, Knoxville, Tenn.: Freddy gives such a good brown job.

brown-nose *n.* [of scatological inspiration but not now considered vulgar] Orig. *Mil.* a toady; an obsequious sycophant. Hence **brown-noser.**

1938 R. McDavid, in *AS* (Feb. 1939) 25: *Brown Nose*…n. a cadet who curries favor. **1941** Kendall *Army & Navy Slang* 2: *Brown nose*…handshaker or army politician. **1946** J.H. Burns *Gallery* 194: Ya know what they call me? Brown-nose. They said that no second lieutenant should be the roommate of his commanding officer. **1946** Bowker *Out of Uniform* 124: To describe what was formerly called an "apple-polisher," the service expression was "brown nose," but its implications were presumably too lurid for general adoption. **1950** Hemingway *Across River* 251: Except the brown-nosers…and all the jerks from wherever who never fought and hold commands. **1958** Plagemann *Steel Cocoon* 119: They took to calling him Brown Nose, and pursed their lips and made loud sucking, kissing noises when he appeared. **1963** Cameron *Black Camp* 95: You're getting to be a brown-nose, Arnold. **1980** *Atlantic* (Dec.) 50: He knew folderol when he saw it…and he was no brown-noser.

brown-nose *v.* Orig. *Mil.* to curry favor (from) in an obsequious way; to toady (to). Also intrans.

1938 R. McDavid, in *AS* (Feb. 1939) 25: *Brown Nose*…To curry favor, especially for rank. [**1945** in Shibutani *Co. K* 119: He's always browning his nose on the colonel's ass.] **1944–46** in *AS* XXII 54: *To Brown Nose.* To toady or play for favors with a superior. **1947** Mailer *Naked & Dead* 230: Brown had always thought, Stanley's brown-nosing me. **1948** J.H. Burns *Lucifer* 126: I hate to say this to you cause you'll say I'm brown-nosin. **1948** Cozzens *Guard of Honor* 115: That's what I'd do, before I went brown-nosing this bastard. **1950** Hemingway *Across River* 65: It is not that I have erected the defense against brown-nosing my superiors and brown-nosing the world. **1953** Harris *Southpaw* 118: But he will not brown-nose. **1953** Paley *Rumble* 11: So what if you got to brownnose the hatch boss or clean out his front yard on a slow day. **1962** Killens *Heard the Thunder* 15 [ref. to WWII]: My man here been brown-nosing ever since he got inside the gate. That's how come his breath smells so bad. **1963** Ross *Dead Are Mine* 13: He's ratted off everything he's seen to Lieutenant Felix…and now he's brown-nosed his way into the platoon radio job. **1964** "Dr. X" *Intern* 265: Most of the time he's brown-nosing Emery or Meadows or one of the other surgeons. **1966** "T. Pendleton" *Iron Orchard* 268: You already got his goddamn bank account. Quit brown-nosin' him! **1975** C.W. Smith *Country Music* 7: The former classmate…had brown-nosed his way into the coveted position. **1979** *L.A. Times Book Rev.* (Sept. 30) 1: Wolfe…[paints] him as a priggish, brown-nosing, ambitious hero-on-the-make. **1991** B.E. Ellis *American Psycho* 387: Bateman's such a bloody ass-kisser, such a brown-nosing goody-goody.

brown-nosed *adj.* Orig. *Mil.* sycophantic. Also **brown-nose.**

1938 R. McDavid in *AS* (Feb. 1939) 25: *Brown Nose*…adj. desirous of rank to the point of currying favor. **1953** Paley *Rumble* 50: What a brown-nose job the bulls can do when you are nice. **1959** Cochrell *Barren Beaches* 313: Drop dead, you brown-nosed bastard. **1974** Univ. Wisc. student: He's more brownnose than that other guy.

brown out *n. Surfing.* an act of exposing one's buttocks, esp. while surfing. *Joc.* [Definition in 1964 quot. is prob. euphem.]

1964 *Look* (June 30) 55: *Brown-out*: riding backwards to shore (very difficult). **1977** Filosa *Surf. Almanac* 183. **1985** Schwendinger & Schwendinger *Adolescent Sub.* 99: Equally astonishing in [the early 1960's] was the "brown-out"—that is, the exhibiting of one's "bare ass" through a car window….This particular stunt…was…identified with [surfers].

brownshoe *n.* **1.** *Navy.* a U.S. naval officer who is an aviator; (now *also*) a submariner. [See 1952 quot. for allusion, and cf. BLACKSHOE.]

1952 Cope & Dyer *Petty Off. Gde.* 424: *Brown shoe* (Slang). A naval aviator; formerly only aviation officers wore brown shoes with khaki. **1962** Quirk *No Red Ribbons* 140 [ref. to WWII]: The Air Belonged to the Brown Shoes. In his Brown Shoe world Paul was the master. **1966** Noel & Bush *Naval Terms* 75: *Brown shoe:* Slang: naval aviator. **1971** Noel & Bush *Naval Terms* (ed. 2) 47: *Brown shoe:* slang: naval aviator or

submariner….The term originally referred to uniforms; only aviators and submariners wore khakis and the brown shoes that went with them.

2. *Mil. Av.* an infantry soldier.

ca1964 K. Cook *Other Capri* 142 [ref. to WWII]: Fly it like we been learning to…and let's give the brownshoes a hand. **1970** in Tamony *Americanisms* (No. 26) 11: It is unusual for a black shoe [military aviator] to get a medal from the brown shoes.

3. (see quots.).

1967 J.B. Williams *Narc. & Hallucin.* 110: *Brown Shoes*—Name for squares. **1980** *Ten-Speed & Brownshoe* (ABC-TV): You know, a *brownshoe*—three-piece vested suit, brown shoes, stockbroker type.

brownshoe *adj. Army. & USAF.* old-fashioned; (*hence*) strict, dedicated, and having had long service. [See 1980 quot. for allusion.]

1971 Vaughan & Lynch *Brandywine's War* 34: In the brown-shoe army, we knew how to handle wise-ass punks like this. The new modern Army with the young punk-ass kids, they don't even know how to sojer, by God! **1978** Truscott *Dress Gray* 47: I never thought I'd see a hard-core, brown-shoe army sergeant with a short-timer's attitude. **1980** D. Cragg *Lex. Militaris* 53: *Brown-Shoe Army.* The Army before black shoes and boots became standard issue [Jan. 1958]. To be called *brown shoe* is to be recognized as hard, tough, dedicated. *a*1981 "K. Rollins" *Fighter Pilots* 105 [ref. to 1950's]: Show him how the brown-shoe Air Force handles punk kids. **1984–88** Hackworth & Sherman *About Face* 286: They called it the Brown Shoe Army, and then it was the Black Shoe Army.

brown stuff *n.* an intoxicating substance that is brown in color; (*specif.*) whiskey or opium.

1943 Seaton *Coney Island* (film): I told him that brown stuff'd get him sooner or later. **1950** *Time* (Aug. 28) 4: Opium (hop, brown stuff).

brown up see s.v. BROWN, *v.*, 3.

bruiser *n.* **1.** a large, muscular, belligerent individual, esp. a hired thug; (*also*) a prizefighter. [These nuances all seem to have been present since the earliest appearance of the word.]

1742 (cited in Partridge *DSUE* (ed. 5) 1016). **1744 H. Walpole, in *F & H* 340: He let into the pit great numbers of bear-garden *bruisers* (that is the term) to knock down everybody that hissed. **1753 in *F & H* I 340: Dick Daylight and Bob Breadbasket, the *bruisers.* **1753 T. Smollett, in *F & H* I 302: An old bruiser makes a good bottle-holder. **1785 Grose *Vulgar Tongue: Bruiser,* a boxer, one skilled in the art of boxing. *a*1815 Brackenridge *Mod. Chiv.* 636: The bruiser…prosecuted the advocate. **1823 [J. Neal] *Errata* I 146: He…was making at me, like an old bruiser. **1836** *Every Body's Album* 93: Ah, Charley, you're a bruiser. **1848 Thackeray *Vanity Fair* ch. xi: At college he pulled stroke-oar in the Christchurch boat, and had thrashed all the best bruisers of the "town." **1859** Matsell *Vocab.* 15: *Bruiser.* A fighter. **1866** *Night Side of N.Y.* 26: The walls are hung on every side with the lithographs of muscular bruisers. **1867** *Nat. Police Gaz.* (Jan. 12) 4: Of the "bruisers" and "burners" of creation, Cincinnati has its share. **1881** in Miller & Snell *Why West Was Wild* 311: The mayor and a "bruiser" from Texas had a kind of prize fight the other night. **1886 Davitt *Prison Diary* 28: The cowardly bully…is known by the term "bruiser" in prison slang. **1894** Bridges *Arcady* 56: That's a lot of guff….about me an' the bruisers. **1905** J. London *Game* 72: Keepin' company vit a bruiser. **1912** *Adventure* (July) 503: She's a decent woman—maybe never saw a bruiser before. **1914** *Amer. Lumberman* (Apr. 25) 106: Paul Bunyan bossed that famous crew:/A bunch of shoutin' bruisers, too. **1925** *Sat. Eve. Post* (Oct. 3) 54: Music wouldn't hurt the bruiser business anyway. *ca*1943 in L'Amour *Over Solomons* 48: A few nights ago in Rio I ran into a big bruiser in a cantina, a drunken prospector with a red beard. And red hair on his chest. **1948** Lay & Bartlett *12 O'Clock High* 75: It's gotten so everybody's afraid to go near him in the club. He's a big bruiser. **1954** Collans & Sterling *House Detect.* 99: A great big hulk-shouldered bruiser lurched in off the street. **1979** F. Thomas *Golden Bird* 150: The bruiser with the slab-sided face. **1985** Sawislak *Dwarf* 85: Listen, I ain't no bruiser.…So I used my teeth.

2. a black eye.

1965–70 in *DARE* I 398.

3. something very difficult.

1973 *TULIPQ* (coll. B.K. Dumas): If course is known to be very hard it might be called a *bruiser.*

brum *n.* [orig. unkn.; perh. alter. of earlier *brim*] a harlot.

1925–26 Black *You Can't Win* 199 [ref. to 1890's]: I'll make the cribs myself. I'm dynamite with them old brums in the cribs.…I go in her joint and drop a hoop to one of her frowsy little brums for nine dollars.

brunette *n.* **1.** a black person. *Joc.*

[**1880** Nye *Boomerang* 188: I nominate him because he is a dark horse. As a candidate he is extremely brunette.] **1884** *Life* (Apr. 3) 186: "Dat ain't none o' yo' bithniss," replied the brunette. **1898** Parker *Gatling Gun* 149: No soldiers ever fought better than the "Brunettes" of the 9th and 10th Cavalry. **1902** Carrothers *Black Cat Club* 58: S'posen dey wuz a lynchin' 'bout to take place, an' de curly-headed brunette whut was to be de pahty acted upon hel' a fust mo'gage uv evah man in de lynchin' party. **1906–07** Ade *Slim Princess* 58: If those two brunettes get me, they'll have to go some. **1910** *N.Y. Eve. Jour.* (Feb. 8) 15: It'll be nightie nightie fer de brunette champ. **1931** R.G. Carter *On Border* 187 [ref. to 1870's]: The open windows filled with "brunettes" ("Buffalo soldiers").

2. an American Indian. *Joc.*

1942 Garcia *Tough Trip* 78: Even Beaver Tom, the squaw Beau Brummel, was saying we had to get away from this bunch of brunettes.

Bruno *n.* ¶ In phrase: **lead Bruno** [poss. ref. to the former practice of itinerant bear trainers, *Bruno* being a name commonly given to circus bears] *Hobo.* (see quot.).

1930 "D. Stiff" *Milk & Honey* 202: *Carry the banner*—to walk the street all night for want of shelter. Sometimes it is called *to lead Bruno*.

brunser *n.* [orig. unkn.] a catamite; (*hence*) a despicable, sneaking man.

1933 Ersine *Pris. Slang* 21: *Brunser*, n. A...punk. **1969** R. Jessup *Sailor* 326: "You brunser," Perry said.

brush *n.* **1.** an act of copulation; (*also*) the penis.

1768–70 in Mead *Shanties* II 623: But save for His sake I venter a Brush/For Love Him I Do I Confes with a Blush. *****1794** in J. Atkins *Sex in Lit.* IV 178: Let her...have a good Brush. I'll give you thirty Guineas for your Brush. *****1841** in J. Atkins *Sex in Lit.* III 216: The brush that lathers two beards at once.

2. whiskers, esp. a mustache.

1824 Paulding *J. Bull in Amer.* 103: A man with such a brush under his nose might reasonably strop his razors...without being suspected of any other intent but to cut up his own stubble field. **1908** in H.C. Fisher *A. Mutt* 39: Detective Tabasco denies emphatically that he ever used curl paper on his brush. **1955** Comden & Green *Always Fair Weather* (film): You haven't changed much, Doug. Except for the brush. **1969** Bosworth *Love Affair* 66: Commander Edward Whitehead, late of the Royal Navy and later president of Schweppes, U.S.A., is known as The Beard, because of his magnificent pink brush. **1976** Hayden *Voyage* 6: That brush the boss wears.

3. a drink of whiskey or other liquor. Also **a rub of the brush**.

1836 *Davy Crockett's Alm.* (1837) 26: Well, now I was just as much interested as if I had come across a couple of men who were going to take a brush. **1915–16** Lait *Beef, Iron & Wine* 106: They call it "the rub of the brush" in that world to which Slim belongs....That's the way it feels when it goes down.

4. BRUSH-OFF.—usu. constr. with *the*.

1940 O'Hara *Pal Joey* 153: She...was glad to see me instead of giving me the brush which was what I was afraid of. **1941** *Slanguage Dict.* 18: *Give the fast brush*...to disregard; to reject; to snub. **1942** Freeman & Gilbert *Larceny, Inc.* (film): An honest citizen like me comes in and all he gets is the quick brush. **1944** M. Chase *Harvey* 595: That's swell of you, Doctor, right after he give you the brush. **1947** Schulberg *Harder They Fall* 27: The ones who had already made up their minds almost always got the brush. **1951** Robbins *Danny Fisher* 113: "You better leave me here, Danny....My father might be waitin' on the steps for me." "That's a good brush," I said coldly. *Ibid.* 114: If I got the brush, I got the brush, that's all. I never expected to bat a thousand. **1956** E. Hunter *Second Ending* 172: I really do have a date for tomorrow. I'm not giving you the fast brush.

brush *v.* BRUSH OFF.

1944 D. Hartman et al. *Princess & Pirate* (film): Some overage crooner kept crabbing my act. I had to brush him. **1956** I. Shulman *Good Deeds* 96: All that time...wasted on a pig who was brushing us as if she were Homecoming Queen. **1981** Sann *Trial* 2: When I raised a question...my old helpmate brushed it.

¶ In phrase:

¶ **brush (someone's) teeth** to punch (someone) in the mouth.

1975–78 O'Brien *Cacciato* 93: No more...next time the toad gets his fuckin' teeth brushed.

brush ape *n.* a person who lives or works in the forest or backwoods.—usu. used contemptuously.

1933 *AS* VIII 53: A derisive name for an unprogressive hillman...*brush ape.* **1933** in *DA* 197: I want to git out of here before a bunch of these *brush apes* swarm down out of the woods an' take him away from me. **1934** Weseen *Slang Dict.* 313: *Brush ape*—A country lad. **1939** in *DARE* I 399: *Brush ape*—one who clears away brush. **1942** *ATS* 480: Logger...*Brush ape.* **1958** McCulloch *Woods Words* 19: *Brush ape*—a logger.

brush cat *n.* (see quot.).

1930 G. Williams *Logger Talk* 12. **1968** R. Adams *Western Words* (ed. 2) 37: *Brush cat.* A sawmill worker's name for a logger.

brushed *adj. Logging.* mentally deranged from living in the woods.

1956 Sorden & Ebert *Logger's* 5 [ref. to a1925]: *Brushed*, Crazy.

brush-off *n.* an abrupt dismissal or rebuff; a snub, spurning, etc.—usu. constr. with *the*.

1938 in Gelman *Photoplay* 224: In Hollywood they have a word for these ultracourteous profitless meetings. They call them "the brush off," meaning you're in and out of some big shot's office before you know what's happened. Ty went through nearly two years of "the brush off." **1940** Wexley *City for Conquest* (film): Givin' me the brush-off, huh? **1941** Macaulay & Wald *Manpower* (film): That blond babe gave me the brush-off. **1941** in W.C. Fields *By Himself* 397: Fields gives her a gay brush-off and crosses over to the director. **1941** in Ruhm *Detective* 257: Like a dog, following her around, talking her up, looking for better bookings, getting her started in radio. And what did he ever get? "The brush-off." *****1945** S.J. Baker *Australian Lang.* 111: *To give someone the brush-off* in modern slang implies rejection or complete dismissal, but this has American antecedents. **1948** in Berg *New Words* 47: All he got was a brush-off. **1952** Brossard *Darkness* 146: If I say hello to you first that gives you the chance to give me the brush-off. **1963** D. Tracy *Brass Ring* 130: This did not look or sound like a brush-off exactly. **1966** *Time* (June 3) 22: I'd go down there, wait three hours to see someone...and I'd get nowhere. I was getting the brushoff. **1985** N.Y.C. man, age 36: I know the brush-off when I see it.

brush off *v.* **1.** to dismiss curtly; to rebuff or disregard deliberately. [*1820–21 quot. is uniquely early.]

*****1820–21** P. Egan *Life in London* 257: A country actor...is liable to be *brushed off* at the end of the first season. **1941** in Ruhm *Detective* 259: Maybe Alma don't like it. Nobody ever brushed her off before. **1941** Schulberg *Sammy* 132: The chances are he'd only brush me off. **1949** Chandler *Little Sister* 114: Cleveland brushed it off. That didn't have anything to do with the Stein killing. **1979** Cassidy *Delta* 165: If the guy was a slob, you brushed him off quickly, even brutally if necessary.

2. to clear out.—used intrans.

1947 *AS* (Apr.) 121: *Brush off* To go away. When one boy wants another to leave he may say, "Brush off man, I'm busy." Or again, "Well let's brush off."

brush-popper *n. West.* a cowboy who works in brushy country.

1928 Dobie *Vaquero* x: The story of the brush and the brush hand has never been written, though the cattle industry of America began in the *mesquitals* along the Rio Bravo, and the first cowboys were "brush poppers." *Ibid.* 86 [ref. to late 19th C.]: Walton knew that I was a brush-popper and that I hankered for ranger service. **1934** Rhodes *Beyond Desert* 24: Listen, fellow, I'm no brush-popper. **1940** F. Hunt *Trail From Tex.* 27 [ref. to ca1880]: I ain't got much sense but I know better'n to wanta be a brush-popper. **1979** Decker *Holdouts* 35: I'm an arena cowboy. I'm no brush popper like you.

brush rat *n.* a logger.

1942 *ATS* 480. **1968** R. Adams *Western Wds.* (ed. 2) 37: *Brush rat.* A logger.

brush-up *n.* a scuffle.

1940 Raine & Niblo *Fighting 69th* (film): Why? Because of that little brush-up?

brutal *adj.* **1.** *Stu.* extremely good; fine; TOUGH.

1964 in *Time* (Jan. 1, 1965) 56: Degrees of superiority at Colorado College begin with *mean*, work up toward *brutal* and *savage*. **1971** Dahlskog *Dict.* 10: *Brutal, a.* Great; extraordinary; marvelous.

2. very bad.

1983 L. Frank *Hardball* 58: Another very common term synonymous with "bad" is "brutal."...A player with poor fielding ability is said to be "brutal in the field,"...a ball that takes a bad hop is said to "take a brutal bounce"...and a player who has had a bad day is said to have had a "brutal game."

brute *n.* **1.a.** a large or unmanageable vessel or vehicle of any sort; now esp. a multiengined aircraft or guided missile.

1860 in C.A. Abbey *Before the Mast* 263: We have all denominated her [the ship] a "*beastly brute.*" **1867** Clark *Sailor's Life* 123: The CHARGER was a one thousand ton ship...composed of as much wood, iron, and canvas as two Yankee ships of the same tonnage, and was, in sailor parlance, "a perfect brute." **1939** Fessier *Wings of Navy* (film): Look at that big brute. **1943** *Newsweek* (Oct. 11) 53: Douglas production of "big brutes" has been on schedule or ahead of schedule, in addition to a fabulous output of more other types of aircraft than any other manufacturer. **1945** Hubbard *R.R. Ave.* 364: *Tease The Brute*—Follow the engine. **1955** Abbey *Brave Cowboy* 136: I've got to stop...got to find a place to park this brute. **1959** *Sat. Eve. Post* (May 2) 67: This morning the pot-bellied brute was really loaded: 17,000 gallons of fuel for its prop-jets. **1962** Harvey *Strike Command* 6: The F-100's came at night. The big shovel-nosed brutes snored around the traffic pattern in the rain at Myrtle Beach. **1963** E.M. Miller *Exile* 137: You can't test-fly those brutes. They're only good for one shot. **1970** S. Ross *Fortune Machine* 156: I drove that big white brute of a car.

b. *Film & TV.* a 10,000-watt arc spotlight.

1968 *CBS Evening News* (June 8) (CBS-TV): The big lights called *brutes.* **1982** T.D. Connors *Dict. Mass Media* 37.

2. (see quot.).

1929–32 in *AS* (Dec. 1934) 289 [Lincoln Univ.]: *Brute.* Anything or anyone that is very good or very bad is described as a brute, thus: That course is a brute (very bad or tough), or that game was a brute (very good).

bruz *n. Black E.* BRO; PAL.

1958 in R.S. Gold *Jazz Talk* 35: No, bruz, that's not my groove. **1961** R. Russell *Sound* 10: Later for you, bruz! **1965–70** in *DARE* I 391. **1989** S. Lee *Do the Right Thing* (film): I gotta smack you around once in a while, bruz.

B.S. *n.* BULLSHIT.

1900 *Howitzer* (U.S. Mil. Acad.) (No. 1) 118: *B.S.*—volubility of discourse, or verbosity. *Ibid.* 138: *Be-esse.*—n....Rough, crude talk. **1905** *Ibid.* (No. 6) 293: *B.S.*—Superfluous talk. **1915** in *DN* IV 232: B.S. Abbreviation of *bovine excrescence*, nonsense, "hot air." **1918** in Wecter *Johnny Comes Marching Home* 257: Altho encouraging, it sounds like B.S. to me. *****1919** Downing *Digger Dialects* 14: B.S. (n.)—See *bullsh.* **1926** [O'Brien] *Wine, Women & War* 316: B.S., "hot air" (very free translation). **1928** Dobie *Drinkin' Gou'd* 56: Why, with B.S., you big windbag, same as that that you have been spouting off. **1928** Bodenheim *Georgie May* 42: They love to haind out that ol' b.s. *****1932** F. Richards *Old Soldiers* 86: We would have been the dullest and most ignorant of men if we had believed some of the B.S. that was dished out to us. **1942** Garcia *Tough Trip* 100: Beaver Tom said he had seen some of my diplomatic work in the Injun camp and it was B.S. stuff. **1958** "R. Traver" *Anatomy* 37: I'll tend to the department of legal B.S. **1958** J. Davis *College Vocab.* 12: Degrees: *B.S.*—Bull Shit. *M.S.*—More Shit. *PhD.*—Piled higher and deeper. **1959** O'Connor *Talked with a Stranger* 162: They give you this line of b.s. and they don't figure on doing anything for you. **1961** Clausen *Season's Over* 222: If b.s. was music, you girls'd be a brass band. **1970** Cole *Street Kids* 171: I gave him a big B.S. story. **1971** Faust *Willy Remembers* 140: You believe what Heatter and Hill and the rest of them b.s. artists tell you you'll wind up crazy. **1989** *Reporters* (Fox-TV) (Feb. 25): He's just a BS artist. Don't believe anything he says.

B.S. *v.* BULLSHIT.

1900 *Howitzer* (U.S. Mil. Acad.) (No. 1) 138: *Be-esse.*—v....To talk crudely. **1930** in D.O. Smith *Cradle* 59: We can B.S. on a spacious porch. **1939** *New Directions* 138: And just what the hell you get out of coming around here and BS-ing about the way I write. **1962** Killens *Thunder* 15: Think they can B.S. around for the whole damn duration. **1963** G. Coon *Short End* 250: I figured there wasn't any sense in BSing him. **1965** Elder *Dark Old Men* 87: I think you're BS'n boy. **1965** Marks *Letters* 58: All we do here is sit around and b/s quite a bit. **1970** Sample *Dirty Ballplayer* 154: Usually on nights before games the team has a little get-together, where we have some sandwiches and BS for a while. **1974** R. Carter *16th Round* 177: There's no further use in me b-s'ing myself any longer.

B school *n. Stu.* a graduate school of business.

1967 *Business Week* (Dec. 9) 118: The B-school is finding that in a jet-sized world, Beirut is not much farther away than Berkeley. **1970** *Harper's* (Mar.) 78: The faculty does not blush when HBS [Harvard

Business School] is called the West Point of capitalism. By design, the "B-School" trains a senior officer class. **1981** *Time* (May 4) 61: The B school even has its own barbershop. **1986** *Newsweek* (May 26) 52: I didn't come out of B school burning with desire to be an entrepreneur....In fact, my education didn't start until I got out of B school. **1988** *Time* (Nov. 14) 50: A shake-up stirs outrage at Yale's humanistic B-school.

BTM *n.* [fr. *bottom*] rump.

*****1919** R. Firbank *Valmouth* 188: She made a sudden dash for his b-t-m. **1937** Binns *Laurels* 265: That's when someone should have taken down their pants and spanked their B.T.M.'s. **1966–67** in *DARE.*

B.T.O *n.* [*big-time operator*] Esp. *Stu. & Mil.* a popular or influential individual who uses flattery or devious means to achieve his ends; WHEELER-DEALER. Also quasi-adv.

1944 in *AS* (Feb. 1945) XX 147: *B.T.O.* Big time operator. **1945** *Yank* (Nov. 2) 15: He thought he was a BTO. **1947** *AS* (Apr.) 110: Widely disseminated is the popular *B.T.O.* In Europe or the Orient this may indicate a soldier who makes a large amount of money by purveying stolen supplies on the black market. **1947** *ATS* (Supp.) 31: *BTO*...a fellow who "gets around," has a way with the girls. **1955** *AS* (Dec.) 302: *BTO* (big-time operator), n. Wolf-type man. **1963** Braly *Shake Him* 131: Randozza nodded, very BTO. **1984–88** Hackworth & Sherman *About Face* 219 [ref. to 1947]: We'd...chased big-time operators (BTOs) who tried to screw us...[on] the black market.

B.U. *n.* [*biological urge*] *Stu.* sexual desire. *Joc.*

1931 Lorimer *Streetcars* 5: They're all alike...when you stir up the old B.U.

bub[1] *n.* a drink, esp. beer or ale. Also as *v.* Now *hist.*

*****1665** R. Head *Eng. Rogue* 23: These four returned laden with bub and food. *Ibid.* 35: Having "bubbed rumly," we concluded an everlasting friendship. *****1707** Cibber *Double Gallant* 129: Neck Beef, and a Pot of plain Bub. *****1781** in W.H. Logan *Pedlar's Pack* 159: For a little bub. **1800** *Amorous Songster* 65: And drink your generous bub. **1805** *Port Folio* (Aug. 24) 261: I smoke my pipe, toss off my bub. **1859** Matsell *Vocab.* 15: "Bubb your lush," drink your grog. **1867** *Nat. Police Gaz.* (Oct. 19) 4: That is, while they "bub their lush." *****1961** Burgess *Dict. Sailing* 39: *Bub and grub.* An old-time expression for meat and drink.

bub[2] *n.* [perh. < South G *Bub,* short for *Bube* 'boy'; or else a childish pronun. of *brother*; cf. BUBBY[2], BUD[1]] boy; young fellow; BUSTER.—now usu. used condescendingly in direct address to a stranger whose name is not known. [Earliest examples are addressed to youths only.]

[*****1698–99** "B.E." *Dict. Canting Crew*: *Bub,* or *Bubble*...one that is Cheated; also an Easy, Soft Fellow.] **1839** Briggs *Harry Franco* II 189: Speak louder, Bub. **1866** G.A. Townsend *Non-Combatant* 251: Where's your pass, bub? **1866** E.C. Downs *Scout & Spy* 99: He...called me "Bub," as he used to do..., though I was forty years old. **1869** Stowe *Oldtown* 176: Hulloah, bub!...Where ye goin'? **1872** "M. Twain" *Roughing It* 51: Well, I shall have to tear myself away from you, bub. **1883** Flagg *Versicles* 30: No siree, Bub, you ain't goin' to! **1897** Hamblen *General Mgr.* 28: Be careful how you pass the signals, bub, or the engineer can't tell what he's doing. **1943** Sherrod *Tarawa* 28: Nobody asked you to be a Marine, bub. **1949** Chandler *Little Sister* 18: No vacancies, bub. Can't you read large print? **1954** G. Kersh, in Pohl *Star of Stars* 27: I don't mind telling you that, bub, because it's already been printed. **1967–68** T. Wolfe *Electric Kool-Aid* 37: Well, bub, I dunno. **1971** Trudeau *A Lot Smarter* (unp.): O.K., Bub, F.B.I.!! **1981** Hathaway *World of Hurt* 60: "Is that a real tattoo?" "That's right bub." **1984** Hindle *Dragon Fall* 42: Hey, bub! This is my ivory chariot. **1990** in Groening *How to Go to Hell* (unp.): Men only, Bub!

bub[3] *n.* usu. *pl.* [fr. BUBBY[1]] a woman's breast.

*****1826** in J. Farmer *Musa Pedestris* 97: Your panting bubs and glist'ning eye. *****1860** Hotten *Slang Dict.* (ed. 2) 105: *Bub,* a teat, a woman's breast. **1928** Bodenheim *Georgie May* 53: Haven't you noticed mah bubs look pretty big. **1936** M. Levin *Old Bunch* 48: He was sizing up her bubs but someone behind pushed him. **1946** I. Shulman *Amboy Dukes* 102: She let me squeeze her bubs. **1967** Ford *Muc Wa* 121: She jumped up and down, setting her rich little bubs to dancing. **1968** Lockridge *Hartspring* 16: One bub. Now two bubs in half-profile. **1972** Swarthout *Tin Lizzie* 6: I remember a girl in Zamboanga had...bubs like ice cream cones.

bubba *n.* [fr. BUBBY[2]] **1.** *So.* brother; (hence) friend.—often in direct address or as a nickname, esp. for a boy.

1864 in N.C. Delaney *J.M. Kell* 152: Poor papa, so far away from his little girl and mama and bubbers. **1922** (cited in Holm & Shilling *Dict.*

Baham. Eng.). **1931** Bontemps *Sends Sunday* 6: "High there, Mistah Steamboat Man!" "He-o, bubba," the captain said pleasantly. **1935** J. Conroy *World to Win* 81: "I'm sorry, bubber," Robert said, using a pet name he had had for Lee when he could not say "brother." *ca***1939** in A. Banks *First Person* 249: Next thing I hear, Bubba huntin a lawyer! **1956** M. Wolff *Big Nick*. 53: Listen to me, Bubber....You've had too many drinks. **1966** K. Hunter *Landlord* 47: My bubba, he run too. **1976** Conroy *Santini* 166: And just what if I don't let go, bubba? **1976** Rosen *Above Rim* 159: My bubba once told me, "Don't never try and bullshit a bullshitter." **1977** Olsen *Fire Five* 71: Well, enjoyed meeting you, bubba. **1980** Conroy *Lords of Discipline* 13: How did you know it was me, Bubba? **1987** W. Georgia State Coll. instructor, age *ca*33: So how's it goin', bubba? **1987** *Wkly. World News* (May 5) 13: Anybody who was a good guy we'd call "Bubba." **1992** Parsons & Nelson *Fighter Country* 156: *Bubbas*: fellow squadron members, cronies.

2. an uneducated southern white male; "good ol' boy"; RED-NECK.

1986 C. Trillin, in *New Yorker* (Dec. 22) 76: She also refers often to a sort of all-purpose Texas ol' boy she calls Bubba. **1988** *Nation* (Aug. 27) 156: George Bush needs the Bubba vote—young Southern white males—and if all else fails, racial animus might get Bubba in the Bush column. **1990** *New Republic* (Oct. 22) 19: Bubba is a rural Texas archetype whose sometimes crude and vulgar culture is an amalgam of male bonding rituals forged on the ranch, in the oil fields, and in the locker room. **1992** *N.Y. Times* (Mar. 1) 22: As Presidential politics move into the states of the Confederacy, the biggest question about Bubba may not be how he will vote but how to find him. **1993** *CBS This Morning* (CBS-TV) (Jan. 21): Real bubbas don't jog.

bubble *n.* [fr. AUTOMOBUBBLE] an automobile. *Joc.*

1905 [Hobart] *Get Next!* 14: Bunch had just tied his Bubble to a tree. **1905** R. Grant *Orchid* 223: It was the largest and most imposing "bubble" which Westfield had gazed upon. **1907** Corbin *Cave Man* 52: What I'm after is a mechanic. My bubble has bust. **1918** in *OEDS*: Gee! He's beat it in my bubble—and it was a hired one! **1939** in *DARE*.

bubble *v.* to drive or ride in an automobile. *Joc.*

1900 *N.Y. Journal* (Nov. 11) 28: Perhaps the most popular fad of the week was "bubbling." This you know is the fashionable slang for auto-mobiling.

bubblebrain *n.* BUBBLEHEAD.

1966 Purdum *Bro. John* 136: What a bubble brain! **1981** Wolf *Roger Rabbit* 18: A bubblebrain like Roger. **1989** Chapple & Talbot *Burning Desires* 177: A pompous network bubblebrain.

bubble-chaser *n.* [see 1945, 1956 quots. for deriv.] *Mil. Av.* an airplane navigator or bombardier. Now *hist.*

1945 in *AS* (Dec. 1946) 310 [AAF]: *Bubble-chaser*. The bombardier on a bomber. In order to drop his bombs accurately, the bombardier has to watch the bubbles in his levelling instrument. **1956** *AS* (Oct.) 227: *Bubble-Chaser*, n. The navigator, who must center a bubble in the sextant in order to use it properly. **1959** Montgomery & Helman *Jet Nav.* 90: You bubble chasers are the number-one guys. **1975** in Higham & Siddall *Combat Aircraft* 58: LORAN...was a new development that greatly eased the work of the bubble-chasers and bolstered the confidence of the pilots in their work.

bubble-dancing *n.* the washing of dishes by hand. Hence **bubble-dancer** a person who washes dishes.

1941 *N.Y. Times* (Sept. 19) 25: [At Maxwell Field, Ala.] bubble dancing is washing dishes. **1941** *AS* (Oct.) 164: *Bubble Dancing.* Dishwashing. **1942** *Sat. Eve. Post* (May 30): *Bubble-dancer*: a dishwasher. **1942** *Good Housekeeping* (Dec.) 11: The Army calls this job K.P. The men have another name...Bubble dancing. **1943** Hunt & Pringle *Service Slang*: *Bubble-dancing*—Pot washing in the cook-house. **1946** Boulware *Jive & Slang* 2: Bubble Dancing....Washing dishes.

bubblegum *n. Music.* popular music that appeals primarily to adolescents. In full, **bubblegum music**. Also adj.

1963 in H. Ellison *Sex Misspelled* 42: Meeting the bubble gum music from the dining room head on. **1970** Landy *Underground Dict.* 41: They like bubble gum music. **1971** Dahlskog *Dict.* 10: *Bubble gum music*, n. A type of music that appeals to the high school or subteen crowd. **1973** *Penthouse* (July) 41: Branded as "bubblegum," for their bouncy hits *She's About a Mover* and *Mendocino*, the group had two strikes against it among the rock tastemakers of the day. *a***1982** Hartwell & Bentley *Open to Lang.* 59: Rock music aimed at very young teenagers is often called "bubblegum music." **1985** *All Things Considered* (Nat. Pub. Radio) (June 10): They've been listening to bubblegum and funk. **1985** Makower *Boom!* 73: Bubblegum groups, including the

Ohio Express and the 1910 Fruitgum Company,....edged into the top ten during [1969]....Bubblegum is a light, simple-minded style aimed at the sub-teen market. **1991** Nelson & Gonzales *Bring Noise* 71: Dre [a rap musician] also produced bubblegum rappers J.J. Fad.

bubblegum machine *n.* the flashing, revolving roof beacon of a police car; (*hence*) a police patrol car having such a beacon. Cf. BUBBLE-TOP; GUMBALL.

1966–68 in *DARE*. **1971** Tak *Truck Talk* 20: *Bubble gum machine*: the flashing light on the roof of a highway patrol car. **1973** Ace *Stand On It* 57: And, sure enough, he turned on the red bubble-gum machine on top of his car and he took out after us. **1974** Phila. man, age 28: A *bubblegum machine* is a police car. I heard it in Philadelphia in 1966. **1975** Gould *Maine Lingo: Bubblegum machine*...a Maine State Police car on the highway. **1976** *Nat. Lampoon* (July) 58: Uh-oh, bubble gum machine. **1980** Eble *Campus Slang* (Mar.) 1: *Bubble gum machine*—police car.

bubblegum man *n.* a policeman. Also **bubblegum boy.** *Joc.*

1978 Univ. Tenn. student: Here come the bubblegum boys. **1980** Eble *Campus Slang* (Mar.) 2: *Bubblegum man* means "policeman."

bubblegummer *n.* a youngster, esp. a silly teenaged girl, who often chews bubblegum; a young teenager or preadolescent.

[**1947** in *AS* (Oct. 1958) 281: A serious bubble-gummer, ambitious to blow the biggest and best bubbles in town.] **1969** *Current Slang* I & II 16: *Bubble gummer*, n. A callow girl; a high school student; young sister.—Air Force Academy cadets; high school students, both sexes, South Dakota. **1970** Wambaugh *New Centurions* 194: You like kids?...I'll bet you got some little bubblegummers of your own. **1975** Wambaugh *Choirboys* 78: It took little or no brains...to drive a high speed chase after some joy-riding bubblegummer. **1979** Hiler *Monkey Mt.* 194: More of Dave's friends arrived, and a carload of giggling bubble-gummers.

bubblehead *n.* a scatterbrain; a person given to flights of fancy. Hence **bubbleheaded,** *adj.*

1952 Bellow *Augie March* 53: He didn't like to see my bubble-headed friends get me in dutch. **1959** Brosnan *Long Season* 202: Some of those bubble-heads interpret that to mean the strike zone is between the lowest button of the shirt to the top button of the pants crotch. **1965** Gallery *8 Bells* 293: World government...may not be the paradise of brotherly love that the bleeding hearts and bubble-heads predict. It will be run by...tough, cold realists. **1968** Cuomo *Among Thieves* 356: Look here, bubblehead—*that* was the cause of the whole goddamn mess. **1971** *N.Y. Times* (Aug. 29) 48: "If they'd just let me do it my way...I could shape up this bunch of bubbleheads—fast," said a master sergeant. **1972** *Nat. Lampoon* (Nov.) 4: Climb down from your ivory tower, bubbleheads! **1976** G. Kirkham *Signal Zero* 11: Bubble-headed intellectuals. **1983** *Rolling Stone* (Feb. 3) 55: Buttons for Bozos, Bubbleheads, and Brains! **1984** W. Murray *Dead Crab* 12: We were afraid she'd...turn out to be just another California bubblehead. **1985** Benson (ABC-TV): I don't even want to hear that bubblehead's name.

bubbles *n.pl.* champagne.

1907 "O. Henry" *Heart of West* 152: I'd like to give him a little whirl after the show this evening— bubbles, you know, and a buzz out to a casino for the whitebait and pickled walnuts. **1908** *New B'way Mag.* (July) 34: I'd rather have foam than bubbles any day.

bubble-shits *n.pl.* diarrhea.—usu. considered vulgar.

1961 Hemingway *Islands in Stream* 357: Eight that could excremente and three of these with the bubbleshits.

bubble-top *n.* a police patrol car having a rotating roof beacon. Cf. BUBBLEGUM MACHINE.

1967–69 in *DARE*.

bubble water *n.* champagne. Also **bubbly water.**

1899 Norris *McTeague* 147: That was how the waiter had spoken of the champagne—"bubble-water." **1943** Wendt & Kogan *Bosses* 265: We had a car full of bubble water. **1951** E. Arcaro, in Woods *Horse-Racing* 41: Me for home and my sweetie—and that bubble water. **1966** Susann *Valley of Dolls* 80: Take some of my bubbly water.

bubbly *n.* champagne.

1920 in *OEDS*: It goes to the head like bubbly. **1971** *Odd Couple* (ABC-TV): You got foam in my bubbly! **1992** *Martin* (Fox-TV): How about a bit of the bubbly?

bubby[1] *n.* usu. *pl.* a woman's breast.

1655 in Burford *Bawdy Verse* 224: Her hands they are red and her bubbies are coarse. **1675** in Duffett *Burlesque Plays* 102: Why, did you ever

feel my Bubbies? *1686 T. D'Urfey, in *F & H* I 346: The Ladies here may without Scandal shew/Face or white Bubbies, to each ogling Beau. *1699 Ward *London-Spy* 141: She was…forc'd to shew her tender Back, and tempting Bubbies. 1744 A. Hamilton *Gentleman's Progress* 140: And handling her bubbies just like an old rake. *1754 in *F & H* I 344: *Bubbys*, a woman's breasts. *1789 in J. Farmer *Musa Pedestris* 64: Thy snowy bubbies e'er appear/Like two small hills of sand, my dear. 1806 M. Lewis *Jrls. Lewis & Clark* in *DARE*: In aged [Indian] women I have seen the bubby reach as low as the waist. *ca1866 *Romance of Lust* 5: Her lovely and beautifully formed bubbies. *1879 *Pearl* (July) 29: He tickled her bubbies, she rubbed up his yard. 1888 *Stag Party* 32: I beside her naked lay,/While each hand held a bubby. 1898 Green *Va. Folk-Speech* 71: *Bubby*, n. A woman's breast. 1902 *DN* II 30: *Bubbies*, n. The breasts. 1927 *Immortalia* 147: And each palpitating bubby/Was so round and firm and chubby. 1940 in Peters *Wisc. Folk Songs* 264: A pretty young mermaid, as naked as Venus/Was washing her bubbies and combing her hair. 1944 Micheaux *Mrs. Wingate* 267: I'd sho lak to hold dem bubbies in mah hand fo' jes a minet. 1958 Camerer *Damned Wear Wings* 146: With their bubbies bouncing and their eyes laughing. 1968 Lockridge *Hartspring* 13: They…tied one another's bubbies back in place. a1973–87 F.M. Davis *Livin' the Blues* 72: A constant contest for bigger and better bubbies.

bubby[2] *n.* [fr. BUB[2] + -IE or < G *Bube* 'boy'; not from Yid] BUB[2]. 1848 [Baker] *Glance at N.Y.* 27: Say, Bubby, what's de matter? 1859 Bartlett *Amer.* (ed. 2): *Bub* and *Bubby*. Contractions for brother, often applied to small boys. 1874 [Pember] *Metropolis* 187: That won't do, bubby, I don't sell such measly apples as that. 1901 H. Robertson *Inlander* 13: No, I ain't made no mistake.…What do you take me for, bubby? 1984 W.M. Henderson *Elvis* 58: As usual, Herbie-bubby, I'm one step ahead of you. 1984 Heath *A-Team* 157: Stick with me, boobie.

bubu var. BOOBOO.

buck *n.* **1.a.** a backwoodsman.
1744 A. Hamilton *Gentleman's Progress* 123: I told him that the most dangerous wild beasts in these woods were shaped exactly like men, and they went by the name of buckskins, or bucks.
b. an American Indian man. [Formerly S.E.; now in racist use only.]
1800 in *OEDS*: When the Peace River bucks look out for women. 1863 in *Iowa Jour. Hist.* LVII (1959) 172: All was a yarn gotten up by the [Santee] bucks down at the agency. 1884 in Lummis *Letters* 20: A big, solemn buck…walked noiselessly up behind the offender. 1905 "W. Hale" *Cowboy & Ranchman* 40: There were…squaws, bucks, and children. a1916 D.E. Conner *Walker* 193: I noticed two "bucks," so called by both men and women of Arizona, playing a…game of something. 1923 J.L. Hill *Cattle Trail* 31: We can slide through without seeing a buck or hearing a shot. 1986 B. Clayton & N. Elliott *Jazz World* 12: When I was about twelve years old [1923] little wild Indian boys were known as bucks. 1986 Dexter *Deadwood* 55: The buck…was desirous to make a papoose with Calamity Jane.
c. fellow; man.
*1821–26 Stewart *Man-of-War's-Man* I 53: Come, Davis, hand round, my buck. 1840 in *DAE*: Pay for your own slug, buck. 1866 C. Hunt *Shenandoah* 202: Blow away, my buck. 1901 Wister *Philosophy* 11: Plato…never caught on to the subjective, any more than the other Greek bucks. 1923 in W.F. Nolan *Black Mask Boys* 49: And he's a buck with uncertain age.
d. a black man.—often attrib. [Now in racist use only.]
1835 in *OEDS*: A buck nigger is worth the slack of two or three hundred dollars. 1859 Bartlett *Amer.* (ed. 2) 51: A "*buck* nigger" is a term often vulgarly applied to a negro man. 1871 in Schele de Vere *Amer.* 209: A big buck negro was found…playing possum. 1909 *DN* III 393: *Buck*…now applied almost exclusively to male negroes as the opposite of *wench*. 1930 Irwin *Tramp & Und. Slang* 37: *Buck*.—A negro. 1944 V.H. Jensen *Lumber & Labor* 78: The workers are most often "buck" Negroes. 1960 Fedoroff *On Side of Angels* 354: Jesus…What you doin' with all them black bucks in there? 1970 Kinoy *Brother John* (film): You can be replaced by any buck with a strong back and a weak mind. 1977 Flusser *Squeal Man* 46: He patrols the colored section.…His first night out he walked right into a bar where all the big bucks hang out.
2.a. a dollar. Now *colloq.*
1856 in *OEDS*: Bernard, assault and battery upon Wm. Croft, mulcted in the sum of twenty bucks. 1896 F.P. Dunne, in Schaaf *Dooley* 130: D'ye mean to say that this buck is worth only fifty cents? 1898 Dunne *Dooley in Peace & War* 177: Carlisle'd hand him out a plunk, a case, a buck. 1930 Rogers & Adler *Chump at Oxford* (film): See, we're down to our last six bucks. 1943 J. Mitchell *McSorley's* 122: He knows he can be certain of at least a couple of bucks of it. 1958 J. King *Pro Football* 4:

Collins…wouldn't have missed a few more bucks. 1970–71 Rubinstein *City Police* 195: Old Jack must have a few bucks tonight. 1992 *TV Guide* (Nov. 21) 3: 500 bucks for that "dream date."
b. usu. *pl.* money.
1928 Pasley *Capone* 56: His guests included persons "not in the bucks." 1929 Sullivan *Look at Chicago* 100: When the ordinary gangster "comes into the bucks." 1940 *Accent* (Autumn) 35: Say Joe, got any bucks? 1955 Graziano & Barber *Somebody Up There* 353: We're going to make a lot of bucks yet. 1963 in A. Sexton *Letters* 203: You are Americans and we like you and your bucks. 1970 Della Femina *Wonderful Folks* 90: Not only was he making big bucks. 1970 Baraka *Jello* 19: Where the hell's the rest of your bucks.…your dough, my man. 1972 T.C. Bambara *Gorilla* 174: Nailed his ass knockin over a bank, but time enough to stash the bucks so his woman and kid could live comfy. 1974 Lahr *Trot* 48: Get that degree and get the big bucks. 1978 B. Johnson *What's Happenin'* 61: He had been offered some pretty nice bucks to wear Pro-Keds. 1992 Mowry *Way Past Cool* 28: He'd made pretty good buck for a while. *Ibid.* 308: What…*we* gonna do with all that buck?
c. a profit or wage. See also FAST BUCK.
1937–40 in Whyte *Street Corner Society* 107: Now I'm out for the buck…Before it was all idealism. 1947 Schulberg *Harder They Fall* 343: Living out all our lives for the easy buck. 1955 Robbins *79 Park Ave.* 261: Same old Joe. Anything to grab a buck. 1971–73 Sheehy *Hustling* 144: It's a steady buck. 1974 Terkel *Working* 122: I make a pretty good buck.
d. *Gamb.* one hundred dollars.
1974 Radano *Cop Stories* 140: "I want a buck and a half for the information."…"A buck and a half!…Look, Gus, this money is coming out of our own pockets." 1976 "N. Ross" *Policeman* 120: Let me tell you, we have five Greek gambling joints, and that's, say, a buck and a quarter a month, right? 1992 Mowry *Way Past Cool* 120: His mom paid the half-buck a month for his room.
e. *Broadly*, one hundred of anything, as points of a batting average or pounds of weight.
1983 L. Frank *Hardball* 12: A player who has a batting average of .150 is often said to be "hitting a buck-fifty." 1984 R. Jackson, in *N.Y. Post* (Aug. 21) 72: They put up with me last year when I couldn't hit a buck ninety. 1993 *N.Y. Times* (Mar. 3) B 17: Kenny weighs about a buck-60.
f. one thousand dollars. Cf. **(d)**, above.
1985 *Fame* (synd. TV series): You know, an actor makes a buck two-eighty every ten years—and that's if he's Robert Redford.
g. one hundred thousand dollars.
1987 *L.A. Law* (NBC-TV): A hundred and fifty thousand for the girl.…She's getting a buck and a half for a scratch. 1990 Dickson *Slang!* 172: *Buck*. In Hollywood, $100,000.
3. *Army & USMC.* BUCK PRIVATE. [Notably common during WWI but increasingly rare afterward.]
1899–1900 Cullen *Tales* 328: There I was…in a buck artilleryman's uniform. 1901 in Remington *Own West* 83: The sergeant…told the old "bucks" to mind their eyes, [and] judiciously scared the "shavetails" into wakefulness. 1902 Remington *John Ermine* 199: Soldiers take to dogs, and it's always "kick my dog kick me" with these bucks. 1905 *Howitzer* (U.S. Mil. Acad.) 293: *Buck*—A private in the ranks. 1907 *Reader* (Sept.) 348: He didn't get so much petting from the officers but he was still the whole thing with the bucks. 1915 Garrett *Army Ballads* 24: I'm only a buck o' the rank and file. 1919 Washburn *One of YD* 7: A cootie shows no preference between the humblest "buck" in the regiment and him who wears a gold leaf on his shoulder. 1919 Small *47th* 58: The next two weeks were certainly ones of unrest for us "bucks." 1925 Thomason *Fix Bayonets!* 86: Don't you know by now how expendable you bucks are? a1949 D. Levin *Mask of Glory* 91: Each in his place—from general to lousy buck. 1960 Bluestone *Cully* 53 [ref. to ca1955]: All right, yo' bucks. Yo' pullin' or talkin'?
4. *Hobo.* a Catholic priest.
1904 *Life in Sing Sing* 246: *Buck*. A priest. 1927 *AS* (June) 387: A priest is known as the *buck*.…It is said that a Catholic vag can usually get a dollar (buck) from the priest if he puts up a good *spiel*. The other [explanation] is based on a popular superstition anent the sexual proclivities of the average priest. 1928 Callahan *Man's Grim Justice* 57: I'll go see the buck (priest) to-morrow and have a Mass said for him. 1931–34 in Clemmer *Pris. Commun.* 330: *Buck*…A Catholic priest. 1966 Kenney *Caste* 101: You sound just like a buck in a gospel shop.
5. responsibility.—alluding to *pass the buck*, below. Now S.E.
1928–29 Nason *White Slicker* 114: Anyway, the buck never travels up but always down. You can't pass any responsibility off onto me. 1952 H. Truman, in *OED2* [ref. to 1946]: On my desk I have a motto which:

says "The buck stops here."

6. *Auto. Sales.* a dilapidated used car.

1973–77 in *AS* (Winter 1980) 309: *Buck.* Car in very poor condition.

¶ In phrases:

¶ **bang for the buck** see s.v. BANG.

¶ **pass the buck, 1.** to give a chance to another. [Despite the poker language, the 1871 quot. is in a nonpoker context; a *buck* 'an object used to indicate the dealer in poker', was formerly used in that game. 1876 quot. illustrates literal use.]

1871 "M. Twain" *Roughing It* 249: I reckon I can't call that hand. Ante and pass the buck. [**1876** in Dwyer & Lingenfelter *Songs of Gold Rush* 190: He'd ante a slug; he'd pass the buck;/He'd go a hat-full blind.]

2. to shift responsibility (to someone else). Now *colloq.* or *S.E.* See also BUCK-PASSER; BUCK-PASSING.

1908 in J. London *Letters* 265: Don't, in good American slang, pass the buck to me. **1912** in *DAE* I 331: The Big Commissioner will get roasted by the papers and hand it to the Deputy Comish, and the Deputy will pass the buck down to me, and I'll have to report how it happened. **1918** in Bowerman *Compensations* 149: The Kaiser and his crowd are trying to "pass the buck"—Germany I believe knows well that Turkey and Austria are going to quit. **1921** *Variety* (Feb. 25) 1: Shuberts Pass Equity Buck. Blame Is Shifted to Managers. **1924** *DN* V 289: *To pass the buck*....To shift responsibility. **1929** A.C. Doyle *Maricot* ch. vii: I guess we can't go out of our way to raise the devil and then pass the buck to the folk that saved us. **1935** S. Lewis *Can't Happen* 80: Buzz'll be able to pass the buck for not creating any real relief for poverty. **1944** Rister *Border Command* 25: He conveniently journeyed westward to Texas, thereby "passing the buck" of meeting the problem to his second in command. **1953** Paul *Wayland* 36: You wouldn't be passing me the buck, by any chance? **1970** Della Femina *Wonderful Folks* 58: Now who's going to stop passing the buck? *a*1989 R. Herman, Jr., *Warbirds* 79: He never makes a decision and always passes the buck.

buck *adj.* **1.** *Stu.* excellent; first-rate.

1856 Hall *College Wds.* 56: At Princeton College, anything which is in an intensive degree good, excellent, pleasant, or agreeable, is called *buck.*

2. [back formation fr. BUCK PRIVATE] *Army & USMC.* new in grade or rank; raw. Also (*vulgar*) **buck-ass.** Cf. BUCK GENERAL, BUCK SERGEANT.

1917 Hunt *Blown in by Draft* 142: Sarge Gregory looked again and then half turned to the freckled red-faced buck second sergeant. **1959** Cochrell *Barren Beaches* 40 [ref. to WWII]: A marine gunner was the platoon...But them buck-ass second looies always want to make points and screw everybody. *ca*1964 K. Cook *Other Capri* 55 [ref. to WWII]: Some squadron commanders and some buck pilots. **1979** McGivern *Soldiers of '44* 332: You're a buck lieutenant and I'm a major. **1989** Zumbro & Walker *Jungletracks* 95: Kind of a big job for a buck sergeant and a buck lieutenant.

buck[1] *v.* to copulate or to copulate with. [Orig. of rabbits.]

***1530** in *OED2*: Konyes buck every moneth. ***1575**, ***1616**, ***1741** in *OED2*. **1888** *Stag Party* 23: Tim and I a-hunting went/On the plains of Timbuctoo,/We found three maidens in a tent,/I bucked one and Tim bucked two. **a*1962** in MacColl & Seeger *Travellers' Songs* 165: I could buck a' the whores in damnation. *Ibid.*: For learnin' young ladies to buck. **1976** in Dundes & Pagter *Alligators* 37: I bucked one/And Tim bucked two!

buck[2] *v.* **1.** to defy; resist; challenge successfully.—usu. trans. or constr. with *against.* Now *S.E.*

1846 in *Utah Hist. Qly.* V (1932) 36: The Mormons would buck against it. **1878** in *Seal & Salmon Fisheries* IV 6: I have taken the names of all Indians that have bucked against my authority. *a*1890 *F & H* I 347: *Buck*...*Verb* (American)—To oppose; to run counter to. **1899–1900** Cullen *Tales* 324: I buck when it comes to going East. **1904** *Life in Sing Sing* 246: *Buck*....to oppose. **1918** Griffin *Ballads of Regt.* 22: There's a non-com placed above you—if you buck him you're a fool. **1920** Weaver *In American* 37: It ain't no use to buck the jinx. **1921** Dos Passos *3 Soldiers* 393: You're crazy. One man alone can't buck the system like that. **1923** Toomer *Cane* 110: I'm not strong enough to buck it. **1923** McAlmon *Village* 59: He...would never actually buck Bull Norton. **1925** S. Lewis *Arrowsmith* ch. xxii: Do you think you can buck the interests and keep a clean city all by yourself? **1928** Wharton *Squad* 145: Oh hell, one guy can't buck the Army. **1934** Wohlforth *Tin Soldiers* 145: I couldn't buck the whole system. **1938** Smitter *Detroit* 163: But you can't buck the system. **1938** Shaw *Brothers in Crime* 167: I'd be

the loser every time if I tried to buck society. **1939–40** O'Hara *Pal Joey* 42: He would think twice about bucking this mouse's old man. **1951** Robbins *Danny Fisher* 145: You know better'n to buck the boys. **1956** in Loosbrock & Skinner *Wild Blue* 101: Start from New York and buck head winds all the way. **1968** Cuomo *Thieves* 144: You can't buck fingerprints. They got them on file at the FBI and everything. **1970** in P. Heller *In This Corner* 100: That calmed him down. He didn't buck me anymore. **1988** Kienzle *Marked for Murder* 255: Bush bucked odds all his life.

2. *Gamb.* to play at a game of chance, orig. faro or monte. Also trans.

1849 in *DA* 200: Several were in their seats, and I left them "bucking" away, desiring only once more to "get even" and then they "would quit." **1855** in Dwyer & Lingenfelter *Songs of Gold Rush* 61: I bucked awhile at Monte. **1856** in Derby *Squibob Papers* 43: I allmost hev a notion to...buck a nite or 2 at farow. **1871** "M. Twain" *Roughing It* 354: About every third Chinaman runs a lottery, and the balance..."buck" at it. **1879** *Snares of N.Y.* 19: I've bucked many a time, but I can't deal. **1885** Siringo *Texas Cowboy* 42: Some of them would "deal" monte while the rest of us "bucked." **1915** Howard *God's Man* 184: It's either buck the double-O, play the big game, or be a piker. **1926** C.M. Russell *Trails* 5: I was winterin' in Cheyenne. One night a stranger stakes me to buck the bank [at faro]. **1935** Lamson *About to Die* 186: He had fifty dollars on 'im, see, an' he starts bucking a crap game.

3. *Esp. Army.* to strive fervently (for a position, promotion, advantage, etc.), esp. by currying favor.—often used with elliptical complement, e.g., *buck for corporal* 'strive for a corporal's rank'. [The orig. army phr. seems to have been *buck for orderly,* explained in 1909 quots.; extended use, often ironic, became common *ca*1940.]

1881 in *DA* 201: I was bucking very strong for the job. **1900** McManus *Soldier Life* 104: Many of the old-time orderly-buckers refused to buck at guard-mount, preferring to take their chances on being assigned to the favorite post down below the old Malate church. **1907** Bush *Enlisted Man* 30: The first sergeant told me to go in and "buck" for orderly. He said the company usually put an orderly "bucker" on their guard detail and generally managed to corral the prize. **1909** J.A. Moss *Off. Man.* (ed. 2) 283: *Bucking For Orderly.*—giving clothing and accoutrements extra cleaning so as to compete for orderly. **1909** M'Govern *Krag Is Laid Away* 92: The men detailed for tomorrow's guard mount were oiling their guns or polishing brass buttons and bullets to "buck for orderly." **1921** *Sentinel* (Feb. 4) 9: Perain, our best and only mechanic, is bucking for the position of Supply Sergeant. **1926** *Sat. Eve. Post* (Oct. 23) 130: Pony Moore is the buckin'est corporal in the outfit. **1941** Hargrove *Pvt. Hargrove* 123: I was impressively busy on my afternoon's assignments. As Busheni says, probably bucking for corporal. **1941** *AS* (Oct.) 164 [Army]: *Bucking for Section 8.* Seeking discharge for military ineptitude. **1943** in Loosbrock & Skinner *Wild Blue* 210: What's the matter with you? Buckin' for Section Eight? **1944** Brooks *Brick Foxhole* 6: Aaaah, he's buckin' for sergeant. **1944–46** in *AS* XXII 54: *Bucking.* Currying favor or making pretense at being a polished soldier, with an eye to advancement. **1948** I. Shaw *Young Lions* 280: The Colonel is bucking for BG. **1948** A. Murphy *Hell & Back* 13: I don't go around reaching for splinters. I'm not bucking for the Purple Heart. **1951** *Amer. Jour. Socio.* 421: There are numerous ass lickers and "buckers" in the Army...To be [called] a bucker is a condemnation. **1953** Russ *Last Parallel* 142: Sir, I didn't buck for corporal. **1960** Leckie *Marines* 61: He...spends his time at sick bay bucking for a medical discharge. **1961** Pirosh & Carr *Hell Is for Heroes* (film): What are you, buckin' for chaplain? **1968** Hawley *Hurricane Yrs.* 182: You bucking for a job? **1971** Contini *Beast Within* 66: I knew he was bucking for parole and I hoped he could make it. **1974** Millard *Thunderbolt* 28: Some eager-beaver cop, bucking for promotion, would spot the license number. **1975** McCaig *Danger Trail* 5: He's bucking for trouble. **1973–77** J. Jones *Whistle* 36: Most of the people around here are bucking their heads off to get shipped back home to the States, and can't. **1978** Wharton *Birdy* 288: Here we are, three guys in a hole, bucking for civilian. **1979** Gutcheon *New Girls* 144: Jesus, she really is bucking for Government, isn't she? **1983** Ehrhart *VN-Perkasie* 144: You buckin' for private? **1987** Norst & Black *Lethal Weapon* 91: You're bucking for a stress disability pension. **1992** *Young & Restless* (CBS-TV): Everybody can see you're bucking for Executive of the Year.

4. [sugg. by *pass the buck* s.v. BUCK, *n.*] *Esp. Mil.* to forward; (*hence*) to pass on responsibility for.

1956 Heflin *USAF Dict.* 93: *Buck*...To forward a *letter, document,* or the like with a buck slip attached. **1958** Camerer *Damned Wear Wings* 206 [ref. to WWII]: I'll put...three carbons on Morrison's desk. He bucks 'em along to Wing, then Air Force. **1959** Webb *Pork Chop* (film): "Think we should buck it up to Corps?" "We'll have to. Maybe they'll have to buck it up higher than that." **1973** Chandler *Captain Hollister* 98: So you read Captain Hollister's things before bucking them to us for signature, Major? **1977** Hynek *UFO Report* 48: Responsibility is a commodity that, especially in the military, one tries to buck up the line.

¶ In phrase:

¶ **buck [against] the tiger** see s.v. TIGER.

buckaroo *n.* [< Sp *vaquero* 'cowboy, cow hand'; not fr. an African language: see extended discussion in *AS* XVII 10–15, XXXV 51–55, and esp. LIII 49–51 and LIV 151–153] **1.** *West.* a cowboy or bronco-buster.

1827 in *DA*: These [*sc.* rancheros] are surrounded by…peons and bakharas, or herdsmen. **1847** in D. Morgan *Overland* I 287: Callifornia…would Just suit Charley for he could ride down 3 or 4 horses a day and he could lern to be Bocarro that [is] one who lases cattel the spanards and Indians are the best riders i ever saw. **1851** Doten *Journals* I 85: Chinn and his buckiero have been gone in pursuit of the [horse and mules] since yesterday morning. **1870** [W.D. Phelps] *Fore & Aft* 303 [ref. to 1846]: Accompanied by an Indian "bucquero," a boy to take care of the horses. **1873** [Perrie] *Buckskin Mose* 172: A large stock of cattle…had been in the charge of five good and trusty *Buccahros* or herdsmen. **1889** in *DA* 201: Our feats were as nothing to what we saw at "Buckaroo" camp some distance from "the Cove." **1900** Wister *Jimmyjohn* 18: "Buccaroos?" "Yep. Cow-punchers. Vaqueros. Buccaroos in Oregon. Bastard Spanish word, you see, drifted up from Mexico." *Ibid.* 26: Five buccaroos entered and stood close. **1907** S.E. White *Arizona*: If you were going to be a buckaroo, you couldn't go into harder training. **1919** in C.M. Russell *Paper Talk* 159: Long ago I ust to hear them senter fire long reatia Buckaroos tell about California rodayos. **1922** Rollins *Cowboy* 39: In Oregon he frequently was called "baquero," "buckaroo," "buckhara" or "buckayro," each a perversion of either the Spanish "vaquero" or the Spanish "boyero," and each subject to be contracted into "bucker." **1926** C.M. Russell *Trails* 3: Cow punchers…west of the Rockies…called themselves buccaros, coming from the Spanish word, *vaquero*. **1931** Z. Grey *Sunset Pass* 46: She always has some buckaroo runnin' after her. **1932** in J.I. White *Git Along Dogies* 120: That part…is lost on all the flat country buckaroos. **1936** McCarthy *Mosshorn* (unp.): *Buckaroo.* One who breaks horses. **1947** Overholser *Buckaroo's Code* 39: You've got to fight, and you're aiming to use the buckaroos who have been doing the work and getting half the wages. **1967** Schaefer *Mavericks* 68: Here's another of them Black Hills buckaroos! **1976** Wren *Bury Me Not* 11: And only five of 'em…are buckaroos. **1979** C. Freeman *Portraits* 546: Okay, buckaroo, let's go home and show mama.

2. a man; BUCKO[2].

*ca*1930 in Bedell *Advert. That Sells* 46: As collegiate [in style] as a college yell…everything that's "It" for young "buckaroos" who know a new style when they see it. **1932** Berg *Prison Doctor* 222: Oh, ho, it's smart you're talking now, is it, me young buckaroo? **1939** O'Brien *One-Way Ticket* 99: That means I got to raise eighty bucks in a week, my buckaroos. *a*1961 Longman *Power of Black* 324: You're a smart buckaroo, Mistah Ashe. **1970** Ebert *Beyond Valley of Dolls* (film): Well, well, old buckaroo. **1978** W. Brown *Tragic Magic* 9: A token black survivor who has never been able to say, like so many of my fellow bronze buckaroos, "I'm a man and a half," and keep a straight face. **1979** Kava coffee ad, WBIR radio (Nov. 26): Good news for you buckaroos who are sometimes bothered by ordinary coffee. **1982** Heat Moon *Blue Hwys.* 206: Let's keep out of each other's way, okay, buckaroo? **1987** *21 Jump St.* (Fox-TV): OK, buckaroos, let's talk about what's goin' down.

buckaroo *v. West.* to work as a cowboy.

1947 Overholser *Buckaroo's Code* 156: He…used to buckaroo for Malloy. **1967** in *DARE*. **1976** Wren *Bury Me Not* 11: Linc and Ted do their share of buckarooin'

buck-ass private *n. Army & USMC.* BUCK PRIVATE.—usu. considered vulgar. Also **buck-ass**.

[**1936** in *Our Army* (Jan. 1937) 19: I'm just a buck-sterned dogface private which is the Orderly Room Punk.] **1945** Huie *Omaha to Oki.* 131: When we wuz sworn into the Regular Army…I had been everything from a buck-ass private to a top kick. **1952** Uris *Battle Cry* 177 [ref. to WWII]: I'm just a buck-assed private, lady. **1961** Plantz *Sweeney Sq.* 6: And what about you, Sidel, a buck-ass private again! **1962** Killens *Heard the Thunder* 14 [ref. to WWII]: You ain't even a private first-damn-class. You ain't hardly a buck-ass private. **1965** Linakis *In Spring* 316 [ref. to WWII]: Otherwise you'll be busted down to buck-ass and cleaning grease pits and doing K.P. for a month. **1967** Ford *Muc Wa* 6:

Lady, I'm just a buck-ass private.

buck-ass sergeant *n. Army & USMC.* BUCK SERGEANT.—usu. considered vulgar. [Quots. ref. to WWII.]

1957 E. Brown *Locust Fire* 93: Lewis, George R., sergeant, buck-ass. Army Air Corps. **1978** Wharton *Birdy* 25: He's liable to lower the boom on this buck-ass sergeant any minute. *a*1982 in Berry *Semper Fi* 23: All these buck-ass sergeants with hash marks up and down their sleeves.

buck-bathing *n.* [BUCK (NAKED) + *bathing*] swimming in the nude.

1931 in *DA* 199: Devotees of "buck bathing" who dance in the nude in and out of the surf are also unwelcome in Brigantine. **1963** D. Tracy *Brass Ring* 90 [ref. to 1930's]: Oh, two or three couples…would come up here with a jug and go buck-bathing.

bucker *n.* [fr. BUCK, *n.*, 2. + *-er*] a dollar; (*pl.*) money.

1979–82 Gwin *Overboard* 246: To make what she called some big buckers. **1989** Univ. Tenn. student: *Buckers* mean *bucks* or money.

buckeroo *n.* **1.** [BUCK + -EROO] a dollar.

1942 *ATS* 559: Dollar…*buck, buckeroo.* **1943–47** in Hodes & Hansen *Sel. from Gutter* 25: Dick gets lucky and gets a 25 buckeroo job. **1948** Manone & Vandervoort *Trumpet* 47: The union paid me back the ten buckeroos they had fined me. **1962** Viertel *Love & Corrupt* 268: Just money. Six or eight million buckeroos. That's all. **1963** Blechman *Omongo* 51: His paintings sell for thousands of buckeroos. **1984** *Good Morning America* (ABC-TV): They're racing their way across the country for a million buckeroos.

2. var. BUCKAROO.

bucket *n.* **1.a.** *Naut.* an old or unseaworthy vessel; TUB.—sometimes used affectionately.

1840 R.H. Dana *2 Yrs. Before Mast* 307: Hurrah, old bucket! **1888** Brooks *Amer. Sailor* 301: The sailor might abuse his vessel as "an infernal old bucket." **1930** Ellsberg *S-54* 225 [ref. to 1918]: This bucket's gonna be our finish, sure. **1930** Buranelli *Maggie* 2 [ref. to 1918]: She was one of a whole armada of similar buckets. **1946** S. Wilson *Voyage to Nowhere* 23: We've got to sail this bucket with just about the same equipment Columbus had. **1962** E. Stephens *Blow Negative* 280: It must be a drag on that bucket without *him* around. **1967** Dibner *Admiral* 18: Once this bucket gets under way I doubt that her damaged deck and hull plates can stand the strain. **1969** Searls *Hero Ship* 163: This goddamn bucket! **1976** S.C. Lawrence *Northern Saga* 117: I wanted to get off this bucket.

b. an old, rickety, or dilapidated motor vehicle or aircraft.

1939 in Hemingway *Fifth Column* 117: It's the noise in these buckets. **1940** in Goodstone *Pulps* 115: I…climbed into my bucket and souped the kidneys out of it. **1946** Boulware *Jive and Slang* 2: *Bucket,*…automobile. **1957** *Sat. Eve. Post* (Aug. 10) 68: What do you suppose he'd give me for a 1948 bucket in beautiful condition? **1960** MacDonald *Slam the Big Door* 93: We should trade in that bucket. **1962** S. Smith *Escape from Hell* 135: Christ only knows if this bucket'll hold together! **1972** W.C. Anderson *Hurricane* 84: Keep this old bucket right side up. **1973** *Roll Out!* (CBS-TV): We been driving them double-clutching buckets all the way to the front. **1979** Abrahams et al. *Airplane!* (film): You know I've never flown a bucket like this.

2. a jail; lockup.

1894 in Ade *Chicago Stories* 94: No more drillin' in the snow; no soup houses; never again in a bucket. **1936** (quot. at BOOB, *n.*). **1947** Boyer *Dark Ship* 10: I was in the bucket about ten days. **1961** Braly *Felony Tank* 98: You can't miss it when you've been around as many of these buckets as I have. **1965** R. Conot *Rivers of Blood* 120: The language…employs the use of such words as "fink," "cop out," "taking a fall," "in the bucket," and so forth. **1968** Spradley *Drunk* 81: Tramps refer to any local city or county jail as "the bucket." **1983** *Nat. Lampoon* (Aug.) 22: Rudy bailed me out of the…bucket.

3. *Basketball.* the act of scoring a basket; a field goal.

1928 Carr *Rampant Age* 152: The upward-twisting arm motion of a basketball player "shootin' a bucket." **1976** Rosen *Above Rim* 236: Score the clutch bucket for Kareem Abdul-Jabbar to tie the game. **1984** *N.Y. Post* (Aug. 11) 44: Last night they improved by one bucket. **1993** *New Yorker* (May 17) 108: A million dollars if he sank the bucket.

4.a. the buttocks; BUTT; anus.

1938 "Justinian" *Americana Sexualis* 14: *Bucket.* n. Posterior. Probably semantically from *buttock*. **1941** Legman *Lang. of Homosex.*: *Bucket.* The anus. **1949** *Gay Girl's Guide* 4: *Bucket*—Posterior (clothed, outlined). **1958** *Hell to Eternity* (film): Get the lead out of your bucket! **1963** Boyle *Yanks* 89: Stick the fish up your bucket! **1969** Smith *U.S.M.C. in*

WWII 113: Suppose this means "up your bucket" in Japanese. **1972** *Life* (Oct. 27) 26: Swinging the buckets of all those sexy dancers who come into mental focus the instant you hear this irresistible party music. **1974** Scalzo *Stand on Gas* 142: I figure I'm going to bust my bucket in one of these damn sprinters anyway. **1984** *Cheers* (NBC-TV): Miss Big-Buckets.

b. a woman.

1954–60 *DAS*: *Bucket*…Any ugly or unpleasant girl or woman. **1968** Mailer *Armies of Night* 98: A plump young waitress with a strong perfume, who looked nonetheless a goddess of a bucket for a one-night stand.

c. (one's) self, life, etc.

1979 *Young Maverick* (Dec. 12) (CBS-TV): I'm beholden to you, ma'am. Your warnin' shout saved my bucket.

5. *Auto.* an engine cylinder.

1942 *ATS* 721: Cylinder. *Barrel*,…*bucket*, [etc.]. **1971** Tak *Truck Talk* 22: *Bucket*: an engine cylinder.

6. a bucket seat.

1943 in J. Gunther *D Day* 26: For seats we have the celebrated "buckets"…there are no arm or back rests, and the shelf…looks like a series of shallow biscuit molds. **1981** Wolf *Roger Rabbit* 12: In the right front bucket of a white Mercedes.

7. *Bowling.* a 2-4-5-6 or 3-5-6-9 leave.

1949 Cummings *Dict. Sports* 52. **1976** *Webster's Sports Dict.* 59. **1982** T. Considine *Lang. of Sport* 84.

8. a dolt; JERK.

1954–60 *DAS*: *Bucket*…A disliked, objectionable, dull person. *Some student use since c1945.* **1969** Cagle *Naval Av. Guide* 390: *Bucket*…A dumbbell.

9. *Mil. Av.* (see quot.).

1969 Cagle *Naval Av. Guide* 390: *Bucket*…a towed target sleeve.

10. *Hosp.* a bedpan.

1980 *AS* (Spring) 47.

11. [prob. sugg. by *kick the bucket* s.v. KICK, *v.*] death.—constr. with *the*.

1983 Helprin *Winter's Tale* 123: When I got up, I couldn't run anymore. I thought it was the bucket.

¶ In phrases:

¶ **go in the bucket** *Baseball.* *put one's foot in the bucket*, below.

1939–40 Tunis *Kid from Tomkinsville* 113: Even the best hitters on the squad began going into the bucket.

¶ **kick the bucket** see s.v. KICK, *v.*

¶ **put one's foot in the bucket** *Baseball.* (of a batter) to move the leading foot away from the pitch while striding to meet it. Also vars.

1922 J. Conway, in *Variety* (June 9) 9: Another guy used to put his foot in the bucket so far that he nearly spiked the visiting bench. **1982** T. Considine *Lang. of Sport* 20: *Foot in the bucket.* The movement of the front foot away from the plate (and toward the dugout water bucket) during the batter's stride into a swing. **1987** *21 Jump St.* (Fox-TV): He steps in the bucket on the inside pitch.

bucket *v.* *Basketball.* to score (a point).

1957 J. Updike, in Cotter *Invit. to Poetry* 33: In '46/He bucketed three hundred ninety points.

bucketfoot *n.* [sugg. by *put one's foot in the bucket* s.v. BUCKET] *Baseball.* a batter who habitually moves his leading foot away from a pitch.

1952 Malamud *Natural* 67: Some are bucket foots and some go for bad throws.

buckethead *n.* a blockhead. Hence **bucketheaded**, *adj.*

1906 in Blackbeard & Williams *Smithsonian Comics* 37: Git out of the way you bucketheaded lunatic. **1954–60** *DAS* 67: *Buckethead*…A stupid person. **1965** in *Nat. Observer* (May 3, 1975) D: The boots are no longer clowns or bucketheads or the earthier terms they still expect to hear in common usage. **1980** Pearl *Slang Dict.*: *Buckethead n.* a fool.

bucketmouth *n.* a person who habitually talks too much; (*specif.*) one who uses foul language.

1975 Dills *CB Slanguage* 21: *Bucket Mouth:* loud mouth or gossip; obscene or profane talker. **1976** Bibb et al. *CB Bible* 65: Number one bucket mouth of the South. **1977** Corder *Citizens Band* 69: What about…the bucket mouth who reads porno over Twenty?

bucket of blood *n.* **1.** a low saloon, dance hall, or similar establishment that is a frequent scene of violence.

1915 H. Young *Hard Knocks* 123 [ref. to Laramie, Wyo., ca1870]: So many disappeared that the saloon was called the "Bucket of Blood." **1917** in Rudwick *Race Riot* 210: The Bucket of Blood. **1926** Dunning & Abbott *B'way* 246: Ease off, Greek, you didn't think I came back to this bucket of blood to work, did you? **1936** Washburn *Parlor* 44: His Frieberg's Hall thrived on its bucket-of-blood notoriety. **1938** Asbury *Sucker's Progress* 329 [ref. to ca1890]: Such notorious resorts as the Palace, the Bucket of Blood, the Morgue. **1947** W.M. Camp *S.F.* 215 [ref. to 1890's]: Pat Ryan's Blue Shades Saloon, also known as the "Bucket of Blood," just above Third Street on Stevenson. **1951** *West. Folklore* X 80: Barroom slang from the Upper Rio Grande.—The setting…[a] bucket of blood. **1967** in Hayes *Smiling Through Apocalypse* 63: The club bruised along, and became known as Dallas' "bucket of blood." **1968** R. Adams *Western Wds.* (ed. 2) 39: The original Bucket of Blood was Shorty Young's notorious dive in Havre, Montana. **1969** Gordone *No Place* 421: It ain't none a yo' business what he does outside this bucket'a blood. **1972** D. Pearce *Pier Head Jump* 24: This joint Tommy has is a real bucket o' blood. Fights and music and broads runnin' in and out all the time. **1982** L. Block *Eight Million Ways* 267: I wanted…to walk through the door of that bucket of blood and put my foot upon the brass rail.

2. a cocktail consisting of vodka and tomato juice.

1985 *USA Today* (Dec. 10) 1D: The first vodka/tomato juice combination, however, is generally attributed to Fernand Petiot, a bartender at Harry's bar in Paris who served his "Bucket of Blood" to fledgling writers such as Ernest Hemingway and F. Scott Fitzgerald in the 1920s.

bucket of bolts *n.* **1.** a ramshackle, noisy, or antiquated vehicle, esp. an aircraft.

1942 in C.R. Bond & T. Anderson *Flying T. Diary* 71: He refers to my ship as a bucket of bolts. [**1944** in Butterfield *Post Treasury* 435: There was something about the Harpy…that made her more than a battling bag of bolts.] **1948** in Galewitz *Great Comics* 280: Let's go see if the old bucket of bolts checks out. **1954–60** *DAS* 67: *Bucket of bolts.* A car, esp. an old dilapidated car that rattles when in motion. **1966** Little *Bold & Lonely* 243: Hell, the ME-109 was your best, and we shot that bucket-of-bolts out of the air, friend. **1968** W. Anderson *Gooney Bird* 41: Do you mean to say we're actually going to ferry that twin-engine bucket of bolts? **1976** *Sci. Mech. CB Gde.* 26: If you have a foreign "bucket of bolts" a check of the electrical system is in order. *****1980** Leland *Kiwi-Yank. Dict.* 19: *Bucket of bolts:* A jalopy.

2. an engine, as of an aircraft.

1945 Hamann *Air Words* s.v. **1956** Heflin *USAF Dict.* 94: *Bucket o' bolts.* An airplane engine. *Slang.*

bucket of lard *n.* a grossly obese person.

1965–70 in *DARE* I 416.

bucket of worms *n.* CAN OF WORMS.

1973 Maas *Serpico* 161: It sounds like a real bucket of worms. *a*1979 Peers & Bennett *Logical Laws* 107: A leap beyond the state of the art may be into a bucket of worms.

bucket shop *n.* **1.** a low saloon that sells beer in buckets. Now *hist.*

1872 Crapsey *Nether Side of N.Y.* 129: The vile liquor of the bucket shop. **1881** in Thornton *Amer. Gloss.* I: A "bucket shop" in N.Y. is a low "gin-mill" or "distillery," where small quantities of spirits are dispensed in pitchers and pails (buckets). **1882** Campbell *Poor* 11: Every other house was a "bucket shop"—a saloon where only the cheapest liquor is sold.

2. *Finance.* an unethical brokerage firm, as one that speculates on its own account against its customers' interests.

1879 *Nat. Police Gaz.* (June 14) 14: Mr. Prowler Discourses…Upon One Kind of Bucket Shop. **1880** in *DA* 202: The failure of the "Produce Exchanges," or bucket shops…caused little excitement. **1883** *Life* (July 19) 40: This is a scene in a "bucket shop." **1886** Nye *Remarks* 40: The exhumist also ran into an Etruscan bucket-shop in one part of the city. **1887** in Ware *Pass. English* 52: Johnson is another victim of bucket-shop speculation. **1888** in *F & H* I 350: Inspector Byrnes was seized with another spasm of indignation against the *bucket-shops* this morning, and, accompanied by detectives and a squad of officers, he swooped down upon the lairs of these enemies of the Stock Exchange that abound on Lower Broadway and New Street. **1908** "O. Henry" *Gentle Grafter* 268: It made Rockefeller's little kerosene speculation look like a bucket shop. **1912** Ade *Babel* 4: A fool with his money!…showy betting at the race-tracks…experiments at the bucket-shops. **1929** "E. Queen" *Roman Hat* 73: He was suspected of negotiating a swindle connected with the bucket-shop scandals. **1950** Spewack

Golden State 19: What was his racket—bucket shop? **1952** Bellow *Augie March* 39: Tommy sent us to his bucket-shop stockbroker on Lake Street. **1989** L. Roberts *Full Cleveland* 57: The Shanes...started their own little bucket shop in the garage, selling advertising.

buckeye *n.* **1.a.** a backwoodsman or settler of the Ohio Valley.

1823 in *DAE* I 334: The indigenous backwoodsman is sometimes called buck-eye, in distinction from the numerous emigrants who are introducing themselves from the eastern states. **1828** in *DAE* I 334: [She] put into his arms a third boy, a fine Illinois buckeye too. **1857** in *DAE* I 334: A handsome young Buckeye Who lived in the West, in the state of Kentucky.

b. (now *cap.*) *Specif.*, an Ohioan. Now *S.E.*

1833 Hoffman *Winter in West* I 210: Nothing was wanting but a "buckeye" from Ohio to render the assemblage as complete as it was select. **1835** in Meine & Owen *Crockett* 45: The lasses of Ohio are all called "Buckeyes."...The "buckeyes" said there was no being up to plaguey Irish "no how." **1837** in R.B. Hayes *Diary* I 16: He was a real Buckeye. **1839** Marryatt *Diary* 271: Ohio...Buckeyes. **1845** in Thornton *Amer. Gloss.* II 974: A smart sprinkling of the inhabitants of Illinois are from New England...and the balance are Pukes...Hoosiers...Buckeyes, [etc.]. **1866** [H.L. Williams] *Gay Life in N.Y.* 20: Mr. Harry Callow, like myself a Buckeye, from Ohio. **1894** H.U. Johnson *Dixie to Canada* 68: "You bist von Yankee, then." "No, I'm a Buckeye."

2. a place of business occupying one or two small rooms, as in a slum; (*specif.*) a cigar factory of this description.

1915 in *DARE* I 417. **1937** *AS* (Dec.) 270: Yet in their day these small factories, or *buckeyes* as they were always called by the cigar-makers themselves, played a rather important rôle. **1947** *New Yorker* (Feb. 15) 59: A buckeye is a small shop in which cigars are made by hand in a back room and sold across the counter out front. **1979** in Terkel *Amer. Dreams* 107 [ref. to Chicago, 1896]: It was a garret with a couple of benches....The place was called a buckeye, the name for a sleazy shop, filthy, no air.

3.a. (see quots.).

1881 (cited in Thornton *Amer. Gloss.*). **1906** *Atlantic Mo.* (Nov.) 640: The despised "buckeye" painter who paints for the department stores and cheap picture shops. **1920** S. Lewis *Main St.*, in *DARE*: The walls of Mrs. Cass's parlor were plastered with "hand-painted" pictures, "buckeye" pictures, of birch-trees, news-boys, puppies, and church-steeples on Christmas Eve. **1942** *ATS* 552: *Buckeye*...a painting of no value, turned out in quantities.

b. *Adver.* an unsophisticated or poorly conceived advertisement.

1982 T.D. Connors *Dict. Mass Media* 37: *Buckeye*...derogatory term for an advertisement visually unsophisticated or lacking in taste.

buckeye *adj.* *Ohio Valley.* second-rate; (*esp.*) unskilled or untrained; JACKLEG.—used prenominally.

1843 in *DARE*: Endowed with our buck-eye-preacher's pathos and unction. **1846** in *DA* 202: The buckeye...as a tree stood very low in the estimation of early settlers [of Cincinnati], and by a figure of speech very forcible to them it was applied to lawyers and doctors whose capacity and attainment were of a low grade.

buck fever *n.* Orig. *Hunting.* nervousness and uncertainty of the sort experienced by a novice hunter at the sight of game. Now *colloq.* or *S.E.*

1841 in *DA*. **1885** E. Custer *Boots & Saddles* 33: One of the officers afforded great amusement...because of an attack of "buck fever." **1890** E. Custer *Guidon* 33 [ref. to 1868]: An attack of "buck fever." At sight of a tree weighed down...with turkeys, he became incapable of loading, to say nothing of firing, his gun. **1893** Casler *Stonewall* 27 [ref. to Civil War]: Some of our men who, evidently, had the "buck fever," commenced, without orders, firing some scattering shots. **1915** D. Collins *Indians' Last Fight* 161: I was influenced by what is called "buck fever." **1971** *Harper's* (Nov.) 128: The buck fever now is terrific. What must I do? **1983** Beckwith & Knox *Delta Force* 174: The German snipers froze. The opportunity was there, but they froze. Was it buck fever? **1986** F. Walton *Once Were Eagles* 133: I'd see a Zero and get buck fever.

buck general *n.* [sugg. by BUCK PRIVATE, BUCK SERGEANT] *Mil.* a brigadier general, esp. if newly appointed.

1944–46 in *AS* XXII 54: *Buck General.* Brigadier general. **1956** *AS* (Oct.) 227: *Buck General* is a brigadier general, lowest in the group of generals, as a buck private or a buck sergeant is lowest in his own group. **1965** W. Beech *Make War in Madness* 74: Thirty buck generals and full

bird colonels sitting and fuming while they waited for a PFC. *ca*1965 IUFA *Folk Speech* [N.Y.]: *Buck general*...(rarely heard) Brigadier General. **1985** former Sp4, U.S. Army, age 35: *Buck general* is a term I heard just a few times [during the 1970's].

buckitis *n.* *Hunting.* BUCK FEVER.
1965–69 in *DARE.*

buckle *v.* to argue; fight.
1970 *Current Slang* V 4: *Buckle,* v. To argue about insignificant things.—College students, Minnesota. **1978** J. Webb *Fields of Fire* 110 [ref. to Vietnam, 1969]: They know the bush, and they can buckle for your dust, Sarge. *Ibid.* 412: *Buckle*: to fight. *Buckle For Your Dust*: To fight furiously. **1990** P. Dickson *Slang!* 234: *Buckle*. To fight.

buckload *n.* [sugg. by SHOT] a large drink of whiskey or other liquor.
1834 *Mil. & Nav. Mag.* 248: The whisky bottle having been set before him, he poured out what in frontier phrase is termed "a buck-load." **1836** *Spirit of Times* (July 9) 162: Colonel, let us have some of your *byled corn*—pour me out a buck load—there—never mind about the water, I drank a heap of it yesterday. *ca*1867 in Harris *Lovingood* 171: He...tuck hissef a buckload ove popskull, an' slip't the bottil intu his pocket. **1898** Green *Va. Folk-Speech* 71: *Buck-load, n.* A large drink of liquor.

buck naked *adj.* stark naked. Also (*vulgar*) **buck-ass naked, bucko naked.**
1928 Peterkin *Sister Mary* 33: You ain' stand up buck naked like dat. **1939** Attaway *Breathe Thunder* 210: Thrown out in the street buck naked. **1952** Randolph & Wilson *Down in Holler* 97: [In the Ozarks] the word *buck-naked* is avoided in polite conversation, although *bare-naked*, *mother-naked*, [etc.] are not offensive. **1955** Willingham *Eat a Peach* 180: What are you, buck naked? **1961** C. Himes *Pinktoes* 113: I'll wrestle you buck-naked. **1962** Killens *Heard Thunder* 291: Buck naked as a jaybird in whistling time. **1969** in *DARE* I 420: Buck-ass naked. **1971** *Newsweek* (Sept. 13) 40: They could hit us right now and all we'd be is a bunch of buck-ass naked fools scrambling like ants. **1973** *Nat. Lampoon* (Mar.) 10: Stark, staring, bucko naked.

buck nun *n.* *West.* a reclusive bachelor. *Joc.*
1907 S.E. White *Ariz. Nights* ch. iii: I might as well go be a buck nun and be done with it. **1944** R. Adams *West. Words* 22: Buck-nun—A recluse, a man who lives alone. **1967** in *DARE* I 420.

Bucko *n.* usu. *pl.* [alter. *bucc*aneer + *-o*] *Baseball.* a member of the Pittsburgh Pirates.
1982 WKGN radio newscast (July 25): The Atlanta Braves lost to the Pittsburgh Buckos this afternoon by a score of 8-2.

bucko[1] *n.* **1.** a bully; a tough; (*esp.*) *Naut.* a brutal ship's officer.—often attrib.
1883 Keane *Blue-Water* 190: After that, no sailor will deny that a "bucko mate" is not sometimes useful, especially when he has a lot of "hang-back, smothered-up-with-dunnage" Dutchmen to drive. **1896** Hamblen *Many Seas* 317: Every man aboard, from the captain down, prides himself on being a "bucko,"—a fighter, that is to say. *Ibid.* 397: Are you de bucko mate of dis bloody hooker, hey? **1897** Kelley *Ship's Company* 155: Brutality was at a premium then, and the sea ruffian was a "bucko" beloved of the state. **1899** Hamblen *Bucko Mate* 36: Sailors are bad; "bucko" officers are tough. *Ibid.* 217: You remember a rule that the bucko sailors used to enforce among the Dutchmen in the old packets, Jack? **1908** J.H. Williams, in *Independent* (Aug. 27) 474: According to the whim of Captain Gammon and his horde of "buckoes." **1908** *Hampton's Mag.* (Dec.) 768: No sailor slugs a bucko mate unless he's drunk. **1925** Farmer *Shellback* 54: Much has been written of the "bucko" mate of American ships...but the bucko was to be found under every flag and on every sea. **1929* Bowen *Sea Slang* 19: *Bucko.* A hard case under sail, particularly a mate. **1932** *Leatherneck* (May) 25: So the bucko went back with a marlinespike. **1937** "L. Short" *Brand of Empire* 49: "It'll take a better bully boy than that."..."No more buckos." **1954** Collans & Sterling *House Detect.* 95: But when it came to the belligerent buckos, there'd be an H.O. call. **1976** Hayden *Voyage* 172: He wasn't born a bucko....Something along the road took him and turned him into a devil.

2. *Army.* BUCK PRIVATE.
1941 (quot. at CRUIT).

bucko[2] *n.* [prob. < Ir *buachaill* 'boy; child'; derivation fr. BUCK + *-o* is less convincing] Esp. *Irish-Amer.* boy; fellow.—used esp. in direct address.
1890 in *F & H* I 346: *Bucco*...(American thieves').—A dandy. **1892** F.P. Dunne, in Schaaf *Dooley* 42: Well, Frank me bucko, an' how ar-re ye?

1898 F.P. Dunne *Dooley in Peace & War* 39: That's where ye'er wrong, me bucko. **1899** Cullen *Tales* 119: "Be careful, my bucko," said the Sergeant. **1902** Norris *The Pit* ch. iii: This time I want to…get a twist on those Porteous buckoes. **1918** in O'Neill *Lost Plays* 38: I'd not have sent for this bucko if Eileen didn't scare me by faintin'. **1938** "E. Queen" *4 Hearts* 177: Listen, me fine bucko, you haven't *got* a private life. **1946** in F. Brown *Angels & Spaceships* 23: Well, my bucko, you don't get the job. **1958** J. Ward *Buchanan* 22: Step aside, bucko, I'm going upstairs. **1958** in C. Beaumont *Best* 67: Anything, my buckos, anything; but not this. **1986** *Miami Vice* (NBC-TV): Guess again, bucko. **1991** *Saved by the Bell* (NBC-TV): You are in big trouble, bucko!

bucko[3] *n.* [BUCK + -o] a dollar.
1983 *Good Morning America* (ABC-TV) (June 2): *Space Hunter* is a big-budget movie—twenty-million buckos.

bucko cap *n. Naut.* a visored cap of a kind worn by BUCKO[1] officers.
1904 J.H. Williams, in *Independent* (June 23) 1432: At the further end of the bar stood a long, lanky gantline, dressed in dirty jean pants, a dungaree jumper and a "bucko" cap.

buck out *v. West.* to die.
1922 Rollins *Cowboy* 55: [The "bad man's"] demise was sometimes referred to as his "snuffing out," "bucking out," "croaking," "cashing in," or "passing in his checks." **1939** in *DARE* I 421.

buck party *n.* a party, as on shipboard, in an army camp, etc., of men only.
1837 J.C. Neal *Charcoal Sks.* 26: It's a buck party, if I may use the expression—a buck party entirely. **1871** Schele de Vere *Amer.* 587: *Buck-party*, like stag-party, denotes a company without ladies.

buck-passer *n.* one who habitually shifts responsibility to others. See also BUCK-PASSING and *pass the buck* s.v. BUCK.
1920 (cited in *W10*). **1924–27** Nason *Three Lights* 150: All right, I'll carry it.…I ain't no buck passer. **1933** in *OEDS*: Why, you lying buck-passer! **1934** Weseen *Slang Dict.* 313: *Buck passer*—A person who evades work and responsibility by passing it on to someone else. **1965** Ward & Kassebaum *Women's Pris.* 21: They seem to be able to give you…facts without being a buck passer. **1966** Young & Hixson *LSD* 70: Kesey is no buck-passer. **1972** B. Harrison *Hospital* 187: You have to be able to pick out the buck passers and stop them.

buck-passing *n.* the shifting of responsibility to others. See also BUCK-PASSER and *pass the buck* s.v. BUCK.
*a*1968 in Haines & Taggart *Ft. Lauderdale* 106: I am opening myself to…charges of buck-passing by leveling responsibility at our elders. **1983** Curry *River's in Blood* 201: A move which occasioned much consternation and buck-passing among various bureaucratic levels. **1986** in Campbell & Moyers *Power of Myth* 45: "The woman said, 'The serpent beguiled me, and I ate.' " You talk about buck passing, it starts very early.

buck private *n. Mil.* a private soldier; (*USAF*) a basic airman. Now *S.E.* [Cf. slightly earlier BUCK SOLDIER; prob. fr. S.E. *buck* 'an impetuous or spirited man or youth'; attempts to derive the term from BUCK 'a dollar' and *pass the buck* s.v. BUCK are untenable.]
1874 *Chicago Inter-Ocean* (in Krause & Olson *Prelude to Glory* 142): I am not a serios Ristocrats. But a comen Bock Private of the 7th U.S. Cavalry. **1874** in D. Jackson *Custer's Gold* 37: And even if an officer did get wet he could go into his tent and change for dry under-clothing, but a poor unfortunate "buck private,"…would have to let the heat of his body evaporate the rain. **1874** Ewert *Diary* 28: A poor unfortunate buck private, unable to boast of…a dry change. **1899** Cullen *Tales* 103: That's what I was—a buck private. **1900** Reeves *Bamboo Tales* 22: Archie Fettin, late of the Queen's Own, but now a "buck" private in Uncle Sam's Service. **1909** J.A. Moss *Officer's Man.* (ed. 2) 283: *Buck private*—term sometimes used in referring to a private. **1915** in White *Amer. Negro Folk-Songs* 289: I'd rather be in the cotton-field/Working hard,/Than be a buck-private in the/National Guard. **1918** Witwer *Baseball to Boches* 55: They was only one buck private…standin' next to me. **1927** J. Stevens *Mattock* 89: But now I was just a buck private. **1941** Hargrove *Pvt. Hargrove* 30: The term "buck private" was explained to us this afternoon. It refers to the Old Army Game, "passing the buck."…The private…can't pass the buck any farther. He keeps it. That makes him a buck private. **1948** Lay & Bartlett *12 O'Clock High* 75: Suddenly he looked more closely at the man, whose sleeves, bare of chevrons, proclaimed that he was a buck private. **1956** Heflin *USAF Dict.* 94: A buck private now corresponds to a basic airman in the AF.

1987 Pelfrey & Carabatsos *Hamburger Hill* 99 [ref. to Vietnam War]: The nest egg ranged from ninety dollars a month for a buck private [etc.].

Buck Rogers [gun] *n. Mil.*, esp. *Navy.* a twin- or quad-mounted antiaircraft battery. [Their appearance fancifully suggested the futuristic weapons used in the science-fiction comic strip "Buck Rogers in the 23rd Century."]
1947 Morison *Naval Ops.* II 85 [ref. to 1942]: Ensign Starts's landing force…set up their "Buck Rogers" guns and stood siege. **1953** Dodson *Away All Boats* 310 [ref. to WWII]: What a target; we could chew him to bits with a few Buck Rogerses. *Ibid.* 416: Round came the gun barrels to open fire in flat trajectory—surely those Buck Rogerses would hit him.

buck sergeant *n.* [sugg. by BUCK PRIVATE] *Army, USMC, & USAF.* an ordinary sergeant of the lowest pay grade; line sergeant. Now *S.E.* [Cf. poss. factitious 1917 quot. at BUCK, *adj.*, 2.; the term was not much used before the 1930's.]
1934 *Our Army* (Nov.) 22: I am a buck sergeant with a chance of being Top Kick later. **1941** Hargrove *Pvt. Hargrove* 107: Well…three stripes means he's just a plain buck sergeant. **1944** *Stars & Stripes* (Rome) (July 1): The [officers] all looked a little sheepish when the tough buck sergeant bawled them out. **1957** E. Brown *Locust Fire* 144 [ref. to WWII]: You'd have your rights and privileges. The same as any other buck sergeant. **1972** Haldeman *War Year* 3: A buck sergeant—three stripes, nothing to be afraid of—was in charge of us. **1983** Van Devanter & Morgan *Before Morning* 53: J.J. was a…buck sergeant. **1992** R. Herman, Jr. *Force of Eagle* 445: The two buck sergeants looked at each other.

buckskin *n.* **1.** a Southern backwoodsman, (*specif.*) one of Virginia.
1744 A. Hamilton *Gent. Progress* 123: I told him that the most dangerous wild beasts in these woods were shaped exactly like men, and they went by the name of buckskins, or bucks,…something…betwixt a man and a beast. **1745** in *DAE*: The Inhabitants on the *Western Shore* are supply'd…from this *Eastern Shore*…to whom they give, also, ironically, the epithet of *Buckskins*, alluding to their Leather Breeches and the Jackets of some of the common People. **1774** in *DAE*: I suppose…[she] has in a merry hour call'd him a Lubber, or a thick-skull, or a Buckskin. **1782** in Bartlett *Amer.* (ed. 4) 73: The name of *Buckskin* is given to the inhabitants of Virginia, because their ancestors were hunters, and sold buck or rather deer skins. **1800** M. Weems, in *DAE*: What! a buckskin! they say with a smile. George Washington a buckskin! pshaw! impossible! he was certainly an European. **1825** J. Neal *Bro. Jonathan* 245: He, a Yankee! he's a Buckskin, every inch of him. **1835** in *DA*: Buckskin is the nickname for Southerns and Westerns.

2. *Logging.* (see quot.).
1938 Holbrook *Mackinaw* 255: *Buckskin.* A log from which bark has fallen off.

buck slip *n.* [prob. sugg. by *pass the buck* s.v. BUCK] *Mil.* a small printed form used for the routing of paperwork.
1943 *Yank* (June 11) 15: Think of the buck slips, pile on pile. **1945** *Yank* (Aug. 3) 15: He handed a yellow buck—er, pardon—yellow slip of paper to Phnar. **1951** *Time* (July 2) 17: An expert use of the buckslip—a small routing slip on which higher authority checks off directions such as "for action," "brief for me," etc.—is an essential Pentagon skill.

buck soldier *n. Army.* a common soldier, esp. a private.
1865 in Springer *Sioux Country* 52: We were—nothing [but] "buck soldiers" in the old First U.S. Regular Cavalry. **1866** in H. Johnson *Talking Wire* 323: As the council was held in the headquarters building, none of us buck soldiers could attend. **1871** *Sioux City Wkly. Times* (Nov. 18) (cited in Athearn *Forts of Upper Mo.* 275): Buck Soldier. **1899–1900** Cullen *Tales* 327: The best I did by switching togs with a buck soldier was to get ditched at Mojave, Cal. **1900** F. Remington *With Bark On* 32: The trumpeter hunted up his instrument while a buck soldier observed, "De old man ull be hotter'n chilli 'bout dis." **1918** *N.Y. Sun* (Aug. 25) V 7: Not a common buck solder any more but a Runner for the Majur. **1930** *Annals of Wyo.* VII 418 [ref. to 1876]: There were two bars in Tillotson's sutler store for officers, the other for white citizens and buck soldiers.

buck-swimming *n.* [BUCK (NAKED) + *swimming*] swimming in the nude; BUCK-BATHING.
1942 Wilder *Flamingo Rd.* 44: I wouldn't be more surprised if I saw the minister's wife buck-swimming in the river.

buckwheat *n.* **1.a.** an ignorant rustic; RUBE; (*hence*) an unpleasant individual. Also **buckwheater.**

1866 *Beadle's Mo.* (Mar.) 248: The most novel and sometimes very funny experiences are with the [Pa.] aborigines, or, as they are called "Buckwheats." **1900** *DN* II 24: *Buckwheat, n.* A green-horn. **1904** *DN* II 395: *Buckwheat, n.* A countryman: a rustic; a "hecker." N.J. **1911** *Hampton's Mag.* (Sept.) 178: The town ought to be full o' buckwheats....Rubes...any guy that comes from the camps. **1942** *ATS* s.v.: Buckwheater. **1956** Sorden & Ebert *Logger's* 5 [ref. to *a*1925]: *Buckwheater,* A novice at lumbering. **1958** McCulloch *Woods Words* 20: *Buckwheater*—A green hand, newcomer to the woods.

b. (used as a disrespectful or jocular term of address to a man).

1987 *Miami Vice* (NBC-TV): Hey, buckwheat, lemme in, man! **1990** Poyer *Gulf* 53: Jus' cool it, Buckwheat.

2. *pl.* nonsense; poppycock.

1924 in Wilstach *Stage Slang* 22: *Buckwheats:* Poppycock, nonsense. **1928** in Wilstach *Stage Slang* (unp.): A "spieler"...is talking "buckwheats."

3. *pl.* Esp. *Pris.* great abuse, esp. in the form of disciplinary action.

1942 Goldin et al. *DAUL* 35: How come you're dishing out buckwheats to me? *Ibid.* 247: Abuse, v....hit with buckwheats. **1955** Graziano & Barber *Somebody Up There* 214: He really give me the buckwheats, this sergeant. **1959** Morrill *Dark Sea Running* 77 [ref. to WWII]: The old Man threw the buckwheats at Hymie today for letting the gun tubs rust.

buckwheat *v.* [fr. the n.] *Pris.* to abuse, as by overwork or severe disciplinary action.

1942 Goldin et al. *DAUL* 35: Them crumby...hacks...are buckwheating me to death. **1955** Graziano & Barber *Somebody Up There* 227: They were out to really buckwheat me....The orders were to keep rubbing it in.

bucky *n.* fellow.—used in direct address.

1845 Smith *Vernon* 41: How much are they, buckey?...No matter, buckey, wait till I come along again.

bud[1] *n.* [perh. an American survival with changed connotation of the Early ModE endearment (which was applied affectionately or sarcastically to either sex): cf. 19th C. Hiberno-E colloq. use of endearments *darling, my jewel,* and *honey* as casual terms of address for either sex; perh. a childish pron. of *brother*]

1. fellow; man; friend.—used in direct address, often to a stranger whose name is not known.

*1614 B. Jonson *Bartholomew Fair* III i: *Over.* What do you mean, [you] sweet buds of gentility? *Cokes.* To ha' my pennyworths out on you, bud. *1675 Wycherley *Country Wife* II 1: 'Tis no matter, bud [i.e., my child]. **1851** in *DAE*: "An't you joking, bud?" asked Polly of her boy brother. **1888** *Scribner's Mag.* (Aug.) 166: Say, bud, you was thar, tell us. **1899** Munroe *Shine Terrill* 99: Look hyar, Bud; yo're too keen on the argue fer me to ketch up with. **1902** Wister *Virginian* 28: "This way, Pard."..."This way, Beau."..."This way, Budd." **1902–03** Ade *People You Know* 88: Here, Bud, open your Eyes! **1903** in "O. Henry" *Works* 155: "Got it pretty bad, bud?"..."Cricket" McGuire looked up pugnaciously at the imputation cast by "bud." **1905** *DN* III 71: *Bud*...Used familiarly [in Arkansas] in addressing a small boy and as a boy's or man's nickname. **1914** Ellis *Billy Sunday* 283: Why don't you use a little, bud, so that something will come your way? **1920** Haslett *Luck* 302: Come on, Bud, let me by. **1930** Botkin *Folk-Say* 78 [In Indiana, 1860's]: All the boys had names...but they were just called...Bud. **1943** J. Mitchell *McSorley's* 10: Won't sell you nothing, bud. Get along home, where you belong. **1952** Himes *First Stone* 9: You talking to me, bud?...Bunch called everybody "bud." **1955** L. Shapiro *Sixth of June* 154: You're out of your mind, bud. **1973** O'Neill & O'Neill *Shifting Gears* 99: Your employer calls you in and says, sorry Bud, but in two weeks it's over.

2. a friend; BUDDY, 2.

1935 E. Anderson *Hungry Men* 17: That bud of mine is a horse's behind. **1945** Dos Passos *Tour* 331: Me and my bud comin' up through France, we had plenty. **1952** E. Brown *Trespass* 124: And I'm your bud, man. **1961** Terry *Old Liberty* 72: Tell me your true bud that you are not going to actually bring her over here. **1962** T.F. Jones *Stairway* 55: Hamlet is big buds with this other cat, Horatio, and he's got a tomato named Ophelia on the string. **1967** in *DARE*: He's my...best bud. **1981** Crowe *Fast Times* 67: Your bud, Stacy. **1982** Leonard *Cat Chaser* 182: I told Jiggs you're my bud, we see eye to eye. **1990** *Teenage Mutant*

Ninja Turtles (CBS-TV): My little bud Maxwell is all right. **1992** Eble *Campus Slang* (Fall) 1: Bud...chum. "She's my bud."

bud[2] *n.* cannabis. Also pl.

1982 Pond *Valley Girl* 53: Bud sesh [i.e. session]—smoking pot. **1984** Glick *Winters Coming* 214: Mingo fashioned a pipe, and they smoked Leo's buds. **1989** P. Munro *U.C.L.A. Slang* 25: Let's smoke some bud. **1989** *Cops* (Fox-TV): I came down here to get some buds...some weed.

buddha *n. Narc.* cannabis, esp. Asian cannabis.

1988 "Rob Base & D.J. EZ Rock" *It Takes Two* (rap song): Don't smoke buddha. **1993** *Source* (July) 69: Songs like "Pass the Ammo," "Fuck 'Em Up," and "Pass the Buddah [*sic*]."

Buddha Belly *n.* [ref. to the large belly of Buddha in conventional representations] a very obese person. *Joc.*

1978 G. Kimberly *Skateboard* 7: Don't try to con me, Buddha Belly. **1980** Cragg *Lex. Militaris* 54: *Buddha Belly.* Any obese person.

Buddhahead *n.* a person, esp. an American, of East Asian ancestry.—usu. used contemptuously. Hence **Buddha-headed,** *adj.*

1945 in Shibutani *Co. K* 104: I hope the Buddhaheads who came before us were on the ball. **1960** Bonham *Burma Rifles* 21 [ref. to 1941]: They're running the slope-heads out....Buddha-heads—Japs! **1960** Buckley *Hiparama* 49: With that wild incense flyin'...and that Buddha-headed moon. **1966** Cameron *Sgt. Slade* 20: Goddamn crazy buddha-headed bastard! **1972** Wambaugh *Blue Knight* 47: Los Angeles policemen are very partial to Buddhaheads because sometimes they seem to be the only ones left in the world who really appreciate cleanliness, discipline and hard work. **1975** Stanley *WWIII* 88: This guy is a Buddhahead. **1967–80** Folb *Runnin' Lines* 57: "What you doin' here, *black boy?*"..."Wait a minute buddhaheads, you talkin' crazy, Jack." **1984–88** Hackworth & Sherman *About Face* 74: You Hawaiian Buddha-heads have enough trouble with the cold.

Buddhist priest *interj.* [sugg. by syn. *Judas priest!*] *Mil. in Vietnam.* (used as a semi-jocular exclam. of annoyance, surprise, etc.).

1978 J. Webb *Fields of Fire* 201 [ref. to Vietnam War]: Well, Buddhist Priest....If anybody dies, I hope it's you. **1980** Cragg *L. Militaris* 54: *Buddhist Priest.* A VN war expression used as an exclamation of surprise or disgust. A play on "Judas Priest."

buddy *n.* [fr. childish or dial. *buddy* 'brother'] **1.** Orig *Black E.* a friend or comrade; (in early use *esp.*) a comrade-in-arms. Now *colloq.* or *S.E.* Also (*obs.*) **butty.**

*1788 in H. Nathan *D. Emmett* 28: Ah how you do buddy....Buddy, buddy,...come to the ribbor....I no tell buddy Tom so. **1863** Mohr *Cormany Diaries* 375: My buddy was shot through the breast at my left. **1864** in Mohr *Cormany Diaries:* A Johnny got my range...."buddy" called my attention, saying "some Johnny is getting range of you." *1873 Hotten *Slang Dict.* (ed. 4) 105: *Butty*...used by the Royal Marines in the sense of comrade. *1875 in *OED* I 1223: *Butty,* a confederate. *1889 Barrère & Leland *Dict. Slang* I 212: *Butty* (cheap Jacks), a partner. (Provincial), a companion or partner in a piece of contract work....(Army), comrade, chum. (Popular), a policeman's assistant. **1896** *DN* I 413: *Buddy*...Intimate companion. "We were always great buddies together." **1901** *DN* II 137: *Buddy, n.* A fellow, comrade [in Pa. & O.]. **1901** *Independent* (Nov. 21) 2766: His companion, with whom the journey from Boston to New York had been made, had...robbed him....The "butty," or "buddy," is by no means the ideal friend. **1904** *Life in Sing Sing* 246: *Buddy.* Companion. **1906** M'Govern *Sarjint Larry* 61: Unless he has swapped with his "Butty" for a quart of Scotch to booth. **1931** Cressey *Taxi-Dance Hall* 123: My "buddy" and I are up here tonight looking for a couple of good "skirts." **1938** Korson *Mine Patch* 41: Say, Butty, is this the only copy ye have of this song?...Call your butties in.

2. *Mining.* a miner's assistant. Also (*obs.*) **butty.**

1877 Pinkerton *Molly Maguires* 125: The place of "butty" or [miner's] helper, even, was not so very easy of acquirement. **1885** "Lykkejaeger" *Dane* 92: My "butty" would drop his drill and refuse to hold it. **1921** U. Sinclair *K. Coal* 66: If you could see your way to let me have that buddy's job, I'd be more than glad to divide with you. *Ibid.* 120: Less than what I'm getting now as a buddy. **1938** in Botkin *American Folklore* 871: Ye bulldozed me butties and I.

3. fellow; man.—used in direct address, esp. to a stranger whose name is not known. [In 1990 quot., used in direct address to a woman.]

1885 Siringo *Texas Cowboy* 33: It's a trade, buddy. **1888** Beers *Memories*

129 [ref. to Civil War]: A big veteran, laying his hand on the shoulder of a small, scared-looking victim,...whined out, "I *say*, buddy, you didn't bring along no sugar-teats, did you?" **1899** Young *Reminiscences of War* 403: "Say, Buddy," said one of them to anyone who chose to consider himself addressed, "did you bring heaps of grub?" **1904** "O. Henry" *Heart of West* 157: "We'll try to make it comfortable for you, buddy," said the cattleman. **1914** *Sat. Eve. Post* (Apr. 4) 10: Dimes, buddie, and most like a quarter or a half. **1918** *Sat. Eve. Post* (Nov. 23) 11: Say, buddy, what's eatin' you? **1922** in Fitzgerald *Stories* I 61: Got an old doughnut, Buddy, or a couple of second-hand sandwiches? **1945** Slesinger & Davis *Tree Grows in Bklyn.* (film): Get back a little bit, buddy, huh? **1990** Bing *Do or Die* 206: It's on, buddy.

buddy *v.* to be friendly or associate; (*hence*) to pair up to provide mutual help or support.—usu. constr. with *up*.

1919 in Wallgren *AEF Cartoons* (unp.): I allus wanted to buddie up with a officer or sumpin. **1930** G. Irwin *Tramp & Und. Slang* 38: Me and Slim buddy up and take a trip. **1932** Lorimer & Lorimer *Like Streetcars* 148: Estelle and I can't buddy up with thin air. **1935** Maltz *Black Pit* 53: Night shift. You can buddy with Anetsky. **1939** Polsky *Curtains for Editor* 15: And you start buddying around with a dull old dodo three times your age. **1940** *AS* (Oct.) 334: *Buddy Up.* Become very friendly. **1961** Granat *Important Thing* 64: I want you men to buddy up with the man next to you.

buddy-buddy 1. *adj.* very friendly; PALSY-WALSY.

1944 in Inks *Eight Bailed Out* 23: I don't like the idea that these people are buddy-buddy with the Krauts. **1950** C.W. Gordon *High School* 70: A girl...who will suddenly become "buddy-buddy" with everyone possible. **1958** Drury *Advise & Consent* 493: In spite of all that buddy-buddy talk last night. **1961** Foster *Hell in Heavens* 49: John Witt...was buddy-buddy with John Nugent. **1966** Brunner *Face of Night* 32: Could Tillman have been buddy-buddy because he wanted something? **1977** Langone *Life at Bottom* 209: No, I was not buddy-buddy with everyone. **1979** in Terkel *Amer. Dreams* 309: I'm ready to go and have a beer with him and to talk and jive and just be buddy-buddy.

2. *n.* an intimate friend.

1947 Schulberg *Harder They Fall* 30: An assistant district attorney...was a buddy-buddy of his. **1963** Rubin *Sweet Daddy* 26: No buddy-buddies, Doc. But there's always a coupla guys hang around together. **1974** (quot. at STICK, *n.*)

buddy-buddy *v.* BUDDY, *v.*

1959 Morrill *Dark Sea* 12: Don't buddy-buddy with the Navy gunners.

buddy-fuck *v.* Esp. *Mil.* to deliberately impose upon or betray (a close friend). Hence **buddy-fucker, buddy-fucking.** All usu. considered vulgar.

1966 in IUFA *Folk-Speech*: Denotes asking a friend for money. *Buddy-fuck.* **1968** Baker et al. *CUSS* 89: *Buddy fucker, play.* Take someone else's date away. *Buddy-fuck.* Take someone else's date away. **1970** N.Y.U. student, age 21: At Fort Gordon [Ga.] last year I kept hearing *buddy-fucker*. It's a guy who turns around and shafts people. **1972** N.Y.U. student, age 25: You *buddy-fuck* a guy like if you start going out with his girl without telling him. *Buddy-fucking* means letting somebody down or ripping them off. **1985** Tate *Bravo Burning* 161: Wash your mouth out...buddyfucker.

buddy-ro *n.* [BUDDY + -*ro* (orig. unkn.; derivation fr. -EROO is phonologically unlikely)] Esp. *Navy.* friend.—used in direct address. *Joc.* Also **-roo, -roll.**

1946–51 J.D. Salinger *Catcher in Rye* 91: You should've seen the way they said hello....Old buddyroos. It was nauseating. **1957** Myrer *Big War* 119 [ref. to WWII]: Aw come on buddy-ro. **1958** Frankel *Band of Bros.* 8: Buddy-roe, you talked me into it. **1960** MacCuish *Do Not Go Gentle* 217 [ref. to WWII]: Sure, buddy-ro, just like that. **1969** Hardy *Ship Called Fat Lady* 140 [ref. to WWII]: That's okay, buddyro, Finster snorted. **1972** C. Gaines *Stay Hungry* 262: Hey...you *look* at me, buddyro. **1972** Hannah *Geronimo Rex* 227: And my buddy-roll, we must be shrewd now, eh? **1980** McDowell *Our Honor* 20 [ref. to Korean War]: This time, buddy-roll, it'll be a different story.

buddy up see BUDDY, *v.*

budge *n.* [orig. unkn.] liquor, esp. whiskey.

***1821** in *F & H* I 352: *Budge*, drink. **1853** [G. Thompson] *Garter* 56: The "*budge*" was prime old stuff. **1863** in J.W. Haley *Rebel Yell* 88: Stimulants going by the colorful names of old budge, tanglefoot, redeye, or bug juice. ***1873** Hotten *Slang Dict.* (ed. 4) 100: *Budge*, strong drink. **1880** Nye *Boomerang* 15: One day Damon got too much budge and told the...old bummer of Syracuse what he thought of him. **1884** in Lummis *Letters* 22: There was some pretty good "budge" there, too.

1888 Field *Sharps & Flats* I 31: Tim...has to do with budge 'til, overcome,/He sinks beneath his jag upon the sod. **1893** Griggs *Lyrics* 27: In every town he'd be the one/To down the most of budge. *Ibid.* 254: *Budge*—whiskey. **1893** in *DARE* I 427: He was full of budge. **1913** Jocknick *Early Days* 903 [ref. to 1875]: That demijohn of "Old Budge!" that booze! which makes all our troubles so light! **1927** *Immortalia* 96: His friends filled him up with villainous budge.

budge *v.* to clear out; to be off. [Cf. S.E. senses.]

***1610** in Partridge *Dict. Und.* 78: Then budge we to the bowsing ken. **1855** Wise *Tales for Marines* 165: Budge, boys, budge! There's a party from the corvette in the other house hot on your scent! **1891** Campbell et al. *Darkness & Daylight* 164: In the spring we had to budge.

buds *n.* see BUD[2].

BUF *n.* [*big ugly (fat) fuck(er)*] USAF. a Boeing B-52 Stratofortress. Also **BUFF.** [Etymologies in 1968, 1972, 1981 quots. are euphemisms.]

1968 Broughton *Thud Ridge* 32: BUF stands for big ugly fellows in polite conversation, but is suitably amplified in [fighter pilot] conversation....The Strategic Air Command general...issued an edict that the B-52 "Stratofortress" was not to be referred to as a BUF. **1972** in J.C. Pratt *Vietnam Voices* 510: 6 "Bufs" came in and rippled that road. **1972** Bob Hope at USAF base in Thailand, on *CBS Evening News* (Dec. 22) (CBS-TV): This is the home of the B-52's. Also known as BUFF's— big ugly friendly fellows [laughter]. **1981** *Time* (Mar. 16) 8: To air crews the B-52 is known as BUFF, a fairly loving acronym that stands for Big Ugly Fat Fellow. **1985** Boyne & Thompson *Wild Blue* 517: The BUFFs—Big Ugly Fat Fuckers to the crews, Big Ugly Fat Fellows to the press. **1990** Poyer *Gulf* 47: Got a wing of fifty Buffs movin' in.

buff *n.* **1.** a buffalo or buffaloes; buffalo meat. Orig. *colloq.* or *S.E.*

***1552**, ***1583**, ***1665** in *OEDS.* **1871** *From Ocean to Ocean* 55: Today we found "buff," so-called, provided for our meals at the various stations on the road. **1876** in *No. Dak. Hist.* XVI (1950) 173: Saw first buf signs today. **1884** in *DA* 205: The ball struck the unsuspecting animal in the thigh....But the old "buff" took the fling as an insult. **1971** T. Mayer *Weary Falcon* 19: I was pretty sure there were more down there than the buff. **1974–77** Heinemann *Close Quarters* 283: And we do it, cranking forward all the time, over hooches and buffs, until everything is run off or dead. **1982–84** Chapple *Outlaws in Babylon* 168: Mrs. McNab...killed this poor buf with one shot.

2. the flesh; bare skin; in phr. **in [the] buff** naked. Now *colloq.*

1654** in *OED*: For accoutrements you wear the buff. **1759** in Silber *Songs of Independence* 146: Each soldier shall enter the [brothel] in buff. ***ca1770** in J. Atkins *Sex in Lit.* IV 86: I'll give you leave her buff to enter. ***1836** *Spirit of Times* (Feb. 20) 3: The pugilist stripped (the flash phrase is "peeled to his buff") to shew "his condition." **1864** in S.C. Wilson *Column South* 165: I missed my "buff" bath in the ocean. **1980** Teichmann *Fonda* 159: Then strip to the buff and I'll send a hand for your laundry. *a1989** R. Herman, Jr., *Warbirds* 8: Cavorting in the buff with the daughter of the...ambassador.

3. see BUF.

buff *adj.* *Stu.* physically attractive; muscular.

1982 Pond *Valley Girls Gde.* 32: Well, dudes have *got* to be totally buf [*sic*], first off, before you even talk to them. **1983** Lane & Crawford *Valley Girl* (film): He's so buff I could die! **1986** Calif. man, age *ca*19, on McCrum *Story of English* (PBS-TV): She was totally buff....Looking good. **1988** Fox-TV advt. (May 15): Hang out with the buffest dudes! **1989** P. Munro *U.C.L.A. Slang* 25: Steve had been pumping weight all year, and now he's buff. **1991** B.E. Ellis *Amer. Psycho* 114: I want Helga to check my body out, notice my chest, see how fucking *buff* my abdominals have gotten. **1992** *N.Y. Observer* (June 15) 26: Would it be possible to...suffer chronic malnutrition and still look, you know, buff?

buff *v.* **1.** *Und.* to incriminate or identify by swearing an oath.

***1812** Vaux *Dict.*: To *buff* to a person or thing, is to swear to the identity of them. **1848** *Ladies' Repository* (Oct.) 315: *Buff*, To swear; to give evidence. *Buff To*, To swear to or against. *Buff For*, To swear in favor. **1867** Williams *Brierly* 12: I'd as leaf have murder as a crack "buffed" to me. **1868** Smith *Sunshine & Shadows* 153: I told him that the man who had lost the money would, in the language of pickpockets, "buff him to death" if he did not restore the money. **1889** Farmer *Amer.*: To *buff it home*—To swear hard and fast to a statement.

2. *Hosp.* to clean (a patient), esp. before discharge or an examination by a consultant.—also constr. with *up*.

1978 Shem *House of God* 61: You got to *buff* the gomers, so that when you *turf* them elsewhere, they don't *bounce* back. *Ibid.* 422: *Buff*...to make look good, as...*buff* a gomer. **1981** in Safire *Good Word* 152: "To buff up" means to prepare a patient for discharge. *Ibid.* 156: "To buff"...means to make a patient look better than he actually is in order that a consultant will take him on his service.

buffalo *n.* **1.a.** Orig. *West.* a heavyset aggressive fellow; (*hence*) a fellow.

1850 Garrard *Wah-to-Yah* 103: 'Tain't often this buffler *is* comfortable, an' when he is, he knows it. *Ibid.* 193: This buffler's called John L. Hatcher. **1947** *Amer. N & Q* (Feb.) 175: *Old buffalo*, an old timer [in the N.Y.C. Fire Dept.]. **1974** Radano *Cop Stories* 73: Some wise guy buffalo with his load on would come into Chinatown to eat and he'd start to push the waiters around....They wanted us available so we could bounce out the buffalo drunks. **1977** Avallone *White Knight* 18: It's guys like Fallon, buffaloes without direction, who make things hairy for the Public. **1979–82** Gwin *Overboard* 152: "And what's the CB slang for men?" "Buffaloes....If I was to call a man [something else] on the CB, they wouldn't know what I was talkin' about."

b. a fat, homely woman.

1962 T. Berger *Reinhart* 371: Being small, he was probably married to one of those buffaloes.

2. Esp. *N.C.* a Southern abolitionist; (*hence*) a Southerner disloyal to the Confederacy.

1856 in Barret *Civil War in N.C.* 174: Buffalo know nothings. **1863** in *Confed. Vet.* XXIV (1916) 93: The commanding general directs that you cause the buffalo Winslow and all other undoubted buffaloes or their aids and abettors to be arrested and sent back for further disposal. **1865** in *DA*: The rebels were very bitter against these "buffaloes," as they called them, for many had been on their side, and left it for the service of the Union.

3. a black person—usu. used contemptuously; (*specif.*) (also **buffalo soldier**) a black soldier. [As the quots. show, *buffalo soldier* has usu. been used as a nickname without offensive overtones.]

1872 Roe *Army Letters* (June) 65: The Indians call them "buffalo soldiers," because their woolly heads are so much like the matted cushion that is between the horns of the buffalo. **1876** Dixon *White Conquest* II 174: Dat 'oman buffal! Hi, hi, hee! Dat 'oman ole gal—dat 'oman nigger wench! **1881** in Miller & Snell *Why West Was Wild* 145: A company of buffalo soldiers was sent to arrest him. **1884** Aldridge *Life on a Ranch* 125: They are mostly garrisoned by coloured regiments, or, as they are called by the Indians, "buffalo soldiers," probably with reference to their dark colour and woolly heads. **1899** Lynk *Black Troopers* 24: This regiment [9th U.S. Cav.], popularly known as the "Black Buffaloes," was with the first division of troops sent to Cuba. **1899** Johnson *Negro Soldiers* 32: *Buffalo Troopers.* The Name By Which Negro Soldiers Are known. **1914** Jackson & Hellyer *Vocab.* 20: *Buffalo*, Noun. General usage in the northern states. A negro. **1919** *Stars & Stripes* (Jan. 24) 3: The Buffaloes [official nickname of the 92nd Division (colored).] **1972** Grogan *Ringolevio* 228: Washington, the buffalo nurse, brought him upstairs. **1973–74** M. Smith *Death of Detective* 30: The buffaloes hardly ever cry, but you dagos always wriggle your way to the bars and start bawling. **1979** in Terkel *Amer. Dreams* 355: My father...was a buffalo soldier in World War One, 370th Infantry.

4. [cf. BULL, *n.*, 12] a buffalo nickel. [The coin stopped being minted in 1938.]

1929 Perelman *Ginsbergh* 187: I suppose you feel like Andrew Carnegie every time you yank a buffalo out of your pants and throw it to me like a fish to a seal. **1942** *ATS*: *Buffalo*, a buffalo nickel. **1950, 1954, 1965–70** in *DARE* I 428.

5. *Mil.* a water trailer; water buffalo.

1981 C. Nelson *Picked Bullets Up* 136: He sat down beside the buffalo [and] removed his shoes and socks.

buffalo *v.* **1.** Orig. *West.* **a.** to intimidate or frighten, esp. by means of mere bluff; to cow.

1891 Lummis *David* 84: The boy's a good boy, 'n' he shain't be buffalered while I'm 'round. **1908** *Atlantic* (Aug.) 229: Shults was buffaloed by Killian and popped to Coughlin [in a baseball game]. **1914** *Collier's* (Aug. 1) 6: He crawfished, Milly....I've got him buffaloed. **1926** C.M. Russell *Trails* 88: He's tryin' to buffalo me. It's the first hoss I ever see that I'm plumb scared of. **1938** Bezzerides *Long Haul* 23: Don't think you've got me buffaloed, because you haven't. **1938** "E. Queen" *4 Hearts* 75: Pshaw, he has you buffaloed. **1942** Kline & MacKenzie *They Died with Their Boots On* (film): You may have buffaloed your way through West Point, but you'll toe the mark here. **1955** Salinger *Roof Beam* 38: He got her so buffaloed that she didn't know whether she was

coming or going. **1958** Cooley *Run for Home* 15: He's got them all buffaloed! **1984** *AP Radio Network News* (May 26): Mr. Reagan said today that despite recent rising interest rates he won't be...buffaloed into changing his economic policy.

b. to confuse or perplex.

1896 *DN* I 413: *Buffalo*...To confuse, "rattle." **1902** Remington *Ermine* 236: The Sioux had your wagon-train surrounded and your soldiers buffaloed. **1907** *Lippincott's Mag.* (Oct.) 501: He'd been posing as a fighter...and he had most of us buffaloed. **1922** Rollins *Cowboy* 261: From the insensate milling of frightened bisons came that picturesque Range word "buffaloed," as a slangy synonym for mentally confused. **1924** Anderson & Stallings *What Price Glory?* 107: Where is the railway station and the two bucks that have got you buffaloed?

2. to allow oneself to be intimidated or bluffed.—used intrans.

1956 Grant & Daves *Last Wagon* (film): I don't buffalo easy!

buffalo piss *n.* weak or warm beer.—used contemptuously.— usu. considered vulgar.

1985 Dye *Between Raindrops* 19: Serving buffalo piss to these guys at the club.

buffarilla *n.* [*buffalo* + *gorilla*] *Stu.* a fat, homely young woman.

1968 Baker et al. *CUSS* 89: *Bufferilla.* An ugly person, female. **1968–70** *Current Slang* III & IV 17: *Buffarilla*, n. Big, ugly girl (bigger than a buffalo, uglier than a gorilla).—College males, New Hampshire. **1975** Univ. Tenn. student: She's a real buffarilla, isn't she?

buffer[1] *n.* [perh. in imitation of a dog's bark; cf. *OED*, esp. the form *bughar*.] **1.** Orig. *Und.* a dog. *Rare* in U.S.

*1610 in Partridge *Dict. Und.* 79: Buffa. ***1698–99** "B.E." *Dict. Canting Crew: Buffer's Nab*, A dog's Head, used in a counterfeit Seal to a false Pass. ***1718** in Partridge *Dict. Und.* 79: Boufer, *alias* Dog. ***1781** G. Parker *View of Society* II 80: He...saw them give...a pound of beef to the Buffer under the table. ***1812** Vaux *Dict.: Buffer*, a dog. ***1842** in *F & H* I 355: Reilly the butcher has two or three capital dogs, and there's a wicked mastiff below stairs, and I'll send for my "buffer" and we'd have some spanking sport. **1848** *Ladies' Repository* (Oct.) 315: *Buffer*, A dog, generally a watch dog. ***1876** in *F & H* I 355: They had a dog belonging to them that would be sure to begin a quarrel with another *buffer*, whenever his master or mistress found a match.

2. a foolish or contemptible fellow; (*hence*) a fellow.

*1749 in *F & H* I 355: You're a buffer always rear'd in/The brutal pleasures of Bear-garden. ***1760** in J. Farmer *Musa Pedestris* 52: Come all you buffers gay,/That rumly do pad the city....For many a buffer has been grab'd. ***1808** Jamieson *Scot. Dict.* I 323: *Buffer, s.* A foolish fellow; a term much used among young people, Clydes. **1840** *Spirit of Times* (Dec. 12) 483: Vot sort of buffers is them hindependents! **1845** Smith *Vernon* 37: How are you old buffer, how are you? **1853** G. Thompson *Gay-Girls* 31: Och! a stout healthy buffer was Paddy the bowld,/And a fine able heifer was she! **1865** *Harper's Mo.* XXX 606: The term buffer...is now common slang, and means a jolly good fellow. **1867** Williams *Brierly* 9: Who is the queer buffer? ***a1927** in Sandburg *Amer. Songbag* 436: Wrap me up in my tarpaulin jacket,/And say a poor buffer lies low.

buffer[2] *n.* [fr. dial. E *buff* 'to hit'] *Boxing.* a prizefighter; (*broadly*) a brawler.

1787 in Thornton *Amer. Gloss.*: Good news, brother dealers in metre and prose,/The world has turned buffer, and coming to blows. [**1799** in Thornton *Amer. Gloss.*: If we were as fond of fighting France as ever buffing Jackson, or big Ben, or the tinker of Cornwall were of entering the lists.] ***1819** Moore *Tom Crib* 7: The *buffers*, both "Boys of the Holy Ground." *Ibid.* 51: Sprightly to the scratch both *buffers* came. ***1834** in *F & H* I (rev.) 404: Bold came each *buffer* to the scratch. ***1859** Hotten *Slang Dict.*: In Irish cant, *buffer* is a boxer. **1859** Matsell *Vocab.* 15: *Buffer.* A pugilist. **a1890** Melville *Billy Budd* 11: The buffer of the gang...must needs bestir himself in trying to get up an ugly row with him.

buffo *n.* [BUFF + -O] BUFFALO, *n.*, 1.

1980 Santoli *Everything* 216: The officers in my unit were these really gung-ho kind of buffos.

buffy *n.* [resp. of *big ugly fucking elephant*] *Mil.* a large ceramic elephant of a kind commonly sold in South Vietnam as a souvenir. *Joc.*

1973 *N.Y. Post* (Jan. 15) 29: A buffy (rhymes with stuffy) is an enormous, glazed ceramic elephant....The name derives from the acronym b-u-f-e, for bloody useless foul-word elephant. **1980** Cragg *L. Militaris*

55: *Buffie*. From the acronym BUFE, *Big Ugly Fucking Elephants*. *Buffies* were large ceramic elephants produced in vast quantities by South Vietnamese craftsmen for sale to Americans. **1982** "J. Cain" *Commandos* 343: He took the roll of bills stuffed inside the white, ceramic "buffy" elephant.

buffy *adj.* [orig. unkn.] tipsy. *Rare* in U.S.

*****1858–59** in *OEDS*: I must have conducted myself with extreme propriety, and not as you did at the Clissolds', when you came in buffy. *****1866** in *F & H* I 358: Flexor was fine and buffy when he came home last night, after you was gone, sir. **1923** McAlmon *Companion Volume* 166: I don't want to get buffy tonight; have to work tomorrow.

bufu *n.* [prob. *butt-fucker*] a homosexual man. Also as *adj.*

1982 Pond *Valley Girls' Gde.* 50: Any dude who'd wear designer jeans *must* be bu-fu, right? **1986** Eble *Campus Slang* (Oct.) 4: Mo—a homosexual or someone who acts like one....Also *Bufu*. **1989** P. Munro *U.C.L.A. Slang* 25: He is so feminine, you can tell he's a bufu.

bug *n.* **1.a.** an enthusiastic supporter; fan. [In early 20th C., applied esp. to sports fans.]

1841 in *OEDS*: Mr. Alford of Georgia warned the "tariff bugs" of the South that...he would read them out of church. **1880** in M. Lewis *Mining Frontier* 103: I reckon he was the peteryodactyle of the geology bugs. **1908** in H.C. Fisher *A. Mutt* 74: Suitable for racing bugs, rent dodgers, commuters, and for use on pay days. **1909** "O. Henry" *Waifs & Strays* 1675: I'm a theatre bug during the season. **1910** *N.Y. Eve. Jour.* (May 31) 15: "Give the other boys a chance," yelled about 15,000 bugs. **1911** Van Loan *Big League* 212: Fifteen thousand delirious baseball "bugs" were pouring into the inclosure with whoops and yells. **1915** in Lardner *Haircut & Others* 156: Doyle scores, o' course, and the bugs suddenly decide not to go home just yet. **1920–21** Witwer *Leather Pushers* 173: One old guy was a...fight bug. **1922** J. Conway, in *Variety* (Jan. 13) 7: The local bugs might get hep. **1939** "E. Queen" *Dragon's Teeth* 185: I'm sort of a camera bug. **1951** Robbins *Danny Fisher* 154: Spritzer was a bug for conditioning. **1958** *N.Y. Times Mag.* (Mar. 30) 21: Collegians, crossword-puzzle bugs and eggheads.

b. an insane, foolish, or eccentric person, esp. a person of bizarre habits, appearance, beliefs, etc.; *(hence)* an amusing eccentric. Also *attrib.*

1884 "M. Twain" *Huckleberry Finn* ch. xxiii: If he didn't shut it up powerful quick he'd lose a lie every time. That's the kind of a bug Henry [VIII] was. **1885** "C. Craddock" *Prophet* 201: Them crazy bugs in N-N-Nashval sent him a book ev'y time they made a batch o' new laws. **1899** Cullen *Tales* 163: The price of a rest in a bug-ward at twenty-five per, with the soothing music of the chapel organ playing down below. **1900** *DN* II 25: *Bug*, n. 1. A stupid person. **1902** [Hobart] *Back to Woods* 94: If I wasn't in a daffy house and him nothin' but a bug, it's the weight of that chair he'd feel over his bald spot. **1907** *Lippincott's Mag.* (Jan.) 96: Th' Moro is a cur'ous bug, a cur'ous bug is he. **1908** in H.C. Fisher *A. Mutt* 151: Why, the poor man is a bug. **1911** O. Johnson *Stover at Yale* 34: I'm going in after that bug myself. **1912** Mathewson *Pitching* 253: It has long been a superstition among ball-players that when a "bug" joins a club, it will win a championship. **1915** Braley *Songs* 80: There's a padded cell awaitin' for your special kind of bug. **1916** *Editor* (June 3) 582: *Bugs*—Persons who call at newspaper offices with visionary schemes, inventions, etc. **1921** O'Neill *Hairy Ape* 244: Hell, look at dat bar bended! On'y a bug is strong enough for dat! **1939** "E. Queen" *Dragon's Teeth* 179: Why, the bug even talks the same way...now that his plate's missing. **1948** Manone & Vandervoort *Trumpet* 9: We played...for the "bugs" in an insane asylum. **1955** Graziano & Barber *Somebody Up There* 125: A famous bug who they wrote books about...the Mad Sculptor who hacked up the model. **1956** N. Algren *Wild Side* 181: New fields is opening and one is the bug field. Hundreds of bugs loaded with gold...willing to pay somebody to make them happy. **1961** C. Cooper *Weed* 15: Yeah, Ruckson wasn't a bug. **1967** in T.C. Bambara *Gorilla* 73: She was a bug about keeping the block informed. **1974** Stone *Dog Soldiers* 64: What about that bug up in Yellowstone Park? He had his pockets full of human finger bones. **1977** Caron *Go-Boy* 61: You're not getting me on some bug ward so you can stick some wires in my head.

2. a hoax; esp. in phr. **to put the bug on** to fool or tease.

1848 [W.T. Thompson] *Jones's Sks.* 126: They say the people...live on fish so much that they...have scales on their backs. This may be a bug what they put on me, but one thing I do know [etc.]. **1853** in *DAE*: I smell a bug. Dave and that ar strannger's only playin' possum. **1908** *Hampton's Mag.* (Oct.) 458: Ain't he the cute one, though?...He's always putting the bug on someone like that. He's the smartest thing! **1924** Anderson & Stallings *What Price Glory?* 98 [ref. to 1918]: Don't try to put the bug on me. I ain't no queen bee. They ain't made one that

could burst alongside of me. **1967** in *DARE*.

3. a defect or imperfection, esp. in a new plan or design. Now *colloq.* or *S.E.*

1878 T. Edison, in Josephson *Edison* 198: "Bugs"—as such little faults and difficulties are called—show themselves and months of anxious watching, study and labor are requisite before commercial success...is reached. **1889** in *OEDS*: Mr. Edison, I was informed, had been up the two previous nights discovering "a bug" in his phonograph—an expression for solving a difficulty. **1909** in Ware *Pass. English* 53: The phraseology of Edison, to judge from his day-book records, is synthetic, strongly descriptive, and quaint....A "bug" is a difficulty which appears insurmountable to the staff. To the master it is "an ugly insect that lives on the lazy and can and must be killed." **1916** in Hall & Niles *One Man's War* 211: If the "bugs" can be detected and overcome it will give us mastery of the air in six months. **1933** Stewart *Speech of Airman* 50: *Bugs*. Mechanical and flying defects. **1937** Parsons *Lafayette Escad.* 148: The first of these [Vickers machine guns], until the bugs were out, were a bit unreliable. **1945** in *DA*: Distribution Bug Blamed for Nation's Meat Shortage. **1946** G.C. Hall, Jr. *1000 Destroyed* 258: They were getting the bugs out of the 51s. **1951** Waggner *Operation Pacific* (film): I've been ordered back home to help 'em find the bugs. **1953** Gresham *Midway* 57: Then follows a further test period of seeing what sandstorms and cloudbursts can do to it and chasing out "bugs" which arise in connection with tearing it down, loading it on flatcar or truck, and putting it up on new locations. **1962** *We Seven* 75: That is what a test pilot is for—to help develop a new system of flight from the ground up and shake the bugs out of it. **1970** in Trudeau *Chronicles* (unp.): Of course, there are still a few bugs in the system. **1981** *Time* (Mar. 16) 8: Kyme manages to work out most of the bugs in the navigational gear.

4. a small object of any kind, including *specif.*:

a. *Cards.* a clip that facilitates the hiding of cards under a card table; *(hence)* the cards thus hidden.

1883 (quot. at RING IN). **1884** Carleton *Poker Club* 41: "Whar—jer—git—dem—jacks?"..."Outen—de—...bug."...Mr. Smith...possessed himself of the extra cards pinned to the table. "*Dis* whadjer call de *bug*?"..."Doan you work de bug no mo?" **1887** Francis *Saddle & Moccasin* 228: A tender-foot got in amongst the gamblers on board one of the boats once, and what with "strippers," and "stocking," and "cold decks," and "bugs," and "reflectors," he hadn't the ghost of a show. **1891** Quinn *Fools of Fortune* 234: The same denomination as the one he has secreted in the "bug." **1961** Scarne *Comp. Gambling Guide* 674: *Bug*...A clip which can be attached to the underside of a card table to hold cards secretly removed from the deck. **1978** Time-Life *Gamblers* 124: As simple as a money clip, the sharply pointed "bug" was jabbed into the underside of the table and gripped the cards in a clamp that was made of watch-spring steel.

b. a small automobile; *(specif.)* (since *ca*1960) a Volkswagen Beetle; a small motor vehicle of any sort.

1919 S. Lewis *Free Air* 21: It was a tin beetle of a car; that agile, cheerful rut-jumping model known as a "bug."...The bug skipped through mud where the Boltwood's Gomez had slogged and rolled. **1940** *Railroad Mag.* (Apr.) 33: *Bug*—...a three-wheeled electric truck that carries mail and baggage around terminals. **1960** D. Hamilton *Death of Citizen* 71: I passed the little bug. **1979** Univ. Tenn. student: You ought to get yourself a bug. **1980** Fry *VW Beetle* 149: Since 1945 the invincible bug has celebrated many happy occasions. **1983** Curry *River's in Blood* 192: A Volkswagen "bug" was...used for running errands. **1991** W. Chamberlain *View from Above* 23: I drove one of the VW Bugs in the commercial.

c. a small, esp. makeshift, lantern or flashlight.

1922 in Avis *Dict. Canadianisms* 90: In front of me danced the vague shadow of Harry and the dim light thrown before him by the "bug." **1933** Ersine *Pris. Slang* 22: *Bug, n.*...a flashlight. **1936** Duncan *Over the Wall* 111: I...sent the bright beam from my "bug" from one end of the car to the other. **1937** *Lit. Digest* (Apr. 3) 22: *Carry the bug*—to carry a lantern on the [circus] lot at night. **1940** *Railroad Mag.* (Apr.) 33: *Bug Slinger*—Switchman or brakeman. **1942** *ATS* 726: *Bug, bug torch*, a flashlight lantern. **1958** McCulloch *Woods Words* 20: *Bug*...a crude lantern made by punching a hole in the side of a can and ramming a candle through it.

d. *Und.* a burglar alarm.

1926 in *AS* (Mar. 1927) 281: *Bug*...Sometimes means a burglar alarm. **1929** E. Booth *Stealing Through Life* 284: He explained further that "keeping 'em from touching off a bug"—that is, preventing any clerk from pressing an alarm button—and getting the money...would be about everything we need do. **1929** Hostetter & Beesley *It's a Racket* 220: *Bug*—Electric automatic burglar alarm. **1931** Wilstach *Under*

Cover Man 177: You knew those doors would close when the bug was pressed. **1979** V. Patrick *Pope* 27: Breaking and entering....They had a bug on one of the inside doors.

e. *Telegraphy.* a transmitting key.

1929 *AS* (Oct.) 48: *Bug*—extra fast type of telegraph key, the "Vibroplex." **1939–40** Tunis *Kid from Tomkinsville* 71: The tap-tap of the telegraph bugs began furiously. **1941** *AS* (Oct.) 164: *Bug.* Speed key on transmitter. (Signal Corps). **1942** in Gould *Prune Face* (unp.): The old lady would never guess that this "typewriter" is a short-wave radio sending "bug." **1945** in *Calif. Folk. Qly.* V (1946) 377: The radioman transmits his messages on a *bug*, a specially constructed wireless telegraph key, so called from the scarab depicted on a trademark plate attached to the device. **1958** Cooley *Run for Home* 126: I better bat this bug awhile!

f. [fr. **(l)** below: the weight allowance is indicated by an asterisk on racing forms] *Horse Racing.* a five-pound weight allowance claimed by an apprentice jockey; (*hence*) standing as an apprentice jockey.

1941 in *DAS* 68: Apprentices get a five-pound allowance in weights—the "bug" it's called. **1968** M.B. Scott *Racing Game* 30: The apprentice jockey is given what is called a weight allowance or "bug." **1982** *N.Y. Post* (Aug. 27) 77: He's just lost his bug. Zaccio's win today was his eleventh. **1984** *N.Y. Post* (Aug. 31) 73: He will come to the Big M without the bug.

g. *Av.* a dead-reckoning tracer; a positional indicator, as on a radar screen.

1941 *AS* (Oct.) 164: *Bug.* Instrument recording performance in Link Trainer. (Air Corps). **1945** J. Bryan *Carrier* 24: Dead Reckoning Tracer—also known as "the bug" (film). **1975** in Higham & Siddall *Combat Aircraft* 92: An interceptor bug on the face of the display continuously locates the aircraft visually in relation to its position over the ground. A target bug is also available.

h. *Mil.* (see quot.).

1946 G.C. Hall, Jr. *1000 Destroyed* 420: *Bug*: Cluster to a decoration.

i. a hidden microphone; (*hence*) a wire-tapping device. Now *colloq.*

1946 Gresham *Nightmare Alley* 162: That would have been a beautiful place to plant a bug if you wanted to work the waiting room gab angle when the doc's secretary came in. **1948** F. Brown, in *OEDS* I 377: There's been a bug on your phone line for three days. **1950** Medford & Weidman *Damned Don't Cry* (film): Then why did they string microphones all over the place and plant that bug in the fireplace? **1955** Q. Reynolds *HQ* 84: Remember, not one word we've heard on the bug could be used in court. **1962** Perry *Young Man* 261: Listen, Harry, there's a bug on the wire. Don't use no dirty words. **1967** Spillane *Delta* 58: We...located two of the bugs planted in the living room and...another in the huge bedroom. **1972** in *Submission of Pres. Conv.* 56: There was a bug found in the telephone of one of the men at the DNC. **1982** WKGN radio news (June 18): The alleged bug placed in the Criminal Court's clerk's office has been found.

j. *Printing.* the label of the International Typographers Union as it appears on printed matter.

1956 *Business Week* (May 19): *Bug*—Name for the Union label on printing. **1982** T.D. Connors *Dict. Mass Media* 37.

k. an electric switch.

1958 McCulloch *Woods Words* 20: *Bug*—An electric switch used by the whistle punk for blowing signals.

l. [cf. **(f)**, above] *Printing.* an asterisk or other typographical device.

1954–60 *DAS* 68: *Bug*...An asterisk. **1982** T.D. Connors *Dict. Mass Media* 38.

5. *pl. Stu.* the study of biology, esp. microbiology; (*specif.*) bacteriology.

1900 *DN* II 25: *Bugs*...the subject of biology. ***1933** Partridge *Slang* 191: *Bugs*, according to the context, bacteria or bacteriology. ***1963** in *OEDS*: "Bugs" may still be used for biology. ***1974** P. Wright *Lang. Brit. Industry* 62: *Bugs*...can stand for the whole bacteriology department ("I work in bugs," "Take this beast to bugs."). **1985** former SP4, U.S. Army: When I was stationed at Dugway [Proving Grounds] in 1977, they called the former bacteriological research center the *bugs* department.

6.a. an urge; a sudden, usu. ill-considered, idea; obsession.

1902 Cullen *More Tales* 73: Don't let that bug run away with you. **1928** MacArthur *War Bugs* 263: The...insistence of the officers on IRON DISCIPLINE, their one bug since the armistice. **1929–31** Runyon *Guys & Dolls* 78: He has a bug that he is a wonderful judge of guys' char-

acters. **1952** H. Grey *Hoods* 314: What?...You still got that bug in your head? **1972** P. Thomas *Savior* 83: Sometimes I'd get a real bug to join the easy living.

b. *pl.* delusions; madness.

1903 in "O. Henry" *Works* 462: Poor Billy. He's got bugs....calling his best friends pseudonyms. **1914** Hawthorne *Brotherhood* 247: Whether the beetle was alive and got away, or whether the prisoner himself had "bugs," as the slang is, at any rate the examiners reported no beetle.

7. a woman.

1904 *Life in Sing Sing* 246: *Bug.* A trollop. **1964** in *Time* (Jan. 1, 1965) 56: Girls search for their *Sam*—sex appeal plus magnetism—and boys prowl for *bugs*.

8. *Circus.* a chameleon sold as a child's pet.

1937 *Lit. Digest* (Apr. 3) 22: *Bug men*—concessionaires who sell chameleons.

9. *Und.* a burglar.

1959 Duffy & Lane *Warden's Wife* 67 [ref. to *ca*1910]: As a rule, my mother refused to have anything to do with housebreakers. A "bug" is usually a selfish character possessed of a mean streak a yard wide.

10. *Pris.* a psychologist.

1954–60 *DAS*: *Bug*...A psychologist. Some prison use.

11. *Jazz.* JITTERBUG.

1962 Killens *Heard the Thunder* 159: Worm was a real gone bug. **1970–71** Rubinstein *City Police* 360: I was comin' through that lot behind the liquor store when one young bug jumped out and knocked me down.

12. *Baseball.* a knuckle ball.

1961 Brosnan *Pennant Race* 158: "That's a hell of a good bug!" A good knuckleball is a pesty pitch to catch. *Ibid.* 198: Ken's got a dandy bug tonight.

13. the vulva.

1981–85 S. King *It* 382: "At the end of it the man pees all over your bug," Greta said, and Sally had cried: "Oh yuck, I'd *never* let a boy do that to me!"

¶ In phrases:

¶ **bug's age** a very long time; DOG'S AGE.

1938 Steinbeck *Grapes of Wrath* 28: I ain't seen ol' Tom in a bug's age.

¶ **have a bug on** to be easily angered; to be in a bad temper.

1931 *AS* (Aug.) 437: *Bug on*—A grouch. "I'm sporting a bug on today."

¶ **have a bug up (one's) ass** [and vars.] **1.** to be uneasy or fidgety.—usu. considered vulgar.

1942 H. Miller *Roofs of Paris* 235: Billie could talk about Jean all afternoon,...but I have a bug up my ass. **1979** T. Baum *Carny* 11: "What's eating her?"..."She's had a bug up all day."

2. to be easily angered; to be in a bad temper.—usu. considered vulgar.

1949 Bezzerides *Thieves' Market* 24: Fire in the mountains, snakes in the grass, the old man died with a bug up his ass. **1949** Van Praag *Day Without End* 75 [ref. to WWII]: That lousy Wormsley...gets a bug up his ass every time he thinks he should make noises like an intelligence officer. **1950** Spillane *Vengeance* 24: [I put] a bug up his behind. Now the captain of Homicide...thinks I'm pulling fast ones on him as a joke. **1957** Atwell *Private* 254 [ref. to WWII]: Aah, he's got a bug up his ass. **1961** Granat *Important Thing* 45 [ref. to WWII]: Captain Harney had a bug up, worse son-of-a-bitch than that other son-of-a-bitch.

3. to have an unreasonable, esp. obsessive or persistent, idea.—usu. considered vulgar.

1951 Spillane *Lonely Night* 37: You have another bug up your behind. *Ibid.* 48: I was the only one who still had a bug up my tail. **1952** Steinbeck *E. of Eden* 492: You've got a bug up your ass. **1958** "Traver" *Anat. Murder* 185: The Legislature is forever getting some unconstitutional bug in its britches. **1960** Sire *Deathmakers* 172: It's going to be tough shit if just one of them gets a bug up his ass. **1961** Sullivan *Shortest, Gladdest Years* 283: You got a bug in your ass, man. Go sleep it off. **1964** "Dr. X" *Intern* 176: I asked him why all the fuss about a sprained ankle, and he said, "Who knows? Sometimes Slater just gets a bug up his ass, that's all." **1970** Wakefield *All the Way* 52: Thanks a lot...for putting that bug up his ass about California.

¶ **put a bug in (someone's) ear** to tell (someone) something, esp. in strict confidence.

1905 *DN* III 72: "I want to put a *bug in your ear*." Common. **1928–29** Nason *White Slicker* 76: An' I'll put a bug in you guys' ears. You know that dressin' station was in the trees? Well, it's gone! **1936** C. Sandburg, in Botkin *Treas. Amer. Folklore* 482: Now let me put one bug in your ear: inside information helps. **1962** H. Simmons *On Eggshells* 110: I got a bug to put in your ear.

¶ **put the bug on, 1.** see **(2)**, above.
2. to put pressure on (someone).
1968 in *DARE* I 433.

bug *adj.* BUGHOUSE. Also as adv.
1899–1900 Cullen *Tales* 212: I've been sitting here listening you talk bug in your sleep. **1908** Green *Maison* 260: He can't stand goin' more'n two drinks without goin' bug! **1908** McGaffey *Show Girl* 101: Kidding me till I was nearly bug. **1972** Swarthout *Tin Lizzie* 13: They will drive me bug. *Ibid.* 59: Going a bit bug, I'll wager. **1984** S. Hager *Hip Hop* 108: *Bug*—strange; weird; crazy. **1989** "Big Daddy Kane" *Another Victory* (rap song): It might sound bug.

bug *v.* **1.** to hoax; to fool.
1843 in *DA* 209: You will first observe the bloom, and the description given, and you will agree with me at once, that Mr. Sears has been *bugged* by an okra flower. **1898, 1966–67** in *DARE* I 434.
2. (of the eyes) to bulge.—often constr. with *out*. Also trans. Also in transf. sense.
1865 in Jackman *Diary* 160: His...eyes "bugged" out. **1866** Locke *Round the Cirkle* 132: My heart bugs out with woe. **1877** "M. Twain," in *Atlantic Mo.* 446: His dead-lights were bugged out like tompions. **1882** "M. Twain" *Life on Miss.* 223: Wouldn't their eyes bug out, to see 'em handled like that? **1889** Reynolds *Kansas Hell* 168: Their eyes bugged out and seemed to stare at him. **1931** *Amer. Merc.* (Dec.) 420: Them little green eyes is buggin' outa his head. **1959** Goodman *Wheeler Dealers* 67: Ah just about bugged out mah pore eyes. **1969** Layden & Snyder *Diff. Game* 138: The kind of a crowd that made a pro owner's eyes bug. **1969** in H.A. Smith *Rude Jokes* 165: His eyes bugged out like a tromped-on toad frog. **1976** Rosen *Above Rim* 117: Reed's eyes bugged with disbelief.
3. *Und.* to bribe (a policeman).
1889 Farmer *Amer.: Bugging* (Cant).—Policemen are *bugged* in criminal class phraseology when bribed by thieves.
4. Orig. *Und.* to equip with an alarm system, hidden microphone, wiretap, or other form of BUG. Now *S.E.*
1919 *Bookman* (Apr.) 209: The possibilities of the joint being bugged. **1927** *DN* V 440: *Bug, v.* To protect a safe with electric alarm devices. **1930** in *Amer. Mercury* (Dec.) 454: The casa's bugged. **1932** in *AS* (Feb. 1934) 26: *Bugged.* Wired with a burglar alarm. **1935** Pollock *Underworld Sp.: Bugged,* a room in which a dictaphone has been installed by the police. **1961** Scarne *Complete Gamb. Guide* 674: *To Bug:* To gimmick....The jackpot is "bugged." **1962** T. Berger *Reinhart* 435: Nuff said, bud, these phones might be bugged. **1968** Lockridge *Hartspring* 47: Who told you we bug our phones around here?
5. *Pris. & Police.* to place under psychiatric treatment; to subject to psychological examination; to commit to a psychiatric hospital.
1929 Panzram *Killer* 222: I don't care what they do to me just so they don't try to prove I am crazy....Let 'em hang me, burn me or anything they want, but I am going to see that they don't bug me. **1932** in Partridge *Dict. Und.* 80: We'll have the Marquis bugged....Settled in the boob house, the nut foundry. **1946** Mezzrow & Wolfe *Really Blues* 54: It finally went to his head and they had to bug him. **1951** D.P. Wilson *Six Convicts* 9 [ref. to 1930's]: These cons have weird ideas of psychiatrists and psychologists, lots of suspicion and resistance about being "bugged." **1974** Radano *Cop Stories* 64: I should have hit him a smash in the mustache. Then he'd have bugged me on the spot.
6. to anger; annoy; pester; bother. Now *colloq.*—rarely constr. with *up*.
1942–49 Goldin et al. *DAUL* 302: These stockholders sure bug me up (get me mad). **1949** in Gold *Jazz Talk* 35: *Bug:* to be annoying [*sic*]. **1950** *Neurotica* (Autumn) 44: A girl. Never stick to anything....I'm always bugged. **1947–52** R. Ellison *Invisible Man* 368: Don't start trying to bug my other customers. **1952** Mandel *Angry Strangers* 354: I didn't want Lizzie bugging him. **1955** Childress *Trouble in Mind* 140: What bugs me is what sends somebody else, if you know what I mean. **1960** Wohl *Cold Wind* 158: So I might as well get out of here and stop bugging you. **1964** *Flintstones* (ABC-TV): Look lady, will you quit buggin' me? **1971** T.C. Bambara *Gorilla* 32: And if I bugged my mother, I could get piano lessons and become a star. **1975** Delaney *Ultra-Psychonics* 34: For weeks his neighbors had been "bugging" him in dozens of little ways. **1976** Haseltine & Yaw *Woman Doctor* 36: It really bugs me you can't let these things lie. **1978** Strieber *Wolfen* 134: You bug me, darling. **1980** Houp & Pearsall *Reporting Tech. Info.* (ed. 4) 146: In a recent survey, a thousand engineers were asked what bugs them most about writing.
7. *Jazz.* to jitterbug.

1962 Killens *Heard the Thunder* 159 [ref. to 1940's]: Worm grabbed one lady and they bugged for a while.
8. to clear out, run away, BUG OUT; (*hence*) to leave; go.
1960 J.H. Williams *Angry Ones* 8: I wasn't alone, but I bugged, and that was something I couldn't tell the folks; there aren't any cowards in our family. **1970** Whitmore *Memphis-Nam-Sweden* 114: You bug on down to the Four Corners and we catch you there. **1971** Rowe *5 Yrs. to Freedom* 409: Grab your stuff and bug! **1971** Cole *Rook* 260: Let's bug. **1993** *Are You Afraid of Dark?* (Nickelodeon TV): Come on. Let's bug.
9.a. to panic; go crazy; FREAK. See also BUG OUT, 3.
1988 Univ. Tenn. student theme: "Buggin' " means to be hyper or anxious. **1990** *In Living Color* (Fox-TV): Cool out! The dude's just buggin'!
b. *Rap Music.* to do something in an audacious or impressive manner.
1993 *Source* (July) 38: Yo, that shit was fly you did with Madonna, you bugged man.

bug barge *n. Naut.* a verminous ship.
1932 Riesenberg *Log of Sea* 112 [ref. to ca1905]: I deserved what I got, going back there on that bug barge.

bug bomb *n.* an aerosol insecticide. Now *colloq.*
1944 Kendall *Service Slang* 35: Bug bombs...canned fog for killing insects in jungles. **1962** Tregaskis *Viet. Diary* 161: I borrowed a bug bomb from Adams. **1981** C. Nelson *Picked Bullets Up* 290: Two dozen bug bombs.

bug boy *n.* [fr. BUG, *n.*, 4.f.] *Horse Racing.* an apprentice jockey.
1969 Hirsch *Treasury* 122: With a hot bug boy, you get both a five-pound pull in the weights and a rider who is going well and is full of confidence. **1973** Haney *Jock:* Working for Pete at that time was a "bug boy" named Johnny Bacon. **1988** Shoemaker & Nagler *Shoemaker* 26: A bug boy making his first start.

bug doctor *n.* **1.** *Army in West.* a field biologist.
1882 *United Services* (May) 587 [ref. to 1860]: Whenever an officer went hunting or fishing he made it a point to find something for our "bug doctor" to name.
2. a psychiatrist or clinical psychologist. Also **bug doc.**
1932 Nelson *Prison Days & Nights* 211: Even these psy-psych-bug doctors that come over here and give us the bug tests. **1940** Lawes *Meet the Murderer* 196: Before the psychiatrist, or "bug doctor," as the men called him, arrived, I interviewed Lester myself. **1941** Algren *Neon Wilderness* 64: They might even send him to a bug doc. **1954** Lindner *50-Min. Hour* 121: They tell me you're the bug doctor. **1958** Schwitzgebel *Street Corner Res.* 15: Say, you're not a bug doctor, are you? **1959** Morrill *Dark Sea* 21: The bug-doctor is gonna drop a net on you, dopey bastard. **1961** Parkhurst *Undertow* 116: An' these bug doctors...are supposed to help you out. **1962** Larner & Tefferteller *Addict in St.* 88: Right away she thinks a psychiatrist means like a bug doctor, you're supposed to be crazy or something. **1968** Heard *Howard St.* 183: A cat goes to a bug doctor and gits his head examined. **1972** *Playboy* (Sept.) 178: So this bug doctor comes in and says, "You know you're on charges!"

bug-eater *n.* a worthless or inconsequential person; (*hence,* applied derisively to a Nebraskan).
1840 *Spirit of Times* (Oct. 3) 366: Now I'm no bug-eater 'bout politics, sartin—and you'll see it. *a*1859 in Bartlett *Amer.* (ed. 2): Congo is a scrouger; he's up a gum, and no bug-eater, I tell you. **1872** *Harper's Mag.* (Jan.) 318: Below will be found a careful compilation of the various nicknames given to the states and people of this republic...Nebraska, Bug-Eaters. **1878** in *DAE* I 344: Our old teamster informed us that in Rocky Mountain parlance, a worthless fellow is called a "bug eater." **1888** in *DAE* I 344: Bug-Eaters...The term is applied derisively to inhabitants of Nebraska by travellers on account of the poverty-stricken appearance of many parts of the State.

bug-eyed *adj.* having staring eyes, as from fear or astonishment.
***1922** in *OED2.* **1934** in *WNID2.* **1936** "E. Queen" *Halfway House* 49: De Jong burst in, bug-eyed with triumph. **1984** Hindle *Dragon Fall* 104: Tribesmen would listen bug-eyed to his...narratives.

bugfuck *adj. Mil.* insane.—usu. considered vulgar.
1970 Ponicsan *Last Detail* 74: You two bastards are trying to drive me bug-fuck in the head, right? **1971** Mayer *Weary Falcon* 11: If Charles doesn't get you, you stand a fine chance of going bug-fuck. **1973** USN veteran, age *ca*28: When you go nuts you go *bugfuck.* **1975** S.P. Smith *Amer. Boys* 130 [ref. to ca1968]: May dead, Irwin dead, Brady bug-fuck. **1979** J. Morris *War Story* 161: My team would go bugfuck when I came

back suggesting that we start bayonet drill. **1983** Ehrhart *VN-Perkasie* 199 [ref. to Vietnam War]: I was gettin' bug-fuck sittin' around the CP all the time. **1987** D. Sherman *Main Force* 83 [ref. to 1966]: We figured you must be going bug-fuck by now, so I came to give you a ride back to Camp Apache. **1991** Nelson & Gonzales *Bring Noise* 167: Law enforcement officials across the country went bug-fuck.

bugfucker *n.* a man with a ridiculously small penis; (*hence*) a contemptible person.—usu. considered vulgar.
   1973 *Zap Comix* (No. 6) (unp.): Needle Dick the Bug Fucker. **1977** Sayles *Union Dues* 20: "Hey, Needledick, check anybody's oil lately?" "Needledick the Bug-Fucker!" **1966–80** McAleer & Dickson *Unit Pride* 345: Then that dirty bohemian bug-fucker…puts the screws to us.

bugged *adj.* [ppl. of BUG, *v.*] **1.a.** obsessed; desperate; enthusiastic.
   1942 Breslow *Blondie Goes to College* (film): That's when I got bugged to go on an arctic expedition. **1956** in Gold *Jazz Talk* 36: Madame Luke, gonna get her a screen test, for these art films she's bugged on. **1959–60** Bloch *Dead Beat* 4: He's bugged for a fix. **1975** Gold *Jazz Talk* 35: *Bugged on*…current *c.*1943–*c.*1953, rare since.
   b. Esp. *Black E.* insane; neurotic.—also constr. with *up* or (more recently) *out*.
   1952 Mandel *Angry Strangers* 175: She's a sad girl; she's bugged up. *Ibid.* 451: "You think I'm really bugged, Carter?"…"Boy, you're a wild man." **1957–58** Lipton *Barbarians* 315: *Bugged*—Bothered, bedeviled, unstrung. **1974** Univ. Tenn. student: He's bugged out. He's nuts. **1988** *Ch. 2 News at Six* (WCBS-TV) (July 6): The kid is bugged out. He really needs help. **1991** Nelson & Gonzales *Bring Noise* 217: Talk about niggers goin' bugged! **1991** in *Rap Pages* (Feb. 1992) 42: They did a lot of bugged-out things.
   2. annoyed; angry.
   1956 M. Wolff *Big Nick.* 7: Ah, I'm really bugged. **1956** S. Longstreet *Real Jazz* 147: Mother is bugged (angry) at me. **1955–57** Kerouac *On Road* 155: Now, man, I know you're probably real bugged; you just got to town and we get thrown out the first day. **1967** Moorse *Duck* 48: Nothing…like those nouveau-hippies…to…tell you how to be bugged at chow-mein packages. **1971** Jacobs & Casey *Grease* 26: Hey, look, uh, I hope you're not bugged about that first day at school. **1972** Kopp *Buddha* 136: God…might well have been bugged with Job. **1974** J. Robinson *Bed/Time/Story* 97: I would have been very bugged with me. **1978** Selby *Requiem* 108: They don't believe in honest mistakes…They can get very bugged. **1992** *Roc* (Fox-TV): I was a little bugged at first that you lucked into this place.
   3. confused; astonished.
   1959 Tevis *Hustler* 40: Both of them were bugged, astonished.

bugger *n.* *North.* usu. /ˈbʌgər/ *So. & West.* /ˈbʊgər/ **1.a.** a despicable person, esp. a man; BASTARD. See also BOOGER. [The S.E. sense 'sodomite' is no longer commonly understood in the U.S.]
   *1719** D. Urfey *Pills* I 59: From every trench the bougers fly. **1780** in Draper *King's Mtn.* 127: [If they did not surrender] every bugger of them would be instantly shot to pieces. **1796** in Long *Nothing Too Daring* 5: Now you bugers we will cool you! **1813** in B. Palmer *Diary* (Dec. 28): I hope they will hang the Bugger. *1833** in Wilkes *Austral. Colloq.* 58: There was a general cry among the party coming down to me, of "*shoot the bugger.*" **1854** in Eliason *Tarheel Talk* 262: You buger you. *ca*1888 *Stag Party* 185: "Phat air ye dooin' thayre?"…"Shitin', ye bugger." **1906** M'Govern *Sjt. Larry* 56: De dhirty bugger! Oi hopes ye'll catch him an' cut his heart out by little bits of inches. **1920** Kelly *Yellowstone Kelly* 105 [ref. to 1870's]: Frow down that axe, you black bugger. **1927** in E. Wilson *Twenties* 399: No, by God, you darn old bugger—I'll stick by ye! **1934** Burns *Female Convict* 177: Serves her right.…[She's] the lousiest goddamn bugger this side of hell. **1934** H. Miller *Tropic of Cancer* 276: I hate those puritanical buggers back home. **1939** Bessie *Men in Battle* 237: Missed the bugger. **1949** Robbins *Dream Merchants* 144: We can't lick the buggers, they're too big for us. **1960–61** Steinbeck *Discontent* 12: The buggers went to work early, didn't they? **1968** Fornes *Promenade* 21: You tricked me, you singing buggers. **1979** Kunstler *Wampanaki Tales* 10: Search me. I never saw the bugger before. **1986** N.Y.C. editor, age *ca*50: Those rich buggers don't care about money.
   b. a fellow; person.
   1839 Briggs *Harry Franco* I 208: I am nothing but an old bugger, it makes no odds whether I've got one leg or two. **1842** in Leyda *Melville Log* I 158: I did not know that you would a bid a poor *bugger* like me good-bye sir. **1854** in *F & H* I 360: If I'd known all you city buggers

was comin', I'd a kivered my bar feet. **1888** *Stag Party* 231: Here lies John Hugger,/A little snugger than that other bugger. **1915** *Report on Colo. Strike* 12: Poor buggers. **1922** Tully *Emmett Lawler* 187: He fell over a railroad tie and the bugger got away. **1928** Callahan *Man's Grim Justice* 133: Poor buggers…how in the hell could anybody stick [them] up. **1934** Burns *Female Convict* 73: Poor bugger, she was poor as a beggar and had seven kids of her own. **1936** J.T. Farrell *World I Never Made* 66: His pride mounted. The cute little bugger! **1940** W.R. Burnett *High Sierra* 117: He was a pretty watchful little bugger. **1942** Algren *Morning* 255: But you drew blood on the bugger. **1945** Colcord *Sea Lang.* 43: *Bugger.* To people who speak by the dictionary, this is a highly obscene word, but as used by sailors, it carries no shade of its actual meaning.…It carries about the meaning of fellow or rascal. **1949** W.R. Burnett *Asphalt Jungle* 95: Bats are sure funny little buggers. **1954** Matheson *Born of Man & Woman* 62: College endowed by a rich old bugger who went off his nut over the Fortean prose. **1962** Tregaskis *Viet. Diary* 164: The little bugger better not fall out. **1967** Moorse *Duck* 3: How much we paying them buggers to sit on the whale? **1975** McKennon *Horse-Dung Trail* 173: The poor buggers ain't never had a decent meal in their lives. **1979** Gutcheon *New Girls* 49: I bet the little bugger wets the bed. **1986** *Hardcastle & McCormick* (ABC-TV): Don't take your eyes off the little bugger.
   c. a thing; object.
   1922 in *DARE.* **1951** in Mailer *Ad. for Myself* 142: You want to take it back?…Well, I'll carry the bugger. **1962** E. Stephens *Blow Negative* 158: Attaboy, Swope, you missed the bugger! **1976** Hayden *Voyage* 184: Inside a factory—one o' the big new buggers like where they're making shoes and rails.
   2. an undertaking that is difficult, dangerous, or unpleasant; a hard task; nuisance.
   *1915–18** in Partridge *DSUE* (ed. 1) 103: It's a bugger making a raid on a wet night. *1936** "G. Orwell," in *OEDS* I 378: This business of class-breaking is a bugger. **1938** Korson *Mine Patch* 236: Dat's a bugger, Mr. Baer. **1944** Liebling *Back to Paris* 12: It is necessary to have a war before you can sell something in this bugger of a department. **1961** R. Russell *Sound* 61: That solo is a bugger to play. **1968** Baker et al. *CUSS* 90: *Bugger.* Difficult exam. **1985** Finkleman *Head Office* (film): This kind is easy to get off but a bugger to get on.
   3. see BOOGER[1], *n.*, 1.

bugger *v.* **1.** to engage in active anal copulation with. Now *S.E.* [Formerly regarded as vulgar; *OED* (1888), for example, does not print the actual exx. it cites.]
   *1598** in *OEDS.* *ca*1625 in J. Katz *Gay Amer. Hist.* 17: The Master would have buggered him. **1682** *Letter from N.E.* 8: His Wife caught him one day buggering a Sow in the Backside. **1840** in Valle *Rocks & Shoals* 169: Asked me to let him bugger me. *ca*1866 *Romance of Lust* 150: Lizzie was…buggered by Mr. M. *ca*1888 *Stag Party* 117: He wound up the clock/With the head of his c—k/And buggared his girl with the key. **1914** T.S. Eliot, in V. Eliot *Letters* 59: But the cabin boy was…bugger'd, in the sphincter. **1966** Braly *On Yard* 186: You look like a monkey trying to bugger a basketball. **1968** Maule *Rub-A-Dub* 140: Go bugger yourself, you toothless old son of a bitch. **1971** Le Guin *Lathe of Heaven* 45: He got arrested for trying to bugger a…boy in broad daylight. **1973** Overgard *Hero* 17: If people wanted to see someone being buggered to Ravel's "Bolero" while eating one of his Hawaiian dinners, why not?
   2. to curse; damn; goddamn.—used optatively. Also **booger.**
   *1794** in *OEDS:* She said, b—st and b—gg—r your eyes, I have got none of your money. *1821** *Real Life in London* I 150: Or b— me if I don't *mill* you. **1852** Hazen *Five Years* 254: "You ort to take ballast aboard to steady you."…"Bugger you an' your ballast," retorted Brown, hiccuping. *Ibid.* 373: Why, bugger his top-lights, what does the fellow mean? **1859** in Huntington *Songs Whalemen Sang* 37: I'll be buggered if the *Rover* isn't sound. *1886** Baumann *Londinismen* 17: *Bugger (you)!* geh' zum henker! **1914** *DN* IV 151: I'll be buggered! **1943** in *DARE* I 437: Bugger it all. **1945** Colcord *Sea Lang.* 43: "I'll be buggered!" an exclamation of mild astonishment. **1954** Crockett *Magnificent Bastards* 193: "Bugger 'em," Rosie said amiably. **1953–55** Kantor *Andersonville* 649: Oh, by God.…I'll be buggered with a cob! **1960–61** Steinbeck *Discontent* 108: "I have to get lunch on." "Bugger lunch." **1963–64** Kesey *Great Notion* 227: Booger these peckerwoods always talkin' about the good old days. **1974** J. Rubin *Barking Deer* 97: Bugger this creep! thought Captain Yancy. **1985** Sawislak *Dwarf* 23: Bugger the policy. I'm the M.E. now. **1991** Marcinko & Weisman *Rogue Warrior* 271: Well, bugger him and screw all diplomats.
   3. [cf. similar sense development of FUCK, SCREW, etc.] **a.** to

confound, ruin, interfere with, doom, confuse, etc.—usu. constr. with *up*.

  1847 in W.R. Garner *Letters* 213 [ref. to 1840]: The said Garner rode up and said to him, tauntingly, "Now you are buggered!" and other words showing that he rejoiced in the approaching death of the deponent. **1856** in C.A. Abbey *Before the Mast* 69: She got all "*buggered*" up main sail & all the courses full & top sails & all the rest aback. ***1903–09** *F & H* (rev.) 408: *To bugger up*...To spoil; to disappoint; to nullify..."He buggered (*or* bitched) up all his chances." ***1915–18** in Partridge *DSUE* (ed. 1) 103: Well, *that's* buggered it. **1924** Wilstach *Anecdota Erotica* 24: What b—d him up was the crust. **1934** Faulkner *Pylon* 204: Buggering up a Sunday feature for Smitty. **1934** J. O'Hara *Samarra* ch. iii: He's probably forgotten about it, and my going there will bugger things up proper. **1939** in Hemingway *Sel. Letters* 485: South...is the one direction that buggars everything; fish won't bite; muggy and rainy; hard to get to work. **1942** *Amer. N & Q* II 143: The expression "buggered up" was in common use in my boyhood days about sixty years ago in Carroll County, Maryland...and it is still used in the sense of "defaced" or "damaged." It was applied to both persons and things. **1948** McHenry & Myers *Home Is Sailor* 207: The shipowners and the fakers got the men all buggered up by yelling Wobbly! **1968** Swarthout *Loveland* 128: You suck the blood out of the trout and bugger up the fishing! **1970–71** Higgins *Coyle* 57: He'll bugger it up fast enough. **1972** Buell *Shrewsdale* 62: The short of it is he buggers things up.

  b. to cheat or victimize.

  *1903–09 *F & H* (rev.) I 408: *Bugger*...(*common*) to cheat at play. **1933** in Niles *Ballad Book* 237: Young John has buggered us all. **1933** J. Conroy *Disinherited* 150: We pay dues for you to represent us, hah? We got to *pay* you to help bugger us!

  4. var. BOOGER.

bugger-all *n.* nothing. *Rare* in U.S.

  *1918 in Brophy & Partridge *Long Trail* 62: Bugger All. ***1936** Partridge *DSUE* 103: Bugger-all. A low variant of *damn-all*. **1968** Cuomo *Among Thieves* 195: Four officers had to remain on duty...and there was bugger-all to do.

buggered *adj.* **1.** damned.—used prenominally.

  1856 in C.A. Abbey *Before the Mast* 43: As soon as we are clear of this "*buggered*" Cape. **1870** *Overland Mo.* (Jan.) 85: Some o' them ...sojers...has a buggered smart eye to pick out a feller as knows his biz. **2.** [BUGGER, *v.*, 3] injured; infirm; deranged.—usu. constr. with *up*.

  *1915–18 in Partridge *DSUE* (ed. 1) 103. **1975** McCaig *Danger Trail* 59: One old bufler hunter [was] too buggered up to take the robe trail any longer. ***1977** T. Jones *Ice* 10: I don't know if they'll take me in my condition, buggered up like this. **1986–91** Hamper *Rivethead* xix: Gazin'...with this buggered glint in his eye.

buggering *adj.* damned; FRIGGING.—usu. considered vulgar. [*****ca1682 quot. is prob. the literal sense.]

  [*****ca1682 in D'Urfey *Pills* II 155: Let *Pilk* and *Shute* be sham'd,/Let Bugg'ring *Oats* be damn'd:/Let cheating *Player* be Nick'd.] **1920** in E. Pound *Letters* 157: Written on the highest pinnacle of Harriet's buggerin rocky mts. **1944** Pennell *Rome Hanks* 21: Four buggering times. **1956** M. Levin *Compulsion* 65: You and your buggering sure-shot hiding place! You and your buggering eyeglasses—. *a*1961 Longman *Power of Black* 43: When the goddamn shells is flyin' and the buggerin' sun is over yo'.

buggerlug *v.* to engage in aimless or trivial activities.

  [**1871** *Overland Mo.* (Feb.) 165: They only make the old buggerlugger stick her round nose in the water, and don't help...a mite.] **1880** Bailey *Danbury Boom* 37: You expect I can prepare myself for the responsibilities of a public station, and empty out slops, and do all kinds of buggerlugging at the same time. **1894** Henderson *Sea Yarns* 50: Doldrums....There ain't no wind at all, an you jess buggalug aroun'. *Ibid.* 78: 'Twarn't no...time fur the skipper to be buggaluggin' aroun' down below.

bugger off *v.* **1.** to run away; depart.—often imper.

  *1914–22 Joyce *Ulysses* 586: Here bugger off, Harry. There's the cops. ***1922** T.E. Lawrence *Mint* 135: Bugger off, lad. [**1929** E.W. Springs *Carol Banks* 202: I gotta beggar off....Ain't you ready to take off?] ***1929** Manning *Fortune* 153 [ref. to 1916]: Then we just buggered off, by some back streets. **1940** in Liebling *Back to Paris* 27: "Then bugger off," Weygand said indignantly and stalked away. **1958** T. Berger *Crazy in Berlin* 112: Bugger off, Wilbur! **1961** Sullivan *Shortest, Gladdest Years* 214: I'd say so long and thanks. Then I'd bugger off. **1967** P.

Welles *Babyhip* 61: Bugger off, jerk. **1984** Hindle *Dragon Fall* 50: "Bugger off!" she yelled back.

  2. to loaf; FUCK OFF.

  1951–52 Frank *Hold Back Night* 10: Every man will take his turn with the jericans. Nobody's going to bugger off on this duty.

bugging *adj.* **1.** FRIGGING.

  1949 Robbins *Dream Merchants* 212: You're supposed to be a buggin' hero, an' yet you're afraid to get out of bed.

  2. crazy or mistaken. Cf. BUG, *v.*, 9.

  1988 *Knightwatch* (ABC-TV): "Derek D's takin' care of me." "Derek D takes care of him*self*!" "You're *buggin'*!" **1990** Univ. Tenn. student: If you think that matters, you're bugging.

buggo *adj.* BUGGY, *adj.*

  1975–78 O'Brien *Cacciato* 36: I told him it's buggo. Sure enough, I says, you bound for doom. **1989** J. Cameron *Abyss* (film): They just go buggo.

buggy *n.* **1.** *R.R.* a caboose, esp. of a freight train.

  1899 in *DA* 210: Estimating the total length of these cars, with engines and buggies, we find [etc.]. **1925** Mullin *Scholar Tramp* 94: The shacks, then, were all back in the caboose, or buggy, as it is known on the road. **1925** in *AS* (Jan. 1926) 250: *Buggy*—Freight caboose. **1953** in Botkin & Harlow *R.R. Folklore* 326: [He] cooned the buggy. **1973** Mathers *Riding the Rails* 34: I have had brakeys invite me to ride in the "buggy" (caboose).

  2. a wheelbarrow. Cf. IRISH BUGGY, GEORGIA BUGGY.

  1934 Weseen *Slang Dict.* 78: *Buggy*—A wheelbarrow.

  3. a motor vehicle; (*hence*) an aircraft.—usu. disparaging or affectionate.

  1926 in *AS* (Mar. 1927) 280: "Buggy bandits" or "joy riders" [automobile thieves]. **1930** Irwin *Tramp Slang*: *Buggy*, an automobile. **1932** J.T. Farrell *Guillotine* 178: I just got my buggy over-hauled and it runs smooth as ice. **1938** Steinbeck *Grapes of Wrath* 188: This buggy been on the road thirteen years. **1943** J.T. Farrell *Days of Anger* 75: I get all the performance I need from this buggy. **1944** *Slanguage Dictionary* 48: *Buggy*—an airplane. **1944** Chase *Harvey* 606: They got no faith—in me or my buggy—yet it's the same cab. **1951** Pryor *The Big Play* 276: I guess you don't give a damn whether you sell these buggies or not. **1965** Yordan & Sperling *Battle of Bulge* (film): All right, let's get these buggies out of here. **1974** Terkel *Working* 165: I hope this buggy lasts till I get out of college.

buggy *adj.* insane; (*hence*) amusingly eccentric; crazy with anger; silly; etc.

  1902 Hapgood *Autobiog.* 168 [ref. to ca1890]: The latter would tell the keepers he was buggy (insane). **1904** *Life in Sing Sing* 246: *Buggy*. Insane. **1905** *DN* III 72: Don't mind him, he's buggy. **1910** *N.Y. Eve. Jour.* (Mar. 26) 9: Those two "buggiest of bugs," Rube Waddell and...Bugs Raymond. **1919** *Lit. Digest* (Mar. 15) 5o: He acts a little buggy. **1919** *DN* V 71: *Buggy*, foolish, silly. "That teacher is *buggy* when it comes to Latin." New Mexico. **1962** T.F. Jones *Stairway* 78: Soon we'll both be as buggy as she is. **1965** Bryan *P.S. Wilkinson* 192: I should think it would drive you buggy. **1975** Univ. Tenn. student: I had two term papers and a final. I'm goin' buggy. **1975–78** O'Brien *Cacciato* 177: He went buggy when he saw the mess. "You stupid so-and-so," he says, "there *isn't* any box." **1982** WKGN radio ad (July 13): It's summertime again. Are bugs driving you buggy?

bughouse *n.* **1.** a verminous lodging house or similar shelter. [The pun in 1852 quot. is apparent in context.]

  1852 Hazen *Five Years* 29: And lodged in a big-bug house, too. **1926** Nichols & Tully *Twenty Below* 6: I'll thank you not to make this bughouse worse'n it is. **1927** C. McKay *Home to Harlem* 78: Any old thing, boh,...to get away from that theah Pennsy bug house. **1979–83** W. Kennedy *Ironweed* 203: Cold's better than this bughouse.

  2. an insane asylum or psychiatric hospital. Also *fig.*

  1899 A.H. Lewis *Sandburrs* 243: I ought to give meself up to d' p'lice right now an' ast 'em to put me in Bloomin'dale or some other bug house. I'm nutty, that's what I am. **1903** in "O. Henry" *Works* 222: I thought he was in the bughouse. **1906** M'Govern *Sarjint Larry* (glossary): *Bug-House*: House for the insane. **1908** in H.C. Fisher *A. Mutt* 50: Of course, the bughouse has its drawbacks. **1911** Sinclair *Plays* 85: The goil's nutty! You got a bughouse patient on your hands! **1938** H. Miller *Trop. Capricorn* 38: I went to his home—a cellar in the Italian quarter. It looked like a bughouse. **1952** Holmes *Go* 46: It's not the police, it's the bughouse boys! **1960** Bannon *Journey* 30: Am I really a case for the bughouse because I want to *escape* once in a while? **1966** Gallery *Start Engines* 21: I wouldn't pull this on a regular guy...because it might put him in the bughouse. **1972** Campbell *Myths to Live By* 221: A paranoid screaming slogans…in a bughouse without walls.

bughouse *adj.* insane; crazy. Also semi-adv.

1891 *Contemporary Rev.* (Aug.) 255: Insanity [is called] "bug-house," etc., etc. **1894** *Century* (Feb.) 521: A fellow had said that "tramps were bug-house" (crazy). **1894** *Atlantic* (Sept.) 324: I'se gettin' sort o' old-like 'n' bughouse. **1896** Ade *Artie* 92: If I don't get mine inside of a week I'll go bug-house. **1904** *Round-Up* (Baylor Univ.) 255: We have one Prof. who studies bugs till he becomes "bug house" and toxins till he becomes intoxicated. **1904** "O. Henry" *Cabbages & Kings* 627: 'Tis a little bughouse he is, on account of losin' his job. **1917** Oemler *Slippy McGee* 98: Some folks talk bughouse these days. **1924** Garahan *Stiffs* 13: *Bughouse*.—Mad or gone wrong. A scheme can go bughouse, so also can a person. **1941** Schulberg *Sammy* 110: That's a helluva way to start a friendship.…I thought mine was queer. But yours is absolutely bughouse. **1948** Kaese *Braves* 131: This club is driving me bug-house. **1961** Granat *Important Thing* 205: Dolce goes off his nut,…starts runnin' around screamin' and wavin' his arms bug-house. **1965** Hersey *Too Far to Walk* 8: John had signed up to room with him during that bughouse fortnight. **1978** Diehl *Sharky's Machine* 313: All he's good for is raisin' hell and drivin' the captain bug-house.

bughouse fable *n.* a wild or highly exaggerated story; a ridiculous untruth.

1923 in Blackbeard *Google* VIII: When Thomas Keating, assistant manager of the St. Francis, read this, he said, "That's a bughouse fable." **1934** Weseen *Slang Dict.* 314: *Bughouse fable*—A highly imaginative story; nonsense.

Bughouse Square *n. Local.* Washington Square, Chicago. [A popular location for street-corner orators.]

1922 N. Anderson *Hobo*: To the "bos" it is "Bughouse Square." **1937** Reitman *Box-Car Bertha* 58: We drifted over to the famous Bughouse Square, in front of the Newberry Library on Walton Place, between Clark and Dearborn Streets. **1948** Chaplin *Wobbly* 71 [ref. to *ca*1905]: We made the acquaintance of the rough-and-ready free-lance orators at "Bughouse Square" near the Newberry Library on the Near North Side. **1958** Motley *Epitaph* 165: Bughouse Square is his neighbor. **1970** Terkel *Hard Times* 13: D.C. Webb organized a group from Bughouse Square to go on this bonus march.

bug hunter *n. Army in West.* a field naturalist. Now *hist.* Hence **bug hunting.**

*1855 in *OEDS* I 377: The naturalist was looked on as a harmless enthusiast, who went "bug-hunting," simply because he had not spirit to follow a fox. *1889 in *OEDS* I 377: It seems sometimes to the bug-hunter as though there would be but very few vacant rooms to rent in Nature's house. **1898** in *DAE* I 345: When the bug hunter was killed on the Little Cheyenne, Captain Miner was acting field officer of the day. **1922–26** Scoggins *Red God* 35: Oh, I could have talked like a bug hunter for a little while. **1966** D. Jackson *Custer's Gold* 52: For the enlisted men, one term sufficed to classify the geologist, zoologist, botanist, and photographer. They were "bug hunters."

bug juice *n.* **1.** cheap potent whiskey.

1863 in J.W. Haley *Rebel Yell* 88: Stimulants going by the colorful names of old budge, tanglefoot, red-eye, or bug juice. **1869** in *OEDS* I 377: Citizens glad to see us—freedom of the city—"bug juice," *ad lib.* **1877** Wheeler *Deadwood Dick, Prince of the Road* 80: They'll h'ist more than a barrel of bug-juice over their defeat. **1878** Nye *Boomerang* 26: I will take about two fingers of bug-juice in mine to sweeten my breath. **1880** J.C. Harris *Uncle Remus* 252: It's the meanest bug-juice in town—regular sorghum skimmings. **1885** Siringo *Texas Cowboy* 101: We passed off the time…by sampling Howard and Reinhart's bug juice. **1887** DeVol *Gambler* 32: When he came aboard he was pretty full of "bug-juice." **1888** Farmer *Amer.*: *Bug-juice*, the Schlechter whiskey of the Pennsylvania Dutch—a very inferior spirit. Also called *bug poison.* These terms are now applied to bad whiskey of all kinds. **1890** C.C. King *Starlight Ranch* 24: Potts is probably stretched out…with…his flask of bug juice. **1897** A.H. Lewis *Wolfville* 43: Thar's the post office for our letters; thar's the Red Light for our bug-juice. **1903** in *DN* II 308: *Bug juice, n.* Whisky (Facetious) [in southeast Mo.]. **1906** C. M'Govern *Bolo & Krag* 31: Drink till you're so sick you'll swear you'll never smell another drop of bug-juice. **1921** *Sentinel* (Jan. 14) 15: He drank up all the bug juice that the whisky man would sell. **1929** Bowen *Sea Slang* 19: *Bug juice.* An American sailor's term for intoxicating liquor. **1937** Parsons *Lafayette Esc.* 35: Under the influence of too much bug juice one eye stared straight ahead, while the other wandered off into space. **1955** M. Kantor *Andersonville* 703: Oh, call it bog juice, bug juice, bull juice, mule juice, white mule or red-eye or forty-rod; it was

all the same. **1975** *Cosmopolitan* (Aug.) 212: Hey, Maginty, drinking that bug juice and laying out all night, you look awful, man. **1978** *Goin' South* (film): You've just had too much bug juice.

2.a. a soft drink, esp. (in recent use) an instant fruit drink.

*1889 Barrère & Leland *Dict. Slang* I: *Bug juice* (army), Ginger ale. *a1890 *F & H* I 360: *Bug Juice*…(common)…Ginger ale. **1920** Mayo *Damn Y* 99 [ref. to 1918]: "Billy's bug juice"—a combination of lime-juice and fruit syrups—was known all over the A.E.F. when thirsty time set in. **1946** *AS* (Dec.) [ref. to WWII]: *Bug juice*, the powdered synthetic lemon juice…very prevalent in K rations. **1950** Calmer *Strange Land* 126 [ref. to WWII]: I don't want the bug juice. **1970** N.Y.U. student: When I was at military school in the early 60's we called any kind of instant drink *bug juice.* **1974** Univ. Tenn. student: They call Kool-Aid *bug juice* [in the army]. **1985** Dye *Between Raindrops* 18: Kool-Aid or the "bug juice" they served in the field messes. **1990** Poyer *Gulf* xvii: But some men had lingered over bug juice…coffee…doughnuts.

b. a sedative or other drug in liquid form.

1942 *ATS* 474: "Knockout Drops."…*bug juice.* **1974** *Time* (June 17) 59 [prison]: *Bug juice*: medicine.

3. an insecticide or insect repellent.

1944 *PADS* II 65: *Bug-juice*…A poison…used to kill insects attacking tobacco [and other plants]. **1952** Himes *First Stone* 77: Neither fire nor water nor bug juice nor anything except burning the bunks could get them out. **1965** Karp *Doobie Doo* 127: He put bug juice in my cereal and I like to had a fit. **1966** *Sat. Eve. Post* (July 16) 35: Put your canteen close at hand and rub on some bug juice to repel the mosquitoes. **1973** Huggett *Body Count* 243: He could use bug juice like hair oil. **1982** Del Vecchio *13th Valley* 394: I need all the bug juice you…can spare.

4. gasoline.

1942 *AS* (Apr.) 103: *Bug Juice.* Gasoline. Also *Push Water.* **1942** *ATS* 72. **1957** Anders *Price of Courage* 229: The Goddamn planes were low on bug juice, or whatever it is they burn. **1983** *NADS* (Sept.) 21: *Bug juice*…gasoline for jalopies.

5. *Av.* (see 1956 quot.).

1945 Hamann *Air Words.* **1956** Heflin *USAF Dict.* 94: *Bug juice.* Propeller deicing fluid. *Slang.*

bugle *n.* **1.** a loud voice.

1877 Wheeler *Deadwood Dick, Prince of the Road* 78: Good heaven! ye hev got a bugle wus nor enny steam tooter frum heer tew Lowell. **1900** Hammond *Whaler* 329: Hain't old Macy got a bugle on 'im, though! I'll bet them niggers…ashore back there could hear 'im when he hollered.

2. the nose.

1865 "M. Twain," in *Calif. Hist. Soc. Qly.* XXI (1942) 147: Maguire…split him in the bugle. **1880** Small *Mother-in-Law* 21: I was sending out my "awful right" for the purpose of giving that imaginary mother-in-law one night on her "bugle." **1881** Nye *Forty Liars* 234: Thy busted snoot…thy fractured bugle. *Ibid.* 259: The tenderfoot would…smite him upon the bugle. **1889** Cox *Frontier Humor* 244: Busting his bugle. **1915** *N.Y. Eve. Jour.* (Aug. 3) 10: A gink with a broken bugle and a cauliflower ear. **1934** H. Roth *Call It Sleep* 251: Stay here, or yuh'll get a bust on de bugle! **1936** Kingsley *Dead End* 688: Fuh dis…right in yuh bugle! **1943** in W.C. Fields *By Himself* 255: Why, bugle-beak,…don't you fill your nose with helium and rent it out as a barrage balloon? **1966** in Perelman *Don't Tread* 231: I almost sliced off the end of my bugle.

bugle oil *n. Army.* an imaginary substance for which raw recruits are sent as a form of hazing; (*hence*) nonsense; **BANANA OIL.**

1921 *DN* V 94: *Bugle oil.* Young recruit [was] sent for [this imaginary substance] at Officer's Training Camp, Fort Benjamin Harrison, Indiana. **1947** *ATS* (Supp.) 21: Fictitious Articles (for which raw recruits are sent)…*bugle oil,*…*cannon report,* [etc.]. **1985** *A-Team* (NBC-TV): Enough of that bugle oil.

bug off *v.* [cf. **BUGGER OFF**] to go away.—usu. in imper.

[*ca*1895 in *EDD*: I shall knock off work now, mister, as I want to bag off home.] **1952** Mauldin *In Korea* 94: They bugged off down that gulley and we lost them. **1963** Morgan *Six-Eleven* 239: If you're too sensitive to appreciate that or accept it, bug off right now. *1966 Shepard *Doom Pussy* 47: Why don't those blokes just bug off? **1966** "Petronius" *N.Y. Unexp.* 63: Has something to say. Bug off. **1968** Lockridge *Hartspring* 149: Bug off, Yoke. **1969** *Rowan & Martin's Laugh-In* (NBC-TV): Now bug off! **1970** *CBS Evening News* (CBS-TV) (Dec. 2): I would tell them to bug off. **1970** R.N. Williams *New Exiles* 299: Why don't you just bug off. **1972** *New Yorker* (Nov. 25) 50: You'll get your forecast. Now bug off. **1977** Univ. Tenn. *Daily Beacon* (Apr. 1) 2: Bugg

Off! **1992** G. Wolff *Day at Beach* 239: I shouted at them to bug off.

bugology *n.* **1.** *Stu.* biology; (*also, specif.*) entomology. *Joc.*

1843 in *DA*: Chemistry, botany, anatomy, conchology, bugology. **1900** *DN* II 25: *Bugology, n.* **1908** *Univ. Tenn. Vol.* (unp.): Did you hear what Professor Bentley told his class in Bugology the other day? **1927** H. Miller *Moloch* 222: Professor of bugology. Roach and rodent exterminator.

2. *Hobo.* an eccentric political, economic, or metaphysical philosophy.

*ca*1915 in Bruns *Kts. of Road* 116: No bugology or socialists, or anarchists [allowed].

bugout *n. Mil.* **1.a.** a hasty retreat; rout.

1951 *N.Y. Herald Tribune* (Dec. 16) II 5: Men talked of "bug-out gas" and "bug-out jeeps" and "bug-out routes." **1958** Frankel *Band of Bros.* 136: We always had a bug-out route in advance. **1958** "Traver" *Anat. Murder* 35: Got there just in time for the big bugout from the Yalu. **1962** Butterworth *Court-Martial* 96: We made the Bug-Out to Hamhung together. **1964** Peacock *Drill & Die* 14: The bug-out trench connected with the deep main-line-of-resistance trench that ran along the crest of the hill. **1965** Donlon *Outpost* 92: And nobody wanted to do a bug-out. **1982** W. Rusher, on WINS radio (Aug. 15): Many Americans began calling for an end to the war on any terms at all, even a bug-out. **1991** Dunnigan & Bay *From Shield to Storm* 282: Nearly 40,000 Iraqi troops tried to flee to Kuwait City. U.S. troopers began to refer to the withdrawal as "The Great Bug-Out."

b. an escape route.

1953 Russ *Last Parallel* 81: There are three points through which a man can run for the hills—rear exits in the trench called "bug-outs."

2. a runaway; deserter.

1956 Hargrove *Girl He Left* 153: We have our own special facilities for bug-outs. **1957** Barrett *D.I.* (film): We've got a bug-out, Owens. **1964** R. Moore *Green Berets* 96: The second CIDG company…had been joined by his own "bug-outs." **1975** Stanley *WWIII* 95: Everyone figured him for a bugout. **1981** Hathaway *World of Hurt* 189: This guy here is a bug-out.

bug out *v.* **1.** see BUG, *v.*, 2.

2.a. Orig. *Mil.* to run away; flee; desert.

1950 *Life* (Dec. 18) 28: The expression "bug out"—taking it on the lam—was used some in the last war, but in Korea it is being spoken many thousands of times a day. **1951** *N.Y. Herald Tribune* (Dec. 16) II 5: But bug-out to the soldiers didn't mean withdrawal. It meant retreat. It meant, "Pull out, because if you stay you'll get killed or captured." **1951–52** Frank *Hold Back Night* 110: It is a terrible thing for a captain to discover that one of his lieutenants has bugged out, although Ekland…had known that Sellers was yellow. **1956** Hargrove *Girl He Left* 153: "What have you been doing up there?"…"Bugging out, sir." **1960** J. Williams *Angry Ones* 8: I was on the line Christmas Day, 1944, with the 92nd Division or what passed for it….but…when the Germans…launched a heavy breakthrough, I bugged out. **1962** G. Ross *Last Campaign* 283: They knew in Seoul three days ago that we were gonna bug out. **1965** *Combat!* (ABC-TV): How do you know I won't bug out like Lennon? **1966** J. Lewis *Tell It to Marines* 24: We had to bug out of there….*Bug out:* Slang for retreat. **1979** Cassidy *Delta* 244: We've got to bug out of here. Can you move?

b. (in weakened sense) to leave; depart.

1955 *AS* XXX 116: Bug Out…Leave suddenly and rapidly. **1958** J. Davis *College Vocab.* 14: Bug out—Leave. **1960** Bluestone *Cully* 140: Okay, bug out. **1961** Coon *Meanwhile at Front* 120: Bug out, Riley. **1967** W. Crawford *Gresham's War* 159: Bug out, Marine.…This ain't your party. **1967** G. Moore *Ngo Tho* 221: I think I'll bug out on the next chopper that comes in. **1983** Eilert *Self & Country* 284: Here you go. Let's bug out.

3. to become insane. Cf. BUG, *v.*, 9.

1972 *Playboy* (Sept.) 178: Bugging out means acting crazy. Getting the doctors to say you're a mental case. Incompetent to stand trial. *a*1974 in *Adolescence* XIII (1978) 476: It's just like bugging you to see if you'll bug out. **1978** *Channel 2 Eye On: Angel Dust* (WCBS-TV): She just smoked one joint and then she started buggin' out. **1978** Cleaver *Soul on Fire* 72: The white guards…locked me up in a padded cell. By that time I had really bugged out. **1984** S. Hager *Hip Hop* 108: *Bug out*—to go wild or turn strange. **1989** *Village Voice* (N.Y.) (Apr. 11) 20: People will be going crazy…bugging out.

4. to treat with psychotherapy.

1972 Kopp *Buddha* 172: Come to bug me out, Doc?

bug poison *n.* BUG JUICE, 1.

*a*1888 in Farmer *Amer.*: Nearly every character introduced by Charles

Dickens…was addicted to drinking…; each and every individual took his bug-poison with surprising regularity and eminent satisfaction.

bugs *adj.* insane; crazy. Cf. BATS.

1903 T.A. Dorgan, in Zwilling *TAD Lexicon* 21: Gee dat's [*sc.* a tooth] a big one. De gas put me "bugs." **1906** M'Govern *Sarjint Larry* (glossary): *Bugs:* Insane. **1907** in H.C. Fisher *A. Mutt* 18: The old man is bugs. **1907** *Reader* (Sept.) 348: I leave it to anyone if that should make him go bugs. **1907** *Lippincott's Mag.* (Oct.) 502: The jackies on the tow thought we was bugs for true. **1908** in Blackbeard & Williams *Smithsonian Comics* 58: I agree…that Mutt is bugs. **1912** Berkman *Prison* 47 [ref. to 1892]: The "Dutchy" there is "bugs." **1912** Mathewson *Pitching* 8: That man was Arthur Raymond, sometimes called "Bugs." He seemed to upset the German by his…"kidding" tactics. **1915** Lardner *Gullible's Travs.* 14: Both o' them's bugs over the same girl. **1918** *Everybody's* (Sept.) 37: It's got ev'body bugs. **1919** O'Brien *Best Stories of '19* 311: Bugs on beauty, I guess. **1924** Marks *Plastic Age* 103: It isn't bugs….it's got sense. **1928** Callahan *Justice* 141: I'm bugs about her. **1929** Burnett *Iron Man* 161: He went bugs out in Omaha and a cop had to slug him.

bug-sharp *n.* an entomologist or field naturalist.

1877 in *DAE* I 345: One…was viewed with emotions too deep for words by jostling crowds of bug-sharps.

bugshit *adj.* BUGFUCK.—usu. considered vulgar.

1978 S. King *Stand* 170: He would go utterly and completely bugshit. **1983** S. King *Christine* 399: That's another thing that used to drive us all fucking bugshit. *Ibid.* 406: The smell drives her bugshit. **1981–85** S. King *It* 127: They drive us bugshit.

Bugsmasher *n. Av.* a Beechcraft Twin Beech light aircraft; (*broadly*) any light plane.

1984 Trotti *Phantom* 113 [ref. to 1966]: An old friend…was flying Bugsmashers for Air America. *Ibid.* 239: *SNB*…the ubiquitous Twin Beech, designated C-45 by the Air Force, used by the Navy and Marine Corps for staff and proficiency flying…Also known as the Bugsmasher. **1987** S. Weiser *Project X* (film): You're talking about fighters and bombers. I've only flown Bugsmashers. **1990** P. Dickson *Slang!* 38: *Bug smashers*…small private planes, especially…in congested areas.

bug trap *n.* **1.** a verminous lodging house or similar shelter; FLEABAG.

1929 Caldwell *Bastard* 20: By God, I cleaned out the bug-trap all right—it burnt to the ground.

2. a bed.

1966 Kenny *Caste* 176: Hey, Mike, you never seen a bug-trap before?

bug up *v.* **1.** to spoil; BUGGER, *v.*, 3.a.

1941 Brackett & Wilder *Ball of Fire* (film): Not now while it would bug up everything.

2. to make or become crazy or nervous.

1952 Mandel *Angry Strangers* 15: I had the real honors….That son-of-a-bitch Stoney bugged me up some more. *Ibid.* 203: It's only when you live too easy…that's when you bug up with ideas. **1968** Cuomo *Thieves* 237: You couldn't go around thinking all the time about getting out. You'd just bug up.

buhow /'buˌhau/ *adj.* [< Mandarin *bu⁴ hao³*] *Mil. in China.* no good; bad.

1921 *Sentinel—15th Inf.* (Jan. 14) 15: Who was the "booze hoister" that wrote to the "Sentinel" about the States being "Boohow"? **1943** R. Scott *God Is Co-Pilot* 59: "Bu-hao"…is a Chinese Bronx cheer, or literally, "you are very bad—you are not 'number one.'" **1953** in Wallrich *A.F. Airs* 143: Buhow. **1962** McKenna *Sand Pebbles* 297: "Bu hao," the little girl said. **1985** former SP4 U.S. Army, age 35: On Taiwan *buhow* was pretty common: "Man, this beer is *buhow*!" "He's one buhow dude."

Buick *v.* [sugg. by fanciful resemblance to *puke*] *Stu.* to vomit. Also **sell a Buick** and vars.

1975 Univ. Tenn. student: To *ralph* is the same as to *sell a Buick.* It means barf. **1978** Eble *Campus Slang* (Apr.) 4: *Sell Buicks*—to vomit: Tony's outside selling some Buicks. **1980** Birnbach *Preppy Hndbk.* 113: Vomiting…[to] Barf…Buick…Heave…Upchuck. **1981** *Bosom Buddies* (ABC-TV): I spent an hour with you in the john last night while you hugged the white wishing well, selling Buicks and calling Rolf… **1984** Algeo *Stud Buds & Dorks:* To vomit…*buick, buy a buick, sell a buick, sell buicks.* **1992** *UTSQ:* He was buying Buicks…after his debauchery.

build *v.* to prepare (food, a drink, a cigarette, etc.).

1900 Cullen *Tales* 382: He'd…built flapjacks for a mining outfit in a Nevada camp. **1967** L'Amour *Matagorda* 71: He pushed his hat back, curled a leg around the saddle horn, and started to build a smoke. **1978** Univ. Tenn. instructor: He can build some good drinks.

¶ In phrase:

¶ **not built that way** not so disposed.

[**1882** in Farmer *Amer.* 100: Even womankind is not built as she was a few brief years ago.] **1888** in Farmer *Amer.* 100: "Why didn't you roll down?" "I wasn't built that way." **1891** in Davidson *Old West* 131: But Uncle Sam…ain't built that way. **1942** in *DA*.

built *adj.* having a muscular or attractive figure or physique; occ. in phr. **built for speed.**

1932 Nelson *Prison Days & Nights* 205: One of these platinum blondes with blue eyes. And is she built! **1938** "R. Hallas" *You Play the Black* 123: He was even a bigger man than I am, and I'm plenty built. **1938** Bellem *Blue Murder* 139: Yeah, you're built all right. **1944** Stiles *Big Bird* 84: She was pretty. She was built. **1949** Maier *Pleasure I.* 148: My God, is that woman built! **1954** Killens *Youngblood* 349: She truly built for speed—ain't she, Youngblood? **1955** Robbins *79 Park Ave.* 211: Yeah, same girl….Blonde and built. **1965** *Dick Van Dyke Show* (CBS-TV): Boy! I wish I was built! **1980** Lorenz *Guys Like Us* 2: He had…necked…with built Italian girls. **1980** *Maclean's* (Feb. 4) 49: He's gorgeous, charming, erudite, multilingual, street-smart, *built*, cocksure and arrestingly self-absorbed.

bulge *n.* **1.** a head start; an advantage of any kind.

1841 *Spirit of Times* (Dec. 18) 498: Kate got the bulge on her at the start. **1860** in Thornton *Amer. Gloss.*: It is in this respect that the South has "the bulge" on the North. **1864** "M. Twain," in *Sks. & Tales* 33: Well, they used to die of conical balls and cold steel, mostly, but here lately erysipelas and the intoxicating bowl have got the bulge on those things. **1871** "M. Twain" *Roughing It* 249: Well, you've ruther got the bulge on me. Or maybe we've both got the bulge, somehow. **1873** Custer *Life on Plains* 237: An' ef we git the bulge on 'em, and keep puttin' it to 'em sort a lively like, we'll sweep the platter—thar won't be nary trick left for 'em. **1880** in M. Lewis *Mining Frontier* 99: That's the time we put the ship ther'—so's to get the bulge on the inland navigation. **1881** Nye *Forty Liars* 70: It marks the crowding years since he got the bulge on his oppressors. **1888** in *F & H* I 362: I saw he had the bulge on you and I got the gun and dropped him. *1891 in Ware *Pass. English* 54: Mr. Dodsley has, to use the new phrase of American slang, "the bulge" on Messrs Longmans. **1906** "O. Henry" *4 Million* 48: I consider that I have the bulge on him as far as you could chase a rabbit. **1971** Cole *Rook* 249: But they had the bulge. Maybe more alert, a little less surprised. **1980** L.N. Smith *Venus Belt* 91: Healers lack the bulge that U.S. doctors throw around. **1982** WINS sports report (Aug. 15): Beth Daniels has an 8-stroke bulge over her competitors.

2. a move forward; a step.

1866 in G.W. Harris *High Times* 167: Unable to make the first bulge towards a run. *Ibid.* 185: As he made his bulge, Boze changed his sneak intu a rush. **1867** G.W. Harris *Lovingood* 121: I wer fear'd tu make a bulge.

bulge *v.* to rush, race, or dash; (*also,* as in 1844 Porter quot.) to leave.

1834 Crockett *Narrative* 105: As soon as we struck, I bulged for my hatchway. **1844** *Spirit of Times* (Sept. 21) 349: She bulged right out on the gallery and clinched one of the gals. **1844** in Porter *Big Bear* 130: "Agreed," says I, and then we bulged. **1854** in G.W. Harris *Lovingood* 36: He buljed squar intu an' thru hit. **1863** in Lyman *Meade's HQ.* 40: Buford…said he thought he could just "boolge" across the river and scare the Rebels to death. **1867** in G.W. Harris *Lovingood* 104: Well, him an' George bulged down that ar ladder like rats wif a tarrier clost tu thar tails. *Ibid.* 268: He tuck me at my word, an' bulged. **1880** J.C. Harris *Uncle Remus* 91: "Yer I come a bulgin'," sez de Tarrypin, sezee. **1882** "M. Twain" *Life on Miss.* 174: When it got ready, it just bulged through it. **1897** A.H. Lewis *Wolfville* 42: I gets that locoed lovin' this girl I goes bulgin' out to make some poetry over her. **1907** S.E. White *Arizona Nts.* 81: This Irishman…comes bulgin' it. *a*1916 D.E. Conner *In Gold Fields* 11: I…made a desperate "bulge" for an alley nearby. **1925** in Faulkner *N.O. Sks.* 206: And then about dark Joe comes bulging in. **1928** in O'Brien *Best Stories of 1928* 106: They jest bulged right erboard.

bulger *n.* something very large; WHOPPER.

1835 in Bartlett *Amer.* (ed. 1) 52: We soon came in sight of the great city of New York, and a *bulger* of a place it is. *1859 Hotten *Slang Dict.* (ed. 1): *Bulger*…synonymous with *buster*. **1871** Schele de Vere *Amer.* 587: *Bulger*…generally designates anything very large. "That's a *bulger* of a story."

bulgine var. BULLGINE.

bulkhead *n. Navy & USMC.* a wall (of any kind).

1942 *Yank* (Nov. 4) 15: Leathernecks always talk as if they were on a ship….The floor is the "deck" and a wall is a "bulkhead." **1943** W. Simmons *Joe Foss* 110: Suck that gut in!…Eyes on the bulkhead! **1957-62** Higginbotham *USMC Folklore* 4: *Bulkhead*—the wall. **1976-79** Duncan & Moore *Green Side Out* 11: Posted on the bulkhead behind the bar. **1984** J.R. Reeves *Mekong* 23: He grinned and waved toward the sandbag bulkhead. **1988** Hynes *Flights of Passage* 22: The wall of a converted women's dormitory…being called a "bulkhead," for God's sake!

bulkhead *v. Navy.* to complain or speak disparagingly with the intention of being overheard by (a superior or other person). Also intrans. Hence **bulkheading,** *n.*

1863 in M. Turner *Navy Gray* 84: Bulkheading. **1875** Sheppard *Love Afloat* 184: Them Britishers…see he was a 'Merican by the cut of his jib, and commenced to bulkhead him, only there wasn't no bulkhead. They was talkin' about the little Potomick, and laughin' at her size…one of 'em said somethin' about her bein' no meaner'n the country she came from. **1900** Benjamin *Nav. Acad.* 59 [ref. to *ca*1860]: They also had the persistent habit of "bulkheading," which meant saying savage things of any officer who had fallen under their displeasure, which, of course, they would not dare to do openly, but which it was intended nevertheless he should hear through the thin bulkhead or partition which separated the ward-room from the steerage. **1941** Maryland WPA *Gde. to U.S. Nav. Acad.* 149: Bulkhead…To gripe loudly, hoping one's superiors will overhear. **1946** Sawyer *Gunboats* [ref. to *ca*1900]: When this "bulkheading," as such conversation is termed in Navy jargon, had almost driven our guest to distraction, the welcome explanation was given him that an Irish hurricane is the Navy term for a flat calm. **1952** Cope & Dyer *Petty Off. Gde.* 424: *Bulkheading*. Navy slang meaning complaining or grumbling within earshot of seniors. **1966** Heinl *Marine Off. Gde.* 591: *Bulkhead*…to complain against or asperse a superior while superficially pretending not to. **1969** Searls *Hero Ship* 283: And when she starts out the way this [ship] did, with everybody bulkheading about what a pig she is….

bulkhead stare *n. USMC.* GOONY-BIRD STARE.

1981 Sledge *Old Breed* 125 [ref. to 1943]: During mid-afternoon as we waited for the army infantry, we sat numbly looking at nothing with the "bulkhead stare."

bull *n.* **1.** a blunder; a botch. [1775 quot. illustrates S.E. sense 'ludicrous jest' or 'self-contradictory proposition'; see *OED*.]

[**1775** in Moore *Songs & Ballads of Revolution* 92: By my faith, but I think ye're all makers of bulls,/With your brains in your breeches, your — in your skulls.] *1785 Grose *Vulgar Tongue*: *Bull*, a blunder, from one Obadiah Bull, a blundering lawyer of London, who lived in the reign of Henry VII. By a *bull*, is now always meant a blunder made by an Irishman. **1812** W. Dunlap *Yankee Chronology* 5: Master Bundle, you've made a bit of a *bull*. **1821** Martin & Waldo *Lightfoot* 96: This was the first *bull* that I made in America. **1837** in Strong *Diary* 73: The best part of him is his father (if that isn't a bull). **1846** Neal *Ploddy* 151: No man ever made a greater "bull." **1862** in H.L. Abbott *Fallen Leaves* 112: I am…afraid that we shall make some terrible bull. **1894** Crane *Red Badge* 96: Oh, thunder, MacChesnay, what an awful bull you made of this thing!…What an awful mess you made! **1900** *DN* III 25: *Bull*, n. Error. **1921** *Variety* (Aug. 5) 9: If you made a bull, you were ripped apart, but if you pulled a smart play, you were lauded to the skies. **1927** Cushing *Doughboy Ditties* 79: Come on you boob. They've pulled a Bull. **1928** Callahan *Man's Grim Justice* 37: She was satisfied that I wouldn't pull any "bulls." **1931** J.T. Farrell *McGinty* 251: Horan, you made another bull puttin' that guy on my wire. **1935** O'Hara *Dr.'s Son* 102: One little bull and phooey! maybe the whole thing goes smack. **1945** Hubbard *R.R. Ave.* 20: The film…proved to be a grade B quickie with the inevitable bulls in railroad operation.

2. an Englishman; JOHN BULL; (*hence,* in 1835 Knickerbocker quot.) a British naval vessel.

1835 *Knickerbocker* (Feb.) 106: Pretty good *gunnery*, Mr. Bull. **1835** in Paulding *Bulls & Jons.* 16: The Bulls would now and then, whenever they could do it safely, revive these pretensions. **1839** *American Joe Miller* 78: Czar wants to spar, but not such a calf as to take the Bull by the horns. **1844** in Haliburton *Sam Slick* 194: Hear old Bull here every day talkin' about the "low Irish." **1858** in *DA*: So the aristocratic senator is half Yankee, half Bull. **1864** in Lyman *Meade's HQ.* 191: I fancy…that he has once been a head servant…in some crack British regiment. He has that intense and impressive manner, only to be got, even by Bulls, in years of drill. **1928** F. Shay *More Pious Friends* 137: The bulls were sure that Heenan would win, which caused them all to fret.

3. an ox.

1859 in Hafen & Hafen *Reports from Colo.* 235: Dougherty's Own Bull Team. **1865** in H. Johnson *Talking Wire* 270: The big "bull wagons" (ships of the desert) are thronged. **1868** J. Chisholm *So. Pass* 156: Two bull teams passed…bearing a large family. **1879** Cody *Life* 64 [ref. to 1857]: One of the best wagon-masters that ever ran a bull train. **1913** Jocknick *Early Days* 84 [ref. to 1870's]: Our lariettes, too, were frequently called into service…to assist "the bulls."

4. *Pris. & Mil.* tough beef; corned beef. Also **bull meat.**

1859 Hotten *Slang Dict.*: *Bull*…a term amongst prisoners for the meat served to them in jail. **1895 Remington *Pony Tracks* 157: To forget that long marches, "bull meat," and sleepless, freezing nights are in the background. **1917** *Wadsworth Gas Attack* (Nov. 27) 23: Bull, gravy, dogs and sinkers are all my long suit. **1918** in Bliss *Victory* 218: Use your thumbs for issue forks and pass the bull about. **1920** Simmons *20th Engrs.* (unp.): A little bull meat, bread, gravy, coffee. **1922** *Leatherneck* (Apr. 22) 5: *Canned Bill*: Canned beef. Also known as canned Willie and canned bull.

5. a railway locomotive; BULLGINE.

1859 Matsell *Vocab.*: Had just touched a bloke's leather when the bull bellowed for the last time.

6.a. a bully fellow; an excellent or high-spirited person.

1867 Clark *Sailor's Life* 165: Come, heave water there, my bulls, and don't have any black looks. **1923** Mills *War Letters* 78 [ref. to 1907]: By virtue of his general achievements, he had already been knighted as a "Bull," a title by which, from time immemorial, the citizenry of that college [Univ. of N.C.] distinguishes the half dozen or so men whose exploits in scholarship, athletics, or forensics appeal to popular approval.

b. Esp. *Logging.* a foreman or boss.

1942 *AS* (Dec.) 220: [logging] *Bull*. As a noun,…any kind of boss. **1956** Sorden & Ebert *Logger's* 5 [ref. to a1925]: *Bull*, The boss of a camp or a logging operation.

7. a bullwhip.

1922 Rollins *Cowboy* 197 [ref. to 1890's]: Of course, a teamster might once have been a cowboy, but no one "teamed" or "threw the bull" so long as he could still sit the buck.

8. *Hobo & Und.* a police officer, police or private detective, or prison guard.

1893 "J. Flynt," in *Century* (Nov.) 103: Even the policemen of this city are often friends of beggars, and I have seldom met a hobo who was very angry with a New York "bull." **1894** *Atlantic* (Sept.) 322: But don't let the bulls* catch you.…*Policemen. *ca*1894 in *Independent* (Jan. 2, 1902) 28: The Police or "Bulls," as they call them…Run them out of town. **1907** J. London *Road* 91: I fought shy of railroad cops, "bulls" and constables as I never had before. **1908** Hopper & Bechholt *9009* 93: Every time a bull or detective passed me, he pinched me fer luck. *a*1904–11 Phillips *Susan Lenox* II 247: The "bull" looked sharply at her. **1912** Berkman *Prison* 130 [ref. to 1892]: It was dat big bull* dere, Pete Hoods.…*Guard. **1915** Howard *God's Man* 365: That's how they came to call him "Pink," copping Pinkerton bulls' watches on the race-track. **1928** Burnett *Little Caesar* 144: Boy, the bulls sure played this one slick. **1931** *Writer's Digest* (May) 41: *Bull*—Special agent or railroad police officer. **1938** in W. Burnett *Best* 504: The L.A. bulls was sure to get me. **1948** Ives *Wayfaring Stranger* 128: I climbed to the top of the boxcar, hoping to walk back and find a flatcar. Just as I reached the top, a railroad bull appeared. **1953** Brossard *Bold Saboteurs* 91: The bulls could never find us. **1960** Larner & Tefferteller *Addict* 65: Each narcotic bull has to make a certain number of arrests to stay in good with the top men at the narcotics bureau. **1963** *True* (May) 41: Giarnella…has been a working bull for 15 years and a detective…for 10. **1965** Yurick *Warriors* 174: A transit bull standing by didn't see a thing. **1966** Elli *Riot* 29: Cool it! Cool it! There's a bull on the walk. **1970** Horman & Fox *Drug Awareness* 464: *Bull*—a Federal narcotic agent, a police officer. **1971** Sorrentino *Up from Never* 3: Wid five guys in the car the bulls might pull us over. **1983** Curry *River's in My Blood* 162: He figured out ways to stump the railroad bulls.

9. lies, flattery, insincerity, nonsense, empty talk, etc.; BULLSHIT. Hence in phr. of the sort **throw the bull** to lie, exaggerate, flatter; (*hence*) to gossip or chat.

1902 T.A. Dorgan, in Zwilling *TAD Lexicon* 21: Harry Hynds listened to a little "bull" from Kid Eagan. **1907** in H.C. Fisher *A. Mutt* 20: That old "sure thing" bull works wonders. **1908** in H.C. Fisher *A. Mutt* 25: Pipe the old man throwing the bull. *Ibid.* 94: At throwing the bull Chinnings Brine will have nothing on Mutt. **1910** T.A. Dorgan, in *N.Y. Eve. Jour.* (Feb. 2) 12: If he goes with Pollock and his brand of bull the dough will roll in again. **1911** Howard *Enemy to Society* 211: I don't

throw any "bull" around like some guys I know. **1912–14** O'Neill *Lost Plays* 37: Aw, shut up! Yuh make me sick with dat line of bull. **1914** *DN* IV 162: *Bull*, talk which is not to the purpose, "hot air." **1915** in Sandburg *Letters* 103: Masters has told me of your aversions to throwing the bull. **1917** in Clover *Suzanne's* 214: These stories of months in the trenches are pure "bull." **1918** Ruggles *Navy* 22: He is "full of bull," savvy? **1919** T. Kelly *What Outfit?* 53: Some Americans…began shootin' the bull. **1921** *Variety* (Nov. 18) 6: The slang word "bull" occasioned a bit of sporadic barring several years ago by the more particular vaudeville managers, but in the last few years has apparently become a part of English language, used without objection regularly at present in the best of vaudeville theaters. **1921** Casey & Casey *Gay-Cat* 191: Cut the bull, Red. **1924** Marks *Plastic Age* 48: You're full of bull. **1928** Wharton *Squad* 195 [ref. to 1918]: Who th' hell'll I sling th' bull wit' now? **1929–30** J.T. Farrell *Young Lonigan* 32: He wished Gilly would choke his bull and let it die. **1930** Nason *Corporal* 199: It may be so for all we know,/But it sounds like bull to us! **1935** Odets *Waiting for Lefty* 11: Stop talking bull! **1938** Steinbeck *Grapes of Wrath* 11: You can sling the bull with the broad behind the counter. **1940** *AS* (Apr.) 216: *Bull*…When the word as making its way into the general…vocabulary [*ca*1915], we knew what it stood for—*bullshit.* **1944** Kapelner *Lonely Boy* 40: You're throwing the bull right in your old man's face. **1950** Stuart *Objector* 266: Isn't that a crock of bull? **1964** *Twilight Zone* (CBS-TV): It certainly sounds like the bull is off the nickel. **1974** in Asimov et al. *Sci. Fi. Short Shorts* 20: I've gotten enough bull from your staff the past year. **1977** Langone *Life at Bottom* 6: You got to sling a little bull, my competing journalist who had been there told me. **1980** J. Carroll *Land of Laughs* 64: One afternoon shooting the bull with Marshal France and maybe talking about books and fantasy. *a*1989 in Bynum & Thompson *Juve. Delinquency* 205: The teachers always gave us that bull about getting an education, working hard, and being successful. **1987–91** D. Gaines *Teenage Wasteland* 63: Telling stories, throwing the bull. **1992** Strawberry & Rust *Darryl* 45: Part of me said, "Total bull."

10. *Circus.* an elephant (of either sex).

1921 *Amer. Legion Wkly.* (Apr. 15) 20: The showman's skepticism increased when he saw Gilvers's "bull" enter the old freight shed. **1921** *Variety* (Nov. 18) 21: It was necessary to shore up the stage, for there are four big "bulls" used. **1923** *N.Y. Times* (Oct. 7) VIII 4: *Bull:* Performing elephant. **1926** Norwood *Other Side of Circus* 62: We're waiting for the bulls to come up. **1961** Clausen *Season's Over* 34: Those are the bull hands. Half of them are rummies and none of them cares about anything…except those elephants. **1978** Ponicsan *Ringmaster* 7: Valencia…had come on the show as a groom, tending to the needs of the cats, bulls, and…horses.

11. (*cap.*) Bull Durham brand of tobacco.

1918 Ruggles *Navy* 22: *Bull*. Generally speaking, it is Bull Durham tobacco.

12. a buffalo nickel; a nickel; BUFFALO, *n.*, 4.

1926 Maines & Grant *Wise-Crack Dict.* 15: *Throw the bull*—Lend a nickel.

13. Esp. *Poker.* an ace; BULLET, *n.*, 1.

1934 Weseen *Slang Dict.* 248: *Bull*—An ace in a card game, especially in bridge. **1936** *AS* (Oct.) 279: *Bull*. Any one of the four aces in a deck of playing cards. **1947** Mailer *Naked & Dead* 12: "Ah got ya in spades with that bull." He pointed to his ace. **1978** Univ. Tenn. student paper: Common phrases [in poker] include "a pair of bulls," or aces.

14.a. a virile, sexually active man; STUD.

1962 T. Berger *Reinhart* 421: Can tell you're a real bull, and I'm sure glad you prefer me over that Grace. **1984** Sample *Raceboss* 24: To enhance her chances at a greater share of the tricks, she and Emma dressed alike to confuse the "bulls" who picked her thinking she was Emma.

b. Esp. *Pris.* an aggressive male homosexual; JOCKER.

1962–68 B. Jackson *In Life* 394: If they catch a homosexual and a bull living together, they can send them back to the penitentiary for unnatural sex acts. **1974** *N.Y. Times Mag.* (Feb. 17) 19: "I'm a bull," he told me, "and I want to stay on that side because I like the queens." **1977** Dunne *Confessions* 86: An old bull, a lifer, had tried to ram him in the ass.

c. BULLDYKE.

1967 Maurer & Vogel *Narc. & Narc. Add.* (ed. 3) 345: *Bull*. An aggressive female homosexual. **1971** Dahlskog *Dict.* 11: *Bull*…a bulldyke. **1977** Dunne *Confessions* 188: "Was she really a les?" "A real bull, Horace." **1979** Gram *Foxes* 82: "Dykes!"…"Hey, butch!" "Check the bulls!"

15. *Boxing.* an aggressive prizefighter.

1970 in P. Heller *In This Corner* 146: Kaplan was one of them bulls. You'd walk inside and he'd body-punch you. **1971** DiPippo *Rhetoric*

126: Yeah, but who's he fought? A few brokendown bulls who were just made for his style—a lot of slow nothings.

16. *Army.* a battle tank.

1976 C.R. Anderson *Grunts* 110 [ref. to 1969]: Bravo! Bravo! Bravo! This is Three! Get that bull off us, over!

17. *Shooting.* a bull's-eye. See also ARTILLERY BULL.

1921 *Sentinel* (May 13) 14: Artillery Bulls [title of joke column]. **1960** Bluestone *Cully* 60: Four bulls and four fours: a nice shot group the first time around. *a*1990 R. Herman, Jr. *Force of Eagles* 251: Three bulls.

¶ In phrases:

¶ **shoot** [or **throw**, etc.] **the bull** see **(9)**, above.

¶ **tie that bull outside!** stop talking rubbish! shut up!

1921 Dos Passos *Three Soldiers* 44 [ref. to 1918]: "Say, tie that bull outside," shouted Bill Grey goodnaturedly. **1925** Dos Passos *Manhattan Transfer* 161: You juss tie that bull outside, I said to him, then I resigned. **1928** Dahlberg *Bottom Dogs* 116: Shrimp…told Mugsy to tie the bull outside. **1930** Bodenheim *Roller Skates* 254: Aw, tie that bull outside! **1930** J.T. Farrell *Calico Shoes* 7: Tie your bull in somebody else's alley. **1947** Willingham *End as a Man* 226: Tie that bull out the door.

¶ (In assorted provs.).

1833 S. Smith *President's Tour* 47: Mr. Calhoun would stand no more chance down east here, than a stump'd tail bull in fly-time. **1846** in Lowell *Poetical Works* 181: Wal, Hosea he com home considerabal riled, and arter I'd gone to bed I heern Him a thrashin round like a short-tailed Bull in fli-time. **1847** in H.C. Lewis *Works* 133: Her mammy…heard the rumption and came to the house, lumbrin' over the high logs like a big bull in…a small pastur' in the worst of fly-time, as she told me arter. **1864** Armstrong *Red-Tape & Pigeon-Hole Generals* 287: Mr. Secretary himself…tossing his head, now on this side and now on that, like a short-horned bull in fly-time. *ca*1895 in Longstreet *Wilder Shore* 83: They still talk of the old days when Senator Broderick ran S.F. "tight as a bull's vent in Flytime." **1945** Monks *A Ribbon and a Star* 48: You couldn't hit the broad side of a bull's ass with a spade…! **1948** Murphy *To Hell and Back* 155: The artillery…couldn't hit a bull in the back with a bass fiddle. **1952** Randolph & Wilson *Down in the Holler* 188: Him? Why, he couldn't *hit a bull in the rump with a fiddle!* **1951** Longstreet *Pedlocks* 106: Gents, all I want to ask you is, have you got a real tight, bull-in-fly-time patent on this copper smelter process? **1960** MacCuish *Do Not Go Gentle* 124: I can't even hit the broad side of a bull's ass with a shotgun at two paces. **1963** Keats *They Fought Alone* 130: He couldn't hit a bull in the ass with a bucket of rice. **1964** Hill *One of the Casualties* 36: That half-witted thang cudden hit a bull in the ass with a banjo, was he aimen to. **1965** Gallery *Eight Bells* 51: About the only thing that these tests really proved was that the army aviators couldn't hit a bull in the stern sheets with a big bass fiddle. **1966** Newhafer *No More Bugles* 22: Maybe you couldn't hit a bull in the ass with a shotgun. **1968** Hooker *MASH* 137: That Hammond is tighter than a bull's ass in Fly-time. **1968** Swarthout *Loveland* 39: I couldn't hit a bull in the behind with a bushel basket. **1969** Maitland *Only War We've Got* 52: Why those SAMs couldn't hit a bull in the ass with a bass Fiddle. **1971** Mayer *Weary Falcon* 165: Sometimes those dickheads can't hit a bull in the asshole boresighted. **1977** Rutgers Univ. student: He couldn't hit a bull in the ass with a bucket of rice. **1981** Jenkins *Baja Okla.* 151: That'd make you richer than six feet up a bull's ass.

bull *adj.* of principal size, power, authority, etc.

1889 J.S. Farmer *Amer.* 101: "Bull" is in America a general prefix for "large." **1929** Barr *Let Tomorrow Come* 164: They make you the bull screw in a place like this. *Ibid.* 207: There's the bull stool pigeon of the dump. **1936–37** Kroll *Share-Cropper* 241: Gus Harkreader…was the bull boss of the works. **1942** *AS* (Dec.) 220 [logging]: *Bull*…As a prefix…the utter superlative in size, power, authority, or virtue. **1942** Sonnichsen *Billy King* 64 [ref. to *a*1900]: He…wanted to know the whereabouts of the "bull gambler," the best man in the house.

bull *v.* **1.a.** to talk emptily; (*hence*) to chat or gossip.

[**1850** in *AS* (1951) (N.C.): Elaborate bulling about a point that has been exploded for years.] **1900** *DN* II 25: *Bull*, v. To spend time in another [student's] room when not working. **1911* O'Brien & Stephens *Australian Sl.* 26: *Bulling*…To talk illogically or ignorantly, wandering in your mind: "You're only bulling." **1914** in J. Reed *Young Man* 53: Always kept bulling around about how wrong it was to fight, and that kind of stuff. **1924** Marks *Plastic Age* 42: Hi, Hugh. Come in and bull a while. **1925** Williams *15th Inf.* 19: You're sitting round a'drinking/Or a'bulling or just thinking. **1956** P. Moore *Chocolates* 14: I can bull through French class.

b. to deceive, cajole, lie to, flatter, etc.; BULLSHIT, *v.*, 1.

1907 in H.C. Fisher *A. Mutt* 16: I wonder if I can bull this pill roller

into selling me a jolt. **1908** in Blackbeard & Williams *Smithsonian Comics* 58: He bulled the loon tenders to drop in at the track long enough to get a chunk down on Wing Ting. **1911** *N.Y. Eve. Jour.* (Jan. 3) 14: There's no use of me bulling the public on the thing. **1911** Howard *Enemy to Society* 304: Don't let him bull you any more!…Take a tumble to yourself! **1915–16** Lait *Beef, Iron & Wine* 169: I done swell lifts for years and bulled the swellest bulls outta the Chief's office. **1918** *Chi. Sun.-Trib.* (Feb. 18) V (unp.): The fact that she wanted you at one time an' didn't at another proves you bulled her. **1919** Johnson *Hoboken* 6: Perhaps there was some Border man "bulling" the newest recruit about his hair-raising experiences in Texas. **1928** Bodenheim *Georgie May* 31: Dopey ain't bulling you. **1930** J.T. Farrell *Calico Shoes* 240: "I know you too well to let you bull me along."…"I'm not bulling you." **1941** Macaulay & Wald *Manpower* (film): Don't bull me, sister. **1956** Yordan *Harder They Fall* (film): Let's not bull each other. **1958** Frede *Entry E* 96: Don't bull me. There's never *that* much work. **1977** *L.A. Times* (Nov. 19) III 2: He's not bulling you. He's not a bull artist. He's real.

2. *Stu.* to fail (an examination). Also intrans.

1851 Hall *College Wds.* 25: Bull. At Dartmouth College, to recite badly; to make a poor recitation. **1936** Monks & Finklehoffe *Brother Rat* 152: I don't reckon there'll be much use…after I bull that chemistry exam in the morning.

3. *Stock Market.* to increase the value of (a stock). Also intrans.

1870 Medbery *Wall St.* 163: He…"bulled" stocks and "beared" gold. **1881** Duffus-Hardy *Cities & Prairie Lands* 146: To "bull" is to send up the stocks; to "bear" is to pull them down. **1885** *Harper's Mo.* (Nov.) 852: Reports of prosperity are prepared…to "bull" the stock. **1934** in *WNID2*.

4. to bungle.

1900 Johnston *20 Yrs.* 584: The telegraph operator at Clyde "bulled" the message and copied it, "Meet us at the noon train with stretcher."

bulladeen *n.* [fr. BULL, *n.* 8, poss. infl. by *bulletin*] *Black E.* a police officer.

1962 Crump *Killer* 200: My old man would have de bulladeens on us in nothin' flat. *Ibid.* 228: And he's probably put the bulladeens on me by now. *Ibid.* 301: Hey! The bulladeens! Cop and blow!

bull artist *n.* a person who habitually exaggerates, lies, or flatters.

1918 in Rossano *Price of Honor* 211: He was, like all marines, a "bull" artist. **1920** Norton *639th Aero. Sq.* 62: Bull artists. **1929–30** J.T. Farrell *Young Lonigan* 77: Is Hennessey the bull artist? **1930** "D. Stiff" *Milk & Honey* 200: *Bull artist*—A hobo with a gift of gab. Becoming a parlor term. **1936** Benton & Ballou *Where Do I Go?* 300: A reputation for being a "bull artist." **1945* S.J. Baker *Australian Lang.* 128: A person given to bragging or empty chatter is known as a *bull artist. ca*1978 *Rockford Files* (NBC-TV): Jim Rockford—the con and bull artist.

bull bitch *n. West.* **1.** a person or thing regarded as unmanageable, recalcitrant, or the like.—often used in comparisons.

1930 Botkin *Folk-Say* 106: I'm a dirty bull-bitch, if I don't see one go in there. **1938** Steinbeck *Grapes of Wrath* 13: Nothin' ain't none of your affair except skinnin' this here bull-bitch [*sc.* a truck] along. *Ibid.* 56: This here's jackrabbit. Tougher'n a bull-bitch. **1960–61** Steinbeck *Discontent* 219: Stoney's mean as a bull bitch.

2. BULLDYKE.

1962 D.W. Maurer, in Mencken *Amer. Lang.* (abr. ed.) 728: The *bull bitch* or *butch pimp* [is] a lesbian who has one or more girls and services them like a man. **1970** Thompson *Garden of Sand* 258: Lousy bullbitch! **1972** R. Wilson *Playboy's Forbidden Words* 54: Bull Dyke…also known as a *bull-dagger* and a *bull bitch.*

bull butter *n.* margarine.

1882 Peck *Peck's Sunshine* 287: Oleomargerine [*sic*], or Bull Butter. **1886** in *DA*: If they personally prefer bull and boar butter to the genuine dairy article, no one can have any objection to their eating it. **1887** in *DAE*: As To Bull Butter….The recent interview with Commissioner Colman on the subject of oleomargarine…has caused considerable excitement. **1948** *Time* (May 10) 20: Farm-area Congressmen had long sneered at margarine as "bull-butter."

bull camp *n.* a camp of laborers engaged in outdoor construction work or the like.

1931 *Amer. Merc.* (Oct.) 168: The place we picked was an old hobo bull-camp.

bull chief *n. Navy.* a chief petty officer.

1961 McKenna *Sons of Martha* 69 [ref. to 1930's]: The bull chief of the black gang was my boss in the fireroom.

bull colonel *n. Mil.* a full colonel. Cf. FULL BULL.

　1980 Cragg *L. Militaris* 56: *Bull Colonel.* A colonel.

bull con *n.* [BULL + CON] exaggerated or lying talk; (*hence*) SNOW JOB. Also **bullcorn.** Also as v.

　1896 Ade *Artie* 26: I may be a farmer, but it takes better people than you to sling the bull con into me. **1904** *Life in Sing Sing* 259: He gave them a bull con and they turned him out. He told a plausible story and they discharged him. **1907** Peele *N.C. to S. Calif.* 109: Allen was a great bull-con man (hot air man). **1919** Hubbell *Company C* 47: They say we're going over the ocean,/They say we're going over the sea,/They say we're going over the ocean,/But it all sounds like "bull con" to me. **1928** Shay *More Pious Friends* 198: It's the old bull con. **1942** *Calif. Folk. Qly.* I 146 [ref. to ca1915]: The boys all…started to throw the bull con. **1959** F.L. Brown *Trumbull Pk.* 195: Now you're bullcorning about "get a white lawyer." **1960** Oliver *Conversations with the Blues* 57: I shot at my woman, 'cause I was tired of so much bull corn. **1967, 1970, 1981** in *DARE*: Bullcorn.

bull cook *n. Esp. Logging.* an employee hired to do odd jobs around a workmen's camp; chore boy.

　1908 Whittles *Lumberjack* 77: The workman who keeps the fires in the bunkhouse and does odd jobs around the camp [is called the] "bull cook," because in the old days when oxen were used his duty was to see to their comfort. **1914** *Amer. Lumberman* (Apr. 25) 33: The bull-cook…hears a sizzlin' in the suds. **1925** *AS* I (Dec.) 137: Once the wood-splitter and the water-carrier of the logging camp was simply the "choreboy"; but this bunkhouse lackey became "bull cook" in the West. **1926** *AS* I (Sept.) 650: *Bull cook.*—camp flunkey. **1929** *AS* IV (June) 338: *Bull cook.* A camp janitor; see "crum boss." **1931** Adamic *Laughing* 209: The [logging] camp was in charge of a bull-cook, to whom the labor boss sent me to get a bunk. **1937** *Lit. Digest* (Apr. 10) 12: *Bull cook.* Camp flunky. **1941** *AS* (Oct.) 232: *Bull cook.* The camptender. He tends fires, sweeps bunkhouses, but never cooks. **1979** Crews *Blood & Grits* 58: Hap…gave me over to a bull cook named Paul.…he explained…that a bull cook was the all-round good guy in camp who made the beds, carried the trash, swept the floors [etc.].

bullcorn var. BULL CON.

bullcrap *n. & v.* (a partial euphem. for) BULLSHIT.

　1935 Algren *Boots* 213: Lyin' Sam the Bullcrap man. **1952** Ellson *Golden Spike* 22: Don't give me that bull-crap. **1960** Hoagland *Circle Home* 68: I ought to stop this one-week bullcrap. **1960** T. Southern, in Rosset *Evergreen* 278: They's a lotta ole *bull-crap* go on in the world. **1963** Cameron *Black Camp* 84: Schooner's just a bull-crap artist. **1970** Gattzden *Black Vendetta* 49: Why had the old man bullcrapped him? **1974** Millard *Thunderbolt* 60: So who do you think you're bull-crapping, Johnny? **1990** *World Today* (CNN-TV) (July 27): That's bullcrap.…You guys believe in lie detectors down there.

bulldag *v.* [back formation fr. BULLDAGGER] to engage in lesbian activity.—used mainly in pres. ppl. Also as n., a lesbian.

　1920–54 Randolph *Bawdy Elements* 47: Two women indulging in any sort of homosexual practice are said to be *bull-dagging.* **1964** in Jackson *Swim Like Me* 149: His bald-head, bulldagging…mammy. *Ibid.* 125: I'm gonna…bulldag you too. **1984** Grahn *Another Mother Tongue* 305: *Bull-dike*…Variations are *bulldagger, bulldag.*

bulldagger *n.* [orig. var. pronun. of BULLDYKER] Esp. *So. & Black E.* BULLDYKE.

　*a*1929 in K. White *First Sex. Revolution* 94: When they want to get married they go to a bull diggar's [*sic*] ball. **1938** *Esquire* (Dec.) 202: It has been given various names—*Squeeze Me, The Little Boy in the Boat* and *The Bulldagger's Dream.* **1952** in J. Blake *Joint* 41: Josie was a "bull-dagger" or active Lesbian. **1920–54** Randolph *Bawdy Elements* 47: An aggressive woman with a passion for her own sex is called a *bull-dagger;* the term is sometimes pronounced *bull-diger,* to rhyme with *tiger.* **1961** J. Baldwin *Another Country* 32: She dresses like a…bull dagger. **1965** Ward & Kassebaum *Women's Pris.* 99: That's more or less a *bull-dagger's*…kick. **1969** Hannerz *Soulside* 130: Your sister a bull-dagger! **1984** Grahn *Another Mother Tongue* 305: *Bulldike*…Variations are *bulldagger, bulldag. a*1973–87 F.M. Davis *Livin' the Blues* 36 [ref. to Kansas, ca1920]: A bulldagger screwed women just like a man.

bull dance *n.* a dancing party attended solely by men, as on shipboard, in a military or workmen's camp, etc.

　1840 in Eliason *Tarheel Talk* 139: A Bull dance was got up on the second story passage. **1843–45** T.J. Green *Tex. Exped.* 316: Some eight or ten were engaged in a "bull dance," being the only one we could perform. **1855** Whitman *Leaves of Grass* 58: At he-festivals with black guard jibes and ironical license and bull-dances and drinking and

laughter. **1867** Smyth *Sailor's Wd.-Bk.*: *Bull-Dance.* At sea it is performed by men only, when without women. It is sometimes called a stag-dance.

bull dick *n. Mil.* bologna.—usu. considered vulgar.

　1988 Fussell *Wartime* 91 [ref. to WWII]: Baloney…*horse-cock* (sometimes *bull-* or *donkey-dick*).

bull dinky *n. & interj.* BULLCRAP. Also **bull dickey.**

　1957 Herber *Tomorrow to Live* 38 [ref. to WWII]: It seems like a lot of bull dickey, Lieutenant. **1972** N.Y.U. student: *Bull dinky* is like hogwash. Kids say it. **1984** Univ. Tenn. student: *Bull dinky* means *incorrect!*

bulldog *n.* **1.a.** a pistol; (*hence,* in later colloq. usage) a snub-nosed revolver.

　*1785 Grose *Vulgar Tongue: Bull Dogs.* Pistols. **1878** [P.S. Warne] *Hard Crowd* 14: His friends had armed him with rib-tickler and bull-dogs. **1893** Wawn *South Sea Islanders* 303: When I felt for my "bull-dog," to send a bullet after him, the holster was empty. **1907** "O. Henry" *Heart of West* 204: No true artist is uplifted by shooting an aged man carrying an old-style .38 bulldog. *ca*1979 in Montell *Killings* 55 [ref. to *ca*1920]: She…pulled out one of them little old double-barrel derringer pistols called the American Bulldog. She said, "I'm going to let my bulldog work some of these days."

　b. *Navy.* a deck-gun.

　1811 in Neesor *Naval Ballads* 84: The yankee bull-dog nobly spoke. ***1815** in Wetherell *Adventures* 335: Up went our Ensign, up our helm, up ports, and out ran our bull dogs. **1823** J.F. Cooper *Pilot* 65: We passed several of the enemy's cutters coming up the Channel, with whom our bull-dogs longed for a conversation.…My little sixes can speak…nearly as loud as the frigate's eighteens. **1827** J.F. Cooper *Red Rover* 128: She is not without a few bull-dogs, to bark in defence of her own rights. **1851** *Harper's Mo.* (Sept.) 470: Let us try if our own throats can not drown the bark of these two bull-dogs of ours! **1863** in Browne & Browne *Fresh-Water Navy* 142: They take very good care to keep out of range of the "Tyler's" "bulldogs," as the darkies call them—our 64-pdrs. **1867** Smyth *Sailor's Wd.-Bk.*: *Bull-Dog*…General name for main deck guns.

　c. *Mil.* an artillery piece.

　*ca*1845 in Botkin *Treas. Amer. Folk.* 28: The barkin o' them big iron bull dogs called cannons. **1871** Crofutt *Tourist's Guide* 207: Beside them are the "Boys in Blue," with ample fortifications, surmounted by the "Bull Dogs" of "Uncle Sam." **1883** Marshall *Army Life* 113 [ref. to Civil War]: The rebels were severely punished with our little bull-dogs (steel guns). **1914** Giles *Rags & Hope* 82 [ref. to Civil War]: We soon saw the white smoke rising…and heard "Pelham's Mountain Bull Dogs" barking and baying at the enemy at the ford.

　2. *Und.* a watchman (*obs.*); a police officer.

　1828 Bird *Looking Glass* 89: We'll have the bull-dogs here in a twinkling, head ratcatchers and all. Come, why don't you stir? **1944** Kendall *Service Slang* 3: *A bull dog*.…Military Police.

　3. *Cards.* a king.

　1900 *DN* II 25: *Bulldog,* n. King, at cards. **1934** Weseen *Slang Dict.* 248: *Bull dog*—The king in playing cards. **1966** Kenny *Caste* 131: Three bulldogs and tenners [in a poker hand].

　4. *Journ.* **a.** (see quot.).

　1918 *Chi. Sun.-Trib.* (June 16) V (unp.): Three of his men were drawn every Friday to write "bull-dog" for the Sunday paper. "Bulldog" is filler of current but not immediate news, differing from "grapevine" in that it still breathes, and differing from news in that it has lost its freshness after the catch.

　b. the earliest morning edition of a daily newspaper. Now *S.E.*

　1926 *Amer. Mercury* (Oct.) 188: Bull-dog editions…dated as of the next day and put on the street as soon as the afternoon papers' sale slowed down. **1926** *Nation* (Oct. 13) 342: This story got into the bulldog edition of one of the papers. **1936** Fellows & Freeman *Big Show* 97 [ref. to 1890's]: An expressman who delivered the "bulldog" edition of the morning *World* to Brooklyn. **1947** M. Davenport *E. Side, W. Side* 201: Until after the bulldog is on the street, one or two in the morning.

　5. *Trucking.* [sugg. by the bulldog trademark on Mack trucks] a Mack truck.

　1971 Tak *Truck Talk* 62: *Follow the bulldog:* to drive a Mack tractor, whose trademark and symbol is a bulldog. **1976** Lieberman & Rhodes *CB Handbook* 125: *Bulldog*—Mack truck. **1977** Avallone *White Knight* 61: Fat Boy led the way in his Bulldog.

bulldog *v.* **1.** *West.* to wrestle (a steer, calf, etc.) to the ground. Now *S.E.*

1905 in Hanes *B. Pickett* 62: Will Pickett, the Texas Negro cowboy, the originator of steer bulldogging, presented at the Calgary Fair the first exhibition of steer bulldogging ever seen outside of [the Southwest]. *a*1940 in Lanning & Lanning *Texas Cowboys* 94: One would bulldog them and the other would mark or brand them.

2. *Horse Racing*. BLAST.

1956 "T. Betts" *Across Board* 240: Touts were allowed to advertise winners they did not have. This was called…"bulldogging."

bulldoze *v.* to intimidate or coerce, as with threats of violence; bully. Now *S.E.*

1876 in Hayes *Diary* 54: The process of intimidation known as "bull dozing." **1903** J. London *Abyss* 10: In order to bulldose me, through fear of exposure, into paying heavily for my purchases. **1927** in Hammett *Knockover* 307: Bulldozing a man who might after all be dying wasn't gentlemanly. **1938** Korson *Mine Patch* 51: For the way that ye bulldozed me butties and I. **1954** L. Armstrong *Satchmo* 207: Baby had been bulldozing us plenty, but he was as tame as a lamb now. **1979** V. Patrick *Pope* 121: Blocks this guy's way and starts to bulldoze him for the money.

bulldozer *n.* **1.** a bully; thug.

1876 in *DA*. **1884** T. Fortune *Black & White* 193: The Bulldozer and White Liner can find but little room to ply their nefarious work. **1907** J.H. Williams, in *Independent* (May 23) 1185: The mates were a pair of huge, unflinching bull-dozers, and they hunted and hounded the crew to desperation. **1966** L. Armstrong *Self-Portrait* 13: He was a bulldozer, a bad character, used to come in and take the money. **1962–68** B. Jackson *In the Life* 181: He's a bulldozer….He wants to throw his weight around.

2. a large pistol, as used for intimidation.

1881 in *DAE*: A Californian bull-doser is a pistol which carries a bullet heavy enough to destroy human life with certainty. **1889** *Century Dict.* 715: *Bulldozer*, a revolver.

bull dust *interj.* [a partial euphem. for] BULLSHIT.

1951 Longstreet *The Pedlocks* 373: Tinker Evans from his table said, "Bulldust."

bulldyke *n.* [*bull* + DYKE] a homosexual woman, esp. one of masculine appearance and behavior. Also **bulldike**.

1931 in Tamony *Americanisms* (No. 31) 8: Bull-dykes Rendezvous….Men are not admitted. **1940** in T. Williams *Letters* 6: A bull-dike named Wanda who is a well-known writer under a male pen-name. **1952** Mandel *Angry Strangers* 364: You lousy bulldike! **1966** S. Harris *Hellhole* 60: This bulldyke, she feel my tits and tried to take my clothes off…in the shower room. **1967** Dibner *Admiral* 333: She belongs to the horniest bull dyke west of Denver. *a*1969 J. Kimbrough *Defender of Angels* 39 [ref. to *a*1920]: You mean…I can't bring his gladness down 'cause I'm a bull-dyke. **1973** Kimball & Bolcolm *Sissle & Blake* 42: It was around 1896 or 1897 when he [*sc.* Eubie Blake] heard Jesse Pickett play his "Dream Rag."…Pickett often called it "The Bull Dyke's Dream" because of its strong impact on the lesbians who worked in [Baltimore] sporting houses. **1982** *Harper's* (July) 61: [He] denounced the raped and butchered Maryknoll sisters as "bull-dyke socialists."

bulldyke *v.* to engage in lesbian activity.—used mainly in pres. ppl. Also **bulldike**.

1921 in J. Katz *Gay/Lesbian Almanac* 402: She had indulged in the practice of "bull diking." **1927** McKay *Home to Harlem* 20: A bulldyking woman and a faggoty man. **1967** deCoy *Nigger Bible* 118: BULL-DIKIN' BLACK MILDRED.

bulldyker *n.* BULLDYKE, *n.* Also **bulldiker**.

1925 Van Vechten *Nigger Heaven* 285: Bulldiker: Lesbian. **1927** C. McKay *Harlem* 68: Lesbian….Tha's what we calls bulldyker in Harlem….Them's all ugly womens. **1929** T. Gordon *Born to Be* 235: Musicians, writers, bull-dikers, hoboes, faggots, bankers, sweetbacks, hotpots and royalty. **1938** H. Miller *Trop. Capricorn* 249: A maiden aunt who looked like a bull-dyker. **1942** in T. Williams *Letters* 53: A sort of literary bull-diker. **1945** Drake & Cayton *Black Metro.* 573: "Bulldiker"—homosexual woman reputed to have male genitalia. **1968** I. Reed *Yellow Back Radio* 92: He rode next to Mighty Dike, bulldyker octoroon. **1969** Pharr *Numbers* 97: So she's a bulldiker, eh?

bullet *n.* **1.** [orig. a technical term in the game of brag] *Cards.* an ace.

1807 W. Irving *Salmagundi* 354: Presently one of them exclaimed triumphantly, "Two bullets and a bragger!" and swept all the money into his pocket. **1827** in *JAF* LXXVI (1963) 291: Ive got too Bragers…ive tu bulits. **1841** *Spirit of Times* (Oct. 23) 402: Two bullets and a bragger. **1844** Porter *Big Bear* 110: Two bullits and a bragger. **1850** J. Greene

Tombs 84: The hands filled each two "bullets" and a "bragger." **1878** Hart *Sazerac* 151: "Here's four bullets," said Brown, as he reached for the pot. **1889** Barrère & Leland *Dict. Slang* I: Bullets (cards) in American brag are aces. **1898–1900** Cullen *Chances* 246: The limit was just what the bank president wanted with his four bullets. **1904** Ade *True Bills* 4: Mrs. Jinkins showed up three Bullets and bumped him for Eighty cents. **1919** Darling *Jargon Bk.* 6: Bullet—A playing card called an ace. **1945* S.J. Baker *Australian Lang.* 180: Bullet, an ace. **1952** Uris *Battle Cry* 142: A bullet, another bullet, six, whore, jack. **1952** Vonnegut *Player Piano* 244: A queen for Charley…And, I'll be go to hell, the Sarge catches a bullet. **1957** Sale *Abandon Ship!* (film): Three lovely aces—the prettiest bullets you ever saw.

2. *Mining*. a nugget.

1889 in *DAE*: In the clay he was…likely to strike "bullets," lumps…or pockets of pure-gold.

3. a biscuit.

1887 N.O. *Lantern* (Nov. 12): And bought some java. With it, they received two bullets each. **1900** *Howitzer* (U.S. Mil. Acad.) 118: Bullet—A mess-hall biscuit, sometimes called "grape shot."

4. a dollar. Cf. SLUG.

1886 *Chi. Tribune* (Mar. 2) 10: He promised me a hundred bullets if I'd spot him any time. **1900** *DN* II 25 [Tufts College]: Bullet, n….2. Money. **1917** *Editor* (Feb. 24) 152: Bullet—One dollar. **1921** Casey & Casey *Gay-Cat* 99: I'd git a thousand bullets in good solid jack fer him. **1970** Landy *Underground Dict.* 41: Bullet…One dollar.

5. *pl.* Esp. *Mil.* beans.

[**1893** Barra *Two Oceans* 49: Salt meat,…beans as hard as bullets.] **1917** *Editor* (Jan. 13) 33: Army Vernacular…"Artillery" or "Boston Bullets"— Beans. **1919** *Lit. Digest* (June 21) 76: The enlisted men did feast on canned "willy" and canned "bullets." **1936** Reddan *Other Men's Lives* 44: Canned horse, gold fish, slum, bullets, etc. **1936** *AS* (Feb.) 42: Bullets. Order of baked beans. **1944** Kendall *Service Slang* 3: Bullets…beans.

6. *Journ.* a brief, forceful editorial.

1923 in Mills *War Letters* 182 [ref. to 1916]: This was what was called in office slang "a bullet" and it hit the bulls-eye fair and true.

7. *Sports.* a ball that has been hit, thrown, or kicked exceptionally hard.

[**1908** *Atlantic* (Aug.) 224: He shoot them bullet-ball straight to breast of Hon. Stop. Hon. Striker swing club for vain effort.] [**1911** in Paxton *Sport USA* 57: The ball sped like a bullet, some twelve feet from the ground, over the third baseman's head.] **1929** *N.Y. Times* (June 2) IX 2: A "bullet" is a ball the batter hits "on the nose" and into the hands of a waiting fielder. **1939** in Paxton *Sport USA* 323: Passes into the flat zone or quick over the line when there are no defenders between pitcher and catcher call for bullets. **1977** N.Y. Yankees baseball (WPIX-TV) (Aug. 23): Big Mike Torrez on the mound for the Yankees—throwing those bullets up there. **1978** H. Cosell on ABC *Monday Night Baseball* (ABC-TV) (June 26): Messersmith has been throwing bullets in practice. **1984** *N.Y. Post* (Aug. 16) 54: Birkenmeier made a spectacular, one-hand save on Ade Coker's rising bullet in the 58th minute.

8. *Constr.* a rivet.

1938 *AS* (Apr.) 156: Bullets. A term for rivets.

9. an ejaculation of semen.

1966 Braly *On Yard* 219: How many bullets did you shoot last night?

10. *Pris.* a one-year term of imprisonment.

1967 Maurer & Vogel *Narc. & Narc. Add.* (ed. 3) 345. **1974** J. Mills *One Just Man* 26: "Will you take a bullet?" A bullet's *und Dict.* 41. a year [in prison]. **1990** *Cops* (Fox-TV): What are you gonna get this time—a bullet? A year?

11. *Stu.* an academic grade of B.

1979 Univ. Tenn. student: A *bullet* is a B. He got a bullet on the exam. I've heard it several times in the past three years here. It's *not* an A.

12. *Music Industry.* a recording that rapidly becomes a hit.

1974 *Night-Stalker* (ABC-TV): A *bullet* is a tune that goes right to the top, that's gonna be a hit. **1979** Homer *Jargon* 119: Bullet. A record believed to be a potential success.

13. *Narc.* a drug capsule.

1966 Brunner *Face of Night* 231: Bullet—a capsule of heroin. **1968* in Spears *Drugs & Drink* 83. **1974** Hyde *Mind Drugs* 151: Blue bullets…Amytal sodium. *Ibid.* 156: Red bullets…Seconal sodium. *Ibid.* 159: Yellow bullets…Nembutal.

14. *pl.* (used in oaths).

1864 "Kirke" *Down in Tenn.* 114: Bullets an' blisters, Tom! but thar's thet outdacious Yankee!

¶ In phrases:

¶ **bite the bullet** see s.v. BITE.

¶ **look bullets** to cast a hostile glance; look daggers.
1846 in *Mo. Hist. Rev.* (July 1928) 8: Capt. Woodside looked bullets.

bullet-eater *n. Mil.* a reckless and aggressive combat soldier.
1918 Gibbons *Thought We Wouldn't Fight* 335: Talk about bullet-eaters—believe me, those Marines sure are.

bullet-launcher *n. Mil.* a firearm. *Joc.*
1980 Cragg *L. Militaris* 56: Bullet Launcher. The individual infantryman's rifle or any individual weapon, including handguns.

bullfeathers *n.* HORSEFEATHERS.
1974 *N.Y. Daily News* (Sept. 5) 74: You are adding apples and oranges and getting bull-feathers. **1980** in *DARE*. **1984–88** Safire *Language Maven* 81: "Horsefeathers"…I have heard "bull feathers" used in the same way, but less often.

bullfest *n.* BULL SESSION.
1917 in Rossano *Price of Honor* 21: A vigorous bull fest. **1924** Marks *Plastic Age* 286: The monthly meetings were nothing but "bull fests." **1932** *AS* VII 400: *Bull-fest*, n. A group conversation or discussion. **1943** Bayler & Carnes *Last Man* 30: The boys would come over and we'd "shoot the breeze" in long bullfests.

bullfighter *n. Hobo.* an empty railway car.
1930 Irwin *Amer. Tramp & Und. Slang: Bull-Fighter.* An empty passenger coach, usually when attached to a freight train or when standing idle in the yards. **1977** R. Adams *Lang. of R.R.* 24: *Bullfighter.* An empty car, especially a passenger car.

bull fuck *n.* cream gravy or custard, fancied to resemble bovine semen; (in 1991 quot.) stew thickened with flour.—usu. considered vulgar. Cf. BULL GRAVY.
[**1942** *ATS* 100: Gravy: *Bull shit, come,…gism.*] **1961** Partridge *DSUE* (ed. 5) 1019: *Bull-fuck.* Custard: Canadian railroad-construction crews: since ca1910. **1966–67** in *DARE* I 445. **1981** Spears *Slang & Euphem.* 53: *Bull fuck…*A thick gravy with chunks of meat. **1991** Killingbeck *U.S. Army* 40 [ref. to 1953]: "Make a bullfuck."…I watched the stew become thicker. "Soldier, that is what is known as a bullfuck."

bull gang *n. Labor.* a labor crew engaged in the manual lifting or moving of heavy objects or materials.
1918 in *St. Lawrence Univ. in War* 144: Afternoon detailed to Bull Gang—worked till 10 p.m. **1931** Gallagher *Bolts & Nuts* 95 [ref. to 1918]: Bull gang (laboring gang). **1951** in J. Blake *Joint* 14: It's rugged back-breaking labor on the bull gang. We work out on the road under three shotgun guards. **1970** Terkel *Hard Times* 30 [ref. to 1930's]: I need two guys for the bull gang. Two guys to go into the hole.

bullgine *n.* [*bull* + en*gine*] a steam engine, esp. a locomotive. Also **bulgine.**
1845 Durivage & Burnham *Stray Subjects* 38: Imitating the "bull-gine." **1848** in *AS* XXI 116: Going ober to Hobuc, in de steamboat,/De bulgine busted and we all got afloat.…Clar de track, de bullgine's coming. **1849** in Doten *Journals* I 4: "Bulgine oberture."…the cars run off the track—smashed the bulgine. **1855** *Crockett Almanac* (unp.): Look out for the Bulgine! **1877** Bartlett *Americanisms* 777: *Bullgine.* A cant term for a locomotive engine. **1889** Barrère & Leland *Dict. Slang* I 196: *Bulljine* (nautical) a locomotive is so called by sailors. **1899** Garland *Eagle's Heart* 151: That's the bull-gine on the Great Western. **1911** Runyon *Tents of Trouble* 42: You hear the gang when the hammers clang an' the bullgines hoist away! **1939** in *DA* 213: His bullgine was new an' shiny, an' there it was with tomater ketchup all over th' boiler an' th' cab. **1962** *AS* XXXVII 132: *Bulgine…*A locomotive.

bull goose *n. West.* a man in charge. Cf. STUD DUCK.
1956 Algren *Walk on the Wild Side* 79 [ref. to 1930's]: "You the bull-goose here?" Dave asked, "I'm lookin' for boat-work." **1962** Kesey *Cuckoo's Nest* 22: Who's the bull goose loony here?

bull gravy *n.* (see quot.).
1949 *PADS* XI 4: *Bull gravy…*Cream gravy. Vulgar.

bull-hauler *n. Trucking.* a truck that is transporting cattle; (*also*) the driver of such a truck.
1972 *N.Y. Times Mag.* (Nov. 12) 95: Trafford waves continually at cattle vans ("bullhaulers"), tankers, Greyhound buses. **1990** Rukuza *W. Coast Turnaround* 37: There was a bull hauler in the space.

bullhead *n.* a buffalo nickel.
1945 in *DAS* 72: Then slip me a bullhead. I need a java.

bullhead clap or **bullheaded clap** *n.* severe gonorrhea. Also vars.

1942 in Randolph & Legman *Blow Candle Out* 600: I got a dose of the bull-headed clap. **1951** in Randolph *Pissing in Snow* 125: He got a dose of the old bullhead clap. **1970** U.S. Army veteran, age 23: In Korea they used to talk about the *bullheaded clap.* The kind you never get over. **1985–90** R. Kane *Veteran's Day* 27: Bullhead syphilis.

bullhead luck *n.* extreme good luck.
1879 in *DA* 216: By exercising skill and judgment or "bull-head luck," as an old veteran of the pass calls it, a little execution may be done.

bull hockey *n.* BULLCRAP. Cf. HORSE HOCKEY.
1968 *Face of War* (documentary film): "He keeps claimin' he's a farmer." "Bull hockey." **1983** *War: A Commentary* (KCTS-TV): Bull! Bullhockey!

bull hook *n. Circus.* an elephant prod.
1926 Norwood *Other Side of Circus* 98: With the point of a bull hook he traced a rude diagram on the ground. **1975** McKennon *Horse-Dung Trail* 149: Scott beat him back with that big "Bull hook" he used to use with old Jumbo. **1978** Ponicsan *Ringmaster* 172: Po Chang was going to work him over with the bullhook.

bull horrors *n.pl.* **1.** *Hobo.* chronic or excessive fear of police.
1927 *AS* (June) 391: *Bull horrors* and *work horrors* are self-explanatory. **1929** *AS* 338: *Bull horrors*—Obsessed with fear of the police. **1933** Ersine *Pris. Slang* 22: *Bullhorrors*, n. Great fear of being arrested or killed by an officer. **1936** Dai *Opium Addiction* 197: *Bull-horrors.* When an addict is full of cocaine, he thinks the police are watching him. This is called *bull-horrors.* **1936** Duncan *Over the Wall* 28: He had just been released from a penitentiary down in Oklahoma, still had the "bull horrors" to a certain extent. **1970** Thackrey *Thief* 288: I finally got the bull horrors, though, reading the newspapers about how there was a crime wave going on. Every single heist they talked about seemed to be me!
2. severe delirium tremens.
1950 in F. Brown *Honeymoon* 36: He was at the stage now where twelve hours without a drink would give him the bull horrors, which are to the D.T.'s as a cyclone is to a zephyr.

bullish *adj. Orig. Stock Market.* optimistic. Now *colloq.*
1924 LeFèvre *Stockbroker* 248: I also became very bullish and put my customers into Dolomite. **1936** *Esquire* (Sept.) 160: The [receipts] in St. Louis happened to be bullish that week. **1947** Schulberg *Harder They Fall* 251: You actually have the public believing this bum's a great fighter. I'm a bullish sort of a guy, but I didn't think the fans would buy him so fast. **1987** *N.Y. Times* (July 17) 25: Mr. Grennan remains bullish, however.

bullissimo *adj.* [BULLY, *adj.* + *-issimo,* It superlative suff.] most excellent.
1865–67 De Forest *Miss Ravenel* 117: Our own regiment, the bullissimo Tenth Barataria.

bulljive *n.* [BULL + JIVE] *Black E.* BULLSHIT.
1971 *N.Y. Post* (Nov. 5) 26: That's a lot of bull jive. **1971** Dahlskog *Dict.* 11: *Bull jive*, n. Insincere talk; lies; flattery. **1984** Ark. man, age ca35: Don't give me none of that bull jive.

bulljive *v. Black E.* to BULLSHIT.
1962 Killens *Heard the Thunder* 340 [ref. to WWII]: Come on, Sergeant Solly, you know I was just bull-jiving. **1969** B. Seale, in Hoffman et al. *Conspiracy* 205: We're not here to be sitting around a jive table vacillating and bull-jiving ourselves. **1972** Casey *Obscenities* 13: I ain't even bulljivin.

bull luck *n.* extreme good luck.
1884 in Lummis *Letters* 44: Sometimes a fellow has what these eloquent sons of the plains call "bull luck." **1914** *Collier's* (Aug. 1) 6: I thought at first it was only bull luck. **1948** J. Stevens *Jim Turner* 121 [ref. to ca1910]: I had bull luck a-running. By midnight I was a hundred and seventeen dollars to the good.

bull merchant *n.* BULL ARTIST.
1915–17 Lait *Gus* 28: Take this back to that spindle-pinned bull merchant. **1956** "T. Betts" *Across the Board* 193: He's my favorite…bull merchant.

bull moose *n. Esp. West.* a big fellow or object; (*hence*) a foreman.
*a***1940** in Lanning & Lanning *Texas Cowboys* 5 [ref. to ca1880]: "Big auger," "bull moose," and similar terms were used when referring to the ranch owner. **1958** McCulloch *Woods Words* 21: *Bull moose*—a. A large anything. b. The push, or head man on a logging show. **1976** Schroeder *Shaking It* 20: Try an' make somethin of it, bullmoose!

bull muffin *n.* also *pl.* BULL HOCKEY.

1981 *Bret Maverick* (NBC-TV): You're really gonna eat this bull muffin, aren't you? **1985** *Night Court* (NBC-TV): "It sounded like a lot of…" "Bull muffins!"

bull nurse *n. West.* a cowboy sent to accompany cattle being shipped by rail.

1922 Rollins *Cowboy* 262 [ref. to 1890's]: The owners of the beasts would send, as caretakers or as not uncommonly called "horse pushers" or "bull nurses," two or three cowboys with the shipment to its ultimate destination, the abbatoirs of Chicago, Omaha, or Kansas City,…to tend the stock en route. **1936** R. Adams *Cowboy Lingo* 22: Cowboys who accompanied a shipment of cattle were also known as "bull nurses."

bullo *n.* [BULL + -O, infl. by BALONEY] BALONEY.

1937 Lay *I Wanted Wings* 168: We had known Wynne back at Randolph as an "expert at slinging the bullo."

bull of the woods *n.* a celebrated or especially powerful or influential person; BIGSHOT; (*specif.*) a foreman, superintendent, or the like; (*occ.*) a formidable thing.

1871 Schele de Vere *Americanisms* 250: [Gen.] Sumner [was nicknamed] the *Bull of The Woods.* [during the Civil War]. **1913** in *DA* 214. **1923** in Kornbluh *Rebel Voices* 93: Any bull of the woods will tell you that Tightline…can handle a yarder with any man that walks on two legs. **1925** J. Stevens *Paul Bunyan* 35: Hels Helsen…the incomparable Bull of the Woods. **1942** *AS* (Dec.) 220: *Bull of The Woods.* The camp foreman, logging superintendent, or bull of bulls of a crew or crews. **1945** *AS* (Oct.) 233: She looked like the bull of the woods.…*Bull of the woods.* Big shot, important person. **1946** Boulware *Jive & Slang* 2: *Bull of The Woods*…College prexy, Dean. **1958** McCulloch *Woods Wds.* 21: *Bull of the woods*—a. A big man, a tough hombre. b. A boss logger, superintendent, or logging manager. c. A top hand. **1974** Terkel *Working* 181: My boss…used to be a real bull of the woods. Tough guy. **1976** Univ. Tenn. professor: This is the big bull of the woods in phonology—the major work you'll have to contend with. **1982** Braun *Judas Tree* 40: Around here, I'm better known as bull o' the woods.

bullpen *n.* **1.a.** a stockade for the confinement of prisoners; (*hence*) a jail.

1809 Weems *Marion* 225 [ref. to 1780]: The tories were all handcuffed two and two, and confined together under a sentinel, in what was called a bull-pen, made of pine trees, cut down so…as to form…a pen or enclosure. **1843** in *DA* 216: All the witnesses…have been taken by force of arms, and thrust into the *"bull-pen"* in order to prevent them from giving their testimony. **1864** Northrop *Chronicles* 85: His wants will grow, like "bull pen" lice. **1864** in *PADS* (No. 70) 24: On guard at the "Bull Pen." **1865** in *Ibid.*: The Captain…said he would put every damd one of us in the bull pen till morning. **1865** in Berkeley *Confed. Arty.* 128: We were duly installed in the "bull pen," which is the name given by our men to what the Yanks call "barracks for enlisted prisoners of war." **1867** Duke *Morgan's Cav.* 465 [ref. to 1863]: It was the custom…in the various prisons for the older inmates to collect about the gates of the "Bull-pen" when "Fresh fish"…arrived. **1884** Triplett *American Crimes* 531: Thompson was kept in a miserable enclosure called a "bull-pen," where, loaded down with irons, he was subjected to many indignities. **1898** F.P. Dunne *Mr. Dooley in Peace & War* 11: Look here…if ye don't lave me counthrymen out iv th' bull-pen in fifteen minyits be the watch…I'll take ye be th' hair iv th' head an' pull ye fr'm th' corner iv Halsted Sthreet to th' r-red bridge. **1899** Skinner *4th Ill.* 276: We had to haul in the "drunks"…and confine them in the "bull pen." **1915** Poole *Harbor* 172: He talked about…the brutality of the militia, the "bull pens" into which strikers were thrown. **1918** in Sherwood *Diary* 123: One thing is sure, our bull (prison) pens are becoming glutted with captured *boches.* **1924** T. Boyd *Points of Honor* 51: You'll fight the war from the bull-pen, Hawthorne. **1927** J. Stevens *Mattock* 3: You tell the rest of your lousy doughboy camp guard they'll get the same if they don't stop sloughin' us engineers in the bull pen! **1930** Dos Passos *42d Parallel* 89: Suppose I'd been a dick, you'd be in the bullpen now, bo. **1933** in R.E. Howard *Iron Man* 53: For a Mexican bull pen is simply a jail with high walls and no roof. **1964** J. Pearl *Stockade* 30: I keep hoping they'll toss you in the bullpen some night when I'm there. **b.** *Police.* a holding cell or detention area within a jail or nearby a courtroom.

1880 Pinkerton *Prof. Thieves & Detective* 576: His companion…had been herded in the "bull-pen" along with the regular daily collection of petty offenders. **1898** *Story of a Strange Career* 290: That part of the building was the "bull pen" for the conscripts. **1934** Berg *Prison Nurse* 44: But those weeks in the county jail had taught him much. Herded in the "bullpen" indiscriminately with old and young, depraved and innocent, he had seen many things. **1952** Viereck *Men into Beasts* 51: The

handcuffs were removed when we entered the bull pen. No one was manacled in the courtroom. **1961** F. Brown *Geezenstacks* 68: He spent a night in the bullpen before they found out he was under age and switched him over to the juvenile authorities. **1971** *Newsweek* (Mar. 8) 18: "The poor mope hardly gets out of the bullpen, and he's got 90 days," says one Chicago lawyer. **1973** Droge *Patrolman* 156: The bridge-man…directs you to sign out the prisoner from the detention cell and into the "bullpen," or waiting pen, where he can be interviewed by either his private attorney or the Legal Aid attorney. **1983** Sturz *Wid. Circles* 32: They boast about it in the bull pen when they get locked up.

c. an enclosed waiting area of any kind.

1903 in "O. Henry" *Works* 438: Unlock him…and let him come to the bull-pen…the warden's outer office. **1944** in *DA*. **1985** Boyne & Thompson *Wild Blue* 317: A waiting area, a bullpen of eight desks.

d. *Pris.* an exercise area in a prison.

1912 Lowrie *Prison* 392: The cells are preferable to the "bull pen" with its fetid miasma. **1954** Gaddis *Birdman of Alcatraz* 63 [ref. to 1920]: Adjoining the cells was a separate, cement-paved "bull pen" about forty feet wide and 120 feet long.…Prisoners were allowed to run, exercise and play handball.

2. a small house or room occupied by a prostitute; (*hence*) a cheap brothel.

1867 *Nat. Police Gaz.* (Jan. 12) 4: They keep a bad old "lush drum," and a couple of "bull pans" [*sic*]. **1935** Pollock *Underworld Speaks*: Bull pen, a cheap crib of prostitution, surrounded by a fence. **1960–69** Runkel *Law* 281: After we got out of the show my uncle took me to a bullpen. *What is a "bullpen"?* A whorehouse, sir. **1970** Winick & Kinsie *Lively Commerce* 162 [ref. to Nevada, 1930's]: The Reno cribs were in a horse-shoe-shaped concrete building known as the bullpen. As the Southern Pacific train entered Reno, many passengers would eagerly go to the windows to look at the bull-pen.

3. *Baseball.* a usu. enclosed area near the playing field where pitchers warm up for a game. Now *S.E.*

1915 *Baseball Mag.* (Dec.) 118 (cited in Nichols *Baseball Termin.*). **1924** in *DA* 216. **1949** Cummings *Dict. Sports* 54.

4. a men's barracks, bunkhouse, sleeping quarters, etc.; (*also*) a men's recreation room.

1936 *AS* (Oct.) 279: *Bullpen.* The men's dormitory. **1937** Burns *Female Convict* 51: Lunch was followed by a session in what we prisoners called the bull-pen. It was a small room, about twenty by thirty.…Here we crowded every afternoon…playing cards,…arguing…smoking. **1945** Hubbard *R.R. Ave.* 335: *Bull Pen*—Crew room. **1956** Sorden & Ebert *Logger's* 6 [ref. to a1925]: *Bull-pen,* the bunkhouse where the lumberjack slept. **1958** McCulloch *Woods Words* 21: *Bull pen*…Any large room where men gather. Sleeping quarters. The recreation room at camp.

5. *Naut.* the steerage.

1960 Jordan & Marberry *Fool's Gold* 25 [ref. to 1899]: Mac explained that the bull pen meant the steerage. **1979** in Terkel *Amer. Dreams* 79: We started off on a wooden ship [in 1906]. They had a bull pen, one big room for most of 'em. The women and children had smaller quarters.

6. *Adver.* an area within an office occupied by low-ranking staff artists.

1979 Kiev *Courage to Live* 21: At the advertising agency…Frank was a member of the "bullpen," one of the lowest positions in the art department.

bull piss *n.* cheap or vile liquor, esp. wine.—usu. considered vulgar.

1917 in Dos Passos *One Man's Initiation* 11: This is Saturday night and everybody is soused on the strong red [French] army wine—nicknamed Pinard (bull piss) of which they dole us in seemingly limitless quantities. **1984** Ark. man, age *ca*35: That [cheap wine] is bull *piss,* man.

bull prick *n. Constr.* a heavy steel drill, spike, pin, or the like.—usu. considered vulgar.

1958 in *AS* (Feb. 1959) 77: Logger Lingo…*Bull prick*…A bar that has a tapered end…A Marlin spike…used in splicing wire rope…A compensating pin which allows for slack between the log trailer and truck. **1959** (cited in Watts *Dict. Old West* 63).

bull pucky *n.* BULL HOCKEY.

1970 *Rolling Stone Interviews* 408: "I am a revolutionary by trade." Bull-fucking puckey. **1974** U.C.L.A. student: Bull puckey! Bull roar! **1978** *Bad News Bears* (CBS-TV): Bull puckey! **1985** *Esquire* (Oct.) 214: That sounds like a lot of bull-pucky. **1986** E. Weiner *Howard the Duck* 142: I never heard such bull pucky.

bull-puncher *n.* **1.** a driver of an ox team. Now *hist.*

*1872 in *OEDS* I 381: The "bull-puncher," as bullock-drivers are familiarly called. **1893** *Scribner's Mag.* (June) 711: A young "bull-puncher" in a Wisconsin logging camp.

2. *West.* COWPUNCHER.

1874 in *DA* 214. **1887** Roberts *W. Avernus* 19: He followed the profession of a "bull-puncher," that is, he went in charge of the cattle destined for slaughter and canning in the distant North, and made money at it.

bull pup *n.* **1.** a pistol.

1855 W.G. Simms *Forayers* 97: I tink, Mass Willie,…dat you better hab dese little bullpups yer. **1876** J. Miller *First Fam'lies* 99: "Gone for his two little bull-pups," said Stubbs. That was what the Parson called his silver-mounted derringers.

2. *Mil.* a small howitzer.

1864 [W.H. Armstrong] *Red-Tape* 307: Good bye, Colonel; these brass bull pups will roar bloody murder at Johnny Reb today. **1867** Duke *Morgan's Cav.* 179: These little guns [mountain howitzers] were attached to the Second Kentucky, and the men of that regiment became much attached to them. They called them familiarly and affectionately, the "bull pups." **1896** in J.M. Carroll *Benteen-Goldin Lets.* 237: I wanted to get some more practice with those little bull pups.

bull-pusher *n.* BULL-PUNCHER, 2.

1879 in *DA* 214.

bull rack *n.* *Trucking.* a truck hauling cattle or other livestock.

1980 Pearl *Slang Dict.*: *Bull rack n.* (Truckers' CB) a truck carrying livestock.

bull-rag *v.* [fr. BULLYRAG] to bully, abuse, harass, etc.

1973 in *Submission of Pres. Convers.* 77: [Pres. Nixon:] And they will haul him up there and bull-rag him around the damn place and it will raise holy hell.

bull ring *n.* **1.a.** *Navy.* (see 1980 quot.). Now *hist.*

1841 [Mercier] *Man-of-War* 144: I'm afraid the old fellow will have you at the *bull-ring*, he looked marlinespikes at you as he picked himself up. **1849** Melville *White Jacket* 132: From the merciless, inquisitorial *baiting* which sailors, charged with offences, too often experience *at the mast*, that vicinity is usually known among them as the *bull ring*. **1980** Valle *Rocks & Shoals* 327 [ref. to *a*1860]: *Bull ring.* Slang. The area just aft of the main mast on the spar deck where captain's mast proceedings were usually held.

b. *Pris.* an exercise area in a prison.

1908 Kelley *Oregon Pen.* 12: The "bull ring" is in the backyard, where the convicts take exercize. **1912** Furlong *Detective* 24 [ref. to 1880's]: Dingfelter was allowed to mingle with the other prisoners on what was called the "bull ring." An allotted time is given to the prisoners each day in this place for exercise. **1912** [Livingston] *Curse* 41: We were turned out to exercise into the "Bull-ring," the open space about the cells.

c. *Pris.* a room or area where prisoners are beaten.

1933 Ersine *Prison Slang* 22: *Bullring, n.* The third degree, *works.* **1934** Lomax *Ballads and Folk Songs* 140 [ref. to late 19th C.]: There's a big bull ring in the middle of the floor,/And a damned old jailer to open the door. **1970** L.D. Johnson *Devil's Front Porch* 18: Up until 1910 when a man escaped, or attempted to do so, he was taken to the "bullring" and given a good working-over….It was situated beneath the tower at the southeast corner of the wall.

2. *Army.* a stockade for the confinement of prisoners; BULL-PEN, 1.a.

1864 in R.G. Carter *4 Bros.* 481: Among the institutions at City Point was the "bull ring," in which were confined deserters and the worst characters being continually sifted from the army.

3. *Army.* a corral for the training of cavalrymen and their mounts; a drill ground.

1899 Prentiss *Utah Vols.* 111: We were put in what is called the "bull ring" and compelled to ride bareback. **1917** Eddy *In France* 45: Just before going into the trenches the British, French, and American troops take a final course for a few weeks in a training school where the expert drill masters put them through a rigorous discipline, and the finishing touches are given to each regiment….The men commonly call this training school, or specially prepared final drill ground, the "Bull Ring." **1920** Moorhead *139th F.A.* 36: Five "bull rings" were laid out, and every man in the regiment who knew anything about horses was tried out and the best horsemen were selected as instructors. **1929** E. Colby, in *Our Army* (Nov.) 27: *Bull Ring.* The closed and fenced corral where horses are exercised, and training is given mounts and men, distinguished from training on the drill ground or across country.

4. *Football.* a ring of players formed to watch a demonstration of blocking.

1923 Wilce *Football* 226: The "bull-ring" is a splendid form of line practice. One or two line-men are played against one another….Other line-men form a ring around the…competing players, study their form and efficiency in blocking. Each line-man in turn performs and practises in the "bull-ring" where every one can see his mistakes and appreciate his good points.

5. a small rural track for horse or (*later*) automobile racing.

1935 Pollock *Underworld*: *Bull ring*, a ½ mile race track. **1959** in Cannon *Nobody Asked* 232: Conditions have improved, but on the county fair bullrings a boy who wouldn't pull a favorite at his owner's suggestion is considered a traitor. **1968** Ainslie *Thoroughbred Racing* 465: *Bull ring*—Small track, because of sharp turns. **1973** Haney *Jock* 57: You might be queen of the bullrings…but you're in New York now. **1973** Roberts *Last American Hero* (film): A couple more runs and I'll set that bullring of yours on fire. **1979** Univ. Tenn. student paper: The sport [of stock-car racing] will never escape its origins: short bullrings, primarily in the South, where virtually every star in the Grand National circuit learned his lessons before rising to the premier series. **1985** *N.Y. Times* (Aug. 31) 12: Forty-lappers on the little dirt bullrings.

6. *Printing.* a composing room.

1875 Hill *Sanctum* 156: Number Eighteen, come up to the bull-ring!

bull-roar *n.* BULLCRAP.

1974 U.C.L.A. student: I heard *bull roar!* in 1961. **1975** Stanley *WWIII* 234: Field of honor, that kind of bullroar. **1982** Knoxville, Tenn., man, age *ca*30: Let's forget all this bullroar and applesauce. **1984** Mason & Rheingold *Slanguage*: *Bull roar*…A nice way to say bullshit.

bull-room *n.* *Naut.* a shipboard cabin.

1868 Macy *There She Blows!* 127: My companions in the "bull-room" were more select and less numerous than in the forecastle.

bull session *n.* an informal discussion, usu. among men, esp. for the purpose of exchanging gossip, stories of sexual exploits, opinions, etc.

1919 Cowing *Dear Folks at Home* 7: Generally, in the evening, just before taps, we hold "bull sessions." **1920** in T. Wolfe *Letters* 11: With no more delightful "bull sessions," I have turned to work. **1924** Marks *Plastic Age* 77: Even religion and sex, the favorite topics for "bull sessions," could not compete with football. **1927** *AS* II 275: *Bull fest* or *bull session*—informal intimate talk of a group of men students. **1931** *AS* (Feb.) 203: *Bull session:* an informal student meeting in which any subject is argued and discussed. **1945** Drake & Cayton *Black Metropolis* 498: Such…images are revealed when men are having "bull sessions" about women. **1951** in Loosbrock & Skinner *Wild Blue* 452: It's good bull-session material. **1956** Moore *Chocolates for Breakfast* 4: She gives me books like *Finnegan's* [*sic*] *Wake* and T.S. Eliot poetry…and in the evenings we discuss them in a kind of a bull session, that's all. **1959** Griffin *Black Like Me* (Nov. 19): They differed completely from the "bull sessions" men customarily have among themselves. These latter, no matter how frank, have generally a robust tone that says: "We are men, this is an enjoyable thing to do and discuss." **1976** Haseltine & Yaw *Woman Doctor* 119: A seventh-grade Boy Scout bull session.

bull-shiner *n.* a truncheon.

1927 Thrasher *Gang* 267: *Bullshiner*—a billy, policeman's club. *Ibid.* 153: A man with a bull-shiner and a 45-automatic said "Stand!"

bullshit *n.* **1.a.** lies, nonsense, exaggeration, or flattery; trickery or tomfoolery, etc. Also in proverb **money talks—bullshit walks**.—usu. considered vulgar.

[**1866** in W.H. Jackson *Diaries* 51: It would amuse and…amaze an Eastern person to hear our first cry when we corrall. It is for fuel and thus spoken—"Bull sh-t, Bull sh-t" in stentorian tones. Since leaving [Fort] Kearney…we have not been able to secure…wood…for cooking purposes. The universal substitute…in dry weather is the manure of the oxen…which ignites & burns readily.] [**1881** Bourke *Diaries* (Oct. 26): The town was then "run" by a crowd of worthless, dissolute and reckless desperadoes, the principals among whom…might be said to be "Slap Jack Billy, the *Pride of the Pan Handle*" and "*Bull Dung* Tommy."] **1914** in E. Pound *Pound/Joyce* 25: I enclose a prize sample of bull shit. **1915** W. Lewis, in Materer *Pound/Joyce* 8: [T.S.] Eliot has sent me Bullshit & the Ballad for Big Louise. They are excellent bits of scholarly ribaldry. **1918** in E.E. Cummings *Letters* 50: The bullshit (to use a forte and accurate expression-du-peuple) of such quality as above quoted I doubt if I stand very long. **1922** in *Ibid.* 84: His mind being unclouded by "The N.Y. Times" and kindred bull-shit. *1922 T.E. Lawrence *The Mint* 207: Wash out all that blarsted bull-shit you've been taught. **1923** *Poems, Ballads & Parodies* 24: Lad, he's handing you

bullshit. **1928** in Read *Lexical Evidence* 75: Bullshit. **1931** in Dos Passos *14th Chronicle* 397: This Is All Bullshit. **1934** H. Roth *Call It Sleep* 249: Dot's a lodd a bullshit. *Ibid.* 337: Aw, bullshit! Yuh know yuh lyin'! **1935** in Hemingway *Sel. Letters* 425: In talk you can winnow out the bullshit. **1961** Brosnan *Pennant Race* 144: Nunn,…if bull— were cement, you could pave a highway from here to Fresno! **1966–67** Stevens *Gunner* 212: You're winding up a mile of bullshit and I can't see the end of it yet. **1968–71** Cole & Black *Checking* 14: He's yelling at one of the guys for running some bullshit and voilà, he's got a flush. **1972** *Life* (Nov. 10) 34: "Bullshit," she said with great force when he finished. **1972** Burkhart *Women in Prison* 3: Money talks, bull-shit walks. **1974** *Nat. Lampoon* (Apr.) 55: My father…used to have a saying, "Money talks, bullshit walks." **1976** Braly *False Starts* 179 [ref. to 1960's]: The Wit told me, "Listen, kid, money talks and bullshit walks." **1984** Kagan & Summers *Mute Evidence* 372: It was a bunch of bullshit. **1992** *Amer. Detective* (ABC-TV): Money talks. Bullshit walks.
b. (in a weakened sense) small talk; chitchat; gossip.—usu. considered vulgar.
1966–67 (quot. at BULLSHIT SESSION). **1975** *Sing Out!* (July) 3: You know, I've never met a railroad man that couldn't listen to a little bit of bullshit no matter how busy they were. **1970–94** [Extremely common in everyday speech.].
2. refuse; rubbish; sludge; junk; inconsequential items; (*specif.*) *Petroleum Industry.* sediment that accumulates at the bottom of petroleum tanks.
[**1945** *AS* (Oct.) 238: About thirty years ago, everything disagreeable was designated in popular slang by two English words of four letters, which in more elegant language would be referred to as the excrement of a male bovine animal.] **1963** Williamson *Hustler!* 142: When we got all this bullshit they marched us back to the cell house. **1966** "T. Pendleton" *Iron Orchard* 157: Git the drain plate off a' that test tank an' clean the bullshit outa the bottom of it. **1975** *Sing Out!* (July) 5: That's a grain car, man, there's going to be dust and bullshit blowing all over the place.
3. absolutely nothing.—usu. considered vulgar.
1956 Neider *Hendry Jones* 70: "What do you believe in, Lon?"…"Bullshit." **1973** Breslin *World Without End* 36: The guys…bitch that they even have to be in court. "For bullshit," they keep saying. **1977** Univ. Tenn. student: Those people don't care bullshit for you.
4. a BULLSHITTER.
1978 Corder *Deer Hunter* 74: He's just a bullshit with angel's wings.
5. marijuana.—usu. considered vulgar.
1969 M. Herr, in *Esquire* (Sept.) 156: We can smoke some bullshit.

bullshit *adj.* [fr. the *n.*] **1.** worthless; contemptible; despicable; trivial.—usu. considered vulgar.
1954 Killens *Youngblood* 134 [ref. to *ca*1930]: I'm going into the medical racket. Make plenty of money. Some of them bullshit doctors. **1968–71** Cole & Black *Checking* 81: Our legs are better than these bullshit horses. **1971** B.J. Friedman, in *Playboy* 336: Bullshit job, credit cards, fag suits, deadlines, time clocks, cocktail parties. **1972** in Bernstein & Woodward *President's Men* 146: You are not going to ask a bullshit question like that. Don't give me that crap. **1973** Schiano & Burton *Solo* 60: Assault or larceny or a bullshit robbery. **1974** V. Smith *Jones Men* 59: First thing is to get Wells off that bullshit duty downtown and get him back in the street. **1974** E. Thompson *Tattoo* 420: It's a bullshit show. **1974** Dubinsky & Standora *Decoy Cop* 20: It's a bullshit idea that won't even last the full ninety days. **1977** Dowd *Slap Shot* (film): You're bullshit! You're really bullshit! **1978** W. Brown *Tragic Magic* 162: "Yeah, but it was my choice." "Then it was a bullshit choice." **1982** D. Williams *Hit Hard* 29: Maybe this isn't such a bullshit outfit after all.
2.a. nonsensical; false.—usu. considered vulgar. Also as *adv.*
1964 in Wepman et al. *The Life* 92: The rest was a bullshit story. **1965** Linakis *In Spring* 27: He made a brief bullshit speech about their sacrifices. **1965** C. Brown *Manchild* 199: Those bullshit promises. **1971** G. Davis *Coming Home* 169: Don't go to jail on a bullshit tip, man. **1974** V. Smith *Jones Men* 32: I sure would hate to get blown away on some bullshit tip. **1976** "N. Ross" *Policeman* 110: I gave him a bullshit name. **1986** Stinson & Carabatsos *Heartbreak* 206: Man, I'm gonna write my congressman about these bullshit alerts! **1980–89** Cheshire *Home Boy* 130: Acting all bullshit contrite.
b. lying; joking.—usu. considered vulgar.
1978 Selby *Requiem* 30: Ya know man, I wasn't bullshit about gettin a piece.
3. Esp. *N.E.* crazy, esp. with rage; out of control.—usu. considered vulgar. Also semi-*adv.*

1962–68 B. Jackson *In the Life* 369: As soon as you bring out some evidence, like the bullets didn't match the gun, all of them pricks they go bullshit. "Man, where'd you hear that?" **1968** Baker et al. *CUSS* 90: *Bullshit, go.* Go wild. **1973** Vermont man, age 25: I must be goin' bullshit. **1973** P. Benchley *Jaws* 97: I think we should know who it is who has enough clout to drive Larry bullshit. **1976** *Verbatim* (Dec.) 16: *I was bullshit.* In effect, "very very angry…upset…terrified." It's necessary to consider the context…e.g.: "I just got my electric bill and I was bullshit."…*My wife was b. with the kid.* *Ibid.*: "The wind blew bullshit last night." The anemometer registered gusts over seventy mph. **1966–80** McAleer & Dickson *Unit Pride* 383: When they shipped my ass back I was so bullshit I wouldn't take any prisoners for a month. **1980** M. Baker *Nam* 280: I was bullshit. I was never like that before I left. **1987** E. Spencer *Macho Man* 112: A Marine colonel on board also goes completely bullshit. **1989** P. Munro *U.C.L.A. Slang* 25: *Bullshit*…angry, mad…Dude, my roommate drank all my beers. I'm so bullshit!

bullshit *v.* [fr. the *n.*] **1.** to lie, deceive, flatter, etc.—usu. considered vulgar.
1937 Weidman *Wholesale* 60: And he comes bullshittin' around here with that crap about we lost the strike! **1948** I. Shulman *Cry Tough!* 63: Stop bullshittin' me. **1965** Linakis *In Spring* 67: I already hand the doctor bullshitted. **1970** Segal *Love Story* 78: Don't bullshit me, Preppie. **1971** Dibner *Admiral* 96: I'm not going to sit here and bullshit you about what's right with this world and what's wrong. **1985** N.Y.C. man, age 36: Don't let her bullshit you.
2. to gossip or talk idly.—usu. considered vulgar.
1926 in Hemingway *Sel. Letters* 203: I've not had one man to talk to or bull shit with for months. **1938–39** Dos Passos *Young Man* 78: Ray was just bullshitting, he didn't mean nothing. **1955** Graziano & Barber *Somebody Up There* 112: Guys…bullshitted all night. **1965** Eastlake *Castle Keep* 38: That's what we talked about yesterday, bullshitted about in that small room of ours. **1978** R. Price *Ladies' Man* 140: We bullshat for a while. **1990** Bing *Do or Die* 4: The kids who are friends engage in a little light bullshitting.
3. to waste time; to act aimlessly.—constr. with *around.*—usu. considered vulgar.
1968 Baker et al. *CUSS* 90: *Bullshit around.* Waste time, not study. **1980** Univ. Tenn. instructor: I'm tired of bullshittin' around. **1991** L. Chambers *Recondo* 149: We'd been drinking and bullshitting around.
4. to make fun of.—used *trans.*—usu. considered vulgar.
1981 Ala. woman, age 27: He's just bullshitting the way she talks. He's doing it deliberately.

bullshit artist *n.* a person who habitually exaggerates, lies, or flatters.—usu. considered vulgar. Cf. BULL ARTIST.
1942 in M. Curtiss *Letters Home* 27: Quite a bull-s— artist. **1951** Morris *China Station* 37: Occupation Bullshit artist. **1955** Graziano & Barber *Somebody Up There* 238: You're a bullshit artist, you don't know what it is to back up your words like a man. **1958** Gardner *Piece of the Action* 65: You're a bullshit artist. ***1965** S.J. Baker *Australian Lang.* (ed. 2) 189 [ref. to WWII]: *Bullshartist…bullsh*t artist.* **1967** Taggart *Reunion* 77: For sure he's some kind of bullshit artist. **1979** McGivern *Soldiers of '44* 16 [ref. to WWII]: "I saw you fight once. You were all right." "Yeah? You're a big bullshit artist." **1979** in Terkel *Amer. Dreams* 391: They never had any money. They were…bullshit artists.

bullshit band *n.* Esp. *Mil.* an unassigned radio frequency that is often used for idle conversation. Also **bullshit freq, bullshit net.**—usu. considered vulgar.
1978 *Nat. Lampoon* (July) 7 [ref. to 1972]: Bullshit freqs…Commonly used frequencies on the PRC-25 FM radio. **1983** Ehrlich *VN-Perkasie* 300 [ref. to 1967]: Get on the bullshit band!…They got tunes on! **1987** Pelfrey & Carabatsos *Hamburger Hill* 120 [ref. to Vietnam War]: Try the bullshit net.

bullshit bomber *n.* *Mil.* an aircraft or airman engaged in psychological warfare operations, as dropping leaflets or broadcasting propaganda messages.—usu. considered vulgar.
1980 W.C. Anderson *BAT-21* 98 [ref. to 1972]: Colonel Black…is the CO of the Bullshit Bombers. *Ibid.* 103: What had been the purpose of this Bullshit Bomber? *Ibid.* 105: Hambleton had assumed the bullshit bombers would be back during the night. **1990** G.R. Clark *Words of Viet. War* 72: *Bullshit Bombers*…were primarily used [in South Vietnam] to drop leaflets and make loudspeaker broadcasts to enemy soldiers and civilians.

bullshit gang *n.* [fr. BULLSHIT, *n.,* 2] *Petroleum Industry.* (see quot.).—usu. considered vulgar.

1972 Haslam *Oil Fields* 96: *Bull Shit Gang*, n. The production crew, which, by maintaining pumping equipment, etc., keeps producing wells in operation.

bullshit session *n.* BULL SESSION.—usu. considered vulgar.
   1966–67 P. Thomas *Mean Streets* 25: It was better to play mysterious with the guys at bullshit sessions.

bullshitter *n.* **1.** one who BULLSHITS.—usu. considered vulgar.
   1933 in Dos Passos *14th Chronicle* 432: He's just the kind of bullshitter who could do it. **1970** *Nat. Lampoon* (May) 48: Doctor, you're a bullshitter. **1974** Univ. Tenn. student: He's such a bullshitter, you can't believe a word he says. **1976** Rosen *Above Rim* 159: Don't never try and bullshit a bullshitter. **1984** Univ. Tenn. instructor: I think he's a big bullshitter.
   2. *Petroleum Industry.* (see quot.).—usu. considered vulgar.
   1972 Haslam *Oil Fields* 96: *Bull Shitter* n. Any member of a *bull shit gang.*

bull-shooter *n.* BULL-SLINGER.
   1927 J. Stevens *Mattock* 286 [ref. to 1918]: Boy, bull-shooter is right. Would you believe anything that old stiff told you? **1959–60** Bloch *Dead Beat* 104: But he was sick of listening to the old bullshooter sounding off.

bull-simple *n.* *Und.* obsessed with fear of or hostility toward police.
   1925–26 Black *You Can't Win* 193 [ref. to 1890's]: He went out on the road "bull-simple," simple on the subject of shooting policemen. **1938** Steinbeck *Grapes of Wrath* 268: "I guess maybe he's bull-simple." "What's 'bull-simple'?" "I guess cops push 'im aroun' so much he's still spinning."

bullskate *v.* *Black E.* to BULLSHIT.
   1946 Boulware *Jive & Slang* 2: Bullskating...Bragging. **1957** H. Simmons *Corner Boy* 11: I've been bull-skating for years with this guy about his ole ladies. **1973** in Sanchez *Word Sorcerers* 24: It was that kind of bullskating that prompted Mother Wit's vigil at the 110th Street entrance to Central Park. **1978** W. Brown *Tragic Magic* 5: Ella...bullskated her way through it with some bodacious makeshift palaver.

bull-slinger *n.* [fr. BULL *n.,* 9] one who habitually exaggerates or pretends to knowledge; BULLSHITTER.
   1930 Bodenheim *Roller Skates* 224: A handsome bullslinger with loads of nerve needed more than that. **1937–40** in Whyte *Street Corner Society* 50: He's a bull-slinger. **1984** Kahane *Logic & Rhet.* (ed. 4) 26: Lots of otherwise fine friends are congenital bull slingers.

bull-thrower *n.* BULL-SLINGER.
   1918 in Braynard *Greatest Ship* I 176: Champion Bull Thrower. **1935** Odets *Waiting for Lefty*: Go pick up that bull-thrower on the corner. **1967** G. Green *To Brooklyn* 221: I had enough of you, you bull-thrower.

bullwash *n.* [sugg. by HOGWASH] BUSHWA.
   1981 *Bret Maverick* (NBC-TV): It's all a buncha bullwash and you know it. **1987** Larson & Heyes *Highwayman* (film): It's a bunch of bullwash.

bullwhack *v.* to drive an ox team. Also *trans.* Now *hist.*
   1866 in W.H. Jackson *Diaries* 81: A good many of the boys in this train will Bull Whack up to Virginia City. **1940** F. Hunt *Trail From Texas* 7: He'd bull-whacked outfits to Santa Fe.

bullwhacker *n.* the driver of an ox team. Now *hist.*
   1858 in *DA.* **1871** Crofutt *Tourist's Guide* 27: How many tremendous jaw-breaking oaths fell from the lips of the "bull-whackers." *Ibid.* 204: Old settlers on the plains call...Ox drivers, "*bull-whackers.*" **1873** Beadle *Undeveloped West* 92: Ranchmen, clerks, "bullwhackers," gamblers and "cappers." **1913** R.M. Wright *Dodge City* 24: In...1859..."Bull Whackers" we were called. **1946** in *DA.*

bully *n.* a good fellow; comrade; (*hence*) a stout fellow, esp. a member of a work crew. Cf. related earlier use as a simple endearment in *OED2.*
   *1605 B. Jonson *Eastward Ho* I i: We are both gentlemen, and therefore should be no coxcombs...eastward, bully. **1676* Wycherley *Plain-Dealer* I: I'll watch your waters, Bully, i' fac. **1688* Shadwell *Squire of Alsatia* I i: But thou must squeeze my Lad: Squeeze hard, and Seal my Bully. **1698–1706* in D'Urfey *Pills* III 131: Fifth-Monarchy must down, Bullies,...This is the life of a...Cavalier. **1827** J.F. Cooper *Red Rover* 332: If a finger is put upon one of my bullies...it will be answered with a blow. **1835** *Mil. & Nav. Mag.* (Feb.) 421: O! long shall our Bullies remember, revere thee. **1847** Downey *Portsmouth* 176: "Fighting

Bob" was a gassy old Cove, and would have "his bullies" as he termed them out every day, drilling, charging, forming hollow squares, and putting themselves in the best possible discipline. **1850** J. Greene *In Tombs* 144: Bullies, your presence in the afterguard. **1851** Ely *Wanderings* 190: Drive her, bullies, drive her. She must walk three hundred miles in the next twenty-four hours. **1898** *Harper's Wkly.* (May 29) 515: Commodore Schley's "bullies" demonstrate their ability to "remember the *Maine.*" **1911** *JAF* (Oct.) 392: Now, let's go, bullies,/Hold-hold-hold. **1928** in Dobie *Drinkin' Gou'd* 50: He had conceived the scheme of soaking his tobacco in corn whiskey and making a "clean-up" by selling it to the oil field "bullies." **1929** Barr *Let Tomorrow Come* 91: Go it, bullies! **1936** Benton & Ballou *Where Do I Go?* 157: All right, Bullies! Out you go! *Ibid.* 166: How these bullies doin' today? **1938** *AS* (Feb.) 70: *Bully.* Any workman in the gang [of R.R. linemen]. **1962–68** B. Jackson *In Life* 272: Raise 'em up old bullies, let's go.

bully *adj.* very fine; splendid; excellent; (*obs.*) best.
   *ca1599 Dekker *Shoemaker's Holiday* V v: Yet Ile shave it off...to please my bully king. **1681* in *OED:* From such Bully fishers, this Book expects no other reception. **1735** in W.H. Kenney *Laughter in Wilderness* 183: Two Hotspurs...To give the World proof they were right bully ranters/Talked big to each other of prowess and fighting. **1841** [Mercier] *Man-of-War* 234: But the launch of the United States Ship Dale took this opportunity of trying *her* speed with the bully boat of the Constitution. **1843** Field *Pokerville* 43: Mr. Wilson's boat...[had] made a "bully trip." **1843** D. Emmett *De Boatman's Dance* (sheet music): For dey whole hoss, an dey a bully crew/Wid a hoosier mate an a captin too. **1845** Durivage & Burnham *Stray Subjects* 72: He was a bully roller—/Spares, ten-strikes, fast as rain. **1846** *Spirit of Times* (May 16) 1: Our "bully" boat sped away like a bird. **1847** Downey *Portsmouth* 7: I have no doubt but that he would have been fully convinced that the *Portsmouth* was the Bully ship. **1850** Garrard *Wah-to-Yah* 225: When they slapped down a bully pair, they 'ud screech an' laff worse 'an fellers on a spree. **1855** in Dwyer & Lingenfelter *Gold Rush* 60: With a bully little pick and a long-handled shovel. **1859** in Botkin *Treas. Amer. Folk.* 590: "Which tree will you take?"..."The bully un." **1859** "Skitt" *Fisher's River* 32 [ref. to 1820's]: It's a bully grave-yard by this time, I s'pose. *Ibid.* 59: They'll make bully pies. **1860** W. Whitman *Correspondence* I 49: Emerson called upon me immediately...gave me a bully dinner, &c. **1860** Olmsted *Back Country* 171: Bigger'n New Orleans? It must be a bully city. **1865–67** De Forest *Miss Ravenel* 77: We'll have the bulliest regiment that ever sprang from the soil of New England. **1872** Holmes *Poet* 282: D'd y' ever see Ed' in Forrest play Metamora? Bully, I tell *you!* **1887** Hinman *Cpl. Klegg* 7: Ye'd make a bully soljer, an' the boys'd like fust rate to have ye 'long. **1899** Ade *Fables* 18: Here was a Bully Chance to act out the Kind-Hearted Pedestrian. **1904** in Opper *Hooligan* 5: Rah for Hooligan. Bully. Do it again, Happy. *a1904–11* Phillips *Susan Lenox* II 161: You feel bully, don't you? **1920** S. Lewis *Main St.* 9: We'd have, Lord, we'd have bully times in Yankton, where I'm going to settle. **1927** "Van Dine" *Canary Case* 133: That's just bully. **1929–30** Dos Passos *42d Parallel* 52: What a dump where we could get a bully breakfast. **1934** Rhodes *Beyond Desert* 180: Roundup next month, steers to sell, debts to pay—bully! **1963–64** Kesey *Great Notion* 156: Give me some bully jacks! **1967** Kornbluth *New Underground* 11: Some double agents paid by the CIA to do studies in sabotage had decided that it was a bully time for fun and games. **1973** Collins *Carrying the Fire* 80: Bully! At least there is some practical advice scattered about.
   ¶ In phrases:
   ¶ **bully boy with a glass eye** *n.* *Mil.* a fine fellow. Now *hist.*
   1863 in *Jour. Ill. Hist. Soc.* XLVIII (1955) 464: To thee Stanton and Wells...do cry, "Bully, bully, bully boy with a glass eye." **1865** in Horrocks *Dear Parents* 150: To use the eulogistic and expressive words of a brother officer, "You are a Bully Boy with a glass eye." **1871** "M. Twain" *Roughing It* 251: He was a bully boy with a glass eye! **1892** Bierce *Beetles* 155: Like a bully boy with an eye of glass. **1910** *Sat. Eve. Post* (July 16) 15 [ref. to Civil War]: He also saluted an officer in spectacles as "Bully boy with a glass eye."
   ¶ **bully for (one)!** good for (one)! Hurray! Now *rare* in U.S.
   *ca1788 Capt. Morris, in Burns *Merry Muses* (ed. 1832): Bully for the great Plenipotentiary. **1858** in C.A. Abbey *Before the Mast* 145: Bully for him. **1862** letter from Lieut. Kilian Frick, 5th Div., Army of the Tenn. (Sept. 21): Bully for Kressen!...Jetzt noch ein guter Schlag in Kentucky u. dann *bully for us!* **1862** Galwey *Valiant Hrs.* 63: Bully for you, by God! **1863** in Bensill *Yamhill* 107: Another fellow sung out, "Christ has washed my sins away." Whereupon a halfwitted disciple sung out, "Bully for Christ." Other...quite as ridiculous moments occurred. **1865** in Andrus *Letters* 131: Bulley for *Andy* (if he did get drunk). **1865** Cooke *Wearing Gray* 427: Bully for us, boys! We are the

boys! ***1977** T. Jones *Ice* 39: Bully for him. Was there free booze? **1979** Kunstler *Wampanaki Tales* 3: "A fly really did land on it." "Bully for him."

bully *adv.* **1.** exceedingly well.

1846 in *F & H* I (rev.) 422: You're doin' the politics bully, as all our family agree. **1863** in G. Whitman *Letters* 89: I shall have my tent fixed up Bully in a day or two. **1869** "M. Twain" *Innocents* I 24: Oh, I'm coming along bully! **1871** "M. Twain" *Roughing It* 251: Put buck through as bully as you can, pard. **1885** *Puck* (Apr. 8) 83: It reads bully. **1887** Hinman *Cpl. Klegg* 71: Ye're stan'in' it bully, bein' it's the fust time. **1906** in "O. Henry" *Works* 1143: I'd like it bully.

2. exceedingly; very.

1863 Heartsill *1491 Days* 148: The "Rangers" will long remember the Negro...who was "Bully lost" last night while we were at rest in the lane. **1898** *Sat. Eve. Post* 19: I had soup, bully hot, too. **1899** Robbins *Gam* 92: "Bully good!" shouted a dozen gruff voices. **1903** Merriman *Letters from Son* 75: The car is bully well stocked with things. **1917** Burroughs *Oakdale Affair* 39: A good fire...will fit us for a bully good sleep. *a***1924** A. Hunter *Yr. on Monitor* 92: He gave me a bully-good tongue-lashing.

bullyrag *v.* to bully, harass, abuse, tease, etc. Also (*obs.*) **ballarag.** Also as *n.* Now *S.E.*

1774 in R.M. Lederer, Jr. *Colonial Eng.* 24: If I can't answer them by ballarag, I can by small sword. **a***1790** in *OEDS*: Ballarag. **1876** "M. Twain," in Bartlett *Amer.* (ed. 4) 79: Here they can't come and pick a feller and bullyrag him so. **1893** Barra *Two Oceans* 139: Because I wouldn't let you bullyrag me on board of your ship.

bum[1] *n.* [fr. ME *bom*, of unkn. orig.] **1.** the buttocks, anus, and rectum; ASS.—often considered vulgar.

1387** J. Trevisa, in *OED*: It semeþ þat his bom is oute þat haþ þat euel. **ca1530** in *OED*: I woold thy mother had kyst thy bum! ***1614** B. Jonson, in *F & H* (rev.) 425: Your breeches sit close enough to your bum. **1666** G. Alsop *Maryland* 26: I must lay double-clothes unto thy Bum. ***1698–99** "B.E." *Dict. Canting Crew*: Bum...one's Breech. ***1706** in *F & H* (rev.) 425: Thought I, for all your pulpit-drumming,/Had you no Hose to hide your bum in. **1746** in Micklus *Comic Genius* 120: The *Sphincter Ani*, or *Bum Muscle*, in him being preternaturally relaxed. **1775** in Moore *Songs & Ballads* 93: But when they got there how they powder'd your pums,/And all the way home how they peppered your —. ***1785** in R. Burns *Selections* 213: And many a tatter'd rag hanging over my bum. **1845** H.C. Lewis *Works* 91: It was *bum*bazine and reminded her by the first syllable of the *seat* of "Cupping on the Sternum." ***1873** Hotten *Slang Dict.* (ed. 4) 102: *Bum,* the part on which we sit. *ca***1888** *Stag Party* 191: Diogenes...was wont to occupy all bums from pupils down to chickens. *Ibid.*: His bum waxed hourly fatter. **1898** Green *Va. Folk-Speech* 73: *Bum, n.* The buttocks. **1916** Cary *Venery* I 28: To *toe one's bum*—An implied threat of physical castigation, rarely, however, carried out literally; to put or chuck out; to show the door to....Sometimes the phrase occurs as "to hoof one's bum." **1927** [Fliesler] *Anecdota* 184: Pearl had a tender bum. **1953** Brossard *Saboteurs* 133: Get your big bum out of my way. **1968** Lockridge *Hartspring* 15: I had seen bare thighs before...and bare bums too. **1969** Cray *Erotic Muse* 13: He can shove them up his bum. **1981–85** S. King *It* 409: Chief Barton'll laugh his bum off.

2. self; ASS.—constr. with possessive pronoun.

***1689** Shadwell *Bury-Fair* II: Now is this Fop setting out his Bum for a smart Bout at Complement. **1973** Crawford *Gunship Commander* 39: You too, sweetheart, get your flaky bum out.

bum[2] *n.* [orig. uncert.; see note at **(2.a.)**]

1.a. a contemptible or despicable person; (*hence*) a worthless animal or useless item. [Extended use not attested before 20th C.]

1806 in Tyler *Verse* 155: Your Bernard's a quiz, and your Twaits is a bum,/Let *me* go on the stage, and I'll show the house fun. **1882** in Leitner *Diamond in Rough* 132: The umpire of to-day is far below that level and properly belongs in the "bum" category. **1904** *Life in Sing Sing* 81: The ungrateful turnkey...calls all convicts "bums." **1907** in H.C. Fisher *A. Mutt* 18: Cloudlight [a racehorse]'s a bum. **1908** Beach *Barrier* 111: I might have known you bums were up to some crooked work. *a***1904–11** Phillips *Susan Lenox* II 160: I'll do the calling myself, you bum. **1915** in Butterfield *Post Treas.* 137: This lucky bum busted two pair. **1918** Grider *War Birds* 156: You, you bum. **1919** in J.A. Lomax *Cattle Trail* 100 [a man addressing a horse]: If John D. Rockefeller shud...want to buy you, you bum, I'd laugh in his face and pat your neck. **1925** Riesenberg *Under Sail* 390: You dirty low-down bum! **1928** MacArthur *War Bugs* 141: The poor bums of E and D batteries main-

tained their fire. **1932** in Runyon *Blue Plate* 357: Mahogany is really not much horse. In fact, Mahogany is nothing but an old bum. **1935** *AS* (Dec.) 270: *Bums.* Almost worthless animals [livestock]. **1961** Brosnan *Pennant Race* 119: You're either a hero or a bum. **1962** *Time* (Dec. 14) 18: Heroes & Bums. **1973** Haney *Jock* 145: Get good horses. Don't take a bunch of bums. **1980** Pearl *Slang Dict.*: Bum *n....*[Post Office] an empty mail sack.

b. a sexually promiscuous woman, esp. a prostitute. [For ***1825** quot., see note at **(2.a.).**]

[***1825** Jamieson *Scot. Dict.* I 329: *Bum,* a lazy, dirty, tawdry, careless woman; chiefly applied to those of high stature; as, "She's a perfect *bum*" i.e. a big, useless, indolent, sluttish woman, Galloway.] **1922** Rice *Adding Machine* 101: The dirty bum! The idea of her comin' to live in a house with respectable people. **1928** Delmar *Bad Girl* 60: You probably should have been married to him months ago, you little bum. **1930** J.T. Farrell *Calico Shoes* 259: A bum came around peddling magazines tonight...and I slipped the blocks to her. **1932** J.T. Farrell *Guillotine* 180: He picks up a bum at the Bourbon Palace. **1934** Appel *Brain Guy* 149: The dames were just bums. **1935** Clarke *Regards to B'way* 87: He hadn't let himself be kidded into testing his masculinity with any bums like Everready Hannah and Surefire May. **1938** H. Miller *Capricorn* 97: He couldn't see why he should waste his money on a couple of bums. **1963** D. Tracy *Brass Ring* 91: Talking as though Hobey's sister was a bum or something. **1966** Susann *Valley of Dolls* 230: What do you think I am? Some kind of a bum? I'm a one-man woman.

c. *Sports.* an unskilled athlete, esp. a prizefighter.

1910 *N.Y. Eve. Jour.* (Feb. 3) 14: Make the bum fight. **1916** D. Runyon, in Paxton *Sport* 96: If it is at a baseball or football game, the delegation that is losing is characterized as a "bunch o' bums." **1929** Hotstetter & Beesley *It's a Racket* 220: *Bum*—A pugilist; prizefighter. **1947** Schulberg *Harder They Fall* 185: My bum and your bum....They fight even. **1970** in P. Heller *In This Corner* 145: A lot of times I had to go out to fight a bum, an ordinary bum. **1978** *N.Y. News World* (Sept. 16) 12B: He's no bum, he's a great fighter and he's gonna be better with experience.

d. *pl.* (*cap.*) *Baseball.* the Brooklyn Dodgers baseball team. *Joc.* Now *hist.*

[**1937** in Paxton *Sport* 239: There was a fan, called by Sid Mercer "The Spirit of Brooklyn," who sat in the same seat behind home plate daily....One day the entire Dodger team so disgusted him that he went plural and cried, "Youse bums, youse!" He never was seen at the park again.] **1942** *Yank* (July 1) 22: Can't Somebody Beat Dem Bums? **1946** J. Adams *Gags* 21: Leo Durocher [is] the famous manager of "dem bums." **1948** Robinson & Smith *J. Robinson* 150: Now...I was one of Brooklyn's beloved Bums. **1950** Cleveland *Great Mgrs.* 245: Gil Hodges, the Bums' first sacker. **1951** Willingham *Gates* 16: "The bums"—that's what they call the Brooklyn team. **1964** Thompson & Rice *Every Diamond* 45: Their nickname of "Bums" was at this time very appropriate. **1969–71** Kahn *Boys of Summer* xiii: The concept of the Dodgers as appealing incompetents—"Dem Bums" in a persistent poor joke—was dying. *Ibid.* 275: What did I hit as a Bum—.032? **1981** Vincent *Mudville* 4: All of Brooklyn fell into a deep funk when the beloved "bums" were robbed of the 1951 pennant by that Bobby Thomson home run. **1984** P. Golenbock *Bums: An Oral History of the Brooklyn Dodgers* (title).

e. *Stock Raising.* a motherless lamb raised by hand.

1931 *AS* VI 358: An "orphan" or a "bum," that is, a lamb whose mother has deserted it. **1938, 1942, 1950, 1954, 1959** in *DARE.*

2.a. a lazy, shiftless person who does not or will not work; a beggar, a tramp, or (*esp.*) a habitually drunken derelict. Now *S.E.* [Although the early Scots quots. (***1540** quot. below and ***1825** quot. at **(1.b.),** above) seem to fall within the semantic domain of the present word, their appositeness here is uncertain; the Scots word—itself of unknown origin—seems never to have been in widespread use. The English term *bum* (short for *bum-bailiff*) (see **(b),** below) may also have exerted some influence on the appearance of the later senses.]

[***1540** D. Lindesay, in *OED*: Quhair Devil gat we this ill-fairde blaitie bum?] **1864** in *DA* 217: The policemen say that even their old, regular and reliable "bums" appear to have reformed, and they have absolutely nothing to do. **1879** *Snares of N.Y.* 82: It would be a waste of time to pass the night here among the cadgers and bums. **1887** *Lippincott's Mag.* (Oct.) 573: The sporting element, or, as they are proud to be termed, the "bums," whose first principle is to do no more work than is absolutely necessary. **1887** M. Roberts *W. Avernus* 239: He fetches a coupling-pin…and…sez: "Take that, you dam bum." **1888** in *F & H* I (rev.) 430: Ten per cent. earn excellent wages, and twenty per cent. are chronic *bums*, who beg or steal the price of their lodgings. **1894** F.P. Dunne, in Schaaf *Dooley* 109: Throwin' lodgin'-house bums into th' patrol wagon. **1901** *Independent* (Nov. 21) 2762: There's just two kinds of people in the world that's really happy—the millionaire and the bum. **1914** Ellis *Billy Sunday* 117: If you're a dirty, low-down, filthy, drunken whisky-soaked bum you'll affect all with whom you come in contact. **1923** H.L. Foster *Beachcomber* 118: So you're another of these bums, are you? **1925–26** J. Black *You Can't Win* 80: He's a railroad bull and he's "bum-simple"—simple-minded on the subject of killing bums. If you run, he'll shoot you. **1943** J. Mitchell *McSorley's* 29: Practically all of her visitors are bums with hangovers who come to her, scratching themselves and twitching, and ask for money with which to get their first drinks of the day.

b. a bailiff.

1797 Brackenridge *Mod. Chiv.* 288: Taking a man wi' a bum. [**1807** W. Irving *Salmagundi* 247: A bum-bailiff whom nobody cares for.] *1820–21* P. Egan *Life in London* 248: A fig for each *Bum**…*Bailiff. *1825* "Blackmantle" *Eng. Spy* I 190: He laughs…at creditors and *Bum*.

c. an itinerant laborer; BOOMER.—used with preceding attrib.

1957 MacDonald *Death Trap* 7: "You don't have to live like a construction bum." "My father was a construction bum, Al."

3. *Hobo.* an act of begging; usu. in phr. **put the bum on (someone)** to beg from (someone).

1923 in N. Cohen *Long Steel Rail* 361: If I make another bum like this I'll be bummin' all the time. **1935** E. Anderson *Hungry Men* 3: I just put the bum on a priest out there. **1947** Motley *Knock On Any Door* 182: A wino came up and tried to put the bum on him. **1957** H. Simmons *Corner Boy* 103: He tried to put the bum on me for a quarter. **1963** Ross *Dead Are Mine* 260: One day he ran into a friend of his from the Regimental Aid Station and he put the bum on him for a box of morphine syrettes.

4.a. a person who is excessively devoted to a particular sport or activity; an obsessive enthusiast.—used with a specifying attrib.

1933 Farrell *To Whom It May Concern* 108: The old man said he didn't want his son to be a football bum. **1956** M. Wolff *Big Nick* 91: "The beach athletes."…"Aaah, them beach bums!" **1968** Kirk & Hanle *Surfer's Hndbk.* 147: *Surf bum*: one who does nothing else but surf. **1981** *AS* (Spring) 64: Computer bum…Person who plays with computers; the "compulsive programmer" described in Joseph Weizenbaum's *Computer Power and Human Reason.*

b. a semiprofessional athlete who avoids steady employment, earning a living chiefly as an instructor at resorts and country clubs and by appearing irregularly in tournaments.—usu. used with a specifying attrib.

1940 in Marx *Groucho Letters* 43: For a tennis bum, you're certainly leading a luxurious life. **1949** Cummings *Dict. Sports* 455: *Tennis bum.* A term applied to an amateur tennis player who appears to have no visible means of livelihood. **1961** Sullivan *Shortest, Gladdest Years* 36: Lectured me on the ski-bum racket once. **1965** W. Crawford *Bronc Rider* 72: In Spain and Mexico bullfighters knew her Latin sisters, in Europe and Australia soccer champs, ski bums and surf boarders are her. **1965** Gary *Ski Bum* 4: The local *Ski Lehrers* hated their guts: the bums were always better looking, they took bigger risks, they had more glamour, there was an air of adventure about them. **1971** *Odd Couple* (ABC-TV): Ray—yeah! Yeah! The ski bum! **1974** L. Gould *Analysis* 48: Lee had at least two professional tennis bums as house guests.

¶ In phrases:

¶ **make a bum out of, 1.** to spoil; ruin.

1918 *Chi. Sun.-Trib.* (June 9) V (unp.): Now you made a bum out o' the whole lesson. **1923** Ornitz *Haunch, Paunch & Jowl* 107: Hey, girlie…you're making a bum outta the rehearsal. **1928** MacArthur *War Bugs* 97: Both sides had made a bum out of the town. Nothing was left but latitude, longitude, and broken brick.

2. to cause to look foolish; to outdo; to surpass.

1925 in Hemingway *Sel. Letters* 157: I got a 8 to 12,000 word bull fight story that makes a bum out of everything I ever did. **1926** in Hemingway *Sel. Letters* 186: Altho he may make a bum out of Mark Twain, Dickens etc. I have never succeeded in re-reading anything by McAlmon. **1958** Camerer *Damned Wear Wings* 84: That town makes a bum out of Kipling's *Never the Twain*.

¶ **on the bum** see BUM³.

¶ **put the bum on, 1.** see **(3)**, above.

2. to ruin.

1930 Graham & Graham *Queer People* 115: I wanted to do extra work, but she put the bum on that, too.

bum³ *n.* [prob. back formation fr. BUMMER¹, infl. by BUM²] a drinking spree; (*obs.*) a celebration.

1863 W. Fisk *Anti-Rebel* 146: One of these nights we are going out on a regular "bum." **1865** Woodruff *Union Soldier* 50: We…make arrangements to go on a Regular Bum in the Evening, but the duties in camp prevent it. *Ibid.* 69: Went to the city on a regular Bum. Got about 7 sheets in the wind. **1871** *Yale Naught-Ical Almanac* 7: February 28 W Phi Theta Psi Anniversary "Bum." **1871** Bagg *Yale* 43: *Bum*, a spree, society supper, or convivial entertainment of any sort, innocent or otherwise. Used also as a verb; whence is derived *bummer*, a fast young man, a fellow who *bums*. *Ibid.* 172: The more depraved Stones men…go off on a "bum"…and afterwards wake the echoes of the college yard with their discordant howlings. **1885** Custer *Boots & Saddles* 160: I intend to celebrate their return by going on a tremendous "bum." **1891** Maitland *Amer. Slang Dict.* 52: *On the bum*, on a drunk. **1891** *Outing* (June) 212: What midnight suppers! What peanut "bums"! What narrow escapes! **1900** *DN* II 25: *Bum*…A spree. On the *bum*…drunk. **1910** Lomax *Cowboy Songs* 255: I spent my money freely and went it on a bum. **1919** S. Lewis *Free Air* 338: Thinks I, lez go off on a little bum. **1978** Dabney *Across Years* 77 [ref. to 1917]: Together we'll get out on a hell of a bum.

¶ In phrase:

¶ **on the bum, 1.** on a drinking spree. [Though historically closer perhaps to BUM³, senses **(2)** and **(3)** below are now gen. felt to derive from BUM², BUM, *adj.*, and BUM, *v.*] (see above for quots.).

2. living as a tramp or vagrant; not engaged in work.

1893 in *Independent* (Dec. 5, 1901) 2886: He had been on the bum for six weeks this time. **1895** *Century* (Oct.) 941: Plans are made also for going "on the bum" the moment they are free. **1896** *Pop. Sci. Mo.* (Dec.) 254: It's gettin' so a respectable 'boe can't get a hand out anywhere no more. The whole d— country is on the bum. **1929** E. Caldwell *Bastard* 69: "And you decided to go on the bum?" "What?" "You decided to walk the streets for a living?" **1929–32** J.T. Farrell *Young Lonigan* ch. vi: He vowed he'd blow the place, and go on the bum. **1947** Schulberg *Harder They Fall* 8: Just as O'Neill spent all those years as a common sailor and Jack London was on the bum. **1961** Kalisher *R.R. Men* 26: Hee Haw Mike he was on the bum one time…playing the stem, that is begging on the streets. **1983** Helprin *Winter's Tale* 429: When Peter Lake had been on the bum, the scars on his face had been covered with soot and grease.

3. in a bad way; unsatisfactory, impaired, injured, out of order, etc.; BUM, *adj.*

1889 *Some Songs at Rochester* 153: He said the place was "on the bum,"/ The faculty was bad. **1896** Ade *Artie* 7: The woman that trifled with the piano for about a half an hour was very much on the bummy bum. *Ibid.* 21: I sized it up that the house was on the bum and she didn't want me to see it. **1899** A.H. Lewis *Sandburrs* 189: D' McGuire household's more or less on d' bum, see! **1908** in H.C. Fisher *A. Mutt* 59: You put my wedding on the bum. **1908** in H.C. Fisher *A. Mutt* 73: Get me another file. This one is on the bum. **1909** in McCay *Little Nemo* 198: Your gun is on the bum, Doc. **1910** G. Rice, in M. Gardner *Casey* 40: Ten thousand fans had come/To see the twirler who had put big Casey on the bum. **1913** W. Wilson *Hell in Nebr.* 185: Prince afterwards stated that he was sorry that he did not have the knife with him, and "I would have put Tom Smith on the bum." **1914** Ellis *Billy Sunday* 35: Cigarettes put him on the bum. **1918** Straub *Diary* (Apr. 24): Our communications has been tampered with or either the wet weather has put our wires on the "bum." **1919** De Beck *Google* 7: They tell me his legs are on the bum from doin' too much road work. **1925** Hemingway *In Our Time* 168: What've I got to go back there to go to school for when everything's on the bum there? **1934** H. Miller *Trop. of Cancer* 128: Her stomach's already on the bum. **1968** Cuomo *Thieves* 357: Tell them the electricity's on the bum. **1973** N.Y.U. student: My TV's been on the bum for a week.

4. without money; broke.

1908 in H.C. Fisher *A. Mutt* 157: Ima, I know you're on the bum, so I'm gonna tell you [a horse to bet on].

bum *adj.* [fr. BUM²] (in general) bad; *specif.*:

1. wretched; despicable; contemptible; unsatisfactory; disagreeable; inferior; poor. Also as adv. [1859 quot. is unlikely to be a true attestation of this sense.]

[**1859** in *DA*: Bum River Ferry, Slight showers on first watch from 8 until 1 A.M.] **1870** in *DA*: McAtee hit a "bum" ball towards Wolters, which rolled along so slowly that the striker secured base ere it was fielded. **1888** *Nation* (May 31) 439: One of them is said to have heard himself called a "bum actor" when he was sauntering through the Lotos [Club] parlors. **1892** Norr *China Town* 17: Get up, you bum prize fighter....What d'ye take this for? A lodging-house? **1894** F.P. Dunne, in Schaaf *Dooley* 79: Th' man...runs that there bum little bank down be Finucane's. **1896** Ade *Artie* 88: All the others is made out o' sheet-iron and bum castin's. *Ibid.* 95: They'll be workin' on bum salaries when they're gray headed. **1900** *DN* II 25: *Bum*...Very poor. **1903** Benton *Cowboy Life on Sidetrack* 12: Dillberry Ike gave it as his opinion that they were the bummest lot of liars he ever see. **1903** Ade *Into Society* 132: Say, I don't like to roast your Establishment, but you have got the bummest lot of Birds I ever listened to. **1905** Hobart *Search Me* 49: That's where Charlie gave us the bum deal. **1908** in H.C. Fisher *A. Mutt* 29: Mutt may be a bum picker but he's a great producer. **1909** in McCay *Little Nemo* 192: I'm getting along very bum. **1909** M'Govern *Krag Is Laid Away* 100: Le Chambre...was always growling about the "bum chow" in the army. **1916** S. Lewis *Job* 35: They'll make bum stenogs. **1922** Colton & Randolph *Rain* 59: Your climate's bum, Mr. Horn. **1927** Benchley *Chips* 3: Any study of the Bayeux Tapestry is made difficult by the fact that the old weavers were such bum draughtsmen. **1946** Gordon *Years Ago* 33: Be kind of bum just sittin' around Wollaston. **1950** Bissell *Stretch on the River* 14: Leave me give you one little nickel's worth of bum advice, kid. **1960** Serling *Stories from Twilight Zone* 9: I've had bum teams before....Real bad outfits.

2. injured; impaired; weak.

1902 Cullen *More Tales* 97: I can see you hunting around for raw steak for two bum lamps. **1908** in Fleming *Unforgettable Season* 39: And who ever said Donlin has a bum leg? **1912** Lowrie *Prison* 60: Y'r haven't got any bum fingers or a broken arm...have y'r? **1918** Hemingway *Sel. Letters* 18: I now have a bum leg and foot and there isn't any army in the world that would take me. **1919** in *Ibid.* 21: The leg is pretty bum. **1947** Schulberg *Harder They Fall* 99: You don't think I'd send one of my boys in with a bum duke, do ya? **1949** Gruber *Broken Lance* 46: You've got a bum leg, Fiore. **1950** Bissell *Stretch on the River* 9: They told me I got bum eyes. **1953** Dibner *Deep Six* 110: It's going to be a little rough on you with that bum gam. **1981** Hathaway *World of Hurt* 107: His leg's still bum. **1984** *Smithsonian* (Apr.) 52: He has a cowlick in his hair and a bum leg.

3. incorrect; erroneous; false.

1896 Ade *Artie* 85: They steered me up against the bum side of the cow. *Ibid.* 104: I'd...spring one o' them bum [musical] notes. *a*1909 Tillotson *Detective* 90: *Bum* or *Phoney*—Spurious gems of jewelry. **1926** *Writer's Mo.* (Dec.) 541: *Bum rap*...a crime which he didn't commit. **1936** H. Gray *Arf* (unp.): Just another bum tip....Bet he ain't within a thousand miles o' here. **1947** Matthews *Assault* 16: Not all of it was bum scoop, however. **1966** Elli *Riot* 13: He'd scream bum beef loud enough to be heard in the warden's house. **1966** Gallery *Start Engines* 48: You guys just made a bum pinch. **1977** *Baa Baa Black Sheep* (NBC-TV): You know how those instruments are always giving you a bum reading. **1983** *Morning Contact* (WKGN radio) (Mar. 24): Maybe they just had some bum information.

4. counterfeit; fraudulent; (*hence*) arousing suspicion.

1903 A.H. Lewis *Boss* 174: They don't amount to a deuce in a bum deck. **1916** *Lit. Digest* (Nov. 11) 1286: He was quite a hand at putting over bum checks. **1931** in Woods *Horse-Racing* 67: He ain't the sort of guy to pull bum checks or rough stuff like that. **1936** Duncan *Over the Wall* 24: We'd just been out four hundred bucks worth of bum paper, that's all. **1937** Johnston *Prison Life* 97: I passed a bum check. **1961** Scarne *Comp. Guide to Gambling* 674: *Bum Move.* A suspicious move.

bum *v.* [prob. fr. BUMMER[1]] **1.a.** to sponge; cadge; mooch.

1857 in *DA* 218: The "Bumming and Gassing Company" were out in full strength, the novelty of labor being a new experience in their existence. **1863** in *DA*: He offered to pay, and didn't undertake to bum a puff out. **1864** in R.G. Carter *4 Bros.* 460: Mose N. is at City Point, bumming on the hospitals. **1868** Macy *There She Blows!* 110: Others had fulfilled their mission by "bumming" considerable quantities of tobacco and literature from the younger lads. **1873** Hotten *Slang Dict.* (ed. 4) 103: Although the term is not much used in [England], the profession of bumming, both literary and otherwise, is freely practised. **1878** Bunner *Letters* 44: Moran bummed on him intellectually and otherwise. **1900** Remington *With Bark On* 186: At evening... we..."bummed" some crackers and coffee from some good-natured officer. **1900** *DN* II 25: *Bum*, v.t. To get from another without work. **1902** *Independent* (Nov. 6) 2635: Each morning each squad [of unemployed seamen] would separate, each man going in a different direction

to see what he could bum. **1908** in Butterfield *Post Treas.* 89: I blowed meself in El Paso...had to beat it to Seattle. I bummed enough there to ship on. **1909** *Miss. A & M Reveille* 45: "Puss" is skilled in Electricity and the art of "bumming" tobacco. **1918** Rendinell *One Man's War* 135: We bummed chow from them. **1928** Hammett *Red Harvest* 63: I...have to bum four bits for breakfast. **1929–30** Dos Passos *42d Parallel* 16: Bumming rides on delivery wagons. **1931** Faulkner *Sanctuary* 14: I have been walking and bumming rides ever since. **1943** J. Mitchell *McSorley's* 38: He bummed cigarettes shamelessly. **1970** N.Y.U. student: Could I bum a cigarette?

b. to accost and beg from (someone).

1893 in *Independent* (Dec. 5, 1901) 2886: He said he was going to bum some Priest for a quarter. **1919** Straub *Diary* (June 13): We stopped at the K. of C. place and there I "bummed" the K. of C. man for...cigarettes, chocolate, pipes and chewing tobacco. **1923** H.L. Foster *Beachcomber* 2: Then he bummed me for the price of a square meal. **1926** Tully *Jarnegan* 65: I hate to bum anybody for a feed. **1928** in Dobie *Drinkin' Gou'd* 60: The men used to...bum him for cigarettes. **1929** Milburn *Hobo's Hornbook* 81: He had bummed every guy up in Portland/And made them come acrost with the goods. **1935** E. Anderson *Hungry Men* 112: I got to bum old Sour Face below for another glass. **1940** O'Neill *Iceman Cometh* 144: He'll be back tonight askin' Harry for his room and bummin' me for a ball. **1958** "Traver" *Anat. Murder* 381: He...was himself bumming my jailer for a smoke. **1970** N.Y.C. derelict: The other day I tried to bum a detective. Those guys are God around here.

c. *Hobo.* to steal a ride on (a freight train); (*intrans.*) to travel by stealing rides or hitchhiking.

1896 *Pop. Sci. Mo.* (Dec.) 254: Several of the "lads" had been "pulled" at the Rapids for "bumming the freights." *ca*1909 in Kornbluh *Rebel Voices* 73: Or else he's bumming a ride [on a train]. **1943** J. Mitchell *McSorley's* 68: He bummed up to Cambridge.

2. *Mil.* to loot; to forage.

1865 Edmondston *Jour.* 710: The system of "bumming," for with Sherman it is a system, is brought as near the perfection of villainy as the human mind can come, Sherman the thief, Sherman the Prince of Bummers. **1871** Schele de Vere *Americanisms* 282 [ref. to Civil War]: The old original bummer was "a man named Jost, belonging to a regiment of Pennsylvania cavalry, whose proficiency in *bumming*, otherwise *looting*,...excited...the envy...of the boldest bushwhackers.

3. to engage in a drinking spree; (now, *esp.*) to frequent saloons or nightclubs.—now usu. constr. with *around.*

1860 in Thornton *Amer. Gloss.*: Another great sham connected with our social life is that of spreeing or "bumming." **1863** in *DA* 217: They are just fit to stay in this city, vegetate in the back slums, read the News and Express, bum round rum-shops [etc.]. **1865** Williams *Joaquin* 55: They "hang" round bars instead of "bumming." **1867** *Nat. Police Gaz.* (Jan. 12) 2: She had been arrested on this occasion for "bumming," having been picked up on the streets in a fearful state of intoxication. **1869** *Carmina Princetonia* 43: For "lazy Billy" is my name, "Bumming," "spreeing" every night my boys. **1955** Robbins *79 Park Ave* 81: That what she learns bumming around to all hours of the night?

4. to be, live, or travel as a tramp or vagrant.

1865 in Hilleary *Webfoot* 143: As I had no money to pay my way with I concluded not to bum and staid at home. **1871** *Overland Mo.* (Sept.) 221: Shakes bummed around here when I fust 'rived, in '52. **1872** Brace *Dangerous Classes* 101: It could be no worse than "bumming," *i.e.* sleeping out. *Ibid.* 102: I say, Jim, this is rayther better an' bummin'—eh? **1874** Alger *Julius* 50: Now I want you boys to leave off bummin', and try to be 'spectable members of s'ciety. **1883** Peck *Bad Boy* 225: He went bumming around the ward settin' 'em up nights. **1895** *Harper's* (Oct.) 776: Bummin' does seem to kill us lads, don't it? **1899** Prentiss *Utah Vols.* 115: I've "bummed" all over the country in every sort of a way. **1911** *JAF* (Oct.) 353: If I could git them good handouts, I'd quit work, bum all the time. **1920** in Fitzgerald *Stories* I 216: Reckon I been bummin' too long. **1924** Howard *Knew What They Wanted* 157: Maybe I was gettin' tired of bummin'. **1948** Ives *Wayfaring Stranger* 183: I bummed to Florida and did a little beachcombing, went to Canada, [etc.].

5.a. to loaf; idle.

1863 in *OEDS*: They are just fit to...bum round rum-ships. **1864** in D. Chisholm *Civil War Notebook* 22: Hezekiah Dean...was reduced to the ranks for bumming. **1880** *Campus Melodies* 39: When Sophomores gay we bum all day/And have no thought of the morrow. **1887** "Bunny" *Cow Boy* 100: In winter so little has to be done [on a cattle ranch] that it goes by the designation of Bumming time! **1900** *DN* II 25: *Bum*...To loaf. **1919** Straub *Diary* (Apr. 7): After class I "bummed" around town.

1926 Hormel *Co-Ed* 10: I got to bumming around with old Fernando Maximos Conde on the Glee Club trip last year. **1971** N.Y.U. students: "What's your sister doing these days?" "Bummin'."

b. to play hooky.

1900 *DN* II 25: *Bum*…To…waste time by cutting a recitation. **1929–31** J.T. Farrell *Young Lonigan* 152: He bummed from school and met Weary and Paulie.

6.a. to irk or annoy; (*also*) to insult.

1969 Mitchell *Thumb Tripping* 15: Wow, but they'd have to turn the kid on somehow. And soon, too, because he was starting to bum everybody. **1984** *TriQuarterly* (Spring) 311: It's the thing about being captain that bums him most. **1985** "Blowdryer" *Mod. Eng.* 8: Bumming…on somebody means insulting them.

b. to spoil.

1978 *Harper's* (July) 31: The town motto, one resident says, should be "Don't bum my trip."

c. to feel irritated or depressed.—used intrans.

1989 P. Munro *U.C.L.A. Slang* 26: *Bum*…to be disappointed, depressed. **1992** N.Y.C. man, age 24 (coll. J. Sheidlower): My girlfriend broke up with me last week. I'm bumming.

bumbazine *n.* [var. BOMBAZINE, punning on BUM¹] the buttocks.

1845 H.C. Lewis *Works* 91: It was *bum*bazine and reminded her by the first syllable of the *seat* of "Cupping on the Sternum." **1867** in Somers *Sport in N.O.* 161: [A hard punch sent Turner] to grass on his bumbazine.

bumbershoot *n.* an umbrella. Also **bumberell.** *Joc.*

1896 *DN* I 413: *Bumbershoot*…umbrella. **1902** Clapin *Americanisms* 83: *Bumberell.* A slang word for umbrella. Also, *bumbershoot.* **1906** *DN* III 129: *Bumbershoot, bumersol, n.* Umbrella. Facetious. **1907** in McCay *Little Nemo* 86: There goes your bumbershoot. **1959** *Sat. Eve. Post* (May 9) 48: Close the bumbershoot, Abby! I've got a sunshade in this car! **1965–70** in *DARE. a***1978** Cooley *Dancer* 356: Hitler…was going to stab Chamberlain in the *tukus* with his own bumbershoot. **1992** *CBS This Morning* (CBS-TV) (Nov. 10): So take the bumbershoot, all the way from Texas to the Great Lakes.

bumbersol *n.* an umbrella or parasol.

1906 (quot. at BUMBERSHOOT). **1911** *DN* III 541: *Bumbersoll, n.* A blend of *umbrella* and *parasol*, used facetiously.

bumblebee *n. Narc.* a capsule or tablet containing an amphetamine.

1977, 1980 (cited in Spears *Drugs & Drink* 83).

bumblebee whiskey *n. So.* potent whiskey.

1867 G.W. Harris *Lovingood* 30: I tuck me a four-finger dose ove bumblebee whiskey. **1968** R. Adams *Western Wds.* (ed. 2) 45: *Bumblebee whisky.* What the cowboy calls a strong whisky with a sting.

bumble dog *n. Cards.* an unskilled player, esp. in bridge.

1934 Weseen *Slang Dict.* 248: *Bumble dog*—A planless player at cards.

Bumblefuck *n.* [alter. of BUMFUCK, EGYPT] a very remote place.—usu. considered vulgar. *Joc.*

1989 P. Munro *U.C.L.A. Slang* 26: *Bumblefuck* any faraway little town. **1990** *UTSQ*: *Bumblefuck*—a word used to describe a location that is very far away or out in the country. "I can't believe we drove all the way to Bumblefuck to go to this party." **1991** Spears *Slang & Euphem.* (abr. ed. 2) 62: *Bumblefuck*…a primitive and rural place; podunk.

bumbo¹ *n.* [orig. unkn.] an alcoholic drink made from brandy, gin, or other liquor mixed with sugar and water. Now *S.E.*

***1748** T. Smollett *Rod. Random* ch. xxxiv: Who were making merry in the ward-room, round a table well stored with bumbo and wine. **1867** Smyth *Sailor's Wd.-Bk.*: *Bombo.* Weak cold punch. ***1882** in *F & H* I 376: The pitmen and the keelmen trim/They drink bumbo made from gin.

bumbo² *n.* [orig. unkn. but infl. by BUM¹] the rump or anus. Also **bombo.** [1785 quot. may be an earlier sense or an error.]

[***1785** Grose *Vulgar Tongue*: *Bumbo*…the negroe name for the private parts of a woman.] **1960** N.Y.C. woman, age *ca*70: When we were children we'd say, "Knock him on his bombo." **1977** Sayles *Union Dues* 237: A sailor went to the Queen of Spain,/His name was Chris Columbo/And every day to pave his way/He'd stick it up her bumbo.

bum-boy *n.* [BUM¹ + *boy*] a catamite; (*hence*) a man who is a lackey; PRATT-BOY.—used contemptuously.

***1929** Manning *Fortune* 190 [ref. to WWI]: I don't see why we

shouldn't have a good time, even if we're not a lot of bum-boys attached to the staff of some general or other. **1959** Burroughs *Naked Lunch* 125: The bum boys fall back in utter confusion. **1967** Schmidt *Lexicon of Sex* 33. **1974** Lahr *Trot* 17: He wears no underwear under those hip huggers. Bum-boy. Fag-bait.

bumf *n.* [short for BUM FODDER] toilet paper; (*hence*) any worthless paper, as official memos; (*hence*) rubbish; nonsense.

***1889** Barrère & Leland *Dict. Slang* I 200: *Bumf* (schoolboys), paper; an abbreviation of "bum-fodder." A *bumf*-hunt is a paper-chase. **1918** E. Pound, in Joyce *Letters* 423: The females have maliciously ruined De Bosscheres drawings by saving 2d. on bumf. ***1934** Yeates *Winged Victory* 11: Sending round reams of bumf. **1978** *Toronto Star* (Oct. 21) The Canadian 2: Our licence plates define the place as "Canada's Ocean playground" and, if you take official tourist bumf seriously, you'd swear we lived in a big, northern Barbados. **1984** *Harper's* (Jan. 1985) 58: He would…fog up the atmosphere with a lot of bumf about his royalty trust.

bum factory *n. Hobo.* (see quot.).

1927 *DN* V 440: *Bum factory, n.* (1) A cheap flop house. (2) A mission.

bumflummux *v.* to dumbfound.

1835 *Mil. & Naval Mag.* (Nov.) 90: That last scrape just bumflummuxed him, perhaps, a little slicker than goose grease.

bum fodder *n.* [BUM¹ + *fodder*] toilet paper.

***1699** Ward *London-Spy* 70: These…were such great Consumers of the *Wicked Weed* in *Snush*, that their upper Lips look'd as if they Excreated thro' their Nostrils, and had forgot to use *Bumfodder.* ***1731** "H. Thrumbo" *Merry-Thought* IV 7: By Swine who nee'r provide Bumfodder. ***1825** Jamieson *Scot. Dict.* I 330: *Bum-fodder.* Paper for the use of the water-closet….This term is often used very emphatically to express contempt for a paltry work. "It is good for nothing but to be *bum-fodder.*" **1940** in *DARE* I 457. **1971** Dahlskog *Dict.* 11: *Bum-fodder*…Toilet paper.

bumfreezer *n.* a short jacket.

***1932** in *OEDS*: An Eton coat, or "bum freezer," as they termed it in Magnolia Street. ***1943, *1955** in *Ibid.* **1973** W. Crawford *Stryker* 72: He straightened his white bumfreezer and shot a look at the driveway.

bumfuck *n.* a hateful person; an idiot; wretch.—usu. considered vulgar.

1979 *Easyriders* (Dec.) 6: A pretty crafty way…to get us bumfucks to read your rag cover to cover. **1981** *Easyriders* (Oct.) 47: Cut loose some of those bumfuck, hardluck losers.

bumfuck *v.* to have anal intercourse with.—usu. considered vulgar.

***ca1866** *Romance of Lust* 269: Bum-fucking his adorable wife. **1967** Mailer *Vietnam*: You…been bum fucking the wrong cunt.

Bumfuck, Egypt *n. Mil. & Stu.* a very remote place.—usu. considered vulgar. *Joc.* See also B.F.E., BUMBLEFUCK.

1972 Sgt. E-6, U.S. Army (coll. J. Ball): They probably sent those records out to Bumfuck, Egypt. **1974** Kingry *Monk & Marines* 31: When they asked…whether he would…volunteer for Vietnam, he said he would volunteer for Bumfuk [*sic*], Egypt, first! **1983** Eble *Campus Slang* (Nov.) 1: *Bumfuck*—the worst place: We had to park in Bumfuck, Egypt. **1986** J. Cain *Suicide Squad* 20: Together, they'll come up with some place beyond Bumfuck, Egypt, to send my sorry ass.

bumfuzzle *v.* **1.** to bamboozle.

1904 Limerick *Villagers* 29: Hezekiah tumbled to the fact that he had been bumfuzzled.

2. to bewilder.

1905 *DN* III 60: *Bumfoozle, bumfuzzle.* **1905** *DN* III 72: *Bumfuzzle, v. tr.* to confuse. "He was just bumfuzzled in that exam." **1971** J. Brown & A. Groff *Monkey* 53: I'm sorry to be so bumfuzzled, fellows. **1983** *Knoxville Journal* (Feb. 17) 1: That's what has me really bumfuzzled, stunned. **1992** S.K. Slocum *Pop. Arthurian Trads.* 87: Arthur…appears bumfuzzled…when he removes the sword from the stone.

bumhole *n.* **1.** the anus.—usu. considered vulgar.

***ca1866** *Romance of Lust* 121: Mrs. Benson's bum-hole. **1961** Gover *$100 Misunderstanding* 18: We jus gittin along like seven crabs in one big bumhole.

2. (see quot.).—usu. considered vulgar.

1980 Pearl *Slang Dict.*: *Bumhole*…a stupid, despicable person.

bum kick *n.* [BUM, *adj.* + KICK] something disappointing or otherwise unpleasant; a bad experience; a bad mood.

1943–47 in Hodes & Hansen *Sel. From Gutter* 12: Some one had robbed me of everything I had. That was one bum kick. **1952** Kerouac *Cody* 150: We'll pass it around in rotation see so we don't get on any bum kicks because of the poor instrument. **1953** in Burroughs & Ginsberg *Yage* 23: The hotel was run by a whorish looking landlady....It was a bum kick. **1956** in Burroughs *Naked Lunch* 250: I once gave marijuana to a guest who was mildly anxious about something ("On bum kicks" as he put it). **1958** Gilbert *Vice Trap* 19: Sometimes, coming off a bum kick, I would get in [my car] and fire hell out of her. **1965** in Cleaver *Soul on Ice* 50: But if the letter is not from you, it's like having two deuces, a three, a four, and a five, all in scrambled suits. A bum kick. Nothing. **1966** Elli *Riot* 312: You tryin' to put me on a bum kick or somethin'?

bumkick *v.* to sadden or annoy. Hence **bumkicked**, *adj.*
    1966 Braly *On Yard* 236: The inhalers bum-kicked him. **1967** Salas *Tattoo* 115 [ref. to 1950's]: Look, man. I know you're bumkicked over your buddy. **1970** Eisen *Altamont* 113: I'm bum kicked about the whole thing. *a***1985** Schwendinger & Schwendinger *Adolescent Sub.* 256 [ref. to 1960's]: Deliberately destroying the sense of peace...or euphoria [caused by marijuana] is known as "bum kicking" a person.

bumly *adj.* depressed; unhappy.
    1908 McGaffey *Show Girl* 235: I naturally felt kind of bumly. **1985** "Blowdryer" *Mod. Eng.* 8: Bumly...Kind of bummed out, real sad. "Why are you so bumly?"

bummed [out] *adj.* **1.** intoxicated by alcohol or drugs.
    1968 Gover *JC Saves* 117: I'm drunk as the lord and gonna get drunker. Bummed out a my mind! **1973** N.Y.U. student: Man, *bummed out*. That means really drunk. Or stoned. Or tired. Or even pissed off. Like, "Man, I was really bummed out," or "That sure bums me out." It's a pretty new expression, I think. Like just this year.
2. depressed or angry; depressing.
    1973 (see quot. at (1), above). **1974** N.Y.C. barmaid, age 22: *Bummed* is California for sad. I was bummed last night. **1978** Groom *Better Times* 21: Hey, man, don't get bummed out—we were just kidding around. **1980** *N.Y. Times Mag.* (Sept. 7) 130: We were bummed out that Mr. Safire skipped over many of the expressions that we use here. **1980** Santoli *Everything* 155: All they told us to do was to kill....It was just a bummed-out trip. **1981** *N.Y. Daily News* (July 24) 41: A few years ago I got very bummed out one night and tried to end it all. I slashed my wrists. **1984** *TriQuarterly* (Spring) 313: Jesse tries his best to look bummed.

bummer[1] *n.* [BUM[1] + *-er*] **1.a.** a shiftless person, as a beggar, vagrant, sponger of drinks, etc.
    1855 in *DA*: Come, clear out you trunken loafer! Ve don't vant no *bummers* here! **1856** in *Ibid.*: A seedy example of the "Bummer" family. **1859** Matsell *Vocab.* 16: *Bummer*. A sponger. **1868** Williams *Black-Eyed Beauty* 47: You're in with a set of bummers, and Matty's the best of them, and she isn't worth shooting. **1869** *Overland Mo.* (Mar.) 273: "Bummers" of the seediest class, who drank at the expense of every stranger who approached the bar. **1871** *Overland Mo.* (Sept.) 221: Shakes...had earned the unenviable reputation of being an inveterate "whisky bummer."...It was seldom that a coin passed from his hands to the bar-keeper's drawer. **1871** "M. Twain" *Roughing It* ch. xxiv: The auctioneer stormed up and down,...and never got a bid—at least never any but the eighteen-dollar one he hired a notoriously substanceless bummer to make. **1872** McCabe *N.Y. Life* 680: The Bummer is simply one who detests work, and who manages to live in some degree of comfort without earning the means of doing so. **1873** Hotten *Slang Dict.* (ed. 4) 103: *Bummer*, literally one who sits or idles about; a loafer; one who sponges upon his acquaintances. **1874** in Bartlett *Amer.* (ed. 4) 80: So long as substantial citizens choose to leave politics to shoulder-hitters, rum-sellers and *bummers* of every degree, so long will they be robbed at every turn. **1875** in *F & H* I (rev.) 429: San Francisco is the Elysium of *bummers*. Nowhere can a worthless fellow, too lazy to work, too cowardly to steal, get on so well. **1878** in *Seal & Salmon Fisheries* IV 6: A gang of rowdies and bummers have, for the past three months, been in the habit of getting on a drunken spree, and then at midnight going about the town making [the] most hideous noises imaginable. **1887** M. Roberts *W. Avernus* 71: Some of the "boys" said it was a regular "hand out" and that we looked like a crowd of old "bummers." **1911** T.A. Dorgan, in *N.Y. Eve. Jour.* (Jan. 7) 8: Get out, you bummer. **1960** Jordan & Marberry *Fool's Gold* 73: Nigger Jim hired a drunken old bummer, sobered him up, supplied him with a clean outfit, and sent him out "missionarying."
b. a worthless or contemptible person, animal, or item.
    1858 in Somers *Sports in N.O.* 57: [Prizefighters were either] "invincibles" or "beaten bummers." *a***1860** Hundley *So. States* 268: Strychnine

whisky,/Sold by some confounded bummer,/At a bit a glass, or cheaper. **1880** Nye *Boomerang* 15: One day Damon...told the...old bummer of Syracuse what he thought of him. **1896** F.H. Smith *Tom Grogan* 90: Begin with Quigg an' some of the bummers as is runnin' the Union. **1918** [Livingston] *Delcassee* 57: Then there were the "bummers," the dregs of dogdom.
c. *Stock Raising.* BUM[2] *n.*, 1.e.
    1940, 1942, 1968 in *DARE* I 455.
2.a. Orig. *Mil.* a straggler, skulker, or deserter; a malingerer or loafer.
    1861 in *DA* 217: We have a fair sprinkling of bummers, but instead of demoralizing their betters by their presence, they are only laughed at. *ca***1863** in K.E. Olson *Music & Musket* 90: Sick men and *bummers*...the bummers far exceed the numbers of genuinely sick. **1864** in Mohr *Cormany Diaries* 484: I have quite an experience cleaning the camp of bummers and sending them out...on Picket. **1866** Brockett *Camp, Battle Field & Hosp.* 406: Suddenly he was confronted by a ragged and bare-footed fellow, whom he instantly recognized as one of the "bummers." **1867** Duke *Morgan's Cav.* 385: We heard cannonading....We saw nothing of it, however, but its effects upon the stragglers and "bummers," who seemed to have unaccountably increased. **1889** Barrère & Leland *Dict. Slang* I 200: *Bummer*...During the war the term was applied to the camp-followers or semi-deserters who followed the Federal army. **1894** Bangs *3 Wks. in Pols.* 75: He had been more or less outspoken on the subject of bummers drawing pensions....The party...gave a pension to every man who lost his breath running away from the enemy in the Rebellion. *a***1910** A. Small *Rd. to Richmond* 187: Early in the war, "hospital bummers" were unknown. **1927** Rollins *Jinglebob* 45: Most of them were graduates of penitentiaries, city slums, and the "bummer" contingent of the armies in the Civil War. **1974** R. Campbell *Chasm* 176: I want them to bug the bummer if they dray him—or her or whatever it is.
b. *Mil.* a forager.
    1862 in R.G. Carter *4 Bros.* 217: Our bummer extracted a hard, sour, indigestible flour pone, which seemed to our astonished eyes as large as a cartwheel. **1865** in *OED* I 1175: If it be asked what a "bummer" is, the reply is easy. He is a raider on his own account—a man who temporarily deserts his place in the ranks...and starts out upon an independent foraging expedition. *ca***1865** in *F & H* I (rev.) 429: Look hyar, Captain, we bummers ain't so bad after all. **1866** *Beadle's Mo.* (May) 390: *Technically* speaking, they are "bummers," who are out thus early to carry out their motto, of "primitias corripere." *Ibid.* 398: We are decided in our opinion that the "Bummer Brigade," as conducted, was neither a credit to the service nor an organization permissible by any known laws of war. **1884** Hedley *Marching Through Ga.* 268: The emergency produced the forager, commonly known as "the Bummer."

bummer[2] *n.* [BUM (TRIP) + *-er*] **1.a.** *Narc.* BUM TRIP, 1.
    1966 (cited in Spears *Drugs & Drink* 84). **1967** Wolf *Love Generation* 276: *Bummer*. A bad drug experience; by extension, anything upsetting. **1967** Yablonsky *Hippie Trip* 215: The Clinic...helped people with so-called "LSD bummers." A "bummer" is a situation where a user has "freaked-out" or gone beyond the pale. He may manifest...hysterical psychosis. **1970** *Playboy* (Sept.) 104: The first part of the [LSD] trip was a real downer; we didn't have the word "bummer" in those days [1965]. **1972** Kopp *Buddha* 59: It is like a person having a "bad trip" when he drops acid. Going on a "bummer." **1974** Hyde *Mind Drugs* 12: Some of the same drugs have produced "bummers" or bad trips. **1980** Luceno *Head Hunters* 15: Follow-up hallucinations from what had been a terrifying, mystifying drug trip, a penultimate bummer.
b. a state of craziness, anger, or depression.—constr. with *on* or *into.*
    1966 Reynolds & McClure *Freewheelin Frank* 10: Anybody who wants to see another Adolph Hitler is definitely on a bummer. *Ibid.* 131: The Berkeley heat were on a bummer and started swinging their clubs. **1967** Wolf *Love Generation* 64: But my marriage failing was really putting me into a bummer. **1974** *Chico and the Man* (NBC-TV): He's really on a bummer today. **1978** Maupin *Tales* 146: Vincent seemed to be on a bummer...."Bad day, huh?"
2.a. something that is unpleasant, difficult, dangerous, or tedious. Also semi-*adj.*
    1966 Thompson *Hell's Angels* 89: Man, it was a bummer, it wasn't right. A lot of people got conned, and now we have to listen to all this crap about us being queers. **1967** *Sat. Eve. Post* (Sept. 23) 28: "Your mother was kind of a bummer," Jeff says to her. **1967** in H. Ellison *Sex Misspelled* 178: Spencer Lichtman was a bummer. **1968** Baker et al. *CUSS* 91: *Bummer*. Difficult exam. A misfortune. Bad. **1972** in H.S. Thompson *Shark Hunt* 122: Nixon...is a serious *politics junkie*...and like

any other junkie, he's a bummer to have around: Especially as President. **1978** Maupin *Tales* 17: Connie's bummer night. **1982** Del Vecchio *13th Valley* 23: Wow, Man,...this dude's a real bummer. **1982** S. Black *Totally Awesome* 58: Way bummer if you miscalculate.

b. an inferior or worn-out device; LEMON.

1972 R. Barrett *Lovomaniacs* 168: Some are bummers; ripoffs peddled around by thieves. **1985** Snapper Lawn Mower ad (WINS Radio) (Aug. 15): "What can I get for this bummer?" Snapper is giving fabulous trade-in allowances on old lawn mowers. **1985** Heywood *Taxi Dancer* 144: You ought to have one of these electric bummers.

bummy *n.* BUM², *n.*, 2.a.

1923 Ornitz *Haunch, Paunch & Jowl* 40: They were unfeminine little bummies. **1949** N. Algren *Golden Arm* 29: Where he got it only the blind bummy called Pig...might have guessed. **1964** N. Algren, in *Sat. Eve. Post* (Sept. 26) 44: Two blind cane bummies were taking up the middle of the sidewalk in an argument. **1970** *Current Slang* V 4: *Bummie*, n. Bum, transient, hobo, tramp.

bummy *adj.* BUM, *adj.*

1896 Ade *Artie* 7: The woman that trifled with the piano for about a half an hour was very much on the bummy bum. **1903** *Pedagog. Sem.* X 379: Isn't that bummy. **1931** in H. Miller *Letters to Emil* 78: Getting into...a bummy condition. **1950, 1970** in *DARE* I 455.

bum out *v.* **1.** to depress or sadden; dispirit; (*intrans.*) to become depressed.

1970 *Current Slang* V 20: *Bum out*, v. To depress.—I just got an F. in Spanish. It really *bums me out.*—He's really *bummed* out because his girlfriend dumped him. **1974** *Odd Couple* (ABC-TV): You're a downer! You bum me out! Telling me I look old. **1982** *Hardcastle & McCormick* (ABC-TV): Don't let it bum you out, Hardcastle. **1984** H. Gould *Cocktail* 197: I never bum out on dope. **1990** *Spring Break* (MTV) (Apr. 17): I'm bumming out 'cause I left my deodorant in the hotel room.

2. to anger or annoy.

1971 *Batman* (Aug.) 20: This really bums me out! Too many cops are getting the short end of the stick these days! **1973** *Nat. Lampoon Encyc. Humor* 87: When we take him home for a visit he'll really bum out our parents. **1974** Hejinian *Extreme Remedies* 194: I didn't mean to bum you out, Joe. Don't be mad. **1976** Univ. Tenn. student: That's what *really* bummed me out.

3. *Stu.* to fail badly.

1968–70 *Current Slang* III & IV 17: *Bum out*, v. To fail a test.—College students, both sexes, Cal. **1973** N.Y.U. student: I did pretty well on the midterm, but if I bum out on this one I'll be in trouble.

bump *n.* **1.** *pl.* USMC. first call for mess.—usu. in phr. **chow bumps.**

1927 Thomason *Red Pants* 186: Then his trumpeter blew two long wails—bumps, that says five minutes to mess-gear. **1930** in *Leatherneck* (Jan. 1931) 11: Rotten chow, rotten this, rotten that, but always first when chow bumps go. **1957** Herber *Tomorrow to Live* 30 [ref. to WWII]: A bugle blew chow bumps. **1973** Krulewitch *Now That You Mention It* 27 [ref. to 1917]: Between "Bumps," first call for chow, and drill, a 20-minute respite was allowed for "the three Sh's"—shave, shower, and shit—and the makeup of bunks for inspection. *a*1989 C.S. Crawford *Four Deuces* 29: Chow bumps sounded.

2. *pl.* hard treatment; hard knocks; (*specif.*) a beating.

1908 in Fleming *Unforgettable Season* 80: He...got his bumps in all four Western cities. **1918** Gibbons *Thought We Wouldn't Fight* 211: I am coming back and get you soon's we give Fritzie his bumps. **1922** Tully *Emmett Lawler* 300: Look at Grant at Valley Forge, he got his bumps, didn't he? **1931** in Galewitz *Great Comics* 19: The Gasoline Alley Rangers passed a resolution...that Emil should be given "the bumps." **1929–33** J.T. Farrell *Young Manhood of Lonigan* 167: They gave him the royal bumps, slamming his can against the sidewalk.

3. *Esp. Und.* a murder; in phrs. **get the bump** to be murdered; **give the bump** to murder.

1919 (quot. at BUMP, *v.*, 3.a.). **1927** Coe *Me—Gangster* 31: When a guy like him gets the bump nobody cares. **1928** Coe *Swag* 43: Whenever anybody gets the bump...[the police] are anxious to pull a quick pinch. **1929** Hammett *Maltese Falcon* 64: That's a...swell system...when I can give somebody else the bump and hang Thursby's on them. **1935** C.J. Daly *Murder* 118: He's overdue for the bump. **1965** "R. Stark" *Jugger* 71: Who else would ease him the bump? **1971** Curtis *Banjo* 204: I'm going to make a fast bump...so fast they won't expect us. **1977** Caron *Go-Boy* 218: Ten will get you nothing says the Russians knew all about the bump, say six months in advance.

4. *pl.* (used as a toast of obscure meaning).

1926 Tully *Jarnegan* 64: "Here's bumps, brother," said Jarnegan, holding the whisky aloft.

5. the act of being dismissed or replaced.—constr. with *the*.

1940 in E. Pound *Letters* 340: If a race neglects to create its own gods, it gets the bump. **1942** *ATS* 67.

6. usu. *pl. Burlesque.* a sudden rapid or repeated pelvic thrust, as during a strip tease.—esp. in phr. **bumps and grinds** erotic pelvic thrusts and rhythmic grinding motions.

[**1936** in Mencken *Amer. Language* (ed. 4) 586: A *hoofer* (dancer) who *grinds, bumps* and *strips* (i.e., rotates her hips, follows with a sharp, sensuous upheaval of her backside, and then sheds all her clothes save a G-string).] **1938** in Botkin *Sidewalks* 304: A third added the bump and the grind. **1941** G.R. Lee *G-String* 247: And these splits in the skirts are swell for my bumps. **1946–51** Motley *We Fished* 343: She twirled her hands above her head....She did bumps and grinds. **1951** Mannix *Sword-Swallower* 2: The Oriental Dancing Girls...turned loose a series of bumps and grinds that began to draw away...the crowd. **1952** MacDonald *Damned* 155: I didn't ask for no bumps and grinds out of those girls. That's cheap stuff. Just a good dignified strip. **1981** C. Nelson *Picked Bullets Up* 298: Throwing a few wicked bumps and grinds.

7. a raise or promotion.

1949 *New Yorker* (Nov. 5) 87: Leave him do a couple pitchas and I guarantee you I'll get him a bump. **1957** Myrer *Big War* 119 [ref. to WWII]: You got a bump to sergeant last night.

8. *pl.* a woman's breasts.

1958 "Traver" *Anat. Murder* 64: Good bumps, too. Boy, oh boy, like...Marilyn Monroe.

9. *Narc.* HIT; TOKE.

1985 Bodey *F.N.G.* 204: How about a quick bump off that bowl?

bump *v.* **1.** to engage in copulation [with].

***1669** *New Academy of Complements* 257: I'z bump thee quoth he..../ How lik'st it quoth he, well *Thomas* quoth she. **1921** McAlmon *Hasty Bunch* 187: He may be getting too much bumping from that widow Brown he knows...or just getting stupid from sitting around on his ass so much. **1974** Univ. Tenn. student: *Bump* or *hump* mean the same thing. "I wonder if she'll bump." **1989** "3rd Bass" *Steppin' to the A.M.* (rap song): You're bumpin' a freak while I'm G'in'. **1990** P. Munro *Slang U.* 49: Bump to have sex...to have sex with.

2.a. to dismiss (a suitor); to discharge (an employee); to remove (something) from a list, schedule, etc.

1899 Kountz *Baxter's Letters* 49: And unless she promises to bump the other fellow, you are going to leave her in a rage, aren't you? **1904** (quot. at TALL GRASS). **1918** *DN* V 23: *To bump*, vb. t. To dismiss from service. General. **1926** *Writer's Mo.* (July) 42: *Bumped.* Discharged, either permanently or temporarily. **1967** Lit *Dictionary* 48: *Bumped.*...the cat was fired; he was sacked. **1978** Univ. Tenn. student: I hear they're bumping him. **1982** WKGN Radio News (June 21): After twenty-five years, the song is being bumped from the Atlantic City event.

b. *Sports & Games.* to defeat.

1901 in Ade *Letters* 23: They prolong the game and double up on the Jack-pots and every one gets sore and tired and the Man that was ahead gets bumped &c.—a typical poker game. **1904** (quot. at BULLET, *n.*, 1). **1942** *ATS* 634.

c. to oust (a person) on the basis of priority or seniority, *specif.* from an assigned seat on an airline flight. Now *S.E.*

1938 *AS* (Dec.) 308: *Got bumped.* A driver loses his run through seniority bidding. **1950** Roeder *J. Robinson* 84: Bumped off the plane, they inched the rest of the way through the South by train and finally by bus. **1958** McCulloch *Woods Words* 23: *Bump*—To take a job away from a man who has less seniority. ***1960** *Times Lit. Supp.* (London) (Nov. 25) 750: The wartime meaning of "bump," forcing a junior to give up his seat on an aircraft to a senior, [has] been forgotten. **1963** D. Tracy *Brass Ring* 381 [ref. to 1940's]: If...he was not bumped (what a strange term) her nephew...would arrive from the West Coast.

3.a. *Orig. Und. & Mil.* to kill, esp. to shoot dead; BUMP OFF.

1914 Jackson & Hellyer *Vocab.* 21: He copped a cuter and got bumped making a getaway. **1919** in F.P. Dunne *Dooley at Best* 282: Th' delay between th' time a criminal bumps some wan an' th' time he gets th' bump...accoordin' to th' law. **1926** *Amer. Legion Mo.* (July) 46 [ref. to WWI]: I won't carry no blankets for some other bozo to salvage after I get bumped. **1930** Fredenburgh *Soldiers* 227 [ref. to WWI]: Who got bumped, Bud? **1943** in Steinbeck *There Was a War* (Oct. 12): Well, anyway, if they bump me our boys will get these three. **1943** Wray & Geraghty *Falcon & Co-Eds* (film): Then he bumps the old lady so his sweetheart can inherit the estate. **1951** Spillane *Lonely Night* 59: What about the guy Oscar bumped? **1962** Spillane *Girl Hunters* 115: Before Dewey got bumped a guy left something with him to give to me. **1974** V.E. Smith *Jones Men* 136: He and Dooney got to arguin' and first thing you know Teddy ups with a roscoe and bumps Dooney. Right there on the street.

b. to die.

1942 *ATS* 132: Die…bump…check out [etc.]. **1988** Knoxville, Tenn., attorney, age 35: Those bastards are old, but there's no telling when one of 'em is going to bump.

4. *Burlesque*. (of a stripper) to thrust the pelvis forward suddenly.

1936 (quot. at BUMP, *n*., 6.). **1979** *Stripper* (CBS-TV movie): Suzy, you still bump when you should grind.

5.a. *Poker*. to raise (a bet or a bettor).

1963 Morgan *Six-Eleven* 39: I'll bump it a dime. **1978** C. Miller *Animal House* 9: "Bump you ten," said the cardplayer. **1985** Heywood *Taxi Dancer* 74: Let's stop bumping each other and lay them down. **1987** S. Weiser *Project X* (film): I see your buck—and I bump your buck.

b. to raise (a numerical figure).

1972 *N.Y. Times Mag.* (Nov. 12) 95: Quite a few drivers say they "bump" weights (cheat on weighing loads). **1983** DeVore *Heart of Steel* (film): They kept bumpin' your pay till the place went broke.

c. to promote in rank.

1860 in *Jour. Ill. Hist. Soc.* XXX (1937) 148: I feel as if he ought to be bumped. **1963** Marshall *Battle at Best* 4: We just bumped him up from private to sergeant today.

¶ In phrase:

¶ **bump (one's) gums** see s.v. GUM[1], *n*.

bump-and-grind *n*. an erotic dance, esp. a striptease, involving bumps and grinds.

1984 J.R. Reeves *Mekong* 224: Watching some…broad doing a bump-and-grind in a G-string.

bumper *n*. usu. *pl*. a woman's breast.

1947 Mailer *Naked & Dead* 378: What bumpers on her. **1963** J. Stearn *Grapevine* 196: The dancing was often cheek-to-cheek and "bumper-to-bumper," as the lesbian expression went. **1970** Rudensky & Riley *Gonif* 102: Babes with Big Bumpers Wanted. **1973** Gwaltney *Destiny's Chickens* 48: All I got's a big set of bumpers.

bumper-jumper *n*. a driver who is tailgating.

1976 Lieberman & Rhodes *CB Handbook* 125: Bumper Jumper—Tailgater.

bumping *adj*. exciting; wonderful.

1989 Eble *Campus Slang* (Spring) 1: Bumpin'—stylish, good looking. "You sure are looking bumpin' tonight, my friend." **1990** Dickson *Slang!* 214: Bump'n…Of the highest quality; such as clothes or music. **1993** *New Yorker* (Mar. 1) 116: This Museum is Bumpin'n [*sic*].

bumpman *n*. *Und. & Police*. a pickpocket; jostler.

1940 O'Hara *Pal Joey* 161: It is also a very fine thing in favor of the light finger gentry and I told Harry…in case he was interested over there was a bump man I use to see out at the track sometimes.

bump-off *n*. a murder.—also attrib.

1920 E. Hemingway, in *N.Y. Times Mag.* (Aug. 18, 1985) 23: Making a play to be bump-off artists.…An exorbitant price for a single bump-off job. **1921** Marquis *Carter* 97: The' was one of them wobblies' bump-off men sayin' he seen Slim in Tacoma. **1926** Dunning & Abbott *B'way* 230: A lot of stuff [in the newspapers] about Scar Edwards' bump off. **1926** Finerty *Criminalese* 10: Bump off—Any premeditated murder. **1929** Sullivan *Look at Chicago* 23: Five shots were fired—all high on the victim—which is typical of gangster bump-offs. **1938** Chandler *Big Sleep* 105: You know the dope on Brody's bump-off. **1945** Fay *Be Poor* 43: Jacques' "bump off"…was hushed up.

bump off *v*. **1.a.** Orig. *Und. & Mil*. to kill, esp. to shoot dead; (*specif.*) to murder.

1907 D. Runyon, in *Lippincott's Mag.* (Oct.) 501: I've seen Fat sit down beside a guy that'd been bumped off and cry like it was his own brother. **1908** Raine *Wyoming* 17: I gathered, ma'am, that they wanted to collect my scalp.…Bump me off—send me across the divide. **1910** Raine *O'Conner* 23: Cheese it, or I'll bump you off. **1912** Lowrie *Prison* 248: I'd let the guy think he was goin' to be bumped off, let him die the million times in his cell. **1913** *Sat. Eve. Post* (May 10) 12: If the bulls come, I hope they bump you off—see? **1915** H.L. Wilson *Ruggles* 299: God bless the trigger finger of the man that bumped him off! **1926** *Amer. Legion Mo.* (July) 46 [ref. to WWI]: I'll bet it made that Frog mad to get bumped off when he had a pack of butts on 'im. **1927** *Vanity Fair*

(Nov.) 134: To "bump off" is to murder or otherwise get rid of a person. **1927** Nicholson *Barker* 69: I reckon she'd be payin' me yet if she hadn't been bumped off in a wreck on th' Sante Fe outa El Paso six years ago. **1938** "R. Hallas" *Play the Black* 23: Now the police were wise, he was trying to bump me off. **1947** Bowers & Millhauser *Web* (film): Kroner gets out of prison one day—and gets bumped off the next. **1957** Myrer *Big War* 92 [ref. to WWII]: They're replacing the ones who already got bumped off. **1989** J. Simon, in *Nat. Review* (Dec. 8) 46: He finally agreed to let his shady brother…have his underworld connections bump her off. **1992** *Inside Politics* (CNN-TV) (Nov. 30): What's going to happen to me [if I inform]? I'll get bumped off.

b. *Mil*. to destroy (a target).

1918 in [J.M. Grider] *War Birds* 202: Bish got one [German plane] about noon and Lady Mary went out and bumped off another one.

c. to die.

1912 Lowrie *Prison* 116: Askin' Almighty God t'…save him a reserved seat when we all bumps off. **1918** O'Reilly *Roving* 237 [ref. to 1901]: Do you know, lad, I believe I'd like to talk to a preacher if I'm going to bump off. **1918** in Niles *Singing Soldiers* 113: Might go out to fly tomorrow and bump off. **1918** in Hall & Niles *One Man's War* 320: Maybe it's my time to bump off. **1929** *AS* (June) 338: Bumped off…died. **1936** Dos Passos *Big Money* 322: The old man bumped off…when I was a little twirp. **1971** Terrell *Bunkhouse* 152: They think I'm liable to bump off any minute.

2. *Sports*. to defeat.

1974 R. Carter *16th Round* 205: They probably thought that he wouldn't have to show up but a minute to bump me off, either. **1984** *Knoxville* (Tenn.) *Journal* (Oct. 6) B4: Cherokee bumped off Rutledge, 42–6.

bum rap *n*. [BUM, *adj*. + RAP] **1.** *Und*. a false accusation or conviction.

1926 *Writer's Mo.* (Dec.) 541: Bum rap…A crime which he didn't commit. **1926** in *AS* (Mar. 1927) 281: Bum rap—sentence imposed upon one who claims to be innocent. **1926** Clark & Eubank *Lockstep* 45: Edgar is…in prison for what I honestly believe is a bum rap. **1927** Murphy *Gray Walls* 42: We got a bum rap (wrongfully accused). **1956** Ross *Hustlers* 8: I was socked in the reform school for a while for a bum rap in the five and dime.

2. an unjust criticism.

1952 W. Brown *Sox* 75: Maybe it was a bum rap for Heinie Zimmerman, but he wasn't the first ball player…who had to take such, and like it. **1970** La Motta et al. *Raging Bull* 13: Harry's a nice guy. He never gave nobody a bum rap. **1982** *N.Y. Post* (Aug. 13) 18: Friday the 13th…has gotten a bum rap, according to Chicago occultists.

3. a misfortune; an unfair action.

1942 Algren *Morning* 177: Ever' one of us is in the law of averages.…That's one bum rap can't nobody beat. **1942** *Big Shot* (film): It wasn't comin' to you. It was a bum rap. **1978** Univ. Tenn. *Daily Beacon* (Jan. 26) 1: This is a bum rap! This apartment is not big enough for two people, let alone three. And now they want to put four in here.

bum-rap *v*. **1.** *Und*. to accuse or convict falsely; FRAME.

1947 Motley *Knock on Any Door* 213: That bastard is going to bum-rap hell out of me. He's going to frame me. **1962–68** B. Jackson *In Life* 169: I can't ever scream about being bum-rapped. **1970** E. Knight et al. *Black Voices* 95: Now, to be sure, it is common to hear a convict say that he or another convict was "bum rapped." **1972** *Playboy* (Apr.) 98: You get bum-rapped by phony evidence. **1982** L. Cohen *Serpent* (film): Nineteen years old—I was bum-rapped by a cop like Powell 'cause he wanted to get a conviction.

2. to disparage or criticize unfairly or harshly; to speak ill of.

1951 Algren *Chicago* 74: Can I keep my job if I bum-rap some people for you? **1954** McGraw *Prison Riots* 193: Man, don't bum rap me. **1964** in L. Bruce *Essential Lenny* 109: They really bum-rapped ya, the I.R.A. **1967** Salas *Tattoo* 229 [ref. to *ca*1951]: Have I ever bumrapped your little girl in any way? **1970** Lincke *Jenny* 57: What one liked, the other bum-rapped.

bum-rush *v*. *Rap Music*. to force one's way into; CRASH; attack.

1987 "Public Enemy" *Yo! Bum Rush the Show* [rap music album title]. **1988** *N.Y. Times* (Aug. 19) C 15: Rap is…bum-rushin' the mainstream. **1990** *New Yorker* (Sept. 17) 63: "The Jungle tried to bumrush my crib"—attack his house. **1991** N. George, in *Village Voice* (N.Y.) (Aug. 13) 24: He walked home from the subway and was bum-rushed by a five-man posse of new jack knuckleheads. **1991** *Source* (Oct.) 33: So, bumrush the door of the store and pick up the album.

bumsquabbled *adj*. [of fanciful orig.] confounded; ruined.

1838 [Haliburton] *Clockmaker* (Ser. 2) 108: If he didn't look bumsquabbled it's a pity. **1871** Schele de Vere *Amer.* 581: *Bamsquabbled,* first used in the "Legend of the American War," and expressing discomfiture, is an evidently manufactured word, and but rarely heard except in humorous writings.

bum's rush *n.* forcible ejection from a place; *(hence)* abrupt dismissal.—usu. constr. with *the.*
1910 T.A. Dorgan, in Zwilling *TAD Lexicon* 21: Suddenly she goes plumb nutty, wallops my noodle and gives me the bum's rush. **1918** E. O'Neill *Dreamy Kid* 30: You can't gimme no bum's rush. I stays. **1919** I. Cobb *Life of Party* 43: The patrolman pushed his prisoner ten feet along the sidewalk, imparting to the offender's movements an involuntary gliding gait, with backward jerks between forward shoves; this method of propulsion being known in the vernacular of the force as "givin' a skate the bum's rush." **1925** Mullin *Scholar Tramp* 140 [ref. to *ca*1912]: The brawny Louie frequently hopped over the bar to collar some belligerent drunk and rush him breathlessly through the swinging doors into the street, using his knees expertly to propel his victim along. This function Louie referred to with great relish as "givin' 'em the bum's rush." **1926** Norwood *Other Side of Circus* 54: It kept Cocky busy giving 'em the bum's rush. **1929–30** Dos Passos *42d Parallel* 357: The bouncer had just vaulted over the bar to give him the bum's rush. **1939–40** Tunis *Kid from Tomkinsville* 119: I'm gonna give you the bum's rush too. **1940** Zinberg *Walk Hard* 333: I ain't going to get heaved out in no ten-second bum's rush. **1954** "Collans" & Sterling *House Detect.* 95: The bouncer can grab the offender by the collar and give him the bum's rush to the street door. **1986** *ALF* (NBC-TV): Why is everyone trying to give me the bum's rush here?

bum steer *n.* [BUM, *adj.* + STEER, *n.* 'advice'] a piece of bad advice or false information.
1924 Henderson *Crookdom* 399: *Bum steer,* poor advice. **1953** R. Wright *Outsider* 148: And if you gave me a bum steer 'bout your name and address—... **1955** Graziano & Barber *Somebody Up There* 331: That means somebody give the books a bum steer. **1958** in Hayakawa *Use & Misuse of Language* 174: You would think that they would turn away in disgust from the voodoo men who gave them such a bum steer. **1963** D. Tracy *Brass Ring* 12: Did I ever give you a bum steer, Kelly? **1968** Cuomo *Thieves* 340: I guess I gave you a bum steer on him. **1972** Ramsay *No Longer on Map* 4: So the Spanish conquerors' usual attitude toward "bum steers" is clear enough. **1992** A. Dershowitz, synd. column in *Daily Beacon* (Univ. Tenn.) (Dec. 4) 4: Journalists with a stake in proving Boesky...had not given them a bum steer.

bum trip *n.* **1.** *Narc.* a terrifying or unpleasant experience induced by a psychotropic, esp. hallucinogenic, drug. [Despite the evidence of the dates, this is prob. the orig. meaning.]
1968 (cited in Spears *Drugs & Drink* 184). **1971** W. Kemp, in *Inter. Jour. Adds.* 351: *Bum trip.* An unpleasant drug experience, particularly a "bad trip" on an hallucinogen. **1974** Hyde *Mind Drugs* 152: *Bummer...Bum Trip...Bad...*[drug] trip.
2. an unpleasant experience or person.
1966 H.S. Thompson *Hell's Angels* 135: It was obviously a bum trip. They...felt deceived and they wanted to retaliate. **1970** *Nat. Lampoon* (May) 6: She says that Homer was a bum trip, and she bad-mouths Christ too. **1970** *Current Slang* V 4: *Bum Trip,* n. A lazy or uninteresting person.—High school students, both sexes, New Mexico. **1973** Overgard *Hero* 55: This whole thing was beginning to shape up like a bum trip. **1988** *Nat. Lampoon* (Apr.) 66: Hey, I know. That was a bum trip. I needed bucks bad.

bum-trip *v.* **1.** to depress, anger, or annoy.
1967 Yablonsky *Hippie Trip* 209: I mean everybody would bum-trip the shit out of me. **1967** Wolf *Love Generation* 69: And they've got a philosophy that...obliges them to love somebody who's bum-tripping them. **1969** *New American Rev.* (No. 6) (Apr.) 211: I don't know how many times I been bum-tripped and burned by poets and I hate the bastards. **1987** *Werewolf* (Fox-TV): Don't bum-trip me, man!
2. *Narc.* to have a BUM TRIP, 1.
1967–68 von Hoffman *Parents Warned Us* 77: Aren't you going to help my friend?...She's bum-tripping bad. **1978** S. King *Stand* 37: A girl...had bum-tripped and gone screaming down the...beach as naked as a jay.

bumwad *n.* toilet paper; *(hence)* newspapers, magazines, etc., supposedly fit only for such use.
1896 in J.M. Carroll *Benteen-Goldin Lets.* 292 [ref. to 1877]: "Yes, General," said I, "bum-wad is good enough for that purpose." **1893–1903** in *JAF* (Apr. 1945) 127: With us the word "bum" never meant buttock

[*sic*] as in England except in the term "bumwad." **1928** *AS* (Aug.) 452: *Bumwad*—The Midshipman's home-town newspaper. **1936** Le Clercq *Rabelais* 42: I cured it by applying my cod-piece for bum-wad. **1941** in Legman *Limerick* 141: Bum-wad's all right in its way. **1958** Cope & Dyer *Petty Off. Gde.* (ed. 2) (glossary): *Bumwad.* Slang for a newspaper or magazine. (Particularly that suitable for use as toilet paper.) **1958** S.H. Adams *Tenderloin* 228: "Well, he's still got his affadavits [*sic*]." "Bum-wad." **1966** Noel & Bush *Naval Terms* 77: *Bumwad:* Slang: a newspaper or a magazine. Also, toilet paper.

bun *n.* **1.a.** a state of drunkenness; esp. in phr. **have a bun on** to be drunk.
1898 Kountz *Baxter's Letters* 15: Oh! But I got a lovely bun on. **1901** "H. McHugh" *J. Henry* 16: You've got another bun on! How dare you trail into my flat with your tide high enough to float a battleship? **1904** in "O. Henry" *Works* 69: Jerry has got a "bun." **1907** *Reader* (Aug.) 250: If you come in here with a bun...don't lean it up against things. **1907** Bush *Enlisted Man* 124: Captain Eight still has a nice little "bun" on. **1910** in McCay *Little Nemo* 240: He's got a bun! The captain has a bun! **1926** E. Springs *Nocturne* 113: Why the bun in the heat of the afternoon? **1940** E. O'Neill *Long Day's Journey* I: And who do you think I met there, with a beautiful bun on? **1950** *New Yorker* (Apr. 29) 30: Getting a bun on from a bottle he was hiding. **1971** Horan *Blue Messiah* 45: I bring up the pint, then when she has a bun on she rings the bell. **1976** Hayden *Voyage* 232: I'm gettin' a nice ol' bun-on outa this booze.
b. a drinking spree; bender.
1915 "High Jinks, Jr." *Choice Slang* 106: Go on a bun. **1927** Shay *Pious Friends* xi: Can you recall those days? The Naughty Nineties? The days when...a bender was called a bun; when a man who was frequently intoxicated was an old toper and not a souse?
c. a fit, as of laughter; JAG.
1918 Witwer *Baseball to Boches* 116: On the level, it was more like havin' a laughin' bun on than anything else!
2.a. usu. *pl.* a buttock; *pl.* (used as a partial euphem. for ASS in most of its idiomatic constructions).
1877 in J.M. Carroll *Camp Talk* 109: The sight of the picture [of a *houri*] in these *hard* times is almost enough to make me want to scrape it from "Bubbies to buns." **1961** L.G. Richards *TAC* 93: My buns are dead. *Ibid.* 138: That was better than dunking my buns in the Pacific. **1962** Cory & LeRoy *Homosexual & Soc.* 262: Buns...Buttocks. **1966** Fariña *Down So Long* 82: And you bet your rosy buns they threw me out, man. **1967** Mailer *Vietnam* 27: Up your buns. **1971** T.C. Bambara *Gorilla* 15: This here the colored matron Brandy and her friends call Thunderbuns. **1971** Woodley *Dealer* 116: You're set up well for the game. Until somebody hits you, catches you correct, really busts your buns. **1972** Andrews & Dickens *Big House* 26: It's colder'n a polar bear's buns out dere. **1972** Wambaugh *Blue Knight* 16: Long ago I decided to admire her big buns from afar. **1977** Corder *Citizens Band* 116: I've been...freezing my buns off waiting for you. **1978** *Nat. Lampoon* (Aug.) 10: We bust our buns all day, every day. **1981** *Nat. Lampoon* (June) 50: I took a breast in one hand and a bun in the other. **1981** *Easyriders* (Oct.) 6: My ol' lady has been bustin' buns on it, too, cleanin', polishin', packin' bearings. **1983** Breathed *Bloom Co.* 84: Let's blast their buns off! **1991** *Sally Jessy Raphaël* (synd. TV): I worked my buns off.
b. the rump; ASS.
1951 [VMF-323] *Old Ballads* 13: She sat down and couldn't get her bun free. **1954–60** *DAS* 76: *Bun...*The human posterior. **1974** E. Thompson *Tattoo* 228: The boy's pale bun.

¶ In phrases:

¶ **butter a bun** [cf. BUTTERED BUN] to engage in copulation.
1957 O. Brand *Bawdy Songs* III (LP): This is number one/And I'm buttering up her bun,/Roll me over, lay me down, and do it again. **1970** *Nat. Lampoon* (Apr.) 56: The Farmer's Daughter Butters Her Bun or "A Roll in the Hay Beats a Turkey in the Straw."

¶ **have a bun in the oven** to be pregnant.
*1951 in *OEDS* I. **1974** N.Y.U. student: She had another bun in the oven at the time. *1980 Leland *Kiwi-Yank. Dict.* 19: *Bun in the oven:* Pregnant. **1990** *Murphy Brown* (CBS-TV): You gals want a leave of absence every time you got a bun in the oven! **1993** *Beyond Reality* (USA-TV): You know, I've got like a bun in the oven.

¶ **take the bun** to take the cake. Also vars.
1882 Miller & Harlow *9'-51"* 146: We are consciensiously at a loss to decide "who yanks the bun." **1887** *N.O. Lantern,* in *AS* XXV (1950) 31: But the "pale and yellow babe of her white sister" takes the bun. **1894** Barnard College *Annual* 67: In short,...in all we take the "bun." **1895** *DN* I 414: *Yank the bun...*to take the cake. **1896** *DN* I 414: "That takes the bun," that's very good...Also *yanks the bun.* **1901** Irwin *Sonnets*

(unp.): "To take the cake," for instance, a figure from the cake-walk of the negroes, becomes to "capture" or "corral" the "bun" or "biscuit." **1907** Corbin *Cave Man* 85: In slickness, I yield you the bun!

bunch *n. Stu.* nonsense; rubbish.

1901 Wister *Philosophy* 15: "Oh, bunch!" exclaimed the second tennis boy, in the slang of his period, which was the early eighties.

¶ In phrase:

¶ **get up in a bunch** to become needlessly excited.

1982 in Terkel *Good War* 3: It's just a story in the past....I don't get myself up in a bunch about it.

bunch *v.* Esp. *West.* to quit (one's job); to leave.—often constr. with *it*.

1927 *AS* (June) 391: To *bunch*, or to *drag it*, means to quit [one's job]. **1936** McCarthy *Mosshorn* (unp.): When a cowboy says I'm going to bunch it...that means he is leaving. **1958** McCulloch *Woods Words* 23: *Bunch the job*—To quit suddenly. **1966** in *DARE*. **1978** in *Ibid.*: "Hey, Joe! You stilla workin' inna schkool?" "No, I bunched dat job."

bunch of fives see s.v. FIVE, *n.*

bunco *n.* [fr. *banco* < var. of Sp *banca*, a kind of card game] **1.a.** a kind of dishonest gambling game played with dice. Now *S.E.* Also **bunko.**

1873 Lening *N.Y. Life* 251: The Banco or Bunco Swindle...is partly a lottery and partly a game of hazard, in which loaded dice are used. **1938** in *DA* 220: Eight-Dice Cloth was introduced into San Francisco by a crooked gambler who made various changes in the method of play and christened it Banco. After a few years this was corrupted into Bunco.

b. the playing of a banco game or other swindle; swindling; fraud. Also attrib.

1904 in "O. Henry" *Works* 329: There's too big a protective tariff on bunco. **1911–12** J. London *Smoke Bellew* 287: The fattest suckers that ever fell for the get-rich-quick bunco. **1935** in Botkin *Sidewalks* 295: Unchallenged King of Bunco throughout the West. **1970** N.Y.U. student: Can't they arrest those people for bunco? **1973** Key *Subliminal Seduction* 26: The one crime not accepted by [prison] inmates is *confidence* or *bunko*. **1981** Wambaugh *Glitter Dome* 106: Charged with a bunco crime. **1989** Kienzle *Eminence* 175: This was some sort of bunco scam.

c. deceit or flattery; bosh.

1914 Jackson & Hellyer *Vocab.* 21: *Bunco*...Deceit. **1940** Zinberg *Walk Hard* 18: Maybe this is bunko and maybe this is it. *Ibid.* 60: That was bunko, anybody would squirm if you got them right. **1943** J.T. Farrell *Days of Anger* 187: What the hell kind of bunco is that?

2. a swindler; BUNCO MAN.

1879 *Nat. Police Gaz.* (July 26) 5: The bunko began, "Why, you d—d fool, you —." **1884** in *DA*. **1900** in Sampson *Ghost Walks* 225: Jim Flimflammer, the bunco. **1929** *AS* (June) 338: *Bunko*—A fakir [*sic*]. **1956** Sorden & Ebert *Logger's* 6 [ref. to a1925]: *Bunko*, A man hired to steer lumberjacks into dives.

3.a. *Police.* BUNCO SQUAD.—constr. without preceding article.

1947 J.C. Higgins *Railroaded* (film): Take these ladies down to bunco. **1959** Burroughs *Naked Lunch* 3: The Bunko people are really carrying a needle for the Rube. **1972** N.Y.U. student: Then they'll turn the whole thing over to bunco. **1978** Diehl *Sharky's Machine* 68: I been in Bunco, six years in Robbery.

b. *Police.* BUNCO COP.

1964–66 R. Stone *Hall of Mirrors* 65: The buncos, the morals, the immigrations, everybody wanted to talk to Farley the sailor.

bunco *adj.* intended to deceive; fraudulent. See also BUNCO GAME and related entries.

1902–03 Ade *People You Know* 66: She had gazed at the Bunco Illustration of the swell Structure with bushy Trees dotting the Lawn.

bunco *v.* to swindle or cheat (orig. at banco); (*hence*) to fool.

1875 in *DAE*: The fugitive is the same person who bunkoed a stranger out of $75 recently. **1889** Barrère & Leland *Dict. Slang* I 205: The writer is well acquainted with an English gentleman who, while travelling in the United States, was "bunkoed" out of several thousand dollars. **1895** Townsend *Fadden Explains* 69: I made a bluff 'bout bein too proud t' bunco de house on no confidence game. **1899** in *DAE*: Mrs. Wells is tired of having these shop-keepers bunco her all the time. **1891–1900** Hoyt *Five Plays* 148: I've been bunced! **1902–03** Ade *People You Know* 157: When buncoing a Relative always be sure that the Knock-Out Drops are Regulation Strength. **1903** A.H. Lewis *Boss* 89: Bunco the foe!...take their money and "con" them! *Ibid.* 106: To throw him for some trick he's really turned will bunco these reform guys into

thinkin' that we're on th' level. **1906** J.W. Pullman in *Army & Navy Life* (Aug.) 33: There is no use talking; we have all been bunced! There is a skin game somewhere! No living chickin can win all the time...! **1911** Fletcher *Up the Trail* 26: It then dawned upon the solicitors that they had been bunced. **1915** in Lardner *Gullible* 12: Genevieve...bunkoed the Chink into settin' her free. **1925–26** Black *You Can't Win* 174: The way to sell a brass brick is to bunko yourself first into the belief that your brick is solid gold—the rest is easy. The most successful bunko man is the one who bunkoes himself before he goes after a sucker. **1927** in Hammett *Knockover* 275: Six years before, this Angel Grace Cardigan had buncoed half a dozen Philadelphia boys out of plenty. **1929** T. Gordon *Born to Be* 24: Billy...[had] twenty years' experience in buncoing lewd women. **1942** Rodgers & Hammerstein *Oklahoma!* 58: Say, young feller, you certainly bunkoed me!

bunco artist *n.* a swindler.

1901 Irwin *Sonnets* (unp.): Sleep, like a bunco artist, rubbed it in,/Sold me his ten-cent oil stocks, though he knew/It was a kosher trick to take the tin. **1946** in *DA*. **1949** *Sat. Eve. Post* (Dec. 10) 22: The last great bunco artist in the profession of publicity. **1978** *Barnaby Jones* (NBC-TV): She's...a bunco artist.

bunco cop *n.* a police officer on a BUNCO SQUAD.

1981 Wolf *Roger Rabbit* 100: Woe to the poor bunco cop snooping around here. **1903** Merriman *Letters from a Son* 214: He would have the biggest bunco artist in town skinned to his last nickel by sundown.

bunco game *n.* a banco swindle; (*hence*) a swindle or confidence game of any kind.

1909 Irwin *Con Man* 160: "Gold brick" had already become slang for a bunco game; and when that happens you might as well quit. **1921** in Handy *Blues Treasury* 129: Love is like a gold brick in a bunco game. **1972** Carr *Bad* 181: Pete McNair...'d been busted for running bunko games on old ladies.

bunco joint *n.* a gambling house where patrons are swindled by means of a banco game; (*hence*) any establishment where swindling regularly occurs.

1889 *Century Dict.* 721: Bunko-joint, a house or rendezvous to which strangers are allured, and in which they are victimized, by bunko-men.

bunco man *n.* a swindler who runs a banco game; (*hence*) a confidence man.

1884 Costello *Police Protectors* 369: Charles P. Miller, "king of the bunko men." **1891** Campbell et al. *Darkness & Daylight* 600: This class of swindlers who are known as "bunco men" or "bunco steerers." **1908** Hopper & Bechdolt *9009* 118: Nichols, that bunco-man, he was the stool-pigeon. **1909** Ware *Pass. English* 56: At Mackinao they took him for a lord, and at Cleveland he was taken for a bunko man. **1989** *Crossfire* (CNN-TV) (Oct. 24): Do you think he's just a bunco man and a fraud?

bunco squad *n. Police.* a squad of detectives who investigate confidence swindling. Now *S.E.*

1949 W.R. Burnett *Asphalt Jungle* 11: You say the bunco squad works with the con men. **1973** I. Reed *La. Red* 35: She was exposed by a supernatural bunko squad. **1984** Univ. Tenn. student: Sounds like a job for the bunco squad. **1992** *Beyond Reality* (USA-TV): He's spent most of his life running from bunco squads.

bunco-steerer *n.* [BUNCO, *n.*, 1 + STEERER] a person who lures prospective victims into a bunco game. Hence **bunco-steering,** *n.* Now *S.E.*

1875 in *DAE*: A "bunko-steerer" seems to be a subordinate confidence-man who...conducts them into a back room of some large building where they are "confidenced" of what money they have about them. **1875** in *DA* 220: Bunko-steering. **1878** McElroy *Andersonville* 103: Decoys, "bunko-steerers" at home, would be on the lookout for promising subjects. **1882** in Miller & Snell *Why West Was Wild* 95: Nearly all the tramps, bunko steerers, bummers and dead beats...know "Bobby Gill." **1883** Peck *Peck's Bad Boy* 126: Pa says he thinks I was cut out for a bunko steerer, and I may look for that kind of a job. **1884** *Life* (Aug. 7) 81: Sir, you are a BUNKO STEERER! **1887** Walling *N.Y. Chief of Police* 328: Look at the "confidence man" or "bunco steerer," for instance. **1889** Barrère & Leland *Dict. Slang* I 205: The *bunko-steerers* or "touts," who seek for victims, are selected from the most gentlemanly-looking, well-educated persons that can be found. **1889** "M. Twain" *Conn. Yankee* 245: I will make short work of these bunco-steerers. **1906** Wooldridge *Hands Up* 96: The outside men, known as bunko steerers, approached unsophisticated strangers. **1945** in *DA* 220: This burg's full of bunco steerers. **1975** Julien *Cogburn* 130: Lookin' for a Bunco steerer named Sawdust Charlie.

bundle *n.* [orig. in dial. E] **1.** a large, unpleasant, or disliked woman; (*hence*, in later use) a young woman.

*1830 in *OEDS* I 387: *Bundle*, an opprobrious term applied to females, equivalent to baggage, which perhaps means strictly, a follower of the camp. ******a***1841** in *OEDS* I 387: *Bundle*, a large fat woman. **1899** A.H. Lewis *Sandburrs* 133: When d' victim takes his little ten spaces, his Bundle mourns 'round for a brace of mont's, see! An' then she marries another guy. **1904** *Life in Sing Sing* 246: *Bundle*....a woman. **1910** Hapgood *Types from City Streets* 34: We're a bunch of blokes and bundles from de Lane. **1924** Henderson *Keys to Crookdom* 406: Girl...tommy, bundle, chippy, creeper. **1931** Harlow *Old Bowery* 426 [ref. to *ca*1900]: Walk it just like you was on de lane wit' yer bundle on yer arm. **1959** Fuller *Marines at Work* 148: I found her. I found her. Wow! What a lovely bundle. **1966** in *DARE* I 461.

2.a. loot, as from a theft.

1899 Willard *Tramping* 392: *Bundle*: plunder from a robbery. **1935** D.W. Maurer, in *AS* (Feb.) 13 [ref. to *ca*1910]: *Bundle*....The loot from a burglary.... Any stolen property.

b. a bankroll; (*hence*) a great amount of money; a fortune.

1879 *Nat. Police Gaz.* (Mar. 15) 11: An' he's got...a bundle bigger'n a book. **1896** Crane *Complete Stories* 317: I'll see if I can't cop out a small bundle. **1899** A.H. Lewis *Sandburrs* 152: Joe win out ten spaces for touchin' a farmer for his bundle. **1903** A.H. Lewis *Black Lion Inn* 306: I've got my bundle on Creole Belle. **1903** Ade *Society* 15: Any one who comes in from the Cockleburr District with a Bundle is known as a Newvo Reash. **1905** "H. McHugh" *Search Me* 15: Did they sting you for the whole bundle? **1906** A.H. Lewis *Confessions* 2: I've made my bundle. **1921** A. Jennings *Through Shadows* 49: We got a little bundle. **1975** Berger *Sneaky People* 44: You got to think up a better way to make your bundle. **1976** N. Meyer *W. End Horror* xiii: He got a bundle on it from some jasper in New Mexico who collects stuff like that. **1980** in McCauley *Dark Forces* 442: But was she really justified in taking him for a bundle under false pretenses? **1982** Rucker *57th Kafka* 110: Marston had made his bundle in oil and uranium.

bundle buggy *n. Trucking.* a delivery truck.

1971 Tak *Truck Talk* 23: *Bundle buggy*: a delivery truck.

bundle stiff *n.* BINDLE STIFF.

1937 Reitman *Box-Car Bertha* 9: The bundle stiffs...their jobs in the wheatfields of Minnesota. **1940** *Time* (Feb. 5) 8: You use "bindle stiff."...Proper term is *bundle* stiff. *a***1949** in Kiskaddon *Rhymes* 25: 'Twas hunger that drove on the bundle stiff's trail.

bun-duster *n. Stu.* CAKE-EATER.

1922 in *DN* V 147: We struck a jazz-garden where a bunch of bundusters were necking it....*Bun duster*—a small salaried male person who frequents teas and other entertainments and never makes any effort to repay his social obligations. Otherwise a cake eater.

bung *n.* **1.** the anus.—usu. considered vulgar. Cf. earlier BUNGHOLE.

*1788 Grose *Vulgar Tongue* (ed. 2): *Bung upwards*. Said of a person lying on his face. **1941** in Legman *Limerick* 98: May I bugger your bung? **1951** [VMF-323] *Old Ballads* 6: The bung of the hedgehog, the hedgehog/Can scarcely be boogered at all. **1959** in Cray *Erotic Muse* 73: He missed her twat and hit her bung. **1959** *41st Ftr. Sq. Songbk.* 13: He can shove them up his bung. **1966–67** Stevens *Gunner:* Right through your guts and out your bung.

2. a bruise, esp. a black eye. Cf. BUNG, *v.*, and BUNGER, *n.*, 1.

1843 Carleton *Logbooks* 20: One eye [was] slightly shadowed by a faint knuckular abrasion remotely resembling a *bung*.

3. *Naut.* a master's assistant.

1854 "Youngster" *Swell Life* 344: But the second master and master's assistants—indeed the *genus* Bung (to use the naval name) were *not* included. *Ibid.* 354: Such was the growl of the Bung, from his hammock in the cock-pit.

¶ In phrases:

¶ **hit the bung** to drink liquor excessively; hit the bottle.

1930 Botkin *Folk-Say* 107: I was hitting the bung and raising hell almighty all of a sudden like I gets the salvation and stops boozing and cussing.

¶ **pull the bung out of** to deflate or cause to collapse; take the wind out of someone's sails.

1905 Phillips *Plum Tree* 27: He's a rotten hypocrite; but then, we can always pull the bung out of these Reform movements that way.

bung *v.* **1.** to close (someone's) eye, esp. with a blow; blacken (someone's) eye.—sometimes constr. with *up*.

*1803 in J. Ashton *Eng. Satires on Napoleon* 160: Rotten eggs will I fur-

nish to bung up his eyes. ***1820–21** P. Egan *Life in London* 23: Bung'd up eyes. **1846** N.J.T. Dana *Monterrey* 146: I got up with a big bunged eye. **1854** in W. Still *Underground R.R.* 59: She is smart, but cannot bung my eye. *a***1860** Hundley *So. States* 240: See, with what...grace Jones bungs up Smith's peepers! **1861** in C.W. Wills *Army Life* 27: Bunged eyes and bloody faces. **1881** H.H. Kane *Opium* 91: The eyes appear swollen or "bunged up," as though one had been drinking.

2. (*broadly*) to injure.—constr. with *up*, often as ppl. adj.

1927 Rollins *Jinglebob* 158 [ref. to 1880's]: Why'd I call that bunged up brute an angel? **1938** Bellem *Blue Murder* 79: They claim...that he was all bunged up when they arrested him. **1975** McCaig *Danger Trail* 12: He's too bunged up to see anyone. **1992** J. Garry *This Ol' Drought* 15: He'd gotten his leg bunged up and was gimping around on crutches.

¶ In phrase:

¶ **bung (one's) eye** to take a drink of liquor; to become or (*trans.*) make drunk. [Although this phr. is attested only in E sources, it does point to the similar Amer. terms.]

*1788 Grose *Vulgar Tongue* (ed. 2): *Bung your eye*, drink a dram. ******ca***1800** in Holloway & Black *Later Broadside Ballads* 261: We Bung'd our Eyes together. *Ibid.* 262: She loves to Bung her Eye Sir....you may gain her Female toy,/If once you Bung her Eye Sir.]

bunged *adj.* (see quot.).—also constr. with *out.*

1984 Univ. Tenn. student: *Bunged* is drunk. *Bunged out* is tired.

bunger *n.* **1.** [fr. BUNG, *v.*; cf. BUNG, *n.*, 2] a bruise, esp. a black eye.

1904 *Life in Sing Sing* 246: *Bunger.* A discolored eye. **1935** D.W. Maurer, in *AS* (Feb.) 13 [ref. to period before 1910]: *Bunger.* A bruise or a black eye.

2. BUNG, *n.*, 1.

1969 Beck *Mama Black Widow* 13: My wand must cry deep in your bunger, my dear boy.

bung-fodder *n.* BUMFODDER.

1889 in *Kans. Hist. Qly.* XIII (1944) 128: That worthless wad of outhouse bung-fodder. **1908** *DN* III 295: *Bung-fodder*...Toilet paper or substitute therefor. **1912** in *DARE* I 463.

bunghole *n.* **1.a.** the anus.—usu. considered vulgar.

*1611 Cotgrave *Dict.*: *Cul de cheval.* A small, and ouglie fish, or excrescence of the Sea, resembling a mans bung-hole, and called, the red Nettle. ***1698** Ward *London-Spy* 44: The Angry *Homunculus*...gathered himself up from his own Dunghill,...turning his unsavoury Bung-hole upon the Company. **1934** "J.M. Hall" *Anecdota* 164: He used his third wish getting it out of his wife's bung-hole. **1938** "Justinian" *Americana Sexualis* 14: *Bung-Hole*, n. The anus....C. 19–20. **1952** Geer *New Breed* 90: We'll be ramming bayonets up their bung holes in a week. **1965** Linakis *In Spring* 31: The army would tear out my bunghole at Le Mans and give me a shithouseful of time besides. **1972** D. Pearce *Pier Head Jump* 5: Right up the old bunghole. **1983** Eilert *Self & Country* 62: A round came up through the floor right in my bung hole.

b. the vagina.—usu. considered vulgar.

1964 J. Thompson *Pop. 1280* 127: That's what makes you so goofy, banging her so much....The way you were banging the bunghole, you damned near fell in!

2. ASSHOLE, 2.—usu. considered vulgar.

1965 N. Daniels *Moments of Glory* 132 [ref. to WWII]: Now there was a real bung-hole. **1968** Baker et al. *CUSS* 91: *Bunghole.* A person without much social or academic ability. **1981–85** S. King *It* 563: You...bunghole. **1993** *Beavis & Butt-head* (MTV): I saw her first, bunghole!

bunghole *v.* to engage in anal copulation [with].—usu. considered vulgar.

1939 in Legman *Limerick* 402: The height of my joys is bung-holing boys. *ca***1942** in *Erotic Verse to 1955* 89: We'll bung-hole his girls. **1965** Beech *Make War* 67: You're liable to get bungholed, Otis, if he's as queer as you think he is. **1971** Cole *Rook* 56: Fat Raymond...liked to bunghole. **1979** Grossbach *And Justice* 62: He said he was going to "bunghole" the short-order chef.

bunghole buddy *n.* ASSHOLE BUDDY.—usu. considered vulgar.

1947 Willingham *End as a Man* 151: Then the Bunghole Buddies come along. **1948** J.H. Burns *Lucifer* 146: I've been noticing you're bunghole buddies with the one boog in this dump.

Bungs *n. Naut.* a ship's cooper.—used as a nickname.

1849 Melville *White Jacket* 80: Why, Bungs, they are all open between the staves.

bung-starter *n.* **1.** *Naut.* (see quot.).

1867 Smyth *Sailor's Wd-Bk.*: Bung-starter....a soubriquet for the captain of the hold. Also, a name given to the master's assistant serving his apprenticeship for hold-duties.

2. a bartender.

1884 in Nye *Western Humor* 117: Men with tears in their eyes and breath like a veteran bung-starter. **1908** Whittles *Lumberjack* 199: Here, bung starter, set up to the house. **1953** *ATS* (ed. 2) 103.

bung up see s.v. BUNG, *v.*

bungwad *n.* BUMWAD, 1.

1927 *Immortalia* 142: Is there plenty of bungwad?

bungy *adj.* drunk.

1736–37 in *AS* (Apr. 1937): He's Bungey.

bun-huggers *n.pl. Surfing.* surfing trunks.

1964 *Time* (June 30) 55: Bun-hugger [*sic*]: too tight trunks. **1968** Kirk & Hanle *Surfer's Hndbk.* 137: Bun-huggers: slang for surf trunks. **1993** *Mystery Sci. Theater* (Comedy Central TV): These Italian bun-huggers give me no room at all.

bunion breeder *n. Army.* an infantryman. *Joc.*

1944 Kendall *Service Slang* 3: Bunion Breeders...infantry, also known as Paddlefeet. **1942–44** in *AS* (Feb. 1946) 31: Bunion Breeder, n. Infantry man.

bunion derby *n.* a cross-country marathon foot race.

1928 *New Yorker* (Dec. 8) 31: C.C. Pyle...invented the bunion derby and lured...Red Grange and Suzanne Lenglen into the gilded cage of professionalism.

bun-joint *n.* [*bun* + JOINT] a coffeehouse.

1895 Townsend *Fadden & Other Stories* 244: Then I took my potential scoop to a coffee-house—a "bun-joint," in his slang—and fed him.

bunk *n.* [fr. *buncombe*, strongly infl. by BUNCO] **1.a.** nonsense; bosh.—also constr. with *the.* Now *S.E.*

1900 Ade *More Fables* 103: He surmised that the Bunk was about to be handed to him. **1901** F.P. Dunne *Mr. Dooley's Opinions* 87: Th' earnest youth in search iv a career in life 'll be taught lyin' individjally an' in classes, lyin' be ear an' be note,...th' con, th' bunk, th' poetic lie, th' business lie, [etc.]. **1914** Jackson & Hellyer *Criminal Slang* 21: If you fall for this bunk, you're a simp. **1916** Clark *Soldier-Letters* (Oct. 6) 47: This nervous strain stuff is a bunch of bunk. **1916** Henry Ford, in *Chi. Trib.* (May 25) 10: History is more or less bunk. **1922** Iowa State College *Bomb* 410: All this talk about prohibition is all bunk. **1928** Panzram *Killer* 160: Honor among thieves is the bunk. **1953** R. Wright *Outsider* 101: That's what this goddamn country says, but it's the bunk. **1954** Matheson *Born of Man & Woman* 216: Superstition....It's the bunk. **1957** Berkeley *Deadly Mantis* (film): People used to think carnivorous plants were the bunk. **1971** *Rowan & Martin's Laugh-In* (NBC-TV) (Feb. 2): I'll say astrology is a bunch of bunk! **1977** Lyon *Tenderness* 47: Some of it was so much macho bunk.

b. something that is worthless or unpleasant.—formerly often constr. with *the.*

1915 Howard *God's Man* 272: How'll you ever know the goods from the bunk? **1921** E. O'Neill *Hairy Ape* 192: Yuh ain't no good for no one. Yuh're de bunk. **1927** *AS* (Mar.) 277: It's the bunk—It's not according to my taste. **1931** Cressey *Taxi-Dance Hall* 42: These white guys that come up here are all the bunk. **1932** *AS* VII 399: Bunk...Anything unpleasant. **1934** Appel *Brain Guy* 157: A frienda mine said he spoke to his girl in your drug store awhile ago. We think he's the bunk. **1972** Smith & Gay *Don't Try It* 198: Bunk. Bad dope. **1987** *21 Jump St.* (Fox-TV): "He sells crack when he's got it, bunk when he don't." "Bunk?" "Soap, wax, macadamia nuts—anything that'll pass for crack."

2. a swindler; BUNCO MAN.

1901 A.H. Lewis *Croker* 64: A lot of bunks who gives me a song an' dance about a tombstone for Dempsey. **1902–03** Ade *People You Know* 180: The Bunk who has the Joint Note already made out and ready to be signed, usually has a Talk calculated to make a Heart of Stone mellow to the Consistency of a Baked Apple. **1911** A.H. Lewis *Apaches of N.Y.* 75: They're a bunch of cheap bunks. **1911–12** Ade *Knocking the Neighbors* 203: He is a prize Bunk, a two-handed Grafter, a Short-Change Artist and a Broadway Wolf.

3. an imposture; a fraud.

1893 F.P. Dunne, in C. Fanning *Dunne & Dooley* 30: I think th' other one...is a sort of bunk. **1902–03** Ade *People You Know* 162: Next to the Miniature painted on Ivory, the modern Photo is the prize Bunk of the Universe. **1906** Green *Actors' Boarding House* 194: All the other places is bunks. **1909** Irwin *Con Man* 117: He looked over the shell-games...and pronounced them a bunk. **1912** *Adventure* (May) 57: It's a

bunc—a con game. **1919** Witwer *Alex the Great* 25: Mutterin' somethin' about Manhattan bein' a well-advertised bunk.

4. BUNKIE.—used in direct address.

1919 Jacobsen *Blue & Gray* 4 [ref. to WWI]: Take it from me, "bunk," you're wrong.

5. a hiding place.

1931 C. Ford *Coconut Oil* 156: It's this dandy "bunk" for ferns. No one knows of this place but you and me, June. **1949** (quot. at BUNK, *v.*, 2).

¶ In phrase:

¶ **shoot the bunk** to talk to no purpose; *shoot the bull* s.v. BULL, *n.*, 9.

1925 J.V.A. Weaver *Collected Poems* 104: Don't go shootin' the bunk, or makin' prayers,/And all that stuff.

bunk *v.* **1.** to fool or trick; impose upon; also (*intrans.*) to tell falsehoods.

1888 *Stag Party* 39: Surely you have not them beguiled,/It cannot be that both you have bunked. **1899** Kountz *Baxter's Letters* 76: Upon learning that he had been bunked, Dick became very dignified. **1908** in H.C. Fisher *A. Mutt* 40: Tobasco bunked her into influencing her nephew to confess. **1908** in Fleming *Unforgettable Season* 40: Mathewson...bunked those Phillies. **1910** *N.Y. Eve. Jour.* (Apr. 16) 11: $1,000 note? Why that's a one dollar bill—you've been bunked! **1926** in Lardner *Haircut & Others* 19: They was no answer and it must of come to her all of a sudden that she'd been bunked. **1929–30** Farrell *Young Lonigan* 81: He's always trying to bunk a guy. **1934** Appel *Brain Guy* 133: It boils down to one thing. No use bunking about it. You want to get hold of my kids. **1988** *Married with Children* (Fox-TV): Bundy's the name; bunking the public's my game.

2. to cache; to hide.

1916 *Rio Grande Rattler* (Sept. 6) 6: Several cautious canteen managers...had "bunked" several hundred copies behind counters and under cracker barrels. **1949** Ellson *Tomboy* 24: "Those cigarettes we bunked in the lot." "Yeah, I'd like to know who copped them." "I don't see how anybody could know they were there. That's a good bunk we have." **1958–60** Freeman *Out of Burning* 54: Where are they bunked?...I looked over every incha the house.

bunk-crusher *n. Army.* a lazy person who likes to lie in bed; SACK RAT.

1919 Law *2nd Army* (unp.): If there are any "bunk crushers" in the A.E.F. that can hold a candle to our specialists, let's hear about 'em. We believe that one of our men holds the world's championship long distance sleeping and snoring record.

bunker plate *n. Navy.* **1.** a large foreign coin of little value.

1917 in K. Morse *Letters* 9: The boys detest the big one and two cent [French] coppers. Known to the Navy as "bunker plates," in the army they pass as "clackers." **1918** Kauffman *Navy at Work* 10: They all want to get rid of their "bunker plates" (the French five and ten centime pieces) and they're spoiling the town's children by tossing these coppers away. **1919** *Our Navy* (Aug.) 61 [ref. to *ca*1913]: We used to lay up in Liverpool trying to bum a few bunker plates to go over on the ferry. **1919** Battey *Sub. Destroyer* 37: The Azorean pennies are the joy of small boys everywhere because of their enormous size, and to sailors are known as "bunker plates."

2. *pl.* pancakes.

1918 Ruggles *Navy Explained* 22: Hot cakes, flapjacks, or pancakes are also called "bunker plates."

bunk fatigue *n. Army & USMC.* sleep.

1915 Garrett *Army Ballads* 31 [ref. to 1899]: The Bowery Boy is fast asleep/Performing Bunk-fatigue. **1918** Crowe *Pat Crowe* 163: After our meager lunch, we lounged around to complete this requisite amount of "bunk fatigue" for the day. **1918** Murrin *With the 112th* 96: Everyone...is taking what "bunk fatigue" he can at the present time. **1919** Duffy *G.P.F. Book* 326: Many were the arms and legs that found relief in "bunk fatigue." **1919** Small *Story of the 47th* 63: Those who didn't care to watch the "choo-choos" could go on "bunk fatigue" or play cards (if you could get a pack). **1919** Stokes *Songs of Services* 69: No more we'll practice bunk fatigue. **1931** *Leatherneck* (Feb.) 13: Mayberry is putting in his bunk fatigue hours. **1942** in *Best from Yank* 64: You're in your barracks now, and you're snatching a little bunk fatigue. **1943** Hubbard *Gung Ho* (film): He's probably so exhausted he's doing bunk fatigue right now. **1982** D. Williams *Hit Hard* 106 [ref. to WWII]: You wonder why the men...do bunk fatigue when they get a chance.

bunk flying *n. USAF.* exaggerated discussion of flying. Also **bunk-room flying.**

1933 Stewart *Airman Speech* 51: Bunk-room flying. **1941** *AS* (Oct.)

164: *Bunk Flying*. Talking aviation in barracks. (Air Corps). **1941** in Wiener *Flyers* 45: *Bunk flying*. A "bull session." **1965** LeMay & Kantor *Mission* 331: Everyone always said in bunk-flying sessions, "There's just one place where I don't want to be wounded."

bunk habit *n. Narc. & Pris.* a tendency or desire to sleep excessively, esp. as a result of addiction to opiates.
   1936 Dai *Opium Add.* 197: One who likes to lie around a lay-out is said to have a *bunk-habit*. **1958** Gilbert *Vice Trap* 88: He had that bunk habit of junkies. **1967** Maurer & Vogel *Narc. Add.* (ed. 3) 346: *Bunk habit*. A tendency to sleep a great deal.

bunkhouse lawyer *n.* [sugg. by GUARDHOUSE LAWYER, SEA LAWYER, etc.] *Logging.* a captious or contentious employee.
   1958 McCulloch *Woods Words* 24: *Bunkhouse lawyer*—A man who thinks he knows all the rules and insists on getting his share and then some.

bunkie *n.* **1.a.** *Army & USMC.* a bunkmate.
   1858 Vielé *Following the Drum* 218: Which triumph over paternal love I rewarded by giving him Jack for his "bunkie" **1865** Springer *Sioux Country* 37: Bugler "Vetter" is my "bunky." **1888** McConnell *Five Years a Cavalryman* 20 [ref. to 1866]: My "bunkie" and I succeeded in getting permission to remain on deck. **1892** Cox *Five Years in Army* 48: My "bunky" would play "Twenty-one," notwithstanding all my advice and protests. **1906** M'Govern *Sarjint Larry* (glossary): *Bunkie*—A bed-fellow; a man who sleeps in the bunk-adjoining; a soldier who pitches his shelter-half with another is his "bunkie." **1909** Moss *Officer's Man.* 283: *Bunkie*—A soldier who shares the shelter of a comrade. **1913** Meyers *Ten Years in the Ranks* 2 [ref. to 1854]: He assigned me to "bunk" with the only boy in the room who had no bedfellow or "bunkie." **1919** T.H. Kelly *What Outfit, Buddy?* 3: Sergeant George Neil, McGee's pal and bunkie... **1934** Wagner *Old Neutriment* 45 [ref. to ca1870]: My bunkie joshed me. He got to callin' me "Old Neutriment." *a*1949 D. Levin *Mask of Glory* 263: He was my bunkie. **1985** Petit *Peacekeepers* 90: Tolbert's bunkie, a staff sergeant named Cummings.
   b. *Stu.* a roommate.
   1918 *DN* V 23: *Bunkie*, n. A roommate. Univ. Idaho and State Coll. of Washington.
   2. *Army.* a friend; comrade.
   1865 in Woodruff *Union Soldier* 20: Corpl. Sherrick arrived...accompanied by my old Bunky, Sergt. Sheeks. **1876** in King *Campaigning With Crook* 149: Wid bunkies shtarvin' by our side, no rations was the rule. **1899** Coston *Spanish-American War Volunteer* 9 [a white soldier speaking to a black]: "Hold on, bunkie, here's my cup." **1907** *Reader* (Sept.) 348: I'd showed 'em I was a good game guy, but I didn't have no bunkies. **1955** Post *Little War of Pvt. Post* 205 [ref. to 1898]: "Bunkie" was the army term for "pal" in those days. To me "buddy" sounds the same, but with a cold in the head. **1980** Hogan *Lawman's Choice* 57: Buck and Travis was bunkies of ours.
   3. (used as a condescending term of direct address to a man).
   1978 Maggin *Superman* 206: Excuse me, bunkie. Don't you have anything useful to do? **1980** *Nat. Lampoon* (Aug.) 70: The sign says *All you can eat*, Bunky. **1984** Heath *A-Team* 138: I gotta tell ya, bunkey, you're hangin' by a thread with me. **1985** WINS Radio News (Dec. 10): Hiya, Bunky; this is the Old Philosopher.

bunk lizard *n. Mil.* SACK RAT.
   1918 Ruggles *Navy Explained* 27: *Bunk Lizard*. That fellow who is always sleeping; never able to get out of his bunk or hammock. **1924** *Amer. Legion Wkly.* (June 13) 6 [ref. to WWI]: "Snap out, you bunk lizards," suddenly yells our sarge's voice.

bunko var. BUNCO.

bunk police *n. Army.* BUNK FATIGUE. [Quots. ref. to WWI.]
   1924 Nason *3 Lights* 89: I hope their friends leave us alone long enough for me to do a bit of bunk police. **1926** Nason *Chevrons* 130: I'm going to do some bunk police. **1928** Nason *Sgt. Eadie* 32: I think it's time to do a little bunk police. I can't keep my eyelids apart much longer. *Ibid.* 130: You guys at the echelon ain't got nothin' to do but bunk police! **1930** Nason *Corporal Once* 61: I wish you'd lay off an' let a man do a little bunk police.

bunk sheet *n.* a sensational newspaper.
   1929–30 Dos Passos *42d Parallel* 284: I got to go back to the daily bunksheet.

bunkum *adj.* excellent.
   1834 *Military & Naval Magazine of U.S.* (Mar.) 24: My companions caused to be put up in parcels, a quantity of candy and cakes; "For" said

Santin,..."these will be *bunkum* about taps." *Ibid.* (May) 203: "Oh, I'm bunkum," replied Dave. "I never enjoyed myself more." **1837** *Spirit of Times* (Feb. 18) 4: We state "upon his word, which is as good as his bond," bunkum both, that [etc.]. **1856** *Ballou's Dollar Mo. Mag.* (Nov.) 424: If Joe Grummet's advice is good at sea, it must be particularly bunkum in Marseilles. **1879** *United Services* (Jan.) 34: Just think of my being here....Ain't it bunkum? **1904** *DN* II 395: *Bunkum*, adj. Fine, good, first-class. "Those buckwheat cakes are just *bunkum*." N.Y. **1905** *DN* 72 [Arkansas]: *Bunkum*, adj. Excellent. Not uncommon. **1918** in Sharp & Karpeles *Songs of So. Appalachians* I 53: I'll set my foot in a bunkum boat/And sail all on the sea.

bunkumsquint *adj.* (see quot.).
   1911 *DN* III 541: *Bunkumsquint*, adj. Fine, excellent. "Say, that looks bunkumsquint." [used in Nebraska.]

bunky *adj.* [BUNK, *n.* + *-y*] full of nonsense.
   1918 in Hemingway *Sel. Letters* 19: Now I'll write you a nice, cheery, bunky letter in about a week, so don't get low over this one.

bunned *adj.* [fr. BUN, *n.*, 1.a.] drunk.
   1908 H. Green *Maison* 206: He was a little bunned. **1922** in *DN* V 148: Shellacked—stewed, bunned, etc.

bunny *n.* **1.** a person.—used mainly in comb.; (*esp.*) **dumb bunny** a simpleton.
   1921 *DN* V 141: *Dumb bunny*, n. A somewhat stupid person, whose stupidity is not so great as that of a *nit-wit*, q.v. *Dumb-bunny* implies a shade of endearment or toleration. "My dear, you are the preshest old dumb-bunny!" (Said to be a corruption of dumb-bell). **1927** Mayer *Between Us Girls* 30: She is a dumb bunny about those sort of things. **1931** *AS* VI 206: *Tough bunny*: hard-hearted or hard-boiled person. **1934** in Ruhm *Detective* 96: They put Kennedy on the dramatic page for a spell and what does the bunny do one night but get tight and go to review a play at the Channock Theatre. **1937** Odets *Golden Boy* 277: Get me some fights—fights with contenders, not with dumb-bunny club fighters. **1971** Curtis *Banjo* 84: Take cover, you dumb bunny! **1974** Millard *Thunderbolt* 54: You *are* a naive bunny...Would *you* announce a find like that to the income tax people, or the cops, or the government, stupid? **1974** Angelou *Gather Together* 88: You dumb bunny.
   2. the buttocks. Cf. BUN, 2.
   1936 Kingsley *Dead End* 727: Go on now, or yuh git dis mickey...red hot...up yuh bunny! **1971** Cole *Rook* 145: Kiss my bunny!
   3. a sexy young woman, esp. one who associates with skiers or surfers. See also BEACH BUNNY, SKI BUNNY. [The 1707 quot. is simply an endearment.]
   [*1707 in Burford *Bawdy Verse* 218: Such Power hath my tripping Doe, my little Pretty Bunny.] **1936** McCarthy *Mosshorn* (unp.): *Cow-bunnies*. n. A cunning name for wives or sweethearts of ranchers. **1942** *ATS* 356, 385. *ca*1950 in *West. Folk.* XVIII (1959) 38: Get six from the ski school to carry my coffin,/Six little bunnies to sing me a song. **1968** S. Ross *Hang-Up* 94: Everybody was out, all the surfers and the bunnies and the ho-dads. **1968** Kirk & Hanle *Surfer's Hndbk.* 137: *Bunny*: non- or beginning girl surfer. **1972** N.Y.C. *Five Boroughs* (Nov.) 19: A heated outdoor pool draws ogling skiers in stocking caps to watch the bunnies in their bikinis.
   4.a. *Basketball.* a short, easy shot.
   1970 in Wimmer *Schoolyard Game* 59: I spun in a little left-handed bunny, using English. **1970** Quammen *Walk the Line* 63: Tyrone would miss the bunny and rebound, miss again, then drop it in. **1974** Univ. Wisc. student: A *bunny* is a real easy shot. **1980** Wielgus & Wolff *Basketball* 41: *Bunny*...Chippie...a very short, simple shot.
   b. *Stu.* (see quot.).
   1984 Algeo *Stud Buds & Dorks*: An easy college course...*bunny*.
   ¶ In phrase:
   ¶ **for the bunnies** very foolish. Cf. *for the birds* s.v. BIRD.
   1961 L.G. Richards *TAC* 163: These inspectors pulled some dillies in their mock war games, but this one was for the bunnies.

bunny boots *n.pl.* tall white felt or insulated boots.
   1954 in F. Harvey *Jet* 117: Fur parkas, felt bunny boots. **1954** in *DARE* I 465. **1977** Langone *Life at Bottom* 197: The best thing we did, though, was get out there with nothin' on, just your bunny boots, and you'd stand there, wavin' bottles of booze, and they'd just about shit, think we'd all gone Asiatic.

bunny hole *n. Army & USMC.* a hole dug in the side of a trench to provide shelter for a single soldier during a bombardment.

1953 Russ *Last Parallel* 81: These caves correspond roughly to our "bunny holes," which are only large enough for one man to huddle in during a mortar barrage. **1969** Scanlan *Davis* 365 [ref. to Korean War]: Bunny holes were one-man caves scooped into the sides of trenches to protect infantry from mortar fire.

bunny slope *n. Skiing.* a beginners' slope.
   1971 *Current Slang* 9: *Bunny slope,* n. The easiest slope at a ski area.

bunny suit *n.* an insulated flight suit or other kind of heavy protective suit.
   1966 Cameron *Sgt. Slade* 14 [ref. to WWII]: Goddam flak tore through my pants and shorted a wire in my bunny suit. ***1978** in Partridge *DSUE* (ed. 8) 159. **1983** Nelkin & Brown *Workers* 39: My boss told us to change these bag-out filters. We had to put on a bunny suit and a respirator. **1991** Marcinko & Weisberg *Rogue Warrior* 48: A bunny suit…is a reinforced, one-piece, hooded jumpsuit, into which is constructed a heavy nylon harness, radio cable, and a microphone in the hood.

bun-on see BUN, *n.,* 1.a.

bunting *n. Naut.* clothing.
   1855 Brougham *Chips* 342: Always purwidin' those savages possessed the blessin's of buntin'.
   ¶ In phrase:
   ¶ **talk bunting** *Naut.* to communicate by means of signal flags.
   1833 N. Ames *Old Sailor's Yarns* 380: The schooner also made an attempt to "talk bunting," or show colors. **1834** *Mil. & Naval Mag.* (Sept.) 18: This is what the sailors call *talking bunting.*

bunting-tosser *n. Navy.* a signalman quartermaster.
   ***1903** in Kipling *Traffics & Discoveries* 51: I'm only a mildewed buntin'-tosser. **1918** *Sat. Eve. Post* (Aug. 24) 9: "What difference, so long's as it's a good idea?" argued the bunting tosser, otherwise the signalman.

bupkis *n.* [Yid, 'beans'] Orig. *Jewish-Amer.* absolutely nothing; (in neg. constr.) anything at all. Occ. as adj.
   1942 Liebling *Telephone* 60: The best you can get there…is a chance to work Saturday night at a ruptured saloon for *bupkis. Bupkis* is a Yiddish word which means "large beans." **1967** Michaels *Women of Green Berets* 127: He made one or two tries through channels and he got *bupkiss* for his troubles. You know what *bupkiss* are, pal, or do you? **1972** Parker *Emotional Common Sense* 125: As a worthless person *you are entitled to bupkis* ("nothing," to those uninitiated in the Jewish tradition). **1976** *Deadly Game* (ABC-TV): One year they make it big, the next they don't sell bupkis. **1985** *Fame* (synd. TV series): The guy hasn't earned bupkis in ten years. **1987** M. Brooks *Spaceballs* (film): The ring is bupkis. I found it in a Cracker Jack box.

buppie *n.* [*b*lack + *yuppie*] *Journ.* a young, urban black professional.
   1984 *People* (Jan. 9) 47: Bryant Gumbel and Vanessa Williams are both Buppies. **1986** *Time* (Aug. 4) 26: He is the clear favorite of the upwardly mobile young blacks, known as buppies, whose BMWs decorate the lot of his sprawling campaign headquarters. **1992** H.L. Gates, Jr., in *N.Y. Times* (Mar. 1) II 12: Abandoning his cold-as-ice, well-educated buppie fiancée, his stiff WASP-manqué manners and Brooks Brothers wardrobe, Daymon does win the working-class woman.

burbs *n.pl.* suburbs.
   1971 (cited in *W10*). **1976** Calif. woman, age *ca*30: We moved from a house in the burbs out into farm country. **1984** *Chicago Sun-Times* (Aug. 8): Cash-rich burbs rank 5th in U.S. **1986** E. Weiner *Howard the Duck* 225: The nice-sweet-kids from the 'burbs. **1992** G. Wolff *Day at Beach* 87: Middle-class hobos on the lam from the burbs.

burg *n.* [back formation from place names such as *Pittsburgh*] a town; a city.—often used disparagingly.
   1835 *Knickerbocker* (July) 63: Susan and Samuel Smith, loafer and loafress of this burgh. **1843** *Spirit of Times* (Mar. 25) 43: Two "individs" in this "burg" will give our friend Greer the "run of his teeth" whenever he visits New York. **1882** "M. Twain" *Life on Miss.* 272: We could have visited that ancient and singular burg, "Pilot-town," which stands on stilts in the water. **1885** Siringo *Texas Cowboy* 136: The little burg would put on city airs. **1889** Univ. Rochester *Rochester Songs* 3: A burg lies on the Erie Ditch Not far from Pittsford town, It bears the name of Rochester And is of vast reknown [*sic*]. **1894** Bangs *3 Wks. in Pol.* 3: Where is this favored burg? **1900** Willard & Hodler *Powers That Prey* 144: He's the meanest grafter in this berg. **1901** Hodder *New Americans* 298: The amount of money I've poured into this "burg" would sink a Spanish galleon. **1903** A. Adams *Log of a Cowboy* 264: We were less than

five miles from the burg, and struck a free gait in riding in. **1903** Merriman *Letters from a Son* 69–70: He's fond of the old burgh, at that. **1907** London *The Road* 53: General Kelly's money was "no good" in their burg. **1908** in H.C. Fisher *A. Mutt* 22: Now I want to take you around to see the nicest little lady in the burg. **1909** "O. Henry" *Options* 799: Bobby,…this old burg isn't such a bad proposition in the summertime, after all. **1910** Livingston *Life* 74: Grafters in this "Burg" [steal]…right here in broad daylight. **1911** D. Runyon *Tents of Trouble* 22: We blew from the burg o' New Orleans. **1915** Lardner *Gullible's Travels* 108: But what can we do all day in this burg? **1920** in Kimball & Bolcolm *Sissle & Blake* 82: Just a note to let you know what kind of burg this is. **1922** S. Lewis *Babbitt* 117: I certainly been seeing some hick towns! I mean…gee whiz, those Main Street burgs are slow. **1929** Milburn *Hobo's Hornbook* 33: The head shack ditched us in a burg/The other side of Fargo. **1936** "E. Queen" *Halfway House* 7: Congress met right here in this little old burg in '84. **1951** *Twist Fort Worth* (film): We're going to delouse this burg. **1952** in Yates *Loneliness* 33: What time we supposed to show up in this Pennsylvania burg tomorra? **1962** Crump *Killer* 227: Everything in this burg is dirty. **1967** "W. Henry" *Alias Butch Cassidy* 106: This burg believed it was something.

burger *n. Sports.* a raw bruise.
   1979 Frommer *Sports Lingo* 192.

-burger *comb. form.* (used as a facetious noun ending to characterize some condition, attribute, etc.).
   1986 Cogan *Top Gun* 61: Maverick's…smile turned his face into an All-American cheerfulburger. **1989** *UTSQ: Psychoburger*—a very strange or frightening person. "Charles Manson is a psychoburger."

Burgh *n. Local.* Pittsburgh, Pa.—constr. with *the.*
   [**1863** in *Ark. Hist. Qly.* XII (1953) 346: We came to the Ohio River…which we crossed at Pittsburgh…After our arrival at the station, the officers were taken off the cars and conducted into the "burgh" and quartered in…a large building.] **1974** Blount *3 Bricks Shy* 14: "That's all people otta ton [*i.e.,* out of town] think of the Burgh as," a local bartender told me: "Soot." **1983** S. King *Christine* 258: "Where did you buy replacement glass, anyway?" "McConnell's…In the Burg."

burglar *n.* a swindler or cheat; a bribe-taker.
   1928 *New Yorker* (Nov. 3) 94: Taxicab Words…*Burglar*—A driver who takes a stranger from Forty-second Street to Seventy-second Street by way of Canarsie, Hoboken, and Van Cortlandt Park. **1935** in R. Nelson *Dishonorable* 273: Bonito rides for that stable, and he's strictly a burglar. **1942** Pegler *Spelvin* 75: There is a judgeship open in Jersey and…they have…recommended a terrible burglar.

burglar hole *n.* a peephole in the front door of a house or apartment.
   1972 M. Rodgers *Freaky Fri.* 27: I peeked through the burglar hole…and almost fainted dead away!

burlap show *n. Logging.* (see quot.).
   1958 McCulloch *Woods Words* 24: Burlap show—A poor logging outfit.

burley *n.* a burlesque show or theater.
   1934 Weseen *Slang Dict.* 137: Burly—A burlesque theater or show. **1941** "G.R. Lee" *G-String* 56: Broadway Burley Pinched on Quick Look by Vice Spy. **1949** Robbins *Dream Merchants* 47: We pay you more here for one day's work than you make all week hustling your ass on a burley line! **1953** in Cannon *Like 'Em Tough* 115: She might have been on the runway of a burley house.

burlycue *n.* burlesque; a burlesque theater. Also **burley-que.**
   1923 *N.Y. Times* (Oct. 14) VIII 4: Burlycue—What vaudeville calls burlesque. **1927** Nicholson *Barker* 85: At least in burley-Q you ain't wadin' knee-deep in soup all the time. **1930** Graham & Graham *Queer People* 188: Usta have a burley-que house right next door to my place. **1942** Rodgers & Hammerstein *Oklahoma!* 15: They got a big theayter they call a burleycue. **1952** Lait & Mortimer *USA* 94: The most famous burleycue on the continent. **1957** J. Jones *Some Came Running* 15: I know these towns. No bar. No burlyque. No racetrack. **1967** Talbot *Chatty Jones* 152: A mixture of burlycue and Satanism. **1992** G. Wolff *Day at Beach* 103: Recollecting burly-que I had seen in Florida and Tennessee as a teenager.

burn *n.* **1.a.** a prank; joke.
   1891 Kirkland *Capt. Co. K* 86 [ref. to Civil War]: A general guffaw burst out at this "burn" on Caleb. **1993** *Real World* (MTV): Oh, my God. This such a burn on me.
   b. a deception or cheat; confidence game.
   1960 C. Cooper *Scene* 59: The junkie…cons somebody out of some money for stuff, and he calls that a burn. **1963** Braly *Shake Him* 13: It's

no burn. There's action in there. **1968–73** Agar *Ripping & Running* 46: In this form of the *burn*,…the *mark* remains interested because of the inexpensive price tag.

c. a great disappointment.

1966 Braly *On Yard* 257: The incentive movie was a burn. **1992** *Mystery Sci. Theater* (Comedy Central TV): Oh, what a burn!

d. *Juve.* (see 1966 quot.).

1942 *ATS* 299. **1966** in *IUFA Folk Speech: Burn:* a deliberate insult to someone. **1990** *Mystery Sci. Theater* (Comedy Central TV): What a burn!

2. a fury; a show of anger; a grudge; esp. in phr. **slow burn** a slowly mounting rage. [The *slow burn* was associated esp. with the comedian Edgar Kennedy.]

1938 *L.A. Times* (Aug. 2) 18: The Saga of the Slow Burn Man [Edgar Kennedy]. **1952** Mandel *Angry Strangers* 138: His father calls him a buttonhole maker and he does a slow burn. **1956** Ross *Hustlers* 35: I like the burn of people in cars and trucks in a big hurry to get somewhere getting nowhere. **1962** Serling *New Stories* 49: "Don't bug me, Sy," he said with a fast burn. **1965** Hersey *Too Far to Walk* 72: By the next afternoon, John had gone into a big burn. **1970** Gattzden *Black Vendetta* 45: I know you got a burn, man. **1980** McAleer & Dickson *Unit Pride* 66: But he was doing a slow burn. **1980** *N.Y. Post* (Mar. 18) 14: Some Carey aides are doing a slow burn over the [film] clip, a shrewd piece of work by Carter media man Gerald Rafshoon. *a***1990** Westcott *Half a Klick* 166: Freddy did a slow burn.

3. a permanent wave.

1957 Simmons *Corner Boy* 146: "Dig the crazy mop, man."…"Where you get a burn like that?"

4. the act of smoking a cigarette.

1971 Dahlskog *Dict.* 11: *Burn*…A cigaret; a smoke, as: to take time out for a *burn*.

5. *Police.* an instance of being exposed as an undercover agent.

1972 Mills *Report* 93: The ultimate disaster is discovery—in undercover language, a "burn." When junkies and pushers…learn or suspect an agent's identity, he has "taken a burn."

6. a penetrating glance.—constr. with *the*.

1981 *Easyriders* (Oct.) 28: All he does is put "the burn" on ya (the look you see above) and that settles it.

7. a feeling of muscle fatigue or pain from intense exercise.

1982 Trudeau *Dressed for Failure* (unp.): I feel a burn—Puff!—but it's a good burn. **1988** Nickelodeon Cable Network spot ad: Working out! Goin' for the *burn!*

8. *Firefighting.* a fire; conflagration; blaze.

1984 *Morning Edition* (Nat. Pub. Radio) (July 24): They really won't be able to determine the cause while the burn is going on.

burn *v.* **1.** to infect with a venereal disease.

*1529 in *OED*: These be they…that be brent wyth one woman, and bere it to another. ***1590** Shakespeare *Comedy of Errors* IV iii 56: Light wenches will burn. ***1686** in Adlard *Forbidden Tree* 95: She vowed if he meddled with her she would burn him. ***1785** Grose *Vulgar Tongue: Burnt.* Poxed or clapped. **1877** in J.M. Carroll *Camp Talk* 105: The "Tads" of the Regt. had all been "codding" Fuller on Annie—i.e., about getting *burnt* by her last winter. **1926** Nichols & Tully *Twenty Below* 12: Nearest 'e ever was to Broadway was to get burned by a dame from there. **1930** J.T. Farrell *Calico Shoes* 261: "And now if I only don't get burned."…"It's no worse than a bad cold." **1937** Steinbeck *Mice & Men* 58: Take your own chance gettin' burned. **1946** J.H. Burns *Gallery* 296: She gave you a nice burning, and she'll do it to others. **1958** S.H. Adams *Tenderloin* 172 [ref. to 1890's]: His kid brother got burned in Georgiana Hastings' place. **1962** Quirk *Red Ribbons* 267: Man gets burned all he wants, they jus' jab…the ass with penicillin, whap, he's out looking for another dose. **1970** Ahlstrom & Havighurst *400 Losers* 177: I got burnt from one of them easy ones. **1990** N.Y. prostitute, on *CBS Evening News* (Jan. 1): Maybe one of these guys…found out he got burnt [with AIDS] and he's takin' these girls out one by one. **1991** *Houston Chronicle* (Oct. 8) 2D: *Burning*, or *Got burnt*—Contracted a sexually transmitted disease.

2.a. to swindle or cheat, now esp. by withholding money or a share of illicit goods. [Precise relevance of 1699–1785 quots. remains somewhat uncertain.]

[***1698–99** "B.E." *Dict. Canting Crew: Burnt the Town,* when the Soldiers leave the place without paying their Quarters.] [***1725** *New Canting Dict.: Burnt the Ken,* when Strollers leave the Ale-house without paying their Quarters.] [***1785** Grose *Vulgar Tongue:* Strollers living in an alehouse without paying their quarters, are said to burn the ken.]

*1808 in *OEDS* I. **1844** in Thornton *Amer. Gloss.*: Two negro burners were arrested in the act of trying to burn two Pottsville boatmen with a plated chain worth about fifteen cents. **1925–26** J. Black *You Can't Win* 106: If you'd burnt Shorty for his end of that coin, you'd been here just the same. **1935** Pollock *Und. Speaks: Burned,* when an addict gives a dope peddler the money for a purchase and the delivery of dope is not made. **1952** Malamud *Natural* 125: They burned me good. **1959** Trocchi *Cain's Bk.* 150: I didn't burn you, Joe, honest. **1960** C. Cooper *Scene* 52: I musta got burnt. **1970** *Newsweek* (May 11) 95: One…social worker…gave police the names of three people who had "burned" friends (that is, who had given them bad-quality marijuana or had failed to make promised deliveries).

b. *Und.* to betray; act treacherously toward.

*ca***1963** in Schwendinger & Schwendinger *Adolescent Sub.* 301: Don't mess with him, man. He's gonna burn you, man!

3.a. to go at great speed; (*hence, joc.*) to leave. Cf. *burn the ground,* below.

1866 *Galaxy* (Nov. 1) 409: Smith lays his forefinger by the side of his long nose, and informs them that…Moseby has burned up White's Ford and blown up the Shenandoah Valley. **1942** *ATS* 60. **1978** *UTSQ:* Leave…Let's *burn, take off, get out of here, split.* **1980** Kotzwinkle *Jack* 158: That's it.…We're ready to *burn. a***1984** T. Clancy *Red Oct.* 155: Just sit tight and let them burn right past us.

b. to perform with great skill and success, esp. in competition.

1964 Gold *Jazz Lexicon* 43: *Burn*…(current since c. 1958) To play music intensely and expertly. **1965** Conot *Rivers of Blood* 219: Let's all get together and burn! **1969** Gordone *No Place* 434: You burned, baby, you burned. **1980** Wielgus & Wolff *Basketball* 41: *Burn* (v.) 1. To score, usually on several shots in succession. **1981** D.E. Miller *Jargon* 230: Freddie's gonna burn in the 220 tonight, just watch!

4.a. to infuriate; annoy.—constr. esp. with *up* or (*vulgar*) *ass*.—used trans.

1922 in S. Smith *Gumps* 14: That'll burn her up. **1922** J. Conway, in *Variety* (Mar. 3) 42: It burned me up but what could I do. **1925** *Collier's* (Sept. 19) 7: That burnt me up. **1926** Maines & Grant *Wise-Crack Dict.* 5: *Burn him up*—Arouse his anger. **1929** in R.E. Howard *Book* 68: I [was] plumb burned up by this deal. **1929** E. Wilson *Daisy* 104: This long range marksmanship of yours burns me up. **1934** in North *New Masses* 91: Sure he was bitter.…All them fools talking their heads off, saying nothing. Them society people burning him up. **1943** Lawson & Korda *Sahara* (film): That crack that guy made…burned me up. **1955** Goethals *Chains* 70: These goddam heroes, they burn my ass. **1953–57** Giovannitti *Combine D* 205: And I don't like it.…It burns my ass. **1956** E. Hunter *Second Ending* 136: Goddammit, this burns my ass. **1967** J. Kramer *Instant Replay* 22: There was no reason, and this burned me up. **1971** T.C. Bambara *Gorilla* 15: Grownups figure they can treat you just anyhow. Which burns me up. **1974** Kurtzman *Bobby* 15: That man burns me. **1988** Barry & Soccio *Practical Logic* 135: Boy, those Muslim terrorists really burn me up.

b. to feel or become furiously angry.—also constr. with *up*. Cf. S.E. *burn with rage*.

1922 *Variety* (July 28) 5: His partner [is] burnin' up all the time. **1932** Hecht & Fowler *Great Magoo* 73: All right. Quit burnin'. **1932** Hawks *Crowd Roars* (film): He's burnin' up. He's plenty sore. **1935** in Paxton *Sport* 203: Boy, did I have Casey Stengel burnin' up! **1941** Schulberg *Sammy* 12: That made me burn. Four dollars was a lot of money to Osborne. **1948** Manone & Vandervoort *Trumpet* 45: Tommy burned up. "What's the matter with you guys?" **1957** Thornton *Teenage Werewolf* (film): I guess I lost my head. I burn easily.

5. to execute or cause to be executed in an electric chair; (*intrans.*) to die by electrocution.

1927 Tully *Circus Parade* 95: I'm willin' to burn in the chair to kill a few cops an' that judge in Alabama. **1928** Coe *Swag* 222: I'll burn you in the chair or I'll shoot you in two right here. **1930** Lavine *3d Degree* 32: You know it is murder if he squawks, and nobody wants to burn for just having a guy knocked off. **1932** R. Fisher *Conjure Man* 273: You rather see me burn. **1934** in Ruhm *Detective* 107: I'm pinching you for the murder of Naomi Penfields.…I'm going to burn you for it, Kennedy. **1942** Algren *Morning* 49: I hope he…burns like poor Andy. **1948** Webb *Four Steps* 161: All I know is I don't want to burn. **1959** O'Connor *To a Stranger* 4: They don't burn you for murder if you're a kid. **1985** Milicevic et al. *Runaway Train* (film): You'll burn for it! You know you will!

6.a. *Orig. Und.* to shoot dead.

1933 Ersine *Pris. Slang* 23: *Burn, v.*…To shoot and kill, especially with a [submachine gun]. **1956** Ross *Hustlers* 111: Burn him! Close the case.

Don't waste time and money. **1961** Coon *At the Front* 299: Ought to burn the son of a bitch where he stands. **1965** C. Brown *Manchild* 176: Do you really want to burn this cat, man? I mean, you want to waste Limpy? **1967** Moorse *Duck* 150: Did he pull out his iron and burn me right there on the spot? **1970–71** Rubinstein *City Police* 329: I could have burned you and nobody would have said a thing. **1976** *S.W.A.T.* (NBC-TV): All the yells and protests when we have to use our weapons. I wonder if anyone's keeping count when one of our own guys gets burned. **1987** *Newsweek* (Mar. 23) 73: Honk came up on him with his own piece, fixing to burn him.

b. to shoot.

1959 W. Miller *Cool World* 103: If you go in burnin it give you an edge. **1988** Dye *Outrage* 8: Practically all...were burning rounds in different directions.

7. *Und.* to stare at.

1930 *Liberty* (July 5) 25: His advice...is "Never round or burn the law," which means, don't go to the other side of the street when you see a bull coming your way and don't turn to look at him after he's passed. **1949** Bezzerides *Thieves' Market* 108: "Get him giving me the eye," the trucker said. "Go ahead, burn a hole in me."

8. *Und.* to rob or steal.

1924 *N.Y. Times* (Aug. 3) VIII 16: "Give Red credit for burning the poke for the four C's."..."Give Red credit for taking the $400 out of the pocketbook." **1960** R. Reisner *Jazz Titans* 151: *Burn, To*: to rob. *ca*1963 in Schwendinger & Schwendinger *Adolescent Sub.* 291: If not I take it back to the Heist who burned (stole) it and we're clean. **1968–70** *Current Slang* III & IV 18: *Burn, v.* To steal.—Watts.

9.a. to punish or cause to be punished; *intrans.* to be punished.

1925 Mullin *Scholar Tramp* 252 [ref. to *ca*1912]: I'll see that you get burnt good and plenty if I catch you loitering around the streets after today. **1928** Nason *Sgt. Eadie* 113 [ref. to 1918]: Won't he burn yuh for beatin' it? **1942** in C.R. Bond & T. Anderson *Flying T. Diary* 183: Someone should "burn" for that mission. **1958** "Traver" *Anat. of Murder* 149: I'll make a damn fool or liar out of you or both. I—I'll burn your ass to a crisp. **1962** Killens *Heard Thunder* 65: All this goldbricking...is going to stop or else I'm going to burn every last damn one of you. **1968** Tauber *Sunshine Soldiers* 207: You open your mouth again and you'll be picking up rocks all afternoon. I'll burn your ass into the ground. **1960–69** Runkel *Law* 103: I know if I do wrong I'm gonna get my ass burnt. **1971** *Playboy* (May) 110: This outfit's gonna have morale or I'll burn a few butts around here. **1986–91** Hamper *Rivethead* 221: Sanders was especially eager to burn my ass.

b. *Specif.*, to file a disciplinary complaint against; place on report.

1938 in *AS* (Feb. 1939) 25: *Burn, v.t.* To report delinquent. **1969** *Current Slang* I & II 16: *Burn, v.* To write up or report for a violation of the rules.—Air Force Academy cadets. **1971** *N.Y. Times Mag.* (Sept. 19) 66: They harass you about haircuts and beards and burn you for sleeping on guard when you've been working all day.

10.a. to cause (someone) to look foolish; humiliate.

1963 *Time* (Aug. 2) 14: *Burned.* Humiliated, rejected. **1981** in Safire *Good Word* 83: First you "burn" someone with a nice move [in a basketball game];...then you say "face job." **1991** Lott & Lieber *Total Impact* 102: I could get badly burned by a receiver.

b. *Journ.* to SCOOP.

1978 *N.Y. Times Mag.* (July 23) 23: The Washington press corps has popularized *burned*, to mean scooped or seriously embarrassed. **1980** Pearl *Slang Dict.: Burned*...(Journalism) beaten by another reporter to the exclusive or first coverage of a news story.

11. *Police.* to expose the identity of (an undercover agent or police informer); to recognize as a detective or the like.

1959 Murtagh & Harris *In Shadow* 154: The police may get rid of him by the practice known as "burning"—revealing him as a stool pigeon to other addicts and peddlers. **1966** Schaap *Turned On* 109: Burned [exposed as a detective]. **1970** Wambaugh *New Centurions* 186: It's no use, I'm burned here. **1972** Mills *Report* 75: So we don't want to burn the undercover and we don't want to mess up whatever he's got goin' in the hotel. **1974** *Kojak* (CBS-TV): They'll be burnt in five minutes. The word'll be out all over Chinatown. **1978** Strieber *Wolfen* 151: [He had been] burned and didn't even know it. **1987** J. Thompson *Gumshoe* 11: I just got seen in the VW. I think the term is "burned."

12. *Narc.* to smoke (a cannabis cigarette).

1964 in Lingeman *Drugs* 32: And burning marijuana, that's just like smoking a cigarette. **1979–82** Gwin *Overboard* 282: Just in case you want to drop by and burn one. **1985** Dye *Between Raindrops* 50: How bad do you want to burn one, babe? Is the high worth the hurt?

13. *Black E.* to prepare by cooking; to cook.

1960 R. Reisner *Jazz Titans* 151: *Burn*: cook. **1962–63** in Giallombardo *Soc. of Women* 201: *Burn.* To cook. **1971** Wells & Dance *Night People* 92: Bill Coleman and his wife threw me a spread, and she can burn, too. *Ibid.* 117: *Burn, v.* To cook. **1971** Dahlskog *Dict.* 11: *Burn, v.* To cook, as food. **1983** *Reader's Digest Success with Words* 84: Black English...*burn*=...to cook food.

14. *Photog.* to overilluminate.

1928 *N.Y. Times* (Mar. 11) VIII 6: *Burning One*—To throw extra strong lights on one in photographing.

15. to produce (a copy) by photocopying, xerography, or the like.

1975 Univ. Tenn. student: Burn me a copy of your paper, will you? **1980** Cragg *L. Militaris* 56: *Burn*...To make a copy of a document. This term originated when Thermofax type reproduction equipment became standard in government offices.

16. *Constr.* to operate an oxyacetylene torch.

1974 Cherry *High Steel* 31: I can burn. *Ibid.* 32: I got sent out to go burning.

17. to place under arrest.

1969 Salerno & Tompkins *Crime Confed.* 153: To be arrested is to be busted, grabbed, burned, or collared. **1977** Dunne *True Confessions* 10: Then he got burned on a Murder One rap and he got life in San Quentin. **1977** Sayles *Union Dues* 151: "When's the last time we burned you, Inez?"..."You turds couldn't burn a one-eyed shoplifter...much less make anything stick on me!"

18. *Sports.* to defeat.

1980 Pearl *Slang Dict.: Burn*...(Sports) to achieve victory over an opponent.

19. to discharge (an employee); to jilt or stand up (a suitor).

1978 *UTSQ:* Fired...*burned, blown away, kicked out, gone for good. Ibid.* Stand up...*burn.*

¶ In phrases:

¶ **burn (one's) collar** to become furiously angry.

1949 Bezzerides *Thieves' Market* 116: Don't burn your collar. I'll move it.

¶ **burn (someone's) ears** [or (*vulgar*) **ass**] to scold (someone) angrily.

1952 Uris *Battle Cry* 182: Bryce knew he'd get his ass burned out by the Major if he fell out. **1963** Morgan *Six-Eleven* 265: I'll burn their ears about it, Charlie. **1967** J. Kramer *Instant Replay* 113: But I got the blame for everything...Vince really burned my ass.

¶ **burn my skin** *So.* (used as an oath).

1836 *Spirit of Times* (Feb. 27) 16: Burn my skin if I had'nt ruther have [a] slave for my father.

¶ **burn rubber** see s.v. RUBBER, *n.*

¶ **burn smoke** to go at great speed.

1972 Casey *Obscenities* 3: He went inta the mile run.../Burnt smoke for the first three laps.

¶ **burn the breeze** see s.v. BREEZE, *n.*

¶ **burn the ground** [or **earth** or **street,** etc.] to go at great speed over the ground (or the like).

1881 in *DA* 223: Burn the prairie. **1894** (quot. at *hit the breeze* s.v. BREEZE). **1900** Wister *Jimmyjohn* 47: Quick now. Burn the earth. **1903** A. Adams *Log of Cowboy* 23: I was...burning the earth like a canned dog. **1906** Wooldridge *Hands Up* 49: The driver was told to "burn the street" to the railroad depot. **1907** Cook *Border & Buffalo* 390: Burn the earth, Cook, to reach Keyes, Cornett and Squirrel-eye.

¶ **to burn a wet dog** [or **mule**] in superabundance.

1895 Townsend *Fadden* 19: Dem folks...got boodle ter burn a wet dog wid. **1895** (quot. at LONG GREEN).

burn artist *n.* Esp. *Narc.* a swindler.

1967–68 (quot. at GEEZER, *n.*). **1972** Smith & Gay *Don't Try It* 198: *Burn Artist.* Someone who makes his living selling phony or heavily adulterated dope. (Has short life expectancy). **1988** T. Logan *Harder They Fall* 10: The packs contained only talcum powder, the property of a burn artist.

burn down *v. Und.* to shoot dead; to kill. Also (*occ.*) in phr. **burn down on.**

1932 in *AS* (Feb. 1934) 26: *Burn down.* To shoot someone. **1936** *Steel College* 313: You burned the janitor down and planted the gun and scrammed. **1942** Faulkner *Go Down, Moses* 235: The negro...outed with a dollar-and-a-half mail-order pistol and would have burned Boon down with it only it never went off. **1952** Bruce & Essex *Kansas City*

Confidential (film): The third guy was Pete Harris—burned down in Tijuana. *Ibid.* That's a sucker move—burning down on your boss. **1956** Ross *Hustlers* 111: Anybody didn't go through with it, he'd get burned down. **1965** Spillane *Killer Mine* 82: He shoots up the guy he started out to get legally. He sure picked a big one to burn down. *a*1970 in Fife & Fife *Ballads of Great West* 67: Do that again, old timer, and I'll burn yuh down.

¶ In phrase:

¶ **burn down the house** *Entertainment Industry*. to excite or dazzle an audience.

1984 *All Things Considered* (Nat. Pub. Radio) (July 20): It's a traditional approach to burnin' down the house with the last tune.

burned *adj.* see BURNED UP.

burned up *adj.* **1.** very angry. Also **burned.**

1923 Witwer *Fighting Blood* 239: The old boy's burnt up. **1927** *Vanity Fair* (Nov.) 132: To be "burned up" is to be angry. **1930** Graham & Graham *Queer People* 117: I got burned up at something one day and told her I'd walk out and leave her if she wanted to be free. **1931** *Amer. Merc.* (Dec.) 414: He was tremblin' all over, he was so boint. **1938** Smitter *Detroit* 177: Russian Bill was burned up because...the whole plant was being moved to Grand Rapids. **1939** Saroyan *Time of Your Life* 413: But every time he comes into this place I get burned up. **1939–40** O'Hara *Pal Joey* 16: Jean was burned because she was afraid her father might see the item. **1961** Terry *Old Liberty* 43: I got to get to the house, or my old lady'll be burned. **1971** T.C. Bambara *Gorilla* 29: I pin number seven to myself and stomp away. I'm so burnt. **1980** WINS radio newscast (Aug. 21): Israel is burned up over our abstention yesterday in the UN.

2. very enthusiastic; excited.

1927 Behrman *Second Man* 336: Austin Lowe. All burned up about Monica Gray....And she's all burned up about you. **1934** H. Miller *Tropic of Cancer* 126: You get all burned up about nothing...about a crack with hair on it.

3. see BURN, *v.*, 4.

burner *n.* **1.** a professional swindler; confidence trickster.

1838 in *DAE*: He pulls out his pocket book, it is seized by the burner, who makes off with it. **1842** in Thornton *Amer. Gloss.*: The burners make better plots than most of our dramatists. **1845** in *DAE* I 361: The Empire Club of New York...consisted of gamblers, pickpockets, droppers, burners, thimble-riggers and the like. **1850** G.G. Foster *Gas-Light* 21: It is easy to pick up a loafer, a pickpocket, a burner, or Bowery blackleg at even the most dashing bowling-saloon. **1854** G.G. Foster *15 Mins.* 28: The fair one...is a pocketbook-dropper, a "burner," a "watch-stuffer." **1867** *Nat. Police Gaz.* (Jan. 12) 4: Of the "bruisers" and "burners" of creation, Cincinnati has its share.

2. (see quot.)

*ca*1855 [G. Thompson] *Road to Ruin* 13: The...gold watch turns out to be one of that class denominated *burners*, with which the watch-stuffing gentry...gull the flats.

3. Esp. *Black E.* a pistol; firearm.

1926 Odum & Johnson *Negro Workaday Songs* 124: I got my col'-iron burner*/Under my ol' left arm....*That is, his pistol. **1935** Hurston *Mules & Men* 322: Cap'n got a burner I'd like to have,/A 32:20 with a shiny barrel. **1961** J. Williams *Night Song* 85: I want to buy me a couple of burners, man....There are two or three cats I want to burn when the shit hits the fan.

4. a cheap cigar.

1940 Zinberg *Walk Hard* 82: They tell me you pick up ritzy cigar bands and stick them on five for a dime burners.

5. a remarkable individual.

1952 Himes *Stone* 76: Oooowah, man, he's a burner, ain't he? **1989** *Newsweek* (July 24) 4: *Burner.* An officer on the fast track.

6. *Av.* a jet engine or jet aircraft.

1955 Archibald *Aviation Cadet* 69: In 1918 they flew planes made of bamboo poles and fabrics, all put together with baling wire, and had no chutes. I'd like to know why more guys don't want the burners.

7. *Baseball*. a fastball.

1942 *ATS* 652. **1978** in Lyle & Golenbock *Bronx Zoo* 30: Goose sailed a burner right past Lou's head.

burn job *n.* **1.** *Mil. Av.* an incendiary bombing.

1956 W. Taylor *Roll Back Sky* 93 [ref. to WWII]: Not the burn-job we were just on; I mean the weather mission.

2. a swindle.

1967–68 von Hoffman *Parents Warned Us* 43: It's a burn job. There isn't enough acid in it.

burnout *n.* Esp. *Stu.* a person whose intellect, sensibilities, etc., have been notably impaired through habitual abuse of drugs or alcohol; (*hence*) a shiftless or ineffectual person; (*later*) a person, usu. an enthusiast of heavy-metal music, who dresses unconventionally and is often pessimistic or antisocial.

1973 *Urban Life & Culture* II 299: One...becomes totally dependent on drugs (a "burn out" who cannot honor commitments to friends [etc.]). **1976–77** in G.A. Fine *With the Boys* 121: [Antisocial boys are labeled] "mental," "rowdies," or "burn-outs." **1980** Lorenz *Guys Like Us* 143: "You know the guys I'm talking about?" "Those burnouts...What about them?" **1984** N. Stephenson *Big U.* 185: An exceptionally tall burnout stood [there]. **1987** *Village Voice* (N.Y.C.) (July 14) 17: "Burnouts" were kids who looked "rock & roll." Guys with earrings, crucifixes, long hair, boom boxes,...blue denim jackets. **1990** Stuck *Adolescent Worlds* 62: There's either the burnouts or the preppies. **1987–91** D. Gaines *Teenage Wasteland* 9: They call themselves burnouts to flaunt their break with the existing order.

burnt *adj.* *Stu.* being or characteristic of a BURNOUT.

1987–91 D. Gaines *Teenage Wasteland* 65: This is really burnt. *Ibid.* 107: "Aren't you afraid somebody will think you're a jock?"..."Hell, no, they know I'm burnt."

burn up *v.* **1.** to overexploit; use up.

1857 in Dressler *Pioneer Circus* 69: I did think we could get a living out of it but...all the country is burnt up [and] the people are poor and tiard of being humbuged. **1922** *Variety* (June 30) 6: A flock of the guns are workin' with the carnivals and burnin' up the territory.

2. to criticize harshly.

1899 Ade *Fables* 74: The way he burned up Magazine Writers, it's a Wonder they didn't get after him for Arson.

3. see s.v. BURN, *v.*, 4.a. & b.

4. to surpass or outdo easily.

1980 Kotzwinkle *Jack* 156: She'll burn up the competition.

burp *n.* [imit.] **1.** a belch. Now *colloq.*

1929 J.M. Saunders *Single Lady* 206: You can have all the beer you like, so long as you don't burp. **1932** Hecht & Fowler *Great Magoo* 72: SAILOR. *Belching as a result of his struggles.* Brrp! **1932** *AS* VII 330: *Burp*—sound made when belching. **1950** in Marx *Groucho Letters* 73: Emitted an effervescent burp. **1958** Frankel *Band of Bros.* 42: Gettin' a feller to volunteer for somethin' like this it'd be hard as sewin' buttons on a burp, sir.

2. *Electronics*. a popping noise, as created by static or other interference.

1941 *Slanguage Dict.* 9: *Burp*...in radio, a superfluous sound heard on long distance transmission levels.

3. *Mil.* BURP-GUN.

1953 White *Down Ridge* 151: The burp has made a deep impression on military thinking, at least at platoon and company level. **1982** Cox & Frazier *Buck* 24 [ref. to 1951]: He's got a burp. I think I know where he is.

burp *v.* [imit.] **1.** to belch. Now *colloq.* or *S.E.*

1932 *AS* VII 330: *Burp*—to belch. **1957** Bannon *Odd Girl* 35: You know, sometimes when you burp, nobody hears you.

2. to cause (an infant) to belch, as to relieve flatulence after feeding. Now *S.E.*

1940 in *AS* (Apr. 1941) 145: Chronic air swallowers should be "burped" three or four times...during each feeding. **1983** Goldman & Fuller *Charlie Co.* 269: Julie [was] burping Jamie on their living room couch.

3. to complain or to speak impudently or arrogantly.

1935 in Hemingway *Sel. Letters* 423: I'll see if I can change it....Unless you think it gives the critics something to burp about...they have to attack me to believe in themselves. **1970** Wertheim & Gonzalez *Talkin' About Us* 128: So the Big Mouth Burped and Priam got up and bopped.

burp bag *n.* *Av.* BARF BAG, 1.

1962 Astronauts *We Seven* 97: John Glenn and Al Shepard decided to follow through on the gag when they spied one of those paper "burp bags" sticking out of the pocket of the seat in front of them. **1972** W.C. Anderson *Hurricane* 142: Two burp bags.

burp cup *n.* BURP BAG.

1945 Hamann *Air Words* 13: *Burp cups.* Vessels installed on airplanes for persons afflicted with airsickness to vomit into.

burp-gun *n. Mil.* **1.** a machine pistol, esp. of a kind employed by the *Wehrmacht* during WWII.

[**1936** D. Runyon, in *Collier's* (Nov. 21) 8: There are occasional bur-ur-ur-urps…that I recognize as machine guns.] **1943** Tregaskis *Invasion Diary* 37: Lots of "burp guns"—machine pistols. **1944** Inks *Eight Bailed Out* 53: A partisan stepped from behind a tree with a burp gun. **1945** Dos Passos *Tour* 332: Two krauts with a burp gun were hidin' behind a big ole apple tree an' they gave it to him. **1949** Van Praag *Day Without End* 47: I think it's a burp-gun. **1960** Matheson *Beardless Warriors* 209: The rattle of a German burp gun. **1980** S. Fuller *Big Red* 47: His nine-pound Schmeisser burp gun.

2. a submachine gun, esp. of a kind manufactured by the Soviet Union during and after WWII.

1950 *Time* (Aug. 28) 24: They come up and stick their burp guns in our stomachs…and…grabbed our rifles. **1951–52** Frank *Hold Back Night* 168: They don't have mortars. All they've got is burp guns. **1953** Russ *Last Parallel* 75: Next…we heard the BRRRRP! sound of one Chinese pp-S or "burp gun" as it is called. **1953** White *Down Ridge* 151: It is the same burp gun the Red Army was shooting joyously into the air when our World War II GIs first met them at Torgau. **1953** in Cray *Erotic Muse* 134: Million Chinks comin' through the pass/Playin' burp-gun boogie all over my ass. **1955** T. Anderson *Your Own Beloved Sons* 114: They were regular Russian "burpguns," and he had recognized their round drums. **1968** W. Crawford *Gresham's War* 20: Hawkins used a Russian burpgun with drum magazines. **1985** M. Brennan *War* 119 [ref. to 1967]: We just made believers out of some dinks in the Tiger Mountains. Haven't seen burp guns since Korea.

burr *n.* a black person; BURRHEAD.—used contemptuously.

1970 Corrington *Bombardier* 177: They had me in a cell, with that…burr with the glasses and the beard.

¶ In phrases:

¶ **burr up (one's) ass** a short temper; (*also*) an obsession.—usu. considered vulgar.

1960 Bluestone *Cully* 25 [ref. to ca1955]: Some guys have a burr up their ass. He's got desert cactus. **1969** Scanlan *Davis* 107: Every now and then the general gets a burr up his ass and we're up half the night running off poop on the mimeograph machine. **1978** Truscott *Dress Gray* 183: Hotheads, young fireballs with a burr up their asses. **1983** Eilert *Self & Country* 99: Does she got a burr up her ass or what?

¶ **off (one's) burr** off (one's) head; crazy.

1912 in W.C. Fields *By Himself* 44: I am thoroughly convinced you are off your Burr.

burrhead *n.* **1.** a black person.—used contemptuously.

1902 P.L. Dunbar *Sport of Gods* 61: Oh, yes, you're done with burr-heads, are you? But burr-heads are good enough fu' you now. **1918** in *AS* (Oct. 1933) 24: Burrhead. A colored prisoner. **1934–41** in Mellon *Bullwhip Days* 307 [ref. to a1860]: He used to…say, "Grandpappy wouldn't take nothing for his little burr-head niggers." **1947–52** R. Ellison *Invisible Man* 127: I say "Yes, suh" as loudly as any burr-head when it's convenient. **1982** D. Williams *Hit Hard* 25: He can whup all these burrheads.

2. a blockhead.

1918 in *AS* (Oct. 1933) 24: Burrhead…a bonehead.

burr-headed *adj.* **1.** stupid.

1948 Faulkner *Intruder* 19: You goddamn biggity stiff-necked stinking burrheaded Edmonds sonofabitch.

2. having rough close-cropped hair.

1955 Scott *Look of Eagle* 18: All those burr-headed guys out there were barely listening to him. **1974** Blount *3 Bricks Shy* 27: A beefy, burr-headed person throughout his youth, Mansfield had by this time…grown hair.

burrito *n.* [< Sp, dim. of *burro* 'jackass, donkey'] a Hispanic person.—used contemptuously.

1987 *Miami Vice* (NBC-TV): Do you believe the stones on this burrito?

burst *n. & v.* **1.** var. BUST, *n. & v.*

2. *n. Army.* a period of enlistment, often for a specified number of years.

1975 former 1 Lt., U.S. Army: "Take a burst of six" means re-enlist for six. I don't think I've ever heard it used with any other numbers. **1984** former Spec. 5, U.S. Army: In 1974 I was in Taiwan and the reenlistment sergeant used to talk about *taking a burst*. **1986** Merkin *Zombie Jamboree* 31 [ref. to 1970]: The Air Force…wanted a three-year burst. *Ibid.* 258: Art had joined the Marines for a burst of three.

burster var. BUSTER.

bury *v.* **1.** to eat voraciously.

1884 in Lummis *Letters* 98: Maybe he didn't help me bury those beans. **1908** in Fleming *Unforgettable Season* 122: The way he buries that double-deck delicacy is a caution.

2. *Pris.* to convict; sentence to a long prison term; to cause to be convicted or imprisoned.

1904 *Life in Sing Sing* 246: *Buried*—Convicted. **1925–26** Black *You Can't Win* 146: That button…is enough to bury us both in Quentin. **1966–67** P. Thomas *Mean Streets* 237: They must have buried him. **1981** Ballenger *Terror* 8: They'd bury you for disobeying a direct order. You'd…[never] get out of the brig. **1987** *Beauty & Beast* (CBS-TV): They tell me you're rehabilitated. But if it were up to me, I'd have buried you.

3. to kill (a person).

1933 Ersine *Pris. Slang* 23: *Bury, v.*…To kill. **1970–71** Rubinstein *City Police* 275: You pull your gun and aim for his chest. If he keeps coming, bury him.

¶ In phrase:

¶ **bury the hatchet** see s.v. HATCHET.

bus *n.* **1.** a busboy.

1915 Lait *Gus* 4: The bus is a figure that fiction has rarely known.

2. an automobile or other motor vehicle.

1914 T.A. Dorgan, in Zwilling *TAD Lexicon* 22: A friend of mine just bought a new car. A flivver…Thats like mine—some bus. **1916** W.J. Robinson *At Front* 121: The old 'bus made the most of what she had. **1917** Imbrie *War Ambulance* 115: A car was a "buss." **1917** in Dos Passos *14th Chronicle* 92: Our ambulance however is simply peppered with *holes*—how the old bus holds together is more than I can make out. **1919** Witwer *Alex the Great* 97: Nice little bus. **1928** Hammett *Red Harvest* 91: Nice work kid. You handle the bus like you meant it. **1928** *Papers Mich. Acad.* [ref. to 1918]: *Bus*, a tank. **1929** Millay *Against Wall* 95: I ain't hurtin' their old bus. **1935** S.I. Miller "G" Men (film): We traced the license, but it was a stolen bus. **1973** *Nat. Lampoon Encyc. of Humor* 74: Hop into the "family bus" with your wife or a friend along.

3. *Av.* an airplane. Now *rare* in U.S.

*1913 in *OED*. **1915** Rosher *Flying Squadron* 65: I pushed the old bus up to 8000 ft. *Ibid.* 68: I flew a Vickers gun bus…the other day. **1917** in Grider *War Birds* 55: These old short-horn Farmans are awful looking buses. **1918** in Hudson *Hostile Skies* 219: I found 36 holes in my bus. **1927** in Thomas *Marines* 208: She was a good bus. **1929** Nordhoff & Hall *Falcons* 87: He'll never admit that any bus is really A-1. **1957** in Loosbrock & Skinner *Wild Blue* 50: Me for staying with the old bus every time. **1958** Hailey & Castle *Runway* 122: Trying to get the bus up as fast as I can. **1961** Joswick & Keating *Cameraman* 97: You plan on riding this bus, Pictures?

4. an elevator.

1934 Weseen *Slang Dict.* 315: *Bus*—A passenger elevator.

¶ In phrase:

¶ **miss the bus** to miss an opportunity. Now *colloq.*

*1915 in *OEDS*. **1944** H. Brown *Walk in Sun* 41: It didn't make sense. It couldn't be that the planes had missed the bus. **1975** Boatner et al. *Dict. Amer. Idioms* 227: *Miss the bus*.…To fail through slowness; to put something off until too late; do the wrong thing and lose the chance; a cliché.

buscar *n.* [fr. the v.] *Mil.* something that is sought or obtained by chance.

1941 Kendall *Army & Navy Slang* 3: *Buscar*.…borrowed money. **1965** Trimble *Sex Words* 33: *Buscar*…a Prostitute or other sexually desirable girl who may unexpectedly or upon chance acquaintance give in freely to sex relations.

buscar *v.* [< Sp *buscar* 'to look for'] *Mil.* to search for and find; SCROUNGE.—also constr. with a prep. Also vars.

1906 *Army & Navy Life* (Oct.) 300 [ref. to 1890's]: Sit quiet. I'll go out and busca up some one. **1913** in A.F. Moe, letter to J.E.L. (7/27/75) 3: Her brother, who was a cochero,/Buscared in Manila dinero. **1922** *Leatherneck* (Apr. 22) 5: *Buscow:* To search for (Spanish, originally). **1924** in Nason *Three Lights* 26 [ref. to WWI]: Come on, get up out of that grass and let's buscar a shovel and see what we can do to get a roof over our heads. **1926** Nason *Chevrons* 269 [ref. to WWI]: Also, when I'm gone, I want you to buscar around and get a couple of blankets to sleep under.

bus-driver *n.* **1.** *USAF.* a pilot of a large multiengine airplane.

1944 Trumbo *Over Tokyo* (film): Come on, you hopped-up bus-drivers. **1954** F.I. Gwaltney *Heaven & Hell* 256 [ref. to WWII]: Oh, how clever you bus drivers are getting these days. **1991** Marcinko & Weisberg *Rogue Warrior* 47: USAF "bus drivers"—transport pilots.

2. *USMC.* a member of the U.S. Air Force.

1956 *AS* (Oct.) 192: An airman is a…*bus driver*, so-called because of his blue uniform.

bush *n.* **1.a.** the pubic hair; *(hence)* the vulva or vagina.—usu. considered vulgar.

ca*1650 in Wardroper *Love & Drollery* 188: There is a bush fit for the nonce/That beareth pricks and pretty stones. **ca*1700 in Pinto & Rodway *Common Muse* 398: But the Bush is the best provocation/If you can but handle your Piercer. **1916 Cary *Venery* I 32: *Bush.* (1) The vagina; and (2) the female pubic hair. **1938** in Legman *Limerick* 29: There once was a Queen of Bulgaria/Whose bush had grown hairier and hairier. **1938** "Justinian" *Americana Sexualis* 14: *Bush.* n. The pubic hair….C.19–20. Most popular American vulgarism for the referent. **1966** S. Stevens *Go Down Dead* 80: They is naked aright except they is got no bush down there. **1970** in *Playboy* (Jan. 1971) 246: Now, there's a nice bush. **1992** N. Baker *Vox* 120: The other pulls out and comes on her bush.

b. women regarded as sexual objects; in phr. **piece of bush** a woman so regarded.—usu. considered vulgar.

1959 *AS* (May) 154: *Blonde bushes* and *brunette bushes* are merely blondes and brunettes. **1971** Rader *Gov't Inspected* 157: A really stacked Movie Actress piece of bush hot after my money. **1981** *Penthouse* (Apr.) 30: Watching all that bush shake on the dance floor was enough to get my blood circulating. **1981** *Nat. Lampoon* (Nov.) 14: Toss a few of those terms around and the bush will think you aced the Bell & Howell home course in two weeks!

2. a beard or mustache.

1908 in H.C. Fisher *A. Mutt* 28: That's a good idea. I'll shed this bush. **1962** Mandel *Wax Boom* 17: Who's that guy with the Buffalo Bill bush on his face?

3.a. usu. *pl. Baseball.* a minor league.

1911 Van Loan *Big League* 77: The freshest young thing…ever hauled out of the baseball bushes…."Bull" Kennedy, one of the Big Chief's scouts, had seen Potts perform with a semi-professional team. *Ibid.* 88: I've been hittin' three-forty out in the bushes. **1921** J. Conway, in *Variety* (Aug. 19) 4: He's tellin' the gang…what he's goin' to do to the pitchers in this bush. **1922** *Variety* (July 14) 5: I have a pretty high-priced club, as payrolls go in this bush.

b. [cf. *colloq.* or *S.E.* sense 'hinterlands'; *(hence)* 'jungle'] rural areas. Also *pl.*

1914 Patten *Lefty o' the Bush* 16: This is true in minor leagues and "out in the bush," where…whole towns…have gone baseball crazy. **1935** H. Gray *Arf* (unp.): I'm not just some movie struck yap from the bushes.

c. *pl. Boxing & Horse Racing.* rural or amateur sports circuits; in phr. **beat the bushes** to compete in such circuits.

1936 Tully *Bruiser* 73: Those were the little days—you're out of the bushes now. **1968** Ainslie *Thoroughbred Racing* 465: *Bushes*—Small-time, bush-league racing. **1973** Haney *Lady Is a Jock* 18: Anything goes in the "bushes," the small racetracks, often situated on fairgrounds, which are not subject to the jurisdictions of state racing commissions. *Ibid.* 19: Mary rode horses in the bushes, in horse shows and in rodeos. *Ibid.* 175: Beat the bushes. To race in cheaper circuits.

4. *Narc.* cannabis; *(occ.)* a marijuana cigarette.

1951 *Sat. Eve. Post* (Mar. 17) 71: Hay, bush, tea…marijuana. **1956** Holiday & Dufty *Lady Sings Blues* 49: They were sure to accuse him smoking somebody's bushes. **1969** Bullock *Watts* 148: But I can't see no turning no brother in for smoking no bush, man. **1970** Cortina *Slain Warrior* 10: He managed everything but junk….Acid, pills, peyote, bush, but no heroin. **1971** *Playboy* (Mar.) 135: He had stayed long enough to unload a stash of Cambodian bush that had been mailed from Tokyo by a spaced-out GI. **1985* in Thorne *Dict. Contemp. Slang* 76: Want some bush, man? **1993** *Village Voice* (N.Y.C.) (June 22) 30: Khyber Bush, an unusually potent hybrid of Mexican sativa and Afghani indica.

5. *Army & USMC.* an ambush; in phr. **blow a bush** to spring an ambush.

1970 *N.Y. Times Mag.* (Feb. 8) 91: My second day out, we blew a bush and four gooks were entirely wiped out. *Ibid.* 94: Charlie started blowin' bushes on us. **1990** G.R. Clark *Words of Vietnam War* 20: A "good ambush"…or "bush" as some GIs called it. **1989** D. Sherman *There I Was* 157: We got a 'bush tonight.

6. BUSH TELEGRAPH.

1991 (quot. at BUSH TELEGRAPH).

¶ In phrases:

¶ **out of (one's) bush** crazy.

1976 Conroy *Santini* 361: What in the hell are you calling me at happy hour for, Lillian? Have you gone out of your goddam bush?

¶ **take the bush** *Army.* to desert.

1872 *Overland Mo.* 53 [ref. to Civil War]: The host himself was conscribed, but soon "took the bush."

bush *adj.* **1.** rustic. [1939 quot. has semantic resemblance to def. 2.]

1910 *N.Y. Eve. Jour.* (Apr. 6) 15: Matty has a new catch throw that he has sprung on several "bush" players this Spring. **1911** Van Loan *Big League* 61: They ain't got no good shows in these bush towns. **1939** *Sat. Eve. Post* (Apr.) 35: The retinues of the more substantial horsemen…refer to the [small stables] as "bush stables" and their nags as "bush horses."

2.a. Orig. *Baseball.* BUSH-LEAGUE; amateurish; childish; second-rate.

1959 Brosnan *Long Season* 116: How bush can you get?…Their trying to make a farce out of the game. *Ibid.* 148: I thought that was real bush, myself. **1960** Meany *Yankee Story* 154: "Domestic champagne!" he sniffed. "That's bush." **1969–71** Kahn *Boys of Summer* 213: Hey, George, *you're* bush. *Ibid.* 232: What are you doing, being suckers for a miserable bush curve? **1971** Coffin *Old Ball Game* 55: "Bush league" has been shortened to "bush," which has become a handy synonym for cheap, for childish, for inexperienced. **1979** B. Veeck, in Terkel *Amer. Dreams* 33: We have an exploding scoreboard in Comiskey Park. At first they declared it…too bush. **1980** Wielgus & Wolff *Basketball* 41: *Bush* (adj) Cheap or without class; dirty. A *submarine* is considered bush.

b. *Stu.* not challenging; easy.

1968 Baker et al. *CUSS* 91: *Bush.* Easy. **1984** Univ. Tenn. student: That course is so bush—anybody can pass.

bush[1] *v.* **1.** [cf. BUSHED] to exhaust.

1862 in A.A. Siegel *For Glory of Union* 91: Acting Gen. Whiting…rode at our head, and seemed bent on "bushing" us….Rests were…few.

2. to lie to; to hoax.

1970–71 Higgins *Eddie Coyle* 165: Don't bush me….Don't hand me that crap.

bush[2] *v.* **1.** to ambush.

1947 Overholser *Buckaroo's Code* 77: Toad Maxon…tried to 'bush me in town the other night. **1975–78** O'Brien *Cacciato* 291: An ambush, Paul Berlin knew and Oscar said it. "Bushed," Oscar whispered…."Fuckin ambushed….Bushed, bushed, bushed!" **1990** G.R. Clark *Words of Vietnam War* 20: Ambush (Bush[ed/ing]).

2. *Army & USMC.* to set up (an ambush). Also intrans.

1971 *Playboy* (Aug.) 206: That's what the enemy wants. You kill him by…bushing at night—selectively. *Ibid.* 200: I bush (ambush) the trails coming out. **1972** O'Brien *Combat Zone* 81: We'll be bushing this trail junction.

bush ape *n.* BRUSH APE.

1942 Hollingshead *Elmtown's Youth* 405: It is reputed to be a hangout for Poles, Italians ("Eye-talians"), "bush apes," "brush monkeys," "yellow hammers," and "reliefers." [**1945* S.J. Baker *Australian Lang.* 75: Bush apes (rural or bush workers; fruit-pickers in South Australia).]

bush beast *n. Mil.* a combat soldier. [Quots. ref. to Vietnam War.]

1985 Dye *Between Raindrops* 20: Shouldn't even let you bush-beasts in here. *Ibid.* 22: You bush-beasts coming in here don't impress me for shit. **1986** Dye & Stone *Platoon* 172: Ain't you the big-time bush-beast?

bushed *adj.* [cf. BUSH[1], *v.,* 1] tired out; exhausted.

1870 *Nation* (July 28) 57: To be "bushed" was to be tired [in E. Pa., *ca*1825]. **1902** Clapin *Americanisms* 87: Bushed. Whipped, tired out. **1910** *DN* III 438: *Bushed, adj.* Tired out, exhausted. **1928** MacArthur *War Bugs* 24: The men were so bushed on their return that they flopped on their cots without removing their haversacks. **1947** Hart *Gentleman's Agreement* (film): I'm bushed. **1952** *I Love Lucy* (CBS-TV): She's really bushed, isn't she? **1958** A. King *Mine Enemy* 59: We're all bushed. **1967** Dibner *Admiral* 15: You better get some shut-eye. You look bushed. **1969** Moynahan *Pairing Off* 126: You look bushed. Come in and have a drink. **1971** Nichols (NBC-TV): Thanks anyway, Nichols, but I'm feeling kind of bushed. **1975** Zezza *Love Potion* 349: I'm really bushed, sweet Gloria.

bush eel *n.* a rattlesnake.

1835 *Davy Crockett's Almanack* (1836) 2: Bush eels fried in butter.

busher *n.* **1.** *Baseball.* a player on a bush-league team.

1910 *Baseball Mag.* (Apr.) 63. **1911** Van Loan *Big League* 98: Here's something pretty soft! Git this busher! **1913** *Sat. Eve. Post* (May 31) 12: Chase him over in the annex, along with the other bushers! **1914** *Collier's* (Aug. 1) 6: They ain't no busher kin eveh play that outfiel' like you. **1939–40** Tunis *Kid from Tomkinsville* 17: Ty tried to run him down as a fresh young busher. **1988** Sayles *Eight Men Out* (film) [ref. to 1919]: We played like a bunch of bushers today. **1993** *Village Voice* (N.Y.C.) (Aug. 24) 142: [Willie] Mays…scans the picture of himself as a busher.

2. BUSH-LEAGUER, 2.

1926 *Variety* (Dec. 29) 5: With my 50-word vocabulary, I'd be a busher in that company. **1952** in Hemingway *Sel. Letters* 772: Maybe because he had won the Nobel prize. It sure was a busher's reaction. **1964** in J. O'Hara *Sel. Letters* 442: This is exactly why I insisted on dealing with you and not with a committee of bushers, and spineless bushers at that. **1981–85** S. King *It* 63: You're being a fucking busher and I don't like it.

bushhead *n.* a person having a bushy head of hair.—used derisively.

1985 *N.Y. Times* (Dec. 16) B 1. **1985** N.Y.C. woman, age *ca*50: When I was a kid there was another little girl in the playground who always called me *bushhead*. I hated it!

bush-hog *n.* BUSH APE.

1984 W.M. Henderson *Elvis* 12: There was no need to hide your bush-hog status in front of rich kids….Here was a true bush-hog with no roots, no culture [etc.].

bush league *n.* a rural, semiprofessional baseball league; (hence) a minor professional league. Now *S.E.*

1908 in Fleming *Unforgettable Season* 95: Three straight defeats, and the local players [were] putting up bush league ball. **1911** Van Loan *Big League* 25: It ain't as if I…had to go back to some bush league. **1914** Patten *Lefty o' the Bush* 129: Hutch ain't handlin' a team in this bush league from choice.

bush-league *adj.* amateurish; unprofessional; juvenile; second-rate.

1908 in Fleming *Unforgettable Season* 260: To avoid duplicating Gill's bush league blunder. **1910** G. Rice, in M. Gardner *Casey* 39: And then to think he'd go and spring a bush-league trick like that. **1912** Mathewson *Pitching* 24: A pantomime…that made *Sumurun* look like a bush-league production. **1912–14** in E. O'Neill *Lost Plays* 185: Everyone in this bush-league army seems all corned up tonight except me. **1915–16** Lait *Beef, Iron & Wine* 194: This bush-league orchestry [is] drawing double for overtime. *Ibid.* 236: I'll move out of this bush-league boarding house. **1920** Ade *Hand-Made Fables* 7: Billy's Bush-League Wheezes would set the whole Table cackling. **1922** J. Conway, in *Variety* (Feb. 24) 9: The stage was about to gain a bush-league hambo. **1926** Wood & Goddard *Amer. Slang* 10: Bush league. Second rate. **1951** Bowers *Mob* (film): Tell your friends their frame was bush-league. **1955** McGovern *Fräulein* 240: They're bush league now, but they were good in those days. **1959** Gault *Drag Strip* 93: You're a real bush-league Socrates. **1968** "Iceberg Slim" *Trick Baby* 134: I was absolutely bush-league as a lover.

bush-leaguer *n.* **1.** *Baseball.* a player on a bush-league team.

1906 *Sporting Life* (Feb. 10) 4. **1911** Van Loan *Big League* 87: Well, good-by, you bush leaguers….The Chief needs me to win that pennant, I guess.

2. a person who is amateurish, inexperienced, or naive.

1942 Horman & Corley *Capts. of Clouds* (film): Nobody but a chump would talk to a girl while he was kissing her. And only a bush leaguer would have to. **1944** C.B. Davis *Leo McGuire* 172: They're going to know Cliff Emerson's no bush leaguer. **1970** Sample *Dirty Ballplayer* 72: "Why don't you shut up, bush-leaguer," he yelled back.

bush parole *n. Pris.* an escape from prison.

1927 *AS* (March) 281: I'm gonna shake a bush parole. **1937** Herndon *Let Me Live* 250: You can bet your roll/A "bush parole"/Will set me free. **1956** N. Algren *Walk on Wild Side* 6: Linkhorn had finally taken bush parole, fleeing his Scottish bondage.

bush rat *n.* a woodsman.

1935 in *DARE* I 478. **1942** *ATS* 365: Backwoodsman. *Brush ape, bush rat,* [etc.]. *Ibid.* 481: Woodsman. *Bush-rat.*

bush telegraph *n.* the spread of information by word of mouth; GRAPEVINE; BAMBOO TELEGRAPH. [Orig. and typically in Australian E.]

*1864 in *Dict. Austral. Eng. *1878, *1893, *1934, *1946, *1951, *1954* in *OEDS.* **1991** K. Douglass *Viper Strike* 115: I had to talk to you before you heard it on the bush….the bush telegraph was slang for the

unofficial lines of shipboard rumor.

bushwa *n.* [prob. < F *bourgeois,* as popularized by the radical movement, esp. in the early 20th C.; now taken as euphem. for BULLSHIT]

1. nonsense; BULL; occ. as adj. fraudulent; bogus.

1906 *Nat. Police Gaz.* (July 7) 6: "Bushwa,"…a term of derision used to convey the same comment as "hot air," drifted East from the plains along with other terse expletives. **1919** in Blackbeard & Williams *Smithsonian Comics* 113: Malaria Boochwa Farina Banana La La. **1920** in Wentworth *ADD.* **1921** Dos Passos *3 Soldiers* 246: Looks to me like it's all bushwa. **1922** Colton & Randolph *Rain* 52: Bush-wa!—You should talk of Sunday. **1923** Ornitz *Haunch, Paunch* 82: You'd make a bum outta us with your classical bushwah. **1927** *AS* (Mar.) 275: *Boosh-wah.* Talking for talk's sake. **1934** H. Roth *Call It Sleep* 272: "Buzjwa!" they chorused. **1939** J.T. Farrell *To Whom It May Concern* 195: The usual boushwah of the Reds, he reflected. **1948** Wolfert *Act of Love* 47: Tell me this in English without any Churchill bushwa to it. **1956** Levin *Compulsion* 138: Bushwah, it's all mechanical reaction. **1961** Rosten *Capt. Newman* 35: Oh, don't give me any of your booshwa. **1973** I. Reed *La. Red* 95: Be quiet, you bushwa bitch! **1977** Olsen *Fire Five* 54: But what's a little bushwah if it'll help save a life? **1987** *Larry King Live* (CNN-TV) (May 14): This is not a bushwa document. It is a genuine document.

2. a bourgeois individual.

1933 Ersine *Prison Slang* 23: *Bushwa, n.* (From the French *bourgeois*) A person hostile to the underworld; a *boosier, yap;* usually one of the middle class who is stern and righteous. "With twelve bushwas on the jury, he didn't have a chance."

bushwhack *n.* **1.** BUSHWHACKER.

1872 *Overland Mo.* (Nov.) 433: Dem bushwhacks pick it up, sartin!

2. an attack from ambush.

1937 Glidden *Brand of Empire* 160: Senator Waranrode is aimin' to hang this bushwhack on me. **1980** S. Fuller *Big Red* 14: Or a welcoming bushwhack. **1985** Tate *Bravo Burning* 74: The first thirty seconds of a bushwhack.

bushwhack *v.* [back formation fr. BUSHWHACKER] **1.a.** to attack from ambush; to ambush. Now *colloq.*

1861 in C.W. Altshuler *Latest from Ariz.* 201: "We will…get ahead of and bush-whack 'em"—i.e., fight them in Indian fashion, from behind rocks and bushes. **1864** in *PADS* (No. 70) 24: Were bushwacked occasionally while on march. **1866** *Galaxy* (Dec. 1) 644: In the language of Sheridan, he "bushwhacked every train, every small party, and every straggler." **1866** Smith *Bill Arp* 116: The Confederate cavalry can fight 'em, and dog 'em, and dodge 'em, and bushwhack 'em, and bedevil 'em for a thousand years. **1891** Lummis *David* 91: Ketched Buxton hid up in the *mal pais* cañon waitin' to bushwhack the boy. **1927** in Hammett *Knockover* 280: They bushwacked the police and made a merry wreck out of 'em. **1984** *Fall Guy* (ABC-TV): When we bushwhack 'em, we gotta make it quick and clean.

b. *Stu.* (see quots.).

1958 J. Davis *College Vocab.* 13: *Bushwhacking*—Searching out parked couples and scaring them. **1970** Wakefield *All the Way* 84: Putting on a show for a bunch of bushwhackers. Sonny used to go bushwhacking himself when he was in high school…sneaking up on some poor couple making out and then flashing a goddam spotlight on them and jeering and yelling a lot of dirty stuff and running away after spoiling things.

2. to travel, as through heavy undergrowth.

1862 in C.W. Wills *Army Life* 61: I'd rather be shot than to bushwhack around in Missouri much longer. **1987** J. Thompson *Gumshoe* 30: I…bushwhacked farther up the bank toward the freeway….*Ibid.* 33: He's not going to want to come bushwhacking up that steep slope.

3. *Stu.* to engage in sexual activity in the seclusion of a wooded area.

1917 in [Grider] *War Birds* 50: One of the boys came in the other night after midnight without his Sam Browne belt. He was last seen walking down the street with a girl and he had it on then. So everybody got to kidding him about bushwhacking. **1943** *Yank* (Sept. 17) 21: We were bush-whacking in the off-limit weeds the night/Your grandpop up and proposed to me.

bushwhacked *adj.* very drunk.

1960 MacCuish *Do Not Go* 79: She's plastered, Normy. Bushwhacked! Taken in the rear by booze.

bushwhacker *n.* **1.** a backwoodsman.

1809 W. Irving *History of N.Y.* II 107: They were gallant bush-whackers and hunters of raccoons by moonlight. [The others were] potent suckers of eggs. **1853** C. Hill *Scenes* 169: Mind what you say to me, you little bushwacker. **1894** Crane *Red Badge* 27: He up an' sed that he was willin' t' give his hand t' his country, but he be dumbed if he was goin' t' have every dumb bushwhacker in th' kentry walkin' 'round on it.

2. a scythe or similar instrument for cutting bushes.
1849 in *DA* 228.

3. *Army.* a guerrilla soldier, esp. of the Confederate Army. Now *hist.*
1861 in C.W. Wills *Army Life* 33: A party of the Iowa 7th were out hunting bushwhackers. **1862** M.V. Victor *Unionist's Dtr.* 91: I'll be chawed up fer bait, ef that ain't the track of a bushwhacker thar in the mud. **1876** *Harper's* (July) 195: "Bush-whackers," as the Kansans and negroes denominated the Confederate guerrilla troops. *ca*1880 Bellard *Gone for a Soldier* 101: A few shots…were fired by the regulars who were on picket at some prowling bushwhackers.

4. Orig. *West.* an ambusher; (*Und., specif.*) a purse-snatcher; (*hence*) any treacherous person.
1926 in *AS* II 280: "Bushwackers" (thieves that steal purses on the streets). **1926** in *DARE* I 479: *Bushwhacker.* **1944** *Amer. N & Q* (Oct.) 101: *Bushwhacker:* in police parlance a "man who lurks in parks for the purpose of attacking unescorted women." **1948** in *DA* 228. **1958** McCulloch *Woods Words* 25: *Bushwhacker*—A man who will do you dirt; not to be trusted. **1985** Dye *Between Raindrops* 288: Fucking bushwhacker disappeared.

business *n.* **1.** the male or female genitals. [Mostly a euphem.; cf. *OED* (used since mid-17th C. to refer in an indefinite way to any material object).]
1942 *ATS* 147. **1951** Elgart *Over Sixteen* 150: A midget was kicked out of the nudist colony because he had his nose in everybody's business. **1972** Swarthout *Tin Lizzie* 45: I'll blow your business off!

2. prostitution.—usu. constr. with *the.*
*a*1904–11 Phillips *Susan Lenox* II 114: You're new to—to the business? *Ibid.* 205: I've got a soft heart for you ladies. I've got a wife in the business, myself. **1929** M. Gold *Jews Without Money* 32: How she drifted into the "business" no one ever learned. **1939** C.R. Cooper *Scarlet* 4: Instead of being a full-fledged "woman in the business"…she was still at its outer fringes. **1966** S. Harris *Hellhole* 180: "How did I get into the business?" she asks with a small smile.

3. a woman.
1928 McKay *Banjo* 107: But I've got this sweet business with me.

4. (in phrs. having the form *give, slip,* or *get the business*):
a. Orig. *Und.* death by murder; (*also*) a beating.
1929–31 Runyon *Guys & Dolls* 107: Many a guy gets the old business on the roads outside Atlantic City. **1939** "E. Queen" *Dragon's Teeth* 118: She admit givin' the other dame the business? **1954** Maurer & Vogel *Narcotics* 264: They finally gave that rat in Chi the business. **1970** N.Y.U. prof., age *ca*33: If anybody said anything against Stalin, they got the business, just like under Hitler. **1974** N.Y.C. man, age *ca*25: [Muhammad] Ali fakes 'em out and then he gives 'em the business [in a prizefight].

b. flirtatious glances.
1940 Hartman & Butler *Rd. to Singapore* (film): Nikkipoo over there is givin' you the business. **1942** *ATS* 335. **1951** Thacher *Captain* 142: But the scuttle has it that some nurse was givin' you the business while you were ashore and finally…you disappeared with her for a while.

c. a close interrogation or cross-examination, esp. by third-degree methods.
1940 in H. Gray *Arf* (unp.): Two days and nights I get th' third degree—th' works—th' business—and now you are *sorry!* **1942** *ATS* 465, 516. **1954** Maurer & Vogel *Narcotics* 264: Everyone gets the business from those dicks in Cincy.

d. a teasing, ridiculing, baiting, or hazing.
1941–42 Gach *In Army Now* 180: If his pet team is getting shellacked…give him the business. **1942** S. Johnston *Queen of Flat-tops* 28: Eventually…they quieted, ceased…casting reflections on Ramsey's ancestors, and proceeded to give the victim "the business." **1947** Schulberg *Harder They Fall* 97: Why you always try to give me the business? **1951** Robbins *Danny Fisher* 115: "You're not givin' me the business?" The last remaining trace of skepticism was in my voice. **1954** Lindner *50-Min. Hr.* 71: They're giving me the business again. **1958** Mayes *Hunters* (film): Everybody's been giving me the business. **1984** Univ. Tenn. instructor, age 32: *Giving someone the business* means teasing them.

e. an act of dismissing or jilting.
1942 *ATS* 67: Oust…Discharge or "Fire."…*give the business.* *Ibid.* 338:

Jilt…*give the business.* **1978** Berry *Kaiser* 239: My fiancée had given me the business and married another guy.

f. a scolding or other form of chastisement.
1942 *ATS* 298, 317. **1961** *Leave It to Beaver* (ABC-TV): He just oughta let the school give him the business. **1984** Univ. Tenn. instructor, age 36: When a little boy or girl *gets the business* that means they get a scolding. That's the only meaning I'm familiar with.

g. a hoodwinking or deceiving.
1942 *ATS* 312: Cheat; defraud…*give* (or *slip*) *the business.* **1963** Rose & Rose *Mad Mad World* (film): Don't let 'em give ya the business! Don't let 'em fool ya!

h. an act of coitus.
1942 *ATS* 342. **1959** Zugsmith *Beat Generation* 37: He liked to give them the business in full daylight. **1959** Tevis *Hustler* 154: Like when you give the business to a woman; you got to give it; don't hold back.

i. destruction.
1945 Atlas et al. *GI Joe* (film): That monastery. It's…an observation post. If you don't want to get us all killed, you better give it the business.

5. *Narc.* paraphernalia for the smoking of opium; (*hence*) a hypodermic syringe for the injection of an opiate or other drug.
1936 Dai *Opium Add.* 197: *Business.* The entire paraphernalia used for smoking opium or for taking drugs hypodermically. **1967** Maurer & Vogel *Narc. Add.* (ed. 3) 342: *Business.* The hypodermic needle, as separate from the syringe.

¶ In phrases:

¶ **do (one's) business** to defecate.
*1645 in *OED* I 1205: Have a…care…that…no birds build, chatter, or do their businesse, or sing there. *1722 [T. Sheridan] *Wonderful Wonder* 14: When in *Office*, (4) no one…*does his Business* better….(4) *Office. Necessary-House.* **1858** in *N. Dak. Hist.* XXXIII (1966) 152: If one of them does its business, instead of wiping [the child] with a stick or grass [etc.]. **1942** McAtee *Supp. to Grant Co. Dial. in '90's* 4: *Do a job, do one's business,* v. phr., defecate. **1942** *ATS* 153. **1962** T. Berger *Reinhart* 14: Deserted except for an impatient man roped to a pet doing its business.

¶ **get** [or **give**] **the business** see (4), above. Also vars.

¶ **like nobody's business** in an extraordinary way; at an extraordinary rate.
[**1839** in *OEDS*: As to eating, jist go to Snowden's and the way you can git good things is nobody's business.] **1935** in M. Crane *Roosevelt* 52: It meant that you wanted to hold your job like nobody's business. **1972** P. Thomas *Savior* 19: They could blend—like nobody's business—into the words of the Holy Scriptures…to uphold their conception of Christianity. **1985** N.O. woman, age 34: He was speeding down the street like nobody's business.

¶ **put out of business** to end the activity of, as by injury, destruction, etc.
1910 Raine *Bucky O'Connor* 155: Would you care if one of their pills happened along in the scrimmage and put me out of business? **1923** in W.F. Nolan *Black Mask Boys* 66: I spotted the weight…which put me out of business. **1980** W.C. Anderson *BAT-21* 116: That's the gun that shot down the…chopper. We're about to put it out of business.

¶ **take care of business** Esp. *Black E.* to do something in an especially effective or vigorous manner.
1965 in Cleaver *Soul on Ice* 37: Home boy, them Brothers is taking care of business!…They walking in fours and kicking in doors; dropping reds and busting heads; drinking wine and committing crime [etc., in Watts riot]. **1977** Sayles *Union Dues* 331: "Take care of *biz*ness, child!" "Whup em, baby, *whup* em!" "Whup they *ass*es!"

business end *n.* **1.a.** the sharp, effective, or dangerous end of a tool, weapon, or the like, as opposed to the butt or handle.
1878 in *DA* 228: The business end of a carpet tack. **1883** in Ware *Pass. English* 57: The joke about the pin in the chair, and the suggestion that the business end of a tin tack would be preferable, are essentially American. **1912** (quot. at KNUCKLE-DUSTER). **1943** J. Mitchell *McSorley's* 65: Striking him in the face with "the business end of a broken beer bottle." **1958** McCulloch *Woods Words* 25: *Business end*—a. The motor end of a power saw. b. The engine end of a train. c. The hind end of a wasp, or mule. d. The most important part of any machine. **1984** Univ. Tenn. instructor, age 32: Looking down the business end of a .45. **1990** Murano & Hoffer *Cop Hunter* 19: Now he realized what it felt like to be on the business end of a gun.

b. the dangerous end of a stinging or kicking creature. *Joc.*
1889 Barrère & Leland *Dict. Slang* I 208: The *business-end* of a mule is

his heels. **1958** (quot. at **(a)**, above). **1984** Univ. Tenn. instructor: The *business end* of a mule is his hindquarters.

2. the genitals. *Joc.*

*ca***1889** Field *Bangin'* st. 9: He spread her on the verdant sward beneath the starlight dim,/And linked his business end to hers, which she turned up to him.

business girl *n.* a prostitute. Also **business woman.** Cf. BUSI-NESS, 2.

1924 Tully *Beggars of Life* 139: I belong to the oldest profession in the world. I'm a business woman. **1964** Crane *Sgt. & Queen* 52: There, she could be artfully blended with "business girls," with the prostitutes who flourished outside the…command post. **1973** D. Peterson *Slaughter* 50: She was a "business girl" and knew it. **1981** Spears *Slang & Euphem.* 57.

busk *v.* [back formation fr. BUSKER] to perform as a busker. Also *trans.* Now *S.E.*

1920 *Variety* (Dec. 31) 26: He decided to pick up a little easy change by "busking." **1962** *N.Y. Times* (Sept. 3): Americans in Paris "Busk" for a Living. **1979** Homer *Jargon* 119: Busking the crowd.

busker *n.* [orig. unkn.] an itinerant entertainer, esp. one who sings or plays music in a street or public house. Now *S.E.*

*****1859** Hotten *Slang Dict.* **1920** *Variety* (Dec. 31) 26: He's not a regular entertainer engaged by the house but a "busker"—a fellow who free lances around, playing in this place and that—and collecting his salary by passing the hat—or his banjo. **1950** *N.Y. Times* (Dec. 25) 11: They heard also the sound of a busker's accordion. **1969** Cray *Erotic Muse* 156: Buskers were audience-wise and ready to please. **1979** Homer *Jargon* 119: Long gone from the theatrical scene, *buskers* are now back in vogue. **1988** Giamo *On Bowery* 25: Irving Berlin started as a "busker" (a freelance performer) at Callahan's dance saloon.

busky var. BOSKY.

busser *n.* the mouth; KISSER.

1865 Byrn *Fudge Fumble* 195: "Smack" went a kiss over her busser.

bussie *n.* a bus-driver.

1967 in J. Flaherty *Chez Joey* 55: Good-bye, bussie—we hate to see you go. **1984** Jackson & Lupica *Reggie* 90 [ref. to *ca*1972]: Hey, bussie, could…we [go] a little faster? **1986** *Morning Edition* (Nat. Pub. Radio) (Mar. 10): Bus drivers are universally called "bussies" by [professional] athletes—but I've never heard the term outside of sports.

bust *n.* [fr. the *v.*] **1.a.** a financial collapse; usu. in phr. **boom and bust.** Now *S.E.*

1842 *Knickerbocker Mag.* 99: A mistake!…It's a reg'lar-bilt bu'st! **1947** in *DA* 229: We had an agricultural "boom and bust" after the other World War. **1979** in Terkel *Amer. Dreams* 80: There was the booms and the busts, we went from one to the other.

b. an utter failure; FLOP.

*ca***1852** in Bartlett *Amer.* (ed. 2) 60: Why is the Whig party like a sculptor? Because it takes Clay; and makes a *bust.* *a***1890** *F & H* I 393: *Bust*…(American.)—A failure; a fizzle. **1917** *N.Y. Times* (Dec. 23) IV 6: I heard some one speak of being a "bust"…[a] failure. **1931** in *DA* 229: We have about came to the conclusion that politics as a means of providing sustenance is a complete "bust." **1935** Odets *Waiting for Lefty* 9: You're a four-star-bust. **1941** *Sat. Eve. Post* (May 17) 86: Rowe was a dreadful bust in two starts. **1953** Gresham *Midway* 79: You've always got to keep enough in the bank to see you through a season that's a complete bust. **1962** T. Berger *Reinhart in Love* 91: I got married, and at this moment that looks like a bust too. **1971** *N.Y.U. prof.*: Despite his careful plugging of it, Petrarch's *Africa* was a bust. **1972** Kellogg *Lion's Tooth* 17: Well, *that* was a bust!

c. *Stu.* a failure in academic work; notice of such a failure.

1894 *Lucky Bag* (U.S. Nav. Acad.) 66: Bust…A failure. Bust, (cold or frigid)…A bad or total failure. **1920** *Howitzer* (U.S. Mil. Acad.) 175: About this time the "busts" came through.

d. a disappointing experience; something that is an utter waste of time; an embarrassing mistake.

1927 C.F. Coe, in Paxton *Sport* 150: The fight was too evidently a bust to hold his interest. **1928** *AS* III 218: The Theta dance sure was a bust. **1930** *Variety* (Jan. 8) 123: Wot the hell, if everyone was honest, life would be a bust. **1933** D. Runyon, in *Collier's* (June 10): You are certainly on a bust if you think you can catch the Orange Blossom now. **1965–70** in *DARE* I 480. **1979** F. Thomas *Golden Bird* 166: I went through that page for page. A bust.

e. *Cards.* a dealt hand that is worthless.

1934 Weseen *Slang Dict.* 249: Bust—A worthless hand in a card game.

1982 Hayano *Poker Faces* 66: Some pros…flaunt their "busts" (useless hands) by turning them face up on the table under the nose of a player who threw away the best hand.

f. a sad or unpleasant thing.

1973 R. Roth *Sand in Wind* ch. 2: "He died in a few minutes…a good kid." "That's a bust." **1978** J. Webb *Fields of Fire* 237: I never heard anything like it. What a bust.

2.a. a drinking spree.

1840 *Amer. Joe Miller* 116: Away with the expense, I say, when a fellow is on a bust. **1845** Hooper *Simon Suggs* 175: And I'll bet he's been down to Wetumpky to sell the cotton—got on a bust thar—and now's on another here. **1847** Robb *Squatter Life* 149: Tom swore that…if a fellar didn't drink he'd bust, and, therefore, it was necessary to take a *bust* now and then to keep out of danger. **1847** in H.C. Lewis *Works* 131: I got on a "bust" in town, an' my critter got loose an' struck for home. **1848** *Life in Rochester* 49: He was acquainted with the gals, and wan't afraid to go out on a bust with the b'hoys. **1852** Hazen *Five Years* 355: Stephens who was out for a "*bust*," refused to mount one step of the "*Jacob's-ladder*," until furnished with a bottle of liquor. **1854** in WPA *S.F. Songster* 34: I'm going to the city to get on a "bust." **1862** Heartsill *1491 Days* 64: Maybe the Editors are on a reglar Old Time "Bust." **1862** in Farley *Soldier Life* 8: Nothing excitable except that a few of the boys got on a bust. **1865** Byrn *Fudge Fumble* 201: Perhaps he might go on a "bust." **1871** Schele de Vere *Americanisms* 216: He is accused of being apt to be on a *bust*, as they call, in California, a great drinking-bout, accompanied with dancing and gambling, or as the West generally says…on a *buster*. **1889** O'Reilly & Nelson *Fifty Years on the Trail* 185: A coach…drove up with half a dozen men out on the "bust." *****1909** in Ware *Passing English* 58: A vulgar critic asserts that Poe must have been on a bust and raven mad when he wrote his famous poem. **1931** Dos Passos *1919* 178.

b. a celebration.

1847 G.B. McClellan *Mex. War Diary* 37: We passed the town, crossed the river and encamped. Sorgo got 19 eggs and we had a "bust." **1944** in *DA* 229: You don't exactly figure that a display of gold sequins and flesh-colored foundations at a Hollywood bust is exactly a contribution toward winning the war.

c. a brief period of unrestrained activity.

1855 in Dwyer & Lingenfelter *Songs of Gold Rush* 46: Old Brigham Young was on a "bust," he swore they'd never die. **1867** in *DA* 229: The darned old thing [a clock] goes on a regular bust when it strikes.

d. a drinking party; esp. in phr. **beer bust.**

1913 J. London *J. Barleycorn* 222: These beer busts were a diversion of these…young fellows. **1928** *AS* (Feb.) 218: Kansas Univ. Slang…*bust.* A drinking party. **1944** Wiener *Flyers* 26: We only got a beer bust. **1949** in Spectorsky *College Years* 187: About time for another beer bust.

3. *Und.* a burglary.

*****ca***1879** in *F & H* I 393: "Fatty Bill, from City Road, rem. for a *bust* ex. two years," means that William…is remanded for a burglary. *****1881–84** Davitt *Prison Diary* I 23: America…is the most difficult and dangerous country in which to do a "burst" (burglary). **1926** Finerty *Criminalese* 7: Bust—A burglary (English slang). **1935** D.W. Maurer, in *AS* (Feb.) 13 [ref. to *a*1910]: *Bust.* Any burglary. (Obs.).

4. *Mil.* a loss of rank or grade.

1918 Griffin *Ballads of Regt.* 46 [ref. to *ca*1905]: The system of "busts" and promotions. **1926** [O'Brien] *Wine, Women & War* 316: *Bust,* reduction in rank. **1953** Russ *Last Parallel* 142: I'm willing to take a bust in order to get out of it, so that I can be with the platoon on line. **1987** Blankenship *Blood Stripe* 162: I got a corporal off with a one-grade bust…in a general court.

5. a hard blow, as with the fist.

1921 in W.C. Fields *By Himself* 112: I'll give you a bust in the eye. **1925** in *OEDS* I 399: *Bust,* a blow; a stroke (in the face). **1933** in R.E. Howard *Iron Man* 120: I…[handed him] a bust that left him standing on his neck in the corner. **1935** Wolfe *Time & River* 107: It's wise guys like you who go around looking for a good bust on the nose, see?

6. *Pool.* the break.

1892 F.P. Dunne, in Schaaf *Dooley* 43: Lawluhr bate thim playin' pool by pocketin' th' fifteen balls from th' bust.

7.a. *Und. & Police.* a police raid or seizure of contraband.

1938 M. Berger, in *New Yorker* (Mar. 12) 37: "One whiff," said Chappy, "and we get a bust." ("Bust" is Harlem for a raid.) **1970** Quammen *Walk Line* 15: He was missing…from the ranks of the Columbia SDS following the Morningside bust. **1977** Butler & Shryack *Gauntlet* 130: *This is a bust!*…Hands up, feet spread, and your balls in your pockets! MOVE! **1977** Bunker *Animal Factory* 1: The attorney had tried to save him from prison, but…two hundred kilos of marijuana and…forty ounces of cocaine was just too big a bust. **1982** *Knoxville Journal* (July 12) 1: Cocaine Bust Biggest in Tennessee History.

b. *Und. & Police.* an arrest.

*ca*1953 Hughes *Lodge* 117: You watch their busts very carefully. **1957** Murtagh & Harris *Cast First Stone* 120: This is my eighth bust. But I only been in the clink four times. **1960** C. Cooper *Scene* 85: There's only so long you can sell [heroin] without getting a bust. **1962** H. Simmons *On Eggshells* 205: That's an automatic bust....That's stealing. **1963** Rubin *Sweet Daddy* 112: This wouldn't be my first bust. **1967** P. Thomas *Mean Streets* 300: Is this your first bust? **1992** *Amer. Detective* (ABC-TV): Anything can go wrong when the bust goes down.

c. *Pris.* a charge of infraction of discipline.

1977 Bunker *Animal Factory* 37: Another bust and I'll never get a parole. I wish I could escape.

d. a criminal charge; RAP.

1965 C. Brown *Manchild* 190: There wasn't so much [prison] time on a drug bust. **1981–85** S. King *It* 22: The boy did not seem to realize just how heavy this particular bust was.

8. *Sports.* a dash; (*also*) a forceful or aggressive move in play.

1942 *ATS* 54: Spurt; burst of speed. *Bust, bust of speed,* [etc.]. **1980** Wielgus & Wolff *Basketball* 41: *Bust* (*n*) A strong move to the hoop.

9. *Black E.* an orgasm.

1965 in W. King *Black Anthol.* 302: I mean he passes out after a bust.

bust *adj.* bankrupt; penniless.—rarely (*obs.*) **burst up.**

1846 Durivage & Burnham *Stray Subjects* 168: Ten pounds [of turkey at seven cents a pound]—I'm bust, by gravy! *ca*1865 Leavitt & Eagan *Dickens* 3: It's no use, I'm burst up, dead broke! **1888** *Outing* (Sept.) 533: I'm sorry he's bust, but who in the mischief is Mary? **1922** Rollins *Cowboy* 20: Thus the West...believed that "going bust"...was not a serious state and was terminable at any time by the insolvent's initiative. **1937** Steinbeck *Mice & Men* 65: The ol' people that owns it is flat bust. **1970** Terkel *Hard Times* 277: We had the first bank to go bust in the early days of the Depression. **1979** G. Wolff *Duke of Deception* 44: My father was down and out..."flat bust" (as he liked to say). **1984** Kagan & Summer *Mute Evidence* 495: Social Security...might go bust.

bust *v.* [fr. dial. pronun. of *burst*; cf. *cuss* and *curse*, (nonstandard) *wuss* and *worse*] Also **burst.**

I. *Intrans.*

1.a. to come to financial ruin; fail in business; go bankrupt; (*broadly*) to meet with defeat or failure.

1833 in *DA*: Two persons who had bursted were sitting vis a vis by the fire-place. **1840** *Amer. Joe Miller* 87: The goods had gone out on a bust long before I busted. **1845** in Durivage & Burnham *Stray Subjects* 56: He had seen the old United States Bank, but, for the life of him, couldn't find the place where it had busted! **1859** in Botkin *Treas. Amer. Folk.* 310: "Pike's Peak or bust."...He busted. **1870** Medbery *Wall St.* 140: "Jones *busted*" passes from mouth to mouth. **1891** F. McCormick *Kans. Farm* 79: One covered wagon had written on it: "In God we trusted, in Kansas we busted." **1897** Ade *Pink* 144: All 'ese heah banks can bust an' 'ey wont eveh touch me. **1908** Opper *H. Hooligan* xvi: De very next day de bank busted an' de depositors never got a cent.

b. *Stu.* to fail an examination or a course of study; to FLUNK.—now usu. constr. with *out.*

1851 Hall *College Wds.* 33: *Burst.* To fail in reciting; to make a bad recitation. This word is used in some of the Southern colleges. **1900** *Volunteer* (Univ. Tenn.) 179: We "busted" in Trig. while at college. **1900** *DN* II 25: *Bust,* v.i. To fail in recitation or examination. **1906** *Army & Navy Life* (Nov.) 498: *Bust* is to fail at a recitation or an examination. **1931** Uhler *Cane Juice* 106: My English, I busted in it at L.S.U. **1957** Gutwillig *Long Silence* 76: Boys who had "busted out" of Cornell. **1972** Hannah *Geronimo* 268: She didn't know I'd busted out of med school.

2. to go at top speed; to tear.

1844 Porter *Big Bear* 131: "Keep them dogs in, and break for the Forkin' Cypress, Sol," says I....."Massa Chunkey *is* risin'," said Sol, and then he busted. **1908** McGaffey *Show Girl* 235: We went busting by the Statue of Liberty. **1929** Caldwell *Bastard* 65: I wish she hadn't gone and busted off like she did. I sorta miss her a lot now. **1955** Graziano & Barber *Somebody Up There* 9: Ma bust out of the house and headed right for her. **1963** E.M. Miller *Exile* 30: Bust over there and see what you can see and call me back. **1977** Avallone *White Knight* 21: All of them must certainly have eyeballed the cowboy busting by.

3. to engage in a drinking bout or spree.

1837 Neal *Charcoal Sks.* 176: For my part, I think this bustin' of yourn looks bad,...'specially when you're goin' it on crab-apple cider. **1858** in *Ind. Mag. of Hist.* XLVII (1951) 277: Heard the Senior Class was about

to bust. Went and brought Miss Lizzie to the party. **1869** in *DAE*.

4. to happen; take place.

1844 Porter *Big Bear* 128: "Chunkey?" says he. "What's busted, Jem?"

5. to break (in various senses).

1926 C.M. Russell *Trails* 126: Wolves...don't like bein' busted in on at meal-times. **1938** Haines *Tension* 213: She busted off quiet a minute or two and then looked me right in the eyes. **1942** L.R. Foster *Mayor of 44th St.* (film): She busted with Kirby same as you did. **1948** Manone & Vandervoort *Trumpet* 53: Then we would bust into some hot jazz. **1962** Kesey *Cuckoo's Nest* 86: They had all busted up laughing fit to kill. **1970** Newman & Benton *Crooked Man* (film): Somebody in this poky must have an idea how to bust out.

II. *Trans.*

6.a. to cause to break (in the simple physical sense); (*hence*) to break up; put the finish to.—also constr. with *up.*

1806 in *DAE*: Windsor busted his rifle near the muzzle. **1845** Hooper *Simon Suggs* 17: You came along and busted up the game. **1865** Sala *Diary* II 57: I learn from the police report of the "busting up" of a disorderly house. **1896** F.H. Smith *Grogan* 22: I'll bust yer jaw, ye sneakin' rat. **1927–30** Rollins *Jinglebob* 28 [ref. to 1880's]: Here's...a busted saddle thong. **1936** R. Adams *Cowboy Lingo* 226: I busted his talk box. **1938** Bellem *Blue Murder* 78: I got a busted finger. **1955** L. Shapiro *Sixth of June* 158: I should've bust him in two. **1990** Costello & Wallace *Sig. Rappers* 3: The gadfly will get his fibula busted.

b. to hit hard; slug.

1873 Bailey *Danbury* 171: I'll bust that goslin' some mornin'. **1874** *Nat. Police Gaz.* (Dec. 5) 3: That's no reason why you should bust your wife in the ear. *ca*1888 *Stag Party* 175: Shut up. I'll bust you again. **1914** Lardner *You Know Me Al* 66: If he had insulted me I would of busted him. **1923** in Truman *Dear Bess* 314: I surely feel like busting a dentist I know of. **1925** Hemingway *In Our Time* 68: A brakeman busted me. **1929** Connelly *Green Pastures* 200: I'd bust anybody what made me de fool. **1944** D. Hartman et al. *Princess & Pirate* (film): I busted him right in the snoot. **1977** in Curry *River's in My Blood* 138: Here, take this damn board and bust him across the rear with it. **1980** N.Y.C. man, age *ca*30: Somebody ought to bust him in the snoot.

c. to break (in various other senses). [For more freq. fig. senses, see phr. entries.]

1863 in C.W. Wills *Army Life* 184: No more alarms...to "bust" the...monotony. **1896** Ade *Artie* 22: Having selected a cue he carefully deposited his cigar at one edge of the table and "busted" the fifteen balls with a fierce stroke. **1922** Rollins *Cowboy* 137: The quirt...was all-important to the man who broke his horses...by "busting their spirit." **1928** in Tuthill *Bungle Family* 45: You have to bust your back for starvation wages. **1934** Berg *Prison Nurse* 115: I suppose the dames gave you such a swell break that it just busts your heart to hear anyone knock them. **1943** *Bataan* (film): Sarge, I'm going to bust one of your orders. **1953** Dibner *Deep Six* 136: Every Jap plane on Kiska and Attu'd hit us if we bust radio silence. **1963** D. Tracy *Brass Ring* 17: The headmaster was looking at him as though he had busted every rule in the place. **1972** W.C. Anderson *Hurricane* 141: Then let's bust out the coffee-pot.

7.a. to bankrupt; to ruin financially.

1829 in *DAE*: For the Aigle Bank was *busted,* and the Cataract of Freedom was stopped. **1870** "M. Twain" in A.L. Scott *Twain's Poetry* 79: If we was playin this fur lucre/You'd bust us sure! **1882** Dodge *Wild Indians* 612: Wall, boys, I was mighty nigh onto busted that time, an' I'll tell you about it. **1882** "M. Twain" *Life on Miss.* 249: And if you work him right he'll bust himself on a single layout. **1917** in R. Peyton *At Track* 152: We've busted Goldfinger Ike at last. **1971** in Cannon *Nobody Asked* 242: Bookmakers are in the business of creating paupers. Their only intention is to bust the player.

b. to get the better of; defeat.—also constr. with *out.*

1842 in J.Q. Anderson *With Bark On* 44: The judge was "busted," "swunk up," and had to give in. He...has never been known to tell a story since that time. **1868** S. Clemens, in *Twain's Letters* II 160: I had the misfortune to "bust out" one author of standing. They had his manuscript, with the understanding that they would publish his book if they could not get a book from me...—so that manuscript was sent back to its author to-day. **1977** Langone *Life at Bottom* 200: You couldn't bust her for nothin', knew it all.

c. *Mil.* to reduce in rank or grade; break.

[**1807** J.R. Shaw *Autobiog.* 69 [ref. to 1782]: Sergeant Pendergrass, you are broken, and to receive 50 lashes.] **1878** Flipper *Colored Cadet* 51 [ref. to 1874]: "Busted," "broken."—These words apply only to cadet officers who are reduced to the ranks. **1899** Cullen *Tales* 104: Jack

Fahey had been busted from post Sergeant-Major at Canby. **1900** *Howitzer* (U.S. Mil. Acad.) 118: *Bust.*—To deprive of rank; to degrade. **1906** Beyer *Amer. Battleship* 83: "Busted"—disrated to a lower rating. **1918** R. Lardner *Treat 'Em Rough* 81: His captain…busted him and I don't mean he cracked him in the jaw. **1918** Ruggles *Navy* 27: Some members of the ship's company may get disrated for some offense, and it is known as being "busted." Very often called "broke." **1920** *Amer. Legion Wkly.* (Jan. 30) 6: The old man is busted down to major, but he stands the gaff. **1922** Paul *Impromptu* 159: If Atwood was pickled…bust him and give him a month's fatigue. **1928** York *Sgt. York* 184: Our sergeant takened forty-eight hours' leave and stayed away ten days. He was busted for that, but later on he got his stripes back. **1947** Lay & Bartlett *12 O'Clock High* 79: Who said anything about busting you or transferring you? **1967** Dibner *Admiral* 27: I'm going to bust him back to seaman second so fast his ears'll whistle. **1981–83** N. Proffitt *Gardens of Stone* 231: The old man busted him down a stripe. **1988** M. Maloney *Thunder Alley* 99: They'll bust him down to paint-scrapper.

8.a. to break into; to burglarize. Cf. BUSTER, 5.

1791 [W. Smith] *Confess. T. Mount* 21: His Peter we did burst. **1891** "Eli Perkins" *30 Yrs. of Wit* 296: I can bust more Pullman coaches on the rail/Than any one who's worked the job before. **1896** Brown *Parson* 42: Did you steal something?…Did you burst a bank?…Did you kill somebody? **1937** E. Anderson *Thieves Like Us* 51: Them are the little snitches that are doing a couple of years for busting a two-bit grocery. **1961** Ellison *Purgatory* 87: The Flyers busted the trade high school…and…worked over the offending Baron with keyhole saws and ball peen hammers.

b. to intrude on without an invitation; CRASH.

1895 Wood *Yale Yarns* 87: Shell we do 'im up, as he'd oughter be did up fer a tryin' fer ter bust de meetin'? **1961** Ellison *Purgatory* 30: I was ready to try and bust a gang.

9.a. *Und. & Police.* to arrest; (*hence*) to turn (someone) over to the police. [Became universally known *ca*1968–70.]

1940 *Current Hist. & Forum* (Nov. 7) 22: The inmates describe…how they *got busted out at* [*sic*] (arrested). **1946** Mezzrow & Wolfe *Really Blues* 63: The police chief was too busy mixing drinks to bust himself under the prohibition act. *Ibid.* 303: *Bust:* arrest. **1952** Brossard *Darkness* 143: He was busted…six months ago. **1952** Mandel *Angry Strangers* 234: Why'n't they like bust the guys which they too big like for anybody? Like Wall Street, I dunno. **1953** W. Brown *Monkey on My Back* 38: Lane and Schonbaum had got busted (arrested). *ca*1953 Hughes *Lodge* 117: If Fran gets busted, then that whole side of town…is going to be out of luck. **1956** A. Ginsberg *Howl* 9: Who got busted in their pubic beards returning through Laredo/with a belt of marijuana for New York. **1959** O'Connor *Talked to Stranger* 23: I got busted two months later for assault. **1960** C.L. Cooper *Scene* 11: I wouldn't bust you, if that's what you're leery about. *Ibid.* 86: He springs me if I get busted. *Ibid.* 265: What'd you get busted for? **1962** Perry *Young Man* 120: He got busted in a stick-up. **1962** H. Simmons *On Eggshells* 163: Charlie had gotten busted on a narcotics rap. **1963** *Time* (Aug. 2) 14: *Busted.* Arrested. **1967** McNeill *Moving Through Here* 30: Soon there was a bail fund to free busted brothers. **1971** H. Roberts *3d Ear* (unp.): I was busted twice that week. **1973** W. Crawford *Stryker* 18: They bust his ass for B & E. **1974** *Police Woman* (NBC-TV): Do tell those guys down at the Morals Unit not to bust me on Saturday night. **1989** Kienzle *Eminence* 176: If the need to bust them arose, he wanted to know what he was doing.

b. to catch in the act; (*broadly*) to discover.

1954–60 *DAS* 79: *Bust*…To catch another in the act of doing something illegal or unethical.…*since c*1955. **1962–68** B. Jackson *In Life* 316: I was busted (somebody recognized me) up there on it. **1970** Landy *Underground Dict.* 43: *Bust*…Catch someone doing something he shouldn't be doing. **1971** N.Y.U. student: He brought a gyp sheet to the exam and the professor busted him when he thought he wasn't looking. *a*1987 Bunch & Cole *Reckoning for Kings* 344: If they bust us now, we're…dead. **1992** *Donahue* (NBC-TV): "He was goin' with a black girl [until] his parents busted him." "What do you mean, they 'busted' him?" "They found out about it!"

c. *Und. & Police.* to raid by force of law.

1971 Simon *Sign of the Fool* 122: As long as a kid had ID proving legal age, the law couldn't bust the house for "contributing to the delinquency of a minor." **1972** *N.Y. Post* (Nov. 3) 2: Several of the parlors…have been busted on prostitution charges…but all were back in business almost immediately.

d. *Pris.* to subject to disciplinary action.

1971 *Intern. Jour. Addictions* VI 10: When I went to jail I never got busted. All them years I have never been in the bing, never had a cop

come sell me ticket, never been in keeper lock, nothing. **1977** Bunker *Animal Factory* 36: I could bust the whole fuckin' mob of you.…Every day the captain [of the guard] gets a dozen snitch letters about those maniacs.

10. *Journ.* to reveal or release (news).

1865 Brown *Ward: Travels* 79: She…sent a boy to Bust the news gently to the afflicted wives. **1930** Graham & Graham *Queer People* 12: If she isn't there call back, and we'll bust the story.

11.a. to kill.

1871 "M. Twain" *Roughing It* 34: Here I've sot, and sot, and sot, a-bust'n muskeeters and wonderin' what was ailin' ye. **1881** Nye *Forty Liars* 79: I…would have been almost childless if little James Abraham Garfield had been busted. **1886** Nye *Remarks* 23: The Eureka bed-bug buster. **1891** *Outing* (Oct.) 84: I run into a hull drove of patridge back yonder, an' if you fellers want to bust 'em, come ahead. **1988** R. Menllo & R. Rubin *Tougher Than Leather* (film): Bust him, Dee.

b. to wreck or ruin; to destroy. [Since WWII used esp. in ref. to air-to-ground combat operations.]

1911 Van Loan *Big League* 63: I bet I bust this business up somehow! If I don't he'll bust the team! **1947** Boyer *Dark Ship* 159: These guys are no good union busting finks. **1956** Heflin *USAF Dict.* 92: *Bridge-busting, n.* The destroying or disabling of bridges by airplane attacks. *Slang.* **1957** Ness & Fraley *Untouchables* 22: I'm going to bust Al Capone and I'm hoping you'll help me. **1966–67** Harvey *Air War* 104: We really busted his ass then. Blew him up like a toy balloon. **1972** *Airman* (Oct.) 37: The AC-130 has accounted for more trucks "busted" than any other aircraft. **1972** DeLillo *End Zone* 225: Then the city-busting begins. Selected population centers…are hit by…ICBMs carrying MIRV warheads. **1979** in Terkel *Amer. Dreams* 210: It makes you feel good to go into a plant and bust heads with professional union busters. **1985** MacLaine *Dancing* 12: A few of my friends had said…[my book] would be a "career buster." *a*1990 R. Herman, Jr. *Force of Eagles* 63: That would have been one busted air patch.

c. to deflower, esp. by rape; to rape.—usu. considered vulgar.

1965 Capote *In Cold Blood* 275: I'm gonna bust that little girl. **1966** King *Brave & Damned* 51: He wanted to bust a virgin who'd screech and claw. **1972** P. Thomas *Savior* 8: Some broad got busted, or says she did and said my brother copped her cherry. **1988** Knoxville, Tenn., paralegal investigator: Once you're actually in the slammer, getting *busted* means getting raped anally.

12. *West.* to break (a horse); (*hence*) to rope and subdue (a cow). Now *colloq.*

1891 *Harper's Mag.* (July) 210: Two rides will usually bust a bronco so that the average cow-puncher can use him. **1897** *Cosmopolitan* (March) 555: His perfesh was bronco-bustin'. **1899** Garland *Eagle's Heart* 88: I don't want him "busted"; I want him taught that I'm his friend. **1905** W.S. Kelly *Lariats* 38: We can "bust" any broncho whatever bucked. **1939** Coolidge *Old Calif. Cowboys* 67 [ref. to *ca*1914]: When a cow-brute is roped and busted he is damaged at least ten dollars' worth the minute he hits the ground. *Ibid.* 79: They were rough on the cattle—they "busted" them and chased them about. **1941** *Nat. Geo.* (Mar.) 300: He's too old now to…bust a bronco.

13. [cf. **(1.b.)**, above] **a.** *Stu.* to fail (a course of study, an examination, etc.).

1931 *AS* (Feb.) 203: *Bust a course:* fail to pass a course of study. *bust a quiz:* fail to pass an examination. **1944** *New Yorker* (June 3) 23: He had busted Meteorology. **1971** Vaughan & Lynch *Brandywine* 88: After we bust this inspection…a lot of us are going to be looking for a new job.

b. *Stu.* to fail (a student). See also BUST OUT, *v.*, 2.

1966 R. Fariña *Down So Long* 51: They can't bust you, Heff.

14.a. to escape from, as by force.

1930 M. West *Babe Gordon* 11: A guy up there busted Sing Sing. **1965** Capote *In Cold Blood* 295: He had decided to "bust jail." **1965** Linakis *In Spring* 325: I didn't bust Loire [stockade]. I didn't have the balls.

b. to enable (someone) to escape, esp. by force.—constr. with *out.*

1950 P. Green *Peer Gynt* 28: "I got the devil all shut up," he says. "Let me at him and I'll bust him out," he says.

15. *Narc.* to smoke (a marijuana cigarette).

1955 E. Hunter *Jungle Kids* 104: He can bust a joint any time he wants. **1956** E. Hunter *Second Ending* 280: Come on, daddy, bust a joint with old Dickie-boy. **1971** *Playboy* (Jan.) 106: It's easier to go back to the apartment, kick off your shoes and bust a joint.

16. *Police.* to pass (a stop sign or signal) illegally.

1967 Hersey *Algiers Motel* 103: Police officers may not bust lights to get to a run in the Brewster projects. **1972** Wambaugh *Blue Knight* 183: Let's see, did I ever tell you about the big dude I stopped for busting a stop sign out front of your place?

17. *Rap Music.* to pay attention to; look at; notice.

1985 "UTFO" *Roxanne Roxanne* (rap song): You gotta be stronger in ways she can't resist,/So, Educated Rapper, huh, bust this! **1990** *Houston Post* (May 24) A3: *Bust this:* watch what I am doing. **1991** *Source* (Oct.) 33: Bust dis, the Bomb Squad ain't doing the beats either.

18. Esp. *Rap Music.* to produce, create, perform, etc.; "knock out."

1981–85 S. King *It* 26: "Was he really working hard on it, then?" ..."Yes—he was busting pages." **1988** "Kid 'n Play" *Rollin' with Kid 'n Play* (rap song): I'll bust a rhyme and a dance. **1989** "The D.O.C." *The Formula* (rap song): Originality is a must whenever I bust/A funky composition. **1989** *Spin* (Aug.) 12: L.L. busts rhymes with unrelenting grace and invention. **1991** Nelson & Gonzales *Bring Noise* 191: Gots to go the studio and bust some raps.

¶ In phrases:

¶ **bust a cap** to fire a bullet; (*hence*) **bust caps** *Mil.* to engage in battle.

1865 in Berlin et al. *Black Mil. Exper.* 463: He cocked it and bursted a cap at some body. **1878** McElroy *Andersonville* 273 [ref. to Civil War]: They'd break their necks runnin' away ef ye so much as bust a cap near to 'em. **1963** Williamson *Hustler!* 112: I shoot you, boy! I'll bust a cap in your ass! **1978** J. Webb *Fields of Fire* 313: Better relax while you can, 'cause in a few days we are gonna be busting some ba-a-ad caps. **1988** S. Lee *School Daze* (film): You get out before I bust a cap in your ass.

¶ **bust a gut** see s.v. GUT.

¶ **bust a move** *Black E.* to make a move; take action; do something.

1984 "Fat Boys" in B. Adler *Rap!* 31: So bust the fresh move—individual raps. **1989** "Young MC" *Busta Move* (rap song): Bust it....So come on, fatso, bust a move. **1990** *In Living Color* (Fox-TV): So why don't you just come up here and bust that rescue move? **1992** *TV Guide* (Dec. 5) 8: Fresh Prince Will Smith is showing the chutzpah to bust another move: lead role in a...Hollywood film.

¶ **bust an oar** *Naut.* to injure oneself through overexertion.

1899 Robbins *Gam* 72: All the dagoes in Talcahuano turned loose and shouting Spanish so I thought they'd bust an oar.

¶ **bust a nut** see s.v. NUT.

¶ **bust ass** see s.v. ASS.

¶ **bust balls** see s.v. BALL, *n.*

¶ **bust bush** [or **jungle**] *Mil.* to cut a trail through a jungle; to move through a jungle, as on a combat patrol.

1970 *N.Y. Times Mag.* (Feb. 8) 91: They "humped the boonies" or "busted bush." **1974–77** Heinemann *Close Quarters* 29: And that kid bustin' jungle in the lead track was busting some bad jungle too. *Ibid.* 68: We busted jungle until we came to a road. **1982** Goff et al. *Brothers* 57: We were busting bush with machetes.

¶ **bust fog** *Constr.* to work on high construction.

1923 in Kornbluh *Rebel Voices* 90: The old fellow took me before a grandstand bigger than the Stadium of the University of Washington that I once busted fog on.

¶ **bust heavies** see s.v. HEAVY, *n.*

¶ **bust (one's) hump** see s.v. HUMP, *n.*

¶ **bust loose** to break free of constraint; (*hence*) to begin acting without restraint; go wild.

1942 *ATS* 311: Abandon Restraint. *Bust loose.* **1955** Q. Reynolds *HQ* 303: His kid has been running around with some rough characters who are about ready to bust loose. **1984** Univ. Tenn. instructor: Sounds like things are getting ready to bust loose in Nicaragua.

¶ **bust open** to sadden greatly; to aggrieve.

1957 Wilbur & Veiller *Monkey on My Back* (film): This is gonna bust the kid wide open.

¶ **bust rocks** see s.v. ROCK.

¶ **bust suds** *Black E.* to wash dishes, esp. as an occupation.

1925 in Leadbitter & Slaven *Blues Records* 404: Suds Bustin' Blues. **1946** G.W. Henderson *Jule* 152: But I ain't going to bust no suds and scrub no floors! **1971** Dahlskog *Dict.* 11: Bust suds, v. To wash dishes. *ca*1979 in J.L. Gwaltney *Drylongso* 68: A woman slinging somebody else's hash and busting somebody else's suds. **1982** Goff et al. *Brothers* 39: You'll mop floors and peel potatoes; you'll scour some pots, and you'll bust some suds down there.

busted *adj.* **1.** penniless; broke.

1836 *Spirit of Times* (July 9) 164: Their pocket change being used up, most of the boys were "busted." **1865** in "M. Twain," *Sks. & Tales* 50: The poor cuss is busted and gone home to the States. **1871** "M. Twain" *Roughing It* 236: It was the wildest mob Virginia had ever seen....To use its own phraseology, it came there "flush" and went away "busted." **1876** in *Contrib. to Hist. Soc. Mont.* I 45: When the outsiders were "busted," they preyed upon one another. **1887** "Bunny" *Cow Boy* 83: I was at last "busted flat," and had not the price of a feed of corn for Pedro. **1893** in J.I. White *Git Along Dogies* 93: A Busted Cowboy's Christmas. **1905** Sinclair *Jungle* 279: No money, either,—a'mos' busted! **1935** in H. Gray *Arf* (unp.): I'm busted and can't land a job. **1946** Heatter *Dim View* 5: I'm busted....You cleaned me at Morobie. **1963** in Cannon *Nobody Asked* 109: Doc died busted. If the guys who owed him had paid off, he would have been wealthy. **1992** N. Cohn *Heart of World* 74: I myself was flat busted.

2. failed; esp. in phr. **busted flush** *Poker.* a worthless hand that is not quite a flush.

1925 in Hammett *Big Knockover* 30: The Princess can give you a fat cut of the profits in a busted caper, with a chance to get yourself hanged. **1927** Rodman *Ky. Admiral* 31: Playing to the gallery is like trying to steal a pot on a "busted flush." It may work once or twice, but in the end it is a losing game if you keep at it persistently. **1982** Hayano *Poker Faces* 61: He was winning on everything—pairs, busted hands.

3. infatuated with.—constr. with *on.* Cf. syn. MASHED.

1929 Caldwell *Bastard* 69: I'm busted on you, kid, and I'll work like hell for you and keep you like a queen.

busted up *adj.* **1.** grief-stricken; depressed.

1892 Gunter *Miss Dividends* 74: The Cap looks as busted up as if he had lost on four aces. **1924** Marks *Plastic Age* 159: This fellow Lavengro was all busted up and depressed. **1930** D. Runyon, in *Collier's* (Jan. 20) 13: Old Doctor Armand Dorval is going to be all busted up if he hears what really happens. **1983** Eilert *Self & Country* 290: I know how busted up you are over Cheryl.

2. insane.

1977 L.A. man, age *ca*30: Man, that cat's busted up.

3. BUSTED, *adj.*, 1.

*ca*1862 *Dodge's Sketches* 11: Dodge was, in fact, literally and metaphorically busted up!

buster *n.* Also **burster.**

1.a. a remarkable person or thing; HUMDINGER.

1831 in *DA* 229: Now he is fairly initiated into the various grades of dissipation, and is looked upon as a "Regular Burster." **1842** *Spirit of Times* (Oct. 22) 402: Blue Dick...is a "buster!"...the fastest horse I ever saw make tracks. **1843** in *DARE* I 481: Applause, laughter, cheers and cries of "go on," "go it, Smith," and "he's a buster, ain't he?" **1845** in *DARE* I 480: Finally I see a country man leading a black colt—wasn't he a buster! **1846** *Spirit of Times* (May 16) 1346: A stump orator for instance, who after making a flaming speech, and knocking his opponent into a "cocked hat" is called a "buster." Or, a man who drinks, swears, fights, and makes himself generally a devilish free and easy, noisy, hearty, clever, and entertaining fellow. **1846** in J.R. Lowell *Works* 176: You *air* a buster ter suppose/I'd eat what makes me hol' my nose! **1852** Stowe *U. Tom's Cabin* 63: "Lor, Pete," said Mose, triumphantly, "han't we got a buster of a breakfast!" **1868** M. Reid *Helpless Hand* 30: Ho, ho, ye young bloods an' busters! I'll make ye pay for this job. **1868** "W.J. Hamilton" *Maid of Mtn.* 65: Warn't she a buster! As pooty as a full-blooded heifer! **1873** in Bunner *Letters* 17: Wasn't that good for a first year? Ain't she a little buster? **1895** Clurman *Nick Carter* 94: The deacon's a buster....He can pray the loudest and the longest of enny man in Cornwall. **1905** *DN* III 4: Buster...A dashing fellow. **1908** in Sandburg *Letters* 78: Capt. Jack's Broncho Book is sure a buster. **1926** Norwood *Other Side of Circus* 76: What do you think of those for a couple of busters? **1957** Lacy *Room to Swing* 132: He seemed...a buster of an idea boy.

b. fellow.—used only in direct address, usu. sarcastically.

1866 G.A. Townsend *Non-Combatant* 262: Halloo! Buster! Keep that bayonit out o' my eye. **1921** U. Sinclair *K. Coal* 52: "Hello, Buster!" said Hal. "Hello yourself!" said the kid. **1953** Chandler *Goodbye* 129: Say that again, buster. **1959** Scott *Flying Tiger* 78: Where were you, buster, where were you fighting from when I was up there getting my ass shot to hell by the Japs? **1962** Astronauts *We Seven* 185: "O.K., Buster," I said to myself, "you volunteered for this thing." **1968** Van Dyke *Strawberries* 172: Look, buster,...I've got a lot of things to do this morning. **1976** Woodley *Bears* 107: Look, buster....I can take care of myself. **1977** F. Wallace *Poker* 119: When you make a stupid play, buster, you pay for it. **1984** Riggan *Free Fire* 97: Not like that, buster.

2. an especially large thing or individual.

1843 Field *Pokerville* 164: Twins—ye gods! a pair of 'em! naked, little, rosy, bawling busters! **1850** in H.C. Lewis *Works* 111: H—l, Doc, but she's a buster! I never seed such a tooth! **1867** in "M. Twain" *Sks. & Tales* 81: He tackled some of them regular busters, tow'rd the middle, you know, and they throwed him. **1891** Bourke *On Border* 331: A fine big fish, "a regular buster." **1900** Hammond *Whaler* 278: Ye-ah, that whale was a buster, that's a fact. **1930** Strickland *Conn. Fights* 137 [ref. to 1918]: Large "busters" from our own and the German guns kept dropping all about with deafening crashes. **1935** J. Conroy *World to Win* 18: Ain't he a buster? Fat as a pig! **1954** Collans & Sterling *House Detect.* 166: A great big buster he was too, with jowls like a lion cub. **1970** Longstreet *Nell Kimball* 6: Later I had a bathroom put in on each floor—on one floor a big buster in marble to hold two.

3. *Naut.* a heavy gale.

1848 Bartlett *Amer.* 57: "This is a buster," i.e. a powerful or heavy wind. **1887** *Outing* (Dec.) 229: We didn't know hard the puff were, but we seed from the damage done that it must have been a buster, and would probably pick a man up like a feather and carry him away. **1898** Stevenson *Cape Horn* 109: They've been having a southerly buster down there. **1903** Sonnichsen *Deep Sea Vagabonds* 18: The gale continued, a regular sou'easter, known by coasters as "the buster," the fiercest wind on that coast. *ca*1940 Harlow *Chanteying* 42 [ref. to 1876]: On the fourth day out, we ran into a "southerly buster."

4. a drinking spree; BENDER; BUST.

1848 Bartlett *Amer.* 57: They were on a buster, and were taken up by the police. **1871** Schele de Vere *Americanisms* 587: Buster…a reckless spree or frolic. **1879** *Puck* (Dec. 3) 635: I'm so darned glad to be in human society like again that I feels like goin' a buster. **1889** Farmer *Amer.*: Buster…a drinking bout accompanied by…dancing, gambling and prostitution.

5. *Und.* a burglar.

1859 Matsell *Vocab.* 16: Burster. A burglar. **1866** *Nat. Police Gaz.* (Dec. 8) 2: A brace of "bursters"…were "pinched to rights" while attempting to "go through" the shoe store of Messrs. C.R. Brooks & Co. **1904** *Life in Sing Sing* 262: But that buster you tipped me to was a raw one.…But that burglar you introduced me to was a novice.

6. *West.* BRONCO-BUSTER.

[**1876** in *Contrib. to Hist. Soc. Montana* II 170: Major Baker…ordered Captain Rawn to get two of his companies in readiness to move, announcing his determination to take them and two companies of his "busters"—as he was pleased to call the cavalry—and pursue.] **1891** *Harper's Mag.* (July) 208: The buster must be careful to keep well away from sheds and timber. **1894** in J.I. White *Git Along Dogies* 92: I want to be a buster/And ride the bucking horse. **1914** in C.M. Russell *Paper Talk* 102: I don't think they would do as well as the old time busters we knew. **1927–30** Rollins *Jinglebob* 39 [ref. to 1880's]: They're called contract busters or flash riders…they'll fork any animal that wears hoofs.

7. *Crab fishing.* a crab or crayfish about to break free of its shell.

1879 in *DA* 219. **1887** in *DARE* I 481: The crabs are separated into two lots, the "busters" and soft crabs going into one compartment, and the "comers" into the other. **1943** in *DA* 219. **1970** Conaway *Big Easy* 81: The remains of a dozen boiled and picked buster crabs.

8. *pl. Gamb.* misspotted dice.

1961 Scarne *Comp. Guide to Gambling* 286: The method of using busters varies with the game being played. *Ibid.* 674: He robbed them by shooting in [i.e., introducing into play] busters.

9. a law-enforcement officer.

1963 *Time* (Aug. 2) 14: Busters,…blue boys, bluebirds…Policemen. **1965** Yurick *Warriors* 126: The buster was about two cars down now, patrolling. **1971** Guggenheimer *Narc. & Drug Abuse* 8: Buster. A narcotics agent (usually FBI).

10. a motor vehicle that gives a very bumpy ride; KIDNEY-BUSTER.

1974 Mayes *Bank Shot* (film): If he thinks I'm going to ride this buster all the way to the West Coast, he's crazy.

11. *pl. Black E.* pleasure; KICKS.

1973 Goines *Players* 131: Now if you want to get your kicks panning me, I'll come back…and let you go for your busters.

¶ In phrase:

¶ **like Buster's gang** *Jazz.* like gangbusters s.v. GANGBUSTER. *Joc.*

1941 Brackett & Wilder *Ball of Fire* (film): Here we go, Krupe, like Buster's gang. **1955** in J. Blake *Joint* 94: The black variety show is coming on like Buster's gang. **1963** Coon *Short End* 213: Winter came on

like buster's gang.

buster *v. Mil.* to hurry; travel quickly.

1988 Coonts *Final Flight* 36: "Get the angel out here buster." …"Buster" meant to hurry, bust your ass. **1990** Poyer *Gulf* 158: We're bustering inbound at a hundred fifty or so.

busthead *n. Esp. So. & Midland.* strong, esp. illicitly distilled, liquor.

1857 in *DA* 229. **1861** in Heartsill *1491 Days* 8: Is there any Bust Head in the Town?…Narry Drap. **1862** in Gilbert *Confed. Letters* 24: The door of a "bust head" establishment. **1865** Sala *Diary* II 394: "Bust-head" whisky, "red-eye" rum. **1874** Wilhelm *Memorandum* 46: That I take to be the finest bust head I have ever seen. **1929** (quot. at THIRD RAIL). **1956** Algren *Wild Side* 8: Satan didn't claim Jesus' mother 'count of wine, ah reckon he won't claim me 'count of a half-pint of busthead. **1956** Gold *Not With It* 205: They sprawled on their porches…with their jugs of busthead and their hatred of the Negro. **1971** Cole *Rook* 206: He better lay off that Korean bust-head. **1971** Horan *Blue Messiah* 337: I got some busthead whiskey from the night man at Regan's. **1985** Dye *Between Raindrops* 173: You…grab for the $3.98 busthead and pass up all the elegant booze.

busting *adj.* very big; (*hence*) splendid. Also as adv.

1847 Henry *Campaign Sks.* 41: I shot a *busting* big buck, and saw it fall, about a hundred yards from me. **1851, 1859** in *DA*. **1862** in Wightman *To Ft. Fisher* 30: He's a bustin' ole feller, ain't he? **1926** Hormel *Co-Ed* 7: It's doing a busting business, too.

bustle *n.* the rump.

1928 MacArthur *War Bugs* 182: Standing in their stirrups they began banging their teams' bony bustles with steel helmets. **1969** M. McCoy *Ride Reckless* 19: You're just beggin' for a burned bustle. **1972** Wambaugh *Blue Knight* 26: I guess even the wienie waggers and bustle rubbers gave up sneaking in the side door of this hole.

¶ In phrase:

¶ **hustle (one's) bustle, 1.** to hurry; to get moving.

[**1941** Macaulay & Wald *Manpower* (film): Hustle your muscle, Scarlett. There's a guy at the bar with a load of dough.] **1971** Faust *Willy* 26: We would hustle our bustle over to the river, strip and dive off the wood piles.

2. to work as a prostitute.

1935 Algren *Boots* 166: You ain't afraid you'll have to start hustling your bustle, is you? **1942** Algren *Morning* 196: Been hustlin' my bustle between here 'n Baton Rouge goin' on fourteen years now.

bust-out *n.* **1.** a breakout; (*specif.*) a jailbreak.

1930 (cited in Partridge *Dict. Und.* 92). **1967** Spillane *Delta* 123: There isn't time for fancy footwork. It'll have to be a straight bust-out. **1982** R. Sutton *Don't Get Taken* 59: It's really not a prison bust-out.

2. a celebration; blowout.

1959 Lederer *Never Steal Anything Small* (film): You can't swing a bust-out for five thousand.

3. a collapse or failure; (*hence*) a smash-up; a person who is a failure.

1963 Rubin *Sweet Daddy* 96: So bang, his heart gives with a bust-out. **1966** H.S. Thompson *Hell's Angels* 98: A maniacal top-speed run at a curve that's a guaranteed bust-out at anything over fifty. **1967** *Playboy* (Nov.) 170. **1971** W. Murray *Dream Girls* 79: "They're not bustouts. They're working actors and directors."…"Bustouts. Losers." **1991** C. Fletcher *Pure Cop* 68: Usually the owner…hires somebody on the street, a bust-out. *Ibid.* 122: Most pimps are bust-outs…Their lives get worse and worse.

4. usu. *pl. Gamb.* a fraudulent die.—often attrib.

1952 Grey *Hoods* 174: Bust-outs.…Nine out of ten times a seven would show up. **1954–60** *DAS* 80: Bust outs. Crooked or loaded dice. **1961** Scarne *Comp. Guide to Gambling* 279: The professional bust-out man, concentrating on the task of switching in his crooked dice. **1962–68** B. Jackson *In the Life* 187: A "bust-out" mob.…You're working with tops or bust-out craps.

5. *Und.* (see quot.).

1958 *N.Y. Times Mag.* 87: Bust-out—High point of a confidence game, when the swindle occurs.

bust-out *adj.* **1.** *Esp. Gamb.* being or connected with a dishonest establishment, esp. a gambling casino or disreputable saloon, at which patrons are routinely fleeced or robbed.

1937 in D. Runyon *More Guys* 215: A bust-out joint being a joint where they will cheat your eyeballs out at cards, and dice, and similar devices. **1953** in *DAS* 80: Percentage dice…common in bust-out joints all over

the country. **1959** in Cannon *Nobody Asked* 147: I once heard an old man in a bust-out joint in Kansas City whisper the anguish of a safe-cracker doing a bread and water bit in an Australian prison far from his girl. **1965** Linakis *In Spring* 281: A real bust-out joint. **1972** Bunker *No Beast* 38: A whore was liable to grab a sucker...and drag him...into a bust-out hotel. **1980** H. Gould *Ft. Apache* 8: Why hit a bust-out saloon where there was no bread? **1988** H. Gould *Double Bang* 27: Hustlers needed a place for their bust-out crap games.
2. penniless; BUSTED.
1976 "N. Ross" *Policeman* 103: Our informant (a bust-out colored guy) told us this might be a pretty big [floating crap] game. **1980** W. Sherman *Times Sq.* 4: The losers, the bustout guys who run...to swipe a watch to pay for that last five-dollar rack. **1984** H. Gould *Cocktail* 126: He took me for a bust-out Viet vet. **1987** R. Miller *Slob* 26: I was...jobless and purposeless, a bust-out drunk about ten cases away from a relief mission.
3.a. unregulated; (*esp.*) blatantly illegal.
1962 in L. Bruce *Essential Lenny* 41: In his name they would do all sorts of bust-out things. **1962** in Cannon *Nobody Asked* 240: There is bust-out action Downtown at night....Agents for prostitutes make whispered pitches from doorways. The waitress who doesn't attempt to shortchange you qualifies as Kentucky's first saint.
b. out-and-out; pure and simple.
1961 in L. Bruce *Essential Lenny* 76: Long...was...a bust-out thief, man, who had relatives who were thieves. **1962** in *Ibid.* 149: I'm a bust-out junkie. Started smoking pot, look at me now. **1980** H. Gould *Ft. Apache* 81: Jealous, jealous, typical bust-out cop reaction.

bust out *v.* **1.** [elab. of BUST, *v.*, 7.a.] Esp. *Gamb.* to ruin financially; bankrupt; (*intrans.*) to go bankrupt.
1962 Fraley & Robsky *Last Untouchables* 11: "I'll see your dollar and raise you two." "I'm busted out." **1962** in L. Bruce *Essential Lenny* 41: In his name they would do all sorts of bust-out things, and bust out people. **1966** "Minnesota Fats" *Bank Shot* 107: Most pool players have a desperate fear of busting out and ending up as a dependent person. **1982** Hayano *Poker Faces* 7: Losing his entire bankroll, busting out, going Tap City.
2. *Stu.* to expel or be expelled from school because of academic failure.
1939 R.A. Winston *Dive Bomber* 18: The fear of "busting out" after only a month of training. **1957** Lacy *Room to Swing* 35: Got busted out of engineering school. **1966** R. Fariña *Down So Long* 51: They busted me out at midterm. **1983** Goldman & Fuller *Charlie Co.* 139: He busted out of college after four shaky terms.

bustskull *n.* BUSTHEAD; POPSKULL.
1942 W. Faulkner, in *DARE:* He...gets himself a whole gallon of bustskull white-mule whiskey. **1960** in *DARE.*

bust-up *n.* an explosion; (*hence*) a collapse, wreck, break-up, etc.
1842 in Bleser *Secret & Sacred* 98: I fear...that there will be another bust up. **1846** *Knickerbocker Mag.* 313: The houdaciousest bust-up I ever seed. **1869** Peyton *Over Alleghanies* 71: I felt I should become practically acquainted with what I had so often heard of—a regular "bust up!" [of a ship's boiler]. **1902** in *DA* 229: I wanted to talk to you about Alan and that bank bu'st-up. **1927** Nicholson *Barker* 45: They had a bust-up over the drink she give Chris. **1989** Zumbro & Walker *Jungletracks* 44: So you were in that bust-up.

bust up *v.* **1.** to break up (in various senses).
1866 in Hilleary *Webfoot* 178: The Getzler theatre troupe bursted up the other day. **1936** Tully *Bruiser* 44: I think we'd better bust up—I ain't worthy of a boy like you. **1945** F. Baldwin *Ariz. Star* 96: It isn't my business. But did you two bust up? **1962** Kesey *Cuckoo's Nest* 253: That busted everybody up. **1977** *Psychology Today* (Oct.) 62: My friends and I didn't think they were funny, but we observed one thing that always busted us up. Almost without exception, they had all their hair.
2. to injure severely.
1978 Pici *Tennis Hustler* 228: Dallas...does not bust people up. **1979** in Terkel *Amer. Dreams* 212: He went back and busted the man up somethin' terrible. It got him a year in [prison].

busy bee *n. Narc.* ANGEL DUST.
1978 *N.Y. Daily News* (Feb. 23) 5: Angel dust goes by dozens of street names...[including] busy bee, hog, elephant tranquilizer, crystal [etc.]. **1979** (cited in Spears *Drugs & Drink* 88).

Busy Bertha *n. Army.* BIG BERTHA.
1917 in Bernheim *Censored* 71: He couldn't have been more shocked 'f a busy Bertha had gone off under him. **1918** in Cowing *Folks at Home*

223: Showers of shrapnel, whizz-bangs, Busy Berthas...bursting on all sides. **1918** R.J. Casey *Cannoneer* 70: It is hard to imagine that busy Bertha might have crumbled most of the house.

but *adv.* (used as an intensive).
1938 in J. O'Hara *Sel. Letters* 140: The bruise will be but terrific. **1942** Bowers & Spence *Seven Days' Leave* (film): If he doesn't come along I'm gonna get good and sore—but definitely. **1954** Yablonsky *Violent Gang* 75: I'll get 'em all but good. **1984** C. Francis *Who's Sorry?* 113: For hours each day, he'd listen to Newark DJ Walter Brenner play country and western music, but real Ozark stuff. **1993** *Sally Jessy Raphaël* (synd. TV series): "So she wanted to get away from that pimp?" "But definitely."

butch *n.* **1.a.** a butcher knife.
1859 "Skitt" *Fisher's River* 72 [ref. to 1820's]: I...jerked out old Butch. **1870** Duval *BigFoot Wallace* 65 [ref. to ca1840]: I loosened "old butch" in the sheath. **1876** in Botkin *Treas. Amer. Folk.* 349: Whar's big butch, little butch, ole case, cob-handle, granny's knife and the one I handled yesterday!
b. a butcher.
1935 (quot. at GUT PLUNGE, *n.*)
2. Esp. *R.R.* BUTCHER, 5.
1919 Darling *Jargon Book* 6: *Butch*—A news dealer on railroad trains. **1945** House *Texas* 20: The news butch came through and the boy bought a banana. In a little while the butch returned and asked the lad if he wanted another. **1953** Botkin & Harlow *R.R. Folklore* 173: The news butcher or "butch," as he is popularly called.
3. *cap.* (used as a nickname for a tough young man).
1942 *ATS* 203: *Buck*,...*Butch, Spike*...nicknames for a "he-man." **1981** G. Wolf *Roger Rabbit* 47: He called all women "Honey" and most men "Butch."
4. [sugg. by (**3**), above] a haircut in which the hair is clipped very short. Now *colloq*
1949 W.R. Burnett *Asphalt Jungle* 29: His white-blond hair [was] disfigured by a butch haircut. **1957** in *DAS* 80: A more radical version of the Crew is the "Butch." **1959** Zugsmith *Beat Generation* 85: She became aware of a girl crowding closer to her. Expensive slack suit, tailored like a man's, butch hair cut. **1978** *Rolling Stone* (Sept. 7) 12 (photo caption): Linda Ronstadt and Mick Jagger compare their new butch cuts.
5. [prob. sugg. by (**3**), above] *Homosex.* a male or (*esp.*) female homosexual who customarily plays a masculine role in a homosexual relationship; a tough or aggressive homosexual, (*esp.*) such a lesbian.
1954 in *OEDS*. **1955** Margulies *Punks* 175: Maybe we aren't full-time Butches like her but we ain't a bunch of Marges, either. **1958** Motley *Epitaph* 248: Billy, the butch, squares off, putting up her fists. **1960** Bannon *Journey* 121: You'd be a butch. You'd cut your hair off real short and live in the Village. **1963** Stearns *Grapevine* 22: "It's up to the butch to make the first move," a femme said gravely. **1966** "Petronius" *N.Y. Unexp.* 97: The New York fag...wants to...mingle with the right butches. **1968** in Giallombardo *Impris. Girls* 151: The butch, she would be found out. **1978** *Nat. Lampoon* (Oct.) 26: Did you get your kicks, you ugly little butch?
6. [poss. sugg. by *botch*, or by BUTCHER, 7] an error; (*esp.*) *Radio & TV* an error made in delivering lines.
1942 *ATS* 194. **1942** B. Morgan & B. Orkow *Wings For Eagle* (film): This is a butch. **1949** Wouk *Caine Mutiny* 190. **1954–60** *DAS* 80: *Butch*...A mistake. **1982** T.D. Connors *Dict. Mass Media* 40.

butch *adj.* **1.** *Homosex.* **a.** (used esp. by female homosexuals) especially masculine in appearance or behavior; virile; tough.
[**1936** Dai *Opium Add.* 111: Here were to be found "Chinatown Whitie," "Butch Turner," "Two Bits," [etc.]...all of them notorious [prostitutes].] **1941** W.H. Auden, in *OEDS*: And culture on all fours to greet/A butch and criminal elite. **1949** De Forrest *Gay Year* 108: You don't have to keep up the butch act with me, Cutie. I know you're gay. **1949** in T. Williams *Letters* 245: He further endeared himself to them by...walking off with the most attractive (butch) sailor. **1950** *Neurotica* (Spring) 37: I no longer remotely resembled a "butch" fairy or "rough trade." **1952** "E. Box" *Fifth Position* 132: They're much more butch than they used to be. **1963** Rechy *City of Night* 328: Butchest damn diesel dyke y'evuh laid yuh gay eyes on! **1966** S. Harris *Hellhole* 217: I went all the way butch—started wearing men's clothes. **1967** Rechy *Numbers* 16: He has been described recurrently in homosexual jargon as "a very butch number."...A supreme accolade in that world, "butch" means

very male and usually carries overtones of roughness. **1971** Rader *Gov't Inspected* 7: They were the butchest, the most rugged...on the street. **1981** Hathaway *World of Hurt* 35: At last I look butch, he thought. **1989** *Nat. Lampoon* (June) 36: I Can Make You a Really Butch Dude.

b. [poss. the orig. sense] (of a man) not homosexual.

1949 *Gay Girl's Guide* 4: *Butch*—not homosexual.

c. (of a woman) mannish; unpleasantly assertive; dominating.

***1971** in *BDNE* 77. **1976** Chayefsky *Network* (film): I don't want to play butch boss with you.

2. Orig. *Pris.* given to or involving violence.

1962 Maurer & Vogel *Narc. Addiction* (ed. 2) 294: *Butch game.* An ultimatum to cooperate or suffer heavy penalty. **1971** Woodley *Dealer* 88: And he's a butch kid....He's just super-violent.

butch-broad *n.* a mannish aggressive lesbian; BULLDYKE.—usu. used contemptuously.

1966 Samuels *People vs. Baby* 34: Those butch-broads are real hard-up if they hafta whistle. **1968** Heard *Howard St.* 225: Moochie, the meanest butch-broad around.

butcher *n.* **1.** a butcher knife.

1834 *Davy Crockett's Alm.* (1835) 26: So I took out a big butcher, and went out and slapped it into him. **1836** *Davy Crockett's Alm.* (1837) 19: I reached his vitals with my big butcher.

2. *S.W.* a bullfighter. [Bullfighting on the Mexican model was popular in New Orleans between the 1840's and the Civil War.]

1848 in Somers *Sports in N.O.* 59: The "butchers" tortured the Bulls...& made them suffer death in an awful manner.

3. *Pris. & Mil.* a surgeon; (*hence*) any physician. Cf. fig. S.E. use.

1849 Melville *White Jacket* 252: Away, butcher! you disgrace the profession. **1889** Barrère & Leland *Dict. Slang* I 210: *Butcher*...(Prison), the *butcher* is a nickname for the doctor. **1917** in Merrill *Uncommon Valor* 302: It appeared as if the butcher must have driven the needle about three inches deep. **1924** Henderson *Keys to Crookdom* 399: *Butcher.* Surgeon. **1944** Kendall *Service Slang* 35: *Butcher*...a medical officer. **1962–63** in Giallombardo *Soc. of Women* 201: *Butcher.* A prison doctor. **1976** Atlee *Domino* 171: I was in the Klamath Falls hospital and the butchers were trying to take my left foot off. **1980** *Easyriders* (May) 54: Anyway,...the butcher got done cuttin'.

4. *Journ.* a copy editor.

1867 in *DA* 229. **1902** Clapin *Americanisms* 88: *Butcher.* In newspaper jargon, a term applied to the copy-reader, who uses mercilessly the blue-pencil in cutting short reporters' stories.

5. a vendor of newspapers, peanuts, candy, etc., esp. aboard a passenger train or at a sporting event.—often used in combs.

1880 Martin *Sam Bass* 58: The "butcher" boy on the train also participated in the fight....The "butcher" shot...Jackson and...Pipes. **1882** in *OEDS* I. **1889** Barrère & Leland *Dict. Slang* I 210: *Butcher, the* (American), a boy who is allowed to pass through the line of "cars" or carriages on a railway for the purpose of selling a great variety of articles. **1902** Swift *Iowa Boy* 113: There were no "peanut butchers" or news agents to annoy passengers. **1920** Conklin & Root *Circus* 18 [ref. to 1870's]: He was what we called a "candy butcher"—that is, he traveled with the show and sold candy to the crowds. **1958** S.H. Adams *Tenderloin* 3: The candy butcher weaved his way in and out among the people.

6. *Mil. & Pris.* a barber.

1906 J.A. Moss *Officer's Man.* 243: *Butcher*—the company barber. **1933** Ersine *Pris. Slang* 23: *Butcher*...A barber. **1947** Mencken *Amer. Lang. Supp. II* 674: The [prison] barber is a...*butcher*. **1984** U.S. Army veteran, age *ca*35: Back in 1971 I remember our old drill sergeant saying, "We gonna take you in to see the butcher now. You wonder why we call him the butcher, you wait an' see when you git out."

7. a clumsy incompetent; a bungler.

1954–60 *DAS.* **1961** Brosnan *Pennant Race* 71: I'm kind of a butcher at times, but I like to play. **1973** *N.Y. Times Mag.* (Apr. 1) 26: He's a real butcher in the outfield. But he can hit the ball.

8. Esp. *Basketball.* an excessively rough defensive player.

1972 N.Y.U. student: A *butcher* is a really vicious fouler. They used to call me The Butcher. **1980** Wielgus & Wolff *Basketball* 41: *Butcher*...A defender who uses force rather than finesse.

butcher *v.* **1.** *Mil.* to give an extremely close haircut to.

1942 *Good Housekeeping* (Dec.) 11: This soldier is getting a haircut.

He'll say he is being: Trimmed—Hot toweled—Cut down to size—Butchered. **1984** U.S. Army veteran, age *ca*35 [ref. to 1971]: The drill sergeant said "We gonna take you in to see the butcher....He gonna butcher you good."

2. to operate on.

1966 Kenney *Caste* 30: You'd be a damned chump to let 'em butcher you.

3. *Sports.* to block (an offensive player) with undue roughness.

1980 Wielgus & Wolff *Basketball* 41: *Butcher*...To inflict physical punishment on another player.

butcherboy *v.* *Baseball.* to bat (a ball) with a sharp downward motion.

1978 P. Rizzuto, on *N.Y. Yankees vs. K.C. Royals* (WINS radio) (July 17): The pitch that Patek hit was way out of the strike zone, but he butcher-boyed it. Like you were chopping down a tree.

butcher cart *n.* see BUTCHER WAGON.

butcher shop *n.* **1.** *Naut.* a whaling ship.—used disparagingly.

1932 Grant *Greasy Luck* 14: The whaler...was held in supreme contempt by the officers and crews of her contemporaneous big sisters the flash clippers, who referred to her as "spouter" and "butcher shop."

2. Esp. *Mil.* an operating room; (*also*) a hospital.—often used disparagingly.

1918 in *Papers Mich. Acad.* (1928) 283: *Butcher shop*, the operating room; the surgical department. **1941** Hargrove *Pvt. Hargrove* 83: *Butcher shop*—a dispensary or hospital. **1953** "L. Short" *Silver Rock* 94: Hi, Doc....What's with you and your butcher shop? **1972–79** C. Major *Emergency Exit* 230: The "butcher shop" was freezing and he was going fast. **1979** D. Milne *Second Chance* 34: The hospital had been aptly nicknamed "the butcher shop." **1985** Dye *Between Raindrops* 129: I just set up the butcher shop somewhere to the rear.

butcher wagon *n.* an ambulance; MEAT WAGON. Also **butcher cart**.

1882 Peck *Peck's Sunshine* 18: The man...dreamed that a smallpox flag was hung in front of his house and that he was riding in a butcher wagon to the pest house. **1926** *Sat. Eve. Post* (Nov. 6) 13: Time, tide, and this here butcher cart waits for no shavetail.

butchy *adj.* resembling or suggesting a BUTCH, 5.

1956 Holiday & Dufty *Lady Sings Blues* 86: Then she started buying...me...suits cut and tailored like a man's with butchy accessories. **1971** G. Davis *Coming Home* 96: The woman is ugly. Big. Butchy.

butt *n.* **1.a.** the buttocks; ASS. [Often considered vulgar, yet it also substitutes freely as a semi-euphem. for ASS in any of its phrasal usages; these are not listed separately.]

***1720** D'Urfey *Pills* VI 91 [in a bawdy song]: And when I set a Butt abroach,/Then shall no Beer run by Sir. ***1744** in Baring-Gould *Mother Goose* 34: Piss a Bed/Piss a Bed/Barley Butt,/ Your Bum is so heavy/You can't get up. **1815** in Merrill *Uncommon Valor* 113: The infernal rascal is patting his butt at us! **1859** Bartlett *Amer.* (ed. 2) 60: *Butt*...The buttocks. The word is used in the West in such phrases as "I fell on my butt," "He kick'd my butt." **1868** in G.W. Harris *High Times* 103: I'd a chuck'd you butt foremos' thru that winder. **1889** Farmer *Amer.*: *Butt*...Common in the West as a contracted form of "buttock" [*sic*]. **1898** Green *Va. Folk-Speech* 75: *Butt n.* The buttocks; the posteriors. *ca*1940 in Botkin *Amer. Folk.* 547: He'll send you butt over appetite to kingdom come. **1942** McAtee *Supp. to Grant Co. Dial. in '90's* 3: *Butt*, n., buttocks. **1944** Liebling *Back to Paris* 114: People who talk like that give me a pain in the butt. **1947** Willingham *End as a Man* 291: You don't know your butt from a bear's ass. **1956** "R. Macdonald" *Barbarous Coast* 43: And drag your butt off of my property. **1956** E. Hunter *Second Ending* 223: Dammit, that's what burns my butt. **1957** Shulman *Rally* 218: You betcher butt. **1963–64** Kesey *Great Notion* 284: Can't you see I'm bustin' my butt hurryin'? **1965** Capote *In Cold Blood* 26: Every time you see a mirror you go into a trance, like. Like you was looking at some gorgeous piece of butt. **1966–67** Harvey *Air War* 150: The U.S. public couldn't care less if they go up over the Red and bust their butts. **1967** J. Kramer *Instant Replay* 101: If he dropped one more pass he was going to send his butt home. **1967** Schmidt *Lexicon of Sex* 34: *Butt*...Sexual intercourse. **1972** Jenkins *Semi-Tough* 109: Me and Shake have bust our butts laughing. **1974** Terkel *Working* 188: If a guy didn't do it they fired his butt. **1974** Widener *N.U.K.E.E.* 153: Drake was now floundering around the Alaskan wilderness...stuffing thermometers up the butts of wolves in a "study" that would take at least five years. **1975** Harington *Ark. Ozarks* 33: Yo're jist workin' yore butt off fer nuthin. **1976** Conroy *Santini* 4: I can see them out there now mincing around like they've got icicles stuck up their butts. **1978** Maupin *Tales* 28: Tell Beauchamp to hustle his butt up here on the double. **1978** B. Johnson *What's Happenin'* 140: Worn smooth as a baby's butt. **1978** Groom *Better Times* 15: Hi, Skinny, how's your butt? **1979** in Terkel *Amer. Dreams* 239: The Environmental Protection Agency gets on their butt about polluting the valleys and streams and air. **1979** Gutcheon *New Girls* 185: It means you have to work your butt off. **1980** *Residence Hall Comp.* 5: Actually, I think a lot of the problems we had stemmed from her resentment of my doing virtually no studying and getting A's while she busted her butt and got C's. **1982** P. Michaels *Grail* 127: And you better get your butt in gear. **1983** *Hour Magazine* (ABC-TV) (May 6): I was gonna get my butt busted anyhow. **1983** *N.Y. Post* (Sept. 2) 68: Get your butt back here! **1983** S. Wright *Meditations* 45: Well, bite my butt. **1984** Nettles & Golenbock *Balls* 205: You have to admire a guy who knew it was his last game with the team and still went out and busted his butt. **1984** *N.Y. Post* (Aug. 9) 80: They just kicked our butts....I ain't gonna make any excuses why. **1984** J.R. Reeves *Mekong* 182: Thicker'n flies on a dog's butt. **1985** Yeager & Janos *Yeager* 1: With so many ways to bust my butt flying research aircraft, I knew better than to think that any test flight was routine. **1988** *Sonny Spoon* (NBC-TV): Look, don't write no check with your mouth that your butt can't cash. **1990** *Simpsons* (Fox-TV): Teacher's pet! Apple-polisher! Butt-kisser!

b. [sugg. by syn. ASS] anger or irritability.—constr. with *the.* **1973** W. Crawford *Gunship Cmndr.* 136: I just had a case of the butt a while ago.

c. a stupid or contemptible person. **1993** *Simpsons* (Fox-TV): I am not a butt! **1993** *Sally Jessy Raphaël* (synd. TV series): She made a total butt outa me.

2.a. a cigarette. **1902** *Our Naval Apprentice* (Apr.) 15: Why, you could light a "butt" between each stroke. **1918** *The Radiator* (July 25) 1: They smoked the first civilized "butt" in two weeks. **1921** Dos Passos *Three Soldiers* 219: Have a butt? **1924** Marks *Plastic Age* 161: Anybody got a butt? **1926** Nason *Chevrons* 179 [ref. to 1918]: Who the hell's got a butt? **1951** in *DAS*: He gave me a pack of butts. **1977** Olshavsky *No More Butts* (title). **1989** Kienzle *Eminence* 92: Don't even take that butt out of your mouth. **1992** *CBS This Morning* (CBS-TV) (Nov. 5): It's a ban on butts in all enclosed public spaces.

b. *pl.* a claim on a partially smoked cigarette. **1963** E.M. Miller *Exile to Stars* 229: "I'm smoking it." "Kin I have butts on it?"

¶ In phrases:

¶ **and a butt** *Mil. & Pris.* and a fractional amount of time to be served, as in an enlistment or a prison term. **1888** Billings *Hardtack* 89 [ref. to Civil War]: Even those troops having nearly three years to serve would exclaim..."It's only two years and a but." **1888** McConnell *Five Years a Cavalryman* 120 [ref. to 1866]: When a fellow has only a little more than a year to serve, he says he has only "a year and a butt," or later on, "a month and a butt." **1906** M'Govern *Sarjint Larry* (glossary): *Butt:*—A short time; "Two months and a butt" means two months and a part of another month remaining on ones enlistment. **1912** Lowrie *Prison* 286: I've only got two months an' a butt left now. **1918** Griffin *Ballads of the Reg't.* 64: A week and a "butt," then my "buzzard"—they'll never enlist me again. **1918** O'Reilly *Roving & Fighting* 49 [ref. to 1899]: Here I am with two years and a butt to serve over in them Chinee islands. **1918** Ruggles *Navy Explained* 28: *Butt.*—commonly used by the sailorman in explaining how long he has to do on a present enlistment. A man will always say "two and a butt," meaning that he has two years and a few months to serve yet. "Two months and a butt will graduate me." we sometimes hear. **1928** Bodenheim *Georgie May* 106: Aw, she'll be out in foah'n a butt if she behaves herself. **1933** Clifford *Boats* 79: Been doin' it now, fifteen years an' a butt. **1945** J. Bryan *Carrier* 128: Roosevelt's three-and-a-butt terms. **1961** Ford *Black, Gray & Gold* 124: Thirty-two days and a butt. **1976** Braly *False Starts* 199: When we were getting short and someone asked how long we had left, we said, "Six days and a butt." "Four days and a butt." The butt is your last morning. **1983** *U.S. News & W.R.* (Sept. 12) 62: There's 98 and a butt...days until Army beats the hell out of Navy at Pasadena!

¶ **crack (one's) butt** to strain (oneself); to exert (oneself) to the limit. **1938** in A. Lomax *Mr. Jelly Roll* 89: I've seen many a one crack their butts trying.

butt *v.* **1.** to give a cigarette to.—used imper. **1944** H. Brown *Walk in Sun* 50: Butt me. **1953** Felsen *Street Rod* 104: "Butt me," Ricky said to Link. **1956** M. Wolff *Big Nick.* 66: Come on, butt me.

2. to crush out (a cigarette or cigar). **1956** Hargrove *Girl He Left* 43: You don't smoke until I tell you! Butt it!

butt-boy *n.* PRATT-BOY. **1981** *Nat. Lampoon* (May) 85: Chuck Barris is looking for a butt-boy....Do you enjoy lighting cigarettes and performing small but important intimate personal services?

butt bucket *n. Mil.* BUTT CAN. **1958** Cope & Dyer *Petty Off. Gde.* (ed. 2) 334. **1966** Noel & Bush *Naval Terms* 79: *Butt bucket, butt kit:* Ash tray.

butt-buster *n.* **1.** a hard-riding vehicle. **1974** *Gunsmoke* (CBS-TV): You'd have to be a fool to ride them butt-busters [sc. wagons].

2. *Army.* an antipersonnel mine; BOUNCING BETTY. **1974** former U.S. Army Specialist, served 1970–73: We called those [antipersonnel] mines *butt-busters* [in Vietnam].

butt can *n. Mil.* a can used as a receptacle for cigarette ashes; (*hence*) a standing ashtray. **1960** Bluestone *Cully* 184: The butt cans had frozen to the ground. **1963** Cameron *Black Camp* 12 [ref. to WWII]: You're on butt cans this morning. **1984** J. Fuller *Fragments* 54: I...knocked down a butt can.

butt-can *v. Mil.* to toss away or aside. *a*1986 D. Tate *Bravo Burning* 42: Bad enough to butt-can his army career for a while.

Butt-End Charlie *n. Mil. Av.* ASS-END CHARLIE. **1942** *N.Y. Times Mag.* (Sept. 27) 16: Butt-End Charlie.

butter *n.* **1.** nitroglycerine or dynamite. **1921** E. O'Neill *Hairy Ape* 251: Gimme de stuff, de old butter—and watch me do de rest.

2. paste. **1929** *AS* (Oct.) 48: *Butter*—soldering paste. **1934** Weseen *Slang Dict.* 166: Radio Slang...*Butter*—soldering paste.

3. paraffin. **1972** Haslam *Oil Fields* 96: *Butter*, n. Paraffin.

butter *v. Gamb.* to double or treble (a bet). ***1698–99** "B.E." *Dict. Canting Crew*: *Butter*,...to double or treble the Bet or Wager to recover all Losses. ***1725** *New Canting Dict.*: *Butter*, to double or treble the Bet or Wager, in order to recover all Losses, used among Sharpers at a Gaming Table or Bowling Green. **1821** Waln *Hermit in Phila.* 29: Every time I *buttered* a bet, it was a *Flemish account.*

butter-and-egg man *n.* a man who is a farmer or small-town businessman and who spends money extravagantly.—used derisively. **1924** T.A. Dorgan, in Zwilling *TAD Lexicon* 22: If you invite Frank that butter and egg man—count me out. **1925** in *DA*: A couple of big butter and egg men from Verona, New Jersey. **1930** in *DAS*. **1954** Botkin *Sidewalks* 370: An earlier song, "The Big Butter and Egg Man," made the "big butter and egg man from the West" synonymous with the sucker or free spender. **1984** Lax & Smith *Great Song Thesaurus* 184: Texas Guinan [N.Y.C. nightclub entertainer]...popularized the description of her best customers as "big butter and egg men" [in 1927].

butterball *n.* a plump individual. [**1860** in L.F. Browne *J.R. Browne* 218: Mrs. Hays' baby...is now as fat as a little butter-ball.] [**1868** G.W. Harris *Lovingood* 304: He was as fat as a butterball.] **1941** Warner Bros. *Merrie Melodies* (animated cartoon): Ya don't get the dough, eh, butterball? **1944** Hartman et al. *Up in Arms* (film): Hey, Butterball. You seen anything of Danny? **1954** Collans & Sterling *House Detect.* 85: He was a roly-poly butterball of a man. **1981–85** S. King *It* 73: I was a regular butterball...I was fat, all right.

butterbar *n. Mil.* **1.** usu. *pl.* one of the two gold bars that are the insignia of the rank of second lieutenant. **1983** Van Devanter & Morgan *Before Morning* 62 [ref. to 1967]: Barbara's father pinned the gold bars—"butter bars"—of a second lieutenant on the collars of our civilian dresses.

2. a second lieutenant. **1973** former U.S. Army M.P., served 1970–73: A *butterbar* is a second lieutenant. **1982** Del Vecchio *13th Valley* 112: That...butterbar lieutenant we got. **1983** Groen & Groen *Huey* 269: In The army, a butter bar was the worst thing you could be. **1984** Former Spec. 5, U.S. Army: *Butterbar* was a well-established term when I went in [the Army] in 1971. The sergeant used to say, "A butterbar ain't nothin' but a private in disguise." That was a common term all over the U.S., and in Taiwan too.

butterbox *n.* **1.** *Naut.* a Dutchman.

  *1698–99 "B.E." *Dict. Canting Crew: Butter-boxes,* Dutchmen. **1771* T. Bridges *Bank-Note* IV 136: You unconscionable son of a butter-box. **1785* Grose *Vulgar Tongue: Butter box,* a Dutchman, from the great quantity of butter eaten by the people of that country. *1867* Smyth *Sailor's Wd.-Bk.: Butterbox….*A cant term for a Dutchman.

  2. *Naut.* a squarish, clumsy vessel.

  1840 R.H. Dana *2 Yrs.* ch. ix: She was the *Loriotte,…*and was engaged in the hide and tallow trade. She was a lump of a thing, what the sailors call a butter-box. *1851* Melville *Moby Dick* ch. xvi: Square-toed luggers; mountainous Japanese junks; butter-box galliots. *1867* Smyth *Sailor's Wd.-Bk.: Butterbox.* A name given to the brig-traders of cumbly form, from London, Bristol, and other English ports. *1899* Robbins *Gam* 49: You're a blarsted ninny if you try to get aout o' this butter-box.

butterbrain *n.* [sugg. by BUTTERFINGERS] a fool.

  1975–78 O'Brien *Cacciato* 57: Twerp, creepo, butter-brain. It wasn't right.…He was not dumb.

buttered bun *n.* sexual intercourse with a woman who has just completed copulation with another man.

  *1698–99 "B.E." *Dict. Canting Crew: Butter'd Bun,* Lying with a Woman that has just been Layn with by another Man. **1785* Grose *Vulgar Tongue:* One lying with a woman, that has just lain with another man, is said to have a buttered bun. *1899* *Memoirs of Dolly Morton* 251: This'll be the first time…that I've ever "had" a buttered bun. *1972* R. Wilson *Forbidden Words* 57: I don't like buttered buns.

butterfingered *adj.* apt to drop things. Now *colloq.*

  *1615 in *OED2:* She must not be butter-fingred…for the first will let everything fall. *1868* Aldrich *Bad Boy* 180: He…called his rescuers "butter-fingered landlubbers" with delicious coolness. **1873* Hotten *Slang Dict.* (ed. 4) 105: *Butter-Fingered,* apt to let things fall; greasy or slippery-fingered.

butterfingers *n.* Esp. *Juve.* a person who drops things. Now *colloq.*

  *1837 C. Dickens, in *OED2:* At every bad attempt to catch, and every failure to stop the ball, he launched his personal displeasure…in such denunciations as…butter-fingers, [etc.]. *1877* Bartlett *Amer.* (ed. 4) 777. *1888* in P. Dickson *Baseball Dict.* 79: And now you know…why they call em "butter-fingers." *1919* *DN* V 62: *Butter-fingers,* one who is clumsy. "That catcher is a regular *butter-fingers.*" New Mexico. *1969* Layden & Snyder *Diff. Game* 8: I wonder which one of us Harry would have called Butterfingers?

butterfly *n.* **1.** *Und.* a worthless check.

  1929 Hostetter & Beesley *It's a Racket* 221: *Butterfly*—A worthless check; a check that is being "kited." *1932* *Writer's Digest* (Aug.) 46: A *butterfly man* makes worthless checks.

  2. *pl.* a feeling of queasiness or tension in the abdomen, esp. as the result of anxiety; jitters; also in phr. **butterflies in (one's) stomach.**

  1940 [W.C. Fields] *Bank Dick* (film): If the gentleman has butterflies in the stomach, I recommend…absinthe. *1941* Kendall *Army & Navy Slang* 3: Full of butterflies…full of burps. *1942* in *Best from Yank* 64: A squadron of butterflies spills into a soft-shoe power dive in your stomach. *1942–44* in *AS* (Feb. 1946) 31: He gets butterflies in his stomach. *1955* Archibald *Aviation Cadet* 39: "No butterflies, Mister?" the instructor asked. *1959* Brosnan *Long Season* 60: It takes a young player a long, long time to get over those opening day butterflies. *1960* Kirkwood *Pony* 51: I've got butterflies about tomorrow. *1971* Sorrentino *Up from Never* 26: I know a lotta guys freeze in the ring because they get butterflies.

  ¶ In phrase:

  ¶ **like a butterfly in heat** Esp. *Homosex.* behaving in a dithering manner.

  1975 Keane *Maximus Zone* 8: One of the Black Satins had once called this high-strung, erratic little man "a butterfly in heat." *1976* N.Y.C. man, age 30: Fags call each other *she.* Sometimes they say, "She was running around like a butterfly in heat!"

butterfly *v.* [trans. of Japn *chocho,* lit., 'butterfly'] *Mil. in Far East.* to be sexually unfaithful (to).

  1945–46 in *AS* (Feb. 1947) 54: *Butterfly.* A term used by Japanese girls and GI's to designate anyone fickle or inconstant in love. *1956* Boatner *Mil. Customs* 114: *Butterfly.* To philander. Japanese pidgin English. A Nipponese "girl san" will assure her current boy friend that she is faithful and does not "butterfly" on him. *1982* J. Cain *Commandos* 435: You no butterfly me, would you, Timmy? *1986* J. Cain *Suicide Squad* 32:

Check on the old lady to make sure she's not butterflyin' on your worthless ass, right?

butterfly kiss *n.* a soft caress given by fluttering the eyelashes against the partner's skin. Also as *v.*

  *1871, *1932 in *OEDS.* *1954* Caprio *Fem. Homosex.* 236: Once she said she was going to give me a butterfly kiss. I didn't know what it was. *1968* Swarthout *Loveland* 224: You claim to be a supersmoocher—well. Butterfly-kiss me. *1970* Sorrentino *Steelwork* 21: I kept thinkin about her an those butterfly kisses she used to give me—you know. He blinked his eyes rapidly. *1976–77* Kernochan *Dry Hustle* 178: Those are the eyelashes…spread your hand and I'll give you a butterfly kiss. *1990* Vachss *Blossom* 208: I…felt her eyelashes flutter on my cheek. "That's a butterfly kiss."

butterhead *n.* a fool.

  1963 *Time* (Aug. 2) 14: Butter head, chili bowl, ditty bob. Terms of contempt, used to refer to Negroes whose behavior embarrasses other Negroes. *1970* Gattzden *Black Vendetta* 49: Butterhead, you've come sneaking around here for some phantom bullets. *1985* Former SP4, U.S. Army, age 35: I heard *butterhead* commonly used in the service when I was in Utah. It meant a fool. It was a term used in public when you couldn't use stronger language. *1986* *Hardcastle & McCormick* (ABC-TV): Just fill 'er up, butterhead.

buttermilk ranger *n. Confed. Army.* a cavalryman.—used derisively. Now *hist.*

  1867 Duke *Morgan's Cavalry* 400: When the "webfeet" called us "buttermilk rangers," we did not get angry with them. *1870* in *DA.* *1885* "Cannon" *Where Men Only* 126 [ref. to Civil War]: There are skeptical people, however, who insist that the infantry, and even the "buttermilk rangers," had a "hand in that fight." *1914* Nisbet *4 Yrs. on Firing Line* 151 [ref. to Civil War]: They answered: "9th Kentucky Cavalry Battalion"….After the departure of the "buttermilk rangers" we had a peaceful sleep.

butternut *n. Army.* a soldier or civilian of the Confederate States; a Southerner. Also attrib. Now *hist.*

  1862 in Keeler *USS Monitor* (Apr. 15) 84: Then the Fortress takes a notion to stir up the "butternuts" in Sewall's point & the 15 in. shells from the Union gun go…like an untamed steam engine. *1862* in McIntyre *Feds. on Frontier* 23: They seem pretty well filled up with about every description of butternut. *1862* in Bartlett *Amer.* 88: We marvelled as we went by that no ambitious *butternut* discharged his rifle or shot-gun at the fleet as it passed. *1863* Connolly *Cumberland* 71: There, on a little stool, in the middle of the bare floor, sat a "butternut,"…about 25 years of age, his wife sitting near him crying. *1865–67* De Forest *Miss Ravenel* 293: The Butternut immediately said…"Halt, you son of a bitch!" *1870* Ludlow *Heart of Cont.* 30: "The peasantry"…a houseful of unfortunate "Pikes" or "Butternuts." *1971* Altman & McKay *McCabe & Mrs. Miller* (film): You goddam butternut muff-diver.

buttface *n.* an ugly or contemptible person.—usu. considered vulgar. Hence **buttfaced,** *adj.*

  1973 Trinity Univ. student: You weirdo!…You buttface! *1973* W. Crawford *Gunship Cmndr.* 78: I'd say it was the buttfaced assistant flight surgeon. *1986* Coonts *Intruder* 76 [ref. to Vietnam War]: Did you hit the goddamn waveoff lights, butt-face?

butt-fuck *n.* **1.** an act of anal copulation.—usu. considered vulgar.

  1971 Dahlskog *Dict.* 11: *Butt fuck, v….*To engage in anal intercourse.—[also] *n.* *1981* *Nat. Lampoon* (Apr.) 39: Let's go to my place for brunch and a buttfuck. *1981* Spears *Slang & Euphem.* 58.

  2. an instance of victimization; an unfortunate event.

  1986 Heinemann *Paco's Story* 128: Iwo Jima was a sloppy, bloody buttfuck.

butt-fuck *v.* **1.** to copulate with anally.—usu. considered vulgar. Also *fig.* Hence **butt-fucker,** *n.*

  1962–68 B. Jackson *In the Life* 324: Everybody was "Old Butt-Fucker" to him. *1971* Rader *Meat* 72: I liked to get buttfucked. *1979* Crews *Blood & Grits* 122: Said if I'd butt-fuck him, he'd take me out there on the train and innerduce me. *1983* Eilert *Self & Country* 272 [ref. to 1968]: You're butt-fucking each other then. *1985* Dye *Between Raindrops* 129: Their…buddy has just been butt-fucked by a B-40 [rocket] or some such nonsense. *1990* Poyer *Gulf* 186: The warriors grab the first missionary…[and] butt-fuck him.

  2. to victimize.—usu. considered vulgar.

  1979 *Maledicta* III 55: Males in particular…who have been denied promotion, given low grades...been fired, jilted [etc.]...commonly relate that they have been *screwed, fucked,...butt-fucked*...and so on. **1981** Wambaugh *Glitter Dome* 240: He'll be back to being butt-fucked by those bogus producers. **1982** Del Vecchio *13th Valley* 491: Gettin butt-fucked.

butt-girl *n.* [sugg. by BUTT-BOY] a young woman who runs errands, as for a fashion model.
   1983 *Nat. Lampoon* (Mar.) 7: Her number-one butt-girl, Frankie, ...travels everywhere with her and runs out for more makeup or eyelashes...when Mean Jill's got a heavy fashion shoot on.

butthead *n.* a blockhead.
   1973 *TULIPQ* (coll. B.K. Dumas): An insincere person...*butthead*. **1985** Zemeckis & Gale *Back to Future* (film) [ref. to 1950's]: What are you looking at, butthead? **1987** Norst & Black *Lethal Weapon* 110: They're butt heads. **1991** *CBS This Morning* (CBS-TV) (May 2): Biff is actually the butthead of all time.

butthole *n.* **1.** the anus.—usu. considered vulgar.—also used in fig. expressions corresponding to those given at ASSHOLE, 1.
   1951 [VMF-323] *Old Ballads* 2: His butt-hole was puckered fit to tie. *a***1969** J. Kimbrough *Defender of Angels* 206 [ref. to 1920's]: Right off, my butt-hole clamped tighter'n a clothes wringer. **1975** C.W. Smith *Country Music* 97: Kissing disease, my aching butthole! **1979** in Terkel *Amer. Dreams* 412: They look up your butt hole. **1980** Univ. Tenn. student: I got women out the butthole [i.e., in great quantity].
   2. ASSHOLE, 2.
   1962 H. Simmons *On Eggshells* 120: Pay attention you little butt hole. **1968** Baker et al. *CUSS* 93: Butthole. An obnoxious person. **1973** Wideman *Lynchers* 110: And gentlemen are buttholes, right. **1981** Jenkins *Baja Okla.* 236: Did those butt-holes score again? **1981** Crowe *Fast Times* 77: Better not, you butthole! **1982** Braun *Judas Tree* 83: I told him there's no room in it for a butthole like Buntline. **1984** Oak Ridge, TN, high-school teacher, age 26: *Butthole* is the big word around school these days. The kids call one another *butthole* all the time. **1993** *Beavis & Butt-head* (MTV): No way he screwed it up, butthole!

butt-hook *n.* an oafish or worthless person.—usu. considered vulgar.
   1981 Hathaway *World of Hurt* 186: You two butt-hooks make NCO?

butt-in *n.* **1.** concern; affair.—used in neg. contexts.
   1902 Cullen *More Tales* 46: I didn't figure that it was my butt-in just at that stage of the journey. **1964** J. Thompson *Pop. 1280* 11: But that wasn't none of my butt-in.
   2. a meddler.
   1917 *Everybody's* (June) 723: She's an old butt-in! **1954–60** *DAS* 81. **1975** Swarthout *Shootist* 62: It was some nobody, some butt-in with a secret compulsion to use a gun once in his life on another human being or to die spectacularly.

butt in *v.* **1.** to intrude or interrupt; meddle.
   1899 Ade *Fables* 49: Whose people butt into the Society Column with Sickening Regularity. **1899–1900** Cullen *Tales* 306: Don't you recall when you butted in here? **1902** Cullen *More Tales* 103: Oi doan't want t'butt in an' make yeez feel bad wit' yeezelf. **1902–03** Ade *People You Know* 68: His apartment had been one of those delectable Man-Joints where women never butted in to hide things and give the whole place a Soapy Smell. **1904** in Opper *H. Hooligan* 51: Happy's butting right into the nobility. **1905** *Lippincott's Mag.* (Nov.) 577: A fellow can't butt in at the beginning of the third year and expect to trot even with fellows who have been there two years. **1907** *Lippincott's Mag.* (Jan.) 128: Don't butt in if you want the story. **1916** Lardner *Gullible's Trav.* 57: He says they butt right in on you. **1949** in *DAS* 81: The Wagner Act forbade any employer to butt in on such matters. **1965** Albert & Grilineks *Diablo* (film): You act like I ought to apologize for butting in. **1975** Boatner & Gates *Dict. Amer. Idioms* 41: John butted in on Bill and Tom's fight, and got hurt.
   2. to arrive.
   1898–1900 Cullen *Chances* 72: You'll never butt in among the first six. **1902** Hobart *Up to You* 88: As soon as we butted-in he picked Mama out as a steady listener.

buttinski or **buttinsky** *n.* **1.** [BUTT IN + *-ski* (final element in many Slavic surnames)] a person who butts in; meddler.
   1902 Ade *Girl Prop.* 70: The Friend belonged to the Buttinsky Family and refused to stay on the Far Side of the Room. **1905** Hobart *Search Me* 54: Sixteen editors...would take a running kick at old Buttinski. **1909** *Miss. A & M Reveille* 54: Kite is a strong man, studious, and is not

a "buttinski." **1920** S. Lewis *Main St.* 40: Suffragettes and God knows what all buttinskis...trying to tell a business man how to run his business. **1930** Bodenheim *Roller Skates* 189: This buttinsky better not try to make him a laughing stock with his girl. **1958** A. King *Mine Enemy* 139: Some were just natural buttinskies. **1975** T. Berger *Sneaky People* 136: He assailed the buttinsky. **1990** Rukuza *W. Coast Turnaround* 177: The buttinskis let go.
   2. [elab. of BUTT] the buttocks. *Joc.*
   1972 *Nat. Lampoon* (July) 84: He's gonna just sit around on his buttinski.

butt into *v.* to meet by chance.
   1931 Z. Grey *Sunset Pass* 47: Anythin' else happen beside buttin' into Mrs. Dabb?

butt kit *n. Navy & USMC.* an ashtray; BUTT CAN.
   1958 Cope & Dyer *Petty Off. Gde.* (ed. 2) 334. **1966** Noel & Bush *Naval Terms* 79: Butt bucket, butt kit: Ash tray. **1971** Tak *Truck Talk* 24: Butt kit: an ash tray in a tractor. **1982** C.R. Anderson *Other War* 203 [ref. to 1967]: A "butt kit" is an empty tin can painted red into which the remains of smoked cigarettes are thrown. **1990** Poyer *Gulf* 216: A Camel smoldered in the butt kit.

button *n.* **1.** *pl.* good sense; sanity.—esp. constr. with *lose*.
   ****1860** Hotten *Slang Dict.* (ed. 2) 109: *Not to have all one's buttons*, to be deficient in intellect. **1911** *Adventure* (Jan.) 444: When a man begins to lose his buttons, it's all off. **1937** Johnston *Prison Life* 71: There is another group...who in the early stages of dementing are referred to as having a few loose buttons. In a more advanced period they are described as having all their buttons off. **1955** O'Connor *Last Hurrah* 102: The trouble with you is you lost all your buttons years ago! You're a loony! **1960** *Twilight Zone* (CBS-TV): Are you missing a couple of buttons?
   2. *pl.* money.
   1859 *Spirit of Times* (Apr. 2) 88: All the "spondulix" and "buttons." **1882** *Puck* (Dec. 27) 261: Six Commercial Brokers/For the "buttons" strive. **1945** Kanin *Born Yesterday* 188: I didn't have the kind of buttons a guy needs for a deal like that.
   3.a. the clitoris.—usu. considered vulgar.
   ****1900** *Horn Book* 15: It is called clitoris, button, etc. **1916** Cary *Venery* I 35: *Button*—The clitoris. *a***1927** in P. Smith *Letter from Father* 135: I rubbed my...sex against her little button. *ca***1939** "M. Hunt" *Vulnerable* 151: Searching out my button, [he] soon had me kissing and hugging him. **1952** Larson *Barnyard Folklore* 75: Clitoris...the "button." **1970** E.W. Johnson *Sex* 86: *Clitoris*—button, clit, switch. **1980** Lorenz *Guys Like Us* 174: He sucked on her button.
   b. a woman's nipple.
   1963 Rubin *Sweet Daddy* 42: Well, they caught me feeling up this broad...I was pushing her buttons a little and she loved it.
   4. *Und.* a uniformed police officer. Also **buttons.**
   1913 Kneeland *Comm. Prost. in N.Y.C.*: "Buttons" (i.e., uniformed police). **1921** (cited in Partridge *Dict. Und.* 94): Button. **1929** Hotstetter & Beesley *It's a Racket* 221: Button...policeman. **1930** J.P. Burke, in *Amer. Mercury* (Dec.) 454: Buttons...A uniformed police officer. "There's the buttons." **1938** Chandler *Big Sleep* 44: Go ahead, call the buttons. You'll get a big reaction from it. **1943** in *Amer. N & Q* (Oct. 1944) 111: Skid, there's a buttons. **1953** Chandler *Goodbye* 6: The buttons in the prowl car were about ready to drop the hook on him. **1969** L. Sanders *Anderson Tapes* 114: It pulled off all the precinct buttons [from their usual duties].
   5. *Boxing.* the point of the chin.
   1920 T.A. Dorgan, in Zwilling *TAD Lexicon* 23: He got one on the button that put him out for four hours. **1920–21** Witwer *Leather Pushers* 7: This bird...smashes a right to the button of Loughlin's jaw. *Ibid.* 70: A well-timed cross to the button gave Williams a one-way ticket to dreamland. **1921** J. Conway, in *Variety* (Mar. 25) 4: The punch [was] right smack on the button. **1925** *Collier's* (Sept. 19) 50: It caught him right on the button and he crashed to the floor. **1931** Uhler *Cane Juice* 180: Sock 'im on the button, Milt. **1942** Liebling *Telephone* 39: I know he ain't got no right to hit me on the button. **1971** *Nat. Lampoon* (Apr.) 72: I let him have it on the button. His legs buckled and he slumped to the floor.
   6. *Police.* a law-enforcement officer's badge.
   1929 Hotstetter & Beesley *It's a Racket* 221: Button—Policeman's star; policeman. **1938** Steinbeck *Grapes of Wrath* 235: You got a tin button an' a gun. *Ibid.* 300: The sheriff tol' 'im he better bring in guys or give up his button. **1968** "Iceberg Slim" *Trick Baby* 44: You got that button?
   7. *West.* a boy. *Joc.*
   1940 F. Hunt *Trail from Tex.* 19 [ref. to *ca*1880]: I'm head wrangler of

you two buttons. **1942** *Yank* (Dec. 16) 18: Even as a button, the jiggle of a Texas cow-gal's walk…fascinated me. **1985** H. Cannon *Cowboy Poetry* 129: He learned this button how to ride.

8. *Und. & Police.* BUTTON MAN.

1966 Samuels *People vs. Baby* 136: Arrowed below them were the "Buttons" or "Soldiers"…the actual triggermen in the stratified structure. **1978** Diehl *Sharky's Machine* 216: Know what a button is, DeLaroza? A shooter. Very loyal people. **1987** Tapply *Dead Meat* 2: "And he's the button from Atlanta."…"You've got the terms down pretty good, Counselor. Watching…*Godfather* flicks, huh?"

9. *Radio & TV.* (see quots.).

1980 Pearl *Slang Dict.*: *Button n.* (Broadcasting) the finalizing bit of music or sound effects on a commercial. **1985** *L.A. Times* (Aug. 3) V 9: Scene after scene trails off indecisively, where a "button" is needed—a note of emotion that will propel us into the next scene.

10. *Army.* a general's star.

*a*1984 in Terry *Bloods* 163: A three-button Army general, Frederick Weyand.

¶ *In phrases:*

¶ **bust** [or **pop**] **(one's) buttons** to swell with pride.

1974 N.Y.C. woman, age 72: I can't bust my buttons about you. **1981** O'Day & Eells *High Times* 21: I was so proud I almost popped my buttons.

¶ **get off the button** to obtain sexual gratification; to experience orgasm.—usu. considered vulgar.

1932 Nelson *Prison Days & Nights* 38: Naturally a guy has got to get off the button now and then. But when I get that way, I'm going out and dig me up a broad for the night. *ca*1935 in Holt *Dirty Comics* 96: Dizzy Lil's cat emporium…it looks as though our hero is at last going to get off the button.

¶ **hot button** see HOT BUTTON.

¶ **on the button** directly; exactly. Now *colloq.*

1903 in F. Remington *Sel. Letters* 344: To judge the other fellows on the button. **1955** Shapiro *Sixth of June* 112: *That* boat caught it smack on the button. **1957** Berkeley *Deadly Mantis* (film): At 0800, sir. Right on the button.

¶ **push (someone's) buttons** to elicit a strongly favorable or unfavorable emotional response (from someone), esp. anger or sexual excitement. Also vars.

1927 H. Miller *Moloch* 22: I must have just touched the button. [**1936** in Garon *Blues* 69: Just press my button, give my bell a ring.] **1964** Smith & Hoefer *Music* 181: When a sharpie winks, presses a button, and spreads the jive, the hip girls will surround him. **1970** Landy *Underground Dict.* 153: *Press someone's buttons*…Verbally make another angry or disturbed; antagonize. [syn.] *push someone's buttons.* **1978** Cleaver *Soul on Fire* 196: I said some positive things about France. This absolutely pushed Genet's button.…He launched into a violent denunciation of France. **1981** *N.Y. Daily News* (Aug. 18) 48: The thing that had pushed his button (I would say "pulled his hair trigger," but he told me he doesn't own a gun) were pictures in the August *Vogue* magazine. **1982** *Morning Line* (WKGN radio) (June 2): Maybe this story about capital punishment will push your buttons. **1983** Sturz *Wid. Circles* 29: Anger can be a therapeutic tool. But never let them push your button. **1984** *N.Y. Post* (Dec. 21) 26: How do you control your temper?…One device is "don't let them push your button." **1986** *ALF* (NBC-TV): All I'm saying is that your mother knows how to push your buttons.

¶ **push the button** to panic; *push the panic button* s.v. PANIC BUTTON.

1967 *N.Y.P.D.* (ABC-TV): If not, I don't want to push the button just because some medical examiner's not sure of himself.

¶ **push the right buttons** to manage to get the desired results, esp. by manipulating another person.

[**1906** A.H. Lewis *Confessions* 22: Now, if you give me any lip, I'll push a button or two and have you sent out to Harlem.] **1970** La Motta et al. *R. Bull* 199: I could always push the right buttons and become as vicious and mean as I had to be. **1975** Delaney *Ultra-Psychonics* 42: Direct suggestion can be very successful, provided you push the right "psychic buttons" in the other person's mind. **1981** *Nat. Lampoon* (Mar.) 59: You've probably heard stratagems like this described as "pushing the right buttons."

¶ *pl.* (used in mild oaths).

*1803 in J. Ashton *Eng. Satires on Napoleon* 172: Dang my Buttons if that beant the head of that Rogue Boney. **1835** Longstreet *Georgia Scenes* 9: "Ding my buttons," said he, "if I didn't know I should stumble over Jim Johnson's foot at last." **1839–40** Cobb *Green Hand* I 60: "I swow," "darn my pluck," "dang my buttons," "I vowny," &c. &c. **1845**

Smith *Vernon* 37: Vell, blow my buttons, if it ain't Alf! **1872** *Overland Mo.* (July) 29: Dern my buttons if you ain't Colonel Bowler. **1879** [Tourgée] *Fool's Errand* 258: Dang my buttons if I ain't ready to kiss the hem of her garments.

button *v.* to close up (the mouth).—now esp. constr. with *nose*, *lip*, or *it.*—usu. imper. Cf. BUTTON UP.

1859 Matsell *Vocab.* 100: Oh, button your bone-box, Peg. ***1868** *N & Q* I 603: At school, it was thought quite an accomplishment in the young gentlemen who were fast of tongue to be able to silence a talkative comrade with the phrase, "button your lip." **1928** McEvoy *Show Girl* 55: Aw, go button your nose! **1928** MacArthur *War Bugs* 32: Brick Bristol told a glittering colonel to button his nose, an unfortunate crack that didn't help matters any. **1929** Sullivan *Look at Chicago* 80: He was told very early to button his lip. **1932** *AS* (June) 330: *Button up your face, lip, or trap*—"Shut up." ***1936** A. Huxley *Eyeless in Gaza* ch. xxv: Mr. Beavis…began to describe his researches into modern American slang.…Horse feathers, dish the dope, button up your face—delicious! **1938** Chandler *Big Sleep* 51: And keep your lip buttoned. **1939** in Galewitz *Great Comics* 122: Aw, button yer yap. **1943** M. Shulman *Barefoot Boy* 4: "Oh, button your lip," Father exclaimed testily. **1960** Leckie *Marines!* 58: …I buttoned my flap and went over to the icebox. **1980** Shue *Nerd* 6: Hey—button it, meathead. **1989** *Baywatch* (NBC-TV): Oh, button it up, Sylvia.

button-chopper *n.* *Army.* a laundry.

1941 *Army Ordnance* (July) 79: Button Chopper…The Laundry.

buttoned up *adj.* emotionally stable; TOGETHER.

1984 *N.Y. Post* (Aug. 29) 54: Polly is one fantastic lady…She is…more buttoned up than most people.…Her spirit is unbelievable.

button jock *n.* [sugg. by DISK JOCK] a console operator, as at a discotheque.

1983 *Judge Dredd* (Nov.) (5): I'm just a harmless button jock.

button man *n.* *Und. & Police.* a low-ranking member of a crime syndicate.

1969 Salerno & Tompkins *Crime Confed.* 93: Ordinary members, "soldiers" or "button men." **1969** Smith & Gay *Don't Try It* 105: The kilo connection may sell to a third line man, known, if a syndicate operation, as a *soldier* or *button man.* **1973** Toma & Brett *Toma* 278: He wants to grow up to be a button man or a lieutenant or a hit man in the organization. **1992** *N.Y. Observer* (Dec. 21) 5: Mafia button-men…planned to dress up as Hasidim for a hit in Brooklyn.

button up *v.* to hold one's tongue; shut up. Cf. BUTTON, *v.*

1859 Bartlett *Amer.* (ed. 2) 61: *Buttoning Up.* A Wall Street phrase.…when a broker…is a loser, he keeps the matter to himself, and is reluctant to confess the ownership of a share. This is called *buttoning up.* **1942** *ATS* 235. **1949** Algren *Golden Arm* 100: If you don't button up I'll sue you for breach of promise even if I *am* married. **1951** West *Flaming Feud* 23: Can I bank on you tuh button up? **1952** Steinbeck *E. of Eden* 387: He heard the parrot say, "Button up, you bloody bastard." **1976** Woodley *Bears* 48: Button up, Engelberg.

butt out *v.* [coined as the antonym to BUTT IN] to refrain from interrupting or intruding.

1906 Beyer *Amer. Battleship* 209: Don't butt in when yer have ter butt out. **1929–30** Dos Passos *42d Parallel* 345: He said it was about time for him to butt out, and picked up his hat and coat and left. **1949** *Life of Riley* (CBS-TV): I'm warnin' you, Gillis! Butt out of this! **1978** J. Webb *Fields of Fire* 167: It's personal.…So butt the hell *out.* **1990** Poyer *Gulf* 314: Won't butt out, huh?

buttplate *n.* *USMC.* an inconsequential or obnoxious person.

1977 Heinl *Marine Off. Gde.* (ed. 4) 692: Corporal Buttplate sure zapped that sniper. **1985** Dye *Between Raindrops* 2: The Southerner: last of the Delta Company Buttplates.

butt plug *n.* a stupid or contemptible person.—usu. considered vulgar.

1993 *Beavis & Butt-head* (MTV): Nice try,…butt plug.

butt-suck *v.* ASS-KISS.—usu. considered vulgar.

1973 *TULIPQ* (coll. B.K. Dumas): Trying to impress a professor, maybe to get a better grade: *butt-suck.*

butt-ugly *adj.* very ugly.

1986 R. Zumbro *Tank Sgt.* 212 [ref. to 1967–68]: A dozen chickens pecked in the dust, while one of those butt-ugly Viet pigs foraged in the garbage heap. **1989** *Night Court* (NBC-TV): What's with that butt-ugly pin you're wearing? **1989** S. Elliott et al. *Slang* 14: *Butt-ugly*…extremely homely. **1990** Costello & Wallace *Signifying Rappers*

38: Butt-ugly dumb drunks. **1993** *Mystery Sci. Theater* (Comedy Central TV): The butt-ugly teen star of today's movie.

butt-wipe *n.* toilet tissue; (*hence*) a worthless, contemptible person; ASS-WIPE, 1.

1971 Dahlskog *Dict.* 12: *Butt-wipe, n.*...Toilet paper. **1990** Univ. Tenn. student: Is there any buttwipe in the next stall? **1991** L. Chambers *Recondo* 180 [ref. to Vietnam War]: You don't give up, do you butt-wipe?

butty *n.* var. BUDDY.

buy *n.* *Police & Und.* a purchase of stolen or illicit goods, esp. narcotics. Now *colloq.*

1906 *Nat. Police Gaz.* (Sept. 15) 6: Will you back up the buy? **1932** L. Berg *Prison Doctor* 64: God, I've seen times when I could have murdered my old lady for dough to make a buy. **1982** J. Cain *Commandos* 353: In her attempts to make a drug buy.

buy *v.* **1.** to accept as satisfactory or true; to approve or believe.

***1926** in *OEDS*: It's rather early in the day for fairy-tales...but I'll buy this one. **1951** Robbins *Danny Fisher* 145: What if I don't buy this deal? **1953** Chandler *Goodbye* 7: I'll buy it this time. **1958** Mayes *Hunters* (film): I'll buy that when I see the goods. **1967** Talbot *Chatty Jones* 11: The chief of police...had advised her where to use a hairbrush. Only Mom hadn't been buying. **1968** "J. Hudson" *Case of Need* 26: I see your analogy...but I don't buy it. **1972** Kopp *Buddha* 178: Tony was far from ready to buy all that. **1976** Dyer *Erroneous Zones* 53: It is just plain easier to buy the stuff that others tell you than to think for yourself. **1983** *Agronsky & Co.* (Mutual Radio Net. news show) (Mar. 13): Do you buy that evaluation?

2. to cause or bring about (for oneself); to inflict upon (oneself).

1932 Berg *Prison Doctor* 221: Them New York wisecracks is going to buy you plenty of grief! **1933–35** D. Lamson *About to Die* 201: An' suppose he does get tough about it, what does it buy him? **1941** *Slanguage Dict.* 9: *Buy v.t.*, accomplish; bring about; result in; bring, as in the phrase, what does that *buy* you? **1953** Chandler *Goodbye* 84: You could buy yourself a lot of grief talking about them. **1959** W. Williams *Ada Dallas* 183: Mrs. Governor Ada Dallas, you just bought yourself a first-class page. **1966** T.V. Olsen *Hard Men* 20: You bought yourself a sack of hell, son, stirring up trouble in my town. **1970** *Adam-12* (NBC-TV): Barstow, you already bought enough trouble. **1976** *S.W.A.T.* (NBC-TV): I got your rap sheet here. A couple of falls. Nothing that tells me you're ready to buy murder one. **1988** Dye *Outrage* 146: The Doc didn't know what he was buyin' into when he hauled Dale's ass out of the line of fire.

3. to be charged for as a result of damaging, losing, etc.

1938 *AS* (Dec.): *Bought A Car* (or *Telephone Pole*, etc.). A driver is to blame for an accident. **1958** McCulloch *Woods Words* 26: *Buy 'er*—To leave or throw away logs or equipment or almost anything else. **1960** N.Y.C. storeowner: Kid, you bust one of them lightbulbs and you bought it. **1984** Knoxville, Tenn., man: You drop that and you just bought yourself a beer mug.

¶ In phrases:

¶ **buy a trunk** *West.* to abscond or depart, esp. permanently.

1934 Cunningham *Triggernometry* 192 [ref. to 1870's]: Outlaws who escaped capture decided to "buy a trunk." *Ibid.* 215: He was not apt to "buy a trunk." *Ibid.* 312: A quiet warning to emigrate—"buy a trunk," was the expressive western phrase. **1944** R. Adams *West. Words*: *Buy a trunk.* to leave the country.

¶ **buy it, 1.** to suffer a serious reverse; to get into a finishing situation. [Continuity of usage cannot be shown between early and mod. use, which prob. arose independently from **(2)**.]

***1825** W.N. Glascock *Naval Sk.-Bk.* I 30: Never mind, in closing with *Crappo*, if we didn't buy it with his raking broadsides. **1957** Myrer *Big War* 148 [ref. to WWII]: You've bought it. You've got a long, long way to go just to see the light of day. **1975** V.B. Miller *Trade-Off* 27: No, baby, this time you've bought it. Ten to twenty on the [prison] farm. **1978** C. Miller *Animal House* 86: You're finished!...You just bought it, brother!

2. [app. in allusion to syn. *buy a packet* (RAF slang of WWI)] Orig. *Mil. Av.* to be killed; (*now also*) to die.

***1920** in *OEDS* I 404 [ref. to WWI]: The wings and fuselage, with fifty-three bullet holes, caused us to realize on our return how near we had been to "buying it." ***1943** Hunt & Pringle *Service Sl.* 39: *He bought it*—he was shot down. **1945** Huie *Omaha to Oki.* 106: A bomb dump

went up...and...Palmer was one of those who "bought it." **1955** Klaas *Maybe I'm Dead* 74 [ref. to WWII]: They thought I'd bought it, back there over Abbeville. **1958** Varnon *Night of the Blood Beast* (film): He bought it all the way. **1963** E.M. Miller *Exile to Stars* 30: Somebody just bought it south of town. It's still burning. **1963** Lester & Gordon *Sgt. Ryker* (film): He took over when Colonel Chambers bought it. **1965** Koch *Casual Company* 14: But I'll be with the Division again; another chicken-colonel's bought it. **1972** *Playboy* (Sept.) 110: Chaucer...seems to disappear from sight around his sixtieth year, but it's been so long now that we can assume that he eventually bought it. **1973** Chandler *Captain Hollister* 52: What if we could do something for the guys who bought it. **1983** Flaherty *Tin Wife* 312: He presumed Sullivan bought it when he was cooping in the club. **1983** Ehrhart *VN-Perkasie* 55 [ref. to 1967]: Moon and Watson bought it. Sergeant Wilson got hit, too, but not bad. **1984** Hammel *Root* 194: Clark's bought it. **1991** *World News Tonight* (ABC-TV) (Feb. 14): In the worst scenario the whole squad could buy it.

¶ **buy one** Orig. *Mil. Av.* to be killed, as in air combat.

1929 in Longstreet *Canvas Falcons* 274 [ref. to 1917]: "The major bought one," I said, climbing out, covered with my own slime. **1970** Corrington *Bombardier* 97:—The cockpit's gone. Finelly and Mitchell have bought one. Junk the sight and bail out. **1973** Salt & Wexler *Serpico* (film): If I buy one, I'm not going to buy it from you.

¶ **buy the farm** Also vars.

1. [orig. in allusion to **(3)**, above] Esp. *USAF.* (of a pilot or airplane) to crash.

1954 *N.Y. Times* (Mar. 7) 20 ["Jet-flight glossary"]: *Bought a plot:* Had a fatal crash. **1954** in F. Harvey *Jet* 117: Those jet jockeys just bought the shop, didn't they? **1955** *AS* XXX 116: *Buy the farm; Buy a plot, v. phr.* Crash fatally. (Jet pilots say that when a jet crashes on a farm the farmer usually sues the government for damages done to his farm by the crash, and the amount demanded is always more than enough to pay off the mortgage and then buy the farm outright. Since this type of crash [i.e., in a jet fighter] is nearly always fatal to the pilot, the pilot pays for the farm with his life.) **1956** Heflin *USAF Dict.* 198: *Buy a farm.* To crash....This expression is in allusion to the notion that the owner of a farm takes advantage of a crash on his land to collect heavy damages. **1963** E.M. Miller *Exile* 29: The police dispatcher says a plane just bought the farm. Went straight in. No one saw a chute. *Ibid.* 169: He was going straight down. Look at the hole he made. He bought the back 40 like a plumb bob. **1973** *CBS Evening News* (Mar. 31): Stewardesses have long been prepared for any emergencies in case the plane "buys the farm," as the pilots jokingly call it.

2. Orig. *Mil.* to be killed; (*hence*) to die.

1958 Davis *Spearhead* 122 [ref. to WWII]: *Panzerfaust!*...One of those in the guts and we've bought the farm, I'll tell you! **1959** Scott *Tiger in Sky* 110: You'll buy the farm, if you keep that up! **1964** Howe *Valley of Fire* 74 [ref. to Korean War]: And in the movie he finally bought the farm. **1964** Peacock *Drill & Die* 90: "Who bought the farm?" one of them asked anxiously. **1965** Beech *Make War in Madness* 67 [ref. to Korean War]: What happened to the father? Did he buy the farm? **1968** K. Cooper *Aerobics* 125: If the clot is in a coronary artery, you've bought the farm. **1968** Barrett *Green Berets* (film): He bought the farm, sir, but he took a lot of them with him. **1969** Eastlake *Bamboo Bed* 135: Five got out. Pike stuck and bought a farm. I got his body out. **1969** Rottmann *Hearts & Minds* 23: I'm thinking, as I hear my chest/Sucking air through its brand new nipple,/I bought the ticket, I hope I drown fast. **1970** Lincke *Jenny Was No Lady* 21: Charlie just got it (meaning he had "bought the lot," i.e., had been killed). **1975** Percy *Message in Bottle* 64: During the Korean War, one way of saying that someone had been killed was to say that he had bought the farm. **1979** Former USAF member, age 45: I remember well the first time I heard *buy the farm.* In 1954 I was at Pax [Patuxent] River and this aircraft went in and they said, "He bought the farm." Right across the river they had the test pilot school. **1980** in McCauley *Dark Forces* 169: "What's your name?"..."Mrs. Mona T. Finch. Mr. Finch bought a farm in Korea." **1983** Eilert *Self & Country* 25: We've been pretty worried about you. You almost bought the farm. **1984** *Prairie Home Companion* (Nat. Pub. Radio) (Oct. 22): I'm not going to stop till the last cricket buys the farm! **1985** Former Spec. 4, U.S. Army, age 35: I've heard *buy the farm, buy the plot, buy the lot.* They all mean the same. **1987** *Tour of Duty* (CBS-TV) [ref. to Vietnam War]: Came pretty close to buyin' the rice paddy, though.

3. to get into a disastrous situation.

1961 L.G. Richards *TAC* 135: Looks like I've really bought the farm and all the livestock this time. **1967** Spillane *Delta* 17: Buddies, you done bought the farm.

¶ **buy the rabbit** to be worsted; to be made to suffer.
*1825 in *F & H* V 356: If that air invoice aint ready soon, thee'll buy the rabbit, I guess. **1830** Martin *Rev. Soldier* 121 [ref. to 1778]: The Indians, with all their alertness, had like to have "bought the rabbit." *Ibid.* 144: I knew that if I was brought before our hotspur of a colonel I should be made to "buy the rabbit."

¶ **buy the rack** see s.v. RACK, *n.*

¶ **buy the ranch** *Mil.* to be killed.
1963 E.M. Miller *Exile to Stars* 52: He'd never "buy the ranch" like Cam had. **1976** C.R. Anderson *Grunts* 154 [ref. to 1969]: They don't do nothing for a guy till after he buys the ranch. **1987** *Tour of Duty* (CBS-TV): Cough real loud, and you've bought the ranch.

¶ **buy [the] real estate** Esp. *Mil.* to be killed.
*1977 T. Jones *Incredible Voyage* 37: Right, Conrad, let's heave to, fast, or we'll be buying Sudanese real estate! **1979** Univ. Tenn. student: We were driving in Dallas [in 1976] and we passed the Book Depository and my friend said, "Here's where JFK bought the real estate." **1985** Former Spec. 4, U.S. Army, age 35: "You don't watch you'll be buyin' some real estate soon!" That means, "I'm gonna kill your ass."

¶ **buy the wad** to be inflicted with the worst.
1968 Myrer *Eagle* 186: I've bought the whole wad. I know....I'm going to check out [die], Sam.

¶ **buy up an orchard** *Trucking.* to have a serious road accident.
1971 Tak *Truck Talk* 24: *Buy up an orchard*: To have an accident by running off the side of the road into the brush or trees. **1976** Lieberman & Rhodes *CB Handbook* 125: *Buying Up An Orchard*—Front tire blowout, or any kind of accident.

buzz *n.* **1.a.** prevailing rumor.
*1820–21 P. Egan *Life in London* 121: A little information respecting the buz [*sic*] on public affairs. **1941** Kendall *Army & Navy Slang* 3: *Buzz*...widespread rumor. **1944** *Slanguage Dict.* 59: *Give with the buzz*—tell me the gossip; dish the dirt. **1983** *N.Y. Post* (Aug. 17) 7: The latest buzz: Some bees work as undertakers. **1984** *N.Y. Post* (Aug. 20) 10: The big buzz around CBS is that Elizabeth Taylor will play Louella Parsons. **1992** *Newsweek* (Dec. 14) 78: If the industry buzz...is to be trusted, multiple Oscar nominations are a sure thing.

b. a quizzing; an interviewing with an ulterior purpose, as by a criminal or a police officer.
1929 Hostetter & Beesley *Racket* 221: In the sinister meaning of visiting and intimidating someone, especially with the ultimate purpose of extorting money..."to put the *buzz* on." **1933** Ersine *Pris. Slang* 24: *Buzz*, *n.* A talk which has as its end the finding out of a person's reactions to some matter. "Give the bull a *buzz* and see if he'll take the grease." **1966** Brunner *Face of Night* 155: I can't even take a peaceful nap without you putting a buzz on me.

c. chatter; conversation.
1930 *Amer. Mercury* (Dec.) 455: Lay off on the buzz. **1933–34** Lorimer & Lorimer *Stag Line* 139: Cut the buzz, boys,...and let your money talk.

2.a. a feeling of mild intoxication, as from liquor or drugs. Also (in recent use) constr. with *on.*
1849 Doten *Journals* I 26: There are some on board so "hard up" as to drink it and so completely the slaves of King Alcohol, as to try to raise a bizz [*sic*] on such stuff as that. [**1882** Campbell *Poor* 34: My head got in a buzz, an' in a week or two I wanted something stronger.] **1935** E. Anderson *Hungry Men* 113: We ought to be gettin' a buzz on this stuff pretty soon. **1948** J.M. Burns *Lucifer* 303: He had now the beginnings of a pleasant buzz on. **1952** Ellson *Golden Spike* 33: You'll get a buzz off it. **1953** Brossard *Bold Saboteurs* 124: He was getting a buzz on from the beer. **1961** Baldwin *Another Country* 22: He had a mild buzz on when he got back to the balcony. **1966** Goldstein *1 in 7* 32: You take another drag as the cigarette is passed again. You can feel the preliminary symptom known as the "buzz." **1967** *Zap Comix* (Oct.) 16: We needed a *buzz!* **1979** Gutcheon *New Girls* 158: I think I'm beginning to get a buzz. **1980** Univ. Tenn. student theme: However, some parties are organized for no other purpose than to "catch a buzz." **1980** Novak *High Culture* xxiii: A smoker might first "catch a buzz," and then get "high." **1993** *N.Y. Times* (May 5) C 12: I had a few drinks, had a buzz on and said, "Let's just do this."

b. a thrill; CHARGE.
1937 *AS* (Oct.) 184: *Buzz.* Thrill derived from hearing good swing music. **1942** *ATS* 282. **1942–44** in *AS* (Feb. 1946) 31: *Buzz* (in *To Get a Buzz*), *n.* To enjoy thoroughly. Probably from alcoholic reaction, a strongly stimulating effect. **1983** Nelkin & Brown *Workers* 99: I get a buzz out of doing a nice job on a nice piece of furniture. **1984** Univ.

Tenn. instructor: Well, if you're one of those people who really gets a buzz out of [John] Milton, go to it.

3. a telephone call. Now *colloq.*
*1930 in *OEDS*. **1933** D. Runyon, in *Collier's* (Aug. 5) 8: She gives the gendarmes a buzz. **1941** Coldewey *Lady Gangster* (film): I'll give him a buzz right now. **1957** Bannon *Odd Girl* 31: I'll give you a buzz. **1963** W.C. Anderson *Penelope* 33: I think I'll give Jaguar a buzz.

4. a close haircut given with electric clippers.
1977 in G.A. Fine *With the Boys* 169: *Buzz*, *n.* Short haircut; crewcut. **1989** *21 Jump St.* (Fox-TV): Chuck, my boyfriend, has a buzz, mostly because he's on the wrestling team.

buzz *v.* **1.a.** *Und.* to rob (a person), as by pickpocketing or purse-snatching. Also intrans.
*1789 G. Parker *Life's Painter* 135: Padding Jack and diving Ned,/With blink-ey'd buzzing Sam. ***1812** J.H. Vaux *Memoirs* (glossary): To *buz* a person is to pick his pocket. ***1821** in Partridge *Dict. Und.* 94: With rolling kiddies, Dick would dive and buz. **1867** *Nat. Police Gaz.* (Mar. 23) 2: He took to "buzzing" on a small scale with some "pals." **1901** *Our Naval Apprentice* (Oct.) 12: The only thing for mine was to conclude that I'd been buzzed for the roll by some San Francisco leatherworker. **1902** Hapgood *Autobiog. of a Thief* 42: Zack and I were grafting, buzzing Molls.

b. *Und.* to engage in theft, esp. pickpocketing, in (a place).
1866 *Nat. Police Gaz.* 3: Not a "clyfaker" could be seen upon the cars, not a "moll" to "buzz" the stages nor a "wire" to "work" the "go-aways."

c. *Hobo.* to solicit handouts from (a person) or on (a street). Also intrans.
1917 *Editor* (Feb. 24) 152: *Buzz*...the main drag...to beg or bum along the main street. **1922** Anderson *Hobo* 20–21: Jungle crimes include...buzzing, or making the jungle a permanent hangout for "jungle buzzards," who subsist on the leavings of meals. **1927** *DN* V 441: *Buzz*, v. (1) To beg. (2) To pilfer. **1930** Irwin *Tramp & Und. Sl.*: *Buzz*...To beg from.

2.a. to chat with, esp. in a cajoling or flirtatious manner; (*hence*) to court; (*also*) to accost or proposition. Also intrans.
1866 G.A. Townsend *Non-Combatant* 299: It is not hard to eschew cognac and claret, but there is no cure for "buzzing." **1867** Eno *Twenty Years* 83: We have been "buzzed" so much this week on political matters that, contrary to our usual custom, we have been led to reflect on party politics. **1870** *Overland Mo.* (Jan.) 89: So candidates mounted their horses, put quart bottles of whisky in the pockets of their linen dusters, and...scoured camp, hill, bar, flat, gulch, and cañon, "buzzing" the aspiring miner. *Ibid.* 90: Sam White...is cornered, confabbed, and "buzzed." **1877** Wonder *Drummer* 26: The great American buzzer commenced. **1878** Mulford *Fighting Indians* 45: An orderly did not have to...do much of anything but buzz the hired girl in the kitchen and eat up all the cold vituals he could find. **1882** in Bunner *Letters* 72: It is a great satisfaction to sit down and buzz you by letter, even as we buzzed face to face over cigarettes and b. floats. **1885** "Lykkejaeger" *Dane* 82: I would have far preferred "buzzing" Sis. **1896** F.H. Smith *Tom Grogan* 76: He['s] up ter de house a-buzzin' Jinnie. **1900** *DN* II 25: *Buzz*, v.t. To entertain, converse with; generally used of a male person at a social function, with reference to the young lady in whose company he is for the time. **1944** Quillan & Bennett *Show Business* (film): When will you quit buzzin' those dames? **1963** Charters *Poetry of the Blues* 127: I buzzed a girl the other day,/I wanted a little thrill. **1968** *N.Y.P.D.* (ABC-TV): She buzzes the first guy that looks at her. **1973** in *DARE*.

b. to question (a person); to interview.
1871 Bagg *Yale* 43: Buzz, to interview and "sound" a man. **1912** Mathewson *Pitching* 45: I could write a book about that guy...after buzzing Cobb. **1912** Stringer *Shadow* 85: He "buzzed" tipsters and floaters and mouthpieces. **1929** Hostetter & Beesley *Racket* 221: *Buzz*—to interview. **1958** A. King *Mine Enemy* 24: Some guy buzzed Panama about me. **1960** Stadley *Barbarians* 91: How do you know she's gonna keep her mouth shut? They'll be buzzin' her all morning.

c. to talk.
1899 Ade *Fables* 88: Gus showed her where to sit on the Sofa, then he placed himself about Six Inches away and began to Buzz, looking her straight in the Eye.

d. to annoy.
1952 Ellson *Golden Spike* 30: I don't want to buzz him, you understand....I ain't looking for trouble from him. *Ibid.* 244: *Buzz*...to irritate someone. **1964** Ellson *Nightmare St.* 14: "You look like a goddam wildman." For the first time he buzzes me, but that passes.

3. to telephone. Now *colloq.* or *S.E.*

1929 in *OEDS* I. **1933** Ersine *Pris. Slang* 23: *Buzz*…To telephone.

4. to throw hard.

1928–29 Nason *White Slicker* 42: Get out o' there…or I'll buzz a grenade at you!

5. *Av.* to fly a plane very low over (a building, field, etc.). Now *S.E.* See also BUZZ JOB.

1944 Solomon & Buchman *Snafu* 31: The roar of a plane "buzzing" the housetop. **1946** *N.Y. Times* (May 1) 9: 2 Russians "Buzz" Gen. Clark's B-17. **1971** Windchy *Tonkin* 137: What is the skipper of a Russian ship to do when he is "buzzed" by an American airplane—open fire? **1984** Jackson & Lupica *Reggie* 246: Why did he buzz the field as close as he did? **1988** Maloney *Thunder Alley* 67: You want to buzz the…admiral's boat?

6. to happen.—used as pres. ppl. only, esp. in phr. **What's buzzin', cousin?** What's the latest news? *Joc.*

1941 Brackett & Wilder *Ball of Fire* (film): What's buzzin', cousin? **1943** in Meyer *Stars & Stripes Story of World War II* 81: A couple of his phrases, "What's buzzin', cousin?" and "What's the action, Jackson?" are by words among the kids all over Tripoli. **1977** Stallone *Paradise Alley* 27: What's buzzin', Lenny?

7. BUZZ OFF, 1.

1968–70 *Current Slang* III & IV 20: Gotta buzz now. **1986** J. Hughes *Ferris Beuller* (film): Gotta buzz.

buzzard *n.* **1.a.** a foolish or despicable person; (now *esp.*) a contemptible old man; GEEZER.—sometimes used as a euphem. for BASTARD.

***1641** R. Brome, in R.G. Lawrence *Comedies* 165: Wizards! Old blind buzzards!/For once they hit, they miss a thousand times. ***1698–99** "B.E." *Dict. Canting Crew*: *Buzzard*,…A foolish soft Fellow, easily drawn in [by swindlers] and Cullied or Trickt. **1714** in Meserve & Reardon *Satiric Comedies* 33: Unsear [*sic*] your Ears, ye Old Buzzard. **1807** in W. Irving *Salmagundi* 13: Shakspeare [*sic*]…sometimes that great poet could talk like a buzzard. **1847** Robb *Squatter Life* 34: We are informed…that the *Buzzard* of the *Eagle* cannot pay his board bill. **1895** *Harper's* (Nov.) 846: I took a look at those buzzards there in Washington. Our Senate and Representatives. *a*1927 in P. Smith *Letter from Father* 75: The buzzard left her at the door of her apartment house. **1927** Hemingway *Men Without Women* 125: What are you buzzards talking about? **1948** McIlwaine *Memphis* 335: Make that buzzard stay in his own bed. **1973** Herbert & Wooten *Soldier* 100: Sergeant Candiotti was about as tough an old buzzard as I'd ever seen in the army. **1983** K. Miller *Lurp Dog* 7: I can see the old buzzard was right.

b. a native or resident of Georgia. *Joc.*

1845 in *DA*. **1902** Clapin *Americanisms* 89: *Buzzards*. A nickname of the inhabitants of Georgia, from a very strict law enacted in that State for the protection of the buzzards, as they act in the capacity of scavengers. **1913** in *DA*.

c. *Army.* a war correspondent.

1914 *Collier's* (May 16) 7: The buzzards—for so are war correspondents named—began to gather.

2. a botched job.

1871 Schele De Vere *Americanisms* 587: *Buzzard* is the half-facetious half-contemptuous term applied in several mechanical professions to a badly-spoiled piece of work.…"Sir, I pronounce that job an unmitigated *buzzard*."

3.a. a representation of the American eagle, as on the U.S. coat of arms, coins, etc.; (*hence*) a gold or silver dollar. See also BUZZARD DOLLAR.

1834 *Military & Naval Mag. of U.S.* (Oct.) 116: He launches out a *golden buzzard* to a coachee for a ride to see the ways of the town. **1902** Clapin *Americanisms* 89: *Buzzard*.…The silver dollar, so called derisively from the buzzard-like eagle on the coin. **1943** in Meyer *Stars and Stripes Story of WWII* 81: Somebody called "Jo-Jo" a sad sack the other day and he came right back with a nifty counterblow, "well, you're a disgrace to the buzzard," he told the ribber, with the gravity of a Supreme Court Justice.

b. *Mil.* a military discharge certificate.

1888 McConnell *Five Years a Cavalryman* 120 [ref. to 1866]: He [*sc.* the U.S. soldier] never says he expects, or has his discharge; he always calls it his "buzzard," presumably owing to the spread eagle which decorates the document. **1899** Cook *Co. B* 108: One day an ex-regular tried to make Louis believe that his "buzzard" (discharge paper) from the Tenth United States Infantry entitled him to go through the lines. **1906** M'Govern *By Bolo & Krag* 20–21: So you bet you yours very sincerely lost no time in attaching himself to the cool end of a brewery the minute he got his buzzard and cashed in his paymaster's checks. **1918**

Griffin *Ballads of the Reg't.* 35: I got my "buzzard" in my hand and cashed my "finals" too. **1918** O'Reilly *Roving and Fighting* 48 [ref. to 1899]: One morning a notice was pasted on the bulletin-board announcing that "General Order Forty" men would "get their buzzard" the following week.…"Eight days and a breakfast!" we would gleefully shout at the old timers. **1921** *Sentinel-15th Inf.* (Mar. 25) 5: You fume and growl and sweat/And wished you had your "buzzard." **1929** *Our Army* (Nov.) 27: *Buzzard*—A discharge from the Army.

4.a. *Navy.* the eagle insigne of a naval petty officer; (*hence*) a naval petty officer.

1894 *Lucky Bag* 66 [U.S. Naval Acad.]: *Buzzard*…A cadet petty officer. **1897** *Lucky Bag* 4 105: *Buzzard*…The insignia of rank of a cadet petty officer—an eagle perched on an anchor. **1898** Allen *Navy Blue* 104: The [Annapolis] cadet petty officers, wearing on their uniforms as insignia of rank an eagle perched on an anchor, are locally known as "buzzards." **1905** *Bluejacket* (Feb.) 157: A buzzard and stripe upon his sleeve. **1906** *Army & Navy Life* (Nov.) 498: A *Buzzard* is the insignia of rank of a cadet petty officer—an eagle perched on an anchor. **1928** *AS* III (Aug.) 452: *Buzzard*—Gold eagle insignia denoting rank of Midshipman Petty Officer. **1938** *U.S. Naval Inst. Proc.* (Aug.) 1131 [ref. to 1882]: The eagles and chevrons of sailor petty officers. We [midshipmen] promptly dubbed these devices "buzzards." **1941** *A Guide to the U.S. Naval Academy* 150: *Buzzard*—The rating badge of a 2 P.O.

b. *Mil.* the eagle insigne designating the rank of a full colonel in the U.S. Army or Marine Corps.

1931 *Our Army* (Mar.) 6: No longer is it necessary for an aspirant to spend four years of his life at the Military Academy, and thirty or more in Army service in order to don the "buzzards" of a colonel. **1941** Downey *Indian-Fighting Army* 226: While both officers now held brevets as generals, each by actual rank still had, in Army parlance, "buzzards up"; that is, wore a colonel's eagles. **1967** Taggart *Reunion of the 108th* 95: Colonel Eggers, you can take those silver buzzards one by one and stick 'em point open —.

5. a worthless horse.

1907 *S.E.* White *Ariz. Nights* 83: He ain't celebratin' that bunch of buzzards, is he?

6.a. *Army.* an enemy airplane. [Quots. ref to WWI.]

1925 Thomason *Fix Bayonets!* 124: No, nor no damn Boche buzzards drop air-bombs on him— **1926** *Sat. Eve. Post* (June 12) 146: Some German buzzard laid a egg in the middle of the road.

b. *Av.* an airplane pilot. *Joc.* [Quots. ref. to WWI.]

1937 Parsons *Lafayette Escadrille* 67: When a buzzard tamed those two ships, if he was still alive and not a nervous wreck, he could fly anything. **1939** Hart *135th Aero Squadron* 119: If I ever saw a buzzard, he's one.

7. *Mil.* chicken or turkey as served in a mess hall.

1941 Kendall *Army & Navy Slang* 3: *Buzzard*…chicken. **1942** *Sat. Eve. Post* (Nov. 28) 65: Buzzard [used for "turkey"]. **1943** Hersey *G.I. Laughs* 171: Buzzard, chicken. **1943–44** in *AS* (Feb. 1946) 31: *Buzzard*, n. Chicken or turkey. **1944** Kober & Uris *In Meantime, Darling* (film): Buzzard again.

¶ In phrase:

¶ **make buzzard talk** (see quot.).

1912–43 *Frank Brown Collection* I 524: *Buzzard talk, to make*…To quarrel. Central and east (N.C.).

¶ (In vulgar prov.).

1952 Randolph & Wilson *Down in the Holler* 179: *Ragged as a buzzard's ass* does not seem to be grounded in anatomical fact, but it is common all through the Ozark country. **1974** Newburgh, N.Y., man, age 24: She's so ugly I wouldn't take her to a buzzard fuck. **1984** Ark. man, age *ca*35: I remember I first heard about somebody *so ugly I wouldn't take her to a buzzard fuck* about 1971 or so. It's a memorable expression. **1984** Ark. man, age *ca*35: The expression I heard was *ragged as a buzzard's asshole*.

buzzard-bait *n.* **1.** Esp. *West.* a corpse left in the open; (*hence*) a dead or doomed person.

1851 in Chittick *Roarers* 184: I'll make buzzard's bait of some on ye fust! **1928** Bradford *Ol' Man Adam* 64: Hit's all accordin' to who playin' de buzzard bait. **1951** West *Flaming Feud* 31: And don't squawk if you end up buzzard bait! **1967** Ford *Muc Wa* 187: We'd all be buzzard bait now if it wasn't for that and that vegetable juice. **1981** *Taxi* (ABC-TV): "What about that little girl?" "She's buzzard bait."

2. *Rural.* CROWBAIT.

1905 *DN* II 72 (Ark.): *Buzzard-bait.* An emaciated horse. **1944** R. Adams *West. Words*.

buzzard-buster *n. Army.* a member of an antiaircraft unit.

1942–44 in *AS* (Feb. 1946) 31: *Buzzard Busters*, n. "Cadets of the Coast

Artillery Regiment; anti-aircraft, a specialty." **1944** Kendall *Service Slang* 4: *Buzzard Buster.*...air corps.

buzzard detail *n. Army.* a graves-registration detail.

1948 Murphy *To Hell and Back* 3 [ref. to WWII]: Then why didn't you get hooked up with a body-snatching outfit? You look like a natural for the buzzard detail. *Ibid.* 95: Tell the buzzard detail not to drive past your station.

buzzard dollar *n. Finance.* a silver or gold dollar as opposed to a trade dollar. Cf. BUZZARD, 3.a.

1889 Barrère & Leland *Dict. Slang* I 213: The waiters...will take anything you give them, from a nickel up to a *buzzard dollar*, and look happy. **1891** Maitland *Amer. Slang Dict.* 54: *Buzzard dollar*...a term applied in derision to the silver dollar, the uncomplimentary allusion being to the buzzard-like eagle on the coin.

buzzard meat *n.* **1.** BUZZARD-BAIT.

1899 Hamblen *Bucko Mate* 124: I pulled my gun, and told him in good plain United States that if he didn't return to the head of his family I'd make buzzard meat of him.

2. BUZZARD-BAIT, 2.

1932 in Runyon *Blue Plate* 365: You are sure this old buzzard meat you are running will win.

3. *Mil.* BUZZARD, 7.

1944 *Slanguage Dictionary* 49: *Buzzard meat*—chicken or turkey.

buzzard roost *n.* **1.** a disreputable gathering place or ramshackle building. Also **buzzard's roost.**

1889 "M. Twain" *Conn. Yankee* 231: The moral and physical stenches of that intolerable old buzzard-roost. **1906** *DN* III 129: *Buzzard-roost*...A dilapidated building. **1945** Hubbard *R.R. Ave.* 336: *Buzzard's Roost*—Yard office.

2. an upper balcony in a theater.

1920 in Drake & Clayton *Black Metropolis* 100: "Don't have to go to the buzzard roost* at shows."...*Semi-humorous colloquial name for the Jim-Crow balcony in southern theaters. **1969** Angelou *Caged Bird* 115: The whitefolks downstairs laughed ever few minutes, throwing the discarded snicker up to the Negroes in the buzzards' roost. **1984** *Walk Through 20th C.* (WNET-TV): Blacks sat up in the balcony—the *buzzard's roost* we called it [in Marshall, Tex., 1930's].

buzzard shit *n. Mil.* vile or unappetizing food.—usu. considered vulgar.

1939 *AS* XIV (Feb.) 25: *Buzzard shit*, n. Roast-beef hash. [**1952** Randolph & Wilson *Down in the Holler* 179: Poor as buzzard dung.]

buzz bomb *n.* a strong cocktail.

1945 Lindsay & Crouse *State of the Union* 497: Mary *(painfully)* what's in those buzz bombs?

buzz boy *n. Mil.* a fighter pilot; a member of an air force.—used derisively.

1944 *Stars & Stripes* (Rome) (Oct. 18): What the hell do they think we are, just a bunch of buzz boys? **1945** in *AS* (Dec. 1946) 310: *Buzz boy.* A single-engine fighter pilot. This term is also used in the Navy Air Force to describe an Army Fighter pilot. **1951** *Merrie Melodies* (animated cartoon): I'm a buzz boy! **1955** Archibald *Aviation Cadet* 154: *Buzz boys:* pilots. **1958** Frankel *Band of Bros.* 46: This here would cost you twenty-five bucks if you bought it from a buzzboy. **1961** Plantz *Sweeney Squadron* 105 [ref. to WWII]: I never would have thunk it. You, a buzz boy.

buzz buggy *n.* BUZZ-WAGON.

1911 T.A. Dorgan, in Zwilling *TAD Lexicon* 23: She offered you her 90 horse power buzz buggy and diamond rings. **1919** *DN* V 64: *Buzz-buggy*, an automobile. "The White family bought a new *buzz-buggy* last week." New Mexico. **1926** Wood & Goddard *Amer. Slang* 10: *Buzz-buggy.* An automobile.

buzzed *adj.* **1.** intoxicated by liquor or drugs.—since *ca*1970 also constr. with *out.*

1952 Steinbeck *E. of Eden* 503: Every time Ethel got a beer in her she would be telling somebody...but they would think she was just a buzzed old hustler. **1955** in *Social Problems* V (1957) 319: High, gay, buzzed,...tight,...drunk. **1973** N.Y.U. student: *Buzzed* means drunk. **1974** U.S. Army Specialist: *Buzzed* or *buzzed out* means drunk. **1979** Univ. Tenn. student theme: [*Drunk:*] Bombed, wasted,...buzzed, flying high.

2. SPACED OUT.—constr. with *out.*

1980 J. Carroll *Land of Laughs* 67: I was so buzzed out by the things that had happened.

buzzer *n.* **1.** *Und.* a pickpocket.

***1821** in Partridge *Dict. Und.* 96. ***1856** in *F & H* I 403: "Buzzers" pick gentlemen's pockets. **1866** *Nat. Police Gaz.* (Nov. 24) 3: Broadway Stage "Buzzers." **1867** *Nat. Police Gaz.* (Mar. 23) 2: He "shook" that and edged into a "school of buzzers" as a "back stall." **1867** in Bartlett *Amer.* (ed. 4) 89: Many were the *car-buzzers* they led captives to police headquarters. ***1881–84** Davitt *Prison Diary* I 106: Hooks.—These individuals, who are also known as "gunns" and "buzzers," in prison slang, constitute the pickpocket class in its various specialties. **1955** Kantor *Andersonville* 175: You dirty buzzers!

2. *Police.* a police or private detective's badge.

1914 Jackson & Hellyer *Vocab.* 22: *Buzzer.*...An officer's badge or star. **1925** in Hammett *Knockover* 80: Pat flashed his buzzer. **1938** Chandler *Big Sleep* 51: I flicked my wallet out and let him look at my buzzer. **1951** Spillane *Lonely Night* 82: I flashed my buzzer. **1966** S. Stevens *Go Down Dead* 167: Like they aint tell him who they is when they show him the buzzer you know.

3. *Army.* a military discharge certificate; BUZZARD, 3.b.

1918 *MacArthur Carry-On* (Dec. 12) 2: A "buzzer"...is simply an honorable discharge. **1946** Bowker *Out of Uniform* 89: A blue [discharge paper], colloquially known as a "blue buzzer," includes most bad character discharges, those for ineptitude, and some for disability incurred through the individual's own misconduct.

buzz job *n. Av.* an instance of flying very low so as to frighten or impress persons on the ground.

1943 in M. Curtiss *Letters Home* 177: They swoop low over the field in a nifty "buzz job." **1944** in *Best from Yank* 85: The crew's request...had been for a "beautiful buzz job" coming in. **1946** G.C. Hall, Jr. *1000 Destroyed* 309: Gentile gave the dispersal the ritualistic buzz job. **1949** Quigley *Corsica* 149: One of the Spitties darted on ahead...to convey to them, by buzz job, that help was on the way. **1953** LeVier & Guenther *Pilot* xii: Even when airplanes fly dangerously low in what is referred to as a buzz job. *a***1986** Muirhead *Those Who Fall* 75: The buzz job was...holding me in a fascinated concentration as I drove her even closer to the ground.

buzz off *v.* **1.** to go away; to leave.—esp. imper.

***1914** in *OEDS* I 405: "Here you!" to the Cub, "you'd better buzz off—quick!" ***1925** in Fraser & Gibbons *Soldier & Sailor Wds.* 41 [ref. to WWI]: *Buzz Off:* Get away. **1940** Hartney *Up & At 'Em* 158 [ref. to 1918]: Why don't you and Freddy Norton buzz off right now? **1942** Chandler *High Window* 364: Buzz off. I just come in from lunch. **1944** in Hemingway *By-Line* 374: Buzz off, you unspeakables. **1955** Robbins *79 Park Ave.* 306: What do you say we buzz off and leave these two to their old-times reunion, honey? **1963** W.C. Anderson *Penelope* 213: Ah'm gonna give y'all a little smacker and buzz off. **1967** Ragni & Rado *Hair* 72: This Indian land, buzz off. **1979** Gutcheon *New Girls* 214: I'll buzz off in a minute, Lisa. **1986** Gilmour *Pretty in Pink* 123: Tell them to buzz off.

2. to send (someone) away curtly.

1967 Spillane *Delta* 16: All he had to do was growl to buzz them off.

buzz-wagon *n.* an automobile. *Joc.*

1903 Ade *Society* 140: Clara met them at the Train with a Buzz-wagon. **1903** McCardell *Conversations of a Chorus Girl* 68: A big red buzz wagon. **1906** M'Govern *Bolo & Krag* 198: Philippine Commissioners draw large fat salaries for hunting bugs, smashing buzz wagons, and climbing high mountains to look for strange savages who don't exist at all. **1918** *DN* V 23: *Buzz-wagon*, n. a cheap automobile. General. **1919** Duffy *G.P.F. Book* 330: "Buzz-wagons" of the Nash-Quad variety...have a particularly bad habit of wandering from the road to the ditches alongside. **1919** Wilkins *Company Fund* 11: His buzz-wagon had a hell of a time to keep from getting stepped on. **1920** Ade *Hand-Made Fables* 4: Piling into the high-powered Buzz-Wagons for a spin. **1930** *AS* V 274: Beneath the level of formal speech are the many slang nouns, some of them surprisingly persistent, as *flivver, buzz-wagon*, and the Afro-American *struggle-buggy.* **1943** J. Mitchell *McSorley's* 76: If all the perverted ingenuity which was put into making buzz-wagons had only gone into improving the breed of horses humanity would be better off.

buzzy *adj.* intoxicated; tipsy.

1736–37 in *AS* (Apr. 1937): The Drinker's Dictionary...He is Addled...Boozy, Bowz'd...Buzzey.

buzzy house *n.* an insane asylum.

1908 Green *Maison de Shine* 65: It's drivin' me to the buzzy house.

B-way *n. N.Y.C.* Broadway, a major avenue in New York City. Also **B'way.**

1850 in Barnum *Letters* 45: Not *Mercer* St., as the entrance is in B-way. **1916** *Variety* (Nov. 3) 21: New...Picture Palace Projected for B'way. **1963** Gant *Queen St.* 11: We hit Amsterdam and down the short hill to B-way. **1986** Stroud *Close Pursuit* 191: B'way at a Hundred and Seventh.

B.W.O.C. *n.* [initialism; cf. B.M.O.C.] *Stu.* a socially prominent college woman; a "big woman on campus."
   1934 Weseen *Slang Dict.* 175: *B.M.O.C.*...*B.W.O.C.* is the corresponding designation for a female student. **1946** Boulware *Jive & Slang* 2: *BWOC*...Big woman on the campus. **1956** I. Shulman *Good Deeds* 55: She's a sophomore and her house is grooming her for a BWOC. **1958** J. Davis *College Vocab.* 5: *B.W.O.C.*—Big Woman on Campus—girl with lots of activities; a campus leader.

by *prep.* in the opinion of. Now *colloq.*
   1923 T.A. Dorgan, in Zwilling *TAD Lexicon* 23: Everytink is wrong by me today. **1932** M. Anderson *Rain* (film): How's it by you today? **1938** in *DARE*: Anything Roosevelt Says or Does is All Right By Him. **1942** L.R. Foster *Mayor of 44th St.* (film): "OK by me." "Swell."

bye-bye *adj. & adv.* away; (*hence*) unconscious or asleep; (*hence*) dead.—usu. constr. with *go*.
   *****1903** in Kipling *Traffics & Discoveries* 52: "Down 'ammicks!"...is our naval way o' goin' to bye-bye. **1904** in "O. Henry" *Works* 1496: Now suppose we trek along and go by-by. **1913–15** Van Loan *Taking the Count* 149: A right hook on the jaw sent him bye-bye. **1928** in Tuthill *Bungle Family* 73: The day when a tenant...[could not] find a vacant flat has gone bye-bye. **1928** MacArthur *War Bugs* 106: A six-inch rifle blew up, and parts of the gun crew clumped past our ears. Seven men went bye-bye with that one. *Ibid.* 181. **1955** Goethals *Command* 135: Christ, that bastard's not slept in days....And you just watch—Regiment'll be on his tail the minute he's gone bye-bye.

by-God *adj. & adv.* **1.** (used as an intensive, often within a phrase).

1884 in Lummis *Letters* 188: To quote an eloquent section-hand, "this is the bigoddest country for water on the face of the earth."...The Rió Puerco is the only stream I have seen in...50 miles. **1935** S. Lewis *Can't Happen* 206: Insulting the whole by God corpo state. **1963** J.E. Grant *Alamo* (film): Who does he think he is, Andy by God Jackson? **1965** Borowik *Lions* 78: In what he referred to as West By God Virginia. **1973** Roberts *Last American Hero* (film): I'll do whatever it by-God takes. **1973** Ace *Stand On It* 47: It's just a by-God good thing that I'm so much better a driver than you, ain't it? **1974** E. Thompson *Tattoo* 246: He said he was from "West-By-God-Virginia," as if it were a challenge. **1980** W.C. Anderson *BAT-21* 167: That was the river, the by-God, ever-lovin' river. **1989** W.E. Merritt *Rivers Ran Backward* 250: A regular by God troop. **1992** Hosansky & Sparling *Working Vice* 69: Like we had just come from West-by-Gawd-Virginia.

2. *n.* (used as a strong standard of comparison).
   1944 in *Best from Yank* 149: Their MI rifles were frozen tighter than a by-god. **1974** E. Thompson *Tattoo* 396: Hotter than a by-God, ain't it?

BYO "Bring Your Own (liquor or the like)." Also adj.
   1966–69 Woiwode *Going to Do* 11: It was a stand-up, BYO, bottle-in-the-hand party. **1981** *L.A. Times* (July 26) IV 4: But walk outside over to a BYO restaurant and you'll dine on more food at half the price.

BYOB "Bring Your Own Bottle (of liquor or the like)." Also adj.
   1970 *Everett* (Wash.) *Herald* (Nov. 3) 10A: The annual "progressive dinner"...—a BYOB affair—is set for Saturday evening. **1976** Angelou *Singin' & Swingin'* 121: I was used to BYOB parties.

BYOL "Bring Your Own Liquor."
   1928 *Variety* (Oct. 24) 59: This type of male patron is not the b.y.o.l. type....He buys where he is. **1975** *DAS* (ed. 3) 763: *B.Y.O.L.*—bring your own liquor.

C *n.* **1.** [the Roman numeral *C* formerly appeared on such bills] a one-hundred-dollar bill; one hundred dollars.

1839 *Amer. Joe Miller* 77: America. Money not to be smelt under cent. per cent....great scarcity of V's, X's, L's, and C's. **1845** in *DAE*: So there's my hundred—and as my pocket-book's out, and my hand's in, there's another C. **1878** Pinkerton *Criminal Reminiscences* 204: Brown...laid a C with the Texan clown. **1899** Cullen *Tales* 169: He tripped me a "C" from his roll. **1930** Irwin *Tramp & Und. Sl.*: C...less frequently, 100 dollars. **1949** Robbins *Dream Merchants* 4: What's five c's a week when you get that kinda dough? **1962** T. Berger *Reinhart in Love* 198: I can get you five C's for it. **1967** Gonzales *Paid My Dues* 82: I'll take the "half-a-C" for Moms. **1968** S. Harris *Puritan Jungle* 152: The ten he promised me. And a C besides.

2. cents.

1896 Ade *Artie* 10: Comrades, it'll cost you fifty c. apiece.

3. *Narc.* cocaine.

1921 (quot. at M). **1922** *DN* V 182: Cocaine...C...Very common. **1929** *AS* (June) 338: C—cocaine. **1929** Tully *Shadows of Men* 189: He knew that an addict "loaded on C" was subject to wild and painful imaginings. **1958** A. King *Mine Enemy* 33: He had used C (cocaine).

4. *pl.* the Civilian Conservation Corps.—constr. with *the.* Now *hist.*

1943 *Yank* (May 28) 9: I belonged to the C's before I came into the Army. **1957** Atwell *Private* 256 [ref. to WWII]: Ah went in the Cs 'cause my parents died. **1961** J. Jones *Thin Red Line* 93 [ref. to WWII]: He had not cooked in the Cs. **1974** *Last Angry Man* (ABC-TV): In the C's.

¶ In phrase:

¶ **hit high C** to utter a shriek.

1940 Wald & Macauley *They Drive by Night* (film): What's that dame hittin' high C for? **1941** G.R. Lee *G-String* 78: "Keeping me?" La Verne hit a high C. "You got a hell of a nerve to say that to me." **1967** Mailer *Vietnam* 48: Hit high C next time you come, Chérie. **1984** *Fall Guy* (ABC-TV): "Can you still hit high C?" "Eeeeeek! Eeeeeeeek! Eeeeeek!"

cab *v.* to work as a cab-driver.

1973 *Playboy* (Sept.) 213: And for me, cabbing isn't work. I only drive this cab when I've got nothing better to do.

cabbage *n.* **1.** bits of cloth left from cutting out garments.

***1698–99** "B.E." *Dict. Canting Crew: Cabbage,* a Taylor, and what they pinch from the Cloaths they make up. **1848** Bartlett *Amer.: Cabbage.* A cant word for shreds and patches made by tailors in cutting out clothes. **1884** Hartranft *Sidesplitter* 59: [A tailor is like] A *Gardner* [because] he *sows his rows* and cultivates his *cabbage.*

2. cheap tobacco; a cigar.

***1843** in *F & H* II 3: The cigar dealers...have made us pay for the *cabbage* ever since. **1932** M. Anderson *Rain* (film): Here, park my cabbage. **1934** Weseen *Dict. Slang* 316: *Cabbage*—cheap tobacco. **1964** Hill *One of the Casualties* 21: Wot if when I git finished burnin' this imported Cuban cabbage I wuz to zip back to town?

3. a simpleton; CABBAGEHEAD.

1870 "M. Twain," in *OEDS*: All this human cabbage could see was the watch was four minutes slow. **1887** in *DARE.*

4. money, esp. paper money. Cf. LETTUCE.

1903 Harriman *Homebuilders* 37: He...drew out a great wad of paper money. "Whew!" ejaculated the humorous Billy, "look at th' cabbage." **1925–26** Black *You Can't Win* 213 [ref. to 1890's]: "You carry this head of cabbage, kid," passing me a pack of greenbacks about the size of a brick. **1935** O'Hara *Dr.'s Son* 101: Some of the biggest restrunts in the city pay plenty cabbage just for good-will. **1939** Calloway *Swingformation:* Could you send a little cabbage my way? **1943** Wolfert *Tucker's People* 65: "Carry your cabbage, boss?"..."Give the money here, boss, save climbing the stairs." **1946** Sherwood *Best Years of Our Lives* (film): Look at that, two hundred leaves of cabbage. **1948** Ives *Wayfaring Stranger* 111: I figured they made a lot of cabbage. **1949** Robbins *Dream Merchants* 167: A million bucks is a lot of cabbage. **1967** Talbot *Chatty Jones* 92: So why part with any cabbage? **1969** Bouton *Ball Four*

288: If we don't draw fans, we're not going to be making the old cabbage. **1991** Univ. Tenn. student: That'll cost a lot of cabbage.

5. *Mil.* (see quot.).

1945 Hamann *Air Words: Cabbage.* Medals and decorations.

¶ In phrases:

¶ **chew** [or **sell** or **boil**] (**one's**) **cabbage twice** to repeat (oneself).—usu. used in negative.

1870 *Overland Mo.* (Apr.) 317: "Won't you say it again, old man?" "It's no use to sell your cabbages twice, says I, and I never repeats." **1902** Clapin *Americanisms* 90: *I don't boil my cabbage twice,* a very common expression in the country towns of Pennsylvania...signifying that the person uttering it does not intend to repeat an observation. **1938** Odets *Rocket to the Moon* 341: I don't chew my cabbage twice, Miss Cleo. **1952** Bellow *Augie March* 508: I don't like to chew my cabbage twice. **1962** T. Berger *Reinhart* 23: "What's that?" "I never chew my cabbage twice." ***1974** P. Wright *Lang. Brit. Industry* 109: *I don't boil mi cabbages twice,* i.e. "I'm not going to repeat myself." **1978** W. Brown *Tragic Magic* 10: "What are you talking about?" "Just what I said. And if you can't figure it out that's too bad cause I don't intend to chew my cabbage twice."

¶ **just fall off the cabbage truck** to be utterly naive or unsophisticated.

1986 *Hunter* (NBC-TV): You think I just fell off the cabbage truck?

cabbage *v.* to pilfer; steal; acquire unethically; SCROUNGE.— also constr. with *onto.* [1806 quot. ref. to CABBAGE, *n.,* 1.]

1806 Webster *Dict.: Cabbage...*to steal in cutting clothes. ***1831** Trelawny *Adv. Younger Son* ch. ix: Don't cabbage books. **1846** in *DAE* I 379: I aint agoin' to let my karacter be *cabbaged* away right before my face. **1848** Bartlett *Amer.: Cabbage.* To steal in a small way. *ca***1880** Bellard *Gone for a Soldier* 161: I took a stroll...to pick up a few ears of corn for a roast (cabbaged of course). **1887** Hinman *Si Klegg* 185: Ef I was you, Johnson,...the next time I went fer a blanket I'd try 'n' cabbage one 't wa'n't marked, er't had a J on it. **1903** Ade *Breaking Into Society* 1: He cabbaged all the Corner Lots and nailed the Main Street Frontage and then held on like a Summer Cold. **1928** MacArthur *War Bugs* 37: One of our gang cabbaged an entire suitcase full of liquor. **1965–70, 1982** in *DARE.* **1987** *Car & Driver* (July) 9: He occasionally uses "cabbage" as a verb, meaning "to acquire by unspecified but very creative methods."

cabbage-eater *n.* a German.—used derisively.

1944 Wecter *Johnny Comes Marching Home* 283 [ref. to 1919]: Cold contempt for Heinies, the cabbage-eaters, the squareheads, was agreed to be the best behavior.

cabbage head *n.* **1.** the head of a simpleton.

1839 *Spirit of Times* (Mar. 16) 24: The "victorious wreath," destined to adorn his "cabbage-head"—we mean his "knowledge box." **1845** in *DAE.* **1896** Brown *Parson* 49: Don't you do it, or I will blow your cabbage head into the next century! **1907** in *DAS*: My poor old cabbage head wobbled about.

2. [cf. G *Kohlkopf* 'blockhead; idiot' (lit. 'cabbagehead'), fr. which this may be borrowed; "Dutch" in 1854 quot. means "German"] a simpleton.

1854 *Harper's Mag.* (Jan.) 269: Do our placid Dutch friends ever make us darkly to understand what may be meant by the term "Cabbage-head?" **1871** Schele de Vere *Americanisms* 588: *Cabbage-head,* a slang term for a fool, is used here as in England. **1888** Tiffany *Rice Pudding* 4: They used to call me cabbage-head, when I wint to school. ***1889** Barrère & Leland *Dict. Slang* I 214: *Cabbage-head*...a soft-headed person. **1910** *Everybody's Mag.* (Feb.) 188: Hello, Cabbage-head. **1919** *DN* V 61: *Cabbage-head,* a witless person. "Charlie is a *cabbage-head,* but he cannot help it." California, New Mexico.

cabbager *n.* [fr. CABBAGE, *n.,* 1.] a tailor.

1744 A. Hamilton *Gentleman's Progress* 58: The cabbager sigh'd and said it was a pagan language.

cabby *n.* a cabdriver. Now *colloq.*

1852** in *F & H* II 6: I'll sit beside *cabby. ca1859** Chamberlain *Confession*

11. *1864–65 in *F & H* II 6: Easy, *cabby*. 1865 *Rogues & Rogueries of N.Y.* 66: Extortion is the great fall back of the "cabby." *1889 Barrère & Leland *Dict. Slang* I 215: No wonder Lord Ronald Gower is popular among *cabbies*. 1904 London *Faith* 80: The cabby'll know where Judge Holmes lives. 1946 in *DAS* 83.

cabeza *n.* [< Sp] *S.W.* the head.
1853 Doten *Journals* I 147: We all felt rather muddy in our cabezas. 1877 in *DAE* 379: He's got more instink, that dog has,...right in that ugly old cabeza of his, [etc.]. 1982–84 Chapple *Outlaws* 237: They suffer a little pain in the *cabeza* and they insist that Doctor Welby prescribe some worthless balm.

cabin *n.* ¶ In phrase: **come in at the cabin window** *Naut.* to be appointed a ship's officer without having had sea experience. Also vars.
1794 in Whiting *Early Amer. Proverbs* 53. 1823 J.F. Cooper *Pioneers* 73: If-so-be that a man wants to walk the quarter-deck with credit...he mustn't do it by getting in at the cabin-windows. 1839 Briggs *Harry Franco* I 166: Hollo! youngster, if you want to get into the afterpart of a ship, you mustn't crawl in at the cabin windows, but come aft as I did, by degrees, through the hawse holes, and through every ring-bolt in the ship's deck. 1898 Stevenson *Cape Horn* 310: What's the matter with the mate is that he came in through the cabin-windows instead o' the hawse-pipes. 1899 Robbins *Gam* 112: I was an old sea-dog even in those days; I didn't come through the cabin windows. 1900 Benjamin *Naval Academy* 6: The midshipmen...expressed contempt for the land-lubbers who had "crawled in at the cabin windows instead of through the hawse-holes."

cab-joint *n.* *Und.* (see quot.).
1930 *Amer. Mercury* (Dec.) 455: *Cab-joint, n.*: A house of prostitution which gets its patronage through taxicab drivers. 1930 Irwin *Tramp & Und. Sl.*: *Cab Joint*—A brothel...to which patrons are driven by taxicab, the drivers...receiving a certain fee or percentage of whatever the patron spends in the "joint."

cable *n.* ¶ In phrases:
¶ **slip cable** *Naut.* to run away; depart.
1805 Brackenridge *Mod. Chiv.* 489: He slipped cable, and shot a-head...before the people were under way to retake him.
¶ **slip (one's) cable** *Naut.* to die. Now *hist.*
1823 J.F. Cooper *Pilot* 195: My orders are to see it done...or Mr. Griffith...slips his cable from this here anchorage. 1841 [Mercier] *Man-of-War* 196: I can't believe he's going to slip his cable yet, for all they say he's so bad. 1868 Aldrich *Bad Boy* 189: My mother slipped her cable for a heavenly port afore I was old enough to hail her. 1869 *Overland Mo.* (Apr.) 354: One night she slipped her cable and put to sea upon...the "ocean of eternity." 1924 Colcord *Roll & Go* 38: He slipped his cable off Cape Horn. 1948 McHenry & Myers *Home Is Sailor* 160: You're not going to slip your cable....You've just got a bad cold. 1986 Wilbur *Tall Ships* 83: "Slipped his cable"—He died.

cab moll *n.* *Und.* a woman who operates or is a prostitute in a brothel.
1859 Matsell *Vocab.* 16: *Cab-Moll.* A woman that keeps a bad house. *1889 Barrère & Leland *Dict. Slang* I 215: *Cab-moll* (common), a prostitute in a brothel.

caboodle *n.* [cf. BOODLE] **1.** lot, pack, or crowd.—usu. constr. with *whole*.
a1848 in Bartlett *Amer.*: The whole caboodle will act upon the recommendation of the Ohio Sun, and endeavour to secure a triumph. 1880 B. Harte *Story of Mine* 253: Down we go, the whole kerboodle of us. 1898 Brooks *Strong Hearts* 200: She's better 'n a whole caboodle of doctors. 1904 London *Faith* 110: Not a genooine miner in the whole caboodle. 1927 Rollins *Jinglebob* 101: 'Peared...like the whole caboodle on 'em might...break int' a hallelujah chorus. 1932 Berg *Doctor* 223: I'm on to ye, the whole damn caboodle of ye. 1950 P. Green *Peer Gynt* 95: We pinch the whole caboodle.
2. the head.
1944 L. Smith *Strange Fruit* 229: They don't reason! Ain't got nothing to reason with in their caboodles.
¶ In phrase:
¶ **the whole kit and caboodle** the whole lot or pack. Now *colloq.*
1888 in *DA* 935: He would wipe out the whole kit and caboodle of them. 1942 *ATS* 24. 1967 *Star Trek* (NBC-TV): I sent the whole kit and caboodle to the Klingon engine room. 1985 N.O. woman, age 33: We packed the whole kit and caboodle and went down to Florida.

caboose *n.* **1.** CALABOOSE.
1865 in *DA* 237. 1929 Bowen *Sea Slang* 21: Caboose...On shore it meant prison. 1940 Chandler *Farewell My Lovely* 10: Where you figure I been the eight years I said about?...In the caboose. 1944 Paxton *Murder, My Sweet* (film): You been in the caboose ever? 1956 Evarts *Ambush Riders* 80: Can't break out of this caboose, can he, George? 1965–70 in *DARE* I 502.
2. the rump.
ca1919 in Winterich *Mlle. from Armentières* (unp.): She waggled her headlights and caboose. 1928 Panzram *Killer* 34: He fell on his big, fat caboose. 1929 Barr *Let Tomorrow Come* 41: He gives me one look an' hauls his caboose back to the stem. 1953 Chandler *Goodbye* 3: Obviously I don't know him from a cow's caboose. 1956 Algren *Walk on Wild Side* 23: You must be connected with the railroads...you got such a purty caboose. 1966 Garfield *Last Bridge* 51: She looked, he thought, like an elephant's caboose. 1983 E. Cunningham *Why Do I Run?* 1: Runnin'...trims my tummy and shrinks my caboose.
3. a slow-witted person.
1932 Lorimer *Streetcars* 31: Don't you realize that you could have had Bill rushing you all evening, caboose?

caboose *v.* to jail.—used trans.
1880 in Lewis *Mining Frontier* 132: I can caboose the whole durned lot under Order No. 6. 1939 in *DA* 237.

ca-ca *n.* [cognate with L *cacare* 'to defecate', M Ir *caccaim*, etc.]
1. excrement.—usu. a nursery euphem. Also as *v.* Also **ka-ka.**
*1879 *Pearl* (Nov.) 174: Mama and de Captain/Are gone to Ca-Ca. 1952 in Cheever *Letters* 152: Do monkeys do ka-ka on the floor? 1976 H. Ellison *Sex Misspelled* 23: Pain, depression, smarmy sex and ka-ka.
2. foolishness; BULLSHIT.
1966–80 McAleer & Dickson *Unit Pride* 232: Cut the ca-ca, Daigle. Toss the dice. 1980 *Bosom Buddies* (ABC-TV): If you ask me, it's ca-ca. 1988 Norst *Colors* 68: Somebody [was] not buying Delauney's...ration of caca.

cack *v.* to fall asleep; (*hence*) to kill.
1959–60 R. Reisner *Jazz Titans* 152: Cack: fall asleep, fall out. a1988 Price & Seaman *Roger Rabbit* (film): The rabbit cacked him last night.

cackle *n.* **1.** chatter; foolish or pointless talk.
*1887 in Partridge *DSUE* (ed. 8) 172: He 'as got to be dabs at the cackle. 1935 S. Lewis *Can't Happen* 20: It's time for you to cut the cackle and join the really responsible citizens. *Ibid.* 236: Cut the cackle, will you, M.J.? I've just come here to tell you that I've had enough. 1945 Casey *Where I Came In* 101: Cut the cackle and let's get on with the killing. 1953 Harris *Southpaw* 79: He gave me a big line of cackle, hoping I had a good night in the sack and what a beautiful day it was. *1961 C.S. Lewis *Exp. in Criticism* 34: The uniterary call [descriptive passages] "padding" and wish the author would "cut the cackle and get to the horses." 1968 Vidal *Breckinridge* 217: Then cut the cackle...and hand over the three hundred fifty G's. 1979 T. Jones *Wayward Sailor* 187: O.K., cut the cackle.
2. usu. *pl.* an egg. *Joc.*
1930 *DN* VI 89: *Two cackles with their eyes open,* two fried eggs. 1939 *Merrie Melodies* (animated cartoon): One coffee and a coupla cackles—coming up right away. 1942–44 in *AS* (Feb. 1946) 31: *Cackle(s).* n. Egg(s).

cackle *v.* **1.** *Und.* to blab.
*1698–99 "B.E." *Dict. Canting Crew*: Cackle,...to discover. *The Cull Cackles,...*the Rogue tells all. 1859 Matsell *Vocab.* 16: *Cackle.* To blab. "The cove cackles"—tells all he knows. *Ibid.* 98: His pal grew leaky and cackled.
2. [cf. S.E. nuance, 'to talk foolishly'] to talk; speak.
1848 Baker *Glance at N.Y.* 17: Now, landlord, if you're game, let's hear you cackle.

cackleberry *n.* an egg.
1916 *DN* IV 272: Pass the cackleberries. 1925 *AS* (Dec.) 139: And he goes forth to eat of "cackleberries and grunts" (eggs and bacon). 1926 Maines & Grant *Wise-Crack Dict.* 12: *Pig's hips and cackle-berries*—Ham and eggs. 1936 *AS* (Feb.) 42: *Cackle Berries.* Eggs. 1948 Lay & Bartlett *12 O'Clock High* 172: "Cackleberries," said Gately, picking up one of the eggs and examining it as though it were an emerald. "A genuine cackleberry." 1956 *Walt Disney's Jiminy Cricket Comics* (#701) (unp.): How's the cackleberry situation? 1978 S. King *Stand* 107: It wasn't breakfast without eggs (which she called "cackleberries" when her humor was good). 1981 Wolf *Roger Rabbit* 190: Cackleberry...was the spitting image of Humpty Dumpty.

cackle crate *n. Trucking.* a truck transporting live poultry.
1942 *AS* (Apr.) 103: *Cackle crate.* Poultry truck. **1971** Tak *Truck Talk* 25: *Cackle crate:* a truck hauling live poultry.

cackle factory *n.* an insane asylum; LOONY BIN.
1942–49 Goldin et al. *DAUL* 39. **1959** Morrill *Dark Sea Running* 87: By midpassage, I was almost a candidate for the cackle-factory. **1980** Ciardi *Browser's Dict.* 34: Some Am. terms for insane asylum are: bat roost, bug house, cackle factory, cuckoo's nest, funny farm, loony bin, nut house.

cacklefruit *n.* eggs.
1966 in *DARE.*

cackle-jelly *n. Army.* a serving of eggs.
1941 Kendall *Army & Navy Slang* 3: *Cackle jelly*…eggs. **1943** D. Hertz *Pilot #5* (film): Pass the major the cackle jelly. **1945** *Sat. Review* (Nov. 24) 14: *Cackle jelly:* eggs.

cackler *n.* **1.** *Hobo.* an office worker.
1926 Finerty *Criminalese* 12: *Cackler*—Office worker. **1927** *DN* V 441: *Cacklers, n.* Office workers;—so called because of their supposed hencoop effeminacy. **1930** "D. Stiff" *Milk & Honey* 201: *Cacklers*—white collar workers.
2. an egg.
1930 Irwin *Tramp & Und. Sl.: Cackler*—An egg. **1933–34** Lorimer & Lorimer *Stag Line* 166: What'll it be: grunt and a couple of cacklers? **1962** Ragen & Finston *Toughest Prison* 793: *Cackler*—An egg.

cacknacker var. COCK-KNOCKER.

cactus *n. Narc.* mescaline.
1969 Fort *Pleasure Seekers* 237: Mescaline. *Cactus.* **1972** C. Gaines *Stay Hungry* 146: He wondered what the hell he was doing here all messed up in the head with cactus.

cactus boomer *n. West. Cattle Industry.* (see quot.).
1928 Dobie *Vaquero of the Brush Country* 210 [ref. to 1880]: A popular nickname for the wild brush cattle was "cactus boomers."

cactus juice *n.* **1.** tequila or mescal.
[**1967** Ravetch & Frank *Hombre* (film): That Apache slop they make out of cactus juice—*tizla.*] **1971** *N.Y. Times* (Dec. 19) II 21: Where men were men and women were women, and everybody slurped a little too much cactus juice. **1971** *Nichols* (NBC-TV): Stop hitting on that cactus juice and you might know the difference between a coyote and a deer track.
2. mescaline.
1971 H.S. Thompson *Las Vegas* 32: And now the fiendish cactus juice took over.

Cactus League *n.* [modeled on BUSH LEAGUE] *Baseball.* major-league teams holding spring training in the Southwest.
1976 *Webster's Sports Dict.* 64. **1980** Pearl *Slang Dict.: Cactus League n.* (sports) major league baseball teams that train in the Southwest, generally in Arizona. **1985** *Time* (Apr. 8) 86: Two hours before a Cactus League game with Milwaukee.

Cactus Patch *n.* Phoenix, Arizona. *Joc.*
1976 Adcock *Not Truckers Only* 45: A hard ankle and his queen bee out of Cactus Patch piled into their old kitty whomper.

Cad *n.* a Cadillac automobile.
1929 Booth *Stealing Through Life* 290 [ref. to ca1920]: There's a Cad parking there now. **1933** Guest *Limey* 25: I usually use this "Cad." **1953** in *DAS* 84. **1963** Lundgren *Primary Cause* 108: The price of Cads jumped to twice what you can buy them for here in the states.

cad *n. Stu.* (see quot.).
1954–60 *DAS* 84: *Cad*…An academy or preparatory-school student. *Common use c1870–c1910.*

Caddy *n.* a Cadillac automobile.
1929 *Jour. Amer. Insurance* (Feb.) 6. **1934** J. O'Hara *App. in Samarra* 30. **1942** *ATS* 82. **1966** Herbert *Fortune & Men's Eyes* 30: I split in the Caddy. **1975** N.Y.C. man, age 27: Would you rather drive a Lincoln or a Caddy? **1990** "Above the Law" in L.A. Stanley *Rap* 1: Rollin' in my Caddy.

caddy *n. Baseball.* a second-string player used esp. as a pinch-runner or substitute fielder in late innings.
1959 Brosnan *Long Season* 269: *Caddie* a player who frequently substitutes for one other particular player, usually in the late innings of games. **1973** Boyd & Harris *Baseball Card Bk.* 194: It is the caddy's sole function to come in as a substitute in the late innings…to act as defensive replacement for an aging power hitter, or to pinch run for a…sec-

ond-string catcher with varicose veins. **1978** in Lyle & Golenbock *Bronx Zoo* 242: Paying him a hundred grand to be Mickey's caddy is too much.

cadet *n.* **1.** [< E Yid *kadet* 'pimp'] *Prost.* a young man who procures women for prostitution; (*hence*) a prostitute's pimp. Now mostly *hist.*
1904 *Life in Sing Sing* 246: *Cadet.* An abductor of young girls. **1906** *Nat. Police Gaz.* (Jan. 13) 3: Three young fellows of the kind known to police as "cadets." *a***1904–11** Phillips *Susan Lenox* II 146: Or you'd work the street for some cheap cadet who'd beat you up oftener than he'd beat up the men who welched on you. **1912–14** in E. O'Neill *Lost Plays* 36: In appearance he is a typical "cadet," flashily dressed, rat-eyed, weak of mouth, undersized, and showing on his face the effects of drink and drugs. **1914** Healy *Delinquent* 253: She willingly began her affairs at 10 years of age, and actually supported a "cadet" by prostitution when she was 12 years old. **1916** Miner *Slavery of Prostitution* 91: They are known as…"cadets." **1921** Woolston *Prostitution in U.S.* I 83: The male procurer, "pimp" or "cadet," as he is often called. **1926** Wood & Goddard *American Slang* 10: *Cadet.* Pimp, pander, procurer. **1942** Davis & Wolsey *Call House Madam* 48: Most of the other girls went out and got tight, hitting the dawn spots with their cadets. **1957** Murtagh & Harris *Cast the First Stone* 218: They hired handsome young men, known as *cadets* in the business, who applied all their energies to seducing suitable girls. **1970** Winick & Kinsie *Lively Commerce* 121: The cadet was a procurer who seduced a young girl, often after promising to marry her. **1982** Rosen *Lost Sisterhood* 76: Sometimes [pimps] were distinguished from cadets, who "sold" women to brothels but did not then continue to make money off them; at other times the terms *pimp* and *cadet* were used interchangeably.
2. *Stu.* SPACE CADET.
1980 in Safire *Good Word* 217.

cadge *v.* to beg. Now *S.E.*
***1812** Vaux *Vocab.: Cadge:* to beg. **1873** Lening *N.Y. Life* 9: They prefer to exist by mendacity and "cadging." **1960** Stolz *Barkham St.* 34: A tramp is…a fellow who never works and usually hangs around cadging handouts.

cadger *n.* a beggar. Now *S.E.*
1859 Matsell *Vocab.* 16: *Cadger.* A beggar; a mean thief. **1888** Bidwell *Forging His Chains* 106: This genteel young man…[was] reduced to the level of a tramp and cadger.

cady *n.* [orig. unkn.] a man's hat or cap; (in more recent use, *specif.*) a straw hat. Also **Katy.**
1846 *Spirit of Times* (June 6) 170: I may be able to discover my lost "Cady." **1848** *The Ladies' Repository* VIII (Oct.) 315: *Cady,* A man's hat. **1859** Matsell *Vocab.* 16: *Cady.* A hat. ***1869** *N & Q* III 406: In Lancashire…a straw hat…[is called] a cady or straw cady. **1871** Banka *Prison Life* 492: Hat,…Tile, or Katey. **1891** Maitland *Amer. Slang Dict.* 56: *Cady*…a hat. **1908** *Hampton's Mag.* (Nov.) 662: I take off my katy to you. You've beat me at my own game. **1930** Pasley *Al Capone* 235: The last bird in Chicago wearing a straw katy in the fall. **1937** Thackrey *Thief* 62: He was a tall, nice-looking kid with a suit on and one of those straw hats, the kind they call Katies, like the dudes wore in those days. **1970** *Western Folk.* XXIX 162: *Kady*—Hat; from brand name K.D.

Caesar *n.* ¶ In phrases:

¶ **bury Caesar** [ref. to Shakespeare's *Julius Caesar* III ii 75] to effect intromission of the penis. *Joc.*
1927 [Fliesler] *Anecdota* 16: I come to bury Caesar, not to praise him.

¶ **Great Caesar's ghost** (used as an exclam. of astonishment).
1871 "M. Twain" *Roughing It* ch. xiii [ref. to 1862]: I'm a liar am I! Grreat Caesar's ghost! **1876** "M. Twain" *Tom Sawyer* 172 [ref. to 1840's]: Great Caesar's ghost! **1883** Peck *Peck's Bad Boy* 236: Well, great Julius Caesar's bald-headed ghost, what's the matter with you? **1952** *Adventures of Superman* (synd. TV series): Great Caesar's ghost, Olsen! **1992** *Simpsons* (Fox-TV): Great Caesar's ghost, a talking Krusty doll!

caf *n.* a café or cafeteria.
1972 *Nat. Lampoon* (Apr.) 32: We asked around the halls and in the caf during fifth lunch. **1981** Peyser & Peyser *Sarah McDavid* (film): It's better than eating in the caf.

cage *n.* **1.** a jail or lock-up. [S.E. in early use.]
1636–1707 in *DAE* I 384. ***1889** Barrère & Leland *Dict. Slang* I 218: *Cage* (thieves), a prison. **1898** Dunne *Mr. Dooley in Peace & War* 234: Col. Hinnery, th' man that sint me frind Cap. Dhry-fuss to th' cage.
2. a hat or cap.

1899 Young *Reminiscences & Stories of the War* 513: So paste this idea in yer cage, wotever else you do. **1898–1900** Cullen *Chances* 109: I'll pass you this cage o' mine...f'r that one o' yours. **1905** *DN* III 73: *Cage*, n. Cap or hat. "Where did you get that *cage*?"

3. *R.R.* a caboose.

1931 *Writer's Digest* (May) 41: *Cage*—Caboose. **1945** Hubbard *R.R. Ave.* 336: *Cage*—Caboose.

4. an elevator.

1938 Korson *Mine Patch* 51: We stepped on the cage, he ding-donged a bell. **1939** Fearing *Hospital* 135: I looked at the operator of the cage. **1974** A. Bergman *Big Kiss-Off* 5: The old cage took the Cape of Good Hope route before reaching nine. **1976** Arble *Long Tunnel* 80: We walked down the main shaft to the cage.

5. *Motorcycling.* an automobile.—used derisively.

1981 *Easyriders* (Oct.) 5: First, some bitch jumped into his cage at a stop light and robbed him of $150. **1985** D. Killerman *Hellrider* 69: Just look at the pigs gettin' out of them cages.

¶ In phrase:

¶ **rattle (someone's) cage** to annoy (someone); provoke (someone).

1980 Algren *Dev. Pocket* 289: "Why were you applying for it then in nineteen seventy-four?" "To rattle Hudson County's cage. I felt Hudson County had gave me the shaft." **1983** *T.J. Hooker* (NBC-TV): I figure we go out there and rattle some cages. **1986** Merkin *Zombie Jamboree* 51: I'd never seen him explode before; nothing...had ever rattled his cage.

cager *n.* *Sports Journ.* a basketball player.

1932 *AS* VII (June) 330: *Cager*—basketball player. **1949** Cummings *Dict. Sports* 57. **1982** Considine *Lang. Sport* 58. **1981** *N.Y. Post* (Dec. 14) 41: Cager dies after collapse.

cagey *adj.* cautious, crafty, or cunning; (*hence*) evasive. Now *colloq.* or *S.E.* Also semi-adv.

1893 in *DA* 239. **1909** in *OEDS*: See, he's cagey about going to 'em. **1917** in Bowerman *Compensations* 8: We're in the danger zone now and I'm going to be real "cagey" tonight. **1927** in *DAS* 84. **1938** Chandler *Big Sleep* 12: I don't see what there is to be cagey about. **1947** Overholser *Buckaroo's Code* 130: He's a cagy galoot. **1952** Steinbeck *E. of Eden* 505: He was cagey. **1985** Ky. woman, age 26: You're being pretty cagey about it.

cahoole *v.* *Stu.* to cajole.

1851 Hall *College Wds.* 40: *Cahoole.* At the University of North Carolina, this word in its application is almost universal, but generally signifies to cajole, to wheedle, to deceive, to procure.

cahoot *n.* [orig. uncert.; perh. < F *cahute* 'cabin, hut'] ¶ In phrase: **in cahoots** [or **cahoot**] in partnership; in league. Now *colloq.*

1829 in *DAE* I 385: Hese in cohoot with me. **1843** Field *Pokerville* 198: He...would "go in with him—in *cahoot*!" **1862** in *DAE* I 384: Mc wished me to go in cahoots in a store. **1902** "J. Flynt" *Little Bro.* 175: To think of Miss Myrtaugh in cahoots with 'em, too. **1928** in Grayson *New Stories* 218: I believe that Christ and Judas were in cahoots. **1942** "E. Queen" *Calamity Town* 60: They're in cahoots. **1956** Neider *Hendry Jones* 27: I don't know if the judge was in cahoots with them. **1962** Berger *Reinhart* 14: A realtor with whom his father was in some kind of cahoots. **1974** E. Thompson *Tattoo* 416: They're all in cahoots, too, you know. **1979** Hofstadter *Gödel* 123: The Evil Majotaur is in cahoots with Bach.

cahoot *adj.* [fr. the *n.*] consisting of a partnership.

1845 Hooper *Simon Suggs* 33: I'd make a *cahoot* business with old man Doublejoy.

cahoot *v.* to go into CAHOOTS.

1857 in *DAE* I 384: They all agree to cahoot with their claims against Nicaragua and Costa Rica. **1886, 1948** in *DA* 240.

cahoots *adv.* [fr. the *n.*] in or into partnership.

1855 in *DA* 240: One or two men...will...as they down South, go "cahoots," that is to say, share the spoil. **1930** Sage *Last Rustler* 188: We decided to throw in cahoots and go there.

Cain *n.* (used as a euphem. for *hell*).

1854 in *DAE*: He didn't know what in cain to do with it. **1855** in *DAE.*

¶ In phrases:

¶ **by Cain** (used as a mild oath).

1819 in *DA* 240. **1839** in *DAE* I 384. **1852** in *DA* 240.

¶ **raise Cain** to create a noisy or unmanageable distur-

bance. [The occasionally repeated sugg. that this expr. derives fr. *raise a cane* is not correct.]

1840 in Thornton *Amer. Gloss.*: Why have we every reason to believe that Adam and Eve were both rowdies? Because...they both raised Cain. **1849** in *F & H* 17: Who'll hinder this child? I'm going to raise Cain! Who's got anything to say agin it? **1858** in G.W. Harris *High Times* 78: Instead of raising Cain generally...he betook himself to zealously writing notes on American customs. **1869** Stowe *Old Town* 116: Without having a boy around raisin' gineral Cain. **1885** in Saunders *Parodies of Whitman* 60: You raise merry Cain. **1887** DeVol *40 Yrs. A Gambler* 16: The Captain went up on deck, cursed the pilot,...knocked down two deck-hands, and raised cain generally. **1922** in W. Burnett *Best* 118: If the locked-up hubbies believe that the boys still at large are raising Cain seven nights a week...let them cease to be envious. **1941** in W.C. Fields *By Himself* 404: Schlepperman raises cain with Fields for the snide trick he played on him. **1960** R. Serling *Stories from Twilight Zone* 135: Sun spots...can raise cain with radio reception all over the world. **1973** Walkup & Otis *Race* 14: Mrs. Nickel...called to raise Cain when she wasn't allowed in the Derby Barn.

caine *n.* cocaine. Also **cane.**

1983 "Grandmaster Melle Mel" in L.A. Stanley *Rap* 156: Cane!...Rock!...Blow!...white lines. **1985** Univ. Tenn. student theme: Cocaine...*blow, caine, nose candy* [etc.]. **1985** "Blowdryer" *Mod. Eng.* 79: Cocaine...*toot, cane, blow.* **1990** Costello & Wallace *Sig. Rappers* 24: How gangs are really families, and 'caine's constant bad news. **1988–92** in Ratner *Crack Pipe* 82: I was scared the way the 'caine did me.

caitiff *n.* *U.S. Mil. Acad.* a third-classman.

1834 *Mil. & Nav. Mag. of U.S.* (Mar.) 27: I felt quite as proud of my being a "plebe," as the third-class-man of his appellation of "*caitiff*," the second-class-man of "*old cadet*" or the first-class-man of "*high private.*" *Ibid.* 23: Groups of "caitiffs" and "high privates" soon assembled to laugh at the awkwardness of the plebes.

caj see CAZH.

cajolerator clamp *n.* (see quot.). *Joc.*

1974 Texas oil pipeliner, age 24: They used to send new hands for things like *cajolerator clamps, muffler-bearings*, and *pipe-stretchers*. Those are all like *left-handed monkey wrenches.*

cake *n.* **1.a.** a soft, foolish fellow; an incompetent.

***1785** Grose *Vulgar Tongue: Cake,* or *Cakey.* A foolish fellow. **1837** Neal *Charcoal Sketches* 164: If...we are...told that Mr. Plinlimmon is a "cake," the word may be derided as a cant appellation; the ultra-fastidious may turn up their noses at it as a slang phrase; but volumes could not render our knowledge of the man more perfect. We have him...weak, unwholesome, and insipid—suited to the fancy, perhaps, of the very youthful, but by no means qualified for association with the bold, the mature, and the enterprising. **1837** in Jackson *Early Songs of Uncle Sam* 34: The silken purse of gold he shakes,/A certain bait for country cakes. **1841** in *F & H* II 18: Vy vot a *cake* I've been! **1859** Matsell *Vocab.* 17: *Cake.* An easy fool of a policeman; a flat cop. **1888** E.L. Thayer, in *S.F. Examiner* (June 3) 4: But Flynn preceded Casey, as did also Jimmy Blake,/And the former was a lulu and the latter was a cake. **1889** Barrère & Leland *Dict. Slang* I 219: *Cake* (American and provincial English), a man without much sense, or one wanting in ideas; not so much a fool as a mere nothing...This expression is most frequently heard in Philadelphia.

b. a fop.

1822 in Damon *Old Amer. Songs* (No. 10): My mammy then sent me to school, for she did intend to make,/A lawyer and a counsellor, but I'd sooner be a cake...with my new suit on a Sunday, to the church I'd strut away,/ The girls they fought, and each bawl'd out, I'll walk with him to day.

2. *pl.* *Theat.* a performer's daily meals.

1906 Green *Actors' Boarding House* 317: Well, I'm draggin' in my old thirty-five an' cakes. **1923** *N.Y. Times* (Sept. 9) VII 2: *And Cakes:* actor's board paid by the manager. **1936** Washburn *Parlor* 117: They paid the [piano player] $50 a week and his "cakes"—the food.

3.a. the head.

1908 *Hampton's Mag.* (Oct.) 458: Show me to him till I knock his cake off.

b. *pl.* a woman's breasts.

1957 Shulman *Rally* 67: A dame leans over 'em with her cakes falling out of her negligee. **1969** N.Y.C. editor, age *ca*30: So she pulled the sheet up over her cakes. She had huge cakes.

c. *pl.* *Black E.* the buttocks; BUNS.

1971 Thigpen *Streets* 20: Hollywood.../Spreads her cakes like the whore/She is. **1972** A. Kemp *Savior* 13: Sweetie, lose three inches off those cakes, pump coupla jolts of silicone in the tits, and I'll make you the cover girl of Nigeria. **1976** Chinn *Dig the Nigger Up* 130: I've been hot on her cakes for years; and the funny thing about it, she wants me as bad as I want her.

4. [cf. *piece of cake*, below] something easy.

1911 H.B. Wright *Barbara Worth* 215: Ye'll be wantin'...wan to handle the greasers, which is cake to me, an' wan to boss the mule skinners, which is pie for Tex. **1942** *ATS* 266: Something easy; "snap." *Breeze, cake*, [etc.]. **1968** Baker et al. *CUSS* 93: *Cake course*. Easy course. **1970** *Current Slang* III & IV 21: *Cake, n.* An easy test.—College students, both sexes, Kentucky. **1982** *Flash* (Dec.) 14: What a haul! This was cake!

5. a fine fellow.—constr. with *the*.—used derisively.

1920 De Beck *Google* 98: Them guys all think they're the cakes with their left hooks—I'll show 'em.

6. CAKE-EATER. [Cf. **(1.b.)**, above.]

1923 *Chi. Daily Trib.* (Oct. 2) 22: Lillums out riding with that cake, Harold Pointe! **1930** Farrell *Calico Shoes* 48: She was with some cake last night at the Neapolitan Room of the Westgate Hotel. **1934** Weseen *Dict. Slang* 176: *Cake*...a male flirter.

7. Esp. *Black E.* a young woman.

1941 *Pittsburgh Courier* (Nov. 15) 7: For a piece of this cake, he'd leave this whole world behind. **1954–60** *DAS* 84. **1968** Heard *Howard St.* 63: Thinkin' 'bout that new cake you pulled from Baxter Terrace?...She a fox, too.

8. [cf. DOUGH] money. Also constr. in pl.

1965 in W. King *Black Anthol.* 308: Let me run this broad down, and I'll give you the cakes. **1967** Colebrook *Cross of Lassitude* 39: I gotta meet this "trick," murmured Opaline...We gonna get us some "cakes." **1972** B. Rodgers *Queens' Vernacular* 137: Money...*cakes* ('70: *in the cakes* = rolling in money; *low in the cakes* = without). **1974** Radano *Cop Stories* 54: You can bet anyone puts up that kind of cake is going to try to get it back one way or the other. **1974** V.E. Smith *Jones Men* 150: He might make a helluva lot of cake...but he's got a lotta cake eaters too. **1989** *New York* (Dec. 11) 36: Handing over the payment [to one's pimp] is called "choosing" or "giving up choosing cake."

¶ In phrases:

¶ **frost** [or **cut**] **cake** to make a difference; matter; *cut ice* s.v. ICE.

1902 Townsend *Fadden & Mr. Paul* 146: It don't frost no cake wedder it is Mark or me dat gets it. **1964** Peacock *Drill & Die* 192: That's what I thought you said....But that don't cut no cake on this other.

¶ **hurry up the cakes** to hasten.

1848 Baker *Glance at N.Y.* 25: But I say, if you want my company, you'll have to hurry up your cakes. **1852** in R.B. Perry *W. James* I 75: He does not imagine the possibility of "hurrying up the cakes" on a large scale. **1865** Williams *Joaquin* 67: You don't seem to be half-civilized the way you hurry up the cakes. **1867** *Galaxy* (Nov.) 871: Some of them, instead of "make haste," say "hurry up the cakes." **1897** in *DA* 240.

¶ **one's cake is dough** one has met with failure.

*1698–99 "B.E." *Dict. Canting Crew: Cake is Dough*, of a Miscarriage or failure of Business. **1830** in [S. Smith] *Letters of Downing* 22: Then up steps the Supreme Court and tells 'em their cake is all dough. **1854** Sleeper *Salt Water Bubbles* 175: As my mother would have said, "My cake is all dough."

¶ **piece of cake** [cf. **(4)**, above] Esp. *Mil. Av.* a task that may be easily accomplished; a BREEZE.

1936 O. Nash, in *OEDS:* Her picture's in the paper now,/And life's a piece of cake. **1942* P. Kinsella *Letters* 26: The Law exam was, in RAF jargon, "a piece of cake." **1944** H. Brown *Walk in Sun* 149: Tyne really cut himself a piece of cake. **1946** G.C. Hall, Jr. *1000 Destroyed* 273: I was a piece of cake for those [enemy planes] behind me. **1955** in Beaumont *Best* 203: "I thought you said it was gonna be difficult."..."Nah. Piece of cake." **1960** Archibald *Jet Flier* 54: Relax. It's a piece of cake. **1961** L.G. Richards *TAC* 126: The air was calm, the hookup was a piece of cake. **1962** Sarlat *War Cry* 84 [ref. to WWII]: "It's no piece of cake," he said earnestly. "I won't kid you about that." **1968** Westheimer *Song of the Young Sentry* 165 [ref. to WWII]: Tell him it's a piece of cake....I mean tell him I'm getting well fast. I'll probably be all right. **1969** Hamill *Doc* 81: It should be a piece of cake. **1979** *Business Week* (May 7) 18: McGoon radioed his wingmate that his situation was "a piece of cake." **1980** *Atlantic* (Feb.) 38: By comparison, antonym questions and reading-comprehension passages were a piece of cake. **1990** *National Review* (May 28) 32: That battle will be a piece of cake compared to the one over Senator Kennedy's Civil Rights Bill.

¶ **pop (one's) cakes** to vomit.

1927 *AS* II (Mar.) 277: *Pop one's cakes:* to vomit.

¶ **take the cake** [or **cakes**] **1.** to be awarded a prize, as in a contest; be victorious. Also **rake the cakes.**

1842 *Spirit of Times* (Apr. 9) 66: The Cymons and Sarpedons [race-horses] will "rake the cakes." **1847** W.T. Porter *Quarter Race* 120: They got up a horse and fifty dollars in money a side....The winning horse [would] take the cakes. **1888** in *OEDS* I 414: Sherriff Moore takes the cake for the first wheat-harvesting in Ransom county.

2. to be a surpassing example, esp. for annoyance, brashness, foolishness, etc.

1864 in J.W. Haley *Rebel Yell* 211: This Brown not only takes the cake, but a whole bake shop. **1882** *Puck* (June 7) 216: The day I acted as scorer in a base-ball match in Weehawken takes the frosted cake. **1882** *Judge* (Dec. 16) 7: Der idea uv stopping the liquor traffic in New York! Dat takes der cake. **1883** Peck *Peck's Bad Boy* 225: The teacher said Bob was the smartest man this country ever produced....He said Bob Ingersoll just took the cake. **1887** Francis *Saddle & Moccasin* 306: Well, when it came to tracking, he believed that he "took the cake." **1888** Dale *Songs of the Seventh* 69: No matter what there was to do, we've always "scooped the cake." **1893** James *Mavrick* 91: The style changed again by '77. The John B. Stetson hat...and the ten-ounce hat took the cake. **1893** Bangs *Coffee* 49: He meant that I took the cake for superficiality. **1894** in J.I. White *Git Along Dogies* 92: At punching cows I know I'll shine;/I'm sure I'll take the cake. **1929** "E. Queen" *Roman Hat* ch. xv 165: All right. You take the cake on that one. Your bloodhound caught me coming out of Morgan's office—what of it? **1968** Kellogg *Junie Moon* 12: Let's not talk about prizes....If we did, you might take the cake. **1977** T. Berger *Villanova* 230: But you take the cake, Rain.

cake and wine *n.* Esp. *Navy & USMC.* bread and water as a punishment diet. Now *hist.* See also ANGEL CAKE AND WINE.

1934 Weseen *Dict. Slang.* **1942** *Yank* (Nov. 4) 15: When a Marine lands in the brig he doesn't get bread and water; he gets "cake and wine." **1952** Uris *Battle Cry* 147: And for Chrisake don't get picked up by the shore patrol or we'll both be on cake and wine for a month. **1966** Noel & Bush *Naval Terms* 80: *Cake and wine:* Slang: bread and water (as a punishment).

cake-cutter *n. Carnival.* a shortchange swindler. Hence **cake-cutting,** shortchanging.

1934 Weseen *Dict. Slang* 158: *Cake cutter*—A short-change man. **1953** Gresham *Midway* 3: *Cake-cutting:* short changing.

cake-eater *n.* Esp. *Stu.* an effeminate fellow; sissy; *(specif.)* an effete young man who attends tea parties or the like; *(hence)* a wealthy young fellow. Hence **cake-eating,** *adj.*

1916 in Hall & Niles *One Man's War* 148: I knew you when you were a snake-stomper back in the Ozark Mountains....They've turned you from a snake-stomper into a cake-eater and soon you'll be a duke or a count or something. **1922** in Ruhm *Detective* 10: They're hard guys, yes, but then I ain't exactly a cake-eater myself. **1923** Jack Yellin & Billy Nosalg *He'll Always Be One of Those Guys* (sheet music) 5: He's just one of those cake-eatin' guys. **1924** *Liberty* (Dec. 27): Jealous males...swore horribly and banded together to denounce Rudolph as a cake-eater and a tea demon. **1925** I. Cobb *Many Laughs* 15: They run me and a lot of other cake-eaters out of town—claimed we was sissified. **1926** Tully *Jarnegan* 171: Who the hell started wearin' neckties, anyhow? Some damn cake-eater. **1929–33** J.T. Farrell *Manhood* 315: Phil Rolfe was one of the best-dressed cake-eaters. **1937** P. Beath, in *Botkin Treas. Amer. Folk.* 230: Febold ain't no lily-livered cake-eater like you. **1948** Wouk *City Boy* 40 [ref. to 1920's]: They wore...soft round felt hats, jeered at by boys too small to wear them as "cake-eaters." **1956** G. Green *Last Angry Man* 84: Brooklyn was for sports in those days, for cake-eaters. **1971** Rader *Govt. Inspected* 34: Nellie cake-eater undergraduates at Northwestern and Garret Seminary. *Ibid.* 102: "Meeting with some righteous cake-eaters tonight," Andrew said, referring to the rich liberals he was trying to hit for coins. **1986** Gilmour *Pretty in Pink* 68: Being asked out by a cake-eater was something she might have dreamed about.

cake-hole *n.* the mouth.

*1943 Hunt & Pringle *Service Slang* 20: *Cake hole*, the airman's name for his or anyone else's mouth. **1979** Ravetch & Frank *Norma Rae* (film): Norma, shut your cake-hole! **1993** *Mystery Sci. Theater* (Comedy Central TV): Shut your cakehole.

cakewalk *n.* Orig. *Boxing.* an easy victory; *(hence)* an easy task.

[**1877** D. Braham *Walking for Dat Cake* (pop. song title).] **1897** Siler & Houseman *Fight of the Century* 46: It's a cake-walk for Jim....Fitz hasn't a chance. **1898–1900** Cullen *Chances* 53: It's a cake-walk fo' dat baby. **1910** *N.Y. Eve. Jour.* (Feb. 7) 10: Joe is the Marathon Kid and Samuel would be a cakewalk. ***1916** in *OEDS* I 414: A fight that would not be a cake-walk. ***1925** Fraser & Gibbons *Soldier & Sailor Wds.* 43 [ref. to WWI]: *Cake Walk, A:* an easy task. **1928** Callahan *Man's Grim Justice* 13: This burglar business was not the cake walk I had pictured it to be. **1958** Camerer *Damned Wear Wings* 188: This'll be a cakewalk if you slow down! **1981** *N.Y. Times* (Aug. 9) IV 20: And as Transportation Secretary Lewis reminds us it will be no "cakewalk" to restore normal service without the dismissed controllers.

cakewalk *v.* to succeed easily; BREEZE.
1936 in R.E. Howard *Iron Man* 156: I reckon I can see good enough to cake walk through [a prizefight].

cakey *adj.* **1.** foolish; soft; suggestive of a CAKE.
1889 Barrère & Leland *Dict. Slang* I 219: *Cakey*…soft, foolish, or empty-headed.
2. *Stu.* being or suggesting a CAKE-EATER.
1931 Farrell *Guillotine Party* 89: Cakey Phil Rolfe, the blond Jewboy, happened in, wearing an oxford gray suit with twenty-two-inch bell bottoms.

Cal *n.* California. Cf. **Cally.**
1860 in E. Marchand *News from N.M.* 14: Cal is gone in ["finished"] for making a fortune quick. **1936** Mackenzie *Living Rough* 118: That's a common procedure in Cal. **1940** Burnett *High Sierra* 275: Every policeman in southern Cal's looking for that Earle guy. **1948** J. Stevens *Jim Turner* 159 [ref. to ca1910]: Sunny Cal! Sunny Cal for me! **1963** Zahn *Amer. Contemp.* 4: The sun was setting over Pomona, Cal, one of those days you could actually see. **1989** Radford & Crowley *Drug Agent* 37: Even in sunny Cal.

calabash *n.* the head.
1723 in *DAE*: You have in the cavity of your Callabash a viscid juice. **1821** Waln *Hermit in Phila.* 31: There was a chance of having his *peepers* plumped by a *bully* or his *calabash* cracked by a Watchman!! **1828** in H.L. Gates, Jr. *Sig. Monkey* 91: Hold your brack jaw…Or soon I break your *Callabash*! **1837** J.C. Neal *Charcoal Sks.* 97: Mind how you chuck, or you'll crack his calabash. **1838** Crockett *Almanac* (1839) 35: Down he shoved her woolly calabash under water. **1847** Downey *Cruise of Portsmouth* 216: I met Sergeant Slim, wending his weary way up the hill with a most colossal [pumpkin] mounted upon his calabash. **1852** in *DA* 241. **1856** in *DAE*.

calabash-cover *n.* a hat. *Joc.*
1886 Abbot *Blue Jackets* 269: "Where will you carry the despatch?"…"In my calabash-kiver, massa," he answered, pointing to his thick, woolly head.

calaboodle *n.* CABOODLE.
1856, 1857 in *DAE* I 386.

calaboose *n.* [< Sp *calabozo* 'dungeon'] a jail; a lockup; (*Mil.*) a guardhouse.
1792 in *DAE*: Their Fate will be confinement…in the Callibouse at Mobile. **1823** *Ibid.*: He was…deposited in a calaboose to await further trial. **1833** Ames *Old Sailor's Yarns* 277: They've been kept this whole week in a snug, warm *caliboose*, and they'll catch cold in the night air. **1837** *Naval Mag.* (Sept.) 471: They walked off with him to that nice little dormitory, the aforesaid *calaboose*, of which *one* is to be found in every Spanish town. **1847** Downey *Cruise of Portsmouth* 140: By getting drunk he would get into the Calaboose where he would remain all night, and next morn be mulcted by His Honor in a fine of $5 and sent on board ship. **1849** *Nat. Police Gaz.* (Sept. 29) 2: He was immediately removed to the calaboose. **1851** in Leyda *Melville Log* I 157: Herman Melville…was lying in the callibiose when I was dragged there. **1852** Stowe *Uncle Tom's Cabin* 116: Why, send them to the calaboose, or some of the other places to be flogged. **1855** in Dwyer & Lingenfelter *Songs of the Gold Rush* 30: And all got drunk as usual, got shoved in the calaboose. **1857** Willcox *Faca* 86: But the guard-house, or calaboose, that was the pleasant, airy, comfortable place! **1874** Carter *Rollingpin* 43: We…were about as tight as men can be and keep out of the calaboose. **1879** Shippen *30 Yrs.* 28: These…had been locked up in the "calaboose" (as sailors call all jails) for riotous conduct. **1882** Cook *Hands Up* 63: As the wagon left the west end of the bridge, a whistle was sounded and immediately answered from the direction of the calaboose. **1902** "J. Flynt" *Little Bro.* 120: The "catch" of a night is thrown promiscuously into the calaboose. **1915** Garrett *Army Ballads* 25 [ref. to 1898]: Oh, yes, *we've* been in the calaboose,/We've done *our* turn in the jug. *Ibid.* 269: Calaboose/Guardhouse or soldier prison. **1956** Rumaker *Gringos* 55: You git in the calaboose down here, buddy, you just rot.

calaboose *v.* to jail.—used trans.
1840 in *DAE*: He calaboosed him…Charley took him in. **1857** in Bartlett *Amer.* (ed. 4) 92: Colonel Titus…was *calaboosed* on Tuesday for shooting at the porter of the Planters' House.

Calamity Jane *n.* [orig. the nickname of Martha Jane Canary Burke (1852?–1903), U.S. frontier markswoman] an exceptionally pessimistic person (of either sex).
1918 *N.Y. Eve. Jour.* (Aug. 7) 16: "I know he won't remember me." (Calamity Jane). **1930** Schuyler *Black No More* 47: Oh, Ah've got all that fixed, Calamity Jane. **1931** Z. Grey *Sunset Pass* 12: "An' now brace yourself for a shock, True." "Fire away, you old Calamity Jane." **1941** Lardner & Kanin *Woman of the Year* (film): He calls you "the Calamity Jane of the fast international set."

Caleb *n. Fur Trapping.* a grizzly bear.
1833 G. Catlin, in *DAE*: All eyes were turned at once upon *Caleb* (as the grizzly bear is familiarly called by the trappers in the Rocky Mountains—or more often "Cale," for brevity's sake).

calendar *n. Pris.* a year spent in prison.
1926 Finerty *Criminalese* 12: *Calendar*—Year and a day. **1932** (cited in Partridge *Dict. Und.* (Add.)). **1966** Braly *Cold* 37: It's rough.…Rough as a cob. 'Specially for you—many calendars as you pulled. **1977** Bunker *Animal Factory* 109: But I've been here eighteen calendars and I know how to get things done.

calf *n.* ¶ In phrase: **have a calf** to have a fit of astonishment or anger. Cf. *have a cow* s.v. COW.
1978 *UTSQ* (Nov. 29): [Get angry]…*have a calf, have a hissy.*

calf around *v.* (see quot.).
1936 R. Adams *Cowboy Lingo* 233: "Calf around" or "soaked" [*sic*] was the cowboy's expression for loafing.

calf-rope *n.* ¶ In phrase: **holler** [or **say**] **calf-rope** *So. & West.* to plead for mercy or admit defeat; say uncle.
1859 "Skitt" *Fisher's River* 87 [ref. to 1820's]: Twelve o'clock he called fur the calfrope. I'd beat him all holler. **1878** in *DARE* I 510: Forced to "hollow calf-rope," that is, to signify by gestures that he was beaten. **1883** in Blair & Meine *Half Horse* 240: Fink called for quarter, or, as he expressed it, "hollered calf rope." **1906** *DN* III 129: I'll give it to him till he yells *calf-rope.* **1928** Bradford *Ol' Man Adam* 146: I jest got to holler "Calf rope." Hit whupped me. **1928–29** Faulkner *Sound & Fury* 166: Now I guess you say calfrope. **1930** Riggs *Green Grow the Lilacs* 135 [ref. to ca1905]: The time you come over of a Sunday a year ago and broke them three broncs all in one evenin', 'thout tetchin' leather er yellin' calf-rope. **1933** *AS* (Feb.) 49: *Holler calf-rope* v. phr. To acknowledge oneself beaten. When one boy throws another down in a wrestling match, the defeated wrestler *hollers calf-rope,* usually by crying "enough" or "I give up." **1934** Cunningham *Triggernometry* 229: All right! Calf rope! **1936** R. Adams *Cowboy Lingo* 206: When the cowboy acknowledged defeat, he was said to "holler calf-rope." **1937** E. Anderson *Thieves Like Us* 17: Anyway, this Dutchman hollers calf rope and he shows me the bottom drawer of a desk there. **1945** Himes *If He Hollers* 99: I bet you be the first one to holler calf rope.

calfskin fiddle *n.* a drum.
***1822** D. Carey *Life in Paris* I 190: Beat the calf-skin fiddle. **1889** Farmer *Amer.*: Calfskin fiddle…a drum.

calf-slobber *n. Texas.* **1.a.** meringue. Also pl.
1927 *AS* II 390: Meringue, on pastry, is called *calf-slobber* [by hoboes]. **1933** *AS* (Feb.) 27: *Calf Slobbers.* Meringue. **1949, 1960, 1966–69** in *DARE* I 511.
b. (see quot.).
1983 K. Weaver *Texas Crude* 64: *Calf-slobber.* Foam on a head of beer.
2. emphatically nothing.
1980 Hogan *Lawman's Choice* 70: That doesn't mean calf slobber to me.

Cali var. CALLY.

calico *n.* [*calico* cloth once widely used to make dresses; cf. SKIRT] a young woman or women.—also constr. with *bit of, piece of,* etc.
1848 Baker *Glance at N.Y.* 28: Only come up to-night, and I'll show you as gallus a piece of calico as any on de floor. **1862** C.F. Browne *Artemus Ward* 32: The gals among you…air as slick pieces of caliker as I ever sot eyes on. **1865** in *PADS* (No. 70) 24: He…had a piece of "calico" in Phila waiting for him. **1868** Williams *Black-Eyed Beauty* 9: Why, the worst bit of calico that ever an engine runner knew would be an angel to that woman! **1883** Peck *Peck's Bad Boy* 105: I shall never allow my

affections to become entwined about another piece of calico. **1895** *DN* I 414: Look at the calico comin'! **1897** Ade *Pink Marsh* 129: I do n' know nothin' 'bout no guhl....I got no money to waste on no piece o' calico. **1900** *DN* II 26: *Calico*, often abb. *calic*, n. 1. A woman, individually as companion to a man, or collectively wherever sex plays a part in social life. **1905** *DN* 72: I'm going to take a bunch of calico to the lecture tonight. **1906** "O. Henry" *Four Million* 98: She says she caught yer dead to rights, huggin' a bunch o' calico in de hot-house. **1907** *Lippincott's Mag.* (May) 675: Out here, you don't see calico for years at a stretch. **1909** *Miss. A & M Reveille* 217: He is very popular with the "calico." **1909** in *DA* 243: What air you calicoes thar a-blubberin' about? **1929** in Goodstone *Pulp* 59: I ain't no gossipin' bit of calico. **1932** "Max Brand" *Jackson Trail* 111: Calico means trouble. **1941** Nixon *Possum Trot* 38: For such occasions an unmarried field hand would sometimes use a week's wages to "hire" a horse and buggy and "haul some calico."

calico *v. So.* to court young women.
1887 in *DAE* I 389. **1909** *Miss. A & M Reveille* 73: Of his "calico"ing career we know nothing. **1915** *DN* IV 181: He's out a-*calicoin'* every Sunday.

Calico Row *n. Army.* SOAPSUDS ROW.
1893 Putnam *Blue Uniform* 4: Their wives were generally laundresses...and gave to this section of the settlement the name of "Calico Row."

California banknote *n.* an ox-hide used in place of currency. *Joc.*
1840 Dana *Before Mast* ch. xviii [ref. to 1835]: [Mexicans] at Monterey...have no circulating medium but silver and hides—which the sailors call "California bank notes." **1850** Buffum *Gold Mines* XV: Money was the scarcest article on the coast,...ox hides having acquired the name and answering to the purpose of "California bank notes." **1947** W.M. Camp *S.F.* 17: When cowhides were called "California banknotes" in the leather markets all over New England.

California bible *n. West.* a deck of cards. *Joc.* Cf. CALIFORNIAN PRAYERBOOK.
1954–60 *DAS*. **1962** *West. Folklore* (Jan.) 29.

California blankets *n.pl. Hobo.* sheets of newspaper used for bedding or warmth. *Joc.*
1926 *AS* I (Sept.) 650: *California blankets*: newspapers, when used for sleeping purposes. **1927** *DN* V 441: *California blankets*, n. Newspapers used by homeless men as a substitute for bedding. **1929** *World's Work* (Nov.) 40: The old-timer who spends his nights on a park bench under California blankets. **1930** "D. Stiff" *Milk & Honey* 201: *California blankets*—Newspapers when used to sit on.

California collar *n. West.* a hangman's noose. *Joc.*
1942 in *DARE* I 513 [ref. to 1870's]: Inexorably the vigilantes put the California collar around his neck. **1942** *ATS* 468. **1949** *AS* XXIV 262: The rope was referred to as a California collar.

California cornflakes *n.pl.* cocaine. *Joc.*
1988 *Atlantic* (Sept.) 102: *California cornflakes* (cocaine).

California moccasins *n.pl. West.* CALIFORNIA SOCKS.
1923 Wheeler *Buffalo Days* 98: I left my boots drying near the fire and from an old grain sack manufactured a pair of "California moccasins." **1936** R. Adams *Cowboy Lingo* 35: When the cowpuncher bound up his feet with sacks to keep them from freezing in cold weather, he called such sacks his "California moccasins."

Californian prayerbook *n. West.* a deck of cards. *Joc.* Cf. CALIFORNIA BIBLE.
1851 W. Kelly *Ex. to Calif.* II 64: By far the greater number were engaged in the study of the "Californian prayer-book"—as a pack of cards are profanely designated.

California overshoes *n.pl.* CALIFORNIA SOCKS.
1952 in *DARE* I 515. **1967** *West. Folk.* XXVI 189: *California overshoes*—footcoverings made of gunny sacks.

California shinplaster *n.* CALIFORNIA BANKNOTE. *Joc.*
1848 in *DA* 245.

California socks *n.pl. West.* rags wrapped around the feet and ankles to provide warmth in cold weather.
1941 in *DARE* I 515. **1942** Garcia *Tough Trip* 385 [ref. to 1890's]: Large-sized rags, called California socks.

California stop *n.* (see quots.).
1978 Univ. Tenn. student (Fla.): A California stop is one where you roll right through a stop sign without stopping. **1986** W. Safire, in *N.Y. Times Mag.* (Dec. 11) 6: *California stop*, frequently localized as a *Hollywood stop*, is what many readers identify as the slight slowing down of a motorist surreptitiously jumping an octagonal stop sign.

California tires *n.pl. West.* (see quot.).
1971 Tak *Truck Talk* 26: *California tires*: tires with little or no tread remaining.

California toothpick *n. West.* ARKANSAS TOOTHPICK.
1856 in *DAE*. **1942** in *DA* 245.

calijumpics *n.pl.* calisthenics.
1944–49 Allardice *At War* 88: "What is the next class?"..."Calijumpics." **1963** Cameron *Black Camp* 44 [ref. to WWII]: They fell out for calijumpics. *Ibid.* 79: Chow came after reveille and calijumpics.

calk var. CAULK.

call *v.* ¶ In phrases:
¶ **call Earl** see s.v. EARL.
¶ **call on the carpet** see s.v. CARPET.
¶ **call (someone's) game** to call (someone's) bluff; to challenge, as to a fight.
1983 Goldman & Fuller *Charlie Co.* 210: The two started snarling at each other when they met at bars, and one night Boxx called his buddy's game....Boxx wound up in the hospital.
¶ **call (someone's) hand** Orig. *Gamb.* to challenge openly; call (someone's) bluff. Now *colloq.*
1857, 1898, 1948 in *DA* 247. **1956** Neider *Hendry Jones* 101: Nobody felt like calling the kid's hand.
¶ **call the shots** see s.v. SHOT, *n.*
¶ **call the turn** [from the game of faro] Orig. *Gamb.* to make an accurate statement or (*esp.*) prediction.
[**1867** in A.K. McClure *Rocky Mtns.* 292: Single turn, gents! Who'll call the turn?] **1876** in Dwyer & Lingenfelter *Songs of Gold Rush* 189: Death stept in and called the turn. **1898** in *DA*. **1908** in Fleming *Unforgettable Season* 65: A rooter...pretty nearly called the turn as he made his way from the grandstand at the conclusion of the contest. "It was 5 to 2 in favor of Hans Wagner." **1912** Mathewson *Pitching* 266: "Didn't I call the turn?" Murray yelled to McGraw as he came to the bench. **1926** C.M. Russell *Trails* 6: "Neighbor, you're a long way from your range." "You call the turn,...but how did you read my iron?" **1935** C.J. Daly *Murder* 5: I'm not saying you didn't call the turn, but after all, it's your business, isn't it? **1956** Neider *Hendry Jones* 74: This was not how he had expected to call the turn. **1975** McCaig *Danger Trail* 19: You called the turn, though I cain't but agree that Cullen's decision was the right one.

call boy *n.* a male prostitute with whom an appointment can be made by telephone. Now *colloq.*
1942 Davis & Wolsey *Call House Madam* 11: And of the call girls and call boys that I employed. **1961** *Social Problems* IX 102: The *call-boy* does not solicit in public. **1971** Rader *Govt. Inspected* 43: I was not so dumb as to think, outside a male trade service for women, a specialized...cake-eater callboy stable, outside of that there was sufficient room to make a life by scoring with broads. **1972** Rodgers *Queens' Vernacular* 111: [Homosexual] Hustlers fall into two categories: the street variety and *models* (call boys). **1981** Wambaugh *Glitter Dome* 70: He made an additional two hundred as a call boy for...gay customers. **1985** D.K. Weisberg *Children of Night* 27: He was also talking about giving up street hustling to become a call boy.

calldown *n.* a reprimand; a scolding; (in 1899 quot.) contradiction.
1895 Tisdale *Behind the Guns* 11: When them guys with the swords and buttons ask you anything, don't know nothing. If you tell them you do, you'll get a call-down, 'cause you see, they'll tell you Uncle Sam is paying them to tell you that. **1899** Cullen *Tales* 87: I think I may say, without fear of call-down, that this...is a pretty hard one to put over the plate. **1903** in Duis *Saloon* 51: Then see how quick he will get a call-down. **1904** *Life in Sing Sing* 255: Call Down—A reprimand. **1910** Munn *Thinks* 5: We may rebel at "call downs," but they are our best educators.

call down *v.* to reprimand, scold, or take issue with.
1894 Gardner *Dr. & Devil* 78: He had been "called down" at police headquarters, and told not to receive any warrants from me. **1896** Ade *Artie* 20: I didn't want to call her down, but, I could tell...that she'd never had any diamonds. **1897** *Chi. Tribune* (July 25) 15: The Kansas Dialect...*Call Down*—To rebuff—"Mrs. Lease recently called down

Queen Victoria." **1910** in McCay *Little Nemo* 256: "Say, Captain, let me tell you, if you want a scrap with me, start to call me down again like that!" "I didn't call you down." **1923** in *DA.*

call flat *n.* CALL HOUSE.
   1916 Miner *Prostitution* 7: "Mrs. Clarke called me up on the phone and I went up to her call flat."…"I have nothing to say," said the call-house keeper. **1923** Ornitz *Haunch, Paunch & Jowl* 187: Now she's old and she keeps a nice respectable call flat. No joint.

call girl *n.* a female prostitute with whom an appointment may be made by telephone; (*broadly*) a prostitute in a brothel. Now *S.E.*
   [*a*1904–11 Phillips *Susan Lenox* II 124: Mrs. Thurston…had a list of girls and married women upon whom she could call. Gentlemen using her house for rendezvous were sometimes disappointed by the ladies with whom they were intriguing.] **1922** E. Paul *Impromptu* 33: For a call girl to be "turned down" (refused after being introduced to a strange man) hurts her professional standing and bruises her vanity. **1937** Reitman *Box-Car Bertha* 198: "Call Girls"…Working girls who take pay for the pleasure they give and are subject to telephone calls by hotel keepers and others. **1956** Holiday & Dufty *Lady Sings the Blues* 24: But I didn't have what it took to be a call girl. **1957** Greenwald *Call Girl* 9: Call girls make almost all their appointments by phone. **1959** W. Williams *Ada Dallas* 114: The call girl, Mary Ellis.

call house *n.* **1.** a house of assignation where appointments with prostitutes can be made, as by telephone. Now *S.E.*
   1913 Vice Comm. of Phila. *Report* 7: A call house is one where the proprietor or proprietress calls or sends for prostitutes, generally using the telephone. **1921** Woolston *Prostitution in U.S.* 139: The call house is really an employment exchange for prostitutes.…Many of the women who are on call live in private apartments or in their own homes. *Ibid.*: Seventy-eight call houses were located in 1912 by vice investigators in [Philadelphia]. **1929** Sullivan *Look at Chi.* 76: The night prowler now had to go to "call houses."…There were no prostitutes in these places, but on the arrival of men the girls were called for [by telephone]. **1940** Fitzgerald *Last Tycoon* 88: "You mean she was a tart?" "So it seems. She went to what you call call-houses." **1959** W. Williams *Ada Dallas* 341: They believe the remains are those of Blanche Jamison, 51, notorious call-house madam. **1959** Egen *Plainclothesman* 99: Call houses are merely telephones maintained by a madam. **1979** P. Goldstein *Prost. & Drugs* 36: The call house…receives [telephone] calls from prospective customers, and…sends the prostitute to the customer.
   2. a brothel.
   1916–22 Cary *Sexual Vocab.* I s.v. *brothel: Call house*…cat house. **1927** Shay *Pious Friends* 34: Frankie went down to the call-house,/She leaned on that call-house bell,/"Get out of the way all chippies and fools/Or I'll blow you straight to hell." **1929** W.R. Burnett *Little Caesar* ch. vii: Sometimes he would go to one of the call-houses…and spend a couple of hours with one of the women. **1951** O'Hara *Farmers Hotel* 52: Not a regular call-house whore. **1952** Uris *Battle Cry* 1: I know every damned port of call and call house in the Mediterranean. **1974** Terkel *Working* 64: During the day I tutored English for fifth- and sixth-grade kids. In the evening, I worked in the call house.

callibogus *n.* [orig. unkn.] *N.E.* a mixture of rum and spruce beer.
   1758 in *DA*: Calabogus club begun. **1785** Grose *Vulgar Tongue: Calibogus,* rum and spruce beer, American beverage. **1861** in *F & H* II 20: *Callibogus,* a mixture of Rum and Spruce-beer, more of the former and less of the latter. **1895, 1947** in *DA* 243.

calliope *n. R.R.* a steam locomotive.
   1929 *Bookman* (July) 524: Before we leave the yards I take a run up to the calliope to match watches with the hoghead. **1931** *Writer's Digest* (May) 41: *Calliope*—steam locomotive.

call joint *n.* CALL HOUSE.
   1937 in *DAS* 86. **1942** Davis & Wolsey *Call House Madam* 78: Run it as a call joint, but keep the standard up.

Cally or **Cali** *n.* California.
   1930 Irwin *Tramp & Und. Sl.*: *Cali:* California. **1942** *ATS* 49: California…*Cali, Cally.* **1985** "Run-D.M.C." *My Adidas* (rap song): We started in an alley/Now we chill in Cally. **1990** Headline News Network (May 26): Milwaukee beat Cally. **1991** *Source* (Oct.) 29: He didn't want to come from Cali to New York.

cally *n. Hobo.* CALABOOSE. Also **callie.**
   1919 *Bookman* (Apr.): Distinguish between…the callie [and] the hoosegow. **1923** *Atlanta Constitution* (Feb. 1) 12: You're running a long chance, kiddo, if you think you're going to land me in the callie. **1926**

AS I (Sept.) 650: *Cally.* police station. **1930** Irwin *Tramp & Und. Sl.*: *Cally*—A police station.

Callyo *adj. Naut.* (see quot.).
   1945 Colcord *Sea Lang.* 47: All Cally-o is a phrase meaning all right, or even better. Callao [Peru] is a port full of delights for seamen.

calve *v.* to vomit.
   1847 in Peskin *Vols.* 24: From many of the bunks the boys are "calfing." *Ibid.* 228: Young men…hanging over the portico…trying (to use a polite expression) "to calve."

Cambo *n. & adj.* **1.** a Cambodian; Cambodian.
   1972 *N.Y. Post* (June 5) 8: Cambo Capital Battered by Rockets. **1973** *N.Y. Post* (Jan. 8) 69: Cambo Factions Fight in Paris. **1979** *N.Y. Post* (Dec. 21) 8: Despot Pol Pot Toppled by Rebel Cambos.
   2. Cambodia. [Quots. ref. to Vietnam War.]
   1985 Bodey *F.N.G.* 69: We were over nearer Cambo, back in March. **1989** R. Miller *Profane Men* 68: Into Laos and Cambo.

Cambode *n. & adj. Mil.* a Cambodian; Cambodian.
   1964 R. Moore *Green Berets* 35: The Cambodes evidently liked the captain. **1967** Calin *Search & Kill* 23: The Cambodes can't be trusted. **1979** J. Morris *War Story* 212: I've heard guys bitch about the Cambodes when they got shot at from across the border. **1986** R. Zumbro *Tank Sgt.* 16: They need the other two companies over on the Cambode border.

camel *n.* **1.** a bustle.
   1882 Sala *Amer. Revisited* II 317: I subsequently discovered…that a "camel" was the popular name for…a "bustle."
   2. *Horse Racing.* an old or worthless horse.
   1898–1900 Cullen *Chances* 34: I couldn't hold down a grin myself when I sized up the poor mutt of a camel.
   3. *Naut.* a floating platform attached to a pier.
   1942 *ATS* 740: *Camel,* a floating landing platform connected to a pier. **1947** Boyer *Dark Ship* 153: A camel is a small floating dock.

camel chaser *n.* CAMEL JOCKEY.
   1968 in Hayes *Apocalypse* 756: "Foreigner," some of the other kids had cried at Demirgian, "Camel chaser," some of the Irish would say.

camel-driver *n.* **1.** *Mil. Av.* a pilot of a Sopwith Camel pursuit plane. Also **camel merchant.** [Quots. ref. to WWI.]
   1926 Springs *Nocturne Militaire* 39: "You Camel merchants can go on with your suicide clubs," he told me; "you all seem to be having a private war of your very own." **1927** Niles *Singing Soldiers* 75: Many of our good boys died trying to fly Camels. They were tricky ships, particularly for the first few hops.…A few, who became quite expert with them, were jokingly referred to as "camel-drivers."
   2. see CAMEL JOCKEY.

camel jockey *n. Esp. Stu.* a native of any country where camels are believed to be customarily ridden; (*specif.*) an Arab.—used contemptuously. Also **camel jock, camel driver.**
   1965 N.Y.C. high-school student: *Lawrence of Arabia.* It's about a bunch of camel jockeys. **1966** in IUFA *Folk Speech: Camel jock*—A name given to a foreign student. **1967** in *DARE* I 521: Camel jock (applied to an Indian national). **1968–70** *Current Slang* III & IV 21: *Camel jock, n.* A foreign student from the near East. **1975** De Mille *Smack Man* 105: His friends called him the Camel Driver. He was…Lebanese by descent. **1977** Schrader *Blue Collar* 79: It's those…camel jockeys.…The…Arabs. **1985** Petit *Peacekeepers* 159: Ragheads and camel jockeys. **1985** A. Naff *Becoming Amer.* 252: Prejudice became more ethnically specific and for Syrian children more frequent in the twenties. The epithets now included "camel jockey"…and more often "Turk."

camera clicker *n.* a photographer.
   1966 J. Lewis *Tell It to the Marines* 43: Where the hell's that new camera clicker?

cammie *n. Mil.* camouflage; (*pl.*) a camouflage uniform.—often attrib.
   1971 Glasser *365 Days* 201: Hey, you…you in the camies. *Ibid.* 242: *Camies.* World War II term for camouflage uniforms. **1983** K. Miller *Lurp Dog* 162: Marvel was…in his spotted cammies. **1984** Hammel *Root* 18: Camouflage utility clothing "cammies." **1987** D. da Cruz *Boot* 17: Recruits are measured, cami (camouflage) "covers" pulled down over bare skulls…*Ibid.* 297: *Cami* camouflage; *camis*: short for camouflage utility uniform, worn in field. **1981–89** R. Atkinson *Long Gray Line* 540: George's face was smeared with green "cammie" stick. **1991** *Leatherneck* (Oct.) 2: Women Marines who become pregnant may adorn maternity cammies with name and service tapes.

camo *n. Mil.* camouflage.—often attrib. Also as v.

1984 J.R. Reeves *Mekong* 134: He'd covered his torso and arms completely with black camo paint. **1986** *Miami Vice* (NBC-TV): You talkin' camo nets and night scopes? **1986** Stinson & Carabatsos *Heartbreak* 206: Highway walked past them, fully decked out and camoed.

camouflage *v. Mil.* to malinger.

1926 *Sat. Eve. Post* (Mar. 6) 14 [ref. to 1918]: Men...were going up to have a fight, and if I catch anyone camouflaging, he'll see a fine Hamburg steak the next time he looks in a mirror.

camp *n.* **1.** *West.* a place.

1915 *N.Y. Eve. Jour.* (Aug. 7) 9: Hotel Insomnia...Quite a camp. **1916** in C.M. Russell *Paper Talk* 127: For snow this camp [N.Y.C.] would make Neihart look like Palm beach. **1926** C.M. Russell *Trails* 5: All this weather makes Cheyenne look small, an' I begin longin' for bigger camps, so I drift for Chicago. **1929** in Blackbeard & Williams *Smithsonian Comics* 106: Here I am in Venice and Boy! What a camp this is— all the alleys in town are flooded. **1977** Bunker *Animal Factory* 27: You can do it....You're the juice man around this camp.

2.a. *Homosex.* a homosexual man who behaves in an exaggeratedly effeminate manner.

1923 McAlmon *Companion Vol.* 214: You old camp. **1931** *New B'way Brevities* (Oct. 5) 1: Drags, Camps, Flaunting Hip-twisters and Reefer Peddlers Run Afoul of Cops on the Lam... **1948** Vidal *City & Pillar* 265: I don't see how you do it. First Shaw and now Sullivan. You really've been a regular little *camp*, haven't you? **1949** De Forrest *Gay Year* 28: You certainly are becoming a camp. **1966** "Petronius" *N.Y. Unexp.* 96: Celebrity fags are [often] full, zany camps. **1967** Crowley *Boys in the Band* 866: Bernard, you're a camp! **1976** in M. Levine *Gay Men* 207: David Kerwin was a camp.

b. (see quot.).

1965 Borowik *Lion's* 69: But he's a camp*, that guy....*"Camp," in the show business lexicon, means an all-round performer, one who can do almost anything and do it well.

3. *Homosex.* a gathering place for homosexual men.

1935 Pollock *Underworld Speaks: Camp*, a meeting place of male sexual perverts where they dress as females. **1942** *ATS* 472: *Camp*...a male homosexual brothel or gathering place. **1942–49** Goldin et al. *DAUL* 39.

4.a. *Homosex.* affected flamboyance in speech or mannerisms displayed by a homosexual man; ironic or exaggerated verbal posturing.

1941 G. Legman, in G. Henry *Sex Variants* II 1160: As a noun, *camp* refers to [homosexual] flamboyance or bizarrerie of speech or action, or to a person displaying it. **1944** in J. Katz *Gay/Lesbian Almanac* 592: The cultivation of a secret language, the *camp*, a tone and a vocabulary...loaded with contempt for the human. **1954** in W.S. Burroughs *Letters* 236: That...is only camp. My real plan he doesn't know.

b. *Entertainment Industry.* a ludicrous parody; a ridiculous or ludicrous occasion.

1956 *Life* (Oct. 27) 91: But they all wanted to kid it...one of those other stars was already in cavalry uniform and about to do the part, but he was going to make a "camp" out of it. (A "camp," as [Mike] Todd explains it, "is something you really can't define, like if Groucho Marx played the train conductor.") **1953–58** J.C. Holmes *Horn* 131: Every time we get on the stand it'll be like an act, a camp, a hype. We'll make the people think we *like* what we're doing. **1966** Susann *Valley of Dolls* 393: Once every month they have a dance [at the mental hospital]. It's a real camp.

c. something that is so affected, outdated, contrived, tasteless, etc., as to be amusing. Now *S.E.*

1964 in Sontag *Against Interpretation* 275: Notes on Camp [title]....One of these is the sensibility—unmistakably modern, a variant of sophistication but hardly identical with it—that goes by the cult name of "Camp." *Ibid.* 290: While it's not true that Camp taste *is* homosexual taste, there is...a peculiar affinity and overlap. **1968** Swarthout *Loveland* 14: To the young...it would seem too quaint to be camp, too intimately out to be in. **1971** Denisoff *Great Day* 95: This song dealt with the attempts of a cripple to join the war-effort....Red Foley's composition "Smoke on the Water,"...advocated making Japan into a graveyard on the glorious day of victory. While these songs, especially today, may be considered "camp," they were manifestations of the mass culture of the war years. **1973** *Drug Forum* II 139: "Sex-crazed dope fiends"..."warped desires"..."killer-weed"—these emotionally charged and outmoded phrases are high camp to the New Generation. **1973** Overgard *Hero* 73: She was so outrageously dressed in such horrible taste that she was amusing. Real, unconscious high camp. **1985** Univ. Tenn. grad. student: Examples of *camp*? *The Rocky Horror Picture Show*,

for one. Some of the humor in *The Avengers.* Grown-ups who weren't hippies who tried to dress like them.

camp *adj.* **1.** *Homosex.* (of a homosexual man) given to often humorously exaggerated feminine mannerisms; blatantly effeminate. [Despite awkwardness of def. in 1909 quot., the adj. is presumably all that is intended.]

*****1909** Ware *Passing English* 61: *Camp*...Actions and gestures of exaggerated emphasis....Used chiefly by persons of exceptional want of character. "How very camp he is." *****1933** in *OEDS.* **1949** *Gay Girl's Guide* 4: *Camp*...equivalent to *gay.* **1965** *Life* (Aug. 20) 84: In fact, the word Camp was '20s slang for homosexual both here and in England.

2. being, relating to, or displaying CAMP.

1966 N.Y.C. high-school student: That is *so* camp. **1966** *Time* (Jan. 21) 40: The "camp" movement, which pretends that the ugly and banal are fun. **1976** W. Safire, in *N.Y. Times Mag.* (Mar. 21) 111: "Camp" means "so banal as to be perversely sophisticated." **1987** *Morning Edition* (Nat. Pub. Radio) (Sept. 3): Generally when songwriters try to adopt that language it comes off as very affected, very camp.

camp *v. Homosex.* to display exaggeratedly effeminate mannerisms.

1925 McAlmon *Silk Stockings* 10: His camping manner, copied from stage fairies in America, sat strangely upon him. *Ibid.* 84: Christ, don't start camping at me this morning. **1931** *New B'way Brevities* (Oct. 5) 10: Boys and men with painted faces and dyed hair flaunt themselves camping and whoopsing for hours each night. **1931** N. West *Balso Snell* 22: On my way back to Broadway I passed some sailors, and felt an overwhelming desire to flirt with them. I went through all the postures of a desperate prostitute; I camped for all I was worth. **1933** Ford & Tyler *Young & Evil* 167: Take them up to the joint and camp like mad! *Ibid.* 179: Don't camp like that.... Or I'll leave. **1944** in T. Williams *Letters* 139: Not camping with a bunch of shrill queens. **1947** Schulberg *Harder They Fall* 167: "Stop staring at me, you naughty boy," he camped in a falsetto and laughed. **1956** J.M. Reinhardt *Perversions* 47: *Camp*—verb. To mimic, consciously or not, the other sex. **1958** Plagemann *Steel Cocoon* 113 [ref. to WWII]: Bullitt went on, in his travesty of a feminine voice, the routine known as "camping,"...which only embarrassed Williams, who didn't know how to respond. "Camping" was familiar to most old Navy hands because of their early exposure to homosexuality, and sometimes, to amuse themselves while they were together, they imitated the speech and the mannerisms of these circles. **1962** in Southern *Red-Dirt* 215: I'm talking about your infernal *camping!* Now just stop it! Right now! **1964** in Sontag *Against Interpretation* 281: To camp is a mode...which employs flamboyant mannerisms [etc.]...with a witty meaning for cognoscenti. **1967** Crowley *Boys in the Band* 827: That's *exactly* what I'm talking about, Emory. *No camping!* **1981** C. Nelson *Picked Bullets Up* 152: He camped outrageously all during supper.

¶ In phrase:

¶ **camp it up** Orig. *Homosex.* to *camp*, above; (*also*) to make an ostentatious or affected display; HAM IT UP.

*****1959** in *OEDS.* **1966–71** Karlen *Sex. & Homosex.* 356: The homosexual camping it up at a gay party is saying, "You see, ladies,...I can play your game more extravagantly than you." **1971** Mishkin et al. *All in the Family* (CBS-TV): Well, he don't camp it up. You know. **1971** Rader *Govt. Inspected* 34: This is what he read, camping it up like a Southern preacher...waving melodramatically and gesticulating in the air. **1971** Dahlskog *Dict.* 12: *Camp it up*, of a man, to behave in an effeminate manner.

camp dog *n.* a camp menial.

1927 *DN* V 441: *Camp-dog*, n. The hobo at construction camps who takes care of the bunks and belongings of hoboes at work. **1968** R. Adams *Western Words* (ed. 2) 52: *Camp dog.* In logging, a helper who looks after the camp sleeping quarters and bunks; a flunky.

camper *n.* [extracted fr. HAPPY CAMPER] an individual; person.

1987 *Beauty & Beast* (CBS-TV): Two of your campers are in a holding cell downtown. **1990** G. Trudeau *Doonesbury* (synd. cartoon strip) (July 9): You know, campers, there's been a lot of debate lately about obscenity.

camp lawyer *n.* [sugg. by SEA LAWYER, GUARDHOUSE LAWYER, etc.] *Logging.* a captious or contentious employee.

1958 McCulloch *Woods Words* 28: *Camp lawyer*—The worst arguer in camp.

camp louse *n. Logging.* (see quot.).

1958 McCulloch *Woods Words* 28: *Camp louse*—Bull cook, handyman, chore boy.

campy *adj.* CAMP.

1941 G. Legman, in G. Henry *Sex Variants* II 1160: *Camp*…Adjective: *campy*. **1942** in Bérubé *Coming Out* 91: Can't you tell when we swish by?/Isn't it campy? Isn't it campy? **1949** *Gay Girl's Guide* 5: *Campy*—Very *gay*, with humorous connotations. **1961** L. Jones, in *Jazz People* (Aug. 28): If I remember correctly, you made some terribly campy remarks about Mr. Gibson's use of the phrase "self-styled," as to the correctness (?) or motive(s) for its use. **1964** in Sontag *Against Interpretation* 277: There are "campy" movies, clothes, furniture, popular songs, novels, people, buildings. **1967** Rechy *Numbers* 40: Almond Joy…he can't bring himself to say the campy name. **1972** *Anthro. Ling.* (Mar.) 3: He was being very campy. **1985** *Kit Parker Cat.* 106: What To Expect from a 3-D Movie—you can expect campy chuckles [etc.]. **1986–89** Norse *Memoirs* 89: He…had a stylized, campy wit.

can *n.* **1.** a dollar.

1859 Matsell *Vocab.*: *Can.* a dollar.

2.a. a lavatory.

1900 *DN* II 26: *Can, n.* water-closet. **1914** Jackson & Hellyer *Crim. Slang* 22: *Can*…Also a lavatory, toilet, urinal. **1928** in Inman *Diary* 387: A room…not up too many stairs, near "the can." **1939** Polsky *Curtains for Editor* 35: Somebody went along the outside edge from Mr. Corey's office to the women's can. **1947** Motley *Knock on Any Door* 163: I had to go to the can. **1970** Hatch *Cedarhurst* 187: Where's the ladies' can?

b. a toilet.

1914 Jackson & Hellyer *Crim. Slang* 22: *Can*…Also a lavatory, toilet, urinal. **1924** in Hemingway *Sel. Letters* 115: I plugged the can…so that the plumbers had to be sent for. **1941** in C.R. Bond & T. Anderson *Flying T. Diary* 54: I was right in the middle of a nature call, on the can near the alert shack. **1962** Gallant *On Valor's Side* 309: If you ain't off the can by then, we are goin' to explode it and you might get blowed off that damned seat. **1968** P. Roth *Portnoy* 128: A full uninterrupted hour on the can.

3. *Stu.* a party; CAN RACKET.

1905 *DN* III 73: *Can, n.* A spread or feast. "We had our Sunday night *can*." "A nickel on the *can*" is five cents to buy food for the *can*. Common among students.

4. [fr. the v.] a dismissal, removal, expulsion, rejection, etc.—constr. with *get the*.

1908 McGaffey *Show Girl* 113: In honor of the prima donna getting the can. **1931** J.T. Farrell *McGinty* 101: I thought sure as Jesus I was gettin' the can. **1933** in Galewitz *Great Comics* 38: You get th' can! **1991** *New Yorker* (Dec. 9) 89: Jim Lefebvre got the can in Seattle after building the Mariners to their first over-.500 finish in the club's…history.

5. a jail or prison.

1912 Lowrie *Prison* 125: I was in th' can ag'in, up against it f'r robbery. **1914** Jackson & Hellyer *Crim. Slang* 22: *Can*, Noun. General usage. A place of confinement; a prison; a cell. **1918** Rowse *Doughboy Dope* 45: J is the jug, otherwise known as the can, the pen or the mill. **1927** Coe *Me—Gangster* 29: He had just got out of the can. **1934** Berg *Prison Nurse* 12: Say, everybody in this "can" knows who I am. **1947** Motley *Knock on Any Door* 179: They're in the can. They caught time for jack-rolling. **1961** Braly *Felony Tank* 22: If he'd ever seen a tight can it was the Penthouse. **1966** Rose *Russians Are Coming* (film): I'll throw you right in the can for disorderly conduct! **1992** *Geraldo* (synd. TV series): So you've been in the can for a while.

6.a. the rump; buttocks.

1914 in Cray *Erotic Muse* 193: Fondle my fat old can. **1920** in Hemingway *Sel. Letters* 39: Dempsey may beat his can off. **1923** in J. O'Hara *Sel. Letters* 12: It's a kick in the can. **1930** J.T. Farrell *Calico Shoes* 30: I always thought that that big can of hers was good for something. **1933** Halper *Union Sq.* 13: Sit down….Rest your weary can. **1934** Halper *Foundry* 118: You've got a big enough can to foal an army, why the hell can't you have a kid? **1967** J.Kramer *Instant Replay* 53: I'll…kick him right in the can. **1985** Tenn. man, age *ca*40: Life knows how to knock you on your can.

b. (used as a euphem. for ASS in various senses).

1930 J.T. Farrell *Calico Shoes* 261: If one of my bosses saw me having a thing like her hang around my station—well, that would be my can. **1934** H. Roth *Call It Sleep* 324: If I'd aknown you wuz such a pain inna can I wouldna let yuh come up hea. **1937** J.T. Farrell *To Whom It May Concern* 150: Well, my can was worked too. Out every night. **1953** Eyster *Customary Skies* 31: Oh, fiddle, fiddle, fiddle/While you can,/Before she lurns to sell 'er can. **1958** in Pohl *Star of Stars* 43: You flatter the cans off the viewers. **1965** Spillane *Killer Mine* 39: That fat slob Reese is after your can, Mr. Scanlon.

7. the head.

1915 *DN* IV 198: *Can, n.* Head. **1967** in *DARE*.

8.a. *Navy.* a depth charge; ASHCAN.

1918 Beston *Full Speed Ahead* 21: I wish I knew where the bird was….I'd drop a can right on his neck. **1918** *Ladies Home Jrnl.* (Nov.): The depth bombs really deserve a eulogy of their own….The Navy always refers to them as "cans." **1918** York *Mud & Stars* 39: We sail the seas and drop the cans,/To keep old Fritzy down.

b. a bomb.

1929 Hotstetter & Beesley *Racket* 221: *Can-maker*—One who manufactures bombs, especially nitroglycerine, black powder, or stench bombs.

c. *Mil. Av.* a canister of napalm.

1966 Shepard *Doom Pussy* 128: Four hundred knots at fifty feet and all cans on target. **1981** "K. Rollins" *Fighter Pilots* 56: She was loaded with four cans of napalm.

9. *Und.* a safe.

1925 in Partridge *Dict. Und.* **1927** McIntyre *Slag* 52: "Do you mean a safe?" "An old can." **1936** Mackenzie *Living Rough* 121: "That's a finger-man" (a safe-blower), "he opens cans." **1942** *Big Shot* (film): Yeah, I opened a can before. It had a combination on the outside and dough on the inside. **1977** Caron *Go-Boy* 262: *Can*—safe.

10.a. a motor vehicle or aircraft, esp. if old or dilapidated.

1923 T.A. Dorgan, in Zwilling *TAD Lexicon* 24: Did you see that old can of his outside? **1928** McCartney, in *Papers of Mich. Acad.* [ref. to 1918]: *Can*: An airplane. **1928** Burnett *Little Caesar* 56: Listen, Bat, can you drive a can? **1933** D. Runyon, in *Collier's* (Dec. 23) 8: The Dutchman gets out of the old can. **1938** in *DAS* 86: Tooling along with the kiddies and the little woman in his costly can. **1943** Siegmeister *American Song* 343: Frankie took a cab at the corner,/Says, "Driver, step on this can." **1951** *New Yorker* (Sept. 8) 81: Guy your age gets ahold of one of these cans and right away he thinks he's a hot-rod. **1963** Lundgren *Primary Cause* 135: That can he's riding has already gulped his fuel reserve. **1970** Landy *Underground Dict.* 46: *Can*…Car.

b. *Navy.* a destroyer; TIN CAN.

1933 *Leatherneck* (Aug.) 12: They have a date on every "can" (destroyer). **1939** O'Brien *One-Way Ticket* 38 [ref. to *ca*1925]: I never heard nothin' about this bein' a lousy can, did you, Kelly? **1940** *Life* (Oct. 28) 99: Torpedoes are *fish*, destroyers *cans*, depth charges *ash cans*. **1942** Casey *Torpedo Junction* 10: *Can*…The familiar name for a destroyer. **1943** Bayler & Carnes *Wake I.* 197: Under escort of a "can"—disrespectful term for a destroyer. **1944** Olds *Helldiver Squadron* 37: Bob…fired a test burst from his forward guns and went after the Jap "can." **1945** J. Bryan *Carrier* 74: We told him to land in the water. A can picked him up. **1945** Dos Passos *Tour* 84: Most of those boys on the cans are new. **1951** Grant *Flying Leathernecks* (film): Flattops, cruisers, cans, transports and barges. **1962** E. Stephens *Blow Negative* 15: I suppose the cans do a lot of antisubmarine work around here. **1968** Blackford *Torp. Sailor* 11 [ref. to 1916]: I found that when a man was too wild for a regulation ship, yet too good a seaman to be kicked out, he was sent to the destroyers. When he was too wild for most cans, he wound up in the old Fifth Division, in which the "*Pauldy*" [USS *Paulding*] was the ship with the wildest reputation. **1974** E. Thompson *Tattoo* 125: I was on an old DE during the invasion of Africa….The can was rollin and pitchin as the captain dodged torpedoes and bombed. *a*1988 Poyer *Med* 9: The Italian can [is] coming up on the Gunnery Coordination Net.

11. *pl. Radio.* headphones.

1929 *AS* (Oct.) 48: *Cans*—head telephones, or receivers. **1939** Fearing *Hospital* 124: Sitting in the shack with…the cans over my ears. **1941** *AS* (Oct.) 164: *Cans.* Headphones. **1969** Crumley *One to Count Cadence* 43: He plugged his cans into Morning's console…. *1974 P. Wright *Lang. Brit. Industry* 84: Headphones are *cans* or *ear-muffs*. **1982** T.D. Connors *Dict. Mass Media* 43.

12.a. *Av.* a cylindrical chamber in an aircraft engine.

1933 Stewart "Airman Speech" 52: *Cans.* Cylinders. **1956** Heflin *USAF Dict.* 100: *Can*…Any one of the individual combustion chambers in a turbojet engine.

b. *Naut.* an engine boiler.

1968 Blackford *Torp. Sailor* 21 [ref. to 1916]: The order for all four cans (boilers) had been belayed as there were not enough firemen aboard to man them.

13. *Narc.* one ounce of an illicit drug.

1933 Ersine *Pris. Slang: Can*…An ounce of morphine. **1963** Braly *Shake Him* 85: Sullivan had hung him up…over a couple of cans of pot. **1970** Cortina *Slain Warrior* 9: A can is a one-ounce package. That'd go for ten dollars.

14. *Army.* a military canteen.

1940 Simonsen *Soldier Bill* 13 [ref. to 1914]: During the day he had learned that about a mile from the post there was a place they call the "Can," where beer and other drinks could be procured, provided you had the price.

15. *R.R.* a tank car.

1942 *ATS* 727. **1954–60** *DAS* 86. **1976** R. Adams *R.R. Lang.* 28: *Can.* A tank car.

16. *pl.* a woman's breasts.

1959 Ellison *Gentleman Junkie* 211: Trouble wore a sheath, and had a pair of cans like the headlights on a fire engine. **1961** C. Cooper *Weed* 12: The smoothest skin, the firmest bouncy cans, the rounded resilient ass, the yielding curve of the stomach. **1968** Baker et al. *CUSS* 93: *Cans*: the female breasts. **1965–70** in *DARE* [7 informants].

17. *Electronics.* a storage battery.

1954–60 *DAS*. **1962** Bonham *War Beneath Sea* 106 [ref. to WWII]: "How's our power holding out?"…"We're running on a nearly flat can right now."

18. *Aerospace.* a space capsule.

1973 M. Collins *Carrying the Fire* 22: Man, they were here to *fly*, not to be locked up in a can and shot around the world like ammunition.…Old Deke must have taken leave of his senses to forsake a fighter test assignment to get shot off somewhere in a tin can.

¶ In phrases:

¶ **carry the can** to take blame or responsibility.

1970 in *BDNE*.

¶ **chase the can** to purchase beer in a can; rush the GROWLER.

*ca*1900 in Harlow *Old Bowery* 426: The old man he ain't working,/But the can he likes to chase. **1902** Mead *Word-Coinage* 167: "Chasing the can," or the "duck," "rolling the rock," and "rushing" or "working the growler" all mean sending the tin can to the corner barroom for beer.

¶ **from can to can't** *So.* without stint; all day long.

1968 J. Lester *Look Out Whitey* 58: You'd still be down on Mr. Charlie's plantation working from can to can't. **1974** Perry & Sudyk *Me & Spitter* 52: Most of the year, a tobacco farmer spent five days a week, "can till can't" (from the time you *can* see the sun till the time you *can't*).

¶ **get the can** see **(4),** above.

¶ **hit the can, 1.** to drink beer or other liquor in excess.

1922 F.L. Packard *Doors of Night* 262: Youse have been hittin' de can, have youse? **1933** *Winners of the West* (Feb. 28) 1: He ain't no temp'rance advocate; he likes to "hit the can."

2. [sugg. by *kick the bucket* s.v. KICK] to die; commit suicide.

1978 *UTSQ* (Nov. 29): [Die]…*kick off, hit the can, kick the bucket.* **1981** *Nat. Lampoon* (July) 55: Maybe he should hit the can and do himself a favor.

¶ **in the can** [cf. CAN, *v.*, 2 and CANNED, *adj.*] **1.** Orig. *Film.* completed.

***1934** in Partridge *DSUE* (ed. 2) 537: When a film is completed it is "in the can." **1942** *ATS* 605: *In the can*…said of a completed picture or scene. **1954–60** *DAS* 87: *Put in the can*…To finish a project or task…*Not common.* **1961** R.L. Scott *Boring Holes* 198: By Christmas the story was on film and "in the cans." **1964** in Marx *Groucho Letters* 280: We all considered the day a triumph if we had one shot in the can by noon. **1969** N.Y.C. editor, age *ca*40: The film version is already in the can. **1981** Univ. Tenn. grad. student: I've got three more chapters of the dissertation in the can. **1988** Breathed *Bloom Co.* (synd. cartoon strip) (Nov. 1): We're up forty points…[The election] is, like,…*in the can!*

2. *Horse Racing.* (see quot.).

1968 Ainslie *Racing Guide* 469: *In the can*—an out-of-the-money finish; "in the crapper," etc.

¶ **rattle the can** to beg money on a public street.

1947 Boyer *Dark Ship* 199: Other seamen were sent to Times Square to "rattle the can" as they solicited contributions from the public.

¶ **rush the can** to drink freely at a bar; *chase the can,* above.

1919 in Braynard *Greatest Ship* I 244: Think of the party we could have if we had this aboard now and we were allowed to "rush the can." **1930** in *DA* 253. **1934** Lomax & Lomax *Amer. Ballads & Folk Songs* 346: I've lived on earth so long/That I used to sing this song/When Abraham and Isaac rushed the can. **1954** L. Armstrong *Satchmo* 112: He would…buy everyone in sight a drink. Then he would really rush the can.

¶ **shut your can!** shut up.

1919 *Blackhawk Howitzer* 50: Shut your —— can!

¶ **tie a can on** to go on a drinking spree; to get drunk. Also vars.

1923 in J. O'Hara *Sel. Letters* 6: I've had one can on since I last wrote…I got nicely fried. **1929** D. Parker, in *DAS* 88: A gal used to throw herself out the window every time she got a can on. **1941** Mahin & Grant *Johnny Eager* (film): Now don't pin another can on, will you? **1951** Mailer *Barbary Shore* 46: They really tie a can on.…He just goes around with her to night clubs and to the beach, the country club. **1956** I. Shulman *Good Deeds* 92: We'll go back to the house and tie on a real can.

¶ **tie a can to** [or **on**] [sugg. by the child's cruel prank of tying a can to the tail of a dog] **1.** to send packing; to get rid of or dismiss; to quit or stop; to CAN (in similar senses).

1899 Ade *Horne* 207: The "little lady" rejected him, or, to use his own language, "tied a can to him." **1901** Ade *Modern Fables* 7: She had tied a can to [husband] No. 2 and come out in Bright Colors. **1903** Ade *Society* 149: If one of those Squabs should begin to pursue you, what would you do?…I think…that I would tie a large can to him. **1906** Ford *Shorty McCabe* 138: Outside of that I'm a stray, and anyone that gets the fit ties a can to me. **1911** Van Loan *Big League* 66: I got a notion to tie a can on you for the rest of the season! **1912** *DN* III 572: To dismiss one summarily…"to tie a can to." **1918** Wagar *Spotter* 89: We tied the can to him yesterday. **1919** *Wadsworth Gas Attack* (Mar.) 20: They've tied the can to Alcohol. **1922** Rice *Adding Machine* 114: Aw, tie a can to that! **1926** Dunning & Abbott *Broadway* 224: Then we'll tie the merry old can to this saloon, eh kid? **1931** Cressey *Taxi-Dance Hall* 41: I used to have a steady boy friend, but he tied the can to me, and now I'm footloose. **1932** J.T. Farrell *Guillotine Party* 181: Did Lillian…tie a can to him? **1939** "E. Queen" *Dragon's Teeth* 184: It's a plant, a frame-up! He's been bribed to say that! You'd better tie the can on him, too, Pop! **1940** O'Hara *Pal Joey* 82: They tied a can to my tail in Ohio. **1941** West *Flying Wild* (film): So they tied a can to you. **1943** in Stillwell, *Papers* 177: So I tied a can to him. Relieved him as deputy chief of staff. **1949** R. MacDonald *Moving Target* 155: Tie a can to it, for Christ's sake! **1958** Gilbert *Vice Trap* 36: Well, there it was. I had the old can tied to me. **1971** Curtis *Banjo* 82: I'm glad to see you tie a can on these crummy thieves.

2. to add a touch to and be done with; to finish up.

1978 Black *Clonemaster* (NBC-TV): To tie a can to it, he's not in any hospital or jail—and he's not in the morgue.

can *v.* **1.a.** to get rid of, expel, discharge, eject, jilt, or dismiss; (now *specif.*) to discharge from employment.

[**1893** Small *Comic History* 29: The Colonists…soon shut him up completely—canned him, so to speak.] **1905** *DN* III 73: *Can, v.tr.*…To expel or suspend. Used by students. "Jim was up before the Faculty and got *canned* for two weeks." Common. **1908** *Hampton's Mag.* (Dec.) 762: I've been canned! Fired! Lost my job! **1910** T.A. Dorgan, in *N.Y. Eve. Jour.* (Jan. 18) 12: They canned poor Sam last night. **1913** *Sat. Eve. Post* (Mar. 1) 38: Breakin' that poor kid's heart by never lookin' once at her all day! I'd 'a' canned you for good if I was her! **1912–14** in E. O'Neill *Lost Plays* 46: I tried to be straight and hold down a job, but as soon as anyone got wise I'd been in a reform school they canned me same as they did you. **1915** Howard *God's Man* 136: He canned her in five months, and grabbed Cleo Darcy. **1916** S. Lewis *Job* 264: I've been fired!…Canned. **1921** in *DAE* I 401: He had trouble in prep school and was canned. **1922** Rice *Adding Machine* 105: Wait a minute, boss.…You mean I'm canned? **1927** Thrasher *The Gang* 34: About twenty Polish boys, "canned" from the settlement, organized a gang they called the "Corporation." **1928** Delmar *Bad Girl* 8: She met someone she knew on the boat and canned me. **1929–30** J.T. Farrell *Young Lonigan* 31: Three naughty little boys who had been canned from school. **1945** Horman & Grant *Here Come the Co-Eds* (film): If he cans Molly we got no basketball team. **1956** Marchant *Desk Set* 35: Well, if we *do* get canned, we won't be the only ones to lose our job through a machine. **1957** Bannon *Odd Girl* 157: If you get caught, we all get canned. **1960** Williams *Angry Ones* 116: He canned me that very day. **1969** Searls *Hero Ship* 125: I'm canning Catlett, for your information, and it could happen to you! **1992** *Middle Ages* (CBS-TV): Canned! Thirty damn years and I'm canned!

b. to stop or give up; leave off.

1906 H. Green *Actors' Boarding House* 187: Can that line o' comedy! **1908** H. Green *Maison de Shine* 60: You can that stuff! **1911** Van Loan *Big League* 136: They'll be a lot more accidents…if these fellows don't "can" the shoulder thing. **1912–14** in E. O'Neill *Lost Plays* 39: Can that chatter, d'yuh hear me? **1918** Witwer *Baseball to Boches* 221: Take this and can that chatter. **1919** Darling *Jargon Book* 7: *Can it*—Stop it, shut up. **1919** Kelly *What Outfit, Buddy?* 15: Can that stuff. You don't need to know anythin' about ridin' a horse in this man's army. **1929–30** J.T. Farrell *Young Lonigan* 102: He climbed up the ladders and slid down…but canned it because the ladders were for young squirts. **1953** E. Hunter *Jungle Kids* 25: Oh, can it and sell it. **1966** Neugeboren *Big Man* 12: Oh, can it already, huh? I don't want to hear. **1971** *Playboy* (Jan.) 255: Gonna can the studying for a bit, Peter, old boy? **1978** Strieber *Wolfen* 169: Can that bullshit.

c. to dispose of as garbage; (*hence*) to cancel (a project or the like).

1930 Irwin *Tramp & Und. Sl.*: *Can*…to dispose of in a can or receptacle for refuse or offal. **1972** N.Y.U. student: When I told my professor that he didn't have to hold on to the final exams more than six months, he said, "You mean now I can can them?" **1985** *N.Y. Times* (Sept. 1) 4 E: Weinberger cans a weapon.…The project was to be killed…because …the gun "didn't work well enough." **1987** in *Black Teen* (Jan. 1988) 10: I wrote the song.…Initially we were going to can it.

2. [cf. CANNED, *adj.*, 1 and *in the can*, 1 s.v. CAN, *n.*] to record phonographically. Now *colloq.*

1918 McBride *Emma Gees* 136: It's a pity some one can not take a phonograph into the lines and "can" some of these things. **1919** Wallgren *AEF Cartoons* (unp.): Get one of his little old morning talks canned to take home with you. **1924** in Charters & Kunstadt *Jazz* 149: The latter was "canned" by them for Brunswick several weeks ago.

3. [fr. the *n.*] *Police.* to imprison; lock up.

1929 in Partridge *Dict. Und.* 102: "Canned for a sleep" means that you are jailed for the night. **1958** *N.Y. Times Mag.* (Mar. 16) 87: *Canned*— Imprisoned. *a*1968 in Haines & Taggart *Ft. Lauderdale* 12: She said that if I touched her, she'd report me to the fuzz and get me canned for rape. **1977** Langone *Life at Bottom* 192: Well, we canned him for three days, and we sent a message out when we locked this dude up. **1990** "Sir Mix-A-Lot" *National Anthem* (rap song): Prosecutor says "Can him."

4. *Golf.* to sink (a putt).

1970 Scharff *Encyc. of Golf* 416: *Can.* To hole a putt.

5. to copulate with anally.

1945–49 Monteleone *Crim. Slang* 43: *Canned* [*sic*]…A sodomite; one having sexual connection by the anus. **1971** Sorrentino *Up from Never* 260: The examining psychiatrist asked him if he would be able to get along without women for a long period. "Oh yeah," he answered. "I seen a lotta sweet lookin' lieutenants I wouldn't mind canning."

Canal *n. Mil.* Guadalcanal.—constr. with *the*. Now *hist.*

1943 Horan & Frank *Boondocks* 33: Ask any Marine who was on the "canal." **1943** in *Best from Yank* 23: Near Lunga Point on the north central shore of the 'Canal. **1951–52** Frank *Hold Back Night* 6: It was just before we sailed for New Zealand to be staged for The 'Canal. **1974** L.D. Miller *Valiant* 6: I was at Kwajalein and Guam, and the 'Canal, too! **1988** Hynes *Flights of Passage* 87: They talked about the 'Canal or the Coral Sea.

canal boats *n.pl.* big or clumsy shoes; (*also*) big feet.

1926 *Sat. Eve. Post* (Nov. 6) 132: Yuh wanta be careful where yuh throw them canal boats o' yours. **1926** Maines & Grant *Wise-Crack Dictionary* 6: *Canalboats*—Large sized shoes. **1929** Segar *Thimble Th.* 45: Blow me down! Canal boats for feet on a lady! **1935** *AS* X 9: Feet…canal boats. **1951** in *DARE* I 527. **1960** Leckie *March to Glory* 94: Hey, Moose, when I die I want you to take my boots to keep those canalboats of yours warm. *a*1961 in R. Goodman *Masterpieces* 271: He had been wearing his father's leather canal-boats, size 14. **1965–70** in *DARE* I 527.

canal wrench *n.* (see quot.). *Joc.*

1972 Haslam *Oil Fields* 97: *Canal Wrench*, n. a long-handled shovel.

canary *n.* **1.** [sugg. by the bosun's whistle] *Naut.* a bosun's mate.

1821 Stewart *Man-of-War's-Man* I 32: But I must belay, my gallant lads, for our time is approaching and our canaries will be chirping for us directly.

2.a. a woman.

***1862** H. Mayhew *London Labour* IV: Sometimes a woman, called a "canary," carries the [burglar's] tools, and watches outside. **1886** in *AS* (Feb. 1950). **1900** *DN* II 26: *Canary*…A servant girl [or] woman student [at Tufts College]. **1934** H. Roth *Call It Sleep* 294: Wod a kinerry we seen! **1945** *Am. N & Q* (Feb.) 171: I thought that you were just perching here with some canary. **1971** Tak *Truck Talk* 35: *Connivin' canary*: a woman trucker who uses her wits and resources…to obtain good loads. **1980** Kotzwinkle *Jack* 235: "Time for the canary exhibit." Crutch pulled Twiller toward the girly tent.

b. *Music Industry.* a vocalist, esp. if female.

***1886** in Ware *Passing English* 62: Chorus singing by the canaries has long been a South London institution. ***1909** Ware *Passing English* 62: Canary (*Music Hall*, 1870). Chorus-singer amongst the public—gener-

ally in the gallery. **1919** Darling *Jargon Book* 6: *Canary*—Singer. **1936** Parker *Battling Hoofer* (film): Come on, canary, get your nose wet. **1936** Darling & Belden *Chan at Opera* (film): I got a personal grudge against that canary. **1937** in *AS* 45: *Canary*, a woman vocalist. **1958** S.H. Adams *Tenderloin* 107: That's all to the good…but it don't make him no canary. **1966** "Petronius" *N.Y. Unexp.* 173: Swell late parties with the best rug cutters and canaries around. **1980** *60 Minutes* (CBS-TV) (June 22): She just barely made enough money to pay the rent as a band singer—a "canary"—in the forties. **1992** (quot. at THRUSH).

3. a burro or mule.—usu. constr. with a place name. *Joc.*

1876 W. Wright *Big Bonanza* 114 [ref. to 1860]: The donkey [was] called by everybody in that region, "The Washoe Canary." **1892** Bierce *Beetles* 24: Washoe canaries on the Geiger Grade/ Subdue the singing of their cavalcade. **1898** in Davidson *Old West* 23: So, moved by notes, most deem scary,/Some dub him now the new canary. *Ibid*: He's a burro—a true canary. **1905** E.F. Langdon *Cripple Creek* 136: They found it to be a burro (Rocky mountain canary) that had been wandering around. **1918** *Stars & Stripes* (Feb. 8) 7: Kindness, the order says in effect, will work wonders with the genus Missouri nightingale, or Indiana canary. **1918** *Stars & Stripes* (Mar. 8) 8: Ye're fine muleskinners, so ye are! Protectin' yerselves and forgettin' the poor canaries! **1919** Wilson *364th Inf.* 46 [ref. to 1918]: The doughboys grumbled some because they had to preserve silence, while the ever-present "Missouri canaries" could sound off whenever they pleased.…The wronged "canaries" were good publicity agents. **1921** Dienst *353rd Inf.* 247 [ref. to 1918]: Their only regret was that the…French horses were not "Missouri canaries." **1930** Nason *Corporal* 134: It was the trill of the old Rocky Mountain canary. **1934** Weston & Cunningham *Old Fashioned Way* (film): Will you sit down, my little Rocky Mountain canary? **1935** Pollock *Underworld*: *Arizona canary*, a burro.

4. *Army.* a Spaniard.—used contemptuously.

1898 *Chicago Record's War Stories* 84: The Spaniards fought well…and tonight the Americans entertain large respect for the "yellow canaries."

5. *Stu.* a cigarette.

1900 *DN* II 26: *Canary*…A cigarette.

6. [sugg. by SING, *v.*] an informer; stool pigeon.

1929 Botkin *Folk-Say* I 110: *Canary*…in the taxi lingo is applied to the tattler and the company spotter. **1929** Hostetter & Beesley *Racket* 221: *Canary*—Informer; especially, one who gives information to the police. **1932** *Writer's Digest* (Aug.) 46: The informer…is put down as a "canary." **1945** *Am. N & Q* (Jan.) 149: *Canary*: New York City Police Department term for any underworld character who "sings." **1954** Schulberg *Waterfront* 257: All I want to know is, is he D 'n D or is he a canary. **1962** Perry *Young Man Drowning* 143: A show-off is only a few steps away from being a canary. **1972** *N.Y. Times* (May 7) 11: A "wheel man" drives the getaway car for his buddies after, say, a bank robbery.…"Singing" is what a stool pigeon (otherwise known as a canary) does. **1984** *N.Y. Post* (Dec. 27) 14: Mob Canary Sings Again For the Feds. **1992** *Married with Children* (Fox-TV): You canaries…can't be trusted!

7. *Pris.* CANARY-BIRD, 1.

1930 Lait *On the Spot* 200: *Canary*…Prisoner. **1933** Ersine *Pris. Slang* 24: *Canary*, *n.* a convict.

8. an unwanted squeak in machinery.

1937–41 in Mencken *Amer. Lang. Supp.* II 724.

9. *P.O.W.'s in Germany, WWII.* a clandestine radio receiver.

1955 Klaas *Maybe I'm Dead* 13: I just got it over the canary.

canary *v.* **1.** *Und.* to turn informer; SING.

1933 (cited in Partridge *Dict. Und.* 102). **1958** Motley *Epitaph* 381: He was going to canary and the pusher went around to jail and told him, "Don't talk."

2. *Music Industry.* to sing as a vocalist.

1944 *Collier's* (Sept. 23) 69: She had to go back to canarying.

canary-bird *n.* **1.** a convict; prisoner.

***1725** *New Canting Dict.*: *Canary-Bird*, a Rogue or Whore taken, and clapp'd into the Cage or Round-house. **1859** Matsell *Vocab.* 17: *Canary-bird*. a convict.

2. a gold coin.

***1842** in *OEDS*. **1889** Barrère & Leland *Dict. Slang* I 221: A goldpiece is also called a "canary-bird" in New York. **1895** Sinclair *Alabama* [ref. to Civil War]: Say, Bill, what are you going to drive at when you fists the "canary-birds"?

canary hatch *n.* LOONY BIN.

1966 Bogner *7th Ave.* 302: You pull yourself together or you'll wind up in a canary hatch.

canasta *n.* the genitals.
1965 Trimble *Sex Words* 37: *Canasta*…1. The Penis. 2. The Vagina. Mainly Homosexual usage. **1973** *Zap Comix* (No. 6) (unp.): You've got a canasta like the transatlantic cable, baby.

cancer *n.* severe rust, as on a motor vehicle.
1977 Philadelphia waitress, age 22: The Penn police won't pass your car if it's got rust spots. They call it *cancer*. They say your car has body cancer. **1978** Hamill *Dirty Laundry* 112: I'll loan you my car. It's got cancer, but it still goes. **1983** S. King *Christine* 300: The Fury's bod…had an advanced case of cancer. **1986–87** K.G. Wilson *Van Winkle's Return* 80: My car has cancer of the fenders.

¶ In phrase: **catch a cancer** [L *cancer* 'crab'] *Stu.* to catch a CRAB while rowing.
*1857 (cited in Partridge *DSUE* (ed. 2) 123). *a*1860 in *DAE* I 405 [at Yale Univ.]

Cancer Alley *n.* an area, esp. a heavily industrialized area, having or presumed to have a high rate of cancer.
1981 N.J. State Health Comm. Joan Finley (WINS radio) (Aug. 7): It was discovered that we no longer need to be dubbed "Cancer Alley" and that we're no worse—and no better—than the rest of the country in regard to the cancer rate. **1984** WINS radio news (Aug. 21): She says, based on this report, that New Jersey's reputation as "Cancer Alley" may be unwarranted. **1985** Univ. Tenn. instructor, age 36: *Cancer Alley* is New Jersey. **1988** *Headline News Network* (Nov. 12): "Cancer Alley" [is] an eighty-five-mile stretch between Baton Rouge and New Orleans.…The…corridor is in the top ten percent of lung cancer deaths for white males. **1992** *Sonya Live* (CNN-TV) (Aug. 10): The place that we're living in [in Texas] is called Cancer Alley.

cancer stick *n.* a cigarette.
[*1919 Downing *Digger Dialects* 17: *Consumption Stick.*—A cigarette.] **1958** J. Davis *College Vocab.* 13: *Cancer Stick*—Cigarette. *1959 in *OEDS* I 425: First cancer stick today. **1961** in *AS* XXXIX (Oct. 1964) 235: *Cancer stick*…A cigarette. **1963** *AS* XXXVIII 276: Cigarettes are called *cancer sticks*. **1964** N.Y.C. high-school student: I quit smokin' them damn cancer sticks. **1966** in IUFA *Folk Speech: Cancer-stick*—cigarette. **1970** *Nat. Lampoon* (Nov.) 40: A bunny hopping cancer stick? **1983** K. Rowell *Outsiders* (film): Hey, you got a cancer stick, Johnny?

can-do *interj.* [pidgin] Orig. *Naut.* I can do it; it can be done. Hence **no can do.** Also *adj., n.*
*1903 R. Kipling, in *OEDS*: "Four hundred and twenty knots."…"Can do," said Moorshed. **1906** *Independent* (Jan. 4) 30: No can do, Johnny, no can do.…Him gloatee too muchee lolry. **1913** *Review of Reviews* (Aug.) 201: "No got" in the [Philippine] islands is the most commonly used expression for "I haven't any." Similarly "no can do" means "I can't." **1921** *15th Inf. Sentinel* (Feb. 11) 4: Among the many suggestions for a regimental motto probably the most popular seems to be the two-word phrase "Can Do." **1922** Rollins *Cowboy* 78 [ref. to 1890's]: Pidgin English contributed…"no can do" [which] definitely expressed personal impotence. **1923** Witwer *Fighting Blood* 141: I've tried everything I know to get this gil to fight us and no can do! **1925** Williams *15th Inf. Annual* 49: "F" Company of the CAN DO outfit. **1930** in Segar *Thimble Th.* 144: No can do! **1933** Thomason *Salt Winds* 150: Can do. Slak, you heard him. **1939** "E. Queen" *Dragon's Teeth* 23: "You'll investigate." "No can do." **1943** *Newsweek* (Oct. 4) 67: "*Can do*" is their motto. **1945** Bellah *Ward 20* 47: I want a midnight pass. Can do? **1952** Himes *First Stone* 133: No can do. **1961** Forbes *Goodbye to Some* 180 [ref. to WWII]: They don't have Yankee know-how and can-do. **1972** Kaplan & Hunt *Coast Guard* 230: The "can-do" spirit. **1977** Langone *Life at Bottom* 176: The can-do spirit of the officers and men assigned to the most arduous peacetime duty the Navy has to offer has reaffirmed my faith in the ingenuity and adaptability of Navymen. **1980** S. Fuller *Big Red* 140: No can do, Sergeant. **1987** M. Hastings *Korean War* 99: Inchon remains a monument to "can do," to improvisation and risk-taking on a magnificent scale.

candy *n.* **1.a.** something that is excellent, easy, or profitable; the best.—usu. constr. with *the.*
1892 in Dobie *Rainbow in the Morning* 163: My baby's a salty dog,/…My baby's the candy. **1908** in H.C. Fisher *A. Mutt* 158: "I'll go now and get a couple of turkeys." "Oh! that'll be the candy." **1908** in Blackbeard & Williams *Smithsonian Comics* 58: Fine and dandy. You're all the candy. **1910** *N.Y. Eve. Jour.* (Apr. 7) 17: Brid was the candy at bat, also. **1931** *Amer. Merc.* (Dec.) 405: I'm the kid that's all the candy. **1942** *ATS* 266: Something easy…*candy*,…*easy pickin's*, [etc.]. **1953** Paley *Rumble* 185: What the hell yuh look so grim about! This is what the big guys called candy!

b. *Baseball.* an easily hit pitch.
1929 *N.Y. Times* (June 2) IX 2: When a batter amasses three or four safe "blows" in one game, he is said to be "hitting candy." *ca*1985 in Random House files: *Baseball:* "[The] pitch was candy."

2. *Narc.* an illicit psychotropic drug of any sort, now esp. capsules of stimulants or depressants.
1931 *AS* VI (Aug.) 437 [ref. to 1920's]: *Candy, n.* Cocaine. **1939** Howsley *Argot* 11: *Candy*—gum opium, hasheesh. Sometimes wrongly used in referring to other narcotics. **1968** Louria *Drug Scene* 208: *Candy.* cocaine. **1968–69** McWhirter *Dunlop Encyc.* 523: Phenobarbitone…*candy.* **1970** Horman & Fox *Drug Awareness* 464: *Candy*—barbiturates. **1976** C. Keane *Hunter* 247: By that time she's ready to eat through a half mile of buffalo shit to get her candy.

candy *adj.* *Labor.* **1.** CANDY-ASSED.
1911 *Hampton's Mag.* (Jan.) 20: Are you going to let a fashion plate, a candy dude, insult us in this way? **1951** in *DAS* 87: I don't like razzin' from any of you candy comics! **1970** *Current Slang* V 4: *Candy, adj.* Cowardly.— High school students, both sexes, New Mexico. **1989** D. Sherman *There I Was* 127: We'd heard…CAPs…were candy duty, sitting in safe villes.

2. (of a job or the like) having pleasant or advantageous conditions; soft; easy.
1930 "D. Stiff" *Milk & Honey* 201: *Candy job* is the pleasant job. **1942** *AS* (Dec.) 220: *Candy Side.* The "side" of a high-lead [logging] camp which has the best equipment; the opposite of *haywire side.* **1958** McCulloch *Woods Words* 28: *Candy side*—The side, or operating unit, which has the best timber or logging conditions. **1976** R. Adams *R.R. Lang.* 29: *Candy run:* A short, easy haul.

candy-ass *n.* **1.a.** a weakling or coward.—usu. considered vulgar.
[**1933** *Leatherneck* (Apr.) 14: Pvt. Bob McCallum, a recruit who looked like a potential fighting man when he enlisted, has been shanghaied into the clerical force and now carries the moniker Candy Ankles.] **1966** Shepard *Doom Pussy* 58: If a new young troop…threatened to behave like a candy-ass, Nails would tell him.…**1968** Tauber *Sunshine Soldiers* 185: "Bye, Cubby, you candy-ass," I call. **1971** Meggyesy *Out of Their League* 56: The rest of you guys are candy asses, you're not fit to be national champions. **1973** Yount *Last Shot* 111: You may be a candy-ass when the chips are down. **1980** *New West* (Jan. 1981) 94: He thought the cars were effete little toys for candy asses. **1992** *Melrose Place* (Fox-TV): "Look at Emily Dickinson—she hardly left her house." "What a candy-ass!"

b. cowardice or weakness.—constr. with *the.*—usu. considered vulgar.
1967 W. Crawford *Gresham's War* 114: You've changed. Got the candyass now, huh?

2. a sweet or sexy young girl.—sometimes used derisively.—usu. considered vulgar.
[**1972** Hannah *Geronimo Rex* 31: Don't you know…that you can't go around giving everybody a smile like your ass was made of candy?] **1973** Pace Univ. student: A *candy-ass* is a sweet-assed, sensual girl. I learned that expression about five years ago [in N.Y.C.]. **1976** Braly *False Starts* 274: I was the sugar daddy, and she almost dangerously young candyass.

candy-assed or **candy-ass** *adj.* **1.** soft; weak; unmanly.—usu. considered vulgar.
1952 Uris *Battle Cry* 182 [ref. to 1942]: And then we began to pass outfits along the route, crapped out and exhausted. "Candy-ass Marines," our boys would shout as we flashed past them. *Ibid.* 188: Come on, Burnside, getting candy-assed? *Ibid.* 209: I whipped that candy-assed gyrene twenty-eight bottles to twenty-three. **1971** *N.Y. Post* (July 8) 33: I wanted to show the Army I wasn't just some candy-assed New York Reservist. **1972** *Nat. Lampoon* (Aug.) 61: Listen, you candy-assed son-of-a-bitch, don't come whining to me. **1972** C. Gaines *Stay Hungry* 249: A three-hundred pound weightlifter turned bodybuilder…still thought posing a little candyass. **1977** S. Gaines *Discotheque* 180: It was a candy assed thing to do, Stella thought, to take a man's drug away from him. **1980** Gould *Ft. Apache* 187: But I ain't freezin' on no candy-ass fuckin' picket line.

2. insufficiently challenging.—usu. considered vulgar.
1974 U.C.L.A. student: That was a real candy-ass exam. **1990** Poyer *Gulf* 50: They're candy-ass…airplanes.

candy-bar punk *n.* *Pris.* a convict who has become a passive homosexual in prison.—usu. used contemptuously.
1962–68 B. Jackson *In the Life* 182: You very seldom catch an outside

fag enter here. Most of what you have in here are known as candy-bar punks.

candy boy *n.* CANDY KID.
1901 Hobart *Down the Line* 82: I was her candy boy for sure.

candy bucket *n. Constr.* (see quot.).
1965 O'Neill *High Steel* 270: *Candy bucket.* A bucket used to raise dirt from a shaft.

candy-cock *n.* CANDY KID.
1925 Mullin *Scholar Tramp* 296 [ref. to *ca*1912]: Well, if ol' Red ain't the candy-cock! *Shavin*'! Kin ye beat that?

candy kid *n.* **1.** a sweet or well-behaved person; (*hence*) a sissy.
1905 T.A. Dorgan, in Zwilling *TAD Lexicon* 24: Smith yer the candy kid. **1906** in McCay *Nemo* 33: Nemo will follow the candy kid any-where....Nemo, this is the candy kid of slumberland, Little Bon Bon. **1912** Lowrie *Prison* 194: I've got him thinking I'm the sweetest candy kid that ever happened. **1924** Henderson *Keys to Crookdom* 400: *Candy kid.*...a pretty boy. **1927** Thrasher *Gang* 216: One day the boys in our crowd were riding their bicycles in a poorer section of town on the other side of the creek. Some of the boys of that part of the town came out yelling "candy kids" and began throwing stones. **1958** McCulloch *Woods Words* 28: *Candy kid.*...A mama's boy.
2.a. a fellow who is lucky, successful, or held in high favor, esp. with women.—*occ.* applied to women.
1906 *Nat. Police Gaz.* (Oct. 20) 10: We used to think Kid McCoy was the "Candy Kid" at getting the coin. **1910** *N.Y. Eve. Jour.* (Mar. 22) 18: Hurray! Kid Biffo wins in th' 16th round! Ain't he th' candy kid? **1910** *Volunteer* (Univ. Tenn.) 26: Orator, scholar, and a leader, but, above all, the "candy kid" with the ladies. **1912** Lowrie *Prison* 153: We're certainly th' candy kids when it comes t' that kind o' work. **1918** *Everybody's* (Aug.) 37: They said that Chicago layout were the Candy Kids. **1919** I. Cobb *Life of Party* 37: Oh, you cutey! Oh, you cut-up!...Oh, you candy kid! **1926** Finerty *Criminalese* 13: *Candy kid*—a fair-haired boy with women. **1936** Cain *Double Indemnity* 393: I was the candy kid in both offices that spring. They were all taking off their hats to me. **1937** in J. O'Hara *Sel. Letters* 124: Regards, The Candy Kid. **1941** Cain *Mildred Pierce* 292: After she's been Mr. Hannen's candy kid? The one that was going to New York and play the pyanner so they'd all be hol-lering for her? **1952** Bellow *Augie March* 62: The candy kid of city politics.
b. a stylishly dressed person.
1913 *DN* IV 16: *Candykid.* A fine fellow; a showy, stylish person...."He's a candykid all right." "She is some candykid." **1934** Weseen *Dict. Slang* 316: *Candy kid*—A stylish youth; a dude. **1944** Bontemps & Cullen *St. Louis Woman* 9: New suit and dicty lid/Call me the candy kid.

candy-leg *n. Stu.* a wealthy fellow who is attractive to women.
1920 McKenna *315th Inf.* 155: "Candy Legs" McHenry. **1934** Weseen *Dict. Slang* 176: *Candy leg*—A male student who is popular with the girls. **1942** *ATS* 770: *Candy leg*, a wealthy ladies' man. **1945** *AS* (Oct.) 233: *Candy leg.* Rich fellow.

candyman *n.* **1.** CANDY KID, 2.
1913 *DN* IV 16: *Candyman.* A dandy fellow; a stylish, showy person. Used in Nebraska. "He's quite a *candyman.*" "There goes a *candyman.*" **1934** in Leadbitter & Slaven *Blues Records* 463: Candy Man Blues.
2. *Narc.* a seller of illicit drugs, esp. in capsule form.
1969 Lingeman *Drugs* 34: *Candy man*...peddler or pusher of drugs. **1975** Sepe & Telano *Cop Team* 65: He might be the candy man. **1981** WCBS-TV editorial (June 24): A high-school reporter interviewed a drug dealer identified only as "The Candyman." **1984** "W.T. Tyler" *Shadow Cabinet* 178: The candy man for that crowd over there, a drug dealer.
3. *CB.* the Federal Communications Commission or one of its field agents.—*constr. with the.*
1976 Bibb et al. *CB Bible* 122: The Candyman Strikes Back....In fiscal year 1975, the FCC issued 1,363 notices of apparent liability.

candy-stripe *v. Hosp.* to work as a CANDY-STRIPER.
1974 Strasburger *Rounding Third* 23: She does stuff like...candy-strip-ing in hospitals. **1976** Price *Bloodbrothers* 108: You come with me, you be makin' more bread in two weeks than you'll make candy-stripin' for two months.

candy-striper *n.* [sugg. by the usu. red and white "candy-cane" stripes on the uniform] *Hosp.* a young woman who is a volunteer nurse's aide. Now *S.E.*
1963 (cited in *W9*). **1968** "Dear Abby" (synd. newspaper column)

(Mar. 14): Mary...is a candy-striper at the local hospital. **1974** *Seattle Post-Intell.* (Aug. 4) C8: The doctor...left home 10 years ago with a 12-year-old candy striper. **1979** Gutcheon *New Girls* 231: Why can't she be a candy-striper at the hospital like all her friends?

candy team *n.* an especially docile or otherwise favored team, as of mules.
1930 "D. Stiff" *Milk & Honey* 201: *Candy team* is the favorite span of mules in the outfit.

candy wagon *n.* **1.** a buggy.
1937 Steinbeck *Mice & Men* 70: Carlson, you get the candy wagon hitched up.
2. a light motor vehicle used in trucking or construction; (*specif.*) a crew truck.
1942 *AS* (Apr.) 103: *Candy Wagon.* Light truck. **1958** McCulloch *Woods Words* 28: *Candy wagon*—a crew truck. **1968** R. Adams *Western Words* (ed. 2) 52: *Candy wagon.* In logging, a station wagon or bus that transports men to and from work. **1971** Tak *Truck Talk* 26: *Candy wagon*: a lightweight truck. **1971** Curtis *Banjo* 130: Gus and Salty...checked out each truck and the tail-end candy-wagon supply truck.

cane *n.* **1.** the penis. Hence **varnish the cane** to copulate.
1879 in J.M. Carroll *Camp Talk* 128: In fact the only use I have for a cane is to have it varnished, and that one I [already] have. *ca*1888 *Stag Party* 227: What is the difference between a dude and a jackass? It is principally a difference in the size of their canes. **1967** Partridge *DSUE* (ed. 6) [Canadian]. **1968** Baker et al. *CUSS* 218: *Varnish the cane.* Have sexual intercourse.
2. var. CAINE.

Canes *n.pl. Sports.* the Univ. of Miami Hurricanes.
1984 *N.Y. Post* (Sept. 3) 34: Kosar's heroics save 'Canes.

can house *n.* Esp. *Chicago.* a brothel.
1906 in Longstreet *Wilder Shore* 323: As for the can houses, Maude Smith told me herself the husbands are staying so close to their wives like they were first married. **1929** in Farrell *Calico Shoes* 145: I don't like can houses. **1930** *Ibid.* 183: Cheap can houses,...ratty saloons. **1938** "Justinian" *Americana Sexualis* 15: *Can-House. n.* A house of prostitu-tion. Most popular C. 20 Americanism for the referent. Derivation unknown. **1946** Mezzrow & Wolfe *Really Blues* 29: The Roamer Inn was like a model of all the canhouses I ever saw around Chicago. *Ibid.* 303: *Canhouse*: whorehouse. **1947** Motley *Knock on Any Door* 85: Down by the railroad tracks and the flop houses and the can houses. **1973** *AS* XLVI 77.

canister *n.* **1.** the head.
***1811** *Lexicon Balatron.*: *Cannister.* The head. *To mill his cannister,* to break his head. ***1821–26** Stewart *Man-of-War's-Man* I 176: 'Twill be beat into your cannister in a twinkling. **1832** *Spirit of Times* (Mar. 3) 3: O'Hegan followed him up to meet a smashing hit on his *countenance* which confused his *cannister* for some moments. **1842** *Spirit of Times* (May 28) 153: Additional raps on the canister. **1870** *Putnam's Mag.* (Mar.) 301: The combatants struck each other...upon the head, the nut, the cone, the conk, the canister.
2. *Und.* **a.** a watch.
1904 *Life in Sing Sing* 247: *Canister.* A watch.
b. a jail; CAN, 5.
1914 Jackson & Hellyer *Crim. Slang* 22: *Canister,* Noun...A prison. **1933** Ersine *Prison Slang* 24: *Cannister, n.* Any jail.
c. a pistol.
1914 Jackson & Hellyer *Crim. Slang* 22: *Canister*...a firearm. Example: "He'll stick his hands up if you flash the canister." **1931** Wilstach *Under Cover Man* 169: Leave your cannister somewhere, not in your room. **1933** Ersine *Prison Slang* 24: *Cannister, n.*...a pistol.
d. a safe or vault. Cf. CAN, 9.
1933 Ersine *Prison Slang* 24: *Cannister, n.*...a safe, *pete.* "It took three blasts to crack the cannister."

canned *adj.* **1.** (of music) recorded phonographically. Now *colloq.*
1903 in "O. Henry" *Cabbages & Kings* 94: We'll export canned music to the Latins. **1915** Braley *Songs of Workaday World* 158: You may say my voice is raucous and the music I make is "canned,"/But you'll hear me singing my carols in every clime and land. **1917** *Lit. Digest* (Aug. 25) 29: That was canned jazz, but you didn't know it then. **1959** Griffin *Black Like Me* (Nov. 14): Canned jazz blared through the street with a monstrous high-strutting rhythm that pulled at the viscera.
2. drunk.—often constr. with *up.*

*1914 in *OEDS*. ***1925** in Fraser & Gibbons *Soldier & Sailor Wds.* 46 [ref. to WWI]: *Canned Up*: Drunk. ***1921** *N & Q* (Oct. 29) 345: *Canned*. Intoxicated. **1927** *AS* II (Mar.) 275: *Canned*. intoxicated. ***1930** Manning *Her Privates We* 35 [ref. to 1916]: They went into Sandby for a spree, and got properly canned there. **1935** E. Anderson *Hungry Men* 88: He must have been canned up. **1943** in Ruhm *Detective* 365: I'm too canned up to think good. **1963** D. Tracy *Brass Ring* 256: If a State trooper had ever found them all canned up at the scene of the wreck it would have been too bad. **1970** Gattzden *Black Vendetta* 38: Sauced….Canned. Don't know nothing.

canned Bill *n. Mil.* see s.v. BILL, *n.*

canned cow *n.* canned condensed milk.
    1925 *AS* I (Dec.) 137: "Chase that Java and canned cow over here, Stub." Asking for coffee and condensed milk. **1928** *AS* III (Apr.) 345: Of latter-day phraseology in Uncle Sam's merchant ships, one discovers at *chow-time* that the current request for the milk is to *pass the canned cow.*

canned goods *n.* a virgin.
    1918 in *AS* (Oct. 1933) 25: *Canned Goods.* Virgin, female or male. **1933** Odets *Awake & Sing!* 57: BESSIE: She don't feel well….MYRON: Canned goods….

canned Willie *n. Mil.* see s.v. WILLIE.

cannibal *n.* a person who practices active oral-genital intercourse.
    1916 Cary *Venery* I 36: *Cannibal*—A person who tongues one of the opposite sex. **1921** Lind *Impersonators* 141: You cannibal! Your nature's…disgustin! **1965** in Fry: This is no place/For cannibals. So stay out! **1967** de Coy *Nigger Bible* 128: Two to one, he is a "cannibal" who ate her before she ate him.

canno *n. USMC.* artillery fire.
    1970 Whitmore *Memphis-Nam-Sweden* 67 [ref. to 1967]: Mortars, rockets, artillery—all kinds of canno coming in on our asses. *Ibid.* 68: Right under all this canno coming in on us.

Cannock var. CANUCK.

cannon *n.* **1.a.** a firearm, esp. a large pistol of heavy caliber.
    1846 *Crockett's Almanac* (unp.): Ben swinged his huntin cannon about thar heads like Pat with a shillelah. **1861** in Harris *High Times* 282: I…seed another feller a rubbin brite a orful cannon; hit were es big es a pump log. **1887** DeVol *Gambler* 92: He handed over his young cannon, and I put up Betsy Jane. **1916** Griffith *Intolerance* (film): The boy tells the boss he won't need the "cannon" any more; he's through with the old life. **1919** S. Lewis *Free Air* 104: Pack a cannon, don't you? **1922** Rollins *Cowboy* 82: Some individual either ducked or "dug for his cannon." **1927** *Amer. Leg. Mo.* (Sept.) 87: A jimmy-legs with a big cannon belted on him. **1931** Armour *Little Caesar* (film): You take it easy with that cannon of yours. **1965** Bonham *Durango St.* 156: You ain't told us what we're going to do with this cannon. **1985** D. Killerman *Hellrider* 15: The large Virginian cannon slid from Heller's holster.
    b. a gun barrel.
    1976 "N. Ross" *Policeman* 41: There it was, a .44 mag with a six-inch cannon staring at me.
    c. a hired gunman.
    1918 in *AS* (Oct. 1933) 25: *Cannon.* 1. Revolver or pistol. 2. The thief who carried it. **1929** *N.Y. Times* (Aug. 22) 25: "A cannon fades a mark."…A gunman holds up a citizen. **1933** Ersine *Prison Slang* 24: *Cannon*….a gunman. "The boss hired a new cannon from Chi." **1955** Bezzerides *Kiss Me Deadly* (film): For a couple of cannons, you guys sure are polite. **1977** *Kojak* (CBS-TV): I told you—I want that cannon's name that hit Lenny.
    d. *Baseball.* a fastball pitcher; a powerful throwing arm.
    1978 K. Jackson, on *Monday Night Baseball* (ABC-TV) (June 26): And you saw his arm last week. Some cannon! **1978** *N.Y. Post* (June 28) 110: Talk about your American League super cannons and the names Ryan, Guidry, and Gossage dominate the conversation. **1988** *CNN Sports* (CNN-TV) (June 18): Barfield, with one of the finest cannons in the major leagues, fires a perfect strike.
    2. [sugg. by GUN] *Und.* **a.** a pickpocket, esp. if highly skilled.
    *a***1909** Tillotson *Detective* 92: *Gun, Cannon or Dip*—A pickpocket. **1921** *Variety* (July 22) 7: A carnival cum to this town with a flock of cannons from New York. **1923** Ornitz *Haunch, Paunch & Jowl* 48: If Archie'd stick to his line…he'd be a Cannon. **1924** *N.Y. Times* (Aug. 3) VIII 16: A pickpocket…is [called a] gun, or [hence] John Cannon. **1937** Reitman *Box-Car Bertha* 113: Most of the cannons (pickpockets) were married. **1955** Q. Reynolds *HQ* 235: I just collared a real live cannon. **1967** Beck *Pimp* 91: A "cannon" took the vacant stool on my right. **1992** N.

Cohn *Heart of World* 17: Serious thieves—*cannons, whizzes…*—did not have greedy hands.
    b. the practice of picking pockets.—constr. with *on the.*
    1933 Ersine *Prison Slang* 24: Blackstone Whitie has been on the cannon since he got out of stir. **1935** Pollock *Und. Speaks*: On the cannon, engaged in pickpocketing. **1956** Resko *Reprieve* 184: A guy that goes out on the cannon.
    3. BIGSHOT.
    1934 Halper *Foundry* 186: I goes up to the Big Shot and I says: "Listen, old cannon."
    4. the penis.
    1968 *Provincetown Rev.* VI 86: With his big cannon and balls. **1975** in *West. Folklore* XXXVI (1977) 359: Fire my cannon.

cannon *v. Und.* to pick pockets. Also trans.
    1925 (cited in Partridge *Dict. Und.* 103). **1946** N. Algren, in *Amer. Merc.* (Jan. 1947): You're too small to cannon the street-cars.

cannonball *n.* **1.a.** *R.R.* an express train. Now *colloq.*
    1894 in J. London *Tramp Diary* 55: We caught the "Cannon Ball." **1897** Hamblen *General Mgr.* 85: This ain't no cannon-ball engine. Set down there 'n' watch out fer signals! *Ibid.* 171: One night the "cannon ball" came along, and…the engineer let her roll slowly through the tunnel. **1906** *DN* III 129: *Cannonball, n.* A fast through train. **1915** White *American Negro Folk-Songs* 271: I'm goin' to ride the cannon ball,/To free my woman from the prison wall. *Ibid.* 298: So if I miss de local I ken ketch de cannon ball. **1921** *DN* V 158: "The happy couple left on the cannonball for St. Louis." Arkansas. **1927** *AS* (June) 388: Fast freights are known as *red balls, cannonballs, hot-shots.* **1948** J. Stevens *Jim Turner* 264: The hardest high-roading…on the decks of the cannonballs.
    b. a powerfully energetic person.
    1962 H. Simmons *On Eggshells* 21: You poppa's a cannonball.
    2. *Und.* a cylindrical safe.
    1925 *Collier's* (Aug. 8) 30: A round manganese safe…is a "cannon-ball." **1933** Ersine *Prison Slang* 24: *Cannonball, n.* A small round safe which is often found within a large safe or vault. "They took two grand out of the V, and six from the cannonball." **1962–68** Jackson *In the Life* 108: Now those big old cannonballs,…all in concrete, I wouldn't fool with one of them….You have to crank the door out and all that kind of stuff.
    3. *Army.* a cantaloupe.
    1941 Kendall & Viney *Army & Navy Slang*. **1945** *Sat. Review* (Nov. 24) 14: *Cannon balls:* cantaloupe.
    4. *Tennis.* a hard-hit serve.
    1942 *ATS* 679: *Cannon ball*…A hard-hit ball. **1949** Cummings *Dict. Sports* 59. **1978** Pici *Tennis Hustler* 90: Both those guys serve cannonballs. **1982** Considine *Lang. of Sport* 297: *Cannonball.* An extremely fast serve. The term was coined at Wimbledon in 1913 to describe the serve of…Maurice McLoughlin.
    5. *Swimming.* (see quot.).
    1949 Cummings *Dict. Sports* 59: *Cannonball. Diving.* A jump into the water with the body curled up in a ball. **1986** *My Sister Sam* (CBS-TV): Suddenly nobody wanted to watch me do cannonballs into the pool any more.
    6. *Army.* an artillery recruit.
    1958 *Nation* (May 10) 417 [ref. to 1955]: At ease, you goddamn cannonballs. At ease!

cannon-cocker *n. Army.* an artillery crewman; artilleryman. Hence **cannon-cocking**, *adj.*
    [**1927** E. Stockwell *Pvt. Stockwell* 122 [ref. to Civil War]: We told him he had never cocked a cannon, and never had been at the front.] **1952** Geer *New Breed* 291 [ref. to 1950]: Several of the artillery positions came under fire from infiltrators and the "cannon cockers" had to fight back with rifles as well as howitzers. **1958** Frankel *Band of Bros.* 117 [ref. to 1950]: Two bats of sloggers [and] some cannon cockers. **1974** Stevens *More There I Was* 77: $40,000 flight training to become a…cannon cocker! **1977** Caputo *Rumor of War* 244 [ref. to 1965]: McKenna…sprayed the artillery officer with imaginary bullets…."You're zapped, you cannon-cockin' Texas shitkicker." **1982** Del Vecchio *13th Valley* 417: He knew the cannon-cockers loved that call.

cannon fever *n. Mil.* a fear of battle. Now *hist.*
    1807 J.R. Shaw *Autobiog.* 123: Some of our party…were immediately seized with cannon fever, and retreated with all possible expedition. **1898** in A.A. Siegel *For Glory of Union* 97 [ref. to 1862]: First our lieutenant-colonel, then our major was smitten with what the men called "cannon fever." Their health failed suddenly…and we were well rid of them. **1987** J.I. Robertson *Blue & Gray* 221 [ref. to Civil War]: Soldiers

usually referred to cowards as men suffering from "cannon fever" or "chicken heart disease."

cannon report *n. Army.* an imaginary written report for which recruits are sent as a practical joke.
　1923 *With the Colors* 16: Many were sent also to get cannon reports, ricochet tape, fixed pivots and other paraphernalia used in the army.

canoe *n.* **1.** *Naut.* a ship.—used derisively.
　1859 in C.A. Abbey *Before the Mast* 229: Unless our *canoe* should sink amidst a school of them. **1942** *ATS* 741. **1963** Keats *They Fought Alone* 17: I'll move your damned canoe. **1965** Harvey *Hudasky's Raiders* 227: The canoe is quiet as a church.
　2. a large automobile.
　1935 Pollock *Und. Speaks* s.v. *hot: Hot duck in a canoe*, a detective in an auto. **1973** *Oui* (Mar.) 110: Used canoes…Pimpmobiles for sale! **1981** D.E. Miller *Jargon* 47: *Ark, canoe, sled.* A large, unwieldy, usually older…car.
　3. *pl.* big feet or shoes.
　1942 *ATS* 146. **1954–60** *DAS.* **1968–69** in *DARE.*
　¶ In phrase:
　¶ **talk to the canoe driver** (see quot.).
　1970 Landy *Underground Dict.* 182: *Talk to the canoe driver*…Have oral copulation of the vagina.

canoe college *n. Navy.* the U.S. Naval Academy.—constr. with *the.* Cf. CANOE U.
　1969 Searls *Hero Ship* 278: Not when a lieutenant commander from the goddamn canoe college went too!

canoe inspection *n. Mil.* (see quots.). Hence **canoe inspector.**
　1965 Trimble *Sex Words* 37: *Canoe Inspection.* Inspection of servicewomen's Genitalia for possible V.D. infection by medical officers or medics…*Canoe inspector* (Gynecologist). **1972** R. Wilson *Playboy's Forbidden Words* 60: *Canoe Inspection.* Inspection of prostitutes' genitalia for venereal disease.

canoe-maker *n. Police.* an autopsy surgeon.
　1970 Wambaugh *New Centurions* 58 [ref. to 1960]: "You'll never believe this," said O'Toole, "but the old canoe maker at the autopsy today claimed that she punctured the aorta with a three and a half inch blade."

Canoe U. *n. Mil.* the U.S. Naval Academy.
　1963 *Sat. Eve. Post* (Nov. 23) 91: The doolie learns to identify Annapolis as Canoe U. and West Point as Hudson High. **1967** Dubus *Lieut.* 74: Well, I'm a Marine. And I know what they taught you at Canoe U. **1969** *Current Slang* I & II 17: *Canoe U.,* n. Annapolis/USNA.—Air Force Academy cadets. **1986** Coonts *Intruder* 45 [ref. to 1972]: Or didn't they cover these fine points of military etiquette at Canoe U?

can of corn *n. Baseball.* a high fly ball that can be easily caught.
　1937 *Pitts. Press* (Jan. 11) (cited in Nichols *Baseball Term.*). **1942** *ATS* 655. **1947** Mencken *Amer. Lang.* Supp. II 735. **1977** P. Rizzuto, on *N.Y. Yankees Baseball* (WPIX-TV) (Aug. 28): Fly ball. That should be a can o' corn for Roy White.

can of worms *n.* a confused, complex, and distasteful state of affairs; a complicated enigma.
　1927–28 in R. Nelson *Dishonorable* 176: But, Lord, it's all like a canful of angle-worms to me! **1954–60** *DAS.* **1968** in *BDNE.* **1974** Stone *Dog Soldiers* 172: My old man is a subtle fella. He's a can of worms. **1978** Groom *Better Times* 384: If we open this can of worms, the whole company's in for it.

canoodle *v.* [orig. unkn.] to hug and kiss; pet; make love; (*hence*) to cajole in such a manner. Now usu. *Joc.*
　1859 in *F & H* II 28: A sly kiss, and a squeeze, and a pressure of the foot or so, and a variety of harmless endearing blandishments, known to our American cousins (who are great adepts at sweet-hearting) as *conoodling* [*sic*]. **1864** in *F & H* II 27: He will *canoodle* the ladies…into the acquisition of whole packages of gimcrack merchandise. **1889** Barrère & Leland *Dict. Slang* I 223: *Canoodle*…to fondle, pet, dally, bill and coo. **1898** B. Harte *Light & Shadow* 189: Only the children still admired her as one who had undoubtedly "canoodled" with a man "a-going to be hung." **1969** *Rowan & Martin's Laugh-In* (NBC-TV): You're beautiful and I'd love to canoodle you. **1973** *Penthouse* (Sept.) 130: I spent the evening reading 200 pages of alfresco canoodling. **1984** *N.Y. Post* (Aug. 29) 35: Never are they caught canoodling in public or even snuggling up to a would-be Romeo.

can-opener *n.* **1.a.** *Mil.* a weapon powerful enough to destroy

an armored target.
　1886 (quot. at TINCLAD).
　b. *Und.* any sort of tool used to break open a safe.
　1912, 1914, 1918 (cited in Partridge *Dict. Und.* 101). **1927** "M. Brand" *Pleasant Jim* 87: With wedges, with heavy hammers, with can-openers, they struggled. **1928** Panzram *Killer* 157: *Can opener*—outfit of tools to rip a safe. **1932** in *AS* (Feb. 1934): *Can Opener.* A device for opening safes.
　2. a cook.
　1918 Wadsworth *Gas Attack* 31: Our chief "can opener," "Lefty Louie," is showing signs of life. **1920** Norton *639th Aero Squadron* 33 [ref. to 1918]: So unexpected was this handout, and so much appreciated, that we voted never to call our cooks "can-openers" again. **1944** *Slanguage Dictionary* 49: *Can opener*—cook.

canopy *n. Naut.* the top of the skull.
　1821–26 (quot. at POTATO-TRAP).

can racket *n.* a beer party.
　1891 Riis *How the Other Half Lives* 29: A man lies dead in the hospital who was cut to pieces in a "can racket" in the alley on Sunday. *Ibid.* 171: Once pitched upon, its occupation by the gang, with its ear-mark of nightly symposiums, "can rackets" in the slang of the street, is the signal for the rapid deterioration of the tenement, if that is possible.

can-shooter *n. Und.* (see quot.).
　1933 Ersine *Prison Slang* 24: *Can shooter.* A safe blower.

Cantab *n.* [shortening of *Cantabrigian*; orig. BrE, ref. to Cambridge Univ.] *Stu.* a student at Harvard College.
　1834 *Knickerbocker Mag.* III 301: Nick was made a cantab at Harvard. **1836** *Harvardiana* III 39: Should all this be a mystery to our uncollegiate friends, or even to many matriculated Cantabs, we advise them not to attempt to unriddle it. **1993** Harvard College grad., class of 1990 (coll. J. Sheidlower): I've heard *Cantab* used to describe Harvard students, but very rarely. It's old-fashioned; an actual Harvard student would never use it.

canteen cowboy *n.* CANTEEN LIZARD.
　1944 Kendall *Service Slang* 57: *Canteen cowboy*.…a soldier who spends time and money at the canteen in order to chat with the uniformed girls who wait on customers.

canteen dispatch *n. Confed. Army.* a rumor.
　1864 in Chamberlayne *Virginian* 255: Rumours the soldiers call grapevine telegraphs and canteen dispatches.

canteen lizard *n. Mil.* an employee or frequenter of a military canteen.
　1918 *Vanity Fair* (July) 45: He acknowledges himself to be a perfect canteen lizard. **1918** in Battey *Sub. Destroyer* 300: Next I went to the Y.M.C.A. and had a row with the lily-fingered "canteen lizard" behind the counter over the price he was charging me for some stuff. **1919** *Vanity Fair* (Jan.) 28: She will stay till the very last canteen-lizard has reeled out into the night.

canteen soldier *n. Army.* (see quot.).
　1941 *AS* (Oct.) 164: *Canteen Soldier.* One who wears non-regulation clothing or insignia.

canto *n. Sports Journ.* an inning of baseball, round of boxing, etc.
　1914 *Collier's* (Aug. 1) 7: Speck Adams limped to the scrap heap in the fourth canto after McCue's line smash to center had gone for a home run. **1920** *N.Y. Times* (Oct. 4). **1933** *AS* (Oct.) 35: *Canto.* Round [of a prizefight]. **1942** *ATS* 651.

Canuck *n.* [perh. var. of *kanaka* 'South Sea Islander' (< Hawaiian), since both French-Canadians and such islanders were employed in the Pacific Northwest fur trade; later reanalyzed as *Cana*dian + arbitrary suffix]
　1. a French Canadian.—sometimes used contemptuously.
　1835 in *DA*: Jonathan distinguishes a Dutch or French Canadian, by the term *Kanuk.* **1840** *Ibid.* **1881–82** Howells *Modern Instance* 119: And Fridays I make up a sort of chowder for the Kanucks; they're Catholics, you know. **1891** *F & H* II 23: Within the Canadian frontier…a *Canuck* is understood to be a French Canadian. **1914** *Amer. Lumberman* (Apr. 25) 33: But Joe, the Cook, a French Canuck,/Said, "Paul, I tink it is ze luck." **1938** Holbrook *Mackinaw* 95: By the time Michigan timber was petering out, Scandinavians were as numerous as Canucks. **1972** in Bernstein & Woodward *President's Men* 132: We don't have blacks but we have Cannocks. **1979** Terkel *Amer. Dreams* XVIII: You room with a French Canuck.

2. a Canadian; (*hence*) a Canadian vessel, animal, etc. Also attrib.

1849 in *OEDS* I 429: Come boys and have some grog, I'm what you call a canuck. **1855** Whitman *Leaves of Grass* 29: Kanuck, Tuckahoe, Congressman, Cuff, I give them the same, I receive them the same. **1871** Schele de Vere *Americanisms* 589: *Canacks, Canucks,* and even *K'nucks,* are slang terms by which the Canadians are known in the United States and among themselves. **1886** *Pap. Mil. Hist. Soc. Mass.* XIII 27: They were…generally "Canucks," as the Canada horse is called. **1889** Barrère & Leland *Dict. Slang* I 224: *Canuck* (American), a Canadian. **1892** Bierce *Beetles* 100: Russians, Italians, Kanucks and Kanaks. **1908** Beach *Barrier* 28: I reckon when a man is too tough for the Canuck police he is tough enough for you to tackle. **1910** *N.Y. Eve. Jour.* (Mar. 28) 10: The Yanks…itched to put it all over the Canucks. **1918** *Lit. Digest* (Apr. 20) 80: The *poilu*, the Tommy, the Canuck, the Anzac. **1925** in J. O'Hara *Sel. Letters* 14: I to appear on your graduation day or thereabouts and force you into the Canuck trip by appealing to your sporting blood or something. **1933–34** "Max Brand" *Mt. Riders* 8: A peevish Canuck one day threw an axe at him. **1938** *AS* (Apr.) 156: *Canuck.* a Canadian Curtis plane. **1954** Boehm *Raid* (film): "I'm Canadian." "We'll take Canucks." **1965** Linakis *In Spring* 34: This didn't include limeys and canucks. **1975** McCaig *Danger Trail* 3: The Canuck government is…closing down the whisky forts. **1984** *N.Y. Times Bk. Review* (Jan. 1) 3: Me? I'm just a Canuck.

Canucker *n.* CANUCK.

1958 McCulloch *Woods Words* 29: Canucker—a logger from north of the border.

canvasback *n. Boxing.* an incompetent prizefighter who is frequently knocked down or out.

1955 Graziano & Barber *Somebody Up There* 178: Yah, you.…I'm talking to you, Canvas Back. **1976** *Webster's Sports Dict.* 67. **1982** T. Considine *Lang. of Sport* 103: *Canvasback*: A fighter who gets knocked down or knocked out often.

canvas inspector *n. Boxing.* CANVASBACK. *Joc.*

1949 Cummings *Dict. Sports* 60: *Canvas inspector*…A boxer who goes down quickly and easily.

canvas-kisser *n. Boxing.* CANVASBACK.

1935 Mackenzie *Been Places* 38: When I get turned loose among the canvas-kissers in this town I'll show them what a little guy from the Coastguard can do. **1942** *ATS* 665.

Canyon *n.* [sugg. by *Steve Canyon*, eponymous hero of comic strip by Milton Caniff, first appearance Jan. 13, 1947] *Mil.* a U.S. Air Force flyer.

1965 Searls *Admiral* (NBC-TV) [ref. to 1950]: Help the Canyons all the way. **1966** *N.Y. Times Mag.* (Oct. 30): Pilots are "Steve Canyons" or "zoomies."

canyon *n.* the vulva or vagina; in phr. of the sort **yodel in the canyon** to perform cunnilingus.—usu. considered vulgar. *Joc.*

1927 Aiken *Blue Voyage* 180: We all have our little p-p-p-p-peculiarities which we don't mention.…Canyon yodeling. Pearl diving. Muff barking. **1960–69** Runkel *Law* 280: I 'member that I finally got my nose warm in 'er canyon. **1973** *TULIPQ* (coll. B.K. Dumas): Sneezing in the canyon. **1977** Flusser *Squeal Man* 99: "He hollers in the canyon." The remark provoked a trumpet of laughter from the group.…"It means he goes down on women."

cap *n.* **1.** (usu. *cap.*) captain; fellow.—used esp. in direct address.

1759 in *AS* (Oct. 1940) 231. **1846** in *Utah Hist. Qly.* V (1932) 99: I and the old Cap (meaning Sutter) locked ourselves up in a room. **1847** Scribner *Camp Life* (May 15) 73: There it is, Cap. **1851** M. Reid *Scalp-Hunters* 111: Why, Cap., I kin surgest my own notion. **1868** "W.J. Hamilton" *Maid of Mtn.* 29: Say, cap.,…we camp here, don't we? **1871** Lee *Army Ballads* 109: Pray tell me, Cap.,—and tell me true,/Why all those officers in blue/Walk up and touch their caps to you? **1886** Wilkins *Cruise* 69: Better have a mite of breakfast with us, Cap. *a*1899 B.F. Sands *Reefer* 119 [ref. to 1839]: Why, cap, you did not stop to take off your watch, did you? **1915** C. Peters *Autobiog.* 6: Hey, Cap,…ain't you got a big load? **1922–24** McIntyre *White Light* 139: Well, Cap, I don't suppose they have music with our meals [in jail]. **1929** Hammett *Maltese Falcon* 106: Hell, Cap, I don't remember that. **1980** Whalen *Takes a Man* 15: Great, Cap. How are you? **1983** Stapleton *30 Yrs.* 64: He's right, cap. **1987** *Smithsonian* (Sept.) 117: She's coming around, Cap.

2. a shot; bullet. See also *bust a cap*, below.

1925 in Hammett *Big Knockover* 229: They can't have a hell of a lot of caps left if they've been snapping them at 'Nacio since early morning. **1944** *Pap. Mich. Acad.* XXX 594: "Caps"…ammunition. **1977** Torres *Q & A* 91: Lanigan put a cap in her.

3. *Narc.* a capsule of narcotic drugs.

1929 *Chi. Tribune* (Oct. 11) 14: A package of drug wrapped in paper is called a "deck," a "check," or a "bundle." If it is in a capsule it is called a "berry," a "bean" or a "cap." **1936** *AS* (Apr.) 119: *Cap.* A bindle of heroin or morphine sold in capsules. **1952** Lait & Mortimer *U.S.A.* 26: The pusher…sells $1 heroin caps for $1.50 in Harlem. **1956** A.J.V. Levy *Others' Children* 78: Some of the boys knew about "caps." They said they gave you a "real lift." **1967–68** von Hoffman *Parents Warned Us* 162: We want to sell them on the street for $2.50 a cap. **1970** Vasquez *Chicano* 216: Now, where'd you get those caps?

4. *Horse Racing.* a handicap race.

1942 *ATS* 694. **1983** *N.Y. Post* (Sept. 5) 31: Pegasus 'Cap set at Big M…the $200,000 Pegasus Handicap.

5. *Black E.* **a.** the mind. Cf. *snap (one's) cap,* below.

1966 Braly *On the Yard* 27: Your cap get pretty loose sometime.

b. the mouth; (*hence*) fellatio; HEAD.

1963 Wepman et al. *The Life* 83: For a lick and a lap from her mellow cap/The tricks would fight a duel. **1974** N.Y.C. man, age 27: Tell the bitch to give you some cap and see what she does.

¶ In phrases:

¶ **bust** [or **pop** or **snap**] **a cap** to fire a shot.

1864 in S.C. Wilson *Column South* 218: He said "To hell with the Yankees," and snapped a cap. **1893** Hampton *Maj. in Washington* 155: He's been a Leftenant Colonel of militia…and he's as game a man as ever snapped a cap. **1899** J.N. Opie *Reb. Cav.* 54 [ref. to Civil War]: Jump down and grab a root, we are going to bust a cap! **1925** in D. Hammett *Continental Op* 172: I had seen his guest snapping caps at a gunman. **1953** in Wepman et al. *The Life* 118: So I popped four caps through his chest with my piece. **1962** Killens *Heard the Thunder* 446 [ref. to WWII]: Goddamn, buddy, you better learn how to talk quicker than that. We almost busted a cap in your ass. **1964** Howe *Valley of Fire* 96: They can step back, cock a bolt, and bust a cap. **1967** Salas *Tattoo* 104 [ref. to *ca*1951]: There ain't no blades nor no blooo-barrulled pistols aroun' to warn big cats away. You know, by bustin' off a few caps. **1970** Thackrey *Thief* 408: I popped a cap. Not at him.…I just fired the gun down between his legs. **1975** Wambaugh *Choirboys* 314: I almost blew the sucker away.…Was ready to bust a cap between his fuckin horns. **1980** M. Baker *Nam* 58: Wow, shit. They're really busting caps at us. **1985** Dye *Between Raindrops* 263: Stop gawking at them and bust caps. **1986** "J. Cain" *Suicide Squad* 28: I thought you two popped a cap on her ass.

¶ **in the cap** *Mining.* (see quot.).

1871 Crofutt *Tourist's Guide* 204: To be out of money, is "*in the Cap,*" "*on the bed rock,*" etc. Ibid. 215: The white…settlers…are…sanguine even in the "cap" after the "grub" fails to "pan."

¶ **on the cap** on the ball s.v. BALL.

1970 Cortina *Slain Warrior* 156: Sometimes they're artistic…in general I'd say they got a lot on the cap.

¶ **snap (one's) cap** to become insane, excited, or angry; go crazy. Also vars.

1941 in Ellington *Music My Mistress* 179: *Blow my top…flip my lid…snap my cap…enjoy.* **1944** in *AS* XX 148: *Snap your cap.* Become excited, flustered. **1946** Mezzrow & Wolfe *Really Blues* 187 [ref. to 1930's]: You snapped your cap long ago. **1948** Manone & Vandervoort *Trumpet* 171: Man, Schertzinger really snapped his cap. **1957** Simmons *Corner Boy* 45: Man, I'm poppin' my cap. Ibid. 203: Man, I'm busting my cap. **1958** Hughes & Bontemps *Negro Folklore* 487: *Snap your cap:* To become very angry. The dozens made him snap his cap. **1960** Mac-Cuish *Do Not Go Gentle* 122: Brain's gone, eh? Snapped your friggin' cap. **1960** Swarthout *Where the Boys Are* 127: I practically snapped my cap. **1961** Rosten *Capt. Newman M.D.* 181 [ref. to 1944]: The Colonel has snapped his cap! **1966** Reynolds & McClure *Freewheelin Frank* 9: He'd blew his cap and gone to the nut house. **1966** Longstreet & God-off *Wm. Kite* 172: That sends me like a kite. I snap my cap. **1985** Benedek *Cocoon* (film): She'd know her old man's finally snapped his cap.

¶ **spin (someone's) cap** *Baseball.* to throw a pitch near a batter's head.

1983 L. Frank *Hardball* 106: He wants to…throw at his chin [or] "spin his cap."

cap *v.* **1.** *Und.* to act as a capper or confederate.—also (*obs.*) constr. with *in*.

*1811 *Lexicon Balatron.: His pall capped*…His confederate assisted in the fraud. **1859** Matsell *Vocab.* 17: *Capper.* One who supports another's assertion, to assist in cheating. "The burner bammed the flat with sham books, and his *pal* capped in for him"—The sharp cheated the country man with false cards, and his confederate assisted (capped) in the fraud. *1889 Barrère & Leland *Dict. Slang* I 224: To *cap*, to assist as a confederate, especially of cardsharpers. **1906** A.H. Lewis *Confessions* 36: Didn't I cap for you, an' square you with the examinin' board? **1912** Quinn *Gambling* 52: Of course I knew that you were "capping" for the game. **1912** Ade *Babel* 72: Now you say they're all out cappin' for this fellow. **1914** S. Lewis *Mr. Wrenn* 39: 'Nother sucker coming, Blaugeld. Now don't do me out of my bit or I'll cap for some other joint. **1933** Ersine *Prison Slang* 25: *Cap, v.* To shill; to act as a come-on man. **1972** Wambaugh *Blue Knight* 144: Herb was fired for capping for a bail bondsman.

2. [cf. S.E. sense] *Black E.* to outdo (someone).
1944 Calloway *Hepster's Dict.* (ed. 6): *Capped*…outdone, surpassed. **1944** Burley *Harlem Jive* 135: *Capped*—Excelled, replied. **1952** Brossard *Darkness* 280: Porter was laughing at something Max had said. "You capped me, man…You capped me." **1968** in *Trans-action* VI (Feb. 1969) 27: His rap was "capped" (Excelled, topped).

3. to place (a drug) in capsules.
1968–70 *Current Slang* III & IV 21: *Cap*…To package heroin for sale.

4. to shoot (a person). Also intrans.
1970–71 Rubinstein *City Police* 188: He ain't kiddin'. He will cap you one night, boy. *Ibid.* 293: Shit, man, he's got an iron. I'm getting…out of here before he caps me. **1972** in W. King *Black Anthol.* 147: Tomorra we gonna' *cap* you, Blood! **1980** M. Baker *Nam* 88: I capped her. That was my first confirmed kill. *Ibid.* 89: Then all of a sudden we heard capping by us. **1983** Spottiswood *48 Hrs.* (film): He broke out of prison a couple of days ago and capped a couple of guards. **1983** P. Dexter *God's Pocket* 65: And then me and the defendant went into the office where he was and, you know, capped him. **1985** E. Leonard *Glitz* 57: They say he got capped by a junkie,…but didn't die. **1988** Norst *Colors* 11: First chance we get…we cap him. **1990** G.R. Clark *Words of Viet. War* 175: The term "bustin' caps" or "capping" was originally credited to the Marines who claimed the…M-16…sounded like a "cap pistol."

5. to KNEECAP.
1978 *N.Y. Post* (July 6) 17: Another Italian exec. is "capped."…The Red Brigades "kneecapped" the president of Turin's Small Industry Assn. today.

¶ In phrase:

¶ **cap on, 1.** *Black E.* to insult or make fun of.
1966 Reynolds & McClure *Freewheelin Frank* 147: Ray capped on me for being last. I said, "Why shouldn't I be? I'm the youngest." **1970** A. Young *Snakes* 19: Some silly stud get to cappin on Cyrano's nose and he don't flinch an inch. *Ibid.* 33: Cut out some of this capping on one another and playing the dozens. **1972–74** Hawes & Asher *Raise Up* 38: One of the older musicians in the house used to cap on me* in a playful way….*Put me down. **1979** Hiler *Monkey Mt.* 282: Sergeant Perfect here says everything is fucked, and then he caps on us when we say the same thing!

2. *Und.* to lure or entice (a prospective victim of a swindle).
1968 Beck *Trick Baby* 120: Both of us could cap on or build up a sucker.

Cape Ann turkey *n. Naut.* CAPE COD TURKEY. *Joc.*
1844 in *DAE* I 417. **1863** in S. Boyer *Naval Surgeon* I 159: Tomorrow we expect to dine on "Cape Ann turkeys" (codfish), as the seafaring men call them. **1947** in *DA* 264.

Cape Cod turkey *n. N.E.* salt cod. *Joc.*
1865 in *F & H* II 32: A salted cod fish is known in American ships as a *Cape Cod turkey.* **1877** Bartlett *Dict. Amer.* (ed. 4) 98: *Cape Cod Turkeys.* Codfish. **1901** Greenough & Kittredge *Wds. & Ways* 331: "Welsh rabbit" is merely a joke, like "Cape Cod turkey" for codfish. **1907** *DN* III 183: *Cape Cod turkey, n. phr.* Salt codfish. **1946** in *DA* 264. **1962** *West. Folklore* 29: *Cape Cod turkey*—codfish.

Cape fever *n. Naut.* CAPE HORN FEVER.
1830 Ames *Mariner's Sketches* 193: The weather was cold…and every thing that was unpleasant, and produced a complaint, jocosely called by our men, "the Cape Fever." Many of them as well as officers "shammed Abraham" or "sogered" as it was called, to get out of the weather. **1856** F.L. Olmsted in *DAE*.

Cape Flyaway *n. Naut.* (see 1942, 1945 quots.).
*1805 J. Davis *Post-Captain* 3: The master…says he can see land broad upon the bow; but I, sir, am of the opinion it is only cape fly-away. **1858** in C.A. Abbey *Before the Mast* 130: Cape Flyaway 5 points on the weather bow at daylight. *1929 Bowen *Sea Slang.* **1942** *ATS* 738: *Cape*

Flyaway…a cloud on the horizon mistaken for land. **1945** Colcord *Sea Lang.* 48: *Cape Flyaway.* A cloud-bank on the horizon having the appearance of land.

Cape Horn fever *n. Naut.* a feigned illness. Also **Horn fever.**
1847 Downey *Cruise of Portsmouth* 34: But after we left Rio and drew near the Cape, he was most violently attacked with the Horn fever, and succeeded in hauling on the [sick] list. **1849** Melville *White Jacket* 314 [ref. to 1843]: What sailors call the "*Cape Horn Fever*" alarmingly prevailed; though it disappeared altogether when we got into fine weather. *1902 Masefield *Salt-Water Ballads* 18: Come none o' your Cape Horn fever lays aboard o' this yer ship. **1908** *Independent* (Apr. 23) 906: He was really dangerously ill, and not troubled with an acute attack of "Cape Horn fever." **1929** Bowen *Sea Slang* 22: *Cape Horn Fever.* Malingering in bad weather under sail.

Cape Misery *n.* Cape Horn.
1866 C.E. Hunt *Shenandoah* 227: We got clear of "old Cape Misery," as it is sometimes aptly called by sailors.

caper *n.* **1.a.** a trick.
1840 in *DAE*: The bizness is a bad one…but I think I understand the caper on't. **1855** Brougham *Chips* 373: They purtend that this here is a hage of henlightenment and hintellect, and all them there capers. *Ibid.* 402: I ain't a goin' to stand no sich capers as that. **1864** in Brobst *Civil War Letters* 72: Pratt…said it was a God damn mean caper after we had been working so hard and just got to sleep and then have the rebs throw shells into us. *1867 in *F & H* II 33: "He'll get five years penal for this little *caper*," said the policeman. **1933** Ersine *Pris. Slang* 25: *Caper, n….*trick. **1968** Myrer *Eagle* 767: Why crawl…when you can do the ozone caper.

b. (see quot.).
1891 *F & H* II 33: *Caper*…occupation. Americans use it in the same sense as *racket, e.g.,* the "real estate racket" or "caper."

2. a course of action; undertaking; in phr. **the proper caper** the right thing to do.
1839 *Spirit of Times* (Nov. 9) 423: A feedin trof is jest the caper. **1885** *Puck* (Apr. 8) 87: It is the fashionable caper now-a-days to go to college. **1888** Bunner *Letters* 127: I can come the modern caper, I think. *a1889* in Barrère & Leland *Dict. Slang* I 225: Mind-reading is now the proper caper. **1893** Friend *Thousand Liars* 106: Dubble whispers to Bings that "the proper caper" would be to "set 'em up." **1899** Norris *McTeague* 52: That's the proper caper. **1899** Lewis *Sandburrs* 189: It's d' fly caper if youse is out to finish wit' d' heavenly squeeze, to honour your father an' mother. **1901** Oliver *Roughing It With Regulars* 61: Ham and eggs will be just the proper caper this evening for supper. **1903** Ade *Society* 8: He learned that the Proper Caper for one who is out of Work and all clogged up with Funds is to build a Cottage overlooking the Sea and work up Features for the Sunday Papers. **1909** "O. Henry" *Options* 778: Go on, Mr. Chalmers…and tell the lady what's the proper caper. **1931** D. Runyon, in *Collier's* (Nov. 14) 8: It is considered the proper caper for this team's boosters to grab the other guy's goal posts. **1976** Hayden *Voyage* 186: There's ten skins in this caper for each of the boys as participates.

3.a. *Police & Und.* a criminal undertaking, esp. a swindle or theft.
1925–26 Black *You Can't Win* 131 [ref. to 1890's]: It was your caper, you located it. **1926** in Ruhm *Detective* 67: The princess can give you a fat cut of the profits in a busted caper, with a good chance to get yourself hanged. **1926** *Writer's Mo.* (Dec.) 541: *Caper*—The crime a man is serving his sentence for. **1929** Barr *Let Tomorrow Come* 149: You're supposed to cut another caper quick as you can so the mugs'll have somethin' to do chasin' you. **1950** Maddow & Huston *Asphalt Jungle* 16: A plan for a caper. And it's a good one.

b. *Police.* a criminal investigation; a case.
1923 in Hammett *Big Knockover* 149: I was glad it was over. It had been a tough caper. **1977** Dunne *Confessions* 97: That's all we need on this caper is a blabbermouth fifteen-dollar hooker. **1981** Wolf *Roger Rabbit* 4: Hardly an earthshaking caper, this one.

c. a notable event; happening.
1933 Ersine *Prison Slang* 25: *Caper, n….*A happening, event, trick. **1959** *Swinging Syllables*: *Caper*—Any experience or incident worth remembering. *a1974* in Fair *New Nonsense* 38: The Mars caper may be too sci-fi-ish and too *visible* for NASA to get involved with.

caper *v. Und.* to do a CAPER, 3.a.
1976 Braly *False Starts* 211: I know you're capering.

caper juice *n.* whiskey.
1888 in *F & H* II 34: Say, fellers, let's take a leetle mo' uv the *caper juice.*

Cape Stiff *n.* [prob. a pun on the phallic senses of *stiff* and *horn*] *Naut.* Cape Horn.

1898 Bullen *Cachalot* 296 [ref. to 1875]: It became necessary to draw down towards "Cape Stiff," as that dreaded extremity of South America, Cape Horn, is familiarly called by seamen. **1900** Kennedy *Adrift* 43: A deep-water vessel that was going to round the Horn—"Cape Stiff," as the sailors call it. **1913–14** London *Elsinore* 13: East to west around Cape Stiff! **1923** Riesenberg *Under Sail* 105: We…headed bravely for old "Cape Stiff." *a*1930 in Tomlinson *Sea Stories* 557: In the bleak…gales off Cape Stiff. **1976** Hayden *Voyage* 155: Off Cape Stiff in the dead of wintertime.

capper *n.* **1.** Orig. *Und.* a person who decoys victims into a crooked gambling game or other swindle; SHILL.

*1753 in *OEDS*: The next is the Capper, who always keeps with the Sailor. **1849** "N. Buntline" *B'hoys of N.Y.* 10: *Ike*, the old capper,…is to play the desperate and *lose* his pile. **1855** in Lewis *Mining Frontier* 58: The dexterous and well-organized gang of hired "cappers," who, disguised as miners, laborers, traders, etc., etc., went from table to table and from game to game making sham bets…and inviting the looker-on to "invest." **1856** in *Calif. Folk. Qly.* I (1942) 271: There's the gambler has his cappers who are looking about,/And where they find a sucker they are sure to pan him out. **1859** Matsell *Vocab.* 109: *Capper*. A man in the employ of the bank, who pretends to be playing against it, and winning large amounts. **1860** L. Barney *Auraria* 85: Those that can afford it, hire "cappers" who the dealer uses when he wishes to feign the loss of his money, that the stranger may the sooner be induced to bet. **1871** in Rosa *Wild Bill* 189: To close up all dead & Brace Gambling Games and to arrest all Cappers for the aforesaid game. **1884** Triplett *American Crimes* 61: He had killed a "capper," as the gambler's decoy is called. **1918** Witwer *Baseball to Boches* 22: What are you—a capper for the army? **1921** Conklin & Root *Circus* 168 [ref. to *ca*1880]: Most of the gamblers used stool-pigeons or, as they were known in circus parlance, "cappers." Not being suspected by the crowd of having any connection with the gamblers, their heavy winnings inflamed the cupidity of the looker-on, while their occasional losses tended to disarm suspicion. **1930** *Variety* (Jan. 8) 123: The cappers gave the mark a peek with the rest of his scratch. **1936** Washburn *Parlor* 151: However, the old levee was replete with "cappers," telling respective customers where to go. **1978** *Gamblers* 63: The gambler's assistant, often called a "capper," steps up to place a bet.

2. B-GIRL.

1915 *Variety* (Oct. 29): A girl who had been a waitress in a mining town and then graduated to a "booze capper" in a western dance hall.

capsule *n.* ¶ In phrase: **out of (one's) capsule** crazy.

1966 E. Shepard *Doom Pussy* 254: "I think she's out of her capsule," Bear said.

captain *n.* **1.** (used in direct address to a man whose name is not known); "buddy."

1845 in *DAE*: I say, capt'n, and Jack, let's have eighteen pence worth of stars. **1851** [G. Thompson] *Jack Harold* 71: It's a d—d purty yarn, captain. **1862** in *F & H* II 35: *Captain* [as a term of address] is very low. **1878** [P.S. Warne] *Hard Crowd* 10: Cap'n, I've got a mite o' business with yeou.

2. *Hobo.* a leader of a gang of tramps.

*1809 (cited in Partridge *Dict. Und.* 105). **1850** "N. Buntline" *G'hals of N.Y.* 39: Have you not learned from the captain, that you must never ask impertinent questions? **1851** [G. Thompson] *Bristol Bill* 27: His reputation as a "cracksman" and as a "captain of the cross." **1925–26** Black *You Can't Win* 197 [ref. to 1890's]: The "captain" of each unit…sent the younger bums…to buy alcohol, beer, and the "makin's" of mulligans. **1933** Ersine *Prison Slang* 25: *Captain*….The leader of a gang of yeggs.

Captain Hicks *n.* [rhyming sl.] *Craps.* two threes on a pair of dice.

1941 *Slanguage Dict.* 9: *Captain Hicks*…six on a pair of dice.

Captain of the Head *n. Navy & USMC.* an enlisted man put in charge of a head or latrine. [Orig. a standard technical term.] Cf. ADMIRAL.

1885 "Lykkejaeger" *Dane* 49: There was still another naval honor I had thrust upon me while on the *Allegheny*,…the position of *Captain of the Head.* **1918** Noyes *Navy Slang*: *Captain of the Head* = man in charge of the head. **1918** *Stars & Stripes* (Mar. 1) 7: Captain of the Head. **1942** *Yank* (Oct. 28) 20: Holding important posts such as "captain of the head" and "sanitary engineer." **1959** Cochrell *Barren Beaches* 225 [ref. to WWII]: "From now on, you're captain of the head," he told Salty.

1961 Coon *Meanwhile at the Front* 233: If this thing gets any worse I'll be made captain of the head in Moon's private john!

Captain Whiskey *n.* whiskey. *Joc.*

1853 "P. Paxton" *In Texas* 201: "Captain Whiskey" has taken him in charge, certainly. **1858** "P. Paxton" *Piney Woods* 84: Captain Whiskey had got a powerful grip on 'em.

carb *n.* a carburetor.

1942 *ATS*: Carburetor, *carb*…juice-pot, [etc.]. **1962** G. Olson *Roaring Road* 84: I don't think the carbs got a fair try, Hardin. **1963** in H. Ellison *Sex Misspelled* 50: Dual carbs. **1983** S. King *Christine* 18: A four-barrel carb as black as a mine shaft.

car-banger *n. Police.* a thief who steals from parked motor vehicles.

1982 De Sola *Crime Dict.* 24.

carbine *v. West.* to cheat or victimize.

1875 Daly *Bonanza* 192: BOB….It was a sell—humbug. I had been carbined. ALL. Robert—carbined? BOB. I mean rifled—cheated. That's the way the miners talk.

carbo *n.* carbohydrates; a food high in carbohydrates.

1976–77 McFadden *Serial* 139: She knew she shouldn't be munching out on carbos like this. **1990** *Bicycling* (Oct.) 80: You can…spend the night in the Comfort Lodge, or stock up on water and carbos…and tackle the remainder of the ride.

carburetor *n.* **1.** the heart.

1924 Anderson & Stallings *What Price Glory?* 123 [ref. to 1918]: And you, the best pistol shot in the corps, would put one through my carburetor as easy as pitching pennies in a well.

2. *Narc.* a water-pipe used for the smoking of marijuana or hashish.

1971 Pvt., U.S. Army (coll. J. Ball): The thing I hate about the military is I don't have my carburetor nearby. **1987** W. Ga. college prof., age 32: A *carburetor* is a marijuana pipe.

card *n.* **1.a.** an odd or remarkable person; customer; character.—often constr. with prec. adj.

*1835 C. Dickens, in *F & H* II 36: Mr. Thomas Potter, whose great aim it was to be considered a knowing *card*. **1840** in *DAE* I 424: Consider me a sure card in that line. *1853 C. Dickens *Bleak House* ch. lxii: You know what a card Krook was for buying…old furniter. **1900** *DN* II 137: *Card*, n. A dissolute fellow; "he was a *card*." **1924** in *DAE* I 424: Jim Harvey's a queer card. **1932** Z. Grey *Robbers' Roost* 175: Happy, you're a card….How in the hell can you whistle and smile when you know this outfit is primed to blow up!

b. an amusing or facetious person; joker.—often used sarcastically. Now *colloq.*

1904 *Life in Sing Sing* 246: Card. Cod. Humorist. *1905 A. Bennett, in *OEDS*: It would be…a topic for years, the crown of his reputation as a card. **1925** Dos Passos *Manhattan Transfer* 28: O Lord, you're a card, you are. **1932** J.T. Farrell *Guillotine Party* 180: Yeah, and was Ike here a card! **1933** in Truman *Dear Bess* 355: These Arkansas boys are cards, but they…do just about the same amount of devilment as any others. **1960** Brooks *Elmer Gantry* (film): Sister, you're a card. **1985** N.O. woman, age 33: I went to Henry's Hardware Store—and Henry was a card, a real card. He called me up the next day and said, "I've got your lamp fixed. And it'll cost you $3000!"

c. an amusing thing.

1943 J.T. Farrell *Days of Anger* 325 [ref. to 1927]: That's a card. There's your democracy for you.

2. a drawing card.

1864 in *DAE*: The curiosity to see him makes him a good card for lecture committees. **1886** F. Whittaker *Pop Hicks* 8: He's a good card; but all they've got sir. We've got four or five. **1936** Tully *Bruiser* 48: Are you sure you ain't be a card for me?

3. (*cap.*) *pl. Sports.* the St. Louis Cardinals or the Chicago Cardinals.

1958 J. King *Pro Football* 26: His Cards…won the West 1947–48.

4. *pl.* sanity; good sense.

1978 L'Amour *Proving Trail* 44: Only some half-baked youngster whose cards were badly mixed would be that crazy.

¶ In phrases:

¶ **call (someone's) card** to stand up to (someone); call (someone's) bluff.

1981 *Penthouse* (Mar.) 159: Pimps seem awful tough…until we call their card.

¶ **give cards and spades** to allow an advantage; to outdo despite an advantage.

1888 in *F & H* II 37: Artie found a Chinaman out in 'Frisco who could give him cards and spades and beat him out. **1903** A. Adams *Log of a Cowboy* 274: That little hole back there could give Natchez-under-the-hill cards and spades, and then outhold her as a tough town. **1903** A.H. Lewis *Boss* 191: That's your game...an'...you've got me beat. But there's other games, like Tammany Hall for instance, where I could give you cards an' spades. **1906** Hobart *Skiddoo* 74: Civilization is a fine idea, but Human Nature can give it cards and spades and then beat it out. **1913** J. London *Valley of Moon* 126: Married folks....We can give 'em cards an' spades an' a little casino an' win out. **1936** J.T. Farrell *World I Never Made* 97: None better. She can deal out cards and spades to most gals.

card *v.* to require (someone) to present proof of legal drinking age before selling an alcoholic beverage to that person.—usu. constr. in passive.

1975 Lichtenstein *Long Way* 90: Peter and I felt like counselors, worrying about the girls getting "carded"—checked for proof of age. **1982** S. Black *Totally Awesome* 21: *Carded*: What you get when you try to buy a six-pack and you've got braces and zits. **1984** N. Bell *Raw Youth* 24: I still get carded at bars. **1987** *Spring Break Guide* 4: To earn your right to a Miller Lite, have at least two valid documents at the ready. Expect to be carded. **1992** G. Wolff *Day at the Beach* 229: I got carded in a convenience store.

cardboard driver *n. Trucking.* (see quot.).

1971 Tak *Truck Talk* 27: *Cardboard driver*: a new driver going through a trial period with a trucking company; so named because the tractor he owns and drives carries cardboard signs instead of the permanent decals affixed by the company.

card-carrying *adj.* [orig. ref. to a *card-carrying* member of the Communist Party] genuine; thoroughgoing. *Joc.*

1963 (cited in *BDNE3*). **1974** Bernstein & Woodward *President's Men* 84: And Magruder really was a card-carrying bicycle freak who had even ridden his 10-speed to the White House every day. **1978** *Harper's* (Sept.) 57: I'm the card-carrying birder in my group. **1981** *Texas Monthly* (Apr.) 234: The only official, card-carrying humanist I know personally [is] a gentle, sensitive, highly ethical man.

card man *n. Labor.* a worker having a union card.

1930 "D. Stiff" *Milk & Honey* 202: *Card man*—A union man or a hobo with a red I.W.W. card. **1968** R. Adams *Western Words* 55: *Card man*. What the loggers call a union man; often shortened to *card*.

card mechanic *n. Gamb.* a person, as a crooked gambler, who is skilled at manipulating playing cards; CARDSHARP.

1906 *Army & Navy Life* (Oct.) 347: As a gambler, "Old Hoss" had no boss, for he knew the game from sun to sun, coming and going. As his pal, Joe Seeley, expressed it: " 'Old Hoss' is the best card mechanic I ever seed!"

card shark *n.* CARDSHARP. Now *S.E.*

1942 *ATS* 699. **1957** McGivern *Against Tomorrow* 82: A big-city card shark. **1960** in Bambara *Gorilla* 53: The sixty-year-old cardshark had insisted.

card-shark *v.* to be a CARD SHARK.

1969 Beard & Kenney *Bored of Rings* 27: Moonlight card-sharking at hick carny shows.

cardsharp *n.* a person who cheats at card games. Now *S.E.*

1884 B. Harte *On Frontier* 273: We ain't takin' this step to make a card sharp out of him. **1980** Hogan *Lawman's Choice* 22: A cardsharp named Stryker.

care *n.* ¶ In phrase: **take care of** [euphem.] Esp. *Und.* to do for (someone), as by beating or killing.

1931 Armour *Little Caesar* (film): I had to take care of a guy. **1935** Odets *Lefty* 23: Take care of him, boys. **1936** in D. Runyon *More Guys* 148: Somebody finally takes care of Dave the Dude himself. **1943–47** in Hodes & Hansen *Sel. From Gutter* 10: It was common gossip that that gang had taken care of her husband. **1970** E.S. Gardner *Cops* 78: The story is that each of the two smugglers was to "take care" of one man. **1975** T. Berger *Sneaky People* 88: I won't beat around the bush....I want to get somebody taken care of. **1984** *Fall Guy* (ABC-TV): We got a tip a guy called "The Wasp" was paid $50,000 to take care of you. **1984** in Terkel *Good War* 147: They had their clubs out. They ran down and really started takin' care of me. **1990** Murano & Hoffer *Cop Hunter* 19: Coleman growled, "I'll take care of you."

care package *n.* [sugg. by *CARE package*, a package of goods distributed to the needy in foreign countries by CARE] a package of sweets or other supplies, esp. as sent from home to a college student or member of the armed forces.

1962 *We Seven* 246: Also, we got a daily "Care" package from Henri Landiwirth....Henri knew that we both liked shrimp—with extra hot sauce—so he sent some out to us almost every day. **1965** N.Y.C. high school student: We're sending Dick a care package at Kent State. **1969** in Van Devanter & Morgan *Before Morning* 131: Six letters in addition to the nicest care package I've ever seen. **1971** Meggyesy *Out of Their League* 203: This guy and I got to know each other during training camp and he told me he was expecting a "care package" from home. **1980** Leland *Kiwi-Yank Dict.* 9: CARE packages sent to World War I N.Z. troops always included some of these. **1980** W.C. Anderson *Bat-21* 82: I'm dropping a CARE package.

car-frisker *n. Police.* a thief who preys on horse-car passengers.

1879 *Snares of N.Y.* 37: Car thieves...known technically as "car-friskers."

carhop *n.* a server at a drive-in restaurant. Now *S.E.*

1939 C.R. Cooper *Scarlet* 88: Beauticians, manicure girls, waitresses, percentage girls, car hops. **1948** in P.C. Berg *New Words* 52. **1973** Lucas, Katz & Huyck *Amer. Graffiti* 16: Terry is pleading with the sexy car hop as she delivers a tray to a car.

carhop *v.* to work as a CARHOP.

1954–60 *DAS.* **1970** N.Y.C. man, age 22: She couldn't make much carhopping.

Carib *n.* the Caribbean Sea.

1964–66 R. Stone *Hall of Mirrors* 68: The rottenest...part on the whole...Carib.

car jockey *n.* a garage or parking-lot attendant.

1956 in *AS* XXXV (1960) 159: My last job was car jockey—I just had to drive the cars wherever the garage told me. **1969** Salerno & Tompkins *Crime Confed.* 47: College kids, car jockeys, salesmen, farmers. **1970** in *OEDS* s.v. *jockey*: Doorman and car jockey. **1988** Cogan & Ferguson *Presidio* 65: The car jockey pulled up from the...lot.

cark *n.* [alter. of COCK] the penis.—usu. considered vulgar.

1976 *Nat. Lampoon* (Jan.) 18: I take out the old cark...and give her one shot. **1978** *Nat. Lampoon* (Aug.) 14: No kosher salami, no Jewish cark for her.

car-knock *n. R.R.* CAR-KNOCKER.

1931 (quot. at CAR-TOAD).

car-knocker *n. R.R.* a railroad-car inspector or repairer.

1916 *Editor* XLIII (Mar. 25) 343: *Car knocker*. Car repairman. **1925** Mullin *Scholar Tramp* 130 [ref. to *ca*1912]: I hammered like hell with my fists and a car-knocker let me out. **1943** Guthrie *Glory* 262: "Checkers." "Car knockers." "Boys—scatter out!" **1951** Kerouac *Cody* 9: Big Diesel whistle by engineer to acknowledge hiball-on-the-air from brakeman or car knocker. **1970** *Current Slang* V 5: *Car Knocker*, n. Railroad car inspector and repairman. **1973** "J. Godey" *Pelham* 23: The shop sends a car knocker; he looks it over, scratches his head.

carny *n.* **1.** a carnival.

1931 D.W. Maurer, in *AS* 330: *Carnifolks*...Persons who engage in the carnival business. **1933** Chipman *Hey Rube* 193: *Carny*, carnival. **1951** Mannix *Sword-Swallower* 5: The carny moves tomorrow. **1951** *New Yorker* (Jan. 27) 21: At a carny, you pitch phonies. **1956** Gold *Not With It* 22: Lucky the carnie got rained out. **1966** R.E. Alter *Carny Kill* 9: Bill Duff and I once worked in a carny together.

2. a carnival performer; a carnival worker.

1939 in Liebling *Telephone Booth* 4: The "carnies"...travel from town to town with carnivals. **1951** Mannix *Sword-Swallower* 47: I was really beginning my life as a carny. **1953** Gresham *Midway* 13: And he was also an old-time carny. **1973** Haney *Jock* 19: I'm by a carny out of a hillbilly. **1979** T. Baum *Carny* 37: Most of the carnies were sleeping late. **1983** *Batman* (Apr.) 11: We carnies stick together, remember?

Carolina racehorse *n.* a razorback hog. *Joc.*

1862 "E. Kirke" *Among Pines* 212: We call them "Carolina racehorses."...Fleet as a deer.

carp *n.* a foolish or obnoxious person; FISH; SUCKER.

1908 in "O. Henry" *Works* 308: The town...[is] stocked full of carp. **1912** *Pedagogical Seminary* (Mar.) 96: "Bonehead"..."you carp," "you're off your perch." **1931** Cressey *Taxi-Dance Hall* 101: They're such easy "carp" I figure that if they hang around long enough somebody's bound to knock them off.

carpenter *n. Wrestling.* a skillful wrestler.
  1980 *AS* (Summer) 143: Good [wrestlers] are also known as *carpenters* because of their ability as craftsmen.

carpet *n.* the grass; the ground.
  1897 Hamblen *General Manager* 88: Ye'll have them all over the d—d carpet. **1899** Hamblen *Bucko Mate* 8: There lay the train, "all over the carpet." **1908** in Fleming *Unforget. Season* 137: Scooping it up with his bare hand an inch from the carpet. **1920** Clapp *17th Aero Squadron* 50 [ref. to 1918]: He was down so near "the carpet"...that he stove in the leading edge of his wings on the branches of trees. **1956** Heflin *USAF Dict.* 103: *Carpet*...The ground. *Slang.* **1972** Jenkins *Semi-Tough* 67: Getting hit and rolling around on the carpet is easy.
  ¶ In phrases:
  ¶ **munch** [or **chew**] **the carpet** to perform cunnilingus.
  1981 *Nat. Lampoon* (Aug.) 22: So, what do you do when you been munching some broad's carpet for a couple years and then all of a sudden the gash demands a $400,000 house for her trouble? **1985** "Blow-dryer" *Mod. Eng.* 74: Homosexual women...*Carpet Chewers.*
  ¶ **on the carpet, 1.** being rebuked or questioned closely by a person in authority; **call on the carpet** to summon for or administer a rebuke or the like.
  1888 *Scribner's Mag.* (Nov.) 548: The mortification of being called into the superintendent's office to explain some dereliction of duty is disguised by referring to the episode as "dancing on the carpet." *1889 Barrère & Leland *Dict. Slang* I 227: To be called upon the *carpet*...to be scolded, reprimanded, to have to give an account of oneself. **1899** Ade *Fables* 55: Next morning she had him up on the Carpet and wanted to know How About It. **1907** Bush *Enlisted Man* 194: You thought that I had been "on the carpet" and your efforts to cheer me up pretty nearly made me tell you all to go to Glory. **1918** *Stars & Stripes* (July 5) 5: The first thing I knew the Loot was on the carpet. **1920** Ade *Hand-Made Fables* 31: The Guv'nor got him up on the Carpet and gave him a quiet Tip to lay off on signing Checks. **1931** J.T. Farrell *McGinty* 101: Ain't he ever had you on the carpet? **1932** Tully *Laughter* 47: Both youths were, in railroad vernacular, "put on the carpet." **1947** Williams *Streetcar Named Desire* 80: Boy, oh, boy, I'd like to have been in that office when Dame Blanche was called on the carpet! **1949** Davies *Happens Every Spring* (film): They had me on the carpet so long I got fallen arches. **1954** Davis & Lay *Strategic Air Command* (film): They had us all on the carpet for that one. **1955** Stern *Rebel Without a Cause* (film): They had him on the carpet for an hour down at headquarters. **1981** Wolf *Roger Rabbit* 184: He called you on the carpet too. **1983** *N.Y. Post* (Sept. 2) 7: Soviet envoy Vladimir Pavlov was called on the carpet in Tokyo yesterday to explain the Korean airliner outrage.
  2. near or at the point of defeat, bankruptcy, or the like.
  1897 Ade *Pink* 158: "Have you got another job?" "No, seh; I'm sutny on 'e edge of 'at cahpet, misteh." **1903** Ade *Society* 94: Most of us are kept so close to the Carpet that we have to buy last year's Magazines to put in the Waiting-Room.
  ¶ **step off the carpet** to get married.
  1843 in Eliason *Tarheel Talk* 297: Cousin Fanny...stepped off the carpet. **1859** in Eliason *Tarheel Talk:* And so Mag is going to step off the carpet tomorrow.

carpet joint *n. Gamb.* a carpeted and well-furnished or well-equipped gambling casino.
  1961 Scarne *Comp. Guide to Gambling* 205: The plush luxury casinos, like those on the Las Vegas Strip, are known as *carpet joints* or *rug joints*. *Ibid.* 210 [caption]: A carpet joint in 1843, the famed Crockford's Club. **1970** S. Ross *Fortune Machine* 7: There are carpet joints on the Strip, sawdust joints downtown. **1981** D.E. Miller *Jargon* 295.

carrier pigeon *n.* a messenger.
  1933 H. Stephenson *Glass* 189 [ref. to ca1905]: Half a dozen boys were engaged in the same work as his own. They were the "carrier pigeons." *Ibid.* 191: The other "carrier pigeons" were duly impressed. **1941** *AS* (Oct.) 164: *Carrier Pigeon.* Officer's messenger. **1983** S. King *Christine* 336: What's happening with our carrier pigeon?

carrothead *n.* a redheaded person. Hence **carrot-headed,** *adj.*
  [**1867** Clark *Sailor's Life* 13: The cook, a carrotty-headed Yankee.] **1867** B. Harte *Sks. of Sixties* 110: You here yet—Carrothead. **1884** Hartranft *Sidesplitter* 196: What carrot-headed, ugly little urchin is that? **1893** Barra *Two Oceans* 167: The mate...entered into conversation with carrot-head. **1932** Riesenberg *Log of the Sea* 108: Did you hear that carrot-head yell at me to come on board?

carrot-top *n.* a redheaded person. Hence **carrot-topped,** *adj.*
  1889 Cox *Frontier Humor* 56: What! Him as the boys in Gosport used

to call Carrot Top Jim? **1941** LeMay et al. *Reap Wild Wind* (film): You lovely little carrot-top. **1948** J. Stevens *Jim Turner* 221: She was a carrot-top, light-complected under a lot of freckles. **1958** Johnson *Henry Orient* 177: O honorable carrot-top...what would we do without you? **1981** Ballenger *Terror* 33: McCurdy [was] a burly carrot top.

carry *v.* **1.** *Und.* to have money in one's possession.
  1933 Ersine *Prison Slang* 25: *Carry, v.* To have money. "Abe's carrying." **1974** Loken *Come Monday Morning* 149: "You...carryin'?" Russ...brought out the rest of his roll.
  2. *Police & Und.* to carry illicit drugs; to have illicit drugs on one's person.
  1961 (cited in Partridge *Dict. Und.* (ed. 2) 803). **1970** Landy *Underground Dict.* 47: *Carry*...Be in possession of a drug. **1971** *Inter. Jour. of Addictions* (June) 352: *Carrying.* to transport drugs; or to keep drugs on one's body. **1972** Smith & Gay *Don't Try It* 199: *Carry.* To possess drugs.
  3. *Police.* to carry a gun or other weapon.
  1955 E. Hunter *Jungle Kids* 102: They talked it up, figuring who was gonna be the first to die, in case Django was carrying....And Django was always heeled. **1970–71** Higgins *Eddie Coyle* 23: They give him a fat three or so for carrying without a permit. **1973** *Playboy* (Apr.) 126: Carries, too, he's got a fuckin' permit. **1983** P. Dexter *God's Pocket* 266: Close enough to the door to be the first one out in case Shellburn was carrying.
  ¶ In phrases:
  ¶ **carry a torch** see s.v. TORCH.
  ¶ **carry me back!** (used to express exasperation or astonishment).
  1877 Bartlett *Amer.* (ed. 4) 778: *Carry me back.* Humorous way of saying, "Take me hence." At first from a negro song..."Oh, carry me back to Ole Virginny."
  ¶ **carry me out!** (used to express exasperation or astonishment). Also in extended vars.
  1857 *N & Q* (May 16) 387: *Carry me out and bury me decently.* Do any of your correspondents recollect to have heard this phrase? **1889** Barrère & Leland *Dict. Slang* I 228: *Carry me out!* (American), an expression of incredulity, or affected disgust. It implies feeling faint and requiring to be carried out into the fresh air....Often preceded by, "Oh, good night," and sometimes intensified by the addition of "and leave me in the gutter." **1927** *AS* III 135: "You could knock me down with a feather" or "carry me out with the tongs!" were expressions of surprise.
  ¶ **carry the banner** see s.v. BANNER.
  ¶ **carry the difference** see s.v. DIFFERENCE.
  ¶ **carry the mail, 1.** Esp. *Sports.* to go at great speed.
  1927 *DN* V 441: *Carry the mail, v.* To run at top speed. **1929** *N.Y. Times* (June 2) IX 2: Stealing bases is "carrying the mail." **1930** Irwin *Tramp & Und. Sl.: Carrying the Mail*—Travelling at high speed; running swiftly. **1934** *Journalism Qly.* (Dec.) 350: *Carry the Mail*—to run with the ball (football). **1940** R. Buckner *Knute Rockne* (film): I'd give my right arm for a halfback who can carry the mail.
  2. to perform or hold responsibility for a difficult task.
  1954–60 *DAS.* **1970–71** Higgins *Eddie Coyle* 87: They...get ahold of Artie Van to carry the mail.
  ¶ **carry the stick** see s.v. STICK.

cart *n.* a tape or other cartridge.
  1982 T.D. Connors *Dict. Mass Media* 45. **1985** Radio disk jockey, age *ca*32: Reel-to-reel usually sounds better than carts, but the cart's fine for the intro.

car-toad *n. R.R.* CAR-KNOCKER.
  1929 (quot. at WHEEL MONKEY). **1931** *Writer's Digest* (May) 41: *Car Toad*—Car repairer; there are many variations of this word: car knock, car tonk, car whack, etc. **1934** *AS* (Feb.) 73: *Car toad.* One who *services* cars when they are at the terminal. *ca*1940 in Botkin *Treas. Amer. Folk.* 537: I'll make you king of all the car toads in hell. **1970** *Current Slang* V 5: *Car toad, n.* A railroad car inspector and repairman.

car-tonk *n. R.R.* CAR-KNOCKER.
  1931 (quot. at CAR-TOAD).

cartoon *n.* a ridiculous person; fool.
  1927 "M. Brand" *Pleasant Jim* 42: D'you think I'm trying to make a crush on this cartoon? *ca*1969 Rabe *Hummel* 69: You're a goddamn cartoon, you know that? *a*1978 Cooley *Dancer* 53: If they ever saw that flat-chested cartoon in the buff, they'd call the coroner!

cartridge *n. Mil.* a sausage.
  1865 in *Civil War History* IV (1958) 24: We sometimes got pork car-

tridges, and milk and soft-tack too.

cartwheel *n.* **1.** a large gold or silver coin, esp. a U.S. silver dollar. [1855 quot. presumably alludes to this sense.]
1855 Barnum *Life* 21: Talk of "cart wheels," there was never one half so large as that dollar looked to me. **1873** Miller *Modocs* 57: I gave you a whole cart-wheel, did I not? a clean twenty dollar. **1880** Pilgrim *Old Nick's Camp Meetin'* 194: Somebody 'ud drap half-a-dozen cart-wheels* in his breeches-pocket….*Mexican silver dollars. **1891** Maitland *Amer. Slang Dict.* 59: Cart-wheel…an American silver dollar. **1900** Greenough & Kittredge *Words & Ways* 141: *Cart-wheel* for "silver dollar." **1919** S. Lewis *Free Air* 107: Say, you haven't got a cartwheel instead of this wrapping paper, have you? I like to feel my money in my pocket. **1930** Bodenheim *Roller Skates* 29: Money…cartwheels…good old iron-men. **1936** Washburn *Parlor* 45: He tossed out a silver dollar to each of the girls…."In case I ain't sure who you are, flash the cartwheel on me." **1953** in F. Brown *Honeymoon* 147: There was a pile of dollar bills in front of him instead of the cartwheels. **1971** *N.Y. Post* (Mar. 31) 37: The first "cartwheels" to be minted in 35 years, first of the new Eisenhower silver dollars, will be struck at the San Francisco mint today. **1977** Monaghan *Schoolboy, Cowboy* 14: Then he handed me two silver "cartwheels."
2. *Narc.* a tablet of a stimulant drug.
1965 in H.S. Thompson *Hell's Angels* 216: Cartwheels, man. Bennies. Eat some. **1971** *Inter. Jour. of Addictions* (June) 352: Cartwheels. amphetamine sulfate (white cross-scored tablets).

carve *v.* **1.** to slash or stab, esp. repeatedly.—also constr. with *up.*
1871 Hay *Pike Co. Ballads* 27: They carved in a way that all admired. **1885** (quot. at LAY OUT). **1897** Ade *Pink Marsh* 153: If 'ey's eveh goin' 'o be any cahvin', misteh, I jus' soon go home an' read 'bout it in 'e papeh nex' mawnin'. *Ibid.* 193: She goin' 'o have him cahved by a light fellow 'at wuhks in a club. **1902** Carrothers *Black Cat* 23: So Jimmy Johnson comes to town (A-purpose to cahve Sambo Brown). **1919** Darling *Jargon Book* 7: Carve—To cut up with a knife or razor. **1923** O'Hare *In Prison* 28: Another "hasher" tried to "cop" her "steady," so Mamie used a steak knife to "carve her map and spoil her mug." **1927** in Hammett *Knockover* 330: I've been choked and carved and shot at tonight. **1931** Bontemps *Sends Sunday* 35: I's a mind to carve you for dat lie. **1932** Berg *Prison Doctor* 135: Lucky the screw came along or the dinge would have carved him. **1946** Petry *Street* 271: Guys built like this one don't let other guys get close enough to carve them with a knife.
2. to defeat decisively; trounce; *(Jazz)* to outperform.
1883 *Life* (Feb. 8) 80: The…Drum-mer said…that if the Dea-con would give him one more Tray, he would carve the Stuf-fing out of Him. **1884** Carleton *Poker Club* 36: An' when yo' ketch 'em, kyarve Smith—kyarve 'im! **1958** in J. Blake *Joint* 193: This cat sits in on all kinds of sessions and carves everybody. **1964** Gold *Jazz Lexicon* 48: Carve…To defeat (someone) in musical competition, or simply to play better than one's contemporaries….Some currency c.1920–c.1940, obs. since except historical. **1971** Wells & Dance *Night People* 23: The best thing, if there was a guy sitting up there you wanted to carve, you'd tell him you'd be waiting outside, and then you'd take him off. *Ibid.* 117: Carve, v. To excel in playing. **1986** Clayton & Elliott *Jazz World* 89: There was nobody in Kansas City who could carve Lester.
3. *Jazz.* to thrill; SEND.
1943 Shulman *Barefoot Boy* 88: Benny Goodman…He carves me. I mean he carves me. Does he carve you?
¶ In phrase:
¶ **carve up scores** *Und.* to reminisce or chat with a friend. Cf. syn. *cut up touches* s.v. TOUCH.
1934 D. Runyon, in *Collier's* (Feb. 3) 9: We are standing there carving up a few old scores.

carver *n.* **1.** a knife used as a weapon.
1907 Siler *Pugilism* 88: He reminded me of his carver by pricking my back and saying: "I'll shove this through you if Bob don't win."
2. *W. Cattle Industry.* a cutting horse.
1913 in *DA.*

carving contest *n. Jazz.* a contest between jazz musicians.
1959 in R. Gold *Jazz Lexicon* 75: In the 1910s…a battle of bands known as a "carving" contest was on. **1964** Smith & Hoefer *Music* 3: What they called a carving contest was when we would try to see who could decorate a well-known melody with the best variations. **1978** W. Brown *Tragic Magic* 5: Their battles are reminiscent of the "carving contests" that went on between musicians during the early days of jazz in New Orleans.

carving horse *n. W. Cattle Industry.* a cutting horse.
1920 in *DA* 276. **1933** *AS* (Feb.) 29: Cuttin' Horse…Variations: *carvin' horse, choppin' horse.*

car-whack *n. R.R.* CAR-KNOCKER.
1931 (quot. at CAR-TOAD).

car-whacker *n. R.R.* CAR-KNOCKER.
1923 McKnight *English Words* 44: To the vocabulary of railroad men belong such words as *car whacker* for "repairer." **1970** *Current Slang* V 5: *Car Whacker,* n. Railroad car inspector and repairman.

casa *n.* [It; Sp] Esp. *Und.* a house.
1855 Doten *Journals* I 220: He has the whole floor of our "casa" for a bunk. **1859** Matsell *Vocab.* 17: *Casa.* A house, "Tout that casa"—mark that house. *1883 in F & H* II 45: From the Italian we get the thieves' slang term *casa* for house. **1889** Barrère & Leland *Dict. Slang* I 228: *Casa*…(Theatrical), a house. **1939** Howsley *Argot* 11: *Casa*—house, home; a joint.

casaba *n.* **1.** a basketball. *Joc.*
1927 *AS* II (Mar.) 275: *Casaba.* basket ball. **1937** in Paxton *Sport* 251: Right now, imagine five tall California basketball players and five not-quite-so-tall University of Southern California casaba chasers on the floor at the Olympic Auditorium.
2. the head.
1954 Schulberg *Waterfront* 191: What was he doing—getting soft in the casaba? **1981** Texas man, age ca20: That stuff'll mess up your casaba.
3. *pl.* a woman's breasts.
1970 S.J. Perelman, in *New Yorker* (Oct. 17) 39: The face was Ava Gardner at nineteen…and the casabas—well. **1986** *Playboy* (Apr.) 20: Breasts…*casabas*…coconuts…[etc.]. **1993** *N.Y. Times Mag.* (Sept. 19) 20: What ever happened to comparing breasts to fruit—casabas, melons, peaches?

cascade *v.* to vomit.
ca1670 Pepys (cited in Partridge *DSUE* (ed. 8) 186). *1805* in *OED:* I had cascaded two or three times. **1848** Bartlett *Amer.:* Cascade. To vomit—from the resemblance to a waterfall. It is a common word in England. **1889** Barrère & Leland *Dict. Slang* I 229: To *cascade,* to vomit. **1943, 1950, 1966** in *DARE* I 552.

case[1] *n.* [perh. < It *casa*] *Und.* a house, shop, or establishment, esp. a brothel or place of low resort; JOINT.
1536 Copland *Spyttel House* iii: Toure the patrying cove in the darkman cace. *1552* (cited in Partridge *Dict. Und.* 108). *1698–99* "B.E." *Dict. Canting Crew:* Case…a House, Shop, or Ware-house; also a Bawdy-house. *Toute the Case…*to view, mark, or eye the House or Shop…*A Case fro…*a Whore that Plies in a Bawdy-house. *1725* New Canting Dict.: Now let's dub the Gigg of the Case, Now…let's fall on, and break open the Door of the House. *Ibid.* And if my Whore be not in Case,/My Hostess' Daughter has her place. *1821* P. Egan *Life in London* II 177: In the motley group are *Coves of Cases* and procuresses. **1859** Matsell *Vocab.* 2: *Casse* [sic]. A house. *1860* Hotten *Slang Dict.* (ed. 2): *Casa,* or *case,* a house, respectable or otherwise. **1867** *Nat. Police Gaz.* (Mar. 30) 2: Roger…keeps a "case" in Howard street, which is well-patronized by "guns." *1890* in Ware *Passing English* 65: Neal kept what is vulgarly known as a case. *1909* Ware *Passing English* 65: He kept a case for years in Panton Street.

case[2] *n.* **1.** a person who is peculiar or remarkable in some way, esp. one who is amusing, pitiable, exasperating, etc.
1833 in *DA:* In the slang of the backwoods, one swore…he would never be "a case"—that is, flat, without a dollar. **1840** in *DAE:* He is quite "a case," I do assure you. **1846** N.J.T. Dana *Monterrey* 41: He is a mighty funny old case. **1912** Ade *Babel* 6: Eddie threw back his head and laughed aloud. "This is one o' the cases," he said, calling to Larry. **1913** in Kornbluh *Rebel Voices* 140: You are a case. **1956** (quot. at YAK, *v.*).
2.a. an infatuation.
1852 in *DA* 276: Young America…voted it "a case." The elderly ladies thought it a "shocking flirtation." **1900** *DN* II 26: "To have a *case,*" to be strongly infatuated. **1963** T.I. Rubin *Sweet Daddy* 79: So I talked about her. That means [I] had a case on her or something? **1970** Landy *Underground Dict.* 47: Case…a crush—e.g. *I've got a case for him.* **1985** *Call to Glory* (ABC-TV): I'm dead serious…she's got a case on you.
b. *So.* a pair of sweethearts.
1976 Crews *Feast of Snakes* 106: Them two used to be a case here in Lebeau County.
3. a state of anger or confusion; a grudge.
1906 *Army & Navy Life* (Nov.) 500: Case, take a. Get confused or angry.

1975 Mahl *Beating Bookie* 42: The officials have too much control of the game. If one of them subconsciously "gets a case" on a coach, player, or team his calls can frustrate a team into a lousy performance.

¶ In phrases:

¶ **get off (one's) case** to quit harassing or annoying (one); *(hence)* **on (one's) case**, harassing or being hostile to (one).
1969 in Safire *Good Word* 205: That creep is always on my case. **1970** Landy *Underground Dict.* 88: Get off my case...leave me alone. **1971** H. Roberts *3d Ear*: Don't get on my case! *a*1972 *Urban Life & Culture* I 83: Everybody's...always on my case. **1972–74** Hawes & Asher *Raise Up* 48: A cracker guard from Mississippi got on my case.*...*Harassed me. **1974** Kurtzman *Bobby* 78: Look bastard, you're not making sense. Stay off my case! **1974** Gober *Black Cop* 212: He wasn't sure that it had done any good to get on Graebo's case. **1978** Selby *Requiem* 81: They're the most despised guys in the joint. Everybody's on their case. **1978** Pilcer *Teen Angel* 12: Will someone get this creep off my case. **1983** *Hour Magazine* (ABC-TV) (May 6): Everybody's gonna be on your case for this. **1989** President G.H.W. Bush, on *CBS This Morning* (CBS-TV) (Aug. 28): Come on, guys, get off my case!

¶ **keep cases on** [sugg. by the S.E. sense as used in the game of faro] Orig. *Gamb.* to watch closely.
1887 *Lantern* (N.O.) (Jan. 22) 5: I'm going to keep cases on the entire crowd. **1895** in J.I. White *Git Along Dogies* 66: I'm going to keep cases on them sky pilots and try to get onto their curves. **1896** Ade *Artie* 24: A Johnny-on-the-spot with a big badge marked "Committee" was tryin' to keep cases on her. **1922** Rollins *Cowboy* 80: Faro's terms permitted one puncher to "keep cases" on another man, rather than prosaically to observe the latter's actions or analyze his plans. **1933** D. Runyon, in *Collier's* (Oct. 28) 7: Ambrose finally becomes so scientific that nobody can keep cases on him.

¶ **on the case** working vigorously; *(also)* on hand.
1971 Goines *Dopefiend* 153: Don't let your fingers get sticky...'cause I'll be right here on the case. **1976** Schroeder *Shaking It* 76: Speakers...blare into Credence Clearwater Revival's raunchy rendition of "Proud Mary." CKLG [radio] is on the case! **1978** W. Brown *Tragic Magic* 9: I thought about all the people I've ever known who were on the case when it came to dipping what was considered up to snuff. **1980** Gould *Ft. Apache* 41: Rest?...Shit, I don't need no rest. I'm on the case, baby.

case³ *n.* [despite evidence of dates, unquestionably a shortening of CASER¹] *Gamb.* a dollar.—often used in comb. with preced. numeral and *note*.
*1839 Brandon *Poverty, Mendicity, and Crime* (glossary): Case...a bad crown piece. *Half a case*—bad half-crown. **1859** Matsell *Vocab.* 17: Case. A dollar. **1871** Banka *Prison Life* 492: One Dollar,...One Case. **1882** *Puck* (Nov. 22) 181: Tell him you came to pay those five "cases" you borrowed of him last month. **1891** DeVere *Tramp Poems* 24: They won't give a case for his chuck. **1891** Maitland *Amer. Slang Dict.* 59: *Case*...one dollar. **1896** Ade *Artie* 34: He...comes over an' touches me for two cases. *Ibid.* 51: I'd give a ten-case note to be out of it. **1906** *Nat. Police Gaz.* (Jan. 13) 3: There ain't a case note among the four of us. **1906** in "O. Henry" *Works* 1275: We got to get that case-note somehow, boys. **1908** McGaffey *Show Girl* 196: He gives me a twenty-case note. **1912** Field *Watch Yourself Go By* 395: You won't get a case from me. **1927** *DN* V 441: *Case, n.* a silver dollar. **1928** J. O'Connor *B'way Racketeers* (glossary): *Case Note*—A dollar bill. **1930** Irwin *Tramp & Und. Sl.*: *Case*—A silver dollar.

case⁴ *n. Und.* an act of looking a place over; an inspection, as for criminal purposes.
1930 Irwin *Tramp & Und. Sl.*: *Case*...An observation or spying. **1943** in Ruhm *Detective* 360: The place is darkened up, and Mr. Dingle gives me a good careful case of the joint.

case *adj. Gamb.* (of money) last in one's possession.—used prenominally.
1908 in H.C. Fisher *A. Mutt* 33: I gotta bet the case 2 bucks today. **1915** T.A. Dorgan, in Zwilling *TAD Lexicon* 24: I'll bet it's the case dime too. **1930** *Amer. Merc.* (Dec.): I'm down to case dough. **1930** in Partridge *Dict. Und.* 108: Case money. **1949** Monteleone *Crim. Slang* 44: *Case Dollar*...one's last dollar. **1959** A. Anderson *Lover Man* 139: You could bet your case ace he'd be there.

case *v.* **1.a.** [prob. sugg. by *keep cases on* s.v. CASE², *n.*] Esp. *Und.* to scrutinize, watch closely, survey, etc., esp. for the purpose of planning a crime.—also constr. with *up*. Hence **casing**, *n.*
1914 Jackson & Hellyer *Criminal Slang* 23: *Case*, verb...To watch, to

observe, to scrutinize. **1929** Booth *Stealing Through Life* 281: I've cased it, on and off for a month. **1929** Hotstetter & Beesley *Racket* 221: *Case*—To search, investigate, look over; *e.g.* "The bulls were casing Feinburg's joint." *Case up*—To look over the situation very carefully. **1930** Conwell *Professional Thief* 5: The thief...made known to the mob that they were being cased (watched). **1939–40** O'Hara *Pal Joey* 53: I cased the mouse and got a look at her kisser. **1944** C.B. Davis *Leo McGuire* 154: This job will take practically no casing. **1949** Monteleone *Crim. Slang* 44: *Case a Mark*...To select a victim. **1952** Chase *McThing* 49: I've cased this burg from end to end and all I bring home is alibis. **1955** Q. Reynolds *HQ* 80: You can spot hoods going into the Harding. Case them good and then go to the B. of I. and look at their mug shots. **1958** S.H. Adams *Tenderloin* 171: There's nothing in his record. We cased it good. **1961** Scarne *Comp. Guide to Gambling* 674: That black-jack player has been casing the deck and knows that there are two live aces left. **1974** E. Thompson *Tattoo* 363: Buck's got this punchboard cased up in Cherryville. Figures it could be hit for a couple of C's. **1976** *S.W.A.T.* (NBC-TV): He's not going to hit you without casing you first. **1980** Kotzwinkle *Jack* 114: Spider's casin' the place. **1991** B.E. Ellis *Amer. Psycho* 32: "Yes?" Price says, casing the room.

b. *Broadly,* to look at.
1944 D. Hartman et al. *Princess & Pirate* (film): Hey! Case this handbill!

2.a. Esp. *Und.* to form a judgment of on the basis of observation; evaluate.
1929 T. Gordon *Born to Be* 125: I began to case every gal and woman I knew in the town. I couldn't place anyone I had been so fly with so much as I should be hanged about. **1933** D. Runyon, in *Collier's* (May 13) 7: They have Lance McGowan pretty well cased. **1956** G. Green *Last Angry Man* 518: You're...a lot smarter than I ever cased you for. **1970** in Cannon *Nobody Asked* 178: They cased Clay as a guy with an angle when he began to preach the doctrines of the Black Muslims.

b. *Police.* to investigate.
1977 Dunne *True Confessions* 29: Two years he had cased stiffs...and it was always the same from Frank: "The butler did it."

3. *Black E.* (see quot.).
1971 H. Roberts *3d Ear*: *Case*...to joke about another's character or foibles; *e.g.* He cased her at lunch. 2. to reprove or reprimand sternly; *e.g.* His mother cased him for being late.

case note *n.* see s.v. CASE³.

caser¹ *n.* [BrE 'crown [a coin worth five shillings]' < W Yid *keser* 'crown [any of a number of coins issued by German-speaking states]', lit. 'one of two ornamental crowns placed on a Scroll of the Law' < Heb *keter-tora*, lit. 'crown of the Pentateuch'] *Gamb.* a dollar. [In BrE quots., a British five-shilling piece.]
*1849 in *OEDS*: A caser (dollar) if you fine him a night of it. ***1879** in Partridge *Dict. Und.*: I did not have more than a caser (5/-) [five shillings]. **1907** *American Mag.* (May) 508: Thirteen casers every month. **1911** Runyon *Tents of Trouble* 96: Thirteen casers every month, pants an' hat an' shirt. **1915** Howard *God's Man* 361: I took out half a caser. **1933** (cited in Partridge *Dict. Und.*).

caser² *n.* [fr. CASE, *v.*] *Und.* a scout for a criminal gang.
1937 Hoover *Persons in Hiding* 148: Kathryn had an underworld reputation as a "locator" or "caser," the person who goes ahead to plan the robbery of a store or a bank. **1970** Rudensky & Riley *Gonif* 94: Talking with casers for Dinty's mob.

Casey *n.* [sugg. by *K.C.* 'Kansas City'] *R.R.* (see quot.).
1916 Livingston *Snare* 68: We rambled southward over the Kansas City Southern, a railroad the hoboes had dubbed "The Casey." **1942** *ATS* 728.

Casey Jones *n.* [nickname of John Luther Jones (1864–1900), U.S. locomotive engineer, folk hero of ballads, stories, and plays]
1. a locomotive engineer.
1929 Tully *Shadows of Men* 107: The railroads'll run right along—the same old freights'll bump over the same old rails—an' all the Casey Joneses'll blow their whistles. **1931** *Writer's Digest* (May) 40: Listen to this about any "Casey Jones." **1958** McCulloch *Woods Words* 30: *Casey Jones*—a locie engineer. **1970** "Grateful Dead" *Casey Jones* (pop. song): Drivin' that train/High on cocaine/Casey Jones you'd better watch your speed.
2. a railroad train.
1945 *Amer. N & Q* (July) 54: *Casey Jones Mission*: a flight undertaken by

U.S. airmen over Japan against railroad installations. **1977** Avallone *White Knight* 5: Four cars of the Casey Jones had been shaken up plenty.

cash *n.* a cashboy or cashgirl.

1876, 1886 in *DA.* **1891** Riis *Other Half* 129: One boy had a place as "cash" in a store.

cash *v.* **1.** to give up; quit; CASH IN, 2.

1905 *Nat. Police Gaz.* (July 15) 6: When a trainer is taken by the eye of an elephant, he may as well "cash."

2. to die; CASH IN, 1.

1908, 1922 in *DAE.*

¶ In phrase:

¶ **cash (one's) pistol** *West.* to rob a bank at gunpoint.

1880 Martin *Sam Bass* 141: What do you reckon the old banker will say, boys, when we tell him we want to cash these old white pistols? *Ibid.* 146: We didn't want any racket until we could make a draw and cash our old white pistols.

cash cow *n.* [cf. *milch cow*, attested since 1601 in *OED2* with same meaning] *Finance.* an investment or other source of money that pays regularly and well.

1974 *Business Week* (Aug. 24) 49: Brown could have considered the old, cyclical businesses…which have always produced handsome returns on minimal investments, merely as "cash cows." **1981** *L.A. Times* (Mar. 29) VI 1: Some of the company's home appliance lines have been milked too heavily as "cash cows" to generate capital for faster-growing GE businesses. **1984** WINS radio ad: We call [such investments] *cash cows.* **1987** *ABC Nightly News* (ABC-TV) (Mar. 30): Home equity loans—are they cash cows or time bombs? **1990** *Nation* (Apr. 16) 511: Any talk of an overall increase in foreign aid is shot down…by the Pentagon's refusal to be seen as a cash cow.

cash down *v.* CASH UP.

1882 Sweet & Knox *Tex. Siftings* 41: Cash down, quick, or I'll bounce you off at the next station we come to.

cash-in *n.* **1.** the end; death.—constr. with *the.*

1926 C.M. Russell *Trails* 147: Several times in my life I've been close to the cash in…but about the nearest I ever come to crossin' the big range is a few years ago, before I move to Montana. *Ibid.* 149: I was with him at the cash in.

2. an act or instance of cashing in financially. [An extension of the technical S.E. sense, 'to redeem a bond or the like'.]

1985 Sawislak *Dwarf* 207: He wanted a quick cash-in.

cash in *v.* **1.** [short for *cash in (one's) chips*, below] to die.—occ. constr. with *it.*

1891 DeVere *Tramp Poems* 63: He/Would not go in/To "the little church round the corner,"/If you or I "cashed in." **1897** A. Lewis *Wolfville* 6: We has, in honor of the dead an' to mark the occasion of his cashin' in, agreed upon a business departure of interest to all. **1899–1900** Cullen *Tales* 291: He's about to cash in for the want of a drink. **1905** in Cather *Short Fiction* 182: Forty's young for a Merrick to cash in. **1907** in H.C. Fisher *A. Mutt* 18: I fear I'm about to cash in. **1911** Fletcher *Up the Trail* 49: Some Texas cowboy on duty had cashed in—had been killed by lightning and was buried beside the body of his faithful horse. **1915** Braley *Songs of Workaday World* 105: But, when I cash in—say, I/Want to take it like that guy. **1972** Wurlitzer *Quake* 99: I won't let you cash it in. **1980** *Nat. Lampoon* (Aug.) 78: Which one of you is going to cash it in? It says here one of you has a fatal congenital disease.

2. [short for *cash in (one's) chips*, below] Orig. *Gamb.* to quit; give up.

1896 Ade *Artie* 30: Now, if you're stuck on him, I'll cash in right here and drop out o' the game. **1905** *N.Y. Times* (May 29) 9: Corbett is a dead one, Fitz [Bob Fitzsimmons, d. 1917] has cashed in, and Hart isn't in my class [as a fighter]. **1918** Bellamy *Diary* (Nov. 6): Austria has cashed in. So has Turkey. Now we are waiting for Germany. **1928** Bodenheim *Georgie May* 5: I'm twenty-three now—seven more years and they'll be ready to cash in.

3. to reap a profit, reward, or advantage of any kind; in phr. **cash in on** to profit from or turn to one's advantage. Now *colloq.*

1928 MacArthur *War Bugs* 52: He hauled Mr. Papolis back to the battery and as nimbly returned to the lady's *maison* to cash in. **1930** in R.E. Howard *Iron Man* 19: I'm going to cash in on my ruggedness. **1942** *ATS* 710: *Cash in big*, to win heavily. **1970** N.Y.U. student: Now's the time to cash in on that experience. **1985** Ark. man, age 35: Stephen

King's really cashing in on the supernatural.

¶ In phrase:

¶ **cash in (one's) chips** [or **checks**] see s.v. CHIP, *n.*, and CHECK, *n.*

cashola *n.* [*cash* + -OLA] cash.

1976–77 Kernochan *Dry Hustle* 84: Anyhow, the deal was I'd make a lot of cashola in a glamorous nightlife of nonstop parties, and for sweeteners Frank would get me a fake ID and a cabaret card.

cash out *v.* **1.a.** to die; CASH IN.

1965 (quot. at (2), below).

b. to commit suicide.

1968 Beck *Trick Baby* 9: You're Iceberg Slim, the pimp. You can't cash out like a square.

2. to kill (a person).

1965 C. Brown *Manchild* 313: Everybody was trying to either cash out on Saturday night or cash somebody else out. **1967** Beck *Pimp* 124: I'm going over there right now and cash them out.

cash over *v.* CASH UP.

1854 in *DAE.*

cash up *v.* to pay; hand over money.

*1837 in *F & H* II 46: For he could not *cash up*, spite of all he could do. **1890** in *DAE* I 438. **1891** Maitland *Amer. Slang Dict.* 59: Cash up…to pay.

casket nail *n.* a cigarette; COFFIN NAIL. Also **casket tack.**

1966–69 in *DARE.*

cast *v.* ¶ In phrase: **cast up (one's) accounts** to vomit.

1887 L.A. Norton *Life* 443: Men, women, and children were "casting up their accounts."

caster *n.* a testicle.

1888 *Stag Party* 61: It cut of one of mi strings and dropped one of mi kasters in the bottom of the sak where hit has been ever since, and my wife says it is a dam shame.

casting *n.* a coin; (*pl.*) cash.

1834 in *DARE.* **1839** *Spirit of Times* (Aug. 10) 267: The greedy thimble player looked with an eager eye towards the handkerchief of Mexican castings before him. **1843** in Harris *High Times* 20: I've got the fastest horse in these United States…and lots of castings to back my judgment. **1844** *Spirit of Times* (Sept. 21) 354: He accordingly forked over the castings, $600 in number. **1851** in *DA.*

casting couch *n. Theat. & Film.* a couch in a director's office, supposedly for use with actresses willing to exchange sexual favors for roles. *Joc.*

1931 in Tamony *Americanisms* (No. 25) 4: This one happened some time ago, long before the casting couches were thrown out of the Shubert Building. **1940** Fitzgerald *Last Tycoon* 70: And you jump up quickly off the casting couch, smoothing your skirts. **1952** Lait & Mortimer *USA* 137: The casting couches of Beverly Hills. **1966** Jarrett *Private Affair* 68: I know bondsmen in Chicago whose offices are equipped with what they call "casting couches"—for the purpose of sampling the wares of girls before the deals are finalized. **1966** "Petronius" *N.Y. Unexp.* 46: Theatrical concerns with the perennial "casting couch." **1968** Moura & Sutherland *Tender Loving Care* 110: You've read too many trashy Hollywood novels. I suppose you were thinking I was going to turn this into a casting couch situation. **1970** Della Femina *Wonderful Folks* 16: As far as he's concerned I'm in Hollywood and the whole world is one big casting couch. **1973** in *Playboy* (Jan. '74) 71: There isn't any casting couch involved, if that's what you mean. **1978** C. Crawford *Mommie* 13: There was no protection from…the famous casting couches. **1990** *Cosmopolitan* (June) 182: Lena Horne later pointed out that she and Ava [Gardner] may have been the only two women on the lot who didn't use the casting couch to get ahead.

cast-iron dog *n. S.W.* a Mexican hairless. *Joc.*

1853, 1882 in *DAE.*

castor *n.* a hat. [In earlier S.E. 'a hat made of beaver or rabbit fur'; *OED* gives English exx. in that sense from 1640 to 1750.]

*1811 *Lexicon Balatron.*: Castor. A hat. *To prig a castor*; to steal a hat. **1812* Vaux *Vocab*: Castor: a hat. **1832** *Spirit of Times* (Mar. 3) 3: McDonnell…threw up his *castor*, amidst the cheers of his friends. **1859** Matsell *Vocab.* 18: Castor. A hat. **1897* in S.J. Baker *Australian Lang.* 117: A "castor" or a "kady"/Is the name he gives his hat! **1909* Ware *Passing English* 66: Any hat is called a castor. **1923** *N.Y. Times* (Sept. 9) VIII 2: *Castor*: A hat, a kelly.

casual *adj. Stu.* **1.** good; satisfactory; acceptable; not worth getting upset over.

1977 Eble *Campus Slang* (Apr.) 1: *Casual*—acceptable, good, fun: I thought I'd study a little then go out with Bill. That's casual! **1982** S. Black *Totally Awesome* 60: Pointed [shoes]. They're like so-o-o casual. **1984** C. Crowe *Wild Life* (film): "Sorry." "That's casual." *Ibid.* "I've been doing your job for two hours. Get to work!" "It's casual."

2. clever; quick-witted.

1979 (quot. at WEENIE, *n.*).

cat *n.* **1.a.** a sexually promiscuous woman; (*specif.*) a prostitute.—occ. with weakened force.

*1675 in Duffett *Burlesque Plays* 66: Heave Cats, heave. **1698–99* "B.E." *Dict. Canting Crew*: *Cat*, a common Whore or Prostitute. **1785* Grose *Vulgar Tongue*: *Cat*. A common prostitute. **1791** [W. Smith] *Confess. T. Mount* 19: Lewd women, *cats*. **1882** in P.M. Ryan *Tombstone Theatre* 68: All sitting around tables drinking promiscuously with the "cats." **1924** Tully *Beggars of Life* 138: None o' these cats care for a fellow's furniture. Never marry a sport, kid. They're bum housekeepers. **1930** Lait *On Spot* 201: *Cat*...a prostitute; a house of ill fame is a cathouse. **1932** *AS* VII 330: *Cat*...a prostitute. **1937** *AS* (Oct.) 240: Negroes use it...to denote...any girl or woman: "Let's go pick up a couple of cats." **1948** J. Stevens *Jim Turner* 233: Thar was cocaine Alice and cocaine Nell/All the cats in the alley give the cocaine hell! **1958** McCulloch *Woods Words* 30: *Cat*...an easy dame. **1961** Gover *$100 Misunderstanding* 41: *I* is the *cat*, you is the *trick*. **1963** Coon *Short End* 75: When she stopped there I figured she was another cat and could be had at the price...but if that was so why wasn't she pushing it? **1966–80** Folb *Runnin' Lines* 232: *Cat*...Female. **1989** "Too Short" *Freaky Tales* (rap song): Once again at the cat, I had it goin' on.

b. the vulva or vagina; PUSSY, 1.—usu. considered vulgar.

[**1629* in J. Katz *Gay/Lesbian Almanac* 72: I [a transvestite or hermaphrodite] go in woman's apparel to get a bit for my cat!] **a1720* in D'Urfey *Pills* II 81: She'd cry...you starve my Cat. **1889* Barrère & Leland *Dict. Slang* I 229: *Cat*...The *pudendum f.* In French, *chat*. **1916** *DN* IV 321: *Get meat for (one's) cat*...To solicit. **1916** Cary *Venery* I 40: *Cat*....The vagina; otherwise a pussy. **1933** in M. Taft *Blues Lyric Poetry* 189: Going to Savannah: make some jack/Hold that cat: till I get back....It's got hair on it....Best little somethin I ever saw. **1938** "Justinian" *Amer. Sexualis* 15: *Cat*. n....Also used to mean the female pudend. **1953** Paley *Rumble* 96: You guys are both cat-crazy! **1965** Trimble *Sex Words* 39: *Cat-Lapper*....a Cunnilinguist [*sic*], usually in reference to a Lesbian. **1971** S. Stevens *Way Uptown* 31: Mindy laid down and jackknifed her legs wide open with her cat to the people. **1974** Miami Univ. student: "Let's get some *cat*" means "Let's get some *pussy*." That's a high-school expression.

2. a cat-o'-nine-tails.

1853 Sketch *Down-Trodden* 17: I'se 'fraid o' de "cat."

3.a. a person, esp. as required for a particular purpose. Cf. *different breed of cat*, below.

1863 in Hay *Lincoln* 91: But politicians are strong yet & he [Lincoln] is not their "kind of a cat." **1885** *Uncle Daniel's Story* 99: Dis darky was done gone when dey comed. I know'd dey'd be dar sometime for dis cat, and Marfa, too....She know how to cook and do things, she do. Be a cole day when dey gits dis cat agin, sho's you born'd...De cat done gone. He-ah! he-ah!

b. Esp. *Black E.* a fellow; a man or boy; (*also*, in recent use) a person of either sex. [Popularized by swing musicians after *ca*1935, when infl. by **(c)**, below; in jazz circles often contrasted with CHICK 'young woman'. The extension of the word to include women, as in 1956 and 1981 quots., is uncommon; cf. earlier and comparable development of GUY.]

1920 F.S. Fitzgerald *Paradise* 45: Oh, it isn't that I mind the glittering caste system....I like having a bunch of hot cats on top, but gosh, Kerry, I've got to be one of them. **1925–26** Black *Can't Win* 67 [ref. to 1890's]: Nix, nix....Buy nothin'....It's you kind of cats that make it tough on us, buyin' chuck. **1930** Botkin *Folk-Say* 107: Knock 'er down to the grit, cats. *Ibid.* 111: *Cats*—[oil] pipeliners. **1931** L. Armstrong, in Driggs & Lewine *Black Beauty* 30: Tell all the cats on the stroll howdy from your boy. **1932** in Leadbitter & Slaven *Blues Records* 389: Cat You Been Messin' Aroun'. **1939** in A. Banks *First Person* 255: I'd sing all night after that cat done give me four bucks. **1944** in Himes *Black on Black* 198: Here come a big Uncle Tomish lookin' cat in starched overalls. **1946** Boulware *Jive & Slang* 2: *Cat*...a boy, fellow. **1946** in Clarke *Amer. Negro Stories* 141: Trouble is...you all cats go bristlin' up when Poke comes round. **1952** E. Brown *Trespass* 20: You cats crazy? **1954** L. Armstrong *Satchmo* 164: Believe me, I was a sharp cat. **1956** in Galewitz *Great Comics* 154: Sally Forth, their top cat, had 'em make me a 'onorary member. **1961** in Himes *Black on Black* 46: I know where some cats are having a reefer party. **1964** R. Kendall *Black School* 173: I wanna bring some cat over to the house to cool her wagon and he wont [*sic*] let me. **1971** Le Guin *Lathe of Heaven* 10: I loan mine, use another cat's, all the time. **1972** C. Gaines *Stay Hungry* 136: Are you cats cowboys? **1973** M. Collins *Carrying the Fire* 403: You cats take it easy on the lunar surface. **1975** Hinton *Rumble Fish* 12: Biff is a mean cat. **1981** O'Day & Eells *High Times* 234: She is a straight cat who doesn't drink hard liquor, drug, or make waves. *a*1982 Hartwell & Bentley *Open to Lang.* 323: Most of us now would find [the phrase] "a real cool cat" to be agonizingly dated. **1989** S. Robinson & D. Ritz *Smokey* 4: The cats would ask me to smoke weed.

c. *Jazz.* a usu. male performer or avid devotee of jazz or swing music.

1931 in P. Oliver *Songsters & Saints* 42: Oh, shout you cats.../Grab your gal and knock 'em dead/...Hey, hey, everybody sing.../Shout you cats. **1932** in *OEDS.* **1935** (quot. at SWING). **1936** Parker *Battling Hoofer* (film): Hit it, you cats! **1937** *New Yorker* (Apr. 17) 27: Dance musicians are known as *cats*. **1940** in Handy *Blues Treasury* 171: The rhythm he beats puts the cats in a trance,/Nobody there bothers to dance. **1945** Drake & Cayton *Black Metropolis* 589: These were the "cats" who, clad in "zoot-suits," stood around and "jived" the women. **1954** W.G. Smith *South St.* 144: "Hell, I'm a *cat*, Uncle Slim." "A cat?" "I can *dance*, Uncle Slim. None of this old-fashioned stuff from me." **1957** in Rosset *Evergreen Reader* 24: Louis [Armstrong] had a lot to do with the popularizing of jazz words. He used certain expressions on the riverboats [*ca*1920], like "Come on, you cats," and "Look out there, Pops," and the like. These were his own ideas. I had never heard such words as "jive" and "cat" and "scat" used in New Orleans....These other terms Louis had a lot to do with. **1959** in Cox *Delinquent, Hipster, Square* 35: Can you imagine—eighteen months—the youngest cat this side of Mars. **1992** *Rolling Stone* (June 11) 58: The conversation turned to jazz...and "the cat" who played the solo on "And the Angels Sing."

d. an object; item.

1972 (quot. at INHALE).

4. *Hobo.* GAYCAT; (*also*) an itinerant laborer or hobo. [The form *cad* in 1894 quot. seems to be a misprint or otherwise erroneous.]

1894 "J. Flynt," in *Century* (Feb.) 518: I'll bet my Thanksgivin' dinner that every cad [*sic*] you meet up the road is bound south. **1925–26** Black *Can't Win* 221 [ref. to 1890's]: They stuck up the cats, took their money, and forced them to jump out...between stations. **1927** *AS* (June) 386: *John*, *cat*, *character* and *stiff* are synonyms for dingbat....a *gaycat* is a greenhorn on the road. **1927** *DN* V 447: *Fresh cat*, n. a neophyte hobo. *Ibid.* 460: *Rank cat*, *n*. The low grade tramp. **1928** *Amer. Mercury* (May): Cats are itinerant workers, the fringe of the hobo, bum, and yegg outfits, who beat their way on freight trains. **1930** Irwin *Tramp & Und. Sl.*: *Cat*—An itinerant worker.

5. *Pris.* an informer.

1926 *Writer's Mo.* (Dec.) 541: *Rat, Fink, Pigeon, Cat*—One who tells on his fellow convicts. **1927–28** Tasker *Grimhaven* 33: "There never was six gees got together in the world without at least one of them being a cat!" "Cat?" "Sure. A fink, stool-pigeon." **1936** Duncan *Over the Wall* 245: He was known as a "cat"—a man who would go to the bulls and betray his associates without batting an eye.

6. *Naval Av.* an airplane catapult.—also attrib.

1962 Quirk *Red Ribbons* 61: The cat sent the fighters careening off the deck. **1966–67** Harvey *Air War* 6: An F-4...was being launched from the....cat. **1981** Mersky & Polmar *Nav. Air War in Viet.* 84: Another Crusader is readied on the starboard "cat." **1984** Trotti *Phantom* 134: [You] signal your readiness with a salute to the cat officer. **1989** J. Weber *Defcon One* 6: He snapped off a salute to the cat officer.

7. (*cap.*) *Mil. Av.* (variously) a Grumman F4F Wildcat fighter plane; a PBY Catalina patrol plane; a Grumman F-14 Tomcat fighter plane.

1943 Bayler & Carnes *Wake* I. 183: I was prejudiced in favor of the scrappy little 'Cats. **1944** E.H. Hunt *Limit* 31: We'll send up a Cat after him. **1983** USAF officer, age *ca*28: The F-14 Tomcats are called *Cats*. **1987** G. Hall *Top Gun* 49: He...reefs the 'Cat into a...vertical climb.

8. a Caterpillar [a registered trademark] tractor or bulldozer; (*hence*) a tractor of any sort.

1918 *DN* V 23: *Cat*, n. Caterpillar traction engine. Farmers. **1919** Duffy *G.P.F. Book* 199: Hence, with the first fall of dusk, the "cats" began their final snorting toward "no man's land." *Ibid.* 210: The Germans mistook ours for tanks and welcomed the cats as tanks are welcomed. **1936** in Pyle *Ernie's Amer.* 153: They said he was driving a "cat" down at the Monument Camp. **1943** Pyle *Brave Men* 66: Campagnone had been a "cat" driver ever since he started working. *a***1944** Binns *Timber Beast* 344: We ought to bring in a couple of "cats" and log it ourselves. **1963–64** Kesey *Great Notion* 346: The state won't let us bring cats and donkeys in. **1968** R. Adams *Western Words* (ed. 2) 56: *Cat*…In logging, any tractor, not necessarily a Caterpillar, though the name comes from that type. **1979** Crews *Blood & Grits* 71: Tractors, Cats, trucks run day and night. *a***1986** K.W. Nolan *Into Laos* 104: One cat could do that in an hour.

9. *Stu.* a grade of C.

1979 Univ. Tenn. grad. student: When I was in college [1964–68] an A was an *ace*, a B was a *bang*, a C was a *cat* or a *hook*, a D was a *dog*, and an F was a *frog*. B+ was a *bang and a half*. C+ was a *hook and a half*.

10. *Okla.* illicitly distilled whiskey.

1965–66 in *DARE*.

11. *Und. & Police.* CAT BURGLAR.

1986 *Miami Vice* (NBC-TV): The guy's a cat…A cat burglar. *Ibid.* It's a cat case.

12. *Narc.* methcathenone, a powerful stimulant.

1993 *Prime News* (CNN-TV) (June 29): Methcathenone—or *cat*— makes cocaine look tame. **1993** *All Things Considered* (Nat. Public Radio) (Oct. 10): Usually inhaled, cat is a stimulant…similar to…cocaine.…It's incredibly popular…it produces a more intense and longer-lasting high than cocaine.

13. usu. *pl.* [orig. a euphem. for *Christ*] (used in various exclamations).

1900 Hammond *Whaler* 203: Jiminy cats! I hain't what you can call *narvous*…but yeh c'n bet I felt shaky enough right then. **1907** in Butterfield *Post Treasury* 8: Holy cats! **1907** S.E. White *Arizona Nights* 131: But, suffering cats, think how that fellow sized us up for…fools. **1909** in O. Johnson *Lawrenceville* 27 [ref. to 1890's]: Holy cats! **1918** *Sat. Eve. Post* (Mar. 30) 89: Sufferin' cats! How did that happen? **1926** Hormel *Co-Ed* 117: And for the cat's sake, she didn't need to be taken care of! **1931** Barry *Animal Kingdom* 346: Holy cats, Red— **1943** in T. Williams *Letters* 81: Holy Cats! **1947** Willingham *End As a Man* 77: Oh, cats, man, that was a hot afternoon. **1973** Savitz *On the Move* 13: "Holy cats…holy cat." He shook his head and laughed. **1992** *New Yorker* (Dec. 28) 105: Holy Cats!

¶ In phrases:

¶ **a cat's tail** (used to express negation or derision).

1862 C.F. Browne *A. Ward* 39: "Betsy, you little appresiate the importance of the event which I this night commemerate." "Commemerate a cat's tail—cum into the house this intstant."

¶ **different breed of cat** a different sort of person.

1899 Garland *Eagle's Heart* 231: These little brown chaps…'re a different breed o' cats from the Ogallalahs. **1928–29** Faulkner *Sound & Fury* 250: She found out pretty quick that I was a different breed of cat from Father. **1973** in *Playboy* (Jan. '74) 47: They are a different breed of cat from my old man.

¶ **higher than a cat's back** very high.

1940 F. Hunt *Trail fr. Tex.* 66 [ref. to 1870's]: The river's higher'n a cat's back an' still risin'?

¶ **in a cat's ass** no indeed.—usu. considered vulgar.

1958 Camerer *Damned Wear Wings* 220 [ref. to WWII]: "You mean you're not going after Ploesti? Just once more?" "In a cat's ass."

¶ **one a cat couldn't scratch** a firm erection of the penis.— usu. considered vulgar.

1968 W. Crawford *Gresham's War* 75: It was so hard a cat couldn't scratch it. **1968** Westheimer *Young Sentry* 157 [ref. to WWII]: It gets so hard a cat couldn't scratch it. **1973** Gent *N. Dallas* 151: I had a hard on a cat couldn't scratch. **1985** Benedek *Cocoon* (film): "Have you got a boner?" "Blue steel! A cat couldn't scratch it."

¶ **on the cat** *Black E.* roaming or staying away from home at night.

1965 C. Brown *Manchild* 69: When I was on the cat, I knew I was going to get caught sooner or later.

¶ **till the last cat is hung** till the very end.

1854 G.G. Foster *15 Mins.* 17: When he leaves the Rotunda, which will not be till the "last cat is hung."

cat *v.* **1.** to vomit.—also trans.

*****1785** Grose *Vulgar Tongue*: *Cat*, or *Shoot the Cat*. To vomit from drunkenness. **1966** Longstreet & Godoff *Wm. Kite* 138: He…knew I was going to be ill, cat my breakfast.

2.a. (of a man) to go seeking after women as sexual partners; to consort with sexually promiscuous women.—usu. constr. with *around*.—occ. trans.

1900 *DN* II 26: *Cat, v.i.* To go with bad women. **1927** J. Stevens *Mattock* 123: One night I was cattin' down Clark Street— **1933** Milburn *No More Trumpets* 302: That would give you a little time to cat around and enjoy your freedom some, huh-huh-huh. **1953** W. Brown *Monkey on My Back* 79: *To go catting* was to go out looking for girls or to visit a brothel. **1953** in *Great Music of D. Ellington* 30: Out cattin' that Satin Doll. **1958** Berger *Crazy in Berlin* 69: Hi, Nate. Goin' out cattin'? **1962** Mandel *Mainside* 125: Bachelor. He cats around a good deal. **1963** Braly *Shake Him* 61: We were out cattin' around most of the night. **1968** Stahl *Hokey* 22: While you're out catting around. **1985** Yeager & Janos *Yeager* 12: Catting around with three or four different gals.

b. (of either sex) to be sexually unfaithful.—constr. with *around*.

1948 J. Stevens *Jim Turner* 89 [ref. to *ca*1910]: Last winter she had wound up there, after a year of catting around and leaving her brats on Aunt Sue Hurd's hands. **1979** in Raban *Old Glory* 379: "Been catting around?" "No, she weren't catting around."

3.a. *Und.* to prowl about, as in scouting an area.—also constr. with *around*.

1925 *Atlantic Mo.* (Dec.) 750: He is taught to look coolly for things and to make no deductions unless he has a fact of value upon which to base his statements. This is known among tramps as "catting" or "cattin' around."

b. *Black E.* to roam or hang about the streets, esp. at night; to stay away from home all night.—also constr. with *out*.

[**1953** W. Brown *Monkey On My Back* 79: *To cat out* was to sneak away.] **1956** Ross *Hustlers* 56: China catting out with her? **1954–60** *DAS* 91: *Cat*…to spend one's time idling on street corners. **1965** C. Brown *Manchild* 18: Catting was staying away from home all night.…Guys catted when they were afraid to go home.…They slept everywhere but in comfortable places. *Ibid.* 19: This was going to be my first try at catting out. **1971** *Inter. Jour. of Addictions* (June) 352: *Catting.* [of drug addicts] living on city rooftops.

catamaran *n.* **1.** a quarrelsome or offensive woman.

*****1785** Grose *Vulgar Tongue*: *Catamaran.* An old scraggy woman; from a kind a float made of spars and yards lashed together, for saving shipwrecked persons. *****1833** Marryat *Peter Simple* 33: "The cursed drunken old catamaran," cried he; "I'll go and cut her down by the head"; but I requested he would not, as she was a lady. **1862** Bensill *Quiet on Yamhill* 25: There was nothing strikingly observable except the fight between to [*sic*] old "catamarans" before the final close. **1883** Peck *Peck's Bad Boy* 188: I took the cage and pointed my finger at the parrot and it looked at the woman and said "old catamaran."

2. a worthless individual.

1836 in Haliburton *Sam Slick* 49: I vow I feel ashamed to be seed with such a catamaran as that. *Ibid.* 62: Now, did you ever see…such a catamaran as that.

catarumpus *n.* [prob. blend CATAWAMPUS + *rumpus*] a commotion; a rumpus.

1848 in Blair & Meine *Half Horse* 176: What's the meaning of all this here catarumpus, eh?

catawampously *adv.* vigorously or completely.

1834 in *DARE*: The giniral was catawampously inclin'd tu the United States' service. **1836** Cather *Voyage* 112: These tarnation bugs will catawampously chaw me up. **1844** *Spirit of Times* (Jan. 27) 572: You will be separately and singly, collectively and jointly catawampously and tetotaciously "chawed" up. *ca***1848** in Bartlett *Amer.* (ed. 4) 105: The bloody ground on which our fathers *catawampously* poured out their claret as free as oil. **1851** M. Reid *Scalp Hunters* 74: Whether we fired symultainyusly, or extraneously, or cattawompously, aint the flappin' o' a beaver's tail to me. **1851** in Chittick *Roarers* 190: He knowed he'd git catawompously chored up ashore. *****1853** in *F & H* II 52: To be catawampously champed up by a mercenary selfish cormorant of a capitalist. **1889** Barrère & Leland *Dict. Slang* I 230: *Catawampously* (American), fiercely, eagerly, violently. **1915** [Swartwood] *Choice Slang* 44: *Catawompously*—Completely. Entirely.

catawamptiously *adv.* CATAWAMPOUSLY.

1857 F. Douglass, in Bartlett *Amer.* (ed. 4) 105: Where is the wealth and power that should make us fourteen millions take to our heels before three hundred thousand slaveholders, for fear of being *catawamptiously chawed up*? **1878** [P.S. Warne] *Hard Crowd* 2: Missouri Bill…kin catawamptiously chaw up any two-legged critter.

catawampus *n.* a peculiar or remarkable thing or person. Often *joc.*

1833 Paulding *Lion of the West* 21: On my way I took a squint at my wild lands along by the Big Muddy and Little Muddy to Bear Grass Creek, and had what I call a rael [*sic*], roundabout catawampus, clean through the deestrict. **1843** in *DA* 282: The tother one what got most sker'd, is a sort of catawampus. **1936** R. Adams *Cowboy Lingo* 236: This old catawampus...orates as how he's got more troubles than a rat-tailed hoss tied short in fly-time. **1947** in *DA* 282.

catawampus *adj.* [orig. unkn.] *Midland.* **1.** ferocious or impressive.

1843 Dickens *Chuzzlewit* ch. xxi: There air some catawampous chawers in the small way too. **1847** *Davy Crockett's Alm.* (unp.): On the back of a catawampus grate wolf.

2. out of shape; diagonal, crooked, or askew. Also *adv.*

1851 *Spirit of Times* (Nov. 8) 453: They sed that he and his wife and children had their faces so wrinkled up an turned catter-wompus like, that the skeeters couldn't lite on um long enuf to bite. **1905** *DN* III 73: *Catawampus, adj.* Drawn out of shape. "This cloth's *catawampus.*" Universal. **1906** *DN* III 116: *Caterwampust*, adj. Diagonally. **1911** *DN* III 542: *Catawampus, cattywampus, adj.* (1) Crosswise, diagonal, (2) Askew, awry. **1931** *Nat. Geo.* (Dec.) 734: A new fence post, set out of line, is "catawampus." **1941** *AS* (Feb.) 21: *Catawampas*. Out of proportion, crooked. **1942** *ATS* 43: Diagonal(ly)...*catawampous, catawampus.* **1963** G. Coon *Short End* 78: But over here things always seem to get balled up, cattywhampus. **1963** E.M. Miller *Exile* 161: She had a nose like a big fat cork and a scar catawampus across her forehead. **1973** Ace *Stand On It* 8: But it is still just a teensy bit sideways or caterwampus, if you follow me.

3. incorrect or out of order.

1884 in *DA*: I kin prove ter ye that ye air all cat-a-wampus on that p'int. **1943** *AS* (Feb.) 66: *Catawampus* (badly out of order) S.C.

4. (see quot.).

1935 Algren *Boots* 13: The townsfolk called him "catawampus," meaning that they thought him violently cross-tempered....Mebbe thet'd learn him to be so derned catawampus all the time.

catawampus *v.* **1.** to confuse, confound, injure, or damage.

1839 in *DA* 282: A catawompussed fix. **1880** in *DA*: May I be cat-a-wampussed. **1906** *DN* III 129: *Catawampus, v.tr.* To warp. "The fire just catawampused this boiler."

2. to move diagonally.

1902 *DN* II 230: *Cattering*...Moving diagonally or obliquely...catter-wampusin, *p.pr.* and *adj.* The same as preceding.

catback *v.* (of a horse) to arch the back, as in bucking.

1922 Rollins *Cowboy* 286 [ref. to 1890's]: The West had its conscious slang, (e.g.) "cat backed" [*sic*] for "(to) buck."

cat beer *n.* milk.—used derisively.

1941 Hargrove *Pvt. Hargrove* 83: Milk is *cat beer*; butter, *dogfat*. **1941** Kendall & Viney *Army and Navy Slang* 3: Cat beer—milk. **1945** *Sat. Rev.* (Nov. 24): Cat beer: milk. **1966** in *DARE*.

catbird *n.* a person in a position of ease or superiority.

1967 Lit *Dictionary* 8: Cat bird—The main man, the leader, top guy, the boss.

¶ In phrase:

¶ **in the catbird seat** in a position of ease or superiority.

1942 in J. Thurber *Thurber Carnival* 10: "Are you sitting in the catbird seat?"...She must be a Dodger fan...Red Barber announces the Dodger games over the radio and he uses those expressions—picked 'em up down South...."Sitting in the catbird seat" meant sitting pretty. **1943** *AS* XVIII 278. **1963** E.M. Miller *Exile to Stars* 44: And with Blair Winsted in the catbird seat, Turk couldn't make any more mistakes. **1964** Howe *Valley of Fire* 217: Then we'll all be sittin' in the catbird seat. **1967** Lit *Dictionary* 8: Cat bird seat—(Fig.) The head of the table. **1968** Myrer *Eagle* 72: Old Reb—Bouncing in the catbird seat. **1968** F. Wallace *Poker* 211: Catbird Seat—A position in high-low poker that assures a player at least half the pot. **1969** Stern *Brood of Eagles* 341: Good old Ned's sitting in the catbird seat. **1971** *CBS Evening News* (CBS-TV) (Aug. 26): Governor George Wallace took the catbird seat in the Alabama Legislature today. **1978** Diehl *Sharky's Machine* 135: You're in the catbird seat there, Victor. **1988** *Headline News Network* (Mar. 12): But the statistics show that sooner or later Middle-East oil producers will be back in the catbird seat. **1991** *N.Y. Times* (nat. ed.) (Jan. 29) A 6: They're in the catbird seat, and they have been since August.

catbird *adj.* excellent; perfect.

1837 Neal *Charcoal Sketches* 138: If you want to feel something like—do you know what "something like" is?—it's cat-bird, jam-up—if you

want to feel so, you must pour a little of the electerizing fluid into you.

cat burglar *n.* a burglar who breaks into upper-story windows. Now *S.E.*

*****1907** in *OEDS* I. **1928** Guerin *Crime* 288: A "cat" burglar gets a...pocketful of jewellery. **1972** Burkhart *Women in Pris.* 76: "Cat burglars" climb up sides of buildings or scale walls to rob safes or break into second- and third-story apartments and offices.

catch *v.* **1.a.** to grasp the meaning of; (*hence, intrans.*) to understand; *catch on*, below.

1881 in Peck *Peck's Sunshine* 85: You catch the idea? **1882** Baillie-Grohman *Rockies* 372: Catch the idea, don't you? **1897** Ade *Pink Marsh* 126: I couldn' ketch 'em boys; not 'ith a laddeh. Too high. **1908** Fletcher *Rebel Private* 11 [ref. to Civil War]: My reply was: "I catch." **1940** B. Reinhardt & M. McCall *Gold Rush Maisie* (film): I do my work in cafés and cabarets. Catch? **1942** Gamet & Trivers *Flying Tigers* (film): Give him time. He'll catch there's a war on. **1947** Schulberg *Harder They Fall* 123: You tell me the smart boys will begin to catch if we let him hang around here. **1951** O'Hara *Farmers Hotel* 65: Oh, I catch. And they invited the gentry for the premeer. **1954** W.G. Smith *South St.* 46: Look, Pete, we got the information from good sources. Catch?

b. to hear; detect.

1923 in W.F. Nolan *Black Mask Boys* 44: I think I catch a shout.

2.a. *Mil.* to be assigned to (duty).

1932 Harvey *Me and Bad Eye* 70 [ref. to 1918]: Caught guard duty tonight.

b. *Police.* to be assigned to handling telephone calls from complainants.

1958 *N.Y. Times Mag.* (Mar. 16): *Catch*—Assignment of a detective to the complaint-receiving desk. One so assigned says: "I'm catching today." **1972** J. Mills *Report* 60: In fact, I was catching, I answered the phone. **1984** Caunitz *Police Plaza* 3: "Who's catching?" "I am."

c. *Police.* (see quot.).

1985 M. Baker *Cops* 236: You start out a tour with him saying, "Are you catching?" That meant if you came across a crime and made an arrest are you willing to be the one who makes the arrest and has to do the paperwork.

3. Orig. *Entertainment Industry.* to make a favorable impression upon; CLICK.

1942 *ATS* 584: Impress audience favorably; "get across." catch,...get over, [etc.]. **1966** Braly *On the Yard* 211: Did I catch good with Candy?

4. to meet casually with (someone). Now *colloq.*

1950 L. Brown *Iron City* 75: Catch you later—for a game.

5. *Pris.* (of a male homosexual) to allow anal copulation.—contrasted with PITCH.

1966 (quot. at PITCH). **1977** (quot. at PITCH).

6. *Prost.* (of a prostitute) to obtain a customer.

1974 Angelou *Gather Together* 33 [ref. to 1945]: Your woman'll catch if she wear these threads. **1989** *New York* (Dec. 11) 36: Getting customers is called "catchin' " or "clockin'."

¶ In phrases:

¶ **catch it, 1.** to be inflicted with trouble or punishment; (now *esp.*) to be scolded or otherwise punished, as by a parent. Now *colloq.*

*****1821–26** Stewart *Man-of-War's-Man* I 8: I would therefore have you stand clear the next time, otherwise you'll catch it. **1843–45** T.J. Green *Tex. Exped.* 123: I *told* you...that when you met these gentlemen you would catch it. **1867** in Foner *Labor Songs* 108: He'll "catch it" soon as Congress sits. **1869** Gough *Autobiog.* 40: One look at my father's face convinced me that "I had done it," and should "catch it," and "catch it" I did. **1879** Thayer *Jewett* 123: The doctor...inquired further...evidently resolved in his mind that the offending dealer would "catch it."

2. *Mil.* to be killed; (*also*) to be severely wounded.

*****1821–26** Stewart *Man-of-War's-Man* I 125: By the Lord Harry! gents, he's caught it seemingly, and rarely, too, if I mistake not. **1883–84** Whittaker *L. Locke* 279: One man's dead....The best of them catches it at last. **1898** *Sat. Eve. Post* (Nov. 5) 295 [ref. to Civil War]: Back there; think he caught it in the lungs. See him spittin' a power of blood as he dropped. **1947** Hart *Gentleman's Agreement* (film): One day we got bombed—and he caught it. **1966** Cameron *Sgt. Slade* 26: Had a hell of a time pulling her out after the skipper caught it. **1970** Whitmore *Memphis-Nam-Sweden* 36: I'd read in the newspaper that fifteen guys caught it in the Nam today. **1971** Cameron *First Blood* 39: He sounded like he'd caught it bad.

¶ **catch on** to become aware; (*hence*) to come to understand. Now *S.E.*

1882 Peck *Peck's Sunshine* 218: Sinners "catch on" better at this time. **1882** in Saunders *Parodies of Whitman* 39: I catch on, my Comrade! **1885** *Nat. Police Gaz.* (Oct. 10) 3: Git 'em, Jimmy, afore the cop catches on! **1890** Janvier *Aztec Treasure House* 168: Do you catch on? **1891** Maitland *Slang Dict.* 195: "Catch on" means to appreciate a point; to be fly to the racket; to tumble. **1893** Friend *Thousand Liars* 75: The Captain was "catching on," as the slang of the street expressed the idea of having one's understanding of a thing developed. **1894** Bridges *Arcady* 22: Do you catch on? His trolley's off the American wire.

¶ **catch one** *Mil.* to be wounded or killed by gunfire.
1898 in Remington *Wister* 249: Get down, old man; you'll catch one! **1943** Nichols *For Whom the Bell Tolls* (film): He caught one. Didn't want to be taken alive.

¶ **catch (one's) lid** (see quot.).
1968–70 *Current Slang* III & IV 23: *Catch one's lid*, v. To leave.—College males, Colorado.

¶ **catch on to** to notice or look at.
1901 A.H. Lewis *Croker* 62: Did you catch on to where the judge lets the killers go with six thousand dollar bonds? **1902** Brenton *Uncle Jed* 10: Oh, look, boys, catch on to ther back of ther hack! **1912** *Pedagogical Seminary* (Mar.) 97: Catch on to the phiz.

¶ **catch out** *Hobo.* to depart, as by stealing a ride on a train.
1973 Mathers *Riding the Rails* 108: We was right there on the Oroville end of the yards, gettin' ready to catch out. **1989** *Harper's* (June) 52: I figger we'll...maybe catch out 'bout midnight.

¶ **catch rays** see s.v. RAY.

¶ **catch wise** to become aware; catch on; *get wise* s.v. WISE.
1930 in Perelman *Old Gang* 156: Why doesn't the dame catch wise to herself? **1933–34** (quot. at MUSH WORKER). **1952** Bellow *Augie March* 463: Oh, I caught wise to this. **1953** Harris *Southpaw* 241: I was a full year catching wise to all this. **1961** Heller *Catch-22* 52: He was driven to make what carnal use of them he could...before Someone caught wise and whisked them away. **1967** Talbot *Chatty Jones* 35: If she catches wise to what we done, she's likely to go screaming to the cops. **1971** *N.Y. Post* (Oct. 15) 42: Willie's wife had already caught wise.

catcher *n.* **1.** a watchman or policeman.
1837 Neal *Charcoal Sketches* 47: The "ketcher" laughed...ketchers...are said to love a joke.
2. *Boxing.* (see quot.).
1945 D. Runyon, in *Collier's* (Aug. 4) 11: He is at one time in his life a prize fighter but strictly a catcher which is a way of saying he catches everything the other guy throws at him.

catcher's mitt *n.* a contraceptive diaphragm.
1984 Caunitz *Police Plaza* 46: The doctor fitted Eisinger with a catcher's mitt.

catch-up *n.* ¶ In phrase: **play catch-up** to attempt to catch up.
1971 (cited in *BDNE2*). **1974** *Business Week* (Apr. 6) 19: The feeling seems to be that labor must be allowed to play catch-up in its 1974 contract demands. **1981** Wambaugh *Glitter Dome* 91: So the cop could personally play a little catch-up. **1989** *Nation* (Dec. 4) 678: Forced to play catch-up, [their] other opponents would then have a much more difficult...task proving that the public should not be forced to pay for billions of dollars of cost overruns.

cat doctor *n.* a mechanic who services track-laying vehicles.
1956 Sorden & Ebert *Logger's* 8 [ref. to *a*1925]: *Cat doctor...Cat skinner*, Man who runs a caterpillar tractor used in logging. **1958** McCulloch *Woods Words* 30: *Cat doctor*—A tractor mechanic.

caterpillar *v.* to depart silently.
1902 Mead *Word-Coinage* 188: I caterpillared.

caterwaul *v.* to roam at night, as in search of sexual partners. Cf. syn. *cat around* s.v. CAT, *v.*, 2 a.
*1785 Grose *Vulgar Tongue: Caterwauling.* Going out in the night in search of intrigues, like a cat in the gutters. **1821** Waln *Hermit in Phila.* 26: Winter *caterwauling* cursed unhealthy;—too cold to *study astronomy*.

cat-eye *n. Labor.* a late-night workshift.
1977 Sayles *Union Dues* 65: They got him workin a ten-to-six cat-eye over there. Damn people won't even run a regular shift.

cat-eyed *adj. West.* (see quot.).
1934 Cunningham *Triggernometry* 8: The consequence of this was to make the average gunman what the oldtimers so expressively called "cat-eyed."...cautious...analytical...before every tiny, ordinary detail of living. *Ibid.* 190: Always armed and "cat-eyed," afraid of arrest.

catface *n. Logging.* a surface scar on a log or tree.
1942 *ATS* 482: *Cat-face*, a mark in a piece of lumber so as to disfigure

it. **1968** R. Adams *West. Words* (ed. 2) 57: *Catface.* In logging, a scar on the surface of a log...or tree.

catfish *n.* **1.** a person.—used derisively.
1858 [S. Hammett] *Piney Woods* 153: A certin man, a most astonishin' big catfish, that I'll call the Ginral. **1864** Hill *Our Boys* 93: You dare to raise that knife to that boy, and off goes your head, cat-fish!
2. (used in mild oaths to express astonishment).
1940 Jones & Houser *Dark Command* (film): Jumpin' *cat*fish! I'm out of the barberin' business! I'm a practicin' physician again! **1950** Bissell *Stretch on the River* 35: Aah, holy catfish, look at that.

cat-fit *n.* a fit of anger, hysteria, or the like, as in a child or a woman.
1905 *DN* III 60: *Catfit...conniption fit.* **1929–33** J.T. Farrell *Young Manhood* 169: He'll throw cat-fits all over the house.

cat food *n. Black E.* copulation.
1978 W. Brown *Tragic Magic* 72: If brothers knew that if they shucked and jived, the sisters wouldn't get up off any cat food, they would get their shit together in a hurry.

catfoot *v.* to walk stealthily, like a cat.—sometimes constr. with dummy-obj. *it.* Also fig.
1916 in *DA* 284: Maybe it's a Blackhander's camp, I think; so I...catfooted. [**1939** Howsley *Argot* 12: *Cat Foot*—a thief who makes no noise, walks silently.] **1948** in *DA* 284: Grif...cat-footed the area topside. **1960** in *OED2*: Crow began to cat-foot it up the stairs. **1993** *Newsweek* (Jan. 18) 39: He'd catfoot around, toying subversively with the chord structure and the rhythm.

catgut *n. N.E.* ROTGUT.
1924 Marks *Plastic Age* 18: You told me yourself that stuff was catgut and that you wouldn't drink it on a bet. **1966–69** in *DARE* I 556.

cath *v. Med.* to catheterize.
1981 in Safire *Good Word* 152.

cathead *n.* **1.** *pl. Naut.* a woman's breasts.
*1805 J. Davis *Post-Captain* 2: Or can any form be more ravishing? Such a pair of cat-heads! And oh! What hair! *Ibid.* 27: She has a good pair of cat-heads. ***1811** *Lexicon Balatron.: Cat-heads.* A woman's breasts. *Sea Phrase.* **1834** *Mil. & Nav. Mag. of U.S.* (Oct.) 116: And only think of her cat-heads! For all the world like two round shot dipt in purser's flour! **1855** Wise *Tales for Marines* 45: "By jingo! such a full, rounded counter the witch had, and such a mass of brown tresses twisted around her elegantly-formed head, over two roguish eyes and a rosy mouth; but such a pair of cat-heads!" "Cat what?" ejaculated Fred's grandmother, as she was listening attentively to this extraordinary narrative. "It's a nautical phrase, ma'am," rejoined the Lieutenant; and he went on rapidly with the thread of his narrative.
2. *So.* a large lumpy biscuit.
1948 Mencken *Amer. Lang.* (Supp. II) 674: Biscuits, *cat-heads.* **1974** Ky. man, age *ca*50: Cathead biscuits and red-eye gravy.
3. a fool.
1952 Bellow *Augie March* 29: My marks showed it, and the old lady give me a going-over when I brought them in, calling me "cat-head" and, in her French, "*meshan.*"

cat hole *n. Mil.* a latrine hole dug by an individual soldier in the field.
1978 J. Webb *Fields of Fire* 169 [ref. to Vietnam, 1969]: Rabbit dug a cathole and squatted in the far weeds. *Ibid.* Digging holes to shit....How many cat holes have *you* dug since you been here? **1985** J. McDonough *Platoon Leader* 89 [ref. to 1971]: My greatest need...was to relieve myself. There was no time to go through the niceties of digging a cathole.

cathouse *n.* a house of prostitution.
*ca*1893 in R.H. Dillon *Shanghaiing Days* 257: Cat House Johnny. **1913** Kneeland *Commercialized Prostitution in N.Y.C.* 114: The only thing we can let the house for is a cat-house (meaning a house of prostitution). **1928** in Randolph *Pissing in Snow* 125: If the people in Joplin want to hang around cat-houses, that's their business. **1928** Hecht & MacArthur *Front Page* 450: Maybe it's another cat-house. Remember when Big Minnie's burned down, and the Mayor of Galesburg came running out? **1933** Odets *Awake and Sing!* 48: What's it, the weekly visit to the cat house? **1937** Steinbeck *Mice & Men* 104: I'll stay all night in some lousy cat house. **1941** Schulberg *Sammy* 241: He started dropping in at the cat-houses on his way home. **1945** Himes *If He Hollers* 21: She might have worked half those years in a cat house. **1956** Levin *Compulsion* 50: At the frat there were those who bragged about their prowess at the cat houses, and those who loudly acclaimed that every girl they took out

"went the whole way." **1966** Jarrett *Sex Is a Private Affair* 5: The police still insist that I'm running a "cat house"—to use their own vulgar term. **1988** Kienzle *Marked for Murder* 255: Her sister…ran a cathouse.

cat-licker *n.* [pun on *Catholicker*, dial. var. of *Catholic*] a Roman Catholic.—used derisively.
  1942 *ATS* 367. **1965–70** in *DARE*. **1970** E. Thompson *Garden of Sand* 377: Goddamn catlicker sonofabitch! **1973** N.Y.C. man, age 27: *Catlicker* is an old term for a Catholic. **1976** Braly *False Starts* 10: My father found a new wife,…a Catholic, who began to convert us. My father called her a "cat licker."

catman *n.* a man who is a CAT BURGLAR.
  1962 Crump *Killer* 110: That's what all you catmen say, especially you spooks. **1980** Pearl *Slang Dict.: Catman n.* (crime) a burglar who gains entrance to premises by climbing through the window.

cat road *n.* a little-traveled road.
  1937 Hoover *Persons in Hiding* 28: And when to slide to the "cat" or back roads in order to skirt a town instead of being forced to stop for traffic lights. *Ibid.* 177: The back or "cat" roads used by bank robbers were choked with snow or filled with ruts.

cat's *n.* something that is superlative.—constr. with *the*. [The dash in 1919 quot. may represent an ellipsis.]
  1919 McKenna *Battery A* 189: My new suit is the cat's — **1923** T.A. Dorgan, in Zwilling *TAD Lexicon* 25: It's the cat's. **1927** [Fliesler] *Anecdota* 187: See that Myrtle girl swim! Ain't she the cat's! **1929** Brecht *Downfall* 73: "Gee, Dick, that's the cat's," Malcolm cried delightedly. **1929** "C. Woolrich" *Times Sq.* 12: My, aren't those the cat's. **1936** Levin *Old Bunch* 99: All you needed was a couple of catchwords, like Oh, yeah? and That's the cats. **1945** Hartman & Grant *Naughty Nineties* (film): It's the cat's. **1968–70** *Current Slang* III & IV 125: *The cat's*, adj. Interesting; superior.—College students, both sexes, New Hampshire.—"This place is the *cat's*."

cats and dogs *n.pl. Finance.* shares in small, poorly financed, or bankrupt companies.
  1879 in *DA* 281. **1900** in *DAE* I 442. **1953** *ATS* (ed. 2) 534: *Cats and dogs*, low-grade or worthless securities. **1970** Terkel *Hard Times* 444: Got rid of all the cats and dogs. I only buy blue chip stocks. **1984** *N.Y. Post* (Aug. 9) 50: "Cats and dogs" is a phrase used in the brokerage business to refer to stock in companies that are marginal and probably have no future of consequence.

cat's ass *n.* **1.** a kink or knot formed in a line or cable; (*hence*) a loop.—usu. considered vulgar.
  1942 *ATS* 487: *Cat's ass*, a kink in a wire cable. **1958** McCulloch *Woods Words* 30: *Cat's ass*…The snarl which results when a choker slips off a log and cinches up tight.…A knot which has been pulled into a line, particularly a full 360 degree kink. **1983** K. Weaver *Texas Crude* 94: *A cat's ass*. A simple single-loop bind made with a tie-down chain.
  2. *Logging.* (see quot.).—usu. considered vulgar. Cf. CAT-FACE.
  1958 McCulloch *Woods Words* 30: *Cat's ass*—a round scar on a tree trunk almost completely healed over.
  3. something that is extraordinarily good or bad.—usu. constr. with *the*.—usu. considered vulgar. Cf. CAT'S, CAT'S MEOW, etc.
  1967 in *DARE*: He seems to think he's…the cat's ass. **1972** U.S. Army S/Sgt., age 26: Man, that's the cat's ass! [i.e., bad]. **1974** Loken *Come Monday Morning* 32: Well, if that ain't the cat's ass. **1979** Gutcheon *New Girls* 65: My dear, she thinks I'm the cat's ass. Which I am, of course. **1981** Yates *Cannonball Run* (film): This infrared's the cat's ass!
  4. a damn.
  1992 *Married with Children* (Fox-TV): Like I give a cat's ass.
  ¶ (in prov. phr.).
  1952 Vonnegut *Player Piano* 199: But Clara'd let one of those jerks at her just about as quick as you could stuff a pound of oleomargarine up a cat's ass with a hot awl. **1974** Millard *Thunderbolt* 10: All b.s. aside, she's cleaner than a cat's ass, son. **1985** Ark. man, age 35: It's cleaner'n a cat's ass.

cat's ass *adj.* splendid; wonderful.
  1970 *Current Slang* V 20: *Cat's ass*, adj. Good, excellent.—Dylan is *cat's ass*.—Jack just bought the most *cat's ass* motorcycle. **1983** N. Proffitt *Gardens of Stone* 230: Hey, cat's ass.

cat's eye *n.* **1.** *USAF.* (see quot.).
  1956 Heflin *USAF Dict.* 105: *Cat's eye*. A fighter equipped for night operations.

2. (see quot.).
  1971 Tak *Truck Talk* 27: *Cat's eyes*: the reflective markers on slender posts that mark the edge of a highway.

cat-shop *n.* CATHOUSE.
  1930 Graham & Graham *Queer People* 182: I don't know all the things they might expect a man to do in a Hollywood cat-shop. **1956** Fleming *Diamonds* 94: Town wide open. Gambling. Legalized catshops.

cat-skinner *n.* [CAT, 8 + SKINNER] a driver of a track-laying construction vehicle, as a tractor or a bulldozer.
  1934 in *Dict. Canadianisms* 136. **1941** *AS* (Oct.) 232: *Cat Skinner.* Operator of caterpillar tractor. **1953** "L. Short" *Silver Rock* 64: We'll pay going wages for a "cat skinner." **1963** J. Ross *Dead Are Mine* 246: Terry showed the cat skinner the place he wanted.

cat's kittens *n.pl.* CAT'S MEOW.—constr. with *the*.
  [**1925** Van Vechten *Nigger Heaven* 207: Dawggone, ef that ain't the cat's kanittans!] **1929** T. Gordon *Born to Be* 204: New York was hot…but London was the cat's kittens.

cat's meat *n.* the lungs.
  *__*1821** in Partridge *Dict. Und.* 111: You must let him have all the *jaw-work* to himself, and give a holiday to your *cat's meat*. **1836** *Spirit of Times* (Feb. 20) 3: His "cat's meat," he complains, has been too long idle. **1935** Pollock *Und. Speaks: Gravel in his cat's meat*, tubercular; weak lungs.

cat-smellers *n.pl.* whiskers.
  1849 *Crockett Almanac* (unp.): Thar war the men with the cat smellers on thar upper lips.

cat's meow *n.* something that is splendid or stylish; the height of excellence.—constr. with *the*.
  1921 *Pirate Piece* (Apr.) 3: A good letter, Quig, one like that every month would be the "cat's meow." **1921** *Variety* (Nov. 18) 1: A general order has been sent out from the Keith office to all Keith, Moss and Proctor (vaudeville) houses, instructing resident managers to hereafter bar the use of the current slang phrases, "That's the Cat's Meow," "Cat's Pajamas," "Hot Dog," "Hot Cat," etc. This means the phrases are not to be used by artists either in dialog form or if occurring in pop songs.…One currently pop song has for its title and catchline, "He's the Cat's Meow." **1926** Maines & Grant *Wise-Crack Dictionary* 6: *Cat's meow*—The latest thing. **1926** *Jour. Applied Psych.* X 259: It's the cat's meow. **1929** J.T. Farrell *Calico Shoes* 228: Will they be the cat's meow. **1930** in Blackbeard & Williams *Smithsonian Comics* 130: Lit'rature is the cat's meow, aint it? **1971** *N.Y. Post* (Aug. 13) 34: I think it's the cat's meow! **1971** *WCBS-TV News* (Mar. 27): Well, the weather today was the cat's meow. **1984** J. Hughes *16 Candles* (film): She thinks you're the cat's meow. **1992** *N.Y. Times Bk. Review* (Aug. 16) 21 [ad]: As a private eye she's the cat's meow.

cat's nuts *n.pl.* CAT'S PAJAMAS.—constr. with *the*.—usu. considered vulgar. Also **cat's balls.**
  [**1918** *Wadsworth Gas Attack* (Jan. 5) 8: I was the cat's mitts, as I doped it out.] **1928** Levin *Reporter* 32: They jumped Catsnuts Maloney for trying to make a…picture. **1930** Dos Passos *42d Parallel* 58 [ref. to *ca*1910]: It's the cat's nuts, Ike. **1936** Levin *Old Bunch* 123: Is she the cat's nuts! Boy, I could go for her! *Ibid.* 189: He forgot his hat! That's the cat's nuts! **1962** E. Stephens *Blow Negative* 236: "Where did you have an art professor, Lydia?" "Radcliffe." "What?" "Isn't that the cat's balls?"

cat soup *n.* catsup. *Joc.*
  1875 *Minstrel Gags* 23: "Wormy celli, wid cat-sup," says de steward. "Wormy soup, cat soup—gid out wid your nonsense!"

cat's pajamas *n.* something that is extraordinary, esp. splendid or delightful.—constr. with *the*. [Unlike CAT'S MEOW, this phrase sometimes expresses annoyance or amazement.]
  1922 in *DN* V 146: Hot dog! It was the cat's pajamas. **1923** O'Brien *Best Stories of 1923* 186: Everything was either "classy" or "swell" or "nobby" or…even "the cat's pajamas." **1924** Marks *Plastic Age* 103: It's a goddamn good poem. It's the cat's pajamas. **1925** S. Lewis *Arrowsmith* 901: Honestly, [I] used to think Pa Gottlieb was the cat's pajamas. **1925** in Lardner *Best Stories* 175: Not used to it! That's the cat's pajamas! [**1926** in *Ibid.* 339: But the cat's nightgown is Tom Stevens and his wife.] **1926** Maines & Grant *Wise-Crack Dictionary* 6: *Cat's pajamas*—Something classy. **1936** Levin *Old Bunch* 28: Is he the cat's pajamas!…I thought I'd die! **1969** in Estren *Underground* 227: Wow! Underground comics are the cat's pajamas out here in Iowa. **1971** Curtis *Banjo* 75: Oh, that's the cat's pajamas! Just the real rich folks can stay there. **1972** *N.Y. Times Bk. Review* (June 11) 9: I'll bet that even Jackie Onassis has

stopped thinking of herself as the cat's pajamas, now that she's reached a certain age. **1972–75** W. Allen *Feathers* 206: She's the cat's pajamas.

cat's water *n.* gin.
　*1859 Hotten *Slang Dict.*: Cat's water…gin. **1891** Maitland *Slang Dict.*: Cat's water, gin. **1930** in *DARE.*

cat's whisker *n.* **1.** *pl.* CAT'S MEOW; CAT'S PAJAMAS.—constr. with *the.*
　1923 *Nashville Banner* (Jan. 4) 14: I must be ze cat's whiskers! **1923** Witwer *Fighting Blood* 39: You think…'at you're the cat's whiskers, now don't you? **1923** O'Brien *Best Stories of 1923* 186-7: Everything was…"the cat's whiskers" or even…"the cat's pajamas." **1925** *Adventure* (Dec. 30) 179: Ain't this the cat's whiskers? **1926** Maines & Grant *Wise-Crack Dictionary* 6: *Cat's whiskers*—Nifty. **1926** Wood & Goddard *American Slang* 10: *Cat's whiskers, cat's pajamas, cat's meaow, elephant's fallen arches, snake's hips, etc.* Something excellent. **1926** Tully *Jarnegan* 119: It's got to be slick as the cat's whiskers before Jarnegan comes on. **1927** Mayer *Just Between Us Girls* 139: This Hotel Excelsior…is supposed to be the cat's whiskers. **1932** *Leatherneck* (May) 37: Ain't that the cat's whiskers? **1933** Odets *Awake & Sing* 84: The cat's whiskers, Mom? **1943** in J. Gunther *D Day* 80: We were the cat's whiskers there. **1948** A. Murphy *To Hell & Back* 104: He is the "cat's whiskers." Ha-ha. **1952** in *DAS* 92.
　2. (see 1986 quot.).
　1952 *Harper's* (Mar.) 59: It contains…two hair-thin wires—"cat's whiskers," in radioman's language. **1961** *Leave It to Beaver* (ABC-TV): I remember bumming twenty cents from my father for a new cat's whisker for my crystal set. **1986** *I'll Buy That!* 201: Semiconductors had seen some use, in conjunction with thin wires called "cat's whiskers," as signal detectors in early crystal sets. *a*1973–87 F.M. Davis *Livin' the Blues* 50 [ref. to 1920's]: I sat up night after night wearing headphones and moving a cat's whisker over a small piece of galena searching for the closest station.

cattawampous var. CATAWAMPUS.

cattawampously var. CATAWAMPOUSLY.

catter *n.* *Hobo.* (see quots.). Now *hist.*
　1916 Livingston *Snare* 32: "Catters"…ride the platforms of the express and baggage cars, the tenders of engines, and similar places. **1976** R. Adams *R.R. Lang.* 30: *Catter.* One who clings to the outside of cars, especially on a blind baggage.

cattle *n.* **1.a.** people.
　*1673 [R. Head] *Canting Academy* 108: The next sort of Cattell I intend to treat of is the *Bawd* and *Whore.* **1848** [W.T. Thompson] *Jones's Sks.* 17: Youna no tell dis nigger nuffin bout dem cattle [Northerners]. **1932** *AS* VII 400: Orphan's Home Argot…*Cattle,* Girls.
　b. *Specif.* (*Prost.*) women who are prostitutes.
　*1677 in D'Urfey *Two Comedies* 208: No place to bring your cattel to but thither? *1698–99 "B.E." *Dict. Canting Crew*: *Cattle,* whores. **1909** (cited in Partridge *Dict. Und.* 111).
　2. *Horse Racing.* racehorses.
　*1821 *Real Life in London* I 10: Go it, Dick—now, Safety—d—d good cattle both. **1854** in Dorson *Long Bow* 86: You'd better believe the cattle they brought to the course…were fast 'uns.

cattle boat *n.* **1.** *Mil.* a troop transport ship.
　1944 Kendall *Service Slang* 35: *Cattle boat….*troop transport. **1945** Huie *Omaha to Oki.* 100: The 13th left Hawaii on a "cattle boat" for the usual long grind to Eniwetok.
　2. *Commercial Fishing.* a party boat.
　1970 in *DARE*: Party boats are called cattle boats by local [Calif.] fishermen.

cattle call *n.* *Theat. & Film.* a casting call; (*also*) a mass audition.
　1952 *New Yorker* (Nov. 8) 24: "Cattle Call" is the actors' name for the weekly assemblage of actors and actresses that one of the television studios holds to see who is available for parts. **1970** *Playboy* (Nov.) 90: From the time I was nine, she dragged me around to cattle calls. **1974** Terkel *Working* 53: Usually you're competing with anywhere from thirty to sixty girls. They're cattle calls. **1976** *N.Y. Post* (July 8) 25: She remembered her resolve to be an actress and headed for a "cattle call." **1977** Sayles *Union Dues* 218: I was at this huge cattle-call, hundreds of summer-stock producers doing a regional audition. **1980** in McCauley *Dark Forces* 434: [Her] actress ambitions [were] discouraged by the cattle calls where she found herself to be merely one of a dozen duplicates. **1984** *Time* (Mar. 25) 7: The rest…wait for "open calls." Known as "cattle calls," they may be publicity stunts.

cattle car *n.* *Mil.* a recruit bus.
　1989 G.C. Wilson *Mud Soldiers* 44: Selvester stood up in Fort Benning's "cattle car" and tried to push…toward the door.

cattle crate *n.* *Mil. Av.* a large troop-carrying airplane.
　1951 Hunt *Judas Hour* 122: I flew the boxcars and the cattle crates—the big slow planes that carried men and equipment.

cattle show *n.* Esp. *Pol.* an event in which numerous contestants or candidates are to be judged.—usu. used derisively.
　1980 *Atlantic* (Feb.) 6: Another of those Saturday Republican "cattle shows" where all the GOP contenders…make brief speeches to the assembled throngs. **1983** *Good Morning America* (ABC-TV) (Sept. 26): Democrats gathered…for the first cattle show of the 1984 campaign. **1983** *Daily Beacon* (Univ. Tenn.) (Nov. 9) 2: The race for homecoming queen is really a beauty *election*—it's not even a pageant. It's a cattle show. **1985** *Time* (Aug. 26) 15: He advised Dole to…stay away from the candidate "cattle shows."

cattle stiff *n.* [*cattle* + STIFF, *n.*] *Hobo.* a cowboy.
　1909, 1910 (cited in Partridge *Dict. Und.* 111).

cat-toe *v.* CATFOOT.
　1951 West *Flaming Feud* 113: You picked one hell of a time to go cat-toeing down dark alleys.

catty *n.* a catfish.
　1845 in Robb *Squatter Life* 66: I had made captive a mammoth *catty.*

cat up *v.* [prob. alter. of GAT UP] **1.** *Und.* to rob at gunpoint; hold up.
　1925–26 J. Black *You Can't Win* 220: Harvest workers were called blanket stiffs or gay cats, and the process of pistoling them away from their money was known as catting them up. *Ibid.*: Others…got "catted up." **1928** Panzram *Killer* 157: Catting up a scatter or ginmill—to hold up a saloon. **1933** Ersine *Prison Slang* 25: He catted up a joint in Elgin.
　2. *Narc.* (see quot.).
　1953 W. Brown *Monkey On My Back* 79: To *cat up* was to hide out, especially from the police.

cat-wagon *n.* **1.** a wagon, van, or the like that serves as transportation or accommodation for a prostitute or prostitutes.
　1930 "D. Stiff" *Milk & Honey* 202: Cat wagon—A brothel on wheels visiting the chaste villages of the middle west or following the harvest crews. **1952** Randolph & Wilson *Down in the Holler* 108: The brothels in the mining camps are called *cat-houses,* and the vans used by travelling prostitutes are known as *cat-wagons.* **1963** Miller & Snell *Why West Was Wild* 15: Attention, too, should be called to the existence of portable brothels or "cat wagons" which seem to have given the military authorities particular trouble.
　2. a police van used to transport prostitutes to jail.
　1972 Pearl *Cops* 67: Driving around in the cat wagon and picking them up in bunches.

cat-yanker *n.* CAT-SKINNER.
　1919 Duffy *G.P.F. Book* 270: This "Cat Yanker" is some Ha-Ha boy. *Ibid.* 275: One of the best "Cat" yankers.

Cauc *n.* *Police.* a Caucasian.
　1986 R. Campbell *In La-La Land* 101: A male Cauc killed in a collision with a pole. **1987** R. Miller *Slob* 78: Same MO…Female Cauc, mid thirties.

cauliflower *n.* **1.** a fellow. *Joc.*
　1837 Neal *Charcoal Sketches* 37: Let go, watchy!—let go, my cauliflower!
　2. CAULIFLOWER EAR.
　1921 J. Conway, in *Variety* (Feb. 18) 8: They get a close-up of his cauliflowers. He's got a set of botanical ears that cover more ground than a tent. **1936** in R.E. Howard *Iron Men* 155: If it hadn't been for my cauliflowers, I'd of looked like a perfessor or something.
　3. fear or cowardice.
　1978 W. Brown *Tragic Magic* 40: So don't feel bad about showing some signs a weakness. Every man in here got some cauliflower in their heart.

cauliflower ear *n.* *Boxing.* an ear that has been deformed by repeated injury, resulting in an irregular thickening of scar tissue. Now *colloq.*
　1896 in A.E. Turner *Earps Talk* 179: I told Sharkey he would have a "cauliflower" ear for sure. **1904** J. London *Sea-Wolf* ch. v: It…was called a "cauliflower" ear by the sailors. **1909** J. London, in M.H. Greenberg *In Ring* 86: A nose, twice broken…and a cauliflower ear. **1915** *N.Y. Eve. Jour.* (Aug. 3) 10: A gink with a broken bugle and a cau-

liflower ear. **1958** J.B. West *Eye* 6: She was contraltoing into my cauliflower ear. **1970** in P. Heller *In This Corner* 90: In fact, he's the one that gave me a cauliflower ear.

caulk *n. Naut.* a sleep; nap. *Rare* in U.S.

> *__*1835__ Marryat *Midshipman Easy* 168: Yes, to your hammock—it's *no go* with old Smallsole, if I want a bit of *caulk.* *__*1917__ in *OEDS* I. *__*1925__ in Fraser & Gibbons *Soldier & Sailor Wds.* 50 [ref. to WWI]: *Caulk, A:* A nap, a short sleep. (Navy.) **1936** Levette *Nav. Customs* (glossary): *Take a caulk*—to take a sleep or nap.

caulk *v. Naut.* **1.a.** to sleep.—sometimes constr. with *off* or *it.*

> *__*1818__ in *OEDS* I. **1841** Mercier *Man-of-War* 258: The watch below [was] stretched at full length busily engaged in what sailors technically term *caulking,* which in the language of folks on shore would amount to *sound sleeping.* **1846** Codman *Sailors' Life* 210: I…volunteered to keep the look-out for the old man, and let him *caulk,* if he could. **1847** Downey *Cruise of Portsmouth* 45: It was my first watch on deck, and at 4 Bells I was relieved from the look out, and stowing myself away underneath the windlass…was soon calking it off quite merrily, and dreaming about my farm, my wife, and no matter what else. **1896** Hamblen *Many Seas* 40: Sleep…is technically called "caulking," and a man will brag of having "caulked" the whole four hours of his watch on deck. **1898** Doubleday *Gunner Aboard "Yankee"* 185: The stress and strain of the night before made the few hours of "calking off"…particularly grateful. **1902** *Our Naval Apprentice* (Apr.) 13: We soon learned the sailor's trick of "calking off" during our watch below. **1937** Thompson *Take Her Down* 66 [ref. to 1918]: Anyhow, there I am a-caulkin' peacefully when I dreams the pilot is comin' down the ladder dressed like a chink. **1977** Heinl *Marine Off. Guide* (ed. 4) 682: *Calk off* (v.)…To take a nap.

b. to loaf.—constr. with *off.*

> **1977** Heinl *Marine Off. Guide* (ed. 4) 682: *Calk off* (v.)…(2) loaf on the job.

2. to kill.

> **1931** *AS* VI (Aug.) 468: Gangsters and racketeers are not the only contributors to our locutions for inflicting violent death. "I'd like to calk him off," I recently heard an American sailor…say of an obnoxious acquaintance. He was following a natural tendency to apply terms of everyday familiarity to figurative uses.

caulked *adj.* weary; exhausted.

> **1936** *AS* (Oct.) 275: *Cawked.* Exhausted. "I'm all cawked."

caulker *n.* **1.** *Naut.* a large drink of liquor.

> *__*1808__ in *F & H* II 60. *__*1836__ in *Ibid.* 60: We…finished off with a *caulker* of good cognac. **1850** in Blair & McDavid *Mirth* 105: "That's the best red eye I've swallowed in a coon's age," said the speaker, after belting a caulker. **1856** Sleeper *Tales* 112: He was…sleeping off the effects of two or three heavy *caulkers* of old Hollands. **1883** Russell *Sailors' Lang.* 28: *Caulker.*—A heavy dose of rum. Also, a lie. **1886** P.D. Haywood *Cruise* 70: He had a chest full of patent medicines, and took a "caulker" every morning. **1889** Barrère & Leland *Dict. Slang* I 232: "Caulker," a stiff dram.

2. an exaggerated story; a lie.

> **1883** (quot. at **(1)**, above). *__*1884__ in *F & H* 60: I also took care that she should never afterwards be able to charge me with having told her a real *caulker.* **1889** Barrère & Leland *Dict. Slang* I 232: *Caulker* (society), a lie.

3. *Boxing.* a hard-punching boxer.

> **1860** in Somers *Sports in N.O.* 58: A caulker at Algiers…[versus] a bruiser from Chicago.

caulk up *v. Naut.* to hold one's tongue; to shut up.

> **1856** *Ballou's Dollar Monthly Mag.* (Oct.) 322: You'd best calk up, Tom Piper, and not expose your ignorance.

caution *n.* a thing or (now *esp.*) a person that causes astonishment, annoyance, or amusement.—also constr. with ref. to assorted animals. Now *colloq.* [1834 quot. may not illustrate this sense; in current use the term retains only mild force.]

> **1834** in *DA* 287: The way I'll lick you will be a caution to the balance of your family. **1835** Hoffman *Winter in West* I 197: The way in which the icy blast would come down the bleak shore of the lake "was a caution." **1837** Strong *Diary* I 69: The way they pulled hair and cuffed ears was a caution. **1845** in G.W. Harris *High Times* 50: The way I *did* sail was a caution to turkles and all the other slow varmints. **1861** Newell *Orpheus C. Kerr* I 230: The way that gal squealed…was a caution to screech owls. **1896** Hamblen *Many Seas* 259: He began to scull himself along at a rate that was a caution to snakes. **1899** Garland *Eagle's Heart* 253: Ain't it a caution to yaller snakes? Must be nigh onto fifteen thousand people there now.

cav *n. Army.* cavalry.

> **1863** in Geer *Diary* 76: Our command called in to line…to repel an expected attack from rebel cav. **1865** in Hilleary *Webfoot* 59: They wish a transfer to the Cav. **1892** in M. Fletcher *Black Soldier* 99: That woman ain't going to want for bread while the 10th Cav has a ration left. **1984–88** Hackworth & Sherman *About Face* 65: An old Horse Cav man.

cave *v.* **1.** to give in or admit defeat.—also constr. with *in.* [Although *cave in* has become S.E., *cave* remains slang.]

> **1844** in *OEDS* I. **1855** [S. Hammett] *Capt. Priest* 64: The one who "caves" first shall pay the shot. **1855** Burgess *500 Mistakes* 49: Avoid using the phrase "*I cave in,*" for "*I give up.*" It savors of slang. **1859** "Skitt" *Fisher's River* 127 [ref. to 1820's]: I soon seen that the jig were up, and I mout as well cave in. **1859** Matsell *Vocab.* 18: *Caved.* Gave up; surrendered. **1861** in Hough *Soldier in West* 46: He "caved" at once. **1865** Sala *Diary* I 111: Then, with a curious alacrity, the despots "cave in." **1868** in G.W. Harris *High Times* 192: *Thar,* by golly, thinks I she's caved. **1872** Burnham *Secret Service* IV: *Cave,* to yield, give in, come down at last. To own up. **1878** Pinkerton *Strikers, Communists* 64: Another [tramp] writes to the Philadelphia *Times* that he may manage to beg his way perhaps two weeks more, but that he has become desperate and will make his mark upon something before he "caves." **1883** Pinkerton *Burglar's Fate* 317: I've got the drop on you, and you might as well cave. **1885** Harte *Snow-Bound* 115: "We cave, Zeenie!" said Rawlins, when their hilarity had subsided. **1885** *Puck* (July 29) 343: "I cave!" good-naturedly responded the first speaker. **1886** Abbot *Blue Jackets of '61* 273: Two huge wheel-houses towered amidships, on each of which was painted…"Deluded Rebels, cave in." **1898** Brooks *Strong Hearts* 63: When I gits cornered, I caves, see? **1900** Willard & Hodler *Powers That Prey* 26: He stood it as long as he could, his face and hands being cut and bruised and smeared all over with blood, and then cried out: "I cave—I cave!" **1901** Calkins *My Host* 218: They've got us under close watch, and we've got to *cave* or fight. **1956** Holiday & Dufty *Lady Sings the Blues* 76: So they finally caved. **1976** *Kojak* (CBS-TV): Being a sensible man, he caved. **1993** *New Republic* (Dec. 6) 9: The Administration caved.

2.a. to collapse or faint, as from exhaustion; to become greatly fatigued.—also constr. with *in.*

> **1861** in *Ark. Hist. Qly.* XVIII (1959) 17: Saturday night I "caved in" sick enough with all the…symptoms. **1863** Heartsill *1491 Days* 136: I think I should "cave," as it is. **1862–64** Noel *Campaign* 35: Our boys were already broken down; our teams were fast "caving." **1887** M. Roberts *W. Avernus* 130: Fritz…had "caved in" at last. He could go no farther. **1938** Bellem *Blue Murder* 69: Look out, boys, he's caving. Catch him.

b. to die.—constr. with *in.*

> **1863** in R.G. Carter *4 Bros.* 225: I have been thinking of what we shall have to endure, and lest we "cave in" on this campaign, I write just before starting.

3. to knock down with a blow.—constr. with *in.*

> **1928** Dahlberg *Bottom Dogs* 148: Mawx was first for caving him in.

cave cop *n. Police.* (see quot.).

> **1974** Terkel *Working* 582: Transit cops are called cave cops because they're in the subway.

caveman *n.* a strong, attractive man who treats women roughly. Also **cave-guy.** [Orig. an allusion to John Corbin's once-popular romantic novel *The Cave Man* (1907).]

> [**1907** Corbin *The Cave Man* (title).] **1914** S. Lewis *Mr. Wrenn* 95: She sent him away with a light "It's been a good party, hasn't it, caveman? (If you *are* a caveman)." **1915** Lait *Gus* 11: The women liked that "cave-guy stuff." **1918** in Grider *War Birds* 149: She started to kid me and said I was her cave man. **1922** *Bomb* (Iowa State Coll.) 398: How To Be A Caveman (In Ten Lessons). **1926** Wood & Goddard *Amer. Slang* 11: *Caveman.* Modern forcible wooer. **1931** Dos Passos *1919* 104: No more caveman stuff, honest injun. **1950** Hartman & O'Brien *Fancy Pants* (film): Women who crave men/ Wanna love cavemen.

caviar can *n.* [most caviar in the U.S. is imported from the former Soviet Union] *Mil.* a Soviet tank.

> **1952** Geer *New Breed* 131: The antitank section men, armed with the 3.5 rockets, wagered considerable sums on who could make the high score on the Russian T-34 "caviar cans." **1958** Frankel *Band of Bros.* 99 [ref. to 1950]: There's the caviar can, Captain.

cayuse *n. West.* **1.** a horse. [In the specific sense "an Indian pony" the term is S.E.]

> **1866** in *Nebr. Hist.* XLVI (1965) 295: We got the "*cayuse*" up at last. **1885** *Harper's Mo.* (July) 190: Quickly his "cayuse" is saddled. **1889** Barrère & Leland *Dict. Slang* I 234: *Cayuse* (cowboys), a horse. **1899**

Garland *Eagle's Heart* 162: I'll take care o' the cayuses. **1901** J. London *God of His Fathers* 81: Mountain cayuses from eastern Oregon. **1916** Knibbs *Riders of Stars* 33: The roan cayuse of the Concho. [**1936** R. Adams *Cowboy Lingo* 81: "Cayuse" was the name of the wild horses of Oregon, so named after the Cayuse tribe of Indians, an equestrian people.] **1948** in *DA* 288.

2. a worthless person.

1905 *Nat. Police Gaz.* (Dec. 9) 7: You show signs of bein' a some inquisitive cayuse. **1929** in Goodstone *Pulps* 63: Tell me what the wall-eyed cayuses figure on doin'!

caz *n.* [fr. earlier E cant *cassan*, of obscure orig.] cheese.

[***1673** R. Head *Canting Academy* 49: Cheese *Cash* or *Cassam.*] **1791** [W. Smith] *Confess. T. Mount* 19: Cheese, *caz.* ***1812** Vaux *Vocab.*: *Caz*, cheese; *As good as caz*, is a phrase signifying that any projected fraud or robbery may be easily and certainly accomplished.

cazh *adj.* CASUAL. Also vars.

1981 Eble *Campus Slang* (Mar.) 2: *Cazh*—casual, laid back, socially optimal, conducive to good time: "I heard that was a really cazh affair." **1982** S. Black *Totally Awesome* 87: Valley guys are totally kazh about everything. **1990** P. Dickson *Slang!* 214: *Caj/cas.* Casual.

CC pusher *n. Army.* a rear-echelon member of the U.S. Army Medical Corps.

1941 Kendall *Army & Navy Slang* 3: *CC pushers.*...medical corps. **1947** *AS* (Apr.) XXII 109: *C.C. pills* give rise to *C.C. pushers*, which is applied to members of the Army Medical Corps.

cedar savage *n. Logging.* (see quots.).

1956 Sorden & Ebert *Logger's* 8 [ref. to a1925]: *Cedar-savage*, A man who cuts or peels cedar logs, poles, or posts. **1958** McCulloch *Woods Words* 31: *Cedar savage*—A logger working in a cedar pole camp, or for a shingle bolt outfit.

ceiling *n.* ¶ In phrases:

¶ **hit the ceiling, 1.** to increase to an excessive level.

1903 Hobart *Out for the Coin* 16: It's a moral that it goes to 10 before it hits the ceiling.

2.a. to become shocked.

1900 *DN* II 41: *Hit the ceiling*, To fail in examination or daily recitation. **1908** Pain *Stroke Oar* 185: He will bounce out of bed high enough to hit the ceiling when he gets my cable. **1929** Hammett *Dain Curse* 189: Collinson hit the ceiling. **1963** Fehrenbach *This Kind of War* 443: Truman hit the ceiling.

b. to fly into a rage.

1914 in *OEDS*: He will..."get warm round the collar," and may even "hit the ceiling." **1936** Miller *Battling Bellhop* (film): Nick would hit the ceiling. **1965** LeMay & Kantor *Mission* 361: So old Fuzz hits the ceiling. He says, "I've done twenty-three missions! I've only got two more to go!...You can't do this to me!" **1980** Berlitz & Moore *Roswell* 73: When Colonel Blanchard learned of this now international news explosion he "hit the ceiling."

¶ **on the ceiling** unduly excited.

1965 C. Brown *Manchild* 411: You're...all up on the ceiling, man, over a little thing like this.

¶ **to the ceiling** to an extreme degree.

1954 Collans & Sterling *House Detect.* 51: She's plastered to the ceiling; I saw her come in half an hour ago; she could hardly hit the floor with her feet.

celeb *n.* a celebrity.

1916 Lardner *Gullible's Travels* 79: It was a little bit thrillin' at first to be rubbin' elbows with all them celeb's. **1929** Millay *Against the Wall* 171: She's a celeb. **1952** in *DAS* 92. **1991** W. Chamberlain *View from Above* 216: Your...garden-variety "celeb."

celebrity-fucker *n.* a person, typically a young woman, who engages in promiscuous sexual intercourse with film stars or other celebrities; (*broadly*) a hanger-on among celebrities.—usu. considered vulgar.

1969 (quot. at BASEBALL ANNIE). **1972** J.W. Wells *Come Fly* 43: I think that was her name, the celebrity fucker. **1984** N.Y.C. man, age 37: Celebrity-fuckers are a distinctively modern phenomenon. **1986** R. Campbell *In La-La Land* 232: I thought he was just a celebrity fucker.

celebrity rot *n. Pub. Relations.* (see quot.).

1983 *USA Today* (Aug. 2) 1D: *Celebrity rot*—what happens when an entertainer ages and is no longer able to perform as well as when younger.

cell *v. Pris.* to live in a cell; to share a cell. Now *S.E.*

1901 "J. Flynt" *World of Graft* (cited in Partridge *Dict. Und.* 112). *a*1945 in Lindner *Stone Walls & Men* 463: I cell in ——. **1971** J. Brown & A. Groff *Monkey* 141: An old guy...who used to cell with Machine Gun Kelly.

cellar *n. Sports.* Orig. *Baseball.* last place in league standing according to games won.—constr. with *the.* Now *S.E.*

1907 Lajoie's *Official Baseball Guide* 166 (cited in Nichols *Baseball Term.*). **1922** in *DA* 290. **1949** Cummings *Dict. Sports* 64. **1985** N.Y.C. man, age *ca*35: If you're in the cellar on the Fourth of July, you can forget about a pennant.

cellie *n. Pris.* a cellmate.

1966 S. Harris *Hellhole* 29: Barbara and Benita shared a cell, while Helena's "cellie" was a young prostitute and narcotics addict named Frankie. **1974** A. Davis *Autobiog.* 35: She would like...to be my "cellie." **1981** *Easyriders* (Oct.) 56: In the four months I'd been his celly, I'd come to know something about bikes and bikers.

cell 13 *n.* a padded cell.

1896 Ade *Artie* 102: They'll put his nobs into cell 13 and send for the doctors.

Cement City *n.* a cemetery.

1975–78 T. O'Brien *Cacciato* 178: *Cement city*—gravestones.

cementhead *n.* a blockhead. Hence **cementheaded,** *adj.*

1949 R.D. Andrews *Bad Boy* (film): The Cementheads against the Dumbbells. **1962** Serling *New Stories* 3: Because you have succumbed to the propaganda of every cement-headed clod up and down this street. **1966** Panama et al. *Not With My Wife You Don't* (film): Now you see, cement-head? Parker's next door! **1969** H.A. Smith *Buskin'* 80: The see-ment-headed cuckold. **1973** *N.Y. Post* (Aug. 3) 68: Now, look here, you cement-headed, male chauvinist dummy. **1977** Dowd *Slap Shot* (film): A real cementhead! **1987** Aykroyd et al. *Dragnet* (film): Some cementhead. **1992** *Heights* (Fox-TV): Tell cementhead here.

cement kimono *n.* CEMENT OVERCOAT.

1952 H. Grey *Hoods* 330: It would be bye-bye for me, in a cement kimona. **1966** Jarrett *Private Affair* 2: I'll admit I'm gun-shy and I know I could wind up in a cement kimona. **1980** *MASH* (CBS-TV): You'll wind up in a cement kimono.

cement-mixer *n.* **1.** a noisy, rickety, rough-riding vehicle or vessel.

1914 T.A. Dorgan, in Zwilling *TAD Lexicon* 97: (Helping a friend sell a car) If he gets four bits for that old cement mixer he's a wonder. **1942** *ATS* 719: *Cement mixer*, a noisy truck. **1943** Lawson & Korda *Sahara* (film): What are we gonna do if we can't get this cement-mixer rollin'? **1943** J. Mitchell *McSorley's* 201: If I was you I'd take that old cement-mixer and set fire to it....I wouldn't be caught dead in that dirty old boat. **1948** Seward & Ryan *Angel's Alley* (film): Now get this cement-mixer outta here! **1959** Gault *Drag Strip* 8: Show 'em the difference between a Woestmann-Ebbert and that cement mixer. **1989** Cassell *S.S.N. Skate* 75: Skate's a cement mixer. You can hear her coming a hundred miles away.

2. an overweight belligerent woman.

1967 Talbot *Chatty Jones* 19: I ain't running from any cement-mixer like Bessie.

cement overcoat *n.* a block of cement in which gangsters have concealed the body of a murdered person.

1969 Crumley *One to Count Cadence* 188: A cement overcoat in the Bay. **1981** *N.Y. Daily News* (Aug. 6) 2: Allegedly threatened...with "cement overcoat" treatment.

cement overshoes *n.pl.* a block of cement used by gangsters to weigh down the feet of a murdered person before disposal in a body of water. Also **cement shoes.**

1962 N.Y.C. high school student: Then there was the time [in a movie] the crooks put [Laurel and Hardy] in cement overshoes. **1967** *Star Trek* (NBC-TV): You mean cement overshoes? **1972** *Five Boroughs* (Nov.) 12: Most people who pick up a skier and who have ski racks on their cars are not the type of people who are going to roll him into the Hudson with cement overshoes on. **1975–76** T. McNally *Ritz* 75: You are gonna end up wearing cement shoes at the bottom of the East River. **1989** *Knoxville* (Tenn.) *Journal* (Sept. 15) 1: Candidate fears "cement shoes." **1993** *Commish* (ABC-TV): He fits people with cement overshoes!

cent *n.* usu. *pl.* a dollar. Usu. *Joc.*

1957 H. Simmons *Corner Boy* 45: Four cents for the plunge and [the heroin is of poor quality]. **1958** Motley *Epitaph* 148: One cent is a dollar. **1966** Samuels *People Vs. Baby* 172: It's a "five cent" bag, good, the best. **1968–70** *Current Slang* III & IV 23: *Cents*, n. Dollars.—Watts— Ten *cents* equals ten dollars. **1980–84** Porter & Dunn *Miami Riot* 121: Cocaine sells on the street in six-, ten-, twenty-five-, and fifty-"cent"— that is, dollar—bags.

¶ In phrases:

¶ **like two cents** worthless.

1929 A.C. Doyle *Maricot* ch. vii: He would make the wardsman of a red-light precinct look like two cents. **1955** N.Y.C. woman, age 40: She made me feel like two cents.

¶ **worth a cent** in the least bit.

1830 in *DA* 292. **1892** L. Moore *Own Story* 354: The fellow on the inside did not scare "worth a cent."

centerfield *v.* to copulate orally with.—constr. with *on*.

1934 "J.M. Hall" *Anecdota* 156: Any son-of-a-bitch that wouldn't cen- ter-field on this dame is a God damned degenerate!

century *n. Gamb.* one hundred dollars; a one-hundred-dollar bill.

1859 Matsell *Vocab.* 3: I fenced the swag for half a century. *Ibid.* 18: *Century*. One hundred dollars; one hundred. **1866** *Nat. Police Gaz.* (Nov. 3) 2: There was a "century" and a half in it at least. **1871** Banka *Prison Life* 492: One hundred Dollars,...Century. Fifty Dollars,...Half Century. **1899** Cullen *Tales* 168: This gyp's worth a century if she's worth two bits. **1917** in R. Peyton *At Track* 139: They need that quar- ter-century entry-money. **1928** Hammett *Red Harvest* 64: That lousy ring wasn't worth no grand. I did swell to get two centuries for it. **1929–30** Dos Passos *42d Parallel* 64: I saved up pretty near a century. **1929** Burnett *Iron Man* 267: I put three centuries on this hot tip. **1930** Bodenheim *Roller Skates* 114: Three centuries ought to cover the hos- pital bill. **1944** C.B. Davis *Leo McGuire* 78: I had to pay a century. **1960** Barber *Minsky's* 244: One hundred smackers. One whole century every lousy week.

century note *n. Gamb.* a one-hundred-dollar bill.

1908 in *DA* 292. **1914** T.A. Dorgan, in Zwilling *TAD Lexicon* 25: Show the man that century note. Make his eyes water. **1928** O'Connor *B'way Racketeers* 250: *Century Note*—A hundred dollar bill. **1929** "E. Queen" *Roman Hat* ch. xv 164: "She tried to slip me a century note....Tried to bribe me, Chief!" **1943** in Ruhm *Detective* 360: He gives me a century note in cash. **1948** Webb *Four Steps* 68: I gave Lawrence change for a century note about one o'clock.

cereb *n.* [fr. *cereb*rum] *Stu.* an overdiligent student.

1980 Birnbach et al. *Preppy Hndbk.* 90: 13 Words For The Person Who *Is* Working—1. Grind 2. Squid 3. Pencil Geek 4. Cereb 5. Grub 6. Weenie 7. Throat 8. Tool 9. Wonk 10. Gome 11. Nerd 12. Spider 13. Conch.

cert *n. Sports.* a sure winner, as a racehorse.

*a***1889** in Barrère & Leland *Dict. Slang* I 234: A man who was burdened with debt/Heard a *cert* and heavily bebt. *****1889** in *F & H* II 64: I hear Pioneer is a cert. for the St. James's. **1949** R. MacDonald *Moving Tar- get* 108: Jinx is a cert in the third tomorrow.

cert *interj.* certainly! yes, indeed!

1879 *Nat. Police Gaz.* (May 31) 13: Why, cert—the perfesh. **1882** A.W. Aiken *Joe Buck* 4: Cert', it's all right. **1892** Garland *Spoil of Office* 339: Cert. That's right, daddy. **1895** Townsend *Fadden* 99: Long time since ye seen me? Cert. **1896** Dunbar *Lyrics* 63: "Cert," said I. **1896** Ade *Artie* 94: Cert. It ain't where a man's born...that puts him in any class. **1899** Lounsberry *Won at West Point* 57: Cert. He'll try and catch us in some out-of-the-way place alone, and then lick us. **1902** "J. Flynt" *Lit- tle Bro.* 47: Cert. And you'll learn how to shoot too. **1906** M'Govern *Sarjint Larry* 56: Cert! Come along, pardner! **1907** *American Mag.* (Sept.) 459: He cert gave me some new ideas about shoe stock. **1936** Connell & Adler *Our Relations* (film): Why, cert!

CFB *adj. USAF.* (see quot.).

1980 W.C. Anderson *Bat-21* 77: Visibility was CFB (clear as a frapping bell).

chabobs *n.pl.* [orig. unkn.] a woman's breasts.

1962 Kesey *Cuckoo's Nest* 159: She's got one hell of a set of chabobs.

cha-cha *adj.* stylish; nifty; chichi.

1967 Mailer *Vietnam* 179: Oh, man, you'd be a cha-cha faggot if you wasn't so ugly.

chain *n.* ¶ In phrases:

¶ **pull (someone's) chain, 1.** to cause (someone) to speak out of turn.—usu. as a sarcastic question. Also vars.

*****1925** Fraser & Gibbons *Soldier & Sailor Wds.* [ref. to WWI]: *Chain, Who Pulled Your*: Who asked you to interfere, to "chip in." (Addressed

to someone intruding on a conversation). **1951** *Amer. Jour. Sociol.* XXXVII 416 [ref. to WWII]: In one unit, soldiers said to a person who interrupted a conversation, "Who pulled your chain?" **1970** Thackeray *Thief* 112: What's this all about, anyway? What the hell pulled your chain, woman? **1970** E. Thompson *Garden of Sand* 314: Who pulled your chain, twirp? **1985** Memphis woman, age 30: When someone pops off with a witticism, you say, "Who pulled your chain?" I always thought it came from those Chatty Cathy-type dolls with the plastic cord you pulled to make them talk.

2. to elicit (someone's) anger or annoyance, esp. deliber- ately; nag; *(also) pull (one's) leg*, s.v. LEG.

1962 T. Berger *Reinhart* 91: You just flush when I pull your chain. **1970–71** Higgins *Eddie Coyle* 129: Hey, Dave,...don't jerk my chain, okay? You know what I mean. **1974** Bernstein & Woodward *President's Men* 41: If there was some reason...just say so. But they had been jerk- ing his chain all day. **1977** Sayles *Union Dues* 167: I wouldn't of spent ten minutes jerking your chain if I couldn't—couldn't *persuade* certain people to see things my way. **1980** Kopp *Mirror, Mask* 98: All I had to do to pull his chain was to talk about my abortions. **1980** Garrison *Snakedoctor* 176: Whose chain do you think you're pulling? I'm talking *evidence. Facts.* **1986** *Head of the Class* (ABC-TV): He's pullin' your chain, man. Don't you get it? **1989** Kellogg's Corn Pops TV ad: There's plenty left. I was just pulling your chain.

¶ **pull the chain** [allusion is to flushing chains on old-fash- ioned toilets] **1.** stop talking rubbish!

1921 Dos Passos *Three Soldiers* 212: "Pull the chain!" "Tie that bull outside!" **1925** Dos Passos *Manhattan Transfer* 170: Aw pull the chain, old man. **1925** Van Vechten *Nigger Heaven* 191: Pull duh chain! one of them cried. Dis heah is duh new boy.

2. to make a decisive end; *(hence)* to take decisive action, esp. against a person.

1935 Pollock *Und. Speaks*: *Pull the chain*, to end all negotiations. **1945** O'Rourke *E Co.* 19: The two had worked crap games together...[but] sooner or later someone caught the drift and pulled the chain, and then the fun was over. **1954** in Botkin *Sidewalks* 490: And when you have finally decided the idea is definitely lousy, you "pull the chain on that one." **1979** Cassidy *Delta* 276: By the time they pulled the chain there was only one smart thing to do, and that was get the hell out.

¶ **slip the chain** *Naut.* to leave.

1846 Codman *Sailors' Life* 181: Now then...we'll get ready to slip the chain.

chain-jerk *n. Juve.* CIRCLE-JERK. Also as v.

1938 "Justinian" *Americana Sexualis* 15: *Chain-Jerk*...n. Masculine group-masturbation in which several males lie adjacent to each other....Each individual grasps another's penis....Post-war American neologism....v. To participate in masculine group-masturbation. **1975** Legman *No Laughing Matter* 111: "Circle-jerks," "chain-jerks," or "pulling parties," in which all the boys masturbate together.

chain lightning *n.* **1.** cheap potent whiskey or rum.

1837 J.C. Neal *Charc. Sks.* (opp. p. 66): Rail-Road Stone Fence chain lightning & other choice Lickers. **1843** in *DA*. **1861** in Lowell *Poetical Works* 224: I know ye ez I know the smell of ole chain-lightnin'. **1870** Keims *Sheridan's Troopers* 45: In the midst of all the frontier...vulgari- ties inspired by oft-repeated charges of "chain lightning," which elec- trified the boisterous crowd, my attempts at slumber were anything but satisfactory. **1871** Schele de Vere *Amer.* 215: The worst of lickers, as the signboards often have it in unconscious irony, is called *chain light- ning*, from its terrible strength and stunning effect. **1896** Brown *Parson* 43: I...bought a barrel of chain-lightning whiskey that would burn the heart out o' a hundred-year-old alligator. **1901** King *Dog Watches* 92: It must have been the worst kind of "chain lightning" (rum). **1905** Blue- jacket (May) 246: "Beno"...acts like "chain lightning."

2. torment or misery, esp. a severe scolding; hell.

1866 Marcy *Army Life* 404: Old Hickry gin um the forkedest sort o' chain-lightnin'.

3. a person who is extremely adept or formidable.

1891 Landon *Eli Perkins* 296: I'm chain-lightning; if I ain't, may I be blessed. **1902** in "M. Twain" *Stories* 456: By jiminy, but he's chain- lightning! **1922** O'Brien *Best Stories of 1922* 296: Charley was chain- lightning.

chain-locker *n. Naut.* a cellar barroom; dive.

1868 Macy *There She Blows!* 271: Liquor is distilled from the sap of the cocoanut tree, which is warranted to "kill at as many yards" as any arti- cle of tangle-foot dispensed over the bar of the most notorious "chain- locker" in New York or London. **1954–60** *DAS* 92.

chair *n.* an electric chair; (*hence*) death by electrocution.—constr. with *the*. Now *colloq.*

1895 Townsend *Fadden* 203: He abused her terrible and the chair is too good for him. **1899** A. Lewis *Sandburrs* 57: Red Mike gets ten spaces in Sing Sing....He oughter get d' chair. **1900** Willard & Hodler *Powers That Prey* 170: He was a copper, and we fly cops have got to send some bloke to the chair for bastin' him. **1910** *N.Y. Eve. Jour.* (Apr. 1) 13: 17-Year-Old Slayer Must Die In Chair. **1918** E. O'Neill *Dreamy Kid* 26: Is you pinin' ter git me kotched an' sent to de chair? **1922** in Ruhm *Detective* 25: Just like the chair looking me in the face was an everyday affair. **1925** *Sat. Eve. Post* (Aug. 29) 137: If some of these hussies got the chair or life, it might not be good for them; it might seem terrible.

chairborne *adj.* [pun on AIRBORNE] *Mil.* sedentary; assigned to rear-echelon clerical or administrative duty.

1943 *Yank* (Nov. 5) 19: Soldiers called him "chairborne company clerk." **1944** *Guide to AAF* 368: Chairborne troops—non-flying AAF personnel. **1953** Michener *Sayonara* 1: I also wanted some solid chairborne duty. **1956** *AS* XXI (Oct.) 227: *Chair-borne Pilot,* n. A pilot whose primary job is administrative. Also *Desk Jockey.* **1957** E. Brown *Locust Fire* 131 [ref. to 1944]: Decisions of chair-borne generals in Calcutta. **1959** Webb *Pork Chop Hill* (film): Chairborne politicians thousands of miles away. **1984** J. Fuller *Fragments* 13: All the chairborne clerks and cashiers. **1985** Former SP4, U.S. Army, age 35: [in the early 1970's] *chairborne* was common in statements like, "I ain't jumpin' out of no planes—I'm goin' *chairborne.*"

chairborne commando *n. Army.* a clerk-typist or administrative officer.—used derisively.

1945 (quot. at COMMANDO). **1948** *N.Y. Folk. Qly.* (Spring) 19. **1957** Myrer *Big War* 140: Probably picked up a couple of chairborne commandos from the Pentagon. **1961** R.L. Scott *Boring Holes* 193: So many chairborne commandos. **1963** Keats *They Fought Alone* 184: If those chair-borne commandos at Headquarters want to come up here and eat cold rice and dodge Japs with me...I'll be glad to arrange it. **1982** Del Vecchio *13th Valley* 546: Chairborne commandos. REMFs. **1988** Dye *Outrage* 131: God save us from chairborne commandos.

chairborne infantry *n. Army.* CHAIRBORNE personnel.—used derisively.

1944 in *AS* XX 147: *Chairborne Infantry.* AST men; desk men in general. **1945** Dos Passos *Tour* 224: We are the chairborne infantry. **1946** Burns *Gallery* 27: They cursed the Pentagon, which (they said) had emasculated old warhorses like themselves into the chairborne infantry. **1949** Van Praag *Day Without End* 32: Pounding a typewriter in the chairborne infantry. **1957** Denker *Time Limit* (film): He wasn't always in the chairborne infantry. **1966** King *Brave & Damned* 182: A fully accredited member of the C.B.I.—the Chair-Borne Infantry. **1971** Faust *Willy Remembers* 14: All the professors of chair-borne infantry.

chairborne ranger *n. Army.* CHAIRBORNE COMMANDO.

1972 U.S. Army admin. clerk (coll. J. Ball): I'm gonna be a chairborne ranger and push pens around. **1983** S.S. Johnson *Cadences* 133: You want to be a Chairborne Ranger. **1989** *Tour of Duty* (CBS-TV) [ref. to Vietnam War]: I'm gonna be a chairborne ranger for the rest of my tour.

chair-pounder *n.* a desk worker.—used derisively.

1919 Duffy *G.P.F. Book* 112: "Chair pounder" has own ambition.

chairwarmer *n.* a person who sits or lounges idly in a chair.—used derisively. Cf. BENCHWARMER.

1896 Ade *Artie* 102: You ain't got nothin'...to live for. You're nothin' but a chair-warmer. **1901** Hobart *John Henry* 65: Did you ever drop in...to play pool under a cross-fire from the chair-warmers? **1904** in "O. Henry" *Works* 1438: He never takes me anywhere. He's a chair-warmer at home for fair. ***1909** Ware *Passing English* 69: Chair Warmer (Theatrical Anglo-Amer.). A beautiful or pretty woman who does nothing on the stage beyond helping to fill it. **1910** Ade *I Knew Him When* 33: Politics was or were the chief Concern of all the Chair Warmers who lined up in front of the Commercial Hotel. **1919** *DN* V 63: *Chairwarmer,* an idle person. "Every bright day all the *chair-warmers* get out in front of the hotel." New Mexico. **1919** Darling *Jargon Book* 7: Chair Warmers—Those who sit around in chairs when they should be out working.

chalk *n.* **1.** a quarter of a dollar.
1796, 1798, 1805 in *DAE.*

2. the fashion.—constr. with *the.*
1840 in *DA.*

3. something that is genuine; truth.—constr. with *the.*

1843 in *DA* 295. **1844** "J. Slick" *High Life in N.Y.* 117: It was the clear chalk, the ginuine thing. **1878** [P.S. Warne] *Hard Crowd* 2: "Hey, fellers? air that the chalk?" "That's about the size of it, ur I'm a liar."

4. milk or cream. *Joc.*

1934 Weseen *Dict. Slang* 6: *Chalk*—Milk. **1941** *Slanguage Dict.* 10: *Chalk*...milk. **1945** in *Calif. Folk Qly.* V (1946) 381. **1978** Truscott *Dress Gray* 231: "How is the cow?"..."Sir, she walks, she talks, she's full of chalk."

5. *Sports.* a chalk talk.

1934 Weseen *Dict. Slang* 226: *Chalk*—A lecture on football by a coach to the players. Short for *chalk talk.*

6. *Black E.* a white person.—used contemptuously.

1945 Mencken *Amer. Lang.* Supp. I 637: The Negroes use various other sportive terms for whites, *e.g., pale-face, chalk* and *milk.* **1966** Ward *Happy Ending* 11: I gave you credit for more integrity. Didn't figger you had chalk streaks in ya. **1971** S. Stevens *Way Uptown* 133: He was with this skinny chalk who was rapping on 'bout how dope kills young kids.

¶ In phrases:

¶ **by a long chalk** by any means; at all.

*1841 (cited in Partridge *DSUE* (ed. 8) 168). **1859** Bartlett *Amer.* (ed. 2) 75: He can't do it by a long chalk. **1871** Schele de Vere *Americanisms* 318: You can't do that *by a long chalk.*

¶ **come up to [the] chalk** to fulfill expectations; be satisfactory.

1836 in *DA* 294. **1871** Schele de Vere *Americanisms* 318: The President, in whom he is disappointed, for one reason or another, does not *come up to chalk.*

¶ **walk (one's) chalks** to go or move, esp. away, quickly; depart quickly.

1840 in *F & H* 68: The way she walks her chalks ain't no matter. She is a regular fore-and-after. **1843** in *Ibid.*: At once I'll walk my chalks. **1859** Matsell *Vocab.* 18: *To walk your chalks;* to run away. *a***1889** in Barrère & Leland *Dict. Slang* I 235: Cut his stick, and walked his chalks.

¶ **walk the chalk** to obey; behave. [1871 quot. seems to confuse this phr. with *walk (one's) chalks.*]

[**1871** Schele de Vere *Americanisms* 318: When [the President] dismisses an official, he is made to *walk the chalk.*] **1886** Field *Sharps and Flats* I 16: You bet your boots I'd l'arn him/In mighty lively fashion heow/To walk the chalk, gol darn him! **1919** in Truman *Ltrs. Home* 66: But that makes no difference. I have to make 'em walk the chalk. **1934–41** in Mellon *Bullwhip Days* 258: He would say, if dat nigger didn't walk de chalk, he would put him on de block and sell him.

chalk *v.* ¶ In phrase: **chalk the lamppost** to pay a bribe.

1857 in *F & H* II 68: *Chalking the Lamp Post.* The term for bribery in Philadelphia.

chalk eater *n. Horse Racing.* a bettor who bets only on favorites.

1937 in D. Runyon *More Guys* 110: A chalk eater [is] a character who always plays the short-priced favorites. **1956** "T. Betts" *Across the Board* 313: *Chalk eaters*: favorite bettors. **1968** M.B. Scott *Racing Game* 94: A man who consistently plays favorites is called a "chalk eater" and is an object of ridicule.

chalk farm *n.* [rhyming slang] the arm.

*1857 "D. Anglicus" *Vulgar Tongue*: Chalk farm. The arm. **1859** Matsell *Vocab.* 18: *Chalk Farm.* The arm. **1928** Sharpe *Chicago May* 287: *Chalk farm*—arm.

chalkies *n.pl.* **1.** the teeth.

1843 "J. Slick" *High Life in N.Y.* 18: He begun to show his chalkies jest as he did before.

2. *Juve.* mere tally marks as opposed to actual stakes.

1982 Braun *Judas Tree* 101: You don't play for chalkies, do you?

chalk off *v.* to leave.
1840 in *DA.*

chalk out *v.* **1.** to kill (a person).

1940 Longstreet *Decade* 357: He chalked out a momser, and the coppers...and G-heat are on him.

2. to die.

1941 in D. Runyon *More Guys* 308: Not long before Rudolph chalks out he looks at O'Toole and says to him like this. **1969** Gordone *No Place to Be Somebody* 426: My ol' man chalked out, Johnny. Heart attack.

chalubbies *n.pl.* CHABOBS.

1972–76 Durden *No Bugles* 125: She wasn't wearin' a bra and had about a thirty-five inch set of chalubbies.

cham *n.* champagne. Also **sham.**
   1867 in Spaeth *Read 'Em & Weep* 97: I'll stand a bottle o' "cham"/For each man round! **1900** Willard & Hodler *Powers That Prey* 14: The chief wants t' ask us to break a bottle o' sham.

champ *n.* Orig. *Boxing.* **1.** a champion; (*broadly*) a person of great skill or excellence. Now *S.E.*
   1868 in *DA* 295. **1906** Ford *Shorty McCabe* 8: Trainin' comers to go against the champs. **1911** T.A. Dorgan, in Zwilling *TAD Lexicon* 25: Slant over at that...chicken—she's a champ sure. **1913–15** Van Loan *Taking the Count* 324: How're you, champ? **1935** Mackenzie *Been Places* 120: She sure is a champ on the chin-music. **1957** in *DAS* 93. **1965** in W. King *Black Anthol.* 309: This doll is a champ on the sheets.
   2. a thing of excellence. Also attrib.
   1919 in De Beck *Google* 40: Golly—this book is a champ. **1981** Graziano & Corsel *Somebody Down Here* 61: And the money...buys us a champ little brick house in Brooklyn.
   3. an admirable, trustworthy person; fine fellow.—often used in direct address to a man or boy.
   1960 C.L. Cooper *Scene* 59: A champ is a junkie who won't snitch or inform. **1964** Peacock *Drill & Die* 146: This is a changed company, champ. I'm not shitting. **1977** Dowd *Slap Shot* (film): I think you're a champ. **1978** De Christoforo *Grease* 146: Pop was a champ. **1978** T. Sanchez *Zoot-Suit* 168: You sure, champ?
   ¶ In phrase:
   ¶ **like a champ** very well; very successfully.
   1968 Heard *Howard St.* 128: By next week I'll be workin' like a champ. **1971** Jacobs & Casey *Grease* 24: Wait till I...soup up the engine—she'll work like a champ! **1972** P. Thomas *Savior* XI: I can shed tears...and smile also, like a champ. **1974** Gober *Black Cop* 84: Don't I always come through like a champ?

champagne trick *n.* *Prost.* a wealthy and generous customer of a prostitute, or a transaction with such a customer.
   1971–73 Sheehy *Hustling* 219: I take only champagne tricks, $100 an hour.

champers *n.* champagne.
   1979 G. Wolff *Duke of Deception* 228 [ref. to 1950's]: Let's get some champers and fish-eggs up here. **1981–85** S. King *It* 440: Champagne..."Champers," some of 'em called it.

champy *n.* champagne.
   1886 E.I. Wheeler *N.Y. Nell* 5: No more champy at his expense.

chance *n.* ¶ In phrases:
   ¶ **down for a chance** *Navy.* on report for captain's mast.
   1895 Tisdale *Behind the Guns* 13: Andy had remarked at breakfast that I was down for a chance, and wanted to know what I was going to do. **1906** Beyer *Amer. Battleship* 83: "*Down for a chance*"—on the report for mast call. **1918** Ruggles *Navy Explained* 50: *Down for a chance.* To be placed on the report; to have a report made against a man. He is down for a chance and has to go before the captain and receive his punishment or, if he can put it over, the captain excuses him.
   ¶ **The customer will take a chance!** *Short-Order.* an order of corned-beef hash or beef stew.
   1981 in Safire *Good Word* 111 [ref. to ca1915]: The customer will take a chance!

chancre mechanic *n.* Esp. *Navy & USMC.* a physician or medical technician engaged in the treatment of venereal disease; (*hence*) a member of a medical corps, (*esp.*) *Navy.* a pharmacist's mate.—used derisively.
   1944 in *AS* (XX) 147: *Chancre Mechanic.* Medic. **1945** in *Calif. Folk. Qly.* V (1946) 384: The pharmacist's mate bears the opprobrious title *chancre mechanic* or the more charitable *pill roller.* **1948** in *N.Y. Folk. Qly.* (Spring) 20: The medical corps boys are now often called "chancre mechanics." **1951** W. Williams *Enemy* 14 [ref. to WWII]: You don't need a doctor, you need a chancre mechanic. **1958** Plageman *Steel Cocoon* 43 [ref. to WWII]: I said we had to handle chancre mechanics like you with kid gloves during wartime because you could lower the boom on any of us. **1964** Peacock *Drill & Die* 116: If anyone else picks up a dose we'll let those chancre mechanics do a little free labor. **1972** Pearce *Pier Head Jump* 142: What am I supposed to be around here? A sea captain or a chancre mechanic? **1982** R.H. Williams *Old Corps* 35 [ref. to 1930's]: In the minds of sailors and marines, the chief occupation of a Navy hospital corpsman was to treat and prevent venereal disease, because they referred to him, jokingly and without malice, as a "chancre mechanic." **1990** Poyer *Gulf* 191: "I'm a corpsman." "The

new chancre mechanic?"

change *n.* **1.** money; cash in hand; (*hence*) in phr. **piece of change** an amount of money.
   1889 Reynolds *Kansas Hell* 167: This human fiend undertook to secure their "loose change," as he called it...over one thousand dollars. **1907** in H.C. Fisher *A. Mutt* 18: Grab this piece of change and go buy yourself a piano. **1907** Siler *Pugilism* 64: I was a bit short of change while loafing around Memphis and requested the fight promoter...to get big Jim Lawler for me. **1910** *N.Y. Eve. Jour.* (Mar. 22) 15: He'll give th' kid a run for his change. **1912** Lowrie *Prison* 192: Every few days I'd slip him a piece of change. **1927** C. McKay *Home to Harlem* 148: But I heard she done beat up anether gal of hisn—a fair-brown that useta hand over moh change than her.... **1942** Algren *Morning* 23: If you guys wanted we c'd always have change. **1958** Gardner *Piece of Action* 70: From this will come loot, change, a piece of change. **1966** I. Reed *Pall-Bearers* 85: I told him to go to da Harry Sam Ear Muffle Factory where they was hirin' and where they makes some good change. **1980** T. Jones *Adrift* 155: Them dudes...sure knew where to look for *change,* man.
   2. Orig. *Pris.* a brief period, as of confinement; (*hence*) a fractional additional amount, as of time.
   1962 Maurer & Vogel *Narc. & Narc. Add.* (ed. 2) 294: *Change.* A short jail or prison sentence. **1984** *Cheers* (NBC-TV): You take your average whale's intestines and stretch 'em out—you're lookin' at three miles and change. **1984** W. Murray *Dead Crab* 12: I clocked her in one-o-two and change. **1985** L. Grizzard, in *Knoxville Journal* (Oct. 30) A7: Anyway, I wound up in the hospital for a month and change. **1985** Bodey *F.N.G.* 37: Four more months and change, and I'll be back in The World. **1989** L. Roberts *Full Cleveland* 155: Followed by a six-pack and change.
   3. usu. *pl.* Esp. *Black E.* marked adjustments of attitude or outlook; (*hence*) anguish, difficulties, unpleasantness, bad treatment, etc.—constr. with *through.*
   1962 H. Simmons *On Eggshells* 185: Aw baby, now you really taking me through some changes. **1962** Maurer & Vogel *Narc. & Narc. Add.* (ed. 2) 294: *Changes.* Adjustments, esp. as *being put through the changes.* **1966** C. Cooper *Farm* 30: It was that little croaker I'd gone through all those changes with on the gallery. **1967** Fiddle *Shooting Gallery* 63: They...freely admit that the life makes no sense. And yet, there they are, day in and day out, going through the same kind of "changes." **1968** I. Reed *Yellow Back Radio* 37: The horsemen dismounted and began to put Loop through changes. **1968** Gover *JC Saves* 77: Man that sure musta put you through some funny-funny changes. **1969** Bullock *Watts* 151: So I go through all kinds of changes. **1971** *Inter. Jour. Addictions* VI 11: I got a thing about needles, man. If you gave me a skin pop, I would cry and go through changes. **1971** Woodley *Dealer* 119: I want to put a phone in [my car], but the telephone company will put you through a change now to do it. **1972** P. Thomas *Savior* 137: "Aye, por Dios, Nita, this is my wedding night and I'm letting myself go through all these changes"..."It's good for me to listen." **1974** *Police Woman* (NBC-TV): You got to quit puttin' yourself through all these changes. **1979** in J.L. Gwaltney *Drylongso* 15: That's why they have to go through so many changes to see that we don't get that even break. **1985** Dye *Between Raindrops* 3: Hué City put me through some righteous changes. **1985** "Blowdryer" *Mod. Eng.* 13: Going *through changes*...queen talk for upset...."Girl, he was just going through all these changes, I begged him not to redecorate that apartment in lime green and pink."
   ¶ In phrases:
   ¶ **piece of change, 1.** see (1), above.
   2. a factor; element.
   1978 Strieber *Wolfen* 43: Carbon monoxide!...That's the crucial piece of change, as far as I'm concerned.
   ¶ **ring the changes** *Und.* to swindle by the substitution of bad money for good. [More general senses are S.E.]
   *1785 Grose *Vulgar Tongue* s.v. *ring:* Ring the Changes. When a person receives silver in change to shift some good shillings and put bad ones in their place. The person who gave the change is then requested to give good shillings for these bad ones. **1891** Maitland *Slang Dict.* 222: *Ring the changes* (Am.), to swindle by substituting bad money for good.

channel *n.* ¶ In phrase: **change channels** [or **the channel**] to change the subject of a conversation.
   1954–60 *DAS* 93: *Change the channel.* To change the topic of conversation. **1978** W. Brown *Tragic Magic* 38: The rap in the dorm...'s a drag cause most folks never change channels.

channel fever *n. Naut.* a restless desire to go ashore, felt as one's ship nears port. [The orig. ref. was to the English Channel.]

*1929 Bowen *Sea Slang* 24: *Channel Fever.* Homesickness. **1939** Fearing *Hospital* 123: I always got channel fever on the downhill run. **1940** *AS* (Dec.) 450: *Channel Fever.* The restlessness shown on shipboard, when the ship is known to be nearing port. **1958** Cope & Dyer *Petty Officer's Guide* (ed. 2) 336: *Channel fever.* The urge for leave and liberty that comes over the crew of a homeward bound ship. **1972** Pearce *Pier Head Jump* 118: What's the matter with you? You got channel fever? **1979** *N.Y. Times Mag.* (Aug. 26) 43: Home port, nevertheless, was on everyone's mind…."Channel fever!" hissed Tim Jenkins, one of the seamen, impatiently. **1983–86** G.C. Wilson *Supercarrier* 248: I don't personally feel this channel fever—the excitement of going home that keeps you from going to sleep at night.

channel-groper *n.* [ref. to the English *Channel*] *Naut.* an English ship.—used derisively.

1837 *Every Body's Album* II 104: Those ten-gun channel-gropers don't run the line off the reel at that rate, in such a catspaw as this.

chant *n. Und.* **1.** (see quot.).

1807 Tufts *Autobiog.* 292 [ref. to 1794]: *Chant*…writing of any kind.
2. a name.

*1812 Vaux *Vocab.*: *Chant*: A person's name, address, or designation; thus, a thief who assumes a feigned name on his apprehension to avoid being known, or a swindler who gives a false address to a tradesman, is said to *tip them a queer chant.* **1845** *Nat. Police Gaz.* (Oct. 16) 51: Altering his "*chant*" (name) to that of Henry T. Erskine, Esq. **1848** *Ladies' Repository* VIII (Oct.) 315: *Chant*, Name, (for instance, "Tip your chant," means give your name). **1859** Matsell *Vocab.* 18: "*Give me your chant,*" give me your name.

chant *v. Und.* to talk or talk about.

1859 Matsell *Vocab.* 18: *Chant.* Talk; to publish; to inform. **1867** *Nat. Police Gaz.* (Apr. 20) 2: Do you charge me with taking that last big thing that's chanted?

chap *n.* [short for *chapman*] a person; fellow; "customer." Now *colloq.* [Now usu. regarded as Brit. usage.]

1704 S.K. Knight *Journal* 23: Perhaps the Chap Reply's Yes. **1797** in Cmiel *Demo. Eloquence* 46: I think this last chap to be of the race of coxcombs. **1831** Seabury *Moneygripe* 63: Thought himself a pretty smart chap. **1850** *Spirit of Times* (Jan. 26) 581: Why, that chap was closer than the bark on a hickory tree. **1864** in J.H. Gooding *Altar of Freedom* 105: You're a brick, old chap. **1870** "M. Twain," in A.L. Scott *Twain's Poetry* 79: Bime by the chap on tother side, sez he "If this was poker…" **1898** in A.P. Hudson *Humor of Old South* 536: Possum is a sly old chap. **1918** E.E. Rose *Cappy Ricks* 97: What kind of a…chap was he?

chap *v.* ¶ **chap (someone's) ass** to irritate or annoy (someone).—usu. considered vulgar. Also euphem.

1961 Terry *Old Liberty* 5: It kind of chapped my rear, if you know what I mean. **1968** Westheimer *Young Sentry* 140 [ref. to WWII]: "Because you're so damn fatheaded it chaps my ass," Moran said. *Ibid.* 152: But I tell you one thing, don't let 'em catch you outside the wall. It really chaps 'em.

chaplain *n.* ¶ In phrase: **see [or tell it to] the chaplain** *Mil.* don't trouble me with your problems or complaints.

1941 *Saturday Review* (Oct. 4) 11: See the chaplain. Shut up. **1941** *AS* (Oct.) 168: See the Chaplain. Stop grousing. **1942** in *Best from Yank* 64: "*Show-down* inspection?…Why, we had 12 of those at the other camp!" "See the chaplain," snaps the sergeant. [**1970** R. Sylvester *Guilty Bystander* 280 [ref. to WWII]: The standard advice to anybody who was bitching…"Tell your troubles to Jesus, the chaplain's gone ashore."] **1980** S. Fuller *Big Red* 43: Tell it to the chaplain. **1985** Bodey *F.N.G.* 80: "I wanna go home." "Tell the chaplain."

chaplain's mate *n. Navy.* a pious sailor.—usu. used derisively.

1914 *DN*: *Chaplain's mate.* A sailor of pronounced religious tendencies. **1941** Kendall *Army & Navy Sl.* 17: *Chaplain's mate*…a sympathetic sailor. A gentle soul.

chapped *adj. S.W.* angry or disgusted.

1968 Baker et al. *CUSS* 95: *Chapped.* Disgusted. **1969** *Current Slang* I & II 18: *Chapped,* adj. Angry.—College students, both sexes, Texas. **1971** Dahlskog *Dict.* 12: *Chapped*…Angry, tee'd off.

chappie[1] *n.* a chap; fellow. *Joc.*

*1882 in *F & H* II 74: A real "dear old chappie," as I needn't perhaps remark. *1883 in Ware *Passing Eng.*: Lord Boodle, a rapid chappie, always ready to bet on everything with everybody. **1886** *Chi. Tribune*

(Mar. 11) 4: Much obliged to you, old chappee. **1888** *Stag Party* (unp.): He heard a chappie get off this sentiment. **1892** *Life* (Dec. 1) 314: My birthday to-day, old chappie. **1896** in Rose *Storyville* 128: The chappies are wondering who is the beautiful girl who is seen with Miss Gertrude Livingston. **1891–1900** in Hoyt *Five Plays* 119: Come 'round to the club, old chappie! **1901** Wister *Philosophy 4* 11: Go on to the next chappie. **1905** Sinclair *Jungle* 278: Poor ole chappie! *a*1904–11 Phillips *Susan Lenox* II 149: I've got quite a line of friends among the rich chappies from Fifth Avenue. **1918** in Truman *Dear Bess* 267: I did help Slagle shut up the chappies. **1924** in Inman *Diary* 248: 'Sthat a go? How 'bout it, chappie? **1941** *Pittsburgh Courier* (Oct. 25) 18: A chappie destined to go places. **1952** E. Brown *Trespass* 119: Okay, chappie.…You entitled to you own attitude. **1990** Poyer *Gulf* 47: Pilots only in here, chappies.

chappie[2] *n. Mil.* a chaplain.

1942 *Life* (Sept. 14) 89: The chaplains who are going to war in 1942 are…apt to be called "Chappie," a nickname indicative of an enlarged relationship.

character *n. Und.* an accomplished professional criminal; (*specif.*) a swindler. Also attrib.

1958 Gilbert *Vice Trap* 111: He's on the highway department. That's a character saying down here. It means a stud who hustles anything. **1964** Ellson *Nightmare St.* 8: With you carrying that kind of weapon, I had you down as a character. You know, some kind of clip artist. **1962–68** B. Jackson *In the Life* 72: Police give us that name, characters. *Ibid.* 127: You might be from out-of-state and a character broad, and it don't take but a few minutes to knock you off as being people.

Charcoal Jemmy *n.* a charcoal peddler.

1837 Neal *Charcoal Sketches* 96: My people's decent people, and I can't disgrace 'em by turning Charcoal Jemmy, or smashing the black stones with a pickaxe. They wouldn't let me into no society at all if I did.

charge *n.* **1.** a stiff drink of liquor.

1834 *Mil. & Nav. Mag. of U.S.* (June) 248 [ref. to 1831]: Measuring the quantity with an experienced eye, ere he replaced the [whiskey] bottle on the counter, he remarked with a knowing cut of the eye, "rather a heavy charge, stranger."
2.a. *Narc.* an injection of a narcotic.

1925 (quot. at HYPO). **1942** *ATS* 475: Narcotic injection…*charge.*
b. a thrill of pleasure; KICK.

1950 *N.Y. Times* (June 20) II 5: I got a big charge out of coming back to U[nited] A[rtists]. **1951** S.J. Perelman, in *New Yorker* (Mar. 3) 28: What kind of an old creep'd get a charge out of this stuff? **1953** W. Brown *Monkey On My Back* 31: [The] reefers were poor stuff, however, and he couldn't get much charge out of them. **1953** E. Hunter *Jungle Kids* 31: I lit up one of the joints, sucking it in with loose lips, mixing it with air for a bigger charge. **1954** Ellson *Harding* 75: They got a large charge out of it. **1959** Scott *Flying Tiger* 116 [ref. to WWII]: Doesn't that give you a charge? **1961** Sullivan *Shortest, Gladdest Years* 140: She'll get a charge out of it. **1963** Braly *Shake Him* 16: Furg's idea of a large charge was three teenagers beating on oil drums in a vacant lot. **1965** Tracy *Bazzaris* 58: I thought you said it gave you more of a charge when we talked rough. **1970** Wakefield *All the Way* 53: He got a real charge out of watching Gunner drive balls. **1992** Hosansky & Sparling *Working Vice* 13: My dad got the biggest charge out of them.
c. a feeling of desire.

1972 R. Wilson *Playboy's Forbidden Words* 14: Have I got a lot of charge for that chick!
3.a. *Narc.* marijuana; a marijuana cigarette.

1941 in Ellington *Music My Mistress* 179: *Charge*…marijuana. **1952** Brossard *Darkness* 10: This is really great charge. **1952** Mandel *Angry Strangers* 162: Nothin like Horse, it's oney jive, but it's good charge. **1956** Ross *Hustlers* 55: Mambo, you got a charge? *Ibid.* 74: The place smelled like it was full of charge. **1960** T. Southern, in Rosset *Evergreen Reader* 274: He call it "charge," too. Sho'. Them's *slang* names. **1961** Baldwin *Another Country* 265: It was great charge. *1967 Glatt et al. *British Drug Scene* 26: In Jamaica,…everybody smokes "charge."
b. *Narc.* narcotics (of any sort).

1957 H. Simmons *Corner Boy* 46: Why don't you let me get my charge from you?

charge *v.* **1.** to celebrate riotously; to act without restraint.

1873 Beadle *Undeveloped West* 369: "Brad. Collins is on a big spree, ain't he?" "You bet he's a chargin'."
2. *Und.* to rob (a bank, store, or the like) recklessly or at gunpoint.

1933 Ersine *Prison Slang* 26: Seven rooters charged the jug. **1937** E.

Anderson *Thieves Like Us* 16: These kids trying to rob these banks are just dingbats. They'll charge a bank with a filling station across the street. **1948** in *DAS*: A little bank just itchin' to be charged.

3. to thrill with excitement.
1965 Trimble *Sex Words* 40: *Charge*...vt to arouse sexually.

charged *adj.* **1.** drunk.
1880 "M. Twain," in *DARE*: The pleasant talk and the beer flow for an hour or two, and by and by the professor, properly charged and comfortable, gives a cordial good night. **1922** T.A. Dorgan, in Zwilling *TAD Lexicon* 25: He's agin' licker ain't he....He's half charged right now too. **1931** Wilstach *Under Cover Man* 77: Charged to the gills, a middle aged man sprawled over a table. **1953** L. Hughes, in *Black Scholar* (June 1971) 19: I believe you are charged now.

2. excited or exhilarated by drugs; (*hence*) excited; enthusiastic.—usu. constr. with *up*.
1922 Murphy *Black Candle* 57: Three of [the murderers] were drug addicts who, before committing the deed, had to be "charged up" with cocaine. **1927** C. McKay *Home to Harlem* 5: I wasn't mahself. I was like man charged up with dope every day. **1939** Howsley *Argot* 12: *Charged*—Full of dope. **1955** E. Hunter *Jungle Kids* 5: You're all charged up, ain't you, Stevie? **1958** Talsman *Gaudy Image* 155: He had to...smoke it away somewhere..., then return, charged, way out, ready for plotzing. **1970** Horman & Fox *Drug Awareness* 464: *Charged up*—under the influence of drugs. **1972** in *Playboy* (Jan. 1973) 208: But if I can't get up in the morning feeling charged about my work, then what's the point? **1986** F. Walton *Once Were Eagles* 140: We were all charged up—scared, but looking forward to it with a certain amount of excitement. **1990** *CBS This Morning* (CBS-TV) (Aug. 27): The people that came over with me are really charged up—keen and ready to go.

charger *n.* Orig. *Mil.* an aggressive, enthusiastic, or competitive person; HARD-CHARGER.
1964 J. Lucas *Dateline* 114: American advisers...arrive as "chargers," eager to tackle the job and help win the war. **1974** Scalzo *Stand on Gas* 65: Under Wally's constant goading, Bobby Marshman...became what Meskowski calls a "charger."

chariot *n.* an automobile or other vehicle. *Joc.*
1935 Odets *Lefty* 8: Honey, I rode the wheels off the chariot today. **1942** Freeman & Gilbert *Larceny, Inc.* (film): He brought me over here in his new chariot. **1958** Gardner *Piece of the Action* 79: Yes, sir, I'm the boss of this chariot. **1959** Hughes *Simply Heavenly* 129: That's the chariot—and I got nobody to ride back there with me. **1963** in S. Lee *Son of Origins* 36: It musta taken a heap of green stamps to buy a chariot like this! **1968** Swarthout *Loveland* 18 [ref. to *ca*1930's]: Our hero and his chariot were parked in front of Al's Drycleanery and it was a darb. **1974** R. Carter *16th Round* 104: How do you dig my new chariot? **1978** Alibrandi *Killshot* 109: I'll see that my old chariot gets sold. **1988** Norst *Colors* 175: I'd still bet this was the chariot old Rocket was driving.

charity ass *n.* an act of sexual intercourse that is not charged for; a woman who grants sexual favors without charge.—used derisively.—usu. considered vulgar. Cf. CHARITY GIRL.
1926 in E. Wilson *Twenties* 254: Charity-ass, eh?—Gives it away! **1952** H. Grey *Hoods* 108: Not bad for the little business woman, especially for a former Delancey Street piece of charity ass.

charity girl *n.* *Prost.* a woman who grants sexual favors without charge. Also **charity worker**, (*vulgar*) **charity cunt**.—all used derisively.
1916 Cary *Venery* I 43: *Charity Cunt*—A woman who distributes her favors without price. **1921** Woolston *Prostitution in U.S.* I 37: The "charity girl"...grants her favors in return for entertainment. **1923** W.I. Thomas *Unadjusted Girl* 119: Girls of the class who...tend to justify sexual intimacy if they are "going to marry"...are called "charity girls" by...prostitutes. **1971** Rader *Govt. Inspected* 13: I ain't no charity worker, dummy.

charity shot *n.* *Basketball.* a free throw. Also **charity toss**.
1942 *ATS* 660: *Charity toss*, a free throw. **1976** *Webster's Sports Dict.* 74: Charity shot.

charity stripe *n.* *Basketball.* the free-throw line.
1934 *Journalism Qly.* (Dec.) 349: *Charity Stripe*—free throw mark (basketball). **1983** Eble *Campus Slang* (Nov.) 1: *Charity Stripe*—the free throw line on the basketball court.

Charles *n.* [sugg. by syn. CHARLIE] *Mil.* Communist Vietnamese armed forces; a Communist Vietnamese soldier.—also constr. with *Mr.*
1966 *N.Y. Times Mag.* (Oct. 30) 104: The troops reduce [Victor Char-

lie] to "Charlie." (Some men use "Charles" as a variation to produce a mock touch of formality.) **1966–67** Harvey *Air War* 104: Charles baby is a little timid this evening. **1968** Corson *Betrayal* 147: Before the initial confrontation, the enemy is disparagingly referred to as "Charlie"; after "Fire Fight One" he is referred to as "Charles." The semantic difference is real. The enemy is recognized as a worthy foe. **1971** Mayer *Weary Falcon* 8: You have to hand it to Charles—he will fuck your program anyway he can. **1972** T. O'Brien *Combat Zone* 193: The ol' soldier's out there messing up Charles. **1973** Huggett *Body Count* 112: Monsoon's coming, Dude. It's gonna rain old Mr. Charles right outta his tennis shoes. **1980** M. Baker *Nam* 205: He was a Charles, you understand. **1983** Ehrhart *VN-Perkasie* 217: That's Mr. Charles country up there. *Ibid.* 271: The Vietcong were collectively called "Charlie"...but the North Vietnamese were called "Charles." **1984** J.R. Reeves *Mekong* 257 [ref. to 1970]: Mr. Charles was a lot more sophisticated than the local recruits.

Charley var. CHARLIE.

Charley horse *n.* [see note] **1.** Orig. *Baseball.* a cramp in an arm or leg muscle resulting from excessive strain or from a blow. Now *S.E.* [Despite investigation, the origin of the term remains obscure.]
1888 in *AS* (1949) XXIV 103: I could dance in those days, because, you see, I never was bothered with "Charley Horse." **1889** in *DA.* **1908** in Fleming *Unforgettable Season* 74: Ball players get charley horses of the legs, but umpires can get the same charley horse in the head. **1911** Van Loan *Big League* 201: Recovering from his chronic Charley horse. **1912** Mathewson *Pitching* 145: Charley horse and the rheumatism have no terrors for you. **1928** Dahlberg *Bottom Dogs* 104: The ball player slung his bat all the way from the plate to the pitcher, getting him rite on the charley-horse. **1940** J.T. Farrell *Father & Son* 346: I got charley horses from football. **1954** Dodd *On Football* 323: The bruising of a muscle, joint, or viscera...is more commonly known as the "Charley horse." **1955** F.K. Franklin *Combat Nurse* 57: Charley horse, varicose veins, flat feet! **1962** Houk & Dexter *Ballplayers* 70: The players suffer sprains, torn ligaments, Charley horses and broken bones. **1972** in *Playboy* (Feb. 1973) 182: I got a Charley horse in my leg. Goes on and off.

2. [sugg. by SALT HORSE] *Army.* canned corned beef.
1919 K. Morse *Letters* 250 [ref. to WWI]: What to do with the "Charlie Horse," as the boys call the canned roast beef, was a puzzle.

charley horse *adj.* (sense uncertain; see quot.).
1896 Ade *Artie* 58: Tommy was all right by that time. He'd got his nerve back, and he was real charley-horse, joshin' me and Mame.

Charlie or **Charley** *n.* **1.a.** [perh. sugg. by CHARLIE-ON-THE-SPOT] a watchman. Now *hist.*
*1812 Vaux *Vocab.*: *Charley*: a watchman. **1837** *Every Body's Album* II 67: "Young 'uns," remarked a passing Charley, "if you keep on cutting didoes, I must talk to you both like a Dutch uncle." **1839** *Amer. Joe Miller* 115: I wonder, if they wouldn't list me for a charley? **1848** *Ladies' Repository* VIII (Oct.) 315: *Charley*, A watchman. **1884** (quot. at LEATHERHEAD). **1981** T.C. Boyle *Water Music* 50: Ned...looks back to see poor Smirke in the grip of two burly Charlies.

b. a police officer. Now *Black E.*
1851 Ely *Wanderings* 157: The "Charley" now advanced and laid hands upon him, for the purpose of arresting him. **1980** *AS* LV 197: Blue coat, bull, Charlie,...cop, copper [etc.].

2.a. (used in direct address to a man, esp. one whose true name is not known). [1868 quot. may be factitious.]
1868 M.H. Smith *Sunshine & Shadows* 427: A woman flitting out from a side street, where she has been watching for her victim, will seize a man by the arm, and cry out, "Charlie, how are you?" **1898** L.J. Beck *Chinatown* 183: [The Chinese man] ambles right up...and says: "H'low, Charlie; how muchee you chargee?" **1919** Klein *With the Chinks* 237: "What's your name, Charlie?" he cries. **1938** *AS* (Apr.) 159: There was also a person who reiterated "Vass you dere, Sharlie?" **1958** Camerer *Damned Wear Wings* 179: How you know? Was you there, Charlie? **1959** J. Rechy, in *Big Table* I (No. 3) 21: If he calls you jack youre hip but if its cholly you dont swing. **1967** "M.T. Knight" *Terrible Ten* 58: You a cop, Charlie? **1975** Mahl *Beating Bookie* 38: Sorry Charlie, you lose unless your other two boys have a super day. **1982** Heat Moon *Blue Hwys.* 138: Don't mess, Charley, or you'll be sorry.

b. (used to personify and identify an individual man on the basis of his most typical characteristic). Cf. similar use of JOE.
1967 Levin *Rosemary's Baby* 142: Do you know what Dr. Hill is? *Charley Nobody*, that's what he is. **1972** *N.Y. Times* (June 25) 15: Listen...don't

get the idea that you're talking to Charlie Saint.

3.a. *pl.* a woman's breasts.

*1873 Hotten *Slang Dict.*: *Charlies*, a woman's breasts. *1909 Ware *Passing English* 71: *Charlies*...women's breasts when well developed. *1911 O'Brien & Stephens *Australian Sl.* 36: *Charlies*: a woman's breasts: variants—dibs, lemons, dairies, bubs. 1974 Strasburger *Rounding Third* 24: And she's got those big charlies...38C. 1977 Dunne *Confessions* 37: Like you never seen a pair of charlies before. 1985 Blumenthal *Tinseltown Murders* 8: A slim waist and a set of charlies that made it into the next room about twenty seconds before the rest of her got there.

b. the penis.

1969 Bartell *Group Sex* 139: I can't understand little Charlie here. He's always up and ready to go, but I've just had a lot on my mind. 1969 Bouton *Ball Four* 163: Also, if you get caught eating at the table after a game with Charley uncovered, that costs a dollar. 1969 *Harper's* (Oct.) 66: His wife had started referring to his sexual organ as "Charlie."

c. [prob. fr. mil. comm. alphabet *Charlie* for *C*] *Navy.* a condom.

a1988 Poyer *Med.* 52: Givens pulled a set of fresh Charlies from the wrappers they had been stowed in since the States.

4.a. *Black E.* white men regarded as oppressors of blacks.—used contemptuously. Also **Mr. Charlie, Boss Charlie.** Also attrib.

[1923 in E. Wilson *Twenties* 164: Mista Charlie, I hear—I hear the niggers is free, is that right?] 1928 Fisher *Jericho* 303: *Miss Anne, Mr. Charlie* Non-specific designation of "swell" whites....."That boogy's got a straight-eight just like *Mr. Charlie's*."—"Yea, and his *mamma's* got a fur coat just like *Miss Anne's*, too." 1928 McKay *Banjo* 217: We have words like ofay, pink, fade, spade, Mr. Charlie, cracker, peckawood, hoojah, and so on—nice words and bitter. 1940 Zinberg *Walk Hard* 244: Put it right there, Mister Charlie, and truck on down. 1945 Drake & Cayton *Black Metropolis* 387: As they phrase it, they have to "Uncle Tom" to "Mr. Charley" a bit to survive. 1948 Cozzens *Guard of Honor* 273: This is Mr. Charlie's War...Japs fight for Afro-Americans' Freedom. 1954 Killens *Youngblood* 21: You got everything right now, Mr. Charlie. 1958 Hansberry *Raisin in the Sun* 271: The Man. Like the guys in the streets say—The Man. Captain Boss—Mistuh Charley. 1960 in T.C. Bambara *Gorilla* 54: On the other hand, if the militant civil liberties unions ever got hold of him, Mr. Charlie was a dead man. 1962 H. Simmons *On Eggshells* 225: You do that you break ole Charlie's rule. 1963 in Clarke *Amer. Negro Stories* 303: They was all beamin' like they had Charley's number. 1965 Conot *Rivers of Blood* 36: "Shit!" a woman said. "Them Charley bastards won't even give you no water." 1969 *N.Y. Times* (Aug. 31) II 13: Charlie can throw too much power for open warfare. 1972 R. Wilson *Playboy's Forbidden Words* 29: An American black caught tampering with Boss Charlie's lady. 1973 Duckett *Raps* 8: And don't raise your voice to Mr. Charlie. ca1974 in J.L. Gwaltney *Drylongso* 16: Now Chahlie knows that he is wrong as two rabbits when he do things like that, so naturally he don't want to hear about these things. 1983 Goldman & Fuller *Charlie Co.* 249: They still don't want us to go to Mr. Charlie's café by the front door.

b. *Black E.* a white man.—used contemptuously.

1964 Brewer *Worser Days* 111: He seed de white man had a fishin' pole slung cross his shoulder, so he say, "Mr. Charlie, is you goin' fishin'?" 1968 Gover *JC* 121: You know how them little chollies sticks t'gether. 1971 Rhinehart *Dice Man* 35: But the brother...came up to that next Charlie. 1972 Sapir & Murphy *Death Therapy* 53: "He a badass,"...said Philander confidentially to the two Charlies. 1984 Sample *Raceboss* 11: You keep this lil' ol' Charlie-lookin devil outta my sight!

5. [sugg. by fictional Chinese detective *Charlie Chan*, created by Earl Derr Biggers] **a.** an Asian man.—used disparagingly.

1938 Bezzerides *Long Haul* 75: He walked to the Chinaman. "Hey, Charlie, what you know?"

b. *Mil.* a Japanese military serviceman; the Japanese armed forces.

1942 *Time* (Feb. 9) 23: The Jap, who is variously "Mr. Moto," "Tojo," "Charlie," or the "Japanzy" to U.S. troops, was beginning to show a heavy preference for night movement, when concealment is best. 1942 Hersey *On Bataan* 98: Those Charlies—we call them Charlies—can't shoot. 1943 in Loosbrock & Skinner *Wild Blue* 213: Two unidentified planes, too, huh? A couple of Charlies pulling a sneak! 1944 E.H. Hunt *Limit* 21: They shelled the hell out of Charlie's airstrip. *Ibid.* 26: First he wants to see how close he can get to Charlie's backyard. *Ibid.* 31: Charlie's coming over...."In force" as the communiqués say.

6.a. [sugg. by *Victor Charlie*, mil. comm. alphabet for *VC*] *Mil.* The Viet Cong or armed forces of North Vietnam; (hence) a person in Communist Vietnamese military service.—also attrib.—also constr. with *Mr.* Now *hist.*

1965 *Newsweek* (Aug. 9) 17: The American GI's...call the enemy simply, "Old Charley." 1965 *Newsweek* (Sept. 20) 26: Don't you tell me Charlie...isn't hiding here! 1965 Adler *Vietnam Letters* 98: They had two fire missions (harassing fire in case Charlie lurks in the nearby glen). 1966 Baxter *Search & Destroy* 99: We...gave them the coordinates, locating the Charlie gunners. 1966 Shepard *Doom Pussy* 28: The Charlies don't alway stay in the jungles. 1969 Marshall *Ambush* 45: I believe we can take these Charlies. 1970 Flood *War of Innocents* 77: We start the day around here by firing a cannon at Charlie out in the hills. 1979 Cassidy *Delta* 38: If the Charlies ever shoot *me* in the ass, they'll have to get under...a bar stool to do it. 1982 "J. Cain" *Commandos* 283: Naw, just some Charlie out there lobbing mortars into downtown. 1989 W.E. Merritt *Rivers Ran Backward* 251: Mr. Charlie ain't scared of nobody.

b. *Mil.* the armed forces of the People's Republic of China.

1966 Tamony *Amer.* (No. 14) 18: Charley is also employed to refer to the Chinese Communists. 1985 Former SP4, U.S. Army, age 34: *Charlie* referred to the [Communist] Vietnamese [in the 1970's], but on Taiwan it also included the Red Chinese, like "Charlie wants this rock ["island"] back." One meaning just blended into the other.

7. [sugg. by the name of popular film comedian Sir Charles S. "Charlie" Chaplin (1889–1977)] *Mil.* a chaplain. *Joc.*

1917 Lord *Boyd's Battery* 24: *Charley*...the Chaplain. 1918 Swan *My Company* 148: Chaplain Edwards (Charlie Chaplin) in the foreground. 1918 Casey *Cannoneers* 270: In the driver's seat, beaming benediction on the wondering cannoneers, sat our chaplain—Charlie Chaplain.

8. *Esp. Black E.* a dollar.

1924 Hecht & Bodenheim *Cutie* 33: Herman handed the man twenty-five charlies and staggered off the premises. [1936 Duncan *Over the Wall* 21 [ref. to 1918]: A two-dollar note was a Hard-Luck-Charlie.] 1944 Burley *Harlem Jive*: And I couldn't dig when they'd want me to knock a scarf or loan them a brace o' chollies. 1958 Hughes & Bontemps *Negro Folklore* 482: *Cholly*: A dollar bill. When you beg for a cholly, you're really down. 1966–67 P. Thomas *Mean Streets* 108 [ref. to 1940's]: Hey, man, you got a couple charlies you can lend me?

9. *Und.* cocaine.

1935 Pollock *Und. Speaks*: *Charley*, cocaine. 1945 in Partridge *Dict. Und.* (ed. 2) 804. 1950 *Time* (Aug. 28) 4: Cocaine...C, Charlie, snow. 1953 Anslinger & Tompkins *Traf. in Narc.* 306: *Charley*. Cocaine. 1972 NYU student: They call cocaine *Charlie* in my neighborhood.

10. *Sports.* CHARLEY HORSE.

1947 Schulberg *Harder They Fall* 155: Just a little Charley. I can rub it out in a few minutes....These muscles...go into a Charley easy.

11. *USAF.* (see quot.).

1956 Heflin *USAF Dict.* 110: *Charlie, n.* A light-weight radar apparatus for warning and fire control against surface craft.

12. Charleston, S.C.

1977 Dills *CB Slanguage* (ed. 1978) 22.

¶ In phrases:

¶ **charlie's dead** your slip is showing.

1942 *ATS* 95: Your slip is showing: *charlie's dead.* 1950, 1967–70 in *DARE* I.

¶ **good-bye, Charlie!** the end; disaster.

1966 Susann *Valley of Dolls* 409 [woman speaking]: They told me...the minute I start with pills or booze, good-by Charlie! 1974 J. Robinson *Bed/Time/Story* 125: They'll take one look at that profile of yours and it's Goodbye-Charlie.

¶ **on the Charlie** being a tramp.

ca1910 Lomax & Lomax *Amer. Ballads & Folk Songs* 38: Dead an' gone, dead an' gone,/Kase he's been on de cholly* so long...*"On de cholly" is equivalent to "out on the hog," or "on the bum." *Ibid.* 40: For I've been on the Charley so long.

Charlie Blow *n.* [CHARLIE, 9 + BLOW, *n.*] *Narc.* cocaine.

1977 *N.Y. Post* (July 8) 15: "Charley Blow"...has been branded a health risk in a report this week by the National Institute on Drug Abuse.

charlie-boy *n.* a soft or effeminate young man.

1896 Ade *Artie* 4: W'y, out there last night I see the measliest lot o' jays—regular Charley-boys—floatin' around with queens. *Ibid.* 33: I'll...tell you why I've got it in for that Charley boy. 1901 Ade *Modern Fables* 20: From the Minute that any Charley-Boy shows up...I talk about Him and nothing else. 1913 J. London *Valley of Moon* 91: It's all right for Charley-boys, but a man that is a man don't like bein' chased by women. **1915** O'Brien *Best Stories of 1915* 86: I wouldn't...run around all hours to dance halls with every sporty Charley-boy that comes along. *Ibid.* 88: Silly ain't no name for him, with his square, charley-boy face and polished hair.

charlie-boy *v.* [fr. CHARLIE in senses ref. to Asians] to work as a busboy.

    1974 Radano *Cop Stories* 70: They'd work twelve, fourteen hours pressing shirts, or Charlie-boy in a restaurant.

Charlie Brown *n.* [alluding to the usu. inept cartoon character created (1950) by Charles M. Schulz in his comic strip *Peanuts*] *Mil.* a blunder.

    1974 Former L/Cpl, USMC, served in Vietnam 1967–69: To really make a mess of something was to *pull a Charlie Brown*.

Charlie-Charlie *n.* [mil. comm. alphabet *Charlie* 'C', redup., for *c*ommand and *c*ontrol] *Mil.* a command-and-control aircraft, esp. a helicopter.—often constr. with *bird*.

    1984 Doleman *Tools of War* 28 [ref. to Vietnam War]: Their airborne operations centers were known in army parlance as command and control ships; to the grunts they were C & Cs, or "Charley-Charleys."...Word...flashed to the hovering brigade Charley-Charley. **1986** Thacker *Pawn* 143: Those Charlie-Charlie birds don't wait for buck sarges. **1987** Pelfrey & Carabatsos *Hamburger Hill* 105 [ref. to Vietnam War]: We got McDaniel's body out on the Charlie-Charlie bird.

Charlie Cong *n. Mil.* the Viet Cong; a member of the Viet Cong. Now *hist.*

    1970 Gattzden *Black Vendetta* 146: He had the choice of playing Charley Cong. **1971** Barnes *Pawns* 82: I wanna go to Vietnam/I wanna kill some Charlie Cong. **1981** Raban *Old Glory* 280: Before I got mistaken for a beer can or Charlie Cong. **1987** "J. Hawkins" *Tunnel Warriors* 142: Fifty-four Charlie Congs.

Charlie Noble *n.* **1.** *Naut.* a galley stovepipe; in phr. **shoot Charlie Noble** to clear the pipe of soot by firing a blank shot inside it.

    1847 Downey *Cruise of Portsmouth* 160: "Charley Noble" as the Cooks funnel was familiarly called. **1881** *United Service* (Aug.) 212: "Charley Noble," the galley funnel is. **1882** Miller & Harlow *9'–51"* 94: I love to feel the silv'ry smoke/Soar up from Charley Noble. **1898** Tisdale *Behind the Guns* 246: He shoots into the galley's smoke-stack, ostensibly to clear it of soot....He has again shot "Charley Noble." **1918** *Lit. Digest* (Aug. 24) 44: Charlie Noble, you know, is the name for the galley smokestack. **1920** *Amer. Leg. Wkly.* (Feb. 13) 34 [ref. to 1918]: "Charlie Noble" was a naval term for the galley or kitchen, smokestack. **1931** Erdman *Reserve Officer's Manual* 429: The expression, "Shooting Charlie Noble," describes a custom once practiced, of loosening the soot in the galley smokestack by firing a blank rifle or pistol cartridge up it. **1939** O'Brien *One-Way Ticket* 37: A wisp of black smoke curled from the Charlie Noble at the galley. **1942** *Leatherneck* (Nov.) 144: *Charlie Noble*—The smoke pipe from galley aboard ship. **1961* Burgess *Dict. Sailing* 49: *Charlie Noble.* The ugly H-type iron chimney-top from a galley or stove.

    2. [allegedly coined aboard *USS Salem* in 1964] *Navy.* a man-overboard dummy used in drills.

    1969 Gallery *Cap'n Fatso* 74: Then how come we call this here dummy a Charley Noble?

Charlie-on-the-spot *n.* JOHNNY-ON-THE-SPOT.

    1805 in Thornton *Glossary* I 162: And I will be upon the spot, as punctual as "Charley." **1942** *ATS* 391: Reliable person...*charlie-on-the-spot*.

Charlie rat *n. Mil.* a C-ration.

    1982 Del Vecchio *13th Valley* 47: Ham and lima beans....Worst Charlie Rat there is. **1992** Reinberg *In Field* 39: *Charlie rats*...Army C-rations.

Charlie's House *n. Mil.* Communist-controlled territory in Vietnam.

    1973 Layne *Murphy* (unp.): Semper Fi, On to Charlie's House/To test what had been learned. *Ibid.*: A year had come and gone at Charlie's House. **1985** Bodey *F.N.G.* 77 [ref. to Vietnam War]: Even though I've been in his house now, he's still not real, just Charlie.

Charlie Taylor *n.* [orig. unkn.] *S.W.* (see quot.).

    1933 *AS* VIII 27: *Charley Taylor.* Syrup or sorghum into which bacon or ham grease from the platter has been poured or stirred. **1939, 1950** in *DARE.*

Charlotte *n.* [sugg. by syn. CHARLIE] *Und.* cocaine.

    1966 Braly *On Yard* 26: I been messin with that charlotte.

charm farm *n. Av.* a school for flight attendants.

    1984 Tiburzi *Takeoff!* 77 [ref. to 1973]: The Stewardess College or Learning Center—affectionately known to irreverent locals as the Charm Farm.

charms *n.pl.* money.

    1871 (quot. at JOHN). **1875** in *F & H* II 76: Money has forty or fifty different names...[including] *charms.* **1889** Farmer *Amer.*: *Charms*...money; not much used now.

charm school *n. Mil.* an officer's training course or other career orientation school.

    1971 Pvt., U.S. Army, Ft. Campbell, Ky. [coll. J. Ball]: Don't talk to Mac. He's going off to charm school to be a big second looie. **1989** Zumbro & Walker *Jungletracks* 10 [ref. to Vietnam War]: I take it you're from the "Charm School"? *Ibid.* 12: The Charm School, formally known as Division Orientation Center.

chart *n.* **1.** *Naut.* the face. Cf. syn. MAP.

    1902 Cullen *More Tales* 43: That peculiar grin of his that overswept his whole chart. *Ibid.* 99: Sleep it off, hey?...I'll sleep you off with a brace o' hot ones on dat chart o' youse's.

    2. *Music.* a musical arrangement.

    1971 in L. Bangs *Psychotic Reactions* 8: They did have one other good chart, "Doctor Stone" it is. **1980** *N.Y. Post* (July 2) 37: The band behind them...worked hard, and the charts they played were excellent. **1989** S. Robinson & D. Ritz *Smokey* 137: Killer charts by cats like Hank Cosby and Gil Askey.

chart-buster *n. Music Industry.* a top-selling song.

    1986 *America: Nissan* (Spring) 26: College students...sang the latest chart busters.

charted *adj.* thoroughly understood.

    1966 Braly *On Yard* 141: You're in serious trouble...you got that charted?

Chas *n. Army.* the Viet Cong; CHARLIE. Now *hist.*

    1982 Del Vecchio *13th Valley* 183: Chas is dug in and got bunkers. **1992** Reinberg *In Field* 39: *Chas* nickname for Charlie, the enemy.

chase *n.* ¶ In phrases:

    ¶ **cut to the chase** [orig. ref. to chase scenes in action movies] get to the point; get on with it. [The 1929 quot. attests a literal use in film.]

    [**1929** McEvoy *Hollywood Girl* 106: Jannings escapes....Cut to chase.] **1983** *Hill St. Blues* (NBC-TV): Cut to the chase. **1987** Mamet *House of Games* (film): Hey, cut to the chase. I'm very busy. **1988** Cogan & Ferguson *Presidio* 64: We can sit here and talk...or...we could just cut to the chase. **1991** *CBS This Morning* (CBS-TV) (June 5): You have cut to the chase in some real essential relationship problems here.

    ¶ **take a chase** to go away.

    1899 Cullen *Tales* 165: So I'll just take a chase.

chase *v.* **1.** to hurry away; leave.

    1898 Hobart *Many Moods* 53: I...chases home to Mame. **1902** Townsend *Fadden & Mr. Paul* 213: We four chases.

    2. *Mil.* to escort (prisoners under guard).

    1917 Morse *Letters* (Dec. 7) 13: If there is one military duty which the doughboy hates above all others, it is this job of chasing prisoners. **1918** in *Papers Mich. Acad.* (1928): *Chasing prisoners*...guarding prisoners employed at labor. **1928** Nason *Sergeant Eadie* 81: In Army parlance a man under guard is chased and one who guards prisoners at work chases them.

    3. to pass (food at a mess table).

    1925 *AS* I 137: Chase us a slab of that bull, will you, Slim? **1926** Maines & Grant *Wise-Crack Dictionary* 6: *Chase the cow down this way*—Pass the milk.

    4. (of a man) to pursue women, esp. in an adulterous fashion.

    1980 *N.Y. Daily News Tonight* (Mag.) (Aug. 20) 2: Three years ago I divorced my husband because he lied, gambled and chased.

    ¶ In phrases:

    ¶ **chase (oneself)** to hurry away; clear out.—esp. in phr. **go chase yourself** go away and stop bothering me!

    1883 Peck *Peck's Bad Boy* 85: O, you go and chase yourself. **1893** Frye *Field & Staff* 175: Go chase yerself off'n de field, Larry....Dis ain't no place for kids. **1895** Townsend *Fadden* 165: It was my night off, and me and de Duchess and Maggie was going t' chase ourselfs down t' de

Bow'ry t' see me friend de barkeep. **1896** Ade *Artie* 68: Aw, go chase yourself. **1928** McKay *Banjo* 36: Go chase you'self. I knowed her long before you did. **1987** *21 Jump St.* (Fox-TV): Hey, go chase yourself. **1993** *Frasier* (NBC-TV): Ah, go chase yourself!

¶ **chase (one's) face** to hurry away.
1900 Patten *Merriwell's Power* 46: If you want to see something…just chase your faces down to the front entrance.

¶ **chase the dragon** see s.v. DRAGON.

chaser *n.* **1.** a philanderer, esp. a married man who habitually attempts to seduce women; SKIRT-CHASER.
1894 in *OEDS.* **1903** McCardell *Chorus Girl* 14: Boozers and chasers do not write. **1936** *New Yorker* (Sept. 12) 34: Boozers, chasers, dopes,…lay off. **1943** Chandler *Farewell, My Lovely* 240: I might have been a little surprised that she would actually marry him, because the man is nothing but a professional chaser. **1953** Gresham *Midway* 52: Need ride help, sober, reliable, no boozers, no chasers.
2. a drink of water, beer, etc., taken after a drink of liquor. Also *fig.* Now *colloq.* or *S.E.*
1897 in *DA:* Everything was 50 cents. a drink, no mixed drinks, and no water for a chaser. **1932** Dos Passos, in *OEDS:* Two guys from Chicago who were drinking whiskey with beer chasers. **1935** in H. Gray *Arf* (unp.): "Let me get a poke at that bird." "And take this for a chaser." **1956** in *OEDS:* He…took the glass of rum…, shot it down in one swallow, and followed it with a chaser of water.
3. a person whose job is to run errands; GOFER.
1901 A.H. Lewis *Croker* 60: One of his "Royal Highness's" chasers comes sprintin' up to me.
4. *Vaud.* (see quot.).
1902 Mead *Word-Coinage* 183: *Chaser*—one who does a turn or an act two or three places of amusement nightly.
5.a. *Mil.* a sentry who escorts prisoners under guard.
1927 Stevens *Mattock* 62: You know that big red-faced Mick who is in the prisoner-chaser detail? **1944** Kendall *Service Slang* 35: *Chaser*…prisoner guard. **1957** Leckie *Helmet For Pillow* 123 [ref. to 1943]: I was elated, and could have hugged the prison chaser when he appeared outside the colonel's office. **1961–63** Drought *Mover* 31: I wish we had the goddam chaser who was guarding him that day in there, too. **1964** Rhodes *Chosen Few* 67: Under the watchful eye of two chasers, the brig detail sat. **1966** Noel & Bush *Naval Terms* 88: *Chaser:* slang for sentry, i.e., Brig Chaser. **1967** W. Crawford *Gresham's War* 111: I'm his chaser. And character witness. **1967** Dubus *Lieutenant* 72: Watched by a Marine chaser, Navy prisoners had swabbed the landings. **1970** Ponicsan *Last Detail* 16: You two dudes pulled temporary duty as chasers.
b. an employee whose job is to urge manual laborers along in their work; straw boss.
1956 (cited in *DAS* 94).
6. *Navy.* a submarine-chaser.
1944 in W.C. Fields *By Himself* 492: I can sympathize with you fellows on the chasers.
7. *Show Bus.* an exit march; music to accompany a performer's exit.
1933 Weseen *Slang Dict.* 137: *Chaser*—An exit march in a theater or variety house. **1954–60** *DAS* 94. **1982** T.D. Connors *Dict. Mass Media* 48.

chassis *n.* a woman's figure, esp. if attractive; (*occ.,* as in 1930 M. West quot.) a man's muscular build.
1930 Farrell *Stories* 106: These dames whose mugs and chassis were in the paper. **1930** Mae West *Babe Gordon* 23: What a chassis you got, Bearcat! **1936** Gaddis *Courtesan* 71: The law says you gotta cover that swell chassis of yours with a few doll-rags. **1940** Wald & Macauley *They Drive by Night* (film): "Nice chassis." "A classy chassis." **1942** "E. Queen" *Calamity Town* 65: She's even got a brain on that swell chassis. **1942** *Yank* (Oct. 14) 19: The Little Scotch Lassie with the Classy Chassis. **1944** *Life* (May 15) 71: New flat-top look is achieved by these four "classy chassis" at Hollywood High. **1946** Gresham *Nightmare Alley* 18: With a chassis like that Cahill kid's got you don't have to do no encouraging. **1958** J.B. West *Eye for an Eye* 5: She knew what I was thinking whenever she paraded that classy chassis in front of me. **1959** Sterling *Wake of the Wahoo* 76: There's a goodlooking babe with a swell chassis across the street. **1966** Ward *Happy Ending* 5: All class and manners, but nothing underneath but a luscious V-8 chassis!—which is a-o-reet wit me since that's all I'm after. **1968** Swarthout *Loveland* 68: Kissable Miller was a Carole Landis-type blonde with a really classy chassis. **1971** *Nat. Lampoon* (Apr.) 70: I couldn't help wondering how a

gal with a swell chassis like hers ended up here.

chatt *n.* usu. *pl.* [poss. fr. *chattel*] *Und.* a louse. *Obs.* in U.S. [The term was well known among British and ANZAC forces during both world wars; see Partridge *DSUE.*]
***1698–99** "B.E." *Dict. Canting Crew: Chatts,…Lice. Squeeze the Chatts,…*to Crack or kill those Vermin. ***1785** Grose *Vulgar Tongue: Chatts.* Lice: perhaps an abbreviation of chattels, lice being the chief live stock or chattels of beggars, gypsies, and the rest of the canting crew. ***1812** J.H. Vaux *Vocab.: Chats,* lice. **1859** Matsell *Vocab.* 18: *Chatts.* Lice. *Chatt,* a louse. ***1974** in *Dict. Austral. Eng.: Chat*…In New South Wales prison argot, it means…"louse."

chatterbox *n.* **1.** an excessively talkative person; chatterer. Now *S.E.*
***1774** in *OED:* But I suppose his father *can,* for he is a fine chatter-box. ***1785** Grose *Vulgar Tongue: Chatter Box.* One whose tongue runs twelve score to the dozen, a chattering man or woman. **1814–18** in *OED.* **1839** *Spirit of Times* (May 11) 120. ***1878** in *OED* 52: A mere political chatterbox.
2. an automobile radio.
1937–41 in Mencken *Amer. Lang.* Supp. II 724. **1941** in *AS* (XVI) 240: *Chatterbox and Fish Pole.* Car radio and aerial.
3. *Mil.* a machine gun.
***1940** in S.J. Baker *Australian Lang.* 152: In the 2nd A.I.F. a Lewis gun is called a *chatterbox.* **1941** Kendall *Army & Navy Slang* 1: Ack-Ack…a machine gun, also known as a scattergun, shot gun, chatterbox. **1943** Hunt *Service Slang* 22: *Chatterbox.* Americanism for machine-gun, now used by pilots and air crews generally. We have to thank the Eagle Squadrons for this and other American phrases. **1942–45** MSU Folklore Coll. (GF2.1) *Army Jargon* 29: *Chatterbox*—Japanese heavy machine gun. **1969** Cameron *Tunnel War* 73: When that chatterbox opened up I headed for the nearest cover.

chattergun *n.* a machine gun or submachine gun.
1931 Wilstach *Under Cover Man* 8: Tracin' that…chatter gun might mean [trouble]. **1961** F. Brown *Geezenstacks* 82: Johnny Dix let go the hot hand-grips of the chatter-gun. **1972** Pendleton *Boston Blitz* 58: It was sheer panic down there when the blitzing black shadow snatched up his chattergun and loped down the road to close on the enemy.

chatter guy *n.* Orig. *Baseball.* a player who helps to maintain team morale by being energetically talkative during a game.
1959 N.Y.C. junior high–school student: We need a chatter guy on this team. **1970** Wakefield *Going All the Way* 48: In baseball they never could hit worth a damn but were terrific chatter guys—C'mon-babe-c'mon-boy-c'mon-Pete.

chattery *n.* *Und.* dry goods.
1791 [W. Smith] *Confess. T. Mount* 19: Dry goods, *chattery.* ***1821** in *F & H* II 79: *Chattery,* cotton, or linen goods.

chat up *v.* **1.** to talk flirtatiously to. [Esp. common in BrE.]
***1963** in Partridge *DSUE* (ed. 7) 1056). **1983** Sturz *Wid. Circles* 44: New enrollees would…go round chatting up the girls. **1983** N. Proffitt *Gardens of Stone* 56: When it comes to chatting up the girls, I might as well be a sophomore in high school. **1987** *Eyewitness News* (WABC-TV) (June 30): Leaving Charles to chat up a former girlfriend. **1988** Lane & Stevens *Mary Phagan* (NBC-TV): Mr. Frank don't like to be disturbed when he chattin' up the young ladies.
2. to interview. [Earlier in Brit. & Austral. use.]
1981 Eyre & Wadleigh *Wolfen* (film): Vander Veer's niece was picked up.…I want you to chat her up.

chaw *n.* **1.** *Stu.* a trick; imposture.
1842 *Dartmouth* IV 117: To say, "It's all a gum," or "a regular chaw," is the same thing. **1856** Hall *College Wds.* 63: *Chaw.* A deception or trick. **1889** Barrère & Leland *Dict. Slang* I 239: *Chaw* (university), a trick.
2. a yokel. Cf. CHAWBACON.
***1856** T. Hughes *Tom Brown's Schooldays* ch. i: There's nothing like the old country-side for me, and no music like the twang of the real old Saxon tongue, as one gets it fresh from the veritable CHAW in the White Horse Vale. **1883** Keane *Blue-Water* 213: His mildest words were, "You chaw! You thing! You dog!"
3. conversation; talk; JAW.
1898–1900 Cullen *Chances* 29: I heard the chaw about it this afternoon. *Ibid.* 46: I had another chaw with his trainer. **1902** Cullen *More Tales* 88: The end of the chaw was that the old man promised to meet O'Brien in Buffalo three days later. **1906** *Nat. Police Gaz.* (Aug. 18) 6: The squeaker…had given up a chaw about getting it into the newspa-

pers how drunken men were being robbed. **1928** Dahlberg *Bottom Dogs* 264: Red Rufus…wasn't much on listening to Davidd's chaw.

4. *West.* an Irish person.—used contemptuously.

*ca***1916** in *Calif. Folk. Qly.* I 228: The scabs come from Joplin,/And the "Chaws" come down from Butte. **1928** Callahan *Man's Grim Justice* 16: He called another big, red-faced "chaw" and told him to lock me up. **1929** in *DARE* I [ref. to early 1900's]: But soon George starts to complain that it was run by a bunch of "red necks," "chaws," "flannel mouths," "Micks"—all names for Irishmen. **1930** "D. Stiff" *Milk & Honey* 205: An Irishman. Sometimes called a *chaw*.

chaw v. **1.a.** to mangle; (*hence*) to defeat utterly; trounce; kill.—often constr. with *up*. Also (emphatic) **chaw up and spit out.**

1835 in Meine & Owens *Crockett Alms.* 54: Mister, I think you are most catawampiously chawed up. **1837** Neal *Charcoal Sks.* 43: I'll chaw up any indewidooal that's fairly my match. **1839** *Knickerbocker Mag.* XIII 65: "I will chaw you up"; a threat involving defeat. **1845** in Robb *Squatter Life* 59: Old Tom Jones…swar he'd "chaw me up." *Ibid.* 64: Jest as I was makin' him a *chawed specimen*, some feller holler'd out. **1848** in Blair & Meine *Half Horse* 200: Don't give 'em no quarter. Chawr 'em up like a Virginia nigger does cabbage. **1848** Judson *Mysteries* 192: I doesn't want to fight. If I did I'd chaw you up and spit you out again afore you knowed whar you was, whiteman. **1862** "E. Kirke" *Among Pines* 21: Massa Seward would hab troops 'nough in Georgetown to chaw up de hull state in less dan no time. **1862** C.F. Browne *A. Ward* 143: We chawed 'em up—that's what we did! **1866** Marcy *Army Life* 365: We chawed um all up; we laid um out cold'r nur a wedge. **1872** "W.J. Hamilton" *Single Hand* 24: We'll only get chawed up if we stay. **1873** J. Miller *Modocs* 156: He…turned to the crowd, ready to "chaw up and spit out," as he called it, the first man who raised a voice against the Judge. **1874** Carter *Rollingpin* 194: To see 'em chaw each other,/ We all enjoyed the sight. **1882** in Sweet *Texas* 31: His tale of the many Indians he had chawed up soon gave him a prominent position among the boys. **1883** "M. Twain" *Mississippi* 26: He flung off a buckskin coat that was all hung with fringes, and says, "You lay thar tell the chawin-up's done."**1889** Alger *Snobden's Office Boy* 78: Mr. Duncan was not so tall as he, and probably weighed twenty pounds less.…"Why," thought Gerrish, "I can chaw him up if I like." **1899** Boyd *Shellback* 74: Do I look as if I could chaw you up, eh?

b. (used in oaths).

1876 J. Miller *First Fam'lies* 100: If Sandy don't go to kingdom come with his boots on, then chaw me up for a shrimp. **1907** S.E. White *Arizona* 82: It was a heap long ways…and I'd be teetotally chawed up and spit out if I was goin' to join these minin' terrapins.

2. *Stu.* **a.** to trick or ridicule.

1842 *Dartmouth* IV 117: Yesterday a Junior cracked a joke on me, when all standing round shouted in great glee, "Chawed! Freshman chawed! Ha! ha! ha!"…When a fellow is *used up*, he is said to be *chawed*; if very much used up, he is said to be *essentially chawed*. **1909** *DN* III 298: *Chaw*…to…guy one.

b. to embarrass.

1952 F.C. Brown *NC Folk.* I 526: *Chaw*…To embarrass. "What that fellow said to you last night certainly did *chaw* you." **1953** *PADS* XIX 9: *Chawed*…Embarrassed. "That compliment sort of chawed me."

3. to scold angrily; BAWL OUT.—also constr. with *up*. Cf. CHEW OUT.

1858 in Law *Citadel Cadets* (Feb. 9) 192: This morning the section that went into Stevens got the Squad Marcher to ask him to stop it. But instead of giving them a direct hearing he endeavored to "chaw" them and sent them out. This of course provoked them more than ever. **1884** in *DARE:* I went *in quest* of him, and I just chawed him up. *ca***1960** (quot. at CHAWED, 1).

4. to converse; to talk.

1899 Cullen *Tales* 165: Got no time t' chaw, anyhow.

¶ In phrase:

¶ **chaw wind** *Naut.* to labor at setting and furling sails.

1883 Keane *Blue-Water* 201: He stood up in an old tattered suit of grey tweed…and no socks under his…boots, to "chaw wind" in the western ocean in the depth of winter.

chawbacon n. a yokel.

*1811 *Lexicon Balatron.*: *Chaw Bacon.* A countryman. A stupid fellow. **1834** in *DARE:* If a few dozen chaw-bacons be us'd up for the public benefit…isn't the glory of the nation increas'd by it. **1869** J.L. Peyton *Over Alleghanies* 318: What does Giniril Tailer care for such chaw-bacons as you! **1898** Green *Va. Folk-Speech* 82: *Chaw-bacon, n.* A countryman. **1899** Cullen *Tales* 48: His pals threw it into him about being a

chaw-bacon and a would-be welcher. **1946** in Botkin *R.R. Folk.* 183: No countrified allusions to "the 9-30" or the "down train" or the "express," as the chaw-bacons in some hick town would call them.

chawed adj. **1.** utterly overcome, as by surprise, embarrassment, fatigue, etc.—often constr. with *up*.

1843 in *DARE:* The Majur was most teetotally discumfisticutted and near about as good as chaw'd up. **1845** T. Thorpe *Mysteries of Backwoods* 28: Miss Patience said she was gratified to hear Mr. Cash was a musician; she admired people who had a musical taste. Whereupon Cash fell into a chair, as he afterwards observed, *chawed up.* **1879** *Puck* (Dec. 3) 635: I feel pretty considerably chawed up—I dew. **1936** *AS* (Dec.) 368: *Chawed up* (adj.). Embarrassed; confused; surprised; as "I surely was chawed up when I found that out." *ca***1960** in *DARE: Chawed up*…Defeated or embarrassed or severely scolded.

2. *So.* angry. Also **chewed.**

1942 *Amer. Merc.* LV 92: I know you feel chewed. **1956** in *DARE:* The American Southernism, "chawed," meaning *mad.*

chawmouth n. a person who boasts or speaks foolishly or complainingly.

1927 Rodman *Ky. Admiral* 41 [ref. to late 19th C.]: Knowing him to be a sea-lawyer, a "chaw-mouth" and trouble breeder,…it was a surprise to me that he had not been on the report for six months. **1964** *PADS* XLII 39: *Chaw-mouth*…refers to the Irishman's talkativeness. **1967** in *DARE:* He's an absolute chaw-mouth and tells everything he knows—and at times even more.

C-head n. *Narc.* a cocaine user.

1982 A. Shaw *Dict. Pop/Rock* 169: [A] "C" head [uses] cocaine. **1982** De Sola *Crime Dict.* 26.

cheap Charlie n. Esp. *Mil.* a stingy man.

1965 C. Brown *Manchild* 168: He'd never worn anything but cheap Charlie's shoes before, but now he started wearing custom-made. *ca***1969** Rabe *Hummel* 76: Hey, GI cheap Charlie, you want one more beer? **1969** Eastlake *Bamboo Bed* 169: You big Cheap Charlie, you buy me nothing else to play with. You number ten. **1973** Huggett *Body Count* 179: Cheap Charlie! **1980** Cragg *L. Militaris* 73: *Cheap Charlie.* Any miserly, stingy person, especially one who will not buy something or who tips in a very niggardly fashion.…As early as 1962 the Chong Nam restaurant on Saigon's Hai Ba Trung Street was being called "Cheap Charlie's" because the prices there were so reasonable.

cheap-Charlie adj. cheap, esp. of inferior quality.

1969 Eastlake *Bamboo Bed* 154: Ho actually came from Kuk Ho just outside of Hanoi but Hanoi sounded like number one, which is the best, Cheap Charlie or number ten is the worst. **1973** Childress *Hero* 124: Blew fifty-seven fifty on that cheap-Charlie suit.

cheapie n. **1.** something that costs little, esp. if inferior in quality.

1942 *ATS* 32: Something poor, mean, contemptible…cheapie. **1950** in *DAS* 95: A couple of real cheapies…1929 Essex sedan…$39; 1930 Chevrolet Tudor…$59. **1952** *Time* (May 12) 103: Low-cost [motion] pictures…known in the trade as "cheapies." **1968** Moura & Sutherland *Tender Loving Care* 139: That's how he gets all these cheapie jobs. **1972** R. Barrett *Lovomaniacs* 185: Talks like some kind of walk-on from a Hell's Angels cheapie.

2. a cheapskate.

1951 *Time* (Apr. 23) 116: We want the rich tourists, not cheapies. *a***1967** Bombeck *Wit's End* 143: Du bist ein cheapie, that's what you are! **1970** N.Y.C. man, age *ca*25: Don't be a cheapie. **1985** J. Green *Dict. Slang* 48.

cheap John n. **1.** a stingy man. [The 1826–27 quot. reflects the S.E. sense.]

[***1826–27** in *OED:* Which cheap-John is offering for next to nothing.] **1905** White *Boniface to Burglar* 282 [ref. to 1865]: The bankers saw that he was no "cheap John"…and that his idea of a recompense was vastly in excess of what they had in mind to pay. **1908** *DN* III 298: *Cheap John*…a niggardly or stingy person, who does things in a cheap style. **1968** in *DARE.*

2. cheap goods.

1944 in *DARE:* Elaborate displays of baubles and "cheap john."

Cheap-John adj. **1.** being an establishment that retails cheap merchandise or provides cheap services.

1855 Hinton R. Helper *Land of Gold* 164 (in *AS* XLIII 92): Notwithstanding all its Peter Funk and Cheap John establishments, it sustains a better character than any other city in the state. **1872** McCabe *New York Life* 752: A Stranger's Exit From A "Cheap John Shop" (an auc-

tioneer's place). **1899** in J. London *Letters* 53: I mean some of these cheap-John publishers. **1928** Wharton *Squad* 16 [ref. to 1918]: That Cheap John shoe store o' yers. **1938** Holbrook *Mackinaw* 183: Cheapjohn stores...stocked with Sunday suits of a particularly bilious and offensive purple-blue color. **1951** in *DAS* 95: Running a Cheap John clinic. **1976** Atlee *Domino* 14: We...rolled past scattered grocery stores and cheap-john liquor drive-ins.
2. cheap in quality; vulgar.
1866 in Hilleary *Webfoot* 210: His dress [is] an old straw hat, Linen duster and Cheap John pants. **1871** "M. Twain" *Roughing It* 244: No, sir! None of your cheap-John turnouts for me. **1905** *DN* III 74: *Cheap John, adj. phr.* In poor taste, low-bred, vulgar. "We don't want any *cheap John* shows in this lecture course."

cheap Johnny *n.* a dealer in cheap merchandise; cheap John.
1866 *Night Side of N.Y.* 26: The front of the bar, like the booth of a cheap Johnny, stares at you with all its trinkets.

cheap liberty *n. Navy.* a look at the shore instead of actual liberty. *Joc.*
1940 *Life* (Oct. 28) 99: *Cheap liberty* is not liberty at all, but a look from ship to shore by spyglass. **1944** Kendall *Service Slang* 21: *Cheap liberty*...to gaze longingly at the shore through binoculars.

cheap-mitt *n.* [*cheap* + MITT 'hand'] *Stu.* a cheapskate.
1919 *DN* V 64: *Cheap-mit*, a shoddy person. "Those old farmers who live in retirement are old *cheap-mits*." New Mexico.

cheapo *n.* [*cheap* + *-o*] **1.** a miser; CHEAPSKATE. [Earliest quot. is factitious.]
1911 in Mager *Sherlocko* 24: Cheapo is the only dealer who handles them. **1956** E. Kovacs Show (NBC-TV): Frugal Productions....Directed by Forrest L. Cheapo...Music by Johan Cheapo [etc.]. **1964** Thompson & Rice *Every Diamond* 69: "Cheapo" was one of the more innocuous words showered upon him. **1972** N.Y.U. student: Don't be such a cheapo.
2. a cheap item.
1972 J. Morris *Strawberry Soldier* 153: Norm didn't want him to jump until he had at least five refresher jumps on a cheapo. **1981** *Rod Serling's Mag.* (Sept.) 80: No more Stein paperbacks....No more cranking out cheapos like sausages for a piddling advance.

cheapo *adj.* cheap.
1972 R. Barrett *Lovomaniacs* 256: Just a little cheap-o pocket transistor. **1974** Lahr *Trot* 202: You want a cheapo...success. **1976** Schroeder *Shaking It* 152: His khaki shirt and his cheapo boots. **1977** *Yosemite Sam* (Aug.) (unp.): We signed up for the cheapo plan—a stick of *gum* for breakfast and a *cupcake* for dinner! **1985** Briskin *Too Much* 200: Let's see how cheapo it is.

cheap shot *n.* Orig. *Sports.* **1.** an act of deliberate roughness against an unprepared opponent; (*hence*) any instance of unsportsmanlike conduct.
1970 Libby *Life in Pit* 87: Crow came back and hit me on the back of the knees. It was a cheap shot....I wouldn't do that to anybody. **1974** Blount *3 Bricks Shy* 107: A guy complained, said I hit him a cheap shot. **1976** *Webster's Sports Dict.* 75. **1976** *U.S. News & W.R.* (Jan. 12) 21: This is the kind of cheap shot that people will use rather than think about the issues. **1978** *Adolescence* XIII 497: If another team member physically abused a jock on the playing field, it was a "cheap-shot."
2. an insult or instance of unfair or malicious treatment.
1971 B.J. Friedman, in *Playboy* (Dec.) 340: But if anybody ever hit him a cheap shot, I'd put two right between the guy's ears. **1972** Grogan *Ringolevio* 264: It was a pretty cheap shot to take at someone. **1973** Flaherty *Fogarty* 164: That's a cheap shot. I've been like clockwork with the kid. **1978** *U.S. News & W.R.* (Aug. 7) 16: I'm a highly partisan politician, but I never take any cheap shots at Republicans. **1992** *Donahue* (NBC-TV): That's kind of a cheap shot...isn't it?
3. a lucky shot requiring little skill.
1986 Coonts *Intruder* 289 [ref. to Vietnam War]: Those lucky fuckers! Smacked us with a cheap shot!

cheap-shot *v.* to take a CHEAP SHOT at.
1970 Libby *Life in Pit* 89: No one's gonna cheap-shot the Deacon and get away with it. **1974** Blount *3 Bricks Shy* 107: I said..."You're not that good, that I have to cheap-shot you." **1988** *N.Y. Post* (June 7) 68: Here we are trying to get the refs on our side and you're cheap-shotting people. **1991** Lott & Lieber *Total Impact* 96: If you cheap-shot me, I'll retaliate.

cheap-shot artist *n.* Orig. *Sports.* a person who takes CHEAP SHOTS at opponents.

1967 (cited in *BDNE3*). **1976** *Webster's Sports Dict.* 75. **1990** *New Republic* (Jan. 29) 12: Carr is a notorious bully, a cheap-shot artist whose columns are filled with ad hominem attacks.

cheap-shotter *n.* CHEAP-SHOT ARTIST.
1974 Blount *3 Bricks Shy* 110: I'm a cheap shotter in a way. **1981** *Psychology Today* (Feb.) 16: He is, after all, a cheap-shotter—one who offends another behind his back but who is afraid to face him directly. **1984** *Chicago Sun-Times* (Jan. 27) 106: It was the same Doug Plank who forged a reputation...around the NFL as a head-hunter, late-hitter, cheap-shotter and loudmouth.

cheapskate *n.* [*cheap* + SKATE] **1.** a low or contemptible individual. [Printed as two words.]
1896 Ade *Artie* 92: A lot o' cheap skates [would be] stoppin' to play horse with her everywhere we go. **1900** Ade *More Fables* 164: No Cheap Skate in a Plug Hat could tell him where to Get Off. **1903** in "O. Henry" *Works* 164: I tumbled to what a cheap skate I been actin'.
2. *Specif.*, a stingy person. Now *colloq.* [Now usu. regarded as one word.]
1903 Harriman *Homebuilders* 35: All right then, you cheap skates. *Ibid.* 36: Say, you're the cheapest lot o' skates I ever laid me eyes on. **1919** *DN* V 64: *Cheap-skate*, a stingy person. "Come across with your money or they will call you a *cheap-skate*." New Mexico. **1939** C.R. Cooper *Scarlet* 15: "We don't take checks," answered the barmaid..."Thinks I'm a cheap skate, eh?" he mumbled. **1950** J. Del Torto, in *Neurotica* (Spring) 15: A "cheap skate" (originally *skite*, British for shit) and a "piker"...has no "guts."

cheapskate *adj.* barely profitable; small-time.
1928–30 Fiaschetti *Gotta Be Rough* 33: It was about some cheap-skate graft that didn't amount to much. **1937** Reitman *Box-Car Bertha* 205: That's all they were, just cheap-skate, petty-larceny bus-boys.

cheap suit *n.* ¶ In phrase: **like a cheap suit** fully and unpleasantly.—constr. with *on* or *all over*.
1978 N.Y.C. man, age 30: I recently heard a guy say some woman was "all over me like a cheap suit." **1981** *Hill St. Blues* (NBC-TV): They've been on me today like a cheap suit. **1990** *Quantum Leap* (CBS-TV): I'd be all over you like a cheap suit.

cheapwad *n.* TIGHTWAD; CHEAPSKATE.
1970 in *DARE*.

cheat *v.* to commit adultery; to be sexually unfaithful. Now *colloq.* or *S.E.*
1927 [Fliesler] *Anecdota* 73: "The reason I don't cheat," said one married man, "is that I find it so hard to keep up with my legitimate screwing." **1929** Booth *Stealing Through Life* 286: If I miss that last boat over, the old woman will think I'm cheating on her. **1930** J.T. Farrell *Grandeur* 217: I don't wanna be mixin' in no brawls over a low, cheatin' frail. **1932** Mahin *Red Dust* (film): If you want to cheat on your husband, that's OK with me. **1933** O'Hara *In Samarra* 110.

cheater *n.* **1.** *pl.* Orig. *Gamb.* eyeglasses.
1908 in H.C. Fisher *A. Mutt* 141: While peeping through a brace of eye cheaters. **1913** *Sat. Eve. Post* (Jan. 4) 26: "De swell mouthpiece wid de gold cheaters"—eyeglasses. **1912–14** in O'Neill *Lost Plays* 185: Better get a pair of cheaters for those bum lamps of yours. **1913–15** Van Loan *Taking the Count* 337: He wears a big pair of black-rimmed cheaters. **1924** H.L. Wilson *Professor* 258: Why the cheaters on Moo-woo, the terrible man-eater? **1928** Lawes *Life & Death* 60: The eye croaker...asked if I ever wore cheaters. **1945** Hartman & Shavelson *Wonder Man* (film): You're not going to fool anybody with those cheaters. **1951** J. Wilson *Dark & Damp* 231: Dockdang it, I got to rid me of these cheaters! They's gettin' so's I can't see over 'em. **1955** Stout *3 Witnesses* 118: Beebe lifted a hand to adjust his cheaters. **1971** Curtis *Banjo* 128: Get him some cheaters, boss! **1982** Sculatti *Catalog of Cool* 121: It wasn't until the late Twenties that exotic "cheaters" actually became stylish.
2. *Gamb.* a device that enables a gambler to cheat; *pl.* marked cards, loaded dice, etc. [Poss. the orig. of (1).]
1942 *ATS* 707: *Cheaters*, any dishonest medium used by a gambler to cheat, such as loaded dice or marked cards. **1968** R. Adams *West. Words* (ed. 2): *Cheaters.* In gambling, marked cards.
3.a. anything that may be used to make a job easier, simplify a process, provide safety or an advantage, etc.
1941 in *AS* (XVI) 240: *Cheater.* Rear view mirror. **1961** *PADS* XXXVI 27: *Cheater*...A short length of pipe which slips over the handle of a wrench to give additional length and leverage. **1963** *AS* XXXVIII 205: When metal skis were first introduced by racers, they were called *cheat-*

ers because of their easier maneuverability. **1969** *AS* XLIV 12: *Cheater*…A paint roller used to apply paint—it cheats men out of hours of work. **1985** Heywood *Taxi Dancer* 4: All the gunner had to do was identify the aircraft, snap his cheater onto his gun, match the silhouette to what he saw, line up the wooden marker with the real aircraft and pull the trigger.

b. *Specif.,* a condom.

1946 in Legman *Limerick* 196: There was a young fellow named Peter/ Who was laying his gal with his cheater.

c. *Specif.* (*pl.*), pads worn inside a brassiere to give the breasts a fuller appearance.

1949 in Partridge *DSUE* (ed. 8) 202: *Cheaters*…make mountains out of molehills. **1963 Reuss & Legman *Songs Mother Never Taught Me* (unp.): And while she was there, [she] adjusted her cheaters. **1971** Dahlskog *Dict.* 12: *Cheaters*…padding worn in a brassiere to improve a girl's figure; falsies.

d. *Specif.* (*pl.*), false teeth.

1950, 1966, 1969 in *DARE.*

e. *Specif.,* *Stu.* a published summary and analysis, as of a literary work, used by a student as an illicit study aid.

1968 Baker et al. *CUSS* 95: *Cheater.* Commercially published subject outline.

4. an act of adultery; (*also*) an adulterer.

1927 *Immortalia* 71: Nothing could be sweeter/Than to have a little cheater/In the morning. **1966** "Petronius" *N.Y. Unexp.* 15: But best for cheaters and would-be cheaters who need privacy.

5. *Logging.* (see quot.).

1948 in *Dict. Canadianisms* 142. **1958** McCulloch *Woods Words* 32: *Cheater*—a. Timekeeper. b. Scaler.

cheat sheet *n.* **1.** *Stu.* a set of notes smuggled by a student into an examination.

1955–57 Felder *Collegiate Slang* 1: *Cheat sheet*—any written material used to cheat in a test. **1961** N.Y.C. high school student: He got caught with a cheat sheet. **1968** Baker et al. *CUSS* 95: *Cheat sheet* Commercially published subject outline (used for cheating). **1987** *News-Sentinel* (Knoxville, Tenn.) (July 17) 1: "Cheat sheet" may void 3,100 civil service tests.

2. *Golf.* a combination course diagram and yardage chart.

1976 *Webster's Sports Dict.* 76. **1979** Cuddon *Dict. Sports & Games* 204.

cheat-stick *n.* **1.** *Logging.* a scale rule.

1942 *AS* (Dec.) 220: *Cheat Stick.* A scaler's rule. A sawyer's pay is gauged by the scaler. **1956** Sorden & Ebert *Logger's* 29 [ref. to *a*1925]: *Scale rule*…cheat-stick,…money-maker, robber-cane, thief-stick. **1958** McCulloch *Woods Words* 32: *Cheat stick*—A stick used by a log scaler in determining log contents. **1972** in *DARE* I.

2. *Stu.* a slide rule. Also **cheating-stick.**

1932 *AS* VII 330: *Cheating-stick*—a slide rule. **1941** *Slanguage Dict.* 10: *Cheating stick*…a slide rule. **1954–60** *DAS*: *Cheat stick.* A slide rule.

cheba var. CHIBA.

check *n.* **1.a.** *pl.* cash; money.

1877 Bartlett *Amer.* (ed. 4) 111: *Checks*, money; cash. A term derived from poker where counters or *checks* bought, as one enters, at certain fixed rates, are equivalent to current coin.

b. a dollar.

1926 Maines & Grant *Wise-Crack Dictionary* 12: One-half check—fifty cents. **1932** *AS* VI 330: *Check*—a dollar. **1934** in Partridge *Dict. Und.* 117: A silver dollar…a buck, check, or slug. **1962** in J. O'Hara *Sel. Letters* 405: A half a check is a half a dollar.

2. *Narc.* (see quot.).

1929 *Chi. Tribune* (Oct. 11) 14: A package of drug wrapped in paper is called a "deck," a "check" or a "bundle."

¶ In phrases:

¶ **cash (one's) check** to die.

1977 in H.S. Thompson *Shark Hunt* 604: Every light in the town went dim when we heard that he'd finally cashed his check. **1978** Truscott *Dress Gray* 43: Suicide? You figure [he] just decided to cash his check?

¶ **get (one's) checks** to die.

1872 G. Gleason *Specter Riders* 60: Dead as a door-nail….Got his checks, sure's shootin'.

¶ **pass** [or **cash, hand, give**] **in (one's) checks** [from gambling games such as faro or poker; cf. *pass in (one's) chips* s.v. CHIP] **1.** to quit or surrender; to admit defeat.

*ca*1863 in Allan *Lone Star Ballads* 27: And the Yankees gave in their cheques,/When the Texians gain'd her decks. **1865** J.H. Browne *Seces-*

sia 236: Hand in your checks, boys, [we are going to be killed]. **1872** in Miller & Snell *Why West Was Wild* 218: Kennedy…walked up in front of Olive and fired at him—telling him "to pass in his checks." **1896** Brown *Parson* 48: He committed suicide the night before….He was a gambler, and when he lost all, he passed in his checks and gave the game up for good. **1939** Howsley *Argot* 23: *Handed in His Checks*—…resigned.

2. to die.

1864 Halpine *Baked Meats* 157: The "Beast" aforesaid hoping to inherit the three stars whenever Grant shall have "cashed in his checks" under the life-compelling sceptre of King Alcohol. **1869** *Overland Mo.* (July) 31: Well now; has he passed in his checks? *Ibid.* 35: Obed Murch had really "handed in his checks." **1872** Crapsey *Nether Side of N.Y.* 96: Any player is free to cease playing at any moment, and at the close of a deal can obtain the money for whatever number of checks he may possess by handing them into the dealer. From this operation, suggestive of a closed career, has come one of the most common of modern slang phrases, "handing in his checks," as a synonyme for death. **1874** Carter *Rollingpin* 169: I've knowed a heap of chaps to hand in their checks there. **1878** [P.S. Warne] *Hard Crowd* 2: I allow the cuss 'ud pass in his checks so powerful suddent, he'd be stiff…afore he made up his mind it was him. **1887** Francis *Saddle & Moccasin* 179: In the shade of the giant cotton-wood…more than one well-known "rustler"…had…passed in his checks. **1887** DeVol *40 Yrs. a Gambler* 20: I…told her…if I handed in my checks she might have all I left. **1888** in Farmer *Amer.* 134: Till death calls upon you to cash in your earthly checks. **1891** Maitland *Slang Dict.* 199: *Pass in one's checks* (Am.), to die, from the practice of cashing in checks or chips at the close of a game. **1896** Hamblen *Many Seas* 134: So it was here in the scuppers…that I was expected to pass in my checks. **1907** McDermott-Stevenson *Lariat Lttrs.* 27: We stayed until four bulls and eight horses had passed in their checks. **1918** Fernald *Expressive English* 251: To "pass in his checks" can never become a good synonym for "die," because it represents the act of the defeated gambler who has lost everything, and no self-respecting person wishes thus to think of the solemn close of life. **1926** Thomas *Woodfill* 296: Sam cashed in his checks just before the Armistice. **1930** J.T. Farrell *Guillotine Party* 138: Or else have a fit and cash in his checks without knowing it.

check *v.* **1.** to look at. Cf. CHECK OUT, 4.

1944 Kendall *Service Slang* 46: *Check your hat.*…means I take note of your hat and very chic. **1953** Paxton *Wild One* (film): Hey, check the hot rod! **1957** Ellison *Web of the City* 46: Check who just dropped in for a chat. **1958** J. Davis *College Vocabulary* 1: "*Check that*"—Look critically at that. **1958** Feiffer *Sick Sick Sick* (unp.): Check the big one in the corner—a possible? **1958** Gardner *Piece of the Action* 72: Check this—the chick on your left. **1960** Swarthout *Where the Boys Are* 8: Biologically, they come to Florida to check the talent. By that I mean to inspect and select. **1962** *The Worst From Mad* 70: A hassled group got all hung up and started in to split:/The other cats there played it cool and stayed to check the bit. **1979** T. Baum *Carny* 20: Check old fat boy. Hey, you know that hat does something for you?

2. to meet again and converse with casually.

1960 Swarthout *Where the Boys Are* 16: He…said he had to cut the scene, he would check us in the afternoon. **1970** in *DARE* I: Check you later. **1974** N.Y.U. student: Check you later. **1985** Univ. Tenn. instructor, age 37: I'll check you guys later.

check *interj.* yes indeed; correct. [Orig. used solely in the oral checking of inventories or equipment.]

1922 in *OEDS.* **1927** in Hammett *Knockover* 323: "Now as I get it, you're counting on landing Papadopoulos…That right?" "Check." **1932** Lorimer *Streetcars* 135: "Check," Jerry said. **1933** O'Hara *In Samarra* 125: Check and double check. **1936** Dos Passos *Big Money* 52: "Didn't you like your soup?"…"Check." *Ibid.* 59: "You call me Bobby, won't you?" "Check." **1938** Chandler *Big Sleep* 54: "You'll take care of Carmen, won't you?" "Check." **1943** Crowley & Sachs *Follow the Leader* (film): "I'll see ya in a minute." "Check." **1947** Schulberg *Harder They Fall* 28: Okay, honey chile…Check, sugar. **1953** "L. Short" *Silver Rock* 17: "You mean if there was any other way to live she wouldn't work for the county?" "Check." **1956** Bellow *Seize the Day* ch. v: When you told him he didn't thank you. He said, "Okay," instead, or "Check." **1967** *Star Trek* (NBC-TV): "Right?" "Check."

checker *n.* the very thing; the CHEESE.—constr. with *the.*

*ca*1850 in *DA*: "That's the checker," said Teeters. **1854, 1911** in *DAE.* **1965** in *DARE*: He said it was just the checker.

checkerboard *adj.* Esp. *Labor.* made up of white and black persons.

1930 "D. Stiff" *Milk & Honey* 202: *Checkerboard crew*—A mixed gang of white and negro workers. **1942** Garcia *Tough Trip* 58: This estimable lady…run a checkerboard house of prostitution where low-down white women and nigger wenches held out under the high-sounding name of Phoebe's Exchange. ***1961** Hugill *Shanties* XIV: Coloured shantymen and "chequerboard crews" were in the main singers of such songs. **1967** Raskin *True Course* 44: There were a few ships which carried both black and white seamen and they were known as "checker-board ships," but on those, Negroes could serve only in the galley crew. **1987** J. Waters *Hairspray* (film) [ref. to 1962]: You two checkerboard chicks?…You know, black and white, salt and pepper?

check in *v.* **1.** to arrive. Now *colloq.*
1918 O'Brien *Wine, Women & War* 35: R. checked in 3.30, more than usually drunk.
2. to die.
1912 in *DARE*. **1918** in York *Mud & Stars* 137: My buddies checked in. **1971** *N.Y. Times* (Feb. 21) 30: If we had gone on the air and broadcast the alert as being from the President of the United States, some old people would have checked in right then.

check out *v.* **1.a.** to die.
1927 McIntyre *Slag* 48: He whimpered like a cold dog. I'll check out to-night.…Honest to God! I'm right on the edge. **1934** L. Berg *Prison Nurse* 52: They say heart cases always know just a little ahead when they're due to check out. **1946** Mezzrow & Wolfe *Really Blues* 24: I landed in the hospital with dysentery and I almost checked out. **1947** Schulberg *Harder They Fall* 315: Nobody would ever believe a guy checked out while trying to take a dive. **1957** Myrer *Big War* 177: When you're old you need it for comfort before you check out. **1970** *The Interns* (CBS-TV): When I was havin' that attack, I thought I was gonna check out for sure. **1971** *Mannix* (CBS-TV): I have heart trouble. And without being dramatic, I could check out very shortly.
b. to kill.
1976 Price *Bloodbrothers* 120: Butler, if I ever got like that, and I asked you to check me out, would you do me the solid?
2. to leave.
1929 Hotstetter & Beesley *Racket* 222: *Check out*—Leave hastily; also, die a natural death. **1933** J.T. Farrell *McGinty* 68: After I get that back pay, I'm checkin' out. **1941** Macaulay & Wald *Manpower* (film): The minute this job is over, I'm still checkin' out. **1941** *Slanguage Dict.* 10: *Check out*…to go away. **1944** Stiles *Big Bird* 83: I gave the captain a blank look and checked out. **1957** H. Ellison *Web of the City* 13: The cop checked out.
3. *Mil.* **a.** to instruct and evaluate; (*hence*) to instruct.
1942 in C.R. Bond & T. Anderson *Flying T. Diary* 121: They have been flying Brewster Buffaloes and now are being checked out in Hurricanes. **1962** T. Berger *Reinhart* 243: In case she hasn't fully checked you out…this was a CCC camp years ago. **1976** (quot. at WHIRLYBIRD).
b. to become fully qualified (in something).
1944 E.H. Hunt *Limit* 35: I'd like to check out in a fighter.
4. to look at; observe with interest; pay attention to. Cf. CHECK, *v.*, 1.
1949 D. Cooper & J. Davis *Duchess of Idaho* (film): Check it out! **1963** Serling *7 Days in May* (film): Check this one [*sc.* a comment] out. **1967** *Black Panther* (Oakland, Calif.) (Apr. 25) 4: Black People must realize that the time is short and growing shorter by the day. Check it out.…Black People…want BLACK POWER. **1969** Crumb *Motor City Comics* (unp.): Check this out, smart guy! **1973** "A.C. Clark" *Crime Partners* 128: Yeah, I noticed him checkin' us out yesterday, Jackie…maybe we ought to lean on him a little. **1983** G. Larson *Beyond Far Side* (unp.): Uh-oh, Lorraine…Someone seems to be checking you out. **1987** E. Spencer *Macho Man* 152 [ref. to 1968]: "Check eet out, Skeeper!" he says excitedly.

cheeba var. CHIBA.

cheek *n.* **1.** a buttock.
*a**1600** in *OEDS*. *1698**–99** "B.E." *Dict. Canting Crew* s.v. *blind: Blind-cheeks*, the Breech. *Kiss my Blind-cheeks*, Kiss my Ar-. *1785** Grose *Vulgar Tongue*: Ask Cheeks near Cunnyborough: the repartee of a St. Giles fair one, who bids you ask her backside, *anglicé* her a-se. **1889** Barrère & Leland *Dict. Slang* I 240: *Cheeks*…the posterior. *1928**–30** in Partridge *DSUE* (ed. 8) 203: "If skirts get any shorter," said the flapper with a sob,/"There'll be two more cheeks to powder, a lot more hair to bob." **1966** L. Armstrong *Self-Portrait* 8: Some of the chicks would…shake everything, slapping themselves on the cheek of their behind. **1974** E. Thompson *Tattoo* 400: He lifted one cheek of his ass and farted resoundingly. **1978** Wheeler & Kerby *Steel Cowboy* (film): I think it's time for Clayton and K.W. to drag their sweet cheeks home.

2. insolence, effrontery, or audacity. Now *S.E.* Cf. CHIN, 1.a.
*1823** (cited in Partridge *DSUE* (ed. 8) 203). *1821**–26** Stewart *Man-of-War's-Man* I 134: The rogue had such an invincible *cheek*, and so smooth and oily a tongue, that he got over them all. *ca*1849** in Jackson *Early Songs of Uncle Sam* 58: I give him some cheek, and I didn't draw it weak. *1851** H. Mayhew, in *F & H* II 82: They'd actually have the cheek to put a blister on a cork leg. **1853** [G. Thompson] *Garter* 47: In view of what she termed, Lydia's "*cheek*." **1856** *Spirit of Times* (Mar. 15) 49: Cheek: In which Lewys was not lacking. **1868** Williams *Black-Eyed Beauty* 43: You always had more cheek than was good for you. I'll knock it off you if you say much! **1869** "Mark Twain" *Innocents* II 61: I admire "cheek." **1872** in "M. Twain" *Life on Miss.* 292: I had not cheak enough to stand that sort of talk. **1877** Bartlett *Amer.* (ed. 4) 111: *Cheek.* Courage; impudence. **1887** Hinman *Si Klegg* 177: He had the cheek ter ax me if we had plenty o' blankets so's we'd sleep warm. **1887** Walling *N.Y. Chief of Police* 316: Well, for clean cheek if you don't get the medal!

cheek *v.* to address with impudence or effrontery.
1871 Bagg *Yale* 43: *Cheek*, brazen audacity. Used also as a verb. **1898** Atherton *Californians* 107: She loves to "cheek" and shock people. **1951** *AS* XXVI 237: He had the nerve to cheek his way into the party.
¶ In phrase:
¶ **cheek it [out]** to overcome a difficulty through insolent or audacious behavior. Also **cheek through.**
*1851** H. Mayhew, in *F & H* II 83: [They] persuaded me to go and beg with them, but I couldn't cheek it. **1863** Hosmer *Color-Guard* 144: We "cheeked" it with a negro driver, and jumped in over the tail-board of a forage wagon. **1866** in W.H. Jackson *Diaries* 73: I'll have no money to speak of and I must "cheek through" a good deal. *1887** in Partridge *DSUE* (ed. 8) 203: Cheek it out. **1900** Doughty *Bradys & Girl Smuggler* 21: "Why, sair, I don't know you. I nevair saw you before een my life." "Come—come. You can't cheek it out that way."

cheeky *adj.* saucy or impudent. Now *S.E.*
*1857** (cited in Partridge *DSUE* (ed. 8) 203). **1891** Clurman *Nick Carter* 32: Cheeky!…I wonder if he thinks I'm a fool? **1941** J.M. Cain, in *DAS* 96.

cheerful earful *n.* a bit of very unpleasant news.
1947 *ATS* (Supp.) 7: *Cheerful earful*, good news [*sic*]. **1964** *Magilla Gorilla Show* (synd. TV series): How's that for a cheerful earful? **1982** N.Y.C. woman, age *ca*65: Then she gave me the cheerful earful.

cheese *n.* **1.a.** the height of style; the fashion.—constr. with *the*.
*1818** (cited in Partridge *DSUE* (ed. 8) 204). **1835** in *F & H* II 85: Whatever is the go in Europe will soon be the *cheese* here. **1895** Wood *Yale Yarns* 252: And I've heard that nowadays [for girls] to talk way down in their boots, like men, was just the cheese. **1908** in H.C. Fisher *A. Mutt* 84: The real cheese in evening gowns.
b. exactly what is correct or required.—constr. with *the*.
1841 *Spirit of Times* (Sept. 25) 360: Talking of *cheese*, your present conduct isn't altogether *the cheshire*. **1842** *Spirit of Times* (Sept. 17) 341. **1854** Avery *Laughing Gas* 126: "Tell me why your scoundrelly master wrote me eighteen letters about that contemptible sum?"…"I think it were because seventeen letters didn't fetch the cheese." **1855** Brougham *Chips* 308: Right's right all the world over, but this here ain't the cheese no how. **1861** in Lowell *Poetical Works* 226: Confed'rit bonds warn't jest the cheese I needed. **1867** *Galaxy* (July) 279: Silver feet are…hardly the cheese, I should say, for dancing. **1883** in F. Remington *Pony Tracks* xii: Papers came all right—are the cheese—man just shot down the street—must go. **1899** in Davidson *Old West* 76: Say, boys, let's find a shepherd,/A herder, that's the cheese. **1905** Belasco *Golden West* 346: That's the cheese. You've struck it. **1924** in E. O'Neill *Letters* 188: If you can pay us a visit…that will be just "the cheese."
c. a splendid person or thing.—usu. constr. with *real*.
1901 Hobart *John Henry* 54: A fish diet is said to be the real cheese for the brain. **1916** O'Brien *Best Stories of 1916* 55: Hey, bo, y' want me, don't y's? Ain't I t' cheese? **1920** O'Brien *Best Stories* 354: This guy's the real cheese. You'll see.…This Evans is the stuff, just like I said. **1929** Milburn *Hobo's Hornbook* 54: I had a cross-eyed daughter,/And she was just the cheese. **1975** Swarthout *Shootist* 128: He was a good criminal, the real cheese.
d. an important or influential person; in phr. **main** [or **head**] **cheese** a boss.—usu. constr. with *the*. See also BIG CHEESE.
1902–03 Ade *People You Know* 34: Give it to the Main Cheese and tell him to have a Laboratory on me. **1905** *Variety* (Dec. 30) 9: I can easily

dope out you don't know what a real cheese a Manager is. **1914** Ellis *Billy Sunday* 252: He's the head cheese of the Philistines. **1928** *N.Y. Times* (Mar. 11) VIII 6: *Head Cheese*—President of company, the business manager, the boss. **1934** Appel *Brain Guy* 207: McMann's chief cheese. **1953** in Cannon *Like 'Em Tough* 38: Take me to the cheese…The head punk. **1966–67** in Loughmiller *Big Thicket* 170: He was the main cheese runnin' the thing. **1974** Eble *Campus Slang* (Mar.) 1: *Cheese*—the head man in an organization.

e. (one's) affair or concern.

1912 Berkman *Prison* 50 [ref. to 1892]: Why, it was none of my "cheese."

2. a foolish, obnoxious, or inept individual.—often constr. with *big*. Also **piece of cheese** and other vars.

*1889 Barrère & Leland *Dict. Slang* I 240: Sometimes *cheese* is used as a derisive nickname for any man who has pretensions to being smart. [**1901** Hobart *John Henry* 16: The old guy looks like a cheese sandwich.] **1903** McCardell *Chorus Girl* 54: Make 'em look like a piece of cheese. **1904** Hobart *Jim Hickey* 37: Didn't I pipe him helping her up the steps—the plate of cheese! **1908** Fleming *Unforgettable Season* 97: McGraw had called him a piece of cheese. **1908** in H.C. Fisher *A. Mutt* 44: You're an awful cheese as a picker. *Ibid.* 73: Say, you big cheese, you ought to be over at the track doin' some good. **1911** *Hampton's Mag.* (June) 743: I'd give my right eye to beat that Dutch cheese. **1913** *Sat. Eve. Post* (May 31) 27: She thinks I'm a great pitcher—and I'm a piece of cheese. **1913–15** Van Loan *Taking the Count* 63: [I'm not] sucker enough to cut off an arm and a leg, just to get a fight with that hunk of cheese that he's managing. **1918** *Stars & Stripes* (July 5) 5: I wrote to the girl's married sister and said that Bill was a big cheese. **1918** *Forum* (Dec.) 690: But s'help me, Joe, if another big cheese didn't put his nib in it. **1918–19** Sinclair *Higgins* 191: When Jimmie persisted, they called him a "nut," a "poor cheese." **1921** Carter *Marine, Sir!* 54: *You big cheese!*…what are *you* doing here? **1926** in Lardner *Haircut & Others* 119: Well, you're an old cheese. To make me dance alone! **1929–33** J.T. Farrell *Young Lonigan* 123: Studs said the Irishman was pretty good. Swan said he was a cheese. **1935** Pollock *Und. Speaks: Piece of cheese,* a racehorse that is not trying to win. **1939** *New Directions* 130: Listen, you big cheese…you can put that in your pipe and smoke it. **1975** Durocher & Linn *Nice Guys* 364: What do you think Santo is, a piece of cheese? He's only been an All-Star third baseman for six–seven years.

3. Esp. *Juve.* smegma; (*also*) grimy matter between or on the toes.

1927 *Immortalia* 161: Cheese…from…her twat. **ca1929** *Collection of Sea Songs* 1: His terrible tool hung down to his knees,/It was wild and wooly and full of cheese. **1938** "Justinian" *Amer. Sexualis* 15: *Cheese.* n. Solidified excreta which has been retained in the folds of the vagina of an unclean female. Medical slang, U.S., C. 20. **ca1943** in Downey *Losing the War* 90: They was baggy at the knees/And the crotch was filled with cheese./Oh, them old red flannel drawers Maggie wore. **1972** *Anthro. Ling.* (Mar.) 100: Cheese…Smegma. **1976** Conroy *Santini* 105: Toe cheese. *Ibid.* 156: I con-sider the Navy the cheese between the Marine Corps' toes. **1978** Pilcer *Teen Angel* 167: You mean cunt cheese?…That's called smegma.

4. [< G *Käse*] nonsense.

1950 Bissell *Stretch on the River* 10: All our lives we been reading Remarque and telling each other what a line of cheese that war stuff is.

5. [sugg. by CHEESECAKE] *Stu.* a young woman or young women.

1959 *AS* (May) 154: *Checking the cheese* (watching the girls go by). **1965** Hersey *Too Far to Walk* 110: He suggested to Breed that they get Margaret and some other volunteer cheese and go skiing. **1969** *Current Slang* I & II 19: *Cheese,* n. a girl. **1970** Segal *Love Story* 2: I got into the habit of studying at the Radcliffe library. Not just to eye the cheese, although I admit that I liked to look. **1974** Lahr *Trot* 223: Gap teeth and bare snatch are surefire signs. This cheese wants to get planked. **1987** (quot. at WOOL).

6. *Petroleum Industry.* (see quot.).

1972 Haslam *Oil Fields* 97: *Cheese,* n. Paraffin saturated with oil.

7. *Baseball.* a fastball.

1984 *N.Y. Post* (Aug. 23) 80: Almost everything [Dwight Gooden] threw was a fastball. Maybe 85 percent. All we had to do was show 'em the hook once in a while because his cheese was that good. **1989** P. Dickson *Baseball Dict.* 182: *Good cheese*…Modern player slang for a blurring fastball.

8. [back formation fr. CHEESY, 1] something tasteless but diverting; CAMP, 4.c.

1992 *N.Y. Times* (Aug. 7) C 1: Lime-green shag carpeting is

Cheese.…Bill Murray's sleazy lounge-lizard impersonation is Cheese. Disco music is Cheese. *Ibid.* C19: Whereas Camp is not necessarily bad art…Cheese willfully focuses on the vulgar, the meretricious, the bogus. **1993** *Mystery Sci. Theater* (Comedy Central TV): Get the cheese you need in half the time.

¶ In phrases:

¶ **cut cheese** see s.v. CUT, *v.*

¶ **cut the cheese** see s.v. CUT, *v.*

¶ **eat cheese** Esp. *Pris.* to inform to authorities; RAT.

1951 in J. Blake *The Joint* 21: To report these unsavory and totally lost creatures is of course a violation of the rigid convict code, and is called "ratting" or "cheese-eating." **1954** Schulberg *Waterfront* 112: People I may know…you mean eat cheese for ya? **1964** Rhodes *Chosen Few* 118: It's only a matter of time 'til somebody gits hip and eats cheese, baby. **1972** A. Kemp *Savior* 6: Not even the usually reliable high-placed stoolies—the bourgeois "rats" that normally ate cheese from what they professed to be a "sense of duty" rather than for gain—could inform anything of value. **1981** in *West. Folklore* XLIV (1985) 10: To inform on someone is "to drop a dime" or "to eat the cheese."

¶ **make the cheese more binding, 1.** to make matters worse.

1927 Shoup *Marines in China* 98: Lt. H—, noting my misstep,…fell atop of me, thus "making the cheese more binding" as per Lt. B—. **1972** Swarthout *Tin Lizzie* 56: And to make the cheese more binding, he knew these things in his very guts.

2. to make circumstances more certain.

1961 *Twilight Zone* (CBS-TV): Well, that makes the cheese a little more binding!

¶ **on the cheese** in a bad way.

ca1895 in *Sat. Eve. Post* (Dec. 19, 1925) 87: Don't get gay with your sassy play,/Or I'll put you on the cheese! **1906** H. Green *Actors' Boarding House* 79: Don't let 'em put this here place on the cheese. **1908** McGaffey *Show Girl* 131: The other two acts may be on the cheese, but the first act is good. **1914** S.H. Adams *Clarion* 68: All newspaper contracts are on the cheese.

¶ **take the cheese** to *take the cake* s.v. CAKE.

1887 in *AS* (Feb. 1950).

¶ **the whole cheese, 1.** everything.

1899 Skinner *4th Illinois* 124: The officers and commissarymen got the whole "cheese." **1907** in H.C. Fisher *A. Mutt* 6: The whole cheese on "Darington" to win—$20.00. **1908** in Fleming *Unforgettable Season* 6: He is the whole Swiss cheese at this meeting.…He is the whole show. **1917** E.R. Burroughs *Oakdale Affair* 61: If you tink you're goin' to cop the whole cheese you got another tink comin'. **1981** Hogan *D. Bullet* 68: The Council's the government—the whole cheese.

2. a pre-eminent individual.

1909 Clivette *Café Cackle* 235: I'll…make him think I'm really the whole cheese. **1910** T.A. Dorgan, in *N.Y. Eve. Jour.* (Jan. 10) 12: This fellow Welsh is the whole cheese on the other side, they tell me. **1914** Ellis *Billy Sunday* 351: He was the whole cheese, the head guy of the opposition party. **1927** S. Lewis *Elmer Gantry* 61 [ref. to 1903]: Here Prexy had said he was the whole cheese; gotten up a big meeting for him.

cheese *adj.* second-rate; CHEESY.

1911 T.A. Dorgan, in Zwilling *TAD Lexicon* 97: The handy manner in which he laced O. Moran, of England, has convinced the sporting world that a "cheese" champion is sort of a regular champion. **1915** T.A. Dorgan, in *N.Y. Eve. Jour.* (Aug. 15) 6: Wait till he pulls the rebel yell with that cheese dialect of his. **1931** Hellinger *Moon* 165: There's no chance in this cheese town. **1978** E. Thompson *Devil to Pay* 40: Such cheese choices.

cheese *v.* [orig. unkn.] **1.** Orig. *Und.* to stop (what one is saying or doing) instantly, esp. (now solely) at the approach of authority.—usu. constr. with *it*; (*hence*) to run away at the approach of authority. Also intrans.

*1811 *Lexicon Balatron.: Cheese It.* Be silent, be quiet, don't do it. *Cheese it, the coves are fly;* be silent, the people understand our discourse. ***1812** Vaux *Vocab.: Cheese it.* The same as *stow it. Cheese That. see* Stow that. **1840** in Botkin *Sidewalks* 236: "Cheese it!" again—always this cry [at the theater] which, though it be…a highly plastic expression, yet…must have come in sometimes with great irrelevance. **1871** Banka *Prison Life* 493: Stop,…Cheese it. **1871** "M. Twain" *Roughing It* 253: Cheese it, pard. You've banked your ball clean outside the string. **1873** Bailey *Newsman* 163: Cheese it, Tompkins, that joke was born before you were. **1874** Pember *Metropolis* 110: The only answer she vouchsafed to my sympathetic inquiry was a hasty *sotto-voce* intimation that !

should "cheese it." **1877** Bartlett *Amer.* (ed. 4) 779: *Cheese it.* What bad boys exclaim to one another when a policeman is seen coming, *i.e.* run, scamper. **1882** *Puck* (Nov. 22) 181: He only murmurs "Cheese it!"—then disappears...two words that mean "Light out, Bill, lively! Here comes Farmer Jones with a shot-gun and bull-dog." **1883** Hay *Bread-Winners* 119: The brothers began to guy him without mercy. They requested him to "cheese it." **1884** Carleton *Poker Club* 43: Cheese dat. **1886** in Fife & Fife *Ballads of West* 188: Cheese yer racket. **1891** Devere *Tramp Poems* 33: Hush! Cheese it! Horace, wait upon the child. **1892** Crane *Maggie* 5: Cheese it, Jimmie, cheese it! Here comes yer fader. **1893** *Life* (Feb. 2) 70: Many a time dey've hollered in your ears to cheese it, but you t'ought dey wuz a givin' you guff. **1896** Ade *Artie* 32: Chee-e-ese it! You know what I mean. **1897** *Harper's Wkly.* (Jan.) 90: "Cheese it, the cop," is the signal that a policeman is coming. **1898** Brooks *Strong Hearts* 5: With loud cries of "Lay bones!" and "Cheese, the cop!" they scattered in all directions. **1901** Atherton *Aristocrats* 173: "Cheese it!" she exclaimed scornfully....."I'm a Noo Yorker born and bred." **1903** Kildare *Mamie Rose* 47 [ref. to ca1875]: The cry—ever and ever familiar to the newsboy—"Cheese it, the cop!" rang out, and...the boys scampered away. **1908** in H.C. Fisher *A. Mutt* 107: Aw, cheese it, Paul. I'm not for this. **1914** in Truman *Dear Bess* 172: Cheese the rain until Monday. **1925** Cohan *Broadway* 70: Cheese it! Here comes the cop! **1969** *Playboy* (Dec.) 157: Cheese it, the cops! **1975** V.B. Miller *Deadly Game* 105: Cheez-it, the fuzz. **1990** G. Keillor, in *New Yorker* (Oct. 20) 36: Cheese it....Amscray. Make tracks.
2. to disregard.
1885 *Puck* (July 29) 343: Cheese the dude!...Lemon is good enough for me.
3. to break wind.
1977 Dunne *True Confessions* 30: Fucking place smells like a sewer, all the guys cheesing on the beer and the eggs and the pickles.

cheese *interj.* [var. *jeez*, *Jesus (Christ) (Almighty)*] (used to express surprise, disappointment, etc.). Also in extended vars.
1911 Howard *Enemy to Society* 182: Aaw, cheese! We've seen it a couple o' times. **1924** *DN* V 260: Cheese and crust. **1942** *ATS* 225: Cheese! Cheese on crackers! **1962** Mandel *Wax Boom* 240: Cheese and crackers, it's too misty to see anything. **1962** Killens *We Heard the Thunder* 10: Cheese and Crackers! Give poor Jody a chance! **1968** in *DARE*: Cheese and crust all maggots.

cheeseball *n.* a stupid or obnoxious person.
1990 *Night Court* (NBC-TV): Listen, cheeseball, your girlfriend's getting married. **1990** *UTSQ*: *Cheeseball*—a word I use every day to define the male species. "Don't touch me, you cheeseball!" **1991** *Capital Gang* (CNN-TV) (Aug. 24): Jim Bakker is a first-class cheeseball, but he's also a human being.

cheesebox *n.* **1.** *Naut.* a naval monitor. Now *hist.* [Orig. applied to the first of these vessels, the *USS Monitor*.]
1862 Keeler *USS Monitor* (June 3) 145: Says one female voice, "Oh here's the Yankee Cheesebox." **1863** in J.H. Gooding *Altar of Freedom* 57: The bombardment...was kept up...by the land batteries...and "cheese boxes." **1871** Schele de Vere *Americanisms* 335: Irreverent [*sic*] Confederates called the hideous-looking vessels *cheese-boxes*. ca1880 Bellard *Gone for a Soldier* 51: The cheese box...sent the Rebel Ram Merimac howling home. **1880** *United Service* (Oct.) 508: They saw the "cheese-box" boldly approach. **1889** Barrère & Leland *Dict. Slang* I 240: *Cheese boxes*...the nick-name given by the irreverent Confederates to the ironclads of the Monitor type.
2. a dilapidated vehicle.
1936 Levin *Old Bunch* 566: Why don't you trade in that cheese-box? I trade my Chevvy in every year.
3. *Petroleum Industry.* (see 1972 quot.).
1942 *ATS* 487. **1972** Haslam *Oil Fields* 97: *Cheesebox*, n. A kerosene still.
4. (see quot.).
1968 G. Edwards *Urban Frontier* 4: A bookie is using a complex electronic device, called a "cheese box," to conceal his telephone number.

cheesecake *n.* **1.** photographs displaying the legs and figures of scantily clad young women.
1934 *Time* (Sept. 17) 30: Tabloid and Hearstmen go after "cheese-cake,"—leg pictures of sporty females. **1940** *AS* (Dec.) 359: *Cheesecake*. Picture [i.e., photograph] in which sex appeal is exploited. **1943** Halper *Inch from Glory* 134: No we can't plug Mary Mason's beautiful legs any more....Cheesecake is out....The photos die on the editors' tables. **1944** Kapelner *Lonely Boy Blues* 6: My culture is pained by the cheese-

cake film at the Rialto. **1950** Duffy *S. Quentin* 100: In the early issues of the paper we used up a lot of space with what newspapermen call cheesecake—pictures of pretty girls displaying prettier legs. **1963** Morgan *Six-Eleven* 73: She has no objection to cheesecake, does she? **1978** J. Reynolds *Geniuses* 21: Former stewardess and cheesecake model. **1985** Ark. photographer, age 35: The magazines have the usual cheesecake, but nothing really *hot*. **1993** *New Yorker* (Oct. 4) 218: She was shot as if posing for a *Playboy* video calendar—cheesecake material.
2. an attractive young woman.
1940 Sturges *McGinty* (film): Your wife—that cheesecake that you married. **1946** Burns *Gallery* 123: All these cheesecakes have bambini. **1955** Mankiewicz *Trial* (film): Every rally needs a little cheesecake [i.e., belly dancers]. **1973** *Playboy* (Mar.) EA2: How To Talk 1920's...Cheese-Cake—A tootsie with beautiful legs.
3. *Bowling.* a bowling lane conducive to high scores.
1976 *Webster's Sports Dict.* 76.

cheesecaker *n.* a photographer or publisher of CHEESECAKE.
1955 Shapiro *6th of June* 121: We're respected—good gracious, when your father attends the publishers' convention he walks like a god among the cheesecakers and the comic-strip Johnny-come-latelies.

cheesecutter *n.* **1.** Esp. *Naut.* a cap having a stiff, orig. straight-edged, bill.
1878 Willis *Our Cruise* 116: Don't boast of your "cheese-cutters"/And your broad-brimmed "Panamas." **1884** Symondson *Abaft the Mast* 176: "Brass buttons" are entirely unknown; and any one wearing even a "cheese-cutter," they call a "lime-juicer." [*1889 Barrère & Leland *Dict. Slang* I 240: *Cheese-cutter*...a large, square peak to a cap.] *a1891 *F & H* II 86: *Cheese-cutter*...the *abat-jour* of the Zouaves. **1905** *Independent* (Nov. 2) 1023: He wore a suit of rough blue serge, a plaid muffler, narrow toed bluchers and a cheesecutter cap. **1932** Bone *Capstan Bars* 72: They wore black cheese-cutter caps that made me think of old London newspapers and pictures of executions at Newgate. **1961** Burgess *Dict. Sailing* 50: *Cheese cutter*...A peak cap. **1992** N. Cohn *Heart of World* 4: A tangled mop of hair spilling out from under a cheese-cutter cap.
2. a bicycle.
1919 *DN* V 63: *Cheese-cutter*, a bicycle. "John's father bought him a new *cheese-cutter*." New Mexico.

cheesed *adj.* Orig. *Mil.* disgruntled, angry, or annoyed; (*occ.*) sad; dejected. Also **cheesed off.**
*1941 *Sat. Rev.* (Oct. 4) 11: *Completely cheesed.* Pretty much fed up with it all. *1941 in Wiener *Flyers* 45: *Brassed off.* Fed up. *Completely cheesed.* No hope at all. *1942 in *OEDS*: *Cheesed off.* **1945** Hamann *Air Words*: *Cheesed.* The ultimate stage of hypochondria; marked depression of spirit. **1976** *Nat. Lampoon* (July) 12: All I'm saying is that if the Pope knew what I know, he'd be *beaucoup* cheesed off. **1982** *Sports Talk* (WKGN radio) (July 22): "Disappointed and a little cheesed off" is how [the] Detroit Lions head coach...expressed it. **1986** Hanson *Stress* 198: Even the loving spouse is beginning to get a little cheesed at him for being around so much. **1992** *Mystery Sci. Theater* (Comedy Central TV): Gee, Joel. You sound cheesed.

cheese dagger *n.* a jackknife.
1926 in Galewitz *Great Comics* 75: Oh boy! *Some* cheese dagger, huh??

cheesedick *n.* a disgusting or contemptible fellow.—usu. considered vulgar. Also vars.
1986 Dye & Stone *Platoon* 9 [ref. to Vietnam War]: Now you cheesedicks listen up and answer when your name is called. **1989** R. Miller *Profane Men* 58: You cheesedix. **1989** P. Munro *U.C.L.A. Slang* 29: *Cheese dong* stupid person/ If that cheese dong makes another stupid comment I will hit him.

cheese-eater *n.* a despicable person, (*esp.*) an informer or sycophant; RAT. Hence **cheese-eating,** *adj.*
1886 F. Whittaker *Pop Hicks* 23: You consarned cheese-eating lummox! **1918** in C.M. Russell *Paper Talk* 139: Im betting when they swarm over on the Kizers men them cheese eaters think somebodys kicked the lid off and all Hells loose. **1954** Schulberg *Waterfront* (film): One lousy little cheese-eater—that Doyle bum who thinks he can go squealin' to the Crime Commission. **1972** Grogan *Ringolevio* 149: You cheese-eatin' motherfucker. **1978** Ponicsan *Ringmaster* 175: I'm still here, cheese-eater. **1981** in Safire *Good Word* 87: "Cheese-eater" ...roughly equivalent to "ass-licker"...[was] in use in the army in the mid-1960's. **1983** *Reader's Digest Succ. with Wds.* 84: Black English...cheese-eater = "toady, apple polisher." **1988** S. Lee *School Daze* (film): Later for you cheese-eatin' niggers.

cheesehead *n.* an obnoxious fool.
1919 *DN* V 61: *Cheese-head*, a green, awkward person. "Anything that

cheese-head says doesn't hurt me." New Mexico. **1924** *Adventure* (Mar. 30) 167: Do you know what that cheesehead did? **1938** Chandler *Big Sleep* 50: You let this cheesehead sit there and insult me, Joe? **1983** S. Wright *Meditations* 171: Every slimy creep and cheesehead…is gonna be after you. **1989** *21 Jump St.* (Fox-TV): As long as I'm not kissing yours, cheesehead!

cheese-knife *n. Mil.* a sword.

    1839–40 Cobb *Green Hand* II 39: The chap that gave you the wipe with his cheese-knife deserves to be kept on three-water-grog, for doing his work so clumsily. **1842** *Ben Hardin's Crockett* (unp.): He blowed like a porpuss, and cum at me with his cheese-knife. **1862** in J.W. Haley *Rebel Yell* 25: Nor have our officers drawn their "cheese knives" in defense of the Union. **1868** Macy *There She Blows!* 159: The other…receives a persuader or two with the flat of the "cheese-knife," a very Spanish substitute for a policeman's baton. **1881** Nye *Forty Liars* 235: Brave men fought with cheese knives long and well. **1887** Hinman *Si Klegg* 551 [ref. to Civil War]: How nice it would be to wear shoulder-straps, and swing a "cheese-knife." ***1889** Barrère & Leland *Dict. Slang* I 240: *Cheese-knife* (army), a sword. **1899** Young *Reminiscences* 512: Wood was there 'long with 'im, with his cheese-knife in his hand. **1932** *Leatherneck* (Mar.) 32: He made a striking appearance in his tunic, spiked helmet, and "cheese-knife," when he appeared…at "Full Dress Parade." **1955** Klaas *Maybe I'm Dead* 463: Where you going with those cheese knives?

cheeser *n. Naut.* CHEESECUTTER. Now *hist.*

    1961 Hugill *Shanties* 591 [ref. to 1920's]: *Blackball cheeser.* A type of peak-cap with no stiffening in the crown worn by seamen of [the]…Blackball Line.

cheese-slicer *n.* a knife. Also **cheese-sticker.** *Joc.*

    1904 in "O. Henry" *Works* 33: Chuck that cheese slicer out of the window. **1957** E. Lacy *Room to Swing* 147: That cheese sticker is going to make me do all this?

cheese-tub *n. Naut.* a monitor; CHEESEBOX.

    1867 in *DAE* I 477 [ref. to Civil War].

cheesy *adj.* **1.** of substandard quality; shoddy; bad; cheap; (*also,* in recent use) tasteless, meretricious.

    1863 Massett *Troubadour* 35: The orchestra consisting of the fiddle—a very cheezy flageolet, played by a gentleman with one eye—a big drum, and a triangle. [**1882** Baillie-Grohman *Rockies* 187: Mutual remarks…that noses and ears "looked cheesy," or in other words were frost-bitten.] **1896** in *OEDS: Cheesy.* Bad. **1904** in "O. Henry" *Works* 257: I reckon we'll fix your clock for a while just to show what we think of your whole cheesy nation. **1911** T.A. Dorgan, in *N.Y. Eve. Jour.* (Jan. 5) 16: I'm tired of reading those cheesey ads. **1915–16** Lait *Beef, Iron & Wine* 177: It's been pretty cheesy fer me. **1918–19** MacArthur *Bugs-Eye View* 98: The cheesy billets of Harricourt…looked like palaces. **1928** McEvoy *Show Girl* 76: We got a cheesy bunch of poets writing our stuff. **1944** Sturges *Conquering Hero* (film): Of all the cheesy songs I ever heard, that one certainly takes the cracker. **1944** Sturges *Miracle of Morgan's Creek* (film): The whole idea sounds pretty cheesy to me. **1951** Mailer *Barbary Shore* 119: Look at it, it's so cheesy. **1961** *Bullwinkle* (NBC-TV): Pretty cheesy disguise. **1964** Faust *Steagle* 165: "Gee, Tall," he said, "these are pretty cheesy-looking sets." **1965** Karp *Doobie Doo* 155: Cheap lampshades and cheezy kimonos. **1973** Overgard *Hero* 9: Fame beckoned in the form of a front man for a cheesy carnival, and she was on her way. **1973–76** J. Allen *Assault* 112: So we got to look at the joint, and it's a cheesy little joint. **1993** *New Yorker* (May 17) 101: Cheesy ceremonies like car-dealership openings.

    2. covered with smegma.

    1934 "J.M. Hall" *Anecdota* 169: This boy's [penis] was extremely cheesy.

chef *n. Und.* an attendant in an opium den who prepares the opium for smoking. Also as *v.* Now *hist.*

    1911 (cited in Partridge *Dict. Und.*). **1922** Murphy *Black Candle* 113: Attendants or "chefs" roll the pills. **1928** Sharpe *Chicago May* 156: I…engaged the services of a high-class chef, to cook the pills. **1936** Dai *Opium Addiction* 197: *Chef.* The person who prepares the opium for smoking. **1937** Reitman *Box-Car Bertha* 117: The "chef" got ready another pill, for some one not adept to prepare his own. **1980** in Courtwright et al. *Addicts Who Survived* 91 [ref. to ca1920]: Somebody in the crowd knew how to chef—they would chef for us. **1982** Courtwright *Dk. Paradise* 74: Those who cooked the opium and prepared the pipe dexterously soon acquired reputations as skilled "chefs."

chemmed up *adj. Mil.* dressed in antichemical protection gear.

    1991 LaBarge *Desert Voices* 105: We got chemmed up.

cher *adj. Stu.* attractive.

    1962 *English Journal* LI 323: Both *bitchin'* and *cher* (with variant, *cherry*) are relatively harmless today, equivalent to *neat* or *swell*, but both have meliorated from less innocent meanings.

cherry *n.* **1.a.** virginity; in phr. **cop** [or **pick**] **(one's) cherry** to take (one's) virginity.

    [***ca1700** in Adlard *Forbidden Tree* 63: Then be not affrighted, for thus we will do:/Thou shalt have my cherry, and cherry-stones, too.] **1918** in *AS* (Oct. 1933) 25: *Cherry.* Virginity of either girl or boy, as in the phrase to cop (filch) 'er cherry. **1927** *Immortalia* 97: But when he's picked your cherry/He'll say, "To hell with you." **1928** Wharton *Squad* 132 [ref. to 1918]: I told him he wuz too young to lose his cherry. He ain't spoke to me since. **1930** J.T. Farrell *Calico Shoes* 44: Girls you would think of only as decent girls…were losing their cherries, one right after the other. **1933** J.T. Farrell *Guillotine Party* 73: We're going to get that cherry of his copped. **1934** Halper *Foundry* 47: Look out, kid, I'll cop your cherry! **1940** J.T. Farrell *Father & Son* 280: He would then be able to say he had lost his cherry. **1947** Willingham *End As a Man* 95: He believed I still had my cherry. **1954** Chessman *Cell 2455* 74: Did you get her cherry? **1956** Metalious *Peyton Place* 190: You busted your daughter's cherry for her, didn't you, Lucas? **1956** Ginsberg *Howl* 26: H.P. graciously took my cherry. **1962** Kesey *Cuckoo's Nest* 245: Not when he's about to cash in his cherry. **1965** S. Harris *Hellhole* 78: I wouldn't tell him and he said, Have you still got your cherry? **1989** "Too Short" *Freaky Tales* (rap song): Took her to the house and I popped that cherry. **1990** P. Munro *Slang U.* 104: *Have one's cherry* to be a virgin (of a woman).

    b. the hymen.

    1938 "Justinian" *Amer. Sexualis* 16: *Cherry.* n. The hymen; maidenhead. Also, any virginal girl….U.S., C. 20. **1946** Gresham *Nightmare Alley* 70: Sailor, you been leaving a trail of busted hearts and busted cherries all along the route. **1969** Corder *Slave Ship* 89: Can't bust her…She's got a cherry like canvas. **1970** Winick & Kinsie *Lively Commerce* 47: By the time I was eighteen, if I still had a cherry it would have been punched so far back I could use it for a tail light. **1976** Floyd *Long War Dead* 40: The other woman had been had so many times…she was using her cherry as a taillight. **1985** Heywood *Taxi Dancer* 75: That [airplane] was as solid as a nun's cherry.

    c. Esp. *Mil.* (one's) condition of inexperience, esp. with risk, hardship, danger, or the like.—used esp. of men.

    1956 in *DAS* 96. **1974** Terkel *Working* 580: I made an arrest….It was petty larceny. The [older] cop said I broke my cherry. **1976** "N. Ross" *Policeman* 132: O'Banion decided that now was the time to break my cherry.…"You try your luck. You figure it out, and I'll back you up." **1983** E. Dodge *Dau* 184 [ref. to Vietnam War]: We took [the replacements] out and broke their cherries, but we didn't get tight with them. **1984** "W.T. Tyler" *Shadow Cabinet* 3: I lost my cherry up near Pleiku, Cambodian border.

    2.a. a virgin. [Bracketed quots. may be erroneously defined.]

    [**1889** Farmer *Amer.: Cherry* (Cant).—A young girl; a full grown woman is…a *cherry ripe.*] [**1916** Cary *Venery* I 44: *Cherry.* A young girl.] **1942** Algren *Morning* 41: Some of them cherries 'r gettin' moldy on the bough these days. **1948** in Legman *Limerick* 165: She was…[an] innocent cherry. **1952** Uris *Battle Cry* 4: Not bad looking, but awfully young. A cherry no doubt. **1958** Talsman *Gaudy Image* 32: I didn't want to miss with the kid 'cause I'm kinda partial to cherries. **1961** Granat *Important Thing* 132: A…little blonde about fifteen, you know, a regular cherry, but built, man, like a brick shithouse.

    b. Esp. *Mil.* a novice or inexperienced person, esp. one who is not inured to hardship.

    1946 Heggen *Mr. Roberts* 124: "On report!" he snarled…."That miserable bastard!…I wonder if he thinks he's getting a cherry!" **1954–60** *DAS* 96. **1966** Braly *On the Yard* 16: Well, they won't be gettin' them no cherry. **1969** Moskos *Enlisted Man* 154: A soldier who has not experienced combat is called a cherry (i.e., virgin). **1971** Glasser *365 Days* 29: "Any ever been here before?" "No, all cherries." **1972** Wambaugh *Blue Knight* 56: You wouldn't be getting a cherry, kid. Guys tried to sue me a dozen times. **1973** Mather *Riding Rails* 74: I been arrested before and you ain't gettin' no cherry. **1975** S.P. Smith *Amer. Boys* 11: His short mustache was a dead giveaway that he was a new guy and a cherry too as far as combat was concerned. **1972–76** Durden *No Bugles* 67: That was a show to see. Man, I'd come here a cherry. I never seen nothin' like that. Napalm, rockets, machine guns. **1973–77** J. Jones *Whistle* 68: You been out and back. You're no cherry. **1979** Homer *Jargon* 76.

c. an old car in nearly perfect condition.

1951–53 in *AS* XXIX (1954) 94: *Cherry* n. A stock car, usually an older model, apparently in as good condition as when it left the factory. **1976** Braly *False Starts* 341: A monstrous old Cadillac convertible—a cherry with only 45,000 miles on the clock. **1978** Alibrandi *Killshot* 107: "You got a car?" "You bet....I'm in the process of restoring it....She's a real cherry, all right." **1982** R. Sutton *Don't Get Taken* 71: For a five-year-old car, this one was a cherry.

d. *Esp. Mil.* an untried newcomer, esp. to a military unit.

1979 Calif. man, age *ca*23: When I first started working construction in San Francisco the other guys on the crew called me *cherry* for the first six weeks. **1979** in R. Carson *Waterfront* 51: You're new/I can tell./A cherry. **1980** Cragg *L. Militaris* 74: *Cherry*. A new man in a unit, a replacement. **1982** Del Vecchio *13th Valley* 88 [ref. to Vietnam War]: Hey, why you comin down so hard on the cherry? **1986** Thacker *Pawn* 135 [ref. to Vietnam War]: Wait until you try a combat assault on a hot LZ with a whole platoon of cherries.

3. *Circus.* a toy balloon.

1926 Norwood *Other Side of Circus* 272: *Balloon*—the cherries.

4. *pl.* a woman's nipples.

1965 Trimble *Sex Words* 72: *Cherries*...The female Nipples. **1971** Dahlskog *Dict.* 13: *Cherry*...n.; pl. the nipples.

5. *Bowling.* an error in which only the front pin is knocked down.

1976 *Webster's Sports Dict.* 76. **1979** Frommer *Sports Lingo* 59. **1982** Considine *Lang. of Sports* 85.

6. a red revolving beacon on the roof of a police car or other official vehicle. Cf. CHERRYTOP.

1971 Dahlskog *Dict.* 13: *Cherry*...the red light on top of a police car. **1974** Univ. Tenn. grad. student: In Ohio they call the red light on top of a police car a *cherry*. **1976** Kans. State Univ. student: The sanitation inspector's sedan even had a cherry on it. **1986** McLoughlin *Jason Lives* (film): Hit the noise and the cherries!

7. *Pool.* an object ball that hangs at the edge of a pocket; (*hence*) an easy shot.

1980 *AS* (Summer) 98.

¶ In phrase: **pick a cherry, 1.** *Bowling.* to fail to knock down all the pins of a relatively simple leave.

1976 *Webster's Sports Dict.* 312. **1979** Frommer *Sports Lingo* 63.

2. see (**1.a.**), above.

cherry *adj.* **1.a.** being a virgin.

1929–33 J.T. Farrell *Manhood of Lonigan* 275 [ref. to *ca*1921]: You see a girl, a nice sweet kid, and she's cherry. **1933** J.T. Farrell *Guillotine Party* 72: He's cherry....And we're going to get him fixed up tonight. **1947** Mailer *Naked & Dead* 96: Even now I don't know if she was cherry. **1952** Bellow *Augie March* 78: I was still cherry. **1956** Levin *Compulsion* 99 [ref. to 1920's]: He'd bet a tenspot half of them were still cherry. "You cherry?" **1958** Motley *Epitaph* 179: She ain't cherry. That's for sure. **1959** Farris *Harrison High* 202: That was explainable when you considered she wasn't cherry. **1975** T. Berger *Sneaky People* 205: You was cherry when we met.

b. *Esp. Mil.* inexperienced; green.

1961 Braly *Felony Tank* 48: He looks cherry. **1964** Faust *Steagle* 120: Poor cherry bastards. Missing a lifetime of excitement. **1972–76** Durden *No Bugles* 63: That's a cheerful twosome. A cherry Ranger lieutenant and a bad-ass lifer. **1981** C. Nelson *Picked Bullets Up* 289: He introduced me to a Dr. Abstein, cherry and gung ho. **1982** Del Vecchio *13th Valley* 196: We was all cherry once. **1989** Leib *Fire Dream* 244: The two men had different feelings about cherry sergeants.

c. naive; ingenuous.

1984 "W.T. Tyler" *Shadow Cabinet* 15: Sore at what? Because Combs isn't cherry and the rest of the Senate is?...I know these people. You're the ones who are cherry.

2.a. (of merchandise) in perfect condition; brand-new or like new.

1951–53 in *AS* XXIX (1954) 94: *Cherry* adj. Attractive, unaltered. Said of a clean-looking stock car, usually an older model, with the original paint job and an undented body. "Man, that car is cherry!" **1954–60** *DAS* 97. **1963** *Little Deuce Coupe* (pop. song): Though it's not very cherry/It's an oldie but a goodie. **1968** Coppel *Order of Battle* 69 [ref. to WWII]: "Well," Chip said, "she's not exactly cherry. Most of the new L-models we been hearing about are going to the Pacific." **1971** Dahlskog *Dict.* 13: *Cherry*...of an object or thing, new or appearing new. **1976** *Nat. Lampoon* (Mar.) 107: Anybody out there interested in a swell 1965 Alfa Romeo GTC convertible....Very rare and practically

cherry. **1981** in Safire *Good Word* 54: A used surfboard or an old car in perfect condition is described as "cherry." **1988** *Supercarrier* (ABC-TV): That MiG was cherry. I mean A-1 condition.

b. *Stu.* very attractive; desirable.

1987 *21 Jump Street* (Fox-TV): Cherry car! '68? Yours? **1990** P. Munro *Slang U.* 57: Cherry...[syns.] sweet, awesome. **1993** *Sharper Image Catalog* (June) 44: Hard to believe something this cherry [*sc.* a portable radio-cassette player] came along in 1993.

3. initiating; first.

1963 Doulis *Path* 317: A cherry jump...is the first unit jump a trooper makes after graduating Airborne School. **1963** Braly *Shake Him* 56: That was going to be my cherry kicks. **1970** Landy *Underground Dict.* 48: *Cherry kicks*...initial injection of drugs after an addict's release from prison. **1972** Bunker *No Beast* 37: It's been a long time. This is like cherry kicks. **1987** Zeybel *Gunship* 96 [ref. to Vietnam War]: The enlisted swine were going to treat new officers one time after their cherry ride [in an aircraft].

cherry-boy *n.* **1.** a boy or man who is a virgin.

1972 Pelfrey *Big V* 115: You're like old Jacobs, goddamned cherry boy. **1974** in J.L. Gwaltney *Drylongso* 164: He might think that I was a cherry boy or that I went with every woman except my own kind.

2. *Army.* a newcomer, esp. one who has yet to see combat. [Quots. ref. to Vietnam War.]

1981 Hathaway *World of Hurt* 96: "How long you been Vietnam?" "Two days." "Ooh. You cherry boy." *a***1984** in Terry *Bloods* 239: I was still a cherry boy—and that's what you stay until you get 90 days in country. **1986** Thacker *Pawn* 10: Jake had stumbled off the helicopter on Charlie Ridge, as cherry as a cherry boy could be. **1989** W.E. Merritt *Rivers Ran Backward* 123: I kind of expected a cherry boy, but I always thought I'd get one who'd been in a fucking boat.

cherry farm *n. Pris.* (see quots.).

1969 *Current Slang* I & II 19: *Cherry farm*, n. A prison for first offenders.—Policemen, Texas. **1971** Dahlskog *Dict.* 13: *Cherry farm*, n. A penal farm for first offenders.

cherry out *v.* to put into perfect condition; make as good as new.

1987 *Oldest Rookie* (CBS-TV): We're looking for unmarked car number 47. I hear it's being cherried out down here. **1990** Bing *Do or Die* xvi: He drives...a cherried-out El Camino.

cherry picker *n.* **1.** a yokel; APPLEKNOCKER.

1929 (quot. at MAT). **1942** *ATS* 735: Inexperienced seaman...*cherry picker.*

2. any of various types of cranes. Now *S.E.*

1945 Huie *Omaha to Oki.* 41: A "cherrypicker" crane. **1953** Dodson *Away All Boats* 51: He returned with a borrowed cherry picker and helped get the stranded craft into the water. **1961** in *OEDS*. **1962** *We Seven* 92: Now that we had the egress tower, we did not need the cherrypicker as much as we had on the Redstone launches. **1974** *Cherry High Steel* 44: All cranes, except for telescoping boom types called cherry pickers. **1974** Terkel *Working* 23: Now they're coming out with a hydraulic crane. Cherry pickers they're called. **1983** P. Dexter *God's Pocket* 22: The cherry picker was a small crane they used to move steel rods or cement blocks, or anything else wasn't in the right place.

3. *R.R.* (see quot.).

1945 Hubbard *R.R. Ave.* 337: *Cherry Picker*—Switchman, so called because of red lights on switch stands. Also any railroad man who is always figuring on the best jobs and sidestepping undesirable ones.

4. one who seduces virgins.

1954–60 *DAS* 97. **1967** Schmidt *Lexicon of Sex* 43: *Cherry-picker*...A seducer of...virgins. **1972** R. Wilson *Forbidden Words* 64: A *cherry picker* is a man with a Lolita complex.

5. *Trucking.* (see quot.).

1971 Tak *Truck Talk* 30: *Cherry picker*: an extremely high cabover tractor. Originally the term referred specifically to the old-time cabover model Mack tractor.

cherrytop *n.* a police car or other official vehicle having a red revolving roof beacon. Cf. CHERRY, *n.*

1966–70 in *DARE*. **1974** Univ. Tenn. grad. students (reported from N.Y. (*ca*1964) and Ohio (1974)).

Cheshire *n.* the correct or best thing; CHEESE, 1.b.—usu. constr. with *the.*

1841 *Spirit of Times* (Sept. 25) 360: Talking of *cheese*, your present conduct isn't altogether "*the Cheshire.*" **1848** G.G. Foster *N.Y. in Slices* 90: Something between a telescope and a pair of goggles is just now "the

Cheshire." ***1909** Ware *Passing Eng.* 71: Cheshire...Perfection. *Ibid.* 72: "She's the Cheshire, I can tell you."...Charles Steyne was very funny as the ratcatcher, who calls everything "the Cheshire."

chest *n.* ¶ In phrase: **play it close to the chest** [alluding to keeping playing cards hidden from other cardplayers] to be secretive about one's intentions.

1955 Shapiro *6th of June* 117: I'm playing it close to the chest. ***1961** in *OEDS.*

chest-cutter *n. Med.* a thoracic surgeon.

1983 Van Devanter & Morgan *Before Morning* 91 [ref. to 1967]: They were calling for a chest-cutter in the OR. *Ibid.* 316: *Chest cutter*: a thoracic surgeon. **1985** Former hospital attendant, age 35: A *chest-cutter* was a thoracic surgeon. A *cutter* was just any surgeon at all [terms heard 1972–75].

Chester *n.* **1.** a sexually aggressive man. Also **Chester Molester.**

1984 Mason & Rheingold *Slanguage: Chester n.* A guy who frequently hits on (tries to pick up) girls. (chester molester). **1989** Munro *U.C.L.A. Slang* 29: *Chester Molester* lecherous man.

2. *Pris.* a child molester.—used contemptuously.

*a***1988** in *AS* 63 (Summer 1988) 133: Prison talk...*Chester*...Child molester. **1991** Marcinko & Weisman *Rogue Warrior* 301: On Sunday we played "Chester Chester Child Molester" with the local police. **1992** *Newsweek* (Feb. 24) 8: *Chester*: A child molester...."Everyone hates the Chesters."

chest-pounder *n.* a Roman Catholic.—used derisively.

1930 *AS* V 238: *Chest-pounder.* A Roman Catholic. **1968** in *DARE* I.

chesty *adj.* boastful; proud.

1899 A.H. Lewis *Sandburrs* 176: On d' level! I feels that chesty about it. **1899** Ade *Fables* 40: All during the seventeen years Zoroaster and Zendavesta continued to walk chesty and tell people how good they were. **1899–1900** Cullen *Tales* 215: I'm not so chesty now as I used to be. **1901** A.H. Lewis *Croker* 60: The English...are too chesty, see! Too much stuck on themselves. **1902** Hapgood *Autobiog. of a Thief* 91: So Johnny became "chesty," began to "spread" himself, to play pool, to wear good linen collars, and to associate with the best young thieves in the ward. **1905** Riordan *Plunkitt* 9: Then I had a followin' of three voters and I began to get a bit chesty. **1912** Mathewson *Pitching* 69: The team had won the championship in 1900, and naturally they were all pretty chesty. **1914** Ellis *Billy Sunday* 282: Being chesty and big-headed is responsible for more failures than anything else in the world. **1915** *N.Y. Eve. Jour.* (Aug. 11) 10: First he motored to the ballpark with a chesty, lordly air. **1928** Scanlon *God Have Mercy On Us!* 301: They began to get chesty and look important. **1970** Boatright & Owens *Derrick* 154: Then he'd get chesty and get drunk and quit. **1974** Radano *Cop Stories* 121: And he's acting chesty, like a lieutenant.

chew *n.* **1.** a discussion; talk.

1926 *Saturday Evening Post* (June 12) 146: What was all the chew about on your side? **1926** Hormel *Co-Ed* 162: It was her first experience at a "chapter chew"—Gamma-ese for those nightly sessions...When the late guests were discussed as potential sisters.

2. a scolding.

1950 *Best Army Stories* 21: I ain't gonna get no chew for being nasty to some officer's kid.

chew *v.* **1.** to eat.

1850 Garrard *Wah-to-Yah* 52: So, reaching around for the blankets, and cutting a piece of dried "buffler" to "chew," I folded my hands over my breast, and...in that state fell asleep. **1889** Barrère & Leland *Dict. Slang* I 242: *Chew it* (cowboys), to eat. **1893** F.P. Dunne, in Schaaf *Dooley* 59: Last winter [he] chewed up be [*i.e.* by] th' Richaloo off chiny plates. **1894** *Century* (Feb.) 518: You can chew all right there, but divil a cent can you beg. **1896** Ade *Artie* 58: You've always got to have one o' them bride-and-groom pictures in the house whether there's anything to chew or not. **1899** Willard *Tramping* 367: Drunk ev'ry day, 'n' so much to chew that I actually had to let my belt out a couple o' notches. **1899** A.H. Lewis *Sandburrs* 59: She's little, an' weak, an' t'in, not gettin' enough to chew. **1900** *Univ. Tenn. Volunteer* 174: I could have towed her down to the hash-room and finished my line of talk while she chewed. **1902** Dunbar *Sport of the Gods* 77: Thought I'd bring it home to chew. **1905** *DN* III 74: *Chew, v. intr.* Eat. Students often say, "Let's go chew."...Students ask each other facetiously, "Have you chewn?" Rare. **1910** Lomax & Lomax *Cowboy Songs* 249: And he chewed enough beans for a hoss. **1925** in D. Hammett *Continental Op* 167: I haven't chewed since breakfast. **1926** Branch *Cowboy* 74: And the cook...called me to chew.

1930 Irwin *Tramp & Und. Sl.*: *Chew.* To eat.

2. to talk or complain.

1894 in Crane *Complete Stories* 206: What's de little Dago chewin' about? **1896** Crane *George's Mother* 174: Say, Kel, hear what dis mug is chewin'? **1911** *Hampton's Mag.* (Oct.) 434: I've been sittin' here half an hour waitin' to get a line on what you're chewin' about. **1913** J. London *Valley of Moon* 8: Lookin' at your brother, a-runnin' around to socialist meetin's, an' chewin' hot air. **1921** A. Jennings *Through Shadows* 50: He chewed on about old times on the Red Fork. **1930** Irwin *Tramp & Und. Sl.*: *Chew*...to talk.

3. Esp. *Mil.* **CHEW OUT.**—occ. constr. with *on.* Also (*vulgar*) **chew ass, chew (someone's) ass** [or **balls**] [**off**].

*1919 *Athenaeum* (July 18) 633: "Chewing a man's ears off" was new to me [in WWI], though ears is not the part of the anatomy generally referred to. ***1922** Lawrence *The Mint* 130: On ceremonial, now, [our officers] are ridiculous, when they first force us into error, and then "chew our balls off." **1937** Lay *I Wanted Wings* 116 [ref. to 1933]: You must be doing all right. He's chewed me plenty lately. **1942** in *Best from Yank* 104: The Old Man...loveth to chew upon thy posterior. **1944** Stiles *Big Bird* 40: Major McPartlin had on his squadron CO look, ready to start chewing. **1945** *Life* (Feb. 5) 99: Mauldin drew a cartoon showing a bearded, weary dogface being "chewed" by an immaculate MP for having some button missing on his blouse. **1950** Stuart *Objector* 83: He'll chew your ass for that every time. **1951** Thacher *Captain* 80: Did he chew my ass!...Boy, you've never heard anything like it! **1955** Goethals *Command* 69: I'll chew him so bad he won't sit down for a week. **1956** I. Shulman *Good Deeds* 84: Let me know if they don't attend meetings...They'll really get chewed. **1945–57** Atwell *Private* 532: General Purvis was always chewin' the ass off the Artillery colonel about the conduct of his men. **1958** F. Davis *Spearhead* 70: I told you Hinky-Dink'd chew your ass if you didn't give him the word. **1967** J. Kramer *Instant Replay* 77: He's riding Gilly every day, chewing him, chewing him, chewing him. *Ibid.* 112: Our line coach chewed me up and down. **1971** Sanders *Family* 209: Charlie was, in the words of De Carlo, "chewing his ass off" about "getting on his case." **1975** C.W. Smith *Country Music* 6: Sidelman had chewed on him twice about lounging during slack times, but he'd had only one customer this morning. **1977** Sayles *Union Dues* 113: And Kulik wasn't even fucking *polite* for Christ's sake, he chewed their asses off down there. **1977** Heinl *Marine Off. Guide* (ed. 4) 682: *Chew out* (or *on*): Reprimand severely. **1978** S. King *Stand* 117: He'll have you on the carpet and chew your ass to a bloody rag. **1979** *N.Y. Post* (June 27) 72: He chewed the kid up one side and down the other. **1984** Riggan *Free Fire* 134: Hargos will chew them up one side and down the other. **1985** Va. man, age 26: He chewed 'em up and down and all around. *a***1991** Kross *Splash One* 60: The...sergeant would...chew his ass.

4. to annoy.—also constr. with *on.*

1926 MacIsaacs *Tin Hats* 41 [ref. to 1917]: What's chewing you, kid?...This ain't none of your business. **1948** Cozzens *Guard of Honor* 428: What's chewing Old Wobbles, Danny? **1960** J.D. MacDonald *Slam the Big Door* 28: I might have some ideas...about what's chewing on you.

¶ In phrases:

¶ **chew ass** see (3), above.

¶ **chew face** *Stu.* to engage in romantic kissing.

1980 Birnbach *Preppy Hndbk.* 218: *Chew face v.* Make out, kiss. **1981** *Nat. Lampoon* (Mar.) 44: Seems one of my mutts chewed face with a little sex kitten uptown and the toms had their tails up over it.

¶ **chew it** *Sports.* to fall or be thrown on one's face.

1979 Frommer *Sports Lingo* 193.

¶ **chew lead** *West.* to be shot to death. Now *hist.*

1951 West *Flaming Feud* 54: Mebbe they hanker to chew lead.

¶ **chew nails** to chew one's fingernails in anxiety.

1976 Wren *Bury Me Not* 9: Oh, thank God, I've been chewin' nails. **1985** Yeager & Janos *Yeager* 154: Yeager here thinks he can make the Navy chew nails by doing a ground take-off in the X-1.

¶ **chew on this!** (used as an obscene retort).—usu. considered vulgar. [The referent is the penis.]

1973 Huggett *Body Count* 210: Chew on this, mother-fucker. **1974** A. Bergman *Big Kiss-Off* 14: "Why don't you chew on this, shamus?" He pointed to...the middle of his body.

¶ **chew (someone) a new one** *Mil.* to scold or rebuke vociferously. ["New one" is "new asshole"; see s.v. **ASS-HOLE.**]

1978 Truscott *Dress Gray* 321: Grimshaw's probably going to chew me a new one.

¶ **chew (someone's) ass [off]** see (3), above.

¶ **chew (someone's) ear off** [or **out**], **1.** to talk to (someone) at length and to no purpose.

1919 Hurst *Humoresque* (ed. 1934) 96. **1934** H. Miller *Tropic of Cancer* 155: She pissed the interval away chewing my ear off. **1958** Gardner *Piece of the Action* 205: I'm sorry I chewed your ear off with all of my problems.

2. to scold.

1934 H. Miller *Tropic of Cancer* 96: She chews my ear off every time I see her. I think the truth is, the mother's jealous. **1974** Former L/Cpl. USMC: The captain really chewed his ear out.

¶ **chew the boot** *chew the fat*, below.

1958 F. Davis *Spearhead* 25 [ref. to 1945]: I wanted to see you too, Lawrence, so I could line your face up with your voice when we got to chewing the boot on the radio.

¶ **chew the carpet** to react with uncontrolled anger or anxiety.

1957 J.D. MacDonald *Price of Murder* 77: The first major setback in your whole life. It must have really rocked you, Paul? Did you chew up the carpets and run around the walls? **1966** Cameron *Sgt. Slade* 119: The guy would be chewing the carpet before he found out. **1984** Univ. Tenn. instructor, age 37: He was so mad he was chewing the carpet.

¶ **chew the fat** to converse, gossip, or chat. [In British use before 1885 as "to grumble" (*OEDS*).]

[**1907** T.A. Dorgan, in Zwilling *TAD Lexicon* 26 (Aug. 8): I have to have these windows washed before Mrs. Chewthefat comes.] **1907** T.A. Dorgan, in *Ibid.* (Nov. 22): Nelson and Gans are chewing the fat again. **1916 in OEDS* I. **1916** *Rio Grande Rattler* (Sept. 27): You chew the fat with the tall gink for half an hour. **1923** Platt *Mr. Archer* 21: I chewed the fat awhile with the engineer. **1926** Nason *Chevrons* 13: You know what a gang they are for lying around and chewing the fat after meals. **1927** Stevens *Mattock* 117: Well, we might as well mosey back to the billet, old kid, I guess, and chew the fat while we got a chance. **1929–30** Farrell *Young Lonigan* 77: They sat around and chewed the fat. **1933** March *Company K* 26: "Come on! Come on!" said Sergeant Dunning. "Get your equipment together, and quit chewing the fat!" **1939** N. West *Locust* 312: Just chinning…Just chewing the fat. **1964** "Doctor X" *Intern* 64: We chewed the fat a while and decided we had exploded the theory that coffee keeps you awake. **1982** Knoxville, Tenn., woman, age *ca*50: This U.N. Peacekeeping Force is just a way to provide a bunch of bureaucrats with the chance to chew the fat.

¶ **chew the rag, 1.** to gossip, talk, or chat.

*ca***1875** in Aswell *Humor* 346: Gents, I could chew the rag hours on end, just spilling out the words and never know no more than a billy-goat what I'd been saying. **1898** Hobart *Many Moods* 53: I heard de kids a "chewin" de rag about…Sandy Claws. **1899** "J. Flynt" *Tramping* 392: *Chew the Rag:* to talk. **1900** Willard & Hodler *Powers That Prey* 103: Guess him an' me'll chew the rag. **1902** "J. Flynt" *Little Bro.* 45: You'll know so much that the other kids'll just have to stand around and listen when you chew the rag. **1914** Patten *Lefty o' the Bush* 43: Play ball, and stop chewin' the rag.…I come here to see a game. **1927** Thrasher *The Gang* 62: Every evening they would get together at their corner or in their shack near by to "chew the rag" and talk over the events of the day. **1928** Scanlon *God Have Mercy* 306 [ref. to 1918]: The next day two fellows from the Twelfth Field Artillery…came over to our positions and we got to chewing the rag. **1942** Garcia *Tough Trip* 306: What the hell are you chewing the rag with them squaws so much for? **1947–52** Ellison *Invisible Man* 139: Just allow me to chew the rag. **1952** Bissell *Monongahela* 21: He came up to the pilothouse to chew the rag for a while. **1960** Jordan & Marberry *Fool's Gold* 122: We were chewing the rag.

2. to grumble, complain, or argue; to speak irresponsibly.

*1885 in Barrère & Leland *Dict. Slang* I 241: Some of the "knowing blokes," prominent among whom will be the "grousers," will, in all probability, be *chewing the rag* or *fat*. **1898** Univ. Tenn. *Volunteer* 158: He…chews the rag with vim,/Yet all are onto him—/He's a jolly fellow all the same. **1899–1900** Cullen *Tales* 210: I told them to go to the devil if they didn't believe me; that I didn't have any time or inclination to chew the rag about it. **1900** Willard & Hodler *Powers That Prey* 25: You've been chewin' the rag all over town, an' somebody's told 'em by this time. **1902** Bell *Worth of Words* 203: *Chewing the rag* is applied to the chatter of a disagreeable and overtalkative person prone to nag and quarrel and find fault. **1906** in "O. Henry" *Works* 178: Now, what's the use of chewin' the rag, boys? **1922** Lewis *Babbitt* 188: The ideal of American manhood isn't a lot of cranks sitting around chewing the rag about their Rights and their Wrongs, but a God-fearing, hustling, successful, two-fisted Regular Guy, who belongs to some church with pep and piety to it.

¶ **chew the rug, 1.** *chew the carpet*, above.

1974 Stone *Dog Soldiers* 250: The shrinks would try to get me so I'd chew the rug.

2. *chew the rag*, 1, above.

1892 F.P. Dunne, in Schaaf *Dooley* 43: They sat there 'n chewed the rug for near an hour. **1973** Lucas, Katz & Huyck *Amer. Graffiti* 18: Nothing I like better than chewing the rug with a pal.

¶ **chew [up] the scenery** *Theat.* to overact.

1895 Foote *Coeur D'Alene* 43: Lads, did ye hear him chewin' the scenery, givin' himself away like a play-actor? **1959** Cox *Delinquent, Hipster, Square* 100: You're overacting, chewing the scenery. **1971** Dahlskog *Dict.* 13: *Chew the scenery,* to overact, to over-emote; to ham it up. **1986** R. Salmaggi, on WINS radio (Sept. 17): And he lets Anne Bancroft, as the simplistic country mother, chew up the scenery with overacting. **1987** *TV Guide* (Nov. 7) A-11: Nick Nolte and Mike the dog both chew the scenery in Paul Mazursky's satire.

chew down *v.* [alludes to JEW DOWN] to haggle down.

1930 Bodenheim *Roller Skates* 148: Semitic vultures allow themselves to be "chewed down" from forty to twenty dollars for a suit worth five dollars and sixty cents. **1936** Levin *Old Bunch* 557: Me, maybe, you can chew down, you old *ganef.* **1969** Hughes *Under a Flare* 59: Paul chewed him down to 150 p. Not bad for a beginner.

chewers *n.pl.* the teeth.

1942 *ATS* 150. **1950, 1965–70** in *DARE.* **1970** Major *Afro-Amer. Sl.: Chewers*…teeth.

chewing *n.* **1.** Esp. *Hobo.* food. Usu. **chewin's.**

1851 M. Reid *Scalp-Hunters* 107: Ye'll be glad to get yur teeth over wuss chawins than wolf-meat. **1891** *Contemporary Rev.* (Aug.) 255: Begging is called "battering for chewing." **1907** *London Road* 51: We went down the river "on our own," hustling our "chewin's," beating every boat in the fleet. *ca***1912** in Kornbluh *Rebel Voices* 73: For the chewings 'round that place are good, they say. **1927** *DN* V 442: *Chewins, n.* Food. **1929** Milburn *Hobo's Hornbook* 228: Dat means a couple of hours or more/Before we get our chewin'.

2. Esp. *Mil.* a scolding.

1961 Crane *Born of Battle* 87: You oughta' hear that colonel hand out a chewin'. **1985** Sawislak *Dwarf* 32: I sure did want to know what Orris had done to deserve the chewing he got.

chewing gum *n.* empty talk.

1927 in Hammett *Big Knockover* 283: That's probably a lot of chewing gum, but anyway this time the police will be ready.

chewing match *n.* a noisy quarrel.

1950, 1960, 1965–70 in *DARE.*

chew-out *n.* a scolding.

1956 Hess *Battle Hymn* 130: I had a brief flash of gratitude that no members of the command were around to hear the impending chew-out. **1986** Univ. Tenn. instructor, age 35: You missed the big chew-out I gave for being bad.

chew out *v.* Orig. *Mil.* to scold harshly. Also (*vulgar*) **chew (someone's) ass out** and other vars. Cf. CHEW, *v.,* 3.

1929 in Longstreet *Canvas Falcons* 380 [ref. to 1917]: H.Q. is chewing out my arse why we're not flying right now. **1937** Lay *I Wanted Wings* 116 [ref. to 1933]: If he's not chewing you out, you must be doing all right. **1943** *Yank* (Oct. 29) 17: Pvt. Graffin was getting "chewed out" by the owner. **1946** Haines *Command Decision* 20: "Go to the hospital and chew his ass out," said Dennis. **1955** Blair *Beyond Courage* 197: Shadduck had never in all his days in the military witnessed such a "chewing-out." **1955** Puzo *Dark Arena* 41: He really got chewed out. **1958** Gay *Run Silent* (film): How 'bout that? Chewin' out an officer in front of *us!* **1965** C.D.B. Bryan *P.S. Wilkinson* 64: Chang was interrupted by Major Kim, who chewed his ass out in rapid Korean. **1969** Whittemore *Cop!* 84: The judge chewed the ass out of the *cops!* The judge! He wanted to know where did they get off arresting these kids with no corroboration to the testimony. **1970** *N.Y. Times* (Mar. 5) IV 3: "Now," said one young career officer, "a commander goes out and gets into a fight and if he loses five men, he gets his ass chewed out." **1971** *N.Y. Post* (Oct. 19) 80: You think I'm a brute for chewing Shirley out that way! **1972** in *Penthouse* (Jan. 1973) 93: He once chewed out an inquisitive interviewer from *Newsweek* for asking him about his sex life. **1973** Gwaltney *Destiny's Chickens* 121: Why don't you get mad and chew his butt out? **1991** K. Douglass *Viper Strike* 26: The tactical frequency was not the place to chew out another pilot.

chew up *v.* **1.** to trounce; vanquish; CHAW, 1.a.

1866 Brockett *Camp, Battlefield and Hospital* 179: Why, dar's a dozen on 'em; dey'd chaw ye up in no time. **1887** Peck *Pvt. Peck* 270: Turn him loose and let me chew him up. **1894** S. Crane *Complete Stories* 209: You're a fine little dirty picter of a scrapper, ain'che? I'll chew yez up, dat's what I will. **1909** in O. Johnson *Lawrenceville* 40: "Chew 'em up, Kennedy." "Hit 'em hard, Buffalo."..."Knock 'em out, boys!"

2. Esp. *Mil.* to scold.

*1918 *Bodleian Qly. Rec.* II 153: To chew up, to reprimand severely. **1921** *N & Q* (Nov. 12) 384 [ref. to WWI]: *Chewed up (to be).* To be "told off," reprimanded. **1945** Hamann *Air Words: Chew up, to.* To bawl out; to reprimand. **1948** Murphy *To Hell & Back* 94: He may chew you up for being trigger-happy, but that's all he'll do. **1950** Girard & Sherdeman *Breakthrough* (film): I understand the old man really chewed up that new lieutenant for pulling that boner...this morning. **1992** *Jerry Springer Show* (synd. TV series): Now, don't chew my father up.

¶ In phrases:

¶ **chew up and spit out** to treat savagely; destroy utterly.

1940 Raine & Niblo *Fighting 69th* (film): I got a good notion to chew you up and spit you out. **1973** N.Y.C. man, age 26: She could chew you up and spit you out. **1977** Butler & Shryack *Gauntlet* 47: The people laying those odds are gonna chew you up and spit you out!

¶ **chew up old touches** to reminisce.

1952 Lait & Mortimer *USA* 396: We were chewing up old touches with a retired Chicago dick.

Chi /ʃaɪ/ *n.* Chicago, Illinois.

1895 *Harper's* (Apr.) 720: Well, ye wan' ter drop in at the Half in State Street when ye strike Chi. **1897** *Harper's Wkly.* (Jan. 23) 86 [ref. to 1888]: We were on our way to "Chi," or Chicago, as polite people call it. **1899** "J. Flynt" *Tramping* 392: Chi (pronounced "Shi")—Chicago. **1903** Merriman *Letters from a Son* 204: "Chi" is the nearest copy of New Jerusalem that's yet been invented. **1907** London *Road* 29 [ref. to *ca*1893]: "Chi (pronounced *shy*)" by the way, is the argot for Chicago. **1908** in Sandburg *Letters* 70: All ready for the trip to Chi again by boat. **1909** M'Govern *Krag Is Laid Away* 48: From good old Chi, sir. **1929–30** Dos Passos *42d Parallel* 52: I'm from Chi. **1949** Maier *Pleasure* I. 36: Quite a town, Chi.

chib *n.* CHIV.

1954 L. Armstrong *Satchmo* 76 [ref. to *ca*1910]: He was...a good man with the big knife called the chib, and most of the hustlers were afraid of him. *Ibid.* 224: She always kept her chib handy.

chiba *n.* [prob. < Puerto Rican or Colombian Sp] *Narc.* marijuana; (*hence*) a marijuana cigarette. Also vars.

1981 *Time* (Oct. 12) 10: He gambles...with men who feed him *chiba chiba,* a Puerto Rican expression for an especially potent kind of marijuana. **1981** in *West. Folklore* XLIV (1985) 18: I got a nickel bag of Cheeba. **1983** Sturz *Wid. Circles* 28: My mother...can't say too much bout me smoking chiba cause I know too much about her. *Ibid.* 405: *Chiba,* marijuana, especially a finer variety grown in Colombia. **1985** Baker *Cops* 100: He sells cheba down on Ninth and Avenue A. **1987** "Schooly D" *Saturday Night* (rap song): He lit up a cheeba and they both took a toke. **1992** *Amer. Detective* (ABC-TV): They're smokin' chiba right now. **1993** *Village Voice* (N.Y.C.) (June 22) 36: Cannabis,...weed, cheeba.

chibbs see JIB, *n.*

Chicago *n.* Orig. *Baseball.* a shut-out. Now *hist.*

1871 in *DA:* They yesterday suffered a defeat which of all others is considered the most degrading which a first-class club can meet with, viz.—a Chicago. **1874, 1886, 1947** in *DA.*

Chicago *v.* Orig. *Baseball.* to shut out (an opponent). Now *hist.*

1874 (cited in Nicholson *Baseball Term.* 14). **1891** Maitland *Slang Dict.:* *Chicagoed...*the equivalent of "skunked" or beaten out of sight. Some years ago Chicago had a baseball team which met with phenomenal success. Other competing clubs which ended the game without scoring were said to have been "Chicagoed." **1894** in *DA: Chicagoed...*a blank score at any game or sport. **1909** *Century Dict.* (Supp.) 234: *Chicago...*v.t. (In allusion to the assumed meaning of *Chicago,* namely, "skunk" (it really means "at the place of the skunk or skunks").) In *card-playing* and other games, to "skunk" or "whitewash" (an opposing side); that is, to prevent it from scoring any runs or points. **1948** Kaese *Braves* 10: Spalding's shutouts [in 1872] inspired the phrase, "to 'Chicago' the opposition."

Chicago atomizer *n. Mil.* (see quots.) *Joc.*

1941 *N.Y. Times* (Sept. 19) 25: *Chicago atomizer...*an automatic rifle. **1955** Reifer *New Words* 45: *Chicago atomizer.* Army Slang. The army's automatic rifle of World War II.

Chicago bankroll *n. Und.* (see quot.).

1966 S. Stevens *Go Down Dead* 44: So thats it. Big George just has a lot

of green paper with a real bill on the outside and one on the inside. The rest worth nothing. Chicago bankroll. Kansas City Bankroll. All the same. What it means is no money. **1986** Ciardi *Good Wds.* 67.

Chicago chicken *n. West.* salt pork or bacon; sidemeat. *Joc.* Cf. CHICKEN, *n.,* 6.

1942 Garcia *Tough Trip* 110 [ref. to 1880's]: This was the proper way for an Indian maid to eat Chicago chicken and it was no time till the greasy chunk had disappeared and they stood around licking their greasy fingers.

Chicago overcoat *n.* CEMENT OVERCOAT.

1938 Chandler *Big Sleep* 105: A Chicago overcoat is what it would get *you,* little man.

Chicago piano *n.* **1.** Esp. *Navy.* a multiple pom-pom gun; a rapid-firing antiaircraft gun. Now *hist.*

1941 Kendall *Army & Navy Sl.* 17: *Chicago piano...*multiple antiaircraft gun. **1942** Casey *Torpedo Junction* 100: They tried out the Chicago pianos this morning for the first time on this ship. **1942** Fetridge *Navy Reader* 420: *Chicago piano.* Multiple pom-pom—a small-caliber, rapid-fire, four-barrelled antiaircraft cannon. **1945** Wolfert *American Guerrilla* 9: Then among the woodpecker chatterings of the cruiser's machine guns sounded the gobbling poomp-poomp—poomp-poomps of their Chicago pianos, the Bofors batteries. **1956** Heflin *USAF Dict.* 112: *Chicago piano.* An antiaircraft weapon, consisting of four automatic cannon mounted together; a kind of pom-pom. *Slang.* **1982** W.R. Dunn *Fighter Pilot* 120: The heavy flak...40-mm rapid-firing "Chicago pianos."

2. a submachine gun.

1944 Kendall *Service Slang* 4: *Chicago piano...*tommy gun. **1961** in *West. Folk.* (Feb. 1962) 29: *Chicago piano*—A Thompson submachine gun....The term was current in 1952. **1976** (cited in J. Green *Dict. Slang* 49). *a*1991 (quot. at CHICAGO TYPEWRITER).

Chicago typewriter *n.* a submachine gun. *Joc.* Cf. TYPE-WRITER.

1963 (cited in Partridge *Dict. Und.* (ed. 2) 805). **1970** *Playboy* (Feb.) 28: The book offers a gun-sight view of the mugs and molls who once wrote headlines with their "Chicago Typewriters." *a*1973 E.G. Robinson & L. Spigelglass *All My Yesterdays* 239: But how can you play Beethoven on a Chicago typewriter? *a*1991 in Safire *Coming to Terms* 156: Your reference to a submachine gun being called a "Chicago piano" was wrong. It was called a "Chicago typewriter."

chi-chi *n.* [< Japn] Esp. *Mil.* *in Far East.* a woman's bosom; (*pl.*) breasts. Also **chichibangas.**

1961 Bosworth *Crows* 79: The blushing process started somewhere down in that entrancing area half concealed and half disclosed by her low-necked evening gown—it began in her chichi, the crew...would have said. *a*1965 Shirota *Lucky Come Hawaii* 140: Her young chi-chis...were sticking out proudly. **1967** in *DARE.* **1972** Wambaugh *Blue Knight* 28: "Oh yeah," I said, seeing only a blur and feeling one of those heavy chi-chis resting on my shoulder. *a*1988 C. Adams *More Straight Dope* 152: Supposedly the gods were so enamored of Helen's chichibangas that they decided to have...Paris make a wax cast, whence to make goblets.

chick[1] *n.* **1.a.** a young woman; a woman or girl. Also **chickie.** [Most common after *ca*1935, esp. in jazz & entertainment circles; in earlier S.E. (e.g., *1677 and 1848 quots.), used only in direct address as an endearment for a young girl (cf. L *pullus* 'chick', also used as an endearment for children).]

[*1677 in D'Urfey *Two Comedies* 163: Chick, prethee [*sic*] let me kiss thee.] [1848 Judson *Mysteries* 206: What's the matter, my little chick?] **1899** Gunter *M.S. Bardford* 56: The "little baggage"...is as pretty a chick as the Casinette Theater boasts. **1910** T.A. Dorgan, in *N.Y. Eve. Jour.* (May 26) 24: Some swell chicks out today—I'll stroll along. **1925** *Sat. Eve. Post* (Jan. 3) 141: This part calls for a chick that can hit the key of Z. **1927** J. Lait, in *Variety* (Jan. 12) 3: These unsent-for chicks...arrive [in Hollywood] practically broke. **1928** Callahan *Man's Grim Justice* 138: I...was making the rounds of the Baltimore dance and music halls looking for a swell chick. I met what I considered...the swellest chick that God ever created! **1930** Bodenheim *Roller Skates* 253: The other, a thin, young chick with a measly face and a pointed nose, was frisking while her husband worked at night. *Ibid.* 259: Those chicks back there are laying an egg. **1938** Ward *Fog* 285: You're a keen little chick all right. **1940** in Goodstone *Pulps* 113: She was an extra chick around the studios. **1940** Zinberg *Walk Hard* 244: What's the matter, chick? **1943** *Newsweek* (Nov. 15) 4: What the chicks like most is beautifying stuff. **1944** Liebling *Back to Paris* 278: He always said that he liked hatcheck chicks. **1946** Petry *Street* 159: Never saw a good-looking chick yet who didn't belong to somebody. **1949** Ellson *Tomboy* 28: We need more members, more guys and more chicks. **1950** Van Ronkel, Heinlein & O'Hanlon *Destination Moon* (film): I got a date with a nice little chick tomorrow. **1954** Collans & Sterling *House Detect.* 211: Yeah…we're takin' the chicks home, jussa few minutes. **1959–60** Bloch *Dead Beat* 126: The world was full of kicks and chicks. **1975** Hinton *Rumble Fish* 9: You leave other guys' chicks alone. **1977** in Mack *Real Life* (unp.): But this was an 80-year-old chick. **1986** *Campus Voice* (Sept.) 25: My biggest fantasy…[is] being a millionaire and having chicks, man.

b. a man; fellow; CHICKEN, 3.a.

1843 [W.T. Thompson] *Scenes in Ga.* 32: I's your boy….I's another chick to Bill Sweeny! **1862** in Geer *Diary* 46: He is the same old chick and doing well. **1864** in Brobst *Civil War Letters* 85: No ragamuffin gal can catch this chick. **1864** in R.G. Carter *4 Bros.* 417: I…almost think the bullet is not made that goes into *this chick*. **1865** in O.J. Hopkins *Under the Flag* 242: The Major…[said] he would tell Mr. Allison what a wild *chick* I was. **1884** in Isenberg *J.L. Sullivan* 159: I'm a chick you must not sass, for I come from Boston, Mass.

2. *Mil. Av.* a friendly aircraft as part of a formation in flight. [Orig. in radio communications.]

1951 Grant *Flying Leathernecks* (film) [ref. to WWII]: This is Red Rock 12, approaching with seven chicks. **1961** L.G. Richards *TAC* 59: How many chicks in your flight? **1971** G. Davis *Coming Home* 14: Roger, four chicks. **1985** Heywood *Taxi Dancer* 164: Spider, our chicks are coming in now. **1989** J. Weber *Defcon One* 83: Have Mother send more chicks.

chick[2] *n.* ¶ In phrase: **keep** [or **lay**] **chick** to *lay chickie* s.v. CHICKIE[2].

1949 Ellson *Tomboy* 4: Yeah, how about me going in first for a change…and letting Mick lay chick? **1953** W. Brown *Monkey On My Back* 100: Hector "lay chic"—standing on the street corner to give the alarm at any sign of danger. **1953–55** Fine *Delinquents* 44: Johnny would stand outside and keep chic (stand guard). **1961** A.J. Roth *Shame* 98: I'll keep chick at this end.

chick *adj.* interesting and fully understandable only to women.—used prenominally. Cf. GUY, *adj.*

[**1993** Ephron et al. *Sleepless in Seattle* (film): That's [*sc. An Affair to Remember*] a chick's movie.] **1993** *CBS This Morning* (CBS-TV) (June 25): Definitely a chick movie…a movie that men were totally mystified by….[*Sleepless in Seattle*] is *not* a chick movie. **1993** *Showbiz Today* (CNN-TV) (June 28): *Rambling Rose* is a chick film.

chickabiddy *n.* CHICK[1], 1.a.

1893 S.F. Batchelder *Hamlet* 36: Tell me, darling chickabiddy. **1943** in Hecht *Charlie* 212: I miss my chickabiddies and it makes me happy to think that every mile…will bring me nearer. **1975** L. Sanders *Stud Horse Flats* 42: Come home, John, don't stay long,/Come home soon to your own Chick-a-biddy.

chickadee *n.* **1.** a young woman.

1939 "E. Queen" *Dragon's Teeth* 101: But now that the funeral's over, chickadees, take me to the New Haven. **1940** *My Little Chickadee* (film title). **1945** in Galewitz *Great Comics* 273: But how did you get so cozy with…a chickadee with such a Rudyard Kipling name? **1970** Grissim *White Man's Blues* 66: Ooooh, mama! Got me a horny chickadee tonight.

2. *Logging.* (see quot.).

1956 Sorden & Ebert *Logger's* 8 [ref. to a1925]: *Chickadee*, A road monkey whose job it was to clean the horse manure from the ice road.

chicken *n.* **1.** [a. dear.—used in direct address to a child or young woman.—formerly also constr. with *my*. [Always colloq. (now uncommon) but app. the basis for several of the following slang senses.]

***1677** in D'Urfey *Two Comedies* 163: Good morrow, Chicken. ***1726** A. Smith *Mems. of J. Wild* 197: *Chucky*, my Chicken…have you not had a child? ***1809** in *OED*: Well! my chicken, said he…are you satisfied? **1880** Bellamy *Dr. Heidenhoff* 22: Come for a walk, chicken. It is much too pretty a night to go in doors. **1963–64** Kesey *Great Notion* 131: I'm broke, Simone, chicken…that's what….For you, chicken. **1985** Briskin *Too Much* 70: Now, chickens, no more arguments.]

b. young fellow; friend.—used in joc. direct address.—constr. with *my*.

1836 *Davy Crockett's Almanac* (1837) 43: Who might ye be, my big chicken, eh? **1849** in R. Moody *Astor Pl. Riot* 81: Go it, my chickens. **1861** Guerin *Mountain Charley* 26: All right my chicken!…count me in

on that air arrangement. **1871** "M. Twain" *Roughing It* 174: Don't you try to come that game, my chicken. **1873** J. Miller *Modocs* 81: Hullo, my little chicken, what's up? **1878** [P.S. Warne] *Hard Crowd* 12: Well, my chicken, I was in hopes of having another opportunity to test your bullet-proof qualities. **1899** Hamblen *Bucko Mate* 31: That's where you are, is it, my chicken?

2.a. a young woman. [Esp. common in U.S. *ca*1905–*ca*1930; earlier exx. are rare, poss. because in earliest use the term was chiefly applied to prostitutes, as in 1788, 1851 quots. (cf. **(b),** below).]

1788 *New Hampshire Spy* (June 10) 54: From visiting *Bagnio's*, those seats of despair,/Where *chickens* will call you *"my duck and my dear,"*/In hopes that your purse may fall to their share,/*Deliver me.* ***1825** "Blackmantle" *English Spy* I 178: Sir *—*—, the *chicken* man,/With pimp *—*a—t in the van…beat up for recruits…/'Mong *little girls*…Of *ages* rather shy….[Note:] The redoubtable general's penchant for *little girls* has obtained him the *tender* appellation of the *chicken* man. ***1851** in D.R. Cox *Sex & Vict. Lit.* 138: Mother Willit…has now turned to the pious dodge, and calls [the prostitutes who work for her] her *darters*, her *chickens*, and kids. **1860** G.D. Prentice *Prenticiana* 97: Call a lady "a *chicken*" and ten to one she is angry. Tell her she is "no chicken," and twenty to one she is still angrier. **1875** *Minstrel Gags* 105: De chicken dat I want's Partheny's self. ***1882** in *OEDS*: Chicken, a Girl (applied to the respectable class). **1896** in Rose *Storyville* 129: Those two very tender spring chickens, Misses Kittie Archer and Lillian Blodgett, have embarked in business on their own account. The chickens have taken Nelly Haley's house. **1908** in H.C. Fisher *A. Mutt* 131: You're a classy little chicken. **1912** Vice Comm. of Phila. *Report* 57: Why don't you go to the Palm Gardens and pick up a chicken—there's bunches of them there. **1913** Kneeland *Prostitution in NYC* 13: I know where there are a lot of chickens. **1912–14** in O'Neill *Lost Plays* 185: Some nerve to that greaser chicken giving a real white man the foot! **1913–15** Van Loan *Taking the Count* 130: Whitey's doin' you dirt with the chicken at the cash register. **1916** Griffith *Intolerance* (film): Say, kid, you're going to be my chicken. **1920** G. Ade, in *American Mag.* (Dec.) 51: I never referred to a young girl as a "chicken." The word originated in the deepest pits of white slavery, and it always gave me the creeps. **1920** Skillman *A.E.F.* 168: French: Bon Jour Mademoiselle What It Means: Howdy, chicken. **1946** Wead & Sheekman *Blaze of Noon* (film): When I chase chickens they wear skirts. **1948** Vidal *City & Pillar* 191: It wouldn't be natural not to have a chicken somewhere. **1954** Lindner *Fifty-Minute Hour* 98: I've tried to hide from myself the fact that he was just no good—a lazy, chicken-chasing, selfish son-of-a-bitch. *a*1968 in Haines and Taggart *Ft. Lauderdale* 12: They were only high-school chickens, but not bad. **1972** Wambaugh *Blue Knight* 149: Another teacher, a curvy little chicken in a hot pink mini. **1974** Terkel *Working* 278: If you got a nice cute chicken, that kinda brightens up your whole day.

b. girls or young women considered sexually; young women collectively; copulation with a woman or women. [Cf. ***1825** quot. at **(a),** above.]

***1851** in D.R. Cox *Sex & Vict. Lit.* 137: French Introducing Houses…[where] importers of French mutton, lamb and chicken set up their shambles. **1934** W. Smith *B. Cotter* 282: I know: they like to think it's chicken. **1958** W. Burroughs *Naked Lunch* 174: Getting that dark chicken meat, Arch? Gettin' that coon pone? **1965** Capote *In Cold Blood* 70: Dick…wanted…a horse to ride, a new car, and "plenty of blond chicken." **1970** Cortina *Slain Warrior* 86: Were you frolicin' tonight…were you out shoppin' for a little bit of chicken? **1986** Jarmusch *Down by Law* (film): I got a piece of chicken for you—the most beautifulest gift I could give you.

3.a. [orig. an allusion to cockfighting] fellow, esp. if spirited or resolute; esp. in phrs. **this chicken** I or me; **gone** [or **dead**] **chicken** a doomed individual.

[***1605–09** Shakespeare *Timon of Athens* II ii: She's e'en setting on water to scald such chickens as you are.] ***1821** *Real Life in London* I 54: The *Gas-light man* appears to be a *game chicken*. **1833** J. Hall *Harpe's Head* 93: Well, if that ain't a droll chicken, I'm mistaken. **1837** *Every Body's Album* II 29: Strike out or you're gone chickens! them as can't swim must tread water, and them as can't tread water must go to Davy Jones! **1841** [Mercier] *Man O'War* 83: I tell you I'll have satisfaction out of your gray jacket if you had fifty *chickens* to back you. **1848** Irving *Hist. of N.Y.* (rev. ed.) 70: A very valiant man, named Hendrick Kip (which being interpreted, meant *chicken*, a name given him in token of his courage). *a*1849 in C. Hill *Scenes* 170: "I don't like to begin fightin, but if I once get at it, I don't mind goin on with the job."…"Well, chicken, you can have a chance." *Ibid.* 179: Joe…was a clear chicken, up to all sorts of didoes. **1853** in Eliason *Tarheel Talk* 140: I wil burn his damd as[s] of[f] with tar and his Boys to[o;] tha cant sker [*i.e.* scare] this chicken. **1863** in R.G. Carter *4 Bros.* 359: I came very near having typhoid fever; I should have been a *gone chicken* if I had. **1870** *Overland Mo.* (June) 515: Well, you are a powerful weak-looking young chicken, for a doctor! **1887** M. Roberts *W. Avernus* 55: Oh no, he can't scare this chicken, bet your life. **1902** Carrothers *Black Cat Club* 40: Dat cat wuz a wahm chicken an' a movin' chile! **1903** A. Adams *Log of a Cowboy* 287: You all can go up the trail that want to, but here's one chicken that won't. **1907** in McCay *Little Nemo* 83: They don't worry this chicken. I'm not afraid of no pirates, no sir! **1918** E. O'Neill *Dreamy Kid* 29: Dey don't git dis chicken alive! Lawd Jesus, no suh. **1927** Niles *Singing Soldiers* 165: Not me—nosser—not dis chicken… ***1931** J. Hanley *Boy* 69: You can do what you like. This chicken doesn't start until he is told off to his job. **1943** in Cheever *Letters* 100: The judo and wrestling instructor for the regiment…calls everybody chicken. "I used to work for the loan sharks in New York, chicken." **1951** Thacher *Captain* 148: Me, carry a torch for a dame! Not this chicken. **1952** in Yates *Loneliness* 58: Not *me*,…not *this* chicken. **1953** Chandler *Goodbye* 35: You're a sick chicken, Marlowe. A very sick chicken. **1957** Myrer *Big War* 210: Not this chicken. You think I'm crazy? **1962** T. Berger *Reinhart* 301: Just give your age, name, and employer, or you're a dead chicken.

b. item; thing.

1846 in *DA*: "Them's the queerest chickens I ever seed in my life any how!" he remarked to himself, as he commenced concocting the juleps.

4.a. *Navy.* a ship's boy, esp. one taken under the tutelage of an experienced seaman.

1840 in Valle *Rocks & Shoals* 169. **1878** McElroy *Andersonville* 176 [ref. to Civil War]: In the [prison] hospital I saw an admirable illustration of the affection which a sailor will lavish on a ship's boy, whom he takes a fancy to and makes his "chicken," as the phrase is.…This old "barnacle-back" was as surly a growler as ever went aloft, but to his chicken he was as tender and thoughtful as a woman. **1879** Shippen *30 Yrs.* 27 [ref. to *ca*1845]: One of the "petty officers"…proposed to me to go off on board the sloop and try to "ship," saying that he would take me as his "chicken." *Ibid.* 30: As Kemp had brought me on board, and was evidently going to make a "chicken" of me, he allowed me to be put into the same mess, with the caution that I was not to be made "steady cook." **1895** Sinclair *Alabama* 58 [ref. to Civil War]: See the older salts eyeing the messenger boys.…You may be assured that the "chicken" gets no punishment that he has not well deserved. *Ibid.* 121: He is engaged in embroidering…the collar of a frock for his "chicken," the sobriquet of the messenger-boy time out of mind.

b. Esp. *Navy & USMC.* a boyish and naive recruit; a raw recruit.

1888 Billings *Hardtack & Coffee* 52 [ref. to Civil War]: A Marblehead man called his chum his "chicken," more especially if the latter was a *young* soldier. **1918** Ruggles *Navy* 33: At one time in the service all new recruits were called chickens. **1942** *Yank* (Nov. 4) 15: They don't even call a young Marine a yardbird, but a fancy "chicken." **1943** Bailey *Boot* 167: *Chicken*—A Marine in his 'teens, usually with a "baby face." **1946** *Amer. Legion Mag.* (Feb.): *Chicken*: a young or puny serviceman. **1950** *Nat. Geographic* (Nov.) 661: No "chicken"—as they call the recruits—dares even so much as speak. **1956** *AS* XXXI 191: An individual who displays a complete, if smug, knowledge of the ways of the Corps is described as *salty* or an *old salt*, while a novice is usually a *chicken*, a *clown*, or a *silly shit*. **1957** Herber *Tomorrow to Live* 59: The kid…the chicken of the outfit. **1965** Koch *Casual Company* 7: I've got retreads, and chickens bloated with fever, but they turn to at reveille. *a*1982 Berry *Semper Fi* 193 [ref. to WWII]: Listen, chicken, you wouldn't get [a 72-hour pass] even if I was fuckin' you. Shove off!

5.a. a weak, naive, or foolish person. [Cf. S.E. *no chicken* 'not a young person, not a novice'; 1971 quot., in a book about homosexuals, has been influenced by (**9.a.**).]

1870 Duval *Big-Foot* 244: My strength (and I am no chicken at ordinary times) was increased fivefold under the excitement. **1891** Clurman *Nick Carter* 57: "But he will starve." "Let him." "At least set him loose." "Bah! Chicken! Climb in, I tell you. I have no time for trifles." **1895** *Ibid.* 76: Oh, I an't any chicken myself, but that Cash Brazen is the worst cuss as hoofs it.…I'm givin' it to you straight now. **1971** Rader *Govt. Inspected* 111: A chicken, Jesus Christ, a chicken at his age, paying before the merchandise was delivered.

b. Esp. *Juve.* a coward. [*OED* shows this to have been literary usage in the 17th and early 18th C.; its mod. currency seems to have arisen independently.]

1936 *AS* XI (Oct.) 279: *Chicken.* A timid soul; a sissy. **1938** C. Wilbur & V. Sherman *Crime School* (film): You guys have turned out to be a fine

bunch of chickens. **1953** Felsen *Street Rod* 106: "Hey, sister," Ricky yelled at the girl. "Why don't you ditch that chicken and ride in something hot." **1957** Laurents & Sondheim *West Side Story* 177: What a coop full of chickens! **1958** Frede *Entry E* 15: Bob went to New York, the chicken. **1973** Childress *Hero* 73: I don't like bein scared-a nothin. My mama didn't have no chickens, you know. **1983** Helprin *Winter's Tale* 224: You may think that I'm a chicken, but I've got to consider Mrs. Freley. **1986** *New Image Teens* (KPBS-TV): You don't want her to think you're a chicken, do you? **1992** Majors & Billson *Cool Pose* 26: If somebody picks on you or something, and you don't fight back, they'll call you a chicken.

c. *Juve.* a contest of nerve in which, typically, a pair of automobiles are driven head-on at high speed in order to see which driver will swerve away first; (hence, fig.) any foolish test of will.

1952 in Brookhouser *Our Years* 147: But meanwhile youngsters had learned to play "chicken," and hot-rod enthusiasts had taken to the road. **1952** Mauldin *In Korea* 16: Willie, you know that game some crazy high school kids play with cars, where they head for each other and the first one that swerves out of the way is called chicken. Well, chicken is a national sport in Japan. **1953** Bradbury *Fahr.* 451 33: We…go out in the cars and race on the streets, trying to see how close you can get to lamp-posts, playing "chicken" and "knock hub-caps." **1959** W. Burroughs *Naked Lunch* 44: They play chicken with passenger planes and busses. **1962** Crump *Killer* 168: I'll bet de double sawbuck that you'll freeze up in a game of chicken. **1967** *Zap Comix* (Oct.) 23: There'll always be the search for the bigger kick! Guys will play "chicken" with suicidal souped-up body rockets! **1972** A.K. Shulman *Ex-Prom Queen* 64: I felt helpless, like a passenger riding in a "chicken" race. **1974** A. Bergman *Big Kiss-Off* 169: Because these guys are apparently playing chicken. They can't believe you'd actually go on the air and expose your daughter. **1976** Knapp & Knapp *One Potato* 81: Chicken requires two players. They stand facing each other, legs wide apart. The boy who has the first turn throws a knife between the feet of his opponent.…The first to chicken—to refuse to continue—loses. **1981** *N.Y. Times* (Aug. 23) IV 2: Most of these actions have been part of a Soviet-American game of confrontation, surveillance and occasional brinkmanship—the pilots wryly call it "chicken of the sea"—that has been in progress in the Mediterranean since at least 1966. **1983** *Good Morning America* (ABC-TV) (May 12): The lawyers were playing a game of chicken, to see which one caved first. **1989** "Captain X" & Dodson *Unfriendly Skies* 21: I've seen the taxiway equivalent of chicken and dragracing in which planes ace each other in an attempt to move up in the takeoff order.

6. bacon or sausage. *Joc.* Cf. CHICAGO CHICKEN.

1903 A. Adams *Log of a Cowboy* 123 [ref. to 1882]: He helped himself to a third piece of "fried chicken" (bacon). **1936** R. Adams *Cowboy Lingo* 148: Fried bacon was "fried chicken" and…"chuck-wagon chicken" was salt pork. **1944** Kendall *Service Slang* 1: *Army chicken*…beans and frankfurters.

7. *Mil. Av.* a friendly aircraft, usu. a fighter plane, as part of a formation in flight.

***1917** *Everybody's* (May) 519: You are beholding that tense ceremony which takes place at sundown on every battle flying-field in Europe—the ceremony of "watching the chickens come home to roost."…When the last chicken had come home they started across the fields like a lot of laughing schoolboys. **1945** J. Bryan *Carrier* 42: "A…chicken is down."…A "chicken" is a fighter plane. **1957** Berkeley *Deadly Mantis* (film): Four chickens heading 015. **1961** Foster *Hell in the Heavens* 42: Fox Base from Red Leader. Have arrived on station with three other chickens. Over. **1964** Newhafer *Tallyho* 168: Move up, Charlie chickens. **1967** Dibner *Admiral* 424: How many chickens still aloft?

8. *Mil.* a U.S. eagle insignie; (specif.) the eagle that is the insigne of rank of a full colonel or Navy captain.

1920 Bissell *63d Inf.* 254 [ref. to WWI]: You ain't no officer, you ain't got no chicken on your shoulders! **1925** Fraser & Gibbons *Soldier & Sailor Words* [ref. to WWI]: *Chicken, The:* the U.S. Army colloquial term for the national "Eagle" badge worn on caps and uniform. **1926** *AS* (Jan.) 244: Chickens are…the eagles…on a colonel's shoulders. **1943** Trumbo *Guy Named Joe* (film): A couple of them chickens wouldn't look bad [on my shoulders]. **1951** Sheldon *Troubling of a Star* 237: Those chickens on your shoulder make you all-wise, don't they? **1956** Rock *Field Service* 127: The new Company's cars were painted with an insignia…chosen after a Company-wide competition—an eagle with a top hat against a red cross. From the first they were known as "chickens." **1959** Fuller *Marines at Work!* 58: Crocker joined them with full colonel's chickens on his shoulder. **1962** Killens *Heard the*

Thunder 64: Look at that soldier with the chicken on his shoulder. If he ain't careful it'll shit all over him. **1964** Rhodes *Chosen Few* 213: Relax and put those chickens away for a while. **1984–87** Ferrandino *Firefight* 115: Ol' Charlie he say, "Beware the soldier with the chicken [eagle's head patch, insigne of the 101st Airborne] on his shoulder." Y'all are Screamin' Eagles.

9.a. *Pris.* & *Homosex.* a catamite; (*hence*) a boy who is or who may be willing to engage in homosexual copulation. Cf. **(4)**, above.

1942 in T. Williams *Letters* 29: Bigelow says it is like me assaulting these little southern chickens. **1948** Kingsley *Detective Story* 357: A kid like this in jail. They toss for him....To see whose chicken he's gonna be! **1949** *Gay Girl's Guide* 5: *Chicken*—Adolescent, homosexual or not. **1959** Burroughs *Naked Lunch* 193: Let your hair down, chicken. **1962** T. Berger *Reinhart* 401: Reinhart...knew this fellow was anything but a queer; on the other hand...he might have been waving at chickens. **1967** Humphreys *Tearoom Trade* 47: Watch out for chicken (teenagers)—they're dangerous game. **1971** Curtis *Banjo* 169: You're my cellmate, and you're goin' to be my chicken. **1973** *N.Y. Post* (Mar. 29) 2: And there were a lot of boys being ordered with a phone call to their pimps. "Chickens," the boys were called. **1975** *N.Y. Post* (July 22) 71: He was a Times Square hustler and "chicken," making a living through shoplifting, mugging, and prostitution on "Forty-Deuce Street."

b. a decoy employed by extortionists or swindlers.

1942–49 Goldin et al. *DAUL* 43: *Chicken.* A catamite, esp. one used as a decoy by extortionists to blackmail susceptible men. **1967** *N.Y.P.D.* (ABC-TV): He's the chicken. He makes the contact....He's the chicken in the shakedown operation.

10.a. *Mil.* CHICKENSHIT, *n.*, 2.a.

1943 Hersey *G.I. Laughs* 186: These guys ain't prepared for that kind of chicken. Are we fighting Japs or Inspection? **1945** *AS* (Dec.) 261: *Chicken,* "unnecessary discipline or regimentation." **1946** Burns *Gallery* 131: But few Americans can play the nobleman without condescension or chicken. **1946** Bowker *Out of Uniform* 124: Throughout the services, personnel complained bitterly about "chicken," which meant abuse of privilege by those in authority, especially officers. **1944–48** A. Lyon *Unknown Station* 256: Resentment against the wholesale showers and all the chicken that surrounded them. **1949** Quigley *Corsica* 19: We give you guys a break and relax the chicken, and somebody screws it up. **1963** *Sat. Eve. Post* (July 27) 26: There's so much chicken...that some guys are more afraid of who's coming out behind them [i.e., on inspection] than who's coming out in front.

b. *Orig. Mil.* a person who abides too closely by petty regulations; CHICKENSHIT, *n.*, 2. b.

1942–44 in *AS* (Feb. 1946) 31: *Chicken, n.*....One who is unfair or takes advantage of another [cadet]. **1963** E.M. Miller *Exile to Stars* 23: You were faced with stopping the whole thing right there by being a chicken and telling him to call you sir. **1972** *Maude* (CBS-TV): Maybe I'm a chicken [for giving you a ticket for a minor traffic violation].

¶ In phrases:

¶ **choke the chicken** (of a male) to masturbate.

1976 Dills *CB* (ed. 2) 23: *Chicken Choker:* one who masturbates....*choking the chicken:* masturbation. **1985** *Maledicta* VIII 106: To masturbate (of males)...*choke the chicken.* **1989** *Nat. Lampoon* (June) 67: The basic reality...is choking the chicken. **1993** *Beavis and Butt-head* (MTV): What are y'all doin'? Chokin' your chicken?

¶ **dead chicken** see **(3.a.)**, above.

¶ **does a chicken have lips?** obviously not. *Joc.*

1974 Newburgh, N.Y., man, age *ca*23: Does a bear shit in the woods? means yes; *does a chicken have lips?* means no. **1974** Univ. Tenn. student: *Does a chicken have lips?*...I heard that a few years ago. **1982** in Bronner *Children's Folk.* 42: Does a chicken have lips? **1985** Bodey *F.N.G.* 191: "Maybe the war will be over by then." "Maybe chickens have lips." **1986** *L.A. Law* (NBC-TV): "That's very short notice. Are you sure you're prepared?" "Does a chicken have lips?" **1986** Dye & Stone *Platoon* 203: Does a chicken have lips?

¶ **gone chicken** see **(3.a.)**, above.

¶ **nobody here but us chickens** (used as a joc. catch phr., orig. the punchline of a joke about a chicken thief surprised in a shed by the farmer).

1963 E.M. Miller *Exile* 50: "Anybody home over there?" "Nobody but us chickens."

¶ **where the chicken got the axe** [in allusion to certain defeat or destruction] in the neck.

1912 (quot. at TOOTSY-WOOTSIE). **1927** Lewis *Elmer Gantry* 12 [ref. to 1902]: Anybody that nominates anybody except Uncle Hell-cat will

catch it right where the chicken caught the ax. **1941** *AS* (Feb.) 25: Where the chicken got the axe. "If he keeps on, he's going to get it where the chicken got the axe." **1952** Sandburg *Young Strangers* 168 [ref. to *ca*1890]: When they quit going together, one kid said, "She gave it to him where the chicken got the axe."

chicken *adj.* **1.** cowardly; afraid.

1933 D. Boehm & E. Gelsey *Jimmy Dolan* (film): Ain't turnin' chicken, are ya? **1929–34** Farrell *Judgment Day* 532: He was the skinny, dark-haired punk around the corner who was so chicken, wasn't he? **1939** *They Made Me a Criminal* (film): Boy, is that guy chicken. **1941** Brackett & Wilder *Ball of Fire* (film): When it comes to leveling off, she gets chicken. **1944** Hubler & DeChant *Flying Leathernecks* 55: The Japanese believed that the Marines regarded the thirteenth of any month as an unlucky day and would, under such circumstances, become chicken, in an expressive Marine phrase. **1945** Kanin *Born Yesterday* 223: You're chicken! **1947** R. Carter *Devils in Baggy Pants* 133: Rumor had it that the officer was chicken and didn't have the guts to lead it. **1949** Ellson *Tomboy* 2: You're afraid. You're chicken. The only one you can beat is Mick. **1953** Elliot *Among the Dangs* 46: By God, come outside and I'll show you who's the man around here. If you're not chicken, that is. **1955** Stern *Rebel Without a Cause* (film): He called me chicken. **1967** Dibner *Admiral* 173: You're chicken. Is that what you're trying to tell me? **1968** Gomberg *Breakout* (film): That's what's eatin' at your guts right now, but you're too chicken to admit it. **1981** G. Wolf *Roger Rabbit* 170: He was so chicken he probably got homesick walking by a Colonel Sanders. **1983** L. Frank *Hardball* 60: Commonly, a person who does not possess a large degree of fortitude or "guts" is said to be "chicken" (i.e., afraid). **1992** *Inside Politics '92* (CNN-TV) (Sept. 30): They don't want to be called chicken any more.

2. CHICKENSHIT, *adj.*, 1.a. [**1936** quot. might as easily illustrate **(1)**, above.]

[**1936** Monks & Finkelhoffe *Bro. Rat* 140: Barney Marcus went chicken. Called up old Ramm, and gave 'im the serial number.] **1937** Steinbeck *Mice & Men* 66: An' I'll wash dishes an' little chicken stuff like that. **1960** Leckie *Marines!* 22 [ref. to WWII]: You know what that chicken bastard told the colonel? **1961** Hemingway *Islands in the Stream* 18: Tom, I want you to be a *big* painter....Leave all that chicken stuff behind. **1963** Ross *Dead Are Mine* 48: Felix, you know this is a pretty chicken deal, don't you? **1977** *Kojak* (CBS-TV): Where do you chicken merchants get off? We're out two hundred thousand bucks! **1979** *N.Y. Times* (July 22) V 1: I'm the only one they don't put up on the scoreboard. It's real chicken.

3. *Mil.* CHICKENSHIT, *adj.*, 1.c.

1944 in Inks *Eight Bailed Out* 40: At times his attitude has been irksome, although he has never attempted to be chicken and does his fair share. **1944** in *AS* XX 147: A person is "chicken" when he abides too closely by army rules and regulations, or when he misuses or abuses authority, especially in minor or petty matters. **1945** *Sat. Rev.* (Nov. 3) 7: "Chicken" is a shortened form of a succinct scatological term meaning excessively spit-and-polish—although chicken is *le mot juste,* expressing a whole body of unpopular attitudes of which spit-and-polish indicates only the bare bones. **1946** Vidal *Williwaw* 39: Yes, he seems to be O.K. At least he's not chicken like some of the ones we've carried. **1944–48** A. Lyon *Unknown Station* 179: You want to be my runner?...Rusty'll tell you that I'm not chicken. **1949** Pirosh *Battleground* (film): "He's really GI since he took over the squad." "Yeah, strictly chicken, that's me." **1953** Michener *Sayonara* 16: He was what enlisted men call chicken because he demanded all the military courtesies, straight caps, shined shoes. **1958** J. Jones *Pistol* 71: I know you'll think it's chicken. But my conscience just won't let me do anything else. It's my responsibility as a noncom. **1960** Duncan *If It Moves, Salute It* 160: The outfit the captain was attached to was one of the most chicken outfits in Japan, and permanent liaisons with Japanese women were strictly forbidden. **1963** Ross *Dead Are Mine* 81: You know General Franks himself called me up last night and said I was to give you every dirty, chicken detail I could find, and when I couldn't find any I was to think up some new ones. **1972** *Maude* (CBS-TV): Would you give me a ticket for a lousy four-mile-per-hour violation? That's really chicken.

chicken *v.* see CHICKEN OUT.

chickenbrain *n.* a fool.

1922 Fitzgerald *Beautiful & Damned* 87: He's a pious ass—a chicken-brain.

chicken-butcher *n. Esp. Stu.* LADY-KILLER.

1930 Lait *On the Spot* 201: A man unusually successful with girls is called a "chicken butcher." **1945** *AS* (Oct.) 233: Everyone knows he is a chicken butcher, a chic sheik, and a candy leg.

chicken button *n. Mil.* a button, to be used in an emergency, that activates any sort of electronic control or escape system; CHICKEN SWITCH; PANIC BUTTON.

1967 *DAS* (ed. 2) 677. **1986** Former SP5, U.S. Army: When I was attached to the USACC in Taiwan [1974] the *chicken button* was a button or a switch that cut down the speed at which incoming communications would be absorbed. It was used when the traffic became too heavy.

chicken colonel *n.* [fr. CHICKEN, *n.*, 8.a.] *Mil.* a full colonel.

1918 in Cushing *Surgeon's Jrnl.* 426: One of our newly arrived "chicken colonels" appeared at breakfast today…with his spurs upside down. **1919** Wiley *Wildcat* 89: "How come dis tin chicken colonel pesterin' roun'?"…The tin chicken colonel addressed the Wildcat. **1945** Dos Passos *Tour* 250: A headquarters like this stuffed with stars and chicken colonels. **1948** Cozzens *Guard* 280: The only reason you have it is that you happen to be married to a chicken colonel. **1954** Davis & Lay *SAC* (film): Say, I just noticed those eagles. When did you make chicken colonel, Dutch? **1960** Bonham *Burma Rifles* 79: Some chicken colonel's flying in to chew us out. **1961** Plantz *Sweeney* 247: But every chicken colonel who ever sat in here made Brigadier. **1971** Flanagan *Maggot* 266: Don't wanna give some chicken colonel a sore ass waiting for us to show.

chicken coop *n.* **1.** *Eques.* an A-shaped wooden obstacle to be jumped by a horse.

1949 Cummings *Dict. Sports* 70.

2. *Trucking.* a weigh station.

1975 Dills *CB Slanguage* 23. **1976** Adcock *Not Truckers Only* 45: On a good trip, all the chicken coops would be out to lunch.…(All the weigh stations would be closed.). **1977** *Sci. Mech. CB Gde.* 161: Are there any chicken coops open up ahead?

chicken corporal *n. Army.* a specialist fourth-class.

1980 Cragg *L. Militaris* 86: *Chicken Corporal.* A specialist fourth class, the specialist equivalent of corporal and from his spread eagle insignia of grade (which was introduced in July, 1955).

chicken crap *n. & adj.* CHICKENSHIT.

1958 McCulloch *Woods Words* 32: *Chicken crap outfit*—a poor show, no place for a good logger to work.

chicken dinner *n. Black E.* an attractive young woman.

1946 Mezzrow & Wolfe *Really Blues* 73: We saw one of our buddies blowing his top over some chicken dinner. *Ibid.* 304: *Chicken dinner*: pretty young girl. **1948** Manone & Vandervoort *Trumpet* 166: Lana Turner…Chicken Dinner.

chicken-eater *n. Black E.* a preacher. *Joc.*

1954, 1966–70 in *DARE*. **1983** *Reader's Dig. Succ. with Wds.* 84: Black English…*Chicken eater* = "preacher, especially black Southern Baptist preacher."

chickenfeed *n.* **1.** a paltry sum of money; something paltry.

1836 [R.P. Smith] *Crockett's Exploits in Tex.* ch. vi: I stood looking on, seeing him pick up the chicken feed from the green horns. **1891** Maitland *Slang Dict.: Chicken-feed*…small change. **1909** "O. Henry" *Roads of Destiny* 452: Halves and quarters and dimes? Not for Sam Turner. "No chicken feed for me." **1919** I. Cobb *Life of Party* 22: A pinch of chicken feed and wot felt like about four one-bone bills. **1924** Marks *Plastic Age* 238: Allen had no time to waste on chicken-feed. **1929** "E. Queen" *Roman Hat* ch. xiii 141: Field had been losing steadily on the stock market—and not chicken feed, either. **1932** Kalman & Perelman *Horse Feathers* (film): Well, here's a little chickenfeed to start with. **1936** Tully *Bruiser* 143: It's not chicken feed I want. **1938** Odets *Rocket to Moon* 342: They burn your ears off around here for sixteen dollars a week. That's chicken feed! **1966** Susann *Valley of Dolls* 228: A star on Broadway. Big deal! That's chicken feed. **1970** Baraka *Jello* 18: I got the chicken feed, now where's the real money?

2. *Army.* cornmeal porridge.

1906 M'Govern *Sarjint Larry* 62: I know that the supper tonight consists mainly of that extremely nutritious but—by the soldiers, at least—as equally despised dish they call "chickenfeed," viz.: cornmeal porridge. **1909** M'Govern *Krag Is Laid Away* 101: The cornmeal is never [called] aught else but "chicken-feed."

chicken-fight *n. Juve.* a test of nerve involving driving two automobiles on a collision course; CHICKEN, *n.*, 5.c.

1938 I. Shaw *Sailor off Bremen* 290: "Get into yer cab, Angelo. I'll drive mine, we'll have a chicken fight."…The two cars spurted at each other, head-on. As they hit, glass broke and a fender flew off.

chickenfight *v. Football.* (see quot.).

1976 *Webster's Sports Dict.* 77: *Chickenfight*…to continually block a defensive lineman from an upright position on a pass play.

chicken-fixings *n.pl.* **1.** trifles; (hence) belongings.

1847 in G.W. Harris *High Times* 71: He had made good his escape, and carried with him every particle of the meek man's "chicken fixens." **1854** in *DA.* **1873** *Slang & Vulgar Forms* 10: *Chicken fixins* is a frivolous expression for which *trifles, small matters* or *little things* may be advantageously substituted.

2. *Mil.* narrow gold trim on the sleeve of an officer's uniform.

1870 Duval *Big Foot* 311: That chap with the gold epaulets on his shoulders and the "chicken fixings" on his coat sleeves.

chicken-fucker *n.* a depraved or disgusting fellow.—usu. constr. with *baldheaded.*—usu. considered vulgar.

1953 in Legman *Rationale* 20: Suddenly two bald-headed men enter, and the parrot says, "You two chicken-fuckers come out in the hen-house with me." **1976–79** Duncan & Moore *Green Side Out* 276 [ref. to ca1960]: All right ya bald-headed chicken fuckers, I want this area policed the fuck up. **1967–80** McAleer & Dickson *Unit Pride* 387 [ref. to Korean War]: Heave in the first shovelful…and run like a bald-headed chicken-fucker.

chicken-gizzard *n.* **1.** a coward.

1851 Webber *Hunter-Naturalist* 85: You d—n pack of chicken-gizzards, niggers!—climb de tree myself! **2.** *pl. Mil.* CHICKENGUT, 1.b.

1918 Griffin *Ballads of the Reg't.* 38: He sees the "chicken gizzards" on the uniform we wear.

chickengut *n.* **1.** *pl.* **a.** *Confed. Army.* narrow gold lace sewn onto the sleeves of an officer's uniform as an insigne of rank. Now *hist.*

1882 Watkins *Co. Aytch* 216 [ref. to Civil War]: And every big bug that I shook hands with put another star on my collar and chicken guts on my sleeve. *Ibid.* 108: Why ain't you with them, then, you cowardly puppy? Take off that coat and those chicken guts. **1903** *So. Hist. Soc. Papers* XXXI 104 [ref. to Civil War]: Oh, Mike, look at that new leftenant! Don't he think he is purty wid the new chicken guts on his arms. **1953–55** Kantor *Andersonville* 128 [ref. to Civil War]: In time he'd have chicken-guts upon his sleeves.

b. *Mil.* aiguillettes.

1943 Wakeman *Shore Leave* 62: "Admirals bring out the worst in me," he claimed. "Especially when one of those smart aleck aides with chicken guts hanging over his shoulder is around givin' him the old Yes, sir. **1958** Cope & Dyer *Petty Officer's Guide* (ed. 2) 336: *Chicken guts.* Slang for aiguilettes. **1965** Hersey *Too Far to Walk* 150: An aide's aiguillettes—a set of those loops of braided colored cord that John had once heard a Marine call chicken guts. **1967** Dibner *Admiral* 334: "Had a sword and all that golden stuff on his shoulder—what'd he call it?" "Chicken guts." **1973** Chandler *Captain Hollister* 7: He wore three rows of ribbons and the chicken guts of a staff officer.

2. *pl.* an ampersand.

1950 *PADS* XIV 19: *Chicken guts*…A child's name for the symbol &.

3. a coward.

1978 Maggin *Superman* 116: Cries of "chickengut" and "waffler" from the chorus.

chicken-gutted *adj.* cowardly.

1959 Sabre & Eiden *Glory Jumpers* 25: Don't go to sleep, you chicken-gutted Okie. **1962** Stone *Ride the High Country* (film): You're too chicken-gutted to finish this thing out in the open?

chicken hat *n. Mil.* a steel helmet. Also **chicken cap.**

1985 Former U.S. Army Spec. 5, served 1972–80: A helmet was a *chicken hat* or a *chicken cap.*

chickenhawk *n.* **1.** *Homosex.* a homosexual man who seeks adolescent sexual partners; CHICKEN QUEEN.

1965 Trimble *Sex Words* 42: *Chicken hawk*…an aggressive chicken fancier. **1966–71** Karlen *Sex. & Homosex.* 42: I'm a chicken hawk, I just like young bodies. **1976** R. Lloyd *Money or Love* 4: In street jargon, the boys are known as "chickens"; their customers as "chickenhawks." **1977** *N.Y. Times* (July 11) 1: It has become a reputed hangout for "chicken hawks," or older men in search of young male prostitutes. **1980** in McCauley *Dark Forces* 440: No holiday halted the perpetual parade of pimps and pushers, chicken-hawks and hookers, winos and heads. **1984** *All Things Considered* (Nat. Pub. Radio) (June 13): The Port Authority Terminal is *filled* with chickenhawks. **1984** *N.Y. Times Bk. Review* (Dec. 23) 14: Had a "chicken hawk," an older homosexual, picked the boy up?

2. a man who seeks adolescent girls as sexual partners.

1986 R. Campbell *In La-La Land* 11: The rain had washed all the baby prostitutes…[and] chicken hawks…off…Hollywood and Vine. **1987** *Beauty & Beast* (CBS-TV): [To a girl:] Without me you got nothin'. You got the chickenhawks out on the street!

chickenhead *n.* a dolt. Hence **chicken-headed,** *adj.*

    1906 *Independent* (Nov. 29) 1271: Any chicken-headed fossil of a perverted judge. **1919** *DN* V 61: *Chicken-head,* a dull person. "How did that *chicken-head* get this far is more than I understand." New Mexico. **1935** *Bedroom Companion* 152: They immediately become chickenheaded, volatile, unstable, incompetent, hysterical, moody. **1952** Steinbeck *E. of Eden* 548: No two of them had the same story, the goddam chickenheads. **1967** Lit *Dictionary* 9: *Chicken head*—a handle for someone who bugs you all the time. **1974** *N.Y. Times Bk. Review* (May 5) 8: The chickenheaded proclamation that a gun is easier to come by than a book. **1991** *Fresh Prince of Bel-Air* (NBC-TV): I been…chasin' all these chickenhead girls around.

chicken hockey *n.* [euphem. for CHICKENSHIT; see HOCKEY] daylights; stuffing.

    1970 A. Young *Snakes* 34: I'll smack the chicken hockey outta you.

chicken inspector *n.* LADY-KILLER. *Joc.*

    1920 Bissell *63rd Inf.* 154: While at Wilmington, the Baldwin brothers spent most of their off-guard time in the sardine cannery; it was impossible to determine whether they were sardine packers or chicken inspectors—or both. **1949** *Looney Tunes* (animated cartoon): Twenty-three skidoo! O you kid! Chicken inspector! **1956** *Phil Silvers Show* (CBS-TV): What does this look like—a chicken inspector's badge? **1956** I. Shulman *Good Deeds* 89: People…wore Chicken Inspector and Oh, You Kid badges. **1975** V.B. Miller *Deadly Game* 116: A "Chicken Inspector" badge from a Johnson Smith catalog.

chicken-lifter *n.* a chicken thief; (*hence*) a petty thief.

    1877 B. Harte, in *DAE*. **1897** Ade *Pink Marsh* 132: Who was 'at cullud rascal 'at tried to make me out [a] chicken-lifteh? **1905** Belasco *Girl of West* 323: Chicken lifter!

chicken liver *n.* **1.** a cowardly streak.

    1909 in O. Johnson *Lawrenceville* 39: He's got a chicken liver….He shuts his eyes when he tackles!

    2. an abject coward.

    *1932 in *OEDS.* **1935** Sayre & Twist *Annie Oakley* (film): You're a downright chicken liver when it comes to women. **1973** Ward *Sting* (film): Butt out, chicken liver.

chicken-livered *adj.* cowardly; chicken-hearted.

    1871 "M. Twain" *Roughing It:* Many a notorious coward, many a chicken-livered poltroon. **1882** "M. Twain" *Life on Miss.* 28: Come back here, you couple of chicken-livered cowards, and I'll thrash the two of ye! **1930** Lait *On Spot* 62: Getting chicken livered, eh? **1951** Pryor *Big Play* 184: I been thinkin' that maybe I oughtn't to touch you with your lily hands, and your chicken-livered soul. **1955** Robbins *79 Park Ave.* 63: Chicken-livered bastard!

chicken money *n.* Navy. (see quot.).

    1914 *DN* IV 150: *Chicken money.* The pay of an enlisted man when retired.

chicken out *v.* to back out, as from fear; renege. Also (in more recent use) **chicken.**

    1934 Weseen *Dict. Slang* 177: College [Slang]…*chicken out*—To fail [sic]. **1941–42** Gach *In Army Now* 142: Old Uncle Sam promised to let me go back…in a year. He can't chicken out on me like this. **1945** Laurents *Home of the Brave* 567: Well, who's going to chicken out in front of anyone else? **1948** Wolfert *Act of Love* 510: We're not going to chicken out on this, are we? **1948** Lay & Bartlett *Twelve O'Clock High!* 218: I know what you're thinking. You think you chickened out. I'll tell you how chicken you are! **1953** Felsen *Street Rod* 62: That's a new way to chicken out. **1956** Poe *Attack* (film): The feeling among the men is that the captain…well, that he *chickened* out there. **1958** Cooley *Run For Home* 38: Listen, you're not goin' to chicken out on me, are you? **1961** Garrett *Which Ones Are the Enemy?* 75: Old Stitch chickened. **1961** Terry *Old Liberty* 74: I ain't chickening. **1962** Shepard *Press Passes* 174: I didn't vote for Ike, but I like a scrapper. I'm glad he didn't chicken out. **1966** Bogner *Seventh Avenue* 354: Naw, he chickened out. I knew he had chicken shit for blood. **1977** J. Pastorius, in *Rolling Stone* (May 5) 26: Most bass guitarists are either frustrated guitarists or guys who played the big bass and chickened out. **1988** *Beauty & Beast* (CBS-TV): Just make sure you're not using ethical considerations as an excuse to chicken out of the relationship. **1988** T. Logan *Harder They Fall* 190: I froze. I chickened. **1992** *TV Guide* (Jan. 2, 1993) 29: Steve…chickened out of shooting Mary Jo.

chicken pie *n. Pol.* (see quot.).

    1871 Schele de Vere *Amer.* 264: A curious term has, of late, sprung up in the South, to designate the necessary expenses for purchasing legislative votes and newspaper influence….These are called Chicken-pie.

chicken-plate *n. Army.* a flak vest. *Joc.*

    1971 Vaughan & Lynch *Brandywine's War* 110: Brandywine took a flak vest, called a "chicken-plate" by the air crews, and put it on over his T-shirt. **1980** Cragg *L. Militaris* 86: *Chickenplate*….flak jacket. **1983** Groen & Groen *Huey* 17 [ref. to 1970]: The captain had on his chicken plate….The chicken plate, made of hardened steel with a thick layer of porcelain on the outside and held in place by a vest, protected you from chin to lap. **1983–88** J.T. McLeod *Crew Chief* 23: He…put on his chicken plate and flight helmet.

chicken-plucking *adj.* COTTON-PICKIN.

    1964 in Gover *Trilogy* 341: Illeagal! I mean, dig that mothahfuggin chickenpluckin—illeagal.

chicken queen *n. Homosex.* CHICKENHAWK, 1.

    1965–72 E. Newton *Mother Camp* 27: There are no feminine counterparts of the male…chicken queens. **1972** *Anthro. Linguistics* (March) 100: *Chicken Queen* (n): A homosexual who seeks out young boys for sexual relations. **1973** R.M. Brown *Rubyfruit* 166: If you were a man, they'd call you a chicken queen. **1978** Maupin *Tales* 113: I hope you're not a chicken queen….I'm twenty-six.

chicken ranch *n.* Orig. *S.W.* a house of prostitution. [Allegedly first applied to a brothel in La Grange, Tex., the subject of the Broadway musical *The Best Little Whorehouse in Texas.*] Cf. HOG RANCH, SNAKE RANCH.

    1973 in *Playboy* (Jan. 1974) 58: The so-called La Grange Chicken Ranch, an east-central Texas house of ill-repute whose lineage stretches back to the 1840s,…was practically a state shrine, like the Alamo. **1982** Savitch *Anchorwoman* 82: By the way, there's some chicken ranch in La Grange that's supposed to be a big deal. **1985** J. Green *Dict. Slang* 49.

chicken roost *n.* the upper balcony of a theater.

    1905 *DN* III 74: *Chicken roost*…Theatre balcony…common [in Ark.]. **1967–70** in *DARE*.

chicken run *n.* CHICKEN, *n.,* 7.b.

    1963 Dwiggins *S.O. Bees* 108 [ref. to *ca*1942]: "Chicken run?" he challenged.

chicken saddle *n. West.* (see quot.). *Joc.*

    1944 R. Adams *West. Wds.*: *Chicken saddle.* A slang name for an unusually small saddle.

chickenshit *n.* **1.a.** something that is worthless, insignificant, or contemptible.—usu. considered vulgar.

    1929 in Longstreet *Canvas Falcons* 278 [ref. to 1917]: He looked very solid and there were flying wings on his tunic and French and English chicken-shit of gold and silver and bronze. **1938** in Hemingway *Sel. Letters* 467: The retreat from Mons was chickenshit alongside of this last show. **1953–55** Kantor *Andersonville* 119: No more chicken shit, but fine sawney and stews, with a swig of pine-top to help it along. **1956** Levin *Compulsion* 122: Maybe he'd let Mac in on some more jobs; maybe they could pull some real stuff together instead of chickenshit. **1972** C. Gaines *Stay Hungry* 154: You know I pull down forty thou a year? I just mess with this chickenshit to keep my hand in. **1977** Olsen *Fire Five* 74: Hot damn, the chickenshit's over for another day.

    b. nonsense; lies.—usu. considered vulgar.

    1947 Willingham *End As a Man* 98: I like a freshman who…says something, instead of this eternal dreary chicken shit. **1971** Dahlskog *Dict.* 13: *Chicken shit,* n.…Nonsense; lies. **1972** Halberstam *Best & Brightest* 436: Asked by reporters why, when he was senate Majority Leader, he had not taken a particular speech of Vice President Nixon's seriously, [Pres. Johnson] said, "Boys, I may not know much but I know the difference between chicken shit and chicken salad." **1972** Wurlitzer *Quake* 14: I'm up to here with that kind of chicken shit.

    2.a. petty details; pettiness; (*specif.*) *Mil.* petty regulations or their zealous enforcement.—usu. considered vulgar.

    1944 in Hemingway *Sel. Letters* 570: We will fight the best one we, or anyone could ever fight…against loneliness, chickenshit, death, injustice, [etc.]. **1945** in Shibutani *Co. K* 225: I try not to pass on any chicken shit to you. **1955** Puzo *Dark Arena* 81: There'll be a hell of a shake-up, the chicken shit will really fly. **1960** Bluestone *Cully* 118: The rumor was that Korean vets…were real good guys who didn't deal out chicken shit to struggling trainees. **1965** Bryan *P.S. Wilkinson* 8: What kind of gung-ho chickenshit is this now? **1967** Dibner *Admiral* 247: "You're waiting for the lieutenant. He gave me an order." "Don't pull that GI chicken shit on me." **1969** Gallery *Cap'n Fatso* 15: But there was only one Navy Regulation on board—"Do your job." There was no more chicken shit than was absolutely necessary. **1970–71** J. Rubinstein *City Police* 104: I'm out there doin' the job and they give us this chickenshit. **1977** Sayles *Union Dues* 42: Always on your back for chickenshit while the important stuff goes right by him. **1983** Ehrhart *VN-Perkasie* 220: Worry about the chickenshit later. **1983–88** J.T. McLeod *Crew Chief* 18: Oh, he's fair enough, doesn't believe in pulling chicken shit on you.

b. *Mil.* a disciplinarian who is overly zealous in the enforcement of petty regulations.—usu. considered vulgar.

1950–53 W. Grove *Down* 100: "You are aware, Colonel, that these quarters are off limits for certain personnel."…"You chicken shit." **1955** Klaas *Maybe I'm Dead* 113 [ref. to WWII]: I'm not a chicken shit. **1968** Tauber *Sunshine Soldiers* 86: Everyone except me agrees that the captain is a chicken-shit. *a*1992 Ambrose *Band of Bros.* 22 [ref. to WWII]: Sobel was the classic chickenshit. He generated maximum anxiety over matters of minimal significance.

3. a contemptible or despicable individual.—usu. considered vulgar.

[**1944** in Hemingway *By-Line* 396: Those chickenspits aren't going to break down this attack….Let's kill these chickenspitters.] **1961** McMurtry *Horseman, Pass By* 26: Would you look at them chickenshits [buzzards]….You couldn't keep 'em scared off with artillery. **1971** Flanagan *Maggot* 250: You mean everybody here knows who that chicken-shit is? **1972** N.Y.U. student: If you really don't like somebody, you can say, "He's a real chickenshit."

4.a. a coward.—usu. considered vulgar.

1947 Willingham *End As a Man* 184: You're both acting like chicken shits. We win a batch of money—you're afraid to take it. **1961** L.E. Young *Virgin Fleet* 25 [ref. to 1941]: The chicken-shits would be afraid to. **1968** Tiede *Coward* 179: The bastard was court-martialed for being a chickenshit. **1977–80** F.M. Stewart *Century* 117: You shouldn't have run…because that proves you're a chickenshit.

b. cowardice.—usu. considered vulgar.

1966 Bogner *Seventh Ave.* 354: I knew he had chicken shit for blood. **1975** S.P. Smith *Amer. Boys* 210: I said to get his ass back in the field, 'cause that's the only way you cure chickenshit. Either that or send him to the nut ward. **1985** Former SP4, U.S. Army, age 35: First Sergeant Porter used to say, "His problem's just chickenshit. The guy's got no balls."

5. *pl.* nervous diarrhea; a feeling of terror.—constr. with *the*.—usu. used contemptuously.

1954–60 *DAS*: Chickenshits…Diarrhea. **1976** Conroy *Santini* 456: If you don't hook onto the last cable, then you get a bad case of the chicken shits.

chickenshit *adj.* **1.a.** insignificant; (*hence*) contemptible; worthless; LOUSY.—usu. considered vulgar.

1934 in Hemingway *Sel. Letters* 409: For Christ sake why not go where I can use them instead of go out here and play around with chicken shit sailfish that I feel sorry for when I catch. **1945** Himes *If He Hollers* 70: You're just a chickenshit nigger, too sad, just too sad for words. **1946** J.H. Burns *Gallery* 76: He was just a base section chicken-shit second looie. **1946** Gresham *Nightmare Alley* 58: Why do I have to frig around with all this chickenshit stuff? **1950** Hemingway *Across River* 293: They haven't enough stuff left even for a chickenshit fire-fight. **1947–52** R. Ellison *Invisible Man* 199: They after my job, the chickenshit bastards! **1953–55** Kantor *Andersonville* 650: Nazareth Stricker! Chicken-shit name for certain. **1958** *Stack A Lee* 2: They killed a motherfucker over a chickenshit dime. **1964** in Jackson *Swim Like Me* 107: I'm gonna to continue to kick you chickenshit whores right in your motherfucken ass. **1980** Gould *Ft. Apache* 15: I been lookin' for a way to get off this chickenshit job anyway. **1984** Sample *Raceboss* 39: You ain' lost but two chicken-shit dollars. **1989** Cassell *SSN Skate* 313: Not a goddamn bit of music in this chicken shit ocean.

b. trivial; niggling; (*hence*) mean-spirited.—usu. considered vulgar.

1934 in Dos Passos *14th Chronicle* 459: Only the little chickenshit middle class attitudes of a bright student in a girl's college. **1968** J.P. Miller *Race for Home* 215: Hell, I bet ole God couldn't give a damn less about all these little chicken-shit details. **1983** K. Miller *Lurp Dog* 15: Seems chickenshit to me, but Pappy runs a tight ship. **1988** Coonts *Final Flight* 327: Don't get caught breaking any of the chickenshit little rules.

c. Esp. *Mil.* overly zealous in the enforcement of petty regulations; characterized by such enforcement. [Early quots. ref. to WWII.]

1945 in Shibutani *Co. K* 239: What a chicken shit place! **1952** Lamott *Stockade* 55: If you smile when you crack the whip, you're a good joe; if you look solemn, you're a chickenshit son of a bitch. **1952** Uris *Battle Cry* 358: "However, as long as you are in my command you will observe all rules and regulations down to the letter. Do I make myself clear?" "Chickenshit outfit." **1953** Dibner *Deep Six* 49: No chicken-shit jaygee is gonna come along and foul things up just like that. **1958** Plagemann *Steel Cocoon* 99: The incident merely served as one more mark against chicken-shit, one-way Cripps. **1959** Cochrell *Barren Beaches* 279: Sure they call us chicken shit if we insist on saluting and all that. But in the long run buddy-buddy stuff doesn't pay off. **1967** P. Roth *When She Was Good* 53: Well, that's the old chicken s—t Army. **1968** W. Anderson *Gooney Bird* 30: How do I get transferred out of this chicken-shit outfit? **1969** Briley *Traitors* 9: Back inside the chopper old chickenshit Pershing was already coming down the aisle, checking equipment, seeing your dog tags were polished, nails clipped—screw him. **1977** Caputo *Rumor of War* 44: How do I get out of this chickenshit outfit? **1990** Rukuza *W. Coast Turnaround* 25: The Connecticut state police, notorious worldwide as the most chickenshit force on wheels.

2. cowardly.—usu. considered vulgar.

1945 in Shibutani *Co. K* 314: That…chicken shit bastard!…he's chicken hearted when he's all alone. **1947** Mailer *Naked & Dead* 10 [ref. to WWII]: What's the matter?…You going chickenshit? **1959** Cochrell *Barren Beaches* 93 [ref. to 1944]: "You're chickenshit," he told the kid. "Get up from there and help pack ammo." **1961** Sullivan *Shortest, Gladdest Years* 216: I never did anything so chickenshit or cynical as to make up an alter ego to take the burden of every instinct I didn't particularly care to admit as my own. **1966** Little *Bold & Lonely* 181: I think you're chicken-shit, and I can whip your ass right now, right here. **1966** Bogner *Seventh Ave.* 348 [ref. to ca1940]: You're not chicken shit are you, Neal? **1966** Elli *Riot* 174: How chickenshit can ya get? **1991** W. Chamberlain *View from Above* 56: Anonymously…is chickenshit.

chickenshit *v.* **1.** to behave in a manner that is CHICKENSHIT.—usu. considered vulgar.

1968 Cuomo *Thieves* 173: Everybody started chickenshitting around then, razzing and blowing off.

2. to hang back out of fear; CHICKEN OUT.—usu. considered vulgar.

1971 S. McQueen in *Playboy* (June) 116: I chickenshitted on the second turn. I just didn't have the balls to hold it side by side.

chicken switch *n.* *Mil.* a switch or button that activates an abort mechanism, a pilot's ejection seat, or the like.

1960 *Britannica Bk. of Yr.*: Chicken switch…An abort button in a man-operated missile. **1967** *DAS* (ed. 2). **1991** O. Stone & Z. Sklar *JFK* (film): He's got his hands on the chicken switch.

chicken-thief *n.* *So.* a small sailing vessel used for minor commerce.

1819, 1828, 1853 in *DAE*. **1855** G.G. Foster *N.Y. Naked* 72: An old Albany packet-schooner, a vessel greatly resembling…the "chicken thieves" that ply up and down the coast to and from New Orleans. **1887** Davis *Sea-Wanderer* 284 [ref. to 1847]: I…purchased a sloop-rigged craft of four tons, decked with a nice cabin. The craft engaged in this "commercial enterprise" are styled "chicken thieves."

chicken tracks *n.pl.* illegible handwriting.

1896 in J.M. Carroll *Benteen-Goldin Lets.* 238: Sorry for troubling you to read so much chicken tracks. **1953** in *DAS*. **1975** Julien *Cogburn* 85: I will rub out your chicken tracks and work them over.

chicken wings *n.pl.* *Mil. Av.* a set of insignia wings worn by military pilots.

1955 Shapiro *6th of June* 87 [ref. to 1944]: Maybe Timmer's getting his chicken wings.

chicken wrangler *n.* *West.* a person who performs odd jobs on a ranch. *Joc.*

1971 Terrell *Bunkhouse Papers* 88 [ref. to ca1920]: They didn't call Fred a chicken wrangler or a handyman…not to his face, anyway. He had the high title of *corral boss.*

chickie[1] *n.* **1.** a girl or young woman.

1919 Darling *Jargon Book* 8: *Chickie*—A young girl. **1936** Gaddis *Courtesan* 12: What's your name, chickie? **1968** Lockridge *Hartspring* 100: Be a good chicky, take my pals' coats. **1970** A. Young *Snakes* 27: OK, that's me posted at the corner digging on all the frozen chickies rushing it home from work. **1980** Kotzwinkle *Jack* 177: More chickies from Gina's gang. **1982** C.R. Anderson *Other War* 179: O-o-o-o, look at that chickee…I'd never kick her out of bed!

2. *Juve.* CHICKEN, *n.*, 7.b.

1964–70 in *Paris Rev.* (No. 50) 96: My cousin in Newark plays "chickie," which is two cars heading toward each other at about 80 m.p.h.

chickie[2] *n.* [fr. the interj.] *Juve. & Und.* a lookout.

1973 *N.Y. Post* (Apr. 24) 33: His "chickie," or lookout, fumbled with a switchblade.

¶ In phrase:

¶ **lay** [or **play** or **keep**] **chickie** Esp. *Juve.* to act as lookout, esp. against the approach of authority.

1934 H. Roth *Call It Sleep* 345 [ref. to *ca*1910]: I'll lay chickee. **1938** W. Sherman & V. Sherman *Crime School* (film): Squirt, play chickie! **1953** Paley *Rumble* 84: He was playing chickie in case the stompers decided to call a rumble. **1957** in Rubinstein *City Police* 181: My job was to be an errand boy…sneak them sandwiches and coffee…and lay chickie for the sergeant while they consumed them. **1962** Perry *Young Man Drowning* 71: All he did was stand there and lay chicky. **1965** C. Brown *Manchild* 31: Not having anyone to lay chickie for me, I had to do it quicker than most of the time. **1968** Heard *Howard St.* 67: They searched for a moneybelt…while Butch and Brother played chickie. **1974** Piñero *Short Eyes* 92: You don't have to take part, play chickie. **1984** D. Smith *Steely Blue* 52: Don't you give me no bullshit about not keeping chickie.

chickie *adj. Juve.* afraid; CHICKEN. Also as quasi-n.

1956 H. Ellison *Deadly Streets* 39: You're not chickie, are you? *Ibid.* 40: To back off was to show yellow, to show chickie. **1961** H. Ellison *Gentleman Junkie* 133: The last one who turns is the winner, the others are chickie. You dig?

chickie *interj.* [fr. CHIGGERS] *Juve.* (used as a warning to indicate esp. the approach of authority).

1934 H. Roth *Call It Sleep* 88 [ref. to *ca*1910]: "Chickee de cop, behin' de rock. De monkey's in de ba'ba shop." And he fled. **1941** in Botkin *Sidewalks* 486: Chickee!…Cant warning of the approach of the janitor's dog. **1954** E. Hunter *Blackboard Jungle* 46: Chiggee! someone shouted. **1983** in *DARE*: Chicky!…was the usual word [of warning] among school children [about 1915–25] in Ramsey [N.J.], when warning others of the approach of a teacher or the principal.

chickie run *n.* CHICKEN RUN.

1955 Stern *Rebel Without a Cause* (film): We'll have a little chickie run. **1961** H. Ellison *Gentleman Junkie* 133: You come on out to the chickie-run tonight, and we'll see you got gut enough to be a Prince.

chicklet *n.* [pun on CHICK, *n.*, 1.a., + -*let*, dimin. suffix and *Chiclets*, a trademark for candy-coated chewing gum] a young woman; girl. Also **chiclet.**

1922 S. Lewis *Babbitt* 172: This is the straight steer, Benny, the painless chicklets of the Wrollicking Wrens are the cuddlingest bunch that ever hit town. **1961** B. Wolfe *Magic of Their Singing* 68: She was…one wild and too balling chiclet. **1965** *Post & Times Star* (Cincinnati) (Nov. 5): A "chiclet" no longer is sugar-coated gum, but a sweet girl. **1968** *Time* (Dec. 27) 47: A trio of pretty chicklets billed as Extraordinary Spooks.

Chiclets *n.pl.* [fr. *Chiclets*, a trademark for candy-coated chewing gum] teeth.

1959 Ellison *Gentleman Junkie* 206: Baby, you want a mouthful of bloody Chiclets, you keep peppering my good nature. **1972** *Nat. Lampoon* (July) 49: You can hand him an earful of patriotism along with that mouthful of bloody Chiclets. **1992** *N.Y. Times* (May 1) B 11: He's lucky somebody didn't grab him during the brawl. He'd be spitting out his Chiclets.

chicom *n. Mil.* **1.** [orig. an official abbr.] a Chinese Communist. Also attrib.

1964 R. Moore *Green Berets* 220: Guess you couldn't snatch a Chicom for us, eh? **1983** K. Miller *Lurp Dog* 44: Capturing some of them sweet Chicom bargirls.

2. a small makeshift grenade or explosive booby trap employed by Communist guerrillas; a grenade of Communist Chinese manufacture.

1970 *Time* (June 22) 34: Homemade devices called "Chicom grenades," which are fashioned from Coca-Cola cans filled with plastique or TNT, rocks and nails. **1973** Browne *Body Shop* 177: I never think about the guy who threw the Chicom. **1973** Huggett *Body Count* 44: Chi-Com! Look out, sir! **1973** Layne *Murphy* (unp.): Chi-coms contain little fragmentation. **1980** Santoli *Everything* 74: The blast from the Chicom set off a smoke grenade that was on his belt. **1982** Del Vecchio

13th Valley 159: He's got two Chicoms an a sachel charge with'm. **1982** R.A. Anderson *Cooks & Bakers* 122: Ran into a minefield…Little ones.…Chi-coms, I'll bet…about the size of a grenade. **1985** Dye *Between Raindrops* 35: The…gooks are…pitchin' Chicoms into the houses.

Chic Sale *n.* [sugg. by the name of the humorist *Chic Sale*, author of *The Specialist* (1929) (a novel about constructing an outhouse) and the self-described "champion privy builder of Sangamon Co. [Ill.]"] an outhouse; (*Mil.*) a latrine.

1943 Pyle *Here Is Your War* 73: Doctors, nurses, everyone but the patients, washed outdoors in cold water, and went to a Chic Sale with a canvas wall around it. **1944** in Eichelberger *Dear Miss Em* 93: I have a screened Chic Sale. **1958** Berger *Crazy in Berlin* 16: An electric-pencil sketch of a pickaninny sitting in a Chic Sale. **1962** Shepard *Press Passes* 30: The contractors had erected two "Chic Sales" at the edge of the lawn for the comfort of the workers. **1963** W.C. Anderson *Penelope* 43: Even if the plumbing facilities had consisted of a one-holed Chic Sale in the rear of the lot. **1967** Mailer *Vietnam* 16: They used rat paper for tar paper on the Chic Sale. **1968** Blackford *Torp. Sailor* 117: The toilet facilities were the crudest…an inside Chic Sale with two or three holes in it on each floor, and a direct drop into some sort of container below. **1977** Berry *Kaiser* 109: Then he'd casually stroll over to this Chic Sales close to a hundred yards away. *Ibid.* 255: We had to build this lady her own Chic Sales. *a*1982 in Berry *Semper Fi* 49: The hell with his Chic Sale.

chief *n.* **1.a.** one's superior.—often used in direct address.

1880 King *Campaigning with Crook* 5 [ref. to 1876]: "Despatch for you, General; thought you'd better have it at once," was all he said, as he handed it to the "chief," and remounting, cantered away. **1903** Ralph *Journalist* 63: My "chief," as we called the editor in supreme control of a newspaper. **1931** Cantor, Ryskind, et al. *Palmy Days* (film): I getcha, chief. **1955** *Adventures of Superman* (synd. TV series): "I'll do it right away, Chief." "And don't call me 'Chief'!"

b. (used in direct address to a man, esp. one whose name is not known).

1935 Wolfe *Death to Morning* 91: Jesus! Yuh got me, chief. **1940** Merrie Melodies (animated cartoon): Say, Chief, where do I deliver this load of oil? **1945–51** Salinger *Catcher in Rye* ch. xiii: How old are you, chief? **1957** J.D. MacDonald *Death Trap* 79: You got a new way to get your kicks, chief? **1972** Buell *Shrewsdale* 127: "I'll settle up later." "Sorry, chief, house rules." **1990** Vachss *Blossom* 42: Don't look so angry, chief. **1992** *Beverly Hills 90210* (Fox-TV): I didn't buy this jacket at an army surplus store, chief.

2. (used in direct address to an American Indian man).—usu. used derisively.

1933 Ersine *Prison Slang* 26: Chief, *n.*…any Indian. **1966–69** in *DARE*. **1968–70** *Current Slang* III & IV 24: Chief, *n.* An American Indian.— New Mexico State.

3. (*cap.*) *USAF.* the Republic F-105 Thunderchief fighter plane.

1961 L.G. Richards *TAC* 234: The Chief will make Mach 2.75.

chief cook and bottle washer *n.* a person having charge of many and varied responsibilities.

1840 in *DA*: Taking it for granted that the Kitchen Orator will be appointed "Chief Cook and Bottle Wash" [*sic*] at the White House. **1865** in *DA*. **1902** Corrothers *Black Cat Club* 136: He wuz…chief cook an' bottle-washah uv a Sunday. **1905** White *Boniface to Burglar* 81: Being the greenhorn of the party, I was detailed the "chief cook and bottle-washer" of our feeding department. **1977** *Wash. Post* (July 7) Virginian 1: Hammond has…no clerical help.…"I'm the chief cook and bottle washer and typist." **1992** *N.Y. Times* (Nov. 7) 24: "I guess this move is a pretty good-sized job," said…Mr. Miller, who described himself as the "president, chief cook and bottle washer" of his company.

chiggers *interj. Juve.* JIGGERS.

1933 Ersine *Prison Slang* 20: Chiggers, *ex.* Look out, there is danger near! **1948** Chaplin *Wobbly* 5 [ref. to *ca*1895]: Sometimes there was the sudden cry, "Chiggers, de cop!" and Clancy, the neighborhood policeman would be upon us.

child *n.* person; in phr. **this child** I, me.

1839 *Spirit of Times* (Mar. 23) 27: You can't stuff dis child. **1843** [W.T. Thompson] *Scenes in Ga.* 23: This child aint to be beat, no how you can fix it! **1847** Ruxton *Life in Far West*: This child remembers that fix. **1892, 1930** in *DA*.

chili *n.* **1.** *S.W.* a Mexican.—usu. used contemptuously. [In 1919 quot. a Chilean.]
[**1919** E. Hemingway, in *N.Y. Times Mag.* (Aug. 18, 1985) 17: They're not a bad lot, those Chillies....But we'll show those dirty Chillies. **1936** R. Adams *Cowboy Lingo* 198: To the cowboy a Mexican was a...."chili" [or] "chili-eater." **1937** E. Anderson *Thieves Like Us* 187: That's one thing them Chilis can do. **1956, 1967** in *DARE*. **1968** J. Miller *Race for Home* 100: She was a spic, a chili. She was a wetback.
2. *S.W.* ire.
1966 "T. Pendleton" *Iron Orchard* ch. v.: Ort, I believe you got your chili up, pardner. I better let you out right here so you won't get mixed up in this.

chili bean *n. S.W.* a Mexican.—usu. used contemptuously.
1976 Braly *False Starts* 224: Split the scene, Chili Bean. **1986** (quot. at CHILI-EATER).

chili-belly *n.* a Mexican.—usu. used contemptuously. Also **chili-gut.**
1967 [Beck] *Pimp* 84: This is light green "pot" from "chili gut" country. **1968** J.P. Miller *Race for Home* 106 [ref. to ca1930's]: Little chili-belly bastard.... **1981** Spears *Slang & Euphem.* 70: *Chili-belly....*A Mexican. **1984** Glick *Winters Coming* 59: I'll remember that, chili-gut. **1986** (quot. at CHILI-EATER).

chili bowl *n. Mil.* a military crew cut.
1942 in *Yank* (Jan. 6, 1943) 14: A G.I. Haircut...No. 1—The Chili-Bowl Special. **1988** Veterans Life Insurance TV ad: And I was issued my chili bowl, too—took the barber fifty seconds flat.

chili-chaser *n. S.W.* a U.S. border patrol officer on the Mexican border.—used derisively.
1956 *AS* XXXI 100: The *chili chasers*, border patrolmen. **1968** R. Adams *West. Words* (ed. 2): *Chili chasers.* The cowboy's name for border patrolmen on the Mexican border.

chili-eater *n. S.W.* a Mexican.—usu. used contemptuously. Also vars.
1911 Fletcher *Up the Trail in '79* 46 [ref. to 1879]: So the chili-eaters, as some cowboys called them, were permitted to resign. **1919** *DN* V 63: *Chili-eater*, low class Mexicans. "I went over to Barellas to a dance and all the *chili-eaters* were there." New Mexico...[also] *chili-picker.* **1935** Pollock *Und. Speaks:* Chili picker, a Mexican. **1968–70** *Current Slang* III & IV 24: *Chili chomper*, n. A Mexican or a Mexican-American (derogatory). New Mexico State. **1970** Wertheim & Gonzalez *Talkin' About Us* 65: Other children call them Frito Banditos, chile chokers and taco vendors. **1970** in *DARE:* Chili choker. *ca*1971 in *DARE:* Chili chompers. **1972** Dozier *When the Legends Die* (film): I buried the old chili-eater out back here. **1973** Tex. man, age *ca*20: Buncha damn chili-shitters. **1978** Univ. Tenn. student: Spics and chili-shitters. **1979** L.A. man, age 35: Mexicans in Southern California are called *chili-stompers.* **1981** C. Nelson *Picked Bullets Up* 143 [ref. to *ca*1970]: You're leaving the land of the Chili Shitters for Aspen. **1986** Univ. Tenn. instructor, age 35: In the army [during the early 1970's] I heard guys from Texas refer to Mexicans with all kinds of *chili* words: *chili-shitter, chili-eater, chili-sucker, chili-maker, chilihead, chili-bean, chili-belly.*

chilihead *n.* a Mexican.—usu. used contemptuously.
1978 Rascoe & Stone *Who'll Stop Rain?* (film): Hey, chilihead! **1986** (quot. at CHILI-EATER).

chill *n.* a spurning; a show of indifference; the cold shoulder.—esp. in phr. of the sort **play the chill.**
1908 *New Broadway Mag.* (July) 80: I knew it was no use trying to save him a chill. **1920** J. Conway, in *Variety* (Dec. 24) 5: He's been playin' the chill for two-dollar broads all his life. **1921** J. Conway, in *Variety* (Feb. 18) 8: Cuthbert and Algy have stopped playing the chill for each other and are warmin' up again. **1928** O'Connor *B'way* 250: Chill— Contempt; "Putting on the chill"—viewing with a scornful eye. **1933** West *I'm No Angel* (film): What are you playin' the chill for all of a sudden? **1941** *Sat. Eve. Post* (May 17) 86: Nobody even spoke to him. They gave him the chill. **1947** Boyer *Dark Ship* 227: I go up to the NMV hall. They're giving me the chill right away. **1956** "T. Betts" *Across the Board* 185: Why does he put the chill on me?
¶ In phrases:
¶ **put the chill on, 1.** see CHILL, *n.*, above.
2. to murder.
1932 in Weinberg et al. *Tough Guys* 49: Then I'll put the chill on both of you. **1949** Chandler *Little Sister* 64: When Weepy Moyer had the chill put on Sunny Moe Stein over on Franklin Avenue last February, the killer used a gun.

3. Esp. *Black E.* to put a stop to; to cease.
1981 in Safire *Good Word* 83: Put a chill on your rap.
¶ **take a chill** calm down; relax; CHILL OUT.
1986 *Outlaws* (CBS-TV): Hey, take a chill! **1989** S. Lee *Do the Right Thing* (film): Y'all take a chill.

chill *adj.* Esp. *Black E.* shrewd; stylish; COOL.
1983 *N.Y. Times*, in *Barnhart Dict. Comp.* VIII 4 130: A "chill" outfit for a girl is tight Sergio Valente...jeans, black loafers and anklets. **1984** Former Spec. 5, U.S. Army: When I was stationed in Taiwan in 1973–74 I used to hear the blacks saying, "He's a chill dude," "That's chill, man." **1984** *USA Today* (Mar. 13) D1: Here at the Roxy Roller Rink, sneakers are called "kicks"...and the look is "chill." **1984** S. Hager *Hip Hop* 108: *Chill*—cool; okay; superior. **1987** Univ. Tenn. student: "That's chill" means "That's so cool." "It's chill. Chill, man!" **1989** Ebbitt & Ebbitt *Index to Eng.* 238: Words of approval...*neat, the most, chill,...rad.* **1991** Nelson & Gonzales *Bring Noise* 169: Open for anyone who wished to shout their chillest rhymes.

chill *adv. Stu.* completely; cold.
1900 *DN* II 26: *Chill.* In phrase, "have anything down chill." To have perfect mastery of anything. **1915** *DN* IV 232: *Have down chill*, to know thoroughly.

chill *v.* **1.a.** to lose interest or enthusiasm (in a matter), esp. suddenly.—used intrans.
1872 *Galaxy* (Feb.) 281: He "sours" on them quick. Don't mean business, Fred don't; he's "spooney," then "chills" all at once!...Fact is, I've "chilled" on last year's operas. **1932** in *AS* (Feb. 1934) 26: *Chill.* To lose interest in a matter. **1935** *Amer. Mercury* (June) 231: Speedy says he flashes a yard and a half a while ago down at the swingers. He chills when them thieves get greedy, though. **1961** Scarne *Comp. Gamb. Gde.* 674: *Chill.* To lose interest. **1988** *N.Y. Times Mag.* (Dec. 11) 22: "She chilled on me," the young man said, after waiting disconsolately for several hours.
b. to snub.
1927 *Vanity Fair* (Nov.) 134: "Ritzed me" or "chilled me"...to be snubbed. **1972** R. Barrett *Lovomaniacs* 389: Even if the ungrateful bastards *did* chill me after they got into office.
c. *Und.* to act or react impassively.
1930 Conwell *Pro. Thief* 6: They chilled for him (pretended not to recognize him) and kept on going, but he turned around and stared after them. He should never have stared after them when they chilled. **1936** *AS* (Apr.) 119: *To chill.* To submit to arrest without struggling or resisting.
d. to calm down; CHILL OUT; relax; lie low.
1979 "Sugar Hill Gang" in L.A. Stanley *Rap* 325: A time to break and a time to chill. **1983** Eble *Campus Slang* (Nov.) 2: *Chill, Chill out*—calm down: Why don't you just chill? It really doesn't matter anyway. **1986** *Newsweek* (July 28) 17: Some woman come out here...barking and woofing and demanding that we get off the street....I flashed her some heat (showed his gun) and she chilled. **1987** *21 Jump Street* (Fox-TV): You'd *best* chill, 'cause he's a business associate of mine. **1987** *Beauty & the Beast* (CBS-TV): Chill a couple of days till the right idea comes to you. **1989** *Life* (July) 29: I like to go over to her house and just chill with her—talk about things, make her laugh. **1990** *New Yorker* (Sept. 10) 66: So I got me another job...and for a while I just chilled [until police pressure ended]. **1994** *New York* (Jan. 10) 21: I be chillin' with my girl.
2. *Und.* to quash (a complaint or the like); put a stop to.
1929–31 D. Runyon *Guys & Dolls* 108: Joe...is in another part of the joint chilling a beef from some customer about a check. **1933** Ersine *Prison Slang* 26: *Chill*...To squash a rap. "The shysters chilled the rap." **1968** Beck *Trick Baby* 151: Goddamnit, I'm going to chill your shit now. *a*1969 J. Kimbrough *Defender of Angels* 192: This rap I'm charged with was supposed to be chilled. **1992** Mowry *Way Past Cool* 195: Deek's shit gotta be chilled.
3. Esp. *Und.* to kill (a person).
1933 Ersine *Prison Slang* 26: *Chill, v.* To kill. **1940** in Goodstone *Pulps* 115: Who chilled him? **1946** Boulware *Jive & Slang* 3: *Chilled*...Killed. **1970** La Motta, Carter & Savage *Raging Bull* 26: If I wanted to chill him, I'da done something more than hit him across the head. **1973** Knopf *Emperor of North Pole* (film): You the guy that chilled Mike? **1987** Santiago *Undercover* 238: The same killer...wanted to chill me.
4. *Boxing.* to knock unconscious; knock out.
1939 Howsley *Argot* 12: *Chill*...To knock unconscious. **1940** P. Gallico, in M.H. Greenberg *In Ring* 36: His boy has been chilled so he will not be up [before Sunday]. **1966–67** P. Thomas *Mean Streets* 60: I'd been aching to chill that *maricon.*
5. to anger or astonish; FROST.

1944 in *DAS*. **1972–76** Durden *No Bugles* 172: A conspiracy between her 'n' me so I could know what *my own father* looked like. Would that chill the ass on a polar bear?

chiller-diller *n.* something frightening. Cf. KILLER-DILLER. *Joc.*

    1964–66 R. Stone *Hall of Mirrors* 96: A real chiller diller for the folks down home.

chilling *adj.* Esp. *Black E.* COOL.

    1987 "Schooly D" *Saturday Night* (rap song): We're most chillin'. **1990** P. Dickson *Slang!* 214: *Chill/Chillin'*…adj. Calm, cool, or laid back.

chill out *v.* **1.** *Black E.* to stop acting foolish; to act COOL.

    1981 in Safire *Good Word* 79.

    2. to take it easy; relax; calm down.—usu. as imper.

    1980 in Safire *Good Word* 79. **1982** Eble *Campus Slang* (Nov.) 1: *Chill out*—relax; calm down: *Chill out!* Don't get so upset! **1983** Sturz *Wid. Circles* 16: Chill out, man.…Nobody at Argus is going to offer you any violence. **1985** M. Baker *Cops* 301: Home…it's like a little oasis, where I can come and chill out for a few days. **1985** *Miami Vice* (NBC-TV): All right. Chill out. **1986** F. Miller et al. *Batman* 22: Chill *out*, Michelle. It's only a block.

chill pill see s.v. PILL.

chilly *n.* a cold can of beer.

    1985 Univ. Tenn. student theme: A six pack is "a pack of chillies."

chilly *adj.* **1.** *Black E.* cool; calculating; (*also*) cold-hearted.

    1971 B.B. Johnson *Blues for Sister* 156: This cat was considered to be a chilly strategist steeped in the law. **1974** Gober *Black Cop* 144: Like, she been messin' around wit' him all this time and she wouldn't tell you. That's awful chilly, I tol' her. **1989** R. Miller *Profane Men* 41: We gonna be *down* with this chilly shit.

    2. COOL.

    1971 Univ. Ark. students (coll. J. Ball): "Man, that's cool." "No, it's *chilly*." **1978** Lieberman & Rhodes *CB* (ed. 2) 289: Better be chilly.…Better cool it—slow down. **1980** N.Y.C. editor, age 27: My brother's starting to say things like, "Stay chilly, man. He's a chilly dude." It means *cool*. **1981** in Safire *Good Word* 79: *Looking chilly* (looks nice). **1985** Eble *Campus Slang* (Oct.) 3: *Chilly*—in order; O.K. "Everything's chilly; don't sweat it." Used predominantly by blacks. **1985** Swados & Trudeau *RapMaster Ronnie* 5: The cat's okay…Yeah…chilly…fresh.

    ¶ In phrase:

    ¶ **lay** [or **sit**] **chilly** to lie low; wait patiently; remain motionless.

    1978 J. Webb *Fields of Fire* 59 [ref. to Vietnam, 1969]: They're laying chilly out there. Wouldn't come back with me. *Ibid.* 96: We could really be in the shit. We better lay chilly til we scope 'em out. *Ibid.* 413: *Lay Chilly*: To freeze, to stop all motion. **1981–85** S. King *It* 559: Make like Kookie…and just lay chilly. **1988** Shoemaker & Nagler *Shoemaker* xiv: Some call it patience and some call it sitting chilly. **1989** R. Miller *Profane Men* 46: You'd best lay chilly till the evil goes away.

chilly down *v.* CHILL OUT, 2.

    1986 Cosby *Fatherhood* 116: He can say "chilly down" so much that he sounds like a short order cook.

chilly mitt *n.* [sugg. by antonymous GLAD HAND] cold treatment or rejection.—constr. with *the*.

    1900 Willard & Hodler *Powers That Prey* 143: Renshaw'll make some old Rube chief o' police, an' we'll all get the chilly mit. *Ibid.* 184: I'm goin' to give you the chilly mit if you don't stop doggin' me 'round to all these joints.

chimes *n.pl.* testicles. *Joc.*

    1960–69 Runkel *Law* 279: Then she started workin' on my chimes.…"Chimes," sir? My balls. You don' know very many words, d'ya?

    ¶ In phrase:

    ¶ **ring (one's) chimes** to arouse (one's) attention; excite.

    1970 *Rowan & Martin's Laugh-In* (NBC-TV): Well, ring my chimes! **1974** V.B. Miller *Girl in River* 25: Something ringing your chimes, Crocker? *a***1986** D. Tate *Bravo Burning* 178: I'm gone [*sic*] ring [her] chimes. **1988** *Day by Day* (NBC-TV): That's the kind of man who can really ring my chimes.

chimney *n.* **1.** *Whaling.* a whale's spout.

    1896 (quot. at FIRE, *n.*). **1899** Robbins *Gam* 79: His chimney's afire! He's spoutin' blood! It's his flurry! **1912** R. Murphy *Logbook for Grace* 102: His spout, formerly so thin and white, reflecting tiny rainbows in

the rays of the low sun, now became first pink and then crimson and gouted. "His chimney's afire!" said Mr. da Lomba, with a heartless chuckle.

    2. [cf. colloq. *smoke like a chimney*] a person who smokes excessively.

    1900 *DN* II 26: *Chimney*. A person addicted to smoking. **1985** Briskin *Too Much* 232: You know her, a regular chimney.

chin *n.* **1.a.** talk, esp. impudent backtalk. Cf. CHEEK, *n.*, 2.

    1862 in J.W. Haley *Rebel Yell* 45: Too much chin of his kind has more than once improved the market for rope. **1877** Bartlett *Amer.* (ed. 4) 779: *Chin, chinning.* Back-talk, impudence. *ca***1880** Bellard *Gone for a Soldier* 259: He was on his feet, and proceeded to give us some chin. **1880** Small *Mother-in-Law* 20: My bristles were up and I disdained "chin" from anybody. **1894** in *Harper's* (Jan. 1895) 421: They have a…language of their own—"de chin dat shows dey're tough"—a lingo all made up of slang and profanity. **1897** *Harper's* (Jan.) 90: Talk is both "yap" and "chin"; impudent talk is "slack." *****1902** Masefield *Salt-Water Ballads* 22: Now quit yer chin/Or I'll smash yer skulls. **1940** Jones & Houser *Dark Command* (film): You keep your chin to yourself.

    b. *Army.* rumor.

    1864 in *PADS* (No. 70) 24: We have had so much of "camp chin" that it is quite refreshing to get something official at last.

    2. a conversation; discussion.

    1894 P.L. Ford *Stirling* 14: I'll wait till I've graduated, and had a chin with my governor about it. **1926** Hormel *Co-Ed* 66: Lucia…perched on the edge of her cot for a "chin." **1929** Burnett *Iron Man* 131: We're all betting on your boy and we came out for a chin. **1940** O'Neill *Iceman* 134: I'll go and have a private chin with the Commissioner. **1957** M. Shulman *Rally* 210: Call me some time and we'll have a good chin.

    3. the mouth as a source of idle talk.

    1929 Perelman *Ginsbergh* 187: If I wanted to open my chin and tell about the time I saw the iceman….

    ¶ In phrases:

    ¶ **lead with (one's) chin** Orig. *Boxing.* to clumsily allow (oneself) to be knocked down by a blow to the chin; (*hence*) to act foolishly in a way that encourages (one's) own defeat.

    1922 in Hemingway *Sel. Letters* 62: I've been teaching Pound to box wit little success. He habitually leads wit his chin and has the general grace of the crayfish or crawfish. **1936** Twist *We About to Die* (film): They sure do a lot of leadin' with their chins. **1949** E.S. Gardner *Negligent Nymph* 34: Me with my binoculars and my damn curiosity, leading with my chin. **1952** Bruce & Essex *K.C. Confidential* (film): "You're leadin' with your chin, Joe." "So I'm leadin' with my chin!" **1990** Ruggero *38 N. Yankee* 37: If they faced an armored force the U.S. Army would be doing what boxers called "leading with the chin."

    ¶ **take it on the chin** Orig. *Boxing.* to be hit squarely on the chin; (*hence*) to suffer serious reversal, loss, etc.

    1922 Tully *Emmett Lawler* 294: You take 'em on the chin, Emmett. I know what that is, no manager's worth a fifty-fifty split. **1927** C.F. Coe, in Paxton *Sport* 147: The kid takes it on the chin and flops. **1928** *Variety* (Oct. 31) 46: Several Chink students…took it on the chin through jacking up prices far in excess of the Broadway scale. **1928** McEvoy *Show Girl* 129: If she walks out Jack Milton won't kick in another nickel. And we're going to take it on the chin for five thousand down here this week. **1932** Berg *Prison Doctor* 55: It's tough to take it on the chin, kid. But don't lose hope. **1938** Adamic *My America* 72: The people were taking the Depression on the chin. **1939–40** Tunis *Kid from Tomkinsville* 161: See where the Dodgers took it on the chin again today? **1990** *U.S. News & W.R.* (Dec. 31) 49: Corporate profits may take it on the chin in 1991.

    ¶ **wipe off your chin!** shut up!

    1876 in Miller & Snell *Why West Was Wild* 129: He commenced one of his long stories. While busily engaged in it, some one remarked: "Oh! Larry, wipe off your chin." Poor Larry had not heard of the late slang phrase and immediately drew forth his bandana. **1877** *Puck* (Mar.) 6: Whenever I talk too much, Jim Gaffney says, "Wipe off your chin." **1883** (quot. at HALL).

chin *v.* **a.** to address or speak to, esp. in a flattering way.—used trans.

    *ca***1871** in *DARE*. **1876** in S.L. Smith *Sagebrush Soldier* 58: Campbell and Smith, came in and chinned me for an hour. **1877** in J.M. Carroll *Camp Talk* 86: Hale is now "chinning" me—wanting to have me go and settle some matters for him with Merrill. **1892** in *OEDS*. **1895** Townsend *Fadden* 158: Mr. Paul…heard me chinning de Duchess about it. **1896** F.H. Smith *Tom Grogan* 76: Didn't I see ye a-chinnin' 'er whin I come over de hill? **1896** Ade *Artie* 34: He…begins chinnin' her and never sees me at all. **1899** A.H. Lewis *Sandburrs* 156: He, an' d' crook who's waitin' for him, is chinnin' each other in whispers. **1900** *DN* II 26: *Chin*, v.t....To "buzz," interrogate, gossip, talk to....To talk to an instructor for the purpose of gaining favor...*chinner, n.* One who tries to curry favor with instructors. **1909** "O. Henry" *Options* 782: Can you chin 'em and make matinee eyes at 'em and squeeze 'em? **1934** J.M. Cain, in *DAS*.

b. to talk; chat.—used intrans.

1872 Crapsey *Nether Side* 158: The three white men were deeply engaged in "chinning" with the black women, as such creatures call the conversation of which they are capable. **1873** Small *Knights of Pythias* 9: Did you ever hear of that man who was talked to death? I am a man more chinned against than chinning. **1883** Hay *Bread-Winners* 115: That's none of your business...and I ain't agoin' to chin about it any more. **1899** A.H. Lewis *Sandburrs* 8: When Mary grows up an' can chase about an' chin, she toins out a dead good kid an' goes to d' Sisters' School. **1922** *Variety* (Aug. 4) 9: Tendler could have knocked out the champion then if he had not stopped to verbally "rag" with Benny....He started "chinning" and Lew gabbed back. **1936** Dos Passos *Big Money* 283: I was expecting to come up and chin with you after dinner. **1958** Swarthout *Cordura* 144: Time we chinned some, Majer.

china *n.* **1.** money.

1940 Longstreet *Decade* 357: Twenty G's is a lot of china.

2. teeth.

1942 *ATS* 150. **1944** Kendall *Service Slang* 35: *Chipping the china*...complaining, beefing. **1950** in *DAS*: Smile and show that china. **1977** Stallone *Paradise Alley* 39: Frankie the Humper set down his beer. "Lookin' to get ya china punched out."

3. tea, as served at a lunch counter.

1967 *DAS* (ed. 2) 677: *China*...a cup of tea. *Lunch-counter use.*

chinaboy *n.* a Chinese man.—usu. used contemptuously.

1850 in A. McLeod *Pigtails & Gold Dust* 35: All the "China boys" are to be assembled...in the Plaza. **1895** Foote *Coeur D'Alene* 128: Where is that Chinaboy? **1979** D. Thoreau *City at Bay* 143: Let's concentrate on catching those crazy China boys.

china chin *n. Boxing.* GLASS JAW.

1940 Zinberg *Walk Hard* 42: You can have a china chin mounted on a ton of muscle, and the muscles will fold like a flat tire when somebody taps the glass kisser. **1950** *New Yorker* (Sept. 30) 52: What is known in the prizefight game as a china chin. **1976** WINS Radio News (July 5): A *china chin* or a *glass jaw* is a boxer who can easily be knocked out.

china clipper *n.* [sugg. by Pan American's *China Clippers*, flying boats offering passenger service to the Far East, and by the 1936 motion picture of the same name]

1. *Army.* a dishwasher. *Joc.*

1941 *AS* (Oct.) 164: *China Clipper.* Dishwasher. **1941** *Amer. N & Q* I (Dec.) 140: *China Clippers:* dishwashers. **1954–60** *DAS.* **1971** N.Y.C. draftsman [ref. to *ca*1940]: A "china-clipper" was a dishwasher.

2. *pl.* false teeth. *Joc.*

1953 Gresham *Midway* 224: Stunt drivers all seem to suffer from a common mishap—getting their front teeth banged out. Most of them wear "china clippers." **1986** Ark. man, age 34: I can't even remember the first time I heard false teeth called *china clippers*. It's real common. **1986** Miss. woman, age 48: My ex-husband always used to refer to his false teeth as *china-clippers.*

Chinaman *n.* **1.** (see quot.).—now usu. considered offensive.

1895 *DN* I 385: *Chinaman*...cup of tea.

2. *Hunting.* a ring-necked pheasant.—usu. considered offensive.

1957, 1966 in *DARE.*

3. *Narc.* an addiction to an opiate; (*specif.*) the withdrawal symptoms associated with such an addiction.—often constr. with *on (one's) back.*—now usu. considered offensive.

1948 in W.S. Burroughs *Letters* 27: I want to stay out of N.O. long enough to get this Chinaman off my back. (Kick my habit.) **1952** Holmes *Go* 81: Win's just about got the Chinaman off her back! **1958** Motley *Epitaph* 91: The Chinaman's riding you, huh?...That Horse won't let me go. *Ibid.* 143: They're rippin' an' runnin' to try to get some money to satisfy that Chinaman. **1962** Maurer & Vogel *Narc. & Narc. Add.* (ed. 2) 295: *Chinaman on my back*...suffering abstinence symptoms. **1963** in Wepman et al. *The Life* 84: The Chinaman spoke, and it wasn't a joke. **1971** Goines *Dopefiend* 116: She just kicked, she ain't got to worry about the Chinaman no more.

¶ In phrases:

¶ **have a Chinaman** Esp. *Chicago.* to have political influence.—now usu. considered offensive.

1973 *AS* XLVI 82.

¶ **play (someone) for a Chinaman** *West.* to treat as a fool.—now usu. considered offensive.

1873 *Overland Mo.* (Feb.) 113: He'd been playing 'em for Chinamen from the word go. **1881** Nye *Forty Liars* 205: Mebbe I can be played for a Chinaman, and mebbe I can't.

Chinaman's chance *n.* an extremely slim chance or no chance at all.—usu. used in negative constructions.—now usu. considered offensive.

1911 *Hampton's Mag.* (June) 746: "Not a Chinaman's chance," repeated Chris quickly. **1913** *Sat. Eve. Post* (July 5) 4: You and me ain't got a Chinaman's chance for a pleasant look from her! **1918** Witwer *Baseball to Boches* 160: Right from the go in, Joe, we all knowed we didn't have a Chinaman's chance. **1927** Nicholson *Barker* 28: A guy in this day an' age without the proper schoolin' ain't got a *Chinaman's* chance. **1930** Waldron *Old Sergeant* 30: It looks to me like a young fellow hasn't got a Chinaman's chance anyway you take it. **1938** McArdle *Collier's* 352: A kid like you ain't got a Chinaman's chance against a man like Regan. **1944** C.B. Davis *Leo McGuire* 164: I frankly can't see how we'd have a Chinaman's chance. **1956** Ginsberg *Howl* 32: I haven't got a chinaman's chance. **1953–57** Giovannitti *Combine* D 181: There isn't a Chinaman's chance once it gets cold. **1966–80** McAleer & Dickson *Unit Pride* 105: We won't have a Chinaman's chance of getting out alive. *Ibid.* 397: We ain't about to take no Chinaman's chances for you or anyone else.

Chinaman's nightmare *n.* an example of uncontrollable confusion; chaos; CHINESE FIRE DRILL.

1982 "W.T. Tyler" *Rogue's March* 41: It was a Chinaman's nightmare up there at GHQ.

China syndrome *n. Nuclear Engineering.* a complete meltdown of fissionable material within the core of a nuclear reactor.

1970 *Esquire* (June) 76: This "fast-breeder reactor" required a large flow of coolant to...prevent the "China syndrome"—a constant worry to technicians, for once she starts melting, she'll melt her all the way down to China. [**1974** Widener *N.U.K.E.E.* 67: The core was in a runaway melt-down condition—the classic "China Accident," so dubbed by a scientist who once said: "In such an accident the fuel would continue to heat and melt all the way to China."] **1978** *N.Y. Times* (Dec. 24) II 11: "The China syndrome" is the wry expression used by physicists to describe the worst of all nuclear plant accidents, in which the radioactive core of the plant could conceivably melt its way through the earth, "all the way to China." **1979** Wohl *The China Syndrome* (title). **1983** S. Wright *Meditations* 227: You familiar with the term "China syndrome"? **1986** *Time* (May 12) 49: When the water boils away, the molten core sinks into the earth in the so-called China syndrome, a term used by scientists, and popularized by the 1979 movie of the same name.

Chinat *n.* [orig. an official abbr.; cf. CHICOM] *Mil.* a Nationalist Chinese.

1961 L.G. Richards *TAC* 179: C-119 Flying Boxcars were turned over to the ChiNats.

China white *n. Narc.* a very powerful synthetic narcotic drug resembling heroin, derived from fentanyl.

1979 D. Thoreau *City at Bay* 166: This ain't that dirty Mexican junk....You're looking at China white. **1980** *L.A. Times* (Dec. 20) II 1: The drug, a synthetic white powder that is known as "China white"...is reportedly powerful enough to cause almost instantaneous respiratory arrest. **1984** *Miami Vice* (NBC-TV): China white—at a price that's right! **1986** *Jour. Drug. Ed.* XVI 289: In December 1979, "China White," or "synthetic heroin," began appearing on the streets. It was later found to be alpha methyl fentanyl, an uncontrolled substance. **1988** *Newsweek* (Mar. 28) 27: Fentanyl: A potent heroin substitute known as China White, the synthetically produced "designer drug" is mostly a West Coast fad. **1989** *21 Jump St.* (Fox-TV): I just scored me some China white.

chinch *n.* [< ME] a miserly or mean person. [Orig. S.E.]

a1300, *ca1325, *ca1386, *a1450, *1570 in *OED.* **1949** *PADS* XI 19: *Chinch, chince*...A stingy person. **1962** Killens *Heard the Thunder* 50: "Come on man!" Bookworm said. "Don't be no chinch!" **1966, 1969** in *DARE.*

chin-chin *n.* [prob. Anglo-Chinese pidgin] talk; CHIN.

1877 "M. Twain," in *OEDS*. **1918** Roberts *Flying Fighter* 289: I went back and resumed the "chin-chin" with Kerr and the other boys.

chinch pad *n.* [*chinch* bug + PAD] *Black E.* (see quot.).
 1958 Hughes & Bontemps *Negro Folklore* 482: *Chinchpad:* A hotel, a cheap rooming house.

chinchy *adj.* [< ME] stingy. [Orig. S.E.]
 ca*1400, **1406, **1653 in *OED*. [1898** Green *Va. Folk-Speech: Chinching*...Miserly, niggardly.] **1906** *DN* III 130: *Chinchy*...Stingy, penurious. **1938** Haines *Tension* 61: The accounting office was chinchy as ever about pay. *Ibid.* 100: It seemed such a chinchy nickel-splitting trick. *Ibid.* 103: The pay's chinchy. **1947** Willingham *End As a Man* 82: They are chinchy...about money. **1953** Peterson *Take a Giant Step* 58: Well, bring it on over—you chinchy skunk. **1963** D. Tracy *Brass Ring* 254 [ref. to 1930's]: Anybody gonna spring for a drink or you gonna be chinchy about it? **1965–70** in *DARE*. **1977** *Santa Barbara* (Calif.) *News Press* (Jan. 11) B6: After shuddering over the prices of next to nothing breakfasts, I tote my own....It sounds chinchy, but makes good sense.

chincy var. CHINTZY.

'chine *n.* [fr. ma*chine*] *Black E.* an automobile or other motor vehicle. Also **sheen**.
 1968 Gover *JC* 63: Puts me in some veddy veddy Brit-tish kinda sheen, carries me away. **1970** *Current Slang* V 12: *Sheen,* n. A car. **1979** in Terkel *Amer. Dreams* 125: My friends are always talkin' about havin' a nice sheen. That's a nice car or van. **1985** Dye *Between Raindrops* 269: Get dis 'chine movin', Reporter-man.

Chinee *n.* **1.** a Chinese person; (as adj.) Chinese.—usu. used contemptuously.
 1853 in McCauley *With Perry* 64: The Chinese have a peculiar odour (not of Sanctity) about them...their calico clothing is perhaps the cause for the Chineys. **1876** Dixon *White Conquest* II 207: Never...have they known a Chinee resent an insult and return a blow. **1890** E. Custer *Guidon* 76 [ref. to 1868]: I ain't no Chinee, general. **1925** Faulkner *N.O. Sketches* 42: And one in the Chinee ocean. **1966** T.V. Olsen *Hard Men* 73: Like Chinee firecrackers. **1968** N.Y.C. man: Those are Chinee vegetables in there. All kinds of Chinee vegetables. **1972–79** T. Wolfe *Right Stuff* 33: Some howling supersonic Chinee. **1979** F. Thomas *Golden Bird* 27: If them heathen Chinee make their way up here, it will cost them.
 2. *Boxing.* (see quots.).
 1932 D. Runyon, in *Collier's* (Jan. 9) 8: A Chinee ducket being a complimentary ducket that is punched full of holes like Chinee money, and which you do not have to pay for. **1931–35** D. Runyon *Money* 211: A guy...gives me a Chinee for a fight at Madison Square Garden, a Chinee being a ducket with holes punched in it like old-fashioned Chink money.

Chinese *adj.* **1.** *Mil.* inferior; clumsy; backward.—usu. considered offensive.
 1898 in S. Crane *War Dispatches* 116: If a torpedo is caught within range in daylight, the fighting is all over before it begins. Any common little gunboat can dispose of it in a moment if the gunnery is not too Chinese. **1919** *Bttry. A* 122: Then to add to the troubles, the lumbering American caisson—or "Chinese caisson" as it was commonly called—went half over a bank near the new echelon, and so the rest of the time before daybreak had to be spent in pulling it onto the road again. **1971** Noel & Bush *Naval Terms* 62: Anything done "Chinese" style is done backward, or the reverse of normal.
 2. *Baseball.* (of a safe hit) gained with little skill; lucky.—esp. in phr. **Chinese home run.**—usu. considered offensive.
 1934 Weseen *Slang Dict.* 206: *Chinese blow*—A lucky hit; a hit ball that is just beyond reach. **1939–40** Tunis *Kid from Tomkinsville* 192: A man could get a "Chinese home run" by merely hitting 257 feet over the right field fence. **1982** Considine *Lang. of Sport* 12: *Chinese homer.* A short or "cheap" home run, as one hit out of a small ballpark or down a particularly short foul line. *a*1984 in Safire *Stand Corrected* 97: A "Chinese home run" is one or more of the following: a home run hit off the handle of the bat; a home run hit to the wrong field...; a very high pop fly home run that just drops into the stands. **1988** Mays & Sahadi *Say Hey* 70: You could hit a "Chinese" home run that didn't even go 260 feet—and you could hit a 450-foot ball for an out.
 3. *Stu.* drunk or high.
 1980 Birnbach *Preppy Hndbk.* 219: Get chinese v. Get really stoned.
 ¶ In phrase:
 ¶ **Chinese home run** see (2), above.

Chinese *adv.* ¶ In phrase **fly Chinese** [see CHINESE ACE] *Av.*

to fly an airplane without being able to maintain horizontal stability. *Joc.*
 1941 *AS* (Oct.) 165: *Flying Chinese.* One wing high—other wing low. (Air Corps).

Chinese ace *n.* [sugg. by the phr. *one wing low,* presumed to resemble Chinese speech-sounds or a Chinese person's name; cf. also CHINESE, *adj.*, 1] *Av.* an inept pilot.—usu. considered offensive. *Joc.*
 [**1925** Faulkner *Soldier's Pay* 1: Lowe, Julian...late a Flying Cadet, Umpteenth Squadron, Air Service, known as "One Wing" by the other embryonic aces of his flight.] **1928** *Pop. Sci. Mo.* (May) 72: That kiwi...washed out the only peppy crate in the outfit. He's a Chinese ace. **1933** Stewart *Airman Speech*. **1945** Hamann *Air Words: Chinese ace.* Pilot who flies with one wing low.

Chinese basket *n. Basketball.* (see quot.).—usu. considered offensive. Cf. CHINESE, *adj.*, 2.
 1980 Wielgus & Wolff *Basketball* 41: *Chinese basket* (*n*) A shot that enters the basket from the bottom of the cylinder before dropping back through. According to "the rules," it doesn't count.

Chinese fire drill *n.* **1.** a state or example of utter confusion.—usu. considered offensive.
 [**1942–45** in *So. Folk. Qly.* XIII (1949) 201: Fouled up like a Filipino at fire-drill.] **1952** Uris *Battle Cry* 132 [ref. to 1942]: You guys have been fouling up those field problems like a Chinese fire-drill. **1957** in J. Blake *The Joint* 183: The kid's as fouled up as a Chinese fire drill. **1958** Frankel *Band of Bros.* 7 [ref. to Korean War]: He's as fouled up as a chink fire drill. **1962** *AS* XXXVII 267: *Chinese fire drill*...An accident scene of great confusion, such as a school bus or cattle truck upset. **1969** *Current Slang* I & II 19: *Chinese fire drill, n.* A confused and unorganized formation; any chaotic event. (applied to doolies marching in parades and to meals.)—Air Force Academy cadets. **1971** Flanagan *Maggot* 54: I've seen Chinese fire drills look better than this herd trying to do a column right. **1984** Trotti *Phantom* 122: The base issues a general recall, turning mere madness into a Chinese fire drill. *a*1984 in Safire *Stand Corrected* 95: "Chinese fire drill" was already a cliché in the decade immediately after World War I among school children in Brooklyn. **1987** Norst & Black *Lethal Weapon* 29: It always happened at these Chinese fire drills.
 2. *Stu.* (see 1981 quot.).—usu. considered offensive.
 1972 N.Y.U. student: A *Chinese firedrill* is when you stop at a red light, everybody hops out, runs around the car and hops back in again before the light turns green. **1976** in *DARE* [ref. to early 1960's]. **1981** *N.Y. Times Mag.* (Sept. 20) 18 [ref. to 1960's]: "Chinese fire drill"...a collegiate prank in which a group of students would jump out of a car as it stopped for a red light, run around the car several times and jump back in just as the light turned to green. **1983** in *DARE* [ref. to *ca*1941].

Chinese gangway *n. Navy.* CHINESE LANDING, 2.—usu. considered offensive.
 1951 "W. Williams" *Enemy* 21 [ref. to WWII]: Moored *soixante-neuf* style. They used to call it Chinese gangway on the Asiatic station, but it's *soixante-neuf* to me.

Chinese home run see s.v. CHINESE, *adj.*, 2.

Chinese landing *n.* [see CHINESE ACE] **1.** *Av.* **a.** a clumsy or disastrous landing made with one wing of an airplane angled acutely toward the ground.—usu. considered offensive. Cf. CHINESE ACE.
 1918 *Yank Talk* 26: First Pilot: He made a Chinese landing. Second Ditto: Howzat? First Ditto: Wing low. **1928** *Pop. Sci. Mo.* (May) 72: "Chinese landing" and "Chinese ace" are derived from the Oriental flavor of the words "one wing low." *Ibid.* 141: A "Chinese three-point landing" is a crash landing, the three points in this case being the propeller hub, one wheel and one wing tip. **1933** Stewart *Airman Speech* 53: *Chinese landing.* A landing made with one wing tip dragging the ground. **1941** *AS* (Oct.) 164: *Chinese Landing.* One Wing Low. (Air Corps). **1944** *AAF Guide* 368: *Chinese landing*—landing with one wing low. **1956** Heflin *USAF Dict.* 113: *Chinese landing. Slang.* 1. A downwind landing. 2. A landing made with one wing of the landing airplane low, named after the mythical Chinese aviator, "Won Wing Low." **1965–66** *Air Officer's Guide* 436: *Chinese landing*—bad landing; named after mythical Chinese pilot, Won Wing Low.
 b. a downwind landing.
 1956 (quot. at 1.a., above). **1958** (quot. at 2, below).
 2. *Navy.* the bringing of a vessel alongside bow-to-stern or down-current.—usu. considered offensive.

1949 Morison *Naval Ops. in WWII* V 57 [ref. to 1920's]: Bagley made a skillful "Chinese landing." **1958** Cope & Dyer *Petty Officer's Guide* (ed. 2) 336: *Chinese landing.* (Slang). Bringing a boat or ship alongside another bow to stern. Bringing a ship alongside down current or landing an aircraft downwind. **1967** Lockwood *Subs* 155 [ref. to 1924]: It had to be done in what we called a "Chinese landing"—bow to stern instead of bow alongside bow—in order to pick up a two-ton spare propeller from the port side of the tender. *a*1984 in Safire *Stand Corrected* 96 [ref. to *a*1949]: Ship's boats in emergencies…sometimes made this "wrong end to" approach to the accommodation ladder and the coxswain's comrades would jeer him for having made a lubberly "Chinese landing."

Chineser *n. Mil.* a U.S. military serviceman on duty in China.
1941 Cruise *Apache Days* 298: This unique organization had been founded during the year [1901], in a spirit of good-humored ridicule of Chaffee's returned "Chinesers."

Chinese rot *n.* a disease of usu. unspecified kind, esp. a venereal disease.—usu. considered offensive.
1940 *AS* (Dec.) 450: *Chinese Rot.* Any social disease. **1942–48** in *So. Folk. Qly.* XIII (1949) 201: A…[sailor] may complain of having *the Chinese rot* (diarrhoea). **1952** Larson *Barnyard Folklore* 84: Venereal Disease…*Chinese rot.* **1968–69** in *DARE*: Imaginary diseases:…*Chinese rot.*

Chinese show *n. Army.* a diversionary demonstration or attack.—usu. considered offensive.
1918 *Sat. Eve. Post* (May 25) 59. **1918** I. Cobb *Glory of the Coming* 61: A feint by infantry…accompanied by…rockets and flares and star shells is a "Chinese show"—to quote the cant or trade name; I think the English first used the term, but our fellows have been borrowing ever since…last year. **1918** *Tex. Rev.* IV (Oct.) 82. [*1948 Partridge et al. *Forces' Slang*: *Chinese attack.* A lot of noise and activity to delude the enemy that an attack was brewing in that spot, and to distract his attention from the real one.]

Chinese tobacco *n.* opium. *Joc.*
1951 Fowler *Schnozzola* 57 [ref. to 1920's]: This was a song about an opium addict. Under the influence of a drug known as Chinese tobacco, or Wyoming ketchup, Willie had a dream, a very long dream. **1970** Landy *Underground Dict.* 49: *Chinese tobacco*…Opium.

chinfest *n.* [modeled on *gabfest* and *songfest*] a period of much talking or complaining.
1940 *AS* XV 204: *Chinfest.* A conference. **1946** *Amer. Leg. Mag.* (May) 26: "Beating the gums" was a "chinfest." **1955** Paxton *Cobweb* (film): You're a good man at a chinfest. **1969** in *DARE*.

Ching *n.* [fr. *Ch'ing* dynasty; cf. CHINK] a Chinese person. Also **Ching Ching.**
1898 Blatchford *Letters* 88: It gave us a very favorable impression of the clean and hard-working Ching-Ching. **1900** Markey *Iowa to Philippines* 193: The "Chings" declined to go further forward.

ching *n.* money; CHINK.
1904 H.N. Brown *Necromancer* 90: It certainly would pay….Yet prayer [is] the thing…/To bring about the ching.

chingus *n.* [alter. of DINGUS; def. 1 poss. infl. by Sp *chingar* 'to fuck'] **1.** the penis.
1953 *ATS* (ed. 2) 121: Male Pudendum…*chingus.* **1967** Schmidt *Lexicon of Sex* 45: *Chingus*…The phallus.
2. thingumajig.
1982 Dickson *Words* 148.

chin-jaw *n.* idle talk.
1942 *AS* (Dec.) 221: *Chinjaw.* Small talk; social conversation; its nearest literary equivalent may be "palaver."

Chink *n.* [perh. alter. of *Ch'ing* dynasty] **1.a.** a Chinese person.—usu. used contemptuously. Also as adj. Also **chinky.** [1790 quot. is an Anglicized proper name.]
[**1790** in E. Snow *Adventures* 294: Chinqui…[a] Chinese.] **1878** Barry *Up & Down* 51: The first Chinese war with Britain had broken out, and there was every appearance of plenty of fun to be shortly had with the Chinkies. *1879 in *OEDS*: Chinkie. **1891** Campbell, Knox & Byrnes *Darkness & Daylight* 569: I can cook a pill just as well as a Chink (Chinaman). **1892** Norr *China Town* 6: T'ell with the Chinks. **1894** Gardner *Doctor & Devil* 40: I'd rather be living with a "Chink," as the Sixth Warders call Chinamen, than be a woman of the town. **1895** Townsend *Daughter of Tenements* 228: You're a pretty slick Chink. I'll see about that reward. **1897** A. Lewis *Wolfville* 43: Among other things, thar's a Chink runnin' a laundry an' a-doin' of our washin'. **1902**

Dunne *Observations by Mr. Dooley* 218: Father Kelly say th' Agyptians done things we cuddn't do an' th' Romans put up skyscrapers an' aven th' Chinks had tillyphones an' phony-grafts. **1908** in H.C. Fisher *A. Mutt* 77: The third day of our journey finds us in this beautiful Chink village. **1911** Runyon *Tents of Trouble* 123: Me and McMurtrie and Masters, sweatin' an army o' Chinks. **1919** Kelly *What Outfit?* 42: They had a Chinese steward named Yung Kow, and that slant-eyed chink hid most of the stuff we were supposed to eat. **1923** H.L. Foster *Beachcomber* 178: If it was not for the Chinks,…this peninsula wouldn't be worth a cent. **1925** in Hammett *Knockover* 159: Maybe those fella's'll swap papers wit' a couple Chink sailors. **1928** Carr *Rampant Age* 121: Learned from the Chinkies. **1940** J.T. Farrell *Father & Son* 203: Drink enough of this and you won't want to be playin' hokum kari, as the Chinkees say. **1959** Mailer *Advts.* 353: A certain Chinkie. **1974** Charyn *Blue Eyes* 14: Chinktown gamblers hired the Chinaman to protect their fan-tan games. **1976** *Nat. Lampoon* (June) 71: The little Chinkies are setting up camps in the national parks out west. **1978** T.H. White *In Search* 17 [ref. to *ca*1922]: The only Chinese I had ever seen was the Chinese laundryman on Erie Street, whom we taunted, as all children did, with the call of "Chinkee, Chinkee, Chinaman." **1980** *N.Y. Daily News* (Sept. 5) 5: Pekin, Ill. (AP)—A decision by school officials to change Pekin High School's [team] nickname from Chinks to Dragons has triggered a student boycott and a pledge by pupils to restore the name. **1984–88** Hackworth & Sherman *About Face* 104: A lot of artillery (both Chink and American).
b. any East Asian person.—usu. used contemptuously.
1942 Algren *Morning* 223: "Why don't you hex Hitler, Polack?"…"I'm doin' that too,…'n what's more, I'm doin' the Chinks too. For free." **1954** in *Social Problems* II (1955) 168: We're proud of our fraternity, and we aren't going to turn it into a rabble for chinks and Niggers. **1963** Blechman *Camp Omongo* 22: "Those Chinks?…They'll never…stand up to the Americans." "They're not Chinks. They're Japs." "What's the difference?…They're yellow, ain't they?" **1964–66** R. Stone *Hall of Mirrors* 317: When your American soldier fighting today drops a napalm bomb on a cluster of gibbering chinks, it's a bomb with a heart. **1970** *Current Slang* V 15: *Chink,* n. and adj. Vietnamese. **1981** Spears *Slang & Euphem.* 71: *Chink*…Recently derogatory for a Vietnamese. **1984** J.R. Reeves *Mekong* 117: How do you know he's not an English-speaking Vietnamese? A Chink that infiltrated us?
2. the Chinese language.—usu. used contemptuously.
1936 Mackenzie *Living Rough* 117: His songs are sung in every language, in Bohunk, in Wop, in Chink, in Spick, in every language.
3. *Hunting.* a ring-necked pheasant.—usu. considered offensive.
1940, 1957, 1966–67 in *DARE*.

chink *n.* cash; money.
*1698–99 "B.E." *Dict. Canting Crew*: *Chink,*…Money, because it chinks in the pocket. *1774 in R. Palmer *Sound of History* 77: Then in comes the farmer with his hands full of chink. *1785 Grose *Vulgar Tongue*: *Chink.* Money. **1812** in Neeser *Naval Ballads* 113: We told 'em then to save their chink. **1821** Waln *Hermit in Phila.* 26: Out with *the chink.* **1833** A. Greene *Duckworth* I 206: They fetch us the chink, the yaller boys and the white. **1834** in Foner *Labor Songs* 28: Till the rattle of the *chink*/Decided him for ever. **1834** *Davy Crockett's Almanack* (1835) 4: I thought that if all the hills there were pure chink, and all belonged to me, I would give them if I could just talk to her as I wanted to. **1841** [Mercier] *Man-of-War* 234: Fork me over that 'ere trifle of chink. **1848** Bartlett *Amer.*: *Chink.* A term for money; used in various parts of England as well as in the United States. *ca*1850 in Jackson *Early Songs of Uncle Sam* 227: Loafing about and spending his chink,/ And…taking too much rum. **1857** Willcox *Faca* 110: Jack…deposits his chink in the hands of this *friend of his'n.* **1859** Matsell *Vocab.* 18: *Chink.* Money. **1861** in Lowell *Poetical Works* 226: Because, ye see, 't's the fashion here to sign an' not to think/A critter 'd be so sordid ez to ax 'em for the chink. **1862** in Davidson *Old West* 171: We've lost sight of the main point—your "chink." **1868** Williams *Black-Eyed Beauty* 22: Well, won't he come down with any more chink? **1884** *Life* (Jan. 17) 33: Y' betcher coldest chink. **1884** Field *Sharps & Flats* I 186: I'm mad to think that you should think/That I am such a greeny/To let you lavish all the chink/On Mrs. Nicolini. **1898** Green *Va. Folk-Speech* 84: *Chink,* n. Money. **1904** *Life in Sing Sing* 246: *Chink*…money. **1938–39** Dos Passos *Young Man* 57: Ain't goin' to be no trouble if you slip me some chink. I can knock the goddam block off either one of you punks if it's trouble you want. **1966** in *DARE*.

chinks *n.* [fr. CHINK] Chinese cuisine; Chinese food.—usu. considered offensive.
1948 I. Shulman *Cry Tough!* 27: Whatever you want. Spaghetti.

Chinks. Steaks. **1951** Robbins *Danny Fisher* 105: Maybe we'll get some chinks. **1956** "T. Betts" *Across the Board* 309: After the show we ate chinks. **1960** Bluestone *Cully* 6: Last night I was eatin' Chinks with my girl. **1967** Flicker *President's Analyst* (film): I thought we could drive into New York tonight and eat Chinks. **1971** Faust *Willy Remembers* 107: First we went out for chinks' on Mott Street.

chin music *n.* **1.** talk, esp. impudent talk.
  1821–26 Stewart *Man-of-War's-Man* I 120: Tuts, man, yon's a' blarney.— mere chin music, that cam in at the tae lug, and gaed out at the ither. **1836** in *DAE.* **1837** *Davy Crockett's Almanack* I (No. 4) 13: Says I, give us none of your chin music. **1873** Small *Douglass & Mule* 84: "Who's shoein' dis yer mule?…" replied Fred, getting tired of his chin-music. **1877** Bartlett *Amer.* (ed. 4) 779: *Chin-music.* Impudent talk; flippant garrulity. **1885** Chadwick *Fielding* 24: Last season an element of weakness…prevailed in the form of "chin-music" and ill-natured "chaffing," in which base-players pretty generally took part. **1909** "O. Henry" *Roads* 395: Of course, I'm awfully obliged to you for making that chin-music to her of evenings. **1936** Sandburg *People* 90: I don't believe a word you say/But I love to listen/To your sweet harmonica/To your chin-music. **1942** *Leatherneck* (Nov.) 144: *Chin Music*—Talking. **1954** Schulberg *Waterfront* 130: Then knock off the chin music. **1955** McGovern *Fräulein* 135: One lieutenant started to give them some chin music.
  2. *Baseball.* a pitch thrown near a batter's chin.
  1969 Bouton *Ball Four* 68: The beanball (it's sometimes called "chin music") is a weapon. Hitters don't like pitchers throwing at them. **1983** L. Frank *Hardball* 106: That is, he wants to "play some chin music" (throw at his chin). **1993** *Seinfeld* (NBC-TV): I threw *inside*…little chin music.

chin-music *v.* to talk or chat.
  1962 in Jackson *The Life* 163: I'm sitting up there chin-musicking with another broad.

chinny *adj.* garrulous.
  1883 Hay *Bread-Winners* 117: He hated these "chinny bummers"…who talked about "State help and self-help" over their beers. **1899** Cullen *Tales* 46: This chinny sport jumped up and yelled, "Twenty to one he don't last the ninth round."

Chino *n.* [Sp] Esp. *Mil.* a Chinese person.—now usu. considered offensive.
  [**1885** in Lummis *Letters* 294: One was called a Chino, which means a certain cross between Indian and negro.] **1898** *Oregon in Philippines* 12: Words added to the regimental vocabulary, "Manana," Googoo, Adios,…Youdamnedchino. **1899** *Harper's Wkly.* (June 17) 592: Now, "Chinos," get along with you. **1900** Reeves *Bamboo Tales* 20: To cap the climax, he taught poor "Chino" to stand at attention. **1900** McManus *Soldier Life* 26: These Chinamen, or Chinos, as they are invariably styled in the Orient…are under contract to the army, specifically as litter-bearers….They are a jolly, rollicksome lot—these Chino coolies. **1905** Devins *Philippines* 51: Every man from the Flowery Kingdom is a "Chino," the Spanish for Chinese, and the word "Chinaman" is never heard in the Philippines. **1915** Garrett *Army Ballads* 82 [ref. to 1900]: A mango knife—or opium/For Chinos bad and bold. **1933** in Thomason *Stories* 288: We agreed that the Chinos had some very clever tricks. **1936** *AS* (Apr.) 119: *Chino.* A Chinese.

chin-skinner *n. Baseball.* a pitch thrown near a batter's chin.
  1961 Brosnan *Pennant Race* 20: Waste all pitches but the fast ball and use it to jam him with "chin-skinners."

chin-splitter *n.* a narrow goatee.
  1906 Ford *Shorty McCabe* 221: A pair of white Chaunceys and a frosted chin-splitter.

chin tackle *n. Naut.* a beard.
  ca1875 Williams *Binnacle Jack* 13: I jist dreamed as little Scratchbook the bos'n had tied me in his chin tackle.

chintz *n.* [var. of CHINCH] a stingy person. Also **chince.**
  1949 *PADS* XI 19: *Chinch, chince*…A stingy person. *a*1989 C.S. Crawford *Four Deuces* 169: Stratemeyer was no chintz when it came to awarding medals.

chintz *adj.* CHINTZY.
  1963 in *Uncle Scrooge* #149 (unp.): Scrooge McDuck is chintz!

chintzy *adj.* [var. of CHINCHY infl. by S.E. *chintz*] **1.** miserly; stingy. Also vars.
  1902 in *OEDS* I. **1940** in Wentworth *ADD*: Chinsy, -cy. **1944** Busch *Dream of Home* 13: Nobody's never been glad to see that chincy son-of-a-bitch. **1947** Schulberg *Harder They Fall* 95: You are a chintzy, turd-

eating butcher! **1949** *PADS* XI 5: Stingy…chintzy. **1960** Stadley *Barbarians* 26: I'll take a hamburger, only don't be so chintzy with the mayonnaise and pickles. **1960** Swarthout *Where Boys Are* 37: She said with all TV's loot it was chintzy of him not to at least give me a blast on the beach. **1961** Brosnan *Pennant Race* 245: How chintzy can they get? **1966–67** Harvey *Air War* 19: There are plenty of customers who aren't chincy about wanting to taste their drinks! **1977** in Curry *River's in My Blood* 136: You just want that damn duck yourself, you chintzy sucker. **1990** *CBS This Morning* (CBS-TV) (Apr. 4): Japan builds up business abroad by being chintzy to the folks back home.
  2. of poor quality; cheap; contemptible.
  1959 Gault *Drag Strip* 51: It's about as chintzy a layout as —. **1960** Bluestone *Cully* 190: Thinking how chintzy it was to bug out on Croman. **1965** Petrakis *Pericles* 128: All that time…you make only one chintzy little bite into that delicious sweet roll. **1965** Spillane *Killer Mine* 60: Hymie used to plan little chintzy jobs and leave them up to Noisy to pull off. **1965–70** in *DARE.* **1970** E. Thompson *Garden of Sand* 59: That's what I give chincy dark meat. **1993** *TV Guide* (Jan. 16) 7: The dramatizations are chintzy.

chinwag *n.* a chat; conversation. Also as *v.*
  1879 in Partridge *DSUE* (ed. 8) 208: I'd just like to have a bit of chin-wag with you on the quiet. **1898** in Ware *Passing English* 73: I have…been…no further from the tent than to the next one for a "chin-wag." **1987** *Daily Beacon* (Univ. Tenn.) (Mar. 4) 4: A bit of chin-wag 'round the oil heater. **1987** Weiser & Stone *Wall St.* (film): I wouldn't be sitting around chinwagging.

chinwork *n.* talk.
  1973 Gwaltney *Destiny's Chickens* 136: Time for the two of us to have a little chin-work, face-to-face, boy.

Chip *n.* [vocalization of initialism CHP] an officer of the California Highway Patrol. Also **chippy.** [The NBC-TV adventure series that popularized the name premiered on Sept. 15, 1977, and ran until July 17, 1983.]
  1977 *CHiPs* (NBC-TV series). **1977** *L.A. Times* (Sept. 15) IV 27: California Highway Patrolmen, in case you didn't know…are called "chippies." **1978** *New West* (Jan. 30) 56: The speeders outnumber the chippies by something like 100,000 to 1. **1992** G. Trudeau *Doonesbury* (synd. cartoon strip) (Sept. 30): How long you been a Chip, babe? **1993** *Donahue* (NBC-TV): "You also have an attitude about Chips." "Triple-A with a badge they call 'em."

chip *n.* **1.** a child; youngster; SQUIRT.
  1698–99 "B.E." *Dict. Canting Crew*: Chip, a child. **1850** Melville *Moby-Dick* ch. iii: That's a purty long sarmon for a chip that rips a little now and then.
  2. a piece of money; (*pl.*) money; now esp. in phr. **in the chips** having much money.
  1840 *Spirit of Times* (Apr. 11) 61: A…horse…on whom he is perfectly willing to "pile the chips" for any distance. **1857** in Thornton *Amer. Gloss.* II 971: All the browns his uncle lent him/All the chips and dust and clinkers. **1859** Matsell *Vocab.* 19: *Chips.* Money. **1880** in M. Lewis *Mining Frontier* 129: But anyhow, he got left without a chip, an' a granger then took him home an' set him to tendin' hogs. **1896** Ade *Artie* 25: Well, where did you get your chips to come in here? **1899** Cullen *Tales* 79: As he'll be the bum outsider I'm going to spin a few chips on him. **1905** Hobart *Search Me* 18: I'm a few chips shy myself. **1935** O'Hara *Butterfield 8* 11: I am in the chips. **1940** in A. Banks *First-Person* 106: Chickenfeed. I could make more chips shooting craps and playing poker. **1940** Zinberg *Walk Hard* 26: This is one racket where they pay off in big chips. **1942** Chandler *High Window* 350: I haven't been in the chips lately. **1942** "E. Queen" *Calamity Town* 173: Q.—Does the defendant owe you a single dollar? A.—Not a chip. **1943** in Ruhm *Detective* 362: I was only trying to get some chips to buy myself something to eat. **1945** Yordan *Dillinger* (film): When the heat cools off I'll be back in the chips. **1949** *The Set-Up* (film): Aaah, dames. They'll only stick by ya when you're in the chips. **1955** Q. Reynolds *HQ* 82: But now he's in the big chips. **1957** Wilbur & Veiller *Monkey on My Back* (film): Are you in the chips? **1985** C. Busch *Vampire Lesbians* 72: Looks like you're in the chips.
  3. *Journ.* (see quot.).
  1889 Barrère & Leland *Dict. Slang* I 244: Local items in newspapers are called *chips*, and sometimes the term is applied to the reporter who collects them.
  4.a. a girl or young woman.
  1892 Norr *China Town* 62: Well, if you're not the luckiest chip in the world to strike "Chuck" Connors to-night! **1895** Townsend *Fadden & Others* 51: Dere is a little chip…wot dusts der rooms, and tings like

dat....But she ain't my size. **1899** A.H. Lewis *Sandburrs* 64: I buy meself an [my] chip d' retoin tickets, see! *Ibid.* 285: Her name's Annie, an' she's a proper straight chip. **1903** in Boni *Gilded Age* 24: She was a Saratoga chip. **1915** Poole *Harbor* 25 [ref. to 1890's]: "The Chips" were three small admiring girls....We got the term from the stout coachman in the barn who used it with a fine sweeping contempt that included all his lady friends. **1959–60** R. Reisner *Jazz Titans* 152: *Chip:* girl.

b. a sexually promiscuous woman, esp. a prostitute.

1892 Norr *China Town* 29: Doctor's got ten new girls from Philadelphia....Why, you can't walk a step without brushing up against some "chips." **1915** Howard *God's Man* 134: Is she a reg'lar looker? No chips, you know. None of your chewing gum broadies. **1917** in Rossano *Price of Honor* 53: Parading around the streets of Paris, drunk as lords, with a vile looking "chip" on each arm. **1924** Wilstach *Anecdota Erotica* 32: Some men have chips on their shoulders; others prefer them on their laps. **1955** Robbins *79 Park Ave.* 41: I can get a thousand cheap chips like you to come with me.

5. *Und.* a till, cashbox, or cash register.

1914 Jackson & Hellyer *Crim. Slang* 23: *Chip*...A cashbox, a till; a cash drawer without belling device. A cash receptacle with belling device is called a "combination chip," or a "damper," or a "dinger." **1927** *AS* II (Mar.) 282: *Chip*—A cash register. **1929** Booth *Stealing Through Life* 300 [ref. to *ca*1920]: Try that chip. See if it's sloughed. Make it snappy!

6. a *chip on (one's) shoulder*, below.

1966 Little *Bold & Lonely* 183: You wearing a chip for me, Roman?

¶ In phrases:

¶ **call in (someone's) chips** to challenge (someone) openly.

1881 Ingraham *Buffalo Bill from Boyhood* 98: "We'll go up and call in their chips, Billy," was the universal decision.

¶ **chip on (one's) shoulder** a belligerent attitude. Now *colloq.*

1830 in *DA* 316: When two churlish boys were *determined* to fight, a *chip* would be placed on the shoulder of one, and the other determined to knock it off at his peril. **1870** in *DA.* **1924** (quot. at (**4.b.**), above).

¶ **in the chips** see (**2**), above.

¶ **pass** [or **hand** or **cash**] **in (one's) chips, 1.a.** to die.

1879 in *OEDS*: If you wish to express the demise of a friend...in Southern Colorado...it would be more elegant to say that he'd "passed in his chips." **1884** in *DA*: He one day passed in his chips. **1890** E. Custer *Guidon* 282 [ref. to 1868]: Such a one will "hand in his chips" soon if he don't leave John Barleycorn alone. **1942** *ATS* 132: Die...*cash in one's checks* or *chips*. **1986** Ark. man, age 33: He's talking like he's ready to cash in his chips.

b. to commit suicide.

1967 [Beck] *Pimp* 299: I've started to cash in my chips a dozen times. **1971** Murphy & Gentry *Second in Command* 213: I'm afraid he's going to try to do something stupid, like cash in his chips. **1986** Middlesboro, Ky., woman, age 29: When you *cash in your chips* you commit suicide.

c. to kill (someone). [1984 quot. is proleptic.]

1984 Caunitz *Police Plaza* 173: I think they've cashed in my chips for me. **1986** Former SP4, U.S. Army, age 34: I was in a bar in Taiwan and a guy was trying to make time with the bar girl. Then her boyfriend says, "You cut in on Fifi and I'll cash in your chips for you." That must have been in 1972.

2. to change (one's) ways.

1895 in J.I. White *Git Along Dogies* 66: I'm going to get [religion]. You had better...cash in your chips with me.

¶ **when the chips are down** at a critical or decisive moment; (*also*) when all is said and done.

1942 in Galewitz *Great Comics* 267: However, when the chips were down, this kid proved herself big league all the way. **1954** in F. Brown *Honeymoon* 69: When the chips are down, though, it was still the foot soldier...that had to take the ground and hold it. **1992** *Good Morning America* (ABC-TV) (Dec. 23): When the chips were down, he...stuck by his principles.

chip *v.* **1.** to utter a word; speak.

1887 Francis *Saddle & Moccasin* 124: Now you let me do the talking...don't you chip! **1972** Wambaugh *Blue Knight* 92: Next time, don't start chipping with them. No speeches, please!

2. *Poker.* to bet; wager.

1876 Cody & Arlington *Life on Border* 41: I'll chip ten dollars. (*Puts up money.*) **1878** Hart *Sazerac* 86: "Wal, you've chipped," observed the Chair, "now make your play." **1890** Quinn *Fools of Fortune* 218: *Chipping, or to Chip.*—Is synonymous with betting. Thus a [poker] player,

instead of saying "I bet" may say "I chip" so much.

3. to filch.

1938 *AS* (Apr.) 151: *Chip.* To steal, kipe.

4. [short for CHIPPY, *v.*, 1] *Narc.* **a.** CHIPPY, *v.*, 1. Also trans.

1964 in Jackson *Swim Like Me* 91: I thought I could chip and never get hooked. **1966** J. Mills *Needle Park* 35 [ref. to 1964]: He was only "chipping," using drugs occasionally when they were handy, and had not yet acquired a habit. **1968** Bloomquist *Marijuana* 157: *Chip.* To play around with a drug; to use drugs sporadically. **1972** Smith & Gay *Don't Try It* 199: I'm not strung out, I'm just chipping. **1986** Merkin *Zombie Jamboree* 213: He chipped smack. **1987** Norst & Black *Lethal Weapon* 127: "Does she use?" "Chips now and again."

b. to inject (heroin or the like) into a muscle rather than a vein; SKINPOP.

1966 Brunner *Face of Night* 231: *Chip*—to inject drugs under the skin instead of into a vein. A "chipper" is an addict who takes drug in this way. **1973** Schiano & Burton *Solo* 151: We only chip junk, no mainlining.

5. to be sexually unfaithful.

1978 Selby *Requiem* 175: She starts chippin with some guy—there aint no cunt in the world that wont chippie onya.

¶ In phrase:

¶ **chip (one's) teeth** [or **china** or **gums**] Esp. *Navy.* to complain; beat (one's) gums.

1944 (quot. at CHINA, 2). **1958** McCulloch *Woods Wds.*: *Chipping their teeth*—said of a group of men sitting around the bunkhouse doing a great deal of talking. **1968–69** in *DARE*: Chip your teeth. **1972** Wambaugh *Blue Knight* 296: Okay, okay, quit chipping your teeth. You complain more than any kid I ever saw. **1982** T.C. Mason *Battleship* 254 [ref. to WWII]: Through it all, the navy enlisted man exercised his right to "chip his gums." **1992** Mowry *Way Past Cool* 228: Seem like...y'all was chippin' your goddamn teeth bout...pizzas.

chiphead *n.* a computer enthusiast.

1982 in *Time* (Jan. 3, 1983) 18: I'm not a chiphead...but if you don't keep up with the new developments...you're not going to have the competitive edge. **1983** in P. Dickson *Slang!* 72: A Chiphead will rhapsodize endlessly about his...[computer]. A Chiphead swears computers are the greatest things since food and sex. **1986** Gilmour *Pretty in Pink* 47: It had to be some chip-head fooling around, and he'd obviously cut into the wrong computer.

chip in *n.* a turn to speak.

1876 in W.A. Graham *Custer Myth* 179: However, 'twasn't my "chip in," so I said nothing.

chip in *v.* **1.a.** to contribute (money). Now *colloq.*

1861 in *DA*. **1880** J.M. Drake *Fast & Loose* 72: We "chipped in" and purchased several instruments. **1887** DeVol *Gambler* 41: The collection amounted to considerable, and I chipped in my share liberally. **1891** McCann & Jarrold *Odds & Ends* 43: The boys chipped in 50 cents a piece every Saturday night. **1893** James *Mavrick* 59: They all chipped in and bought one of the best to be had. **1895** in Ade *Chicago Stories* 155: Ev'y hotel an' resta'nt 'roun' here chips in a few dollahs. **1897** *Cosmopolitan* (Mar.) 558: A number of them...chipped in to have him buried decent. **1917–20** in J.M. Hunter *Trail Drivers* I 286: They passed an empty cigar box and all "chipped in."

b. to give (advice, a suggestion, or the like).

1903 A.H. Lewis *Boss* 71: I'll chip you in this piece of advice.

2. to contribute a remark, a service, etc.; to take part; to have a say.

1871 "M. Twain" *Roughing It* 253: Pard, he was a great loss to this town. It would please the boys if you could chip in something like that and do him justice. *Ibid.* 268: I'll be there, and chip in and help. **1878** B. Harte *Drift* 208: If he'd missed her, I'd have chipped in. Thar warn't no sense in my doing his duty unless he failed. **1884** in Lummis *Letters* 5: A...fellow came around the corner and chipped in. **1912** Lowrie *Prison* 145: Did this guy chip in and get y'r t' come after them sheets, too?

chipper *v. Narc.* CHIPPY, *v.*, 1.

1971 *Go Ask Alice* 74: We're certainly not going to chipper around any more.

chippy *n.* **1.a.** a youngster.

1877 Wheeler *Deadwood Dick, Pr. of Road* 77: Not all owing to that, chippy. **1937** Di Donato *Concrete* 92: "Such a sad little chippie is he," said Nazone.

b. a novice; a beginner; a greenhorn. See also 1924 and

1926 quots. at **(c)**, below.

1899 *Sat. Eve. Post* (July 1) 3: What'll she do to this chippy runner [a locomotive engineer on his first run]? **1961** Scarne *Comp. Guide to Gambling* 675: *Chippy* (1) A sucker (2) An inexperienced player. **1970** Rudensky & Riley *Gonif* 50: They had so many damn clay-assed, two-bit chippies in Atlanta [Federal Penitentiary], the screws actually seemed to welcome a con with a reputation.

c. *Narc.* an occasional user of morphine, heroin, etc., who is not yet addicted.

1924 Henderson *Keys to Crookdom* 400: *Chippy-user*—one who uses narcotics moderately. **1926** *N.Y. Times* 8:20: If they are wise, they will be content to be "chippy" users or those who only "play with the white stuff" instead of addicts. **1936** Duncan *Over the Wall* 21 [ref. to 1918]: Chloroform sniffers...belonged to the riff-raff element of the dope chippeys. **1957** in Rosset *Evergreen* 115: She's no chippie, man!...She takes all she can get, man. **1966** S. Harris *Hellhole* 94: You're a lousy junkie, Joyce. You're not a chippy any more. **1971** *Inter. Jour. Addictions* VI 6: So it is not the same feeling when you come out of the joint as it was when you were a chippy.

d. [elliptical for *chippy habit*] *Narc.* a mild or incipient addiction to heroin or a similar drug.

1964 Larner & Tefferteller *Addict* 93: I still got a small habit, which we call a chippy. **1966** Mills *Needle Park* 43: At the moment...he had only a chippy and got most of the heroin he needed by hanging around other addicts who occasionally turned him on with a taste. **1971** *Inter. Jour. Addictions* VI 6: What is a "chippy?"...A chippy is a mild mental sickness. You say I am going to try one shot and there is nothing going to happen because it is only one shot. *Ibid.* 7: It's like when you have a chippy, it's in your mind. **1974** Dubinsky & Standora *Decoy Cop* 65: The question is whether he's got a chippy or has a Jones.

2.a. a young woman; a girl.—now *esp. Black E.*

1890 in *DA:* The leading dudes and chippies of Europe had [the influenza] and pulled through all right. **1891** Maitland *Amer. Slang Dict.* 64: *Chippy*, a young girl; not a complimentary term. **1895** Townsend *Fadden & Others* 93: Down where I useter live I was de boss jollier wid de chippies, but dis time I was nottin but a farmer. **1904** *Life in Sing Sing* 247: *Chippy*. A young girl. **1929** T. Gordon *Born to Be* 227: I can't understand what you men want with these little chippies. They ain't no woman who knows what love is all about until she's at least thirty. **1944** Burley *Hndbk. of Jive* 25: The cats and the chippies were all knocking a nod. **1964** Rhodes *Chosen Few* 148: She goes pretty deep for a chippy, you know? **1970** Quammen *Walk the Line* 57: Isn't it no wonder them chippies crave your body? **1972** P. Thomas *Savior* 3: I measured them against the cats and chippies from my time. **1981** N.Y.C. woman, age 56: You certainly don't look your age. You look like a chippy!

b. a sexually promiscuous woman; *(esp.)* a prostitute.—occ. constr. with *piece of.* [Prob. the orig. sense.]

1886 in *AS* (Feb. 1950) 31: This class of females are known by the gang as "Chippies," and most of them come from the slums. *ca***1889** E. Field *Bangin' on Rhine* st. iii: Full many a chippy had he banged, and many a whore, 'tis said. **1897** Norris *Vandover* 300: I shook those chippies. I sized them up right away....They were no good. **1898** Atherton *Californians* 36: "Why do they wear so many frizzes, and sailor hats on one side?" "They're chippies....They work all day and promenade with their beaux all evening." **1902** Clapin *Americanisms* 111: *Chippy*. A derogatory name for a young girl or woman of a questionable character. *a***1904–11** Phillips *Susan Lenox* II 155: I manage to pick up a living in spite of the damn chippies. I don't see why the hell they don't go into the business regular and make something out of it, instead of loving free. **1930** Fredenburgh *Soldiers March* 16: That lousy Navy of ours is all at Hingham chasing chippies. **1942** McAtee *Supp. to Grant Co. Dial.* 3 [ref. to 1890's]: *Chippy*, n., prostitute. **1952** H. Grey *Hoods* 166: I spent more than that every night, on a piece of chippy. **1953** R. Wright *Outsider* 97: They all think you're dead, and here you are in a cat house with the chippies. **1954** L. Armstrong *Satchmo* 94: I had been brought up around the honky-tonks on Liberty and Perdido where life was just about the same as it was in Storyville except that the chippies were cheaper. **1956** Metalious *Peyton Place* 195: Running out every night to go see that little chippy. **1958** J. Ward *Buchanan* 27: Plucked one of Maude's chippies right outta the coop! **1958** Frankel *Band of Bros.* 17: Y' smell like a Honolulu chippie after a Satiddy-night shore leave! **1962** T. Berger *Reinhart* 330: No sooner do I turn my back than you bring in your chippies. **1964** Warburg *Long Road* 46 [ref. to *ca*1918]: Not with a prostitute...but with some "chippie," meaning some little working girl whom he might pick up and seduce. **1967** Taggart *Reunion* 81: Who was it? Some little chippy you picked up hitchhiking? [**1984** G. Legman, in *Maledicta* VIII (1985) 79: Every French slang dictionary for

two centuries back...and every French-speaking person today, is aware of the common French word *chippie* (or *chipie*) for an evil-tempered (formerly immoral) woman.] **1992** N. Cohn *Heart of World* 235: *Chippy*, her father called her. *Go pull a train.*

c. (see quot.).

1938 in A. Lomax *Mr. Jelly Roll* 23 [ref. to N.O., 1890's]: There were women standing in their cribs with their chippies on—a crib is a room about seven feet wide and a chippie is a dress that [whores] wore, knee length and very easy to disrobe.

3. *R.R.* a narrow-gauge track, car, or train.

1918 *DN* V 23: *Chippy*, n....a narrow gauge railroad track or the train that runs on it. General in the Coeur d'Alenes. **1945** Hubbard *R.R. Ave.* 337: *Chippies*—Narrow-gauge cars.

4. *Basketball.* an easy shot made unopposed from near the basket.

1976 *Webster's Sports Dict.* 77. **1980** Pearl *Slang Dict.: Chippie n....*(Basketball) an unblocked shot.

5. see CHIP.

chippy *v.* **1.** *Narc.* to use heroin, cocaine, or similar drugs occasionally and without becoming addicted.

1924 Henderson *Keys to Crookdom* 400: *To chippy with coke*—To use cocaine occasionally. **1952** in W.S. Burroughs *Letters* 104: I chippy around but haven't been hooked in a year now. **1959** in Blake *Joint* 225: Pseudo-hipster, digs jazz musicians if not their music, aspires to the jee-sunk and chippys with it. **1959–60** R. Reisner *Jazz Titans* 152: *Chippie*: to dabble with narcotics; to take subcutaneous injections once in a while. **1966** Braly *On Yard* 199: He had been chippying with heavy. **1966** S. Harris *Hellhole* 94: I chippied before this—as many pills as I was taking, I wasn't an addict before I got cut. But then, after, I wanted to be high all the time.

2. to be sexually promiscuous or unfaithful; *(also)* to whore. [Used fig. in 1991 quot.]

1930 in *DARE:* You can't chippy on me. **1936** Duncan *Over the Wall* 144: Aren't you afraid that if I get down there alone with Gwen, I'll chippey on you? **1942–49** Goldin et al. *DAUL* 43. **1958** Gilbert *Vice Trap* 23: Thinking she was chippying on somebody was so funny. **1963** Bruce *Essential Lenny* 195: I'm honest, and when I chippy on her I just *gotta* tell her. **1970** Thackrey *Thief* 59: At first, after the two of us got busted up, I thought it was just because of my chippying around, you know? **1986** Univ. Tenn. grad. student: To *chippy around* means to whore around. **1991** *N.Y. Times Mag.* (May 5) 69: We had hired KKR and we should stay married. Why chippy around and get somebody else?

3. to work halfheartedly or without serious purpose.

1974 Angelou *Gather Together* 24 [ref. to 1945]: Don't chippy at anything. Anything worth having is worth working for.

chippy-chaser *n.* a whoremonger or philanderer.

1891 Maitland *Amer. Slang Dict.* 64: Chippy-Chasers are the well-dressed loafers who lie in wait for shopgirls and school children. **1913** W. Wilson *Hell in Nebr.* 359: Nor have I been a "chippy-chaser" on the dark streets of Lincoln. **1928** Dahlberg *Bottom Dogs* 18: He was sometimes a pimp, always a chippie-chaser. **1928** MacArthur *War Bugs* 206: Mr. Papolis was a Greek chippy-chaser. **1938** "E. Queen" *4 Hearts* 18: Gambler, chippy-chaser, dipsomaniac. **1942** McAtee *Supp. to Grant Co. Dial.* 3 [ref. to 1890's]: *Chippy-chaser*, n., one addicted to whoring. **1962** Crump *Killer* 73: That chippie-chaser! **1966** Gallery *Start Engines* 50: He is a chippy chaser and a fanny pincher, too, he is. **1974** Price *Wanderers* 107: Chippy chaser!

chippy-chasing *n.* whoring or philandering.

1915 Howard *God's Man* 138: While regular fellows are young, they have a hell of a time chippy-chasing—glorious jags with the ladies down the line.

chippy house *n.* a brothel. Also **chippy joint.**

1924 Anderson & Stallings *What Price Glory?* 104 [ref. to 1918]: It was old Smoke Plangetch, who was killed in 1913 in a chippie joint in Yokohama. **1929** T. Wolfe *Angel* xii 254: Chippy-house. **1938** Holbrook *Mackinaw* 107: It was a combination saloon...and...chippy house.

chips *n. Naut.* a ship's carpenter.—usu. used as a nickname.—occ. cap.

***1805** J. Davis *Post-Captain* 117: Be it so! Mr Chips. **1847** Downey *Cruise of the Portsmouth* 16: A conversation with our Chips was any thing but agreeable. **1884** Symondson *Abaft the Mast* 54: Our "chips," however, was allowed by the captain to carry his grub to the steward's berth. **1888** Spear *Old Sailor* 40 [ref. to 1830's]: I was "chips," and had all night in when I could get it. **1898** Stevenson *Cape Horn* 24: Next comes the carpenter whose only name aboard ship is "Chips." **1906** Beyer *Amer. Battleship* 82: "Chips"—a carpenter's mate. *__1929__ Bowen *Sea Slang* 26: Chips...the ship's carpenter. **1930** Buck & Anthony *Bring 'Em Back* 124: One day I said to the carpenter, "Chips, I've got a real job for you." **1932** Riesenberg *Log of the Sea* 37: Mr. Christiansen, late "chips" of the...*Roanoke*. **1953** Dodson *Away All Boats* 140: "Bring in the shoring, Chips," he yelled to his carpenter. **1976** S.C. Lawrence *Northern Saga* 93: Chips and Hickson made plans.

chiquita *n.* [< Sp; dim. of the fem. sg. form of *chico* 'small'] a girl or young woman.
  1942 Bowers & Spence *Seven Days' Leave* (film): "Who's he talkin' about, Sarge?" "His little *chiquita*, I suppose." **1964–66** (quot. at SOUND, *v.*).

chirp *n. Jazz.* a female vocalist; CHIRPER.
  1944 *New Cab Calloway's Dict.*: Chirp: female singer. **1959–60** Bloch *Dead Beat* 4: "The boss's wife, stacked." "Peeler?" "Chirp. Being the boss's wife, she don't hafta belt it out too good."

chirp *v.* **1.a.** *Und.* to inform. Hence **chirper.**
  *__1839__ in Partridge *Dict. Und.* 121: Oh! who would chirp to dishonor his name,/And betray his pals in a nibsome game./To the traps?—Not I for one! *__1891__ *F & H* II 95: *Chirp*...To inform. **1926** Finerty *Criminalese* 12: Chirrup [*sic*]—Evidence, to talk. **1935** Pollock *Und. Sp.*: Chirp, to squeal; to tell the police. **1936** in D. Runyon *More Guys* 150: I am by no means a chirper.
  b. to speak, esp. loudly or out of turn.
  1878 B. Harte *Drift* 199: I saw you a minnit ago standin' over in yon box—chirpin' with a lady. **1883** in B. Harte *Writings* IV 88: "I've chirped," said the sheriff gravely. "Drive on." **1918** *N.Y. Eve. Jour.* (Aug. 11) 11: You chirped it, Julius. **1919** in De Beck *Google* 33: Come on—play the game an' quit chirpin'. **1920** Ade *Hand-Made Fables* 93: He sat over there by himself and never chirped. **1938** Haines *Tension* 61: So I just let this bird chirp a while and then I taken him with me. **1938** Chandler *Big Sleep* 99: "Want to hear it or not?" "Go ahead and chirp."
  2. *Jazz.* (esp. of women) to sing. Hence **chirper.**
  *__1891__ *F & H* II 95: *Chirper*...A singer. **1935** in R. Nelson *Dishonorable* 290: Come in, Loretta, and chirp a little. **1937** in *AS* (1938) 46: Chirping. Feminine singing. **1944** in Hodes & Hansen *Sel. from Gutter* 76: I'm tellin' you, I usta really chirp. **1962** Crump *Killer* 145: "Ah! chirp, lady, chirp." I encouraged the vocalist. **1969** B. Beckham *Main Mother* 62: She was chirping a...soft ballad. **1981** O'Day & Eells *High Times* 72 [ref. to *ca*1940]: I was "the young chirper whom Teddy Wilson...swore was Billie Holiday."
  3. *Stu.* to vomit.
  1980 in Safire *Good Word* 304.

chirper *n.* **1.** [cf. syn. CANARY] a female vocalist.
  (see quots. at CHIRP, *v.*, 2.).
  2. [cf. CHIRP OUT] *Stu.* (see quot.).
  1978 *Adolescence* XIII 499: He could "pull a chirper,"...a loud squealing noise caused by giving the car more gasoline than necessary while releasing the clutch.

chirp out *v.* [cf. CHIRPER, 2] *Stu.* (see quot.).
  1972 N.Y.U. student: You never heard of *to chirp out?* It's when you drive off in a car so fast the tires go skreeeee! and you look like a real idiot.

chirpy *adj.* cheerful.
  *__1837__ in *F & H* II 95: It makes me chirpy to think of Roseland. *__1879__ in *F & H*: To Charlton this appeared gravely ominous...Paulina, on the other hand, was what she would herself have called *chirpy*. **1899** A. Lewis *Sandburrs* 152: Joe don't feel no sort chirpy.

chisel *n.* a method of cheating or swindling.
  1941 Lees *Hold That Ghost* (film): That's the oldest chisel in the world! The wildcat bus racket.
  ¶ In phrase:
  ¶ **full chisel** at top speed.
  1826 in *JAF* LXXVI (1963) 281: So I'me goin tu hev mi liklynes takon full chizel. **1830** in [S. Smith] *Letters of Downing* 37: T'other [chased] arter [*sic*] him full chisel. **1838** [Haliburton] *Clockmaker* (ser. 2) 23: If you don't travel that road full chisel it's a pity. **1839–40** Cobb *Green Hand* II 114: Off I started full-chisel. **1855** Burgess *500 Mistakes* 51: "He was *going at full chisel:*" say, *at the top of his speed*. **1873** *Slang & Vulgar Forms* 12: "He went full chisel" is an absurd expression. Say "as fast as he could," or, "he ran his best."

chisel *v.* **1.a.** to cheat.—usu. constr. with *out of.*

*__1808__ Jamieson *Scot. Dict.* I 424: To *Chizzel*...To cheat, to act deceitfully. **1833** in [S. Smith] *Letters from Downing* 197: Now...you can chizzle them out of their property. *__1844__ in *F & H* II 96: They have chiseled the peaman and no mistake about that. **1846** Neal *Charc. Sks.* (Series 2) 64: They traded—bargained, sold, swopped, exchanged, and "chiselled." **1848** Bartlett *Amer.*: *Chisel*. To cheat; the same as *to gouge.* A Western word. **1858** [S. Hammett] *Piney Woods* 264: If you'd a chizzled me clean out of...the fifty, I'd have said the same. *__1861__ H. Mayhew *London Labour* III 78: I think they *chiselled* me. **1871** Schele de Vere *Americanisms* 298: Stockholders would be *chiseled* out of a pretty considerable sum. **1889** Farmer *Amer.*: *Chisel, to*—To cheat; defraud; swindle. Said to be a Western phrase. **1935** Coburn *Law Rides Range* 108: He sees where he can chisel Bull outa da game. **1936** Mencken *Amer. Language* 567: In the sense of to cheat, as in "He *chiseled* me out of $3," it goes back to the first years of the Nineteenth Century, but with the advent of the N.R.A., in the late Summer of 1933, it took on the new meaning of to evade compliance with the law by concealment or stealth. **1941** Schulberg *Sammy* 32: I never saw a man so pleased about getting chiseled in all my life. **1942** Chandler *High Window* 350: We were in the same racket. So I wouldn't chisel him. **1943** in *Best from Yank* 36: Don't try to chisel him out of his rights.
  b. to be unfaithful.
  1943 Wakeman *Shore Leave* 190: You impress me as the type who wouldn't chisel on his wife. Would you?
  2. to obtain by begging or underhanded means; MOOCH.
  1927 Lindbergh *We* 107: When we did have a few spare moments... they were usually spent in trying to "chizzle" a hop from one of the instructors on the line. **1934** Berg *Prison Nurse* 132: Why, there are hacks in this joint cheap enough to chisel four bit pieces from the "fish" for some lousy privilege. **1961** R.L. Scott *Boring Holes* 50: The parts we hadn't been able to chisel, he either "borrowed"...or actually manufactured.
  3. to insinuate oneself.—constr. with *in.*
  1926 Finerty *Crim.* 12: Chisel in—Butt in without bid. **1935** *AS* (Feb.) 52: To chisel in (to intrude). **1941** F. Ryan & W. Hamilton *Call Out Marines* (film): But no. You couldn't wait. You had to chisel in. **1952** Himes *Stone* 116: You mean he wanted to chisel in on that special diet?

chiseler *n.* **1.** one who cheats, swindles, or uses unethical practices.
  1918 in *OEDS:* You know I won the toss. We tossed up which should tell and I won. You *are* a chiseller. **1923** *N.Y. Times* (Sept. 9) VIII 2: *Chiseler:* a theatrical promoter who fails to keep his promise. **1926** Finerty *Criminalese* 14: Chisler—Petty bargainer who tries to cheat. **1932** *Writer's Digest* (Aug.) 46: A chisler is a gangster or one who lives by his wits. **1960–61** Steinbeck *Discontent* 23: Who's a chiseler? That's good business. **1965** Spillane *Killer Mine* 25: Hating the politicos and the chiselers and the punks. **1975** T. Berger *Sneaky People* 30: You're a goddam chiseler.
  2. Esp. *Und.* a small-time criminal; (*hence*) a no-account.
  1928 O'Connor *B'way Racketeers* 250: Chiseler—One who works at any racket as long as there is a dollar in it. **1930** *Amer. Merc.* (Dec.) 455: Chisler, *n.*: A small operator; a petty thief. "We got to run the chislers out. They ruin the racket." **1931** *AS* VI (Aug.) 437: Chisler, *n.* A petty larceny thief, a minor gangster. **1933** Ersine *Prison Slang* 26: Chiseler, *n.* A petty thief, tin-horn gambler, or pool-room hanger-on. **1934** Berg *Prison Nurse* 125: What are you trying to do, you chiseler, drive us bugs? **1961** Scarne *Comp. Gamb. Gde.* 675: Chiseler...A person who would like to be a gambler but lacks the money and class.

chitlin circuit *n. Music Industry.* (see 1982 quot.). Also **chitlins circuit.**
  1974 Abdul *Black Entertainers* 61: Aretha...made the dreary round of rhythm and blues nightclubs along the "chitlin circuit." **1982** A. Shaw *Dict. Pop/Rock* 74: "Chitlin Circuit." A term first used by singer Lou Rawls...to describe the bars, lounges, clubs, dives, and honky-tonks...at which black artists perform before a hit recording opens the door to major white outlets. **1985** *Maledicta* VIII 188: As recently as 1950, many...black comics on the TOBA [Theater Owners Booking Association] or "chittling" circuit still blackened up. **1987** *Campus Voice* (Winter) 8: The RCA Victor Blues and Rhythm Revue sounds like a traveling show that did the chitlins circuit in the '40s.

chitlins *n.pl.* Now *So.* the human intestines. Usu. **chitterlings** in earlier print.
  *__1785__ Grose *Vulgar Tongue: Chitterlins.* The bowels. There is a rumpus among my chitterlins, i.e. I have the colic. **1840** in *DARE:* My soul if I don't jump down his throat, and gallop every chittering out of him. **1848** in *DARE:* If my *sow*-licitude is hurtin' yer chitterlings, why, be

smashed into a hog's pudding. **1933, 1938** in *DARE*.

Chitlin Switch *n. Black E.* any small, rural southern town.
1926 Odum & Johnson *Negro Workaday Songs* 173: Way down yonder on chit'lin' switch…Bull frog jump from ditch to ditch. **1970** in Jackson *Swim Like Me* 111: Now if you ever think about going back home to Chitlin' Switch. **1971** Wells & Dance *Night People* 66: When we went South before, do you remember that little bundle that was standing by the stand when we played Chittlin' Switch, Georgia? **1974** in D.C. Dance *Shuckin' & Jivin'* 236: If you *ever* think about goin' back home to Chitlin' Switch.

Chi-Town *n.* [cf. CHI] Chicago, Illinois.
1922 Tully *Emmett Lawler* 281: He's the best boy in Chi-town. **1990** Rukuza *W. Coast Turnaround* 39: He had to be in Chi-town in two days.

Chiv *n.* [fr. *chivalry*] *West.* a white southerner.—used derisively.
1860 in *DA.* **1866** *Beadle's Mo.* (May) 395: No wonder the "chivs" at the house exclaimed against violating the sanctity of the tomb! **1877** Bartlett *Amer.* (ed. 4) 116: Chiv. The California term for a Southerner,—an abbreviation for Chivalry. **1890** *Overland Mo.* (Feb.) 113: The high-toned chivs proved there was genuine chivalry in them.

chiv *n.* [< Romani *chiv* 'blade'] Orig. *Und.* a knife or straight razor used as a weapon; (*also, obs.*) a saw or sharp file; (*Mil.*) a bayonet. Also vars.
*__1673__ in *OED*: He takes his Chive and cuts us down. *__1698–99__ "B.E." *Dict. Canting Crew*: Chive,…a knife. **1791** [W. Smith] *Confess. T. Mount* 18: A knife, *a chive*. **1807** Tufts *Narrative* (gloss.) [ref. to 1794]: Chiv…a knife. *__1812__ Vaux *Vocab.*: Chiv: a knife. **1848** *Ladies' Repository* VIII (Oct.) 315: Chiv, A knife. **1859** Matsell *Vocab.* 19: Chive. A file or saw. *__1873__ Hotten *Slang Dict.* (ed. 5): Chive, a knife.…the word is pronounced as though written chiv or chivvy. **1897** in J. London *Reports* 320: Shiv, knife. **1907** Siler *Pugilism* 9: The gang were there to see that he did win, even if it was necessary to stick a "chiv" into the westerner's back. **1911** A.H. Lewis *Apaches of N.Y.* 233: I never could stand for a chive. **1912** Lowrie *Prison* 82: I always carried a shive myself. **1914** Jackson & Hellyer *Crim. Slang* 23: Chiv…A knife; a sharp-edged tool or weapon. **1919** Hamilton & Corbin *Echoes From Over There* 28 [ref. to WWI]: A queer sound the bayonet makes when it takes the flesh, and queerer still is the feel of the gun in your hand when you have the old "shiv" in a human body. **1928** Sharpe *Chicago May* 287: Shive—knife. **1929** Hammett *Dain Curse* 274: The spick's got a chive. **1936** Dai *Opium Add.* 203: Schive. A knife is always called this, both in prison and out. **1938** Bellem *Blue Murder* 15: She acted like a dame who wouldn't hesitate to jam a shiv into the ribs of somebody she didn't like. **1939–40** O'Hara *Pal Joey* 27: She gets this annonamous letter sticking the shiv in my back. **1947** Motley *Knock on Any Door* 176: "Have you got a shieve?" Squint said. **1948** Webb *Four Steps* 103: Pull [that] ol shive. **1953** Paley *Rumble* 27: The dock bosses with their shiv men and trigger boys. **1961** Braly *Felony Tank* 23: No one was tough with a shiv in his belly. **1978** Strieber *Wolfen* 80: The bastard was about to pull a hidden shiv on me. **1984–87** Ferrandino *Firefight* 165: Now clean that sticky stuff off my shiv, okay?

chiv *v.* **1.** *Und.* to cut, saw, or file. Also **chive.**
*__1714__ in Partridge *Dict. Und.* 121: *Chiving* Bags or Port-mantles from behind Horses, that's cutting them off. *__1724__ in Partridge *Dict. Und.*: He chiv'd his Darbies in twain. *__1725__ *New Canting Dict.*: To Chive his Darbies: to saw asunder his irons. *__1785__ Grose *Vulgar Tongue* 78: To *chive the darbies*, to file off the irons or fetters. *To chive the boungs of the frows*; to cut off women's pockets. **1848** *Ladies' Repository* VIII (Oct.) 315: Chiv, To cut. **1859** Matsell *Vocab.* 19: "Chive your darbies," file your irons off.

2. Orig. *Und.* to knife.—in later use also constr. with *up.* Also **shiv.**
*__1812__ Vaux *Vocab.*: To chiv a person is to stab him or cut him with a knife. *__1816__ in Partridge *Dict. Und.* 121: They will chiv me; that means stabbing him; putting a knife into him. *__1827__ in Partridge *Dict. Und.*: Now, Bill, chiv the b—r. *__1870__ in Ware *Passing English* 73: I've had to be chivved. **1914** Jackson & Hellyer *Crim. Slang* 23: Chiv, verb…To cut; to slash; used only in regard to an attack upon a human. **1932** D. Runyon, in *Collier's* (June 11) 8: He dies from being shivved by Johnny Mizzoo. **1933** Ersine *Prison Slang* 66: Shiv Up. To stab. **1953** T. Runyon *In for Life* 91: Hardly a week passed without someone getting shivved up.

choad *n.* [orig. unkn.] **1.** the penis. Cf. CHOAN.
1968 *Zap Comix* No. 3 (unp.): What a find…a giant choad! **1969** in Estren *Underground* 67: Club Choad Charlie and Wes the Geek.

2. DINGLEBERRY, 1.
1991 *UTSQ*: Chode—a particle of fecal matter or something on an animal's behind. **1993** *Beavis & Butt-head* (MTV): Choad encounters of the turd kind!

choan *n.* [orig. unkn.] Esp. *Stu.* copulation. Also **chome.**
1974 N.Y.C. banker, age 27: [At Princeton, 1965–69] we used to talk about *choan* and *poontang.* **1974** N.Y.U. student: "Go lookin' for chome" is one I haven't heard in years. It means looking for cunt. It's from Quincy, Mass., about 1960, maybe earlier. **1968–77** Herr *Dispatches* 29: They never heard a grunt talk about anything except cars, football and chone.

Choatie *n. Stu.* a student or graduate of the Choate School.
1979 G. Wolff *Duke of Deception* 206: There were Choaties at Princeton, but I kept apart from them. **1980** Birnbach *Preppy Hndbk.* 52: If you can't get a girl, get a Choatie.

chocha *n.* [< Sp 'doddering woman'] *Hispanic.* the vulva or vagina; (*hence*) copulation with a woman; CUNT.
1967 *DAS* (ed. 2) 677: Chocha…cunt. **1980** Gould *Ft. Apache* 130: He means he ain't gettin' any *cho cha.* **1986** *NDAS*: Chocha…the vulva.

cho-cho *n.* [alter. F *Chauchat*] *Army.* a French Chauchat automatic rifle. Now *hist.*
1918 Casey *Cannoneers* 256: From every gun position came the chatter of Cho-cho, Hotchkiss, Maxim or Lewis. **1929** *Our Army* (Dec.) 34 [ref. to WWI]: Besides the regular equipment of machine guns to each battery, the men had salvaged numbers of German guns and French "cho-chos," with unlimited amounts of ammunition, and it required constant supervision to keep them from opening on anything that appeared in the air.

chocolate *adj.* racially black, esp. very dark-skinned.—often used derisively. Also as *n.*
1906 *Nat. Police Gaz.* (Nov. 3) 6: George Dixon…"Little Chocolate," as he was known. **1909** in Sampson *Ghost Walks* 495: I'm…Chocolate to the Bone. **1915** White *Amer. Negro Folk-Songs* 268: I'm going to build me a railroad from Burmingham to Rome,/Ain't nobody going to ride but a chocolate baby to the bone. **1923** O'Brien *Best Stories of 1923* 157: My full onshortened name is the Chawklate Hyena. **1923** in Kimball & Balcolm *Sissle & Blake* 160: When it comes to shufflin' feet/These chocolate dandies can't be beat. **1927** McKay *Home to Harlem* 3: In the winter he sailed for Brest with a happy chocolate company. **1932** McKay *Gingertown* 27: You sings that theah song jest like a…chocolate that useta sing at Fearon's cabaret. **1969** Crumley *One to Count Cadence* 200: This soft-spoken chocolate cat.… **1970** Baraka *Jello* 15: Well my chocolate friend, what are you gonna do for money? **1981** C. Nelson *Picked Bullets Up* 333: A ringleader among the 7th Battalion's uppity chocolate bloc. **1991** Nelson & Gonzales *Bring Noise* 254: Sipping champagne with the chocolate honeys.

chocolate baby *n.* CHOCOLATE DROP.—used derisively.
1908 in Fleming *Unforgettable Season* 23: The "chocolate babies" delegation, the darkies.

chocolate bunny *n.* CHOCOLATE DROP.—used contemptuously.
*a*__1984__ in Terry *Bloods* 5: And then we had a Southerner from Arkansas that liked to call you chocolate bunny and Brillo head.

chocolate chips *n.pl. Mil.* a desert camouflage uniform. Also attrib.
1991 G. Trudeau *Doonesbury* (synd. comic strip) (June 24): You might want to change into those chocolate chips. **1992** Cornum & Copeland *She Went* 189: Troy…was wearing chocolate-chip fatigues.

chocolate drop *n.* a black person.—usu. used contemptuously.
1900 *DN* II 27: *Chocolate-drop*, a young negress. **1910** *N.Y. Eve. Jour.* (May 7) 10: I'm no nurse-girl for chocolate drops! **1912** *Pedagog. Sem.* (Mar.) 97: "Chocolate drop" (negro). **1918** *Scribner's* (Aug.) 178: He might have stayed to let us handle these chocolate drops. **1926** Odum & Johnson *Negro Workaday Songs* 64: Slim Jim wus a chocolate drop/From dark-town alley. **1944** L. Smith *Strange Fruit* 144: Those words and the white children's *chocolate drop* hurled at you on your way to school…you'd never forget. **1953** Eyster *Customary Skies* 49: A real blowout, not a mugging party with a chocolate drop. **1962, 1964,** etc., in *DARE.* **1986** Churcher *N.Y. Confidential* 33: I saw nothing but Japs and chocolate drops.

chocolate highway *n.* [cf. syn. HERSHEY HIGHWAY] the rectum.—usu. considered vulgar. Also vars. *Joc.*

1977 L. Jordan *Hype* 76: I want to put it up your chocolate speedway. **1983–86** Zausner *Streets* 76: Your...chocolate tunnel. **1989** R. Miller *Profane Men* 65: Up the old chocolate highway.

Choctaw *n.* any baffling or unintelligible language; "Greek."
1839 in *DA*. **1853** "P. Paxton" *In Texas* 211: No choctaw, sir—use plain English. **1900** *DN* II 27: *Chocktaw, n.* Spanish [as an academic subject]. **1907** McDermott-Stevenson *Lariat Letters* 35: We roped in all the chuck we wanted without having to read the darned French program, which was all Choctaw to me. **1921** in *DA*.

choff *n.* [var. earlier Brit. slang *chuff,* of unkn. orig.] food.
1971 Sanders *Family* 103: The bulk of the choff was garbage. Part of the "rent" the family paid at the ranch was the preparation of food. **1985** J. Green *Dict. Slang* 50.

chogi *n.* [< Korean] *Mil.* a Korean laborer working esp. for U.S. armed forces. Also **chogi boy.** Also vars.
1951 *N.Y. Herald-Tribune* (Dec. 16) II 5: *Chogi* (Korean): Human supply trains, native Koreans lugging food, ammunition and other supplies on their backs up the hills to the front-line U.N. troops. **1966–80** McAleer & Dickson *Unit Pride* 145 [ref. to Korean War]: Armand pulled the jeep into the sector where the choggie-boy pool was located. **1984–88** Hackworth & Sherman *About Face* [ref. to Korean War]: The Korean *chogi* party, our resupply train, had gotten lost...*Chogi* was our nickname for the Korean laborers who worked for the Eighth Army. **1989** P.H.C. Mason *Recovering* 88 [ref. to Vietnam War]: A chogey boy was a guy from the ville...For one dollar a day he'd carry your backpack and dig your hole and cook your meal.
¶ In phrase:
¶ **cut a chogi** Orig. *Mil. in E. Asia.* to clear out; to run. Also vars.
1953 in *IUFA* (IU: GI: Army Songs Misc. 32): Ah'm cuttin' a chogie, brutha. **1961** Peacock *Valhalla* 106 [ref. to 1953]: Cut a choge. **1964** Peacock *Drill & Die* 79: You can cut a choge any time you want—you're relieved. **1969** Spetz *Rat Pack Six* 64: Well, they seem to think we cut a chogie and let the others sink. **1980** D. Cragg *Lex. Mil.* 114: *Cut a choggie.* To run, retreat, bug out. **1983** Knoxville, Tenn., woman, age *ca*35: All them peoples came a-cuttin' a chogi up that hill. **1991** *UTSQ*: Let's "cut a choagie"...means let's...leave.

chogi *v.* [< Korean; also reflecting E *chug (along)*] *Mil. in E. Asia.* to move along quickly. Also **choggie.**
1964 R. Moore *Green Berets* 88: Instead of being on an azimuth of 225 degrees we're choggying along at 240 degrees. **1970** N.Y.U. student: To chogi means to walk or get over there, over that way. **1978** U.S. Army enlisted man: He was chogi-in' like a motherfucker. **1980** Cragg *L. Militaris* 88: *Choggie.* To run or move, as "choggie down the street." From the Korean *chogi*, to go. **1981** Hathaway *World of Hurt* 179: We...went into the bushes and waited till they chogied by. **1982** Cox & Frazier *Buck* 37: We'll chogie over to this other bunker and have breakfast with Sergeant Delaino.

chogi boy see CHOGI, *n.*

choice *adj.* great; wonderful; (*also*) very attractive.
1958 *AS* (Oct.) 225: Hip expressions...expressing warm approval: *choice, tremendous,...crazy, cool.* **1964** R.S. Gold *Jazz Lexicon* 56: *Choice*...with esp. currency among jazzmen c. 1947–c. 1952...Excellent. **1975** in D.C. Dance *Shuckin' & Jivin'* 201: She said she thought it [*sc.* an anecdote] was choice! **1982** Pond *Valley Girls Gde.* 54: *Choice*—A choice babe is like Tom Selleck or Rick Springfield, like that. **1986** J. Hughes *Ferris Beuller* (film): I love driving it. It is *so* choice. **1989** S. Elliott et al. *Slang* 7: *Choice* well-liked, pleasing...That dinner was choice. **1992** *Northern Exposure* (CBS-TV): "Are you OK?" "Oh, I am *choice*!"

choirboy *n.* a fellow who is naive and self-righteously good or honest; (*hence*) an innocent person.—used derisively.
1977 Sayles *Union Dues* 165: He's a fuckin choirboy. Mitch, he don't want any part of it. **1977** Hamill *Flesh & Blood* 8: Who's the fuckin' choirboy with the jigaboo? **1978** Schrader *Hardcore* 39: Hey, I'm a private detective, Van Dorn. If you want a choirboy, you can go back to Grand Rapids. **1989** L. Roberts *Full Cleveland* 124: A guy fixes your car good, do you really give a damn whether he's a choirboy?

choke *adj. Sports.* characterized by a tendency to CHOKE, 2.
1976 Rosen *Above Rim* 4: The Stars' coach was...raging at one of the officials..."You fucken asshole! You blew the call! You choke bastard!"

choke *v.* **1.** to put a stop to (chatter).
1912 *Pedagogical Seminary* (Mar.) 96: "Shut your beak,"..."choke it."... "cut out the ruff,"..."drown it,"..."ring off,"..."souse it,"..."button your lip." **1948** A. Murphy *Hell & Back* 202: Aw, choke de chatter.

2. Esp. *Sports.* to become tense or lose one's composure in a critical situation. Also **choke up.**
1941 Kendall *Army & Navy Slang* 3: *To choke up*...to have the mind leave the body. **1950** Roeder *J. Robinson* 141: In one of the vital pennant battles in St. Louis, Robinson grabbed at his throat to signify that Bill Stewart, the umpire, was "choking up." Stewart threw him out of the game. **1961** Brosnan *Pennant Race* 80: The Reds really choked again today....They'll never win the pennant. **1982** G. Larson *Far Side* (unp.): Go for it, Sidney! You've got it!...Don't choke! *a*1991 Kross *Splash One* 8: The kid [might] choke at the moment of truth.
¶ In phrase:
¶ **big enough to choke a cow** (of a bankroll) very thick. Also vars.
1897 A. Lewis *Wolfville* 13: An' yere Cherokee lugs out a roll of bills big enough to choke a cow. **1899** A. Lewis *Sandburrs* 152: D' roll Joe gets is big enough to choke a cow—'leven t'ousand plunks, if it's a splinter. **1903** Ade *Society* 48: I've got a Roll here that would choke a Horse. **1919** Z. Grey *Desert of Wheat* 21: Why, one of them had a wad of bills that would choke a cow. **1925** Faulkner *New Orleans Sketches* 137: Mebbe they'll think I'm a racing man, with a roll on my hip would choke a ox. **1966** Herbert *Fortune & Men's Eyes* 30: I split in the Caddy with a roll that would choke a elephant an' had me a ball. **1974** Radano *Cop Stories* 120: His bankroll...was big enough to choke an elephant.

choke-and-chew *n. CB.* CHOKE-AND-PUKE.
1976 Bibb et al. *CB Bible* 80: Anyone looking for a choke and chew or a place to go bowling just has to get on [channel] 11.

choke-and-puke *n.* Esp. *Trucking.* a cheap, esp. roadside, restaurant; GREASY SPOON.
1971 Tak *Truck Talk* 30: *Choke and puke:* a run-down truck stop. **1976** Lieberman & Rhodes *CB Handbook* 125: *Choke And Puke*—Restaurant. **1980** *Nat. Lampoon* (Sept.) 62: All night choke-and-pukes, where you eyeball pretty waitresses over bottomless cups of thirty-weight mud.

choke artist *n.* Esp. *Baseball.* a player who habitually CHOKES.
1975 Durocher & Linn *Nice Guys* 301: I had waited for him to pass me on his way back to the dugout so that I could let him know what a choke-artist he was.

choke-ass *n. Army.* cheese; CHOKE-DOG, 2.
1988 Fussell *Wartime* 91 [ref. to WWII]: The two most common kinds of sandwiches, baloney and cheese, are designated respectively *horsecock*...and *choke-ass*.

choke-dog *n.* **1.** rum or grog.
1821 J.F. Cooper *Spy* ch. xxi: Replenishing the mug with a large addition of the article known to the soldiery as "choke-dog," she held it towards the peddler.
2. Esp. *Naut.* strong cheese.
***1870** in *F & H* II 99: Bread and *choke-dog*, as he calls his county's cheese. **1883** C. Russell *Sailors' Language* xii: "Lobscouse," "dandyfunk," "dogsbody," "seapie," "choke-dog," "twice-laid," "hisheehashee" are among some of the delicate entrées which the sailor contrives to get out of his kids.

choke in *v.* to hold one's tongue.
1843 in *DA*.

chokem *n.* cheese.
1928 in *DARE: Chokem, choke'm*...(army) cheese. **1958** McCulloch *Woods Words* 33: *Chokem*—Cheese.

choke off *v.* **1.** to stop; cease.
1843 "J. Slick" *High Life in N.Y.* 37: He seemed mortal loth to choke off. **1899** Norris *McTeague* 122: Say, for God's sake...choke off on that pipe! If you've got to smoke rope like that, smoke it in a crowd of muckers. **1900** Willard & Hodler *Powers That Prey* 79: Choke it off, Dutchy, you're excited. **1921** E. O'Neill *Hairy Ape* 188: Choke off dat noise! Where d'yuh get dat beer stuff?
2. to stop (a person) from talking or complaining.
1883 Peck *Peck's Bad Boy* 226: But if a boy tries to branch out as a statesman [in his speech], they choke him off. ***1881–84** Davitt *Prison Diary* I 64: I have known the governor to have "choked off" (successfully humbugged) dozens of these frequently complaining and contemptible impostors by expressing his surprise at "*an educated man*" giving such trouble without cause." **1889** King *Marion's Faith* 424: Shut up, you idiot! Choke him off, somebody! **1905** *DN* V: *Choke off,* v. phr. Slang, to stop a person talking. **1911** E. Howe *Sayings* 30: When a man once gets a start holding office, it is nearly always necessary to finally choke him off. **1935** Saunders *Standard* 128: He started squealing like a pig, but I choked him off pronto.

choker *n.* **1.a.** a cravat. Now *hist.*
*1848 in Partridge *DSUE* (ed. 8) 213: The usual attire of a gentleman, viz., pumps, a gold waistcoat, a crush hat, a sham frill, and a white choker. **1859** Matsell *Vocab.* 19: *Choker:* a neckerchief. **1869** Graham *Words* 176: A boy will sometimes puzzle his sisters at home, by asking them if they do not find his "toggery" absolutely "stunning;" or what they think of his "tile" or white "choker." **1872** Burnham *Secret Svc.* iv: *Choker,*—a dominie, a white cravat. **1875** *Minstrel Gags* 108: A straight collared coat and a white choker. **1877** Bartlett *Amer.* (ed. 4) 117: *Choker.* A cravat. **1901** Dunne *Mr. Dooley's Opinions* 181: Ye take a man with small side whiskers, a long coat an' a white choker, a man that wudden't harm a spider....
b. a high, stiff collar; (*hence*) a clergyman.
1869 in *F & H* II 100: A choker collar of enormous size. **1872** Burnham *Secret Svc.* iv: *Choker.* A parson. **1875** in *DAE.* ***1886** in Partridge *Dict. Und.* 122: *Gulling a choker*...Deceiving a Minister. ***1889** Barrère & Leland *Dict. Slang* I 247: *Choker*...a clergyman. **1889** King *Marion's Faith* 90: The white tie and stiff "choker" of conventionality. **1896** F.H. Smith *Tom Grogan* 131: Cully had taken off his "choker," as he called it, and had curled it outside his hat. **1906** *Independent* (Apr. 19) 913: Then my shoes must be polished, my clothes brushed and my choker adjusted—even tho it cut my throat—and I would start off for school. **1911** Howard *Enemy to Society* 8: His collar [was] what those of the last two decades called a "choker." **1922** *Harper's* (Mar.) 530: Shiners and claw-hammers and stiff choker, and bear grease on his hair.
c. *Police.* a high-collared winter blouse.
1973 Droge *Patrolman* 25: A winter blouse, called a choker.
2. a hangman's noose.
1862 M.V. Victor *Unionist's Dtr.* 105: They'd a had a choker on him in the morning.
3. a snugly fitting necklace. Now *S.E.*
*1928 in *OEDS.* **1949, 1956** in *DAS.*
4. cheese.
1925 *AS* I (Dec.) 137: Cheese is "choker." **1930** Irwin *Tramp & Und. Sl.:* *Choker*—cheese. Largely used in the harvest fields and in the lumber camps, and so called from its effect on the bowels.

choke rag *n. S.W.* a cravat or necktie. *Joc.*
1840 *Spirit of Times* (Mar. 7) 8: I've got on the red coat..., black choke-rag round my neck, and lambs-wool hose. **1952** Randolph & Wilson *Down in Holler* 234: *Choke rag*...An old-fashioned necktie. **1954** in *DARE*: *Choke rag*: A necktie. Humorous.

choker-hole *n.* a doughnut.
1925 *AS* I (Dec.) 137. **1936** *AS* (Feb.) 42: *Choker Holes.* Doughnuts.

choke strap *n. West.* a necktie. *Joc.*
1944 R. Adams *West. Words*: *Choke strap*...a necktie, something for which the cowboy has little need. **1969** in *DARE*: *Choke strap*—A necktie.

choke up *v.* **1.** to shut up.
1903 Hobart *Out for Coin* 74: Aw, choke up! choke up!...What do you t'ink I am—a wax works? **1907** in *DA.*
2. see CHOKE, 2.

choky *n.* [< Hindi *chauki*] *Naut.* a prison; jail.
*ca1840 (cited in Partridge *DSUE* (ed. 8) 213). **1867** Clark *Sailor's Life* 162: Say, bully, who keeps the Home now? Has Bill got out of chockey yet? **1875** Sheppard *Love Afloat* 180: Yes; he languishes in choky. **1884** Symondson *Abaft the Mast* 202: The older seamen swore...they would rather be put in "choky" than sail under him.

chola *n.* [< MexSp: fem. of CHOLO] a girl who is a member of a Chicano street gang.
1976 *L.A. Times* (Aug. 9) II 1: There's...Sandy, not long ago a *chola*— a young girl who hangs out with male gang members. **1979** *New West* (Jan. 29) 42: Chica is the least *chola* looking of the three girls, and also the...most likely to "straighten up." **1983** *L.A. Times* (Mar. 29) II 1: There were about 65 young women, many of them *cholas*, or gang girls. **1988** Norst *Colors* 120: Are you a *chola*?...a gang girl.

cholo *n.* [< MexSp: 'mestizo, peasant'] a boy or man who is a member of a Chicano street gang. [See *OED2* for earlier citations of different senses.]
1978 *L.A. Times* (July 30) Calendar 90: It is like the ultimate fantasy of the Cholo low riders that cruise Whittier Blvd. ceremonially on weekend nights. **1979** *L.A. Times* (Mar. 23) IV 20: The actor who plays the *cholo* (gang member). **1984** *N.Y. Times* (July 16) A 16: A cholo is...a member of the youth culture that centers on modified low-riding motorcycles.

chomp *v. Stu.* to be disgusting, unsatisfactory, or inferior; BITE.
1983 Naiman *Computer Dict.* 31: This new editor really chomps.

chomper *n.* **1.** *pl.* teeth.
1950, 1954, etc., in *DARE.* **1988** *Highwayman* (NBC-TV): Do you get the feeling we're swimming straight into the pearly chompers of a great white [shark]?
2. *Stu.* something or someone regarded as disgusting, unsatisfactory, or inferior.
1983 Naiman *Computer Dict.* 31: A *chomper* is a loser.

chomp on *v. USAF.* to apply (wheel brakes).
1956 Heflin *USAF Dict.* 113: *To chomp on the binders,* to apply the wheel brakes of an airplane. *Slang.*

chooch *n.* [shortening of Southern It *ciuccio* 'blockhead, fool'; lit. 'ass, donkey'] *Ital.-Amer.* a fool.
1971 Sorrentino *Up from Never* 18: C'mon, what size, *jooche* (oaf)? **1978** N.J. man, age *ca*30: Italian-Americans call each other *chooch*. It means idiot. Literally, it means "donkey." **1988** R. Menlo & R. Rubin *Tougher Than Leather* (film): He's been robbin' you blind for over a year, you big chooch!

choo-choo *n.* [imit.] a railroad train.—mainly used in addressing young children.
1898 Bangs *Ghosts* 103: Only two days' ride on the choo-choo. **1902–03** Ade *People You Know* 110: Percy M. Piker was hanging on the rear end of the Choo-Choo with $7 sewed up in the inside Pocket of his Vest. **1923** G. Wells & B. Cooper *Papa Better Watch Your Step* (sheet music) 3: You'd better catch a choo-choo leavin' town. **1983** Ephron *Heartburn* 34: My mother was singing, "When that midnight choochoo leaves for Alabam."

Choo-Choo Town *n.* [sugg. by pop. song "The Chattanooga Choo Choo"] Chattanooga, Tennessee.
1975 Dills *CB Slanguage* (1976 ed.) 23: *Choo Choo Town.* Chattanooga, Tennessee. **1976** Lieberman & Rhodes *CB Handbook* 125: *Choo Choo Town*—Chattanooga.

choogle *v.* [orig. unkn.; perh. blend of *choo-choo* and *chug*] to go; drive; progress.
1970 Landy *Underground Dict.* 50: *Choogle v.*...Progress; continue what has been started...*choogle on* or *choogle down the highway.* **1977** *New West* (Oct. 24) 89: The session choogled on a mite too long. **1984–87** Ferrandino *Firefight* 119: You choogle around town in this short?

chookee *n.* [fr. regional *chookee* 'the orchard oriole'] *Miss. Valley.* a rustic person, JAY.—used derisively.
1968 in *DARE* [La.]: *Chookee*—a country hick. **1977** S. Foote *September September* 71 [Miss.]: One of those hungry little nineteen-year-old chookies—hair ironed flat, pullover sweater a couple of sizes too small, white socks.

choose *v.* to challenge to a fight.—now usu. constr. with *out.*
1934 Cunningham *Triggernometry* 41: A...canvasman of the John Robinson show "chose" Wes at Horn Hill...He "slapped leather" with the canvasman and left him dead. **1933–35** D. Lamson *About to Die* 205: Of course if you get choosed by a hophead or a nut, then all bets is off an' anything might happen. **1956** R. Ellison, in W. King *Black Anthol.*: He's choosing 'em...offering to fight 'em. **1967** W. Crawford *Gresham's War* 162: You chose us out: now do something with us. **1971** in L. Bangs *Psychotic Reactions* 53: All right, punk. This is it. Choose ya out. We're gonna settle this right here.

chooser *n. Vaud.* a performer who pirates the material of others.
1913 *Sat. Eve. Post* (Mar. 29) 8: Some other act, of the breed called "choosers" in vaudeville, had stolen his specialties. **1924** *Sat. Eve. Post* (July 12) 15: *A Chooser*—a performer who steals material from other acts which have been watched for that purpose.

chop[1] *n.* [pidgin] Esp. *Naut.* food.
*1805 in *OEDS*: Their food is chop made of yam cut in slices, cayenne pepper [etc.]. **1840** in Dillard *Amer. Talk* 15: The hominy is nothin' but Ingin chop. **1935** *AS* (Feb.) 78: *Chop.* Food. Also used as a verb. Possibly from the lingua franca of the West coast of Africa, where the expression is common among the Kru boys. **1942** *Yank* (Dec. 23) 23: The chop (food) is excellent. **1968–77** Herr *Dispatches* 7: Freeze-dry rations, three-star war food, the same chop they sold at Abercrombie & Fitch. **1980** Cragg *L. Militaris* 89: *Chop*..."Let's get some chop" ...Food.

chop² *n.* **1.** a marked reduction, as in salary or financing; cut. **1942** *ATS* 531: *Chop*…a wage cut. **1985** Univ. Tenn. instructor, age 34: They told him he'd have to take a chop in his housing allowance.
2. *Juve.* a cutting insult. **1957** H. Ellison *Web of the City* 45: It was the worst. It was a chop low like no other he'd ever heard. **1970** Landy *Underground Dict.* 50: *Chop*…*n.* an insult. **1973** Lucas, Katz & Huyck *Amer. Graffiti* 100: All right, very funny. What a chop.
3. CHOPPER, 8.a. **1970** *Playboy* (Sept.) 88: It was a photograph from *The Wild Angels* of me and actor Bruce Dern on a chop. *Ibid.* They get on these chops, these wild far-out bikes.

¶ In phrases:

¶ **get the chop** *Orig. Mil. Av.* to be killed. **1945* in *OEDS.* **1968** Coppel *Order of Battle* 60 [ref. to WWII]: "Oh, Man," Harry yelled breathlessly into my ear. "I thought you'd had it, Dev! When I saw that Goddamn main gear fold up, I thought you'd really got the chop!" **1969** Coppel *Little Time* 181 [ref. to WWII]: What were you doing the night he got the chop? **1972** *Penthouse* (Aug.) 27: And Gerald Sim gets the chop in *Dr. Jekyll and Sister Hyde.* **1979** *N.Y. Times Mag.* (Dec. 23) 15: The ghost story celebrates the experience of death. In Dickens, the hero is usually given a reprieve; in M.R. James, he gets the chop.

¶ **give (someone) the chop** to drop; eliminate from consideration. **1977** Dunne *True Confessions* 12: The Pope gave the chop to Saint Philomena a few years back. **1986** Univ. Tenn. grad. student, age 34: She just gave him the cold chop.

chop¹ *v.* [pidgin] to eat.—also constr. with *down, up.* [Earliest recorded use seems to have been among English seamen on the West Coast of Africa.] **1833* in *OEDS.* **1935** *AS* (Feb.) 78: *Chop.* Food. Also used as a verb. **1967** Riessman & Dawkins *Play It Cool* 54: *Chop down v.* to eat: *I'll chop down any time, and you know it. Ibid.* 56: *Chop up* (same as *chop down*). **1980** Cragg *L. Militaris* 89: *Chop*…To eat.

chop² *v.* **1.a.** to stop, cease, or give up.—also (*obs.*) constr. with *on.* See also CHOP OFF. **1880** in M. Lewis *Mining Frontier* 127: He's chopped on all his old rackets. *Ibid.* 129: I'll just take a grand tumble to myself, an' chop on this racket at once. **1896** Ade *Artie* 43: Chop the laughin'. **1903** Ade *Society* 18: Rule No. 1 of the Smart Set is to chop any Diversion that has caught on with the working classes. **1908** Beach *Barrier* 143: I'm goin' to chop all them prodigal habits. **1911** T.A. Dorgan, in *N.Y. Eve. Jour.* (Jan. 7) 8: Been on the wagon six days now, Harry….I promised my girl I'd chop the stuff and I did. **1912** Ade *Babel* 107: It did look for a while as if I'd have to chop on these [cigarettes] for fair. **1913** Z. Grey *Desert Gold* 58: Chop it. *Ibid.* 249: Chop that kind of talk with me, you ——! **1913–15** Van Loan *Taking the Count* 29: If you mean business, we'll chop the tobacco and booze right here. **1915** Howard *God's Man* 279: Chop the dear old Picadilly stuff. **1927** J. Stevens *Mattock* 128 [ref. to 1918]: Lay off Johnny Hard. Chop 'er [it]. *Ibid.* 286: Chop the old guff. **1956** Hargrove *Girl He Left* 82: Chop it….Here comes the government. **1957** E. Brown *Locust Fire* 122: Chop it, Lewis.
b. to cut short or stop what one is saying or doing. **1898** Kountz *Baxter's Letters* 20: Johnny was shaking his head and motioning for me to chop. **1902** Cullen *More Tales* 33: To chop, I wanted to make New York, and I wanted to do it bad. *a***1909** Tillotson *Detective* 90: *Chop*—To stop.
c. *Av.* to reduce power to (a throttle); to reduce (power) by means of a throttle. **1939** R.A. Winston *Dive Bomber* 21: The check pilot…chopped the throttle. **1943** Mears *Carrier* 105: The motor died as soon as I chopped the throttle. **1944** Stiles *Big Bird* 71: A ground-gripper would never…see the high squadron leader chop his throttles and almost pile his wingmen into his trailing edges. **1964** Newhafer *Last Tallyho* 171: He dropped his flaps and chopped his throttle all the way off. **1964** Caidin *Everything But Flak* 17: He chopped the throttle to Number One, feathered the propeller. **1975** in Higham & Siddall *Combat Aircraft* 14: I should have chopped power immediately. *a***1984** T. Clancy *Red Oct.* 375: Propulsion sounds are down some. She just chopped power.
d. to drop from a list, roster, or the like; cut; dismiss. **1957** E. Brown *Locust Fire* 83 [ref. to 1944]: "Most of you R.O.'s are washouts," said Shultz. "Where'd you get chopped?" "In primary," I told him. **1976** SP5, U.S. Army [coll. J. Ball]: We had to chop Mac.

2. to shoot (someone) [dead], esp. with an automatic weapon.—also constr. with *down.* Also intrans. **1929–33** Farrell *Young Manhood of Lonigan* 161: I ain't afraid of death, and before they get me, I'll chop down a few goddamn sausage-eatin' Dutchmen. **1933** Ersine *Pris. Slang* 26: *Chop, v.* To kill with a *tommy-gun.* **1958** Gilbert *Vice Trap* 130: When he chops you with the riot piece they have in the car, come back and see me. **1961** Davis *Marine at War* 196 [ref. to 1945]: You got ten seconds to think of the password. Get it up or I'll begin to chop! **1971–72** Giovannitti *Medal* 163: A trooper chops down the mother and then tears the pajamas off the girl. **1980** Gould *Ft. Apache* 110: "Why didn't you just chop the bastard?"…"Shoot a purse snatcher, right?"
3. to remove (the top or other parts of a motor vehicle) in order to customize; to strip down and customize (a car or motorcycle). **1953** Felsen *Street Rod* 53: Fat lot any of those profs would know about souping up a V-8 or chopping a top! **1954–60** *DAS: Chopped top.* A convertible car. **1981** *Easyriders* (Oct.) 80: I…still have a chopped Sporty. **1982** R. Sutton *Don't Get Taken* 366: *Chopped Car:* A car reconstructed from two wrecked and/or stolen cars. **1990** Vachss *Blossom* 62: Three bikers went by on chopped hogs.
4. to criticize; insult with sarcasm.—also constr. with *down.* **1957** in Hogan & German *Chronicle Reader* 215: Don't believe what you read in those scandal magazines….They're really choppin' me and it ain't true. **1957** Kohner *Gidget* 51: That chopped him royal. **1964** Gregory *Nigger* 133: Unless you're well-known as an insulting comedian you can't chop hecklers down too hard or the crowd will turn against you. **1970** Landy *Underground Dict.* 50: *Chop*…Insult someone with a remark, a dig or a criticism….[Also] *chop down.* **1976** H. Ellison *Sex Misspelled* 31: Lori and I were talking about what a prick I am when someone tries to chop me conversationally. **1977** Schrader *Blue Collar* 8: It was bad enough for some sucker to chop his union, but absolutely nobody said nothing about his family.
5. *Narc.* to adulterate; cut. **1960** C.L. Cooper *Scene* 182: He had…nearly a kilo of pure [heroin], and if he had to make his getaway money by chopping it, he'd chop it! **1977** S. Gaines *Discotheque* 38: You can't snort this stuff without chopping it first.

chop-chop *n.* [pidgin, cf. CHOP] *Mil. & Naut.* food. **1951** *N.Y. Herald-Tribune* (Dec. 16) II 5: *Chop chop:* food or any allusion to food or eating. **1956** H. Gold *Not With It* 26: "Chop-chop?" Grack asked, handing a sandwich toward me. **1969** Spetz *Rat Pack Six* 203: We'll have chop-chop soon enough. **1970** Whitmore *Memphis-Nam-Sweden* 51: Chop-chop. You give chop-chop? **1971** *Army Reporter* (Feb. 1) 5: Little Red Riding Hood is leaving her hootch with a basket of chop-chop to take to her sick grandma-san. **1975** S.P. Smith *Amer. Boys* 34: Come here, Lang. Good chop-chop. **1978** Hasford *Short-Timers* 66: The kid says that our chop-chop is number ten.

chop-chop *adv.* [pidgin] *Naut. & Mil.* immediately; quickly. **1836* in Partridge *DSUE* (ed. 8) 213. **1878* in *F & H* II 102: *Chop-chop*…means directly. **1898** Norris *Moran* 54: Come back chop-chop. **1922** Colton & Randolph *Rain* 51: We'll have that bird on his feet and down to the dock—chop-chop pronto! **1942** in *Yank* (Jan. 6, 1943) 18: *Chop-chop*—on the double. **1952** Haines & Krims *One Minute to Zero* (film): You fix these up right away. *Chop-chop.* Hubba-hubba…Pronto. **1952** Lamott *Stockade* 16 [ref. to WWII]: Out of my way, chop-chop! **1964** "Doctor X" *Intern* 368: I told the nurse to get an oxygen tank in there chop-chop. **1976** Atlee *Domino* 115: I want this to get to Kaettong, chop-chop. **1990** *ALF* (NBC-TV): Come on. Chop chop!

chop-chop *v.* [pidgin] **1.** *Naut. & Mil.* to hurry. **1946** Bowker *Out of Uniform* 181: There was a great deal of: "Chop-chop and wait." **1949** McMillan *Old Breed* 257: All right, knucklehead,…let's see ya chop-chop. **1959** Cochrell *Barren Beaches* 235: Now gimme that BAR and chop-chop to sick bay.
2. *Naut. & Mil.* **a.** to eat. [1951 quot. may not exemplify this sense.] **1951** *N.Y. Herald-Tribune* (Dec. 16) II 5: *Chop chop:* food or any allusion to food or eating. **1970* Partridge *DSUE* (ed. 7).
b. [cf. identical development of EAT] to perform fellatio. **1975** S.P. Smith *Amer. Boys* 408 [ref. to 1967]: "Boom-boom four hundred p." "You chop-chop too?" "No chop-chop. Chop-chop number ten."

chop line *n.* a cut-off line. **1981** Ballenger *Terror* 6: The line behind which ships could travel without escort was now the 130-degree north chop line.

chop off *v.* to stop or put a stop to.

1897 Siler & Houseman *Fight of the Century* 57: When he began to recover he asked the doctor to "chop off that dope," as he called the morphine injections. **1899** in J. London *Letters* 58: Having done nothing but lecture, I shall now chop off. **1901** Ade *Modern Fables* 155: They had agreed to chop off at Eleven. **1901** in J. London *Letters* I 249: Well, must chop off. **1933** Ersine *Prison Slang* 26: *Chop…off.* To stop, quit work. At three we chop off and go scoff.

chopped liver *n.* something trivial; something to be scoffed at.—usu. in negative.

1954 *Jimmy Durante Show* (CBS-TV): Now that ain't chopped liver. **1983** *Family Feud* (ABC-TV) (May 6): Now this is not exactly chopped liver. **1989** *N.Y. Times Mag.* (Dec. 3) 102: That hurt me in the industry…and it ticked me off. I thought, "What was I—chopped liver or something?" **1990** H.L. Gates, Jr., in *N.Y. Times Bk. Review* (Mar. 25) 37: The literary canon—now that ain't chopped liver.

chopper *n.* **1.** a backhand blow to the face.

***1819** [T. Moore] *Tom Crib* 30: A *chopper* is a blow, struck on the face with the back of the hand. Mendoza claims the honor of its invention, but unjustly. **1821–26** Stewart *Man-of-War's-Man* I 138: Every chopper the skipper gave him made the poor mulatto smell the deck whether he would or not.

2. a ticket-taker.

1899, 1904 in *DA*. **1954–60** *DAS*: *Chopper*…one who tears a ticket in two parts to show that it has been used.

3. *West.* a cutting horse.

1913 in *DA*.

4. *Radiocommunications.* (see quot.).

1929 *AS* (Oct.) 48: *Chopper*—interrupter used in sending.

5. usu. *pl.* a tooth; (*also*) (*pl.*) a set of false teeth.

1944 (quot. at IVORY). **1952** Mandel *Angry Strangers* 134: The choppers show up missin and I sound like a chicken's ass. **1953** Dodson *Away All Boats* 463: They sure fixed him up with store choppers in a hurry. **1960** Jordan & Marberry *Fool's Gold* 77: Unlike most people in Alaska, he had good choppers. **1961** in C. Beaumont *Best* 94: What do you imagine happens to us when our choppers start to go? **1966** I. Reed *Pall-Bearers* 16: What's the crust doin' in you greasy choppers if he ate it? **1966** Kenney *Caste* 22: A man should be born without choppers—like a bird. **1977** Hagerman *Odd World* 39: They export over thirty million sets of choppers a year. **1982** in Ehrhart *Carrying Darkness* 22: For popping a loud-mouth punk in the choppers. **1987** S. Stark *Wrestling Season* 23: Bad skin, beady eyes, them big yella choppers. **1992** F. Mills *Overkill* (film): Those ain't your real choppers, are they?

6.a. a TOMMY GUN or machine gun.

1929 *Harper's Mag.* (Oct.) 535: Johnny Hand…had met the "chopper," *i.e.* machine-gun. **1929** Hotstetter & Beesley *Racket* 222: *Chopper*—Machine gun. **1931** Armour *Little Caesar* (film): Give me that chopper. **1940** Burnett *High Sierra* 104: A chopper in there and two or three rods. **1947** Spillane *I, the Jury* 18: Time was when you stood behind a chopper yourself, now you let a college kid do your blasting. **1959** *Swinging Syllables*: *Chopper*—Tommy gun, or any fast firing gun. **1976** Berry *Kaiser* 41: The Germans did get me at Soissons, though, only with shrapnel, not a chopper.

b. *Und.* a gunman who uses a CHOPPER.

1929 Sullivan *Look at Chicago* 11: Seven of the toughest booze operatives Chicago ever knew…were lined up and mowed down by "choppers"—that is, machine gun killers. **1930** Lait *On the Spot* 201: *Chopper*…Machine gunner. **1932** in *AS* (Feb. 1934) 21: *Chopper.* A machine gunner.

7. Orig. *Mil.* a helicopter.

1951 *N.Y. Herald-Tribune* (Dec. 16) II 5: *Chopper*: Helicopter. **1951** Sheldon *Troubling of a Star* 247: We have two choppers in the vicinity returning from an abort. **1953** White *Down the Ridge* 43: The first choppers to arrive in Korea were Bell helicopters with a 75–100 mile range. **1955** in Loosbrock & Skinner *Wild Blue* 495: The chopper might be plenty useful up there. **1960** *One Step Beyond* (ABC-TV): If you can spare a chopper, McCord, we'll vector him in. **1964** Dillon *Muscle Beach Party* (film): Come on, get in the chopper. **1964** in J. Lucas *Dateline* 16: Day after day he sat at the open door of his chopper as it took off and landed. **1969** Eastlake *Bamboo Bed* 16: The choppers came in with ear-hurting noise like enormous insects from another planet. **1975** J.P. Smith *Amer. Boys* 210: Chopper jockey dumped four WP's on him at once.

8.a. a customized motorcycle.

1966 H.S. Thompson *Hell's Angels* 97: A chopped hog, or "chopper," is little more than a heavy frame, a tiny seat and a massive 1,200-cubic-centimeter…engine.

b. any motorcycle, esp. if large and powerful.

1971 N.Y.U. student: Jeez, you look like you just got off of your chopper. Vroom, vroom!

9. the penis.

1973 *TULIPQ* (coll. B.K. Dumas): Dick, peter,…chopper, weenie.

¶ In phrases:

¶ **beat (one's) choppers** *beat (one's) chops* s.v. CHOPS.

1945 Bellah *Ward 20* 11: You start beating your choppers…and I'll slug you.

¶ **get the chopper, 1.** *Mil. Av.* to be killed. Also vars.

1955 L. Shapiro *Sixth of June* 117 [ref. to WWII]: Missing, eh? Well nothing's happened [to me] yet. I'm still waiting for the big chopper to hit me. **1963** E.M. Miller *Exile to Stars* 76: You heard Mom say….He bought the chopper.

2. *Mil.* to be dismissed; get the AX.

1969 Whiting *St.-Vith* 149: Bedell Smith would probably give him the boot, or in more American jargon, he would "get the chopper."

chopper *v.* to go or transport by helicopter.

1968 Hayes *Apocalypse* 783: He lay out on the stretcher while the doctor explained how he would be choppered back to the Phubai hospital and then put on a plane for Danang. **1968** Cameron *Dragon's Spine* 23: A…Team would chopper in. **1971** Glasser *365 Days* 107: He was choppered to his unit. **1968–77** Herr *Dispatches* 21: We can chopper you back to base-camp hospital in like twenty minutes. **1983** T. Page *Nam* 26: I…choppered out to a company plugging the paddies on an anti-rocket patrol. **1988** *Highwayman* (NBC-TV): Why hasn't this thing been choppered over there?

chops *n.pl.* [orig. dial. and colloq.; cf. early S.E. sense, 'jaws']

1.a. Now esp. *Black E.* the mouth or lips; (*occ.*) teeth.

***1589** in *OED*: Whose good names can take no staine, from a bishops chopps. ***1655** in *OED*: The sight of this egg…caused our monarchymen…to lick their chops. **1666** G. Alsop *Maryland* 48: The lawyer…might button up his Chops. ***1750** *Exmoor Scolding* 28: Chell gi'en a Strat in tha Chops [*sic omne*]. ***1811** *Lexicon Balatron.: Chops.* The mouth. I gave him a wherrit…across the chops; I gave him a blow over the mouth. ***1824** in *EDD*: Now each worried his chops (bit his lips). **1843** "J. Slick" *High Life in N.Y.* 13: A slap over the chops that made my teeth rattle. **1851** [G. Thompson] *Briston Bill* 14: What makes you look so down in the chops? **1864** in Horrocks *Dear Parents* 70: I…planted my right hand glove fairly in his chops. ***1889** Barrère & Leland *Dict. Slang* I 248: *Chops*…the mouth. A "wipe on the chops," a blow on the face. ***1894** in *EDD*: Shut yer chops an' keep yer belly warm. **1908** in Fleming *Unforgettable Season* 201: Take a punch at his chops in the dressing room. **1939** in Gold *Jazz Talk* 48: Louis…silently fingers the valves, while "getting his chops set." **1945** Himes *If He Hollers* 99: Man, I dared them chumps to open their chops. **1946** Mezzrow & Wolfe *Really Blues* 184: You never smacked your chops on anything sweeter. **1946** Boulware *Jive & Slang* 2: *Chops*…Lips. **1954** L. Armstrong *Satchmo* 112: If anyone made the mistake of passing that growler to him first he would put it to his chops and all we could see was his Adam's apple moving up and down. **1960** R. Reisner *Jazz Titans* 152: *Chops*: Lips. **1967** Lit *Dictionary* 11: *Cool your chops*—Shut your mouth. **1974** Weisman & Boyer *Heroin Triple Cross* 40: Dig your chops into the chateaubriand.

b. (used to receive the action of usu. intrans. verbs).—usu. constr. with *off*. [Cf. similar use of ASS; also *bust chops*, below.]

1970 N.Y.U. student: Man, I'm freezin' my chops off! **1971** N.Y.U. student: I was sweatin' my chops off in that place. **1986** Raven Den, Ark., man, age 35: *Workin' my chops off, freezin' my chops off*—those go back as far as I can remember. I'd say early '60's for sure.

2.a. *Jazz.* a trumpet player's strength of embouchure.

1947 in Gold *Jazz Talk* 48: He might not have the chops he used to have, but his ideas are always fine. **1962** H. Simmons *On Eggshells* 187: You'd need…practice to get your chops…back. **1966** Armstrong *Self-Portrait* 40: I'd go wild in those solos—up there in the high register all the time, and if I had some more chops left, just use 'em some more. **1972** *Nat. Lampoon* (Sept.) 67: A real musician should be able to "get off" on his own chops! **1993** *Newsweek* (Jan. 18) 39: Others would've killed to have his [Dizzy Gillespie's] chops.

b. Orig. *Jazz.* musical ability or skill; (*hence*) ability or skill of any sort.

1968 in A. Chapman *New Black Voices* 147: Maybe you could get your chops together on this horn. **1973** Ellington *Music My Mistress* 247: Musicians…who like to get together once or twice a week to try out their chops. **1977** in L. Bangs *Psychotic Reactions* 245: Where bands like the Iron Butterfly...got their *chops* together. *a*1979 Pepper & Pepper *Straight Life* 199: Those early fears and feelings of musical inadequacy...seem now dreamlike....He "got his chops back." **1989** *New Yorker* (May 8) 7: He had discovered the blues...and pretty soon he was saying "great chops" a lot. **1990** *Nat. Lampoon* (Apr.) 43: But his pickup chops remain rusty.

c. *Jazz.* a singer's tone or strength of voice.

1981 O'Day & Eells *High Times* 52 [ref. to 1930's]: Even though you haven't got much chops, you have other qualities to create excitement. **1989** *CBS This Morning* (CBS-TV) (Dec. 7): In my opinion, he's the best singer of the decade, in terms of pure vocal chops.

3. desire; appetite.

1968–77 Herr *Dispatches* 62: Sometimes your chops for action and your terror would reach a different balance.

4. *Black E.* (in sexual contexts) the thighs or legs.

1954–60 DAS: *Chops*...The legs, esp. the thighs; the hips. *Negro use.* **1967** P. Roth *When She Was Good* 62: All you have to do to make a girl spread her chops...is to tell her you love her.

¶ In phrases:

¶ **beat [up] (one's) chops** Esp. *Black E.* to talk or complain, esp. to no purpose.

1946 Boulware *Jive & Slang* 2: Beating Your Chops...Talking. **1946** Mezzrow & Wolfe *Really Blues* 146: They were beating up their chops like mad. **1954** L. Armstrong *Satchmo* 60: I turned around to continue beating my chops with Ponce. **1957** in *Tom & Jerry* (comics) (Dec. 1969) (unp.): You're not just beatin' your chops, chum! **1958** Hughes & Bontemps *Negro Folklore* 481: *Beating one's chops.* Talking a lot. *Stop beating up your chops, gal.* **1958** Russell *Permanent Playboy* 69: He had the spirit—the thing that you can beat up your chops about it for two weeks straight and never say what it is. **1960** Leckie *March to Glory* 22: Barber knew that gum-beating Marines are hard to lick. He knew, because he had beat his chops in ranks himself.

¶ **break [or bust] (someone's) chops, 1.** to harass by the forcible exertion of one's authority; (*also*) to make a nuisance of oneself; to anger, annoy, or frustrate.

1953 Paley *Rumble* 254: Rocky is breakin' our chops. **1970** Zindel *Your Mind* 17: And the two ladies in room 409...busted my chops about regulating the oxygen. *Ibid.* She'd say "How was school?" and I'd say it busted my chops. **1971** Sorrentino *Up from Never* 3: "The bulls might pull us over." "Yeah, jus' ta break chops." Jerry illustrated by cupping his crotch in his hands. *Ibid.* 40: Don't bust my chops. Cut out da bull. **1973** Maas *Serpico* 125: Somebody's trying to break my chops, and I think I know why. **1976** *Kojak* (CBS-TV): Billy Joe's been breaking chops. **1976** Price *Bloodbrothers* 184: He was breakin' my chops about me wantin' to do hospital work when I could be makin' triple the bread with the electricians. **1977** Olsen *Fire Five* 52: Hey...quit breaking her chops. **1980** Gould *Ft. Apache* 51: Will you stop breakin' my chops and just get outta here? **1982** Castoire & Posner *Gold Shield* 144: Tough...He breaks your chops.

2. to work to exhaustion; *bust (one's) ass* s.v. ASS.

1966 Neugeboren *Big Man* 62 [ref. to 1950's]: If Thorpe can get ten for busting his chops way back in 1930, I can get more than five from Louie. **1974** Lahr *Trot* 112: You spend eight weeks bustin' your chops for a newspaper. **1985** N.Y.C. man, age 37: I'm tired of bustin' my chops on this damn deal.

¶ **run (one's) chops out** *Black E.* to talk or complain.

1964 Rhodes *Chosen Few* 27: All he's gotta do is run his chops out and roll his eyes and Pearson would court-martial his own mammy if he's got one.

chop shop *n.* Orig. *Police.* a place where parts are stripped from stolen vehicles for unlawful resale.

1977 (cited in *W10*). **1979** Kilian, Fletcher, & Ciccone *Who Runs Chicago?* 68: The chop-shop operation, in which luxury cars are stolen, taken apart, and resold as separate, untraceable parts. **1979** *N.Y. Times* (Feb. 14) B 9: A police stakeout team saw a car with JSC license plates roll into an alleged auto "chop shop." **1982** WINS Radio News (Dec. 30): Chop shops [are] places where stolen cars are taken to be broken down into component parts. **1989** L. Roberts *Full Cleveland* 163: A chop shop...takes in stolen cars, strips the parts off, and sells them. **1993** *N.Y. Times* (Sept. 19) XIII 11: Most nearly new stolen cars are taken to chop shops, cannibalized and sold for parts.

chop-socky *adj.* [pun on *chop suey*] *Film.* (of a motion picture) primarily concerned with sensational adventure involving the use of Asian martial arts. Also as *n.*

1978 in *Barnhart Dict. Comp.* VII 89. **1982** in "J.B. Briggs" *Drive-In* 15:

The name of the flick is *Mad Monkey Kung Fu*. We're talking serious chopsocky here. **1986** *TV Guide* (July 26) 23: Martial-arts master Sho Kosugi in a chop-socky tale about a peace-loving Japanese immigrant forced to do battle with...ruthless criminals. **1988** *N.Y. Daily News* (June 8) 35: *Blood Kick*, a rickety 1970s chopsocky flick.

chopstick *n.* *Baseball.* a baseball bat.

1908 in Fleming *Unforgettable Season* 52: The ball shot off his chopstick on a loop-the-loop message for the clubhouse.

chopsticks *n.* a Chinese person.—used derisively.—used in direct address.

1939 *Detective Comics* (May) (unp.): Here, here, chopsticks, and where do you think you're going? **1955** B.J. Friedman, in *Antioch Rev.* XV 376: "You refueled, chopsticks?" he asked the mechanic. **1964** R. Moore *Green Berets* 226: Hey, Chopsticks! Bring the captain and his guest some chow.

chop up *v.* to divide.

1859 Matsell *Vocab.* 19: *Chopped Up.* When large quantities of goods are sold to a receiver, they are divided into small lots, and put into various houses, and this is called "chopping up the swag."

¶ In phrase:

¶ **chop it up** to discuss.

1956 H. Gold *Not With It* 192: Don't make me chop it up tonight. **1962–68** B. Jackson *In the Life* 252: I don't enjoy talking to people that I don't believe are my peers. But I do enjoy just chopping it up, kicking it around and seeing what other people seem to think.

chorine *n.* *Theat.* a chorus girl.

1922 in *OEDS*. **1934** Weseen *Dict. Slang* 138. **1935** O'Hara *Dr.'s Son* 151: It is estimated that the professional life of a chorine is ten years. **1952** "E. Box" *Fifth Position* 38: He got her into ballet when she was just another chorine. **1948** Lait & Mortimer *New York* 35: About this time, too, chorines and musicians are getting off. **1974** Robinson *Comics* 100: The snappy chorine theme was dropped. **1977–80** F.M. Stewart *Century* 102: It's Doreen the Chorine. **1985** C. Busch *Vampire Lesbians* 77: We're the youngest chorines in town. **1992** N. Cohn *Heart of World* 232: Evelyn Nesbit...was a chorine in the hit show *Floradora*.

chow[1] *n.* [fr. CHOW-CHOW] **1.** Orig. *Naut. in E. Asia.* food; provisions. Now *colloq.*

1856 in *DA*: *Chow*, something good to eat. **1882** Miller & Harlow *9'-51"* 259: Pork and beans have made us thin,/"Johnny rick-shaw-chow," *chin-chin;*/Town ahead, fresh grub anew. ***1886** Yule & Burnell *Hobson-Jobson* 164: *Chow* is in "pigeon" applied to food of any kind. **1898** *Amer. Soldier* (Manila) (Nov. 26) 1: The resources of the latter financially and in the matter of "chow" evidently was at low water mark. **1902** Swift *Iowa Boy* 255: They busied themself in silence in preparing the evening "chow." **1904** in J. London *Reports* 11: And my foreign food is giving out, and I was compelled to begin on native chow. *Ibid.* 33: Whitemen's chow. **1908** J.H. Williams, in *Independent* (Aug. 27) 472 [ref. to *ca*1890]: "Mama give plenty chow—velly good chow."...I gave "old mama" three more [dollars] for chow. **1916** *Army & Navy Jour.* (Sept. 30) 135: I...do not blame the sick man for making a complaint about the "chow." **1918** Ruggles *Navy Explained* 32: Chow...used as much if not more than any other slang navy word. **1919** Kauffman *Lost Squadron* 18: Chow call became insistent. **1921** Casey & Casey *Gay-Cat* 45: He can...git money fer his chow out of any old safe he meets. **1923** Weaver *Finders* 31: I grabbed some chow, and put the glad rags on. **1926** Mazzanovich *Trail of Geronimo* 169 [ref. to 1886]: We were compelled to omit our "chow" that evening and go hungry. **1940** *AS* (Dec.) 450: *Chow.* The words *chow* and *grub* are as common afloat as ashore. Mealtime is *chowtime.* **1942** *Leatherneck* (Nov.) 144: *Chow*—Food. **1945** Dos Passos *Tour* 57: How about chow? **1948** Ives *Wayfaring Stranger* 120: I sang lots of songs in lots of places for a great variety of chow. **1976** J.W. Thomas *Heavy Number* 91: Should we get chow? **1984** in Ehrhart *Carrying Darkness* 95: I...soon pass on/To chow, and sleep. **1984** "W.T. Tyler" *Shadow Cabinet* 102: A buck-fifty worth of rabbit chow.

2.a. *Mil.* mess; mealtime.

1898 in O.K. Davis *Pacific Conquests* 151: The soldier's house-building gets a welcome break at noon with "chow." **1898** Tisdale *Behind the Guns* 178: The zest of the brine savors everything, and a man no longer eats his meals or goes to "chow," but "scoffs his scouse." **1907** *Army & Navy Life* (Nov.) 559: We went to chow and met some more officers and came home and B-ached again. **1918** in Merrill *Butler College in War* 41: Early "chow" always follows these religious services. **1928** Scanlon *God Have Mercy* 114 [ref. to 1918]: I got orders to pack tonight and be ready to shove off right after chow tomorrow. **1961** Pirosh & Carr *Hell Is for Heroes* (film): "You seen Homer?" "Not since chow."

1964 Peacock *Drill & Die* 106: I want to talk to the troops at afternoon muster after noon chow. **1971** *Playboy* (May) 110: After morning chow, the second section will meet in front of the supply room. **1991** in LaBarge *Desert Voices* 29: We had breakfast and evening chow.

b. *Mil.* mess call.

1926 Nason *Chevrons* 116 [ref. to 1918]: He'll blow chow right on top of recall like he did yesterday.

¶ In phrase:

¶ **chow down!** Orig. *Navy.* (used to announce mess). Cf. CHOW DOWN, *v.*

1939 O'Brien *One-Way Ticket* 10 [ref. to *ca*1925]: Chow down, sailors! Come and get it! **1940** *Life* (Oct. 28) 99: Chow down! (soup's on). **1944** Kendall *Service Slang* 57: *Chow down*...dinner is served. **1955** Abbey *Brave Cowboy* 84: Chow down! The good word passed along. *Ibid.* 90: Chow! someone shouted. Chow down! [**1959** Sterling *Wake of the Wahoo* 181 [ref. to WWII]: Chow's down. You hungry?] **1963** Ross *Dead Are Mine* 111 [ref. to 1944]: Chow down, Lewis. If you want some you better get with it. **1968** Blackford *Torp. Sailor* 115 [ref. to 1917]: At ten the cook would cry, "Chow down!" The bunks emptied...[and] the men fell to.

chow² *n.* a Chinese person.—usu. used contemptuously. *Rare* in U.S.

*****1872** in *OEDS.* *****1876** in Wilkes *Austral. Colloq.* *****1888** *Sydney Bulletin* (Apr. 14) 8. **1910** Lomax *Cowboy Songs* 209: My boots are number eleven,/For I swiped them from a chow. *****1916** in *OEDS.* *****1966** Baker *Australian Language* 10.

chow *v.* **1.** Esp. *Mil.* to eat.

1900 Williams *Odyssey* 53: They must go and *chow.* **1906** M'Govern *Bolo & Krag* 110: I proceeded to Bill's residence to take possession, bathe and chow. **1907** *Army & Navy Life* (Oct.) 430: He was always lookin' around to find somethin' to chow, too. **1918** *Stars & Stripes* (May 3) 8: Chowing En Route to the Line. **1919** *307th Field Arty.* 34: Kept moving all day without "chowing" till evening. **1921** Casey & Casey *Gay-Cat* 54: We'll go in and chow first. **1924** in Hemingway *Sel. Letters* 130: We'll have an extra room and we'll chow together. **1930** Nason *A Corporal Once* 130 [ref. to 1918]: We chowed high in those days. **1942** *Yank* (Nov. 11) 5: They are convinced the Army doesn't chow as well [as the Navy]. **1968** W. Crawford *Gresham's War* 154: Might as well chow with us, Marine. **1986** Stinson & Carabatsos *Heartbreak* 44: You chow with Helen and me tonight, Tom. **1991** Coen & Coen *Barton Fink* (film): Let's chow.

2. *Mil.* to feed or provision.

1951 Thacher *Captain* 25: I'll chow my men in camp.

chow call *n. Mil.* mess call.

1918 *Lit. Dig.* (Sept. 28) 48: We sounded another chow call. **1919** Emmett *Give 'Way* 110: After chow-call that evening I met King going up the street. **1922** *Amer. Leg. Wkly.* (Jan. 13) 10: Here, take this "juice harp" to blow chow-call.

chow-chow *n.* **1.** Orig. *Naut.* in *E. Asia.* food.

*****1795** in *OEDS: Chow-chow...victuals or meat.* **1856** *Ballou's Dollar Mo. Mag.* (Sept.) 246: We want something to eat; savey? all the same as chow chow...Yes, chow-chow, grub, feed, victuals. **1868** in Boyer *Naval Surgeon* II 49: Satsuma is getting hard up for chow-chow. **1899** Gatewood *Smoked Yankees* 277: $1 a week and their chow-chow. **1979** McGivern *Soldiers* 68: I'm serving chow-chow right here.

2. a meal.

1868 in Boyer *Naval Surgeon* II 84: Am invited to a grand Japanese chow chow given by the Prince's Prime Minister in...honor of my services.

chow-chow *v.* [pidgin] to eat.

1854 in McCauley *With Perry* 121: But give, oh give me some dunderfunk,/And I'll chow-chow it joyfully——.

chowderbrain *n.* CHOWDER-HEAD.

1960 MacCuish *Do Not Go Gentle* 119 [ref. to WWII]: Don't let chowderbrain scare ya, Normy.

chowder-faced *adj.* white-faced.—usu. used contemptuously.

1898 in S. Crane *Complete Stories* 518: Of course I know you, you chowder-faced monkey.

chowder-head *n. N.E.* a fool. Hence **chowderheaded,** *adj.*

*****1819** Sir W. Scott, in *F & H* II 104: A very chowder-headed person. **1833** J. Neal *Down-Easters* I 119: If taint I'm a chowderhead. **1845** Durivage & Burnham *Stray Subjects* 49: O! you darn'd old chowderhead! **1851** Melville *Moby Dick* ch. xv: What's that stultifying saying about chowder-headed people? **1960** in Marx *Groucho Letters* 144: The

current administration [is] largely composed of ineffectual chowderheads. **1967** G. Moore *Killing at Ngo Tho* 55: I've got a lot of things you should know that I wouldn't tell just any chowderhead that came down the pike. **1980** McAleer & Dickson *Unit Pride* 66: Hey, you two chowderheads. **1988** C. Dillon et al. *Return of Killer Tomatoes* (film): "Guest room" is a euphemism for dungeon, Chowder-head.

chow-dog *n. Mil.* CHOWHOUND.

1920 *Latrine Rumor* (unp.): Mess was procured at a galley on the after deck....In two or three days of rather rough weather which occurred on the trip, the "chow-dog's" mission was a precarious one, as the pitfalls and backslidings were numerous and unexpected between galley and mess table.

chowdown *n.* [fr. the *v.*] a meal.

1942–45 Caniff *Male Call* (unp.): I'm tossing a chow-down tonight. **1957** Myrer *Big War* 306 [ref. to WWII]: Royal chow-down. *Ibid.* 325: Have us a little roast pig chow-down. **1965** Capote *In Cold Blood* 24: Three aspirin, cold root beer, and a chain of Pall Mall cigarettes—that was his notion of a proper "chow-down." **1966–67** W. Stevens *Gunner* 217 [ref. to WWII]: Little chowdown....Don't look like you brought any. **1981** *N.Y. Post* (Dec. 14) 25: None of the dishes listed below is considered a full meal, just something to tide you over until the next scheduled chow-down. **1990** *Bill & Ted's Adven.* (CBS-TV): All in favor of a chowdown say "Aye."

chow down *v.* [shift of phr. *chow down!* s.v. CHOW¹] **1.** Orig. *Navy.* to eat. See also CHOW¹, *n.*

1945 in *Calif. Folk. Qly.* (Oct. 1946) 19: Let's knock off...and chow down. **1951** Pryor *The Big Play* 9: Brock shoved Tom's pail along the bench. "Chow down!" **1958** J. Davis *College Vocab.* 14: *Chow down—* Eat. **1960** Leckie *Marines!* 4 [ref. to WWII]: But when I squatted in the slop to chow down, the boys crowded around me and started firing questions at me. **1961** Boyd *Lighter Than Air* 63 [ref. to WWII]: "Chow down!" yelled Cooper a short time later as he apportioned the soup into containers. **1965** Linakis *In Spring* 52 [ref. to WWII]: We chowed-down in the ward. **1965** Beech *Make War in Madness* 115 [ref. to Korean War]: "Yes, sir," Price said. "Just as soon as we get Paige's luggage and chow down." **1970** Wakefield *Going All the Way* 106: We might as well chow down.

2. to perform cunnilingus or fellatio; EAT.

1951 Leveridge *Walk on Water* 125 [ref. to WWII]: Chow down, you bastard. Chow down. **1974** *Penthouse* (Nov.) 161: Going down—giving head, eating pussy, chowing down, cunnilingus, oral sex—is still illegal in a few of the more backward states of the U.S. **1976** Univ. Tenn. student: Can't wait till I'm chowing down on that little honey. **1979** Hiler *Monkey Mt.* 75: You want to chow down?...You want to eat Lucy?

chow fight *n. Army.* a dinner party. Cf. TEA FIGHT.

1933 *Forum* (Dec.) 367: After we pull that chow fight for the Johnsons.

chow gun *n. Army.* a mobile field kitchen. [Quots. ref. to WWI.]

1925 *Adventure* (Dec. 20) 2: I see the chow gun smokin' away like a fire engine. **1926** *Sat. Eve. Post* (Oct. 23) 134: Just then the boche chow gun comes into the square. **1927** *Amer. Leg. Mo.* (Aug.) 93: I suppose I'll be assigned to the watercart or the chow-gun in this outfit. **1928–29** Nason *White Slicker* 201: Let's pray it's to get the coördinates of the nearest chow gun! **1931** Ottosen *Trench Arty.* (caption opp. p. 177): Exit of the Chow Gun (rolling kitchen) from Fort de la Bonnelle to the Front.

chow-hall *n. Mil.* a mess hall.

1919 Cowing *Dear Folks at Home* 6 [ref. to 1918]: Chow-hall. **1933** *Leatherneck* (July) 7: This Marine...usually says, "Follow me," leading them off to the chow hall.

chowhook *n. Mil.* a hand; GRUBHOOK.

1986 Former SP4, U.S. Army (coll. J. Ball): I remember a Mess Sergeant E-7 [in 1971] telling people "Get your chow-hooks off them biscuits."

chowhound *n.* [CHOW¹ + HOUND] *Mil.* an overenthusiastic eater.

1917 *Marines Magazine* (Oct.) 15: Weinstein...keeps unsullied his well-known record...as chow hound. **1918** in Cowing *Dear Folks* 5: The next scene is necessarily a short one, for I'm not master enough to describe a "chow-hound" in action. **1921** *Pirate Piece* (May) 3: A "chow hound" from "C" was as cross as could be. **1933** *Leatherneck* (Jan.) 19: Looks like all the "chow hounds" are on the move. **1922** *Amer. Leg. Wkly.* (Mar. 3) 11: The chow hound who was always first in line for seconds enjoyed a proud distinction. **1926** Nason *Chevrons* 118 [ref. to 1918]: "The chow hounds have got too much in their mess-kits to run around to the rear of the line still eatin'," remarked Ham. **1941** Hargrove *Pvt. Hargrove* 52: Its number-one chow hound, Buster Charnley, would drop around after supper. **1953–57** Giovannitti *Combine D:* Chow hound.…All you think of is your gut. **1960** Sire *Deathmakers* 45: Old chow-hound Nicholson. **1972** *N.Y. Post* (June 3) 4: Chow Hound.

chow-line *n.* **1.** *Mil.* a mess-line.
     1917 in Peat *Legion Airs* 84: Oh the chow line's the place that we mean. **1918** Morse *Letters* (Apr. 18) 114: Chow line. **1927** Stevens *Mattock* 1 [ref. to 1918]: Chow-line. **1928** Wharton *Squad* 3 [ref. to 1918]: They form up into a platoon file—the chow line. **1960** Bluestone *Cully* 175 [ref. to ca1955]: I mean I been on more pay lines than you been on chow lines, so I know what I'm talking about. **1971** Cameron *First Blood* 93 [ref. to WWII]: I've spent more time in the chow line than you have in this man's army! **1985** Former 1LT, U.S. Army, age 36 [ref. to 1968]: In basic the drill sergeant used to say, "You know-nothin' 'cruits, I got more time in pay lines than you got in chow lines."
     2. *Mil. Av.* (see quot.).
     1956 Heflin *USAF Dict.* 113: *Chow line*…A line formation, used by Japanese fighter pilots during WWII, above and parallel to a formation to be attacked. In such a formation the fighters were readily able to attack one by one in diving turns. *Slang*.

chow out *v.* to overindulge in food; PIG OUT.
     1978 *UTSQ:* Eat…*munch out, chow down, chow out, stuff my gut.* **1984** Algeo *Stud Buds & Dorks:* To eat a lot…*chow out.*

chow rag *n. Navy.* a meal pennant.
     1921 *Amer. Leg. Wkly.* (Apr. 22) 7: Loomis, what do you mean by flying the meal pennant (slang for chow rag) when the crew is no longer at its meal?

chow-slinger *n. Mil.* a cook.
     1917 in Bernheim *Passed as Censored* 67: Mr. Sarasati and Mr. Salvatore are at present chow-slingers at Base Hospital No. 18, A.E.F.

chowtime *n. Esp. Mil.* mess time; mealtime.
     1926 Nason *Chevrons* 116 [ref. to WWI]: It's getting near chow-time. **1943** Crowley & Sachs *Follow the Leader* (film): Hey, Ma, we're past chowtime.

chow up *v. Esp. Mil.* to eat. [Early quots. ref. to WWII.]
     1948 Wolfert *Act of Love* 512: Have you men chowed up? **1955** Klaas *Maybe I'm Dead* 128: Chow up while you've got a chance. **1957** E. Brown *Locust Fire* 96: Come on now…wet your face and we'll chow up at the shack. **1963** Lundgren *Primary Cause* 176: Better chow up, you guys. **1979** McGivern *Soldiers* 281: Let's chow up. **1981–85** S. King *It* 284: Bill…had been chowing up a piece of…cake.

Christ *n.* daylights; stuffing; BEJESUS.
     1977 (quot. at QUAIL). **1984** in Terkel *Good War* 100: They see us movin' up, they're gonna beat the Christ out of us.
     ¶ In phrases:
     ¶ **Christ on a crutch** (used as a vulgar, semijocular oath). Also vars.
     1928 J.M. March *Set-Up* 124: Christ on a raft!—/What a sock that Sailor had! **1930** Fredenburgh *Soldiers March!* 225 [ref. to 1918]: "Christ on a raft," Zorn groaned. **1937** Weidman *Wholesale* 34: "Jesus Christ on a raft!" I said. **1942** *ATS* 225: Christ-on-a-crutch! **1947** in Botkin *Sidewalks* 95: Kee-rist-on-a-bicycle, look at 'em! **1952** Uris *Battle Cry* 4 [ref. to WWII]: Christ on a crutch! Right off the farm, a barefoot Rav. *Ibid.* 104: Jesus H. Christ on a crutch. **1960** MacCuish *Do Not Go Gentle* 144 [ref. to WWII]: Christ on a crutch, your men shoulda spotted 'em. **1961** Sullivan *Shortest, Gladdest Years* 15: Christ on a crutch, man. They're not worth five. **1962** Harvey *Strike Command* 198: Christ in a basket! She's heading straight for us! **1971** "R. Stark" *Lemons* 18: Good Christ on a crutch! **1973** R.M. Brown *Rubyfruit* 154: Jesus H. Christ on a crutch, I've just been picked up by a spectacular six-foot woman. **1983** Wambaugh *Delta Star* 22: Jesus Christ on Roller Skates! **1987** *Nat. Lampoon* (June) 80: How dare you barge in here without knocking? Christ on a crutch!
     ¶ **since Christ was a corporal** *Army.* since time immemorial. Also vars.
     [*ca1595* Shakespeare *Twelfth Night* III ii: They haue beene grand Iury men, since before Noah was a Saylor.] [**1900** Reeves *Bamboo Tales* 20: Private McCoy…had been in the service since George Washington was a "lance jack."] **1921** Dos Passos *3 Soldiers* 75 [ref. to WWI]: Ain't had any pay since Christ was a corporal. I've forgotten what it looks like. **1933** Clifford *Boats* 132: Old Pop-Eye Johnson [had been] sergeant in the regiment since "Christ was a lance corporal," as the men said. **1963** Doulis *Path* 332: Those of us who been in the Army since Christ was a corporal know what we're gonna be doing tomorrow.

1970 *N.Y. Post* (Apr. 7) 5: Dana Stone had been in Vietnam since Christ was a corporal, as the grunts in the field would say. **1982** Del Vecchio *13th Valley* 113: Man, Egan was a cherry way back when Christ was a corporal. **1986** Stinson & Carabatsos *Heartbreak* 1: Yeah,…since Christ was a corporal.

Christ-awful *adj.* god-awful.
     1942 Algren *Morning* 120: The fellas begun givin' me a Christ-awful razzin'. **1975** Larsen *Runner* 40: And don't bring none of that Christawful pork and applesauce shit.

Christ-bitten *adj.* (used as an expletive); (also, in 1948 quot.) holding strong Christian beliefs.
     [**1935** S. Anderson *Winterset* 5: These Jesus-bitten professors!] **1938–39** Dos Passos *Young Man* 257: Now here was this christbitten hell-bound party line f—g them proper. **1948** McHenry & Myers *Home Is Sailor* 95: She's Christ-bitten. She thinks I need saving. **1958** Cooley *Run for Home* 187: Nuthin' to do and nuthin' to drink on Sunday in this Christ-bitten place!

christen *v. Und.* (see 1859 quot.).
     *1781** in *F & H* II 105: This alteration is called *christening*, and the watch thus transformed faces the world without fear of detection. **1859** Matsell *Vocab.* 19: *Christening.* Erasing the name of the maker from a stolen watch and putting another in its place. *1872** in *F & H* II 105: The tools found in his possession he used for *christening* stolen watches and putting new bows to them.

Christer *n.* **1.** a self-righteous Christian.—usu. used contemptuously.
     1921 McAlmon *Hasty Bunch* 263: I don't give a Christer's damn. **1927** S. Lewis *Elmer Gantry* 21 [ref. to 1902]: Heh! I suppose you're a Christer, too! **1927** Hemingway *Men Without Women* 210: You're a regular Christer, big boy. **1928** *AS* (Apr.) 346: Regarding "Christer,"…I can testify that it was a term in common use when I was a student in the Boston University Medical School in 1893–97. It was always used in a disparaging way of narrow, pious, sanctimonious students. **1934** Minehan *Boy & Girl Tramps* 152: How do those Christers get so fat if it ain't off our lean shanks? **1935** in Horowitz *Campus Life* 83 [ref. to ca1917]: Included…the "grinds" and "Christers." **1942** Hollinghead *Elmtown's Youth* 257: The boys who attend church socials…are often looked down upon by the boys "wise in the ways of the world" as…"a bunch of Christers." **1956** Grant & Daves *Last Wagon* (film): Now look here, you Christers! This here's Comanche Todd!…An Injun-lovin' murderer! **1958** S.H. Adams *Tenderloin* 204: Oh, I just thought I'd like to take a slant at the old Christer's…mug. **1963** D. Tracy *Brass Ring* 191: And where do you get off calling me a christer? **1979** McGivern *Soldiers* 25: Korbick had pounded on him…all through basic just because he wasn't a Christer. **1981–85** S. King *It* 175: Run by people Ben's mother called the "Christers."
     2. *N.E.* something very large or excessive.
     1956 H.P. Beck *Folklore of Maine* 168: A large deer which was "a regular old Christer." **1976** Hayden *Voyage* 26: Let the boys rest. This trip had been a Christer. *Ibid.* 229: One Christer of a hurricane. **1979** in *DARE: Wan't* that thunderstorm a *christer!*

Christian *n.* ¶ In phrase: **make a Christian [out] of** to force (a recalcitrant person) into a demanded pattern of behavior. Cf. *make a believer out of* S.V. BELIEVER.
     1943 W. Simmons *Joe Foss* 35: Bet that makes a Christian out of you. You won't pull that stunt again. **1943** *Reader's Digest* (Dec.) 111: But it sure made Christians out of the others. **1947** Blankfort *Big Yankee* 102: The court-martial made a "Christian" of Carlson. **1982** D. Williams *Hit Hard* 15: Kinda hate to see you go, Williams. I think I'da made a Christian out of you before long. **1988** *Reaching for Skies* (TNT-TV): That happened often enough to make a Christian out of you.

Christ-killer *n.* **1.** a Jew.—usu. used contemptuously.—usu. considered offensive. Hence **Christ-killing,** *adj.*
     *1851–61** H. Mayhew *London Labour* IV 223: They was mostly Christ-killers, and chousing a Jew was no sin. **1865** in Harris *High Times* 157: Whar's my breetches, yu durned close clipt, Ch—st killin, hog hatin, bainch laiged son av a clothes hoss? **1878** in Glanz *Jew in Folklore* 10: Get out, you bloody Christ-killer. **1893** Macdonald *Prison Secrets* 64: Ye d— Chroist-killin' son av a ——. *1909** Ware *Passing English* 74: *Christ-killers*…Jews. Passing away—chiefly used by old army men. "What can you expect?—he's a Christ-killer." **1917** Cahan D. *Levinsky* 9: Boys would descend upon him with shouts of "Damned Jew!" "Christ-killer!" and sick their dogs at him. **1923** Ornitz *Haunch, Paunch & Jowl* 27: The Irish lads shouted, "Kill the Christ killers!" **1937** E. Anderson *Thieves Like Us* 48: I called him a Christ-killer and a few other

things. **1944** Brooks *Brick Foxhole* 31: Them Christ-killers. You know they're running this country, don't you? **1951** Longstreet *Pedlocks* 374: Where I come from, we don't mix with niggers or Christ-killers. **1965** in H. Ellison *Sex Misspelled* 318: Dirty little Christ-killers! **1971** *N.Y. Times* (Oct. 10) 17 [ref. to 1933]: And at 11, why was I sent to the principal for fighting another kid who all but tore my heart out by calling me a "Christ-killer"? **1981–85** S. King *It* 65: Hey, you fuckin Christ-killer! Where ya goin? **1988** *New York* (Aug. 29) 50: The Christ-killers...have struck again: The *Jews* are responsible.
2. see CHRIST-KILLING.

Christ-killing *n. Hobo.* noisy, esp. radical, political oratory, esp. from a soapbox orator. Hence **Christ-killer.**
1930 "D. Stiff" *Milk & Honey* 202: *Christ killing*—To speak from the soap box giving the *economic argument*. **1931** Adamic *Laughing* 208: Now and then I stopped to listen to the argufiers or "nuts" in Pershing's Park and on the Plaza, most of them professional atheists, or "Christ-killers," full of sound and fury, as fanatical in their way as the religionists were in theirs.

Christless *adj. & adv.* goddamned.
1912 Murphy *Logbook for Grace* (July 16) 14: That usually leads to a gentle admonition that he'll be goddamned if he'll stand for one such word from any Christless bastard on board, afore or abaft the mainmast. **1968** "R. Hooker" *MASH* 108: We wouldn't be going out of our way for a Christless Regular Army Colonel if we didn't mean it! **1978** S. King *Stand* 85: The desert was taking a Christless long time to bloom. **1980** in *N.E. Folklore* XXVIII (1988) 43: He got this christless big book and opened it up.

Christly *adj. & adv.* CHRISTLESS.
1925 Nason *Top Kick* 188 [ref. to 1918]: Aw, how the hell can I fire if the christly aimin' point blew out? **1944** H. Brown *A Walk in the Sun* 24: "We'll never find that christly road," Porter said. **1949** "F. Bonnamy" *Blood & Thirst* 146: Ladies gettin Christly scarce. **1955** Goethals *Command* 147: It was so christly dark in there ——. **1966** W. Wilson *LBJ Brigade* 54: The copter makes a Christly racket as it violently shivers along. **1967** Dibner *Admiral* 20: A Christly mess. **1968** "R. Hooker" *MASH* 100: And get that Christly gas-passer in here! **1973** in A. Sexton *Letters* 401: I've just been too Christly busy. **1980** in *N.E. Folklore* XXVIII (1988) 23: The christly dooryard was full of them.

Christmas *n.* ¶ In phrase: **So's Christmas!** (a sarcastic retort to the promise that someone or something is coming).
1938 H. Miller *Trop. Capricorn* 255: Not coming any more than Christmas was coming. **1977** L. Jordan *Hype* 18: "I'm coming." "So's Christmas!"

Christmas tree *n.* **1.** *Petroleum Industry.* an assembly of valves and flow connections at the top of the casing of an active oil well.
1925 Dobie *Hunting Ground* 66: The "Christmas tree" is a group of fittings consisting of several valves of different sizes used to cap a well after it is completed. **1944** Boatright & Day *Hell to Breakfast* 147: The well is finally closed with a manifold of valves and connections universally known as the "christmas tree." It may consist of only one valve or a dozen valves and other elaborate control equipment. **1951** Pryor *The Big Play* 97: That's the Christmas tree....See those pipes running out from it?
2. Esp. *Navy.* any of various control panels that utilize red and green indicator lights.
1945 Trumbull *Silversides* 8: The neat rows of rectangular green and red lights called the "Christmas tree" which by their color tell the current state of all the submarine's valves and hull openings. **1949** Morison *Naval Ops. in WWII* IV 194: In these up-and-down operations, the diving officer kept a careful eye on the "Christmas tree," a vertical panel of red and green lights, which told him at a glance the status of the hatches, valves and other openings. **1952** Cope & Dyer *Petty Off. Gde.* 337: *Christmas tree.* Any control panel featuring red and green indicator lights. Examples are found in submarine conning tower and on magnetic sweepers. **1958** Grider *War Fish* 39: In front of him, at face level, was the Christmas Tree, a board with red and green lights for every vital opening in the hull and all the ballast-tank vents. **1959** Chambliss *Silent Service* 154: *Christmas tree* A display of lights on a board fixed to the bulkhead of a submarine for the purpose of indicating key situations throughout the boat involved in diving. In earlier (i.e., pre-1941) boats, the lights were green to indicate correct diving situations, and red to indicate if any given situation was not correct. **1984** Holland *Let Soldier* 184: The Christmas tree lit up and the engine quit.

3. *Mil. Av.* (see quot.).
1945 Hamann *Air Words: Christmas trees.* Triangular-shaped cluster rocket-launchers that are installed under the wings of airplanes.
4. *Bowling.* (for a right-handed bowler) a 3-7-10 split or (for a left-handed bowler) a 2-7-10 split; (*occ.*) a 1-7-10 leave.
1949 Cummings *Dict. Sports* 72. **1976** *Webster's Sports Dict.* 78.
5. *Narc.* a red and green capsule containing a barbiturate, esp. Tuinal.
1963 Braly *Shake Him* 24: Bennies, redbirds, yellow jackets, christmas trees. **1965** Vermes *Helping Youth* 119: Barbiturates...have colorful slang names like "redbirds," "Christmas trees," and "yellow jackets." **1968** Louria *Drug Scene* 208: Christmas trees, tuinal (secobarbital and amobarbital). **1976** Braly *False Starts* 267: A Christmas Tree, a cap filled with red and green spansules.
6. *Pol.* a legislative bill carrying a number of usu. unrelated riders. Also as *v.*
1968 Safire *New Language* 382. **1971** *U.S. News & W.R.* (Mar. 8) 44: Result, legislators say, may well be a "Christmas tree" bill, with something for everybody on it. **1979** Homer *Jargon* 36: *Christmas-treeing* that bill. **1986** WINS Radio News (Sept. 14): It's called a Christmas-tree bill because legislators tack on all sorts of ornaments. **1992** *Capital Gang* (CNN-TV) (May 16): This bill is in danger of becoming a Christmas tree.

Christopher *interj.* [euphem. for *Christ*] (used as a mild oath). Also extended vars.
1834 Caruthers *Kentuck. in N.Y.* I 188: O Christopher! what a stump speech he could make. **1895** Wood *Yale Yarns* 65: Christopher Hemlock! Two coppers...grabbed me by the arm. **1930** Sage *Last Rustler* 103: By the land-thirsty-sea-rovin' Christopher Columbo—you will!

chrome-dome *n.* **1.** a bald person.
1962 in IUFA *Folk Speech*: "Chrome Dome" is used to describe a bald person. **1974** Univ. Tenn. student: A chrome dome is a baldheaded person. We called our high school math teacher *chrome dome* in 1965. **1978** *N.Y. Post* (Dec. 26) 3: MacLeod—"Lots of women think chrome domes are irresistible. We all think Gavin is." **1980** Santoli *Everything* 62: Good old Chrome Dome. I named her that because she was bald on top of the head. **1981–85** S. King *It* 466: Bill...went for the chrome dome look.
2. *Mil.* a lightweight, highly reflective helmet used in various drills and displays.
1968 Mares *Marine Machine* 116: For the first time, they dressed like Marines, exchanging their "chrome domes" for steel helmets. **1986** Former SP4, U.S. Army, age 34: I actually wore a *chrome dome* as a color guard in 1977. That's the only term I've ever heard applied to them—it was in common use. **1987** D. da Cruz *Boot* 188: Recruits perform PT in the cool morning hours, wear aluminum-coated "chrome dome" helmets to reflect the sun's heat.

chromo *n.* an obnoxious person.
1935 Miller "G" Men (film): Take care of all those old chromos with the mumps. **1937** in D. Runyon *More Guys* 223: She is the chromo sitting behind him.

chronic *n. Narc.* marijuana.
1993 *Source* (July) 65: A fat puff of the chronic. **1993** *Village Voice* (N.Y.C.) (June 22) 36: Cannabis, ganja, kaya, weed, cheeba, chronic.

chub *n.* a chubby person. Also **chub-chub.**
***1838** J. Hogg, in *EDD*: When the bishop flung the water on your boy's face, how the little chub looked at him! **1869** *Overland Mo.* III 129: For the Texan soubriquet "Chub" I know of no explanation, unless it be found in the size of the Eastern Texans. **1876** *Harper's Mo.* (Dec.) 30: The *Chub*...is round, rosy-cheeked, and omnivorous. **1967–70** in *DARE.* **1971** T.C. Bambara *Gorilla* 8: She was a chub-chub like me and not very pretty. **1985** Univ. Tenn. instructor: You're turning into a real chub.

chubbo *n.* a chubby person.
1977 *Muppet Show* (CBS-TV): Knock it off, chubbo! **1982** *Diff'rent Strokes* (ABC-TV): So long, chubbo! **1987** Kent *Phr. Book* 153: A chubbo.

chubby-chaser *n.* a man who is attracted to chubby women.
1975–76 T. McNally *Ritz* 27: *Tiger:* You trying to tell me he's a chubby chaser?...Someone who likes (*He gestures, indicating great bulk*). **1986** Churcher *N.Y. Confidential* 214: Scrawny chubby-chasers (admirers). **1992** *Sally Jessy Raphaël* (synd. TV series): Do you consider yourself a chubby-chaser?

Chuck *n.* [sugg. by syn. CHARLIE] **1.** *Black E.* a white man;

white persons generally. Also attrib.—usu. used contemptuously.

1965 C. Brown *Manchild* 333: That's the same thing that Mr. Chuck's been doing all these years. **1967** *Time* (May 26) 17: The Negro G.I. can get away from "Chuck," the white man. **1968** J. Lester *Look Out Whitey* 19: It went from "white man" to "whitey"; from "Mr. Charlie" to "Chuck." **1970** *Current Slang* III & IV 25: He sings pretty good for a chuck. **1971** G. Davis *Coming Home* 21: The average mother-fucking Chuck doesn't feel anything. **1973** R. Roth *Sand in Wind* 225: When they see some chuck they don't know, they just assume he's a bigot. **1973** Huggett *Body Count* 99: I think you got a kindly father-image of all the Chuck officers....He just couldn't understand all the fuss Wilson and the others made about Chucks. **1978** J. Webb *Fields of Fire* 194: He don't wanna see any Chuck dudes. **1979** Hiler *Monkey Mt.* 155: The people that like King was the Toms and the Chucks. You dig it? *a***1987** T. Wolfe *Bonfire of Vanities* 3: Chuck come up to Harlem and gonna take care a business for the black community.

2. *Mil.* the Viet Cong or North Vietnamese armed forces; a member of such forces.

1981 C. Nelson *Picked Bullets Up* 327: Dropped old Chuck like a bad habit, I tell you what. *Ibid.* 348: Two dead Chucks. **1990** G.R. Clark *Words of VN War* 164: GIs had many names for their Vietnamese enemy...[including] *Charlie, Charles, Chuck* [etc.]. **1991** Reinberg *In Field: Chuck*...the enemy.

chuck[1] *n.* **1.** Esp. *West.* food; provisions; GRUB.

****1850** in *F & H* II 105: The prisoner, upon coming to his cottage door had tried hard to get some *chuck* out of him, but had failed. **1865** in *DA.* **1872** in "M. Twain" *Life on Miss.* 295: I wish i was nere you so i could send you chuck (refreshments) on holidays. ****1873** Hotten *Slang Dict.* (ed. 5): *Chuck*...anything to eat. **1874** Pember *Metropolis* 259: They had cooked their "chuck," as they called their bit of supper. **1879** in Miller & Snell *Why West Was Wild* 392: plenty of chuck and $3 a day from the railroad company. **1881** Dodge *Wild Indians* 302: Chuck is a word in almost universal use among the Plains Indians of all tribes and languages. It means food. **1885** Siringo *Texas Cowboy* 40: I used to get my chuck from the cook who thought I was a bully boy. **1887** Andrews *Mountebanks* 12: Haul your chair up to supper, and eat your chuck. **1890** Finerty *War-Path & Bivouac* 151 [ref. to 1876]: You fellows look as if you didn't have any chuck (the frontier word for rations) in a month. **1894** *Century* (Feb.) 519: You can batter for clothes, chuck, and booze all right enough. **1894** Putnam *Offensive* 241: The cooks, around the little fires...uttered one word, "Chuck!" and the men drifted toward them in glad obedience. **1895** *Harper's* (Oct.) 780: We have good luck/In bumming our chuck./To hell with the man that works. **1897** *Cosmopolitan* (Mar.) 554: I want you to look out not to kick up the dust so that it falls into the chuck I'm a cookin'. **1901** Oliver *Roughing It with Regulars* 11: The soldiers...were feasting upon government "chuck," hard tack, canned beef and coffee. **1905** W.S. Kelly *Lariats* 19: We ain't got a bite of chuck in the house cooked yit. **1921** Z. Grey *Mysterious Rider* 14: Jake has been hollerin' thet chuck was ready. Now we can eat. **1929** "M. Brand" *Beacon Creek* 7: What kind of chuck you throw to the boys in the hoosegow? **1952** Bonham *Snaketrack* 17: Why don't you go uptown and get some chuck? **1973** Mathers *Riding the Rails* 38: He'll treat you right—always give you some chuck. **1979** Terkel *Amer. Dreams* xviii: A Dutchman cooks your chuck.

2. mealtime.

1915 in J.I. White *Git Along Dogies* 144: I stays until...after chuck.

chuck[2] *n.* a woodchuck.

1957 *Sat. Eve. Post* (Aug. 10) 69: From 'chucks to charging lions. **1972** M. Kumin, in J.P. Hunter *Norton Intro. Poetry* (ed. 2) 43: There's one chuck left. Old wily fellow.

chuck[1] *v.* **1.a.** to toss or pitch; hurl. Now *S.E.*

****1593** in *OED*: Yes, this old one will I give you (chucks him old hose and doublet). **1798** T. Jefferson, in *OED*: To chuck a stone, etc. = to throw. ****1808** Jamieson *Etym. Dict. Scot. Lang.* I 426: To *chuck*...To toss or throw any thing smartly out of the hand. **1813–18** Weems *Drunk. Look. Glass* 63: Let's chuck these carts into the River. **1861** in C.W. Wills *Army Life* 35: They are talking of chucking us into Cairo and making us garrison it this winter. **1868** Aldrich *Bad Boy* 72: "Threw it into the river!" shrieked the smaller boys....One luckless urchin said, "Chucked it," for which happy expression he was kept in at recess. **1891** Clurman *Nick Carter* 19: Better chuck him into the river now. **1895** *Harper's* (Dec.) 962: Do they chuck in a policy for that. **1900** White *Westerners* 17: He chucked it down on the prairie, an' called it the Black Hills. **1939–40** Tunis *Kid from Tomkinsville* 202: Attaboy, Raz, tha's chucking, that is.

b. to hurl (a rider) to the ground.—also constr. with *off*.

****1841** in *OEDS* I 521: My horse...tore off with me...there was a fair chance of my being chucked off. **1922** Rollins *Cowboy* 125: Many a tenderfoot...has...been "spilled," "chucked," or "dumped" (by a horse).

c. to pass (food) at table.

1867 Clark *Sailor's Life* 111: Chuck the beef along this way; do look alive for once, man.

d. to vomit up.

*ca***1877–89** in *EDD.* **1942** *ATS* 159. **1971** Dahlskog *Dict.* 13: *Chuck*...to vomit, as: to chuck one's dinner. **1977** Dunne *True Confessions* 33: The first thing Bingo did when he saw the body was chuck his Wheaties.

e. *Sports.* to lose (a game) through clumsiness or connivance; throw.

1906 *Independent* (Nov. 29) 1259: I always said he was a stiff...Now Duffer chucked the game.

f. to throw away; discard.

1911 in Mager *Sherlocko* 106: Chuck that butt you're smoking. **1980** Univ. Tenn. instructor: Never chuck your first draft.

2. to hit, as with the fist.

1864 Northrop *Chronicles* 79: Peacable men occasionally get "chucked in the mug" as they call it, for attempting a friendly interference.

3.a. to give up; abandon; quit.—also constr. with *up* or (in recent use) *in*.

****1878** in *OEDS*: A stalwart navvy...declared he must "chuck it up" if he could not be a Turk. **1896** F.H. Smith *Tom Grogan* 98: Shall I chuck up the job or stick? **1903** A.H. Lewis *Boss* 125: You must chuck sentiment. **1908** J. London *M. Eden* 52: When'd you chuck the cannery? **1914** Kreymborg *Edna* 25: We chucked our jobs. **1923** in Hammett *Knockover* 136: I'd made up my mind that he was going to tell me all I wanted to know, or I'd chuck the job. **1923** O'Brien *Best Stories of 1923* 78: I've chucked the stuff. **1926** Hormel *Co-Ed* 83: Oh, chuck the venerable-old-grad stuff, Tobey! **1927–30** Rollins *Jinglebob* 37: He cut loose from his father and chucked college. **1949** Bezzerides *Thieves' Market* 53: He hated to quit any other way. He had to win; then he would chuck it. **1966** Susann *Valley of Dolls* 48: Suppose...someone...asked you to marry him and chuck the show before it even opened. **1970** Gattzden *Black Vendetta* 49: He just chucked it in. **1980** Ciardi *Browser's Dict.* 76: *Chuck the habit* To break off an addiction or a habituated behavior. **1984** W. Murray *Dead Crab* 217: I know I'll feel better tomorrow, but right now I could chuck it all in.

b. to refrain from considering or speaking.—constr. with *it.*—used imperatively.

****1888** in *OEDS*: *Chuck it.* **1906** Ford *Shorty McCabe* 165: "Why, her lip was tremblin' like a lost kid's." "Chuck it!" **1928–30** Fiaschetti *Gotta Be Rough* 255: You're just wasting your time looking for him. It's no use. Chuck it. **1940** *AS* (Oct.) 334: *Chuck It.* Be quiet. **1967** *Lit Dictionary* 48: *Chuck It*—a command to shut up.

4. to dismiss, jilt, etc.

****1883** in *OEDS* I: Look how easily she chucked you up because she did not think you good enough. **1914** Patten *Lefty o' the Bush* 151: It'll be tough if you're really chucked off your college team. **1926** in Gelman *Photoplay* 95: She chucked Irving Berlin and ran away to marry John Pialoglov. **1961** (quot. at FINK).

5.a. to perform (acrobatics).

1883 Needham *Arabs* 69: You wouldn't say so if you was to see him chuckin' handsprings and somersets a-side of the 'buses.

b. to have (a fit or spell).

****1881–84** Davitt *Prison Diary* I 116: What you saw the other day was what we call "chucking a dummy," or, as you might name it, in your less expressive manner of speaking, "counterfeiting a fit." ****1889** Barrère & Leland *Dict. Slang* I 251: To "chuck" a fit is a common slang expression for counterfeiting one. **1927** in Hammett *Knockover* 324: She'll chuck a convulsion. **1931** D. Runyon, in *Collier's* (Nov. 14) 8: The chances are she will start chucking faints one after the other.

6. to put on; assume.

1931 D. Runyon, in *Collier's* (Sept. 26) 7: Many a party...chucking quite a swell is nothing but the phonus bolonus. **1931–35** D. Runyon *Money* 167: He always chucks a good front, and has a kind face. **1935** in R. Nelson *Dishonorable* 245: I've got to keep chucking a front if I'm going to try to...raise the money.

7. to throw (a party).

1934 Appel *Brain Guy* 8: Since when did Paddy chuck parties? **1949** Ellson *Tomboy* 72: Of course, I'd chuck some real parties.

chuck[2] *v.* to eat.—usu. constr. with *up.*

1881 Nye *Forty Liars* 205: Probably you have never chucked up at the Thornburgh. **1933** Ersine *Prison Slang* 27: We chuck up in here. **1944** *Pap. Mich. Acad.* XXX 598: *Chuck up*, to eat. **1964** Harris *Junkie Priest* 65: Starting to chuck. Eating all they give me. *Ibid.* 120: I see you're chucking. That's a junkie word. It means eating well.

chuck horrors *n.pl. Und. & Narc.* an abnormal craving for food, esp. as the result of drug withdrawal.
1925–26 J. Black *You Can't Win* 39 [ref. to 1890's]: They were "fresh fish," new arrivals, who had not yet acquired the "chuck horrors," that awful animal craving for food that comes after missing half a dozen meals. **1936** Dai *Opium Addiction* 197: *Chuck-horrors*. When an addict is breaking the habit, he develops what is called the chuck-horrors. He is always hungry and will eat anything at any time and in any amount. **1966** Brunner *Face of Night* 231: *Chuck horrors*—the tremendous appetite an addict gets when he has stopped using narcotics. **1980** Manchester *Darkness* 59: The withdrawal routine would start again: yawning, shaking, sweating, cramps, nausea…and the chuck horrors.

chuck house *n. West.* a cookhouse or boarding house.
1908 Raine *Wyoming* 97: If y'u miss it, y'u'll feed at some other chuckhouse. **1910** in *DA* 323. **1918** *DN* V 23: *Chuck-house,* n. A boarding house, in connection with a mine or mill. Coeur d'Alenes.

chucklehead *n.* a fool; a silly person.
*****1731** in *OED.* *****1808** Jamieson *Etym. Dict. Scot. Lang.* I 427: *Chuckle-Head, s.* A dolt, Aberd[eenshire]. *Chuckle-Headed, adj.* Doltish, *Ibid.* **1848** Bartlett *Amer.: Chucklehead.* A fool. Not peculiar to America. **1863** in Beatty *Memoirs of Volunteer* 176: McCook is a chucklehead. **1899** Munroe *Shine Terrill* 43: You've let go the line, you blamed chucklehead! **1981** *Rod Serling's Mag.* (Sept.) 19: Don't count on it, chucklehead! **1986–91** Hamper *Rivethead* 162: Hey, you chuckleheads!

chuckleheaded *adj.* foolish; simple-minded.
*****1764** in *OED.* *****1808** (quot. at CHUCKLEHEAD). **1821** Waln *Hermit in Phila.* 28: *Beetle headed—Bottle-headed—Buffle-headed—* and *Chuckle-headed!!!* **1849** Melville *White Jacket* 234: Our chuckleheaded reefers on board here. **1889** "M. Twain" *Conn. Yankee* 63: Of all the childish, idiotic, chuckle-headed, chicken-livered superstitions. **1907** S.E. White *Arizona* 9: The whole thing was a trap-for-me—and I'd walked into it, chuckle-headed as a prairie dog!

chuckline *n.* ¶ In phrase: **ride [the] chuckline** *West.* to ride from ranch to ranch seeking board and odd jobs. Hence **chuckline rider,** *n.*
1903 A. Adams *Log of a Cowboy* 280 [ref. to 1882]: He was riding the chuckline all right, but Miller gave him a welcome as he was the real thing. **1925** in Botkin *Treas. Amer. Folk.* 95 [ref. to late 19th C.]: No, he didn't work for me. Just lived with me. Riding the chuck line. **1928** Santee *Cowboy* 48: But I rode the chuck-line from then till spring before I got another job. **1931** Raine *Beyond R. Grande* 12: I'm riding the chuck line. **1936** R. Adams *Cowboy Lingo* 27: The appellation of "chuck-line rider" was applied to anyone who was out of a job and riding through the country. Any worthy cowpuncher may be forced to "ride chuck-line" at certain seasons, but the professional "chuck-line rider" was just a plain "range bum" or "saddle tramp."

chucks *n.pl.* CHUCK HORRORS.
1952 W. Burroughs *Junkie* 13: *Chucks.* Excessive hunger often for sweets. This comes on an addict when he has kicked his habit far enough so that he starts to eat. When an addict is cut off the junk he can't eat for several days. **1956** Holiday & Dufty *Lady Sings the Blues* 134: When you're kicking, you get what we call the chucks, and after that you're hungry all the time. **1970** Landy *Underground Dict.* 50: *Chucks, the…*Intense craving for food, usually sweets.

chuck wagon *n.* **1.** *West.* a cook wagon. Now *S.E.*
1887 [C.C. Post] *10 Yrs. Cowboy* 302: This ain't my chuck wagon of course. **1890** in *OEDS.* **1891** Lummis *David* 81: The big canvas-covered "chuck-wagon" was grumbling over the jagged lava fragments that strewed the road to Agua Frio. **1918** *DN* V 23: *Chuck-wagon,* n. A cooking-wagon that follows a gang of harvest hands about a great ranch. General. **1921** in *Calif. Folk. Qly.* I (1942) 272: The old chuck-wagon'd run. **1922** Rollins *Cowboy* 218: "Chuck wagons," as mess wagons were called.
2. a food or snack cart.
1972 Haldeman *War Year* 83: Here comes the chuck wagon.

chug *n.* a long swallow, as of beer.
1968–69 in *DARE.* **1979** G. Wolff *Duke of Deception* 141 [ref. to 1950's]: Hand me that beer. Want a sip? I said a sip, not a whole goddamned chug. **1979** *Nat. Lampoon* (July) 47: The guy with the four-digit score gets four chugs…and the whiz gets two pops. **1979** Hiler

Monkey Mt. 141: Steve took a big chug.…"You're gonna have a nice red wine hangover tomorrow."

chug *v.* to CHUGALUG.
1958 J. Davis *College Vocab.* 15: *Chug down*—Drink a whole measure of a beverage without stopping. **1961** Terry *Old Liberty* 136: He would chug with us. **1966** in IUFA *Folk Speech: Chug your beer*—drink your beer all in one gulp. **1972** N.Y.U. student: You *chug* a bottle of beer when you drink it all at one gulp. **1978** B. Johnson *What's Happenin'* 141: Everybody…[was] chugging their OJ and Coke. **1979** J. Morris *War Story* 72: I tried to chug it all down at a gulp. **1980** Univ. Tenn. student: We were sitting around chugging beer.

chugalug *v.* to drink (a bottle of beer, glass of soda, or the like) without pausing for breath. Also attrib.
*ca***1936** in Reuss *Field Collection* 173: So drink chug-a-lug, chug-a-lug. **1946** Burns *Gallery* 33: I'm almost afraid to chugalug a drink. **1953** R. Matheson, in Pohl *Star of Stars* 192: Come on, *drink* girl!…Chuggalug! **1954** MacDonald *Condemned* 32: The person knocked into the lake had to chugalug a drink. **1955** Harrington *Dr. Modesto* 70: At the other tables the college boys were already chug-a-lugging. **1958** Frede *Entry E* 102: Chugalug it! **1968** Cuomo *Thieves* 10: He poured some milk in. "Chug-a-lug, kid. Make you strong." **1974** Lahr *Trot* 7: I chugalugged a Ballantine. **1977** Olsen *Fire Five* 89: The cop chugalugs his coffee. **1983** K. Miller *Lurp Dog* 25: The first to drain his mug in chugalug contests.

chuggerhead *n.* CHUCKLEHEAD.
1979 Charyn *7th Babe* 39: He was contemptuous of all the chuggerheads he had to meet day after day, country boys who had trouble with their own signatures.

chugs *n.pl.* [var. JUGS] a woman's breasts.
1968 Baker et al. *CUSS* 96: *Chugs.* The female breasts. **1973** N.Y.U. student: I know a guy from Massachusetts who calls tits *chugs.* Not *jugs, chugs.*

chug-wagon *n.* an automobile.
1928 Burnett *Little Caesar* 123: I could buy and sell guys that's got three homes and a couple of chugwagons.

chum *n.* [prob. alter. of *cham,* clipping of *chamber fellow* 'roommate'] Orig. *Stu.* a close friend or companion, esp. *(obs.)* a roommate. Now *colloq.* or *S.E.*
*****1684** in *OED2:* To my chum Mr. Hody of Wadham College. *****1698–99** "B.E." *Dict. Canting Crew: Chum,* a Chamber-fellow, or constant Companion. **1748** in *AS* (Oct. 1940) 231. **1807** W. Irving *Salmagundi* 28: My cousin and old college chum. *****1811** *Lexicon Balatron.: Chum.* A chamber fellow, particularly at the universities and in prison. **1819** A. Pierce *Rebelliad* 17: But his chum/Had wielded in his just defence,/A bowl of vast circumference. **1849** Melville *White Jacket* 232: I'm your old chum, Mandeville. **1850** in Eliason *Tarheel Talk* 265: My chumb…old chums. **1856** Hall *College Wds.* 65: *Chum* is used…with the more extended meaning of companion, friend. **1858** in Eliason *Tarheel Talk* 265: I…came…to my room and asked my chum. **1867** Clark *Sailor's Life* 113: But come, chum, the air is too close here. **1871** Bagg *Yale* 43: *Chum,* a room-mate or particular friend. Sometimes called *chummy.* Chum is used also as a verb. **1873** Payne *Behind Bars* 116: Thump on your lock when the Guard passes your cell after the lights are out, chum. **1904** in "O. Henry" *Works* 29: Anna and Maggie…were the greatest chums ever. **1904** in A. Adams *Chisholm Trail* 83: This chum of mine was queer in his drinking. **1911–12** Ade *Knocking the Neighbors* 125: The two Chums had made a Pact. **1942** Pegler *Spelvin* 76: How are you doing, chum? **1962** *Dennis the Menace* (CBS-TV): Why don't you spend the day with Dennis and his little chums? **1978** Diehl *Sharky's Machine* 3: You're not gonna choke up on me, are you, chum? **1982** Heat Moon *Blue Hwys.* 225: What's up, chum?

chum *v.* to share a room (*hence*) to be friends. Now *colloq.*
*****1730** in *OED2:* There are…some honest fellows in College, who would be willing to chum in one of them. **1831** *Harvardiana* I 324: Such is one of the evils of chumming. **1871** (quot. at CHUM, *n.*). *****1884** in *OEDS.*

chummo *n.* [CHUM + -O] CHUM. *Joc.*
1947 Schulberg *Harder They Fall* 166: Okay, chummo. I was only kiddin'.

chummy *n.* Esp. *Naut.* CHUM; PAL.
1841 [Mercier] *Man-of-War* xxi: Should they chance to fall in with any of their old topmates or *chummies.* **1847** Downey *Cruise of Portsmouth* 50: I got [the birds] home with the assistance of my chummy. **1849** Melville *Mardi* ch. iii: For be it known that, in sea-parlance, we were *chummies.*

1849 Melville *White Jacket* 319: Pierre…had been a *"chummy"* of Shenley's. **1875** Sheppard *Love Afloat* 44: The captain's steward was a chummy o' mine. **1879** Shippen *30 Yrs.* 35: Little more is thought of the poor fellow who is gone, except, perhaps, by his "chummy," who laments him for a time, but with no outward show. **1900** *N.Y. Eve. Post* (Dec. 1) 15: Ah, cheese it, chummy, I on'y got to holler fer *one* leg. **1902** in "M. Twain" *Stories* 419: Been chummies ever since.

chummy *v. Naut.* CHUM.
  1849 Melville *Mardi* ch. iii: Now this *chummying* among sailors is…a co-partnership…a bond of love and good feeling. **1903* in Partridge *DSUE* (ed. 7) 1064: He chummied for a few weeks with a squatter.

chump *n.* **1.** the head.—now soley in phr. **off (one's) chump** crazy.
  1859 Matsell *Vocab.* 19: *Chump.* Head. **1864* Hotten *Slang Dict.* (ed. 3): *Chump,* the head or face….A half-idiotic or daft person is said to be off his chump. **1870** Greey *Blue Jackets* 42: Bill was off his chump. **1891** Maitland *Slang Dict.* 193: *Off his chump,* foolish, insane, off his head or "his base." **1933** Witherspoon *Liverpool Jarge* (unp.): Which shewed he was off his chump. **1938** Steinbeck *Grapes of Wrath* 204: Ya Granma's off her chump. **1968** Myrer *Eagle* 427: You're off your chump, buddy.
  2. a fool; dolt; sucker.
  1876 Grover *Boarding House* 204: COL.…Shouter is a chump. WALT. A what? COL. A chump, a regular chump. **1883* in *F & H* II 112: Such a long-winded old chump. *ca*1888 *Stag Party* 155: A chump who thought he knew just how a paper should be run—/He's at the county poor house now. *Ibid.* 186: I am but a girl…but I am not a chump. **1890** Quinn *Fools of Fortune* 197: The unwary [are] called among the [gambling] fraternity "chumps," or…"suckers." **1892** L. Moore *Own Story* 59 [ref. to *ca*1860]: The Chief will call us "chumps" or say you have been giving us "sugar." **1895** Foote *Coeur D'Alene* 55: A set av bullheaded chumps that never did an honest day's work in their lives. **1896** Ade *Artie* 14: W'y, that chump had a full house, nines on somethin'. **1899** *Sat. Eve. Post* (July 22) 57: Those red and gray chumps can't take care of themselves, and we must protect 'em. **1902** *N.Y. Eve. Jour.* (Dec. 8) 1: Senator Hanna…called Colonel L.T. Michener a "chump."…"This man Michener," said the Senator, "is a chump—a big chump.…I used to think he was a politician, but I don't now. He's a chump." **1904** in Opper *Hooligan* 2: Chump! He scalded me with hot coffee. **1910** Hapgood *Types from City Streets* 37: A chump is slang for a sucker. **1946** in Himes *Black on Black* 256: A coupla beat-up colored mamas sat in the window booth awaiting chumps. **1949** Cuppy *Decline & Fall* 143: Korsakov [was] a chump who lasted only fifteen months. **1958** Hailey & Castle *Runway* 14: Don't make life hard for yourself, you chump. **1970** Scharff *Encyc. of Golf* 416: *Chump.* An easy opponent. **1980** Wielgus & Wolff *Basketball* 41: *Chump*…a weak opponent.

chump *adj.* typical of, fit for, or being a CHUMP, 2.
  1932 Nelson *Prison Days & Nights* 23: And the chump kid's only nineteen years old. **1929–33** J.T. Farrell *Manhood* 310: It's chump stuff, drinking that way. **1940** Burnett *High Sierra* 93: Robbing banks is a chump profession now. **1944** N. Johnson *Casanova Brown* (film): But this is a chump idea!

chump *v.* **1.a.** to make a fool of; trick; hoodwink.
  1930 in Partridge *Dict. Und.* 125: Every once in a while I chump a guy for some real dough. **1970** *Current Slang* V 20: *Chump,* v. To cheat; to defraud. **1972** *Alias Smith & Jones* (ABC-TV): Don't try to chump me again. **1978** Fisher & Rubin *Special Teachers* 1: No, I can't believe you'd chump yourself that way. **1987** *Daybreak* (CNN-TV) (June 27): And here is the guy who chumped the champ.
  b. *Black E.* to belittle or make fun of.
  1979 "Sugar Hill Gang" in L.A. Stanley *Rap* 325: Sucker M.C.s try to chump my style.
  2. *Pris.* to trump up (a charge).
  1968 in Andrews & Dickens *Big House* 16: "Not guilty," said Bud, the hip-cat stud./"The charges were chumped from the jump."

chump change *n. Black E.* a small amount of money; CHICKENFEED; (*hence*) a triviality.
  1967 Beck *Pimp* 285 [ref. to 1940's]: Western whores were lazy and satisfied with making "chump change." **1968–70** *Current Slang* III & IV 26: My chump change is running low. **1970** Cain *Blueschild Baby* 32: The toughs stand at the entrances…jingling chump change in their pockets. **1970** Winick & Kinsie *Lively Commerce* 120: Some pimps even have part-time "legitimate" jobs and receive only "chump change" or pocket money from their prostitutes. **1973** I. Reed *La. Red* 62: To be a man was easy; chump change. Antigone was after bigger game. **1974** Blount *3 Bricks Shy* 10: And Joe Greene once referred to $50 as "chump change." **1978** B. Johnson *What's Happenin'* 63: Who else out there

wants to give me some chump change? **1987** *Newsweek* (Mar. 23) 61: He wasn't going to be like his daddy, slaving for chump change. **1992** *Daybreak Sunday* (CNN-TV) (Mar. 8): If I had five million and chump change, I'd do it myself. **1993** C. Vandersee *Dictionaries* 3: *Chump change*…Houston Baker [former MLA president] told me he remembered the term in Louisville as far back as the 1950s or 1960s. [Economist] James Steward at Penn State says he knew it growing up in Cleveland in the late Forties and early Fifties.

chump off *v. Esp. Black E.* **1.** to act like a chump; DOPE OFF.
  1935 E. Anderson *Hungry Men* 247: He had chumped off and spent twenty cents. **1967** in *DARE.* **1969** Beck *Mama Black Widow* 219: All them whores got in the wind when they got hip how he chumped off.
  2. to lose (money) foolishly.
  1952 Himes *Stone* 188: It was better to toss away a few dollars than go to the hole. And we got ours too.…But we'd chump it off like all the others.
  3. to treat (someone) like a chump; play for a fool.
  1978 W. Brown *Tragic Magic* 6: Once during a show at the Apollo the headliner tried to chump the audience off by playing bad imitations of the imitators of his own work. **1978** Sopher & McGregor *Up from Walking Dead* 103: Should never let no nigger chump you off that way.

chump-twister *n. Carnival.* a merry-go-round.
  1961 Scarne *Comp. Guide to Gambling* 456: If he had to depend on the income derived from the Ferris wheels, *chump twisters* (merry-go-rounds), Dodge'ems, fun houses…and similar amusement devices, the owner would be lucky to break even.

chumpy *adj.* doltish; stupid.
  1900 *DN* II 27: *Chumpy,* adj. Foolish. **1902** Clapin *Americanisms* 115: *Chumpy.* In college slang, foolish, stupid. **1937** E. Anderson *Thieves Like Us* 211: You're just…chumpy as hell.

chum up *v.* to be or become friendly.
  1903 Hobart *Out for Coin* 30: Hank…chummed up with yo' all at Gravesend. **1920** Cheley *Fifty-Minus* 21: Give every boy a chance to chum up with a real man. **1931** Dos Passos *1919* 151: [He] sits down an' starts to chum up. **1952** MacDonald *Damned* 33: Chum up with a correspondent, no less, who can fix you precisely in the time and place.

chunk *n.* a portion or share, as of money; WAD.
  1855 (quot. at SLICE, *n.*). **1881** Nye *Forty Liars* 116: You can…make him think he is having a chunk of luxury ladled out to him such as no other living man ever got. **1908** in H.C. Fisher *A. Mutt* 22: When you find an affinity, bet the chunk. **1917** C.E. Van Loan, in Woods *Horse-Racing* 292: Parker is going to set in a chunk on him at post time. **1979** Hiler *Monkey Mt.* 104: Luck had little to do with the chunk he had lost.
  ¶ In phrases:
  ¶ **from who laid the chunk** *West.* since time immemorial; from way back. Also vars.
  1909 "O. Henry" *Roads of Destiny* 435: He can shore holler a plenty, and he straddles a hoss from where you laid the chunk. *ca*1938 in D. Runyon *More Guys* 174: A character who will bet on baseball games from who-laid-the-chunk. **1977** Monaghan *Schoolboy, Cowboy* 20 [ref. to 1908]: He's…a real windjammer from who laid the chunk.
  ¶ **tear off a chunk** (of men) to copulate.
  1972 Wambaugh *Blue Knight* 117: I used to tear off a chunk every night.
  ¶ **throw** [or **blow**] **chunks** *Stu.* to vomit.
  1984 Algeo *Stud Buds & Dorks*: To vomit…blow beets, …chow, …chunks, …[etc.]. **1987** Univ. Tenn. student theme: *Dump groceries, toss cookies,* and *throw chunks* are a few other interesting examples.

chunk *v.* **1.** CHUCK.
  1872 *Overland Mo.* (Nov.) 439: Chunk 'em inter de smoke-house.
  2. [fr. *throw chunks* s.v. CHUNK] *Stu.* to vomit.
  1989 P. Munro *U.C.L.A. Slang* 30: *Chunk*…to vomit. **1994** *Mystery Sci. Theater* (Comedy Central TV): Look out! She's gonna chunk!

chunker *n. Army.* a grenade launcher. [Quots. ref. to Vietnam War.]
  1975 S.P. Smith *Amer. Boys* 53: Ennis had an automatic chunker that fired three grenades in rapid succession. **1980** Cragg *L. Militaris* 89: *Chunker*…The M-79 grenade launcher. **1987** Chinnery *Life on Line* 228: An M-79 Chunker (grenade launcher).

chunky *adv.* ¶ In phrase: **take chunky** *Und.* to cover with a gun.
  1847–49 Bonney *Banditti* 207: Fox turned to fly, when John Long cried out to him, *"Take him chunky!"* Fox, turning, drew a pistol and said to Davenport, "Stand, sir!"

church *n.* the end; CURTAINS.
   1978 in Lyle & Golenbock *Bronx Zoo* 119: Even right now, if he starts messing with the curve ball, he'll lose something off his slider and it'll be church. *Ibid.* 177: When George found out about that, it was church.

church key *n.* a bottle opener or can opener.
   1951 *Western Folk.* X 170: *Church key.* A bottle opener. **1955** Margulies *Punks* 174: You got the church keys? **1958** J. Davis *College Vocab.* 13: *Church key*—Beer can opener. **1967** Morris & Morris *Word & Phrase Origins* II: The expression *church key* is old in the brewing business....I worked in a brewery for about 35 years and everybody carried a bottle-opener or *church key*, perhaps so called because it looked like the top end of the kind of heavy ornate key used to unlock church doors. **1968** Hayes *Smiling Through Apocalypse* 765: One soldier who didn't have a "church key" to open a can of orange soda at the Coke stand had tried unintelligently with a 50-caliber bullet instead. **1971** Tak *Truck Talk* 31: *Church key:* an oil can opener. **1974** E. Thompson *Tattoo* 385: There's a church key in the glove compartment. **1989** T. Blackburn *Jolly Rogers* xii: *Church key* beer-can opener.

churn *v. Stock Market.* (of a broker) to trade (a customer's securities) specifically to generate commissions.—also intrans.
   1953 *Time* (July 20) 48: The "fraudulent practice known...as 'churning,' by means of which a large part of the customers' invested capital was taken...in the form of repeated commissions, charges and profits." **1959** *Sat. Eve. Post* (Feb. 7) 80: You can be sure [a broker] won't "churn" your portfolio just to earn a commission. **1968** *Business Week* (Nov. 30) 96: Brokers are just interested in churning your account. **1979** *Business Week* (July 23) 206: Churning the investor's account—encouraging needless transactions to generate brokerage commissions. **1987** R.M. Brown *Starting* 168: If you're making enough to hire a stockbroker, okay. But they'll churn. (Churn: keep turning over stocks to generate commissions.) **1991** *Daywatch* (CNN-TV) (Apr. 30): There's a saying on Wall Street, "churn 'em and burn 'em."

churnbrain whiskey *n.* BUSTHEAD.
   *a***1867** in G.W. Harris *Lovingood* 40: I...then live tu spen' the las' durn cent, fur churnbrain whiskey.

'Chusetts *n. Esp. Stu.* Massachusetts.
   1967 Brandeis Univ. student: Massachusetts is always called 'Chusetts. **1972** Brandeis Univ. student: Up at Brandeis we call it 'Chusetts.

chute[1] *n.* **1.** *Av.* a parachute. Also as *v.* Now *colloq.* or *S.E.*
   *****1920** in *OEDS.* **1926** *Writer's Monthly* (Nov.) 395: *Chute*—a parachute. **1929** Springs *Carol Banks* 177: George...yelled to his passenger to jump and count four, and then open his 'chute. **1931** in Loosbrock & Skinner *Wild Blue* 161: I realized that my chute had not opened! **1934** Faulkner *Pylon* 33: I'll help you put the 'chutes on. **1936** Steel *College* 254: Busted my ankle when I landed in the chute. **1943** Twist *Bombardier* (film): The chutes are down here, so let's get 'em on. **1955** in Loosbrock & Skinner *Wild Blue* 38: In World War I you flew without a chute and had no choice. **1980** W.C. Anderson *Bat-21* 19: There was no longer any doubt about which side of the lines he had chuted into.
   2. *Sailing.* a parachute spinnaker.
   1981 D.E. Miller *Jargon* 254.

chute[2] *n.* the rectum.
   1976 R. Price *Bloodbrothers* 152: "We did it up the chute."..."You banged her in the ass!" **1986–90** in Ratner *Crack Pipe* 62: So I turned her over and put it in her chute (anus). *a***1990** Westcott *Half a Klick* 155: Sounds like she got a bar stool up her chute!

¶ In phrases:

¶ **down the chute** *Baseball.* into the strike zone.
   1972 World Series (NBC-TV) (Oct. 14): Vida starts off with a fastball right down the chute.

¶ **get the chutes** to be dropped or dismissed.
   [**1899** Ade *Horne* 170: If you don't, you'll be runnin' errands for her, an' some other geezer won't do a thing but pull the handle an' let you through the chute.] [**1903** Ade *Society* 99: "Don't start into this Life," he said. "It's only a Tread-mill, and after your Legs give out you are dropped down the Dark Chute."] **1918** in Carey *Mlle. from Armentieres* I (unp.): The regulars furnished a lot of lieuts,/But after the war they'll get the chutes.

¶ **go down the chute** [or **chutes**] to come to ruin; (*specif.*) to die. Also vars.
   1899 in Davidson *Old West* 154: If a man should scoot down the final chute that leads to the by an' by,/After leakin' his soul through a pistoled hole, there wasn't no hue an' cry. [**1931** Hellinger *Moon* 103: He

hit the chutes in a beautiful manner. If ever a man slid downward faster than he, I've never encountered him in real life.] **1946–51** Jones *Eternity* 75: "By the books, I should have let this outfit go on down the shutes," Warden said.

¶ **on the chute** *on the skids* s.v. SKID.
   1913 in M. Gardner *Casey* 89: Oh, yes, I must admit it; the poem is a beaut. Been runnin' through my thinker since our team got on the chute.

¶ **take a chute** *West.* to leave in a hurry.
   1877 Bartlett *Americanisms* (ed. 4) 689: *To take a Shute.* In the West, a person running away, or leaving in a hurry, is said to have "*taken a shute.*"

chute up *v. Av.* to put on a parachute. Now *colloq.*
   1974 J. Rubin *Barking Deer* 194: The Americans were all chuted up.

chutist *n.* a parachutist.
   1974 E. Thompson *Tattoo* 449: Chutist's wings on his cap.

chutzpah *n.* [< Yid *khutspe* < Heb *huspa*] **1.** unmitigated effrontery or impudence. [In use among non-Ashkenazim only since the 1960's.]
   *****1853** in *Jewish Lang. Rev.* 6 (1986) 150: No Chootspers Allowed. *****1892, 1945** in *OEDS.* **1965** Borowik *Lions* 132: And he's got the hutzpah to con people into thinking he thinks. **1970** Hatch *Cedarhurst* 168: The Greeks call that chutzpa. **1970** Cole *Street Kids* 25: Samson was the leader of a bunch of spic troublemakers who had the chutzpah to take policemen's badge numbers when the policemen broke the law. **1980** Manchester *Darkness* 326: For Magellan to rage over Chamorro larceny was chutzpah, since his countrymen were exterminating them.
   2. [the positive connotation is an E innovation not found in Yid] nerve; guts.
   1966 I. Reed *Pall-Bearers* 71: He may be a crackpot but he's got a lot of chutzpah. **1972** *Five Boroughs* (Nov.) 18: Finding a place to crash should be no harder than getting up the chutzpah to ask. **1990** *Cosmopolitan* (Apr.) 126: I auditioned with newfound chutzpah [and] landed a role in an off-Broadway musical.

ciao *interj.* [< It] so long; goodbye. Now *colloq.* [In use among non-Italians only since the 1960's.]
   1919 Hemingway *Sel. Letters* 30: See what you can do and Merry Christmas old cock. Ciaou, Stein. **1956** M. Anderson & MacPhail *Wrong Man* (film): "Ciao, ma." "Ciao." **1973** N.Y.C. bartender, age 26: O.K. Ciao. **1990** C. Trillin, in *Nation* (Dec. 31) 829: Kurt Waldheim said ciao.

cig *n.* **1.** a cigar.
   *a***1889** in Barrère & Leland *Dict. Slang* I 252: A *cig* of confounded bad tobacco. **1915** *DN* IV 236: *Cig*...Cigar.
   2. a cigarette.
   1894 *Century* (Feb.) 518: Cig, you've not been in the sick lugger all this while. **1903** Jackson *Third Degree* 204: I told him where I got my cigs. **1918** *The Radiator* (June 6) 1: Cig?—Coffin nail? **1960** Stadley *Barbarians* 33: I stop by the cig machine which is in the corner. **1978** *Rolling Stone* (May 18) 85: A man who...smoked "too many cigs."

cigar *n.* ¶ In phrase: **[close, but] no cigar** (used to indicate a near miss).
   1935 Sayre & Twist *Annie Oakley* (film): Close, Colonel, but no cigar! **1938** O'Hara *Hope of Heaven* 6: It was no cigar; she was in one of her moods. **1940** O'Hara *Pal Joey* 111: The mouse with me is strictly no cigar. **1945** *Yank* (Nov. 30) 11: The official verdict reads: "Close, but no cigar." **1959** Brosnan *Long Season* 147: Anyway, Haddix *almost* pitches a perfect game for twelve innings, and this sports editor...wants to give him a seat in the Hall of Fame. What ever happened to the old saying, "Almost but no cigar." **1974** WINS Radio News (July 22): As they say—close, but no cigar.

cigarette *v.* to give (someone) a cigarette.—usu. in imper. Cf. BEER, *v.*
   1975 *Salt Day of Locust* (film) [ref. to 1930's]: Cigarette me.

cigarette bed *n. West.* a bedroll. *Joc.*
   1977 Monaghan *Schoolboy, Cowboy* 91 [ref. to 1908]: If them cigareet beds don't beat all!

cigarette roll *n. Parachuting.* a parachute canopy that has not opened.
   1962 Harvey *Strike Command* 27: A cigarette roll is trooper talk for an unopened parachute. If you get one of these, get the reserve parachute out fast, or you'll be dead. **1980** Cragg *L. Militaris* 90: *Cigarette Roll.* An improperly deployed parachute. **1982** Goff, Sanders & Smith *Bros.* 44:

A cigarette roll…was when the chute would be rolled up like a cigarette and it wouldn't open at all.

cigaroot *n.* a cigarette. *Joc.*

1897 F.P. Dunne, in Schaaf *Dooley* 99: A steady dite iv cigaroots. **1899** in Ade *Chicago Stories* 247: But you're game enough to hit the cigaroot. *a***1907** J.C. McNeill *Cotton Land* 124: Wid a cigaroot rollin' aroun' in my mouf. **1907** Hobart *Beat It!* 37: Smoke Yellowfinger's Cigaroots. **1947–53** Guthrie *Seeds* 276: "I'd just hire you ta…roll cigarootes up fer me."

ciggie *n.* a cigarette.

1915 *DN* IV 236: *Cig*.…*Cigar*;…*cigarette*. Also *ciggy*. **1921** Dos Passos *Three Soldiers* 14: The corporal likes fancy ciggies and so does the sergeant. **1929** Brecht *Downfall* 29: She called…cigarettes "ciggies." **1948** Manone & Vandervoort *Trumpet* 69: He kept staring at that pack of ciggies. *****1962** in *OEDS*. **1979** Gutcheon *New Girls* 54: Well, then, have a ciggy for me!

ciggy-boo *n.* a cigarette. Also **ciggy-poo.** *Joc.*

*****1958** in Partridge *DSUE* (ed. 8) 219: Cigaboo. **1966** in *IUFA Folk Speech*: Folk Speech, Negro *Ciggyboos*. Cigarettes. **1968** Baker et al. *CUSS* 96: *Ciggie-boo*.…Cigarette. *a***1988** M. Atwood *Cat's Eye* 248: "I need a ciggie-poo," Cordelia says.

cinch *n.* **1.a.** a certainty; sure thing. See also LEAD-PIPE CINCH.

1890 *DN* I 60: *Cinch*, a sure thing. **1893** in Ade *Chicago Stories* 10: I've followed him a dozen times and it was always a cinch, and I never win but once. **1898** Dunne *Mr. Dooley in Peace & War* 101: An' that was a cinch. **1899** Cullen *Tales* 75: But it was Stockton, for a cinch. **1903** A. Adams *Log of a Cowboy* 248 [ref. to 1880's]: He thinks it's a dead immortal cinch. **1903** A.H. Lewis *Boss* 96: At this time of day it's a cinch he's takin' a snooze. **1905** in "O. Henry" *Works* 1461: It's tough to be alone in New York—that's a cinch. **1912** Beach *Net* 155: "Are you sure?"…"It's a cinch!" **1985** *N.Y. Times* (Sept. 3) A 18: Americans, the general said, don't like…long wars. Thus, his advice on using military force: "Don't go if you don't have to; that's a cinch."

b. *Specif.*, a sure winner, as in a race or contest.

1888 in *F & H* II 114: The bettor…has a *cinch* bottled up for a particular race. **1905** *Nat. Police Gaz.* (Aug. 19) 14: Reno "Phenom" a Cinch. **1907** in H.C. Fisher *A. Mutt* 7: I'll put you on to a cinch for this afternoon.

2.a. something accomplished with little effort; an easy task. See also LEAD-PIPE CINCH.

1891 *Outing* (Nov.) 138: It was now a "regular cinch." **1896** Ade *Artie* 25: Just shut your eyes every time and you've got a cinch. **1899** Ade *Fables* 78: It began to resemble a cinch. **1933** Weseen *Dict. Slang* 319: *Cinch*—An easy task. **1947** in *DA*: It sounds like a cinch—and it is a cinch, too, in one way. **1957** in *DAS*: It's a cinch to get a husband. The trick is getting the right one. **1986** Univ. Tenn. instructor: That Latin exam's a cinch.

b. an easy or enviable office or position; sinecure.

1896 Ade *Artie* 82: Says I to myself: "This is a cinch." **1908** H. Green *Maison de Shine* 242: I think you got a cinch. *ca***1910** Upson *With Sherman to the Sea* 170: While we were eating dinner the orderly told me I had a cinch with the old Man, as he called the [Provost] Marshall, that he never saw him take to anyone like that before. **1956** N.Y.C. man, age *ca*70: I tell you, you've got a cinch.

3.a. a person who is easily overcome or imposed upon.

1894 in S. Crane *Complete Stories* 206: Say, if yeh pick me up for a cinch, I'll fool yeh.…Don't take me for no dead easy mug. **1895** S. Crane *George's Mother* 174: Youse is dead easy, 'e says. He says he kin punch holes in you.…Youse is a cinch, Kel' says. **1906** Ford *Shorty McCabe* 264: I'm a cinch.…Every panhandler…knows he can work me for a beer check. **1910** *Bluejacket* (June) 356: They may separate the bluejacket from his money. But the old idea that "Jack's a cinch" as embodied in the song is rapidly passing.

b. *Specif.*, a woman who can be easily seduced.

1942 *ATS* 395: Woman of easy morals…(*cute*) *cinch*. **1966** "Petronius" *N.Y. Unexp.* 12: Thus, once established as a "cinch," a girl is free to pursue any course she desires. **1974** E. Thompson *Tattoo* 49: "Gotcherself a cinch there, mate," Glenn told the sailor knowingly.

¶ In phrase:

¶ **have a cinch on** to have a tight grip on or complete control over.

1888 in Farmer *Amer.*: The Dwyers have a cinch on both great events. **1891** Maitland *Slang Dict.* 155: *Cinch* (Am.), "to have a cinch on" anything is to have "a dead pull." The word comes from the "cinch," or saddle-girth that properly manipulated, holds the saddle or load in

place. A "leadpipe" or "grapevine" cinch are superlatives. **1895** Townsend *Fadden Explains* 25: What mug has de dead cinch on bein de dandiest dresser on de avnoo? **1896** Ade *Artie* 20: I asked her if the boy with the badge owned her and she laughed. I see that he didn't have no cinch on it, so I just started in. **1899** Thomas *Arizona* 9: A woman that's married to a fellow has a pretty tight cinch on him. **1905** in J. London *Short Stories* 213: I've got the almighty cinch on you…an' you can't lose me.

cinch *adj.* **1.** assured; certain.

1890 Quinn *Fools of Fortune* 562: The bookmaker's agent assumes the role of a gentleman who…has secured a "cinch tip" (meaning a sure thing). **1918** *Chi. Sun.-Trib.* (Mar. 17) V (unp.): I ain't waitin' for a cinch hand. But I can't stake it all on the blind. **1944** in *DA*.

2. easy or easily gained.

1931 Hellinger *Moon* 52: Glad you're in with us on this cinch dough. **1952** Mandel *Angry Strangers* 365: It's a cinch hyste. **1977** Caron *Go-Boy* 229: See for yourself what a cinch heist this is.

cinch *v.* **1.a.** to defeat or get the better of; check.

1873 *Overland Mo.* (Feb.) 110: He told me where to overtake him, and I outfitted a party, and—well, we all got "cinched." **1873** J. Miller *Modocs* 62: On the square—how on earth did you get sinched, anyhow? and did you really have four aces? **1875** in *F & H* II 114: A man is *cinched* = he is hurt in a mining transaction (San Francisco localism). **1881** in *F & H*: Thus it is unfairly said that the Northern Pacific Company intends to *cinch* the settlers by exacting large prices for its lands. **1894** O. Wister, in Remington *Wister* 90: In cinching somebody or something you may mean that you hold four aces, or the key of a political crisis; and when a man is very much indeed upper-dog, then he is said to have an air-tight cinch. **1908** in H.C. Fisher *A. Mutt* 35: A. Mutt…the notorious desperado…was cinched this morning. *Ibid.* 37: I would rather cinch Mutt than have my picture in the paper. **1910** T. Roosevelt, in *DA*: If the rich man strives to use his wealth to destroy others, I will cinch him if I can.

b. to impose upon.

*a***1889** in Barrère & Leland *Dict. Slang* I 252: My father is wealthy, and I think I can cinch him for five hundred dollars.

2. to secure or guarantee (a victory or other accomplishment).

1900 *DN* II 27: *Cinch*, v.t. To make sure of anything. **1904** Limerick *Villagers* 16: He had her cinched, but he didn't know it. **1910** Raine *O'Connor* 25: That extra hour and a half cinches our escape. **1915** Lardner *Haircut* 156: He's so lucky…that if they traded him to the St. Louis Browns they'd have the pennant cinched by the Fourth o' July. **1925** Hemingway *In Our Time* 47: That ought to cinch it for them. **1980** Univ. Tenn. grad. student: That's what cinched the deal.

3. *Army.* to take the last full portion or serving of (food or drink), as at a mess table.

1941 Kendall *Army & Navy Slang* 4: He cinched the bread…took last piece and didn't refill the dish. **1942** in *Best from Yank* 104: Damned be he who standeth first in the line of chow and…cincheth the coffee. **1956** Boatner *Military Customs* 124: *Cinch*. Unforgivable breach of mess-hall etiquette, "cinching" consists of taking the last or next to last piece of food from a platter without holding it up for the DRO (dining room orderly) to replenish. Good for a fight in the Old Army.

4. to determine exactly.

1966–67 W. Stevens *Gunner* 26: But by the time we make our run they'll have the range cinched.

cinchers *n.pl.* brakes.

1942 *AS* (Apr.) 103: *Cinchers*. Brakes. **1971** Tak *Truck Talk* 31: *Cinchers*: the brakes of a truck.

cinchy *adj.* **1.** certain.

1898–1900 Cullen *Chances* 21: Are you cinchy about the one you've got turning the trick? **1908** in Fleming *Unforgettable Season* 227: That looks cinchy enough, doesn't it?

2. easy.

1937 *Esquire* (Nov.) 172: Such assignments are regarded by the rank-and-file cops as "cinchy." **1960** N.Y.C. child: It'll be cinchy.

Cinci *n.* see CINCY.

Cincinnati *n. Bowling.* an 8-10 split.

1949 Cummings *Sports Dict.* 73. **1976** *Webster's Sports Dict.* 79.

Cincinnati doubloon *n.* a penny. *Joc.*

1858 in *Coll. Kansas State Hist. Soc.* XIV 99: Nothing smaller than [a] five-cent piece is in circulation [in Kansas]. A cent they call a "Cincinnati doubloon" and a three-cent bit is totally disregarded.

Cincinnati oysters *n.pl.* pickled pig's feet. *Joc.*

1877 Bartlett *Amer.* (ed. 4) 121. **1938** Asbury *Sucker's Progress* 271: For some forty years hogs and Cincinnati were so nearly synonymous...that pigs-feet were called "Cincinnati oysters," and in many places were so listed on restaurant menus.

Cincinnati quail *n.* pork or bacon. *Joc.*

1884 in *AS* XX 71: "Cincinnati quail—have it fat," was the next order. The cook cut off a large slice of fat pork and put it on a plate. **1886** Nye *Remarks* 163: Cincinnati quail, as we miners call bacon.

Cincinnati turkey *n. West.* salt pork. Also **Cincinnati chicken.**

1864 in Tilney *My Life* 85: Boiling our coffee and frying a slice of "Cincinnati turkey" (commonly called salt pork). **1963** Rickey *Beans & Hay* 266 [ref. to 1890's]: Cincinnati chicken.

Cincy *n.* Cincinnati, Ohio.

1899 "J. Flynt" *Tramping* 392: *Cincie:* Cincinnati. **1906** H. Green *Actor's Boarding House* 127: I knows him in Cincy (Cincinnati). **1922** Tully *Emmett Lawler* 138: I go far's Dayton, and my mate here goes on to Cincy. **1932–34** Minehan *Boy & Girl Tramps* 152: They takes buddy from the train in Cinci. **1935** J. Conroy *World to Win* 88: Outside Cinci. **1961** Himes *Pinktoes* 15: Yeah, man, I'm from Cincy, how could you tell?

cinder bull *n.* [*cinder* + BULL] *Hobo.* a railroad detective.

1930 Irwin *Amer. Tramp & Und. Slang.* **1933** Weseen *Dict. Slang* 51: *Cinder bull*—A railroad policeman. **1981** in Safire *Good Word* 119.

cinder-cruncher *n. R.R.* (see quots.).

1936 Mencken *American Lang.* (ed. 4) 583: A switchman is a *cinder-cruncher*. **1945** Hubbard *R.R. Ave.* 337: *Cinder Cruncher*—Switchman or flagman.

cinder dick *n.* [*cinder* + DICK] *Hobo.* a railroad detective.

1925 *Collier's* (Aug. 8) 30: A railroad detective is a "cinder dick." **1945** Hubbard *R.R. Ave.* 282: Presently a flashlight approached and the voice of a cinder dick called out. **1980** Bruns *Kts. of Road* 42: The cinder dick whose sole mission in life seemed to be to exterminate the hobo and tramp infestation.

Cinderella liberty *n. Navy & USMC.* a short liberty that ends at midnight.

1961 L.E. Young *Virgin Fleet* 59 [ref. to 1941]: I've got Cinderella Liberty....If I'm not back aboard ship by midnight, I get turned into a pumpkin. **1972** Poniscan *Cinderella Liberty* 49: I'm on Cinderella liberty. I got to get moving now...or I'm going to be AWOL. **1977** Caputo *Rumor of War* 129 [ref. to 1965]: Ten percent of the battalion would be allowed Cinderella liberty (ending at midnight) at Da Nang. **1991** *CBS Evening News* (CBS-TV) (Sept. 28): A Cinderella liberty—they have to be back by midnight.

cinder-gabbler *n.* a maidservant.

*1785 Grose *Vulgar Tongue:* Cinder garbler [*sic*]. A servant maid, from her business of sifting the ashes from the cinders. *Custom-house wit.* **1821** Waln *Hermit in Phila.* 26: Had an assig with a *Quicunque Vult*—a snug little *cinder-gabbler.*

cinder grifter *n.* [*cinder* + GRIFTER] *Und.* a tramp or hobo.

[**1927** *DN* V 442: Cinder sifter, n. a tramp.] **1929** Milburn *Hobo's Hornbook* 71: Come all you cinder grifters/And listen while I hum—/A story I'll relate to you/Of the great American bum. **1965** Wallace *Skid Row as a Way of Life* 204: *Cinder grifters*—hoboes.

circle-jerk *n.* **1.** an instance of group, esp. mutual, masturbation.—usu. considered vulgar.

1958 Salisbury *Shook Up* (gloss.): *Circle jerk*...Mass masturbation. **1960** in Cray *Erotic Muse* 35: They were too old to firk,/So they sat around the table and had a circle jerk. **1963** Rubin *Sweet Daddy* 11: Sure, we had circle jerks—everything. **1967** Dubus *Lieutenant* 64 [ref. to 1956]: What should I call it—a circle jerk, McKittrick? **1968** P. Roth *Portnoy* 194: He is also a participant in...circle-jerks. **1972** Pelfrey *Big V* 103: You guys havin a circle jerk? **1976** Braly *False Starts* 30: Yardstick...liked to organize circle jerks. **1983** W. Walker *Dime to Dance* 144: Because the two of you did your first circle jerk together or something. **1986** "J. Cain" *Suicide Squad* 128: In a back room conducting a circle jerk.

2. a pointless or frustrating discussion among several individuals.—usu. considered vulgar.

1973 Flaherty *Fogarty* 25: Even the jargon of these circle jerks tormented him. **1978** S. King *Stand* 540: Public meeting? Public circle jerk.

3. the runaround; any unpleasant situation; mess.—usu. considered vulgar.

1973 in Flaherty *Chez Joey* xxii: Publishers: "Please submit through an agent." Agents: "We only handle published writers." In the classic Mailer canon, a circle jerk. **1983** N. Proffitt *Gardens of Stone* 88: Top company in this here circle jerk gets free beer in the mess hall every Sunday for a month. **1989** R. Miller *Profane Men* 122: Some hairbrained field circle jerk. **1991** *UTSQ*: Circle jerk—situation where you are being led by people who don't know what is going on.

circle-jerker *n.* a participant in a CIRCLE-JERK.

1968 P. Roth *Portnoy* 196: Whom do I run in to...but the old circle-jerker himself.

circular file *n.* a wastebasket. *Joc.*

1947 *West. Folk.* VI (1947) 161 [ref. to WWII]: Papers thrown in the wastebasket are *given the deep six*, or filed in the *circular file.* **1942–48** in *So. Folk. Qly.* XIII (1949) 203: Something to be jettisoned, forgotten, or ignored is filed in the *circular file* (waste-paper basket), the *blue room* (the sea), or the *outboard locker* (sea). **1955** Ruppelt *Report on UFOs* 114: UFO reports were about as popular as sand in spinach, and I would guess that at least a few wound up in the "circular file." **1962** Quirk *Red Ribbons* 143 [ref. to 1946]: I sent it on through channels, but apparently it ended up in somebody's circular file. **1967** Lockwood *Subs* 252: This news, of course, I wrote back to the Navy Department but some bespectacled plank-owner probably filed my report in the "great circular file" (wastebasket). **1980** *N.Y. Daily News* (Sept. 10) 20: Anyway, you figure, some clerk would probably just throw your letter into the circular file. **1982** *Psychology Today* (Jan. 1983) 13: Every day literally tons and tons of these strips are thrown into the circular file.

circus *n.* **1.** *Prost.* an obscene exhibition by prostitutes.

1878 in Asbury *Gem of Prairie* 133: The Circus House, 70 Wells Street,...performances take place any hour of the day or night. **1894** Gardner *Doctor & Devil* 53: She motioned us toward a parlor...and...asked us if we had come to the place to see a "French circus." *Ibid.* 54: After the "circus," I ordered drinks for the party. **1899** in J. Katz *Gay/Lesbian Almanac* 298: You have never heard of them giving circuses around that neighborhood? **1913** Kneeland *Prostitution* 15: In the more exclusive parlor houses "circuses" or "shows" are also given....These exhibitions are too vulgar and degrading to be described. *a*1927 in P. Smith *Letter from Father* 61: For $50 you could see a circus—men and women fornicating [etc.]. **1938** Holbrook *Mackinaw* 107: Upstairs..."circuses" often were staged and were reported to cover all forms of perversion. **1938** in A. Lomax *Mr. Jelly Roll* 50 [ref. to N.O., 1890's]: They put on naked dances, circuses, and jive. **1939** C.R. Cooper *Scarlet* 346: A "circus" includes two girls and a man in a parlor exhibition of the perversions. **1952** Steinbeck *E. of Eden* 446: We'll go to Kate's place....They got a circus down there. Ever seen a circus, Harry? **1961** Rubin *In the Life* 116: Circuses, you know, a bunch eating it, whatnot, all at once.

2. a matter, state of affairs, or undertaking.

1899 Willard *Tramping* 377: What's that got to do with this circus? **1900** Willard & Hodler *Powers That Prey* 121: "This's my circus," he said defiantly. **1925** *Adventure* (Dec. 20) 8: I hope it's a order callin' this circus off.

3.a. *Mil. Av.* a wide-ranging air combat unit consisting of both bombers and fighters.—often constr. with *flying* or *traveling.* Now *hist.*

1916 in Roy *Pvt. Fraser* 86: The "Travelling Circus" under Baron Von Richtofen. **1917** Hall & Nordhoff II 58: He's to be in a *groupe de combat* ("traveling circus," as the British call them). **1919** Rickenbacker *Fighting the Flying Circus* (title). **1920** *American Legion Weekly* (Jan. 30) 16: A flying circus to liven things up, crab Fritz some! **1920** Clapp *17th Aero Squadron* 42: The enemy had thrown in prodigally his best and largest "circuses."

b. *Mil.* a combat unit, such as a storm battalion, that engages in hit-and-run attacks or that is transferred from area to area in support of other units.—often constr. with *traveling* or *flying.*

1918 *N.Y. Sun* (Aug. 19) 8: The traveling circus is the name given by Yanks to the Prussian veterans...who are rushed from one point of the line to another wherever there is being a relief made so that they can throw a scare into the Yanks. **1918** *Wadsworth Gas Attack* (Dec. 25): We're on the hike again, boys,/Our travelling circus moves. **1919** *Being Narr. of Btty. A* 93: On April 20th Hun "Flying Circus" launched its vicious assault against Seichesprey. **1920** *Marine Gaz.* (Mar.) 104: The Hindenburg Circus attacked with flame-throwers, grenades and knives. **1930** Nason *Corporal* 177: An outgrowth of this was the formation of special [German] units known vulgarly as traveling circuses…The circuses went up and down the front spreading trouble, here today, the other side of France a week later. They were not supposed to hold ground.

circus bee n. Carnival. a louse.

1929 *AS* IV (June) 339: *Circus bees*—Lice, crabs, and bed bugs. **1938** in W.C. Fields *By Himself* 312: Down to the common circus bee and (*scratches himself*) the seam-squirrel.

circus-simple adj. Circus. enamored of circus life.—also as n.

1975 McKennon *Horse Dung Trail* 36: Guess we are both sort of "circus simple" and we are stuck with it. *Ibid.* 487: *Circus Simple:* Anyone who ran away and stayed with a circus.…Any person with an obsession about circuses.

circus squirrel n. Carnival. a louse; SEAM SQUIRREL.

*ca*1928 in Wilstach *Stage Slang* (unp.): "Circus squirrels," cooties. **1962** Ragen & Finston *Toughest Prison* 794: *Circus Squirrels*—Body lice.

circus try n. a game attempt.

1949 W.R. Burnett *Asphalt Jungle* 145: Give it a circus try. I'm counting on you.

cissy var. SISSY.

cit n. a citizen; an ordinary or undistinguished person; (hence) Mil. a civilian.

*1669 *New Academy of Complements* 243: These Citts are subtle slaves. **1701* in D'Urfey *Pills* I 87: Fops, Bullies, and Cits, all set up for Wits. **1703* E. Ward *London Spy* 302: The *Bulky Cits* March'd after in a Throng. **1709* in R.J. Allen *Tatler & Spectator* 23: In a word, *Paulo* is a Citizen, and *Avaro* a Cit. **1773** in Trumbull *Satiric Poems* 89: Fops, scholars, dunces, cits, together. **1833** *Mil. & Nav. Mag. of U.S.* (Oct.) 85: Another asked the "loan of my cit's pants and vest." **1839** Briggs *Harry Franco* II 88: The high basilica, if placed beside the mighty model to his eye revealed, would dwindle to the cottage of a cit. **1864** Lyman *Meade's HQ* 214: Captain Fay took out the cits today…and showed them the lines. **1871** Gould *Maine Regt.* 106 [ref. to Civil War]: The "cit's" took kindly to us. **1878** Flipper *Colored Cadet* 155 [ref. to 1874]: Some "cit" wanted to see a cadet and asked C…if he could do so. **1888** King *Deserter* 153: Any girl who will go East and marry a "cit" and leave six or seven penniless subs sighing behind her, I have no opinion of. **1894** King *Cadet Days* 250: Well, the other one's a cit, who's doing something for us. **1894** *U.S. Nav. Acad. Lucky Bag* No. 1 66: Cit…A civilian. **1901** *Our Naval Apprentice* (July) 3: There was…cits squinting and peeping at em from all sides. **1889** *United Service* (Aug.) 138: They felt that with the "swell cit." out of the field they would stand a better chance. **1909** Moss *Officer's Manual* 283: Cit, A civilian. **1916** *Editor* XLIII (Mar. 11) 297: "Cit" is the word for citizen or civilian and a very contemptuous word at that. **1920** Lewis *Main Street* 132: But I can't be so very enthusiastic over the smug cits like Jack Elder. **1927** Cushing *Doughboy Ditties* 93: Now the War long since quit/And you're back as a "cit."

cits n.pl. Mil. civilian clothes; CIVVIES.

1829 in Wood *West Pt. Scrap Book* 47: My uniform I've taken off,/My "cits" I've just put on. **1877** Lee *Fag-Ends* 19: My dusty "cits" still graced my form. **1888** King *War-Time Wooing* 115: He wore his uniform coming to the city, but would soon turn out in "cits." **1894** *Lucky Bag* (U.S. Naval Acad.) No. 1 66: *Cits*…Civilians' clothes. **1909** Moss *Officer's Manual* 283: Cits, civilian clothes. **1917** Hunt *Blown In By Draft* 215: An overgrown boy in worn "cits"…was lazily shovelling snow from the sidewalk. **1918** Crowe *Pat Crowe* 202: I can take my lordly ease again in "Cits." **1921** *15th Inf. Sentinel* (Jan. 7) 13: You toy with your collar as you don your suit of cits. **1930** Deitrick *Parade Ground* 281: They won't catch me this time. I'm in cits.

City n. & comb. form. (used as an intensive in combination with various parts of speech):

1.a. (used after a noun) a place, person, condition, or state of affairs having or strongly characterized by ——; a time of ——. [The expression FIST CITY seems to have been a set phrase; the 1930 quot. does not imply the free use of *city* in combinations at that date.]

1930 (quot. at FIST CITY). [**1948** Lay & Bartlett *Twelve O'Clock High!* 56: There had been raucous boos at the briefing upon the announcement that three groups [of bombers] were going over St. Nazaire—"Flak City" to the crews.] **1960** Buckley *Hiparama* 16: With that wild incense flyin' all over the place.…It was Romance City. **1961** B. Wolfe *Magic of Their Singing* 77: This man, he's from Drag City, he's the mayor of Nowheresville. **1962** H. Simmons *On Eggshells* 202: Don't go

to Nut City on me now, Jack. **1964** R.S. Gold *Jazz Lexicon* 57: *City*…according to jazzmen, first used by either Lester Young or Emmett Berry c.1938, but has been widely current only since c.1947. **1966** *Sat. Eve. Post* (July 2) 22: Businessmen [now] talk about "losing their cool," and use phrases like "wipe-out city," which is a mega-cool version of "hubba-hubba." *a*1971 in Bullins *Hungered One* 27: Yeah…Action city. **1978** Rascoe & Stone *Who'll Stop Rain?* (film): We're in Tree City, man [i.e., lost in the woods]. Who the hell knows where we are? **1978** Maupin *Tales* 16: Hot damn!…This place is Pickup City tonight! **1980** Grizzard *Billy Bob Bailey* 19: In flight it is Terror City at 30,000 feet. **1980** *Penthouse* (Jan. 1981) 170: Be cool, folks, it's entrapment city. **1981** Univ. Tenn. students: The party last night was Excitement City.…It's Crowd City down there.…It'll be Disaster City. **1983** S. King *Christine* 2: Arnie was Pimple City. **1990** *Time* (Sept. 10) 78: Triceratopses can be had cheap hereabouts. [Paleontologist Jack] Horner picked his way through the litter ("Rib city," he remarks).

b. (used esp. after an adjective) (used as a simple or joc. intensive).

1968 D.H. Hampton *Young Runaways* (film): "How'd you make out this afternoon?" "Cheap city." **1971** Georgia man, age *ca*28: Man, you ain't just dumb—you *Dumb City!* **1976** Price *Bloodbrothers* 25: Romance-wise, Mott was nowhere city. **1977** Sayles *Union Dues* 280: Were they all Schizo City too? **1981** Univ. Tenn. students: I'm Broke City.…This guy was Dull City.…You're lookin' Sharp City. **1981** Rogan *Mixed Co.* 149: The WAC was strac city. You know…that "strac" stands for super giant good military bearing with everything right. **1986** Univ. Tenn. instructor: It's Dull City. **1992** *Garfield* (CBS-TV): Yuck City! Who in the world would be stupid enough to like this food!

c. (used after an uninflected verb) a time or state of affairs characterized by ——ing; a time to —— or of ——ing; (constr. with *go*) to ——.

1946 Mezzrow & Wolfe *Really Blues* 58: All these chicks went to Weep City when they heard the words to *The Curse of an Aching Heart. Ibid.* 145: Josh really went to Beef City.…"The hell with everything." **1958** Russell *Perm. Playboy* 65: Came Honker's trip to Slice City along about then: our sax man got a neck all full of the sharpest kind of steel. **1967** Hamma *Motorcycle Mommas* 150: The guys turn on their 'cycle lights, and it's Panic City for the dudes. **1970** M. Brennan *Drugs* 59: "Burn City": when a situation looks bad enough to stay away from because of possible robbery. **1971** Ind. man, age 19: He is so fuckin' weird, man—he's gonna go Freak City. **1972** Wells *Fly With Us* 124: I know one girl who was skyjacked three times.…The first time it's Panic City. **1978** J. Webb *Fields of Fire* 114: The Bridge was a skating place.…Skate City [i.e., everyone could SKATE (loaf)]. **1981** *Rod Serling's Mag.* (Sept.) 39: Then number one engine starts to miss. That's bad. That's Sweat City. **1981** Univ. Tenn. student: Everybody failed. It was Flag City [i.e., they had FLAGGED (failed)]. **1986** Former SP5, U.S. Army: "He started goin' Yak City." He was talking incessantly.…In basic training [in 1971] the drill sergeant said, "You're gonna be on a extended trip to Hurt City!"

2. (used with various parts of speech as above but in more highly allusive combinations).

1971 Wells & Dance *Night People* 70: But don't ever tell her so or you'll be in Hung City [i.e., HUNG UP]. **1977** Langone *Life at Bottom* 177: I didn't like the dark, either. All that black: coalsack city. **1977** *Nat. Lampoon* (Aug.) 34: They find you and pump your stomach and then it's priest city. **1983** S. King *Christine* 126: "Want a Trip to Loose-Tooth City?" Garfield was inquiring over one cocked paw. *a*1984 C. Adams *Straight Dope* 205: If you get stuck in a falling elevator.…Pancake City. **1986** Univ. Tenn. instructor: A guy was snoring away and somebody said, "Freight Train City, man." **1987** Chicago woman, age *ca*40: Truly, you could have been crushed. It was Sardine City.

¶ In phrases:

¶ **night on the city** [i.e., at the expense of the city government] a night in jail.

1977 Sayles *Union Dues* 152: Wouldn't follow up on the chodge, just give you a night on the city.

¶ **one on the city** [i.e., at the expense of the city government] *Short-Order.* A glass of water.

1926 Maines & Grant *Wise-Crack Dict.* 11: *One on the city*—A glass of water. **1945** *Calif. Folk. Qly.* IV 56: *Pull one on the city*: Glass of water.

city college n. Police & Und. a city prison, esp. the Tombs in New York City.

*1796 Grose *Vulgar Tongue* (ed. 3): *City College.* Newgate. **1859** Matsell *Vocab.* 19: *City College.* The Tombs. **1930** Lait *On the Spot* 201: *City*

College…The Tombs. **1933** Ersine *Prison Slang* 27: *City College.* A city jail, lockup.

civilian *n.* a layperson; a nonmember of the speaker's group.

1946 J. Adams *Gags* 221: Show gals are smarter and keener than most "civilians."…*Civilian.* Show-business vernacular for anybody outside of the entertainment world. **1967** *World of Acid* (film): This is probably why so many civilians [i.e., nonhippies] have no concept. It's a whole different way of thinking. **1978** Ponicsan *Ringmaster* 25: I heard the civilian had money. *a***1981** in S. King *Bachman* 640: I don't deal in metaphysics anymore. I'm a civilian. **1989** *Dream St.* (NBC-TV): Friends are for civilians. You got your family; you got your crew [gang]. Period. **1991** *Geraldo* (synd. TV series): Are you a biker or a civilian?

civil serpent *n.* a civil servant. *Joc.*

1980 Cragg (letter to J.E.L., Aug. 10) 3: When I retire from the Army I'll become a *civil serpent.* **1986** Former SP5, U.S. Army: I heard *civil serpent* at *least* fifty times in the Army [during 1970's].

civs *n.pl.* CIVVIES.

1939 M. Levin *Citizens* 234: Two cops, in civs, walked through.

civvies *n.pl. Mil.* civilian clothes. Also **civies.**

***1889** Barrère & Leland *Slang Dict.* I 253: A suit of *civvies,* i.e., civilian's clothes. **1916** *Editor* XLIII 297: "Civies" is a set of civilian clothes. **1920** Herr *Company F* 12: We were still in Civies. ***1921** (quot. ref. to 1874 at CIVVY). **1922** Jordan *Battery B* 11: Instead of drilling in "civies," as we did at first, the boys wore khaki. **1928** Nason *A Matter of Business* 244: We won't have to hide out so much if we're in civies. **1930** Nason *A Corporal Once* 131: A striker's a great job! You get the Old Man's civvies to wear, and handouts from the cook! Hahaha! **1943** Pyle *Brave Men* 133: The average soldier will get into civvies the moment he is discharged. **1949** *Harper's* (June) 93: An occasional soldier in civvies. **1952** Uris *Battle Cry* 32: Two minutes to dress and a minute to weep over your civvies. **1957** Hall *Cloak & Dagger* 55: You were a paratroop lieutenant then, you're in civvies now. **1968** Crawford *Gresham's War* 26: The girls in civvies giggled, heads bowed. **1991** K. Douglass *Viper Strike* 123: They were all wearing civies and looked like typical tourists.

civvy *n. Mil.* a civilian. Also as *adj.*

***1895** (cited in Partridge *DSUE* (ed. 8) 221). **1917** Depew *Gunner Depew* 53: There were no civvies to be seen; only mules and horses bringing up casks of water, bags of beans, chloride of lime, barbed wire, ammunition, etc. **1918** in Merrill *Butler College in War* 131: Things have to be done which a "civi" never dreams of. **1919** *Our Navy* (Sept.) 21: There's nothing in our looks to rouse the cheers/Of gazing "civie" crowds. **1919** Duffy *G.P.F. Book* 268: He was a butcher In his "civvy" days. **1920** *American Legion Weekly* (Dec. 24) 10: Well, "normalcy" is just Ohio civvie talk for "as you were." ***1921** *N & Q* (Nov. 5) 379: *Civvy.* A civilian. Was in use when I joined the Army in 1874. "Civies" meant "plain clothes." **1926** *Sat. Eve. Post* (May 1) 18: Some of these Frog civvies don't even wear gas masks. **1961** Pirosh & Carr *Hell Is for Heroes* (film): It's like when you were a civvy. **1977** Langone *Life at Bottom* 77: I mean those civvies up there are at least gettin' good dough from the oil companies. **1978** T. Sanchez *Zoot-Suit* 192: You civvies think you got it bad.

Civvy Street *n. Mil.* civilian life.

1944 Patrick *Hasty Heart* 519: How did you manage to avoid work in civvy street? **1945** *Yank* (June 15) 18: They seem to be doing *beaucoup* for the GI who intends to go back to civvy street. **1949** Lowry *Wolf That Fed Us* 108: Back on civvy street all these guys would be thinking about was money. **1971** Waters *Smugglers of Spirits* 43: One, a little Russian who had been a ballet dancer in Civvy Street, did a lively sailor's hornpipe which was received with wild applause. ***1984** Partridge *DSUE* (ed. 8) 221: *Civvy Street*…was first used *ca*1917 by the [British] army.

clack *n.* the tongue.

***1675** in Duffett *Burlesque Plays* 64: Pry'thee old Goat, tye up thy Clack. **1800** *Amorous Songster* 58: I eat, I scold, I scold, I eat,/My clack is never quiet.

clacker *n.* [< MexSp *claco* 'a large copper coin equivalent in value to three centavos'] **1.** *Mil.* a large foreign copper coin of little value, such as a Philippine centavo, British penny, or French centime. Now *hist.*

[**1833** A. Pike *Prose Sks.* 100: Not ten clakos—not ten jolas!] [**1843** in *Texana* (spring 1963) 108: The huxter women…sold…15 or 16 peaches for a *clacko.*] [**1897** in *Ala. Hist. Qly.* (1957) 453: These drinks are very cheap, usually selling for a "claco" (one cent) per glass.] **1899** Gatewood *Smoked Yankees* 277: You can get about fifty for four clackers, which equals one cent in our money. **1906** M'Govern *Bolo & Krag* 40:

He…doled out the last clacker. **1917** Morse *Letters* 3: Next to the paper money that comes to pieces in their fingers, the boys detest the big one and two cent coppers. Known to the Navy as "bunker plates," in the army they pass as "clackers." **1919** Ashton *F63* 45: A Frog let them sleep in his hay mow for the compensation of a few clackers. **1920** *Inf. Jour.* XVII (Dec.) 557: Private Strang laboriously counted out a little pile of old nickel "chinee money" and copper "clackers" and silently departed. **1932** *Leatherneck* (May) 7: For a Chink clacquer I'd put a bullet through his worthless hide. **1937** Thompson *Take Her Down* 148 [ref. to 1918]: I threw down my last *milreis,* or clacker. **1942** Herman *42nd Foot* 107 [ref. to 1898]: As the mining operations only netted one small earthenware pot of clackers (large copper pennies), amounting to probably fifty cents—the cache of some child—the teamsters and packers saw the error of their ways.

2. a dollar.

1918 Ruggles *Navy Explained* 102: Iron men, washers, clackers, jack, cart wheels, simoleons, [etc.]. **1951** (cited in *DAS*).

clackers *n.pl.* the teeth.

1950, 1965–70 in *DARE.*

clag *n. Av.* heavy overcast.

***1967** Partridge *DSUE* (ed. 6) 1056: *Clag.* Cloud; a cloud: R.A.F.: since *ca*1935 (?). Ex dial. *clag,* clay. ***1981** *Macquarie Dict.* 352: *Clag*…*Aeronautics Colloq.* clouds. (Trademark for a brand of glue; from Brit. d[ialect].) **1986** Coonts *Intruder* 51 [ref. to 1972]: We're in the clag.…Do you want us to find the tops, over? *Ibid.* 68: Stay at about 250 feet, underneath the clag.

clam *n.* **1.a.** the mouth; *pl.* the lips or jaws.

1825 in *DA*: Shet your clam. **1833** J. Neal *Down-Easters* I 93: Hush your jaw there!…Shet your clam…hold your yop! **1914** Lardner *You Know Me Al* 119: As for her husband the first time he opens his clam to me I will haul off and bust him one in the jaw. **1928** Hammett *Red Harvest* 116: I'll give you fifty bucks now and a split of whatever I get from McGraw if you'll keep your clam shut till I can put it over and grab a rattler. **1929** Hammett *Maltese Falcon* 85: You know I'll keep my clam shut. **1940** E. O'Neill *Iceman Cometh* 153: Close that big clam of yours, Hickey. **1957** Simmons *Corner Boy* 200: You'd better open your clams and talk. **1958** S.H. Adams *Tenderloin* 330: All I'm asking you to do is keep your clam shut.

b. the vulva or vagina; *(also)* the hymen. Cf. BEARDED CLAM.

1916 Cary *Venery* II 20: Opening a clam—To copulate. *Ibid.* 45: *Clam*—The vagina. **1928** in Oliver *Blues Tradition* 178: Oh how that boy does open clams,/No one else is gonna touch my hams. **1938** "Justinian" *Amer. Sexualis* 16: *Clam.* n. An older and less popular term for the maidenhead. Generally refers to a hymen which is difficult to pierce; an unusually thick membranous surface. Obsolescent, U.S., C. 19–20. Low coll. **1974** Price *Wanderers* 37: I was gobblin' her clam like it was the last supper.…An' I'm tellin' you I musta hit the bullseye because I never got hit with as much clam juice in my life.

2. a foolish, worthless, or useless individual.

1866 in *DA*: That lets you out, you know, you chowder-headed old clam! **1891** Townsend *Negro Minstrels* 44: He was a regular tough old clam,/He lived on hominy, hash and ham. **1901** Hobart *Down the Line* 17: The favorite galloped into port…six hours ahead of the other clams [horses]. **1903** Townsend *Sure* 181: De riddles dat kiddie asks makes a clam of me many a time. **1908** Sullivan *Crim. Slang* 5: *Clam*—An easy mark. **1928** in Tuthill *Bungle Family* 49: The multitude of clams who are Browns in name only. **1975** *Knoxville* (Tenn.) *News-Sentinel* (Apr. 2) 5: Among the names Eanes was accused of calling were "dummy," "yo yo," "clam" and "hotdog." **1991** *Simpsons* (Fox-TV): I been bustin' my hump all week for that withered old clam.

3. a dollar.

[**1881** Nye *Forty Liars* 236: Reck not one cold, careless clam that all thy limbs are knocked into a shapeless mass.] **1886** E.L. Wheeler *N.Y. Nell* 12: Bet a clam…he'd like to shut off my wind. **1915–17** Lait *Gus* 53: That there is wort' t'ree hundred clams. **1929** Perelman *Ginsbergh* 71: Izzy's grandpaw…left him a half million clams in cash. **1939** O'Hara *Files* 159: Last night cost me…about fifteen clams. **1942** Freeman & Gilbert *Larceny, Inc.* (film): Ten clams. **1948** Manone & Vandervoort *Trumpet* 146: Here's your twenty-five clams, Bud. **1959** *Phil Silvers Show* (CBS-TV): This adventure into science has already cost me thirty-five clams. **1970** *Playboy* (Apr.) 168: Took that old coot for his old wad—eight hundred clams. **1972** *N.Y. Post* (Mar. 22) 47: We give them 11 billion clams a year in taxes. **1992** *CBS This Morning* (CBS-TV) (Dec. 23): *Clams* is another synonym for money.

4.a. a stingy person; tightwad.

1901 Ade *Modern Fables* 9: Then permit your Affections to center on some Tractable Person who is neither a Prospective Pauper nor a close-fisted Clam. **1901** *Chi. Tribune* (July 28) 38: "Don't be a clam," means...[do] not put a time lock on the pocket containing...money.

b. a silent or close-mouthed person; one who will not betray a confidence.

1908 Raine *Wyoming* 121: I'm a clam till y'u give the word. **1934** Appel *Brain Guy* 138: The prop had a reputation for being a clam. **1948** I. Shulman *Cry Tough!* 122: I'm a clam. You still want me to tell them you want them to call you up? **1949** "J. Evans" *Halo in Brass* 111: "It's not like him to talk so much." "Stu...is a clam." **1974** Millard *Thunderbolt* 48: The word almost leaked out, there, before you went clam. *What* money.

5. *Entertainment Industry.* a mistake; BONER; (*Jazz*) a misplayed note.

1952 in *DAS.* **1955** *Down Beat* (Nov. 30) 47: I'd say that was a band that doesn't work together regularly...because there were a few clams in the ensemble. **1964** *New Yorker* (Apr. 25) 195: Clams proliferate. **1991** *N.Y. Times* (Dec. 1) H 33: Bing Crosby...always said, "Leave the clams in, let 'em know I'm human."

6. *pl.* the hands.

1969 in *DARE.*

7. a gob of phlegm. Cf. syn. OYSTER.

1970 T. Veitch, in Padgett & Shapiro *N.Y. Poets* 164: The clam/...which I spit/there. **1970** Zindel *Your Mind* 19: She cleared her throat again and dropped a clam into her cuspidor. **1977** Bredes *Hard Feelings* 4: He coughs up clams into a hanky. **1980** Gould *Ft. Apache* 99: "That was some clam you laid on him," Corelli said. Murphy wiped his chin.

¶ In phrase:

¶ **happy as a clam** very happy; quite contented.

1834 in *DA.* **1841** *Spirit of Times* (July 17) 229. *a*1870 in *DA:* Happy as a clam (in the mud at high water). **1961** Barbeau *Ikon* 21: Mom's happy as a clam to have me home.

clam *v.* to cease or refrain from talking, esp. under questioning.—usu. constr. with *up*, occ. with *down*. Occ. refl.

1916 in *OEDS:* When I ask for details he just clams up. **1925** *Sat. Eve. Post* (Jan. 3) 142: Clam yourselfs. **1925–26** J. Black *You Can't Win* 97: Just clam up, kid...till you get a lawyer. **1929** Hotstetter & Beesley *Racket* 222: *Clam*—To keep absolutely quiet; to refuse to talk. **1932** Berg *Prison Doctor* 85: Clam down and get to bed or I'll throw you in the bing! *Ibid.* 127: Clam down, you guys. **1937** Johnston *Prison Life* 35: Nix, you guys....Clam. Dummy up. **1948** Lay & Bartlett *Twelve O'Clock High!* 16: Everybody from cooks, M.P.'s, ground crews and officers, to you and me, have got to clam up more. **1958** "R. Traver" *Anatomy of a Murder* 182: His buddy had purposely clammed up so that he wouldn't get in a jam with this young officer. **1962** Perry *Young Man Drowning* 126: Deny everything and clam up. **1978** Strieber *Wolfen* 76: You shouldn't clam up on us. **1980** Druffel & Rogo *Tujunga Contacts* 64: Emily immediately clammed up again and continued denying that she knew anything pertaining to what had happened. **1988** T. Harris *Silence of Lambs* 4: Four...with appeals pending clammed up.

clambake *n.* **1.** a lavish social affair; party; (*Jazz*) a jam session.

1937 *AS* 46: *Clambake.* Same as jam session. **1941** Schulberg *Sammy* 160: No more trying to angle invitations to Harry Godfrey Wilson's clambakes. **1946** Mezzrow & Wolfe *Really Blues* 117: Life was going to be one long clambake. **1950–52** Ulanov *Hist. Jazz* 350: *Clambake:* earlier used synonymously (and honorifically) with "jam session," later descriptive of an improvised or arranged session which doesn't come off. **1953** Rodgers & Hammerstein *Me and Juliet* 464: That was quite a clambake going on when I came in here.

2. *Radio.* an unsuccessful radio broadcast.

1937 in *AS* (Apr. 1938): A *clambake* is radio's slang for a program which becomes a definite failure due to errors and lack of rehearsals. **1941** *Slanguage Dict.* 10: *Clambake*...an elaborate radio program which fails due to lack of preparation or poor performance.

3. an undertaking, esp. if elaborate or enjoyable.—now often ironic.

1939 in W.C. Fields *By Himself* 330: When this clam-bake folds up in the Fall, I'm going to Leadville and open a honky-tonk. **1944** N. Johnson *Casanova Brown* (film): They're not gonna suck me in on this clambake. **1949** Beloin *Conn. Yankee* (film): You got a mighty nice turnout for the clambake. **1955** F. Harvey *Jet* 28: If we lost the elevators...it was going to be quite a clambake trying to land the airplane. **1958** Frankel *Band of Bros.* 142: Last time everybody was involved. Not this Korean clambake. **1969** in Tuso *Vietnam Blues* 126: Till this clambake is done. **1985** C. Busch *Vampire Lesbians* 71: And that goes for everyone in this clambake. Get me?

clam-basket *n.* the stomach; belly.

1832 *Spirit of the Times* (Mar. 21) 2: One fish, a "real screamer," had no less than fifteen nutmegs in his clam basket, and others nearly as many.

clam-catcher *n.* a New Jerseyite.—used as a derisive nickname.

1845 in *DA:* The inhabitants of...New Jersey [are called] Clam-Catchers. **1902** Clapin *Americanisms* 119: *Clam-catchers.* A nickname applied to the inhabitants of New Jersey.

clam gun *n.* a shovel.

1927 *AS* (June) 392: A long-handled shovel is a *muck-stick* and a short-handled one is a *clam-gun.* **1942** *AS* (Dec.) 221 [logging]: *Clam Gun.* A shovel, used by a *gopher, gandy dancer,* or *road monkey.* **1956** Sorden & Ebert *Logger's* 9 [ref. to *a*1925]: *Clam gun,* A power shovel. Originally a steam shovel that opens and closes. **1965** O'Neill *High Steel* 270: *Clam gun.* Shovel.

clammed *adj.* silent; not divulging information.—also constr. with *up.*

1936 R. Chandler, in Ruhm *Detective* 139: Think he'll stay clammed? **1936** Duncan *Over the Wall* 72: Remember that I know how to keep clammed up. **1944** C.B. Davis *Leo McGuire* 21: Listen, Leo, you can keep your mouth clammed, can't you?

clam-mouthed *adj.* close-mouthed.

1951 Pryor *The Big Play* 167: Oil men's wives have got to be as clam-mouthed as doctors' wives.

clamp *v.* to seize or apprehend.

1834 Caruthers *Kentuck. in N.Y.* I 66: Then the real officers come up and clamped me. **1925** in D. Hammett *Continental Op* 164: I'm going to clamp him some day, though.

clampers *n.pl.* the hands. Also **clamps.**

1880 J.C. Harris *Uncle Remus* 119: W'en Brer B'ar got his clampers on 'im good, he sot down en talk at 'im. **1986** Univ. Tenn. grad. student, age 35: "Get your clamps off of me" means get your hands off me.

clamshell *n.* **1.** the mouth; (*pl.*) the lips.

1832 in [S. Smith] *Letters of Downing* 104: Shut up your clack, or I'll knock your clam-shells together pretty quick. **1856** Sleeper *Tales* 257: Open your clam-shell, and give us a yarn. **1859** Bartlett *Amer.* (ed. 2) 85: Shut your clam-shell. **1862** H.J. Thomas *Wrong Man* 73: Oh, keep your old clam-shell shut. **1871** De Vere *Americanisms* 70: The expression, quite common wherever slang is heard, "Shut your clamshell," for: Keep your own counsel." **1877** Bartlett *Americanisms* (ed. 4) 590: *Shut up your clam-shells.* Close your lips together; be silent. Common along the shores of Connecticut and Rhode Island, where clams abound. Same as *shut up your head.*

2. a dollar.

1927 Nicholson *The Barker* 102: *Clam shells*—Silver dollars.

clam trap *n.* the mouth.

1800 in *DA.* **1941** LeMay, Bennett, & Lasky *Reap Wild Wind* (film): Shut your clam traps. You boys'll like whalin'.

clanger *n.* a blunder; esp. in phr. **drop a clanger** to commit a faux pas. Also **clangeroo.**

***1957** in Partridge *DSUE* (ed. 8) 221: A real old-fashioned clangeroo. **1973** *Oui* (May) 10: "I am afraid you have dropped a big, outsized clanger in your March *Openers*"..."*Oui* clanged." **1985** J. Green *Dict. Contemp. Slang* 81: *Drop a clanger*...To make a social error, the awfulness of which reverberates around the assembled gathering.

clank *n. USMC.* a battle tank.

*a*1982 Dunstan *Viet. Tracks* 143: Marine tanks in Vietnam were called..."clanks." **1982** Former U.S. Marine: In Vietnam we called the tanks *clanks.*

clank *v. USAF.* to become jittery, disconcerted, or the like.—usu. constr. with *up.*

1955 *AS* XXX 116: *Clank up; Get the clanks,* v. phr. Become nervous. **1961** *Sat. Eve. Post* (Oct. 14) 82: Should a doolie apologize for "clanking up" (flubbing), [etc.]. **1961** *AS* (May) 148: *To clank* or to *clank up* means "to freeze up," to make errors because of fright or temporary shock. **1969** *Current Slang* I & II 20: *Clank,* v. To fail to perform under pressure.

clanked up *adj. USAF.* very nervous; frightened; rattled.

1953 in Loosbrock & Skinner *Wild Blue* 471: At first he thought it was a kid on his first mission, a little nervous and "clanked up." **1955** *AS* XXX 16: *Clanked up*...Nervous; excited; disconcerted; rattled. **1956** in Harvey *Air Force* 65: The guy who got all clanked up the first time you spotted some MIGs over Sinuju? **1973** M. Collins *Carrying the Fire* 17:

But how about some poor second lieutenant in bad weather, at night for the first time, when he's clanked up anyway?

clanker *n.* a silver dollar.

> **1927** *AS* (June) 390: A dollar [is] a *clanker* or *slug*.

clanks *n.pl.* **1.** *USAF.* jitters; (*also*) combat neurosis.—usu. constr. with *the.*

> **1943** *Life* (Aug. 9) 44: By the summer of 1942 he was so sore about being kept out of the war that he developed a case of the "clanks," a Cochran term that is roughly synonymous with the jitters. **1955** Salter *Hunters* 16: All the damned kids got the clanks when they heard about it. **1955** Reifer *New Words* 48: Clanks *n. Slang.* A nervous state, as in "He's got the clanks." **1957** Wallrich *Air Force Airs* 101: Once I was a civilian and flew on weekends,/No sweat about clanks and no sign of the bends. **1959** Scott *Flying Tiger* 104: What gave me the "clanks" for the first time was that I now knew too much. **1962** *We Seven* 65: Obviously, I succeeded, although the test engineer who was with me suffered slightly from the "clanks," which is pilot talk for the shakes. **1963** E.M. Miller *Exile* 134: I think you're still suffering from the Korean Klanks.

2. (see quot.).

> **1980** Pearl *Slang Dict.: Clanks, the n.* delirium tremens.

clanky *adj.* *USAF.* nervous; jumpy, esp. as a reaction to air combat.

> **1974** Stevens *More There I Was* 36: I get clanky when I'm in the sky.

clap *n.* [akin to MF *clapoir* 'bubo', *clapier* 'brothel'] gonorrhea.—usu. constr. with *the.*—usu. considered vulgar. Also (now *Black E.*) **claps.**

> ***1587** in *F & H* II 119: Before they get the clap. ***ca1650** in Wardroper *Love & Drollery* 205: She caught a clap. ***1672** in Burford *Bawdy Verse* 155: Lechers whom *Drink* or *Clapp* disable. ***ca1680** in Adlard *Forbidden Tree* 39: May he die…of claps. ***1698** Ward *London-Spy* 11: My *Patients*…are seldom free from *Clap, Pox, Thumps, Cuts* or *Bruises*. ***1741** in J. Atkins *Sex in Lit.* IV 184: Dread fore-runners of a *Clap*! **1826** in Bleser *Secret & Sacred* 5: The Clap…pale faces among the raking youth of town evince its existence. **1845** in Eliason *Tarheel Talk* 71: Take my advice and touch nothing in the shape of a prostitute when you come through Raleigh, for in honest truth the clap there is of luxuriant growth. **1864** in Wiley & Milhollen *They Who Fought* 192: Not…the clap, but…something worse. **1888** *Stag Party* 41: For fear that he'd give 'em the clap or the pox. **1917** Moss *Non-Com's Manual* 190: Should you discover that you have clap or other venereal disease, report to the hospital *at once* for treatment. **1919** O'Brien *Wine, Women & War* 306: Physical exam—crabs, cooties and clap. **1921** in Randolph *Pissing in Snow* 31: He gave Collins some clap-medicine. **1925** in Hemingway *Sel. Letters* 182: I didn't know whether clap had two p's or one, so I changed it to gonoccoci. **1930** Dos Passos *42nd Parallel* 71: He was particularly glad he hadn't got the clap off that girl in Seattle. **1939** in J. Jones *Reach* 5: Men who had the "clap" as it is called in the army. **1952** Sandburg *Young Strangers* 240 [ref. to *ca*1890's]: I remember one barber going on and on about fools he had heard saying, "A case of the clap is no worse than a bad cold," and what had happened to them and how they learned better. **1965** C. Brown *Manchild* 147: Cats who mess around wit faggots usually come out wit claps or somethin' like that. **1988** DeLillo *Libra* 114: Ozzie had the clap. **1991** C. Roberts *Combat Medic* 53: Gonorrhea, or the "clap," as we called it, took its…toll.

clap *v.* to infect with gonorrhea.—now usu. constr. with *up.*—usu. considered vulgar.

> ***1658** in *F & H* II 119: Atropos clapt him, a Pox on the Drab! ***1675** in Duffett *Burlesque Plays* 61: It does not vex me to be Clapp'd by her: Gad she was handsome. ***a1700** in J. Atkins *Sex in Lit.* IV 170: They clap all their cullies, and their pockets pick. **1934** "J.M. Hall" *Anecdota* 34: A clapped up prick. **1938–39** Dos Passos *Young Man* 26: Well, Toby, here's to the clapped up ladies of Paree. **1939** C.R. Cooper *Scarlet* 81: With your damned respectable wives going out in the bushes for four bits a shot and clapping up everybody that's fool enough to fall for 'em. **1952** in Hemingway *Sel. Letters* 780: *La puta mar* that we have loved…has clapped us and pox-ed us too. **1962** T. Berger *Reinhart in Love* 180: Aw, we know he got clapped up. **1972** Jenkins *Semi-Tough* 47: She's a gotch-eyed, hump-backed, clapped-up Cambodian hooker. **1979** McGivern *Soldiers* 179: Stay alert, keep your rifle clean, and trench-foot, don't get clapped-up.

clapped-out *adj.* worn-out.

> **1980** *Nat. Lampoon* (Apr.) 40: And his brand-new Sportster was probably faster and certainly safer than Jack's old clapped-out chopper. **1985** Boyne & Thompson *Wild Blue* 17: A clapped-out '31 Chevy he'd stolen

from his uncle for fifty bucks.

clapper[1] *n.* the tongue; mouth; (*hence*) the tendency to speak.

> ***1609** in *F & H* II 119: And to let that *clapper* (your tongue) be tost so high, that all the house may ring of it. ***1698–1706** in D'Urfey *Pills* IV 126: Where…our Wives Clappers never sound. ***1750** Fielding *Tom Jones* VII ch. xv: No *clapper* could be heard there but her own. **1838** [Haliburton] *Clockmaker* (ser. 2) 80: A-lettin' of her clapper run away with her. **1847** Robb *Kaam* 9: I speculate I'd silence his clapper. **1872** G. Gleason *Spirit Riders* 58: Hold yer clapper, boy! **1900** Willard & Hodler *Powers That Prey* 102: Can he keep his clapper quiet? **1901** *DN* II 137: *Clapper, n.* The mouth; used in iron foundries; "shut your clapper." Buffalo, N.Y. **1902** "J. Flynt" *Little Bro.* 128: You tie that little clapper o' yours to the top of your mouth till court is over. **1927** J. Stevens *Mattock* 147: But he got Madam Rose shut up, the Busons'll keep quiet, and it's up to you to hush the clapper of that fat madam of yours. **1962** Maurer & Vogel *Narc. & Narc. Add.* (ed. 2) 296: *Clapper.* The tongue.

clapper[2] *n.* a gonorrheal infection; (*hence*) a person having gonorrhea.

> **1750** in Breslaw *Tues. Club* 233: Why is a man with a moderate pox like a finished church bell?…Because it is not without a Clapper. **1956** H. Gold *Not With It* 17: I used to join out the odds, had myself a stable of clappers for the gash-hounds too dumb to do their own howling.

clappy *adj.* infected with gonorrhea.—usu. considered vulgar.

> **1937** Reitman *Box-Car Bertha* 163: She was a no-account clappy little chippy when I found her. **1964** in Jackson *Swim Like Me* 124: Before I'd touch your slimy thighs I'd…suck a clappy dick. **1982** Downey *Losing the War* 101: Poor food, terrible merchandise, clappy pussy.

clap shack *n.* *USMC & Navy.* a venereal-disease ward. [Quots. ref. to WWII.]

> **1952** Uris *Battle Cry* 131: Suppose you get a dose and they throw you in the clap shack and make you do G.O. time without pay? **1959** Cochrell *Barren Beaches* 38: Haven't you spent enough time in the clap shack? **1968** W. Styron, in *Esquire* (Oct.) 123: In 1944, as a Marine recruit, I was shanghaied into the "clap shack," the venereal disease ward of the Naval Hospital at Parris Island, South Carolina. **1988** Hynes *Flights of Passage* 73: The flight…couldn't function…with one member in the clap shack.

claret *n.* Esp. *Boxing.* blood, esp. from the nose.

> ***1604** in *OED.* ***1803** in Wetherell *Adventures* 72: Pug…kick'd Burchel in the mouth…made the claret fly. ***1821–26** Stewart *Man-of-War's-Man* I 192: We…can both take and lose a trifle of what is called *claret* on occasion without twitching. **1831** *Spirit of Times* (Dec. 10) 4: And well with their mawleys they bustle about,/For the claret they're tapping in streams from the snout. **1832** *Spirit of Times* (Mar. 3) 3: *Claret* was observed to flow from Mc's *snout.* **1847** Downey *Cruise of Portsmouth* 91: Hurra said Spouter—give it to him—that's your sort—once more—just under his fin—Hurra—there he spouts the claret. **1859** Matsell *Vocab.* 19: *Claret.* Blood. **1864** Hill *Our Boys* 240: The "claret" was rushing profusely from his "mug." **1869** *Overland Mo.* (Aug.) 121: He…exhorted him…not to be over-particular as to a few slices of skin, or a few ounces of flesh, or a pint or so of "claret." **1870** *Putnam's Mag.* (Mar.) 301: The combatants struck each other… upon…the nose…drawing the blood, the claret, the ruby. **1873** Small *Joining the Grangers* 60: The swingle…struck him on the nose, and scattered the claret in all directions. **1910** T.A. Dorgan, in *N.Y. Eve. Jour.* (Jan. 18) 12 (headline): Claret flowed freely. **1933–34** Lorimer & Lorimer *Stag Line* 86: Get that nose again, Bat. Spill that claret. **1942** Garcia *Tough Trip* 432: In-who-lise…gave him a swinging back-hander across his face that brought the claret dripping from his nose. **1942** Algren *Morning* 259: Looka that claret! I'll take mine in a small glass!

claret jug *n.* Esp. *Boxing.* the nose, esp. when bloodied. Also **claret bottle.**

> ***1859** in *F & H* II 120: A man's broken nose, is his *claret-jug* smashed. **1873** Scammon *Marine Mammals* 267: Haul ahead, and I'll tap his claret-bottle! **a1889** in Barrère & Leland *Dict. Slang* I 253: On his *claret-jug*, I ask you, what's that variegated rise?

clarry *n.* *Jazz.* a clarinet.

> **1942** *ATS* 558. **1964** R.S. Gold *Jazz Lexicon* 58.

class *n.* **1.** Orig. *Sports.* elegance of style, behavior, taste, etc.; excellence; refinement.

> ***1874** Hotten *Slang Dict.* (ed. 5): *Class*, the highest quality or combination of highest qualities among athletes. "He's not class enough," *i.e.*, not good enough. "There's a deal of class about him," *i.e.*, a deal of good quality. ***1884** in *F & H* II 120: The elasticity necessary for any-

thing like class at sprinting departs comparatively early. **1893** *Chi. Daily Tribune* (Sept. 1) 7: Racing Lacks Class…Racing at Hawthorne yesterday was rather common…Cyclone was the opening favorite. **1898–1900** Cullen *Chances* 30: Mazie V., a clean-limbed filly that never showed a particle of class. **1907** in H.C. Fisher *A. Mutt* 16: Some class, huh? I'll need a club to keep the dames away. **1911** Runyon *Tents of Trouble* 98: The soldier man…/Must think a little for himself an' show a lot o' class. **1916** S. Lewis *Job* 296: Some class, eh? **1920** Ade *Hand-Made Fables* 51: It never occurred to her that Joe was among those who had shown Class. **1922** S. Lewis *Babbitt* 74: Oh, shoot, that's just because you never tried a sedan. Let's get one. It's got a lot more class. **1932** Berg *Prison Doctor* 13: Trouble with you is, you ain't got no class. **1969** Gardner *Fat City* 148: He's got all the moves. He's got class.

2. an individual or individuals displaying class. Hence quasi-adj.

*1874 (quot. at (1), above). ***1897** in Ware *Passing Eng*. Soldiers ain't no class. **1913** Light *Hobo* 24: Jack…was sitting in an observation chair arranged by himself and termed "some class." **1913–15** Van Loan *Taking the Count* 76: He looks like class. **1918** *Ladies Home Journal* (Jan.) 27: But this one woman, she's class. **1934** Berg *Prison Nurse* 43: This dame was class. **1936** Gaddis *Courtesan* 39: You're class, baby. **1964** *Flintstones* (ABC-TV): Look at that walk. You can tell he's *real* class. **1970** Rudensky & Riley *Goniff* 11: These were class cons, the best, brainiest, and most dedicated cons behind walls.

class A *adj.* first-rate; topnotch.

1922 G. Ade in W. Burnett *Best* 113: Each of whom looks up to Class A women with…worshipful adoration. **1924** H.L. Wilson *Professor* 237: He's a Class-A press agent for me too. **1938** "E. Queen" *4 Hearts* 9: What the hell did you expect—a class A assignment your first week on the lot? **1951** Fowler *Schnozzola* 67: I know you are a class-A drummer. **1960** Bannon *Journey* 27: Vega…is a class-A bitch. **1963** Morgan *Six-Eleven* 129: That part of Connecticut is Class A all the way. **1964** Pearl *Stockade* 222: And me with class-A heartburn! **1972** Jenkins *Semi-Tough* 9: I was gonna give her my Class A boomer.

class act *n. Entertainment Industry.* a classy person.—also used ironically.

1976 L.A. man, age 32: She sounds like a real class act. **1977** Stallone *Paradise Alley* 55: You're a real class act, Nickels! **1987** *Beauty & Beast* (CBS-TV): Boy, this guy's a class act all the way. **1988** *N.Y. Post* (June 6) 50: I pray that Lou Piniella, a class act, is soon able to escape [the N.Y. Yankees] and secure a managerial position.

class up *v.* to make classy.

1983 *Good Morning America* (ABC-TV) (Apr. 20): I gotta class up my act. **1993** *Young & Restless* (CBS-TV): You wouldn't mind if I classed up my act for you.

classy *adj.* having or displaying CLASS, 1. Now *colloq.*

1891 in *OEDS*. **1915** Howard *God's Man* 134: Nothing coarse, nothing rough, nothing not classy. **1906** H. Green *Actor's Boarding House* 108: Say, Annabelle, d'yuh think yuh oughter be wearin' yer diamonds in the mornin' this classy, dear. It ain't classy. **a1904–11** Phillips *Susan Lenox* I 126: He'd give up a lot to you, because you're classier than I am. **1914** Dale *Songs of 7th* 86: Perhaps you think those mentioned are quite a classy lot,/But the Captain of our Company is really twice as hot. **1914** S. Lewis *Mr. Wrenn* 148: Well, it's no wonder I had a classy hang-over. **1914** Lardner *You Know Me Al* 75: She ain't nowheres near as big as Hazel but she's classier al and she will make me a good wife. **1917** Morse *Letters* 33: That's a real classy letter, ain't it? **1920** S. Lewis *Main St.* 52: I hear the house is getting to be real classy. **1952** Sandburg *Young Strangers* 240 [ref. to *ca*1895]: Harry and the other porter used to dress in their fanciest clothes and Sunday noon walk into the Brown's Hotel dining room and order and eat a fifty-cent dinner. They called it "classy."

clatter *n.* **1.** time; instance.

1913 J. London *J. Barleycorn* 165: It meant forty to fifty cents a clatter. **1918** E.E. Rose *Cappy Ricks* 13: Cost me twenty thousand dollars at a clatter! **1978** Ponicsan *Ringmaster* 15: A girl would come by soon to cop your joint, twenty bucks a clatter.

2. *Und.* a police patrol wagon.

1914 Jackson & Hellyer *Criminal Slang* 24: *Clatter*, Noun General usage. A patrol wagon. **1942–49** Goldin et al. *DAUL*.

claustro *adj.* claustrophobic.

1968 Swarthout *Loveland* 134: You get claustro sometimes, living on a yacht, and lonesome.

claw *n.* **1.** a finger or hand.

1752 in Breslaw *Tues. Club* 381: Towards the Chair Strech'd forth one

of his claws. **1851** M. Reid *Scalp-Hunters* 76: Take care o' my claws, d'yur hear! Them Injuns has made 'em scace. **1854** Sleeper *Salt Water Bubbles* 77: What has become of those missing claws? **1868** M. Reid *Helpless Hand* 22: Le's lay my claws on't. **1883** Keane *Blue-Water* 192: They can't lay a claw on you. **1898** Green *Va. Folk-Speech* 88: *Claw, n.* The human hand. **1904** in "O. Henry" *Works* 849: Most anybody but me would have popped you when you wouldn't hoist that left claw of yours. **1975** Schott *No Left Turns* 56: They caught him with his claw in the tambourine. **1977** B. Murphy, on N.Y. Mets baseball (WOR-TV) (Aug. 21): Milner almost had it in the claw, but he couldn't hold it.

2. *Und.* (see quot.).

1914 Jackson & Hellyer *Crim. Slang* 24: *Claw*, Noun. Current amongst pickpockets. The "tool," the "jerve," the "wire," or the expert operator in a "gun mob" who lifts the money and valuable collateral from the victim's person. Example: "Our mob is working under one of the speediest claws in the country."

claw *v. Esp. Carnival.* to seize or snatch; *(hence)* to place under arrest.

1833 in [S. Smith] *Letters of Downing* 116: They run into Mr. Harris's room and clawed the money off of his table. **1914** Jackson & Hellyer *Crim. Slang* 24: *Claw*, Verb. General usage. To snatch; to appropriate; to annex. **1927** *DN* V 442: *Claw*, v. To arrest. **1929** Milburn *Hobo's Hornbook* 255: The bulls they made them halt,/And they all got clawed in Gettasford for a mangy bag of salt. **1933–34** Lorimer & Lorimer *Stag Line* 160: He'll claw me for running a Chuck-Luck game.

clawhammer *n.* a man's dress coat. Now *colloq.*

1863 N. Hawthorne, in *F & H* II 120: Sea-captains call a dress-coat a *claw-hammer*. **1868** Macy *There She Blows!* 19: A "claw-hammer" or "dress-coat." **a1867** G.W. Harris *Lovingood* 55: Off went the clawhammer coat. **1891** Maitland *Slang Dict.* 68: *Clawhammer* (Am.), a dress-coat; otherwise known as a "steel pen" or "swallow tail." **1894** Bangs *3 Wks. in Politics* 7: Cut-aways is bad enough…but claw-hammers is ruin. **1895** Townsend *Fadden Explains* 82: I says nottin but just sneaks me clawhammer wid us. **1899** King *Found in Philippines* 162: Prime's was the only black "claw hammer" in the room.

claw off *v.* to come away.

1897 A. Lewis *Wolfville* 130: Cimarron Pete claws off all sound.

clawthumper *n.* var. crawthumper.

1863, 1888 in *DA*.

clay[1] *n.* ¶ In phrase: **moisten the clay** to slake one's thirst, esp. with whiskey. Also vars.

1800 *Amorous Songster* 92: With honest old stingo [he] was soaking his clay. **1808** in Whiting *Early Amer. Proverbs* 74: And when he thus has wet his clay. **1829** J. Hall *Winter Eves.* 48: Soaking Sam…ev'ry day/Went to Sot's Hole to soak his clay. **1836** *Spirit of Times* (July 16) 169: Two are gardeners, who had been *moistening* their *clay* with a little mountain dew. **1838** [Haliburton] *Clockmaker* (ser. 2) 182: Won't you moisten the clay, eh? **1840** *Spirit of Times* (Oct. 10) 378: One might "moisten his clay" without drinking "rank *pysen*." **1848** *Life in Rochester* 68: I think a brandy punch would moisten my clay to about the right consistency.

clay[2] *n. Army.* a claymore mine. [Quots. ref. to Vietnam War.]

1978 *Nat. Lampoon* (July) 67: Claymore(s) or Clays…electronically detonated land mines (U.S.). **1989** Leib *Fire Dream* 246: Four Clays [are] on this side of the road.

clean *adj.* **1.** being without money; broke.

1897 Ade *Pink* 168: When she gets th'ough 'ith him he's so clean he don' need to take no bath faw [a] month. **1908** in H.C. Fisher *A. Mutt* 28: I hope she don't steer me where it costs anything. I'm clean. **1922** Paul *Impromptu* 17: I'm clean—unless you can give me back my dollar for the dance. **1925** Mullin *Scholar Tramp* 225: "Sorry," I said, "I'm clean." **1932** Riesenberg *Log of the Sea* 167: I was broke, wiped clean as an eel's tail. **1953–58** J.C. Holmes *Horn* 56: I'm clean. I haven't worked for three weeks. **1959–60** R. Reisner *Jazz Titans* 152: *Clean*: Free from money.

2. *Police.* free of contraband or incriminating evidence, esp. drugs or weapons; *(hence)* unarmed.

1887 Walling *N.Y. Chief of Police* 455: He is always "clean" when the hand of the law is laid on him, having thrown his plunder away. **1925–26** Black *You Can't Win* 155 [ref. to 1890's]: I…thought of my room and was thankful that it was clean. **1927** McIntyre *Slag* 48: Ain't I told you I'm clean! What more do you want? **1952** Bruce & Essex *K.C. Confidential* (film): I don't get it! This man tried to reach for a gun and he's clean! **1962** H. Simmons *On Eggshells* 104: They're clean, Sarge. **1975** V. Miller *Trade-Off* 7: Somebody like Maurie Steiner, a nondrug user, who's so "clean" we haven't been able to hang so much as a parking ticket on him. *Ibid.* 23: Not even a weapon. He's cleaner than a streaker in a carwash. **1976** Hoffman & Pecznick *Drop a Dime* 206: They'd be "clean"—unarmed.

3.a. *Police.* innocent of wrongdoing; free of suspicion.

1925–26 Black *You Can't Win* 131: We are clean so far as the coppers are concerned. **1927–28** in R. Nelson *Dishonorable* 139: Lis'en, Lieutenant, I'm clean on that [stolen] car. **1957** MacDonald *Price of Murder* 49: If he wants to make trouble for me, he can…As long as we stay clean, he won't bother. **1961** Scarne *Guide to Gambling* 227: Dealer and croupier schools are turning out hundreds of formally trained dealers who are *clean* (without police records). **1963** E. Hunter *Ten Plus One* 82: At the end of their session, they were convinced he was clean. **1968** Simoun *Madigan* (film): I been clean for two years. What do I know about Brooklyn? **1973** in *Submission of Pres. Convers.* 81: He is just as clean as a whistle. **1978** Strieber *Wolfen* 112: You know damn well I'm not clean.

b. *Narc.* not using illicit drugs.

[**1913** J. London *J. Barleycorn* 239: Now I was…clean of alcohol.] **1949** in W.S. Burroughs *Letters* 47: I doubt if you will ever be bothered, but best keep clean. **1959–60** R. Reisner *Jazz Titans* 152: *Clean*: not to have any [drugs] on one's person or free from the habit. **1960** C.L. Cooper *Scene* 8: I haven't had no stuff for four days; I'm clean. I'll never get hooked again. **1965** in Sanchez *Word Sorcerers* 192: I can get clean, babee. I mean, I don't have a long jones. **1982** Rucker *Kafka* 168: "Sounds like…drug psychosis." "Hey!…I'm, clean!" **1988** T. Logan *Harder They Fall* 66: She's on crack…I'm clean, but she won't quit.

c. (of a communications system) free of a wiretap or other eavesdropping device.

1978 Truscott *Dress Gray* 421: You on a clean phone? **1983** Flaherty *Tin Wife* 291: Is your phone clean? Not bugged?

4. *Esp. Black E.* **a.** stylishly and attractively dressed; stylishly attractive.

1954 in Wepman et al. *The Life* 36: And believe me, Jim, we were both real clean. **1966** Braly *On Yard* 72: I hope you looked real clean in that hot suit. **1969** *Black Panther* (Oakland, Calif.) (Sept. 20): Some of you would be blowing joints, and drinking and carrying on and being sharp, trying to get you some clean clothes. **1971** *Essence* (Aug.) 47: We definitely some clean muthas. **1973** *Black World* (Apr.) 63: Lawd, but you was clean! **1977** Filosa *Surf. Almanac* 183: *Clean*…Neat, nice, attractive. **1978** Wheeler & Kerby *Steel Cowboy* (film): I do admire a tractor all dolled up like that. It looks so *clean* you could eat off it. **1989** *21 Jump St.* (Fox-TV): That's clean! Where'd you get that? **1994** *Newsweek* (Feb. 7) 46: When we were dressed in blue jeans…babes wouldn't give us the time of day. But when we were clean we got all the phone numbers we wanted.

b. superior; excellent.

1968 H. Ellison *Deadly Streets* 104: She found…my stash and cut out…with about three pounds of really clean stuff.

¶ In phrases:

¶ **clean and green, 1.** *CB.* (of a highway) free of heavy traffic, stop signals, police radar, etc.

1976 Lieberman & Rhodes *CB Handbook* 126: *Clean And Green*—All clear. **1976** Whelton *CB Baby* 14: I just came through the tunnel and it was clean and green all the way to Jersey.

2. *USAF.* having all dials and indicators on a control panel indicating readiness for takeoff.

1985 Heywood *Taxi Dancer* 160 [ref. to Vietnam War]: Okay, Blazers, make sure you're clean and green.

¶ **come clean, 1.** to pay up, as with all of one's money.

1914 Ellis *Billy Sunday* 208: Come across with the mazuma, come clean, divvy. **1928** Fisher *Jericho* 31: Damage suit—ten thousand berries…Claim' he was go'n' bring in my occupation and lots o' other stuff if I didn' come clean—forcin' my hand, see? Knew I had hard cash and knew he could make me pay off by threatenin' to squeal.

2. to divulge all one knows, esp. in a confession of guilt.

1918 E.E. Rose *Cappy Ricks* 105: Now, don't stall—come clean! **1919** Darling *Jargon Book* 8: *Come clean*—to confess everything. **1920–21** Witwer *Leather Pushers* 197: Why not come clean with the old man and be done with it, kid? **1922** in S. Smith *Gumps* 29: I'll make these four-flushers come clean. **1925** *Collier's* (Feb. 3) 30: I'm coming clean with you, kid. I'm a bad girl and I admit it. **1929** "E. Queen" *Roman Hat* ch. v 59: Aw, cut it out, Madge…Come clean, Madge! **1931** Uhler *Cane Juice* 55: Come clean now…Who's the man? **1932** Berg *Prison Doctor* 211: All right; I'll come clean. No reason why I should. But I will. **1990** *U.S. News & W.R.* (Oct. 15) 136: Our political leadership won't come clean with the people.

clean *v.* **1.** to deprive of all one's money, as through gambling or theft.—also (formerly usu.) constr. with *out.*

***1812** Vaux *Vocab.*: *Cleaned Out*: said of a gambler who has lost his last stake at play; also, of a *flat* who has been stript of all his money by a coalition of *sharps.* ***1823** "J. Bee" *Slang* 52: "*Cleaned out, quite*"—lost every farthing—at gambling, is commonly understood. **1840** *New Yorker* (Mar. 21) 7: I've been down upon my luck, cleaned out, everything gone, and my body in quod. **1848** in Smith & Judah *Chronicles of the Gringos* 311: The soldier is "cleaned out." **1855** Dwyer & Lingenfelter *Songs of Gold Rush* 110: I played all night and cleaned them out. **1857** Smith *Chili Con Carne* 324: He is a good judge of human nature, and knows who to "clean out" at once. **1866** *Nat. Police Gaz.* (Apr. 21) 3: One of them knocked him down while the other "cleaned him out." **1876** Cody & Arlington *Life on Border* 40: They've got him drunk and they are cleaning him out. **1883** in Rosa *Wild Bill* 79: They gambled…and…Tutt effectually "cleaned out" Bill. **1907** in H.C. Fisher *A. Mutt* 10: A. Mutt Is Cleaned So Often That He Don't Need the Bathtub. **1912–14** in E. O'Neill *Lost Plays* 38: I got into a game at Tony's place and they cleaned me. **1915–16** Lait *Beef, Iron & Wine* 175: That…crook…would'a' cleaned me if I hadn' beat him to it. **1929** Bodenheim *60 Secs.* 236: The girl always manages it so's the guy gets cleaned *after* he's left them, so's they can't be blamed for it. **1935** West *Goin' to Town* (film): Yeah, they cleaned me. **1946** Heatter *Dim View* 5: I'm busted….You cleaned me at Morobie. **1953** Gresham *Midway* 20: Those folks will clean you like a Thanksgiving turkey. **1981** Ballenger *Terror* 8: That shyster she hired cleaned me like a chicken.

2.a. to drub or vanquish.—also (formerly usu.) constr. with *out*, occ. with *off.* Also as *n.* Hence **cleaning,** *n.*

***1819** [T. Moore] *Tom Crib* 38: [At] a *round* of odes…Bobby's the boy would *clean* them *out!* **1858** in *DA*: I could clean you out quicker than greased lightning would pass a funeral. **1864** in Hough *Soldier in W.* 235: Old "Tom" has cleaned out Hood and a messenger starts immediately from here to join him. **1862–65** C. Barney *20th Iowa Vols.* 265: He had enjoyed seeing the "Yanks *cleaned out*" at Bull Run. **1865** in Andrus *Letters* 128: We have now commenced the grand forward move, which is going to result in the capture of Mobile, or a *cleaning out* to ourselves. **1866** Marcy *Army Life* 365: We fout at the battle of the Hoss-shoe, whar we and ole Hickry cleaned out the Ingines. **1869** in J. Chisholm *So. Pass*: I can beat old Uncle Snow…I can clean the whole caboodle. **1871** "M. Twain" *Roughing It* 252: He *went* for 'em! And he *cleaned* 'em, too! **1874** in Miller & Snell *Why West Was Wild* 141: He undertakes to "clean out" everyone who asserts the facts. **1883** Peck *Peck's Bad Boy* 143: Me and my chum thought that if Pa was such a terror on skates we could…enter him as the "great unknown," and clean out the whole gang. **1885** Siringo *Texas Cowboy* 22: If he is from Texas I'll bet two to one that he can clean out any two boys of his size in the crowd. **1909** "Clivette" *Café Cackle* 69: I'm a lightweight pugilist…and I can clean the bunch without perspiring a drop. **1915** in Grayson *New Stories* 567: Clean him, Tony! Clean him, kid! **1929** in R.E. Howard *Book* 62: Our skipper took their captain to a cleaning on the wharfs of Zanzibar. **1929–30** J.T. Farrell *Young Lonigan* 77: Nearly every guy his size in the neighborhood has cleaned on him. **1930** J.T. Farrell *Calico Shoes* 12: Yes, if Dick had started something, he would have cleaned the guts out of him. **1935** Coburn *Law Rides Range* 19: I'll take you to a cleaning that will linger in your memories for many a year. **1938** Smitter *Detroit* 205: What chance has a rat got to clean off a cat? **1970** Wakefield *Going All the Way* 197: Gunner would clean his ass. **1974** Loken *Come Monday Morning* 75: Russ…caught him out at the…truckstop and cleaned his ass…good.

b. to make short work of (a person); do for.

1872 Burnham *Secret Service* 185: They'll clean him out, sure…They've been thrusting these threatening letters under the door of his hotel room all day long. **1887** Francis *Saddle & Moccasin* 83: A lieutenant and half a company was despatched in search of him, but he "cleaned them out."

3. to win or earn.

1910 T.A. Dorgan, in *N.Y. Eve. Jour.* (May 28) 12: Hi George—just cleaned $6,000 on the street.

¶ In phrases:

¶ **clean house** to inflict punishment; administer a beating.

1910 *N.Y. Eve. Jour.* (Feb. 5) 6: He got very nasty and abusive, calling me twenty different names, and even pulled off his coat and started to clean house. **1929** Segar *Thimble Th.* 115: G'wan, ya hick! I'll clean house on ya in about a minute! **1968** Gover *JC* 21: Man, they're out t'clean house with each other's nappy haids.

¶ **clean out (one's) pipes** see s.v. PIPE.

¶ **clean (someone's) canyon** *S.W.* to thrash (someone).

1935 Algren *Boots* 13: Som'un ort to clean thet Stub McKay's canyon up proper for him jest once.

¶ **clean (someone's) clock, 1.** to thrash (someone); to trounce.

1959 Cochrell *Barren Beaches* 225 [ref. to WWII]: "Don't give me that guff. You're not a corporal anymore." "I don't have to be a corporal to clean your clock." **1965** Adler *Vietnam Letters* 37: I wish these little SOB's would come out in the open so we could "clean their clocks" for them. **1966** Braly *On Yard* 172: Turnipseed had gotten his clock cleaned in his own cell. **1966–69** in *DARE.* **1984** *N.Y. Post* (Aug. 3) 87: Chapman cleaned a few clocks during a bench-clearing brawl. **1992** *Donahue* (NBC-TV): We're getting our clock cleaned by sending all these jobs overseas.

2. (see quot.).

1971 Tak *Truck Talk* 32: *Clean his clock*: to pass another vehicle…at great speed.

¶ **clean (someone's) greens** *So.* to thrash (someone).

1972 C. Gaines *Stay Hungry* 262: But when I get out I'm gon come around to see you and I'm might gonna clean your greens.

¶ **clean (someone's) plow** to thrash (someone).

1919 *DN* V 37: *plow, to clean one's*, v. phr. To give one a whipping. **1974** E. Thompson *Tattoo* 111: If Gorilla wanted to clean those loud-mouthed farmers' plows, he was ready to help him.

cleaner *n.* ¶ In phrase: **send** [or **take**] **(someone) to the cleaners** to CLEAN, 1 & 2.

1907 Siler *Pugilism* 31: He not only knocked you down, George…but he sent you to the cleaners. **1908** in H.C. Fisher *A. Mutt* 21: You'll send us to the cleaners yet, you big stew. *a***1921** Sandburg *Slabs of the Sunburnt West* 7: Put it over, shoot it across./Send 'em to the cleaners. **1928** MacArthur *War Bugs* 196: The foe started some rough-house stuff that nearly sent us to the cleaners'. **1928** Hammett *Red Harvest* 30: The people you want taken to the cleaners were friends of yours yesterday. **1933** in Galewitz *Great Comics* 10: This wily old gambler takes them one and all to the cleaners! **1942** "E. Queen" *Calamity Town* 173: Maybe some broad may have took him to the cleaners while he was feeling happy, but he never shelled out one cent in my place except for drinks. **1960–61** Steinbeck *Discontent* 213: If…he's a crook, you could be taken. Taken to the cleaners. **1964** Maibaum & Dehn *Goldfinger* (film): Goldfinger's been taking him to the cleaners every day for a week. **1974** A. Bergman *Big Kiss-Off* 117: Men I genuinely admired for the job they had done in taking the Axis to the cleaners. **1983** Ehrhart *VN-Perkasie* 367: And now they steal our stuff while out there [in combat] gettin' taken to the cleaners.

clean out see S.V. CLEAN, *v.*

cleansleeve *n. Mil.* a cadet private in a military academy; (*hence*) a member of the armed forces in the lowest enlisted grade. Cf. SLICKSLEEVE.

1909 *Miss. A.&M. Reveille* 101: In the fall of 1906 there were assembled…about a hundred and ninety "clean sleeves" and "ring-tails" to stand the strain of the hardest year in the College course. **1978** Truscott *Dress Gray* 103: An enlisted man, a GI, a clean-sleeve grunt trooper. **1985** Former SP4, U.S. Army: A *clean-sleeve* was a person who either had no rank at all or had his rank stripped off of him. It was relatively common [in the 1970's].

clean-up *n.* **1.** a decisive defeat.

1866 H.J. Harris *So. Sketches* 14: Suppose you represent your feelings…on an occasion of a clean up of our army by…the Yankee forces. **2.** a great profit; a windfall.

1867 in A.K. McClure *Rocky Mtns.* 242: The miners…gather in their week's wages or "clean-up" in their pockets. **1878** Hart *Sazerac* 21: At the same time make a nice little clean-up for himself. **1907** in H.C. Fisher *A. Mutt* 4: Mr. A. Mutt Makes a Clean-Up. He had $25 Both Ways on Sugarmaid. **1913–15** Van Loan *Taking the Count* 33: You're going to make a clean-up in the betting. **1920** Weaver *In American* 17: I'd make a clean-up at it. **1923** Witwer *Fighting Blood* 223: I saw a chance for a clean-up on that infernal nag. **1929** Burnett *Iron Man* 12: "What do you say we all make a clean-up?"…"Well, we ain't passing up no ready money."

3. a thorough job.

1873 *Overland Mo.* (Feb.): I didn't mean to tell this part of this story; but now that I am at it I may as well make a "clean-up."

clean-up *adj. Baseball.* (in a batting order) fourth. Also adv. or quasi-n.

1911 Van Loan *Big League* 171: "Hardy had been moved up into the "clean-up" position. **1960** N.Y.C. man, age *ca*45: He usually bats in the

clean-up spot…Sometimes Berra bats clean-up. **1982** Considine *Lang. of Sport* 13: *Cleanup.* The fourth position in the lineup.

clean up *v.* **1.** to gain (a profit); win (money).

1831 in *DA.* **1884** Shinn *Mining Camps* 119: Another miner "cleaned up" eighteen thousand dollars in one day's labor with pan and pick. **1907** in H.C. Fisher *A. Mutt* 7: I cleaned up 4000 today on the 2d race. **1921** J. Conway, in *Variety* (Dec. 30) 97: I know a guy who…cleaned up a lot of kale. **1929–33** J.T. Farrell *Manhood* 278: I cleaned up twenty bucks. **1963** D. Tracy *Brass Ring* 117: Hobey said you cleaned up all the prizes.

2.a. to defeat decisively; thrash.—also constr. with *on.*

1862 in J.M. McPherson *Chrons. of Civil War* V 133: If we all had guns like these we would clean the Yankees up in six months. **1882** Watkins *Co. Aytch* 195: Well, Fed was a trained rooster, and would "clean up" a big-foot rooster as soon as he was put in the pit. **1898** in A. Charters *Ragtime Songbk.* 40: Shot craps last night, got cleaned up right. **1908** Barron *Lone Star* 35 [ref. to Civil War]: We'll clean 'em up and drive 'em from the state of Missouri. **1919** in DeBeck *Google* 11: You heard me, you big stiff—I said I was gonna clean you up!! **1928** Dahlberg *Bottom Dogs* 135: Kum aroun to my allie an I'll klean yu all up, shoes an' everything. **1929–31** J.T. Farrell *Young Lonigan* 143: He pretended that he had cleaned up all the tough guys on Fifty-eighth Street. **1933** Milburn *No More Trumpets* 103: He was big enough to clean up on any two of us. **1937** Reitman *Box-Car Bertha* 94: Every time she got stewed in a joint called Cassidy's Saloon, she wanted to "clean up" the place. **1947** Willingham *End As a Man* 259: I hear you boys cleaned up on Gatt. **1958** S.H. Adams *Tenderloin* 4: Cleaned up Syracuse and Colgate that fall.

b. to kill in revenge.

1951 West *Flaming Feud* 156: My paw cleaned up three of the Rourke clan.

3. to meet with great, esp. financial, success.

1910 *Variety* (June 18) 19: Fred Niblo, following the dogs, "cleaned up" with his rapid fire monolog, once started. **1916** in Paxton *Sport* 92: If we'dah on'y had sense to lay in some raincoats too, we'dah cleaned up. **1925** Faulkner *New Orleans Sketches* 69: It's four hundred ahead today I am, and tomorrow we'll clean up, see? **1938** Bezzerides *Long Haul* 86: Paul and me are going to clean up.

clear *n.* ¶ In phrase: **in the clear** above the amount of money needed to break even.

1928 O'Connor *B'way Racketeers* 185: When we counted up the final night we figured nearly sixty grand in the clear.

clear *v.* to be off; CLEAR OUT.

1805, 1827, 1839 in *OEDS.* **1868** Williams *Black-Eyed Beauty* 50: That's what broke me! I had to clear for California!

¶ In phrase: **clear the track** get out of the way; get ready.

1877 Wheeler *Deadwood Dick, Prince of the Road* 84: Clear the track and we'll take him out and boost him to a limb.

clear out *v.* to leave or run away. Now *S.E.*

1818 in Royall *Letters from Ala.* 182: *First Guest.* Who's run away. *Second Guest.* Bill Cheatum's cleared out. **1821** Martin & Waldo *Lightfoot* 15: I found the business was rather serious, and thought it would be best for me to *clear out. Ibid.* 50: As soon as they had gone back, "*I cleared out like a rigger." Ibid.* 115: I immediately mounted my horse, and *cleared out like a white head.* **1839** Marryatt *Diary* 266: *Clear out, quit,* and *put—* all mean "be off." "Captain, now you *hush* or *put*"—that is, "Either hold your tongue or be off." **1848** Thompson *House Breaker* 5: Clear out, shorty—if you've lost all your money, you've no business here. **1853** Lippard *New York* 50: Just give 'em to me, and clear out. **1856** Wilkins *Young N.Y.* 20: Clear out, before I break your head.

clem *n.* [orig. unkn.; perh. fr. the given name *Clem,* taken as characteristic of rural people] *Carnival.* a brawl, esp. with townspeople. Also (repr. a dialect pron.) **clim.**

1891 De Vere *Tramp Poems* 88: "Gawks," "guys" and "Rubes," another day,/When e'er a circus comes your way,/Are you spilein' for a "clim,"/Be sure they haven't learned to sing… **1924** Isman *Weber & Fields* 100 [ref. to 1880's]: Clems, such shindigs were known in circus argot, and their battle cry, "Hey, Rube!" **1925** Robinson *Wagon Show* 62: "Hey rube," primarily a cry for help in a fight, or, as a circus man would say "a clem." "Hey rube" has been in use among circus men for over a century. **1947** T.W. Duncan *Gus the Great* 446: So Plains City had started a clem. The bastards. **1951** Mannix *Sword-Swallower* 54: There's going to be a clem here, sure as Christ…A clem is a fight with the town people. **1975** McKennon *Horse Trail* 117: Another "Clem" resulted in several show people being beaten up.

clerk and jerk *n. Army.* an enlisted soldier engaged in administrative or support duty.

1975 S.P. Smith *Amer. Boys* 268: A former clerk—a clerk and jerk, as the combat soldiers called them. *a***1986** D. Tate *Bravo Burning* 11: We have pulled in every clerk and jerk and gold-bricking flake. **1988** *Tour of Duty* (CBS-TV): Some clerk and jerk.

click[1] *n.* [var. of *clique*] a street gang.

1879 *Puck* (Sept. 20) 451: I ain't no slouch on grammar meself—no, nor none of the b'yes in me gang—that is, click I would say. **1961** A.J. Roth *Shame* 49 [ref. to 1930's]: Our gang is all the time scrapping with the Eastside click. *Ibid.* 50: If anybody picks on you, you tell the click and we take care of him. **1966–67** P. Thomas *Mean Streets* 57: There's a lot of streets where a whole "click" is made out of punks who can't fight one guy unless they all jump him for the stomp.

click[2] *n.* a successful undertaking; (now *esp.*) a popular theatrical success.

1919 in Niles *Singing Soldiers* 128: I've fingered the roll and made many a click.../But never used a jimmy or a loaded stick. **1938** in Botkin *Sidewalks* 303: The tease must've been a click the first time out. **1945** Fay *Be Poor* 22: A "click," and—bingo, I was "in the chips" again. **1953** Gresham *Midway* 165: The show opened at Chicago in '32 and was an instantaneous click. **1966–72** Winchell *Exclusive* 282: I could not imagine it not being as big a click as...the *Untouchables* sagas.

click[3] *n. Mil.* **1.** a kilometer. Also **klick, klik.**

1962 Tregaskis *Viet. Diary* 180: We are 30 clicks (kilometers) from the area of operations. **1964** J. Lucas *Dateline* 81: There's a hell of a battle going on 10 clicks (kilometers) north of Kien Long. **1966** Shepard *Doom Pussy* 81: We're now four clicks from the Laotian border and ten miles from the demilitarized zone. **1968** Schell *Military Half* 172: O.K., well there's one hootch down there about a klik south of us that we want you to get. **1969** Spetz *Rat Pack Six* 37: The distance was six clicks (kilometers). **1980** Cragg *L. Militaris* 92: *Clicks*...Kilometers...It was used...particularly in Germany during the '50s. **1980** Santoli *Everything* 57: I...sailed a couple of kliks north of the American compound. **1982** Del Vecchio *13th Valley* 61: That's only ten klicks from where we're going. **1988** M. Maloney *Thunder Alley* 295: Gomers now twenty-two clicks out. *a***1993** Rishell *Black Platoon* 31 [ref. to Korean War]: Sangju was at least a hundred "klicks" (kilometers) northwest of Taegu.

2. (see quot.).

1991 J.T. Ward *Dear Mom* 84 [ref. to Vietnam War]: While a "click" usually meant a kilometer, in the [USMC] snipers we understood it as 1000 yards.

click *v.* **1.a.** to successfully strike up acquaintance, esp. with a person of the opposite sex; hit it off.

******1915** in *OEDS.* ******1918** (quot. at (b), below). **1928** in J. O'Hara *Sel. Letters* 33: This time I clicked and on Thursday for the first time...I slept with her. ******1930** Brophy & Partridge *Songs & Slang* 111 [ref. to WWI]: *Click.*—To strike up a temporary acquaintance for sentimental purposes with a stranger of the opposite sex in the street or other public place...*Clicking* always began with a mingling of glances. **1933–34** Lorimer & Lorimer *Stag Line* 107: But it isn't so much fun unless you click with the girls too. **1941** *Slanguage Dict.* 10: *Click*...to become friends on sight. **1968** S. Ross *Hang-Up* 34: And maybe if they clicked, they'd make it stick.

b. Esp. *Theat.* to meet with success; do well.

******1918** in Fraser & Gibbons *Soldier & Sailor Wds.* 58: *Click, To:* To meet with good (or bad) luck...To "click" might mean for instance, that a man had succeeded in something, had secured a good job, had made good his advances or "got off with a girl." **1923** *N.Y. Times* (Oct. 14) VIII 4: *Click*—To achieve precise and dependable success with the act, scoring at the right times and places as a time lock clicks. **1924** H.L. Wilson *Professor* 251: It certainly clicks. **1924** Garahan *Stiffs* 10: Tomorrow "something" will turn up; he will touch, he will click, he will finger the dough. *Ibid.* 109: Whether he "clicked" or not, he always demanded the return of his appeal. **1926** Finerty *Crim.* 12: *Click*—Success, make good. **1927** *Vanity Fair* (Nov.) 67: He doesn't hope that he "makes good." He hopes that he "clicks." He trusts that he doesn't "flop" or "brody" meaning that he hopes he will not fail. And when he "wows 'em" or "panics 'em," he has been a "hit." **1927** *Variety* (May 4) 45: "The Barker" [a play] failed to "click." **1929** *Our Army* (Feb.) 34: It clicks—and how!...The Hippodrome Arena is packed to the doors every week. **1931** Hellinger *Moon* 99: So George went to Hollywood. And he clicked. **1933** in Sandburg *Letters* (Jan. 24) 286: Even more than Eugene O'Neill I have failed to "click" in Europe. **1936** Tully *Bruiser* 22: You got a hundred bucks on yourself—three to one—suppose you

click. **1936** R. Chandler, in Ruhm *Detective* 127: And the twenty grand, if you click. Of course you won't. **1939** Goodman & Kolodin *Swing* 259: It's the kind of teamwork that makes a band click. **1942** Liebling *Telephone* 47: They might as well write a play, and if it clicks, they might also eat. **1946** Dadswell *Hey, Sucker* 76: Stage shows, radio shows, circuses and what-not—all dish out whatever the producers believe will "click." **1950** Cleveland *Great Mgrs.* 30: But the team continued to click. **1961** *Car 54* (NBC-TV): Boy, are we clicking tonight! Let's keep going while we're hot. **1983** *Rolling Stone* (Feb. 10) 23: Cannon...clicked in the Fifties with "Tallahassee Lassie." **1991** Lott & Lieber *Total Impact* 232: The running game wasn't clicking.

c. to have a stroke of good luck.

******1918** (quot. at (2), below). **1939** Goodman & Kolodin *Swing* 133: There was a job open if I could click.

d. to function smoothly.

1930 *Liberty* (July 19) 26: For more than a year my business clicks without a miss. **1936** Dos Passos *Big Money* 278: If every department don't click like a machine, we're rooked. **1982** Rucker *57th Kafka* 50: Everything was clicking. I *knew* that Jack was going to be standing in that window.

e. to be compatible; get along well.

1938 Chandler *Big Sleep* 74: He married General Sternwood's older daughter and...they didn't click. **1941** Schulberg *Sammy* 200: And they seem to feel that Keeler and I are clicking as a writer-director team. **1967** Yablonsky *Hippie Trip* 179: I want to click with people so they look at me and I can smile back at them. **1971** Dahlskog *Dict.* 14: *Click*...to be compatible with (someone).

2. [cf. *click it,* below] *Mil.* to get or be given (something), esp. unexpectedly.—also constr. with *for,* rarely with *off.*

******1917** in Lee *No Parachute* 43: I clicked for a new kind of job the Wing has started. ******1918** *Bodleian Qly. Rec.* II 152: *To click, to click for,* to be lucky enough to get a good job: "To click a good job," i.e. Be lucky. "Did you click," i.e. Any luck? **1918** Burton *Letters* (Apr. 19) 329: In fact I think I have "clicked" for about the best job in the whole Allied Army. **1919** *Amer. Leg. Wkly.* (Sept. 19) 27: A squad from a famous Irish regiment "clicked" the job of burying some Boche dead. **1919** in Niles *Singing Soldiers* 129: We wangle fur a little and touch a lot less/ And damn seldom clik [*sic*] much real happiness. **1923** Witwer *Fighting Blood* 106: I have to work...for *two* years to click off twelve hundred smackers.

3. to suddenly make sense; fall logically into place; add up.

1928 Hammett *Red Harvest* 85: That doesn't click with me. Try another. **1929** in Hammett *Knockover* 59: That [suggestion] clicks. **1929** Hammett *Dain Curse* 249: You've got to sit down to all the facts you can get and turn them over and over till they click. ******1939** in *OEDS.* **1981** Hofstadter & Dennett *Mind's I* 21: Then, at a certain moment, after the description has gotten quite specific, something suddenly "clicks."...Doesn't it all suddenly "click"? **1983** *Rolling Stone* (Feb. 3) 22: And that's when it clicked: Allentown, yeah, iron and steel.

¶ In phrase:

¶ **click it** [cf. (2), above] *Mil.* to become a casualty.

1917 Empey *Over the Top* 151: "Clicked it." Got killed; up against it; wounded. **1918** *Wadsworth Gas Attack* (Jan. 26) 26: Being killed...is referred to delicately as being "huffed," or having "clicked it," or "gone West." **1919** Murrin *With the 112th* 168: The Huns rained gas and H.E. shells in the valley most of the night...and...it seemed surprising that our fellows, under such a terrific barrage, did not "click it" more heavily.

clicker *n.* a knockdown blow.

1859 Matsell *Vocab.* 19: *Clicker.* A knock down.

click up *v. Und.* to join a clique.

1932 Lawes *Sing Sing* 272: Don't click up too easily with fellows you don't know.

clicky *adj. Theat.* likely to appeal to an audience.

1961 Swarthout *Where the Boys Are* 170: In the interim he would call upon his muse and see if he couldn't create something clickier.

cliff ape *n.* a crude or brutal man; GORILLA.

1919 Wilkins *Company Fund* 46: Cliff ape. **1942** Algren *Morning* 63: Who's *that* cliff-ape? **1956** Algren *Wild Side* 143: "I've taken all the insults I'm going to off that cliff-ape," she warned Gross aloud. **1986** Coonts *Intruder* 192: Paint him as an insensitive cliff ape who didn't care who he killed.

cliffhanger *n.* **1.** *Cinema.* a cheaply made motion-picture serial having individual episodes that end showing the hero or the female lead in imminent deadly danger, such as hanging from the edge of a cliff; (*hence,* in recent use) a suspenseful story. Now *S.E.*

1937 *AS* (Dec.) 318: *Cliff-hangers.* Types of serial melodrama. **1944** *Amer. N & Q* (Nov.) 127: *Cliff Hanger.* Detective story in serial form. **1955** Reifer *New Words* 48: *Cliff hanger. Radio Slang.* A serial story of highly pitched excitement. **1975** Boatner et al. *Dict. Amer. Idioms* 57: Did you see The Guns of Navarone? It's a real cliffhanger. **1982** Hieatt *Beowulf* xii: The history of *Beowulf*'s physical preservation is, then, something of a cliff-hanger.

2. a suspenseful situation, such as a narrowly decided sporting event. Now *colloq.*

1952 in *OEDS.* **1969** Layden & Snyder *Diff. Game* 103: By cliff-hangers, he meant games that were not decided until the closing minutes.

Cliffie *n. Stu.* a student at or graduate of Radcliffe College.

*a***1961** Boroff *Campus U.S.A.* 16: The lowliest Cliffie can command a senior. **1970** Segal *Love Story* 3. **1985** Westin *Love & Glory* 200: I'll have to leave the analysis to you Cliffies.

clim *n.* see CLEM.

climb *v.* **1.** to attack or drub; beat up.—also constr. with *all over.*

1882 A.W. Aiken *Joe Buck* 2: He made up his mind to "climb" the fust "tenderfoot" he struck. **1886** Nye *Remarks* 219: The most tropical...dude can climb him with the butt-end of a sunflower. **1969** Sidney *For Love of Dying* 150: The lieutenant's set to climb all over your ass. **1970** Wambaugh *New Centurions* 97: Somebody that's so pissed off at his landlord or tenant that he's ready to climb the ass of anybody that comes through the door.

2. *Mil.* to scold angrily; rebuke.—also constr. with *on* or *all over.*

1918 Griffin *Ballads of the Reg't.* 34: He would "climb" a slouchy rookey till he straightened out his back;/Then he'd "crawl" him from his shoe-strings to the rifle in the rack. **1954** Bissell *High Water* 124: Well they are gonna climb on me over this. **1963** Coon *Short End* 165: He's chicken and he's climbing us like a ladder, but he's right about this. **1964** Newhafer *Tallyho* 78: Crowley would just love to climb all over his back after last night.

3. to mount and copulate with.

1927 *Immortalia* 4: She said she'd been climbed by a stud. **1977** Stallone *Paradise Alley* 56: Let's climb a hooker at the Sunset Hotel. **1981** *Time* (Apr. 6) 83: A tourist rape case...Indeed, before their arrests some of them gave a group interview to a Honolulu reporter, in which they admitted they "climbed her."

¶ In phrases:

¶ **climb down** [or **climb [down] off it**] to stop one's pretentious behavior; come off it.

1938 "E. Queen" *4 Hearts* 131: "Go peddle your eggs somewheres else. I ain't done nothin'." "Climb down, buddy. What kind of business do you run?" **1960** *Twilight Zone* (CBS-TV): Come on, dear, climb off it. **1972** in H. Ellison *Sex Misspelled* 119: "I don't know where he is." "Climb down off it, Princess."

¶ **climb out of** to cease.

1876 "M. Twain" *Sawyer* 45 [ref. to *ca*1845]: Now you shut up that nonsense and climb out of this.

¶ **climb (someone's) frame** to attack or thrash (someone).

1938 Wolfe *Web & Rock* 45: I'll come right over there and climb your frame. **1960** Leckie *Marines!* 22: "Gallagher, Ah'm gonna climb youah frame. On youah feet!"...They fought for fifteen minutes and it must have been a good scrap because both of them had to turn into sick bay.

¶ **climb the walls** to be beside oneself with impatience, frustration, anxiety, or the like.

1972 Kopp *Buddha* 195: It made his...wife climb the walls. **1990** *Cosmopolitan* (Nov.) 114: I think it's I who need another man....After two years, I'm ready to climb the walls.

climb-a-pole *n.* a self-important person; (*hence,* as adj.) highfalutin.

*a***1866** in G.W. Harris *High Times* 166: Hit warnt long afore she coaxed old climb-a-pole outen the kitchen. *Ibid.* 167: That war another climb-a-pole idea she'd picked up some whar.

climber *n. Und.* a porch climber.

1900 Willard & Hodler *Powers That Prey* 64: I say that we hunt up a good sneak an' climber (sneak-thief and burglar) an' jump over there. *****1934,** *****1942,** *****1943** (cited in Partridge *Dict. Und.* 130).

clinch *n.* a passionate embrace.

1901 Hobart *John Henry* 25: A love clinch from Laura Jean Libbey's latest. **1915** *Variety* (Oct. 24): The final "clinch" with the hero and heroine in each others' arms. **1922** in C.M. Russell *Paper Talk* 185: Most of the ladyes that have gon to a clinch with men use their paint more artistick then thair red sisters. **1928** *N.Y. Times* (Mar. 11) VIII 6: *Clinch*—Final love scene in a picture. **1933–34** Lorimer & Lorimer *Stag Line* 68: It's only natural for Sam to go into a clinch. **1938** "E. Queen" *4 Hearts* 50: We're filming the clinch tomorrow. **1951** Robbins *Danny Fisher* 120: She was there all right. So was the guy. They were in a hell of a clinch. **1962** Fenin & Everson *Western* 31: As the "clinch" approached, the camera would pan to Champion, Autry's horse.

clinch *v.* to embrace passionately.

1894 F.P. Dunne, in Schaaf *Dooley* 81: An' with that they clinched. **1899** Ade *Fables in Slang* 26: George was sitting on the Front Porch with a good Side Hold on Mabel...While they were Clinched, Mabel's Father...came down the Stairway and out to the Veranda. **1938** Smitter *Detroit* 37: "My snookie-um-u-m-m-ums." They clinched. **1962** Fenin & Everson *Western* 31: On the few occasions when he did "clinch" right in front of the camera, Autry emerged a trifle shamefaced.

clink *n.* **1.** money.

*****1729** in *OEDS*: The World is rul'd by Asses,/And the Wise are sway'd by Clink. *****1781** in R. Palmer *Sound of History* 285: I'll bring all his clink to my sodger laddie. *****1808** Jamieson *Scot. Dict.* I 452: *Clink*...Money; a cant term. **ca***1817** in *OEDS*: Such young ladies as were particularly beautiful...and had the clink. **1848** Judson *Mysteries* 76: "Down with the clink, then," replied one of the dirty-looking fellows behind the counter. *Ibid.* 527: *Clink.* Clink or chink, money.

2.a. jail or prison; a lockup.—usu. used with *the.* [In earlier use, the nickname of a particular prison in Southwark, London; see Partridge, *Dict. Und.*]

*****1785** Grose *Vulgar Tongue*: *Clink*...A gaol, from the clinking of the prisoners' chains or fetters: he is gone to clink. *****1821** *Real Life in Ireland* 196: His master was in the *Clink.* *****1835** in *F & H* 724: We've a nice *clink* at Wandsworth to lock you up in. *****1889** Barrère & Leland *Dict. Slang.* I 255: *Clink* (military), another term for guard-house, derived evidently from the *Clink,* one of the ancient London prisons, that of Westminster. **1893** in F. Remington *Sel. Letters* 178: They would lock me in the "clink". **1899** Cullen *Tales* 104: Monk and I got a month and a month each—which means the month in the clink and the loss of a month's pay. **1902** Cullen *More Tales* 131: The back room off a precinct clink. **1915** Braley *Songs of Workaday World* 15: A spree on pay day night/A day or two in the clink. **1938** O'Hara *Hope of Heaven* 39: I'm giving you all the chance in the world to get me thrown in the clink. **1938** "E. Queen" *4 Hearts* 60: I'll put you in clink for this. **1939** Polsky *Curtains* 109: Chad's words when I got him out of the clink. **1940** Burnett *High Sierra* 113: A guy gets lonesome in clink. **1942** Wylie *Vipers* 168: If your grocer did a tenth as much to you, you would have him in the clink. **1946** Michener *So. Pacific* 148: But if I ever see you doing it, I'll throw you in the clink! **1950** in Daley *Sports of Times* 55: The cops throw everyone into the clink—the innocent along with the guilty. **1954** Arnow *Dollmaker* 166: The Red Squad would have us both inu clink. **1968** "J. Hudson" *Case of Need* 26: They'll toss you in the clink and take away your license.

b. *Ice Hockey.* a penalty box.—constr. with *the.*

1949 Cummings *Dict. Sports* 76.

clinker *n.* **1.** a remarkable or excellent individual.

*****1673** [R. Head] *Canting Academy* 37: *Clincker* A Crafty Fellow. **1836** *Spirit of Times* (Feb. 27) 13: "I will just take him to beat anything that Col. Johnson can start. He is a clinker, I tell you. **1842** *Spirit of Times* (Feb. 26) 614: Reel...is a clinker, and no mistake; but Boston is a whole team. *****1869** in *OEDS.* **1891** *Outing* (Oct.) 17: The competitors are rejected or selected for further trial according to the excellence of the work actually done, whether drawn against a "duffer," "bolter," or a "clinker," to use dog parlance. **1905** *DN* III 75: *Clinker, n.* 1. An industrious or diligent person. "He's a *clinker* to work."

2. *pl. Pris.* irons or chains.

*****1698–99** "B.E." *Dict. Canting Crew*: *Clinkers,*...the Irons Felons wear in Goals [*sic*]. **1934** Weseen *Dict. Slang* 7: *Clinkers*—A prisoner's chains. **1942–49** Goldin et al. *DAUL* 45: *Clinkers.* Shackles, especially for fettering the ankles.

3. a coin; (*hence*) a dollar.

1857 (quot. at CHIP, 2). **1934** Weseen *Dict. Slang* 295: *Clinkers*—Coins; money in general. **1950** Jacoby & Brady *Champagne* (film): Our sixth question pays...150 clinkers!

4. a hard biscuit.

1900 *DN* II 28: *Clinker*, A biscuit. **1936** *AS* (Feb.) 42: *Clinker.* Biscuit.

5. a stoker. Also **clinker boy.**

1905 *Independent* (Mar. 2) 488: I pray that my readers may ever be spared such a maddening experience as mine was for the first two weeks of my life as a clinker. *Ibid.* 489: The head crimp came to me and asked me—*me*, an able seaman—to ship as a clinker. ***1923** (cited in Partridge *DSUE* (ed. 8) 226). **1929** *Bookman* (July) 525: The fireman is a Tallow-pot, a Smoke-agent, a Clinker-boy or a Bakehead.

6. jail or prison; CLINK.—constr. with *the.*

1935 *Jour. Abnorm. & Soc. Psych.* (Oct.) 362: In the clinker. **1983** Knoxville (Tenn.) pharmacist, age *ca*50: Armed robbery of drugs from a drugstore or hospital or a physician's office'll get you ten full years in the clinker—no pardon, no parole.

7.a. *Jazz.* an off-pitch or misplayed note.

1937 in R.S. Gold *Jazz Talk* 51: Hey, you dope, watch them there clinkers. **1941** H.A. Smith *Low Man* 127: Somebody in the band hit a clinker near the end. **1953–58** J.C. Holmes *Horn* 209: He blew three clinkers in a simple phrase. **1969** Gordone *No Place to Be Somebody* 430: The part calls for a guitar player. Cain't you hear these clinkers? **1971** Wells & Dance *Night People* 104: Second tenor, watch your part. I heard some clinkers.

b. a blunder; (*Baseball*) an error.

1937 *Sporting News Record Book* 64. **1954–60** *DAS.* **1961** in R.S. Gold *Jazz Talk* 51: Egregious clinkers in our foreign policy.

c. Esp. *Entertainment Industry.* something or someone of inferior quality, esp. a show, performance, or the like.

1961 *Dick Van Dyke Show* (CBS-TV): Is it going to be a good show? I hate to…see a clinker. **1969** [Garrity] *Sensuous Woman* 105: Weeding out the clinkers before intimacy is kinder to you both. You save his male pride from being demolished…and you save yourself from a less than happy experience. **1979** R. Salmaggi, on WINS radio (Dec. 9): "Star Trek: The Motion Picture" is a supercolossal clinker. **1982** *N.Y. Post* (Dec. 30) 54: The normally smooth-shooting King had an 0-12 clinker. **1983** *Good Morning America* (ABC-TV) (May 10): Of course, the *Original Amateur Hour* did put on a few clinkers—acts that nobody would want to see.

d. a difficulty; hitch.

1968 Spooner *War in General* 29: But we've got some sort of clinker this year. There's someone from Washington coming up to observe us.

clinking *adv.* exceptionally; RATTLING.

*1868 in *F & H* II 126: Vermouth was a *clinking* good horse. ***1887** in *F & H*: Prince Henry must be a clinking good horse. **1898–1900** Cullen *Chances* 7: He was a clinking good talker.

clip *n.* **1.** a sharp blow.

*1830 Marryat *King's Own* ch. xxvi: The master fires and hits the cat a *clip* on the neck. **1838** [Haliburton] *Clockmaker* (Ser. 2) 172: She fetched me…a clip on the side of the face. **1905** *Nat. Police Gaz.* (July 8) 10: That clip in the eye…put Joe out of the running. **1920–21** Witwer *Leather Pushers* 25: A clip on the jaw…staggered Roberts. **1943** in Steinbeck *Once There Was a War* (Sept. 1): "You'd like maybe a clip in the kisser," said Sligo.

2. a lively or unconventional individual, esp. a young woman.

1901 *DN* II 138: *Clip*…A lively girl; "she's a clip." **1906** H. Green *Actors' Boarding House* 7: Them piano players is like sailors—a gell in every town! Oh, they're the clips! But that ain't sayin' he ain't on the level with you. **1922** in *DARE:* I like a girl that's quite a "clip." **1932** in *AS* (1933) VIII 72: A *clip.* A shrewd girl.

3. a theft.

1941 G. Legman, in Henry *Sex Variants* II (gloss.): *Make a clip* is to rob a homosexual or other client.

4. a male Jew.—usu. used contemptuously.

1942–44 in *AS* (Feb. 1946) 31: *Clip*, n. Jew. From "clipped dick," one who has been circumcised.

5. CLIP JOINT.

1949 W.R. Burnett *Asphalt Jungle* 151: I'm in that clip on Baxter Street.

¶ In phrases:

¶ **on the clip** *Und.* engaged in swindling.

1962 in Cannon *Nobody Asked* 240: But this pitch has been on the clip every spring for eighty-eight years.

¶ **put the clip on** to CLIP (in any sense).

1938 Haines *Tension* 28: When they put the clip on Shelly for a drink, he figured as how he had to be polite and buy 'em one. **1942** *ATS* 566:

Put the clip on the jive. **1954–60** *DAS.*

clip *v.* **1.a.** to hit; (now *esp.*) to punch.

1855 "P. Doesticks" *Doesticks* 99: 97's engineer clipped one of 73's men with a trumpet. ***1880** Couch *E. Cornwall Gloss.* 90: *Klip*, to strike or cuff. **1928** in E. Ferber *One Basket* 332: So I clip him one in the jaw. **1930** Buck & Anthony *Bring 'Em Back* 123: I'll clip him on the snoot. **1942** Casey *Torpedo Junction* 27: So the guard put down his rifle and clipped him on the chin. **1947** Boyer *Dark Ship* 157: Don't just smile and walk away. Clip the son-of-a-bitch! **1955** Graziano & Barber *Somebody Up There* 45: I was ready to clip the guy. Who was he trying to kid? **1962** Houk & Dexter *Ballplayers* 16: I felt like someone clipped me on the jaw.

b. *Und.* to shoot dead; kill.

1928 *AS* III (Feb.) 255: *Clip.* To shoot dead. **1930** Lait *On the Spot* 112: He spilled…who clipped Kinky King, why and how. **1986** Philbin *Under Cover* 60: Everyone's afraid of them. They'll clip your family and then go out and have a…night on the town. **1987** Norst & Black *Lethal Weapon* 35: Remember…the hooker we thought for a while clipped Tyrone the Bone.

c. *Und.* to place under arrest.

1942 *ATS* 464: Arrest…*clip*, collar [etc.]. **1962** Maurer & Vogel *Narc. & Narc. Add.* (ed. 2) 296.

d. to strike with a bullet, antiaircraft shell, etc.

1945 Bellah *Ward 20* 20: He was a part of it because he was clipped. **1956** Lockwood & Adamson *Zoomies* 133: And if they clip you—we'll pick you up.

2. to steal.

1931–35 Runyon *Money* 185: They are clipped too. **1945** Beecher *All Brave Sailors* 105 [ref. to *ca*1935]: "Clipping"…was breaking into stores. **1949** Ellson *Tomboy* 54: Where'd you clip that? **1951** Robbins *Danny Fisher* 56: You think somebody clipped it, Papa? **1955** Graziano & Barber *Somebody Up There* 25: Somebody clipped my box. **1962** Perry *Young Man Drowning* 122: I want you to clip a car for me. **1968** S. Harris *Puritan Jungle* 152: I bet you never even clipped his wallet. **1990** *Flash* (CBS-TV): This ain't clippin' cigarettes from the Minimart.

3.a. to rob; rob of.—often constr. with *for.*

1922 *Variety* (July 14) 8: We clipped a couple of monkeys for their whole roll. **1928** O'Connor *B'way Racketeers* 15: The sharpshooter who aimed to clip him for anything beyond the right time would be wise to padlock his own poke. **1932** Nelson *Prison Days & Nights* 26: "I'd like to see anybody try to steal anything off of me." "Huh!…I'd like to see you get clipped for something." **1934** Appel *Brain Guy* 127: Neither was very excited about clipping a speak. **1939** Brecher *At the Circus* (film): Where were you when Jeff got bopped on the conk and clipped for his ring? **1942** Liebling *Telephone* 73: By the time the scalper noticed the ring was gone, he thought a bosko he knew had clipped him for it. **1950** Maddow & Huston *Asphalt Jungle* 13: I wouldn't go parading around with a suitcase. Some of these young punks would clip you. **1968** Heard *Howard St.* 97: She learned how to clip a trick as he concentrated on his kicks, or was drunk. **1965–70** J. Carroll, in *Paris Rev.* (No. 50) 103: Just yesterday I got clipped for a five. **1979** D. Thoreau *City at Bay* 45: Coupla those Nob Hill hotels, clip me some of them farmers with white shoes.

b. to cheat or swindle; (*hence*) to overcharge.

1927 W. Winchell, in *Vanity Fair* 134: When a patron in a night club is "clipped" he isn't punched, he's "taken" or "gypped" out of some currency or he is overcharged. **1930** *Variety* (Jan. 8) 123: So I used a last come on and popped out with that old store that clips everybody—the peek 'em store. **1931** *Amer. Merc.* (Dec.) 418: She'll clip him for a flock of dough or a present. **1932** Nelson *Prison Days & Nights* 95: We…clipped her for the thirty grand worth of stocks. **1941** G.R. Lee *G-String* 186: If a candy butcher could clip Moey he certainly had it coming to him. **1945** Gerraghty & Frank *Whiplash* (film): Sam, you clipped her! **1963** Morgan *Six-Eleven* 119: I think he's clipping us. **1963** D. Tracy *Brass Ring* 166: Then you get lousy service and they clip you every way they can think of. **1965** Himes *Imabelle* 107: The gamblers [were] clipping chumps. **1982** *N.Y. Post* (Aug. 24) 26: He claimed he had been clipped for $12,000 in a dice game.

4. to circumcise.

1942–44 in *AS* (Feb. 1946) 31: *Clipped dick*, one who has been circumcised. **1970** *Playboy* (Aug.) 38: The unclipped stud who took the ad out for his services is [an]…uncircumcised male hustler.

clip artist *n.* a petty thief or swindler.

1941 G. Legman, in Henry *Sex Variants* II (gloss.): A prostitute who is accustomed to robbing the client, usually before any sexual act occurs, is called a *clip artist.* **1956** in *DAS.* **1967** in H. Ellison *Sex Misspelled* 131: A forty-five day marriage to a clip artist.

clip joint *n.* a night club, bar, restaurant, or other establishment that makes a practice of overcharging or cheating customers.

1932 Nicholson & Robinson *Sailor Beware!* 58. **1933** in *OEDS*. **1934** Appel *Brain Guy* 17: Down the street of speaks, garages, clip joints, and tenements. **1936** Dos Passos *Big Money* 209: He'd been rolled in a clip-joint. **1937** *Life* (Apr. 19) 49: The five girls above are "clip joint" hostesses. **1938** "Justinian" *Amer. Sexualis* 16: Clip-Joint. n...Late 1920's: an expensive night club or gambling casino which charges prices far out of proportion to its services. **1950** Maddow & Huston *Asphalt Jungle* 22: They knocked over that clip joint—the Club Royal. **1959–60** Bloch *Dead Beat* 1: A hot, stuffy clipjoint bordered by tiny tables and mismatched chairs. **1973** J.E. Martin *95 File* 18: They sped toward the garish lights of the clip joints lining Eureka. **1987** Blankenship *Blood Stripe* 29: That place was a clip joint from day one. **1992** *Seinfeld* (NBC-TV): What kind of clip joint are you running here?

clipper *n.* **1.** a clam.

1832 in *DA*.

2.a. a lively, splendid, or remarkable individual; (*specif.*) a fast horse.

1835 in *F & H* II 126: A perfect pictur' of a horse, and a genuine *clipper*; could gallop like the wind. **1836** in Haliburton *Sam Slick* 47: Why,...that's a rael clipper of your'n, I vow. **1836** in *DARE*: She was a real handsum looking gall...a real clipper, and as full of fun and frolic as a kitten. **1840** in *Amer. Qly. Church Rev.* (Jan. 1866) 551: A real...clipper of a horse. *1846 Thackeray *Vanity Fair* ch. xvi: I never saw your equal, and I've met with some *clippers* in my time. *1848 (cited in Partridge *DSUE* (ed. 8) 226). **1900** Willard & Hodler *Powers That Prey* 123: No very definite ideas are attached to these words, but they both express admiration, and "corker" is more nearly extreme than "clipper." **1908** in Botkin *Treas. Amer. Folk.* 620: Bob was a clipper. He made his living by his superior marksmanship. **1930** in *DARE*: Clipper—A fast or forward girl.

b. Esp. *Naut.* a stylish or attractive woman.

1858 [S. Hammett] *Piney Woods* 124: Let him...not be...deceivin that A No. 1 little clipper. **1872** (quot. at HULL). **1891** Maitland *Slang Dict.* 69: Clipper...a showy, handsome woman. **1895** Barentz *Woordenboek* 59: Clipper...mooie, knappe vrouw. **1932** Bone *Capstan Bars* 81: As I was a walkin' down Paradise Street....A smart little clipper I chanced for to meet.

c. a philanderer.

1942 Hollingshead *Elmtown's Youth* 218: John's bunch are "clippers;" none of our group [Lutheran girls] will go with them. *Ibid.* 311: On Friday and Saturday nights the "clippers" and "wolves" hang around them like flies around sugar. *Ibid.* 422: One clique takes great pride in its members' ability to seduce girls. The high school students refer to them as "clippers" and "wolves."

3. *Boxing.* the point of the chin.

1944 in *Best from Yank* 102: A idea jess give me a clip on the clipper.

4. *Meteorology.* an especially cold air mass or storm system.

1985 *WINS Radio News* (Dec. 18): One of those big storms, commonly known as an "Alberta clipper," is rushing in from western Canada.

clipper-built *adj. Naut.* having a slender build; slim; (*also*) wiry.

1834 in *DA*. **1864** in C.W. Wills *Army Life* 280: Some fine fat ones,...but they are not "clipper-built," and lack "get up" and "figure heads." **1871** Thomes *Whaleman* 207: He is clipper-built, and I'm on the old style, bluff and square. I can't run with such a feller. **1873** in *DA*.

clipper-rigged *adj. Naut.* stylishly dressed.

1891 Maitland *Slang Dict.* 69: Clipper-rigged means stylish, well-arranged.

clip queen *n. Homosex.* a homosexual prostitute who thieves from customers.

1949 *Gay Girl's Guide* 5: Clip-Queen: A second cousin to *dirt* and usually a young, commercially-inclined homosexual without any desire for violence, i.e., a sneak thief.

clipster *n.* a swindler.

1942 *ATS* 425. **1961** H. Ellison *Purgatory* 25: The age of the clipster and the fast, hard sell.

clit *n.* the clitoris. Also **clitty.**—usu. considered vulgar.

*ca1866 *Romance of Lust* 386: I sucked her clitty. **1958–59** Southern & Hoffenberg *Candy* 53: Why, I've only to give my clit a...flick. **1970** in L. Williams *City of Angels* 123: Gloria fingered her clit. **1977** L. Jordan *Hype* 49: He could tickle her clit. **1980** M. Harris *Why Nothing Works* 114: Comic books for teenagers extolled the virtues of "Tits 'n' Clits." **1980** DiFusco et al. *Tracers* 14: He's...suckin' on her clitty. **1992** *Letters to Penthouse* III 6: I could feel my clit swelling.

cloak-and-dagger *adj.* [cf. earlier use in *OED*] Orig. *Mil.* pertaining to, engaged in, or characteristic of espionage operations or the like. Now *S.E.*

1944 *Am. N & Q* (July) 54: *Cloak and Dagger*: phrase generally used as an adjective, applied to a person "engaged in some form of activity that is at once secret, exciting, dangerous, and highly important."...In use in the Army, particularly the British Army. **1944** *N.Y. Herald-Tribune* (July 20). **1946** Sevareid *Wild Dream* 237: The latter was from the Office of Strategic Services—one of the "cloak and dagger boys." **1946** *Britannica Bk. of Yr.* 832: *Cloak and dagger.* Office of Strategic Services; pertaining to OSS.

clobber *v.* [orig. unkn.] **1.a.** to strike heavily or repeatedly; bash; batter; pound. [This word came to prominence and may have originated in the RAF and USAF during WWII. The n. use in the 1934 quot., in an autobiographical novel about RAF flying in 1918, means 'equipment; gear' and has been attested in BrE since the 1890's; but the nuance here seems to be 'rubble', and a functional shift might possibly account for the development of the v. The suggestion (see, e.g., R.S. Kissel in *The Playing-Card* XVIII 3 (Feb. 1990) 94) that the word developed from a supposed call in the card game *Klabberjass* (also called *clobber* and found in a variety of other spellings) is unsupported by the early evidence and is unlikely on sociolinguistic grounds.]

[*1934 Yeates *Winged Victory* 152: Amid all the clutter and clobber of the battlefield.] **1944** in Inks *Eight Bailed Out* 45: At least here the grapes are ripe. We're clobbering the vineyard. **1945** in Gellhorn *Face of War* 160: "We sure clobbered the Herman." This means we definitely shot up the Germans. **1946** G.C. Hall, Jr., *1000 Destroyed* 355: Don't...go saying "Deacon" on the R/T. Don would clobber me. *Ibid.* 420: FDR said of the enemy, "We'll hit him again, again and again." He might have said: "We'll *clobber* him." **1948** Wolfert *Act of Love* 223: You don't pick a cumulus for sight-seeing, Doc. There were three Zeroes on my tail clobbering me into it. **1950** Spillane *Vengeance* 14: I hope you clobbered him good! **1950** M. Shulman *Dobie Gillis* 206: "Poor loser!" they kept yelling as they clobbered me. **1952** S. Bellow *Augie March* 46: He was clobbered by his father. **1954** E. Hunter *Runaway Black* 8: He...clobbered him on the back of the head with both hands squeezed together. **1958** J. King *Inside Football* 202: Our quarterback [is] being rushed and clobbered successfully. **1961** L.G. Richards *TAC* 25: The German commander...sent through an offer to surrender upon condition the Air Force would quit clobbering him! **1962** Dougherty *Commissioner* 122: Just for effect I clobbered a gorilla he had with him. Nice punch, too, went right down. **1967** Dibner *Admiral* 35: I almost had my mitts on it when your OD clobbered me. **1974** L.D. Miller *Valiant* 152: They're really clobbering us. **1990** Poyer *Gulf* 11: So we got clobbered.

b. to crash into.

1959 [*41st Ftr. Sq. Songbk.*] 8: At altitude zero he clobbered a tree.

c. *Mil. Av.* to crash or make a crash landing.—also constr. with *in.*

1951 *Air Cadet* (film): Nobody did clobber, did they? **1951** Sheldon *Troubling a Star* 10: He'd watched the F-80s that were struck by flak, and sometimes small-arms fire, clobber into the earth like falling stars. **1956** Heflin *USAF Dict.* 119: *To clobber in*, to make a crash landing.

2. *Mil. Av.* to shoot down (an enemy aircraft).

*1944 in *OEDS*. **1946** G.C. Hall, Jr., *1000 Destroyed* 231: The 109 rolled over and Godfrey clobbered him. He watched the German bail out. **1964** in Asimov, Greenberg & Olander *Great Sci. Fi. Short Shorts* 42: The Martians got...the astronauts in their sights and clobbered them like sitting ducks.

3. *Mil.* to kill or wound.

1946 G.C. Hall, Jr., *1000 Destroyed* 420: Marshal Stalin ended his orders of the day with, "Death to the Nazi invader!" He could have said, "*Clobber* the Jerry!" **1948** Wolfert *Act of Love* 475: They're all going to get themselves clobbered out there, and do no good. **1953** White *Down the Ridge* 169: If you got clobbered in the leg—with maybe a fractured femur—at Mash they still hoped it could be saved. *Ibid.* 28: It can happen that a veteran will get clobbered and a green man survive. **1955** Scott *Look of Eagle* 95: There's the Frank Luke of this war, if he doesn't clobber himself trying to prove it too soon. **1957** Aarons *Stella*

Marni 17: They've killed and tortured and pulled out all stops. They'll clobber you first. **1959** Searls *Big X* 32: George Welch got killed...Nobody'd ever *heard* of a "coupling effect" until he got clobbered. **1963** D. Tracy *Brass Ring* 377 [ref. to WWII]: I'll get killed...You'll probably get clobbered too, but you stand a chance. **1977* T. Jones *Ice* 9: Heard you got clobbered. Singapore, wasn't it?

4.a. to defeat decisively; trounce.

1946 G.C. Hall, Jr., *1000 Destroyed* 376: Blakeslee had clobbered the female vanity of America. *Ibid.* 420: Monty *clobbered* Rommel at El Alamein. **1956** J. Brown *Kings Go Forth* 175: Boy! Did we ever clobber the bastards! **1956** *Walt Disney's Jiminy Cricket* (No. 70) 5: Have you ever come out ahead...No! Every time you get clobbered. **1978** B. Johnson *What's Happenin'* 88: The Sonics...[had gotten] clobbered by the Spurs. **1983** *WKGN Radio News* (Apr. 13): The Tigers clobbered the Yankees 13–2.

b. to treat harshly, as through severe criticism.

1955 Reifer *New Words* 49: *Clobber v.*...to berate. **1956** in *OEDS*. **1970** Hersh *My Lai 4* 123: If they prosecute somebody for this, the Army's going to get clobbered.

5. to suppress (a story); scotch.

1954 MacDonald *Condemned* 51: It was an article on Wilma Ferris...My friend wasn't placed high enough to clobber it.

clobbered *adj.* drunk. Cf. SMASHED.

1951 J. Thurber, in *New Yorker* (Sept. 29) 27: Those who are, to use a word presently popular with the younger set, clobbered. **1959** Searls *Big X* 126: He and I sat around and got half clobbered. **1961** Terry *Old Liberty* 40: Mrs. P.J. looks pretty clobbered. **1982** P. Dickson *Words* 257: Clobbered...corned...crocked [etc.].

clock *n.* **1.** [cf. earlier Brit. syn. *dial*] the face. [In 1908 quot., the head.]

[**1908** T.A. Dorgan, in Zwilling *TAD Lexicon* 98: Help—Police—Murder—My clock. [Man with a bandage around his head].] **1918** in Grider *War Birds* 145: She slipped her toga's shoulder strap, and displayed a fancy clock. **1923* Manchon *Slang* 87: Clock...la tête, le ciboulot. **1934** Weseen *Dict. Slang* 51: Clock—The face. **1961* in *OEDS*. **1986** Univ. Tenn. grad. student: Your face is your clock, especially if it's ugly. It could stop an eight-day clock, I guess.

2. a taxi meter. Now *colloq.*

1939 in Botkin *Sidewalks* 290: "What's on the clock?" "Eighty-five, madame."

3. the heart; TICKER.

1942 *ATS* 149: Heart...clock, ...pump, ...ticker [etc.]. **1942–49** Goldin et al. *DAUL* 45.

4. a punch in the face.

*a***1986** in *World Book Dict.* (1986 ed.) I 388: He would give the daughter a clock on the jaw.

¶ In phrases:

¶ **by the clock** manifestly.

*ca***1920** in C.M. Russell *Paper Talk* 163: Your a liar by the clock.

¶ **clean (someone's) clock** see s.v. CLEAN, *v.*

¶ **fix (someone's) clock** to finish (someone); to do for.

1904 in "O. Henry" *Works* 257: I reckon we'll fix your clock for a while. **1906** H. Green *Actor's Boarding House* 130: Youse fixed me clock, ain't youse? **1909** M'Govern *Krag* 121: I'll fix his clock in the morning! I'll sling enough charges against the fellow to sink a transport! **1923** *Chi. Daily Trib.* (Oct. 5) 22: Now's my chance to fix his clock. **1924** in Galewitz *Great Comics* 138: My big brudder'll fix your clock for that. **1928** O'Brien *Best Stories of '28* 215: The Kid said he'd fix his clock for him. **1942** Algren *Morning* 243: I was s'pose to get you drunk 'n the barber's boys was s'pose to come in 'n fix your clock. **1971** Rader *Govt. Inspected* 108: I saw the fat white man who had called Andrew a nigger faggot. Fix the pig's clock.

¶ **stop (someone's) clock** to stop or defeat (someone); (*hence*) to kill (someone).

1947 R. Carter *Devils in Baggy Pants* 74: Why, those chicken sons of bitches are killing our boys down there! I'll stop their goddamned clock. **1958** J. Ward *Buchanan* 80: Did ye stop Hynman's clock fer 'em? **1971** Curtis *Banjo* 122: They'd come a thousand mile just for the pure pleasure of stopping your clock...I mean they got guns. **1976** *Kojak* (CBS-TV): When they stopped Grimaldi's clock, my life expectancy dipped to zip. **1982** in *Fury of Firestorm* (Jan. 1983) 20: We'd better stop his clock, Professor—same as we did last time!

¶ **wind (someone's) clock, 1.** to trounce.

1958 Camerer *Damned Wear Wings* 148: Remember the last game you played against Princeton? You wound those bastards' clock real good.

2. (of a woman) to copulate with (a man).

1972 C. Gaines *Stay Hungry* 58: She's got a hundred ways to wind your clock. **1992** G. Wolff *Day at the Beach* 105: Wind your clock.

¶ **wipe** [or **clean**] **the clock** *R.R.* to apply the emergency brakes.

1929 *Bookman* (July) 525: I wipe the clock but my train is shakin' too many ties. *Ibid.* 526: Should an engineer "wipe the gauge" or "clean the clock," it means that he has brought the train to a sudden stop by setting the air brakes. **1945** Hubbard *R.R. Ave.* 101: Ernest "wiped the clock" (made an emergency application of the air brake) with one hand and shut his throttle with the other. **1958** McCulloch *Woods Words* 35: *Clean the clock*—To apply emergency air brakes. This causes the indicator needle on the gauge (or clock) to drop back to zero and the "clock" is then empty.

clock *v.* **1.a.** to watch.

1929 Gill *Und. Slang: Clock him*—Look him over. **1942** *ATS* 446: Look at; see. *Clock...gander...lamp.* **1943** *N.Y. Times* (May 9) II 5: Some alligators clocking the action started for the stage. **1942–49** Goldin et al. *DAUL* 45: *Clock*...To watch the movements of a prospective victim of crime, especially a watchman on his rounds. **1949** Monteleone *Crim. Slang* 52: *Clock*...to look at. **1965** in H. Ellison *Sex Misspelled* 316: Y'wanna go up to the Big Boy and get something to eat, clock the action? **1966** Pei *Language* (ed. 2) 185: *Clock the kid,* "Look at me!" **1966** "Petronius" *N.Y. Unexp.* 17: Girls and boys who seek impromptu adventure or a nightcap to clock the late action. **1976** Rosen *Above Rim* 192: "The redhead?" "Yeah...I've been clockin' her too." **1968–77** Herr *Dispatches* 37: We watched them, the wasted clocking the wasted. **1978** W. Green *Sorcerer* (film): I been clockin' you since you first put your nose in this town. **1991** Simon & Mazursky *Scenes from Mall* (film): He was clocking you in the elevator.

b. to plan.

1959 in H. Ellison *Sex Misspelled* 102: He had it all clocked, of course. Slug the kid, grab his dough.

c. to count up or evaluate.

1961 Scarne *Guide to Gambling* 675: *Clock.* To count. "I clocked the money bet for the evening." **1978** Truscott *Dress Gray* 90: I finish clocking my stocks, Slaight, let's you and me go on over to the late movie, how 'bout it?

d. to catch sight of; see; (*hence*) to recognize; identify.

1976 H. Ellison *Sex Misspelled* 29: She'll test him by drawing his attention to a girl he's already clocked and turned away from. **1977** Hamill *Flesh & Blood* 9: Wait till Kingsize clocks this dinge. **1980** Gould *Ft. Apache* 77: Let's get outta here before I get clocked with you two assholes. **1989** R. Miller *Profane Men* 48: Everybody clocks him for an idiot. **1990** Univ. Tenn. student theme: If someone states that he "clocked Joe the minute he walked in," he is really saying that he knew Joe was gay.

e. *Und.* to reconnoiter (a place to be robbed); CASE. Cf. 1942–49 quot. at **(a)**, above.

1978 *N.Y. Times Mag.* (Dec. 17) 106: Persons with criminal records are [often] apprehended while "clocking" the galleries.

2. to strike sharply or heavily.

1932 *Baseball Mag.* (Oct.) 496. **1941* S.J. Baker *Austral. Slang* 18: To *clock,* to strike with the fist. **1950** in *DAS*: [The one] who clocked me when I wasn't looking. **1973** in J. Flaherty *Chez Joey* xxiv: The cop promptly clocked me an overhand right, driving me to my knees. **1976** Price *Bloodbrothers* 78: You got clocked on the head. **1979** V. Patrick *Pope* 111: Finally the fool clocked a sergeant in the locker room at the end of a shift. Knocked him cold. **1989** *Cops* (Fox-TV): The car...clocked him, kept on going.

3.a. (see quot.).

1989 *New York* (Dec. 11) 36: Getting customers is called "catchin'" or "clockin'" [by prostitutes].

b. Esp. *Black E.* to acquire; earn; "rack up."

1990 "Above the Law," in L. Stanley *Rap* 2: To clock big G's I'd be definitely certain. **1990** P. Dickson *Slang!* 215: *Clockin'.* Bringing in; acquiring. **1991** Nelson & Gonzales *Bring Noise* 38: Fresh Prince is bouncing around on television, clockin' dollars.

clock-setter *n. Naut.* a complainer or busybody.

1856 Sleeper *Tales* 95: He seems to delight in complaining of the persons and things around him, and to make others as unhappy as himself. Such "clock-setters"...are sources of incalculable mischief on shipboard. **1868** Macy *There She Blows!* 24: A white American of some intelligence—one of those sea-lawyers or "clocksetters," who are to be found in all sorts of ships, and who make more mischief than can well be imagined by people not conversant with matters of this sort. *Ibid.* 27: "I do!" shouted the clock-setter, from the recesses of his bunk.

clod *n.* a stupid person; dolt. Orig. *S.E.* [Slang use of this term arose in the 20th C.]

*1605 B. Jonson, in *OED2:* Not bred 'mongst clods and clodpoles.
*1645, *1793, *1852, *1869 in *OED2.* **1908** J. London *M. Eden* 10: He was not wholly a stupid clod. **1950–53** W. Grove *Down* 270: He's a real clod, you know. **1963** *AS* XXXVIII 170: A rather stupid student...*clod.* **1978** Pici *Tennis Hustler* 111: I love that...clod. **1985** Schwendinger & Schwendinger *Adolescent Sub.* 65: Certain names, such as Clod, Weirdo, Square, Lame, and Spaz...simply refer to youngsters defined as worthless human beings. **1991** K. Douglass *Viper Strike* 60: You two clods are just jealous!

clodbuster *n. West.* a farmer or plowman. Cf. SODBUSTER.

1950 in *DARE.* **1952** Overholser *Fab. Gunman* 64: It don't make sense that he'd want to fetch in a swarm of clodbusters. **1954** in *Dict. Canadianisms.* **1972–76** Durden *No Bugles* 78: A big, strappin' corn-fed clodbuster. **1977** Univ. Tenn. student: The rest are just clodbusters like me.

clod-crusher *n.* a big foot.

1889 Barrère & Leland *Dict. Slang* I 256: Clod-crushers...an epithet used by Americans to describe the large feet which they believe to be the characteristics of English women as compared with those of their own country.

clodhop *v.* to walk heavily and clumsily.

1966–69 in *DARE:* To walk heavily, making a lot of noise...*Clodhopping.* **1985** MacLaine *Dancing* 94: She just couldn't have Cinderella "clodhopping" across the stage.

clodhopper *n.* **1.** a plowman; (*hence*) rustic; yokel.

*1698–99 "B.E." *Dict. Canting Crew:* Clod-hopper, a Ploughman. *1721 in *OED2.* **1815** Brackenridge *Mod. Chiv.* 624: Warrior or...clod-hopper. **1849** Melville *Redburn* ch. vi: A parcel of farmers and clodhoppers. **1899** Green *Va. Folk-Speech:* Clod-hopper...A farmer's labourer. **1912** *DN* III 573: Clod-hopper...a rustic; a hayseed. **1950** in *DARE.* **1965–70** in *DARE:* A rustic or countrified person...*Clodhopper.*

2. a big shoe or foot.

*1836 in *OED* II 512: Purser's shoes...a hybrid breed, between a pair of cast-off slippers and the ploughman's clodhoppers. **1912** *DN* III 573: Clodhopper...A coarse kind of shoe. **1919** *Blackhawk Howitzer* 21: Whose clodhoppers are these here? **1934** Burns *Female Convict* 184: These clod-hoppers are terrible! **1936** Dos Passos *Big Money* 279: Flies went up right from under his black clodhoppers. **1962** Gallant *On Valor's Side* 42: Our shoes were heavy clodhoppers of rough leather that had tops high enough to reach just above our ankles, and thick soles with rubber heels. **1965** Karp *Doobie Doo* 67: Why don't you keep your clodhoppers where they belong. **1972** P. Thomas *Savior* 81: There were four young black men dressed in prison clodhoppers, uniforms. **1990** McDowell *Our Honor* 10: Get those clodhoppers off and be quick about it.

clod-jumper *n.* a yokel; CLODHOPPER.—used derisively.

1917, 1960 in *DARE.*

clod-knocker *n.* **1.a.** a big foot.

1918 *DN* V 20: Clod-knocker...foot. **1942** *ATS* 935: Clod-knockers...large feet.

b. a heavy shoe.

1946 *PADS* VI 9: Clod-knocker...A heavy shoe. **1968–70** in *DARE.*

2. a country person; CLODHOPPER.—used derisively.

1946 *PADS* VI 9: Clod knocker...In some parts of the South also applied to a countryman in a derogatory sense. **1970** in *DARE.*

clod-masher *n.* CLOD-CRUSHER.

1970 in *DARE:* Clod mashers.

clomp *n.* a blow; CLONK, *n.*

1961 *Many Loves of D. Gillis* (CBS-TV): I gave him a slight clomp on the ear just last week.

clomp *v.* to hit; CLONK, *v.*

1966 Kenney *Caste* 44: I was prayin' to God right there on the Bulge when I got clomped. I got clomped right in the middle of prayin'.

clomper *n.* a heavy boot or shoe; CLUMPER.

1903 *DN* II 296 [ref. to 1850's]: Clomper...heavy boot. **1916** *DN* IV 265: To take his great "clompers" off before he walks on the new "settin'-room mattin." **1973** *TULIPQ* (coll. B.K. Dumas): Footwear...*clompers.*

clone *n.* a worthless person, esp. a boring conformist.

1980 Univ. Tenn. instructor: What a bunch of clones! **1984** D. Jenkins *Life Its Ownself* 58: Barbara Jane's reviews knocked them off like 21-point underdogs....Dede Aldwyn? "Clone." **1989** Kanter & Mirvis *Cynical Amer.* 29: Often they surround themselves with yes-men and clones.

clonk *n.* a sharp or heavy blow.

1943 (quot. at CLONK, *v.*). **1978** E.F. Thompson *Devil to Pay* 49: Until Carlson wanted to give them a clonk.

clonk *v.* [var. CLUNK, infl. by CONK] to strike hard.

1943 *Sat. Eve. Post* (Mar. 20) 86: One clonk on the knuckle...One crack on the head...Clonk yourself once. [**1943** Hersey *G. I. Laughs* 48: Something goes "clonk" on my head.] *1949 in *OEDS.* **1963** E. Hunter *Ten Plus One* 94: I'll clonk you right on the head with my shoe. **1968** Myrer *Eagle* 353: Brand must have really klonked him.

clonker *n.* CLUNKER.

1972 *N.Y. Times Mag.* (Nov. 12) 37: Trucks aren't the clonkers they were years ago.

clop *n.* [imit.] a smart blow.

1940 in D. Runyon *More Guys* 358: A few good clops on the chops. **1985** C. Busch *Times Sq. Angel* 49: I'll give you a swift clop in the chops. **1985** Ann Landers (synd. column) (Feb. 12): Tell him...you will give him a clop in the chops.

clop *v.* to strike smartly.

1956 G. Green *Last Angry Man* 48: I should be a decoy and get klopped on the head so you can come rescue me? **1988** Dietl & Gross *One Tough Cop* 182: If I clopped this little punk here, I would knock him into tomorrowland.

clopper *n.* a big shoe.

1959 Morrill *Dark Sea* 103: How about a pair of cloppers, Admiral?

close *adj.* ¶ In phrase: **that's close** *Stu.* that's absolute nonsense; (*also*) (see 1973 quot.).

1965 in *IUFA:* "Bill, I heard you ask my girl for a date"..."That's close. I wouldn't take that pig out." **1968** Baker et al. *CUSS* 209: *That's close.* Extraordinary, unusual, hard to believe. **1973** Eble *Campus Slang* (Nov.) 1: *That's close:* spoken in a sarcastic tone, this expression is used to discourage an unreasonable request or to refute an outrageous statement. Literally, it means "that is not close to the actual situation." *That's close* could be used as a reply to a request like, "Lend me ten dollars."

close-reef *n. Naut.* rum.

1843 J.R. Browne *Whaling Cruise* ch. ii: "What d'ye say, shipmates, close-reef or sea-breeze?" "Close-reef," said we at a guess...and we discovered, when we emptied our glasses, that "close-reef" was something very strong. **1899** Robbins *Gam* 93: "Take 'nother turn around the capstan an' give us nex' versh!" "Close-reef, first," replied the Cockney singer. "Ware's the bloody bottle?" *Ibid.* 99: Then they...laid in a new bottle of "close-reef," drank the health of the cast-away cooper, and toasted his many virtues. *Ibid.* 154: It was worth a bottle o' close-reef to see it.

closet *n.* ¶ In phrases:

¶ **come out of the closet** [elab. of earlier COME OUT] Orig. *Homosex.* to acknowledge having been an unadmitted homosexual; (*hence*) to come into the open. [The 1963 quot. does not illustrate this sense.]

[**1963** S. Plath, in *OED2:* Come here, sweetie, out of the closet.] **1971** *Ramparts* (Nov.) 52: My journey out of the closet had its beginnings during...college. **1971** N.Y.U. student: When's he coming out of the closet? **1974** *N.Y. Times* (Aug. 25) II 1: I hate to say that science fiction has come out of the closet...but there is no question that it has come to be regarded as respectable. **1979** Kiev *Courage to Live* x: Suicide has only recently come out of the closet, so to speak, to become a possible topic of conversation. **1981** *Film Comment* (May) 23: "Wir Sind Schwül"...featured interviews with homosexuals from many walks of life who had decided it was time to come out of the closet.

¶ **in the closet** being an unadmitted homosexual.

1967 Crowley *Boys in the Band* 891: Have you heard the term "closet queen?" Do you know what that means? Do you know what it means to be "in the closet?" **1978** Truscott *Dress Gray* 301: You're in the closet. I shoulda known. **1993** *Sonya* (CNN-TV) (Mar. 9): I was in the closet for the longest time.

closet *adj.* unadmitted; secret.—used prenominally, esp. in contexts alluding to homosexuality. See also CLOSET QUEEN. Now *colloq.*

1952 in *Qly. Jour. Studies on Alcohol* XIV (1953) 481: The "silent" or "closet" drinker...has withdrawn from social participation. **1961** *Social*

Problems IX 108: "Secret"...homosexuals...in the..."gay world"...are known as "closet fags." **1966** "Petronius" *N.Y. Unexp.* 96: Discreet, closet fags. **1966–71** Karlen *Sex. & Homosex.* 525: The steady bar crowd complained of "closet queers." **1971** Rader *Govt. Inspected* 49: I, playing closet fuzz, convincing no one, not even myself. **1971** in H.S. Thompson *Shark Hunt* 203: Failed dingbats and closet-junkies. **1972** R. Wilson *Playboy's Forbidden Words* 69: Closet Queen. The lesbian equivalent is *closet dyke*. **1976** *L.A. Times* (Nov. 23) "You" 12: You may be one of those closet country-western fans. **1981** *N.Y. Times Mag.* (June 21) 78: Ever since chuckling with my toddlers over "The Mellops Go Flying"...in the calm corner of our local library in 1959, I've been a closet fan.

closet case *n.* **1.** *Stu.* a socially inept, embarrassing or unattractive person.
1958 J. Davis *College Vocab.* 6: *Closet case*—An unattractive person whom you would like to hide. **1959** Maier *College Terms* 6 [ref. to U. of Ill., 1957]: *Closet* or *Attic Case*—That is where he belongs. **1968** Baker et al. *CUSS* 97: *Closet case.* A person who studies a great deal. **1978** C. Miller *Animal House* 13: Unless, of course, the pledge in question turns out to be a real closet case.
2. CLOSET QUEEN.
1969 S. Harris *Puritan Jungle* 139: The ones who can help you...won't because they don't want to be identified. They're what we call "closet cases," hiding and scared to death of exposure. **1970** Landy *Underground Dict.* 52: *Closet case n.*....One who engages in homosexual activities yet firmly believes he or she is not a homosexual. **1979** in Fierstein *Torch Song* 169: The guy keeps tellin' you he's Bi and all you keep doin' is callin' him a closet case. **1985** J. Dillinger *Adrenaline* 226: I was a real closet case in high school. **1993** *English Today* 35 (July) 9: *Closet case* A gay term for someone who is still in denial over his Gay [*sic*] sexual identity.

closet queen *n. Homosex.* a man who conceals his homosexual proclivities.
1959 ISR Graffiti: You closet queens are full of shit. **1964** Selby *Brooklyn* 46: All the fairies in her town were closet queens or pink teas. **1964** L. Jones *Blues People*: Hollow Men, Paper Tigers, Closet Queens of the Universe. **1967** Ragni & Rado *Hair* 54: Tell them you're a closet queen. **1968** Vidal *Breckinridge* 238: You were in love with him, you God-damned closet-queen. **1969** *Playboy* (Aug.) 26: Cruising closet queens in business suits. **1971** *N.Y. Times Bk. Review* (Sept. 5) 23: After a lurid 10-year life as a "flaming fag," Mr. Stanhope decided to become a "closet queen" again. **1973** Billy Joel *Captain Jack* (pop. song): You stare at the junkies and the closet queens.

close-up *n.* a close look.
1921 J. Conway, in *Variety* (Feb. 18) 8: They get a close-up of his cauliflowers.

clothes *n.pl. Police.* plainclothes; a plainclothes division.
1970-71 Rubinstein *City Police* 398: When a man goes "into clothes," his relationship to former colleagues changes immediately..."He's in clothes, ain't he?" **1973** Salt & Wexler *Serpico* (film): They think everybody in clothes is on the take. **1973** Droge *Patrolman* 185: I decided to attend the course and spend my last few months in "clothes." *Ibid.* 189: You'll still go to clothes.

clotheshorse *n.* **1.** a person who wears showy or fashionable clothes.
1850, 1889 in *OEDS.* **1930** *Outlook* (Sept. 3) 6: Along Broadway, O. O. McIntyre and Mayor Jimmy Walker are the most striking clothes horses. **1941** *Slanguage Dict.* 10: *Clotheshorse*...a motion picture actress whose ability to wear clothes well exceeds her histrionic talent; an actress who frequently appears in pictures in which her costumes are more interesting than the action. **1985** Briskin *Too Much* 73: Is he making love to that skinny clotheshorse? **1990** *Cosmopolitan* (Aug.) 158: A clotheshorse and avid tie collector, Bielecki is known locally as The Stylemaster.
2. a fashion model.
1939 "E. Queen" *Dragon's Teeth* 97: It was that woman back there...ex-clothes-horse! **1950** Spillane *Vengeance* 31: You see, the agency is divided into two factions, more or less...the clotheshorses and the no-clotheshorses. **1972** *Nat. Lampoon* (Feb.) 31: So this is where she lives? Not bad for a two-bit clotheshorse. **1982** *Chicago Sun Times* (Oct. 5) 39: The idea that the smartly dressed Savitch could be a clotheshorse would be another anachronism.

clothesline *n.* **1.** *West.* a lariat.
1922 Rollins *Cowboy* 138 [ref. to ca1890]: "Lariat"..."lasso"..."rope." ..."Clothes-line," ..."lass rope," and occasional alternates.

2. *Baseball.* a hard line drive. Also as v., to hit a hard line drive.
1937 *Phila. Record* (Oct. 11) (cited in Nichols *Baseball Term.*). **1946** *N.Y. Times Mag.* (July 14) 18: *Clothesline:* low line drive. **1971** Coffin *Old Ball Game* 55: "Hang a clothesline" (hit a line drive). **1981** *Detroit Free Press* (Oct. 26) F1: He clothes-lined a single to left.
3. see CLOTHESLINE, *v.*, 1.

clothesline *v.* **1.** Esp. *Sports.* to knock down by a usu. horizontal blow to the head or throat. Also as *n.*
1964 (cited in *W10*). **1965** *Time* (Nov. 26) 80: A...tackle tried to clothesline Jimmy, clubbing him across the throat with a rigid arm. **1970** Sample *Dirty Ballplayer* 134: The ball was overthrown, but I clotheslined him right there by catching him in the head with my forearm. **1970** Libby *Life in Pit* 85: In the 1967 Playoff Bowl...Deacon drove at Browns' quarterback Gary Lane and "clothes-lined" him, wrapping a straight arm under his head. **1972** *Amer. Leg. Mag.* (Apr.) 21: Also, unlike cars, snowmobiles are driven in field and wood where there's no highway engineering. As a result, they have a special brand of accident of their own—"clotheslining"—in which the vehicle or operator gets conked by some overhanging thing. **1978** G. Trudeau *Doonesbury* (synd. cartoon strip) (Sept. 15): That's the second quarterback in a *row* he's clotheslined! **1992** *N.Y. Times* (May 17) (Sports) 1: Fined $5000 for his dangerous midair clothesline of Scottie Pippin. **1992** *Closer Look* (NBC-TV) (July 14): Bouncers were clotheslining 'em—knocking 'em down.
2. see CLOTHESLINE, *n.* 2.

clothesliner *n. Und.* a thief who steals from clotheslines; petty thief.
1887 Walling *N.Y. Chief of Police* 475: Brady went back to Sing Sing prison under a heavy sentence for a miserable little theft of which a "clothes liner" would have been ashamed.

clothespin vote *n.* [sugg. by the cartoon-inspired idea that voters must use a clothespin to protect their noses from the supposed stench of such candidates] *Pol.* a vote or votes made unenthusiastically for a candidate who is regarded as the least objectionable. *Joc.*
1980 (quot. at KANGAROO TICKET).

cloud *n.* a black person.—used contemptuously. Cf. BLACK CLOUD, DARK CLOUD.
1928 Fisher *Jericho* 298: *Cloud.* See *boogy.* **1944** *PADS* (No. 2) 55: *Cloud:* n. A Negro. Randolph Co. [Mo.] Used mainly by uneducated whites.
¶ In phrase:
¶ **push clouds** to be dead.
1922 Tully *Emmett Lawler* 175: He's an honest to God man, but he'll be pushing the clouds before another year, he's almost dead now.

cloud-buster *n.* an aviator.
1936 in Goodstone *Pulps* 55: Buzzards, kiwis, peelots, ack emmas and cloudbusters!

cloud-cleaner *n. Naut.* a hypothetical sail set above a skysail.
1884 Symondson *Abaft the Mast* 303: Above her main-royal she carried a skysail, moonsail, cloud-cleaner, star-gazer, sky-scraper, and an angels' footstool. *1889 Barrère & Leland *Dict. Slang* 257: *Cloud-cleaner* (nautical), an imaginary sail carried by a Yankee bottom.

cloud-hopper *n. Av.* an aviator. *Joc.*
1929 Springs *Carol Banks* 101 [ref. to WWI]: I'll just tell you what she is, you half-baked cloud-hopper. **1959** in *Dict. Canadianisms.*

cloud nine *n.* a state of elation or great happiness; (in 1956 Ross quot.) great excellence.—usu. constr. with *on*. Also constr. with other numbers. Also attrib.
1935 Pollock *Und. Speaks: Cloud eight*, befuddled on account of drinking too much liquor. **1954** *Time* (Nov. 8) 73: He's way out on Cloud 7. **1956** Ross *Hustlers* 19: That stuff is way up on Cloud Thirty-nine. **1956** in R.S. Gold *Jazz Lexicon*: Oh, she's off on cloud seven—doesn't even know we exist. **1957** in Elliott *Among the Dangs* 180: I waited awhile, but he was off on cloud nine. **1961** in Bruce *Essential Bruce* 122: Oh, yeah, he's right on it now. Cloud seven. **1963** Braly *Shake Him* 138: See if I can ease up on that cloud-nine kick Kovin's always riding. **1964** Larner & Tefferteller *Addict in the Street* 113: If the clinic was giving just enough to keep them satisfied and not on cloud nine, they'd want a little extra so they could get up to cloud nine. **1970** Wertheim & Gonzalez *Talkin' About Us* 38: Shorty had just come from a drinkin party and he was on cloud nine. **1970** Rudensky & Riley *Gonif* 13: I

drifted away to Cloud Nine. **1975** *N.Y. Post* (Dec. 22) 32: When he asked me out, I was on cloud nine! **1978** *N.Y. Times* (Aug. 6) V 3: Allen considers this the greatest honor of his life, he says it puts him "on cloud ten." **1992** *Donahue* (synd. TV series): I'm on cloud seven. Leave me alone. **1993** *New Yorker* (Oct. 6) 214: Moving slightly further toward Cloud Nine.

clout[1] *n.* **1.** *Und.* a cotton handkerchief. *Rare* in U.S. Orig. *S.E.* **ca*1380, **ca*1440 in *OED2.* **1621* in Partridge *Dict. Und.* 132. **1698–99* "B.E." *Dict. Canting Crew: Clout*, a Handkerchief. **1791** [W. Smith] *Confess. T. Mount* 21: A clout he'll nap unseen. **1807** Tufts *Autobiog.* 292 [ref. to 1794]: *Clout*...a handerchief [*sic*]. **1811 Lex. Balatron: Clout*...also means a handkerchief. **1839* Brandon *Poverty, Mendicity, & Crime* (gloss.): *Clout*—a cotton handkerchief. **1859** Matsell *Vocab.* 19: *Clout*. Handkerchief.
2.a. *Und.* a theft; the crime of theft.
1928 (cited in Partridge *Dict. Und.* 132). **1929** Booth *Stealing Through Life* 297 [ref. to *ca*1920]: This is a fast clout. You ain't got more than a minute after you start, and you got to make every second count. **1965** Bonham *Durango St.* 59: I been busted for aggravated assault, car clout, and more raps than you ever see on one sheet of paper. **1976** R. Daley *To Kill* 95: This wasn't an ordinary car clout. I mean the thief didn't just grab a car parked on the street.
b. *Und.* the practice of theft.—constr. with *the*.
1936 (quot. at BOOST).
c. *Und.* a shoplifter; thief.
1941 in Partridge *Dict. Und.* 132. **1981** *L.A. Times* (Oct. 28) I 23: Police do arrest suspected car clouts.

clout[2] *n.* **1.a.** *Pol.* political influence; (*hence*) power. [The provenance of the remarkably early 1868 quot. sugg. that the term arose in New York; though it is now of national distribution, journalists often associate it with Chicago politics.]
1868 in T. Whitman *Dear Walt* 127: I suppose the political boiling is really more heard than felt in regard to office holding—I know lost [*sic*] of fellows in Brook[lyn] (and it is the same with Engineers) that always think they are going to be deprived of office and "*clout.*" **1937** in *DARE*: No one...gets anywhere in politics or business on his merits. He has to have the "clout" from behind. **1948** Kingsley *Detective Story* 338: What plays between you two guys? What's he got on you? What's the clout? **1959** *AS* (Oct.) 229: *Clout*, meaning political influence, is a term which has been known to Chicago newspapermen for more than ten years and which apparently originated in the familiar conversation of local politicians. **1959** F.L. Brown *Trumbull Pk.* 386: Oh, well, he's got a better clout, I guess. **1966** Jarrett *Private Affair* 8: They had money, clout, social status and a child. **1967** Terkel *Division St.* 4: In those days it was a new idea. You had to fight the politician who saw clearance and change as a threat to his power, his clout.* [Note:] *Clout: a Chicago idiom for "drag," "pull," "political power." **1968** Safire *New Language of Politics* 82: *Clout*. political power, or political influence.... The political use of the word is believed to have originated in Chicago in the 1940's, taken from the baseball phrase, "What a clout!" **1970** in Cannon *Nobody Asked* 286: He knows how to win. It is not a common trait and only guys such as Vince Lombardi, Casey Stengel and Red Auerbach had the same kind of clout. **1981** Centi *Positive/Negative* 17: I used to hang around with the nonathletes and we had no clout in school. **1981** Rucker *57th Kafka* 12: He had the clout to get the necessary components and materials.
b. *Police.* a politically influential friend or ally.
1955 Deutsch *Cops* 50: The "rabbi" in New York police parlance is the "clout" in Chicago. *Ibid.* 51: "The man with a clout...is ruined for police work. He owes his sponsor a loyalty higher than that to his department or to the public. And there are too many clout-owned men on this force." **1976** "N. Ross" *Policeman* 124: First thing he had to do was see his political clout...We can't hang the clout because all they really did was help a little guy with a headache. **1980** in *DARE*: Who's her clout? City Hall contracts for $25,000 don't just come down the chimney with Santa.
c. liveliness.
1973 Flaherty *Fogarty* 21: But this place had no clout.
2. *pl.* a beating.—constr. with *the*.
1929–30 J.T. Farrell *Young Lonigan* 76: The guys told Muggsy that just for that he would get the clouts. *Ibid.* 144: All they ever wanted to do was...give guys the clouts.

clout *v.* **1.** *Und.* to steal. Hence **clouter**. [In earliest use app. restricted to the stealing of silk or silk handkerchiefs; see CLOUT[1], *n.*]
*1708 in Partridge *Dict. Und.* 132: *Clouters.* Such as take Hankerchiefs

out of Folks Pockets. **1734* in Partridge *Dict. Und.* 132: *Clouting.* Picking Handkerchiefs out of Pockets. *a*1909 Tillotson *Detective* 90: *Clouter*—A shoplifter. **1914** Jackson & Hellyer *Crim. Slang* 24: *Clout*...To purloin any kind of valuables in any manner. **1924** Henderson *Keys to Crookdom* 401: *Clouting*...stealing from stores or homes. **1927–28** Tasker *Grimhaven* 32: I'm going to...clout a five-ton Mack truck, load it with sand, and fix it so it can be operated from the tailboard. **1929** Booth *Stealing Through Life* 291: Maybe we can clout a heap and get back in time. **1933** Ersine *Pris. Slang* 27: *Clout v.*...To steal, usually to shoplift. **1954** Chessman *Cell 2455* 102 [ref. to *ca*1940]: Where'd ya get this crate, clout it? **1970** Thackrey *Thief* 105: Well, don't forget about clouting that car. **1970** Terkel *Hard Times* 171: Tony went over and clouted two of the Chez Paree's best blue spotlights. **1973** Toma & Brett *Toma* 46: His kid brother...was clouting cars...the kid was stealing cars and taking fast rides.
2. *Und.* to place under arrest.
1929 Booth *Stealing Through Life* 193: Say! why didn't you send word to Dan or me after you was clouted in that house prowl! **1935** Pollock *Und. Speaks: Clouted*, arrested.
3. to exercise political influence (for).
1958 *AS* XXXIV 230: He clouted himself a job. **1980** in *DARE*: I did not clout for her. **1982** *Chicago Sun Times* (Aug. 11) 51: Investigated by the FBI (for clouting for a nursing home operator who later gave business to [his] pharmacy).

clover-eater *n.* a Virginian.
1869 *Overland Mo.* (Aug.) 129: For no particular reason that I am aware of, a Virginian is styled a "Clover-eater."

clover-kicker *n.* a yokel.
1918 *Wadsworth Gas Attack* 15: Clover-Kicker's Waltz. **1937** *Lit. Digest* (Apr. 10) 12: *Clover kicker.* Farmer, rube. **1938** Haines *Tension* 31: We knowed if Parker just cut [the telephone line] down for an hour some clover kicker along the line would choose that hour to call the doctor. **1968–69** in *DARE*.

clown *n.* **1.** a troublemaking fool; idiot; wiseacre. Now *colloq.*
1898 Dunne *In Peace & War* 137: "They'll be no such thing as givin' a girl in marredge to a clown an' makin' her depindant on his whims," she says. **1920** in De Beck *Google* 96: "Yeh. I had me new bonnet on the seat and this clown waltzed in an' set down on it." **1914–21* Joyce *Ulysses* 342: Jesus, there's always some bloody clown or other kicking up a bloody murder about bloody nothing. **1929–30** J.T. Farrell *Young Lonigan* 97: He felt that he was a Goddamn clown. **1929** Williamson *Hunky* 137: Say, Teena, who is this clown, anyway? **1937** Hellman *Dead End* (film): What are you talkin' about, clown? **1941** J.T. Farrell *To Whom It May Concern* 40: "Who's that clown?" Patsy asked, looking after him. **1954** Schulberg *Waterfront* (film): These two clowns can't fight. **1954** Chessman *Cell 2455* 157: You flat-footed clowns couldn't catch a cold. **1955** O'Connor *Last Hurrah* 43: The only ones who buy the booze are the musicians and a few clowns who come in to get warm. **1957** McGivern *Against Tomorrow* 10: I mean, is he a dependable guy? I don't want to get mixed up with any clowns. **1965** Cassavetes *Faces* 245: I'll tear that clown apart, and put him together again.
2. *Carnival & Und.* a constable or police officer. Cf. TOWN CLOWN.
1929 Barr *Let Tomorrow Come* 266: *Clown*—A policeman; specifically, a small-town policeman. **1930** Irwin *Tramp & Und. Sl.: Clown*...A sheriff, constable or town marshal. **1936** Duncan *Over the Wall* 143: The clowns in this burg believe in that "Cherchez la femme" stuff. **1944** *Pap. Mich. Acad.* XXX 598: *Clowns*, police. **1956** Sorden & Ebert *Logger's* 9 [ref. to *ca*1925]: *Clown*, A city policeman. **1965** in Jackson *Swim Like Me* 14: I only stood until the smoke was clear and the village clown lay dead.

clown wagon *n. R.R.* a caboose.
1931 *Writer's Digest* (May) 41: *Clown Wagon*—Caboose. **1939** *Sat. Eve. Post.* (Apr. 15) 26: When they got near the gate at the end of the alley, he swung off the clown wagon. **1945** Hubbard *R.R. Ave.* 337: *Clown wagon* is caboose.

club *n. Av.* a two-bladed propeller.
1918 Roberts *Flying Fighter* 337: *Prop* or *Club*. The propeller of a flying machine. **1933** Stewart *Airman Speech* 55: *Club*. propeller.

Club Fed *n.* [after *Club Med*, trademark name for a chain of vacation resorts] a Federal prison, esp. a minimum-security prison.
1986 *Miami Vice* (NBC-TV): An extended vacation at a Club Fed. **1988** *N.Y. Times* (May 29) E 4: The camps are often called country-club prisons or "Club Feds." **1990** *Time* (Aug. 20) 49: Set on 42 cam-

pus-like acres, Club Fed, as it was called, had neither walls nor armed guards. **1993** *L.A. Times* (Oct. 13) B 1: They are officially known as Security Level No. 1 institutions; inmates sometimes refer to them as country club prisons or Club Fed.

clubhouse lawyer *n.* [sugg. by GUARDHOUSE LAWYER] Esp. *Baseball.* a contentious player.

1946 *N.Y. Times Mag.* (July 14) 18: *Clubhouse lawyer:* player who gives opinion freely. **1970** Scharff *Encyc. of Golf* 416: *Clubhouse lawyer.* An over-officious caller of the Rules of Golf; or a self-appointed arbiter. **1971** *WCBS-TV News* (Apr. 7): Baseball's most outspoken clubhouse lawyer. **1974** Terkel *Working* 370: "Don't be a clubhouse lawyer." A clubhouse lawyer was a troublemaker. **1980** *N.Y. Post* (June 17) 56: Maybe the Yankees don't read the paper…We don't need no clubhouse lawyers around here. We don't need nobody talking about how good they are.

cluck *n.* **1.** *Und.* a counterfeit coin.

1904 *Life in Sing Sing* 246: *Cluck.* Counterfeit coin. **1927** (cited in Partridge *Dict. Und.* 133).

2. a fool; dolt.

1906 T.A. Dorgan, in Zwilling *TAD Lexicon* 28: This guy O'Brien is a "cluck." Take it from me. **1908** McGaffey *Show Girl* 69: That worthy cluck had stretched a rope from the blacksmith shop. **1915-16** Lait *Beef, Iron & Wine* 270: Gene…ain't nobody's cluck. **1921** *Variety* (June 17) 7: But them two clucks like the glory…that goes with the four baggers. **1928** McEvoy *Show Girl* 137: Clucks, back to your corners. **1930** *Amer. Merc.* (Dec.) 415: This baby's the champion cluck of all time. **1934** H. Miller *Tropic of Cancer* 113: That cluck! Did you see her face? **1936** Steel *College* 170: That cluck's back there wit' Greta? **1938** "E. Queen" *4 Hearts* 125: Your contract wasn't…drawn up by a cluck. **1942** Wylie *Vipers* 18: The integrity of thinking and acting that enters into the radio set on the common man's bedside table is a thundering rebuke to the reliability of the cluck beside it and the macaroon singing over it. **1950** Cleveland *Great Mgrs.* 170: I'd have been a dumb cluck if I hadn't taken advantage of the situation. **1961** Wolfe *Magic of Their Singing* 19: Did you listen to those two clucks in the bus? **1962** Kesey *Cuckoo's Nest* 126: Don't a one of you clucks know what I'm talkin' about enough to give us a hand? **1966** Lehman *Virginia Woolf* (film): What a cluck you are! **1973** Droge *Patrolman* 28: A fat man whose lack of common sense made him the "class cluck."

3. an egg.

1947 *ATS* (ed. 2). **1981** in Safire *Good Word* 111: A cluck and a grunt on a burned British.

4. a wearying situation.

1979 Terkel *Amer. Dreams* 300: I said I'm gonna get out of this cluck if it's the last thing I do.

cluck *v.* to speak.

1888 in *AS* XXXVII (1962) 76: *Did you hear me cluck?* Did you hear what I said?

cluckhead *n.* fool; CLUCK, 2.

1949 *New Yorker* (Nov. 5) 82: First thing they're gonna do, they'll kick a certain cluckhead…right the hell outa Hollywood. **1989** *Comments on Ety.* (Jan.) 5 [ref. to 1956]: Piloted by your fellow terrorized student "cluck heads."

clucking hen *n. Nuclear Engineering.* a Geiger counter.

1955 Reifer *New Words* 49: *Clucking hen.* A contamination meter.

clue *n.* an idea; (*hence*) a piece of information.

***1948** Partridge et al. *Forces' Slang* 43 [ref. to WWII]: "He simply hasn't a clue"—he is completely ignorant of his job, or of what is going on. **1957** E. Brown *Locust Fire* 85 [ref. to 1944]: "Let me give you a clue," I said. "You'll see mountains over here that are pretty damn high." **1957** Gutwillig *Long Silence* 241: "Any new clues for the box?" Translation: Did anyone come up with some original program ideas? **1959** Zugsmith *Beat Generation* 56: Give me the clue. **1991** *Time* (Nov. 11) 71: The U.S. economy is in a mess and no one in Washington seems to have a clue how to get out of it.

¶ In phrase:

¶ **get** [or **catch**] **a clue** to become alert, intelligent, or efficient.—used imper.

1981 Eble *Campus Slang* (Oct.) 3: *Get a clue*—pay attention, get the right information: Get a clue, Tom. You were supposed to come over last night. **1985** Univ. Tenn. student theme: "Catch a clue" and "clue in" are two phrases that are often addressed toward these people. **1986** Univ. Tenn. student: *Get a clue!* means "Start acting intelligently! Don't be such a fool."…*Catch a clue* means the same thing. **1992** *Herman's Head* (Fox-TV): Get a clue, Herman! He dumped me!

clue *v.* to inform; tell.—often constr. with *in*, occ. with *up*.

***1948** in *OEDS:* We've got to jump at this decision, now….We can clue up the official side later. **1951** Sheldon *Troubling of a Star* 121: You can really clue us on that. *Ibid.* 128: I'll clue you something. You're just jealous, boy. **1952** Mauldin *In Korea* 65: "Let me clue you, these static wars will fool you sometimes," a corporal who looked about nineteen said. **1955** Scott *Look of Eagle* 163: I'll clue you right now…that I'm not going into North Korea. **1957** Kohner *Gidget* 40: I thought I'd better clue you in. **1957** M. Shulman *Rally* 231: I'll clue you…There's gotta be a rumble. **1957** E. Brown *Locust Fire* 154 [ref. to 1944]: "I'll clue you," Benedict said. "We been going up every day the last two weeks. Moving a whole damn army to Peking." **1957** H. Ellison *Deadly Streets* 111: I'll clue 'em in not to bother ya. **1958** Frankel *Band of Bros.* 6 [ref. to 1950]: I clue you, I had my work cut out for me. **1958** J. Davis *College Vocab.* 3: *Clue me in*—Tell me what this is all about. **1959–60** Bloch *Dead Beat* 3: Say, Fox, you sure you're clued in for the floor show? *Ibid.* 77: Like clue me. **1960** MacCuish *Do Not Go Gentle* 85 [ref. to *ca*1940]: Okay, now let me clue you in. **1960** Swarthout *Where the Boys Are* 4: You may be very sophisticated and have been to Florida before but let me clue you. **1962** G. Ross *Last Campaign* 188 [ref. to 1950]: Let me clue you in, Bidley; we're all fucked up. **1964** Hill *One of the Casualties* 70: He's a mess, but like I clued you, he could maybe get a wrecker in case we ever need one. **1970** N.Y.U. professor: You begin to wonder, why wasn't Leontes ever clued in? **1979** *N.Y. Post* (Dec. 13) 7: How Clued Up Are You On Frankie? **1980** *N.Y. Times* II (July 27) 26: Laughing the in-laugh that only one who has been clued in by a critic can laugh. **1989** Kanter & Mirvis *Cynical Amer.* 1: Self-interest and opportunism mark today's clued-up person. **1992** *CBS This Morning* (CBS-TV) (Oct. 20): The American people are clued in and they're watching [the candidates] carefully.

clueless *adj.* ignorant, incompetent, or baffled; stupid.

***1943** in *OEDS:* "I'm clueless"—I don't know; or, "He's a clueless type"—the opposite of a gen wallah. **1946** G.C. Hall, Jr. *1000 Destroyed* 60: Luftwaffe pilots were thus very hot in some cases and very clueless, or incompetent, in others. *Ibid.* 153: We'll show those jokers at Halesworth, the clueless bastards. **1957** N. Frye *Anat. of Crit.* 101: He is, in the current slang, clueless. **1979** N.Y.C. man, age *ca*30: I'm clueless about this. **1981** Eble *Campus Slang* (Oct.) 2: *Clueless*—confused, puzzled: Harvey was so clueless that we had to explain the whole situation to him again. **1985** Univ. Tenn. student theme: A "clueless" person is someone who just can't grasp reality. **1986** *New Gidget* (synd. TV series): And Gidget, I was absolutely clueless [on the surfboard]. **1992** Carrie Fisher, in *N.Y. Times Mag.* (May 24) 24: Penny [Marshall] acts like she's clueless.…But she is a very sane kind of crazy.

clumper *n.* a clumsy shoe or boot.

***a*1825, ***1835** in *OEDS:* Stilton made me ten pairs of "clumpers." **1859** Elwyn *Glossary:* Shoes with thick soles we called a "real pair of *clumpers.*" **1966** in *DARE.*

clunk *n.* **1.** a dolt; CLUCK, 2.

1929 Hotstetter & Beesley *Racket* 222: *Clunk*—Stupid; slow-witted; foolish. Also, a fool. **1936** Steel *College* 175: You dumb klunks! **1942** in Galewitz *Great Comics* 267: Normandie remained loyal to this clunk. **1943** Holmes & Scott *Mr. Lucky* (film): The guy came over and punched the clunk in the snoot. **1956** G. Green *Last Angry Man* 199: You better be nice to this big clunk. **1956** Bellow *Seize the Day* ch. i: You fool, you clunk! **1959** Davis *Spearhead* 111: You hate to think of something like that, his going thinking you're a clunk. **1963** Morgan *Six-Eleven* 144: You won't have to with these clunks I play with. **1977** *Texas Monthly* (July) 124: Good-looking clunks…hang back like boys at their first dance.

2. a slow-moving or dilapidated motor vehicle or aircraft; a worthless device, CLUNKER.

1938 *AS* (Dec.) 307: *Clunk.* A bus, usually old and worn-out. **1956** Lockwood & Adamson *Zoomies* 155: One of the five Mitchells…was "The Klunk." **1957** *AS* XXXII 193: *Clunker*…An old, dilapidated, or poorly rebuilt handgun.…[also] *old clunk.* **1966** Adler *Vietnam Letters* 153: This old clunk of an airplane. **1971** *Playboy* (Jan.) 51: I see some joker wearing blue jeans and driving a real klunk. **1974** Scalzo *Stand on Gas* 68: I was profoundly impressed that the old clunk was still running at all. **1983** S. King *Christine* 13: So worked up over an old clunk. **1991** Linnekin *80 Knots* 230: Pilots, man your clunks.

3. a blow, esp. on the head.

[**1929** McEvoy *Hollywood Girl* 86: Hit…with a custard pie klunk.] **1941** West *Flying Wild* (film): What's a clunk on the head?

clunk *v.* [imit.] to strike, esp. on the head; (*hence*, in 1942 quot.) to kill.

1934 in *DAS* 111. **1941** "G.R. Lee" *G-String* 171: I wanted to clunk her. **1941** West *Flying Wild* (film): I got clunked too and I wasn't even playin'. **1942** *Leatherneck* (Dec.) 57: I was out there after dark and discovered at least five klunked Huns. **1943** Wolfert *Tucker's People* 265: Sit down or I'll clunk your other ear. **1961** A. J. Roth *Shame of Wounds* 30: Clunk him on the noodle with a rock. **1982** R.M. Brown *So. Discomfort* 142: Rhonda clunked him on the head. **1992** Mowry *Way Past Cool* 133: Lyon had seen Gordon get clunked with a…bottle.

clunker *n.* **1.a.** an inferior machine or device, esp. an old, slow, or worn-out vehicle.
1942 in C.R. Bond & T. Anderson *Flying T. Diary* 122: Swapped a couple of good P-40s for our two clunkers. **1943** in Ruhm *Detective* 360: So about midnight we get in his clunker and go over to this other farmhouse. **1950** in *DARE*: *Joking names for a pocket watch*…Clunker. **1952** Bissell *Monongahela* 217: Pilot on this decrepit excuse of an old clunker with its lousy internal combustion. **1952** Cope & Dyer *Petty Officer's Guide* 429: *Clunker*. (Slang). An old slow ship or plane. **1954** Arnow *Dollmaker* 397: They whooshed right by th curb in that ole clunker. **1954** Chessman *Cell 2455* 170 [ref to ca1940]: I can dump this clunker as soon as we can get hold of my car. **1961** Hall *Stowaway* 141: She's some clunker. **1965** Gallery *Eight Bells* 166: But the decrepit old clunker just dropped both wheels into the catwalk and stuck there. **1972** *New Yorker* (Nov. 18) 121: Clever Swiss engineering…makes our typewriter just about half the size of the usual office clunkers. **1974** Millard *Thunderbolt* 55: Just start this klunker and drive out the road, away from town. **1972–79** T. Wolfe *Right Stuff* 159: Old clunkers that will hardly go Mach 1.
b. [infl. by CLINKER] a poor performance; a blunder; error.
1976 *L.A. Times* (Nov. 7) III 2: The red-hot Kings turned in a clunker here Friday night and coach Bob Pulford was baffled as to why. **1976** *L.A. Times* (Apr. 12) I 16: The ballot measure is an ill-conceived step backward. "This initiative is a real clunker." **1981** *Atlantic* (Apr.) 115: That's an easy position for a director to take after manufacturing two or three clunkers. **1989** W. Safire, in *N.Y. Times Mag.* (Oct. 8) 18: Add to these clunkers the use of *respectively*, an unnecessary word. **1992** *TV Guide* (Nov. 14) 33: And the production has as many scenes that click as it does clichés and clunkers.
2. a clumsy person; dolt.
1951 in *DAS* 112. **1968–71** Cole & Black *Checking* 10: Nuny comes in and tells these guys are a bunch of clunkers. **1978** *Business Week* (May 22) 164: It's a battle between the "clunkers" in Cleveland who make all the money and the "weirdos" in California who think they're financial hot dogs.
3. a hard blow.
1968-70 in *DARE*.

clunkhead *n.* a dolt; CLUCKHEAD.
1952 in *DAS* 112. **1973** Farb *Word Play* 94: Clunkhead, Dummy, Jerk and Smartass. **1974** *AS* XLIX 205. **1982** Northrup Frye, in *Maclean's* (Apr. 5) 43: Scientists who consider the study of humanities worthless are just clunkheads.

clunky *adj.* clumsy; (*hence*) stupid.
1965 *My Three Sons* (CBS-TV): I can't ask Mary Lou to do a clunky thing like that. **1968** Kirk & Hanle *Surfer's Hndbk.* 18: It may look clunkier because it's heavier and thicker. **1976** *L.A. Times* (Nov. 14) V 20: All the identity was in the clunky shoe. **1983** *L.A. Times* (Jan. 16) (Calendar) 20: The San Francisco Chronicle's Peter Stack called the acting, screenplay and direction "clunky, clunky, clunky."

clusterfuck *n.* **1.** an orgy.—usu. considered vulgar.
1966 "Petronius" *N.Y. Unexp.* 242: Zoothageous Klusterfux. **1967–68** von Hoffman *Parents Warned Us* 182: Oh, those big cluster fucks! I can't stand them. **1969** Bartell *Group Sex* 134: One advantage of open versus closed swinging, according to most of our informants, is the possibility of "three-on-one" or "gang bang" (sometimes called "cluster fuck") activity. **1972** R. Wilson *Forbidden Words* 69: *Cluster Fuck*—Two men copulating simultaneously with the same woman. **1975** Legman *No Laughing Matter* 754: The cheap hippie "group-grope" and "Mongolian cluster-fuck." **1977** *Nat. Lampoon* (Aug.) 50: Well, they're usually pretty wrapped up in a cluster-fuck with the photo models.
2. *Mil.* a bungled or confused undertaking or situation; mess; (*also*) a disorganized group of individuals.—usu. considered vulgar.
1969 in B.E. Holley *Vietnam* 143: These are the screwups that the American public rarely hears about. They happen often enough over here that we have a term for them—"cluster-fuck"! **1974** NYC man, age 27: A *clusterfuck* was a big expression in [the N.Y. National Guard] in 1969. It meant any time people were standing around outside of a regular formation. They'd say, "What the hell is this clusterfuck?"

"Break up this clusterfuck." **1982** Del Vecchio *13th Valley* 42: This place looks like a giant cluster fuck. *Ibid.* 137: We goina get this clusterfuck in the air? **1983** K. Miller *Lurp Dog* 222 [ref. to Vietnam War]: Shame to pass up a clusterfuck target like this. **1985** Dye *Between Raindrops* 42: The rest is up for grabs. This place is a cluster-fuck. **1986** Thacker *Pawn* 135 [ref. to 1970]: What you're going to have is an A number one clusterfuck. **1986** Stinson & Carabatsos *Heartbreak* 146: "What's your assessment of this alert?"…"It's a cluster fuck!…Marines should be fighting, not…filling out request forms for equipment they should already have, Sir." **1990** Poyer *Gulf* 141: Yeah, but which one's which? What a clusterfuck.
3. *Mil.* a bungler; idiot.—usu. considered vulgar.
*a***1987** Bunch & Cole *Reckoning* 284 [ref. to Vietnam War]: He's a clusterfuck.

cluster-fuck *v. Mil.* to congregate in a disorganized or offensive manner.—usu. considered vulgar.
1983 Ehrhart *VN-Perkasie* 162 [ref. to 1967]: All those amtracs clusterfuckin' around the CP yesterday—Charlie knew *somethin'* was up.

cluster-screw *n.* CLUSTERFUCK, 2.
1976 C.R. Anderson *Grunts* 48 [ref. to 1969]: The big man is still seeing a cluster-screw. Now get them damn people…either moving or spread out. *Ibid.* 65: You saw what a cluster-screw that outfit was.

clutch[1] *n.* Orig. *Baseball*. a crucial moment, as in a game.—often attrib.
1929 *N.Y. Times* (June 2) 2: When a batter produces a safe "blow" at an opportune moment, his fellow-players say that he has hit "in the saddle" or "in the clutch." **1949** *N.Y. Daily News* (Oct. 2): They won this clutch game from the Phillies—won it 9-7 in 10 agonizing innings…Jack whiffed Seminick on the clutch pitch. **1949** Cummings *Dict. Sports* 78: A good performer comes through in the "clutch." **1950** Cleveland *Great Mgrs.* 42: The best "clutch" pitcher he ever had. **1951** *N.Y. Daily News* (Sept. 30): But they will never be able to say the Brooks of 1951 lacked clutch guts. **1956** M. Wolff *Big Nick*. 94: Now in the clutch, when I need everything that I've got. **1956** in Woods *Horse-Racing* 49: They are cool in the clutches. **1962** Houk & Dexter *Ballplayers* 131: Johnny is cool in the clutch. **1967** J. Kramer *Instant Replay* 69: He's a great clutch performer. **1990** *New Republic* (Mar. 12) 28: The UAW…may feel that, in the clutch, it must support that industry even when it treats workers ruthlessly.

clutch[2] *n.* a clumsy person; KLUTZ.
1974 *Nat. Lampoon* (Aug.) 57: Anyone who is ashamed of her…own recycling system must be a drag at modeling clay class and a stone clutch at mudpies.

clutch[3] *n.* a Kaffeeklatsch.
1977 Olsen *Fire Five* 7: He…gets in every clutch we got: breakfast, lunch, dinner and late snack. He doesn't miss a clutch.

clutch *v.* to become frozen in panic or indecision.—often constr. with up.
1955 *Science Digest* (Aug.) 34: "Clutch"…is a verb…meaning to be nervous or upset before, during or after any occasion of importance. **1957** Anders *Price of Courage* 88: Lieutenant Felty tried hard, but he had been known to clutch. **1969** *Current Slang* I & II 20: *Clutch*, v. To panic; to become tense; to fail.—College students, both sexes, Minnesota, South Dakota. **1978** Matthiessen *Snow Leopard* 135: It is…the tightness of panic that gets people killed: "to clutch." **1993** *Oprah* (synd. TV series): You clutch. You get nervous.

clutch artist *n.* a professional driver.
1971 Tak *Truck Talk* 33: *Clutch artist*…generally speaking, any truck driver.

clutch-butt *n.* copulation. *Joc.*
1966 Shepard *Doom Pussy* 130: "That big old gal is ready for some rib-rattling clutch butt," said Nails.

clutched *adj.* **1.** frightened and tense.—also constr. with *up*.
1952 Cope & Dyer *Petty Officer's Guide* 427: *Clutched*. (slang). All tensed up. **1958** Frankel *Band of Bros.* 7 [ref. to 1950]: You're clutched up…I don't see a thing. **1960** Swarthout *Where the Boys Are* 138: I was double-clutched. I had no clue whether to laugh…or cry. **1970** Wakefield *Going All the Way* 244: He wasn't clutched up at all. **1977** Heinl *Marine Off. Guide* (ed. 4) 683: *Clutched-up*: Nervous, panicky. **1982** E. Leonard *Cat Chaser* 160: If that's what's got you clutched up, don't worry about it.
2. angry.
1956 in *DAS* 112.

cly *n.* [orig. unkn.] **1.** *Und.* a pocket.

*1698–99 "B.E." *Dict. Canting Crew: Cly*...a Pocket. *Filed a Cly*...Pickt a Pocket. ***1785** Grose *Vulgar Tongue:* He has filed a cly. **1807** Tufts *Autobiog.* 293 [ref. to 1794]: *Touching a cly*...robbing a pocket. **1859** Matsell *Vocab.* 19: *Cly*...A pocket. **1866** *Nat. Police Gaz.* (Nov. 3) 3: A "century" and a half of "queer" in his "cly." **1871** Banka *Pris. Life* 492: Pocket...*Clye*...Upper Vest Pocket...*Chimney Clye.*
2. *Und.* the practice of picking pockets.—constr. with *the.*
1866 *Nat. Police Gaz.* (Nov. 10) 3: Jimmy Mack...bids fair to rival his brother on the "cly."

Clyde *n.* **1.** [fr. the given name *Clyde* regarded as esp. old-fashioned or provincial; cf. HICK, RUBE, and others] a contemptible man; jerk; SQUARE.—usu. used in direct address. Also as adj.
1950 C.W. Gordon *High School* 114: Positively rated persons who are "hep"...and "george" [versus]...the negatively rated "fruits" and "clydes." *Ibid.* 126: Disapproved behavior was "fruit," "drippy," or "clyde." **1962** *Mad* (Dec.) 22: Hi, Clyde! Frank Sinatra here, with a ring-a-ding home movie. **1964** Hill *One of the Casualties* 53: On my side of the crick...it's just the sophisticated ring-a-ding cats that go around callin people Clyde. **1967** Taggart *Reunion of the 108th* 102: "You got a place, Clyde?" she said to Henry. **1966–69** Woiwode *Going to Do* 25: One look at me and they decided I was a wastrel, a Clyde. **1969** *Current Slang* I & II 20: *Clyde,* n. A real clod; a nothing.—Air Force Academy cadets. **1970** Gattzden *Black Vendetta* 68: This Clyde's a schmuck. **1975** S.P. Smith *Amer. Boys* 157: Mother fuck you, Clyde. **1976** *Daily Beacon* (Univ. Tenn.) (Nov. 10) 8: Well, Clyde, you say you have a date for the game today with a girl who thinks a football is a Podiatrists' Convention. **1981** *Daily Beacon* (Univ. Tenn.) (Nov. 13) 2: "Where do I go to complain about your service?" "Right through that door, Clyde." **1986** *Miami Vice* (NBC-TV): What's your problem, *Clyde?* **1990** Vachss *Blossom* 273: What was I gonna do with the ride, Clyde?
2. [sugg. by the hat worn by the character Clyde Barrow (Warren Beatty) in the film *Bonnie and Clyde* (1967)] a wide-brimmed fedora.
1973 Droge *Patrolman* 11: A weasel-like countenance, covered by an overly long-brimmed "Clyde."

cly-faker *n. Und.* a pickpocket.
*1823 (cited in Partridge *Dict. Und.*). **1845** *Nat. Police Gaz.* (Oct. 11) 59: Two other "*cly fakers*" and "*tilers.*"

cly-faking *n. Und.* the picking of pockets.
1845 *Nat. Police Gaz.* (Nov. 8) 91: For the purpose of facilitating his "clyfaking" operations. **1846** *Lives of the Felons* 84: The "clyfaking" operations of Master Dowling had commenced. **1859** Matsell *Vocab.* 19: *Cly-faking.* Picking pockets. **1866** *Nat. Police Gaz.* (Apr. 21) 3: George Harrison, a member of the "cly-faking" fraternity.

C-man *n.* (a partial euphem. for) COCKSMAN.
1943 J.T. Farrell *Days of Anger* 133 [ref. to 1925]: Carberry thinks he's a C-man. O'Neill thinks he's an intellectual.

C-note *n.* [C + NOTE] *Gamb.* a one-hundred-dollar bill.
1930 *Liberty* (Oct. 11) 30: We gave him five C notes and two tens. **1954** Schulberg *Waterfront* 8: He was always good for fifties and C-notes peeled off the fat roll. **1956** Algren *Walk on Wild Side* 136: Finnerty's C-note still waited to be spent. **1972–75** W. Allen *Feathers* 35: I laid a C-note on her. **1987** Norst & Black *Lethal Weapon* 96: He had a C-note riding on the play-offs.

co *n. Av.* a copilot.
1972 Carpenter *Flight One* 61: For co, anyway. **1985** Heywood *Taxi Dancer* 308 [ref. to 1973]: Where are your manners, co? **1987** Zeybel *Gunship* 27 [ref. to Vietnam War]: Major Ed Holcomb was so good that he could have done it without a co.

coach *n. Whaling.* (see quot.).
1873 Scammon *Marine Mammals* 75: The bone of the upper jaw [of the sperm whale] is termed the "coach" or "sleigh."

coachie *n.* a coachman.
*1819 [T. Moore] *Tom Crib* 79: This song...in which the language and sentiments of *coachee* are transferred so ingeniously. **1834** *Mil. & Nav. Mag. of U.S.* (Oct.) 116: He launches out a *golden buzzard* to a coachee for a ride to see the ways of the town. **1895** Townsend *Fadden* 15: Miss Fannie wanted ter cry, an' coachy was struck dead dumb.

coachwheel *n.* a dollar coin. Cf. CARTWHEEL.
[***1785** Grose *Vulgar Tongue: Coach Wheel.* A half crown piece is a fore coach wheel, and a crown piece a hind coach wheel; the fore wheels of a coach being less than the hind ones.] **1859** Matsell *Vocab.* 19: *Coach-wheel.* A dollar.

coachwhip *n. Naut.* a long narrow pennant, as carried by a war ship. Now *hist.*
1841 [Mercier] *Man-of-War* 199: There fluttered the *coach-whip* where the broad blue pennant was wont to expand to the breeze. **1849** Melville *White-Jacket* 32: The *long pennant,* or *coach-whip,* a tapering, serpentine streamer worn by all men-of-war. **1867** Clark *Sailor's Life* 205: The Union banner danced from her spanker-gaff, and the long "coach-whip" proclaimed her a Yankee gunboat.

coal *n.* **1.** black persons.—esp. in phrs. of the sort **haul, burn,** or **deal in coal** to associate with black persons, often in a sexual context.—used contemptuously.
1833 in Dillard *Lexicon of Black Eng.* 7: "She go for bring coal"...a Negro cargo. **1909** in Sampson *Ghost Walks* 490: And the curtain falls on the second act of "Mr. Lode of Koal." **1916–22** Cary *Sexual Vocab.* I s.v. *copulation: Shoveling coal.* To copulate with a negress. **1930** Huston *Frankie & Johnny* 98: Damn his soul, he was mining in coal. **1930** Schuyler *Black No More* 4: You aint thinkin' o' dealin' in coal, are you? **1938** *AS* (Apr.) 151: *Deal in Coal.* To associate with one who is of darker hue than the speaker, connoting a very black negro and used by one sex in reference to the other. A very insulting expression...Never is it used in the hearing of a white person. **1968** *Sat. Eve. Post* (Sept. 16) 57a: After dark the only white people one usually sees on the main streets are punks and thrill-seekers, young men out to buy dope, and aggressive young prostitutes known as "coal-haulers." **1969** Pharr *Numbers* 95 [ref. to 1930's]: Does that mean that you don't deal in coal, Mr. Greene? **1970** Landy *Underground Dict.* 42: *Burn coal* v. Date a Black person. **1971** *N.Y. Times Mag.* (Nov. 28) 94: Make no difference. She don't burn no coal. **1969–71** Kahn *Boys of Summer* 110: Say, you guys going out to see the coal?...The coal is taking over...Where I grew up there's all these fucking cannibals. **1974** S. Stevens *Rat Pack* 146: She don't burn no coal. **1976** Braly *False Starts* 222: Listen, punk, you keep hauling coal and one day you'll wake up dead. **ca1979** in J.L. Gwaltney *Drylongso* 81: Girl, I didn't know you dealt in coal.
2. *Mil.* bombs or shells exploding with black smoke. Now *hist.* [Quots. ref. to WWI.]
1918 Adler *77th Div.* 44: "Tons-of-coal," "Jack Johnsons," "G.I. Cans"...are some of the names adopted for the German...eight-inch and ten-inch...shells. **1924–27** Nason *Three Lights* 236: Jerry c'n see us comin' over the hill...We don't want him to throw no load o' coal at us. **1940** Carter *101st Field Arty.* 167: No sign of the Boches. A little coal being dumped in the field to our left ("Coal" was the accepted lingo to describe incoming shell fire). *Ibid.* 211: Each day the enemy dumped "coal" into the empty positions of the previous night.
¶ In phrases:
¶ **pour on the coal** Esp. *Av.* to accelerate, esp. by applying full throttle. Also vars.
1937 Parsons *Lafayette Escadrille* 233 [ref. to WWI]: I poured coal into the old Hispano and lit out like a scared jack rabbit. **1943** *Newsweek* (Oct. 11) 15: The trainee, behind a 175 or 200 horsepower Ranger engine, just "pours on the coal" and he's quickly in the air with a lot of runway to spare. **1955** Klaas *Maybe I'm Dead* 63: Point the Stearman down the field. Gently pour the coal. **1956** *AS* XXXI (Oct.) 229: *Pour the Coal to It*...To throttle on take-off. **1959** Scott *Flying Tiger* 147: I even considered "pouring the coal" to the engine and taking off. **1961** Foster *Hell in the Heavens* 58: He poured the coal to his plane and banked to avoid passing too close. **1962** Robinson *Barbara* 25: Pour on the coal, Lee. **1962** Quirk *Red Ribbons* 38: Wave off! Pour the coal to it!...Bank left, pull up, bank right, level off. **1991** Jenkins *Baja Okla.* 121: When you're shovelin' in the coal on them freeways, think about somebody shovelin' in the dirt on your casket.

coal barge *n. Army.* COAL-BOX.
1919 Kelly *What Outfit?* 116: Hadn't put over eight rounds before the coal barges—that's the big shells that Fritz throws at us—began sailin' right in.

coal-box *n. Army.* a heavy German artillery shell. [Quots. ref. to WWI.]
*1914 in *OEDS.* **1916** in Roy *Pvt. Fraser* 83: The enemy opened up rather violently with coal boxes, whiz-bangs and aerial torpedoes. **1917** Empey *Over the Top* 23: Then about two hundred yards to our left in a large field, four columns of black earth and smoke rose into the air, and the ground trembled from the report,—the explosion of four German five-nine's, or "coal-boxes." **1919** Kuhn *Co. A* 47: Suddenly Jerry sent over a few "coal-boxes" as we termed the overhead shrapnel and in a few minutes everything movable was in a mad rush for shelter. **1919** Tomlinson *Sgt. Ted Cole* 85: *Coal-box.* A heavy artillery shell which, when exploding, sends up a cloud of thick black smoke. **1920** *Amer.*

Leg. Wkly. (Sept. 3) 8: Over came a "coal-box" a-screamin' through the air. **1924** Barker *Along the Road* 138: I realized a coal box was coming straight for me. **1928** Harrison *Generals Die in Bed* 215: They say those "coalbox" shells cost five thousand dollars each.

coal-chute *n.* *Navy.* (see quot.).
   1920 *Amer. Leg. Wkly.* (Feb. 13) 33: A coal-chute's a dirty hammock, mom.

coal-bucket *n.* *Army.* a shako.
   1939 *AS* XIV (Feb.) 26: *Coal Bucket,* n. Cadet shako (full-dress headgear).

coal hole *n.* *Stock Market.* the bidding floor of a stock market.
   1865 *Harper's Mag.* (Apr.) 618: [He] soon became a prominent figure at the "coal-hole."...When he rose in the coal-hole to bid..."seller three or thirty"...by-standers looked on with admiration.

coalie *n.* a stoker.
   *1880 in *F & H* II 133: The grateful coaley takes his departure. **1889* in *Ibid.*: The coalies demonstrated last night in right novel fashion. **1977** R. Adams *Lang. R.R.* 34: *Coaly:* A fireman.
   2. Usu. *Coaly.* the devil.—esp. in phr. **black as Coaly's ass** very black.
   1950 Bissell *On the River* 56: I was black as Coaly's ass, so I didn't much care. **1953** Randolph & Wilson *Down in Holler* 177: Any black object may be described as...*black as Coaley's butt.* Coaley is an old-time name for the Devil. **1975** in *DARE*: Black as Old Coaly...black as Old Coaly's ass.

coal-puncher *n.* *Naut.* a stoker.
   1918 E. O'Neill *Moon of the Caribees* 38: Blarsted coal-puncher!

coal-scuttle blonde *n.* *Black E.* a very black woman. *Joc.*
   1938 *AS* XIII 151: *Coal-skuttle blonde.* A dark negro girl. **1942** Z.N. Hurston, in *Amer. Merc.* LV 88: Dat broad...wasn't no peola. She was one of them coal-scuttle blondes.

coal-slinger *n.* *Naut.* a coal-passer; stoker.
   1878 Willis *Our Cruise* 10: There was a row about her in one of the firemens' messes; one coal-slinger saying that she had engines of a certain pattern and mounted four funnels.

Coastie *n.* *Navy.* a member of the U.S. Coast Guard.
   1971 Sheehan *Arnheiter* 46: She sailed under Coast Guard officers and men—"the Coasties," in derisive Navy slang. **1973** Overgard *Hero* 83: We've been hove-to by the Coasties a couple of times, but what do they find? **1977** Langone *Life at Bottom* 74: Oh yeah, I been to Kodiak or Newfoundland with the Coasties, those fuckin' shallow-water sailors, Hooligan's Navy. **1985** Dye *Between Raindrops* 321: [A] Coastie [is] rolling up the ramp. **1989** *New Yorker* (Aug. 7) 50: In the eyes of most Americans—and of most Coasties—the service's first function was search and rescue on the water.

coast-to-coast *n.* a pill containing a strong stimulant.
   1969 Geller & Boas *Drug Beat* 239: "Copilots," "truckdrivers," "cartwheels," and "coast-to-coasts" originate with the habit of truck-drivers using speed to stay awake on long overnight hauls.

coat *n.* ¶ In phrase: **pull (someone's) coat** *Black E.* to alert, warn, or advise (someone).
   1960 C.L. Cooper *Scene* 85: I been tryin to pull your coat, man. **1962** Crump *Killer* 292: Never pull a sucker's coat to the things he don't know. **1965** C. Brown *Manchild* 236: He was the cat who pulled my coat to this brand-new, hip way of life. **1967** Gonzales *Paid My Dues* 48: He pulled my coat to all the aspects of royalties I never knew existed. **1968** Cleaver *Soul on Ice* 182: Look here, baby, pull my coat to what's going down! **1970** Conaway *Big Easy* 90: I'm going to pull your coat about something so big, so wonderful.... **1970** A. Young *Snakes* 51: I might can...introduce you to some of the people that's on the set that can maybe pull your coats to some good things. **1971** T.C. Bambara *Gorilla* 5: Look here Mama...We just tryin to pull your coat. **1973** E. Knight *Belly Song* 44: This poem is to pull your coat to who/your enemy is. **1992** Perl & Lee *Malcolm X* (film): Pull my coat on this, man.

coat-holder *n.* *Pol.* a political follower.
   1972 in Bernstein & Woodward *President's Men* 206: Mr. Bradlee [is] an old Kennedy coat-holder.

coat-tail *n.* ¶ In phrase: **make a straight coat-tail** to run; hurry.
   1834 Caruthers *Kentuck.* I 195: I'm for making a straight coat-tail out of this place. **1843** (quot. at CUT A STICK). **1925** Bailey *Shanghaied* 105 [ref. to 1899]: I jest made a straight coat-tail up the lane to her heart.

cob *n.* the penis.

1920–54 in Randolph & Legman *Blow Candle Out* 787: Other common names [in the Ozarks] for the male organ are cob, cock, dick, dinger, dink, dood, doodle, ducey, family organ, goober, gun, hammer, hammer-handle, hoe-handle, horn, jemson or jimmison, jock, john, jong, okra, pecker, peter, pintle, pood, poodle, poodle-dink, prick, rhubarb, robin, stalk, tackey, tail, tallywhacker, thing, tickler, tilly-whacker, tool, and ying-yang. **1958** Cooley *Run For Home* 334: She'd never be able to get his cob up! **1960–69** Runkel *Law* 141: I'd never so much as stuck my cob in a girl's shuckings.
   ¶ In phrases:
   ¶ **off** [or **on**] **the cob** CORNY; poor.
   1935 *Vanity Fair* (Nov.) 71: All that is ornate or out-of-date comes under the terms *corny, corn-fed, on the cob,* or sometimes *strictly union.* **1937** *New Yorker* (Apr. 17) 27: Those not up on current idioms are *corny, on the cob,* or...*icky.* **1941** (quot. at HAMOLA). **1944** Trumbo *30 Sec. over Tokyo* (film): That landing was strictly on the cob. **1944** Kendall *Service Slang* 54: *Right off the cob...*a rural recruit. **1944** *Slanguage Dict.* 60: *Off the cob*—corny; countrified. **1951** Mannix *Sword-Swallower* 227: What I saw tonight was sure straight off the cob. **1950–52** Ulanov *Hist. Jazz* 350: *Corny:* stale, insipid, trite, usually the worse for age; and so too "corn" (noun), "cornfed," "cornball," and "off the cob."
   ¶ **rough as a cob** very rough (in any sense).
   1945 *Yank* (Apr. 20) 14: A good law-enforcement officer had to be "rough as a cob and slicker'n a school teacher's elbow." **1945** Bryan *Carrier* 13: Thienes "had it rough as a cob on a cold morning." **1948** Cozzens *Guard of Honor* 76: And here I am, at fifteen thousand feet, flying upside down...Rougher than a cob, pal! **1961** L.G. Richards *TAC* 64: Refueling...in air as rough as a cob. **1963** Boyle *Yanks Don't Cry* 152 [ref. to WWII]: Sure, our language was rough as a cob and some of the things we did were crude and coarse.... **1969** Apollo II Communication, in *N.Y. Times* (July 21) 4: Sounds like it looks a lot better than it did yesterday. At that very low sun angle it looked rough as a cob then. **1972** C. Gaines *Stay Hungry* 19: But some of those boys are rough as a cob. Uneducated. **1975** T. Berger *Sneaky People* 67: Lester's as rough as a cob; he'd kick him in the nuts.

cob *v.* **1.** to steal; COP.
   1969, 1969, 1980 in *DARE*.
   2. *Av.* to accelerate; in phr. **cob it** to go at full throttle. Cf. FULL COB.
   1969 Cagle *Naval Av. Guide* 391: *Cob It* Full throttle; also *two-blocked, firewall.* **1974** J.C. Pratt *Laotian Fragments* 82: Cob this old mother.
   3. (see quot.).
   1976 J.L. Dillard *Amer. Talk* 14: The vulgar "Cob you!" (the older and more rural predecessor of "Up yours!").

cobber *n.* [orig. unkn.] **1.** Esp. *USMC in Pacific WWII.* friend; buddy. [Adopted from Australian and New Zealand usage.]
   *1895 in S.J. Baker *Austr. Lang.* 116: She's my cobber and I'm her bloke. **1897* in *Ibid.* 117: And a bosom friend's a "cobber." **1944** E.H. Hunt *Limit* 123: It's no fun when your cobbers are killed. **1944** in *Best from Yank* 37: He was clever at sniping, but my cobber resented him. **1949** McMillan *Old Breed* 151: Their cobbers pulled them away. **1958** Frankel *Band of Bros.* 100: Don't miss, cobber. **1959** Cochrell *Barren Beaches* 42 [ref. to 1943]: It's my birthday, so a bunch of my cobbers is throwin' a whing-ding at my in-laws. **1981** Sledge *Old Breed* 285: Wish I could light that cigar for you, Cobber, but the smokin' lamp is out. **1986** F. Walton *Once Were Eagles* 63 [ref. to WWII]: The men...don't let their "cobbers" (pals) down.
   2. (*cap.*) a New Zealander.
   *a*1982 in Berry *Semper Fi* 146 [ref. to WWII]: I know you're curious about what the Cobbers were doing here.

cobble *v.* *Juve.* (see quot.).
   1986 Ciardi *Good Words* 76: To cobble is the gang act of seizing a boy and ripping his fly open (or pulling down his pants) to examine his genitals....It is often concluded by spitting on his genitals....It was standard slang in Boston in the 1920s and 1930s.

cocabola *n.* [orig. unkn.] a black person.—usu. used contemptuously.
   1942 *Pittsburgh Courier* (Jan. 10) 11: I don't mind tellin' you, brother, I am a scared coca-bola by then. **1958** Frankel *Band of Bros.* 52 [ref. to 1950]: "We called this cocabola."..."What's a cocabola?" "Nigger."

cocinero *n.* [< Sp] *West.* a cook.
   1843–45 T.J. Green *Tex. Exped.* 258: Presiding as chief *cocinero* (cook).

cock *n.* **1.a.** the penis.—usu. considered vulgar. [The double entendre in the familiar *ca*1450 quot. is inescapable.]

[*a1325 in *MED:* Mi pilkoc pisseþ on mi schone.] *ca1450 in R.H. Robbins *Lyrics of XIVth–XVth C.* (No. 46): I haue a gentil cook...his comb is of reed corel,/his tayil is of get ["jet"]...& euery nyȝt he perchit hym/in myn ladyis chaumbyr. [*a1475 in *MED:* Owre syre fydecoke ffayn wold I skyfte [i.e. change].] *ca1510 in *Folklore* CII (1991) 194: And whyte nonnes with whyte vayles/That was full wanton of theyr tayles,/To mete with Cocke they asked how to do. *1607 in *Folklore* CII (1991) 194: Commendation of Cockes. *1618 in *OEDS:* Oh man what art thou? when thy cock is up? *1647 Beaumont & Fletcher, in *F & H* II 135: The mainspring's weakened that holds up his cock. *1708 in D'Urfey *Pills* VI 201: Oh that my Belly it were a Tun of stall,/My Cock were turn'd into a Tap, to run when I did call. *1743 in Burford *Bawdy Verse* 259: E'er his small *Cock* were yet a fortnight old,/How with majestick Vigour it should rise. *ca1866 *Romance of Lust* 336: Let her see your great big cock. 1867 (quot. at (3.a.), below). [1868 Bache *Vulgarisms* 35: It is a shame that excellent words...should be driven out of familiar use by prurient imaginations...Why then should we substitute *rooster* for *cock*?] 1877 in J.M. Carroll *Camp Talk* 114: Did you dream...That I had *two* cocks? 1888 *Stag Party* 22: The cordee and the thousand cursed pains/Sore cocks are heir to. 1918 in Carey *Mlle. From Armentières* II (unp.): The little Marine went over the top,/And circumcized the Kaiser's cock. *a1927* in P. Smith *Letter from Father* 46: I looked at her cunt and she at my cock. 1928 in Read *Lexical Evidence* 42: Piss here.../Shake your cock and disappear. 1929 in J. O'Hara *Sel. Letters* 40: So much for affaires de cock. 1934 H. Miller *Tropic of Cancer* 93: I thought she'd tear the cock off me. 1963 in Cheever *Letters* 237: Daddy, my cock is stuck in a zipper. 1968 in Walker *Rights in Conflict* 157: Your wife sucks cock! 1972 Jenkins *Semi-Tough* 43: They're going to get your cock knocked off Sunday. 1987 Taubman *Lady Cop* 201: I started a discussion on why some men wear their cocks on the right side of their pants and some on the left. 1992 N. Baker *Vox* 84: The cock of the man underneath me slid right inside.

b. copulation with a man.—usu. considered vulgar.
*a1890–93 *F & H* III 206: To have...a lot of...beef...cock...cunt. *ca1888–94 in Karlen *Sex. & Homosex.* 171: Servants and women of the humbler class...all took cock on the quiet. 1936 Dos Passos *Big Money* 124: Well, you've had the last piece of c—k you get outa dat baby.

c. BASTARD, 1.a.; PRICK.—usu. considered vulgar.
1961 Sullivan *Shortest, Gladdest Yrs.* 21: Cocks. Bastards. Smart Bastards. *Ibid.* 22: The cock's got a knife, guys, get 'em. Kill 'em. 1964 Gelber *On Ice* 165: You cock! 1967 Aaron *About Us* 107: Benny, you half-cocked Hebrew cock, you're sober. 1970 La Motta, Carter & Savage *Raging Bull* 234: I know I'm a suspicious, treacherous bastard...I know I acted like the prize cock of all time. 1974 E. Thompson *Tattoo* 59: He could be dead. I mean, I really pasted that old cock. *Ibid.* 199: Kiss off, cock! 1974 Kurtzman *Bobby* 12: "The police brought me too!" a fat cock says.

2. a usu. spirited fellow.—usu. constr. with *old*.
*1639 in *F & H* II 135: He has drawn blood of him yet: well done, old cock. *1684 Bunyan, in *OED:* Thou art a Cock of the right kind. *1725 in *OED:* An old club of merry cocks. 1767 "A. Barton" *Disappointment* 112: Ne'er fear, old cock. *ca1777 in Silber *Songs of Independence* 164: Come listen, my cocks, to a brother and friend. 1786 in W. Dunlap *Diary* 4: Hearty fellows! staunch cocks! jolly dogs! *1786 in Partridge *DSUE* (ed. 8) 823: Well, father, you sent for me: now, what do you want, my old cock. 1787–89 Tyler *Contrast* 71: You are a d—d hearty cock, smite my timbers! *1814 in Wetherell *Adventures* 300: "Vive Louis dix huit," says the hearty old cock. 1835 Longstreet *Georgia Scenes* 15: Well, fetch up your nag, my old cock. 1838 [Haliburton] *Clockmaker* (Ser. 2) 107: Rum-lookin' old cocks them saints. 1853 Lippard *New York* 92: "To think o' sich ingratitude from an old cock like you, when I've come to keep that throat o' yourn from bein' cut by robbers." 1872 *Galaxy* (Mar.) 297: Know the old cock? 1872 *Overland Mo.* (May) 466: The old cock's puttin' on frills. 1885 "Lykkejaeger" *Dane* 118: Sold 'em of course, old cock. 1893 W.K. Post *Harvard* 130: An interesting old cock. *Ibid.* 260: He used to be the jolliest old cock in college. 1919 in Hemingway *Sel. Letters* 30: See what you can do and Merry Christmas old cock. 1938 "E. Queen" *4 Hearts* 15: *My* m'stake, El, ole cock. 1938–39 Dos Passos *Young Man* 257: Hello, Sandy, old cock, have a drink. 1958 S.H. Adams *Tenderloin* 351: That's the old cock over there. *a1961 Longman *Power of Black* 271: Be seein' yo', ol' cock. 1972 Jenkins *Semi-Tough* 63: And take it from an old advertising cock that if no one knows what you're *saying*, you couldn't sell welfare in Harlem. 1976 Hayden *Voyage* 199: Yonson, old cock, there's a busted batten up in them topmast shrouds. 1989 D. Sherman *There I Was* 48: All cocks in second team [are] shooting.

3. [perh. fr. obs. Eng. dial. *cock* 'cockle, shell-fish' (*OED2* "rare," but cites are given for *ca*1000 and 1661); cf. esp.

bracketed 1892 quot.] *So. & Black E.* **a.** the vulva or vagina; CUNT.—usu. considered vulgar.
1867 Doten *Journals* II 957 [In cipher]: We felt of each other's cocks...and then she got on and fucked me bully. [*1892 Northall *Eng. Folk-Rhymes* 156: It is significant that the *labia minora* are still termed "cockles" in vulgar parlance.] *ca*1905 in Logsdon *Whorehouse Bells* 158: And I saw my Lula's cock. 1928 in Read *Lexical Evidence* 42: Ashes to ashes dust to dust if it wasnt for your/cock my prick would rust. 1942 McAtee *Supp. to Grant Co. Dial.* 3 [ref. to 1890's]: Cock, n., applied to both the female pudendum and the male penis. Also meant the "deed of kind," as in "plenty of good —." 1944 *PADS* (No. 2) 18: Cock: n. ((Pudenda muliebra.)) Always a vulgar term among the highlanders, no matter what it is used for. In the vulgar sense, it is always applied to females, never to males, as in England. 1956 in Oliver *Blues Trad.* 240: Jumped through you mammy's cock and never touched a hair. 1964 Abrahams *Down in Jungle* 209: Ever since you came out of your mammy's cock. 1968 Legman *No Laughing Matter* 118: Cock...the female genitals...The actual linguistic origin is the French *coquille*, cockleshell, as referring to the female genitals...in the 18th century. 1976 Knapp & Knapp *One Potato* 188: Picked up a rock and hit her in the cock. *a*1973–87 F.M. Davis *Livin' the Blues* 36 [ref. to Kansas, *ca*1920]: A woman...had a "cock." When we learned whites used that term for the male organ, we felt contempt for their dumbness.

b. copulation with a woman.—usu. considered vulgar.
1927 in Randolph *Pissing in Snow* 136: He was looking for a piece of cock, but the girls didn't want no part of Ambrose. 1930 in *Ibid.* 7: But I come here to pull my pud,/Cause the cock in this town ain't no good. 1930 *Lyra Ebriosa* 24: The crew demanded rum and cock, which drove Columbo frantic. 1942 (quot. at (a), above). 1950 in Randolph & Legman *Blow Candle Out* 603 [rhyme learned *ca*1900]: Before I'd pay a dollar for cock,/I'd let my prick get hard as a rock. 1954 in *DARE:* She's a good piece of cock. 1962 T. Berger *Reinhart* 401: "What I need is a piece of cock."...Reinhart...knew this fellow was anything but a queer. 1963 Reuss *Field Collection* 242: "I want some cock," said Barnacle Bill the sailor. 1966 Bullins *Goin' a Buffalo* 179: I ain't buyin' no cock. 1966 Braly *On Yard* 23: His woman holdin' out on him...No cock can sure make a man red-eyed. 1971 N.Y.U. student: I was in South Carolina once with my friend and we were sitting in this bar, and we heard this one guy say, "I'm gonna go get me some cock," and we jumped up and ran outta there, thinking that was the wrong place to be. Then we found out that's their word for the female genitals. Wow. 1972 Jenkins *Semi-Tough* 23: T.J. wrote on a magazine that a little boy had given him, "Hope...you get yourself lots of cock when you grow up." 1975 S. P. Smith *Amer. Boys* 170: Going up to Frankfurt to see the town and try for a shot of cock. 1981 C. Nelson *Picked Bullets Up* 29: Unless one hails from the Deepest South where cock means pussy.

4. nonsense; poppycock. *Rare* in U.S.
*1945 in S.J. Baker *Australian Lang.* (ed. 2) 189: *Hot cock*, nonsense, boasting empty talk. 1966 Gass *Omensetter's Luck* 247: Told Furber of lot of cock, I bet—a lot of shit.

¶ In phrases:

¶ **down the cock** *Baseball.* directly into the strike zone.—usu. considered vulgar.
1969 Bouton *Ball Four* 271: *Down the cock* is the quintessence of the hitting zone. 1978 in Lyle & Golenbock *Bronx Zoo* 65: I tell you, if I had been pitching against them and it was extra innings, I'd have thrown the ball right down the cock...just so we could get the hell out of here.

¶ **drop your cocks and grab your socks!** *Naut. & Mil.* wake up! (addressed to sleepers in a forecastle or barracks).—usu. considered vulgar.
[1922 *Amer. Leg. Wkly.* (July 28) 27: Hit the deck you sailors! Rise and shine, you gobs! Lift your block and grab a sock!] 1942 H. Miller *Roofs of Paris* 7: Drop your cocks and grab your socks. 1952 Uris *Battle Cry* 456 [ref. to 1943]: Hit the deck, drop your cocks and grab your socks. Half the day gone and not a drop of work done. 1958 Cooley *Run for Home* 52 [ref. to *ca*1920's]: He delighted in turning out the first watch each morning by coming into the fo'c'sle with the top of a pot, banging it loudly and hollering the traditional mustering call: "Let go your cock and grab a sock!" [1961 Coon *Front* 175: Drop 'em and grab 'em.] 1961 J. Jones *Thin Red Line* 41 [ref. to WWII]: All right! Off and on!...Drop your cocks and grab your socks! 1962 Kesey *Cuckoo's Nest* 192: Hit the deck. Drop your cocks and grab your socks....Outa the sack and into the sea. 1970 Ponicsan *Last Detail* 101: "Now, reveille, reveille!" he shouts. "Drop your cocks and grab your socks!" 1978 C. Miller *Animal House* 18: Everybody up!...Drop your cocks and grab your socks! Move it, move it, move it! 1983 Ehrhart *VN-Perkasie* 215: Drop your cocks and pull up your socks, boys. 1991 J.T. Ward *Dear Mom* 7: Reveille,

reveille, reveille! Drop your cocks and grab your socks!

¶ **get the cock** *Mil.* to be mistreated, victimized, or ruined.—usu. considered vulgar. Also vars.

1957–62 Higginbotham *Folklore of U.S.M.C.* 24: You've had the cock, buster. **1970** Ponicsan *Last Detail* 28: Well, they sure put the cock to you. *Ibid.* 144: Yeah, well they court-martialed the old man and put the cock to him. Negligent, der'liction of duty and like that. **1972** Ponicsan *Cinderella Liberty* 119: I don't think they'll put the cock to me once I explain the circumstances. **1986** Univ. Tenn. instructor, age 36: To wind up *getting the cock* means to wind up screwed. That's a Navy expression. **1988** Dye *Outrage* 96: Lead APC has had the cock! Burning like a bitch.

¶ **keep (one's) cock up** to remain cheerful and optimistic.—usu. considered vulgar. Cf. sim. phr. at PECKER.

1970 E. Thompson *Garden of Sand* 332: Keep your cock up, pardner.

¶ **(one's) cock is on the block** (of a man) to be close to defeat, failure, or collapse.—usu. considered vulgar.

1972 in Bernstein & Woodward *President's Men* 152: Our cocks are on the chopping block now. **1978** Truscott *Dress Gray* 375: We got his cock on the block, mister.

¶ **pull (someone's) cock** to hoax, fool or tease (a man); pull (someone's) leg.—usu. considered vulgar.

1938 in P. Smith *Letter from Father* 417: Whether she was "pulling my cock" or not I do not know.

¶ **step on** [or **trip over**] **(one's) cock** (of a man) to blunder seriously.—usu. considered vulgar. Cf. sim. phrs. at PRICK.

1974 Stone *Dog Soldiers* 277: That shot was some nark tripping over his cock. **1977** Torres *Q & A* 18: One of these days he'll step on his cock. Don't be there. **1980** *Oui* (Aug.) 50: John's gonna step on his cock if he ain't careful. It's a jungle out there. **1981** *Nat. Lampoon* (Aug.) 53: Mozart...was very self-destructive...He was a schmuck who stepped on his own cock. He had nobody else to blame.

cock *adj.* **1.** pornographic; erotic; FUCK, *adj.*—used prenominally.—usu. considered vulgar.

*ca***1964** K. Cook *Other Capri* 127 [ref. to WWII]: [Europa and] the bull....I've heard a lot of cock stories, but that one —. **1968** Lockridge *Hartspring* 98: I knew then why...cockbooks like *Playboy* always manage to hide something important. **1975** S.P. Smith *Amer. Boys* 246 [ref. to 1960's]: That cat put away some cock books. Some of 'em pretty good too. *Ibid.* 250: I found out that he's been reading cock books at division all the time. **1978** J. Webb *Fields of Fire* 124 [ref. to 1969]: And I don't want all these magazines and cock books just laying around. **1982** Del Vecchio *13th Valley* 43: Now you wanta hear a cock story...Let me tell you bout the tattooed lady. **1983** S. Wright *Meditations* 85: Hometown newspapers, cock books, stale food,... obscene...calendars.

2. *Stu.* (see quots.).—usu. considered vulgar.

1968–70 *Current Slang* III & IV 28: *Cock*, adj. Attractive; "cool"; desirable.—College males, South Dakota. **1971** Dahlskog *Dict.* 14: *Cock*...a. *Vulgar.* Impressive; very big or good, as: a *cock* sports car.

cock *v.* **1.** to copulate with (a woman).—usu. considered vulgar.

***a*1891** *F & H* II 136: *Cock*...To copulate. Usually employed by women in the passive sense: e.g., "to want cocking," or "to get cocked." **1941** in Legman *Limerick* 115: Never go off till you're cocked. **1962** Simmons *Powdered Eggs* 1: The hen gets cocked. **1967** Schmidt *Lexicon of Sex* 46: *Cock*...To give the female pudendum a dose of phallus erectus.

2. to strike hard, esp. on the head. Cf. COLDCOCK.

1923 *Chi. Dail. Trib.* (Oct. 2) 22: I'd sock him, knock him, cock him— poke him, choke him, croak him. **1960, 1968** in *DARE*. **1971** *Playboy* (May) 78: So I pick up this pick handle and I yell, "Hey!" and cock him across the head. **1986** P. Markle *Youngblood* (film): Yeah, he cocked me.

3. *USAF.* to ready (a combat aircraft) for takeoff. Cf. COCKED, *adj.*, 2.

1985 Boyne & Thompson *Wild Blue* 261: The crews were...preflighting the airplanes, "cocking" them for instant take-off.

cock-a-dandy *n.* a sweetheart.

1767 "A. Barton" *Disappointment* 103: I t'ink she lobes [*sic*] me, an she wouldn't call me her Coony and her cock-a-dandy.

cockadau *v. Mil. in Vietnam.* [< Vietnamese] to kill.

1987 "J. Hawkins" *Tunnel Warriors* 112: "How many VC *you* kill?"..."Hell, I ain't *cocka-dau'd* a single Victor Charlie, baby." **1968– 90** Linderer *Eyes of Eagle* 11: VC numba ten. Trow grenades in bus. Cockadau (kill) beaucoup GI. *Ibid.* 222: Cockadau—Vietnamese slang

derivative meaning "kill."

cock-a-doodle-doo *n.* a self-important person; a boss.

1922 Rollins *Cowboy* 165: The [ranch] foreman...sometimes was referred to as the "cock-a-doodle-doo."

cockalize *v. Juve.* **1.** (see 1975 quot.).

1936 Kingsley *Dead End* 689: Let's cockalize him! **1975** Legman *No Laughing Matter* 111: The boy's penis is also sometimes struck with a knotted handkerchief, or smeared with paint, or is urinated upon by one or all of the other boys, under the name of "cockalizing"... him....The humiliating intention of such forms of "cockalizing" is perfectly evident.

2. to drub; destroy.

1967 G. Green *To Brooklyn* 38 [ref. to 1930's]: Ya crazy or somethin'? They'll cockalize ya!

cockamamie *n.* **1.** a crazy or ridiculous person.

1936 Kingsley *Dead End* 725: Haf an hour wid at cockamamee yuh'd be dead! **1944** Kapelner *Lonely Boy Blues* 6: A terrible curse on that cockamamee, Emily Post and her goddamn Bible on Formal Introductions. **1967** G. Green *To Brooklyn* 177 [ref. to 1930's]: *He's* stupid!...Look at his *teacher!* A coupla cockamamies. **1979** Oleg Cassini, in *St. Louis Post-Dispatch* (Oct. 17) 2H: Those cockamamies cover the models with unwearable stuff.

2. a crazy situation; foolish nonsense.

[**1956** Shelley Winters, in *N.Y. Times* (Apr. 29) II X 3: "Most of the pictures I made in the seven years I was a Hollywood Star...were like cockamamies." (This word, translated from the Brooklynese, is the authorized pronunciation for decalcomania. Anyone there who calls a cockamamie a decalcomania is stared at.)] **1963** *Car-54* (NBC-TV): What are you tryin' to do? You're gonna start a cockamamie here! **1969** *Harper's*, in *BDNE3*: Arlen characterized the drama as "a ninety-minute uninterrupted cliché...the most asinine and inept piece of cockamamie that I'd seen all year."

cockamamie *adj.* ridiculous or absurd; (in 1941 quot.) second-rate; inferior.

1941 Lardner & Kanin *Woman of the Year* (film): Don't give 'em none of that cockamamie bar stock, you hear? **1950** *New Yorker* (Oct. 7) 33: They're all strickly [*sic*] from hunger, all cockamamie outfits. ***1960** in *OEDS*. **1961** Rosten *Capt. Newman, M.D.* 80 [ref. to *ca*1940's]: He got into the ward with some cockamamy story Hammerhead fell for. **1968** W. Anderson *Gooney Bird* 71: As a result we've got the goddamndest, screwiest, cockamamie war you ever heard of. **1968** P. Roth *Portnoy* 211: Some cockamaimy story he is making up for the fun of it. **1971** *Interns* (CBS-TV): I had you pegged as a good intern, conscientious, bright—then you come up with a cockamamy story like "you don't remember." **1971** *Odd Couple* (ABC-TV): I'm not going to say anything about your cockamamie costume. **1980** Ciardi *Browser's Dict.* 82: *Cockamamie.* Cheap. Ridiculous. Unbelievable. *He gave me some cockamamie story.* **1982** Knoxville, Tenn., woman, age *ca*60: Now they got it all cockamamie and confused and turned around and you don't know what. **1982** *Daily Beacon* (Univ. Tenn.) (May 6) 2: The new flock of cockamamie schemes to shoot down incoming warheads with...laser beams in outer space. **1983** *Batman* (Apr.) 11: I...tried to put her off with some cockamamie story. **1992** *Crossfire* (CNN-TV) (July 18): I thought it was a cockamamie idea.

cock-and-hen *adj.* admitting both men and women.—used prenominally.

***1819** [T. Moore] *Tom Crib* 78: A Masquerade, or *Fancy* Ball, given lately at one of the most fashionable Cock-and-Hen Clubs in St. Giles's. ***1828** in *F & H* II 139: Introduced him to one of the *cock-and-hen* houses near Drury Lane Theatre well primed with wine. **1859** Matsell *Vocab.* 19: *Cock And Hen Club.* A place frequented by thieves of both sexes.

cockbite *n.* a despicable or contemptible person.—usu. considered vulgar.

1970 Landy *Underground Dict.* 53: *Cock bite*...Disagreeable female; bitch. **1976** Kalamazoo, Mich., man, age 27: About 1962 or '63 I had a friend from Tennessee who always called people he didn't like "cock-bites." **1988** *Lame Monkey* (Univ. Tenn.) (Mar. 21) 8: Belligerent cockbite SOB. Doesn't belong to the human race.

cockblock *v.* to thwart the sexual advances of (a third person). Hence **cockblocker**. Also as *n.*

1971 N.Y.U. student: A *cockblocker* is someone who tries to get between you and your girlfriend. He tries to take her away from you. You say, "That cockblocker!" I just heard it recently. **1967–80** Folb *Runnin' Lines* 139: Like somebody wanna do they thing and neither one o' you gonna give up....So you both jus' gonna set dere and cock block and neither one o' you gonna get nothin'. *Ibid.* 139: Sometimes the cock block is more overtly disruptive. *Ibid.* 232: Cock block Interrupt, sabotage, or otherwise interfere with another's advances toward a member of the opposite sex (used mainly by males). **1991** Eble *Campus Slang* (Fall) 2: I was talking to Jenny, and James cockblocked me by calling her to him.

cockbook see s.v. COCK, *adj.*

cockcited *adj.* excited.—usu. considered vulgar.
    1971 Faust *Willy Remembers* 151: "Jesus," I said, patting the air, "don't get so cockcited." She looked briefly at me, then back to the window.

cock collar *n. Black E.* CUNT COLLAR.—usu. considered vulgar.
    1978 W. Brown *Tragic Magic* 13: I considered what it would be like to fuck all the women I knew. By the time I reached my block my cock collar had grown to the size of a turtleneck sweater.

cock-diesel *adj.* (of a man) muscular; (*hence*) tough; aggressive. [The 1988 quot. is probably in error.]
    1988 Eble *Campus Slang* (Fall): Cog-D—muscular, solid: The boy is cog-d." (stated with approving tone of voice) D = diesel. **1991** *Source* (Oct.) 18: I had listened to NWA all week and was feeling cock diesel. **1993** *N.Y. Observer* (June 28) 11: In street terms "cock-diesel" means well-built....We never thought the term "cock-diesel" was offensive. **1993** *Village Voice* (N.Y.C.) (June 29) 18: The wannabe cock-diesel William "Don't Call Me Billy" Baldwin.

cocked *adj.* **1.** drunk.
    1737 *Penna. Gazette* (Jan. 6) 1: He's in his Cups...Non Compos...Cock'd...Cut. **1837** Strong *Diary* I 59: Magnificently drunk...pugnaciously cocked, fought everyone, swore like a trooper....Walsh was philanthropically cocked...running over with the milk of human kindness. **1840** *Spirit of Times* (Sept. 26) 360: The Squire's cocked as a musket. **1854** in Dorson *Long Bow* 86: He wasn't *very* drunk, but *pooty* drunk....Half-cocked. **1927** *New Republic* (Mar 9.) 71: Half screwed, half cocked, half shot, half seas over. **1928** Carr *Rampant Age* 11: Big fellows who smoked and had hot dates and even got cocked on corn liquor. *Ibid.* 25: We could all get cockeder'n hell. **1929** *Our Army* (Nov.) 15: It was a custom, then, to get cocked to the eyebrows every payday. **1935** O'Hara *Dr.'s Son* 128: Paddy wouldn'ta moved. Not Paddy when he's cocked. **1968** Baker et al. *CUSS* 98: Cocked. Drunk. **1965–70** in *DARE*: Half-cocked...Cocked...Cocked as a log...Cocked to the gills. **1979** Pennsylvania man, age 32: He was so cocked he couldn't even sit straight. **1982** Univ. Tenn. grad. student: Up around Binghamton [N.Y.] I used to hear the word *cocked*, meaning drunk, almost every day. But I can't say I've heard it anywhere else.
    2. *USAF.* (of a combat aircraft) ready for takeoff; on fifteen-minute alert.
    1955 Scott *Look of Eagle* 174: The ChiNat jet man would stay where he was—cocked and ready. **1961** Barr & Howard *Combat Missileman* 25: Many more of the jet bombers are "cocked" on runways on a 15-minute alert. **1967** D. Robinson *B-58* 54: Their aircraft standing "cocked" and ready, weapon pods slung beneath. **1975** in Higham & Siddall *Combat Aircraft* 30: The above procedures were followed for routine training flights but were altered drastically when the aircraft was "cocked" on alert. **1983** M. Skinner *USAFE* 7: The...F-15s are kept "cocked"—ready to fly and fight at any moment.
    ¶ In phrase:
    ¶ **cocked and locked** *Mil.* ready for action.
    1983 Beckwith & Knox *Delta Force* 259: By early Saturday night, Delta was cocked and locked. **1984–88** Hackworth & Sherman *About Face* 234: He said the battalion was cocked, locked, and ready to go. **1989** *Newsweek* (Oct. 2) 15: You've got to be cocked, locked and ready to rock. That means clean living.

cocked hat *n. Naut.* a triangular spot formed by a plotting error on a nautical chart.
    1961 Burgess *Dict. Sailing* 55: *Cocked hat.* The small triangular position indicated on a chart by three positional lines that should meet at one spot but do not quite do so.
    ¶ In phrase:
    ¶ **knock into a cocked hat** to trounce, injure, ruin, confound, etc. Now *colloq.*
    1833 in *OEDS*. **1842** in Jackson *Early Songs of Uncle Sam* 64: The coach it got upside quite flat...And knocked into a cocked hat/Was my sweet Betsey Baker. **1842** *Crockett Almanac* 18: She has knocked me into a cocked hat with those black eyes of hers. **1843** Field *Pokerville* 62: The Great Small Affair banquet was essentially knocked into a cocked-hat. **1848** Hartman *Own Jour.* 26: Our whole calculation is knocked into a

"cocked hat." **1884** Bruell *Sea Memories* 41: The target...had been "knocked into a cocked hat" the first fire. **1898** Bellamy *Blindman's World* 161: For Goethe to have married then would have knocked his art-life into a cocked hat. **1899** Willard *Tramping* 370: Red...knocked a policeman into a cocked hat. **1960** N.Y.C. woman, age 72: That knocked his plans into a cocked hat.

cocked up *adj.* cocky.
    1940 Zinberg *Walk Hard* 146: Don't be too cocked up either because a front runner isn't worth a....

cocker *n.* **1.** [COCK, *n.* + *-er*, strongly infl. by Yid *alte kakker*; cf. A.K.] a man.—usu. constr. with *old.*—used derisively.
    1946 I. Shulman *Amboy Dukes* 102: Them other suits you picked out for me are for old kockers. **1949** Bezzerides *Thieves' Market* 138: Even...that old cocker with the rooster-look stiffening his face at the sight of the girl. **1964–66** Kirstein *Rhymes* 85: Why can't the little cocker scram? **1969** Tynan *Oh! Calcutta* 131: So long, you old cocker. **1974** Charyn *Blue Eyes* 68: Maybe eight, nine at night you'll see the old cockers with boutonnières. **1976** Price *Bloodbrothers* 155: You believe this old cocker?
    2. (used as a term of abuse).
    *ca*1953 Hughes *Lodge* 196: "You rotten bitch! You lousy cocker!" I'm screaming at her. **1981** *Nat. Lampoon* (Aug.) 15: Actually, the broads weren't bad for a bunch of old cockers. They got more energy than most of the young ones.

cockeyed *adj. & adv.* **1.** drunk. Also **cockeyed drunk.**
    1737 *Penna. Gazette* (Jan. 6) 1: [syn. for *drunk*] He's Cock-Ey'd. **1927** Benchley *Early Worm* 160: It is the day of the bull fight in Madrid. Everyone is cock-eyed. **1927** Hemingway *Men Without Women* 207: The three Roman soldiers are a little cock-eyed. **1931** Hellinger *Moon* 279: He...opened a bottle of brandy. When dawn came he was cock-eyed. **1933** Halper *Union Square* 15: You've got to get cock-eyed every once in a while. **1942** Epstein & Epstein *Male Animal* (film): How did you guys get so cockeyed? **1942** "E. Queen" *Calamity Town* 58: He's settin' in my back room right now, cockeyed...I mean drunk. **1967** Terkel *Div. St.: America* 12: When I get blue and disgusted, I go get me some beer and get cockeyed drunk, stay at home.
    2.a. askew; awry; (*hence*, in 1931 quot.) unconscious.
    1918 in Truman *Ltrs. Home* 50: That little cockeyed cap stuck over one ear. **1931** D. Runyon, in *Collier's* (Apr. 25) 7: Izzy Cheesecake taps him on the noggin with the butt of a forty-five, and knocks him cock-eyed. **1936** Cain *Indemnity* 365: It was built cock-eyed. The garage was under the house, the first floor was over that, and the rest of it was spilled up the hill any way they could get it in. **1942** E.S. Gardner *Drowning Duck* 63: Either you're lying to me, or everything is cockeyed. *a*1988 D. Smith *Firefighters* 180: I had a minor shoulder bruise from landing cockeyed.
    b. crazy; irrational; (*hence*) wrong.
    1918 in Truman *Dear Bess* 249: I can't waste my time on a bunch of cockeyed lieutenants that are not professionals. **1928** Delmar *Bad Girl* 29: "I thought you'd like to go, too." "You thought cock-eyed." **1928** Dahlberg *Bottom Dogs* 96: Shrimp was thinking how they could get into that washroom after those cock-eyed graders had locked themselves in. **1935** in H. Gray *Arf* (unp.): I told you this is a cockeyed business, Annie. **1936** McCarty & Johnson *Great Guy* (film): I'd say you were cockeyed. He's as honest as the day is long. **1944** Sherrod *Tarawa* 2: War correspondents lived such interesting, cockeyed lives. **1970** in P. Heller *In This Corner* 28: Bob Edgren's judgment of him was cockeyed. *a*1988 Poyer *Med* 384: Just plain cockeyed luck. **1991** "R. Brown" & R. Angus *A.K.A. Narc* 112: In a cockeyed kinda way it all fits.
    3. confounded; damned.—in phr. **I'll tell the cockeyed world!** most certainly!
    1919 in Carey *Mlle. From Armentières* I (unp.): The M.P.'s won the cockeyed war. **1922** in Cornebise *Amaroc News* 62: By being so cockeyed sure of itself. **1922–24** McIntyre *White Light Nights* 190: I'll tell the cock-eyed the [sic] world he does. **1925** Heyward *Porgy* 404: Dem's de same cock-eye bones whut clean de gang out las' week. **1928** in Hemingway *Sel. Letters* 283: It seemed Swell—cockeyed wonderful. **1931** Adamic *Laughing* 57: Say, you're some fighter, Steve. I tell the cock-eyed world! **1931** Dos Passos *1919* 304: It all hit him cockeyed funny. **1935** Wolfe *Time & River* 117: Is it cold! I'll tell the cockeyed wuhld! **1936** in N. Cohen *Long Steel Rail* 398: I've been around this cockeyed world a dozen times or more. **1938** Wolfe *Web & Rock* 457: You bet your cockeyed life that's what's worrying me! **1945** Dos Passos *Tour* 335: I'd like to see us show the cockeyed world. **1962** Shepard *Press Passes* 44: We both knew cockeyed well there was a little more to it than that.... **1963** Gant *Queen St.* 7: But not half light enough, I'll tell

the cockeyed world. **1966–80** McAleer & Dickson *Unit Pride* 337: Not that I give a cockeyed fuck.

¶ In phrase:

¶ **look cockeyed** to look with a squinting or hostile glance. [***1821** Byron, in *OED* II 572: A merry, cock-eyed, curious looking sprite.] [***1863** in *OED* II 572: Cock-eyed Tom.] [***1891** *F & H* II 141: *Cock-Eyed*…(common).—squinting.] *a***1904–11** Phillips *Susan Lenox* I 149: I'll knock anybody down that looks cockeyed at you. **1934** H. Roth *Call It Sleep* 104: W'y, I hardly looked at 'im cock-eyed! **1956** N.Y.C. man, age *ca*70: If you looked cockeyed [the teacher] would smack you with a ruler.

cockface *n.* (used as a term of abuse).—usu considered vulgar.
1969 graffito in N.Y. Public Library: You cockface. **1981** Hathaway *World of Hurt* 174: Tell cock-face here to get some mortar fire into those trees.

cockhead *n.* FUCKHEAD.—usu. considered vulgar.
1972 Hannah *Geronimo Rex* 255: I wonder if that cockhead remembers me.

cock-high *adj.* Baseball. (see quot.).—usu. considered vulgar.
1983 L. Frank *Hardball* 91: The [batter's] description of a pitch in the most desirable spot of the strike zone (at about the height of the waist)…[is] "cock high."

cockhound *n.* Esp. *So. & West.* a lecher.—usu. considered vulgar.
1947 Mailer *Naked & Dead* 160: You're jus', jus' an old *cock-hound*, Wilson. You're the goddamnedest ole lecher. **1947–53** W. Guthrie *Seeds* 99: Whore-time gold…three-way gold….cock-hound gold. **1965** Linakis *In Spring* 210: He'd tell you things like George Washington was a cocksman, and when Johnny said, "What's that?" I said "Cockhound." **1960–69** Runkel *Law* 139: That was a breeding farm for every cockhound in town. **1969** Crumley *Count Cadence* 119: The first guy, a real cockhound lover boy, couldn't get a hard-on. **1971** in Sanchez *Word Sorcerers* 37: The Avenue was jumpin', a drunk's delight and a cock-hound's carnival. **1977** L. Gordon *Hype* 243: He's a cockhound and he might just want to get into your pants. **1984** Sample *Racehoss* 50: He was a cock-hound from way back.

cock-knocker *n.* a contemptible fellow.—usu. considered vulgar.
1959 Morrill *Dark Sea* 73 [ref. to WWII]: I'll be a cock-knocker! **1962** Dougherty *Commissioner* 22: I'm goin' to kill that cacknacker. I'm goin' to kill him. *Ibid.* 255: Every precautionary measure will be taken, Commissioner, but this cacknacker will probably play for keeps. **1974** Murray *Train Whistle Guitar* 154: They say you ain't nothing but some little old granny-dodging cock knocker. **1978** S. King *Stand* 170: Shut up, cock-knocker! **1983** S. King *Christine* 329: Let's grease the little cock-knockers, kid, what do you say?

cock-knocking *adj.* damned.—usu. considered vulgar.
1980 Gould *Ft. Apache* 169: He's takin' the risks, ain't he! He don't have no cock-knockin' Civil Service job like you do.

cockles *n.pl.* ¶ In phrase: **cry cockles** to be executed by hanging. Now *hist.*
1977 Coover *Public Burning* 334: We hadn't even got around to makin' them Jap warlords cry cockles.

cock-locker *n.* the vagina.—usu. considered vulgar. Cf. SHOT-LOCKER, SNOT-LOCKER.
1987 *Nat. Lampoon* (Oct.) 21: You got a wife…[with] a hungry cock-locker that's clean as a whistle.

cockpit *n.* the vagina.—usu. considered vulgar. *Joc.*
*1891 *F & H* II 138: The female *pudendum*:…*cock-pit.* **1941** in Legman *Limerick* 47: There was a young harlot named Schwartz/Whose cockpit was studded with warts. **1969** Searls *Hero Ship* 140: "How come you ain't on a carrier? Can't you climb into them cockpits no more?" "I can get into any cock pit you can," Horseman said. "Including your old lady." **1981** *Penthouse* (Apr.) 26: My face worked its way toward her…cockpit.

cockroach *n.* Navy. (see quot.).
1847 Downey *Cruise* 20: They were sure to have a certain dryness…seize from meat, which nothing but a "Cockroach" (the cant name for a Gin Toddy) could be found to allay.

cock-rot *n.* venereal disease.—usu. considered vulgar.
1983 R.C. Mason *Chickenhawk* 117 [ref. to 1960's]: Rumors of the dreaded Vietnamese cock-rot came to mind. **1984–87** Ferrandino *Firefight* 146: At least we won't have to worry about catching cockrot. **1989**

R. Miller *Profane Men* 88: Cock rot [and] immersion foot.

cock-shop *n.* Logging. a lumber-camp office.
1942 *AS* (Dec.) 221: *Cock Shop.* The camp office. **1956** Sorden & Ebert *Logger's* 9 [ref. to *a*1925]: *Cock-shop*, camp office. **1975** Gould *ME Lingo* 54.

cocksman /ˈkɑksmən/ *n.* a sexually promiscuous man; STUD.—usu. considered vulgar.
*a***1896** E. Field, in *Immortalia* 9: It made us cocksmen fairly sick. **1916** Cary *Venery* I 48: *Cocksman*—A whoremonger. **1931** Dos Passos *1919* 11: Research proves R. L. S. to have been a great cocksman. **1951** Kerouac *Cody* 57: He was a big drinker, big fighter,… big cocksman. **1958** Cooley *Run for Home* 272 [ref. to *ca*1925]: Warndahl, either you're the greatest cocksman in the world—which I doubt—or you're the sickest—which I think! **1963** T.I. Rubin *Sweet Daddy* 127: A chick knows a guy wants to feel like a big coxman. **1970** Wakefield *Going All the Way* 26: Gunner was known throughout the town as a great cocksman. **1976** Arble *Long Tunnel* 70: Kurtz…had a reputation as a cocksman when I was young. **1979** C. Martin *Catullus* 14: May she have…pleasure from her cocksmen. **1991** J. Cheever, in *New Yorker* (Jan. 28) 56 [ref. to 1960's]: She's left her husband, and had, I guess, several affairs with celebrated cocksmen. **1992** Jernigan *Tin Can Man* 68: We also had people who were real smart about girls; we called them "cocksmen."

cocksmith *n.* COCKSMAN.—usu. considered vulgar.
1959 W. Miller *Cool World* 73: "Maybe you right." Cowboy say. He standin in the door comin back from Lu Ann. Cowboy a cocksmith. **1969** Cray *Erotic Muse* 9: "The Tinker" is a cocksmith's delight. **1976** *Nat. Lampoon* (July) 98: You guys think you got a way with women?…You think you're real cocksmiths?

cock-stand *n.* an erection of the penis.—usu. considered vulgar.
*1866 *Romance of Lust* (passim). ***1891** *F & H* II 144: *Cock-Stand*…An erection of the *penis*. **1938** "Justinian" *Amer. Sexualis* 17: *Cock-stand*, an erection, is obsolescent.

cocksuck *n.* **1.** an act of fellatio.—usu. considered vulgar.
1940 Del Torto: Yours for a good cock suck. **1981** *Nat. Lampoon* (June) 50: You've *earned* a good cock suck.

2. a despicable person; COCKSUCKER.—usu. considered vulgar.
1969 *Esquire* (Oct.) 120: Hey, c…suck, you just told me to turn it off. **1983** S. Wright *Meditations* 84: You're…a real cocksuck. **1987** R. Miller *Slob* 256: He boogies. That's why we never saw the cocksuck.

cocksucker *n.* **1.a.** a person who performs fellatio.—often used contemptuously.—usu. considered vulgar.
*a1891 *F & H* II: *Cocksucker.* A feliatrix. **1916** Cary *Venery* I 348: *Cock Sucker*—A feliatrix. Said of either sex. **1918** Lind *Androgyne* 170 [ref. to 1890's]: He is a c—. I found him down on 26th Street wid this young feller. **1930** J.T. Farrell *Guillotine Party* 253: I'm a c…. **1934** "J.M. Hall" *Anecdota* 67: He called me an old whore and a cocksucker. **1942** H. Miller *Roofs of Paris* 131: She's a cocksucker if I ever met one. **1946** M. Cowley, in Jay *Burke-Cowley Corres.* 273: I'm working on Whitman, the old cocksucker. **1965** Friedman *Totempole* 274: Cocksuckers…fairies…fags. **1971** R. Polanski, in *Playboy* LV (Dec.) 110: But I know one women's lib leader who, friends tell me, is a great cock-sucker.

b. *So. & Black E.* a person who performs cunnilingus.—often used contemptuously.—usu. considered vulgar.
1942 McAtee *Supp. to Grant Co. Dial.* 3 [ref. to 1890's]: *Cock-sucker*, n. Could be of either sex operating on either sex. Also used as a term of reprobation not to be understood literally. **1969** Crumley *Count Cadence* 124: The term "cocksucker," certainly a vile implication across America, in the South refers not to fellatio but cunnilingus, linguistically. *a***1973–1987** F.M. Davis *Livin' the Blues* 36 [ref. to Kansas, *ca*1920]: A cocksucker engaged in cunnilingus.

2.a. (used as a contemptuous epithet, usu. for a man); SON OF A BITCH.—usu. considered vulgar.
1918 in Dos Passos *14th Chronicle* 219: Muttered oaths and shouted imprecations—God-damned bastards—cocksuckers every one of them—were sincere. **1920** in Sandburg *Letters* 183: In a mobbing, the event reaches a point where all rationale is gone; such a term as "anarchist" or "traitor" or "Boche" or "Englander Schwein" disappears and they babble hysterically only one or two epithets, in our language usually a tenor of "Son of a Bitch" with a bass of "Cocksucker." **1927** [Fliesler] *Anecdota* 6: "Who called my picollo player a cock-sucker?" he demanded. A voice in the rear of the theatre yelled back, "Who called that cock-sucker a picollo player?" **1928** E. Hemingway, in M. Reynolds *First War* 63: So do you, you cocksucker. **1931** Dos Passos *1919*

409: Atten'SHUN suck in your gut you c—r wipe that smile off your face eyes right. **1942** (quot. at **(1.b.)**, above). **1952** Bellow *Augie March* 221: Shut up!…C—sucker! **1955** Caprio *Sexual Behavior* 110: During this period he convinced himself that all women were c—ks—s as he put it. **1959** W. Burroughs *Naked Lunch* 82: Gold-bricking cocksuckers! **1967** Fiddle *Shooting Gallery* 155: Listen, you little cocksucker, don't be sayin' I lied. **1970** M. Thomas *Total Beast* 186: Snitching cocksucker! **1980** Kotzwinkle *Jack* 11: Hey! Hey, you little cocksuckers. **1984** D. Jenkins *Life Its Ownself* 44: You think you're a slick cocksucker. **b.** (with weakened force) rascal; scamp; fellow.—usu. considered vulgar. *Joc.*

1935 Read *Lexical Evidence* 43: *Cock sucker.* Frequently applied jocularly to children. **1938–39** Dos Passos *Young Man* 26: Come in, Toby, you old c—r…Jesus Christ, it does me good to see you.

3. an annoying or infuriating thing or place.—usu. considered vulgar.

1941 G. Legman, in Henry *Sex Variants* II 1161: *Cock-sucker*…is applied to inanimate objects in irritation at their innate perversity. **1965** Eastlake *Castle Keep* 100: I work my ass off to build these cocksuckers. **1971** *Playboy* (May) 176: It's an overloaded system…and the only reason the cocksucker works is because the guys who control it *make* it work. **1975** T. Berger *Sneaky People* 304: Today has been some cocksucker. **1977** Bunker *Animal Factory* 97: I'll be in this cocksucker [i.e., prison] a year! **1984** Jenkins *Life Its Ownself* 164: I don't know what pea-brain scheduled that cocksucker! **1989** Radford & Crowley *Drug Agent* 216: England's easy but Germany's a real cocksucker.

4. (used as an interj. of pain or angry surprise).—usu. considered vulgar.

1967 Taggart *Reunion* 140 [ref. to 1941]: "*Cock-sucker!*" said McGowan in pain. **1970** Woods *Killing Zone* 135: Cocksucker—hold up! That shit stings, man.

cocksucking *adj. & adv.* performing fellatio or cunnilingus; (*hence, usu.*) despicable; goddamned; FUCKING.—usu. considered vulgar.

ca1911 in Cray *Erotic Muse* (ed. 2) 113: A cocksucking son of a bitch. **1923** in Cummings *Letters* 99: Members…of the cocksucking leisure class. **1927** [Fliesler] *Anecdota* 19: That dirty son-of-a-bitch, that lousy cock-sucking bastard, that whoremaster fairy. **1931** Dos Passos *1919* 22: I want to get out of the c—g life and get a job that pays something. **1939** Bessie *Men in Battle* 144: The goddamn c…s… bastards….They killed all the good guys. **1963–64** Kesey *Great Notion* 128: *Cock*suckin', *ass*lickin', *fart*knockin', *shit*eatin' [bastard]. **1969** Cassill *Intro #2* 9: The cocksucking son of a bitch. **1970** in Jackson *Swim Like Me* 110: I'll make you jump over there and swim some cocksucken more. [*1972 "A. Burgess," in *N.Y. Times Mag.* (Oct. 28) 28: I have already had several abusive phone calls, telling me to eff off back to effing Russia, you effing corksacking limey effer.] **1972** Hannah *Geronimo Rex* 193: I want to crack your cocksucking bones. **1992** Mowry *Way Past Cool* 8: Been bustin my goddam ass all cocksuckin week.

cocktail *n.* **1.** *Trail Herding.* the final watch of the day or night. Often attrib. Now *hist.*

1891 in *DARE*: Half-past 2 and the boys are counting the minutes before calling the "cocktail guard" that relieves them. **1926** W. James *Smoky* 153: Four riders on "cocktail" (hours between the last meal of the day and the first night guard) got on their horses and rode to "relieve" the riders holding the herd. **1961** R. Adams *Old-Time Cowhand* 278: There were several periods of guard durin' the night, and "cocktail." **1965** D.G. Moore *Log of 20th C. Cowboy* 188: This was the cock tail guard for the old-time cattlemen.

2. *Narc.* the butt of a marijuana cigarette combined with a tobacco cigarette. Also as *v.*

1959 Gilbert *Vice Cop* 40: She clipped the holder to the cocktail and touched her lighter to it. **1960** R. Reisner *Jazz Titans* 152: *Cocktail:* to take a roach…and fit it into a regular cigarette so as to smoke it without burning your fingers. **1966** Bogner *7th Ave* 282: When they finished, he emptied some tobacco out of a cigarette and carefully fitted the remainder [of the marihuana cigarette] into it with a matchstick. "Cocktail?" he said. **1967** Rosevear *Pot* 158: *Cocktail:* The short butt of a marihuana cigarette inserted in the end of a regular cigarette for the purpose of consuming it. *Ibid.* 70: The cocktail method is one of the most popular means of consuming roaches. **1970** A. Young *Snakes* 66: Extinguishing the last of the joint…and twisting all three butts into the end of a regular cigarette from which tobacco had been removed. "Anyone for cocktails?"

3. a Molotov cocktail.

1968 K. Hunter *Soul Bros.* 205: How are the cocktails coming? **1970**

Wambaugh *Centurions* 328 [ref. to 1965]: A mob of fifty young Negroes appeared from nowhere and a cocktail had bounced off the door but failed to burst. **1976** Arble *Long Tunnel* 148: Then they threw them cocktails in there. **1977** *N.Y. Post* (July 23) 2: He could burn a whole block down by running on the roofs of the buildings tossing cocktails through the skylights.

cocktail *v.* **1.** see COCKTAIL, *n.*, **2.**

2. to work as a cocktail waitress.

1986 Stinson & Carabatsos *Heartbreak* 58: She's cocktailin' over at the Palace.

cocktease *v.* to act as a COCKTEASER; (*hence*) to tantalize cynically.—usu. considered vulgar.

*1957 in *OEDS.* **1972** *Nat. Lampoon* (June) 14: We Earth people have an ancient term—"cockteasing"—to describe her approach. **1975** Brownmiller *Against Our Will* 312: The popularity of the belief that a woman…"cock-teases" a man into rape. **1978** Selby *Requiem* 39: Ya rotten pricks, cockteasin me along with ya goddamn shows. **1993** *New Yorker* (Apr. 5) 80: They hardly ever went to bed with anybody…and they called each other late at night after dates and giggled. They cockteased.

cockteaser *n.* a woman who engages in provocative sexual behavior, esp. foreplay, with a man but will not engage in sexual intercourse or allow him to have an orgasm.—usu. considered vulgar. Also **cocktease.**

*1891 *F & H* II: *Cock-teaser,* or *Cock-chafer,*…A girl in the habit of permitting all familiarities but the last. **1934** "J.M. Hall" *Anecdota* 163: Boy to cock-teaser…: "Thanks for the ostrich party…all neck and no tail." **1942** H. Miller *Roofs of Paris* 52: Even if she is a cockteaser. **1943** in Legman *Limerick* 387: There was a cock-teaser named Jeanie. **1961** Baldwin *Another Country* 42: What are you, anyway—just a cock teaser? **1964** Faust *Steagle* 116: She twisted her head slowly toward him while Mendy croaked in his ear: *Cock tease, Hesh, cock tease.* **1965** Friedman *Totempole* 218: If there's one thing I can't stand, it's a cock-tease. **1967** Dibner *Admiral* 350: The sly conniving bitch. The cunning cockteaser. **1969** Pharr *Numbers* 286: Delilah looked into his eyes and read the hated epithet…"Cock-teaser." **1971** Rader *Govt. Inspected* 138: Playing cocktease to the basketeers. **1990** L.B. Rubin *Erotic Wars* 28: We had a name for those girls: cock-teasers.

cock wagon *n.* a flashy automobile meant to impress young women.—usu. considered vulgar.

1975 C.W. Smith *Country Music* 36: You see this fancy *cockwagon* of yours?

coco *n.* the head. Also **cocoa.**

*1828 in *OEDS:* He would give him a *pelt on the cocoa.* **1836** *Every Body's Album* I 93: Your cocoa's near a hammer—it may get cracked. **1837** Neal *Charcoal Sks.* 37: Your coco is very near a sledge hammer. If it isn't hard, it may get cracked. **1899** A. Lewis *Sandburrs* 11: She…boins all d'hair off her cocoa doin' it. **1901** Hobart *John Henry* 53: Does he have to rush around with a mop on his koko? **1904** Hobart *Jim Hickey* 70: Gee! Look at that crack on the coco. **1906** Ford *Shorty McCabe* 284: It had saved a lot of wear on his koko. **1910** *N.Y. Eve. Jour.* (Mar. 5) 9: It soaked McGraw a resounding whack full on the top of his cocoa. **1914** Ellis *Billy Sunday* 252: He soaked Goliath in the coco between the lamps. **1920** S. Lewis *Main St.* 150: I'm glad we have such dainty romances as "Right on the Coco" instead. **1923** W. Hall *It Ain't Gonna Rain No Mo'* (sheet music) 5: If your cocoa's cold/Put on your hat. **1928** Panzram *Killer* 35: I got a wallop alongside of the coco that floored me. **1933** D. Runyon, in *Collier's* 8: I personally tap him over the coco with a blackjack.

¶ In phrase:

¶ **screw (one's) coco** to leave in a hurry; *screw (one's) nut* s.v. NUT.

1899 A. Lewis *Sandburrs* 191: I only sees Bridgy onct [*sic*] after that, before she screws her cocoa.

coco *v.* to knock (on the head).

1927 *AS* II (May) 351: A falling limb cocoed him on the bean.

coconut *n.* **1.a.** the head.

1828 in H.L. Gates, Jr. *Sig. Monkey* 91: Wid club you *cocanut* we smash! ***1829** Marryat *Frank Mildmay* 203 [ref. to ca1810]: Thinks I to myself, "If ever I saw 'lodgings to let, unfurnished,' it is in that cocoa-nut, or pumpkin, or gourd of yours." **1834** Caruthers *Kentuck. in N.Y.* 66: I rather suspicion he thought a two year old colt's heel had got a taste of his cocoanut. **1838** *Crockett Almanac* (1839) 6: I give him a sogdolager over his coco nut. **1841** [Mercier] *Man-of-War* 137: You had better look sharp, old boy, or you may lose that woolly *cocoa-nut* of yours before you reach *Yankee-town*. **1854** Sleeper *Salt-Water Bubbles* 205: Felled by a blow on his cocoa-nut. **1881** Nye *Forty Liars* 151: I plead with my hard-hearted parent to prevent him from mashing the cocoa-nut of the original Smith. **1883** Hay *Bread-Winners* 232: If I was you, the first thing I did with that hammer, I'd crack Art Farnham's cocoa-nut. **1891** Maitland *Slang Dict.* 71: *Cocoa-nut*…the head. **1901** Irwin *Sonnets* (unp.): Oh! would I were the ice man for a space,/Then I might cool this red-hot cocoanut. **1957** Willingham *Strange One* (film): He's what the coconut doctors call a schizophrenic. **1962** T. Berger *Reinhart in Love* 151: That's what you just can't get through your coconut. **1980** F. Healey on *N.Y. Yankees Baseball* (Sept. 6) (WINS): It's like getting hit on the coconut with a fist. **1990** *Twin Peaks* (ABC-TV): "How's that coconut?" "Kinda tender."

b. *pl.* intelligence.

1931 D. Runyon, in *Collier's* (Apr. 25) 7: He is a smart guy at his own dodge, and everything else, and has plenty of coconuts.

2. a dollar; *(pl.)* money.

1929 *AS* III (Feb.) 254: *Coconuts, String of.* Money. **1929** *Sat. Eve. Post* (Oct. 12) 29: *Coconuts:* Money. **1929-31** D. Runyon *Guys & Dolls* 140: The Brain's ever-loving wife…has a society bug and needs plenty of coconuts at all times to keep her a going concern. **1930** *Amer. Merc.* (Dec.) 420: He shoots the bankroll on the brewery, the whole hundred thousand coconuts. **1933** Odets *Awake & Sing!* 60: Still jumping off the high buildings like flies—the big shots who lost all their cocoanuts. Pfft! **1943** J. Mitchell *McSorley's* 129: Anyway, he seen to it I had plenty of coconuts. **1944** Pyle *Brave Men* 204: I've got three thousand coco-nuts in the bank, and I'm going to get some education after the war and be a salesman.

3. *pl.* a woman's breasts.

1944 Kendall *Service Slang* 53: GI cocoanuts…brassieres. **1986** *Playboy* (Apr.) 20: Breasts…casabas…coconuts…[etc.]. **1993** N.J. man, age 26 (coll. J. Sheidlower): *Coconuts* for breasts is pretty common, but not as much as *melons*.

4. *Army.* a hand grenade.

1979 McGivern *Soldiers* 3 [ref. to WWII]: He had already booted Spinelli hard for rolling a rock at him and shouting, "Think fast! Live coconut!"

5. *Pol.* a Hispanic person who has adopted the values of white American society.—used derisively. Cf. APPLE, BANANA, OREO.

1980 *Mother Jones* (Dec.) 31: Blacks have their "oreos"; Hispanos have "coconuts" and so on. **1984** J. Wambaugh *Lines & Shadows* 29: And yet even this might be refuted by those people living south of the imaginary line who feel they are nothing like the northern "coconuts," who are brown on the outside but white within. **1989** *N.Y. Times Bk. Review* (July 9) 16: Huero Maldonado…ridicules him for selling out—for being "a coconut.…Brown on the outside, white on the inside."

coconut-dodger *n. Black E.* an African or South American black person.—used derisively.

1928 C. McKay *Banjo* 162: I'll slap the sass outa you, you mean little cocoanut-dodger.

cocum *adj.* [< Yid *chochem*] *Esp. Und.* clever; smart; (hence) proper. Also *adv.*

*1839 in *OEDS* I 565: *Cocum*, very cunning and sly. *To fight cocum*, to be wary. **1859** Matsell *Vocab.* 19: *Cocum.* Sly; wary. ***1861** in *F & H* II 146: No one was to get drunk, the governor said as how it wasn't *cokum*, and he wouldn't have it. **1867** *Nat. Police Gaz.* (Jan. 12) 3: The "fly cops" have something to learn when they are not "fly" to the "mug" of so "cocum" a "moll." ***ca1886** in *F & H* II 147: I once was a Member-for-Slocum young man…A know-pretty-well what-is-*kocum* young man.

cod *n.* [< OE *cod* 'a bag'] **1.a.** usu. *pl.* a testicle.—usu. considered vulgar. [In earlier S.E., 'the scrotum'.]

*1527 in *OEDS* II 581: Good for a mannes yarde or coddes. ***1632** in *OEDS*: The…cods of a man or beast, *couillon, testicule.* ***ca1684** in R. Thompson *Unfit for Modest Ears* 184: Quidling and Dandling their Codds. ***ca1775** *Frisky Songster* 34: He snatch'd at his cods. ***1785** Grose *Vulgar Tongue: Cods.* The scrotum. ***1788** R. Burns, in Seldes *Great Thoughts* 60: Every one, more or less, in the words of the old Scots Proverb, "Has his cods in a cloven stick, and must wyse them out the best way he can." ***ca1866** *Romance of Lust* 120: With one hand she tickled my cods. **ca1888** *Stag Party* 225: And gently takes up/Your cods in their bag. **1889** Barrère & Leland *Dict. Slang* I 262: *Cods* (common), the testicles. **1908** *DN* III 299: *Cod*…A testicle. **1938** "Justinian" *Amer. Sexualis* 17: *Cod. n.* The scrotum. Generally in the plural, *cods*, the testicles. **1947** Willingham *End As a Man* 97: Go shoot off Hitler's cods. **1961** in Cray

Erotic Muse 143: Hobo Bill was riding the rods/When ninety-nine cars rolled over his cods. **1971** *Blushes & Bellylaffs* 42: He shot both his wads,/His cash and his cods. **1974** E. Thompson *Tattoo* 162: She stepped aside, reaching out and cupping his cock and cods in her…hand. **1983** K. Weaver *Texas Crude* 74: I kicked him in the cods twice.

b. *pl.* courage; BALLS.—usu. considered vulgar.

1962-68 B. Jackson *In the Life* 209: You really want to let your hair down, but you just haven't got the cods (balls). **1970** M. Thomas *Total Beast* 200: I didn't think the motherfucker had the cods!

2. a fool. Cf. CODFISH.

*1698-99 "B.E." *Dict. Canting Crew: Cod*…a Fool. *A meer Cod*, a silly, shallow fellow. **1867** in Foner *Labor Songs* 109: He always makes himself a "cod." ***a1891** *F & H* II 147: *Cod*…A fool. ***1931** J. Hanley *Boy* 49: You watch. This dozy looking cod'll be put on. **1964** Gallant *Friendly Dead* 75: You're just as lucky as hell, you dumb cod.

3. the penis.—usu. considered vulgar.

*ca1775 *Frisky Songster* 25: She…was often delighted to play with his cod. ***ca1835-40** in Speaight *Bawdy Songs* 22: So he asked her, quite bold, if she didn't want *cod*. **ca1888** *Stag Party* 153: 'Twill be very odd,/But he'll find something better than nursing his —. **1902** "M. Twain" *Mammoth Cod:* The word "cod" is frequently used in ancient literature to signify penis, and I take it you use it in that sense. **1939** in *DARE: Cod*…penis. **1954** in Randolph & Legman *Blow Candle Out* 788: I have never heard an Ozarker use *cod* to mean penis. **1975** Oliver Springs, Tenn., man, age 27: Your cod is your dick, also known as your hog. Or your dog. I first heard it called a cod last year. Cods are your balls. **1976** graffiti, Univ. Tenn. library: A woman has a cock, a man has a cod. [In another hand:] You fool! A woman doesn't have a cock, a man does!! *a*1986 Muirhead *Those Who Fall* 37: She couldn't bear to let go of his goddamn great cod.

4. (see quot.).

1892 in *DARE: Cod:* a bit of deceit, as in, "He gave the teacher a cod."

cod *v.* to trick or tease. Now *rare* in U.S.

1859 in C.A. Abbey *Before the Mast* 204: They are…"codded" as they come on deck. ***1865** in *F & H* II 147: Codding a Town Council. **1866** in W.H. Jackson *Diaries* 90: Their credulity is amusing. I sometimes feel like "codding" them. ***1873** Hotten *Slang Dict.* (ed. 4). *Cod*, to hoax, to take a "rise" out of one. **1878** *Funny Fatherland* 32: They "cod" us until we are entirely out of herring. **1883** Russell *Sailors' Lang.* 32: *Cod.*—To cod a man is to gull him. **1883-84** Whittaker *L. Locke* 179: He's a-coddin' yer. **1888** Nye & Riley *Railway Guide* 25: We managed to *use* him, though,—/Coddin' the gilley along the rout'. **1890** *JAF* III 311: Oh, you're just codding me! **1930** Raine *Valiant* 216: Spinnin' a yarn to cod the other fellow. **1932, 1941, 1950** in *DARE.*

code brown *n. Hosp.* (see quot.).

*a*1990 in *Maledicta* X 31: *Code Brown* copious, foul-smelling bowel movement deposited in an inappropriate place.

codfish *n.* a fool; PILL; COD, 2.

1776 in Meserve & Reardon *Satiric Comedies* 90: Did he not make cod-fish of them all at Boston! **1842** in R.B. Hayes *Diary* I 106: Ill calculated to enliven the spirits of the "codfish" of Kenyon.

codger *n.* [prob. var. of obs. *cadger*] a fellow; (usu., and now solely) an old man, esp. if odd or eccentric. Now *S.E.*

*1756 in *OED* II 583. ***1760** in *F & H* II 148: The old codger's gone, and has locked me up with his daughter. **1798** *Amer. Musical Misc.* 57: It set the old codger agog. **1819** Clopper *Bawlfredonia* 93: The old codger and his troops run to extinguish the flames. **1821** Wetmore *Pedlar* 5: I suppose the old cogger [*sic*] is not up yet. ***1830** in *EDD* I 691: The Sharperton codgers are cunnin'. **1842** in Jackson *Early Songs of Uncle Sam* 234: "No, no, my old codger," said Harry with speed, "I'm not to be caught by that gammon indeed." **1850** in Eliason *Tarheel Talk* 186: The State impannelled 12 old codjers/To try a man, with Fanny Rogers. **1889** Field *Western Verse* 2: A codger who has lived a life out West. **1904** *Life in Sing Sing* 246: *Codger*—A fellow. **1935** D.W. Maurer, in *AS* (Feb.) 14 [ref. to *a*1910]: *Codger.* One of the boys; a cove; a companion in crime. (Obs.) **1940** F. Hunt *Trail fr. Tex.* 147 [ref. to 1870's]: They're awful nice little codgers.

co-driver *Av.* copilot.

1963 E.M. Miller *Exile to Stars* 57: But I've always thought you career co-drivers ought to develop this technique.

codshead *n.* a fool; COD, 2.

*1566 in *OED2:* This coddes heade…This asse, doth wante his comon sence. ***1675** in Duffett *Burlesque Plays* 100: Alas poor Codshead. **1793** Brackenridge *Mod. Chiv.* 187: Many of the cod-heads…Who did not shew themselves so brave. *a*1815 Brackenridge *Mod. Chiv.* 777: Any cod-head may do that. *1886 in *OED2:* If he had not been what is called in familiar parlance a cod's-head-and-shoulders himself.

codswallop *n.* [orig. unkn.] nonsense; foolishness. *Rare* in U.S.
*1963 in *OED2:* Just branding a programme as "rubbish," "tripe," or—there are a lot of these—"codswallop," gives little indication of what moved the viewer to write. *1966 in *OED2:* All that stuff about mutual respect between police and criminal was a load of old codswallop. **1978** *Vancouver Sun* (Oct. 28) B1: It is, by the way, also a load of codswallop…that Vancouver ditched the ward system in the 1930s because of the fear of a left-wing takeover. **1982** Randi *Flim-Flam!* 215: But a number of qualifying truths were cunningly dropped among the codswallop. **1982** in Safire *Language Maven* 81: What we said [was] so much codswallop.

co-edna *n. Stu.* a coed. *Joc.*
1926 Hormel *Co-Ed* 18: "We've got some classy co-ednas over there."

coff *n.* coffee.
1884 in *AS* XX 70: Three up, coff.

coffee *n.* ¶ In phrases:
¶ —— **and a dime** [or **quarter**, etc.] **will get you a cup of coffee** ——is worthless or meaningless.
1957 McGivern *Against Tomorrow* 175: The medal…That and a dime buys a cup of coffee. **1960** Archibald *Jet Flier* 60: That medal and a dime got them a cup of coffee. **1964** Thompson & Rice *Every Diamond* 106: "Sportsmanship and ten cents will get you a cup of coffee," I scoffed. **1980** Univ. Tenn. grad. students: "He's having his diploma mounted and framed." "Tell him a Ph.D. and a quarter'll get him a cup of coffee." **1986** NYC woman, age *ca*50: My father used to say, "That and a nickel will get you a cup of coffee." He was saying it in the forties.
¶ **cool coffee** *Army.* to shirk or idle. See also COFFEE COOLER.
1902 Remington *John Ermine* 105: New faces appeared as came in from the hills to "cool coffee." **1925** Nason *Three Lights* 74 [ref. to 1918]: How do I know you men haven't been cooling coffee over in the wheat all day? This yarn sounds a little high.
¶ **grind coffee** to grind the hips in a manner suggestive of copulation.
1933 W. March *Co. K* 52 [ref. to 1918]: I walked over to her and put my hands on her thighs, and she came up to me with her hips and started to grind coffee. **1965** Trimble *Sex Words* 46: *Coffee grinder*…1. A Stripper…who grinds her hips and belly in a dance descriptive of Copulation. 2. A Prostitute or other adept sex partner who grinds her body stimulatingly during Intercourse.
¶ **grind (someone's) coffee** *Black E.* to copulate with (someone).
1928 in Oliver *Meaning of Blues* 148: He could grind my coffee, 'cause he has a brand new grind.
¶ **settle (someone's) coffee** to settle (someone's) hash.
1843 in Haliburton *Sam Slick* 177: Don't call me names…or I'll settle your coffee for you.

coffee-and *n.* **1.** a cheap meal consisting of coffee and cakes or rolls or doughnuts.
[**1869** "G. Ellington" *Women of N.Y.* 218: The "coffee-and-cake" saloons, always a peculiar institution of the metropolis, are largely patronized by the middling class of the *demi-monde.* They are cheap, and coffee-and-cake is a cheap dish.] **1901** in *OED2.* *ca*1912 in Kornbluh *Rebel Voices* 134: Count your pennies…and get your coffee an'. **1913** Brown *Broke* 29: I can get along without my "coffee and." **1922** N. Anderson *Hobo* 40: Old men who do not move around much will live a long time on "coffee-an'," which they can get at the average restaurant for a nickel. **1929–33** J.T. Farrell *Manhood* 323: They had coffee an' in the Greek restaurant. **1935** Odets *Waiting for Lefty* 8: I had "coffee and—" in a beanery. **1940** *AS* (Dec.) 450: *Coffee an', Coffee and.* Coffee and *sinkers* (doughnuts) or coffee and *snails* (cinnamon rolls). **1964** Selby *Last Exit* 26: He'll set us up to coffee an'. **1972** *U.S. News & W.R.* (Sept. 11) 9 [advt.]: She serves "coffee and" before her guests drive home, rather than the proverbial "one for the road."
2. a cheap eating place where COFFEE-AND is mainly served.
[**1940** *AS* (Dec.) 450: Cafés on the waterfront often have no other name or sign than *Coffee And.*] **1953** Paley *Rumble* 169: What the hell yuh think this is—a coffee an'!
3. just enough money to purchase COFFEE-AND; money for necessities.
1958 in *DAS* 113.

coffee-and *adj.* earning or providing only enough money for

COFFEE-AND; small-time; cheap.
1937 Reitman *Box-Car Bertha* 174: The girls called him a "coffee and" pimp, because Irene just gave him a dollar a day. **1946** Mezzrow & Wolfe *Really Blues* 29: That coffee-an' mac you got.

coffee-and-cake *adj.* Esp. *Und.* COFFEE-AND, *adj.*; small-time. Also **coffee-and-doughnut.**
[**1869** (quot. at COFFEE-AND, *n.*).] **1927** in Hammett *Knockover* 310: These coffee-and-doughnut guns [i.e., crooks] are going to rub Red out, and that won't get us anything. **1932** Berg *Prison Doctor* 103: They ain't got the brains to know you can knock off a big touch just as easy as a coffee-and-cake job. **1954–60** *DAS* 113: Coffee-and-cake-job (—joint, —layout, —place, —spot, *etc.*)

coffee-and-cakes *n.pl.* a small salary.
1925 *Collier's* (Sept. 19) 7: I'm never going to make my coffee and cakes on the weaknesses of my fellow clowns. [**1927** *Vanity Fair* (Nov.) 134: "Coffee and cake money" is small salary.] **1950** A. Lomax *Mr. Jelly Roll* x: 1938 found him playing for coffee and cakes in an obscure Washington nightspot.

coffee bag *n. Hobo.* a coat pocket.
1925 Mullin *Scholar Tramp* 188 [ref. to *ca*1912]: What he liked was "ridin' the cushions wid a ducat in yer coffee-bag"; that is, riding inside a coach with a ticket in one's coat pocket.

coffee-boiler *n. Army.* a straggler or shirker.
1864 Northrop *Chronicles* 74: Innocent liars tell…that Secretary Stanton has said that "none but dead beats and coffee boilers are taken prisoners, and the army is better off without them." **1872** *Overland Mo.* (Oct.) 331: Passing rapidly down among the lazy coffee-boilers. **1886** F. Wilkeson *Recoll.* 76: When I was well to the rear, I for the first and last time became a "coffee boiler." *ca*1890 Stearns *Co. K* 86 [ref. to 1862]: We commenced to meet those…who in a later period of the war were called "Bummers," "Coffee boilers," those who never under any circumstances or consideration would be found in a battle.

coffee brigade *n. Army.* a group of stragglers or shirkers.
1872 *Overland Mo.* (May) 400 [ref. to Civil War]: We laughed at the rage of the fellows we disturbed, for you know how we all despised the "coffee brigade."

coffee-cooler *n. Army.* a straggler or loafer; (*occ.*) a coward. Now *hist.*
1876 in *DA* 353. **1876** in J.M. Carroll *Camp Talk* 26: 3 "Coffee Coolers" are made Captains. *ca*1880 Bellard *Gone for a Soldier* 172 [ref. to Civil War]: We had to drive before us all stragglers who were resting in the woods (coffee coolers). **1886** Lummis *Ft. Bowie* 56: One coffee-cooler whom I watched gambling, had 15 rings on his left hand. **1887** Hinman *Si Klegg* 202 [ref. to Civil War]: It was…enough to prove to both himself and his comrades that he wouldn't be one of the "coffee coolers" when there was business on hand. **1892** Cox *5 Yrs. in Army* 36 [ref. to 1873]: One of the first visitors to our quarters was an old "coffee cooler," who managed to let us know that the Twenty-second Infantry boys, whom we had relieved, had employed him [an Indian] to chop wood and do their chores. **1898** Brooks *Strong Hearts* 27: Think me coffee-cooler (the Indian name for a coward). *Ibid.* 61: Red Cloud has turned coffee-cooler. **1906** M'Govern *Sarjint Larry* (gloss.): *Coffee-Cooler.*—A soldier or officer with a sinecure. **1909** Moss *Officers' Manual* 283: *Coffee-Cooler.*—One who seeks easy details away from troops; one who is always looking for an easy job. **1913** Meyers *10 Yrs. in the Ranks* 304 [ref. to Civil War]: Some of our stragglers, or "coffee coolers," as they were also called. **1918** O'Reilly *Roving & Raking* 67 [ref. to 1899]: We didn't want to be "coffee coolers" behind the lines. **1918** *Camp Meade Herald* (Feb. 1) 3: Some men in the army have easy jobs and very little to do. These men are called "coffee coolers." **1918** Griffin *Ballads of the Reg't* 6: He's watching out for "coffee coolers"—you, too. **1926** C.M. Russell *Trails* 142: Barrin' some old coffee-cooler mumblin' a prayer, or a pony clearin' his nostrils, these riders are joggin' along pretty near as noiseless as a band of ghosts. **1927** Liggett *AEF* 209: When I was a young lieutenant on the plains [*ca*1880] we still called them [shirkers] by their Civil War name: "coffee coolers," or "coffee boiler." **1927** Breddan *Under Fire* 72: A few coffee coolers broke the spirit and ambition of their betters. **1936** R. Adams *Cowboy Lingo* 201: Prospectors were sometimes called "coffee coolers." **1957** O'Connor *Co. Q* 67 [ref. to Civil War]: Get up on the tracks where you belong, you coffee-coolers! **1977** T. McCoy *Remembers* 38 [ref. to *ca*1910]: Staying in the vicinity of the mess wagon, staring…into a cup of hot coffee…qualified one for the derisive title of "coffee-cooler."

coffee-grinder *n.* **1.** *Mil.* a Gatling gun or machine gun. Now *hist.*

1898 *Chicago Record's War Stories* 112: "How do you like our coffee-grinder?" was the derisive inquiry shouted…when the Gatling gun section…unlimbered and turned a stream of bullets loose. **1935** Cobb *Paths of Glory* 59: Keep your fingers off that coffee grinder [machine gun] till we get out of the way. **1958** Freidel *Splendid Little War* 161 [ref. to 1898]: Against San Juan Hill the "coffee grinders" were as spectacularly successful as the artillery had been a failure. **1970** Dierks *Leap to Arms* 105 [ref. to 1898]: The physical effect of the eight-barreled "coffee grinders" was no less timely than the moral lift it gave the Americans.

2. a rough or unreliable engine; (*hence*) a vehicle, aircraft, etc., having such an engine.

1911-12 Ade *Knocking the Neighbors* 54: Whenever he ran up behind a Pewee Coffee-Grinder he went into the High and made the Cheap Machine look like a Fish. **1915** T.A. Dorgan, in Zwilling *TAD Lexicon* 28: I wouldnt care if I wuz hit by a good car but sh—What kind of a cofee-grinder was it? **1933** in Dos Passos *14th Chronicle* 431: Anxious to find out how much it costs to rent a Citröen or Peugeot or some little cheap coffeegrinder. **1944** *AAF* 368: *Coffee grinder.* aircraft engine. **1944** Mellor *Sank Same* 57: And no chance to glide to safety if your coffee-grinder conks out. **1956** Heflin *USAF Dict.* 123: *Coffee grinder.* Slang…A piston-type aircraft engine. **1958** in Loosbrock & Skinner *Wild Blue* 230: I can get a little altitude out of this coffee-grinder. **1971** Waters *Smugglers* 54: The patrons would wave at our old Coast Guard relics of Spanish-American War vintage as they lumbered by, their old "coffee-grinder" type steam engines straining flat out to make all of ten knots or so.

3.a. (see quot.).

1934 Weseen *Dict. Slang* 166: Radio Slang…*Coffee grinder*—A synchronous rectifier; also a rotary gap.

b. *Av.* a hand-cranked radio-direction finder.

1943 Rochester (N.Y.) *Times-Union* (Jun. 24) 1. **1956** Heflin *USAF Dict.* 123: *Coffee grinder.* Slang. A kind of radio-direction-finder tuning device. **1975** in Higham & Siddall *Combat Aircraft* 58: VHF radio was a fine substitute for the old "coffee-grinders" but it did not immediately replace them since some ground stations were very tardy in updating their transmitters. **1991** Linnekin *80 Knots* 52: We [had] primitive medium-frequency radios, with broad-band "coffee-grinder" receivers.

4. *Sailing.* a kind of large two-handed winch.

1981 D.E. Miller *Jargon* 254. **1990** P. Dickson *Slang!* 154: *Coffee grinder.* Winch for controlling yacht sails.

coffeehouse *v.* to gossip. *Rare* in U.S.

*****1878** in *OEDS*. **1955** L. Shapiro *Sixth of June* 259 [ref. to 1944]: Those damned coffeehousing gunners. Don't know a war from a pink tea.

coffee-mill *n.* **1.** *Mil.* a Gatling gun or the like.

1861 in McClellan *Civil War Papers* 145: Fifty of the "Coffee Mill" guns. **1862** in Norton *Army Letters* 87: Don't you think one of those coffee mills would "weed out" a *secesh* regiment about as quickly as any tools they have? **1864** in Church *Civil War Mar.* 32: Captain Breese fired at geese with the Coffee Mill gun. *ca***1880** Bellard *Gone for a Soldier* 69 [ref. to Civil War]: The Excelsior Brigade had a patent gun that was calculated to annihilate an entire regt. at once. By the manner in which it worked, it was nicknamed the coffee mill. **1893** Hill *20 Yrs. at Sea* 201: Mr. Bailey had…a small Butler machine gun mounted in the bow of the boat…"Hurrah! There's Taylor down there with his Butler coffee-mill!" **1913** Meyers *10 Yrs. in Ranks* 248 [ref. to 1862]: The soldiers named it the "coffee-mill battery." It really looked like a large coffee-mill mounted on wheels, except for the barrel.

2. a pistol or rifle having revolving chambers.—used derisively.

1886 *Pap. Mil. Hist. Soc. Mass.* XIII 27: The Michigan brigade had the Spencer magazine seven-shooters [rifles];—"coffee-mills," the Confederates called them. **1887** in *DA* 353: One of the old-pattern Colts, with the barrels revolving, the ancient "coffee-mill" or "pepper-box," laughed at all over the West in the present day.

3. an engine, esp. if old.

*****1929** Bowen *Sea Slang* 29: *Coffee Mill.* A marine engine. **1936** in *Esquire* (Jan. 1937) 120: I didn't want to get mixed up in that coffee mill when we crashed. **1961** Hemingway *Islands* 182: There were water-splashed faces as the old coffee-mills revved up.

coffee pot *n.* **1.** Esp. *N.Y.C.* a small lunchroom or diner.

1928 in E. Ferber *One Basket* 330: A near-by lunchroom whose sign said Jack's Coffee Pot. **1930** *Time* (May 19) 76: *Coffee Pot.* A cheap quick lunch emporium, usually greasy and smelly; frequently called a "greasy spoon." **1930** *Amer. Merc.* (Dec.) 416: The boss of the coffee pot is all burnt up over the amount of grub he wrecks. **1933** Ford &

Tyler *Young & Evil* 46: Four gangsters…had come out of a coffee pot on Fourth and Sixth. **1934** Appel *Brain Guy* 27: On the corner of Leroy and Hudson, there was a coffee-pot. **1948** I. Shulman *Cry Tough!* 3: The same coffee-pots with their dirt-streaked windows. **1951** *Time* (Dec. 31) 29: They…ate in coffee pots and greasy spoons. **1961** Parkhurst *Undertow* 261: When I had money, I bought eggs an' threw 'em all over the street outside the coffeepot. **1971** Horan *Blue Messiah* 337: I went into this coffeepot on Columbus Circle.

2. a small or weakly powered steam engine or steam locomotive.

1958 McCulloch *Woods Words* 36: *Coffee pot*—A mill, a locomotive, or a donkey unusually small or low powered. **1954–60** *DAS* 114.

coffee up *v.* to drink much coffee eagerly, as a means of refreshment.

1965 D.G. Moore *20th C. Cowboy* 120: The Drag boss was coffeeing up. **1974** Terkel *Working* 208: Coffee up, tell all the stories, about how badly you're treated in the steel mill, [etc.]. **1990** M. Blake *Dances with Wolves* (film): Let's coffee up.

coffin *n.* **1.** a clumsy boot or shoe.

1851 Hall *College Wds.* 51: *Coffin.* At the University of Vermont, a boot, especially a large one. **1880** "M. Twain" *Tramp Abroad* ch. xlvii: That woman's majestic coffin-clad feet.

2.a. Orig. *Naut.* a ship or (*later*) aircraft that is dangerously out of repair.

[*****1829** Marryat *Frank Mildmay* 145: We had a four-oared gig, a small narrow thing (nicknamed by the sailors a "coffin"), to make our escape in.] **1883** C. Russell *Sailors' Lang.* 53: *Floating coffin.*—A rotten vessel. **1966** Little *Bold & Lonely* 193: Know what I make for ferrying this coffin? Ten grand a year.

b. *Av.* a plane that is extremely dangerous to fly. Cf. ANGEL-MAKER.

1984 J. Dailey *Silver Wings* 266 [ref. to WWII]: Pilots loathed missions in the "coffin," as they called the A-25 Curtiss Helldiver.

coffin box *n.* *Trucking.* (see quot.).

1971 Tak *Truck Talk* 33: *Coffin box:* a sleeper added onto a conventional cab.

coffin corner *n.* **1.a.** *Football.* a corner of a football field within ten yards of a goal line.

1933 *Leatherneck* (Dec.) 39: It was indeed something to see the famous "Coffin Corner" Paglia outmatched in booting skill. **1946** L.H. Baker *Football* 71: What is a coffin corner kick? **1954** Dodd *On Football* 250: Is he kicking from either hash mark or is he kicking for the "coffin corner?" **1976** *Webster's Sports Dict.* **1988** *Daily Beacon* (Univ. Tenn.) (Mar. 1) 4: I really enjoy my "coffin corner" seats they give me. **1989** *Newsweek* (Oct. 2) 79: Buried in the Coffin Corner?

b. *Basketball & Tennis.* an area on a court bounded by the intersection of a sideline and a baseline.

1976 Rosen *Above Rim* 82: Bingo! From the coffin corner this time. **1976** *AS* LI 293.

2. *Mil.* an exposed area that is especially vulnerable to enemy attack.

1945 Monks *Ribbon & Star* 117 [ref. to 1943]: The shift toward the northeast "Coffin Corner" began in earnest. **1949** Morison *Naval Ops. in WWII* V 192 [ref. to 1942]: Along "Coffin Corner," as the soldiers named this point where their lines came out of the woods, the Japs tried all their tricks and fought savagely all night. **1956** Morison *Naval Ops. in WWII* X 270: The first wave was coming in on the usual "coffin corner," the port bow. **1959** Morrill *Dark Sea* 35 [ref. to WWII]: The tail spot [on shipboard] was known as "coffin-corner" or "torpedo junction."

coffin-dodger *n.* *Stu.* (see quot.).

1900 *DN* II 28: *Coffin-Dodger.* A person much addicted to cigarette smoking.

coffin meat *n.* a corpse.

1837 Bird *Nick of Woods*: He arn't hurt much to speak on, for all of his looking so much like coffin-meat at the first jump.

coffin nail *n.* a cigar (now *rare*) or cigarette. Cf. COFFIN TACK.

[**1867** *Galaxy* (Mar. 15) 609: Pamela…tries to persuade me, that every puff of smoke…is a nail in my coffin.] [**1873** B. Harte *Skaggs's Husbands* 6: Bill…touched glasses with him, and after saying "Here's another nail in your coffin,"—a cheerful sentiment, to which "And the hair all off your head" was playfully added by the other,—he "threw off his liquor."] **1888** *Tex. Siftings* (Feb. 18) 8: A youth…puffed at an ill-smelling coffin nail. **1900** *DN* II 28: *Coffin-nail* or *coffin-tack, n.* A cigarette. **1906** in "O.

Henry" *Works* 182: Say, sport, have you got a coffin nail on you? **1913-15** Van Loan *Taking the Count* 38: There's more nicotine in those coffin nails that you smoke than in cigars. *****1919** Downing *Digger Dialects* 17: *Coffin Nail.*—Cigarette. **1920** S. Lewis *Main Street* 78: Hey, gol darn your hide, don't you go sticking your coffin nail in my i-scream. **1930** Dos Passos *42nd Parallel* 53: Have a coffin nail, Mac? **1930** "D. Stiff" *Milk & Honey* 202: *Coffin nail*—A vanishing term for a cigarette. **1935** Pollock *Und. Speaks: Coffin nail*, a cigar. **1952** Uris *Battle Cry* 132: Give me a coffin nail. **1965** Schmitt *All Hands* 4 [ref. to 1917]: At school we had been taught that smoking cigarettes, sometimes referred to as "coffin nails," was a habit that once acquired could never be broken. **1966** Young & Hixson *LSD* 6: No smoking of coffin nails until you were…at least fourteen. **1967** Dibner *Admiral* 299: You should knock off those coffin nails, Mom. **1977** M. Franklin *Last of Cowboys* 8: You know the doctor took me off coffin nails. **1981** Wolf *Roger Rabbit* 79: Coffin nails at two bucks a pack. **1992** G. Wolff *Day at the Beach* 124: Bogey in *Casablanca*, a coffin nail dangling from his lower lip.

coffin ship *n. Naut.* an unseaworthy or otherwise dangerous ship.
  1838 [Haliburton] *Clockmaker* (Ser. 2) 195: Them coffin ships ain't sent out for nothin'. Ten of them gun-brigs have been lost already. **1918** "M. Brand" *Harrigan* 101: This is a coffin ship, Harrigan, an' Henshaw he's the undertaker. **1947** W.M. Camp *S.F.* 324: The dangerous conditions aboard…the notorious "coffin ships" in the Pacific. **1951** Doerflinger *Shantymen* 40: Older windjammers, vessels considered by their crews to be of doubtful seaworthiness…were "known to sailors as 'coffin ships.'"

coffin tack *n.* a cigarette. Cf. COFFIN NAIL.
  1897 in *DA* 354. **1900** (quot. at COFFIN NAIL). **1943** Stuart *Pvt. Tussie* 96: I think they are coffin tacks. **1935** Pollock *Und. Speaks: Coffin tack*, a cigarette. **1951** Willingham *Gates of Hell* 117: Please give me another of those cigarettes…Or should I say, "coffin tacks?"

coffin varnish *n.* liquor, esp. cheap whiskey.
  1881 Nye *Forty Liars* 16: We gather about the camp fire…with the inspiration of six fingers of agency coffin varnish. **1884** in E. West *Saloon* 31: A single bottle of coffin varnish. **1891** Bourke *On the Border* 71: Some of the vilest coffin varnish on the mundane sphere was to be found there by those who tried diligently. **1908** Sullivan *Criminal Slang* 5: *Coffin varnish*—Bad whiskey. **1926** Maines & Grant *Wise-Crack Dict.* 6: *Coffin varnish*—Bad whiskey. **1926** *N.Y. Times* (Dec. 26) VIII 3: Bootleg whiskey [is known] as "coffin varnish." **1927** Rollins *Jinglebob* 58 [ref. to 1880's]: Do you reckon your boys'd be offended if we rustled 'em a little coffin varnish when they rolls in? **1972–76** Lynde *Rick O'Shay* (unp.): Didn't you tell me…you were going to swear off that coffin varnish?

cog *n.* [clipping of *cognomen*] a name.
  1885 S.S. Hall *Gold Buttons* 3: Very appropriate "cogs," they are indeed. **1886** E.L. Wheeler *N.Y. Nell* 9: If you want to exchange cogs, my name is Nell Niblo.
  ¶ In phrase:
  ¶ **slip a cog** to lose one's good sense.
  1937 *AS* (Dec.) 316: You've got a screw loose…you've slipped a cog.

cog box *n.* a gearbox or transmission.
  1938 *AS* (Dec.) 308: *Cog box*. The transmission of a bus. *****1979** in Partridge *DSUE* (ed. 8) 237.

cognacked *adj. Mil. in France.* intoxicated by cognac.
  1919 Lindner *Letters* 121: I'll stay cognac-ed [until] we start home. **1930** *AS* V 383: *To be cognacked.* To be drunk. *Ibid.* 373: I do not think that this use of the word was brought back to America.

cog-stripper *n. Trucking.* (see quots.).
  1942 *AS* (Apr.) 103: *Cog Stripper.* Driver who makes noise when shifting gears. Also *Gear Fighter.* **1971** Tak *Truck Talk* 33: *Cog stripper*: a trucker who shifts gears noisily.

cogue *v.* [fr. Scots *cogue* 'a dram'] to drink (brandy or the like).—also constr. with dummy obj. *it.*
  *****1730–36** in *OED2: Cogue*, to drink Brandy. *****1775** in *OED2: Cogue*, to drink Brandy, to drink drams. **1821** Waln *Hermit* 24: No harm to *cogue a few.* **1877** Bartlett *Americanisms* (ed. 4) 779: To *coge* or *coag* [*sic*] *it.* One of the many phrases signifying the habitual and excessive use of ardent spirits.

coguey *adj.* drunk.
  1722 B. Franklin, in *AS* XV (Feb. 1940) 103: *Boozy, cogey, tipsy, fox'd,* [etc.]. *****1823** "J. Bee" *Dict. of Turf.*

cohogle *v.* (see quot.).

1829 in M. Mathews *Beginnings of Amer. Eng.* 103: To *cohogle.* "To bamboozle." *Kentucky.*

coil *v.* to curl up asleep.—constr. with *up.*
  1862 in Norton *Letters* 50: At 9 o'clock the "taps" are beaten and all lights must be extinguished. It is rather uninteresting sitting in the dark, so that hour generally finds us "coiled up," as the boys express it. **1895** Sinclair *Alabama* 119: Jack is coiled up under the weather bulwarks, dreaming perhaps of days long gone by.
  ¶ In phrase:
  ¶ **coil [up] (one's) ropes** [or **cables**] *Naut.* to die.
  *****1929** Bowen *Sea Slang* 29: Coil up One's Cables, To. To die. **1941** Kendall *Army & Navy Sl.* 18: He coiled up his ropes…passed on. **1975** Gould *ME Lingo: Coiled His Ropes*—Died.

coin *n.* money. Also (*Black E.*) pl.
  *****ca1820** in Holloway & Black *Later Ballads* I 260: For all her search was to find out my coin. **1836** (quot. at PLANK). *****1874** Hotten *Slang Dict.* (ed. 4) 124: "To post the coin"…a sporting phrase meaning to make a deposit of money for a match of any kind. **1876** W. Wright *Big Bonanza* 378: The best man is the man for my coin. **1878** Hart *Sazerac* 167: More coin and less hyperbole is my motto. **1880** in M. Lewis *Mining Frontier* 128: The Prodigal Son had an old man who put up the coin every time the kid struck him for a stake. **1891** *Munsey's Mag.* 235: Displaying a handful of coin, "dar's fo' dollahs an' sixty fo' cents." **1893** F.P. Dunne, in Schaaf *Dooley* 55: Musha, it's a little old Bill Shakespeare iver cared f'r th' coin…An' he cud write pothry like a wild man. **1896** Ade *Artie* 7: If they put the same turns on at any variety house the people'd tear down the buildin', tryin' to get their coin back. **1922** Rice *Adding Machine* 112: You'll be scrubbin' floors in about a year, if you go blowin' your coin like that. **1927** McKay *Home to Harlem* 33: "But all these sociables—and you spend so much coin on gin," Miss Curdy had said. **1959–60** R. Reisner *Jazz Titans* 152: One asks for coins instead of a specific amount of small change. **1966-67** P. Thomas *Mean Streets* 206: I've been thinking about the things that some good coins could bring. **1970** Wambaugh *New Centurions* 82: I jist got to make me some coin tonight. **1970** Conaway *Big Easy* 44: On days they got the coins, they drink a dozen pops apiece. **1971** Horan *Blue Messiah* 35: Wow! That's a lot of coin! **1989** *21 Jump St.* (Fox-TV): Morty just likes sittin' on his butt collectin' coin.

coin-heaver *n.* an embezzler of small change.
  1918 Wagar *Spotter* 56: The interurbans are supposed to be the most vulnerable point of any large system to attack by "coin heavers."

coinkydink *n.* [intentional malapropism] a coincidence. *Joc.*
  1969 *Rowan & Martin's Laugh-In* (NBC-TV): Isn't that a coinkydink? **1989** P. Munro *U.C.L.A. Slang* 30: What a coinkidink [*sic*] that we have two classes together. **1992** *Donahue* (NBC-TV): It's a little coinkydink.

co-jockey *n. Av.* a copilot.
  1959 Montgomery & Heinan *Jet Nav.*: I end up here as a B-52 co-jockey. **1963** E.M. Miller *Exile* 54: Well, one of the other co-jockeys puts me up to this.

cojones /kɔ'hɔnes; *Eng.* kə'houniz/ *n.pl.* [< Sp] the testicles; (*hence*) courage; BALLS.
  1932 Hemingway *Death in Aft.* ii 28: It takes more cojones to be a sportsman where death is a closer party to the game. **1966** T. Capote *In Cold Blood* iv 274: The baseball field was mud up to your *cojones.* **1984** N. Bell *Raw Youth* 7: It's yet to reach my cojones. *a*1989 R. Herman, Jr. *Warbirds* 264: I don't think your average [MiG pilot] has the *cojones* to…mix it up with a Phantom. **1993** *Sally Jessy Raphaël* (synd. TV series): Any man with cojones, any man that is not a wimp.

coke[1] *n. Narc.* **1.** cocaine. Also attrib.
  *ca*1903 (cited in *W10*). **1908** *Sat. Eve. Post* (Dec. 5) 46: I gave Sawyer [$10] to go down on Park Row and hunt up a coke jag. *****1908** in *OEDS:* They buy the "coke" in the form of powder and snuff it up the nose. **1911** *Hampton's Mag.* (May) 596: Many…were confirmed users of "coke." *Ibid.* 600: He had become a "coke fiend" and his life was irretrievably ruined. **1911** *JAF* (Oct.) 359: Sign on the door, "There's no more coke." **1912–14** in E. O'Neill *Lost Plays* 52: Looks to me as if this doll was full of coke or something. **1914** Spencer *Jailer* 118: "Coc" [a] word in the hop-head's vocabulary meaning cocaine. **1921** McAlmon *Hasty Bunch* 186: Takes coke, doesn't he? **1928** Bodenheim *Georgie May* 5: What did a coke-sniffer know about being decent? **1950** A. Lomax *Mr. Jelly Roll* 50: A lot of them smoked hop or used coke. **1975** V.B. Miller *Deadly Game* 127: Go buy yourself a new coke spoon. **1990** J. Updike *Rabbit at Rest* 132: I don't do needles and I don't fuck coke whores. **1991** B.E. Ellis *Amer. Psycho* 207: She was drunk [and] wasted on coke.

2. an opiate, such as morphine or heroin; (*hence*) any illicit drug taken by injection.

1926 Nason *Chevrons* 166 [ref. to WWI]: Give him a shot of coke and a bucket of water over his head and let him wait for the doctor. *Ibid.* 282: I hope I don't get the coke habit from this. **1928** O'Connor *B'way Racketeers* 250: Coke—any type of narcotic. **1928–29** Nason *White Slicker* 49: If it begins to hurt too badly they can give him a shot of coke. **1929** *AS* IV 338: *Coke*—Dope.

3. a drug addict.

[**1912** *Hampton's Mag.* (Jan.) 748: He's called Coke Morgan...because he's a cocaine-fiend.] **1929** Zorbaugh *Gold Coast* 123: Then there are the "cokes," "snowbirds" they call them, who will pawn everything they have for a shot. **1934** Appel *Brain Guy* 177: For two days the coke spied on McMann. *Ibid.* 189: Maybe he'd like that coke poking a knife a foot long at him. **1935** *Our Army* (May) 34: It's like "snow" to needle-hungry "cokes." **1936** Duncan *Over the Wall* 21 [ref. to 1918]: Hopheads or cokes—the cocaine addicts on the snow.

coke² *n.* [fr. COCONUT, 1.a.] the head.

1920 Ade *Hand-Made Fables* 69: Some of our Fellow-Beings...still have the idea...in their Cokes that running a Whizzer is a legitimate Pastime and Nobody's Business, except the Ike that gets hooked.

coke *v.* to take or be under the influence of cocaine.—usu. constr. with *up.* Hence **coker.**

1971 Woodley *Dealer* 64: I coke up and then go to sleep. **1975** *Daily Beacon* (Univ. Tenn.) (Apr. 28) 2: They were all sitting around in a circle coking. *Ibid.* Mr. Kung Fu...died of overcoking. **1976** Braly *False Starts* 278: You coke up on those devil drugs, and you're liable to come crashing through the wall. **1979** *New West* (Oct. 8) 96: A young white male cops a plea to possession....A show business coker. **1982–84** Chapple *Outlaws in Babylon* 192: Watching color television while they coke up. **1989** S. Robinson & D. Ritz *Smokey* 4: A semi-regular smoker and a once-in-a-while coker.

coke-blower *n. Narc.* a sniffer of cocaine.

1924 (quot. at HOPPY).

coked *adj.* under the influence of cocaine or (*loosely*) another drug (including alcohol). Also **coked up,** (in recent use) **coked out.**

1924 Henderson *Crookdom* 307: When "coked up" he will murder and rob and steal. **1925** McAlmon *Silk Stockings* 39: She was "coked to the eyeballs." **1930** Lavine *3d Degree* 227: "Coked" or "hopped up" gunmen. **1944** Stiles *Big Bird* 114: He was like the others, a little coked-up and sunstruck. **1952** Mandel *Angry Strangers* 257: Well they're all coked-up, the whole screwy world. **1952** J.C. Holmes *Go* 121: I was real hung up on it two years ago...—coked most of the time. **1968** J. Kerr *Clinic* 134: He's an alcoholic and a drug addict...drunk or coked one day a week. **1977** A. Patrick *Beyond Law* 27: I could see she was pretty coked out. **1981** Wambaugh *Glitter Dome* 43: Every coked-out tenant of the building. **1979** *L.A. Times* (Aug. 27) IV 14: They seen him when he was coked up. **1989** Hynes & Drury *Howard Beach* 276: So coked out he could have been hit by a jet.

coke fiend *n.* a habitual user of cocaine.

1911 (quot. at COKE, *n.*). **1912** in *OEDS.* **1956** in *DAS* 114: This Sherlock Holmes...[was] a coke fiend. **1984** McInerny *Bright Lights* 43: All us coke fiends sneezing—it adds up.

cokehead *n.* a habitual user of cocaine or (*obs.*) another drug.

1922 Anderson *Hobo* 67: These who are transient are often cocaine users who are able to do without the drug for considerable periods of time. Not infrequently "coke heads" or "snow-birds" are found among the hobo workers. **1927** *DN* V 442: *Coke heads,* n. Cocaine addicts, and, by extension, the users of any drug. **1930** "D. Stiff" *Milk & Honey* 38: A hop head or user of dope may earn the monicker of "Dopey" or "Coke Head." **1936** R. Chandler, in Ruhm *Detective* 121: And then a cokehead to turn it up. **1970** Landy *Underground Dict.* 53: *Coke head*...Cocaine addict. **1983** *Time* (Apr. 11) 25: A room full of cokeheads, bristling with that hard, artificial arrogance, can be an unsettling place. **1992** *Rolling Stone* (June 11) 140: I called cokeheads, junkies and speed freaks.

cokehound *n.* COKEHEAD.

1936 R. Chandler, in Ruhm *Detective* 121: He's a cokehound and he talks in his sleep.

coker *n.* see s.v. COKE, *v.*

coke up see s.v. COKE, *v.*

cokey *adj.* foolish; DOPEY.

1929–32 in *AS* (Dec. 1934) 289: *Cokey.* Dopey (figuratively or liter-

ally); not all there; sleepy-looking; unambitious. **1947** Schulberg *Harder They Fall* 315: It may sound cokey, but we could go as high as two million with this fight. **1956** Hargrove *Girl He Left* 92: Who gets five minutes for anything around this cokey outfit?

cokie *n.* Orig. *Narc.* a habitual user of cocaine; (*loosely*) (*obs.*) a drug addict.

1916 *New Republic* (Apr. 22) 173: A period...referred to by the "cokies" as "the panic." **1917** in Ireland *Med. Dept.* X (1929) 69: Heroin takers...have a characteristic vocabulary and will talk much more freely about their habit if the examiner in his inquiries uses such words as "deck," "quill," "package," "an eighth," "blowers," "cokie," etc. **1917** *Forum* (Dec.) 686: You're a kokie. Cold feet my eye. **1918** *N.Y. Times* (Dec. 18) 14: A world of "cokeys" and "hop fiends." **1922** Murphy *Black Candle* 20: Cocainomaniacs are commonly called "cokies." **1932** Daly *Not Only War* 56 [ref. to 1918]: What the hell's the matter with you, Roscoe?...You act like a cokie. **1936** Dai *Opium Add.* 197: In the East the term cokie refers to all users except smokers. **1941** "G.R. Lee" *G-String* 33: See that the women aren't put in a cell with a lot of cokies. **1953** Anslinger & Tompkins *Traffic in Narc.* 307: Cokie. An opium addict. **1956** Algren *Wild Side* 78: Cokies and queers and threadbare whores. **1957** Murtagh & Harris *Cast the First Stone* 5: The girls never bother the alkies and cokies of the street with their joke, but save it for the others... *Ibid.* 304: *Cokies* Cocaine addicts. **1970** *Sat. Rev.* (Nov. 14) 21: *Cokie* Cocaine addict. **1971** Faust *Willy Remembers* 135: Wally Reid was taking that stuff before all these cokies were a gleam in their old man's eyes.

Cokie Joe *n.* a man who is a habitual user of cocaine.

1933 *Kokey Joe* (blues rec. by Mills Blue Rhythm Band). **1948** Webb *Four Steps* 4: Cokey Joe gave Ditto a dirty look. **1951** Algren *Chicago* 97: Whiskey-heads and hop-heads, old cokey-joes and musclemen.

cold *n. Black E.* a burned-out cigarette stub.

1983 Harris & Weingrod *Trading Places* (film): Who's been puttin' out their colds on my floor?

¶ In phrase:

¶ **give (someone) the cold** [sugg. by COLD SHOULDER] to receive (someone) with hostility.

1896 F.H. Smith *Tom Grogan* 79: "Afore I could tell her she opens the front door and gives me the dead cold." "Fired ye?" exclaimed McGaw incredulously.

cold *adj.* **1.** (of a sum of money) actual; "cool." Cf. COLD CASH.

1914 in Handy *Treasury of Blues* 73: Gwine to ask him for a cold ten spot.

2. (of a check) worthless or fraudulent.

1927 in *DA.* **1928, 1939, 1970** in *DARE.*

3. *Gamb.* (of dice, cards, etc.) unlucky.

1931 Wilstach *Under Cover Man* 79: Dice...if they're not cold I'm right at home. **1987** Mamet *House of Games* (film): Damn cards. Cold as ice.

4. *Black E.* **a.** markedly unfair or unpleasant; bad. Cf. *not so cold*, below.

1934 in M. Taft *Blues Concordance* III 1328: That jive you...shooting: coldest stuff in town. **1963** (quot. at COLD SHOT). **1968** Heard *Howard Street* 12: You musta thought I was a real lame, pullin' some cold shit like this on me, huh? **1973** Goines *Players* 145: Now, I want to know, man, if you went along with that cold shit? **1972–74** Hawes & Asher *Raise Up* 18: You still sound like a little kid playing at being an adult...And that's some cold shit. **1983** Eilert *Self & Country* 165: Three dressing changes and three Keflin shots a day. Man, that's cold.

b. extremely good; wonderful; (*hence*) stylish. Cf. COOL.

1942 Z.N. Hurston, in *Amer. Mercury* LV 94: He was cold on that trumpet! **1974** (quot. at COLD-BLOODED). **1977** in *DARE:* Thass *cold,* Baby, thass *cold.* **1967–80** Folb *Runnin' Lines* 233: Cold...Fine, exceptional. **1985** "Run-D.M.C." *My Adidas* (rap song): My Adidas...funky-fresh and yes, cold on my feet.

c. brutal; cruel.

1962 in Jackson *Swim Like Me* 115: He was the sharpest junkie, Jack, to ever hit the streets. And the coldest too. He'd work his whores in snow and rain. **1962–63** in Giallombardo *Soc. of Women* 202: *Cold Blow.* A shock or disappointment of any kind. **1966** Braly *On Yard*: That was cold, man. **1974** Gober *Black Cop* 68: You're coming on awful strong, my man. A dude that's that cold has got to walk awful hard. **1978** B. Johnson *What's Happenin'?* 51: Russell told him, "Just keep...out of my face." That's cold, man. *a*1984 in Terry *Bloods* 13: I was against nuclear weapons, because I thought what they did to Hiroshima and Nagasaki was totally cold. **1992** L. Johnson *My Posse* 157: That's cold!...They didn't have to do that.

5. *Mil.* not defended by or under enemy fire.

1970 Hammer *One Morning in the War* 119: I reported the LZ is cold. Immediately thereafter the helicopter pilot broke in and reported, "Negative, negative, negative." LZ is hot. You are receiving small arms fire. **1984–87** Ferrandino *Firefight* 12 [ref. to Vietnam War]: Relax....It's a cold landing zone. **1989** D. Sherman *There I Was* 9: Those LZs were what is called cold.

¶ In phrase:

¶ **not so cold** quite good.

1897 Ade *Pink* 165: Gawge Dixon's [a] puhty wahm boy, an' 'at Misteh Joe Woolcott ain't so cold.

cold *adv.* **1.** completely; with finality. Now *colloq.* or *S.E.*

1889 in *OEDS*: A. D. Taylor...trailed a variety actress...with whom he was infatuated...She shook him cold yesterday. **1891** Maitland *Slang Dict.* 71: *Cold* (Am.), certain, positive; as, "I give it out cold" that I will do so and so. **1896** Ade *Artie* ch. X: Then I quit cold. **1900** *DN* II 29: *Cold*, adj. Perfect, complete. In phrase: *to have down cold* = to be perfectly prepared, as on a lesson. **1905** R. Beach *Pardners* 79: We were liable to get turned down cold. **1925* in Fraser & Gibbons *Soldier & Sailor Wds.* 60 [ref. to WWI]: *Cold, To Have Someone:* To be master of the situation, e.g., "We had Jerry cold in that last affair." **1929** in Hammett *Knockover* 39: We've got them cold for conspiracy to defraud. **1942** Casey *Torpedo Junction* 232: Those boys had us cold. **1944** H. Brown *Walk in the Sun* 96: If they catch us on this road they've got us cold. Like mackerel. **1949** Leahy *Notre Dame* 84: Whenever such a play is stopped "cold," try to find out why. **1976** Hayden *Voyage* 178: I'd nail him colder'n a gravedigger's ass. **1984** Univ. Tenn. instructor: You've got to know this stuff cold.

2. *Rap Music.* indeed; just.—used for emphasis.—used pre-verbally.

1986 "Beastie Boys" *Rhymin' & Stealin'* (rap song): I fought the law an' I cold won. **1988** *Spin* (Oct.) 47: *Cold* adv., intensely. **1988** "Slick Rick" *Treat Her Like a Prostitute* (rap song): They...cold hurt your feelings. **1993** *Sally Jessy Raphaël* (synd. TV series): If you hadda been my daughter, I'd a cold whipped your butt!

cold-blooded *adj. Black E.* **1.** out-and-out; absolute.

1962 in Wepman et al. *The Life* 145: You couldn't pull a fast one on a cold-blooded lame.

2. striking; exceptional; splendid.

1969 Bullock *Watts* 275: As one youngster explains, "When I say, 'That's a cold-blooded automobile,' that means I want this car and I'm gonna get it." **1974** Blount *3 Bricks Shy* 214: "Cold-blooded," or "cold," was a term of radical approval among the players, as in "this cheese is cold-blooded," or "*Twilight Zone* is *cold*." **1984** Algeo *Stud Buds & Dorks*: Very good...cold-blooded. **1985** *A-Team* (NBC-TV): Is he [a rock musician] cold-blooded or what?

cold bottle *n.* COLD JUG.

1947 *ATS* (Supp.) 2. **1956** (quot. at COLD JUG).

coldcock *n.* a knockout blow.

1942 *ATS* 460: *Cold-cock*...a knockout blow. **1972** R. Wilson *Forbidden Words* 74: Wyatt Earp...usually managed to avoid gunfights by moving in quickly with a coldcock before the other party was ready to draw a pistol.

coldcock *adj.* unconscious.

1918 in *AS* (Oct. 1933) 25: *Coldcock*...adverbial objective, as in So I up an' knocked 'im coldcock.

coldcock *adv.* absolutely; cold.

1982 W. Wharton *Midnight Clear* 111: Krauts jumped us, had us cold cock,...then didn't shoot.

coldcock *v.* to render unconscious, as with a sudden blow to the head; (*hence*) to take by surprise; stun.

1918 in *AS* (Oct. 1933) 25: *Coldcock*. To knock unconscious usually with a blackjack. "'F dat goddam orderly rats on us, we'll colecock 'im sure." **1927** *AS* II (May) 351: Tom was cold cocked when that rock hit him. **1930** Botkin *Folk-Say* 110: Then I cold-cocks him and he...flops and sprawls out on the ground like a country girl on an organ stool. **1934** Weseen *Dict. Slang* 231: *Cold cocked*—Knocked senseless. **1952** Uris *Battle Cry* 209: Andy,...you go up and coldcock him. **1957** E. Lacy *Room to Swing* 68: I'd been had, been set up....I was cold cocked. **1962** Ragen & Finston *Toughest Prison* 795: *Cold Cock*—To render insensible with a blow from a bottle. **1970** Wohl & Brackett *Rio Lobo* (film): Chester'd been coldcocked pretty bad. **1970** Landy *Underground Dict.* 53: *Cold cock*...Hit someone mentally, leaving him with no comeback. **1976** Whelton *CB Baby* 4: I coldcocked him with a left hand to the head. **1990** Ruggero *38 N. Yankee* 109: They'd been...cold cocked like an

unsuspecting high school kid in his first bar fight.

coldcocked *adj.* outright.

1967 Dibner *Admiral* 141: I watched those Nips joy-ride in and out, machine-gunning the men. Cold-cocked murder.

coldconk *v.* COLDCOCK.

1961 J. Flynn *Action Man* 137: She cold-conked herself. **1974** Cherry *High Steel* 98: You got to cold-conk him.

coldcut *n. Stu.* an unfriendly or obnoxious individual.

1944 *Slanguage Dict.* 59: *Cold cut*—a "junior jerk." **1956** Hargrove *Girl He Left* 16: Any other girl half as responsible would have impressed Andy Sheaffer as a real cold-cut, a mothball.

cold deal *n. Gamb.* a dishonest deal, as from a COLD DECK.

1919 in C.M. Russell *Paper Talk* 145: Romance...can pull aney thing from a cold deel to murder and get away with it.

cold deck *n.* **1.** *Gamb.* a stacked deck.

1857 in *DA* 355: He's got the thing all set to ring in a "cold deck." **1858** [S. Hammett] *Piney Woods* 83: Them no 'count chaps that foller poker for a livin' is mighty apt to wring in a cold deck. **1859** Matsell *Vocab.* 20: *Cold Deck.* A prepared deck of cards played on a novice or "sucker." **1870** in "M. Twain" *Sketches & Tales* 134: I never have gambled from that day to this—never once—without a "cold deck" in my pocket. **1887** Francis *Saddle & Moccasin* 225: To "ring in a cold deck" is to order in and substitute a fresh deck, in which the cards are prearranged. **1891** Maitland *Slang Dict.* 71: *Cold deck* (Am.), a pack of cards so arranged that the dealer knows what kind of a hand he is giving his opponent. **1925** Cobb *Many Laughs* 76: I've been running cold decks into poker games for nearly forty years but, by heavens, this is the first one I ever struck that was froze solid! **1929** T. Gordon *Born to Be* 18: He put out a couple of cold decks. Then the gang of gamblers got wise to him. **1960** Jordan & Marberry *Fool's Gold* 189 [ref. to 1899]: In the States it was easy to ring in a cold deck...a pack of cards that had been stacked. **1978** *Gamblers* 127: I handled a cold deck only once, and that for a joke.

2.a. any kind of fraudulent substitution or unfairly manipulated situation.

1890 Quinn *Fools of Fortune* 229: The use of "cold decks" in almost all card games has become so common, among the professionals, that the term, "ringing in a cold deck," has achieved a recognized place in the vocabulary of American slang. Almost every one knows that the expression refers to a substitution of one thing for another, yet not every one knows whence the phrase has its origin. **1934** Berg *Prison Nurse* 60: After all, what can you do when you're up against a cold deck?

b. a deceitful or treacherous individual.

1891 C. King *By Land & Sea* 132: I put him up fer kind of a cold-deck. He's got some tuff ones guarding in the "Lidyer," which he claims.

3. *Logging.* a pile of logs to be held in storage.

1938 in *Dict. Canadianisms.* **1941** *AS* (Oct.) 232: *Cold Deck.* A pile of logs stored for transportation later. **1942** *AS* (Dec.) 221: *Cold Deck.* A pile of logs left for later loading and hauling.

cold-deck *v.* **1.** Orig. *Gamb.* to cheat by means of a COLD DECK; (*hence*) to swindle.

1884 in *AS* XVII (1942) 125: The miller...kicked because said Serna was trying to cold deck said Sanches. **1887** DeVol *40 Yrs. a Gambler* 25: I used to make it a point to "cold deck" a sucker on his own deal. **1893** Hampton *Maj. in Washington* 159: I did cold deck him a couple of times. **1897** A. Lewis *Wolfville* 107: Nellie...did you cold-deck this yere Red Dog sport this a-way? **1909** Irwin *Con Man* 18: Cold-decking was his specialty. By "cold deck," I mean the substitution of a deck, already stacked, for the one which has just been shuffled and cut on the table. **1939** N. West *Locust* 379: You're trying to cold-deck us! **1972** Pendleton *Vegas Vendetta* 121: Don't you believe it, Joe. Nobody cold-decks Bolan. **1975** W. Salt *Day of Locust* (film): You think you're the only guy that's been cold-decked by a dumb blonde? **1981** Hogan *D. Bullet* 61: Hell, he was cold-decking me!...stinking card sharp.

2. to knock down; DECK; COLDCOCK.

1976 Price *Bloodbrothers* 96: If a big kid was tormenting Albert, you wouldn't hesitate to cold-deck him, right?

cold feet *n.* a lack of courage or confidence; uncertainty or fear. Now *colloq.* or *S.E.* [The "1893" ex. in *OED2*, from second ed. of S. Crane's *Maggie*, is actually from 1896; the term does not appear in the 1893 first ed.]

1896 Ade *Artie* 63: He's one o' them boys that never has cold feet and there's nothin' too good for a friend. **1898** in S. Crane *Complete Stories* 412: Get cold feet! **1898** Doubleday *Aboard "Yankee"* 75: This sort of business would give him a bad case of "cold feet." **1898** Markey *Iowa to*

Philippines 102: We have few in M Company that have this new disease, "cold feet." **1896–1900** in *DN* II (1901) 138: "To get *cold-feet* in a subject," abandon it for weariness. Ithaca [N.Y.] **1906** Moss *Officers' Manual* 284: *Cold feet, have.* To be afraid, to lack courage. **1910** Stirling *Midshipman in Philippines* 115: What is it, O'Neil, just pure cold feet? **1950** Maddow & Huston *Asphalt Jungle* 11: Our witness got cold feet and backed down. **1981** Wambaugh *Glitter Dome* 264: Thought I was getting cold feet.

cold fish *n.* an unfriendly or emotionally cold person. Now *colloq.* Cf. FISH², *n.*
   1924 (cited in *W10*). **1926** S. Lewis *Mantrap* 149: And you *are* a cold fish, too. **1941** in *OED2*: He's a cold fish. No, fish isn't the right creature—I believe they are quite affectionate. **1956** (quot. at COLD JUG). **1954–60** *DAS* 115. **1965** N.Y.C. woman, age 50: What I don't like about her is she's a cold fish. She doesn't have any likes or dislikes. She's a cold fish. **1975** Ky. high-school student: She's such a cold fish. She doesn't care how the *students* feel. **1986** Ark. man, age 34: That one over there, he's really a cold fish. **1986** R. Walker *AF Wives* 134: She was a cold fish sexually.

cold-iron watch *n. Navy.* (see quot.).
   1958 Cope & Dyer *Petty Officer's Guide* (ed. 2) 337: *Cold Iron Watch.* (Slang). A security patrol in the engineering spaces of a ship whose machinery is not used or tended.

cold-jaw *n. Eques.* (see quot.).
   1933 *AS* (Feb.) 28: *Cold-Jaw.* A horse that does not respond to bridle signals, however harsh they may be.

cold jug *n.* (see quot.).
   1956 Boatner *Military Customs* 125: *Cold jug* (or *cold bottle, fish*): A person without humor, who appears to get no joy out of living.

cold meat *n.* **1.** a corpse or corpses.—often used proleptically.
   *****1780** *Town & Country Jester* 17: There's no cold meat like a dead wife. *****1788** Grose *Vulgar Tongue* (ed. 2): A dead wife is the best cold meat in a man's house. *****1819** [T. Moore] *Tom Crib* 25: Left him all's one as cold meat for the Crowner. **1838** [Haliburton] *Clockmaker* (Ser. 2) 132: The doctors are dissectin' of a carcase of cold meat (for that's the name a subject goes by). **1873** Badger *Little Thunderbolt* 62: You'd 'a' been cold meat, fer all we could 'a' done. **1877** *Puck* (Apr.) 6: I'll make cold meat of you all; I'll knock you all into the middle of next week. **1882** in Smith & Smith *Police Gazette* 35: They will give exhibitions of how they did up Jesse James and sold his cold meat for the reward of $10,000. **1885** "Lykkejaeger" *Dane* 97: If I had gone to sleep…that night, there would have been "cold meat" there the next morning. **1928–29** Nason *White Slicker* 175: If anything had started they'd have made cold meat out of you and me in about two seconds. **1930** *Amer. Mercury* (Dec.) 455: *Cold meat, n.:* A corpse. "Get me, sucker: lay off or you'll be cold meat." **1951** C. Lederer *Thing* (film): If he thinks too long, we're cold meat. **1960** Sire *Deathmakers* 87: Just one sliver of flak and you will be cold meat. **1973** W. Crawford *Gunship Cmndr.* 123: He looked like cold meat some doctor was trying to Frankenstein. **1982** Braun *Judas Tree* 101: You'd be cold meat the minute you hit the street. **1983** Eilert *Self & Country* 197: If you let it go after that you'll be cold meat. **1986** Coonts *Intruder* 29: You think about this stuff too much and you'll be cold meat, just like McPherson.
   2. Esp. *Mil.* an easy target or victim. [Early quots. ref. to WWI.]
   1918 Grider *War Birds* 206: I expected…to watch him go down in flames. It looked like cold meat. **1926** Springs *Nocturne* 39: Don't let me cheat the Fokkers out of their daily cold meat, but I have business to attend to after the war is over. **1929** Nordhoff & Hall *Falcons of France* 135: Another of those photographic buses….Selden, there's some cold meat for us. Let's go after it! **1933** Stewart *Airman Speech* 55: *Cold Meat.* A term used in English combat flying during the war, and meaning easy pickings. **1937** Codman *Contact* 72: Alone at four thousand metres with a dead motor. Cold meat for the veriest novice among Boches. **1937** Parsons *Lafayette Escadrille* 167: Stragglers were cold meat for Hun pursuit pilots. **1943** *Corvette K-225* (film): Keep guard. We're cold meat at the speed we can make. **1961** Foster *Hell in the Heavens* 80: "This is going to be cold meat," I breathed into my oxygen mask as I ruddered into a left *chandelle* and dived for the unsuspecting Jap.

cold-meat *adj.* absolute; certain; COLD.—used prenominally.
   1936 Mulholland *Splinter Fleet* 137 [ref. to *ca*1918]: Three times we had a "cold-meat-fix" on him.

cold-meat box *n.* a coffin.
   *****1845** (cited in Partridge *DSUE* (ed. 8) 238). *****1889** Barrère & Leland

Dict. Slang I 263: *Cold meat box* (popular), a coffin. *****1889** in *F & H* II 151: I should just come in where you were lying in the cold-meat box, and I should whisper in your ear. **1926** Maines & Grant *Wise-Crack Dict.* 6: *Cold meat box*—A coffin.

cold-meat cart *n.* a hearse. [Cf. MEAT WAGON]
   *****1820** in *F & H* II 151: He's gone—how very muddy some folks die!—He's for the *cold-meat cart*, and so am I. **1930** *Amer. Merc.* (Dec.) 455: Ambulance hell! It's the cold-meat cart you want.

cold-meat party *n. Irish-Amer.* a wake or funeral.
   1908 Sullivan *Criminal Slang* 1: *A cold meat party*—A wake. **1924** *N.Y. Times* (Aug. 3) VIII 16: If I was the D.A. there'd be a cold meat party for you. **1946** in *DAS* 115: You were at that cold-meat party, I spotted you coming out of the cemetery.

cold mitt *n.* (see quot.).
   1924 Henderson *Keys to Crookdom* 411: *Cold mitt.* Cold welcome.

cold nose *n.* COLD MITT; cold shoulder.
   1962 Kesey *Cuckoo's Nest* 226: What's everybody in this place givin' me the cold nose about?

cold one *n.* **1.** a dollar.
   1908 McGaffey *Show Girl* 223: I just lost five hundred cold ones by the deal.
   2. a cold bottle, glass, can, etc., of beer.
   1927 Shoup *Marines in China* 101: Each person having enjoyed the refreshment of a "cold one." **1928** in *DARE*: *Cold one*…euphemism for a bottle of beer kept on ice or otherwise cooled. **1933** J. Conroy *Disinherited* 220: Let's go…lap up a few cold ones. **1973** W. Crawford *Stryker* 26: Let's get a cold one. **1986** Univ. Tenn. instructor: Let's get a couple of cold ones. **1986–91** Hamper *Rivethead* 141: Several tall cold ones.

cold pack *n. Boxing.* a knockout blow. *Joc.*
   1934 Weseen *Dict. Slang* 231: *Cold pack*—A knockout. **1980** Pearl *Slang Dict.*: *Cold pack* n. (Boxing) A knockout.

cold potato *n.* a tedious or obnoxious person; PILL.
   1879 Sala *America Revisited* 50: Should the Rebellion Bore persist in invoking phantoms…the chances are that his indignant hearers will vote him a "cold potato" and "run him out." **1928** T.A. Dorgan, in Zwilling *TAD Lexicon* 28: (Trying to lose an awful pest before going on with the party) Cold potato. **1942** *ATS* 772: "Flat tire" (a poor companion on a "date"; a bore.)…*clunk…cold potato* [etc.].

cold prowl *n. Und.* (see quot.).
   1926 in *AS* LVII (1982) 261: *Cold prowl.* Ransacking a house while the occupants are away.

cold quack *adv. Und.* COLD TURKEY, 1.c.
   1963 Braly *Shake Him* 97: "What they got you for?" "Possession." "Stuff?" "No, just pot."…"That still do it. They got you cold quack?" "Cold enough."

cold shake *n.* an act of rejection or dismissal. [1892 quot. may mean 'betrayal' or 'rotten deal'.]
   1880 *Comic Bio. of Hancock* 24: Will you cast your vote for a man who rescues a widow and then gives her the cold shake? **1892** L. Moore *Own Story* 288: I am sorry you have given me such a cold shake.

cold shot *n.* a treacherous or offensive act or remark; an unpleasant surprise or situation.
   1963 Braly *Shake Him* 99: This is a cold shot. **1970** Landy *Underground Dict.* 54: *Cold shot* n. 1. Verbal insult; put-down. 2. Act that would bring dissension. **1972** Smith & Gay *Don't Try It* 199: *Cold Shot.* A bad deal; a "dirty trick." **1973** W. Crawford *Stryker* 33: Bellon's cold shot at Seamon…had been no idle jab. **1978** Selby *Requiem* 160: Harry and Tyrone were hit with a cold shot…Brody couldn't score any uncut weight. **1967–80** Folb *Runnin' Lines* 233: *Cold shot.* Uncalled for or belligerent behavior.

cold turkey *n.* **1.** *Narc.* the extreme physical and emotional suffering accompanying the sudden withholding, from an addict, of heroin, morphine or the like; withdrawal sickness; (hence, in recent use) sudden and complete cessation of a habit or addiction of any kind.
   1925 *Amer. Mercury* (Feb.) 197: I…favor full withdrawal—the process known as "cold turkey." **1931** in Partridge *Dict. Und.* **1936** *AS* (Apr.) 120: *Cold turkey.* Treatment of addicts in institutions where they are taken off drugs suddenly without…"tapering off." **1956** E. Hunter *Second Ending* 311: No, this is cold turkey, friend, that's what it is. There ain't a doctor in the world can help me. **1960** R. Reisner *Jazz Titans* 152: *Cold Turkey:* a narcotics cure in which the removal is sudden and

complete rather than gradual diminution. **1968** "J. Hudson" *Case of Need* 287: "Ten milligrams of this stuff will shove her into cold turkey so fast—" **1972** Burkhart *Women in Pris.* 235: She died in the hospital...of complications—not the cold turkey. **1978** Hamill *Dirty Laundry* 2: Cold turkey is never pleasant, not if you've come to love the habit. **1980** Manchester *Darkness* 59: Morphine...An army doctor had cut it off completely, leaving me to cold turkey.

2. the most basic level; bedrock.

1927 Coe *Me—Gangster* 237: He was not afraid of Flop when it came right down to cold turkey. **1993** Albany, N.Y., man, age 70: In the forties, maybe even the thirties, people would say, "Let's get down to cold turkey," meaning let's get down to business.

3. an easy target; a helpless victim.

1928 in E. O'Neill *Letters* 302: I am sure [the scandal]...will be cold turkey for the news boys from now on. **1937** Parsons *Lafayette Escadrille* 184 [ref. to *ca*1917]: The German, his motor functioning perfectly, sliced in heedlessly in a long screaming dive, anxious to make his kill. It was apparently cold turkey. **1942** Wylie *Vipers* 135: All the rest of mankind was cold turkey, to be preyed upon. **1956** Heflin *USAF Dict.: Cold turkey*...cold meat. **1958** Johnson & Caidin *Thunderbolt* 164: I would too quickly become cold turkey for a Focke-Wulf's cannon. **1966** Olsen *Hard Men* 24: Then Angus was cold turkey like the rest.

cold turkey *adv. & adj.* **1.a.** outright; directly; without preparation or warning; without mincing words.

1910 Service *Trail of '98* 43: I'd lost five thousand dollars..."cold turkey." **1920** T.A. Dorgan, in Zwilling *TAD Lexicon* 28: Now tell me on the square—can I get by with this for the wedding—don't string me—tell me cold turkey. **1922** in Sandburg *Letters* 212: I'm going to talk cold turkey with booksellers about the hot gravy in the stories. **1925** in Partridge *Dict. Und.: Cold turkey*—a departure without explanation. **1926** Maines & Grant *Wise-Crack Dict.* 7: *Cold turkey*—Definite statement of facts. **1928** Levin *Reporter* 70: The reporter put it to La Mouche cold turkey, asking, "Can we rid this district of the Culex?" **1937** C.B. Davis *Anointed* 207: 1 asked her cold turkey whether she believed in God. **1957** Myrer *Big War* 306: And you were planning on sashaying up there cold turkey. **1972** *Newsweek* (May 8) 22: Campaign manager Berl Bernhard spoke to the candidate "cold turkey," according to one witness, saying that Muskie had no money and no serious hope of bettering himself in any future primary. **1973** Haney *Jock* 36: She'll walk on a track cold turkey and say, "Boys, here I am! I want to ride!" **1974** Terkel *Working* 402: I call my customers cold turkey. I look in the book and call ten people. **1983** Rossner *August* 328: He was going to break with her cold turkey. **1991** Linnekin *80 Knots* 87: He...shot...32 percent—cold turkey, after having not been in a gunnery pattern for months.

b. with absolute certainty; COLD.

1952 Uris *Battle Cry* 57 [ref. to 1942]: Shannon had them cold turkey...brig for the whole bunch. **1959** Sterling *Wake of Waboo* 116: We've got them cold-turkey in the water. **1966–80** McAleer & Dickson *Unit Pride* 398: As I said, he catches them cold turkey. **1985** J.M.G. Brown *Rice Paddy Grunt* 281: We had these three Viet Cong cold turkey.

2. completely without narcotics or other addictive substances.

1922 Murphy *Black Candle* 264: This method of sudden withdrawal...is described in the jargon of the jail as "the cold turkey" treatment. **1932** L. Berg *Prison Doctor* 62: "Whitey" Allen was a "junkie"...in the days of "cold turkey cures." **1933** *Newsweek* (Aug. 5) 26: Mention of the "cold turkey treatment" gives a chill of horror to a drug addict. It means being thrown in jail with his drug supply completely cut off. **1947** Spillane *I, the Jury* 28: I doubt if you can comprehend what it means to one addicted to narcotics to go "cold turkey" as they call it. **1953** W. Brown *Monkey On My Back* 204: He sweats it out in prison "cold turkey." **1964** W. Stringfellow *My People* 48: They commonly have to endure going "cold turkey." **1981** D. Burns *Feeling Good* 98: I don't really feel like going cold turkey, and cutting down [on cigarettes] gradually would be slow torture. **1987** *Miami Vice* (NBC-TV): He talked about going cold turkey in the joint.

3. *Und.* (of a criminal charge) based on incontrovertible evidence.

1927–28 Tasker *Grimhaven* 68: It was a cold-turkey rap. Right on the main street, and a hundred people saw him go in with the gun in his hand. **1932** L. Berg *Prison Doctor* 233: "How the hell would you beat a cold turkey rap?"..."Easy. Don't get caught." **1931–34** in Clemmer *Pris. Comm.* 331: *Cold turkey*...caught in the act; a right charge, an open and shut case.

4. dead. Cf. COLD TURKEY, *n.*, 1.

1939 Appel *Power-House* 168: Suppose one of the kids did kill Ross....Kerrigan might squeeze him out of the syndicate the minute Ross was cold turkey. **1956** Fleming *Diamonds* 110: Out, Limey, or your friend's cold turkey.

5. emotionless; cold.

1936 Darling & Belden *Chan at Opera* (film): I tell you the dame is cold turkey. I saw her...yesterday. **1938** H. Miller *Trop. Capricorn* 106: The haughty one with the statuesque figure is probably a cold turkey fuck, a sort of *con anonyme*. **1962** Butterworth *Court-Martial* 30: He was a cold turkey sonofabitch, with cold eyes and a mind like a razor.

cold-turkey *v.* **1.a.** to address without mincing words.

1934 W. Smith *B. Cotter* 77: If I wanted a dame I'd cold-turkey her. **1949** Monteleone *Crim. Slang* 55: Cold Turkey (v) To speak frankly.

b. to resist flatly and completely.

1952 Mandel *Angry Strangers* 244: You gonna cold-turkey any squallin you get inside for it—like?

2.a. *Narc.* to effect a cure of narcotics addiction by the sudden and complete withholding of or abstention from the addicting drug. Also trans.

1949 Monteleone *Crim. Slang* 55: Cold Turkey (v)...to quit using drugs without tapering off to relieve the withdrawal. **1952** Ellson *Golden Spike* 47: I'm going to cold turkey it. **1952** Mandel *Angry Strangers* 238: You gonna cold-turkey it!...See? **1968** Gover *JC* 35: Maybe one a the black nashional brothers'll help you cold-turkey. **1990** Poyer *Gulf* 102: Cold turkeyed it. And really got clean.

b. to effect (a cold-turkey cure).

1961 H. Ellison *Gentleman Junkie* 38: He had started to "cold turkey" a cure. **1971** Curtis *Banjo* 209: The tough stretch of health she'd cold-turkeyed while she was with Gus had been wiped out.

cold wire *n.* [sugg. by LIVE WIRE] an unsuccessful or unlikable person.

1941 Macaulay & Wald *Manpower* (film): I'm a cold wire when it comes to the dames.

cole *n.* [poss. alter. of *coal*] *Gamb. & Und.* money.

*1592, *1665, *1676, *1688, *1692 (cited in Partridge *Dict. Und.* 138). *1724 in J. Farmer *Musa Pedestris* 41: He had tipt the cole. *1785 Grose *Vulgar Tongue: Cole*. Money. *Post the cole;* pay down the money. **1839** *Spirit of Times* (Mar. 30) 43: The parties coming down with their dust pretty *fully*, having been previously lucky in getting the *cole*. **1872** Burnham *Secret Service* 80: Spose you put me to the "queer cole maker" himself, and let me try my luck with *him*.

collar *n.* **1.a.** *Police & Und.* an arrest.—esp. in phrs. **get the collar** to be arrested; **give the collar** to arrest. Cf. *put the collar on*, below.

1871 in Burnham *Secret Service* 371: I would have gone right to your rescue, and risked all the "collar" I would get. **1889** Bailey *"Crook's" Life* 40 [ref. to *ca*1870]: "Yaller"...had exposed himself, and had got the "collar" in a down-town bank. **1890** Roe *Police* 220: The foregoing are only one or two of the good "collars" made by Dan Callahan. **1891** Davis *Galleger* 52: The driver's got the collar—he's 'rested. **1893** Riis *Nisby* 47: Once he had caught them at it and "given them the collar." **1904** A.H. Lewis *President* 432: Neither you...nor any of the pals you'll put into this game will get the collar. **1911** A.H. Lewis *Apaches of N.Y.* 31: It was for that stick-up in Mersher's the two made the collar. **1913** Kneeland *Prostitution* 151: She got a "collar" (*i.e.*, arrest) in the bargain. **1930** *Amer. Merc.* (Dec.) 455: What do you think? The lousy bull makes a collar on me. **1936** Dai *Opium Add.* 197: *Collar*. An arrest. **1955** Q. Reynolds *HQ* 31: An arrest was a "collar." **1962** Dougherty *Commissioner* 16: By the way,...do you guys have a warrant? Is this a collar, or ain't it? **1982** WINS radio news report (Aug. 15): The first collar came Friday...in Brentwood. **1988** Norst *Colors* 22: I just made a righteous collar.

b. *Police.* a person who is under arrest or who is to be arrested.

1974 *Kojak* (CBS-TV): We thought Petaki was an important collar. **1975** V.B. Miller *Deadly Game* 74: I grab the first uniformed policeman I can find...and hand over my collar. **1980** Gould *Ft. Apache* 33: When you saw him beat up on a collar in the back of a radio car, you knew there was something sick behind his humor. **1984** *N.Y. Post* (Aug. 2) 48: Cop Saves "Collar" in River. **1987** Taubman *Lady Cop* 4: They went to the hospital and I took the collar...I took him downtown.

2. a police officer.

1887 *N.O. Lantern* (Jan. 22): I t'ink de collars could jam him for somethin' else. **1891** Maitland *Slang Dict.* 72: *Collar* (Am.), (as a noun) a policeman. **1904** *Life in Sing Sing* 246: *Collar*...an officer. *Ibid.* 259: He *busted the collar's smeller.* He broke the officer's nose.

3. the foam on a glass of beer.

1891 McCann & Jarrold *Odds & Ends* 84: Just the color o' beer when you looks at it under the white collar o' foam. **1894** F.P. Dunne, in Schaaf *Dooley* 110: Fetch in a tub iv beer an' lave th' collar off. **1929** Shay *Drawn From the Wood* 26: The old man says less collar and more beer this time. **1940** O'Neill *Iceman* 108: He would as soon blow the collar off a schooner of beer as look at you. **1943** in Ruhm *Detective* 358: I'll send back this beer for another collar and I'll tell you. **1973** Layne *Murphy* (unp.): So let's blow the collar off a schooner of beer.

4. *Baseball.* the experience of being held hitless by an opposing pitcher.

[*a***1891** *F & H* II 154: *To be Collared*…(gaming).—To be unable to play one's usual game owing to temper, "funk," or other causes.] **1978** F. Messer *N.Y. Yankees vs. Texas Rangers* (WINS radio) (July 6): Graig took the collar last night—0 for 4. **1978** *N.Y. Times* (Aug. 6) V 5: But the thing [Pete Rose] will remember most about the night of Aug. 1, 1978, is the collar he got from McWilliams and Garber—0-for-4. **1980** Lorenz *Guys Like Us* 141: Stretch and Herman [were] taking the collar.

¶ In phrase:

¶ **put the collar on** *Police.* to arrest.

1872 Burnham *Secret Service* 99: Kennock was the man who sprung the trap and "put the collar" upon Dow at Hookset, N.H. **1927** Coe *Me—Gangster* 26: You can't put the collar on me! **1970** Gattzden *Black Vendetta* 39: Next thing…McCasker is putting the collar on me. **1982** *Ask Jack Anderson* (Mutual Radio Network) (Oct. 4): Last year, agents put the collar on over one thousand suspected counterfeiters.

collar *v.* **1.a.** [cf. earlier S.E. 'to seize (a person) by the collar'] to take hold of or grab; (*esp.*) to steal.

*ca***1700** in *OED* II 615: *Collar the Cole,* lay hold on the money. *****1838** Dickens *Nicholas Nickleby* ch. xv: Another gentleman comes and collars that glass of punch. *****1841** in *F & H* II 153: Ve *collar'd* the blunt, started off for town. **1859** Matsell *Vocab.* 20: *Collar.* To seize or take. **1866** *Nat. Police Gaz.* (Nov. 24) 3: No "cross cove" can collar my "super" or go "through" me for my "soft." **1882** "M. Twain" *Life on Miss.* 173: *What* are you sucking your fingers there for? Collar that kag of nails! **1884** "M. Twain" *Huck. Finn* 154: S'pose people left money laying around where he was—what did he do? He collared it. **1885** *Puck* (June 17) 252: I'd shell out a few dollars and collar the check. **1889** Trumble *Mott Street* 27: Collar the plunks, Chinay! **1891** Devere *Tramp Poems* 71: Don't collar these apples—beware of the snake! **1891** *Harper's* (Sept.) 624: Make out he's a sneak dat collars overcoats an' lifts door-mats in de brownstone deestrict. **1895** Townsend *Daughter of the Tenements* 230: How do you know he collared the boodle? How do you know Teresa didn't get it? **1906** *Nat. Police Gaz.* (Aug. 11) 6: The crook who had collared it simulated a look of…surprise. **1938** in Gelman *Photoplay* 209: A studio scenarist passed by our table. Mickey collared him.

b. to obtain; get.

1848 *Yale Banger* (Oct.): By that means the oration marks will be effectually collared, with scarce an effort. **1889** Field *Western Verse* 153: Can't ye see it is yer game/To go for all the votes ye kin an' collar uv the same? **1895** Townsend *Fadden* 3: How'd I collar it? Square. See? Dead square, an' easy. **1901** in "O. Henry" *Cabbages & Kings* 14: We need the spondulicks. You collar it. **1902** Remington *John Ermine* 134: When I fight, it's only glory which I collars. **1948** Manone & Vandervoort *Trumpet* 122: Then…I collared an idea.

2. *Racing.* to draw abreast of; catch up to.

1835 *Spirit of Times* (Dec. 26) 5: Gautier…went up on his fiery steed and collared the horse, and by a free use of the persuaders, finally passed. **1839** *Spirit of Times* (May 11) 115: David collared him, and a severe struggle ensued, which resulted in the Fylde winning by a half a neck only. **1880** *N.Y. Clipper Almanac* 44: Turf Directory…*Collar.*—To catch up with the leading horse…To draw up on an antagonist. **1898–1900** Cullen *Chances* 16: He collars the two in front of him as if they were munching carrots in their stalls. **1931** Harlow *Old Bowery* 203: Now one company would draw ahead for a few yards, then the other would "collar" it. **1949** Cummings *Dict. Sports* 79: The runner collars his opponent on the home stretch.

3. to catch or apprehend; (*specif.*) to place under arrest.

*****1853** (cited in Partridge *Dict. Und.* 139). **1859** Matsell *Vocab.* 20: *Collared.* Taken; arrested. **1865** Sala *Diary* II 19: What little vagrants there are the police likewise collar and sweep away to the "Institutions" on Deer Island. **1866** *Nat. Police Gaz.* (Nov. 10) 3: The Captain had been "collared" and locked up by McMullen. **1872** Burnham *Secret Service* v: *Collar,* to arrest, or seize with legal authority. *Ibid.* 319: Wright was quickly "collared" with $6000 worth of these stamps upon him. *****1881–84** Davitt *Prison Diary* I 200: I was constantly being interrogated as to

where I had been "collared," what I had "boned," and where I had done my "last bit." **1888** in *Amer. Heritage* (Oct. 1979) 20: And thought that they'd collar me/Never oh! never. **1895** *Harper's* (Oct.) 777: I told his mother I'd fetch 'im back if I collared him. **1903** Kildare *Mamie Rose* 45: To be "collared" by a "cop" at this hour meant a stay in the station house and a visit to the police court. **1908** *New Broadway* (Aug.) 141: Collared, he couldn't talk a word of English. **1930** Irwin *Tramp & Und. Sl.: Collar*…To arrest. **1955** Q. Reynolds *HQ* 11: He collared me twice.

4.a. to master.

*****1859** in *OED* II 615. **1877** *Puck* (Aug. 22) 13: The Hartfords could not collar Cummings's curves. **1948** Manone & Vandervoort *Trumpet* 116: When morning came I had that tune collared.

b. [perh. cf. COLLY] *Black E.* to comprehend.

1938 in R.S. Gold *Jazz Talk* 52: Do you collar this jive? **1942** *Pittsburgh Courier* (July 18) 7: Just sit tight and collar my ditty. **1946** Mezzrow & Wolfe *Really Blues* 47: I began to collar that all the evil I ever found came from ounce-brain white men. *Ibid.* 186: He collars all jive. **1946** Boulware *Jive & Slang* 2: *Collar The Jive?*…Do you understand?

5. to catch out.

1896 in S. Crane *Complete Stories* 308: If you hadn't lied to me in one thing, and I hadn't collared you flat in it, I might believe all the rest.

¶ In phrase:

¶ **collar a nod** *Black E.* to take a nap.

1934 Lomax & Lomax *Amer. Ballads & Folk Songs* 46: This ain' no place to collar no nod,/White folks wants you on de lumber yard.

collar-and-elbow joint *n.* a cafeteria or boardinghouse where patrons sit close together at long dining tables.—used derisively.

1933 Ersine *Prison Slang* 28: *Collar and elbow joint.* A restaurant in which all patrons sit close together at one long table. **1945** Hubbard *R.R. Ave.* 338: *Collar and elbow joint*—Boardinghouse. (There isn't too much room at dinner table).

college *n.* **1.** *Und. & Police.* a prison, reformatory, or the like. *Joc.*

*****1699** Ward *London-Spy* 112: Let him but enter in this *College*…and if he does not come out Qualified to take any *Degree of Villany,* he must be the most *Honest Dunce* that ever had the advantage of such Eminent Tutors. *****1703** in *F & H* II 155: The History of Whittington's *Colledge* otherwise (Vulgarly) called Newgate. *****1785** Grose *Vulgar Tongue: College,* Newgate, or any other prison. *****1836** C. Dickens, in *F & H* II 155: Welcome to the college, gen'l'mem. **1859** Matsell *Vocab.* 20: *College.* A State prison. *****1889** in *F & H* II 155: But only one other has stopped me to remind me that we were at "college" together. **1903** McCardell *Chorus Girl* 110: The college her brother is in is the Elmira Reformatory. **1906** H. Green *Boarding House* 59: "Pretty Sammy" was just out of "college", and he had money. **1922** T. Dreiser, in Riggio *Dreiser-Mencken Letters* II 482: My old college friend—Sing Sing college. **1928** Panzram *Killer* 158: Big house—hoosegow, stir or college. **1930** *Amer. Merc.* (Dec.) 455: *College, n.:* A reformatory. "Say, I'm no punker. Wasn't I in college?" **1933** Tannenbaum *Osborne of Sing Sing* 38: That's a trick I learned at "College." **1936** in D. Runyon *More Guys* 149: He is finally lumbered in 1931 and sent to college…He is in college at Dannemora…until…1936. **1941** Root & Burnett *Get-Away* (film): I'm gonna crash out of this college. **1960** Carpenter *Harlot* 107: "I'm a graduate of the college at Warwick," he said bitterly. **1967** Lit *Dictionary* 9: *College*—Jail.

2. NUT COLLEGE.

1937 in Goodstone *Pulps* 11: Are you his keeper, mister?…If you are, you'd better take him back to the college and lock him up.

college try *n.* a worthy or plucky effort, esp. with only limited hope of success.—usu. constr. with *the old.* Now *colloq.*

1927 *N.Y. Sun* (July 18) (cited in Nichols *Baseball Term.*). **1942** *ATS* 256. **1950** *Sat. Eve. Post* (Oct. 28) 136: This is the college try for me….I'll sell my franchise…if I don't finish near the top this year. **1962** *Time* (Dec. 21) 56: Everyone was gunning for the Packers, giving it the old college try.

college widow *n.* *Stu.* (see quots.).

1900 *DN* II 29: *College-widow, n.* A girl whom new men meet from year to year but whom no one ever marries. **1934** Weseen *Dict. Slang* 177: *College widow*—A noncollege girl or woman who flirts with students.

collision mat *n.* usu. *pl.* Esp. *USMC & Navy.* a pancake or waffle. *Joc.*

1926 in *AS* III (1927) 451: *Collision mats*—Waffles. **1940** *Life* (Oct. 28) 99: Collision mats (pancakes). **1942** *Leatherneck* (Nov.) 144: *Collision-Mats.*—Pancakes. So called because they are about the size and consistency of the mats hung over the side of a boat or ship for protection in docking or coming alongside another. **1944** Sturges *Hero* (film): Won't you join us in a stack of collision mats [pancakes], as they say in the Marine Corps? **1944** E.H. Hunt *Limit* 22: Your favorite—collision mats and lube oil. **1958** Cooley *Run For Home* 53 [ref. to *ca*1922]: The little messman had never forgotten the name an ex-Navy seaman had given the cakes—"collision mats." **1977** Avallone *White Knight* 55: I could always meet them…at a collision-mat house on the Jersey Turnpike.

colly v. [cf. COLLAR, v., 4.b.] *Und.* to understand.
1932 in *AS* (Feb. 1934) 26 [as pris. slang]: *Colly*. To understand. **1941** *AS* XVI 245: There's fuzz in the back. Don't you colly?

collywobbles n.pl. [poss. alter of *cholera morbus*] a stomachache; (*hence*) jitters; (*also*) an imaginary illness of any sort.
***1823** Egan *Grose*: *Collywobbles*, the gripes. **1834** in *DARE*: There was a general depression of spirits; the people seem'd to have taken the collywobbles, and every one was afear'd to speak his mind to his neighbor. ***1889** Barrère & Leland *Dict. Slang* I 264: *Colly-wobbles* (popular), rumblings in the intestines; the belly-ache. **1942** *Sat. Eve. Post* (Oct. 10) 103: It's a wonder Larry don't get the collywobbles, playin' around Mud Lake after varmints. **1950, 1965–70** in *DARE*. ***1980** Leland *Kiwi-Yank. Dict.* 27: *Collywobbles*: A nervous upset stomach.

color v. to regard as.—usu. imper. *Joc.*
1962 ABC-TV ad for series *I'm Dickens He's Fenster* (Oct.): "Color her married." "Yeah, color her very married." **1966** Young & Hixson *LSD* 6: Color the current scene "psychedelic." **1974** WINS Radio News (May 26): American youth and the job market: color the future bleak. **1975** V.B. Miller *Trade-Off* 105: I shrug. "Color me kinky." **1980** Eble *Campus Slang* (Mar.) 2: *Color me gone*—to declare the intention to leave immediately. **1982** Rucker *Kafka* 144: Give me my money…and color me gone! **1985** Dye *Between Raindrops* 317: Well, let 'er rip, man…Color me gone. **1986** Franzoni *Jumpin' Jack Flash* (film): Well, color me so surprised! **1992** *Middle Ages* (CBS-TV): Color me bad!

Colorado Kool-Aid n. [sugg. by *Kool-Aid*, trademark for a sweetened soft-drink mix; Coors beer is brewed in Colorado] Coors brand of beer. *Joc.*
1972 Jenkins *Semi-Tough* 33: Big-un would drink himself a lot of that Colorado Kool-Aid. **1977** Univ. Tenn. student: In Texas, Coors is Colorado Kool-Aid. **1983** K. Weaver *Texas Crude* 66: *Colorado Kool-aid*. Coors beer. **1990** *Newsweek* (Jan. 29) 14: *Colorado Kool-Aid*: Coors beer.

color-blind adj. given to embezzlement or other thievery.
1943 *AS* XVIII 164: One who is color-blind is an employee who cannot distinguish between his own money and that of the company. **1966** in *DARE*.

colors n.pl. [cf. earlier uses in *OED2* since *ca*1400 and *1873 quot. below] identifying insignia, as of a motorcycle club or street gang; (*hence*) an article, as of clothing, bearing such insignia.
[***1873** Hotten *Slang Dict.*: *Colour*, a handkerchief worn by each of the supporters of a professional athlete on the day of a match.] **1967–68** T. Wolfe *Kool-Aid* 25: He has on the Hell's Angels "colors," meaning a jacket with an insignia, a jacket with the sleeves cut off and the skull with the helmet on it and the wings and a lot of other arcane symbols. **1971** Sanders *Family* 151: The bikers are famous for their elaborate funerals with single-file lines of motorcycles forming the funeral procession. The woman's "colors"—her club garb—are often buried with the "colors" of "her man" in the grave. **1972** *N.Y. Post* (Jun. 26) 27: Being forcibly stripped of your "colors," as the youths call their jackets, is a humiliation which spreads like a stain to the other members of the clique. **1977** Butler & Shryack *Gauntlet* 134: Bikers pulled on their identifying "colors." **1978** *N.Y. Post* (Dec. 9) 14: The *Roman Queens* are on one side and the *Kings* are on their side and everybody flies their colors. **1988** Norst *Colors* 11: They're flying their colors. **1990** *Daily Beacon* (Univ. Tenn.) (Sept. 6) 5: None wear recognizable "colors," such as jackets or bandannas.

colossal adj. [sugg. by the hyperbolic use of the word in cinema promotions] wonderful.
1942 *ATS* 32: Magnificent…*colossal*. **1977** Coover *Public Burning* 433: Which is fuzzbeard lingo for the "colossal" of [the 1930's].

colt n. **1.** a novice, esp. a professional athlete in his first year; ROOKIE.
***1725** *New Cant. Dict.*: *Colt*, a Lad newly initiated into Roguery. ***1823** "J. Bee" *Slang* 55: "A *colt*" is he who enters upon a new avocation, as an apprentice, or juryman for the first time. **1869** *N.Y. Herald* (July 13)

(cited in Nichols *Baseball Term.*). ***1885** in *F & H* II 157: A match arranged for the benefit of the young players of the county was commenced yesterday at Manchester, when the Lancashire Eleven were opposed to Twenty-six *colts*. ***1889** Barrère & Leland *Dict. Slang* I 265: *Colt*…(Cricketers), a young inexperienced player, a professional at his first season. **1891** Maitland *Slang Dict.* 72: *Colt*, a professional cricketer or baseball player during his first season. **1908** in Fleming *Unforget. Season* 38: A doubleheader was the opening attraction of the season, the colts, or young recruits, playing the New York Athletic Club, and the real Giants lining up against Yale. **1911** Van Loan *Big League* 19: To-day, in that game with the colts, he kept pegging low.
2. a young or spirited fellow.
1833 J. Hall *Soldier's Bride* 239: He extolled Colonel J— as "a severe colt." **1834** *Davy Crockett's Almanack* (1835) 6: I now found I had a pretty severe colt to deal with. **1836** *Davy Crockett's Almanack* I (No. 3) 40: Goliah was a pretty hard colt but I could choke him. **1944** C.B. Davis *Leo McGuire* 168: Maybe I was careless sometimes when I was a colt.

colyoons n.pl. [< Early ModE *cullions*] the testicles.
1977 Bredes *Hard Feelings* 12: Belt him with a stick. Knee him in the colyoons.

com n. **1.** a commissioned officer. Cf. NONCOM.
1887 W. Watson *Life in Confed. Army* 156 [ref. to 1861]: The "coms," (as we called the commissioned officers) were still asleep.
2. an intercom. Cf. COMM.
1981 *Rod Serling's Mag.* (Sept.) 38: Skeet Mahoney does a Bugs Bunny over the 'com.
3. var. COMM.

comb v. to thrash; (*hence*) to scold.—usu. in phr. **comb (someone's) head** [or **hair**].
***1596** Shakespeare *Taming Shrew* I i: To combe your noddle with a three-legg'd stoole. ***1600** in *OED*. ***1679** in *OED*: He would have…combed his head with a Bunch of Keys. ***1783** (cited in Partridge *DSUE* (ed. 8) 241 in phr. *comb (someone's) hair*). **1795** in *DARE*: If I don't comb his head with a three-legged stool, there is no snakes in Ireland. **1847** in Blair & Meine *Half Horse* 123: I jest gin old aunty an idee that Jabe was the man, and lor didn't she comb him! He ain't got the creases out'n his face yet! ***1858** in *OED*: Till I find you a wife who will comb your head for you. **1891** in *DARE*: To comb a man's head—to give him a thrashing. ***a1891** *F & H* II 157: *Comb One's Hair*…Sometimes to thrash, and generally ill-treat. **1926** C.M. Russell *Trails* 174: He gets his own barker first and combs this puncher's hair. Of course this finishes the fight with some spillin' of blood, but there's no powder burnt. **1928** in *DARE*: *Comb, comb (one's) hair*…to scold. **1968** R. Adams *West. Words*: *Comb his hair*. To hit someone over the head with the barrel of a pistol.

combat-happy adj. *Mil.* afflicted with combat neurosis; (*hence*) crazy.
1962 *Our Army at War* (Apr.) 1: The combat-happy Joes of Easy Co.! **1971** Cole *Rook* 216: They were combat-happy, everyone said, but whatever they were, they were fighters. **1975** S.P. Smith *Amer. Boys* 79: A squad leader in D Company had gone "combat-happy."…That could mean anything from turning chicken to killing forty prisoners. **1966–80** McAleer & Dickson *Unit Pride* 240: The Commies? You're combat-happy.

combat zone n. Orig. *Boston.* a crowded city area characterized by tawdry small businesses, esp. disreputable bars, adult theaters and bookstores, etc.; red-light district.
1970–71 Higgins *Eddie Coyle* 87: The Combat Zone sounded like there was a war going on there for a while. **1978** Schrader *Hardcore* 134: San Diego's "combat zone," four square blocks of adult bookstores, peep shows, and flophouses. **1980** Algren *Dev. Stocking* 136: A combat zone where prostitutes, pimps and johns can frolic freely without let or hindrance by the police. **1983** Stapleton *30 Yrs.* 126: Who were mugged or who contracted a slight social disease in the Combat Zone. *Ibid.* 202: The Boston Combat Zone is nowhere near as large as Times Square or even North Beach in San Francisco. **1984** W.M. Henderson *Elvis* 11: Scollay Square honky-tonks and "combat-zone" joints like the Hillbilly Ranch. **1985** *USAir* (Mar.) 97: Ironically, Lafayette Place is now seen as a key to cleaning up the "Combat Zone. **1989** Radford & Crowley *Drug Agent* 54: At the Combat Zone intersection of Washington and Essex Streets [in Boston].

combination n. a syndicate of gamblers or criminals; gang.
1880 *N.Y. Clipper Almanac* 44: *Combination*.—A pool formed by jockeys or drivers to fix an event. **1943** Wolfert *Tucker's People* 383: We know

Leo is in the combination. **1961** Scarne *Gamb. Gde.* 206: The operators are usually a *combination* (syndicate) of neighborhood toughs, one of whose members is the racket boss of the area. **1970** in Cannon *Nobody Asked* 246: Them days a combination out of Pittsburgh was betting all big offices a ton of money.

¶ In phrase:

¶ **lose the combination** to miss the point; become forgetful. *Joc.*

1889 Barrère & Leland *Dict. Slang* II 30: *To lose the combination* (American), to miss the meaning or point of anything. **1906** in *OEDS*.

combo *n.* **1.** a combination (in any sense), as a betting combination, combination sandwich, partnership, etc.

1921 *Variety* (Dec. 30) 97: A guy who knew the combos could…grab himself enough jack [shooting craps]. **1926** Dunning & Abbott *Broadway* 252: Well, I used to think we'd make about the best combo I could imagine. **1931** *AS* VII 105: *Combo*, the combination of a safe or vault. **1933** Ersine *Prison Slang: Combinations, Combo, n.* The ingredients of a meal, ready for cooking; a meal. **1936** *AS* (Feb.) 42: *Combo.* Combination sandwich or salad. **1959** in *AS* XXXVII (1962) 79: Take chicken-rice combo. **1959** De Roo *Young Wolves* 130: I got a winning combo. **1970** Southern *Blue Movie* 169: Combo of surprise and indignation.**1965** Spillane *Killer Mine* 45: If he talks the upstate combo will fall. **1978** J. Reynolds *Geniuses* 56: It's a snap—a one-two combo to the kidneys, a left hook to the jaw. **1980** Whalen *Takes a Man* 22: We're priceless. What a combo! **1981** *N.Y. Daily News* (Aug. 12) 70: It was then that Dave Kingman and Ellis Valentine proved what a potent combo they can be…Valentine's single sent Kingman to third. **1988** *Superior Court* (ABC-TV): She gave me the combo to the safe.

2. a small jazz band. Now *S.E.*

1924 *Variety* (Dec. 24) 14: An all-male string combo. **1935** in *OEDS*: As a soft fiddle-sax combo, it clicks. **1950–52** Ulanov *Hist. Jazz* 350: *Combo*: short for "combination" of musicians, usually a small band. **1952** Uris *Battle Cry* 147: There was a Negro combo slapping out sixteen jazz on the bandstand at one end. **1962** E. Stephens *Blow Negative* 293: The combo…played in the little dancing area that adjoined the circular bar. **1964** R.S. Gold *Jazz Lexicon* 61. **1970** *Playboy* (Sept.) 60: A combo that includes bassist Ron Carter keeps things moving. **1977** Harnack *Under Wings* 49: "Good-Night, Ladies" from the three-man combo.

come or **cum** *n.* **1.a.** semen.—usu. considered vulgar.

1923 Manchon *Le Slang* 90: *Come,* Sperme. **1934** "J.M. Hall" *Anecdota* 28: The come…landed gracefully at the ladies' feet. **1941** G. Legman, in G. Henry *Sex Variants* II 1161: *Come*…The semen, a term commonly used by homosexuals. **ca1949** in Holt *Dirty Comics* 173: Oh Daddy, there it is. Red hot com! **1959** Kerouac *Dr. Sax* 70: Zaza has an endless supply of come. **1967** Rechy *Numbers* 197: Johnny comes readily, his cum spurting on the other's face. **1967** Mitchell *Thumb Tripping* 18: He'd piss and see…dried cum on his cock. **1968** Heard *Howard St.* 20: Well, dammit, it was full of his come! **1970** W.C. Woods *Killing Zone* 118: The lieutenant is out in the parking lot wiping the come off his bucket seats. **1974** Angelou *Gather Together* 32: A heap of come-filled rubbers. **1991** C. Fletcher *Pure Cop* 87: I'll tell you what's romantic today. If the whore swallows your come. That's about as romantic as it gets.

b. vaginal fluid.—usu. considered vulgar.

1945–48 *USMC Marianas Coll.* (unp.): With cum running down my legs. **1964** in Jackson *Swim Like Me* 99: She said, "I wouldn't let him suck the come from my drawers."

c. energy; spirit.—usu. considered vulgar.

1988 Norst *Colors* 108: When I was young and dumb and full of come as you, *loco!*

2. Esp. *Mil.* cream gravy, mayonnaise, or the like.—usu. considered vulgar.

1937 *AS* (Feb.) 74: *Come*—gravy. **1942–44** *AS* (Feb. 1946) 32: *Cum,* n…Salad dressing or mayonnaise.

3. an orgasm.—usu. considered vulgar.

1967 Salas *Tattoo* 178: As if he were at the peak of a come. **1967** Hamma *Motorcycle Mommas* 108: I think you ought to lick it for her. Until she has a come! **1968** in L. Williams *City of Angeles* 104: What has more…value than a good come anyway? **1970** Peters *Sex Newspapers* 6: This gives Jane her greatest "come" of all.

come *v.* **1.a.** to experience sexual orgasm.—also (rarely in U.S.) constr. with *off*.—usu. considered vulgar. Also **cum.**

***ca1600** in Burford *Bawdy Verse* 57: "I come, I come…" "Not so, my Dear and Dearest," she replied,/"From us two Sweet, this pleasure must not glide." ***1604** Dekker & Middleton *Honest Whore Pt. I* I ii 4:

Theres for thy paines, godamercy, if euer I stand in neede of a wench that will come with a wet finger, Porter, thou shalt earne my mony. ***a1650** in Furnivall *Loose Songs*: Then off he came, & blusht for shame soe soone that he had endit. ***1672** *Covent Garden Drollery* 31: Though I spent a full share,/Yet by *Cupid* I swear,/I came off with a ha ha ha ha ha [etc.]. ***1691** in Adlard *Forbidden Tree* 29: She gave him a lift for his thrust/And catched him as he was a-coming. ***1714** in *OEDS*: Just as we *came,* I cried, "I faint! I die!" ***1698–1720** D'Urfey *Pills* V 108: But being call'd by Company,/As he was taking pains to please her;/I'm coming, coming Sir, says he,/My Dear, and so am I, says she, Sir. ***ca1835–40** in Speaight *Bawdy Songs* 24: "There—I told you," says she, "There was somebody coming." ***ca1866** *Romance of Lust* 85: He spent twice before giving me time to come once. *ca***1888** *Stag Party* 208: Oh-h! I'm coming—I'm coming—I'm coming! **1899** *Memoirs of Dolly Morton* 250: Though nature forced me to "come," I had no feeling but one of loathing. ***1909** in Joyce *Selected Letters* 182: Did you come? **1916** Cary *Venery* I 50: Come—To experience the sexual spasm; to achieve emission; to spend. The expression…is common to both the sexes. **1919** in Dreiser *Diaries* 289: Helen…comes off with me now very quickly. Didn't at first. **1934** "J.M. Hall" *Anecdota* 28: Just then Little Willie came off. **1935** in Oliver *Blues Trad.* 231: I got somethin' 'tween my legs'll make a dead man come. **1946** in Inman *Diary* 1310: When he became excited, did he "come off"? **1963** Davenport *Carmina Archilochi* 15: He comes, in bed,/As copiously as a Prienian ass. **1965** Linakis *In Spring* 120: Naked, she was Aphrodite…Christ, she could make a dead man come. **1967** Rosenthal *Sheeper* 88: Have you ever run across the type who apologize when they come off? **1972** in E. Knight *Essential* 21: My Father grunted and comed. **1973** *TULIPQ* (coll. B.K. Dumas): Damn! That's enough to make a dead man come! **1978** Strieber *Wolfen* 157: She came. Like a…freight train. **1978** Wharton *Birdy* 33: Bango, I come off. **1991** B.E. Ellis *Amer. Psycho* 101: In the time since I've started licking and sucking on her pussy she's already come twice.

b. to ejaculate.—used. trans.—usu. considered vulgar.

1967 W. Crawford *Gresham's War* 157: Don't that make you come a quart? **1968** P. Roth *Portnoy* 23: It is my fourth orgasm of the day. When will I begin to come blood?

c. to induce orgasm in (someone).—usu. considered vulgar.

1973 Gwaltney *Destiny's Chickens* 17: Wail, I comed that little old gal, then I crawled off.

d. to be overcome by excitement, enthusiasm, eagerness or delight; usu. in phr. **come in (one's) pants.**—used derisively.—usu. considered vulgar. Cf. sim. devel. of GET OFF.

1926 in Hemingway *Sel. Letters* 199: Walsh's poem or coming in his pants or whatever you want to call it made me vomit again. **1939** M. Levin *Citizens* 38: What's the matter with Baldy, what's he coming in his pants for? **1952** Landon *Angle of Attack* 171: I'll tell you something else you been just coming in your pants to know. **1971** Dahlskog *Dict.* 14: *Come*…to become highly excited.

2.a. to accomplish, perpetrate, or do; PULL; in phr. **come it strong** exert oneself to the limit, esp. in pretense or exaggeration. [Bracketed exx. illustrate an earlier meaning, itself prob. elliptical for *come forth with*, from which the present sense seems to have arisen.]

[***1698–99** "B.E." *Dict. Canting Crew: Has he come it?*…has he lent it to you?] [***1823** "J. Bee" *Dict. Turf.: To come it*—to comply with a request, as lending money.] ***1823** "J. Bee" *Dict. Turf.*: Come it strong. ***1825** in *OEDS*: Let him come that, and I shall be satisfied. **1833** J. Hall *Soldier's Bride* 226: I don't want to strike such a *mean white man* as you, but if you *come over* them words agin, drot my skin if I don't try you a cool dig or two. **1836** *Spirit of Times* (July 9) 162: Hurra my Popcorn—…come it strong—lumber—go it with a looseness—root little pig or die. ***1837** C. Dickens, in *OEDS*: The inimitable manner in which Bill Thompson can come the double monkey. ***1839** in Partridge *Dict. Und.* 141: The fellows sing psalms vigorously, and if they "come it strong," as they call it, they calculate upon a remission of their sentence. **1842** *Spirit of Times* (Oct. 29) 409: He "couldn't come it." **1843** Greene *Exposure of Gambling* 192: And the way this pad, already stocked is introduced on the table, is as follows (it is called *coming the change*). **1847** Robb *Squatter Life* 74: You aint comin' a hoax over a fellar? *Ibid.* 143: Arter a spell,…I cum it strong about affecshun. **1848** Baker *Glance at N.Y.* 5: I think you can come the drop game there. **1852** in Eliason *Tarheel Talk* 265: Who [the senatorial nominee] will be it will be difficult to predict, but my opinion is Old — will not "come it." **1854** G.G. Foster *15 Mins.* 6: Mr. Sandford came a great democratic dodge in going to Louis Napoleon's fête in plain black coat and trowsers. **1862** C.F. Browne *A. Ward* 157: He didn't cum it, as the sekel showed. **1864** Hill

Our Boys 37: Can't come it, captain. **1868** Williams *Black-Eyed Beauty* 8: He has a flat, round face, and tries to come the English side-whisker with his light-brown hair. **1869** B. Harte, in *F & H* II 160: In his sleeves, which were long,/He had twenty-four packs, which was coming it strong. **1888** Bunner *Letters* 127: I can come the modern caper, I think. **1895** Coup *Sawdust* 118: I declined to receive it…telling him not to come any of his "funny business over me." **1908** *DN* III 300: He tried hard, but he couldn't quite come it. **1915–16** Lait *Beef, Iron & Wine* 233: Don't come that stuff on me. **1916** Lardner *Know Me Al* 156: I sent $25.00 to Florie so she can't come no none support business on me. **1917–20** in J.M. Hunter *Trail Drivers* I 63: I said, "You can't come that on me. Give me back my ticket." **1932** Berg *Prison Dr.* 86: Trying to come the insane gag on me, Ripper, eh? *1959 Behan *Borstal Boy* 29: Don't you come that stuff here, Behan. **1962** L'Amour *Killoe* 24: You folks come it mighty big around here. **1972** in *DARE*: I can't come it— I can't eat more.

b. to act the part of; play.

*1837 C. Dickens, in *OED*: That man, sir…has comic powers that would do honor to Drury Lane Theatre…Hear him come the four cats in the wheelbarrow. *1841, *1850 in *Ibid.* **1854** G.G. Foster *15 Mins.* 89: Feeling quite grand at having come the fashionable swell so loud. **1979** Edson *Gentle Giant* 102: Don't come the innocent with me…!

¶ In phrases:

¶ **come again?** what did you say? Now *colloq.*

1884 G.W. Peck, in *OED2*: "After diagnosing the case—" "Come again, please," said the old man, when she struck the college word. "You *whiched* the case?" **1920** S. Lewis *Main Street* ch. xxiii.

¶ **come clean** see s.v. CLEAN.

¶ **come it** *Und.* to confess or inform. *Obs.* in U.S.

*1812 Vaux *Vocab.*: *Come It*: to divulge a secret; to tell anything of one party to another; they say of a thief who has turned evidence against his accomplices, that he is *coming* all he knows, or that he *comes it as strong as a horse*. *1835, *1839 (cited in Partridge *Dict. Und.*). **1846** *Nat. Police Gaz.* (Mar. 21) 241: He…would be induced to "come it,"* on the whole business…. *To reveal to officers, or become States' evidence. *1857 in *F & H* II 160: To inform = to come it. *1881, *1889, *1932, *1935 (cited in Partridge *Dict. Und.*).

¶ **come it on, 1.** to manhandle; drub.

1848 *Life in Rochester* 67: We came it on him right and left, hit his right hind wheel, smashed his concern all to flinters.

2. *come it over*, below.

1888 Bidwell *Forging His Chains* 80: You are trying to "come it" on us.

¶ **come [it] over** to fool, trick, swindle, take advantage of.

*1785 Grose *Vulgar Tongue*: To come over anyone; to cheat or over-reach him. *1827 in *OEDS*: They try to come it over us venhever they have a tunity. **1845** in Robb *Squatter Life* 163: Tom had "come it" over him for…many odd dinners. **1852** Stowe *Uncle Tom's Cabin* 45: Don't you think to come it over me! **1862** Browne *Art. Ward* 49: You can't cum it over me, my boy! **1865** *Rogues & Rogueries of N.Y.* 42: The above is but a sample of the many methods adopted by the "members of the profession" to "come it over" strangers. **1868** Macy *There She Blows!* 54: Well, I come it over him once. *ca*1875 Williams *Binnacle Jack* 36: There's a bastely fellow in the cisspool who wants to come over me wid his blarney. **1936** Lipscomb & Ferris *Under Two Flags* (film): Don't try to come it over me with your soft ways.

¶ **come off the grass** to stop talking foolishly.

*a*1891 *F & H* 161: Come off the Grass or the Tall Grass!…(American) "None of your airs!" "Don't put it on so!" "Don't tell any more lies!" **1894** in Remington *Wister* 115: Hence the expression, "come off the grass." *1936 Partridge *DSUE*.

¶ **come off the roof** to stop behaving foolishly or pretentiously.—constr. in imper.

1883–84 Whittaker *L. Locke* 260: Oh, come off the roof…Position be blowed! **1884** *Life* (Jan. 17) 35: Now, alas! my hopes are broken—/I could bear reproof—/But those accents lowly spoken/"O! Come off the roof." **1895** Foote *Coeur D'Alene* 173: Oh, come off the roof, and do as you are told! *1895 (cited in Partridge *DSUE* (ed. 8)).

¶ **come the old dog** to *come the old soldier*, below.

1848 (quot. at *come the old soldier*, below).

¶ **come the old soldier** Esp. *Mil.* to act in an insolent, deceptive, sly, or bullying manner. *Rare* in U.S.

*1818 in Partridge *DSUE* (ed. 6) 1064: Come the old soldier over [someone]. *1824 Sir W. Scott, in *OED* IX 385: I should think he was coming the old soldier over me, and keeping up his game. **1848** J. Scott *Encarnation* 52: The fastest fellow got the best one, and the sick and lame got none…Those who were guilty of this act of meanness called

it "coming the old soldier." Some called it "ringing in," and some, "coming the old dog." *1861 in *OED* IX 385: But you needn't try to come the old soldier over me. I'm not quite such a fool as that. *1925 Fraser & Gibbons *Soldier & Sailor Wds.* 61 [ref. to WWI]: To Come the Old Soldier…To attempt to shirk anything. To try to bluff someone. Also, to be domineering.

¶ **come [the] —— over (someone)** to have the effect of (——) on (someone). Cf. *come Paddy over* s.v. PADDY.

1845 in Blair & McDavid *Mirth* 82: But our animal knowed how to come the giraffe over *him*—so round he turns and gives him the stern view again! **1845** in Oehlschlaeger *Reveille* 119: Jake come *bar* over him [i.e. hugged him like a bear]. **1858** in G.W. Harris *High Times* 154: How does that chicken cock rest on yer bowels what yer cum the boar-constructor over? **1861** in McClellan *Civil War Papers* 50: They are strongly entrenched, but I think I can come the Cerro Gordo over them.

¶ **come the possum** to play possum; feign ignorance.

1848 in R.L. Wright *Irish Emigrant Ballads* 521: But he cum de possum, and got free. **1862** "E. Kirke" *Among Pines* 88: Pshaw, Scip, you're "coming de possum."

¶ **come up roses** to turn out in a way that is exceedingly favorable, pleasant, profitable, or the like.

1963 D. Tracy *Brass Ring* 276: I thought everything was going to come up roses. **1969** L. Sanders *Anderson Tapes* 242: What luck! Everything was coming up roses. **1974** Leggett, Mead & Charvat *Prentice-Hall Handbook* 353: I asked him how he was making out with the car and he told me everything was coming up roses. **1974** Millard *Thunderbolt* 50: An old veteran bank robber…taught Red…about safes and bank vaults and how to crack them and come up roses. **1978** Selby *Requiem* 127: All of a sudden, or so it seemed, the world had turned around and they were coming up roses. **1979** McGivern *Soldiers* 101: So after more than three months of looking like somebody who slept in a slit trench, Gelnick comes up roses. [**1983** W. Walker *Dime to Dance* 28: Yeah, well, it was one of those things where he fell in a shit pile and came up with a rose in his mouth.]

¶ **make come** (see quot.).

1853 "P. Paxton" *In Texas* 118: [The Texan] does not kill his game, he *saves* or *gets* it, or *makes it come*.

¶ **not coming** Black E. not interested.—constr. with *on*.

1948 Manone & Vandervoort *Trumpet* 109: I ain't comin' on that riff right now, 'cause I got a taste of the shorts. So you gotta help me blow the joint.

¶ **where (someone) is coming from** (someone's) precise meaning, intention, or character.

1969 Ark. State Univ. student: I get what Nietzsche's saying but I'm not real sure where he's coming from. **1971** N.Y.U. student: Find out where he's coming from with that stuff. **1974** Gober *Black Cop* 24: Ain't no way! You dig where I'm coming from? **1974** Goines *Eldorado* 62: Even a blind man can dig where I'm coming from, Buddy. **1973–76** J. Allen *Assault* 123: Now, most of the time when a dude is very quiet in jail, he be left alone, 'cause you don't never know where a quiet dude coming from unless he show a lot of feelings within his face. **1986** NYC man, age 37: Yeah, I know just where he's coming from. **1989** Geraldo (synd. TV series) (Apr. 27): Walter, I understand where you're comin' from.

come across *v.* **1.** to provide, hand over, pay or (*later*) tell or do, esp. what has been demanded or agreed to.—usu. constr. with *with*. Now *colloq.*

1878 Mulford *Fighting Indians* 17: The said proprietor would come across with a bite and a drink. **1908** McGaffey *Show Girl* 214: Waiting for the angel to come across with the necessary funds. **1909** T. Dreiser, in Riggio *Dreiser-Mencken Letters* I 26: Won't you come across with something real snappy? **1912** Lowrie *Prison* 143: Make 'em come across with what's comin' t' y'r. **1914** Ellis *Billy Sunday* 208: Come across with the mazuma. **1914** S. Lewis *Our Mr. Wrenn* 47: "Coming across" with ten dollars for a bribe. **1914** London *Jacket* 62: Standing, you're going to come across with that dynamite, or I'll kill you in the Jacket. Harder cases than you have come across before I got done with them. **1918** T.A. Dorgan, in *N.Y. Eve. Jour.* (Aug. 6) 12: Come across like a ferryboat, kid. **1931** Hellinger *Moon* 67: When I asked this guy his name, he wouldn't come across. **1931** Uhler *Cane Juice* 54: What's that you're trying to hide from me, daughter?…Come across, girl.

2. (of a woman) to engage in sexual intercourse at the urging or demand of a man.

1921 McAlmon *Hasty Bunch* 237: You could fuss your damned head off, and they'd go so far and no further, and then because they'd want to see you again, say that maybe they'd come across another night. **1927** [Fliesler] *Anecdota* 168: "That's a brand-new Buick, what you want to paint it up like a boat for?"…"Last night a puritan came across in it." **1929** E. Caldwell *Bastard* 41: Why didn't you let her out, if she came across? **1932** J.T. Farrell *Guillotine Party* 180: Did you hear how she screamed because Hugh made her come across even if she was sick? **1934** H. Miller *Tropic of Cancer* 209: First she wouldn't come across because she had the monthlies. **1937** Reitman *Box-Car Bertha* 230: One of the other girls told how hard it was to hitchhike without "coming across" to the men who gave the rides. **1941** Halliday *Tickets for Death* 65: I call this old jalopy of mine the Mayflower…because so many puritans have come across in it. **1946** I. Shulman *Dukes* 22: Look, babe…If you go out with me you've got to come across. I'm one guy that don't like passion cramps. **1956** Levin *Compulsion* 68: Only you see, officer, these girls wouldn't come across, so about ten o'clock we told them to get out and walk. **1957** H. Simmons *Corner Boy* 21: To think he'd gone with this babe a whole month before she came across.

comeback *n.* **1.** a response, (*specif.*) an effective retort. Now *S.E.*

1889 in *OEDS*: He shouldn't thus invite a sarcastic "come-back." **1896** Ade *Artie* 35: I never will be able to give him the right kind of hot comeback for what he done to me. **1912** Mathewson *Pitching* 34: He was there with the "come-back." **1936** in *DA* 365: "Some people have no ear for music," was Pete's come-back.

2. *Und.* repercussions, esp. in the form of a complaint to authorities, resistance on the part of a victim, etc.

1894 in Partridge *Dict. Und.* **1902** Hapgood *Autobiog. of Thief* 210 [ref. to ca1890's]: It seemed easy, with no come-back in sight. **1904** *Life in Sing Sing* 255: Come back. Vehement complaint; quick detection. **1922** F.L. Packard *Doors of Night* 27: No, there won't be no come-back. **1935** *AS* (Feb.) 14: *Comeback*. Resistance on the part of the victim.

come bubble *n. Mil.* an insignificant contemptible person, as a trainee.—usu. considered vulgar.

1973 R. Roth *Sand in Wind* 79: Listen, come bubble, what did I tell you? **1982** S. P. Smith *Officer & Gentleman* 51: "Run, come-bubble!" the D.I. said.

come bucket *n.* a despicable wretch; SCUMBAG.—usu. considered vulgar.

1975 Wambaugh *Choirboys* 33: "How about…[the word] cumbuckets?" "Too long." **1986** "J. Cain" *Suicide Squad* 24: One of you comebuckets fucked up.

come down *v.* **1.** to pay.

1849 [G. Thompson] *Venus in Boston* 37: She would "come down" handsomely. **1853** G. Thompson *Garter* 38: If they think it worth their while to *come down* handsomely.

2. *Und.* to confess.

1872 Burnham *Secret Service* v: Come down, owning up to having committed wrong.

3.a. *Black E.* (of love or luck) to grow or develop.

1931 Bontemps *Sends Sunday* 12: I feels ma luck comin' down. **1944** Bontemps & Cullen *St. Louis Woman* 9: A lucky horseshoe/Flew up and hit me…/I feel my luck comin' down. **1970** NYC street musician, age ca40: Oh, yeah, she make my love come down.

b. Esp. *Black E.* to occur; GO DOWN.

1966 Braly *On Yard* 284: I don't say that's the way it came down. **1967** Salas *Tattoo* 228 [ref. to ca1951]: "Now, what's coming down?" Skip asked. **1967** Wolf *Love Generation* 16: The more positive you can be the more things come down. The more you give the more you get. **1976–77** McFadden *Serial* 12: Something *weird* had to be coming down. *Ibid.* 128: Hey, look, what's coming down here, anyway? **1981** O'Day & Eells *High Times* 55: A lot has come down since those happy days.

c. to talk or behave.

1972 Sapir & Murphy *Death Therapy* 53: Oh, you come down real badass, man….Maybe I ain't coming down too clear. But this is a holdup.

4. *Narc.* to recover from drug-induced intoxication.

1959 (cited in R.S. Gold *Jazz Lexicon*). **1960** R. Reisner *Jazz Titans* 152: Come Down: wearing off of a high. **1964** R.S. Gold *Jazz Lexicon*: *Come down*…current among jazzmen since c. 1935. **1970** Landy *Underground Dict.*: *Come down*…Lose the drug-induced exhilaration as the drug wears off.

comedy *n.* foolish or impertinent talk or behavior.

1915–16 Lait *Beef, Iron & Wine* 23: "Nix on the comedy," said Kelly. **1918** *N.Y. Eve. Jour.* (Aug. 13) 13: Aw, cut the bum comedy! **1919** Witwer *Alex the Great* 146: Pay *you* off?…Save that comedy for Cousin

Alice! **1925** Dos Passos *Manhattan Transfer* 121: Cut de comedy, yous guys. **1926** *Sat. Eve. Post* (Oct. 23) 130 [ref. to 1918]: You know who I am! Lay off the comedy! **1931** Armour *Little Caesar* (film): Aw come on now, cut the comedy.

come freak *n.* a person obsessed with sexual intercourse.—usu. considered vulgar.

1966 Braly *On Yard* 272: Maybe I'm turning into a come freak. **1973** Schulz *Pimp* 110: She is a little bit of a come freak, wanting to have sex all the time and always bothering me about it. **1977** Sayles *Union Dues* 180: Body have to be struck with a mean case of horniness to even *think* about it in this weather…Have to be a stone come-freak.

come-off *n.* a result. Orig. *S.E.*

***1634, *1690, *1716** in *OED*. **1887** J.W. Nichols *Hear My Horn* 111: Thats a dam prety come off. **1889** *Century Dict.*: Come-off…Issue; conclusion. **1926** Norwood *Other Side of Circus* 266: As funny a come-off as I ever saw! **1932** Nelson *Prison Days & Nights* 27: The four coons wind up getting twenty to twenty-five years! Ain't that a swell comeoff? **1950, 1960** in *DARE*. **1970** La Motta, Carter & Savage *Raging Bull* 29: I didn't want to tell you before…but there were a couple of the boys there tonight to see the come-off.

come off *v.* **1.** see s.v. COME, *v.*, 1.a.

2. to desist, *specif.* from pretending, talking foolishness, or the like. Also (the only current form) **come off it.** Also in obs. phr. **come off your perch.** [The early *OEDS* ex. dated "1870" must now be correctly dated "ca1895."]

1885 *Puck* (Sept. 9) 20: Say, young fellow, come off! **1888** Pierson *Slave of Circumstances* 80: "Come off, Dutchy," irreverently shouted some of the younger men in the group. **1889** *Century Dict.* 73: *Come off*, to cease (fooling, flattering, chaffing, or humbugging); desist: chiefly in the imperative…(Recent slang, U.S.) **1891** Maitland *Slang Dict.* 73: *Come off* (Am.), go slow, let up, stop your conversation or tricks. **1892** S. Crane *Maggie* 11: Ah, come off! **1895** J.L. Williams *Princeton* 5: Aw! Come off! That was over the line! **1896** Ade *Artie* 30: "Come off," I says, "he wouldn't be…comin' 'round here unless he had some pull." **1899** Garland *Eagle's Heart* 110: Oh, come off! It can't be true. **1901** in "M. Twain" *Stories* 403: Oh, come off! What are you giving me? **1904** in "O. Henry" *Works* 1210: Oh, come off your perch! **1912** Field *Watch Yourself* 268 [ref. to ca1890]: Come off, come off your perch, you poll parrot! **1914** London *Jacket* 182: Aw, come off. **1918** Morse *Letters* 43: "Aw, come off," rises the incredulous jeer. **1926** Hemingway *Sun Also Rises* 63: "Oh, come off it," Brett said. **1950** Felsen *Hot Rod* 66: "Come off it, Bud!" the usually mild Mr. Cole exploded. **1958** S.H. Adams *Tenderloin* 233: "Aw, come off!" Tommy protested. **1968** L. Davis *Whence All Had Fled* 103: "Come off it, baby," Stark said wearily. **1975** Boatner et al. *Dict. Amer. Idioms* 62: Fritz said he had a car of his own. "Oh, come off it," said John. "You can't even drive." **1991** K. Douglass *Viper Strike* 60: Come off it, Batman, you don't know what the hell you're talking about.

3. to get the effrontery; GET OFF.—constr. with *where* as interrogative only.

1929 "E. Queen" *Roman Hat* 56: Where do you come off saying you don't know Monte Field? **1958** *26 Men* (syndic. TV series): Where do you come off tellin' me what to do?

4. to hand over reluctantly.

1961 Braly *Felony Tank* 48: He's got to come off that watch.

5. *Black E.* to make a profit; be successful.

1983 Sturz *Wid. Circles* 30: I really came off last night. Look at my stash.

come-on *n.* **1.** *Und.* a victim or prospective victim of a swindle; SUCKER.

1897 Townsend *Whole City Full* 172: He's got a come-on from New Jersey that I'm to steer to the turning joint. **1898** L.J. Beck *Chinatown* 257: These "come-ons" wore long whiskers and had large rolls of…money. **1901** Ade *Modern Fables* 67: He is a Come-On for any Bunco Game in the List. He is a Ninny. **1901** Hobart *Down the Line* 31: Tod's main hold…is to throw salve at the come-ons. **1902** Cullen *More Tales* 153: Some Come-Ons I have met. **1903** A.H. Lewis *Boss* 182: The City's a come-on—a sucker—an' it belongs to whoever picks it up. **1904** A.H. Lewis *President* 422: Don't you think now you're a bit of a come-on? **1905** Riordon *Plunkitt* 59: Talk about come-ons from Iowa or Texas—they ain't in it with the childlike simplicity of these papers. **1908** Train *Crime Stories* 12: What do you think I am, anyhow?…I must look like a "come-on." a**1904–11** Phillips *Susan Lenox* II 152: She never lifts it till the "come on" has given up his cash. **1922** *Variety* (Aug. 11) 8: Peoria…would stuff a white card in Mr. Comeon's hatband. **1927–28** in R. Nelson *Dishonorable* 170: You used to stall—tease along the come-ons—for Beauty Parker's mob. **1958** S.H. Adams *Tenderloin* 313: What an easy mark he had been! A softie, a come-on, a pushover.

2.a. STEERER.

1905 in *OEDS*. **1906** (quot. at HOOK). **1947** in W.S. Burroughs *Letters* 13: He actually had the gall to come on hurt because I had doubted his "integrity." **1970** Winick & Kinsie *Commerce* 171: A B-girl (also called a "come-on" or "percentage girl" or "drink rustler") often spends six or seven hours in a bar every evening.

b. a lure or inducement, as in a swindle.

1902 in *OEDS*. **1920** (quot. at WET GOODS). **1922** in Ruhm *Detective* 18: Yes, she was this gang's come on. **1939** "E. Queen" *4 Hearts* 83: The come-on…. What a clumsy trick! **1962** T. Berger *Reinhart* 398: I'm Harry. There ain't no Psycho. Just a name, get it? Kind of a come-on. **1970** Terkel *Hard Times* 36: Our speak-easy had a candy store front. That was the come-on. **1971** J. Turley *Empire of Ants* (film): Cheap scotch. I think it's all a come-on.

c. a sexual advance or invitation.

1942 *ATS* 341: Sex Appeal…come-on. **1949** Monteleone *Crim. Slang* 56: Come-On…sex attraction employed to entice or decoy. **1954** Collans & Sterling *House Detect.* 51: We could ask her if she hadn't given him the old come-on over at L—'s bar, on School Street. **1971** Rhinehart *Dice Man* 41: I think she might once have given me a housewifely come-on. **1979** *Playboy* (Aug.) 168: This is the *weirdest* come-on I've had all week.

d. a dare.

1955 Graziano & Barber *Somebody Up There* 237: It's about time I got a come-on for a fight in this joint.

come on *v.* **1.** Orig. *Theat. & Jazz.* to perform before an audience, esp. energetically. [1899 quot., referring simply to vaudeville entertainers coming out on stage, represents the kind of locution from which this and related senses arose.]

[**1899** Ade *Fables* 40: Zoroaster and Zendavesta came on very Cocky.] **1925** *AS* I (Oct.) 37: Then I dressed up my ac'…I comes on rube, see? I gets me some good business and props. **1939** in R.S. Gold *Jazz Talk* 53: Bauduc…really comes on with some very fly and superb drumming. **1946** Mezzrow & Wolfe *Really Blues* 53: It used to tickle Rapp…to hear a Yankee really come on with the blues. **1959** in Russell *Perm. Playboy* 419: How did he come on, Baby? Fairly great or so? **1961** Russell *Sound* 11: They really came on then, man!

2.a. Orig. *Jazz.* to behave, act, speak, or appear to be.—usu. constr. with following adv. (in form of adj.) or adj.

1942 Z.N. Hurston, in *Amer. Merc.* (July) 89: Man, I come on like the Gang Busters. **1944** in Himes *Black on Black* 196: "Pour me some mo' of that licker." He come on so fast I done…poured him a shot…'fore I knew what I was doin.' **1946** Mezzrow & Wolfe *Really Blues* 23: When he finally showed himself he came like a funky rat. *a*1953 in *Amer. Jour. Sociol.* LIX 237: I came on like I had turned on many times before, you know….I just came on cool, as though I knew exactly what the score was. **1956** in R.S. Gold *Jazz Talk* 53: He's a good guy…just comes on weird sometimes. **1958** Gilbert *Vice Trap* 41: Don't come on crutty to Nick. **1959** Burroughs *Naked Lunch* 2: A square wants to come on hip. **1962** Kesey *Cuckoo's Nest* 68: If I come on as nice as pie to her…she ain't gonna get in a tizzy and have me electrocuted? **1963** Coon *Short End* 122: Don't come on dumb. **1963** Hayden *Wanderer* 350: The chief of the Bureau comes on smooth. **1964** Howe *Valley of Fire* 104: You hear what he's been comin' on with? **1964** Rhodes *Chosen Few* 176: Then she comes on with some shit about she can't accept what? **1965** Hentoff *Jazz Country* 130: You're coming on like a child. **1968** P. Roth *Portnoy* 221: To wear old clothes and no make-up and not have to come on tough all the time? **1968** Kirk & Hanle *Surfer's Hndbk.* 122: Surfers will have more of the high cards if they come on as reasonably well-behaved, mature people. **1970** A. Young *Snakes* 61: You aint got no business comin on to me with that bad attitude of yours. **1979** W. Safire, in *N.Y. Times Mag.* (Dec. 23) 9: "I'm getting an image of coming on tough," candidate John Connally [said]…"I'm only coming on candid."…It is possible to come on soft, to come on uptight, to come on flaky, to come on sincere…"He comes on smart." **1983** Univ. Tenn. instructor: Students are coming on a lot more conservative these days.

b. Orig. *Jazz.* to behave or speak in a forward, aggressive, or heated manner.—now usu. constr. with *strong*. [Became widespread in early 1960's.]

1940 Zinberg *Walk Hard* 181: Damn, but this baby comes on all at once. **1952** E. Brown *Trespass* 63: She really comes on, man [in reject-

ing an advance]. **1952** Mandel *Angry Strangers* 290: I'm like gangbusters. Watch me come on. **1953** W. Fisher *Waiters* 44: Man, he comes on with the girls. **1956** in R.S. Gold *Jazz Talk* 54: "These cats come on so strong," a musician…says. **1960** R. Reisner *Jazz Titans* 152: *Comes On:* attitude, approach. Example: He comes on strong. **1963** Rubin *Sweet Daddy* 106: Like she comes on strong and then kind of fades out of the scene. *Ibid.* 154: Come On Strong: to present oneself with intensity or enthusiasm. **1965** Cassavetes *Faces* 223: You're coming on awfully strong. **1971** B.B. Johnson *Blues for Sister* 76: If he begins to come on wrong. **1971** DiPippo *Rhetoric* 125: What did you think of the Muhammed Ali fight last night?…He sure did come on strong. **1974** Stone *Dog Soldiers* 4: He said that drugs condition the intellect to fascism and came on about C. Manson. **1975** Boatner et al. *Dict. Amer. Idioms* 63: Joe came on very strong last night about the War in Indochina; most of us felt embarrassed.

c. *Specif.* to make a sexual advance.

1959 A. Anderson *Lover Man* 130: After the chick came on so strong the Chief Stud copped a plea. **1963** in H. Ellison *Sex Misspelled* 42: He was coming on with Rooney because he knew it would make me feel tall. **1964** Rhodes *Chosen Few* 50: Th' way she was comin' on, any other time would be th' wrong time. **1967** Rosenthal *Sheeper* 165: I wouldn't think of coming on to any intelligent boy. **1969** in R.S. Gold *Jazz Talk* 54: To say that someone "comes on strong" means that he has an overdeveloped personality. Also, to make sexual overtures. **1984** Univ. Tenn. student: You can't come on to a chick the first or second date. But the *third!* **1986** R. Walker *AF Wives* 471: The girls at school must be coming on to you all the time.

d. to jest.

1959 "D. Stagg" *Glory Jumpers* 64: What? Jump in France? Man, you're coming on. A cat could get himself messed up that way.

3. *Narc.* **a.** (of a drug) to take effect.

1946 Mezzrow & Wolfe *Really Blues* 92: Muta never came on like that. **1970** A. Young *Snakes* 58: I aint never smoked nothin come on this strong!

b. to begin to experience the effects of a hallucinogenic drug.

1970 Landy *Underground Dict.* **1972** *Playboy* (Apr.) 80: When we got up there, we were just starting to come on.

come out *v. Homosex.* to openly acknowledge one's homosexuality, esp. by beginning to engage in homosexual acts. See also *come out of the closet* s.v. CLOSET, *n.*

1941 G. Legman, in G. Henry *Sex Variants* II 1161: *Come out* To become progressively more and more exclusively homosexual with experience. **1949** *Gay Girl's Guide* 5: *Come Out:* To be initiated into the mysteries of homosexuality. **1963** Stearn *Grapevine* 5: The phrase "coming out" ironically indicated a lesbian's sexual debut: being "brought out" reflected the same result. **1972** Wells *Fly With Us* 74: It was only after I "came out" that I was able to identify myself consciously as a lesbian. **1973** Tennessee Williams, in *Playboy* (Apr.) 74: That was my coming out and I enjoyed it. **1978** Maupin *Tales* 114: I didn't come out until three years ago. I was a eunuch in high school. **1986** Calif. man, on *Story of English* (PBS-TV series): When did you come out?…When did you admit you were gay? **1993** *N.Y. Times* (June 30) A 10: We've seen an explosion of organizing for gay rights in rural states….People are coming out because so much is at stake.

come-pad *n. Mil.* a mattress.—usu. considered vulgar.

1984 J. Fuller *Fragments* 56 [ref. to Vietnam War]: Up and out of the fartsacks…Crawl offa them cum pads.

comer *n.* Esp. *Sports & Pol.* a person, animal, or thing that shows great progress or potential. Now *colloq.*

1879 in *OEDS*: A crab…is always very poor to begin with; but he eats everything he gets hold of, which…fattens him up some. Then he is called a "comer." **1902** *Sporting Life* (July 12) 13. **1913** *DN* IV 10: He's a comer in politics. **1934** Weseen *Dict. Slang* 138: *Comer*—A show or an actor that has good prospects; a prospective success. **1947** Schulberg *Harder They Fall* 272: He's a comer, Mr. Lewis…a comin' champ if I ever seen one. **1949** in *DAS*: He said the [baseball] club is a comer. **1993** *N.Y. Times* (July 7) A 3: He was obviously picked by his superiors as a comer.

comet *n. Hobo.* an experienced tramp or hobo who travels long distances, esp. on express trains.

1894 in J. London *Tramp Diary* 59: The slow pokes & the comets. **1907** London *Road* 26 [ref. to 1892]: The Road had gripped me and would not let me go; and later,…I returned to The Road to make longer flights, to be a "comet" and a profesh. *Ibid.* 27: I was a "comet" and "tramp-royal." **1917** Livingston *Coast to Coast* 123: At Reno, every hobo, ranging from the aristocratic "comet" down to the lowliest of low "grease balls," registered his moniker. **1930** Irwin *Tramp & Und. Sl.: Comet*...A tramp or hobo...riding only fast trains, and for long distances.

come through *v.* **1.** to hand over, pay up, or provide, esp. that which is expected or demanded; COME ACROSS, 1.

1875 in Ownby *Subduing Satan* 158: When one of their friends "came through" [by being converted,] the women could not hold themselves still. **1907** in H.C. Fisher *A. Mutt* 6: "Telegram for you." "Well, come through with it." **1910** *N.Y. Eve. Jour.* (Feb. 2) 18: We'll touch Tightwaddo for a dollar...He'll come thro' like a prince. **1911** A.H. Lewis *Apaches of N.Y.* 29: Come through wit' that ten! **1959** Farris *Harrison High* 85: You know, I think ol' Jean will come through one of these nights.

2. to confess; *come clean* s.v. CLEAN.

1907 *American Mag.* (Sept.) 497: He "gets them right," makes them "come through" (as he calls confessing). **1911** Van Loan *Big League* 55: Come through!...Is she a chorus girl? **1912** Lowrie *Prison* 229: Brown was placed in the jacket and told that he would be kept there until he "came through." **1923** *Atlanta Constitution* (Feb. 1) 12: Come t'rough clean. **1930** Lavine *3d Degree* 63: Go at him again and see if he won't come through.

come-to-Jesus coat *n.* (see quots.).

1930 G. Williams *Logger-Talk* 20: *Come-to-Jesus coat*. A frock, Prince Albert, morning, or any long official or ministerial looking coat. **1942** *ATS* 91: Dress coat...*come-to-Jesus coat*.

come-to-Jesus collar *n.* a high detachable collar.—used derisively. Also vars.

[**1919** Johnson *Heaven, Hell or Hoboken* 40: Judging by the angle of his cute little "come to Jesus" cap, the Colonel had a snootful of that light wine himself.] **1924** Tully *Beggars of Life* 330: The good man wore a "come to Jesus" collar, a shoe string black tie and a Uriah Heep expression. **1925** S. Lewis *Arrowsmith* 638 [ref. to *ca*1910]: I never thought I'd have to live up to a man with a dress suit and a come-to-Heaven collar. **1927** Tully *Circus Parade* 113: A black string tie was crooked on his "come to Jesus" collar. **1930** "D. Stiff" *Milk & Honey* 144: The hobo is never seen in any shirt upon which a detached collar is worn. These...are known as "come to Jesus bands." *Ibid.* 202: A *come-to-Jesus collar* is one worn by a preacher. **1984** Partridge *DSUE* (ed. 8) [as a Canadian term].

comfies *n.pl.* comfortable clothes; pajamas.

1898 *Chicago Record's War Stories* 43: Then comes supper, the clean clothes are laid away, the blue jackets get into their "comfies" and play-time lasts until "hammocks" is sounded.

comical stupid *n. Navy.* commissary steward. *Joc.*

1930 Buranelli *Maggie* 59 [ref. to 1918]: The commissary steward, who the gobs called the Comical Stupid, was the petty officer responsible for supplies in the larder.

comical warfare *n. Army.* chemical warfare. *Joc.*

1942–44 in *AS* (Feb. 1946) 32: *Comical Warfare*, n. Chemical warfare. **1980** Cragg *L. Militaris* 100: *Comical Warfare.* A play on chemical warfare. **1982** D. Williams *Hit Hard* 27 [ref. to WWII]: Comical Warfare School...They ain't gonna use no poison gas in this war.

comm *n.* communication. Also **com.**

*a***1988** Poyer *Med* 238: After that message all comms with the embassy were lost. **1988** Dye *Outrage* 93: It's a satellite link that puts us in direct comm with anyone in the chain of command. **1991** LaBarge *Desert Voices* 25: Com was excellent.

comma-hound *n. Pub.* a proofreader.

1942 *ATS* 492.

commando *n. Mil.* a military serviceman assigned to noncombat duty, esp. far from danger.—used in comb. with prec. n.—used derisively. See also REAR-ECHELON COMMANDO and USO COMMANDO, prob. the most freq. attested forms.

1943 Trumbo *Guy Named Joe* (film): Probably listenin' to some small talk from that jukebox commando. **1943** Daves & Maltz *Destination Tokyo* (film): I don't see this Market Street Commando hove up alongside. **1944** Brooks *Brick Foxhole* 71: Come on you Hollywood Commandos. Get your tail off that bed. **1944** in *AS* XX 147: *Boudoir commando.* Homefront hero. **1945** *Yank* (Nov. 2) 15: This fountain-pen commando. **1945** *Yank* (Nov. 9) 15: Damn swivel-chair commandos. **1945** Trumbull *Silversides* 75: He spoke scathingly of fighting a war with "Market Street commandos." **1944–46** in *AS* XXII 55: *Red Cross*

Commando. Any soldier who hangs out at Red Cross clubs; a term used by Marines for all soldiers. **1946** Burns *Gallery* 339: I thought ya was one of these PBS commandos. **1951** Morison *Nav. Ops. in WWII* VII 38 [ref. to 1943]: To strengthen gunfire support, Admiral Nimitz assigned three of the older battleships, *Pennsylvania, Idaho,* and *Nevada.* Their crews, nicknamed the "Market Street Commandos" during the months of frustration when based on San Francisco, were delighted with the prospect of action. **1955** Goethals *Chains of Command* 5: He still had to be careful with these headquarters commandos. **1957** Myrer *Big War* 147: You gutless stateside garrison commando. **1962** Mandel *Wax Boom* 272: Those two PX commandos couldn't get near him. **1965** Linakis *In Spring* 112: I saw her...with a Chanor Base major, one of those desk commandos. **1968** Myrer *Eagle* 587: Anybody in this hell hole with a monkey suit *that* clean is either a Slopey or a rear-area commando. **1969** Linn & Pearl *Masque of Honor* 9: I shouldn't give you barracks commandoes anything more than a weather report. **1972** Haldeman *War Year* 110: Well, Farmer, how do you like bein' a base-camp commando?

Commie *n. & adj.* Communist.

1939 M. Levin *Citizens* 352: The Commies can be just as perverse. **1940** in G. Marx *Letters* 21: I see...Commies under my bed. **1946** in J. O'Hara *Sel. Letters* 198: This, on May Day, is what the Commies consider a defeatist attitude. **1949** J.H. Burns *Lucifer* 159: A bunch of Commie intellectuals. **1949** Grayson & Andrews *I Married a Communist* (film): I'd make a bet she's a practicing Commie. **1950** in F. Brown *Honeymoon* 17: Somehow, he hadn't thought it possible for a Commie to have a sense of humor. **1951** Spillane *Lonely Night* 29: Some of them even looked like Commies, the cartoon kind. **1952** Grant & Taylor *Big Jim McLain* (film): That's how he got that broken nose—fighting Commies. **1954** Arnow *Dollmaker* 253: "They'd be called a commie." "What's that?"..."A red, I reckon." **1957** M. Shulman *Rally* 114: Are you some kind of commie rat bastard? **1961** L.G. Richards *TAC* 27: We did take a few days to knock out the Commies in the air. **1963** in S. Lee *Son of Origins* 51: The Commies would give their eyeteeth to know what he's working on now! **1968** L. Davis *Whence All Had Fled* 63: It's run by a bunch of atheist commie professors. **1972–75** W. Allen *Without Feathers* 144: You're all a bunch of...commie pinkos. **1978** Hasford *Short-Timers* 86: On the back of the helmet: *Kill a Commie for Christ.* **1982** Woodruff & Maxa *At White House* 163: "That just goes to show you that you can't trust the Commies," declared [Pres. Reagan]. **1992** *New Yorker* (Dec. 28) 150: I am just trying to protect the President from Commie advisers like you.

commish /kə'mɪʃ/ *n.* **1.** a commission (in var. senses).

1862 in C.W. Wills *Army Life* 93: Told her we'd give her a commish as chief taster. **1885** *Puck* (Apr. 8) 83: I'll enter the commish before he forgets it. **1910** O. Johnson *Varmint* 71: Doc wants to make his commish. **1913** J. London *Valley of Moon* 455: It's horse-buyin' on commish. **1947** Schulberg *Harder They Fall* 295: All I need now is for the Commish to smell a rat and tie up our purses. *****1949** P.G. Wodehouse, in *OEDS*: I thought she might be glad of the commish. **1958** S.H. Adams *Tenderloin* 284: At the toe of the Commish's boot.

2. a commissioned officer.

1863 in J.H. Gooding *Altar of Freedom* 18: The high "comish"...will have to follow the unheroic paths of commerce or law once more. **1863** in C.H. Moulton *Ft. Lyon* 151: We boys...[eat] as respectable as a "comish." In fact our Captain boards at the same place. **1864** in O.J. Hopkins *Under the Flag* 208: No noisy "Commish" disturbs me, though there is no telling when...Capt. Burke, or...Lieutenant W—, or Major West, will come in. **1865** in *Lincoln Herald* LXXX (1978) 81: Two comish officers and about twenty-five enlisted men.

3. a commissioner.

1910 in McCay *Little Nemo* 256: Hello Jim! Howdy, Commish! **1912** in *DAE* I 331: The big Commissioner will get roasted by the papers and hand it to the Deputy Comish, and the Deputy will pass the buck down to me, and I'll have to report how it happened. **1921–25** J. Gleason & R. Taber *Is Zat So?* 31: The commish here will stake you. **1931** Wilstach *Under Cover Man* 86: The commish might...be urgin' me to leave town. **1965** Spillane *Killer Mine* 100: Argenio took it, called the commissioner because the tipster said to do it, and the commish in person directed Argenio to get to your place. **1983** *N.Y. Daily News* (Aug. 31) 37: It would be a blunder for the commish to ignore the accusations...Go to it, commissioner. **1992** *The Commish* (ABC-TV series).

commissary department *n.* the stomach.

1873 in Rosa & Koop *Rowdy Joe* 75: A derringer was held against his commissary department. **1898** Bullen *Cachalot* 186 [ref. to 1875]: I guess that ar bomb o' yourn kinder upset his commissary department. **1908** *Independent* (Apr. 30) 956: Anything...has always served me for food, and I have never had the slightest quarrel with my commissary department yet as long as I could manage to secure sufficient ammunition of some kind for filling.

commo *n.* **1.** *Navy.* commodore.

1853 McCauley *With Perry* 65: The Commo. is not here.

2. *Mil.* **a.** a communications officer.

1922 Thompson *Minute Men* 161 [ref. to 1918]: Maj. Howard C. Smith, Commo. Louis M. Josephtal. **1956** Boatner *Mil. Customs* 115: *Commo* Communications Officer (from abbreviation "Comm. O.")

b. communications.

*1925 Fraser & Gibbons *Soldier & Sailor Words* 62 [ref. to WWI]: *Commo:* Communication Trench. **1964** R. Moore *Green Berets* 68: He's in the commo bunker. **1967** Ford *Muc Wa* 38: Behind the commo shack. **1970** Flood *War of Innocents* 277: Maybe his commo went to pieces and he couldn't call them off. **1973** Karlin et al. *Free Fire Zone* 10: Commo check, over. **1975** S.P. Smith *Amer. Boys* 296: I work in commo. **1979** Cassidy *Delta* 270: Jerry was shaking a set of liar's dice with Russ, the commo man. **1979** J. Morris *War Story* 225: I was cross-trained in commo and demo. **1983** K. Miller *Lurp Dog* 59: Nobody liked being without commo. *a*1987 Coyle *Team Yankee* 72: Bannon...tried to establish commo with Uleski.

3. COMMIE.

*1942 in *OEDS.* *1945 S.J. Baker *Australian Lang.* 265: Communist becomes *commo.* **1972** *Nat. Lampoon* (Feb.) 84: Bite the dust, Commo creeps! **1976** *Nat. Lampoon* (July) 72: Show me a Commo and I'll drive a wedge in his crack.

commode-hugging drunk *adj.* drunk and nauseated; extremely drunk.

1973 *TULIPQ* (coll. B.K. Dumas): *Commode-hugging drunk;* blasted; shitfaced. **1979** Univ. Tenn. student: *Commode-hugging drunk* is about as drunk as a human can get. **1987** Nichols & Tillman *Yankee Stadium* 46: They got knee-walking, commode-hugging drunk the first couple of days.

communists *n.pl.* the menses.—constr. with *the. Joc.*

1931 J.T. Farrell *Calico Shoes* 118: He asked her if the "communists" had come, and she blushed, telling him that was not a nice way to talk.

comp *n.* **1.** *Printing.* a compositor.

1842 *Spirit of Times* (May 7) 116. *1870 in *F & H:* I stood before the world a journeyman comp. *1899 in *OED.* **1929–33** J. Lowell *Gal Reporter* 6: The comp will set it in the first slug. **1982** *L.A. Times* (May 27) I-D 11: Then veteran Sorg "comps"...sit down and punch out the copy on the Linotypes.

2. a compliment.

1864 in O.J. Hopkins *Under the Flag* 217: He...said "give her my Comps." **1914, 1967–68** in *DARE.*

3.a. a complimentary or free pass or ticket; (*hence*) a person given complimentary admission or service.

1887 (cited in *W10*). **1902** *Sporting Life* (Oct. 4) 7. **1909** *DN* IV 133: "Rag" Elliott gives comps to the Majestic. **1939** *AS* (Oct.) 239: *Comp.* Non-paying guest [in a hotel]. **1953** *St. Louis Post-Dispatch* (Aug. 16) (Parade) 7: For each game, players usually get at least four "comps"— free tickets to the best seats. **1977** *L.A. Times* (July 25) III 3: DiMaggio said he never received a free game ticket in all his years with the Yankees. You can imagine what today's primas and donnas would do if they didn't get their dozen comps per.

b. a complimentary gift as given by a hotel or the like.

1982 *Santa Barbara* (Calif.) *News-Press* (Dec. 23) C12: Baccarat, blackjack, craps or roulette players may be given "comps" ranging from free parking to an expensive suite. **1985** E. Leonard *Glitz* 77: "Wha's...a comp?" "Like the champagne, a gift."

4. *Stu.* **a.** (a course in) composition.

1942 *ATS* 776. **1954–60** *DAS.* **1957** Kohner *Gidget* 9: That's what my English comp teacher says. **1970** N.Y.U. student: He tested out of freshman comp. **1982** Carolyn See, in *L.A. Times* (July 19) V 8: The syllabus for a very good and imaginative course in freshman comp. **1985** Univ. Tenn. instructor: Teaching two sophomore [classes] and two comp.

b. usu. *pl.* a comprehensive examination taken before graduation.

1974 Univ. Tenn. student: She's studying for comps. **1986** Univ. Tenn. student: When are you taking comps?

5. a compass.

1942 *ATS* 76.

6. *Music.* accompaniment.

1946 Mezzrow & Wolfe *Really Blues:* The piano...sticks to a rhythmic

function, with either a four-four tempo or strictly comp. **1981** O'Day & Eells *High Times* 229: If a song had an upbeat he played "comp" style.

7. compensation. Now *S.E.*

1953 *Portland Oregonian* (Oct. 4) I 18: The comparatively low benefits they will receive under "workmen's comp." **1970** *Everett* (Wash.) *Herald* (Jan. 24) 2A: Joe has two more years to get an unemployment comp law through here. **1977** *Business Week* (Nov. 14) 161: Careless administration of workers' comp systems is partly to blame. **1983** *Business Week* (July 25) 42: The coming executive "comp" technique of the 1980s.

8. *Sports.* competition; competitors.

1980 Wielgus & Wolff *Basketball* 70: Checking out the comp at a new park, before breaking a sweat. *Ibid.* 77: They're just waiting for comp to come by.

comp *v.* **1.** *Music.* to play an accompaniment; (*trans.*) to accompany.

1949 in *OEDS:* The guitar...is employed like the piano to "feed" or "bop" the soloists by "comping" with irregularly accented chords. **1955** Shapiro & Hentoff *Talkin'* 274: Count is also just about the best piano player...for comping soloists. **1953–58** J.C. Holmes *Horn* 27: All who comped with funk.

2. to give a complimentary pass, ticket, or gift to; (*hence*) to obtain (something) free of charge.

1961 *Sat. Eve. Post* (Nov. 11) 21: Volume is encouraged by "promotion," such as the big-name shows, or by "comping"—giving things away on a complimentary basis. **1977** *L.A. Times* (Apr. 14) I 26: Records show Argent "comped" Payvlikowski $2,800 on the old bill. **1978** in *Barnhart Dict. Comp.* III (1984) 103: During trips to Las Vegas, Ritchie was often "comped" by Caesar's management. Ritchie acknowledges accepting free dinners and drinks. **1983** *L.A. Times* (Feb. 23) I 1: His meals and drinks, and those of his friends or family, often were "comped" and he cashed checks up to $10,000 at the casino cage. **1985** E. Leonard *Glitz* 152: You comped him to everything but the ice-cream parlor. *Ibid.* 153: Yeah, we comp him. **1986** Stinson & Carabatsos *Heartbreak* 30: The...brothers get their drinks comped by the house.

compadre *n.* [< Sp] *West.* a close male friend.

1833 A. Pike *Prose Sks.* 102: Buy some tobacco, compadre. **1834** in *OEDS:* Nay, compadre, an American cannot steal. **1850** Garrard *Wah-to-yah* 77: I had apprehensions he would lie in wait with his *compadres.* **1883** in Miller & Snell *Why West Was Wild* 550: Deager is an old "compadre" of Webster's. **1894** *DN* I 324: *Compadre:* friend, companion. **1948, 1966–69** in *DARE.* **1974** *Police Woman* (NBC-TV): The grievance of our compadre...has been duly noted—and will be filed in the men's room. **1982** Goff, Sanders & Smith *Bros.* 123: I just could not leave the field without telling my black compadres. **1984** Sample *Raceboss* 137: Some of my compadres...saw me at the same bar several times. **1986** B. Breathed, in *Daily Beacon* (Univ. Tenn.) (Apr. 21) 7: Nothing better to lift the spirits of a man in physical crisis than by a show of loyalty by his *compadres!* **1991** Coen & Coen *Barton Fink* (film): Don't worry about that, compadre.

companero *n.* [< Sp *compañero*] *West.* a male friend or companion; PAL.

1845 in *DA.* **1848** in *DARE.* **1929** Panzram *Killer* 211: Yes, I read about the demise of one of my old companeroes, Frank Marlow of Silver Slipper fame. **1931** in *DA.* **1948** J. Stevens *Jim Turner* 76: Then we'd be fixed for life, *compañero.* **1968** *AS* XLIII 217: Trail companions were *companyeros.*

Company *n.* [sugg. by *Cia.*, Sp abbrev. of *compañía* 'company'] *Pol.* the U.S. Central Intelligence Agency.—constr. with *the.*

1967 *DAS* (Supp. ed) 678. **1976** Atlee *Domino* 31: He was right about "The Company" falling on hard times, however. *a*1984 T. Clancy *Red Oct.* 138: It was time to leave the "Company." **1984** Kagan & Summers *Mute Evidence* 370: When you work for the Company you've got to get approval if you want to join any sort of organization.

company clown *n.* **1.** *Army & USMC.* a company clerk.

1933 *Leatherneck* (Apr.) 34: Cpl. H. S. Morris, the company clerk (Note: I am being different; anyone else would have written "Company Clown"). *Ibid.* 21: You know it is fatal to contradict a company clown. **1933** *Leatherneck* (July) 17: The company clown'll fix 'em up when they get back though. **1944** Kendall *Service Slang* 5: Company clown...the company clerk.

2. *Army & USMC.* a bungler or jester in a military unit.

1952 Uris *Battle Cry* 2 [ref. to WWII]: There was the company clown, the farmer, the wanderer, the bigot, the boy with the mission, the Texan. **1963** Coon *Short End* 53: Not that I was the company clown. Willie Feeley already had a lock on that.

company man *n. Labor.* a male employee who behaves subserviently toward his employer, esp. by informing on fellow employees. Cf. COMPANY STIFF.

1942 *AS* (Apr.) 103: *Company Man.* Squealer. **1957** in *DAS.*

company monkey *n. Army.* a company clerk.

1931 *Our Army* (Oct.) 18. **1936** *AS* (Feb.) 60: A conscientious clerk is the *company monkey* or the *punk.*

Company Q *n. Army.* (see quots.).

1848 in Peskin *Vols.* 248: Company "Q" (as the guard house inmates are called). **1882** F.W. Dawson *Confed. Service* 98 [ref. to Civil War]: "Company Q" (the stragglers, and the disabled men with the trains)...drove them back. **1883** *Harper's Mag.* (Sept.) 644 [ref. to Civil War]: He was in fact a Company "Q" man—negroes and the guardhouse. **1899** J.N. Opie *Reb. Cav.* 158 [ref. to Civil War]: When a cavalryman lost his horse, in battle or otherwise, he was put in what, in soldier parlance, was called Company "Q." This was a quasi organization of dismounted men, who followed the cavalry like a nightmare.

company stiff *n.* COMPANY MAN.

1954 Mirvish *Texana* 223: "This is gonna louse up the whole day's work." "What are you? A company stiff?"

compree *v.* [< F *compris*] *Mil. in France.* to understand.

1918 Woollcott *Command is Forward* 6: Everyone swore that Belle could "compree" English. **1918** in *Ohio History* XCVII (1988) 36: They don't seem to "compree." **1919** Johnson *Heaven, Hell, Hoboken* 49: I succeeded in making them "compri" that I wanted something to eat. **1925 in Fraser & Gibbons *Soldier & Sailor Wds.* 62 [ref. to WWI]: *Compree*...Understand! See! **1928** [quot at DAISY FOOD]. **1930** Nason *Corporal* 260 [ref. to WWI]: I *compree,* all right. **1944** in Litoff et al. *Miss You* 228: Anyway that is the bargain—compree? **1955** F. K. Franklin *Combat Nurse* 55 [ref. to WWII]: I damn well don't *compris* it!

comprendo *v.* to understand.

1987 Kent *Phr. Book* 153: You comprendo? **1988** *New Adven. of Pooh* (ABC-TV): I'm really gonna clean up this town. Comprendo?

compute *v.* to make sense; add up.—constr. in negative. [Introduced as a catchword by the television series cited in 1964 quot.]

1964 *My Living Doll* (CBS-TV): I'm sorry, but that does not compute. **1973** N.Y.U. student: That doesn't compute. *a*1979 in Feldman et al. *Angel Dust* 166: I'd read, but it wouldn't compute right, you know? I wouldn't understand it. **1983** *L.A. Times* (Sept. 4) V 4: You can't...say that he's too artsy-craftsy to run a business. It doesn't compute. **1986** R. Walker *AF Walker* 392: It doesn't compute—as we computer freaks say. **1986** Wilson & Maddock *Short Circuit* (film): "Alive" doesn't compute.

Comrade *n.* **1.** a Soviet Communist.

1937 in Goodstone *Pulp* 9: If I never see a Comrade again, that will be far too soon for Pat Morgan. **1939** M. Levin *Citizens* 215: "He's not a comrade, is he?..."If he is, it'll be a surprise to me." **1948** I. Shaw *Young Lions* 21: It is the one thing the Comrades have taught Europe—the end justifies the means.

2. [< G *Kamerad*] *Mil. in W. Germany.* a German. Cf. syn. RAD.

1959 A. Anderson *Lover Man* 135 [ref. to 1945]: I figured if that was a Comrade it might be my last challenge. *Ibid.* 149: Comrade is OK by me, and I hope we never have to fight one another no more. **1964** Rhodes *Chosen Few* 122 [ref. to *ca*1950]: Man, I never thought I'd...come across a bunch of Aryan spooks...Just like comrade's youth movement durin' th' war.

con *n.* **1.** *R.R.* a railway conductor. Cf. CONNIE, 2.

1887 M. Roberts *W. Avernus* 240: If the "con" had found us on the other side, the dollar and the ride would have both been lost. **1893** *Century* (Nov.) 106: Soon the "Con." appeared. **1899** A.H. Lewis *Sandburrs* 25: An' what wit' squarin' a con or brakey if youse are graftin' on a train, there ain't...much left for Mollie. **1902** "J. Flynt" *Little Bro.* 222: The con won't see me here, so what's the odds? **1907** *London Road* 75 [ref. to *ca*1894]: A "con" (conductor) was poking his head inside the door. **1912** in Truman *Dear Bess* 105: A man will whip the con with his transfer if it is overdue. **1913** *Light Hobo* 15: That engineer will put the "con" (conductor) wise to us.

2. *Orig. Pris.* a convict or ex-convict.

1888 in *Amer. Heritage* (Oct. 1979) 20: A merry, merry Christmas! to

each old Con up here. **1893** in Partridge *Dict. Und.* 143: Prisoners are known as "con," which is short for convict, and the whole body of prisoners is designated "condom"—short for convictdom. **1907** *London Road* 126 [ref. to *ca*1894]: He was a huge, illiterate brute, an ex-Chesapeake Bay oyster pirate, an "ex-con" who had done five years in Sing Sing. **1908** Hopper & Bechdolt *9009* 11: The guards, they're bad enough...But the cons—they're devils. **1913** T.M. Osborne *Pris. Walls* 57: He got in line with the rest of the cons. **1921** *Variety* (July 15) 5: An S.O.S. From An Ex-Con. **1950** Duffy *San Quentin* 24: Warden Holohan had always been a firm believer in the "con boss" system, because he thought seasoned prisoners could handle the men as well as some civilian guards on the work projects. **1972** Burkhart *Women in Pris.* 48: No one could stereotype her visually as a "con" or a "rough, hard-talking broad in prison."

3.a. a confidence swindle; CON GAME; swindling in general; in phr. **on the con** engaged in confidence swindles. [Despite the evidence of the dates, this is probably the original sense.]

1904 in Partridge *Dict. Und.:* It's not easy to throw the religious con (confidence game) into a convict. **1930** Conwell *Pro. Thief* 56: The second class of con rackets are called "short con" because they can be played in a very short time, in almost any place, and are designed merely to get the money the sucker may have on his person at the time. **1930** *Variety* (Jan. 8) 123: He'll do anything in the way of short con that will not cop his liberty...And the short con artist breezes off. **1952** Himes *Stone* 164: The old slide game, the old short con. **1956** Resko *Reprieve* 248 [ref. to 1940's]: I turned out on the con and worked everything from the Rumanian box to shaking queers. **1967** Spillane *Delta* 112: If you're on the con, cut out, friend. They're worse than the cops in Vegas. **1969** Crumb *Motor City Comics* (unp.): So lay offa me with your cheap cons! **1979** in Terkel *Amer. Dreams* 5: There's a gesture the characters use which means the con is on. **1983** Helprin *Winter's Tale* 32: There was...talk...about stealing and the state of the con. **1992** *Knoxville* (Tenn.) *News-Sentinel* (Aug. 14) (Detours sec.) 11: A con man who sets up a big con on [a] crooked businessman.

b. deception; flattery, etc.; (*hence*) nonsense; BULL. Also attrib.

1896 Ade *Artie* 83: I'd been readin' them con story-books about pickin' flowers and goin' fishin' and dubbin' around the woods out in the country. **1897** Ade *Pink* 134: Yes, seh, she's full o' 'at 'ol con. **1902** Hapgood *Autobiog. of Thief* 48: Some of them escaped because they knew how to throw the innocent "con" so well. **1902** Corrothers *Black Cat* 69: "C'on" in negro dialect stands for "corn." Negroes did not like corn because they were compelled to eat *corn bread* in slavery until they were disgusted with it. So, now, when disgusted with a subject, or when they wish to say, "You are giving me taffy," they say instead, "You're feedin' me 'co'n.'" A "co'n man," then, is a taffy-feeder who lives by his wits—a "confidence man." **1919** Cober *Bttry. D* 23: Even though we had never seen the front, we figured that there was lots of "con" in their stories. **1929** Milburn *Hobo's Hornbook* 194: We chewed the rag for quite a while, I shot con for fair. **1942** Freeman & Gilbert *Larceny, Inc.* (film): Givin' me that con about goin' straight. **1965** in Jackson *Swim Like Me* 131: We chewed the rag for quite a while and shot the con for fair. **1971** Caillou *Evel Knievel* (film): That's a bunch of con! He's conning you.

c. a confidence swindler.

1897 in D. Cohen *Airship* 78: The Con was further surprised at seeing the girl...wind a large purple and white anaconda about her neck just as if it were a feather boa. **1902** Mead *Word Coinage* 165: A "con" is an abbreviation of confidence man. **1912** Field *Watch Yourself* [ref. to 19th C.] 396: He's a saint and that's what makes him successful as a con. **1928** Sharpe *Chicago May* 286: *Pay-off Men,* or *Cons*—confidence men (or women). **1975** Earp & Boyer *Wyatt* 170: The confederate, or capper as he would be called by the cons, was always the only winner. *a*1978 J. Carroll *B. Diaries* 89: Some junkie con and his partner did a fast take on one of them. **1992** *Hard Copy* (synd. TV series): Bob decided to give up his career as a con.

4.a. *Med.* consumption.—often constr. with *the.*

1912 Berkman *Prison* 130 [ref. to 1890's]: I've got the con bad, spittin' blood every night. **1917** *DN* IV 357: *Con.* Consumption: among doctors. **1917** Grider *War Birds* 23: Bob Kelly was...in Arizona for a while...trying to shake off the con. **1926** *AS* I (Dec.) 651. **1928** Bodenheim *Georgie May* 10: Emmy Lou...coughing her head off with the con. **1929–33** Farrell *Manhood of Lonigan* 270: Might he not die on a mattress grave from con in the charity ward of a hospital. **1945** *Calif. Folk. Qly.* IV 322: *The con:* silicosis. **1989** Emmons *Butte Irish* 150 [ref. to *ca*1900]: TB...the con....."rocks in the chest," as it was also known.

b. *Hobo.* a consumptive.

1930 "D. Stiff" *Milk & Honey* 202: A *con* is a tubercular person.

5. *Av.* a condensation trail.

1955 Salter *Hunters* 31: It's usually like that when the flight is in the cons. **1963** E. M. Miller *Exile to Stars* 22: Worland, there's a bogie at two o'clock high...Freck, got that con at ten-thirty? ***1984** Partridge *DSUE* (ed. 8) 247.

con *v.* to swindle; *(hence)* to fool; hoax; lie to. Now *colloq.* or *S.E.*

1892 in Dreiser *Jour.* I 9: He has "conned" McClaughry into believing otherwise. **1896** Ade *Artie* 25: Don't try to con me with no such talk. **1903** Townsend *Sure* 129: "Oh, no," I says, wondering wedder he was bug house, or only conning me. **1904** Limerick *Villagers* 87: Such was the case with every dame who stacked the cards so that she could con Kelsey into thinking he was real intelligent. *a***1904–11** Phillips *Susan Lenox* II 176: I'll not let any woman con me. **1939–40** O'Hara *Pal Joey* 34: I...had to con the tailor into letting me have it for only the down payment. **1973** O'Neill & O'Neill *Shifting Gears* 29: Society has conned them. **1975** V.B. Miller *Trade-Off* 36: And yet he could con a teacher as easily as he could con an upper-classman.

con artist *n.* a confidence swindler (now *S.E.*); *(hence)* a deceiver.

1937 in D. Runyon *More Guys* 251: He was a natural-born con artist. **1949** Monteleone *Crim. Slang* 56: *Con Artists*...Swindlers anxious to get something for nothing. **1957** N.Y.C. man, age *ca*70: He's a regular con artist. **1980** Pearl *Slang Dict: Con artist n.* One adept at winning favor in a deceitful manner. This term is sometimes used affectionately when applied to an appealing child. **1981** D. Burns *Feeling Good* 139: A con artist might sell you a fake ancient coin at an antique shop. **1987** *TV Guide* (Nov. 7) A-2: He played a con artist named Harry the Hustler.

conbobberation *n.* a disturbance.

1845 in *DA*: There was something aflouncin' and sloshin', and makin' a devil of a conbobberation at the end of the line. **1852** in *DARE*.

conbobbolate *v.* to think. *Joc.*

1846 in Botkin *Treas. Amer. Folk.* 29: So I combobbolated on the subject and last I resisted that I would explunctificate my passions by axletrissity.

Conch /kɑŋk/ *n.* an inhabitant of the Bahamas, the Florida Keys, or the coast of North Carolina; *(also)* a West Indian. Also **conk.**

*1804 in Holm *Dict. Bahamian Eng.* ***1833** in *OEDS*. **1855** Wise *Tales for Marines* 150: Pop was a Marblehead man, and the old woman was a conch from the Beheymees, where Pop got her on a wrackin' vyge; and it's ginerally considered 'long our shore to be kinder good for the breed to cross; it sorter makes the grizzil hard and fibry. **1861** in Bartlett *Amer.* (ed. 4): A Negro on this Key...is a more successful cultivator of the soil than all the rebel concks together. **1870** in *DARE*: The North Carolina "Conch" is unquestionably the lowest specimen of the race known. He has absolutely no virtues, and is dirtier, if possible, than the negro. **1871** Schele de Vere *Americanisms* 45: A *cracker*...appears as *Conch* or *Low Downer* in North Carolina, and as *Sandhiller* or *Poor White Trash* in South Carolina and Georgia. **1876** J. Wilkinson *Blockade-Runner* 123: The inhabitants [of Nassau]...are known among sailors by the generic name of "Conchs." **1878** Shippen *30 Yrs.* 304: The "conchs," as the natives of Key West are called, are not a very interesting race. **1899** Abbot *Blue Jackets of '98* 94: The little town [was] deadly dull usually and given over to Cuban cigar-makers and the native "conchs" who lead an amphibious life. **1910** *Everybody's* (June) 824: "I wish 'e was in 'ell," growled the lean rum smuggler, a real "Conch," who had been on a spree in Havana. **1937** Hemingway *Have & Have Not* 32: It certainly would make some Conchs happy. **1960** in T. Williams *Letters* 309: Frank and another wild young Conch...went over there and took him to our house. **1962** in *OEDS*: Keys natives are nicknamed "Conchs." **1984** *U.S. News & W.R.* (Apr. 9) 64: Booms and busts have shaped the natives [of Key West]—who call themselves "Conchs"...after the tough and tasty sea snails they eat—into supreme opportunists. **1992** *World News* (CNN-TV) (Nov. 12): With all the garbage around here, I'm ashamed to tell people I'm a Conch.

conch /kɑntʃ/ *n.* [clipping of *conscientious*] *Stu.* an overdiligent student.

1980 (quot. at CEREB).

conchie *n.* a conscientious objector to military service. Also **conshie.**

*1917 in *OEDS*. **1918** *Stars & Stripes* (Aug. 30) 7: We're "conchys"—but we don't work at it. **1919** Ashton *F,63* 18: The first "conchy" arrived about this time. **1924** *Amer. Leg. Wkly.* (Feb. 8) 16: Conchies Refunded $9840 of Pay They Weren't Entitled To. **1927** Stevens *Mattock* 234 [ref. to 1918]: We tamed a few conshies in the old outfit. Made good soldiers out of 'em, too. **1945** in *DAS* 118: Denies That His Son Was a Conchie. **1949** *Harper's* (June) 96: Our country, we only lock them up as conchies, as yet. **1957** Atwell *Private* 201 [ref. to WWII]: That Conchie! **1985** *Civil War Times Illus.* (June) 12: Perhaps the most fascinating is the diary of the "conshie," a drafted Vermont Quaker's account of his efforts...to get a discharge.

Conchy *n.* *Hobo.* Connecticut.

1916 Livingston *Snare* 95: "Conchy* Slim"...*"Conchy" is the hobo argot for Connecticut. **1927** *DN* V 442: *Conchy*, n. The tramp's abbreviation for Connecticut.

concho *n.* CONCHIE.

1969 Maitland *Only War* 95: But how can you hate me if you're a pacifist—a concho.

conch-shell *n.* a nose; CONK, 1.

1850 Melville *White Jacket* ch. xxxix: And Lord Wood's Nose—a lofty eminence said by seamen to resemble his lordship's conch-shell.

concrete elbow *n.* *Tennis.* the production of stiff or weak racket strokes.

1976 *AS* LI 293.

concrete overcoat *n.* CEMENT OVERCOAT.

1971 Waters *Smugglers of Spirits* 190 [ref. to *ca*1930]: Erring rummies were given what was quaintly called the "Concrete Overcoat" treatment...After being liquidated by members of the "enforcing squad," generally by shooting, their bodies were encased in concrete, taken out into the Gulf Stream at night and dumped overboard. **1974** *Playboy* (Feb.) 188: History does not record the inventor of the concrete overcoat, but the practice of putting a corpse in concrete and dumping it into a lake or river apparently came into fashion in New York in the late Twenties or early Thirties. **1979** R. Foster *Concrete Cowboys* (film): Take this punk out and fit him for a concrete overcoat.

concrete overshoes *n.pl.* CEMENT OVERSHOES.

1976 R. Daley *To Kill* 196: That would mean concrete overshoes for you, wouldn't it?

condish *n.* condition.

1862 in C.W. Wills *Army Life* 57: You'll understand my "condish." **1915** *N.Y. Eve. Jour.* (Nov. 23) (comics): "The Cyclone Kid"...is already in the pink of condish. **1919** in De Beck *Google* 7: I wanna tell him Dempsey's legs are in purty good condish.

cone *n.* the head.

1870 *Putnam's Mag.* (Mar.) 301: The combatants struck each other...upon the head, the nut, the cone. **1874** Carter *Rollingpin* 188: Well, it wa'nt a fly that lit/On the side of his convex cone that day.

conehead *n.* [sugg. by "the Coneheads," a farcical family of space creatures introduced on *Saturday Night Live* (NBC-TV) in 1976] a foolish or bizarre person.

1983 S. King *Christine* 131: Is there any more juice, or did you two coneheads drink it all? **1985** *Miami Vice* (NBC-TV): That conehead! **1989** *Night Court* (NBC-TV): Conehead!

coneroo var. CONNEROO.

coney[1] *n.* var. CUNNY.

coney[2] *n.* [orig. unkn.; cf. CONIACKER] *Und.* counterfeit banknotes.

1846 J. Greene *Secret Band of Brothers* 113 [ref. to 1798]: The word *Coney* means Counterfeit paper money. **1859** Matsell *Vocab.* 49: *Kone* [sic]. Counterfeit money. **1872** Burnham *Secret Service* v: *Coney*, counterfeit notes of any denomination. *Ibid.* 47: The manufacture and circulation of "coney" must be stopped. **1876** Pinkerton *Model Town* 80: Are you doing anything in the "coney" line now?

Coney Island whitefish *n.* *N.Y.C. area.* (see 1980 quot.).

1980 Univ. Tenn. grad. student: A *Coney Island whitefish* is a used condom seen floating near a dock or washed up on the beach. We used this term in Brooklyn around 1969 or '70. **1988** H. Gould *Double Bang* 27: They washed up at the doors of the River Royale like Coney Island whitefish on a Sunday morning. **1990** P. Dickson *Slang!* 196: *Coney Island whitefish*. Condom. **1993** *Mystery Science Theater* (Comedy Central TV): Aaah, just some syringes and Coney Island whitefish.

coney-man *n.* *Und.* a man who is a counterfeiter.

1872 Burnham *Secret Service* v: *Coneyman*, one known as a bank-note counterfeiter. *Ibid.* 47: He carried on his nefarious practices, in company with his friend and pal, Fred Biebusch, another famous western "coney-man." 1876 Pinkerton *Model Town* 78: Counterfeiters are called "coney" men or "coniackers," the terms being applied only to those who manufacture bogus coin for others to pass. They rarely handle it themselves. 1880 Pinkerton *Prof. Thieves & the Detective* 24: You helped break up the "coney men" and horse-thieves on "Bogus Island."

confab *n.* [clipping fr. *confab*ulation] a conversation, chat, conference, or the like. Now *colloq.*
    *1701 in *OED*: I will enter into a confab with you. 1763 T. Jefferson, in *OED*: The whole confab I will tell you word for word. *1789, *1836 in *OED*. 1833 A. Pike *Prose Sks.* 23: They held a long confab. 1840 Strong *Diary* I 149: Had a confab of an hour or so and then came home. 1880 J.C. Harris *Uncle Remus* 4: "I wanter have some confab wid you, Brer Rabbit," sez Brer Fox, sezee. 1934 Weseen *Dict. Slang* 322: *Confab*—A conversation; a conference; an interview; a convention; a meeting. 1945 in *DAS* 119: The infamous Munich confab. 1986–91 Hamper *Rivethead* 22: A small confab was held and I was…immediately expelled.

confab *v.* to chat or confer. Now *colloq.*
    *1741, *1778, *1795 in *OED*. 1880 J.C. Harris *Uncle Remus* 49: Dey had plenty er time fer confabbin' 'long de way.

Confed *n.* Confederate currency. Now *hist.*
    1863 in *Jour. Ill. State Hist. Soc.* LVI (1963) 323: I paid $2 Greenback for $8 "Confed." 1864 in *Civil War Hist.* VIII (1962) 221: 35 dollars…in Confed. 1865 in J.M. Williams *That Terrible Field* 151: Ten dollars is my amount of "Confed" at present. 1893 Casler *Stonewall* 205: We would then charge five dollars in "Confed."

Confederate *adj. So.* fine; decent.
    1869 *Overland Mo.* (Aug.) 128: When a Texan wishes to express the strongest possible approval…he will exclaim, "You're mighty Confederate!"

confetti *n.pl.* bullets; shrapnel. *Joc.*
    1923 Platt *Mr. Archer* 324: We used tons of Krag confetti, north an' south of the Lunetty,/Givin' lessons to the Gugus. 1928 MacArthur *War Bugs* 141: After standing in the roads all night, dodging confetti, the drivers were ordered up. 1935 Pollock *Und. Speaks: Confetti*, machine gun bullets. 1943 Fetridge *2nd Navy Reader* 74: Immediately, four Hellcats…sprinkled them with .50-caliber confetti. 1943 Hunt *Service Slang* 24: Confetti. American name for machine gun bullets.

conflab *n.* CONFAB.
    1864 in *Coll. Kans. State Hist. Soc.* XIV 331: General Curtis…had a *conflab* with Blunt. 1873 in *OEDS*: "Conflabs" lively among the lawyers. 1914 *DN* IV 104: *Conflab…Confab*, conversation. 1928 in *DARE*. 1934 Weseen *Dict. Slang* 322: *Conflab*—A conference; a conversation. 1942 *AS* XVII 283: To attend…conflabs with other schools. 1965–70 in *DARE*.

confo *n.* a conference.
    *1953 S.J. Baker *Austral. Lang.* 1956 Chamales *Never So Few* 195 [ref. to WWII]: Then the big confo with all the brass.

con game *n.* a swindle. Now *S.E.*
    1899–1900 Cullen *Tales* 227: This is no con. game…. It's on the level. 1903 in *DA*. 1906 in "O. Henry" *Works* 175: How far a "con" game would go. 1906 Wooldridge *Hands Up* 92: A hundrd [*sic*] varieties of "con" games. 1907 London *Road* 40 [ref. to ca1894]: His advice was good, and I followed it, prepared, however, if it was a "con game" the shack had given me, to take the blind as the overland pulled out.

congrats *n.* congratulations. Also **congratters.**
    1906 in "O. Henry" *Works* 153: "Congrats," says I. 1916 T.S. Eliot, in V. Eliot *Letters* 126: Congratters on the new book. 1919 Rickenbacker *Fighting the Flying Circus* 235: "Congrats, Cookie!" said Crocker triumphantly. 1928 H.P. Lovecraft *Mtns. of Madness* 23: Congrats, Pabodie, on the drill that opened up the cave. 1949 Loos & Sales *Mother Is a Freshman* (film): Congrats, Mom! You're a freshman! 1952 Chase *McThing* 57: You're in—congrats—shake! 1959 De Roo *Young Wolves* 23: Congrats, man.

coniacker *n.* [orig. unkn.; cf. CONEY²] *Und.* a counterfeiter. Hence **coniacking** counterfeiting.
    1845 *Nat. Police Gaz.* (Nov. 15) 100: The "King of the Koneyackers." 1846 in Partridge *Dict. Und.* 144. 1866 *Nat. Police Gaz.* (Nov. 3) 2: Bill Cregar…the life-long "koniacker." 1867 *Nat. Police Gaz.* (Mar. 23) 2: Jim was doing pretty well…in the "koniacking" business. 1871 Schele de Vere *Americanisms* 296: The makers [of false coins] are curiously

called *coniackers.* 1876 (quot. at CONEY-MAN). 1888 in *Amer. Heritage* (Oct. 1979) 21: I have known great "Koniackers," and greater still "Crib Crackers."

con job *n.* a swindle; a hoax; a deception.
    1942 *ATS* 457. 1955 in *DAS*: He was being taken in by a sharp con job. 1972 Madden *Bros.* 112: It sounded like one of Traven's con jobs. 1973 W. Crawford *Gunship Cmndr.* 102: Are you putting the con-job on me? 1978 Kopp *Innocence* 99: Flattery, con jobs, and intimidation. 1982 People's Court (ABC-TV): He says he knows what the plaintiff is doing, and he isn't going to let him get away with a con job. 1992 This Week with D. Brinkley (ABC-TV) (Oct. 25): You say that Social Security is a "con job."

conk¹ *n.* **1.** the nose. [The predominant 19th century sense.]
    *1812 Vaux *Vocab.*: *Conk*: the nose. 1832 *Spirit of Times* (Mar. 31) 2: The Kangaroo again hit out with his right, which caught Larkins on his conk, and floored him, the claret flowing profusely. 1841 [Mercier] *Man-of-War* 182: You don't appear now as if you had gentility enough about you to pick up a lady's handkerchief that she might chance to drop on the sidewalk, and present it to her without first bringing it in contact with that pretty carbuncled *conch* of yours. 1859 Matsell *Vocab.* 20: *Conk.* The nose. 1866 *Night Side of N.Y.* 80: His nose is a "conk," his chest a "bread-basket," his mouth a "potato-trap." 1870 *Putnam's Mag.* (March) 301: That conk,* with its delicate aquiline curve…*Nose. 1966 in *DARE*.
    2. the head; in phr. **off (one's) conk** crazy. [Although context of 1870 quot. would seem to suggest this meaning, the quot. fr. identical source at **(1)**, above, renders sense ambiguous.]
    1870 *Putnam's Mag.* (March) 301: The combatants struck each other…upon the head, the nut, the cone, the conk, the canister, the noddle. *1873 in *OEDS*: Isaac and Peter and the like of them, That's allis got conks like turkey's eggs. 1879 *Snares of N.Y.* 81: I've got to bunk here to-night if I hits you on the conk wid this paving stone. 1895 Townsend *Fadden Explains* 101: She'd yell murder when she'd jolt her conk. Eh? Don't you cop dat?…Why, dat's bump her head. 1906 *Nat. Police Gaz.* (Sept. 22) 6: Well, don't get it into your conk that I'm [heartless]…just because I'm a fly-cop. 1922 Rollins *Cowboy* 105: These other [cowboy] names [for a hat] included "lid," "war bonnet," "conk cover," [etc.]. 1924 Nason *Three Lights* 61: Up on your feet or I'll blow your conk off! 1926 *Sat. Eve. Post* (Mar. 6) 154: The Old Man said you were off your conk. 1928 Nason *Sgt. Eadie* 340: If he ain't off his conk I'm a chiropractor! 1940 O'Hara *Pal Joey* 98: What they did was lop her conk off for saying it. 1944 Olds *Helldiver Squadron* 3: You're off your conk. This is going to be something easy. 1953 Freeman *Destination Gobi* (film): There's just one thing for you guys to get in your conks. 1971 Curtis *Banjo* 220: She's bonked on the conk ever since she went east. 1976 Hayden *Voyage* 420: The top of his konk. 1985 Baker *Cops* 241: Listen to the way his head sounds. Listen to that conk…It's hollow, man.
    3. a blow on the nose (*obs.*) or head.
    *1898 *EDD*: A'll catch ye a conk in a minute. 1983 *Comedy Store* (WKGN radio) (Mar. 5): A conk with a…hammer ought to do it. 1993 N.Y.C. woman, age 59: I can remember "a conk on the head" from the funnies in the forties.
    ¶ In phrase:
    ¶ **bust (one's) conk** *Jazz.* to go wild with delight.
    [1939 Cab Calloway, in Gold *Jazz Lexicon* 16: Bust your conk: apply yourself diligently, break your neck.] 1939 West *Locust* 392: Truck on down to the candy store,/Bust your conk on peppermint candy! 1941 in Ellington *Music My Mistress* 179: Bust my conk…enjoy. 1946 Mezzrow & Wolfe *Really Blues* (gloss.): Bust your conk: become extremely happy and carefree.

conk² *n.* [fr. the v., infl. by CONK¹, *n.,* 2] *Black E.* a hairstyle in which the hair has been chemically straightened and flattened; (*hence*) the hair preparation for a conk.
    1942 *Yank* (Dec. 23) 18: The glare from his konk brought all the cats down. 1945 Himes *If He Hollers* 43: Even the solid cats in their pancho conks didn't ruffle me. 1969 L. Sanders *Anderson Tapes* 97: A negro…with long black greased hair combed in a high "conk" (pompadour). 1986 Clayton & Elliott *Jazz World* 47: I think the formula for conk is about seventy-five percent pure lye. 1990 *Nat. Lampoon* (Apr.) 14: All that stinking hair conk.

conk³ *n.* var. CONCH.

conk¹ *v.* **1.a.** to hit on the nose (*obs.*) or the head, esp. to knock unconscious. Also transf.

*1821 in *OEDS:* Spring, however, *conked* his opponent, when they closed. **1928–29** Nason *White Slicker* 190: He couldn't have run around like that…after being conked! **1930** Irwin *Tramp & Und. Sl.* 54: *Conk.*—To strike on the head. **1933** D. Boehm & E. Gelsey *Jimmy Dolan* (film): He conks me in the jaw and down I go. **1938** Baldwin & Schrank *Murder* (film): What do you think you are? Ya wanna get conked? **1941** in Thomason *Stories* 453: They conked him too! *a*1946 in W.C. Fields *By Himself* 149: They give him his milk bottle. He tried to conk me with it. **1947** Motley *Knock On Any Door* 145: They konked him over the head. They took all his money and his wrist watch. **1958** Swarthout *Cordura* 69: I been conked before, with chairs and bottles and suchlike. **1960** Garagiola *Funny Game* 47: Jocko was conked on the elbow. **1966–80** McAleer & Dickson *Unit Pride* 128: The gook I'd conked was coming to.

b. *Mil.* to strike (with a bullet or fragment).

1929 Niles, Moore & Wallgren *Songs* 77 [ref. to 1918]: But I wouldn't a minded gettin' concked if they hadn't took my tunic off me.

c. to knock.

1962 Crump *Killer* 9: I konked ya off my hill cause I'm the king o' dis hill!…So you better keep de hellie off if yas don't wanna get konked off again!

2.a. to kill.

1918 Roberts *Flying Fighter* 334: *Conked.* A new word which is taken from the Russian language and which means stopped or killed. **1926** Finerty *Crim.* 13: *Conked*—killed. **1936** Steel *College* 311: The janitor wasn't conked with Strike's gun…He was shot with a Smith and Wesson.

b. to die.

1942 *ATS* 132. **1965** Capote *In Cold Blood* 154: Because I caught pneumonia. I almost conked.

3. (of an engine or other machinery) to stop suddenly; stall; break down during operation.—also (now *usu.*) constr. with *out.*

*1917 in Lee *No Parachute* 110: My engine conked right out. **1918** Grider *War Birds* 88: The motor conked all right, but he made a nice landing in the field with a dead stick. **1918** Paine *Fighting Fleets* 228: Tried to zoom, engine konked,—side-slip—nose-dive. **1927** in Thomason *Marines* 202: Can't see why she conked. **1936** Mulholland *Splinter Fleet* 175 [ref. to 1918]: This damned mag has conked on us! **1942** T. White *Expendable* 105: The other engine conked out. **1943** Mears *Carrier* 105: I added throttle and the engine conked again astern of the ramp. **1952** Uris *Battle Cry* 419 [ref. to 1944]: Dammit, the generator conked! **1957** E. Brown *Locust Fire* 27: "What do you do when your engines conk?" "Get the hell out." **1971** *N.Y. Times* (Feb. 14) 3: Last week, part of the Con Ed system simply konked out.

conk[2] *v.* [fr. *congolene*, chemical application for straightening hair] *Black E.* **1.** to treat (hair) with congolene so as to straighten it.

1944 Burley *Harlem Jive:* Blessings on Thee, Little Square,/Barefoot cat with the unconked hair. **1957** H. Simmons *Corner Boy* 13: The straight, sticky patches of his conked hair. **1958** Hansberry *Raisin* 256: He ain't but 'bout five feet tall and he's got a conked head and his eyes is always closed and all his music. **1959** Griffin *Black Like Me* [entry for Nov. 8]: We're old Uncle Toms to our people, no matter how much education and morals we've got. No, you have to be almost a mulatto, have your hair conked and all slicked out and look like a Valentino. Then the Negro will look up to you…Isn't that a pitiful hero-type? **1968** Heard *Howard St.* 154: He looked upon hair-conking with scorn. **1974** Drafts *Bloodwhispers* 14: Damn, you still/got your hair conked! **1977** Torres *Q & A* 27: Wasn't but yesterday you was conkin' yo' head with a steam iron. **1980** in *Nat. Lampoon* (Jan. 1981) 51: Long, lacquered, conked, processed hair is still the rage with Negroes who hang out in the liquor line at Kinsell's all-nite drugstore. **1986** Clayton & Elliott *Jazz World* 47: The way Jimmy conked your hair.

2. to wear a CONK[2].

1992 Perl & Lee *Malcolm X* (film) [ref. to 1940's]: Everybody conks.

conk-buster *n. Black E.* see quot.

1946 Boulware *Jive & Slang* 2: *Conk Buster*…Cheap whiskey.

conked *adj.* drunk.

1957 Lacy *Room to Swing* 53: More fun getting conked in a night club. *Ibid.* 54: Conked? Oh, drunk, looped.

conked up *adj.* incapacitated.

1972 Pendleton *Vegas Vendetta* 159: That is, until he got all conked up with the siff.

conk off *v.* **1.** to kill; KNOCK OFF.

1943 *Destination Tokyo* (film): If anything happened to us on patrol, if we got conked off, do you think we'd see our folks in the hereafter?

2.a. to fail; break down.

1943 in Kluger *Yank* 64: Only to have [the engines] conk off again.

b. to fall asleep; sleep.

1945 in *Calif. Folk. Qly.* (1946) 387: Whoever *knocks off* work in order to rest or sleep *conks out, conks off, caulks off,* or *flakes out.* **1951** in *DAS:* You been conking off for eight hours. **1963** Morgan *Six-Eleven* 276: Conk off and get some sleep. **1969** Whittemore *Cop!* II 120: But John would work the average man to death. He'll konk off after twenty-four hours, but he won't complain. **1973** *Nat. Lampoon* (Mar.) 10: I am going to…hide under your bed, and, when you finally conk off, slit your throat…with a chain saw. **1984** J. McNamara *First Directive* 91: I got out before konking off.

c. to die.

1966 Susann *Valley of Dolls* 395: He thought she'd conk off in a few years. **1975** Phila. man, age *ca*28: When a roach conks off you'll notice you don't see them lying around very long…The other little bastards eat 'em.

conk-out *n.* an instance of conking out; failure; breakdown.

1942 *ATS* 160. **1959** R. Scott *Tiger in Sky* 42: Lufberry circles, Immelmann turns, loops and rolls and "conk-outs" were an integral part of my life. **1970** *New Yorker* (Nov. 14) 103: Delays, derailments, engine conkouts. **1979** *N.Y. Times* (July 1) II 28: "The Great Sioux Massacre" (1965) Joseph Cotten…Custer's conk-out. Less than memorable.

conk out *v.* **1.** CONK[1], *v.*, 3.

2.a. to faint or collapse, as from exhaustion.

*1924 R. Kipling, in *OEDS* [ref. to WWI]: The man was vi'lently sick an' conked out. **1948** A. Murphy *Hell & Back* 198: I'm sorry I conked out. I know you need men badly. *ca*1953 Hughes *Fantastic Lodge* 52: I konked out on the street…on the way to my doctor's office. **1963** Rubin *Sweet Daddy* 113: I took one look and conked out. **1969** Crichton *Andromeda Strain* 257: He wouldn't take his insulin…We almost put him off the force, because we were afraid to let him drive a car—thought he'd go into acidosis at the wheel and conk out. **1993** *CBS This Morning* (CBS-TV) (May 10): They conk out and watch television.

b. to die.

1929 L. Thomas *Woodfill* 28: But some of those rookies just about konked out. *Ibid.* 125: He just sat down in a drift and was all ready to konk out and have St. Peter punch his ticket. **1943** Steinbeck *Once There Was a War:* What size shoe you wear, Brown? I get them if you conk out. **1949** Gresham *Limbo Tower* 142: Why don't they put rubber sheets under these guys, they got a chance of conking out any minute? **1955** Ellson *Rock* 97: That's the way he conked out, with his eyes open. **1957** *Leave It to Beaver* (CBS-TV): Then when [the hamsters] conked out, I got blamed. **1966** Elli *Riot* 34: If Malaski konks out, we're facin' a murder rap. **1977** Dunne *Confessions* 231: What was he now? Eighty?…He's going to conk out soon. **1981** P. Sann *Trial* 69: If I knew I was going to see you again I might have conked out even sooner. **1989** *48 Hours* (CBS-TV): Before I conk out, I want to do something for the city.

c. to fall asleep.

1945 (quot. at CONK OFF, 2.b.). **1952** Mandel *Angry Strangers* 244: Whatta you wanna do? When she's conked out? **1955** Goethals *Chains* 135: Howley doesn't want him going out again tonight, so it's just as well the guy's conked out. **1967** Spradley *Drunk* 15: He was conked out on the ballroom floor with a hangover. **1968** Kirkwood *Good Times* 33: Headmaster conked out early, but there's lights on over there. **1976** Rosen *Above Rim* 73: I'll watch the news, catch the scores and then conk out.

3. to render (someone) unconscious, esp. by a blow to the head.

1943 in Guthrie *Bound for Glory* 364: Only you don't hafta swing that there pump aroun' so much here in th' car. You don't want to konk none of yer own soldiers out, do you? **1952** Mandel *Angry Strangers* 256: You want to conk me out and diddle me while I'm helpless, you big degenerate?

con man *n.* **1.** Orig. *Und.* a confidence man. Now *S.E.*

1886 *Chi. Tribune* (Mar. 2) 3: A good union man informed the reporter that they were "scabs" and con men. **1888** in *Amer. Heritage* (Oct. 1979) 21: I know the "Con-man" stately, who has left rich pastures lately. **1889** in *OEDS:* It does not take an unsophisticated countryman to get swindled by the "con man." **1891** Maitland *Slang Dict.* 74: *Con man* (Am.), or confidence men, swindlers, bunko steerers. **1892** Norr *China Town* 41: It's a good state for "con" men to keep away from. **1902** Corrothers *Black Cat* 29: Then there was Prof. Lightfoot Johnsing, the "con man." **1906** Wooldridge *Hands Up* 92: The most notorious and best organized gangs of "con" men. **1927** H. Miller *Moloch* 79: This individual had failed...as a "con" man.

2. a man given to insincere flattery.

1899 Cullen *Tales* 139: Well, he was a pretty good con man, and he nailed me for that positively last and final appearance.

3. *So.* a convict or ex-convict.

1930 "D. Stiff" *Milk & Honey* 203: *Con man*...It may [also] mean exconvict.

con merchant *n.* CON ARTIST.

1963 T.I. Rubin *Sweet Daddy* 21: Some of these con merchants—really made a buck at it. **1965** Horan *Seat of Power* 19: He's a con merchant with women. **1978** *N.Y. Times* (July 9) V 3: The day this con merchant joined the horsemen for dinner they had...one thing in common. **1986** R. Campbell *In La-La Land* 29: Warsaw didn't have to be friendly to anybody he suspected was a con merchant.

connect *n. Und.* a connection (in any sense).

1962 (quot. at WING, *n.*) **1972** Grogan *Ringolevio* 51: The "connect" would give him half the price marked on the packages of meat in exchange for heroin. **1974** V. Smith *Jones Men* 19: So youall fixing to make a big connect. **1986** Jarmusch *Down by Law* (film): Check it out— I got the right connects, I'm organized.

connect *v.* **1. to meet or find (someone).—constr. with *with.***

1903 A.H. Lewis *Black Lion* 121: The first local sport I connects with is the padre. **1922** Murphy *Black Candle* 158: The problem [of the drug smuggler] is to "connect" with his patrons. **1925–26** J. Black *Can't Win* 177: I'll send you word. Don't try to connect with me. **1931** Hellinger *Moon* 221: All I connect with is lousy people and lousier tips. **1952** Brossard *Darkness* 13: I felt sorry for her that she ever had connected with Porter. **1981** P. Sann *Trial* 160: Leander had to swim across a whole river to connect with that chick.

2. to gain.—constr. with *with.*

1904 Ade *True Bills* 4: They should have connected with all the Coin. **1908** *Independent* (July 23) 200: He doesn't seem to have any idea of how he came to..."connect" with those notions. **1920** Ade *Hand-Made Fables* 41: He got into Practice and began to connect with the Currency.

3. *Sports.* to hit a baseball hard; land a heavy blow. Now *S.E.*

1905 *Sporting Life* (Sept. 2) 14 (cited in Nichols *Baseball Term.*). **1912** Mathewson *Pitching* 4: When Tinker...connects, he hits 'em far. **1933 in OEDS.*

4. to succeed (in a specific endeavor).

1925–26 J. Black *Can't Win* 144 [ref. to 1890's]: Did you connect, Kid? **1928** Dahlberg *Bottom Dogs* 197: Funny he had never been able to connect as campflunkey. **1933** J.T. Farrell *McGinty* 186: My wife and I want a kid, and we do plenty of homework, but, goddamn it, Dutch, I just can't connect. **1937** in D. Runyon *More Guys* 128: He will move himself in for a few dibs if the good thing connects. **1958** Frankel *Band of Bros.* 6 [ref. to 1950]: I got booted in the family jewels playin' football, so maybe it's my fault we can't connect [i.e., succeed in having a child]. **1977** Olsen *Fire Five* 6: Easier for him to connect, he don't even have a bald spot.

5. *Und.* to make a purchase of illicit goods, esp. narcotics.

1938 in *OEDS*. **1947** in W.S. Burroughs *Letters* 13: I am not sick and I do not want you to even try and connect. **1967** Kolb *Getting Straight* 143: Help me. You gotta help me connect.

connected *adj. Und. & Police.* being a member of or closely connected with an organized crime syndicate.

1977 B. Davidson *Collura* 24: The population of Union Street was split into "those who are straight," the majority, and "those who are connected." **1983** P. Dexter *God's Pocket* 4: The truth was, he didn't think the kid's stepfather was connected. **1989** Radford & Crowley *Drug Agent* 135: He constantly portrayed himself as "connected." **1990** Murano & Hoffer *Cop Hunter*: These thugs had to be extremely brazen to...[rob] a connected guy.

connection *n.* **1. *Und. & Police.* the act of purchasing, or (*later*) a purchase of, illicit goods, esp. narcotics.**

1927–28 Tasker *Grimhaven* 164: He'll tell you where you can make a connection. **1930** M. West *Babe Gordon* 10: Where coke peddler and sniffer made their "connection" in safety. **1930** V.H. Brightman *Vice Exposures* 72: *Making a connection*— finding a drug seller. **1936** Dai *Opium Add.* 91: Addicts generally "hang around" and make their "connections," that is...secure their supply of drug from peddlers. **1972** P. Thomas *Savior* 89: Tired of walking miles for a connection and tired of getting beat out of it.

2. *Und. & Police.* a supplier of illicit goods, esp. narcotics.

1927–28 Tasker *Grimhaven* 165: Walk around till a Mexican comes to you and asks what you want. That's the connexion. **1931** B. Niles *Strange Bro.* 275: My connection was drunk that morning. **1936** Dai *Opium Add.* 172: All of them have this code in common that no one should betray the other or give away one's "connection," that is, the peddler. *Ibid.* 197: *Connection.* A drug peddler. Also called *a pusher* or *a shover.* **1948** Schwartz *Blowtop* 27: "What about his tea connection?"..."He's been getting that stuff from some seaman who hangs around the 16 Bar." **1950** *Neurotica* (Autumn) 45: Duke [was] his connection. **1955** Q. Reynolds *HQ* 274: But the junkies and the connections (big operators) and the pushers usually keep active until 2 or 3 a.m. **1960** R. Reisner *Jazz Titans* 153: *Connection:* One's source of supply. **1979** in Terkel *Amer. Dreams* 218: Now there's a connection on every block.

¶ In phrase:

¶ **have a loose connection** to be crazy.

1973 *Penthouse* (Aug.) 14: Anybody who would rather pack up...and go...has to have a loose connection. **1976** Ark. man, age *ca*26: Somebody's got a loose connection around here.

conneroo *n.* [CON + -EROO] CON ARTIST.

1949 Algren *Golden Arm* 77: This mild-looking, white-haired ...coneroo. **1951** N. Algren *Chicago* 54: His harlots and hopheads, his coneroos and fancy-men. **1964** N. Algren, in *Sat. Eve. Post* (Sept. 26) 44: Fireships, finks, and coneroos. **1974** E. Thompson *Tattoo* 13: The boy's narrow face split into a beautiful Hamite conneroo's grin.

connie or **conny** *n.* **1. *Army.* a conscript.**

1865 in Andrus *Letters* 118: He singled out old Jimmy Fleming, one of our $700.00 Connies. **1884** Hedley *Marching Through Ga.* 407 [ref. to 1865]: You —— "connie" (conscript), come on and fight!

2. a conductor, as on a streetcar or railroad train. Cf. CON, 1.

1904 *Life in Sing Sing* 246: *Conny*—Conductor. **1930** Irwin *Tramp & Und. Sl.* 54: *Conny.*—A railroad conductor. **1931** J.T. Farrell *McGinty* 81: He looked quizzically at the connie's outstretched hand.

3. a consumptive.

1904 *Life in Sing Sing* 246: *Conny*...consumptive. **1925** in Partridge *Dict. Und.* 145.

4. (*cap.*) *Navy.* the frigate and training ship USS *Constellation*; (*later*) the aircraft carrier USS *Constellation*.

1915 in *OEDS* s.v. *gob*: Us "gobs" were on the "Conny" standing by. **1966** F. Elkins *Heart of Man* 121: He turned up...over the *Connie.* **1967** Harvey *Air War—Vietnam* 1: The movies shift very frequently, however. The *Connie* trades movies with *Ranger* and *Ranger* trades with *Oriskany*, which trades with *Intrepid*, and so on. **1984** Cunningham & Ethell *Fox Two* 1 [ref. to 1971]: *Connie*, as we knew her, left San Diego harbor with an escort designed to protect the ship. **1989** J. Weber *Defcon One* 49: I sure hope the "Connie" is listening.

5. (*cap.*) *Av.* a Lockheed Constellation aircraft.

1953 Chandler *Goodbye* 25: Nobody...wants to ride a DC-3 over mountains when he can take a Connie and make it in seven hours to Mexico City. **1956** Heflin *USAF Dict.* 137: *Connie, n.* A nickname for the Constellation. **1959** Russell *Perm. Playboy* 478: For instance, that Connie could have been a B-47 with the big boy aboard. **1959** Searls *Big X* 143: The Connie falls on the City Hall and wipes it out.

6. (*cap.*) a Lincoln Continental automobile.

1978 S. King *Stand* 82: A big white Connie was roaring north on US 180.

connive *n. Und.* a share of illicit profits.

1961 Parkhurst *Undertow* 71 [ref. to *ca*1950]: If you deliver half a piece, that's eight spoons, you get $30 plus your cut or "connive." That's how you get paid.

conshie var. CONCHIE.

consolation *n.* alcoholic liquor, esp. whiskey. *Joc.*

1863 "E. Kirke" *So. Friends* 87: The young planter bade the bar-tender..."trot out the consolation."

Constan *n. Naut.* Constantinople.

1922 in Hemingway *By-Line* 53: Old timers always call it Constan, just as you are a tenderfoot if you call Gibraltar anything but Gib.

consy *n. Auto Racing.* a consolation race.

1976 *Webster's Sports Dict.* 88.

contact high *n. Narc.* a mild feeling of intoxication induced by the smoke of another person's marijuana cigarette; (*also*) a feeling of exhilaration induced by interaction with someone who is high on drugs, or with any exuberant individual. Also **contact.**

1954–55 in *Social Problems* VII (1959) 244: A "contact high." **1958** Kerouac *Subterraneans* 40: I was getting, every time they turned on, a kind of a contact high. **1962** Maurer & Vogel *Narc. & Narc. Add.* (ed. 2) 297. **1966** Goldstein *1 in 7* 21: Somewhere in between are those who find a vicarious pleasure in the "contact high." **1969** Mitchell *Thumb Tripping* 20: He was fascinated. A contact high? **1969** *New Amer. Rev.* 7 (Aug.) 115: You trying to avoid a contact high, man? **1978** W. Brown *Tragic Magic* 7: We hadn't known each other very long but with the rocking train nudging us toward one another, I was beginning to get a contact high. **1982** Eble *Campus Slang* (Nov.) 1: *Contact*—effect of inhaling marijuana smoke without actually smoking a joint: I got a *contact* just walking into the bathroom. **1989** *ALF* (NBC-TV): I was just...hoping for a contact high. **1986–91** Hamper *Rivethead* 152: I used to get contact highs just lookin' at his eyes.

con talk *n.* the misleading talk that is part of a confidence game; *(hence)* insincerity; lies.
    1896 Ade *Artie* 7: One on each arm, see?—and puttin' up the large, juicy con talk. *Ibid.* 30: Mame tried to give me a con talk and that made me sore. **1909** Irwin *Con Man* 39: With him to pull things off and me to work the line of con-talk which I acquired...we should have made one of the greatest combinations in the country.

continental damn *n.* [*continental* 'a small amount' + *damn*] a damn.
    1847 in Somers *Sports in N.O.* 64: [Not] for the outside shadow of a continental d—n. **1869** *Galaxy* (May) 666: My mere passing allusion to the slang phrase, "a continental damn"...a tinker's damn, a trooper's damn. **1899** Barrère & Leland *Dict. Slang* I 269: *Continental damn*...Not to care a *continental*, not to care a damn. **1899** Hamblen *Bucko Mate* 129: I don't care a continental damn whether I ever get up again or not. **1968** N.J. man, age *ca*50: I don't give a continental damn.

contract *n.* **1.a.** *Und.* an offer of payment for the commission of a crime, esp. murder; a command to murder someone.
    1941 in Tyler *Org. Crime* 71: "The contract is to 'take' a fellow by the name of Puggy Feinstein."...The reason for the contract? "Well, he crossed Vince." **1951** in Partridge *Dict. Und.* 808: He had such a lust for bloodletting that he would volunteer to handle "contracts" even when it was not his turn to work. **1952** H. Grey *Hoods* 49: People came to us with what we called "contracts." From all over town...came unsolicited propositions to heist big payrolls...Bootleggers and racketeers came to us with contracts to murder their business partners. **1962** *Mad* (Sept.) 27: My Most Memorable Contract, Heart-Warming Nostalgia By Professional Killer Oogie Freuchen. **1969** Salerno & Tompkins *Crime Confed.* 102: As an enforcer, having accepted a "contract" to see to the performance of a violent crime, he must now...get the right people for the job. **1974** in J.L. Gwaltney *Drylongso* 162: They might run a contract on him. **1976** Schroeder *Shaking It* 107: They put a contract out on you, man. Fifteen [candy] bars to beat up, not to kill. **1983** E. Dodge *Dau* 36: Some say the CIA had a contract on him.
    b. the intended target of a crime carried out under such a contract, esp. a person to be murdered.
    1930 Lavine *3d Degree* 188: A dinner...was held up by gunmen in search of a murder contract.
    2. *Und. & Police.* a mutually beneficial arrangement, esp. if illicit; *(hence)* a service or favor done under such an arrangement; *(broadly)* a favor done with the expectation of repayment.
    1958 *N.Y. Times Mag.* (Mar. 16) 87: *Contract*—Any favor one policeman says he'll do for another. **1962** Dougherty *Commissioner* 27: For one thing he did not believe in doing favors, or "contracts," as they were called. **1972** J. Mills *Report* 121: It's a contract, a politician's kid or something like that, so someone has to make a show, go through the motions. **1985** Baker *Cops* 251: "We have a number of contracts. There's money to be made...Now, do you guys want in on them or not?"..."No, we want to stay clean. We like not having to worry about being crooked."

contrib *n. Journ.* contributor.
    1942 *ATS* 491. **1958** S.H. Adams *Tenderloin* 224: I'm a regular contrib to the funny papers.

control freak *n.* a person having a neurotic need to control his or her surroundings.
    1968–77 Herr *Dispatches* 13: I got to hate surprises, control freak at the crossroads....one of those people who always...had to know what was coming next. **1979** Washburn *Deer Hunter* (film): You're a control freak. **1986** *TV Guide* (Aug. 2) 27: "I'm a control freak," Spielberg has said. **1987** *Us* (Nov. 30) 20: So would you describe yourself as a control

freak now? **1991** G. Piaget *Control Freaks* (title). **1992** *Bold & Beautiful* (CBS-TV): You're a powermonger! You're a control freak!

contwisted *adj.* confounded; darned.
    1834 Caruthers *Kentuck.* I 23: I wish I may be contwisted if you ain't one of the queerest men...I have clapped eyes on this many a day. **1845** in *DARE.*

convent *n.* a brothel. Cf. ABBESS, NUNNERY.
    1759 in Silber *Songs of Independence* 146: Each soldier shall enter the convent in buff.

conversation water *n.* Champagne. Also **conversation fluid.** *Joc.*
    1903 Ade *Society* 34: The highest-priced Caterer in Town would deal out the sparkling Conversation Water as if Brut and Buttermilk cost about the same. **1926** C.M. Russell *Trails* 55: They're sure whooping her up, singin', and I get a little of that conversation fluid in me.

convict *n. Circus.* a zebra. *Joc.*
    1926 (quot. at HUMP, *n.*). **1931** *Nat. Geo.* (Oct.) 467: The animal keepers call the zebras "convicts."

convincer *n.* Esp. *Und.* an effective means of inveiglement or intimidation, esp. a pistol or other deadly weapon.
    1930 *Variety* (Jan. 8) 123: [The victim of a crooked card game] is permitted to win ("thrown the convincer") until considered ripe for picking. **1935** Pollock *Und. Speaks: A convincer,* a pistol. **1942** Algren *Morning* 20: Use it fer a jimmy first 'n fer the convincer later.

con-wise *adj.* **1.** *Pris.* familiar with the attitudes and behavior of convicts.
    1912 in Partridge *Dict. Und.* 144: He had been a prison officer nearly all his life, and was what is known as "con-wise." **1966–71** Karlen *Sex. & Homosex.* 553: He is not yet con-wise.
    2. *Und.* having a professional knowledge of swindling.
    1965 Ward & Kassebaum *Women's Pris.* 50: Criminally mature or *con-wise* persons.

con woman *n.* a woman who is a confidence swindler. Now *S.E.*
    1906 *Nat. Police Gaz.* (Aug. 18) 6: A foxy con woman. **1978** *Barnaby Jones* (NBC-TV): You wouldn't con a con woman would you?

con work *n.* CON TALK.
    1917–20 Dreiser *Newspaper Days* 69: Cut the gentle con work, Theodore.

coo *n.* [cf. COOZIE] the vulva or vagina; *(hence)* a woman or women, esp. regarded sexually.—usu. considered vulgar.
    *1879 *Pearl* 174: Though perfect all the charms may seem,/That famed Apelles drew./Not half so sweet are they, I deem,/As fair Cecilia's Cu. **1954–60** *DAS* 125: *Cou.* A girl. **1962** Quirk *Red Ribbons* 67: I think we better haul ass and see Damascus before VBF gets all the good coo lined up. *Ibid.* 97: I'm here to have some booze and coo. *Ibid.* 200: Coo is scarce in this town. At least good-looking coo. *Ibid.* 214: I think I'll marry that coo. **1964** in Gover *Trilogy* 218: One coo named Wanda...she say this Friday night crowd's the roughest any place. *ca*1965 IUFA *Folk Speech*: *Coo* = Girl. **1967** W. Crawford *Gresham's War* 169: This is life and death and history...not a piece of coo. *Ibid.* 190: She wasn't just another piece of coo?

cooch[1] *n.* a hootchy-kootchy dance. Often attrib. Also **kootch.**
    1910 *Variety* (Sept. 10) 20: Her "cooch"...is also suggestive. **1913** *Billboard* (Mar. 24) 4: A mighty good-looking and shapely dancer of the "cooch" variety. **1921** *Variety* (Feb. 18) 11: The "cooch" dance [is] under its latest name of "shimmy." **1924** Wilstach *Anecdota Erotica* 35: There were naked women doing kootch dances and the like. **1928** *AS* III (June) 414: *Cooch.* A contraction of "hoochie coochie," the famous Turkish muscle dance. Barred from nearly all the carnivals of the better class. Supplanted in some cases by the Hawaiian hula, which is somewhat similar. **1931** Hellinger *Moon* 92: Two drinks of brandy would bring on a cooch dance that made Mr. Volstead wish he was a kid again. **1934** North *New Masses* 93: With a ballet of cooch dancers. **1937** Reitman *Box-Car Bertha* 224: Polly, the cootch dancer. **1940** in A. Banks *First-Person* 176: You don't have to do much [actual] dancing in a kootch tent anyway. **1977** T. Berger *Villanova* 212: She entered in the mode of a Casbah cooch-dancer. **1979** T. Baum *Carny* 38: Cosmo Baptiste [was] the kootch show agent.

cooch[2] *n.* [cf. COO, COOZIE] the female crotch. *Not common.* **1969** *Current Slang* I & II 21: *Cooch*, *n.* An attractive female.—Air Force Academy cadets. **1972** R. Wilson *Forbidden Words* 76: *Cooch*…In the South, the vagina.

cooch[3] *n.* [alter. of HOOCH] liquor, esp. whiskey.
1965–68 in *DARE*.

coocher *n.* a hootchy-kootchy dancer.
1927 in Charters & Kunstadt *Jazz* 219: One coocher…does the Harlem River Quiver. **1967** Zeidman *Amer. Burlesque Show* 38: These had a tiny cast of two or three coochers, a comedian or two, little if any scenery.

coochie *n.* a hootchy-kootchy dance. Also redup. Also fig.
[**1893** W.C. Robey *Naughty Doings on the Midway Plaisance* (Chicago: Will Rossiter) (sheet music): On the Midway, the Midway, the Midway Plaisance,/Where the naughty girls from Algiers do the "Kouta Kouta" dance.] **1921** Conklin & Root *Circus* 261: A beautiful black stallion named Eagle, whose especial accomplishment was to dance the "couchee-couchee" with John O'Brien on his back. **1942** *ATS* 589: Hootchy-cootchy or shimmy dance…*coochy*.

cook *n.* a person who prepares opium; CHEF; *(hence)* a chemist who makes illegal drugs.
1933 (cited in Partridge *Dict. Und.* 146). **1990** *21 Jump St.* (synd. TV series): If he was the cook, why would he…draw attention to himself?

cook *v.* **1.a.** to falsely manipulate or adjust (facts, figures, accounts, or the like). Orig. *S.E.*
*****1636** in *OED*: The Proof was once clear, however they have cook'd it since. *****1848** J.S. Mill, in *OED*: These accounts, even if cooked, still exercise some check. **1885** *Harper's Mo.* (Nov.) 852: Accounts are "cooked" so as to exhibit decreased earnings [etc.]. **1909** *WNID* 494: *Cook*…*Math. Slang.* To adjust (observations and calculations) arbitrarily so as to render them apparently harmonious. **1942** *ATS* 534: Falsify accounts…*cook the accounts.* **1972** *Harper's* (Mar.) 88: With respect to some of the other figures, she appears to have been cooking her data. **1986** Cash & Epps *Legal Eagles* (film): The three partners were cookin' the books. **1988** in Safire *Coming to Terms* 33: The way a crooked bookkeeper "cooks" books.

b. *Und.* to illicitly prearrange or influence, as through bribery.
1872 Burnham *Secret Service* IV: *Cooked*, fixed up desirably for the occasion. *Ibid.* 71: He had sought out the Government witnesses and "cooked" all he could find access to.

2.a. to ruin, finish, do for.—now usu. in past. ppl.
*****1851** in *F & H*: When…the cabs that carry four came in, they cooked the hackney-coachmen in no time. *****1857** in Partridge *Dict. Und.*: Come on. He's cooked. He wants no more. **1865** Byrn *Fudge Fumble* 215: The thirteenth of December cooked my love box so that it was not open to the reception of anything mortal until the following spring. **1883** *Life* (Aug. 30) 105: He only said "I'm cooked" and passed away. **1896** Ade *Artie* 42: "My Dear Madam." Wouldn't that cook you, though? **1903** Townsend *Sure* 48: Dey cooks deir college standing by such weaknesses. **1918** Grider *War Birds* 218: It's afternoon now and no word has come from him so I guess he's cooked. Requiescat in pace. **1929** Burnett *Iron Man* 96: That cooked it. **1939–40** Tunis *Kid from Tomkinsville* 31: It was the continual speed which cooked a guy. **1949** J. O'Hara, in *New Yorker* (July 16) 17: I don't care how big a star is, if he gets temperamental, that cooks him. **1952** Chase *McThing* 120: Boss, the cops—we're cooked! **1953** *New Yorker* (Mar. 7) 51: Nowadays, if the big record companies don't go for you, you're cooked. **1957** Yordan *Men in War* (film): Then we're really cooked.

b. Esp. *Und.* to murder.
*****1856** (cited in Partridge *Dict. Und.* 146). **1906** A.H. Lewis *Confessions* 25: If I was to be "cooked," I was set to do some "cooking" in return. **1908** Hopper & Bechdolt *9009* 91: Fer stealin'? Fer killin'? Fer snuffing a gofe? Fer cookin' a bull? **1908** *New Broadway* (Aug.) 142: Those Dagos meant to cook me. **1917** *Editor* (Feb. 24) 152: *Cooked*, or *Croaked*—killed. **1931** Harlow *Old Bowery* 506: While half drunk, they decided to "cook" Kelly. **1934** Garrett & Mankiewicz *Manhattan Melo.* (film): I tell ya, it was me cooked that guy—not Blackie Gallegher! **1951** Fowler *Schnozzola* 122: Link, somebody is going to get cooked, and you'll wind up on the front burner.

c. *Pris.* to execute or be executed by electrocution.
1932 Eleson *Last Mile* (film): They'll only sew him up so they can cook him. **1931–34** in Clemmer *Pris. Commun.* 331: *Cook*…To kill by legal electrocution. **1965** C. Brown *Manchild* 220: When they cooked Lollipop…—just before he left, he said, "Well, looks like Lolly's had his last lick." *****1966–72** Winchell *Exclusive* 9: A police lieutenant named Becker also cooked in the same chair. **1971** Dahlskog *Dict.* 15: *Cook*…to elec-

trocute, as in the electric chair, or to be electrocuted.

3.a. to do very well; in phr. **cook with gas** [or **on the front burner**] to do superlatively well. [*Cook with gas* appears to be the original form; gas stoves became common in the U.S. just before WWI, but these expressions gained national currency only during the 1940's.]
[**1918** *Inf. Journal* XV (Oct.) 344: It's all right to "cook with gas"/But who wants to croak with it? Get that mask on *Quick*.] [**1922** in Galewitz *Great Comics* 1: Supper's all ready…I don't know how good it's going to be because I'm not used to cooking with gas.] **1942** *Time* (Jan. 12) 44: "Cooking with gas" meant perfect understanding. **1943** *N.Y. Times* (May 9) 11: Brother, when you are cooking with both burners the fiddle is out. **1945** in *OEDS: Cooking on the front burner*, tops. **1946** G.W. Henderson *Jule* 107: "How you doing?" "O.K.…Cooking on the front burner." **1947** *ATS* (Supp.) 5: Now you're cooking with gas. **1954** Ellson *Owen Harding* 54: If he feels good he'll…say, "I'm cooking on the front burner, woman." **1960** R. Reisner *Jazz Titans* 153: *Cook:* to play well. **1963** in Clarke *Amer. Negro Stories* 309: He knew he had to cook. **1965** Hentoff *Jazz Country* 19: I don't mean they make mistakes, but they're not "cooking." You're cooking when you can play everything that jumps into your mind. **1974** N.Y.C. man, age *ca*76 [ref. to 1918]: We'd see these old worn-out planes, these *crates*, we called them. We'd say, look at that old crate. But when a new, fast-flying plane went over, we'd say, "Now they're cookin' with gas! Now that's a *plane!*" **1976** Rosten *To Anywhere* 302: Now you're cooking. **1976** Mich. man, age 29: My father used to say, "Now you're cooking with gas on the right front burner." **1983** *Bon Appetit* magazine ad, WINS Radio (Dec. 30): Other recipe magazines are just coffee table books, but *Bon Appetit* really cooks! **1985** *Maxie* (film): Now you're cookin' with gas. **1987** *Time* (Feb. 9) 16: The band cooked, dig? It was tight.

b. (of an engine) to run smoothly.
1955 Scott *Look of Eagle* 144: The big J-57 engine [was] "cooking" serenely along. **1959** Scott *Tiger in Sky* 43: Nor did it do anything commonplace like *run*, either. It "cooked."

4. to be developing; go on; happen.
1940 Hartman & Butler *Rd. to Singapore* (film): What's cookin' here? **1941** Chodorov & Fields *Louisiana Purchase* (film): What's cooking, fellas? **1941** Boardman, Perrin & Grant *Keep 'Em Flying* (film): I don't know what's cookin' here. **1941** in Ruhm *Detective* 250: Wait a minute….What cooks? **1942** in T. Williams *Letters* 47: What's cooking at your end of the line? **1942** Algren *Morning* 19: I don't know what you guys got cookin'…but I'm still takin' care of number one. **1943** Chandler *High Window* 424: What's cookin'? **1944** *Slanguage Dict.* 60: Hi, good lookin'; what's cookin'? **1947** *ATS* (Supp.) 9: What's cookin', good lookin'? **1951** *Sat. Eve. Post* (Apr. 21) 10: It would be a good idea to let the American people in on what's cooking. **1953** Dibner *Deep Six* 14: I figure you're entitled to know what cooks. **1957** Ness & Fraley *Untouchables* 37: We don't have too much cookin' around here right now. **1958** Hailey & Castle *Runway* 7: A deal is cooking that involves maybe thirty to a hundred trucks. **1967** Steiger & Whritenour *Saucers Are Hostile* 103: The possibility that other races have…been systematically investigating this…planet…to see what cooks.

¶ In phrase:

¶ **cook (someone's) goose** to ruin, do for, or undo (someone); *(obs.)* to kill. Now *colloq.*
*****a1851** in *OED*: If they come here we'll cook their goose/The Pope and Cardinal Wiseman. *****1860** A. Trollope *Framley P.* ch. xlii: Chaldicotes, Gagebee, is a cooked goose, as far as Sowerby is concerned. *****1863** in *OED*: If you worry or excite your brain, you will cook your own goose—by a quick fire. **1866** *Night Side of N.Y.* 72: What cooked my goose to a turn was Sarah Jane. *****1873** Hotten *Slang Dict.* (ed. 4): "To cook his goose," to kill him…or "settle his hash." **1882** A.W. Aitken *Joe Buck* 14: Don't you p'int that we'pon…or I'll cook your goose. **1887** DeVol *Gambler* 84: I grabbed my gun and…said, "Don't come one step more towards me, or I will cook your goose." **1900** Patten *Merriwell's Power* 76: That cooks his goose. **1906** in McCay *Little Nemo* 68: I can see my finish. My goose is cooked. It's all over with me now but the shouting. **1913** Jocknick *Early Days* 145: It'll cook his goose O.K. any how, I'll bet. *ca*1920 in *Civil War Times Illus.* (Feb. 1966) 37: Later had a backset, and the flu which almost cooked my goose. **1935** J. Conroy *World to Win* 40: My daddy'll kick *your* goose!…Wait and see, smart aleck! **1942** Garcia *Tough Trip* 152: They would have cooked the Squaw Kid's goose for him good and brown. **1953** Wicker *Kingpin* 291: And if that doesn't cook Anson's goose for sure, nothing ever will. **1983** Hofstadter & Dennett *Mind's I* 32: My goose may soon be cooked just as *his* was!

cookbook *n. USAF Acad.* the book of regulations of the U.S.

Air Force Academy.
1965 *Life* (Feb. 12) 68: There's a whole volume of regulations, known as the "cookbook."

cooked *adj.* drunk.
1930 J.T. Farrell *To Whom It May Concern* 72: Another bum cooked on canned heat.

cooker *n.* **1.** *Jazz.* that which is exciting or attractive, as a young woman, jazz tune, or the like.
1943 *AS* (Apr.) 154: *Some cooker.* An attractive girl. **1971** *Playboy* (Aug.) 34: [The record album] includes the Jones-Bergman cooker *In the Heat of the Night.*
2. *Med.* a heat lamp.
1980 *AS* (Spring) 48.

cookie *n.* **1.** a cook or cook's helper.
***1825** "Blackmantle" *English Spy* I 278: Then by the powers, cookey, you had better pay for one and a half. **1846** in *DAE:* We embarked…in company with…a cookie who was lord and master of the culinary department. **1867** Clark *Sailor's Life* 151: Good bye, Cookie. **1886** Nye *Remarks* 147: I…smoked the…tobacco of the cookee. **1888** Billings *Hardtack & Coffee* 287 [ref. to Civil War]: Not at all daunted by this experience, the cookey harnessed the mule again as before. **1926** Kephart *So. Highlanders* 232: The cookee banged his poker on a piece of iron swung from a string to call all hands to dinner. **1930** *DN* VI 86: *Cookee,* cook in camp. **1938** Holbrook *Mackinaw* 256: *Cookee.* Any sort of cook's helper in Lake States and Northeast. **1973** Overgard *Hero* 83: That's all, square shooters, Americans, except for the cookie.
2. person.—usu. with prec. modifier.
1917 in Truman *Dear Bess* 235: He's a hard-boiled cookie. **1918** in Hall & Nordhoff *Lafayette Flying Corps* II 185: One of the Lieutenants was very proud of his men. They were tough and hard-boiled; in short, to use his own words, "Rough Cookies." **1920** Ade *Hand-Made Fables* 96: I have seen countless hordes of first-time Cookies going through the deadly Routine. **1933** in Galewitz *Great Comics* 34: What's th' matta with you cookies? **1939** Stegner *Darkling* 8: That cookie's a deserter. I'll bet you on it. **1940** in H. Gray *Arf* (unp.): He's a tough cookie. He'll sit tight and wait for us to make another pass. *Ibid.* Yeah, reckon I will keep an eye on that cookie, like Nick said. **1944** Paxton *Murder, My Sweet* (film): How'd you get mixed up with these cookies? **1944** *Life* (May 15) 68: A girl with less than two bracelets feels like a "homely" or a "shot cookie." **1947** Bowers & Millhouser *Web* (film): He's a smart cookie. **1953** Freeman *Gobi* (film): Why didn't they just let those cookies knock us off? **1955** Q. Reynolds *HQ* 11: A real smart cookie…A decent guy, too. **1965** Karp *Doobie Doo* 32: She's a smart cookie. **1968** Hawley *Hurricane Yrs.* 63: Oh, he was a smart cookie, all right. **1970** Trustman & Webb *Mr. Tibbs* (film): I think you're a scared cookie trying to figure out what to do. **1974** *Odd Couple* (ABC-TV): You're a cold cookie—you know that? **1975** V.B. Miller *Deadly Game* 95: He's playing the cool cookie. **1978** Barry *Ultimate Encounter* 48: Travis was a smart cookie. **1980** *N.Y. Post* (June 20) 79: Duran is a tough cookie. **1993** *Donahue* (NBC-TV): I can be one tough little cookie.
3.a. an attractive young person of the opposite sex, esp. a young woman.
1920 *Collier's* (Mar. 6) 42: That girl friend of yours is a cookie—hey, what? **1930** Lait *On The Spot* 201: *Cooky*…sweetheart. **1951** *N.Y. Times* (Sept. 30) VII 20: The general met and passed several nights in Paris with a cookie named Dottie Peale. **1972–79** T. Wolfe *Right Stuff* 139: The most marvelous lively young cookies were materializing also.
b. (among lesbians) a lesbian who takes a passive role in homosexual activity.
1978 *N.Y. Post* (Dec. 9) 14. Some girls don't like gay…They won't turn cookie for nothing.
4.a. *pl.* the contents of the stomach.—usu. used in var. phrs. meaning "to vomit."
1927 *AS* II (Mar.) 278: *Shoot one's cookies*…vomit. **1927** Mayer *Between Us Girls* 104: Vile-looking people…snapping their cookies at every roll of the ship. **1930** Weaver *Collected Poems* 233: He…turns green as a catfish two days dead,/And shoots his cookies, and has to go on sick-call. **1941** *Slanguage Dict.* 11: *Cough up one's cookies*…to vomit. **1941** in C.R. Bond & T. Anderson *Flying T. Diary* 24: He usually ended up tossing his cookies. **1945** in *Calif. Folk. Qly.* V (1946) 389: Part one's cookies. **1954** Ellson *Owen Harding* 43: He heaved his cookies all over the front steps. **1959–60** Bloch *Dead Beat* 58: I guess you heaved your cookies when you saw him, didn't you? **1962** Robinson *Barbara* 61: The colonel was sick as hell last night, tossing his cookies all over the place! **1963** Coon *Short End* 55: "Crazy," I yelled back at him, and just about

flipped my cookies from the effort. *Ibid.* 58: He threw his cookies all over the floor. **1964** Howe *Valley of Fire* 209: Every time I pop my cookies over one of Comrade Mao's literary bonbons. **1968** Coppel *Order of Battle* 144: He remembered getting sick…and popping his cookies. **1968** J.P. Miller *Race for Home* 174 [ref. to ca1930]: She didn't know how her daddy could have such a walleyed ole heifer for a sister, and the whole idea made her want to woof her cookies. **1968** Swarthout *Loveland* 113: And what a howl to see from the pier, her joining the Navy and you tossing your cookies. **1968** Baker et al. *CUSS* 99: *Cookies, snap your.* Vomit. **1970** Landy *Underground Dict.* 122: *Lose your cookies* v. Vomit. **1972** Ponicsan *Cinderella Liberty* 15: Your education doin' you any good now, lying there about to chuck your cookies? **1972** *Nat. Lampoon* (Oct.) 82: Virgin Mary/Shot her cookies in his face! **1972** Kerr *Dinky Hocker* 41: They're not religious songs, so don't look like you're going to toss your cookies. **1973** Overgard *Hero* 89: He keeps shipping out with us every time, like he's going to hang onto his cookies, but when we land he's always five pounds lighter. **1976** Conroy *Santini* 382: You got to have a light meal, otherwise you'll blow your cookies all over the place. **1985** Briskin *Too Much* 203: I just tossed my cookies. *a*1989 R. Herman, Jr. *Warbirds* 94: Trying with diminishing success to keep his cookies down.
b. *pl.* daylights; stuffing.
1984 *Prairie Home Companion* (Nat. Pub. Radio) (Nov. 10): The team was getting the cookies knocked out of them.
c. *pl.* BUNS; (*hence*) (one's) life, reputation, etc.
1986 *Heart of the City* (ABC-TV): You did it all, man. You saved my cookies. *a*1987 Bunch & Cole *Reckoning* 127: You better start listening or somebody's gonna toast your cookies out there in the boonies. **1990** *Murphy Brown* (CBS-TV): This Rocket fellow just steams my cookies [infuriates me].
5. *Mil.* an explosive device; bomb.
1942 Hersey *On Bataan* 106: He designed the Casey Cookie for counter-sniping order…a hollow joint of bamboo with a dynamite stick in it. **1943** in *DAS.* **1956** Heflin *USAF Dict.* 142: *Cookie, n.* A large bomb. *Slang.* **1979** A. Hopkins *Front & Rear* 42 [ref. to WWII]: Each one has a bomb—a 4,000 pound "cookie"—carried beneath it.
6. usu. *pl.* a dollar.
1954 R. MacDonald *Condemned* 27: There's a tax matter pending. She put too many cookies in this layout. She's living too high.
7. the vulva and vagina. *Joc.*
1954–60 *DAS.* **1968** Legman *Dirty Joke* 100. **1972** *Nat. Lampoon* (Dec.) 48: It was Della's wont to clout her cookie whenever life began to overwhelm her. **1978** T. Sanchez *Zoot-Suit* 70: If you can't get a boner, I'll let you cop a feel of my cookie.
8. a cigarette. *Joc.*
1977 Avallone *White Knight* 17: So I smoked a cookie. **1978** Lieberman & Rhodes *CB* (ed. 2) 296: *Cookie box*—Pack of cigarettes.
¶ In phrases:
¶ **eat the cookie** to be vanquished; endure defeat.
1978 *Black Sheep Sqdn.* (CBS-TV): I'm afraid we'll have to eat the cookie on this one. Without help—we're stuck!
¶ **get (one's) cookies (off)** to experience orgasm; (*hence*) to experience intense pleasure, esp. in a perverse way.
*ca*1952–56 in Reuss *Field Collection* 101: If we want our cookies off,/We call up SDT's. **1966** Elli *Riot* 72: Let's castrate the ol' bastard…Fix him so he can't get his cookies. **1966** I. Reed *Pall-Bearers* 130: He wouldn't even let my generals get *their* cookies, he was carryin' on so. **1968–70** *Current Slang* III & IV 54: *Get…cookies off* v. To reach a sexual climax.—High school males, Ohio. **1971** Altman & McKay *McCabe & Mrs. Miller* (film): If you want to get your cookies, I got three girls up here who can do more tricks than a monkey on a hundred yards of grapevine. **1972** in *Playboy* (Jan. '73) 250: This how you get your cookies, Father? Asking people [about their sex lives]? **1973** *Shaft* (CBS-TV): Are all your wives in the hospital, or is this how you get your cookies? **1984** D. Smith *Steely Blue* 169: That'll be enough to get my cookies. **1992** *Donahue* (NBC-TV): Do they get their cookies off when you're beating them?
¶ **have a cookie in the oven** to be pregnant.
1960–69 Runkel *Law* 270: They c'n do the same thing I do but the women they do't with can't end up with a cookie in 'er oven.
¶ **pop (someone's) cookies** to induce orgasm in (someone).
1972 R. Wilson *Forbidden Words* 200: Man, did she pop my cookies!
¶ **take the cookie** to surpass all others; *take the cake* s.v. CAKE.
1882 in Miller & Snell *Why West Was Wild* 214: He comes to the front

with a remarkable display of adamantine cheek…Pass him the cookie. **1886** in *AS* XXV 31: For keeping away from trouble a peeler takes the cookie.

¶ **that's the way the cookie crumbles** that's the way things are and nothing can be done to change it.
1956 Hargrove *Girl He Left* 50: There's people up front going to chew me, and then I'm going to chew you, because that's the way the cooky crumbles. **1957** *Sat. Eve. Post* (Sept. 7) 59: From then on, that's the way the cooky crumbled. **1960–61** Steinbeck *Discontent* 181: That's the chance you take—the way the cooky crumbles. **1972** Madden *Bros.* 154: So you get your money…any way the cookie crumbles, huh?

cookie-cutter *n.* **1.** *Carnival.* a sheriff's star-shaped badge.
1926 Norwood *Other Side of Circus* 155: Against the law to pack a cookie cutter without a license in a lot of states.
2. *Garment Industry.* a manufacturer of cheap, mass-produced clothing.
1963 *N.Y. Post* (Sept. 21) 34: The mass-production houses, with offices on Broadway, are known as "cookie cutters."

cookie-dipper *n.* COOKIE-PUSHER, 1.
1958 Camerer *Damned Wear Wings* 66 [ref. to WWII]: He was being cut out for a "cookie dipper," a gravel cruncher in the Air Force.

cookie-duster *n.* a mustache; (*rarely*) a person with a mustache.
1930 J.T. Farrell *Grandeur* 203: Mary…always says she wouldn't trade me for these cookie-dusters that try to sneak feels off of her while she's serving them lunch. **1934** in Wallechinsky & Wallace *People's Almanac* 54: College Boys!/Your Courage Muster/Shave Off/That Fuzzy/ Cookie Duster/Burma-Shave. **1943** Burnett *Nobody* 151: He wasn't a bad guy at that…in spite of the cookie-duster. **1959** *Swinging Syllables: Cookie duster*—Mustache. **1961** Peacock *Valhalla* 140: More cosmoline for your goddam cookie duster…Why the hell didn't you use mustache wax. **1971** Dahlskog *Dict.* 15: *Cookie duster, n.* A mustache. **1974** Mayes *Bank Shot* (film): Your cookie-duster's loose again. **1992** *Simpsons* (Fox-TV): I shaved off the old cookie-duster.

cookie-pusher *n.* **1.** an effete man who frequents tea parties or the like; CAKE-EATER; (*hence*) *Pol.* (used as a derisive term for State Department officials).
1934 Weseen *Dict. Slang* 178: *Cookie pusher*—A male student who seeks female companions; a tea hound. **1943** *Sat. Rev. Lit.* (July 24) 18: "Cookie pushers" is a newspaper men's term for thwarted "career men" in the State Department…who wear striped trousers and know the proper gambits for unattractive wives of foreign secretaries. **1946** *Word Study* (May) 2: State Department officials have long been called "cookie pushers." **1950** *N.Y. Times* (Sept. 14) 11: He said…that attachés were only "cookie pushers," anyway. **1967** Michaels *Women of Berets* 40: Mr. Honeybone was a State Department specialist in Asian affairs…The people who didn't like him would sometimes call him a cookie-pusher. **1973** M. Collins *Carrying the Fire* 467: The foreign-service officer is the most maligned person in government, invariably depicted as a "striped-pants cookie-pusher." **1977** Coover *Public Burning* 418: It's gonna be no place for skonks and cookie pushers. **1981** *N.Y. Times* (Aug. 2) IV 3: People say we're not just cookie pushers, and that's healthy in a foreign policy. **1989** *Capital Gang* (CNN-TV) (Feb. 18): The striped-pants cookie-pushers in the State Department.
2. a waitress.
1936 McCarthy *Mosshorn* (unp.): Cookie Pushers. A waitress. **1950** in *DARE*. **1958** McCulloch *Woods Words* 38: *Cookie pusher*—A hasher, same as biscuit shooter.

cookie-snatcher *n.* a child. *Joc.*
1962 IUFA *Folk Speech:* Term for children *Cookie snatchers.*

cookie truck *n.* FUNNY WAGON.
1976 *Barney Miller* (ABC-TV): This is…[the] 42d Precinct. Send over a cookie truck, will you? **1984** Hindle *Dragon Fall* 61: Somebody, anybody, get the cookie truck up here, pronto!

cookie wagon *n.* a police patrol wagon; PIE WAGON.
1929–31 (cited in Partridge *Dict. Und.* 147).

cooko *n.* a cook.
1919 Beston *Full Speed Ahead* 28 [ref. to 1918]: The cook was a child of Brooklyn, and could talk…"Give it to 'em, cooko," said one of the crew…"We're with you."

cookoo var. CUCKOO.

cool *n.* **1.** Orig. *Black E.* composure. [Became a fashionable term nationally 1964–66.]

1953 in Wepman et al. *The Life* 119: Dig yourself, creep, don't lose your cool. **1959** A. Anderson *Lover Man* 129: Anyway I kept my cool. **1961** H. Ellison *Gentleman Junkie* 143: I'd wee-wee'd all over myself…I was really beginning to blow my cool. **1962** Larner & Tefferteller *Addict in the Street* 80: Now if I blew my cool—if I got up and said I was going and they knew what was happening—they couldn't stop me. **1962** Crump *Killer* 41: A cat can't allow hisself to lose his cool in dis day 'n' age. **1964** in Redfield *Let. from Actor* 160: In fact, it would indicate a mass loss of New York cool. *Ibid.* 184: Momentarily blowing my cool, I asked Burton what would happen to yours truly of the not-so-hot performance. **1964** Faust *Steagle* 36: It so happens I greatly admire his cool. **1965** Summers *Flunkie* 49: Thats how you catch fish though. You can't afford to blow your cool. **1966** *New Yorker* (June 18) 37: I'll bet that old guy has never blown his cool. **1970** Segal *Love Story* 53: I kept my cool long enough to pull into the parking lot of a seafood diner. **1972** Madden *Bros.* 159: So I try to match his cool. **1973** Childress *Hero* 90: They got a steam table that'll blow your cool. **1982** P. Michaels *Grail* 129: But at least I kept my cool. **1984** J. McCorkle *Cheer Leader* 199: He must laugh it off and keep his cool. **1988** *N.Y. Daily News* (June 9) 74: John…simply didn't have his customary icy cool. **1992** Pres. G. Bush, on *World News* (CNN-TV) (July 24): I didn't blow my cool, I just made an emphatic point.
2. *Und.* a period of truce, as between street gangs.
1958 *N.Y. Times* (Apr. 30) 26: Following this shooting efforts were made to establish a "cool" or truce between street gangs in the area. **1959** Salisbury *Shook-Up* ch. iii: A "cool" was negotiated by street club workers, but it was an uneasy truce, often broken. **1959** E. Hunter *Matter of Conviction* 199: There was a cool on at the time, until this thing with the girl happened. **1966** Samuels *People vs. Baby* 152: I'm trying to work out a cool between these two groups.
3. stylishness; fashionable sophistication.
1961 Sullivan *Shortest, Gladdest Years* 72: It was the final unqualified quintessence of Cool. **1965** *N.Y. Times* (May 30) II X 3: You have to play it with a certain degree of cool. **1966** *Sat. Eve. Post* (May 21) 60: Nobody uses drugs out in the open, and no one flaunts it around for cool. **1966** *Time* (Apr. 22) 87: He has neither Batman's flair nor James Bond's cool. **1971** Sonzski *Punch Goes Judy* 43: Sally, for instance, had a lot of cool. **1972** Chipman *Hardening Rock* xviii: We were weaned on the concept that material goods were the criteria of success, of "cool." **1973** *Odd Couple* (ABC-TV): You've got cool, that's what you've got. **1973–76** J. Allen *Assault* 4: I dug his cool. I dug his manner, his nonchalant way of dealing with people. **1982** Suffolk Co. Honda ad (WINS radio) (Aug. 12): We are the *kings* of cool. **1993** *Newsweek* (July 26) 46: He reminds one of the young Ike Turner, he of the pencil-thin mustache and the dangerous cool.

cool *adj.* **1.** insolent; impudent; unabashed; (*hence*) daring.
*1825 "Blackmantle" *English Spy* I 69: [At Eton] A *dapper dog,* a *right cool fish*…takes his dish In [*sic*] private with his tutor.…*A right cool fish,* one who is not particular what he says or does. **1839** Briggs *Harry Franco* I 39: "That's right cool," said my neighbor, fixing his keen eyes upon me. **1844** Porter *Big Bear of Ark.* 142: Prodigiously cool! Enough to make the *cannonized* leg of the Presidential Unipede…burst its cerements. **1846** Durivage & Burnham *Stray Subjects* 173: *You are the coolest specimen of a genuine scamp that it has ever been my ill luck to meet with.* **1848** Bartlett *Amer.: Cool.* Used in familiar language, in England and the United States, in the sense of impudent. **1850** *Spirit of Times* 235: Well, hand me, if that ain't cool! **1852–55** C.G. Parsons *Inside View* 147: Then each took a pistol in the right hand, [and] pointed it directly at the other's heart.…When the "ten" was uttered, the pistols were fired and…they were both dead! "Now, that was pretty cool all around," said the Colonel [approvingly]. ***1863** Cheadle *Journal* 224: He…said, "Look here, I've got no money for the road," in the coolest manner, as if it was my duty to supply anything he liked to order. **1865** in Hilleary *Webfoot* 99: A huge rattlesnake crawled out, rather cool! ***1873** in *OED*: He certainly knew that such a request was a trifle cool. **1879** in M. Lewis *Mining Frontier* 8: Well, Jake, ef that ere ain't the dog-rotted, coolest thing I ever seen a human critter do, you can shoot me. **1880** J.M. Drake *Fast & Loose* 119: The horseman smiled again, and broke the silence by saying, "That's —— cool, any way." **1887** W. Watson *Life in Confed. Army* 261: Hold your tongue, you impudent scoundrel.…Well, that is a cool scoundrel. **1890** in Hoppenstand *Dime N. Detective* 26: Well, upon my life, boy, this is about the coolest business I ever saw. **1895** *Confed. War Jour.* (Feb.) 176: "Come," said Smith.…"I must take you to headquarters." "That's cool," said the Yankee—"from a prisoner, too!" **1943** Kurnitz *They Got Me Covered* (film): "Cozy little nook. What time do the bats fly out?" "You're a cool one, ain't ya?" **1946** in D. McKay *Wild Wheels* 38: There's been some talk about the lad being a little too cool, too sure [as a race car driver].

1992 Hosansky & Sparling *Working Vice* 61: This guy—he's cool, he's tough. **1993** *Front Page* (Fox-TV): Fictional [football] players, to show how cool and tough they are, lie down in traffic.

2.a. shrewd; clever; (*hence*) urbane; suave; sophisticated, esp. in ways attractive to the opposite sex.—occ. (in recent use) used in direct address to a man. Also adv.

*1918 *Bodleian Qly. Rec.* II 152: *A case, a lad, a head, a cool kid*, all words for expressing admiration for another's cleverness or cunning. **1924** in Leadbitter & Slaven *Blues Records* 155: Cool Kind Daddy Blues. **1925** in P. Oliver *Songsters & Saints* 73: Some cool kind daddy stole my heart away. **1944** Burley *Hndbk. Jive* 101: Portrait of a Cool Stud Hyping His Chick. **1944** Stiles *Big Bird* 51: We flew it on three missions, and we named it the *Cool Papa*....The *Cool Papa* was Sam's name. When we were in school everyone called him cool papa because he was such a major operator. **1945** T. Anderson *Come Out Fighting* 115: "Cool Stud," the rooster-mascot of Sergeant Dan Cardell's Charlie tank. **1946** Boulware *Jive & Slang* 3: Cool Papa...Nonchalant fellow. **1952** E. Brown *Trespass* 14: Man, you never seen such fine chicks in your whole life...But Hopalong, he cool. These chicks come call on him, where you think he at? Out. That where...He roping up some old cow, or shooting up some fine saloon. I mean, he *real* cool. It ain't hardly natural for no man to be cool as old Hopalong. **1953** W. Fisher *Waiters* 106: As cool a hustler as he is, he wouldn't let a sweet racket like this slip through his fingers. **1963** Gant *Queen St.* 40: He started off, walking cool. **1967** Taggart *Reunion of 108th* 183: "Did you think I was that cool?" she said lightly, squeezing his arm. **1965–68** McCord et al. *Life Styles in Black Ghetto* 71: Some men become "cool cats." **1973** Duckett *Raps* 21: Me?/O.D?.../I'm much too cool for that. **1982** Del Vecchio *13th Valley* 76: Watch yourself, Cool. **1983** Leeson *Survivors* (film): You're so cool you piss ice cubes.

b. fashionable; stylish. Also adv.

1946 Boulware *Jive & Slang* 3: Cool...neatly dressed. **1952** Ellson *Golden Spike* 144: I'll have money, be dressed all cool. **1954** *St. Louis Post-Dispatch* (Jan. 17) (Pictures) 2: As students move into the upper years of high school, their taste in clothes becomes something that only they can understand....They follow modes...that are either "cool" or just not admissible. **1958** *N.Y. Times* (July 27) IV 6 E: Driving a two-toned convertible that teenagers would call "real cool." **1962** H. Simmons *On Eggshells* 221: They go for what they figure it's supposed to be cool to go for. **1969** D.L. Lee *Think Black* 16: Or are u too busy tryen to be cool/like tony curtis & twiggy? **1979** in Terkel *Amer. Dreams* 447: Nobody cool ever changed the world. Nobody cool ever wrote great literature. **1980** Kotzwinkle *Jack* 212: The outfit looked unbelievably cool. **1989** *CBS This Morning* (CBS-TV) (Apr. 26): Tomorrow we start our series on who and what's cool. **1992** Majors & Billson *Cool Pose* 22: Black males often use alcohol and drugs...to be cool—part of the "scene."

3.a. Orig. *Black E.* superlative; exciting; enjoyable; (esp. later, with weakened force) satisfactory; acceptable; OK. [Pop. by jazz musicians after WWII.]

1933 in Clarke *Amer. Negro Stories* 67: Sho wisht it [*sc.* his wealth] wuz mine. And whut make it so cool, he got money 'cumulated. And womens give it all to 'im. **1935** Hurston *Mules & Men* 33: Man, you know Ah don't go nowhere unless Ah take my box [guitar] wid me...And what make it so cool, Ah don't go nowhere unless I play it. **1944** Kendall *Service Slang* 57: *Cool*...good. **1950** *Neurotica* (Autumn) 46: This is a cool pad man. **1950** *Harper's* (Apr.) 92: The Bop musician's use of "cool" instead of "hot" as a word of highest praise. **1951** *New Yorker* (Aug. 4) 15: Described here and there as the coolest drummer alive ("cool" being, of course, the current word for "hot" in musical terminology). *ca*1953 Hughes *Lodge* 96: How is it? Is it cool, man? Everything is always cool, everything is all right. **1954** *Harper's Mag.* (Nov.) 36: Anything nice was crazy or cool. **1960** R. Reisner *Jazz Titans* 153: *Cool:*...a word of assent. **1964** Gold *Jazz Lexicon* 65. **1973** Eble *Campus Slang* (Mar.) 1: *Cool as shit!*—That's fantastic! **1973** Childress *Hero* 27: When Mr. Cohen got holda our class, he was mad cause our readin was not cool a-tall. **1972–74** Hawes & Asher *Raise Up* 91: I'd pull into a station, the attendant would check it out, assure me the tire was cool. **1975** *Wond. World of Disney* (NBC-TV): Running away wasn't too cool either. **1978** Maupin *Tales* 111: It's cool if you don't want to talk about it. **1980** Univ. Tenn. freshman theme: There are a couple of cool guys on my floor. The rest are a bunch of shit heads. **1982** Del Vecchio *13th Valley* 23: It's cool, Man, ya know. It's okay. **1990** *Simpsons* (Fox-TV): Cool! **1992** Majors & Billson *Cool Pose* 45: "Is he cool?" is frequently the first question one adolescent asks concerning another.

b. on friendly terms; cooperative.

1973 Goines *Players* 8: If someone who didn't know us heard you talk-

ing, they wouldn't believe we was real cool with each other. **1975** Sepe & Telano *Cop Team* 27: "Be cool....Get over to that car and spread yourself." The suspect was searched. **1988** T. Logan *Harder They Fall* 49: "Can you wait for us a couple of minutes?" "Long as you give me some green to keep me cool."

4. *Und.* no longer being sought by police. Cf. HOT.

1937 Hoover *Persons in Hiding* 176: He possesses a million dollars' worth of buried bonds awaiting a time when they can be "cool" enough to place on the market.

5. under control; cautious; discreet; in phr. **stay** [or **be**] **cool** (used as a valediction). Also adv. [Cf. S.E. literary sense 'not heated by passion or emotion', in *OED* with cites fr. *Beowulf*, Chaucer, Shakespeare, Tennyson, etc., and with parallels in other languages; the main difference is that the S.E. sense is used in a privative sense, in implied comparison with *hot* 'passionate; emotional', whereas the slang sense is used in a semantically absolute sense.]

[**1862** in C. Brewster *Cruel War* 161: Cal...is as cool as a cucumber.] [**1882** in Sweet *Sweet's Texas* 32: Hush!...lie low, be cool, and wait for orders.] **1952** Mandel *Angry Strangers* 104: I like things should stay cool; you got it? Real cool. **1955** *AS* XXX 87: *Cool*, adj. Quiet. **1968** Cameron *Dragon's Spine* 16: Just move forward, friend, and move *cool* until I see what you look like. **1971** T.C. Bambara *Gorilla* 72: Elo, be cool a minute. **1972–73** in M.J. Bell *Brown's Lounge* 12: You don't have to worry about Mike, he's cool. **1980** D. Hamill *Stomping Ground* 91: You just be cool with that bread. **1980** T. Jones *Adrift* 185: Thanks for the coffees...stay cool! *a*1984 Sereny *Invisible Children* 4: I believe all I have to do is just talk to you cool, you know. **1987–91** D. Gaines *Teenage Wasteland* 17: The park closes after dark....But if...you're cool about it, you can have some privacy.

6. safe or well.

1952 Mandel *Angry Strangers* 251: Dinch, go on home to the Bronx, Dinch. You'll be cool up there. **1954** in *Social Problems* III (1955) 43: Nothing happened. So I knew it was cool (alright). **1975** Sepe & Telano *Cop Team* 177: Everything's cool....These guys are the Lone Ranger and Tonto. **1980** Gould *Ft. Apache* 44: Just see if they ain't movin' or makin' any noise, and wave to us if it's cool, you understand. **1982** "J. Cain" *Commandos* 173: "You okay, mister?" "Yeah, I'm cool." **1983** *Nat. Lampoon* (Feb.) 46: Her whole family's going to be out of town, so it's cool.

¶ In phrases:

¶ **cool as a moose** *Stu.* especially COOL, 3.a.

1969 *Current Slang* I & II 21: *Cool as a mouse* [*sic*] *and twice as hairy*, adj. Tremendous; handsome.—College females, New York State. **1975** Univ. Tenn. student: That's cool as a moose. **1978** Katz *Folklore* 231: Cool as a moose. **1981–85** S. King *It* 648: "Is that cool?" "Cool as a moose."

¶ **play it cool, 1.** to act in a manner that is cautious, shrewd, wary, calculating, or the like.

1942 *Pittsburgh Courier* (Jan. 3) 7: All this time I have been trying to play it cool, but suddenly realized that I was the fool. **1945** in M. Chennault *Up Sun!* 137: McGoon and I thought we'd better not do any bragging and better play it cool. **1947–52** R. Ellison *Invisible Man* 418: Play it cool, ole man, play it cool! **1953** in *Great Music of D. Ellington* 31: I'm playing it cool as can be. **1953** W. Brown *Monkey on My Back* 31: Of course there had been a row with both his mother and father, but Dave had "played it cool," making believe it was really the older boys who had led him on. **1955** Ellson *Rock* 107: I play it cool this time. Cut across the street, come down the block and cross over. **1958** H. Ellison *Deadly Streets* 19: Avoid cops. Play it cool. **1959** in Cox *Delinquent, Hipster, Square* 15: I don't antagonize nothing. I play it cool. **1970** LaMotta, Carter & Savage *R. Bull* 57: When I got into the warden's office, there was nothing I could do except play it cool. **1972** Buell *Shrewsdale* 38: Light a smoke and play it cool. **1980** W.C. Anderson *Bat-21* 129: He was going to have to play it cool. Real cool. **1993** *TV Guide* (Aug. 28) 26: At the moment, that means playing it cool.

2. to become or remain calm; take it easy; relax.

1942 *Pittsburgh Courier* (Jan. 17) 7: We don't do nothing but play it cool....Play it cool—Don't become ruffled. **1944** Burley *Hndbk. Jive* 105: To play it cool with some mellow fool. **1953** in T. Williams *Letters* 280: Have a good Summer and "play it cool" as they say. **1959** Gault *Drag Strip* 77: Don't get nervous, now. Cool, cool, cool—play it cool. **1959–60** Bloch *Dead Beat* 134: Nobody was going to know, not if he played it cool. In the movies, they always get panicky. **1991** B.E. Ellis *Amer. Psycho* 59: Without complaining, playing it totally cool, I pull out my gazelleskin wallet and hand her a fifty.

¶ **take it cool** to take it easy; remain unruffled; relax.

1841 [Mercier] *Man-of-War* 211: Don't hurry me whatever you do....I want to take it cool, Garnet; I always take dese sort of tings as coolly as possible. **1850** "N. Buntline" *G'hals of N.Y.* 17: Do you want me ter lay off and take it cool, while we're all a-starvin'? **1862** M.V. Victor *Unionist's Dtr.* 47: Don't be scart, boys, take it cool; I've been bit before. **1864** Northrop *Chronicles* 30: Though we had not gone a rod an officer came along and in a kindly manner said, "Sit down, boys and take it cool." *a***1881** G.C. Harding *Misc. Writings* 155: But Lize took it cool, an' told me to keep my shirt on. **1906** in S.C. Wilson *Column South* 320 [ref. to Civil War]: Boys, just take it cool, for you gave them all they wanted. They won't bother us anymore. **1944** Stiles *Big Bird* 99: Take it cool. **1958–59** Lipton *Barbarians* 110: Sit tight. Take it cool. **1992** Mowry *Way Past Cool* 5: Well, you for sure be takin' it cool, man.

cool *v.* **1.** Esp. *Und.* to kill.

1920–22 in *DN* V 328: Newfoundland Dialect Terms...*cool* v.t. Kill. **1930** in Partridge *Dict. Und.* 147: Eight stick-up Johnnies out of ten aren't so hot about coolin' a cop. **1937** in H. Gray *Arf* (unp.): Th' cops know we cooled old Ginger. **1943** Mears *Carrier* 62: On the other hand, I'd hate to be "cooled" in my first engagement just because I was unprepared in some way. **1956** H. Ellison *Deadly Streets* 39: I'll bet Cherry against your killin' a cop. You cool a harness boy, you get Cherry. **1969** D.L. Lee *Don't Cry* 22: That was befo pee wee/Was cooled by a cop's warning shot.

2.a. to knock unconscious.

1927 Niles *Singing Soldiers* 165 [ref. to 1919]: I won't git myself cooled fur nobody's 25 francs. *ca***1936** in R.E. Howard *Iron Man* 177: Old Dennis here cooled both your prize [fighters]. **1937** Hemingway *Have & Have Not* 204: "Cool the son-of-a-bitch," he said. **1939** Hemingway *Fifth Column* 130: Try it...I'd like to cool you, you rummy fake Santa Claus. **1945** Himes *If He Hollers* 34: I'll cool the nigger! **1952** E. Brown *Trespass* 118: "I should cool you," said Gus rising slowly to his full height. **1959** Lederer *Never Steal Anything Small* (film): "You sure it won't kill him?" "No, just cool him for about twenty minutes." **1966** *Batman* (ABC-TV): That twin brother of yours—I had to cool him, Harry. **1971** *Batman* (Aug.) 13: I cooled Two-Face's henchmen.

b. to deliver a finishing blow against; defeat.

1944 Stiles *Big Bird* 108: There had been a lot of talk about the RAF tagging along behind on this ride, and really cooling [the target] this time for all time. **1958** F. Davis *Spearhead* 128 [ref. to 1945]: I sure cooled that son of a bitch. **1966** Bullins *Buffalo* 162: Those Toms we were really out to cool.

c. *Stu.* to do well on.

1955 *Science Digest* (Aug.) 33: "Cool"...has become a verb whereby one "cools" a thing by doing it well. **1964** R. Kendall *Black School* 34: "How are you doing in all your school work?"..."I'm coolin' it, man," he grinned.

d. to subdue (a person).

1957 O'Rourke *Bravados* 31: Cooled him. [Tied him up with] the sheets. He can't wiggle his toes.

3.a. to mollify, calm, or appease (a person), as with flattery, a bribe, or the like.

1952 Mandel *Angry Strangers* 434: You cool Dincher; you hear? I give you the loot 'n you cool him off; you hip? **1970–71** Rubinstein *City Police* 320: So I had to call an assist and go back in there and cool them all. **1972–75** W. Allen *Feathers* 35: "The house dick can usually spot an intellectual." "A five-spot cools him."

b. *Narc.* to administer or sell heroin to.

1973 Childress *Hero* 71: "You lookin for somebody round here?"..."Cool me, that's what."

4.a. [extended from *cool it*, below] to put a stop to; halt; abstain from.

1956 H. Ellison *Deadly Streets* 184: I cooled the idea fast. **1958** *Life* (Apr. 28) 83: Cool that jive. **1959** De Roo *Wolves* 164: Cool that horn! **1962** Riccio & Slocum *All the Way Down* 127: Nobody's going to cool this. **1966–67** P. Thomas *Mean Streets* 114: The guy...started to say something and I cooled him. **1968** Spooner *War in General* 176: Cool the noise! **1971** Wells & Dance *Night People* 69: Russ Procope cooled my blackjack playing when we were with Teddy Hill, and I think his cooling was the most brutal. That cat took my whole week's salary in just four hands. **1972** *WCBS-TV News* (June): Last year he took a bullet in the head from a 17-year-old boy while trying to cool a rumble. **1975** R. Davis *Pilot* 77: Mike, I think you ought to cool the booze. **1981** C. Nelson *Picked Bullets Up* 295: Nonetheless, I decided to cool the scene the third night.

b. to put off; keep in abeyance.

1962 *New Yorker* (July 28) 24: His girl friend, Flo, had been cooling him of late. She had always cooled him, in fact; she was practically not a girl friend at all. **1964** in Gover *Trilogy* 244: Gonna cool that messinger till I'm dam good an ready.

5. to die.

1960 in J. O'Hara *Sel. Letters* 324: I think I know my place in Am. Lit., as of five or ten years after I cool.... **1964** J. O'Hara, in *Sat. Eve. Post* (Feb. 8) 32: He cooled about a year ago. Don't you read the obituary columns? **1972** *Nat. Lampoon* (July) 76: The next you know, he up and cooled on me. **1974** Hejinian *Extreme Remedies* 76: My technicians would get upset if he cooled here. **1976** J.W. Thomas *Heavy Number* 39: His dad...had cooled three years ago.

6. to relax; enjoy oneself; *cool it,* 2, below.

1986 Clayton & Elliott *Jazz World* 165: We would go over to Central Park on our intermission and "cool" between sets. **1988** in Nelson & Gonzales *Bring Noise* 227: Coolin in Cali. **1989** "Tone Loc" in B. Adler *Rap!* 99: Cold coolin' at the bar and I'm lookin' for some action. **1990** *Yo! MTV Raps* (MTV): And we are coolin'!

¶ In phrases:

¶ **cool in** to tell; CLUE in.

1957 Kohner *Gidget* 74: Let me cool you in on something. **1961** Kohner *G. Goes Hawaiian* 2: To cool you in, I wouldn't be surprised if [etc.]. *Ibid.* 76: They usually cooled me in on their itinerary.

¶ **cool it, 1.** to quit what one is doing, esp. to stop talking.—often imper.; *(hence)* to begin behaving less conspicuously; lie low. [Gained nationwide currency in the mid 1950's.]

1952 Ellson *Golden Spike* 14: No, let's cool it for a while. *Ibid.* 154: Cool it, people will hear. **1955** Ellson *Rock* 15: Man, you got to cool it...You be killed. **1956** E. Hunter *Second Ending* 138: He's a bull. He's lookin' for some damn stupid fool like you, so just cool it. **1959** J. Rechy, in *Big Table* I (No. 3) 23: I'll cool it by the parking lot. **1960** R. Reisner *Jazz Titans* 153: *Cooling It:* tapering off. **1961** J. Williams *Night Song* 8: That's right, Jimsey, cool it. **1965** Yurick *Warriors* 13: Man, we have to cool it here for a while. **1976** Dyer *Erroneous Zones* 60: Perhaps you've "cooled it" in order to placate someone. **1976** Woodley *Bears* 20: Hey, Engelberg...Cool it. **1978** J. Webb *Fields of Fire* 167: Come on. Cool it, turkey. **1983** *Good Morning America* (ABC-TV) (Sept. 20): The extension of the War Powers Act ensures that the warring factions won't just cool it till the Marines leave. **1989** *Harper's* (June) 55: Hey, think you guys could cool it with the cigarettes for a few minutes? **1992** *CBS This Morning* (CBS-TV) (Dec. 7): The word is that senior [Somali] gang leaders have told their gunmen to cool it and make the Americans feel welcome.

2. to relax.

1953 in Cannon *Like 'Em Tough* 38: Cool it, man. Cool it...What's your gripe? **1954** *Time* (Nov. 8) 70: I cooled it at a table for a while. **1961** Gover *$100 Misunderstanding* 119: Jimmy Honey take a seat an cool it. **1964** Gold *Jazz Lexicon* 66. **1966** H.S. Thompson *Hell's Angels* 40: Man, we'd be sitting over there in the bar...just coolin' it around the pool table with a few beers. **1970** Kinoy *Brother John* (film): I'm going to cool it for a few days before I split.

3. to die.

1963 Braly *Shake Him* 130: They fix a hex and the cat cools it. **1966** Braly *On Yard* 228: "How is he?" "He's cooled it."

4. to leave a place.

1968 Baker et al. *CUSS* 99: *Cool it.* Leave a place.

¶ **cool (one's) jets** to take it easy; become less agitated or excited.

1973 Eble *Campus Slang* (Nov.) 1: *Cool your jets*—settle down and relax: Cool your jets or the cops will think you're the guilty one. **1978** UTSQ: Get off my case, cool your jets, take a hike. **1980–89** Cheshire *Home Boy* 310: Martinez...bops him one....Cruise cools his jets. **1989** *Dream Street* (NBC-TV): Cool your jets, man. He's my brother.

cool breeze *n. Black E.* a shrewd, likable, or fashionable fellow.—used in direct address.

1961 Garrett *Which Ones* 48 [ref. to *ca*1952]: There was Clayton, called Cool Breeze. **1962** H. Simmons *On Eggshells* 114: Aw that's all right, papa cool breeze. **1966** Bullins *Buffalo* 187: You let me and Deeny worry about that, cool breeze. **1967–68** Wolfe *Kool-Aid* 3: That's good thinking there, Cool Breeze. **1972** *Sanford & Son* (NBC-TV) (Nov.): What's up, Cool Breeze? **1979** E. Thompson *Golden Pond* 128: Smooth move, Norman...Thanks, cool breeze. **1992** *In Living Color* (Fox-TV): Hey, cool breeze!

cool-breeze *adj. Black E.* cool; calm; excellent.

1966–67 P. Thomas *Mean Streets* 55 [ref. to 1940's]: Be down, cool breeze, smooth. *Ibid.* 56: Good when I'm cool breeze and bad when I'm down. *Ibid.* 105: "And I'm in!" "Cool breeze!"

coolcock *v.* COLDCOCK, *v.*

1950 *PADS* (No. 14) 21: *Coolcock*...To knock out, knock cold, with a connotation of knocking with a blunt instrument on the side or back of the head.

coolcrack *v. Black E.* to kill. Cf. COLDCOCK.

1947–52 Ellison *Invisible Man* 422: Pull your switch blade!...Cool-crack the motherfouler!

cooled out *adj.* COOL, *adj.,* 2.

1978 De Christoforo *Grease* 89: Danny was steamed...Sandy was cooled out. *Ibid.* 169: But our part of town was just too cooled out for that.

cooler *n.* **1.** a finishing blow or retort.

1821 Waln *Hermit* 25: "Don't *claw off,* Bill"—"That's a *cooler*"—"Don't *crow* yet"—"That's a *damper.*" ***1823** (cited in Partridge *DSUE* (ed. 8)). [**1832** in [S. Smith] *Letters of Downing* 83: I guess we shall have a caucus and try to put a cooler on the Bangor Republican.] **1865** Byrn *Fudge Fumble* 134: The last scrape which I had gotten into was a "cooler" for my sympathies. **1900** *DN* II 29: *Cooler*...A sharp retort.

2.a. a jail or lockup.

1872 in Miller & Snell *Why West Was Wild* 123: The point in dispute seemed to be the proper way to go to the cooler. **1880** Nye *Boomerang* 134: I hunt up the penitentiary, if there be one, and if not, I go to the cooler. **1885** Siringo *Texas Cowboy* 27: If he caught me out again so late at night he would put me in the cooler. **1887** Francis *Saddle & Moccasin* 145: They came near socking him in the cooler* the other day...*Putting him in prison. **1891** Maitland *Slang Dict.* 75: *Cooler* (Am.), the calaboose or police station. **1898** Kerlin *Camp Life* 37: They were glad to get out of the "cooler" on any terms. **1907** in H.C. Fisher *A. Mutt* 4: To the cooler for yours. **1919** Hubbell *Company C* 157: Several of the boys...[got] into arguments with the M.P.s which resulted in incarceration in the cooler. **1922** Jordan *Btty. B* 139: As the Germans were still far away...we couldn't start a real first class scrap without landing in the "cooler." **1938** Smitter *Detroit* 273: Hadn't been for me you'd been spending a few days in the cooler. **1938** Chandler *Big Sleep* 31: We had him in the cooler on a Mann Act rap. **1961** Rosten *Capt. Newman* 94: Twenty-four hours in the little old cooler will cool off that joker. **1967** Spillane *Delta* 41: The cops picked him up and slapped him in the cooler.

b. *Pris.* a solitary confinement cell.

1899 "J. Flynt" *Tramping* 388: Got the cooler (dark cell) ev'ry time I did en'thin'. **1904** *Life in Sing Sing* 224: The one least to blame...is sent back to the shop and the other goes into the "cooler" for a few days. **1913** in Tannenbaum *Osborne of Sing Sing* 331: The series of dark cells...is called "The Cooler." **1918–19** Sinclair *Higgins* 67: If you even so much as hummed, they took you out and shut you up in a dark hole called the "cooler"! **1922** *In the Clutch of Circumstance* 53: He told me about the terrible "cooler," or punishment cell, where recalcitrant inmates were locked up on bread and water for weeks at a stretch. **1928** Panzram *Killer* 72: In some you stay a day, others a week, and there have been times when I have been in the cooler a month or more. **1932** Nelson *Prison Days & Nights* 24: Don't shoot off your mouth to me, or I'll run you down to the cooler and let you try some bread and water! **1955** Klaas *Maybe I'm Dead* 157: I sat in the cooler—the tiny solitary cell at Dulag Luft—for days because I wouldn't answer questions. **1956** Holiday & Dufty *Lady Sings the Blues* 28: This little scuffle cost me my fifteen days off for good behavior and caused me to get tossed in the cooler. **1953–7** Giovannitti *Combine D* 286: Popeye went right on breaking guys in the cooler. **1977** Caron *Go-Boy* 6: Two minutes after morning light came on a guy was out of bed or he got the bum's rush to the cooler.

3. *Gamb.* COLD DECK.

1935 Pollock *Und. Speaks: Cooler,* a cold deck of arranged (stacked) playing cards. **1961** Scarne *Gambling Gde.* 676. **1978** *Time-Life Gamblers* 123: One pair of Seattle sharpers...tried to "ring in a cooler."...A cold deck. **1984** W. Murray *Dead Crab* 104: You want me to run a cooler in on him?

4. *Horse Racing.* a horse entered into a race which it is not intended to win.

1931–35 D. Runyon *Money* 235: They are going to shoo in Never Despair. Everything else in the race is a cooler. **1949** Cummings *Dict. Sports* 432. **1968** Ainslie *Racing Guide* 466: *Cooler*...horse that is restrained to prevent it from running well.

¶ In phrase:

¶ **in the cooler** in safe reserve; *on ice* s.v. ICE.

1895 *Harper's* (May) 917: I've got a steady job, wit' t'ree hundert dol-

lars in ter cooler—see? **1906** in *DA.*

cool hand *n.* a dispassionate, self-assured or highly skilled individual.

*a1845 in *OED:* A fact which has stamped him a rather "Cool hand." ***1855** in T. Taylor *Plays* 42: I'm a cool hand, I flatter myself. ***1863** in T. Taylor *Plays* 193: Well, you *are* a cool hand. **1870** in Hay *Lincoln* 306: The General is what we call in the West a "cool hand" and takes everything in the most matter-of-fact manner. **1891** Maitland *Amer. Slang Dict.* 136: A "cool hand," a person with plenty of assurance. Sometimes a "cool bird." **1908** Raine *Wyoming* 312: You're a cool hand, my friend. **1970** Pearce *Cool Hand Luke* (title). **1986** Coonts *Intruder* 265: "Cool Hand? Why's he called that?" "Because he's cool when the shooting starts. Real cool."

coolie[1] *n.* a Chinese; *(loosely)* an East Asian.—usu. used contemptuously.

1854 Soulé, Gihon, & Nisbet *Annals of S.F.* 380: The white miner...could not pretend to compete with the..."coolie," as so John Chinaman was now called by many. *ca*1870 (quot. at JOHN). **1871** *Overland Mo.* (July) 94: 'E tuk to drinkin' harder an' harder, an' got rabider an' rabider anti-coolie. **1898** Norris *Moran* 62: Now, nothing about this to the coolies. **1907** Johnson *Discrimination Against Japanese* 56: The name "coolie"...is applied to all...Orientals.

coolie[2] *n.* a COOL individual; *(specif.)* a youth who is not a member of a teenage street gang.

1958 Salisbury *Shook-up Generation* 30: I thought you might be a coolie, man. **1959** De Roo *Wolves* 88: I'm a coolie, Cliff. **1959** E. Hunter *Conviction* 73: I mean, there are some spics I know who are coolies, and really, you know, okay. **1959** W. Miller *Cool World* 12: The coolies look at me. Coolies don't swing with the gang. They are out by themselves alone. **1965** Yurick *Warriors* 96: We're not coolies. We're warriors. **1966** Harris & Freeman *Lords of Hell* 128: Coolies...got nothing behind them, so it easy to push them to the wall. **1966–67** P. Thomas *Mean Streets* 56: I hear you 104th Street coolies are supposed to have heart.

coolie[3] *n.* [< Sp *culo*] anus.

1976 "N. Ross" *Policeman* 87: He pulled my peepee. Then he put his finger in my coolie.

cool off *v.* **1.a.** to kill (someone).

1863 in A. Cook *Armies of Streets* 117: You shut up, or we will cool...[you] off. **1933** D. Runyon, in *Collier's* (July 8) 8: Nobody knows how many guys Cheeks cools off in his time, not even himself. **1935** in R. Nelson *Dishonorable* 248: When Bill got cooled off his people thought I had something to do with it. **1968** "H. King" *Box-Man* 28: They'll cool 'em off (kill them) if they catch him.

b. to subdue (someone) with blows; knock unconscious.

1931 D.W. Maurer, in *AS* (June) 330: "Take that monkey for a walk and cool him off."...The "cooling" process sometimes consists of blackjacking. **1962** Quirk *Red Ribbons* 184: I can't afford a night in the jug or I'd cool you off...I could do it, too. Cool you off...I was intercollegiate light heavyweight champion.

2. *Und.* to lie low until police interest has cooled.

1937 Hoover *Persons in Hiding* 283: Now, however, Doll was "cooling off," to use an underworld expression...There was no word from him for days, no explanation. **1937** (cited in Partridge *Dict. Und.* 147).

cool one *n.* a cold bottle, glass, can, etc., of beer; COLD ONE.

1959 *AS* (May) 157: Take a long, tall cool one. **1965–70** in *DARE.* **1974** J.C. Pratt *Laotian Fragments* 195: I go back to the bar for a cool one. **1981** in *DARE.* **1983** Flaherty *Tin Wife* 226: A nice walk along the water's edge and then some lunch and a cool one.

cool out *v.* **1.** to subdue; *(also)* to kill.

1832 [M. St.C. Clarke] *Sks. of Crockett* 145: I can kill more lickur, fool more varmints, and cool out more men than any man you can find in all Kentucky. **1980** L. Heinemann, in *Harper's* (June) 69: That's how you cool out gooks.

2.a. to cool off; calm down. Also trans.

1836 *Davy Crockett's Alm.* (1837) 24: Resting a while, just long enough to cool out a little. **1906** *Nat. Police Gaz.* (Sept. 22) 3: "It's a good thing he's not in the big events, Judge," I said, trying to cool him out. **1917** C.E. Van Loan, in Woods *Horse-Racing* 293: I was crazy for a minute...I thought you'd double-crossed me. I've cooled out since then. **1929** in Runyon *Guys & Dolls* 67: Well, Johnny is so excited it is some time I can get him cooled out enough to explain. **1930** D. Runyon, in *Sat. Eve. Post* (Apr. 5) 6: He cools out the minute he sees Rusty Charley. **1926–35** Watters & Hopkins *Burlesque* 27: Well, you can stop blowin' off steam and cool out, 'cause I ain't goin'. **1963** in Cannon

Nobody Asked 110: Jack's hot as you…Let him cool out and it'll straighten out. **1968** Hoffman *Revolution* 95: Besides, I was the only one who tried to cool out the scene. **1968** I. Reed *Radio* 148: I'm a come to cool tings out and get rid of this maleficiem. **1972** *Nat. Lampoon* (June) 89: Can't you cool out your mind a little?…I'm getting a headache trying to follow you. **1978** B. Johnson *What's Happenin'* 130: Things cooled out a little. **1983** Walford *Max. Life-Span* 128: I found that India…had cooled me out. **1986** *Stingray* (NBC-TV): Hey, cool out! **1991** LaBarge *Desert Voices* 187: We trying to cool [the captured Iraqis] out.

b. *Sports.* to cool off (a racehorse or prizefighter) after heavy exertion.

1911–12 Ade *Knocking Neighbors* 118: His Seconds would cool him out and rub him with Witch Hazel and pin Medals on him. **1954–60** *DAS: Cool out…*to reduce exercise slowly so that one does not become suddenly chilly; esp., to walk a horse after a race so he will calm down slowly. **1961** *WNID3: Cool out…*to cause (a horse) to move about quietly after heavy exercise until sweating has ceased and relaxation is attained. **1984** W. Murray *Dead Crab* 41: Get him cooled out now and we'll call it a day here.

c. *Und.* to pacify or appease (the victim of a swindle or theft).

1940 D.W. Maurer, in *AS* (Apr.) 116: *To Cool (A Mark) Out.* To pacify a *mark* after he has been fleeced. **1956** in Woods *Horse-Racing* 50: I can't tout. I can't cool out a sucker. **1977** Schrader *Blue Collar* 120: Bald Eddie's gonna be cooled out. Charlie T.'s already on ice.

d. to make manageable or satisfactory.

1963 in Bruce *Essential Bruce* 285: Well, we must have some laws to restrict the behavior, to cool the people out. **1968–77** Herr *Dispatches* 5: He told me that [barbiturates and stimulants] cooled things out just right for him, that he could see that old jungle at night like he was looking at it through a starlight scope.

e. to take it easy; relax.

1983 Goldman & Fuller *Charlie Co.* 26: More privileged boys…were skipping to Canada, or cooling out on college deferments.

3. to become fashionably COOL.

1973 *Penthouse* (July) 42: She…sounds like a cooled-out Streisand and writes her own material. **1979** in Terkel *Amer. Dreams* 447: I don't want to cool out…I don't want to be like them.

coon *n.* **1.** Esp. *So. Midland.* a man; fellow, esp. a sly or otherwise remarkable fellow.

[**1821** Wetmore *Pedlar* 26: Did that raccoon [a person] hurt you?] **1832** in *OEDS:* I was always reckoned a pretty slick koon for a trade. **1832** [M. St.C. Clarke] *Sks. of Crockett* 144: He was a right smart koon. **1835** Longstreet *Georgia Scenes* 15: "Well, my old coon," said he, "do you want to swap hosses?" **1839** Marryatt *Diary* 266: I should like to see the 'coon. **1843** Field *Pokerville* 23: "Put it into him, hoss!" "Look out old coon!" **1844** in Porter *Big Bear* 82: None of your tricks, for I've heard that your city fellers are mity slip'ry coons. **1847** Reid *Rangers* 77: The "old coon" turns round, and sez he, "That bullet never was made for Martin Scott." **1849** Windeler *Gold Rush Diary* 30: Our second M[ate] is a queer coon, tried to work up Nic for last night growling by letting him grease the foregallantmast. **1850** Garrard *Wah-to-yah* 39: Hyar's the doins, and hyar's the coon as *savvys* "poor bull" from "fat cow." *Ibid.* 104: How are ye, Smith old coon. **1851** Burke *Peablossom's Wedding* 150: Lay thar, ole Methodist, till I learn this coon some sense. **1851** M. Reid *Scalp-Hunters* 112: Wal—so the ole coon thinks. **1852** Stowe *Uncle Tom's Cabin* 42: "So now, old coon," he said to the man at the bar, "get us hot water, and sugar, and cigars, and plenty of the *real stuff,* and we'll have a blow-out." **1859** in Botkin *Treas. Amer. Folk.* 586: They can't fool this old 'coon, fur I know whut I know. **1861** in *Civil War Times Illus.* (Nov. 1972) 22: Two regiments have already passed. The Fire Zouaves was one of them. They are *coons* and will be a great help to this Division. **1864** "E. Kirke" *Down in Tenn.* 95: The old coon'll be watchin' on it ter night. **1878** Pinkerton *Reminiscences* 189: Them cussed coons has worked some all-fired charm on that durned keerd. **1879** Dacus *Frank & Jesse* 163: You seem to be a sort of jolly coon, anyhow. *Ibid.* 199: Come now, old coon, dry up. **1887** Francis *Saddle & Moccasin* 246: [There is] free admission of the right of "a coon to do as he durn pleases" in the States. **1889** Cox *Frontier Humor* 333: One singular-lookin' old coon with a weed on his hat got up. **1896** Brown *Parson* 44: He drank it dry…He did, the old coon! **1899** Green *Va. Folk-Speech: Coon…*a sly, knowing person. **1939** in *DARE:* He was a bad old coon; he was a fighter. **1963–64** Kesey *Great Notion* 320: Hey, what's happening, Hank, you old coon? **1965–70** in *DARE.*

2. a black person.—used contemptuously. [Undoubtedly popularized—and perhaps introduced—by the minstrel

song quoted in 1834 quot.; orig. pub. date may have been as early as 1829.]

1834 in Damon *Old Amer. Songs* (No. 20) [sheet music]: O ole Zip Coon he is a larned skoler. **1848** in Blesh & Janis *Ragtime* 86: Dey may talk ob dandy niggers/But dey neber see dis coon/A prombernading Broadway/On a Sunday afternoon. **1852** Stowe *Uncle Tom's Cabin* 130: Well, Tom, yer coons [escaped slaves] are fairly treed. **1862** in R. Mitchell *Civil War Soldiers* 122: The little coons were delighted. **1877** in Asbury *Gem of Prairie* [opp. p. 136]: Prospect of a Prize Fight Between Two Noted Coon Sluggers. **1879** Campbell *Fairfax* 153: The next time I find that coffee-colored coon here, I'll put a hole in him. **1882** D. Cook *Hands Up* 149: Dan Diamond, the Negro, was one of the worst "coons" that ever came to Denver. **1890** *DN* I 64: *Coon:* for negro. **1895** Heskett *Jake & Snow* 4: I expect it's some of those coons that are always loafing around here. **1894** Peirce *Man from Corpus Christi* 93: There's a good job, but the next coons that come along 'll pitch the whole thing into the mud again. **1896** in Cather *Short Fiction* 557: I used to play the banjo in there with a couple of coons. **1901** Dunne *Dooley's Opinions* 207: What ails th' prisidint havin' a coon to dinner at th' White House? **1927** Aiken *Blue Voyage* 311: Suppose you had a sister—…Suppose she wanted to marry a coon, would you let her? **1928** Dahlberg *Bottom Dogs* 134: "No fair," said the coon. **1968** J.P. Miller *Race for Home* 57: Occasionally a lawman would resent his easygoing lack of timidity and…dress him down with a few old standbys like "stinkin' nigger" and "black bastard" and "coon." **1969** Pharr *Numbers* 4: Thirty thousand coons in this city and only one lousy block for them to fuss and fight on. **1982** D. Williams *Hit Hard* 18: You got to have a mean coon like Brooks to keep these boys in line. **1992** *CBS Morning News* (CBS-TV) (Oct. 7): It was a classic coon hunt [by racist authorities].

3. [alludes to the raccoon emblem of the Whigs] *Pol.* a member or supporter of the Whig Party. Now *hist.*

1842 in *DA.* **1848** in Lowell *Poetical Works* 213: Agetherin' public sentiment, 'mongst Demercrats and Coons. **1931** Harlow *Old Bowery* 299: Down with the coons and up with the Young Hickories!

¶ In phrases:

¶ **gone coon** a person who is doomed or beyond help; DEAD DUCK.

1837 *Spirit of Times* (June 10) 132: If they didn't do something for him, he was a gone 'coon. **1839** *Spirit of Times* (July 27) 247: There is no getting around a widder, when one takes a hankering arter a feller he's a gone coon. **1839** Marryatt *Diary* 266: "I'm a gone 'coon" implies "I am distressed—or ruined—or lost." **1850** Garrard *Wah-to-yah* 163: Sez I, hyar's a gone coon if they keep my gun. **1853** "P. Paxton" *In Texas* 309: If he onst gits thar he's a gone coon. **1889** Meriwether *Tramp at Home* 95: If you blow on us, you're a gone coon. **1894** S. Crane *Red Badge* 26: I'm a gone coon this first time. **1968, 1970** in *DARE.*

¶ **go the whole coon** (see quot.).

*a***1891** *F & H* II 178: *To go the whole coon…*(American) = "To go the whole hog."

coon *adj.* sly.

1852 in *DA:* I know it's a humbug afore I commence: cause that ere Barnum lays the hose of the whole concern…May be he aint coon!

coon *v.* **1.** to crawl or scamper across or climb up in the manner of a raccoon.—also constr. with *it.*

1833 A. Pike *Prose Sks.* 77: Irwin…was obliged to straddle the log, and as they quaintly call it in the west, "Coon it across." **1863** Heartsill *1491 Days* 178: We soon come to a stream which detains us some time, at last we find a log, that extends across yet we must "Coon it." **1881** Ingraham *Buffalo Bill* 92: Let us coon up into the loft. **1903** *DN* II 310: He cooned up the tree. **1907** Moore *Cannoneer* 44: I was able to reach a fence and "coon it" to a hill above. **1917** *DN* IV 410: I cooned across on a log. **1915–18** *Coll. Kans. State Hist. Soc.* XIV 343: I walked over the narrow place…but he got down and "cooned" it. **1934** in Botkin *Treas. Amer. Folk.* 431: The singing master…decided that he would just hunker down and 'coon across [the log bridge]. **1939** *Sat. Eve. Post* (Apr. 15) 26: The car-knocker cooned it over the gons. **1945** Hubbard *R.R. Ave.* 338: *Coon it*—Crawl. **1953** in Botkin & Harlow *R.R. Folklore* 326: [He] cooned the buggy.

2. to pilfer, esp. fruit.

1890 in *DA:* One of our lads while "cooning" apples in town this week was caught and badly scared. **1901** *DN* II 138: To go cooning melons. **1966** in *DARE:* Yesterday somebody cooned my watch.

coon-ass *n.* [perh. folk ety. of F *conasse* 'vulva or vagina', used as an insult] *La. & Tex.* a Cajun.—usu. used derisively.—usu. considered vulgar.

1943 in M. Curtiss *Letters Home* 234: I have lots of laughs at the expense of and with a coon ass by the name of Clark. **1959** "D. Stagg" *Glory Jumpers* 26 [ref. to WWII]: Why that mean ol' coon-ass is the barehand pisshouse champion of lower Mississip'. **1962** Atwood *Vocab.* 73: For a person of Acadian French origin…In keeping with their tendency to avoid "bad words," only five Texas informants gave *Coonass*, a term that I have personally heard many more times than that. **1972** Hannah *Geronimo Rex* 318: "Is she coon-ass?" This means Cajun in downhome Louisiana idiom. **1972** Jenkins *Semi-Tough* 125: I don't see how you can be any kind of coon ass legend when you ain't got no *x*'s or *u*'s in your name. **1976** Bumper sticker at Knoxville, Tn.: Coonasses Have More Fun Because They'll Eat Anything. **1977** Bascom *Frontiers of Folklore* 127: The Texan called the Cajun a *coonass*, a common derogatory epithet for Cajuns. **1979** in Raban *Old Glory* 299: We had it figured for some kinda crazy coon-ass voice. **1981** in Wilder *You All* 160: The [Louisiana State] Legislature concluded that this word came into use after World War II by the accidental commingling of sound with the French noun *conasse*…an ignorant or stupid person [etc.]. **1979–82** Gwin *Overboard* 36: The coast-correct, if vulgar, term for the Acadian-French immigrants to Louisiana is *coonass*. *Ibid.* 37: Wait fo' I teachin' you coonass talk. Den you see I ain' so dumb like I soun', no. *Ibid.* 164: Not for nothing do they call rice "coonass ice cream." **1983** in G.R. Conrad *Cajuns* 229: Those who proclaim themselves [on bumper stickers, T-shirts, etc.] "Proud Coonasses," or "Registered Coonasses." **1983** Dormon *Cajuns* 87: The term "coonass," originally a term of ethnic derision introduced by "outsiders" to apply to Cajuns…may have been a racial allusion suggesting a Cajun-black genetic mixture. **1991** *Prime News* (CNN-TV) (Nov. 13): I am a *coon-ass!* I am a *Cajun!*

coonie *n.* **1.** COON, 1.
1864 Hill *Our Boys* 186: Now, old cooney, you waddle out o' this!
2. *Tex. & La.* COON-ASS.
1969, 1970 in *DARE*. **1980** *AS* (Fall) 199. **1983** Dormon *Cajuns* 88: The pervasive in-group use of coonass or "coonie" is a prime example. **1984** Jenkins *Life Its Ownself* 315: Oh, say does dat music wail, boy,/ O'er dat land by the coonie's Bayou?

coon out *v.* to leave surreptitiously.
1962 in B. Jackson *In the Life* 154: Ole So-and-So cooned out the other night and he went to Tulsa.

coon's age *n.* a very long time; DOG'S AGE.
1843 *Spirit of Times* (Sept. 9) 326: We had not seen the amount of cash mentioned as lost, in a "coon's age." **1845** in G.W. Harris *High Times* 48: They've been gone a coon's age. **1845** in Eliason *Tarheel Talk* 266: Kicked so far I would hardly get back in a coons age. **1853** "P. Paxton" *In Texas* 201: Hello, old hoss, whar hev you been this coon's age? **1855** in Eliason *Tarheel Talk* 266: I haven't heard of him in a *coons-age.* **1897** Fox *Hell-for-Sartain* 85: Hit ud take a coon's age, I reckon, to tell ye. **1922** Tully *Emmett Lawler* 138: Lord, I got to get a front one of these days…I ain't had a suit in a coon's age. **1952** "E. Box" *Fifth Position* 56: Not in a coon's age. **1956** Lee & Bradley *Passed for White* 82: Haven't seen you in a *coon's* age! **1973** Yount *Last Shot* 117: I haven't seen anybody from school in a coon's age. **1993** *N.Y. Observer* (Oct. 18) 3: We've been so busy we haven't seen each other in a coon's age.

coon squall *n.* *So.* loud senseless talk.
1884 Beard *Bristling with Thorns* 358: I don't like dat resolution of the brother's…It's all coon squall.

coony *adj.* sly.
1899 A.H. Lewis *Sandburrs* 93: It's at d' table I'm rattled, wit' all d' glasses an' dishes an' d' lights overhead. But I'm cooney all d' same…I puts it up on d' quiet I'll pick out some students who knows d' ropes an' string me bets wit' his. **1903** in *DA*. **1947** *Time* (Jan. 27) 20: Ezell ran a coony eye over the new Georgia constitution. **1952** Lamott *Stockade* 50: He's a coony old bastard isn't he? **1961** *WNID3*: A coony candidate remaining mum. **1964–66** Kirstein *Rhymes* 142: This racketeer/Is kinda-cooney, in-a-way.

coop *n.* **1.a.** a prison; jail; a lockup.
***1785** in Partridge *Dict. Und.* 147: He has been *in coop* for a week. **1887** Walling *Chief of Police* 387: To the residents of my precinct the station-house occupies the same place as the "coop," "cooler," "jug," etc., do to the inhabitants of a country town. **1899** A.H. Lewis *Sandburrs* 60: But when dey takes dad to d' coop, tell her to run her lamps over d' plunder, an' she has her pick, see! **1907** Bush *Enlisted Man* 18: I got up from my labors with the scrub-brush and sleeping on the hard bed in the "coop." **1912–14** in E. O'Neill *Lost Plays* 46: They got me and this time I went to the coop fur five years. **1919** Penner et al. *120th Field Arty.* 491: The whole regiment's in the coop! Jugged. **1929** in Goodstone *Pulps* 63: They'd have the Sheriff pay you a little visit and stick you in the coop.

1932 Pagano *Blue-jackets* 128: This is the coop, isn't it? **1941** in Mailer *Ad. for Myself* 86: Why aren't they put in the coop where they belong? **1958** Chandler *Playback* 4: Been in the coop.
b. a jail cell.
1920 in De Beck *Google* 55: What about that guy in the first coop? **1928** in Partridge *Dict. Und.* 147.
2.a. a small or makeshift shelter; dugout.
1862 in R.G. Carter *4 Bros.* 211: Each seemed to vie with the other…as to who should get up the best "coop." **1909** *American Mag.* (May) 405.
b. *Police.* a small place where an on-duty patrolman may go, usu. illicitly, to rest or relax.
1958 *N.Y. Times Mag.* (Mar. 16) 88: *Coop* also *heave*—Any shelter used by a policeman to avoid the elements. **1968** Radano *Walking the Beat* 13: A coop is a shelter where cops go to sit down. **1974** Radano *Cop Stories* 12: A coop might be a garage, a park house, the back of a store, the basement of an office building. **1977** Sayles *Union Dues* 367: What's the cop doing?…Drinking coffee…Cooping, they call it in the city, in New York. We disturbed his coop.
3.a. a cabin, house, or other building.
1877 Wheeler *Prince of Rd.* 80: There's my coop, pilgrim…Owns this coop and two or three other lots in Deadwood…. I'll take you over to my coop, and you can lay low there until this jamboree blows over.
b. a small or disreputable establishment.
1940 Chandler *My Lovely* 9: How long's this coop been a dinge joint?
4. the head or mind.
1909 T.A. Dorgan, in Zwilling *TAD Lexicon* 98: He's the only player in the league with a solid mahogany coop—Can you beat it? **1920** in Sagendorf *Popeye* 16: Some people say he's off in the coop. Talk to him and see if you think he's batty.
5. *Av.* (see quot.).
1956 Heflin *USAF Dict.*: *Coop, n.* A cockpit or cockpit canopy. *Slang.*
6. *Trucking.* a weigh station; CHICKEN COOP.
1978 Lieberman & Rhodes *CB* (ed. 2) 296: *Coop*—Same as "chicken coop."
¶ In phrases:
¶ **clear the coop** to clear out.
1836 *Spirit of Times* (Feb. 27) 16: But he hid, and the fust chance he got, didn't he cleer the koop, I wonder? **1839** in *AS* XXI 116: A tin pedlar has cleared the coop, hook and line, bob and sinker, without being able to square his accounts! **1845** in *Ibid:* "Clear the coop!" cried all hands. **1855** in *Ibid:* The dandy very sensibly "cleared the coop," and vanished up-stairs.
¶ **fly the coop** to clear out; to escape suddenly from confinement.
1895 Townsend *Fadden* 182: Dey bote jumped up, real saucy, and flew de coop widout so much as saying "s'long." **1899** Dunne *Mr. Dooley in the Hearts* 66: I see be th' pa-apers…that Boss have flew th' coop. **1903** *DN* II 313: *Fly the coop, v. phr.* To leave suddenly; to run away. "He got in debt to everybody and then *flew the coop.*" **1960** Kirkwood *Pony* 197: I knew my mother had flown the coop. **1976** Haseltine & Yaw *Woman Doctor* 43: Mr. Witowski had flown the coop.

coop *v.* **1.** to stay or lodge.
1877 Wheeler *Prince of Road* 80: The "toughs" are after you, and you cannot find a better place to coop than in here.
2. *Police.* (of a patrolman) to evade duty while loafing in a store, parked car, or the like.
1962 Dougherty *Commissioner* 28: Random stops were made to see if a given post was covered or if the cop assigned was "cooped" and having a nap in the back of a store. **1974** Radano *Cop Stories* 99: Anyway, these two rookies are trying to figure out where's the best place to eat and a warm place to coop. **1980** Gould *Ft. Apache* 125: That might cut into their cooping time a little. **1991** J. Dwyer *Subway Lives* 92: Were you cooping, Callahan?

cooper *v.* [orig. unkn.; perh. alter. of *comprehend*] to understand.
a**1889** in Barrère & Leland *Dict. Slang* I 270: Why on earth nature made you in the shape she did is more than I can cooper.

cooshay *v.* [< F *coucher* 'to sleep'] *Mil. in France.* to sleep.
1919 (quot. at MOPE, *n.*).

coosie *n.* [alter. & abbr. of COCINERO] *West.* a cook on a ranch or a cattle drive.
1903 A. Adams *Log of Cowboy* 157 [ref. to 1882]: How soon will supper be ready, cusi? **1933** *AS* (Feb.) 27: *Coosey.* Variation of *cocinera.* **1933** J. V. Allen *Cowboy Lore* 60: *Coosie,* Cook—from the Spanish word *cocinero.*

1967 in S.O. Barker *Rawhide Rhymes* 9: The chuckbox is the cupboard where the coosie keeps the gear. **1969** L. Hoffman *Loco* 23: The coosie stepped up to prod Loco in the ribs.

coot[1] *n.* a foolish or unpleasant (esp. old) person; (*rarely*) a person.

*1766 in *OEDS*: A very coot, or fool. **1794** in Thornton *Amer. Gloss.*: But Satan was not such a coot/To sell Judea for a goat. **1843** "J. Slick" *High Life in N.Y.* 1: The lazy coot did nothing…but eat raw turnips and drink cider brandy. *Ibid.* 2: To see a feller make such an eternal coot of himself. **1856** [Burwell] *White Acre* 199: Why you lazy impudent coot! **1877** Wheeler *Prince of Road* 79: Feller coots and liquidarians [i.e., drinkers], behold before ye a lineal descendant uv Cain and Abel. **1907** in H.C. Fisher *A. Mutt* 19: Chris was a wise old coot. **1914** Ellis *Billy Sunday* 304: Those old stingy coots. *ca*1929 *Collection of Sea Songs* 35: Rebecca was a floozy coot/A prostitute of ill repute. **1938** "E. Queen" *4 Hearts* 166: I asked the old coot yesterday. **1966** R.E. Alter *Carny Kill* 59: Ex knife-thrower marries kindly rich old coot. **1976** Schroeder *Shaking It* 133: What do you think I should say to the old coot? **1982** D. Williams *Hit Hard* 25: That old coot just trying you out. **1984** W.M. Henderson *Elvis* 1: In the days when the old coot could still think straight. **1992** G. Wolff *Day at the Beach* 109: The young bravos shoulder aside the old coots.

coot[2] *n.* Orig. *Mil.* COOTIE, 1. Now *hist.*

1918 *Stars & Stripes* (Apr. 26) 4: *A Coot May Look At A King.* **1918** in York *Mud & Stars* 102: A soldier boy should never swear/When coots are in his underwear. **1920** *Amer. Leg. Wkly.* (Jan. 23) 8: Since the last doughboy paused in No Man's Land to brush a coot into new quarters, poets have thrown a halo about the dugout. **1920** Skillman *A.E.F.* 171: Hard hunting 'twas true, but far harder to do,/Was to find the last "coot" in your shirt. **1926** Nason *Three Lights* 144 [ref. to 1918]: All they do is talk about their coots. **1966** in *DARE*.

cooter *n.* **1.** COOTIE, 1.

1968 in *DARE*.

2. COOT[1].

1970 A. Walker *Copeland* 219: That sly old cooter!

3. the vulva or vagina; COOZIE.—usu. considered vulgar.

1986 Eble *Campus Slang* (Nov.) 2: *Cooter*—female genitals. Also *Box, Cat, Coot, Snatch.* **1987** *UTSQ*: Vagina…*cooter.*

cootie *n.* [orig. unkn.; Malay *kutu* 'biting louse' has been suggested, but no early connection of the word with S.E. Asia has been demonstrated]

1.a. a louse, esp. a body louse. [The word was popularized in the press during World War I as a result of its wide currency in the military at that time; its earlier history—if any—is unclear; cf. 1930 quot. at COOTIE CAGE, 1.]

*1917 Empey *Over the Top*: "Cooties" or body lice are the bane of Tommy's existence. **1917** Depew *Gunner Depew* 46: Of course you know what the word "cooties" means. Let us hope you will never know what the cooties themselves mean. **1918** *Nat. Geo.* (June) 497: The American soldiers speak of the pest as "cooties." *ca*1920 in F.A. Bailey *Confed. Generation* 97 [ref. to Civil War]: About one million or more Cooties Chas[ed] Each other up and down my Spine. **1923** Fishman & Perlman *Crucible* 38: It has…more than the usual quota of bed bugs and "cooties." *ca*1940 in Botkin *Treas. Amer. Folk.* 524: A crumb is what you might call a louse. They was called "cooties" by the soldiers during the war. **1942** *Time* (Feb. 2) 30: Death Rides a Cootie. **1945** Peeples *Swing Low* 127: Chinch bugs began to bite him and there seemed to be cooties in here and fleas. **1949** Robbins *Dream Merchants* 209: Those Goddamn cooties are drivin' me nuts! **1951** Willingham *Gates of Hell* 53: They had…conducted cootie hunts the one upon the other. **1957** Bradbury *Dandelion Wine* 83: Get the flies, boys, kill the cooties! **1960** H. Lee *Mockingbird* 32: There ain't no need to fear a cootie, ma'am. Ain't you ever seen one? **1971** *Laugh-In* (Feb. 15) (NBC-TV): I ran a finger through his hair and a cootie bit my finger! **1978** *Saturday Night Live* (NBC-TV): It's about a girl with cooties!

b. *Juve.* an imaginary microbe or repulsive quality thought to be transmitted by slovenly or obnoxious people.

1971 Jacobs & Casey *Grease* 19 [ref. to 1950's]: Just drink it out of the bottle, we ain't got cooties. **1972** *N.Y. Times Mag.* (Apr. 23) 79 [ref. to 1964]: Westill screamed when the boys came near us (which they rarely did) and said they had cooties. **1973** Lucas, Katz & Huyck *Amer. Graffiti* 44: Get your cooties off me. **1976** Knapp & Knapp *One Potato* 78: Cooties are "imaginary germs" or "contaminated bugs." All a child does to start a game is touch someone and say, "You've got cooties!"…At that, everyone scatters, screaming in mock panic. *Ibid.* 79:

Watch out, here comes the Cootie Queen! **1986** Watterson *Calvin* 46: "And you get all woozy." "Heck, that happened to *me* once, but I figured it was *cooties*!!"

c. *Juve.* a particle of nasal mucus.

1979 Pilcer *Teen Angel* 47: They picked their noses…Then they stuck the cooties under the desk.

2. Orig. *Mil.* a worthless individual; parasite; upstart.

1918 in *JAF* XXXIV (1921) 388: Tady, have you a daughter fine,/Fit for a cootie right off the line? **1919** MacGill *Dough-Boys* 8: "A damned insolent cootie!" said the other cook, who was in the kitchen. **1920** (quot. at LOUSE). **1924** *Adventure* (Dec. 10) 107: Why, you—old cooties, I think you thought I was going to throw you down. **1925** Stallings *Big Parade* (film): I'd like to see that cootie try to break me. **1972** Hannah *Geronimo Rex* 165: You fellows help me get these cooties out of the hotel. **1990** *Married with Children* (Fox-TV): Face it, Bud. You're a cootie.

3. a small vehicle. *Joc.*

1921 *15th Inf. Sentinel* (Mar. 18) 13: I taken the road cootie [tin lizzie] of the skipper's over to the M.T.C. **1945** Hamann *Air Words: Cootie.* A very small airplane or light plane.

cootie cage *n.* **1.** a berth or bunk. *Joc.*

*ca*1928 in Wilstach *Stage Slang* (unp.): "Cootie cage," sleeping car berth. **1930** Irwin *Tramp & Und. Sl.* 55: *Cootie cage.* A berth in a carnival or circus sleeping car. A bunk in a construction camp or logging camp. The term was used before the World War had made the word "cootie" so familiar.

2. COOTIE GARAGE. Now *hist.*

1986 NYC woman, age *ca*50: *Cootie cages* were those puffs of hair over the ears in hairstyles women used to wear in the '30's and '40's…I've never heard them called *cootie garages.*

cootie drill *n. Army.* examination of one's clothing for COOTIES.

1920 Riggs & Platt *Btry. F* 7 [ref. to 1918]: There was a group of "Selects" out over the hills learning to talk by signs, dots, dashes, flags (which later on proved to be a great help in "Cootie Drill") and to talk over the field telephone.

cootie drapes *n.pl. Black E.* (see quot.).

1966 I. Reed *Pall-Bearers* 100: Trousers known in the forties as "cootie drapes."

cootie garage *n.* a puff of hair, esp. over the ears, in a woman's hairstyle. *Joc.*

1922 S. Lewis *Babbitt*: Hey, leggo, quit crushing me cootie-garage. **1953** S.J. Perelman, in *New Yorker* (Jan. 3) 15: A hairdress of those unlovely puffs we used to call "cootie garages." **1975** Gould *Maine Lingo* 107: In the early 1920's the ladies and girls affected a new hairdo which was inelegantly dubbed the "cootie garage."

cootie mill *n. Army.* a delousing station. [Quots. ref. to WWI.]

1919 *Amer. Leg. Wkly.* (Aug. 8) 14: The Mill. Check Your Cooties Here. **1919** Hawke *E Btry.* 111: Cootie Mill down by Bordeaux. **1919** York, in *Co. A* 145: All packed up and through the "cootie mill." **1920** Norton *639th Aero Sq.* 116: Pushin them thru the cootie mill. **1929** Coles *37th Div.*, II, 463: Trips to the "cootie mill" were frequent.

coozie or **cooze** *n.* [Cf. COO] **1.a.** the vulva and vagina.—usu. considered vulgar.

*a*1927 in P. Smith *Letter from Father* 136: As I touched her cuze, she…kissed me. **1934** "J.M. Hall" *Anecdota* 112: It serves to stuff coozies. **1920–54** (quot. at HOG-EYE). **1969** L. Sanders *Anderson Tapes* 148: Almost bare-ass naked with your cousy hanging out. **1970** *Southern Blue Movie* 132: You're going to get a shot at Arabella's fabulous cooze. **1971** Wilson *Bent* (unp.): Lap away at my captain's kooze.

b. copulation with a woman.—usu. considered vulgar.

1937 Weidman *Wholesale* 4: What's more important than cuzzy? **1977** Olsen *Fire Five* 58: What's more important than cooze? You crazy?

2. a sexually promiscuous or contemptible woman; CUNT, 2.—usu. considered vulgar.

1921 Dos Passos *Soldiers* 15 [ref. to 1917]: I guess it's better to go with coosies. Ye don't have to say good-by to them. **1922** Paul *Impromptu* 17 [ref. to *ca*1915]: Dutch, let's go to the beach and see if we can pick up a couple of couzies. **1928** Bodenheim *Georgie May* 38: What the hell was coming off—couldn't hit a coosie giving *him* back-talk? **1931** Stevenson *St. Luke's* 238 [ref. to *ca*1910]: The coosey-looking little waitress. **1934** H. Roth *Call It Sleep* 412: Say, listen O'Toole, dere's a couple o' coozies in de back. **1945** Bellah *Ward 20* 52: That big guy just grabbed off a coosey, wait'll his wife finds out. **1954** Schulberg *Waterfront* 94: Think of Melva, the neighborhood's favorite teen-age cooze. **1957** Kohner *Gidget* 22: Who's that fine-looking coozy? **1965** Pollini *Glover* 46: Oh ho, you are some coozie. **1967** P. Welles *Babyhip* 17: What a bore! The old couze was just a fake gypsy, not the real thing at all. Why was she wearing rhinestone rings on every finger if she weren't a gypsy? **1970** S. Ross *Fortune Machine* 20: He shacked up with an Italian cooze. **1974** R. Stone *Dog Soldiers* 54: When I saw you last you were as skittish as a cooze. **1976–77** Dry *Hustle* 77: Whose habit are you supporting, you clever little cooze? **1977** T. Berger *Villanova* 234: Got some pair, that cooze. **1978** Rascoe & Stone *Who'll Stop Rain?* (film): You dumb cooze!

coozy *adj.* [perh. fr. *cozy*; but perh. simply a misprint for *boozy*] intoxicated; drunk.

> **1821** Wetmore *Pedlar* 27: 'Twill cost one of your city dandies, five dollars to get *coozy*, as they call it.

cop[1] *n.* [prob. fr. COPPER] **1.a.** Orig. *Und.* a police officer; in phr. **on the cops** on a police force.

> **1859** Matsell *Vocab.* 124: Oh! where will he…all the cops and beaks so knowin',/A hundred stretches hence? **1866** *Nat. Police Gaz.* (Apr. 21) 3: The "cops" made a double case in "pinching" Petter, as there is also a charge of forgery to be preferred against him. **1867** Alger *Ragged Dick* 216: Look out for the "copp." **1867** Williams *Brierly* 20: I ought to have given the "cop" the same dose. **1872** Burnham *Secret Service*: Cop, or Copper, a U.S. Detective, or Police officer. *Ibid.* 219: She…kept a sharp eye for the "cops." **1872** McCabe *New York Life* 241: Look out, Billy; there's a big cop. **1877** *Puck* (Aug. 8) 6: That's what I said to the cop. **1878** *Scribner's Mo.* (July) 351: An anecdote or two will show what it meant to be a "cop" in the Points twenty years ago. **1883** Peck *Peck's Bad Boy* 110: Pa was mad and tried to jerk away, and another cop choked him, and another cop came along and helped. **1883–84** Whittaker *L. Locke* 186: I don't need to holler for the cops. **1884** Costello *Police Protectors* 122 [ref. to N.Y.C., 1848]: When he looked out he said to his companions, "The cops are here." *Ibid.* 127: The only insignia of office worn by the Police after [*ca*1845] was a star-shaped copper shield, from which they received the name of "cops." **1889** *Harper's Mo.* (Mar.) 629: That's always the way of it whin the cops take a hand. **1889** Bailey *"Crook's" Life* 52: It strikes me you are pretty fresh coming around with a gang of cops at this time in the morning looking for a man. **1895** Townsend *Daughter of the Tenements* 230: Besides, if de letters didn't show Waters was crooked would he be offerin' de cops a thousand dollars for 'em? **1904** in Opper *Happy Hooligan* 40: Maybe that cop won't be mad when he comes up. **1928** Santee *Cowboy* 28: I finally asked a cop. **1930** Lavine *3d Degree* 10: Most of the men "went on the cops" because they were square pegs who weren't succeeding in their respective positions. **1943** Wolfert *Tucker's People* 250: Guess you can't be on the cops then. **1949** in F. Brown *Honeymoon* 71: Cops came running, too…and kept people from going too close to the alien object. **1955** Q. Reynolds *HQ* 4: He thinks of himself as a working cop, and is known and respected in the Department as such. **1962** Link & Levinson *Prescription: Murder* 58: Cops aren't the brightest guys in the world. **1970** Thompson *Garden of Sand* 149: He's going to start crying cop. **1991** Hasburgh *NYPD Mounted* (film): When did you ever hear of a horse cop gettin' killed? **1992** M. Gelman *Crime Scene* 11: Sneaking out of class to play…cops and robbers.

b. *Ice Hockey.* ENFORCER, 2.

> **1976** *Webster's Sports Dict.* 89.

2. *Pol.* COPPERHEAD.

> **1864** in Jackson *Letters* 218: I expect the "Cops" will begin to think they had no man in the field. **1864** in O.J. Hopkins *Under the Flag* 169: 'Twould be worse than an old Cop. *1864 in *PADS* (No. 70) 28: A Captain from our regiment…could not control himself on hearing the traitors spout…I do not know how much harm he did to the cops. **1865, 1875** in *DA*.

3. *Gamb.* a bet to lose; COPPER.

> **1866** *Night Side of N.Y.* 75: Bet nine loses, gentlemen, and the ace wins—not a cop on the ace.

cop[2] *n.* [fr. the v.] **1.** *Gamb.* winnings; (*specif.*) small winnings employed to entice the victim of a swindle.

> **1930** *Variety* (Jan. 8) 123: I threw him out a half a C cop, re-hashed him and clipped him for about 5 yards, or half a grand, when he got hip to the out-count. **1940** *AS* (Apr.) 116: Cop…n. The money which a *mark* is allowed to win. **1969** Beck *Trick Baby* 93: Blue is gonna gaff that wheel on your number and heave you a heavy cop to excite the mark.

2. *Und.* a purchase of illicit drugs.

> **1961** (cited in Partridge *Dict. Und.* 808). **1967–68** von Hoffman *Par-*

ents Warned Us 81: The dealers were rushing around talking about monumental cops. **1973** "A.C. Clark" *Crime Partners* 9: Remember on the last cop we were short on the man's money.

3. *Und.* an acquisition.

> **1966–67** P. Thomas *Mean Streets* 255: You're to him like a virgin would be on the outside, a first cop. **1967** [Beck] *Pimp* 225: I had three original girls and three new cops.

4. *Und. & Police.* a guilty plea, esp. as the result of plea-bargaining; a plea bargain.

> **1973–76** J. Allen *Assault* 120: The D.A. offered me a cop to a robbery charge, but I wasn't accepting nothing. *Ibid.* 150: He didn't take a cop to attempted robbery. **1979** Homer *Jargon* 77: A guilty-as-charged cop.

cop *v.* [orig. unkn.; perh. < D *kapen* 'to take' via Early ModE *cap* in similar senses; relevance of *OED*'s uniquely early (1704) ex. (in form *cop up* 'to catch or snatch up') is problematical, for the word is otherwise attested only after 1840] **1.** *Und.* to apprehend or place under arrest; catch; NAB.

> *1844 in *OED2*: Waiting until the patrol should pass to commence my robbery…in order to be copped. *1857 (cited in Partridge *Dict. Und.* 148). **1859** Matsell *Vocab.* 21: Copped to Rights. Arrested on undoubted evidence. **1866** [quot. at LIFT, *n.*] *1869 in Davitt *Prison Diary* I 150: Copped while boning the swag. **1871** Banka *Prison Life* 493: Caught….Coped. **1872** Burnham *Secret Service* v: Copped, arrested or secured by a "Cop," or Detective. *Ibid.* 81: He was "copped" two years previously, as a "boodle carrier." **1879** *Nat. Police Gaz.* (Jan. 4) 11: Copped Dead to Rights. **1888** Bidwell *Forging His Chains* 63: The most of us are no sooner out than we are "copped." **1902** Hapgood *Autobiog. of Thief* 225: I'm copped. **1906** London *Moon-Face* 52: The whole push was *copped* by an overwhelming array of constables. **1924** in D. Hammett *Continental Op* 52: Jamocha is copped. **1928** Guerin *Crime* 25 [ref. to *a*1880]: I can't do it, Eddie, I'll sure be copped. **1954** E. Hunter *Jungle Kids* 51: You'll find out the first time we cop you with a package of H. **1957** Gelber *Connection* 28: Cowboy went to cop and got copped. **1965** in W. King *Black Anthol.* 308: He loses everything if the bagman gets copped.

2.a. Orig. *Und.* to steal (something).

> *1879 *Macmillan's Mag.* (Oct.) 500: I was taken by two pals…to an orchard to cop (steal) some fruit. **1906** in "O. Henry" *Works* 1275: Say we go up and punch 'er and stick a towel in 'er mouth and cop the coin. **1906** H. Green *Actors' Boarding House* 150: Susy, if Coppit & Blow, them acrobats…. starts tuh set down, tell 'em I said they gotta settle or nothin' doin. **1918** in E. O'Neill *Moon of the Caribbees* 47: I was goin' to turn one loose on the jaw of any guy'd cop my dame. **1924** *Sat. Eve. Post* (July 12) 15: Her routine's just a lotta apple sauce she's copped off other comics. **1933** Hammett *Thin Man* 288: Who do you think copped the stuff? **1945** Slesinger & Davis *Tree Grows in Brooklyn* (film): Take your hat and get out of here before someone else cops that job. **1948** in Marx *Groucho Letters* 191: A phrase I copped out of Bartlett's book of quotations years ago. **1955** O'Connor *Last Hurrah* 189: The bum was a…scene stealer. He tried to cop the act at his own brother's wake. **1971** *New York Mag.* (Nov. 22) 36: One steal-to-order group cops fur while another deals in diamonds. **1978** Hamill *Dirty Laundry* 22: In other words, somebody could have copped the handbag? **1979** De Christoforo *Grease* 131: The top was down, which would make it a snap to cop the windshield. *a*1985 in Schwendinger & Schwendinger *Adolescent Sub.* 136: If I don't cop it, *somebody else* will. **1987–91** D. Gaines *Teenage Wasteland* 104: We…went "copping" (shoplifting).

b. to take for oneself, esp. unfairly.—formerly also constr. with *off*; (*hence*) take (in var. familiar trans. senses).

> **1901** T.A. Dorgan, in Zwilling *TAD Lexicon* 28: None of the Telegraph Hill booze would go to waste if Mrs. Nation copped it. *a*1909 Tillotson *Detective* 90: Cop—To take. **1917** Hunt *Draft* 172: Guess them early birds copped 'em all off. **1919** Law *Air Service* (unp.): Adj. Olds cops off the Cadillac every day and rides around trying to look as much like a colonel as possible. **1919** Hawke *E Btry* 28: Copping off some swell uniforms! **1928** MacArthur *War Bugs* 140: We waited, snoring, copping a smoke or biting our nails. **1933** D. Runyon, in *Collier's* (Dec. 23) 8: Blondy also cops a little snooze now and then. **1936** Levin *Old Bunch* 81: I ain't saying you're going to cop off the big dough. **1963** in Clarke *Amer. Negro Stories* 297: And Pa's tryin' to cop a snooze in the next room. **1963** in Clarke *Amer. Negro Stories* 299: I copped a hack to Ray's Barbershoppe. **1964** in Jackson *Swim Like Me* 96: Joe the Grinder was coppin' a snooze. **1966–67** P. Thomas *Mean Streets* 156: We can cop a Greyhound bus for Norfolk, Virginia. **1972** P. Thomas *Savior* 155: I copped a look from the corner of my eye…to dig his reaction. **1980** in *Nat. Lampoon* (Jan. 1981) 10: Cop a look-see at the knockers on that honey.

c. *Und.* to execute a theft successfully.

1921 Casey & Casey *Gay-Cat* 157: Before they gits here, we'll have copped an' be skeedaddlin' along the road. **1936** Dai *Opium Addiction* 198: *Cop and blow.* An expression meaning "take it and go quickly." This expression is generally applied to drugs, but it may be applied to anything. **1941** *Pittsburgh Courier* (Nov. 15) 7: The driver looked away to give Dagwood a chance to "cop." **1972** Grogan *Ringolevio* 46: He had no…excessive style of stealing like his two partners—his way was simply to cop and blow.

d. *Esp. Pros.* to fellate (the penis). Also absol.

1941 G. Legman, in Henry *Sex Variants* II 1161: *Cop a bird* To perform fellation. (Prostitutes' and Negro slang.) Also: *to cop.* **1942–49** Goldin et al. *DAUL*: *Cop a doodle.*

e. *Esp. Und.* to perform, carry out, do.—used mainly in idiomatic phrs. defined at the end of this entry or separately under the object, usu. a nominalized v., that heads the phrase. [The earliest ex. appears to be *cop a sneak* s.v. SNEAK.]

1938 W. Sherman & V. Sherman *Crime School* (film): Cop a gander, Joe. I found these keys in Braden's office. **1966–67** P. Thomas *Mean Streets* 78: Naw, if we cop a steal, we may as well go all the way.

f. *Sports.* to defeat.

1907 T.A. Dorgan, in *N.Y. Eve. Jour.* (Feb. 7): Ryan copping Barry in five rounds speaks well for him, considering that he has been out of the ring for two years. **1922** Tully *Emmett Lawler* 303: He'll cop Emmett in less than that. I hate to see a good Irish boy licked.

3.a. to get (in most familiar trans. senses), as: to obtain, receive, purchase, be inflicted with, etc.

1867 *Nat. Police Gaz.* (Jan. 12) 3: They were soon "pulled to rights" and "copped" two "stretches." ***1868** in *OED*: The privileged driver, on dropping his fare…almost invariably "cops" a job on his way back. **1911** A.H. Lewis *Apaches of N.Y.* 243: Then all of a sudden I cops a shock. **1929** Bodenheim *60 Secs.* 22: Copping 95 in some [academic class]. **1930** Weaver *Poems* 232: Maybe you can figger the answer out,/ And write it up, and cop a piece of jack. **1948** McHenry & Myers *Home Is Sailor* 41: You can always cop a washup at the "Y." **1953** Paley *Rumble* 252: I got enough dough to take us all to Gennaro's *pizzeria* and cop a couple of *pizzas.* **1960** R. Reisner *Jazz Titans* 153: *Cop, To Cop:* to obtain either by stealing or buying or permanent loan. **1966–67** P. Thomas *Mean Streets* 211: Most of our jobs copped us more like $250. **1967** Gonzales *Paid My Dues* 23: All I had to do was show up at his pad and cop my salary from the butler. **1970** A. Young *Snakes* 44: You might even be able to cop some ideas. **1991** Univ. Tenn. student: Man, cop a new look. **1993** *Donahue* (NBC-TV): In Harlem trying to cop some smoke.

b. Now *Black E.* to comprehend; understand.

1895 Townsend *Fadden* 165: Don't you cop dat? Steady comp'ny. Yes, dat's right. **1903** Townsend *Sure* 44: Cop me right, son. **1936** in Partridge *Dict. Und.* 148. **1942** *Pittsburgh Courier* (Mar. 14) 7: You don't know your way around.…you can't cop the gals use. **1956** Holiday & Dufty *Lady Sings the Blues* 95: By the time the ofays got around to copping "swing" a new-style music was already breaking out all over uptown. **1962** Crump *Killer* 93: Only remember, what goes around comes around, cop? **1968** Cleaver *Soul* 69: Do you cop that? **1970** Quammen *Walk the Line* 20: All they cop is that they own that room.

c. Now *Black E.* to look at, see, or hear.—formerly also constr. with *off.*

1895 Townsend *C. Fadden* 170: Den I takes off me silk dicer, and when dey seen de middle varnish part t' me hair one mug yells out: "Cop de dude wig Chimmie has got on Fift' Avenue!" *Ibid.* 171: Say, while de crowd was yelling I was trying t' cop off de real swell what was chinning on de odder truck. I couldn't hear a word he said for de noise, and dere was a torch what kep me from getting a good look. **1895** Townsend *Fadden Explains* 96: I cops his Whiskers come waltzin in like a two-year old. **1969** H. Brown *Die Nigger Die* 87: We were copping some t.v. **1970** Quammen *Walk the Line* 52: So le's me and you fall on up there and cop what they're saying.

d. *Specif.* (*Narc.*) to obtain illicit drugs.—occ. constr. with *up.*

1951 *Conf. on Drug Addiction* 11: Words and phrases such as *scoring, copping, going after the stuff, on the nod, straightened,* et cetera, are particularly related to the addiction field. **1952** Ellson *Golden Spike* 13: Who did you cop from? **1955** in Wepman et al. *The Life* 171: I got to cop. **1966** J. Mills *Needle Park* 12: Once the addict has bought his fix (has "copped" or "scored"), he is faced with the risky business of getting it to his cooker and into his arm without getting caught and "busted"

(arrested). **1968** *N.Y. Post* (July 15) 12: Large amounts are brought in…by people who "cop" (buy dope) in small two- or three-pound lots. **1972** Kopp *Buddha* 202: The very act of *copping* (of buying grass) was itself an elaborate time-consuming adventure. **1974** Dubinsky & Standora *Decoy Cop* 198: I got the money. I just wanna cop up, that's all. **1988–92** in Ratner *Crack Pipe* 105: Joy has *copped* (bought crack).

e. *Specif.* (now *Black E.*) to gain the favor or affection of a young woman; (*hence*) (*Und.*) to recruit a woman for purposes of prostitution. Also (orig. solely) trans., and formerly also constr. with *off.*

1899 Ade *Horne* 211: He'd…copped the princess. **1909** Chrysler *White Slavery* 70: Oh, how easy to go out and "cop a quim" and peddle her. **1924** in Boyd *Points of Honor* 139 [ref. to WWI]: An' boy, did I cop her off! Well, did I! **1964** Smith & Hoefer *Music* 184 [ref. to 1920's]: There was once a phrase we used to have in the tenderloin, "Did you cop?"…When a guy said he had copped, it meant he had made the grade and his woman thought the world of him. **1967** Colebrook *Lassitude* 174: "Heard you copped Alice last night…She's a good girl. There's nice money there." "I took a shot at her myself, but she wouldn't give me any action," complains the one who has not been lucky enough to "cop." **1970** A. Young *Snakes* 19: He…let her old lame boyfriend move on into the picture and cop.

f. *Specif.* (*Black E.*) to accomplish a seduction or engage in sexual intercourse; SCORE. Occ. trans.

1965 in Knight *Black Voices* 153: This one gray cat sent his buddy, who had made parole, by his ol' lady's house, and his buddy copped righteous. Then his buddy came back on parole violation…and this cat busted the Lothario's head with a baseball bat. **1965** in W. King *Black Anthol.* 302: It don't take too long to cop Glorie. **1967** in Wepman et al. *The Life* 136: She said, "You look like you ain't copped in quite a time." **1967** Colebrook *Lassitude* 103: Listen Baby he's only tryin' to cop. He satisfies her, he'll sock it to her, but later on she'll get him when she can. **1972** Andrews & Dickens *Big House* 33: "He summoned Jezebel." "Did he cop?" "He not only copped, but he planted a human seed in Bel." **1976** Chinn *Dig Nigger Up* 130: I might not cop the next time I see her, but believe me, I'm goin' to cop, and I ain't goin' to pay!

g. *Esp. Black E.* to take or put on (a manner or appearance).

1966–67 P. Thomas *Mean Streets* 19: Moms copped that wet-eyed look and began dream-talk about her *isla verde.* **1976** Braly *False Starts* 20: I would be copping an attitude which never occurred to me. **1992** *N.Y. Times* (July 16) C 10: I am trying to straighten this out—but *you*…are copping an attitude. So, chill with me for a minute.

4. *Esp. Sports.* to win (a game, championship, or the like). Also intrans.—formerly often constr. with *off.*

***1889** Barrère & Leland *Dict. Slang* I 271: *Cop*…(Sporting) to win. **1900** Ade *More Fables* 18: The other Girl might not have copped off many prizes at a Beauty Contest…yet she caught a Majority of the Callers. **1906** *Nat. Police Gaz.* (July 21) 6: Tommy Foster "copped" at Benning…[at] 200 to 1. **1907** in H.C. Fisher *A. Mutt* 3: I see here where a guy copped a million on the track. **1908** in H.C. Fisher *A. Mutt* 152: Let's see…. Amada ought to cop. **1908** in Fleming *Unforgettable Season* 274: [Philadelphia] copped the second [game] by whaling the horsehide. **1910** T.A. Dorgan, in *N.Y. Eve. Jour.* (Jan. 10) 12: Yes, it's a cinch. Go and bet your lead pencils even that I'll cop. **1912–14** in E. O'Neill *Lost Plays* 174: And I suppose you copped her and dated her up? **1914** Patten *Lefty o' the Bush* 135: Kingsbridge 'u'd like to win the pennant…[or] keep us from coppin' it. **1915** Lardner *Haircut & Others* 150: The Cubs copped the pennant and Speed got in on the big dough. *Ibid.* 152: Because, even if the Cubs didn't cop again, they'd have a city serious with the White Sox. **1919** Johnson *321st Inf.* 84: It was a man from the 321st, Sergt. James B. McIntosh, that copped the heavyweight wrestling championship of the Eighth Army Corps. **1922** *Bomb* (Iowa State College) 336: The Cyclones…determined to cop first honors in the Iowa track classic. **1925** *Sat. Eve. Post* (Oct. 3) 52: Isn't it yellow…for a bimbo to quit cold when he's copping? **1929** in E. O'Neill *Letters* 338: A Guggenheim [*sic*] F'ship….Hope he copped. **1931** Wilstach *Under Cover Man* 215: The Giants should cop from the Phillies to-day. **1939–40** Tunis *Kid from Tomkinsville* 92: I'd like to have copped that game, but we can't win 'em all. **1949** Davies *Happens Every Spring* (film): With one more top notch pitcher, Dolan might cop that pennant.

5.a. to strike; to hit hard; to catch with a blow or missile. Also constr. with *it.*

***1883** in *OED*: A cricket ball is copt; so is a bird if hit with a stone. ***1898** in *OEDS*: Copped 'im one under the chin. **1899** A.H. Lewis *Sandburrs* 207: As she toins, he cops her one in d' neck, wit'out a woid. Down she goes like ninepins! **1906** *Nat. Police Gaz.* (Nov. 10) 3: Nelson will…cop him one with that right haymaker of his. **1910** *N.Y. Eve. Jour.* (Feb. 3) 14: He copped Tommy with a fast right in the second round that shook the Harlemite from toes to dome. **1912** *Adventure* (July) 503: He copped it too hard on Al Rafferty—six pile-drivin' smashes over the heart. **1913–15** Van Loan *Taking Count* 9: You copped him nice with that right swing…It set him back on his heels. **1921** *Variety* (Sept. 2) 5: Tomato copped him on the button. **1922** Tully *Emmett Lawler* 300: It's just that lucky bump Ryan copped you on the jaw, that's all. **1921–25** J. Gleason & R. Taber *Is Zat So?* 13: The set-up cops him on the button for a clean K.O. **1925** in Hammett *Big Knockover* 217: He copped me with his right again—but not so hard. **1927** Shay *Pious Friends* 99: The way he staggered made me sick,/I stalled, McGee yelled "cop him quick!"

b. to shoot (someone), esp. to death; kill.

1911 A.H. Lewis *Apaches of N.Y.* 153: It's time to dig up black!…They've copped Phil. **1923** in W.F. Nolan *Black Mask Boys* 64: He ain't dressed like the bird I copped in the doorway. **1928** Nason *Sgt. Eadie* 306 [ref. to 1918]: I guess they was so busy tryin' to cop you two that they never seen us.

6. to tell (something) (to someone).—formerly also constr. with *off*.

1895 Townsend *C. Fadden* 166: Den he cops off de game t' me right. It was like dis: [etc.] **1895** Townsend *Fadden Explains* 102: "What t'ell," I says like dat; not bein on t'what he was coppin me. **1978** Sopher & McGregor *Up from Walking Dead* 19: I copped some phony excuses and bowed out of the game. **1985** Ponicsan *Vision Quest* (film): Hey, cop me a clue, man.

7.a. *Und.* to cop a plea, below.

1929 (quots. at *cop a plea*, below, and *go over* s.v. GO).

b. Orig. *Und.* to confess (to wrongdoing); admit.

1961 Braly *Felony Tank* 39: You wouldn't cop to something you didn't do, would you? **1967** Yablonsky *Hippie Trip* 178: Would you cop [admit] to that? **1970** *N.Y. Post* (Apr. 14) 43: "I don't know. Maybe it's what I copped [confessed] to the other night…" "They got me to cop to prostituting myself to fags and stealing from my mother." **1968–71** Cole & Black *Checking* 115: There was a definite time gap on a lot of things between us in our cars. We copped to it and saw it when it was there. These leaders cop to no gaps between them and their followers. **1973** NYC film producer, age *ca*40: What I want to know is, did these two guys ever cop and say it was all a hoax. **1973** W. Crawford *Gunship Cmndr.* 98: "What did they do with this other kid?"…"He just copped." **1986** *Miami Vice* (NBC-TV): "He admitted it?" "Copped to the whole thing."

8. *Police.* to work as a police officer. Cf. earlier COPPER, *v.*, 5.

1953 Manchester *City of Anger* 199: Bull Hoover was a cop…When neighbors asked him what he did,…Bull always answered, "Copping." **1971** Freeman *Catcher* (film): Mind if I ask you a question? Why'd you quit coppin'?

¶ In phrases:

¶ **cop a buzz** to get drunk or high.

1973 Calif. man, age *ca*20: Man, I'm so fucking bored I'm gonna go out and cop me a buzz. **1978** Univ. Tenn. student: Let's go cop a buzz. **1978** *N.Y. Post* (Dec. 9) 20: We're listening to Brian, a 12-year-old school boy whose life revolves around "copping a buzz" on marijuana.

¶ **cop (someone's)** [or a] **cherry** to deflower a virgin.—usu. considered vulgar.

1933 J.T. Farrell *Manhood* 311. **1954–60** *DAS* 123: Cop a cherry. **1970** Longstreet *Nell Kimball* 85: Their sons came to visit us to get their cherries copped—give up their virginity. **1984* J. Green *Dict. Contemp. Slang* 59.

¶ **cop a feel** to fondle someone in a sexual manner, esp. surreptitiously. Cf. FEEL, *n.*

*ca*1935 in Holt *Dirty Comics* 85: David Coppafeel. **1935** Pollock *Und. Speaks:* Cop a feel, a presumptuous man, who will not let his hands behave when with an attractive girl. **1936** Levin *Old Bunch* 40: Boy, I'd like to cop a feel off that one. **1943** M. Shulman *Barefoot Boy* 77: "Sure you don't want to cop a feel?" she said suspiciously. **1956** H. Ellison *Deadly Streets* 188: He copped a cheap feel off me. **1966** Shepard *Doom Pussy* 58: The fifth one copped a feel from the blond and the Moose backhanded him across the room. **1973** Lucas, Katz & Huyck *Amer. Graffiti* 33: Hey, is this what they call copping a feel? **1985** Sawislak *Dwarf* 16: Doralee…announced that no ape from Chicago was going to cop a feel from her. **1990** *Night Court* (NBC-TV): Made a lewd assault on his wife by telekinetically copping a feel.

¶ **cop a goose** to GOOSE someone.

1967 Mailer *Vietnam* 190: Like a businessman copping a goose on a

bare-ass nightclub waitress, yum!

¶ **cop a joint** Esp. *Prost.* to perform fellatio. Cf. **(2.d.)**, above.

1962 Riccio & Slocum *All the Way Down* 91: I got my joint copped and five bucks. Is that bad? **1967** Rechy *Numbers* 65: This guy kept following me in the showers, wanting to cop my joint. **1970** Southern *Blue Movie* 169: How about if I cop your joint instead?…Well, you know, give you some head, blow you. **1977** Dunne *Confessions* 135: Brenda was copping the judge's own joint twice a week. **1978** Ponicsan *Ringmaster* 15: A girl would come by soon to cop your joint, twenty bucks a clatter. **1978** Hamill *Dirty Laundry* 47: He's been copping joints in men's rooms all over town.

¶ **cop a nod** *Black E.* to get some sleep.

1946 Boulware *Jive & Slang* 3: Cop A Nod…Get some sleep. **1958** Hughes & Bontemps *Negro Folk.* 482: Between acts he cops a nod. **1962** Crump *Killer* 198: No, you better cop you some nods. **1964** Rhodes *Chosen Few* 212: Everybody else is coppin' some nods. **1966–67** P. Thomas *Mean Streets* 67: Each cat makes it to his pad to cop a nod. **1971** Wells & Dance *Night People* 99: He would start rehearsing when I was trying to cop a nod.

¶ **cop a plea** *Police & Und.* **1.** to plead guilty to an offense as the result of plea bargaining; (*hence*) to plead guilty (under any circumstances); confess. Now *colloq.*

[**1904** *Life in Sing Sing* 14: He's comin' up next week. Goin' to take a plea.] **1929** Hostetter & Beesley *Racket* 222: Cop a plea—To plead guilty to a lesser crime…in order to escape a heavier sentence. **1929** Barr *Let Tomorrow Come* 151: No guy that cops a plea is a good guy, an' Greasy copped. **1932** Berg *Prison Doctor* 53: Butch copped a plea to manslaughter and got off with a twenty-year jolt. **1938** R. Chandler *Big Sleep* 62: You're going to cop a plea, brother, don't ever think you're not. And you're going to say just what we want you to say and nothing we don't want you to say. **1940** Lawes *Meet the Murderer!* 226: It was a cinch for me to cop a plea. **1940** in H. Gray *Arf* (unp.): Tell him to cop a guilty plea…I'll see he's taken care of. **1942** Breslow *Blondie Goes to College* (film): If you think you're gonna cop an insanity plea, you're crazy. **1949** Algren *Golden Arm* 100: You're goin' to cop a plea 'n get paroled to me—if I ain't gonna be your wife I'll just be your dirty guardian. **1950** Rackin *Enforcer* (film): "What would he be doin' in church?" "Robbin' the poorbox and coppin' a plea." **1953** Q. Reynolds *Sutton* 72: When the ordinary fences are nabbed, the police immediately tell them, "Just name who you got this stuff from and we'll let you cop a plea."

2. to ask for leniency or plead for mercy; (*hence*) to make excuses.

1941 in O'Day & Eells *High Times* 307: "Coppin' a Plea" [title of jazz recording]. **1953** in Wepman et al. *The Life* 117: There won't be no crying or copping no pleas,/Hanging on the bars or begging on my knees. **1955** Graziano & Barber *Somebody Up There* 60: We played it innocent and copped a plea. **1959** O'Connor *Talked to a Stranger* 219: I'm not coppin' a plea. It is my fault. **1960** R. Reisner *Jazz Titans* 153: *Cop A Plea:* ask forgiveness, beg. **1965–68** E.R. Johnson *Silver St.* 114: Me, Frenchie Labiche, copping a plea to get away from a nut! **1970–71** Rubinstein *City Police* 404: He cops a plea about not knowin' the neighborhood. **1976** "N. Ross" *Policeman* 122: One call from the nervous bartender brought the owner to the scene within moments, ready to cop a plea with the "hero" cop…"Listen, officer, can't we talk this over?" **1977** Coover *Public Burning* 387: She was using his slender boyish body as I had used Pat's cloth coat—to cop a plea.

3. *Und.* to admit defeat.

1966–67 P. Thomas *Mean Streets* 30: Yeah, man, I cop a plea. Now will you get the fuck outta here?

4. to make a request.

1970 Wertheim & Gonzalez *About Us* 128: All the cats got some wine and copped a plea for a ride…And all the men copped a plea…to Apollo the pusher.

¶ **cop a slave** see s.v. SLAVE, *n.*

¶ **cop a sneak** see s.v. SNEAK, *n.*

¶ **cop a squat** *Black E.* to take a seat; sit down.

1944 Burley *Handbk. Jive* 136: *Cop a squat*—To be seated, to sit down. **1958** Hughes & Bontemps *Negro Folk.* 482: Cop a squat and stay awhile. **1972** Claerbaut *Black Jargon* 61: *Cop a squat v.* to take a seat; sit down. **1973** L.I. high school student: *Cop a squat* means to sit down, have a seat.

¶ **cop a Sunday** [sugg. by SUNDAY PUNCH] Esp. *Pris.* to deliver a punch or blow, esp. without warning.

1935 Pollock *Und. Speaks:* Cop a sunday, to assault from behind. **1941**

Kendall *Army & Navy Slang* 4: *Cop a Sunday*...sock somebody without warning. **1954** Chessman *Cell 2455* 91 [ref. to *ca*1938]: He ran it without "copping Sundays," catching any who attempted to escape, or telling the man anything, and not as a policeman. **1966** Elli *Riot* 125: The half-wit copped a Sunday on me. **1976** Braly *False Starts* 46: The first he knew he was in a fight was when someone copped a Sunday.

¶ **cop a walk** to take a walk; (esp. imper.) to clear out, go away, "get lost."

1952 Mandel *Angry Strangers* 244: Go on, Dinch, cop a walk. **1953** W. Brown *Monkey On My Back* 153: Cop a walk, will you, Iggy. **1966** N.Y.C. high school student: *Cop a walk!* means Go to hell. **1967** Talbot *Chatty Jones* 106: If you want to chicken out, Albert, just cop a walk. **1970** E. Thompson *Garden of Sand* 294: Cop a walk, kid!

¶ **cop it, 1.** to be hit with a blow or missile.

1911 A.H. Lewis *Apaches of N.Y.* 23: "What was the shooting?..." "One of 'em cops in th' leg. Th' other blew."

2. to surpass comparison; take the cake.

1966 Moran *Faster, Pussycat* (film): I've seen some funny scenes before, but this cops it.

¶ **cop (someone's) drawers** to seduce (a woman).

1966–67 P. Thomas *Mean Streets* 23: I...copped girls' drawers and blew pot. **1976** Selby *Demon* 32: Who might find out if he copped her drawers and what might happen.

¶ **cop Z's** see s.v. z.

copacetic *adj.* [orig. unkn.; not, as sometimes claimed, fr. Heb, It, or Louisiana F] **1.** fine; all right.

1919 in *OEDS*: "As to looks I'd call him, as ye might say, real copesetic." Mrs. Lukins expressed this opinion solemnly. It's last word stood for nothing more than an indefinite depth of meaning. **1930** Franklyn *Knights of Cockpit* 205: Gone loco, that's all—I had to sock him in the jaw, but he'll be copasthetic. **1934** in J. O'Hara *Sel. Letters* 100: "Copacetic" is a Harlem and gangster corruption of an Italian word...In American it means all right. **1943** *Amer. N & Q* (Aug.) 72. **1944** Gould *Snowflake* (unp.): Everything's copacetic! Why feel low? **1944** Kapelner *Lonely Boy Blues* 7: That's copacetic with me. **1950** Funk *Hangs a Tale* 83: "Well, Bill, how do you feel this morning?"..."Oh, jes' copesetic, boss; jes' copesetic!"...just fine and dandy. **1955** F. Harvey *Jet* 28: He...gave the old "copacetic" signal with the thumb and fingers. **1959–60** Bloch *Dead Beat* 108: Everything was still copacetic, everything was fine. **1968** Barrett *Green Berets* (film): Everything copacetic, sergeant? **1969** *Playboy* (Dec.) 94: All was copacetic for Namath. **1969** Apollo II Mission Control, in *N.Y. Times* (July 21) 4: All your consumables are solid. You're looking good in every respect. We copy the DPS venting. Everything is copacetic. Over. **1972** *N.Y. Times Bk. Review* (Apr. 30) 40: How long will liberals go on believing in the eventual benevolence of our capitalist system? Or—once Vietnam is really behind us and Nixon replaced—that everything will be copacetic in the Land of the Free? **1978** W. Brown *Tragic Magic* 33: I tried to maintain the fiction that everything was copacetic. **1982** *Morning Line* (WKGN radio) (July 9): We'll see if everything is still copacetic and cool in the Middle East. *a***1988** C. Adams *Straight Dope* 452: The thumbs-up sign, in Rio as in the U.S., signifies everything's copacetic. *a***1991** J.R. Wilson *Landing Zones* 160: These sons of bitches ain't acting right. Something ain't copasetic here.

2. confidential.

1959 NYC grade-school student: Let's keep this copacetic. **1978** MacKillop & Cross *Speaking of Words* 147: Fewer still would remember the youth-oriented word from the 1940s and 1950s "copacetic" (confidential, between only us).

copasetty *adj.* COPACETIC, 1.

1921 J. Conway, in *Variety* (May 6) 11: To make everything copesetty he put one arm around Tomato's neck and kissed him on the forehead. **1922** *Variety* (June 30) 6: Of course, some of the towns is copesetty, especially where the [pickpockets] have been rippin' and tearin' and cuttin' their bit up with the local authorities. **1925** Van Vechten *Nigger Heaven* 285: *Kopasetee:* an approbatory epithet somewhat stronger than *all right.* **1926** Finerty *Criminalese* 19: Everything is copsetty— O.K, settled. **1930** Lait *On the Spot* 32: Gee, that's hot. Is it all copesettee? *Ibid.* 201: *Copesettee*...Safe, O.K., all right.

cop-caller *n.* *Trucking.* (see quots.). *Joc.*

1938 in *AS* (Apr. 1942) 103: *Cop Caller.* Truck with squeaking brakes. **1971** Tak *Truck Talk* 37: *Cop caller:* 1. a truck with squealing brakes...2. a recapped tire with an unbroken tread line that creates an exceptional amount of road noise.

cop house *n.* a police station.

1928 Coe *Swag* 57: Just what did they ask you over there at the cop house? **1956** H. Ellison *Deadly Streets* 42: They stay in the cop house and play poker. **1958** Chandler *Playback* 127: I have to go to the cop house just about now. **1970** Conaway *Big Easy* 137: This is your man at the cop house...I'm quitting. **1985** Sawislak *Dwarf* 98: By the time they got to the cop house, one of them got through to Swift.

copilot *n.* **1.** *Narc.* an amphetamine tablet.

1965 Vermes *Helping Youth* 119: Benzedrine drugs...are also known as..."co-pilots." **1967** *Time* (May 5) 69: He calls them "bennies" or "co-pilots." **1971** *Go Ask Alice* 94: Jackie slipped me a couple of co-pilots in English when she passed out the test papers. **1975** *Atlantic* (May) 44: A couple of Co-Pilots in the morning orange juice.

2. *Trucking.* (see quot.).

1971 Tak *Truck Talk* 37: *Copilot:* a second driver on a long haul.

cop-killer *n.* a bullet that can pierce a protective vest as worn by a police officer.—often used attrib.

1985 *WINS Radio News* (Dec. 17): The House has passed a bill outlawing so-called "cop-killer" bullets. **1988** B. Breathed *Bloom Co.* (syndic. cartoon strip) (May 17): It's a cheap plastic machine gun loaded with Teflon coated "cop-killer" bullets. **1992** *Cops* (Fox-TV): Teflon-coated bullets are commonly referred to as "cop killers." **1993** *New Yorker* (Nov. 1) 8: Mr. Giuliani lobbied against a bill to ban armor-piercing, or "cop-killer," bullets.

cop man *n.* *Narc.* a seller of illicit drugs; DEALER, 2.

1962 Maurer & Vogel *Narc. & Narc. Add.* (ed. 2): *Cop-man*...A narcotics dealer. **1993** *Donahue* (NBC-TV): I just went over to the cop man and [bought heroin].

cop off *v.* **1.** to die.

1898 Norris *Moran* 73: If I thought he stood in our way...I'd shut him in the [gas-filled] cabin with the old man a spell, till he'd copped off. *Ibid.* 80: Old woman copped off...so much the better for us...no heirs to put in their gab.

2. to rob.

1921 Casey & Casey *Gay-Cat* 160: It'll be a cinch fer him ter cop off this place!

3. to meet (someone) at a later time.

1922 in Ruhm *Detective* 17: Then I'll cop you off at breakfast tomorrow morning.

4. see COP, *v.* (various defs.).

cop-out *n.* **1.** an instance of picking up a chance acquaintance, as by a prostitute.

1909 Chrysler *White Slavery* 51: Good girls...run with bad girls, girls...that make "cop outs" or mashes.

2. [cf. COP OUT, *v.*, 4] Orig. *Jazz & Und.* a pretext or means of evading or backing down; excuse; (*hence*) an act or instance of reneging or evading; evasion. [Gained nationwide currency *ca*1965–68.]

1956 in Ellington *Music My Mistress* 507: Cop-Out. **1960** R. Reisner *Jazz Titans* 153: *Cop Out:* Evasiveness. Excuse. **1964** in Redfield *Let. from Actor* 76: It's a cliché, a cop-out, a confession of helplessness. **1966** *Time* (Apr. 8) 83: God is an infantile fantasy, which was necessary when men did not understand what lightning was. God is a cop-out. **1966** M.T. Moore, in *Lompoc* (Calif.) *Record* (Dec. 2) 3B: They thought about making an announcement that I had a cold but that sounded like a cop-out. **1966** H.S. Thompson *Hell's Angels* 88: Any attempt to explain the Hell's Angels as an essentially homosexual phenomenon would be a cop-out, a self-satisfied dismissal of...reality. **1969** *Harper's* (Feb.) 81: *2001* is a celebration of cop-out. It says man is just a tiny nothing...and it's all out of your hands anyway. **1970** *Atlantic* (Jan.) 38: The blacks have become "purist," any contact with whites other than violence is a "cop-out." **1971** Sorrentino *Up from Never* 70: I mumbled cop-outs until right up to him. **1972** Kopp *Buddha* 126: Easy cop-out solutions are of no...help. **1975** Boatner et al. *Dict. Amer. Idioms* 66: Joe's answer to the question of forced bussing in Boston was a regular copout. **1977** Avallone *White Knight* 3: After the big cop-out in Nam, I came back Stateside. **1979** in M. Adler *Drawing Down the Moon* 134: I wished to become a nun and enter a contemplative order. My parents were radically against it. They felt it would be a copout. **1990** Rep. Henry Hyde, in *Nat. Review* (Nov. 5) 52: Blaming "the system" for the moral failures of individual Americans is a cop-out.

3. a person who evades an issue, reneges on a commitment, or the like.

1965 *N.Y. Times* (Dec. 5) VI 102: Like the characters in their plays, they are "cop-outs" from their assigned seats on the gravy train of an affluent society. **1966** *New Yorker* (Dec. 31) 28: I know the whole giftie bit is for Grant Wood copouts and all. **1967** in *BDNE* 167: The cop-out is like a fink-out, only more graceful. **1968** Bullins *Wine Time* 402: Goddamn what a collection of cop-outs. **1970** Zindel *Your Mind* 111: He threw me out of the house because he's a commercial artist and I called him a cop-out. **1971** Dahlskog *Dict.* 15: *Cop-out, n.* One who or that which is noncommittal. **1989** Charleston, S.C., woman, on *CBS This Morning* (Sept. 27): I'm not gonna be a cop-out. I'm gonna stay here and…try to help my husband.

cop out *v.* **1.a.** to get or take for oneself; COP, *v.*, 2.c.

1896 Ade *Artie* 4: I see the measliest lot o' jays—regular Charley-boys— floatin' around with queens. I wish somebody'd tell me how they cop 'em out. *Ibid.* 60: He'll see that I got a good job in the town offices, where I can cop out about twice what I'm gettin' now. **1903** Ade *Society* 32: But when I plugged for the lowly Wage-Earner I never had been in the Director's Office to see that beautiful Tableau entitled "Virtue copping out the Annual Dividend." **1904** in "O. Henry" *Works* 30: Cop him out if you want him.

b. to steal or snatch; COP, *v.*, 2.a.

1905 in "O. Henry" *Works* 1271: I'll step down and cop one out for you—see? **1906** *Variety* (Jan. 6) 7: Some other fellow on the same bill had copped out his fake drama.

c. *Und.* to apprehend or place under arrest; COP, *v.*, 1.

1900 Willard & Hodler *Powers That Prey* 14: A number of gentlemen…made themselves invisible; but the majority of those that he had mentioned were "copped out." **1924** Henderson *Keys to Crookdom* 401: *Copped out*—Taken into custody…. **1927** *DN* V 443: *Cop out, v.* To arrest. **1935** D.W. Maurer, in *AS* (Feb.) 14 [ref.to *ca*1910]: *Copped Out.* Arrested. **1946** (cited in Partridge *Dict. Und.* 149).

2. COP, *v.*, 4.

1916 in M. Gardner *Casey* 141: And how this bunch cops out the games is easy to explain.

3.a. *Und. & Police.* to plead guilty, esp. to a lesser charge as the result of plea-bargaining. Also *trans.*

1938 in Partridge *Dict. Und.* 149: It was a bum beef, but I copped out for a deuce because I was hot on a jug heist that called for a double saw-buck. **1951** in J. Blake *Joint* 13: I copped out on the larceny charges, figuring to get six months at the most. **1955** in Wepman et al. *The Life* 74: He copped out to Subdivision Two. **1958** "Traver" *Anatomy of Murder* 52: I will either find a sound and plausible legal defense in your case or else advise you to cop out. **1959** W. Burroughs *Naked Lunch* 8: The Vigilante copped out as a schizo possession case. **1967** Fiddle *Shooting Gallery* 154: You know, during the hearing, the cop kept tellin' me, why don't you cop out, you know, he'll give you a break. **1970** *Evergreen Review* (Apr.) 47: Marty was represented by a Legal Aid lawyer, fresh out of Fordham night school, who told him to "cop out." **1971** *Newsweek* (Mar. 8) 29: And he knows the most he will be able to do for 90 per cent of them is "cop them out"—plead them guilty—"and look for the best deal you can get." **1987** Santiago *Undercover* 80: If he was a juvenile he'd cop out to Daytop Village or some other halfway house. **1994** *New Yorker* (Jan. 31) 61: They tried to get him to cop out, to take a sentence of two to four years.

b. *Orig. Und. & Police.* to confess; make full admission.

1958 A. King *Mine Enemy* 17: Then, quite unexpectedly, one day he copped out to me. *Ibid.* 33: Aw, this guy King is a cool stud…We can cop out to him. **1958** Motley *Epitaph* 173: He copped out. He told his guts. It's jail for me. **1961** Braly *Felony Tank* 59: They probably thought you were going to cop out to every job pulled in this country in the last fifteen years. **1962** Quirk *Red Ribbons* 241: She was so damn mad she copped out to me when I told her I was a reporter after Green's skin. **1964** in Bruce *Essential Bruce* 59: Who copped out they're here? **1970** L.D. Johnson *Devil's Front Porch* 45 [ref. to *ca*1920]: I figured if I copped out to being an idiot, he might have a little mercy on me. **1971** B.B. Johnson *Blues for Sister* 10: Both of us refrained from copping out to either my daddy or Mama Franny. **1967–80** Folb *Runnin' Lines* 233: *Cop out*…Inform the police. **1984** McNamara *First Directive* 225: He cops out for seven jobs in the area. We think he's good for ten times that many. **1994** *New Yorker* (Jan. 31) 61: They can make you cop out to something you didn't even do.

4. *Orig. Und.* to back down or surrender; (*hence*) to back out of a responsibility or commitment; (*also*) to give up crime, drug-taking, or an unconventional lifestyle.—often used derisively. [The def. given in 1955 quot. cannot be corroborated and is prob. a nonce use.]

[**1955** Feather *Encyc. Jazz* 346: *Cop out*—go to sleep.] **1957–58** Lipton *Barbarians* 315: *Cop Out*—To settle down, go conventional, in the sense of "sell out" or "cop a plea." In some circles you may be charged with copping out if you shave off your beard. **1958** Gilbert *Vice Trap* 5: Cop

Out—…to back out of a responsibility. *Ibid.* 150: I wouldn't have copped out on him. **1961** Anhalt & Miller *Young Savages* (film): Just don't cop out on us! **1962** in Ricks & Marsh *Patterns in English* 47: [Among NYC gangs] to *cop out* means to avoid conflict by running. **1965** Borowik *Lions* 17: She played [the role] for eight months and then copped out claiming illness. **1965** Mathiessen *Fields of Lord* 87: You really mean you'd cop out on your only chance because [of] some lunatic? **1965** Hardman *Chaplains Raid* 14: So if any of you are too fat to make it is this the time to cop out. **1966** Young & Hixson *LSD* 77: He can "cop out" of the hip world and go straight. **1966** H.S. Thompson *Hell's Angels* 172: Or what if a girl wants to cop out sometime and get married? **1966–67** P. Thomas *Mean Streets* 30: "I'm gonna punch you in the mouth."…"You cop out?" "Yeah, I cop out" *Ibid.* 40: I ain't gonna cop out. I'm a fighter, too. **1968** Bloomquist *Marijuana* (gloss.). **1969** *Harper's* (July) 60: You can have a good life doing anything in the world, if you want it badly enough and don't cop out to your paranoias. **1971** in Sanchez *Word Sorcerers* 112: Dig how smooth she copped out…"You got it all wrong baby, I wasn't trying to sell you none." **1986** *New Image Teens* (KPBS-TV): Are you coppin' out? Are you a man or a mouse?

5.a. to evade an issue, esp. by making excuses; take the easy way out. [Gained nationwide currency 1965–69.]

1960 *Down Beat* (Oct. 13) 6: One of the grossest examples of ambiguity, copping out, padded writing and incompetency that I have ever read. **1961** J. Baldwin *Another Country* 346: Now, come on, baby, don't try to cop out that way. **1961** H. Ellison *Gentleman Junkie* 28: Cool it, man. No one's asking you to cop out. **1964** R. Dillon *Muscle Beach Party* (film): You always cop out. **1964** *New Yorker* (Dec. 19) 30: Even the satirists who cop out are helping to build a sympathetic climate for those people who don't cop out, who do get to the core. **1965** Hentoff *Jazz Country* 26: I'm not trying to cop out, but I was playing it too safe that afternoon at your house. **1966** Mandel *Mott the Hoople* 128: You're copping out!…Stay here. Answer me! **1967** Crowley *Boys in the Band* 817: It's easy to cop out and blame Evelyn and Walt and say it was *their* fault. **1970** A. Young *Snakes* 15: I got into the habit of copping out of whatever games we kids happened to have going whenever he came over. **1972** Kopp *Buddha* 44: Adam…copped out: "The woman…gave me the fruit of the tree, and I ate." **1990** *Regardie's* (June) 99: I copped out, saying that I didn't have the authority.

b. to yield to the authority or views of someone else.

1970 *Playboy* (Sept.) 279: I've got to defer to Christ on that one…I cop out to Christ. Do we know enough about today to ask about tomorrow?

6. to depart; leave.—also constr. with *of*.

1965 Borowik *Lions* 61: Anyway he's run out on the tour!…Just packed his bag and copped out. **1965** *N.Y. Times* (Dec. 5) V 100: He cops out of the social scene….They don't try to make him join them. **1967** Riessman & Dawkins *Play It Cool* 56: *Cop out v.* 1. to take a powder; leave: *When Rocky heard Teach say there was going to be a surprise test, he copped out of the room.* **1970** E. Thompson *Garden of Sand* 315: I need a drink. Get me one or cop the hell out.

copper *n.* **1.** an American Indian. Cf. COPPERHEAD, 2.

1772 in *DARE*: He said there would be Copers [*sic*] and White people present at the meeting. **1966** in *DARE*.

2. *pl.* dryness of the mouth or throat, esp. as the result of a hangover.—often constr. with *hot*.

1842 *Spirit of Times* (July 16) 231: They…had escaped from the hot atmosphere of the city, to cool their coppers amid rural scenes. **1849** Melville *White Jacket* 220: There were more *hot coppers* in the *Neversink* than in the ship's galley. **1854** Doten *Journals* I 181: Most of the boys were troubled with swelled heads and hot coppers today. **1863 in T. Taylor *Plays* 211: Suppose we begin with a little brandy and soda, to cool the coppers? **1896** Ade *Artie* 45: I've got a set o' coppers on me this g.m. that'd heat a four-room flat and my mouth tastes like a Chinese family'd just moved out of it. **1907** Corbin *Cave Man* 322: To drown the hot coppers in my gullet.

3. *Orig. Und.* a police officer; **holler** [or **yell**] **copper** (*Und.*) to call for the police.

*1846 in *OEDS*. **1846** *Nat. Police Gaz.* (Feb. 21) 210: Dick White has been playing the "dog,"* and he and the "coppers"† are now within ten minutes of the house!…*Traitor….† Officers. **1846** *Lives of the Felons* 58: If we follow your plan, the "*coppers*" (officers) will know that there are others into it, and…perhaps suspicion will fall upon us. **1848** Judson *Mysteries* 36: In Boston the coppers there aint half so keen with their peepers as they are here! *Ibid.* 527: "Coppers." Officers of the police; also termed "pigs," "nabs," &c. **1849** "N. Buntline" *B'hoys of N.Y.* 33: Who's wanted now, Coppers? **1871** Banka *Prison Life* 493: Policeman,…*Copper.* **1886** *Chi. Tribune* (Mar. 2) 3: The gratified copper was a Celt with a Munster brogue. **1893** F.P. Dunne, in Schaaf *Dooley* 48: He's acquainted with all th' coppers. **1894** Bridges *Arcady* 56: The coppers chased me into the Press office. **1899** Dunne *Hearts of His Countrymen* 84: "Polisman," he said. "Copper," he says. **1908** J. London *M. Eden* 27: That copper thought I was drunk. **1918** in Gibbons *Floyd Gibbons* 120: Perhaps it was the sight of his "copper" friends blowing their lungs out to the tune of "Over There" for his benefit. **1921** J. Conway, in *Variety* (Dec. 30) 97: They would holler copper right off the reel if any other stranger was to suggest the same thing to them. **1923** *Chi. Daily Trib.* (Oct. 3) 16: Copper Wounds Man He Saved From Sluggers. **1927** in Brookhouser *Our Years* 210: Mrs. Snyder and Gray have been "hollering copper" on each other lately, as the boys say. **1928** Ruth *Baseball* 4: There in those crooked winding streets...I learned to fear and to hate the coppers. **1928–30** Fiaschetti *Gotta Be Rough* 187: I knew she would treat me O.K., although I was a copper. **1938** in H. Gray *Arf* (unp.): How's that crazy young copper? **1946** Gresham *Nightmare Alley* 168: You don't dare yell copper on me. **1950** *Time* (Oct. 9) 24: The pattern which Chicagoans expect of their police captain—a rich man's life on a copper's pay. **1965** Tavel *Lady Godiva* 184: So what's your pitch, copper? **1978** Pilcer *Teen Angel* 118: We pass another copper. **1979** in Terkel *Amer. Dreams* 217: You said something to a copper, he'd whack you across the ass with his club. **1982** *N.Y. Post* (Aug. 24) 26: Six months later...a sucker...hollered copper. **1985** *Lady Blue* (ABC-TV): I got nothing to say to you, copper. Nothing. **1992** *Batman* (Fox-TV): Freeze, copper! I got ya covered!

4. *Pris.* time to be deducted from a convict's sentence, as for good behavior.

1908 Hopper & Bechdolt *9009* 10: Keep to yourself and hang on to your good-time; hang on to your copper. **1914** Jackson & Hellyer *Vocab.* 25: Copper, Noun. Current amongst prison habitues. The commutation or good time allowed prisoners for good behavior. Example: "You grab one month copper off the first year." **1927–28** Tasker *Grimhaven* 158: Good time credits—*copper* in the vernacular. **1937** Johnston *Prison Life* 87: I'm trying to get my "copper" back. **1944** C.B. Davis *Leo McGuire* 177: So we went through the winter keeping our copper, which is an old prison word meaning keeping your record clean. *Ibid.* 178: There's about an eighty-twenty bet that they'll catch you and you've lost your copper. *Ibid.* 242: I was going to keep my good behavior, or what good old Danny Ashland...used to call holding your copper. **1959** Duffy & Lane *Warden's Wife* 326: Their behavior had cost them their "copper"—their prison credits for good conduct.

copper *v.* **1.** to arrest or apprehend. *Obs.* in U.S.

1866 *Nat. Police Gaz.* (Nov. 17) 3: Mose Sargent, the "shadow" that "coppered" the "jug crackers"...was their keeper in "sturbin." **1872** Crapsey *Nether Side of N.Y.* 17: They are more frequently "coppered"—that is, arrested. **1877** in *Contrib. Hist. Soc. of Montana* II 270: I was ahead and was "coppered" (captured, taken in) by one of the pickets. ***1962** in *OEDS:* "Arrest" has many Cant synonyms including...*copper*.

2.a. *Gamb.* to bet against; to hedge (a bet or expectation). [Orig., as in 1897 quot., a technical term in the game of faro.]

1882 "M. Twain" *Life on Miss.* 175: I reckon the safe way...is to *copper* the operation, and at the same time buy enough property in Vicksburg to square you up in case they win. [**1897** A.H. Lewis *Wolfville* 12: Thar's fifty dollars on the king coppered.] **1904** in A. Adams *Chisholm Trail* 98: He simply coppered the play to win. **1907** London *Road* 46: Our intention was to take the first train out, but the railroad officials "coppered" our play—and won. **1912** Stringer *Shadow* 40: Yet at times he had what he called a "coppered hunch." **1934** in Fenner *Throttle* 56: There was always a chance of that, and...he was coppering all bets. **1950** *Sci. American* (Dec.) 2: Gamblers copper all bets and never take a chance, even a good one. **1959** in J. O'Hara *Sel. Letters* 291: We may have had them so often that we kind of copper our bets.... **1966–67** Harvey *Air War* 180: "He realizes that nobody can be without God, particularly near death." "You mean he's coppering his bets?" **1968** M.B. Scott *Racing Game* 94: The rule is "copper the public," that is, play against it.

b. *Gamb.* to disbelieve.

1856 in *DA:* It is a safe bet to "copper" all that comes from the immaculate [Vigilance] Committee. **1896** Ade *Artie* 79: Pay no attention to what she says about me, Miller. Just copper it. **1903** Ade *Society* 148: You are a Mere Child of 19, with...a Simple Faith in Mankind, and you are due to be Strung unless you Copper about four-thirds of all that is said to you. **1906** *Nat. Police Gaz.* (Dec. 22) 10: Some students of form would "copper" this tip. **1917** T.A. Dorgan, in Zwilling *TAD Lexicon* 98: (Greeting unexpected company...) Hello—ha—ha—I wondered

who it could be...Come right in—So glad to see you. [Arrow pointing at words:] Copper the whole spiel.

3. to steal or embezzle.

1884 in *DA:* He's been in office a long while an' never coppered a d—n cent.

4. to make certain of getting; get; COP.

1901 Irwin *Sonnets* (unp.): All the chronic hand-claspers came/To copper invites for the wedding day. **1915–16** Lait *Beef, Iron & Wine* 159: Youse newspapers guys...is tryin' to copper the lowdown on the bad boy problem. **1927–30** Rollins *Jinglebob* 20 [ref. to 1880's]: We'll copper a snake for your bonnet later.

5. to work as a police officer. Cf. COP, *v.,* 8.

1923 in W.F. Nolan *Black Mask Boys* 80: Three days of hotel-coppering.

copperbelly *n. R.R.* a veteran telephone lineman.

1938 Haines *High Tension* 48: After we got the job well started the yard was full of hopeful kids...They was hospital bait...We put the best of them to work as grunts and second-class linemen and divided what few old copper bellies we had around through the trains and went to work and hoped for the best.

copperhead *n.* **1.a.** a despicable person.

1809 W. Irving, in *DA.* **1853** in *Ibid.* "Come, copper-head! march!" and Millhouse, planting himself on one side of the captive. **1866** *Nat. Police Gaz.* (Nov. 3) 2: The latter...said Farley deserved death because he was "a d—d old copperhead."

b. *Pol.* a Northerner who sympathized with the Confederacy. Now *S.E.* and *hist.*

1862 E.H. Rhodes *All for the Union* (Feb. 6) 54: All Copperheads should be punished, for they are too cowardly to fight us in front so they stop us in the rear. **1862** in *DA.* **1864** W. Whitman, in *F & H* II 182: Exciting times in Congress. The Copperheads are getting furious, and want to recognise the Southern Confederacy. **1892** in E. Ellis *Dooley's Amer.* 46: I don't believe any copperhead should be made president of the United States. **1893** Casler *Stonewall* 170: He was a "copper-head" and a Rebel sympathizer. **1901** Dunbar *Fanatics* 7: You damned copper-head, you! **1928** Lonn *Desertion* 205: It was feared a California deserter would be warned and abetted by Copperheads of Oregon. **1965** Catton *Never Call Retreat* 104: Vallandigham in short was speaking for those numerous war-weary Northerners who were already becoming known as Copperheads. **1982** Bowman *Civil War Almanac* 232: Confederate agents and Copperhead sympathizers.

2. an American Indian.—used contemptuously.

1838 in *DA:* He said...it would be a sin to kill one, but if he was to go he should want to kill one of the damned copper-heads. **1845** in *OEDS:* First Mexicans, then Indians, come on. Brush the Yellow-Bellies. Then the Copperheads come sneaking down. **1859** Avery *Comical Stories* 57: Look here, old copperhead...none of that. *a*1861 in *OEDS:* Five foul cop- perheads...lurked among the plunder of that noisome spot. **1871** Schele de Vere *Amer.* 22: Along the frontier line [the Indian] was perhaps as frequently called a Copperhead, an ancient term of contempt of which W. Irving makes frequent use in his quaint History of New York.

copper-hearted *adj. Und.* having the nature of an informer; treacherous.

1927 Murphy *Gray Walls* 39: This copper-hearted rat had quietly drifted among these men. **1930** *Amer. Mercury* (Dec.) 455: *Copper-hearted, adj.:* To be by nature a police informer. "Is that broad copper-hearted? And how!" **1933** Ersine *Pris. Slang* 29: *Copper-hearted,* adj. Instinctively mean; vicious; resembling a cop in behavior. "The bull who is not copper-hearted is a rare exception." **1935** Pollock *Und. Sp: Copper hearted,* by desire and character an informer; stool pigeon. **1967** [Beck] *Pimp* 41: He wasn't copper hearted. He never tipped my name to the heat.

copperhide *n.* an American Indian.—used contemptuously.

*ca*1900 *Buffalo Bill* 210: When he git this call from the copper-hide.

copper-plated *adj.* utter; absolute.

1886 Nye *Remarks* 362: He...called me a copperplate ass. **1924** in Hemingway *Sel. Letters* 137: He has been hooked and married by the most absolutely copper plated bitch in the world.

coppers *n. Navy.* coppersmith.

1906 Beyer *Amer. Battleship* 82: "Coppers"—the coppersmith. **1917** Ruggles *Navy Explained* 33: *Coppers.* The coppersmith of a navy vessel.

copper-shy *adj. Und.* afraid of the police.

1930 Conwell *Pro. Thief* 30: The suggestion of a certain thief to fill in may bring forth the fact that he is a drunkard, lazy, a dope fiend, copper-shy, late for meets.

copperskin *n.* an American Indian.—used contemptuously. Hence **copper-skinned.**

1840 in *DARE:* "Go on, go on, Kit; d'ye say a dozen Injuns?" "Yes, uncle, not a Copperskin less." **1846** *Crockett's Almanac* (unp.): The copper-skinned, painter-blooded, hog-stomached varmints. **1876** Cody & Arlington *Life on Border* 45: I will fight it out with that copperskin. **1904** in *DA.* **1966** in *DARE.*

cop shop *n.* a police station.

1941 in *OEDS.* **1961 J. Flynn *Action Man* 80: It'll jam the band every time the cop shop…tries to transmit. **1970** Thackrey *Thief* 436: And headed over to the cop-shop, to see about the dough. **1971** Dahlskog *Dict.* 15: *Cop shop, n.* Police station. **1984** McNamara *First Directive* 236: We were back in the…cop shop. **1987** *Ampersand's Entertainment Guide* (Summer) 3: His one-time adversaries from the Beverly Hills cop shop. **1989** L. Roberts *Full Cleveland* 125: Sitting around a cop shop.

cop-spotter *n.* (see quot.). *Joc.*

1971 Tak *Truck Talk* 37: *Cop spotter:* a rearview mirror.

copter *n.* a helicopter. Now *colloq.*

1947 in *OEDS.* **1949** *N.Y. Times* (Mar. 22) 20: The pilot…landed the 'copter in a desolate high-altitude hollow. **1949** in Conklin *Sci. Fic. Omnibus* 124: Behind him the technicians were unloading the apparatus from the 'copter. **1953** "L. Padgett" *Mutant* 9: The copter's laid up today, though. **1961** L.G. Richards *TAC* 66: A whole network of ships, planes, and 'copters. **1964** *L.A. Times* (Dec. 8) IV 1: He is trying to put a copter in the area to ferry food. **1978** S. King *Stand* 696: Hangar 9, where two other skimmers and three large Baby Huey copters were stored. **1984** Kagan & Summers *Mute Evidence* 332: They couldn't control their own copter jockeys.

copy *v.* [fr. radiocommunications jargon 'to receive a message'] *Mil.* to understand.

1984 Glick *Winters Coming* 200: I'm okay, Mingo. You copy? **1985** Heywood *Taxi Dancer* 219 [ref. to 1967]: I'll lay you five to one that you can't hit the deck before me. You copy?

coral sandwich *n.* *Surfing.* an instance of being thrown from a surfboard face-first onto a reef, a beach, or into the shallows. *Joc.*

1981 in Safire *Good Word* 111: You bounced off the bottom and had a coral sandwich.

cord *n.* a large amount; a lot.

1842 *Spirit of Times* (Jan. 8) 531: He could make a cord of money in Old Kentucky. **1842** *Spirit of Times* (Nov. 5) 421: He was thought to be worth "a cord." **1843** in *DARE.* **1846** (quot. at WET, *n.*). **1871** in *DARE.*

cords *n.pl.* corduroy clothing, esp. trousers.

1926 in *AS* (Feb. 1927) 276: *Cords*—corduroy trousers. **1952** *N.Y. Times* (July 20) I 39 (adv.): Corduroy coverall…Watch these cords steal the limelight anywhere. **1954** in D. McKay *Wild Wheels* 96: He was…seventeen. Leather jacket and cords. **1958** J. Davis *College Vocab.* 11: *Cords*—Senior Corduroy trousers. **1965 S.J. Baker *Austral Lang.* (ed. 2) 259: *Cords,* corduroy trousers. **1979** *N.Y. Times Mag.* (Sept. 23) 12: "Corduroy" [is] clipped to "cords." **1981** Wolf *Roger Rabbit* 65: I found a pair of baggy cords. **1983** Univ. Tenn. student theme (Apr. 8): Blue jeans or cords are the pants worn by jocks everywhere. **1987** J. Thompson *Gumshoe* 303: My dirty cords [were] in a pile by the door.

corduroy *n.* hash.

1866 (quot. at SIAMESE TWINS).

cork *n.* **1.** (see quot.). Cf. CORK, *v.,* 2.

1851 Hall *College Wds.* 85: *Cork.* Calk. In some of the Southern colleges, this word, with a derived meaning, signifies a *complete stopper.* Used in the sense of an entire failure in reciting; an utter inability to answer an instructor's interrogatories.

2. the penis.

1938 in Randolph *Pissing in Snow* 86: Pretty soon the Yankee says, "Boys, I can feel my cork a-bobbing already!" **1975** *Nat. Lampoon* (Oct.) 109: I shoved my limp cork at Rocky.

¶ In phrase:

¶ **draw a cork** *Boxing.* (see 1891 quot.).

1818 in *F & H* II 184: Several blows exchanged, but no corks were drawn. **1837 in *F & H* II: Tap his claret cask—draw his cork! **1891 Maitland *Slang Dict.* 77: *Cork, "to draw a"* (P[rize] R[ing]), to give one a bloody nose.

¶ **pop** [or **blow**] **(one's) cork, 1.** to lose (one's) temper; become very angry.

1938 *AS* (Apr.) 156: *Pop your cork.* Loose [*sic*] your temper. **1947** Boyer *Dark Ship* 283: The captain blew his cork. I thought he was going to shoot us. **1954** Schulberg *Waterfront* 232: I guess I did blow my cork and I hit' em with that stuff about Christ in the shape-up. **1955** Klaas *Maybe I'm Dead* 120: You can't pop your cork every day or so living in a room full of men. **1964** "Doctor X" *Intern* 345: Well, I blew my cork…I told her that if this was a temper tantrum, it was high time somebody threw one about something like this. **1970** Thackrey *Thief* 420: The judge had just blown his cork over that and called me a lot of fucking names from the bench and all. **1985** Boyne & Thompson *Wild Blue* 222: When I saw what was happening, I just blew my cork.

2. to lose (one's) mind or composure; go crazy. Also vars.

1952 Uris *Battle Cry* 213: I'll blow my cork if I stick around this hole any more. **1953** in Cannon *Like 'Em Tough* 24: You've flipped your cork, Cannon. **1958** Talsman *Gaudy Image* 90: You remember when Serioso popped his cork over Minerva? He was wild on her. **1960** Leckie *Marines!* 118 [ref. to WWII]: "Gawd," Pete breathed when he saw him. "He's popped his cork." **1968** in Rowe *Five Yrs. to Freedom* 363: Locals will never know how close to popping my cork I have been at times. **1967** Yablonsky *Hippie Trip* 263: She looked into a mirror and her face turned almost to that of a mummy and she just blew her cork right there. She had panic reactions—screaming, yelling. **1970** *Nat. Lampoon* (Sept.) 60: Many silver screen veterans would pop their corks if they could own "Exhibit A" from the gala murder trial. **1971** Horan *Blue Messiah* 587: He blows his cork some night and works over a dame. **1971** Faust *Willy Remembers* 71: You would blow your cork too if Dietrich waved her Frankies under your nose. **1978** Karl *13th Outpost* 140: Christ Almighty, Mac, you've popped your cork.

¶ **pull (one's) cork, 1.** to exhaust; (*hence*) put a stop to.

1918 *Stars & Stripes* (Feb. 8) 3: Gee, though, that was some clip he run us at on the way up that hill! It pulled my cork all right, I'll tell the world. **1960** Leckie *Marines!* 13 [ref. to WWII]: I didn't have my gun or my helmet or the stuff for pulling Pistol Pete's [a heavy gun] cork and I didn't even know where I was.

2. to make (one) insane.

1960 Leckie *Marines!* 103 [ref. to WWII]: We looked at him like we thought the battle had pulled his cork….

¶ **pull the cork, 1.** to get busy.

1937 Lay *I Wanted Wings* 280: Pull the cork, Murphy,…we aren't going to work for you.

2. *Navy.* to begin to submerge (in a submarine); *pull the plug* s.v. PLUG.

1959 W. Anderson *Nautilus* 98: If [the ice] closed in we would simply "pull the cork" and descend beneath it.

3. to make an end; *pull the plug* s.v. PLUG.

1974 Terkel *Working* 147: They canceled the following day. The big bosses were the ones that pulled the cork.

¶ **put a cork in it** shut up!

1982 "J. Cain" *Commandos* 287: Put a cork in it, Marvin! **1983** N. Proffitt *Gardens of Stone* 150: Put a cork in it Willow. **1984** Glick *Winters Coming* 114: What say you put a cork in it, killer? **1988** *It's Garry Shandling's Show* (Fox-TV): Put a cork in it, Shandling.

¶ **slip (one's) cork** to lose (one's) mind.

1968 *Rowan & Martin's Laugh-In* (NBC-TV): He's slipped his cork!

¶ **snap (one's) cork** *snap (one's) cap* s.v. CAP.

1954 E. Hunter *Jungle Kids* 60: I was ready to really snap my cork when the goddamn cops pulled up.

cork *v.* **1.** to hit hard. Cf. CORKER, 1, 2.

1876 *Chi. Inter-Ocean* (May 1) (cited in Nichols *Baseball Term.*). **1883** Peck *Peck's Bad Boy* 205: When Ma corks herself, or has a pain anywhere, she just uses liniment for all that is out. **1909** *DN* III 394: *Cork one's self*…To injure one's self. **1961** Gover *$100 Misunderstanding* 19: That bundle cork my ass! Yeah! It knock me clean off my feet! **1971** Sorrentino *Up from Never* 214: I was five feet away when Jackie corked him.

2. to get the better of; (*hence*) in phr. **wouldn't that cork you?** Doesn't that astound or irritate you?

1888 Nye & Riley *Railway Guide* 4: Never talk back! sich things is ripperhensible;/A feller only "corks" hisse'f that jaws a man that's hot. **1906** *DN* III 132: *Cork, v. tr.* To get the better of. "It certainly did *cork* me." **1912** *Pedagogical Sem.* (Mar.) 96: Wouldn't that "jar," "frost," "cook," "cork," "stump," etc., you. **1918** *Sat. Eve. Post* (Jan. 19) 65: Wouldn't it cork you? **1920** in *DARE:* The student who flagrantly failed to reply correctly to the questions of his professor in the classroom was said to have been *corked.* **1960** in *DARE:* Wouldn't that cork you?

3.a. to cause to stop talking; CORK UP.

1889 "M. Twain" *Conn. Yankee* 147: But you can't cork that kind; they would die. Her clack was going all day.

b. to quit talking; CORK UP.—also constr. with (*imper.*) *it* or (*occ.*) (*vulgar*) *ass.*

1899 A.H. Lewis *Sandburrs* 132: Say! d' Face wasn't doin' a t'ing but put up a roar all d' mornin', till a cop shows up an' lays it out cold if d' Face don't cork, he'll pinch him. **1935** Pollock *Und. Speaks: Cork it,* shut up, keep quiet. **1961** Gover *$100 Misunderstanding* 36: An then I cork ass an start in considerin all over agen. **1975–78** O'Brien *Cacciato* 118: "Please…" "Cork it." **1989** *ALF* (NBC-TV): Cork it, eh Jake.

4. to copulate with (a woman).

1974 Strasburger *Rounding Third* 168: I had always thought about how great it would be to play strip poker with a girl before you corked her.

5. [sugg. by CORK OFF] to loaf.

1982 Lisberger *Tron* (film): Come on, Flynn, quit corking.

6. *Stu.* (see quot.).

1978 Dabney *Across Years* 80 [ref. to 1918]: A student [at the Univ. of Va.] who flunked a course was said to have "corked," while one who made a high mark was said to have "curled."

corked *adj.* **1.** drunk.

1895 Gore *Stu. Slang* 13: *Corked*…Drunk. **1912** *DN* III 572: *Corked, adj.* Drunk. **1927** *AS* II (Mar.) 276: *Corked.* Intoxicated. **1971** Sloan *War Games* 152: If I eat nuoc-man I have to be corked. **1979** W. Cross *Kids & Booze* 14: And if we get corked we got a big headache the next day and serves us right. **1981** Univ. Tenn. student: *Corked* is drunk.

2. tired out; BUSHED.—also (*later*) constr. with *out.*

1938 Bezzerides *Long Haul* 26: Listen to that guy snore…He must be corked. **1952** Uris *Battle Cry* 256 [ref. to 1942]: I know, Sam…but my boys are kind of corked out. **1953** Dodson *Away All Boats* 398: Hey, you look corked…There's a pot of hot joe over there. **1955** Klaas *Maybe I'm Dead* 208: Well, my feet hurt, and my back aches, and I'm plenty corked. **1957** Myrer *Big War* 318: The rest of them were corked out, too. **1970** in *DARE*: Corked.

corker *n.* **1.** a hard or finishing blow; (*hence*) (*obs.*) that which settles an issue. Cf. CORK, *v.*, 1.

1835 in *F & H* II 184: Then I lets him have it, right, left, right, jist three corkers, beginning with the right hand, shifting to the left, and then with the right hand ag'in. *****1873** Hotten *Slang Dict.* (ed. 4): "That's a corker," i.e., that settles the question, or closes the discussion. *a*1888 in J.A. Applegate *Cow Column* 56: This, I suppose, was generally regarded as a "corker." **1908** *DN* III 301: *Corker*…A knock-out blow, a good blow. **1968, 1969** in *DARE*.

2.a. a stiff drink of liquor.

1842 *Spirit of Times* (July 23) 243: Come, let me give you a *corker* this time; so—there now; drink that. **1875** *Minstrel Gags* 136: He bolted another corker.

b. a person or thing of extraordinary size, effectiveness, quality, etc.; a remarkable person or thing.

*****1882** in *OEDS*: We look over our boat-side and see the big "corkers" rising out of the marl and sand in which their roots lie buried. **1884** in Lummis *Letters* 68: Some of the names of towns out in this country are real "corkers." **1885** *Puck* (June 17) 251: Some on 'em was corkers, too. **1888** Gunter *Miss Nobody* 86: Florence being, to use a Western expression, a "corker." *****a*1889 in Barrère & Leland *Dict. Slang* I 272: The Crown Prince's lunch-bill was rather a *corker*. **1889** in *Ibid.*: Jake Kilrain is a *corker*, and ought to have the championship of the world. **1889** "M. Twain" *Conn. Yankee* 193: For just a modest little one-line ad., it's a corker. **1893** Frye *Staff & Field* 122: That man Woodleigh, of yours, is a corker! **1896** F.H. Smith *Tom Grogan* 23: He's a corker, he is; reads po'try an' everythin'. **1898** Stratemeyer *Young Volunteer* 86: My, but this is a corker! **1900** *DN* II 29: *Corker.* 1. Anybody or anything all right. 2. Severe, as an examination. 3. An accomplished person (often ironical). 4. A perfect recitation. **1903** in "O. Henry" *Works* 651: By Heavens! that dictator chap is a corker! He's a dictator clear down to his finger ends. **1913** Jocknick *Early Days* 142 [ref. to 1870's]: Well, I'll be d—d if this doesn't beat the band for a corker. **1934** Weseen *Dict. Slang* 322: *Corker*—A name for any thing or any person regarded as superlatively good or bad. **1952** in *DAS*: Honestly—you're a corker! **1960** in *DARE*. **1971** Keith *Long Line Rider* 166: "You guys sure are corkers," I said finally. **1976** T. Walker *Ft. Apache* 81: That guy's a corker. **1986** Knoxville, Tenn. attorney, age 33: I don't know what her excuse will be, but it *will* be a corker!

c. *Specif.* an attractive young woman; KNOCK-OUT.

1895 in Kisseloff *Must Remember This* 386: I am de belle dey say ov Avenoo A,/…I'm a "Corker." **1895** Townsend *Fadden* 58: Say, de Duchess is a corker, sure. **1899** Norris *McTeague* 88: And this girl she

was a corker. **1906–07** (quot. at PIPPIN). **1938** in *DARE*. **1963–64** Kesey *Great Notion* 112: Ain't she a corker? I'm gonna marry that girl, Hank.

3. *Baseball.* a fly ball. Cf. CORK, *v.*, 1.

1867, 1868, 1900 in *DA.*

corkhead *n.* a fool.

1942 Freeman & Gilbert *Larceny, Inc.* (film): You corkhead, banks aren't made out of cellophane.

corking *adj.* **1.** splendid; wonderful. Also quasi-adv. [Most freq. *ca*1895–1915.]

1891 McCann & Jarrold *Odds & Ends* 82: They knowed Jack was a corkin' singer. **1894** *Harper's* (Oct.) 699: Dat'll be corkin' wid dis song. **1895** Townsend *Fadden* 99: It was der corkin'est weddin' dere ever was. **1899** Cullen *Tales* 108: I never put in two more corking weeks of solid comfort. **1891–1900** in Hoyt *Five Plays* 120: A corking supper, my boy! Nothing's too good! **1900** Greenough & Kittredge *Words & Ways* 313: Of the same sort are the genuine slang words *bang-up, rattling good, tip-top, first-rate, immense* (cf. German *Kolossal*), *stunning, corking.* **1903** Townsend *Sure* 75: It was de corkingest play dat was ever acted. **1907** Corbin *Cave Man* 44: That's a corking fine moon. **1910** *Variety* (July 23) 13: It is a corking good act. **1917** in E.E. Cummings *Letters* 17: I got one corking letter from Sears, a perfect bird, right off. **1921** *Variety* (July 1) 15: The 'phone bit was…corking. **1922** S. Lewis *Babbitt* 20: But say, this is corking!…New York Assembly has passed some bills that ought to completely outlaw the socialists! **1926** Hormel *Co-Ed* 20: Corking of you to come, Miss Leigh. **1935** H. Gray *Arf* (unp.): This is going to make a corking picture, Mr. Gamble. **1936** "E. Queen" *Half-way House* 151: Corking day, isn't it? **1983** Flaherty *Tin Wife* 26: And she was a corking dancer.

2. extraordinary; unsurpassed.

1891–1900 in Hoyt *Five Plays* 148: What a corking lie!

cork off *v.* [var. CAULK OFF] **1.** *Orig. Naut.* to go to sleep; take a nap; fall asleep; rest. [Early quots. ref. to WWI.]

1918 in York *Mud & Stars* 41: Everyday we have two smoking lamps and we cork off in the sun. **1919** T. Kelly *What Outfit?* 62: There's a chance to lay down and cork off a bit. **1922** *Leatherneck* (Apr. 22) 5: *Caulk-off:* To sleep. Generally pronounced "cork-off." Originally, to sleep on the deck, from the process of *caulking,* or stuffing the cracks, in the deck flooring of a ship. **1922** Jordan *Btty. B* 17: The rest "corked off." **1926** *Amer. Leg. Mo.* (July) 46: I'm going to cork off so you can do the same. **1929** Hemingway *Farewell to Arms* 190: I'm going to sleep where the old man corks off. **1942** *Leatherneck* (Nov.) 144: *Corking off*—Taking it easy; resting or sleeping. **1958** Cooley *Run for Home* 317: If you want to cork off for a little while, I'll keep an eye on Laughing Boy here! **1964** Faust *Steagle* 181: Stewardess on lap. Corked-off tower man. **1970** Lincke *Jenny Was No Lady* 41: They weren't intrepid, they just corked off once too often. **1974** Terkel *Working* 104: After being outside all day and walkin' into a warm house, I can cork off in a minute. **1974** Millard *Thunderbolt* 37: Try to cork off for a little bit.

2. to lose one's mind.

1942 (quot. at NUT FACTORY).

3. to produce rapidly or easily; KNOCK OFF.

1961 H. Ellison *Gentleman Junkie* 45: He had started writing…hoping to cork off a solid five thousand words that day.

4. [prob. alter. *cook off*] to set off, detonate.

1984 (quot. at WINDER, *n.*).

cork opera *n. Theat.* a minstrel show.

1857, 1869 in *DA.*

cork out *v.* **1.** to fall exhausted.

1955 Klaas *Maybe I'm Dead* 241 [ref. to 1945]: First thing he did when the rest of us were corking out nine-tenths dead was get ahold of a wheelbarrow…and gather up most of these guys where they dropped.

2. to go to sleep.

1960 MacCuish *Do Not Go Gentle* 74 [ref. to 1940]: Naw! I put them over my face to keep out the light when I cork out. **1968** Spradley *A Drunk* 99: *Flopping* is the most common word, but such synonyms as *sleeping, corking out,* and *crapping out* are also used.

cork up *v.* **1.** to fall silent; shut up.

1855 in Meserve & Reardon *Satiric Comedies* 146: Demmy John, cork up! **1859** Tayleure *Boy Martyrs* 22: Cork up!…Here's the young lady. **1892** Frye *From HQs* 71: Cork up, will you, and don't let these sailors carry away wrong impressions of us. **1895** J.L. Williams *Princeton* 22: Oh, cork up, you big cow! **1900** Patten *Merriwell's Power* 45: Cork up, and come on! **1903** in F. Remington *Sel. Letters* 340: I will cork up even on that with my very good plea. **1959** Morrill *Dark Sea* 40 [ref. to WWII]: That

big wind of yours has been going for months. Now cork up.
2. to silence.

1884 "M. Twain" *Huck. Finn* 16: Jim would happen in and say, "Hm! What you know 'bout witches?" and that nigger was corked up and had to take a back seat. **1895** J.L. Williams *Princeton* 17: Oh, cork up that laugh.

3. to get drunk.

1961 H. Ellison *Memos* 86: Her boy friend was out corking up on Sneaky Pete.

corky *adj.* ebullient.

1872 O.W. Holmes *Poet* 96: They danced as if they…couldn't help dancing; they looked as if they felt so "corky" it was hard to keep them down. **1987** *News Night* (CNN-TV) (Apr. 9): A marvelously corky supporting cast.

corn *n.* **1.** money, esp. in small amounts.

1837 *Spirit of Times* (June 10) 134: Blood and hard-starving until two years old, is the only thing now-a-days I would venture "corn" on. **1892** L. Moore *Own Story* 366 [ref. to 1870]: He then asked me where the rest of the property was, saying that he had all the "corn." *ca*1928 in Wilstach *Stage Slang* (unp.): "Corn" is small change. **1930** Irwin *Tramp & Und. Sl.* 55: Corn.—Small change. **1933–34** Lorimer & Lorimer *Stag Line* 160: Get me some corn for pikers and plenty of scratch to pay off with. **1969** in *DARE*. **1970** Major *Afro-Amer. Sl.: Corn:* (1940's) money.

2. a drunkard.

1847 Downey *Portsmouth* 227: Wall now, I swan to man, you are what I call a touch of the entire swine, tail and all, you've gone and drunk a half a pipe of wine, and not content with that, you've got in all over and gone swimming in it. Don't you think you are a Corn? Why you are a regular tank and if you don't bust after this I'll give up. **1971** *PADS* (No. 52) 28: *Corn, n.* One who drinks heavily off the job. "Jim surely is a corn."

3. *Black E.* flattery; deception; CON.

1897 Ade *Pink* 171: She's took a lot of at co'n fom 'em cullud boys, an' she's beginnin' to give ev'y man 'at bad look when he tells huh how good she is. Misteh, you can't feed it to 'em feveh.

4. Orig. *Jazz.* triteness, esp. old-fashioned or mawkishly sentimental entertainment material.

1936 *Variety* (June 24) 63: The B.B.C. doesn't understand that the great English public loves corn, loves a waltz. **1937** *AS* 46: That chorus reeks of corn. **1944** in T. Williams *Letters* 155: I screamed over the footlights, "My God, what corn!" **1948** J.H. Burns *Lucifer* 275: When Mr. Hudson wants to show us in class that something is mystical nineteenth-century corn, he says it's Alfred Lord Tennysonish. **1962** T. Berger *Reinhart in Love* 174: At some instance of corn she had wept, unnoticed by him. **1993** *New Republic* (Sept. 20) 36: Ford is in a bus taking him and some other prisoners to a penitentiary for execution when an accident overturns the bus. (Predictable corn.)

5. *Baseball.* CAN OF CORN.

1980 Lorenz *Guys Like Us* 145: They were hitting corn, swinging like a bunch of tired old Moose.

¶ In phrases:

¶ **acknowledge the corn** to admit defeat or error; (*hence*) to admit the truth. Also vars.

1839 *Spirit of Times* (Nov. 16) 439: The modest Quaker being compelled to acknowledge "the corn," and give up the heat to the chesnut colt. **1839** in *DARE*: We "acknowledge the corn."…The people there do not drink one-tenth part of what they do in this state. **1842** *Spirit of Times* (Mar. 16): Your honor, I confess the corn. I was royally drunk. **1845** in Robb *Squatter Life* 107: I acknowledge the corn, boys, that when I started my track warn't anythin' like a *bee-line*. **1858** in *N. Dak. Hist.* XXXIII (1966) 305: I had been regularly *"sold."*…I came quietly back to the Fort and "acknowledged the corn." **1872** Burnham *Secret Service* iv: *Acknowledge the corn*, to make a full frank confession. *Ibid.* 99: The Chief had hardly been in conclave with him fifteen minutes before he "acknowledged the corn." **1887** L.A. Norton *Life* 84: I "acknowledged the corn," and was ever after known as the veritable "green sucker." **1936** *AS* (Dec.) 316: *Own the corn*, v. phr. To admit an error, same as "acknowledge the corn."

¶ **have (one's) corn ground** to have sexual intercourse.

1800 *Amorous Songster* 91: Sir, I must have my corn ground, I must and I will.

¶ **take the corn** to become the center of attention.

1839 *Spirit of Times* (July 27) 247: Well, what has got into the people of Arkansas?—they are getting jist as bad as they used to be before Mississippi and Texas took the corn.

cornball *n.* Orig. *Show Business.* a person given to CORNY performances, remarks or the like; an unsophisticated or sentimental person, esp. from the country. Also as v., to behave like a cornball.

1952 Chase *McThing* 68: Don't be a cornball. **1952** Brossard *Darkness* 12: Too many cornballs go there. **1955** Graziano & Barber *Somebody Up There* 243: You ignorant cornballs!…You dumb country bastards! **1957** E. Lacy *Room to Swing* 25: It's too early for cornballing. **1961** J. Jones *Thin Red Line* 89: Pfc Marl, a Nebraska cornball. **1962** T. Jones *Stairway* 83: It was dark inside, and in the back a victrola was cranking Bach or some other cornball. **1963** Coon *Short End* 107: Billyjo was a real cornball. **1969** Nat. Guard ad, WINS Radio (Jan. 3): Some people say patriotism is old-fashioned—for cornballs. **1976** "N. Ross" *Policeman* 40: "That's a fact…yessiree, bob." This was a number one cornball. **1986** *TV Guide* (Oct. 4) 37: There's still some lingering image, because of the early rural humor, as some sort of cornball, but the guy is sharp as a tack.

cornball *adj.* CORNY.

1948 Manone & Vandervoort *Trumpet* 38: So all the bands stunk, and a cornball band wound up getting the job. **1953** "L. Short" *Silver Rock* 77: You'd make a damn good cornball heroine. **1960** Swarthout *Where Boys Are* 170: We could not, he said, do anything in public as cornball as sing school songs. **1971** Dibner *Trouble With Heroes* 258: Heroes are cornball. Out of style, Jarv. **1989** J. Simon, in *Nat. Review* (Dec. 8) 46: Some jokes are cornball, but still funny. **1993** *New Republic* (Nov. 15) 35: There's something cornball about [Anaïs] Nin's high-priestess act.

Corn Binder *n. Trucking.* (a nickname for) a truck built by International Harvester Corporation.

1971 Tak *Truck Talk* 37: *Corn binder:* any tractor manufactured by International Harvester. **1977** *Sci. Mech. CB Gde.* 162: That Corn Binder is some rig.

cornbread *n.* **1.** *Black E.* an unsophisticated Southern black person.

1954 *Harper's Mag.* (Nov.) 36: *Corn-bread, bread:* a fellow with a Southern accent. **1974** Matthews & Amdur *My Race* 77 [ref. to 1960's]: Billy Johnson…always called Southerners "Cornbreads." He'd go around saying, "I'm not gonna let these Cornbreads push me around."

2. *Black E.* CORN, 4.

1957 H. Simmons *Corner Boy* 143: Scar was not in the mood for digging corn bread.

corncake *n.* a dollar.

1961 in Cannon *Nobody Asked* 141: You'd think we heisted a poor box instead of trying to make a few corncakes.

corncob *n.* corn whiskey.

1848 in Blair & Meine *Half Horse* 183: A gallon o' the rale corn-cob.

corncob *v.* **1.** CORNHOLE.

1975 Knoxville, TN man, age *ca*32: There've been many inmates attacked down at the jail. They call it *corncobbin'*.

2. to punish or victimize.

1979 Decker *Holdouts* 134: Sam'll corncob you. Not only that, he'll dip that cob in turpentine first.

corncobber *n.* a rustic.—used derisively.

1970 Gaddis & Long *Killer* 29: The significance of this was lost upon the overworked, morally indignant staff, which consisted mainly of local native "corncobbers," who gravitate to such work.

corncob oil *n.* corn whiskey.

1856 in *DA:* The old man had gone out to procure some "corn-cob oil" wherewith to regale his guest.

corncracker *n.* **1.a.** a poor white native of Kentucky.—usu. used derisively.

1835 A.A. Parker *Trip* 87: Those…of Kentucky, corn-crackers. **1835** in *OEDS:* There is neither wit nor meaning in the terms *Hoosier, Sucker, Corncracker,* and *Buckeye* which have become so current. **1839** Marryatt *Diary* 271: Kentucky…Corn Crackers. **1853** in *Western Folk.* VII (1948) 22: A promiscuous assemblage of suckers, hoosiers, buckeyes, corncrackers, etc. **1909** *WNID: Corn-cracker*…A native of Kentucky. **1940** in *OEDS:* I never in my life heard a Buckeye get into his voice that quiver of ecstasy that is second nature to a Corncracker when he mentions his bluegrass and his mountains and his folks.

b. a poor white native of Georgia.

1884 Hedley *Marching Through Ga.* 111 [ref. to Civil War]: Georgian and Carolina troops, "Corncrackers" and "Tar Heels," as they were known. **1908** *DN* III 302: *Cracker*…A Georgian. Sometimes called *corn-cracker.*

2. Esp. *So. Broadly*, a poor white rustic; HILLBILLY; RED-
NECK.—used derisively.

1848 in *DARE:* Amongst them big bands of corncrackers to Missoura.
1862 "E. Kirke" *Among Pine's* 231: I'll fight the d—d corn-cracker, and
his whole race, at once. **1901** King *Dog-Watches* 209: Numerous
saloons and dancehalls, overcrowded, not only with black women, but
also with the lowest "corn-crackers." **1919** J. Harris *Dizzed to a Million*
30: What are these boys from the South? Are they cotton-pickers,
corn-crackers, stump jumpers, ridge-runners or bog-leapers? **1920**
26th Engrs. 69: 600 Signal Corps recruits, "corn-crackers" from Arkansas and Missouri. **1938** *AS* XIII 22: *Corn-crackers*, the poor whites of
Florida, Georgia, Kentucky and Tennessee. **1968** in *DARE: Corn-
cracker*, a person from Delaware.

corn-cutter *n.* a sword.

1906 in A. Adams *Chisholm Trail* 208: When it was brought into camp,
no one would have the old corn cutter.

corndog *v.* CORNHOLE.

1985 "Blowdryer" *Mod. English* 72: *Corn dogged*…To be sodomized.

corned *adj.* drunk.—occ. constr. with *up*.

*1785 Grose *Vulgar Tongue: Corned.* Drunk. **1821** Waln *Hermit in
Phila.* 23: *Blue as razors*, no doubt; —*drunk as wheel-barrows*, —*fuddled*,
—and *corned*. **1827** in *JAF* LXXVI (1963) 295: I nevver sea so menny
fellers cornd in awl me born dase. **1832** *Spirit of Times* 2: So forward
comes the witness, a fat, chuffy looking man, "*a leetle corned*." **1832**
Wines 2½ *Yrs. in Navy* I 153: Many of the men were "pretty well
corned," as they call it. **1839** Marryatt *Diary* 265: When a man is
tipsy…they generally say he is *corned*. **1841** [Mercier] *Man-of-War* 5:
I…[was] pretty well *corned*. **1867** *Galaxy* (Mar. 15) 640: Hell hath no
fury like a woman *corned*. **1907** *DN* III 184: He was *corned* all right.
1912 Field *Watch Yourself* 148: I never dreamed ye wus jus corned.
1912–14 in E. O'Neill *Lost Plays* 185: Everyone on this bush-league
army seems all corned up tonight but me. **1918** Richards *War Diary*
(June 23): Steve Jocelyn and Fitz come in every night "corned." **1924**
Raine *Desert's Price* 198: Say, I got kinda corned up an' I got a hangover.
1931 Rynning *Gun Notches* 19: He'd been pretty well corned when he
took me on.

corner *n.* **1.** *Und.* a share (of loot).

1889 Barrère & Leland *Dict. Slang* I 273: *Corner*, (Thieves), a share—
generally a share in the proceeds of a robbery. **1904** *Life in Sing Sing*
48: I have to hustle pretty sharp to get my corner out of it when the bigger thieves get through. **1908** Sullivan *Crim. Slang* 4: *Bigger corner*—
Larger share of the spoils.

2. (*cap.*) *Naut.* Cape Horn.

1898 Stevenson *Cape Horn* 49: How'd you like to do this when we're
turnin' the Corner with two feet of water on deck? **1899** Hamblen
Bucko Mate 90: Captain Bramley was an old Cape Horner, and kept her
well to the westward, "so as to dodge around this infernal corner the
first chance I get." **1923** in Tomlinson *Sea Stories* 565: That we might
slip by the "corner" in record time.

corn-fed *n.* **1.** [pun on *Confed.*] **a.** a Confederate soldier or
sailor. *Joc.*

1864 Fosdick *Frank on a Gun-Boat* 118: Come, you corn-fed, march.
*ca*1864 in Allan *Lone Star Ballads* 141: But the "Corn-Fed" is proof to
all evils. **1867** Clark *Sailor's Life* 238: Jest as true as I am a corn-Fed.

b. Confederate money.

1865 Dennett *South as It Is* 232: This "corn-fed," as we used to call it,
I never had no confidence in it. **1883** Gerrish & Hutchinson *Blue &
Gray* 303: The Union troops were often supplied with a bogus issue of
"corn-fed," which they very liberally circulated whenever an opportunity allowed.

2. a country person.—used derisively.

1916 in O'Brien *Best Stories of 1916* 265: Say, ain't these corn-feds a
nice bunch?

corn-fed *adj.* **1.** plump; husky.

1796 in *OEDS:* Brown corn-fed nymphs, and strong hard-handed
beaus. **1840** *Spirit of Times* (Nov. 21) 447: She was a most beautiful
piece of woman flesh, fine corn-fed, and showed her back. **1853** C. Hill
Scenes 95: There was two fat Sals in our town, Sal Stebbins and Sal
Babit, real corn-fed gals I swow. **1891** Maitland *Slang Dict.* 77: *Corn-fed*
(Am.), stout, plump, in good condition. **1938, 1967, 1972** in *DARE*.

2. countrified; rustic and unsophisticated.

1924 Tully *Beggars of Life* 70: A guy don't get the right kind of girls in
this country. They're all corn-fed. **1929** in *OEDS*. **1944** Sturges *Miracle of Morgan's Creek* (film): I hope you weren't such a cornfed dope!
1947 Willingham *End As a Man* 165: He's a corn-fed son-of-a-

bitch…just as stupid and snotty as the day is long. **1964** Rhodes *Chosen
Few* 53: I'm what Marines refer to as a corn-fed chick. **1972** A. Kemp
Savior 68: Yes, that is it, a corn-fed accent. **1975** De Mille *Smack Man*
117: They talk a lot of the cornfed chicks into trying skag.

3. CORNY.

1933 (quot. at CORNY). **1950–52** Ulanov *Hist. Jazz* 350: *Corny:* stale,
insipid, trite, usually the worse for age; and so too "corn" (noun),
"cornfed," "cornball," and "off the cob."

cornfield meet *n.* *R.R.* a head-on collision between trains.

1931 *Writer's Digest* (May) 41: *Corn Field Meet*—Where two trains
meet head-on, both trying to use the same mainline. **1939** *Sat. Eve. Post*
(Apr. 15) 26: He didn't want any cornfield meet on the main iron. **1943**
AS XVIII 164: *Cornfield meet*. Head-on collision between two trains
using the same track. **1945** Hubbard *R.R. Ave.* 226: John was killed in
a "cornfield meet," technically known as a head-on collision. **1969** *AS*
XLIV 255.

corn-grinders *n.pl.* the teeth. *Joc.*

1844 "J. Slick" *High Life in N.Y.* 115: I grinned jest enough to show my
corn-grinders. **1859** "Skitt" *Fisher's River* 254: We've wore our corn-
grinders down to the gums.

cornhole *n.* **1.** the anus.—usu. in the context of homosexual
anal copulation.

1916–22 Cary *Sexual Vocab.* III s.v. *human body:* The Anus…ass
hole…corn hole. **1969** Corder *Slave Ship* 210: Try one of the bucks'
cornholes. **1977** Coover *Public Burning* 115: McCarthy's got such a
cactus up his cornhole. **1980** in *Nat. Lampoon* (Jan. 1981) 10: And if he
ever gets out there won't be an unviolated cornhole between here and
Philadelphia.

2. an act of anal copulation.

1970 Southern *Blue Movie* 132: How's about a *quick cornhole?*

cornhole *v.* **1.** to engage in active anal copulation with.—occ.
intrans. Also **cornhaul.**

1938 "Justinian" *Amer. Sex.* 17: *Corn-Hole.* v. U.S. 1920– for *bugger.* To
practise pederasty. Low coll. *ca*1942 in A. Hopkins *Front & Rear* 153:
They corn-holed one another. **1949** Monteleone *Crim. Slang* 59: *Cornhole* (v) To have sexual relations by the anus. **1953–55** Kantor *Andersonville* 260: They talked of corn-holing, browning and other mysteries
unknown to Floral Tebbs. **1958** Cooley *Run for Home* 278 [ref. to
*ca*1922]: I think you and your ass-hole buddy, Ioway, are corn-holin'
together. **1959** W. Burroughs *Naked Lunch* 196: Does the Man cornhole you? **1959** in *So. Folklore Qly.* XL (1976) 171: You'll be corn-
hauled if you won't! **1957–62** Higginbotham *U.S.M.C. Folklore* 21:
Quit jumping around like a corn-holed chicken. **1970** Longstreet *Nell
Kimball* 13: They horsed around a lot, with pecker pulling and talk of
cornholing and country buggery. **1972** Wurlitzer *Quake* 67: I believe
they were cornholed as well. **1983** *N.Y Review of Bks.* (Oct. 27) 52: Bar-
tley had corn-holed the Irish maid in full view of wife and child. *a*1973–
87 F.M. Davis *Livin' the Blues* 36: Anal intercourse was [called] "corn-
holing" [in Kansas, *ca*1920].

2. to defraud; victimize.

1974 Loken *Come Monday Morning* 141: If he hadn't let that slimy bastard cornhole 'im with that policy he'd be clear now. **1976** Conroy *Santini* 68: Of all the group commanders in the world, I get cornholed with
that pussy son of a bitch.

cornhusker *n.* a farmer; rustic.

*a*1904–11 Phillips *Susan Lenox* II 163: Most of the cornhuskers are
married men, too. **1955** *Disneyland* (ABC-TV): Them cornhuskers!
1973 in *DARE*.

corn juice *n.* corn whiskey; (*obs.*) whiskey.

1845 in Robb *Squatter Life* 107: He was too full of corn juice to cut
carefully. **1845** in Porter *Quarter Race in Ky.* 83: He can belt six shillins
of corn-juice at stillhouse rates and travel. **1848** Bartlett *Americanisms:
Corn-juice.* Whiskey. A Western term. *ca*1867 in G.W. Harris *Lovingood* 78: I hed got about a fox squirril skin full ove boiled co'n juice
packed onder my shut. **1871** Schele de Vere *Americanisms* 43: *Corn-
juice* is the poetical name which Western men are fond of giving to
whiskey, because it is frequently made of corn. **1884** Beard *Thorns* 23:
Turn up him snout at cawn juice. **1936** in *DA*.

corn mule *n.* (see 1942 quot.).

1929 (quot. at MULE). **1942** *ATS* 114: *corn mule*,…raw corn whisky, esp.
illicit.

corn plantations *n.pl.* the feet. *Joc.*

1902 Corrothers *Black Cat Club* 80: S'I, "Feet, he'p de body!" An' de
way I to'e up sidewalk wid ma co'n plantations an' bu'nt de air wid ma
coat-tails wuz a caution!

corn pone *n. & adj.* **1.** Southern; a rustic Southerner.

1919 *Variety* (Apr. 4) 16: His dog-gone corn pone town back home. **1964** in Gover *Trilogy* 368: Get that through you cornpone skull. **1964–66** R. Stone *Hall of Mirrors* 220: You see that, you cornpone Savonarola? **1967, 1970** in *DARE*. **1974** R. Stone *Dog Soldiers* 281: Every cornpone cop down here knows the way in. **1984** "W.T. Tyler" *Shadow Cabinet* 13: The guy's a...corn pone. **1981–86** R. Parker & R. Rashke *Capitol Hill* 92: Bobby kept saying that he'd rather lose than have that "cornponed bastard" on the ticket. **1986** *TV Guide* (Oct. 4) 38: It wasn't so much that the character was corn pone, it was that he was *so* honest and dedicated to doing right.

2. *Pol.* (see quot.).

1968 Safire *New Language* 93: *Corn pone* has come to mean "sweet talk," and gentle persuasion. Non-Southerners tend to consider it synonymous with "corny" or "cornball," cloyingly folksy, but in the South there is a more gallant political connotation.

cornpopper *n.* **1.** a large truck.

1940 Chandler *Farewell My Lovely* 47: On the highway the lights of the streaming cars made an almost solid beam in both directions. The big cornpoppers were rolling north growling as they went and festooned all over with green and yellow overhang lights.

2. a cheap car.

1972 Swarthout *Tin Lizzie* 10: You pulled good stock all the way from El Paso behind those corn poppers?

cornshucking *n. Pol.* LOG ROLLING.

1813 in Eliason *Tarheel Talk* 266: *Log rolling or corn shucking* on Capitol Hill.

corn-shucking *adj. So.* damned; COTTON-PICKING.

1835 Longstreet *Georgia Scenes* 3: Now, blast your corn-shucking soul,...come cutt'n your shines 'bout me agin, next time I come to the Courthouse, will you! **1884** Beard *Thorns* 34: Ding blast yer corn-shuckin' hide!

corn squeezings *n.* corn whiskey; CORN JUICE.

1989 T. Blackburn *Jolly Rogers* 152: A liberal ingestion of corn squeezings.

cornstalk *n.* a lanky person.

1823 J.F. Cooper *Pioneers* 251: What's that, old corn-stalk! you sapless stub!

cornstealer *n.* a hand.

1838 in A.P. Hudson *Humor of Old South* 304: My cornstealers were *nat'*rally used for other purposes. **1838** *Crockett Almanac* (1839) 35: The methodizer laid his cornstealers on a wench blacker than the ace of spades. **1835–40** in Barrère & Leland *Dict. Slang* I 273: "How is you been, my old Bullock?" and he squeezed his *corn-stealers* till the old gineral began to dance like a bear on red-hot iron. **1841** *Spirit of Times* (July 3) 211: "Give us your corn-stealer," said the Missourian, and they locked fists. **1845** in Eliason *Tarheel Talk* 266: Hoping the time is not far distant when I shall have the exquisit pleasure of shaking your corn stealer. **1876** J.M. Reid *Old Settlers* 143: You old hoss thief,...give me a shake of your corn-stealer.

corn up *v.* to get drunk.

1899 Cullen *Tales* 88: It got so that every time I corned up I just longed to get on a train and ride to the middle of the country.

corn willy *n.* see WILLY.

corny *adj.* extremely trite or sentimental; hackneyed. Also quasi-adv.

1932 in *OEDS*. **1933** *Fortune* (Aug.) 46: *Cornfed* or *corny* is the jazz musician's term for what is old-fashioned. **1937** *New Yorker* (Apr. 17) 27: Those not up on current idioms are *corny, on the cob,* or...*icky.* **1937** *AS* 46: *Corny.* Playing...in an outmoded style. **1938** O'Hara *Hope of Heaven* 21: "I imagine it's...Utopian. I don't mean Utopian Sinclair Utopian." "Oooh!...And you talk about corny!" **1939** Goodman & Kolodin *Swing* 94: We were just kidding around, playing "St. Louis Blues" corny. **1940** O'Hara *Pal Joey* 70: Sousa had this big corny band. **1941** Cain *Mildred Pierce* 240: "What's banality, sir?" "I mean it sounds corny. Cheap...Play it an octave higher and put a couple of trills in it, it would be 'Listen to the Mocking Bird' almost before you knew it." **1941** Schulberg *Sammy* 89: The supervisor keeps throwing out [script ideas] but the producer plays tough. All he says is *corny, stinks,* or *1902.* **1942** Chandler *High Window* 334: I love my wife...A corny touch, but it's true. **1942** Liebling *Telephone* 174: "Corny" is a cultural term meaning crude, obvious, and the antithesis of what Noel Coward would do in a given situation. **1945** Drake & Cayton *Black Metropolis* 370: Nothing is too "corny" or sentimental to "pull" on the electorate. **1950** F.

Brown *Space* 76: You needn't even tell me you wouldn't have me if I was the last man on Earth; it would be corny under the circumstances. **1951** *Amer. Journ. Socio.* 37:141: That's why I don't mind playing corny too much...I guess I'm kind of a ham. **1958** Drury *Advise and Consent* 280: "I know it sounds kind of corny." "Just corny enough to be true." **1959** Morrill *Dark Sea Running* 78: He's cornier than a hog full of succotash. **1963** D. Tracy *Brass Ring* 13: The jokes were dopey, the slang corny. **1965** Karp *Doobie Doo* 131: You *could* say it's a mite corny if you went and declared undying love to each and t'other. **1973** J.E. Martin *95 File* 118: That's when I woke up, in prison. I found Jesus there—or he found me. Isn't that corny? **1983** *Hour Magazine* (ABC-TV) (Apr. 21): I don't mean to sound corny, but those are my feelings. I love life and I love my children and I love my husband. **1993** *New Yorker* (Jan. 11) 64: "Macbeth"...was corny. It was nothing like as good as "The Wizard of Oz." **1993** *N.Y. Times Mag.* (July 25) 26: This is a man...so corny that he proposed to his current wife at Disney World.

corp *n. Army.* a corporal.

1862 in Jackman *Diary* 15: The "corp" let the water-hunters through. **1863** in C.H. Moulton *Ft. Lyon* 117: One of our corp's did fire at one. **1883** G.H. Holliday *On Plains* 37: All right, corp., what's up? **1887** Peck *Pvt. Peck* 136 [ref. to Civil War]: Hello, Corp. **1909** *Century Dict. Supp.* **1920** *Amer. Leg. Wkly.* (Jan. 23) 33: Hey, fellows, here's the old corp. **1921** Dos Passos *Three Soldiers* 61: "Ole Corp. looks sort o' sick himself," said Fuselli. **1944** H. Brown *Walk in the Sun* 130: Say, Corp, do you think I'll make Pfc. by the Battle of Tibet? **1989** (quot. at JODY).

corporal *n.* the penis.

[**1916–22** Cary *Sexual Vocab.* I: *Corporal love.* The penis.] **1974** Lahr *Trot* 209: They've got a knife in one hand and their corporal in the other...At my age, rape would be the last straw.

corporation *n.* a paunch.

1823 in Spectorsky *College Years* 59: To display the Chest, draw in the Corporation, draw the Chin in perpendicular to the Chest.... **1842** *Spirit of Times* (Aug. 6) 270. **1852* in J. Farmer *Musa Pedestris* 150: But Peg had sich a corporation,/He dropp'd her like a red hot brick. **1856** in *Civil War History* X (1964) 299: His sword belt...surrounded his immense "corporation." **1921** Schauble *First Bn.* 63: "Squad" McKinney, formerly a commercial clerk, lost his "corporation." **1933** in Clarke *Amer. Negro Stories* 67: He ain't puzzlegutted, honey. He jes' got a corperation. **1967–69** in *DARE*.

corporosity *n.* **1.** (one's) body or health. *Joc.*

1838 *Crockett Almanac* (1839) 35: He coodent get her whole corporosity under no how he could fix it. **1838** Neal *Charc. Sks.* 100: Should he, however, chance to trip...his "corporosity" touches the ground with his hands in vain attempt to reach. **1843** in Eliason *Tarheel Talk* 266: How does your corporosity seem to sagaticate. I will now conversate a little upon the proximorities of nonsense. **1891** Maitland *Slang Dict.* 77: *Corporosity* (Am.), supposed to have some reference to the human form. "How does your corporosity sagaciate?" is a supposedly comic inquiry after one's health. **1916** in Botkin *Treas. Amer. Folk.* 663: How is yer copperosity segashuatin, Brer Coon? **1945, 1950, 1960, 1979** in *DARE*.

2. a paunch; CORPORATION.

1890 Crook *Autobiog.* 27: His corporosity shook like a bag of jelly.

corpse *n. Mil.* corps. *Joc.*

*1838 Glascock *Land Sharks* II 24: The [marine] corps are invariably called the *corpse* by the foremast men. **1924** Nason *3 Lights* 190 [ref. to WWI]: Air corpse. **1941** Kendall *Army & Navy Slang* 4: The corpse...affectionate term for the corps. **1943** *Yank* (May 14) 18: I'm a ole Signal Corpse man. **1959** Groninger *Run from Mt.* 21: The big baby is the headquarters building...where Corpse is. *Ibid.* 25: Corpse MP's?

corpse *v.* to kill. *Rare* in U.S.

*a*1881 G.C. Harding *Misc. Writings* 224: Telescopic rifles, with which a man might be "corpsed" at a greater distance than he could be distinguished with the naked eye. **1884* in *F & H* II 187: To *corpse*...is one of many customary and coarse ways of menacing the infliction of death. It is horribly familiar in London. **1887* in *Ibid.*: And is he thunderingly well corpsed? **1956** Neider *Hendry Jones* 17: I jammed the gun away, wondering if they would corpse me now.

corpse-cutter *n. Med.* a forensic surgeon.

1983 S. King *Christine* 329: Let's hit them so fucking hard the corpse-cutter down at city hospital will have to pull the paint-chips out of their carcasses with pliers.

corpse-reviver *n.* a strong drink, esp. taken for a hangover.

1865 Sala *Diary* II 313: Mint juleps, egg noggs, cobblers, smashes,

Windsor-coolers,...corpse revivers, [etc.]. **1871** in *OEDS*. **1877** [quot. at FLY POISON].

corral *v.* to seize; secure. Now *colloq.*
    1860 in *OED2*: I want to "corel" [*sic*] you for a little chat. **1862** in S. Clemens *Twain's Letters* I 203: Raish is a great manager, and must be "corraled" [*sic*] into this arrangement. **1867** A.D. Richardson *Beyond Miss.* 134 [ref. to Mo., 1858]: "I have him in my power." "I have him *corraled*" [*sic*]...bore exactly the same signification. **1877** in J.M. Carroll *Camp Talk* 90: As I have but a few hours for sleep—I must corral them. **1885** S.S. Hall *Gold Buttons* 3: A number of them would...order Fresh Frank to "set 'em up" and..."corral" each a pair of bottles besides. **1945** Gerraghty & Frank *Whiplash* (film): You remember that gal you took a shellackin' over? Did you ever corral her?

corroded *adj.* very drunk.
    1986 *Knoxville* (Tenn.) *Journal* C1: *Corroded:* Drunk.

corset *n.* a bullet-proof vest; (*Mil.*) a flak jacket. *Joc.*
    1933 Ersine *Pris. Slang* 29: *Corset, n.* A bullet-proof vest. **1939** in Galewitz *Great Comics* 165: We'll put on the old bullet-proof "corsets," Pat. **1959** Webb *Pork Chop* (film): I feel like a packhorse with all this gear— this bullet-proof corset.

cosh *n.* a bludgeon.
    1869** in *OEDS*: The coshman (a man who carries a "cosh" or life preserver). **a1889** in Barrère & Leland *Dict. Slang*: The officer sought to give the finishing *coup de grâce* with his cosh. ***1925** in Fraser & Gibbons *Soldier & Sailor Wds.* 64 [ref. to WWI]: *Cosh*, the bludgeon carried by night patrols men and trench raiders. **1950** in *DAS*: He might first have been hit on the head with a cosh. **1989** *Harper's* (June) 53: And the sun like a cosh in their eyes.

cosh *v.* to bludgeon. *Rare* in U.S.
    ***1889** in *OEDS*. ***1896** in *OEDS*: With a sudden blow behind the head, the stranger was happily coshed. **1931–34** in Clemmer *Pris. Comm.* 331: *Coshed*...To be knocked out, especially by a blow on the head.

cosmic *adj.* of profound and surpassing excellence; (*also*) exciting wonder.
    1935 H. Gray *Arf* (unp.): It's prodigious—world-wide appeal—why, it's *cosmic!* Absolutely *cosmic!* Call it "Cosmic Curse"—what a title! [**1945** M. Miller *Joe Louis* 155 [Lou] Nova's insistence that through...Yoga...he had developed a "cosmic" punch...had gained headlines [in 1941].] **1972** in L. Bangs *Psychotic Reactions* 112: Ain't nothin' cosmic anymore. **1976–77** McFadden *Serial* 107: She said she needed a good rap, too, and it was cosmic of Kate to flash on it like that. **1986** Univ. Tenn. student: It's *cosmic*, man! **1986** Eble *Campus Slang* (Mar.) 3: *Cosmic*—very good, terrific: "My date last night was cosmic." *a***1990** R. Herman, Jr. *Force of Eagles* 65: One of the most cosmic jets...twenty-nine million dollars a copy. *Ibid.* 181: The APQ-146 radar in the F-111F is cosmic.

cosmoline or **cosmolene** *adj.* [see 1928 quot.] *Army.* being or belonging to a coast artillery unit; (*hence, n.*) a coast artilleryman.
    1925 Nason *Three Lights* 15 [ref. to 1918]: If you really want to see some fine shootin' all over the lot, you want to watch some o' them cosmoline anti-aircraft outfits. **1926** *Marine Corps Gazette* (Dec.) 241: Yuh were a cosmolene humbree when I knew yuh last. **1928** *Our Army* (Dec.) 28: A Cosmolene and Doughboy/Are sent here to inspect. **1928** in *Papers of Mich. Acad.* 286 [ref. to 1918]: *Cosmolene soldiers*, heavy artillery, so called from the oil used on the guns. **1929** *Our Army* (Dec.) 25: *Cosmoline Gang:* A derisive name for the Coast Artillery, also called "cosmoline slingers," because their big guns are kept constantly coated with a heavy oil or grease called cosmoline as protection against rust and weather. **1941** *AS* (Oct.) 164: *Cosmolines*. Artillery.

cot *n.* an apricot.
    1921 *DN* V 109: *Cot*...Apricot. **1966, 1967, 1968** in *DARE*.

cotics *n.pl. Und.* narcotics.
    1942 *ATS* 473. **1953** Anslinger & Tompkins *Traf. in Narc.* 307: *Cotics.* Narcotics. **1970** M. Thomas *Total Beast* 42: They'd have to need a man bad to keep him here if he had 'cotics on his record.

cot jockey *n. Army.* one who enjoys sleeping while others work; SACK ARTIST.
    1919 J. Harris *Dizzed* 48 [ref. to 1918]: We had some birds whose only fatigue consisted of doing bunk fatigue. This is easy to learn and once learned hard to forget. The real genuine Cot Jockey started at Seagirt when he was inoculated. He took a high dive, was carried to his cot and finding it easier to ride the cot than drill he cultivated the acquaintanceship...we wish we were able to print the names of our cot jockeys—look

over the Battery roster—the list is the same.

cotton *n.* ¶ In phrases:
    ¶ **have had the cotton** to be doomed.
    1971 Sheehan *Arnheiter* 220: You've bought it, you bastard...you've had the cotton. They finally caught up with you.
    ¶ **in tall cotton** *So.* in an easeful or advantageous situation. Also vars.
    1949 Bartlett & Lay *12 O'Clock High!* (film): Just livin' in the tall cotton, sir. **1968** in B.E. Holley *Vietnam* 76: We are in hog heaven....We will all be sleeping in high cotton tonight! **1977** Bunker *Animal Factory* 119: I shit in tall cotton the whole four years. Vegas, Acapulco, Miami, the whole tamale. **1978** Alibrandi *Killshot* 190: By the time they hit Ann Arbor, Coldiron was up to his ass in cotton. **1983** Curry *River's in My Blood* 256: They thought they were up in high cotton, but pilots was gettin' $315.
    ¶ **spit cotton** to be very thirsty.
    1825 in *OEDS*: We'll see who spits cotton first. **1866** in *DA*: To *spit cotton* is, I think, American. **1887** J.W. Nichols *Hear My Horn* 28: It was a hot day and som[e] of the men already spitting cotton. **1899** F.E. Daniel *Rebel Surgeon* 140: I was nearly famished for water. I was "spittin' cotton." **1920** in Randolph *Church House* 70: For God's sake, take me somewhere I can buy a drink, as I am spitting cotton all day and I got to stay here while they are fixing my buggy. **1928** Harlow *Sailor* 41: I was "spitting cotton" just the same.
    ¶ **up to picking cotton** *So.* drunk.
    1813–18 Weems *Drunk. Look. Glass* 60: Boozy—groggy—blue...*up to picking cotton* [Georgia].

cotton-chopper *n.* a rural Southerner.—used derisively.
    1970 *FBI* (ABC-TV): Why, you thick-headed cotton-chopper! Just how far do you think you'd get on that job without me?

cotton-eyed *adj. So.* (see 1905 quot.).
    1905 *DN* III 75: *Cotton-eyed*...Having the whites of the eyes prominent. **1952** Steinbeck *E. of Eden* 228: The crooked little cotton-eyed piano player stood in the entrance.

cotton freak *n. Pris.* a person addicted to the use of amphetamine-saturated cotton, as removed from nasal inhalers.
    1966 Braly *On Yard* 63: He was Big Dad to all cotton freaks.

cottonhead *n.* a dull-witted person. Hence **cotton-headed,** *adj.*
    1937 E. Anderson *Thieves Like Us* 10: Come on, you cotton-headed old soldier! **1958** Johnson *Henry Orient* 46: To Val I was something, anyway, if only a cotton-head. **1968** Poe *Riot* (film): You dumb cottonhead loudmouth punks.

cotton-jammer *n. Naut.* a vessel engaged in the cotton trade.
    1909 *Independent* (July 8) 76: All these originated in the old Cotton Jammers, which were so famous just before the Civil War.

cotton-knocker *n.* [perh. euphem. for COCK KNOCKER] a contemptible fellow.
    1946 G.C. Hall, Jr. *1000 Destroyed* 362: "There, you cotton-knocker," growled Glover.

cottonmouth *n.* dryness of the mouth, esp. accompanying a hangover.
    1978 Maupin *Tales* 112: Michael woke with cottonmouth. **1985** Heywood *Taxi Dancer* 25: And he'd been thirsty all the time with an endless case of cottonmouth. **1986** Univ. Tenn. instructor: I remember one guy [in early 1972] saying, "I got the cottonmouth so bad I'm spitting up socks."

cottonpicker *n.* **1.** *So.* a contemptible fellow. Often *Joc.*
    1919 J. Harris *Dizzed* 30: What are these boys from the South? Are they cotton-pickers, corn-crackers, stump jumpers, ridge-runners or bog-leapers? **1937** Coolidge *Texas Cowboys* 15: Eastern Texas, according to the punchers, is given over to cotton and corn; and their favorite term of reproach is to call a man a cotton-picker. **1959** Montgomery & Heiman *Jet Nav.* 47: The cotton pickers have got it down to a science. **1962** Harvey *Strike Command* 93: That cotton picker would sure have been delayed if he *hadn't* hit the drogue. **1976** Whelton *CB Baby* 14: You follow that cotton-picker...northbound.
    2. a black person.—used contemptuously.
    1930 G. Williams *Logger-Talk* 15: *Cotton-picker.* A negro. **1938** Smitter *Detroit* 110: A lot of good mechanics got laid off when that bunch of cotton-pickers went to work on that line. **1973** graffito, NYC: Niggers Cotton-pickers spearchuckers Jungle Bunnies.
    3. *pl.* the hands.

1966, 1969 in *DARE*. **1976** *N.Y. Post* (July 6) 33: Keep his cotton-pickers off that island.

cotton-picking *adj. & adv.* Orig. *So.* confounded; damned.

1952 *Looney Tunes* (animation): Get your cotton-pickin' hooks offa me! **1953** in Algren *Lonesome Monsters* 154: Lousy cotton-pickin' fog! **1954** *I Love Lucy* (CBS-TV): Now you got arrested. Ain't that the cotton-pickin' end? **1959** Cochrell *Barren Beaches* 139 [ref. to WWII]: You're a cotton-pickin' liar. **1962** Dougherty *Commissioner* 148: You lost your cotton-pickin' mind? **1963** Breen *PT 109* (film): It's not you, sir. It's that cotton-pickin' enlisted man. **1968** J.P. Miller *Race for Home* 231 [ref. to *ca*1930]: "Laddy Buck!" Mr. Burns roared. "Git your cotton-picking little ass out here, God damn you, where we can see you, see the whites of your eyes!" **1966–70** in *DARE*: I was so cotton-picking mad! **1971** NYC bus rider: Two-fifty! Are they out of their cotton-pickin' minds? **1979** *Business Week* (May 7) 82: Anyone who is less than guarded on China is out of his cotton-picking mind. **1982** Knoxville, TN man, age *ca*40: Now they've given me some tickets and I deserved every cotton-pickin' one of them. **1992** O. Kelly *Brave Men* 196: That's the wrong cotton-pickin' signal.

cottontail *n.* an attractive young woman; BUNNY, 3.

1962 in B. Jackson *In the Life* 160: I was in high school and I got strung out behind some old cottontail, you know. **1966** NYC high-school student: She's a good-lookin' little cottontail. **1978** Lieberman & Rhodes *CB* (ed. 2) 296: Cottontail—Female hitchhiker.

cottontop *n.* a person having white or very light blond hair.

1921 *DN* V 160: Cotton-top, n. A white-haired man. **1930, 1935, 1960** in *DARE*. **1963** G. Abbott *Mr. Abbott* 27 [ref. to *ca*1905]: I had blondish, dishwater-colored hair, white on top where the son [*sic*] had bleached it; sometimes I was called Cottontop.

cottonwood *n.* ¶ In phrase: **have the cottonwood on** to *have the deadwood on* s.v. DEADWOOD.

1888 in Farmer *Amer.*: I jess reckoned she was blowin' around, an' yere she had de cottonwood on me all de time!

couch *v.* to lounge on a couch while watching television, esp. for a long period.

1987 Coors beer TV ad: So get ready to couch—like you've *never* couched before! **1990** *CBS This Morning* (Jan. 2) (CBS-TV): Who says couching can't be *chic*?

couch case *n.* a person in need of psychiatric treatment.

1969 *Current Slang* I & II 22: Couch case…A psychotic.—College males, California. **1971** Dahlskog *Dict.* 16: Couch case, n. An emotionally disturbed or psychoneurotic person.

couch checkers *n.pl.* lovemaking on a couch. *Joc.*

1966 Shepard *Doom Pussy* 55: What sports do you like? Couch checkers?

couch cootie *n.* LOUNGE-LIZARD.

1918 *Vanity Fair* (July) 43: Exterminating the Couch Cootie. Languid Lawrence and Lads of His Type Have Seen the Awful Writing on the Wall. **1922** *Bomb* (Iowa State Coll.) 418: Leisurely, loafing, lusty lounge lizards; coy, captivating, crusty couch cooties—that's us.

couch pirate *n.* a bedbug. *Joc.*

1872 Marcy *Border Reminiscences* 70: But if there was one thing that was more repulsive to him than all others, it was a bedbug…and if by chance one of these "couch-pirates" ever invaded his dormitory, it disturbed his slumbers for a good while.

couch potato *n. Trademark.* an indolent person whose leisure time is chiefly spent watching television. Also as v., to act as a couch potato. ["The US trade mark registration for the term…claims that it was first used on 15 July 1976"— *Oxford Dict. New Words*; it gained nationwide currency 1985–86.]

1980 in Safire *Coming to Terms* 47: The Doo Dah Parade…[featured] the All-City Waitress Band and the World-Famous Couch Potatoes. **1982** *The Tuber's Voice: The Couch Potato Newsletter* (title). **1982** Armstrong & Mingo *Dr. Spudd's Etiquette for the Couch Potato* (title). **1983** Mingo & Armstrong *Couch Potato* 64: Tom Iacino [of Pasadena, Calif.] coined the term "couch potato." It was shortly adopted as the name of their organization. *Ibid.* 67: Then, in 1979, the Couch Potatoes surfaced in Pasadena's famous Doo Dah Parade. **1985** *Nat. Lampoon* (Sept.) 83: The Couch Potatoes. **1986** *Daily Beacon* (Univ. Tenn.) (Apr. 16) 7: Great! Just what I need…A patch of couch potatoes! **1988** *Newsweek* (Feb. 8) 60: Couch potatoes: off your duffs. **1990** *Newsweek* (Oct. 15) 65: Mike Doonesbury, America's first couch potato. **1992** D. Mar-

lette *Kudzu* (synd. cartoon strip) (Mar. 19): Cuomo *couch-potatos* it, avoiding media scrutiny.

cougar den *n. Logging.* (see quot.). *Joc.*

1956 Sorden & Ebert *Logger's Wds.* 10 [ref. to *a*1925]: *Cougar-den*, A term used for the bunkhouse of a logging camp.

cougar milk *n.* strong liquor. *Joc.* Cf. PANTHER PISS.

1937 Parsons *Lafayette Escadrille* 90: Bill was constantly on the jump, squaring us with the brass hats; setttling squabbles among the boys resulting from strained nerves or too much cougar milk. **1958** McCulloch *Woods Wds.* 39: *Cougar milk*—Any kind of stout home brew or other raw liquor.

cough *v.* **1.** *Und.* to inform or confess; SQUEAL.

1899 A.H. Lewis *Sandburrs* 81: While dey gets d' collar, not one of 'em coughs on me, an' me name ain't never in it from start to finish. **1901** Willard *World of Graft* 102: They put him in the sweat-box, made him cough, an' you know the rest. **1917** *Editor* (Feb. 24) 152: *Cough*…to give information to the police. **1921** Casey & Casey *Gay-Cat* 89: Now try to cough on Scar-face! **1962, *1970* in *OEDS*.

2. to pay or hand over money. Also trans. See also COUGH UP, 1.

1898–1900 Cullen *Chances* 128: The bookies…had to cough. **1901** Ade *Modern Fables* 28: He…said that inasmuch as 95 per cent of the Voters had Declared for him, he did not see the Necessity of Coughing so Frequently. **1902** Cullen *More Tales* 99: Its eight bones youse'll cough on de spot. **1904** Hobart *Jim Hickey* 16: Buy, and the gang is with you…Proceed to cough.

coughing tack *n.* COFFIN TACK.

1973 Jackson *Fall Out* 87 [ref. to 1918]: He did not intend to be without "coughing tacks" in France.

cough medicine *n.* whiskey. Also **cough syrup**. *Joc.*

1910 *Adventure* (Nov.) 162: The chief source of Henry's pull with the screws is "cough medicine"…*booze*. **1919** Small *Story of 47th* 128: Everybody invests in a little "cough medicine." *Ibid.* 128: No more "cough syrup."

cough up *v.* **1.** (esp. of money) to produce, provide, or hand over; to pay. Also intrans.

1890 in F. Remington *Sel. Letters* 92: I will be glad to "cough up" the dues. **1894** in *DA*: Cough up a nickel, read the paper, and get the latest of camp doings. **1895** *DN* I 415: Cough up. v. phr. to produce, as of money. "I *coughed up* a V." **1895** *Harper's* (Sept.) 622: I want you to cough up a hundred. **1895** Townsend *Fadden* 60: I coughs up me fiver. **1900** Willard & Hodler *Powers* 15: If you don't cough up, Jim, I'll put a dead-line around this whole town. **1902** Cullen *More Tales* 53: Coughing up $150 for the rent of the op'ry house. **1906** London *Moon-Face* 49: "Better cough up, eh?"…"Make it cash." *a*1904–11 Phillips *Susan Lenox* II 157: That makes him cough up. **1918** Stringer *House of Intrigue* 298: Then who'd you s'pose coughed up for all that convent life of yours? **1927** Rollins *Jinglebob* 63: Where's them three extry bottles?…Cough 'em up. **1949** *Time* (Nov. 21) 27: He fumbled when the airport bus driver asked for the $1.25 fare until a kindly passenger coughed up. **1983** Breathed *Bloom Co.* 32: Just cough up some dough, Mac! **1983** Beckwith & Knox *Delta Force* 188: Occasionally the army coughed up a small prop aircraft, but a T-39 was more expensive than flying a commercial airline. **1991** Sachar *Let Lady Teach* 16: Cough up every dollar you got.

2. to tell or divulge; (*intrans.*) to speak frankly; in phr. **cough up (one's) guts** to confess or divulge all one knows, esp. under questioning. [*OED* demonstrates similar use of the phr. in ME, but no continuity of usage is evident between *ca*1485 and 1896; mod. use seems to stem from **(1)**, above.]

1896 Ade *Artie* 56: Miller, you're the only man that I'd tell some things to, and I cough up to you because I know that you're a good fellow. **1899–1900** Cullen *Tales* 194: He never coughed up anything about himself, however. *Ibid.* 201: Don't cough up who put you next to this scheme. **1912** Furlong *Detective* 171: The St. Louis officers…used every art known to them to make the prisoner "cough up." **1930** Lait *On the Spot* 112: We nailed one of Goldie's outfit last night, and he coughed up his guts. **1937** Johnston *Prison Life* 33: The lousy skunk is always coughin' up his guts. Somebody better put him wise or…he'll queer the whole gang. **1957** Atwell *Private* 40: He was a high-ranking officer, and he coughed up his guts. He said they knew they were licked. **1958** Johnson *Henry Orient* 54: Come on, Val…Cough it up. What is it? **1961** Sullivan *Shortest, Gladdest Years* 290: So cough up, f'crissake. Whatsa story?

count *n.* ¶ In phrases:

¶ **down for the count** [sugg. by the boxing phr.] nearly or utterly defeated; dead. Also vars.

1908 in H.C. Fisher *A. Mutt* 22: Kid Cupid Had Mutt Down For The Count Again, But He Stalled The Round Out. **1911** A.H. Lewis *Apaches of N.Y.* 148: I'll put him down in Bellevue for the count! **1929–33** J.T. Farrell *Manhood* 233: Death is a funny thing…You never think about it until it puts your best friend out for the count. **1973** Boyd & Harris *Baseball Card* 18: Polio is down for the eight count. **1975** S.P. Smith *Amer. Boys* 100: He had this big board with razors stuck in the end of it and bip! he hit Johnny Law right in the neck…The pudgy white chump looked like he was down for the big count.

¶ **take the count** [sugg. by the boxing phr.] to die or be vanquished.

1904 Hobart *Jim Hickey* 98: You're not going to take the count, don't worry! **1908** in H.C. Fisher *A. Mutt* 22: A. Mutt almost took the count this morn. **1914** Ellis *Billy Sunday* 185: Give [the devil] the Word of God and he will take the count mighty quick. **1931** Rynning *Gun Notches* 8: I never did get the right of how many of the Dodge men took the long count, but the casualties included quite a bunch of officers and tin-horns.

count *v.* ¶ In phrase: **count ties** *Hobo.* to tramp along a railroad track.

1885 *Puck* (Mar. 11) 22: With weeping eyes I count the ties,/And swear I'll no more roam. **1891** Maitland *Slang Dict.* 78: *Counting ties* (Am.);…Tramps and others compelled to walk for lack of railroad fare speak of having "taken a contract to count ties," which is done one at a time. **ca1909** in Kornbluh *Rebel Voices* 73: He's counting the ties with his bed on his back,/Or else he is bumming a ride. **1912** *DN* III 573. **1927** *AS* II (June) 385: *Counting ties* and *beating trains*, now well-known phrases, probably originated in the days of the young railroads.

counter *n.* *Naut.* the buttocks. Also pl.

1846 Codman *Sailors' Life* 167: Her counters was rounded off, just enough to be handsome. **1855** Wise *Tales for Marines* 45: By jingo! such a full, rounded counter the witch had, and such a mass of brown tresses twisted around her elegantly formed head, over two roguish eyes and a rosy mouth. **1872** (quot. at HULL). **a1900** in Shay & Wilson *Amer. Sea Songs* 40: Blow the Man Down…She was round in the counter and bluff in the bow. **1942–48** in *So. Folk. Qly.* XIII (1949) 204: The physical description of one's dream girl may be accompanied by the phrase *she's bluff in the counter.*

counter-hopper *n.* a sales clerk.

1845 in *DARE*: The ardent apprentice and the constant counter-hopper indite their amatory lays. **1851** [Byrn] *Ark. Doctor* 24: I could never flourish…as a "counter hopper." **1858** Pollard *Diamonds* 57: The counter-hoppers and fast young gents…for whom they pimp. **1865** Springer *Sioux Country* 24: What would some of those…counterhoppers think if they had to crawl into our dog-houses in such weather? **1887** DeVol *Gambler* 221: You look like a nice, smart counter-hopper. **1911** H.B. Wright *Barbara Worth* 214: Ye danged counter-hopper. **1935** J. Conroy *World to Win* 161: Clerks and counter hoppers.

counter-jumper *n.* a sales clerk. Hence **counter-jumping**, *adj.*

1829 in *OEDS*: In the conceited towns he is held in abhorrence by the *clerk* and *counter-jumper.* **1849** Melville *White Jacket* 228: You counter-jumping son of a gun. *1855 in *F & H* II 190: It seems free enough to every counter-jumper in the town. *1860, *1864, *1876 in *Ibid.* **1859** Bartlett *Amer.* (ed. 2): *Counter-jumper.* A clerk in a retail "store," whose place is behind a counter. **1860** Victor *Alice Wylde* 54: Alice will never be the wife of that counter-jumper. **1899** Green *Va. Folk-Speech*: *Counter-jumper*…A salesman in a dry goods store. **1935** S. Lewis *Can't Happen* 197: Just a plain hired man, another counter-jumper in the Marked-down Classics Goods Department. **1975** McCaig *Danger Trail* 174: You little counterjumper, you're lying to me. **1980** Hogan *Lawman's Choice* 43: Him and the rest of the counter-jumpers in this town.

counter-snatcher *n.* *Police.* a shoplifter.

1915–16 Lait *Beef, Iron & Wine* 163: I was the son of a tough boxcracker an' a whiskey-drinkin' counter-snatcher.

country *n.* **1.** (used derisively in direct address to a countryman).

1834 Caruthers *Kentuck. in N.Y.* I 32: One of 'em popped his head out of the window, and says to me as they went by, "Country," says he, "there's something on your horse's tail." **1884** Blanding *Sailor Boy* 32 [ref. to Civil War]: Go in, Country. **1892** Bunner *Zadoc Pine* 159: Hi,

country. Where are you?

2. *Navy.* a specified area in a large ship.—used in combinations.

[**1832** Wines *Two Years and a Half in the Navy*, I, 25 [ref. to 1829]: The open space between the steerage and the mess rooms is familiarly called the "country."] **a1899** B.F. Sands *Reefer* 135 [ref. to 1842]: In the wardroom "country" some of the officers sat round the mess-table reading, writing or playing chess. **1919** Fiske *Midshipman* 164 [ref. to 1891]: My bureau stood in the wardroom "country" outside my door. **1951** Thacher *Captain* 7 [ref. to WWII]: What are you doing in officers' country, Rinehart? **1956** Wier & Hickey *Navy Wife* 103: J.O. Country. The area in a ship where junior officers live and eat—found only in large ships. **1958** Cooley *Run for Home* 22 [ref. to 1920's]: This was "officer's country," where only the exalted were at home. **1960** Bonham *Burma Rifles* 66 [ref. to WWII]: A sign beside the ladder read: Officers' Country. **1966** Noel & Bush *Naval Terms* 106: *Country:* Definite area of ship such as admiral's country, wardroom country, chief's country. Rarely used alone. **1967** Lockwood *Subs* 18 [ref. to 1912]: We were a proud lot of 13 ensigns…who were quartered in her Junior Officers' Country…we J.O.'s disliked him heartily. **1968** W. Crawford *Gresham's War* 32: Officer's country is full of houndfaces and pilots. **1980** S. Fuller *Big Red* 10: What do you hear in officer's country, Demps?

country way *n.* *Craps.* the combination of 3 and 4 on the dice.

1961 in Himes *Black on Black* 103: Seven!…four-trey, the country way.

county hotel *n.* a county jail. *Joc.*

1965–70 in *DARE*. **1971** Simon *Sign of Fool* 84: Tattoo had indeed spent the night in the "county hotel."

county mountie *n.* a county sheriff or police officer.

1975 *Nat. Lampoon* (Nov.) 52: We gotta county mounty up ahead checkin' out a hippie van. **1976** Whelton *CB Baby* 95: That County Mounty…is one bad Bear. **1976** Cookin' Good Chicken ad (WINS radio): I'm what they call a county mountie. **1976** Univ. Tenn. student: A county mountie is a local trooper. **1980** Eble *Campus Slang* (Mar.) 2: *County-mounty*—sheriff [sic]. **1985** D. Killerman *Hellrider* 127: The town [was] crammed full of Smokies, county mounties, and local heat. **1988** Norst *Colors* 25: Except the county mountie. **1991** "R. Brown" & R. Angus *A.K.A. Narc* 167: Remember that county mountie that chased you near Nogales?

coupling pin *n.* the penis. *Joc.*

1916 Cary *Venery* I 54: *Coupling Pin*—The penis.

course *n.* ¶ In phrase: **have had the course** *Mil.* to have suffered greatly; be done for.

1955 L. Shapiro *6th of June* 255 [ref. to 1944]: The marine…dealt him two crushing punches to the face and a third to the side of the head…The gunner went down…."Think he's had the course?" "Yep." **1959** H. Ellison *Gentleman Junkie* 204: Derry Maylor had had the course. **1962** Tregaskis *Vietnam Diary* 27: His father…was, with the 11th Marines on Guadalcanal and "had the course" of malaria, dengue, [etc.]. **1962** Harvey *Strike Command* 93: I thought old dad had had the course…I thought we'd blown up. **1963** Doulis *Path* 143: 'Cause if you ain't got mental alertness, you've had the course.

court *n.* ¶ In phrase: **hold court in the street** *Und.* (of a fugitive) to engage in a gun battle to the death rather than be sent to prison.

1966 Elli *Riot* 110: I'm not goin' the pistol route. I doubt if I could hold court in the street. **1971** *Adam-12* (NBC-TV): Not this time cop! I'm holdin' court right here in the street. **1972** Bunker *No Beast* 83: If you're gonna get busted, hold fuckin' court right on the street. **1973** *CBS Eve. News* (CBS-TV) (Aug. 31): He's gonna hold court right there in the street 'cause he's got nothin' to lose.

cousin *n.* **1.** friend.—used in direct address to a man.

1876 *Harper's Mo.* (Dec.) 21: "That's so, cousin!" exclaims a grim old Californian adventurer. **1947** *ATS* (Supp.) 9: What's buzzin, cousin? **1964–66** R. Stone *Hall of Mirrors* 87: Steady, cousin…You must not be up to a day's honest work yet.

2.a. *Baseball.* a pitcher who is habitually ineffective against a particular batter or batters.

1928 Ruth *Ruth's Own Bk.* 299. **1929** *N.Y. Times* (June 2) IV 2: A pitcher easy to hit is termed a "cousin," the expression that such-and-such a pitcher is "my cousin" being a common one. **1946** *N.Y. Times Mag.* (July 14) 18: *Cousin:* easy pitcher for some batters. **1980** Pearl *Slang Dict.: Cousin n.* (Baseball) a pitcher whose pitches are so easy to hit that one assumes him to be the batter's cousin.

b. *Boxing.* an easily defeated opponent; pushover.
1958 Heinz *Professional* 95: I get him…guys that he can learn on, but no cousins.

Cousin Jack *n. West. Mining.* a Cornish miner; Cornishman.
1899 Norris *McTeague* 326: "Are you a 'cousin Jack'?"…This prejudice against Cornishmen he remembered, too. **1925–26** Black *You Can't Win* 185: The mines were worked by Irishmen and "Cousin Jacks" (Cornishmen). **1926** *AS* (Nov.) 88: The only foreign element [in the coal country] being usually "Cousin Jacks" from the coal mines of Cornwall. **1930** "D. Stiff" *Milk & Honey* 203: *Cousin Jack*…a Cornish miner. **1938** in A. Banks *First-Person* 81 [ref. to 1880's]: I saw one poor galoot of a Cousin Jack—that's a Cornishman. **1963** R.W. Paul *Mining Frontiers* 69: Cornishmen [in Nevada in the 1870's]…were known by the nickname of "Cousin Jack" (and their women folk as "Cousin Jennies").

Cousin Jenny *n. West. Mining.* a Cornishwoman.
1918 *DN* V 24: *Cousin Jennie*, n. A Cornishwoman. Companion to the universal Cousin Jack for a Cornishman. Coeur d'Alenes. **1929, 1965–70** in *DARE*.

Cousin John *n.* see CUZ JOHN.

Cousin Sally Ann *n.* [sugg. by *C.S.A.*] *Confed. Army.* the Confederate States of America. Also **Cousin Sal, Cousin Sally.**
1863 in Tapert *Bros'. War* 118: Your kind and interesting letters…were both received through the obliging mails of "Cousin Sally" in good season. **1865** Sala *Diary* II 242: C.S.A.—I guess it means Cousin Sally Ann. **1869** *Overland Mo.* (Aug.) 128: "Cousin Sal" is pretty generally lamented throughout the South as the only daughter of…"Uncle Sam." **1885** Cannon *Where Men Only* 200: Especially was "Cousin Sallie" careful to feed her champions when they stood in line of battle.

couthed up *adj. Stu.* having become neat, stylish, polite, etc.
1969 *Current Slang* I & II 39: *Get couthed up*, v. To get cleaned up.—College students, both sexes, Michigan. **1971** Dahlskog *Dict.* 16: *Couthed up, get,* to get dressed up; to make oneself neat and presentable. **1986** Univ. Tenn. instructor, age *ca*33: Let's get couthed up.

couze var. COOZE.

cove *n.* [< Romani *kova* 'thing, person'] a man; fellow. [Increasingly rare in U.S. after *ca*1885.]
[*1567 in *F & H* II 192: *Cofe:* a person.] *1609 in *OED:* The word Cove, or Cofe, or Cuffin, signifies a Man, a Fellow. &c. *1698–99 "B.E." *Dict. Canting Crew: Cove*…a Man, a Fellow…*The Cove has bit the Cole*…The Rogue has Stolen the Money. **1791** [W. Smith] *Confess. T. Mount* 18: A man, *a cove*….A young lad, *a young cove. Ibid.* 19: The devil, *the crimson cove.* **1807** Tufts *Autobiog.* 291 [ref. to 1794]: *A cove,* signifies…a man. **1834** *Mil. & Nav. Mag. of U.S.* (Sept.) 41: "What coves have ye troll'd here, Sal?" asked a voice near us. **1836** *Spirit of Times* (Feb. 27) 16: The heditor is a knowing cove. **1839** *Spirit of Times* (Apr. 27) 87: Twig the cove in the yellow turban. **1841** in Valle *Rocks & Shoals* 198: I have a particular regard for some of you coves. **1846** *Lives of the Felons* 58: We're out o' harm's way, so long as they think they've got the right coves. **1855** Wise *Tales for Marines* 159: There's been some suspicious coves about the crimping houses. **1859** Matsell *Vocab.* 21: *Cove or Covey.* A man. **1860** J.G. Holland *Miss Gilbert* 173: You are the most sensible-looking old cove…on this boat. **1872** Crapsey *Nether Side of N.Y.* 185: The cove what blowd the safe away with the ham. **1875** Daly *Pique* 309: It's a dangerous place—and particularly for a cove what can't move through the streets without a peeler at his heels. **1893** Coes *Badly Sold* 3: Mr. Jollycove is a drummer who stops here, and a right jolly cove he is, too. **1879** *Snares of N.Y.* 82: If that cove gets it in his eye, who's to know? **1898** Blatchford *Letters* 23: Say, dat cove must 'a' taut a lot on us fellers to blow us to grub like dat, see! **1903** A.H. Lewis *Boss* 16: These two coves are under arrest. **1919** Darling *Jargon Book* 9: *Cove*—Used in place of the word "man." **1920** Ade *Hand-Made Fables* 112: Once upon a Time an ambitious Cove separated himself from his native Shire and made a long Trek. **1926** G. Rice, in *N.Y. Herald Tribune* (June 1) 23: I know a cove who'd never heard of Washington and Lee. **1950** *N.Y. Times* (Sept. 10) VI 4: He occasionally gestures in the direction of the bull pen to the cove elected to turn the hose on the fire. *1977 T. Jones *Ice* 40: Funny little cove, effeminate-like. *1993 *Times* (London) *Magazine* (Sept. 25) 3: *McVicar* was written—and directed—by a bluff old Yorkshire cove called Tom Clegg.

cover *n.* an act of coitus.
*ca*1889 Field *Bangin'* (st. 2): He had not had a cover since he left his native land./For months his tool had stranger been to touch of velvet hand.
¶ In phrase:

¶ **put a cover on** to stop (one's talking or foolishness) immediately.
1976–79 Milius & Coppola *Apocalypse Now* (film): Clean, put a cover on that. Now.

cover *v.* ¶ In phrase: **have (someone) covered** to understand and be willing to comply with (someone).
1953 W. Fisher *Waiters* 282: "An' tell 'em I want it on the double-quick." "Gotcha covered, man." **1969** *Current Slang* I & II 42: *Got you covered,* v. To understand.—College females, New York. **1973** Andrews & Owens *Black Lang.* 76: When you understand someone, you got them *covered.* When you got a situation *covered,* everything is all right. **1977** Bunker *Animal Factory* 150: "Send me some smokes and something to read." "Got you covered." **1989** Leib *Fire Dream* 248: "Put the taped ones on the battery box." "Gotcha covered."

covered wagon *n.* **1.** *Navy.* an aircraft carrier.
1933 Stewart *Airman Speech* 55. **1942** *Time* (Apr. 13) 25: The old "covered wagon"…set off on the highest adventure of her career. **1944** Kendall *Service Slang* 21: *Covered wagon*…aircraft carrier, also a flat-top. **1969** Bosworth *Love Affair* 94 [ref. to *ca*1923]: It was true that during Force exercises we could look out and see an especially unlovely ship, a converted collier renamed the U.S.S. *Langley* and nicknamed "The Covered Wagon," horsing around to launch and recover a handful of biplanes on her perilous flight deck. *Ibid.* 184: The *Langley* quickly became known as the "Covered Wagon"—after a very popular motion picture of the era. **1982** T.C. Mason *Battleship* 129 [ref. to 1941]: They're all big-gun men. They don't give a shit about them covered wagons you see out there.
2. *R.R.* a cableless locomotive.
1970 *Current Slang* V 5: *Covered Wagon,* n. A streamliner type locomotive with no cab used as a booster locomotive.

covess *n.* [COVE + -*ess* (fem. nominal suffix)] *Und.* a woman.
*1789 in *OED:* He was well acquainted with the cove and covess. *1819, *1827 in *OED.* **1848** *Ladies' Repository* VIII (Oct.) 315: *Covess Dinge,* A negress, sometimes called *Dinge Blowen.*

covey *n.* COVE.
*ca*1811 (cited in Partridge *Dict. Und.*). *1821 in *OED:* The covey was no scholard, as he asserted. **1835** *Mil. & Nav. Mag. of U.S.* (Dec.) 295: I, and some of the long shore coveys, got into conversation. **1839** Briggs *Franco* I 206: None of your gammon, my coveys. **1840** Dana *Before the Mast* 269: This old covey knows the ropes. **1846** Durivage & Burnham *Stray Subjects* 174: Wal—she hain't done it *yit,* old covey. **1848** *Ladies' Repository* VIII (Oct.) 315: *Cove, or Covey,* A man in general. **1853** Lippard *New York* 57: Besides, I was arter these two covies this very night. **1856** A.D. Hall *Christmas Trot* 98: Rum covey, that! but it's useless to foller him. **1864** Armstrong *Red-Tape* 1: He is a strange-looking old covey any how. **1864** in S. Boyer *Naval Surgeon* I 329: But all right, my covey, such are the fortunes of war and love. **1865** Springer *Sioux Country* 32: That is the way I spent my 25th birth-day. Time is gaining on me. I am geting to be an old covey. *a1870 *Coon-Hunt* 1: Bill Sweeney and Tom Culpepper is the two greatest old coveys in our settlement for coon-huntin'. **1885** Byrn *Greenhorn* 48: Two of the most sour-tempered old coveys on the face of this earth. **1887** Hinman *Si Klegg* 278 [ref. to Civil War]: Ef that old covey loves his country's much's he says he does…I guess he kin 'ford ter give her a bar'l o' cider!

cow *n.* **1.** a woman; *specif.* a prostitute.—usu. used derisively. Cf. COW-BOY.
*1696 in *OED2:* Cow…the Emblem…of a Lazy, Dronish, beastly Woman, who is likened to a Cow. **1859** Matsell *Vocab.* 21: *Cow.* A dilapidated prostitute. *1891 *F & H* II 194: *Cow*…a prostitute. **1913** J. London *Valley of Moon* 60: It's what a man needs in his wife—and not these fat cows of women. **1928** Callahan *Man's Grim Justice* 138: There never was a grifter who had a steady cow that didn't land in the boob. *Ibid.* 139: But you ought to see this cow…She's a darb, a wonder, a pip. **1938** *AS* (Apr.) 152: *Cow.* A girl. **1933** Ersine *Prison Slang* 30: *Cow,* n. A woman. **1942** S.J. Perelman in *New Yorker* (Nov. 21) 17: My arms are so tired from flailing these cows that I can hardly mix my pigments. **1953** W. Fisher *Waiters* 163: But not no cow like that…bitch. **1957** Murtagh & Harris *First Stone* 151: Her tricks, when she functioned as an independent instead of a cow, had been hundred-dollar babies who came highly recommended. *Ibid.* 304: *Cow* A prostitute; one of a group of girls in a pimp's stable. **1962** T. Berger *Reinhart* 47: I got me a stable of cows. **1969** L. Sanders *Anderson Tapes* 10: The hotel room. The money. The booze. And that cow you sent over. **1972** Cleaves *Sea Fever* 262: That miserable cow! **1976** *Saturday Night Live* (NBC-TV): It's a dessert topping, you cow! *a1990 Westcott *Half a Klick* 67: Some white

cow spaced to the gills. **1991** B.E. Ellis *Amer. Psycho* 147: Two dumb-looking fat girls…, one of the cows wrapped in what I'm guessing is the Irish flag.

2.a. milk; cream; *(also)* a milk pitcher.

1895 J.L. Williams *Princeton* 39: At the eating clubs they call the milk-pitcher the "cow." **1900** *DN* II 30: *Cow*, n. 1. Milk. 2. Milk pitcher. **1906** H. Green *Boarding House* 58: "Throw the cow acrost!" said Mr. Rant…indicating the milk jug. **1911** T.A. Dorgan, in *N.Y. Eve. Jour.* (Jan. 7) 8: Order me a glass of cow. **1920** Edwards *Doniphan to Verdun* 120 [ref. to WWI]: It was interesting to see how boys from the farm, who a year ago would have scorned "canned cow" would eagerly drink a can of condensed milk. **1929** Brecht *Downfall* 212: At the table when he wanted the milk Dick had said, "Drive the cow this way." **1934** *Our Army* (Nov.) 8: The Captain slowly added "canned cow" and sugar to the cup. **1936** R. Adams *Cowboy Lingo* 148: Canned milk was "canned cow." **1936** *Our Army* (July) 32: The G.I. coffee, the condensed cow. **1942** Horman & Corley *Capts. of the Clouds* (film): Will you pass the cow, please? **1944** Brooks *Brick Foxhole* 81: Down the canned cow. **1990** *Knoxville News-Sentinel* (Oct. 5) 37: Have some cow, man!

b. beef.

1918 Griffin *Ballads of the Reg't* 4: Hash and mush, and slum and coffee,/Slabs of beef and corned cow. **1945** in *Calif. Folk. Qly.* V (1946) 381: *Cow*. beef.

3. *Gamb.* a gambling pot; KITTY.

1903 A. Adams *Log of a Cowboy* 260: My bunkie had shown no inclination to gamble, but now he was the first one to suggest that we make up a "cow," and let him try his luck at monte…I…contributed my five to the general fund.

4. *U.S. Mil. Acad.* a second classman.

1930 in D.O. Smith *Cradle* 44: Just before the Cows come home (2nd class) we take a week hike. **1947** *ATS* (Supp.) 15. **1961** N.R. Ford *Black, Gray & Gold* 150: Rah! Rah! Rah! Cows! Cows! Cows! **1970** Ward *Just*, in *Atlantic* (Oct.) 73: For yearlings to attend the hearings of cows (second classmen). **1978** Truscott *Dress Gray* 10: They were cows. Juniors.

5. *Mil.* a blimp; *(hence)* a barrage balloon.—sometimes constr. with *rubber*.

1933 Stewart *Airman Speech* 87: *Rubber Cow.* A blimp. **1942** *Sat. Eve. Post* (Dec. 5) 40. **1943** Wakeman *Shore Leave* 67: But that didn't prove BBs were worthless. It did prove that we had to put AA on them, so that today any Jap pilot crazy enough to dive down on one of our big cows is damn near committing suicide.

6. *pl.* a woman's breasts.

1968–70 in *DARE.*

¶ In phrases:

¶ **dark as the inside of a cow** exceptionally dark. Also vars.

1871 "M. Twain" *Roughing It* 41: We…made the place as "dark as the inside of a cow," as the conductor phrased it. **1964** Peacock *Drill & Die* 78: Don't matter if it's darker than the inside of a black cow's ass, he could still find his way around.

¶ **have a cow** to become foolishly and unduly upset, astounded, or the like; have a fit.

1966 IUFA *Folk Speech:* He's going to have a cow (Become unduly upset). **1968** Baker et al. *CUSS* 100: *Cow, have a.* Astonished. **1969** *Current Slang* I & II 49: Sue had a hairy cow when the teacher caught his tie in the drawer. **1974** Strasburger *Rounding Third* 110: Then, whenever he and I are going to do something, Carol always has a cow. **1976** Conroy *Santini* 405: You know he must have had a cow when he got that note. **1978** C. Miller *Animal House* 9: She was up on the piano and down to her underwear. I about had a cow. **1979** Haas & Hunter *Over the Edge* (film): If I don't get home my mom's gonna have a cow. **1988** Groening *Childhood* (unp.): Jeez, don't have a cow. **1992** *Freshman Dorm* (CBS-TV): Fab! My mom is gonna have an absolute cow!

¶ **holy cow!** (used to express astonishment or disappointment). Cf. earlier cow, *interj.*

1934 Appel *Brain Guy* 74: Holy cow, where's your whisky? **1937** in Gelman *Photoplay* 235: Actors? Holy cow. **1938–40** Clark *Ox-Bow* 25: "Holy cow," he said, and worked his hands in and out from his head to show how it was feeling. **1942** in F. Brown *Angels & Spaceships* 52: "Holy cow, five hundred dollars a day!" **1944** Davis *Leo McGuire* 151: Holy cow…don't tell me they took you for all of yours and four grand of mine! **1946** Michener *S. Pacific* 6l: Holy cow! It's hot over here! **1950** Felsen *Hot Rod* 51: Holy Cow! **1965** Hersey *Too Far to Walk* 5: Holy cow, Breed, aren't you going to stop? **1968** Baker et al. *CUSS* 138: Holy moo cow!

¶ **my cow!** heavens!

1963 D. Tracy *Brass Ring* 122: My cow, I'm just about able to drag one

foot after the other. **1968** in *DARE.*

¶ **rain like a cow pissing on a flat rock** to rain heavily.—usu. considered vulgar. Also vars.

1946 Michener *S. Pacific* 326: The skies opened torrentially every morning, afternoon, evening, and night. "Like a cow on a flat rock," old Navy hands said. **1951** in Cassill *Writing Fiction* 73: Going to rain like hell…Like a cow pissing off a flat rock. **1952** Uris *Battle Cry* 132 [ref. to 1942]: My gawd, it's raining harder than a cow pissin' on a flat rock. **1969** L. Sanders *Anderson Tapes* 247: We had a rainy spell….Four solid days like a cow pissing on a flat rock. **1971** Flanagan *Maggot* 72: Now here's the Pig sweating like a double-cunted cow pissing on a flat rock. **1977** Indiana man, age *ca*40: It's raining harder than an old cow pissing on a flat rock in Arkansas. **1979** Knoxville, TN man, age *ca*35: The correct phrase is "raining like a *double-cunted* cow pissing on a flat rock." **1986** Ark. man, age *ca*35: Raining like a bull pissing on a flat rock.

¶ **Why buy a cow when milk is so cheap?** Why take a wife when many women are sexually available?

1935 O'Hara *Butterfield 8* 178: Once Nancy had heard the French wisecrack: that you can walk in the Bois without buying it. (It sounded better than the American: why keep a cow when milk is so cheap?). **1942** Garcia *Tough Trip* 100 [ref. to *ca*1878]: As Beaver Tom said…only a damn fool would buy a cow when milk was so cheap. **1948** Vidal *City & Pillar* 184: Well, they say there's nothing like a wife but not for me. I think it's a lot cheaper to buy milk than to keep a cow—that's what I think. **1967** Dibner *Admiral* 210: What the unmarried sailors said: Why buy a cow when milk's so cheap? **1970** Ponicsan *Last Detail* 149: Why buy a cow when milk is so cheap?

¶ (In various vulgar proverbs).

1938 Steinbeck *Grapes of Wrath* 197: Ya stickin' it out like a cow's ass. **1971** Meggyesy *Out of Their League* 193: He went down like a bag of wet cowshit and didn't make the necessary yard. **1971** S. Stevens *Way Uptown* 44: That mob was madder'n a cow's tit on a cold day but there wasn't nothin' they could do. **1980** Bruns *Kts. of Road* 147: The workers could "tie up any job tighter'n a cow's ass in fly-time."

cow *v. Narc.* (see quot.).

1972–74 Hawes & Asher *Raise Up* 45: Well, I'm low myself, make it two dimes and we'll cow.*…*Pool resources to buy dope.

cow *interj.* (used to express astonishment). Cf. *holy cow* s.v. cow, *n.*

1863 in *Jour. Ill. State Hist. Soc.* LVI (1963) 161: O cow, the…drums ain't worth much. **1865** in J.I. Robertson *Blue & Gray* 112: Wall, ain't that nice, Oh Cow! **1930** Sage *Last Rustler* 129: Cow hell! I was duded up.

cowabunga *interj.* [of fanciful origin; see 1975 quot.] Esp. *Surfing.* (used to express enthusiasm or astonishment).

1955 Kurtzman *Inside Mad* 39: Gosharootie…I mean *Kowabunga*, Clarabella!…Kowabunga! Him got woman's *name!* **1963** *Time* (Aug. 9) 49: Shouting the surfer's cry "Cowabunga!" **1964** Dillon *Muscle Beach Party* (film): [Graffiti] Cowabunga. **1964** *Look* (June 30) 57: As surfers say, "*Cowabunga*," Only they know just what *that* exultant cry means. **1968** Kirk & Hanle *Surfer's Hndbk.* 137: *Cowabunga:* old-fashioned expression meaning "wow!" **1969** Bouton *Ball Four* 314: Gene Brabender sometimes walks around bellowing "cowabunga!"…[The first person to use this word] was, as almost everyone knows, Chief Thunder Thud on the "Howdy Doody" show. **1975** John Algeo (priv. commun.) (Sept. 19): "Buffalo Bob" Smith tells me that he believes the word was invented by a Howdy Doody writer, Eddie Kean, for Chief Thunderthud. Buffalo Bob spells it *kawabonga*, and says it indicated bad things. There was a companion, joyous term *kawagoopa*. The fact that the distressful word has survived and the joyful one not, I suppose is paradigmatic. **1987** *Nat. Lampoon* (Oct.) 91: Cowabunga!

cowbay *n.* a cheap brothel or prostitute's room.

1851 in *DA:* It takes one more than ten years to find out all the nokes and corners and cow-bays in this modern Sodom. [**1856** "H. Hazel" *Jack Waid* 8 [ref. to Five Points, N.Y.C.]: "Cow Bay," "Murder Lane," "Black Alley."] [**1884** Costello *Police* 77 [ref. to N.Y.C. *ca*1825]: The well-known names of Cow Bay and Murderer's Alley were suggestively characteristic of the place.]

cowboy *n.* **1.a.** (in a general sense) a rash, reckless fellow.

1935 C. Odets, in Baym et al. *Norton Antho.* (ed. 2) II 1686: You got the committee here. This bunch of cowboys you elected. **1961** Scarne *Gamb. Gde.* 676: *Cowboy* A reckless and fast gambler. **1962** Barron *Pro. Gambler* 137: *Cowboy*—a wild bettor. **1975** Mostert *Supership* 136: The Basque commanding my ship had taken no evasive action as Tucker had done. "He must have been a real cowboy," Tucker observed. **1980**

Santoli *Everything* 201: The Green Berets...They got all kinds of cowboys in there, and the cowboys wanted to go out and shoot and kick down doors and beat up people. **1984** *N.Y. Post* (Sept. 4) 31: As moderates in the White House and Congress see it, the administration will be losing a "cowboy" who has launched some overly risky operations—like the mining of Nicaraguan harbors.

b. *Specif.* a man who drives recklessly at high speeds; *(hence, Mil.)* a dispatch rider.

1928 *New Yorker* (Nov. 3) 94: *Cowboy*—A taxicab driver who makes speed through traffic and around fenders; term used derisively. **1928** *N.Y. Times Mag.* (Nov. 11) 21: A driver who is constantly dashing in and out—a reckless driver—is called a "cowboy." **1937** *Rev. of Reviews* (June) 43: *Cowboy*—reckless driver. **1946** *Amer. Leg. Mag.* (May) 26: "Cowboy" was a dispatch rider with more nerve than sense. **1953** Gresham *Midway* 69: In this business [of motorcycle stunt-riding] the "cowboys" are either pushing up the dandelions or else they are too stove-up to ride. **1958** Simonson & Philips *Blob* (film): Hey, who's the cowboy? **1958** *N.Y. Times Mag.* (Mar. 16) 88: *Cowboy*—A motorist given to "moving violations"—jumping lights, weaving, speeding, etc. **1968** "R. Hooker" *MASH* 84 [ref. to 1951]: Come to think of it, get somebody to start rounding up donors, and send some cowboys to Seoul for all the goddam blood they can get.

c. *Specif.* *(Und. & Police)* a man who is a reckless, impulsive or violent criminal, esp. a gunman.

1926 Finerty *Crim.* 15: *Cowboy*—Noisy, amateur hold-up man. **1930** Lait *On the Spot* 201: Cowboy....One quick to shoot. **1931–34** in Clemmer *Pris. Comm.* 331: Cowboy, n. A young inexperienced gangster. **1935** in Thompson & Raymond *Gang Rule in N.Y.* 348: He was a cowboy in one of the seven days a week fights. No business, no hangout, no friends, nothing. **1942** Algren *Morning* 118: Did you 'r him have the rod? Whose turn was it to be the cowboy? **1952** Bellow *Augie March* 163: Gorman...was cowboy enough to shoot. **1962** Perry *Young Man Drowning* 203: I can't take no more of this cowboy. **1971** Guggenheimer *Narc. & Drug Abuse* 12: Cowboy. independent drug dealer. **1972** Grogan *Ringolevio* 51: O'Keefe stole a real pistol someplace and became a cowboy, sticking up gas stations, delicatessens, candy stores, anything. **1980** Gould *Ft. Apache* 10: The three were known "cowboys," small-time heist guys who stick up four or five places a night. **1984** *CBS Evening News* (Jan. 2): These individuals are definitely cowboys to say the least—they are very dangerous. **1985** *WINS Radio News* (Dec. 18): Federal and local authorities are looking for the leader of the so-called "cowboy" faction [of an organized crime syndicate].

d. *Specif.* *(Pol.)* a rash undisciplined politician.

1968 Safire *New Language* 95: Cowboy. a political rebel, usually one opposed to party discipline. **1977** Coover *Public Burning* 60: I had to cool the barnburners, soften up the hardshells, keep the hunkers and cowboys in line.

2. a contemptible fellow who frequents or lounges about a particular area, esp. in hopes of impressing women with his manliness or sophistication.—used in combinations. See also DRUGSTORE COWBOY.

1928 MacArthur *War Bugs* 119: Often, of course, these S.O.S. cowboys [M.P.'s] would bump into the wrong guys. **1929** Bodenheim *60 Secs.* 182: He was...a cake-eater and a lunch-room cowboy. **1945** Hamann *Air Words: Canteen cowboy.* Aviator who spends his free time at the counter of the canteen to ogle or flirt with the waitresses. **1974** A.F. Moe (letter to J.E.L., Aug. 18): *Cowboy*...was a popular catch-word [in the 1930's] and was tacked onto any word that would convey the thought...that the individual so designated was...a "phony" who "looked good." He was usually intent on using the area as a backdrop for his "posturing" to impress the "fair sex."...*Drugstore cowboy, soda fountain cowboy*, had currency during that...period.

3. *Poker.* a king.

1951 *AS* (May) 98: Cowboys. Kings. **1963** *Sat. Eve. Post* (Mar. 23) 35: Eight, Lady...Twin cowboys. Ah can't play no more. *ca*1965 in IUFA *Folk Speech*: King = Cowboy. **1973** Ward *Sting* (film): Three cowboys. **1981** *Bret Maverick* (NBC-TV): "Call." "Cowboys over nines."

4. [sugg. by advertisements featuring a cowboy smoking a Marlboro] a Marlboro cigarette.

1968–70 *Current Slang* III & IV 31: Cowboys, n. Marlboro cigarettes. **1977** Univ. Tenn. student: I heard Marlboros called *cowboys* back in '75 or earlier. In Virginia.

5. *Army in Vietnam.* (see quot.).

1971 Polner *No Victory Parades* 113 [ref. to 1963]: Cowboys is an affectionate name for Montagnards.

6. *Mil. in Vietnam.* SAIGON COWBOY. Now *hist.*

1982 Del Vecchio *13th Valley* 72: She says the cowboys trade medical supplies for it.

cowboy *adj.* rash; reckless.—used prenominally.

1936 *Pop. Sci. Mo.* (Apr.) 37: He indulged in what he calls "cowboy flying," diving twice on the field to scatter a herd of burros. **1937** Reitman *Box-Car Bertha* 205: It was just a cheap cowboy drunken stunt. **1954–60** *DAS*: Cowboy job...a robbery staged recklessly. **1980** *Mother Jones* (Sept./Oct.) 43: Allen has already displayed a genius for profiting from the cowboy foreign policy spirit now prevailing in the United States. **1982** *N.Y. Post* (Sept. 2) 3: They kept telling me it was a real "cowboy move." Then they read me my rights.

cowboy *v.* **1.** *West.* **a.** to work as a cowboy. Now *S.E.*

1925 W. James *Drifting Cowboy* 174: How's the chances of getting a job *"cowboying"* on this ranch? **1960** in *Dict. Canadianisms.* **1972** Bercovici & Prentiss *Culpepper Cattle Co.* (film): Kid, cowboyin's somethin' you do when you can't do nothin' else.

b. to subdue (a horse) by hard riding.

1925 W. James *Drifting Cowboy* 117: If you're lucky enough to draw him and *cowboy* him to the finish you're pretty near sure of first money.

2. *Und.* **a.** to commit reckless or daring armed robberies or similar crimes; *(trans.)* to rob at gunpoint in a reckless manner.

1941 Algren *Neon Wilderness* 61: You were out cowboyin' with Benkowski. **1942** Algren *Morning* 83: I guess you been hearin' 'bout a little cowboyin' I done up around the powerhouse. **1950** *Harper's* (Feb.) 75: The mob are calm and polite on the job. "Cowboying," or the wild brandishing of pistols...is frowned upon. **1968–69** *Current Slang* III & IV 31: Cowboy, v. To commit an especially daring crime.—Watts—He cowboyed a bank.

b. to murder in a reckless fashion.

1946 in *DAS:* He had had an assignment to kill a man and his bodyguard "even if we had to cowboy them." "What does that mean?"..."That means we were to kill them any place we found them even if it was in the middle of Broadway." **1959** W. Burroughs *Naked Lunch* 207: The Gimp [was] cowboyed in the Waldorf. (*Cowboy:* New York hood talk means kill the mother fucker wherever you find him). **1973** *Toma* (ABC-TV): Cowboy him and I'll see it's the last job you ever do!

3. to drive in a reckless manner. Also trans.

1949 *New Yorker* (Nov. 19) 92: "I'll show you something we call cowboying."...He threw the clutch out and we went rushing almost silently down a long hill as the speedometer crept up to seventy-two miles an hour. **1963** *Wash. Post* (Aug. 29) C3: They cowboy onto the sidewalks without warning and dart nonchalantly in front of buses 20 times their size. **1966** *L.A. Times* (Jan. 16) (Ford adv. section) 4: Just imagine what roads would be like if everyone tried to "cowboy" the other fellow out of his way. **1980** in *DARE* [ref. to 1953]: Fred had to let him go; he got caught cowboying the customers' cars.

cowboy bible *n. West.* a book of cigarette papers. *Joc.*

1980 *Ariz. Highways* (Feb.) 8: Roll-your-own cigarettes were so popular that the little books of paper were called "cowboy bibles."

cowboy Cadillac *n. S.W.* a pickup truck or open-backed automobile. *Joc.*

1976 Lieberman & Rhodes *CB Handbook* 126: Cowboy Cadillac—An El Camino or Ford Ranchero (open-backed cars). **1977** Avallone *White Knight* 20: This Cowboy Cadillac came hammering by...The open-backed Ford Ranchero was making like the Roadrunner. **1982** Heat Moon *Blue Hwys.* 115: A parking lot full of pick-ups, Cadillacs, and El Caminos ("cowboy Cadillacs"). **1985** *Miami Vice* (NBC-TV): Cowboy Cadillac. **1990** *Newsweek* (Jan. 29) 14: Cowboy Cadillac: Any fully loaded pickup truck that isn't Japanese.

cowboy coffee *n.* (see quot.).

1943 J. Mitchell *McSorley's* 68: He tells people that he lives on "air, self-esteem, cigarette butts, cowboy coffee, fried-egg sandwiches, and ketchup." Cowboy coffee is black coffee without sugar. **1967** in *DARE.*

cowboy hat *n. Army & USMC.* a campaign hat.

1941 Kendall *Army & Navy Slang* 4: Cowboy hat...campaign hat. **1980** Cragg *Lex. Militaris* 112: Cowboy Hat. The campaign hat.

cowboy's delight *n. West.* whiskey.

1885 Siringo *Texas Cowboy* 50: Mr. Burkheart kept a store at the "Point" well-filled with Cow Boys delight.

cowcatcher *n.* **1.** a full beard.

1869 in G.W. Harris *High Times* 212: Eny vile cuss in tight britches, an' a biled shut, a totin a cow catcher, or a cattipillar mustach, com-

mences a consultin ove you...tell him...to go to h—l.
2. a prominent bosom.
1945 Lindsay & Crouse *State of the Union* 484: The Head Incorruptible is the fat dame with the big cowcatcher. **1968** W. Crawford *Gresham's War* 36: She was short with thick ankles and a preposterous bosom. She was called CC, which I learned meant cow-catcher, like on a locomotive.

cow college *n. Stu.* an agricultural college; (*hence*) any small rural college.
   1906 London *Moon-Face* 120: They could have stumped any chemistry or "cow college" professor in the institution. **1923** *Bomb* (Iowa State Coll.) 422: Might as well...get back to the cow college. **1930** *AS* VI (Oct.) 92. **1943** Pyle *Here Is Your War* 87: They called him the boy from "Cow College," the nickname for the University of New Hampshire. **1963** *Time* (Feb. 1) 84: A hapless Manhattan teacher's exile at a cow college in the Northwest. **1965** W. Crawford *Bronc Rider* 44: A cow college in West Texas remembered him. **1970** A. Lewis *Carnival* 34: The first time I met Jimmy I was a senior at a little cow college. Class of '14. **1983** in "J.B. Briggs" *Drive-In* 130: Tarleton State cow college in Stephenville.

cow coroner *n. Cattle Industry.* a claim agent.
   1905 in A. Adams *Chisholm Trail* 288: That measly job of claim agent, commonly called "cow coroner."

cow-crate *n. R.R.* (see quot.).
   1948 Mencken *Amer. Lang.* (Supp. II) 714: A cattle car is a *cow-crate*.

cow-crazy *adj.* foolishly infatuated with a woman or women.
   1928 Callahan *Man's Grim Justice* 139: Take a tip from an old timer, Jack, don't get cow-crazy.

cow-cunted *adj.* having a large vagina.—used contemptuously.—usu. considered vulgar.
   1891 F & H II 195: *Cow-Cunted*...A term of opprobrium applied to women deformed by parturition or debauchery. **1943** in P. Smith *Letter from Father* 388: That cow-cunted bitch.

cow dog *n. West.* a cowboy.
   1919 in C.M. Russell *Paper Talk* 141: This spaeces [*sic*] of cow dog generly drifted north...trailing bands of horses. **1921** Thorp *Songs of Cowboys* 12: And all us cowdogs are in hell/With a "set" joined hand in hand. **1926** C.M. Russell *Trails* 5: Barrin' Mexicans, he's the fanciest cow dog I ever see.

cow grease *n. So. & Midland.* butter.
   1891 F & H II 195: *Cow-Grease* or *Cow-Oil*...Butter. **1930** *DN* VI 87: *Cow grease,* butter. **1944** *PADS* (No. 2) 55: *Cow-grease: n.* Butter...Vulgar...[Mo.] Va., N.C., S.C., Tenn. **1944** Kendall *Service Slang* 21: *Cow grease*...butter.

cow-hearted *adj.* fearful; timid.
   1698–99 "B.E." *Dict. Canting Crew*: *Cow-Hearted,* Fearful or Henhearted. **1845** G.H. Barnum *Life* 14 [ref. to *ca*1805]: Now, my boys, don't be cow-hearted, there is something for us in these seas yet.

cowhunky *n. West.* a cowboy. *Joc.*
   1971 Terrell *Bunkhouse Papers* 170: There's an old cowhunky from up north some place after Suzie.

cow juice *n.* milk.
   1788 Grose *Vulgar Tongue* (ed. 2): *Cow juice.* Milk. **1846** in *DA*. **1859** Matsell *Vocab.* 21: *Cow Juice.* Milk. **1861** in C.W. Wills *Army Life* 23: Don't you think they ought to mix clean water with the cow juice? **1885** "Lykkejaeger" *Dane* 90: I absorbed what "hen fruit" and "cow juice" I considered necessary for my health and strength. **1900** *DN* II 30: *Cow-juice, n.* Milk. **1911** in C.M. Russell *Paper Talk* 87: My Pardner...couldn't think of coffe without milk so we blew for som caned cow juice. **1928** Dahlberg *Bottom Dogs* 39: The milk...was more watery than Missouri dairy grade B cow juice. **1941** Macaulay & Wald *Manpower* (film): I just had a glass of that cow juice an hour ago. **1959** Montgomery & Heiman *Jet Nav.* 47: Pass the cow juice. **1971** Curtis *Banjo* 136: Reckon I'll have a sup [*sic*] of coffee and cow juice.

cow-killer *n.* an incompetent physician.
   1899 Norris *McTeague* 197: Ah, one-horse dentist...Ah, zinc-plugger, cow-killer, I'd like to show you once, you overgrown mucker, you—you— cow-killer!

cow-pie *n.* a piece of cow dung.
   1977 *Texas Mo.* (Feb.) 99: Setting up tennis camps in spots once marked by nothing except cow pies. **1983** *N.Y. Post* (Sept. 2) 31: How about entering a cow-pie throwing contest? **1985** Siefert *Coyote Ugly* 6: Waltzing...past your mama like she's a cowpie.

cowpoke *n. West.* COWPUNCHER. [Wentworth *American Dialect Dictionary* (1944), and hence all other standard sources, erroneously cites Croffutt *Grip-Sack Guide to Colorado* (1881); the word *cowpoke* is not found in that work.]
   *ca*1925 in Logsdon *Whorehouse Bells* 68: A cow-poke's boss had got to pay his fine. **1928** in *DA*: A cowpoke told me why they were named that. *a*1940 in Lanning & Lanning *Texas Cowboys* 45: All the cowpokes were right anxious to learn me to ride. **1947** Overholser *Buckaroo's Code* 17: I reckon she'd never have any use for a thirty-a-month cowpoke like me. **1958** Bard & Spring *Horse Wrangler* 229: 1904...is probably the year that [we first heard of] "cowpokes"...Up to this time we only had our cowhands, the cowboy or cowpuncher. There was no such thing as a cowpoke or cowpoker...[but now] we read about them in books and newspapers. **1966** *Dick Van Dyke Show* (CBS-TV): Last night a couple of cowpokes really broke up the joint. **1968** S.O. Barker *Rawhide Rhymes* 25: Something most all cowpokes know, most everywhere out West. **1968** I. Reed *Yellow Back Radio* 21 : You can't have many cowpokes left behind. **1969** Turner *Mayberly* 82: Half a dozen young cowpokes were pestering the women out there. **1978** *Gamblers* 7: Prospectors and dance-hall girls, cattle barons and cowpokes. **1992** G. Wolff *Day at the Beach* 164: Jose is tall and ropy thin, with a cowpoke's easy lope.

cow-prod *n. West.* COWPOKE.
   1942 *ATS* 822: Cowboy...*cow-poke, cow-prod, cowpuncher*. **1961** R. Adams *Old-Time Cowhand* 91: Most all good cow prods love their hosses.

cowprodder *n. West.* COWPOKE.
   1930 in *DA*.

cowpunch *n. West.* COWPUNCHER.
   1934 Lomax & Lomax *Amer. Ballads & Folk Songs* 408: And them was the days that a good cow-punch'/Could ile up his inside. *a*1940 in Lanning & Lanning *Texas Cowboys* 18: I was hired as a cow punch at twenty dollars a month and chuck. **1977** Monaghan *Schoolboy, Cowboy* 61 [ref. to 1909]: Once a cowpunch, alus a cowpunch.

cowpunch *v. West.* to herd cattle; work as a cowboy.
   1881 in *DARE*. **1903** in *Dict. Canadianisms*. **1905** in A. Adams *Chisholm Trail* 117: I...got a job cowpunching with this through man. **1928** Dahlberg *Bottom Dogs* 144: Skinny...had cowpunched and played yukon in Cheyenne, Wyoming.

cowpuncher *n.* a cattle drover. Now *S.E.*
   [**1874** McCoy *Cattle Trade* 115: The Illinois "Bovine Puncher," dressed in a style that was greatly contrasted with the official's garb.] **1879** in *AS* (Dec. 1941) 269: Cow puncher, mule skinner, and bull whacker each expresses honorable callings. **1881** A.A. Hayes *New Colo.* 63: The life of the "cow-puncher," as he calls himself, riding his spirited horse in the company of his fellows. **1883** *Life* (Feb. 1) 56: Oh, the cowpuncher Budge has come in from the West;/In all Colorado his ranch is the best. **1887–89** in C.M. Russell *Paper Talk* 13: I would rather be a poor cow puncher than a poor artist. **1907** Wells *Life* 157: There are three distinct grades of the cowboy: first, the range herder, second, the cow-puncher (trailman), and the cowboy proper. **1911** Fletcher *Up the Trail* 6: I...expressed a desire to make a trip up the trail as a cowpuncher. **1917** in Bowerman *Compensations* 20: Our cabby had one time been a cow puncher near Fort Worth Texas. **1922** Rollins *Cowboy* 39: He was [called] a cowboy or cowpuncher whether his charges were cattle or horses. There were no such terms as horse-boy or horse puncher.

cow salve *n.* COW GREASE.
   1940 *AS* (Apr.) 211: Butter, *cow salve*; sliced peaches, *gold fish*. **1976** *N.Y. Folklore* II 238: A common synonymy for butter is *cow salve*.

cow's baby *n.* veal.
   1883 *United Service* (Feb.) 198: You are not in Connecticut, where they live on cow's baby all the year through.

cow's breakfast *n.* (see 1901 quot.).
   1900 in *Dict. Canadianisms*. **1901** *DN* II 138: *Cow's breakfast, n.* A large straw hat for farmers.

cowshit *n. & adj.* **1.** *West.* a despicable or contemptible person.—usu. considered vulgar.
   1962 McMurtry *Cheyenne* 69: Here come two cowshits.
   2. *West.* BULLSHIT.—usu. considered vulgar.
   1965 W. Crawford *Bronc Rider* 203: "That's a cowshit lie, Howdy, and what's it make you?...what's it make a man who tells a cowshit lie, Howdy?" "I don't have to take that off'n you." **1969** Hamill *Doc* 35: You talkin' cowshit, Ike Clanton. **1970** J. Howard *Please Touch* 82: That cowshit little town you come from! **1972** A. Kemp *Savior* 207: All this

whimpering about man's inhumanity to man, and human morality and all the rest of that cow shit.

cow-simple *adj.* COW-CRAZY.
  1928 Callahan *Man's Grim Justice* 138: We young fellows began to cultivate the ladies. The old-timers...said we were "cow-simple." **1954–60** *DAS: Cow-simple adj.* Girl-crazy; in love with a girl. *c1935 underworld use.*

cowskin *n.* a whip.
  1838 [Haliburton] *Clockmaker* (Ser. 2) 53: He shook the cowskin over the tailor's head to show him he intended to be obeyed.

cowskin *v.* to whip.
  1838 [Haliburton] *Clockmaker* (Ser. 2) 25: I'll cow-skin him, till this riding-whip is worn up to shoe-strings. *Ibid.* 31: I teach 'em how to cow-skin de black villains.

cow's tail *n. Naut.* a frayed rope end.
  1965 Schmitt *All Hands Aloft* 108 [ref. to 1918]: Back home, if we had occasion to cut a rope, we simply tied a knot in each end to keep it from unraveling. Aboard ship this was strictly taboo; in order to prevent those frayed, untidy ends known as "cows' tails," we used a process called whipping. **1966** Noel & Bush *Naval Terms* 107: *Cow's tail:* Frayed end of a rope; also called a Fag or Fag End. **1970, 1975** in *DARE.*

Cow Town *n.* Fort Worth, Texas.
  1976 Dills *CB* 27: *Cow Town:* Ft. Worth, Texas. **1979** Edson *Gentle Giant* 145: Somebody...in Cowtown found this one out.*...*"Cowtown": a colloquial name for Fort Worth, Tarrant County, Texas.

cow-waddie *n. West.* WADDIE.
  1923 in *DARE:* Trouble would come to the "cow waddie" who had caused it. **1928** in *DARE* [ref. to 1880's]. **1930** Sage *Last Rustler* 82: Some drifting cow-waddies had told of a country...where cow-punchers run in herds. **1940** *AS* (Apr.) 220: The "cow-waddie" could be relied on. **1940** F. Hunt *Trail fr. Tex.* 40 [ref. to 1870's]: You ain't got no more sense 'an a cow waddie. **1973** in *DARE.*

cow-west *adv.* GALLEY-WEST.
  1930 Sage *Last Rustler* 192: Squealing and jumping cow-west and crooked.

cowyard *n.* a cheap brothel.
  1964 Gentry *Madames* xii [ref. to *ca*1890]: In the nature of its business, the parlor house differed not at all from the bawdy house, brothel, crib, cow yard, bull pen, rookery, and other more explicitly designated houses of prostitution. **1965** Schmitt *All Hands* 229 [ref. to 1918]: The men outside the railing made vulgar and lewd remarks; occasionally, one would beckon to a girl to come up close to him. If she met with his approval, he would pay the woman at the gate an amount equivalent to an American dollar. He would be admitted and would follow the girl up a stairway to the upper floor of the building. The place was called a "cow yard" by Laurence and the older fellows. It was the cheapest and roughest type to be found in the town. **1982** Rosen *Lost Sisterhood* 94 [ref. to 1913]: A "cowyard whorehouse" was a three- or four-story tenement with long halls lined with cubicles or closets. Sometimes as many as 250 women crowded into these separate small cubicles.

cox *v. Naut.* to act as coxswain to. Now *S.E.*
  *1881 in *OEDS.* **1895** Wood *Yale Yarns* 5: Find some other...coxswain! I've coxed my last crew. **1909** *WNID.*

coxs'n *n.* (a partial euphem. for) COCKSMAN.
  1951 Robbins *Danny Fisher* 311: You're the original college coxs'n...I ran into a certain little blonde dancer yuh got stashed in a hotel across town.

coxy *n.* coxswain.
  1966 Fariña *Down So Long* 32: He's coxy on the Olympic crew.

coyote *n.* **1.a.** *West.* a contemptible or despicable fellow.
  1872 in *DA.* **1878** [P.S. Warne] *Hard Crowd* 8: Drop every coyote that proposes to take a hand in the game. **1902** in "O. Henry" *Works* 1641: A-livin' with a sore-headed kiote like me. **1905** *Nat. Police Gaz.* (Dec. 9) 7: You mangy coyote. **1941** G. Fowler *Billy the Kid* (film): I told you. We ain't servin' that coyote.
  b. an extremely homely woman. *Joc.* Cf. COYOTE UGLY.
  1985 M. Baker *Cops* 192: You see policemen with coyote dates. When you wake up in the morning and she's laying on your arm, you chew your arm off so she won't wake up as you leave. That's a coyote date. Who do you think a guy meets in topless bars and strip joints and hooker bars? **1988** Univ. Tenn. student theme: A "coyote" refers to a woman...so unattractive that if she were laying on your hand or arm you would chew it off rather than risk waking her in your attempt to escape.

2. a Dakotan.
  *ca*1900 in Fife & Fife *Ballads of West* 74: Some folks they call us "Coyotes," but that we do not mind,/We are just as good as Badgers.
3. *Police. S.W.* a labor contractor or other person who brings illegal immigrants into the U.S. from Mexico.
  1929 Gill *Und. Slang: Coyotes*—Labor agents. **1970** S. Steiner *La Raza* 300: "Coyote!" is what the campesinos say of a man like Corrilio Macias. **1973** *U.S. News & W.R.* (July 23) 32: Smugglers, known as "coyotes" in the Mexican-American community in Los Angeles. **1974** Martinez & Longeaux y Vásquez *La Raza* 127: A worker in Mexico would be picked up by a labor smuggler—called a coyote. **1977** *L.A. Times* (Jan. 15) II 5: His name was Roberto and he paid a "coyote" 300 American dollars to smuggle him across the border. **1979** in Terkel *Amer. Dreams* 7: A coyote is a smuggler of people. *Ibid.* 8: Coyotes advertise...If [an immigrant has] a lot of money, the coyote will bring him from Tijuana all the way to Chicago and guarantee him a job. **1984** *L.A. Times* (Feb. 1) V 1: She crossed the border with a coyote, a man who smuggles people through the fence. **1987** *Time* (July 13) 21: He promised to pay $400 to a "coyote" (the term for smugglers who grow wealthy by sneaking Mexicans into the U.S.).

coyote *v.* **1.** *West.* to abscond (*obs.*); to sneak.
  1857 in *DA:* And I, why I cayotied. *ca*1860 in R.W. Paul *Mining Frontiers* 163: I did as I had done before,/Coyoted out from 'neath the floor [of the makeshift jail]. **1861** in *DA.* **1964** in *DARE.* **1968** R. Adams *West. Words* (ed. 2): *Coyotin' round*—Sneaking.
  2. *West.* to trick; hoodwink.
  1895 in *Calif. Folk. Qly.* I (1942) 273: Wunst I catch him coyotein' me now!
  3. *West.* to wander about; drift.
  1928 Santee *Cowboy* 17: Now don't go a-layin' out...an' coyote along the way, but stop at some farmhouse an' spend the night, an' pay for what you get. **1948, 1964, 1968** in *DARE.*

coyote hole *n.* a mining tunnel dug for the introduction of explosives.
  1851 in Caughey *Mob* 53: The prosecutors...fancied that the gold was hidden in a "coyote hole" near the camp from which it had been taken. **1851** in *AS* (Oct. 1951) 225: A piece of wood taken from a cayota hole...sixty-two feet below the surface. **1856** in *Calif. Folk. Qly.* I (1942) 273: Oh! cayote holes, oh! high bed-rock without a bit of blue clay to be seen. **1858** in *Ibid.*: While I jump down a deep coyote-hole. **1876** W. Wright *Big Bonanza* 133: Substantially constructed tunnels took the place of the "coyote holes" which were at first run into the hills. **1948** J. Stevens *Jim Turner* 245 [ref.to *ca*1915]: He had driven a four-foot coyote along through the canyon wall...This tunnel had been loaded with seventy-five hundred kegs of black powder and thirty-five hundred boxes of giant, all for a single blast.

coyote ugly *adj.* extremely ugly. *Joc.* Cf. COYOTE, 1.b. Also fig.
  1985 Siefert *Coyote Ugly* (title). **1989** P. Munro *U.C.L.A. Slang* 31: *Coyote ugly*...so ugly that if you were to find yourself waking up next to such a person...sleeping on your arm, that you would...bite your own arm off to escape. **1989** S. Elliott et al. *Slang* 14: *Coyote ugly*...so ugly one would chew his own arm off before choosing to date the ugly one. **1990** *Cosmopolitan* (Nov.) 256: There was a year or so of public kissyface, then things got coyote ugly.

coz var. CUZ.

cozy *adj.* crafty; cunning. Also *adv.*
  1936 Monks & Finklehoffe *Brother Rat* 28: Why is she down here on Harrington's bid? Think she's playin' me cozy? **1956** Fleming *Diamonds* 56: If you're planning anything cosy you'd better start taking harp lessons.
  ¶ In phrase:
  ¶ **play [it] cozy** to behave in an especially cautious or secretive manner.
  1959–60 Bloch *Dead Beat* 33: He could stay here and play it cozy until he decided what to do about LaVerne. **1961** Hall *Stowaway* 80: Do what you have to, play it cozy. **1963** Gidding *Haunting* (film): You're playing this whole thing so cozy, like this was a jailbreak or something. **1965** *Time* (June 18) 69: Atlanta's Stadium Authority has been playing it cozy, says only that no decision on rental rights will be made until July 1. **1967** *N.Y.P.D.* (ABC-TV): You just keep on playin' cozy and I'll throw everything in the book at you. **1980** W.C. Anderson *Bat-21* 165: He'd play it cozy, just sit down, relax and think.

cozy up *v.* to try to ingratiate oneself.—*constr. with to.*
  1965 *L.A. Times* (May 30) C2: Johnson cozied up as much to the Republicans as to the Democrats. **1965** *Time* (Sept. 17) 47: Russia, as worried

as the U.S. by China's cozying up to Pakistan. **1975** Boatner et al. *Dict. Amer. Idioms* 69: John is cozying up to Henry so he can join the club. **1986** *World Book Dict.* I 480: *Cozy up to*…to attempt to gain favor with.

C.P. *n.* [*cunt pensioner*] a man who lives off his wife's money.—usu. considered vulgar.

*ca***1835–40** in Speaight *Bawdy Songs* 32: With red-haired Moll, the fat a—e mot,/He soon was a C.P. **1894** in J.M. Carroll *Benteen-Goldin Lets.* 223: Squiers married a Miss Fargo of Ex[press] Co[mpany] fame, and besides being a "C.P." he was a "B.F." [i.e. bloody fool] of first water. *1923 (cited in Partridge *DSUE* (ed. 1)).

C.P.T. *n.* Esp. *Black E.* "colored people's time."—used contemptuously by non-blacks, otherwise joc. Also **C.P. time.**

1925 Van Vechten *Nigger Heaven* 98: Perhaps he's keeping C.P.T. *Ibid.* (glossary) 286: *C.P.T:* Coloured people's time, *i.e.,* late. **1954** Killens *Youngblood* 47: She wasn't going to have any *CPT* (Colored People's Time) in her classroom. **1966** in *Trans-action* IV (Apr. 1967) 10: Mr. Jones arrived "CPT" (colored people's time). **1965–68** McCord et al. *Life Styles in Black Ghetto* 128: The middle-class [black] person often talks jokingly of CPT (Colored People's Time), referring disparagingly to a presumed Negro tendency to be late for appointments. **1972** R.L. Williams *BITCH* 2. **1973** Andrews & Owens *Black Lang.* 91: *C.P.T.*— Colored People Time—Late. **1983** Eble *Campus Slang* (Nov.) 2: *CP Time*—late. Colored People's Time. **1990** *In Living Color* (Fox-TV): I guess you think we're on CP time. **1992** Darryl Pinckney, in *New Yorker* (Jan. 20) 32: I settled at a table outside and prepared for a long wait, but she wasn't on C.P.T. Through my glass I saw [her] stride toward me.

crab *n.* **1.** a sour or ill-tempered person. Orig. *S.E.* [No continuity of usage is evident between the early 17th C. and the early 19th.]

*1580 in *OED.* *ca***1593** Shakespeare *Two Gent. Verona* II iii: LAUNCE. I think my dog be the sourest-natured dog that lives. *1594 Shakespeare *Taming of Shrew* II i. *1605 in *OED:* And that sowre crab do but leere at thee I shall squeeze him to vargris. *1826 "Blackmantle" *English Spy* II 158: I know that crab Gambier. **1869** Stowe *Oldtown* 127: Whose character had caused the name he bore to degenerate into another which was held to be descriptive of his nature, namely, "Crab"; and the boys of the vicinity commonly expressed the popular idea of the man by calling him "Old Crab Smith." **1891** Maitland *Slang Dict.* 79: *Crab,* a sour, disagreeable person, no doubt from the crab or wild apple, which is a very ill-tempered fruit. **1902-03** Ade *People You Know* 23: They rather fancied "Parsifal" and were willing to concede that Vogner made good in Spots, but Mascagni they branded as a Crab. **1911** Howard *Enemy to Society* 210: I'm helping to support a no-good, fault-finding crab of a cripple, ain't I? **1928** MacArthur *War Bugs* 192: They were getting to be regular crabs. **1929–30** J.T. Farrell *Young Lonigan* 19: Was he a first-rate crab! **1930** Lavine *3d Degree* 174: He would…apologize for being such a "crab."

2. a louse, esp. a pubic louse. Orig. *S.E.*

*ca***1707** in Farmer *Merry Songs* IV 110: *Crabs* were the only Fruit on't. *a***1796** R. Burns, in Legman *Horn Book* 155: A Crab Louse is still but a Crab/Tho' perch'd on the Cunt o' a Queen. **1888** (quot. at STONE, *n.*). **1918** B. Miller *Diary* [entry for Nov. 1]: They give us a crab inspection that afternoon and they found a few. But you couldn't've been losey as we didn't have a bath since Oct. 12. **1924** in Hemingway *Sel. Letters* 133: The Wasserman test showed he only had crabs. **1928** in Read *Lexical Evidence* 44: Look out for the crabs. Better not shit here. **1933** Hemingway *Winner Take Nothing* 76: Many of them never had crabs, wonderful chaps. **1940** *New Directions* 61: Jackson has the crabs. **1942** McAtee *Supp. to Grant Co. Dial.* 3 [ref. to 1890's]: *Crab, crab louse,* n., the pubic louse. **1957** Greenwald *Call Girl* 170: Crabs was the worst I ever got. **1974** Radano *Cop Stories* 25: If you're going to use my toilet the least you can do is sit down, like everyone else.…What do you think I have, crabs? **1966–80** McAleer & Dickson *Unit Pride* 194: The bullets around us became thick as crabs on a whore's snatch. **1993** *Oprah* (synd. TV series): Good God, I'm glad you don't have crabs!

3. *pl.* shoes or feet.

1791 [W. Smith] *Confess. T. Mount* 18: Shoes, crabs. **1807** Tufts *Narr. Life* 292 [ref. to 1794]: *Crab*…a shoe. *1821 in *F & H* II 196: *Crabs* = shoes. **1848** *Ladies' Repository* VIII (Oct.) 315: *Crabs,* Shoes. **1859** Matsell *Vocab.* 22: *Crabs.* Feet. *1984 Partridge *DSUE* (ed. 8) 262: *Crabs.* Shoes.…still current in Aus[tralia] for "boots" so late as 1898.

4. a naval seaman.

1837 *Every Body's Album* II 241: If I'm a *Lobster*, Master *Crab,*/By the information on your nab;/In some scrimmage or other they've cracked your shell.

5. *Horse Racing.* a racehorse; (*later,* derisively) horse; nag.

1839 *Spirit of Times* (July 27) 246: A pair of very "fast crabs" will command from $1200 to $1800. **1841** *Spirit of Times* (Oct. 30) 409: [He] had been in the habit of riding a "fast crab," the DREAD of all the *trotting cattle* of the west. **1845** Durivage & Burnham *Stray Subjects* 31: *Bill Sikes,* in his new trotting sulky, with the brown horse he bought for a fast crab…good for a rush, but hain't got nigh so much bottom as the mare. *Ibid.* 108: And though ven he struck the pavement,/The "crab" began to fail,/I got another mile out—/ By twisting of his tail. **1846** in Harlow *Old Bowery* 190: And though ven he struck the pavement,/The "Crab" began to fail,/I got another mile out/By twisting of his tail. **1848** G.G. Foster *N.Y. in Slices* 46: Calling with whip or voice upon his "crab" to "go it or break a leg." **1898–1900** Cullen *Chances* 13: How cheap, he'll make a crab like Bowling Brook look! **1907** in H.C. Fisher *A. Mutt* 3: They must have been feeding that crab of mine on birdseed and snails. *Ibid.* 21: Mutt…is back again, dallying with the Emeryville crabs.

6.a. *U.S. Nav. Acad.* a naval ship on which a summer training cruise is made.

1922 Taylor *Nav. Acad. Song Book* 15: We've sailed in half-raters, destroyers also, We've cruised in the crabs, and cutters we row. **1934** Weseen *Dict. Slang* 126: *Crab fleet*—The battleship squadron on which midshipmen make a summer practice cruise.

b. *U.S. Nav. Acad.* a civilian inhabitant, esp. a young woman, of the city of Annapolis, Md.

1922 *DN* V 189: At Annapolis, the natives are *crabs.* **1928** *AS* III (Aug.) 452: *Crab.* An Annapolis girl.

c. *Mil.* a midshipman of the U.S. Naval Academy. [The *1916 quot. reflects an earlier comparable use in the Royal Navy.]

[*1916 in *OEDS:* The sub, assisted by the senior "snotties," had drilled the Crabs into a high state of discipline and efficiency.] **1980** Cragg *L. Militaris* 63: West Point cadets call their Naval Academy counterparts *crabs* and those of the Air Force *zoomies.*

¶ In phrases:

¶ **catch a crab** *Rowing.* to make a faulty stroke, so that the oar becomes jammed in the water.

*1804, *1806 in *OED2.* **1867** Benjamin *Shakings* (unp.): Boat Exercise.—Supernumeraries catching "crabs." **1882** F.W. Dawson *Confed. Service* 25: Abused, by the rest of the crew, for "catching crabs" in the most awkward manner as we rowed back. **1883** C. Russell *Sailor's Lang.* 27: *Catch a crab.*—To miss striking the water with your oar when rowing, the usual result of which is that you fall heels over head backwards. **1898** Bullen *Cachalot* 16: As before noticed, there were two greenies in each boat, they being so arranged so that whenever one of them "caught a crab," which of course was about every other stroke, his failure made little difference to the boat's progress. *1902 Masefield *Salt-Water Ballads* 30: For you're the juggins who caught the crab and lost the ship the Cup. **1975** Gould *Maine Lingo* 46. **1986** *Newsweek on Campus* (Sept.) 33: If a rower fails to release his oar on count, he can be catapulted into the water (known in the trade as catching a crab).

¶ **put the crab on** to ruin or spoil.

1930 *Am. Leg. Mo.* (Feb.) 17: That put the crab on the whole system.

crab *v.* **1.** to filch; steal.

1798 in Greene *Secret Band* 113: The word *Coney* means Counterfeit paper money…The word *Crabbing* means Robbing, Stealing, &c. **1848** *Ladies' Repository* (Oct.) 315: *Crab,* To pilfer trifling articles. **1918** Stringer *House of Intrigue:* At eight I was crabbing drop-cakes from…cooking class.

2. Orig. *Und.* to spoil, as by interfering; hinder; thwart. See also *crab the act* s.v. ACT, *n.,* 1.

*1812 Vaux *Vocab.:* To prevent the perfection or execution of any…business, by saying any thing offensive or unpleasant, is called *crabbing it.* *1849 in Partridge *Dict. Und.* 154. *1899 Whiteing *John St.* 191: We was crabbed…The mugs might ha' wrecked the show. **1901** in *Century Dict.* (Supp.): The use of foreign tires of course crabbed the deal. **1903** Ade *Society* 94: If you acquire a Reputation, they work the Night-Bell on you; and if you arrange a Dinner-Party, it's a cinch that some Old Lady, three miles away, will ring in an Epileptic Fit and crab your whole evening. **1904** McCardell *Show Girl & Friends* 127: Dopey McKnight says that it's a sure sign that something's going to come up to crab you if your cigarette keeps going out. **1908** *Hampton's Mag.* (Oct.) 458: Where's the fresh mutt that tried to crab me song? **1911** Howard *Enemy to Society* 291: We've just got one chance…and we ain't goin' to have you "crab" it. **1915** Lardner *Gullible's Travels* 31: But the Missus crabbed it a few minutes after her. **1918** Witwer *Baseball to*

Boches 55: What d'ye know about them damn big…stiffs crabbin' a guy's supper! **1919** Witwer *Alex the Great* 49: Well, you crabbed any chance you might of had. **1923** *N.Y. Times* (Oct. 7) VIII 4: *Crabbing the Turn*—Gumming the act with malicious intent. **1930** Graham & Graham *Queer People* 90: What do you care if they crab the Madame's shindig? **1926–35** Watters & Hopkins *Burlesque* 19: Why, that bird crabbed me number again. **1949** *N.Y. Times* (July 21) 2: I think they (the Government) have crabbed a real chance of getting a resumption of work.

3. to run away.—constr. with *off*.

1846 N.J.T. Dana *Monterrey* 145: Our volunteers are crabbing off in great numbers.

4.a. to criticize adversely. Cf. 1812 quot. at **(2)**, above.

*1862 in *OED*: Owners…will not send their horses to be crabbed and consequently lowered in value because they cannot pass a strict veterinary inspection. *1891 in *OED*: And you "crab" the girl because she is able to take care of herself. **1932** Mahin *Red Dust* (film): They sit around crabbing the government for not stamping out malaria. **1969** in *DARE*.

b. to complain, esp. without justification.

*1891 in *OEDS*: Shice…"crabbed"…as the case might require. **1906** in *OEDS*. **1910** *N.Y. Eve. Jour.* (Mar. 16) 15: A scrub game can breed just as much bitterness and "crabbing" as one in the championship series…A grouchy ball player has been dubbed "crab." **1917** in Bowerman *Compensations* 7: Crabbing is rampant and the spirit of mutiny runs thru Section 585. **1930** in Perelman *Old Gang* 111: Some people have a crust, crabbing all the time. **1938** Smitter *Detroit* 27: What are you crabbing about…You're drawing your wages. **1938** Bezzerides *Long Haul* 23: He never crabs. I give him a job and he does it. **1950** in F. Brown *Honeymoon* 17: So quit crabbing. **1950** O'Brian & Evans *Chain Lightning* (film): What are you crabbin' about? **1976** Woodley *Bears* 127: You musta figured I'm not calling you in here to crab about that. **1982** R.M. Brown *So. Discomfort* 23: That…did not stop her from crabbing about sports, especially boxing. **1992** N. Cohn *Heart of World* 233: "Another dumb male thing to say," Sadie crabbed.

¶ In phrase:

¶ **crab the act** see *s.v.* ACT, *n*.

crabapple *n.* a sour-tempered person ; CRAB, *n.*, 1.

1859 Tayleure *Boy Martyrs* 18: Hark'ee, old crab-apple. I'm after provisions and fodder for our troops, and if you make the *slightest* offer of resistance, I'll hang you and burn down your miserable hovel. **1918** Judy *Diary* 114: We all yelled "sour crab apple" at him. **1921** McAlmon *Hasty Bunch* 164: You shriveled up crabapple.

crab-ass *n.* CRABAPPLE.—usu. considered vulgar.

1939 M. Levin *Citizens* 274: "Why don't you fix this bottom?" "I'll fix your bottom, you old crab-ass."

crabbed *adj.* CRABBY, 1.

1843 "J. Slick" *High Life in N.Y.* 13: It's kinder natural for woman folks to get a little crabbed once in a while.

crabby *adj.* **1.** bad-tempered; cross.

1908 in Fleming *Unforgettable Season* 223: Roger Bresnahan…can be just as "crabby" and unreasonable as the worst umpire that ever lived. **1909** *WNID*: *Crabby*…Cross; churlish; ill-natured. **1956** Metalious *Peyton Place* 85: She's not crabby like some teachers. *a*1986 in *World Book Dict.* I 481: He is brought up under the…Puritan maxims of a crabby maiden aunt. **1990** *U.S. News & W.R.* (Feb. 5) 40: Why voters are so crabby in California.

2. infested with crab lice.

1942 McAtee *Supp. to Dial. of Grant Co.* 3 [ref. to 1890's]: *Crabby*, adj., infested by "crabs."

crab cruise *n.* U.S. Nav. Acad. an annual summer training cruise for midshipmen.

1912 *Lucky Bag* (U.S. Naval Acad.) No. 19 298: The boys still gather in Smoke Hall and tell tales of the old Crab Cruise. **1918** "Commander" *Clear the Decks!* 50: But let them talk of "Crab Cruises," and like rot, no Armada ever put to sea with such swelling hope and spirit as let Migg's…crowded mess.

crabfat *n.* Naut. (see quot.).

1958 Cooley *Run for Home* 77 [ref. to *ca*1925]: Pulley wheels were "shivs" and cable grease was "crabfat."

crabkin *n.* [CRAB, *n.*, 3 + *kin* var. of KEN, *n.*] *Und.* a shoemaker's shop.

1807 Tufts *Autobiog.* 293 [ref. to 1794]: *To crack a crabkin*…to break a shoemaker's shop.

crabshell *n.* a shoe. Cf. CRAB, *n.*, 3.

*1785 Grose *Vulgar Tongue: Crab Shells*. Shoes. *Irish.* **1846** in H.L. Gates, Jr. *Sig. Monkey* 93: "Crab-shells" mean shoes. **1852** *Harper's Mo.* (Dec.) 90: When shoes is shoes, they're good for those as likes 'em, which I don't; but when they're "crab shells," and leaky and gammy in the soles,…the sooner you get shut of 'em, the better.

Crabtown *n.* U.S. Nav. Acad. the city of Annapolis, Md.

1922 Taylor *Nav. Acad. Song Book* 31: Blow the men down right here in Crabtown. **1928** *AS* III (Aug.) 453: *Crabtown*. Annapolis. **1978** Dills *CB* (ed. 4) 28: *Crab Town:* Annapolis, Maryland. **1993** *Reader's Digest* (May) 108: Annapolis, Md., [is]…nicknamed Crabtown.

crabwalk *n.* (see quot.).

1975 Legman *No Laughing Matter* 321: The perinaeum is vulgarly denominated "*the crabwalk*" as purposely crude humor.

crack *n.* **1.a.** a boast. Orig. *S.E.*

*1523, *1550, *1590, *1621–51 in *OED*. **1775** in Moore *Songs & Ballads of Revolution* 93: And is it not, honies, a comical crack,/To be proud in the face, and be shot in the back.

b. the current fashion or style.—constr. with *the*.

*1788 Grose *Vulgar Tongue* (ed. 2): *The Crack*, or *All the Crack*. The fashionable theme, the go. **1807** *Port Folio* (June 6) 356: He determined to be quite the crack o/…And he call'd for his gin and tobacco. **1821** Waln *Hermit in Phila.* 28: All *the crack*, pon honour.

2.a. *Horse Racing.* an exceptionally fast racehorse; a favorite.

*1637 in *OED*: The crack o' the field's against you. **1837** *Spirit of Times* (Mar. 4) 20: The "Cracks" of the Day. Pedigree, Characteristics, and Performances. **1839** *Spirit of Times* (Mar. 16) 18: This formidable Kentucky bred "crack"…is doing finely…From what we hear of the Mississippi and Alabama "cracks," winning at New Orleans, the ensuing Spring, won't be the thing it "used to was." **1859** *Spirit of Times* (Apr. 9) 104: The favorite…the "crack" rose at the hurdles. **1906** *Nat. Police Gaz.* (Sept. 22) 3: The crack he put in my keeping was entered for all the year's great stakes. **1963** in Woods *Horse-Racing* 99: Trainers…through whose hands had passed most of the cracks of the previous thirty years.

b. something or someone that is preeminent or superior, esp. a person having outstanding skills; CRACKERJACK.

*1868 in *OED*: They were the "cracks" of the regulars, as the Scottish and the London were the "cracks" of the volunteers. **1913** J. London *Valley of Moon* 31: He's their crack, an' there's a lot of bets up. **1918** in Rossano *Price of Honor* 106: He may be a crack and all that, but he's got twenty-eight more of us to deal with. **1925** *Collier's* (Sept. 19) 7: Left Hook O'Brien—the lightweight crack. **1925** Z. Grey *Vanishing Amer.* 16: He's the Indian crack. You saw him play today. **1958** S.H. Adams *Tenderloin* 5 [ref. to 1890's]: "You're a Park Row crack." "I'm a newspaperman, if that's what you mean." *Ibid.* 49: At…Tennis. You were one of the cracks and I a small and adoring brat.

3.a. a prostitute or lewd woman; (*hence*) a woman.—used contemptuously.

*1675 in Duffett *Burlesque Plays* 80: Thou pretty, pocky, well-favor'd Crack. *1676 in D'Urfey *Two Comedies* 119: He that you quarrel'd with about your crack there. *1707 in Burford *Bawdy Verse* 204: Yet *Cracks* are Saints compar'd with them. *1785 Grose *Vulgar Tongue: Crack*, a whore. **1939** *AS* (Oct.) 239: *Crack*. A prostitute. **1968–70** *Current Slang* III & IV 32: *Crack*, n. A girl who is particularly sexually desirable.—College males, South Dakota. **1970** Landy *Underground Dict.* 59: *Crack*…Female. **1981** *Nat. Lampoon* (July) 54: The two cracks were about to go nuts. **1984** *TriQuarterly* (Spring) 307: They said that was a filthy crack, and speaking of filthy cracks how's your ma? **1986** Ark. man, age 36: I can remember my father using the word *crack* as an insult for a woman since at least 1956. He'd say, "You damn crack!" *a*1987 Bunch & Cole *Reckoning* 349: This is DeeJay here,…cats and cracks.

b. the vulva or vagina.—usu. considered vulgar. [Undoubtedly prior to **(a)**, but early cites are lacking.]

ca*1775 *Frisky Songster* 31: She up'd with her cloths [*sic*] and discover'd her crack. *1879 *Pearl* (July) 4: I felt her crack deluged with a warm, creamy spend. **1888 *Stag Party* 223: As she gasped your prick gently/ Right up her crack. *1891 *F & H* II 197: *Crack*…The female pudendum. **1916** Cary *Venery* I 56: *Crack*—…The female pudendum. **1921** *John's Gun* 1: Her…hand guided his prick in her crack. **1927** *Immortalia* 164: She filled up her crack/With cement and shellac. **1930** *Lyra Ebriosa* 20: She had a most capacious crack. **1934** H. Miller *Tropic of Cancer* 225: If anyone knew what it meant to read the riddle of that thing which today is called a "crack" or a "hole." **1934** H. Roth *Call It Sleep* 326: She letcha see it?…De crack? **1970** Longstreet *Kimball* 38: I can still feel…the moisture in my crack.

c. copulation with a woman.—usu. considered vulgar.

1962 Ark. high-school students (coll. J. Ball): Let's go out, get us some crack.

4.a. the cleft of the buttocks; in phr. **out the crack** in excessive amounts; *out the ass* s.v. ASS, *n.*

***1716** in "H. Thrumbo" *Merry-Thought* I 21: The Crack of your B—m. **1858** Doten *Journals* I 410: I have a terrible *big boil* on behind—a whopper, right in the crack. [**1928** C. McKay *Banjo* 113: You think Ise gwine be everything like you because use Ise on the beach? Not on you' crack!] *ca*1935 in Barkley *Sex Cartoons* 65: In the crack of my ass. **1968** Standish *Non-Stand. Terms* 9: Man who kisses wife's behind gets crack in face. **1974** E. Thompson *Tattoo* 378: Jack simply reached out and goosed the old man in his khaki-clothed crack. **1982** Rucker *57th Kafka* 155: Uli is crouched behind her,…his face pressed into her crack. **1983** S. Wright *Meditations* 20: We got lieutenants falling out our crack. **1992** *Donahue* (NBC-TV): It goes right up the crack of your butt.

b. the cleavage between a woman's breasts.

1974 Kurtzman *Sweet Bobby* 3: She's got on a low cut top and I can see her crack.

5.a. *Und.* CRACKSMAN.

***1749** in *OED:* No strange Abram, ruffler crack. **1866** *Nat. Police Gaz.* (Dec. 8) 2: Wilson is a jig-dancer as well as a "crack." **1867** *Nat. Police Gaz.* (Jan. 5) 2: The "cracks"…have been before the "flute" and convicted. **1870** *Comic Songster* 41: The Cracksman's Chaunt…Now, vy did this throw them [the police] off the track,/Cos Frenchman and Dutchman was Coll the Crack.

b. *Und.* a burglary; in phr. **the crack** the practice of burglary.

1791 [W. Smith] *Confess. T. Mount* 21: We did set out/Upon the crack. ***1812** Vaux *Flash Dict.: The crack* is the game of house-breaking; *a crack* is a breaking any house or building for the purpose of plunder. **1846** *Lives of the Felons* 27: The robbery had been what thieves, in their peculiar parlance, would call "a neat *crack*." *Ibid.* 35: Making a "*crack*" (burglary). **1847** *Nat. Police Gaz.* (Jan. 16) 149: They will then secure the keys by a "crack" of the premises. **1848** *Ladies' Repository* VIII (Oct.) 315: *Crack Lay*, An expedition for the purpose of house-breaking. **1851** [G. Thompson] *Jack Harold* 106: I do a little in the *crack* line myself, occasionally. **1855** Brougham *Chips* 177: I had to establish a crack on my own account, and a jolly good swag I got. **1867** Williams *Brierly* 12: I'd as leaf have murder as a crack "buffed" to me. **1927** *DN* V 457: *On the crack*, adj. Out for burglary. Also *on the grift.*

6. a remark; *(specif.)* one that is impudent, bitter, sarcastic, or ironic. [The 1884 quot. might as easily illustrate **(7.a.)**, below.]

1884 Hedley *Marching Through Ga.* 109: Both "swapping lies" the while…; the Yankee…losing no opportunity to take a crack at his captive's relatives and friends. **1895** in J.I. White *Git Along Dogies* 66: That last one is a hard crack. **1896** Ade *Artie* 13: After that first saucy crack with the half I laid low three or four hands. **1901** A.H. Lewis *Croker* 63: Priests and preachers are all right, an' I would be the first to call down a duck who made a crack the other way. **1901** Ade *Modern Fables* 74: She never made any of these unwelcome Cracks about being Second Choice. **1902** Cullen *More Tales* 112: I'm not making any such crack. *Ibid.* 128: I experience…neurasthenia…whenever I hear those O-gladsome-happy-days cracks from members of this organization. **1903** A.H. Lewis *Boss* 120: That crack about bein' a taxpayer is more of a public utterance. **1904** Hobart *I'm from Missouri* 45: Jefferson had handbills…with cracks like these in big black type:…When Was Peter Grant Born? And Why? **1905** *Variety* (Dec. 30) 7: He makes as many funny cracks as James Richmond Glenroy, but…he won't tell 'em on the stage. **1908** Kelley *Oregon Pen.* 68: Of course he was put up to make that crack. **1911** A.H. Lewis *Apaches of N.Y.* 112: I don't like them cracks about startin' somethin'. **1912** Mathewson *Pitching* 71: When he made that crack, I guessed that he was trying to cross me by telling the truth. **1914** Ellis *Billy Sunday* 275: I would not know what to do if I didn't get some cracks from people now and then. **1918** in Grider *War Birds* 128: Then he took a couple of nasty cracks at a few of our friends and regular callers. **1920** Witwer *Kid Scanlan* 33: If Scanlan hears him make any cracks about him like he just did now—well, he'll practically ruin him, that's all! **1928** Fisher *Jericho* 155: He…makes another crack. **1931** Hellinger *Moon* 255: I was sorry for that crack because I really liked the girl. **1936** Miller *Battling Bellhop* (film): "Is that a crack?" "Now, why would it be a crack?" **1952** Felton & Essex *Las Vegas Story* (film): I'll ignore the crack. **1962** L'Engle *Wrinkle in Time* 7: When cracks were made about anybody in the Murry family, they weren't made about Sandy and Dennys. **1978** Strieber *Wolfen* 17: It was a nasty crack, and she was sorry for it. **1993** N.Y.C. man, age 44: What kind of a crack was that?

7.a. an attempt or opportunity; in phr. **first crack out of the box** the very first opportunity. Now *colloq.* [The phrase *get a crack at* was orig. colloq. or S.E. and ref. to 'getting a shot at (a game animal)', as in an 1844 quot.]

[**1844** *Spirit of Times* (Feb. 3) 583: Get a crack at him.] **1893** F.P. Dunne, in Schaaf *Dooley* 232: I want to get just wan crack at Balfour before I die. **1896** *Ibid.* 249: Th' American people will name their Prisidint in their own way, an' I may take a crack at it mesilf. **1906** *Nat. Police Gaz.* (Sept. 1) 3: We knew they would pounce down upon us the first crack out of the box. **1911** Van Loan *Big League* 121: All I want…is one crack at him. **1912** Mathewson *Pitching* 104: All I want…is another crack at that Buttermilk after what I learned about him this afternoon. **1918** in *St. Lawrence U. in War* 144: Intend to plug along until I know the supply to be here and then make a crack for something better. **1920** Ade *Hand-Made Fables* 43: He could get at least one more crack at real American Chow. **1938** Bezzerides *Long Haul* 94: Let's give the chain store supply houses a crack. **1939** Goodman & Kolodin *Swing* 66: They took me on to have a crack at the hot work in the reeds. **1969** Layden & Snyder *Diff. Game* 39: A crack at coaching and a chance at law.

b. an instance; a time.

1937 Steinbeck *Mice & Men* 58: Clara gets three bucks a crack and thirty-five cents a shot. **1980** N.Y.C. man, age *ca*32: Selling tickets at five dollars a crack.

8. a line of talk.

1912 Field *Watch Yourself* 268 [ref. to 19th C.]: Just listen to that crack; he'll make them think he's going to take up a collection for the foreign missions. *ca*1920 in Bruns *Kts. of Road* 81: I was lookin' for work, oh judge, he said./Said the judge, "I've heard that crack before."

9. something or someone that is extremely amusing.

1971 Winterfilm *Winter Soldier* (film): This thing is a crack, you know? **1976** Eble *Campus Slang* (Nov.) 1: *Crack*—n. a funny or witty person: Jones is such a crack.

10. *Narc.* an especially potent form of solidified freebase cocaine. Now *S.E.*

1985 *USA Today* (Dec. 10) 1A: A superpotent, superdangerous but cheap form of cocaine is hooking teens and young adults…The new form, called crack, produces an almost instant "high."…88 percent felt extremely paranoid while high on crack…Crack is sold in small glass vials. **1985** WINS Radio News (Dec. 28): Police have arrested eight people who were allegedly selling a super-cocaine known as *crack.* **1986** *Miami Vice* (NBC-TV): Wants to move eight pounds of crack. **1986** *Time* (Sept. 15) 63: Crack…was first imported from the Bahamas around 1983. **1988** H. Gould *Double Bang* 209: [A] crack-freak burglar.

¶ In phrase:

¶ **get [(one's) tail** or **ass] in a crack** to get into trouble or difficulty.

1926 in *AS* LVII (1982) 261: *Crack.* Tight place. **1933** J. Conway *Disinherited* 109: You had the company in a tight crack then. **1941** Crane *Born of Battle* 42 [ref. to Korean War]: Heroism is gettin' your tail in a crack where you got to do somethin' to get it out. **1966** Shepard *Doom Pussy* 59: Unless the friendlies have their ass in a crack, no target is worth a man or a bird. **1967** Talbot *Chatty Jones* 86: You got your Goddamn friggin' ass in a crack this time. **1967** W. Crawford *Gresham's War* 212: Y'all're only going to get your asses in one big crack. **1970** *Just Military Men* 10: In every great American battle, the United States has had its ass in a crack. Bataan, Corregidor, the Marne.

crack *adj.* **1.a.** first-rate; exceptionally good; *(occ.)* fancy; high-class. Now *colloq.* or *S.E.*

***1793** in *OED:* [Sheep] called here [in Suffolk] a crack flock, which is a provincial term for excellent. ***1807** in *OED:* Crack regiments. **1841** Strong *Diary* I 170: Some of his crack songs,…though superbly sung, were spoiled by clap-trappery. **1846** Oehlschlaeger *Reveille* 169: Carrying on a *smashing* trade of a very *crack* character. **1848** *Life in Rochester* 13: We'll have a crack tragedy after all! **1848** G. G. Foster *N.Y. in Slices* 120: The Bowery is celebrated for its drinking and gambling-houses, its poultry-raffling shops, and its "crack" ice-cream saloons. **1851** F.B. Mayer *Pen & Pencil* 49: Left Cincinnati on the Ben Franklin, a "crack boat." **1853** Lippard *New York* 139: Have drank much champagne at a "crack" hotel. **1873** Scammon *Marine Mammals* 219: If half their number are really "crack whalemen," the voyage will usually be a successful one. **1891** Maitland *Slang Dict.* 79: *Crack*, first-rate; excellent; the favorite horse in a race. A crack hand, a crack article, a crack regiment. *a*1914 in McIlvaine *Chi. in Civil War* 33: The regiment [was] then considered the most "crack" of any…in the country. **1929** T. Gordon *Born to Be* 128: We were hooked on the tail end of a crack train, north bound. **1955** in Loosbrock & Skinner *Wild Blue* 43:

Crack German fighter outfits were often ordered to fresh locations. **1958** J. King *Pro Football* 91: These aides are crack football men. **1973** *Playboy* (Sept.) 12: Huzzah to Smith for a crack job in bringing Albert Einstein's film career to life. **1978** in Curry *River's in Blood* 166: He was a crack towboat man. **1979** in Terkel *Amer. Dreams* 289: She became a crack typist. **1984** Bane *Willie* 103: Willie also signed up Dan "Bee" Spears, a crack bass player. **1985** Sawislak *Dwarf* 2: The paper's "crack news staff."

b. finest; best.

***1837** in *OED:* My sleeping-room…was the crack apartment of the hotel. **1840** *Spirit of Times* (June 27) 192: The Crack Story of the Month…the very best story contained in any of the English Magazines. **1843** Field *Pokerville* 121: He was the "crack" amateur of the place. **1881** Ingraham *Buffalo Bill from Boyhood* 93: They say you are the crack shot in the fort. **1889** Reynolds *Kansas Hell* 88: The Sunday dinner is the "crack" meal of the institution. **1890** Roe *Police* 249: It will be the "crack" company of horsemen in the country. **1952** in Fenner *Throttle* 17: Frank was the son of his crack engineer.

2. favorite; (*also*) celebrated; famous.

1835 *Spirit of Times* (Dec. 12) 2: It was election-day, and they were qualifying themselves to give plumpers for their crack candidate. **1838** [Haliburton] *Clockmaker* (Ser. 2) 164: Never buy a crack horse; he's done too much. Never buy a colt; he's done too little.

crack *v.* **1.a.** Orig. *Und.* to break open or into for the purpose of theft; burglarize.—formerly also constr. with *up*.

***1725** *New Canting Dict.: Crack,* is also used to [mean] break open; as, *To crack up a Door.* **1791** [W. Smith] *Confess. T. Mount* 19: *Cracking a ken,* breaking into a house. ***1812** Vaux *Flash Dict.: Crack,* to break open. ***1838** Dickens *Oliver Twist* ch. xix: The crib's barred up at night like a jail; but there's one part we can crack. **1848** *Ladies' Repository* VIII (Oct.) 315: *Crack,* To enter a house by violence. **1851** [G. Thompson] *Jack Harold* 60: Likewise each gallant burglar, that cracks his cribs at night. **1859** Matsell *Vocab.* 22: *Crack.* To force; to burst open. **1865** *Rogues & Rogueries of N.Y.* 19: Ike, we will "crack" (slang for "break into") the store in Reade…street. **1872** Crapsey *Nether Side of N.Y.* 60: "Stutter Jack," "G'immer George," and sundry others…had arranged the preliminaries for "cracking" the house. **1882** Campbell *Poor* 54: I cracked a place not long after I come out. **1892** Bierce *Beetles* 259: You crack a crib…and…explore the dining room for plate. **1932** L. Berg *Prison Doctor* 223: Why, Little Red Moran worked eighteen months as repair man for a safe company just to learn how to crack the Eastern Savings Bank! **1943** *School & Soc.* LVIII 169: *Crack the joint:* break out of a place or into it. **1965** in J. Mills *On the Edge* 100: For burglary and "cracking shorts"—breaking into cars. **1968** E. Knight, in J.P. Hunter *Norton Intro. Poetry* 59: The next day in Memphis I cracked a croaker's crib for a fix. **1970** Rudensky & Riley *Gonif* 96: I…decided to crack the speak…at 3:00 a.m. **1973** Schiano & Burton *Solo* 83: I'm looking to crack a short. **1985** T. Wells *444 Days* 9: So when the armories were cracked, a huge number of guns and lots of ammunition hit the street in a hurry.

b. *Pris.* to break (jail); escape from (prison).

1791 [W. Smith] *Confess. T. Mount* 21: To rob a church or crack a gaol. *Ibid.* 22: Now I've crack'd the quod again. **1807** Tufts *Autobiog.* 293 [ref. to 1794]: *Crack the qua*…break the jail. **1944** Kendall *Service Slang* 46: *Crack the joint*…get out of a place by force or into one. **1970** Rudensky & Riley *Gonif* 82: I'd cracked two top pens.

2. to deflower.—usu. considered vulgar.

***ca1725** in Pinto & Rodway *Common Muse* 383: And when they are Crack'd, away they are pack'd/for Virgins, away to the City. **1938** "Justinian" *Americana Sexualis* 17: *Crack. v.* To deflower a virgin.

3.a. to open (a bottle or can) for the purpose of drinking; (*hence, occ.*) to open (a container of a drug). [Earlier *OED* exx. appear to be colloq. or S.E., but it is difficult to judge without additional evidence.]

***1773** H. Kelly *School for Wives* 146: When shall we crack a bottle together? ***1775** in *OED.* **1849** G.G. Foster *Celio* 48: Let's crack another bottle. **1854** St. Clair *Metropolis* 94: We must crack a bottle of champagne before you go. *ca*1900 *Buffalo Bill* 204: Perhaps he cracks a bottle now, perhaps he's had his fill. **1929** "C. Woolrich" *Times Sq.* 209: Crack a bottle of fire-juice and let's pretend we're alive. **1931** *Amer. Merc.* (Sept.) 22: I just been thinkin' about beer myself…Sure, boys, we'll crack a bottle. **1943** in P. Smith *Letter from Father* 225: Champagne was "cracked." **1952** "M. Roscoe" *Black Ball* 82: We stopped at the bar finally and Big Joe cracked a new bottle of scotch. **1968–73** Agar *Ripping & Running* 68: Here, crack some of these bags [of heroin]. **1973** Turbeville *Buster & Billie* (film): I've been known to crack a cool one now and then. **1977** in Lyle & Golenbock *Bronx Zoo* 16: We didn't crack

the champagne because we had to wait to see whether the Tigers would win or not. **1978** Truscott *Dress Gray* 182: The two cracked beers and took long drafts. **1979** Hiler *Monkey Mt.* 307: Wanna crack that new bottle and have another nightcap? *a*1983 Newby *Target Ploesti* 27: We cracked the jug and toasted our fallen comrades.

b. to open (a book) for the purpose of studying. Now *S.E.*

1934 Weseen *Dict. Slang* 178: *Crack a book…Crack the books*—To study. **1962** Quirk *Red Ribbons* 155: He was a smart aleck and enjoyed his reputation as a man who scarcely cracked the books and could still get passing grades. **1973** Flaherty *Fogarty* 112: He wasn't one of those lazy teenagers who read Classic comic books, no, sir, he cracked Mickey Spillane in the original. **1977** *Nat. Lampoon* (Jan.) 91: Crack our hot new stereo catalog and discover the straight scoop and low prices. **1988** Kienzle *Marked for Murder* 4: She had become a 4.0 student…without cracking a book.

c. *USAF.* to open (sealed orders).

1958 Camerer *Damned Wear Wings* 67 [ref. to WWII]: Forty-five minutes out Casey had cracked the orders.

4.a. *Sports.* (of a racehorse or human competitor) to lose a lead as the result of loss of stamina; (*hence*) to lose one's combative or competitive spirit. Also trans. [This and the following sense are specialized developments of the S.E. sense 'to collapse or give way under pressure'; see *OED*.]

1880 *N.Y. Clipper Almanac* 44: *Crack (To).*—This is said of a horse that gives way and falls behind the moment he is caught up with. ***1884** in *OED:* The first named [of the racing horses]…"cracked" some distance from home. ***1891** in *OED:* Twice, however, the Dublin crew looked like "cracking." **1913–15** Van Loan *Taking the Count* 52: "That sort of pace will crack him if anything will."…But Wade did not crack. **1915** *N.Y. Eve. Jour.* (Aug. 5) 12: The veteran had gone along splendidly for six innings, holding the Cards runless and allowing them but four hits. He bent a little in the seventh and in the eighth he cracked all to pieces. **1928** J.M. March *Set-Up* 10: All fighters crack./…And they never come back.

b. to suffer an emotional breakdown; (now *esp.*) to become insane.—often constr. with *up*.

***1917** in Lee *No Parachute* 8: If he's not rested then, he begins to crack up under the strain. ***1918** in F.M. Ford *Letters* 86: I wrote about half a novel in the Salient, but I got tired of it when I cracked up. **1925** Faulkner *Soldiers' Pay* 47: To hell with kee-wees, anyway…Rather be a sergeant. Rather be a mechanic. Crack up, Cadet. Hell, yes. Why not? War's over. Glad. Glad. Oh, God. **1928** *Amer. Mercury* (Feb.) 88: You'll go goofy, kid!…You'll crack! **1930** in R.E. Howard *Iron Man* 19: You'll crack…and wind up in the booby hatch. **1933** Creelman & Rose *King Kong* (film): Bang! He cracks up. **1938** Smitter *Detroit* 153: What are you trying to do? Make the poor guy miserable? Trying to make him crack up? **1942** "E. Queen" *Calamity Town* 144: The old boy is cracking. **1943** Perrin & Mahoney *Whistling in Brooklyn* (film): Writer of murder stories cracks up, goes berserk! **1952** *I Love Lucy* (CBS-TV): I never thought I'd see *you* crack up. **1966** Harrington *Swinger* 104: Pectin's cracked up.

5. [ult. a survival, with added sense developments, of ME and Early ModE senses (*OED2* defs. 5–8) related to speaking and boasting; cf. survivals in colloq. or S.E. idioms *to crack a joke* and *not all that it's cracked up to be*]

a. Esp. *Und.* to say; (*intrans.*) to talk; speak; speak up.

1897 in Hoppenstand *Dime N. Detective* 72: Don't "crack" it so loud. **1898** L.J. Beck *Chinatown* 158: Cook the hop and don't be cracking so much. **1904** *Life in Sing Sing* 247: *Cracking*…speaking. **1911** *Adventure* (Mar.) 903: Soupbone cracked that no 'bo could ride his division. **1911** *Hampton's Mag.* (June) 743: Dutch Henkel cracked the other night that he hopes you're the judge this time. **1914** Jackson & Hellyer *Crim. Slang* 26, 31: *Crack,* verb General usage. To talk…"Quit crackin." **1921** J. Conway, in *Variety* (Feb. 4) 7: "Tomato" cracks to me about what happened. **1927** Coe *Me-Gangster* 38: I never cracked about Fletch or the foreman. **1929** Hammett *Maltese Falcon* 19: And then you birds cracking foxy. **1931** *AS* (June) 330: He tried to crack to the copper, but the cop cut him short. **1938** Baldwin & Schrank *Case of Murder* (film): Don't crack, but I think I know who stuck up the bookies' truck. **1956** Resko *Reprieve* 124: Don't crack ta him, *I'll* talk ta him! **1958** Camerer *Damned Wear Wings* 134: He don't crack a word all night. **1964** in Jackson *Swim Like Me* 111: This is what I cracked:/"Shut up whore and let a man have the floor." **1971** Hilaire *Thanatos* 14: I don't know why I'm cracking to you. **1974** Piñero *Short Eyes* 57: You're on it second.…Cupcakes cracked already. **1987** Mamet *House of Games* (film): You cracked out of turn.

b. *Und.* to divulge (a confidence); (*also*) (*intrans.*) to inform. [In later use infl. by the S.E. sense alluded to at (**4.a.**), above.]

1922 *Variety* (July 21) 4: I wouldn't crack it to anybody in the world but yourself. **1927** Coe *Me—Gangster* 26: I'll crack the works on the kid, here. **1934** W. Smith *Bessie Cotter* 129: You can rely on me not to crack. **1953** in Loosbrock & Skinner *Wild Blue* 485: I nearly cracked…I'd known two of the men they said confessed. **1991** C. Fletcher *Pure Cop* 88: Or you make an arrest and the arrestee cracks.

c. to utter a wisecrack; speak in a jesting or sarcastic manner. [The trans. sense, constr. with *joke*, as in early quots. below, is S.E.; see *OED2*.]

[**1811** in W. Dunlap *Diary* 426: Comes out and cracks his jokes.] [**1861** in M. Lane *Dear Mother* 21: Many are the good jokes cracked around the table.] [**1864** in D. Chisholm *Civil War Notebook* 51: Are doing nothing but roasting our shins and cracking jokes.] **1930** J.T. Farrell *Grandeur* 221: No bastard is crackin' like that about my sister. **1930** M. West *Babe Gordon* 189: Listen to dat gal crack! **1936** Miller *Battling Bellhop* (film): She got sore because I cracked about the bellhop. **1961** L.G. Richards *TAC* 44: "You should have been here when it was hot," they cracked. **1983** M.J. Bell *Brown's Lounge* 22: Talking shit, telling lies, rapping, or cracking.

d. Esp. *Black E.* to taunt or insult, as with a wisecrack.—also constr. with *on*.

1942 Z.N. Hurston, in *DARE*: She demanded that Papa "handle" some of the sisters of the church who kept cracking her about it. **1957** Simmons *Corner Boy* 121: Yeh, I'm cracking, and I'm facting. **1970** Ahlstrom & Havighurst *400 Losers* 70: Now look, I'm going to begin cracking you in front of the boys, and I mean hard. **1970** in *DARE*: He's always…cracking me. **1972–73** in M.J. Bell *Brown's Lounge* 26: If *you* do I wish you'd tell me unless you're just crackin' on me. *a***1978** J. Carroll *B. Diaries* 8: Herbie wasn't cracking on him for a goof. **1966–80** Folb *Running Lines* 233: Crack on (someone). **1980** Eble *Campus Slang* (Oct.) 2: *Crackin'*—Belittling, criticizing: "Hey! Stop crackin' on me." **1991** *True Colors* (Fox-TV): Why are you crackin' on me so hard? **1992** *Wash. Post* (June 10) D1: I wasn't going to crack on Eddie, I really wasn't.

6. [sugg. by *break*] to change (money); cash (a check).

1927 T.A. Dorgan, in Zwilling *TAD Lexicon* 29: I cracked a $20 bill when I got into the game. **1951** in *DAS*: Twenty bucks? Gee, I can't crack that. **1968** Spradley *Drunk* 30: I'll give you thirty the minute I crack a check.

7. *Und.* to ask; make a demand (of).—often constr. with *on*.

1928 Coe *Swag* 17: "Whose uncle?" I remember cracking. **1953** in Wepman et al. *The Life* 118: When I cracked for seconds, the hack stood there looking. **1967** [Beck] *Pimp* 135: You can cop a "spike" at any drug store. You gotta crack for insulin with it. **1969** Smith & Gay *Don't Try It* 109: He may hear that a certain dealer has a good bag and, on a speculative basis, steer customers to him and then go to him later and ask to be taken care of for the service. This is known as *cracking* on a dealer.

8. [poss. sugg. by *crack a case* 'solve a case'] *Und.* to seize or place under arrest.—occ. constr. with *out*.

1952 Mandel *Angry Strangers* 378: It's what they cracked a banker guy for, he run away to Florida with all that loot. **1962** Crump *Killer* 323: What did they crack you for? **1966** Brunner *Face of Night* 232: Crack—to arrest. **1967** C. Cooper *Farm* 50: Did you know that was the time I got cracked? That the Man swooped down on me? **1974** "A.C. Clark" *Death List* 37: Shit, Red, as slow as you were moving, I'd have thought you kind of wanted to get cracked out.

9. to surpass or exceed (a limit, record, or benchmark number).

*****1953** in *OEDS*: I was fortunate…to see him crack the one-mile record in the Futurity Stakes. **1961** L.G. Richards *TAC* 136: He was one of the first…pilots to crack 1000 hours in tactical jets. **1980** *Nat. Lampoon* (June) 90: I betcha didn't crack 225 on your friggin' SATs, neither.

10. to proposition; HIT ON.—constr. with *on*.

1974 Piñero *Short Eyes* 68: He's the one you should be cracking on. **1973–76** J. Allen *Assault* 126: Man, everybody else cracking on the whore. Why don't you? **1992** Hosansky & Sparling *Working Vice* 187: One tried to crack on Cynthia for sex.

¶ In phrases:

¶ **crack (one's) jaw** *Black E.* to talk, esp. boastfully. Cf. earlier sense of *crack* 'boast' in *OED2*.

1932 in *AS* (Feb. 1934) 26: *He's just cracking his jaw*, i.e., he's boasting. **1946** Mezzrow & Wolfe *Really Blues* 88: I figured I'd be out of line if I cracked my jaw.

¶ **crack wise** Orig. *Und.* to speak in a knowing or sardonic manner; offer insults; wisecrack.

1921 J. Conway, in *Variety* (June 24) 7: Mead kept crackin' wise about cover up Lux, he ain't bleedin', he's stallin'. **1924** *Sat. Eve. Post* (July 12) 15: She cracked wise to the stage manager to be ready for a lotta bows, but she did a mean flop. **1929** "C. Woolrich" *Times Sq.* 55: How would you like to get canned for cracking wise? **1929–33** Farrell *Young Manhood of Lonigan* 195: If he cracks wise…I'll just blow. **1942** Pegler *Spelvin* 74: I have heard you crack wise about some of the activities of Mr. Roosevelt's wife. **1955** Graziano & Barber *Somebody Up There* 319: I was cracking wise with the bulls…about my bouts. **1960** Stadley *Barbarians* 27: Neil still cracks wise. **1971** Faust *Willy Remembers* 85: I think of my poor Henry. Happy-go-lucky, cracking wise. **1983** S. King *Christine* 11: Are you cracking wise on me, son? **1992** *Nation* (Nov. 16) 608: Enjoying a Coke with his friend Petronius…and cracking wise about the Emperor.

¶ **get cracking** to get busy; get going. [This phr. came into U.S. speech through contact with British armed forces during WWII.]

*****1936** Partridge *DSUE* 324: *Get cracking*, to begin work. *****1940** in *AS* XVI (1941) 76: *Get Cracking On Something*. Showing action on a job. *****1941** in Wiener *Flyers* 45: *Get cracking*. Get going. **1950** *New Yorker* (Oct. 14) 116: Now, then…we'd best get cracking, hadn't we? **1963** *Time* (Jan. 4) 37: Then the boarders get cracking again. The boys polish floors, mow lawns, [etc.]. **1973** J.E. Martin *95 File* 230: We've got to get cracking. **1977** Coover *Public Burning* 519: So we gotta get crackin', children! **1981** Wolf *Roger Rabbit* 69: We've got to keep cracking. **1984** Glick *Winters Coming* 47: We'll be right behind them—let's get crackin'.

crackbrain *n.* a crazy person. Orig. *colloq.* or *S.E.*

*****ca1570** in *OED*: Such a crackbrain as thou art. *****a1661** in *OED*: Sure, once thou wast No crack-brain. *****1831** in *OED*: If the unhappy crackbrain has any handicraft. **1984** W.M. Henderson *Elvis* 150: You get these crackbrains running around.

cracked *adj.* **1.** crazy; insane. Orig. *S.E.*

*****1692** J. Locke, in *OED*. *****1705** in *OED*: You are as studious as a cracked Chymist. *****1775** S. Johnson, in *OED*: I never could see why Sir Roger is represented as a little cracked. **1804** Brackenridge *Mod. Chiv.* 431: He seems to be a little *cracked*. **1809** W. Irving *Hist. of N.Y.* I ix: The poor old gentleman's head was a little cracked. **1833** J. Hall *Soldier's Bride* 125: Impossible! the man's sartainly cracked! **1840** *Spirit of Times* (Sept. 26) 360: You're ither cracked…or else you're blind drunk. **1848** in Borden *Dear Sarah* 150: He believed that the fellow was "cracked" as he acted rather strangely. **1863** in J.H. Gooding *Altar of Freedom* 26: He must have been cracked or drunk. **1876** W. Wright *Big Bonanza* 82: He was considered…to be "a little cracked" in the "upper story." **1909** in *DAS*. **1911–12** J. London *Smoke Bellew* 103: You're gettin' cracked on systems. **1918** in Rossano *Price of Honor* 139: A cracked bloke tried to see how badly he could smash my bus. **1931** Dos Passos *1919* 118: People around her seemed so cracked. **1934** Weseen *Dict. Slang* 323: *Cracked*—Mentally unbalanced; crazy. **1955** N.Y.C. woman, age *ca*65: You must be cracked! **1977** in Rice *Adolescent* 272: Slang expressions…compiled by high school and college youths on the East Coast…*Cracked*—crazy.

2. intoxicated by CRACK, *n.*, 10.—often constr. with *up* or *out*.

1988 N.Y.C. man, age 40: *Cracked up* or *cracked out* has come to mean being on *crack*. **1988** *DayWatch* (CNN-TV) (June 7): In his cracked state, he decided [to hire a killer]. **1992** *World News Tonight* (ABC-TV) (May 12): Who's cracked up, who's cracked out, and who's dead?

cracked up *adj.* **1.** delighted; happy.

1977 Langone *Life at Bottom* 33: He's not too cracked up over it, though, he says, it'll give him something to wow 'em back home with it in the Cordillera.

2. CRACKED, 2.

crack-'em-up *n.* an automotive accident.

1978 Lieberman & Rhodes *CB* (ed. 2) 296: *Crack 'em up*—Accident (noun).

cracker *n.* **1.** [see 1766 quot.] **a.** a backwoods Southern white person regarded as ignorant, brutal, loutish, bigoted, etc.; REDNECK.—used contemptuously. Also attrib., adv.

1766 in *DA*: I should explain to your Lordship what is meant by Crackers; a name they have got from being great boasters; they are a lawless set of rascals on the frontiers of Virginia, Maryland, the Carolinas, and Georgia, who often change their places of abode. **1772** in McWhiney

Cracker Culture vii: The People I refer to are really what you and I understand by *Crackers*...persons who have no settled habitation, and live by hunting and plundering the industrious Settlers. **1780** in Draper *King's Mountain* 593: But those that led us on that day of "Crackers" had no fear. **1801** in *Ibid.* 70: I speak only of backwoodsmen, not of the inhabitants in general of South Carolina...I speak only of that *heathen race* known by the name of *Crackers*. **1828** Cooper *Notions of Amer.* II 175: In Georgia you find a positive drawl among what are called the "crackers." **1840** *Spirit of Times* (Dec. 19) 499: The dancing was peculiarly "cracker." **1843** Field *Pokerville* 188: Exclusive of the driver—an "up-country cracker." **1865–67** De Forest *Miss Ravenel* 8: They remind me of a Cracker...a red-nosed, tobacco-drizzling, whiskey-perfumed giant. *ca***1875** Bemrose *Seminole War* 42: There were the Georgian and Floridian crackers (country farmers) with their nasal twang in answer to queries. **1891** C.H. Smith *Farm & Fireside* 9: There is really but little difference between the Georgia cracker and the Alabama or Tennessee cracker. **1891** Powell *Amer. Siberia* 30: Most of them were "Cracker" outlaws. **1908** Sullivan *Crim. Slang* 5: *Cracker*—A poor Southerner. **1924** in Clarke *Amer. Negro Stories* 25: They's a thousand shines in Harlem would change places with you in a minute jess f' the honor of killin' a cracker. **1927** C. McKay *Harlem* 26: I won't scab on nobody, not even the ornriest crackers. **1929–30** Dos Passos *42d Parallel* 357: Ah'm nutten but a lowdown cracker from Okachobe City. **1934** L. Hughes *Ways of White Folks* 62: Hell, I'm from Arkansas where the crackers lynch niggers in the streets. **1955** Robbins *79 Park Ave.* 224: She's probably some cracker without a thought in her head except for the sun and the sand. **1957** Mayfield *Hit* 43: He looks colored, but he talks cracker. **1965** C. Brown *Manchild* 44: The crackers down South is white people, real mean white people. **1970** Kinoy *Brother John* (film): You redneck cracker—get out of my house. **1976** Conroy *Santini* 63: I want these crackers to wake up and wonder what in the hell just blew into town. **1978** Price *Ladies' Man* 29: Yeah! I'm talking a *you!* Yah cracker bastad! **1983** R. Thomas *Missionary* 128: He was a cracker, damn near white trash. **1985** *Campus Voice* (Apr.) 27: The University of Florida journalism dean banned students with "black, cracker, New York, or ethnic accents" from being radio announcers on the student radio station. **1986** Ark. man, age 36: To me, a *redneck* is somebody who does outdoor labor, but a *cracker* is just plain trash...A redneck'll hit you in the face but a cracker'll stab you in the back.

b. *Black E.* a white racist.

1924 White *Fire in the Flint* 235: That's the way "Crackers" always fight colored folks! **1927** C. McKay *Harlem,* in *DARE*: He bitterly hated the whites he served ("crackers" he called them all). **1942** in P. McGuire *Jim Crow Army* 109: He...is a...Negro hating cracker from Louisiana. **1965** C. Brown *Manchild* 248: The jails, man, are all run by Northern crackers. You might as well be down in Alabama. **1979** in J.L. Gwaltney *Drylongso* 15: I did not tell these crackers to go over there and mess with these Arabs and Vietnam people! *Ibid.* 20: Let's not sell anything to those South African crackers, too, until they let some of our people go. **1994** *Newsweek* (Feb. 14) 48: Calling Jews "bloodsuckers"...and the pope a "no-good cracker."

2. *pl.* beans.

1900 *DN* II 30: *Crackers,* n. Beans. **1919** Darling *Jargon Book* 9: *Crackers*—Beans.

3. a remarkable individual; an outstanding example of a particular kind.

***1863** in *F & H* II 201: That was a *cracker* of those fellows. **1898** Green *Va. Folk.-Speech* 101: *Cracker, n.* A long foreskin. **1914** *DN* IV 70: *Cracker*...A fine-looking, stylish, lively person. "She's a cracker!" **1938** *AS* (Feb.) 5: "He's the cracker on this team." That is, he is the player who inspires the team to do its best. **1970** in *DARE*. **1979** in Raban *Old Glory* 133: He's a cracker. He's not one of those milk-and-water priests. He makes you think.

4. a dollar.

1933 in Goodstone *Pulps* 105: When I pay sixty-seven crackers for a cardboard box...I want to see what I'm stung with!

5. *Skiing.* BASHER.

1949 Cummings *Dict. Sports* 88.

6. *Black E.* (see quot.).

1967–69 Foster & Stoddard *Pops* 74 [ref. to N.O., *ca*1920]: Tom Turpin was a cracker, that's what we called a very light-colored person back then.

¶ In phrase:

¶ **by cracker** (used as a mild oath).

1972 T. O'Brien *Combat Zone* 143: But, by cracker, those guys better keep their eyes open.

cracker-ass *n.* a skinny person; (*hence*) a weakling.—used deri-

sively.—usu. considered vulgar.

1968 Maule *Rub-A-Dub* 65: Some cracker-ass ordinary...[and] a fat-ass first assistant. **1970** *Current Slang* V 5: *Crackerass,* n. A slender or skinny person.—Hurry up, *crackerass!* **1983** Eilert *Self & Country* 58 [ref. to 1967]: Don't be a cracker ass. *Ibid.* 150: Man, what a cracker ass.

cracker-assed *adj.* skinny.—used derisively.—usu. considered vulgar.

[**1935** J. Conroy *World to Win* 12: Somebody...'lowed yo' hinder parts looked like two sody crackers stuck together.] *ca***1937** in Holt *Dirty Comics* 50: Come on you flubber-cunted cracker-assed bitch.

cracker boss *n.* a straw boss.

1986 Kubicki *Breaker Boys* 36: Turning, he confronted the "cracker boss."

crackerbox *n.* **1.** *Mil.* a truck or tracked vehicle used as an ambulance.

[**1932** W. Smith *Lost Sqdrn.* (film): I could fly this old crackerbox blindfolded.] **1950** *Collier's* (Nov. 4) 24: A "cracker box" (ambulance) makes a slow haul from the 2d Division's front toward the rear. **1953** in *History of Chaplain Corps USN* 187: The pilot who was all right was sent out by ambulance (crackerbox). **1973** N.Y.U. student [ref. to 1971]: The Air Force uses two kinds of ambulances—the regular Packard and a truck which has room for four or six stretcher cases at once. It's a very square, box-like truck and it's called a *crackerbox*. **1991** C. Roberts *Combat Medic* 131: Get back to the cracker box and take cover.

2. a crazy or eccentric person.

1983 *A-Team* (NBC-TV): Don't worry. I'll find out who these crackerboxes are.

cracker factory *n.* [sugg. by CRACKERS] a hospital for the insane.

1981 "A. Landers," in *NY Daily News (Tonight)* (June 18) 58: Send her to the cracker factory. **1984** *N.Y. Post* (Aug. 15) 43: The people responsible for *Dreamscape* must be ready for the cracker factory. **1989** Radford & Crowley *Drug Agent* 149: If you can't accept the things you cannot change, you'll soon be...[in] the cracker factory.

crackerjack *n.* [cf. CRACKER, *n.,* 3] **1.** an individual of superior excellence or ability; *esp.* one who is especially expert or skillful; (*occ.*) a thing of excellence.

1895 in F. Remington *Sel. Letters* 272: You are a crackajack. **1895** in *OEDS*: He got a crackerjack when he bought that horse...As a pitcher he's a crackerjack. **1895** *DN* I 415: *Crackerjack*...A person of remarkable ability. **1897** Siler & Houseman *Fight of the Century* 34: With a little development and training you should become a crackerjack. **1902** K. Harriman *Ann Arbor Tales* 71: We can depend on him, fellows. He's a regular crackerjack! **1903** A. Adams *Log of a Cowboy* 265 [ref. to 1880's]: I know your man is a cracker-jack. **1905** W. S. Kelly *Lariats* 180: She is a warm baby, a regular "crackerjack," you know. **1905** *DN* III 61: His new gun is a crackajack. **1905** Hobart *Get Next!* 104: To Admiral...Togo, the Japanese crackerjack. **1905** in "O. Henry" *Works* 1313: "That's a crackerjack," said Sammy admiringly. **1909** *WNID*: He is a *crackajack* in tennis. **1906–07** Ade *Slim Princess* 53: I have seen Parisian beauties...and...so-called cracker-jacks that ought to be doing the mountain-of-flesh act in the Ringling side-show. **1909** *Sat. Eve. Post* (July 3) 32: The Mexican crackajack was comin' like a flushed quail. **1911** *JAF* (Oct.) 352: De womens in Jackson all dressed in black,/Said, in fact, he was a cracker-jack. **1928** Weaver *Collected Poems* 200: I got to be a cracker-jack, even if I/Say it as shouldn't. **1958** E. Hunter *Killer's Choice* 7: We're his top men...Crackerjacks. **1965–70** in *DARE*.

2. a cocky, insolent individual; (*also*) a foolish or useless person.

1919 MacGill *Dough-Boys* 11: If the Colonel didn't wash your mouth out, you crackerjack, I will! **1979** Eble *Campus Slang* (Mar.) 2: *Crackerjack*—oaf, fool (synonyms: nerd, turkey.).

crackerjack *adj.* **1.** of marked excellence; first-rate; splendid.

1899 Ade *Fables* 60: Gabby Will, the Crackerjack Salesman. **1906** Carter *Old Army Sketches* 17 [ref. to 1898]: God, Curly, what a crackerjack horse that fellar's got! **1907** London *Road* 19 [ref. to 1892]: Their ring-leader was a crackerjack road kid named Bob. **1909** *WNID*: *Crackajack, adj.* **1910** O. Johnson *Varmint* 43: Look out—he's a crackerjack boxer. **1949** *Time* (Sept. 5) 38: Had he lived longer, the crackerjack art student, playboy and plaything of society might have known disappointment. **1966** in *DARE*: crackerjack condition. **1968** J. Kerr *Clinic* 110: Things used to go smoother...when he was doing our anesthesia. He was crackerjack. **1969** *Playboy* (Mar.) 23: When would you like to pal up with Dustin for a crackerjack story? **1979** T. Baum *Carny* 93: She's a crackerjack dancer. **1981** *N.Y. Daily News* (July 24) 49: The

Grand Rapids Press did a crackerjack job of rounding up some revealing sentiments from the scattered Detroit ballplayers. *a*1991 Kross *Splash One* 223: I bet you'd make a crackerjack strategist.
2. worthless; two-bit.
   1970 in *DARE:* An unprofessional part-time lay preacher…*Crackerjack preacher.* **1976** *Nat. Lampoon* (July) 98: Maybe if we print more arty stuff…we can blow this crackerjack mag and get real jobs over at the *New Yorker.* **1981** Crowe *Fast Times* 243: Good luck to all you rats coming back to this crackerjack joint…I laugh in your face.

cracker line *n. Army.* a supply line. Now *hist.*
   1864 Andrus *Letters* 103: We fortified our position within ½ mile of the Rebls last & only Cracker line. **1864** in C.W. Wills *Army Life* 319: The cracker line is cut now. **1885** *Uncle Daniel's Story* 225: When this line was opened the boys christened it "Silent's cracker line." **1887** Hinman *Si Klegg* 453 [ref. to Civil War]: Ye know our cracker-line's all cut off. **1900** Remington *With the Bark On* 179 [ref. to 1898]: Shafter…sent his personal aide on a fast horse with positive orders to halt until the "cracker-line" could be fixed up behind them. **1900** Reeves *Bamboo Tales* 119: The water buffalo, the beast of burden that formed the American "cracker-line" in the Philippines before the introduction of the ever-faithful mule.

crackers *n.pl. Army.* supplies of rations.
   1898 in Remington *Wister* 245: We got *"three days"* crackers ahead.

crackers *adj.* crazy; insane.—used predicatively.
   [*1925 in Fraser & Gibbons *Soldier & Sailor Wds.* 65 [ref. to WWI]: *To get the crackers,* to go off one's head. Mad.] *1928 in *OEDS:* I shall go "crackers," (meaning mad) if anything happens to Ted. *1928, *1938, *1940, *1941, *1943, *1956 in *OEDS. *1948 *N.Y. Times* (Nov. 15): "England will…be going crackers tonight." An American reporter, unfamiliar with the English synonym for "daffy," asked [etc.]. **1957** Hall *Cloak & Dagger* 141 [ref. to WWII]: The C.O. happens to be a deeply religious man, he'll go crackers when I hand him the roll. **1960** *Sat. Eve. Post* (Apr. 2) 76: Have you gone crackers, doc?…Want to get us all killed? **1965–66** Pynchon *Crying* 146: The lad is crackers with grief. **1967** P. Welles *Babyhip* 212: She had been told that when you took LSD with another person, unless you were altogether crackers, you would instantly, irretrievably, fall in love. **1968** P. Roth *Portnoy* 263: There was her cutesy-wootsy boarding school argot…"Barf" for vomit, "ticked off" for angry, "a howl" for funny, "crackers" for crazy. **1968** Kirkwood *Good Times/Bad Times* 200: "Yes, a little, but only because he's crackers," he said, using the English term we both got a kick out of. **1970** Corrington *Bombardier* 31: I'm in the great Texas desert one lousy afternoon and evening and I'm crackers. *Ibid.* 116: Boy, did they make a mistake with this guy. He is crackers… **1975** Wambaugh *Choirboys* 114: He was driving Wolfgang crackers. **1976** *N.Y. Times Bk. Review* (Aug. 29) 6: If I'd worked on the book much longer I would have gone crackers. **1982** *N.Y. Post* (Aug. 13) 18 [headline]: Parrot Goes Crackers.

crackhead *n.* a habitual user of CRACK, *n.,* 10.
   1986 *Time* (June 2) 17: More than half the nation's so-called crackheads are black. **1987** *21 Jump St.* (Fox-TV): Unaffiliated dealers, crackheads with no place to go. **1988** *Newsday* (N.Y.C.) (July 1) 41: You expect behavior like this from crack heads. **1989** in *Harper's* (Mar.) 73: She's being called "prostitute, crackhead, a liar." **1994** *Newsweek* (Jan. 10) 22: He's turning in the …handgun he bought for $30 from "a crackhead."

crackhouse *n. Police.* a building, apartment, etc., often fortified by drug dealers, where someone may purchase or use CRACK, *n.,* 10.
   1985 *S.F. Chronicle* (Dec. 6), in *Oxf. Dict. New Words* 73: Drug dealers have opened up drug galleries, called "crack houses." **1985** WINS Radio News (Dec. 30): Police say the "crackhouses" operate out of private apartments. **1988** *Daily Beacon* (Univ. Tenn.) (May 20) 1: Bush's speech followed a tour of a recently raided "crack house" in South Central Los Angeles. **1989** *U.S. News & W.R.* (Apr. 10) 29: Crack house can mean…a place to use, a place to sell or a place to do both, and the location may be an apartment, bungalow or abandoned building. **1994** *Newsweek* (Feb. 14) 29: [The] west Philadelphia neighborhood is loaded with crack houses and crackheads.

cracking *adj.* excellent; splendid; rattling.
   1833 S. Smith *President's Tour* 46: If you don't hear of cracking work done there, that will make 'em all stare, I'm mistaken. **1833** in [S. Smith] *Letters of Downing* 109: The President's Message to Congress makes cracking work here. **1842** *Spirit of Times* (May 28) 151: This was a cracking race. **1873** in *AS* XLVIII (1973) 90: Popped a proud whip over a pair of crackin blood bays. **1896** Ade *Artie* 36: He had 240 acres of crackin' Corn Land. **1902** Cullen *More Tales* 22: They sell 'em fr

real antiques, y'see, and they get crackin' prices.

cracking *adv.* exceedingly.
   1916 Livingston *Snare* 110: Ain't this some cracking fine road, sir? **1963** W. C. Anderson *Penelope* 72: That's a cracking good idea. **1978** E. Thompson *Devil to Pay* 52: I think you have the bones of a cracking good novel.

crackling *n.* a fellow.
   1834 in *DA:* I looked like a pretty cracklin ever to get to Congress! **1884** Beard *Thorns* 44: I hain't the skeery sort o' a cracklin'.

crackman *n.* CRACKSMAN.
   1853 Lippard *New York* 93: There's two crackmen—burglars, you know,—hid up-stairs in your son's room.

crack off *v.* to WISE OFF.
   1986 Univ. Tenn. instructor: If a student cracks off in class, you *kung fu* him.

crack out *v.* CRACK, *v.,* 4.b.
   1985 M. Baker *Cops* 275: A police officer has too much stress and cracks out.

crackpot *n.* a person who is crazy, markedly eccentric, or fanatical. Now *colloq.*
   *1883 in *F & H:* My aunty knew lots, and called them crack-pots. **1889** Barrère & Leland *Dict. Slang* I 278: *Crack-pot* (American), pretentious, petty, a small person of little account. *1919 in *OEDS:* He felt it would annoy this Toplofty Crackpot. **1929** Hammett *Maltese Falcon* 134: I'm damned tired of being called things by every crackpot on the city payroll. **1932** Hecht & Fowler *Great Magoo* 137: You little crack-pot! Who told you you could sing and dance? **1941** in Truman *Ltrs. Home* 157: All the Missourians in this part of the world are trying to see me, and so are the California crackpots. **1945** in Truman *Dear Bess* 515: But it has possibilities as appeasement for the crackpots. **1953** in Marx *Groucho* 35: The local gendarmes might regard me as a crackpot. **1976** *Barnaby Jones* (CBS-TV): Some crackpot's trying to ruin this town. **1982** Nicholas *World's Greatest Cranks & Crackpots* (title). **1992** Pres. G. Bush, campaign speech in Gainesville, Ga. (Oct. 19): You have a debate, you say what you think. And then two seconds later some crackpot comes on and tells you what you think.

crackpot *adj.* (of a person, idea, or the like) crazy; irrational. Cf. 1889 quot. at CRACKPOT, *n.*
   1934 in *OEDS.* **1968** P. Roth *Portnoy* 11: A medical procedure like this (crackpot though it may be) takes time. **1977** *Oui* (Apr.) 129: The Air Force had also hired a psychologist to see how many of the reports were strictly crackpot. **1989** J.M. Ellis *Against Deconstruction* 152: Genuinely shocking as opposed to dismissibly crackpot.

crackskull *n.* POPSKULL.
   1842 *Spirit of Times* (Sept. 17) 341: Sufficient to debar his fellow beings from the use of the "crack-skull," i.e., whiskey…a quart of real *crackskull.* **1956** Longstreet *Real Jazz* 103: And the piano chords rode up and down and somebody ran out to get another bottle of crackskull. And the chippie he was dating hitched up her rolled stockings and said, "Play it, Daddy."

cracksman *n. Orig. Und.* a housebreaker or safecracker. Now *hist.*
   *1797 in Partridge *Dict. Und.* *1811 *Lexicon Balatron.:* The kiddy is a clever cracksman. **1845** *Nat. Police Gaz.* (Oct. 18) 66: Any "cracksman" or lock-picker. **1846** *Lives of the Felons* 15: The daring and successful "cracksmen." **1848** *Ladies' Repository* VIII (Oct.) 315: *Cracksman,* One who breaks houses open. **1859** Matsell *Vocab.* 22: *Cracksman.* A burglar who uses force instead of picklocks or false keys. **1866** *Night Side of N.Y.* 60: It is kept by an old "cracksman," or house-breaker. **1869** *Overland Mo.* (Aug.) 116: Not every day you find a Dublin cracksman to practice on. **1882** Pinkerton *Bank-Robbers* 90: Two noted "cracksmen," or professional burglars. *1881–84 Davitt *Prison Diary* I 23: I have conversed with several cracksmen who have been in Egypt, Russia, Turkey, and other foreign lands. **1899** A.H. Lewis *Sandburrs* 274: The cracksman took a drink. **1911** Howard *Enemy to Society* 147: Say a "house man" or a "sneak" or a "second-story" man or a "peteman"—anything but "cracksman." You see that in novels and that's about the only place where you do see it. **1916** *Editor* XLIII (May 6) 487: *Cracksman,*…safeblower. **1925** *Atlantic Mo.* (Dec.) 747: I attended their seances, listened to their jargon about "boxes" and "screws" and "obies" and "cracksman" and "hog's-eyes." **1979** F. Thomas *Golden Bird* 29: We followed the master cracksman as he led us over the roof of the warehouse. **1980** Bruns *Kts. of Road* 96: They could look forward to certification as master cracksmen.

crack troops *n.* [pun on CRACK, *n.*, 3.b.] *Mil.* female members of the armed forces.—usu. considered vulgar. Occ. sing. *Joc.*

1947 *ATS* (Supp.) 14: *Crack troops*, Women's Army Corps. **1980** McDowell *Our Honor* 81 [ref. to *ca*1952]: He never missed an opportunity to refer to the Women Marines...as "crack troops." **1980** Univ. Tenn. grad. student, age 32: *Crack troops* was commonly used to refer to WAFs at Lackland Air Force Base, Texas, in 1971 and at Tyndall Air Force Base, Florida, 1971–75. There was a pun on "elite military unit"—elite in some physical capabilities, that is. **1986** Former SP4, U.S. Army: When I was at Ft. Jackson, S.C., in 1972 I was an ad man, and I was told, "You ad men are lucky—you'll hook up with some *crack troops*. Ha ha ha ha!" And between 1972 and 1976 I heard it almost daily, whenever a new WAC was assigned to us: "We got a new crack troop."

crack-up *n.* **1.** an emotional breakdown, nervous collapse, or onset of insanity.

1938–39 Dos Passos *Young Man* 270: Dr. Blumenthal says you are heading for a crackup. **1964** Thompson & Rice *Every Diamond* 52: A rabid fan...seemed headed for a nervous crackup. **2.** a lunatic; one who has cracked up.

*a*1949 D. Levin *Mask of Glory* 229: I don't want him to go back as a crack-up. **1965** *Munsters* (CBS-TV): Don't do that, dad, or the fellas'll think you're some kind of a crack-up.

3. a cause for hilarity.

1961 Braly *Felony Tank* 59: Isn't that a crack-up? I bet he gave those two clowns a fit? **1975** *Cocaine Comix* (unp.): That's the *funniest*...goddam thing I've ever seen!! Wotta crack-up!!! **1985** Baker *Cops* 123: Working massage parlors [undercover] is a crack-up. *a*1990 Westcott *Half a Klick* 164: That Gilligan's a real crack up.

crack up *v.* **1.** to praise (*obs.*); in phr. **not what (it's) cracked up to be** not as good as (it's) said to be. Now *colloq.*

1829 in *OEDS*: He is not the thing he is cracked up for. **1837** Strong *Diary* I 60: Byron...is not such an incarnate Satan as he's cracked up to be. *1844 Dickens *Chuzzlewit* ch. xxxiii: You'd better crack us up, you had! **1847** Robb *Squatter Life* 143: It *did* tickle his fancy to have her cracked up, 'cause he thought her creation's finishin' touch. **1848** Judson *Mysteries* 246: This 'ere losin' time, isn't vot its cracked up to be! **1862** O.W. Holmes, Jr., in M.D. Howe *Shaping Years* 120: Local regiments...get cracked up like thunder. **1868** J. Chisholm *So. Pass* 141: The...springs...had been much "cracked up" to me by certain parties. **1884** in *OED*: Mexico...is not what it has been cracked up to be. **1896** Ade *Artie* 88: Every guy cracks up his own wheel. **1914** in J. Reed *Young Man* 53: Well,...you can crack up your pretty señoritas all you want to. But for *me*, give me a clean little American girl. *ca*1930 in Gardner *Casey* 123: But what's the use of crackin' up the mutt that lost the game?

2. see CRACK, *v.*, 4.b.

3. to laugh or cause to laugh unrestrainedly.

1942 in C.R. Bond & T. Anderson *Flying T. Diary* 131: We got the funniest...story out of Moose Moss...We cracked up. *Ibid.* 160: The guys cracked up when they saw it. **1954** Ellson *Owen Harding* 42: All we had to do to start in laughing again was look at each other's faces and we almost cracked up. **1964** R. Gold *Jazz Lexicon* 71. **1966** Goldstein *1 in 7* 41: I said, "What's the matter, haven't you ever seen a gentleman before?" and that really cracked them up. **1973** Wideman *Lynchers* 35: She cracked up laughing all over the place. **1974** Kurtzman *Bobby* 77: "What's so funny, Coral." "I don't know. He cracks me up. Always." **1976** Schroeder *Shaking It* 94: Both of us just crack up, just let go and convulse with laughter. **1980** Grizzard *Billy Bob Bailey* 41: He cracked me up. **1990** *Atlanta Jour.* (July 28) B6: You know what cracks me up? Ants *run* everywhere!

cradle *n.* a saddle. *Joc.*

1906 M'Govern *Sarjint Larry* 66: Hell, dis craddle (saddle) of "Red's" with your blouse trun over it'll make [a] comfortable...piller.

¶ In phrases:

¶ **rob the cradle** to keep company with or marry a much younger person.

1942 *ATS* 339. **1975** Boatner et al. *Dict. Amer. Idioms* 286: When the old woman married the young man, everyone said she was robbing the cradle. **1986** *World Book Dict.* I 482: His friends teased him about robbing the cradle when he proposed, at 40, to a girl of 20.

¶ **rock the cradle** *Naut.* to stand watch during the night.

1851 Ely *Wanderings* 190: I must now go on deck. It is eight o'clock, and I shall have to "rock the cradle" till twelve o'clock.

cradle robber *n.* a person who keeps company with or marries a much younger person of the opposite sex.

1926 Tully *Jarnegan* 262: You lousy, cradle robber. **1975** Boatner *Dict. Amer. Idioms* 286: The Judge died when he was seventy. He was a real cradle-robber because he left a thirty-year-old widow. **1992** *Geraldo* (synd. TV series): Is he permanently branded as a cradle-robber? **1993** *Wkly. World News* (July 13) 23: I'm a 28-year-old man...in love with a 17-year-old girl. Please don't think I'm a cradle robber.

cradle-snatcher *n.* **1.** CRADLE ROBBER.

1907 Corbin *Cave Man* 314: Some men are never too old. What is that they call them—cradle snatchers? **1913** J. London *Valley of Moon* 56: "Cradle-snatcher," was the final sting that sent the angry blood into Saxon's cheeks. **1925** in *DA*. **1942** *ATS* 772. **1949** *Life of Riley* (CBS-TV): That cradle-snatcher! **1950** in Conklin *Sci. Fi. Omnibus* 39: You don't want to go around looking twice as old as your wife and having people calling you a cradle snatcher, now do you? **1967** Talbot *Chatty Jones* 101: "Chatty, I'm no cradle-snatcher. How old are you really?" "Eighteen." **1992** *Sally Jessy Raphaël* (synd. TV series): You're a cradle-snatcher!

2. a child molester.

1942 H. Miller *Roofs of Paris* 11: I've never seen myself as a cradle snatcher....those men you watch being hustled away in the public parks...explaining that the child had dust on her dress and they were brushing it off.

craft *n.* *Naut.* a person, esp. a young woman.

1836 *Spirit of Times* (Feb. 20) 7: Ned Curtis had a wife; a strapping craft, broad in the beam, with a high starn, and very bluff in the bows. **1838** *Crockett Almanac* (1839) 24: He said she was a slick craft...as sweet as honey. **1848** in Ely *There She Blows* 24: Aye, boy, I tell you, she was a trim craft. **1853** [J. Jones] *Jack Junk* 5: Kate Markham is a craft that any man might be proud of. **1867** *Nat. Police Gaz.* (Oct. 26) 2: I had the pleasure of finding myself...alongside of a full-rigged craft. **1872** Thomes *Slaver* 96: How would you like to sail with such a craft? **1895** Sinclair *Alabama* 337: Nor do I imagine he has mastered French and returned to his "little craft." **1916** in *DARE*: Respect or contempt are expressed by such terms as "She's quite a craft," or "He's a poor craft." Eccentricity is implied in the term "a queer craft."

cram *n.* *Stu.* (see quot.).

1900 *DN* II 30: *Cram*, n. 1. One who does much extra work before an examination. 2. A course requiring hard study. 3. A lecture course.

cram *v.* **1.** *Stu.* to study hastily and intently, as for an academic examination. Now *S.E.*

*1810 in *OED*. **1865** *Harper's Mo.* XXX 605: To "cram" for an examination. **1871** Bagg *Yale* 44: *Cram*, to prepare for an examination on a subject, rather than to really master it. **1872** O.W. Holmes *Poet* 72: I suppose you do a little of what we teachers used to call "cramming" now and then? **1880** Sprague *Campus Melodies* 38: For exams we cram. **1979** J. Morris *War Story* 225: I'd really have to cram for a while. **1981** Pagel *Cosmic Code* 10: In 1900, Einstein graduated from the university, but only by cramming for final exams. **1983** Wambaugh *Delta Star* 195: My...daughter's cramming for a history test and I'm supposed to quiz her.

2. to copulate with (a woman).

*a*1896 in *Immortalia* 15: I dearly delighted to fondle and cram her,/This old-fashioned harlot whose surname was Belle. **1942** McAtee *Supp. to Grant Co.* 4 [ref. to 1890's]: *Cram*, v., to fuck a woman.

3. away with; be done with; SHOVE.—used imperatively or with imperative force.—usu. constr. with *it*.

1957 Kohner *Gidget* 112: Cram it, Gidget, this is nothing for you. **1962** W. Crawford *Give Me Tomorrow* 78 [ref. to 1951]: Cram your dice! *Ibid.* 100: Cram it! **1964** *AS* (May) 117: *Cram it* or...*up yours*. **1964** *Social Problems* XI 357: He better quit riding me or I'll tell him to take this job and cram it! **1971** Jacobs & Casey *Grease* 9: ROGER. Nice job! KENICKLE. Hey, cramit! I'm savin' up to get me some wheels. **1973** *Nat. Lampoon Encyc. of Humor* 50: Cram it, clown! **1974** E. Thompson *Tattoo* 394: Oh, cram you and your goddamn *mistake*! **1988** *N.Y. Daily News* (June 14) 54: It's obvious no one at NBC feels it's safe to tell their Mr. Baseball Broadcasting Legend to cram it.

crammer *n.* **1.** a lie.

1837 *Every Body's Album* II 235: Oh, he loved this pastry cook, too, and told her many a *crammer*. **1859** Matsell *Vocab.* 22: *Crammer*. A falsehood. **1870** *Comic Songster* 25: That there's a jolly crammer!

2. the stomach.

1848 *Ladies' Repository* VIII (Oct.) 315: *Crammer*, The Stomach.

cramp *n.* [prob. sugg. by menstrual *cramps*] *Black E.* an unpleasant or contemptible woman.

1992 Mowry *Way Past Cool* 32: Stupid cramp, man! She just like I tellin you.

¶ In phrase: **put a cramp on** to coerce.

1966 in Young *UFO Top Secret* 52: The Air Force is putting a cramp on Hynek for a press release.

cramp *v.* **1.** *Und.* to execute or kill.

1859 Matsell *Vocab.* 22: *Cramped.* Killed; murdered; hanged. *Cramping Cull.* Executioner; hangman.

2. *Army.* to steal; SCROUNGE.

1862 in *Civil War Hist.* XIV 24: Whatever else we got we had to press or cramp & keep it kind of shy. *Ibid.:* We have lots of fun here, cramping from the Secesh, milk their cows, eat their peaches, etc. etc. **1862** in Andrus *Letters* 43: I cramped a blanket the other day, & then I cramped another & sold it for $40.00, Confederate scrip, which is the same as nothing at all. **1862** in Bear *Civil War Letters* 5: They say we will Cramp enough of wagons to carry the extra load. **1884** Hedley *Marching Through Ga.* 448 [ref. to 1865]: Chickens and buttermilk were now being bought...instead of being "cramped."

3. to annoy.

1886 Nye *Remarks* 21: It cramps your mother and me like Sam Hill to put up the money. **1969** in *DARE*.

¶ In phrase:

¶ **cramp (someone's) style** to hinder (someone), esp. from doing his or her best; thwart. Now *colloq.*

1917 in *OEDS*: I think the very fact of a censorship cramps one's style. *1925** in Fraser & Gibbons *Soldier & Sailor Wds.* 65 [ref. to WWI]: *Cramp One's Style, To:* To render useless. To put off one's stroke. **1929** Burnett *Iron Man* 4: Don't say I'm always trying to cramp your style. **1929–30** in *DAS* 127. **1934** Weseen *Dict. Amer. Slang* 323: *Cramp one's style*—To restrain a person; to hamper; to restrict.

cram session *n.* *Stu.* a brief period of intensive study, esp. shortly before an examination.

1939 M. Levin *Citizens* 83: He had gone through a cram session, spent an entire week in his room sunk in his texts.

Cranberry *n.* *USAF.* the Martin B-57 Canberra bomber and reconnaissance aircraft.

1966 Shepard *Doom Pussy* 45: Old Charlie harbors a special hatred for the Cranberries.

cranberry eye *n.* (see quot.). Cf. CAULIFLOWER EAR.

1889 Barrère & Leland *Dict. Slang* I 279: *Cranberry eye* (American). When a man's eye is bloodshot, generally from drinking alcohol, he is often called a boy with a *cranberry eye.*

crank *n.* **1.** a person who is insane (now *rare*), eccentric (now *colloq.*), or possessed of irrational or uninformed views on a particular subject (now *S.E.*); in phrs. **crank call, crank letter** a telephone call or letter from a crank.

1833 in *OEDS*: Uncle Sam's "Old Mother Bank" Is managed by a foreign crank. **1874** *Nat. Police Gaz.* (Dec. 5) 3: He is a "crank" since coming down the river. **1885** *Nat. Police Gaz.* (Nov. 28) 2: New York Prohibitionists have expelled a member of one of their societies for being a "crank." It is seldom that the beam in one's own eye is perceived. **1886** in *F & H* II: I know perfectly well that I shall probably be called an old fogy, if not a *crank*, for presuming to think that anything in the past can be better than in the present. **1889** Reynolds *Twin Hells* 121: He was placed in the "Crank House" with the cranks. Those prisoners, who have either lost their mind or are suffering with temporary insanity...are classed as "cranks," and have an apartment by themselves. **1891** Maitland *Slang Dict.* 80: *Crank* (Am.), an erratic person; one of ill-balanced mind. **1893** in F. Harris *Conklin* 207: Roberts was plainly a "crank," book-mad. **1902** in Tomlin *H. Tomlin* 135: Q.—You said you were locked up with a crank on each side; what do you mean by that? A.—Crazy people, yelling and squalling. Q.—How many cranks have they got? A.—Ten or twelve. **1903** A. Adams *Log of a Cowboy* 128: What kind of a crank is that you ran me up against? **1918–19** Sinclair *Higgins* 271: He's a Socialist and a crank, you know, and you'd be surprised how ugly some of them fellows can be. **1938** "E. Queen" *4 Hearts* 137: The writer was sane, not a crank. **1948** in *DA* 429: He gets a lot of crank letters and these I threw away. **1967** J. Kramer *Instant Replay* 29: I don't pay any attention to those crank calls. **1984** *Chi. Sun-Times* (Mar. 25) 8: *Crank*—A mentally unstable person.

2. an enthusiast; (*specif.*) a sports fan. Now *hist.*

1882 Sweet *Sketches* 58: *Fire cranks.* There are a number of stereotyped characters who attend all fires. *Ibid.* 75: The statistical crank can give figures on anything. **1887** (cited in Nichols *Baseball Term.*). **1890** Kerbey *War Path* 191: I have already confessed to being an amateur photo

crank. **1892** Bierce *Beetles* 236: To marshal the vinophobe ranks...I anoint thee.../As King of aquatical cranks! **1893** *Chi. Daily Tribune* (Sept. 3) 7: The New Yorks won a regular old-time slugging match from the Louisvilles today in the presence of 5,000 cranks. **1894** in Ade *Chicago Stories* 63: "You two fellows have got hearts too big for your bodies," remarked the ball crank. **1894** in P. Levine *Spalding* 66: Baseball cranks are peculiar. **1895** C. C. King *Trooper Ross* 133: I've been a baseball crank for twenty years. **1906** *Nat. Police Gaz.* (Oct. 20) 10: This fight is...the biggest treat the pugilistic cranks are looking forward to. **1907** Siler *Pugilism* 191: "Crank"—Follower and close student of the game. (See also "Fan," "Fiend.") *a*1911 in Spalding *Base Ball* 52: Two Brooklyn cranks had a wager of $100 a side on John Holden's making a home run. **1944** Mellor *Sank Same* 34: Aviation "cranks" from every state in the Union, members of the Civil Air Patrol. **1949** J. Durant *Baseball* 19: Thousands of cheering *cranks* (yesterday's word for fans). **1973** H. Peterson *Man Who Invented Baseball* 79: Early fans...were called cranks. **1981** Vincent *Mudville* 94: The knowledgeable baseball "crank" became the prototype of the "hipster."

3. a craze; fad.

1884 in Smith & Smith *Police Gaz.* 55: Society has developed a new crank. It is the worship of its favorite operatic tenors.

4. a grouchy or ill-tempered person. Now *colloq.*

1893 W.K. Post *Harvard* 2: You old crank. **1921** *Variety* (Dec. 30) 4: But God, what a crank!...He blustered, he fumed and he raved about/ Everything under the skies. **1986** N.Y.C. man, age 38: I guess I'm just becoming a crank.

5. the penis.

1968 *Zap Comix* (No. 3) (unp.): Bite my crank. *Ibid.* Your crank is as warm as toast. **1972** *Nat. Lampoon* (July) 33: Bite my clank [pseudo-Chinese]. **1975** T. Berger *Sneaky People* 45: Ralph always inspected his face carefully after yanking his crank. **1978** Price *Ladies' Man* 33: All I could think about was her hand on my crank in the deli. **1981** Crowe *Fast Times* 166: He didn't often use the word [*penis*]. Dick, cock, cock, wang, pud, pecker, schlong, weiner, or frank—they all came much more easily. **1985** Dye *Between Raindrops* 16: Just say the word and my crank looks like a boa constrictor with a turtleneck sweater on. **1992** N. Baker *Vox* 57: That's a fair description of my...crank. [Ellipses in original.]

6.a. *Narc.* methamphetamine; SPEED.

1969 *Esquire* (July) 65: I'm still a little wired from the crank I shot a couple days ago. **1971** Simon *Sign of Fool* 17: I asked Chuck if he could spare a small taste of crank as I needed the speed in order to work the rest of the day. **1972** Smith & Gay *Don't Try It* 68: Some guys shoot crank for the same reason. **1979** *N.Y. Times* (June 24) IV 22: The large-scale manufacture and mass distribution of methamphetamine, also known as "speed" and "crank." **1986** *New Image Teens* (KPBS-TV): Speed, amphetamine, crystal, crank! **1987** R. Miller *Slob* 202: They could go over [to Australia] and sell crank free from any laws. **1989** *48 Hours* (CBS-TV) (May 4): "I can't tell you how many truckers use crank. I don't know."...*Crank*—what city folks call "crystal."

b. a thrill of excitement; charge.

1973 in H.S. Thompson *Shark Hunt* 85: The NFL is a molasses farm compared to the fine sense of crank that comes on when you get locked into watching a team like the Montreal Canadiens or the Boston Celtics. **1974** in *Ibid.* 361: For me there is no real crank or elation in having been a front-row spectator at the final scenes.

¶ In phrase:

¶ **turn (someone's) crank** to interest or stimulate (someone) greatly; TURN ON.

1987 Univ. Tenn. student: Oh, well. Whatever turns your crank.

crank *adj.* proud.

1843 "J. Slick" *High Life in N.Y.* 9: Standing up on...top...as crank as could be. *Ibid.* 12: The old woman began to brag about Samuel, for she's felt mighty crank about him ever since he had that great dinner give to him.

crank *v.* **1.a.** to activate or put into operation (a motor or similar mechanical device) without the use of an actual crank.—usu. constr. with *up*. Also *fig.* Also intrans. [Esp. common after *ca*1970.]

1930 J.T. Farrell *Calico Shoes* 53: When he cranks his jaw up, the story's ended. **1942** in C.R. Bond & T. Anderson *Flying T. Diary* 122: We started cranking...[the planes] up. *Ibid.* 162: We decided to crank up and make a reconnaissance flight. **1961** G. Forbes *Goodbye to Some* 131: Crank something up, mate, if you want your ass in ribbons. *ca*1964 K. Cook *Other Capri* 128 [ref. to WWII]: I'm ready to crank up [*sc.* start an aircraft engine]. **1964** *Newsweek* (Sept. 28) 46: It led Wilson to crank up his campaign pace too soon in anticipation of an earlier election. **1972** W.C. Anderson *Hurricane* 37: Especially when…Clark cranks up his banjo. **1980** W.C. Anderson *Bat-21* 3: Crank up your jamming equipment. *__1984__ Partridge *DSUE* (ed. 8) 265: So right on the button we crank [jet] engines.

b. to get ready or go into operation.—constr. with *up.*—also constr. with *it.*

1968 *Business Week* (Jan. 13) 42: NASA will be hard-pressed to crank up any new programs to follow its initial Apollo moon landing. **1970** *New Yorker* (Dec. 5) 112: Bayh instructed his staff to crank up for an all-out fight against the nomination. **1972** H.S.F. Cooper, Jr. *Thirteen* 43: Kranz requested…that additional computers…be what he called "cranked up"—made ready for use. **1976** Crews *Feast of Snakes* 69: Just a bunch of crazy people cranking up to git crazier. **1977** Shryack, Butler & Slade *The Car* (film): "You better step on it." "I'll crank it up." **1978** *Monday Night Baseball* (ABC-TV) (June 27): Sparky Lyle is also cranking up in the bullpen for the Yankees. **1982** *N.Y. Times Mag.* (Aug. 29) 66: While watching the batter crank up and swing. **1984** Hammel *Root* 25: A speaker truck would crank up and further incite the gathering crowd with brave exhortations. **1989** Berent *Rolling Thunder* 62: Crank up the paperwork to…do a Top Secret Plus background on him.

c. (of an engine) to respond to the ignition; start.

1970 *Pop. Sci.* (Aug.) 20: Once again I am having difficulties getting this engine to crank. **1983** Beckwith & Knox *Delta Force* 277: We all knew the eccentricities of choppers. There was a good chance two of them would not crank tomorrow. *Ibid.* 285: In special ops when a chopper doesn't crank, it's usually a matter of life and death. *a*1990 R. Herman, Jr. *Force of Eagles* 410: I wish to hell my jet would crank.

2. (esp. of a small child) to be cranky or sullen.

1942 *ATS* 291. **1985** Kalamazoo, Mich., man, age 38: He's cranking again.

3. to engage in energetic activity; do well. Hence **cranking** exciting. See also CRANKED UP.

1981 Eble *Campus Slang* (Oct.) 3: *Crank*—to study intensively: She's really cranking for that mid-term. **1982** S. Black *Totally Awesome* 21: *Cranking*: Something that kicks butt, gets down, goes all out. A good band *cranks* totally. **1984** Eble *Campus Slang* (Sept.) 2: *Crank*—party, get wild. **1985** "Blowdryer" *Mod. Eng.* 8: Something that's really happenin' can be cranking. A band or a club, par example. **1985** on *Story of English* (PBS-TV): The waves were totally cranking! *a*1988 C. Adams *More Straight Dope* 313: Your metabolism is really cranking. **1988** *Rage* (Univ. Tenn.) (Mar. 30) 31: Things get cranking when he walks in the door. **1988** Univ. Tenn. student: I guess I better get cranking. **1986–91** Hamper *Rivethead* 128: A few days later, we were crankin'. **1992** G. Wolff *Day at the Beach* 91: Cranked by the music,…I drank rye-and-ginger by the yard.

4. to be under the influence of CRANK, *n.*, 6.a.

1987–91 D. Gaines *Teenage Wasteland* 189: I spent several months cranked on "crystal meth." **1992** *Amer. Detective* (ABC-TV): Does he look loaded at all? Were they crankin'?

¶ In phrases:

¶ **crank in** to key or factor in.

1961 L.G. Richards *TAC* 235: You can crank in a "map" of the route and she'll…sniff her way along, eight hundred feet above the ground. **1969** *U.S. News & W.R.* (Nov. 24) 77: Conclusion to crank into year-end planning: While most investors will pay lower taxes on next year's capital gains, the reverse will be true for many wealthy people. **1972** W.C. Anderson *Hurricane* 154: They'll crank in…the weather information and shoot you your computerized flight plans. **1977** Kleinberg *Live With Computer* 119: I decided to assign a value factor to that, and to crank it into the equation. **1981** *Business Week* (June 1) 73: As farmers pay ever-higher rates of interest, that gets cranked into the cost of production.

¶ **crank off** to fire (a round). Also intrans.

1961 Coon *Front* 114: It's like if you take a walk, and somebody cranks one off at you. **1962** in H.S. Thompson *Shark Hunt* 428: If I hadn't sold my pistol I'd whip up the blinds and crank off a few rounds at his feet. **1963** Coon *Short End* 183: And if they start to shoot at us, you crank off at them without waiting to hear from me. **1977** Caputo *Rumor of War* 98: A rifleman cranks off a couple of rounds at something he has seen or heard. *a*1989 C.S. Crawford *Four Deuces* 70: He cranks off just two shots from his M1.

¶ **crank up** see **(1.a., b.),** above, and CRANKED UP.

crankcase *n.* the head; the mind.

1960 C. Cooper *Scene* 54: You're not responsible to desk sergeants any more…can't you get that through your crankcase?

cranked *adj.* **1.** mentally unbalanced.

1881 in *DA* 429. **1890** *Overland Mo.* (Feb.) 124: The boys have deviled him about the loss of his ear, until he's cranked about it, sure!

2. see CRANK, *v.* 4.

cranked up *adj.* enthusiastic; excited; revved up.

1957 Myrer *Big War* 324: I'm a five-alarm fire when I'm cranked up. **1968** Myrer *Eagle* 116: You're pretty cranked up, Reb. **1971** H.S. Thompson *Las Vegas* 14: He's probably all cranked up on speed. **1972** in *Penthouse* (Jan. 1973) 95: I went there, you know, all cranked up. Finally…Shanghai! Front row seats. **1977** *L.A. Times* (Nov. 2) III 7: Right now I'm cranked up more than I ever have been. **1984** *N.Y. Post* (Aug. 18) 39: Fouts will go in there just as cranked up as if he were playing the whole game. **1988** A. Gould *Double Bang* 54: He's all cranked up and he wants some more. **1988** Frazier & Offen *W. Frazier* 101: By the time you're starting to relax, it's time to get cranked up again.

cranker *n.* a physician.

*a*1946 in W.C. Fields *By Himself* 152: The cranker informed me…[to] lay off the vile stuff.

cranking *adj.* see CRANK, *v.*, 3.

crankster *n. Narc.* a user of CRANK, *n.*, 6.a.

*a*1990 E. Currie *Dope & Trouble* 93: Cranksters tend to go on…binges.

crank up *v.* see CRANK, *v.*, 1.a., b.

cranky *adj.* **1.** irritable; crotchety. Now *S.E.*

1812 in Howay *New Hazard* 113: Being very drunk and cranky had offered abuse to captain. *__1821__ in *OED*. *__1840__ C. Dickens *Curiosity Shop* ch. VII: His friend appeared to be rather cranky in point of temper. **1880** G.L. Vanderbilt *Flatbush* 55 [ref. to 1830's]: A child who was querulous was said to be "krankie," from [Dutch] "krank," weak, sick. **1903** *Independent* (Nov. 26) 2791: The excited bawling of cranky officers on deck. **1929** Hammett *Maltese Falcon* 22: "Don't be cranky, Sam," she said wearily. **1986** Yolen *Merlin's Boke* 79: The dragon sounded just a bit cranky.

2. insane.

*__1850__ in *OED*. **1859** Matsell *Vocab.* 22: Cranky. Mad; insane. **1889** Reynolds *Kansas Hell* 186: He thought I was going "cranky."

cranky-hutch *n. Und.* (see quot.).

1859 Matsell *Vocab.* 22: Cranky-Hutch. An insane asylum.

crap[1] *n.* [fr. E. dial. *crap* 'a scrap or remnant', ME *crappe* 'chaff', later 'a crackling', and related senses. In the light of these meanings, **(1.b.)** may be the orig. sense. The earliest attested form clearly identical with current senses is CRAPPY (1846), q.v. *Crap* is usu. regarded as a euphemism for SHIT in corresponding senses, but speakers strongly offended by the latter word often find the "euphemism" almost equally offensive. See also note at CRAP, *v.*]

1.a. excrement.—sometimes considered vulgar.

*__1846__ (implied by quot. at CRAPPY, 1). *__1889__ Barrère & Leland *Dict. Slang* I 279: *Crap*…(Printers), applied to "pie," or mixed-up type, that a compositor neglects to clear away; equivalent to the popular name for excrement. *__a__1898__ in *EDD* I 776: *Crap*…Ordure. Also used as a term of gross insult. **1927** C. McKay *Harlem* 89: Or I'll throw this heah garbage in you' crap-yaller face. **1931** Dos Passos *1919* 128: The regulars…were digging trenches and shovelling crap and fighting malaria and dysentery and yellowjack. **1938** "Justinian" *Amer. Sexualis* 18: *Crap*…In U.S., C. 20, becoming euphemism for *shit*. **1942** McAtee *Supp. to Grant Co.* 4 [ref. to 1890's]: *Crap*, n. feces. *Crap*, v. defecate. **1951** Salinger *Catcher in Rye* ch. xvi: There didn't look like there was anything in the park except dog crap. **1952** Himes *First Stone* 82: They were busy as cats covering up crap. **1970** A. Joyce *5 Easy Pieces* (film): I am *not* a piece of *crap*! **1981** D. Burns *Feeling Good* 113: You'll show him what a no-good piece of crap he is! **1992** F. Mills *Overkill* (film): They just started comin' like flies on crap.

b. muck; filth; vile stuff.

[*__1879__ in *OED*: *Crap*…the settlings of ale or beer at the bottom of a barrel.] **1919** *Our Navy* (Aug.) 19: Thou mixture of Sea and Crap/Not one bean will I dish. **1932** L. Berg *Prison Doctor* 40: They know that crap that Sam cooks ain't fit for a dog to eat. **1932** *AS* VII (June) 332: *Crap*—dormitory food. **1929–33** J.T. Farrell *Young Manhood of Lonigan* 173: I'll stay home if it means eatin' all that crap. **1939** Appel *Power House* 12: What kind of greasy crap you put on your hair? *ca*1964 K. Cook *Other Capri* 8: Get that crap shaved off your face!

c. trash, junk; litter; inferior merchandise; (*broadly*) belongings; gear.

1916 *Chicago Defender* (July 1) 4: Anyhow, the films themselves are what is commonly called "crap." **1928** McKay *Banjo* 54: It's the same crap to me whether there was a dozen or a thousand. **1928** Dahlberg *Bottom Dogs* 262: Take your krap, Pett, and come right up. **1930** Bodenheim *Roller Skates* 30: I take the damn crap and what happens? **1932** in Hemingway *Sel. Letters* 366: I never have received a copy of the book of Faulkner's early crap. **1934** H. Miller *Tropic of Cancer* 104: Can you picture her moving in here with her big trunks and her hatboxes and all that crap she drags around with her? *1935 Amer. Mercury* (June) 229: *Crap:* cheap prizes. **1940** Zinberg *Walk Hard* 32: Always rush my fighters along and they all end up on the crap pile. **1947–53** Guthrie *Seeds* 366: I'll throw my crap an' gear up on it. **1954** Mirvish *Texana* 219: Ah, it's probably just some damn paper or crap that got caught in behind there. **1959** Groninger *Run from Mt.* 17: Got your crap? **1972** *N.Y. Times Mag.* (Nov. 26) 30: New York City is the capital of the world when it comes to crap. **1984** J. McNamara *First Directive* 254: Selling defective computer components to the Defense Department and charging them three times for the same crap.

d. an act of defecation.

1926 Finerty *Criminalese* 11: *Crap*—Idle talk; Using toilet. **1928** Dahlberg *Bottom Dogs* 134: He was never interested in anything except taking a krap. **1934** H. Miller *Tropic of Cancer* 111: I wish I could take a crap in the bureau drawer. **1936** J.T. Farrell *World I Never Made* 202: It isn't every day that I get a chance to have a smoke and take a crap in comfort like this. **1938** Steinbeck *Grapes of Wrath* 299: Goin' to take a crap, I guess. **1942** McAtee *Supp. to Grant Co.* 4 [ref. to 1890's]: *Take a crap,* v. phr., defecate. **1945** Himes *If He Hollers* 15: If somebody'd take a crap on deck Kelly'd come and get our gang to clean it up. **1957** J. Jones *Some Came Running* 11: Without mealtimes, and without bedtimes, without a morning crap somewhere, and without running water. *1959 Behan *Borstal Boy* 60: And then, God of war, did I want a crap. **1972** in P. Heller *In This Corner* 287: I told the guy to go take a crap for himself.

e. daylights; stuffing.

1929–30 J.T. Farrell *Young Lonigan* 106: He'll kick the crap out of you. **1931** J.T. Farrell *Guillotine Party* 105: We would have cleaned the crap out of them if we hadn't been outnumbered. **1940** J.T. Farrell *Father & Son* 62: I'll kick the crap out of you! **1947** Motley *Knock On Any Door* 351: They'll make you talk, all right, all right…they'll beat the living crap out of you. **1944–48** A. Lyon *Unknown Station* 258: If you want to knock the crap out of me, okay. **1959** E. Hunter *Conviction* 82: And that night we waited for him, and we beat the crap outa him. **1978** Wharton *Birdy* 3: Sometimes it'd scare the crap out of me. **1984** Eisen & Farley *Powertalk!* 18: Kick the crap out of him.

f. (used as an expletive); the hell.—constr. with *the.*

1947 Willingham *End As a Man* 79: What the crap do I care. **1947–51** Motley *We Fished* 215: What the crap's the big idea? **1985** Boyne & Thompson *Wild Blue* 339: What the crap were you doing out there, Charlie? **1988** Norst *Colors* 196: What the crap do I mean, first time?

g. emphatically nothing.

1949 Ellson *Tomboy* 72: Big people think they know everything and they know crap—less than that. **1949** Mende *Spit & Stars* 60: "I know ten times more'n you any day." "You know crap." **1951** (quot. at POWDER). **1959** E. Hunter *Conviction* 199: Like this girl didn't mean crap to them, you know what I mean? **1963** Lundgren *Primary Cause* 89: "We're gonna get us some Russians."…"We're gonna get crap."

h. a damn.

1951 Kerouac *Cody* 64: Nobody made a move to notice or even gave much of a crap. **1968** P. Roth *Portnoy* 9: Don't they give a single crap for the loved ones they leave behind? **1992** *Mystery Sci. Theater* (Comedy Central TV): I give not a crap for thee.

2.a. nonsense; humbug; drivel. Cf. **(1.c.),** above.

*a1898 EDD: What crap's that y'er talkin'? **1914** Jackson & Hellyer *Crim. Slang* 26: *Crap*, Noun. General usage…See "Bunk," "Bull," "Con." **1918** O'Brien *Wine, Women and War* (unp.): Like last day of school. Valedictories, inspirational talks and usual crap. **1920** H.L. Mencken, in Riggio *Dreiser-Mencken Letters* II 415: All the other new novels I have seen are crap. **1923** McAlmon *Companion Volume* 90: Don't listen to the crap I'm saying. **1924** in Hemingway *Sel. Letters* 137: If all this sounds too much like crap, remember that I ain't written a letter in your direction for a long time. **1925** Dos Passos *Transfer* 93: None o' that crap Jess, I know your kinda promises. **1928** Hecht & MacArthur *Front Page* 457: You made that up! And all that other crap about my being his soul mate and having a love nest with him! **1929** Bodenheim *60 Secs.* 22: A girl calling you handsome (cra-ap, but you still ate it up). **1935** Odets *Lefty* 7: What's this crap about goin' home to hot suppers? **1940** O'Hara *Pal Joey* 178: I wasn't satisfied with the crap I handed her but had to put it on thicker. **1941** in Stilwell *Papers*

20: The wild, farcical and fantastic stuff that G-2 Fourth Army pushes out! The latest is a two-pound bundle of crap. **1942** Wylie *Vipers* 131: The statements and figures on which Hitler bases his monstrous accusation are simply crap. **1954** Lindner *50-Min. Hour* 52: "I think that's a lot of crap," Mac said. **1956** Levin *Compulsion* 183: Aaw, cut the crap. **1959** Morrill *Dark Sea Running* 68: This crap has got to come to a screeching halt. **1978** Diehl *Sharky's Machine* 198: "Sounds like a lot of crap shootin' to me." "No,…it's deduction." **1980** Albrecht *Brain Power* 15: *Crap detecting* is the skill of critical observation. **1993** *New Republic* (Oct. 25) 18: Does this crap ever end? someone wondered aloud.

b. insolence; (*also*) underhanded acts or behavior.

1914 Jackson & Hellyer *Vocab.* 26: *Crap*, Noun. General usage. Treachery. **1927** J. Stevens *Mattock* 236 [ref. to 1918]: "Chris," the crap that's pulled— **1933** Young *Over the Top* 103 [ref. to 1918]: I am not trying to knock the regular army in any way, but they tried to hand us a lot of crapp. **1929–34** J.T. Farrell *Judgment Day* 530: I don't…take nobody's crap. **1945** in M. Chennault *Up Sun!* 105: I don't plan to take any crap from him. **1947** Willingham *End As a Man* 24: You run crap on me every time I come in here. **1948** Mailer *Naked & Dead* 16: He'd do no man harm if he could help it, and he'd take no crap. **1949** Bezzerides *Thieve's Market* 166: The crap I've pulled…I'm going to pull it on Nick. **1952** Vonnegut *Player Piano* 69: I don't have to take no crap from nobody no more. **1965** N.Y.C. high-school student: I don't take crap from nobody. **1987** Univ. Tenn. instructor: They give me any crap, I flunk 'em. **1992** L. Johnson *My Posse* 83: Crocker doesn't take any crap.

3. *Narc.* heroin; SHIT. [The "1942" quot. adduced by Spears, *Drugs and Drink*, is not found in the work cited.]

1952 (quot. at WHITE GOD). **1956** E. Hunter *Second Ending* 130: You got an itch for a couple of caps of the crap? **1969** Lingeman *Drugs A to Z* 51: *Crap*…heroin.

4. trouble.

1954 Faulkner *Fable* 330: Going to live in Chicago soon as this crap's over. **1966** Herbert *Fortune & Men's Eyes* 29: Fruits always get ya in the deep crap. **1971** Rowe *5 Yrs. to Freedom* 302: The thought of how much crap I could have gotten myself into was enough to dull the ache. **1991** "R. Brown" & R. Angus *A.K.A. Narc* 215: I was in deep crap, and I knew it.

¶ In phrases:

¶ **eat crap** see *eat shit* s.v. EAT, *v.*

¶ **for crap's sake** for heaven's sake.

1936 Dos Passos *Big Money* 195: For crap's sake, Charley,…the war's over. **1966** B. Cassiday *Angels Ten* 32: Oh, for crap sake.

¶ **full of crap** talking rubbish; contemptible.

1932 *AS* VII (June) 332: *Full of crap*—expression of disbelief or contempt. **1938** Steinbeck *Grapes of Wrath* 197: Ya full a crap. **1948** Vidal *City & Pillar* 33: "She's full of crap," he said. **1991** Sachar *Let Lady Teach* 52: You know who's full of crap and who's telling the truth.

¶ **have crap in (one's) blood** to be a coward.

1956 Ross *Hustlers* 64: We'll show everybody the Hustlers ain't got crap in their blood.

¶ **holy crap!** (used to express astonishment or the like).

1965 Toland *Last 100 Days* 208: Holy crap! **1991** "R. Brown" & R. Angus *A.K.A. Narc* 24: Holy crap….Don't shoot! **1993** *Simpsons* (Fox-TV): Holy crap!

¶ **like crap** indeed not! like hell!

1946 Gresham *Nightmare Alley* 7: Like crap you're doing okay.

crap[2] *n.* [fr. E cant *crap* 'to hang', prob. dial. var. of *crop* 'to cut off, etc.'] *Und.* a gallows; in phr. **knock down** [or **up**] **for the crap** to be sentenced to the gallows.

*1789 G. Parker *Life's Painter* 137: He was knocked down for the *crap* the last sessions. **1791** [W. Smith] *Confess. T. Mount* 19: *Knocked down upon the crap,* condemned. *1812 Vaux *Vocab.: Crap:* the gallows. *1854 Bulwer-Lytton, in *F & H:* I'll go to the crap like a gentleman.

crap[3] *n.* **1.** *pl.* dice used in the game of craps. [Undoubtedly the original sense.]

1968 Heard *Howard St.* 122: Ain' nothin' wrong wid dem craps. **1984** Sample *Raceboss* 28: She became a whiz with the craps.

2. *pl.* Navy. sugar cubes.

1928 *AS* III (Apr.) 395: Should you then need the sugar, it is *sand* if granulated; *craps* if cubed; and *dominoes* (an obvious derivation) if in the familiar form originated not so many years ago.

¶ In phrase:

¶ **throw craps** to lose or fail.

1908 McGaffey *Show Girl* 37: Providence has got to throw something besides "crap" some time or other. **1957** H. Simmons *Corner Boy* 150: Looks like I threw craps.

crap *interj.* [infl. by CRIPES] (used as an exclamation of disgust, disbelief, or surprise). Also **craps.**

1886 F. Whittaker *Pop Hicks* 19: Seventy-five dollars a week, by the jumping Jerushy Crambo Crap! **1899** Gunter *M.S. Bradford* 50: By craps, some big affair? **1922** in O'Brien *Best Stories of 1922* 24: Craps amighty. **1928** Harrison *Generals* 19 [ref. to 1918]: Aw, crap. **1932** *AS* VII (June) 330: *Crap*—explanation [*sic*] of disgust. **1935** Read *Lexical Evidence* 45: A favorite ejaculation of disapprobation with many is *craps!*...[or] as often, *crap!* **1947** Willingham *End As a Man* 249: Well, by crap, they're going to transfer me too. **1954** Faulkner *Fable* 328: "Sweet crap," Buchwald said, "Come on." *Ibid.* 335: "He slipped!"..."Slipped my crap...You didn't hold him." **1993** *Mystery Sci. Theater* (Comedy Central TV): Crap, here come our dads!

crap *v.* [the v. probably derives fr. the n., and, as the evidence demonstrates, no historical connection exists between this word and the name of the English sanitary engineer Thomas Crapper (1837–1910); see K.J. Grabowski, "Crap, Crapper, and Thomas Crapper," in Edward Callary, ed., *Festschrift in Honor of Virgil J. Vogel* (DeKalb, Ill.: Illinois Names Society, 1985), pp. 199–240), and J.P. Maher, "Out of the Closet," *Ibid.*, pp. 190–98. The early bracketed forms of the type *croppin(g) ken* 'a privy', all from cant glossaries, are unlikely to represent a participial use of the v. (see quots. that define obs. cant *croppin*, of unkn. orig.). The late form *crapping ken* (perh. surviving as or influencing CRAPPING CAN in the U.S.) presumably resulted fr. the infl. of CRAP, *n.*, upon the earlier idiom]

1.a. to defecate.—usu. considered vulgar.

[***1673** R. Head *Canting Acad.* 36: *Croppinken.* A Privy or Boghouse. *Ibid.* 38: *At the Cropping of the Rotan*...at Carts-arse.] [***1676** in Partridge *Dict. Und.* 158: *Croppin-ken*, a privy.] [***1725** *New Canting Dict.*: *Croppin*, the Tail of any Thing....*Croppin-ken*, a Privy or Bog-house.] [***1796** Grose *Vulgar Tongue* (ed. 3): *Croppen.* The tail. *The croppen of the rotan*; the tail of the cart. *Croppen ken*; the necessary house. *Cant.*] ***1846** in *OEDS s.v. dunny*: What? Fenced in a crapping ken [a privy]? ***1859** Hotten *Slang Dict.* 26: *Crapping case*, a privy, or water closet. ***1874** Hotten *Slang Dict.* (ed. 5) 132: *Crap*, to ease oneself by evacuation. ***1889** Barrère & Leland *Dict. Slang.* I 279: *Crap*...(Popular) to ease oneself. ***1891** *F & H* II 206: *Crap...Verb*...(common).—To ease oneself by evacuation. ***1896** Northall *Warwickshire Word-Book* 57: *Crap*...To discharge excrement. **1918** in Carey *Mlle. from Armentières* I (unp.): The sailors liked the pork and beans,/So they could crap on submarines. **1927** [Fliesler] *Anecdota* 159: The Englishman...crapped with precision. **1928** in Read *Lexical Evidence* 45: Please do not crap on the seat. **1929–33** Farrell *Manhood of Lonigan* 205 [ref. to ca1919]: He was goddamn near crapping in his pants. **1936** J. T. Farrell *World I Never Made* 201: I got to go and crap. **1937** Weidman *Wholesale* 90: There goes another rule, I said to myself...And a good one, too. Never crap where you eat. **1938** Steinbeck *Grapes of Wrath* 193: Pa'd crap a litter of lizards if we buy beers. **1938** "Justinian" *Amer. Sexualis* 18: *Crap.* v. To defecate. U.S. low coll., late C. 19–20. **1943** G. Biddle *Artist at War* 25: By God, if some bloody A-rab hasn't crapped into it. **a1949** D. Levin *Mask of Glory* 131: He got so scared he didn't know whether to crap or go blind. **1952** Mandel *Angry Strangers* 112: I don't crap where I eat. **1954** Arnow *Dollmaker* 249: "Yu dirty lyen son uv a bitch"..."Go crap on yu mama's neck." **1960–61** Steinbeck *Discontent* 27: Wonder what Saint Francis would say if...a bird crapped on him. **1962** T. Berger *Reinhart* 22: "Joe around?"..."He went to crap and the hogs ate him." **1972** *N.Y. Times Mag.* (Nov. 26) 32: A lot of psychiatrists and philosophers talk about why people let their dogs c— in the street...The owners would like to c— in the streets themselves, but society won't let them. **1982** Heat Moon *Blue Hwys.* 138: I saw in the bushes a great white rump. A woman crapping. **a1989** in Kisseloff *Must Remember This* 31: You used to crap in the pot instead of going downstairs. **1991** Ganz & Mandel *City Slickers* (film): I *crap* bigger'n you.

b. to soil with excrement.

1986–91 Hamper *Rivethead* 135: Heroes couldn't go around crappin' themselves.

2. to lie to; to attempt to deceive by lies or flattery.—also constr. with *up.*

1927 McKay *Harlem* 69: "Don't crap me," Jake interrupted. "Aintchu...one of us, too?" **1930–31** J.T. Farrell *Grandeur* 148: Don't

crap me! You're still in love with her. **1932** Halyburton & Goll *Shoot and Be Damned* 301 [ref. to 1918]: Let's see whether you've got real leadership or whether you just crapped your way up from the ranks. **1937** Weidman *Wholesale* 208: Crap me easy, kid, I thought. **1941** J.T. Farrell *Whom It May Concern* 50: Listen, Johnny, I know you. You can't crap Patsy Gilbride. **1946** Gresham *Nightmare Alley* 7: Just because I'm your pal I ain't going to crap you up. **1947** Willingham *End as a Man* 287: Don't crap me...You've got plenty of money. **1949** Ellson *Tomboy* 121: "You don't have to give me any crap." "Well, for Christ's sakes, who's crapping you up?" **1951** Robbins *Danny Fisher* 224: Don't crap us, bud. You know who we mean. **1956** G. Green *Last Angry Man* 80: Don't crap me up about Rumanians or any of those other lice. **1959** Searls *Big X* 191: Who are you trying to crap? **1972** R. Barrett *Lovomaniacs* 458: And you don't have to crap the troops anymore.

3. to talk volubly, esp. to complain. Cf. CRAB.

1939 M. Levin *Citizens* 302: He was...crapping about how he didn't say any of that stuff. **1943** *Corvette K-225* (film): Why don't you take that twenty-eight days' leave you're always crapping about? **1954** Arnow *Dollmaker* 428: You're young an alive, kid; quit th crappen an leave this damned alley. *Ibid.* 511: Bender's got a right to crap; he's on a grievance committee. **1956** Resko *Reprieve* 68 [ref. to ca1940]: You guys! Stop the crappin till I get this pass made, willya?

¶ In phrases:

¶ **crap a smoke** to smoke surreptitiously in a rest room.

*ca*1940 N. Algren, in Botkin *Treas. Amer. Folk.* 541: It was goodbye crapping a smoke or drinking a rest.

¶ **crap on, 1.** away with; to hell with.—used imper.

1947 Willingham *End As a Man* 109: Oh, crap on the whole thing. **a1949** D. Levin *Mask of Glory* 140: Crap on fate....You got to try your best. **1958** Frankel *Band of Bros.* 272 [ref. to 1950]: Bastard Chinks...crap on 'em. **1981** Gilliland *Rosinante* 3: Crap on that stuff, Charlie!

2. to treat contemptuously or unfairly.

1964 *AS* (May) 118: He was *crapped on*, or "dealt with unfairly." **1970** E. Thompson *Garden of Sand* 358: If you crap on me, I'll take it out of *his* ass. **1976** Woodley *Bears* 188: All season long you've been laughed at, crapped on. **1983** *Rolling Stone* (Feb. 3) 10: It's much easier to crap on the kids. There's something in human nature that wants someone to step on.

crap around *v.* **1.** to waste time; act to no purpose; fool about; loaf.

1935 Algren *Boots* 41: Y'all been...crappin' roun' heah since mo'nin' now. **1936** Kingsley *Dead End* 695: Come on! Stop crappin' aroun'. **1936** Levin *Old Bunch* 521: Aw, why crap around? **1937** Weidman *Wholesale* 29: We've decided to show these guys that we mean business. No crapping around. **1949** Robbins *Dream Merchants* 342: Stop the crappin' around and tell me what happened. **1956** Levin *Compulsion* 37: It's nearly summer, you sonofabitch. We'll never do it if you keep crapping around! **1957** Gutwillig *Long Silence* 141: So let's stop crapping around. **1961** Rosten *Capt. Newman* 158: Naw, I'm just crappin' around. I know. **1962** Killens *Heard the Thunder* 191: Listen, Baker, I'm not going to stand for no crapping around. **1971** N.Y.U. student: All we did was crap around for an hour and fifteen minutes.

2. to trifle or fool (with).

1941 Schulberg *Sammy* 69: What good do you think it's gonna do you to crap around with stuff like that? **1965** C.D.B. Bryan *P.S. Wilkinson* 397: I don't like them crapping around with my life when if they only did their jobs this sort of call-up wouldn't be necessary. **1971** *Nat. Lampoon* (May) 19: Man will stop crapping around with the environment and the environment will have a shot at him.

crap artist *n.* one who hoaxes, lies, or exaggerates.

1934 in J.T. Farrell *Coll. Stories*: I want to tell you what a goddamn crap artist you are! **1954** E. Hunter *Blackboard Jungle* 59: He's exaggerating...Solly is a big crap artist. **1956** G. Green *Angry Man* 39: A good little crap artist, that kid. **1967** Michaels *Women of Green Berets* 86: Don't shit a crap artist, man. **1970** Gattzden *Black Vendetta* 40: That doesn't qualify me as a crap artist.

crap-ass *n.* a despicable fellow; SHIT-ASS.—usu. considered vulgar.

1975 C.W. Smith *Country Music* 210: You sorry crap-ass! Just *read* this! **1976** Rosen *Above Rim* 40: You lazy crap-asses, get back to work.

Crapaud var. CRAPEAU.

crap can *n.* CRAPPING CAN.

1942 *ATS* 87: Toilet...*crap can.* **a1969** J. Kimbrough *Defender of Angels* 154 [ref. to 1920's]: Crap-can poetry.

crap course *n. Stu.* an easy course of study.

1956 I. Shulman *Good Deeds* 243: A one-hour crap course entitled Egyptian Band Instruments. **1986** Univ. Tenn. student: It's a crap course.

crap creek *n.* ¶ **up crap creek** [euphem. for SHIT CREEK] in a hopeless or nearly hopeless predicament.

1977 Univ. Tenn. student: If I don't come up with three bucks, I'm up crap creek.

crape *n.* CRAPE-HANGER.

1943 Halper *Inch from Glory* 10: Jeepers, Frank, don't be a crape.

¶ In phrases:

¶ **hang crape** to be gloomy and pessimistic.

1922 Tully *Emmett Lawler* 218: There you go…hanging crepe. Was your dad a grave digger?

¶ **knock for a crape** to destroy.

1925 Nason *Three Lights* 43: It knocks everything within twenty yards for a crape.

Crapeau *n.* [< F *crapaud* 'a toad'] *Esp. Naut.* the French; a Frenchman; (*hence*) a French vessel. Often constr. with *Johnny.* Also **Crapaud, Crappo.** Now *hist.*

*1803 in Wetherell *Adventures* 88: What the devil were you all about to let the damn'd Croppoes give you such an infernal drubbing? **1815* in Wetherell *Adventures* 340: Crappo took the advantage of poor Nelson. **1818* (cited in Partridge *DSUE* (ed. 8) 626): Jean Crappeau. **1825* Glascock *Nav. Sk.-Bk.* I 25: Crappo. **1830** Ames *Mariner's Sks.* 222: "Johnny Crapaud" did not seem to forget or forgive. **1834* Glascock *Nav. Sk.-Bk.* (Series 2) II 137: Johnny Crappo. **1835** *Mil. & Naval Mag.* (July) 379: Old England will ever be called "John Bull"; the French, "Johnny Crappo." **1836** *Spirit of Times* (Oct. 22) 284: Jim Crow Rice has been to Paris, gallivanting and poking fun and High-Dutch at Johnny Crapeau! **1836** *Every Body's Album* I 168: Johnny Bull and Crapeau fell out about some trifling matter, and agreed to settle the dispute with swords. **1839** in *AS* XXIX (1954) 120: The Crapeau then commenced picking a wild turkey and some prairie chickens. **1839** *Spirit of Times* (Aug. 31) 312: Poor Johnny Crapeau has been the favorite mark for every shaft of ridicule. **1841** [Mercier] *Man-of-War* 162: Now, *Crapeau*, is your chance. *Ibid.* 164: I tell you, *Johnny Crapeau* is no *slouch* at killing a whale. **1842** *Spirit of Times* (Feb. 19) 598: The infernal *low flung liquor* swilled at the *Crapeau cafés.* **1847** Downey *Portsmouth* 65: Crapeau manned yards whenever the barges came in sight. **1848** in Leyda *Melville Log* I 281: She was…ironing the Crapeau's trowsers. **1850** Melville *Moby Dick* ch. xci: I well know that these Crappoes of Frenchmen are but poor devils in the fishery…Here's a Crappo that is content with our leavings. **1854** Brackett *Lane's Brigade* 230: It was amusing to hear Crapeau give an account of the occurrence. **1863** in Allan *Lone Star Ballads* 77: For we can grow de cotton—wool—/For John Crapeau and Johnny Bull. **1865** Edmondston *Jour.* 699: I can only…hope that Johnny Crapeau and Bro Johnathan have in fact fallen out in Mexico. **1873** *Galaxy* (Mar.) 412: Johnny Crapaud and Oncle Sam. *ca***1875** Bemrose *Seminole War* 42: Johnny Crappeau would ejaculate, "Ah, le pauve Indian! He be one grande coward." **1887** Davis *Sea-Wanderer* 49 [ref. to 1831]: He is a "Johnny Crapeau," as they call it. **1893** Barra *Two Oceans* 59: To stand around with them Johnny Crapauds trying to learn to speak their jawbreaking lingo. **1918** Griffin *Ballads of Reg't* 42: The English, the Irish, the "Johnny Crapeauds." **1929* Bowen *Sea Slang* 76: *John Crappo.* The old British name for a Frenchman (Jean Crapeau).

crape-hanger *n.* a person who is constantly pessimistic, complaining, or critical. Also **crepe-hanger.**

1915 T.A. Dorgan, in Zwilling *TAD Lexicon* 29: I don't want to knock the old boy or be a crepe hanger or nothin like that. **1917** in Mills *War Letters* 250: He is more or less of a crape-hanger. **1918** *Chi. Sun.-Trib.* V (unp.): You're a regular crêpe hanger the way you mope around. **1918** *N.Y. Eve. Jour.* (Aug. 2) 15: But our hero passed up the crape hanger's advice and made a million in his new location. **1918** Day *Camion Cartoons* 99: Yes, you Crape Hanger, and in the *second place*, if you don't dry up you're going to get *crowned.* **1919** Darling *Jargon Book* 9: *Crape Hanger*—One who is always saying something to make things look gloomy. **1919** T. Kelly *What Outfit?* 40: "Bet we'll get torpedoed," shouted one crape-hanger. **1920–21** Witwer *Leather Pushers* 170: Don't be a crape hanger *all* your life. **1924** Wilstach *Stage Slang* 21: *Crape Hangers.* Fault finders. **1925** S. Lewis *Arrowsmith* 593: Ordinarily Encore would have suggested, with amiable malice, that Gottlieb was a "crape-hanger" who wasted time destroying the theories of other men instead of making new ones of his own. *Ibid.* 673: Gottlieb's gods are the cynics, the destroyers—crape-hangers, the vulgar call 'em. **1926**

Reader's Digest (June) 115: Are You a Crape-Hanger? **1944** Micheaux *Mrs. Wingate* 233: You're a crepe hanger. Why are you so hard to please? **1963** W.C. Anderson *Penelope* 21: Hi, yuh, O'Leary, you old crepe-hanger. **1966** "T. Pendleton" *Iron Orchard* 94: I never welshed on a deal yet. What are you, one of these natural-born crepe-hangers? **1980** "Ann Landers," in *N.Y. Daily News* (Sept. 5) 22: Dear Buffalo: Sorry to be a crepe-hanger, but it sounds to me as if your marriage has had it. **1981** Ballenger *Terror* 42: Suppose you two crepe-hangers are right. **1989** Kanter & Mirvis *Cynical Amer.* xix: It will be easy to…conclude that we are crape-hangers. Gloom and doom tend to permeate our analyses.

craperoo *n.* [CRAP, *n.*, 2 + -EROO] arrant nonsense; absolute rubbish.

1940 Zinberg *Walk Hard* 313: The ole craperoo! **1947** Schulberg *Harder They Fall* 8: Ladling out the old craperoo. **1949** in Hemingway *Sel. Letters* 679: You can see it is not craperoo. **1958** Camerer *Damned Wear Wings* 120: So the kid brother gives us the old craperoo. **1963** Ross *Dead Are Mine* 66: Element of surprise and all that craperoo. **1972** R. Barrett *Lovomaniacs* 50: What a lot of juvenile crapperoo! **1974** A. Bergman *Big Kiss-Off* 128: Strictly craperoo.

crap-happy *adj.* silly; SLAP-HAPPY.

1961 Gover *$100 Misunderstanding* 65: Then he give me this crap-happy smile. [**1984* Partridge *DSUE* (ed. 8) 266: *Crap-happy pappy.* "Young father who takes incidentals of fatherhood in world-view stride."]

craphead *n.* (a partial euphem. for) SHITHEAD.

1952 Uris *Battle Cry* 31 [ref. to WWII]: "Pick up that butt, craphead." "Don't you call me craphead." **1957** H. Ellison *Web of the City* 17: You call me spick, craphead? **1958** S.H. Adams *Tenderloin* 365 [ref. to 1890's]: Spill it, you old craphead. **1965** Daniels *Moments of Glory* 20: I got that way from all the crapheads who kept needling me.

craphole *n.* a filthy or unpleasant place.

1939 in A. Banks *First-Person* 55: Reminds me of Wilson's. Boy, what a craphole! **1951** Jones *Face of War* 166: Jesus, what a craphole this is! **1971–72** Giovannitti *Medal* 36: If there were more I'da been long gone from this craphole.

craphouse *n.* a lavatory; (*broadly*) a filthy or unpleasant place.

1934 Appel *Brain Guy* 49: Two, three, six months and they'll be feedin' outa your mitt. King of the crap-house. **1938** Steinbeck *Grapes of Wrath* 29: We'll maybe get a litter of crap houses. *a***1944** Binns *Timber Beast* 191: It looks like a crap house, because I didn't care. **1960** Carpenter *Harlot* 107: They made us march together everyplace. To school, to work, to recreation, to cottage, to drill ground, to the crap-house. **1961** Rubin *In the Life* 7: But you got a nice place here. I'll be back, what the hell. Better than the rest of this crap house [prison]. **1966** in L. Williams *City of Angels* 20: Lavatory,…toilet,…can, or crap-house. *a***1988** Poyer *Med* 54: Some enlisted-man's off-limits crap-house.

craphouse luck *n.* surprisingly good luck.

1966 Cameron *Sgt. Slade* 63: Quick reflexes and crap-house luck had kept him going, so far.

craphouse mouse *interj.* (used to express surprise).

1952 Uris *Battle Cry* 241 [ref. to 1942]: Craphouse mouse, hot chow!

craphouse rat *n.* (used in var. similes).

1942 Algren *Morning* 12: I got the ol' experience, I'm smart as a crap-house rat. **1958* in *OEDS:* As cunning as a crap-house rat. **1966** Herbert *Fortune* 52: If I had a choice, I'd be dirty as a craphouse rat before taking a shower with Rocky.

crapless *adv.* SHITLESS.

1973 Toma & Brett *Toma* 86: It's got her and her girlfriend scared crapless. **1990** in M. Chennault *Up Sun!* 85: I was scared crapless.

crap list *n.* SHIT LIST.

1959 Sabre & Eiden *Glory Jumpers* 16: Who wants to start buddying around with a guy that's right on top of the lieutenant's crap list? **1963** D. Tracy *Brass Ring* 28: He'll have me on his crappo list soon enough, anyways.

crapola *n.* [CRAP, *n.*, 2.a. + -OLA] CRAP, *n.*, 2.a., & *interj.*

1961 G. Forbes *Goodbye to Some* 102 [ref. to WWII]: Crapola! **1971** *All in the Family* (CBS-TV): And all that Commie crapola. **1972** R. Barrett *Lovomaniacs* 106: This new sound—acid rock, all that crappola [*sic*]. **1983** *Rolling Stone* (Feb. 3) 6: The…American Crapola Dream. **1986** Heinemann *Paco's Story* 135: I don't want no chickenshit Marine Corps crapola.

crap-out *n.* a person who has CRAPPED OUT, (*specif.*) a quitter, welsher, or the like; (*also*) an instance of failure.

1966–67 Stevens *Gunner* 111 [ref. to WWII]: It's a rest camp for all the crap-outs. *Ibid.* 247: There was a file...his name in red letters on the crapout list. **1974** Kingry *Monk & Marines* 167: Monasteries are full of crap-outs from regular life. **1991** K. Douglass *Viper Strike* 266: Another crap-out, guys.

crap out *v.* [orig. a technical term in the game of craps] **1.** to lose; to fail. [Despite the specific context, 1992 quot. is figurative.]

1908 *DN* III 302: *Crap out, v. phr.* To fail to make good in the game of craps. Also used in college slang of failing on examination. **1932** *AS* VII (June) 330: *Crap out*—to lose at dice; to fail. **1934** Appel *Brain Guy* 79: "The breaks is with us. Seven eleven." "We almost crapped out." **1938** *AS* (Apr.) 152: *Crap out.* To lose, or to be unable to keep up. **1953** Manchester *City of Anger* 276: When he crapped out with $50...he had won $1,200. **1980** *N.Y. Post* (June 17) 58: It was a gamble I had to take...But I crapped out. **1981** *Nat. Lampoon* (Feb.) 75: Coontown is a bad spot if you just crapped out at the dog track. **1992** G. Wolff *Day at the Beach* 186: We'd rolled snake eyes, crapped out.

2.a. to back down or renege; to lose one's nerve; to quit ignominiously.

1929 in Longstreet *Canvas Falcons* 277 [ref. to 1917]: Half of them crap out—mental. **1938** (quot. at (1), above). **1945** in *Calif. Folk Qly.* V (1946) 380: *Crap out*...may also signify to renege on a previously given promise. **1944–46** in *AS* XXII 54: *To crap out.* To run out on some assigned duty. **1961** H. Ellison *Memos* 76: My eyes started to unfocus...Now was no time to crap out. **1965** Eastlake *Castle Keep* 184: I...know people, the kind you can depend on and the kind that crap out. **1966** Adler *Vietnam Letters* 53: I guess everyone wonders what he will act like in one of these situations, and wonders if he will be one of those who will crap out in a bad spot. **1966–67** Stevens *Gunner* 93: Is that what that bastard put down, that I wanted to crap out?

b. to die.

1929 in Longstreet *Canvas Falcons* 280 [ref. to 1918]: Both of us likely to crap out on any flight. Odds against us ever meeting again. **1951–52** Frank *Hold Back Night* 198: They were all thinking what he was thinking—the captain was going to crap out. **1957** Myrer *Big War* 368 [ref. to WWII]: He's got dengue and he's got it bad. He could crap out anytime. **1962** T. Jones *Stairway* 54: It seems [Hamlet's] old man crapped out and his old lady jumped for his uncle right away. **1964** "Doctor X" *Intern* 93: It just goes to show that you don't have to have a typical picture of a coronary to have a patient just up and crap out on you.

c. (of machinery) to break down; to malfunction; CONK OUT.

1951 Morris *China Station* 186: That TBS been crapping out on and off for a week. **1969** Coppel *Little Time* 134 [ref. to ca1940]: Can I borrow your radio? Mine's crapped out. **1976** Fuller *Ghost of Flt. 401* 206: That damn thing crap out again? **1986** Coonts *Intruder* 225: The computer had crapped out. **1988** *Daily Beacon* (Univ. Tenn.) (Mar. 1) 7: Battery-operated toilet seats crap out. **1990** Poyer *Gulf* 51: Then the landing lights crapped out.

3.a. to go to sleep.

1944 Kendall *Service Slang* 21: *Crapping out*...sleeping during work hours, or shooting craps. **1945** Wolfert *Amer. Guerrilla* 5 [ref. to 1941]: Crap out, boy, you look like you need it. **1957** Yordan *Men in War* (film): I'm crappin' out. **1958** Frankel *Band of Bros.* 12: I saw where they been crapped out. But they wasn't there. **1959** Cochrell *Barren Beaches* 217 [ref. to WWII]: "It's my turn to crap out." "Okay. Sleep fast." **1960** MacCuish *Do Not Go Gentle* 119 [ref. to WWII]: "Hey, Norm, you crapped out?" "No, I'm awake." **1963** Ross *Dead Are Mine* 14 [ref. to 1944]: Well, why the hell don't you try getting some sleep? It's liable to be a long spell before you get another chance to crap out. **1963** Boyle *Yanks Don't Cry* 2 [ref. to 1941]: What's your hurry? I thought you said you were all crapped out and didn't feel like making a night of it? **1964** Howe *Valley of Fire* 141: Daddy was still crapped out. **1965** Marks *Letters* 134: I feel a little tired now, so I think I'll crap out, so adios. **1971** Cole *Rook* 258: Why don't you crap out for awhile on the cot back there?

b. Esp. *USMC.* to loaf or relax, esp. while shirking duty; rest.

1944 E.H. Hunt *Limit* 185: He's standin' on the fantail by himself when the Old Man walks by and sees him crapped out. **1956** *AS* XXXI (Oct.) 190: If any of them had been caught *crapping out* during the day, the whole platoon may get...a forced march the following morning through the *boonies*. **1958** Frankel *Band of Bros.* 99 [ref. to 1950]: We won't be fit to do any shootin', we don't crap out a few minutes. **1959** Cochrell *Barren Beaches* 110 [ref. to WWII]: "Crap out," he said. "But don't go near them dames." **1989** D. Sherman *There I Was* 12: We

crapped out a bit before we dug in again.

c. to faint, as from exhaustion.

1966 Elli *Riot* 40: Nobody hit him. He just crapped out. **1974** Kingry *Monk & Marines* 80: I had two guys crap out from exhaustion.

4. to do for; kill.

1960 Sire *Deathmakers* 252: You had no right to come up here where they could crap you out.

crapper *n.* [see ety. note at CRAP, *v.*] **1.a.** a lavatory.

1927 *Immortalia* 142: She beshiteth herself in the crapper. **1928** Read *Lexical Evidence* 45: It shows only people with brains use this crapper. **1932** *AS* VII (June) 330: *Crapper*—...a lavatory. **1935** J. Conroy *World to Win* 41: Couldn't go to the crapper...without asking somebody to unbutton his pants. **1937** Weidman *Wholesale* 56: But if they had as much luck in the crapper as they had with their strikes, they must've been good and constipated. **1950** Stuart *Objector* 19: Salute the son of a bitch no matter where you are, even in the crapper. **1951** Morris *China Station* 35: I don't know Chinese for "bathroom," but I can say "crapper" eight ways. **1955** Abbey *Brave Cowboy* 51: This soap we use for washin up our hands and so on. In the crapper. **1958** Motley *Epitaph* 304: Let's go to the crapper. **1968** J.P. Miller *Race for Home* 156: Yonder she goes, into the crapper.... **1972** Tamony *Americanisms* (No. 32) 7: It is assumed that *crapper* stems from the name of Thomas Crapper, a London plumber who had much to do with the development of the modern [flush toilet]. Crapper was issued Patent No. 4,990 for his "Crapper's Valveless Water Waste Preventer" [in the 1870's]. **1993** *Beavis & Butt-head* (MTV): You wouldn't know about a couple of kids blowin' up the crapper with a stick of dynamite.

b. a toilet commode.

1938 Steinbeck *Grapes of Wrath* 368: They got ten crappers for the whole shebang. **1942** H. Miller *Roofs of Paris* 83: She's sitting on the crapper. **1961** Coon *Front* 19: I might as well shove them down the crapper with the rest of the toilet paper! **1966** Longstreet & Godoff *Wm. Kite* 189: "*What* a crapper," she said, admiring the throned fixture with its high overhead tank. **1969** Moynahan *Pairing Off* 228: Go down the line of crappers to the fifth booth, where the coin locks been taken off so the door swings free. **1972** Ponicsan *Cinderella Liberty* 2: The crappers are all in service, two facing rows of three each. ***1977*** T. Jones *Incred. Voyage* 356: Inside [the cell] there were thirty-two men and boys, plus one crouching over the crapper in the back corner.

2. *Und.* a jail or prison. Cf. syn. CAN.

1924 Henderson *Keys to Crookdom* 401: *Crapper.* Jail, prison. **1926** Finerty *Criminalese* 13: *Crapper*—State prison.

3. (used as a term of abuse for) a liar or other detestable person; (*broadly*) a detestable place or thing.

1896–1900 in *DN* II (1901) 138: *Crapper, n.* A wealthy but stingy man. Oswego Co., N.Y. **1932** *AS* VII (June) 330: *Crapper*—a user of empty, boastful terms. **1935** Algren *Boots* 214: I'm callin' you the Texas *Crapper*. **1939** M. Levin *Citizens* 160: The director of personnel—that crapper. *Ibid.* 274: If that crapper goes through...she'll go through in your lap. **1957** H. Ellison *Deadly Streets* 111: I'm sick and tired of this little crapper, anyhow. **1956** Levin *Compulsion* 67: I ought to kill you first, you crapper. **1958** Gardner *Piece of the Action* 158: We'd still be here snailing along while this crapper up ahead blasts exhaust in our face. **1964** Howe *Valley of Fire* 130: Y'know, for an old crapper you do pretty well. **1971** Rader *Govt. Inspected* 5: New York...choked with foreign crappers, you know the type, in her mind, fish carts,...prayer shawls,...spade rapists in Central Park. *Ibid.* 44: I decided to find a job, no nine to five crapper but some smooth slot to bring me closer to my friends. **1965** Herlihy *Midnight Cowboy* 91: See this crapper they call a room?

¶ In phrase:

¶ **in the crapper** finished; ruined; (of a racehorse) out of the money.

1942–49 Goldin et al. *DAUL* 51: *In the crapper*—lost, hopeless, profitless. **1949** Mende *Spit & Stars* 67: If Peanuts belted you one, you'd be in the crapper. **1968** Ainslie *Racing Guide* 469: *In the can*—an out-of-the-money finish; "in the crapper," etc. **1987** Blankenship *Blood Stripe* 136: Morale was in the crapper.

crapping *adj.* damned; SHITTING, *adj.*

1957 E. Brown *Locust Fire* 174 [ref. to 1944]: "It's the works," said Shellbarger. "The whole crapping works." **1966** Herbert *Fortune* 93: You crapping fink! **1987** Pedneau *A.P.B.* 229: And he took a crappin' handful.

crapping can *n.* CRAPPER, 1. [See note at CRAP, *v.*]

1935 J. Conroy *World to Win* 215: This part o' town stinks like a crappin' can...anyhow. **1965–70** in *DARE* [7 informants, W. of Mississippi R.].

Crappo var. CRAPEAU.

crappo *n., interj., & adj.* CRAP, *n.*, 2. & *interj.*; (*also*) CRAPPY.
a1949 D. Levin *Mask of Glory* 87: On Crappo Island. **1953** Manchester *City of Anger* 223: "Same old crappo," he muttered. **1977** S. Stallone *Paradise Alley* 152: What if I ain't satisfied with this crap-o arrangement? **1986** Gilmour *Pretty in Pink* 77: "Crappo!" Duckie hollered. *****1990** T. Thorne *Dict. Contemp. Slang* 114: Crappy...adj....Crappo is a more recent variant. **1993** N.Y.C. editor, age 45: That's a pretty crappo attitude.

crappy *adj.* **1.** befouled with excrement or filth.—sometimes considered vulgar.
*****1846** in *OEDS*: Which of us had hold of the crappy (sh-ten) end of the stick? **1986–91** Hamper *Rivethead* 17: Six kids...to...clean crappy diapers for.
2. despicable or contemptible; shoddy.—sometimes considered vulgar.
1928 Dahlberg *Bottom Dogs* 211: The krappy cigarettes them social secs. palmed off on the fellas in the trenches. **1929** in *OEDS*: Some crappy oil stock. **1932** *AS* VII (June) 31: Crappy—boastful; nonsensical; no good. **1936** in E. O'Neill *Letters* 455: Very superior and crappy cracks indeed! **1943** Wakeman *Shore Leave* 220: Just think, the lousiest books have not been written, the crappiest plays are yet unacted, the stupidest poems still not printed. **1963** Boyle *Yanks Don't Cry* 208: Good Christ! You'd think they could find something better to blast than one crappy machine gun! **1970** *N.Y. Times* (Mar. 22) 24: The crappiest decade in history, all our best men murdered, what's fascinating about it? **1979** in Terkel *Amer. Dreams* 214: I've done some crappy things, some good things.
3. in poor condition; unwell.—sometimes considered vulgar.
1942 *ATS* 10: In poor condition...*crappy*. **1965** N.Y.C. high-school student: Still feelin' pretty crappy. **1972** W.C. Anderson *Hurricane* 97: God, I feel crappy!

crapshoot *n.* a gamble; risky situation. Also as v., to take risks.
1971 (cited in *W9*). **1975** *Business Week* (July 7) 60: Investing in commodities is strictly a crapshoot—some 85% of speculators lose money at it. **1978** *Business Week* (Sept. 25) 131: We were crap shooting...taking the risk mostly because we had to do something. **1978** *L.A. Times* (Sept. 27) II 8: I'd rather crapshoot on getting the dollars from somewhere. **1982** *N.Y. Times* (Dec. 9) B 14: Senator Laxalt himself has occasionally called the Reagan economic program a "crap shoot." **1984** Caunitz *Police Plaza* 262: Whenever you go into court it's a crap shoot. **1985** Dye *Between Raindrops* 175: Like everything else in this fucking city; it's a crapshoot, man.

crap-slinger *n.* CRAP ARTIST.
1930 Bodenheim *Roller Skates* 151: A lot of crapslingers wind up in the ashcan when they blow themselves up too much.

crap up *v.* **1.** to burden or clutter with foolish ideas or items.
1946 Gresham *Nightmare Alley* 47: Why do they have to crap it up with all that stuff? **1952** H. Grey *Hoods* 156: Who writes crapped-up stories to mislead the public? **1957** Atwell *Private* 238: Crap it up with a lot of big, fancy words, make it real literary. **1961** J. Jones *Thin Red Line* 270: He was not here for any crapped up West Point heroics. **1963** Braly *Shake Him* 47: She *was* looking wistfully at the big crapped-up merry-go-round. **1965** Lurie *Nowhere City* 174: Their yards are all crapped up with stuff, rock gardens and birdbaths and iron flamingoes plugged into the grass.
2. to ruin; FOUL UP.
1953 Paley *Rumble* 85: I don' want you crappin' up the neighborhood. **1958** Gardner *Piece of the Action* 119: I'm too old and too well off to take a chance on crapping things up and changing my style. **1972** Kellogg *Lion's Tooth* 13: One rotten troop will crap up the whole platoon.
3. CRAP, *v.*, 2.

crap work *n.* CRUD WORK.
1973 N.Y.U. student: The first part is crap work. **1993** *Real World* (MTV): I saved some work for you. Some crap work....He's doing all my crap work.

crash *n.* **1.** a great success; hit.
1894 in Remington *Wister* 108: You have an air tight cinch on the West—Others may monkey but you arrive with a horrible crash every pop. **1918** *Stars & Stripes* (May 17) 7: I gotta date with a classy frail tonight and I wanta make a crash with her.
2. *Stu.* an infatuation; CRUSH.
1900 *DN* II 30: *Crash*, n. 1. Strong infatuation.

3. *Stu.* a complete failure in a course or examination.
1900 *DN* II 30: *Crash*, n...2. A complete flunk.
4.a. *Pris.* a jailbreak.
1942 *ATS* 462. **1959** Farris *Harrison High* 450: There's a crash at the state farm.
b. *Und.* a burglary involving forced entry.
1971 Goines *Dopefiend* 144: He had been around too long not to know what a crash meant...When you crashed, the whole thing depended on speed, if you didn't want to get caught in a freak bust.
5. the return to a normal state after a drug-induced or other emotionally intense experience.
1969 (cited in Spears *Drugs & Drink*). **1971** Woodley *Dealer* 59: As the quality of the cocaine "high" is an individual matter, so is that of the "crash"—the descent from the "high." **1979** Kiev *Courage to Live* 28: Such a letdown used to be known in the 1960's, as the "crash" after a "high." **1983** *Time* (Apr. 11) 25: But the "crash" from coke, the letdown when the drug wears off...is grim.

crash *v.* **1.a.** to force one's way into; (*hence*) to enter (a party, dance, sporting event, social group) uninvited, without a required ticket, or the like. Also absol.
1921 *Variety* (Dec. 30) 4: I want to crash in around here, for makin' good in Denver don't mean a thing. **1922** *Variety* (July 28) 5: Cuthbert...has crashed into the magazines disguised as a pug. **1926** Finerty *Criminalese* 14: *Crashing*—Getting past the gate without paying. **1927** *N.Y. Times* (Oct. 30): *Crashing*—Getting into a theatre gratis. **1928** MacArthur *War Bugs* 242: They ate like ostriches and crashed the mess line five or six times a meal. **1930** Lavine *3d Degree* 11: With the gold shield he can crash dances, parties, theaters, ball games or the races. **1936** in Weinberg et al. *Tough Guys* 513: Being...a cocking enthusiast, he'd "crashed." **1941** in Boucher *Werewolf* 120: Not that I guess you're important enough to crash the paper. **1952** E. Brown *Trespass* 93: You sure Jack's is the right place for crashing society? **1966** Braly *Cold Out There* 27: You trying to crash the leisure class? **1984** W. Murray *Dead Crab* 18: Crashing the races was a point of honor with Jay.
b. *Orig. Und.* to force entry into; break into (a place to be robbed).
1924 Henderson *Keys to Crookdom* 401: *Crash*. Break into. As, crash a joint. **1927** in Hammett *Big Knockover* 283: They seem to think their mob will crash the prison and turn 'em loose. **1928** Levin *Reporter* 323: Larchkin says crash the joint. **1930** *Liberty* (July 19) 22: One night we crash eleven stores. **1935** Pollock *Und. Speaks*: *Crash*, police breaking into an unlawful place. **1971** Goines *Dopefiend* 144: We goin' crash a joint this morning, baby.
2. *Pris.* to break out of (prison).
1932 in *AS* (Feb. 1934) 26: *Crash A Stir*. To escape from prison. **1955** D. Stern *Swamp Women* (film): We been in here three lousy years. What makes you think you can crash this joint? **1970** Rudensky & Riley *Gonif* 47: Howinhell are you going to crash this place?
3.a. to pass out, as from intoxication.
1927 in E. Wilson *Twenties* 393: He "crashed" upstairs, came back to say that he couldn't come with us. **1967** *DAS* (ed. 2): *Crash*...To pass out drunk. **1970** Landy *Underground Dict.* 59: *Crash*...Pass out. **1979** Hiler *Monkey Mt.* 24: Everything was spinning...*Got to sit up or I'll crash.*
b. *Hosp.* to suffer cardiac arrest. Cf. CRASH CART.
1983 *Santa Barbara News-Press* (Dec. 18) 1: Courtney...had "crashed." Five nurses and the doctor were bent over the baby, trying to restart her failing heart. **1985** Univ. Tenn. student theme: To *crash*, in the health-care profession, is to have a cardiovascular collapse.
4. to strike sharply; punch.
1927 C.J. Daly *Snarl of Beast* 137: But it takes a peculiar mental twist to make a man crash a woman. **1931** in H. Miller *Letters to Emil* 83: Can you imagine that little son-of-a-bitch saying that to me?...I don't know why I didn't crash him. **1984** Toop *Rap Attack* 158: *Crash*: to hit or cause bodily harm...."If you keep messing with my car, I'm gonna crash you."
5. to go to sleep; go to bed; sleep; (*hence*) to spend the night.—in recent use occ. constr. with *out*. [Popularized in U.S. in late 1960's, when widely associated with hippies.]
*****1943** (cited in Partridge *DSUE* (ed. 8) 266). *****1945** S.J. Baker *Australian Lang.* 162: *Crash*. To sleep. **1965** (quot. at WASTED). **1967** *Time* (July 7) 19: Last weeks the sidewalks and doorways were filling with new arrivals...just off the bus and looking for a place to "crash" (sleep). **1970** Landy *Underground Dict.* 59: *Crash*...Sleep for one or two nights at someone's house. **1970** *Playboy* (Dec.) 288: I could crash. **1972** in *Atlantic* (Jan. 1973) 62: Whenever you want to crash, there's plenty of

room up on the dorm floor. **1975** *Sing Out!* (July) 5: Probably where the engineers crash out while waiting for their trains. **1982** Goff, Sanders & Smith *Bros.* 186: So I crashed, and couldn't even fall asleep. **1986** *Night Court* (NBC-TV): Thanks for lettin' me crash with you for a while. **1993** *As World Turns* (CBS-TV): Why don't you crash on my couch tonight?

6. *Narc.* to return to a normal state after a drug-induced, esp. hallucinatory, experience.

1967 J.B. Williams *Narc. & Hallucin.: Crash*…come down hard and fast from a high or a trip. **1969** Lingeman *Drugs A to Z* 51: *Crash*…to return abruptly to normal from a state of drug intoxication. **1970** N.Y.U. student: I'm crashing.

¶ In phrases:

¶ **crash and burn** to fail utterly.

1978 in *Atlantic* (May 1988) 98: The Bullets were no longer speeding. They were crashing and burning. **1979** Molly Ivins, in *Quest* (Sept.) 20: The show recently bit the dust in the ratings battle, or, as they say in television, it crashed and burned. **1984** Glick *Winters Coming* 201: Don't crash and burn on me, *hombre*. I need you. **1988** *Atlantic* (May) 98: O'Grady…crashed and burned 17 times before finally qualifying for the [P.G.A. golf] Tour four years ago.

¶ **crash the gate** to enter uninvited or without a required ticket of admission. Now *colloq.* Cf. GATE-CRASHER.

1922 in *DN* V 147: We crashed the gate at a swell joint like some finale-hoppers.…*Crashing the gate*—to go to a place uninvited or without paying admission. **1923** *N.Y. Times* (Oct. 7) VIII 4: *Crashing the gate*: Getting by the doorman without pass or ticket. **1927** *Vanity Fair* (Nov.) 132: To "crash the gate" is getting into a place without paying. **1928** Burnett *Little Caesar* 121: Ain't none of us ever been asked to eat with the Big Boy at his dump…Nobody's ever crashed the gates before but Pete Montana. **1958** J. King *Pro Football* 90: You're not the first coach who isn't going to crash this gate today!

crash box *n. Auto.* an unsynchronized transmission.

1976 *Webster's Sports Dict.* 96.

crash cart *n. Hosp.* an instrument cart used to carry emergency resuscitation equipment.

[*1974 P. Wright *Lang. Brit. Industry* 85: In the hospitals…the container with all necessary equipment for resuscitating a patient is the *crash-wagon*.] **1982** Huttmann *Code Blue* 28: Another nurse rushes the crash cart (a mini-operating room in a cabinet, with all the drugs, equipment and supplies for retrieving life) to the bedside. **1983** Van Devanter & Morgan *Before Morning* 42 [ref. to 1967]: Get a crash cart. He needs blood. Somebody get an IV and a tourniquet. **1985** *Newsweek* (June 17) 21: Someone who delivers the crash cart when there is a cardiac arrest. **1985** Former hospital attendant, age 35: The *crash cart* was an instrument cart. They made a lot of noise when you rolled them down the hall. **1985** Frede *Nurses* 61: Two crash carts…contained the medications and equipment for addressing cardiac arrest.

crasher *n.* an undesirable person who makes his or her way into a party without invitation. Now *colloq.* Cf. GATE-CRASHER.

1922 in *DN* V 147: *Crasher*—anyone who goes to parties uninvited. *1924 in *OEDS: Crasher*—A man who comes in without an invitation. **1926** Finerty *Criminalese* 12: *Crasher*—No pay or invitation. **1967** "M.T. Knight" *Terrible Ten* 72: By midnight the place was…packed with guests, at least a quarter of which were crashers. **1982** Univ. Tenn. student: Uh-oh. These guys look like crashers.

crash-out *n. Pris.* a jailbreak.

1940 Burnett *High Sierra* 50: But all I thought about was a crash out.

crash pad *n.* **1.** Esp. *Narc.* a room, apartment, or other place where people may stay temporarily.

1967 *Time* (July 7) 22: Galahad maintains a "crash" pad and returns runaways to their parents. **1968** *Atlantic* (Mar.) 59: Allowing them to use one part of the church building as a "crash pad," which is hippie language for a temporary place to sleep. **1970** Grissim *White Man's Blues* 46: There was even an adjacent apartment of sorts which served as a C & W crash pad for anyone who happened to just come into town without a place to stay. **1973** Droge *Patrolman* 60: Many of the residents form "crash pads" that consist entirely of wall-to-wall mattresses. **1974** *Harper's* (July) 27: One platoon leader's apartment became a sort of crash pad for men in the company who needed a place to stay on weekends. **1980** Gould *Ft. Apache* 37: Working-class families struggled to maintain apartments next to burnt-out shooting galleries, crash pads and numbers drops.

2. *Gymnastics.* a safety mat.

1979 Frommer *Sports Lingo* 116.

crash wagon *n.* Esp. *Av.* a crash ambulance. Now *colloq.*

1934 Boylan & Baldwin *Devil Dogs of the Air* (film): We'll get the station crash wagon over. **1942** *AS* (Apr.) 103: *Crash Wagon.* Ambulance.

C-rat *n. Army.* C-ration. [Quots. ref. to Vietnam War.]

1965 *Time* (Dec. 24) 20: An estimated 70% of the troops in Viet Nam are still eating canned C-rations ("C-rats" to the G.I.s). **1973** Huggett *Body Count* 10: Flak jackets, helmets, canteens, C-rats. **1980** Santoli *Everything* 92: The C-rat stock went down rapidly when we all started eating.

crate *n.* **1.** an old or worthless horse; PLUG.

1869 "Mark Twain" *Innocents* II 155: We were to select our horses at 3 P.M. At that hour, Abraham, the dragoman, marshaled them before us…Blucher shook his head and said: "That dragon is going to get himself into trouble fetching those old crates out of the hospital the way they are, unless he has got a permit. **1969** in *DARE*.

2.a. *Av.* an aircraft, esp. if old or of little value.

1918 Grider *War Birds* 62: Springs and DeGamo were duly ordered to go up and spin those ancient crates. **1925** in Faulkner *New Orleans Sketches* 205: Whatcher going to do with your crate? **1926** *Writer's Mo.* (Nov.) 394: *Crate*—Like "ship" and "plane," used as a synonym for "airplane." **1928** in Thomason *Stories* 462: Sergeant, we better burn the old crate. **1928** Hall & Niles *One Man's War* 119: And the old "crates" we flew at that training school would give any self-respecting pilot the willies. **1931** Springs *Carol Banks* 43: He must have a ton of bombs in that crate. **1933** Stewart *Airman Speech* 56: A very common name for a plane. A "hot" crate or a "peppy" crate usually signifies a fast ship. **1934** Boylan & Baldwin *Devil Dogs of the Air* (film): Get that crate out of here before I place you under arrest! **1938** *N.Y. Sunday News* (Sept. 4) 11: Douglas took off for the National Air Races at Cleveland in his $900 trans-atlantic "crate." **1938** "E. Queen" *4 Hearts* 47: I'll fly 'em down in my own crate. **1940** Hartney *Up & At 'Em* 69: "Wish you hadn't ruined that crate of yours," said the adjutant. "We need it badly." **1942** *Time* (Apr. 27) 93: You'd laugh today at the planes the pilots flew in the last war. Flimsy, cloth-covered fighting planes that flew only 130 miles an hour. Heavy, inefficient engines. No wonder pilots called them "crates." **1955** in Loosbrock & Skinner *Wild Blue* 32: A Royal Flying Corps airman, nursing his crate toward enemy lines. **1958** Hailey & Castle *Runway* 113: What's the story on the passenger who's flying the crate? **1965** Matthiessen *Fields of Lord* 113: Get that crate gassed up and oiled. **1977** Langone *Life at Bottom* 232: This here crate isn't one of the new LC-130R models.

b. a motor vehicle, esp. if old or of little value; a vehicle.

1927 *AS* II (Mar.) 276: *Crate.* An old Ford. **1932** Hawks *Crowd Roars* (film): What've you been doin' with this crate? **1938** Bellem *Blue Murder* 154: I've got to have another crate right away—with gas in it. **1949** Bezzerides *Thieves' Highway* (film): What keeps that crate together? **1952** Kahn *Able One Four* 30: Can't you move that damn crate without so much damn noise? **1955** Rumaker *Stories* 11: Get the crate rolling! **1958** Gilbert *Vice Trap* 7: There was something familiar about the crate. **1961** Ellison *Gentleman Junkie* 128: He wouldn't bother with just swiping Mestman's crate either. **1971** Keith *Long Line Rider* 9: Nobody's going to spot the crate buried in these elms.

c. *Naut.* an old or unseaworthy vessel.

1933 Deleon & Martin *Tillie and Gus* (film): I'll put that old crate back in service and make a fortune. **1942** Casey *Torpedo Junction* 20: If the Japs should hit this crate she'd sink like a shot.

3. a coffin.

1925 McAlmon *Stockings* 53: I thought I wuz going home in a crate the next day. **1954–60** *DAS* 128.

4. *Pris.* a prison.

1927 *AS* (June) 391: *Hoosegow* and *can* are quite common names for jail but *crate* is rarely used except by vags. **1970** Rudensky & Riley *Gonif* 59: They say I'm a big rich slob, but where the hell does it show up in this crate?

crater *n.* **1.** *Narc.* an abscess caused by repeated intravenous injections.

1966–67 P. Thomas *Down Mean Streets*: I had cultivated a crater and always shot through the same hole. **1969** *New Amer. Rev. #7* (Aug.) 115: I'm not wearing any craters on my forearm. **1981** (cited in Spears *Drugs & Drink* 127).

2. an acne scar. See also CRATERFACE.

1987 J. Waters *Hairspray* (film) [ref. to 1962]: I've got craters!

craterface *n. Juve.* a person having a scarred or acned complexion. Hence **craterfaced,** *adj.*

1983 W. Safire, in *N.Y. Times Mag.* (Aug. 7) 6: A person with a proliferation of *zits* is called by his kind playmates a *crater-face* or *pizza-face*. **1984** Hindle *Dragon Fall* 19: Wimpy, crater-faced, sewer-mouthed Richard.

crave *n. Stu.* a person of the opposite sex with whom one is infatuated.

1987 Univ. Tenn. student theme: When this person becomes a more serious romantic prospect, he or she becomes the person's *crave*. **1987** Univ. Tenn. student theme: When there is someone I have a desire to go out with, I usually refer to this person as my latest *crave*.

craw *n.* **1.** the stomach (of a human being).

1859 "Skitt" *Fisher's River* 86 [ref. to 1820's]: "My craw's full," says he. **1909** *DN* III 394: I feel sick at the craw this morning. **1967** in *DARE*.

2. nerve.

1958 Swarthout *Cordura* 139: Pullin' a gun like you had tha craw to use it. **1974** E. Thompson *Tattoo* 491: Bull! They's *lots*-o-people you *like* to kill. You jes don have that kinda craw. **1985** Boyne & Thompson *Wild Blue* 64: Breaking eye contact gave him enough craw to sneer.

crawfish *n.* **1.** a weak-willed person who backs out of commitments; a coward.

1847 in Blair & Meine *Half Horse* 110: "If you're determined to stay, I must leave you, Captain Fink,…it's late." "You can slope, old *crawfish*." **1865** Byrn *Fudge Fumble* 67: The old lady was none of your *chicken*-hearted, craw-fish lookin' women. **1908** in H.C. Fisher *A. Mutt* 21: So, you broke your New Year's pledge…you big crawfish. **1951** Wilson *My Six Convicts* 165: I didn't want you to go yellow on me. Can't have any crawfish on this deal.

2. a French person.—used derisively.

1964 E. Green *Ely* 460 [ref. to 1918]: The Americans would cast verbal slurs at the men of other nations as if they were superior to them…: the Limies, Frogs, Fritzies, Poles, Bohunks, Crawfishes. **1968** in *DARE*.

crawfish *v.* **1.a.** to move away backwards; retreat; turn tail.

1842 in *DA* 430: I crawfished out of that place monstrous quick, you may depend. **1844** in *DARE*. **1848** *Ladies' Repository* (Oct.) 315: *Craw-fish*. To back out; refuse to do anything after starting to do it. **1850** Garrard *Wah-to-Yah* 23: Others slowly "crawfished," hiding, by their singular way of crouching the back, until nothing but their heads and tails could be seen. **1863** in Heartsill *1491 Days* 93: The sharp shooters pepper us quite lively, so much so that we are again compelled to "crawfish," for it is impossible for Cavalry to compete successfully with Infantry. **1863** in Allan *Lone Star Ballads* 48: And altho' some laugh'd as I crawfished,/I could not discover the fun. *a*1867 in G. W. Harris *Lovingood* 85: He crawfish'd back durn'd quick. **1877** in *DARE*.

b. *West.* (of a horse) to buck backwards.

1933 *AS* VIII 28: *Crawfish.* To pitch backwards. **1961** in *DARE*.

2. to back out of a commitment; to renege.

1844 in Oehlschlaeger *Reveille* 56: Well, gentlemen, I crawfish! What will you take? **1850** in *DA* 430: The council met the next day and "craw fished"—withdrawing the resolutions by an almost unanimous vote. **1855** Derby *Phoenixiana* 208: If you don't allow that there's been no such publication, weekly, or serial, since the days of the "Bunkum Flag-staff," I'll *craw fish*, and take to reading Johnson's Dictionary. **1889** Harte *Dedlow Marsh* 58: So ye've been crawfishin' agin?…What's this backen out o' what you said yesterday? **1928** Bradford *Ol' Man Adam* 80: Old King Pharaoh crawfished about lettin' de Hebrews go. **1930** Franklyn *Take Off* 26: Horleigh promised us our jobs back…and I don't think he'd crawfish. **1936** Levin *Old Bunch* 171: So they want you to crayfish, huh? **1940** Busch & Swerling *Westerner* (film): You ain't gonna crawfish! **1953** Chandler *Long Goodbye* 32: You're crawfishing and you know it. **1965–70** in *DARE*. *a*1977 in S. King *Bachman* 100: I might have to fight him or crawfish before the day was over. **1986** Jarmusch *Down by Law* (film): When you get enough of it, you gotta crawfish and back out out of it.

crawl *n.* **1.** a dance.

1921 in Cray *Erotic Muse* 194: Frankie…went out to the nickel crawl. **1926** Maines & Grant *Wise-Crack Dict.* 8: *Give us a crawl*—May I have the pleasure of the next dance.

2. *Film & TV.* a display of credits or other information that moves up or across a screen.

1967 in Rowan & MacDonald *Friendship* 21: Our producer partner…"forgot" to give us writer credit on the crawl. **1976** *Sat. Review* (Sept. 18) 12: The names of the people responsible for this reverse masterpiece go on like the "crawl" preceding a pornographic movie, constituting a list of individuals eagerly seeking credit for the discreditable. **1981** (quot. at TALKING HEAD).

3. *pl.* CREEPS.—constr. with *the*.

1970 Cortina *Slain Warrior* 129: This place gives me the crawls.

crawl *v.* **1.** to be well or overly supplied (with).

*1821–26 Stewart *Man-of-War's-Man* II 195: Portsmouth is…absolutely crawling with them. **1879** in M. Lewis *Mining Frontier* 180: Bodie's just crawlin' with lucre, but the people there ain't got no energy. **1902* R. Kipling, in *OEDS:* The starboard side's crawlin' with 'em. **1925* in Fraser & Gibbons *Soldier & Sailor Wds.* 66 [ref. to WWI]: The place fairly crawled with Staff Officers. **1928** McEvoy *Show Girl* 74: He is…crawling with jack. **1928** Nason *Sgt. Eadie* 149 [ref. to 1918]: The place is crawling with Boche! **1956** Poe *Attack* (film): The place is crawling with krauts. **1987** Univ. Tenn. instructor, age 38: His folks are crawling with bucks.

2.a. to leave stealthily.

1885 in Wister *Out West* 35: The would-be squatters have crawled. **1894** (quot. at MOOCH, *n.*).

b. to renege; to back out.

1907 Siler *Pugilism* 132: Twenty-fi' dollars if me backer don't crawl.

3.a. to mount (a horse).

1893 Remington *Pony Tracks* 46: Anything and everything is his work, from the negotiation for the sale of five thousand head of cattle to the "busting" of a bronco which no one else can "crawl." *Ibid.* 53: Hyar, crawl some horses, and we'll go out and meet 'em. **1926** C. M. Russell *Trails* 7: Charley crawls him again kinder careful and rides him sixty miles. **1928** Santee *Cowboy* 69: By the time I'd saddled an' crawled a bronc I'd be circulatin' good. **1931** in Fife & Fife *Ballads of West* 96: I crawls him just like he was gentle.

b. to engage in sexual intercourse with.

1947 Willingham *End As a Man* 144: I finally crawled Mary Jane Cummings last night. She meeowed like a kitty. **1965** Trimble *Sex Words* 55: *Crawl*…*vt.*…To take an Active Homosexual role.—*Crawler.* **1972** PFC, U.S. Army, age *ca*20 (coll. J. Ball): Boy, I'd like to crawl that.

4.a. *Army.* to scold harshly; reprove.—occ. constr. with *on* or *over.*

1878 Flipper *Colored Cadet* 66 [ref. to 1874]: He'll be "crawled over" for a certainty, and to make his crimes appear as bad as possible, will be reported for "neglect of duty while a sentinel, [etc.]." *Ibid.* 51: "To crawl over."—To haze, generally in the severest manner possible. **1893** in F. Remington *Sel. Letters* 205: Did the Chiefs crawl all over Weiss for having his…exploits published? **1900** *Howitzer* (U.S. Mil. Acad.) *No. 1* 118: *Crawl*—To chide; to scold; the act of teaching "plebes" their duties as Cadets. **1905** *DN* III 76: *Crawl*…to reprove. "The professor crawled him for cutting recitations." **1907** Moss *Officer's Manual* 243: *Crawl*, to admonish. **1928** Nason *Sgt. Eadie* 47 [ref. to 1918]: And then to have his hump crawled by the first sergeant! **1929** *Our Army* (Dec.) 25: *Crawl*: To reprimand in a thorough and emphatic manner, often with profanity for additional decoration, is to "crawl" a person. It is much like to "bawl out" or "climb" a man. **1930** *Our Army* (Dec.) 27: I'm crawled on/If I let'm sit or lag. **1935** *Our Army* (Nov.) 32: I Hear the Skipper Crawled the New John Because He Scratched His Nose in Ranks. **1975** Univ. Tenn. student: That bitch crawled my ass Friday. **1976** Univ. Tenn. grad. student: She crawled my tail. She just chewed me out. **1981** C. Nelson *Picked Bullets Up* 189: [The] manager…crawled up my ass for every mistake.

b. to attack physically.

1899 A. Lewis *Sandburrs* 20: "Which a gent don't have to have no reason for crawlin' you!" said Cook. "Anyone's licenced to chase you 'round jest for exercise!" **1905** *DN* III 76: *Crawl*…To whip. **1925** Mullin *Scholar Tramp* 126: He kicked me one day, and I crawls 'im. When they pulled me off muh meat, I had 'im bloody as a hawg. **1960** in *DARE*: I'll crawl the bastard as soon as I see him. **1972–79** T. Wolfe *Right Stuff* 65: Don't cross that line or I'll crawl you. **1986** Ark. man, age 35: To *crawl somebody's ass* is to beat them up.

5. *Stu.* to dance.

1924 Hecht & Bodenheim *Cutie* 39: Come on,…let's crawl.

6. to go from nightclub to nightclub; (*trans.*) to go from establishment to establishment on (a street that is the location of numerous bars, casinos, or the like); to frequent (numerous such establishments).

1959 *Swinging Syllables: Crawling*—Nightclubbing, moving from hole to hole. **1965** Capote *In Cold Blood* 244: As Captain Tracy Hand, smartly clothed in a made-to-order uniform, Dick intended to "crawl the strip," Las Vegas's street of never-closed casinos.

¶ In phrases:

¶ **crawl heads** to work as a barber.

1897 Ade *Pink* 143: I can't une'stan' why all 'ese wahm boys…is all down heah in 'is ol' shop, crawlin' heads faw tow [*sic*] bits.

¶ **crawl (someone's) frame** CRAWL, 4.a., b.

1905 *DN* III 76: The professor *crawled* him for cutting recitations. *Ibid.* 79: He crawled his frame. **1918** "Commander" *Clear the Decks!* 100: Old Man will crawl your frame if he sees so much as a sailor cross it. **1928** in E. O'Neill *Sel. Letters* 317: I'll bet you'll have a large section of infuriated fairies crawling your frame for that one. **1940** E. O'Neill *Iceman Cometh* 142: And every time dey'd crawl my frame wid de same old argument. **1949** in *PADS* (No. 14) 78: *Crawl your frame.* To give one a beating or a thrashing. [Fla.]

¶ **crawl (someone's) hump** *West.* to attack (someone).

1907 S.E. White *Arizona* 104: Here I…save your worthless carcass and the first chance you get you try to crawl my hump. **1922** Raine *Fighting Edge* 141: Crawl his hump sudden. Go it like a wild cat. **1936** R. Adams *Cowboy Lingo* 226: He…was liable to "crawl yo' hump at any moment."

crawler *n. Hobo.* a legless beggar.

1925–26 Black *You Can't Win* 197 [ref. to 1890's]: "Crawlers" with cut-off legs swung themselves along on their hands drunkenly, like huge toads. **1927** *DN* V 443: *Crawlers,* n. Legless beggars. **1927** Tully *Circus Parade* 6: Among the trailers with this circus were legless men called crawlers, who traveled with their bodies strapped to small wheeled platforms.

crawloid *n. U.S. Mil. Acad.* an upperclassman who notably rebukes new cadets.

1900 *Howitzer* (U.S. Mil. Acad.) *No. 1* 118 [ref. to *ca*1890]: *Crawloid.*—One who crawls a great deal.

crawl out *n.* an evasion.

1903 A.H. Lewis *Boss* 184: That's a crawl-out…an' it ain't worthy of you.

craw-thumper *n.* a devout Roman Catholic; (*broadly*) (*obs.*) an inhabitant of Maryland.—used contemptuously. Hence **craw-thumping,** *adj.*

***1785** Grose *Vulgar T.: Craw Thumpers.* Roman catholics, so called from their beating their breasts in the confession of their sins. **1845** in *DA* 430: The inhabitants of…Maryland [are called] Craw-thumpers. **1889** in *F & H* II: Wanted a servant-maid. No pulings or *craw-thumpers* need apply. **1895** Barentz *Woordenboek* 71: *Craw-thumper,* Roomsch Katholiek. **1918** Griffin *Ballads of the Reg't* 16: One day big Tim Fagan—his Irish was up—/Called bunkie a "psalm-singin', craw-thumpin' pup." ***1959** Behan *Borstal Boy* 12: The left-wing element [of the IRA]…would be delighted, and the others, the craw-thumpers, could not say anything against me. *Ibid.* 344: *Craw-thumper:* breast-beater, a religious person. [**1987** in *N.Y. Times Bk. Review* (Mar. 22) 12: In Chicago in the 1880's Patrick (Pagan) O'Leary…called upon Irish-Americans to abandon their Roman Catholic religion, which, he said…, had made them good for nothing but "thumping their craws and telling their beads."]

crazo *n. & adj.* a person who is crazy or eccentric; (as *adj.*) crazy.

1972 *Playboy* (April) 82: DeVreer had sort of a running open house for crazos over there, all the local eccentrics like Vampira. **1984** D. Jenkins *Life Its Ownself* 28: Those cities were perfect for your "mondo, craze-o, leftist derelicts."

crazy *n.* an insane or wildly eccentric person; lunatic. [Rare before late 1960's.]

1867 Goss *Soldier's Story* 30: I was addressed as "old crazy" by my companions, and told to keep still. **1889** *Harper's Mag.* (Oct.) 702: The doctor from the crazies…tried all kinds o' brainy tricks on her. **1913–14** London *Elsinore* 142: A crazy lashed down in his bunk and harmless. **1951** in *Neurotica* (Winter 1952) 3: There are more "crazies" than "sanes" now. **1968** Gover *JC* 100: Johnlaw took him for a crazy. **1970** *Playboy* (Aug.) 174: The hippies—now called freaks or crazies—have spread out. **1972** Kerr *Dinky Hocker* 9: Crazies…talk to themselves in corners and warm themselves by radiators. **1973** I. Reed *La. Red* 35: They took her where they put the crazies. **1978** Strieber *Wolfen* 154: Those two crazies were right then? **1981** D. Burns *Feeling Good* 76: They must be "crazies" with whom you would have little in common. **1982** P. Michaels *Grail* 93: The crazy is revving himself up. **1983** R. Thomas *Missionary* 53: The radicals, the dopers, the crazies.

crazy *adj.* Orig. *Jazz.* excitingly unconventional; (*hence,* in gen.) exciting; impressive; wonderful; fine; good.

1948 *Life* (Nov. 1) 106: It's crazy [terrific] up there. You get steak and chicken and potato salad. **1950** *Neurotica* (Autumn) 46: And Jack we got some crazy shit. **1952** Holmes *Go* 111: Lotsa weed tonight and crazy

music! *ca*1953 Hughes *Lodge* 72: They carried some of the craziest Mexican pot with them that I have ever smoked in my whole life. **1954** *Harper's Mag.* (Nov.) 36: Anything nice was crazy or cool. **1956** Kubrick & Thompson *Killing* (film): O.K., crazy. Now tell me what's your angle, John. **1958** Landau & Yates *Frankenstein—1970* (film): Yeah, that's real crazy. **1960** J.A. Williams *Angry Ones* 16: "Say, I just had dinner with Lint Mason." "Crazy," Obie said. **1971** in Sanchez *Word Sorcerers* 115: You've got a crazy crib, girl. **1976** *Kojak* (CBS-TV): Are we in business? Crazy! **1978** Selby *Requiem* 247: Lets split. Crazy. Good. I'm dying to get home. **1980** Kotzwinkle *Jack* 266: It's a crazy set of wheels. **1990** *New Yorker* (Sept. 17) 73: He carry the coke but I be carrying crazy paraphernalia. **1991** *Source* (Oct.) 41: This kid has crazy skills and…can…rap in Arabic.

¶ In phrases:

¶ **crazy like** [or **as**] **a fox** seemingly foolish but in fact extremely cunning.

1908 in Fleming *Unforget. Season* 107: Showing the doubting tommies that he was crazy like a fox. **1935** in *OEDS*: "Crazy as a fox," I said glumly. **1944** S.J. Perelman *Crazy Like a Fox* (title). **1987** *TV Guide* (Apr. 4) A-48: Still Crazy Like a Fox. **1992** Ross Perot, campaign speech in Pittsburgh, Pa. (Oct. 25): These fellas up there might say, "They were crazy like a fox."

¶ **like crazy** with great energy; without restraint.

1924 Marks *Plastic* 288: She has been…tearing around like crazy. **1936** in Fenner *Throttle* 142: Gondola of scrap iron's out on the main line and goin' like crazy. **1944** Busch *Dream of Home* 69: The machine guns opened up, chattering like crazy. **1950** *Sat. Eve. Post* (Jan. 7) 70: You live when you're at home…like crazy in order to get them free. **1960** *N.Y. Times* (Feb. 21) II 1: A supervisor once came to Hollywood, laughing like crazy. **1974** *Business Week* (Aug. 10) 46: People are trying like crazy to save money. **1990** *Cosmopolitan* (Nov.) 256: Her lawyers tried like crazy to prove that…the couple was married.

crazy farm *n.* FUNNY FARM.

1967 N.Y.C. man, age *ca*20: Next thing, you'll wind up at the crazy farm.

crazyhead *n.* a very eccentric person.

1979 Charyn *7th Babe* 150: But those crazyheads could draw a crowd.

crazyhead whiskey *n.* very potent whiskey.

1885 "Lykkejaeger" *Dane* 114: He had gotten outside of too much tangle foot, crazy head whiskey.

crazy house *n.* an insane asylum or psychiatric hospital.

1887 *N.O. Lantern* (July 16) 2: To keep him from being sent to a crazy house. **1891** Riis *How Other Half Lives* 50: The "old man"…had been taken to the "crazy-house," and the woman who was his neighbor…had simply disappeared. **1898** Brooks *Strong Hearts* 140: Say! Where do you live when you're at home—in a crazy-house? What did they let you out for? **1912** Ade *Babel* 110: I figured that I was booked for the crazy-house or the bone-orchard, I couldn't tell which. **1915** in Kornbluth *Reb. Voices* 152: Should be locked up in the crazy house as a menace to society. **1935** T. Wolfe *Time & River* 211: They may have to send you to the crazy-house to take the cure. **1950** A. Lomax *Mr. Jelly Roll* 60: Anyhow he died in the crazy house. **1958** Gardner *Piece of the Action* 77: I'm sitting on top of the crazy house. **1962** in Hayakawa *Use & Misuse of Lang.* 206: He has come from a "crazy house." *a*1990 E. Currie *Dope & Trouble* 147: This crazy house…insane-asylum house or something.

crazy-water *n.* [orig. pidgin] whiskey.

1933 Clifford *Boats* 10: Man cain't drink that crazy-water an' do his drill. **1936** *Chrons. of Okla.* XIV (Sept.) 331: The Comanche word for [whisky] was *Bosah-pah*, meaning "crazy water." **1950** in *Dict. Canadianisms.*

creaker *n. Black E.* (see quot.).

1958 Hughes & Bontemps *Negro Folklore* 482: *Creaker:* An aged person.

cream *n.* semen; (*also*) the coital secretion of the vagina.

***ca*1866** *Romance of Lust* 208: She delighted to break her fast on cream. ***1900** *Horn Book* 98: But they must not lose their head when they lose their cream. **1916** Cary *Venery* I 57: *Cream*—The seminal fluid…A single drop is called a snowball. **1921** E. Pound, in V. Eliot *Letters* 499: His foaming and abundant cream/Has coated the world. *a*1927 in P. Smith *Letter from Father* 47: To keep the cream from getting all over the furniture when she jerked me off. **1938** "Justinian" *Amer. Sexualis* 18: *Cream.* n. The sexual fluid of the male…Low coll., C. 19–20. **1967** Mailer *Vietnam* 17: Get that drop of cream off your jeans before you grow hair on your hand. **1972** *Anthro. Linguistics* (Mar.) 100: *Cream* (n): Semen.

cream *v.* **1.a.** to experience sexual orgasm.

*ca*1915–20 in Cray *Erotic Muse* 88: Oh, she laid a-dreaming/While he laid a-creaming. **1916–22** Cary *Sex. Vocab.* I s.v. *copulation*: *Creaming.* To have an emission. **1939** in *So. Folk. Qly.* XL 105: Then kiss me, kid, for I'm about to cream. **1943** in Legman *Limerick* 183: Her drawers cream at the mere thought of it. **1952** Mandel *Angry Strangers* 42: He loves that…He prob'ly creamed on the floor is right. **1958** W. Burroughs *Naked Lunch* 125: Another horrible old character just sits there…and creams in his dry goods. **1961** Gover *$100 Misunderstanding* 93: Her lil ol pussy jes a-creamin fer her…boyfrien'. **1964** Faust *Steagle* 107: He sings "Cheeribeeribee" and the girls cream in their pants. **1972** C. Gaines *Stay Hungry* 145: I had this monster flash, like creamin' off in my head. **1973** "J. Godey" *Pelham* 175: Opening and closing her legs as if she was creaming at the very sight of him.

b. to become ecstatic.—usu. used derisively. See also *cream (one's) jeans*, below.

1955 Robbins *79 Park Ave* 64: That blonde you were creamin' over this afternoon? **1961** Wolfe *Magic* 89: Sure, you're a knockout, Mar. Worthington'll cream. **1966** Neugeboren *Big Man* 79: And these smiling blond chicks creaming over their dicks. **1970** Wakefield *Going All the Way* 93 [ref. to 1950's]: He really creamed for her. **1978** De Christoforo *Grease* 72: The chicks are gonna cream for [a ride in my new car]. **1985** J. Dillinger *Adrenaline* 253: The guy had practically creamed when he'd seen the MP5 submachine gun, but Dewey had been unwilling to trade it.

2.a. *Stu.* to pass (a course or examination) easily.

1934 Weseen *Dict. Slang* 178: *Cream*—To pass an examination with a high mark. **1941** in *DAS*: Boy, did I cream that exam! **1986** Cosby *Fatherhood* 125: Not *Driver's Ed!* I'm *creaming* that!

b. to defeat soundly; (*broadly*) to ruin.

1940 O'Hara *Pal Joey* 80: I got creamed out of the hotel spot in Ohio & came here and made this connection. **1945** in *DARE*. **1946** J.H. Burns *Gallery* 283: We're gettin creamed on the rate of exchange for the lira. **1947** Mailer *Naked & Dead* 217: I bet some of those rich kikes in the party are the ones that creamed the CU. *Ibid.* 265: Don't cream it for me. I mean a fellow's chances can be hurt by his roommate. **1948** J.H. Burns *Lucifer* 406: I think we've been given one helluva creaming. **1959** Gault *Drag Strip* 61: Arky really creamed him; Juan was never in it from the drop of the flag. **1970** Segal *Love Story* 11: We creamed them 7–0. **1983** WKGN radio news (Mar. 10): The Bruins flexed their muscles, creaming Arizona 111–57.

c. to kill; (*hence*) *Mil. Av.* to destroy (an enemy aircraft).

1940 in Goodstone *Pulps* 116: Sooner than give him up to another woman, you creamed him. **1944** Olds *Helldiver Squadron* 166: An Army motion picture…was summarized by someone as being "about various ways to sneak through a bush and cream a guy." **1944** *N.Y. Times* (Mar. 6): I was just about ateam this Jap Zeke and going for a ninety-degree deflection shot…He made a tight inside turn, so I flipped over, tailed and creamed him. **1958** Frankel *Band of Bros.* 51 [ref. to 1950]: Anybody did that much thinkin', he'd deserve to get creamed. **1963** Dwiggins *S.O. Bees* 171: Chasnoff…let the Zekes overshoot, then creamed two in succession. **1964** Howe *Valley of Fire* 37: They'd give him the business, polish him off, cream his ass. *Ibid.* 164: An' when the gooks creamed him, the whole camp fell apart. **1970** Thackrey *Thief* 228: But if you ain't topped—who the hell was it got creamed in that Caddy? The one that spun off the road and burned up? **1985** Sawislak *Dwarf* 80: I'll kill you. Lemme down and I'll cream ya all! **1990** Ruggero *38 N. Yankee* 206: Our guys will get creamed if they try to move.

d. to hit or strike hard, esp. to beat up; BELT.

1942 *ATS* 318: Bash…cream,…lam,…sock, [etc.]. *Ibid.* 674: *Knock out*…cream,…kayo [etc.]. **1959** Morrill *Dark Sea* 111: Every port we stopped at Joe Parker got creamed. A Limey paratrooper in Naples broke his nose. A Swede sailor in Abadon tore out a piece of his scalp. I was afraid he wouldn't live through the war. **1959** Brosnan *Long Season* 168: But eventually he'd hang [a pitch] and I'd cream it. **1962** Shepard *Press Passes* 104: Get down or I'll cream you. **1965** W. Crawford *Bronc Rider* 237: I'll cream you, you go at me again. **1965** Spillane *Killer Mine* 28: You ought to see your face, it's all screwed up red and tight and if I wasn't a broad you'd cream me, huh? **1969** *Playboy* (Dec.) 114: Georgia Tech really creamed me in a game…just about crunched every bone in my body. **1978** P. Rizzuto on *NY Yankees baseball* (WPIX-TV) (June 16): That was a high-rising fastball he creamed.

e. to smash at great speed.—also constr. with *into*.

1951 Sheldon *Troubling a Star* 55: Lieutenant Rossi…couldn't pull out and knew he was about to cream into a mountain. **1976** J.W. Thomas *Heavy Number* 85: She could see the speeding cars creaming one another. **1980** Whalen *Takes a Man* 225: The truck rolled down the street and creamed about five cars.

3. *Education.* to accept or attend to only the cream of a crop of students or applicants.

1983 Sturz *Wid. Circles* 84: They claimed that since our participants were orderly and studious, we had to be "creaming," that is, taking in those without serious problems.

¶ In phrase:

¶ **cream (one's) jeans** to be overcome with shock, enthusiasm, or delight.—used derisively.—usu. considered vulgar. Also vars.

1942–45 in Campbell & Campbell *War Paint* 207: Jean Creamer. **1951** Morris *China Station* 52: We busted right in, that M.P. creamed in his jeans when he sees this colonel. **1951** Mailer *Barbary Shore* 88: I've never creamed m'pants over the beauties of the land across the sea. **1960** MacCuish *Do Not Go Gentle* 225: Tell me, darlin', afore I cream my jeans. **1969** Sidney *Love of Dying* 48: She'll just cream her pants over that handle-bar moustache of yours. **1970** Siciliano *Kill Me First* 174: I have to laugh when I hear about somebody creaming his jeans over law and order. **1974** Kingry *Monk & Marines* 38: He was just about to cream his jeans, whether from glee or indignation I wasn't sure. **1979** Gutcheon *New Girls* 46: Mother would absolutely cream in her pants if she knew…what happened…last night. **1980** McAleer & Dickson *Unit Pride* 85: He'll really cream his jeans when he hears we screwed Miller out of eleven [cases of beer]. **1985** Dye *Between Raindrops* 197: Don't cream your jeans, Captain. This won't last long. **1992** Mowry *Way Past Cool* 78: Creamin their jeans over that goddam car.

creamed *adj.* very drunk.

1966 (quot. at SNAKED UP). **1975** (cited in Spears *Drugs & Drink*).

cream of the valley *n.* whiskey or gin.

1850 in H.C. Lewis *Works* 160: Pat imagined he was going to be out in a more stimulating course of treatment. His eyes fairly glistened, and his leg was, if possible, drawn still more closely to his body as he took a mental view of his situation—no work, good lodgings, pleasant medicine, liberal diet, and at last, to cap the climax of his earthly felicity, the pure "Crame of the Valley." *1858 in *F & H* II: Is it cream o' the walley or fits as has overcome the lady?

creampuff *n.* **1.** a weakling; PUSHOVER; also in phr. **rough tough creampuff.**

1913–15 Van Loan *Taking the Count* 105: He ain't a creampuff boxer, if that's what you mean. He don't know anything about sparrin' for points. **1923** *Amer. Leg. Wkly.* (Jan. 26) 20: You said it, ole creampuff. **1933–34** Lorimer & Lorimer *Stag Line* 70: It looked like those two he-men were going to meekly obey Davy, the cream puff. **1936** in Leadbitter & Slaven *Blues Records* 383: You're Just A Cream Puff (You Can't Take It). **1937** Wexley & Duff *Angels* (film): What do ya think we are, a buncha creampuffs or somethin'? **1940** W.R. Burnett *High Sierra* 63: I'm beginning to get the idea that our boy-friend is no cream-puff. **1952** Chase *McThing* 50: This kid is a cream puff. **1959** N.Y.C. schoolboy: Oh, a rough-tough creampuff, eh? **1962** in IUFA *Folk Speech*: Roughtough cream puff. **1963** *N.Y. Times Mag.* (Nov. 24) 52: One 11-year-old pointed out contemptuously that "rough, tough creampuff," was by now so archaic "it belongs in the dictionary." **1967** Spillane *Delta* 9: If he could [break out] there, this place would be a cream puff, so the cuffs stay on him, Doctor. **1967** Colebrook *Cross of Lassitude* 72: He thinks I'm a ruff-tuff cream puff and that the only way I'm goin' to learn my lesson is by puttin' me away. **1974** Lahr *Trot* 99: LeRoi Jones is a cream puff compared to what I have inside. **1975** Kangas & Solomon *Psych. of Strength* 77: People who show weakness are labeled variously as creampuffs, fags, or sissies. **1979** T. Baum *Carny* 83: Come on, creampuff, my old lady throws harder than that! **1986** C. Freeman *Seasons of Heart* 98: A cream puff…He'll last a week.

2. *Mil. Av.* a cloud of white smoke resulting from the bursting of an antiaircraft shell.

1918 *Stars & Stripes* (Feb. 8) 8: "The sky was full of cream puffs," he said, "but…most of the stuff was breaking above or below us." *1919* Downing *Digger Dialects* 18: Cream-Puffs.—Shellbursts. **1928** in *Papers of Mich. Acad.*: Cream-puffs. Airman's term for spherical clouds of white smoke caused by bursting shells.

3.a. a person or thing of excellence.

1920 Ade *Hand-Made Fables* 53: He was a Cream Puff that should have been served Day before Yesterday.

b. (among automobile salesmen) a used car in excellent condition.

1949 in *DAS*. **1963** *Time* (May 17) 105: Used-car dealers can usually sell a "cream puff"—the car in good condition with a good paint job.

1972 *Motor Trend* (Oct.) 128: No prices on cream puffs, right? **1974** Millard *Thunderbolt* 9: You happen to be looking at a little cream puff I hoped nobody'd swipe before I could buy it myself. **1982** R. Sutton *Don't Get Taken* 366: *Cream puffs:* Extremely nice used cars. **1986** Heinemann *Paco's Story* 97: Drives a mint-condition, cream-puff 1948 Mercury.

cream-stick *n.* the penis.

   *1891 *F & H* II 208: *Cream-stick*...(common).—The penis. **1938** "Justinian" *Amer. Sexualis* 18: *Cream-stick,* the *membrum virile*...obsolescent in U.S.

creamy *adj.* delightful; attractive.

   *1889 Barrère & Leland *Dict. Slang* I 280: *Creamy* (common), excellent. **1891** *F & H* II: *Creamy, adj.* (general).—Excellent; first-rate. **1895** Gore *Stu. Slang* 13: *Creamy.* Very nice. **1947** Greene & Macauley *Born to Kill* (film): Helen's a creamy dish. **1953** Paley *Rumble* 92: That's what you call a creamy job! **1959** E. Hunter *Conviction* 54: Agatha's expecting me at eight-thirty, and she's got some creamy new records. **1969** R. Beck *Black Widow* 25: Mike is creamy and cute as always. **1973** *Oui* (June) 118: The creamiest set of gears in Paris...the most exquisite bicycle in the world. **1984** W. Gibson *Neuromancer* 153: Up the hill...just the creamiest crib.

creature var. CRITTER, 1.

credentials *n.pl.* genitals or breasts. *Joc.*

   1968 in *DARE*. **1977** Caputo *Rumor of War* 140: When I saw it down between my legs, all I could think of were my credentials. "It's going to blow my balls off." **1980** J.S. Young *Rumor of War* (film): "He lost his foot!" "Yeah, but he's still got his—credentials."

creek *n.* ¶ In phrase: **up the** [or a] **creek** [**without a paddle**] in a serious predicament. See also SHIT CREEK.

   1918 in Truman *Ltrs. Home* 50: Then if some inquisitive nut asks me a question, I'm up a creek. **1918** in Rossano *Price of Honor* 88: [If] the motor stops...you're "up the creek." **1930** in Perelman *Old Gang* 142 [caption]: "I'm Up A Creek Without A Paddle," Fluttered the Phoney Baloney. **1941** in *OEDS*. **1944** C.B. Davis *Leo McGuire* 22: I'd have laid down on the job...but I didn't want to get Albert up the old creek. **1951** Robbins *Danny Fisher* 61: Papa's business was really up the creek. **1958** Frankel *Band of Bros.* 201: No jawin' about what you wanna do, not when you're up the creek without a paddle, like us. **1961** Heller *Catch-22* 78: You really are up the creek, Popinjay. **1975** Boatner et al. *Dict. Amer. Idioms* 366: I'll be up the creek if I don't pass this history test. **1976** A.W. Moffat *Maverick Navy* 69: We were..."up the creek without oars." **1992** *Golden Palace* (CBS-TV): We're up the creek.

creep *n.* **1.** *pl.* a sensation of horror or anxiety.—constr. with *the.* Now *colloq.*

   [***1849** Dickens *Copperfield* ch. iii: She was constantly complaining of the cold, and of its occasioning a visitation in her back which she called "the creeps."] ***1870** in *F & H* II: Talking about bodies, I could give you the creeps with what I've seen. **1889** Pierson *Vagabond's Honor* 91: He's playin' agin. Always sad as the wailin' of a banshee. It gives me the creeps sometimes to hear him. *a*1904–11 Phillips *Susan Lenox* II 190: Don't laugh that way...It gives me the creeps. **1923** Boyd *Through Wheat* 255 [ref. to 1918]: "Let's get out of here. Hicks is crazy." "Yeah. He gives me the creeps." **1931** Hellinger *Moon* 15: I hate them damn corpses...They give me the creeps. **1933** Hammett *Thin Man* 316: Dorothy shuddered. "He gives me the creeps." **1938** Bellem *Blue Murder* 15: She sort of gave me the creeps. **1941** Schulberg *Sammy* 15: I don't know what it is about that kid, he's a hard worker and I think he's good to his mother but he gives me the creeps. **1990** Vachss *Blossom* 233: You're giving me the creeps.

   2. *Und. & Police.* CREEPER, 3.

   [***1877** E. Leigh *Dial. of Cheshire* 52: A *Creep*...A creeping fellow.] [***1898** *EDD*: *Creep n....*a sneak. [Lancashire].] **1913** (implied at CREEP JOINT). **1914** Jackson & Hellyer *Crim. Slang* 26: *Creep,* Noun. Current amongst crooked pimps. A creeper, a crawler who searches the clothes of a victim while the latter is abed with the creep's paramour. **1928** (quot. at PAY-OFF). **1951** in J. Blake *Joint* 21: We also have a group of prisoners called "creeps" or "night-crawlers," who prowl the dormitory at night and steal from the other sleeping prisoners. **1954** Collans & Sterling *House Detect.* 47: A Corridor Creep...operates...in the early hours of the morning, getting into guests' rooms while they are asleep...The Creep only becomes genuinely dangerous if and when discovered.

   3. *pl. Black E.* the feet.

   1927 McKay *Home to Harlem* 32: She ain't got 'em from creeps to crown, and her trotters is B flat, but her gin is regal.

4. [perh. sugg. by **(2)**, but commonly assoc. with **(1)**] a worthless, contemptible, offensive, or despicable person.

   1926 in J.M. March *Wild Party* 111: "The son-of-a-bitch—he wants to sleep!"/"Jesus Christ, what a stupid creep!" **1934** in *Jour. Ab. & Clin. Psych.* XXX (1935) 362: *Creep*—a worthless person [term used at Sing Sing Prison.] **1935** in Thompson & Raymond *Gang Rule in NY* 346: Okay. I won't be such a big creep. **1941** Macaulay & Wald *Manpower* (film): Get out of here, you creep! **1942** Freeman & Gilbert *Larceny, Inc.* (film): Aw, some creep named Hotchkiss. **1944** N. Johnson *Casanova Brown* (film): And you can't marry that creep you've dug up. **1947** Schulberg *Harder They Fall* 143: He...fell in with those creeps who have connections with the clubs. **1949** Ellson *Tomboy* 62: Did you hear him talk? That guy's a bloody creep. **1952** Chase *McThing* 99: Why, you little creep. **1953** Chandler *Goodbye* 145: I've got to go out there and smile at those creeps. **1954** Matheson *Born of Man & Woman* 219: That janitor gives me the creeps...I'm serious. The man is a creep. **1955** Graziano & Barber *Somebody Up There* 4: You creep, you don't know how bad I feel. **1961** in Cannon *Nobody Asked* 142: All they learn them is that a manager is nothing but a creep looking to heist them. **1966** Shepard *Doom Pussy* 73: Why don't those creeps who write crank letters to American widows have the guts to put on a return address? **1970** Baraka *Jello* 23: Shutup, creep. How'd you get all this loot in the first place? **1973** Lucas, Katz & Huyck *Amer. Graffiti* 57: Don't let those creeps bug you. **1975** V.B. Miller *Deadly Game* 9: If all the cops in the City were as good or as dedicated as Ben Keller, the creeps wouldn't stand a chance. **1976** Rosten *To Anywhere* 298: Tourist creeps from the States. **1978** Strieber *Wolfen* 252: That little creep! Leave him where he is! **1982** Whissen *Way with Wds.* 24: He was the creep who popped her balloon. **1983** *Good Morning America* (ABC-TV) (June 2): You lying, filthy, disgusting creep!

   5. *Black E.* a stealthy departure or (*occ.*) arrival.

   1946 Mezzrow & Wolfe *Really Blues* 116: The Chicagoans were pulling a creep in a dozen different directions. **1957** H. Simmons *Corner Boy* 177: "I mean everybody loves and hates and has babies and pulls creeps—" "Creeps?" "Yeh, sneaks in the back door when the ole man goes out the front." **1963** Charters *Poetry of Blues* 89: It was early this morning, I was 'bout half asleep,/I heard somebody making a 'fore day creep.

   ¶ In phrase:

   ¶ **holy creeps!** CRIPES.

   1958 R. Wright *Long Dream* 23: "Holy creeps!" the woman exclaimed, then broke into a laugh.

creep *v.* Esp. *Black E.* to escape stealthily; to abscond.

   1942 Liebling *Telephone* 49: You cannot let a tenant creep on you. **1966** Braly *On the Yard* 174: Still even those who managed to creep were reapprehended with stifling regularity. **1966–80** Folb *Runnin' Lines* 233: *Creep*...Steal away. **1983** *Reader's Digest Success with Words* 85: Black English...*creep*...to leave, depart.

creepazoid *n.* CREEP, 4.

   1987 Hauser & DeCoteau *Creepazoids* (title). **1990** *Teenage Mutant Ninja Turtles* (CBS-TV): That creepazoid is more of a rat than Splinter will ever be.

creeper *n.* **1.** usu. *pl.* a louse.

   *1785 Grose *Vulgar T.: Creepers....*lice. **1883–84** Whittaker *L. Locke* 138: Are you sure you're clean, Larry? Got any creepers about you? **1899** Green *Va. Folk-Speech* 133: *Creepers*...Head-lice. **1950, 1965–70** in *DARE*.

   2. *pl.* **a.** the feet.

   1889 Barrère & Leland *Dict. Slang* I 280: *Creepers*...(American), the feet. **1941** *Pittsburgh Courier* (Nov. 29) 7: These guys always have their *peepers* on just what they want and their *creepers* on the path that leads up to it. **1966** Kenney *Caste* 73: The damn dirt's so soft my creepers's sinkin' in deeper and deeper.

   b. sneakers.

   1904 *Life in Sing Sing* 246: *Creepers*—Soft shoes worn by burglars, sneak thieves, and prison guards. **1930** Irwin *Tramp & Und. Sl.: Creepers.*—Felt or rubber-soled shoes worn by prison guards and sneak thieves.

   3. *Und.* a sneak thief; (*specif.*) a person, esp. a prostitute, who robs sleeping or drunken individuals.

   1906 *Nat. Police Gaz.* (June 9) 6: She acted as "creeper," explaining that the "creeper" did not really creep, but walked to the victim's clothes. **1924** Henderson *Keys to Crookdom* 406: Girl...tommy, bundle, chippy, creeper. **1926** Finerty *Criminalese* 13: *Creeper*—A woman thief who steals from drunken men. **1929** Hostetter & Beesley *Racket* 222: *Creeper*—A sneak thief who robs garments. **1935** *AS* (Feb.) 14 [ref. to a1910]: *Creeper.* A prostitute who robs inebriated patrons. *ca***1940** in Botkin *Treas. Amer. Folk.* 536: Some creeper may come sneaking up and cabbage onto castings or nails [etc.]. **1962** Mencken & McDavid *Amer. Language* (rev. ed.) 728: *Creepers* or *panel workers* are girls who specialize in robbing customers. **1968** Heard *Howard St.* 36: Bill had been a creeper at one time, who made his living by breaking into homes and apartments. **1970** Winick & Kinsie *Lively Commerce* 27: Some prostitutes have associates ("creepers") who do not need the second door of the panel house to tiptoe into the prostitute's room. The "creeper" quietly goes through the client's trousers and takes his money without the client knowing that anyone else is present. **1972** Wambaugh *Blue Knight* 24: He was a daytime hotel creeper and hitting maybe four to six hotel rooms in the best downtown hotels every time he went to work…This guy would shim doors…and…burgle the place whether the occupants were in or not. **1976** Chinn *Dig Nigger Up* 52: He was an expert…creeper (sneak thief).

4. *Black E.* a man who commits adultery with another man's wife.

1911 *JAF* (Oct.) 354: The "creeper" watches his chance to get admittance into a home, unknown to the husband. **1925** Odum & Johnson *Negro & His Songs* 190: I keep rappin' on my woman's do',/Lak I never had been dere befo';/She got a midnight creeper dere,/An' I couldn't git in. **1925** Van Vechten *Nigger Heaven* 286: *Creeper.* a man who invades another's marital rights. **1929** Connelly *Green Pastures* 204: Dey tell me las' night you was talkin' to a creeper man, baby. **1940** Lomax & Lomax *Singing Country* 305: Guitar players, however, have the reputation of being midnight creepers. **1942** *Pittsburgh Courier* (July 18) 7: This…creeper…tried to do a fast Clark Gable. **1977** Dillard *Lexicon* 36: The man doing the cuckolding may be [called] a *creeper.*

5.a. *Gamb.* (see quot.).

1927 Nicholson *Barker* 103: *Creeper*—A dishonest roulette wheel.

b. *Und.* CREEP JOINT, 2.

1933 Ersine *Pris. Slang* 30: *Creeper, Creep Joint.* A gambling joint which, to avoid police raids, changes its location often.

6. (among sidewalk pitchmen) a small collapsible table on which wares are exhibited.

1930 *Variety* (Jan. 8) 123: What's a mug gonna do? He can't set up his spindle or creeper on a street corner in winter.

7. the lowest gear in a motor vehicle.

1937 *Review of Reviews* (June) 43: *Creeper*—low gear. **1939** *Chi. Tribune* (Jan. 22) (Graphic Sec.) 9: *In creeper*—In low gear. **1978** Dills *CB* (ed. 4) 29: *Creeper gear:* lowest gear, or combination of gears, to get extra power.

8. *Black E.* a policeman or detective.

1945 Drake & Cayton *Black Metropolis* 568: "Shet up, you bitch," Mr. Ben bawled. "I wisht they'da let them creepers take you to the station!"

creepers *interj.* [euphem. for *Christ;* cf. CRIPES] (used to express astonishment).

1944 in Gould *Snowflake* (unp.): Creepers! At least he's got dough. **1948** J.H. Burns *Lucifer* 98: Made us memorize a whole sonnet. Creepers!

creep game *n. Und.* BADGER GAME, 1.

1967 Gonzales *Paid My Dues* 90: "The Creep game" where one girl actually does the physical work while another would rob the victim's pockets.

creep house *n. Und.* CREEP JOINT, 1.

1913 Kneeland *Prostitution in NYC* 77: A "creep house" is a place where women take men to rob them. **1943** in P. Smith *Letter from Father* 367: It was a creep house where men took rooms and…the night manager sent them girls to assuage their sexual appetites. **1970** Winick & Kinsie *Lively Commerce* 28: A "creep house" is a place to which men are taken by prostitutes to be robbed. A client approaching orgasm is usually so preoccupied that he is relatively uninterested in what is going on around him.

creepie-peepie *n.* [sugg. by WALKIE-TALKIE] a hand-held television or video camera. Also **creepie.**

1952 *Time* (Oct. 6) 30: There would be no prying TV eyes, no creepie-peepies to eavesdrop on unrehearsed moments. **1956** *Sat. Eve. Post* (June 16) 105: The "creepie-peepie," a lightweight TV camera and transmitter. **1972** *Harper's* (May) 70: Television newsmen armed with hand-held "creepy-peepy" cameras. **1978** J. Garagiola, on *World Series* (NBC-TV) (Oct. 10): Take a look at this high shot [of Dodger Stadium] from our creepy. **1988** *TV Guide* (Aug. 13) 5: In 1960, "creepie-peepie" hand-held cameras [were used in covering the national political conventions]. **1991** *Donahue* (NBC-TV): How are you supposed to know there's a guy out there with a creepie-peepie?

creepies *n.pl.* CREEP, 1.—constr. with *the.*

1972 Wambaugh *Blue Knight* 302: This place…gives me the creepies.

creeping Jesus *n.* **1.** a sneaking, cringing, or (esp. in later use) sanctimonious person. Also as interj. of amazement.

ca*1818** W. Blake, in *OEDS:* If he had been Antichrist, creeping Jesus, He'd have done any thing to please us. *****1827,** *****1871** in *OEDS.* **1920** E. O'Neill *Diff'rent* 209: Oh golly, there you go agen makin' a durned creepin'-Jesus out of him! What d'you want to marry, anyhow—a man or a sky-pilot? **1922** in H. Miller *Letters to Emil* 4: Maybe, Creeping Jesus, I'm another Lindsay or Masters or Bodenheim, eh? *****1959** Behan *Borstal Boy* 80: You dull scruffy old creeping Jesus. **1970** E. Thompson *Garden of Sand* 379: Dink had *checked* on him—*checked on him!* That creeping Jesus sonofabitch. **1970** Cortina *Slain Warrior* 133: You're another one of them creepin' Jesuses. **1981–85** S. King *It* 614: Malloy…was called "Creeping Jesus"…because he was nearsighted but wouldn't put on his specs. **1987** in *N.O. Review* (Spring, 1988) 23: My mother always called her "Creeping Jesus" because she was so quiet. **1992** N. Cohn *Heart of World* 79: What I couldn't stand was the mealymouths,…the creeping Jesuses, the *smooth* men.

2. a maddeningly slow or lazy person.

1976 Price *Bloodbrothers* 149: It's like creepin' Jesus in here [a store] today, man. **1983** S. King *Christine* 152: You're riding with the original Old Creeping Jesus anyway.

creep joint *n.* **1.** *Und.* BADGER JOINT, 1.

1921 Woolston *Prostitution in U.S.* I 111 [ref. to 1917]: Negro "panel houses" and "creep joints," where systematic robbery was carried on, were reported but not investigated. **1928** Sharpe *Chicago May* 46: New York was full of creep joints at that time. **1938** in A. Lomax *Mr. Jelly Roll* 50 [ref. to 1890's]: Creep joints where they'd put the feelers on a guy's clothes. **1946** Mezzrow & Wolfe *Really Blues* 13: Creep joints and speakeasies and dancehalls. **1955** Tarry *Third Door* 235: We walked in the direction of a "creep joint" I had overheard the boys talking about. They said it was across the street from the "pro" (prophylactic) station. **1965** Conot *Rivers of Blood* 338: The former operator of a creep joint, she is recalled by police officers on the vice squad not without a certain fondness as "good old Black Annie."

2. *Und.* (see quots.).

1930 *Amer. Merc.* (Dec.) 455: *Creep joint, n.:* A gambling house that moves to a different apartment each night. "Nothing's going but creep-and steer-joints." **1931** *Saturday Rev.* (July 18) 978: *Creep-Joint*—Gambling joint that moves nightly. **1933** (quot. at CREEPER, 5.b.). **1933** Guest *Limey* 163: A "creep joint" is a gambling saloon which moves on from place to place.

3. an establishment run or patronized by CREEPS; a despicable or CREEPY place.

1929 McEvoy *Hollywood Girl* 18: The Fuzzy-Wuzzy…a creep joint in Harlem. **1930** M. West *Babe Gordon* 29: They parked around the…creep joints. **1948** I. Shulman *Cry Tough!* 154: Whaddaya going to that kind of a creep joint for? When they lay out stiffs in coffins they dress them in clothes from there. **1963** Rubin *Sweet Daddy* 141: Tomorrow night and out of this creep joint. **1965** Horan *Seat of Power* 12: "The Automat across from the Library." "Christ! You can find more creep joints!" **1966** Susann *Valley of Dolls* 368: Protect the patient! You mean protect this creep joint! **1984** W. Gibson *Neuromancer* 4: What kinda creepjoint you running here? Man can't have a drink.

creepo *n.* [CREEP + *-o*] CREEP, 4. Also adj.

1954–60 *DAS* 623. **1970** E. Thompson *Garden of Sand* 446: It's an *honest* livin, creep-o! **1978** Maggin *Superman* 230: This is private property, Creepo. **1980** *Nat. Lampoon* (Aug.) 10: Wendy Slauson thinks you're a creepo. **1984** D. Smith *Steely Blue* 157: "Hey, creepo," he called. He called everybody creepo. **1988** T. Harris *Silence of Lambs* 29: Creepo son of a bitch.

creepola *n.* [CREEP + *-OLA*] CREEP, 4.

1983 *Nat. Lampoon* (Apr.) 5: Total scumbags and creepolas.

creep out *v.* to give the CREEPS to.

1983 Univ. Tenn. student: Just thinking about nuclear war creeps me out. **1993** *Simpsons* (Fox-TV): You're creepin' me out!

creep pad *n. Und.* CREEP HOUSE.

1946 Mezzrow & Wolfe *Really Blues* 81: A creep pad turns into a confession booth as soon as I squat in it. *Ibid.* 304: *Creep pad:* a whorehouse where the girls are pickpockets.

creeps see s.v. CREEP, *n.,* 1.

creepy *adj.* Esp. *Juve.* obnoxious.

1919 S. Lewis *Free Air* 135: The creepy jack ass, I don't believe he's ever been on a horse in his life! He thinks riding-breeches are the…last word in smartness. Overdressing is just ten degrees worse than underdressing. **1940** Wexley *City for Conquest* (film): That's what I been gettin' ever since that creepy cake-eater horned in. **1949** Loos & Sales *Mother Is a Freshman* (film): He's pretty creepy, but I was desperate. **1962** *Leave It to Beaver* (ABC-TV): I didn't know it was over some creepy sweater. **1988** P. Peck & P. Massman *Rich Men, Single Women* 123: The "creepy stockbroker" and the "fat-but-funny" surgeon.

creepy-crawly *n.* usu. *pl.* **1.** a crawling insect, spider, centipede, or similar creature.

*1858, *1891, *1960 in *OEDS.* **1986** Merkin *Zombie Jamboree* 314: Nah, don't take a flashlight, Julie. You'll just attract the creepie-crawlies. **1989** Pini *Portrait of Love* (unp.): Keep dust and creepy-crawlies off.

2. CREEPS.

1971 *Batman* (Aug.) 4: This place gives me the creepy-crawlies!

creepy Pete *n.* SNEAKY PETE.

1950 *New Directions* 315: Or describing the sweet inward/upward of "creepy Pete"*…*wine.

crepe-hanger var. CRAPE-HANGER.

crew *n.* **1.** a gang of criminals, now esp. a small juvenile street gang. [In S.E.—as in **1641* quot.—a disreputable group of persons.]

[**1641* R. Brome, in R.G. Lawrence *Comedies* 225: Where's all the rest of the crew?] **1946** R. White & E. Taylor *D. Tracy* (film): How many men in the stickup crew? **1957** *New Yorker* (Sept. 21) 128: We told the guy he didn't kick the habit, he was out of the crew. *Ibid.* 137: You're swinging with another crew. **1976** T. Walker *Ft. Apache* 68: The crew we followed that night had come to watch and cheer a rerun of the movie version [of *West Side Story*]. **1976** N.Y.C. man, age 37: Up in the South Bronx, the kids call their gangs *crews* now. **1981** in *West. Folklore* XLIV (1985) 9: The boys refer to a gang as a "crew." **1983** Sturz *Wid. Circles* 4: Alton boasted…that he was the author of the crime and asked if they had heard him and "his crew." **1984** Toop *Rap Attack* 14 [ref. to 1970's]: In the transition from outright war the hierarchical gang structure mutated into comparatively peaceful groups called crews. **1988** H. Gould *Double Bang* 13: Their crew [was] the Jokers. **1988** *N.Y. Newsday* (June 20) 34: A Westchester-based crew of the Genovese [crime] family. **1990** Costello & Wallace *Sig. Rappers* 80: Any crew naturally wants its own distinctive game and face. **1991** Jankowski *Islands in Street* 29: "Crews"…are small groups (usually fewer than ten and generally around three to five individuals) organized solely for the purpose of committing crime.

2. (see quots.).

1990 Thorne *Dict. Contemp. Slang* 114: *Crew*…American. a group of young people…usually refers to hip-hop artists, break dancers or scratch musicians. **1991** *New York* (Aug. 5) 24: Children call their circle of friends "crews" or "posses," just like the dealers do.

crib *n.* **1.a.** *Orig. Und.* a room, house, or apartment; (one's) place of residence. [Now mostly Black E; in earlier S.E., 'a hut or hovel'; see *OED.*]

*1809 (cited in Partridge *Dict. Und.* 160). **1811* *Lexicon Balatron.*: *Crib.* A house. *To crack a crib:* to break open a house. **1812* Vaux *Vocab.* 234: *Crib:* a house, sometimes applied to shops, as, a *thimble-crib*, a watchmaker's shop; a *stocking-crib*, a hosier's, &c. **1838* Glascock *Land Sharks* I 202: Bobson…knocked gently at Leary Davis's "crib." **1846** J. Greene *Secret Band* 113 [ref. to 1798]: The word *Coney* means Counterfeit paper money…The word *Crack* means Break. As crack a crib. The word *Crib* means House, trunk, desk, &c. **1848** *Ladies' Repository* VIII (Oct.) 315: *Crib*, A house in general. **1859** Matsell *Vocab.* 22: *Crib*, A house. **1866** *Nat. Police Gaz.* (Nov. 17) 3: Toward his "moll's" "crib" in Rector street. *Ibid.* (Nov. 24) 3: Nelly gets the "kid" that opens the store in "hock," while Alick "weeds" the "crib." **1867** Williams *Brierly* 13: This won't do!…The crib's alive! **1869** Graham *Words* 175: The Universities also have their slang terms. The graduates use "crib" for a house; "deadman" for empty wine-bottles; "governor" or "relieving-officer" for a father; "plucked," for defeated or rejected in an examination. **1871** Banka *Prison Life* 492: House,…*Crib.* **1873** Murdoch *Crockett* 132: EL. Is this your hunting lodge? DAVY. Yes, this is my crib. This is where I come and bunk when I'm out on a long stretch arter game. **1876** Cody & Arlington *Life on Border* 13: Set fire to the infernal crib if you can't get them out any other way. *Ibid.* 14: This crib was made to stand a siege. **1891** King *By Land & Sea* 131: Here's the crib!…Pap, I've fetched a boarder! **1895** F. P. Dunne, in Schaaf *Dooley* 97: She cud see

th' blue wather iv th' la-ake an' th' crib that Tom Gahan built. **1899** A.H. Lewis *Sandburrs* 80: Wit' that she steers herself in to take a squint an' size up d' crib. **1918** Stringer *House of Intrigue* 123: And if Bud had ever seen that room, he would undoubtedly have said, "Some crib, believe me!" **1921** Marquis *Carter* 116: You likely don't realize how many of those big swell millionaires' cribs uptown are in the hands of caretakers…the best part of the year. **1928** Bodenheim *Georgie May* 64: You might take a crib in this shack heah. **1944** Burley *Hndbk. Harlem Jive* 25: 'Twas the dim before Nicktide, and all through the crib,/You could hear Joe Hipp spieling that righteous ad lib. **1953** "L. Short" *Silver Rock* 306: You know, this is what I need for my crib—a touch of the female. **1957** H. Simmons *Corner Boy* 35: You got a swell crib. **1958** Hughes & Bontemps *Negro Folklore* 482: *Crib:* House, home, wear you can not only hang your hat, but raise hell. **1963** Williamson *Hustler!* 33: Do you want to come up to my crib for a drink? **1965** C. Brown *Manchild* 109: They'd go down there and loot the cat's crib. **1970** Quammen *Walk the Line* 131: The old man threw me out, see…I need a crib. **1978** R. Price *Ladies' Man* 105: I gotta crib on the upper West Side. Nice. **1982** Rucker *57th Kafka* 54: "Where's your crib?" she was asking. **1994** N. McCall *Wanna Holler* 94: Me and my partner kick in cribs and make a killin'.

b. a narrow compartment set aside for some activity; stall.

*1838 Glascock *Land Sharks* II 133: Ready-made mechanics were…knocking down the bulkheads belonging to the officers' "cribs" in the ward-room. **1847–78* in *OED.* **1886* in *OED.* **1944** Ind *Bataan* 161: From Colonel Willoughby's "crib" in the G-2 Section, I go to G-3.

c. a lockup or cell.

1907 Bush *Enlisted Man* 207: One of them "got heavy" with one of the sergeants and was put in the "crib" for the night. **1938, 1969** in *DARE.* **1992** *Newsweek* (Feb. 24) 8: Cell…"crib."

d. *R.R.* a caboose.

1931 (cited in Partridge *DSUE* (ed. 8) 269). **1945** Hubbard *R.R. Ave.* 338: *Crib*—Caboose.

2.a. *Und.* a drinking saloon, dancehall, or gambling den; (*later*) a nightclub; (*broadly*) JOINT.

*1823 "J. Bee" *Dict. Turf*: *Crib* implies a single place, as a tap-room, a drinking-booth, coffee-shop, &c. **1848** Baker *Glance at N.Y.* 15: I'm a-goin' to have a fight in this crib—I am! *Ibid.* 23: Let's have a drink; there's a crib open. **1848** Thompson *House Breaker* 4: John Carr…had requested to be conveyed to Boy Jack's *crib*, (the name of a thieves' den). *ca*1849 in Jackson *Early Songs of Uncle Sam* 252: Here's a crib out of sight,/Let's go get a drop on the sly. **1853** G. Thompson *Gay Girls* 29: Nearly all of the "cribs" were still open. **1865** *Rogues & Rogueries of N.Y.* 61: So let us leave the murky atmosphere of the "crib," and once more breathe the pure air of Heaven. **1866** *Night Side of N.Y.* 32: Are there many robberies committed in these cribs? **1867** *Nat. Police Gaz.* (Apr. 6) 2: Apropos of "gonnoffs" lush drums,…none of this city can compare to Pete Tracey's "crib" in the Bowery. **1872** Crapsey *Nether Side of NY* 60: One of them went to the house with a story of a conversation he had overheard in a "crib," during which "Stutter Jack," "Glimmer George," and sundry others…had arranged the preliminaries for "cracking" the house. **1876** Dixon *White Conquest* II 260: Hereabouts lie the tan cellars and thieves' gaming cribs. **1893** Hill *20 Yrs at Sea* 265: Why, captain, this looks more like a young ladies' boarding-school than a bush-whackers crib. **1899** "J. Flynt" *Tramping* 393: *Crib:* a saloon or gambling-place; more or less synonymous with "joint" and "hang-out." **1900** (quot. at MEXIE). **1912** Quinn *Gambling* 283: From that time on little that comes from the gaming crib sticks to the Captain's fingers. **1919** *DN* V 41: *Crib*, n. Dive. **1939** in J. O'Hara *Sel. Letters* 144: Crib is a derogatory term for a night club, like flea-bag for hotel. **1939–40** O'Hara *Pal Joey* 45: I am singing for coffee & cakes at a crib on Cottage Grove Ave. here. *Ibid.* 51: I am getting by in this crib in Chi. **1959** in Cannon *Nobody Asked* 146: The tune's gone, as that old crib on 12th Street must be, as the old piano player certainly is. **1974** in D.C. Dance *Shuckin' & Jivin'* 228: He come to a crib they call the Bucket o' Blood.

b. a shack, room, or apartment occupied by a prostitute; (*hence*) a brothel.

1846 in M.W. Hill *Sisters' Keepers* 57: A Black "Crib" Broken Up. **1881** [Trumble] *Man Traps of N.Y.* 17: One or two cribs, as these places are called, though they also enjoy the euphonious appellation of "badger houses"—are quite notorious. **1882* in *OEDS: Drum*, or *crib*, house of ill repute. **1908** in McArdle *Collier's* 147: Down one street from this saloon runs a row of gaudy houses of prostitution; down the other two blocks of those little apartments known in the South and West as "cribs." **1912** D. Runyon *Rhymes* 90: George has a line o' cribs an' twenty gals or more. **1925–26** Black *You Can't Win* 198: He detailed a couple of them to take the main "drag," another to make the railroad men's boarding houses, another to the saloons. "I'll make the cribs myself." **1929** T. Gordon *Born to Be* 20: Her house was the Palace on the line. In all the other cribs, the girls worked in gingham gowns, kimonas, Spanish shawls [etc.]. **1929–30** Dos Passos *42d Parallel* 281: Barrow wanted to go into one of the cribs, so they…talked to one of the girls. **1932** Halyburton & Goll *Shoot & Be Damned* 4 [ref. to 1916]: Remember those pay-day nights in Casas Grandes, Mexico—those nights around the cribs an' twenty gals or more. **1933** Ersine *Prison Slang* 30: *Crib*…A one-room brothel. **1934** Cunningham *Triggernometry* 41: The saloon and the crib were his hangouts. **1934** L. Hughes *Way of White Folk* 122: She's probably on the crib-line now. **1939** E. O'Brien *One-Way Ticket* 4: You make more money in the cribs with the sailors. **1942** Wilder *Flamingo Road* 229: I was afraid he'd wind up in some crib along the line. **1960** Jordan & Marberry *Fool's Gold* 217 [ref. to 1899]: This crib was just large enough to hold a bed and a washstand. The girls always loitered outside their door while promoting business. **1970** S. Ross *Fortune Machine* 25: Madam…of the biggest crib in the world. **1990** Vachss *Blossom* 204: Mama started with a little crib on Water Street.

3. *Und.* a trunk, desk, or similar object to be broken into; *(now solely)* a safe or vault.

1846 J. Greene *Secret Band* 113 [ref. to 1798]: The word *Crib* means House, trunk, desk &c. **1876** Pinkerton *Model Town* 35: I'll bet he's a high-toned "crib-cracker," for he's too well educated to be after small game. I shouldn't wonder if the explosion he spoke about took place in a safe door. *a***1906** Burke *Prison Gates* 10: The last crib I cracked was the Schrage $53,000 bond case. **1916** Marcin *Cheaters* 14: Good manners don't crack no cribs. **1918** in *AS* (Oct. 1933) 26: *Crib*. Safe or vault. **1929** *AS* IV (June) 338: *Crib*. A safe. **1933** *Forum* (Dec.) 369: *Crib*—safe. **1970** Rudensky & Riley *Gonif* 20: I was…even better at blowing cribs.

4. a bed.

*****1827** in *F & H* II: You may have a crib to stow in. **1874** Pember *Metropolis* 256: My "crib," as Mrs. Casey called it, was in the middle room. **1944** Burley *Hndbk. Jive* 136: *Crib*…bed. **1960** MacCuish *Do Not Go Gentle* 83: Thanks for the crib for the night. *ca***1965** in IUFA *Folk Speech*: *Crib*—bed. **1967** Lit *Dictionary* 10: *Crib*—Bed. **1983** Flaherty *Tin Wife* 299: But dying in the crib, during the actual act, was another matter. **1986** G. Brach *Pirates* (film): Out of your crib!

5.a. *Stu.* a translation, list of correct answers, or other illicit aid used by a student. Also attrib.

*****1841** in *F & H* II: He has with a prudent forethought stuffed his *cribs* inside his double-breasted waistcoat. *****1853**, *****1855**, *****1856** in *Ibid.* **1856** J. Hall *College Wds.* 144: *Crib*. Probably a translation; a pony. **1900** *DN* II 30: *Crib*, n. A paper, book, or other means to be used unlawfully in a recitation or examination, or in the preparation for the same. **1924** Marks *Plastic Age* 106: Those who did cheat spent…time evolving ingenious methods of preparing cribs. **1953** Manchester *City of Anger* 75: Before an examination she would carefully ink crib notes on the inside of her thigh. **1986** Univ. Tenn. instructor, age 35: A *crib* is a *cheat sheet*, but I don't think I've heard the word used since I was in the sixth grade. **1987** R.M. Brown *Starting* 68: To hell with Thucydides. I reached for the crib.

b. *Stu.* an instance of plagiarism. Now *colloq.* or *S.E.*

1868 Williams *Black-Eyed Beauty* 23: You will notice it is a bit of a "crib" from the sensation novels.

c. *Stu.* a student who cheats on an examination.

1915 *DN* IV 233: *Crib*…One who cheats. "He's a dirty crib."

crib² *n.* the game of cribbage.

1944 E.H. Hunt *Limit* 15: Play crib last night?

crib *v.* **1.** to pilfer; steal; *(hence, now esp.)* plagiarize.

*****1748** in *F & H* II: *Crib*…to withhold, keep back, pinch, or thieve a part out of money given to lay out for necessaries. *****1772** in *F & H* II: There are a brace of birds and a hare, that I cribbed this morning out of a basket of game. *****1785** Grose *Vulgar Tongue: To Crib*. To purloin, or appropriate to one's own use, part of anything intrusted to one's care. **1839–40** Cobb *Green Hand* I 112: To such an extent had the Loafer carried this cribbing process, that the crew had already given him the distinctive cognomen of the turkey-buzzard of the brig. *****1841** in *F & H* II: Cribbing his answers from a tiny manual of knowledge…which he hides under his blotting paper. **1845** in Oehlschlaeger *Reveille* 174: You hay-hookin', corn-cribbin', fodder-fudgin', [etc.]. **1881** [Trumble] *Man Traps* 30: Cribbed it you know, 'fraid I'll be bagged if I hock it. **1882** in Botkin *Folk-Say* 93: I had a chance…to crib the overcoat of the infernal Chinaman who had given me away. **1900** *DN* II 30: *Crib*. To steal. **1979** W. Cross *Kids & Booze* 16: But how do you get…whiskey if…you

can't crib an I.D. card?

2.a. *Stu.* to prepare (a lesson) by means of a CRIB, 5.a.

1897 Norris *Vandover* 300: He found Geary alone in their room, cribbing "Horace" again. **1900** *DN* II 30: *Crib*, v.t. 1. To interline.

b. *Stu.* to cheat (on an examination or the like) by plagiarism or the use of a CRIB, 5.a. Now *colloq.*

*****1891** *F & H* II: *Crib*…To use a translation; to cheat at an examination; to plagiarise. **1895** J.L. Williams *Princeton* 175: I feel more like a fellow cribbing in exams. **1900** *DN* II 30: *Crib*…To cheat in a recitation or examination. **1930** *AS* V (Feb.) 238: *Crib* (noun and verb): a paper or set of notes used in cheating in an examination; also, the act of cheating. "He brought a crib to class in order to crib in the quizz." **1931** Stevenson *St. Luke's* 59: Lots of fellas cribbed. **1948** J.H. Burns *Lucifer* 153: I've caught you two cribbing. Red-handed! **1951** in *DAS* 130.

3. Esp. *Black E.* to reside; to dwell.—now also constr. with *out.*

1967 Beck *Pimp* 12: The hotel where Kim…was cribbing. **1968** in *Trans-action* VI (Feb. 1969) 27: Gene was cribbin (living) over here. **1970** Quammen *Walk the Line* 142: Where you cribbing now? **1974** S. Stevens *Rat Pack* 50: Where I'm cribbin' in that ratty basement there's so many rats they asked the people upstairs to move out so's they could move in. **1992** Mowry *Way Past Cool* 226: I know where Deek be cribbin out.

cribbage-faced *adj.* having a pockmarked face.

*****1785** Grose *Vulgar T.: Cribbage-Faced*. Marked with the small pox, the pits bearing a kind of resemblance to the holes in a cribbage-board. **1821** Waln *Hermit in Phila.* 28: Bacon-faced—Bran-Faced…Cribbage-faced. **1929** Bowen *Sea Slang* 31: Cribbage faced. Marked with smallpox.

cribber *n.* **1.** a horse that is a crib-biter.

*****1889** Barrère & Leland *Dict. Slang* I 280. **1942** *ATS* 687. **1968** Ainslie *Racing Guide* 466: Cribber—Horse that bites parts of its stall, sucking air into lungs; "wind-sucker;" "crib-biter." **1969** Hirsch *Treasury* 182: A horse who clings to an object, such as a stall door, with his teeth, and who sucks air into his lungs, is known as a cribber.

2. *Und.* a safecracker.

1925, **1938** in Partridge *Dict. Und.* 161.

cribbey *n.* (see quots.).

*****1785** Grose *Vulgar T.: Cribbeys*…Blind alleys, courts, or bye-ways; perhaps from the houses built there being cribbed out of the common way or passage. **1848** Judson *Myst. of N.Y.* 113: *Cribbeys*, blind alleys, dark narrow ways.

crib course *n.* *Stu.* a very easy academic course.

1970 N.Y.U. student: I'm looking for crib courses this semester. **1972** G. Shaw *Meat on Hoof* 78: Access to these crib courses was aided by the fact that we had the advantage of registering before the other students. **1987** Univ. Tenn. student theme: The easy courses are called *crib courses* because even a baby could pass them.

crib-cracker *n.* *Und.* a housebreaker or safecracker.

1867 *Nat. Police Gaz.* (Jan. 5) 3: A burglar or "crib-cracker," went into Tommy's house with a big "swag." *****1879** in *OEDS*. **1888** in *Amer. Heritage* (Oct. 1979) 21: I have known great "koniackers," and greater still "Crib Crackers."

cribhouse *n.* a whorehouse, esp. if small or dirty.

1916 Miner *Slavery* 154: A large "crib house" containing separate rooms for 300 prostitutes. **1923** in Kornbluh *Rebel Voices* 92: They had the string of crib houses where the girls were brought in about pay day. **1926** Spaeth *Read 'Em & Weep* 33: Frankie lived down in a crib-house,/ Crib-house with only two doors. **1928** Bodenheim *Georgie May* 66: Georgie and Clara visited other women in the cribhouse. **1931** Dos Passos *1919* 47: The doors of all the cribhouses were open. **1937** C.B. Davis *Anointed* 174: Then the ocean began to paint herself up like an old crib-house woman getting ready for a hard day at the window. **1946** Gresham *Midnight Alley* 12: She looked like something from a crib house—and jail bait at that. **1958** J. Ward *Buchanan* 26: The so-called High Sheriff…preached the wrath of God and helped stock a crib-house, all in one day.

crib job *n.* *Und.* an easy theft.

1980 WINS Radio News (Sept. 11): Police say that muggings of senior citizens are known among criminals as "crib jobs" because the elderly can do little to resist an attack.

crib joint *n.* CRIBHOUSE.

1927 *Immortalia* 50: Frankie worked in a crib-joint. **1942** Davis & Wolsey *Call House Madam* 79: This place is…gonna make the other parlor houses look like crib joints, Jimmie.

crib sheet *n.* a sheet of paper on which examination answers are written, used by a student to cheat on a test; (*hence*) a page of notes for use in an emergency.

1960 N.Y.C. high-school student: He got caught with a crib sheet. **1981** G. Wolf *Roger Rabbit* 19: A crib sheet...taped to his nose. **1984** *TriQuarterly* (Spring) 308: I made a crib sheet for my history test. **1992** Hosansky & Sparling *Working Vice* 222: Bright kept a crib sheet....A folded piece of paper, a running log of the information.

cricket *n.* an unwanted squeak in machinery.

1937–41 in Mencken *Amer. Lang. Supp. II* 724.

cricket *adj.* fair; according to the custom or rules.—used predicatively in negative contexts only. Now *colloq.* [Cf. earlier lit. sense 'cricket as it should be played', in *OED2*.]

*1900 in *OED2*. **1935** J. Conroy *World to Win* 270: That wouldn't be ethical, it wouldn't be Rotary, it wouldn't be cricket. **1942** Davis & Wolsey *Call House Madam* 122: I saw it was not cricket to go without them. **1955** L. Shapiro *6th of June* 67: This ain't cricket, don'cha know. **1984** McInerny *Bright Lights* 33: This is not cricket on his part.

crimey *n.* **1.** *Pris.* a partner in criminal activity.

1969 Smith & Gay *Don't Try It* 104: Sometimes a distinction is made between a hustling partner and a crime partner (*crimey*), where it is suggested that the latter is more dependable. **1971** Guggenheimer *Narc. & Drug Abuse* 12: Crimey, a partner in crime. **1992** *L.A. Times Mag.* (Oct. 18) 6: Joe's crimey...was a bead-wearing, apple-capped, paintbrush-totin', long-haired flower child in the '60s.

2. *Pub.* a crime novel.

1987 *Unicorn Ltd.* (catalog no. 62) 7: Hailed when published as the best "crimie" ever written with a Scottish setting.

criminy *interj.* (used to express surprise or the like).

*1694 in Partridge *DSUE* (ed. 8) 269: Oh! crimine! ***1700** in *F & H* II 213: Murder'd my brother! O crimini! **1848** Bartlett *Amer.: Crimany.* Interj. of sudden surprise.—*Forby's Vocabulary.* **1942** *ATS* 225: Criminy!

crimp *n.* ¶ In phrase: **put a crimp on** [or **in**] to injure, hamper, or spoil; (*occ.*) to defeat.

1896 Ade *Artie* 63: They'll put a crimp in him if things come their way. **1899** Kountz *Baxter's Letters* 56: Never mind, Jim, old pal, we have all had a crimp put into us at one time or another. **1899** A.H. Lewis *Sandburrs* 58: Mike puts a crimp too many in his Norah—that's his wife—an d' city 'tories plants her in Potters' Field. **1901** Hobart *Down the Line* 80: I figured that the picture...would put a crimp in Clarence. **1901** Ade *Modern Fables* 5: It put a Sickening Crimp in his Visible Assets. **1908** in Fleming *Unforget. Season* 274: Another crimp was put in [the Giants'] pennant aspirations. **1908** in H. C. Fisher *A. Mutt* 38: Damaging Evidence...Puts Crimp in Defense. **1920** in De Beck *Google* 63: An hour or two practise every day and I can put a crimp in 'em all around here. **1923** Ornitz *Haunch, Paunch & Jowl* 80: Do you want to put a crimp on us? **1927** C. McKay *Home to Harlem* 29: "Who was it put the krimp on me?" asked Zeddy. **1969** *New Yorker* (Dec. 27) 26: A giant black panther...puts a terrific crimp in my evening. **1974** A. Bergman *Big Kiss-Off* 10: The smell is going to put a real crimp in...business.

crimp up *v.* to put a crimp on s.v. CRIMP, *n.*

1929–33 Farrell *Manhood of Lonigan* 264: He felt that that rat, Arnold, would crimp up all the plans.

crimpy *adj.* (of weather) cold.

1905 *DN* III 76: How's this for crimpy weather? **1907** J. London, in *DAS* 130: I could expect "crimpy" weather. **1914** Jackson & Hellyer *Crim. Slang* 27: Crimpy...Cold, applied to the weather. **1930** Irwin *Tramp & Und. Sl.: Crimpy Weather.*—Inclement weather. **1983** in *DARE.*

crimson *n.* *Boxing.* blood from the nose.

1870 *Putnam's Mag.* (Mar.) 301: The combatants struck each other...upon...the nose...drawing the blood, the claret, the ruby, the crimson.

crimson rambler *n.* a bedbug. *Joc.*

1906 *DN* III 132: Crimson rambler...Bed-bug. **1918** Beston *Full Speed Ahead* 248: True, the "Toto," alias greyback, alias "Cootie," or his occasional but less famous accomplice, the "crimson rambler" does not infest a Navy ship. **1921** *DN* V 160: Crimson rambler, n. phr. Bed-bug. "At that hotel they have beds of crimson ramblers." Arkansas. **1933** Ersine *Prison Slang* 30: Crimson Rambler. A bedbug. **1967** in *DARE.*

crink *n.* *Narc.* CRANK, 6.a.

1968 Legman *Dirty Joke* 774: I never come down, man. I just shoot crink and fuck, shoot crink and fuck. Can you dig it? **1974** Hyde *Mind Drugs* 153: Crank...Crink...Cris...Cristina...methamphetamine in powdered form.

crinkum-crankum *n.* *Whaling.* a whale that is impossible to catch. Now *hist.* Cf. *OED.*

1849 Melville *Redburn* ch. xxi: "I tell ye, men, them's Crinkum-crankum whales." "And what are they?" "Why, them is whales that can't be cotched." ***1929** Bowen *Sea Slang* 31: Crinkum-Crankum...The old whaler's term for a whale which knows too much to be caught.

crinkums *n.pl.* syphilis.

*1618 in *OED:* Crincums. ***1698–1699** "B.E." *Dict. Cant. Crew: Crinkums*, the French Pox. ***1719** D'Urfey *Pills* I 147: The Old Queen has got the Crincums. ***1725** *New Canting Dict.: Crinkums*, the foul disease. ***1811** *Lexicon Balatron.: Crinkums.* The foul or venereal disease. **1935** Algren *Boots* 175: She give ya buboes an' crinkums an' the bloody-blue flux is why ya doin' it.

crip[1] *n.* **1.** a crippled person or animal.

1893 in Wister *Out West* 153: A man lame from being shot in the leg is "Crip" Jones. **1906** *Nat. Police Gaz.* (Sept. 22) 3: He was a...counterfeit crip. **1906** in A. Adams *Chisholm Trail* 179: The rear guard of crips and dogies passed this impromptu review. **1907** *McClure's Mag.* (Jan.) 327: Be you a crip with some new-fangled lung cure. **1908** in McCay *Little Nemo* 129: Look! He has cured Cripp! **1916** Thompson *Round Levee* 45: [Nicknames such as] Water-head, Chisel-head, Flop, Nubby, Fingers, Lips, Crip, Peg, Boots, Hump, Slim, Shorty, and a host of others describe some noticeable physical peculiarity. **1918** Livingston *Delcassee* 84: Going to play the "phoney crip" act for a spell, Dallas Bob? **1925** Mullin *Scholar Tramp* 242 [ref. to ca1912]: But hell! wot's the use o' makin' a crip out o' yerself when ye don't haffta? **1937** *AS* (Apr.) 103: A crippled horse is a *crip*. **1942** Algren *Morning* 148: Her old man was a crip. **1934–43** F. Collinson *Life in Saddle* 172 [ref. to 1870's]: The old stock and "crips" were always at the tail of the herd. **1972** *Nat. Lampoon* (Oct.) 64: We gave dem slant crips da *works.*

2.a. an easy task; CINCH.

1923 *DN* V 243: Crip...A cinch; a set up. **1970** in *DARE.* **1978** *UTSQ* (Easy job): This job'll be a *breeze* [or] *crip.* **1986** Univ. Tenn. student theme: A student who maxes out will brag that it was a crip test.

b. *Stu.* an easy course of study. Also attrib.

1926 in *DAS* 130: Crip has about driven snap into oblivion...it seems...probable that the word came into collegiate use via the poolroom. **1959** *AS* XXXIV 156: A crip is an easy course. **1970** N.Y.U. student: I only try to sign up for crip courses. **1974** Univ. Tenn. student: Education courses are always a crip. **1980** in *DARE.*

crip[2] *n.* an apartment; CRIB.

1976 "N. Ross" *Policeman* 55: This is the last straw. Yesterday you had me burglarizing that crip, and today this. *Ibid.* 60: I hit him with a warrant and found four spoons of dope in his crip.

crip *adj.* *Stu.* (of a course or examination) requiring little study; easy.

1977 Univ. Tenn. student: It should be crip. And the exams ought to be crip, too.

cripes *interj.* [euphem. alter. of *Christ*] (used to express amazement, disappointment, etc.). Also vars.

*1910 in *OEDS.* **1914** *DN* IV 69: By cripes. **1936** "E. Queen" *Halfway House* 24: Well, for cripe's sake why didn't he say *anything* about it? **1937** P. Beath, in Botkin *Treas. Amer. Folk.* 230: Want to know! Cripes, I do know! **1938** Bellem *Blue Murder* 188: Oh, cut it out, for cripe's sake. **1938** Korson *Mine Patch* 236: Cripes a'mighty, dat's no fair. **1958** P. O'Connor *At Le Mans* 40: And for cripe's sake stop calling me sir. **1963** Cameron *Black Camp* 7: For cripe's sake, doll, it's not like we're strangers. **1965–70** in *DARE.* **1974** Blount *3 Bricks Shy* 245: Good cripe! **1982** Huttmann *Code Blue* 119: Kripes...this is like being in a James Bond movie. **1993** *Daily Beacon* (Univ. Tenn.) (Dec. 2) 4: For cripe's sake, keep him away from Death Row!

cripple *n.* **1.** *Baseball.* an easily hit pitch; (*hence*) a pitch made when the count is three balls and fewer than two strikes and which consequently must be made into the strike zone to avoid walking the batter.

1914 *N.Y. Tribune* (Oct. 13) (cited in Nichols *Baseball Term.*). **1929** *N.Y. Times* (June 2) IX 2: Balls that are pitched with little or no curve and require no great effort to hit solidly are called "cripples." **1939–40** Tunis *Kid from Tomkinsville* 137: Kelley went for the cripple and knocked it over the fence. *Ibid.* 229: Three and one. The cripple. Should he hit? **1953** M. Harris *Southpaw* 156: He throwed him 3 balls...and then he throwed the cripple.

2. *Basketball.* an easy lay-up made from near the basket.

1974 Univ. Wisc. student: A *cripple* is an easy lay-up shot. **1982** Considine *Lang. Sport* 59.

crisis *v. Journ.* to sensationalize or otherwise play up (a news story).

1979 Homer *Jargon* 103: We gotta find some way to *crisis* this piece.

crispy *n.* **1.** *Mil.* CRISPY CRITTER, 1.

1970 in L. Williams *City of Angels* 92: Twenty crispies out of a dirigible were...more fun than a trench full of bodies. **1970** Calley & Sack *Lt. Calley* 122 [ref. to 1968]: A crispy would come and be given a casualty card so Quartermaster wouldn't say, "God. What is this body's name?" **1981** C. Nelson *Picked Bullets Up* 80 [ref. to Vietnam War]: Crispies (burn victims) go to Yokasuka, Japan.

2. *Army.* CRISPY CRITTER, 2.

1982 F. Hailey *Soldier Talk* 16: Crispies. New replacements. (As crisp as a newly-minted dollar bill.)

crispy critter *n.* **1.** Esp. *Mil.* a person who has burned to death or has suffered extensive third-degree burns.

1967 U.S. Army E-2: Crispy critters are burned up people. **1968** in Tuso *Vietnam Blues* 157: Forty crispy critters. **1970** *Current Slang* V 15: *Crispy Critter,* n. Napalm victims. **1973** Huggett *Body Count* 431: Hey, look, here's a Crispy Critter, a napalm-fried-gook. **1977** Sayles *Union Dues* 257: Weasel took it like a big joke and was giggling about crispy critters and like that. **1978** Hasford *Short-Timers* 123: I find...Rafter Man looking at some crispy critters. It's impossible to determine which army the men were from. **1978** J. Webb *Fields of Fire* 2: Get some, tank. Half a dozen crispy critters in there, now. **1982** Univ. Tenn. grad. student: If that fire alarm had been real you'd have wound up as a crispy critter. **1982** Huttmann *Code Blue* 212: "Listen, Crispy Critter...." Loren...used...graphic words to incite riot in Bill—the riot that fueled his determination to survive...all the skin grafting. **1983** Van Devanter & Morgan *Before Morning* 100: In the middle of the darkest humor, the doctors and nurses would call these patients crispy critters. **1990** Poyer *Gulf* 165: We all go crispy critter then. *a***1991** J.R. Wilson *Landing Zones* 175: They called the ones who got killed "crispy critters."

2. *Army.* a combat replacement.

1970 Calley & Sack *Lt. Calley* [ref. to 1968]: To be around death took a while getting used to. It was hard on the crispy critters: replacements, who we began getting in Charlie [Co.] now...The first of the crispy critters came in April. **1982** F. Hailey *Soldier Talk* 16: New replacements...Crispy critters.

critter *n.* [orig. dial. var. of *creature*] **1.** liquor, esp. whiskey. Also **creature.**

1737 *Penna. Gaz.* (Jan. 6) He's been too free with the Creature. **1830** Martin *Narr. of Revolutionary Soldier* 94 [ref. to 1777]: We left one man in the fort who had taken too large a dose of "the good creature." **1835** *Spirit of Times* (Dec. 12) 2: Glass after glass of the *crittur* went down their throats with the accompaniment of oaths and yells. **1840** in A.P. Hudson *Humor of Deep So.* 280: Small and delicate juleps...with but little of the *live critter* in them. **1841** *Spirit of Times* (Nov. 6) 421. **1847** Henry *Campaign Sketches* 282: A drop of the "critter" with which to drink a "Happy New Year." **1853** P.H. Skinner *Ragged Ten Thousand* 61: There is some of the "good critter" in you yet. **1858** in G.W. Harris *High Times* 79: He went to the still house in his neighborhood and had his jug filled with the critter. **1859** "Skitt" *Fisher's River* [ref. to 1820's]: Few men in that social region...would not take some of the "good critter." **1863** "E. Kirke" *So. Friends* 49: Th' clar juice, th' raal, genuwine critter...Come, take a drink. **1865** Springer *Sioux Country* 16: He gave me a good horn of the "critter," which went like living fire through my body. **1871** Still *Underground R.R.* 542: How about the "crittur?" do you take a little sometimes? **1883** G.H. Holliday *On Plains* 19: I've got a wee drop of the critter by me now, boys. **1885** Siringo *Texas Cowboy* 70: Jack...couldn't resist the temptation of taking a "wee drop of the critter" every fifteen or twenty minutes.

2. an animal, esp. a horse. Now *colloq.*

1815 in *OEDS.* **1874** Pinkerton *Expressman* 38: I'll jist take this yar lady hum, git my critter, and come in to Montgomery.

3. a person, esp. a man—usu. constr. with qualifying adj.

1826 in *JAF* LXXVI (1963) 285: Thee fust kritter I sea was old Haze. **1836** in Haliburton *Sam Slick* 45: [He] is an ugly-grained critter; he'll break his wife's heart. **1838** [Haliburton] *Clockmaker* (Ser. 2) 21: I...seed this critter alivin'...on the fat o' the land. **1843** "J. Slick" *High Life in N.Y.* 2: You wouldn't know the critter, he's altered so. **1848** in

T. Whitman *Dear Walt* 9: The ladies in N.O....are something like the "critters" in N.Y. except they were [*sic*] one or two more "flonces"...&c &c &c. **1862** "E. Kirke" *Among Pines* 227: The lawyer was a "stuck-up critter." **1868** "W. J. Hamilton" *Maid of Mtn.* 20: There's Chinamen there, the queerest critters! **1878** Hart *Sazerac* 87: The bar-creetur don't mind takin' my face for the drinks. **1969** in B. Edelman *Dear Amer.* 155: I's a lonely critter. **1978** Truscott *Dress Gray* 45: The crusty old critter was stomping around the halls like a caged opossum.

4. an object; item; thing.

1834, 1843 in *DARE.* **1874** McCoy *Cattle Trade* 311: What's this hur trick? I guess I'll try the critter. **1958** McCulloch *Wds. Words* 41: *Critter*...Any machine or piece of equipment.

¶ In phrase:

¶ **go the whole critter** to go whole hog.

1834 Caruthers *Kentuck.* I 188: If that ain't what I call goin the whole cretur.

critterback *adj.* mounted on horseback.

1866 Vale *Minty & the Cavalry* 331: The "critter back" boys of the Fourth Michigan and Seventh Pennsylvania. **1890** in *DARE.*

critter company *n. Army.* a unit of cavalry. Now *hist.*

1864 Connolly *Army of the Cumberland* 223: I suppose they imagine their "critter companies" are making havoc with our railroad line which supplies us with rations. **1865** in C.W. Wills *Army Life* 348: It was the Kentucky brigade of Wheeler's "Critter Co." **1893** Casler *Stonewall* 70 [ref. to Civil War]: General Jackson sent a foot company and a critter company to ramshag the Blue Ridge and capture them. **1931** Lytle *Bedford Forrest and His Critter Company* (title).

croak *n.* a person who complains unreasonably; CROAKER.

1918 Dodge *Yellow Dog* 58: "Spot the main croaks, fellers," he admonished them. "Get after 'em. Slip 'em the yellow card."

¶ In phrases:

¶ **do** [or **pull**] **a croak, 1.** to die; in phr. **do a gun croak** to shoot oneself.

1902 Mead *Word-Coinage* 167: "To croak" is to die; whereas "to do a croak" and "to do a gun croak" mean to be shot. **1903** McCardell *Chorus Girl* 38: You'd wonder I wouldn't get off in despair and do a gun croak. **1926** *Sat. Eve. Post* (Nov. 6) 12 [ref. to WWI]: He'll pull a croak if he don't get out quick.

2. *Und.* to carry out an assassination; murder someone.

1920 E. Hemingway, in *N.Y. Times Mag.* (Aug. 18, 1985) 23: Occasionally reports filtered back to the city about him. He was in New York. He'd done a croak there. He'd left New York. [Etc.].

¶ **on the croak** dying.

1899 A.H. Lewis *Sandburrs* 155: D' last will an' test'ment of a galoot he says in o' croak, an' can't wait for mornin'.

croak *v.* **1.a.** to die.—in later use also constr. with *off* or (still later) *out.*

***1812** Vaux *Vocab.* 234: *Croak*: to die. ***1823** "J. Bee" *Dict.* 59: To *Croak*—to die. **1853** [G. Thompson] *Garter* 76: Yes, she *croaked,* and was carted off in a pine coffin. **1859** Matsell *Vocab.* 22: *Croake.* To murder; to die. ***1870** Greey *Blue Jackets* 74: She says her missis av bin werry dicky and likely to croak. **1877** *Puck* #3 (Mar.) 14: A bi-weekly journal has been produced in Paris called *The Grenoville—The Frog.* One need not be a prophet to announce that, like a good many of its London contemporaries, this new paper will speedily croak. **1878** *Nat. Police Gaz.* (Apr. 24) 6: Another man "croaked" in the same place. **1888** in *AS* XXXVII (1962) 76: He's gone and croaked long ago. **1895** *Harper's* (Oct.) 776: Ev'ry day I hear o' some stiff croakin' or gettin' ditched. **1895** in J.I. White *Git Along Dogies* 66: We've got to croak some day. **1897** *Harper's Wkly.* (Jan. 23) 86: He'll croak for it, an' don' cher forget it. **1907** in H.C. Fisher *A. Mutt* 11: I fear he is going to croak. **1914** London *Jacket* 58: Go ahead and croak, but don't make so much noise about it. **1920** S. Lewis *Main Street* 229: Why she'd simply turn up her toes and croak if she found out how much she doesn't know about the high old times a wise guy could have in this burg on the Q.T. **1926** Nason *Chevrons* 269: You big bum! I thought you'd croaked! **1942** Garcia *Tough Trip* 48: He thought that Beaver Tom was going to croak. **1957** Myrer *Big War* 330: Don't waste the water, Danny...He'll croak off in five minutes. **1958** S.H. Adams *Tenderloin* 108: And see to it you don't catch cold and croak out like...Bamberg did. **1973** Browne *Body Shop* 151: I kept telling myself not to pass out 'cause I'd surely croak off. **1977** Univ. Tenn. prof.: Let's hope I don't croak out today. **1993** *New Yorker* (Oct. 6) 187: I don't care if he croaks.

b. *Stu.* to fail an academic course.

1900 *DN* II 30: *Croak, v.i.* 1. to flunk.

2. to kill.—in later use occ. constr. with *off*.

*1823 Egan *Vulgar T.*: *Croaked*, hanged. A flash term among keepers of prisons, who, speaking of a thief that was executed, observe, "He was *croaked*." **1848** *Ladies' Repository* VIII (Oct.) 315: *Croak*, To murder. **1859** Matsell *Vocab.* 22: *Croake*. To murder; to die. **1867** *Nat. Police Gaz.* (Jan. 12) 3: The ball…went cracking through Whalen's saloon,…nearly "croaking" old Tom. **1871** Banka *Prison Life* 128: That hospital will "croak" you in two weeks. **1880** in M. Lewis *Mining Frontier* 130: I am going to maintain a proper respect for the gospel if I have to croak every son-of-a-gun of a sinner in the mines. **1899** A.H. Lewis *Sandburrs* 47: Mother Worden always told me that if we was lagged, d' p'lice guys would croak me. **1913** *Sat. Eve. Post* (Jan. 4) 26: They just told me somebody had croaked her. **1921** Casey & Casey *Gay-Cat* 99: He tried to croak him off by drownin' him. **1928** Hammett *Red Harvest* 110: You didn't croak her, did you? **1938** Wolfe *Web & Rock* 530: Honest, kid, if I thought some other guy was goin' with you, I'd croak the both of you.

3. to speak; (*hence*) **to inform.**

1899 Cullen *Tales* 72: You know not whereof you croak. **1900** *DN* II 30: *Croak, v.i.*…To make a speech, especially of a pessimistic turn. *Ibid. Croak*…To play the informer, disclose secrets.

croaker *n.* **1.** Esp. *Mil.* **a grumbler.**

1847 Downey *Cruise of Portsmouth* 85: The "Old Croakers" found plenty of food to growl on. **1861** in Frank & Reaves *Seeing Elephant* 43: A liar…a croaker and coward. **1865** Cooke *Wearing of the Gray* 34: Gloom could not live in his presence, and the whole race of "croakers" were shamed into hopefulness by his inspiring words and demeanour. **1867** [S.B. Putnam] *Richmond During War* 330: We would not listen to them;…we called them "croakers." **1893** *Our Navy* (Dec. 27) 2: From the inception of the Club Scheme, the promoters have been badly handicapped by the great number of "croakers" who infest the United States Navy.

2. *Pris.* **a newspaper.**

1859 Matsell *Vocab.* 22: *Croakers.* Newspapers.

3. Esp. *Pris.* **a physician.** Cf. CROCUS.

*1879 in Partridge *Dict. Und.* 162: I have scores of men…who used to chuckle to their pals over their success in hoodwinking the "croker." **1885* (cited in Partridge *Dict. Und.*). **1889* Barrère & Leland *Dict. Slang* I: *Croaker*…(Prison), the doctor. **1897** *Pop. Sci. Mo.* (Apr.) 833: *Croaker*…means doctor. **1903** in "O. Henry" *Works* 571: I thought I'd strike the croaker for a handful of the little sugar pills. **1904** *Life in Sing Sing* 246: *Croaker*—A doctor. **1908** in H.C. Fisher *A. Mutt* 122: It's a wonder the croakers don't have their offices on the ground floor. **1912** Lowrie *Prison* 73: I saw the croaker…but he stuck a thermometer in my mouth and then called me a faker. **1930** D. Runyon, in *Collier's* (Jan. 20) 13: I get her…the best croakers in Montreal. **1933** Milburn *No More Trumpets* 34: After a while the croaker started sawing. **1937** Reitman *Box-Car Bertha* 99: For Christ's sake, send me a croaker. **1957** Fenton & Haines *Wings of Eagles* (film): These croakers around here'll tell you it can't be done, but I tell ya it can. **1968** "R. Hooker" *MASH* 111: As far as I'm concerned, you're just another Regular Army croaker, and you all give me the red ass. **1970** in E. Knight *Black Voices* 87: The next day in Memphis I cracked a croaker's crib for a fix. **1975** *Inter. Jour. Addictions* X 429: The Croaker saw him, shook his head and said,/"Here comes one walking in dead." **1982** *Nat. Lampoon* (Sept.) 6: Don Martin Infantima, chief croaker to the court of Ferdinand and Isabella.

croaksman *n. Und.* **a hired assassin.**

1848 *Ladies' Repository* VIII (Oct.) 315: *Croaksman*, One who will murder.

croc *n.* **a crocodile.** Now *colloq.*

*1884 in *OEDS*. **1907* (cited in Partridge *DSUE* (ed. 8) 270). **1921*, **1925* in *OEDS*. **1928** Panzram *Killer* 118: The crocs done the rest. *ca*1943 in L'Amour *Over Solomons* 27: Crocs in the streams and sharks in the bay. **1960** Leckie *Marines!* 20: The croc, Cap'n—get the croc!

crock *n.* **1.a. an old or worthless horse.**

*1876 in *OEDS*. **1879* in *OED*: I was riding a broken-kneed old crock. **1887* in *F & H* II: The wretched crocks that now go to the post will be relegated to more appropriate work. **1889* in *Ibid.*: For five minutes that crock went about twice as fast as it had ever done. **1909** *WNID*.

b. an old or infirm person.—used derisively.—now usu. constr. with *old*.

*1889 in *F & H* II: "I say," said the Lumberer to the Old Hermit…"You are getting a bit of a crock—failing fast, I should say." **1918** Roberts *Flying Fighter* 335: *Crock.* Any soldier who is disabled for life through the European War. **1929** in Longstreet *Canvas Falcons* 285: By 1917 we tired rummies and crocks were aware of how dreadful a war it

was. **1931** Lubbock *Bully Hayes* 68: We must ha' been a queer lookin' lot o' crocks to the eye. **1932* F. Richards *Old Soldiers* 175 [ref. to WWI]: I remember one draft some months later who were very nearly all crocks. One man had a double rupture and was soon sent to hospital. **1937** Barry *Clowns* 560: If my cause is a lost one, it's none the less my own, you old crock! **1944** N. Johnson *Woman in Window* (film): I don't think I like being described as an old crock. **1958** F. Davis *Spearhead* 29: They don't want anything out of an old crock like me anyway. **1958** A. King *Mine Enemy* 87: He was an old crock. **1966** in Asimov, Greenberg & Olander *Sci. Fiction Shorts* 230: The old crock in front of me, she was ninety if she was a day! **1967** Taggart *Reunion* 154: You came here—we came here—to see each other again, not listen to some old crock. **1967–68** Wolfe *Kool-Aid* 83: Playing games with old crocks at gas stations. **1977** Rusk *World to Care for* 93: A crock…is a patient for whom the doctors have run out of theories and prescriptions…There was nothing we could do for him except get him placed in a nursing home. **1983** R. Thomas *Missionary* 118: We didn't do too bad last night for a couple of old crocks.

c. *Hosp.* **a patient who complains unreasonably about real or imagined illnesses; hypochondriac.** Cf. CROCK, *v.*, 2.

*1880 in *OEDS*: *Crock*…a derisive term [in Ireland] for a person who fancies himself ailing or delicate. **1961** *AS* XXXVI 146: *Crock*…A patient who complains continually of multiple symptoms, many of which are either imaginary or of psychic origin. **1964** "Dr. X" *Intern* 141: Every now and then a patient turns up that nobody can stand, not even his own attending physician; these are the ones that the profession speaks of as the "crocks"—usually old, cantankerous, complaining, uncooperative people who seem to go out of their way to make themselves especially repulsive to everybody. **1972** *Nat. Lampoon* (July) 76: *Crock* A hypochondriac, as in: "Nurse, if this crock buzzes, don't break a leg getting there or he'll drive you nuts all night." *a1982* Medved *Hospital* 215: We get plenty of crocks at this hospital.…A crock is somebody who's not really sick but who wants to get attention, so they come into the hospital. **1984** in *Maledicta* VI (1985) 15: Nine crocks a-moaning…*Crock*, hypochondriac. **1985** *Daily Beacon* (Univ. Tenn.) (Feb. 3) 6: The doctor labels the person as a "crock" or complainer. **1992** *Doctor Dean* (synd. TV series): *Crocks*…are complaining all the time.

d. a drunkard. Cf. CROCKED.

1939 *AS* XIV 239: *Crock*…drunken person. **1941** in *DARE*. **1950** in *DAS*. **1969** in *DARE*.

2. an old or dilapidated ship, motor vehicle, or airplane.

*1903 R. Kipling, in *OEDS*: But if those cruisers are crocks, why does the Admiral let 'em out of Weymouth at all? **1905* G.B. Shaw, in *OEDS*: An old crock of a…car. **1917* Lee *No Parachute* 8: It's a damn scandal that such dangerous crocks are still being sent to France. Compared with a Pup, every variation of the B. E. is like flying a mangle. *Ibid.* 13: I'd been given the oldest crock in the flight. **1918** "Commander" *Clear the Decks!* 50: That was Migg's luck…when he packed his duffle bag and hammock aboard the old *Massachusetts*. He had heard the fleet term of "Crocks" for such relics. And he knew this particular one was classed a "Pre-Crock," as against the modern *Kansas* type, which was a "Super-Crock." **1933** Stewart *Airman Speech* 56: *Crock.* A common name for a plane. **1950**, **1969** in *DARE*. **1985** Boyne & Thompson *Wild Blue* 104: We're flying clapped-out old crocks with two thousand hours on a one-thousand-hour airframe.

3. *Stu.* **an unattractive or obnoxious person.**

1927 *AS* II (Mar.) 276: *Crock.* A good-for-nothing girl. **1934** Weseen *Dict. Slang* 322: *Crock*—An unattractive girl. **1944** Sturges *Morgan Creek* (film): By dropping the charges, you dumb crock!

4. the head; in phr. **off (one's) crock** crazy.

1923 McKnight *Eng. Words* 60: *Dome*,…*coco*, *crock*, *cranium*,…*bean*, only begin the list of names for the head. **1928** Scanlon *God Have Mercy* 109 [ref. to 1918]: I heard a voice yell, "I'm hit in the crock! I'm hit in the crock!" **1929** Barr *Let Tomorrow Come* 27: Listen, Joe, you're off your crock on that. **1952** *I Love Lucy* (CBS-TV): I believe you've finally cracked your Cuban crock. **1960** Leckie *Marines!* 90: "Except what?" I snapped. "If you got some buts or excepts in your crock, let's hear 'em now before we move out."

5. an injury or blow.

1922 *Variety* (July 28) 5: The old soup bone was bad.…I fixed his crock up by takin' him to a local osteopath who unraveled the twisted ligaments. **1932** Ward *Between Big Parades* 161 [ref. to 1918]: That was a whale of a "crock," you handed him, "Smitty."

6. a bottle of whiskey.

1935 Pollock *Und. Speaks*: *Crock*, a bottle of bootleg whiskey. **1939** *AS* XIV 239: *Crock*: Bottle. **1958** McCulloch *Woods Words* 41: *Crock*—A bottle of whiskey. **1971** *Qly. Jour. Studies on Alcohol* XXXII 725: *Crock*.

Jug or bottle of an alcoholic beverage. **1979** W. Cross *Kids & Booze* 16: A bottle of wine and a crock of whiskey.

7. CROCK OF SHIT, 1, 2.

1944 in *Best from Yank* 30: This was a crock of extremely erroneous information. **1945** *Yank* (Aug. 3) 14: That…is a crock. **1947** Heggen & Logan *Mr. Roberts* 427: Well, I thought that over and I've decided that's just a crock, Doug—just a crock. **1948** Vidal *City & Pillar* 181: You may've heard stories that we weren't as tough as some other branches but that's just a crock. *a*1949 D. Levin *Mask of Glory* 194: Wouldn't it be a crock if some damn gook got us now? **1949** Pirosh *Battleground* (film): "Merry Christmas." That's a crock. **1950** Shulman *Sleep Till Noon* 76: Communism is…a crock…It's a nonesuch—a bubble and a chimera. **1956** Poe *Attack* (film): It could be a real, real crock, sir. **1958** Frankel *Band of Bros.* 5: All this snoopin' and poopin' on your belly. What a crock! **1961** Rubin *In the Life* 156: *Crock*. phony. **1965** Bonham *Durango St.* 93: Claims he was sponsoring the Moors! Now, ain't that a crock? **1967** *N.Y.P.D.* (ABC-TV): His story's a crock but he'll get to believing it himself if he's not careful. **1968** Westheimer *Young Sentry* 58: You ever hear such a crock? I was over here on a visit when the war started and it was join their army or go to jail. **1972** West *Village* 17: I think it's a crock…He's just trying to cover up for that guy screwing up. **1974** *N.Y. Daily News* (Sept. 5) 74: That crock about 13-year-olds being allowed to smoke and drink is strictly for the birds. **1975** C.W. Smith *Country Music* 211: This letter's a real crock, Ginger. **1978** in Lyle & Golenbock *Bronx Zoo* 178: But what Reggie is saying really is a crock. **1983** Goldman & Fuller *Charlie Co.* 211: What a crock…They get the hero treatment and we get treated like dirt. **1983** Naiman *Computer Dict.* 37: *Crock*…A program…[or] anything [else] that isn't well designed. **1983** G. Larson *Beyond Far Side* (unp.): These new uniforms are a crock!

crock *v.* **1.** to hit (on the head); injure; (*also*, in 1918 Rossano quot.) to kill.

1918 in Rossano *Price of Honor* 100: Flying…is all luck….If I'm going to get crocked, that's that. **1918** in Hemingway *Sel. Letters* 20: Bill this is some girl and I thank God I got crucked [*sic*] so I met her. **1940** Chandler *Farewell, My Lovely* 183: I crocked the orderly with a bed spring. **1955** Abbey *Brave Cowboy* 75: By the way, which one of you crocked me on the back of the head? **1960** in *DARE*. *1990 T. Thorne *Dict. Contemp. Slang* 116: *Crocked*…broken or injured; used particularly of sportsmen incapacitated through injury.

2. to have a breakdown. [Perh. simply an error for *crack*.]

1929 in E. O'Neill *Letters* 336: The doctor, fearing I was going to crock completely, ordered me to the hospital, where I spent two weeks.

crocked *adj.* drunk.

1917 in C.H. Burton *Letters* 270: I fancy he is "crocked." **1927** *New Republic* (Mar. 9) 71: Crocked loaded leaping screeching lathered plastered soused. **1952** Uris *Battle Cry* 74 [ref. to 1942]: I want to get crocked. **1956** I. Shulman *Good Deeds* 90: I was crocked and feeling mean. **1959** Zugsmith *Beat Generation* 1: Oh, he was just a little crocked. **1963** Stearn *Grapevine* 22: She's half crocked most of the time. **1965** Gallery *Eight Bells* 16: My memory certainly isn't the result of hearsay, for I never told anyone about it except my wife, when I git a little bit crocked one time. **1969** Zelver *Honey Bunch* 137: Old Buzz was crocked. **1971** Cole *Rook* 179: Boy, are you crocked! **1980** Eble *Campus Slang* (Mar.) 2: *Crocked*—drunk. **1993** *New Yorker* (Feb. 8) 104: Many Americans…seem determined to die half crocked.

crockery *n.* teeth. *Joc.*

1910 *N.Y. Eve. Jour.* (May 17) 12: He has a fine set of store crockery, and the gap in the front of his mouth is not noticed. **1915** *N.Y. Eve. Jour.* (Aug. 2) 13: That tooth tearin'…crockery cloutin' joint of yours won't lamp me no more. **1919** *Lit. Digest* (Mar. 8) 59: "The Colonel?" chuckles a dusky dough-boy from the Harlem jungles showing his entire expanse of white crockery up-stairs and down. **1932** D. Runyon, in *Collier's* (Mar. 6) 8: Regret…sticks his finger in her mouth to get a peek at her crockery. **1942** Hurston *Dust Tracks* 136 [ref. to *ca*1917]: Mouth looking like a dish-pan full of broke-up crockery!

crockery fleet *n. Navy.* (see quot.).

1945 in *Calif. Folk Qly.* V (1946) 379: Noteworthy is the novel *crockery fleets* or group of *crocks*, or barge-like freight-bearing ships constructed—with the exception of the machinery, fittings, and fixtures—entirely reinforced concrete.

crockful *n.* CROCK OF SHIT, 1.

1985 Briskin *Too Much* 325: "He has your eyes."…"What a crockful."

crockhead *n. West.* a stubborn or stupid animal or person.

1942 *ATS* 141. **1966** "T. Pendleton" *Iron Orchard* 99: We *ort* to have let them fuckin' bulls cart you off to the stout house is what we *ort* to done, you ol' crock-head.

crocko *adj.* CROCKED.

1922 in E. Wilson *Twenties* 116: Crocko, squiffy, boiled to the ears. **1942** *ATS* 122.

crock of shit *n.* **1.** a pack of lies.—usu. considered vulgar. [The 1944 quot. is clearly euphemistic.]

[**1944** *Stars & Stripes* (Oct. 18): "I think it's a crock of sugar," said 1st Lt. Charles House…"Most of the folks back home have been seeing too many movies."] **1945** in Shibutani *Co. K* 254: Dat's a crock of sheet! We no get racial equality een Hawaii. **1946** J.H. Burns *Gallery* 13: Ya know it's all a crocka shit. **1947** Mailer *Naked & Dead* 361: To himself he thought, "What a crock of shit!" **1950–53** W. Grove *Down* 21: It's nothing but a crock of shit from A to Z. **1958** Cooley *Run for Home* 108: I think that's a crock of shit, kid, but it's okay. **1961** Forbes *Goodbye to Some* 180: That's a crock of shit about how the Japs don't have decent radar. **1965** C.D.B Bryan *P.S. Wilkinson* 388: Question: "What do you think of this call-up?" Answer: "I think it's a crock of shit." **1967** Yablonsky *Hippie Trip* 212: And it's a crock of shit. It's not true. **1972** C. Gaines *Stay Hungry* 144: Sounds like a crock of shit to me. **1984** Kagan & Summers *Mute Evidence* 427: That experiment was a crock of shit. **1993** N.Y.C. man, age 45: It's a crock of shit, that's why.

2. that which is hateful or disgusting, esp. a wretched state of affairs.

1951 Kerouac *Cody* 91: America's a lonely crockashit. **1970** Wexler *Joe* (film): Ever get the feeling that everything you do, your whole life, is just one big crock of shit? **1980** T. Jones *Adrift* 96: Hell, when we heard what you were doing in London, stoking a goddam boiler, hey, that's a crocka bull, man! *Ibid.* 271: 'At Welfare's a crocka shit, Cap'n.

crocky *adj.* infirm; shaky.

*1921 (cited in Partridge *DSUE* (ed. 8) 270). **1944** in Giles *G.I. Journal* 5: With my crocky knees, it wasn't platoon sergeant. **1980** Algren *Dev. Stocking* 159: Vince was always crocky, of course. Now he's punchy.

crocodile *n.* an extended double line of people, esp. of schoolgirls on a class outing.

*1890–91 F & H II 215: *Crocodile*…(University).—A girl's school walking two and two. **1905** Brainerd *Belinda* 36: Trailing up and down the street at the tail of the "crocodile" was one of the features of the boarding-school which she particularly disliked.

¶ In phrase:

¶ **in a while, crocodile** (used in parting as a response to *see you later, alligator* s.v. ALLIGATOR). Also vars.

1962 N.Y.C. high school students: "See you later, alligator." "In a while, crocodile." **1966** IUFA *Folk Speech*: Children's saying: After-while, crocodile! **1980** N.Y. woman, age *ca*25: Someone says, "See you later, alligator," and *you* say, "On the Nile, crocodile."

crocodile scam *n. So. Und.* (see quot.).

1980 Garrison *Snakedoctor* 59: They've been working the old crocodile scam…They get some joker in the motel room…then the husband or boyfriend shows.

crocus *n.* a physician. Cf. CROAKER.

*1785 Grose *Vulgar T.*: *Crocus*, or *Crocus Metallorum*. A nick name for a surgeon of the army and navy. **1859** Matsell *Vocab.* 22: *Crokus*. A doctor. *"The cove sold a stiff un to a crokus for twenty cases,"* the rogue sold a corpse to a doctor for twenty dollars. **1895** *Harper's* (July) 776: Anyhow, the crocus* says so, 'n' I s'pose he knows…*Doctor. **1899** "J. Flynt" *Tramping* 393: *Crocus*: a doctor. **1926** *AS* I (Jan.) 251: *Crocus*. A doctor, derived from croak, to die. **1930** "D. Stiff" *Milk & Honey* 203: *Croaker* or *crocus*—A member of the medical fraternity.

cro'-jack-eyed *adj. Naut.* crosseyed or squinting. Hence **cro'jack eye** a strabismic eye.

*1828 *Night Watch* II 88: *Cro'-jack-eyed.* *1834 in Partridge *DSUE* (ed. 8) 270: Cro'-Jack-eyed. **1903** *Independent* (Dec. 31) 3104: The bar…was presided over by a sinister looking "cracker" with a freckled face and a "Cro' Jack" eye. *1929 Bowen *Sea Slang* 31: *Cro' Jack Eyed.* Squinting. **1961** Burgess *Dict. Sailing* 64: *Cross-jack-eyed.* Squinting.

crony *n.* a close friend or associate; chum (now *colloq.*); fellow (*obs.*); (*occ., obs.*) lover. [In 19th–20th C. S.E., restricted to a close political associate or a partner in wrongdoing, with opprobrious connotations not present in earlier use.]

*1663, *1665 in *OED2*. *1671 in Adlard *Forbidden Tree* 37: She that for love with her crony lies/Is chaste: But that's the whore that kisses for prize. *ca*1682 in D'Urfey *Pills* II 285: He told the King like a Croney. *1698–99 "B.E." *Dict. Canting Crew*: *Crony*, a Camerade or intimate Friend; an *old Crony*, one of long standing; used also for a tough old Hen. *1726 A. Smith *Mems. of J. Wild* 43: For desperately wounding

One of his Cronies in a Tavern-Fray. **1797** in Tyler *Verse* 54: All long'd to catch the fusty crony. **1805** Brackenridge *Mod. Chiv.* 527: Come shake hands, my cronies. *****1815** T. Carlyle, in C.R. Sanders *Carlyle Letters* I 53: The spirit-stirring *crack* of our jocund cronies. **1845** in Oehlschlaeger *Reveille* 247: The widder…sent for…an old maid croney [of hers]. **1943** in Botkin *Sidewalks* 325: Favored spots of Joe and his cronies, next to the saloons, were the city's bathhouses. **1950–53** W. Grove *Down* 77: An old crony who's close to Al Faber. **1986–91** Hamper *Rivethead* 16: My…cronies from St. Luke's.

crook *n.* a thief or swindler; a dishonest person. Now *S.E.*

1877 in W. Parker *Deadwood* 203: Crooks of all kinds—gamblers, confidence men, pickpockets, thieves, highwaymen and murderers. **1879** *Nat. Police Gaz.* (June 21) 12: The Sharp "Crooks" of the Far West. **1879** in *DA.* *****1887** in *F & H* II: A crook whose methods are exposed is a second-rate crook. **1888** in *Amer. Heritage* (Oct. 1979) 21: I've talked…with…the wittiest and dryest of the Crooks I've met by chance. **1891** Maitland *Slang Dict.* 82: *Crook* (Am.), a thief. **1891** Campbell, Knox & Byrnes *Darkness & Daylight* viii: He knows the methods and characteristics of "crooks" of high and low degree. **1913** A. Palmer *Salvage* 149: He had come near wasting his life among "crooks and bums." **1916** in Truman *Dear Bess* 197: The superintendent we have is a crook I believe. **1916** MacBrayne & Ramsay *One More Chance* 44: I did not plan to turn professional crook. **1918–19** Sinclair *Higgins* 42: What do you take us for? A bunch of crooks? **1927** C.J. Daly *Snarl of Beast* 12: The police don't like me. The crooks don't like me.

¶ In phrase:

¶ **on the crook** *Und.* dishonestly; (*also*) being a professional criminal.

*****1879** *Macmillan's Mag.* XL 503: Which he had bought on the crook (dishonestly). *****1889** Barrère & Leland *Slang* I: On the *crook*, by dishonest means. **1909** *WNID.* **1927** *DN* V 457: *On the crook*, adj. Committed to the life of the underworld.

crook *v.* **1.** to cheat; ROOK. Also absol.

1841 R.W. Emerson, in *DARE*: Shuffle they will, and crow, crook, and hide, feign to confess here, only that they may brag and conquer there. **1925** *Sat. Eve. Post* (Jan. 3) 142: Say,…are you guys crooking me? **1927** "M. Brand" *Pleasant Jim* 43: Your brother crooked me with a dirty deal! **1928–30** Fiaschetti *Gotta Be Rough* 137: He was a stool pigeon who had crooked me. **1930** Sage *Last Rustler* 160: He figured them a yeller bunch to crook a kid fighting the game alone. **1939** in *DARE*. **1948** in *DA* 437. **1966–69** in *DARE*.

2. to steal.

1882 in *DA*: He would once have gone to jail on the charge of "crooking" six hens. **1928** Dahlberg *Bottom Dogs* 45: Stale doughnuts they had crooked from Becker's Bakery. **1942** in *Jour. Gen. Psych.* LXVI (1945) 131: He went in my locker and crooked my socks. **1945** in *DAS* 131. **1949** Neumayer *Delinquency* 141: In the beginning, John did not like to "crook."…He never "crooked alone." **1966–69** in *DARE*. **1979** Kunstler *Wampanaki Tales* 13: A little good-by present.…They'd kill you if they found out you crooked it.

¶ In phrase:

¶ **crook (one's) elbow** see s.v. ELBOW.

¶ **crook (one's) little finger** see s.v. FINGER.

crooked *adj.* **1.** dishonest; criminal. Now *S.E.*

1859 *Spirit of Times* (Mar. 5) 44: Don't be crooked, my son,…bekase you ain't gwine to gaither me. **1876** in *DA* 437. *****1877** in *F & H* II: He immediately saw how he could pay off the crooked officer. **1878** *Nat. Police Gaz.* (Apr. 28) 2: The "Crooked" Governor. **1880** Pinkerton *Prof. Thieves & Detective* 58: He did not, however, discontinue his operations in the "crooked" line. **1888** Bidwell *Forging His Chains* 79: A buyer who is "crooked" always pays his first bill in order to get a bigger shipment afterwards. **1903** A.H. Lewis *Boss* 106: He's as crooked as a dog's hind leg. **1912** Ade *Babel* 40: You had to go crooked at last, did you? **1952** W. Brown *Sox* 100: Don't tell me that game today wasn't crooked. **1960** J. Mitford *Daughters* 218: Racing…is…as crooked as a nine-dollar bill.

2. stolen; illicit.

*****1864** Hotten *Slang Dict.* (ed. 3): *Crooked.* A term used among dog-stealers…to denote anything stolen. **1875** *Chi. Tribune* (Nov. 17) 3: He was…suspected, by the Internal Revenue Collector at St. Joe, of keeping "crooked" tobacco. *****1879** in Partridge *Dict. Und.* 163: One scamp…requested me to carry a "crooked message" to this brother. **1888** Bidwell *Forging His Chains* 130: Is there anything "crooked" going on to-day? *****1889** Barrère & Leland *Dict. Slang: Crooked*…stolen. **1891** Maitland *Slang Dict.* 82: *Crooked* (Am.), anything stolen…*Crooked whisky* (Am.), that upon which the government tax has not been paid.

1896 Ade *Artie* 64: He won't never let on that he's handled any crooked money.

crooked stick *n.* an obnoxious or good-for-nothing person.

1828 in *DARE*. **1848** in Lowell *Poetical Works* 213: So, ez I aint a crooked stick…I'll go back to my plough. *Ibid.* 458: *Crooked stick*, a perverse, froward person. **1923** *DN* V 234: *Crooked stick*…A man who has turned out to be more or less a failure in life. No dishonesty of character is implied. **1960, 1965** in *DARE*.

croot var. CRUIT.

croppy *n.* a corpse.

1929 *Bookman* (July) 525: That kid needs a doctor…If you don't want a croppy on your hands, start feedin' this goat black diamonds!

croppy *v.* to kill (someone).

1918 Casey *Cannoneers* 132: I don't want no red-head fuse to croppy me. *Ibid.* 188: Lieut. Wertz captured a machine gun nest. And he shot it out with the Kraut who was running it an' croppied him.

cross *n.* **1.** *Und.* a carefully arranged swindle, (*esp. in early use*) a fixed prizefight; a swindle or method of swindling; a betrayal.

*****1823** Egan *Vulgar Tongue*: *Cross*…Any collusion or unfair dealing between several parties. *****1834** in *F & H* II: Both kids agreed to play a cross. *****1836** *Spirit of Times* (Feb. 20) 3: I have seen…a prize fight between two ruffians, who had made what is called "a cross," and thus gulled the aristocracy.…The backers…arranged…that the best man should *lose* the battle. *Ibid.*: I remember an instance, however, where there was "a cross" resumed…"Friend Ikey, 'tis *no* cross." **1880** *N.Y. Clipper Almanac* 44: Barney.—A race in which there has been a "cross" or "sell-out." **1891** Maitland *Slang Dict.* 82: *Cross*, in the sporting world, is an arrangement for a fight or any contest to be won or lost irrespective of the merits of the contestants. A "double cross" is where the man who "put up the job" plays straight at the last and swindles his associate swindler. *****1894** in Partridge *Dict. Und.* 164: He at once suspected a "cross"; that is, to use his own language, he had been put away, betrayed, sold either by the "blokes" or his "pals." **1911** *Hampton's Mag.* (June) 747: Why, it's the cross!…It's the cross! You guys have handed it to me! **1911** A.H. Lewis *Apaches of N.Y.* 129: She's givin' you the cross, Jackeen. **1914** London *Jacket* 22: The Captain of the Yard did not know that the cross was being worked on him. **1936** Tully *Bruiser* 144: When Shane answered the gong for the seventh, Tim whispered to Blinky, "It's a cross."…"We thought we might win in the sixth." **1963** Westlake *Getaway Face* 37: She's going to try a cross. **1967** [Beck] *Pimp* 61: Here was a hardened ex-whore who knew all the crosses, all the answers, who handled lots of scratch. **1969** L. Sanders *Anderson Tapes* 145: They must put their own man in to make sure there's no cross.

2. *Und.* criminal activities; the criminal underworld; in phr. **on the cross** being a professional criminal.

*****1812** Vaux *Vocab.* 234: *Cross*: illegal or dishonest practices in general are called *the cross*, in opposition to *the square*…Any article which has been irregularly obtained, is said to have been *got upon the cross*, and is emphatically termed *a cross article*. *****1823** "J. Bee" *Turf*: To "live upon the cross" is to exist by dishonest means. *****1830** in *F & H* II: A firm ally and generous patron of the *lads of the cross*. **1845** *Nat. Police Gaz.* (Dec. 6) 122: He squared his moral doctrine by every proposition of the strictest code of the "cross." **1846** *Lives of Felons* 36: Stevens was "*on the cross*," i.e. a professional rogue. **1848** Judson *Mysteries* 89: You know me, Sam, I'm on the *cross*! *Ibid.* 326: To be "on the cross" is to be dishonest. **1851** [G. Thompson] *Jack Harold* 60: I went upon the cross, and began to rob and steal. **1872** Crapsey *Nether Side of NY* 58: He made the acquaintance of these outlaws, and…represented himself as "on the cross." **1872** in "M. Twain" *Life on Miss.* 292: You told me if I would shake the cross (*quit stealing*), & live on the square for 3 months, it would be the best job I ever done in my life. **1884** Triplett *American Crimes* 49: Don't hang back, man, we are all on the cross together*…*A cant saying for "We are brother thieves."

¶ In phrases:

¶ **in a cross** *Black E.* in trouble; at a disadvantage.

1954 in Wepman et al. *The Life* 40: But don't think you can ever put me in a cross. **1967** [Beck] *Pimp* 245: I'm in a cross.

¶ **on the cross, 1.** see (**2**), above.

2. fraudulently; dishonestly; criminally.

*****1802** in Partridge *Dict. Und.* 164: I got it on…the cross. *****1836** *Spirit of Times* (Feb. 20) 3: He…beat [the other boxer] on the cross, and so the game went. **1865** Sala *Diary* II 172: The games played are roulette and faro. Whether they are played on the "square" or on the "cross" I do not undertake to determine. **1878** Bellew *Tramp* 12: "I don't mind doin' a little bit on the cross" (here he crossed his forefingers) "now and then, in case of necessity, or for a lark."

3. engaged in a doublecross.

1941 Mahin & Grant *Johnny Eager* (film): So you *were* on the cross, huh?

cross *adj. Und.* being a professional criminal; related to or involving crime or criminals; criminal.

*1811 Lexicon Balatron.: *Cross.* Dishonest. *A cross cove;* any person who lives by stealing or in a dishonest manner. **1812 Vaux Vocab.* 234: *Cross-Cove,* or *Cross-Mollisher,* a man or woman who lives *upon the cross. Ibid. Cross-Crib:* a house inhabited or kept by *family* people [i.e., criminals]. **1845** *Nat. Police Gaz.* (Nov. 8) 89: Many of the new "cross" friends...had helped him to his secret gains...Thieving gangs...made that "cross-crib," or thieves' den, a place of resort. **1848** *Ladies' Repository* VIII (Oct.) 315: *Cross,* Not honest. *Cross Cove,* a dishonest man. **1859** Matsell *Vocab.* 22: *Cross.* Dishonest. *Ibid. Cross-Cove.* A thief; any person that lives in a dishonest way is said to be "on the cross," from the fact that highwaymen were in the habit of waiting for their victims on the cross-roads. **1873** Sutton *N.Y. Tombs* 184: I was put in with a notorious old criminal, who soon initiated me into the mysteries of a "cross life."

cross *v. Esp. Und.* to betray or cheat; DOUBLECROSS. Now also constr. with *up.*

*1821 Real Life in London II 338: Up to all the manoeuvres of the race course...*betting, hedging off, crossing* and *jostling, sweating* and *training.* **1823* Egan *Vulgar Tongue.* **1910** Z. Grey *Heritage of the Desert* 1: Don't cross Dene. **1914** London *Jacket* 28: Winwood crossed us and squealed. **1925** in Partridge *Dict. Und.* **1927** in Hammett *Big Knockover* 295: You're a thief among thieves, and those who don't double-cross get crossed. **1933** in R. E. Howard *Iron Man* 78: So you was the smart boy that crossed us! **1936** S.I. Miller *Battling Bellhop* (film): Has he been crossing me up with you? **1936** Steel *College* 311: Fusil hissed, "You crosser." **1938** E.S. Gardner, in Ruhm *Detective* 227: How do I know you wouldn't cross me to the bulls if anybody came along and offered a reward? **1947** Schulberg *Harder They Fall* 12: He was the boy who crossed the wise money by [winning the boxing title]. **1948** L. Allen *Reds* 150: Burns insisted...that after the second game the guilty players, not having received their money in full, tried to cross the gamblers and win the series. **1953** Manchester *City of Anger* 151: If a rival boss crossed him he would rub him out or have him deported. **1959–60** Bloch *Dead Beat* 132: Larry, listen to me. I wouldn't cross you...I was going to tell you. **1966** in Cannon *Nobody Asked* 131: I only showed them to you because you're my friend. What a dirty rotten bum you'd be to cross. **1970** R. Vasquez *Chicano* 338: Don't cross me, man. **1984** *Tales of Gold Monkey* (ABC-TV): Cross me for one instant and *he* gets the paper. **1993** *Are You Afraid of Dark?* (Nickelodeon TV): Crossing him will lead to your destruction.

crossback *n.* a Roman Catholic.—used contemptuously.

1964 *PADS* (No. 42) 34: The Catholic is identified by multiple responses of *papist, cross-back, Turk,* and *Roman*...All three...informants...remember the expression from childhood. **1965–70** in *DARE.*

crossbar hotel *n.* a jail, prison, or lockup.

1865 Woodruff *Union Soldier* 80: I...sent a large escort of Bayonets to conduct him to the Provost Martials who put him in what we call a cross bared hotel showed him a snug little room & turned a key on him. **1866** in Hilleary *Webfoot* 155: Hall...has took up his abode...[in] the "Hotel de Crossbar." **1941** *Army Ordnance* (July) 79: *Cross Bar Hotel.* Guardhouse. **1942** Lindsay & Crouse *Strip for Action* 20: "Where's Nutsy Davis?" "He's in the cross-bar hotel." "With a dame, I'll bet." "Mister, the cross-bar hotel is the guardhouse." **1959** *Swinging Syllables: Cross Bar Hotel*—Jail or prison. **1970** Ponicsan *Detail* 181: You take static from some "officer and gentleman"...while the poor jerk from Camden you take up the river to the Crossbars Hotel. **1974** *Playboy* (Apr.) 132: Sheriff T.J. Flournoy would...suggest...overnight lodgings in Fayette County's crossbar hotel. **1990** Rukuza *West Coast Turnaround* 49: Julio was doing fifteen to life in the crossbar hotel.

crossbones *n.* a physician; SAWBONES.

1919 Darling *Jargon Book* 9: *Crossbones*—A doctor.

cross-cut *n.* a prank; SAW.

1850 *Spirit of Times* (June 8) 234: The captain...thought he'd run a small "cross cut" on the old joker.

cross-drum *n. Und.* a tavern or similar establishment frequented by criminals.

1859 Matsell *Vocab.* 22: *Cross-Drum.* A drinking-place where thieves resort. **1872** Burnham *Secret Svc.* v: *Cross-Drum.* A country tavern, upon the road. *Ibid.* 98: I made for the "cross-drum" lively, you can bet.

crossfire *n. Orig. Vaudeville.* rapid repartee.

1901 Hobart *John Henry* 65: Did you ever drop in...to play pool under a cross-fire from the chair-warmers? **1921** *Variety* (Mar. 11) 24: The clever crossfire quickly thawed-out the hard-boiled attendants. **1923** *N.Y. Times* (Oct. 7) VIII 4: *Crossfire*—Fast gag lines between comedians. **1929** *Bookman* (Apr.) 150: Brisk gagging between comedians [is called] "crossfire." **1930** in Perelman *Old Gang* 98: A brillant bit of cross-fire between Sacher Masoch and the Marquis de Sade. **1959** M. Harris *Wake Up* 55: Unsupervised debate...Dr. Youngdahl merely engaging in this "cross-fire" waving his hands and shouting. **1981** McKee & Chisenhall *Beale* 165: They started it with some "cross firing," a cousin of the minstrel show patter.

cross-jack-eyed var. CRO'-JACK-EYED.

crossman *n. Und.* a man who is a professional criminal.

1845 *Nat. Police Gaz.* (Oct. 16) 51: Reed's great reputation among "crossmen." **1846** *Lives of Felons* 12: The City and the Phoenix banks...two institutions which might easily be entered by any burglars and "crossmen" of address. **1848** Judson *Mysteries* 33: For many a year it has been known to the "crossmen" and "knucks" of the town as "Jack Circle's watering place" and "fence." *Ibid.* 526: "Crossmen." The professional term for thieves. **1871** Banka *Prison Life* 493: Thief,...*Cross-man.*

crossroader *n. Gamb.* an itinerant criminal, usu. a cardsharp or swindler.

a1889 in Barrère & Leland *Slang* I: For the simple purpose of being introduced to the club, there to "fleece the suckers," who never suspect they are playing against a *cross-roader.* **1897** (cited in Partridge *Dict. Und.* 810). **1926** C.M. Russell *Trails* 115: The old lady's shakin' hands, and, between sobs, thankin' this old cross-roader. **1961** Scarne *Gambling Gde.* 343: Sometimes it is the casino operators themselves who complain that they have been cheated by *hand-muckers* or *crossroaders* (card sharps). **1966** Braly *Cold* 69: I been a tramp and a crossroader and a nothing-minus-nothing since the day I slipped out of the barn. **1968** "H. King" *Box-Man* 76: Most thieves are crossroaders—they travel around. **1977** Laxalt *Nevada* 111: In the gambling industry, cheating customers are known as "crossroaders," and there are literally hundreds of them moving from one casino to another.

cross-up *n. Und.* a betrayal or swindle.

1963 D. Tracy *Brass Ring* 269: This last he considered a stinking cross-up.

crot *n. U.S. Mil. Acad.* CRUT.—usu. constr. with *dumb.*

1961 N. Ford *Black, Gray & Gold* 3: Get a move on, Dumbcrot! **1978** Truscott *Dress Gray* 260: He was a...dullard and a crot and...worthless. **1981–89** R. Atkinson *Long Gray Line* 17 [ref. to 1962]: Wrong, you dumb crot.

Crotch *n. USMC.* the U.S. Marine Corps.—constr. with *the.*—used derisively.

1953 in Russ *Last Parallel* 145: Pfc. Dunbar Bloomfield...is a twenty-year man, who loves the Crotch, as we call it. **1962** W. Crawford *Give Me Tomorrow* 34 [ref. to 1951]: "No, Sergeant. You are in the Maahreen Kore. Otherwise known as the Crotch." "That's her. U-S-M-C. Uncle Sam's Moldy Crotch." **1964** Peacock *Drill & Die* 161: Maybe he would make a career out of the Crotch after all. **1967** W. Crawford *Gresham's War* 45: This here member of the Crotch is possessor of the Navy Cross. **1970** *Playboy* (Apr.) 208: Thirty years in the Crotch...with a few more stripes than when I came in. **1973** *N.Y. Times* (Sept. 16) II 13: Don pumps him for 15 minutes about life in the Crotch, as the Corps is called by those who are in it but who wish to be out of it. **1977** Caputo *Rumor of War* 133: Man, I been busted so many times I couldn't make lance corporal if I stayed in the Crotch for thirty years. **1983** Eilert *Self & Country* 36: Rick, you're nuts...How...did you ever get in the Crotch?

crotch *adj.* erotic or pornographic.—used prenominally.

1971 Murphy & Gentry *2nd in Command* 297: Actually the latter was a "crotch" novel that Sterling had written. **1973** in *Playboy* (Jan. 1974) 52: On nuclear submarines, the men are keen consumers of X-rated movies and what they call "crotch novels." **1980** Key *Clam-Plate* 15: Having always believed these crotch magazines dealt with real, live women, I was stunned. **1986** R. Campbell *In La-La Land* 95: The attendant looked up from his crotch magazine.

crotch-buster *n.* a very difficult task; BALLBUSTER.

1986 Univ. Tenn. grad. student, age 35: That was a real crotch-buster.

crotch cricket *n.* a crab louse. *Joc.*

1971 *Blushes & Bellylaffs* 16: How to get rid of crotch crickets: Rub yourself with alcohol and sit in the sand…they'll get drunk and kill each other throwing rocks. **1971** *Coming, Dear!* 122: That's what I've got…all the crotch crickets in Kansas.

crotch pheasant *n.* a crab louse. *Joc.*
   1967, 1969 in *DARE*. **1975** Legman *No Laughing Matter* 118: Crab lice or "crotch-pheasants" (*pediculus pubis*).

crotch rocket *n.* a motorcycle. *Joc.*
   1974 Univ. Tenn. grad. student, age 22: A *crotch rocket* is a damn motorcycle. I heard that about two years ago in North Carolina. **1978** Dills *CB* (ed. 4) 29: *Crotch Rocket:* motorcycle. **1979** *Easyriders* (Dec.) 8: Two squirrels on crotch rockets came burning between the two lines of Harleys. **1980** Univ. Tenn. student: A *crotch rocket* is a motorcycle. I learned that term between '73 and '75. **1988** *West 57th* (CBS-TV): They're called everything from "super bikes" to "crotch rockets."

crotch rot *n.* **1.** any of various fungal infections of the groin.
   1967 Partridge *DSUE* (ed. 6) [as a Canadian term]. **1971** Dahlskog *Dict.* 16: *Crotch rot*…A fungus infection of the scrotum; any itch in the groin; itching testicles. **1973** Jong *Flying* 49: You've given me indigestion! You've given me crotch rot! **1973** Karlin, Paquet & Rottmann *Free Fire Zone* 141: Bouquets of crotch-rot. **1968–77** Herr *Dispatches* 62: A fire ant would fly up your nose or you'd grow a crotch rot. **1980** Gould *Ft. Apache* 38: He's an orthodox Jew…which makes him about as popular as crotch rot. **1983** S. Wright *Meditations* 64: And McFarland had crotch rot and Ellis malaria again. **1986** Thacker *Pawn* 130: Insect repellent and crotch-rot powder.
   2. venereal disease.
   1977 Schrader *Blue Collar* 54: I mean like crotch rot.

Croton cocktail *n.* [ref. to the *Croton* reservoir, which supplies much of New York City's drinking water] *N.Y.C.* a glass of water. *Joc.* Also **Croton highball.**
   1908 in Fleming *Unforgettable Season* 122: Croton cocktails and cow juice is my limit. **1981** in Safire *Good Word* 111 [ref. to *ca*1915]: Croton highball.

crow *n.* **1.** a crowbar.
   ***1699** N. Ward *London-Spy* 112: The Light-Finger'd Subtlety of *Shop-Lifting;* the excellent use of *Jack* and *Crow*. **1983** Helprin *Winter's Tale* 31: They…dropped their hammer and crow, and made for the exit.
   2. a black person.—used contemptuously.
   1823 J.F. Cooper *Pioneers* 199: Kirby turned fiercely to the black, and said—"Shut your oven, you crow!" **1852** B.R. Hall *Freeman's Barber Shop* 109: You black crow. **1855** Wise *Tales for Marines* 76: *Calla-boca!* silence, you crow! **1863** "E. Kirke" *So. Friends* 191: Shet up, you brack crows! **1869** *Galaxy* (Jan.) 112: You look like that ol crow you were talking of, Mammy. **1924** *Amer. Mercury* (Feb.) 130: Dey'd call you Crow den—or Chocolate—or Smoke. **1968** I. Reed *Yellow Back Radio* 115: I understand you got some wild and woolly crow over here that's about to worry you to death. **1968** *Gunsmoke* (CBS-TV western series): You know, if we don't find Dillon, I'm gonna go find me that camp and I'm gonna roust me a smart-mouthed crow. **1969** Angelou *Caged Bird* 106: It was a dangerous practice to call a Negro anything that could be loosely construed as insulting because of the centuries of their having been called niggers, jigs, dinges, crows, boots, and spooks.
   3. *Und.* a person who acts as a lookout for thieves.
   ***1839** Brandon *Poverty, Mendicity, Crime* (gloss.) (s.v. *sneak*): While another, who is called a *crow*, watches. **1859** Matsell *Vocab.* 23: *Crow.* The crow is the fellow that watches outside when his accomplices are inside, and gives them warning of the approach of danger. **1866** *Nat. Police Gaz.* (Dec. 8) 2: Sheehan and Lambert stationed themselves inside the store, while the other man remained outside to "hock the crow."…The "crow" was also "pinched," and turned out to be Cunningham. **1886, 1930** (cited in Partridge *Dict. Und.* 166).
   4.a. an old or unattractive woman.
   1866 *Night Side of N.Y.* 98: And this crow picked you up? **1889** Field *Western Verse* 143: In a passing wittie jest he dubbeth her ye crow. **1926** MacIssac *Tin Hats* 88 [ref. to 1918]: "I kind of thought it would be pretty girls."…"There ain't none over here," declared Jack. "Member the crows we saw in Boulogny?" **1932** Hecht & Fowler *Great Magoo* 119: What's that old crow writing you for? **1944** Caldwell *Tragic Ground* 62: You can't make me marry that old crow! **1944** Kendall *Service Slang* 21: A *crow*…a female ashore who lacks pulchritude. **1956** Levin *Compulsion* 67: The girls went into a building. "Crows, anyway," Artie said, but his spirits had lifted. **1956** *Honeymooners* (synd. TV series): She's not such a bad old crow at that. **1972** W.C. Anderson *Hurricane* 122: You're a lovable old crow.

b. a young woman; woman.
   1891 McCann & Jarrold *Odds & Ends* 10: Hello, Mag, me jim-dandy crow, what're ye doin' here lallygaggin' agin de wall? **1924** *Century Mag.* (Nov.) 124: It was still a sure way of gaining public disfavor to be seen too often in the company of girls, who, as in old days [*ca*1909], were still ungallantly referred to as "crows." **1930** Shoemaker *1300 Wds.* 13 [ref. to *ca*1900]: *Crow*—A rather attractive girl. **1942** Algren *Morning* 39: Ol' Fireball gets this crow t' come up 'n look at his books you—like a Nort'western co-ed she looked. ***1945** S.J. Baker *Australian Lang.* 156: *Crow.* A girl or sweetheart. **1968** in *DARE*.
   c. an unpleasant man, esp. one who is old.
   1922 Colton & Randolph *Rain* 74: There's something about that crow that isn't human. **1935** F.H. Lea *Anchor Man* 275: A bunch of stuffed shirts…a flock of nine old crows in a star chamber proceeding. **1952** "R. Marsten" *So Nude* 112: Look, man, don't be a crow.
   5. *Navy & USCG.* the eagle that is part of a petty officer's rating badge; (*hence*) such a rating.
   1905 *Bluejacket* (Feb.) 157: I'm goin' to sport a "crow" of my own. **1914** *DN* 150: *Crow. n.* The eagle on petty officers' sleeves. **1917** *Lit. Digest* (Apr. 14) 113: The rating-badge consists…of a spread eagle, commonly called by the bluejackets a "crow," which is placed above a special mark or chevron. **1918** Ruggles *Navy Explained:* The rating badges of the service [Navy] have an eagle spread over the designated insignia of the wearer and when a man gets rated, it is said that he got the crow—buzzard, bird, or hawk. **1919** Battey *Sub. Destroyer* 298: He broke the news in the classic phrase that he was "putting me up for a crow"—the crow being the eagle which is a prominent part of a petty officer's rating badge. **1927** *Amer. Leg. Mo.* (Sept.) 26: Used to have a crow, didn't you Rollins? **1943** Chase *Destroyer* (film): I'll show you how fast that crow can fly off your arm. **1953** Dodson *Away All Boats* 191: I had a lot of that crow on my sleeve! **1959** Sterling *Wake of the Wahoo* 66: I…had a yeoman's "crow" sewed on. **1982** T.C. Mason *Battleship* 34: Now if you flunk, you don't get your third-class crow. **1986** L. Johnson *Waves* 156: Guess I'm gonna have to hold my punches a little bit when I tack a crow on a Wave. **1991** K. Douglass *Viper Strike* 140: When they go up before the Old Man, I'll lay you odds Bentley and Paterowski lose their crows.
   6. *Mil.* chicken served in a messhall.—used derisively.
   1941 Kendall *Army & Navy Slang* 4: *Crow*…chicken. **1943** *Amer. Mercury* (Nov.) 553: Chicken [is] *crow* or *buzzard*; and turkey, *seagull*. **1945** *Sat. Rev.* (Nov. 24) 14 [ref. to WWII]: *Crow.* chicken.
   7. *USAF.* an electronic warfare officer.
   1980 W.C. Anderson *Bat-21* [ref. to 1972]: "Roger. You crows in back wake up."…"Crows"…electronic warfare officers.
¶ In phrase:
¶ **Holy crow!** (used to express astonishment).
   1965 Pollini *Glover* 126: Holy crow, all her troubles. **1973** *TULIPQ* (coll. B.K. Dumas): If something very good happens, you might say *Holy Crow!* **1974** in Asimov, Greenberg & Olander *Sci. Fi. Short Shorts* 213: "Holy Crow!" Tommy said in a loud whisper. **1975** Witchell *Loch Ness Story* 153: "Holy crow," I thought, "that looks like a cabbage." **1983** S. King *Christine* 449: Holy crow! I bet they ain't there anymore anyway, though. I bet one of them cops got it. **1989** *CBS This Morning* (CBS-TV) (Dec. 19): Your first reaction is "Holy crow! I'm alive!"

crowbait *n.* **1.** a worthless or decrepit horse or mule.
   1851 W. Kelly *Ex. to Calif.* II 98: Such an animal is called a "Crowbait" in Yankeeland. **1865** in Tilney *My Life* 202: A horse…what, in army phraseology, is termed a "crow-bait." **1891** Bourke *On the Border* 16: The joke would be on the deluded savage who might sneak down to ride away with such a crow-bait. **1891** Maitland *Slang Dict.* 83: *Crow-bait*, an aged and decrepit horse, only fit to feed the crows. **1900** White *Westerners* 25: Yore hosses are a lot of crowbait. **1906** in "O. Henry" *Works* 1397: I think I like your horses best. I haven't seen a crowbait since I've been in town. **1910** *N.Y. Eve. Jour.* (Apr. 4) 16: That crow bait can't pull. Get the other horse. **1912** Field *Watch Yourself Go By* 436: Didn't your crow-baits ever see a gas wagon before? **1918** Casey *Cannoneers* [entry for Aug. 27]: Fall down and break your damn neck, you crazy crowbait. **1925** Nason *Three Lights* 117 [ref. to 1918]: You old crow bait, you cheat the sausage maker every day of your life. **1929** Barr *Let Tomorrow Come* 216: A skinner chides a mule: "Giddap, crow bait." **1930** Fredenburgh *Soldiers March!* 193 [ref. to 1918]: Look at those goddamned crow-baits. **1958** McCulloch *Woods Words* 41: *Crow bait*—A poor logging team, horses or bulls. **1982** F. Hailey *Soldier Talk* 16: *Crow bait.* Old cavalry horse or pack mule.
   2. a corpse exposed to the elements.
   [***1681** in Otway *Works* II 150: He shall be Crows meat by to morrow night, I tell you he shall be Crows meat by midnight.] **1857** in *DA*.

1892 Bierce *Beetles* 274: [Epitaph:] Here's crowbait! **1948** Faulkner *Intruder* 19: Keep on walking around here with that look on your face and what you'll be is crowbait. **1969** Sidney *Love of Dying* 153: You guys'll learn…else you'll be crowbait.
3. a contemptible person.
1944 Bellow *Dangling Man* 119: Do you think you can get away with it forever…you crowbait? **1951** J. Reach *My Friend Irma* 56: A hunk o' crow-bait like her.

crowbar *n.* penis.
*a*1927 in P. Smith *Letter from Father* 135: The old crow-bar was standing up quite rigid.

crowbar hotel *n.* CROSSBAR HOTEL.
1941 Kendall *Army & Navy Slang* 4: Crow bar hotel…the dear old army jail. **1965–68** E.R. Johnson *Silver St.* 113: It would be good for about five years in a crowbar hotel. **1968–70** in *DARE*. **1975** *Nat. Lampoon* (Aug.) 61: I'll…ask if they have a honeymoon sweet…at the Crowbar Hotel. **1991** *Current Affair* (synd. TV series): [He] had to spend his wedding night in the old crowbar hotel.

crowd *n.* a group of people; a circle of friends, coworkers, or the like; clique. Now *S.E.*
1840 in *OEDS:* I became satisfied that Democracy had but few charms for that crowd. **1871** Bagg *Yale* 44: *Crowd*, a common synonym for clique, coterie, or set, especially with reference to society connections. **1929** Dobie *Vaquero* 12: The "crowd"—as a cow outfit was then generally called.
¶ In phrase:
¶ **Join the crowd!** (ironically) others are suffering similar misfortunes.
1973 P. Benchley *Jaws* 25: "I think I'm going to be sick."…"Join the crowd."

crowd *v.* **1.** to put pressure on (someone).
1836 *Spirit of Times* (July 6) 208 (cited in Weingartner *Slang Dict.*). **1867** [S.B. Putnam] *Richmond During War* 197: General Stuart was redeeming his promise to "crowd 'em" with artillery. **1867** "M. Twain" in A.L. Scott *Twain's Poetry* 57: She crowded Lewis till he swore. **1908** *New Broadway* (Aug.) 142: At last I crowded Giuseppi a little. I told him…that the plate used to engrave the forged check blanks had been made in his place. **1929** Hammett *Maltese Falcon* 14: Don't crowd me. **1958** Chandler *Playback* 45: He looked like a nice guy if you didn't crowd him. **1967** Talbot *Chatty Jones* 59: Take it easy. I wasn't crowding you. I was just trying to break the ice.
2. to give forcibly.—constr. with *on*.
1899 Ade *Fables* 64: And every Saturday Evening…the Boss met her as she went out and crowded three Dollars on her.
3. *Baseball.* to load (the bases).
1912 *N.Y. Tribune* (Sept. 5) (cited in Nicholson *Baseball Term.*).
¶ In phrases:
¶ **crowd (one's) luck** to press (one's) luck.
1928 MacArthur *War Bugs* 239: The last statement was crowding his luck somewhat. **1937** "L. Short" *Brand of Empire* 107: Pete is a man who knows how to crowd his luck. **1953** T. Runyon *In for Life* 150: I was wondering if I could crowd my luck far enough to leave him. **1986** F. Walton *Once Were Eagles* 28: I didn't want to crowd my luck too far.
¶ **crowd the mourners, 1.** to add to one's difficulties; (*also*) to create resentment.
1841 *Spirit of Times* (Mar. 20) 25: It *crowds the mourners* exceedingly to "stand and deliver" when I appear to them; particularly if they are obliged to "just *step*" next door to borrow the amount. **1842** in *OEDS:* In the second mile, however, Fashion commenced "crowding the mourners" by brushing down both straight sides. **1848** in *DA:* He rather "crowded the mourners" in his historical illustrations. **1859** Bartlett *Amer.* 282: "Crowding the mourners" in political slang, means adding some further embarrassment to politicians laboring under difficulties. **1868** in *DARE:* Sir, this is "crowding the mourners." **1905** *DN* III 14: "Crowding the *mourners*," i.e. putting some further embarrassment on a person already laboring under difficulties.
2. to push forward precipitately; (*hence*) to act in haste; be overeager.
1845 Ade *Spirit of Times* (June 21) 194: I have travelled from Maine to Mexico…and never heard that [phrase] "Don't Crowd the Mourners" anywhere but in East Tennessee…Others of the old brethren were engaged clearing the ring, begging the people *not* to "crowd the mourners"—occasionally patting a mourner on the back and telling him to "agonize!" **1859** in L.F. Browne *J.R. Browne* 205: The Major talked with so much enthusiasm…and in short "crowded the mourners" so

hard, I was forced to promise him I would try and do it. **1885** in Lummis *Letters* 267: But when my dog has to go over the range, it strikes me it's rather crowding the mourners. **1912** *DN* III 574: *Crowd the mourners…*To be in a hurry. Used only in the expression "Don't crowd the mourners," *i.e.,* don't be precipitate. **1936** *AS* XI 314.
3. to be remarkable.
1845 in G.W. Harris *High Times* 45: Dick Harlan tells of one [frolic] that took place somewhere in the neighborhood of Stock Creek that "crowds the mourners."

crowder *n. Horse Racing.* a very fast horse.
1839 in *DA*. **1839** *Spirit of Times* (Apr. 20) 78: [The horse] Portsmouth is a "crowder" for two miles at least, and if he had been called upon, could have made time "mighty low down in the forties." **1856** in *DA*.

crowd-pleaser *n.* a weapon that is efficacious in controlling or dispersing crowds.
1983 Neaman & Silver *Kind Words* 169: The most efficacious of these is still the gun, also known as a *crowd pleaser* (U.S., 1970's).

crowfoot *n. Army.* a chevron designating enlisted rank.
[**1935** *Our Army* (June) 12: A man spends his life getting from Buck to Sergeant and his fondest dream meant the day he could crow-foot top-sergeant chevrons on his blouse.] **1967** W. Stevens *Gunner* 183 [ref. to WWII]: Each wore a PFC crowfoot on his arm.

crowhop *v. West.* (of a horse) to jump about stiff-leggedly, as in an attempt to throw a rider.
1922 Rollins *Cowboy* 280 [ref. to 1890's]: A few [horses] might for a while "crowhop," i.e. jump about with arched back and stiffened knees. **1930** Sage *Last Rustler* 191: Some of them bucked pretty hard, while others just crow-hopped around.

Crow Jim *n.* [inversion of JIM CROW] *Jazz.* (see 1964 quot.).
1956 in Tamony *Americanisms* (No. 20) 9: A form of racial bias known in the trade as "Crow Jim." **1964** Gold *Jazz Lexicon* 73: *Crow Jim*. Racial discrimination by Negroes against whites…some currency esp. among white jazzmen since *c.* 1957. **1968** R.B. Browne et al. *Frontiers* 161: Crow-Jim remains a mute point: Shepp and his friends may hire white jazz men but they infer that skin color somehow limits the potential of the whites. **1973** Buerkle & Barker *Bourbon St. Black* 111: A new form—Crow Jim, black rejection of the white musician—became prevalent.

crown *v.* to hit sharply on the head. Now *colloq.* [OEDS exx. are from Eng. dialects.]
*1746, *1866 in *OEDS*. **1878** Willis *Our Cruise* 10: With that he crowned old Tangent with a pan of cracker hash. **1911** Howard *Enemy to Society* 149: Gee! I wanted to crown him with a cuspidor. **1912–14** in E. O'Neill *Lost Plays* 179: Now blow before I crown you! **1918** *Forum* (Dec.) 695: Saay, Corporal,…lemme crown this guy. **1919** T. Kelly *What Outfit?* 123: An M.P. got crowned on the bean. **1920** in De Beck *Google* 93: Cause his watch was outta commish he crowned me. **1925** Dos Passos *Transfer* 320: I crowned one of em good wid a piece of pipe. **1940** Lawes *Meet the Murderer!* 5 [ref. to 1905]: I could crown you with this piece of hardware before you could reach for your gun. **1972** Hannah *Geronimo Rex* 256: I'll crown him. I'll lay some kind of dent in that buckaroo hat for him.

crown jewels *n.pl.* FAMILY JEWELS.
1971 Rader *Govt. Inspected* 123: Coretta the Transsexual once stomped with me…soon after the crown jewels were first dumped into a dustbin.

crow's nest *n.* the upper balcony of a theater.
1965–70 in *DARE*. **1982** L.I. woman, age *ca*29: Why sit in the crow's nest if you can afford the orchestra? **1986** B. Clayton & N. Elliott *Jazz World* 15 [ref. to *ca*1920]: Black people had to sit in what we called the "crow's nest," which were seats way up in the balcony where…you could hardly see the screen.

crowtrack *n.* **1.** *pl.* illegible handwriting.
1875 Hill *Sanctum* 102: Some sort of characters which he intends for certain letters of the English alphabet, and which should never be termed "crow-tracks," for the reason they are not half so symmetrical. **1875,** *ca*1960, **1967–69** in *DARE*.
2. CROWFOOT.
1941 *AS* (Oct.) 164: *Crow Tracks*. Chevrons. **1942** Colby *Army Talk*.

crud *n.* [a semantic extension in Scots dial. of ME *crud* 'curd, curdled matter' (hence, as in *a*1508 quot.) 'clotted or congealed filth'; yet modern U.S. use of *crud* appears to be a back formation from CRUDDY rather than a direct survival; cf. also CRUT]

1.a. disgusting matter; filth; (*specif.*) a deposit, incrustation, or coating of filth, grease, or impurities. [Definition in 1954–60 quot. is overly specific.]

a*1508 in Henryson *Poems & Fables* 159: The crud of my culome [*sc.* fundament], with your teith crakit. [1896–1900** in *DN* II 138: *Crud, n.* Curd. Detroit.] [**1903** *DN* II 350: *Crud, n.* Curdled milk, as in "cruds and whey." Penn[sylvania].] **1943** *AS* (Apr.) 153: *Crud.* Food, usually unpalatable. **1948** J.H. Burns *Lucifer* 99: Consecrated to dust, ashes, and crud! **1950** in *OEDS: Crud,* a slang term referring to an undesirable impurity or foreign material arising in a process. **1954** Ellson *Owen Harding* 22: The food was complete pure crud. **1954–60** *DAS: Crud*…(taboo) Dried semen, as sticks to the body or clothes after sexual intercourse. **1960** Hardy *Wolfpack* 41: There was some crud fouling the injection nozzle, but it's okay now. **1961** Rossen & Carroll *Hustler* (film): Get all this crud out of your system. **1963** Hayden *Wanderer* 240: I'd…try to peel off a few layers of crud. **1963** Davenport *Carmina Archilochi* 12: Slime and crud…Snot. **1966** Rumaker *Stories* 172: It stinks like sneaker crud in here. **1967** Dibner *Admiral* 5: Why must it always be like this on land, filthy and clinging with crud? **1971** *Playboy* (Mar.) 22: He demonstrates his radicalism by calling everything either crap or crud. **1974** Univ. Tenn. grad. student: Deposits on the inside of cooling pipes of nuclear reactors are officially called *crud.* It comes from the name of one particular reactor, the Cross River reactor. It stands for "Cross River Undetermined Deposits." **1980** Ciardi *Browser's Dict.* 47: Am. child's usage *booger*, dirty thing, as snot, toe crud. **1989** *ALF* (NBC-TV): Wipe the crud out of your eyes and wake up!

b. rubbish; arrant nonsense; CRAP.

1951 in Mailer *Ad. for Myself* 129: "What crud," someone muttered. **1951** Leveridge *Walk on the Water* 211: Don't give me that Christian Endeavor crud. **1954** Gaddis *Birdman* 27: Just give me a pencil and turn off the crud. **1959–60** Bloch *Dead Beat* 28: He'd picked up a line of crud…which might go well here. **1961** Granat *Important Thing* 156: I heard a lot of crud, but what's the real story? **1971** Lundwall *Sci. Fiction* 25: Ninety percent of all science fiction is crud, the SF writer Theodore Sturgeon once said; but, on the other hand, ninety percent of *everything* is crud! **1975** Hynek & Vallee *Edge of Reality* 203: You just couldn't take the good [U.F.O.] cases seriously when you saw all this crud, all this noise, all the junk. **1984** "W.T. Tyler" *Shadow Cabinet* 9: It's the holier-than-thou crud that gets me. **1986–91** Hamper *Rivethead* 126: Music…mainly sixties…crud.

c. daylights; stuffing; CRAP.

1958 Frede *Entry E* 77: God, he scared the crud out of me. **1961** Lehman *West Side Story* (film): I'll beat the livin' crud outta ya!

2.a. a despicable person.

1930 in Perelman *Old Gang* 89: How Love Came to Dudley Crud… Dudley Crud, the brilliant young surgeon, was to perform a compound parsimony. **1932** Mankiewicz & Myer *Million Dollar Legs* (film): He'll resent anything I call him. The crud! **1941** Wald, Macauley et al. *Navy Blues* (film): Shut up, you crud! **1945** Laurents *Home of the Brave* 580: He's a first-class crud, anyway. **1947** Heggen & Logan *Mr. Roberts* 421: I don't trust that crud. **1951** W. Williams *Enemy* 149: If those cruds are so hot on us knowing, why don't they come out here? **1953** Freeman *Gobi* (film): You could call it *How I Became a Crud.* **1956** I. Shulman *Good Deeds* 67: The cruds in your house…go around looking at freshmen's cards. **1959** Morrill *Dark Sea Running* 191: It was cruds like you that sold paper-bottomed shoes to the U.S. Army in the Civil War. **1967** Dibner *Admiral* 53: Krueger sent a smashing kick to Wilson's ribs. "That's the down payment, you crud." **1972** N.Y.U. student: David comes off as a real crud in that. **1986–91** Hamper *Rivethead* 81: A guy void of defects mustered no challenge. Send in the cruds.

b. Esp. *Mil.* a habitually unwashed person.

1940 *AS* (Apr.) 212: A "crud" is a fellow who is slovenly in his personal appearance and with his possessions. **1970** Wambaugh *New Centurions* 191: Get the hell out of here, you old crud! **1980** McDowell *Our Honor* 34: There will be no cruds in this platoon…You will shower each night, you will clean your teeth morning and night, and you will shave each morning whether you think you need it or not. *a*1989 C.S. Crawford *Four Deuces* 78: I had given my hands and face a quick wash….I mean, no one wants to be a consummate crud.

3.a. Esp. *Mil.* a hypothetical or unidentified ailment; disease.—often elaborated with *creeping, crawling,* etc.

1932 *AS* VII (Feb.) 232: At Stanford University…*Crud* means illness. "I've got the crud," means "I'm ill." **1951** Mauldin *Up Front* (film) [ref. to WWII]: I gotta get him outa here! He's got the crud! **1951–52** Frank *Hold Back Night* 18: Mackenzie spoke of malaria, and dysentery, and jungle rot, and the crud. **1958** Cooley *Run for Home* 417 [ref. to

*ca*1922]: It don't itch or nuttin', but I want to get it looked at just in case I got some sorta crud. **1958** Frede *Entry E* 27: You got the crud or something, Bogard? **1961** R. L. Scott *Boring Holes* 108 [ref. to 1942]: Everybody who came there was doomed to stagnate and die of something they called familiarly, "Karachi krud." **1962** Tregaskis *Vietnam Diary* 27: Malaria, dengue, and all the other tropical cruds we encountered in the…South Pacific. **1966** Derrig *Pride of Green Berets* 206: If your resistance gets low, you sure as the devil will pick up some kind of crud. **1969** Thompson *They Shoot Horses* 153: Maybe the Mongolian crud. **1970** Sugarman & Freeman *Serenity* 23: He continued to use the phrase "creeping crud" to describe the crawling, uncomfortable, all-pervasive feeling of the anxiety within him. **1973** Hirschfeld *Victors* 17: It's the tropics is what it is, gives you everything from a dripping cock to the Mongolian crud. **1966–80** McAleer & Dickson *Unit Pride* 172: It's a wonder they didn't all die of the creeping crud. **1993** Knoxville, Tenn., woman, age *ca*50: I'm still fighting this crud [*sc.* a bad cold].

b. Specif. Esp. *Mil.* any of various usu. ulcerous skin diseases.—usu. constr. with *the.*

1945 *Reader's Digest* (Apr.) 109: We…have some cases of malaria, dengue and dysentery. We also have what the men [in the Pacific] call "crud," a skin outbreak like ringworm caused by excessive perspiration and too few chances to bathe. **1945** *Time* (Aug. 13) 76: "Jungle rot," "New Guinea crud" or "the creeping crud" are U.S. servicemen's names for any & every kind of tropical skin disease. **1942–48** in *So. Folk. Qly.* XIII (1949) 201: The *crud,* an all-inclusive term for athlete's foot, the hives, impetigo, ring-worm, etc. **1951** D. Duncan *This is War!* [ref. to WWII]: The mildew which ruined equipment; the crud which cut like acid into our flesh and stank like death. **1958** Craven & Cate *AAF in WWII* VII 448 [ref. to 1943]: Fungus infections ("Guinea Crud," "Jungle Rot"). **1973** Huggett *Body Count* 382: The cut wasn't so bad as the inevitable Jungle-crud infection which got into it. **1981** C. Nelson *Picked Bullets Up* 276: Scungy skin diseases…ringworm, eczema, creeping Congo crud, etc.

c. Specif. a venereal disease, esp. gonorrhea.—usu. constr. with *the.*

1951 Willingham *Gates of Hell* 176: He later discovered he had gotten a case of a social disease, the creeping crud. **1958** Plagemann *Steel Cocoon* 68 [ref. to WWII]: Jesus, Doc, even if I get the clap it was worth it. But have you sure as hell got my names down in the book? If I get the old crud I sure as hell don't want to lose pay. **1954–60** *DAS* 132: *Crud*…Any venereal disease, esp. syphilis. Orig. Army use since c1925. **1968** Tauber *Sunshine Soldiers* 36: Many of the men look somewhat vacant as the lecturer discusses "venereal diseases" until he clarifies the subject by mentioning that they are also called "the clap," "the crud," "the crabs" and such. **1975** De Mille *Smack Man* 79: Maybe some john got a case of the galloping crud from one of them. **1984** Riggan *Free Fire* 124: Hey, Doc! I think I got the crud from babysan here.

d. Specif. Esp. *Mil.* diarrhea or dysentery.—usu. constr. with *the.*

1952 Randolph & Wilson *Down in Holler* 237: Crud (krud): n.…Here in the Ozarks some hillfolk say crud when they mean hives, others tell me it means diarrhea. **1952** Uris *Battle Cry* 235 [ref. to WWII]: Wish my gut would stop jumping. Crapped nine times tonight. Musta got the crud. **1952** Randolph & Wilson *Down in Holler* 237: In Fayetteville, Ark., it is said that when a man has the *crud* "everything he eats turns to dung." **1957** E. Brown *Locust Fire* 117 [ref. to WWII]: He had caught all of it in his time…Everything. From the rice-paddy rot to the crawling crud. **1962** Gallant *Valor's Side* 304 [ref. to WWII]: "He acts like a sick cow. Down on his side and has vomited in the new slit trench"…"Maybe it's the crud." **1966** Shaw & Spiegl *Scouse* 56: I got Bombay crud. *I am suffering from looseness of the bowels.* **1971** N.Y.U. student: The *crud* means dysentery. **1985** *Maledicta* VI 99: The [Ohio] student slang term, *Chinese creeping crud*…suggests the…unexpected onset of diarrhea.

crud *interj.* [fr. the n., mainly euphem. for SHIT or CRAP] (used to express disappointment, exasperation, or the like).

1946 J.H. Burns *Gallery* 189: Ah, crud. They'll do as they're tole. **1955–57** Felder *Collegiate Slang* 4: Oh! Crud!—an exclamation of disgust. **1968** C. Victor *Sky Burned* 66: "Crud," said Private Cummings as he threw off his pack and sat down. **1978** Buchanan *Shining Season* 128: Oh crud, Coach…We're all wrung out. *a*1988 D. Smith *Firefighters* 164: Oh, crud, here I am trapped.

crudball *n.* a filthy or offensive person; SCUZZBALL.

1968 in B. Edelman *Dear Amer.* 178: I feel like a crudball leaving my men. **1986** R. Walker *AF Wives* 41: That crudball Henderson.

crudball *adj.* filthy; disgusting.

1970 Thackrey *Thief* 245: And I was fucking well tired of living in crud-ball hotels.

crud detail *n.* Esp. *Mil.* a demeaning or objectionable task.

1957 Myrer *Big War* 191 [ref. to WWII]: He…gives me every crud detail he possibly can. **1964** Pearl *Stockade* 27: How come I get stuck with your squad on that crud detail, White? *a***1986** E. Bombeck, in *NDAS*: It's in your ballpark, since you love the crud detail.

cruddy *adj.* **1.** filthy. [The 1877 quot., by far the earliest available, sugg. this sense arose in Hiberno-E dial.; it is not of Celtic orig. Cf. CRUD.]

1877 Pinkerton *Molly Maguires* 157: Sure an' you needn't take me for a *gomersal*, *cruddy* from the bogs! *Ibid.* 285: An' is it yourself that ye are, or some *cruddy gorsoon*, right from the auld sod? *a***1949** D. Levin *Mask of Glory* 150: We get the cruddy end of the stick again. **1953** Felsen *Street Rod* 38: He looked around the inside of his car with less than pleasure. It was pretty cruddy. **1957** E. Brown *Locust Fire* 89 [ref. to 1944]: "How was it in Assam?" "Muddy and cruddy," he said. **1960** in Rosset *Evergreen Reader* 326: The little man with the cruddy vest opened his eyes. **1963** Coon *Short End* 22: He was pretty cruddy. Not exactly personally. It was his clothes.

2. contemptible or despicable; wretched; bad.

1947 Heggen & Logan *Mr. Roberts* 419 [ref. to WWII]: Look at that cruddy island. **1950** G. Legman, in *Neurotica* (Autumn) 12: Please do not patronize our cruddy competitors. **1956** Poe *Attack* (film) [ref. to 1944]: Them cruddy Krauts. **1959** in A. Sexton *Letters* 63: Got an acceptance from *Accent*…two old rather cruddy poems. **1960** Duncan *Salute It* 21: And it's a pretty cruddy deal, if you ask me, taking all the doors down. Pretty cruddy. **1965** Hersey *Too Far to Walk* 30: You're a Gutwillig boy and don't know about all that cruddy bunch? Those dormitory Maoists? **1970** Cortina *Slain Warrior* 133: I never hung around with them cruddy bastards who ain't got no backbone and no balls to do nothin'. **1982** Castoire & Posner *Gold Shield* 161: Why were you so cruddy to me before? **1986** Coonts *Intruder* 67: The weather gets cruddy.

crudhead *n.* CRAPHEAD.

1984 Hindle *Dragon Fall* 55: This scuzzball crudhead did!

crud-sucking *adj.* SCUM-SUCKING.

1966 Braly *Cold* 65: Stop shoving, you crud-sucking slobs!

crud up *v.* to make CRUDDY; (*hence*) to spoil.

1963 Rubin *Sweet Daddy* 75: More horse shit that society…wants to crud themselves up with. **1968** Myrer *Eagle* 622: They only crudded everything all up with sentimental notions of pedestals and undying devotion. **1968** S. Ross *Hang-Up* 115: "Wouldn't you like shoes with that dress?"…"No. That'd crud everything up."

crud work *n.* menial labor or drudgery.

1959 on *Golden Age of TV* (A & E TV) (1987): Why does a guy like you give up pool playing and do crud work?

crudzoid *n.* *Stu.* a contemptible person.

1984 Hindle *Dragon Fall* 23: You little crudzoid!

cruel *adv.* exceedingly.

1849 Melville *White Jacket* 133: *Dunderfunk*; a cruel nice dish as ever man put into him.

crufty *adj.* [infl. by *crusty*, CRUDDY] disgusting or inferior; CRUDDY.

1983 Naiman *Computer Dict.* 37: *Crufty*…Poorly built…Also, disgusting—especially to the touch. **1990** P. Dickson *Slang!* 73: *Crufty.* Bad, poorly built, yucky.

cruise *n.* **1.** Orig. *Naut.* a walk or trip, esp. for the sake of amusement; stroll.

*****1808** in Wetherell *Adventures* 167: An hours cruise among the Girls in Petit Givet. **1821** Waln *Hermit in Phila.* 30: Come, boys, for a *cruise?* **1845** Corcoran *Pickings* 156: I was on a bit of a cruise…your honour. **1848** in *AS* X (1935) 40: *Going on a cruise.* About to ride or walk. **1852** Hazen *Five Years* 352: Rather too long a cruise, to go on foot. **1855** Brougham *Chips* 306: You must take a cruise about this here city by yourself. **1887** Davis *Sea-Wanderer* 302: Ben Barney and I were on a cruise uptown in a Madison avenue 'bus.

2. *Navy & USMC.* a term of enlistment or tour of duty whether on land or sea.

1884 Blanding *Sailor Boy* 9 [ref. to 1862]: What say you boys to our taking a cruise?…Let's enlist in the navy…for a term of service, or during the war. **1899** Cullen *Tales* 111: He concluded that a three-year cruise in the navy was about as good as anything else. **1918** *Lit. Digest* (Sept.

28) 45: A Cruise Among the "Leather-Necks" On the Firing Line. **1918** Ruggles *Navy Explained* 142: The term of all enlistments is four years unless a man is doing a minority cruise (until he is twenty-one) or the duration of the war. **1924** *Amer. Leg. Wkly.* (Jan. 18) 23: Down in the marine barracks at Portsmouth, Virginia, there's a leather-neck…doing a second cruise. **1928** *Our Army* (Nov.) [back cover]: [The sailor's] "hitch" is a "cruise" and his "bunk" is a "hammock." **1945** Monk *Ribbon & Star* 116: How many years you done on your cruise? **1947** W. M. Camp *S.F.* IX: I returned to California after my first "cruise" in the Marines. **1964** Rhodes *Chosen Few* 14: You're going to be the assistant DI on this cruise, right? **1965** Hardman *Chaplains Raid* 31: They're Navy Reserves on the base for a six weeks' summer cruise.

3. *Homosex.* a significant glance or other expression of interest made toward a prospective sexual partner.

1966 Herbert *Fortune* 15: Look at the girls givin' the new boy a fast cruise. **1978** R. Price *Ladies' Man* 240: A long-haired guy in a leather jacket hooked glances with me…"Your first cruise." *Ibid.* 244: Most of the guys passing by gave him a heavy cruise.

4. an act of CRUISING (CRUISE, *v.*, 3.a.).

1989 *Dream St.* (NBC-TV): We're takin' a cruise. Wanta come?

cruise *v.* **1.a.** (of a prostitute) to solicit customers by walking the streets; (*hence*, esp. in homosexual use) to look for sexual partners, as in a bar. Also transf.

*****1674** in Duffett *Burlesque Plays* 34: Little cruising punk and first-class Harlot. **1865** *Rogues & Rogueries of N.Y.* 58: Mary French…is known in Boston by the name of Mary Floyd…She is in the house all day, and "cruises" at night. **1869** "G. Ellington" *Women of N.Y.* 624: These wretched girls…go nightly "cruising" upon Broadway. **1925** McAlmon *Silk Stockings* 51: We spent more time makin' up to go out cruisin' than we did in makin' up for the show. **1927** Rosanoff *Manual of Psych.* (ed. 6) 208: *Cruising*, going out in search of a [homosexual] partner. **1928** *N.Y. Times Mag.* (Nov. 11) 21: A driver…looking for fares is said to be "cruising." **1945** in T. Williams *Letters* 159: She could at least tell him where to cruise. **1946–51** Motley *We Fished* 366: A few fairies cruise in there. **1958** Talsman *Gaudy Image* 51: She's probably cruising on Decatur. **1962** T. Berger *Reinhart* 122: You give in like that and they won't cruise all week. **1973** I. Reed *La. Red* 126: Women rarely cruise or rape. **1976** Haseltine & Yaw *Woman Doctor* 157: If there was prostitution, there wasn't much cruising.

b. to cruise in (an area). [In *****1803 quot., simply 'to stroll'.]

[*****1803** in Wetherell *Adventures* 92: We cruised the Market up and down.] **1872** Crapsey *Nether Side of N.Y.* 143: The chief difference between the inmates [of the brothels] and the street-walkers is that the former do not cruise the streets to entice strangers to their dens. **1943** in T. Williams *Letters* 89: I go out and cruise the Palisades and fetch in a pretty little belle. **1946** J.H. Burns *Gallery* 157: Done any one nice lately? What a town to cruise this is.

c. Esp. *Prost. & Homosex.* to seek, watch, or flirt with (a prospective sexual partner).

1925 McAlmon *Silk Stockings* 51: This show ain't to be used for cruising your trade while you're on stage at least. **1927** [Fliesler] *Anecdota* 145: Two friends, one of them the owner of a car, used to go "chippy-cruising" every night. **1943** in Legman *Limerick* 96: There was a young pansy named Gene/Who cruised a sadistic Marine. **1946** J.H. Burns *Gallery* 215: He was going out into the streets of Algiers to cruise up a little lovin'. **1949** *Gay Girl's Guide* 5: *Cruise*—As a transitive verb, to seek to catch the eye of someone in whom one is interested, after placing oneself in his vicinity. **1953** Brossard *Saboteurs* 117: Dead-faced young government clerks expressed the deepest depravity by cruising other young government clerks. **1957** Murtagh & Harris *First Stone* 4: Although there are individual streetwalkers who cruise their tricks in other places, there are four principal areas that are known as street-walker hangouts…. **1960** Bannon *Journey* 107: She's been cruising you like mad since we came in…Looking you over, sizing you up. **1967** Rechy *Numbers* 117: What if they're cruising each other—and not me! **1985** J. Dillinger *Adrenaline* 247: He probably just cruised the wrong guy. **1992** *Herman's Head* (Fox-TV): We can sneak out and cruise chicks.

d. *Und.* to look for potential victims (in).

1962 T. Berger *Reinhart in Love* 124: I could cruise a few saloons, but I tell you, don't look for much.

2. *Naut. & Und.* to travel and associate (with).

1847 Downey *Cruise of the Portsmouth* 11: Why…you see, when the old *States* come home, I was on a spree and used to cruise with the Sailors. **1851** [G. Thompson] *Jack Harold* 60: The pal I cruis'd with did to me unfaithful prove.

3.a. Esp. *Stu.* to amuse oneself by driving or riding in a car, esp. in a small group, for the purpose of drinking beer, picking up girls, etc.

1957 M. Shulman *Rally* 59: Let's do some cruisin'. **1970** in S. King *Christine* 67: I would buy me a Mercury/And cruise up and down this road. **1979** Gram *Blvd. Nights* 42: We've cruised enough tonight, Raymond. **1983** *Portfolio* (WKGN radio) (Mar. 13): He'd written this tune about teenage cruisers in Seattle **1986** *USA Today* (June 21) 1: Teen Cruisin' Gears Up For Summer.

b. Esp. *Stu.* to leave.

1980 Birnbach *Preppy Hndbk.* 233: Exit Lines…"Let's cruise."… "We're out of here." **1981** Eble *Campus Slang* (Oct.) 3: *Cruise*—to leave. **1985** Hartman et al. *Pee-Wee's Big Adventure* (film): Let's say we cruise, dudes. **1986** *St. Elsewhere* (NBC-TV): "Let's cruise." "Are you kidding? We can't just get up and walk out of here."

4. *Sports.* to win easily.

1984 *N.Y. Post* (Dec. 12) 78: Brooklyn's Roger McCready scored 19 points…as the Eagles…cruised.

¶ In phrase:

¶ **cruisin' for a bruisin'** [or **bruise**] inviting a beating; heading for trouble.

1947 *ATS* (Supp.) 4: *Cruisin' for a bruisin'*, riding for a fall. **1960** Bluestone *Cully* 11: You are definitely cruisin' for a bruise, Private. **1966** Herbert *Fortune* 18: You're cruisin' for a bruisin', bitch! **1972** 7-Up TV Commercial (June): In those days [1957], if a guy let on he was even *thinkin'* of that kind of stuff he'd 'a' been cruisin' for a bruisin'. **1975** Univ. Tenn. student: You're cruisin' for a bruisin' and you'll be hurtin' for certain.

cruisemobile *n. Stu.* a stylish automobile that is especially suitable for CRUISING (CRUISE, *v.*, 3.a.).

1978 *UTSQ* (Nov. 29): Automobile…ride, wheels, cruisemobile. **1982** Pond *Valley Girls' Guide* 55: *Cruisemobile*—A totally cool car, like a 'Vette.

cruiser *n.* a streetwalker.

1868 *Detective's Manual* 148: On nearing the cruiser, he hailed her thus. **1869** "G. Ellington" *Women of N.Y.* 298: They differ…in being what is called "street-walkers" or "cruisers." **1902** Hapgood *Autobiog. of Thief* 35 [ref. to ca1882]: Even the Bowery "cruisers" (street-walkers) carried [silk handkerchiefs]. **1910** Hapgood *Types from Streets* 139: There are, roughly speaking, two metropolitan classes of these miserable beings—the Tenderloin Girl and the Bowery "Cruiser." **1958** S.H. Adams *Tenderloin* 12: Its…sexual advertisements…would have made a West Third Street cruiser blush. **1972** R. Wilson *Forbidden Words* 81: In New York…a *heavy cruiser* is a case-hardened and tough-looking prostitute.

cruise widow *n. Navy.* the wife or sweetheart of a sailor away at sea.

1987 Nichols & Tillman *Yankee Sta.* 43: The women left behind at Miramar or Lemoore—"cruise widows"—had their own effect on morale.

cruisy *adj. Homosex.* (see 1949 quot.).

1949 *Gay Girl's Guide* 6: *Cruisy*—N.Y.C.…adjective for any kind of place in which it's fun to cruise or fool around. **1962–65** Cavan *Liquor License* 177: Some homosexual bars are known as "cruisy gay bars." **1971–74** in *West. Folk.* XXXIII (1974) 218: *Cruisy:* Adjective describing a place to find sexual partners. **1975** in M. Levine *Gay Men* 160: One of the "cruisiest" spots within one hundred miles of Los Angeles. **1985** J. Dillinger *Adrenaline* 69: This area starts to get real cruisy about this time of day.

cruit *n. Mil.* a recruit; (hence, esp. in mod. use) an inexperienced private soldier.

1897 *Cosmopolitan* (Feb.) 351: Now you see that black feller just turnin' his head; well, he's a 'cruit, and he thinks I been abusin' him for a long time…Says I to that 'cruit, "Blame yer eyes, I don't have to get along wid you; you have to get along wid me. Understand?" **1941** Kendall *Army & Navy Slang* 4: *Croot*…recruit, also known as a yearo, rookie, trainee, draftee, selectee, bimbo, bozo, dude, John dogface, bucko, poggie. **1950** L. Brown *Iron City* 216: You can tell all the 'cruits that you are an *old* soldier. **1960** Bluestone *Cully* 55: Just one less thing to worry about, 'cruit. **1962** Killens *Heard the Thunder* 11 [ref. to WWII]: Anything a poor Crute's heart could desire. **1973** Karlin, Paquet & Rottmann *Free Fire Zone* 4: You got a ways yet, Cruit.

cruitie *n.* CRUIT.

1847 Downey *Portsmouth* 136: Sergeant Slim…"guessed"…that the

heads we saw, were those of the "Cruities" who were to take our Ship while we were to go home in the *Brooklyn.*

cruller *n. N.E.* the head.

1942 Goldin et al. *DAUL* 53: *Cruller.* The head. **1948** McHenry & Myers *Home Is Sailor* 112: The cruller's a little soft.…A cop came down on it with a stick. **1960** in *DAS.* **1967** Weiss & Lawrence *Easy Come* (film): I shall be forced to clobber you on the cruller. **1974** Radano *Cop Stories* 37: Mack beat the cruller off the bum.

crumb *n.* **1.** the head.

1832 *Spirit of Times* (Feb. 4) 1: Hit him in the bread basket—paste up his eyes—give it to him in the crumb.

2. a body louse.

1863 in Norton *Army Letters* 137: The other night I was sitting by the fire smoking a cigar when I felt something twitch at my pants' leg. I looked down and there was one of the "crumbs" with a straw in his mouth, standing on his hind legs and working his claws round like a crab on a line. **ca1885** A.C. Stearns *Co. K* 225: Some of the boys discovered that pest of the soldier "Army Crums." **1898** *Scribner's Mag.* XXIII 440: Just then I felt something crawling on my neck. It was a crumb. **1905** Sinclair *Jungle* 256: He even scrubbed his head with sand, and combed what the men called "crumbs" out of his…hair. **1916** Cary *Venery* I 58: *Crumb*—…A crab louse. **1919** Streeter *Same Old Bill* 49: He might think he was a crum some night and try to choke somebody. **1929** *AS* IV (June) 339: *Crumb.* Body vermin. **1930** "D. Stiff" *Milk & Honey* 195: There are crums upon the ceiling, on the side walls and the floor,/They are drowning in the toilet crying, "Pull, boys, for the shore." **ca1940** in Botkin *Treas. Amer. Folk.* 524: A crumb is what you might call a louse.

3.a. a filthy person.

1914 *DN* IV 150: *Crumb.* A dirty sailor. **1931** *AS* VI (Aug.) 437: *Crum, n.* A filthy person. **1963** D. Tracy *Brass Ring* 30: The man who evaded his daily shower…risked being labelled a crumb. **ca1930-73** E. Mackin *Suddenly Didn't Want to Die* 211 [ref. to 1918]: Hey, crumbs! Why don't you wash your dirty necks?

b. an obnoxious, useless, or despicable person; (*occ.*) a worthless item.

1919 *DN* V 66: *Crumb*, a small insignificant person. Sometimes used in disgust. "You poor *crumb.*" New Mexico. **1919** in *OEDS*: A couple of crumbs want to kill you. **1922** Colton & Randolph *Rain* 75: There was I jumping with the shakes…just because that dismal crumb Davidson wouldn't let me go to Apia. **1923** *N.Y. Times* (Oct. 7) VIII 4: *Crumb*—A very bad act or actor. **1927** Faulkner *Mosquitoes* 257: I won't hardly see him, he's such a damn crum. **1928** Hecht & MacArthur *Front Page* 457: You cheap crumbs have been making a fool out of me long enough. **1937** Hellman *Dead End* (film): Hey, crumb! Duck! **1944** H. Brown *Walk in the Sun* 128: He's a crumb, ain't he, Judson? **1953** Cain *Galatea* 205: You lying crumb. **1955** O'Connor *Last Hurrah* 321: There's no use giving anything classy to little crumbs like this and her old man. **1965** Bonham *Durango St.* 71: You're going to rehabilitate this crumb, eh? **1968** L.J. Davis *Whence All Had Fled* 85: Why did we ever have a crumb like Morris for a son? **1969** Maitland *Only War We've Got* 58: Get this crum outa here! **1983** *Judge Dredd* (Nov.) [14]: Where would a small-time crumb like Monks get access to this kind of information?

c. a cruel or despicable person; no-good; LOUSE.

1970 La Motta, Carter & Savage *R. Bull* 26: C'mon, you crumbs, which one is Curly? **1976** *Esquire* (Sept.) 70: What I'm talking about is your Unmitigated Crumb, your really *inexplicably rotten* person. **1982** Castoire & Posner *Gold Shield* 252: I really believed the conniving crumb.

4. the penis.

1927 in E. Wilson *Twenties* 365: The clap…What's the matter with you? I was just thinkin' that must have been some puddle where you dropped your crumb!

5. *Black E.* a small child; CRUMB-CRUSHER.

1963 Williamson *Hustler!* 101: I didn't want to have no kids. I said, "We ain't able to take care of no crumbs around here!"

crumb *v.* **1.** to spoil.—also constr. with *up.*

1916 Thompson *Round Levee* 45: "To crumb a parole" is to forfeit it in some way. **1918** in *AS* (Oct. 1933) 26: *Crumb The Deal.* Spoil a plan. **1928** *AS* III (Feb.) 220: *Crum.* One who backs out, or crums the deal, or spoils the party. **1951** Bowers *Mob* (film): You had to crumb things up and pick my wife. **1962** Crump *Killer* 292: I'm going to…crumb this deal. **1987** Mamet *House of Games* (film): You crumbed the play.

2. Esp. *Navy.* to clean up; wash.—usu. constr. with *up.* Also trans.

1919 *Our Navy* (Oct.) 18: Scrub the old packet up, flop your coaling clothes out in front of the salt water hose and generally "crumb up." **1926** *AS* I (Dec.) 651: *Crum Up.* Washing one's under clothing. **1929** *AS* III (June) 339: *Crum Up.* To clean up. **1939** O'Brien *One-Way Ticket* 100 [ref. to 1920's]: Snap out of it and get this place crumbed up. *Ibid.* 116: Tony, don't you think you ought to kind of crumb up a little? **1969** Bosworth *Love Affair* 97 [ref. to ca1923]: So they decide to crumb up the joint for inspection. *ca*1930–73 E. Mackin *Suddenly Didn't Want to Die* 170 [ref. to 1918]: C'mon, let's police this place up....Crumb this place!

3. to make filthy.—constr. with *up.*

1961 *Leave It to Beaver* (ABC-TV): I'm trying to crum it up so it'll look like the old one.

crumb *interj.* (used to express mild annoyance); phooey.

1957 Kohner *Gidget* 96: Oh, crum, I forgot my bag. **1960** Stolz *Barkham St.* 5: "Oh, crums," said Edward in a gloomy voice. **1966** Harrington *Swinger* 27: Oh, crumb. Let's dance then. **1972** M. Rodgers *Freaky Fri.* 58: Oh ook, oh cripes, oh crum, what to do now?

crumb boss *n. West.* a janitor or cleanup man.

1926 *AS* I (Dec.) 651: *Crum Boss.* A janitor in a camp "bunk-house." **1927** *DN* V 443: *Crum boss,* n. The janitor of a bunk house. **1929** *AS* (June) 339: *Crum Boss.* Camp porter in Western construction camps. **1930** "D. Stiff" *Milk & Honey* 203: *Crum boss*—Man who builds fires in the bunk houses. **1942** *AS* (Dec.) 221: *Crumb Boss.* Insulting name for a *bullcook.* **1964** *Social Problems* XI 376: The Skid Row term for the post [of night superintendent at a rescue mission] was "crumb boss," so named because the person had charge of delousing operations. **1970** Boatright & Owens *Derrick* 159: They had crumb bosses. He tended to all the making up the beds and everything, putting on the clean sheets whenever they had them.

crumb-bum *n.* a filthy, worthless, or contemptible person.

1934 Appel *Brain Guy* 138: None of the leaders were there, only a dozen or so of the crumbums and chisellers. **1944** Brooks *Brick Foxhole* 79: "Now listen to me, you crumb-bums," said the mess sergeant. **1946** H.A. Smith *Rhubarb* 95: "That crumb bum!" he said. **1946** J. Adams *Gags* 18: Toots Shor has called me a crum-bum and many other names. **1950** *Sat. Eve. Post* (Mar. 18) 36: Them crumbums are a part of every water front. **1953** Eyster *Customary Skies* 28: Don't wait for those crum bums. **1971** *Qly. Jour. Studies on Alcohol* XXXII 725: *Crumb bum.* Any derelict who appears to have lice on his person. **1979** Kunstler *Wampanaki Tales* 10: "We're the worst there is." "Crumb-bums!"

crumbcatcher *n.* **1.** a comb. *Joc.*

1942 *ATS* 78.

2. CRUMB-CRUSHER, 2.

1962 in B. Jackson *In the Life* 162: I got a dough-roll (wife) and two crumb-catchers (children), you know.

crumb-chaser *n. Logging.* (see quot.).

1958 McCulloch *Woods Words* 42: *Crumb chaser*—A cook's helper.

crumb-crusher *n. Black E.* **1.** *pl.* the teeth, jaws, or lips. Also **crumb cruncher.**

1940 in Driggs & Lewine *Black Beauty* 80: Our Meals are a Solid Sender Right in the Groove....We'll swing your crumb-crushers right in the groove. **1942** *Pittsburgh Courier* (Jan. 17) 7: *Crumb crushers*—Teeth. **1944** Calloway *Hepster's Dict.*: *Crumb crushers*...Teeth. **1944** Burley *Hndbk. Jive* 136: *Crumb crunchers*—The teeth, molars. **1957** Simmons *Corner Boy* 195: Just keep your crumb crushers shut, Monk said. **1971** Dahlskog *Dict.* 16: *Crumbcrushers*...The teeth. **1972** Claerbaut *Black Jargon* 62: *Crumb crushers* n. lips.

2. a baby or small child. Also **crumb cruncher.**

1959 in R. Gold *Jazz Talk* 62: *Crumb crusher:* baby. **1966** Ward *Happy Ending* 11: I never heard your shedding such tragic tears when your own lil crumb-crushers suffered through fatherless periods! **1970** Major *Afro-Amer. Sl.: Crumb cruncher*...a child, an infant. **1970** *N.Y. Times* (Dec. 27) 19: Once upon a time, in the year 1970, there was an old woman who lived in a shoe, who had so many crumcrushers, she didn't know what to do. Especially around bedtime, when they liked to dig music. **1972** Claerbaut *Black Jargon* 62: *Crumb cruncher* n. a child; an infant. **1978** Dills *CB* (ed. 4) 29: *Crumb Crushers*...Children.

crumb-grabber *n.* CRUMB-CRUSHER, 2.

1962 IUFA *Folk Speech:* Term for children *Crumb grabber.*

crumb hunt *n. Army.* (see quots.).

1941 *AS* (Oct.) 164: *Crumb Hunt.* Kitchen inspection. **1944** *N.Y. Times Mag.* (Sept. 17) 32: *Crumb Hunt.* Kitchen inspection by a mess officer.

crumb joint *n.* a filthy lodging house or other establishment.

1936 Mackenzie *Living Rough* 116: Where are you going to flop—in some crumb joint or some mission?

crumbo *n.* CRUMB, 3.

1937 in D. Runyon *More Guys* 99: He is regarded as...a crumbo around the race tracks. **1960** in *DAS.* **1983** *Judge Dredd* (Nov.) (unp.): Who's that crumbo in the cab?

crumb roll *n.* a bedroll.

1918 *DN* V 24: *Crumb-roll,* n. A bed roll; sometimes a bed. Etymology obvious. Woodsmen; ranchmen. **1930** Irwin *Tramp & Und. Sl.: Crum Roll.*—A bed roll or "balloon." **1980** *CBS Mystery Theater* (CBS-Radio) (May 14): I got my own crumb-roll and I'll doss down in my wagon.

crumb-snatcher *n. Esp. Black E.* CRUMB-CRUSHER, 2.

1958 in R. Gold *Jazz Talk* 62: *A crumb snatcher:* a baby. **1959–60** R. Reisner *Jazz Titans* 153: *Crumbsnatcher:* child. **1962** H. Simmons *On Eggshells* 160: All the crumb-snatchers...looked at the movie houses with bulging eyes. **1972** Bunker *No Beast* 253: I've got an old lady and crumb snatchers. **1973–76** J. Allen *Assault* 158: She could go, yeah, and hurt me enough; but if she had took one of the crumb snatchers, then it really would have been something. **1977** Univ. Tenn. student: My little brother's still at the crumbsnatcher stage. **1967–80** Folb *Runnin' Lines* 233: *Crumbsnatcher.* Baby. **1986** Univ. Tenn. grad. student: *Crumbsnatcher* means *rug rat.* *a*1986 D. Tate *Bravo Burning* 42: I...got married and had some li'l crumbsnatchers.

crumb up see CRUMB, *v.*

crummy *n.* **1.** a louse; CRUMB.

1863 in Johns *49th Mass.* 86: Hunting seams and hems of garments for "crummies" and showing *them* no quarter, is an occupation that... genius...cannot invest with the beautiful.

2. *R.R.* a caboose.

1916 *Editor* XLIII (Mar. 25) 343: Crummy, hack, dog house, van, caboose. **1926** *AS* I (Dec.) 651: *Crummy.* A caboose. **1927** *AS* (June) 388: A caboose is called a *crummy,* from the fact that in the early days of the *boomer* railroader, cabooses were cursed with *crums* (lice). **1929** *Bookman* (July) 524: G'wan back to the crummy and bury your head! **1930** "D. Stiff" *Milk & Honey* 203: *Crummy*...the caboose on a train. **1934** *AS* (Feb.) 73: *Crummy.* Caboose. This name is applied because of the vermin that sometimes infest the caboose. **1935** E. Anderson *Hungry Men* 194: Catch her back toward the crumby, though, 'cause there's always a bunch of empties up forward. **1937** *AS* (Apr.) 154: *Crummy.* Caboose. **1952** in Fenner *Throttle* 16: I could see Whitey Jones, our rear-end brakie, working forward from the crummy. **1968** Spradley *Drunk* 116: "Crummies," or cabooses, are often kept heated for those who travel in them at the end of the train. **1976** Hayden *Voyage* 456: Tell him Georgie Argall's waitin' ta see him back in th' crummy. **1982** D.A. Harper *Good Company* 9: They ride in the crummy.

3. *Logging.* a railroad car, truck, or bus used to transport logging crews to and from a work site.

1946 in *DARE.* **1958** McCulloch *Woods Words* 43: *Crummy*...applied first to a closed box car used to haul men to work out in the woods, later applied to a closed-in truck or bus used for the same purpose. **1963–64** Kesey *Great Notion* 335: Anybody want to try to take a crummy up to Pacific Camp or Feeny Creek? **1975** *Sing Out!* (July) 8: Here comes the crummy carrying two cabooses. **1979** Toelken *Dyn. of Folklore* 55: *Crummy* the crew van or truck that carries loggers back and forth to their jobs.

crummy *adj.* **1.a.** infested with lice; verminous.

***1859** Hotten *Slang Dict.* 27: *Crummy-doss,* a lousy or filthy bed. **1863** in Wightman *To Ft. Fisher* 99: One of the sergeants with whom I bunked was (not to put too fine a point on it) *crumbie.* ***1891** *F & H* II: *Crummy*...(thieves' and soldiers').—Lousy. **1907** *Reader* (Sept.) 344: They call me Crummy Collins, because I got crumbs when I first took on. Crumbs? Why lice—graybacks. **1918** *DN* V 24: *Crummy,* adj. Full of, infested with, body-lice. Lumbermen. **1919** Hinman *Ranging in France* 239: You lay down on your straw tick/That's so crumby it crawls. **1928** Bodenheim *Georgie May* 40: Dopey ses youah gettin' crummy. *ca*1940 in Botkin *Treas. Amer. Folk.* 524: In Bunyan's day the camps was crummy, the bunks was crummy, and the men were so used to being crummy they wouldn't of knowed what to do without 'em. **1943** J. Mitchell *McSorley's* 34: You may get up stiff, but you won't get up crummy. **1960** Krueger *St. Patrick's Bn.* 17: My guess is, you're so crummy they none of them couldn't look at you twice without vomiting.

b. filthy.

***1859** (quot. at (a), above). ***1889** Barrère & Leland *Dict. Slang* I 283: *Crummy* (army), dirty; applied amongst soldiers to a man's appearance. **1919** Piesbergen *Aero Squadron* 61: The barracks looked crummy. ***1925** in Fraser & Gibbons *Soldier & Sailor Wds.* 68 [ref. to WWI]:

Crummy: Dirty (Navy). **1931** *AS* VI (Aug.) 437: *Crummy,* adj. Filthy. **1940** Burnett *High Sierra* 35: I guess we look kind of crummy. We been fishing all day. **1953** R. Wright *Outsider* 98: Kind of crummy here, but the gals are nice. **1972** Wambaugh *Blue Knight* 153: I almost expected the second story to have a dirt floor, the place was so crummy. **1983** Stapleton *30 Yrs.* 195: One guy…scooped out the spaghetti with his filthy hands…They were appalled, he was so crummy.

c. infected; diseased.

1917 in K. Morse *Letters* 32: Outside! You're one of the crumby ones!

2. bad; inferior; unpleasant; LOUSY; (*hence*) (used as an intensive). Also adv. [The sense intended in 1903 quot. is not clear; prob. a sense of **(1)**, above, is meant.]

[**1903** *Pedagog. Sem.* X 373: Back to the breadbox, you're crumby.] **1915** [Swartwood] *Choice Slang* 46: *Crummy stunt*…A mean trick. **1921** E. O'Neill *Hairy Ape* 213: I'll cut yer guts out for a nickel, yuh lousy boob, yuh dirty, crummy, muck-eatin' son of a —. **1925** Dos Passos *Manhattan Transfer* 355: There's nowhere you can go in the whole crummy city without people watchin you. **1925** in Faulkner *New Orleans Sketches* 96: And so I fixed it up with the least crummy of them rats I was with. **1931** Armour *Little Caesar* (film): Listen, you crummy flat-footed copper! **1932** Halyburton & Goll *Shoot & Be Damned* 297 [ref. to 1918]: Get back there, you crummy son of a bitch! **1940** Goodrich *Delilah* 18 [ref. to 1916]: "You crummy bastards!" he waved at the ship in general. **1941** Hargrove *Pvt. Hargrove* 24: No kidding, though, our platoon makes all the others look crummy. **1942** "D. Ormsbee" *Sound of American* 34: Jesus, I feel crummy. **1969** Postman, Weingartner & Moran *Language in America* 100: People only brushed their teeth to get the crummy early-morning taste out of their mouths. **1978** Wharton *Birdy* 16: I…tell him to keep his crummy hands off my knife. **1978** in Lyle & Golenbock *Bronx Zoo* 132: His arm felt sore and crummy. **1979** Norwood *Survival of Dana* (film): How come if I'm so good your coach treated me so crummy? **1993** *New Yorker* (Jan. 11) 61: All of Laura's Moms are Crummy Poets.

crump *n.* **1.** *Mil.* a heavy artillery shell.

*1915 in *OEDS.* **1919** Kauffman *Victorious* 344: A German "crump" shattered the earth nearby.

2. *Hosp.* a patient in extremely critical condition.

1972 *Nat. Lampoon* (July) 76: *Crump* A patient requiring intensive care, incapable of movement, and apparently unaware of his surroundings.

crump *v.* [poss. fr. *crumple,* infl. by CRAP OUT] **1.a.** *Stu.* to pass out or fall exhausted; (*also*) to quit from fatigue, boredom, lack of resources, or the like; CRAP OUT.—usu. constr. with *out.*

1950–53 W. Grove *Down* 243: Old man crumped out? **1958** Frede *Entry E* 46: Just a question of who has the money when everyone else crumps out. **1954–60** *DAS* 132. **1961** G. Forbes *Goodbye to Some* 244 [ref. to WWII]: Everyone was loaded…Dames were crumped out all over the place. **1965* J. Nichols *Sterile Cuckoo* ch. vi: "You crumped," she accused. "I was tired."…"Crumper!" she giggled. **1980** in Safire *Good Word* 213: In the late fifties [at Nazareth College, Rochester, N.Y., we] used the expression crumped out often. When we were tired, we would "crump out."

b. to die.

1953–58 J.C. Holmes *Horn* 133: Man, you kill me, I'll die, I'll crump. **1978** Shem *House of God* 77: The Yellow Man and the Runt [are] both about to crump.

c. *Med.* (of a patient) to lapse into extremely critical condition. Also constr. with *out.*

1980 in Safire *Good Word* 211: "How's our patient doing?"…"Fine until midnight…when suddenly he crumped out. I've been with him all night." *a***1982** Medved *Hospital* 117: If you say that a patient is crumping, it means…he's turning bad, he's getting into trouble. It doesn't mean he's going to die; it just means he's going the wrong way. **1984** *N.Y. Times* (Oct. 11) 20: We don't say or think, "Mrs. Hawthorne's cancer is making her sicker." We say, "Mrs. Hawthorne's crumping on me." *a***1990** in *Maledicta* X 34: *Poot, to* to take a turn for the worst quickly and often irreversibly….Also known as *To Crump* and *To Go Poopoo.*

2.a. to kill.

1962 T.F. Jones *Stairway* 55: All [Hamlet] can think about is the way his uncle crumped his old man.

b. to destroy.

1984 M. Skinner *Red Flag* 96: So you think you shacked the target, crumped it, waxed it?

3. (of machinery) to break down; CONK OUT; fail.—often constr. with *out.*

1973 M. Collins *Carrying the Fire* 284: If the Saturn V crumped, it was a whole new ball game. **1980** in Safire *Good Word* 213 [ref. to late 1950's]: Once in a while…some mechanical apparatus would also "crump out."

crunch *n.* **1.** a critical situation, esp. a test; a showdown. Now *colloq.* or *S.E.*

*1939 W.S. Churchill, in *OEDS.* **1968** Vidal *Breckinridge* 190: Now we are at the crunch. **1983** Van Devanter & Morgan *Before Morning* 50: We…[were] headed for a cash crunch.

2. *Stu.* (see quot.).

1976 Eble *Campus Slang* (Nov.) 2: *Crunch*—mass noun: girls, especially girls responsive to sexual advances: Bill and Tom went out on the town to hunt crunch; Al met some crunch at Murphy's.

crunch *v. Av.* to crash in an aircraft.

1972–79 T. Wolfe *Right Stuff* 3 [ref. to 1950's]: Jane had heard the young men…talk about other young men who had "bought it" or "augered in" or "crunched."

cruncher *n.* **1.** *pl.* feet.

1946 Mezzrow & Wolfe *Really Blues* 90: You feel it way down to your crunchers.

2. *Jazz.* a sidewalk or street.

1944 Burley *Hndbk. Jive* 136: *Cruncher*—The street, sidewalk, road. **1946** Mezzrow & Wolfe *Really Blues* 188.

3. *Surfing.* a heavy breaker.

1968 Kirk & Hanle *Surfer's Hndbk.* 138: *Cruncher:* see *bomber.* **1977** [quot. at SAND-BUSTER].

4. *Tennis.* a hard-hit volley that bounces outside the court and cannot be returned.

1976 *AS* LI 293.

5. *USMC.* CRUNCHY.

1977 Heinl *Marine Off. Guide* 683: *Cruncher:* Aviation term for a Marine assigned to a ground unit; contraction of "gravel cruncher."

6. the decisive instant; last straw.

1987 Zeybel *Gunship* 5: The cruncher came when I refused to meet her…in Hawaii.

crunchy *n. Mil. Av.* a foot soldier; infantryman.

1951 [VMF-323] *Old Ballads* 2: You ask the crunchies who's the best they yell 323. **1969** Broughton *Thud Ridge* 71: The crunchies from the ground were shooting at the entire gaggle. **1983** C. Rich *Advisors* 438: The word crunchy comes from the sound made by an infantryman when run over by a tank. **1988** Clodfelter *Mad Minutes* 53 [ref. to 1965]: Another 13 crunchies (infantrymen).

crupper *n.* a person's rump.

*1594, *1630, *1664 in *OED.* **1731* "H. Thrumbo" *Merry-Thought* II 22: After a tedious Journey, and my Supper,/And dam—d uneasy with my Crupper. **1838** [Haliburton] *Clockmaker* (Ser. 2) 25: What…was them…rolls o' canvass for, I seed…tied to your crupper?

crush *n.* **1.** a social gathering.

*1854 (cited in Partridge *DSUE* (ed. 8)). **1890* in *F & H* II: And we settled…to give a crush at nine. **1900** *DN* II 30: *Crush,* n…A reception.

2. an infatuation (now *colloq.*); a person with whom one is infatuated (*obs.*).

1884 in *DA* 443: Wintie is weeping because her crush is gone. **1900** *DN* II 30: *Crush,* n….A liking for a person. **1942** "E. Queen" *Calamity Town* 21: Frank had a crush on Nora. **1965** Gary *Ski Bum* 79: And I'd better stop looking at him or he'll think I have a crush on him. **1985** D. Steel *Secrets* 170: She looked as though she had a crush on Zack.

3. *Und.* a set of persons; gang.

1904 *Life in Sing Sing* 247: *Crush.*—A crowd; to escape; to force. **1924** in *DA* 443: Any one of that crush would do murder for no more than 500 dollars reward.

¶ In phrase:

¶ **make a crush on** to impress favorably.

1927 "Max Brand" *Pleasant Jim* 42: D'you think I'm trying to make a crush on this cartoon?

crush *v.* **1.** to force one's way, (*esp.*) *Pris.* to break prison, escape.—usu. constr. with *out.*

1908 in H.C. Fisher *A. Mutt* 89: I have no special desire to crush into the president business. **1924** in D. Hammett *Continental Op* 49: Rooney…had crushed out of…Leavenworth. **1925–26** Black *You Can't Win* 232: The thought of our getting anything to "crush out" with never entered his foggy mind. **1929** Hotstetter & Beesley *Racket* 223: *Crush out*—To escape from custody or prison, using bribery or violence or murder if necessary. **1932** Berg *Prison Doctor* 81: When the warden found out how they crushed out, he sent screws to look for Fatty. **1933** Mizner & Holmes *20,000 Yrs. in Sing Sing* (film): With the connections I got he doesn't have to crush out. **1944** N. Johnson *Casanova Brown* (film): You've still got time to crush out of this booby trap.

2. *Pris.* to escape from (prison).

1904 *Life in Sing Sing* 247: *Crush*...to escape. *Ibid.* 258: *Crushing the jungle.* Escaping from prison. *ᵃ***1909** in Ware *Passing English* 100: My two "fly" friends had "crushed the stir," and were at large. **1931** *AS* VI (Aug.) 437: *Crush, v.* To escape. "This poem deals with a con who crushes Sing Sing."

crushed *adj. Stu.* infatuated; stuck.

1895 *Harper's* (Apr.) 787: "I think Cordelia's a pretty name."..."I don't...I'm not all crushed on it." **1895** *Harper's* (May) 921: I'll show you how much I'm crushed on dancing. **1896** in S. Crane *N.Y.C. Sks.* 169: He's crushed on Dollie Bangle. ****1909** Ware *Passing English* 100: *Crushed*...Spoony, in love with.

crusher *n.* **1.** *Und.* a police officer.

****1835** in *OEDS:* "Here are two *crushers.*"...I looked out of the window, and saw both the policemen. **1859** Matsell *Vocab.* 23: *Crusher.* A policeman. **1867** Williams *Brierly* 20: The crushers are getting to know too much. I believe the best of our trade join the blues. **1927** *DN* V 443: *Crusher,* n. A policeman.

2. a crush hat.

1915–16 Lait *Beef, Iron & Wine* 113: From time to time [he] would take off his worn and shiny crusher and caressingly comb his shock.

crushout *n. Pris.* a jailbreak.

1925 (cited in Partridge *Dict. Und.* 168). **1927** in Hammett *Knockover* 354: Papadopoulos had arranged a crush-out for Flora. **1928** Hammett *Red Harvest* 78: What do you think of the crush-out? **1932** Halyburton & Goll *Shoot & Be Damned* 385 [ref. to 1918]: The crush-out had excited the camp authorities but little. **1954** Gaddis *Birdman* 185: Unknown to Stroud, this was the prearranged tip-off for a "crush-out."

crust *n.* effrontery.

1900 *DN* II 31: *Crust, n.* Forwardness. **1908** in H.C. Fisher *A. Mutt* 72: You've got a crust to speak to me without an introduction. **1915** *DN* IV 233: That guy certainly has some crust. **1929** in Galewitz *Great Comics* 117: Say, Emmy you got a lotta crust blabbin' to Mamie that you heard Uncle Willie talkin' about bein' out with Mrs. Smokehouse on the Coast. **1929–31** Farrell *Young Lonigan* 54: "And the crust of May!"...Mrs. Lonigan said. **1934** H. Roth *Sleep* 60: An' wattayuh t'ink he had de crust to tell me? **1938** W. Sherman & V. Sherman *Crime School* (film): Don't you think he's got a crust puttin' us down in this hole or has he got a crust? **1941** Wead & Buckner *Dive Bomber* (film): Now you've got the crust to ——. **1956** Childress *Like One of Family* 96: Girl, people have got some crust! **1962** G. Olson *Roaring Road* 63: Look, Mr. Flagg, maybe I got a crust asking a favor from you but dog-gone. **1965–79** in *DARE.* **1988** *N.Y. Newsday* (July 6) 11: Pie-tosser has dropped routine, but crust remains.

¶ In phrase:

¶ **bust** [or **cave in**] **(someone's) crust** to thrash and injure; (*hence*) to ruin.

1853 Lippard *New York* 266: I broke a jaw for one of 'em an' *caved the crust in* for another. **1865** Harte *Sk. of Sixties* 34: Let us bust the crust of this Perfect Gent and black his eye. **1870** *Overland Mo.* (Dec.) 518: Dick said, bust his crust if he had ever had a breakfast set so comfortable-like as that one did. **1880** Small *Mother-in-Law* 21: I tumbled over that dog and burst the crust of several of her bandboxes. **1886** Nye *Remarks* 362: He used to...intimate...that if I did not produce that copy p.d.q., or some other abbreviation or other, that he would bust my crust, or words of like import. **1886** Harte *Tasajara* 65: Then it ain't a free fight, nor havin' your crust busted and bein' robbed by black combers, eh? **1907** *Reader* (Sept.) 345: If he ever tried to hand me anything again I'd bust his crust. **1911** *Hampton's Mag.* (June) 744: You do anything to that woman and I'll cave in your crust!

crustbuster *n. Black E.* a small child; CRUMB-CRUSHER.

1953 in Clarke *Amer. Negro Stories* 214: You tell 'em, little crust busters. **1974** A. Murray *Train Whistle* 27: What I got a good mind to do is whale the sawdust out of both you little crustbusters.

crusty *adj. Juve.* unpleasant; bad.

1985 in M. Groening *School is Hell* (unp.): 6 guys got in trouble today....Isn't that crusty? *Ibid.* Today was crusty. Annie got in trouble today.

crut *n.* [app. var. CRUD] **1.** a despicable person.

1925 in Hemingway *Sel. Letters* 177: Now don't be a lousy crut and not

answer this because letters are worth millions of dollars down here. **1925** Hemingway *In Our Time* 65: That lousy crut of a brakeman. He would get him some day. **1937** Hemingway *To Have & Have Not* 131: You miserable little crut. **1940** Hemingway *For Whom Bell Tolls* 369: The dirty rotten crut.

2. filth.

1940 Hemingway *For Whom Bell Tolls* 150: Goat crut. ****1955** in *OEDS:* Two years in Ireland....Land of crut. **1958** Gilbert *Vice Trap* 10: You're still crut in my book. **1964** Abrahams *Deep Down in Jungle* 265: *Crut*—Variant of *crud*...anything base. ****1990** Thorne *Dict. Contemp. Slang* 118: *Crut*...dirt, distasteful material or unpleasantness in general. A version of *crud* (normally felt to be less offensive than that word).

3. disease.

1947 *AS* XXII 304 [ref. to WWII]: *Crut* (the). A variant of *Crud....*The most common form is *the Senegambian Crut.* **1948** La Farge *Eagle in Egg* 147 [ref. to WWII]: An irritated cough, known as "the Maidaguri crut," was endemic.

4. rubbish; arrant nonsense.

1958 Gilbert *Vice Trap* 17: Crut...And what was it you're supposed to be?

crutch *n.* a pin, clip, or similar device used for holding the stub of a marijuana cigarette.

1938 (cited in Spears *Drugs & Drink*). **1952** Kerouac *Cody* 167: I'll get the crutch, men. **1963–64** Kesey *Great Notion* 273: Roaches, crutches, and burnt paper matches. **1967** Rosevear *Pot* 158: *Crutch:* A device for holding a short, burning marihuana cigarette. It can be a hair clip, bobby pin, forceps, etc. **1972** Smith & Gay *Don't Try It* 200: *Crutch.* Device used to hold the last part of a marijuana cigarette; also called "Roach Clip."

¶ In phrase:

¶ **funny as a crutch, 1.** decidedly funny.

1919 T. Kelly *What Outfit?* 114: Funny as a crutch the way we looked gettin' out o' the mademoiselle's riggin's. **1925** Dos Passos *Transfer* 401: Didn't you read about it? It was funny as a crutch. **1962** T. Berger *Reinhart in Love* 146: Genevieve misunderstood clichés....she used "funny as a crutch" for something that really *was* comical.

2. (used ironically) decidedly not funny.

1916 in Dreiser *Diaries* 125: Say Andy. Your as funny as a crutch. Your as funny as a cry for help. **1934** Appel *Brain Guy* 164: "You're funny as a crutch." This...was n.g. **1948** Seward & Ryan *Angel's Alley* (film): 'Bout as funny as a crutch. **1962** Killens *Heard the Thunder* 68: You're a real funny fellow, Office Boy...Funny as a broken crutch.

crutty *adj.* CRUDDY, 1, 2. Also **crutting.**

1925 Hemingway *In Our Time* 66: That son of a crutting brakeman. **1956** P. Moore *Chocolates* 16: Oh, that crutty publication is only a mechanism of social approval. **1958** Gilbert *Vice Trap* 41: Don't come on crutty to Nick.

cry *v.* ¶ **for crying out loud!** [a euphem. for *for Christ's sake*] (used to indicate exasperation). Now *colloq.*

1924 in *OEDS.* **1925** Kearney *Man's Man* 25: Oh, for cryin' out loud! **1925** *Collier's* (Feb. 14) 30: Well, for cryin' out loud!...a euphemism. **1928** in Segar *Thimble Th.* 22: For Cryin' out loud don't be like that! **1931** *AS* VI 204: *For crying out loud:* an exclamation of surprise or anger. **1937** Odets *Golden Boy* 280: For crying out loud! Where do you come off to make a remark like that? ****1945** S.J. Baker *Australian Lang.* 250: Strike me handsome!...for crying out loud! **1993** *Real World* (MTV): You gotta stir that thing around, for cryin' out loud. **1993** *Frasier* (NBC-TV): Aw, for cryin' out loud!

crying *adj.* single (used emphatically, esp. of a coin).

1942 Algren *Morning* 96: I ain't got a cryin' dime. **1966** in Jackson *Swim Like Me* 129: Not one cryin' penny in her pocket. **1970** E. Thompson *Garden of Sand* 72: Leave you alone for a goddamn cryin minute and you tear the sonofabitchin place apart! **1970** Boatright & Owens *Derrick* 133: It'd got every crying nickel we had. **1971** J. Brown & A. Groff *Monkey* 97: I...didn't have a cryin' dime. **1974** Gober *Black Cop* 105: Without a cryin' ass quarter in my pocket.

crying jag *n.* see s.v. JAG.

crying towel *n.* a supposed or actual towel used to wipe the tears of a self-pitying person.—used derisively.

1928 T.A. Dorgan, in Zwilling *TAD Lexicon* 29: [Caption:] Passing by a bunch of big operators who have just joined the I Shoulda Club...That oughta be a good spot to sell cryin' towels. **1943** *Yank* (Oct. 8) 21: Crying Towel Pays Off. **1946** I. Shulman *Amboy Dukes* 14: "Cut out the crying towel," Larry said. **1951** in Paxton *Sport* 400: I was never one to call for the crying towel. **1982** Hayano *Poker Faces* 53:

Regulars often sarcastically request the floorman to bring "crying towels" for the losers when complaints are heard.

crypto *n. & adj. Mil.* cryptography; cryptographic.

1979 Ennes *Liberty* 85 [ref. to 1967]: They destroyed a crypto machine.

crystal *n. Narc.* methamphetamine in powdered form.

1966 Reynolds & McClure *Freewheelin Frank* 56: Geezin crystal is an amphetamine trip. **1967** *Sat. Eve. Post* (Sept. 23) 89: All the amphetamines, or "speed"—Benzedrine, Dexedrine and particularly Methedrine ("crystal")—were in common use. **1967** Wolf *Love Generation* 203: I had dropped some crystal and later someone brought over some DMT. **1967–68** von Hoffman *Parents Warned Us* 80: The old-time psychedelic heads inveighed against crystal. **1968** *CBS Evening News* (CBS-TV) (Feb. 26): Methedrine—known on the street as *crystal*. **1970** *Sat. Review* (Nov. 14) 21: *Crystal*—Methedrine, an amphetamine. **1983** S. Wright *Meditations* 152: I took a lot of crystal in LA back in 'sixty-seven. **1988** *Newsweek* (Apr. 25) 25: 10 pounds of "crystal meth," one of the most…sought-after forms of amphetamine on the street. *Ibid.* 66: "How much can you spend?" "Cash or crystal?"

crystal ball *n. USAF.* a radar set. *Joc.*

1956 *AS* XXXI 227: His radar set is sometimes referred to as the *crystal ball* because he spends large amounts of time looking into it.

C.S. *n. & adj.* (a partial euphem. for) CHICKENSHIT.

1944 in *AS* XX 147: *C.S.* See *Chicken*. **1945** *Yank* (July 27) 18: To…give our officers more time to dream up C.S. **1948** *N.Y. Folklore Qly.* (Spring) 20. **1951** *Amer. Jour. Socio.* LI 420: In this case the authority exceeds being GI, it becomes "chicken s—," sometimes abbreviated to "CS" or "chicken." **1971** Faust *Willy Remembers* 211: C.S. Tom. The lieutenant. The captain. **1973** Lucas, Katz & Huyck *Amer. Graffiti* 54: C.S.….Chickenshit.

C-speck *n.* C-NOTE.

*a***1846** in *DA* 235: Sol. Lauflin matched his bay four year old colt…to run a quarter…for a C speck.

C.T. *n.* COCKTEASER.—usu. considered vulgar.

*****1923** Manchon *Le Slang* 97: C.T., cf. *cock-teaser.* **1967** Roth *When She Was Good* 102: A professional virgin—a c.t., if she knew what that was. **1970** L. Gould *Friends* 74: You're a lousy C.T.! **1972** A. Burgess, in *N.Y. Times Mag.* (Nov. 19) 30: One ought not to pass an essay [by a U.S. student] that describes Shakespeare's Cressida as "kind of a C.T." or Ophelia as "going crazy because of her dad's being wiped out." **1975** W. Salt *Day of Locust* (film): She's a C.T., isn't she?

cu *n. Av.* a cumulus cloud.

1961 Forbes *Goodbye to Some* 84 [ref. to WWII]: I can see the dark masses of the really big cus.

cub *n.* **1.** a child or youngster; a young man. Orig. *S.E.*

*****1601** Shakespeare *12th Night* v i 167: O thou dissembling Cub. *****1687** Congreve, in *OED:* But, oh gad! two such unlicked cubs! *****1723** Steele, in *OED:* He thinks it necessary to be civil to the young cub. *****1773** Goldsmith *She Stoops to Conquer* IV: A mere boy…An insensible cub. **1780** in *DA* 444. **1828** Bird *Looking Glass* 106: Death and hell!—Oh! 'tis only the cub! **1840** in *OEDS:* Awaiting the arrival of "a cub" (a young speculator). *****1855** Thackeray, in *OED.* **1860** Victor *Alice Wilde* 10: "And who's 'herself'?"…"My cub, sir." **1867** S. Clemens, in *Twain's Letters* II 130: She had another pup under her charge, younger than myself, whom I always called the "cub." **1882** Sweet *Sketches* 82: Jedge, has you been a parent of a wuflers yaller boy like dat ar cub of mine? **1882** "M. Twain" *Life on Miss.* 35: He's nothing but a cub. I'll paint the man that tetches him! **1885** "Lykkejaeger" *Dane* 9: Make that big, lazy cub earn his bread! **1890** Kerbey *War Path* 75: The "cubs"—as the younger officers are familiarly termed. **1928** in Botkin *Treas. Amer. Folk.* 840: There ain't no cub as neat as him/Dandy, handy Raftsman Jim!

2. a novice or apprentice; (now *esp.*) **cub reporter** a novice reporter. Now *colloq.*

1845 in Oehlschlaeger *Reveille* 152: Expressing his wishes to some of his brother "cubs." **1859** in "M. Twain" *Selected Shorter Writings* 8: Sergeant Fathom, one of the oldest cub pilots on the river…Sergeant Fathom is a "cub" of much experience. **1875** "M. Twain" *Old Times* 47 [ref. to *ca*1860]: An't the new cub turned out yet? *Ibid.* 80: The pilot…takes his "cub" or steersman and a picked crew of men. *Ibid.* 100: It was nice to have a "cub," a steersman, to do all the hard work. **1879** Dacus *Frank & Jesse* 242: The "cub" robber, Hobbs Kerry, was scarcely shrewd enough to evade capture. **1908** J. London *M. Eden* 333: The cub reporter was perplexed.…"That's right…" the cub announced. **1912** Ade *Babel* 18: He had been a "cub" machinist in his youth. **1919** Bates *Fighting to Win* 13: Robert Dalton, after the death of his parents,

had become a "cub" reporter. **1952** in C. Beaumont *Best* 18: Look, you're still a cub, but you do swell work. **1961** in Cannon *Nobody Asked* 193: The modern cubs I run into are sober young men who cover the news with a funless intensity. **1992** G. Wolff *Day at the Beach* 14: Every cub has a novel.

cub *v.* to work as a novice or apprentice, esp. as a novice reporter.

1951 *Time* (Dec. 10) 102: James first cubbed for the Baltimore *Sun*. **1960** H. Carter, in *Sat. Eve. Post* (June 4) 58: Shelby Foote, who cubbed on the *Democrat-Times*, has six books to his credit. **1983** Curry *River's in My Blood* 48: Ben Burman…cubbed on the [riverboat] *Tennessee Belle* in the 1920's.

Cube *n.* a Cuban.—used derisively.

1980 in *Penthouse* (Jan. '81) 169: How'd the…Cubes find out he was carrying? **1986** Knoxville, TN, man, age *ca*35: *Cubes* are Cubans.

cube *n.* **1.** *pl.* dice.

1918 *Sat. Eve. Post* (Aug. 3) 73: He was shaking the cubes himself. **1919** Wiley *Wildcat* 92: Le's you an' me have a r'ar at de cubes whilst we's waitin'. **1958** Frede *Entry E* 44: Bogard is gonna deign to wager on the cubes with us. **1967** Spillane *Delta* 63: Once more the stickman…spoke hurriedly to his assistant to run in fresh cubes. **1972** Pendleton *Vegas Vendetta* 142: The guy pushed him a stack of chips and announced, "The cubes are hot." **1977** Bredes *Hard Feelings* 297: "Where'd you get seven hundred dollars?"…"Game of cubes, man."

2. *Stu.* a cubicle.

*****1936** Partridge *DSUE:* Cube. A cubicle: at certain Public Schools, e.g., Charterhouse. **1979** Hiler *Monkey Mt.* 16: Steve's cube was just inside the door. *Ibid.* 17. Oh, some lifer decided that the cubes should all be exactly the same size. **1984** *N.Y. Post* (Jan. 6): A cube…a library cubicle. **1986** L. Johnson *WAVES* 23: My cube mate…walked in.

3. [sugg. by SQUARE, *n.*] *Stu.* a foolish, unsophisticated, or very tiresome person.

1957 MacDonald *Death Trap* 78: Work was for the cubes—the quintessence of a square. **1957** Margulies *Punks* 149: "Don't be a cube. Nobody owns little Rita." **1958** J. Davis *College Vocab.* 6: Cube—Same as square, only to a greater degree. **1959** Frank *Alas, Babylon* 53: A cube is a square anyway you look at him, hah, hah—. **1960** Swarthout *Where Boys Are* 69: Compared to you, Big Ten boys are cubes. **1967** P. Welles *Babyhip* 23: List for Academic Slobs, Sarah mused. The worst cubes were on top of the list. **1969** *Current Slang* I & II 23: Cube, *n.* One who does not follow current trends, a "square."—College females, New York. **1970** Horman & Fox *Drug Awareness* 465: Cube—non-user of drugs. **1973** I. Reed *La. Red* 46: That man is a square. A cube. **1977** Olsen *Fire Five* 267: There's a guy that's really square, like a cube, ya know? **1986** E. Weiner *Howard the Duck* 129: We think of ourselves as a street gang…We do a prime number on the squares and cubes.

4. a cubic foot; cubic centimeter.

1958 *N.Y. Times* (Feb. 16) I 88: The "cube"—that is, the space occupied by a shipment expressed in cubic feet. **1971** Tak *Truck Talk* 39: Cube: short for cubic feet [*sic*], the measure of a trailer's carrying capacity. **1981** *Easyriders* (Oct.) 3: 100 cubes, an' they ain't square.

5. [sugg. by BALLS] *pl.* the testicles. *Joc.*

1968 Baker et al. *CUSS* 102: Cubes. The testicles. **1970** *Nat. Lampoon* (May) 49: Tell 'em plain…You want to see your cubes. **1978** in *Maledicta* VI (1982) 23: Testicles…cubes.

cubehead *n. Narc.* a frequent user of LSD-25 in sugar-cube form. Also **cubie.**

1966 Young & Hixson *LSD* 152: "Acid-heads," hippies, druggies, cubies. **1970** Landy *Underground Dict.* 61: Cubehead…Regular user of LSD sugar cubes. **1970** *Sat. Rev.* (Nov. 14) 21: Cubehead. Frequent user of LSD.

cubistic *adj.* [sugg. by CUBE] *Stu.* stilted and old-fashioned; very SQUARE.

1961 Anhalt & Miller *Young Savages* (film): Mother, you're such a drag. So utterly cubistic.

cuckaboo see KOOKABOO.

cuckoo *n.* **1.** a foolish or insane person; (*hence*) an amusing eccentric; (*hence*) an enthusiast; (*rarely*) a person.

*****1889** Barrère & Leland *Slang* I: Cuckoo (society), a fool. **1903** Hobart *Out for the Coin* 15: Peter Grant wasn't the only cuckoo on the curb in those days! **1911** T.A. Dorgan, in *N.Y. Eve. Jour.* (Jan. 12) 16: Why you poor cheese. You're a cuckoo an' don't know it. **1918** *Wadsworth Gas Attack* 2: Any one who has lamped a covey of camp Marathoners operating their ambitious ankles in the snow drifts knows that we have plenty of cuckoos right here in camp. **1919** Darling *Jargon Book* 8: *Coo Coo*—A person who has done something foolish. **1919** in DeBeck *Google* 37: Those relations of my wife are gonna make a cuckoo out of me. **1919** *Lit. Digest* (May 17) 50: Familiarity...makes a cuckoo contemptuous of danger. **1920–21** Witwer *Leather Pushers* 4: On account of this cuckoo forgettin' he was a box fighter...we lose five other bouts. **1923** Witwer *Fighting Blood* 72: You act like you was a cuckoo and trade rights and lefts with the air. **1926** Lardner *Haircut* 19: The poor cuckoo, as Jim called him, he was here in the shop one night when Jim was still gloatin' over what he'd done to Julie. **1937** Steinbeck *Mice & Men* 43: He ain't no cuckoo...He's dumb as hell, but he ain't crazy. **1943** Chandler *High Window* 419: When a guy gets like that...he's a lost cuckoo. ***1958** P. O'Connor *At Le Mans* 15: Next time...'tis you will go down and argue wi' yon customs cuckoo. **1958** A. King *Mine Enemy* 98: It handled only genuine cuckoos. **1972** Ponicsan *Cinderella Liberty* 47: What "walking the dog" is to a Yo-Yo cuckoo. **1985** M. Baker *Cops* 294: I wouldn't go to a shrink. Shrinks to me were the fucking cuckoos.

2. a remarkable example of its kind; a remarkable person or thing.

*a***1938** in Adamic *My America* 225: To retreat again to hay. I put up my first stack today and it's a cuckoo. **1918** in Bliss *805th Pioneer Inf.* 213: She's a Lulu, she's a cuckoo! She's the goods! **1921** *Amer. Leg. Wkly.* (Mar. 11) 2: Oh, boy! This idea is a cuckoo—It'll knock 'em dead. **1928** McEvoy *Show Girl* 77: Well baby, this week has been a cuckoo.

3. *Army.* a body louse. [Quots. ref. to WWI.]

1918 Swan *My Co.* 81: "Cuckoos" or "cooties," as we afterwards called them, were proven to be of pro-German proclivities, and our common enemy. **1920** Norton *639th Aero Squadron* 73: Regarding his experiences at Ourches, he never tired relating stories regarding the numerous wild times he spent in search of "coo-coos." **1923** LaBranche *Amer. Btry.* 59: Looka here, wen we was in siwilian clothes, we didn't know wot coo-coos was, now we come to France and we find out what coo-coos is.

cuckoo *adj.* **1.** insane; crazy. Also **cuckooed.**

1906 Hobart *Skiddoo* 98: In presenting these Cuckoo Recipes for the Chafing Dish to his friends, Mr. Jefferson wishes it distinctly understood that all doctors' bills arising from a free indulgence in any of the dishes suggested herein must be paid by the indulgee. **1918** in Bowerman *Compensations* 71: We must have been "cookooed" coming down. **1918** Ruggles *Navy Explained* 120: A place to put those men who are crazy, loco or coocooed, men with bats in their belfry. **1918** O'Brien *Wine, Women & War* 75: Fell for her 100%. Wish my daughter would grow up like that. Oh—cuckoo!* *Seen her since. Certainly must have been cuckoo! **1918–19** Sinclair *Higgins* 191: They told him that he was "cuckoo," that his "trolley was twisted." **1923** Witwer *Fighting Blood* 78: A wild idea come to me to tell her how cuckoo I am over her and get either kissed or canned, but...be done with it! **1925** Dos Passos *Manhattan Transfer* 222: The police department is cookoo, absolutely cookoo treating us a rape and suicide case. **1925** in Faulkner *New Orleans Sks.* 206: Joe must be coo-coo. **1928** Hammett *Red Harvest* 40: You were cuckoo over the girl. **1938** "R. Hallas" *You Play the Black* 139: That's cuckoo. **1970** Newmann & Benton *Crooked Man* (film): You gotta figure out some way to keep from goin' cuckoo.

2. markedly out of the ordinary; odd; funny.

*a***1938** in Adamic *My America* 225: Poverty forces the children...to wear "coo-coo" clothes. **1963** Hayden *Wanderer* 148: I don't get it. Something's wrong. Cuckoo. **1993** *Mystery Sci. Theater* (Comedy Central TV): A richly cuckoo fantasy world of love.

¶ In phrase:

¶ **knock cuckoo** to render unconscious; (*hence*) to dazzle (an audience).

1927 Shay *Pious Friends* 97: And I was champ in the U.S.A.,/And knocked 'em cuckoo every day. **1928** in Tuthill *Bungle Family* 123: The lightning of love knocked him cuckoo. **1931** Uhler *Cane Juice* 121: A drink like that would a knocked me cuckoo. **1929–33** Farrell *Manhood of Lonigan* 247: Because you won't get knocked cuckoo if you keep your heads up.

cuckoo academy *n.* CUCKOO HOUSE. *Joc.*

1968 Swarthout *Loveland* 232: I loved her too much to commit her to the Cuckoo Academy.

cuckoo bird *n.* a crazy or eccentric person.

1942 Davis & Wolsey *Call House Madam* 282: This same cuckoo bird threw a stag party one night. **1948** McIlwaine *Memphis* 25: Not like the old-fashioned coo-coo bird called "prexy." **1960** Bannon *Journey* 31: Cleve says they're a trio of cuckoo birds. **1979–83** W. Kennedy *Iron-*

weed 3: You goddamn cuckoo bird, you don't talk about the weather that way.

cuckoo farm *n.* CUCKOO HOUSE. *Joc.*

1980 Algren *Dev. Stocking* 175: You ought to be on the cuckoo farm. You're nutty as a fruitcake.

cuckoo house *n.* an insane asylum; CRAZY HOUSE.

1930 Sage *Last Rustler* 27: Enough to send him to the cuckoo house. **1941** in *Time* (Jan. 5, 1942) 50: Current favorite among her recordings: *Doin' a War Dance Down at the Cuckoo House.* **1968** Mailer *Armies of the Night* 239: Watch it, old buddy, they put junior reverends in the cuckoo house for carrying on. **1971** Horan *Blue Messiah* 119: He goes to the cuckoo house and we starve. **1972** N.Y.U. student: The *cuckoo house.* When I was a kid in Brooklyn that was one of the real big expressions.

cuckoo juice *n.* strong liquor. *Joc.*

1970 La Motta, Carter & Savage *Raging Bull* 226: I nursed that beautiful container of cuckoo juice carefully.

cuckoo's nest *n.* **1.** the vulva or vagina.

ca1835–40** in Speaight *Bawdy Songs of Music Hall* 27: Such thighs.../ And a black little cuckoo's nest right in between! ***1891** *F & H* II: *Cuckoo's Nest*...The female *pudendum.* **1920–54** (quot. at HOG-EYE).

2. a psychiatric hospital. [In 1960 quot., a crazy place.]

[**1960** *Many Loves of D. Gillis* (CBS-TV): Well, you *belong* in a cuckoo's nest like this!] **1962** Kesey *One Flew Over the Cuckoo's Nest* (title). **1984** Jackson & Lupica *Reggie* 234: We all felt like we'd landed in the cuckoo's nest. **1981–89** R. Atkinson *Long Gray Line* 327: Funny farm, loony bin, cuckoo's nest, booby hatch, nut house.

cucumber *n.* the penis. *Joc.*

1888 *Stag Party* 9: The young man...asked, "How's that for a cucumber?" **1916–22** Cary *Sexual Vocab.* I: *Cucumber.* The penis. **1972** *Nat. Lampoon* (July) 74: Is your cucumber getting ripe? [**1992** N.Y.C. novelty T-shirt: 15 Reasons Why a Cucumber Is Better than a Man: 1. A cucumber is always hard [etc.].]

cuda *n.* **1.** a barracuda.

1949 Cummings *Dict. Sports* 94. **1974** E. Thompson *Tattoo* 237: Men counseled each other to watch out for the 'cuda.

2. (*cap.*) a Plymouth Barracuda automobile.

1975 Dills *CB* (rev. ed.) 27: 'Cuda. Plymouth Barracuda. **1982** in "J.B. Briggs" *Drive-In* 89: Walks around breathin' like a Hemi 'Cuda. **1990** Vachss *Blossom* 272: The 'Cuda catapulted forward.

cuddle-bunny *n.* an affectionate, passionate, or sexually attractive young woman.

1950 Bissell *Stretch on the River* 27: This Toots would probably turn out to be one of these cuddle bunnies with a baby voice. **1955** Reifer *New Words* 56: *Cuddle-bunny. Slang* Delinquent girl.

cueball *n.* a bald person.

1941 Kendall *Army & Navy Slang* 4: *Cueballs*...the lads the student barber works on. **1943** *Amer. Mercury* (Nov.) 552: Cueballs, the barber's clients. **1946** S. Wilson *Voyage to Somewhere* 234: Two seamen shaved each other's heads for a lark. They called each other "cue ball" and "eight ball." **1967** G. Green *To Brooklyn* 263: Who's that?...What a cueball! **1983** *Mork & Mindy* (ABC-TV): Easy for you to say, cueball! *a***1990** Westcott *Half a Klick* 196: Bet you can't count that high, cueball.

cues *n.pl. Music Industry.* headphones.

1979 Homer *Jargon* 121.

cuff[1] *n.* CUFFY. [The 1755 and 1867 quots. are proper names; see note at CUFFY.]

[**1755** in *DARE* 876: An Indian freewoman wife to Mr. Tilley's Negro Cuff died.] **1860** Whitman *Leaves* 29: Kanuck, Tuckahoe, Congressman, Cuff, I give them the same. **1864** in A.P. Hudson *Humor of Old So.* 498: Some of the..."cuffs" [were] "dead-blowed" with heeling it. [**1867** in *DA* 445.] **1964** *PADS* (No. 42) 29: Most of the terms collected exclusively from Negro informants are rare within the Caucasian social dialects of Chicago, e.g., *Cuff.* **1971** H. Roberts *3d Ear: Cuff*...a black man.

cuff[2] *n.* credit.—usu. in phr. **on the cuff,** 1, below.

1896 in J.M. Carroll *Benteen-Goldin Lets.* 248: "No limits" is apt to make pretty steep [poker] game, and...no "cuff" went. **1916** T.A. Dorgan, in Zwilling *TAD Lexicon* 29: Anytime you're broke and wanna "swing the cuff" for a round of drinks mention my name—an' you're in right.

¶ In phrases:

¶ **off the cuff** impromptu. Now *S.E.*

1938 in *OEDS.* **1941** *Time* (Sept. 8) 4: A powerful "off-the-cuff orator." **1979** Kiev *Courage to Live* 17: An impulsive person will make more than the usual quota of rapid-fire, off-the-cuff decisions.

¶ **on the cuff, 1.** on credit; in phr. **put on the cuff** to extend credit to or (*rarely*) ask credit from.

1927 Nicholson *Barker* 149: On the cuff, a charged account. **1933** Ersine *Prison Slang* 30: Joe's trying to hire a mouthpiece on the cuff. **1934** Berg *Prison Nurse* 95: A buck thirty-five cash a pint…and nothing on the cuff. ***1938*** in *OEDS*. **1940** Wald & Macauley *They Drive by Night* (film): On the cuff. You'll get it on the trip back. **1947** Schulberg *Harder They Fall* 46: Put it on the cuff. **1950** Duffy *S. Quentin* 117: Do you suppose I could go on the cuff for a big block of soft wood? **1953** Gresham *Midway* 25: We had to put the landlord on the cuff for the winter's board. **1957** Townley *Up in Smoke* (film): Maybe you could put us on the cuff till we get back on our feet.

2. free of charge; "on the house."

1927 *Vanity Fair* (Nov.) 134: "On the cuff" is "on the house" or "free." **1939–40** O'Hara *Pal Joey* 52: The press agent gets no pay but only a certain am't of drinks on the cuff. **1941** "G.R. Lee" *G-String* 54: Take a swig of this…It ain't like the champagne we drank last night, but it's on the cuff anyhow. **1961** Scarne *Gamb. Gde.* 686: On the Cuff Bet A free bet for the player. **1976** C. Keane *Hunter* 198: "I'll pay you anything."…"This one's on the cuff." **1977** Dunne *True Confessions* 4: A meal on the cuff and a twenty in a fortune cookie and Frank would let the Mah-Jongg game in the back survive for another month.

cuff *v.* to extend credit to.

1939 *AS* (Oct.) 239: To cuff…to extend credit. **1966–80** McAleer & Dickson *Unit Pride* 182: "Wanna cuff us till payday for another twenty-five?" "What do you mean 'cuff'?" "Credit, an IOU."

cuffer *n. Naut.* a tall tale.

1878 (quot. at HOLY JOE). ***1887*** in *OEDS*. ***1888*** in *F & H* II: The Australian youth can develop the art of *spinning cuffers* very successfully on his own account. ***1889*** Barrère & Leland *Dict. Slang* I: *Cuffer* (military), a lie; spinning a *cuffer*, telling an exaggerated, grossly improbable story. **1898** Bullen *Cachalot* 108: They will talk by the hour of trivialities about which they know nothing; they will spin interminable "cuffers" of debaucheries ashore all over the world.

cufferoo *adj.* [*on the cuff*, 2, s.v. CUFF² + -EROO] free of charge.

1940 O'Hara *Pal Joey* 132: It was not a spending party, strictly cufferoo.

cuffo *n.* [fr. CUFF², *n.*] credit.

1974 Sann *Dead Heat* 50: And no cuffo, buddy. [He]…pays a tab.

cuffo *adj.* [*on the cuff*, 2, s.v. CUFF² + -o] free of charge.

1942 in *DAS*: Concerteers like a cuffo concert once in a while. **1951** A. Green & J. Laurie, Jr. *Show Biz* 14: A 40-minute monolog…on the inalienable rights of American citizens…evoked tumultuous applause from the cuffo customers. **1955** Reifer *New Words* 56: *Cuffo. Adv. Show business slang.* Without any charge; for nothing. **1981** Sann *Trial* 17: You put away too much booze before you caught your cuffo flight? **1989** *TV Guide* (June 17) 20: Free. Gratis. El cuffo.

cuffy or **cuffee** *n.* [< Twi *Kofi* (day name for males born on Friday)] **1.** (used as a generic name for a black man); a black man.—usu. patronizing or derisive. [The 1763 and 1767 quots. are proper names.]

1713 in *OEDS*: I…obliged Cuffee to call for him. [**1763** in Windley *Runaway Slave Advs.* IV 1: Another NEGROE FELLOW NAMED CUFFE.] [**1767** in Windley *Runaway Slave Advs.* IV 22: TWO NEGROE FELLOWS, named GEORGE and CUFFEE.] **1833** J. Neal *Down-Easters* I 95: Mind your eyes, cuffee….*Colored* Americans are called *cuffees*. **1837** in *OEDS*: The song ceased, and the cuffee advanced in silence. **1839** *Spirit of Times* (June 8) 159: He did not, as a Cuffee said, "shine like any glissen." **1843** "J. Slick" *High Life in N.Y.* 29: A leetle…cuffy boy. *Ibid.* 95: I begun to feel…streaked to think I'd been a talking sich things to a cuffy. **1844** in *OEDS*: Jest as I was a thinking this, the cuffy come into the room. **1855** Wise *Tales for Marines* 246: In burst a laughing-eyed little cuffee, as black and shining as his master's varnished boots. *Ibid.* 253: The little cuffy. **1859** Bartlett *Amer.* (ed. 2) 110: *Cuffy*. A very common term for a Negro. **1865** Dennett *South as It Is* 248: If the general don't tell them cuffees they're to have their share o' our land…you'll see a hell of a row today. ***1889*** Barrère & Leland *Dict. Slang* I: *Cuffy, cuffee* (West Indian), a word generally applied to negroes, and which was at one time a very common name among them. Literally it means "Thursday [*sic*]."…[among] the Guinea and Dahomey negroes. **1950** *PADS* (No. 14) 24: *Cuffey*…A Negro. Patronizing, sometimes with a shade of derision. Obsolete.

2. a bear.

1824 in *DA*. **1860–61** R.F. Burton *City of Saints* 212: Under the promise that "cuffy" should previously be marked down so as to save a long ride and a troublesome trudge over the mountains. *Ibid.* 255: In the Himalayas many a sportsman…has enjoyed a grill of "cuffy." **1892** in *DA*.

3. a young boy.

1871 Wood *West Point Scrapbook* 128 [ref. to 1859]: A large moustache we each will raise,/We'll strike the "cuffies" with amaze./They'll rub their beardless chins, you know,/And wonder why their hairs don't grow.

cuke *n.* a cucumber. Now *colloq.*

1903 in *OEDS*. **1950** *Pop. Sci.* (Jan.) 106: The old stoop-and-squat technique of harvesting cucumbers….close to the ground—and the cukes. **1958** *N.Y. Times* (Aug. 24) I 61: A daily average of 1,400 bushels of salad "cukes" for fresh markets. **1968** *Business Week* (Mar. 2) 63: This machine uproots the entire vine, separates the "cukes" from the plants. **1981** Romero *Knightriders* (film): Cukes. Zukes. Eggplants. Tomatoes. **1984** *N.Y. Post* (Aug. 18) 27: Cukes for salads are ready when they're about eight inches.

cull¹ *n.* [prob. fr. *cullion* 'a contemptible fellow'] [**1.** [These senses are not attested in AmE, but are the origin of **(2)**, below, and are related to comparable senses of CULLY.]

a. a foolish fellow; dupe; SUCKER. [The 1665 quot. is erron. dated "1671" by Farmer & Henley.]

1665 in *F & H* II: Culle, a sap-headed fellow. ***1698–99*** "B.E." *Dict. Canting Crew*: Cull, Cully,…a Man, a Fop, a Rogue, a Fool or silly Creature that is easily drawn in and cheated by Whores or Rogues.

b. *Specif.* a customer of a prostitute.

1680 in Burford *Bawdy Verse* 172: Yet if a Cull they by chance should meet/At him they will be bobbing. ***1748*** in *F & H* II: Cull…a cant word for a man, either good or bad, but generally means one that a wench has picked up for some naughty purpose. ***1818*** in Partridge *Dict. Und.* 169: Cull, the dupe of prostitutes. ***1823*** "J. Bee" *Slang* 61: Formerly a cull was a prostitute's favourite; now, however, 'tis a customer of any sort who *pays* for "favors secret, sweet, and precious."… *Cully* is but a variation.

2. a man; fellow; (*later*) comrade.—in more recent use, only in direct address, esp. to a man whose name is not known. Now *hist.*

1665 in Partridge *Dict. Und.* 169: The Cul Snylches…The man eyes you. ***1698–99*** (quot. at **(a)**, above). ***1717*** in Partridge *Dict. Und.* 169: The Cull looks as if he had the Blunt. ***1748*** (quot. at **(1.b.)**, above). ***1785*** Grose *Vulgar Tongue*: Cull, a man, honest or otherwise. **1859** Matsell *Vocab.* 23: Cull. A man; sometimes a partner. **1882** *Judge* (Dec. 9) 7: By the way, cull, want to buy my trotter? **1902–03** Ade *People You Know* 88: What's the matter, Cull? Here, Bud, open your Eyes! **1904** in "O. Henry" *Works* 1212: Say, cull,…wot's doin'? **1906** H. Green *Actors' Boarding House* 130: Don't bodder me, cul. **1906** in McCay *Little Nemo* 65: Go ahead! Tell me what you are going to do! See, Cull? **1914** S. Lewis *Mr. Wrenn* 165: He…frequently said, "Ah there, cull," in general admiration. **1923** Ornitz *Haunch, Paunch & Jowl* 102: Well, culls, look out dat don't happen to youse. **1926** Mac Issac *Tin Hats* 47: It's this way, cul. **1926** *Marine Corps Gaz.* (Dec.) 243: Forgit it, cull, I was doin' fatigue the hull time. **1952** Sandburg *Young Strangers* 167 [ref. to *ca*1890]: John MacNally met a hobo near the Q. switchyards, a New York Bowery boy who said, "Kuh-hay, Cull, wot's duh chance fer duh next cab over duh rails—huh?"

cull² *n.* [fr. S.E. sense 'something rejected as worthless'] Esp. *Stu.* a stupid, inept, or obnoxious person.

1939 in *Calif. Folk. Qly.* I 292: You have to be a *whole man* before you can switch wells. *It won't work for no culls.* **1955** Salter *Hunters* 24: It's probably some cull, but it might be old Casey himself. **1964** in *Time* (Jan. 1, 1965).

cully *n.* **1.a.** CULL¹, *n.*, 1.a.

1656 in Partridge *Dict. Und.* 169: Pinched the Cully of a Casket of Jewels. ***1673*** R. Head *Canting Acad.* 36: Cully, a Fool or Fop. ***1676*** in *F & H* II: We bite the *culley* of his cole. ***1676*** in D'Urfey *Two Comedies* 124: As dull as a rifl'd cully. ***1693*** Congreve, in *F & H* II: Man was by nature woman's *cully* made: We never are but by ourselves betrayed. ***1698*** N. Ward *London-Spy* 108: They were some of the Shallow-Brain'd *Cullies*, who were drawn in by the *Land-Bank*, and were fumbling out a method of licking themselves whole by cheating of other people. ***1698–99*** (quot. at CULL¹, *n.*, 1.a.). ***1708*** *Modern World Disrob'd* 96: If Men of Honour must be lewd,/And will be Women's Cullies/Let 'em not mix their noble Blood/With Scoundrels bred in Alleys.

*1726 A. Smith *Mems. of J. Wild* 116: Whilst the Cully was feeling what Gender she was of, she in the mean Time was feeling for his Watch. ***1785** Grose *Vulgar Tongue: Cully*, a fop or fool. **1826** Flint *10 Yrs.* 310: [To the gambling houses] the raw cullies from the upper country come, lose all, and either hang themselves, or get drunk, and perish in the streets.

b. CULL[1], *n.*, 1.b.

*1698 N. Ward *London-Spy* 72: On the East side...sat a parcel of Women, some looking like Jilts who wanted Cullies. ***1698–99** (quot. at CULL[1], *n.*, 1.a.). **1792** Brackenridge *Mod. Chiv.* 112: Old bauds, and strumpets, and cullies. ***1823** (quot. at CULL[1], *n.*, 1.b.).

2. CULL[1], *n.*, 2.

1846 J. Greene *Secret Band of Brothers* 112 [ref. to 1798]: If you wish to ascertain if a Brother be present, you can easily do so by *Sounding*. *Sounding* signifies *Feeling*, or *Ascertaining*; and if you wish to do, use the word *Culley*, which signifies Brother, Friend, Partner. **1848** *Ladies' Repository* VIII (Oct.) 315: *Cully*, A partner. **1854** *Crockett Almanac* (unp.): Where are you going with that baggage, Cully? **1867** Harte *Sk. of Sixties* 111: Cully! how's his nibs? ***1873** T. Frost *Circus Life* 280: "Cully" is the circus man's equivalent for the mechanic's "mate" and the soldier's "comrade." **1883–84** Whittaker *Locke* 178: Skip, cully, skip. *a*1889 in Barrère & Leland *Dict. Slang* I: "Where's your wife, old boy?"..."Don't know, *cully*." **1889** Alger *Snobden's Office Boy* 42: Say, cully, you're too fresh! **1892** Frye *From HQ* 166: Sa-ay, cully, w'at's de taxes on dese 'freshments? **1894** Bridges *Arcady* 56: And say, cully, can't ye give me a box of cigarettes? **1899** A.H. Lewis *Sandburrs* 108: Well, Cully, you don't miss much. **1902** Raine *Raasay* 67: A black night, my cullies. **1904** in "O. Henry" *Works* 1665: Come on, Cully...You're in on the feed. **1912** Lowrie *Prison* 41: We never stands f'r dat, do we, cullies? **1913–15** Van Loan *Taking the Count* 124: Dat's all right, cully....We don't charge you for dat. **1925** Mullin *Scholar Tramp* 113: "Here, Cully," he said, handing me a bottle of whisky.

culture vulture *n. Stu.* an overdiligent student; *(also)* an intellectual person interested in the humanities.

[**1931** Nash *Free Wheeling* 67: There is a woman—/There is a vulture/Who circles above/The carcass of culture.] [**1945** J. Bryan *Carrier* 35: "The Vulture for Culture," as Joe calls himself.] **1947** in *DAS* 134: Everybody can't be a culture vulture. **1952** Sandburg *Young Strangers* 292: The Standishes were what my friend Tom Ferril of Denver calls "Culture Vultures." **1955–57** Felder *Collegiate Slang* 1: *Culture vulture*—an intellectual. **1963** Behan *N.Y.* 42: Stuff of that sort for the culture vulture. **1969** Crumley *Count Cadence* 202: He grew a beard to go with his long hair, and was soon a minor rage among new rich, pseudo liberals, culture vultures in Phoenix. **1971** *Playboy* (Apr.) 105: All right, culture vultures, here's a list of heavy dudes and sisters. **1972** *N.Y. Times* (Apr. 2) 13: Fiedler is also aware of the members of the public who dismiss him as a charlatan, hooting at his symphonic versions of Broadway and Tin Pan Alley tunes. He calls these people "culture-vultures" and returns the disdain. **1973** Flaherty *Fogarty* 175: His son [was] doomed to these culture vultures, being endlessly dragged about a museum on a Sunday afternoon. **1983** *New Yorker* (Aug. 8) 21: Shelley Winters is Charlotte Hazard, the culture vulture rampant.

cultus *adj.* [< Chinook Jargon] *N.W.* worthless; despicable.

1851 in *DA*. **1900** Wister *Jimmyjohn* 210: He can't bile water without burnin' it, and his toes turns in, and he's blurry round the finger-nails. He's jest kultus, he is. **1904** in *Dict. Canadianisms*. **1922** Rollins *Cowboy* 79: "Cultus" (despicable, worthless). **1954** Voorhees *Show Me a Hero* 146: A no-good character....A no-good cultus man without manners or morals. **1972** Bercovici & Prentiss *Culpepper Cattle Co.* (film): They're plum cultus. Just as mean as they come.

cum var. COME, *n. & v.*

cume *n.* **1.** a cumulative figure; *specif.* (*Stu.*) a cumulative grade-point average.

1968 Baker et al. *CUSS* 102: *Cume.* Overall academic average. **1976** Univ. Tenn. student: I'll lose financial aid if I can't boost my cume. **1980** in Safire *Good Word* 304: It could shoot my cume (...cumulative GPA). **1986** R. Walker *AF Wives* 54: Her grades...had been very high—a lofty 3.9 cum.

2. *Adver.* the cumulative audience reached by an advertising campaign.

1979 Homer *Jargon* 88.

cumshaw *n.* [pidgin < Amoy *kam siā* 'grateful thanks'] **1.** *Naut., esp. in Far East.* a present or gratuity; *(broadly)* a bribe.

*1818 (cited in Partridge *DSUE* (ed. 8) 277). **1840** in *Essex. Inst. Hist. Coll.* LXXXIV (1948) 311: About $100 worth of Cumsha teas. **1868** in

Boyer *Naval Surgeon* II 85: The city doctor gave me a kumshaw consisting of 5 fans and a saki cup. **1906** Beyer *Amer. Battleship* 83: "Cum shaw"—a rake-off. **1908** J.H. Williams, in *Independent* (Aug. 27) 471: "Cummshaw"...is pigeon English for "commission." **1935** Pollock *Und. Speaks: Cumshaw*, the pay off; bribe money; shakedown. **1936** *ISU Pilot* (Aug. 14) 1: Every bona fide seaman who goes to sea for a living and who doesn't expect some "comshaw" from Scharrenburg & Co. has voiced his disapproval of this bill. **1940** *AS* (Dec.) 450 [sea]: *Cumshaw*. This Chinese word is used along the seaboards of various countries as well as throughout the Orient. It means *boodle* or bribe rather than just reward. **1951** Morris *China Station* 19: You give one of them brats cumshaw, you get every one in town down our necks. **1957** Campbell *Cry for Happy* 29: Can't you slip the cook some cumshaw to keep him interested. **1958** McCulloch *Woods Words* 42: *Cumsha*—A handout (from Indian); also spelled cumshaw.

2. *Naut.* anything obtained unexpectedly, free of charge, or through means that are devious, ingenious, unofficial, etc.

*1925 in Fraser & Gibbons *Soldier & Sailor Wds.* 69 [ref. to WWI]: *Cumshaw:* Naval slang for something "extra"; something gratis; a perquisite; a gift, equivalent to Buckshee. ***1929** Bowen *Sea Slang* 32: *Cumsha.* Anything extra or unexpected...It is generally applied to money which comes unexpectedly. **1931** Erdman *Reserve Officer's Manual* 431: *Cumshaw.* Something for nothing...Synonymous with "baksheesh" (Arabic), "jawbone," and "squeeze." **1951** Morris *China Station* 86 [ref. to WWII]: Any job he could induce the tender to accept without an approved work request,...was known as cumshaw, and the engineering officer's service reputation was largely computed by the amount of cumshaw he was able to produce. **1971** Sheehan *Arnheiter* 61: Belmonte was the *Vance's* acknowledged "cum shaw" expert, the man...who does the semilegal horse trading for items the ship...cannot obtain through regular supply channels. **1971** Noel & Beach *Naval Terms* 81: *Cumshaw*...In the U.S. Navy the term now relates to unauthorized work done for or equipment given to a ship or station, and usually no connotation of personal gain exists. A "cumshaw artist" is a man who is adept at getting cumshaw work done, frequently by liberal handouts of food and coffee to the shipyard workers.

cumshaw *v.* **1.** (in the Far East) to give a gift or gratuity to; *(broadly)* to bribe.

1868 in Boyer *Naval Surgeon* II 85: He kumshawed me with a piece of dress goods. **1870** Greey *Blue Jackets* 77: Hi! you dogs. I'm pilot here. If you don't cumshaw me (i.e., fee me) I'll get these red-haired devils to burn your town about your ears.

2. *Orig. Navy.* to obtain by devious or ingenious methods; scrounge.

1918 Ruggles *Navy Explained* 33: *Cum Shaw.* The Chinese merchant's name for come ashore. When he tells you to come ashore, it means to kick loose or come across. Also, to get money from some person as a bribe, or graft from a shipmate. **1961** Bosworth *Crows* 32: I need to cumshaw a pickup truck, or a jeep, next weekend. Got any wheels in your department? **1964** Peacock *Drill & Die* 35: There was only a cumshawed wooden desk, two field chairs against the wall, the three flags...behind the desk. **1962–68** B. Jackson *In the Life* 132: You can comshaw—or steal—comshaw is a much better word—a $25 chip from a table. **1971** Dibner *Trouble with Heroes* 15: Cumshaw what you can and steal the rest. **1971** Murphy & Gentry *2nd in Command* 28: "Cumshawing," more politely defined as "appropriating" and less politely as "stealing," was also essential in providing seating in the research spaces.

Cunnuck var. CANUCK.

cunny *n.* CUNT, 1.a., b.—usu. considered vulgar. Also (*obs.*) **coney.**

*ca1615 in Farmer *Merry Songs* IV 3: There traffique is of coney. ***1622** in *Folklore* CII (1991) 197: [Whores] cry, like poulterer's wives,/"No money, no coney!" **1666** G. Alsop *Maryland* 61: Their Virginity...a deed of Gift of it to Mother Coney. ***1731** "H. Thrumbo" *Merry-Thought* III 4: Yet I ne'er knew a C—y that savour'd of Civet. ***1879–80** *Pearl* (passim). ***a1890–91** *F & H* II 230: The female pudendum...cunny. **1972** Friday *Secret Garden* 85: In and out of her exposed cunnie. **1974** *Coq* (Apr.) 46: Can't you tell cock from cunny, you little bitch?

cunny-thumper *n.* a rascal. *Joc.*

1978 in Lyle & Golenbock *Bronx Zoo* 239: 'Bout time you won twenty, you cunny thumper.

cunt *n.* [ME *cunte*] **1.a.** the vulva or vagina.—usu. considered vulgar. Also in prov. phrs.

*ca1230, *a1325, *a1400, *a1425 in *OEDS.* ***a1425, *ca1440,**

*a**1450**, *ca**1500** in *MED.* *ca**1650** Hales & Furnivall *Loose Songs* 99: Vp start the Crabfish, & catcht her by the Cunt. **1748** in Breslaw *Tues. Club* 105: To the pious memory of Sally Salsburys ****. **1778** in Connor *Songbag* 116: In war we'll stand the brunt:/Here's a health to that good thing boys/Which mortals call a c—. *1818** J. Keats, in Partridge *Vulgar Tongue* 112: After which there was an enquiry about the derivation of the word C—t. *ca**1866** *Romance of Lust* 229: I saw Aunt's hand steal down to her cunt. **1888** *Stag Party* 41: And to her astonishment tickled her cunt. **1919** in Dreiser *Diaries* 291: Theo is fucking Helens cunt. **1928** in Read *Lexical Evidence* 46: Ashes to ashes and dust to dust/if it wasn't for cunts your cock would rust. *Ibid.* 47: I…eat cunt. **1942** McAtee *Supp. to Grant Co. Dial.* 4 [ref. to 1890's]: c—n, the female pudendum. **1950** in Randolph *Pissing in Snow* 43: A fellow that spells CUNT with a K ain't got no business in the Congress of the United States! **1952** Himes *Stone* 115: "Kiss my ass!" "Kiss your mother's—" There was the usual fight. **1974** Loken *Come Monday Morning* 6: The whole damn works froze up tighter'n a nun's cunt. **1982** Hayano *Poker Faces* 55: I've played with tight players, but you're tighter than a nun's cunt. **1983** K. Weaver *Texas Crude* 18: Flat as a mule cunt. **1991** B.E. Ellis *Amer. Psycho* 101: Her cunt is tight and hot and wet.

b. copulation with a woman.—usu. considered vulgar.

*ca**1670** Lord Rochester, in Burford *Bawdy Verse* 147: I to Cunt am not a foe. *ca**1680** in R. Thompson *Unfit for Modest Ears* 120: C—t was the Star that rul'd thy Fate,/C—t the sole business and Affair of State. *1791** R. Burns, in Barke & Smith *Merry Muses* 140: I tell you even c— has lost its power to please. **1918** in Carey *Mlle. from Armentières* II (unp.): The soldier who wants a piece of —/In France will never have far to hunt. *ca**1929** *Collection of Sea Songs* 22: We love our rum and cunt. **1931** Dos Passos *1919* 43: Hart…whispered to Joe did he want some c—t. **1931** in H. Miller *Letters to Emil* 82: Everything is futile to him. Everything but cunt. **1934** H. Roth *Call It Sleep* 411 [ref. to ca1915]: An' w'en it comes t' booze, I says, shove it up yer ass! Cunt fer me, ev'ytime, I says. **1947–52** Ellison *Invisible Man* 323: A pat on the back and a piece of cunt with no passion? **1960** Sire *Deathmakers* 170: *I* got some cunt here you should try. **1965** C. Brown *Manchild* 170: But some of their daughters were giving away more cunt than Dixie was selling. **1972** C. Gaines *Stay Hungry* 72: They're sweeter'n cunt. **1972** A.K. Shulman *Ex-Prom Queen* 105: He cares only for cunt.

c. a woman or women considered solely as objects of copulation; (*occ.*) a woman or women.—usu. considered vulgar.—usu. used contemptuously.

*1674** in R. Thompson *Unfit for Modest Ears* 123: She came to set up C—ts to Fifth Monarchy. *1675** in Burford *Bawdy Verse* 170: Citty Cunts are dangerous sport,/Who…/Trudge to Moseley's where ye fatt things/Fuck with Shaftesbury and Judge Atkins./…Whitehall Cunts are…fitt for no man. **1916** Cary *Venery* 161: *Cunt*—The female pudendum…The word is also generic for women. **1918** in K. White *First Sex. Revolution* 88: Twenty cunts hanging around here. **1923** *Poems, Ballads & Parodies* 43: I went on a bunt/With a damn swell cunt. **1924** Wilstach *Anecdota Erotica* 35: McDonald story of the Colorado Sheriff saying, after a discussion of the evils of permitting women to drink,—"A drunk c— has no guard." *a**1927** in P. Smith *Letter from Father* 56: Larry and I…would…have the cunts lift their skirts. **1931** in H. Miller *Letters to Emil* 86: Interviews with distinguished cunts. **1934** H. Roth *Call It Sleep* 414 [ref. to ca1915]: I sees a pretty cunt come walkin' up de street…wit' a mean shaft an' a sweet pair o' knockers. **1934** H. Miller *Tropic of Cancer* 22: A cunt who can play as she does ought to have better sense. **1936** Dai *Opium Addiction* 141: The cunt I was living with had gone away with this other fellow. **1947** in J. Jones *Reach* 113: Dan…was at Condon's last night with two gorgeously decked out cunts. **1950** in Randolph & Legman *Roll Me in Your Arms* 275 [song learned in 1898]: I'll go hunt a new cunt. **1958** Cooley *Run for Home* 47: It was that red-headed cunt at the hotel last night. **1961** in Rose *Storyville* 159: All dem cunts was talkin' about Marie Laveau was dead. **1962** W. Crawford *Tomorrow* 33: Francis. A cunt's name. **1965** Pollini *Glover* 91: Nice cunt, brunette, you know her. **1966** W. Wilson *LBJ Brigade* 68: You ain't fightin' for liberty or America or the cunt next door. You're fightin' ta stay alive. **1968** Smart *Long Watch* 37: What cooks? You got a piece of cunt down there? **1970** *Harper's* (Feb.) 51: We break out [of puritan restraint] by posting pictures of cunt on the street. **1974** Charyn *Blue Eyes* 25: The cunt are scarier in Queens.

d. *Specif.* a despicable or contemptible woman, esp. one who is sexually promiscuous; BITCH.—usu. considered vulgar. [Not always easily distinguishable from (c), above.]

1916–22 Cary *Sexual Vocab.* II s.v. *female: Cold cunt.* An indifferent woman….*Stingy cunt.* A woman chary of her favors. **1933** Ford & Tyler *Young & Evil* 146: You ought to know those cunts. **1937–40** in Whyte

Street Corner Society 7 [ref. to 1920's]: He called her a ——. I saw her going down the stairs crying. **1959** J. Rechy, in *Big Table* I (No. 3) 33: You dizzy silly cunt. **1961** J. Baldwin *Another Country* 316: Answer me, you bitch, you slut, you *cunt!* **1965** Linakis *In Spring* 19: You know what the bastard, no good, sonofabitchin', redheaded, whorin' cunt wanted me to do? **1968** P. Roth *Portnoy* 120: The cunt! I'm lucky really that I came out of that affair *alive.* **1970** Cortina *Slain Warrior* 186: You stupid cunt. **1970** in J. Flaherty *Chez Joey* 17: The regular Joe's wife was bitching at him…until he told her to stop being a cunt. **1985** D. Steel *Secrets* 107: He called her a "dumb cunt," and as he said the words she could feel something snap inside. **1985** Briskin *Too Much* 47: You dumb English cunt. Ain't I taught you nothing? **1991** B.E. Ellis *Amer. Psycho* 59: I leave the cunt no tip.

e. an infuriating object or mechanical device.—usu. considered vulgar.

*1931** Partridge *Vulgar Tongue* 111: [British soldiers in 1914–18] if displeased with rifle or knapsack or indeed almost any object, occasion or person would describe it as "a c—." **1978** E. Thompson *Devil to Pay* 31: Those things are cunts. **1983** S. King *Christine* 120: Come loose, you cunt. **1985** Univ. Tenn. grad. student: I've heard "You cunt" addressed to bicycles, machine parts, anything like that. Certainly by the [early 1960's].

f. that which is extraordinarily difficult or unpleasant; BITCH.—usu. considered vulgar.

1963 Ark. gas station attendant (coll. J. Ball): It's gonna be a cunt gettin' this done.

2. a despicable, contemptible, or foolish man.—usu. considered vulgar. Occ. adj.

1860 in Neely *Lincoln Encyc.* 154: And when they got to Charleston, they had to, as is wont/Look around to find a chairman, and so they took a Cu—. *1922** T.E. Lawrence *Mint* 50: You're silly cunts, you rookies, to sweat yourselves. *Ibid.* 69: Stiffy was laughing like a cunt. **1928** in Read *Lexical Evidence* 48: Why fuck me when thers [*sic*] a cunt like you hanging around. *1929** Manning *Fortune* 37 [ref. to 1916]: Wouldn't you've thought the cunt would 'a' give me vingt frong for 'em anyway? *1929** Aldington *Death of a Hero* 243 [ref. to WWI]: Bloody old c—. **1939** Bessie *Men in Battle* 233: Where is that c… Garfield? **1962** Crump *Killer* 154: I ought to hit you in the head, cunt. **1964** Rhodes *Chosen Few* 17: Contrary to what they told you in that cunt recruiting office, this does not make you a Marine. **1966** Terry *Keep Tightly Closed* 184: You first-class prick…You second-class cunt. **1967** Crowley *Boys in the Band* 822: Donald, you are a real *card-carrying cunt.* **1969** S. Harris *Puritan Jungle* 44: That cheap cunt Mann is always late. For all he pays us, you wouldn't think he'd have the gall to keep us waiting. **1970–71** J. Rubinstein *City Police* 108: That fuckin' rookie prick. Making me look like a cunt. **1973** R. Roth *Sand in the Wind* 78: TAKE CARE OF THIS GUTLESS CUNT. **1974** Blount *3 Bricks Shy* 106: Some guys I like to mouth off to. Say, "Old Cunt. You must be having your period." **1973–77** J. Jones *Whistle* 176: That cunt Baker had called him a "guardhouse lawyer." **1966–80** McAleer & Dickson *Unit Pride* 137: I'll be a dirty cunt if I want my kids fighting a war. **1983** N. Proffitt *Gardens of Stone* 145: Let's cover this cunt and get on the bus. **1987** E. Spencer *Macho Man* 10: The worst thing you could call a fellow Marine was a cunt.

3. *Narc.* (see 1974 quot.).—usu. considered vulgar.

1970, 1971 (cited in Spears *Drugs & Drink*). **1974** Hyde *Mind Drugs* 153: *Cunt*…An area of vein favored for injection [of heroin, etc.] usually in the arm.

4. *Navy.* a yeoman.—used derisively.—usu. considered vulgar.

1972 Ponicsan *Cinderella Liberty* 166: "What rate did you finally get, by the way?" "Yeoman second class."…"A cunt! I shoulda knew!"

cunt *adj.* pornographic; erotic.—used prenominally.—usu. considered vulgar. Cf. COCK, *adj.*, FUCK, *adj.*

1950 in J. Jones *Reach* 162: The word "cunt-pictures"…is as much a common term in the Army as "latrine."…That term, and not…"pin-ups," was the term used [in 1941]. **1974** R. Carter *16th Round* 165: The worthless luxuries that most of the inmates craved—the cunt books, the fags, the cigarettes, the movies.

cuntbreath *n.* COCKBREATH.—usu. considered vulgar.

1991 Marcinko & Weisman *Rogue Warrior* 141: He was a stupid asshole cuntbreath.

cunt cap *n. Army & USMC.* an overseas or garrison cap.—usu. considered vulgar. Also **cunt hat.**

[*1923** Manchon *Slang* 97: *Cunt-hat*…chapeau de feutre.] *1945** in Baker *Austr. Lang.* (ed. 2) 170: C*nt cap, forrage cap issued to A.I.F. till about 1942. ***1948** Partridge, Granville & Roberts *Forces' Slang* 51: C**t *cap* or *hat*. Synonymous with *splitarse cap;* i.e., a forage cap. **1956** *AS* XXXI (Oct.) 108: *Cunt cap* (garrison hat; so called because of the grooved top). **1964** Rhodes *Chosen Few* 27 [ref. to 1950]: Garrison cap, otherwise known as a cunt cap or piss cutter. **1969** Groninger *Run* 14: With his cunt cap square on his head. **1971** in *AS* XLVII (1972) 39 [ref. to 1918]: The overseas cap...made you look like a fool. Some of the boys would call it a *cunt cap*. **1974** E. Thompson *Tattoo* 100: A white soldier, his cunt cap crosswise on his dome, staggered along happily. *a***1982** in Berry *Semper Fi* 282 [ref. to WWII]: They gave us the globe and anchor to put on our piss cutters (also called cunt hat...and garrison cap). **1982** Downey *Losing the War* 45 [ref. to WWII]: At least get your fuckin' cunt cap on right. **1988** Fussell *Wartime* 92: The...overseas cap...[was] called [during WWII] a *cunt cap*.

cunt collar *n. Black E.* sexual desire for women.—usu. considered vulgar.

    1965 C. Brown *Manchild* 193: Even cats with long cunt collars would get tired of screwing these cold junkie bitches. **1968** Heard *Howard St.* 176: She'd have no trouble putting a cunt-collar on Franchot. **1970** Cain *Blueschild Baby* 63: He let his cunt collar overrule his reason.

cunt-eyed *adj.* having narrow or squinting eyes.—usu. considered vulgar.

    *1916 Cary *Venery* II 123: English bullies have a pet term: "You cunt-eyed sod." **1980** Conroy *Lords of Discipline* 93: Bawl, you fucking cunt-eyed baby.

cuntface *n.* an ugly or despicable person.—usu. considered vulgar. Hence **cuntfaced,** *adj.*

    *1948 Partridge *DSUE* (ed. 3) 1025: C*nt *face* is a low term of address to an ugly person: late C. 19–20. **1962** Mandel *Wax Boom* 37 [ref. to WWII]: Get the hell out of here, you cunt-faced son of a bitch! **1970** Sorrentino *Steelwork* 6: Semper Fidelis, shape up, cuntface bastards! **1974** Charyn *Blue Eyes* 149: Manfred, you got to be a cuntface and a snot from your mother. **1977** Bredes *Hard Feelings* 223: I can't hear you, cuntface. **1980** M. Baker *Nam* 51: Hanoi Hanna....The little cunt face. But I liked listening to her. **1981** *Nat. Lampoon* (Aug.) 16: His...cunt-faced, slut girl friend. **1991** Sachar *Let Lady Teach* 67: "Say it!...9 x 2 is 18." "Cuntface."

cunt hair *n.* a minute distance or margin; a hair.—usu. considered vulgar. Also **cunt's hair.**

    [**1958** McCulloch *Woods Words* 27: "C" *hair*—A unit of measurement used in forest surveys.] **1963–64** Kesey *Great Notion* 468: So's the tree would fall so cunthair *perfect* that he could put a stake where he aimed for it to fall, then...drive that stake into the ground with the trunk! **1970** Whitmore *Memphis-Nam-Sweden* 43: But I ain't moving a cunt's hair. **1973** N.Y.U. prof.: Have you ever heard the military expression a *cunthair?*...It means something very, very fine, very small. That's from the Korean War or maybe World War II. **1974** Pine Plains, N.Y., man, age 24: Last year I was working on construction. If they were measuring and it was just a little bit off, they'd say, "It's just a cunt hair off." **1976** Price *Bloodbrothers* 47: I was a cunt hair away from runnin' you through. **1974–77** Heinemann *Close Quarters* 45: You yank the ring and pull the pin all but half a cunt hair. **1984–88** Hackworth & Sherman *About Face* 37 [ref. to 1947]: Sergeant...Oller...gave his gunner corrections in phrases like "down a crack" and "left a cunt hair." *a***1989** C.S. Crawford *Four Deuces* 88: Trip wires...aren't but a cunt's hair thick.

cunthead *n.* an idiot.—usu. considered vulgar.

    1971 *Nat. Lampoon* (June) 8: I...beat the c—p out of the little c—thead until he about p—d in his pants. **1974** Univ. Tenn. student: Whatcha doing in San Antonio, ya cunthead? **1974–77** Heinemann *Close Quarters* 30: An' that fucken Trobridge is a *prime* cunt-head, too. **1983** N. Proffitt *Gardens of Stone* 292: No, that's too far, cunthead!

cunthound *n.* a man who obsessively seeks opportunities for sexual intercourse.—usu. considered vulgar.

    1960 Peacock *Valhalla* ch. 9 [ref. to 1953]: "I'm a cocksman from the word go," Poke said. "Me and Stack here...we are truly a couple of cunt-hounds." **1967** C. Cooper *Farm* 195: I knew Joe was 1 helluva cunthound, or so he said, and was having a lot of trouble with his wife. **1969** Pharr *Numbers* 101 [ref. to ca1930]: Fact is, if you weren't such a cunt hound you'da noticed her walk instead of her butt. That gal is built like a champ. *Ibid.* 160: Everybody said us sailors were drunks and cunt hounds. **1971** Dahlskog *Dict.* 17: *Cunt hound, n.* A man who is sexually very active; one who is always looking for a female sex partner.

cuntish *adj.* womanish.—used contemptuously.—usu. considered vulgar.

    1975 Wambaugh *Choirboys* 53: Don't go cuntish on me!

cunt-lapper *n.* a person who performs cunnilingus; (*hence*) a despicable person.—usu. considered vulgar. Also **cunt-licker.**

    1916 Cary *Slang of Venery* I 63: *Cunt Lapper*—A name given to a man who tongues a woman. Also applied to women who follow the same practice. **1934** "J.M. Hall" *Anecdota* 29: He insulted her by calling her a cheap little cunt-lapper. *Ibid.* 168: Calling him a cunt lapper for interfering with his sport. **1938** "Justinian" *Americana Sexualis* 19: *Cunt-Lapper.* n. A male who participates in *cunnilingus.* Sometimes, merely a derogatory term for anyone disliked: a fop, effeminate male, or concupiscent person. Vulgarism, U.S., C. 19–20. **1942** H. Miller *Roofs of Paris* 263: That cunt licker. **1955** Caprio *Variations* 239: Cunnilingus is a very repulsive act as far as a man's conception of a man who would practice it. He is called a "c—t lapper."...Men look on a "c—t lapper" as they would a "c—ks—r." **1971** Dahlskog *Dict.* 17: *Cunt lapper, n. Vulgar.* One who performs cunnilingus; one who prefers cunnilingus to other forms of sexual activity; any disliked person. **1980** Kotzwinkle *Jack* 205: We'll smoke those cuntlappers! **1988** C. Roberts & C. Sasser *Walking Dead* 210 [ref. to ca1966]: That's just in case the slant-eyed cuntlickers cut us off here and we can't be resupplied from Da Nang.

cunt-lapping *adj.* degenerate or despicable; goddamned.—usu. considered vulgar. Also **cunt-licking.**

    1923 M. Cowley, in Jay *Burke–Cowley Corresp.* 135: I'm not ashamed to...tell these cunt-lapping Europeans that I'm an American citizen. **1947–53** W. Guthrie *Seeds* 99: Cunt-lappin' gold. **1967** Styron *Nat Turner* 285: You is a sonabitchin' cuntlappin' fuckah! **1974** Terkel *Working* 525: What a cunt-lapping society we've become! **1975** S.P. Smith *Amer. Boys* 198: I don't care. I don't care about no cunt-lapping monkey either. **1985** *Maledicta* VIII 244: Of all the cocksucking, cuntlicking, asshole ideas I've hever heard of, this is the most unfuckinbelievable.

cunt show *n. Wrestling.* (see quot.).—usu. considered vulgar.

    1980 *AS* (Summer) 145: A [wrestling] match between women is called a *cunt show.*

cunt-struck *adj.* infatuated with sexual desire for a woman or women.—usu. considered vulgar.

    ca*1866** *Romance of Lust* 476: He...became in fact cunt-struck upon her. ***1879** *Pearl* 139: By no means am I so cunt-struck now. **1916** Cary *Venery* I 64: *Cunt struck*—Enamored of women. **1923** Manchon *Le Slang* 97: *Cunt-struck*...porté sur les femmes. ***1929** Manning *Fortune* 116: Seems to me you're getting a bit cunt-struck. **1934** H. Miller *Tropic of Cancer* 4: He is cunt-struck, that's all. **1943** in P. Smith *Letter from Father* 362: Was I just cunt struck—could that have been my trouble I wonder? **1920–54** Randolph & Legman *Blow Candle Out* 785: At Granby, Mo., they were talking about a young man who was *cunt-struck,* interested in nothing but running after women. **1972** McGregor *Bawdy Ballads* 48: You cunt-struck simp of a Yankee pimp. **1975** S. Bellow *Humboldt's Gift* 204: Were we to end our lives as cunt-struck doddering wooers left over from a Goldoni farce?

cunt-sucker *n.* **1.** a person who performs cunnilingus.—usu. considered vulgar.

    *1868 in *OEDS:* A satire on Baeticus, who was a priest of Cybele, and a cunt-sucker. **1940** Del Torto: The greatest cunt sucker. **1942** H. Miller *Roofs of Paris* 277: You dirty little cunt sucker! **1967** Schmidt *Lexicon of Sex* 58: *Cunt-sucker*...The male counterpart of a fellatrice. **1972** R. Barrett *Lovomaniacs* 355: I don't mean cuntsuckers or other specialists like that.

    2. a despicable person; COCKSUCKER.—usu. considered vulgar. Hence **cuntsucking,** *adj.*

    1964 W. Burroughs *Nova Express* 56: You stinking...cunt sucking...bastards. **1964** in Gover *Trilogy* 251: Hello, you confederit cunsugger. **1970** Thackrey *Thief* 252: Hell, the least she could have done was date some 4-F cuntsucker who could pay his own freight. **1971** S. Stevens *Way Uptown* 221: Goddam right, that's what those colorless cuntsuckers in Washington need.

cunt-tickler *n.* a mustache; PUSSY-TICKLER.—usu. considered vulgar. *Joc.*

    1967 Mailer *Vietnam* 15: I wish you...had a cunt-tickler of a mustache.

cunt wagon *n.* a fancy automobile intended by its owner to aid in impressing and seducing young women.—usu. considered vulgar.

    1974 E. Thompson *Tattoo* 360: A real cunt wagon...A real gem...Been up on blocks in a garage since forty-two. **1985** Ark. man, age 35: Man,

I've heard *cunt wagon* so many times! *Cunt wagon, pussy wagon.* My brother even used it back in the '60's.

cup *n.* a cup of coffee.
   1984 Knoxville, Tenn., businessman, age *ca*50: I'd like two scrambled eggs and a cup. **1986** R. Campbell *In La-La Land* 173: You want a cup? How about a glass of water?

cupboard *n.* the stomach; BREADBASKET.
   1842 *Spirit of Times* (Nov. 5) 421: Bell buttons…marked the graceful outward sweep of his "cupboard."

cupcake *n.* a sweet or attractive young woman.
   1939 D. Runyon, in *Collier's* (May 6) 9: I never see a prettier little cupcake than this nurse. **1946** Boulware *Jive & Slang* 2: Cup-Cake…Girl. **1970** Gattzden *Black Vendetta* 110: A cupcake like Ingebord. **1977** Hamill *Flesh & Blood* 40: Does this cupcake speak for you?

Cupid's itch *n.* gonorrhea or infestation with crab lice.
   1930 Irwin *Tramp & Und. Sl.: Cupid's Itch.*—Any venereal disease. **1944** Kendall *Service Slang* 50: *Orange-pop man…*a patient with Cupid's itch. **1967** Schmidt *Lexicon of Sex* 110: *Have cupid's itch…*To be venereally infected. **1976** *N.Y. Folklore* II 240: *Cupid's itch* is the eponym-synonymy for venereal disease. **1982** *East of Eden* (NBC-TV): There are many names for it—*Cupid's itch* will do well enough.

Cupid's measles *n.pl.* secondary syphilis; (*hence*) syphilis.
   1947 Schulberg *Harder They Fall* 32: A full set of *spirochaete pallida*, known to the world as syphilis and to the trade as Cupid's measles. **1959** Morrill *Dark Sea* 176 [ref. to WWII]: A couple of days after we burned the Japs, I started getting pains in my groin. "Cupid's measles," said the Steward.

cup of coffee *n. Baseball.* a brief trial as a major-league player.
   1908 in Fleming *Unforgettable Season* 92: A young player just getting his "cup of coffee" in the league. **1921** *Variety* (Aug. 19) 4: He once had a cup of coffee with the White Sox and had all the palaver of a big leaguer droppin down into the bushes for a short vacation. **1943** *Yank* (Oct. 8) 23: *Cup of coffee.* Short trial in the Majors. **1960** Garagiola *Funny Game* 89: The minor leaguer who never had that "cup of coffee" in the major leagues. **1971** Coffin *Old Ball Game* 55: "A cup of coffee" (a brief stay in the majors). **1984** Jackson & Lupica *Reggie* 57: In June of '67, I got called up to the Kansas City A's for a cup of coffee.

cupola *n.* the head.
   1899 A.H. Lewis *Sandburrs* 10: Mebby it's because he ain't used to woik, or mebby he gets funny in his cupolo, bein' up so high; anyhow he dives down to d' pavement, an' when he lands…Billy's d' deadest t'ing that ever happened. **1908** in H.C. Fisher *A. Mutt* 41: I am thoroughly convinced that the old man has a breeze in his cupalo. **1918** *Wash. Post* (June 2) (Mag. Sec.) 1: I'll bust your cupola like a blue-rock. **1924** H.L. Wilson *Professor* 142: That bird must be all curdled in his cupola. **1952** in *DAS* 134.

cuppa *n.* [informal pron. of *cup of*; orig. Brit. slang] a cup of tea or coffee.
   [*1925 P.G. Wodehouse, in *OED2*: Come and have a cuppa coffee.] *1934 (cited in *W9*). **1962** *N.Y. Times* (Sept. 30) VII 4: A chipper cuppa now and then is refreshment truly grateful for. **1972** Rossner *Any Minute* 135: You and me,…we can have a cuppa, huh? **1984** *New Yorker* (Nov. 19) 187: Pull up a chair, prop up your feet, pour yourself a cuppa. **1986** E. Weiner *Howard the Duck* 181: Anyway, I could sure use a shower and a cuppa.

curbie *n.* (see quot.).
   1937 *AS* (Dec.) 320: At roadside *drive-ins…*the waitresses are now being called *curbies* or *car-hops.*

curbstone canary *n. Hobo.* a whining beggar. *Joc.*
   1937 *Lit. Digest* (Apr. 10) 12: Sightseeing punks, mission stiffs, out-and-out bums, curbstone canaries, psychopaths and heat artists.

cure *n.* an eccentric, peculiar, or amusing individual.
   1856 in *F & H* II: The sweeper muttered, "He's a *cure.*" *1874 Hotten *Slang Dict.* (ed. 5): *Cure*, an odd person; a contemptuous term, abridged from *curiosity…*Of late years it has…been used to denote a funny, humorous person, who can give and receive chaff. **1889** Barrère & Leland *Dict. Slang* I: *Cure* (common), a curious, eccentric, odd person. Imported from America; was used with that sense twenty-five years ago. More generally now a humorous, comical person. Derived from an eccentric American popular song called "The Cure."

cure-all *n.* whiskey.—constr. with *the. Joc.*
   1848 *High Private* 11: So out the soldier goes after his whiskey, returning pays toll by giving the sentinel a *smack* at the welcome *cure-all.*

curious *adj.* amazing; notable; excellent.
   1832 J. Hall *Legends of West* 25: The way we'd fix these seven Indians would be curious. **1873** *Slang & Vulgar Forms* 10: Curious, for *excellent*; as, "These are *curious* apples." "This is *curious* wheat."

curl *v.* **1.** (see quot.).—constr. with *up.*
   1839 Marryatt *Diary* 266: "Curl up"—to be angry—from the panther and other animals raising their hair.
   2. (see quot.). Now *hist.*
   1856 B. Hall *College Wds.* 146: *Curl.* In the University of Virginia, to make a perfect recitation; to overwhelm a Professor with student learning. **1978** Dabney *Across Years* 80 [ref. to 1918]: A student [at the Univ. of Va.] who flunked a course was said to have "corked," while one who made a high mark was said to have "curled."
   3. *West.* to kill (someone).—constr. with *up.*
   1936 R. Adams *Cowboy Lingo* 171: When one killed another, he…"curled him up." **1951** West *Flaming Feud* 82: First you had to prove you were the Big Casino. How? By curling up Rock.

curlyhead *n.* a black person.—used derisively.
   1819 Clopper *Bawlfredonia* 69: A brace of curley heads*…*A name by which they called their black slaves.

curly whoop *n.* a boisterous cry.
   1834 Caruthers *Kentuck. in N.Y.* I 68: Then with a curly whoop, and a hurrah! for old Kentuck, I got to my own door.

curly wolf *n. West.* a tough, wild, or pugnacious fellow.
   1910 T.A. Dorgan, in Zwilling *TAD Lexicon* 29: He's supposed to be the curly wolf among the lightweights, eh, but he won't start. **1919** in *DA* 448: Alex was a curly wolf, they's no question about that. **1929–31** Runyon *Guys & Dolls* 93: When it comes to pool, the old judge is just naturally a curly wolf. **1931** Rynning *Gun Notches* 102: A curly wolf hombre come in the door shooting at the barkeep. **1944** R. Adams *West. Words: Curly wolf.* A tough character. **1967** Decker *To be a Man* 55: He was quite a boy, old Buck. A regular curly wolf. **1968** S.O. Barker *Rawhide Rhymes* 16: Charley…with his .45 ablaze/Rode squallin' into town with us, a shootin' in the air/To show the world we're curly wolves with cactus in our hair. **1969** L'Amour *Conagher* 71: Conagher…was an old curly wolf from the high country. **1981** Hogan *D. Bullet* 55: I ain't swallowing all this talk about him being such a curly wolf. Gets wet in the rain same as I do. **1982** WINS radio news report: They call him [Alabama football coach Bryant] "The Bear," but he's part fox and part curly wolf.

curse *n.* a menstrual period; menstruation.—constr. with *the.*
   1929–30 Dos Passos *42d Parallel* 147: She'd only had the curse a few times yet. **1942–43** C. Jackson *Lost Weekend* 74: Feigns headaches, falls asleep the minute she hits the hay, has the curse practically every day in the month—. **1963** Horwitz *Candlelight* 150: It's called the curse…, but I don't know if it is. **1979** Gutcheon *New Girls* 90: Christ! I've got the curse!

curtain climber *n.* a small child; toddler. *Joc.*
   1962 IUFA *Folk Speech*: Term for children: *Curtain climber.* **1986** *NDAS* 91.

curtains *n.pl.* **1.** Orig. *Theat.* the finish, esp. as by death or destruction. Cf. BIG CURTAIN.
   1901 T.A. Dorgan, in Zwilling *TAD Lexicon* 29: I got tired and tried to hold on, but I couldn't find anything. Gee whiz; I thought it was curtains. **1907** in H.C. Fisher *A. Mutt* 3: If my wife finds out…it's curtains. **1912** Lowrie *Prison* 80: It would 'a' been curtains fr all of us. **1914** London *Jacket* 62: Standing, you're going to come across with that dynamite, or I'll kill you in the jacket…You've got your choice—dynamite or curtains. **1918** *Sat. Eve. Post* (Jan. 19) 66: But when they're caught doing same it is curtains. **1919** in Gelman *Photoplay* 54: If she discovers he has told the truth, it's generally "curtains" for him. **1936** Cain *Double Indemnity* 450: Another eighth of an inch, and it would have been curtains for you. **1941** Schulberg *Sammy* 31: In court it looks like curtains for her until they clinch and decide to get married. **1944** C.B. Davis *Leo McGuire* 118: When a burglar gets greedy it's a disease and it's curtains. **1944** Gould *Tracy* 11: Okay, copper, brace yourself! This is curtains! **1963** Packer *Alone at Night* 21: One day he'll put a bug in Oliver Percy's ear, and it'll be curtains for me. **1978** Severin *Brendan* 123: I hope the mast doesn't go. That really would be curtains.
   2. *Homosex.* the foreskin.
   1971 Rader *Govt. Inspected* 12: "He still got his curtains?" meaning foreskin.

curve *n.* **1.** *pl.* peculiarities; ways.—usu. constr. with *onto.*
   1891 in Leitner *Diamond in Rough* 155: We'll just get onto the devil's curves/And knock him out of the box. **1894** Bridges *Arcady* 22: He's

lived with you so long that we're not onto his curves. **1895** Wood *Yale Yarns* 217: Just get on to my curves! **1895** in J.I. White *Git Along Dogies* 66: I'm going to keep cases on them sky pilots and try to get onto their curves. **1895** Townsend *Fadden* 31: I was dead crazy 'cause I couldn't git onto 'is curves. **1898** Doubleday *Gunner Aboard "Yankee"* 13: The next time you try to size up a new shipmate be sure you are on to his curves. **1898** Dunne *Mr. Dooley in Peace & War* 74: Day be day he had his pitchers took, an' still th' people didn't get onto th' cur-rves iv him. **1901** Wister *Philosophy* 11 [ref. to *ca*1882]: Yep...you've put us onto their curves enough. Go on. **1906** Ford *Shorty McCabe* 215: Anyway, I ain't losin' my eyesight, tryin' to follow his curves. **1910** Service *Trail of '98* 15: Oh, I'm onto their curves all right.

2. a development; wrinkle.

1899 Thomas *Arizona* 35: Funny, though, to run up against a new curve, 'way out here.

3. a shapely young woman.

1927 *DN* V 443: *Curve*, n. A beautifully formed woman. **1933–34** Lorimer & Lorimer *Stag Line* 143: There's a pretty cute little curve. *Ibid.* 170: You're a nice little curve. I could learn you a lot.

4. an instance of surprisingly unfair treatment; CURVE-BALL.—usu. in phr. **throw a curve** to surprise and outwit, trick, etc.

1947 Willingham *End As a Man* 37: The goddamn bastard treats me like a hound...What have I done to rate a godblasted curve like that? **1953** M. Harris *Southpaw* 3: Think of somebody that would never throw you a curve come thick or thin. **1969** *Star Trek* (NBC-TV): "What did they do, Jim?" "Threw me a few curves. I'll explain later." **1971** Dibner *Trouble with Heroes* 105: You threw him one hell of a curve.

curveball *n.* a tricky or unexpected question or action.

1944 in *AS* XX 147: *Curve Balls.* Tricky questions on an examination. **1962** Perry *Young Man* 163: It's just like my Uncle Max used to say, you always got to be looking for the curve ball! **1966** Gallery *Start Engines* 105: All eyes now turned to the Captain, curious as to how the Old Man would handle this unheard-of curve ball. **1968** W. Crawford *Gresham's War* 32: He never came on like this before. He was aces up north...These were curve balls.

curve-buster *n. Stu.* a student whose grades are significantly higher than the average.

1969 *Current Slang* I & II 23: *Curve-buster*, n. Someone who is substantially over the mean on a test.—Air Force Academy cadets. **1985** Univ. Tenn. student: Somebody who wants to study all the time and get those high grades is a *curve-buster*.

cush *n.* **1.** money.

1898–1900 Cullen *Chances* 20: I need the cush, being several shy of paying my feed bills. **1899** Cullen *Tales* 76: "Go to the devil," said I. "I'd already went, until I struck this...graft," said he..."Now I'm getting the cush. Want to come in?" *Ibid.* 84: Two hundred dollars of my cush in the hands of a hotel clerk...! **1904** *Life in Sing Sing* 246: *Cush.* Money. *Ibid.* 261: Everything was rosy, the cush was coming strong. **1904** Ade *True Bills* 83: I have been discouraged at times to think that I had to get my Cush by such slow and painful Methods. **1904** Hughie Cannon *Little Gertie Murphy* (NY: Howley-Dresser Co., 1904) sheet music: Goitie's got all of de cush. **1905** Hobart *Search Me* 63: They've put up their good cush to send me on tour. **1906** *Nat. Police Gaz.* (Nov. 10) 3: Has this guy you call Red got any cush? **1907** in H.C. Fisher *A. Mutt* 16: $448.00 in Uncle Sam's koosh. **1918** *Chi. Sunday Tribune* (Feb. 10) V (unp.): You may speak yourself out of a reasonable amount of green dough, cush, so to say. **1928** Burnett *Little Caesar* 62: There's a little cush for you. **1936** Levin *Old Bunch* 456: His mob is even short-changing on beer trying to scrape up some cush. [**1938** Bezzerides *Long Haul* 75: We work velly hard, alla time, but no make cush-cush, money, see?] **1945** Fay *Be Poor* 3: The "Cush" (meaning "money.").

2. (see 1965 quot.).

1954–60 *DAS* 135: *Cush*...Sex or sexual gratification. **1965** Trimble *Sex Words* 57: *Cush*...1. Copulation. 2. The Vagina. 3. A female as a Sex Object. **1967* Partridge *DSUE* (ed. 6): *Cush*...Female genitalia...Ex Arabic. **1967** Beck *Pimp* 40: A flaming itch for black "Cush." **1972** R. Wilson *Forbidden Words* 84: *Cush.* The female genitalia.

cush *adj.* CUSHY.

1931 Dos Passos *1919* 282: He got this cush job in the Post Dispatch Service. **1934** in Dos Passos *14th Chronicle* 454: It's quite a different thing than just having your cush job at stake. **1965** Koch *Casual Company* 12: Any sane man would settle for this cush home-away-from home, but not you. **1968** Pearce & Pierson *Cool Hand Luke* (film): I work on the top—real cush job. **1969** Moynahan *Pairing Off* 65: There

was no real reason to suppose that the fatuous Pee-Pee Pinkham would ever let him take over Petkov's cush job. **1987** *Tour of Duty* (CBS-TV): We finally got ourselves a cush gig.

cushions *n.pl. Hobo.* the upholstered seats of a passenger car as opposed to the inside of a boxcar.—usu. in phr. **ride the cushions.**

1913 Light *Hobo* 10: You look as if you're going to "ride the cushions." **1922** N. Anderson *Hobo* 12: The labor exchanges facilitate this turn-over of seasonal labor. They enable a man to leave the city "on the cushions." **1930** "D. Stiff" *Milk & Honey* 203: *Cushions, Riding the—* Riding *de luxe* in a passenger train. **1937** Reitman *Box-Car Bertha* 36: Not a nickel. If I had I'd be riding the cushions. **1941** in Fenner *Throttle* 168: Passenger conductors...hadn't been obliging with free rides on the cushions. **1944** C.B. Davis *Leo McGuire* 175: A year or so ago I'm riding the cushions with Shorty Donaldson. **1946** Mezzrow & Wolfe *Really Blues* 25: Riding the cushions on the way home made me think of another train ride I once took. **1971** Terrell *Bunkhouse Papers* 121: That gives me enough to ride the cushions out to Oregon.

cushion-thumper *n.* a ranting clergyman.—used derisively.

*a1643 in *OED*: Thou violent cushion-thumper, hold thy tongue. **1785* Grose *Vulgar Tongue: Cushion Thumper*...A parson; many of whom, in the fury of their eloquence, heartily belabour their cushions. **1821** Waln *Hermit in Phila.* 28: Promised to call in the cushion-thumper when Dick sowed his wild oats. **1849* Thackeray, in *F & H* II 233: Cushion-thumpers and High and Low Church extatics. **1889* in *F & H*: On a recent occasion a cushion-thumper received a challenge from the miserable sinner whom he so volubly denounced.

cushy *adj.* [< Hindi *khush* 'pleasant'] **1.** Orig. *Mil.* comfortable and easy. Now *S.E.*

*1915 in *OEDS*. **1917* Empey *Over the Top* 48: So making bombs could not be called a "cushy" or safe job. **1918** *Lit. Digest* (Oct. 5) 62: I am tempted to go after a "cushy" job myself. **1918** O'Brien *Wine, Women & War* 123: He supposed to have gotten himself a cushy job in the A.M. **1921** Dos Passos *Three Soldiers* 112: Or do you think you're goin' to get a cushy job in camp here? **1925* Fraser & Gibbons *Soldier & Sailor Wds.* 69 [ref. to WWI]: *Cushy:*...Comfortable. Easy. Pleasant. **1930** Fredenburgh *Soldiers March!* 302 [ref. to 1918]: But, hell, you're lined up for a cushy berth for three months. **1935** in *Americans vs. Germans* 26: A nice, cushy wound is a free ticket to the hospital. **1955** L. Shapiro *6th of June* 84: I've got what they call a cushy job. **1970** *N.Y. Times* (Mar. 22) 24: It's a big joke you know, you're an actor, you only work three hours a night, what a cushy deal! **1974** Radano *Cop Stories* 49: On late tours he was always getting cushy assignments. **1986** Thacker *Pawn* 81: An' everybody thinks this is a cushy job.

2. fancy; high-toned; posh.

1935 Odets *Waiting for Lefty*: Stop at some cushy hotel downtown. **1941** in *DAS* 135: I may not know a lot of cushy words. **1988** *Daily Beacon* (Univ. Tenn.) (May 24) 5: A cushy Illinois suburb.

3. friendly; intimate.

1979 Charyn *7th Babe* 102: If you're so cushy with them, why don't you ask the sockamayocks if they want to play?

cuss *n.* [fr. *customer*] a person.—usu. in a disparaging context.

1775 in *OEDS*: A man that was noted for a damn cuss. **1845** in *DA*. **1853** Lippard *New York* 199: What a treat it 'ud be to pitch this here cuss down stairs. **1859** in Eliason *Tarheel Talk* 267: Have 93 mules to feed and any "cuss" who happens to have an armful, can only be induced to sell it by the *sight of money*. **1862** G. Whitman *Letters* 55: I would go myself to Burlington on purpose to give that little Cuss Heyde a good square kicking. **1871** Banka *Prison Life* 103: Take this miserable lazy cuss to the office. **1878** [P.S. Warne] *Hard Crowd* 10: The leetle cuss air a tearer! **1880** Pilgrim *Old Nick's Camp Meetin'* 47: Powerful relijus the ole cuss pertends to be. **1904** in A. Adams *Chisholm Trail* 83: He was a big, ambling, awkward cuss. **1912** in J.I. White *Git Along Dogies* 149: He was the bravest cuss that ever pulled a gun. **1918** in Bowerman *Compensations* 100: I...[was] about the most unhappy cuss in the world. **1918** in Truman *Ltrs. Home* 46: Some low-down cuss burned up most of it in 1789. **1921** U. Sinclair *K. Coal* 231: Well, you're an enterprising cuss! **1927** Rollins *Jinglebob* 49: Glad you like the onery cuss...He's my twin brother. **1931** Z. Grey *Sunset Pass* 48: You always was a mysterious cuss. **1943** in Fenner *Throttle* 158: You know, I sort of admire the cuss. **1949** Maier *Pleasure I.* 124: He's a gentlemanly old cuss.

cuss in *v. Army.* to swear into service.

1864 in *PADS* (No. 70) 28: Succeeding getting "cussed in" about 12 M.

cuss out *v.* **1.** to curse soundly; (*hence*) to scold or reprove, esp.

with the use of profanity. Also **curse out.** Now *colloq.*

1863 in W. White *Diary of War* 224: We devote ourselves to "cussin out" the whole business. **1878** Flipper *Colored Cadet* 52: "To curse out." To reprimand, to reprove, and also simply to interview. This expression does not by any means imply the use of oaths. **1881** in *F & H* II: He cussed that fellow out. **1889** Barrère & Leland *Slang* I: *Cuss out, to* (American), to subdue or silence an opponent by overwhelming severity of tongue. *ca***1905** Dolph *Sound Off!* 225: But when the papers "cuss him out," and lay him on the shelf,/I only ask the privilege of saying to myself. **1911** Funston *Memories* 231: I had lost my temper and "cussed out" an officer of the offending regiment, who bristled up and told me he took no orders from outsiders. **1918** in Patton *Papers I* 623: I have just been in to cuss out the surgeon but it does no good. **1928** Bodenheim *Georgie May* 152: Ah've bin cussing mahself out. **1948** in Levine *Black Culture* 246: I've knowed guys that wanted to cuss out the boss and was afraid to go up to his face and tell him what they wanted to tell him. **1961** G. Forbes *Goodbye to Some* 50: He even apologizes to Cunningham for "gettin' a little excited and cussin' you out." **1986** Knoxville, Tenn., service station attendant: Man, the boss gave me a real cussin' out.

2. [sugg. by cuss in] *Army.* to muster out of service.

1864 in *PADS* (No. 70) 28: Today we were "cussed" out of the service of "Uncle Sam."

cut *n.* **1.** *Stu.* a failure of a class to meet (*obs.*); (*hence*) an absence from class. Now *colloq.*

1851 B. Hall *College Wds.* 90: *Cut.* An omission of a recitation. This phrase is frequently heard: "We had a cut to-day in Greek," i.e. no recitation in Greek. **1915** *DN* IV 233: *Cut, n.* Unexcused absence from class. **1975** Univ. Tenn. professor: Five cuts and you fail automatically.

2. a share, esp. of loot or profits.

*****1911** O'Brien & Stephens *Australian Sl.* 47: *Cut:* /slang/ share, commission, bribe. **1912** Lowrie *Prison* 282: I'll see that you get a cut. **1925** in D. Hammett *Continental Op* 198: A fat two-way cut. **1928** Guerin *Crime* 98: Bill...came on the scene and demanded his "cut." **1949** *Sat. Eve. Post* (Oct. 22) 52: He returned me two hundred the dealer had given him...what he called Sergeant Pulham's "cut." **1956** L. Samuels *Great Day in the Morning* (film): He did me out of a hunk of my cut.

3. a swing, as with the fist.

1978 *Barney Miller* (NBC-TV): The guy took a cut at me.

4. an insult. Cf. cut, *v.*, 11.

1982 S. Black *Totally Awesome* 54: You should hear what Babette said about you and Todd. It's like the biggest cut. **1988** *Cheers* (NBC-TV): Was that a cut?

¶ In phrases:

¶ **lay [back] in the cut** *Black E.* to relax; take it easy; (*also*) to lie low; keep out of sight.

1971 N.Y.U. student: *Laying back in the cut* means taking it real easy. **1987** *Tour of Duty* (CBS-TV): I'm gonna be layin' in the cut up till tomorrow afternoon. **1990** Vachss *Blossom* 16: Lay in the cut, work in the shadows.

cut *adj.* drunk. Also in elaborated vars.

*****1650** in Partridge *DSUE* (ed. 7) 1458: No man must call a Good-fellow Drunkard....He is Foxt, He is...Cut in the Leg or Back. *****1698–99** "B.E." *Dict. Canting Crew:* Cut, Drunk. *Deep Cut,* very Drunk. *Cut in the Leg or Back,* very Drunk. **1722** B. Franklin, in *AS* XV (Feb. 1940) 103: *Boozy, cogey,...groatable, confoundedly cut.* *****1748** in *F & H* II: He is deeply *cut,* that is, he is so drunk, that he can neither stand nor go. **1813–18** Weems *Drunk. Look. Glass* 60: Boozy—groggy—blue—damp—tipsy...cut—cut in the craw. **1821** Waln *Hermit in Phila.* 27: [He's] *A little cut over the head.* **1857** in *DA* s.v. eye: You are as balmy as a summer evening, as shiny as a new boot; you are sprung and cut in the eye; come, rouse yourself. **1859** Matsell *Vocab.* 23: *Cut.* drunk; "Half cut," half drunk. **1861** in W.H. Russell *My Diary* 46: Tom is a little cut, sir; but he's a splendid fellow. **1927** *AS* II (Mar.) 276: *Cut.* Intoxicated. *****1971** in *OEDS* s.v. *half-cut: Inebriation...is the sport of all ranks. How many executives can work reasonably effectively unless they are half-cut? *****1980** Leland *Kiwi-Yank. Dict.* 50: *Half cut:...More than half drunk.

cut *v.* **1.a.** to run; (*esp.*) to run away; (*hence*) to desert or decamp.

*****1793** in Partridge *DSUE* (ed. 7) 1087: She cut—I chac'd. *****1821–26** Stewart *Man-of-War's-Man* II 128: "Did you cut for it?"..."At the time I cut, Ned, there was due me better than some eighteen months' pay as captain of the forecastle...but what then, I ran for my life." **1835** in Meine & Owens *Crockett Alm.* 51: I cut for home like a cane-brake on fire. **1853** Lippard *New York* 234: Run for your life...The very devil's to pay and no pitch hot. Cut! **1856** Cozzens *Sparrowgrass* 269: Omar

Pasha...drove the rowdy Muscovite back.../With an intimation exceedingly plain,/That they'd better cut! and not come again! **1861** Berkeley *Sportsman* 54: But if I come across an insolent puppy like yourself, I just about lap into him uncommon; so you'd better cut! **1871** Thomes *Whaleman* 253: Hadn't I better jump and cut for it? *Ibid.* 257: You look so much like a boy what cut from us one night, that I thought it was him. **1884** "M. Twain" *Huck. Finn* 22: And then the teacher charged in, and made us drop everything and cut. **1884** Hartranft *Side-splitter* 20: A shopkeeper in the Bowery advertised...for a *sharp boy.* One applicant grounded his qualification of sharpness on the fact of having "cut" from four places. **1898** Norris *Moran* 145: Sometimes I don't wonder the beasts cut. **1899** Boyd *Shellback* 32: Cut for the bottle while there's a chance.

b. to leave or desert.—used trans.

1836 *Spirit of Times* (July 16) 170: I was compelled to bolt, and *cut* the sermon, in order to prevent behaving ill towards the minister. **1851** W. Kelly *Ex. to Calif.* II 123: I used to meet numbers...wending back to the coast "damning the infernal gold," and "cutting the beastly diggins" in disgust. **1852** Hazen *Five Years* 183: Want to run two days among strangers—get drunk, and then cut the service altogether, like your thirty-eight shipmates, a'nt it so, you canvass-covered lubber? **1853** Ballantine *Autobiog.* 66 [ref. to 1845]: I was born and brought up within the sound of the famous bells of Bows, whose voice, speaking through the legends of childhood, has warned many an incipient mayor and alderman to turn again, when half inclined to "cut" the paternal mansion, and the precincts of their guardians' influence. **1928** Bradford *Ol' Man Adam* 73: Moses cut de county after killin' de man in Egypt.

c. to leave, esp. abruptly.—used intrans. [S.E. in 16th & 17th C.; see *OED* def. 19.a. See also cut out.]

*****1796** Grose *Vulgar Tongue* (ed. 3): *To cut;* to leave a person or company. *****1823** "J. Bee" *Slang* 62: To *cut,* to quit and go away—from *cutting* the cable. *****1821–26** Stewart *Man-of-War's-Man* II 236: Here comes Ogilvy...I do not like him, therefore, let us cut at once—I'll tell you more to-morrow—Good-by. **1856** Wilkins *Young N.Y.* 13: This will be dangerous, so I'll cut. [*Exit,* R.] **1868** Williams *Black-Eyed Beauty* 47: Make a ten-strike if you know how, and cut! **1944** Burley *Hndbk. Jive* 95: Cut! Cop a trot you rugcutters. **1952** E. Brown *Trespass* 117: Hell, let's cut, man. *Ibid.* 131: I guess I'll be cutting. **1958** Ferlinghetti *Coney Island* 9: And I says/Dad let's cut. **1974** Hejinian *Extreme Remedies* 133: He was ready to take Billy and cut. **1977** Butler & Shryack *Gauntlet* 183: Let's cut. *a***1990** E. Currie *Dope & Trouble* 223: And so like we'd cut, you know.

2. Esp. *Stu.* to absent oneself from, usu. without good cause. Now *S.E.*

*****1794** in *OEDS:* I was told of men who cut chapel,...cut lectures,...cut examinations [etc.]. **1846** in Eliason *Tarheel Talk* 76: My only anxiety [was] to drop, take leave, cut, whichever expression may be suitable, mathematicks. **1851** B. Hall *College Wds.* 89: *Cut.* To be absent from; to neglect. Thus, a person is said to "cut prayers," to "cut lecture," &c. **1871** Bagg *Yale* 44: *Cut,* to absent one's self from a college exercise. **1871** *Yale Naught-Ical Almanac* 15: Cut church and cram! **1897** Norris *Vandover* 294: He cut his lectures as often as he dared.

3. to act in the manner of; play the part of.

*****1833** Marryat *Peter Simple* 121: I used to dress very smart, and "cut the boatswain" when I was on shore; and perhaps I had not lost so much of the polish I had picked up in good society. **1962** Killens *Heard the Thunder* 123: You gon show me your pass, boy, or you gon cut the goddamn fool?

4. to cease (foolishness or the like). Occ. (*obs.*) absol.

*****1820–21** P. Egan *Life in London* 277: *Cheese* it!...Cut it....*Slang.* **1836** *Nav. Mag.* (Nov.) 541: But for poesy—cut it Grum, 'tis a starvling. **1842** *Spirit of Times* (Oct. 29) 416: But here I cut, or you may...say my verse is...too *long.* **1848** Baker *Glance at N.Y.* 23: Oh, none of your nonsense! Come along—cut your poetry and play-acting stuff for a little while, or I'll change my mind. *****1859** Hotten *Slang Dict.* 28: *Cut...*to cease doing anything...*Cut that,* be quiet, or stop. *****1863** in *F & H* I: "Cut that," said Green sternly, "or you'll get into trouble." *****1871** in *OEDS:* Oh, cut that; you told me all about that. *****1889** Barrère & Leland *Dict. Slang* I: *Cut that* (popular), be quiet. **1890** Janvier *Aztec Treasure House* 182: Cut that, Rayburn. I'm too dead in earnest about my being thirsty to stand any foolin'. **1891** Maitland *Slang Dict.* 85. "*Cut it,*" to desist; "*cut that,*" be quiet. **1898–1900** Cullen *Chances* 195: That...is the reason I've cut card-playing on trains. **1903** Townsend *Sure* 59: Cut de gammon...and get to de evidence. **1906** H. Green *Actors' Boarding House* 81: She might as well cut that smile. I don't fall for that old gag. **1915** Poole *Harbor* 59: "Oh, cut it, J.K.," I said pettishly. "I tell you I don't care what he believes." **1921** Dos Passos *Three*

Soldiers 50: "Cut that," said someone else. **1923** Bellah *Sketchbook* 82: Cut it! **1928** Benchley *20,000 Leagues* 198: Come on now! Cut the fooling! **1932** *AS* VII (June) 331: *Cut the crap*—"stop the nonsense." **1949** Van Praag *Day Without End* 27: "Cut the crap!" said Roth. **1958** Frede *Entry E* 8: Cut the crap, Bogard! **1989** Cassell *S.S.N. Skate* 38: Cut the crap, Mead.

5.a. to attack and wound with a knife.

1860 Olmsted *Back Country* 56: "As 't is, they often get cut pretty bad." (Cutting is knifing—it may be stabbing, in south-western parlance.) **1925** Hemingway *In Our Time* 77: I was in [jail] for cuttin' a man. **1963** J.A. Williams *Sissie* 150: They say it's bad, with cuttings going on all the time. **1972** Wambaugh *Blue Knight* 307: Jesus, Slim'll cut Jake wide, deep, and often. **1985** Dye *Between Raindrops* 229: Fuck wit' Philly Dog, dudes, and you get cut every way but loose.

b. *Homosex.* to circumcise.

1916 Cary *Slang of Venery* I 64: *Cut Cock*—A Jew. From the fact of circumcision. **1971** Rader *Govt. Inspected* 13: You *know* I don't like cut joints. **1987** E. White *Beautiful Room* 66: Inches? Cut or uncut? Body hair?

6. Esp. *Black E.* to outdo; surpass.

[**1899** J.S. Wise *End of Era* 48: To keep her from "cutting me down" in the spelling class.] **1937** *AS* (Oct.) 182: Musicians vie with one another to see who can blow the hotter lick. The winner is said to have *cut* the loser. **1948** Manone & Vandervoort *Trumpet* 129: I knew Louis was a fly cat and would come on draped in style and try to cut *me*. **1950** A. Lomax *Mr. Jelly Roll* 160: Nobody playing piano I can't cut. **1954** L. Armstrong *Satchmo* 149: Bunk cut everybody for tone, though they all had good tones. **1956** E. Hunter *Second Ending* 141: Cuts this Italian and Lebanese stuff all to hell. **1962** H. Simmons *On Eggshells* 12: That lady piano player...some insisted could cut Lil. **1972** Jenkins *Semi-Tough* 13: And I think I'll be that Sidney Poitier cat so I can cut all of your asses with white chicks.

7.a. to manage or tolerate.

1899 Cullen *Tales* 62: Hello, there, pal...how're you cuttin' it this morning? **1928** Burnett *Little Caesar* 137: "Can't cut it," said the turn-key. **1937** in *AS* (Oct.) 46: This arrangement is so tough my band can't cut it. **1965** in *DARE*. **1969** *Current Slang* I & II 24: *Cut*...to manage..."I can't cut biology." **1972** Hannah *Geronimo Rex* 254: I can't think right off of any band that could *cut* this. **1975** H. Ellison *Gentleman Junkie* 182: He doesn't look like he can cut three, four hundred miles of hard driving and still stay alert.

b. to accomplish or perform.

1906 *Independent* (Nov. 29) 1270: He can't cut that game with me, your Honor...He ain't wanted aboard till tomorrow. He kin see the captain then. **1934** O'Brien *Best Stories 1935* 192: After he caught on he'd cut it fine. **1938** Steinbeck *Grapes of Wrath* 227: If a fella's willin' to work hard, can't he cut 'er? **1955** Doud *Hell & Back* (film): You think that squad of yours can cut it?

8. Esp. *So.* to copulate with (a woman).

1927 [Fliesler] *Anecdota* 72: Here's where ah cuts de gash dat nevah heals. **1930** in Oliver *Blues Trad.* 210: You ain't cut my meat yet and my range is still hot. **1936** in *Ibid.* 173: I can do your cuttin' until the butcher-man comes. **1938** *AS* (Apr.) 152: *Cut*...To have sexual intercourse. **1958** R. Wright *Long Dream* 86: Hell, yes. I cut Laura Green. *Ibid.* 88: Man, I *cut* her and was she *glad*. **1959** Farris *Harrison High* 85: I guess if ol' Buck isn't cutting them, they just don't want it. **1971** *Blushes & Bellylaffs* 146: *Song Title:* She Was Only The Admiral's Daughter, But All the Coast Guard Cutter. **1970** Ebert *Beyond Valley of Dolls* (film): I'd like to cut that! **1975** S.P. Smith *Amer. Boys* 47: He got him the blackest hole he could find and cut that bitch till her pussy hurt. **1992** *AS* LXVII 410: Did you cut her yet?

9.a. to record phonographically. Now *colloq.* or *S.E.*

1937 in *OEDS*: *Cut a disk*, to make a recording. **1948** *Newsweek* (July 19) 38: Bernard Baruch cut a record of "Yankee Doodle." **1953–58** J.C. Holmes *Horn* 66: That swings....Maybe I'll cut that next time. **1960** in T.C. Bambara *Gorilla* 47: To cut records for the new blues series. **1970** Corrington *Bombardier* 17: We were cutting six new sides.

b. to film.

1967 J. Kramer *Instant Replay* 113: I've got to go cut a few commercials for...Pepsi and Citgo. **1970** Della Femina *Wonderful Folks* 188: They cut the commercial at a great deal of money.

10. Esp. *Mil.* to type on a stencil; (*hence*) to set down on paper prior to issuance.—usu. constr. with *order.* Now *S.E.* [Early quots. ref. to WWII.]

1949 Bartlett & Lay *Twelve O'Clock High!* (film): When the old man cuts a field order, he's thought about it. *a***1950** P. Wolff *Friend* 146: Cut an order relieving Asmur from command. **1952** in Yates *Loneliness* 54:

The orders are cut. Tomorrow's his last day. **1963** D. Tracy *Brass Ring* 378: I didn't cut the order. Take it up with headquarters. **1964** R. Moore *Green Berets* 245: Just as soon as they'll cut my orders. **1977** Butler & Shryack *Gauntlet* 35: They're still cutting her papers. **1978** J. Webb *Fields of Fire* 236: I talked Top into cutting orders to Land Mine Warfare School for me and Ogre.

11. *Gamb.* to supervise (gambling) in return for a CUT, *n.*, 2; (*also*) to take (money) as one's CUT, *n.*, 2.

1950 *Sat. Eve. Post* (July 15) 36: To "cut" crap games—supervise them for a percentage of each pot. **1950** *N.Y. Times* (Dec. 7) 68: [He] placed the blame for juvenile delinquency on..."cops cutting card games and crap games." *a***1989** in Kisseloff *Must Remember This* 193 [ref. to 1930's]: I used to run card games, and I used to cut a lot of money....I cut five percent.

12. *Stu.* to insult (someone).—usu. constr. with *down.*

1965 in *AS* XLI (1966) 72: *Cut someone down*...To insult someone. **1989** *UTSQ: Slam*—to cut down someone. **1989** *ALF* (NBC-TV): Whoa! Cut you *low*, bro!

13. to expel (intestinal gas). Cf. *cut the cheese* and *cut (one's) finger*, below.

1967 G. Green *To Brooklyn* 176: Don't nobody cut one. **1965–70** in *DARE*. **1972** Jenkins *Semi-Tough* 190: He finally stood up and licked his fingers and bent over with his butt toward me, and he cut one that must have been the color of a Christmas package. **1977** Sayles *Union Dues* 60: Somebody kept cutting killer farts. **1978** J. Webb *Fields of Fire* 243: Cut farts and light 'em. That's cool. **1984** W.M. Henderson *Elvis* 90: Bruno...cut a fart. **1984** J. McCorkle *Cheer Leader* 14: "Why do cherry trees stink?"..."George Washington cut one." **1988** Groening *Childhood* (unp.): Who cut one?

14. to be satisfactory or convincing.

1970 *Adam-12* (NBC-TV): Well, it just won't cut. I want results. **1983** Helprin *Winter's Tale* 225: You can't see the future...It just doesn't cut.

15.a. to favor with; to give.

1972 C. Gaines *Stay Hungry* 153: Crump said he [usually] made five hundred dollars...but...today...they'd probably try to cut him a C. **1972–76** Durden *No Bugles* 8: Aw, Sarge, cut us a break. **1987** D. Sherman *Main Force* 27 [ref. to 1966]: I'm going to cut you people a break. You're not going to have to hump those packs back to Camp Apache. **1987** *ALF* (NBC-TV): Hey, cut me a break! **1987** S. Stark *Wrestling Season* 130: Cut us a break, will ya?

b. to offer or arrange (a compromise or agreement).

1979 *N.Y. Times Mag.* (July 22) 15: And so we may have to cut a deal with the Soviets. We do not like this, because cutting deals with the Soviets is hazardous—and often the Soviets end up holding all the cards. **1980** D. Rather, on *CBS-TV News* (July 16): Walter, the number of sources on the floor who say a deal has been cut is increasing. **1981** WHEL radio (ad) (Apr. 20): Reeder [Chevrolet dealer] will cut you a little cheaper deal on the truck of your choice. **1985** B. Breathed, in *Knoxville Journal* (Feb. 12) C9: Relax...I think we can cut a deal.

16. *Football.* (see quot.).

1974 Blount *3 Bricks Shy* 105: One of the things defensive linemen hate is to be "cut"—hit low, around the knees, and cut down.

¶ In phrases:

¶ **cut a hog** *Black E.* to make an embarrassing mistake; to blunder.

1935 J. Conroy *World to Win* 169: You think you cuttin' a fat hog in the ass, don't you? **1937** in *DARE*. **1940** Zinberg *Walk Hard* 76: Near cut a hog with her, acted like a jerk. **1957** Lacy *Room to Swing* 54: "Barbara sure cut a hog with that detective remark."..."But you handled it beautifully." **1966** in *DARE*. **1984** Wilder *You All* 58: *Cut a hog:* Make a mess of things. *a***1973–87** F.M. Davis *Livin' the Blues* 45 [ref. to *ca*1920]: Ev'ry time a bunch of us gits out in public, somebody's gotta cut a hog.

¶ **cut and run** Orig. *Naut.* to clear out precipitately; flee; desert. Now *S.E.*

*****1704** in *OEDS*. **1788** in Whiting *Early Amer. Proverbs* 91: I was among the first who were obliged to cut and run. *a***1815** Brackenridge *Mod. Chiv.* 772: Go to jail or, as the phrase is, *cut and run.* **1833** S. Smith *President's Tour* 58: At that we all cut and run. *****1833** Marryat *Peter Simple* 10: "There's cut and run," cried the sailor, thrusting all the money into his breeches pocket. "That's what you'll learn to do, my joker, before you have been two cruises to sea." **1835** *Mil. & Nav. Mag. of U.S.* (July) 355: The first luff allowed the visitors fifteen minutes to cut and run. **1846** Codman *Sailors' Life* 97: I don't see no other way then, but for her to cut and run....Yes, 'lope. **1848** Judson *Mysteries* 12: Cut and run, my darling. Hays is the word, and off you go. **1848** *Life in Rochester* 67: If you know when you're well off, you'd better cut and run. **1848** in Lowell *Poetical Works* 216: Pomp…yelled to me to throw away my pistils an' my gun,/Or else thet they'd cair off the [wooden] leg, an' fairly cut an' run. **1849** Melville *White Jacket* 30: "Jack Chase cut and run!" cried a sentimental middy. "It must have been all for love, then; the signoritas have turned his head." **1853** Ballantine *Autobiog.* 126: Our only chance was to "cut and run," as the sailors term it. **1953** in Loosbrock & Skinner *Wild Blue* 487: There is always the small minority who cut and run the first time they hear a shot fired in anger. **1957** O'Rourke *Bravados* 67: He's thinking right now how to cut and run on his own.

¶ **cut a rug** *Jazz.* to dance, esp. to swing music.
1941 Horman & Grant *In the Navy* (film): Did you cut a rug? **1942** Tregaskis *Guadalcanal Diary* [entry for Aug. 6]: After a few moments two sailors joined in the fun, themselves cut a rug or two. **1958** Hughes & Bontemps *Negro Folklore* 482: *Cut Some Rug:* To dance. **1960** Leckie *Marines!* 54 [ref. to WWII]: I jumped up and grabbed Bonny and we went off to cut a rug or two, Australian style. **1980** Coast deodorant soap TV ad: That's what we call cuttin' the rug! **1984** N. Bell *Raw Youth* 17: We'd cut a few rugs. **1990** *Donahue* (NBC-TV): "Probably a good dancer?" "I cut the rug."

¶ **cut ass** to clear out.—usu. considered vulgar. See also quots. with *cut A* s.v. A, *n.*, 1.
1954–60 *DAS* 136. **1965** Eastlake *Castle Keep* 232: Be ready with a grenade when Jerry cuts ass out. **1969** Eastlake *Bamboo Bed* 60: Sarge,…you guys cut ass. I'll cover your withdrawal.

¶ **cut cheese** to *cut ice*, below.
1895 Gore *Stu. Slang* 17: *Cut no cheese.* To have no weight or value. Used with reference to an idea or argument. **1896** *DN* I 414: "That don't cut any cheese." That has no weight. **1921** *DN* V 158: "That don't cut any cheese." i.e., that has no weight. New York, Nebraska.

¶ **cut dirt** to run or go quickly; gallop; take off.
*ca*1829 in Barrère & Leland *Dict.* I 287: He jump use fo' sartin—he cut dirt and run. **1833** in Damon *Old Amer. Songs* No. 18 (sheet music): I look I see, he only stun im,/…De Niggar he cut dirt an run im. **1838** *Crockett Almanac* (1839) 18: So cut dirt, by gum, or I'll bark you clean from the end of your nose to the tip of your tail. **1843** Field *Pokerville* 132: Now cut dirt, d—m you! **1844** in Haliburton *Sam Slick* 190: When he is mounted on Old Clay, the way he cuts dirt is cautionary. **1856** in Harris *High Times* 236: Seaward cut dirt as soon as that awful jack was turned. **1863** in Heartsill *1491 Days* 177: You may imagine we "Cut dirt" for the next five miles.

¶ **cut gravel** to go at great speed.
1843 Oliver *Illinois* 33: Look at him—see how he cuts gravel—whoop, halloo, &c.

¶ **cut ice** to make a difference; influence; matter.—usu. used in negative contexts.
1893 Frye *Staff & Field* 175: Huh! w'at youse say cuts no ice wid me! It's clean nutty dat youse. **1894** in Ade *Chicago Stories* 34: What you say cuts no ice with me. **1895** Wood *Yale Yarns* 12: Eloquence cut no ice at *that* dinner! It was just fun and give and take. **1896** Ade *Artie* 56: We didn't break into the sassiety notes, but that cuts no ice in our set. *Ibid.* 67: Anyt'ing you say cuts no ice wit' me. **1897** *Critic* (Sept. 18) 153: Two of the slang phrases now in gallingly frequent use are, "that's right" and "that won't cut much ice." **1899** Ade *Fables* 10: A New York Man never begins to Cut Ice until he is west of Rahway. **1904** "O. Henry" *Cabbages & Kings* 591: That man cut ice in Anchuria [*sic*].…He was the Royal Kafoozlum. **1918** *Chi. Sun. Trib.* (Mar. 24) V (unp.): "He cuts a lot of ice around here," meaning he is some pumpkins, or "He cuts no ice," meaning he is small potatoes. **1935** Odets *Lefty* 17: Sure, we know he's serious, that he's stuck on you. But that don't cut no ice. **1948** Kingsley *Detective Story* 331: What the hell ice does that cut? **1974** Stone *Dog Soldiers* 292: Real life don't cut no ice with me. *1984 G. Jones *Hist. of Vikings* 353: Law and tradition are hardly mentioned; religion…cuts little ice.

¶ **cut it, 1.** see (7), above.
2. to dance; *cut a rug*, above.—formerly constr. with *down*.
1869 W.H.H. Murray *Adv. in Wilderness* 100: The way he "cut it down" revealed a wonderful aptness for the "double-shuffle." **1944** Busch *Dream of Home* 136: Pris's dance routine was entirely different.…She could really cut it.
3. to *cut the mustard*, 1.
*a*1990 E. Currie *Dope & Trouble* 191: I hate it. This…don't cut it at all.

¶ **cut it fat** to overdo or exaggerate.
1837 Neal *Charcoal Sketches* 65: "If that ain't cutting it fat, I'll be darned!" growled Salix. **1843** in Haliburton *Sam Slick* 166: "Come," sais I to myself, "this is cuttin' it rather too fat." **1848** [G. Thompson] *House Breaker* 43: The Captain is *cutting it fat*, living in this *flash crib*,

and having that pretty little girl for a *blowen*. **1867** in Rosa *Wild Bill* 83: But Nichols "cuts it very fat" when he describes Bill's feats in arms.

¶ **cut loose, 1.** to abandon all restraint. Now *colloq.*
1809 in *DA:* The enemy…all at once cut loose upon them with a thundering clap. **1840** *Spirit of Times* (Feb. 1) 570 (cited in Weingarten *Dict. Slang*). **1897** Siler & Houseman *Fight of the Century* 21: With his trainers thus equipped he can "cut loose" to his heart's content. **1909** in McCay *Little Nemo* 169: Come on! Let's inspect this pond! Cut loose! **1920** Ade *Hand-Made Fables* 115: The Kids would cut loose and have a regular Lark. *ca*1963 in Schwendinger & Schwendinger *Adolescent Sub.* 302: He only did three months and he was cut loose.
2. to clear out.
1968 Van Dyke *Strawberries* 176: Aw, Mitch, we scored. Let's cut loose. **1979** D. Milne *Second Chance* 151: Hey, when are you cuttin' loose from this joint?
3. *Black E.* to give up; quit; (*also*) jilt.—used trans.
1968 Cleaver *Soul on Ice* 182: You know what, man, I'm gon' cut that fucking weed aloose. **1978** Selby *Requiem* 39: When that happens ah gotta cut loose this shit and split jim. *Ibid.* 140: Hey ma, ya gotta cut that stuff loose. **1979** D. Milne *Second Chance* 181: Word soon circulated that so-and-so's "old lady" had cut him loose.
4. Esp. *Und.* to release (someone) from custody; (*hence*) to exonerate.
1966 Braly *Cold Out There* 37: So they finally cut you loose? **1970–71** Rubinstein *City Police* 193: If we cut you loose, will you stay…away from the house? **1972** Bunker *No Beast* 33: He got on the stand and cut Joe loose, but the fuckin' narks didn't go for it.

¶ **cut mud** *So.* to run or go quickly.
1936 *AS* (Dec.) 314: *Cut mud,* v. To make haste…"You jest *cut mud* for home, afore I take a hick'ry to you!"

¶ **cut (one's) finger** to break wind. *Joc.*
1899 Green *Va. Folk Speech: To cut one's finger*, is to break wind. "Somebody has cut his finger." **1909* Ware *Passing English* 102: *Cut a finger* (lower classes). To cause a disagreeable odour; *e.g.*, "My hi! some cove's cut 'is finger."

¶ **cut (one's) lucky** to clear out; to make (one's) escape; to abscond.
*1834 in Partridge *DSUE:* You'd better cut your lucky. **1877** Bartlett *Americanisms* (ed. 4) 596: *To skedaddle*…is synonymous with "to cut stick," "to vamose the ranch," "to slope," "to cut your lucky," "to clear out," "to absquatulate." **1882** A.W. Aiken *Joe Buck* 2: Durn the leetle cuss, ef he hasn't cut his lucky. **1884** Blanding *Sailor Boy* 184: We'll have them, then cut our lucky.

¶ **cut one's [or a] stick[s]** to run away; to make off; (*hence*, *occ.*) to die.
*1821–26 Stewart *Man-of-War's-Man* II 24: He…has cut his stick, mayhap until we sail. **1836** *Spirit of Times* (Feb. 27) 16: Where do you 'magine you'll die when you go to, if you don't give a slave liberty to cut his stick and be Gemmen like you? **1837** Neal *Charcoal Sks.* 190: Marry or cut stick. *Ibid.* 217: Cut you' stick, 'cumbent.—take you'sef off. **1843** in G.W. Harris *High Times* 20: He waited a few minutes longer, then cut a stick and made a straight coat tail for Little Shinbone. **1853** Lippard *New York* 122: Dis meetin' stand adjourn…Niggas, I tink you'd bettaw cut stick. **1858** [S. Hammett] *Piney Woods* 55: With the advice…that he should cut stick directly. **1863** Root *Bugle-Call* 27: They heard a distant cannon, and then/Commenced a cutting their sticks, sticks, sticks. **1864** *Old Abe's Jokes* 58: De folks round yer began to cut dar stick mitey short. **1868** "W.J. Hamilton" *Maid of Mtn.* 75: So I cut stick for Californy. **1871** Thomes *Whaleman* 275: Let me get clear of this, and you see if I don't cut stick. **1871** Schele de Vere *Americanisms* 594: *To cut one's stick*…often means to die. "I'm blowed if he cut stick." (N. Hawthorne). **1872** G. Gleason *Specter Riders* 91: I reckon thar's no danger of your cuttin' sticks while we've got our peepers on you. **1893** Coes *Black Blunders* 6: I've got his money, now I'll cut my stick. **1902** "J. Flynt" *Little Bro.* 87: An' thet wuz only two days afore the boy cut stick. **1904** in "O. Henry" *Works* 1404: There was a little row at home and I cut sticks just to show them. **1928** Raine *Texas Man* 262: Soon as we reach the cache he can cut his stick.

¶ **cut (one's) suspenders** *West.* to head; hasten.
1934 Cunningham *Triggernometry* 338: They…"cut their suspenders" for Hanksville, down in Utah.

¶ **cut shit** to *cut ice*, above.—usu. considered vulgar.
1978 Hasford *Short-Timers* 119 [ref. to Vietnam War]: That don't cut no shit out here. **1983** W. Walker *Dime to Dance* 140: That don't cut no shit anymore.

¶ **cut (someone) a huss** see s.v. HUSS.

¶ **cut the buck** [orig. ref. to a dance step, as in 1927 and 1936–38 quots.] to *cut the mustard*, below.

[1927 E. Adams *Congaree Sks.* 52: You ought er seen some of dem niggers cut de buck and de buzzard lope.] [1936–38 in Emery *Black Dance* 89 [ref. to ca1860]: Any darky dat could cut de buck and de pigeon wing was called up to de platform to perform fer ev'ybody.] **1938** Haines *Tension* 80: And you tell him if he's lazy or a boozer or can't cut the buck, he'll get fired just like anyone else. **1952** Uris *Battle Cry* 288 [ref. to WWII]: "Don't go advertising that you were drafted into the Corps or you'll make your life miserable."..."I'll cut the buck." "I hope so. We're going to work your ass till it drags." **1957** McGivern *Against Tomorrow* 105: Make 'em toe the mark and cut the buck, I say. **1961** Terry *Old Liberty* 90: He was...making us read all these poems, and I couldn't cut the buck on that. **1975** McCaig *Danger Trail* 22: You can be assured that I will *cut the buck*, as you say out here.

¶ **cut the cheese** to break wind.

[*1811 *Lex. Balatron.* sv. *Cheeser.* A strong-smelling fart.] **1959** N.Y.C. grade-school student: Who cut the cheese? **1973** Lucas, Katz & Huyck *Amer. Graffiti* 97: Hey, man, who cut the cheese?...He who smelt it, dealt it. **1977** Bredes *Hard Feelings* 49: Harlan...sorted of shifted up on one cheek and cut the cheese. **1980** *Nat. Lampoon* (Oct.) 48: If I was still in the mood for fun, I'd call our minister and cut the cheese. **1981** in Safire *Good Word* 87: "Cutting cheese" as an expression for farting...[was] in use in the army in the mid-1960's. **1982** in Bronner *Children's Folk.* 41: Who cut the cheese?

¶ **cut [the] mustard, 1.** to do what is required; prove satisfactory. [Discussed in W. Safire, *I Stand Corrected*, pp. 245–47.]

1902 in "O. Henry" *Works* 190: So I looked around and found a proposition that exactly cut the mustard. **1905** *DN* III 76: *Cut the mustard,...*To succeed. "But he couldn't *cut the mustard.*" Rare. **1921** *DN* V 160: *Cut the mustard,* v. phr. To succeed. "But he couldn't cut the mustard." Arkansas. **1922** Hough *Covered Wagon* 96: Kansas City...didn't cut no mustard, an' I drifted to the Bluffs. **1930** Raine *Rutledge* 12: I come mighty nigh not cuttin' the mustard, as it was. **1948** Lay & Bartlett *12 O'Clock High!* 88: Each one of you was assigned to me on the assumption that you didn't know your jobs. Or that if you knew them, you hadn't been cutting the mustard. **1955** Scott *Look of Eagle* 169: I couldn't have cut the mustard unless I had had all day just to experiment. **1961** McMurtry *Horseman* 67: You're too old to cut the mustard any more. **1973** J.E. Martin *95 File* 74: That won't cut mustard in court. **1983** K. Miller *Lurp Dog* 156: Unless I know he can cut the mustard.

2. to show off.

1950 Bissell *Stretch on the River* 67: He really cuts the mustard around his home town.

3. to carry weight; *cut ice*, above.

1980 Lorenz *Guys Like Us* 229: It doesn't cut any mustard with me.

¶ **cut the rust** *West.* to *cut the mustard*, 1, above.

1931 Raine *Beyond Rio Grande* 23: When I don't cut the rust to suit her, Miss Lee will gimme my time, I expect.

¶ **cut under** *Black E.* to disparage.

1954 L. Armstrong *Satchmo* 212: I sort of felt he should have treated me like a man, and I did not like the way he cut under me. But I did not want to jump him up about it.

cut-and-shoot *n. TV.* the practice of rapidly filming, recording, and broadcasting a news report.

1982 N.Y.C. reporter, age ca33: A lot of TV news is cut-'n'-shoot.

cutbones *n. So.* SAWBONES.

1947 Willingham *End As a Man* 66: There is no liking between Miss Frune and that cut-bones. **1966** in *DARE.*

cut buddy *n. Black E.* a close male companion; crony.

1954 Killens *Youngblood* 342: This is my real cut-buddy. I don't want nobody messing with him. **1959–60** R. Reisner *Jazz Titans* 153: Cut-Buddy: Your closest friend, your ace. **1962** Killens *Heard the Thunder* 52 [ref. to 1943]: Tried to get my cut-buddy here to go with me. **1969** H. Brown *Die Nigger Die* 24: We greeted each other like we were ol' cut-buddies. **1969** Pharr *Numbers* 144 [ref. to ca1932]: He's a good friend of mine. He's always talking about Blueboy. They're cut-buddies. **1978** W. Brown *Tragic Magic* 72: There is no way that the demogogic politicians and their cut buddies, the avaricious businessmen, can mess with us.

cute *n.* CUTER, 2.

1915 (quot. at MEG). **1926** Maines & Grant *Wise-Crack Dict.* 13: *Qute*—Twenty-five cents.

cute *adj.* **1.** devious; underhanded; shrewd; tricky; skillful and cunning.

1787–89 Tyler *Contrast* 74: Scandalization!...New-York folks are...cute at it. **1815** in M. Mathews *Beginnings of Amer. Eng.* 58: *Cute,* acute, smart, sharp. **1833** J. Neal *Down-Easters* I 18: But he knows how the cat jumps, I tell ye—cute as nutmeg—brought up on ten-penny nails, pynted at both ends. **1835** in Paulding *Bulls & Jons.* 67: These travelling pedlers...were about the 'cutest fellows you ever saw. **1840** in Haliburton *Sam Slick* 135: That man lives by tradin', and bein' a cute chap, and always gettin' the right eend of the bargain. *a*1849 in C. Hill *Scenes* 172: I am sharp as a briar, and cute as a lawyer. **1855** in Barnum *Letters* 90: I want some *cute* lawyer. **1867** Macnamara *Irish Ninth* 172: "Cute" men...resolved to start opposition bakeries. **1947** Schulberg *Harder They Fall* 329: Stein had been around; he was very cute. **1955** Graziano & Barber *Somebody Up There* 2: I've put a scare in the bastard and he's turned cute to protect himself. **1973** Wagenheim *Clemente!* 135: A...rookie pitcher tried to get "cute," making Clemente lunge for bad pitches. **1974** R. Novak *Concrete Cage* 25: This town's not big enough for you to hide from me if you try to pull anything cute. **1976** Hayden *Voyage* 474: A tough nut what's some cute with his mitts.

2. impudent.

1974 A. Bergman *Big Kiss-Off* 57: When Duke got cute, it just meant he got the payoff first.

cuter *n.* **1.** *Poker.* a joker.

1877 in *Gamblers* 169: Four aces laid over four kings and a "cuter."

2. a twenty-five-cent piece.

1927 *AS* (June) 390: A quarter [is] a *kyuter.* **1951** Robbins *Danny Fisher* 212 "What's your ceiling?" "A cuter." **1954** Collans & Sterling *House Detect.* 219: *Cuter.* Quarter; one who habitually tips two-bits. **1959** *Phil Silvers Show* (CBS-TV): A dollar and a cuter.

cutesy *adj.* self-consciously cute. Now *S.E.*

1914 (cited in *W9*). **1978** B. Johnson *What's Happenin'?* 2: When Zinkoff isn't being dramatic, he's cutesy.

cutesy-cutesy *n.* coyness; preciosity.

1984 D. Young, in *N.Y. Post* (Aug. 13) 31: TV wants cutesy-cutesy, not sports.

cutie *n.* **1.** a cute individual; (*specif.*) a cute or sexy young woman.

*a*1904–11 Phillips *Susan Lenox* II 204: Evening, cutie...What'll you have? **1915–16** Lait *Beef, Iron & Wine* 193: Welcome to Broadway, cutey. **1918** in Janis *Big Show* 31: The hotel is full of "cuties." **1919** S. Lewis *Free Air* 108: Pretty lil feet, ain't they cutie? **1925** S. Lewis *Arrowsmith* 897: I've never seen a nicer cutie than you anywhere. **1929** E. Wilson *Daisy* 64: She's proud and snooty—But she's my cutie! **1928–30** Fiaschetti *Gotta Be Rough* 66: Women...But try to get a cutie to come clean. **1938** "E. Queen" *4 Hearts* 134: He'll tell his wife and his cuties and his pals. **1939** M. Levin *Citizens* 140: So a bunch of profiteers could ride around in private trains with their carloads of cuties. **1972** Ponicsan *Cinderella Liberty* 2: Ten of the little cuties [i.e., cockroaches] dash away from the light, which they hate.

2. COOTIE, 1.

1918 *Variety* (Aug. 16) 7: I finally gave myself up to the "Cuties" in a dugout 40 feet underground. **1919** *U.S.A. Ambulance Co. 33 La Trine Rumor* (Jan.): What cher looking for Doc, got a cutie? **1926** *AS* I (Dec.) 651: *Cuties*—lice. **1929** *AS* IV (June) 339: *Cuties*—Lice.

3. a formidably shrewd person.

1964 Redfield *Let. from Actor* 63: Like the baseball pitcher who would rather outsmart hitters than mow them down with speed, he was what ball nuts call a "cutie."

cut-in *n.* a share or interest.

1915–16 Lait *Beef, Iron & Wine* 183: You...gits your cut-in...on his two bits. **1931** in *DA.*

cut in *v.* **1.a.** to take a share in a business deal or the like.—usu. constr. with *on.*

1890 in *OEDS:* You don't cut in for any of it. **1911** *Hampton's Mag.* (Feb.) 194: We're giving you a chance to cut in on the play. **1930** *Bookman* (Dec.) 397: Swamis cut in heavy on the big dough. **1943** Crowley & Sachs *Follow the Leader* (film): I'd like to cut in on a soft deal like that.

1960–61 (quot. at LOOT).

b. to include in a business deal; grant a share or interest to.

1915 Howard *God's Man* 379: You oughta be mighty grateful to me for cutting you in on it. **1931** *AS* (June) 330: Business was good, so we cut him in for a couple of days. **1936** Tully *Bruiser* 22: Cut me in on another hundred of that—and another century if there's a knockout Rory here'll land it in. **1953** *I Love Lucy* (CBS-TV): Especially if we cut her in…to the tune of 3¢ a bottle. **1958** S.H. Adams *Tenderloin* 108: He cut Tommy in on the Guttenberg race-track book. *ca*1978 *Rockford Files* (NBC-TV): I'll even cut you in on the real estate deal.

c. to provide with information.—usu. constr. with *on*.

1946 Heggen *Mr. Roberts* 129: Come on, Red, cut me in on the dope. **1957** Myrer *Big War* 147: Let me cut you in, hero. **1958** Frankel *Band of Bros.* 216: I'm gonna cut you in [to] all the hot poop. **1980** Berlitz & Moore *Roswell* 129: Although we weren't cut in on it…we know that the AF was secretly test-flying a real alien spacecraft. **1986** B. Kalb, former U.S. Asst. Sec'y of State (public lecture) (Nov. 18): State wasn't cut in; Defense wasn't cut in; Congress wasn't cut in.

2.a. to meet; run into.

1930 Conwell *Prof. Thief* 236: *Cut Into*, v.—Make contact with, interfere with. **1965** C. Brown *Manchild* 246: He wasn't drinking when I cut into him about six months before. **1994** N. McCall *Wanna Holler* 104: The best thing that happened to me that year was that I cut into Elisabeth Miller.

b. to introduce (a person) (to someone or something).

1965 C. Brown *Manchild* 118: I had cut Tito and Dunny…into Johnny too. **1972** Bunker *No Beast* 78: Cut me into one. **1978** W. Brown *Tragic Magic* 97: I'll cut you in to some stone freaks.

cutlery *n.* an edged weapon or weapons.

1846 in Oehlschlaeger *Reveille* 215: *Cutlery*—Each party to carry…two bowie knives, and…two short swords. **1866** *Night Side of N.Y.* 35: The negro…seldom shows any fight unless he has "cutlery" about him. *Ibid.* 43: The "cutlery" is always on hand, and not a night passes but bright blades reek with human blood. **1902** Corrothers *Black Cat Club* 14: Come on wid yo' cutlery. **1904** in W.C. Fields *By Himself* 25: They would have cutlery with them, and after they were finished with me, as an encore, they would stuff me in sausage skins.

cut of (one's) jib *n.* Orig. *Naut.* (one's) features or appearance. Now *colloq.*

1796 in Whiting *Early Amer. Proverbs* 91: By the cut of your jib. *1821 *Real Life in London* I 139: She knew he was a *trump* by the cut of his *jib*. *1823 R. Southey, in *OED:* Their likeability…depends something upon the cut of their jib. **1833** A. Greene *Nullifiers* 100: I know you're a Yankee by the cut of your jib. **1903** *Independent* (Dec. 31) 3103: By the cut of his jib I took him at first for a commercial drummer, or a professional "con" man. **1933–35** D. Lamson *About to Die* 35: You soon get so you can recognize a man as far away as you can see him, just by the cut of his jib, he says. **1956** Lockwood & Adamson *Zoomies* 205: Frankly, until we got the cut of your jib we had…trigger fingers at the ready.

cutor *n.* /'kjutər/ *Crim.* a prosecutor or district attorney.

1925–26 Black *You Can't Win* 227: "He'll appear when you go an trial…," said the "cutor." **1927** *DN* V 443: *Cutor*, n. A prosecuting attorney. **1928** Hammett *Red Harvest* 66: You'll have the 'cuter get a stiff out of here? **1933–35** D. Lamson *About to Die* 194: An' the 'cutors put on these three witnesses. **1936** Duncan *Over the Wall* 28: The 'cutor held me for a rap. **1937** E. Anderson *Thieves Like Us* 13: District 'Cuter shouting that all over the Court House won't sound so good, boys. **1938** Holbrook *Mackinaw* 204: The prosecuting attorney was the *cutor*. **1938** Chandler *Big Sleep* 31: Then next day she comes down to the D.A. and gets him to beg the kid off with the U.S. 'cutor.

cut out *v.* **1.a.** to take off in a rush.

1834 *Davy Crockett's Almanack* (1835) 26: I now cut out for a creek, called the Big Clover. **1836** *Davy Crockett's Almanack* (1837) 2: I am now about to cut out to that country, to help give the Mexicans a licking. **1871** "M. Twain" *Roughing It* 59: You ought to have seen the bull cut out after him, too.

b. to run away, clear out; (*hence*) to leave; to be on one's way. [In general currency esp. since *ca*1950, but now less freq. than *split*.]

1827 in Shackford *D. Crockett* 81: Old Maj. Henry has cut out for Orleans in the hooks. **1835** in Meine & Owens *Crockett Alms.* 74: I'll just go and wash out my…petticoat, and I'll be ready to cut out for to hear the sarmont. **1848** in Lee *Genl. Lee* 52: Several of your naval boys are here who will be obliged to "cut out." *ca*1851 in J.Q. Anderson *Bark On* 139: D—n me if old Parson Roberts—the old fox—hadn't cut out and gone, clear as mud. **1919** S. Anderson, in Woods *Horse-Racing* 31: We fixed it all up and laid low until…some of our men, the sportiest ones, the ones we envied the most, had cut out—then we cut out too. *Ibid.* 33: After the race that night I cut out from Tom and Hanley and Henry. **1927** "M. Brand" *Pleasant Jim* 56: We got to cut out of this town. **1937** in Leadbitter & Slaven *Blues Records* 297: I'm Cuttin' It Out. **1942** Wilder *Flamingo Road* 239: Then, win or lose…he'd cut out.

1942 *Pittsburgh Courier* (July 18) 7: She…cut out that very day. **1944** Burley *Hndbk. Harlem Jive* 13: The stud cuts out to drop a flat in the piccolo. **1945** Himes *If He Hollers* 147: I cut out. I'd listened all I could. **1946** Mezzrow & Wolfe *Really Blues* 35: I put my horn under my arm and cut out for the South Side. *Ibid.* 304: Cut out: leave. *Ibid.* 111: We…cut out fast. **1946** Boulware *Jive & Slang* 2: Cut Out…Leave. **1950** *Neurotica* (Autumn) 46: We just cut out of a gone session and they're still blowin'. **1952** J.C. Holmes *Go* 98: Now, look, man, we ought to be cutting out. **1953** R. Wright *Outsider* 53: Well, guys, I've got to cut out and get some shut-eye. **1954** L. Armstrong *Satchmo* 165: I took the boys' advice and let her cut out. **1958–59** Lipton *Barbarians* 315: Cut Out—To take one's leave. **1961** J.A. Williams *Night Song* 22: You haven't cut out for good? **1967** Spillane *Delta* 16: Supposing I get to this hypothetical country and decide to cut out? **1970** A. Young *Snakes* 16: Lemme hear you play a little taste of it back before I cut out. **1984** "W.T. Tyler" *Shadow Cabinet* 3: I've got to cut out early, quarter to seven at the latest. **1987** Santiago *Undercover* 41: They musta jumped onto the next building and cut out.

c. to die.

1967 Gonzales *Paid My Dues* 49: If I "cut out," at least I'll go happy. **1990** Lenkov *Parker Kane* (film): Hey, you ain't cuttin' out.

2.a. to supersede or surpass.

1836 *Spirit of Times* (Oct. 1) 257: If they would "cut out" the three "Girls Up-Town," however, they must be merry as grigs, and gay as larks.

b. to replace (in the affections of another).

1846 in Blair & McDavid *Mirth* 88: No sooner did this cussed serpent see me sidlin up to Sophie than he went to slickin up too, and sot himself to work to cut me out. **1854** "Youngster" *Swell Life* 181: "My affections are unalterably plighted to another." "Who may she be?" "I'll tell you if you won't try to cut me out." **1856** Wilkins *Young N.Y.* 24: Married that tenor, who cut out our sweet, pious friend, Crawl. **1868** Williams *Black-Eyed Beauty* 13: Getchem was all aboard. How could he cut out her companion? **1875** "M. Twain" *Old Times* 40: No girl could withstand her charms. He "cut out" every boy in the village. **1892** Garland *Prairie Folks* 277: She's in the other room there. Milt Jennings has cut you out. **1908** *DN* III 303: *Cut out*…To supplant in someone's affections. "She *cut* Mary *out* of her beau." **1929** Kaufman *Cocoanuts* (film): Is Bob Adams cutting you out of Polly Potter? **1934** Hughes *Ways of White Folks* 64: I loved her, boy!…Some black buck had to come along and cut me out. **1934** Weston & Cunningham *Old Fashioned Way* (film): Looks like he's cut you out.

c. to deprive (of something).

1907 *Lippincott's Mag.* (Jan.) 229: Four days, now, he's tried to cut me out of my meal ticket.

3. to release (one).—constr. with *of*.

1855 Brougham *Chips* 352: We…cut ourselves out o' that are small paradise of Palmo's. **1966** Brunner *Face of Night* 232: Cut out—to drop criminal charges.

4. to cease; to quit; to abstain from.—often constr. with *it*. Now *colloq.*

1895 Tisdale *Behind the Guns* 4: Cut it out, boy!—the past, home, and all that sacred word implies. **1898–1900** Cullen *Chances* 79: I'll just cut out the worry about him. *Ibid.* 134: Why don't you cut it out? **1901** Hobart *Down the Line* 64: Cut it out! **1901** Irwin *Sonnets* (unp.): Rats! cut this out. **1903** *Munsey's Mag.* (May) 270: Aw, cut it out. **1903** Kildare *Mamie Rose* 171: I'd like to cut this all out and go to work some place. **1905** in "O. Henry" *Works* 1416: I'm going to cut out the gang. **1907** Bush *Enlisted Man* 14: An older private nudged me and told me it was not military and to "cut it out." **1911** Howard *Enemy to Society* 76: It smells like the devil and it's ruined your career. Why don't you cut it out? **1911** *Hampton's Mag.* (Oct.) 434: Cut that out. You know I've got to have help. **1914** London *Jacket* 42: Cut that out, Morrell!

5. to identify; to recognize.

1899 Garland *Eagle's Heart* 99: Only the closest observer was able to "cut out" Mose as a "tenderfoot."

cut-rate *adj.* contemptible; cheap; unsatisfactory. Also *adv.*

1944 Calloway *Hepster's Dict.:* Don't play me cut rate, Jack. **1947** *ATS* (Supp.) 5. **1972** Grogan *Ringolevio* 148: The cut-rate parasitical prick!

cutter *n.* **1.** *Naut.* an attractive young woman.

1839–40 Cobb *Green Hand* I 267: So trim built a cutter, must be the daughter of a sailor.

2.a. an extraordinary person.

1911 *DN* III 537: *Cutter*, n. A term of approval, applied to persons…"He's a *cutter*," meaning "a good fellow." Cf. *humdinger*. **1937** E. Anderson *Thieves Like Us* 55: I was a cutter then. **1961** Plantz

Sweeney Squadron 233: How's Ole Bucket? A real cutter, ain't he?

b. an extraordinary item or occurrence.

1967 W. Crawford *Gresham's War* 150: Ain't that a cutter? *Haw!* **1971** *Playboy* (May) 254: Boy—sure is a cutter! Get these [storms] often around here?

3. *West.* a pistol.

1908 Thorp *Songs of Cowboys* 18: When he meets a greener he…makes him dance a jig,/Waives a loaded cutter, makes him sing and shout. **1926** Branch *Cowboy* 26: The Colt pistol was referred to as a gun, sometimes as a "cutter." **1927** Dobie *Tex. & S.W. Lore* 200: The cowboy…/ Totes a "cutter" and Winchester to boot. **1934** Cunningham *Triggernometry* 39: His sack coat…covered the "cutter's" bulge. **1952** Overholser *Fab. Gunman* 40: Right hand on his gun…"The first thing you think about is your damned cutter." **1971** Heckelmann *Durango* 69: Check your cutter with me, mister.…No guns permitted inside.

4. a knife or other edged weapon.

1978 Ponicsan *Ringmaster* 172: Rufus put his hand in his pocket. If it came out with a cutter, Po Chang was going to work him over.

5. *Hosp.* a surgeon.

1985 Dye *Between Raindrops* 307: I got some antibiotics here but you need a good cutter in an operating room to work on that thumb.

cut-up *n.* **1.** a person given to pranks and jokes. Now *colloq.*

1899 Kountz *Baxter's Letters* 71: His Chickens was the village cut-up. **1900** Ade *More Fables* 147: The Subject of this Fable started out in Life as a Town Cut-Up. **1901** Ade *Modern Fables* 106: These Town Cut-Ups had only one Accomplishment. **1905** *DN* III 76: *Cut-up, n.* Wag, joker. "He's a great *cut-up.*" **1919** Glock *316th Inf.* 10: Farmers, miners, steel-workers, mechanics, clerks, village cut-ups and ministers' sons, teachers, and laborers unsullied by contact with the alphabet. **1919** in Gelman *Photoplay* 7: Now the little dramatic yearn has died, leaving Mabel again content as a cut-up.

2. a division of profits.

1928 Guerin *Crime* 99: The cut-up wasn't going to be anything like as good as it promised.

3. *Pris.* a knife fight; a knifing.

1975 *N.Y. Post* (July 22) 3: There have been two attempted escapes recently, and five "cut-ups"—knife battles between black and Hispanic inmates.

cut up *adj.* saddened; sad.

1862 in H.L. Abbott *Fallen Leaves* 112: We are cut up about Frank Bartlett's loss. **1906** Ford *Shorty McCabe* 310: Well, I was havin' too good a time to feel cut up about it. **1914** in Truman *Dear Bess* 159: I am very much cut up over auntie's death. **1926** Springs *Nocturne Militaire* 165: And the poor little kid sure was cut up. **1928** Dahlberg *Bottom Dogs* 36: She carried on a little, acted all cut up, cried a dab. **1938** H. Miller *Trop. Capricorn* 317: I felt a bit cut up about the incident. **1953** Kerr *Daisies* 93: I reached for a butt. I was pretty cut up. **1959** Cochrell *Barren Beaches* 292: I know him. A nice little guy—all cut up over what happened. I gave him a sedative that night afterwards.

cut up *v.* **1.** to show off, esp. in a boisterous fashion; to clown. Now *S.E.*

1846 in Dolph *Sound Off!* 416: The Mexicans have cut up high,/And we have let 'em do it,/Till they have got our "dander riz"/And now they'll have to rue it. **1847** Field *Pokerville* 198: One of them fellers that tumbles!—seen 'em once, more'n half naked, cuttin' up down to Madison! **1871** Small *Parson Beecher* 90: He…[is] still disposed to "cut up" with the hostler and his companion racers. **1879** Thayer *Jewett* 34: Can you tell me about his pranks? Such a boy as he must have been inclined to "cut up." **1915** Braley *Songs of Workaday World* 76: Rowin' around the shebang,/Cuttin' up ugly an' rough.

2.a. *Und.* to yield up booty for distribution.

1859 Matsell *Vocab.* 24: *Cut Up.* "The jug cut up very fat, and the gonniffs all got their regulars; there was no sinking in that mob," the bank was very rich, and the thieves all received their share; there was no cheating in that gang.

b. to divide (profits).

1908 in H.C. Fisher *A. Mutt* 100: He cut [the money] up with Tobasco. **1914** *Collier's* (Aug. 1) 5: And if we do cut up that dough, you bet Speck will get his share of it. **1955** Graziano & Barber *Somebody Up There* 309: You and Zale are going to cut up half a million bucks. **1955** Q. Reynolds *HQ* 192: They had nearly half a million dollars in small bills to cut up.

3. to discuss; (*esp.*) to exchange reminiscences about.

1929 T.A. Dorgan, in Zwilling *TAD Lexicon* 30: Cutting up the latest scandal from the local barber shop. **1930** Irwin *Tramp & Und. Sl.: Cutting Up.*—Discussing an absent person's actions or morals. **1946** Gre-

sham *Nightmare Alley* 267: We were cutting up old times. **1949** in *Harper's* (Feb. 1950) 76: Such is the considered opinion of the heistmen with whom I have cut up this situation. **1956** H. Gold *Not With It* 284: We been cutting up old times, friend Nancy here and me. **1966** Elli *Riot* 221: You been cuttin' this up with other guys? **1972** Bunker *No Beast* 30: Same old shit. We'll cut it up when I get there. *Ibid.* 88: Me and the Horse were cutting you up last night.

¶ In phrases:

¶ **cut up extras** to misbehave.

1842 in L.F. Browne *J.R. Browne* 14: But if you show any obstinacy or cut up any extras, I'll be d—d if it won't be worse for you!

¶ **cut up [old] scores** see *s.v.* SCORE, *n.*

¶ **cut up rough** to act in a rough, rowdy, or violent manner.

1888 Pierson *Slave of Circumstances* 132: I knowed that you'd had some trouble with old Tillinghurst—that he'd been cuttin' up rough with you. **1890** Quinn *Fools of Fortune* 294: There's no use in your cutting up rough. Of course you can have your money. **1891** in F. Harris *Conklin* 81: Williams cut up rough with Johnson, and drawed a knife on him. *ca*1895 G.B. Sanford *Rebels & Redskins* 144: The "boys" were a little doubtful about our character and *might* "cut up rough" if they took the notion. **1915** (quot. at (1), above). *1959 Behan *Borstal Boy* 20: They could easily kill you. Say you cut up rough.

¶ **cut up touches** see *s.v.* TOUCH.

cut-water *n. Naut.* a sharp nose.

*1821–26 Stewart *Man-of-War's-Man* II 97: See the sharp cut-water of the skipper standing on the quarter-deck yonder, sure, and…Liftenant Fyke, cheek for jowl beside him? **1834** Caruthers *Kentuckian* II 16: [Eyes drawn in like a turtle's head; nose sticking out…like the cutwater of a ship.] **1839** *American Joe Miller* 62: Her nose is constructed on the cut-water principle. **1839–40** Cobb *Green Hand* II 38: I must bid the audience to direct their attentions to the cut-water in your face. **1845** Appleton *Miser's Daughter* 11: His nose, which he contended was a beautiful *cut-water*, was long and hooked. **1849** Melville *White Jacket* 227 [ref. to 1843]: Your nose is a pug, and mine is a cut-water. **1933** Witherspoon *Liverpool Jarge* (unp.): I'll bust your blasted cutwater. **1964** McKenna *Sons of Martha* 172 [ref. to *ca*1935]: He had a huge and sharply curving nose, which he called his *cutwater*.

cuz or **coz** *n.* **1.** cousin. [Formerly S.E.; see *OED2* for early exx.]

1807 W. Irving *Salmagundi* 33: Old-fashioned, indeed, coz. **1821** Wetmore *Pedlar* 9: Don't hurt him, coz. **1860** Shipley *Privateer's Cruise* 22: Fear not, sweet coz. **1962** H. Simmons *On Eggshells* 114: Hey, wait a minute, cuzz. **1967–74** in R. Rosenthal *Diff. Strokes* 83: Like my cousins…I'll see them out in the street, I'll say, "Hey cous." **1979** L. Heinemann, in *TriQuarterly* (Spring) 183: Well okay, Cuz. **1981** C. Nelson *Picked Bullets Up* 27: It was good to see you, gentle cuz. **1982** Cox & Frazier *Buck* 19: Hi, Cuz! **1985** Briskin *Too Much* 432: How's my little coz? **1988** Norst *Colors* 132: Hoping to…make his way back to his cuzzes.

2. *Black E.* friend.—used in direct address.

1979 "Fatback Band" in L.A. Stanley *Rap* 122: Yo, little old cous'. **1967–80** Folb *Runnin' Lines* 234: *Cuz*…Form of address, especially among black males. **1986** Eble *Campus Slang* (Fall) 2: *Cuz*—noun of address for a friend, generally of the same race. **1988** *Spin* (Oct.) 47: *Cuz n.*, homeboy or homegirl. *a*1990 E. Currie *Dope & Trouble*: Hey cuz…you don't be selling my mom no dope.

cuze var. COOZE.

Cuz John *n. Stu.* a privy. Also **Cousin John.** Cf. syn. JOHN.

1734 in B. Hall *College Wds.* (1856) 216: No Freshman shall mingo against the College wall, nor go into the Fellows cus john. **1741** in *Ibid.* 217: No Freshman shall call or throw anything across the College yard, nor go into the Fellows' Cuz-John. **1856** B. Hall *College Wds.* 216: *Cus john*…Abbreviated for Cousin John, i.e. a privy.

cuzy, cuzzy vars. COOZIE.

C.Y.A. *interj.* Esp. *Mil.* "cover your ass," i.e., "protect yourself from the possible consequences of your actions."

1959 Heflin *Aerospace Glossary: CYA* (abbr.) "Keep your skirts clean." Pentagon *slang.* **1970** Just *Military Men* 207: I said that was an old bureaucratic principle, widely known as CYA—cover your ass. **1971** *N.Y. Times Mag.* (Sept. 5) 34: In World War II, the Army coined its special code word—SNAFU, or, politely translated, Situation Normal All Fouled Up. Today's Army has its code word too—CYA, or Cover Your Ass. **1973** Herbert & Wooten *Soldier* 34: Cover Your Ass…CYA. **1977** Olsen *Fire Five* 107: "C.Y.A.!" I says. "C.Y.A." Cover your ass. Fireman's Rule No. 1, 2 and 3. **1981** Gilliland *Rosinante* 166: "What does CYA mean?" "Cover Your Ass." **1982** Del Vecchio *13th Valley* 464: Uncle Tony said CYA—you'd understand. **1987** *McLaughlin Group* (WTTW-TV) (July 26): Is he a hero…[or] a CYA practitioner?

cycle /ˈsɪkəl/ *n.* a motorcycle.

1913 *Sat. Eve. Post* (June 7) 26: Study your cycle…before you buy it. **1937** E. Anderson *Thieves Like Us* 122: Ninety is about all I want to push that 'cycle over there. **1975** Hinton *Rumble Fish* 29: He had stolen a cycle and left. **1988** Kienzle *Marked for Murder* 66: The passenger on the 'cycle opens up with automatic fire.

D *n.* **1.** *Und.* a detective.
*1879 in *F & H* II 244: I have a few friends among the D's (detectives), who give me the job to watch a house occasionally. **1891** Maitland *Slang Dict.* 91: *Dee or D*, a pocketbook; a detective. **1933** Ersine *Prison Slang* 31: *D*. A detective. **1992** M. Gelman *Crime Scene* 126: My forced introduction to the Chief of D's…taught me a lot about how detectives think.

2. *Narc.* Dilaudid, trademark for a brand of dihydromorphinone.
1954 (cited in Spears *Drugs & Drink*). **1962–68** B. Jackson *In Life* 234: We was just gonna shoot this little bitty bottle of D.

3. *Sports.* defense.
1967 J. Kramer *Instant Replay* 113: The offense against the Big D. I think the D stands for dummies instead of defense. **1977** in G.A. Fine *With the Boys* 148: Tough on D now. **1978** B. Johnson *What's Happenin'* 220: You can't play no d and you can't talk. **1980** Wielgus & Wolff *Basketball* 11: The player who does nothing but rebound and play D. *Ibid.* 43: *D…Defense.* **1983** *N.Y. Post* (Sept. 2) 73: And new LA offense is still unsettled, with rookies…up against NFL's best "D." **1992** *Sports Close-Up* (CNN-TV) (June 30): The Bombers threw in some gold-gloved D.

4. *Mil.* a demilitarized zone; DMZ.
1983 Ehrhart *VN-Perkasie* 293 [ref. to 1967]: How the hell are we supposed to keep the gooks from infiltratin' the D.

D.A. *n.* [initialism of DUCK'S ASS] a ducktail haircut. Also *adv.*
1951 (cited in *Oxf. Dict. Mod. Slang*). **1956** E. Hunter *Second Ending* 343: He sported a D.A. in the back. **1956** H. Ellison *Deadly Streets* 180: He had one of those half crew-cut, half d.a. haircuts. **1961** H. Ellison *Purgatory* 31: The hair d.a., the black jacket, the boots, the insolent curl to the lips. **1961** *New Directions* 17 216: Pushing their d.a.'s gently and patting them in place. **1963** Stearn *Grapevine* 187: You can tell those butch haircuts—D.A. they call them. **1966** Neugeboren *Big Man* 131: He got black greasy hair, combed back into a d.a. **1970** Dunn *Attic* 54: Her hair is short, slicked back in a D.A. **1978** Maupin *Tales* 21: Her hair was done in a salt-and-pepper DA. **1980** *New West* (July 28) 63: Hair greased back in the time-honored DA.

dab *n.* [orig. unkn.; cf. DABSTER] **1.** Orig. *Und.* a skilled or adept person; expert.
*1698–99 "B.E." *Dict. Canting Crew: Dab*,…expert exquisite in Roguery…*He is a Dab at it*, He is well vers'd in it. ***1733** in *F & H* II 244: Known dabs at finding out mysteries. ***1748** in *F & H: Dab*…an expert gamester is so called also. ***1759** in *F & H.* ***1785** Grose *Vulgar Tongue: Dab.* An adept; a dab at any feat or exercise. **1821** Waln *Hermit in Phila.* 27: [He's] *A poor dab.*

2. a try; crack.
1861 in *Civil War Times Illus.* (Nov. 1972) 22: It won't be likely to give us a chance to have a *dab* at the rebels. **1900** *DN* II 31: *Dab.* "to make a *dab*," to make an attempt at a thing.

dabster *n.* an expert; master; DAB, 1.
*1708 in *OED:* Ye Dabsters at Rhime. ***1770–86** in *OED. a1824* in *DARE:* I…went so much beyond my expectations that I thought I soon would be a dabster. **1838** Crockett *Almanack* (1839) 2: A dabster at Mathewmattocks. **1842** *Spirit of Times* (Feb. 12) 591: I became…as we used to term it at school, "a dabster at it." ***1877** in *F & H* II 245: Not in the least like the performance of an amateur dabster. **a1910** Bierce *Shapes of Clay* 233: Here's Dabster if you won't give in to me. **1928** in Botkin *Treas. Amer. Folk.* 753; I will take you along if you…can prove to me that you have the guts to stay with a dabster like myself. **1968** R. Adams *West. Wds.* (ed. 2) 88: *Dabster hand.* A cowboy expert in his work; used in eastern Washington. **1968** in *DARE.*

dad[1] *n.* DADDLE.
1791 [W. Smith] *Confess. T. Mount* 18: Hands, *dads.* ***1826** in J. Farmer *Musa Pedestris* 97: Come tip's your dad.

dad[2] *n.* **1.** (used in direct address to a much older man).
1847 in Blair & Meine *Half Horse* 91: Well, old dad, if you allays raise *h—ll* in this 'ere way fur a little laffin' that's done in your court, I'll cussed ef I gin you any more of my cases! **1865** Dennett *South as It Is*

258: Dad, lend me your knife and I'll cut it for you. **1885** Cannon *Where Men Only* 204: This man planted himself in front of General Lee, and, looking up into his face, grinned and said, "Howdy do, dad?" General Lee…answered, "Howdy do, my man?" and rode on. **1933** J. Conroy *Disinherited* 129: How old a man are you, dad? **1936** R. Chandler, in Ruhm *Detective* 158: All right, Dad. Shed the heater. **1944** Busch *Dream of Home* 135: Cliff beckoned to the ancient waiter. "Bring me a slug of rum for this coke, Dad."

2. *Jazz.* fellow; friend.—used in direct address to a man regardless of age. [Usage applied to a woman in 1966 quot. is rare.]
1928 C. McKay *Banjo* 294: "Let's get on to it, too, dad," she had said. **1942** R. Chandler *High Window* 378: Don't kid yourself, dad. All those cuties do is push buttons. **1954** F.I. Gwaltney *Heaven & Hell* 256: All right, dad. We will buzz your position in precisely thirty seconds. **1956** E. Hunter *Second Ending* 21: Well, those guys knew the score, dad, said we were all sick. **1959** Brosnan *Long Season* 221: Breaks are going our way, dad. **1966** in *OEDS:* Altoist Bruce Turner even called his wife "dad." **1967** W. Murray *Sweet Ride* 153: I'm telling you, dad, Collie and I here, we have nothing to lose, and there ain't a cop in the world who's going to bust us or anyone for working you over. **1985** *Newsweek* (Apr. 22) 83: How bad is "Leader of the Pack?" Not that bad, dad.

dad *interj. & comb. form.* (a euphemistic alteration of) God.—used in various mild oaths. *Obs.* except in combs., as listed below. Cf. DOD.
*1678 in *OED:* But by Dad he's pure company. ***1681** in *ibid.:* Say'st thou so, Neighbour? dad, you have very much revived my heart. **1890** *DN* I 64: *Dad, dod,* for *God* in certain curses…"Dad drat your hide."

dad-bing *v.* DAD-BLAME.
1877 Burdette *Mustache* 222: He *would* be dad binged. **1899** Hamblen *Bucko Mate* 13: Wal I'll be dad binged!

dad-blame *v.* to confound; darn; (used as a mild oath).
1844 *Spirit of Times* (Apr. 13) 73. **1844** in *DA:* I'm dad blamed if there's any fun in any sich doin'. **1883** "M. Twain" *Huck. Finn* ch. xxxviii: Dey's de dadblamedest creturs. **1933** J. Conroy *Disinherited* 72: A dadblamed crawdad's hole. **1946** in *DA:* Dad blame it, I've taken all I can from you. **1966** F. Elkins *Heart of Man* 23: They're cycling the dadblamed catapults. **1987** *Daily Beacon* (Univ. Tenn.) (May 13) 4: Son, I've seen gals in here who could outmarch a dadblamed Marine.

dad-blast *v.* DAD-BLAME.
1840 *Spirit of Times* (Dec. 19) 499: Dadblasted. **1917** in Truman *Ltrs. Home* 30: That dad blasted mine has been sold twice. **1936** in Botkin *Amer. Folk.* 215: These dadblasted blizzards! **1987** *RHD2:* What makes you so dad-blasted stubborn?

dad-bloom *v.* DAD-BLAME.
1912 in Truman *Ltrs. Home* 20: I waited fully ten minutes…for that dad bloomed car.

dad-burn *v.* DAD-BLAME.
1829 in *OEDS* I 831: Dod burn the boy! **1839** *Spirit of Times* (May 18) 129: If I don't now, dad burn me! **1839** *Spirit of Times* (Sept. 21) 341: I'll be dad burn'd if it does, they said. **1864** J.R. Browne *Apache Country* 50: You git, dodburn you! **1901** in *DA.* **1940** F. Hunt *Trail fr. Tex.* 39: You dad-bern, inbred, Arkansas throwoffs! **1942** *Cyclone Kid* (film): "You got running water?" "Oh, you dadburn betcha." **1987** *RHD2:* I ruined the whole dad-burned batch.

daddle *n.* usu. *pl.* [orig. unkn.] a hand or fist.
*1773 (cited in Partridge *Dict. Und.* (rev. ed.) 811). ***1781** in W.H. Logan *Pedlar's Pack* 159: And they've got nimble daddles. ***1785** Grose *Vulgar Tongue: Daddles.* Hands; *tip us your daddle,* give me your hand. Cant. ***1789** G. Parker *Life's Painter* 134: You're afraid to thrust your daddles in 'em. **1791** [W. Smith] *Confess. T. Mount* 21: His daddles [are] clean. ***1819** T. Moore *Tom Crib* 23: Poor Georgy, at last, could scarce hold up his *daddle*. **1821** Waln *Hermit* 23: "Tom, *my old boy, tip us your daddle*." "Tom, *my old crabby, give us a shake*." "Tom, *my old hearty, hand us your paw*." **1823** [J. Neal] *Errata* I 146: Tip us your daddle, boy. ***1827** W. Scott *Two Drovers* ch. ii: Men forget the use of their daddles.

*1842 in *F & H* II 246. **1844** in Haliburton *Sam Slick* 186: They jist up and give you a shake of the daddle. **1859** Matsell *Vocab.* 126: ["Technical Words and Phrases in General Use by Pugilists"] *Daddles.* The hands. *1862 in Ware *Passing Eng.* 103: The men having shaken daddles, the seconds retired to their corners. **1870** *Putnam's Mag.* (Mar.) 301: I kissed the signature again and again, for the sake of the dear little daddle that will one day make me the happiest buffer going.

daddy *n.* **1.** (used esp. in direct address to refer to an older man). [The speakers of *1681 quot. are prostitutes who also use the word *papa*; cf. **(3.a., b.),** below.]
*1681 in Otway *Works* II 106: We might be dead for all of you, you naughty *Dady*, you....Oh Law, where *Dady*, where?...Shan't I be in Love with him, *Dady?* **1774** in *DA:* I saw her at Daddy Gumby's. *1785 Grose *Vulgar Tongue: Old daddy*; a familiar address to an old man. **1866** E.C. Downs *Scout & Spy* 91: Well, daddy, you don't look like a man with a clear conscience. **1889** in *DA:* Well, old daddy, how did you like the preaching?

2.a. the finest, largest, or most striking example.
1865 Byrn *Fudge Fumble* 72: The terrapin...no doubt was the mammy and daddy of terrapin creation. **1907** Siler *Pugilism* 109: Fitz traveled around the country as "daddy of them all." **1909** O'Neill *Irish Folk Music* 34: We learned that Kennedy's father was a violinist of celebrity; in fact, "the daddy of them all" around Ballinamore, in the County of Leitrim. **1943** Horan & Frank *Boondocks* 163: It was terrific. It was the daddy of all explosions.

b. a man who is an important influence in a field; doyen; (*also*) a forerunner or progenitor.
1925 in *OEDS:* The Daddy of Sunday Painters. **1954** Huff *Statistics* 66: The daddy of the pictorial chart...is the ordinary bar chart. **1964** Gold *Jazz Lexicon* 77: *Daddy.* A profound musical influence or a musical progenitor; by extension, one who is a seminal influence in any art form or in any activity.

3.a. a male lover, boyfriend, or husband, (*esp.*) the lover and protector of a prostitute; pimp. [See also note at **(1),** above.]
1909 in *DARE:* [A song] I've got a lovin daddy/Who cert'nly can love sweet. **1913** T.A. Dorgan, in Zwilling *TAD Lexicon* 30: [Singer:] Here comes my daddy now. **1921** in Leadbitter & Slaven *Blues Records* 313: I Wonder Where My Brown Skin Daddy's Gone. *Ibid.* 496: Sweet Daddy. **1923** Ornitz *Haunch* 185: Say,...sweet daddy, I wisht somebody would take me off on a drunk. **1924** *Adventure* (Apr. 20) 143: Elizabeth's "daddy" was "Hi-Jack" Holmes. **1926** Odum & Johnson *Workaday Songs* 32: How Can I Be Your Sweet "Mama" When You're "Daddy" to Some One Else. *Ibid.* How Long, Sweet Daddy, How Long? **1926** Van Vechten *Nigger Heaven* 285: *Daddy,* husband or lover. **1932** C. McKay *Gingertown* 25: Maybe it was daddy Rascoe done experience a change o' heart. **1936** Gaddis *Courtesan* 132: You're a swell guy and an all-right daddy. **1948** Wilder & Monroe *Song Is Born* (film): The man on the wire said it's from your "daddy." **1959** J. Rechy in *Big Table* I (No. 3) 20: Shes made it three years with the same rich daddy. **1974** Angelou *Gather Together* 137 [ref. to ca1950]: So my daddy brought me down to this crib. **1980** W. Sherman *Times Square* 58: All those girls are lookin' for a new daddy.

b. Esp. *So.* & *Black E.* sweetheart.—used in direct address to a man.
1923 in *DARE:* [A blues song] Tell me pretty daddy: what's the matter now/Are you trying to quit me: and you don't know how. **1925** L. Hughes *Weary Blues* 27: Kiss me...daddy. **1927** in Oliver *Blues Tradition* 34: You know I loved you daddy, that's why we couldn't get along. **1927** C. McKay *Harlem* 7: But there wasn't no boat in with soldiers today, daddy. **1928–29** Faulkner *Sound & Fury* 240: Dear daddy wish you were here. No good parties when daddys out of town I miss my sweet daddy. **1930** Botkin *Folk-Say* 326: You been a good ole wagon, daddy, but you done broke down. **1935** Algren *Boots* 48: Look daddy, y'all like to sleep with me tonight?

c. *Pris.* the partner who plays the dominant or masculine role in a homosexual relationship. Cf. JAILHOUSE DADDY.
1932 Nelson *Prison Days & Nights* 150: The active participants [in homosexual intercourse] are known as "wolves," "jockers," "daddies," etc. **1937** in Karlen *Sex. & Homosex.* 306: You are a real wife and I think I am showing you I am a real daddy. **1974** Piñero *Short Eyes* 66: Ask me like a daddy should be asked. *a*1988 in *AS* 63 (Summer 1988) 133 [Tennessee prison talk]: *Daddy n.* Protector of a *boy.*

4.a. *Jazz.* fellow; friend.—used in direct address to a man regardless of age.
1948 *New Yorker* (July 3) 28: The bebop people...call each other Pops, Daddy, and Dick. **1965** Bonham *Durango St.* 57: He live right across

the street though, daddy. **1978** Strieber *Wolfen* 126: You got fifty cents, daddy? That's fifty cents in advance.

b. a fellow; "customer."
1964 in Gover *Trilogy* 265: This daddy got *some*thin crankin away inside his head. **1969** B. Beckham *Main Mother* 14: The cool daddy swung around the corner without breaking. **1972** Gover *Mr. Big* 6: This daddy's from somewhere up there in the Great American Bald Eagle's Nest. **1979** Gram *Foxes* 91: The gross daddy in the black leather vest and blood-red boots lurked by the...stage. **1986** D. Tate *Bravo Burning* 43: You ain' gotta sacrifice your black nuts for nunna them white daddies. **1986–91** Hamper *Rivethead* 164: Jimbo babbled on in the kinda cool-daddy corporate jumble-thump that...you and me...could never...untangle.

daddy-o *n.* **1.** a boyfriend, male lover, or husband.
1944 Burley *Harlem Jive* 103: I'm your daddy-O, you're my baby-O, and Queen Bee, that's what she wrote! **1952** Mandel *Angry Strangers* 294: "Come on, Daddio," she whispered in a travesty of slow passion. "Rock it for me, snag me good." **1961** T.I. Rubin *In the Life* 156: *Daddy-o.* Pimp or kept man. **1963** T.I. Rubin *Sweet Daddy* 22: Reminds 'em they really got a daddy-o. You know—a man. **1966–67** P. Thomas *Mean Streets* 251: He [a homosexual] wants to buy a daddy-O.

2. *Jazz.* fellow.—used esp. in direct address.
1948 Wilder & Monroe *Song Is Born* (film): Daddy-o, I'm gonna teach you some blues. **1948** in R.S. Gold *Jazz Talk* 66: Daddy-o, friend, buddy. **1949** in *OEDS:* Daddy-o, friend, buddy. Originated with Negro musicians. **1951** *Amer. Jour. Socio.* XXXVII 138: Be cool, daddio, everything'll be real gone, you know. **1947–52** R. Ellison *Invisible Man* 153: Wait a minute, daddy-o, I'm going your way! **1953** Paxton *Wild One* (film): Let me tell you about Johnny, daddy-o. **1961** Gover *$100 Misunderstanding* 16: She think alla time this daddio been smilin at her. **1962** Killens *Heard the Thunder* 22 [ref. to 1943]: I'm with you, daddy-o. **1966** Manus *Mott the Hoople* 30: I'm going all the way, daddy-o. **1970** Southern *Blue Movie* 239: Not *you,* daddy-O. **1971** Trudeau *A Lot Smarter* (unp.): Like what's happening, daddy-O? **1980** Algren *Dev. Stocking* 49: Congratulations, daddy-O. **1982** Univ. Tenn. student: What's happening, daddyo? **1992** *As the World Turns* (CBS-TV): If you get my drift, daddyo. **1992** Perl & Lee *Malcolm X* (film): Talk, daddyo!

3. *Black E.* thing; item. *Joc.*
1961 Gover *$100 Misunderstanding* 183: I ain never gonna fergit that mothahless word...I git me so godam fuss up bout that daddio, I bout flip.

4. *Jazz.* a person's father.
1962 in J. O'Hara *Sel. Letters* 387: Well, bedtime for Daddy-o. **1964** *Twilight Zone* (CBS-TV): We're monsters from space, daddyo. **1965** *N.Y. Times* (Dec. 27) 20: Daddy-O...was "in the groove" back in the class of '40. **1968** Cuomo *Thieves* 116: The men played Daddy-o and the women took turns taking care of each other's children. **1983** Breathed *Bloom Co.* 71: Well, catch *this* one, daddy-o!

dad-fetch *v.* DAD-GUM.
1839 *Spirit of Times* (Dec. 28) 512: Dad fetch him...he jumped right into me. **1912** in *DA.*

dad-gast *v.* DAD-GUM.
1892 Bunner *Runaway* 158: He was a dod-gasted dunder-headed fool jackass. *ca*1900 *Buffalo Bill* 211: It all happened so dad-gasted quick. **1922** Rollins *Cowboy* 192: Look here, you dodgasted, pale pink, wall-eyed, glandered, spavined cayuse, pull down that injur rubber-neck of yourn. *a*1946 (quot. at SARDINE).

dad-gum *v.* to confound; darn; DAD-BLAME.
1887 in *F & H* II 245: Dadgum ye! **1901** S.E. Griggs *Overshadowed* 196: Naw, dad gum it, she ain't dead. **1912, 1944** in *DA.* **1976** Ark. man, age 24: Well, dad*gum*it! **1984** Nettles & Golenbock *Balls* 208: Dad-gummit.

dad-rat *v.* DAD-GUM.
1844 *Spirit of Times* (Apr. 6) 67. **1864** J. R. Browne *Apache Country* 40: Now git, dodrot ye! **1984** in Terkel *Good War* 263: It didn't do a dadratted thing.

dad-shave *v.* DAD-GUM.
1867 in G.W. Harris *High Times* 175: I wishes I may be dad shaved if I minds sayin' any thing 'bout *that.*

dad-shim *v.* DAD-GUM.
1839 *Spirit of Times* (Aug. 24) 294: I'll be "dad-shim'd" if you could find another man like this Old Isham for management.

dad-swamp *v.* DAD-GUM.
1863 in C. Smith *Bill Arp* 47: I'll be dad-swamped if the commissary didn't keep his flour in 'em.

daffodil *n.* an effeminate young man; PANSY.

1935 A. Dubin *Lullaby of Broadway* (pop. song): The daffydils who entertain/At Angelo's and Maxie's. **1938** "R. Hallas" *You Play the Black* 3: He said it mocking, in a high voice, like a daffodil. ***1952** (cited in Partridge *DSUE* (ed. 7) 1090).

daffy *n.* (see quot.).

1893 Macdonald *Prison Secrets* 65: "Whoi wusen't ye on hand ter saa the daffie* the wardin lit in far the new confidence-boarder?"...*"Daffie"—a cant word for a light woman.

daffy *adj.* [var. *daft*] daft; crazy; silly; (*esp.* in recent use) amusingly eccentric.

***1884** in *OEDS*: *Daffy*, simple, soft. **1895** Townsend *Fadden* 28: I'd gone clean daffy. **1896** F. P. Dunne, in Schaaf *Dooley* 242: They're crazy, plumb daffy, Jawnny. **1896** Ade *Artie* 19: She'd make anybody daffy. *a**1898** in *EDD* s.v. *daff*, adj: He is a bit daffy. **1898** in Crane *Stories* 490: Man! man!...have you gone daffy? **1899** in Cather *Short Fiction* 393: Let's go and get this poor, daffy, tealess widow and wine and dine with her and make it all up. **1903** *Pedagog. Sem.* X 379: You're daffy. **1908** Beach *Barrier* 200: He's the kind most women go daffy over. **1908** in Blackbeard & Williams *Smithsonian Comics* 58: I think the old man is daffy myself. **1912** Lowrie *Prison* 123: I was in love with th' gal...clean daffy over her. **1913** *Sat. Eve. Post* (Mar. 1) 18: She's daffy over bein' catered to. **1914** Ellis *Billy Sunday* 415: That Noah bunch is getting daffy on religion. **1915** in Grayson *New Stories* 563: I'm hearing that he's gone just a little bit daffy. **1917** *Crisis* (Sept.) 253: "He's daffy," laughed the first group he encountered. **1926** Tully *Jarnegan* 45: Poor old daffy dad. **1928** in Galewitz *Great Comics* 100: He's daffy over Babe Ruth. **1931** Hellinger *Moon* 26: The kids...were daffy about his voice. **1938** "R. Hallas" *You Play the Black* 18: I was feeling daffy. **1949** Beloin *Conn. Yankee* (film): You're daffy! **1968** I. Reed *Yellow Back Radio* 50: A daffy cat a really daffy cat, started saying spooky things about magic. **1978** J. Reynolds *Geniuses* 22: The daffy ingenue.

daffy house *n.* an asylum for the insane. Also **daffy joint.**

1902 Hobart *Back to Woods* 94: If I wasn't in a daffy house and him nothin' but a bug, it's the weight of that chair he'd feel over his bald spot. **1908** in H.C. Fisher *A. Mutt* 49: I will be able to get any kind of odds I want in the daffy joint. **1909** "Clivette" *Café Cackle* 81: Every cook in town was nearing the "daffy" house.

dagged *adj.* drunk.

1737 *Penna. Gaz.* (Jan. 6): He's...Boozy...Cut...Dagged.

dagger *n. Black E.* BULLDAGGER.

1967–80 Folb *Runnin' Lines* 234. *a***1990** Bérubé *Coming Out* 43: Working-class lesbian slang...during [WWII]...called the masculine partner the "dyke," the "lesbian," the "butch," or—among black servicewomen—the "dagger."

daggone *v.* var. DOGGONE.

dagnab *v.* DAD-GUM.

1942 *ATS* 224. **1975** T. Berger *Sneaky People* 49: "Dagnab it!" Even when hurt she would not curse. **1987** S. Stark *Wrestling Season* 59: Dagnabit, Kleeve!

Dago *n. Esp. USMC.* San Diego, Calif.

1931 *Leatherneck* (May) 21: In Dago the troops have their sunshine and wonderful barracks. **1939** E. O'Brien *One-Way Ticket* 67 [ref. to 1920's]: Knockin' a guy's teeth out for makin' a pass at a whore in Dago when she didn't mean a damn thing to me. **1944** Wakeman *Shore Leave* 21: But we seduced a four-striper into wangling us a shore leave in San Francisco until they call us down to Dago. **1948** Manone & Vandervoort *Trumpet* 158: I was on my way to Dago to play this one-nighter. **1957** Herber *Tomorrow* 17: If you think you had it bad at Dago, you should have come through Parris Island. **1962** E. Stephens *Blow Negative* 213: Look me up when you're in Dago. **1976** Lieberman & Rhodes *CB Handbook* 127: Dago—San Diego.

dago *n.* [< Sp male given name *Diego*, equiv. to E *James*] **1.** Orig. *Naut.* a Spaniard, Portuguese, or other Caucasian of southern Europe or Latin America; (*broadly*) a foreigner.—usu. used contemptuously. Often attrib.

1832 Wines *In Navy* I 101 [ref. to 1829]: These *Degos*, as they are pleasantly called by our people, were always a great pest when we were in the harbour of Mahon. **1833** Ames *Old Sailor's Yarns* 265: We shan't be called away till ten or eleven o'clock when all the Degos are asleep. **1835** *Mil. & Nav. Mag. of U.S.* (Sept.) 47: The sailors, secure in their hammocks, laughed, and as often as a diego* would grasp a hammock to support himself by, as often would he be saluted with a box from its inmate...*Diego is an appellation given by our seamen to foreigners,

but can be more properly applied to the natives of Minorca. **1847** Downey *Cruise of Portsmouth* 31: "Ah begar," chimed in my friend the Dago, "It makes but a very leetle diffrance to him, how he lay, for I bleive he got so mush brain in one end as the other." **1849** Judson *Life-Yarn* 27: In this outlandish [South American] country, among a lot of cowardly Diegos. **1858** *Knickerbocker* (Jan.) 7: And so, Bill, you served as a ingineer with these ere blamed dagos, you say. **1863** in I. Berlin et al. *Wartime Genesis* 443: There are a lot of Greeks, Sicilians, Maltese & Corsicans in New Orleans....These men from the Mediterranean isles are all known by the general name of "Dagos." It is the commonest phrase in the world. **1867** *Galaxy* (Apr. 1) 728: "Dagos"...includes the natives of the countries bordering upon the Mediterranean. **1868** Macy *There She Blows!* 28: I don't know what you Dagoes [Portuguese] mean to do, but I'll have my rights. **1877** Bartlett *Amer.* (ed. 4) 167: *Dagos*. Originally people of Spanish parentage, born in Louisiana, now applied there to all Italians, Sicilians, Spanish, and Portuguese. **1889** *United Service* (Sept.) 274: Dago is universal sailor language for a native of Southern Europe, the islands, and South American States. **1893** in Matthews *Manhattan* 104: I've seen Dagoes you could tie to. **1895** Townsend *Fadden Explains* 55: You remember dat Ulalu was over here from some dago country de time me and de Duchess was married. **1897** *Harper's Wkly.* (Jan.) 90: Our townsfolk call every black-haired, swarthy-skinned foreigner (except the Chinese) all "dagoes." **1898** Stevenson *Cape Horn* 334: At sea Frenchmen, Spaniards, and Italians are Dagos; Scandinavians, Hollanders, and Germans are Dutchmen. **1898** Dunne *Mr. Dooley in Peace and War* 21: "Surrinder," he says. "Niver," says th' Dago. **1899** in A. Naff *Becoming Amer.* 219: We call them "dago" down there...I think they are [Syrians]. **1899** Stratemeyer *Cuban Waters* 260: Those dagos ain't going to give ground without a big fight, that's certain. **1900** Gilder *Tom-Boy* 282 [ref. to 1862]: "Thet theer frog-eatin' dago o' theers had sassed her."..."Never...was I called sich names as I've been called to-day by that French dago o' your'n." **1906** Stewart *N'th Foot* 10: The men...longed for a chance at "them damn dagoes." **1910** in "O. Henry" *Works* 1684: Then I reflected that to George all foreigners were probably "Dagoes." **1914** Nisbet *4 Yrs. on Firing Line* 19 [ref. to Civil War]: To them the sight of soldiers who understood French was a spectacle. They listened in wonder to Colonel Polignac on battalion drill. "That-thur furriner *he* calls out er lot er gibberish, an them-thur Dagoes jes maneuvers-up like Hell-beatin'-tanbark. Jes' like he wuz *talkin' sense!*" **1927** Finger *Frontier Ballads* 54: Dagoes such as Mexicans, Japanese, and more of 'em. **1939** Howsley *Argot* 56: Italian:...Dago...Greek: Dago. **1945** Colcord *Sea Lang.* 63: *Dago*...A person belonging to any of the Latin races, except Frenchmen; at sea they are "Frenchies." **1970** Rudensky & Riley *Gonif* 38: A...Cuban tried to use a scissors on me...I growled, "Remember Dago punk, I'm still King of the Coup!" **1972** Carr *Bad* 141: Up to that point gambling had been handled completely by the dagos [Mexicans]. **1973** *Nat. Lampoon* (Sept.) 25: If it's O.K. with all you dagoes, we'll fly straight for a while.

2. *Specif.* an Italian.—used contemptuously. Often attrib. [The predominant 20th C. sense.]

[**1867** (quot. at (1), above).] **1875** Sheppard *Love Afloat* 406: Our band is all broke up. Arrowson has got every Dago, and Greaser, and nigger against me. **1877** (quot. at (1), above). **1882** Baillie-Grohman *Camps in Rockies* 372: I waited until a lot of Dago immigrants passed through this town. **1885** Clark *Boy Life in U.S.N.* 241: Them Dagoes is snatchin' from one another, sir. **1889** Barrère & Leland *Dict. Slang* I 291: *Dago* (American), an Italian. **1891** Maitland *Slang Dict.* 87: *Dago* (Am.), a name given in the United States to the low-class Italians and Sicilians. Said to be derived from the Spanish *Diego*. *Dago-shop*, a low saloon or resort for depraved men and women, conducted by a Dago. **1896** F.H. Smith *Tom Grogan* 8: "Come now, ye blatherin' dagos,"—this time to two Italian shovellers filling the buckets. **1900** Greenough & Kittredge *Words & Ways* 66: *Dago* is a queer misnomer. It must come from the Spanish Diego, yet it is usually applied to Italians. **1904** "O. Henry" *Cabbages* 621: There was two hundred men workin' on the road—mostly Dagoes, nigger-men, Spanish-men and Swedes. **1915** Braley *Workaday World* 16: Dago an' French, an' Russ,/Irish an' English, too. **1915** Poole *Harbor* 281: I am Italian man! You call me Guinney, Dago, Wop—you call another man Coon, Nigger—another man a Sheeny! Stop calling names—call men fellow workers! **1954** Arnow *Dollmaker* 188: What was you expecten—a castle in Grosse Pointe where them rich dagoes live? **1959** Brosnan *Long Season* 208: The double-crossing Dago. **1969–71** Kahn *Boys of Summer* 372: Tonight we get you, dago. **1977** Brennan *Prejudiced Man* 98 [ref. to 1945]: Somebody hooted "Prego, dago!" and got the standard echo, "Grazie Nazi!" The soldiers meant it kindly. **1979** in Terkel *Amer. Dreams* 352: I lost my temper, and my Dago blood came out...."If I hadda be alderman with your help,

I don't wanna be." **1977–80** F.M. Stewart *Century* 89: Wop. Dago. Guinea. Take your pick. **1984** Nettles & Golenbock *Balls* 114: You can tell the *New York Times* to kiss my dago ass.

3. a southern European language, esp. Italian; (*broadly*) a foreign language.—used contemptuously.

1895 Townsend *Fadden* 23: De kind er dago dat French folks talk when dey talks English. **1900** *DN* II 31: *Dago*, n. The Italian language. **1901** Hobart *John Henry* 14: The track-walkers...were talking Dago [French]! **1902** J. London *Dazzler* 192: I couldn't speak Dago [Italian]. **1911** in Truman *Dear Bess* 20: Perhaps if I could understand Dutch and Dago I could appreciate it better. **1912** *Lucky Bag* (*No. 19*) 33: Dago— meaning any foreign language—is the same the world over. **1928** *AS* II (Aug.) 453: *Dago*. Department of Modern Languages: applied to either French or Spanish. **1943** Hersey *Bell for Adano* 202: Goddamit, I'm going to have to start taking lessons in dago. **1947** Motley *Knock on Any Door* 98: Angelo meant "angel" in dago. **1962** in *Harper's* (Jan. 1963) 52: Midshipmen dismiss the humanities as "Bull" and foreign languages by the unspeakable term "Dago." **1963** *Time* (Feb. 8) 49: At Annapolis...foreign language study...is known as "dago."

4. Italian food, esp. pasta.

1942–44 in *AS* (Feb. 1946) 32: *Dago*, n. Macaroni. **1948** Mencken *Amer. Lang.* (*Supp. II*) 674: Macaroni [is called] *dago*.

5. DAGO RED.

1965–71 in *Qly. Jour. Stud. Alcohol* XXXII (1971) 728: *Dago*. Italian-type red wine.

dagoed *adj.* [fr. DAGO, 1] *Army in Spanish-Amer. War.* killed by a Spaniard.

1899 Young *Reminiscences* 43 [ref. to 1898]: If he was killed, cause of injuries unknown, the soldiers will tell you he was "dagoed," and let it go at that.

Dagoland *n.* Southern Europe, esp. Italy.—used contemptuously.

1976 Hayden *Voyage* 142: Which ships...were from northern Europe and which hailed from Dagoland.

dago red *n.* cheap red wine, esp. of Italian origin.

1906 in *OEDS*: Casks of wine (real "Dago red"). **1912** Lowrie *Prison* 340: Everybody took Dago Red. **1915** Garrett, in *Army Ballads* 66 [ref. to 1899]: Just the "Barbary Coast" of 'Frisco,/Just a taste of "Dago Red." **1921** in McArdle *Collier's* 230: "Dago red" flows plentifully at many restaurants. **1925** Dos Passos *Manhattan Trans.* 318: Bettern Dago Red, eh Meester 'Erf? **1927** *DN* V 443: *Dago red*, n. Cheap wine. Also *red ink* and *rooje*. **1930** "D. Stiff" *Milk & Honey* 43: There to bask in California sunshine in the land of Dago red. **1950** *Sat. Eve. Post* (Sept. 9) 150: We had a jug of Dago red the plumber gave us years ago. **1952** Uris *Battle Cry* 118 [ref. to 1942]: "Dago red," I repeated, pouring the wine down the front of his shirt. **1958** Motley *Epitaph* 63: I brought along a small sampling of dago red. **1963** Zahn *Amer. Contemp.* 56: She got tanked on dago red wine. **1965–70** in *DARE* [104 informants]. **1972** Kopp *Buddha* 174: I reach for some Dago red.

Dagwood *n.* [sugg. by the character *Dagwood* Bumstead, often portrayed eating such sandwiches, in the comic strip *Blondie*, by Chic Young] a huge, usu. multilayered sandwich. In full, **Dagwood sandwich.** [The 1947 def. is either very limited or else erroneous.]

[**1947** *ATS* (Supp.) 11: *Dagwood special*, a banana split.] **1948** *Ladies' Home Jour.* (Sept.): All the makings on hand for giant three-inch Dagwood sandwiches. *Ibid.:* A serve-it-yourself menu for a "soda fountain" or a "Dagwood sandwich" party. **1953** *Pop. Sci.* (May) 213: Let each picnic guest stack his own favorite Dagwood. **1954–60** *DAS.* **1973** *Everett* (Wash.) *Herald* (Jan. 27) 12A: Hot chocolate, hard boiled eggs, Dagwood sandwiches and cookies. **1979–82** Gwin *Overboard* 183: A lusty triple-decker sandwich, a super-Dagwood. **1986, 1988** in *DARE.*

daily-daily pill *n. Army.* (see quot.).

1982 Del Vecchio *13th Valley* 221 [ref. to Vietnam War]: Doc McCarthy came by with the daily-daily (anti-malaria) pills.

daisy *n.* **1.** a prime or superior example of its kind.

1836 in Haliburton *Sam Slick* 48: I raised a four-year-old colt once...could gallop like the wind; a rael daisy, a perfect doll. **1880** in Sweet *Sweet's Texas* 108: He wears a 96-inch undershirt, and has had the small-pox on both sides. He is a daisy. **1882** in Francis *Saddle & Moccasin* 32: "Is [the elk] down, Dick?" "You bet yer. He's a daisy!" **1883** Peck *Peck's Bad Boy* 253: The baby is a daisy. **1886** Wilkins *Cruise* 22: "Is that man in a boat?" "Yes! and danged if he ain't got a daisy too!" **1887** Hinman *Si Klegg* 22 [ref. to Civil War]: I tell ye he's a daisy, too;

must be a big gin'ral or suthin' like that. **1888** in *F & H* II 248: Jack Dempsey is beyond compare a pugilistic daisy. **1921** U. Sinclair *K. Coal* 380: Ain't he a daisy, hey? **1936** Connell & Adler *Our Relations* (film): Isn't that a daisy? **1952** MacDonald *Damned* 40: Lots of times it's better if they kick off when they have a daisy like that one, because they come out of it paralyzed.

2. an attractive young woman.

*ca*1876 in *F & H* II 248: She's such a daisy, she sets me crazy. **1881** Trumble *Man Traps of NY* 9 (caption): Speeling the Daisies. **1885** Carleton *City Ballads* 31: Aw, auyn't she a daisy! **1891** Maitland *Slang Dict.* 87: *Daisy*, a young girl. **1895** Townsend *Fadden Explains* 106: She's a doisy, and just seventeen. **1897–99** Heth *Memoirs* 57 [ref. to Mexican War]: "Oh, Heth, she is a daisy!" ("So was the sutler's daughter at Fort Hamilton a daisy," I said.)...One Mexican daisy is enough at a time. **1942** Davis & Wolsey *Call House Madam* 161: Small-town daisies, street-corner pushovers or trailer-camp floozies. *Ibid.* 216: You wouldn't want those pretty daisies to sail into town with the spinach showing. **1944** E. Caldwell *Tragic Ground* 47: Mac, you sure are nuts if you think I'd marry one of those daisies!...I'll take my beating some other way.

3. a mule.

1887 Hinman *Si Klegg* 227 [ref. to Civil War]: Si pointed with a proud and gratified air to where the six "daisies" were standing...with their noses in the feed-box quietly munching their natural rations.

4. an effeminate man, esp. an effeminate homosexual man; PANSY.—used derisively.

1944 Kendall *Service Slang* 7: A fluff, a fairy, a daisy or a fuff. **1952** Lait & Mortimer *USA* 27: Acheson's dumb daisies reply that we cannot do that. **1965** Trimble *Sex Words* 59: *Daisy*...A Passive Male Homosexual. **1970** Newman & Benton *Crooked Man* (film): You wouldn't want to run with them two old daisies now, would ya? **1973** *TULIPQ* (coll. B.K. Dumas): Male homosexuals...fags, queers, gay, daisies. **1985** *Miami Vice* (NBC-TV): "Still keepin' in touch with the Casiodores?" "That bunch of daisies?"

¶ In phrases:

¶ **flog** [or **beat**] **the daisy** to masturbate.

1956 Whittington *Across That River* 95: Petters! Oh, my God, some fool and his woman, stopping down there to flog the daisy! **1971** Selby *Room* 238: I don't care if i go crazy/Just so i can beat my daisy.

¶ **push up daisies** see s.v. PUSH, *v.*

daisy *adj.* excellent; superior; fine. Also adv.

[***1757** in *OED*: Oh daisy; that's charming.] **1879** Burt *Prof. Smith* 77: Byron is good. Anacreon a fine fielder. Tom Moore belongs on first base. Longfellow is a first class short stop. Crabbe a daisy clipper. **1880** in F. Remington *Sel. Letters* 27: Havanna...segars...are...the "daisy thing." **1885** *Puck* (Apr. 22) 115: A daisy old prophet, a spy has just come in from the English. **1887** Francis *Saddle & Moccasin* 189: Well, if he can kick anything out of a Government mule, he's a daisy *burro*. **1889** Farmer *Amer.*: Daisy Beat. The euphonious name applied to a swindle of the first water. ***1889** in *F & H* II 248: Big scenes of boats ascending Nile cataracts...and chances for daisy effects in the desert. **1890** Atherton *Los Cerritos* 226: What a daisy place he could make of it! **1891** *Puck* (Jan. 21) 370: This is the daisiest beanshooter out—it's got a terrible lot o' force. **1894** *Lucky Bag* (No. 1) 21: We have a daisy "cinch." **1898** Kountz *Baxter's Letters* 9: He would have got it fine and daisy. **1898** *Univ. of Tennessee Volunteer* 164: My father was a daisy fencer, and he taught me when I was a boy. **1903** Ade *Society* 42: It is true that she starved the Household for six months in order to give the Young Couple a daisy Send-Off. **1906** *Independent* (Nov. 29) 1259: I think those lace wraps are just the daisiest—.

daisy chain *n.* **1.a.** Orig. *Prost.* a line or rough circle of individuals engaged in copulation in which the participants serve as active and passive partners to different people simultaneously.

*a*1927 in P. Smith *Letter from Father* 56: Houses [of prostitution]...where they staged shows, daisy-chains, etc. **1938** "Justinian" *Amer. Sexualis* 19: *Daisy-Chain*. n....a melange of normal and perverted sexual conduct in an extremely heteromorphous manner...until each person in the group is engaged in duofunctional sexual activities...American C. 20 neologism. **1949** *Gay Girl's Guide* 6: *Daisy Chain*—Homosexual activity, anal, oral or in combination involving more than two persons. **1954** Caprio *Female Homosexuality* 99: In still another lesbian house in Havana, the show wound up with what is known in slang as a "daisy-chain" arrangement, whereby each prostitute is engaged in simultaneous mouth-genital contact. **1959** in Russell *Perm. Playboy* 461: One of those pornographic finger rings where a man and a woman or a daisy chain wickedly romp in engraved idleness. **1966** Longstreet & Godoff *Wm. Kite* 79: "Daisy chain or one by one?" she asked. **1967** P. Welles *Babyhip* 70: "Hi, Jan," she said, "how's the daisy chain gang-bang scene?" **1972** in *Penthouse* (Jan. 1973) 112: It was her first orgy…Maybe there would be…threesomes, foursomes, daisy chains. **1974** N.Y.C. social worker, age *ca*28: A daisy chain, as it was explained to me, is a group of people, all facing the same direction, all engaged in anal intercourse with the person in front.

b. a group of homosexual men in close association.—used derisively.

1942 *ATS* 473: *Daisy chain,* a group of active sodomites. **1952** Lait & Mortimer *USA* 46: There is an active daisy chain…on every ship. **1981** Hathaway *World of Hurt* 38: Yes, they discovered a whole ring of the little sodomites. A regular daisy chain.

2.a. a group of individuals engaged in unfair collaboration.—used derisively.

1969 *Reader's Digest* (Aug.) 126 [ref. to WWII]: It's time to bust up this daisy chain.

b. *Specif.* (*Finance*) a collaborative fraudulent scheme for the evasion of corporate or other taxes.

1985 WINS Radio News (Aug. 8): These individuals created what is known as a "daisy chain,"…a device in which individuals try to conceal non-payment of tax in a maze of paper flow and fictitious corporations. **1985** *N.Y. Times* (Aug. 9) B 2: State officials said the defendants had operated a "daisy chain" scheme, involving a maze of paper transactions and bogus corporations, that enabled large amounts of gasoline to be sold to retailers without payment of taxes. **1990** *New Republic* (Oct. 8) 16: S&Ls would hide such loans by selling them to each other at inflated prices in a daisy-chain network.

c. *Specif.* (*Commerce*) a series of transactions designed to create the appearance of active trading, as in a particular stock, in order to manipulate the price.

1987 *RHD2.*

3. *Mil. Av.* a single-file formation of three or more aircraft; (*also*) an aerial dogfight that briefly assumes a similar shape.

1966 Newhafer *Bugles* 60 [ref. to WWII]: And so they went at the guns of Majon-ni in a daisy chain, a continuous chain of attacking aircraft peeling off, making their attack, then climbing to altitude to initiate another attack. **1968** Meyerson *Vinh Long* 82: Gordon proposes to Meehan that all gunships in the area link up in a long tactical trail formation like a daisy chain. **1969** Cagle *Naval Av. Guide* 391: *Daisy Chain.* A group of airplanes, usually four, descending in single file from altitude to make an instrument approach or a CCA aboard ship. Sometimes the planes are in pairs. **1986** F. Walton *Once Were Eagles* 25 [ref. to WWII]: Rinabarger saw a "daisy chain": a Corsair had a Zero on its tail, another Corsair was on the Zero's tail, and another Zero was on the second Corsair's tail.

daisy-chain *v.* to engage in a DAISY CHAIN, 1.a.

1966 Longstreet & Godoff *Wm. Kite* 336: There was smart wife-swapping in Westchester and daisy-chaining in the Village. **1968** Lockridge *Hartspring* 49: The…bastards must have been looking in to see if we were all daisy-chaining.

daisy-clipper *n.* **1.** DAISY-CUTTER, 3. Now *hist.*

1874 (cited in Nichols *Baseball Term.*). **1973** H. Peterson *Man Who Invented Baseball* 52: That was a real daisy clipper.

2. *Army.* DAISY-CUTTER, 4.a.

1918 in Gow *Letters* 402: I have been continually running through Jerry's counter-barrages, machine gun fire and shells of every description and calibre, whizz-bangs, wooley-bears, Jack Johnsons, pound wonders, Tock Emmas, minnies, daisy-clippers, iron foundries and gas. These are all trench slang names for various types of Jerry's shells.

daisy-cutter *n.* **1.** *Horse Racing.* a horse that does not step high in trotting or running.

*1785 Grose *Vulgar Tongue: Daisy Cutter.* A jockey term for a horse that does not lift up his legs sufficiently, or goes too near the ground, and is therefore apt to stumble. ***1791** in *OED:* I luckily picked up a Daisy-cutter, by his throwing me down on the smoothest part of the grass. ***1817** W. Scott, in *F & H* II 248: I should like to try that daisy-cutter of yours upon a piece of level road (barring canter) for a quart of claret at the next inn. ***1847** in *OED:* The careless daisy-cutter, however pleasant on the turf, should…be avoided. ***1866** in *F & H* II 248. **1880** *N.Y. Clipper Almanac* 44: *Daisy-cutter.*—A horse that keeps his feet near the ground in trotting or running. **1949** Cummings *Sports Dict.* 98: *Daisy-cutter*…A term applied, by the breeders of saddle horses, to racing thoroughbreds and standardbreds. Reason: saddle horses raise

their feet high, but race horses barely skim the ground—the emphasis being on length of stride. **1978** *N.Y. Post* (June 29) 68: Too Young: Vastly-improved daisy-cutter seeking bigger game after taking last two. Will be flying down the lane.

2. a fine fellow.

1840 *Spirit of Times* (May 2) 99: Spake to that, my daisy-cutter.

3. *Baseball.* a batted ball that skims along just above the ground. [Earlier in England in the game of cricket; see *OEDS.*]

1866, 1869 (cited in Nichols *Baseball Term.*). **1872** Chadwick *Dime Base-Ball* 25: A "daisy-cutter" is a ball hit sharply and close along the ground from a ball pitched low to the bat. **1877** *Puck* (Aug. 22) 13: Strikes, fair balls, base hits, daisy-cutters. **1880** in *DAE* II 720: He knocked a daisy-cutter over to Pel Snelgro. **1889** "M. Twain" *Conn. Yankee* 534: My peerless short-stop! I've seen him catch a daisy-cutter in his teeth! **1891** Maitland *Slang Dict.* 87: *Daisy-cutter,* applied…in the baseball field to a straight "liner" which does not rise high.

4. *Mil.* **a.** an antipersonnel fragmentation bomb that explodes slightly above ground level.

1917 Cushing *Surgeon's Jrnl.* 192: At No. 61 five bombs had been dropped, four with so horizontal a spread—"daisy cutters"—that lying down did not suffice to escape fragments. **1919** *With the 114th* 133: "*Daisy Cutter.*"—Shell exploding on top of ground and spreading. **1945** Jensen *Carrier War* 47: 2,000-pound bombs, fragmentation "daisy-cutters" and incendiaries suddenly rocked all of the little island. **1945** in *Calif. Folk. Qly.* V (1946) 378: The [aviators] display a macabre humor in dubbing particularly effective anti-personnel bombs as *daisy-cutters.* **1961** Forbes *Goodbye to Some* 124: One Jap begins dropping daisy-cutters in the tent area. **1963** Boyle *Yanks* 18: A daisy-cutter, an antipersonnel bomb designed to spread its lethal fragments low above the ground, exploded ten yards in front of him.

b. a special-purpose high-explosive bomb of tremendous power.

1966–67 Harvey *Air War* 56: These special bombs were known as "daisy cutters," and if the VC were…underwater…a daisy cutter would float their bodies to the surface like corks. **1971** *Newsweek* (Apr. 26) 46: A gigantic, 15,000 pound bomb called the "daisy-cutter" because its explosion creates instant clearings in the jungle. **1978** Groom *Better Times* 225: Every few days the Air Force would drop a "daisy-cutter" bomb…that would blow an enormous hole in the jungle, through which helicopters could descend to resupply them. **1983** Groen & Groen *Huey* 172: John flew into an LZ cleared by one of these "daisy-cutters." **1984** Doleman *Tools of War* 127: The 15,000-pound BLU-82B "Daisy Cutter"…floated earthward on a parachute and exploded twenty feet above the ground…Its purpose was to level all vegetation…to create an instant helicopter landing zone. **1991** *War in Gulf* (CNN-TV) (Feb. 12): 15,000-pound bombs dubbed "daisy-cutters"…[will] clear land mines for advancing ground troops.

daisy-pusher *n. Army.* a dead person. Also **daisy-shover.** [Quots. ref. to WWI.]

1919 *With the 114th* 133: *Daisy Pusher*—One who becomes mere fertilizer. **1928–29** Nason *White Slicker* 140: If they were really on the offensive we'd have been all daisy shovers by now.

daisy roots *n.pl.* [rhyming slang] boots or shoes. *Rare* in U.S.

1859 Matsell *Vocab.* 24: *Daisy-roots,* boots and shoes. **1928** Sharpe *Chicago May* 288: *Daisy Roots*—boots. ***1943** in *OEDS.*

Daisyville *n.* [folk ety. of much earlier *Dewse a vyle* (of unkn. orig.); see Partridge *Dict. Und.*] *Und.* the country.

1859 Matsell *Vocab.* 24: *Daisyville.* The country. **1866** *Nat. Police Gaz.* (Nov. 24) 3: The "guns" thought it best to take a trip to "Daisyville."

damage *n.* cost; price.—constr. with *the.*

*1755 in *OED.* **1843** "J. Slick" *High Life in N.Y.* 69: "Wal, what's the damage." "Only a dollar." **1845** Durivage & Burnham *Stray Subjects* 57: "Wo-wot's the damage?" "Three levies, sir." **1848** Judson *Mysteries* 349: Well, wot's to pay? Wot's the damage? **1852** Stowe *Uncle Tom* 98: Well, now, my good fellow, what's the damage, as they say in Kentucky: in short, what's to be paid out for this business? **1881–84** Davitt *Prison Diary* I 45: He would rush into a public-house or gin palace…call for a glass of beer or spirits, and pay the "damage" with a half sovereign or half-a-crown. **1895** Townsend *Fadden* 82: "Wot's de damage?" "Fifty cents fer hat check." **1926** *Writer's Mo.* (Mar.) 198: If you do a man a service, he usually asks, "What's the damage?" **1928** Scanlon *God Have Mercy* 168: Wait until you hear what the damage is. **1938** *Test Pilot* (film): "What's the damage [for a new nightgown]?" "Fifty dollars, sir." **1971** Sorrentino *Up from Never* 51: "What's the damage?" "T'oity cents." **1985** N. Kazan *At Close Range* (film): "What's the damage?" "Forty." **1986** *Miami Vice* (NBC-TV): Just give me the damage on these two.

damaged *adj.* tipsy.

1859 Bartlett *Amer.* (ed. 2) 114: *Damaged.* Intoxicated. **1891** Maitland *Slang Dict.* 87: *Damaged...*intoxicated.

damaged goods *n.* a person, esp. a woman, who is no longer a virgin.

1916 S. Lewis *Job* 257: She had reason to suppose that her husband was damaged goods. **1929–34** J.T. Farrell *Judgment Day* 665: Still, when he got married, he'd be getting damaged goods. **1942** *ATS* 395. **1971** *Nichols* (NBC-TV): Maybe these boys don't like damaged goods. **1990** L.B. Rubin *Erotic Wars* 5: A word from my past [1940's], when a girl who "slipped" was considered "damaged goods." **1991** *Nation* (June 24) 851: Many believe that a woman can't be raped against her will and that damaged goods are damaged goods.

dame *n.* a woman or girl.—often used disparagingly. [Ironic in earliest use.]

*****1698–1720** D'Urfey *Pills* V 107: As Oyster *Nan* stood by her Tub,...A Vintner of no little Fame,...Beheld the little dirty Dame, As she stood scratching of her Belly. **1744** A. Hamilton *Gentleman's Progress* 138: This house was well furnished with women of all sorts and sizes...tall and short, fat and lean, ugly and pritty dames. *ca*1786 in S. Rodman *Amer. Poems* 45: One whorish dame I fear to name/Lest I should give offense. *****ca1835** in Holloway & Black *Broadsides* II 61: The sight of my glutton [penis] so pleased the dame,/She seem'd in a hurry to be at the game. **1850** in M.W. Brown *Dan Rice* 437: Ain't she a thrifty dame? **1865** Woodruff *Union Soldier* 16: Imagine me & a creole Dame... sporting over a fine shell road behind a lame Mule. **1866** in Hilleary *Webfoot* 188: The fair dames from Emerald Isle who compose the laundress corps. **1885** *Puck* (Apr. 8) 83: That's tough luck; not more than two hundred per cent profit! Did you have any trouble with the dame? **1887** DeVol *Gambler* 274: I'd spent more'n a half-bushel of 'em for dames afore they got on to 'em. **1888** Bangs *Katharine* 16: Now Katharine—that's the lady's name—/For Petrucio is just the dame! **1897** Ade *Horne* 173: I've got a swell dame here from the south side. **1904** Hughie Cannon *Little Gertie Murphy* (N.Y.: Howley-Dresser Co., 1904) (song): Wid me she's a mighty swell dame. **1918** Witwer *Baseball to Boches* 10: They're battin' .1000 with the dames on board just the same. **1920** S. Lewis *Main Street* 228: There's still a few dames that think the old man isn't so darn unattractive! **1923** T. Boyd *Through the Wheat* 69: Now if some of them dames we seen at Meux was here. **1949** Rodgers & Hammerstein *South Pacific* 289: There is nothin' like a dame. **1952** in C. Beaumont *Best* 18: The dames will start asking questions. **1967** Deutsch & Kingsley *Valley of Dolls* (film): Ted Casablanca is not a fag! And I'm the dame that can prove it! **1973–76** J. Allen *Assault* 22: There were also some dames that were counsellors and some of them was pretty hot mamas too. **1980** *N.Y. Post* (June 7) 5: "She's a feisty dame," said officer Bill Scully. "And a knockout too." **1982** *N.Y. Post* (Dec. 30) 16: That's why so many women have accidents! Dames are a disaster behind the wheel!

damfino *interj.* "damned if I know."

1882 Peck *Peck's Sunshine* 148: Damfino what it is. **1883** Peck *Peck's Bad Boy* 40: Pa said, "damfino" and "it's no such thing." **1903** Benton *Cowboy Life on Sidetrack* 31: We asked him where our car was that we would go out on, and he said, "Damfino." *****1909** Ware *Passing Eng.* 103: Damfino (*Anglo-Amer.*)..."I am damned if I know." **1918** McNutt *Yanks* 41: "Where is he now?" I asked. "Damfino," he replied without interest. "I didn't take notice of where they sent him." **1970** N.Y.U. students: "What did it say?" "Damfino. I forget." **1975** McCaig *Danger Trail* 33: "Where's the poor girl now?" "Damfino." *a*1987 Bunch & Cole *Reckoning* 7: Damfino, but good guess.

damn *infix.* (used as an intensifier). [1865–67 quot. is the earliest known example of infixing in English; cf. similar use of BLOODY, FUCKING, and GODDAMN.]

1865–67 De Forest *Miss Ravenel* 272: "He is, by Jove! a dam incurdam-able dam coward." (When Van Zandt was informed the next day of this Feat of profanity he seemed quite gratified). **1950** Bissell *Stretch on the River* 56: I guarandamtee ya I ain't agoing to wheel no mo' coal. **1959** W. Anderson *Nautilus* 219: Fan-damn-tastic. **1961** H. Ellison *Memos* 49: I was not...anydamnbody but me. **1971** G. Davis *Coming Home* 144: I gar-and-damn-tee you that. **1980** Grizzard *Billy Bob Bailey* 4: The University of Aladambama. **1985** Bodey *F.N.G.* 2: Ungoddamnly hot here. **1986** R. Zumbro *Tank Sgt.* 232: The Executioner's crew was dog-damn-tired and ready for a break.

damn-all *n.* emphatically nothing; anything; (*occ.*) a damn.

*****1914–22** J. Joyce *Ulysses* 417 [ref. to 1904]: Proud possessor of damn all. *****1930** Brophy & Partridge *Songs & Slang* 114 [ref. to WWI]: *Damn all*, nothing. Used to give emphasis...A bowdlerisation of a foul expression. **1959** Trocchi *Cain's Book* 120: Milk? I got damn-ass all. **1971** "L. Short" *Man from Desert* 11: He lifted his glass and set, "Here's damn all to every banker." **1975** Swarthout *Shootist* 142: My life has not amounted to a damn-all. **1975** Larsen *Runner* 43: I don't care damn-all what Lieutenant Carter said. *Ibid.* 50: So don't act like you know damn-all.

damn-damn *n.* [resp. of *dam-dam*, echoic pidgin] *Mil. in Vietnam.* bombardment; gunfire. Now *hist.*

1982 Del Vecchio *13th Valley* 22: Without worryin about Charlie doin a damn-damn on yer heads. *Ibid.* 194: Chas don't like them fast-movers. They bring in the damn-damn. **1984–87** Ferrandino *Firefight* 126: Or I put boo-coo damndamn on your ass.

damn-my-eyes *adj. Naut.* flashy; ostentatious.

1849 Melville *White Jacket* 293 [ref. to 1843]: You may put that man down for what man-of-war's men call a *damn-my-eyes tar*, that is a humbug. And many damn-my-eyes humbugs there are. **1899** Boyd *Shellback* 16 [ref. to 1860's]: A tall complexioned hat and a "d—n my eyes" necktie.

damp *adj.* **1.** slightly intoxicated. Cf. DRENCHED, SOAKED, WET.

1813–18 Weems *Drunk. Look. Glass* 60: Boozy-groggy-blue-damp-tipsy.

2. foolish; crazy; "all wet."

1928 Segar *Thimble Th.* 17: G'wan you're all damp in the head!...all damp between the ears. **1929** *Ibid.* 101: Anything damp about my face?

damp *n.* a drink of liquor.

*****1836** C. Dickens *Pickwick Papers* ch. xxvii: "So we'll just give ourselves a damp, Sammy." Saying this, Mr. Weller mixed two glasses of spirits and water. **1891** Maitland *Slang Dict.* 87: *Damp...*a drink. **1899** Cullen *Tales* 108: As for the damps, I've got kags of it.

¶ In phrase:

¶ **slice of damp** copulation with a woman.

1977 Butler & Shryack *Gauntlet* 99: Bet you had ideas of gettin' a little gash for yourself, hunh?...Nothin' like a slice of damp, is there?

damper *n.* **1.** *Und.* a cash drawer; till; (*also*, in more recent use) a cash register.

*****1848** in Partridge *Dict. Und.* 175: *Draw a damper...*take a money drawer. *****1857** (cited in *F & H* II 250). **1892** Norr *China Town* 50: I went to the damper to see if she had taken the roll, but there wasn't a cent gone. **1893** F.P. Dunne, in Schaaf *Dooley* 226: "Turn down the damper" [was] a current phrase along the Archey road for robbing a cash drawer. **1904** *Life in Sing Sing* 247: *Damper.* Money-drawer. **1906** *Nat. Police Gaz.* (Mar. 31) 3: I could have got the damper alone if it hadn't been for the man's wife...sitting behind the counter. **1911** A.H. Lewis *Apaches of N.Y.* 28: Give me ten dollars out of the damper. **1914** Jackson & Hellyer *Vocab.* 28: *Damper...*A combination cash drawer or register. **1926** *AS* I (Dec.) 651: *Damper.* A cash register. **1931** *Amer. Merc.* (Dec.) 417: And maybe you think *that* didn't put a hole in the damper. **1933** Ersine *Pris. Slang* 31: *Damper...*a cash register. **1961** in Cannon *Nobody Asked* 352: Toots grabbed the tab when you were empty and often he had to put a marker in the damper against his salary to straighten out a guy with the shorts.

2. *Und.* a safe or safe-deposit box.

1872 Crapsey *Nether Side of N.Y.* 16: Damper-sneaks are...not more than one hundred in number. By "damper," a thief means a safe, for the reason that it is supposed to put a damper upon his hopes. **1872** McCabe *N.Y. Life* 529: The safe...in the thief language, is called a "Damper." **1967** (quot. at (3), below).

3. *Und.* a bank.

1932 in *AS* (Feb. 1934) 26: *Damper.* A bank. *Damper pad.* A bank book. **1967** [Beck] *Pimp* 314: *Damper...*a place holding savings, bank, safe deposit box, etc.

¶ In phrase:

¶ **turn (one's) damper down** *Black E.* to cool (one's) ardor or enthusiasm.

1924 in M. Taft *Blues Lyric Poetry* 242: All I need is some good daddy: turn my damper down. **1937** in M. Taft *Blues Lyric Poetry* 10: Now if you mess with me, mama: I'm sure going to turn your damper down. *a*1969 J. Kimbrough *Defender of Angels* 198 [ref. to 1920's]: You would come here and turn my damper down.

damper-getter *n. Und.* a robber of tills.

1904 *Life in Sing Sing* 255: *Damper getter.* A thief who robs money drawers. **1921** "M. Brand" *Black Jack* 107: As a damper-getter he was just an amateur. **1935** *AS* (Feb.) 14.

dan *n.* *Und.* dynamite.

*a***1909** Tillotson *Detective* 91: Dan—Dynamite. **1925–26** Black *You Can't Win* 109 [ref. to 1890's]: Extracting the explosive oil, nitroglycerine, from sticks of "dan" or dynamite. **1928** Guerin *Crime* 160 [ref. to 1901]: He…was one of the greatest "dan" men in the States. **1944** C.B. Davis *Leo McGuire* 127: You can't tell about dan. Buy it in a store and maybe it's so old it's starting to crystallize.

dance *n.* ¶ In phrase: **do a dance on** to kick and stomp. [Fig. in 1981 quot.]

1974 Dubinsky & Standora *Decoy Cop* 88: The lover did a tap dance on the husband's eye then ran him out the door. **1981** *N.Y. Daily News* (July 10) 65: It just sounded like the guy got roasted totally. They were doing a dance on his head.

dance *v.* **1.** to kick and stomp.—now constr. with *on*.

*****1821–26** Stewart *Man-of-War's-Man* I 52: Blast your day-lights, you lubber!…I'll dance your rascally ribs into powder. **1984** Caunitz *Police Plaza* 240: If you don't, my large friend here will come back and dance the tarentella [*sic*] on your nuts.

2. (of a hanged person) to make involuntary spasmodic movements while being hanged; (*hence*) to be executed by hanging.

1859 Matsell *Vocab.* 24: *Dance at his death.* To be hung. "May he dance when he dies," may he be hanged. **1864** in I. Jackson *Civil War Letters* 196: One of our boys said, "I do wish Ben Butler was President—he would make some of them dance in the air." **1929** Hotstetter & Beesley *Racket* 223: *Dance*—To die by hanging. **1932** in *AS* (Feb. 1934) 26: *Dance.* To hang from the gallows.

3. to send (someone) away with deceptive or delaying action.

1978 Black *Clonemaster* (NBC-TV): "Why would Harry bug our office?" "Because we danced him."

¶ In phrases:

¶ **dance on air** to be executed by hanging. Cf. AIR DANCE.

1873 [De Witt] *Dundreary* 12: Use plenty of *slang* phrases.…You may "bet your boots" when at last you are "dancing a jig on air," folks will exclaim "How is that for high?" **1902** Raine *Raasay* 299: I see your old rival Montagu is to dance on air to-morrow. **1933–34** "M. Brand" *Mt. Riders* 100: You've got the range talkin'. It'll keep on talkin'…after you've danced on air, son.

¶ **dance on nothing** to be executed by hanging.

1807 *Port Folio* (June 6) 357: How we wept…to see them dance upon nothing at all. [**1827** J. F. Cooper *Red Rover* 499: Pipe the rogues to prayers, before they take their dance on nothing!] **1832** in S. Smith *Letters of Downing* 103: Shooting is too good for him. He must dance upon nothing. **1836** W.G. Simms *Millichampe* 41: What! they pardoned him—and so many people as was guine [*sic*] to see him dance upon nothing? **1842** *Ben Hardin's Crockett* (unp.): Into [Havana], where they danced on nothing. **1864** "E. Kirke" *Down in Tenn.* 159: I knowed whot thet meant—a short prayer, a long rope, an' a break-down danced on the top o' nothin'. *ca***1875** Williams *Binnacle Jack* 14: Better to turn a windlass here than turn out under the smoke of a gun to dance upon nothing. **1884** in Lummis *Letters* 80: Give them $50 a piece…or you'll dance on nothing in two minutes.

dancehall *n.* **1.** *Pris.* a pre-execution cell; (*occ.*) an execution chamber; (*rarely*) a death house. Also **dancehouse**.

1928 Lawes *Life & Death* 162: The "dance hall" (pre-execution chamber)…is connected by a corridor with…the execution chamber and the "ice box," or morgue, adjoining. **1928** Panzram *Killer* 158: *Dance hall—* death house. **1929** Hotstetter & Beesley *Racket* 223: *Dance hall—*Cell or cell block in prison where criminals sentenced to death are confined before execution. **1931** *AS* VI (Aug.) 437: *Dance-hall.* The execution chambers of a prison. **1932** L. Berg *Prison Doctor* 53: Once a day I was allowed to exercise so that I would be in good condition when my turn came to walk into the "dance hall." **1939** Howsley *Argot* 15: *Dance Hall, Dance House*—prison death house; electric chair or lethal (otherwise) chamber. **1944** C.B. Davis *Leo McGuire* 232: On a Thursday they took Sokolsky into the dance hall. **1956** Resko *Reprieve* 18: A passageway connects the two wings to the "Dance hall" with its last-minute cells where the condemned spend their final day. **1977** Coover *Public Burning* 512: The convicts here call it the Dance Hall. **1981** P. Sann *Trial* 166: The other five were in the Dance Hall up there on the river.

2. (see quot.).

1944 Boatright & Day *Hell to Breakfast* 148: Among the transportation

equipment, a tractor is a "cat" and a large flat bed semi-trailer truck is a "dance hall."

dancer *n.* **1.** *pl.* stairs.

*****1665–71** in *F & H* II 251: *Track up the Dancers*, go up the stayres. *****1673** R. Head *Canting Acad.* 37: *Dancers.* Stairs. *****1698–99** "B.E." *Dict. Canting Crew: Dancers…*Stairs. *****1707**, *****1718** (cited in Partridge *Dict. Und.* 176). *****1828** in Partridge *Dict. Und.* 176: I thinks as how I hear a bit of a scrummage below the *dancers.* *****1812** Vaux *Vocab.* 235: *Dancers:* stairs. **1859** Matsell *Vocab.* 65: *Up the dancers…*up stairs. **1926** Finerty *Criminalese* 15: *Dancers*—Steps. **1965** O'Neill *High Steel* 270: *Dancers.* Stairs. **1986** *AS* LXI 212: American Angloromani…contains some Cant words—*dancers* 'stairs,' for example.

2. *Boxing.* a boxer who relies heavily on footwork in the ring.

1949 Cummings *Sports Dict.* 98. **1971** Torres *Sting Like a Bee* 141: Liston is flat-footed, but me and Sugar Ray are two pretty dancers.

3. *Baseball.* a knuckleball.

1978 K. Jackson, on *ABC Monday Nt. Baseball* (July 3): Maybe if Jimmy Spencer—if he can get the dancer under control—'ll get a chance.

D and D *adj. & n.* **1.** *Police.* being drunk and disorderly; a charge of being drunk and disorderly; one who is drunk and disorderly.

*****1889** in *F & H* II 251: The old man was up for D and D, trying to break a window with his broom. *****1892** in Franklyn *Rhyming Sl.* 184: A slop pinched him for "d. and d." **1917** *DN* IV 357: *D & D.* Drunk and disorderly: in the Navy. **1957** J.D. MacDonald *Price of Murder* 105: One of the beat cars…had brought in an early…D and D they had netted. **1958** S.H. Adams *Tenderloin* 113: "Soliciting in a public place," the cop says. Or maybe dee and dee if they want to make it hard.…Drunk and disorderly. **1960** J.D. MacDonald *Slam the Big Door* 38: He was charged with D and D. **1986** R. Campbell *In La-La Land* 112: Chances were, an old drunk told them, they'd give him two days on the D and D.

2. (among beggars) deaf and dumb; a beggar who is or who pretends to be deaf and dumb.

1937 Reitman *Box-Car Bertha* 139: The deaf and dumb ones my informer called "D and D's." **1954** Schulberg *Waterfront* (film): All I want to know—is he D and D or is he a canary? **1969** *Time* (Mar. 21) 21: Playing D. & D. (deaf and dumb) with cops was a lesson taught in the quiet back rooms of precinct houses. **1983** Flaherty *Tin Wife* 294: She had played D & D to the extravagances.

dandery *adj.* irritated; angry.

1838 [Haliburton] *Clockmaker* (Ser. 2) 20: It made me feel kinder dandry at him.

dandruff *n.* [either a joc. alter. of *dander* in this phr. (itself historically an alter. of *dandruff*) or a survival of the orig. form] ¶ In phrase: **get (someone's) dandruff up** to anger (someone). Sometimes *Joc.*

1902 Townsend *Fadden & Mr. Paul* 12: Carrie Nation's a boarding school goil alongside him when he gets his dandruff up. **1958** "R. Traver" *Anatomy of a Murder* 295: Instead of talking Maida got her "dandruff" up, as Sulo Kangas might put it. **1966–69** in *DARE.* **1984** Sample *Raceboss* 237: So don' gitcha dandruff up. **1988** *Perfect Strangers* (ABC-TV): Now I understand what got your dandruff up!

dandy *n.* [app. of Scots orig. rel. to obs. *jackadandy, dandilly,* and *Dandy* (a hypocoristic form of *Andrew*)] **1.** a man who dresses fashionably and ostentatiously; fop; DUDE. Now *S.E.*

*****ca***1780** in *SND*: I've heard my granny crack/O' sixty-two years back/ Where there were sic a stock of Dandies O. **1817** in Royall *Letters from Ala.* 87: One old farmer, and one of your dandies. *****1818** in *F & H* II 252: When I walk along the streets I see fair women…and fops (or dandies as they are called in current slang), shaped like an hour-glass. *****1818** in *OED*: They've made him a Dandy,/A thing, you know, whiskered, great-coated, and laced,/Like an hour-glass, exceedingly small in the waist. **1821** in *So. Folk. Qly.* XIX (1955) 172: You little dandies and other big folks…enjoy the fruits of our hardships. **1850** Melville *Moby-Dick* ch. xxxii: No town-bred dandy will compare with a country-bred one. **1866** W.D. Howells *Venetian Life* ch. xx: He is a dandy, of course,—all Italians are dandies,—but his vanity is perfectly harmless, and his heart is not bad. *****1873** Hotten *Slang Dict.* (ed. 5) 139: *Dandies* [of *ca*1816] wore stays, studied a feminine style, and tried to undo their manhood by all manner of affectations which were not actually immoral. Lord Petersham headed them.

2. one that is most attractive, neat, skillful, or stylish.—formerly constr. with *the*; (*hence*, now solely) a stylish or first-class example (of anything). Now *colloq.*

*1784 in *OED:* Her breath is like the rose, and the pretty little mouth/ Of pretty little Tippet is the Dandy O! **1787–89** Tyler *Contrast* 77: Marblehead's a rocky place...Boston is the dandy. **1796** in Thornton *Amer. Gloss.* I 236: At that sport sure now Ireland's not the dandy. ***1811** *Lexicon Balatron.:* That's the dandy; i.e. the ton, the clever thing. **1812** in Shay *Sea Songs* 162: Oh, the Yankee boys for fighting are the dandy, oh! *Ibid.* 163: If we take this boasting Briton we're the dandy, oh! **1822** in Thornton *Amer. Gloss.* I 237: The reader will suppose this was a *dandy* of a thing, since it was on writing paper, two columns with a border. **1835** in *F & H* II 253: [This] liquor...here. It's the dandy, that's a fact. **1838** [Haliburton] *Clockmaker* (Ser. 2) 219: That's it—that's the dandy! **1847** in Oehlschlaeger *Reveille* 193: Of course we brag on our St. Louis Legion, as having been the dandy. **1882** in Farmer *Amer.:* Officer Finley...was caught under the chin with a dandy from the specimen's left that staggered him. **1888** in *F & H* II 253: The animal...is said to be a dandy. **1948** L. Allen *Reds* 175: Garry Herrmann...put on a party that was a dandy. **1956** M. Wolff *Big Nick.* 69: It's a dandy, all right. **1975** McCaig *Danger Trail* 4: Speaking of whiners, here comes a dandy. **1987** *Daywatch* (CNN-TV) (June 29): It was a dandy of a baseball game.

dandy *adj.* fancy; fashionable; (*hence*) splendid; first-class. Now *S.E.*

1792 in *DAE:* An old woman...dressed out with dandy finery. **1794** in *OEDS:* My uncle Cuthbert blew out a prodigious puff of my dandy tobacco. ***1821** *Real Life in Ireland* 189: Amongst these dandy ladies Brian threw away money by handfuls. **1842** in Eliason *Tarheel Talk* 128: I now have a real dandy suit of clothes. **1843** Field *Pokerville* 43: Mr. Wilson's boat...with...Mr. Tom Sky, her "dandy clerk." **1884** Bunner *Letters* 96: Riley—J.W.—...a dandy Hoosier. Trim, neatly dressed, polite, nasal, Western, with a face that might mean twenty-five and might mean seventy. **1889** Barrère & Leland *Dict. Slang* I 294: *Dandy-rig* (West American), fashionable attire. **1899** Garland *Eagle's Heart* 5: He's a dandy ball player and skates bully. **1921** *Variety* (Nov. 18) 21: I'll give you the dandiest punch in the nose, dear. **1933** J. Conroy *Disinherited* 31: I just been thinking if you wouldn't make a dandy pit boss. **1953** *Manchester City of Anger* 309: I'm fine and dandy. **1956** M. Wolff *Big Nick.* 22: "How've you been, Mrs. Stacey?" "Just fine and dandy." **1962** G. Olson *Roaring Road* 106: It was a dandy party. **1992** G. Wolff *Day at Beach* 122: The lodgings were dandy.

dandy *adv.* well, satisfactorily.

1908 in *OEDS.*

dandyfunk *n.* DUNDERFUNK. Now *hist.*

1849 in *AS* LXIII (1988) 114: If mush runs low or dundyfunk [*sic*], We eat our fill of cold salt junk. **1856** in C.A. Abbey *Before the Mast* 98: The "*duff*" was baked in a large pan & called in that state "*Dandy Funck*." I liked it as well if not better than the boiled. **1883** in *AS* XXXIV (1959) 28: *Dandy funk*—A mess made of powdered biscuit, molasses and slush. **1887** Davis *Sea-Wanderer* 288: When scouse is made without either meat or potatoes (but with vegetables)...it is called dandyfunk. **1893** Barra *Two Oceans* 76: Dandyfunk...is very palatable to a sailor. **1904** *Independent* (Mar. 24) 655: And through the week good lobscouse, slumgullion, dandy funk, and American hash alternated each other with pleasing regularity. **1909** in *Calif. Hist. Soc. Qly.* VI (1927) 267 [ref. to 1849]: We had..."dandy funk," a dish consisting of ship-biscuit and molasses, baked in the oven. **1945** Colcord *Sea Lang.* 63: *Dandyfunk.* A sailor's term for a pudding made of cracker crumbs, slush, and molasses.

dandy-trap *n.* a loose paving stone.

1842 *Spirit of Times* (Feb. 19) 598: The immense number of "dandy traps" (loose flag stones) which, on the slightest pressure, will cover you with mud and water. **1877** Bartlett *Amer.* (ed. 4) 168: *Dandy-Trap.* Loose brick in the pavement; when stepped upon, the muddy water underneath gushes up and soils boots or clothing.

dang *n., v., adj.* [euphem.] damn or damned. Also (as adj.) **danged.**

*1821 W. Scott, in *SND:* Dang it. ***1821–26** Stewart *Man-of-War's-Man* I 54: Dang it, Tummas! that's always thy way. **1840** *Spirit of Times* (Jan. 25) 557. **1845** Corcoran *Pickings* 10: Dang it, the legislature won't come to my relief. ***1906** in *OEDS:* He wouldn't give a dang for them. **1959** in Harvey *Air Force* 78: You're danged right you wouldn't. **1962** E. Stephens *Blow Negative* 328: This...job is a dang good one. **1982** Heat Moon *Blue Hwys.* 202: Dang him!...He played that dang song.

dangerous *adj.* extremely effective or impressive.

1984 R. Daniels *Be Dangerous on Rock Guitar* (title). **1987** *21 Jump Street* (Fox-TV): Judy, you are really getting *dangerous!* **1990** *World*

Tonight (CNN-TV) (May 10): Join us for Sports Tonight, the world's most dangerous sports broadcast.

dangle *n.* the penis. Also **dangler.**

1927, 1930 (implied by DANGLER, 1. b.). ***1936** Partridge *DSUE* 207 [ref. to WWI]: *Dangle-parade*, a "short-arm" inspection: New Zealand soldiers' [slang]. **1968** Baker et al. *CUSS* 103: *Dangle.* Male sex organ. **1977** Monaco *Parsival* 161: So...you never even guessed what your dangler was for?

dangle *v.* [perh. sugg. by the practice of "riding the rods"; cf. DANGLER, 2.a.] Esp. *Hobo.* to travel or depart, esp. in a hurry.

1927 *AS* (June) 390: To *take a jump* or *dangle up the line* signifies journeying. **1929** Barr *Let Tomorrow Come* 40: Me an' him an' a gunsel dangles into this burgh...in the belly of a drag. **1936** McCarthy *Mosshorn* (unp.): I'm Goin' to Dangle. When a cowboy shouts that expression or says I'm going to bunch it, draw my time or sell out, that means he is leaving. **1936** R. Chandler, in Ruhm *Detective* 139: Let's dangle. **1958** McCulloch *Woods Words* 45: *Dangle*—To travel in a hurry. *a*1979 Toelken *Dyn. of Folklore* 61: Oh, I've dangled afar with a big stick and a small bundle.

¶ In phrases:

¶ **dangle the cat** (see quots.).

1918 *DN* V 29: *To dangle the cat for a living*, vb. phr. To drive a caterpillar engine. Farmers. **1971** Tak *Truck Talk* 40: *Dangle the cat*: to drive a truck with an engine manufactured by Caterpillar.

¶ **got it dangling!** (used as a vulgar retort).

1983 K. Miller *Lurp Dog* 8: "Got that?"...He hefted an imaginary foot-long penis in his hand and shook it at the doorway..."Got it *dangling*, you fuckin' Lifer Pig."

dangler *n.* **1.a.** (see quots.).

*1785 Grose *Vulgar Tongue:* Dangler. One who follows women in general, without any particular attachment. **1859** Matsell *Vocab.* 24: *Dangler.* A roué; a seducer. **b.** (see quots.).

1927 *DN* V 443: *Dangler*, n. An exhibitionist. **1930** Irwin *Tramp & Und. Sl.:* *Dangler*—An exhibitionist.

2. *Hobo.* **a.** (see quots.).

1916 Livingston *Snare* 32: "Danglers"...suspend themselves on the rods upholding the coach bodies, straddle trucks of brakebeams, or attach themselves to other hazardous holds beneath the passenger equipment. **1930** Irwin *Tramp & Und. Sl.:* *Dangler*...A "rambler" riding the "rods" or brake beams, in both of which cases he more or less dangles from his perch.

b. an express or freight train.

1926 Finerty *Criminalese* 16: *Dangler*—An express train. **1928** in Partridge *Dict. Und.* 177: A freight train is a "rattler." An express train is a "dangler." **1933** Ersine *Prison Slang* 31: *Dangler*, n. A freight train.

3. *Und.* a beggar or criminal.

1928 Callahan *Man's Grim Justice* 34: Kelly's a raw-jawed dangler...Most of the crooks are afraid of him. *Ibid.* 26: A crook wasn't a regular hard-boiled underworld dangler unless he was addicted to drugs in some way or other. **1934** in Partridge *Dict. Und.* 177.

4.a. *pl.* the testicles.

1934 "J.M. Hall" *Anecdota* 104: D stands for danglers/More coarsely termed nuts. ***1961** Partridge *DSUE* (ed. 5).

b. see DANGLE, *n.*

5. *Circus.* a trapeze artist.

1934 Weseen *Dict. Slang* 158: *Dangler*—A trapeze performer. **1944** in *DAS* 140: He started rushing a dangler.

daniel *n.* *Black E.* the buttocks.

1946 Mezzrow & Wolfe *Really Blues* 78: Just before she went to fall on her daniel. *Ibid.* 304: *Daniel:* buttocks.

dap *n.* **1.** (see quot.).

1938 *AS* (Apr.) 152: *Dap.* A white person. Indiana Univ.

2. *Black E.* **a.** any of various elaborate handshakes used esp. by young black men to express solidarity or enthusiasm.

1972 Claerbaut *Black Jargon* 62: *Dap*, *n.* a rather sophisticated or complicated hand greeting used by many black people. **1982** Del Vecchio *13th Valley* 288 [ref. to *ca*1970]: Doc greeted Jax with an abbreviated field dap. **1983** "J. Cain" *Dinky-Dau* 147: That handshake nonsense...they had the audacity to call it a "dap," which in Vietnamese means "beautiful." **1984** Eble *Campus Slang* (Sept.) 2: *Dap*—handshake: "Yo, man, give me some dap." **1985** Bodey *F.N.G.* 42 [ref. to Vietnam War]: Peacock knows more daps than Callme. **1985** Boyne & Thompson *Wild Blue* 450: Catlin did a diddibop dap routine that left

Shields…bewildered. **1987** Pelfrey & Carabatsos *Hamburger Hill* 32: Each of the three black troops gave him the intricate ritual handshake normally reserved only for fellow bloods—the "dap," the universal gesture of brotherhood. **1993** *Martin* (Fox-TV): Gimme dap!

b. a warm welcome; (*hence*) affection or respect from peers.

1985 Eble *Campus Slang* (Spr.) 3: *Dap*—any kind of physical affection. **1990** Eble *Campus Slang* (Fall) 2: *Dap*—influence, admiration. "Rob has absolutely no dap on the yard." **1993** *Source* (July) 40: Girls was in love with Kid Frost. Me and Rakim got no dap.

dap *adj. Black E.* dapper; well-dressed; (*broadly*) pleasant. Also **dapt, dapped [down].**

1956 in R.S. Gold *Jazz Talk* 66: The word now is *dap*. You want somebody to know a man is sharp, is au reet, you say he's dap. **1959–60** R. Reisner *Jazz Titans* 153: *Dap*: dapper. **1965** in W. King *Black Anthol.* 306: Sweet Mac was very dap that night. Sharper than Logan X because he was wearing more jewels. **1967** Riessman & Dawkins *Play It Cool* 58: *Dapt, adj.* stylish. "That Chester is a real dapt dresser." **1968–70** *Current Slang* III & IV 34: *Dap, adj.* Nice…He is really dap when it comes to doing favors. **1974** in D.C. Dance *Shuckin' & Jivin'* 245: But I too was like you, I was *dap*. **1976** Braly *False Starts* 316: You think you look dap in that tux? You look like a waiter in a failing restaurant. **1967–80** Folb *Runnin' Lines* 111: Well dressed…*dapped down*.

dap *v. Black E.* to greet with a DAP.—also used absol. [Quots. ref. to Vietnam War.]

1973 *U.S. News & W.R.* (Feb. 19) 91: Nonmilitary gestures such as "passing the power" or "dapping" are disruptive, serve to enhance racial polarization, and should be discouraged. **1982** "J. Cain" *Commandos* 67: A black rookie MP…had started to "dap" a black suspect they had just arrested for burglary. **1985** Boyne & Thompson *Wild Blue* 455: The five blacks crowded around…excited, cheering, dapping. **1987** Pelfrey & Carabatsos *Hamburger Hill* 34: The three bloods again dapped.

darb *n.* **1.** Esp. *Und.* DARBY, 2.

1904 *Life in Sing Sing* 247: *Darb.* Money. *Ibid.* 259: *He pigged with the darb.* He absconded with the money. **1924** *N.Y. Times* (Aug. 3) VIII 16: Darb is still used for money. **1928** Sharpe *Chicago May* 42: Say, kid,…I've got the darb (stolen money).

2. a person or thing that is superior, remarkable, or attractive; peach.—in early use often constr. with *the.* Occ. **darbs.**

1915 in Grayson *New Stories* 553: Your right cross is a darb. **1915** Howard *God's Man* 129: Pink's playing was the darb. **1918–19** MacArthur *Bug's Eye View* 102: The dinner…was a darb, in army patter. **1919** Johnson *Heaven, Hell or Hoboken* 118: In other words, he was a "Darb." **1922** in *DN* V 147: Darbs—usually used with the definite article, i.e., "The Darbs," a person with money who can be relied on to pay the checks. **1922** *Variety* (June 30) 6: They say the carnivals are the darb. **1924** P. Marks *Plastic Age* 9: We're going to have a swell joint here. Quite the darb. **1926** Norwood *Other Side of Circus* 54: He certainly was a darb. **1926** Dunning & Abbott *Broadway* I: Ain't he a darb? **1934** Weseen *Dict. Slang* 179: *Darb*—A popular girl. **1944** in *Best from Yank* 98: Is she a darb? **1945** Hemingway *Sel. Letters* 589: The other night bellied up against the bar was a darb. **1945** Bellah *Ward 20* 125: Gee, Mahon—you're a darb. **1968** Swarthout *Loveland* 18 [ref. to ca1930's]: Our hero and his chariot were parked in front of Al's Drycleanery and it was a darb.

darb *adj.* DARBY.

1930 Irwin *Tramp & Und. Sl.*: *Darb*—Unusually skilled or able; excellent.

darby *n.* **1.** [earlier (a1576) *Father Derbie's bands*, allegedly sugg. by the name of a noted usurer] usu. *pl.* Orig. *Und.* a fetter, shackle, or handcuff. Now *hist.*

*1665 (cited in Partridge *Dict. Und.* 177). ***1676** in *F & H* II: But when that we come to the Whitt/Our darbies to behold. ***1698–99** "B.E." *Dict. Canting Crew: Darbies*…Irons, Shackles, or Fetters. ***1796** Grose *Vulgar Tongue* (ed. 3): *Darbies.* Fetters. *Cant.* ***1812** Vaux *Vocab.* 235: *Darbies:* fetters. ***1819** [T. Moore] *Tom Crib* 77: Thus a new set of *darbies*…Makes the jail-bird uneasy. ***1821–26** Stewart *Man-O'-War* II 110: I rather wish to keep my trotters clear of the darbies. **1836** *Naval Magazine* (Nov.) 520: His feet have never been lashed to a "grating," or his wrists adorned with a pair of "darby's." **1842** *Spirit of Times* (June 11) 173: He felt like a felon with a darby to his leg. **1848** *Ladies' Repository* VIII (Oct.) 315: *Darbies*, Manacles; fetters; irons. **1849** Melville *White Jacket* 228: You'll be getting us all into darbies for this. **1854** Mayer *Capt. Conot* 196: The Frenchman…ordered the mate to strike off my "darbies." **1865** Sala *Diary* II 354: It is scarcely feasible to put

the "darbies" on the delicate wrists of a fair Secesher. **1873** Perrie *Buckskin Mose* 29: I…placed in the pockets of my disguise a pair of darbies, (handcuffs), a revolver, and a brass knuckle. **1888** Gunter *Mr. Potter* 121: Them darbies is cold.

2. *Und.* cash; money. Also **derbies.**

*1688 Shadwell *Squire of Alsatia* (gloss.): *Darby.* Ready money. *Ibid.* 211: Thou shalt [not] want the *Ready*, the *Darby.* ***1698–99** "B.E." *Dict. Canting Crew: Darby*…Ready Money. ***ca1712** in *F & H* II 255: Come nimbly lay down *darby*;/Come, pray sir, don't be tardy. ***1725** *New Canting Dict.*: The Cull Tipp'd us the Darby. ***1785** Grose *Vulgar Tongue: Darby.* Ready money. *Cant.* ***1796** Grose *Vulgar Tongue* (ed. 3): *To come down with the Derbies;* to pay the money. **1821** Waln *Hermit in Phila.* 26: Down with the *derbies*—down with *the dust*—rouse out your gelt. **1859** Matsell *Vocab.* 24: *Darby.* Cash. "Fork over the darby," hand over the cash. **1928** Callahan *Man's Grim Justice* 127: Kate'll be tickled to death when I git back with all this darby (money). **1934** Weseen *Dict. Slang* 295: *Darby*—Money in general.

darby *adj.* excellent; great.

1918 in Hemingway *Sel. Letters* 11: I took some darby pictures of the Piave and the Austrian trenches. **1925** (cited in Partridge *Dict. Und.* 177). **1933** Ersine *Pris. Slang* 31: *Darby, adj.* Good, fine. "Everything is darby now."

darby kelly *n.* [rhyming slang] (see quot.).

1925 T.A. Dorgan, in Zwilling *TAD Lexicon* 30: An de ole soupfaw to de darby kelly. He don't like 'em down dere. **1928** Sharpe *Chicago May* 287: *Darby Kelly*—belly.

dark *n.* DARKY, 2.—now usu. considered offensive.

1862 in *DA:* Two venerable old darks…were sitting cross-legged on the floor. **1864** in Thornton *Amer. Gloss.* I 239: He immediately dispatched a "*dark*" to get [the book]. **1864** in S.C. Wilson *Column South* 157: The darks commenced leaving the church pretty fast. **1879** *Nat. Police Gaz.* (July 19) 14: No other "dark" was ever so particular about his linen. **1913** R. G. Carter *4 Bros.* 285 [ref. to Civil War]: A twenty-five cent scrip was transferred to the delighted "dark."

¶ In phrase:

¶ **in the dark** (of coffee) black.

1885 (quot. at DUMP). **1891** Maitland *Slang Dict.* 98: *Draw one in the dark* (Am.), a cheap restaurant order for a cup of coffee. **1900** (quot. at DRAW ONE).

dark *adj.* ¶ In phrase: **keep [it] dark** to keep silent.

1835 in Meine & Owens *Crockett Alms.* 73: But says I to myself, Crockett keep dark and squat low. **1845** in Robb *Squatter Life* 113: "Keep dark!" said one. "Mum is the word!" said the other. ***1857** "Ducange Anglicus" *Vulgar Tongue:* Keep it dark! *a*1867 in G.W. Harris *Lovingood* 52: He et her cookin, he promised her he'd keep dark—an' then went strait an' tole her mam. ***1868** in *F & H* IV 90: I always thought it was a pity she kept it so dark. ***1888** in *F & H*: I'll keep dark.

dark cloud *n.* a black person.—used derisively or contemptuously.

1909 in Sampson *Ghost Walks* 488: A moment later Big Smoak is called a big, dark cloud. **1913** *DN* IV 163: *Dark cloud*…A negro. **1931** J.T. Farrell *Guillotine Party* 86: I smell dark clouds around here. ***1945** S.J. Baker *Australian Lang.* 185: For the aboriginal: *abo, black,… darkie,…dark cloud.*

dark meat *n.* [sugg. by MEAT] copulation with a black person; a black person, esp. a woman, regarded as a source for sexual gratification.

1888 *Stag Party* 38: I prefer the *dark meat* always. **1931** Dos Passos *1919* 136: I'm not much on the dark meat. **1931** Farrell *Guillotine Party* 85: "If you ask me, I turn down nothing."…"Not even dark meat?" **1936** Levin *Old Bunch* 47: Maybe dark meat tonight. They were supposed to be swell. **1938** H. Miller *Trop. Capricorn* 178: The one thing he couldn't tolerate was dark meat. **1966** Neugeboren *Big Man* 6: Which you like best—white meat or dark meat? **1985** J. Dillinger *Adrenaline* 6: "If she ain't prejudiced 'gainst dark meat," a black guy joked.

dark-thirty *n. Mil.* a time shortly before dawn. *Joc.*

1985 Petit *Peacekeepers* 33 [ref. to 1983]: Before dawn—zero dark thirty in Marine Corps language. **1989** P.H.C. Mason *Recovering* 74: We got up at dark-thirty and take off at the first hint of day.

Darktown *n.* a neighborhood inhabited principally by blacks. —now usu. considered offensive.

1916 *The Dark-Town Strutters' Ball* (pop. song). **1975** T. Berger *Sneaky People* 13: Clarence…presumably lived in Darktown. **1980** R.L. Morris

Wait Until Dark 70: Every town had its own circumscribed "darktown."

darky *n.* **1.** *Und.* night; evening. *Rare* in U.S.

    *1753 in Partridge *Dict. Und.* 178: At *Darky*...at Night. ***1781** G. Parker *View of Society* II 133: About *Darkey**...*Twilight. ***1789** G. Parker *Life's Painter* 132: I don't come here every *darkey.* **1791** [W. Smith] *Confess. T. Mount* 19: A fit night for stealing, *a good darky. Ibid.* 20: Day-light being over and darky coming on.***1820–21** P. Egan *Life in London* 73: Only for a single *darkey!*

2. a black person.—usu. used patronizingly or (now solely) contemptuously. Orig. *colloq.*

    1775 in Moore *Songs of Revol.* 100: The women ran, the darkeys too. **1829** in *DA:* The darky's skip. **1840** Dana *Two Yrs.* ch. xvii: It almost broke our poor darky's heart. **1849** [J.B. Robertson] *Remin.* 112: Mind, darkie, who you spatter your water upon. **1850** Melville *Moby-Dick* ch. xcix: Some old darkey's wedding ring. **1856** in Thornton *Amer. Gloss.* I 238: Ouch! an awkward darkey's basket/Hit him a thump in the eye. **1870** in *F & H* II 256: Walk in, darkies, troo de gate. **1871** Schele de Vere *Amer.* 594: I wish de legislatur' would set dis darkie free. **1887** E. Custer *Tenting* 26: There was a good many other darkeys from all about our place. *a***1889** in Barrère & Leland *Dict. Slang* I 296: Before the darky of antebellum times quite disappears. **1901** S.E. Griggs *Overshadowed* 157: You must play "darky" to the last. **1907** in Sampson *Ghost Walks* 408: "Nigger"...grossly insults the colored race....The word "darky" is not at all objectionable. **1908** in Fleming *Unforget. Season* 23: The darkies [were] rolling...in paroxysms of laughter. **1937** in Botkin *Treas. Amer. Folk.* 799: Smarty, smarty,/Had a party,/And nobody came/But an old fat darky. **1943** in P. McGuire *Jim Crow Army* 68: We are subject to all kinds of abusive languages. Such as Nigger, darkie, son of a b—, and everything mentionable. **1954** Killens *Youngblood* 114: I know where Harlem darkies to a tee. **1994** N. McCall *Wanna Holler* 247: Yeah, I was born down by the river in a little shack, just like every other darky you've read about!

darky *adj. Und.* (see quot.).

    1807 Tufts *Autobiog.* 292 [ref. to 1794]: *Darky*...cloudy.

dart *n.* ¶ In phrase: **tough darts!** that's your misfortune! tough luck!

    1973 *N.Y. Times Bk. Review* (Oct. 21) 44 [ref. to 1950's]: I win, you lose, tough darts. **1975** V. B. Miller *Trade-Off* 42: Tough darts, Theo. Take it up with the commissioner. **1979** Radio ad (WBIR): "But the train is leaving!" "Tough darts!" **1989** *Tracey Ullman Show* (Fox-TV): Tough darts!

dash *n.* an attractive young woman; DASHER.

    1814 in Eliason *Tarheel Talk* 268: Miss — was there. I expected she would be a *dash*, but she is very coarse.

dasher *n.* a fashionable, attractive person who often attends parties, dances, etc.

    *1790 in *F & H* II 257: My Poll, once a dasher, now turned to a nurse. ***1802** in Barrère & Leland *Dict. Slang* I 296: These young ladies were *dashers.* **1807** W. Irving, in *OED*: To charter a curricle for a month...as is done by certain dashers of my acquaintance. **1807** in Eliason *Tarheel Talk* 268: I had the superlative pleasure of dancing with Mr. Hosler one of the dashers there. **1833** in Eliason *Tarheel Talk:* We have now some of the greatest bells lately come among us...and they make a greate display but since the revivle such great dashers look to be out of season in Charlotte. ***1843** C. Dickens *Martin Chuzzlewit* ch. xxix: Why, you look smarter by day...than you do by candle-light. I never see such a tight young dasher. ***1887** in *OED*.

date *n. Pros.* a sexual transaction with a prostitute; (*hence*) a prostitute's customer; TRICK. Also as *v.*

    1957 H. Danforth & J. Horan *D.A.'s Man* 221 [ref. to 1942]: There were four girls, one named Ruth, who gave me her address for a "date" before I left. *a***1976** Roebuck & Frese *Rendezvous* 162: Party girls insist that they will stop "dating" (tricking) when they "eventually find the right man." **1979** in E.M. Miller *Street Woman* 57: My first "date" (trick) was my first time having sex. **1985** Kasindorf *Brothel Wars* 188: There was a Shamrock customer waiting for "a date." **1985** D.K. Weisberg *Children of Night* 107: First, the girl attracts a customer on the street, and the pair agree to a sexual encounter (a "date"). **1990** Rukuza *W. Coast Turnaround* 43: Wanna date? **1993** *New Yorker* (Apr. 26) 64: "No way my dates will know?" (A "date" is a john.)

date bait *n.* **1.** *Stu.* an attractive person whom one would like to date.

    1944 *Slanguage Dict.* 59: *Date bait*—an "alreet" girl. **1948** *AS* (Dec.) 248: *Date bait, n.* A desirable girl. **1957** in *DAS* 140: How to Be Date Bait. **1966** in IUFA *Folk Speech*: *Date Bait*: a girl many boys are attracted

to and one who always has a date. **1985** *N.Y. Post* (Aug. 17) 28: Your interest in him as date bait is something else.

2. *Stu.* something that will entice a member of the opposite sex to accept the offer of a date.

    1986 *Campus Voice* (Sept.) 58: He...sold [cocaine] to moneyed fraternity men who used coke as "date bait."

daub *n. Circus.* an advertising poster.

    1923 Revell *Off the Chest* 203: One of the best circus advance agents that ever stole a "daub" or "ditched a bundle of snipes" under the culvert on a country route. **1975** McKennon *Horse Dung Trail* 29: The wagon passed a big barn they had pasted a "daub" on the day before.

dauber *n.* spirit; enthusiasm. Also **dobber.**

    1915 in Butterfield *Post Treasury* 142: I don't want to knock my own ball club, but it looks like a one-man team, and when that one man's dauber is down we couldn't trim our whiskers. **1926** J. Conway, in *Variety* (Dec. 29) 5: I've conned myself back to normal and the dauber isn't down. **1953** White *Down the Ridge* 50: So now, the psychiatrist from the Snake Pit starts to work on you, anything, as they say in the trade, to "dispel your negative outlook" or, to put it more simply, to prop your dobber back up again. **1989** *CBS This Morning* (CBS-TV) (Oct. 17): He has a favorite expression: Don't get your dauber down.

Davy *n.* [orig. alluding to DAVY JONES] *Naut. & Mil.* a power or spirit controlling rain and storms; DAVY JONES. Also **David.** *Joc.*

    1800 *Amorous Songster* 5: And if to old Davy I should go. ***1803** in J. Ashton *Eng. Satires on Napoleon* 161: Davy will have him, as sure as a gun. ***1889** Barrère & Leland *Dict. Slang* I 297: *Davy putting on the coppers for the parsons* (nautical), the brewing of a storm. ***1918** in Fraser & Gibbons *Soldier & Sailor Wds.* 72: *David* (or *Davy*), *Send It Down:* A soldiers' greeting to a shower of rain likely to postpone a parade. **1926** Nason *Chevrons* 202 [ref. to 1918]: Let Davey do his damnedest...Rain an' snow ain't nothin' to us. **1972** Cleaves *Sea Fever* 129 [ref. to 1920's]: You won't need your bit o' pay/For Davy'll take you far away. **1980** W.C. Anderson *Bat-21* 72: Rain! Bring 'er down, David!

davy *n.* [fr. *affidavy*, dial. pronun. of *affidavit*] a sworn oath; affidavit.

    *1764 in *F & H* II 258: And I with my *davy* will back it, I'll swear. ***1796** Grose *Vulgar Tongue* (ed. 3): *I'll take my davy of it*; vulgar abbreviation of affidavit. **1835** in *F & H* II 258: "I'll take my davy," says the captain, "it's some Yankee trick." **1838** [Haliburton] *Clockmaker* (Ser. 2) 171: I'll take my davy I didn't mean no offence at all. **1859** Matsell *Vocab.* 25: *Davy.* Affidavit; to witness upon oath. **1866** Meline *On Horseback* 263: I'll take...my davy—on a Mormon bible. **1867** *Nat. Police Gaz.* (Jan. 12) 3: The two "cops" made their "davy" that Johnny...had no visible means of support. **1912** *N.Y. Tribune* (Apr. 21) (magazine) 5: And he's no native, either, you can take your davy on that. **1918** Griffin *Ballads of Regt.* 49: A Sergeant made his "davey" that he...took away...a Sibley stove. **1930** Irwin *Tramp & Und. Sl.:* *Davy*—An affidavit, and now seldom heard except among the older tramps.

Davy Jones *n.* **1.** *Naut.* the demon of the sea; (*hence*) the bottom of the sea; DAVY JONES'S LOCKER. Now *S.E.*

    *1751 Smollett *Peregrine Pickle* ch. xiii: "I'll be damned if it was not Davy Jones himself. I know him by his saucer eyes, his three rows of teeth, and tail, and the blue smoke that came out of his nostrils"...This same Davy Jones, according to the mythology of sailors, is the fiend that presides over all the evil spirits of the deep. **1774** in Whiting *Early Provs.* 94: We would certainly have thought it was Davy Jones the terror of all sailors, come to fetch us away. ******ca***1790** in *OED*: The great bugbear of the ocean is Davie Jones....At the crossing of the line...[they call] out that Davie Jones and his wife are coming on board and that everything must be made ready. **1850** Melville *Moby-Dick* ch. lxxxi: This is the way a fellow feels when he's going to Davy Jones. ***1891** *F & H* II 258: *Davy Jones*...The spirit of the sea; specifically, the sailor's devil. **1893** Barra *Two Oceans* 76 [ref. to 1849]: They cook me up and pick my bones,/And throw the rest to Davy Jones. **1939** Willoughby *Sondra* 3: The men have no mind to be blown to Davy Jones, Cap'n. **1962** Quirk *Red Ribbons* 61: Two others [*sc.* planes] were consigned to Davy Jones alongside the carrier.

2. (a personification of death).

    1860 in *Ala. Hist. Qly.* XLIV (1982) 102: Disease...has carried a great many of them over to Davy Jones.

Davy Jones's locker *n. Naut.* the bottom of the sea, esp. regarded as the grave of those who perish at sea. Now *colloq.* or *S.E.*

    *1774 in Partridge *DSUE* (ed. 8) 293: "D—m my eyes," says he, "they are gone to Davy Jones's locker." This is a common saying when anything goes overboard. **1774** in Whiting *Early Provs.* 94: And every thing else gone to Davy Jones' locker, that is to the Devil. **1776, 1783, 1792, 1796, 1803** in Whiting *Early Provs.* *1803** in *OED* III 47: The...seamen would have met a watery grave; or, to use a seaman's phrase, gone to Davy Jones's locker. *1836** Marryatt *Mr. Mid. Easy* ch. xxvii: That terrible sort of gale the other day....I tink one time we all go to Davy Jones's locker. *1842** in *F & H* II 258: Consign'd to Davy Jones's locker. *1851** *N & Q* (Series 1) III 478: If a sailor is killed in a sea-skirmish, or falls overboard and is drowned, or any other fatality occurs which necessitates the consignment of his remains to the "great deep," his surviving messmates speak of him as one who has been sent to Davy Jones' locker. **1857** Willcox *Faca* 61: Then you think your profession is going to Davy Jones' locker? **1873** F. Whittaker *Sea Kings* 48: You'd drive his blessed majesty into Davy Jones' locker for not clearin' the says of that...pirate. **1929** Bowen *Sea Slang* 34: *Davy Jones' Locker.* The bottom of the sea. **1956** Moran & Reid *Tugboat* 103: The tug...grabbed the dog...from a certain end in Davy Jones's locker. **1961** Forbes *Goodbye to Some* 231: Blasted to oblivion....Consigned to Davy Jones' Locker, man. **1973** Flaherty *Fogarty* 235: But first, an intermezzo in Davey Jones' locker. **1990** Cogill *When God Was a Sailor* 82: Anything that wasn't wanted was "deep-sixed" immediately. Davy Jones's locker must have been bulging.

Davy's locker *n. Naut.* DAVY JONES's LOCKER. Now *colloq.*
1802 in Whiting *Early Provs.* 94: Rowan has gone to Davie's Locker at last: he died in the West Indies. *1803** in J. Ashton *Eng. Satires on Napoleon* 183: Eleven a.m. Bonypart in *Davy's locker.* *1839** Marryatt *Phantom Ship* ch. xli: I thought you had gone to Davy's locker. **1917** Depew *Gunner Depew* 143.

day *n.* ¶ In phrases:

¶ **all day, 1.** yes indeed. *Joc.*
1978 W. Brown *Tragic Magic* 37: "Is that 'Straight, No Chaser'?" "All day."
2. *Pris.* (see quot.).
1992 *Newsweek* (Feb. 14) 8: *All day:* A life sentence.

¶ **all day with** the end for.
1853 W.W. Brown *Clotel* 200: Otherwise it would have been "all day" with Bruin at the first pass.

¶ **back in the days** [or **day**] *Rap Music.* formerly; long ago.
1988 "Biz Markie" *Vapors* (rap song): Back in the days, he was nothin' like that. **1991** Nelson & Gonzales *Bring Noise* 116: Back in the days, he was ridiculed for being wack. **1992** *Martin* (Fox-TV): About your size twenty years ago—way *back* in the days. **1993** *Source* (July) 16: Reminds me of the...melodies we heard back in the day. *Ibid.* 52: My pops was a disco DJ back in the day.

¶ **for days** extensively; strikingly; emphatically.—also used as adj.
1968–70 *Current Slang* III & IV 50: *For days, adv.* The truth. **1971** Carr *Bad* 26: We'd gotten together over three hundred birds...Man, we had pigeons for *days!* **1971** in Sanchez *Word Sorcerers* 179: The coooool-cooooool Marcy Chaplains...was bad for days. **1978** Maupin *Tales* 253: A chrome bin for the fireplace logs. Travertine marble for *days.* **1978** W. Brown *Tragic Magic* 35: He had a well-stocked torso and arms and legs for days. *Ibid.* 48: I'm gonna be macking with Anita for days. **1980** M. Baker *Nam* 112: That's got to be the hairiest thing in the world. Adrenaline for days. **1981–89** J. Goodwin *More Man* 16: "Lipstick for days!" means, "She's wearing a really thick layer of lipstick."

¶ **ruin (someone's) whole day** *Mil.* to kill (someone). *Joc.*
1961 L.G. Richards *TAC* 44: "A blowout on takeoff can ruin your whole day," as Lieutenant Lorentzen put it. **1963** E.M. Miller *Exile* 147: There was always the problem of fast airplanes tending to run over them in flight, which—the pilots grinned—"can ruin a guy's whole day." **1974** Vietnam veteran, N.Y.C.: Those CBU's, man, they can ruin your *whole* day! **1991** *Etc., Etc.* (Cable TV Travel Channel): A Spanish cannonball ripped through his cabin and ruined his whole day. **1992** *CBS This Morning* (CBS-TV) (Dec. 8): An explosion [resulting from an asteroid impact] to ruin your entire day.

daylight *n.* **1.a.** [cf. L *lumen* 'eye', lit. 'light'] usu. *pl.* Esp. *Naut.* an eye.
*1752** H. Fielding, in *F & H* II 259: If the lady says such another word to me, d—n me, I will darken her daylights. *1785** Grose *Vulgar Tongue: To darken his day lights,* or *sew up his sees;* to close up a man's eyes in boxing. *1823** "J. Bee" *Slang Dict.:* The hero in his tent they found,/ His day-lights fixed upon the cold, cold ground. *1821–26** Stewart *Man-of-War's-Man* I 39: If my own day-lights could come over the spalpeens that hoisted me...if I wouldn't be after serving them a ticket

or two in the bread-baskets. **1833** A. Greene *Duckworth* I 156: Dody...resolved not to open his day-lights until he should be pretty certain of being right beyond the borders of Cornbury. **1900** Hammond *Whaler* 205: Put 'is daylights out, boys! **1921** *DN* V 116: *Daylights...*eyes. **1944** *PADS* (No. 2) 26: *Daylights...*The eyes.
b. usu. *pl.* wits, consciousness, "stuffing," etc. Now *colloq.*
1819 in Whiting *Early Provs.* 97: And knock the rulers' daylights out. **1848** E. Bennett *Mike Fink* 10: That'll shake the day-lights out o' us. **1853** Lippard *New York* 139: I have a cry for 1848 that will knock their daylights out of 'em. **1866** C.H. Smith *Bill Arp* 43: One day might be while enough for my daylights to be shelled out. **1884** Nye *Baled Hay* 79: The mule...is ostensibly pulling his daylights out. **1885** Byrn *Greenhorn* 7: I have often run down a fox a fair chase in an open field, and knocked his daylight out in no time. **1929** in *DARE* [ref. to ca1905]: He will "thump the living daylights out of the next varmint that makes a swing." **1934** G.W. Lee *Beale St.* 87: Dat's one nigger whose daylights I's gwine put out...de fust time he crosses me. **1936** "E. Queen" *Halfway House* 7: George Washington licked the daylights out of those, now, Hessians. **1955** Funk *Heavens* 94: In my own span of life someone...has tried to scare the daylights out of me from the time I was two...Some people amplify it to "the living daylights." **1960** N.Y.C. woman, age 45: It nearly scared the daylights out of me! *1984** Partridge *DSUE* s.v. *frighten:* Frighten the living daylights...out of someone.

2. a hole, esp. a fatal wound, made by a sword, a knife, or (now usu.) a bullet; in phr. **let daylight through** to shoot or stab, esp. fatally. Also vars.
1774 in Thornton *Amer. Gloss.* I 239: [He] drew forth a Sword declaring he would make Daylight shine thro' em, but he would carry his Point. **1777** in Whiting *Early Provs.* 97: The Ensign having his sword Drawn, says he would make the Day Light shine true [*sic*] him. **1833** S. Smith *President's Tour* 48: One of the wads come within six inches of making daylight shine thro' the President. **1839–40** Cobb *Green Hand* II 39: I let daylight into his weasand before it was fairly out of my left blinker. **1846** in Lowell *Poetical Works* 182: Wen cold lead puts daylight thru ye/You'll begin to kal'late. *Ibid.* 186: They'd let daylight into me to pay me fer desartin! **1847** Furber *12 Months Volunteer* 206: Take yourselves off, or I'll send daylight through your d-m-d liver, and that quick. **1848** Judson *Mysteries* 356: "Get out of the way, or by Heaven I'll let daylight through you!" said Whitmore,...drawing a dirk from his bosom. **1861** in W.H. Russell *My Diary* 115: If ye prod me wid that agin, I'll let dayloite into ye. **1868** "W. J. Hamilton" *Maid of Mtn.* 17: I'll let daylight through you, if yer don't answer. **1868** Macy *There She Blows!* 105: I'd have let daylight through him! **1879** *Puck* (Dec. 10) 654: Hands up, darn ye, or I'll let daylight through ye! **1882** D.J. Cook *Hands Up* 90: Pull that pistol one inch, and I'll blow daylight through you. **1885** Harte *Snow-Bound* 20: He's...let daylight through a dozen chaps afore now for half what you said. **1887** C. Coffin *Days & Nights* 275 [ref. to 1862]: Step in, I say, or I'll let daylight through you. **1929–30** Dos Passos *42d Parallel* 306: Their own kin are shootin' daylight into each other at the front.

3.a. a clear or open space, esp. for one in competition.
1902–03 Ade *People You Know* 113: Sassafras had a piece of Daylight between himself and the Bunch. **1909** *WNID: Daylight...*A clear or open space, as between boats in a race. **1974** Price *Wanderers* 56: He saw daylight every time he got the ball and...racked up over 120 yards. **1982** Considine *Lang. Sport* 135: *Daylight:* A gap or open space between defensive players.
b. enough space for light to shine through, esp. as between a rider and his saddle.
1922 Rollins *Cowboy* 290 [ref. to 1880's]: An expert...kept his seat and legs so closely to the saddle as never to bounce upward, and thus, even for an instant, to "show daylight" beneath his body. **1944** R. Adams *West. Words:* Riding so that daylight can be seen between the rider's seat and the saddle. **1967** *Hondo* (ABC-TV): There's a little daylight between your britches and the chair. *1984** Partridge *DSUE* 293: Daylight...A space between a rider and his saddle: from ca1870.

¶ In phrase:

¶ **daylight in the swamp** [or **swamps**] *Logging.* time to wake up.
1936 Partridge *DSUE: Daylight in the swamp!* Time to get out of bed! Can[adian catch-phrase]. **1942** *Yank* (Nov. 4) 8: Yelling "Daylight in the swamps" or "Grab your socks"...at 6 a.m. **1958** McCulloch *Woods Words* 45: *Daylight in the swamp*—Time to get up. **1976** Braly *False Starts* 202: Rise and shine. It's daylight in the swamps.

day one *n.* see -ONE.

dayside *n. Labor.* a day shift.—also attrib., adv.

1985 WINS Radio News (Aug. 16): Dayside crews say they'll be working all morning to get the job done. **1989** *48 Hours* (CBS-TV): Dan Green and Phil Stevens work dayside.

DB *n. Finance.* a DEADBEAT.

1974 Terkel *Working* 92: *DB*...Deadbeat.

D.D. *n.* (among beggars) a beggar who is or pretends to be deaf and dumb. Also as *v.* Cf. D AND D.

1925–26 Black *You Can't Win* 69 [ref. to 1890's]: I...went down to Denver to do a little D.D.ing...Imitatin' a deaf an' dumb man. D.D.ing, see? **1929** Zorbaugh *Gold Coast* 138: There were...beggars, "dingers," "D.D.'s" and "T.B.'s." **1929** *AS* IV (June) 339: *Dee Dee*— Deaf and dumb; or someone faking to be deaf and dumb. **1935** Algren *Boots* 198: She had bought the house with the proceeds of twenty years of work as a "D.D." **1992** Schrader *Light Sleeper* (film): I figure you can tell a DD anything.

DDT *interj.* [facetious use of *DDT*, the name of an insecticide] *Stu.* "drop dead twice."

1949 *Time* (Oct. 3) 37: In Chicago, last year's "D.D.T." (drop dead twice) is still fashionable. **1959** *Encyc. Britannica* XX 768: D.D.T., drop dead twice. **1981–89** R. Atkinson *Long Gray Line* 14: Sons of the 1950s...knew that DDT meant "drop dead twice."

deac *n.* a deacon. Also **deke.**

1742, 1821, 1913 in *DA*.

deacon *v.* **1.** (see 1889 quot.).

1855 in *DAE*: The only change it was known to produce in the farmer's practice was to make him careful afterward to "deacon" both ends [of the barrel]. **1869** Alcott *Little Women* 168: The blanc-mange was lumpy, and the strawberries not as ripe as they looked, having been skillfully "deaconed." *a*1870, 1882 in *DAE*. **1889** *Century Dict.*: *Deacon*...To arrange so as to present a specious and attractive appearance; present the best and largest specimens (of fruit or vegetables) to view and conceal the defective ones: as, to *deacon* strawberries or apples. (Slang, U.S.) **1891** Maitland *Slang Dict.* 89: To deacon berries is to place the best fruit on top, a practice not entirely unknown outside of church circles. **1975** Gould *Maine Lingo* 70: *Deacon*...to arrange apples in the top of a box or barrel so the customer presumes the same quality runs to the bottom.

2. (see quot.).

1889 *Century Dict.*: *Deacon*...To sophisticate; adulterate; "doctor": as, to *deacon* wine or other liquor. (Slang.)

dead *n.* [cf. DEAD, *v.*] *Stu.* a complete failure in recitation; DEAD-SET.

1827 *Harvard Register* (Nov.) 287: And sad it is to take a *screw*/Or *dead* in recitation. *Ibid.* (Dec.) 312: I have a most instinctive dread/Of getting up to take a *dead*. **1835** in B. Hall *College Wds.* (ed. 2) 149: He, unmoved by Freshman's curses,/Loves the *deads* which Freshmen make. **1851** B. Hall *College Wds.* 92: *Dead*. A complete failure; a declaration that one is not prepared to recite. **1889** *Century Dict.* **1900** *DN* II 31: *Dead*, *n.* A complete failure in recitation.

¶ In phrase:

¶ **on the dead** [short for *on the dead level*, var. of *on the level* s.v. LEVEL] honestly; truthfully.

1888 in F. Remington *Sel. Letters* 62: On the dead—Clark, I have it at the place of honor. **1896** Ade *Artie* 7: On the dead, I don't believe any o' them people out there ever saw a good show. **1899** A.H. Lewis *Sandburrs* 96: On d' dead! I was farmer enough to t'ink I'd t'ank him for bein' me guide before I shook d' push an' quit. **1906** H. Green *Boarding House* 127: On the dead, I t'ink I'm off me nut for fair. **1926** Dunning & Abbott *Broadway* 231: No Steve, on the dead, why'n't you go out of town till this blows over.

dead *adj.* **1.** tired to exhaustion. Now *colloq.*

*1813 in *OEDS*. **1883** Flagg *Versicles* 26: My sakes, I'm most dead! **1897** Hamblen *General Mgr.* 184: I was too dead to look at my watch. **1934** in *DAS*: For two days after that I was dead.

2. perfect; genuine; veritable; unmistakable; absolute.—used prenominally. Now *rare* in U.S. except in set phrs. *dead giveaway, dead ringer.*

*1819 [T. Moore] *Tom Crib* 36: As dead hands at a [prizefight] as they, and quite as ready after it. **1852–55** Ingraham *Sunny South* 151: You must not publish it...for it is a "dead secret." **1859** Matsell *Vocab.* 72: *Rabbit.* A rowdy. "Dead rabbit," a very athletic rowdy fellow. ***1860** in *F & H* II 260: A dead take-in is swipes too thin. **1871** Bagg *Yale* 44: *Dead*, complete, perfect; as a *dead* rush, a *dead* flunk. **1877** Bartlett

Amer. (ed. 4) 543: A *rush* is a glib recitation, but to be a *dead rush* it must be flawless, polished, and sparkling like a Koh-i-noor. **1882** in *DA*: It would be a dead give away. **1891** *Outing* (Oct.) 87: Yure in dead luck, you are! **1891** *F & H* II 262: Dead-Give-Away. **1891** in *DAS*: Homan is a "dead-ringer" for Anson. **1892** Moore *Own Story* 546: He made the remark that Grady was a "dead shark." **1895** *Harper's* (Apr.) 788: Cordelia, I heard you was a dead fraud. **1895** *Harper's* (Sept.) 620: I'd bank all I ever get dat you'll be a dead lady. **1895** Townsend *Fadden & Other Stories* 167: Me friend hadn't got on t' his being a dead swell 'till just before we meets him. **1895** in J.I. White *Git Along Dogies* 66: Lately we've been on the dead square. **1902–03** Ade *People You Know* 86: I'm supposed to be a Dead Swell that's come to take her to a Masquerade. **1974** *Gunsmoke* (CBS-TV): It's a dead cinch we can't walk clean to Santa Fe. **1987** N.Y.C. woman, age 53: Robert DeNiro is a dead ringer for my lawyer.

3. ample; great in number or quantity.

1866 in "M. Twain" *Letters fr. Hawaii* 242: I can buy dead loads of just such for six bits. **1869** *Overland Mo.* III 131: A great quantity..."dead oodles." **1869** "M. Twain" *Innocents Abroad* ch. lvii: The old man's got dead loads of books. **1883** Bunner *Letters* 76: My boy, malaria is dead loads of fun, if you hanker after that style of humor. **1884** Sweet & Knox *Through Tex.* 100: When I kem here in '46 thar was dead-oodles of game all around here. **1894** in *DAE*: Dead loads of other things. **1902** Clapin *Amer.* 154: *Dead load*, a great quantity of anything.

4. *Und.* being no longer a tramp or criminal; reformed.

1899 "J. Flynt" *Tramping* 387: The word "dead" is practically synonymous with "squared it."..."Dead" means that he has left the fraternity and is trying to live respectably. *Ibid.* 388: I've be'n dead now about ten years...I learned my trade in the pen, 'n' when I got out I decided to square it. *Ibid.* 393: *Dead:* reformed. A "dead" criminal is either discouraged or reformed. **1902** Hapgood *Thief* 259 [ref. to 1898]: Some of the old pals I did meet again had squared it, others were "dead" (out of the game) and some had degenerated into bums. **1918** *Everybody's* (Sept.) 37: Big Annie...was "dead."...Big Annie had "squared it"...had turned straight and quit the game. **1926** *AS* I (Dec.) 651: *Dead one*—hobo who has retired from the road.

5. exceedingly stupid; dense.

1900, 1901, 1904, 1931 (in Partridge *Dict. Und.* 179).

¶ In phrases:

¶ **dead for** in desperate need of; "dying for."

1876 "M. Twain" *Sawyer* 163 [ref. to *ca*1845]: I'm dead for some sleep!

¶ **dead from the neck up** exceedingly stupid. Also vars.

1911 T.A. Dorgan, in Zwilling *TAD Lexicon* 30: You're dead from the neck up. **1918** in Cummings *Letters* 47: Another man dead—if not from the neck upward, at least downward. **1924** Hecht & Bodenheim *Cutie* 38: He was dead from the neck both ways. **1939** Fearing *Hospital* 92: Ninety per cent of the personnel are dead, at least from the neck up. **1952** Malamud *Natural* 34: I shoulda farmed instead of playing wet nurse to a last place, dead-to-the-neck ball team. ***1963** P.G. Wodehouse, in *OEDS*: Dead from the neck up. **1963** *Travels of J. McPheeters* (ABC-TV): Sounds to me like you're dead already—from the neck up! **1971** *All in the Family* (CBS-TV): You know, I think you're dead from the neck up.

¶ **dead on (one's) feet** tired to exhaustion. Now *colloq.*

*ca*1890 Green *Orphan Battery* 142: I was dead on my feet here, could hardly mount guard & do my other duties. **1896** Ade *Artie* 84: Well, I put on my clothes and went downstairs, dead on my feet. ***1962, *1970** in *OEDS*.

¶ **dead to rights** see s.v. RIGHTS, *n.*

¶ **get dead** to be killed.

1961 J. Flynn *Action Man* 49: You can get dead if you let it get around you were in on this. **1966** B. Cassiday *Angels Ten* 147 [ref. to WWII]: That's the way to get dead quick. **1967–79** in S. King *Bachman* 292: Beats the hell out of getting dead, am I right? **1982** Basel *Pak Six* 82 [ref. to Vietnam War]: Trying to find a way to do what we were ordered to do, not get dead, not get hung. **1988** *N.Y. Newsday* (May 20) 26: I don't want to get dead....I don't want no one to know it was me.

¶ **keep dead** to remain silent.

1900 "J. Flynt" & Walton *Powers:* I can keep as dead about that as you can.

¶ **make dead men chew tobacco** *Naut.* (of a purser) to falsify accounts in order to conceal the embezzlement of funds or stores.

*1805 J. Davis *Post-Captain* 5: And now you will be occupied *in making dead men chew tobacco*. **1836** *Nav. Mag.* (Sept.) 434: I hope to stand on the credit side of the log, unless the sly Gabriel is in the habit of doing that, which Jack sometimes charges the purser's steward—*"making dead men chew tobacco!"*

¶ **too dead to skin** being of no value whatsoever; worthless.

1873 Beadle *Undevel. W.* 214: [The projected city of] Quindaro was, in the classic language of the "jayhawkers," "too dead to skin." **1893** in F. Remington *Sel. Letters* 200: The people…fell on the bosses and they are too dead to skin.

dead *adv.* thoroughly; absolutely; completely; wholeheartedly; with no mistake; (with weakened force) very. [Orig. S.E., now rare in U.S. except in several colloq. collocations, esp. *broke, calm, certain, tired, even, right, wrong, serious, sure, set (on), last*; in S.E. phrs. *dead drunk* and *dead tired* the word continues to carry its 16th C. meaning "in a manner, or to a degree…suggesting death" (*OED2* s.v. *dead* C.1.a.).]

1807 Tufts *Narr.* [ref. to 1794]: *I'm dead up to the cove*…I know the man well. **1851** in Blair & Meine *Half Horse* 224: The dogs led off fust, "dead" bent for the old deacon's. **1852** in [Clappe] *Shirley Letters* 191: To use a phrase much in vogue here [*sc.* California], "dead broke." **1854** Yellow Bird *Murieta* 57: We have them, boys! We have got them *dead!* **1863** in Stanard *Letters* 18: I was *dead* broke at the time. **1865** G.W. Nichols *Great March* 24: We are going in, and we are just dead sure to whip the Rebs every time. **1873** Beadle *Undeveloped West* 140: He thinks the gambler ignorant…and goes in on what he considers a "dead sure thing." **1875** Burnham *Counterfeits* 36: The government had got "a dead sure thing" on poor Furber. **1875–80** Kwong *Dict. Eng. Phr.* 747: *Dead-broke* = ruined; bankrupt. **1886** N.O. *Lantern* (Apr. 30) 2: I'm dead onto them. **1886** N.O. *Lantern* (Nov. 20) 2: George Juet…is dead gone on a coon. **1887** Francis *Saddle & Moccasin* 226: Look here, Frank! I've got a dead sure thing on—can't lose! **1890** Howells *Hazard* 305: He's dead gone on you, Chris. **1895** *Harper's* (Oct.) 778: I've trained 'im dead fine. **1895** in J.I. White *Git Along Dogies* 65: The good Lord [is] dead onto every angel in the herd. **1896** Ade *Artie* 16: The old man's dead with me. **1899** Cullen *Tales* 154: That was too dead easy for anything. **1900** *DN* II 31: *Dead, adv.* Very. Used generally [by college students]. **1900** Patten *Merriwell's Power* 9: That ought to be dead easy. *Ibid.* 24: I'm not dead sure that I know you now! **1900** Willard & Hodler *Powers That Prey* 48: I'll be dead obliged to you if you'll get it for me. **1904** in Opper *Hooligan* 31: Aw, this is dead slow. *a***1904–11** Phillips *Susan Lenox* II 42: I'm dead stuck on you—and that's a God's fact. **1914** Ellis *Billy Sunday* 347: A good fellow and a dead-game sport. **1930** D. Runyon, in *Collier's* (Mar. 22) 20: Bad Basil Valentine is one dead tough mug. **1940** E. O'Neill *Long Day's Journey* I: They're a great bargain too. I got them dead cheap. **1947** Overholser *Buckaroo's Code* 20: Her hair's the color of wheat when it's dead ripe. **1953** Paley *Rumble* 24: Every man in the ship today had to be dead game all right! **1960** L'Amour *Sacketts* 106: I'd timed things dead right. **1980** Birnbach et al. *Preppy Hbk.* 219: *Dead attractive*…Same as completely cute. **1984** Mason & Rheingold *Slanguage*: *Dead grotty*…Nasty.

¶ In phrase:

¶ **dead to rights** see S.V. RIGHTS.

dead *v.* [cf. DEAD, *n.*] *Stu.* **1.** to make a complete failure in recitation.

1847 in *DAE*: In fact, he'd rather dead than dig; he'd rather slump than squirt. **1848** in B. Hall *College Wds.* (ed. 2) 148: Be ready…to cut, to drink, to smoke, to dead. **1856** *Ibid.*: *Dead.* To be unable to recite; to be ignorant of the lesson; to declare oneself unprepared to recite. **1876** in *DAE*: I didn't relish the idea of deading. **1889** *Century Dict.*

2. (of a teacher) to cause (a student) to fail in recitation.

1837 *Harvardiana* III 255: Have I been screwed, yea, deaded morn and eve…And not yet taught me to philosophize? **1856** B. Hall *College Wds.* (ed. 2) 148: *Dead*…*Transitively*; to cause one to fail in reciting. Said of a teacher who puzzles a scholar with difficult questions, and thereby causes him to fail. **1884** *Harper's Mag.* LXIX 386: Was it Dr. Peabody, whose…inquiry, "What is ethics?" had deaded so many a promising…student? **1889** *Century Dict.*

dead ass *n.* **1.** the seated rump.—usu. considered vulgar. Also **dead butt.** [Early quots. ref. to WWII.]

[**1924** T. Boyd *Point of Honor* 137 [ref. to 1918]: If you hadn't laid back there on your dead hams ever since March, you wouldn't be so soft; you'd be able to stand a little hike.] [**1945** *Best from Yank* 175: The rest of the time we set on our dead hams.] **1950** Stuart *Objector* 75: Get your dead ass moving. **1946–51** J. Jones *Eternity* ch. ix: You sit around here all morning on your dead ass working a crossword. **1952** Uris *Battle Cry*

124: Headquarters! Hit the road! Off your dead asses and on your dying feet! **1952** Bissell *Monongahela* 10: Get up off yer dead ass and turn that line loose. **1959** Russell *Playboy* 40: Get off'n yo' dead butt and answer thet cotton-pickin' phone, y' heah? **1961** Crane *Born of Battle* 63 [ref. to Korean War]: Off your dead asses and on your dyin' feet! **1961** Plantz *Sweeney* 67: We aren't going to operate, Top. We're going to sit on our dead asses and rot. **1971** Contini *Beast Within* 126: He'd better get off his dead ass and do something.

2. a lazy or stupid person.—usu. considered vulgar.

1959 Morrill *Dark Sea* 142 [ref. to WWII]: Look lively, you deadasses. We're running for the South Seas! **1967** J. Kramer *Instant Replay* 53: There's too many deadasses out there! **1967** Mailer *Vietnam* 18: Us women know which man…is the unfortunate dead ass. **1976** Hayden *Voyage* 626: That dead-ass husband of hers. **1991** *Get a Life* (Fox-TV): You fat-brained dead-ass!

3. GONER; DEAD DUCK.—usu. considered vulgar.

1968 Heard *Howard St.* 207: Try somethin' slick and you a dead ass.

dead-ass *adj.* lacking animation, energy, or spirit; lifeless.—usu. considered vulgar. Also **dead-butt.**

1958 Gilbert *Vice Trap* 22: I was pretty sore at that dead-butt grease monkey. **1961** Brosnan *Pennant Race* 78: We're dead-ass, that's all. Swing the damn bats! *Ibid.* 207: On day games following night games we all have looked logy, tired, dead-ass. **1971** in S.J. Perelman *Don't Tread on Me* 274: It's very dead-ass. **1976** Univ. Tenn. instructor, age 28: Then they'll go dead-ass on you.

dead-ass *adv.* utterly; absolutely.—usu. considered vulgar.

1971 *Playboy* (Dec.) 338: He would rather be "dead-ass broke in New York than rich in Mississippi." **1983** Goldman & Fuller *Charlie Co.* 208: He's dead-ass wrong. **1985** Dye *Between Raindrops* 291: Them gooks is dead-ass stupid.

dead-bang *adj.* **1.** (of a criminal case) open-and-shut; irrefutable.

1934 in Partridge *Dict. Und.* 179: If he…figures they have the evidence on him he says it is a dead bang rap. **1935** Pollock *Und. Speaks*: *Dead bang rap*, caught red handed; a slight chance to escape conviction. **1975** Wambaugh *Choirboys* 125: They said it was a "dead bang" case. A cinch. The evidence was overwhelming. **1987** R. Miller *Slob* 166: "It's dead bang, Jack," another cop says.

2. certain; absolute.

1985 *Morning Edition* (Mar. 4) (Nat. Pub. Radio): That is a dead-bang winner. **1986** *L.A. Law* (NBC-TV): [This case] is a dead-bang loser.

dead-bang *adv.* **1.** *Police.* absolutely; without doubt; (*hence*) in the act; redhanded.

1919 *Amer. Legion Wkly.* (Sept. 12) 29: Come clean!…We have got you dead bang right! **1952** J.B. Martin *Life in Crime* 54: The cops knew just about who was doing it but they couldn't catch anybody dead bang. **1973** W. Crawford *Stryker* 50: But I want the job *done*, dead-bang. **1983** S. King *Christine* 412: They caught me dead-bang. **1987** Blankenship *Blood Stripe* 96: Those guys are dead-bang guilty. **1988** *21 Jump St.* (Fox-TV): We got him! We got him dead bang! **1992** Hosansky & Sparling *Working Vice* 331: We had him, dead bang.

2. squarely; smack.

1978 S. King *Stand* 89: Got him dead-bang between the eyes. **1982** in S. King *Bachman* 895: We had him dead-bang over Albany.

deadbeat *n.* **1.a.** Esp. *Mil.* a malingerer or loafer; GOLDBRICK.

1862 in Galwey *Valiant Hours* 72: The really sick and the habitual deadbeats, anxious to escape duty, are marched from each company by a sergeant to the Surgeon. **1862** in W. Whitman *Whitman & Civil War* 68: "*Healthy beat*" a man who would shirk and make something up; "*dead beat*"—a man who would shirk and not make something up. **1863** in G. Whitman *Letters* 87: There is a lot of dead beats that get off by playing sick. **1869** *Putnam's* (Sept.) 318: Beside him lags a dead-beat, who five minutes hence will complain of sore feet.…and look for every chance to drop out and straggle. **1882** in K.E. Olson *Music & Musket* 89 [ref. to Civil War]: The cronic [*sic*] "dead-beats,"—the most contemptible vermin…that could encumber ambulance, hospital, or barracks…day after day limped to the tune of the surgeon's call. **1905** *Howitzer* 293: *Dead Beat*…One who avoids exertion in any form. **1974** R. Campbell *Chasm* 176: I want them to know what a teacher is and not settle for some ordinary deadbeat. **1976** Hayden *Voyage* 158: Mr. Mate, tell them two deadbeats come into the cabin. **1977** Lyon *Tenderness* 68: The so-called deadbeats…invariably joined the sick-call ranks to escape military training, even among the elite airborne paratroopers.

b. *Broadly,* a worthless or unsociable person.

1872 Burnham *Secret Service* v: *Dead-beat,* a "dead-beat" is an utterly worthless fellow. *Ibid.* 372: He was the friend of Sam Felker, and others of that stamp, dead-beats, so-called "private Detectives," and unscrupulous lawyers. **1883** Peck *Bad Boy* 222: I know more than some of the dead beats that lay around the court to get on a jury. **1893** Corby *Chaplain Life* 98: "Dead-beat" is the worst term that can be applied to a soldier. It is a generic term, implying everything worthless and mean. *Ibid.* 231: Many…thought some "dead beat" had stolen my horse. **1959** *Encyc. Britannica* XX 768: *Dead beat*, a worthless fellow. **1978** Eble *Campus Slang* (Apr.) 2: *Dead-beat*—one who opposes the wishes of the majority: a party-pooper or one who is considered a wet blanket; Ben doesn't want to go out for a few beers, what a dead-beat!

2. a fraudulent or worthless item; *(also)* a deception or disappointment.

1866 Williams *Gay Life in N.Y.* 87: The best way to treat such missives whenever, or however received, is to put them in the fire. They are, to use an expressive phrase, "Dead Beats" one and all. **1867** in A.K. McClure *Rocky Mtns.* 204: But the…breakfast was a "dead beat" on all of us. The coffee was…water…, the fat bacon was stale, [etc.]. **1872** Burnham *Secret Service* 130: "It's a counterfeit…" "A what!"…"A 'dead-beat,' old fellow. Not worth a penny." **1956** Ross *Hustlers* 81: The movie was a dead beat.

3. a cadger or sponger; parasite; one who will not or cannot pay debts; FREELOADER; *(often)* derelict.

1871 *Galaxy* (Nov.) 730: I lit right on that proposish like a dead-beat on a nip. **1874** Pember *Metropolis* 43: He thought I was a "dead beat" and wanted a drink for nothing. **1877** E.L. Wheeler *Deadwood Dick* 79: It only remains for you to aim straight and rid your country of an A No. 1 dead-beat swindler! **1890** Quinn *Fools of Fortune* 210: No sober applicant (unless a chronic "dead beat")…is ever refused a drink, a cigar, a square meal, or a night's lodging. **1891** Maitland *Slang Dict.* 89: *Dead-beat* (Am.), a fellow who borrows money or obtains credit on all kinds of pretenses and pays nobody…he keeps just outside of the statutes against fraud, and he seldom possesses the qualities of a first-class swindler. **1894** *Century* (Feb.) 517: Not being at all sure that I should be successful in making the journey from New York to Albany in one night as a "dead-beat" on a freight train, I felt safer in buying a second-class ticket on the steamboat. **1914** Ellis *Billy Sunday* 133: You booze-fighter, you libertine, you dead-beat. **1944** Bellow *Dangling Man* 86: To be perfectly frank, I've been a deadbeat all my life. **1950** P. Green *Peer Gynt* 10: Able to support me in my weakness and old age—if you would. But you won't…you deadbeat. **1953** Manchester *City of Anger* 65: Railroad police chased ten deadbeats from Holden Station. **1970–71** Rubinstein *City Police* 194: "Bums," "winos," "deadbeats" are common in many neighborhoods. *a***1985** in K. Walker *Piece of My Heart* 399: Most of the donors were alcoholics and deadbeats out of the Tenderloin district. **1987** *Univ. Tenn.* instructor: He's a deadbeat who's just sponging off his relatives.

4. an imposter or pretender; fraud; cheat.

1873 *Overland Mo.* (Feb.) 113: Well, Hal, here's to the great American dead-beat. **1882** D. J. Cook *Hands Up* 136: We have our share of the pretenders and dead beats and they do us more harm than good. **1884** "M. Twain" *H. Finn* 185: They're a couple of frauds—regular dead-beats.

5. a kind of cocktail.

1877 Bartlett *Amer.* (ed. 4) 170: *Dead-Beat*…A mixture of ginger-soda and whiskey, taken by hard drinkers after a night's carousal.

dead beat *adj.* **1.** thoroughly defeated.

***1820–21** P. Egan *Life in London* 71: So *dead beat*, as to be compelled to cry for quarter. ***1845** in *F & H* II 260: The general opinion is that the Premier is dead beat. **1846** in G.W. Harris *High Times* 66: I mite get to ravin…an go off [i.e., fire] afore you want me to, an then ye'll be *dead beat* sartin! **1854** in Somers *Sports in N.O.* 31: They still think Lex. had Lcte. [racehorses] dead beat at the end of three miles in the 2d heat of the 2d race. **1859** Matsell *Vocab.* 25: *Dead Beat.* Without hope. **1880** *N.Y. Clipper Almanac* 44: Turf Directory…*Dead Beat.*—Beaten to a standstill.

2. thoroughly exhausted.

***1843** Dickens *M. Chuzzlewit* ch. xvii: I wish you would pull off my boots for me…I am quite knocked up. Dead beat. ***1873** Hotten *Slang Dict.* (ed. 5): *Dead-beat*, utterly exhausted, utterly "done up." **1900** Flandrau *Freshman* 232: The horse was "dead beat," he said. **1911–12** J. London *Smoke Bellew* 215: I got some dogs out there—dead beat. **1960** *N.Y.C* child, age 12: I was dead beat after playing ball. **1980** Algren *Dev. Stocking* 80: We'd hit the hay, dead beat, about four A.M.

3. (see quot.). Cf. DEAD-BANG.

1859 Matsell *Vocab.* 25: *Dead Beat*…certain.

deadbeat *v.* to loaf, sponge, malinger, or defraud.

1881 in *DA:* He's dead beated on you. **1888** in Farmer *Amer.:* No party can dead-beat his way on me these hard times. **1900** *Howitzer* (No. 1) 118: *Dead Beat.*—To save all superfluous energy for another time; to avoid any work or duty without being hived. **1904** *Howitzer* (No. 5) 220: *Dead-Beat*—To avoid doing a thing. **1905** *Howitzer* (No. 6) 293: *Dead Beat*—To avoid working. **1914** Ellis *Billy Sunday* 304: He is dead-beating his way to hell. **1946** Cooke *Me & Thee* 135: How many men from this outfit have dead-beat their way into a hospital? **1986** *NDAS:* Living off interest is not exactly deadbeating.

dead card *n.* something that is hopeless or out of favor.

1899 A.H. Lewis *Sandburrs* 60: One of d' city's jackleg sawbones is there mendin' Emmer wit' bandages. But he says himself he's on a dead card, an' that Emmer's going to die. **1901** Ade *Modern Fables* 23: If any one had to be spared, they preferred that it should be some Dead Card who wore Congress Gaiters and Throat Warmers. **1903** Ade *Society* 16: I started to play Golf this year, not knowing that it was a Dead Card with the 400.

dead dog *n. Navy.* a drained liquor bottle; DEAD SOLDIER.

1918 Ruggles *Navy Explained* 50: *Dead dog*…dead soldier.

dead-dog *adv. So. Midland.* exceedingly.

1984 *Univ. Tenn.* student: *Dead-dog drunk* is real drunk. **1985** *Univ. Tenn.* instructor, age *ca*30: I mean, he was dead-*dog* stupid!

dead duck *n.* **1.** a person or thing that has become useless, worthless, powerless, or passé.

1829 in *DA:* There is an old saying, "never waste powder on a dead duck"; but we cannot avoid flashing away a few grains upon an old friend, Henry Clay. **1844** A. Jackson, in *DA:* Clay [is] a dead political duck. **1867** in *DAE:* His merit won the approval of both President and Congress, notwithstanding the "powerful" efforts of certain "dead ducks" to prevent his appointment. **1888** in *F & H* II 262: Long Branch is said to be a dead duck. But for the investments made at Elberton, the Branch proper would probably have been abandoned long ago. **1890** in *DAE:* A man, taking up the labor question…will say, "I am to be true to justice and to man: otherwise I am a dead duck." **1893** M. Philips *Newspaper* 6: Newspaper men are not given to retrospection; they call a printed paper a "dead duck"; and after twelve hours it is "ancient history." **1948** Lait & Mortimer *N.Y. Confidential* 27: The hotel grills and [roof restaurants]…were dead ducks by now. **1950** F. Brown *Space on My Hands* 95: Sector Three was proud of that record, or had been until the record became a dead duck. **1955** Funk *Heavens* 42: "Dead duck"…anything—person or article—that is no longer worth a straw, that is done up, played out.

2. one whose case is hopeless; GONER. [Now the usual U.S. sense.]

1944–48 A. Lyon *Unknown Station* 39: Don't move!…if you get up…you're a dead duck. **1949** Gruber *Broken Lance* 9: You're a dead duck right now. **1953** R. Wright *Outsider* 102: I was sick with a fever of one hundred and four for three days. I thought I was a dead duck. **1968** M.B. Scott *Racing Game* 40: If your horse went with the favorite for half a mile…the favorite would be a dead duck. **1978** S. King *Stand* 536: And if Tom won't kill, he's apt to be a dead duck. **1984** J. McCorkle *Cheer Leader* 261: Life is like a cardiogram…If your beep beep turns into a low droning monotone…then you are a dead duck. **1992** *CBS This Morning* (CBS-TV) (Aug. 31): Two Oriole runners were dead ducks at second base.

deadener *n.* one that is stunning; KNOCKOUT.

1870 Duval *Big-Foot* 303: She was a "deadener," I tell you, and a regular "knee-weakener," in the bargain.

deader *n.* a dead or utterly exhausted person.

***1890–91** *F & H* II 262: *Deader*…(common).—A corpse. **1895** *DN* I 415: *Deader.* An exhausted person. **1909** *WNID.* ***1936** Partridge *DSUE: Deader*…A corpse: from *ca*1880. Conan Doyle. **1975** McCaig *Danger Trail* 16: You can scoop dirt on my coffin, for I'll be a deader. **1967–79** in S. King *Bachman* 231: Nobody loves a deader.

deadeye *n.* **1.** *Naut.* a worthless fellow; dolt.

1849 Melville *White Jacket* 28 [ref. to 1843]: Why, you dead-eye!…your ambition never mounted above pig-killing.

2. Deady brand gin; gin.

***1890–91** *F & H: Deady* (modern American, *Dead-Eye*)…Gin; a special brand of full proof spirit. **1942** *ATS.*

3. a skilled marksman.

1942 *ATS* 392. **1986** "J. Cain" *Suicide Squad* 51: Take your best shot, dead-eye.

4. *Esp. Naut. & Pris.* the anus; BROWNEYE.

[*a1890–91 F & H I 231: *Blind Eye*…(common).—The podex.] *a1961 Hugill *Shanties fr. Seven Seas* 269 [ref. to a1925]: "Dead-eye" [had] both a [technical]…and an obscene significance. **1983** in J. Green *Dict. Contemp. Slang* 69: *Deadeye* [the anus]. **1991** Randolph & Legman *Roll Me in Your Arms* 401: *Hog-eye* means…the vagina, not to be confused with "dead-eye," meaning the anus.

deadeye *v.* to stare at coldly or intently.
1965 Pollini *Glover* 321: Pause, dead-eyeing Glover. **1978** De Christoforo *Grease* 109: Danny walked up to the plate shouldering his bat, and dead-eyeing the pitcher.

deadfall *n.* a disreputable saloon or similar establishment. Cf. DEADHOUSE, 1.
1837 in *DA*: At a small pot-house grocery or dead-fall of the village…there was a lingerer. **1856** in A.P. Hudson *Humor of Old So.* 463: So we adjourned over to the nearest dead-fall, tuck a whoppin' horn of Ball Face, [etc.]. **1866** in Hilleary *Webfoot* 170: The lovers of "red-eye" were loth to leave the "dead falls." **1867** *Harper's Mo.* (June) 131: In California, old Judge C— kept *a little dead fall*, as they call a rum-mill out there. **1886** Nye *Remarks* 327: Old Blackhawk…is sawing wood for the Belle of the West deadfall. **1903** A.H. Lewis *Boss* 273: His [hangout] is this deadfall on Barclay Street. **1903** A. Adams *Log of Cowboy* 251: There's a deadfall down here on the river…that robs a man going and coming. *a*1916 D.E. Conner *In Gold Fields* 94: A drinking saloon or more properly speaking, in miner's parlance, a deadfall. **1930** D. Runyon, in *Sat. Eve. Post* (Apr. 5) 5: The Bohemian Club is nothing but a deadfall where guys and dolls go when there is positively no other place in town open. **1951** Lait & Mortimer *Washington* 5: The sailors' deadfalls of Port Said have nothing on it. **1958** Camerer *Damned Wear Wings* 61: We're in Havana this night. Mike gets hung up in some deadfall. **1970** Thompson *Garden of Sand* 420: The movie version of a waterfront deadfall came to life. **1970** A. Hawk *Gunfighter* 33: You'll be back where you came from—in a Tombstone deadfall! **1992** N. Cohn *Heart of the World* 239: Deadfalls like the Haymarket and the Cremorne, Dan the Dude's and Paddy the Pig's.

dead fish *n. Baseball.* a weakly thrown pitch.
1964 Thompson & Rice *Every Diamond* 140: *Dead fish*…A slow pitch.

deadhead *n.* **1.** a person admitted free to a theater, sporting event, hotel, etc.; (now *esp.*) a person carried free on a train, bus, or similar conveyance. Also attrib.
1841 *Spirit of Times* (Jan. 23) 564: The house…was filled as far as $300 could fill it, barring "the dead heads." **1843** *Knickerbocker Mag.* XXII 496: Not fifty persons in the room?—and half of those "dead heads." **1848** Bartlett *Amer.* (App.): Persons who drink at a bar, ride in an omnibus or railroad car, travel in steamboats, or visit the theatre, without charge, are called *dead heads*. These consist of the engineers, conductors, and laborers on railroads; the keepers of hotels; the editors of newspapers, etc. **1849** in Thornton *Amer. Gloss.* I 241: The term "dead-head" was applied by the steamboat gentlemen to passengers who were allowed to travel without paying their fare. **1854** *Knickerbocker Mag.* XLIV 96: On the Little River Road they don't allow no *dead-heads.* **1871** Schele de Vere *Americanisms* 363: The class of *dead-heads* is almost endless, every favor being returned, every adverse criticism averted, and every service acknowledged by a *free ticket.* **1872** Holmes *Poet* 281: The *Caput mortuum* (or dead-head, in vulgar phrase) is apt to be furnished with a Venter vivus, or, as we may say, a lively appetite. **1873** Small *Knights* 50: A sort of theatre; the galleries of which were occupied exclusively by dead-heads. **1877** *Puck* (May) 2: There will be "deadheads" in such numbers as would make Stephen Fiske a raving maniac. **1882** Nye *Western Humor* 79: I've…handled the passes of our most eminent deadheads. **1891** Maitland *Slang Dict.* 90: *Deadhead* (Am.), one who has free admission to theatres or free rides on railroads, etc. **1896** in J.M. Carroll *Benteen-Goldin Lets.* 302: Well, he had about twenty dead-heads as audience! **1918** Wagar *Spotter* 14: The "dead-heads" include policemen, firemen, postmen, and employees in uniform, or carrying badges. **1925** Robinson *Wagon Show* 136: Altogether we passed in about seventy-five "deadheads." **1937** *Review of Reviews* (June) 43: *Deadhead*—a non-paying passenger. **1939** *AS* (Oct.) 239: *Dead Head.* Non-paying guest. **1943** J. Mitchell *McSorley's* 123: I don't allow no deadheads, and you know it. **1976** J.G. Fuller *Flt. 401* 181: No deadhead pilot was found on the passenger manifest list.

2. a sponger or loafer; DEADBEAT, 3.
1847 *Nat. Police Gaz.* (Feb. 20) 186: The usual local loungers of a village tavern…"Dead heads!" said the stranger, motioning his head derisively towards the trio at the stove. **1863** in *DAE*: The milch cow which barely pays the expense of keeping and care is a "dead head," yielding no profit. **1864** C.H. Smith *Bill Arp* 68: My daddy sold goods on credit

about forty years ago, and when a customer run away, he used to codicil his name with "G.T.A." *gone to Arkansaw.* What a power of dead heads must have roosted in them woods on the other side of Jordan! **1871** Banka *Prison Life* 499: Among the "dead heads," at the corner grocery, he was a "hale fellow, well met." **1889** Barrère & Leland *Dict. Slang* I 298: *Dead-head* (American), one who stands about at a bar to drink at the expense of others. **1897** Siler & Houseman *Fight of the Century* 45: Have you been bothered much by the deadheads? **1942** Garcia *Tough Trip* 29: Hell, no, what use could we have for that drunken deadhead?

3. a corpse. *Joc.*
1857 in Bartlett *Amer.* (ed. 2) 116: No, no, doctor…You send too many *dead heads* through here as it is. **1882** in Smith & Smith *Police Gazette* 35: Manger Starr will…be seated on a Gatling gun while taking tickets. Any suspicious person attempting to pass him will be put on the dead-head list.

4. *Army.* a noncombatant accompanying a military unit; camp-follower.
1864 in *OEDS*: The real fighting men did little injury, sneaks and dead-heads being the principal plunderers. **1867** in *OEDS*: Accompanied by at least five hundred "dead-heads," loafers, and amateur cavalry gentlemen.

5.a. *R.R.* an empty railway car, esp. in transit; (*also*) a train without freight or passengers.
1897 Hamblen *General Manager* 24: He was a car-repairer and was at work between two cars on the "dead-head." **1938** Beebe *High Iron* 220: *Deadhead*…empty passenger car. **1963** Morgan *Six-Eleven* 13: We have a full load and we have to sit and wait for the goddamned deadhead empties and one lousy carload of passengers to arrive. **1964–66** R. Stone *Hall of Mirrors* 128: Linked freight cars and deadheads stood motionless in the heat. **1977** R. Adams *Lang. Railroader* 42: *Deadhead*…Unused empty cars [*sic*] on a train being sent to another point.
b. *Transport.* a portion of a trip without passengers or freight.
1985 R. Harrison *Av. Lore* 110: In charter flying as in railroading, a "deadhead" is that portion of a trip made without paying passengers or cargo. **1990** L. Nieman *Boomer* 19: We got paid…just for going there (a "deadhead") and also for coming back.

6. *Logging.* **a.** a sunken or partially sunken log.
1896 *DN* I 415: *Dead-head*: a log so soaked with water that it will not float. **1902** in *DA*. **1938** in *DARE*: Old, nearly submerged floating logs, called deadheads, remnants of lumbering days. **1956** Sorden & Ebert *Logger's* 11 [ref. to a1925]: *Deadhead*, A water soaked log lying on the bottom of a river or lake, or a partly sunken log. **1992** G. Wolff *Day at Beach* 241: The channel bristled with snags and deadheads.
b. (see quot.).
1958 McCulloch *Woods Wds.* 45: *Deadhead*…A tree with a dead top.

7. a dull or lazy individual; (*specif.*) a person who is present at a meeting, party, or the like, but who does not participate or contribute.
1907 Wells *Life* 45: The loose cattle were called the "Kavy-Yard," which the extra men took turns in driving. My day came…and the "Dead-Heads" (lazy cattle), as they are called, gave me much trouble straying from the road. **1911** in Bierce *Letters* 182: Misses C. and S. will be "no deadheads in the enterprise"—to quote a political phrase of long ago. **1921** *Ohio Doughboys* 81: "Who the hell is this guy?" "Yah, some dead-head." **1923** McAlmon *Village* 58: All the youngsters in town, except the deadheads, were ready to steal fruit, candy. **1926** C.M. Russell *Trails* 86: If I can only get my string on him I'll be all right, but with this dead-head [*sc.* a horse] between my legs, how am I goin' to do it? **1929** *Bookman* (July) 525: I'm no deadhead, brother, and I'm always good for a job on the C. & M. **1936** Levin *Old Bunch* 447: I had to let go a couple of deadheads. **1941** Schulberg *Sammy* 89: I'm thinking I know from nothing about what I'm supposed to be doing and any minute the producer who's no deadhead is going to find out. **1946** J.H. Burns *Gallery* 192: Reading letters…was a job for a deadhead. **1953** Dodson *Away All Boats* 38: Look at that fat deadhead. **1955** *Phil Silvers Show* (CBS-TV): I want these deadheads to look at a real live wire. **1960** Oster *Country Blues* 153: You ain't got nothin' but deadheads in yo' lot,/They don't know right from wrong. **1965** Hersey *Too Far to Walk* 19: A mid-morning sidewalk deadhead muttering to himself. **1974** Terkel *Working* 107: I know live ones…from deadheads. **1982** Eble *Campus Slang* (Nov.) 2: *Deadhead*…one who seems dead when those around him are very much alive: Joe was a *deadhead* at the party (and therefore no fun).

8. (*cap.*) an enthusiastic fan of the Grateful Dead, a rock group.

1973 (Sept. 4), in Brandelius *Grateful Dead Family Album* 114: Dear Fellow Dead Head, [etc.]. **1973** *Rolling Stone* (Nov. 22) 52: The Dead fan club dates from [1971]....There are Dead Heads in every part of the country...and the rate of new memberships has reached 50 a day. **1977** *Wash. Post* (Aug. 31) B8: There is probably no other band in rock that inspires the loyalty and affection accorded the Grateful Dead. Lovingly dubbed the "Dead Heads," these legions fill concert halls around the country. **1982** A. Shaw *Dict. Pop/Rock* 103: "Dead heads." That's what fans of the Grateful Dead called themselves. **1982** Eble *Campus Slang* (Nov.) 2: *Deadhead*...Grateful Dead fan: After seeing the Grateful Dead in concert, I became a *Deadhead.* **1987** *Daily Beacon* (Univ. Tenn.) (Nov. 11) 5: Besides, we're not punks anymore. We're Deadheads. **1987–91** D. Gaines *Teenage Wasteland* 183: He's a Deadhead. Like some kids, he respects the old bands, trusts them more than the newer ones. **1993** *New Yorker* (Oct. 11) 101: The average Deadhead had attended seventy-five Dead concerts in his or her lifetime.

deadhead *adv.* **1.** free of charge.
1873 "M. Twain" & Warner *Gilded Age* ch. xxx: Senators and Representatives always traveled "dead-head" both ways. **1875** Hill *Sanctum* 144: Not only did the Dead-head...travel over the road at the expense of the corporation that owned it, but his chairs, tables, bedsteads [etc.]...also enjoyed the stately privilege of "going dead-head." **1888** in Farmer *Amer.*: [A few letters] had to do with the stage business and went dead-head. **1968** R. Adams *West. Words* (ed. 2) 90: Freight... shipped without charge was said to *go deadhead.*
2. *Transport.* without cargo. Also as adj.
1990 Rukuza *W. Coast Turnaround* 39: He had to be in Chi-town in two days, but there was no law that said he had to do it deadhead. *Ibid.* 41: Eddie quoted his empty or deadhead, weight.

deadhead *v.* **1.a.** to convey (a passenger) or admit (a guest or spectator) without charge.
1854 in *DA*: I will not be deadheaded. **1858** in Thornton *Amer. Gloss.* I 241: The conductor concluded that it was the intention of the trio to *dead-head* one party through. **1871** in Farmer *Amer.*: He is reported to have advertised that he would furnish a free pass to glory, but very few of the unrighteous population seemed anxious to be dead-headed on this train. **1875** A. Pinkerton *C. Melnotte* 14: In like manner he is "dead-headed" at the hotels, theatres, restaurants and elsewhere, until he becomes...one of the greatest "sponges" in the community. **1889** *Century Dict.*: *Deadhead*...To provide free passage, admission, etc., for; pass or admit without payment, as on a railroad or into a theater; as, to *deadhead* a passenger, or a guest at a hotel. **1897** in *DAE.* **1921** Wiley *Lady Luck* 58: Don't know kin I dead-head 'at goat. **1955** G.W. Allen *Sol. Singer* 8: Petted and "deadheaded" by the gatekeepers and deckhands of the ferries, he amused himself by riding back and forth across the river.
b. to allow nonpaying passengers or guests.
1860 in *DA*: This line and two others have entered into a compact not to "dead head."
c. to secure on a complimentary basis.
1867 Clark *Sailor's Life* 265: I shared my money with him, and then took my chance of dead-heading my way on the steamer. This was the only time I ever was what is called "hard up," and I was bound to make the best of it. **1886** Nye *Remarks* 163: He got into the mines, and the way he dead-headed feed and sour mash, on the strength of his relations with the press, made the older miners weep.
2.a. *Transport.* to travel as a nonpaying passenger.
1873 in *DA*. **1889** *Century Dict.*: *Deadhead*...To travel on a train, steamboat, etc., or gain admission to a theater or similar place, without payment. **1935** Faulkner *Pylon* 126: He must have deadheaded out somehow. **1975** R.P. Davis *Pilot* 117: Mike...left for the airport where he deadheaded back to JFK. **1976** J.G. Fuller *Flt. 401* 166: There was an Eastern captain in uniform in one of the seats, and obviously he would be one who was deadheading back after bringing in another plane to Newark. **1985** Boyne & Thompson *Wild Blue* 438: He hated to dead-head; the boredom was intolerable.
b. to enter a show without paying, esp. using a complimentary ticket; (*broadly*) to receive complimentary service of any kind.
1855 in *DA*: The "fast boys" of Chicago prefer to be members of the police force, by virtue of which they "dead head" at all the unlicensed taverns. **1881** Howells *Mod. Instance* ch. vii: Marcia regarded dead-heading as a just and legitimate privilege of the press. **1889** (quot. at (**2.a.**), above). **1929** Caldwell *Bastard* 29: Fork out your jack and the show will start right off....There ain't going to be no deadheading tonight like there was last time.

3. *Transport.* **a.** *Trans.* to drive, dispatch, or pilot (an empty vehicle, train, aircraft, etc.).
1911 in *OEDS:* Only O'Leary and the conductor...were in the car, which was deadheaded. **1983** R. Thomas *Missionary* 166: Oxy was deadheading one of its 727s back out. **1986** *NDAS*: I'll deadhead your hack back to the garage. **1987** Norst & Black *Lethal Weapon* 142: It made no sense to dead-head a cargo plane out of the Golden Triangle.
b. *Intrans.* (of a vehicle, train, aircraft, etc., or its crew or driver) to travel without cargo or passengers.
1929 Botkin *Folk Say I* 111: A guy don't make no jack on a *long-haul* when he has to *dead-head* all the way back...*Dead-Heading*...suggests...that there is no possibility of picking up a fare. **1931** Wilstach *Under Cover Man* 156: Nick may have to deadhead on the return trip. **1942** *AS* (Apr.) 103: *Deadheading.* Going from place to place without a load. **1956** in *OEDS:* Kyle had flown up to Berlin...as a check pilot and now had forty-eight hours before deadheading back. **1958** in *DAS.* **1968** *Everett* (Wash.) *Herald* (Apr. 6) 7C: Some buses already are deadheading (traveling without students) during these hours. **1975** McCaig *Danger Trail* 2: Then we dead- headed back to Whoop-Up and loaded with coal. **1988** *Highwayman* (NBC-TV): "So what are you carrying tonight?" "Tonight we're deadheading."
4. *Publishing.* (see quot.).
1972 *N.Y. Times Mag.* (Dec. 10) 104: Although the magazine "deadheads" into the college audience (its readers' average age is 22), many people love it into their late 20's.

dead horse *n.* **1.** [sugg. by the S.E. provs. illus. by 1638, 1668 quots., suggesting 'something no longer of value'] Esp. *Naut.* work that has been paid for in advance; an obligation to work off an advance in pay; (*hence*) an advance in pay; a financial debt that must be worked off.
[***1638** in *OED2* s.v. *horse*, *n.*, 19: His land...'twas sold to pay his debts; All went That way, for a dead horse, as one would say.] [***1668** in *ibid.*: Sir Humphry Foster had lost the greatest part of his estate, and then (playing, as it is said, for a dead horse) did, by happy fortune, recover it again.] **1832** Wines *Two Years and a Half* I 73 [ref. to 1829]: Unfortunately, most of us had not "worked out our dead horses."...*Dead horses* are debts to the purser on account of advances of pay. **1855** Wise *Tales* 110: I was only three months pay in arrears to the purser on my "dead horse." ***1857** *N & Q* (Series 2) IV 192: When he charges for more...work than he has really done...he has so much unprofitable work to get through in the ensuing week, which is called "dead horse." **1859** Bartlett *Amer.* (ed. 2) 116: *Dead Horse.* Work for which one has been paid before it is performed. When a printer, on Saturday night, includes in his bill work not yet finished, he is said, on the following week, to "work off a *dead horse*." Also used in England. **1864** in Boyer *Naval Surgeon* I 310: My "dead horse" is worked out. **1882** Miller & Harlow *9' 51"* 11: The long service required for his pay to cancel the indebtedness he called "working off his dead horse." **a1899** B.F. Sands *Reefer* 19 [ref. to ca1830]: Not wishing to have too much "dead horse" (as our advanced pay is called) to work out. **1901** *Our Naval Apprentice* (July) 16 [ref. to ca1870]: This eighty dollars charged against them was a "dead horse" which had to be worked off before any liberty was given. **1903** *Independent* (Nov. 26) 2791: The ship dropped out to an anchorage in the stream, to forestall any lurking inclination on our part to desert, before our "dead horse," or price, per head had been worked up. **1924** Colcord *Roll & Go* 18: After one month at sea, it was considered that this "dead horse" had been worked off. **1931** Erdman *Reserve Officer's Man.* 432: *Dead horse.* This term now signifies the advance of pay which is authorized when an officer is transferred from shore to sea and vice-versa. [**1946** *Am. Leg. Mag.* (Apr.) 71 [ref. to WWII]: Dead Horse, Oats For A: Allotment home.] **1988** Poyer *The Med* 61: He was still paying off a dead horse he'd drawn for his PFC drunk.
2. (see quot.).
1942 *ATS* 407: *Dead horse*, a workman who receives pay in advance.
3. merchandise that cannot be sold.
1942 *ATS* 540: Unsaleable merchandise...*dead horse. Ibid.* 619: *Dead horse*...goods that cannot be disposed of.
4. *Printing.* matter typeset in duplication of already prepared type or copy, usu. to comply with a union requirement.
a1986 in *World Book Dict.*: The printer looks up sullenly. "Give me some live copy, not that...dead horse."

deadhouse *n.* **1.** a disreputable saloon. Cf. DEADFALL.
1894 Gardner *Doctor & Devil* 33: The place is over a 5-cent whiskey saloon, or "dead house," as the poor wretches who frequent it call it.

1897 in *DAE*: War on the cheap drink saloons…The initial step against the "dead houses" was taken last Saturday. **1906** Kildare *Old Bailiwick* 35: Low gin-mills—"dead houses"—will spring up like mushrooms. *Ibid.* 62: "Nick's Dead-House" and "The Morgue" were our names for the place. **1925** (cited in Partridge *Dict. Und.* 179).
2. a place for the storage of vehicles.
1951 Shidle *Clear Writing* 94: Dead house…Car storage.

deadie *n.* a dead person.
1973 Karlin, Paquet & Rottmann *Free Fire Zone* 85: You laugh at the deadies. Look at *this* stupid son of a bitch.

dead Indian *n.* an empty liquor bottle; DEAD SOLDIER.
1965 Borowik *Lions* 42: It's looking for old wine in new bottles which is a waste of time and if there are a lot of bottles it can get pretty dull…hence the expression "dead Indians."

deadlight *n.* usu. *pl. Naut.* an eyelid; (*hence*) an eye.
*1821 *Real Life in Ireland* 178: His *dead lights are up*, and *sky lights clos'd*. **1860** Shipley *Privateer's Cruise* 32: Shut your dead-lights, you young jackanapes. **1866** in "M. Twain" *Let. from Hawaii*: Three sheets in the wind and his deadlights stove in. **1871** "M. Twain" *Roughing It* 288: She was always dropping [her glass eye] out, and turning up her old deadlight on the company empty. **1877** in "M. Twain" *Sketches & Tales* 312: Well, sir, his dead-lights were bugged out like tompions. ***1890–91** F & H II 263: Dead-lights…(nautical) The eyes. **1918** *Everybody's* (Nov.) 20: And I'm a son of a sea-cook if I don't plant me hooks in his deadlights for it, too!

dead line *n.* an urban district of saloons and brothels.
1910 *Everybody's Mag.* (Jan.) 118: He nodded toward the city's "dead line." "The women down there don't sink so low as them."

dead man *n.* **1.** usu. *pl.* a bottle or similar container of liquor that has been emptied of its contents. Cf. syns. DEAD SOLDIER, DEAD MARINE.
*1698–99 "B.E." *Dict. Canting Crew*: Dead-Men, empty-Pots or bottles on a Tavern-table. ***1738** J. Swift, in F & H: Come, John, bring us a fresh bottle…Ay, my lord; and pray, let him carry off the dead men, as we say in the army. ***1825** in F & H: Surrounded by a regiment of *dead men* (empty bottles). **1844** in R.H. Dana *Journal* I 243: Why, Stockton, this is a *dead* man. **1854** The *"Fourth"* 6: Another dead man overboard…At this time all hands were thirsty. **1869** (quot. at CRIB, *n.*). ***1871, *1879, *1888** in F & H.
2. *pl. Naut.* gasket, reef, or rope ends carelessly left dangling, esp. under a yard when a sail is furled; IRISH PENNANTS.
*1825 Glascock *Nav. Sk. Bk.* I 11: Why don't they tuck-in those *"dead men"* out of sight! ***1867** Smyth *Sailor's Wd.-Bk.*: Dead Man. The reef or gasket-ends carelessly left dangling under the yard when the sail is furled, instead of being tucked in. **1909** *WNID* 573 [with note *Obs.*]. **1961** Burgess *Dict. Sailing* 67: Dead Men. Odd yarns or rope ends, etc., left hanging about untidily.
3. a large, heavy object, such as a log, fallen tree, boulder, concrete block, etc., that, esp. when buried in earth or ice, can anchor a cable, guy wire, rope, or the like.
*1840 in *OEDS* I 744: Deadman, a piece of timber buried in the earth, to secure posts, or other timbers by. **1867** in *DA*: After they had found the spars would do no good, the mate and four men went ashore and made a "dead man." **1887** E. Custer *Tenting* 34 [ref. to 1860's]: When it dawned upon me that "tying up" was called, in steamer vernacular, "burying a dead man," my eyes returned to their…sockets. **1909** *WNID* 573: Dead man…A buried log, or the like, serving as an anchor for something, as a guy rope. **1944** Mellor *Sank Same* 63: The pilots made "deadmen" by burying logs or gasoline tins to which were attached mooring cables…to prevent the planes from blowing over. **1956** Sorden & Ebert *Logger's Wds.* 11 [ref. to a1925]: Dead-man, A fallen tree on the shore, or a timber to which the hawser of a boom is attached. **1963–64** Kesey *Great Notion* 5: The trees…have supporting guy wires of their own running to wooden deadmen buried deep in the mountainside. ***1974** P. Wright *Lang. Brit. Industry* 64: Deadman…a quayside iron bollard. **1979** Cuddon *Dict. Sports & Games* 279: Dead man. Mountaineering. A snow anchor. **1983** R.C. Mason *Chickenhawk* 452: A dead man is something you tie a rope to and bury.

dead man's hand *n. Poker.* a poker hand made up of a pair of eights and a pair of aces, kings, or jacks, with one indifferent card. [Alleged by tradition to be the hand held by former U.S. marshal James Butler "Wild Bill" Hickock when he was murdered by a shot from behind in Deadwood, Dakota

Terr., Aug. 2, 1876; his biographer, Rosa, remarks (*Wild Bill*, 298), "The actual cards [held by Hickock] are disputed."]
1908 *Century Dict.* (Supp.): Dead man's hand, in poker, two pairs, jacks and eights. **1926** in Botkin *Treas. Amer. Folk.* 90: Bill's hand read "aces and eights"—two pair, and since that day aces and eights have been known as "the dead man's hand" in the Western country. **1935** Pollock *Und. Speaks*: Kings and eights, dead man's hand (poker). **1940** F. Hunt *Trail fr. Tex.* 163: The hand he held—kings and eights—was forever to be known as [the] "dead man's hand." **1944** R. Adams *West. Words* 49. **1974** Rosa *Wild Bill* 298: Aces and Eights—The Dead Man's Hand.

dead marine *n. Naut.* an empty liquor bottle. Cf. DEAD MAN, DEAD SOLDIER.
[*1831 in *OED* s.v. *marine*, n., 4.d.: To see their case bottles properly filled,—no marines among them,—with plenty of grog in their lockers.] **1854** Doten *Journals* I 176: We slayed the last bottle of wine, [and] threw the "dead marines" under the table. **1855** Nordhoff *Merchant Vessel* ch. i: The old topers took a final swig at their jug, and it being emptied, declared it a "dead marine" and tossed it into the chain locker. **1868** Baer *Champagne Charlie* 15: And now let's rid our boat of the dead marines. ***1880** in *OED* s.v. *marine*, n., 4.d.: We filled a dead marine, Sir, at the family watering-hole. **1883** *United Service* (Mar.) 311: The dead "marine" is a variety of mankind that always tells tales. **1889** *United Service* (Apr.) 400: There were a lot of empty bottles standing round and the admiral…said, "Take away those dead marines." **1903** Sonnichsen *Deep Sea Vagabonds* 34: Empty bottles were strewn about—dead marines. **1969** Bosworth *Affair with Navy* 43 [ref. to ca1920]: Nobody ever mentioned the "dead Marine" in the double-bottoms. I had already learned that a "dead Marine" was an empty bottle.

dead meat *n.* **1.a.** a corpse; (*hence*) a person facing certain death; GONER.
1865 Williams *Joaquin* 44: Drop your belts on the ground, or you're dead meat! ***1890–91** F & H: Dead-Meat…(common).—A corpse. **1974** Gober *Black Cop* 126: Without his magnum he would be dead meat in a fire fight. **1977** Butler & Shryack *Gauntlet* 164: You draw one drop of blood from her and you're all dead meat. **1981** *Hill St. Blues* (NBC-TV): You're dead meat! Rats are gonna eat your eyes!
b. an utterly exhausted person.
1987 *Wkly. World News* (June 9) 24: If I don't get to bed by 1 a.m., I'm dead meat the whole next day.
2. *Horse Racing.* a horse intended to lose a race; DEAD ONE, 1.
*1922 *N & Q* (Ser. 12) XI 206: Dead meat. Horses which are not out to win are so described. **1979** Cuddon *Dict. Sports & Games* 280: Dead meat. In *horseracing* circles, a horse not entered to win a race.

deadneck *n.* a dull person.
1929–31 Farrell *Young Lonigan* 133: They were awake and lively; they weren't deadnecks.

dead-nuts *adv. & adj.* **1.** unalterably; perfectly; dead.—usu. considered vulgar.
1887 *Lantern* (N.O.) (May 21) 4: No doubt other policemen are dead-nuts against it. **1984** Trotti *Phantom* 171 [ref. to Vietnam War]: Your dive angle and air speed were dead nuts on. **a1987** Bunch & Cole *Reckoning* 420: Mosby was dead-nuts wrong.
2. *Mil. Av.* (see quot.).
1987 Zeybel *Gunship* 31 [ref. to 1970]: I allowed the cameras to settle to the "dead nuts" position, staring forty-five degrees downward and straight off the left wing. *Ibid.* 37: The gun firing at us was aft of dead nuts.

deado *n.* a dead person.
1919 *Ladies Home Jour.* (Sept.) 114: "Who's your commanding officer?" "Me…all the rest are 'deados.'" ***1976** (cited in Partridge *DSUE* (ed. 8)).

deado *adj. & adv.* dead; (*also*) dead drunk.
*1890 F & H II 265: Dead-oh…(naval).—In the last stage of intoxication. **1913** J. London *Valley of Moon* 23: The thing is they're deados. *Ibid.* 80: It finishes me deado. **1913–14** J. London *Elsinore* 13: The second mate killed deado an' no one to know who done it.

dead-on *adj.* perfectly accurate; (*hence*) correct; exactly right. Now *S.E.*
[*1889 Barrère & Leland *Dict. Slang* I 300: A rifle-shot talks of the aiming being dead-on when the day is so calm he can aim straight at the bull's eye instead of having to allow to the right or left for wind. He is said to be dead-on himself when he is shooting very well.] **1955** L. Shapiro *Sixth of June* 178 [ref. to WWII]: Dead on! How'd you guess?

1982 P. Michaels *Grail* 290: "Try it now"..."Dead on." **1984** in Partridge *DSUE* (ed. 8): *Dead on*...Absolutely right: since *ca*1945. **1985** O'Neil *Lady Blue* (film): Your hunches are usually dead on. **1993** *CBS This Morning* (CBS-TV) (Jan. 15): Phil Hartman does a dead-on imitation of Clinton.

dead one *n.* **1.** *Horse Racing.* (see 1880 quot.).
*1864 in *F & H* II 265: These *al fresco* speculators have their dead 'uns...like their more civilised brethren. *1868 in *OEDS* I 741: The stable and owners might safely lay against what was technically a "dead 'un" from the first. **1880** *N.Y. Clipper Almanac* 44: *Dead One*—A horse that will not run, or has no chance to win, or is not meant to win. **1891** Maitland *Slang Dict.* 91: *Dead 'un*, a horse which it is known is not meant to win. **1898–1900** Cullen *Chances* 16: They look into each other's mugs and chew about being on a dead one. **1906** *Nat. Police Gaz.* (July 7) 6: Racing men...used it to designate a horse that was considered a "dead one." **1918** McNutt *Yanks* 225: Seeing horses they had looked upon as mere goats—dead ones—...flashing around the first turn.

2. GONER.
1899 Kountz *Baxter's Letters* 34: I might have known I was a dead one...Because Mr. Percy Harold was talking to her. **1910** Hapgood *City Streets* 108: It had changed management, and the new men were looking about for something which would give the newspaper, which was a "dead one," a new lease on life. **1912** Lowrie *Prison* 11: We've got y'r right. You're a dead one. The name don't cut no ice. **1930** in Perelman *Old Gang* 101: A false move and you are a dead 'un. **1978** De Christoforo *Grease* 102: He's a dead one.

3.a. a person who is penniless, inept, useless, obnoxious, unsociable, or the like; LOSER.
1899 Cullen *Tales* 77: My man in Sacramento has proved himself a dead one by running it up all the time and neglecting business. **1898– 1900** Cullen *Chances* 25: He went broke, and has been a dead 'un for a good many years now. **1903** T.W. Jackson *Slow Train* 109: If you don't catch [a girl] there you are certainly a dead one. **1904** *Life in Sing Sing* 255: *Dead one.*—A person who has ceased to be of any use. **1906** *Nat. Police Gaz.* (Jan. 13) 3: And you turn around...and declare those two dead ones in on the play. **1907** in Fleming *Unforget. Season* 9: Mathewson is by no means a "dead one," but...[certainly not] the best twirler in the league. **1910** *N.Y. Eve. Jour.* (Feb. 1) 14: Paul is going with a lot of dead ones now...He wants to say whether or not, in his opinion, Jeff [Jim Jeffries] is a dead one or [Jack] Johnson is a dead one. **1913** J. London *Valley of Moon* 60: These fat cows of women. They're the dead ones. Now you're a live one. **1912–14** in E. O'Neill *Lost Plays* 36: Yuh're a fine-lookin' mess!...Yuh look like a dead one. Put on some paint and cheer up! **1917** McCann *On the Border* 270: They are not "dead ones," either, but are full of..."pep." **1924** Henderson *Keys to Crookdom* 402: *Dead one*—person who is broke or incompetent. **1926** *AS* I (Dec.) 651: *Dead One.* A stingy person. **1930** "D. Stiff" *Milk & Honey* 203: *Dead one*—...a hobo who has just spent all his money. **1939** *AS* (Oct.) 239: *Dead One.* Non-tipping guests.

b. a fool.
1914 Atherton *Perch* 138: And it's copper carbonate or I'm a dead 'un. **1931** Wilstach *Under Cover Man* 177: Standing there like a couple of dead ones.

4. *Und.* a person who is no longer a tramp or criminal.
1901 "J. Flynt" *Graft* 193: What the Dead Ones say should be Done. The Dead Ones are the inhabitants of the Under World who have "squared it." **1930** Irwin *Tramp & Und.:* *Dead one*...A reformed criminal; a former tramp.
¶ In phrase:
¶ **on a dead one** betting on a horse that is sure to lose; (*hence*) engaged in a hopeless pursuit.
1896 Ade *Artie* 26: When any o' you blokies try to push into a game where I am and get me to put up any dough against your shark combinations—w'y, you're on a dead one. **1898–1900** (quot. at (1), above).

dead pan *n.* [*dead* + PAN] Orig. *Theat.* a face or facial expression that displays no emotion, animation, or humor.
1927 *Vanity Fair* (Nov.) 132: A "poker-face" or a "dead-pan" is a lifeless facial expression. **1928** MacArthur *War Bugs* 234: Freddie Smith...told us with a dead pan that an armistice had been signed. **1929** *Bookman* (Apr.) 150: A "dead pan" is an expressionless face, and "mugging," facial pantomime. **1931** Wilstach *Under Cover Man* 9: He tried to keep a dead pan, an expressionless face. **1933** N. West *Miss Lonelyhearts* 72: He practiced a trick used much by moving-picture comedians—the dead pan. No matter how fantastic or excited his speech, he never changed his expression. **1938–40** W.V.T. Clark *Ox-Bow* 19: He was just sitting

there with a sullen dead-pan. **1942** Algren *Morning* 262: Not a flicker. A dead pan. **1950** *Sat. Eve. Post* (Aug. 5) 35: When expounding, the colonel wears a froglike dead pan. **1993** *New Yorker* (June 14) 28: [Actress] Valeria Golino has developed a fetching deadpan.

deadpan *adv. & adj.* Orig. *Theat.* displaying no humor or emotion. Now *S.E.*
1928 *N.Y. Times* (Mar. 11) VIII 6: *Dead-Pan*—Playing a rôle with expressionless face as, for instance, the work of Buster Keaton. **1930** in Hemingway *Sel. Letters* 324: I wrote Maxie (Dead-Pan) and asked him if it was true that the publishers were all in the s—t house now...I guess publishing is a thing of the past. **1950** F. Brown *Space* 193: He looked at Candler and Candler wasn't kidding. Candler was strictly deadpan. **1952** Brossard *Darkness* 8: He looked deadpan at us, and went to the bar for my beer. **1955** Q. Reynolds *HQ* 96: Act deadpan and get down here when you can. **1960** Serling *Stories from Twilight Zone* 12: Casey stared at him deadpan. **1966–67** Harvey *Air War* 143: He was a quiet, deadpan guy. **1966–69** Woiwode *Going to Do* 25: Listened deadpan to everything they said.

deadpan *v.* to speak, act, or utter in a DEADPAN manner; to maintain a DEAD PAN. Now *S.E.*
1942 *Life* (Sept. 14) 28: A Jap press officer dead-pans the news that Singapore is fallen. **1952** H. Grey *Hoods* 205: Max deadpanned. "Never heard of the guy." **1955** Robbins *79 Park Ave.* 8: "You know Alec." Joel deadpanned in return. **1974** Foster *Star Trek Log One* 73: "No, sir," deadpanned Sulu in return. **1987** *Campus Voice* (Spring) 9: "We may make more trips to the bathroom than any other club members on campus," he deadpans.

dead-picker *n.* *Hobo.* a robber of sleeping drunks.
1930 "D. Stiff" *Milk & Honey* 203: *Dead picker*—A yegg who robs a drunk. **1949** Algren *Golden Arm* 102: That crummy deadpicker left the downstairs door open again.

dead pigeon *n.* DEAD DUCK, 2.
1919 V. Lindsay *Golden Whales* 92: Your Daniel is a dead little pigeon. **1940** Hartman & Butler *Rd. to Singapore* (film): Gloria hits you with a little of that billing and cooing and you're a dead pigeon. **1944** H. Brown *Walk in the Sun* 93: Those guys are dead pigeons. High mortality rate. *ca*1947 in L'Amour *Over Solomons* 146: He'll have his sights set on that open place, and I'm a dead pigeon. **1954** in Marx *Groucho Letters* 59: The male is a dead pigeon. **1958** Frankel *Band of Bros.* 15: We're dead pigeons we try to cross all that open ground. **1958** J. King *Pro Football* 130: One weak halfback...on defense is enough to make his coach a dead pigeon. **1987** Univ. Tenn. instructor: If you get guys like that mad at you, you're a dead pigeon.

dead president *n.* [U.S. law prohibits the likeness of a living person from appearing on its currency] a U.S. banknote.
1944 Burley *Harlem Jive* 136: *Dead President*—A dollar bill, paper money of any denomination. **1946** Boulware *Jive & Slang* 3: *Dead President*...Dollar bill. **1959** *Life* (Nov. 23) 45: *Dead Presidents*—$20 bills with Andrew Jackson portrait, $50s with Ulysses Grant portrait, etc., used in payoffs. *Ibid.* 46: How many dead presidents are there for me? **1977** Sayles *Union Dues* 181: I see you again...it better be behind a pile of dead Presidents. Take a load of Jacksons and Grants get you off my shit list, girl. **1986** *Morning Call* (Allentown, Pa.) (Aug. 18) D3: *Dead Presidents:* Money. **1989** *Newsweek* (Aug. 14) 6: We found a briefcase full of dead presidents in the trunk of the Caddie.

dead rabbit *n.* [from a gang of roughs who paraded in N.Y.C. in 1848, carrying a dead rabbit as a standard, the dead rabbit meaning "a conquered enemy."—Barrère & Leland *Dict. Slang* (1889) s.v.]
1. a member of a criminal street gang; hoodlum. Now *hist.*
1857 in *DA.* **1859** Matsell *Vocab.* 72: *Rabbit.* A rowdy. "Dead rabbit," a very athletic rowdy fellow. **1862** Norton *Army Letters* 48: The Twenty-Fifth New York is composed of New York roughs, Bowery boys, "Dead rabbits," etc. **1931** Harlow *Old Bowery* 187 [ref. to 1850's]: For in the slang of the day...a dead rabbit was a very prince of rowdies.
2. DEAD DUCK, 2.
1944 C.B. Davis *Leo McGuire* 94: When he yelled out I thought we was dead rabbits and no fooling.

dead ringer *n.* see s.v. RINGER.

dead-set *n.* *Stu.* a complete failure in recitation; DEAD.
1819 A. Pierce *Rebelliad* 52: Now's the day and now's the hour;/See approach Old Sikes's power;/See the front of Logic lower;/Screws, dead-sets, and fines. **1837** *Knickerbocker Mag.* IX 123: The next week came Greek. I knew nothing of the Grammar—I took *dead set* after *dead*

set, that is, I was set down. **1856** B. Hall *College Wds.* (ed. 2) 149: One…is *taking a dead-set*.

dead shot *n.* vile whiskey.

1865 in *DAE*: A negro saloon on Cherry street, where dead-shot is retailed…by the rod.

dead soldier *n.* **1.** an empty wine, liquor, or beer bottle; (*recently*) an empty beer can. Cf. earlier syns. DEAD MAN, DEAD MARINE.

1899 Robbins *Gam* 98: Beside him lay the bottle (a "dead soldier") entirely empty. **1899** Norris *McTeague* 149: A row of empty champagne bottles—"dead soldiers," as the facetious waiter had called them. **1906** Beyer *Amer. Battleship* 84: "Dead soldier"—an empty bottle. **1917** Batchelder *Watching & Waiting* 112: We walk slowly along, picking here a tin-can, here a "dead soldier," there a cigarette butt. **1918** Ruggles *Navy Explained* 50: *Dead soldier.* An empty bottle which had contained liquor or beer. Very often called a "dead dog." **1938** in W.C. Fields *By Himself* 304: I am going up to Soboba over Decoration Day to put flowers on the graves of some of the dead soldiers I buried there just prior to my stubborn attack of D.T.'s. **1940** Chandler *Farewell, My Lovely* 22: I held up the dead soldier and shook it. **1942–43** C. Jackson *Lost Weekend* 165: The empty sticky bottles, the dead soldiers. **1946** Gresham *Nightmare Alley* 30: Then he drew the cork out, finished it, and heaved it into the night. "Dead soldier." **1965** Eastlake *Castle Keep* 230: Bring all your empty bottles, all the dead soldiers, and line them up on the bar. **1972** in J. Flaherty *Chez Joey* 220: All that could be heard from the hatch was the sound of "dead soldiers" breaking and loud cursing. **1974** *Police Woman* (NBC-TV): Another dead soldier. **1985** Briskin *Too Much* 120: "Dead soldier," he said, setting the empty bottle [of Scotch] on the window ledge. **1987** Eble *Campus Slang* (Apr.) 3: *Dead soldier*—empty beer can.

2. *pl.* (among waiters) food left on a plate; (*also*) (*sing.*) a dirty plate.

1954 L. Armstrong *Satchmo* 215: When [the waiters] would pass the bandstand on the way to the kitchen with the dead soldiers, or leftovers, they would look me in the eye and I would give them the well known wink.

dead-stick *adv.* [sugg. by *dead-stick landing*] *Av.* without engine power.

1977 J. Wylie *Homestead Grays* 71: You'll have to bring it in dead stick, Carl. **1972–79** T. Wolfe *Right Stuff* 54: He was now faced with the task of landing the ship both deadstick and blind. **1981** Bill Land, Space Shuttle official, on *Larry King Show* (Mutual Radio Network) (Mar. 6): It'll be coming down what the pilots call "dead-stick." In other words it won't have any power at all.

dead-stick *v. Av.* to land an aircraft without engine power.

1962 S. Smith *Escape from Hell* 130 [ref. to WWII]: Captain George wanted to "dead stick" into Candler Field. **1987** Robbins *Ravens* (photo caption): Beside an 0-1 he "dead-sticked" into a rice paddy after the engine quit.

dead tank *n. Police.* a holding cell for prisoners awaiting sentencing.

1981 O'Day & Eells *High Times* 197 [ref. to *ca*1950]: While you're sitting in the "dead tank" waiting to find out…how long you're going to serve, that's really hard time.

dead turkey *n.* DEAD DUCK, 2.

1941 in Ruhm *Detective* 268: Stay here and you're a dead turkey.

deadwood *n.* **1.** a coffin. *Joc.*

1845 Durivage & Burnham *Stray Subjects* 71: And I was took to my last home,/And in the dead wood laid.

2. *Gamb.* a sure bet.

1855 in M. Lewis *Mining Frontier* 58: Others were enslaved and relieved of many an ounce by his counterfeiting intoxication, and recklessly tossing his money around, and exhibiting "deadwoods" (certainties of winning) to their temptation. **1857** in Thornton *Amer. Gloss.* I 242: Let such men but have a sure thing, or, as Californians say, the *deadwood*, and they will bet their last farthing.

3. *Theat.* unsold or complimentary tickets.

1934 Weseen *Dict. Slang* 139: *Deadwood*—Unsold tickets. **1942** Liebling *Telephone* 164: Tickets that have been paid for—known in the trade as "the hardwood"—and…complimentaries, or "deadwood."

¶ In phrase:

¶ **have the deadwood on** to have a critical advantage over; have at one's mercy; (*hence, specif.*) to have incontrovertible evidence against.

1851 in *DA*. **1867** A.D. Richardson *Beyond Miss.* 134 [ref. to Mo., 1858]: "I have the dead wood on him" was used familiarly, meaning: "I have him in my power." **1862** in S. Clemens *Twain's Letters* I 175: I've got that learned author cornered at last—got the dead-wood on him, Ma. **1870** *Overland Mo.* (Dec.) 517: 'Taint much of a story, but it gives the Georgetown boys the deadwood on Dick Irwin and me, and they hain't let up on us yet. **1871** Banka *Prison Life* 468: He has what they call the "deadwood" on him. **1871** Bagg *Yale* 48: To have a *soft thing* on, or the *dead wood* on, any object, to hold the "inside track," the best opportunity for gaining it. **1872** Crapsey *Nether Side of N.Y.* 185: You cant get the dead wood on nobody. **1872** Burnham *Secret Service* V: *Deadwood*, the material for certain conviction. *Ibid.* 99: You've got the "dead wood" on me, Colonel. **1877** Wheeler *Deadwood Dick* 78: Look out that ther allies uv Sittin' Bull don't git ther *dead wood* on ye. **1878** [P.S. Warne] *Hard Crowd* 3: I reckon t'other'n has got the deadwood on him. **1890** Janvier *Aztec Treasure House* 236: If they don't know enough to corral our guns…we've got a pretty good-sized piece of dead-wood on 'em. **1891** Kirkland *Capt. of Co. K* 258: But seein' I got the dead wood on ye, I let ye know that the bet's off. **1936** Green *Johnny Johnson* 163: I got the deadwood on you this time— **1941** in Randolph *Church House* 21: "Now you little varmint," says the heron, "I've got the deadwood on you!" **1956** *So. Folk. Qly.* XX 175: Now I guess I got the dead wood on you. **1966** Purdum *Bro. John* 88: I wanted to…find out if he really did have the deadwood on Belknap.

deadwood *adj.* genuine; DEAD, 2.

1876 "M. Twain," in Barrère & Leland *Dict. Slang* I 301: Are you in real dead-wood earnest?

deal *n.* **1.a.** an act of buying or selling; business agreement; bargain. Now *S.E.*

1838 [Haliburton] *Clockmaker* (Ser. 2): Six dollars apiece for the picturs is about the fair deal for the price. **1847–49** Bonney *Banditti* 86: He is more honorable in his deal with the boys than Jack is. *1861 in OED*: He wanted to have a deal with me for [the mare]. *1876 in F & H* II 266: I shall be back again shortly, when we will wet the deal [i.e., ratify it by taking a drink]. **1889** *Century Dict.* *1890–91 F & H* II 266: To do a deal…(common).—To conclude a bargain.

b. *Specif.* Esp. *Pol.* a secret or underhand agreement for mutual advantage; scheme.

1881 in *OED*: [The party boss's] power of making "deals." **1882** in *Century Dict.*: The President had definitively abandoned the maxims and practices of…machine politics in New York, with the shifts and expedients and *deals* which had illustrated his rise to political prominence. **1889** *Century Dict.*: They made a *deal* for the division of the offices. **1909** *WNID*: Deal…A secret arrangement, as in business or political bargains, to attain a desired result by a combination of interested parties. Cant, U.S. **1988** *21 Jump St.* (Fox-TV): Now is this one of your deals—or is it serious?

2. an action; (*hence,* usually) treatment received; sort of treatment.—constr. with an evaluative adj.

1876 in *OEDS*: That was a square deal, Mis Brown. **1881** Crofutt *Gde. to Colo.* 132: The motto being "a fair profit, but a square deal." **1882** in Sonnichsen *Billy King* 59: I…demanded of the prison-keeper a "square deal." *Ibid.* 60: Muttering something about a "rough deal." **1885** in Lummis *Letters* 196: Say, Lummy, you're having a rough deal out there. **1892** L. Moore *Own Story* 288: I had not intended to give "Slippery" such a rough deal quite so soon. **1901** Irwin *Sonnets* (unp.): O scaly Mame to give me such a deal,/To hand me such a bunch when I was true. **1903** A.H. Lewis *Black Lion* 117: Doc Peets is the one white gent…willin' to mete out to Mexicans a squar' deal from a squar' deck. **1909** in McCay *Little Nemo* 187: The Princess surely does not think much of you, giving you a deal like this. **1912** in *OEDS*: Raw deal, a bare-faced swindle. **1912** Mathewson *Pitching* 12: The roughest deal that I got from Baker in the 1911 series was in the third game. **1912** Lowrie *Life in Prison* 104: He's goin' down to "get" some waiter what's given him a dirty deal in the dinin'-room. **1913** T.M. Osborne *Pris. Walls* 132: It was a "pretty raw deal." **1915** Poole *Harbor* 81: They've had a raw deal since the world began. **1926** Nason *Chevrons* 281: I been gettin' a raw deal everywhere. **1928** Callahan *Man's Grim Justice* 158: He confessed that he had given me a "dirty deal" because he had taken a dislike to me. **1928** Scanlon *God Have Mercy* 6: The Third Battalion always gets a dirty deal. **1930** Sage *Last Rustler* 112: He'd had a pretty rough deal. **1932** Tully *Laughter* 54: It's all a hell of a muddle, Barney—most women stick to men who beat 'em blue as ink and you git a deal like this. **1933** in R.E. Howard *Iron Man* 81: Where I come from,…there's only one answer to the deal they gave me. Get out of my way. **1935** E. Anderson *Hungry Men* 241: Some cops gave him a dirty deal up there. **1946** I. Shulman *Dukes* 27: Any guy who became drunk and started a fight got a fast deal and was thrown out. **1980** Hogan *Lawman's Choice* 24: Well, the way I see it…you got a mighty raw deal.

3.a. situation; business; state of affairs. See also *real deal* and *What's the deal?*, below.

1892 L. Moore *Own Story* 104: This is a pretty tough deal…you have placed me in such a position as to make me appear to be the owner of this counterfeit money. **1895** in J.I. White *Git Along Dogies* 65: Well, this deal about the sweet bye and bye. Do you think a couple of toughs like us would stand any kind of a show way up there among these angels? **1896** Ade *Artie* 58: I'd never said nothin' to Mame about the marry deal, and he was takin' it for granted. **1899–1900** Cullen *Tales* 308: So we landed here linked-arms…Queer deal, ain't it? **1903** Ade *Society* 31: Once there was an Employee who was getting the Nub End of the Deal. **1906** Tomlin *H. Tomlin* 263: It's a pretty hard deal when you're held responsible for what somebody else does. **1916** Livingston *Snare* 42: Hoboing is a rather rough deal, bo! **1929** "E. Queen" *Roman Hat* 74: He was mixed up in a dirty deal with a girl. **1929** in R.E. Howard *Book* 68: "All right," I says, plumb burned up by this deal. *Ibid.* 69: What kind of a deal have I got into? **1941** Macaulay & Wald *Manpower* (film): Why don't you stop tryin' to crab our deal? **1944–48** A. Lyon *Unknown Station* 34: You boys have a rough deal. **1950** Spillane *Vengeance* 41: Then the whole deal will get boring. **1979** T. Baum *Carny* 7: That's the deal…He wasn't even drunk.

b. a development; turn of events. [In 1989 quot., "emergency."]

1929 "E. Queen" *Roman Hat* 65: Sorry, Inspector. Lost my temper. But of all the rotten deals—. **1948** Manone & Vandervoort *Trumpet* 167: By some screwy deal, the fire had only reached one side of it. **1957** J.D. MacDonald *Price of Murder* 104: "That your [dead] wife?" "Yes." "Rough deal, mister." **1966** I. Reed *Pall-Bearers* 12: You'd better get on the right side, brother, because when the deal goes down, all the backsliding Uncle Toms are going to be mowed down. **1989** "Capt. X" & Dodson *Unfriendly Skies* 111: When a beeper goes off, the controllers…call it a "deal."

c. (one's) concern or business.

1957 H. Ellison *Web of the City* 27: You guys wanna do it, that's your deal, but leave me alone.

4. an individual or thing (in the broadest sense).

1944 *Slanguage Dict.* 59: *A good deal*—an "alreet" gal; "the kind you'd like to come home to." **1966** in IUFA *Folk Speech*: *Deal*—object. *Ibid.*: *Deal*—A layout, usually applied to clothing as in, "I'm wearing the green deal."

¶ In phrases:

¶ **cut a deal** see s.v. CUT, *v.*

¶ **good deal!** excellent! fine! O.K.!

1944 in Butterfield *Post Treasury* 434: "Good deal," Watts grinned. **1944–46** in *AS* XXII 55: *Good Deal.* Fine, glad to hear it, okay by me. **1949** Quigley *Corsica* 71: "You got a ride." "Good deal." **1950** Felsen *Hot Rod* 47: Good deal. We'll shove in a minute. **1958** Meltzer & Blees *H.S. Confidential* (film): In half an hour? Good deal. I'll be there. **1962** McElfresh *Jill Nolan* 31: "Good deal!" Dr. Armistead applauded verbally. **1979** J. Morris *War Story* 214: Good fucking deal. An entire battalion of NVA had pulled out of here about two hours before.

¶ **new deal** a fresh start; new beginning. [This phr., orig. from card playing, has infl. the development of defs. 1, 2, and 3 above.]

1834 in *OEDS*: A new bank and a New Deal. **1838** [Haliburton] *Clockmaker* (Ser. 2) 62: Folks thought a new deal now would give 'em more fair play. **1863** in *OEDS*: The war is prolonged, and but little chance of its ending until we have a new deal. **1898** Kountz *Baxter's Letters* 3: They asked me to go with them. It was [a] new deal for me, so of course I was for it. **1900** Hammond *Whaler* 105: Look here, boys, there's got to be a new deal.…I'll not have one of those fellows in with me. **1908** in H.C. Fisher *A. Mutt* 134: If [your suitor] has a can full of coin and a weak chin, grab him! If not, shuffle the cards and wait for a new deal. *a*1904–11 Phillips *Susan Lenox* II 113: "Baggage lost—eh?"…"No…I'm beginning an entire new deal." **1954** A. Cohn *Fighting Lady* (film): That was the last war. This is a new deal. **1962** McKenna *Sand Pebbles* 443: I'm dealin' you birds a new deal down here!…Get off your asses and get to work!

¶ **real deal** the genuine article; the truth.—constr. with *the.*

1971 Goines *Dopefiend* 138: This bullshit Smokey was mumbling about better be the real deal. **1989** *CBS This Morning* (CBS-TV) (Dec. 11): This is not just lake-effect snow. This is the real deal. **1993** *Jerry Springer Show* (synd. TV series): OK, you want the real deal, right?

¶ **What's the deal?** What's going on? (*also*) What's the plan or situation?

1941 Hargrove *Pvt. Hargrove* 73: "What's the deal?" I asked. "Where do I go and what do I do?" **1941–42** Gach *In Army Now* 141: He usually prefaces all his remarks with "What's the deal?" **1944–48** A. Lyon *Unknown Station* 239: "What's the deal?" "Sick call." **1949** Grayson & Andrews *I Married a Communist* (film): What's the deal this time? **1952** in Yates *Loneliness* 33: So what's the deal?…What time we supposed to show up? **1960** *Father Knows Best* (CBS-TV): Mom didn't talk much about her driving lesson yesterday. What's the deal? **1971** Cameron *First Blood* 152: What's the deal? We…hit them with all we've got? **1987** Univ. Tenn. student: So what's the deal with all the questions? **1993** *CBS This Morning* (CBS-TV) (Feb. 11): What's the deal on the President's signature?…Sometimes he's just plain "Bill" and sometimes he's "William J."

deal *v.* **1.a.** *Und.* to pass (fraudulent currency or paper).

1880 Pinkerton *Prof. Thieves* 34: I sold Foster a big pile the last time I was in Chicago…"Did you ever 'deal' any?"…"Yes, Mr. Craig, but only when I could get a first-class article." **1924** (implied by quot. at DEALER, 1).

b. *Und.* to sell (drugs) illegally. Also absol. Now *colloq.* or *S.E.*

1931–34 (implied by quot. at DEALER, 2). **1958** Motley *Epitaph* 122: I know they used to deal but I don't know if they're dealing now. **1963** Williamson *Hustler!* 106: He said this broad's dealin' and that she got some nice stuff on. **1965** C. Brown *Manchild* 153: If you were dealing horse, junkies were always around you. **1966** J. Mills *Needle Park* 149: And also because sometimes these guys won't deal to her. **1966** Brunner *Face of Night* 33: The peddler was set up, ready to deal, and suddenly at the very last second, he backed away as if he'd been tipped off somehow. **1970** Landy *Underground Dict.* 64: *Deal*…Make a living by buying and selling drugs. **1970** E. Knight *Black Voices* 67: His brothers dealt reefers around the neighborhood. *a*1989 E. Currie *Dope & Trouble* 27: I used to deal. It was…[cocaine and methamphetamines].

c. to give; hand over.

1921–25 J. Gleason & R. Taber *Is Zat So?* 14: The army [was] only dealin' him thirty a month!

2.a. *Und.* to deal with, esp. with violence.

1942 Goldin et al. *DAUL*: *Deal, n.* A severe beating…*Deal, v.* To give one a *deal.* **1970** La Motta, Savage & Carter *R. Bull* 29: "You find Curly?"…"Jake found a couple of Curlys…Why?" "You deal 'em?"… "Jake dealt 'em."

b. *Und.* to fight; brawl.

1966–67 P. Thomas *Mean Streets* 57 [ref. to 1940's]: He got heart when it comes to dealing. *Ibid.* 59: You ain't got no heart for dealing on fists alone. *Ibid.*: We deal with our *manos. Ibid.* 60: Everybody was dealing hard.

3. to treat.

1957 H. Ellison *Web of City* 28: He dealt me right all along. **1971–73** Sheehy *Hustling* 67: Get out of this racket while you still can, honey…It deals women hard.

4. to strike a bargain; make a deal.

1963 Westlake *Getaway Face* 56: You ready to deal? **1981** in *Nat. Lampoon* (Jan. 1982) 12: Remember, $3.00 is our firm and final offer. Call us when you are ready to deal. **1982** P. Michaels *Grail* 147: Now it's your turn. Do we deal?

5. *Baseball.* to pitch (a baseball) to a batter. Also absol.

1978 F. Messer, on N.Y. Yankees vs. Boston Red Sox (WINS radio) (June 27): Drago ready—and deals. **1986** *NDAS*: The big left-hander deals a smoker.

6. to trade (a professional athlete); to sell the contract of (a person under contract).

1981 G. Wolf *Roger Rabbit* 3: Why won't they deal me away? **1987** *RHD2*.

¶ In phrases:

¶ **deal (one) a hand** to include.

1889 O'Reilly & Nelson *Fifty Years on Trail* 182: Thinking it about time to have a look in, I yelled out, "Deal me a hand, boys!"

¶ **deal off** [or **from**] **the bottom [of the deck]** to act deceptively, as by perpetrating a swindle.

1918 *Chi. Sun.-Trib.* (Feb. 17) V (unp.): You dealt off the bottom after you got her to sit in. **1934** Weseen *Dict. Slang* 96: *Deal from the bottom*—To cheat. **1947** in Hemingway *Sel. Letters* 628: Looks as though our Heavenly Father was perhaps dealing off the bottom of the deck. **1976** Wren *Bury Me Not* 12: He's the county sheriff, and I've never had any reason to think he was dealin' off the bottom.

dealer *n.* **1.** *Und.* (see quot.).

1924 Henderson *Crookdom* 402: *Dealer.* Wholesaler of bogus currency.
2. *Narc.* a person who sells illegal drugs; PUSHER.
1931–34 in Clemmer *Pris. Community* 331: *Dealer*, n. A narcotic peddlar [*sic*]. **1936** *AS* (Apr.) 120: *Dealer.* A [drug] peddler. **1952** Ellson *Golden Spike* 244: Dealer...a pusher. **1958** Motley *Epitaph* 143: All the pushers and dealers done took off. **1958–59** Lipton *Barbarians* 315: *Dealer*—Drug-seller, pusher. **1960** R. Reisner *Jazz Titans* 154: *Dealer*: Pusher or drug vendor. **1960** C. Cooper *Scene* 60: That's a guy called Ace. He's one of the biggest dealers on the Scene. *a*1989 E. Currie *Dope & Trouble* 205: They're big-time—big-time dealers.

deal under *v. Black E.* to do for; victimize.
1963 L. Jones, in *Blues People*: Sonny Liston is the big black Negro in every white man's hallway, waiting to do him, deal him under for all the hurts white men, through their arbitrary order, have been able to inflict on the world.

Dear Jane letter *n.* [fr. DEAR JOHN] a letter from a man informing his wife or sweetheart that he is ending their relationship.
1984 J. Dailey *Silver Wings* 305: He wrote his wife a Dear Jane letter. **1994** *Harper's* (Feb.) 43: One thing you should know about a Dear John/Dear Jane letter....She's going to hate you.

Dear John *n.* Orig. *Mil.* a letter from a woman informing her husband or sweetheart that she is ending their relationship; (*broadly*) a similar letter sent by a man to a woman. Also *fig.* In full, **Dear John letter.**
1942–45 in Campbell & Campbell *War Paint* 206: "Dear John." **1945** in *OEDS.* **1947** Mailer *Naked & Dead* 143 [ref. to WWII]: Leave a girl friend behind? Get a Dear John? **1948** Taylor *Lang. of WWII* 63: *Dear Johns*: Name given by soldiers to letters from wives or sweethearts "calling it all off." Name came from a current radio program made up of letters addressed to "Dear John."—*Democrat & Chronicle.* Rochester, N.Y. Aug. 17, 1945. **1951** Thacher *Captain* 77: You think Mr. Gilchrist is tapped for the "Dear John?" **1952** Uris *Battle Cry* 145 [ref. to 1942]: "A Dear John letter," Andy hissed. **1959** Hunter *Conviction* 31: I got a Dear John while I was overseas. **1960–61** Steinbeck *Discontent* 43: It might have ended with the traditional Dear John letter. **1969** Crumley *Cadence* 42: His parents had replied to his honest confession and plea for understanding with a Dear John asking him not to return, ever. **1972** Burkhart *Women in Pris.* 266: If...she gets a Dear John letter, she might get hysterical. **1982** Del Vecchio *13th Valley* 137: Somebody said yer ol gal sent ya a Dear John. **1991** J.T. Ward *Dear Mom* 190: I took the letter from Laura as a Dear John.

death *n.* ¶ In phrases:
¶ **death on** especially effective against, at, or in; passionately fond of or having a great capacity for.
1839 *Spirit of Times* (Oct. 5) 368: There is a chap in this city whose nose is so red that no musquito can stand the blaze of it. It's death upon gallinippers, too. **1842** in Thornton *Amer. Gloss.* I 243: This medicine is death on colds. **1843** Field *Pokerville* 131: Yes,...you're death on teeth,...but ken Mesmerism come the re-*mee*-jil over rheumatiz? **1846** *Spirit of Times* (Apr. 25) 101: He is death on anything pure, imbibes liquids as the parched earth does the dews. **1847** Robb *Squatter Life* 30: A long, lanky cadaverous lawyer, who was death on a speech. **1853** "P. Paxton" *In Texas* 44: He's death on a quarter [mile race]. **1859** Bartlett *Amer.* (ed. 2) 117: To be *death on* a thing, is to be completely master of it, a capital hand at it, like the quack doctor who...was, as he expressed it, "*death on* fits." Vulgar. **1862** "E. Kirke" *Among Pines* 212: They make excellent bacon, and are "death on snakes." **1889** Barrère & Leland *Dict. Slang* I 302: *Death on* (Australian), good at..."*Death on* rabbits," would mean a very good rabbit shot; "*death on* peaches," greedy of peaches. The phrase is common in the United States, where a lady over fond of finery is said to be *death on* dress. **1889** *Century Dict.*: He *was death on* the sherry. **1890–91* F & H II 266: *To be death on*...(common) Very fond of, or thoroughly master of. **1912** Mathewson *Pitching* 84: He is a wonderful fielder and sure death on bunts. **1987** *RHD2*: The third baseman is death on pop flies.
¶ **go (one's) death** to bet everything; do (one's) utmost; go all-out.
1832 [M. St.C. Clarke] *Sks. of Crockett* 39: Sal...swore she could "go her death" upon a jig. *Ibid.* 40: Now, Dick,...didn't I go my death? **1833** in *OEDS*: My little boys at home will go their death upon my election. **1835** in *OEDS*: I'll go my death upon you at the shooting match. **1878** in *OEDS.*
¶ **like death to a dead cat** with unyielding tenacity. Also vars., some ethnically offensive.

1804 in Whiting *Early Am. Prov.* 100: He stuck to him like grim Death to a dead cat. [**1845** Durivage & Burnham *Stray Subjects* 78: But they hung on to him, "like Mortality to a deceased African," as my friend expressed it, determined not to give out.] **1862** C.F. Browne *Art. Ward* 70: My tung would...stick thar, like deth to a deseast Afrikan. **1865** in Horrocks *Dear Parents* 141: I...held on to the lower rigging, like grim death to a dead nigger. **1866** Dimsdale *Vigilantes* 97: Cased in a suit of frozen clothes, which, as one of them observed, "stuck to them like death to a dead nigger." **1928** Nason *Sgt. Eadie* 11 [ref. to 1918]: I've held on to 'em like grim death to a dead chink for nearly a year and I'd hate to lose 'em now.
¶ **like death warmed over** [or **up**] very ill or exhausted, often as the result of a hangover.
*1939 in *OEDS* I 746: To feel like death warmed up, to feel ill. **1966** Jarrett *Private Affair* 188: She looked like death warmed over. **1972** in *Playboy* (Jan. 1973) 122: You're too old for staying out like that. No wonder you look like death warmed over.
¶ **look like death eating a sandwich** to look extremely angry, ill, or exhausted. Also vars. Usu. *Joc.*
1947–52 R. Ellison *Invisible Man* 486: That crazy sonofabitch...look[s] like death eating a sandwich. **1974** Terkel *Working* 62: You must look presentable, not like death on a soda cracker. **1974** R.H. Carter *16th Round* 79: Its inhabitants looked like death standing on the street corner eating lifesavers. **1976** A. Walker *Meridian* 11: I must look like death eating a soda cracker.
¶ **to death** to an extraordinary degree. [In early use restricted to phr. *dressed to death*.]
*1859 in *F & H* II 326: "He was got up very extensively," said of a man who is *dressed within an inch of his life* or *dressed to death.* **1873* Hotten *Slang Dict.* (ed. 5) 141: "To dress to *death*," i.e., to the very extreme of fashion. **1887** DeVol *40 Yrs. a Gambler* 13: You ought to have seen me when I stepped on the wharf boat...dressed to death, with my gold watch and chain. **1987** Univ. Tenn. student: I just love that movie to death! **1987–91** D. Gaines *Teenage Wasteland* 76: Hair like Heather Locklear, fierce, nails to death.

death *adj.* [see note at DEF, *adj.*] Esp. *Black E.* superlative. Cf. DEF. See also *death on* s.v. DEATH, *n.*
1965 in W. King *Black Anthol.* 309: This doll is a champ on the sheets! She is brutal; death on sheets, man! **1980** W. Safire, in *N.Y. Times Mag.* (Jan. 18, 1981): [In black slang] *death* is the liveliest. **1982** Levinson *Diner* (film): She's death! **1983** Sturz *Wid. Circles* 35: "But this looks like a death little workshop to me, run by...cool people." ("Death" is a term of high praise in the South Bronx.) **1984** Mason & Rheingold *Slanguage: Death* n./adj. Gorgeous person...."She's death." **1985** N. George et al. *Fresh* 22: The rapper tells you how pretty he is, how well he loves, how "bad" he dresses, how "death" his rapping and scratching are. **1988** Univ. Tenn. student theme: "Death"...means the same as "bad," that something is favorable to a person.

death seat *n.* [because a person in this seat is the most likely to be killed if the vehicle is hit while making a left-hand turn across traffic or runs off the road into an obstruction] the right front seat of a passenger car. Mostly *Joc.*
[**1933** Stewart *Airman Speech* 58: *Death Chair.* The appellation given to the front seat in old ships; a crash nearly always resulted in the motor's being projected back into the front cockpit.] **1962** *What Every Young Man Should Know* 41: Which is the Death Seat? **1978** R. Price *Ladies' Man* 110: I tossed my case in the rear and sat in the death seat. **1987–91** D. Gaines *Teenage Wasteland* 220: Heather is in the "death seat" place of honor.

death trip *n.* **1.** something considered to be lethally dangerous.
1967 Kornbluth *New Underground* 118: He is...doing up smack, doing your death trip super. **1978** S. King *Stand* 473: Rationalism....It's a death trip. **1986** Spears *Drugs & Drink* 137: *Death trips* L.S.D. mixed with Datura or some other drug.
2. a vivid fantasy about death, esp. for psychotherapeutic purposes.
1969 Gustaitis *Turning On* 319: It's a death trip. You see yourself in a coffin. **1971** S. Miller *Hot Springs* 67: Haven't you heard about the death trip?...We're all going to die on Sunday....We were all to spend the weekend preparing for death...and imagining that Sunday night we were to die.

Death Valley *n. Baseball.* deep center field in Yankee Stadium, N.Y.C. Now *hist.*
1978 in Lyle & Golenbock *Bronx Zoo* 164: He hit a ball 430 feet—

where it was caught by Amos Otis in the deepest part of Death Valley. **1984** *N.Y. Post* (Aug. 15) 76: Willie Randolph rapped a 410-foot Death Valley triple. **1992** N.Y.C. man, age 31 (coll. J. Sheidlower): I know I heard *Death Valley* for deep center in Yankee Stadium in the early 70's. Only old-timers would use it now, though; they redesigned the stadium and moved the fences in years ago.

death wish *n. Narc.* (see quot.).

1980 Pearl *Slang Dict.*: Death wish *n.* (Drug Culture) an hallucinogenic drug, originally used in veterinary medicine as a tranquilizer.

deb *n.* **1.** a debutante.

1920 (cited in *W10*). **1914–22* Joyce *Ulysses* 437 [ref. to 1904]: Josie Powell, that was, prettiest deb in Dublin. **1926** in *DA*. **1982** S.P. Smith *Officer & Gentleman* 46: I reckon you debs do talk, don't you? *Ibid.* 64: You better stop dreamin' about those Puget debs, Mayo. **1984** W. Gibson *Neuromancer* 154: You some kinda closet deb?

2. *Und.* a girlfriend of a member of a street gang; a girl who is a member of such a gang.

1946 *Amer. Mercury* (Apr.) 482: The "debutante" or "sub-deb" divisions are the girl friends of the senior boy members of some gangs. **1946** *Life* (Apr. 8) 89: A "deb" is a girl [gang] member who by a willingness to fight alongside the boys and, sometimes, sexual promiscuity has proved her worth. **1948** Lait & Mortimer *New York* 121: The Debs and Sub-debs are usually from 50 to 500 feet behind the warriors. **1949** Ellson *Tomboy* 2: Why isn't she like the rest of the debs in the gang, or any other girl? **1954** *Harper's Mag.* (Nov.) 36: *Debs:* gang members' girls. **1956** Ross *Hustlers* 20: The Debs with them began to giggle. **1957** Simmons *Corner Boy* 30: Girls who were debs for teen-age gangs wore berets…and sweaters. **1959** Dee Roo *Wolves* 63: Your deb's looking for you. **1966** S. Stevens *Go Down Dead* 23: Shirley & Jo Jo they is debs what belong to the Playboys. **1993** *Showbiz Today* (CNN-TV) (Mar. 11): Teenage Gang Debs [title of fanzine].

deball *v.* to castrate.—*usu.* considered vulgar.

1961 Forbes *Goodbye to Some* 82 [ref. to WWII]: The chute harness is too big. I don't want to be deballed. **1965** Hersey *Too Far to Walk*: Slit, gutted, de-balled, salted, and laid out to dry. **1987** Pedneau *A.P.B.* 284: Like a bull about to be deballed.

debbie *n.* DEB, 1.

1920 Fitzgerald *Paradise* 212: Tom…had outgrown the passion for dancing with…New Jersey debbies.

debug *v.* **1.** to eliminate faults from (a design or equipment). Now *colloq.*

1945 in *OEDS*. **1956** Heflin *USAF Dict.* 156: Debug, *v. tr.* To eliminate *bugs* from AF equipment. *Slang.* **1961** L.G. Richards *TAC* 234: The job of "debugging" a new aircraft from the first production model to squadron use. **1973** *Business Week* (May 19) 98: We went into the marketplace before we had the technology totally debugged.

2. to remove clandestine listening devices from. Now *S.E.*

1970 *WNWD*: Debug…(Slang) to find and remove hidden electronic listening devices from (a room, building, etc.). **1974** *U.S. News & W.R.* (May 6) 8: So many members of Congress are asking Capitol police to scrutinize their offices for electronic eavesdropping devices that plans are afoot to train and equip a special "debugging" squad of six officers. **1987** Univ. Tenn. instructor: Now they're going to spend millions to debug the new [U.S.] embassy in Moscow.

dece *adj. Stu.* excellent. Also **dees.**

1979 in *RHD* files: Dece. **1987** *RHD2*: Dece…great, wonderful. Also, *dees.* **1990** *Mystery Sci. Theater* (Comedy Central TV): "Then I'm gonna give her a kiss." "Dece!"

decent *adj. Stu.* excellent.

1969 *Current Slang* I & II 25: Decent, *adj.* Very appealing.—Air Force Academy cadets. **1968–70** *Current Slang* III & IV 35: Decent, *adj.* Good…(understatement).—College students…New Hampshire.— "What did you get on that exam?" "A." "*Decent.*" **1987** *RHD2*. **1990** P. Dickson *Slang!* 215: Decent. Excellent. **1990** *Mystery Sci. Theater* (Comedy Central TV): Colombian! Decent!

deck *n.* **1.a.** Orig. *Naut.* the floor or ground.

*1836 *Spirit of Times* (Feb. 27) 15: You mustn't…keep rolling your eyes about the deck; and when people gets up and sits down, mind you get up and sits down, too. **1899** Cullen *Tales* 54: Nine has now got the deck. Nine, shoot it out. **1918** Kauffman *Navy at Work* 199: Though he falls on a country road out of sight of the sea, he "hits the deck." **1921* *N & Q* (Dec. 24) 502 [ref. to WWI]: *Deck (off the).* Leaving the ground. **1942** *Leatherneck* (Nov.) 144: Deck—Any floor. **1946** Veiller *Killers* (film): You were on the deck when the bell rang. **1947** Boyer *Dark Ship* 155: Everybody'll get a chance who wants to take the deck

[to speak]. **1952** Ellson *Golden Spike* 102: I might beat you flat to the deck. **1958** in Loosbrock & Skinner *Wild Blue* 231: Good luck! See you on the deck. **1976** C.R. Anderson *Grunts* 26: Keep your head and ass close to the deck, Sweetheart—Ha! **1978** Hasford *Short-Timers* 12: I collide with the sandy deck.

b. *Av.* the surface of land or water; (*also*) minimum altitude. Now *S.E.*

1942 *Yank* (Sept. 30) 3: When I say "on deck" I mean it—our planes were skimming…only 10 feet over the water. **1946** G.C. Hall, Jr. *1000 Destroyed* 62: The two fighters were flat-out on the deck, down by the railroad track, the German on the American's tail, firing. **1964** Newhafer *Tallyho* 168: Go in on the deck at max speed. **1965** LeMay & Kantor *Mission* 56: We flew awhile, and the next thing I knew we were right down on the deck. (In old AC parlance, that doesn't mean we were actually *on* the ground; it means merely that we were still flying, but too close to the planet Earth for comfort.) **1971** Cameron *First Blood* 22: We're going in, three hundred feet above the deck. **1978** in Higham & Williams *Combat Aircraft* 16: The first 60 miles outbound were "on the deck" at full power. **1986** Cogan *Top Gun* 88: The hard deck for this hop was ten thousand feet. **1991** K. Douglass *Viper Strike* 10: The ROEs for the op established a hard deck of ten thousand feet, a lower limit below which they were not allowed to fly.

2. *Theat.* a stage.

1942 *ATS* 578. **1984** J. Green *Newspeak* 65.

3. [fr. *deck* 'a pack of playing cards'] **a.** *Narc.* an envelope or packet of narcotics.

1916 *New Republic* (Apr. 22) 314: One of the number produces a "deck" or "package" of heroin and tells the others that the taking of it is wonderfully enjoyable. **1917** Depew *Gunner* 97: Gimme a deck of the stuff. Dope out the coke, Doc, dope out the old coke. **1921** in E. Murphy *Black Candle* 214: We would call these "decks," but some people call them "bindles." **1922** in *ibid.* 52: Cocaine is usually retailed in small paper packages about the size and shape of a postage stamp. These are called "decks" and contain a couple of "sniffs." **1923** Fishman & Perlman *Crucibles* 122: A "deck" is a small package of opium, a "stem" is a pipe. **1925** McAlmon *Silk Stockings* 22: A German boy…took her aside, to sell her cocaine.…We decided to invest in a deck each. **1925** in Moriarty *True Confessions* 24: I can fix you up with a coupla decks of morphine. **1929** *Chi. Tribune* (Oct. 11) 14: A package of drug wrapped in paper is called a "deck," a "check," or a "bundle." If it is in a capsule it is called a "berry," a "bean" or a "cap." **1955** Q. Reynolds *HQ* 275: They may cache their decks of heroin within the inner tube of the spare tire. **1963** *Sat. Eve. Post* (July 27) 74: Lipscomb first asked him to get him a "deck" of heroin about six months ago. **1966** Samuels *People vs. Baby* 4: She usually needed three or four decks of horse. **1983** Sturz *Wid. Circles* 31: They've got decks of heroin in their shopping bags.

b. a pack (of cigarettes).

1923 in W.F. Nolan *Black Mask Boys* 53: I…killed nearly a double deck of butts. **1942** *ATS* 128: Package of cigarettes…*deck.* **1950** Spillane *Vengeance* 21: I slid my deck of Luckies across the table to him. **1958** J.B. West *Eye* 15: I…picked up a fresh deck of Luckies. **1971** Allen *Getting Even* 104: I opened a deck of Luckies and a pack of gum. **1977** Berry *Kaiser* 85: "Do you have any Lucky Strikes?"…"Sure, boys, here you are," and he gave both men a deck. **1978** *Nat. Lampoon* (July) 66: Deck of Luckies with a couple of sticks of [marijuana] inside.

c. *Narc.* several marijuana cigarettes.

1943 *Time* (July 19) 54: "Gimme an ace" (meaning one reefer), "a deuce" (meaning two), or "a deck" (meaning a large number).

¶ In phrases:

¶ **fuck the deck** *USMC.* to perform push-ups on command.—*usu.* considered vulgar.

1983 Ehrhart *VN-Perkasie* 32 [ref. to 1966]: Fuck the deck, piggy!…Push-ups!

¶ **have only fifty cards in (one's) deck** to be stupid or crazy. Cf. *not playing with a full deck*, below.

1929 Hammett *Dain Curse* 256: How do you figure her—only fifty cards to her deck? **1929–33** Farrell *Young Manhood* 223: Say, that punk has only got fifty cards in his deck. **1949** Algren *Golden Arm* 42: "There's only fifty cards in your deck tonight, honey" Frankie reproached her gently. "I think you got a little repercussion again today."

¶ **hit the deck, 1.** Orig. *Navy & USMC.* to jump out of bed, as at reveille; wake up.

1917 *Marines Mag.* (Oct.) 23: Come on! Hit the Deck! It's 4 o'clock. **1918** *Stars & Stripes* (Aug. 30) 7: Hey lad—reveille! Hit th' deck! **1919** Cober *Btry. D* 38: The gun squads "hit the deck" at 4 A.M. **1920** *Our*

Navy (Mar.) 37: Show a leg! Hit th' deck! **1928** Nason *Sgt. Eadie* 18 [ref. to 1917]: Get up!…Hit the deck! **1928** Wharton *Squad* 13 [ref. to 1918]: Come up, you guys, hit th' deck, th' day's on! **1952** Uris *Battle Cry* 30: "Hit the deck!" The light went on. **1964** *Flintstones* (ABC-TV): Come on, Tubby, hit the deck, rise and shine!

2. Orig. *Navy & USMC.* to get going; get busy.

1924 Anderson & Stallings *What Price Glory?* 91 [ref. to 1918]: You win. Hit the deck. **1928** Wilstach *Motion Picture Sl.* (unp.): *Hit the deck!* means it is lunch hour, or quitting time at night. **1942** *Leatherneck* (Nov.) 146: Hit-the-Deck.—Get ready for action. **1964** Pearl *Stockade* 71: If he starts acting up again…you boys better hit the deck. "Cause I ain't tolerating any more of his rampages."

3. Orig. *USMC.* to throw oneself to the ground for protection.

1925 Thomason *Fix Bayonets!* 121 [ref. to 1918]: Boche! Hit the deck! **1957** Yordan *Men in War* (film): Hit the deck! Take cover! **1957** in Vallee *Anatomy of a Phenomenon* 136: I jumped out and hit the deck as the thing passed directly over the truck with a great sound and a rush of wind. **1966** Adler *Vietnam Letters* 21: Bullets started sailing through the air around us so we hit the deck. **1969** *Playboy* (Mar.) 43: "Hit the deck," the terrified dentist cried, not knowing who was shooting into his house or why.

4. Orig. *Navy.* to lie down to sleep.

*1935 W. de la Mare, in *Proc. Brit. Acad.* XXI 247: He hit the deck; he slung his hammock; he went to bed; he retired for the night; [etc.]…they all signify much the same thing. **1942** *Good Housekeeping* (Dec.) 11 (caption): What every soldier does every night, gladly. He calls it: Hitting the deck—Haying it—Bunk Fatigue—20 winks. **1961** Burgess *Dict. Sailing* 115: Hit the deck. Take an upper-deck siesta. **1977** Univ. Tenn. grad. student: I'm tired. I'm going to hit the deck.

5. *Av.* to descend rapidly to a low altitude.

1956 Heflin *USAF Dict.* 252: *To hit the deck*…to come down to a low or minimum altitude.

¶ **not playing with a full deck** crazy or extremely foolish. Also vars. Cf. *have only fifty cards in (one's) deck*, above.

1968–70 *Current Slang* III & IV 93: *Playing with a full deck of cards*, v. To evidence high intelligence…—College males…New Hampshire. **1972** Wambaugh *Blue Knight* 164: That broad…ain't got a full deck even now. **1972** Beech-Nut Gum TV commercial (June): Anybody playin' with a full deck'd take Beech-Nut, right? **1973** *Penthouse* (Aug.) 38: People who gain sexual gratification from such an ordeal are not playing the game with a full deck. **1974** Blount *3 Bricks Shy* 5: Being three bricks shy of a load…is comparable to playing with less than a full deck. **1976** Price *Bloodbrothers* 117: I swear she wasn't playin' with a full deck, you know? **1977** Bunker *Animal Factory* 128: He's…schizoid. He's lost some cards from the deck lately. **1978** W. Brown *Tragic Magic* 32: Anybody that laughs behind gettin' the shit slapped out of em definitely ain't dealin' with a full deck. **1981** Ballenger *Terror* 139: You've got to be playing with a short deck to even think of such a stupid thing. **1988** Dietl & Gross *One Tough Cop* 33: Nobody with a full deck thinks he can get away with it. **1994** *N.Y. Times* (Jan. 21) A 13: They are like children and neither one plays with a whole deck.

¶ **on deck, 1.** *Baseball.* scheduled to bat next; (*specif.*) waiting near home plate to bat. Now *S.E.*

1867 in *DA*: Well, I went on deck and took up a bat. **1881** *N.Y. Herald* (Aug. 23) (cited in Nichols, *Baseball Term.*). **1886** Nye *Remarks* 197: Where glory waited, there you would always find Arnold Winkelreid at the bat, and William Tell on deck. **1893** *Funk & Wagnalls Stand. Dict.* 476: On deck…standing next in batting order.

2. alive.

1873 in Miller & Snell *Why West Was Wild* 208: The readers of the *Democrat*…will be glad to learn from his own pen that he is still "on deck." **1888** Pierson *Slave of Circumstances* 111: He thinks I'm dead…If he knew I was still on deck, it 'ud spoil some of his sleep o' nights. **1889** in *DAE*: Ex-Sheriff A. H. Moore…was kicked by a horse, a cow and a colt, and has had numerous other mishaps happen to him, but is still on deck. **1901** Irwin *Sonnets* (unp.): Vanity is still on deck/And humble virtue gets it in the neck.

3. present and in readiness; available; (*imper.*) come here at once!

1878 *Nat. Police Gaz.* (Apr. 24) 6: The "joint" is interviewed by a special "dittal," a divy is arranged and the squealer is not on deck when the case is called. **1881** in Saunders *Parodies of Whitman* 31: I am all on deck! Come and loaf with me! **1882** Field *Tribune Primer* 45: One of the Lungs takes a Rest while the Other runs the Shop. One of them is always On Deck all of the Time. **1884** *Life* (Jan. 31) 63: Whoop-la, pard! I'm all on deck! **1928** J.M. March *Set-Up* 57: Third bout!…Mun-

sey on deck! **1947** *Merrie Melodies* (animated cartoon): Hey, Smokey! On deck! **1958** J. King *Pro Football* 115: The Detroit Lions obviously could not have won the NFL title with Layne hurt, if Rote hadn't been on deck. **1984** Caunitz *Police Plaza* 60: "On deck," Malone said into the mike. *Ibid.* 300: I'm on the way. Who's on deck?

4. scheduled.

1885 *Puck* (Apr. 8) 83: What's on deck this aft?

deck[1] *v.* [prob. of Romani orig.; cf. DEEK, DICK[2] *n.*, DICK[1], *v.*] *Und.* to see; look at.

1859 Matsell *Vocab.* 35: "*Deck the gage,*" see the man.

deck[2] *v.* **1.** *Hobo.* to ride illicitly on the roof of (a freight car).—also constr. with *it*.

1894 in J. London *Tramp Diary* 35: Two of us jumped the palace cars and decked them while the third went underneath on the rods. **1907** London *Road* 19 [ref. to 1892]: Following Bob's advice, I immediately "decked her," that is, climbed up on the top of the roof of one of the mail-cars. **1907** in Bruns *Kts. of Road* 38: I'll take the third blind and deck her. **1925** Mullin *Scholar Tramp* 7: I had "decked a cannon-ball on the fly"—and from the middle of the train, too! **1929** Hotstetter & Beesley *Racket* 223: *Deck*—To ride on top of, *e.g.* "Deck a Rattler." **1937** Reitman *Box-Car Bertha* 24: They had decked a Pullman on the fastest passenger train, climbing up on top while it waited in the station. *Ibid.* 33: You'll have to ride the bumpers or deck it.

2. *Und.* (see quot.).

1928 Callahan *Grim Justice* 54: I could stem them, or punch them, or deck them…."Decking"…means drilling through the top of the safe.

3. to knock (a person) down; floor.

1945 Huie *Omaha to Oki.* 99: I goosed one of them big Russian broads, and she *decked* me! **1952** Uris *Battle Cry* 205 [ref. to 1942]: Use your football training, play rough, gouge his eyes, kick his nuts, deck him and finish him. **1957** M. Shulman *Rally* 252: He was forced…to deck quite a number of prominent citizens. **1960** Wohl *Cold Wind* 183: Why'd you deck Frankie? **1961** J.A. Williams *Night Song* 48: An hour after it happened, Eagle was laughing about it, telling how he had "decked that cat." **1961** Brosnan *Pennant Race* 196: Larry Sherry had decked Robinson with a fast ball. **1962** Quirk *Red Ribbons* 96: If you lay a hand on her, I'll deck you. **1967** *Look* (Nov. 14) 116: He decked John with one punch right to the chest. **1968** P. Roth *Portnoy* 97: And slug her if you have to! Deck her, Jake! **1968** G. Edwards *Urban Frontier* 31: That's the way we teach them respect. Now I'll pick one for you and you deck him. **1969** A. Hoffman, in Hoffman, Seale, et al. *Conspiracy* 57: Don McNeil…got decked real bad [by police] in Grand Central Station. **1971** *Nichols* (NBC-TV): My son here gives you any salt, deck 'im. **1972** *Rookies* (ABC-TV): If he doesn't get off my back, I'll deck him. **1993** *TV Guide* (Jan. 16) 19: Doherty allegedly decked a fellow dance-floor diva.

4. to press (a gas pedal) to the floor.

1961 Ellison *Gentleman Junkie* 134: He decked the gas pedal and fed all the power he had to the engine.

5. to copulate with (a woman).

1968 Radano *Walking the Beat* 49: I made up my mind I was going to deck her that night…Well, to make a long story short I take her to her joint and I deck her. She was good.

6. *Naut.* to work as a deckhand.

1977 in Curry *River's in My Blood* 135: I was deckin' on a boat and we were double-trippin'. **1979–82** Gwin *Overboard* 57: Decking was probably too heavy a job for a woman.

deckaneer *n. Naut.* a deckhand or roustabout.

1840 in *DA*.

deck ape *n. Navy.* a deckhand; (*Mil.*) a sailor. Cf. DECK MONKEY.

[**1942** *Leatherneck* (Nov.) 144: *Deck-Ape*—A man who sweeps and swabs the floor.] **1944** Kendall *Service Slang* 21: A deck ape is a seaman. **1946** S. Wilson *Voyage* 47 [ref. to WWII]: Come on, you deck apes, let's get this mess cleaned up. **1951** Morris *China Station* 252: Some, the "deck apes," entered the unceasing toil of the gunnery divisions. **1952** Uris *Battle Cry* 101 [ref. to 1942]: Say, deck ape. I'm really sorry. **1964** Howe *Valley of Fire* 57: They teach you deck apes all that in boot camp? **1964** McKenna *Martha* 120: First tell me how come you picked being a snipe instead of a deck ape. **1966** Noel & Bush *Naval Terms* 117: Deck hand…Slang: swab jockey, deck ape. **1971** *U.S. Naval Proceedings* (Jan.) 69 [ref. to 1930]: Marines were assigned to Navy duties as signalmen, radiomen, deck apes, and boat crews. **1971** Sheehan *Arnheiter* 71: Belmonte's deck gang, the "deck apes" in nauticalese, were repeated objects of the captain's irritation. **1972** Pearce *Pier Head Jump* 121.

The *entire* crew. Not just the deck apes. **1974** E. Thompson *Tattoo* 257: Deck apes worked in *whites*, not dungarees. **1983–86** G.C. Wilson *Supercarrier* 42: The deck force…the "deck apes." **1990** *Newsweek* (Apr. 9) 8: *Deck ape*: A boatswain's mate who works abovedeck.

deckaroo *n. Naut.* a deckhand.

1937 C.B. Davis *Anointed* 102: We were a couple of deckaroos off a freighter. **1942** *ATS* 734. **1965** E. Hall *Flotsam* 279: With the enemy on the run, the deckaroos came running, ostensibly to our rescue.

deck dud *n. Naval Av.* (see quot.).

1969 Cagle *Naval Av. Guide* 392: *Deck Dud* An airplane, readied and manned for flight, which is unable to be launched.

decked[1] *adj.* [prob. past ppl. of DECK[1]] *Und.* guarded by a watchman.

1919 *Am. Leg. Wkly.* (Sept. 12) 8: See if it is decked, bugged, or under the Eye's protection. **1925** (cited in Partridge *Dict. Und.* 181).

decked[2] *adj.* asleep or unconscious from the effects of alcohol or narcotics.—also constr. with *out*.

1961 Ellison *Memos* 102: Pooch caught sight of Mustard, half decked-out with a reefer in his jaw…They…dragged him to his feet. **1974** *TULIPQ* (coll. B.K. Dumas): Drunk…plastered, decked.

deckhand *n.* **1.** a menial laborer, esp. a domestic worker.

1903 A.H. Lewis *Boss* 199: The next day one of th' deck hands will come to see me. I'll turn him down; th' Chief of Tammany don't deal with deck hands. **1908** Sullivan *Criminal Slang* 8: *Deckhand*—A domestic. **1926** Finerty *Criminalese* 17: *Deckhand*—A domestic.

2. *Theat.* a stagehand.

1937 *AS* (Dec.) 317: *Deckhand*. Stagehand. **1984** J. Green *Newspeak* 65.

deckie *n. Naut.* a deckhand.

*1913 in *OEDS*. **1922** *Amer. Leg. Wkly.* (Oct. 6) 8: The Deckies were led…by a boatswain's mate. **1979–82** Gwin *Overboard* 67: A small crowd of deckies and rigrats.

deck monkey *n. Naut.* a deckhand. Cf. DECK APE.

1941 *AS* (Oct.) 164: *Deck Monkeys*. Deck crew of Army Mine Planter. **1972** Pearce *Pier Head Jump* 46: You and the Second Mate go down and help those deck monkeys swing the lifeboat out.

deck swab *n. Naut.* a deckhand.

1906 Ford *Shorty McCabe* 236: It is, eh, you wall-eyed deck swab? **1908** J. London *M. Eden* 31: A deck-swab like him. **1937** C.B. Davis *Anointed* 198: It ain't anybody but a long-legged deck swab.

deck-walloper *n. Naut.* a deckhand.

1841 [Mercier] *Man-of-War* 280: Now, Mr. Deckwolloper [*sic*], she is from the port she *left last.* *ca*1856 in Whipple *Whaler* 81: William Henry Royce, Second Officer…Too ignorant to catch a bow-head, and afraid as death of a right whale. Would make a good deck walloper…Charles Bushnell, Third Officer…Would make a good blubber room hand. **1943** *Yank* (Mar. 5) 9: As a deck-walloper on the Staten Island ferry.

decon *n.* decontamination.—often used attrib.

1986 *Daily Beacon* (Univ. Tenn.) (July 15) 6: Check your equipment! Make sure all the seals on your decon suits are tight.

decorate *v.* **1.** to lay money on a bar or table, as to pay for drinks or as a wager; usu. in phr. **decorate the mahogany.**

1908 in H.C. Fisher *A. Mutt* 29: Decorate!…Now kick in with the rest of it. **1912** T.A. Dorgan, in *N.Y. Eve. Jour.* (July 6) 8: Come back and decorate the mahogany. **1922** *Amer. Leg. Wkly.* (Jan. 20) 23: All hands had to "decorate the mahogany" as the phrase was put. **1926** Maines & Grant *Wise-Crack Dictionary* 7: *Decorate the mahogany*—Lay the money on the bar. **1930** "D. Stiff" *Milk & Honey* 203: *Decorate the mahogany*—To buy the drinks. **1935** S. Kingsley *Dead End* II: I'll open fuh two….Come on, decorate da mahogany! **1950** *West. Folk.* IX 117: *Decorate the mahogany*. To gamble.

2. to give a black eye to; bruise or injure badly. *Joc.*

1919 Darling *Jargon Book* 10: *Decorate*—To give another a black eye or a cut face. **1952** H. Grey *Hoods* 84: So who decorated you so fancy, your mother-in-law? **1957** E. Brown *Locust Fire* 86: "Georgie got decorated in St. Louis," said Hannibal. "By a colonel's daughter."

3. *R.R.* (see 1934 quot.).

1931 *Writer's Dig.* (May) 41: *Decorate*—The act of riding on top of freight cars as required on mountains or passing stations on certain railroads. **1934** Weseen *Dict. Slang* 69: *Decorate*—To ride on top of a freight car. **1945** Hubbard *R.R. Ave.* 93: A peremptory call for "down brakes!"—the signal for trainmen to "deckorate and tie 'em down" (Walk the freight-car tops, or decks, and set hand brakes). *Ibid.* 339:

Deckorate—Get out on top of freight cars to set hand brakes or receive or transmit signals. Derived from *deck*.

deduction *n.* [because dependent children are among federal income-tax deductions] a small child. *Joc.*

1962 T. Berger *Reinhart* 97: Go get your ball and chain and your deductions, if they haven't been eaten up by the vermin in this dump.

deed *n.* ¶ In phrase: **do the deed** [euphem.] *Stu.* to engage in coitus. See also *do the dirties* s.v. DIRTY.

1969 *Esquire* (Aug.) 71 [ref. to 1950's]: Does she put out?…Do the deed? **1976** Conroy *Santini* 296: Oh boy, I'll tell you about the first time I did the evil deed with ol' Ansley. **1992** *Simpsons* (Fox-TV): I did the deed with Uta. **1993** Danoff *Superpotency* 13: I was just about to do the deed when my dick…folded up like an umbrella.

deedee[1] var. D.D.

deedee[2] var. DIDI.

deedonc var. DIDONK.

deejay see DJ.

deek *n.* [prob. fr. the v.; cf. DICK[2], *n.*] *Und.* a detective, police officer, or watchman.

1933 Ersine *Pris. Slang* 31: *Deek, n.* A detective. **1946** Severeid *Wild Dream* 42 [ref. to 1934]: Cities were judged on the basis of their citizens' generosity with handouts and the temperament of the railway "deeks" who guarded the freight yards. **1982** Auletta *Underclass* 110: The regulars had long since recognized them as "deeks"—street slang for cops.

deek *v.* [prob. < E Romani *dik* 'to look, see'; see DICK[1], *v.*] *Und.* to see; look at. [The Scots exx., while synonymous, do not represent slang usage.]

[***1784** in *SND*: Slee Ægle deek'd her lover cumin'.] [***1825** Jamieson *Scot. Dict.:* To deek…To spy out, to descry. I deekit him, I descried him, Lanarks[hire].] **1859** Matsell *Vocab.* 25: *Deek The Cove*. See the fellow; look at him. **1964** *AS* (Oct.) 280: *Deek*, v.t. To notice. [In use in Boonville, Calif.]

deemer *n.* **1.** Esp. *Carnival.* a dime.

1926 Maines & Grant *Wise-Crack Dict.* 7: *Deemer*—Dime. **1927** *AS* (June) 390: A dime is a *deemer*. **1930** Lait *On the Spot* 202: *Deemer*…Dime. **1935** *Amer. Mercury* (June) 229: *Deemer*: a dime [among carnival workers]. **1939** *AS* (Oct.) 239: *Deemer*…a dime tip. *ca*1940 in Botkin *Treas. Amer. Folk.* 536: It'd put a deemer extra on his time slip. **1953** Gresham *Midway* 24 [ref. to 1918]: But the best thing with Wonderland was an annex—a dime extra in those days, what we called a "deemer" show. **1968** Beck *Trick Baby* 12: If I…played Santa Claus to my last deemer.

2. (see quot.).

1938 *AS* (Apr.) 156: *Deemer*. Referring to ten—as a number or size.

3. *Restaurant.* a patron who leaves a dime tip.

1939 *AS* (Oct.) 239: *Deemer*. One who tips a dime. **1954** Collans & Sterling *House Detect.* 219: *Deemer*. One who gives dimes as gratuities.

deep end see s.v. END.

deep freeze *n.* **1.** a place of incarceration; a prison or jail.

1958 Chandler *Playback* 62: Even if the cops didn't grab him and toss him into the deep freeze.

2. an ostracism; (*also*) a position of marginality.

1966 B. Cassiday *Angels Ten* 53 [ref. to WWII]: The Deep Freeze…involved isolating a man by not talking to him…[or] associating with him. **1974** *Business Week* (Jan. 12) 15: "We're in the deep freeze, but not yet in the deep six," says one of the lonely band of 11 professionals still serving on the National Commission on Productivity. **1975** *L.A. Times* (Oct. 31) II 5: There is no reason to believe that Franco's deep freeze of political life did anything to alter the fact that excess is the distinguishing mark of the Spanish spirit. **1980** Pearl *Slang Dict.: Deep freeze, n.* (Politics) a disdainful treatment; ostracism, particularly of a former ally.

deepie *n. Film.* a three-dimensional motion picture.

*1953, 1954 in *OEDS*.

deep pockets *n.pl.* an inexhaustible source of revenues; abundance of money. Also sing.

1976 *Business Week* (Nov. 1) 64: Loews was a new, deep pocket. **1976** (cited in *W10*). **1977** *Wash. Post*, in *Barnhart Dict. Comp.* V 11: He knows all his alumni with the big bucks and those deep pockets are watchin' and they'd be mighty upset to lose to us. **1984** *U.S. News & W.R.* (Dec. 3) 63: For those with deep pockets, Neiman-Marcus has a handmade, wooden desk...for $65,000. **1991** *N.Y. Times* (June 23) III 1: Boeing officials say they are competing not just against a company—but against the deep pockets of the French, German, British and Spanish governments.

deep sea *n*. Army. (see quot.).
1940 Simonsen *Soldier Bill* 11 [ref. to 1914]: Bill learned at his first meal that "java" meant coffee and "punk," bread; "deep sea" meant stew; "hash with overcoats," meant meat balls with pie crust around them; "slum" meant a thick meat stew.

deep-sea turkey *n*. *Mil.* salmon. *Joc.*
1921 *DN* V 111: *Deep-sea turkey, n.* Salmon....Navy, and army. **1923** McKnight *Eng. Words* 56 [ref. to 1918]: *Gold fish* and *deep sea turkey* for "salmon."

deep six *n*. **1.** *Navy.* the act of being sunk to the bottom of the sea.—usu. constr. with *give* or *get*. [The orig. sense is often alleged to be 'burial at sea', and although this is not improbable no early documentation is available.]
1919 *Our Navy* (May) 39: As usual the balance of the crew did all in their power to save the crew and chaser, but it was too late for the chaser so they took the "Deep Six." **1930** Buranelli *Maggie* 50 [ref. to 1918]: "We nearly got the 'deep six' all right," one of the *May*'s crew signalled. **1945** in *Calif. Folk. Qly.* V (1946) 381: A *honey barge* gets *the deep six.* **1949** Daves *Task Force* (film): Made fast landing. And in for a deep six. **1953** Dibner *Deep Six* 105: You drop dead out here and they give you the deep six. I ain't ending up on the bottom of this frigging cold sea. **1958** Gay *Run Silent* (film): You've just given a Jap tin can the deep six in thirty-three seconds. **1967** Dibner *Admiral* 230: He also gave...the deep six to a shipful of men. **1974** *Everett* (Wash.) *Herald* (Feb. 23) (Panorama) 26: There was the young kayaker...who tried for Japan...and got maybe as far north as Umatilla Reef when he took the deep six.
2. Orig. *Navy.* a toss overboard; (*hence*) the act of being discarded, disposed of, rejected, or the like.
1929 Bowen *Sea Slang* 58: *Given the Deep Six, to be.* To be heaved overboard. **1937** Thompson *Take Her Down* 69 [ref. to 1918]: Within a few months all hands had heaved those outfits overboard—"given them the deep six," in navy parlance. **1943** *Destination Tokyo* (film): Give that gear the deep six. **1944** Kendall *Service Slang* 23: *Give it the deep six*...toss overboard. **1947** *West. Folk.* VI (1947) 161 [ref. to WWII]: Papers thrown in the wastebasket are *given the deep six*, or filed in the *circular file.* **1980** *N.Y. Daily News* (Sept. 9) (Inside Manhattan) 2: My advice is to give Mr. Hot Pants the deep six. *a*1986 in *World Book Dict.*: In the Navy Department...the wastebasket is referred to as the Deep Six.
3. the grave; death and burial, esp. at sea; usu. in phr. **give (someone) the deep six** to kill. [Perh. the orig. sense if the customary six-foot depth of the grave is alluded to; cf. note at (1), above.]
1929 Gill *Und. Slang: Deep six*—Grave. **1942** *ATS* 132: Grave...*deep six.* **1944** Burley *Harlem Jive* 42: When thou hast been stashed/In thy deep six. *Ibid.* 136: *Deep six*—A grave. **1957** T. Williams *Orpheus* 18: "I don't think half as many married men have committed suicide...as the Coroner says..."..."You think it's their wives that give them the deep six?" **1963** Braly *Shake Him* 139: A lot of them hit the deep six. **1965** Longstreet *Sportin' House* 140: If they had to take the deep six [death in a grave] they'd just as leave be found in bed with a whore and doing what a man seems to want more than anything else when he feels Ol' Scratch is at his heels. **1980** Eble *Campus Slang* (Oct.) 7: *Take the deep six*—Die (usually said jokingly): "If I hadn't gotten out of the way of that car, I would have taken the deep six." **1983** Ehrhart *VN-Perkasie* 135: Kablooie! Deep six.
4. the depths of the sea.
1962 Robinson *Barbara* 98 [ref. to WWII]: If you're worryin' about launchin' those tanks of yours into the deep six, forget about it. We're taking you in.

deep-six *v.* **1.** *Navy & USMC.* to toss overboard. [1949 quot. is in a nautical context, and it seems likely that it refers to this, rather than the broader sense.]
1949 *N.Y. Times* (Oct. 9) VI 54 (ad for Rose's Lime Juice): You mean I can "deep-six" this squeezer...? **1952** Cope & Dyer *Petty Officer's Guide* (gloss.): *Deep-six.* A term meaning dispose of by throwing over the side. **1959** Sterling *Wahoo* 62 [ref. to WWII]: Don't deep-six it...but somehow get it lost while I am Skipper. **1962** Bonham *War Beneath Sea* 87 [ref. to WWII]: Put the old exploder in a weighted bag and deep-six it. **1966** Noel *Naval Terms: Deep-six.* To throw an object away or over-

board. **1990** Cogill *When God Was a Sailor* 82: Anything that wasn't wanted was "deep-sixed" immediately. Davy Jones's locker must have been bulging.
2. Orig. *Navy & USMC.* **a.** to get rid of; drop.
1952 *U.S.M.C.* 2/Lt., in *Time* (Dec. 15) 4: I suggest...that you "deep six" such terminology as "gaudy" (Marine) uniforms. **1956** *AS* XXXI (Oct.) 190: *Deep-sixed*...Thrown out or disposed of...."get rid of." **1959** *Swinging Syllables: Deep-six:* Dispose of, get rid of. **1964** Peacock *Drill & Die* 221: But to see Holland get deep-sixed, and Bizal reign supreme, went beyond personal feelings. **1970–71** J. Rubinstein *City Police* 116: If it wasn't for that lieutenant going on the air, you know we'd deep six this one. **1974** in H.S. Thompson *Shark Hunt* 366: No sooner had the priest been deep-sixed than he unveiled another holy man. **1976–77** Kernochan *Dry Hustle* 133: Your mother...got Mister Wilder fired...She didn't let up until the school deep-sixed him. **1979** G. Wolff *Duke of Deception* 238 [ref. to 1960]: Only a couple of friends *took gas,* were *deep-sixed* from Princeton prematurely and against their wishes. **1987** *TV Guide* (Nov. 28) A- 12: A lovesick teen-ager...is mortified when his girl friend deep-sixes him for someone more popular.
b. to reject, negate, or abandon.
1954 *New Yorker* (Oct. 16) 44: "We must analyze....We must experiment. And we must deep-six." (Weaver served in the Navy...nowadays everyone...knows that "deep-six" is a nautical way of saying "abandon.") **1969** *Everett* (Wash.) *Herald* (Apr. 18) 2B: Rep. John O'Brien's predicted pitch for a super marine and airport authority...was deep-sixed yesterday by the House of Representatives. **1978** *Business Week* (Mar. 20) 126: Carter lost prestige and some of his "good guy" image when Congress deep-sixed the proposal. **1981** *Business Week* (Jan. 12) 121: Communications industry interests...are likely to deep-six any 1981 effort to rewrite the communications law. **1990** *Nation* (Mar. 5) 8: Gorbachev and the Central Committee deep-sixed Article Six.
3. Orig. *Navy & USMC.* to kill.
1957 Myrer *Big War* 156 [ref. to WWII]: Should have let her deepsix herself. **1959** in Russell *Perm. Playboy* 317: So you might as well have fun right up to the minute they deep-six you. **1972** B. Rodgers *Queens' Vernacular* 158: If one has been killed, he has been *deep-sixed.* **1977** Caputo *Rumor of War* 55 [ref. to 1965]: Jesus, if I'da been a couple inches the other way, I'da been deep-sixed sure as shit.
4. *Naut.* (of a ship) to sink.
1981 Ballenger *Terror* 59: If they leak, we have got nothing to keep us from deep-sixing.

deep-throat *n.* [fr. the title of the popular pornographic film *Deep Throat* (1973), in which this was demonstrated; see 1973 quot.] an act of accepting the penis into the throat during fellatio.
1973 *Deep Throat* (film): Like deep-throat....Have you ever taken a penis all the way down to the bottom of your throat? **1987** *Penthouse Letters* (Oct.) 54: If you don't want to give deep-throat, there's no way you possibly can without choking.

deep-throat *v.* to accept the penis of into the throat during fellatio. Also absol.
1979 *Playboy* (Aug.) 52: She proceeded to deep-throat me in about 15 seconds. **1981** *Nat. Lampoon* (Feb.) 51: All the other girls I've slept with can deep throat. **1986–89** Norse *Memoirs* 237: He deep-throated me.

deevy *adj.* [by alter.] divine; delightful. *Rare* in U.S.
*1900 in *OED2.* ***1905** in Partridge *DSUE* (ed. 8): "O Mums?...do look at this *sweet* little monkey...Isn't he deevie?" "Deevie" is, I believe, short for "divine" with certain sets. **1915** Howard *God's Man* 162: Oh, you absolutely must. It's too deevy...What a ripper! Topping. ***1930, *1942** in *OED2.*

def *adj.* [prob. < W Ind E pron. of *death* as intensifying adj. (see 1907 quot. and DEATH, *adj.*); deriv. fr. *definite* is less likely] *Rap Music.* splendid; superlative.
[**1907** in Cassidy & LePage *Dict. Jamaican Eng.*: "I never do him one def ting," a single thing. "Def" is emphatic, but is not a "swear-word."] **1979** "Sugar Hill Gang" in L.A. Stanley *Rap* 319: Drive off in a def OJ. **1980** W. Safire, in *N.Y. Times Mag.* (Jan. 18, 1981): *Deaf* [*sic*]...is the current superlative. **1982** in S. Hager *Hip Hop* 89: Another Def Bet. **1983** *N.Y. Daily News* (Mar. 25): Teentalk glossary...*def*—short for definite, excellent. **1984** S. Hager *Hip Hop* 109: *Def*—cool; okay; superior; short for "death." **1984** Toop *Rap Attack* 158: *Def*: an adjective used to describe anything that is unquestionably cool. **1988** R. Menllo & R. Rubin *Tougher Than Leather* (film): Up comes this big black-and-gold def Benz. *Ibid.* That's stupid, deffest. **1988** *Right On!* (June) 12: Rappers...use bits and pieces of...his hit songs to create def jams for

themselves. *Ibid.* 62: Heavy D is def. **1990** *Kid 'n' Play* (NBC-TV): You missed a def party at Play's house.

def *adv.* definitely; without question.

1942 *ATS* 25: *Def,* definitely. **1947** *Tomorrow* (Aug.) 28: But def! **1970** in L. Bangs *Psychotic Reactions* 36: Morrison, def, does not get a pie in the face! **1984** W. Gibson *Neuromancer* 134: They're def triff, huh?

defi or **defy** *n.* a defiant challenge.

1886 Lummis *Ft. Bowie* 68: About as pithy a *defi* as could be desired. **1897** *Harper's Mag.* (Jan.) 231: He sent out the last defy to the enemy in 1800. **1906** *Nat. Police Gaz.* (Mar. 24) 10: John L. Sullivan issues a defi to fight again. **1910** in Warren & Warren *Everybody Works* 70: It has been a custom of years' standing for the rival student bodies to offer a "defi" in support of their team in the great annual game. **1930** Lavine *3d Degree* 90: A Hip Sing was sent to paste, on a signboard, a defi to the On Leongs. **1933** S. Lowell *Gal Reporter* 15: I sent a defy back to the night sounds. **1978** *Gamblers* 104: Two rival ice-dealers..."hurled the defi" at each other—to use the then-current slang expression for a challenge.

definootly *adv.* definitely. *Joc.*

1985 Heywood *Taxi Dancer* 11: Defin-oot-ly not a Mig.

defunct *v.* to die. *Joc.*

1837 (quot. at KEEL UP, *v.*). **1846** Neal *Ploddy* 179: He gives me as much as I want now, and a great deal more when he defuncts riggler.

degenerate *n.* Esp. *Gamb.* one who gambles compulsively or is easily taken in by swindlers.

1942 Goldin et al. *DAUL: Degenerate* (Eastern Carnival). A fool; sucker....any...prospective swindle victim. **1970** in Cannon *Nobody Asked* 246: I know a cop who is a horse degenerate...He was in hock up to here. **1984** W. Murray *Dead Crab* 21: To him we were obviously horse degenerates. **1989** Cincinnati police detective, on *World News Tonight* (ABC-TV) (June 27): To me, it would be a degenerate if he bet this way.

dehorn *n.* **1.** *I.W.W.* **a.** a worker opposed to syndicalism.

1919 in Kornbluh *Rebel Voices* 270: The De-Horn's nose is deepest red. **1948** J. Stevens *Jim Turner* 211 [ref. to ca1910]: I know...you for a grayback bastard dehorn, a traitor to your fellow workers! *Ibid.* 216: I was...a dehorn and fink in her sight.

b. beliefs, attitudes, practices, or the like that blunt workers' desire for radical social change. Often attrib.

1927 *DN* V 444: *Dehorn, adj., v.* and *n.* Anything which tends to...[make] the worker forget the oppression of capital, is regarded as "dehorn." **1942** *AS* (Dec.) 221: *Dehorn*...Old-time Wobblies used the word to mean anything that diverted the worker's mind from the class struggle. **1948** J. Stevens *Jim Turner* 93 [ref. to ca1910]: Lay off that dehorn song!...The old dehorn! It's the stuff to disable the natural revolt in you and soften you into a dumb ox who'll toil along willin' in the yoke of the master class!

2. denatured or adulterated alcohol drunk in place of liquor; (*also*) a drink made from denatured or adulterated alcohol; (*broadly*) a drink cheap or bootlegged liquor. Also attrib.

1926 *Amer. Mercury* XXX (Apr.) 2: *Dehorn*...bootleg booze and its users. **1929** *AS* IV (June) 339: *Dee horn*—Denatured alcohol. **1933** Ersine *Prison Slang* 31: *Dehorn, n.* Canned heat, smoke. **1932–34** Minehan *Boy & Girl Tramps* 150: A filthy old drunk, full of dehorn moon. **1942** *AS* (Dec.) 221: *Dehorn.* Any kind of drinking liquor. **1944** Huie *Can Do!* 190: If you will add three fingers of paint-thinner to a small bottle of beer, you'll get a Dehorn that will blast the top of your head off. **1953–58** J.C. Holmes *Horn* 159: He lived on dehorn alcohol, mulligan, day-olds, misery.

3. (esp. among tramps) a derelict made chronically ill by the drinking of denatured or adulterated alcohol; (*hence*) a drunken tramp; drunkard. [The 1919 quot. at (**1.a.**) might possibly belong here.]

1926 (quot. at (**2.**), above). **1936** R. Adams *Cowboy Lingo* 229: A hard drinker, especially one who was inclined to fight while drunk, was sometimes called a "dehorn." **1965** Wallace *Skid Row* 204: *Dehorn*—one who does not drink anything but non-beverage alcohol. Also, *rubby-dub.* **1968** Spradley *Drunk* 141: Many other discrediting labels such as "you wino son-of-a-bitch," "ding bat," "fucking dehorn," "drunken bum,"...were among those reported by the informants. **1976** Hayden *Voyage* 655: Deadbeats and dehorns, mostly, hired for a dollar a day.

dehorn *v.* **1.** to denature or adulterate (alcohol).

1958 McCulloch *Woods Words* 46: *Dehorn*...To water down alcohol,

particularly if it is bad. **1980** Bruns *Kts. of Road* 193: Decrepit bums puking on dehorned alcohol.

2. [cf. HORNY] to render sexually impotent; deprive of sexual desire.

1953 in Randolph *Pissing in Snow* 36: Maybe some of the young fellows has not been dehorned yet.

3. *Mil.* (see quot.).

1956 Heflin *USAF Dict.* 159: *Dehorn, v. tr.* To defuse a bomb. Slang.

dehorner *n.* DEHORN, 3.

1958 McCulloch *Woods Words* 46: *Dehorners*—Thirsty guys who would drink canned heat or anything else that smelled like alcohol.

Deke *n. Stu.* a member of the Delta Kappa Epsilon fraternity.

1871 Bagg *Yale* 138: DKE men are often called "Deaks" by the others, but as this word is somewhat akin to an epithet it is not employed in their presence...Similarly, in sophomore year, Beta Xi men are called "Dead Beats," or simply "Beats." **1936** Levin *Old Bunch* 161: Have those Dekes got any option on all the hot stuff? **1947** Mailer *Naked & Dead* 188: A Cornell man, a Deke, a perfect asshole. **1963** D. Tracy *Brass Ring* 18: Wick [was] a Deke at Wallington. **1972** *Nat. Lampoon* (Dec.) 33: A "Deke" House complete with..."brew blasts."

deke *n.* **1.** *Hunting.* a decoy.

1950 Hemingway *Across River* 6: I offered to put the dekes out with him.

2. *Sports.* a feint made to deceive a player and draw him out of position. Also as *v.*

1960 *Time* (Can. ed.) in *Dict. Canadianisms*: Moore is one of the league's best players in the split-second art of faking a goalie out of position...."It's a kind of fake shot—we call them 'deeks' for decoys." **1971** *New Yorker*, in *BDNE3*: He gave them...a fantastic series of dekes....They crashed into each other and knocked each other down. **1977** *Webster's Sports Dict.* 111: *Deke* To fake an opponent out of position. **1984** J. Green *Newspeak* 66. **1991** *New Yorker* (Dec. 9) 109: Knoblauch and...Gagne feinted a force-play peg to second—the trifling everyday deke maneuver, without the ball, that once or twice in a month will make a careless base runner pause.

delayer *n. R.R.* a train dispatcher.

1942 *Sat. Eve. Post* (June 13) 27: Dispatchers are "delayers."

Delhi belly *n. Mil.* diarrhea or dysentery contracted in India. *Joc.* Cf. GYPPY TUMMY.

1944 *Newsweek* (Feb. 28) 76: He got "Delhi belly" (a form of dysentery). **1945** *AS* (Feb.) 77: "Delhi Belly," the name given by our troops in India to a form of dysentery. **1958** Craven & Cate *AAF in WWII* VII 448 [ref. to 1944]: Afflictions like malaria, dengue fever, scrub typhus, diarrhea and dysentery ("Karachi Crouch," "Delhi Belly"). **1977** *L.A. Times* (Aug. 24) IV 1: Where else can one get hepatitis, jungle rot, and Delhi-belly, all in one convenient package?

delink *n.* a juvenile delinquent.

1959 in A. Sexton *Letters* 57: I failed most things. (a real juvenile delink).

delish *adj.* delicious.

***1920** in *OEDS*. **1927** Mayer *Between Us Girls* 173: They are actually delish. **1948** McIlwaine *Memphis* 381: They were simply delish. **1948** in M. Shulman *Dobie Gillis* 52: Gee, that was a delish dinner. **1965** Cassavetes *Faces* 65: The cakes are delish. **1967** R. Morris *Modern Millie* (film): Delish! **1987** Red Lobster, Inc., TV ad: Three different tastes, each one delish! **1992** *Batman* (Fox-TV): They're...also delish.

Delta Sierra *adj.* [mil. comm. alphabet *Delta* 'D' for *dumb* or *dog* + *Sierra* 'S' for *shit*] *Mil. Av.* DOGSHIT.

1987 in Safire *Coming to Terms* 21: The phrase used in blistering criticism is *Delta Sierra.* **1989** Berent *Rolling Thunder* 127: "And the weather is going to get delta sierra"—that meant dog shit. **1992** Parsons & Nelson *Fighter Country* 157: *Delta Sierra:* Phonetics for "dumb shit"; describes a stupid action.

delts *n.pl. Bodybuilding.* the deltoid muscles.

1981 D.E. Miller *Jargon* 230. *a***1984** in *AS* LIX (1984) 199: *Delts n* Deltoid muscles. **1990** *L.A. Times Mag.* (Mar. 11) 6: The popularity of body building in the decade popularized such terms as *pecs, delts, lats* and *steroids.*

deluxe *adj.* wonderful; superlative.

1973 Savitz *On the Move* 35: Some school...Delux. **1975** Univ. Tenn. student: She is definitely deluxe. **1976** Eble *Campus Slang* (Nov.) 2: *Deluxe*—superb, excellent, fantastic: The play was deluxe.

deluxe *adv.* to an extraordinary degree.

1981 Ballenger *Terror* 26: Rough…They laid it on us deluxe.

Dem *n. Pol.* a Democrat. Now *colloq.* Cf. DEMMY, DEMO[1], 1.
1875 Hayes *Diary* 6: Dems oppose discussion, agitation of this topic. 1897 in Schaaf *Dooley* 146: Dooley on the County "Dems."

demento *n.* [sugg. by *Dr. Demento*, synd. radio program of mid-1970's] a demented person.
1977 *N.Y. Times Mag.* (Jan. 1, 1978) 19: All the electronic gear…could not replicate the effect of 60,000 live dementos in Little Rock's War Memorial Stadium. 1978 Price *Ladies' Man* 225: Christ, man, you wouldn't believe what these dementos can get into. 1980 in *Barnhart Dict. Comp.* I (1982) 37: Can she have been peering through her curtains at some other lone demento?

Demmy *n.* **1.** *Pol.* a Democrat.
1840 in *DAE*: We had dubbed our parties Feds and Demies—that is, Federalists and Democrats. 1849 in *DAE*: Malicious "demmys" did say he preached for hire. 1884 in Lummis *Letters* 75: There is a general impressions [*sic*] that the Demmies "got thar." 1892 in F. Remington *Sel. Letters* 156: We will have to lick the Demmies.
2. a capsule or tablet of Demerol.
1956 Stearn *Sisters of Night* 39: That's a synthetic. We call them demmies. If you can't buy H & M, why, demmies will do the trick.

demo[1] /ˈdɛmoʊ/ *n.* **1.** (usu. *cap.*) a Democrat.
1795 in Whiting *EAP* 105: The devil is to pay among the demo's. 1796 in Tyler *Verse* 48: Southern Demos…represent our brother negroes. 1798 in *DAE*: In vain each Demo spouts and bellows. 1803, 1804 in *DAE*. 1804, 1805 in *OEDS*. 1806, 1808 in *DAE*. 1821 in *DA*. 1857 in *Calif. Hist. Soc. Qly.* VI (1927) 10: It turns the "Demos" blue. 1862 Strong *Diary* III 203: The *Demos* begin to carp at McClellan. 1948 in *OEDS*: The program chairman kept peace between GOP and Demos. 1987 *Daily Beacon* (Univ. Tenn.) (Jan. 7) 1: Demos rule reconvening Congress.
2.a. a protest demonstration.
*1936 in *OEDS*: The anti-war demo last week. 1964 *Time* (Dec. 18) 27: The name of this activity is "demo"…demonstration. That, at least, is what it is called by the U.S. embassy personnel who are its…victims.…The demo is actually a carefully prepared propaganda device. *1965 S.J. Baker *Australian Lang.* (ed. 2) 368: *Demo*, a demonstration, especially a demonstration in the form of a public protest. 1978 *N.Y. Post* (Dec. 15) 5: Iran bans street demos after more bloodshed. 1980 Gould *Ft. Apache* 177: I'll get out and organize a demo.
b. a demonstration model, item, performance, etc.
1963 Dwiggins *S.O. Bees* 23 [ref. to WWII]: Chance Vought's final demo flight. 1978 S. King *Stand* 35: They wanted to release his demo as a single. 1979 G. Wolff *Duke of Deception* 260: He could get one with only a thousand miles on it, a "demo." 1982 *N.Y. Post* (Aug. 27) 74 (ad): Our Company Cadillac Demo Inventory is limited! 1983 *Rolling Stone* (Feb. 3) 57: Best rates for tunes and demos. 1984 C. Francis *Who's Sorry?* 54: I was hired to make demonstration records—"demos"—for music publishers.
3. demolition or demolitions; a demolition charge or charges.—often attrib.
1943 Twist *Bombardier* (film): "Don't I get to play with these demos?" "No demolition bombs for you." a1949 D. Levin *Mask of Glory* 194: They don't need no demo men along. 1967 Ford *Muc Wa* 14: "He's a demolition expert." "Demo!" 1969 in Lanning *Only War* 108: We…set off demo to blow a hole. 1973 Browne *Body Shop* 68: He was our demo man. 1979 J. Morris *War Story* 225: I was cross-trained in commo and demo. 1982 P. Michaels *Grail* 289: The demo man picked out the holes bored into the walls. 1983 K. Miller *Lurp Dog* 15: We got to turn in all our demo and grenades and special weapons. 1983 S. King *Christine* 23: Like a refugee from the demo derby at Philly Plains. 1990 Costello & Wallace *Sig. Rappers* 52: What maybe a demo derby is to a Vermeer.

demo[2] /ˈdimoʊ/ *n.* **1.** a dime. Cf. DEMON.
1926 Norwood *Other Side of Circus* 272: A dime—a demo.
2. *U.S. Mil. Acad.* a demerit.
1930 in D.O. Smith *Cradle* 116: "Five demos," says no. 3. 1941 *AS* (Oct.) 165: Demo. (pronounced "deemo"). A demerit. (West Point).

demo *v.* to demolish.
1987 *Rage* (Univ. Tenn.) I (No. 2) 13: Demo—to smash or destroy.

demob *v. Mil.* to demobilize.
*1920 in *OEDS*. 1922 Eliot *Waste Land* 34: Lil's husband got demobbed. 1925 *Am. Leg. Wkly.* (Jan. 2) 11: Aw, they demobbed our M.P. company in Paris, and I'm going home as a casual. 1968 E.M. Parsons *Fargo* 37: With the army de-mobbing getting out had been the easiest part. a1973 E.G. Robinson & L. Spigelglass *All My Yesterdays*

54: What with…the world…safe for democracy…I was ready to be demobed.

Democrat gloves *n.pl.* men's white gloves. *Joc.* Now *hist.*
1977 Monaghan *Schoolboy, Cowboy* (opp. 116) [ref. to *ca*1910]: The man wearing glasses and "Democrat gloves" is the Mexican spy in this book.

demon *n. Black E.* a dime; DEMO[2].
1944 Burley *Orig. Hndbk. Harlem Jive* 12: All the stud's laying down is a deuce of demons. *Ibid.* 137: *Demon*—Dime.

Dennis *n.* ¶ In phrase: **(one's) name is Dennis** (one) is done for.
1839 J. Reynolds, in *Knickerbocker* (May) 383: "Carry me on, and his name's *Dennis*[*]!" cried the boat-steerer, in a confident tone. *[Note] A whale's name is "Dennis," when he spouts blood. 1878 Mulford *Fighting Indians* 64: When he did get after a man, his name was *Dennis*. 1884 in Lummis *Letters* 47: He was just mulish enough not to budge, and would have been named "Dennis" in a brief time. 1899 F.E. Daniel *Rebel Surgeon* 90: It's unnecessary to say that our name was "Dennis."

denso *n.* a dense person; dullard.
1987 S. Stark *Wrestling Season* 54: Who we talking about, denso?

dent *n.* [shortening of Sp *aguardiente*] *Naut.* a strong native liquor.
1868 Macy *There She Blows!* 53: I'd half a bottle of that blackguard potteen what they call *dent*. *Ibid.* 271: The exhilarating cordial (distilled from the sap of a coconut tree) [is] known among seamen by the name of "dent" (…a contraction of the Spanish aguardiente [*sic*]).

dentist *n. Logging.* (see quot.).
1956 Sorden & Ebert *Logger's* 11 [ref. to *a*1925]: *Dentist*, One who files saws.

de-nut *v.* [*de-* + NUT] to castrate.—usu. considered vulgar. Cf. DEBALL.
1950 in *DARE*: Words for castrating an animal…*De-nut*. 1959 F.L. Brown *Trumbull Pk.* 213: The boys say that a guy like that has been de-nutted. 1973 in *DARE*: Castrate…*de-nut*.

dep *n.* a deputy.
*1890–91 F & H: *Dep*…(common)…A deputy. 1905 Belasco *Girl of Golden West* 385: Help yourself, Dep. 1929 Barr *Let Tomorrow Come* 21: He was some kind of a one-barreled gambler before he was made dep. 1955 Graziano & Barber *Somebody Up There* 155: The warden buzzed for the dep. 1976 R. Daley *To Kill* 55: I can't fight the First Dep.

depresso **1.** *adj.* depressing.
1976 Price *Bloodbrothers* 126: It's too depresso up there.
2. *n.* a chronically depressed person.
1978 Price *Ladies' Man* 237: I mean, I wasn't no depresso, was I?

depth bomb *n.* **1.** *Navy.* an egg. *Joc.*
1918 Ruggles *Navy Explained* 22: Eggs are "gas bombs" and "depth bombs."
2. *Army.* (see quot.). *Joc.*
1944 *N.Y. Times Mag.* (Sept. 12) 32: *Depth Bomb and Worms.* Wac term for meatballs and spaghetti.
3. DEPTH CHARGE.
1963 W.C. Anderson *Penelope* 199: Mike, two depth bombs, please.

depth charge *n.* Orig. *Navy.* a drink consisting of a shot glass of whiskey dropped into a glass of beer.
1956 W. Brinkley *Don't Go Near Water* 230 [ref. to WWII]: Help yourself to a depth charge, Calvert. 1969 Searls *Hero Ship* 170 [ref. to WWII]: They ordered depth charges, a shot of bourbon dropped, glass and all, into a stein of Carta Blanca beer so that greenish tendrils of liquor formed above the sunken whiskey, and coiled mysteriously. 1983 DeVore *Heart of Steel* (film): Hey, watch out! They're droppin' depth charges here! 1984 D. Smith *Steely Blue* 145: Steely picked up the shot glass and dropped it in the middle of the glass of beer. He stared at it, a depth charge. 1987 D. Sipos et al. *Mind Killer* (film): We're doin' depth charges tonight.

derail *n.* **1.** *Hobo.* DEHORN, 2.
1934 Kromer *Waiting* 15: So these guys make derail and drink it. *Ibid.* 16: A guy who will drink derail is lower than a skunk. 1940 in Inman *Diary* 955: He starts drinking derail (denatured alcohol). 1942 *ATS* 112: Illicit liquor…*derail*. 1951 Algren *Chicago* 98: To toast man's earth derisively with earth's last can of derail.
2. *Hobo.* a habitual drinker of derail; DEHORN, 3. [1934 quot. is evidently erroneous.]
1934 Weseen *Dict. Slang* 179: *Derail*—A person disliked. 1935 E.

Anderson *Hungry Men* 261: If I couldn't whip a derail like him I'd kiss anything you say.

derby *n.* **1.** [metonymy] the head.
1930 Lavine *3d Degree* 109: Two billiard cues bounced on his derby, shoulders and body until the detectives became tired. **1966–80** McAleer & Dickson *Unit Pride* 328: You don't think I'd sit by doin' nothin' while Billy gets his derby kicked in?
2. [fr. **(1)**, above, alluding to HEAD] *Prost.* oral copulation, esp. fellatio; an act of oral copulation.
1967 "Iceberg Slim" *Pimp* 177: If she ain't too shy to show what her "Derby's" like…I might give her a break. **1970** Winick & Kinsie *Lively Commerce* 207: Today the single most requested service is fellatio ("French" or "derby"). **1972** R. Wilson *Playboy's Forbidden Words* 86: *Derby.* Oral copulation, usually a blow job, as in "She gave me a derby."

derk var. DIRK.

derm *n. Med.* dermatology.
1984 J. Green *Newspeak* 68.

DEROS *v.* [official acronym for *date of estimated return from overseas*] *Army.* to return to the United States from duty overseas. Also **deros.**
1968 in B.E. Holley *Vietnam* 82: Lots of them have DEROS'd (rotated or returned back home), but quite a few have been wounded or killed. **1975** Former U.S. Army lieut., age *ca*25: "When does he *DEROS*?" means "When does he return to the States?" **1979** Homer *Jargon* 160: "I'm *derosing*" means "I'm going home." **1983** Van Devanter & Morgan *Before Morning* 187 [ref. to Vietnam War]: He DEROSed at Christmas. **1986** "J. Cain" *Suicide Squad* 252: His old partner DEROSed back to The World.

derrick *n. Und.* a shoplifter, esp. if adept or successful.
1911 A.H. Lewis *Apaches of N.Y.* 128: As a derrick, she's got the Darby Kid…beat four ways from th' jack. **1914** Jackson & Hellyer *Vocab.* 28: *Derrick*, Noun. Current amongst shop lifters chiefly. A "hoister"; a "lifter," a "booster," an "elevator." **1925** *Collier's* (Aug. 8) 30: A thief whose hauls are large is a "derrick." **1930** Lait *On the Spot* 200: *Booster…*Shoplifter. (Var.: *Derrick*). **1941** (cited in Partridge *Dict. Und.* 183).

derrick *v.* **1.** *Sports.* to remove (a player) from a game.
1925 T.A. Dorgan, in Zwilling *TAD Lexicon* 31: The humiliation of being derricked in his first World's Series. **1942** *ATS* 633. **1949** Cummings *Sports Dict.* 104. **1952** in *DAS.* **1973** C. Gowdy on *World Series* (NBC-TV) (Oct. 14): They've derricked Kranepool—he was removed.
2. *Und.* to steal, esp. to shoplift; LIFT.
1934, 1936 (cited in Partridge *Dict. Und.* 183).

derrick monkey *n. Petroleum Industry.* (see quot.).
1934 Weseen *Dict. Slang* 89: *Derrick monkey*—A well driller's helper who handles drill pipe in the top of the derrick.

desecrated *adj.* [intentional malapropism] (of vegetables or eggs) desiccated; dried or powdered.
1887 Hinman *Si Klegg* 210 [ref. to Civil War]: They were "desiccated vegetables" for the human stomach…Its scientific name was immediately changed to "desecrated" or "consecrated" vegetables, and it was rarely called by any other. **1906** H. Green *Boarding House* 298: We call 'em desecrated eggs out West. **1907** Mahan *Sail to Steam* 177 [ref. to Civil War]: "Desecrated" (dessicated) potatoes. **1963** Cameron *Black Camp* 82 [ref. to WWII]: Don't you love desecrated eggs with your Spam?

desert rat *n. West.* a person who lives in the desert; (*specif.*) a desert prospector.
1907 in *DA.* **1914** Knibbs *Outlands* 6: The desert rat with color on the brain. **1919** Sabin *Pacific R.R.* 274: Paiutes, Diggers, Greasers, Mongolians, desert rats, stage-drivers, freighters and millionaires. **1927** *Amer. Mercury* (July) 362: The desert rats…applauded the show. **1936** R. Adams *Cowboy Lingo* 200: A veteran prospector…was often spoken of as a "desert rat." **1938** in W. Burnett *Best* 503: I got picked up by a old what they call desert rat. **1987** *Sunday Morning* (CBS-TV) (Mar. 22): The people who live here [in the eastern Mojave Desert] call themselves "desert rats."

desi *n. Baseball.* a designated hitter.
1976 *Webster's Sports Dict.* 112. **1980** Pearl *Slang Dict: Desi n.* (Sports) in baseball, the designated hitter.

desiccate *v.* to be quiet; DRY UP. *Joc.*
1877 *Puck* (May) 6: "Albion will please desiccate." "Desiccate?" "Dry up."

desk *n.* ¶ In phrases:
¶ **fly a desk** *Mil. Av.* (see 1956 quot.). [Early quots. ref. to WWII.]
1946 G.C. Hall, Jr. *1000 Destroyed* 378: He was…to return to the Z. of I. to fly a desk. **1948** Lay & Bartlett *12 O'Clock High!* 107: "Gately," said Savage, "is not available to fly a desk." **1954** Davis & Lay *S.A.C.* (film): Don't forget, you're still flying a desk for me. **1956** Heflin *USAF Dict.* 213: *To fly a desk*, to perform clerical or administrative duties (said esp. of rated persons). **1959** Scott *Flying Tiger* 103: I sat there "flying" my Training Command desk. **1971** G. Davis *Coming Home* 114: Seems like the older you get, the more the Air Force looks over your shoulder, looking for an excuse to make you fly a desk for the rest of your career. **1979** J. Morris *War Story* 274: I was flying my desk up there in the headquarters.
¶ **ride a desk** to be a DESK JOCKEY; *fly a desk*, above.
1966 (implied at DESK-RIDER). **1986** *Heart of the City* (ABC-TV): He's a guy lookin' to make sergeant so he can ride a desk somewhere.

deskateer *n.* [*desk* + *-ateer*, extracted fr. *musketeer*] a desk clerk. *Joc.*
1981 (quot. at DESKIE).

desk commando *n. Mil.* DESK JOCKEY.
1958 Frankel *Band of Bros.* 24 [ref. to 1950]: The desk commandos tell him what they think he wants to hear.

desk cowboy *n.* DESK JOCKEY.
1942 Wylie *Vipers* 242: They…hie themselves to Washington and persuade some desk cowboy to try Professor Pusspocket's theory of negative money on a test area in the Middle West.

desk-hooks *n.pl. Mil. Av.* spurs.
1928 *Papers Mich. Acad.* 288 [ref. to 1918]: *Desk Hooks.* (Am), spurs, an expression employed in the air-service, because the only use an officer had for spurs was to keep his feet from sliding off the desk.

deskie *n.* a desk clerk.
1981 Eble *Campus Slang* (Mar.) 2: *Deskie* or *deskateer*—a night attendant in a dorm; "I'm a deskie at James."

desk jockey *n.* [*desk* + JOCKEY] *Esp. Mil.* a person who works at a desk and typically holds administrative or clerical responsibilities only. [The term's currency may owe something to its phonetic resemblance to DISK JOCKEY.]
1953 in *DAS.* **1956** *AS* XXI (Oct.) 227: *Chair-borne Pilot,* n. A pilot whose primary job is administrative. Also *Desk Jockey.* **1958** Whitcomb *Corregidor* 268 [ref. to WWII]: Being a "desk jockey" and listening to the fliers' tales…did not suit my fancy. **1959** E. Hunter *Killer's Wedge* 55: He was a trained policeman who happened to be a desk jockey. **1968** K. Cooper *Aerobics* 38: This category catches all the do-nothings, the desk jockeys, the TV watchers, the over-eaters, the over-smokers. **1971** *Adam-12* (NBC-TV): That was quite a running tackle for a desk jockey and a man of your seniority. **1978** Truscott *Dress Gray* 71: That gaggle of desk jockeys. **1987** *Science News* (Sept. 5) 147: The degree of difficulty is measured and tested…to the point observed by the desk jockey.

desk pilot *n. Mil. Av.* DESK JOCKEY.
1955 Salter *Hunters* 49: If you want to get anything out of those desk pilots at Fifth, you practically have to squeeze it out of them. **1956** Heflin *USAF Dict.* 163: *Desk pilot.* A rated pilot assigned duty at a desk. *Slang.* **1966** Gallery *Start Engines* 208: By the time I come back, I'll be a chairborne desk pilot. **1966–67** W. Stevens *Gunner* 117 [ref. to WWII]: You think some desk pilot…is going to run me through like a number?

desk rider *n.* DESK JOCKEY.
1966 Longstreet & Godoff *Wm. Kite* 60: There were assorted officers of all nations with that fine smooth look of desk riders.

desperado *n. Gamb.* (see quots.).
1961 Scarne *Guide to Gamb.* 677: *Desperado* A gambler who bets big with bookmakers and cannot pay off when he loses. **1986** *NDAS: Desperado…*A person who gambles or borrows more than he can pay, and is certain to default.

destroyed *adj.* extremely intoxicated from a narcotic drug; WRECKED.
1966 (quot. at SNAKED-UP). **1969** Geller & Boas *Drug Beat* xvii: *Destroyed:* Worn out, exhausted, from the use of drugs. **1970** Landy *Underground Dict.* 65: *Destroyed…*So high on a drug that one cannot move, think or talk well. **1972** *Nat. Lampoon* (Feb.) 6: I mean, we were really *destroyed,* you know?

detail *n. Army.* the situation at hand; things.—constr. with *the.*—constr. with such verbs as *mess up, screw up,* etc. [Early quots. ref. to WWI.]

1919 Fox *What Boys Did* 45: The pill roller put the glass tube in my mouth, which always "balled the detail up." **1919** Emmett *Give Way* 268: Whenever things seem to be going best there is always somebody or something to "mess up the detail." **1930** Graham & Graham *Queer People* 228: Jane…please keep quiet…You'll only mess up the detail. **1932** Halyburton & Goll *Shoot & Be Damned* 206: That…[idiot] will jazz up the detail for all of us. You better dust off a court martial for him. **1948** Wolfert *Act of Love* 183: You're just lousing up the detail. **1962** G. Ross *Last Campaign* 27: Der first vuns dot screw up der detail gonna be pretty damn quick long gone. **1966** Rose *Russians Are Coming* (film): You're gonna foul up the whole detail!

detainer *n. R.R.* a train dispatcher. *Joc.*

1931 *Writer's Digest* (May) 41: *Detainer*—Usually applied to the train dispatcher. **1934** *AS* (Feb.) 73: *Train detainer.* Train dispatcher. A sarcastic term; railroaders contend that the dispatcher holds up trains instead of helping them on.

detec *n.* a detective.

1866 *Nat. Police Gaz.* (Dec. 29) 2: Detective "Hawkshaw"…says he is going to do the same thing that the "detecs" do up above. *1884 (cited in Partridge *DSUE* (ed. 8)).

detox *n.* detoxification.

1973 *Everett* (Wash.) *Herald* (Apr. 12) 8A: Counselors working with the alcoholism detox centers keep track of people and can pick up the "pattern" of a person who drinks. **1979** (cited in J. Green *Dict. Slang*). **1984** *L.A. Times* (Jan. 13) V 1: A Weingart employee—herself a former alcoholic…—asked if the woman was ready to go into "detox." **1985** Univ. Tenn. instructor: Grade enough of these [student themes] and you feel like you're ready for detox. **1990** *U.S. News & W.R.* (Jan. 15) 27: Typically, a homeless alcoholic goes through detox dozens of times. **1994** *New Yorker* (Jan. 31) 62: We finally got him in, for five days of detox.

detox *v.* to detoxify.

1972 in *BDNE3*. **1976** *L.A. Times* (Apr. 20) III 1: Slowly he has begun taking a smaller dose in the hope that he can detox and get off parole. **1980** *N.Y. Times* (Sept. 22) C 15: I've had six businessmen from New York fly out here to "detox" from heroin. **1983** Sturz *Wid. Circles* 69: When the monkey on his back got too bad, he would check himself into the hospital and detox. **1987** B. Ford & Chase *Awakening* 23: Number one, we've got to get her detoxed. **1994** *New Yorker* (Jan. 31) 63: He really hadn't detoxed long enough, so it didn't work.

Detroit iron *n.* an American-made motor vehicle.

1950 *Amer. Qly.* (Winter): The hot-rod culture is committed to the everlasting modification of what it casually calls "Detroit iron"—the American production car. **1962** *West. Folklore* 30: *Detroit iron*—Any American-built automobile…(Los Angeles, 1961). **1970** in H.S. Thompson *Shark Hunt* 99: But no Fords or Chevvys. "Detroit iron" didn't make it in that league. **1980** *Easyriders* (May) 54: Some bitch in a piece of Detroit iron pulled out in front of me.

Detroit vibrator *n. Trucking.* a Chevrolet, esp. a Chevrolet truck. *Joc.*

1971 Tak *Truck Talk* 43: *Detroit vibrator:* a Chevrolet tractor. **1976** Dills *CB 1977* 29: *Detroit Vibrators:* Chevrolets.

detuned *adj. Auto Racing.* out of control; awry.

1979 Frommer *Sports Lingo* 164.

deuce *n.* **1.a.** *Und.* twopence or two cents.

***1698–99** "B.E." *Dict. Canting Crew: A Duce…*two Pence. **1859** Matsell *Vocab.* 28: *Duce.* Two cents; two.

b. a two-dollar bill; two dollars.

1898–1900 Cullen *Chances* 108: This super's good fr a deuce in any hock shop. **1929–31** Runyon *Guys & Dolls* 78: He offers to compromise with me for a deuce. **1935** *Amer. Mercury* (June) 229: *Deuce:* two dollars [among carnival workers]. **1940** O'Hara *Pal Joey* 185: Something for a fin or a deuce. **1942** in *Best From Yank* 65: You've dropped a fast deuce in a friendly crap game. **1956** Algren *Wild Side* 94: The driver in turn was victimized by the device of deducting two dollars from his regular salary in lieu of that same housewife's deuce. **1961** Clausen *Season's Over* 156: If you can't get a sawbuck, take a deuce, baby. **1971** D. Smith *Engine Co.* 18: A deuce is a lot of money. **1973** Duckett *Raps* 22: But could you lay a deuce on me for a bag? **1980** Kotzwinkle *Jack* 111: "I'll give you a buck for it."…"A deuce…or stop wastin' my time." **1983** Stapleton *30 Yrs.* 216: Eight guys a week at a deuce a week came to sixteen bucks a week.

c. *Gamb.* two hundred dollars.

1974 Angelou *Gather Together* 33 [ref. to 1945]: For you, four dresses for a deuce. **1979** V. Patrick *Pope* 56: Grabbing themselves an easy deuce apiece each week.

2.a. Esp. *Black E.* a pair; two.

1859 Matsell *Vocab.* 30: "*The cull equipped me with a deuce of finifs,*" the man gave me two five-dollar bills. **1943** *Time* (July 19) 54: "Gimme an ace" (meaning one reefer), "a deuce" (meaning two), or "a deck" (meaning a large number). **1960** C.L. Cooper *Scene* 10: I *couldn't* get hooked with a deuce (two capsules of heroin), could I? **1963** in Clarke *Amer. Negro Stories* 304: Wonderin' where I could cop myself a deuce of African drums. **1964** Rhodes *Chosen Few* 102: Bring me a deuce a' double bourbons. **1969** Cagle *Naval Av. Guide* 395: *Loose Deuce.* A two-section flight of aircraft flying in such a way as to be able to give each other support. **1981** *Nat. Lampoon* (Mar.) 45: I muscled over to the cathouse and tied up a deuce of felines. **1992** *Seinfeld* (NBC-TV): Because you look like a nice guy—a thousand bucks for the deuce [i.e., pair of tickets].

b. the second in sequence or rank.

1921 *Variety* (July 8) 6: She was in the "deuce" spot at this show. **1958** McCulloch *Woods Words* 46: *Deuce*—Number two locie. It would also be called the two-spot.

c. (the number) two.

1959 Montgomery & Heiman *Jet Nav.* 111: In World War Deuce. **1984** *CNN Network News* (May 29): California 6, New York deuce. **1986** Zeybel *First Ace* 7: World War Deuce.

3. Orig. *Gamb.* a worthless individual. [The *deuce* is the least-valued card in most card games.]

1897 Ade *Pink* 171: When it comes to playin' faw huh…I'm jus' a deuce in a duhty deck. **1901** A.H. Lewis *Croker* 59: Shakspere right now ain't a deuce in a bum deck. **1914** Lardner *Al* 97: So I am going to give it to her for a New Year's present and I guess that will make Allen feel like a dirty doose. **1922** Tully *Emmett Lawler* 166: You may only be a deuce now, but you might grow into a ten-spot. **1935** Coburn *Law Rides Range* 70: She'll have to listen to the drunken bragging of that unwashed pair of deuces. **1952** Overholser *Fab. Gunman* 51: I'd say you were just a deuce, but you fill out his hand. **1963** E.M. Miller *Exile* 188: We call ourselves the Deuces because none of us was an ace.

4. *Pris.* a two-year prison sentence.

1925 (cited in Partridge *Dict. Und.* 184). **1932** *Writer's Mo.* (Aug.) 46: Two-year men hold a "deuce." **1952** Bruce & Essex *Kansas City Confidential* (film): Pete Harris and me did a deuce together at Joliet. **1958** A. King *Mine Enemy* 200: He was a first offender doing a "deuce" for pushing junk. **1972** P. Thomas *Savior* 86: I owe 'em a deuce, two years. **1975** *Kojak* (CBS-TV): He went upstate, pulled a deuce, I think.

5. *Restaurant.* a table that seats two patrons; (*hence*) a party of two. Cf. ACE, *n.*, 13.

1935 O'Hara *Dr.'s Son* 72: In Childs she went to a "deuce," or table for two, in the bay window. **1938** in Himes *Black on Black* 145: Fill those glasses for that deuce over there. **1954** Collans & Sterling *House Detect.* 219: *Deuce.* Table set for two. **1959** A. Anderson *Lover Man* 126: I was working three tables for two—"three deuces." **1972** A.K. Shulman *Ex-Prom Queen* 97: At my five-table station [were]…three "deuces" and two "squares."…I expected the deuces to be perturbed. **1979** Gutcheon *New Girls* 268: The dinner party at the Wrights' was so crowded, Marge had to set up a deuce in the powder room.

6.a. *Hot Rodding.* a 1932 Ford, esp. a Model A coupe rebuilt as a hot rod.

1959 Kellogg & Simms *Giant Gila Monster* (film): You want to sell that Deuce?…That '32 is the ideal stock car to turn into a bomb. **1963** in Chipman *Hardening Rock* 49: Just a little deuce coupe with a flat head mill. **1973** Lucas, Katz & Huyck *Amer. Graffiti* A yellow '32 Ford deuce coupe. **1986** Oddo *Street Rod. Hndbk.* 13: The Deuce roadster will always be The Classic. **1993** *Smithsonian* (July) 52: It is a '32 Ford roadster, the hot rod favorite, a Deuce. *Ibid.* 53: His shop is full of Deuce roadsters and coupes.

b. [fr. DEUCE-AND-A-QUARTER] a Buick Electra 225.

1968 in D.L. Lee *We Walk* 57: The stang & the deuce hit the corner of 39th & Cottage/at the same time.

c. (*cap.*) *USAF.* an F-102 Delta Dagger fighter airplane.

1970 *Current Slang* V 15: *Deuce,* USAF F-102 fighter aircraft. **1974** Stevens *More There I Was* 36: Red lights in the cockpit of the Deuce/ Are out to clobber me. **1975** in Higham & Siddall *Combat Aircraft* 83: The Deuce jockey fought my kind of dogfight. **1986** Zeybel *First Ace* 118: He banked the Deuce into a one-hundred-eighty degree turn.

7. [ref. to the *2 of 502*, police code for a drunk-driving infraction] *Calif. Police.* a charge of driving while intoxicated; (*hence*) a drunken driver.

1965 Conot *Rivers of Blood* 11: "A deuce!" he replied, using police slang for a 502. **1977** *L.A. Times* (Sept. 5) IV 1: He often finds "speeders, jay-walkers and 'deuces'" (drunk drivers) quoting and misquoting the Bible. **1984** *Santa Barbara News-Press* (Dec. 21) A4: The image of the entire county bar could be damaged if any of the partygoers received a "deuce" or drunken driving citation on the way home.

8. *Army.* a black soldier.

1966 (quot. at ACE, *n.*, 16).

9. [the catcher's sign to the pitcher for a curveball is customarily two extended fingers] *Baseball.* a curveball.

1978 *N.Y. Post* (June 28) 110: Nolan Ryan is Nolan Ryan because he's got a 104-mile-an-hour heater and a 104-mile-an-hour deuce that drops off the table. **1992** Strawberry & Rust *Darryl* 231: Bobby O throws deuces, curving down and in.

10. [ref. to the *2* of *42nd* Street; cf. earlier syn. FORTY-DEUCE] (*cap.*) *N.Y.C.* (see quots.).—constr. with *the*.

1984 Toop *Rap Attack* 159: *Deuce:* Forty-second Street or the Times Square area....."Those drugs I got on the Deuce are whacked." **1986** Churcher *N.Y. Confidential* 156: The Deuce, a block of Forty-second Street in the Times Square area. **1990** *Houston* (Tex.) *Post* (May 24) A3: The Deuce: 42nd Street in New York City. **1992** M. Gelman *Crime Scene* 232: The Deuce, the street name for the stretch of 42nd Street from Seventh to Eighth Avenue.

¶ In phrase:

¶ **cop a deuce** *Pris.* DEUCE OUT.

1974 Andrews & Dickens *Over the Wall* 151: No copping deuces for him. No, he would not sign any papers for the governor!

deuce *adj. Navy.* having apprentice or second-class rating.—used postpositively.

1958 Frankel *Band of Bros.* 23: You're a First Class. The others are H.A. Deuce. **1959** Sterling *Wahoo* 51 [ref. to WWII]: Gerlacher, Seaman "duce" to Seaman. **1972** Ponicsan *Cinderella Liberty* 3: Some poor seaman deuce, lower than whaleshit, is given the repair detail. **1974** E. Thompson *Tattoo* 30: You don't have to call me sir. I'm just a Bosun Deuce. **1981** Ballenger *Terror* 90: A metalsmith deuce.

deuce *v.* **1.** *Entertainment Industry.* to appear second in a programmed presentation.

1923 *N.Y. Times* (Oct. 14) VIII 4: *Deucing*—Appearing in No. 2 spot. **1924** *Sat. Eve. Post* (July 12) 15: *Deucing*—appearing second on the bill. **2.** see DEUCE OUT.

deuce-and-a *n.* DEUCE-AND-A-HALF.

1986 Merkin *Zombie Jamboree* 87: I can use the deuce-and-a to drive us out....The armorer's deuce-and-a tarpaulined truck.

deuce-and-a-half *n.* Esp. *Mil.* a two-and-a-half-ton truck.

*ca***1944** in Kaplan & Smith *One Last Look* 82: Deuce-and-a-half. **1962** in *Harper's Mag.* (Feb. 1964) 45: A group of men...were brought back...in a deuce-and-a-half. **1963** Doulis *Path* 57: Clarke...saw a Deuce-and-a-Half parked on the company street. *Ibid.* 321: He directed the planeload to a pair of Deuce-and-a-Halves. **1967** Sadler *Lucky One* 143: Conlon's "A" team fitted up a "deuce-and-a-half," an Army two-and-a-half ton truck, as a rolling dispensary. **1978** Downs *Killing Zone* 17: We loaded aboard deuce-and-a-halfs to ride across town to the camp. **1989** "Capt. X" & Dodson *Unfriendly Skies* 55: I was in the back of a deuce-and-a-half, and we were driving through a wasteland of wreckage. **1992** Cornum & Copeland *She Went* 3: Our 2½-ton truck, known in the army as a deuce-and-a-half.

deuce-and-a-quarter *n.* Esp. *Black E.* a Buick Electra 225.

1968 in D.L. Lee *We Walk* 57: Noticeably driving/down cottage grove in a gold & black deuce & a quarter. **1970** in C.M. Rodgers *Ovah* 20: A man/in a deuce and a quarter/is staring daggers at me. **1970** *Current Slang* V 6: *Deuce and a quarter*, n. An Electra 225 Buick. **1972** Claerbaut *Black Jargon* 62: The cat's got a bad Deuce and a Quarter. **1975** Univ. Tenn. student: A deuce-and-a-quarter is a Buick 225. **1982** *Las Vegas* woman, age *ca*25: When I've heard it, it's always been pronounced /ˈduzənˌkwɔtə/. **1986** *Morning Call* (Allentown, Pa.) (Aug. 18) D3. **1988** Norst *Colors* 27: Crip-killers in their Buick deuce-and-a-quarters.

deuce ball *n. Baseball.* DEUCE, *n.*, 9.

1985 D. Young, in *N.Y. Post* (Aug. 31) 89: He'll have to work on hitting the ol' deuceball.

deuce-high *adj.* [the deuce is the lowest-ranked card in many card games; cf. ACE-HIGH] Orig. *Gamb.* in very low esteem.

1896 Ade *Artie* 50: If she'd ever see me with that fairy I wouldn't be deuce-high with her now. **1901** Irwin *Sonnets* (unp.): One who with his

---

landlord stands deuce-high. **1918** *Independent* (May 11) 260: Say, Fred Harvey wouldn't be deuce high with that little Frenchman.

deuce of clubs *n.* the fists as used in fighting; usu. in phr. **play the deuce of clubs** to inflict a beating.

1942 Goldin et al. *DAUL* 160: That beef...has got to be chilled...play the deuce of clubs if you gotta. **1947** *AS* (Apr.) 121: *Deuce of clubs.* Both fists.

deuce out *v.* to back down, esp. from cowardice. Also **deuce.**

1949 Ellson *Tomboy* 3: You deuced. Admit it. You deuced. **1953** W. Brown *Monkey On My Back* 32: Dave had been scared but he sensed that if he "deuced out," Vesta would be through with him. **1979** in J.L. Gwaltney *Drylongso* 232: It's the blackest and the baddest ass that makes the others deuce out.

deucer *n.* a two-dollar bill; DEUCE, *n.*, 1.b.

1937 in D. Runyon *More Guys* 102: I am feeling so good about my success at the track that I slip him a deucer.

deuce-spot *n.* a two-dollar bill; DEUCE, *n.*, 1.b.

1917 *Editor* (Feb. 24) 152: *Deuce-Spot*—two dollars. **1921** (cited in Partridge *Dict. Und.*; date given erron. as 1914).

deuceways *n. Black E.* a pair.

1958 Hughes & Bontemps *Negro Folk.* 482: *Cop a deuceways:* To buy two dollars worth of something. "Let's cop a deuceways of barbecue."

Deusey *n.* a Deusenberg automobile.

1936 "E. Queen" *Halfway House* 11: As soon as I can breathe life into the old Deusey again.

devil *n.* **1.** *Printing.* a printer's apprentice or office boy. Now *S.E.*

1683** in *OED*: The Press-man sometimes has a Week-Boy to Take Sheets, as they are Printed off the Tympan: These Boys do in a Printing-House, commonly black and Dawb themselves: Whence the Workmen do Jocosely call them Devils; and sometimes Spirits, and sometimes Flies. ***1754** in *F & H*: Our publisher, printer, corrector, *devil*, or any other employed in our service. **1784** in St. G. Tucker *Poems* 46: Christmas Verses for the Printer's Devil....Next, tho' I'm a devil, I drink and I eat. **1838, 1853, 1856, 1857,** etc., in *DAE*. **1868** M.H. Smith *Sunshine and Shadow* 102: He was the "devil" in the printing-office. **1895** Coup *Sawdust* x: He...left home [*ca*1850] and took the position of "devil" in a country newspaper office. **1903** Ralph *Journalist* 13: Horace Greeley, Mark Twain, and scores of others began as printers' "devils." **1935** in Alter *Utah Journ.* 267: We wanted to rest as the editor, as the compositor, as the "devil." *ca1940** in Botkin *Treas. Amer. Folk.* 550: Green hands, such as a new devil, would always be asked to look at the type louse at the bottom of a type case. **1947** T.W. Duncan *Gus the Great* 149: That's why they call him a devil—because he has such a hell of a time. **1958** S.H. Adams *Tenderloin* 5: A short...spell as a printer's devil.

2. *Narc.* RED DEVIL; BLUE DEVIL.

1970 Landy *Underground Dict.* 65: *Devil*...A pill, usually Seconal.

¶ In phrases:

¶ **black as the devil's arse** as black as can be; pitch-black.—usu. considered vulgar.

1774 in Whiting *EAP* 102: I have at this time, a great high Gire Carline as Black as the D[evil]s A-se spinning for me.

¶ **the devil to pay [and no pitch hot]** severe trouble as a consequence. [Despite freq. assertions to the contrary, the shorter form appears to be the original.]

***1711** J. Swift, in *F & H*: And then there will be the devil and all to pay. **1744** in Whiting *EAP* 105: It was *the devil to pay and no pitch hot?* An interrogatory adage metaphorically derived from the manner of sailors who pay their ship's bottoms with pitch. **1747** in Whiting *EAP* 104: I have had ye devil and all to pay here. ***1761** in *F & H*: There's the devil to pay in meddling with them. **1843–45** T.J. Green *Tex. Exped.* 231: [Pulque] will get in your heads, and then the devil will be to pay. **1849** G.G. Foster *Celio* 89: I'll have an explanation...or there'll be the devil to pay and no pitch hot, in somebody's camp. **1951** *N.Y. Times Mag.* (Dec. 16): The forenoon watch opens, in the words of an old seagoing term, "with the devil to pay and no pitch hot."

¶ **up jumps the devil** an unexpected reverse or problem suddenly appears. Also vars.

1935 Pollock *Und. Speaks:* Up pops the devil, a 7 in craps...when attempting to make a point. **1942** *ATS* 705: Up jumped the devil!, exclaimed at a loss (in craps). **1952** Bruce & Essex *K. C. Confidential* (film): Uh-oh, the devil jumped up. He went away with the seven. **1955** Wilbur & Mainwaring *Phenix City* (film): Up jumped the devil again.

1970 L.D. Johnson *Devil's Front Porch* 50: Then up jumped the devil*...*Prison expression meaning "here came trouble." **1985** Dye *Between Raindrops* 191.

¶ **whip the devil around a stump** [or **the meeting-house**] to accomplish one's ends in a roundabout or indirect way.

1776 in Whiting *EAP*: It was only an artifice to whip the devil round the stump. **1786** in *DAE*: What the Virginians call "whipping the devil round a stump." **1798** in Whiting *EAP* 107: The House of Representatives sit...whipping the devil round the post. **1799, 1809, 1822** in Whiting *EAP*. **1834** Caruthers *Kentuck.* I 189: There's no whippin the devil round the stump with him; he jumps right at him, tooth and toenail. **1835** *Mil. & Navy Mag. of U.S.* (Sept.) 44: The motive for creating me an officer...was to "whip the devil round the stump," and purchase six gallons of New England rum from the Yankee captain. **1847** in Blair & Meine *Half Horse* 104: Benson had been in the pirate business before he cum up to Monongahela to whip the devil around the meeting-house. **1863, 1871, 1891** in *DAE*. **1912** Quinn *Gambling* 206: It creates a peculiar situation, and is nothing more nor less than "whipping the devil round the stump."

devil-dodger *n.* **a.** a Christian clergyman, esp. a chaplain or evangelist.

*1791 in Barrère & Leland *Dict. Slang* I 305: These devil-dodgers happened to be so very powerful (that is, noisy) that they soon sent John home crying out, he should be damn'd. *1873 Hotten *Slang Dict.* (ed. 4) 142: *Devil dodger*, a clergyman. *1886 in *OED*. **1889** in *F & H*: He's...a gambler or a devil-dodger. I reckon...he's a preacher. **1889** *Century Dict.*: *Devil-dodger*...A ranting preacher. (Humorous.) **1902** J. Williams, in *Independent* (Nov. 6) 2635: Sailors, as a rule, are prejudiced against "sky pilots" and "devil dodgers." **1917** Oemler *Slippy McGee* 31: Devil-dodger,...are you just making a noise with your face, or is that on the level? *1929 Bowen *Sea Slang* 35: *Devil Dodger*. Chaplain, R.N. **1933** Ersine *Pris. Slang* 32: *Devildodger, n.* A preacher.

b. a zealous or sanctimonious Christian.—used derisively.

*1857 "Ducange Anglicus" *Vulgar Tongue* 6: *Devil-Dodger*—A religious person. *1890–91 *F & H*: *Devil Dodger*...(common). A clergyman. Also, by implication, anyone of a religious turn of mind. **1966** Kenney *Caste* 79: Don't you understand, you devil-dodger, that if you improved you'd start from the top? **1976** Hayden *Voyage* 515: Here comes them devil dodgers now.

devil-dog *n.* [the often repeated assertion that the term translates a hypothetical G *Teufelhund* allegedly applied at the battle of Belleau Wood or Château-Thierry is unsubstantiated] a member of the U.S. Marine Corps.

1918 *N.O. Times Picayune* (Aug. 24) 1: This is one of the first photographs to reach the United States of the battle of Chateau Thierry, where the now famous Devil Dogs (U.S. Marines) covered themselves with glory. **1918** in Gibbons *Floyd Gibbons* 123: American marines...have earned the name of "Devil Dogs" from the Germans and "Saviors" from the French. **1919** *Devil Dog* (Co. B, 11th Marines, La Pallice, France) (May 3) 2: Jim Bones and His Devil-Dogs. **1925** *Amer. Leg. Wkly.* (Jan. 2) 12: You're goin' to lift the laurel off'n that devil dog's brow like the lid off'n a G.I. can. **1929–33** Farrell *Young Manhood of Lonigan* 170: "I'm all for joining the Marines," said Red. "Me too, the devil dogs." **1961** Coon *Front* 58: I would be delighted, you hard-bitten devil-dog. **1978** Hasford *Short-Timers* 13: At Belleau Wood the Marines were so vicious that the German infantrymen called them *Teufel-Hunden*—"devil dogs." **1984** Hammel *Root* 134: The others punctuated the epithet with a solid "Oorah" Devildog grunt. **1987** D. da Cruz *Boot* 263: "Devildogs aren't surgeons," he says, "but they don't need a medical degree to operate on the enemy with the bayonet." **1992** *Amer. Gladiators* (synd. TV series): You old Marine, you. We call you The Devil Dog around here.

devil-fish *n. Whaling.* a California gray whale.

1860 in *DA*. **1873** Scammon *Marine Mammals* 25: "Devil-fish" is significant of the danger incurred in the pursuit of the animal.

devil's bedpost *n. Cards.* the four of clubs. Also **devil's bedposts**.

*1837 (cited in Partridge *DSUE* (ed. 8)). *1873 Hotten *Slang Dict.* (ed. 5): *Devil's bed-posts*, the four of clubs. *1879 *N & Q* (Series 5) XII 473: In London I have always heard the four of clubs called the *devil's bedpost*, and also that it is the worst turn-up one could have. **1935** Pollock *Und. Speaks*: *Devil's bedpost*, 4 of clubs (playing cards). **1949** G.S. Coffin *Winning Poker* 176: *Devil's Bedpost*—The four of clubs. **1968** F. Wallace *Poker* 213: *Devil's Bedposts*—A four of clubs.

devil's box *n.* a fiddle.

1976 *N.Y. Folklore* II 240: *Devil's Box*...is a common synonymy for fiddle.

devil's brew *n.* whiskey. *Joc.*

1947 Goffin *Horn of Plenty* 84: How 'bout a shot of devil's brew?

devil's claw *n. Naut.* (see quot.).

1966 Noel & Bush *Naval Terms* 123: *Devil's Claw*: Slang: Compressor, device used to hold anchor chain.

devil's dandruff *n.* cocaine. *Joc.*

1981 Wambaugh *Glitter Dome* 244: Beware the devil's dandruff, he'd heard an actress warn.

devil's dye *n.* whiskey. *Joc.*

1863 (quot. at RIFLE WHISKY).

devil's piano *n. Army.* a machine gun. *Joc.*

1941 *AS* (Oct.) 165: *Devil's Piano.* Machine gun.

devil's pitchfork *n. Petroleum Industry.* (see 1934 quot.).

1934 Weeseen *Slang Dict.* 89: *Devil's pitchfork*—A fishing tool used to recover pieces of bits or under-reamer lugs lost in a drilled hole. **1972** Haslam *Oil Fields* 99: *Devil's Pitchfork, n.* A fishing tool that resembles a pitchfork.

devil's smile *n. Naut.* (see 1882 quot.).

1882 *United Service* (Feb.) 161: "Devil's smiles" are the deceptive gleams of fair weather or the scowl on an angry captain's face. *1890–91 *F & H*: *Devil's Smiles*...(common). April weather with alternations of sunshine and rain.

devil's swill *n. Naut.* gin.

1855 Wise *Tale for Marines* 130: Preventing the boat's crew from lacing their coffee with too much gin, which they called "devil's swill."

devil's table-cloth *n. Naut.* lowering rain clouds.

1881 *United Service* (July) 161: The "devil's table-cloth" is...still seen spread in threatening weather.

devil-teaser *n.* a Christian minister.

1914 *DN* IV 150: *Devil Teaser*...Chaplain.

devoon var. DIVOON.

dew *n.* **1.** whiskey; MOUNTAIN DEW.

*1836 in *OED*: Then came the whiskey—the real dew. *1841 in *EDD*: We'll have the "dew" now. **1846** *Spirit of Times* (Apr. 18) 92: He had solaced himself with a few bumpers of the "dew." **1847** *Davy Crockett's Alm.* (unp.): I...brought him out a horn of the best dew. *1891 in *EDD*: Oh man, gie me a drap o' the real dew. **1950** in *West. Folk.* (Jan. 1951) 80: Give me a shot of Kentucky dew.

2. Esp. *Mil.* marijuana.

1971 *Newsweek* (Jan. 11) 31: And as the Iron Butterfly sang "In the Time of Our Lives," the grunts passed around a glowing pipe of "dew," the GI slang for marijuana. **1971** *N.Y. Times Mag.* (Sept. 19) 66: The air in the little room in the back of the hangar is heavy with the sweet smell of "dew." **1982** Del Vecchio *13th Valley* 24: I'm clean out a dew. **1985** J.M.G. Brown *Rice Paddy Grunt* 132: We got our weed, our dew, all stuffed into American cigarettes.

¶ In phrase:

¶ **shake the dew off the lily** (of a boy or man) to urinate. *Joc.*

1963 Ark. man, age *ca*20 (coll. J. Ball): I got to shake the dew off the lily. **1966** N.Y.C. man, age *ca*45: Gotta shake the dew off the lily. **1970** Seelye *Finn* 44: I'll be along in a minute, soon's I shake a little dew off the lily. **1970** E. Thompson *Garden of Sand* 262: Jack shook the dew off his wienie and zipped it back into his...slacks. **1983** Neaman & Silver *Kind Words* 50: *Shake the dew off the lily*....This popular expression is from about 1930 and is still in use. Our informant, an Irish-American cleric, reported that it was often used humorously by clerics; it may be Irish in origin. **1989** *Tracey Ullman Show* (Fox-TV): Excuse me, fellows. I've got to shake the dew off the lily.

dewdrop *n. Baseball.* a spitball.

1974 Perry & Sudyk *Me & Spitter* 16: The old dew drop takes total dedication, like any new pitch you learn. **1975** *Urban Life* IV 239: The umpire suspected he was throwing the "dew drop."

dewdrop *v. Hobo.* (see quots.).

1907 London *Road* 67 [ref. to *ca*1894]: If I remain on the roof after the train stops, I know those shacks will fusillade me with rocks. A healthy shack can "dew-drop" a pretty heavy chunk of stone on top of a car. **1927** *DN* V 444: *Dewdrop, v.* To heave lumps of coal in the air so as to fall at high angles upon the heads of hoboes riding between cars. This is usually done from the tinder and by the fireman. When a hobo is riding the rods or gunnels, pieces of coal are dropped between trucks so that striking the ties they may rebound with sufficient violence to knock the hobo under the wheels. This is called *bombing a bum*. **1930** Irwin *Tramp & Und. Slang*: Dewdrop. To hurl lumps of coal back over the train in hopes of striking a tramp riding between the cars.

dex *n. Narc.* dextroamphetamine sulfate, a stimulant; (*also*) a tablet containing it.
1961 Rubin *In the Life* 156: *Dex.* Stimulant, usually Dexedrine. *Ibid.* 50: Well, maybe a dex or something. **1966** Goldstein *1 in 7* 202: "Bennies" and "dex" are shorthand for Benzedrine and Dexedrine, two stimulants. **1969** Mitchell *Tripping* 83: Dex is smooth. **1983** K. Miller *Lurp Dog* 205: Five tablets of dex.

dexie *n.* DEX.
1951 Kerouac *Cody* 106: I...just took dexy. **1956** in J. Blake *Joint* 134: I had a couple of Dexies. **1959** Trocchi *Cain's Book* 148: I...took a couple of dexies and felt better. **1966** Susann *Valley of Dolls* 409: I'd take a Dexie—or a drink. **1970** Landy *Underground Dict.* 65: *Dexy...Dexamyl...Dexedrine.* **1971** N.Y.U. student: You should have taken Dexies. *a***1987** Bunch & Cole *Reckoning* 361: He regretted having taken the dexies.

dexter *n.* [fr. poin*dexter*] *Stu.* an overly studious or offensively intelligent student.
1987 *Village Voice* (N.Y.C.) (July 14) 17: The archenemies of jocks [and] dexters. **1990** P. Dickson *Slang!* 216: *Dexter.* Nerd.

D.F. *n.* damned fool.
1918 Griffin *Ballads of Reg't.* 25: For he's no "DF" martinet. **1919** Fiske *Midshipman* 101 [ref. to 1887]: I said: "Greene, we're a couple of d.f.'s." **1920** Smith *Leathernecks* 90: You d— f—, that's the North Star! **1924** LeFèvre *Stockbroker* 256: Two classes of customers—the wise and the d.f. **1926** in Lardner *Haircut* 59: Maybe I'm a D.F. not to know, but would you tell me what a B.F. and G.F. are? **1935** in Truman *Dear Bess* 367: But I'm just a d.f. I guess. **1938** *Amer. Mercury* (Oct.) 246: The poor D.F. with the radio voice.

dial *n.* [cf. DIAL PLATE] the face. [The "1811" ex. cited without quotation in *OED* is an error for DIAL PLATE.]
1842 *Spirit of Times* (May 28) 152: Broome in with his left [hand] on the dial. **1842** *Spirit of Times* (Sept. 3) 322: The upper part of his dial was quite *eyerascible*, his nose inflamed, his lip cushioned, and the war paint trickling (though scantily) down his chin. **1882** in "M. Twain" *Stories* 193: Whenever I perceive this sign on this man's dial, I...give him opportunity to unload his heart. **1889** in *F & H*: An absinthe tumbler...caught him a nasty crack across the dial. **1902–03** Ade *People You Know* 92: His Dial suggested a Map of the Bad Lands and he was just out of kind Words. **1908** McGaffey *Show Girl* 113: Pipe my dial! Get onto the scratch! **1927** C.F. Coe, in Paxton *Sport* 147: You'll quit with the first paste on the dial. **1928** Shay *More Pious Friends* 136: Heenan made a pass at him, which slightly bruised his dial. **1936** Mackenzie *Living Rough* 242: His beak is plastered all over his dial. *****1958** in *OEDS* I 791.

dial-a-clap *n.* [sugg. by telephone services such as *Dial-A-Joke, Dial-A-Prayer,* etc.] *Army.* a kind of medical reference chart in the form of a pair of rotatable cardboard disks that match symptoms to the names of specific venereal diseases.
1985 Former SP5, U.S. Army, age 35: They had *dial-a-claps* posted on the bulletin boards everywhere I was stationed [in the U.S. and Taiwan, 1971–78]. People would steal 'em for ready reference. The word was already in widespread use when I was in basic training.

dial plate *n.* [cf. DIAL] the face.
*****1811** *Lexicon Balatron.*: Dial Plate. The face. *To alter his dial plate;* to disfigure his face. **1836** in Haliburton *Sam Slick* 42: That will...make her dial plate as smooth as a lick of copal varnish.

diamond *n.* **1.** usu. *pl.* a lump of coal. Cf. BLACK DIAMOND.
1863 in Boyer *Nav. Surgeon* I 67: The coal brig is unloading her cargo of "diamonds." *****1889** Barrère & Leland *Dict. Slang* I 307: In England, *diamond cracking* refers to working in a coal mine. **1900** in Botkin & Harlow *R.R. Folklore* 314: *Cracking diamonds...breaking coal.* **1929** Bookman (July) 524: He's spadin' diamonds with his feet together and hittin' everythin' but the firebox. **1942** *Sat. Eve. Post* (June 13) 27.
2. *Pris.* an ax.
1934 Lomax *Amer. Ballads* 77: Wid his di'mond blade/Got it in his han'. **1934** in Lomax *Singing Country* 392: I'm gonna preach to my diamond, hammer ring. **1967** *JAFL* LXXX 93: I got a diamond in my hand/Now you know I'm a lonesome man.

3. *pl.* the testicles. Cf. FAMILY JEWELS.
1954–60 *DAS.*

diamond-cracker *n. R.R.* a locomotive fireman.
[*****1889** cf. quot. at DIAMOND, 1]. **1936** Mencken *Amer. Lang.* (ed. 4) 583: A fireman is a...*bakehead, fireboy,* or *diamond-cracker.*

diamond-cutting *n. Hobo.* commercial ice-cutting. Now *hist.*
1930 "D. Stiff" *Milk & Honey* 35: The art of cutting ice in the winter is called "glass blowing" or "diamond cutting." **1980** Bruns *Kts. of Road* 8: From diamond cutting in the winter waters of Minnesota...to working the mines in Montana, the boomer workers filled enormous labor needs. [*a***1989** in Kisseloff *Must Remember This* 283: Then I got a job as an assistant to an iceman. That was a thrill, because you stuck a pick in the ice, and it split so perfectly. It was like being a diamond cutter.]

diamond-pusher *n. R.R.* a locomotive fireman.
1926 *AS* I (Jan.) 250. **1945** Hubbard *R.R. Ave.* 340: *Diamond Pusher*—Locomotive fireman.

diarrhea *n.* garrulous nonsense.
1881 C. Guiteau, in *Amer. History Illus.* (Feb. 1969) 21: Is there any limit to this diarrhea? **1915** in Pound *Pound/Joyce* 43: The futuristic taint, i.e. spliced cinematography in paintings and diarrhoea in writing.
¶ In phrase:
¶ **diarrhea of the mouth** [or **jawbone**] offensive loquacity.
1944 R. Adams *Western Words:* Diarrhea of the jawbone. **1948** A. Murphy *Hell & Back* 19: "Aw shadup," the Italian replies, "you got diarrhea of the mout." **1952** Lait & Mortimer *USA* 115: Senator Byrd described Humphrey as "constipated of brain with diarrhea of mouth." **1965** Horan *Seat of Power* 90: Cops get diarrhea of the mouth sometimes. **1971** Flanagan *Maggot* 252: What d'you respect him for, huh? Diarrhea of the mouth? **1987** Frumkes *Street Trash* (film): This fuckin' rat—he's got diarrhea of the mouth again.

diarrhea gun *n. Army.* (see quot.). Cf. SHIT PISTOL.
1944 *Nat. Geo.* (Nov.) 524: He must be able to handle captured weapons, such as the German machine pistol, or "diarrhea gun," as the men call it.

diarrhea-mouth *n.* an excessively talkative person.
1976 Lieberman & Rhodes *CB* 127: *Diarrhea Mouth*—Constant talker. **1978** Pilcer *Teen Angel* 40: Hey, diarrhea mouth!

dib *n.* [prob. fr. *dibstones,* a type of child's jacks] **1.a.** *pl.* money.
1807 *Port Folio* (June 6) 357: You must put some more cash in your pocket./Make Nunky surrender his dibbs. *****1821** *Real Life in London* II 57: *The dibs are in tune*—There is plenty of money. *****1837** in *F & H:* One of their drummers.../Had brush'd with the dibs. *****1842** in *F & H:* Science can't be purchased without *dibbs.* **1855** Brougham *Basket of Chips* 80: The dollarum dibs will hold paramount sway. **1859** Matsell *Vocab.* 25: *Dibs.* Money. **1859** *Spirit of Times* (Apr. 2) 88: All the cash and all the "rhino,"/...All the "dibs" he did discover. *****1867** Smyth *Sailor's Wd. Bk.: Dibbs,* a galley term for ready money. **1889** *United Service* (Sept.) 279: The best we [American seamen] can wish is an accumulation of "addlings" (pay), plenty of "dibbs" (ready cash), and no "dead horse" (back debt) to work off. *****1909** Ware *Passing Eng.* 117: Dibs [is] the [bootmaker's] trade term for money. **1923** (quot. at IRON). **1949** R. Chandler *Little Sister* 31: What's your racket?...How do you make your dibs? **1958** S.H. Adams *Tenderloin* 110 [ref. to 1890's]: The dibs. The dollars. Mazuma. Spondulix. Cash.
b. a dollar.
1936 in D. Runyon *More Guys* 151: The best I can do is to stake him to few dibs. **1951** *New Yorker* (Dec. 8) 81: Fifty sweet dibs!
2.a. a share; portion.
*****1829** in J. Farmer *Musa Pedestris* 107: If you'd share the swag, or have one dib...[i.e.] the least share. **1859** Matsell *Vocab.* 25: *Dib.* Portion or share. **1927** in Hammett *Knockover* 311: By rights, I ought to collect the kid's dib, too. **1929** in *Ibid.* 51: And I was to get my dib.
b. *pl.* Esp. *Juve.* a first claim on an item.
1932 *AS* VII 401: Dibs on that magazine when you're through. **1934** Weseen *Dict. Slang* 327: *Dibs*—an option; a first chance. **1956** N.Y.C. schoolchild: I got dibs! Dibs on that! **1954–60** *DAS.* **1975** McCaig *Danger Trail* 69: And I'll give ye dibs on the first shot. **1981** Wolf *Roger Rabbit* 90: I knew who had first dibs on it. **1986** E. Weiner *Howard the Duck* 131: I got dibs on the laser first.

dibby *adj.* (see quot.).
1901 *DN* II 138: *Dibby, adj.* Fine. Brooklyn (school girl expression).

dic *n.* a dictionary; (*hence*) difficult words; highflown language. Also **dick.**
1831 Seabury *Moneygripe* 63 [ref. to 1815]: Was always reading when

he got a chance and could talk *dic* (dictionary words) equal to any fellow. **1841** [Mercier] *Man-of-War* 138: If that ain't going the whole figure on *dick* I wonder at it. **1860** in *F & H* II 280. **1895** Gore *Stu. Slang* 6: *Dic* n. Dictionary. **1928** Dahlberg *Bottom Dogs* 264: Walsh said Lorry packed a mean mitt at Webster's *dic*. **1979** Univ. Tenn. grad. student: I had a teacher [in grade school] who referred to our dictionaries as *dics*. None of us could keep from laughing and she never could figure out why.

dice *n.* **1.** DICER[1].

1891 Maitland *Amer. Slang Dict.* 92: *Dice* or *Dicer* (Am.), a silk hat.

2. [fr. DICE, *v.*] *Auto. Racing.* a close contest for position between two racing-car drivers.

1962 G. Olson *Roaring Road* 14: Man, what a dice!…Great driving there, buddy boy! **1965** *Time* (July 9) 80: He drove the…Lotus Elite in a ten-lap race…[and] found himself involved in "a whale of a dice" with another Elite. **1987** *RHD2*.

¶ In phrase:

¶ **no dice, 1.** worthless.

1929–31 D. Runyon *Guys & Dolls* 76: I never have much truck with him because he is a guy I consider no dice. In fact, he does not mean a thing. **1932** D. Runyon in *Collier's* (Jan. 9) 8: When it comes to looks, Mary Marble is practically no dice…She has a large beezer and large feet. **1952** W. Pegler, in *DAS:* We have been paying a disguised subsidy to a little no-dice paper called the Rome American.

2. an utterly unsuccessful attempt; (*hence*, as *interj.*) no luck; absolutely not.

1928 in J.M. March *Wild Party* 172: No dice/We ain't got nothin' at that price. **1934** L. Berg *Prison Nurse* 51: He tried, but it was "no dice." **1936** Steel *College* 338: "But if you'll talk to her quietly and—"…"No dice." **1937** Weidman *Wholesale* 268: Sorry, Bogen, it's no dice. **1939** "E. Queen" *Dragon's Teeth* 114: No dice. Think of something else. **1946** Haines *Command Decision* 127: No dice, Casey. Schweinhafen's mine. **1949** Grayson & Andrews *I Married a Communist* (film): It's no dice, baby. I've got no use for you. **1953 Fleming *Casino Royale* 82: He wasn't going to fall for this childish trick. No dice. **1954** Schulberg *Waterfront* 11: Charley wastes his best arguments and comes back with no dice. **1960** J.A. Williams *Angry Ones* 101: "What'd he say, your boss?" "No dice." **1961** Sullivan *Gladdest Yrs.* 10: I searched for a switch: no dice. **1962** Shepard *Passes* 200: Just as we left the Bando Hotel, back came the reply "no dice." **1968** Broughton *Thud Ridge* 58: Roger, Lincoln—Pintail. It's negative, negative, negative. No dice. We're on our way out. **1981** Wolf *Roger Rabbit* 89: I wanted to kid myself, but no dice. **1991** B.E. Ellis *Amer. Psycho* 208: "Any luck?" I ask. "No dice," he says.

dice *v. Auto. Racing.* to contend closely for position with another driver during a race.

1941 in *OEDS:* Racing motorists usually referred to driving in a race as either "cracking" or "dicing," the latter word having been derived from the journalists' former habit of writing about their being "speed demons dicing with death." **1965 *N.Y. Times* (July 25) VI 22: Ferrari does not seem to mind crashes…which befall pros dicing for the lead. **1970 Partridge *DSUE* (ed. 7) 1096: *Dicing*…a "duel" between two drivers…since *ca*1955. **1976** *6000 Words*.

dicer[1] *n.* a top hat or derby; (*broadly*) a man's hat of any sort. [The dating "*ca*1800–40" in Partridge *DSUE* (ed. 7) is due to a typographical error.]

1887 *N.O. Lantern* (July 9) 2: Now Lehman wears his dicer down over his eyes. **1889** Bailey *Ups & Downs* 23 [ref. to 1871]: I wore a high silk dicer and carried a gold watch and chain. **1890** in *DA*. **1896** Ade *Artie* 56: New suit, new white necktie, new dicer, new shoes. **1899** "J. Flynt" *Tramping* 393: *Dicer:* A hat. **1904** Limerick *Villagers* 17: The…visitor removed his weather-beaten dicer. **1918** in Blackbeard & Williams *Smithsonian Comics* 28: "Off wit' the dicer you hornswoggled galoot!" **1926** *AS* I (Dec.) 651: *Dicer.* A hat.

dicer[2] *n.* [fr. mer*chandise* + -*r*] *R.R.* a freight train.

1927 *DN* V 444: *Dicer, n.* A fast freight. **1930** Irwin *Tramp & Und. Slang: Dicer*…A fast freight. **1980** Bruns *Kts. of Road* 195: The men reel off their stories of the road, of holding down dicers and rattlers, of mean bulls and hostile towns.

dicey *adj.* [dice + -*y*] Orig. *Mil. Av.* risky or difficult; dangerous; tricky; unpredictable; delicate. Now *colloq.* or *S.E.*

[**1917** in Rossano *Price of Honor* 24: Some of our men got out the dice….You never saw a "dicier" crowd in your life.] **ca*1944 in Kaplan & Smith *One Last Look* 82: Dicey…Dodgy. **1950 in *OEDS.* **1964** *Time* (Dec. 4) 81: Filming wildlife in the veld is dicey business at best. **1966**

Shepard *Doom Pussy* 58: I think I should warn you. These are our diciest missions. It's your decision, but you know, the boys don't always come back. *Ibid.* The dicier the sortie, the louder he bellowed bawdy ballads. **1967 Partridge *DSUE* (ed. 6) (Add.): *Dicey.* Risky; dangerous: RAF 1940+; by 1946, common among civilians. **1968** Coppel *Order of Battle* 79 [ref. to 1944]: It's going to be dicey getting back to the bar, you know. **1969** Briley *Traitors* 152: The atmosphere was a little dicey, but Hill had a talent for irreverent humor that must have driven the stoutest teachers up the wall. **1972** *N.Y. Post* (Oct. 20) 44: In Bedford-Stuyvesant…life is dicey at best. **1975** Lichtenstein *Long Way* 72: Every week it's been kind of dicey whether we're going to get meals. **1975** in Higham & Siddall *Combat Aircraft* 43: Neither pilot could see the wing on the opposite side of the aircraft, which made taxiing very dicey. **1978** *N.Y. Post* (Dec. 9) 11: That's the kind of thinking that makes the passage of a SALT treaty a dicey affair. **1984** J. Michener, in *N.Y. Times Mag.* (Aug. 19) 82: I know that survival is a very dicey affair. **1985** Dye *Between Raindrops* 122: It was dicey there for a minute. **1990** *CBS This Morning* (CBS-TV) (Jan. 3): We have a rather dicey [satellite] signal this morning.

dick[1] *n.* [fr. *Dick*, hypocoristic form of *Richard*] **1.** a fellow, esp. if foolish or peculiar; man. [1968, 1971 quots. have been infl. by SWINGING DICK.]

1553 in *OED:* Desperate Dickes borowes now and then against the owners will all that ever he hath. **1588 Shakespeare *Love's Labors* V ii: Some Dick that smiles his cheeke in yeares, and knowes the trick/To make my Lady laugh. **1659 in Partridge *Dict. Und.* 185: Her part is to pick up a Dick that is full of money, whom she invites to her house. **1822 in *OED:* He's a gone dick, a dead man. **1914 S.H. Adams *Clarion* 125: You're a queer Dick, Ellis. **1925** Nason *Three Lights* 135: See what the old Dick wants. **1928–29** Nason *White Slicker* 234: That old dick is only a jawbone colonel, anyway. **1938** Burt *Powder River* 350: The sheep-herder…If an American, likely to be a queer sort of dick. **1940** Farrell *Father & Son* 310: But McCormack there, an ordinary dick, he didn't. **1968** Just *What End* 169: Goddamnit I want forty hard-charging fuckin' dicks. And if anybody ain't a hard-charging fuckin' dick I want him out. **1971** *Playboy* (Aug.) 200: I want ten guys for patrol…ten hard-charging dicks.

2.a. the penis.—usu. considered vulgar. Also in semi-prov. phr.

*ca*1888 *Stag Party* 208: Student (turning her fairly around and putting his dick where his finger was)—Nice, isn't it, ducky? **1889 Barrère & Leland *Dict.* I 307: *Dick* (military), the penis. **1916** Cary *Venery* I 66: *Dick*—The penis. **1928** in Read *Lexical Evidence* 49: She sucked my dick. **1929 Manning *Fortune* 53: Dost turn thysen to t' wall, lad, so's us'ns shan't see tha dick? **1930** *Lyra Ebriosa* 17: He kept on letting out his dick. **1934** H. Miller *Tropic of Cancer* 52: It feels exactly as if he had taken out that dick of his and was peeing on us. **1936** Farrell *World I Never Made* 124: And Pa puts his dick into Ma's hole. **1942** McAtee *Supp. Grant Co.* 4 [ref. to 1890's]: *Dick, n.* Penis. **1961** Granat *Important Thing* 157: He just folds up like a tired dick. **1962** Killens *Heard the Thunder* 38: More pussy over there than you can shake a dick at. **1966–67** P. Thomas *Mean Streets* 193: I wouldn't touch that…bitch with a ten-foot dick. **1970** A. Walker *Copeland* 96: You been out all Saturday night swinging your dick. **1974** E. Thompson *Tattoo* 242: "I wouldn't fuck her with *your* dick!" was the consensus. **1976** Selby *Demon* 17: A stiff dick ain't got no conscience, right? **1977** Bunker *Animal Factory* 131: I've been watchin' you an' watchin' you an' my dick stays hard as Chinese arithmetic! **1973–77** J. Jones *Whistles* 103: There's more worthless commissions floating around…than you can shake your dick at. **1980** Gould *Ft. Apache* 113: He was out on the street freezing his dick off. **1980** DiFusco et al. *Tracers* 13: That's right, maggot, you do [push-ups] till my dick gets hard. *Ibid.* 78: "You smoke?"…"Does Pinocchio have a wooden dick?" **1983** Wambaugh *Delta Star* 23: Some days…I don't know my dick from a dumplin'. **1988** Poyer *The Med* 539: We was busy as a dog with two dicks.

b. the clitoris.—usu. considered vulgar.

1964 in B. Jackson *Swim Like Me* 148: She had a dick so long she had to be circumcised.

3. the least bit; anything; (in nonnegative constructions) nothing.—usu. in negative constructions.—usu. considered vulgar.

1915–25 in Fraser & Gibbons *Soldier & Sailor Wds.* 76: *Dick, Money for:* Money for nothing. **1951–52 Frank *Hold Back Night* 162: "It isn't going to work, Sam. We haven't got dick." This was a strange and fatherless expression birthed by the Korean war. **1966** Neugeboren *Big Man* 52: He's fifteen months, going on sixteen and still can't do dick for himself. *Ibid.* 132: They couldn't get dick out of you. **1968** I. Reed *Yel-*

low Back Radio 40: Man they didn't know from dick. **1974** Price *Wanderers* 161: You can't fight wort' dick. **1975** S.P. Smith *Amer. Boys* 220: He figured that the bosses must know about the habits of the people, then he realized that the bosses didn't know dick. **1978** Price *Ladies' Man* 8: I wasn't going to say dick. **1985** M. Baker *Cops* 210: That's just verbiage. It doesn't mean shit. It doesn't mean dick, because nothing is going to change. **1987** Mamet *House of Games* (film): All the time you say you want to help me—you don't do dick. **1992** *Vanity Fair* (Sept.) 102: I didn't have any money, the Feds wouldn't do dick, nobody was helping out.

4. copulation with a man.—usu. considered vulgar.

1956 in Oliver *Blues Tradition* 240: She's out on the street catchin' dick, dick, dick. **1958** Motley *Epitaph* 210: They peddle anything from watches, rings, dope, all the way down to dick. **1964** Rhodes *Chosen Few* 77 [ref. to *ca*1950]: If you hafta give up some dick to do it, GIVE IT UP! **1965** C. Brown *Manchild* 207: The first time somebody put some good dick to her, she'd be giving him money. *1976 in Partridge *DSUE* (ed. 8): She was crazy for dick. **1985** E. Leonard *Glitz* 320: Old women don't get a lot of dick.

5. a stupid or contemptible man or boy; PRICK.—usu. considered vulgar.

1966 Bogner *7th Ave.* 389: He's a dick. I don't know from respect, except for my parents. **1967** Kolb *Getting Straight* 83: "Dick's an old classmate from pre-med."...He looked the type. A dick, all right. **1968** Baker et al. *CUSS* 104: *Dick.* A person who always does the wrong thing. **1970** Whitmore *Memphis-Nam-Sweden* 36: Slick dicks who thought they could hustle and bullshit their way out of the Army. **1974** Strasburger *Rounding Third* 130: I was (if you'll pardon my French) a crude little dick. **1978** S. King *Stand* 564: Take it from me, the original dipstick, oilslick, and drippy dick. **1979** *Nat. Lampoon* (Aug.) 41: [You] Really feel like a dick for traveling around with your mom and dad in a camper. **1980** Conroy *Lords of Discipline* 180: Piss all over these tight-assed dicks. **1981** Crowe *Fast Times* 28: You dick.

¶ In phrases:

¶ **beans and dicks** *Mil.* beans and frankfurters.—usu. considered vulgar. [Quots. ref. to Vietnam War.]

1980 DiFusco et al. *Tracers* 43: You can have all the spaghetti and meatballs, and the beans 'n dicks, and I get all the fruit. **1983** Van DeVanter & Morgan *Before Morning* 20: The crazy fucker just finished eating six cans of beans and dicks before we got hit.

¶ **buy the dick** (see quot.).—usu. considered vulgar.

1970 Landy *Underground Dict.* 43: *Buy the dick*...Get into trouble; get hurt...Die—eg. He bought the dick through an overdose.

¶ **holding (one's) dick** stupidly unaware or unprepared.—usu. considered vulgar.

1982 "W.T. Tyler" *Rogue's March* 91: Don't tell me they caught you holding your dick too, like the rest of these birds.

¶ **knock** [or **put**] **(someone's) dick in the dirt** to knock (a person) down; (*hence*) to overwhelm or punish.—usu. considered vulgar.

1970 in D.C. Dance *Shuckin' & Jivin'* 197: The Elephant.../Knocked his dick in the dirt and knocked his nuts out of place. **1972** Jenkins *Semi-Tough* 50: Don't that mother [a song] knock your dicks in the dirt? **1973** W. Crawford *Stryker* 34: He wants to, he can knock your dick inna dirt. **1987** W.Ga. College prof.: I got an American lit exam that's gonna knock their dick in the *dirt*!...Yeah, I first heard that on Okinawa in 1977. **1988** Norst *Colors* 106: I will put your dick in the dirt right now. **1990** R. Herman, Jr. *Force of Eagles* 9: Snake was...telling anyone who would listen how he had "knocked their dicks in the dirt."

¶ **my dick!** (used to express disbelief or anger).—usu. considered vulgar.

1979 Gram *Blvd. Nights* 104: "It's gotta seep, man."..."Seep my dick." **1980** Manchester *Darkness* 109 [ref. to 1942]: A cascade [on Guadalcanal] which we called Mydick Falls—christened by...the point man who saw it first and gasped, "My dick!" **1981** Wambaugh *Glitter Dome* 19: Irish whiskey, my dick. **1992** Mowry *Way Past Cool* 217: "Twenty bucks an hour!" "My dick!"

¶ **pull (someone's) dick** see s.v. PULL, *v.*

¶ **snap (one's) dick** (see quot.).—usu. considered vulgar.

1972 Haslam *Oil Fields* 112: *Snap Your Dick, v.* To hurry.

dick² *n.* [prob. by reanalysis of Hiberno-E travelers' cant *dicked* 'being watched,' der. fr. DICK¹, *v.*; cf. DECK¹, *v.*; DECKED¹; DEEK, *v. & n.*]

1. *Und.* a police officer.

1908 Sullivan *Criminal Slang* 8: *Dick*—A cop, detective (Canadian slang). *a*1909 Tillotson *Detective* 90: *Dick*—A county policeman, constable, sherrif [*sic*], or any officer. **1928** Sharpe *Chicago May* 281: A dick may mean a detective, or a policeman. A harness-bull, however, is, properly, only a policeman in uniform. **1931** in A.E. Wood *Hamtramck* 155: Each gang changes its headquarters as the "dicks" get wise to the old one. **1939** Hixson & Colodny *Word Ways* 136: A banker would scarcely call...policemen "dicks" or "bulls."

2. *Orig. Und.* a detective.

[*1896–1900 *EDD* s.v. *dick, n.* (Co. Antrim, N. Ire.): To *keep dick*, to keep watch.] **1908** (quot. at **(1)**, above). **1909** C. Chrysler *White Slavery* 70: "No dick has anything on you."...No detective can make a case against you. **1911** A.H. Lewis *Apaches of N.Y.* 95: Those plain-clothes dicks did not despair. **1911** Howard *Enemy to Society* 162: The "dicks" ain't givin' him no protection, see? **1918** *Everybody's* (Sept.) 36: Why don't you send a coupla dicks over there an' pull the joint? **1922** in Ruhm *Detective* 4: He ain't got none of the earmarks of a dick. **1926** Clark & Eubank *Lockstep* 23: There sure enough stood a "Dick," Tom Myler by name. **1927** C. McKay *Harlem* 29: Soon as this heah kind a business stahts, the dicks will sartain sure git on to us. **1927** in F.S. Fitzgerald *Stories* I 364: He got in a row at the station in Pittsburgh and a dick got him. **1930** Lavine *3d Degree* 13: One of the more ambitious ones would go in the Detective Bureau and become a "dick." **1939** "E. Queen" *Dragon's Teeth* 114: The other was the the house dick. **1939** Rossen *Dust Be My Destiny* (film): Don't kid me, he's going to get the dicks. **1951** J. Wilson *Dark & Damp* 412: Get on that car before one of these railroad dicks picks you up. **1960** C.L. Cooper *Scene* 233: I got 'em from a lady store-dick in California. **1970** N.Y.U. student: These two dicks were waiting for us as we came out of the alley.

dick³ *n.* see s.v. DIC.

dick¹ *v.* [< E Romani *dik* 'to look, see' < Hindi *dekkhna*; cf. DEEK, *v.*; DECK¹, *v.*; DECKED¹] *Und.* to watch.

*1864 Hotten *Slang Dict.* (ed. 3): "Look, the bulky is dicking," i.e. the constable has his eye on you. **1935** Pollock *Und. Speaks: Dicking*...a guard is watching (prison).

dick² *v.* [fr. DICK¹, *n.*, 2.a.] **1.** to botch; ruin; SCREW UP.—usu. constr. with *up*.—usu. considered vulgar. [The appositeness of the 1811 quot. is perh. more suggestive than real.]

[*1811 *Lexicon Balatron.*: *Dicked in the Nob.* Silly. Crazed.] **1951** Morris *China Station* 223: I want you to stay, sure, but if it dicks everything up for you, if we leave Tsingtao, maybe you better go now. **1966** Shepard *Doom Pussy* 52: He...claimed his schedule was "dicked up like a Mongolian shot card." **1969** *Current Slang* I & II 25: *Dicked up, adj.* In serious difficulty, often the result of thoughtlessness; in any serious state or condition.—Air Force Academy cadets. **1972** C. Gaines *Stay Hungry* 129: I'm sorry Stewart had to dick it for you. **1983** P. Dexter *God's Pocket* 130: We ran a story yesterday,...and somehow we got it all dicked up. **1983** M. Skinner *USAFE* 70: Ten other guys...go in and dick the strike flight. *a*1990 Poyer *Gulf* 42: You flyboys can dick 'em up a lot faster than us.

2. to copulate with (a woman; *rarely* a man).—usu. considered vulgar. [Asserted kinship with ME *dight* is untenable on the basis of phonological problems and of the unlikeliness of unrecorded survival for many centuries.]

1942 in Randolph & Legman *Roll Me in Your Arms* 327: She ought to be dicked. **1962** Mandel *Mainside* 357: Not beat off in your sack or cut classes or dick the commandant's daughter. **1966–67** W. Stevens *Gunner* 245 [ref. to WWII]: All he'd be able to give in return would be a dicking. Wham, bam, thank you ma'am. **1970** Whitmore *Memphis-Nam-Sweden* 165: That son of a bitch is coming back with a cop and I'm getting ten years for dicking his wife! **1970** in J. Flaherty *Chez Joey* 22: He didn't believe in alimony because of all the great dicking he had given his woman. **1971** *Nude, Blued & Tattooed* 58: You know you should never argue or fight with a lady—just dicker. **1977** Bredes *Hard Feelings* 59: I actually saw Zeke dicking some mutt over by the spruce tree. **1978** Rascoe & Stone *Who'll Stop Rain?* (film): I think he's dickin' her in there. **1982** "W.T. Tyler" *Rogue's March* 302: You're off in the bush, dicking some French babe. **1985** N. Kazan *At Close Range* (film): Julie started dickin' some grease monkey from Willard.

3. to victimize; ruin; cheat; deceive.—usu. considered vulgar.

1964 *AS* (Oct.) 280: *Dick, v.t.* To cheat. **1970** Whitmore *Memphis-Nam-Sweden* 127: He was stateside and I was dicked! **1971** Dahlskog *Dict.* 18: *Dicked*...Screwed; taken advantage of; double-crossed. **1987** J. Hughes *16 Candles* (film): Jake, would I dick you?

4. Esp. *Mil.* to master; often in phr. **have** [or **get**] **it dicked**

to have it easy; have it made.—usu. considered vulgar. [Quots. ref. to Vietnam War.]

1972 Pelfrey *Big V* 100: These guys got it dicked…Nothin to do but write letters and read *Playboy.* **1975** S.P. Smith *Amer. Boys* 250: You ought to stay on. We'd have it dicked. **1982** Del Vecchio *13th Valley* 2: You REMF…candyasses sure got it dicked. **1986** Merkin *Zombie Jamboree* 204: A rite of passage that any shmuck could dick.

¶ In phrases:

¶ **dick with** to interfere with or harass; fool with.—usu. considered vulgar.

1978 Texas man, age 34: But the best Texas expression is "Do yourself a favor, boy—don't dick with me." **1979** Gram *Blvd. Nights* 49: C'mon, you assholes, don't dick with me! **1984** "W.T. Tyler" *Shadow Cabinet* 309: That's federal merchandise you're dicking with.

¶ **I'll be dicked!** (used as an oath).—usu. considered vulgar.

1966 Neugeboren *Big Man* 181: "I'll be dicked," Morgan says. **1969** in *DARE*: Well, I'll be dicked!

dick around *v.* **1.** to be sexually promiscuous or unfaithful.—usu. considered vulgar.

1969 Girodias *New Olympia Reader* 629: I had been dicking around with an absolutely frenzied little grass widow with a cottage by the Pacific. **1977** Bredes *Hard Feelings* 237: I think my *father* might dick around some, or else he might like to.

2. to loaf or waste time; fool around; FUCK AROUND.—usu. considered vulgar. Cf. poss. euphem. DICKY AROUND.

1947 Mailer *Naked & Dead* 276 [ref. to WWII]: The only reason you been dicking around is there ain't anything big enough for you to get your teeth in. **1966** Neugeboren *Big Man* 134: Don't dick around with me, huh? **1975** Wambaugh *Choirboys* 281: She was getting sick and tired of dicking around with the little creep. **1984** H. Searls *Blood Song* 249: "Don't dick around," Jeff threatened, "get us there!" **1987** J. Thompson *Gumshoe* 3: Some kind of college professor dicking around as a detective.

3. to impose upon contemptuously; victimize.

1983 Spottiswood *48 Hrs.* (film): You been dickin' me around ever since we started this turd-hunt.

dickbrain *n.* DICKHEAD.—usu. considered vulgar.

1971 Drill sgt., U.S. Army, age *ca*22 (coll. J. Ball): How're we gonna win Best Platoon when they send us a bunch of dickbrains like this? **1974** U.C.L.A. student: He's a real dickbrain. **1977** Bredes *Hard Feelings* 229: You dickbrain. It wasn't me that killed your dog. **1982** S.P. Smith *Officer & Gentleman* 30: You laughing at me, dick-brain? **1986** *NDAS.*

dick-breath *n.* a contemptible fellow; COCKSUCKER.—usu. considered vulgar.

1972 Bunker *No Beast* 12: Look, dick breath motherfucker. **1974** Univ. Tenn. student: Who asked you, dick-breath? **1979** Univ. Tenn. grad. student: The phrase "Hey, dick-breath!" was used to impugn one's sexual orientation. This was at Davidson College, 1965–69. **1988** R. Snow *Members of Committee* 1: What names do you think non-gay people use to describe your sexuality?…Faggot…Queen…Pansy…Dickbreath.

dickey *n. Naut.* mate, esp. second mate; lieutenant.—often constr. with *first, second,* or *third.*

***1805** J. Davis *Post-Captain* 124: They called him Acting Dickey. ***1829** (cited in Partridge *DSUE* (ed. 8)). **1836** *Knickerbocker* (Aug.) 203: Jack Marlinespike, who had been first dickey of an Indiaman, couldn't get a situation afore the mast of a Ballyhoo coasting-brig. **1841** [Mercier] *Man-of-War* 51: I was taken into the cabin as *first dickey.* **1844** J.F. Cooper *Afloat* 44: I heard the chief mate tell the dickey that the parson's son was likely to turn out a regular "barber's clerk" to the captain. *Ibid.* 311: I went to work regularly, and have been ever since sarving as dickey, or chief mate, on board some craft or other. **1846** Codman *Sailors' Life* 164: I…borrowed one or two white shirts from the second dickey. **1856** *Ballou's Dollar Mo. Mag.* (Oct.) 324: The second dickey came forward to rouse all hands to wash decks. *ca*1856 in Whipple *Whalers* 81: And finally 3d dickey of the "Lancaster." **1899** Boyd *Shellback* 36: The dickey began his tramp between the wheelhouse and the break of the quarter-deck. ***1929** Bowen *Sea Slang* 36: *Dicky.* The second mate.

dickey *adj.* [orig. unkn.] ruined; gone; finished.—constr. with *all.*

***1796** Grose *Vulgar Tongue* (ed. 3): *It's all Dickey with him;* i.e., it's all over with him. **1821** Waln *Hermit* 25: It's *all Dickey* with you. ***1873** Hotten *Slang Dict.* (ed. 4): "It's all *dickey* with him," *i.e.,* all over with him.

dickface *n.* (used as a term of abuse).—usu. considered vulgar.

1975 Univ. Tenn. student: Hey, dickface! **1983** S. King *Christine* 143: How did you like that, dickface? **1985** N. Kazan *At Close Range* (film): Your daddy's a dickface. Don't want me to have no money, don't want me to have no fun. **1987** D. Sherman *Main Force* 186 [ref. to 1966]: Both of you dickfaces better get a good night's sleep because tomorrow your ass is grass. **1988** H. Stern (synd. radio program) (Nov. 22): Rick! Dickface! What are you doing?

dick-fingered *adj.* (see quot.).—usu. considered vulgar.

1983 K. Weaver *Texas Crude* 108: Dick-fingered. Maladroit.

dickhead *n.* [DICK[1] + *head;* cf. CUNTHEAD, FUCKHEAD, PECKERHEAD] **1.** something difficult to deal with.—usu. considered vulgar.

1962 B. Jackson *In Life* 165: But this bit here, man, aw, it's a dickhead. **1974** R. Carter *16th Round* 291: Ray Brown was…trying to outthink their next moves, but then they threw a real dickhead at us. *Ibid.* 306: Judge Larner added one other small note which I thought was the dickhead of all. *Ibid.* 319: The verdict was the dickhead that really seemed to blow Hogan's mind the most. **1985** Dye *Between Raindrops* 287: This Goddam adrenalin high was a dickhead.

2. a blockhead; dolt.—usu. considered vulgar.

1964 R. Moore *Green Berets* 82: I just don't like that little crook to think we're absolute dickheads. **1966** Shepard *Doom Pussy* 164: Gahdam dickhead. **1969** Crumley *Cadence* 70: That dickhead needs to learn he can't get away with that nineteenth century Capt. Bligh shit. **1969** Maitland *Only War* 37: Yeah, only because he's the only dickhead stupid enough to get involved in such a mess. **1970** *Current Slang* V 7: *Dickhead, n.* One who has a peculiarly shaped head; a very stupid person. **1971** N.Y.U. student [ref. to 1961–62]: "Dickhead" was "idiot." **1971** Mayer *Falcon* 27: "Don't be a dickhead," I said. **1987** G. Matthews *Rooster* 220: What a bunch of dickheads people are. **1991** B.E. Ellis *Amer. Psycho* 271: Boasting, arrogant, cheerful dickhead who constantly weaseled his way out of checks.

dick-jacket *n.* a condom.—usu. considered vulgar.

1974 SP6, U.S. Army, age *ca*30 (coll. J. Ball): I need to…get some dick-jackets so I won't get the clap this time.

dick job *n. Mil.* an easy job.—usu. considered vulgar.

1972 SP4, U.S. Army, age *ca*20 (coll. J. Ball): Man, I wish I could get *me* a dick job like that. **1985** (quot. at SKATE JOB).

dickless *adj.* (used as a term of abuse).—usu. considered vulgar. Cf. DICKLESS TRACY.

1984 Aykroyd & Ramis *Ghostbusters* (film). **1990** *Tenn. Ling.* X (Winter) 39: [Insults]…"Prick" "Bastard"…"Dickless pimp."

Dickless Tracy *n.* [pun on DICK 'penis' and the name of *Dick Tracy,* a popular comic-strip detective introduced (1931) by Chester Gould] *Police.* a woman who is a police officer.—used contemptuously.—usu. considered vulgar.

1963 D.W. Maurer, in McDavid *Amer. Lang.* 730: *Dickless Tracy,* a police woman. **1971** Sonzski *Punch Goes Judy* 142: No comment from Dickless Tracy. **1978** Dills *CB* (ed. 4) 31: *Dickless Tracy:* police woman. **1979** *Playboy* (Aug.) 51: I refer to the sexual harassment by the "Dickless Tracy" division of all local police departments, whereby policewomen entrap helpless males into soliciting them for acts of prostitution…The man is…convicted…on the word of a Dickless Tracy. **1983** Wambaugh *Delta Star* 88: You dickless Tracys.

dicklicker *n.* a fellator; *(hence)* a despicable person; COCKSUCKER.—usu. considered vulgar. Also **dick-lick.**

1968 Heard *Howard St.* 236: Ahm sho'nuff glad they got that dicklicker, man! **1971** 2/Lt. U.S. Army, age 23: Another expression you hear a lot is "you sorry-assed dicklicker!" **1971** N.Y.U. man [ref. to U.S. Army, 1969]: Another common expression is "you sorry-assed dicklicker!" **1975** T. Berger *Sneaky People* 30: I'll kill that dicklicker. **1977** Monaco *Parsival* 147: Yield yourself, and maybe I won't crack your head for you, you red dick-licker. **1987** *Penthouse Letters* (Oct.) 54: There must be at least a few cock-crazy dick-lickers out there! **1988** Norst *Colors* 145: You did okay…for a dick-lick.

dicklicking *adj.* despicable; COCKSUCKING.—usu. considered vulgar.

1978 J. Webb *Fields of Fire* 19: Cocksuckin', dicklickin' mohfucka.

dicknose *n.* DICKFACE.—usu. considered vulgar.

1974 Matthews & Amdur *Race Be Won* 4: Nothing, dick-nose. **1976** in L. Bangs *Psychotic Reactions* 196: Which makes him *more* human than the rest of those…dicknoses. **1985** Loeb & Weisman *Teen Wolf* (film):

What are you looking at, dicknose?

dick off *v.* to loaf; FUCK OFF.—usu. considered vulgar.

1947 Mailer *Naked & Dead* 110 [ref. to WWII]: But when it comes down to a little goddam work, you're always dicking off. **1961** Forbes *Goodbye to Some* 27 [ref. to WWII]: I say don't let him dick off any longer. **1968** Baker et al. *CUSS* 104: *Dick off.* Waste time, not study. **1972** Hannah *Geronimo Rex* 172: Get out there and perform...no dicking off! **1979** Univ. Tenn. student: They're dickin' off again.

dickotomy *n. Hosp.* surgery of the male genitals.—usu. considered vulgar.

1983 Eilert *Self & Country* 110 [ref. to 1968]: There he is...his pecker all bandaged from this dickotomy.

dick out *v.* to endure; stick out.—usu. considered vulgar.

1976 N.Y.C. bartender, age 28: If I can dick it out for eighteen months I'll be rich.

Dick's hatband *n.* (used in various similes, esp. with *tight*). [Despite speculation, the allusive orig. is unkn. and likely to remain so.]

*1788 Grose *Vulgar Tongue* (ed. 2): *I am as queer as Dick's hatband;* that is, out of spirits, or don't know what ails me. **1835** *Knickerbocker* (May) 436: When a person is eccentric, he is pronounced "as odd as Dick's hat band." The origin of this native apothegm is buried in obscurity. ***1856** *N & Q* (Series 2) II 238: As tight as Dick's hat-band. **1892** in *EDD* (U.S. usage): As odd as Dick's hat-band. As contrary as Dick's hat-band. **1909** *DN* III 389: Tight as Dick's hat band. *Ibid.* 414: Odd as Dick's hat band. **1952** Randolph & Wilson *Holler* 176: *Tighter than Dick's hatband* does not refer to drunkenness, but is said of a door or window that is difficult to open, or of anything else that fits very tightly; some hillfolk regard this expression as vulgar, and won't let their children use it. **1953** W. Fisher *Waiters* 69: He's got this place sewed up tighter than Dick's hatband. **1967** Colebrook *Lassitude* 124: I'm gonna sit here tight as Dick's hatband. *ca***1974** in J.L. Gwaltney *Drylongso* 17: So they can help themselves when times get tight as Dick's hatband a person bucks. **1980** Algren *Dev. Stocking* 303: They're crazy as Dick's hatband. **1986** *Story of English* (PBS-TV): "Tight as Dick's hatband" means you're real cheap.

Dick Shit *n.* JACK SHIT.—usu. considered vulgar.

1983 Eilert *Self & Country* 256: I owe those American brothers Dick Shit. **1984** in *Maledicta* VIII (1985) 236: You can't do dick-shit in this town.

dick-shriveler *n.* an offensive or obnoxious person.—usu. considered vulgar.

1983 P. Dexter *God's Pocket* 251: There were as many dick shrivelers that wanted to ban nuclear sites...as there were that wanted to bomb Russia.

dick-skinner *n. Mil.* a hand.—usu. considered vulgar.

1971 Drill Sgt., U.S. Army, age *ca*45, Ft. Campbell, Ky. (coll. J. Ball): Raise them dick-skinners so's I can see 'em! **1985** Dye *Between Raindrops* 84 [ref. to 1968]: This particular [camera] is worth about a thousand bucks. Or it was before you got your dick-skinners on it. **1986** Dye & Stone *Platoon* 23 [ref. to Vietnam War]: Hey, White Boy, get yer dick-skinners back on that E-tool. **1988** Dye *Outrage* 83: [He had] a dick-skinner in every scam afloat.

Dick Smith *n.* [P. Tamony's suggestion (in *S.F. News Letter & Wasp* (Sept. 15, 1939) 12) that this derives fr. Richard Penn Smith (1799–1854), American playwright known for his plagiarism, seems unlikely] a solitary drinker; an unsociable fellow.

1876 in *DARE*: Provide that out of that fund this House may receive that pittance which shall enable it to supply the necessary wants of its members, without...playing "Dick Smith" on the Senate. **1919** T.A. Dorgan, in *S.F. Call & Post* (Mar. 25) 15 (Tamony Coll.): Whenever he buys a shot it's all for himself—a Dick Smith y'know. **1923** T.A. Dorgan, in *S.F. Call & Post* (June 4) 21 (Tamony Coll.): Dick Smith was an old ball player who never drank except by himself. **1930** Williams *Logger Talk* 22: *Dick Smith:* A drink of liquor taken privately; suggested by the famous Dick Smith who was given to such a sneaking practice to avoid buying a round. **1940** D. Runyon, in *S.F. Examiner* (Feb. 5) 8 (Tamony Coll.): A chap who walked up to a bar...and ordered and drank a drink without asking any one to join him, was a "Dick Smith." **1942** *ATS* 646: *Dick Smith,* a quiet, self-centered [baseball] player. **1955** *AS* XXX 87: *Dick Smith,* n. An addict who is a lone wolf. **1957** *Social Problems* V 311: It is the "Dick Smith" or "chiseler" who will accept a drink and not give one or who...will go off and drink by him-

self. **1969** in *DARE*: A Dick Smith spends his money by himself.

dicksmith *n. Navy.* a hospital corpsman.—used derisively.—usu. considered vulgar.

[***1967** Partridge *DSUE* (ed. 6) (Add.): *Prick-smith.* Medical officer: army: 1939+.] **1974** Ward *Folklore Coll.* 7: "Pecker-checker" is one of several names given to the hospital corpsman...Other names are "pill-roller," "pill-pusher," "dicksmith," and "chancre-mechanic."

dick-stepper *n.* [sugg. by *step on (one's) dick* s.v. STEP] *Mil.* a bungler; oaf.—usu. considered vulgar.

1983 K. Miller *Lurp Dog* 6 [ref. to Vietnam War]: I don't take no stumbling dicksteppers out on my team. **1991** L. Chambers *Recondo* 228: I just don't want any dick-steppers.

dick-string *n.* Esp. *Black E.* a man's ability to get or maintain an erection.—usu. considered vulgar.

*ca***1965** Walnut Ridge, Ark., teenager (coll. J. Ball): I'll clip that motherfucker's dick-string! **1966–67** P. Thomas *Mean Streets* 156 [ref. to WWII]: Ah hopes yuh busted his dick string. **1969** Pharr *Numbers* 181 [ref. to *ca*1935]: Keep your women off balance! If you ever let her get set, she'll knock your dick-string loose. **1972** P. Thomas *Savior* XI: I'll break your dick-string. **1985–90** R. Kane *Veteran's Day* 158: Then I dam up...something puts a knot in my dick string.

dicksucking *adj.* despicable; contemptible; COCKSUCKING.—usu. considered vulgar.

1972 Wurlitzer *Quake* 94: Which one of you dick sucking creeps is going to make a break for it?

dick-teaser *n.* COCKTEASER.—usu. considered vulgar. Also **dick-tease.**

1962 in *AS* (Dec. 1963) 273: A girl who will go so far as to arouse a male, but who will go no further is a *dick teaser* or a *prick teaser.* **1969** Mitchell *Thumb Tripping* 166: Are you all right, you little dick-tease? **1974** Angelou *Gather Together* 17: I didn't want him to think of me as a dick teaser.

dick up see s.v. DICK², *v.,* 1.

dickwad *n.* DICKWEED.

1989 P. Munro *U.C.L.A. Slang* 33: *Dickweed/dickwad* jerk, idiot, *asshole.* **1990** Rukuza *W. Coast Turnaround* 11: Listen to me, you dickwad!

dickweed *n.* a contemptible or stupid person.—usu. considered vulgar. Also **dinkweed.**

1980 Rimmer *Album* 40 [ref. to 1965]: How much time before dinner, dinkweed? **1984** Algeo *Stud Buds* 5: Dick, dickweed, dildo, [etc.]. **1985** J. Hughes *Weird Science* (film): Listen, dickweed! **1989** C. Matheson & E. Solomon *Excellent Adventure* (film): You killed Ted, you medieval dickweed! **1991** Ellis *American Psycho* 319: You're dating the biggest dickweed in New York.

dicky *n.* [dim. of DICK¹] the penis, usu. of a small boy.

*1890–91 *F & H*: *Dickey...*(schoolboys') The *penis.* **1962** Perry *Young Man* 37: The hair around my dicky has been there since I was fourteen. **1968** P. Roth *Portnoy* 229: Look what I'm sticking my dicky into.

dicky around *v.* [perh. euphem. for DICK AROUND] to fool around.

1926 Nichols & Tully *Twenty Below* 32: Quit dickying around that girl and listen to me!

dicky bird *n. Und.* (see quot.).

1902 Hapgood *Thief* 193: I was tipped off to you by a Dicky Bird (stool pigeon), damn him!

dicky-licker *n.* DICKLICKER.—usu. considered vulgar.

1934 "J.M. Hall" *Anecdota* 181: A dozen synonyms for male homosexuality...Fairy, pansy, queen, floosie, cock-sucker, gobbler, queerie, dickie-licker, femmie, Nancy, fruit, lapper. **1973** *AS* XLVI 382. **1986** *NDAS.*

dicky-waver *n.* Esp. *Police.* a man who exposes his genitals in public; male exhibitionist.

1973 Maas *Serpico* 107: The arrest of a "dicky-waver," a man who exposed himself. **1980** Key *Clam-Plate* 129: The artist subliminally portrayed the author as a maternally dominated dickie waver. **1980** Gould *Ft. Apache* 60: You guys collar a dicky-waver at seven o'clock in the morning in the South Bronx.

dicty *n. Black E.* a DICTY person; snob.

1928 Fisher *Jericho* 8: Hyeh's a dickty tryin' his damnedest to be fay—like all de other dickties. **1945** Drake & Cayton *Black Metropolis* 521: People with slight education, small incomes, and few of the social graces are always referring to the more affluent and successful as "dic-

ties," "stuck-ups," "mucktimucks," "high-toned folks," "tony people."
1951 J.S. Redding *Being Negro* 40: The incumbents who, in the common phrase, were "dickies," found their following split. **1958** Hughes & Bontemps *Negro Folklore* 482: The dicties live on Riverside. **1964** Smith & Hoefer *Music* 38: Our dictys* had some fancy cabarets and cafés...*Harlem sophisticates.

dicty or **dickty** *adj.* [orig. unkn.] *Black E.* **1.** wealthy or fashionable; (*hence*) snobbish; haughty.
1923 Toomer *Cane* 47: So that's how th' dictie nigger does it...Mus' give 'em credit fo' their gall. **1923** in R.S. Gold *Jazz Talk*: Dicty Blues. **1924** in Handy *Blues Treasury* 144: He [a tomcat] ain't gaycattin' round with dicty cats. **1926** Walrond *Tropic Death* 90: Indeed, Miss Buckner, a lady of sixty, would have been *wordless* at the idea of having to go beyond the dickty rim of Jamaica in quest of *manners*. **1927** C. McKay *Harlem* 14: Nevah befoh I seed so many dickty shines in sich swell motor-cars. *Ibid.* 46: My God!...Working with white folks so dickty and high-and-mighty, youse think theyse nevah oncet naked and them feets nevah touch ground. **1928** Fisher *Jericho* 4: Fifth Avenue's shame lies in having missed these so-called dickty sections. **1929** T. Gordon *Born to Be* 99 [ref. to Chicago, *ca*1915]: The railroad porter who introduced me to him told me he was a dickty spade, and that all dickty spades loathed the word NIGGAH, and for me never to use it in his presence. **1929** Larsen *Passing* 141: One day I went to an awful tea, terribly dicty. **1946** Mezzrow & Wolfe *Really Blues* 14: Dicty Washington embassies and Park Avenue salons. *Ibid.* 304: *Dicty:* snooty, high-class. **1956** Holiday & Dufty *Lady* 79: A Rolls is...only good for one thing...that's to be dicty. **1961** in Rose *Storyville* 160: All dem dicty people use t' hang by d' Frenchman's. **1967–69** Foster & Stoddard *Pops* 2: Some of those critics and dicty teachers should see the first bass I had. *Ibid.* 41: A band like John Robichaux's played nothin' but sweet music and played the dicty affairs. **1973** Ellington *Music My Mistress* 175: Sweet-and-low, scuffling-type Negroes, and dicty Negroes as well (doctors, lawyers, etc.). *a*1989 in Kisseloff *Must Remember This* 282: That sounds like me in my monkey suit, looking like all of those other dickty niggers.
2. fancy; (*hence*) very attractive; nifty.
1925 Van Vechten *Nigger Heaven* 285: Dicty: swell, in the slang sense. **1944** Bontemps & Cullen *St. Louis Woman* 9: New suit and dicty lid/ Call me the candy kid. **1961** *New Yorker* (Oct. 28) 167: A few dicty arpeggios. **1966** S. Harris *Hellhole* 109: He was seventeen and "dicty-looking" and Bertha would have done anything he wanted. *a*1986 *New Yorker*, in *World Book Dict.*: Dicty...excellent:...*a dicty cure for spasms.*

diddies *n.pl.* a woman's breasts; TITTIES.
1989 *Maledicta* X 52: Bazooms...diddies.

diddle[1] *n.* [orig. unkn.] Orig. *Und.* gin; (*broadly*) liquor.
ca*1700 in *OED: Diddle,* Geneva. **1724* in Partridge *Dict. Und.* 185: Had he not Bowz'd in the Diddle Shops*...*Geneva Shops. **1725 New Canting Dict.: Diddle,* The Cant Word for *Geneva,* a Liquor very much drank by the lowest Rank of People. **1785* Grose *Vulgar Tongue: Diddle.* Gin. **1728 View of London* 36: Twelve *Sneaking-Budge* Men, with Cags and Rundlets of *Diddle.* **1791 [W. Smith] *Confess. T. Mount* 21: A jorum of diddle. **1809* in Partridge *Dict. Und.* 185: *Diddle,* Rum, brandy, gin, &c. **1859** Matsell *Vocab.* 25: *Diddle.* Liquor.

diddle[2] *n.* [fr. the v.] **1.** an act of copulation.
1864 in R. Mitchell *Vacant Chair* 90: You could get a good *diddle.* *ca*1915 in Logsdon *Whorehouse Bells* 54: She'd gave him a little diddle that fairly made him dance.
2. a swindle or act of swindling.
*1885 in *F & H* II 283: And something whispered me...It's all a diddle! **1890–93 F & H* II 283: *Diddle...*(common).—A swindle or "do." **1980** Lorenz *Guys Like Us* 95: Noselli wondered what was life if not one big diddle after another.

diddle *v.* [orig. uncert.; see *OED*] **1.a.** to copulate or copulate with. [The early date of 1767 quot. makes the meaning problematic; the song, however (to the tune of "Yankee Doodle"), is addressed to "*Moll Placket,* a woman of the town."]
[**1767** "A. Barton" *Disappointment* 65: Oh, how joyful shall I be/When I get de money,/I will bring it all to dee;/Oh, my diddling honey.] **1870** in Rosa & Koop *Rowdy Joe* 24: Diddles in the dark. **1888** Field *Socratic Love* st. 2: It was the usual thing for horny Greeks to diddle/This gummy vent, instead of that with which the ladies piddle. *ca*1889 Field *Bangin'* st. 13: In far away Chicago, on that calm summer night,/Did Smith's soubrette diddle from dusk till morning light. **1889* Barrère & Leland *Dict.* 308: *Diddle, to* (vulgar), to have sexual commerce. **1908**

DN III 304: *Diddle...*To copulate. **1918** in Carey *Mlle. from Armentières* II (unp.): Oh, the Louey diddled a dame named Lou,/And now his nerts are painted blue. **1930** *Lyra Ebriosa* 12: She kept fiddlin', I kept diddlin'.../Till she got my watch and pocket-book. **1940** Faulkner *Hamlet* 144: Just out of curiosity to find out for certain just which of them was and wasn't diddling her? **1942** McAtee *Supp. to Grant Co.* 4 [ref. to 1890's]: *Diddle,* v., copulate. **1952** Randolph *Holler* 111: The verb *diddle...*signifies copulate in the Ozarks and is not mentioned in the best family circles. **1963–64** Kesey *Great Notion* 75: Leave *off* this diddlin' of your cousins and sisters an' the like. **1966** R.E. Alter *Carny Kill* 91: Diddling an ape? Is he some kind of a nut or what? **1970** Gaffney *World of Good* 76: If you're old enough to diddle, you're old enough to marry. **1975** S.P. Smith *Amer. Boys* 35: First pregnant girl I ever diddled.
b. to masturbate.
1934 H. Miller *Trop. of Cancer* 110: He may not have fucked her...but she may have let him diddle her. **1938** "Justinian" *Amer. Sexualis* 20: *Diddle,* v. To play with one's penis. **1961** Himes *Pinktoes* 141: Keep so drunk they can't even diddle. **1987** G. Matthews *Rooster* 170: She's masturbating! Diddling herself!
2. to swindle; cheat; take advantage of; fool.
[**1803* J. Kenney *Raising the Wind* I i: I wasn't born two hundred miles north of Lunnun, to be done by Mr. Diddler.] **1806* in *OED:* That flashy captain...may lay all London under contribution...but he can't diddle me. **1809* in *OED:* We shall soon find ourselves completely diddled and undone. **1811 Lexicon Balatron.: To Diddle.* To cheat. To defraud. *The cull diddled me out of my dearee;* the fellow robbed me of my sweetheart. See Jeremy Diddler in Raising the Wind. **1819* [T. Moore] *Tom Crib* I: *Diddling* your subjects, and *gutting* their *fobs.* **1842** Strong *Diary* I 180: How the *cognoscenti* will diddle people tomorrow at the [races]. **1845** Corcoran *Pickings* 171: The Danger of Diddling a Barber. **1889* Barrère & Leland *Dict.* I 308: *Diddle, to...*also to cheat in an artful way. **1944** M. Shulman *Feather Merchants* 63: A Eurasian who diddled her out of the bulk of her substance. **1962** Arnold *Hands of a Stranger* (film): I suspect you of some premeditated diddling on the hillside. **1980** Lorenz *Guys Like Us* 84: His motto was: nobody diddles the kid. **1982** "W.T. Tyler" *Rogue's March* 218: They diddled us, diddled us good. **1985** Sawislak *Dwarf* 40: Phil, this sounds like a runaround. Is he really doing this much traveling or are you diddling?
3. to waste time; trifle; fiddle.
1840 in Strong *Diary* I 122: Diddled and dawdled about all morning. **1908** *DN* III 304: *Diddle...*Dawdle. **1980** Lorenz *Guys Like Us* 86: Individuals...had diddled with him. **1981** Wolf *Roger Rabbit* 103: I'm not diddling with you any more. **1983** in "J.B. Briggs" *Drive-In* 187: [A bowling alley] where the geeks and weirdos go to diddle around in their Danskins.
4. to kill.
1986 Heinemann *Paco's Story* 127: This kid...reaches his M-1 up to diddle the guy.

diddlebop *n.* **1.** see DIDDYBOP.
2. *Black E.* a gang fight.
1956 E. Hunter *Jungle Kids* 158: This is how the club said we should settle it. Without a big street diddlebop, you dig?

diddle-cove *n.* [DIDDLE[1] + COVE] *Und.* a tavern-keeper.
*1797 in Partridge *Dict. Und.* 185: *Diddle cove,* The keeper of a gin shop. **1858* A. Mayhew, in *F & H:* And there's a first-rate "diddle-cove" keeps a gin-shop there. **1859** Matsell *Vocab.* 25: *Diddle Cove.* A landlord.

diddly *n.* Esp. *So.* the least bit; a damn; (in nonnegative constr.) nothing.—esp. in negative constr.
1964 *AS* (May) 117: Bull- and *diddly-shit* become *bull* and *diddly.* **1969** Coppel *Laughter* 270: Not that I give a diddley about what Reeder thinks. **1978** E. Thompson *Devil to Pay* 144: He doesn't know diddly. **1978** Selby *Requiem* 16: Dont mean diddly to me. **1982** in "J.B. Briggs" *Drive-In* 8: A bunch...that didn't know diddly about the movie business. *Ibid.* 46: I didn't give a diddly. **1984** "W.T. Tyler" *Shadow Cabinet* 277: He doesn't know diddly. **1985** Sawislak *Dwarf* 15: That doesn't tell us diddley about what's going on. **1987** N. Bell *Cold Sweat* 7: I couldn't give a good diddly, pal.

diddly *adj.* **1.** unbalanced; crazy.
1968 Cuomo *Thieves* 212: One con...was kind of diddly in the brain. **1987** *Oprah Winfrey Show* (synd. TV series): He thought I was just an elderly lady who was diddly.
2. inconsequential; petty.
1970 Whitmore *Memphis-Nam-Sweden* 38: None of that diddly Army infantry shit for a gung-ho, red-blooded American boy like me.

diddlybop *v.* [prob. fr. *diddly bop! diddly bop!*, expressive of bebop rhythm] **1.** Orig. *Black E.* to strut, saunter, or swagger. Also vars. See also DIDDYBOP, 2.

1964 Larner & Tefferteller *Addict* 143 [ref. to ca1952]: The diddley-bops would come from 4th Street and they would walk in doubles or triples, walking tough, diddleybopping, and they would talk loud and wise sometimes. And that would start a fight. **1965** *N.Y. Times* (Dec. 27) 20: To "diddlybop"...to the corner pizzeria. **1966** Manus *Mott the Hoople* 63: Leroy went off, diddledy bopping along like the Harlem hippie he once was. **1967** Duncan *New Legions* 72: Crossing those streams and diddlybopping past the VC. **1975** V.B. Miller *Deadly Game* 34: Andrews come diddly-bopping in through the right-hand glass door. **1980** Di Fusco et al. *Tracers* 14: You're beginning to wish you were back on the block, diddly-boppin' around.

2. *Black E.* to engage in a gang fight; (*also*) to assault.

1955 Yablonsky *Violent Gang* 63: All this diddley-boppin' bullshit is just a waste, man. **1965** Conot *Rivers of Blood* 11: Can't you see I'm a good fellow who wouldn't diddledybop nobody?

diddlybopper *n. Black E.* one who diddlybops; (*hence*) a young street hoodlum. Also **diddlybop.** See also DIDDYBOP.

1958 Salisbury *Shook-Up* 28: *Diddley bop*...First-clas gang fighter. **1964** (quot. at DIDDLYBOP.). **1966** Manus *Mott the Hoople* 41: Leroy's stance was that of a two-fisted, hard-swinging, ex-Harlem diddledybopper.

diddly-dick *n.* DIDDLY-SHIT, 2.b.—usu. considered vulgar.

1972 DeLillo *End Zone* 117: I'll waste that diddly dick before this thing's over.

diddly-shit *n.* [prob. var. of DOODLY-SQUAT] **1.** absolutely nothing; (*hence*) a damn.—often in double-negative constrs.—usu. considered vulgar. Also vars., some euphem., esp. **diddly-squat.**

1963 Doulis *Path* 274: No skin off my ass, as the man says...who gives a diddly-squat? **1964** *AS* (May) 117: *Bull-* and *diddly-shit* become *bull* and *diddly.* **1967** *DAS* (ed. 2): *Diddlyshit.* **1966–69** Woiwode *Going to Do* 143: As if I gave a diddly shit. *ca*1970 in *DARE*: Not worth a diddly-damn. **1972** *Nat. Lampoon* (Aug.) 60: So many of the candidates...just don't know didilly squat, if you'll pardon my French. **1975** Larsen *Runner* 52: Rumors...don't mean diddley-shit. **1972–76** Durden *No Bugles* 118: I don't think you know diddly-dork. **1977** Langone *Life at Bottom* 178: You know, that psychiatric screening we give, it's not worth diddly-doo. **1979** R. Foster *Concrete Cowboys* (film): You don't know diddly-damn! **1983** Breathed *Bloom Co.* (unp.): Truth, objectivity and fair play mean diddly-squat to this crowd. **1985** Sawislak *Dwarf* 75: I personally didn't give a diddley-damn what either was doing. **1986** Univ. Tenn. instructor, age 35: I *have* heard "I don't give a diddly-fuck" and "Not worth a diddly-fart," but I can't tell you when. **1986** *A-Team* (NBC-TV): You been goin' to school here ten years, music man, and you ain't learned diddly jack.

2.a. anything trivial.—usu. considered vulgar.

1967 *DAS* (ed. 2): *Diddlyshit.* **1978** Truscott *Dress Gray* 185: It took me a week to get hold of anything. Even then it was diddlyshit, rumors and stuff.

b. (see 1968 quot.).—usu. considered vulgar.

1965 C.D.B. Bryan *Wilkinson* 9 [ref. to ca1960]: Which diddly-squat down at Headquarters is responsible for this latest bit of idiocy? **1967** *DAS* (ed. 2). **1968** Baker et al. *CUSS* 104: *Diddly shit.* A small or insignificant person.

3. (used as an expletive); HELL; FUCK.—constr. with *the.*—usu. considered vulgar.

1984 J.R. Reeves *Mekong* 121: They don't know what the diddlyshit they're protesting about.

diddly-shit *adj.* paltry; contemptible.—usu. considered vulgar.

1967 *DAS* (ed. 2). **1972** Wolf *Dream of Dracula* 8: There is nothing diddlyshit about the Hell's Angels. They are the wandering outlaws of our own dark minds. **1987** Univ. Tenn. instructor: More of his diddly-shit ideas.

diddlywhacker *n.* [cf. DILLYWHACKER] the penis.

[**1942** *ATS* 74: Contrivance; indefinite object; "gadget"...*diddledy-whacker*...*diddlewhacker.*] **1964** in Cray *Erotic Muse* 10: With his long dong diddly-whacker,/Overgrown kidney-cracker.

diddybop or **dittybop** *n.* **1.** Esp. *Black E.* a foolish or worthless person; a nobody; (*also*) a juvenile delinquent. Also **diddlebop.**

1959 J. Rechy in *Big Table* I (No. 3) 12: Tough teenage chicks—"ditty-

bops." **1963** C. Wright *Messenger* 60: Look blank like a diddy bop, fake a cool walk, a sort of bounce on the balls of your feet. **1963** in Clarke *Amer. Negro Stories* 298: You slick-headed ditty-bop. **1963–64** Kesey *Great Notion* 214: Then maybe somebody gets to dance except them little dittybops. **1967** in Wepman et al. *The Life* 114: I was like a ditty bop lost in a fog. **1974** Beacham & Garrett *Intro 5* 69: A young diddy-bop called Poochie ran down the sidewalk toward us.

2. *Black E.* (see 1982 quot.). Also as adv. Also **diddlebop.**

1964 Larner & Tefferteller *Addict* 143 [ref. to ca1952]: Just because of that diddlebop walk, there were always fights, too. **1973** Duckett *Raps* 11: No matter how/Diddy bop/You walk...that jail/.../Is a very tough mother! **1982** C.R. Anderson *Other War* 150 [ref. to 1967]: First was a style of walking called the ditty-bop...The ditty-bop was accomplished by exaggerating the normal roll and swing of hips, shoulders, and arms, and locking one knee.

diddybop *adj.* Esp. *Black E.* offensive or foolish.—used prenominally.

1969 *Current Slang* I & II 25: *Diddy-bop*, adj. Ugly.—College females, New York. **1972** N.Y.C. grocery clerk, age ca25: They ain't payin' you to walk around wearin' that diddybop hat on your head.

diddybop or **dittybop** *v.* **1.** DIDDLYBOP, 1.

1968 Mares *Marine Machine* 88: I'm sure you've all seen John Wayne movies where he kills 10,000 gooks, then slings the barrel over his shoulder and ditty-bops away. Bull shit! **1969** H. Brown *Die Nigger* 97: Those young brothers came out there woofing, diddy-bopping and raising hell. **1970** N.Y.U. student: There was this rabbit diddyboppin' down the road. **1982** C.R. Anderson *Other War* 150 [ref. to 1967]: Two blacks were ditty-bopping toward each other. **1987** Norst & Black *Lethal Weapon* 32: He wouldn't show himself if some psycho diddy-bopped into his field of fire.

2. *Black E.* to keep time to music, esp. jazz or rock and roll, by gesturing and moving the body rhythmically.

1987 *Nat. Lampoon* (Oct.) 80: Black dudes jived and diddybopped. **1988** J.S. Young *China Beach* (film): Diddyboppin' white chicks?

diddybopper or **dittybopper** *n.* **1.** DIDDLYBOPPER.

1959 Stearn *Wasted Years* 45: Nobody would know you guys were diddyboppers...You look like bank presidents. **1962** in Wepman et al. *The Life* 23: Now the lion jumped up full of rage,/Like a ditty bopper ready to rampage. **1968** Bullins *Wine Time* 393: How would you want him to be like...one of the Derby Street Donkeys? Or one of the ditty boppers or an avenue hype...or...a drug addict...or what?

2. an immature or inconsequential young person.

1969 *Current Slang* I & II 27: *Ditty bopper*, n. Someone having a high school appearance or attitude.—College students, both sexes, Michigan. **1985** Frede *Nurses* 275: Day...characterized Diana...as a diddy-bopper because of the rock that...emanated from a radio...where Diana was...the charge nurse.

diddywaddle *adj.* [of fanciful orig.; cf. DIDDYBOP] paltry; worthless.

1972 Jenkins *Semi-Tough* 26: My defense ain't give 'em nothin' but one diddywaddle pass.

didi *n.* ¶ In phrase: **make (one's) didi** *Mil. in Vietnam.* to DIDI.

1978 J. Webb *Fields of Fire* 59 [ref. to 1969]: But they only got an hour before they have to make their *didi.* **1985** Bodey *F.N.G.* 88: Charlie...has made his *didi.*

didi *v.* [fr. DIDIMAU] *Mil. in Vietnam.* to flee. Also vars.

1964 R. Moore *Green Berets* 135: He say we must dee-dee quick. VC come again. **1968** Schell *Mil. Half* 28: "So we would go up there on a chopper an hour before the strike and tell the people to *didi* on out of there." "*Didi* is Vietnamese for get out," and is a standard word in American pidgin Vietnamese. "And you'd see 'em puttin' their little sticks on their shoulders, and gettin' their buffalo, and *didi*-in' out." **1969** *Esquire* (Oct.) 205: Sir, there's a Gook di-di-ing down the trail into Laos. **1971** Mayer *Falcon* 22: They're running...They're DD-ing. **1972** *West Village* 194: Let's didi on out of here. We're wasting time. **1973** Huggett *Body Count* 93: You sure dee-deed off that hill three weeks ago when we caught the shit. **1975** S.P. Smith *Amer. Boys* 63 [ref. to Vietnam War]: Hell, sir, we got our prisoner. Let's deedee out of here. **1977** Caputo *Rumor of War* 132: "Di-di, you little bastards...Di-di mau." (Get out of here and quickly.) **1981** Hathaway *World of Hurt* 170: If we get hurt during the night, we gotta be ready to di-di. **1982** Del Vecchio *13th Valley* 74: Man, the dinks have dee-deed. They've split, man.

¶ In phrase:

¶ **didi it up** *Mil. in Vietnam.* to hurry.

1966 *N.Y. Times Mag.* (Oct. 30) 102: "Di di" ("dee dee") means "go," and sometimes becomes "di di it up" for "hurry it up."

didimau *v.* [< Vietnamese đi đi mau] *Mil. in* Vietnam. to flee. Also vars.

1971 Morris & Morris *Wd. & Phr. Origs.* III 81: They'll didi mow—which means bug out or run away. **1978** Hasford *Short-Timers* 87: The Arvins started *didi-mauing* for the rear. **1986** Thacker *Pawn* 114 [ref. to 1970]: Why don't you *didimau* over to the aid station. **1989** W.E. Merritt *Rivers Ran Backward* 17: You'll have thirty seconds to diddy mao the area.

dido *n.* [orig. unkn.] an antic; often in phr. **cut [up] didoes** to engage in mischievous or uncontrolled behavior.

1807 in *OEDS:* A jolly Irishman, who cut as many didos as I could for the life of me. **1835** in *F & H:* A real conceited lookin' critter…all shines and didoes. **1837** Neal *Charc. Sks.* 201: If you keep a cutting didoes, I must talk to you like a Dutch uncle. **1847** Neal *Charc. Sks.* (Series 2) 16: Never cut up shindies, or indulge in didos. **1869** Stowe *Oldtown* 146: They'll be a consultin' together, and cuttin' up didos. **1873 Hotten *Slang Dict.* (ed. 5): *Didoes,* pranks or capers; "to cut up *didoes*," to make pranks. **1899** Thomas *Arizona* 14: Whenever he begins that tom-fool dido, you kin know Henry's had his full gauge. **1936** C. Mack, in Paxton *Sport U.S.A.* 9: One of those bits of folklore was that a curve-ball pitcher must have a cast in eye, and that in some mysterious way this gave him the power to make the ball cut up didoes in mid-flight. **1944** *PADS* (No. 2) 28: *Dido, to cut a*…To have a fit of anger or drunkenness, or to show any uncommon behavior. "Your pa'll *cut a dido* when he finds out about this." (Also: *to cut up didoes.*). **1945** Colcord *Sea Lang.* 66: *Dido, Cut A.* Now completely a shore phrase; said to come from H.M.S. *Dido,* a very fast ship, whose commander used to sail her in circles around other vessels of his squadron to show off her fleetness. **1963** W.C. Anderson *Penelope* 182: Well, these didoes of the submarine made us kind of curious. **1987** S. King *Misery* 148: When he was sure she was gone and not hanging around to see if he was going to "get up to didoes" he rolled the wheelchair over to the bed.

didonk *n.* [< F *dis donc!* 'say!'] a French person.—used derisively.

[**1886* Yule & Burnell *Hobson-Jobson* 439: In Java the French are called by the natives *Orang deedong,* i.e., the *dîtes-donc* people.] **1918** in *Papers Mich. Acad.* X (1929) 280: *Deedonc:* (Am), Frenchman. **1919** *Lit. Digest* (May 25): To the Americans, the *poilu* has become a *didonk,* and the term is used quite affectionately. **1926** Traven *Death Ship* ch. xliv: We were at anchor off Dakar. Dakar is a decent port. Nothing doing. Full of…French didonks. **1936* Partridge *DSUE: Dee-Donk.* A Frenchman: Crimean War.

die *n.* ¶ In phrase: **make a die of it** to die.

1825 in *DAE:* I wonder…[the dog] didn't go mad; or make a die of it. **1837** Bird *Nick of Woods* III: Why, Tom, you don't mean to make a die of it. **1883** in *DAE.*

die *v. Theat.* to fail utterly to satisfy an audience.—often constr. with *standing up.*

1917 *N.Y. Times* (Dec. 23) IV 6: A comedian "dying on his feet." **1920** Ade *Hand-Made Fables* 57: The…Loon had tried to compete…in the Fields of Literature, Music, Art…and he had Died standing up. **1924** *Sat. Eve. Post* (July 12) 15: *To Die*—playing to no applause. **1925** in *DAS:* The performers have "flopped."…They have "died standing up." **1929** *Bookman* (Apr.) 150: We died last night in New Orleans. **1953** B. Crosby, in *Sat. Eve. Post* (Feb. 28) 31: In New York, with the same songs, sung the same way, we died. **1970* Partridge *DSUE* (ed. 7): My gags didn't mean a thing…I died!

¶ In phrases:

¶ **die on base** *Baseball.* (of a runner) to be called out or (now usu.) be left on base without scoring.

1880 (cited in Nichols *Baseball Term.*). **1891** in Leitner *Diamond in Rough* 155: You seem doomed to die on a base. **1914** Ellis *Billy Sunday* 274: Some of them are dying on second and third base.

¶ **to die** [fr. colloq. *to die for*] extraordinary.

1983 *Nat. Lampoon* (Mar.) 70: "It's to die!" cried a lanky brunette. "Yves is throwing an outrageous…snit." **1993** Kitty Carlisle Hart, in *New Yorker* (July 5) 40: Has anyone seen "Saint Joan" at the Roundabout? It is to die! The ideas are profound.

diesel *n.* **1.** an aggressive female homosexual of decided masculine appearance and behavior. Also **diesel dyke.**

1958–59 Lipton *Barbarians* 316: *Dyke*—A highpower Lesbian. Variants: diesel-dyke, bull-dyke. **1963** in Bruce *Essential Lenny* 216: A real obvious diesel dike with…leather zipper jacket, short hair, no nails,

army shoes. **1963** Stearn *Grapevine* 3: Actually, there were all types of lesbians, and the masculine stereotype, known as the "butch" or "dike," had many variations—the "bull-dagger," the "bull-dike," the "big diesel," the "stompin' butch," and the "baby butch." **1973** *Wacky World of Jonathan Winters* (CBS-TV): We've got a word for *you*—diesel! **1977** Olsen *Fire Five* 128: They're only hiring straights, no diesels need apply. **1984** Grahn *Another Mother Tongue* 305: *Bulldike*…in the Gay bar slang of the fifties, *Dieseldike.*

2. *Stu.* (see quot.). Cf. COCK-DIESEL.

1991 *Houston Chronicle* (Oct. 8) 2D: *Diesel*—A man with a great body, or particularly muscular build.

diesel digits *n.pl. CB.* a citizens-band channel reserved for the use of commercial truckers.

1976 Bibb et al. *CB Bible* 29: Everybody else on the "diesel digits" takes a back seat. *Ibid.* 92: *Diesel Digit* [*sic*]. channel 19, truckers' channel.

diff or **dif** *n.* difference.

1896 Ade *Artie* 19: "What's the diff?" I says. **1904** *Round-Up* (Baylor Univ.) 233: One day won't make much diff. **1908** in H.C. Fisher *A. Mutt* 21: So what's the diff? **1928** Benchley *20,000 Leagues* 198: Oh, well, what's the diff? **1936** "E. Queen" *Halfway House* 64: Oh nuts. What's the diff? **1949** Ellson *Tomboy* 63: What's the dif? **1972** *Nat. Lampoon* (Dec.) 34: You pocket the dif. **1973** *Oui* (Feb.) 113: One roll's as good as another. No diff, it's all cosmic. **1992** *Newsweek* (Dec. 28) 31: Gaining power, losing weight; liberation, liposuction—what's the diff?

diff *adj.* different.

1919 *Amer. Legion Wkly.* (Aug. 22) 28: This Legion is diff. **1968** Spradley *Owe Yourself a Drunk* 39: I'm a diff person when drinking.

diffabitterence *n.* [intentional spoonerism] a bit of difference. *Joc.*

1864 in Silber *Songs of Civil War* 241: Oh! it don't make a diff-a-bitt'rence to neither you nor I. **1923** *DN* V 245: *Diffabitterence* Transposition of *bit of difference,* used by [Kansas] boys as far back as 1883. *ca1960* in *DARE: Diffabitterance* [*sic*]…A humorous transposition of *bit of difference,* usually said to indicate one's utter lack of interest.

difference *n.* a decisive advantage, esp. as provided by a concealed weapon such as a pistol.—constr. with *the.* Cf. EQUALIZER.

1903 T.W. Jackson *Slow Train* 70: "Yo' is twice as big as him." "Yes, but Charlie carries de diffunce 'round in his pocket." **1931** D. Runyon, in *Collier's* 9: They let them have it…with the good old difference in their dukes…such as a dollar's worth of nickels rolled up tight. **1935** Pollock *Und. Speaks: The difference,* a pistol. **1941** Mahin & Grant *Johnny Eager* (film): If you're gonna fool around with that guy the way he is now, don't you think you oughta carry the difference?

dig *n.* **1.** *Stu.* an overdiligent student; GRIND. Now *hist.*

1830 in B.H. Hall *College Wds.* 159: The many honest digs who had in this room consumed the midnight oil. **1850** in *Ibid.:* That humbug of all humbugs, the staid, inveterate *dig.* **1851** in Bartlett *Amer.* (ed. 2) 120: There goes the *dig,* just look!/How like a parson he eyes his book! **1863** in Thornton *Amer. Gloss.* I 251: A "dig" may at times be a genius, but a genius can never be a "dig." **1871** Bagg *Yale* 44: *Dig,* a close, mechanical student. Used also as a verb. Used also as an abbreviation for *dignity.* **1871** Schele de Vere *Americanisms* 597: *Dig,* in college slang, represents a hard-working student, who is supposed to *dig* deep into his books. **1887** *Lippincott's Mo.* (Nov.) 737: How shall I picture the daily life of an Amherst student? Let us follow one—an average man, no "dig," and yet no idler. **1890** Munroe *Orders* 51: The same class "dig" with whom he had been barely on speaking terms only the morning before. **1891** *Outing* (July) 317: I'll make them think you're a sort of a hard-working dig. **1895** Wood *Yale Yarns* 76: Deacon…had assumed the usual "grouch" of a hard-working "dig." **1900** *DN* II 32: *Dig,* n.…One who studies hard. [Reported from 28 colleges.]. **1933** *Decisions of U.S. Courts Involving Copyright* XX 871: A bookworm whom they respected for his scholastic accomplishments, but "scorned" as a "dig." **1987** Horowitz *Campus Life* 30 [ref. to 19th C.]: They labeled a studious classmate a "dig," a "fag," a "grub," or a "blue."

2. [fr. DIGGINGS, 2] a locality.

1842 *Spirit of Times* (Sept. 3) 318: You will frequently see a crowd at some particular "dig" [on Long Island]…playing…"All Fours."

3. a dignitary.

1847 Downey *Cruise of Portsmouth* 151: Some old grudge had existed between our Purser and one of the Dignitaries of the Town and high words ensued, but suddenly, slap, bang, went a blow and down went the dig.

4. *Und.* a theft.

1909 Warner *Lifer* 57 [ref. to *ca*1891]: We took what money we had secured from the first "dig," $9,800, and left the scene.

dig *v.* **1.** *Stu.* to study diligently. [Now subsumed by the general colloq. sense, "to search for information."]

1827 *Harvard Register* (Dec.) 303: Here the sunken eye and sallow countenance bespoke the man who dug sixteen hours "per diem." **1869** Alcott *Little Women* II: Then he...gave out that he was going to "dig," intending to graduate in a blaze of glory. **1902** J. London *Dazzler* 5: I can't come....I've got to dig. **1907** *DN* III 211: *Dig*...To study...*Digging*...Studying hard. **1915** *DN* IV 233: *Dig*...To study. "I'm going to dig some German."

2. to depart in a hurry; clear out; (*obs.*) leave.—constr. with *out* or *it*; (*hence*) to go at top speed.

1842 *Spirit of Times* (Oct. 22) 398: Away he went....And then we dug also. **1852** Furber *Ike* 33: [The crab] was "digging it" round and round the old man's body at a rapid rate. *a*1855 in *DA*: Mad and furious, the young chaps made a general onslaught on the people present, who "dug out" very quick, leaving the bacchanalians to their glory. **1855** *Crockett Almanac* (unp.): He was ordered in mining phrase to "*dig out*," or in other words "be off." **1864** in Northrop *Chronicles* 161: We have been using "disrespectful language" to the Corporal. He don't take it to heart, and "dug out." **1884** "M. Twain" *Huck. Finn* 269: Well, thinks I, that looks powerful bad for Tom, and I'll dig out for the island right off. **1906** *DN* III 133: *Dig, v. intr.* To leave at once. "He'd just better *dig* and never come back." **1907** S.E. White *Arizona Nights* 8: It was surely a funny sight...to see them trying to dig out on horses too tired to trot. **1909** in McCay *Little Nemo* 167: Keep right on, kid! Dig! **1910** *DN* III 440: *Dig out*...To start; to leave. **1910** in *DAE*: If it wasn't for you, Davy, I'd cut in a minute and dig for the wooly West. **1918** *Lit. Digest* (Mar. 4) 56: The trawler's skipper..."dug out" with all the speed he had. **1919** Darling *Jargon Book* 10: *Dig out*—To go away. **1926** Wood & Goddard *Amer. Slang* 14: *Dig out.* To leave suddenly. **1931** Tak *Truck Talk* 44: *Dig out*: To make a fast start. **1975** L. Nelson, on N.Y. Mets vs. Pittsburgh Pirates (WOR-TV) (June 21): Sanguillan's digging, but he can't get it.

3. to reach down in search of, esp. of money in one's pocket or purse; (*hence*) to pay. See also DIG UP.

1908 McGaffey *Show Girl* 106: You didn't have to dig once. Everything paid for ad lib. **1922** Rollins *Cowboy* 148 [ref. to 1890's]: He "dug for" his own [pistol]. **1932** in *AS* (Feb. 1934) 26: *Dig deep.* To hand over. **1958** S.H. Adams *Tenderloin* 28: Brace yourselves, girlies. You gotta dig.

4. *Und.* to pick pockets; rob.

1925 (cited in Partridge *Dict. Und.* 186). **1933** Ersine *Prison Slang* 33: *Dig, v.* To pick pockets in a clumsy manner. **1949** Monteleone *Crim. Sl.* 68: *Digging*...A pickpocket operator working a crowd.

5. [The development of these senses has aroused some interest. R.S. Gold, a knowledgeable commentator, asserts (*Jazz Talk*, p. 68) that *dig* in these senses was "introduced into jazz speech by Louis Armstrong, c. 1925, but [has become] widely current only since c. 1935"; this implies that the word was unfamiliar to black jazz performers before this period. D. Dalby's suggestion in 1972 that *dig* is a reflex of some African word (e.g., Wolof *deg, dega* 'to understand; to appreciate') has not been substantiated; nor has the assumed earlier currency in Black E. in the U.S. or elsewhere been documented in surviving representations of early Black E. Derivation from (**1**), above, is most unlikely on sociolinguistic grounds. The resemblance to Hiberno-E cant DICK[1], *v.*, 'to watch', is striking, yet *dick* was never common in U.S. use. A more likely source semantically, if not phonologically, may be the well-documented syn. TWIG. Derivation directly fr. S.E. *dig* 'to excavate' is perh. least problematic.] Esp. *Black E.* Orig. *Jazz.*

a. to understand; comprehend.—now also constr. with *on.*

1934 in M. Starks *Cocaine Fiends* 101: You dig—she's flipped her wig. **1936** *N.Y. World-Telegram* (Oct. 6) 16: "You dig?" is a short cut for "You understand?" **1940** in Oliver *Meaning of Blues* 319: Do you dig just what I mean? **1940** *Current Hist. & Forum* (Nov. 7) 22: *Do you dig the play?*...(Do you understand me?) **1941** *Life* (Dec. 15) 89: Dig me? **1944** Burley *Hndbk. Jive* 18: They don't dig that this is 1944, and not 1844. **1947–52** Ellison *Invisible Man* 155: You digging me, daddy? **1952** E. Brown *Trespass* 122: But you still not diggin' my point. **1959** Lederer *Never Steal Anything Small* (film): Now I dig you. **1960** *Twi-

light Zone (CBS-TV): To use the vernacular—frankly, I don't dig you. **1961** C. Cooper *Weed* 21: He can't understand you...He don't dig English. **1966** Fariña *Been Down So Long* 190: It's true man, dig it, it's a real fact. **1967** *Lit Dictionary* 7: *Can you dig it*—Do you like it; do you know what I mean; showing or telling something; to make a point. **1967** Kornbluth *New Underground* 44: And it was really, really strange...Can you dig it? **1968–71** Cole & Black *Checking* 105: But Larry was hot and I really dug on why. *a*1987 Bunch & Cole *Reckoning* 70: You dig what I be layin' down, honey? **1993** *Beyond Reality* (USA-TV): It's your job, dig?

b. to pay close attention to, as by listening or watching; notice; see; look at; (*broadly*) experience.—now often constr. with *on.*

[**1929** in Leadbitter & Slaven *Blues Records* 296: Dig It, Digger.] **1935** in *OEDS*: If you listen enough, and dig him enough, you will realize that that...riff is the high-spot of the record. **1941** in Ellington *Music My Mistress* 179: *Dig this*...get this. **1941** G. Legman, in Henry *Sex Var.* 1163: *Dig* is a Negro slang verb meaning look, see, or notice. **1942** *Pittsburgh Courier* (Jan. 17) 7: I haven't dug you since Ol' Unc' called you in. **1944** Calloway *Hepster's Dict.*: *Dig*...look, see. Ex.: "Dig the chick on your left duke." **1944** Burley *Hndbk. Jive* 15: I dug a skull...putting down a spiel...on a heavy hen. **1944** in Galewitz *Great Comics* 50: Dig it—she says. *Ibid.* Dig it! Com'on babe! **1952** in Botkin *Sidewalks* 532: Never mind the arrangement...Dig that crazy music stand. **1954** L. Armstrong *Satchmo* 142: I nudged Ory, as if to say, "You dig what I'm diggin'?" Ory gave me a nod, as if to say yes, he digged. **1960** R. Reisner *Jazz Titans* 154: *Dig*:...to listen. **1966–67** P. Thomas *Mean Streets* 22: [We] huddled around the radio digging the All-American Jack and his adventures. *Ibid.* 128: Dig it, man, the Indian fought the paddy and lost. **1970** A. Young *Snakes* 38: "You dig on much modern jazz?" "I kinda go for jazz, unh-hunh." **1968–71** Cole & Black *Checking* 56: Hey, dig on this, man! This white kid wants to fight me.

c. to discover; find out.

1940 in Oliver *Meaning of Blues* 319: I been throwed in the hole, black baby, ain't been able to dig no gold. **1946** Mezzrow & Wolfe *Really Blues* 30: It didn't take her long to dig where I hung out.

d. to imagine; think; consider.

1944 Burley *Hndbk. Jive* 26: And you'll never dig what it was pulled by. **1952** Mandel *Angry Strangers* 428: You ain't the boy, like—you dig you the boy but you ain't. **1973** Childress *Hero* 11: For a time I was even diggin bein a social worker, a block organizer or somethin like that.

e. [perh. infl. by *dig for gold*, below] to like, love, enjoy, appreciate, or admire.—now also constr. with *on.*

1939 in A. Banks *First-Person* 242: Make you dig your fish on the mellow side. **1944** Burley *Hndbk. Jive* 55: Dig a chick that's fine and yellow/Then thy gold thou must then spend! **1957** in *DAS*: That's why I dig Italy. **1959** *Swinging Syllables*: *Dig*...enjoy; like. **1970** A. Young *Snakes* 44: She dont dig on people just up and fallin by. **1973** Childress *Hero* 18: I took *his* advice, cause I dug it the most. **1972–74** Hawes & Asher *Raise Up* 23: I had dug working with those guys, but the caliber of the music just wasn't the same. **1988** Eble *Campus Slang* (Fall): *Dig*—like. "I dig the guy Ginny set me up with."..."I dig chocolate ice cream."

f. to come together with, usu. later; meet; "see."

1938 in R.S. Gold *Jazz Talk*: Dig. Meet. **1943** *N.Y. Times* (May 9) II 5: Plant me now and dig me later. **1944** Burley *Hndbk. Jive* 17: And that's that...Dig you. **1951** in *DAS*: Where did you dig her, kid? **1966** Fariña *Down So Long* 11: We'll dig you later. **1968** Heard *Howard St.* 42: He doffed his hat to them..."I'll dig y'all later."

g. to put in an appearance at; visit.

1946 Mezzrow & Wolfe *Really Blues* 31: The first place we dug was the De Luxe Café at 35th and State. **1961** (quot. at BASH, *n.*).

h. to discuss.

1953 W. Brown *Monkey On My Back* 53: Look, I didn't come here to dig the cat with you.

¶ In phrase:

¶ **dig for gold** to associate with or marry (a man) for material gain. Cf. GOLDDIGGER.

1931 Hellinger *Moon* 157: Joan did not know what it meant to dig a man for gold. **1963** in J. Blake *Joint* 327: Pubescent [homosexuals] who were either digging for gold or hollering for fuzz or both.

digester *n.* the digestive tract, esp. the stomach.

1851 Melville *Moby Dick* 83: Like the dyspeptic old woman, he must have "broken his digester." **1882** Miller & Harlow *9'-51"* 59: There was a young man of *Jamestown*/Whose digester was all up and down.

1886 in Nye *West. Humor* 183: Now we fill our digesters with…the canned peach.

digger *n.* **1.** a fingernail. *Joc.*

1859 Matsell *Vocab.* 3: *Diggers.* Finger-nails.

2. *Cards.* a spade.

***1859** Hotten *Slang: Diggers,* spurs; also the spades in cards. **1935** Pollock *Und. Speaks: Digger,* a spade in playing cards.

3. *Stu.* an overdiligent student; DIG.

1901 *DN* II 139: *Digger, n.* A grind. Wellesley. **1969** in *DARE:* Somebody who studies too hard or all the time…*Digger.*

4. (usu. *cap.*) [orig. Austral. army slang, sugg. by Austral. slang *digger* 'buddy'] a member of the armed forces of Australia or New Zealand, esp. an enlisted soldier. Now *hist.*

***1917** in *OEDS:* He ain't no digger; that's the colonel or the sergeant-major. **1918** in Bowerman *Compensations* 83: The main remark of the "Diggers" is that "these xx—*! Woodbines let us down again." **1919** *With 114th M.G. Bn.* 133: "Digger."—Australian. **1943** *Yank* (Aug. 20) 6: The 26-year-old digger has two ambitions. **1960** Leckie *Marines* 61 [ref. to WWII]: He didn't land in the brig for goofing off in the ordinary way—fighting with the Diggers or shipping aboard too much beer or missing reveille. *a*1982 in Berry *Semper Fi* 83 [ref. to WWII]: Our generals decided to give a joint beer party for the Diggers at the cricket grounds. **1986** F. Walton *Once Were Eagles* 69 [ref. to WWII]: I watched a Digger (Aussie) and his girl one day.

5. GOLDDIGGER.

1922–24 McIntyre *White Light Nights* 188: "Do it now!" is the digger's favorite slogan. *Ibid.* 189: Many of the most successful diggers are not out of their 'teens. **1932** W.R. Burnett *Iron Man* 32: She was just a plain digger. **1949** Monteleone *Crim. Sl.* 68: *Digger*…a prostitute; a whore.

6. *Theat.* a scalper or a person hired by a scalper to buy tickets to a show or performance for resale at inflated prices.

1927 *N.Y. Times* (Oct. 30): *Rats* or *Diggers*—Sidewalk speculators [in tickets]. *a*1986 in *NDAS:* They use diggers, dozens of guys who stand in lines and buy the maximum. **1988** Barrow & Munder *Joe Louis* 46: He moved quickly from being a "digger," a boy who bought opera or theater tickets for scalpers, to being a scalper.

7. *Und.* a pickpocket.

1931 *AS* (Aug.) 438: *Digger*—The modern term for pick-pocket. *a*1990 P. Dickson *Slang* 103: *Digger.* A pickpocket.

8. *Stu.* an academic grade of D.

1968 Baker et al. *CUSS* 104: *Digger.* The grade "D."

diggety ¶ In phrase: **hot diggety** (used to express enthusiasm). Also vars.

1928 Bodenheim *Georgie May* 14: Diggedy dog, ah wish you'd brained her! **1941** *Birth of Blues* (film): Hot diggety dog! **1967** Rose *Flim Flam Man* (film): Hot diggety damn! **1969** B. Beckham *Main Mother* 42: Hot diggity….Today's the day.

diggings *n.pl.* **1.** locality; place.

1834, 1837 in *DAE.* **1839** *Spirit of Times* (Nov. 9) 423: Wall now, the way they git along in these diggins I guess ain't to be sneezed at. **1841** in Eliason *Tarheel Talk* 268: You request…an epitome of the times about here. *There is no times in these diggins.* **1841** Porter *Big Bear* 16: It means chippen-birds and shite-pokes; maybe such trash live in my diggins, but I ain't noticed them yet. *Ibid.* 88: There hayn't no skunk hole in these 'ere diggins. **1842** in Blair & Meine *Half Horse* 78: The Choctaw live in these diggins. **1845** in Robb *Squatter Life* 59: I promised to tell you how I cum to git out in these Platte diggins. **1845** in Leyda *Melville Log I* 196: He has a prospect of *striking a lead,* as we say, "in these diggins." **1845** Durivage & Burnham *Stray Subjects* 67: Ther was a certain lawyer on the Cape a long time ago, the only one in those "diggin's" then. **1846** in Blair & McDavid *Mirth* 86: I…am the first white man ever seed in these here diggins. **1862** C.H. Smith *Bill Arp* 26: What makes cotton sell at 67 cents a pound in your diggins. **1867** Clark *Sailor's Life* 224: Well, Ned, it was the cutest game that I have seen played in these diggins. **1876** in Botkin *American Folklore* 349: Stranger, you won't git out'n these diggins for six weeks. **1932** Z. Grey *Robbers' Roost* 17: Wal, for thet matter, all men in these diggin's have got to be riders.

2. lodgings; place of residence.

1837 Neal *Charc. Sks.* 119: Look here, Ned, I reckon it's about time we should go to our diggings; I am dead beat. **1858** [S. Hammett] *Piney Woods* 112: All the women folks a leavin' their own diggins, and gittin into the main cabin. ***1888** in *F & H* II 286: "Diggings" I call my dwelling, according to the prevalent slang. **1926** W.H. Wright *Benson Case* 170: I've often had 'em to little affairs at my humble diggin's.

digithead *n.* an enthusiast of computers, math, etc.

1983 Univ. Tenn. student: Computer freaks are called *digitheads.* **1990** Dickson *Slang!* 216: *Digithead.* One who…works too long in front of a computer. **1993** *N.Y. Times* (July 1): The 21-year-old accounting student laughs about being called "a digithead."

digs[1] *n.pl.* [fr. DIGGINGS, 2; cf. DIG, 2] lodging; residence. Now *colloq.*

***1893** in *OEDS:* "Being in the know" regarding the best "digs" can only be attained by experience. ***1916** in W. Owen *Letters* 414: I like this digs far better. **1951** *New Yorker* (Sept. 8) 35: We'll probably find digs more suited to the family needs. **1975** *Sing Out!* (July) 5: Engineers is the elite. They wouldn't have no humble digs like that. **1979** F. Thomas *Golden Bird* 166: I went over the Barker digs and gave it the full treatment. **1987** *Wkly. World News* (Sept. 8) 12: She hosted a starbrite bash at her Tinseltown digs. **1992** *Stand By Your Man* (Fox-TV): Whoa! Great digs, Lorraine!

digs[2] *n.pl.* [prob. alluding to *dig in!* (invitation to begin eating)] (see quot.).

1968–70 *Current Slang* III & IV 36: *Digs, n.* Food.—College males, Negro, California.

digs[3] *n.pl.* [var. of DIBS] *Juve.* first claim on something.

1971 Cole *Rook* 94: The other boys…clamored for digs on the butt.

digs[4] *n.pl.* [fr. DIG, *v.*] information.

1973 S/Sgt., U.S. Army, age *ca*37 (coll. J. Ball): You mean you got the *digs* on this guy? **1986** *Daily Beacon* (Univ. Tenn.) (May 13) 3: Micki Free, guitarist for Shalamar, takes a minute to give the digs on the group Monday.

dig up *v.* **1.** to find. Now *S.E.*

1863 [Fitch] *Annals of Army* 542: He obtained their confidence and sympathies, and "dug up" some items of much interest to the Union cause. **1910** Raine *O'Connor* 192: If it's a show-down he'll dig the dough up. **1911** A.H. Lewis *Apaches of N.Y.* 149: Shall I go dig him up? **1929** "E. Queen" *Roman Hat* ch. ii 32: I dug up the refreshment boy who had this section of the theatre. **1932** in Runyon *Blue Plate* 358: He digs me up in Mindy's. **1965** N.Y.C. woman, age 50: Where'd you dig *her* up?

2. [cf. DIG, *v.*, 3] to pay up or hand over. Also absol.

1894 in J. London *Tramp Diary* 57: Dig up. How much stuff have you got? **1904** in "O. Henry" *Works* 837: Like hiding a wad of money in his shoe and forgetting to dig up. **1910** Raine *O'Connor* 21: Dig up, Mr. Pullman, go way down into your jeans. **1914** Ellis *Billy Sunday* 208: Dig up…Come across with the mazuma. **1928** (quot. at UNLOAD).

3. *Black E.* DIG, 5.a.

1970 A. Young *Snakes* 50: Dig up…Tell you, here's how I feel about you guys' music. **1970** Wertheim & Gonzales *Talkin' About Us* 61: I was diggin' up on the radio when it came.

D.I. house *n.* *USMC.* a drill instructor's office.

1987 D. da Cruz *Boot* 39: To the left is the *D.I. House,* not the office.

dike[1] *n.* [prob. fr. DIKE OUT] *So.* (see 1871 quot.).

1864 in Stanard *Letters* 29: Commenced in a great hurry to get on what the boys *here term, a "big dike."*…I *would certainly captivate* "those young ladies." **1871** Schele de Vere *Amer.* 597: *Dike,* denoting a man in full dress, or merely the dress, is a peculiar American cant term as yet unexplained. To be *out on a dike* is said of persons, mainly young men, who are dressed more carefully than usual, in order to pay visits or attend a party. **1936** Monks & Finklehoffe *Bro. Rat* 36: Get all shined up in your full dike.

dike[2] var. DYKE.

diked up *adj.* **1.** see DIKE OUT.

2. intoxicated.

1903 Ade *Society* 18: The Night before the Departure he dropped into the Tavern to say Good-Bye. He became all diked up and overslept himself…That one Jag is what put our whole Family to the Bad.

dike out *v.* Esp. *So.* to dress up. Also **dike, dike up.**

1851 B. Hall *College Wds.* 100: At the University of Virginia, one who is dressed with more than ordinary elegance is said to be *diked out.* **1901** Irwin *Sonnets* (unp.): Mame and Murphy, diked to suit the part. **1901** H. Robertson *Inlander* 55: He would rather do a day's ploughing than "dyke" himself up for an evening call. **1902** Cullen *More Tales* 11: It's not necessary for any member of this club to get real Oriental and dike himself out in figurative loose red trousers and a bum fez. **1906** *DN* III 133: She was all *diked out* for the party. **1914** Giles *Rags & Hope* 70 [ref. to Civil War]: I had an idea that we would be diked out in barrel shirts and labeled "Grand Reviewers" and marched up and down in front of the guard house for the remainder of the war. **1920–23** in J.M. Hunter *Trail Drivers* II 860: When diked out in this garb a man was supposed to be ready for all kinds of weather. **1930** Riggs *Green Grow Lilacs* 141: You git yerself over here to supper all diked up and fancy.

dikey var. DYKEY.

dilbery var. DILLBERRY.

dilbert *n.* Esp. *Navy.* a fool; in phr. **pull a dilbert** to blunder. Also **delbert**.
    1944 Olds *Helldiver Squadron* 3: His poker face cracked for no man, unless Moe himself willed it. And on those occasions it was usually because he wanted to grin about the antics of some "Dilbert" or "Zoot." **1944** in Rea *Wings of Gold* 172: It was a sort of stinky ride and I played Dilbert a couple of times. **1945** in *Ibid.* 271: Each man pulling a "Dilbert," that is something dumb, contributes $1. **1945** Hamann *Air Words: Dilbert*. A stupid flyer or any stupid person. Pulling a Dilbert is a common expression among Navy flyers. **1958** Cope & Dyer *Petty Off. Gde.* 341: *Dilbert.* Aviation slang for a person who dopes off, acts stupidly. **1964–66** R. Stone *Hall of Mirrors* 304: You dopey dilbert. **1980** *Daily Beacon* (Univ. Tenn.) (Dec. 2) 2: Do you realize some greeks and some non-greeks are really nice people and others are some real delberts?

Dilbert dunker *n. Naval Av.* a training device used to teach pilots to escape from a submerged cockpit.
    1969 Cagle *Naval Av. Guide* 392: *Dilbert dunker.* A training device to teach pilots to escape from an underwater cockpit. **1979** Former USN av. mech.: When I was at Norfolk, Va., in 1955, at one of the air training schools, they had *Dilbert dunkers.* Basically it was an SBD airframe mounted on rails going down into a pool of water, and when it hit the bottom of the rails it flips over and you're under water. Instant panic. Very effective. **1982** S.P. Smith *Officer & Gentleman* 73: You been through the Dilbert Dunker yet? **1984** Trotti *Phantom* 120 [ref. to 1960's]: The Dilbert Dunker…is a makeshift cockpit section attached to rails that run from a high platform steeply down into a training pool.

dildo *n.* a clumsy or stupid person; dolt.
    1954–60 *DAS: Dildo*…A foolish, stupid person; a prick. *Common among boys between 10 and 14 who do not know the primary meaning of the term.* **1968** Baker et al. *CUSS* 105: *Dildo.* A person who always does the wrong thing. **1971** Dahlskog *Dict.* 18: *Dildo*…a stupid, slow-witted, or silly person. **1973** Maas *Serpico* 75: Old dildo got caught, but fuck *him.* **1976** Schroeder *Shaking It* 190: The dildo who runs this camp is still tryin' to learn to chew bubblegum and hit his ass with both hands at the same time. **1978** Alibrandi *Killshot* 109: You have the sale the weekend before we leave, dildo. ***1990** Anderson & Trudgill *Bad Language* 89: "Stupid Person"…*dildo*…*dunce*, [etc.].

dildobrain *n.* a dolt. Also **dildohead**.
    1974 Univ. Tenn. student: He's a dildobrain. **1975** graffito, Univ. Tenn.: That's a left arm, dildo-head! **1980** DiFusco et al. *Tracers* 43 [ref. to Vietnam War]: Okay, okay, dildo-brain. **1984** Ehrhart *Marking Time* 39: What's that got to do with anything, dildo brain?

dildock *n.* [alter. of *dildo*, perh. infl. by COCK or PRICK] **1.** a clumsy, stupid, or offensive person. [1934 def. is app. erroneous.]
    1919 Lincoln *Co. C* 56: Dilldock Easley came back and was given the job again. However, Dilldock's inability to express himself clearly regarding orders to the company resulted in a great many ludicrous situations. [**1934** Weseen *Dict.* 10: *Dildock*—A gambler who uses a dishonest pack of cards.] **1944** *Yank* (Feb. 18) 22: I know you never try to push yourself ahead, you dildock. **1971** N.Y.U. student: A dildock is the kind of person who watches *Hee-Haw* because he likes the jokes. **1993** N.Y.C. woman, age *ca*55: A dopey dildock was a goofy person. That was a teen expression around 1950.
    2. a dildo. [Prob. the earlier sense.]
    1949 *Gay Girl's Guide* 7: *Dill-Dock:* Artificial penis strapped on by active Lesbian partner.

dill *n.* [fr. DILDO, DILL PICKLE, or DILLY] a foolish or offensive person.
    *1942 S.J. Baker *Austral. Lang.* 156: The common use of *dill* for a simpleton or fool. ***1949** (cited in Partridge *DSUE* [ed. 8]). **1969** *Current Slang* I & II 26: *Dill*, n. A party-spoiler; bore; dullard….—Air Force Academy cadets. **1985** in Dundes *Parsing* 184: Kill the Dill.

dill *v. Stu.* to spoil (a party, fun, etc.).
    1969 *Current Slang* I & II 26: *Dill*…v. To kill pleasure…"You really know how to *dill* a blast."—Air Force Academy cadets.

dillberry *n.* DINGLEBERRY, 2.a.; FARTLEBERRY. Also vars.

*1811 *Lexicon Balatron.: Dilberries.* Small pieces of excrement adhering to the hairs near the fundament. *Dilberry maker.* The fundament. **1888** E. Field "Socratic Love" st. 3: And gather from that excrement a rank dilberric bordure. ***1890–91** *F & H* II 286: *Dilberries*…(common).—Faecal and seminal deposits in the hair of the anus and the female *pudendum.* **1916** Cary *Slang of Venery* III 109: The anus:…dilberry creek. **1916–22** Cary *Sexual Vocab.* III (s.v. *human body*): The Anus…dilberry creek, dilberry patch. **1942** in Legman *Limerick* 215: Till they got some fairies with pretty dillberries. **1950** *PADS* (No. 14) 26: *Dillberries*…The small lumps of excrement clinging to wool on the hindquarters of sheep at certain seasons. **1920–54** Randolph *Bawdy Elements* 101: *Dill-balls* or *dill-berries.*

diller *n.* DILLY¹, 1.
    1962 Algren *Sea Diary* 83: We called him "Hippo"—now ain't *that* a diller? **1968** in *DARE*: That cabbage is a diller.

dill pickle *n.* a foolish or obnoxious person.
    1908 in H.C. Fisher *A. Mutt* 47: Shortribs Enlivens Court Proceedings by Calling Beany A "Dill Pickle." ***1984** Partridge *DSUE* (ed. 8) s.v. *dill: Dill-pickle*…is also used as a general term of abuse.

dilly¹ *n.* [orig. unkn.] **1.** an extraordinary specimen or example; LULU.
    1908 in Fleming *Unforget. Season* 161: Pittsburgh may be a one-man team, but that man is a "dilly." **1923** *Bomb* (Iowa State Coll.) 418: They are a bunch of dilly birds for fair. **1935** *Amer. Merc.* (June) 229: Ain't that a *dilly* (or *honey*)! **1939–40** Tunis *Kid from Tomkinsville* 239: That was a wonderful catch, what the boys call a "dilly." **1942** Algren *Morning* 106: The guy's a dilly….He's forgot what he's here for. **1943** in F. Brown *Honeymoon* 126: And I thought that yarn Charlie just told was a dilly. **1947** Schulberg *Harder They Fall* 110: Danny talked a kind of slang that sounds archaic nowadays. He still said things like "dilly," and he was inclined to refer to beautiful babes as "stunners." **1951** Spillane *Lonely Night* 28: They were a fine pair, those two, a brace of dillies. **1952** J.D. MacDonald *Damned* 51: We came through a dilly of a dust storm up in the mountains. **1961** L.G. Richards *TAC* 150: Northwest Territory, mother of storms, had whipped up a dilly. **1981** E. Keyes *Double Dare* 19: First offense, and a dilly. **1985** *Lady Blue* (ABC-TV): If it's excitement you want, we've got this dilly of a DB.
    2. a Dilaudid tablet.
    1971 Guggenheimer *Narc. & Drug Abuse* 16: *Dillies.* Opium derivatives. **1972** Smith & Gay *Don't Try It* 200: *Dillies.* Dilaudid.

dilly² *n.* [prob. fr. DILLYWHACKER, infl. by DILLY¹] the penis.
    1941 in Legman *Limerick* 37: The end of his dillie/Was shaped like a lily. **1962** T. Berger *Reinhart* 399: He'll buy anything and kiss your dilly for it.

dilly-dick *v.* [elab. of DICK AROUND] to loaf or waste time.—constr. with *around*.
    1984–89 Micheels *Braving the Flames* 113: We got in there and…they were dilly-dicking around the door.

dillywhacker *n.* [cf. TALLYWHACKER] the penis. *Joc.*
    1927 *Immortalia* 93: Oh, his long, long dillywhacker.

dim *n. Jazz.* evening; night.
    1944 Burley *Hndbk. Jive* 137: *Dim*—Evening; night. *Dims and brights*—Days and nights.

dimbo *n.* [infl. by BIMBO] *Stu.* DIM BULB.
    1978 Truscott *Dress Gray* 41: That dimbo couldn't squint and spit at the same time. **1989** *Larry King* (CNN-TV) (Sept. 6): You dimbo!…You may have written books, but you are dumb as they come! ***1990** Andersson & Trudgill *Bad Lang.* 88: "Stupid Person"…*dimbo.*

dimbrain *n.* DIMWIT.
    1936 Monks & Finklehoffe *Brother Rat* 181: "You dimbrain!" **1949** "R. MacDonald" *Moving Target* 114: How many jails you seen the inside of, dimbrain? ***1990** Andersson & Trudgill *Bad Lang.* 89: "Stupid Person"…*dimbrain, dingbat,* [etc.].

dim bulb *n.* DIMWIT.
    1927 T.A. Dorgan, in Zwilling *TAD Lexicon* 31: She's dead from the neck up—A dim bulb—She thinks Pearl Harbor is a night club hostess. **1934** Weseen *Dict.* 328: *Dim bulb*—An uninteresting person. **1951** Bowers *Mob* (film): If you mean that dim bulb that pushed me around—. **1955–57** Felder *Collegiate Slang* 2: *Dimbulb*—stupid. **1959** Lederer *Never Steal Anything Small* (film): How long does it take those dim bulbs to add up one and one? **1981** *Rod Serling's Mag.* (July) 31: Figuring isn't your job, dimbulb. **1986** *Newsweek* (May 26) 69: The cant charge against Ike's presidency was that…[he] was a superannuated dim bulb too fond of golfing to take note of the alarming "Bomber Gap."

dime *n.* **1.** *pl.* money. [Esp. common *ca*1845–60.]

1843 *Spirit of Times* (Jan. 21) 560: Times are hard, and dimes are scarce. **1848** Baer *Life in Baltimore* 80: I told you I'd raise the dimes. **1848** Judson *Mysteries* 248: "He was dressed well, and looked as if he toted dimes about." "*Toted dimes?*"…"He looked as if he had money." **1853** Lippard *New York* 56: I caught the young'un examinin' the valise—I seed the dimes with my own eyes. **1859** *Spirit of Times* (Apr. 2) 88: All the "dough"…All the "dimes." **1859** in Davidson *Old West* 19: Been to Pike's Peak, lost all my dimes. *ca*1860 *Startling Discoveries!* 9: The goods is here, and we've got the dimes…an' that's all you need know about it. *a*1867 G.W. Harris *Lovingood* 60: Bake dwelt ontu the crop ove dimes tu be gethered frum that field. **1871** Schele de Vere *Americanisms* 309: A young lady was said to *have the dimes*, when she was reputed rich. **1904** H.N. Brown *Necromancer* 89: Go on my friends and make the dimes/And save for harder times. **1920** Witwer *Kid Scanlan* 9: It made him enough dimes in five years to step out of the crowd.

2.a. Orig. *Gamb.* a ten-dollar bill; ten dollars; ten dollars' worth; (*Narc.*) ten dollars' worth of an illicit drug. See also DIME NOTE.

1958 Motley *Epitaph* 148: A dime is ten dollars. **1958** in Droge *Patrolman* 109: A spidery black man…would come out and give you the "dime." **1962** in Wepman et al. *The Life* 143: She came to see me and left me a dime. **1962** H. Simmons *On Eggshells* 192: A bill and a dime for a whole pound. **1970** *Life* (Feb. 20) 26: Eight or nine dime bags. **1979** in Feldman et al. *Angel Dust* 95: The standard "dime" of buzz is the amount of powder measured by a level McDonald's coffee stirrer spoon. **1981** *Penthouse* (Mar.) 174: And now people think they can endear themselves to me by offering me a dime bag [of heroin]. **1983** *Good Morning America* (ABC-TV) (June 2): Come on, baby, just a dime bag. **1986–90** in Ratner *Crack Pipe* 46: You only came there to buy a nickel (five-dollar rock) or a dime (ten-dollar rock). **1991** Nelson & Gonzales *Bring Noise* 15: Leaving behind a trail of…misplaced dime bags of skunk weed.

b. *Gamb.* one thousand dollars.

1974 Mayer *Bookie* 201: "You know if there's over $5,000 in action here, this is a felony rap."…Since I had more than five dimes bet on the White Sox–Tiger second game, I didn't comment on the charge. *Ibid.* 253: Dime: $1,000. **1974** Sann *Dead Heat* 14: Haven't we still got those fourteen dimes if our track action stands up? **1989** *Donahue* (NBC-TV): Five dimes…In betting parlance that means five thousand dollars.

3. *Pris.* **a.** a ten-year prison sentence.

1962 in Wepman et al. *The Life* 105: You can bet he had to do that dime. **1965** C. Brown *Manchild* 411: If…the bench man throws a dime on me, I'll walk with that too. **1966** C. Cooper *Scene* 75: I'll be 50 when I get the dime done. **1972–74** Hawes & Asher *Raise Up* 115: Next day I pleaded guilty and got a dime. **1981** Ballenger *Terror* 102: I may be busted…and get a big dime at the Portsmouth brig. **1985** *Knoxville* (Tenn.) *Journal* (Jan. 29) C3: That means you're looking at a dime and a half mandatory. **1985** *Miami Vice* (NBC-TV): He's lookin' at a dime and a half if he messes up.

b. ten years.

1968 I. Reed *Yellow Back Radio* 76: Like those old guys in Club Harlem.…drop a dime of their lives just to sniff me.

4. an unwished-for opinion; TWO CENTS.

1978 Diehl *Sharky's Machine* 193: Just keep your dime out of it, Twiggs.

¶ In phrases:

¶ **behind a dime** at all; to any degree.

1981 Safire *Good Word* 81: I wouldn't trust him behind a dime (i.e., under any circumstances). **1983** *Reader's Digest Success with Words* 84: Black English.…*behind a dime* = "at all"; used in expressing distrust: *I wouldn't trust him behind a dime*.

¶ **drop a dime** Esp. *Und.* to place a telephone call; (*specif.*) to inform on someone by making a phone call to police; (*hence*) to inform or betray.

1966 (implied at DIME-DROPPER). **1967** Lit *Dictionary* 12: *Drop the dime*—To fink, tell, crack on, squeal. **1968** Wiseman *Law & Order* (film): Now you gonna try an' drop a dime on me! **1970–71** J. Rubinstein *City Police* 43: Betraying, "dropping the dime," is the last resort of the persecuted, the ambitious, the threatened, the fearful, and occasionally the honest. **1972** Smith & Gay *Don't Even Try It* 201: *Drop a dime*. To phone police, turn someone in. **1974** *Police Woman* (NBC-TV): Where you cats been? I been droppin' dimes all night. **1978** Lieberman & Rhodes *CB* (ed. 2) 298: *Drop a dime*—Make a phone call. **1983** Sturz *Wid. Circles* 110: At first they see it as "ratting," "snitching," or "dropping a dime." **1991** D. Anderson *In Corner* 96: Another num-

bers guy dropped a dime on me.

¶ **get off the dime, 1.** to move from a stationary position.—used esp. of dancers in a dancehall.

1925 Van Vechten *Nigger Heaven* 15: Sometimes a…[dancing] couple…would scarcely move from one spot. Then the floor manager would cry, Git off dat dime! **1931** Cressey *Taxi-Dance Hall* 13: "Get off that dime," good-naturedly shouts a taxi-dancer to a girl chum and her over-zealous patron. [**1945** Drake & Cayton *Black Metro.* 610: They will "dance on the dime" and "grind" around the juke-box in taverns and joints.]

2. to take action after a period of indecision or procrastination; to act.

1926 in *AS* (Mar. 1927) 276: *Get off the dime*—start. *Ibid.* 277: *Off the dime*—started hurrying. **1938** *AS* (Apr.) 156: *Get off the dime*. To quit loafing. **1951** D.P. Wilson *6 Convicts* 119: Well, somebody in this goddam Gover'ment better get the hell off the dime. Doc's suit ain't gonna hold out much longer. **1955** Wilbur & Mainwaring *Phenix City* (film): Maybe you'll help get your dad off the dime. He's gone stubborn on us. **1971** *N.Y. Times Mag.* (Nov. 7) 74: We've had a copout by the Federal Government, and, frankly, if they don't get off the dime we're going to have syphilis in epidemic proportions. **1973** in *Submission of Pres. Convers.* 178: I think he helped to get the thing off the dime. **1978** Rep. Griffin Bell (R.-Mich.) (WINS radio): I think it's time to get off the dime. This session of Congress is drawing to a close. **1982** Pres. R. Reagan, national radio speech (May 8): Congress [should] get off the dime and adopt the…budget proposal before it. **1985** WINS Radio News (Aug. 7): It's time we either get off the dime and [go on strike] or else accept an unsatisfactory contract, which we will not do. **1985** Finkleman *Head Office* (film): All we have to do is get off the dime and get the show on the road.

¶ **have a nickel in that dime** *Black E.* to have an interest in a certain state of affairs.

*ca*1974 in J.L. Gwaltney *Drylongso* 20: I didn't have no nickel in that dime.

¶ **play on a dime** *Baseball.* (see quot.).

1929 *N.Y. Times* (June 2) IX 2: A fielder who fails to cover much ground is said to be "playing on a dime."

¶ (In prov. phr.):

[**1881** A.A. Hayes *New Colo.* 38: The well trained horse "turns on a five-cent piece."] **1915** in J.I. White *Git Along Dogies* 145: He could turn on a dime and give you back change. **1962** L'Amour *Killoe* 16: That bronc of mine turned on a dime. **1984** Weaver *Texas Crude* 22: Shining like a dime in a goat's ass.

dime *v.* [sugg. by *drop a dime* s.v. DIME, *n.*] *Und. & Police.* to inform or inform on.—also constr. with *out*.

1970 Scott-Heron *Vulture* 38: He wanted it badly enough to take the chance of being dimed on by some punk. **1970–71** Rubinstein *City Police* 324: Policemen still resort to force when they are challenged and feel that they will not be "dimed" by the people involved. **1979** *Atlanta Constitution* (Feb. 2) 8A: These ridge runners—you just don't dime on one another. **1985** E. Leonard *Glitz* 180: So he says I dimed out on him. Bullshit. **1987** Wambaugh *Echoes* (NBC-TV): His prison buddies dimed him.

dime bag *n.* see s.v. DIME, *n.*, 2.a.

dime-dropper *n.* [sugg. by *drop a dime* s.v. DIME, *n.*] an informer.

1966 *N.Y. Post* (Aug. 24) 30: Words like "muska" and "dime dropper" don't show up on middle class-oriented intelligence tests. **1970** *Current Slang* V 20: *Dime-dropper*, n. An informer; a tell-tale; a "stool-pigeon." **1986** *NDAS*.

dime-grind *n.* a taxi-dance hall.

1937 *AS* 46.

dime-nickel *n. Army.* a 105 mm. howitzer.

1982 Del Vecchio *13th Valley* 231 [ref. to Vietnam War]: You had a secondary with that last dime-nickel. **1990** G.R. Clark *Words of Vietnam War* 303: The "Dime-Nickel" fired a wide variety of rounds.

dime note *n.* Esp. *Gamb.* a ten-dollar bill; in phr. **double-dime note** a twenty-dollar bill.

1938 *Better Eng.* (Nov.) 51: *Dime note.* $10. **1944** *Slanguage Dict.* 59: *Dime note*—a ten dollar bill. **1946** Mezzrow & Wolfe *Really Blues* 188. **1959** Zugsmith *Beat Generation* 43: Why would anyone who wanted to pay off a ten-buck handout of bread suggest a check instead of a dime note? **1961** Russell *Sound* 31: It cost mother a double-dime note only this morning.

dime store *n*. [sugg. by *five and ten* 'a dime store'] **1.** *Pris.* a five- to ten-year sentence. *Joc.*

1939 C.R. Cooper *Scarlet* 18: "What did you draw?"..."Oh, a dime store." "You kids catch the slang pretty quick, don't you?...He means five to ten."

2. *Poker.* a variety of poker in which fives and tens are wild cards.

1985 Westin *Love & Glory* 379: "We don't need girls to play poker...They play dime store." "What the hell's dime store?"..."Fives and tens are wild."

dimey *n*. a glass of beer costing ten cents.

1961 Sullivan *Shortest, Gladdest Years* 124: A dollar-fifty...represents fifteen fine cold draughts at Bill Karl's dimies. **1970** *Playboy* (Feb.) 16: A 16-year-old with a fake I.D. ran down to Bubba's Cafe, coughed down a "dimey" and passed out. **1986** G.V. Higgins *Impostors* ch. 43: Implying that because I had a couple dimies with my lunch, I was a beer drunk.

dimmer[1] *n*. Esp. *Carnival.* a dime; DEEMER; DIMMO.

1925 *Writer's Monthly* (June) 485: "Dimmer—A dime." **1933–34** Lorimer & Lorimer *Stag Line* 141: *A dimmer*—a dime. **1935** J. Conroy *World to Win* 57: Most he got was a dimmer in cash at a time. **1936** Dai *Opium Add.* 198: *Dimmer.* A ten-cent piece. **1943** D. Hammett, in *DAS*: Neither of us can make a thin dimmer.

dimmer[2] *n*. *Und.* an electric light, esp. a small light such as a flashlight.

1932 in *AS* (Feb. 1934) 26: *Dimmer.* An electric light. **1942** Goldin et al. *DAUL*: Choke...that dimmer, Slim. **1970** La Motta, Carter & Savage *R. Bull* 21: Salvy cut the La Salle lights to the dimmers.

dimmo *n*. a dime.

1915 (quot. at MEG).

dimmy *n*. [app. fr. Br E cant *dimmock*] money.

1879 in *Real West* (Nov. 1979) 17: Some crack shots are found amongst these men, and many handsful of the "dimmy" change hands over the scores on the target.

dimp *n*. [perh. var. DINK[2]] *Stu.* a foolish person; WIMP; DIP[3].

1964 (quot. at ZILCH, *n.*).

DIM syndrome *n*. *Med.* (see quot.).

1970 *Interns* (CBS-TV): Have you checked her for the DIM syndrome?...DIM, D-I-M, means "Doctor Is Mystified."

dimwit *n*. a stupid or slow-thinking person. Now *colloq.*

1921 *DN* V 141: *Dim-wit, n.* A person of small common sense; a stupid person. "She's the worst dim-wit on campus." **1933–34** Lorimer & Lorimer *Stag Line* 142: Good golly, dimwit, don't you see? **1938** *Amer. Mercury* (Oct.) 137: I was too much of a dim-wit to realize the editors were exercising unfair discrimination against me.

dinah *n*. [by shortening and resp.] dynamite.

1929 *Sat. Eve. Post* (Apr. 13) 54: Dinah is dynamite. **1930** *Amer. Mercury* (Dec.) 455: *Dinah, n.*: Nitroglycerine. "We got to get dinah for them pineapples." **1933** Ersine *Pris. Sl.* 32: *Dinah*...Dynamite.

dinch *n*. [orig. unkn.; cf. syn. Br E sl. *dimp*] the stub of a cigarette or cigar.

1927 *DN* V 444: *Dinch, n.* The butt of a cigar or cigarette.

dinch *v*. [fr. the *n.*] to crush out (a cigarette).

1935 O'Hara *Dr.'s Son* 61: He lay back and dinched the cigarette in an ashtray on the night table that stood between his and Nancy's beds.

dincher *n*. DINCH, *n*.

1926 Maines & Grant *Wise-Crack Dict.* 14: *Slip the dincher*—Give one a half-smoked cigarette. **1934** Weseen *Dict.* 328: *Dincher*—An unsmoked part of a cigarette. **1962** Carr & Cassavetes *Too Late Blues* (film): Still smokin' dinchers?

dinero *n*. [< Sp] Esp. *West.* money.

1856 in *DA*: They pungled the dinero. **1903** A.H. Lewis *Black Lion* 116: Every sport who's got the dinero does. **1907** S.E. White *Arizona Nights* 159: If he never gets back...his dinero'll be there. **1913** *Sat. Eve. Post* (July 5) 4: It's the dough that counts...—the dinero; the iron men. **1922** Knibbs *Saddle Songs* 42: His sack of dinero. **1925** in Hammett *Big Knockover* 204: Try him out and we'll talk dinero. **1947** Overholser *Buckaroo's Code* 47: The dinero she was talking about looked awful good. **1952** Overholser *Fab. Gunman* 120: Have him send to Cheyenne for my dinero. **1966** C. Ross *N.Y. After Dark* 18: The girls know how lightly they part with *mucho* dinero. **1982** Del Vecchio *13th Valley* 26: Mama-san makes beaucoup dinero off my orders. **1986** *Hardcastle &*

McCormick (ABC-TV): Next time, you come with the dinero.

ding *n*. **1.a.** Esp. *Pris.* a simple-minded, useless, or crazy person.

1929 Booth *Stealing* 66 [ref. to ca1916]: He's an awful harmless ding...He can't steal because he ain't got the guts. *Ibid.* 257: All of us have a spot here, and the dings and odds-and-ends don't get into our spot at any time. **1957** *N.Y. Times* (Sept. 8) 6 108: Tommy had been a "ding"—boy terminology for an extreme behavior problem—hostile and disruptive. *a*1969 B. Jackson *Thief's Primer* 144: One of these old country dings. **1970** Thackrey *Thief* 133: One cat I know, he's a real ding! I mean, nuts! **1970** Gaddis & Long *Killer* 80: Regarded as a "ding" ("crazy," mentally unstable convict) he was left alone. **1971** Hilaire *Thanatos* 31: The dings walking the prison yard...ain't known where they been for 20 years. **1973** Trinity Univ. student questionnaire: A naive person...dumbshit, ding.

b. [prob. fr. syn. DINGBAT] *Hobo.* a beggar.

1933 Ersine *Prison Slang* 32: *Ding, n.* An able-bodied beggar. **1968** Spradley *Owe Yourself* 75: I was with a ding one time and he made $30 begging while we walked back to town from West Seattle.

2.a. a dent, nick, or scratch.

*ca*1945 (cited in *W9*). **1951** (quot. at DINGMAN). **1962** in *OEDS* I 804: *Dings*, dents or holes in surfboard. **1968** Kirk & Hanle *Surfer's Hndbk.* 19: Larger dings or slits...can be covered with a patch of fiberglass and the resin then applied. *Ibid.* 138: *Dings*: damage to board—nicks, gouges, breaks, holes. *Ibid.* 17: The two-layer covering is more ding-proof. **1975** *Nat. Lampoon* (Feb.) 77: A small ding on the left rear fender. **1981** in Safire *Good Word* 54: My '40 Ford Woody has a ding in the fender.

b. a bruise or minor injury.

1968 Kirk & Hanle *Surfer's Hndbk.* 32: Immediate care of body nicks, dings, stings, burns, and bruises. **1972** *Harper's* (Feb.) 64: Collecting my third Purple Heart. I got a couple of little dings in my leg. **1978** J. Webb *Fields of Fire* 58 [ref. to 1969]: Homicide has a ding up the side of his head. **1981** C. Nelson *Picked Bullets Up* 117 [ref. to Vietnam War]: Stokes...had already been wounded twice. "Minor dings." **1991** Marcinko & Weisberg *Rogue Warrior* 70: Sure, you take a certain number of dings in the pursuit of these unruly activities.

3. [fr. DING[1], *v.*, 5] a statement or notice of rejection, as for a fraternity membership or a job; (*hence*) a notation of criticism or disapproval.

1950 in M. Daly *Profile of Youth* 110: A "ding" is a statement by one fraternity member that he does not want a particular boy in the fraternity. **1981** in Safire *Good Word* 56 [ref. to 1976–80]: "I'm papering the wall beside my desk with dings"..."Two more dings today." **1983** *Wall St. Journ.*: They use their job-rejection letters—known as dings—to paper their poolroom. *a*1987 Bunch & Cole *Reckoning* 317: Who was he...to cast the first ding on a man's 201 file? **1988** *Campus Voice* (Spring) 46: The bottom line is not to judge your performance until you receive either a job offer or a ding letter from the person who's doing the hiring.

4. *Pris.* (see quot.).

1954 Maurer & Vogel *Narcotics & Narc. Addiction* 270: *Ding.* Marihuana.

5. [cf. DINGDONG, DINGUS, DINGWALLACE] the penis.

1967 Mailer *Vietnam* 158: Do you have hard-on enough...to put your...ding into a cake of ice? **1969** Cray *Erotic Muse* 38: Inviting the king to bring his ding/And spend the week with her. **1973** *TULIPQ* (coll. B.K. Dumas): Male sexual organ...ding. **1974** *Nat. Lampoon* (Oct.) 26: When my friend Bruno here gets through with your ding you'll have to pee through your ear.

6. a drinking spree.

1965–71 in *Qly. Journ. Stud. Alcohol* XXXII (1971) 728: *Ding.* A drinking bout.

7. a thrill of pleasure; BOOT; KICK.

1981 O'Day & Eells *High Times* 13: Gee, this is good! This is the most! What a ding! Wow!

¶ In phrase:

¶ **put the ding on** (among beggars) to beg from.

1936 Mackenzie *Living Rough* 206: I was just starting to put the ding on another bird when I got pinched for panhandling. **1970** in *DARE*: An old tramp...put the ding on me.

ding[1] *v*. [orig. dial. < ME *dinger* 'to strike'] **1.a.** to hit hard; strike; knock.

1688 E. Taylor, in *DARE*: Hells Nymps [*sic*] with spite their Dog's sticks threat ding/To Dash the Grafft off. **1698–99* "B.E." *Dict.*

Canting Crew: *Ding*...to knock down. *Ding the Cull*...knock down the Fellow. **1859** Matsell *Vocab.* 26: *Ding*...to strike. **1912** Runyon *Rhymes* 148: Get up there an' ding it, an' be sure to ding it a mile! **1942** *Calif. Folk. Qly.* I 220: "Dinger" Williams acquired his nickname [around 1900] because of his expertness at "dinging" the 14 ball into the pool pocket. **1971** Meggyesy *Out of Their League* 108: Getting "dinged" means getting hit in the head so hard that your memory is affected, although you can still walk around and sometimes even continue playing. **1973** Roth *Sand in the Wind* 424: A few pieces dinged his helmet. **1974** *Time* (June 17) 59: *Ding him:* swing sneakily at him. **1972–79** T. Wolfe *Right Stuff* 45: I sorta...dinged my goddamned ribs. **1984** J. Green *Newspeak* 69.

b. to dent, nick, or scratch.

1968 Kirk & Hanle *Surfer's Hndbk.* 15: They don't soak up much water if the fiberglass skin is "dinged" or nicked. **1981** in Safire *Good Word* 54: I dinged my board on the rocks. **1988** in *DARE* [ref. to 1960's]: Watch out or you'll ding that fender.

c. *Mil.* to shoot or kill.

1966 *N.Y. Times Mag.* (Oct. 30) 102: A soldier on the battlefield is..."dinged," not wounded. *ca***1969** Rabe *Hummel* 99: Poor ole Ryan gets dinged round about Tay Ninh. **1971** Turque *Viet Vet* (NBC-TV): If you go out on a patrol and you see a South Vietnamese out there, you try and ding 'im, 'cause he could be a VC, and that's a kill. **1971** T. Mayer *Weary Falcon* 31: If you make your runs parallel to the friendlies there is considerably less chance of dinging a few by mistake. **1972–76** Durden *No Bugles* 129: The other [was] dinged right through his legs with an AK-round. **1977** Caputo *Rumor of War* 237: Then I'm your son, and if you get dinged I'll be an orphan. **1984** Holland *Let Soldier* 20: I've brought in three dinged aircraft commanders in two months, and two were evacuated to Japan. **1988** C. Roberts & C. Sasser *Walking Dead* 45: Orders were we didn't ding anybody until we spotted a weapon.

d. *Esp. Mil.* to shoot a gun.

1970 Whitmore *Memphis-Nam-Sweden* 62: I'm dinging away at this herd on the hill. **1980** M. Baker *Nam* 107: He's still dinging at you, the cocksucker. **1984** Ehrhart *Marking Time* 19: There they'd be again, one or two guys, dingin' away at you.

e. *Av.* to crash in an aircraft. Also *trans.*

1965 Adler *Vietnam Letters* 34: The 1st lost a pilot doing a low altitude roll with rocket pods on the aircraft. Dished out of the bottom and dinged—very senseless. **1985** Yeager & Janos *Yeager* 169: That airplane was a tricky bastard to fly cold. If he dinged it, the old man would have him for supper. **1989** Berent *Rolling Thunder* 55: But then I didn't ding on the runway either.

2. *Und.* to discard or get rid of (usu. stolen goods); (*hence*) to pass (stolen goods) to an accomplice.

***1753** in Partridge *Dict. Und.* 187: We...ding the empty [purse], for fear it should be found. ***1781** G. Parker *View of Society* II 174: A highwayman will *ding* his *Upper-Benjamin*. ***1789** G. Parker *Life's Painter* 161: Another thief...*prigs* your *reader*, [and] *dings* it to another. ***1820–21** P. Egan *Life in London* 220: It would have been *dinged* into the *dunagan*. **1859** Matsell *Vocab.* 26: *Ding.* To throw away. **1935** Pollock *Und. Speaks*: *Ding*, to get rid of contraband (usually dope) when fearful of arrest. **1955** in D. Maurer *Lang. of Und.* 239: *Ding*...To throw (a wallet) onto the ground under duress...To discard (an empty wallet).

3. [sugg. by syns. *hit, strike*] *Hobo.* to beg (money or food); steal (a ride on a train); BUM.—also constr. with *it*.

*ca***1920** in Bruns *Kts. of Road* 81: Oh, he's counting the ties with a bed on his back/Or else he is dinging a ride. **1927** *AS* (June) 390: Dinging the stem is known as *mooching, stemming* and *plinging*. **1929** *AS* (June) 339: *Ding*—To beg. **1933** Ersine *Prison Slang* 32: *Ding, v.* To beg money. **1934** E. Anderson *Hungry Men* 189: He dings the salt and bacon if you agree to get the pepper and bread. **1935** Algren *Boots* 199: He was only "dinging it" to get a gambling-stake together. **1953** Gresham *Midway* 305: Another beef...is the angle of always getting "dinged" for a contribution to something. **1981** in Safire *Good Word* 55: Some time ago I met people who were street hustlers. They used to...ask for donations. Those fellows used the term "I'll ding him" or "I'll ding this side of the street; you ding the other side."

4. to nag, harass; or rebuke; (*also*) to file a negative evaluation of.

1942 *ATS* 299: Nag...*ding*,...*jaw*,...*rag*. **1951** *Harper's* (June) 87: He was always dinging at other people to write books. **1955** Klaas *Maybe I'm Dead* 398: I'll ding you all down the line—and you know I can do it. **1957** Campbell *Cry for Happy* 48: I don't want Chiyoko raising hell with me. She dings me enough as it is. **1981** Safire *Good Word* 52: "I

dinged him" means "I communicated my desire to have this straightened out"..."I made known my displeasure." *a***1986** in *NDAS*: If we dinged people, very seldom did they get jobs.

5. *Stu.* to reject or turn down (someone); (*specif.*) to blackball. Cf. DING, *n.*, 3.

1950 in M. Daly *Profile of Youth* 111: One kid who was dinged out at the first meeting kept pretending he was a pledge. **1954–60** *DAS*: *Ding*...To vote against a candidate for fraternity membership; to blackball; to veto. *Student use since c1930.* **1968** Baker et al. *CUSS* 105: *Ding.* Turned down when asking for a date...Reject someone for a membership in a club, frat., etc. **1981** in Safire *Good Word* 56 [ref. to 1976–80]: I got dinged by U. of Y. **1987** *TV Guide* (Dec. 12) 44 [ref. to 1960's]: There'd be votes on whether to accept or reject new fraternity members. Some of them dinged this Japanese guy, blackballed him, for no reason than that he didn't have blond hair and blue eyes.

ding² *v.* [euphem.] to damn; dang.

1821 in Royall *Letters From Ala.* 202: And some dinged ugly ones, too. **1878** [P.S. Warne] *Hard Crowd* 5: Dinged ef I don't! **1884** Beard *Thorns* 20: Ding my buttons! *Ibid.* 26: An' dinged pooty! **1942** "E. Queen" *Calamity Town* 31: I'll be dinged.

ding-a-ling *n.* **1.** [sugg. by the stereotype that crazy people hear imaginary bells] a crazy or foolish person; (*also*) an amusing eccentric.

1935 Pollock *Und. Speaks*: *Ding-a-ling*, brainless [person]. **1944** *AS* XIX 104: [Among merchant seamen, a] man who acts up...is...a *squirrel*, or some kind of *ding-a-ling.* **1954** Gaddis *Birdman* 29: How you gonna know when some ding-a-ling's gonna choose *you*? **1973** Lucas, Katz & Huyck *Amer. Graffiti* 88: Hawkins, a real ding-a-ling. **1983** Univ. Tenn. *Daily Beacon* (May 16) 2: Play it smart, you dingalings. **1993** *TV Guide* (Feb. 6) 86: Including Goldie Hawn, as the giggling ding-a-ling.

2. the penis.

1968 Bullins *Wine Time* 389: Pour yourself a drink, Ray. Put some hair on your...ding-a-ling. **1974** Lahr *Trot* 18: I was a six-penny man; he can't even balance three on his ding-a-ling. *a***1990** in Costello & Wallace *Sig. Rappers* 26: I think with my dingaling. **1992** Jernigan *Tin Can Man* 27 [ref. to 1941]: A doctor and nurse came in to look at my ding-a-ling.

3. a telephone.

1971 Woodley *Dealer* 14: I can't talk problems, not over the ding-a-ling.

ding-a-ling *adj.* crazy or eccentric.

1970 *Playboy* (Aug.) 37: How do I handle...her utterly ding-a-ling sex views? **1972** Sapir & Murphy *Death Therapy* 29: Who taught you that dingaling move? **1972** Wambaugh *Blue Kt.* 30: Everyone was acting a little ding-a-ling when I mentioned my retirement.

dingbat *n.* **1.** a stiff drink.

1838 in *AS* XXXVIII (1963) 10: We can take a "Quaker" before we start—apply a "Ding Bat" at Providence.

2. [semantically, cf. PLUNK, SMACK, SMACKER] a coin or banknote; (*pl.*) money.

1861 in Bartlett *Amer.* (ed. 4) 177: It has been found necessary to expend the *dingbats*...to bring our unruly relatives to their P's and Q's. **1865** Sala *Diary* II 280: I paid...a five-cent "dingbat," or "spondulick"—two of the many names given to the fractional currency. **1894** *DN* I 387: *Dingbats, n.* Pieces of money; money. (Reportedly used in Maine, 1855.).

3. a missile or projectile.

1877 Bartlett *Amer.* (ed. 4) 177: *Dingbat.* A bat of wood that may be thrown (dinged);...a cannon-ball; a bullet. **1895** *DN* I 387: *Dingbat*...Flying missile.

4.a. a crazy, eccentric, or foolish person. [Popularized by George Herriman's comic strip "The Dingbat Family"; repopularized 1971 in the CBS-TV situation comedy *All in the Family.*]

1879 Burt *Prof. Smith* 132: To what end are these observations of Coriolanus Dingbat tending? **1909** G. Herriman *The Dingbat Family* (title). **1911** G. Herriman, in *N.Y. Eve. Jour.* (Jan. 3) 15: The Dingbats' "Bird of Peace" Gets No Further Than Their Door. **1923** Toomer *Cane* 118: Who is that coming in? Blind as a bat. Ding-bat. Looks like Dan. **1929–33** Farrell *Young Manhood* 368: He...was acting and talking like a goddamn dingbat. **1937** E. Anderson *Thieves Like Us* 16: These kids trying to rob these banks are just dingbats. They'll charge a bank with a filling station across the street. **1944** D. Runyon, in *Collier's* (Jan. 15) 49: His daughter...is a dingbat and so is her mamma. **1962** Kesey

Cuckoo's Nest 106: What they should do with that whole bunch of dingbats up there is toss a couple of grenades in the dorm. **1971** *All in the Family* (CBS-TV) (Jan. 12): *You* are a dingbat! **1985** Kasindorf *Brothel Wars* 218: And what a "dingbat" Joni…was. **1986** Heinemann *Paco's Story* 200: Calls Myrna a dingbat. **1990** *CBS This Morning* (CBS-TV) (May 30): He's competent. She's a dingbat.

b. *Und.* a tramp or beggar; DING, 1.b.

1912 *Railroad Man's Mag.* (Apr.) 493: The lingering sunset…shone on the passing track close by/Where a dingbat sat on a rotten tie. **1918** Livingston *Delcassee* 74: Dingbat…The dregs of vagrantdom. **1925–26** Black *You Can't Win* 65 [ref. to 1890's]: If you was some kind of a rank dingbat you wouldn't have been invited down here. **1926** Nichols & Tully *Twenty Below* 37: D'you hear that, you bloody dingbats? **1929** Barr *Let Tomorrow Come* 40: I meet a happy-lookin' dingbat an' start to tell him the news, but I get a rumble from Dick. **1929** *AS* (June) 339: *Dingbat*—An itinerant beggar. **1968** (quot. at DYNO, 2).

5. [prob. dial. *ding* + *bat*, both meaning 'a sharp blow, esp. with the hand'] a slap or sharp blow with the hand; (*specif.*) a slap on the buttocks.

1895 *DN* I 387: *Dingbat*…Blow or slap on the buttocks. **1969** in *DARE:* I got the dingbats for that.

6.a. thingamabob; DINGUS.

1931 J. Thurber *Owl* 78: It was sitting on a strange and almost indescribable sort of iron dingbat. **1944** in F. Brown *Angels & Spaceships* 208: It was his dingbat. I mean, he made it, and he thought he knew what it was. **1949** in Botkin *Sidewalks* 261: It's got a gizmo that hooks onto the dingbat in the slot.

b. *Specif. Stu.* a muffin or biscuit.

1894 *DN* I 387: *Dingbat.* In some of the N.E. schools, the word is student slang for various kinds of muffins or biscuits…Phillips Academy (Mass.), Wilbraham Academy (Mass.), Suffield Literary Institute (Conn.).

c. *Specif.* a clinging bit of excrement; DINGLEBERRY.

1895 *DN* I 387: *Dingbats.* Balls of dung on buttocks of sheep or cattle.

d. (a nonspecific term of admiration or derision). Cf. DINGER, 1.a.

1895 *DN* I 387: *Dingbat*…Term of admiration. "They are regular *dingbats*" (speaking of girls). **1923** in *OEDS:* That blasted "ding bat" of a Ford, as Stubs calls it. **1944** *AS* XIX 104: [Among merchant seamen, a] woman who is neither your sister nor your mother is a *dingbat.*

e. *Specif. Printing.* any of various typographical symbols or ornaments. Now *S.E.*

1904 (cited in *W9*).

f. *Specif.*, the penis; (*pl.*) the male genitals.

1916–22 Cary *Sexual Vocab.* IV s.v. *penis:* Dingbat. **1930** *Lyra Ebriosa* 9: Her husband is feeble, his dingbat is limber. **1942** *ATS* 147: Genitals…dingbats. **1969** Girodias *New Olympia Rdr.* 627: Do not withdraw your ding-bat, for in grinding you will be shifting your weight this way and that.

g. (used as an indefinite standard of comparison).

*1967 Partridge *DSUE* (ed. 6) 1087: *Go like a dingbat,* to travel very fast: RAF: since *ca*1950. **1968** Broughton *Thud Ridge* 41: [The F-105] would go like a dingbat on the deck and she would haul a huge load. **1974** Kingry *Monk & Marines* 144: Two were dead as a dingbat.

7. heck; DING-DONG.—used as an expletive.

1968 Swarthout *Loveland* 58: Still…figuring what the dingbat to do with me, he said that the orch was downtown.

dingbat *adj.* **1.** fit for a DINGBAT, 4.a.

1970 J. Levin, in *N.Y. Post* (Apr. 14) 43: At first, Daniel is given a "dingbat" job, such as cleaning toilets or washing dishes.

2. crazy.

1970 Thackrey *Thief* 48: I know this sounds dingbat to anyone else, but this is how it really was.

dingbatty *adj.* crazy; BATTY.

1911 *DN* III 542: *Dingbatty, adj.* Half crazy, imbecile. "That fellow is dingbatty." **1937** E. Anderson *Thieves Like Us* 22: You're going to go dingbatty out here.

dingbust *v.* to darn; damn.—used in imprecations.

1881 Nye *Forty Liars* 32: I don't know the first ding busted thing you have said to me. **1884** "M. Twain" *Huck. Finn* 84 [ref. to *ca*1850]: Well, now, I be ding-busted! **1977** Coover *Public Burning* 569: The whole dingbusted United States guvvamint.

ding-dang *v.* to darn; doggone.

1942 *ATS* 224. **1951** Davidson *Old West* 28: The purtiest gal in this

hull ding danged town. **1963–64** Kesey *Great Notion* 210: Oh, you dingdang right!

ding-ding *n.* DINGALING, 1.

1970 Rudensky & Riley *Gonif* 15: All you have to fear is getting castrated by the ding-ding's knife. *a***1986** in *NDAS:* Or have that dingding of a driver inform the cops.

dingdong *n.* **1.** a gong or bell.

1925 Odum & Johnson *Negro & His Songs* 253: Get up in mornin' when ding-dong rings,/Look at table—see same damn things. **1948** J. Stevens *Jim Turner* 239: Mind that dingdong—rise and shine!

2. a fool; a scatterbrain.

1929 Shay *Drawn from Wood* 74: I'm just a dumb ding-dong,/Walking my poor life away. **1976** Whelton *CB Baby* 145: Bringing dingdongs like Whatley…onto the airwaves. **1988** Univ. Colo. student: Don't get too close, you ding dong!

3.a. the head. *Joc.*

1929 in *DARE:* He sho rap on yo' ding-dong!

b. the penis. *Joc.*

1944 *PADS* (No. 2) 29: *Ding-dong*…In some parts of Va. and N.C., the penis. **1956** *Ky. Folklore Record* II 20: In western Kentucky, one finds…*pecker, dick, peter, prick, pintle, pizzle, rod, tool, yard* (*yerd*), *jock, talliwhacker,* and *ding-dong.* **1958–59** Southern & Hoffenberg *Candy* 216: I dug the defrocked ding-dong of his. **1963** Horwitz *Candlelight* 230: I think she was silly to get involved in painting. It's not a business for women. You need a ding dong to paint. **1967** Ragni & Rado *Hair* 52: They're hot for my ding dong. **1982** "J. Cain" *Commandos* 359: You're telling me dope is more important than my ding dong?

c. *pl.* the testicles. *Joc.*

1957 E. Brown *Locust Fire* 98 [ref. to WWII]: Some stalls…A man gets his ding-dongs kicked off going up to the cockpit. **1972** B. Rodgers *Queens' Vernacular* 27: No, these levis are too tight—There's no room for m' ding-dongs t' breathe.

4. *R.R.* (see quot.).

1945 Hubbard *R.R. Ave.* 340: Ding-dong—Gas or gas-electric coach, usually used on small roads or branch lines not important enough to support regular trains; name derived from sound of its bell. Sometimes called *doodlebug.*

5.a. the devil; the heck.—used as a mild oath.

1956 *Walt Disney's Jiminy Cricket* (unp.): What the ding dong?

b. emphatically nothing; emphatically anything.—usu. in neg. constr.

1978 Groom *Better Times* 335: We don't have ding-dong to show for it.

6. SHINDIG.

1966 Longstreet & Godoff *Wm. Kite* 344: We have another half of Scotch to kill before the big dingdong.

7. *pl.* see DING-DONG PANTS.

ding-dong *adj.* **1.** exciting; snappy.

1899 Cullen *Tales* 172: There was a ding-dong drive all the length of the stretch. **1923** P. Baxter *I'm a Ding Dong Daddy* (song): I'm a ding-dong daddy from Dumas,/You ought to see me do my stuff. **1952** in *DAS.*

2. damned; goldarned. Also as adv.

1906 London *White Fang* 17: I'll be ding-dong-danged if I do. *ca***1938** in Rawick *Amer. Slave* II (Pt. 1) 172: Too much ding-dong do-nuttin' foolishness. **1958** in C. Beaumont *Best* 74: Made me so dingdong mad. **1961** Forbes *Goodbye to Some* 104: You're ding-dong right it does! *Ibid.* 154: I don't owe anybody a ding-dong thing any more. **1989** *ALF* (NBC-TV): What the dingdong heck are you doing down there? **1993** *Village Voice* (N.Y.C.) (June 29) 6: I felt like a ding dong spazmo.

3. crazy.

1961 *Many Loves of Dobie Gillis* (CBS-TV): It made women go as dingdong as a clock shop. **1975** S.P. Smith *Amer. Boys* 11: Most dingdong place he'd ever been.

ding-dong *v.* **1.** *Hobo.* to ring the doorbells of private houses looking for handouts.

1925–26 Black *You Can't Win* 211: He…bewailed…having to "dingdong" his way about the country for a few "lousy dimes." **1929** Barr *Let Tomorrow Come* 40: I start ding-dongin' an' collect a few dimes.

2. to rant or argue.

1925–26 Black *You Can't Win* 119: He dingdonged away till the judge ordered him to stop.

ding-dong pants *n.pl.* bell-bottomed trousers. Also **dingdongs.**

1929–33 Farrell *Young Manhood of Lonigan* 226: They look goofy in their ding-dong pants. **1972** B. Rodgers *Queens' Vernacular* 22: Prone to unfastening all thirteen buttons on his...ding-dongs.

dinge *n.* **1.** *Und.* (see quot.).

1807 Tufts *Autobiog.* 292 [ref. to 1794]: *Dinge*...a dark night.

2. [back formation fr. *dingy* 'dark'] Orig. *Und.* a black person.—used contemptuously.

1848 *Ladies' Repository* VIII (Oct.) 315: *Dinge*, A negro man. *Dinge Kinch*, A negro child. **1904** *Life in Sing Sing* 247: *Dinge*. A negro. **1908** Beach *Barrier* 151: You can't blame a dinge for stealing...Hogs and chickens are legitimate prey. **1910** *N.Y. Eve. Jour.* (May 4) 15: Now, which way did that dinge go? **1912** Berkman *Prison* 48 [ref. to 1892]: Say, Berk, you don't want to be seen walking with that "dinge." **1917** *Lit. Digest* (Aug. 25) 29: Some laughed at this "daffy-dinge" music. **1920–21** Witwer *Leather Pushers* 19: A big dinge...was workin' out. **1922** S. Lewis *Babbitt* 145: The old-fashioned coon was a fine old cuss—he knew his place—but these young dinges don't want to be porters or cotton-pickers. **1940** R. Chandler *Farewell* 5: You say this here is a dinge joint? **1959** P. Frank *Babylon* 66: But he does say we'll have to watch out for the dinges. Keep 'em under control. **1969** Pharr *Numbers* 69 [ref. to ca1930]: Probably the only dinge on the campus, but he was a star on a losing football team. **1973** Breslin *World Without End* 277: See this dinge standin' there like he's made of ice.

dinged *adj.* drunk.—constr. with *out*.

1969 *Current Slang* I & II 26: *Dinged out, adj.* Intoxicated. College males, South Dakota.

dinge queen *n. Homosex.* a white homosexual man who habitually seeks black men as sexual partners; (*hence*) a white woman who seeks black men as sexual partners.—usu. considered offensive.

1965 Trimble *Sex Words* 64: *Dinge Queen*...A male Homosexual who prefers Negro love partners. **1967** Rosenthal *Sheeper* 41: Calling all dinge queens and size queens. **1965–72** E. Newton *Mother Camp* 27: There are no feminine counterparts of the male...dinge queens, [etc.]. **1972** B. Rodgers *Queens' Vernacular* 63: *Dinge queen*...white homosexual who prefers black men sexually. **1990** *Nat. Lampoon* (Apr.) 34: After one of them called me [a woman] "dinge queen," I passed out.

dinger *n.* [fr. dial. *ding* 'to strike'] **1.a.** a striking or extraordinary specimen; CORKER. [The "1809" date of the first quot. may be erroneous (for 1890?); no other pre-1892 cites are available.]

1809 in *DA* s.v. *scad*: This land of our dads...is a dinger at nailing the scads. *1892 in *OEDS*. **1909** *DN* III 395: *Dinger*, n. Anything particularly liked. "The lecture course this year is a *dinger*." **1911–12** Ade *Knocking the Neighbors* 100: He knew that he was a Dinger. **1930** Riggs *Green Grow Lilacs* 145: Yeah, that shore *is* a dinger. **1930** Weaver *Coll. Poems* 240: She *is* a dinger! **1931** Lorimer *Streetcars* 13: She's a ding-er, what I mean. **1936** Tully *Bruiser* 129: It was a dinger of a fight. **1938** Breslow & Patrick *Moto Takes a Chance* (film): I know another that's a dinger. **1938** Steinbeck *Grapes of Wrath* 28: Been a dinger of a crop. **1951** Kerouac *Cody* 84: I thought by gawrsh it was going to be one big dinger of a night. **1962** Perry *Young Man* 103: It was a dinger of a fight.

b. a daunting task.

1940 Burnett *High Sierra* 282: Brother, it's a dinger to drive even in the summer!

2.a. an alarm bell.

1931 (cited in Partridge *Dict. Und.* 188).

b. *R.R.* a yardmaster; (*also*) a conductor.

1929 *Bookman* (July) 524: Do you think the Dinger is goin' to put you in their class? *Ibid.* 526: A yardmaster [is] known from coast-to-coast as a Dinger or a Ringmaster. **1939** *Sat. Eve. Post* (Apr. 15) 26: The dinger handed the hoghead the flimsy. **1945** Hubbard *R.R. Ave.* 318: *Dinger*—Conductor (man who rings the bell). **1972** *Urban Life & Culture* I 373: "Dingers"...yardmasters.

3. the penis.

1952 Randolph & Wilson *Down in Holler* 101: The noun *dinger* means penis, too, but I don't think it as old, or as widely used [in the Ozarks] as the other names here listed.

4. a beggar or tramp, esp. (among beggars) a beggar who is or pretends to be disabled; DINGBAT, 4.b.

1927 *AS* III 141: [In Maine, years ago, a] "dinger"...meant a tramp. **1929** Zorbaugh *Gold Coast* 138: There were...beggars, "dingers," "D.D.'s" and "T.B.'s." **1935** Algren *Boots* 199: There was Anthony Brown, known as a "dinger"; he twisted his right arm out of shape every morning, and returned, his arm back in position and his pockets jingling, when the day was done.

5. *USMC.* a sniper.

1972 West *Village* 60: You two dingers can come home now. **1982** E. Leonard *Cat Chaser* 24: The dinger would fire a round, then disappear...We're chasing the dinger. **1985** Dye *Between Raindrops* 163 [ref. to Vietnam War]: He must have a scope because he places his shots like a real dinger.

6. *Baseball.* a home run.

1976 *Webster's Sports Dict.* 113. **1979** (quot. at TATER). **1984** *N.Y. Post* (Aug. 20) 27: Dave Winfield...got his 250th career dinger yesterday. **1984** Jackson & Lupica *Reggie* 2: I could make the difference if I could hit enough dingers. That's what I call home runs. Dingers. **1985** WINS Radio News (Sept. 5): Those dingers manage to find his bat on a regular basis. **1991** Headline News Network (Apr. 18): A pair of two-run dingers...in a 19-run shellacking.

ding-how *adj. & interj.* [< Mandarin *ding²hao³* 'of the greatest excellence; wonderful'] *Mil. in Eastern Asia.* perfect; wonderful; excellent; O.K.

1921 *Sentinel-15th Inf.* (Jan. 14) 15: As Speedy describes it, "Dinghow chow." **1931** *Leatherneck* (Apr.) 24: He was one "Ding How" shipmate, and carries the best wishes of all the detachment with him. **1941** *AS* (Oct.) 165: [Army] *Ding How*. Everything O.K. **1942** *Leatherneck* (Nov.) 144: *Ding Hau*—Chinese word meaning "All right" or "O.K." **1943** R. Scott *God Is Co-Pilot* 59: Ding-hao—you are "number one." **1959** McKenna *Sons of Martha* 39: Brown tried in his own way to become an Asiatic sailor. He said "maskee" and "ding hao" too often and in the wrong context. **1960** Morrison *Hellbirds* 10 [ref. to WWII]: I held up the thumb of my right hand, grinned, and said, "Ding Hao." **1961** Coon *Back at Front* 96: You stay, ding hao. You run, boo hao. **1981** *Rod Serling's Mag.* (Sept.) 38 [ref. to WWII]: "Copilot." "Check." "Bombardier-navigator." Sweeney in the greenhouse: "Ding-how." *Ibid.* 39: "Bombs away!" "Ding-how! Let's go home."

dingle[1] *n.* [cf. DANGLE, DINGLE-DANGLE] the penis.

1916–22 Cary *Sexual Vocab.* IV (s.v. *penis*): Dingle. **1957** Rumaker *Pipe* 72: You think I'm hot to see a boogie's dingle, the way Billy is? **1966** Susann *Valley of Dolls* 260: You stand there with your dingle blowing in the breeze.

dingle[2] *n.* [prob. fr. DINGLEBERRY] *Stu.* (see quot.).

1938 R.I. McDavid, in *AS* (Feb. 1939) 26: *Dingle*, n. The favor of superiors; principally in such idioms as *to get a dingle*, or *to have a dingle with someone*. *Ibid.* 29: *Pluck dingles*, v.i. To curry favor with superiors.

dingleberry *n.* [var. of DILLBERRY; cf. earlier FARTLEBERRY] **1.** a doltish or contemptible person.

[**1915** *N.Y. Eve. Jour.* (Aug. 28) 9: Him say ubigloock snivers chapski-nolvitch dingleberry skivolow wonjib.] **1924** Hecht & Bodenheim *Cutie* 12: This pious dingleberry had only one eye. **1938** (quot. at **(2.a.)**, below). **1968** Baker et al. *CUSS* 105: *Dingleberry*. A person who always fools around. An effeminate male. **1973** Eble *Campus Slang* (Mar.) 1: *Dingleberry*—nerd, jerk. **1973** *TULIPQ* (coll. B.K. Dumas): A naive person:...dumbo,...dingleberry, dildo. **1974** Strasburger *Rounding Third* 67: One "for instance" for the dingleberry in the front row, James. **1976** Conroy *Santini* 225: A lot of officers are a bunch of dingleberries going along for the ride. **1986** Eble *Campus Slang* (Fall) 3: You're a real...dingleberry. **1988** *Nat. Lampoon* (Feb.) 25: White trash...dingleberry...wussy.

2.a. (see **1938** quot.). [Prob. the orig. sense.]

1938 "Justinian" *Amer. Sexualis* 20: *Dingleberry*. n. Tiny globular pieces of solidified excreta which cling to the hirsute region about the anal passage. Usually a term of opprobrium designating a mean, petty, or insignificant individual...U.S. C.[entury]. 19–20. **1966** IUFA *Folk Speech*: *Dingle berry*—Piece of crap hanging on a hair. **1966** Bogner *7th Ave.* 358: Money dripping from his asshole like dingleberries. **1970** Byrne *Memories* 42: Dingleberries...were the beads of dried fecal matter that hung on the hairs around the bunghole. **1970** graffito, N.Y.C. bus: You eat dinkle berries. **1972** Pearce *Pier Head Jump* 161: In comes the Dingleberry Kid. *1984 Partridge *DSUE* (ed. 8).

b. *Mil.* a decoration.—used derisively. Also **dingleberry cluster.**

1953 Russ *Last Parallel* 95: Then he left, to receive his combat pay and Dingleberry Cluster for valor in action. **1961** Peacock *Valhalla* 21: Maybe in the next war you can get another Silver Star....Or even a dingleberry cluster. **1977** Olsen *Fire Five* 159: We don't recognize the hero concept, with ribbons and dingleberries all over your chest.

c. (see quot.).

1984 J. Green *Newspeak* 69: *Dingleberries*...splattered molten particles around a metallic weld on a pipe or vessel.

3.a. *pl.* the testicles.
1912–43 *Frank Brown Collection* I 533: *Dingle-berry n.* A testicle. **1986** Knoxville (Tenn.) lab technician, age 32: *Dingleberries* are testicles *or* little pieces of shit.

b. the clitoris or vagina.
1974 Strasburger *Rounding Third* 182: And diddle your dingleberry until your boobs quiver.

dinglebody *n.* DINGLEBERRY, 1.
1959 Zugsmith *Beat Generation* 21: The world is full of dinglebodies. The crumbbums who…just vegetate. All dinglebodies were walking dead who didn't go.

dingle-dangle *n.* the penis. *Joc.*
1938 "Justinian" *Amer. Sexualis* 20: *Dong.* n. The *membrum virile*…Similar terms…are *dingle-dangle, dingus, dink, dornick*, etc. **1961** Peacock *Valhalla* 251: Sitting on his bunk…bitterly soaking his dingledangle in a beer can which contained a beautiful purple liquid. **1964** J. Thompson *Pop. 1280* 37: Probably you ain't got as long a dingle-dangle as he has—they tell me them idjits are hung like a stud-hoss.

dingman *n.* (see quot.).
1951 Shidle *Clear Writing* 93: *Dingmen*…Fender repairmen.

dingo *n.* [cf. DING; DINGBAT; DINGY²] **1.** *Hobo.* a beggar; tramp.
1926 *AS* (Dec.) 651: *Dingoes*—those [tramps] who wander about and live without working. **1939** *New Yorker* (Mar. 11) 43: "Dingos"…really are small-time confidence men rather than beggars…All he needs, he says, is a few more pennies to make up the carfare.
2. a foolish or crazy person. Also redup.
1953 R. Chandler *Goodbye* 128: Dingoes who park their brains with their gum. **1968** Myrer *Once an Eagle* 586: Come on, Chief. Don't be a dingo. **1970** Cortina *Slain Warrior* 134: They is tryin' to break me down into some kinda dingo-dingo…a dingo-dingo starin' at my belly button all day. **1971** N.Y.U. student: Don't be a dingo. **1973** *TULIPQ* (coll. B.K. Dumas): A naive person…*dumbo*,…*dingo*. ***1990** Andersson & Trudgill *Bad Language* 88: "Stupid Person"…*dingo*…*dodo, drip* [etc.]. **1993** *CBS This Morning* (CBS-TV) (May 25): Because you're a professional and I'm a dingo.
3. a thing; DINGUS.
1978 Diehl *Sharky's Machine* 21: We oughta go in there, blow the whole dingo outa the pond with an A-bomb.

dingo *adj.* [cf. DINGY] crazy.
1971 N.Y.U. student: I think I'm going dingo. **1978** Truscott *Dress Gray* 39: You're not going to believe what's come down from…dingo Grimshaw, Slaight.

dingswizzled *adj.* (see quot.).
1894 *DN* I 396: *Dingswizzled.* Expression of surprise, consternation, etc. A person who is at a loss how to act says, "I'll be *dingswizzled.*" N.Y.

dingus *n.* [< New Netherland Du *dinges*] **1.** a thing; device; whatchamacallit. Now *colloq.*
1876 in *DA.* **1882** Peck *Peck's Sunshine* 21: They pull out a dingus and three joints of fish-pole come out. **1886** Nye *Remarks* 170: A new self-cocking weapon that had an automatic dingus for throwing out the empty shells. **1921** Bucklew *Orphan Battery* 58: These three-eyed "Dingusses" with curly tails. **1929** Hammett *Maltese Falcon* 115: Then you think the dingus is worth two million?
2.a. the penis.
*ca***1888** *Stag Party* 218: All he's got on, too, is a fig-leaf, and that aint big enough to hide his damned old dingus. **1923** *Poems, Ballads & Parodies* 44: I went to the doctor,/He said I had the clapp./He gave me a little bag/So my dingus wouldn't flap. **1952** in Legman *Limerick* 38: There once was a horse named Lily/Whose dingus was really a dilly. **1958** Frankel *Band of Bros.* 9: I'll feed your dingus to the gooney birds! **1961** Coon *Meanwhile At Front* 128: You need fifteen bucks like I need a four-foot dingus. **1966** Gass *Omensetter* 269: Meng's got diarrhea of the dingus and all his strength's leaked out. **1972** R. Wilson *Playboy's Forbidden Words* 89: To copulate…*dunk the dingus* or *dunk the love muscle.* **1973** *Best From Screw* (No. 4) 22: Playing with your "dingus" causes baldness. **1986** Kubicki *Breaker Boys* 18: How his "dingus" had grown.
b. a dildo.
1958 W. Burroughs *Naked Lunch* 92: She greases the dingus…and works it up his ass.
3. the rump.
1929 Milburn *Hobo's Hornbook* 150: He tapped me on the dingus—and mashed me on the dome.

dingus *adj.* crazy; DINGO.
1979 *MASH* (CBS-TV): Has everybody here gone dingus?

dingwallace *n.* the penis.
1927 *Immortalia* 40: Young man, will your old dingwallace stand?

dingy¹ *n.* [dimin. of DINGE] a black person.—used contemptuously. Cf. DINGY COVE.
1895 *DN* I 415: *Dingy*, n. A negro. **1903** McCardell *Chorus Girl* 15: Dingies…billed…as "Octoroon Odalisques." **1904** in "O. Henry" *Works* 509: What's your report on the dingy I told you to watch? **1905** in *Ibid.* 424: These dingies will cheat you out of the gold in your teeth. **1919** *Amer. Legion Wkly.* (Aug. 22) 23: "Good boy, dingy," the crowd sang out in approval of Sam's luck. **1945** Drake & Cayton *Black Metro.* 267: Epithets like "nigger," "darky," "shine," "smoke," "spade," "dingy,"… used as short-cut symbols to express all the contempt concentrated in the popular estimate of the Negro.

dingy² *n. Hobo.* DING, n., 1.b.
1956 Algren *Wild Side* 78: And coasted…past broken men and breaking ones; wingies, dingies and lop-sided kukes.

dingy *adj.* **1.** crazy. Also vars.
1907 *Reader* (Sept.) 351: I hikes out of that car for fear I might get dingey and bust out crying myself. **1911** in Truman *Dear Bess* 36: Sometimes they go dingy or get two or three divorces. **1912** *DN* III 550: *Dingy*…foolish, not quite right in the mind; about the same as "batty." "He's dingy." **1919** Darling *Jargon Bk.* 54: If one acts foolish say: He is…Dingie. **1927–28** Tasker *Grimhaven* 32: You're dingy. Why take a chance like that? **1936** Duncan *Over the Wall* 57: We all get dingier'n a pet coon inside these dumps. **1958** Gilbert *Vice Trap* 54: Is he dingie? **1971** *Interns* (CBS-TV): She was dingy, but she wasn't that dingy.
2. groggy; dazed.
1981 O'Day & Eells *High Times* 36: But as to whether I'd been given extra sleep, I was too dingy to ask anyone.

dingy cove *n. Und.* (see quot.).
1807 Tufts *Autobiog.* 292 [ref. to 1794]: *Dingy cove*…a negro man.

dink¹ *n.* [prob. fr. *dinkus*, infl. by *dick*] the penis.
*ca***1888** *Stag Party* 62: A knot hole he happened to see/So he stuck his dink through it to pee. *ca***1889** Field *Boastful Yak:* [She] took the versatile dink. **1923** *Poems, Ballads and Parodies* 13: Two pimples pink/Are on his dink. **1928** in Read *Lexical Evidence* 49: I come here to pull my dink. **1942** McAtee *Grant Co. Dial.* 4 [ref. to 1890's]: *Dink*, n., penis, especially the small one of a boy. **1956** Metalious *Peyton Place* 75: That is, if he's got a dink to pee with. **1962** Quirk *Red Ribbons* 80: The old lady asked me why sailors have two flies on their pants…Because we all have two dinks. **1978** in *Maledicta* VI (1982) 23: Penis…*dick, dink, dong, dork.*

dink² *n.* [prob. fr. DINKY, *adj.*] **1.a.** a young man who dresses in a showy fashion, esp. in order to impress women; DUDE.
1900 *DN* II 32: *Dink*, n…Dude. [In use at Tufts College.]. **1935** D.W. Maurer, in *AS* (Feb.) 14 [ref. to *a*1910]: *Dink*. A dude…one who dresses in the latest manner; one especially successful with women.
b. *Stu.* a skullcap worn by freshmen at certain colleges. Now *hist.*
1919 in Horowitz *Campus Life* 122: Remove your dink when passing a superior. **1951** Lampell & Buchman *Saturday's Hero* (film): Freshmen will wear the dink at all times. **1966** Young & Hixson *LSD* 74: A symbolic Oxford gown or an absurd Princeton "dink." **1971** Cole *Rook* 3: There are frosh in dinks…and seniors in racy convertibles. **1992** *Princeton Alumni Wkly.* (Dec. 9) 3: In September 1947, sophomores resurrected a defunct tradition that required freshmen to wear beanies, or "dinks," as signs of their lowly status.
2.a. a jerk; TWERP.
1962 in *AS* (Oct. 1963) 171. **1965** Ark. auto mech., age *ca*65 (coll. J. Ball): You goddamn dink, pick up the wrench! **1968** Baker et al. *CUSS* 105: *Dink.* An obnoxious person; a person without much social or academic ability. **1968** Lockridge *Hartspring* 69: You poor dink, your art is excremental. **1972** N.Y.U. student: In New England, if you're really stupid they call you a dink. **1976** Schroeder *Shaking It* 25: It's only important if it's important, ya little dink. **1978** Maupin *Tales* 13: Safeway, dink. As in supermarket. **1980** Rimmer *Album* 11 [ref. to 1963]: Stay out there and suffer, you dinks! **1982** E. Leonard *Cat Chaser* 233: It's an anonymous call, you dink. **1983** B. Breathed, in *Daily Beacon* (Univ. Tenn.) (Nov. 9) 2: Do ya think we can keep our incredible profit margin if all we do is sit around looking up numbers for dinks like you? **1987** *21 Jump St.* (Fox-TV): Yeah, he *is* a bit of a dink. **1989** *Roseanne* (ABC-TV): The truth is, you're a dink.
b. *Rodeo.* a worthless, esp. spiritless, horse or bull.
1930 (quot. at SLOUCH, *n.*). **1965** W. Crawford *Bronc Rider* 58: Blaze ain't as much as you'd like. Not plumb dink, but no money horse 'less

you really fit a ride on him. *Ibid.* 76: No money ridin' dinks! **1992** *New Yorker* (Sept. 14) 96: A dink [is] a [rodeo] bull known for low scores.

dink³ *n.* **1.** *Stu.* (see quot.).

1900 *DN* II 32: *Dink*, n. 1. Failure to pass an examination.

2. *Tennis.* a weakly hit ball that drops just beyond the net; drop shot.

1939 in *OEDS.* **1975** Lichtenstein *Long Way* 23: The man played a woman's style—strategy, dinks, chips and lobs. **1987** Sevierville (Tenn.) tennis player: A *dink* is a shot that's very soft and easy and it hardly bounces up. They were using the term when I was taking tennis lessons twenty years ago.

¶ In phrase:

¶ **on the dink** in a bad way; on the blink.

1904 McCardell *Show Girl & Friends* 115: It ain't in New York alone that the drama's on the dink. **1911** in J. London *Short Stories* 510: Los Angeles must be on the dink when this is the best you can scare up.

dink⁴ *n. Naut.* a dinghy.

1903 (cited in *W9*). **1949** Cummings *Sports Dict.* 105. **1964** *Coast Guardsman's Manual* 856: *Dink.* A dinghy.

dink⁵ *n.* [poss. alter. of DINGE, DINGY] a black person.—used contemptuously. Also **dinky**.

1928 R. Fisher *Jericho* 263: Knew I'd turn the bug on you dinkies this time! **1942** *ATS* 360: Negro...dinge...dink. **1945** Mencken *Amer. Lang. Supp. I* 634 [ref. to 1890's]: *Dinkey*, in the Baltimore of my nonage, meant a colored child.

dink⁶ *n.* [orig. unkn.] **1.** an East Asian.—usu. used contemptuously. [Orig. Austral. slang; in current U.S. usage generalized from (**2.a.**), below.]

*1938 (cited in Partridge *DSUE* (ed. 8)). **1970** in H.S. Thompson *Shark Hunt* 188: When the Japs went into Olympic volleyball they ran a blitz on everybody using strange but maddeningly legal techniques like the "Jap roll," the "dink spike" and the "lightning belly pass."

2. [infl. by DINKY, *adj.*, 2, RINKY-DINK, CHINK, and DINK², 2.a.] *Mil.* **a.** a Vietnamese, esp. a Communist Vietnamese soldier.—usu. used contemptuously.

1967 in B. Edelman *Dear Amer.* 68: The dinks divided into two groups and took off up the mountain to our front. **1967** in Schell *Military Half* 44: I've seen about forty dinks get zapped in the field, and I can tell you that I want to get out there and pop some more dinks! **1968** in B. Edelman *Dear Amer.* 48: Another man mistook him for a dink and shot him....Every man we pick up says "Me Vietnamese Numbah 1, VC Numbah 10," so we have to let him go....We know damn well that they're dinks but we can't do anything to them until we catch them with a weapon. **1969** M. Herr, in *Esquire* (Sept.) 152: Run it over to the Dink compound. **1970** Hersh *My Lai* 8: You can't help these dinks. They like to live like pigs in hovels. **1970** *CBS Evening News* (May 4): It's better'n just sittin' around, waitin' for the dinks, I guess. **1972** Pelfrey *Big V* 105: Ye must spare the gook, even as I hath bade you to smite the dink. **1978** Downs *Killing Zone* 32 [ref. to 1967]: It turned out that the enemy had started calling us "dinks" first, because it was an insulting or demeaning term that meant "hairy man from the jungle." We had just turned the word around and started calling them dinks. At least, that was the story. **1982** Del Vecchio *13th Valley* 138: Theah was fifteen dink reg'ments out theah. **1986** Dye & Stone *Platoon* 132: This fucker's a dink for sure.

b. the Vietnamese language.—usu. used contemptuously.

1983 S. Wright *Meditations* 137: What an opportunity. See the country. Brush up on your dink.

dink⁷ *n.* [*double income, no kids*] either partner of a married couple having two incomes and no children.

1987 *New York* (Jan. 12), in *OEDS* I 84: A friend referred to two young professionals as "a couple of dinks."...Double Income, No Kids. **1987** *L.A. Times* (Feb. 8): Someone I work with accused me of being a dink...I got so tired of being called a yuppie. **1988** *World News Tonight* (ABC-TV) (Oct. 13): Then came the "double-income, no kids [people]," the *dinks*. **1990** *Newsweek* (Mar. 19) 43: They were little dinks setting up their world, thinking everything's beautiful, then, all of a sudden—wham.

dink *v.* [prob. var. of DING¹, *v.*, 1.a.] **1.a.** to strike; poke.

1980 Lorenz *Guys Like Us* 41: She dinked him...in his...nuts.

b. Esp. *Tennis.* to hit (a ball) weakly.

1981 (quot. at PUSHER). **1984** Nettles & Golenbock *Balls* 79: The batter will hit it, bloop it, dink it, ping it, and you can see his frustration.

2. *Mil.* DING¹, *v.*, 1.c.

1984 Trotti *Phantom* 22 [ref. to 1966]: I...don't want to be the one...to explain to Seventh Air Force why another Marine got dinked doing flak suppression.

dinkbreath *n.* [partial euphem.] DICKBREATH.

1988 *21 Jump St.* (Fox-TV): Great move, dinkbreath!

dinker *v.* [perh. alter. of *dicker*] to swindle; cheat.

1887 DeVol *Gambler* 274: You...look just like a chap what dinkered me out of $1000 when I got off at Cincinnati.

dinkum¹ *n.* [see DINKUM, *adj.*] truth. *Rare* in U.S.

1960–61 Steinbeck *Discontent* 209: Don't you want to know what the investment is?...The fiscal dinkum and all that?

dinkum² *n.* the penis.

1975 T. Berger *Sneaky People* 175: I'd chop his dinkum off with a cleaver.

dinkum *adj.* [fr. Austral. slang *(fair) dinkum* 'genuine; true' < dial. E (Lincolnshire) 'fair play' < *dinkum* 'a share of work'] **1.** Esp. *Mil. in Pacific.* true; authentic; genuine.

*1894 (cited in Partridge *DSUE* (ed. 8). **1959** Cochrell *Barren Beaches* 41 [ref. to 1943]: "Fair dinkum," Chick said. **1961** R. Davis *Marine at War* 143 [ref. to 1944]: I tell you this is *dinkum*:...The attack will go right up the face of a cliff.

2. fine; satisfactory.

*ca*1938 in D. Runyon *More Guys* 379: Things are by no means dinkum with Fatso and me at the moment.

dinkus *n.* DINGUS, 1.

1902–03 Ade *People You Know* 126: What are those Iron Dinkuses sticking out from the wall? **1942** *ATS* 74.

dinkweed var. DICKWEED.

dinky¹ or **dinkey** *n.* **1.** *R.R.* **a.** a small engine or locomotive, esp. a switch engine or logging locomotive.

1905 in *OEDS* I 806: *Dinkey*, a small logging locomotive. **1918** *Stars & Stripes* (Feb. 22) 5: Dinkey. **1927** *AS* II 506: *Dinkey*...a small locomotive. **1948** J. Stevens *Jim Turner* 137 [ref. to *ca*1910]: Dinkies and dump cars wheeled the diggings away on their little tracks.

b. a small railroad car; (*also*) a trolley car.

1923 McKnight *English Words* 44: The interurban railroad...has its own vocabulary such as: *dinkey*, for "city car"; *high ball* for "limited"; *steel boy* for "steel car." **1928** Dahlberg *Bottom Dogs* 192: Lorry went for the boxcar rite behind the coaldinky. **1942** *ATS* 727: Trolley Car...*dinky*, a one-man car. **1945** Hubbard *R.R. Ave.* 340: *Dinky*...a four-wheeled trolleycar. **1955** Tarry *Third Door* 220: It's hard to hope...in a Jim Crow dinky.

c. (see quots.).

1905 *DN* III 77: *Dinky*, n. short branch railway. **1927** *AS* II 506: *Dinkey*—A short train.

2. *Trucking.* (see quot.).

1942 *AS* (Apr.) 103: *Dinky.* Short coupled truck.

3. *Journ.* a brief newspaper story.

1963 Hecht *Gaily* 74 [ref. to *ca*1915]: "If you can figure out what this Vienna hypnotist is trying to say, give me a dinky on it." A dinky was three hundred words.

dinky² *n. Juve.* the penis; DINK¹.

1935 Read *Lexical Evidence* 49: The penis...A child's term is *dinkie*. **1962** Perry *Young Man* 176: They start...grabbing at his dinky. **1981** Wolf *Roger Rabbit* 10: Here I sit with a thirty-six-year-old lust and a three-year-old dinky.

dinky³ var. DINK⁵.

dinky *adj.* [Scots] **1.** attractive; natty; fancy; nice.

*1788 in *OEDS* I 806: *Dinkie*, neat, handsome. **1895** *DN* I 415: "A *dinky* time," a nice time. **1895** Townsend *Fadden* 114: I couldn't spell your dinky name. **1896** Ade *Artie* 87: I'll come hot-footin' in here with my knee-pants and a dinky coat, and do the club yell. **1919** T. Kelly *What Outfit?* 37: Sure enough, two hours later, me, my white flannels, silk shirt and dinky Panama was on board a flat ridin' toward Boxford, Massachusetts. **1921** Marquis *Carter* 203: Where is my dinky clothes to eat dinner in?

2. small; undersized; puny; (*hence*) insignificant.

1895 Townsend *Fadden* 12: I just natur'ly swipes one under me dinky apron. **1898** *Harper's Wkly.* (Feb. 5) 138: The Governor said that Wall Street was nothing but a lot of "dinky little alley, anyway." **1902** Mead *Word-Coinage* 164: "Dinky" is something cheap, defective, not first-class. **1903** Ade *Society* 24: Just above one Ear he wore a dinky Cap about the size of a Postage Stamp. **1912** in Truman *Lttrs. Home* 20: I am almost tempted sometimes to get papa to agree to sell the black horses and buy a dinky Ford. **1922** in Ruhm *Detective* 31: I ain't offering you a dinky coupla thousand dollars. **1985** Wells *444 Days* 313: Little cots...Those cots were real dinky.

dinky-dau *adj.* [< Vietnamese *diên c'ai dau*] *Mil.* in Vietnam. crazy. Also vars. Now *hist.*

1967 Sack *M* 114: Girlsan, I no dinky dow! *You* dinky dow. **1967** in B. Edelman *Dear Amer.* 105: And they call me "dinky dow" (crazy). **1969** Maitland *Only War We've Got* 50: You dinky-dao, G.I. **1969** Hughes *Under a Flare* 21: The sign read, *Dink-a-Dow Club.* **1971** Vaughan & Lynch *Brandywine's War* 24: You beaucoup dinky-dau. **1978** J. Webb *Fields of Fire* 3: You know how it is in the bush, Lieutenant. Sometimes things go *dinky dau. Ibid.* 60: He's gone a little *dinky dau,* man. **1983** "J. Cain" *Dinky-Dau Death* (title). *a***1990** Westcott *Half a Klick* 41: The Dutchman...is a little dinky-dow sometimes.

dinky-dau cigarette *n. Mil.* in Vietnam. a marijuana cigarette. Hence **dinky-dau smoke.**

1985 J.M.G. Brown *Rice Paddy Grunt* 53: The use of "dinky-dau smoke" had spread. **1984–87** Ferrandino *Firefight* 33: You got *dinky-dau* cigarettes? **1989** Berent *Rolling Thunder* 270: Dinky-dau cigarettes?

dinky-dink *n.* [infl. by RINKY-DINKY] an act of ignoring or dismissing.—constr. with *the.*

1899 Whiteing *John St.* 288: We just let it all roll by, and gave all the bounders that preached it the dinky-dink. **1901** Irwin *Sonnets* (unp.): I could not draw/My last week's pay. I got the dinky dink.

dinky skinner *n. R.R.* the engineer of a DINKY[1], 1.

1930 "D. Stiff" *Milk & Honey* 203: *Dinky skinner*—The man who runs a dinkey engine on construction jobs. **1965** O'Neill *High Steel* 270: *Dinky skinner*—one who drives a dinky engine—a small locomotive used in tracklaying and tunneling.

dinner *n.* **1.** *Black E.* an attractive young woman; DISH.

1946 Mezzrow & Wolfe *Really Blues* 186: This is my new dinner and she's a solid viper. **1962** Killens *Heard the Thunder* 52 [ref. to 1940's]: Two *fine* delicious dinners.

2. *pl.* a woman's breasts.

1952 Randolph & Wilson *Down in Holler* 120: The real old-time [Ozark] term for female breasts is not bosom but *dinners.* **1969** Kimbrough *Def. of Angels* 130 [ref. to ca1920]: She's got a broad ass and big soft dinners. **1979** Dallas man, age 27: She's got quite a pair of dinners on her.

dinner bucket *n. Bowling.* a 2-4-5-8 or 3-5-6-9 leave.

1949 Cummings *Sports Dict.* 105.

dinner-crushers *n.pl.* teeth. *Joc.*

1920 *Hicoxy's Army* 19: When the war *was* over...the Government presented Al with a fine set of enamelware dinner-crushers two sizes too large for him.

dinner plate *n. West.* a large saddle. *Joc.*

1936 R. Adams *Cowboy Lingo* 43: [Saddles of the 1870's] had a large flat "horn" the size of a tin plate...and were slangily called "dinner plates."

dinner pot *n. Army.* a large artillery shell.

1847 *Life of Gen. Worth* 183: Let's see which way that big dinner pot comes! Whiz-z-z!—there it comes! *ca***1910–19** J.H. Smith *War with Mex.* II 34 [ref. to 1847]: It was...quite annoying to have one of the big "dinner-pots," as the soldiers called them, explode close by.

dino[1] *n.* [< It male given name *Dino*] *R.R.* an Italian or Hispanic laborer.—usu. considered offensive.

1918 in *AS* (Oct. 1933) 26: *Dino* (pronounced dee-no). Wop or Spic (Mexican) section-hand.

dino[2] *n.* var. DYNO.

dinosaur *n.* **1.** Esp. *Pol.* a person who clings tenaciously to conservative or outmoded beliefs.—used derisively.

1970 *Playboy* (Sept.) 56: Hidebound conservatives..."Give us an insight into the needs of these men," says one of the local dinosaurs. **1984** *L.A. Times* (Feb. 21) I 1: President Reagan...called his challengers "captives of an anti-growth, dinosaur mentality." **1987** Taubman *Lady Cop* 74: Some of the dinosaurs in the precinct teased them. *Ibid.* 268: *Dinosaur:* Derogatory term used to describe an old-fashioned cop. **1987** C. Joyner *Prison* (film): Joel, the man is a dinosaur.

2. a large outdated piece of equipment.

1980 *Maclean's* (Sept. 1) 35: Ford committed $313 million toward a special automatic transmission plant designed solely for V-8s, the industry's instant dinosaur. **1981** *Rod Serling's Mag.* (Sept.) 80: "The machine you loaned me the other day...." "Sure. Big old dinosaur.

They don't make 'em anymore." [A typewriter]. **1982** *Business Week* (June 14) (ad) 75: Unlike those metal-cabinet dinosaurs eating up space in your office now, with OFISfile you don't have to know how it was filed.

D.I.O. *interj.* damn it, I'm off!—used at parting. *Joc.*

1821 Waln *Hermit in Phila.* 26: D.I.O.!—The *blood made his leg* and staggered out of the rooms. **1859** Matsell *Vocab.* 26: D.I.O. Damn it! I'm off.

dip[1] *n.* **1.a.** *Und.* a theft; robbery; *(specif.)* the act of picking a pocket.

1821 Martin & Waldo *Lightfoot* 10: But finding that this money was never missed, I thought I might as well have a *brighter dip. Ibid.* 30: There he expected me to make my first *dip.* **1859** Matsell *Vocab.* 26: *Dip*...the act of [a thief's] putting a hand into a pocket. **1931** Steffens *Autobiog.* 266 [ref. to 1890's]: He made his dip and...got caught. *Ibid.* 227: That was not a dip. I didn't mean to steal the watch. **1988** *Sonny Spoon* (NBC-TV): She's doin' dips in front of the Chadway Arms Hotel...She's usin' the dog as a stall.

b. *Und. & Police.* the practice of picking pockets.—constr. with *the.*

1866 *Nat. Police Gaz.* (Nov. 3) 2: Tommy Ryan, the well known knight of the "dip." **1867** *Nat. Police Gaz.* (Feb. 16) 3: Though "pinched dead to rights" on the "dip." **1872** in "M. Twain" *Life on Miss.* 292: I...was thinking I would have to go on the dipe [*sic*] (*picking pockets*) again. **1896** Ade *Artie* 63: When it comes to doin' the nice, genteel dip he belongs with the smoothest of 'em. **1900** Willard & Hodler *Powers That Prey* 65: Fifteen per cent. goes with some of 'em if you ain't on the dip. *a***1906** Burke *Prison Gates* 9: I then got settled for the "dip" (picking pockets) and got a "three spot" in Joliet. **1935** Pollock *Und. Speaks: On the dip,* engaged in the pickpocketing racket. **1949** Monteleone *Crim. Sl.* 166: On the *dip*...Working at picking pockets.

c. *Und. & Police.* a pickpocket.

1859 Matsell *Vocab.* 26: *Dip.* Pickpocket. **1866** (quot. at school). **1899** in Ade *Chicago Stories* 262: An' you didn't know Eddie was a dip? **1902** Hapgood *Thief* 36: One acted as the "dip," or "pick," and the other two as "stalls." The duty of the "stalls" was to distract the attention of the "sucker," or victim, or otherwise to hide the operations of the "dip." **1904** *Life in Sing Sing* 247: Dip—Pickpocket. **1923** Ornitz *Haunch, Paunch & Jowl* 48: I...makes him the best little dip...in the business. **1928** Bodenheim *Georgie May* 25: You ain't a dip, far's I know. **1958** S.H. Adams *Tenderloin* 33: At twenty he was a fairly skilled "dip." **1965** Spillane *Killer Mine* 22: Until now it was all juvenile. Wouldn't even put me out in the field where the dips were working. **1973** *N.Y. Post* (Apr. 16) 36: One time I was following a dip...in Grand Central.

d. *Und.* a lowlife.

1925 *Sat. Eve. Post* (Oct. 3) 52: Now listen, dip...you've got to give 'em raw meat.

2. [alluding to tipping the hat as a gesture of respect] a man's hat.

1906 M'Govern *Sgt. Larry* 64: Some Greaser fellow...wouldn't take off his "dip" when he passed the Stars and Stripes in the street. **1910** Service *Trail of '98* 17: Plant that in your dip. **1913** *DN* IV 4: *Dip,* n. A hat. **1918** *Stars & Stripes* (Feb. 8) 7: You're too good a soldier, old dip, to cuss or cry...goodby, old hat, goodby. **1970** Major *Afro-Amer. Sl.* 46: *Dip:* a hat.

3. a share of graft. Cf. **(1.a.),** above.

1988 H. Gould *Double Bang* 215: Vinnie figured he'd take a little dip along with everybody else.

¶ In phrases:

¶ **lose (one's) dip** to lose (one's) composure or sanity.

1907 *McClure's Mag.* (Jan.) 335: What with the crowd growin' personal, he lost his dip.

¶ **off (one's) dip** insane.

1901 Hobart *John Henry* 19: I went off my dip. **1901** Ade *Modern Fables* 71: Some Poor Man who was off his Dip on Matchless Mazie. **1903** McCardell *Chorus Girl* 29: You are off your dip. **1903** Hobart *Out for the Coin* 66: I fo'got for the moment that he is off his dip, suh. **1908** H. Green *Maison* 1: It's enough to drive a party off their dip. **1920** Ade *Hand-Made Fables* 256: Either the Orchestra had forgotten to tune up or he was going off his Dip. **1925** *Amer. Leg. Mo.* (June 5) 8: Who else sends a guy clean off his dip?

dip[2] *n.* **1.** *Stu.* a diploma.

1895 Gore *Stu. Slang* 6: *Dip*...Diploma. **1900** *DN* II 32: *Dip,* n. A diploma. [Reported from 13 colleges.]. **1941** in *DAS.* *****1971** in *OEDS* I 808.

2.a. a diplomatic passport.

1977 *N.Y. Times* (Jan. 9) IV 3: Starting last Jan. 1 all "dips," as the documents are called in the trade, must carry a five-year expiration date. **b.** a diplomat.

1991 *Newsweek* (Sept. 2) 8: J. Matlock…ex-dip rakes in TV bucks.

3. *cap. pl. Soccer.* the Washington Diplomats of the NASL.

1978 *Wash. Post* (Apr. 24) D1: Dips Beat Kicks via Shootout.

dip³ *n.* [back formation from DIPPY] a crazy, foolish, or obnoxious person.

1932 *AS* VII 401: *Dip, n.* A person who lacks good sense. **1934** Weeseen *Dict.* 328: *Dip*—Mentally unbalanced; a person who is so. **1939** Appel *Power-House* 330: You're dippy! Only a dip'd chase out to Slagtown. **1965** (quot. at GRUNGE). **1968** Baker et al. *CUSS* 105: *Dip.* A person without much social or academic ability. An ugly person. Any small or insignificant person. **1969** *Current Slang* I & II 26: *Dip, n.* A dull, stupid person.—College females, Minnesota. **1970** N.Y.C. man, age *ca*35: No, he means *you*, ya dip! **1973** Lucas, Katz & Huyck *Amer. Graffiti* 18: You little dip! **1987** Univ. Tenn. student: She's such a dip!

dip⁴ *n. Med.* (see 1937 quot.).

*****1937** Partridge *DSUE* 979: *Dip, n.*…Diphtheria; a patient suffering from diphtheria. **1942** *ATS* 510. **1954–60** *DAS.*

dip⁵ *n.* a dipsomaniac.

1942–43 C. Jackson *Lost Weekend* 41: He was a drunk, that's all: a soak and a dip. **1958** J.B. West *Eye* 33: Benny was most rightfully called the Dyp—not from dope, but short for dypsomaniac. **1964** in Dane & Silber *Vietnam Songbook* 122: If you want to beat the draft…/You don't have to be a fairy, a dip, or a head;/All you got to do is be a red.

dip *adj.* DIPPY.

1917 *Forum* (Dec.) 688: Those guys are going dip, coming out in the open like that. **1925** in *AS* (Feb. 1926) 266: The Jane's dip.

dip *v.* **1.** *Und.* to steal by pickpocketing; (*occ.*) to pick the pocket of.

*****1857** "Ducange Anglicus" *Vulgar Tongue* 6: Dip, to pick pockets. **1859** Matsell *Vocab.* 26: *Dip.* To pick a pocket. **1866** *Nat. Police Gaz.* (Dec. 1) 2: He "dipped" a woman of $8 on Tenth Avenue. **1890** Quinn *Fools of Fortune* 212: He's one of the finest "dips" in the country…Hope he'll "dip" some more. **1902** Hapgood *Thief* 60: Sometimes Mamie or Lena would dip and I would stall. **1904** *Life in Sing Sing* 247: *Dipping.* Picking pockets. **1912** Lowrie *Prison* 150: "Cockey" dipped you for them. *****1925** in *OEDS:* If you don't want to get "dipped," buy…small nuts and put them in your pocket with cash. There isn't one of the boys can dip you then. **1931** Steffens *Autobiog.* 228 [ref. to 1890's]: I saw them look at…the fellow I was dipping. **1968–73** Agar *Ripping & Running* 49: *Dipping* ("pickpocketing"). **1973** Goines *Players* 39: I've been trying to teach her how to dip. **1983** R. Thomas *Missionary* 105: He was living off an American Express gold card he'd dipped off some tourist. **1992** N. Cohn *Heart of World* 19: Picking pockets was an art, a…discipline. *Dipping*, he called it. *Ibid.* 21: So he just dipped.

2. to hurry away; DUCK. [1984 quot. perh. reflects an independent use.]

1903 Hobart *Out for the Coin* 14: He…grabbed his lid…and dipped for the woods. **1984** Toop *Rap Attack* 158: *Dip*, or *buff*: terms for leaving.

¶ In phrases:

¶ **dip into** to attack vigorously; pitch into.

1862 in R.G. Carter *4 Bros.* 109: They "dipped into" that fellow and beat him shockingly.

¶ **dip (one's) wick** see s.v. WICK.

¶ **I'll be dipped [in shit]!** (used to express astonishment).—usu. considered vulgar.

1955 Kantor *Andersonville* 683: I'll be dipped in shit! **1961** Coon *Front* 2: I'll be dipped in shit. I'll be the only man in history to get a Purple Heart on the way to a whorehouse. **1973** Roberts *Last American Hero* (film): "Well, I'll be dipped!" **1976** Freeman & Cohen *Big Bus* (film): Well, I'll be dipped! It's Torrance! **1968–77** Herr *Dispatches* 40: Helpless amazement on his face, "Well I'll be dipped in shit!" **1978** Gann *Hostage* 443: I heard him say softly to Kane, "Well I'll be dipped in shit." **1983** Groen & Groen *Huey* 135: Well, I'll be dipped! *a*1986 in *NDAS:* I will be dipped in shit.

diphead *n.* DIP³.

1975 Univ. Tenn. student: The person who thought it up must have been such a diphead. **1980** J.S. Young *Rumor of War* (film): What are you doing, diphead?

diploma *n. R.R.* (see quots.).

1945 Hubbard *R.R. Ave.* 183: In [the 1890's] you could buy a "diploma," or false clearance, made out on the stationery of almost any road you cared to mention, at prices ranging up to $25 apiece. *Ibid.* 340: *Diploma*—Clearance or service letter; fake service letter.

dipper *n.* **1.** *Und.* a pickpocket; DIP¹.

*****1889** Barrère & Leland *Dict. Slang* I 311: *Dipper*…(thieves), a pickpocket. **1924** H.L. Wilson *Professor* 72: Any dipper that tries to frisk you will have his work cut out.

2. *Pol.* a government employee who enjoys more than one source of governmental income.

1979 Homer *Jargon* 38.

¶ In phrase:

¶ **get (one's) dipper wet** (of a man) to engage in copulation.

1980 W. Sherman *Times Square* 127: I didn't see you getting your dipper wet.

dipping bird *n. Petroleum Industry.* a pumping jack.

1985 *All Things Considered* (Nat. Pub. Radio) (Mar. 14): This giant pumping-jack, or "dipping bird," rocks back and forth continually.

dippy *adj.* crazy or silly.

1899 Kountz *Baxter's Letters* 33: Enough to drive a person dippy. **1903** Merriman *Letters* 119: Whatever the cause, I was dippy for fair. **1904** McCardell *Show Girl & Friends* 171: Green and yellow stripes that would drive you dippy. **1907** in H.C. Fisher *A. Mutt* 3: That poor rum must be dippy. **1908** *Hampton's Mag.* (Oct.) 457: Say, you'd oughter to see me in Joisey City last week. I sure knocked 'em cold…They went dippy. **1911** *DN* III 542: *Dippy*…Foolish, idiotic…"He was *dippy* about her." **1917** in Handy *Blues Treasury* 108: They get you dippy, with their strange melodies. **1925** Bailey *Shanghaied* 110 [ref. to 1899]: Don't mind his goldarn dippy rot. **1927** C. McKay *Harlem* 114: Order that theah ovah-water liquor you useter be so dippy about. That theah Scotch. **1952** Sandburg *Young Strangers* 169 [ref. to *ca*1890]: It wasn't an insult among us kids to say, "You're off your nut," or "You're dippy." **1959** *Untouchables* (ABC-TV): You know I'm dippy about you. **1970–71** Rubinstein *City Police* 320: You know that dippy broad. **1978** S. King *Stand* 537: He complimented me on my sneakers…Isn't that dippy? **1983** Flaherty *Tin Wife* 191: Well, I guess we're all dippy.

dipshit *n.* **1.** a stupid or offensive person.—usu. considered vulgar.

1962 in *AS* (Oct. 1963) 172: Pejorative expressions traditionally directed at the…rural resident: *country bumpkin, dipshit, farmboy, lout* [etc.]. **1962** N.Y.C. teenager: Don't listen to that dipshit. **1968** Baker et al. *CUSS* 105: *Dipshit.* An obnoxious person. **1969** M. Lynch *American Soldier* 21 [ref. to 1953]: Come again here, dip shits, Jackson shouted. **1970** *Playboy* (Dec.) 278: She's bumming around with some dipshit from the Piggy Club now. **1972** Hannah *Geronimo Rex* 272: He knows what a dipshit he is.

2. emphatically nothing.—used in double negative constructions.—usu. considered vulgar.

1980 Garrison *Snakedoctor* 108: Cobb didn't know dipshit about Lee Ann's personal life. *a*1989 C.S. Crawford *Four Deuces* 66: I don't know dip-shit about a Haggler.

dipshit *adj.* [fr. the *n.*] stupid or offensive.—usu. considered vulgar.

1968 I. Reed *Yellow Back Radio* 102: The Preacher backed away…with a dipshit grin on his face. **1975** S.P. Smith *Amer. Boys* 102: LaMont had scored the highest in the regiment on all the dipshit Army tests. **1976** Univ. Tenn student: Now they're making him take additional courses. Isn't that dipshit? **1968–77** Herr *Dispatches* 26: He was about the biggest dipshit fool of all time. **1983** S. King *Christine* 310: A dipshit little freshman Arnie had never even heard of. **1986** D. Tate *Bravo Burning* 33: Not…the individual dipshit enlisted swine. **1989** S. Robinson & D. Ritz *Smokey* 214: Then they called disco dipshit. **1993** L. McMurtry, in *New Republic* (June 7) 18: He mainly liked to preach, fuck and play the guitar, preferences that are hardly unique in the annals of dipshit gurus.

dipshitting *adj.* damned; contemptible.—usu. considered vulgar.

1973 Conn. man, age *ca*22: Now I got to do the dipshittin' paper.

dip shop *n. Finance.* (see 1973–77 quot.).

1973–77 in *AS* (Winter 1980) 309: *Dip shop.* Finance company. **1982** R. Sutton *Don't Get Taken* 143: If you are constantly supporting your local dip shop…what can you do?

dipso *n.* a dipsomaniac; drunk. Also as *adj.*

*****1880**, *****1923** in *OEDS.* **1943** *Sat. Eve. Post* (Sept. 25) 12: Many become dipsos. **1958** Cooley *Run for Home* 422: The…apparently reformed "dipso"...rattled down the gangway. **1961** Sullivan *Shortest, Gladdest Years* 160: Gimme your tie, Dipso. **1968** I. Reed *Yellow Back Radio* 11: He's really gone dipso this time. **1971** *All in the Family* (CBS-TV): Doorbells ringin' in the middle of the night, I got a dipso on the phone, this is a nightmare! **1973** Flaherty *Fogarty* 225: Dipso Druggist Gets Hooked on Cough Medicine.

dipstick *n.* **1.** [partly euphem.] DIPSHIT, *n.*
1963 Walnut Ridge, Ark., high-school student (coll. J. Ball): He's such a dipstick. **1969** *Current Slang* I & II 26: *Dipstick*, n. Someone to be avoided; a dull, stupid person.—College students, both sexes, Kansas. **1971** Jacobs & Casey *Grease* 24: All right, put those things back on the car, dipstick! **1974** Stone *Dog Soldiers* 279: What are you thinking about, dipstick? **1978** S. King *Stand* 564: Take it from me, the original dipstick. **1978** Truscott *Dress Gray* 369: You two dipsticks. **1988** *Straight Up* (synd. TV series): Who needs that dipstick, anyway?
2. the penis. *Joc.*
1973 N.Y.U. student: *Getting lipstick on your dipstick* means getting a blow job. **1978** in *Maledicta* VI (1982) 23: Penis...dipstick. **1985** *Campus Voice* (Apr.) 41: Lipstick on the Dipstick versus the Fabulous Jets.

dipsy *n.* [orig. unkn.] *Hobo.* a sentence to confinement in a workhouse.
1926 *AS* (Dec.) 651: "Hobo Lingo"...*Dipsey*—workhouse sentence. **1927** *DN* V 444: *Dipsy*, n. A workhouse sentence. **1930** "D. Stiff" *Milk & Honey* 204: *Dipsy*—Workhouse sentence.

dipsy *adj.* **1.** tipsy.
1971–73 Sheehy *Hustling* 45: Nothing but dipsy drunks. *a*1986 in *NDAS*.
2. eccentric; DIPPY.
1984 *N.Y. Post* (Aug. 14) 78: Featuring a display of bawdy laughs, dipsy costumes and impressionistic special effects. *a*1986 in *NDAS*.

dipsy-do *n.* [fanciful elab. of *dip*] **1.** *Baseball.* a deceptive sinking curveball; screwball.
1932 *Baseball Mag.* (Oct.) 496. **1943** *Yank* (Dec. 31) 23: Cobb warned Hubbell that he would ruin his arm if he continued to throw "that dipsy-do." **1946** *N.Y. Times Mag.* (July 14) 18: *Dipsydo:* tantalizing curve. **1974** Perry & Sudyk *Me & Spitter* 163: Willie Stargell laughed when he saw my dipsy-do.
2. *Boxing.* (see quot.).
1980 Pearl *Pop. Slang* 38: *Dipsy-do*...a prizefight in which the two combatants have illegally agreed to pre-determine the outcome.
3. *Basketball.* (see quot.).
1980 Wielgus & Wolff *Basketball* 42: *Dipsy-do* (*n*) A short double-pumped shot, usually let go underhanded.

dipsy-doodle *n.* **1.** trickery.
1943 Chandler *High Window* 438: I wasn't going to work any dipsy-doodle in this place.
2. *Baseball.* DIPSY-DO, 1.—often attrib.
1954–60 *DAS*. **1969** Layden & Snyder *Diff. Game* 51: I fumbled one of Kolls' dipsy-doodle passes from center. **1974** Perry & Sudyk *Me & Spitter* 165: I had served up two straight dipsy-doodles to Tony Taylor of the Phillies. **1982–84** Safire *Take My Word* 333: "Dipsy Doodle" was a song composed by Larry Clinton in 1937...As baseball fans know, the *dipsy doodle* was taken up as the name for a sinking curve ball....According to George Simon's *The Big Bands Songbook*, Larry Clinton named his [song]...after the...screwball thrown by...Carl Hubbell. **1991** D. Anderson *In Corner* 76: He came back with the dipsy-doodle.

dipsy-doodle *v.* **1.** to trick; fool.
1951 in *DAS:* Now all I've got to figure out is whether we've been dipsy-doodled.
2. to amble.
1983 S. Wright *Meditations* 156: He'd dipsy-doodle on back to his room.

dipwad *n.* [partly euphem.] *Stu.* DIPSHIT, 1.—often attrib.
1976 Univ. Tenn. student: It's such a dipwad city. **1984** Algeo *Stud Buds* 7: Dip,...dipwad, dope,...dork, [etc.]. **1987** Univ. Tenn. student theme: *Dipwads*...lack intelligence. **1991** *Amer. Funniest Videos* (ABC-TV): Take that, dipwad!

dirk *n.* [alter. of DICK] **1.** the penis.
1964 *AS* (May) 118: Two variants [of *dick*] which are probably Midwestern, *dirk* and *dork*, also meaning "penis."
2. a foolish, peculiar, or obnoxious person; JERK; DORK.
1964 *AS* (May) 118: On at least one [Midwestern] campus, a *dirk* may be an "oddball" student. **1979** *N.Y. Post* (Aug. 30) 18 ["Crock" cartoon]: I wanna see what those Legion dirks are up to. **1984** Algeo *Stud*

Buds 7: An absent-minded or inattentive person...*dingbat...dip...dirk* [etc.]. ***1990** Andersson & Trudgill *Bad Language* 89: "Stupid Person"...*derk, dick, dimwit* [etc.].

dirt *n.* **1.** mischief; underhandedness; a mean action or actions.—now usu. constr. with *do* or *play*.
1835 *Mil. & Naval Mag. of U.S.* (Apr.) 102 [ref. to 1812]: He deserted from the army in Spain, out of love for "Ameriky;" and wasn't he up to all manner of dirt? I swear, if you wanted to know how to bring down a hen from the roost without noise, or to catch a goose with a fishhook, or the quickest way to ease a pig of his yoke, and forty more such tricks, you needn't go any further. **1865** J. Pike *Scout & Ranger* 278: The enemy must be up to some "dirt." **1865** in Hilleary *Webfoot* 80: Poker playing was all the "go" in camp & almost resulted in a little "dirt." **1866** in H. Johnson *Talking Wire* 342: The officers are afraid the Indians will "play dirt" on them. **1883** Peck *Peck's Bad Boy* 220: But I think my chum played dirt on me. We sold the gold plates to a jewelry man, and my chum kept the money. **1884** "M. Twain" *Huck. Finn* 90: En trash is what people is dat puts dirt on de head er dey fren's en makes 'em ashamed. **1889** Bailey *Ups & Downs* 18 [ref. to 1871]: I was very much afraid that Billy was going to "do me dirt" by giving me the slip after I had got the boodle. **1892** S. Crane *Maggie* 11: I got dis can fer dat ol' woman an' it 'ud be dirt teh swipe it. See? *Ibid.* ch. xiv: Yer doin' me dirt, Nell! **1893** in *DAE:* Ef I tek ter doin' dirt, den Ise willin' ter be jacky-me-lantuhn—an' sarve me right, too! **1899** Norris *McTeague* 46: Has any duck been doing you dirt? **1902** *DN* II 233: *Do one dirt, v.phr.t.* To injure by mischief or rascally tricks. **1907** Corbin *Cave Man* 84: You wouldn't dare to do me dirt. **1912–14** in E. O'Neill *Lost Plays* 41: But yuh wouldn't have me pinched, would yuh, Steve? Yuh wouldn't do me dirt like that? **1914** Ellis *Billy Sunday* 53: You are going to play me dirt again! **1924** Marks *Plastic Age* 200: You're turning the fraternity down; you're playing us dirt. **1929** Ferber *Cimarron* 89: But I suspect they're the boys that did Pegler dirt [killed him]. **1935** Coburn *Law Rides Range* 115: But I never done you no poisonal doit. **1942** Garcia *Tough Trip* 115: To hell with you. You ain't going to unload your dirt on me any longer. **1948** Ives *Stranger* 95: Someone must have done me dirt because she turned up her nose at me.
2. embarrassing or scandalous information; (*hence*) current, esp. malicious, gossip.
1844 Strong *Diary* I 249: But this dirt...may fall on the head of him who aims it. **1886** *N.O. Lantern* (Sept. 22) 2: But the [political] dirt will come to the surface. **1908** J. London *M. Eden* 309: Come on,—I'll show you the real dirt. **1919** in E. O'Neill *Letters* 85: But let me hear all the "dirt" as I haven't talked with anyone from New London in a century, it seems. **1922** in E. Wilson *Twenties* 116: What's the dirt? Spill the dirt! **1923** in Hemingway *Sel. Letters* 80: McAlmon has given us the dirt on everybody. It is all most enjoyable. **1924** Marks *Plastic Age* 224: Everybody seems to be digging dirt about Norry's friend. **1926** Hemingway *Sun Also Rises* 10: Do you know any dirt? None of your exalted connections getting divorces? **1928** Hecht & MacArthur *Front Page* 452: Come on...what's the dirt? **1931** Hellinger *Moon* 296: We'll write to each other all the time and spill all the dirt. **1935** Wolfe *Time & River* 20: Now we'll get it!...What do you call it?...the low down?—the dirt? **1954** Matheson *Born of Man & Woman* 136: What's new?...Give me the lowdown. Give me the dirt. **1959** Strunk & White *Elements of Style* 59: Here I am again with my bagful of dirt about your disorderly classmates. **1978** Strieber *Wolfen* 153: Somebody turned up a little dirt, Dick. Nothing really. *a*1988 C. Adams *More Straight Dope* 7: I want the *dirt*. Is Mrs. Mantis *really* guilty...?
3. money.
1871 Schele de Vere *Amer.* 296: Among the less generally known terms [for money] are...*spondulics, dooteroomus,...dirt.* **1933–34** Lorimer & Lorimer *Stag Line* 145: Plenty of scratch, I mean...You know, dirt...Money.
4. *Mil. Av.* aerial bombs.
1918 *N.Y. Times* (July 21) 3: Far ahead we knew our objective lay, where we would leave our "dirt" and settle a few reckonings.
5. *Homosex.* a man or group of men who will assault, rob, or inform on homosexuals.
1927 Rosanoff *Manual of Psych.* (ed. 6) 208: *Dirt*, a pretended homosexual whose motive is blackmail. **1932** Nelson *Prison Days & Nights* 105: Soon the word passed among the "fag" community that the Green mob was "dirt." **1935** Pollock *Und. Speaks: Dirt*, one who informs about a sexual pervert. **1949** *Gay Girl's Guide* 7: *Dirt*—...a criminally psychopathic youth, self-appointed nemesis of...homosexuals..., who guilefully leads on a homosexual interested in him until in a position to do him dirt, rolling and/or beating him up. **1963** in J. Blake *Joint* 327: He had a penchant for picking up pubescent finks (generic term, "Dirt")

who were either digging for gold or hollering for fuzz or both. **1965** Trimble *Sex Words* 64: Dirt…A man who submits to a sex act with a homosexual male, then robs him.

6.a. pepper. [1931 quot. may be erroneous.]

[**1931** *AS* (Aug.) 438: *Dirt*—Prison term for sugar.] **1942–44** in *AS* (Feb. 1946) 32: *Dirt*, n. Black Pepper.

b. tobacco, esp. chewing tobacco.

1970 Landy *Underground Dict.* 67: *Dirt*….Tobacco cigarette. **1985** Univ. Tenn. student theme: For smokeless tobacco users, *dip* and *chew* were changed to *lip dirt* or simply just *dirt*.

dirtbag *n.* a filthy or contemptible person.

1941 Kendall *Army & Navy Slang* 4: *Dirt bag*….a soldier on the garbage detail. **1968** Baker et al. *CUSS* 106: *Dirt bag*. An obnoxious person. **1969** *Current Slang* I & II 26: *Dirt bag*, n. A somewhat less than acceptable person.—Air Force Academy cadets. **1977** B. Davidson *Collura* 41: I was convinced I had blown it anyway because I looked like such a dirt bag and everyone else was all dressed up. **1980** Gould *Ft. Apache* 92: You don't buy me, dirtbag, you understand? **1985** M. Baker *Cops* 257: He was a dirtbag. No money. No insurance. No job. Just a dirtbag. **1985** Hallmark Christmas greeting card: Santa is a Dirt-Bag! **1986** *TV Guide* (Aug. 2) 30: Hey, Murray, you old dirtbag! **1991** *Donahue* (NBC-TV): They're more caring about people than most of the dirtbags you meet on the street.

dirtball *n.* DIRTBAG.

1974 Strasburger *Rounding Third* 21: Some dirtball is liable to come up and ask me why I didn't try out for such-and-such. **1976** Akron Univ. student [ref. to 1972]: We used to call each other *dirtballs*. **1977** Stallone *Paradise Alley* 55: It was a strain for her to even give the Irish dirtball the time of day. **1978** Groom *Better Times* 229: You dirtballs heard the First Sergeant. **1980** Garrison *Snakedoctor* 49: I'm gonna get you, you dirtball. **1984** Hindle *Dragon Fall* 23: Hey, hey, dirtball? I really liked your bike. **1987** *21 Jump Street* (Fox-TV): Don't move, dirtball!

dirt chute *n.* [fr. *dirt* 'excrement'] the rectum.

1942 *ATS* 150: Anus…*dirt chute* or *road*. **1979** (cited in Partridge *DSUE* (ed. 8)). **1981** C. Nelson *Picked Bullets Up* 353: Up the old dirt chute, huh? **1982** in *Nat. Lampoon* (Feb. 1983) 61: Excuse me for shanking you up the dirt chute like this.

dirt-dobber *n. So.* a dirt farmer; (*hence*) a worthless man.

1947 Willingham *End As a Man* 75: He dressed okay, not like a dirt-dobber, or the way a nigger'll dress. **1958** Frankel *Band of Bros.* 242: A dirt farmer…a dirt dauber. **1962** Crump *Killer* 9: Hey, dirt-dobber!…Who are you?

dirt-eater *n.* **1.** *So.* a poor white Southerner.—usu. used contemptuously.

1840 in *DARE.* **1844** in *DAE.* **1845** Hooper *Suggs* 88: "Whar' do you aim to bury your dead Injuns, Cap'en?" sarcastically inquired the little dirt-eater. **1865, 1866, 1871, 1902** in *DAE.* **1908, 1913, 1941** in *DARE.*

2. *Auto Racing.* a driver who races on a dirt track.

1962 G. Olson *Roaring Road* 36: Why, that old dirt eater!…Buck, hike across the track and flag him in on this lap!

dirt-eating *adj.* despicable.

1940 F. Hunt *Trail fr. Tex.* 130 [ref. to 1870's]: Why don' ya tell this bunch a' dirt-eatin' shorthorns ta go ta hell?

dirt hider *n. Constr.* a road grader.

1958 McCulloch *Woods Words* 47: *Dirt hider*—A road grader.

dirt nap *n.* death; esp. in phr. **take a dirt nap** to die. *Joc.*

1981 *Bosom Buddies* (ABC-TV): We've got to convince him that Hildy's taken a dirt nap. **1981** *Bosom Buddies* (ABC-TV): "Are you sitting down?…Isobel's a goner." "So: who else took the dirt nap?" **1986** *It's a Living* (synd. TV series): Take a dirt nap, creep! **1988** *ALF* (NBC-TV): Takin' a dirt nap. **1992** Mowry *Way Past Cool* 7: "Then…you end up with jack." "Or a dirt nap."

dirt road *n.* [fr. *dirt* 'excrement'] the rectum, esp. in ref. to anal copulation.

1916–22 Cary *Sexual Vocab.* IV s.v. *human body:* The Anus…*dirt road.* **1931** *AS* (June) 332: Go up the dirt road, v.phr. To practice pederasty. **1940** Del Torto: To be screwed up the old dirt road. **1949** Monteleone *Crim. Sl.* 69: *Dirt Road*….The posterior; the rectum. **1980** *Penthouse* (Dec.) 51: I decided that the dirt road was the right road. **1982** *Nat. Lampoon* (Sept.) 56: Anal sex…Dirt Road Delights.

dirt-scraper *n. Law.* (see quot.).

1889 Barrère & Leland *Dict.* I 311: *Dirt-scrapers* (American), lawyers who in examining witnesses…inquire closely as to all their relations

with women, etc., either with a view to making them appear immoral and discreditable, or…to afford to the court and spectators the exquisite pleaure of seeing a [witness] tortured and put to shame.

dirt-scratcher *n. West.* a poor farmer.

1942 Rodgers & Hammerstein *Oklahoma!* 52: Whyn't those dirt-scratchers stay in Missouri where they belong? *ca*1969 *Gunsmoke* (CBS-TV): My old man…was a farmer. Just a dirt-scratcher.

dirt slinger *n.* a pick-and-shovel worker.

1926 Tully *Jarnegan* 87: Fellow dirt slingers—you've got nothing to lose but your pick and shovel.

dirt-track *n.* DIRT ROAD.

1967 Mailer *Vietnam* 20: Putting it in the young lady's vagina rather than going up her dirt-track. **1976** Crews *Feast of Snakes* 68: Ain't he sweet? Looks like a dirt track specialist to me.

dirty *n.* ¶ In phrases:

¶ **do (one's) dirty** to defecate.

1970 Thompson *Garden of Sand* 58: You do your dirty and be quick about it!

¶ **do (someone) the dirty** to cheat, betray, or victimize. *Rare* in U.S.

*1914, *1915, *1929, *1930, *1942 in *OEDS.* *a*1961 Longman *Power of Black* 121: Do you the dirty as soon as look at you. **1971** Dahlskog *Dict.* 19: *Dirty on (someone), do the*, to do something mean and malicious to someone; to doublecross someone. **1985** Briskin *Too Much* 132: Gideon…fired Curt for doing him the dirty.

¶ **do the dirties** [or **dirty deed**] *Stu.* to engage in copulation.

*a*1968 in Haines & Taggart *Ft. Lauderdale* 140: We got around to doing the dirty deed a couple of times on the beach. **1968–70** *Current Slang* III & IV 37: *Do the dirties, v.* To act promiscuously (applies only to girls).—New Mexico State. **1974** Strasburger *Rounding Third* 40: Come on, baby, let's do the dirties.

dirty *adj.* **1.** very; very great.

1858 in G.W. Harris *High Times* 128: Then they dus thar dirty best. **1925** Loos *Prefer Blondes* 27: I overheard her say…that she really liked to become intoxicated once in a "dirty" while.

2.a. *Naut. & Av.* stormy, squally, or foggy.

1869 in *Seal & Salmon Fisheries* IV 57: We had promise of what sailors call a "dirty night." **1956** Heflin *USAF Dict.: Dirty weather*…Bad weather. **1959** Duffy & Lane *Warden's Wife* 137: Dirty weather, isn't it, Miss Carpenter?

b. *Meteorology.* (of clouds) extremely moist.

1984 WINS Radio News (Aug. 2): This storm is high and dirty—in other words, loaded with moisture.

3. having money; flush.—usu. constr. with *with.*

1896 Ade *Artie* 82: They cleaned me in two days, but then, as they say down on State Street, I wasn't very dirty when I landed. **1908** McGaffey *Show Girl* 237: These two boobs are dirty with the evergreen. **1930** Irwin *Tramp & Und. Sl.* **1931** Bontemps *Sends Sunday* 22: I'm jes' dirty wid money.

4. *Jazz.* characterized by strong blues elements, esp. a raw or husky tonal quality. Also as adv.

1926 in R.S. Gold *Jazz Talk* 70: Fine "hot" record, with a special "dirty" piano solo. **1936** in *ibid.:* His tone almost always has a pronounced rasp, the effect of which is magnificently "dirty." **1939, 1959** in *ibid.* **1982** A. Shaw *Dict. Pop/Rock* 106: "Dirty" tone. An alteration in the texture of a note played by the brasses or reeds that gives it an erotic…quality. **1986** B. Clayton & N. Elliott *Jazz World* 44: He could play "dirty" when he wanted to.

5. *Police.* **a.** in possession of contraband, esp. narcotics. Cf. earlier CLEAN, 2.

1927 in Hammett *Knockover* 320: Paddy was dirty with fifteen thousand or so [in stolen money]. **1966** J. Mills *Needle Park* 13: He is at that moment "dirty"—carrying drugs. **1969** Whittemore *Cop* 159: If we catch him dirty…with some reefers in his pocket or something, we'd really have him. **1971** Woodley *Dealer* 34: He had a pistol on him when he took the fall, you know, he was dirty. **1973** Schiano & Burton *Solo* 87: Listen, this guy's got stuff, too, he's dirty as well. It's in his…pocket! **1976** *Deadly Game* (ABC-TV movie): You were caught dirty with heroin, Doyle. That's heavy time. **1985** *Newsweek* (Apr. 22) 64: You can tell if a guy's dirty by looking at him.

b. taking bribes; corrupt.

1958 Appel *Raw Edge* 78: Honest Johns, and dirty Johns. **1985** O'Neil *Lady Blue* (film): There's some evidence that he was dirty…Was he ever on the take? **1986** Philbin *Under Cover* 102: He quickly realized that his reputation as a dirty cop had preceded him. **1989** *Beauty & Beast* (CBS-TV): Moreno's *dirty*, Joe!

c. *adv.* in the act of committing a crime; red-handed.

1966 Brunner *Face of Night* 232: Dirty—to be caught by a policeman…while committing a crime. **1976** "N. Ross" *Policeman* 21: I don't really know why, but when I catch them dirty [having violated a traffic law]…they don't beef very often.

d. (see quot.).

1987 Taubman *Lady Cop* 227: Those kids coming up out of the park look dirty. *Ibid.* 268: *Dirty*: Suspicious, usually used by cops to describe potential suspects.

6. *Med.* involving infected tissue.

***1950** Partridge *DSUE* (ed. 3) 1031: *Dirty one*…1914–18…a wound that turns septic. **1976** Haseltine & Yaw *Woman Doctor* 121: It was an infected case, a "dirty" operation.

¶ In phrase:

¶ **do the dirty deed** see *do the dirties* s.v. DIRTY, *n.*

dirty *adv.* **1.** exceedingly.

1894 Bunner *More Sixes* 48: He's dirty well, and it's devilish little you care! **1942** in *Jour. Gen. Psych.* LXVI (1945) 132: "Boy, that was a dirty nifty show." "I returned that book a dirty long time ago."

2. *Av.* (see 1973 quot.).

1973 W. Crawford *Gunship Cmndr.* 145: The Skyhawk came in low and "dirty"—that is, with flaps and wheels and speedbrakes extended to slow the airplane's speed as much as possible. ***1979** in Partridge *DSUE* (ed. 8): He's coming past dirty now.

¶ In phrase:

¶ **do** [or **play**] **(someone) dirty** to cheat, victimize, or betray (someone).

1910 G. Rice, in M. Gardner *Casey* 55: Sayin' we had done 'em dirty and it wuzn't on the square. **1927** McIntyre *Slag* 155: I never played anybody dirty. **1933** E. Caldwell *God's Little Acre* 6: They can do him dirty and he won't know about it till it's too late to stop the clock. **1942** Wilder *Flamingo Road* 102: Why couldn't you have had sense enough to keep away from Semple even if he has done you dirty. **1952** "E. Box" *Fifth Position* 129: He was…all the time doing somebody dirty. **1962** T. Berger *Reinhart* 103: He had assumed Humbold would try to do the Clendellans dirty. **1972–76** Durden *No Bugles* 110: You think there's slopes layin' up out here waitin' to do us dirty?

Dirty D *n. Navy.* the U.S.S. *Denver*. Now *hist.*

1930 in *Leatherneck* (Jan.) 8: Since we last broadcast from the "Dirty D" much water has flowed under the bridge.

Dirty Dozen *n. Mil.* the Twelfth U.S. Infantry.

1919 *12th U.S. Inf.* 51: "The Dirty Dozen," they were called in those days.…The Twelfth was known from one end of the Union armies to the other.

Dirty Gertie *n.* **1.** (a nickname applied to a sexually forward or promiscuous woman).

1928 Carr *Rampant Age* 42: Lookit young Skeeter Brown steppin' out with Dirty Gertie. **1931** Dos Passos *1919* 305: Dirty Gertie. **1944** Posselt *G.I. Songs* 72: Dirty Gertie from Bizerte. **1945** *Sat. Rev. Lit.* (Nov. 3) 7: Dirty Gertie from Bizerte…Filthy Fanny from Trapani.

2. *Navy.* (see quot.). Now *hist.*

1945 Dos Passos *Tour* 112: The solution was to keep floating tank farms—Dirty Girties, they called them, old cargo boats condemned for one reason or other and turned into tankers—as far forward as possible as a margin of safety.

dirty laundry *n.* [sugg. by colloq. phr. *air (one's) dirty laundry* (earlier *linen*) *in public*] embarrassing personal or confidential information. Also **dirty linen.**

1982 D. Henley *Dirty Laundry* (pop. song title). **1987** *USA Today* (Aug. 12) 1: Yanks Hang Out Dirty Laundry. Piniella in Trouble? **1993** *N.Y. Times* (Jan. 15) B 4: Their Day on "Donahue": Dirty Linen on the Air.

dirty-leg *n. Esp. Texas.* a sluttish woman.

1962–68 B. Jackson *In Life* 192: A dirty leg is just for a guy that comes in, a drunk, maybe and wants a $5 to $10 piece of ass. **1968–70** *Current Slang* III & IV 36: *Dirty leg, n.* A prostitute; a promiscuous girl.—College males, Kansas. **1972** D. Jenkins *Semi-Tough* 100: A Dirty Leg…waited tables or hopped cars, was truly hung, might chew gum, posed for pictures, and got most of her fun in groups. **1975** Texas man, age 30: A *dirty-leg* is a lascivious or promiscuous girl. I remember very distinctly hearing that in 1962 in Austin, Texas. **1976** W. Texas man, age 33: In 1960 or '61, in Texas and Oklahoma, a *dirty leg* meant a

woman of *loose* virtue—but not a pro.

dirty-neck *n.* a sluttish woman.

1918 in *AS* (June 1930) 383: *Dirty-necks*. French girls. **1962** T. Berger *Reinhart* 413: Reinhart…saw no good reason why they should know more about man on the basis of drunks, dirty necks, and addresses of ill repute.

Dirty-Plate Route *n. Hobo.* the San Joaquin Valley of southern California.

1926 *AS* (Dec.) 651: *Dirty Plate Route*—the Lux and Miller ranches of California. **1939** McWilliams *Factories in the Field* ch. xvii: The California growers…foster[ed] the "Dirty Plate Route" along which the tramps…and hobos of former years used to plod their way on foot and by freight cars.

dirty pool *n.* unfair or unsportsmanlike conduct.

1940 (cited in *W9*). **1942** Swerling & Mankiewicz *Pride of Yankees* (film): That's dirty pool! **1947** Hart *Gentleman's Agreement* (film): All right, I'm a cat. And this is dirty pool. *a***1967** Bombeck *Wit's End* 126: She told us you hid our skateboard.…She said that was dirty pool. **1972** J. Pearl *Cops* 21: I'm not talking about pay-offs.…That's dirty pool. **1982** R.M. Brown *So. Discomfort* 171: I'd call it dirty pool. **1983** Ehrhart *VN-Perkasie* 194: I'm sorry…That was dirty pool. **1992** *Rolling Stone* (Apr. 30) 64: It's dirty pool to reveal what happens next [in a movie].

dirty private *n.* confidential or inside information.—constr. with *a.*

1903 Benton *Cowboy Life on Sidetrack* 12: Each one took each of us aside and gave us a dirty private as to what they would do for us.

Dirty Side *n. CB.* the East Coast; (*specif.*) New York City and its environs.—constr. with *the.*

1975 Dills *CB* 28: *Dirty Side*: New York; New Jersey; the East coast. **1977** Corder *Citizens Band* 33: You say how-do to all my boys at K&L when you hit the Dirty Side, all right?

dirty spoon *n.* GREASY SPOON.

1908 *Hampton's Mag.* (Oct.) 528: Gallo's…"The Dirty Spoon" is what some chorus girl nicknamed it on a happy night. **1915** Poole *Harbor* 73 [ref. to *ca*1905]:That cafe endeared to so many youths of all nations under its name of "The Dirty Spoon." **1970** Boatright & Owens *Derrick* 124: We were in one of the cafés, the dirty spoons, down at Humble one day.

Dirtytown *n. CB.* New York City.

1976 Whelton *CB Baby* 8: We're definitely looking for that Holland Tunnel westbound out of this Dirtytown.

dirty tricks *n.pl. Pol.* undercover or clandestine operations; (*hence*) deceitful stratagems intended to subvert an opponent's campaign for office; in phr. **department of dirty tricks** the Plans Directorate of the Central Intelligence Agency.

[**1945** Jensen *Carrier War* 156: To his flagship he [Adm. W.F. Halsey] brought a large and brilliant staff (including…Commander Harold Stassen, ex-governor of Minnesota, and a group of others who soon dubbed themselves the "dirty-trick department" because of their facility at thinking up nasty surprises for the Japanese).] **1963** in *OED2*: In the "Department of Dirty Tricks"…our Intelligencers behave like babes in the wood. **1966** *The Times* (London) in *BDNE3*: The more serious question is whether the very existence of an efficient C.I.A. causes the United States Government to rely too much on clandestine and illicit activities, back-alley tactics, subversion, and what is known in official jargon as "dirty tricks." **1968** Safire *New Language* 112: *Department of Dirty Tricks*. Nickname for the plans division of the Central Intelligence Agency, which handles espionage and other covert, undercover operations. **1971** Waters *Smugglers* 134: Until that is, we set up our own "dirty tricks department." **1973** *N.Y. Times Mag.* (Jan. 28) 4: Cord Meyer…has…ended up grubbing among the muckrackers at the department of dirty tricks over at the C.I.A. **1974** *N.Y. Times* (Dec. 29) IV 1: Mr. Helms became head of the Plans Directorate, sometimes known as the C.I.A.'s "department of dirty tricks." **1983** *Business Week* (May 9) 50: The Newfoundlander has injected this plain talk into a…campaign otherwise dominated by dirty tricks on the part of the two front-runners. **1990** *Nation* (Sept. 17) 261: As though…the revelations over the years of dirty tricks…by the Central Intelligence Agency were all a bad dream, the Senate…concludes that "Congress should expressly authorize covert action as a legitimate foreign policy instrument."

dirty up *v. Av.* to extend flaps, speedbrakes, etc., in flight.

1989 J. Weber *Defcon One* 233: Karns swore, watching the wily Russian simultaneously "dirty up" and pull into his Tomcat.

dis *n.* [fr. the v.] Esp. *Black E.* an expression of disrespect, disparagement, or rejection.

1990 *Village Voice* (N.Y.C.) (July 3) 61: As the rap score reflects his increasing frustration…, the women get colder, the "dis" becomes ever more explicit. **1990** Costello & Wallace *Sig. Rappers* 49: They'll look you up coldly from loafers to eyes and then turn very deliberately to look somewhere else. It's a "dis." **1991** *Fresh Prince of Bel-Air* (NBC-TV): She just gave you a pretty hard dis. **1992** *Rolling Stone* (Feb. 6) 90: The answer to both questions is no—with no dis intended.

dis *v.* [extracted fr. such words as *disrespect, dismiss, disparage*] Esp. *Black E.* **1.** to disparage; belittle.

1982 "Crash Crew" in L.A. Stanley *Rap* 57: Guaranteed to get dissed if you tell me I'm wrong. **1987** "Public Enemy" *Bring the Noise* (rap song): A magazine or two is dissin' me and dissin' you. **1989** *Village Voice* (N.Y.C.) (Nov. 28) 80: Unbelievers dis their sincerity. **1990** *Rolling Stone* (July 12) 29: [Rap artist Hammer]'s an overtly religious man who refuses to dis other artists even as they dis him. **1991** Gaines *Teenage Wasteland* 91: There was not one conversation among the outcast [*sic*] that did not include de rigueur dissin' the jocks. **1992** *Melrose Place* (Fox-TV): I would never dis a good machine.

2. to disrespect; affront.

1984 *Miami Vice* (NBC-TV): Tell 'em what you know, man! You're dissin' me! **1988** *Atlantic* (June) 110: The victim…made the mistake of irritating Nuke at a party. "He *dissed* him," Sergeant Croissant said, using the street term. **1989** *New Republic* (May 29) 29: Those young black male writers [Alice] Walker chastised…for dissing their black sisters. **1991** *N.Y. Newsday* (June 11) 7: Vallone was visibly angry when he was turned from the more exclusive [restaurant]. He even said he had been "dissed." **1992** M. Gelman *Crime Scene* 135: They had been "dissed," shown disrespect in public, which was a slight worth dying for. **1993** *Newsweek* (Jan. 18) 4: Early Oscar Picks…Malcolm X…Denzel [Washington] solid for Actor nomination. But Hollywood always disses Spike [Lee].

disc *n.* a dollar.

1919 *Amer. Leg. Wkly.* (Jan. 11) 24: I've got a job waiting for me that pays thirty moons a week instead of thirty a month…Thirty discs. That's sure beaucoup l'argent.

discharge *n.* ¶ In phrase: **get (one's) discharge** *Mil.* to die; be killed.

1893 Corby *Chaplain Life* 237 [ref. to Civil War]: Very early that morning a colonel of the Twenty-eighth Massachusetts…called on me and told me that he *felt* he should get his "discharge" that day. He was a very brave officer, and up to this time had no serious misgivings.

disc jock *n.* DISC JOCKEY.

1952 MacDonald *Damned* 13: He's my favorite disc jock. **1952** Lait & Mortimer *USA* 37: Through disc-jocks, kids get to know…"hot" musicians.

disc jockey or **disk jockey** *n.* [*disc* + JOCKEY] a person who conducts a program featuring recorded music (and, now, informal conversation) on a radio station or at a discotheque. Also as *v.* Now *S.E.*

1941 *Variety* (Aug. 13) 36: Gilbert is a disc-jockey who sings with his records. *Ibid.* 51: Art Green disc-jockeys from Manhattan Beach. **1943** *Newsweek* (Oct. 4) 50: But Martin Block, station WNEW's king "disk jockey," got a priority of 1,000 "Mamas." **1948** Lait & Mortimer *New York* 30: Band leaders and disk jockeys…"plug" the latest publications of the companies in which they are interested. **1952** Brossard *Darkness* 126: He dialed…to a fairly good disk jockey's program. **1977** S. Gaines *Discotheque* 23: He…made his way back across the dance floor to the disc jockey's booth.

discombobberate *v.* [fanciful alter. of *discompose, discommode,* or *discomfit*] to confound, confuse, or spoil; (*intrans.*) to fall apart. Also vars.

1834 in *OEDS*: May be some of you don't get discombobracated. **1837** Neal *Charcoal Sketches* 14: While you tear the one, you'll discombobberate the nerves of the other. **1838** *Crockett Almanac* (1839) 35: The methodizer was discombobberated a few and shoved her starn down agin. **1839** in *DAE*: The lad doesn't love to have his hunting tools discomboborated. **1840** in *DAE*: Let me tell you now that this discovery discomboberated me considerably. **1846** Codman *Sailors' Life* 189: Cook, I feels a little discomboberated, but I'm not gwoin to be 'timidated. **1854** *Spirit of Times* (May 13) 152: *Persist!* gentle*men*, I say by

G-d, *persist!* or I'll *discomborbirate* the whole d—d possum-cum-it-at-us of you. **1860** in Saunders *Parodies of Whitman* 19: The entire system of the universe discomboberates around us with a perfect looseness. *a***1889** in Barrère & Leland *Dict.* I 312: An' when he seen I'd killed a deer as slick as grease he was so discombobberated he couldn't speak. **1916** (quot. at DISCOMBOBULATE).

discombooberate *v.* [alter. of DISCOMBOBBERATE, infl. by BOOB] DISCOMBOBBERATE.

1948 in *DA*: The introduction of radio to the conventions discombooberated the speechmakers terribly. **1960** *Twilight Zone* (CBS-TV): Mr. Bevis is a little confused, a little discombooberated.

discombobulate *v.* DISCOMBOBBERATE. Hence **discombobulation,** *n.*

1916 *DN* IV 322: Discomboberate…In N. Eng., *discumbobulate*…Medina Co., Ohio, in the nineties, *discombobelate*. **1970** Zindel *Your Mind* 98: I hadn't been so discombobulated and hurt since Jackie Kohild did you-know-what in my insectarium. **1977** Coover *Public Burning* 78: Our crool and onrelentin' inimy…has damn near discombobulated us. **1984** W. Safire, in *N.Y. Times* (Sept. 3) 25: Con Con II might discombobulate the permanent political power structure, but it would reflect the popular muscle-flexing intended by the Founders. **1987** R. Miller *Slob* 38: To be assaulted by some prickless FREAK only added to her overwhelming nausea, terror, and discombobulation. **1991** J. Lamar *Bourgeois Blues* 44: Discombobulated, the Jehovah's Witness quickly gathered up his magazines.

discon *n. Police.* disorderly conduct. Also vars.

1963 E. Hunter *Ten Plus One* 133: "What can we book him for? Vagrancy?"…"Dis cond." **1966** Samuels *People vs. Baby* 61: "Discon" (disorderly conduct, such as loitering or using abusive language). **1966** J. Mills *Needle Park* 115: "Bobby got busted," she said excitedly…"What for?" I asked. "Discon. For nothing. He was out there in the phone booth…and some lousy bluecoat came along and just busted him for discon, for nothing, for just *being* there." **1968** Radano *Walking the Beat* 75: We'll hit him with dis con also—loud and boisterous, causing a crowd to collect. **1972** J. Mills *Report* 78: There was people up there in those days'd rather kill you than take a collar for attempted discon. **1976–77** Kernochan *Dry Hustle* 84: Here I was in jail for the first time for dis-con and soliciting.

dise *n.* merchandise; goods.

1914 Jackson & Hellyer *Vocab.* 29: *Dise*…A contraction of merchandise. Loot; plunder…"There's a mob riding the rattlers between here and the jungle who have a dise plant stashed (cached) in the jungles." **1927** *AS* (June) 388: A freight is called a *drag*. *Dise-drag* (merchandise), *silk-drag*, [etc.] result from this word.

disguised *adj.* [sugg. by earlier S.E. *disguised in liquor*] drunk.

*****1622** in *F & H* II 291: *Harp.* I am a prince disguised. *Hir.* Disguised! How? Drunk! *****1663** J. Dryden, in *F & H*: I was a little disguised, as they say. **1737** *Penna. Gazette* (Jan. 6): He's…Boozy…in his Cups…Disguiz'd. **1844** in L.F. Browne *J.R. Browne* 46: There were a few stragglers in the street, most gloriously "disguised." **1859** Bartlett *Amer.* 122 (ed. 2): *Disguised.* Intoxicated.

disgusto *adj. Stu.* disgusting.

1981 *Dark Room* (ABC-TV): How disgusto! A dirty old bat! *a***1986** in *NDAS*: Disgusto special effects.

dish *n.* **1.** something exactly suited to one's liking or abilities.

[*****1599** Shakespeare *Much Ado* II i: Heeres a dish I loue not, I cannot indure this Lady tongue.] **1904** T.A. Dorgan, in Zwilling *TAD Lexicon* 32: A scribe. That's the dish for me. **1908** in H.C. Fisher *A. Mutt* 109: Ah, this is the dish. Away from the tempters. **1910** T.A. Dorgan, in *N.Y. Eve. Jour.* (Apr. 13) 20: Automobilin' is my dish. **1918** Witwer *Baseball to Boches* 106: They ought to of been my dish, seein' what a notorious pitcher I was. **1920–21** Witwer *Leather Pushers* 25: The rough-house stuff was DuFresne's dish. **1940** R. Buckner *Knute Rockne* (film): "Ever play football?" "Some. Baseball's my dish." **1942** in H. Gray *Arf* (unp.): Nice work, Doc. But from here on, he's *my* dish! **1947, *1955, *1957** in *OEDS*.

2. an attractive young woman.

[*****1606** Shakespeare *Antony & Cleo.* II vi: He will to his Egyptian dish againe.] [*ca***1888** *Stag Party* 197: The bride—that dainty dish/Of female flesh.] **1921** J. Conway, in *Variety* (Nov. 25) 9: She ought to be a swell-lookin' dish in tights. **1926** Maines & Grant *Wise-Crack Dict.* 13: *Swell dish*—Very beautiful girl. [**1928** MacArthur *War Bugs* 200: She certainly was an elegant dish of beans.] **1940** O'Hara *Pal Joey* 86: She was…dumb…but willing to learn. So all the time I was thinking this was going to be my favorite dish. **1941** Schulberg *Sammy* 274: She looks like quite a dish. **1946** Wead & Sheekman *Blaze of Noon* (film): Not a bad dish at that. **1948** Lay & Bartlett *12 O'Clock High!* 23: "She's a real dish?" "On the plus side of a knock-out." **1951** O'Hara *Farmers Hotel* 52: She was quite a dish. **1952** Felton & Essex *Las Vegas Story* (film): With a dish like that, I'd probably park first. **1957** Bannon *Odd Girl* 38: Gee, I knew a lovely dish over there a couple of years ago. **1960–61** Steinbeck *Discontent* 63: Margie is what Joey-boy would call a "dish." **1969** Jessup *Sailor* 243: I saw that dish you had in for the night. **1971** B.B. Johnson *Blues for Sister* 99: She had no knowledge of my prior encounter with that swinging Norwegian dish. **1990** Updike *Rabbit at Rest* 216: The kid has a big tall hippy dish to boff.

3. nothing; zero.

1884 *Life* (June 19) 342: His bank stopped to pay/With assets amounting to "Dish."

4. *Baseball.* home plate.—constr. with *the.*

1907 *N.Y. Eve. Jour.* (Apr. 17) (cited in Nichols *Base. Termin.*). **1910** *N.Y. Eve. Jour.* (Feb. 3) 14: There is something odd…about a pitcher who can cut the dish with curves and fast ones propelled by the sinister wing. **1964** Thompson & Rice *Every Diamond* 141: Dish: the home plate. **1974** J. Garagiola, on *World Series* (NBC-TV) (Oct. 16): He couldn't find the dish. **1978** F. Messer, on N.Y. Yankees–Boston Red Sox (WPIX-TV) (June 27): He hangs over the plate a lot. He crowds the dish. **1980** Lorenz *Guys Like Us* 67: He came to the dish.

5. Orig. *Homosex.* gossip; spiteful or malicious comments. Cf. DISH, *v.*, 3.c.

1976 in M. Levine *Gay Men* 209: Calculated camp, packaged so that people will think she's bringing them the real "dish" from the inside. **1992** *L.A. Times* (Jan. 22) F2: The end result is said to be gossip, "dish" and anecdote to the max. **1992** *CBS This Morning* (CBS-TV) (Nov. 10): All the latest dish on Diana.

dish *v.* **1.** to ruin or finish; defeat; thwart; discomfit.

*1788 Grose *Vulgar Tongue* (ed. 2): He is completely dished up; he is totally ruined. *1797 in J. Ashton *Eng. Satires on Napoleon* 40: May now be considered as completely dished. *1811 in *F & H*: He was completely dished—could never have appeared again. **1821** Waln *Hermit in Philadelphia* 25: I'm dished—done-up. **1834** Caruthers *Kentuck. in N.Y.* I 96: I'm a Turk if I aint tetotally dished. **1854** Avery *Laughing Gas* 155: Scuffle for life, as the result of which, one chicken gets *dished*, and the other is very much *cut up.* **1873** *Galaxy* (Apr.) 438: Can't I make you understand that I am dished and must study a profession? **1891–1900** Hoyt *Five Plays* 115: We're dished on going to the ball, and we've got to put in a night toting that old fool all over Chinatown. **1901** Ade *Modern Fables* 33: They had dished many a Bright Prospect. **1912** Stringer *Shadow* 134: I'm dished!…I'm dished for this coast! **1913** *Sat. Eve. Post* (Mar. 29) 9: I stood for bein' the goat an' openin'. The result is I'm dished for the week! **1936** Dos Passos *Big Money* 284: Well, you're dished this time. **1963** Rechy *City of Night* 334: Never try to dish a queen, babes. **1982** "W.T. Tyler" *Rogue's March* 157: [You mean] that someone planted Russian guns on those bimbos…just to dish the Sovs?

2.a. *Cards.* to deal.

1898–1900 Cullen *Chances* 194: How many is the dealer dishing himself?

b. *Basketball.* to pass.—occ. constr. with *off.*

1980 Wielgus & Wolff *Basketball* 137: He dishes well, shoots like a trooper. **1988** Frazier & Offen *W. Frazier* 23: He could penetrate and then dish off, but…there was no way he was going to make the team.

3.a. to retail (gossip or scandal).—also constr. with *out.* Cf. DISH OUT.

1926 Maines & Grant *Wise-Crack Dict.* 7: *Dish out the dirt*—Tell the latest scandal. **1929** in Galewitz *Great Comics* 110: She'll dish you all the dirt. **1932** *AS* VII (June) 331: *Dish the dope*—"Let's hear the gossip." **1934** in Ruhm *Detective* 107: The dame—this Penfields dame—dish us the dirt and I don't care how dirty you dish it. **1936** Levin *Old Bunch* 236: The seven wise virgins…proceeded to dish the dirt.

b. to disparage, orig. (and esp.) in a gossipy or spiteful manner.

1941 "G.R. Lee" *G-String* 16: Boy, did they start dishing us. **1946** J.H. Burns *Gallery* 145: Their conversation was a series of laments and groans and criticisms of everyone else present. They called this dishing the joint. **1973** *New Yorker* (Jan. 27) 66: Conservative columnists…had at first gone along with the President out of a certain pleasure at his "dishing the Whigs." **1992** *Newsweek* (Nov. 23) 55: She…dished rival model Kate Moss for going topless. **1992** *New Yorker* (Dec. 28) 150: Strauss loves to dish people to their faces or behind their backs.

c. *Homosex.* to gossip.

1963 Cory & LeRay *Homosex. & Soc.* 263: *Dish*…To gossip about someone, usually in a derogatory manner; often used when such gossip involves the person's sexual activities and amative interests. **1965** *Fact* (Feb.): *Dish.* To talk at length; relate; describe. **1965** Selby *Last Exit* 225: She sat and dished with the girls. **1978** Maupin *Tales* 121: O.K., if you don't wanna dish, we won't dish. **1981–89** J. Goodwin *More Man* 8: He would occasionally drop gay terms into the conversation, words like *dishing*, meaning "gossiping" or "insulting."

4. to provoke; goad; JIVE.

1987 *21 Jump St.* (Fox-TV): Hey, man, don't dish me. Pay me or give it back.

dish of chat *n.* a talk.

1834 Caruthers *Kentuck. in N.Y.* 28: He would…die of the solemncholies, if…he and I couldn't have a dish of chat together.

dish out *v.* to deal out (something, esp. abuse or punishment) with force; in phr. **dish it out** to deal out abuse or punishment.

[**1666** G. Alsop *Maryland* 39: The sawce that dish'd out of the muzzle of a Gun.] **1908** McGaffey *Show Girl* 27: They commence to dish out this Emporia humor. **1930** Pasley *Capone* 69: Johnny's the same as a lot of fighters in the ring…He can dish it out, but he can't take it. **1931** Armour *Little Caesar* (film): Sam, you can dish it out, but you're gettin' so you can't take it no more. **1933** Thurber *Life and Hard Times* 3: Not being able to see, I could take it but I couldn't dish it out. **1934** L. Berg *Prison Nurse* 57: I'm wondering if you can take it—like you dish it out! *Ibid.* 59: Any mugg can dish it out. But I ain't had my turn at bat yet. **1950** F. Brown *Space* 11: I can take it, Lieutenant. Dish it out. **1954** Gruber *Bugles* 67: I can take anything that damn Shuba can dish out. **1955** Goethals *Chains* 104: You bastard—who's dishing the shit out now, for chrissakes? **1962** Sarlat *War Cry* 46: You can dish out plenty of rough treatment to rookies, but I don't think you can take it. **1964** Kaufman *Down Staircase* 82: You teachers are all alike, dishing out crap and expecting us to swallow it and then give it back to you. **1982** Castoire & Posner *Gold Shield* 128: Can't take it, can you? You can only dish it out.

dishrag *n.* DOORMAT.

1976 A. Walker *Meridian* 30: He ain't nothing but a dishrag for those crackers downtown.

¶ In phrase:

¶ **chief of the dishrag** a cook.

1864 in McKee *Throb of Drums* 165: I am still Chief of the Dish Rag but I am getting duced tired of it.

dishy *adj.* [sugg. by DISH, *n.*, 2] sexually attractive; good-looking.

*1961 in *OEDS*: The dishy St. Tropezienne. *1967 in *BDNE*. **1969** R. Welch, in *Playboy* (Jan. 1970) 82: If you're separated from a dishy guy or a dishy lady for three months or more, he might really fall for somebody else. **1974** Lahr *Trot* 37: These dishy boys with bangs and collarless Pierre Cardin suits. **1976** *S.W.A.T.* (NBC-TV): I've got to admit—he's kind of dishy. **1981** *Nat. Lampoon* (Apr.) 10: Those guys are really dishy, compared to our nerdy boyfriends.

disk jockey var. DISC JOCKEY.

dismiss *v.* to leave.

1845 in *DAE*: Bein as my kumpny aint acceptable here, I'll dismiss.

Disneyland East *n.* [sugg. by *Disneyland*, amusement park in Anaheim, Calif., opened 1955] **1.** *Mil.* Washington, D.C.; (*specif.*) the Pentagon Building.

1963 E.M. Miller *Exile* 132: What…is Honcho Turko doing in Disneyland East? **1969** N.Y.C. man, age 21: They call the Pentagon *Disneyland East* down at Fort Gordon. **1980** D. Cragg *Lex. Mil.* 124: *Disneyland East*…the Pentagon Building.

2. *USAF Acad.* the United States Air Force Academy.

1963 *Harper's* (Feb.) 87: Cadets…call the Air Academy "Disneyland East." **1963** *Sat. Eve. Post* (Nov. 23) 92: Disneyland East, as the cadets call [the U.S.A.F. Academy]. **1969** *Current Slang* I & II 27: *Disneyland east, n.* The United States Air Force Academy.—Air Force Academy cadets.

3. *Mil.* (see 1980 quot.). Now *hist.*

1966 *Time* (May 6) 29: Disneyland East…Ankhe Plaza…or "Disneyland," as the G.I.'s call it, is a 25-acre sprawl of [saloons and brothels]. **1980** D. Cragg *Lex. Mil.* 124: *Disneyland East*…The name given to a number of sprawling business enterprises…in the vicinity of American base camps in South Vietnam. Originally applied to the complex of bars and bordellos which sprang up around An Khe, the base camp of the

1st Air Cavalry Division.

4. *Av.* the headquarters of the Federal Aviation Administration.

1966 *Flying* (Dec.) 6: Our FAA friends down at Disneyland East/Didn't help matters any.

5. *Mil.* the headquarters of the U.S. Military Assistance Command, Vietnam. Now *hist.*

1980 D. Cragg *Lex. Mil.* 124: *Disneyland East*…The Military Assistance Command Headquarters, formerly located in Tan Son Nhut Air Base, Saigon. **1982** "J. Cain" *Commandos* 390 [ref. to Vietnam War]: MACV headquarters. Yeah, Disneyland East. **1984–88** Hackworth & Sherman *About Face* 730: "Disneyland East," as MACV was known.

dispatchers *n.pl. Gamb.* fraudulent dice. Now *hist.*

*1811 *Lexicon Balatron.: Despatchers.* Loaded or false dice. **1978** *Gamblers* 136: The mis-spotted dice were called "dispatchers"—because they sent the sucker to the cleaners with such dispatch.

disposish *n.* disposition. *Joc.*

1908 in Fleming *Unforget. Season* 113: He of the shrinking, retiring disposish.

disreps *n.pl. USAF Acad.* (see quot.).

1969 *Current Slang* I & II 27: *Disreps,* n. Poor or bad (disreputable) shoes.—Air Force Academy cadets.—Wear your *disreps* to the parade because the ground is muddy.

distribber *n.* a distributor.

1984 *Nat. Lampoon* (Dec.) 84: Prexy scores distribber woes.

disturbance *n.* liquor. *Joc.*

1898 Dunne *Peace & War* 174: All this time ye've been standin' behind this bar ladlin' out disturbance to th' Sixth Wa-ard.

ditch *n.* **1.a.** the Atlantic Ocean.—constr. with *the.* Cf. Big Ditch.

1841 *Spirit of Times* (Feb. 13) 595: "Low down in the forties" (as we say over the ditch). **1841** *Spirit of Times* (Mar. 6) 6: Should not we,—on this side of the ditch,—have a say? **1909** Ware *Passing Eng.* 110: Ditch (*Anglo-Amer.*). The Atlantic.

b. the sea; (*Av.*) a body of water in which a damaged aircraft is forced to land.—constr. with *the.*

*1918 in Fraser & Gibbons *Soldier & Sailor Wds.* 78: "He fell into the ditch," i.e., overboard. ***1922** in *OEDS*: A smart seaman would not talk officially of the sea by a favourite slang expression, "the ditch." **1942** Horman & Corley *Capts. of the Clouds* (film): We're heading for the ditch! Are you ready?

2.a. a canal, esp. the Erie, Panama, or Suez canal.

1878 (quot. at KNOCK). **1881** in *DA*. **1956** Moran & Reid *Tugboat* 4: The Irish have most of the jobs on the Ditch—they're laborers and masons and drivers! **1983** LaBarge & Holt *Sweetwater Gunslinger* 113: We can get some practice too…before the Nimitz enters the Ditch.

b. [punning on *canal*] *USMC.* Guadalcanal.—constr. with *the.* Now *hist.* Cf. Big Ditch.

1943 Horan & Frank *Boondocks* 75: And now, Guadalcanal. Guadalcanal, the "ditch."

3. an instance of being abandoned or betrayed.—constr. with *the.*

1898–1900 Cullen *Chances* 19: A plunger…got the dump-and-the-ditch at the hands of a poor-but-honest-not owner at Alexander Island.

4. *Narc.* (see quot.).

1968–70 *Current Slang* III & IV 36: *Ditch,* n. The inside of the elbow where large veins can be found. (Drug users' jargon)—Watts.

ditch *v.* **1.** *Hobo.* to put (a tramp) forcibly off a railroad train.

1894 in J. London *Tramp Diary* 31: They were forced to stop the train twice before they succeeded in ditching us. **1895** *Harper's* (Oct.) 777: Well, 'bout a year 'n' a half ago I got ditched there one night in a little town not far from the main line. **1897** *Harper's Wkly.* (Jan. 23) 86: The brakeman tries to ditch the tramp, and the latter tries to "beat" the brakeman. **1899** "J. Flynt" *Tramping* 393: *Ditch,* or *Be Ditched:* to get into trouble, or to fail at what one has undertaken. To be "ditched" when riding on trains means to be put off, or to get locked into a car. **1899–1900** Cullen *Tales* 324: When they do get wise that you ain't me, they can't do no more than ditch you. Are you on? **1902** Cullen *More Tales* 80: D'ye think I'd have been ditched if I'd been a monte? **1930** Irwin *Tramp & Und. Sl.: Ditch*…to put off a train by force or threat.

2.a. to get rid of; abandon; discard; (*also*) to get away from (pursuers); elude.

1899–1900 Cullen *Tales* 344: The old man couldn't stand for your win that time…and he ditched me the next morning. **1908** in H.C. Fisher *A. Mutt* 24: Oh! If he would only speak and forgive me for ditching him. **1914** *Sat. Eve. Post* (Apr. 4) 12: Yuh was to ditch him.…Kid…you ditch that dorg. **1914** *Amer. Lumberman* (Apr. 25) 33: Beside the spring he ditched his load. **1921** T. Wolfe *Lttrs.* 22: C. is going to see a girl in Brookline that he met in the bank last summer and it seems the Ohio girl has been ditched. **1929–30** Farrell *Young Lonigan* 79: They ditched the gang. **1934** H. Miller *Trop. of Cancer* 96: I thought first I'd get drunk and ditch her. **1944–48** A. Lyon *Unknown Station* 42: "Four blankets?"…Tomorrow…I'll ditch two of them. **1982** Reiner & Martin *Dead Men* (film): She took off her brooch and ditched it. **1989** E. Currie *Dope & Trouble* 188: They was following us and…we'd ditch 'em. **1990** *Nation* (Dec. 3) 48: The Tories have ditched a three-time election winner for the unknown.

b. *Stu.* to absent oneself from (school or a class) without a compelling reason; (*intrans.*) to play hooky.—also constr. with *off.*

1926 Hormel *Co-Ed* 13: Used to ditch off summers and work on the lake boats. **1936** Farrell *World I Never Made* 218: But, say, Delaney, ditch school, and come along downtown with me. **1939** in A. Banks *First-Person* 222: I'd ditch school and go out there. **1947** Motley *Knock on Any Door* 28: She never caught on and before September was out they were able to cut class almost half the time. They'd ditch and go roaming over the city. **1972** Wambaugh *Blue Knight* 301: "How you gonna pass if you cut classes like this?" "I don't ditch too often, and I'm pretty smart in school." **1973** *TULIPQ* (coll. B.K. Dumas): I'm going to ditch a class. **1978** Buchanan *Shining Season* 83: That shithead's dropping me from class for ditching. **1987** *21 Jump St.* (Fox-TV): Hey, you guys, wanna ditch? **1992** *Roseanne* (ABC-TV): I can call the school and find out if you ditched too.

3. to ruin; thwart. Cf. DISH, 1.

1899 (quot. at (1.), above). **1900** Willard & Hodler *Powers That Prey* 103: Ever known him to ditch any o' the guns [thieves] here? **1911** in *DAE*: Its enactment into law would have ditched them in their present reciprocity campaign. **1918** in *DAE*: Ditched! We're ditched! Lost our map after all this trouble.

4. *Av.* to land (a damaged aircraft) in a body of water. Also absol. Now *S.E.*

*1941 in *OEDS*: The pilot…must "ditch" his aircraft in the sea, near enough to a ship for him to be picked up. **1943** *Life* (Nov. 29) 75: Didn't see her ditch. **1944** *Life* (May 1) 112: Ditching is primarily the art of getting a big, fast plane down on the water in one piece. **1945** Dos Passos *Tour* 77: If they can give us their position when they ditch, we can usually find 'em, if they haven't drifted too far. **1961** Forbes *Goodbye to Some* 161: He figures maybe there's a chance that Dougherty ditched.

ditch hog *n. Naut.* a canal or freshwater sailor. Now *hist.*

1961 Hugill *Shanties* 269: A "Ditch-Hog" was a sarcastic phrase used by American deep-watermen to denote sailors of inland waterways such as the Mississippi and Missouri as opposed to foreign-going Johns.

ditch out *v.* to leave hurriedly or furtively.

1924 Henderson *Crookdom* 403: To ditch out before an arrest. **1926** Hormel *Co-Ed* 325: She and Jack "ditched out" in the midst of the prophecy. **1973** Browne *Body Shop* 22: I couldn't ditch out, it would tear the old man apart.

dit-da artist *n.* [*dit-da* (imit. of the sound of Morse code being transmitted) + ARTIST] *Army.* a radio operator.

1941 *Army Ordnance* (July) 79: Dit Da Artist…Radio operator. **1945** Hamann *Air Words: Dit-dah artist.* Radio operator.

dit-happy *adj. Mil.* crazy or eccentric from the extended study, copying, or transmission of Morse code.

1942 *Yank* (Nov. 4) 16: They call us the AACS/Dit happy guys are we. **1944** in *AS* XX 147: *Dit Happy.* "Batty" because of copying too much radio code. **1945** (quot. at CODE-HAPPY). **1952** Uris *Battle Cry* 132 [ref. to 1942]: Come on, Mac, have a heart and let's knock off. I'm going dit happy at this damned key.

dits *var.* DITZ.

ditso *n.* DITZ. Also attrib. Also **ditzo.**

1976 Price *Bloodbrothers* 185: Look, I was gonna go down to this ditso school in Louisiana in the fall, then I figure, screw that. **1988** Eble *Campus Slang* (Fall): She can be such a ditzo sometimes.

ditsy *var.* DITZY.

dittybop *var.* DIDDYBOP.

dittybopper var. DIDDYBOPPER.

ditty wagon *n.* [perh. alter. DIDI + *wagon*] *Mil. in Vietnam.* a three-wheeled Vietnamese bus. Now *hist.*

    1986 R. Zumbro *Tank Sgt.* 20: These vehicles, called "ditty wagons," were the bane of high-speed traffic. **1989** Zumbro & Walker *Jungletracks* 163: Ditty wagon drivers.

ditz or **dits** *n.* [fr. DITZY] a person who is DITZY, 2. Cf. DIZZ.

    1982 (cited in *W10*). **1984** Eble *Campus Slang* (Mar.) 2: Dits, Ditsy—a scatter-brain, scatter-brained. **1984** D. Jenkins *Life Its Ownself* 58: Sally Anthony? "Dits." **1987** *Nat. Lampoon* (Dec.) 86: Her category would have been "Luscious Blonde Ditz." **1988** *Boys Will Be Boys* (Fox-TV): No way! She's a ditz! **1990** S. Shapiro & R. Glass *Running Against Time* (film): He thinks I'm a ditz.

ditzy or **ditsy** *adj.* **1.** wonderful; remarkable.

    1975 in *DARE*: Ditz, ditzy…common among boys in Akron, Ohio [*ca*1920], e.g. "Look at my new knife." "Gee, that's a ditz!" Or, "That's ditzy!" **1986** in *DARE*: I vaguely recall the word *ditzy*—It was used [in Akron] to describe anything first class.

    2. [perh. alter. *dizzy*] (of a woman) silly; scatterbrained; flighty.

    1973 (cited in *W10*). **1976** *New Yorker* (Dec. 6) 182: He thinks women who want equality are ditsey little twitches. **1978** *L.A. Times* (Aug. 6) (Calendar) 1: The series concerns "a strong woman, not a ditsy dumb blonde, who is in charge of a Las Vegas revue and bringing up a kid sister." **1984** *Rod Serling's TZ Mag.* (Oct.) 40: Actress Nancy Allen, whose brassy, somewhat ditzy charm has yet to find the role in which she'll leave a mark. **1986** *TV Guide* (Aug. 16) 28: A sexy, ditzy blonde [on a situation comedy]. **1989** *Village Voice* (N.Y.C.) (Apr. 11) 47: I always feel if I'm flirting with a guy I have to be…ditzy. **1992** *TV Guide* (Nov. 28) 8: She's not ditzy—she's just a liberal-arts graduate.

    3. nervous; jumpy.

    1986 R. Campbell *In La-La Land* 96: No need to get ditsy…I'm not asking you to rent to me. *Ibid.* 127: They was very ditsy so I drove with him, and Jickie drove the girl so they'd think they could leave when they wanted.

dive *n.* [cf. DIVING-BELL; poss. a back formation fr. *diver* in 1785 quot.] **1.** a filthy cellar apartment, esp. a drinking den; (*hence*) a filthy or disreputable resort of any kind; DUMP.

    [***1785** Grose *Vulgar Tongue: Diver.* One who lives in a cellar.] **1867** *Nat. Police Gaz.* (Jan. 12) 4: This "moll" keeps a "dive" on Plumb street, in "Nigger Row." The inhabitants of this place being both white and black of the lowest class. **1867** *Nat. Police Gaz.* (Oct. 26) 3: Clara Hudson's "dive" at No. 463 South Clark street, was emptied of its inmates. **1871** in *OEDS*: One of the gayly decorated dives where young ladies…dispense refreshment to thirsty souls. **1872** Crapsey *Nether Side* 159: Let me explain that in detective parlance every foul place is a "dive," whether it be a cellar or garret, or neither. **1873** in H.N. Smith *Popular Culture* 202: The Sanitary Inspectors…have commenced a good work in cleaning out the vile under-ground dens—"dives," in the slang of the street—in which hundreds and thousands of the lower classes…herd together in filth and squalor too dreadful to be described. **1875** Lloyd *Lights and Shades in S.F.* 124: The low dives are thronged with cut-throats and ruffians. **1884** Triplett *American Crimes* 63: A dive is a low drinking den. **1887** "Bunny" *Cow Boy* 23: We visited the various saloons and "dives," the name given to a sort of "café chantant" built under the ground, and where there is much drinking and dancing going on. **1887** Francis *Saddle & Moccasin* 227: It occurred to him to drop into a little "dive" on Jin Street. **1891–1900** Hoyt *Five Plays* 129: Your place is a dive, and I'll never set foot in it again. **1929** *AS* IV (June) 339: *Dive.* Any place of evil repute. **1939** Saroyan *Time of Your Life* IV: I've got a dive in the lousiest part of town. **1955** in C. Beaumont *Best* 175: No more meeting at midnight dives, feeling shame, feeling dirt. **1959** Duffy & Lane *Warden's Wife* 147: He had struck up an acquaintance with the man in a bootleg dive. **1975** McCaig *Danger Trail* 59: I scoured the dives and the cathouses. **1987** *Cheers* (NBC-TV): "This isn't a dive." "By a dive I meant below street level."

    2. a speakeasy, nightclub, or similar establishment. [Orig. ironic.]

    1930–31 Farrell *Grandeur* 140: It would be…an exclusive dive whose members would be all filthy with dough. **1934** Appel *Brain Guy* 140: And now a regular dive where a feller could drink his beer or play cards or line up a dame. **1951** J. Reach *My Friend Irma* 28: What Automat? This was a very ritzy dive.

    ¶ In phrases:

    ¶ **take** [or (*obs.*) **do**] **a dive**, **1.a.** *Boxing.* to be knocked down; (*hence*) (now solely) to feign a knockout; lose a bout deliberately. Cf. DIVE, *v.*, 2.

    1916 T.A. Dorgan, in Zwilling *TAD Lexicon* 32: In the first three rounds [he] took five dives. **1921** J. Conway, in *Variety* (Feb. 4) 29: Smack began to kid him in the clinches, askin' him why didn't he take a dive now and then and not keep the crowd up later than necessary. **1927** C.F. Coe, in Paxton *Sport* 147: The referee is countin' over him an' I know he's done a dive…He musta seen me, cause he winked once. **1928** Hammett *Red Harvest* 47: Going to the fights tonight?…I hear Bush takes a dive in the sixth. **1930** Farrell *Calico Shoes* 185: This time he would have to fight. No taking a dive in this fight. **1933** in R.E. Howard *Iron Man* 88: So Lynch says for you to take a dive in the fifth. **1947** Schulberg *Harder They Fall* 6: Boxers who've taken so many dives they've got hinges on their knees. **1964** in S. Lee *Son of Origins* 123: Sure, I'll get ya some fights! And you won't have to take a dive, either! **1970** in P. Heller *In This Corner* 21: Gans took a dive. It was a fixed fight.

    b. (*fig.*) to compromise one's artistic standards for profit.

    1981 *N.Y. Times Mag.* (June 21) 26: "I wouldn't sing the garbage they were peddling," [Tony] Bennett said in a recent interview. "The record companies were forcing artists to take a dive, and I resisted."

    2. to suffer blame or consequences.

    1969 Gordone *No Place* 428: Way I see it, was like you took a dive for me once. Figger I owe ya.

    3. to fail; come to grief; (*Sports.*) (of a team) to go into a losing streak.

    1984 *N.Y. Post* (Aug. 31) 74: For seven more days, the Mets will live with eyes fixed upon the scoreboard, wondering, "Will Chicago ever take a dive?" **1990** *Bill & Ted's Adven.* (CBS-TV): United you stand, divided you take a dive!

    ¶ **take the big dive** to commit suicide.

    1974 *Happy Days* (ABC-TV): Hamlet…is thinkin' of takin' the big dive. **1977** *Nat. Lampoon* (Aug.) 34: Dr. Sam, a certified suicide doctor, answers your questions about the Big Dive…I'm ready to take the Big Dive. Should I?

dive *v.* **1.** *Und.* to pick pockets; (*trans.*) to steal from (a pocket).

    *1604 in Partridge *Dict. Und.* s.v. *nim*: I give and bequeath to you *Benedick Bottomlesse*, most deepe Cut-purse, all the benefitte of…Playhouses, to Cut, Dive, or Nim, with as muche speede, Arte, and dexteritie, as may be handled by honest Rogues of thy qualitie. ***1621** B. Jonson, in Partridge *Dict. Und.*: Using your nimbles/in diving the pockets. ***1665** in Partridge *Dict. Und.* s.v. *diving*: One of our diving companions picked their pockets. ***1698–99** "B.E." *Dict. Canting Crew: Dive*…to pick a Pocket. ***1726** A. Smith *Mems. of J. Wild* viii: Rogues, and Whores, Young, and Old, that are employ'd in the *Diving Trade*. ***1785** Grose *Vulgar Tongue: To dive*; to pick a pocket. **1791** [W. Smith] *Confess. T. Mount* 19: Picking pockets, *diving*. **1859** Matsell *Vocab.* 26: *Diving.* Picking pockets. **1933** Ersine *Prison Slang* 32: *Dive, v.* To pick pockets.

    2. *Boxing.* to feign a knockout; to lose a bout deliberately. Hence **diver**, *n.* Cf. **take a dive** s.v. DIVE, *n.*

    1921 *Variety* (July 1) 5: I…warned him not to let his bimbo dive as we would both get run out of town. **1922** J. Conway, in *Variety* (Mar. 31) 8: Whatever his plans were about divin', Tomato copped him on the old button in the seventh and he didn't need to quit after that. **1923** *Chi. Daily Trib.* (Oct. 3) 17: Down in Memphis A Boxing "Diver" Even "Crosses Up" Himself…When Freddie Roth went into the ring…he firmly intended to be knocked out. **1928** Hammett *Red Harvest* 50: Everybody in town seems to know that Bush is going to dive. **1929** Hostetter & Beesley *Racket* 223: *Dive*—To take a knockout, in a prizefight. **1930** Farrell *Calico Shoes* 185: Lissen, now, that ring ain't no swimmin' pool. See! No divin'. **1937** *Esquire* (July) 80: They want you to dive…before the seventh.

    3. to perform cunnilingus. Hence **diver**, *n.* Cf. MUFF-DIVE.

    1939 *AS* (Oct.) 239: To *Dive.* To indulge in unnatural intercourse. **1976** Atlee *Domino* 146: He was a diver, and rimmer, and very possibly the most enthusiastic onanist in Asia.

    ¶ In phrase:

    ¶ **dive for pearls** to work as a dishwasher. Cf. PEARLDIVER.

    1948–51 J. Jones *Eternity* ch. ix: Keep on like you're goin and watch. You'll find yourself divin for pearls in the kitchen.

diver *n.* **1.** *Und.* a pickpocket. Cf. DIVE, *v.*, 1.

    *1611 in Partridge *Dict. Und.* 191: A diver with two fingers, a pickpocket. ***ca1663** in Partridge *Dict. Und.*: The Divel of hell in his trade is not worse/Then Gilter, and Diver, and Cutter of purse. ***1698–99** "B.E." *Dict. Canting Crew: Diver*…a Pick-pocket. ***1785** Grose *Vulgar*

Tongue: Diver. A pickpocket. *1818 (cited in Partridge *Dict. Und.*).
1846 *Nat. Police Gaz.* (Dec. 26) 121: New-York "Divers," or Street
Thieves, at Work. **1847** *Nat. Police Gaz.* (Jan. 2) 133: This juvenile
female "diver," observing the man's condition, immediately froze fast
to him. **1859** Matsell *Vocab.* 26: *Diver.* A pickpocket. **1925, 1926** (cited
in Partridge *Dict. Und.*).

2. a beggar who forages in trashcans.

1939 *New Yorker* (Mar. 11) 43: "Divers" [are beggars who] dig hungrily
into ashcans when they see a prospect approaching.

3. see DIVE, *v.*, 2 & 3.

Divide *n.* [alluding to the Continental (or Great) *Divide*] *West.*
the boundary between life and death.—constr. with *the.*—
sometimes constr. with qualifying adj.

1872 in *DA.* **1881** Nye *Forty Liars* 217: We will slay the governor. We
will send him across the divide. **1898–1900** Cullen *Chances* 168: When
I heard the…gun I…figured that I was already three-quarters of the
way over the Big Divide. **1901** J. London *God of His Fathers* 207: There
was no reason for us to…get hustled over the divide before our time.
1908 Raine *Wyoming* 113: He'll still be sailing awful close to the divide.
I'll bet a hundred plunks he'll cash in, anyway. **1922** Rollins *Cowboy* 23:
About to "cross the Divide," with body amid the grama grass, and with
thoughts apportioned between the hereafter and some great country
house in England [etc.]. **1926** Siringo *Riata & Spurs* 48: The hereafter
on the other side of the great divide.

diving-bell *n.* **1.** Esp. *Und.* a saloon or brothel in a cellar; DIVE,
n., 1.

1859 Matsell *Vocab.* 26: *Diving-Bell.* A rum-shop in a basement. **1872**
Burnham *Secret Service* 401: Proprietors of sailor dance-houses, and
underground "diving-bells," where women and whiskey were the mar-
ketable wares. *a1890–91 F & H: Diving-bell…*(common).—A cellar-
tavern.

2. *Naut.* (see quot.).

1896 Hamblen *Many Seas* 180: Iron ships are proverbially wet. Some
call them "diving bells."

diving canoe *n. Navy.* a submarine. *Joc.*

1930 Buranelli *Maggie* 85 [ref. to WWI]: Bring on your diving canoes,
and we'll show 'em.

divoon *adj.* [intentional alter. *divine*] divine; DREAMY.

1944 Kapelner *Lonely Boy Blues* 51: Oh, say, that soldier boy was utterly
divoon! **1947** in *DAS:* "Pretty snazzy weather we're having, eh?"
"Devoon," said Jeanie languidly. **1955–57** Felder *Collegiate Slang* 2:
Divoon—divine. **1987** N.Y.C. woman, age 53: "It's simply *divoon*!" was
a schoolgirl expression around 1950.

divot *n.* (see quots.). *Joc.*

1934 Weseen *Dict.* 139: *Divot*—A toupee. **1939** *Time* (Dec. 25) 2: He
wears a toupee (hairpiece or divot in Hollywood).

divvy *n.* **1.** *Mil.* a military division.

1864 in Malone *Whipt 'Em Everytime* 109: Mr. Carrol preaches to our
Divi which is the 8th. **1918** *Nat. Geographic* (Mar.) 300: Two more
"birds" from our "divvy" came to town day before yesterday. **1919**
Wadsworth Gas Attack (Mar.) 32: I was with the Divvy in Belgium.
*1919 Downing *Digger Dialects* 19: *Divvy.*—…A division. **1974** L.D.
Miller *Valiant* 156: Harmon got into a fight with one of the First Divvy
gunners.

2.a. a dividing of spoils.

1872 Burnham *Secret Service* 170: He agreed to make a fair "divvy" of
the funds then in his hands. **1878** Bardeen *Hume* 188: Now, the point
is, there hasn't been a fair divvy. Those of us who have done most of
the work have got the least of the spoils. **1882** D. Cook *Hands Up* 184:
But before the time for the meeting of the robbers and their "divy" had
come around, Saegar stole the whole amount from the hiding place.
1889 Bailey *Ups & Downs* 79: After a long argument, it was finally settled between them and a divy was made, after which Scotty left. **1958**
S.H. Adams *Tenderloin* 34: But there's so much damn divvy. Gotta pay
off everybody from the Commissioners on down.

b. a share or portion of money that has been divvied.

1872 in *AS* XXVII (1952) 77: A fraudulent "divy." **1880** in M. Lewis
Mining Frontier 129: He'd no sooner got his divy in his fist than he
shook the old man an' struck out to take in some of the other camps.
1883 Hay *Bread-Winners* 164: To strike Saul for a divvy? Nothing of
the sort. **1891** Maitland *Slang Dict.* 94: *Divy* (Am.), an abbreviation of
dividend; the share coming to each person. **1906** in A. Adams *Chisholm
Trail* 216: I got my divvy of the prize money. **1915** Lardner *Haircut*
167: They told me they'd intended to give me five hundred bucks for
my divvy. **1932** Berg *Prison Doctor* 107: A screw who takes a chance

wants his divvy. **1953–58** J.C. Holmes *Horn* 111: Ah get divvies
though. **1978** G. Shirley *W. of Hell's Fringe* 58: The divvy amounted to
a little more than $400 per man.

divvy *v.* **1.** to divide; share.—now usu. constr. with *up.*

1876 Grover *Boarding House* 203: We divvy a cool $20,000. **1880** Pink-
erton *Prof. Thieves & the Detective* 212: I guess we can *divvy* on this.
1881 A.A. Hayes *New Colo.* 156: The two men were "divvying up the
spoils." **1892** Garland *Spoil of Office* 98: Brother John…gets twelve dollars for it, and then they "divvy" on the thing. **1895** Townsend *Fadden
Explains* 64: I felt like a tree-time winner wid no one t' divvy wid. **1899**
Willard *Tramping* 374: He had no right to change his mind without
divvyin' that boodle. **1902** Wister *Virginian* 137: Divvy, won't you?
1928 Wharton *Squad* 171: We'll divvy with you, Sarge. **1951–52**
Frank *Hold Back Night* 8: You goin' to divvy that up with us, captain?
1956 O'Rourke *Last Chance* 13: I'd divvy the skim milk so every customer of mine got a fair share. **1990** *U.S. News & W.R.* (Sept. 10) 70:
Britain and France were negotiating to divvy up the bountiful oil riches
of the Mideast.

2. to part company; separate.—constr. with *up.*

1934 Appel *Brain Guy* 54: Bill said…this weather was a blizzard, and he
was going to divvy up or know why.

Dixie *n.* [orig. unkn.; associated with the song "Dixie's Land"
(popularly "Dixie") written by the Ohioan Daniel D.
Emmett (1815–1904), a celebrated blackface minstrel, and
first performed April 4, 1859, in New York City; the form
Dixie Land had appeared without explanation or elaboration in Emmett's song "Jonny Roach," performed in February of the same year. Of various proposed etymologies,
that sugg. by Hotze in the 1861 quot. below is perh. to be
favored on phonological as well as historical grounds. The
assertion (1872 *N.Y. Weekly* quot. below) that the phrase
Dixie's Land had been part of a N.Y.C. children's game for
many decades cannot be substantiated and even if true
would not explain the phrase's origin. See H. Nathan, *Dan
Emmett*, pp. 243–75 for a full discussion. (The existence of
a minstrel showman named *Dixey* (1951 quot. below) and a
blackface character called *Dixie* in a skit of 1850 (Nathan, p.
265) is intriguing, but neither can be shown to have influenced the development of the present word; see also 1872
Emmett, below.)]

1. the southern states of the United States, esp. those that
were part of the Confederacy. Now *colloq.* or *S.E.* [The
word was colloq. or S.E. soon after the Civil War but was
slang in earliest use.]

1859 (Feb.) D. Emmett "Jonny Roach" (minstrel song), in H. Nathan
Dan Emmett 358: Gib me de place called Dixie Land,/Wid hoe and
shubble in my hand. **1859** (Apr.) D. Emmett, in *Ibid.* 249: *Dixie's
Land*…In Dixie Land whar I was born in….Den I wish I was in
Dixie…To lib an die in Dixie…away down south in Dixie. **1861** H.
Hotze, in Harwell *Confed. Reader* 27: This tune of "Dixie"…we shall be
fortunate if it does not impose its very name on our country. *Ibid.* 29:
The word "Dixie" is an abbreviation of "Mason and Dixon's
line."…Years before I heard the tune I have heard negroes in the North
use the word "Dixie" in that sense, as familiarly as we do the more
lengthy phrase from which it is derived. **1863** in Theaker *Through One
Man's Eyes* 62: This is about the finest country that I have seen since I
came into "Dixie." **1863** [Fitch] *Annals of Army* 531: Said articles were
ready to be sent to "Dixie." **1864** in A.W. Petty *3d Mo. Cav.* 62: We
resumed the march to Dixie in better spirits. **1865** in Blackett *Chester*
253: They…must bid farewell to "Dixie." **1870** F.M. Myers *Comanches*
375: There was no longer a "Dixie" banner to be true to. **1872** D.
Emmett, in Nathan *D. Emmett* 287: "Dixie's Land" is an old phrase
applied to the Southern States…lying south of Mason and Dixon's line.
In my traveling days amongst showmen [before 1859], when we would
start for a winter's season south, while speaking of the change, they
would invariably ejaculate [*sic*] the stereotyped saying:—"I Wish I was
in Dixie's Land," meaning the southern country. **1872** *N.Y. Weekly*
(Dec. 30) 6: Its origin has been described as Southern, but such is not
the case. During any time within the last eighty years the term "Dixie's
Land" has been in use with the New York boys while engaged in the
game of "tag." **1951** M.M. Mathews in *AS* (Dec.) XXVI 288: A minstrel named Dixey…was at the Arch Street Theater in Philadelphia on
28 December 1856….There is no evidence of the use of *Dixie* as a name
of a region, either the South or an earthly paradise…or as the name of

a ten-dollar bill, before the appearance of [Emmett's] song.

2. *Pop. Music.* Dixieland jazz; (*also*) (*obs.*) a song about the South.

1948 in Botkin *Sidewalks* 406: A pretty fair idea of the difference between bop and Dixie. **1948** Lait & Mortimer *New York* 31: Tin Pan Alley has its own glossary…All songs of regret and revenge and love's bitter grief are "torches." All crazy songs, which make no sense, are "freaks."…War songs are "flag wavers." All songs about the south are "Dixies."

¶ In phrase:

¶ **whistle Dixie** see s.v. WHISTLE, *v.*

dixie cup *n.* **1.** [sugg. by a fancied resemblance to a *Dixie Cup* (trademark for a disposable drinking cup)] **a.** *Navy.* the round white uniform cap worn by U.S. Navy enlisted men.

1973 Former QM, USN [ref. to 1967–69]: Those little white hats are called *dixie cups.* **1977** *L.A. Times* (Jan. 27) I 2: 86% of the service's sailors favor returning to the old uniform of bell bottom trousers, jumper and "Dixie cup" hat. **1982** "J. Cain" *Commandos* 126: The seaman's white floppy dixie-cup-and-bell-bottom uniform.

b. *Mil.* an enlisted sailor in the U.S. Navy.

1968 Stuard (unp.) (USMC): *Dixie Cups*…naval personnel.

c. a nurse's small white cap.

*a***1985** in K. Walker *Piece of My Heart* 70 [ref. to 1967]: Our little blue uniforms…and our little Dixie cup hats.

2. [DIXIE + *cup*cake] a Southern girl. *Joc.*

1978 Lieberman & Rhodes *CB* (ed. 2): *Dixie cup*—Female CBer with drawl.

dizz *n.* [fr. DIZZY] a silly or eccentric person. Also **diz.** Cf. DITZ.

1963 D. Tracy *Brass Ring* 169 [ref. to 1930's]: *A real dizz,* Kelly told himself unhappily. *Ibid.* 172: Heels would take advantage of her being such a dizz. **1972** B. Rodgers *Queens' Vernacular* 65: What's takin' that diz so long? **1984** Algeo *Stud Buds* 7: An absent-minded or inattentive person…*diz, dope,…dork,* [etc.].

dizz *adj.* dizzy, esp. tipsy.

1987 Univ. Tenn. student theme: He or she may first become *buzzed, slaphappy, dizz,* or *lifted.*

dizzy *n.* **1.** a lunatic.

1918 *Lit. Digest* (Mar. 23) 79: Take him away, Sergeant, he's a dizzy.

2. a cigarette.

1918–19 MacArthur *Bug's-Eye View* 64: Ken Hoy…was apprehended taking a last drag at a "dizzy." **1919** Wilkins *Co. Fund* 45: Twist a dizzy. **1922** *Bomb* (Iowa State Coll.) 417: The girls have all sworn off smoking now, even though we can roll a mean dizzy.

dizzy *adj.* **1.a.** silly; foolish; crazy; wildly enthusiastic.

1878 *Funny Fatherland* 64: She has seen many a dizzy Blond in America, and don't think they are so wonderful. **1878** Beadle *West. Wilds* ch. xxxv: Dance houses and saloons multiplied and "dizzy doves" gave an air of abandon to the streets. **1882** in Smith & Smith *Police Gazette* 34: A beauty from a dizzy blonde troupe has demoralized things in Yankton, Dakota. **1885** *Puck* (Aug. 5) 355: I must say, though, that John's canoes are a pretty dizzy-looking lot. **1893** F.P. Dunne, in Schaaf *Dooley* 50: Isn't this better than thim dizzy pictures? **1918** *Wadsworth Gas Attack* 36: What are you laughing at, you dizzy son-of-a-gun? **1918** in Truman *Lttrs. Home* 52: You must think I'm clean gone dizzy sure enough. **1922** *Am. Leg. Wkly.* (June 16) 4: Zeke's dead gone on the pitcher of a dizzy blonde. **1923** Weaver *Finders* 14: That dizzy gink there, 'way up on the roof,/What is he doin'? **1925** Nason *Three Lights* 178: One of my dizzy operators came down with the message. **1931** Hellinger *Moon* 31: You ain't goin' dizzy, are you? **1933** March *Co. K* 145: I hate cops! Something burns me up and I get dizzy every time I see one. I bumped that cop, all right. Why not? **1960** C. Cooper *Scene* 66: Don't be dizzy! **1963** D. Tracy *Brass Ring* 15: He was still wearing the dizzy cloth hat Dad had made him promise to keep on his head. **1968** Tauber *Sunshine Soldiers* 191: It might look like we're saluting some dizzy-assed civilians. **1992** *N.Y. Times* (July 26) H 16: We may not be blond—and dizzy may be beyond our behavioral repertory— [etc.].

b. odd; peculiar.

*ca***1896** McCloskey *Across Continent* 83: "This coat…it's queer." "It is a dizzy coat."

2. fancy; attractive.

1885 *Puck* 251: We paid out twenty cases for a dizzy check-book for him, too. It was magnif'. **1896** Ade *Artie* 29: I know boys that went down there [to a formal ball] and put on a dizzy front, and the next day they had to make a hot touch for a short coin so as to get the price for

a couple o' sinkers and a good old "draw one." **1942** A.C. Johnston *Courtship of A. Hardy* (film): She said that nightgown I gave her was so dizzy she was going to wear it as an evening dress.

¶ In phrase:

¶ **knock dizzy** to knock unconscious.

1935 in Conklin *Sci. Fi. Omnibus* 23: I must 'a sprawled in a heap and was knocked dizzy. Because when I came to, the thing was gone.

dizzy-o *adj.* tipsy.

1971 N.Y.C. man, age *ca*40: Last night I was kind of dizzy-o.

dizzy-stick *n. Police.* a nightstick.

1929 E. Wilson *Daisy* 35 [ref. to 1918]: The first morning, when he was led out in lockstep with the other prisoners, the ranks fell in disorder, and the sergeants set upon the men and clubbed them with what were known as "dizzy-sticks." **1929** Hotstetter & Beesley *Racket* 223: *Dizzy-stick*—Police officer's club or nightstick.

dizzy-water *n.* liquor. *Joc.*

1920 *Hicoxy's Army* 41: Was she not from Chambey, where her father served dizzy-water to soldiers?

DJ *n.* **1.** an agent of the U.S. Department of Justice.

1935 *Lit. Digest* (June 22) 38: "G men" have also been called "Feds," "Dee Jays," and "Whiskers" (*Uncle Sam's* Agents).

2. DISK JOCKEY. Now *colloq.*

1950 (cited in *W10*). **1954–60** *DAS.* **1961** J.A. Williams *Night Song* 67: All the spade deejays, they playin' rock 'n' roll. ***1978** Gribbin *Time-warps* 22: Messages from our local deejay.

3. *Mil.* DEAR JOHN.

1961 Forbes *Goodbye to Some* 100 [ref. to WWII]: His D.J. was a pip…She told him all the things he never had been for her. **1987** Pelfrey & Carabatsos *Hamburger Hill* 153 [ref. to Vietnam War]: The grief and shock on Bienstock's face were the G.I.'s ultimate nightmare: the DJ, Dear John letter, from the girl back home. **1989** Care *Viet. Spook Show* 114 [ref. to *ca*1968]: He got a Dear John letter….Christmas brings out the best in the folks back home, huh? Packages, tinsel, and DJs. *Ibid.* 119: Still bummed out over that DJ letter.

DJ *v.* to work as a disk jockey.

1985 B.E. Ellis *Less Than Zero* 33: Are you deejaying anymore? **1991** Nelson & Gonzales *Bring Noise* 285: Teddy's younger DJing brother.

DK *interj. & v. Stock Market.* (see quots.).

1931–47 in Mencken *Amer. Lang.* Supp. II 773: Stockbrokers…*D.K.* The opposite of O.K. **1987** Weiser & Stone *Wall St.* (film): Some jerk tried to DK me…DK—"didn't know."

D.L. & W. *n. R.R.* (see quots.). *Joc.*

1936 Sandburg *People, Yes* 149: The Delay Linger and Wait is the D.L.&W., the Delaware,/Lackawanna and Western. **1965** Hersey *Too Far to Walk* 130: This is old Ninety-Six of the D.L. and W.; what we used to call the Delay, Linger, and Wait…Delaware, Lackawanna, and Western.

do *n.* **1.a.** a social affair.

*1824 in Partridge *DSUE* (ed. 8): A generally profitable *do.* **1947** *ATS* (Supp.) 28: Social affair: *do* (Australia). **1952** in *DAS.* **1971** H. Roberts *3d Ear* (unp.): Are you going to the do tonight? *a***1986** in *NDAS.*

b. *Mil. Av.* a combat mission. [In Brit. mil. slang of WWI 'an attack; an offensive' (Partridge *DSUE*).]

1946 G.C. Hall, Jr. *1000 Destroyed* 155: They could…open a bottle and talk about the first Big "B" do. *Ibid.* 420: *Do*:…mission.

2. a hairdo. [The 1901 quot. seems to be imprecise or erroneous.]

1901 *DN* II 139: *Do*…In phrase, "a great *do*," a child's word for a mass of woman's back hair. **1966** in *OEDAS* I 90: *Do*, shortened form of Hairdo…*Slang.* **1971** H. Roberts *3d Ear* (unp.): *Do*…slick, processed hair. **1980** WINS Radio (Aug. 19): He sports an outrageous do—a big bushy fro. **1986** *NDAS.* **1992** G. Wolff *Day at Beach* 229: Girls with a lot of bouffant to their dos.

3. excrement, esp. of dogs or infants. Also **doo.**

1930 *Lyra Ebriosa* 21: Now the old woman rose for to do a little do/And the sea-crab grabbed her by the flue. **1972** C. Gaines *Stay Hungry* 126: I'm gonna get on that bastad like baby doo on a wool blanket. **1973** Layne Murphy (unp.): You Can Smell Dog Do. **1974** Strasburger *Rounding Third* 123: All of this stuff about *falling in love* is a lot of dog-do. **1981** C. Nelson *Picked Bullets Up* 151: My eyes…are the color of doggy doo. **1983** Neaman & Silver *Kind Words* 51: It is one of a number of terms common to human or animal excrement, as in *do, dog-do,* [etc.].

4. *Narc.* a dose of an illicit drug, esp. a FIX.

1971 Goines *Dopefiend* 134: What we goin' do about a do? My nose is already running, man. *Ibid.* 193: I hope you saved me a do, Snake, 'cause I'm sure gettin' sick.

do *v.* **1.a.** to cheat; swindle; take advantage of.—now rare except in colloq. phr. **do out of.**

*1641 in *OED*: And I can doe, My master too, when my master turnes his backe. ***1768** in *OED*: If the man comes from the Cornish borough, you must do him. ***1789** in *F & H* II 293: Who are continually looking out for flats, in order to *do* them upon the *broads*, that is, *cards*. **1807** Tufts *Autobiog.* 293 [ref. to 1794]: *To do him of his blowen...*to rob him of his wife. **1842–44** Kendall *Santa Fé Exped.* I 255: His success in "doing" the green-horn out of his supper. **1846** in Eliason *Tarheel Talk* 76: A woman done me out of $5.00 for a silk shirt & scarf. **1848** Baker *Glance at N.Y.* 16: Don't you remember the chap we did at the foot of Barclay Street? **1849** Mackay *Western World* I 7: 'Cute as he thought himself, I've done him slick. **1861** Berkeley *Sportsman* 150: Rather than let a lot of thieves think they had "done" a gentleman. **1875** Daly *Bonanza* 213: You've been done—sold—swindled! **1898–1900** Cullen *Chances* 23: "Do others or they'll do you" isn't the way they used to teach it when I went to Sunday-school. **1902** Carrothers *Black Cat* 109: De Chicago Golden Rule—"Do de other feller befo' he do you." *a***1904–11** Phillips *Susan Lenox* II 95: I don't blame you for trying to do me. You're right to try to buy your way out of hell. **1922** in Ruhm *Detective* 4: It's enough to say that I've been in card games with four sharpers and did the quartet. **1986** R. Campbell *In La-La Land* 20: They get a chance to do you, they'll do you.

b. to rob.

*1774 in *OEDAS* I 91: I...went to go to *do* a jew ladies; to break the house open. **1791** [W. Smith] *Confess. T. Mount* 19: *Doing the cove of a trick*, taking a gentleman's watch. **1879** (quot. at STAGE BUZZER). ***1881–84** Davitt *Prison Diary* I 116: We sometimes...make good use of this dodge when a number of us go to "do" a chapel. **1972** Wambaugh *Blue Knight* 33: You did a few gas stations, right? **1994** *New Yorker* (Jan. 31) 59: Martin does cars. He doesn't rob *people*....He does the same cars on the same streets, every night.

2. to copulate with, now esp. orally or anally.

*ca1650 in Burford *Bawdy Verse* 70: But hee knewe not how to woo me nor do me. **1888** Field *Socratic Love* st. 3: Like some sweet bird it nested there.../Old Socrates more madly longed to do it. **1949** *Gay Girl's Guide* 8: Do: To fellate, blow, bring to an orgasm orally. **1957** Simmons *Corner Boy* 163: Well, all the fellows hang around in the hall and ask all the girls who have they been doing. **1966** Mandel *Mott the Hoople* 119: She cried out as all good whores do, "Do me, baby. Do me good." **1966** Braly *On Yard* 244: I was done more ways than I thought was possible. **1966** H.S. Thompson *Hell's Angels* 192: She...proceeded to do him on a pool table in a back room. **1970** Landy *Underground Dict.* 67: *Do*...Suck a penis. **1974** Lahr *Trot* 20: She likes performing this unnatural act. The first time Irene did me, she made me wear a Trojan. That must have been as big a treat as licking a Good Humor in its wrapper. **1991** B.E. Ellis *Amer. Psycho* 207: I recognize Alison as a girl I did last spring. **1992** *N.Y. Rev. of Books* (July 16) 31: They were forced to "do" between a half-dozen and a dozen clients a night.

3.a. to kill. See also DO IN.

*1780 in *OEDS*: He...got one of our cutlasses, which was drawn;...and said, "D—n my eyes, here is one of Akerman's bloody thieves, let us do him first." **1791** [W. Smith] *Confess. T. Mount* 19: *I have done the cove out and out*, I have killed a man. **1848** Judson *Mysteries* 356: Mose, you've done him! **1891** Riis *How Other Half Lives* 166: The more notorious he is, the warmer the welcome, and if he has "done" his man he is by common consent accorded the leadership in his new field. **1899** A.H. Lewis *Sandburrs* 58: Naw, Mike does Norah by his constant abuse, see! Beats d' life out of her by degrees. **1900** Willard & Hodler *Powers* 186: You got the wrong bloke in that Hooper business. Slifer didn't do Hooper. **1919–21** Chi. Comm. Race Rel. *Negro in Chi.* 14: If you open your mouth...we will not only burn your house down but we will "do" you. **1925** Robinson *Wagon Show* 71: He had come to kill a showman and was bound to "do" one before he left for home. **1957** H. Ellison *Web of the City* 140: Rusty [was] hot to find out who had done his sister. **1971** Nichols (NBC-TV): Remember the time they tried to do each other about six years ago? **1985** E. Leonard *Glitz* 179: They say here's the name of the fink, do him. **1986** *Miami Vice* (NBC-TV): Oh, no! They're gonna do him now, Rico! **1992** F. Mills *Overkill* (film): What if we lose her and she does someone else?

b. Orig. *Boxing.* to vanquish, as in a prizefight; (*hence*) to thrash; (*specif.*) to beat up.

*1794 in *OEDS*: Much skill was displayed by both the combatants...Dame Fortune...at length favoured the tin-man, who, in the language of the schools, *did his man*. ***1796** Grose *Vulgar Tongue* (ed. 3):

Do,...to overcome in a boxing match. **1844** Strong *Diary* I 232: Clay's as sure of [being elected]...as ever he was of doing his man at brag or poker. **1888** Pinkerton *Scaffold* 40: The youngster is dead game, and I'll do him myself, or pile in and help him! ***1890–91** *F & H* II 294: *Do*...(pugilistic).—To "punish." **1894** Ade *Chicago Stories* 30: He says he kin do you. **1895** Townsend *Fadden* 3: When I useter sell poipers, wasn't I a scrapper?...Was der a kid on Park Row I didn't do? **1897** Ade *Pink* 139: Englan' got mo' ships 'an us an' mo' soljahs, an' might do 'iss country if it come to [a] show-down. **1918** in Dolph *Sound Off!* 169: Bill, old dog, we're going to do yah. **1966** H.S. Thompson *Hell's Angels* 277: None of those who did me were among the group I considered my friends. **1978** J. Webb *Fields of Fire* 62: Fairchild, get your ass up here or I'm gonna *do* you. I shit you not. **1991** in *Rap Masters* (Jan. 1992) 60: If a White man, anybody touch me, they're gonna get done.

c. to bring about the ruin of; (*Mil.*) to destroy.

1905 Riordan *Plunkitt* 5: I had a sort of monopoly of this business for a while, but once a newspaper tried to do me. **1987** Zeybel *Gunship* 77 [ref. to Vietnam War]: Ten-wheeler...Let's do him.

4. to serve (a specified period of time, esp. a prison term). Now *S.E.* Cf. *do time*, below.

*1870 in Davitt *Pris. Diary* I 151: I was in quod, doin 14 days. **1933** Ersine *Pris. Slang* 32: Do, *v.* To serve time in any jail. "What are you *doing*?" **1933–35** D. Lamson *About to Die* 184: I done eight years in the Navy. **1969** *Rowan & Martin's Laugh-In* (NBC-TV): "I haven't seen you in twenty years. What have you been doing?" "Twenty years."

5.a. Orig. *Narc.* to use or take (a psychotropic drug). Now *S.E.* Also absol.

1967 Baraka *Tales* 60: "What is it, horse [i.e. heroin]?"..."Uh huh."..."I didn't know you did that." **1970** R.N. Williams *New Exiles* 215: I was dropping acid, things like that. I was doing acid in high school. **1972** *Penthouse* (Aug.) 68: I don't want to do speed tonight. **1974** V.E. Smith *Jones Men* 144: The dope man is...wondering why I ain't doing too. **1963–78** J. Carroll *B. Diaries* 14: Do reefer and sniff glue. **1978** Maupin *Tales* 31: I did mescaline last night. **1981** *N.Y. Times* (July 19) 38: In my sophomore year, I did a lot of acid and pot. **1993** *New Yorker* (Jan. 11) 60: Do you do reefer here?

b. to consume; eat or drink.

1970 Della Femina *Wonderful Folks* 21: Those guys who do booze...they're all bagged by noon. **1972** Eble *Campus Slang* (Oct. 1972) 2: Do *v.*—general, all-purpose action verb: Let's do a few beers. **1978** R. Price *Ladies' Man* 139: I took a bus down to the diner and did some oatmeal with the boys. **1982** *All Things Considered* (Nat. Public Radio) (July 8): So you'd recommend staying away from all fizzy stuff and you'd just do low-fat milk, orange juice, and so forth. **1991** TV ad: Yoo-Hoo. The cool way to do chocolate. **1992** *Donahue* (NBC-TV) (Dec. 16): I was doing some soda and things like that.

c. to meet for (a meal), esp. for the purpose of conducting business.

1978 R. Price *Ladies' Man* 101: "Kenny, whata you doin' now?" "Now? I was gonna do lunch; you wanna do lunch?" **1980** *McCall's* (Mar.) 162: As you know, I don't do dinner. **1985** *Los Angeles* (June) 16: Most of these meetings involve "doing lunch." **1990** *U.S. News & W.R.* (Sept. 17) 21: Bush can jet off to...do lunch with Prime Minister Charles Haughey.

¶ In phrases:

¶ **do a** [or **the**] —— (esp. of people) to behave in the characteristic manner of ——; act like ——. See also BRODIE, *n.*

1899 Kountz *Baxter's Letters* 76: K.C....did a Brodie out of his chair and lit on his eye. **1908** in H.C. Fisher *A. Mutt* 37: I absolutely refuse to do a Morris Levy. **1914** S. Lewis *Mr. Wrenn* 18: Me, I ain't never got the sense to do the traffic cop on the booze. **1921** J. Conway, in *Variety* (Oct. 7) 9: The fliv [automobile] did a Gilda Grey all over the driveway. **1928–29** Nason *White Slicker* 35: O'Nail, the next time you do a Kellerman...pick Mackintosh to do it on. **1932** R. Fisher *Conjure-Man* 170: He done done a Lazarus! ***1934** in *OEDS*: "To do a Gaynor."..."To do a Garbo." **1944** in Himes *Black on Black* 202: Well, all root...You don't have to do no Joe Louis. **1986** *Morning Call* (Allentown, Penn.) (Aug. 18) [Court slang]: Do *a train*: Leave. **1991** *Village Voice* (N.Y.C.) (Aug. 13) 11: Falsely claiming a history as a lesbian liberationist insults the work of activists who have taken considerable risks...."We've lately coined the phrase 'doing an Abzug' to mean being an opportunist."

¶ **do for** to bring about the death of. Cf. S.E. *done for*.

*1740 in *OEDS*: D-mn you, I'll *do for* you. **1864** "E. Kirke" *Down in Tenn.* 54: They feel they's doin' God service...when they does fur a secesh.

¶ **do it** to copulate. Cf. IT.
*1914–22 J. Joyce *Ulysses* 724: Not that I care...who he does it with. 1929–31 Farrell *Young Lonigan* 151: The newspapers were full of stories about people who did it. Millionaires did it with chorus girls, and got sued. 1962 T. Berger *Reinhart* 256: Fedder and his wife Doing It. Extraordinary. 1976 Hayden *Voyage* 35: They did it on the rug. 1979–82 Gwin *Overboard* 153: Misguided male vanities from passing bumper stickers: "Divers Do It Deeper," "Welders Can Do It in Any Position."

¶ **do it all** *Pris.* to serve a life sentence.
1912 Lowrie *Prison* 24: I afterward learned that he was "doing it all" and had twenty-two years' service behind him. 1913 W. Wilson *Hell in Nebr.* 194: No man who is "doing it all" should be administering medicine to his fellow convicts. 1920 Murphy *Gray Walls* 20: I'm doing it all on the installment plan. I'm on my third stretch in this stir. 1923 Fishman & Perlman *Crucibles* 196: The "trusty" who found the guns and turned them in was "doin' it all" as the prisoners say of a "lifer." 1928 *AS* III (Feb.) 255: *Doing it all*—Serving a life term in prison. 1948 Chaplin *Wobbly* 265: Smith was sent up for a train robbery and murder in Woodlawn. He is "doing it all" and incidentally learning "dentistry."

¶ **do it to** *Mil.* to kill.
1973 Kingry *Monk & Marines* 105: The marines claimed they'd done it to six gooks, though.

¶ **do it to it** to get busy; get going.
1976 Lieberman & Rhodes *CB* 127: *Do It To It*—All clear ahead, pick up speed. 1980 Gould *Ft. Apache* 261: Do it, baby. Do it to it! 1982 Del Vecchio *13th Valley* 24: Let's do it to it.

¶ **do (one's) stuff** see s.v. STUFF.

¶ **do (one's) thing** see s.v. THING.

¶ **do over, 1.** to tire to exhaustion.
1789 in *DAE.* 1807 J.R. Shaw *Autobiog.* 115: Our jolly group...late at night broke up, pretty well done over. 1853 "P. Paxton" *In Tex.* 96: [The dogs] were completely done over and used up.

2. to cheat; fool; ruin; destroy; get the better of.
*1781 G. Parker *View of Society* II 43: And now, Hostler, can't you tell me how you have *done 'em over*? 1789 in Meserve & Reardon *Satiric Comedies* 113: He hopes the *pit critics*—will nor do him over....Till death does him over. *1789 G. Parker *Life's Painter* 138: And that's what *did him over* [i.e., led to his conviction]. 1807 J.R. Shaw *Autobiog.* 115: Finding myself completely done over.

¶ **do time** to serve a prison sentence. Now *S.E.* Cf. (4), above.
*1865 in *OED*: "I was doing time"...(a cant term for serving a sentence in prison). 1866 *Nat. Police Gaz.* (Nov. 10) 3: Tommy has "done time" in Dover, N.H., and Charlestown, Mass. 1884 Triplett *American Crimes* 54: Doing time for the State, means being sentenced to the penitentiary. 1891 Maitland *Slang Dict.* 153: *Jail-bird*, one who has "done time." 1893 Riis *Nisby* 49: Most of them had "done time" up the river. 1897 in J. London *Reports* 313: Many...have "done time" and are...worthy of doing more. 1899 A.H. Lewis *Sandburrs* 24: As swell a mob as ever does time. 1902 Hapgood *Thief* 48: I know some thieves who, although they have grafted for twenty-five years, have not yet "done time." 1913 A. Palmer *Salvage* 187: The after delinquencies of men who have "done time." 1925 S. Lewis *Arrowsmith* 768: They've done time for selling licker to the Indians. 1929 "E. Queen" *Roman Hat* ch. ix 103: Where did you do time, Michaels? 1965 Spillane *Killer Mine* 34: You ever do time, kid?

¶ (For phr. not found in this list look under the next main word of the expression; e.g., for *do brown* see s.v. BROWN.)

D.O.A. *v. Police.* to die before arrival at a hospital emergency room.
1975 DeMille *Smack Man* 124: And if I had my way, all your worthless hookers could D.O.A. *Ibid.* 143: They say a pimp has D.O.A.'ed in his pad.

dob *n.* the penis. Also **dobber.**
1974 Newburgh, N.Y., man, age 23: *Dob* is short for *dobber*, meaning *dick*. An insult is *Suck my dob.*

dobber[1] var. DAUBER.

dobber[2] see DOB.

dobbin *n.* [orig. unkn.] *Und.* ribbon; a ribbon.
*1781 G. Parker *View of Soc.* II 151: On the Dobbin Rig. *1789 G. Parker *Life's Painter* 162: Dobbin is ribbon. 1791 [W. Smith] *Confess. T. Mount* 19: Ribbons, dobbins. *1812 Vaux *Vocab.: Cant of Dobbin*, a roll of riband.

dobe /'doubi/ *n.* dobe dollar.

1903 *Our Naval Apprentice* (Nov.) 129: He has plenty of "Dobies," he's out for sport. 1906 M'Govern *Bolo & Krag* 33: I planked down the sixty dhobes I knew to be the price of the fare to Talisayan. 1931 Rynning *Gun Notches* 58: They even called the Mexican silver dollars "dobies." 1933 Ersine *Pris. Slang* 32: Dobe, *n.* A dollar.

dobe biscuit *n. Army.* a hardtack biscuit.
1931 R.G. Carter *Border* 41 [ref. to *ca*1870]: Our supper at night consisted of broiled wild turkey thighs, larded with bacon slivers, and buffalo sweetbreads, with "doby" biscuits and coffee.

dobe dollar *n.* [*adobe* + *dollar*] *Army & S.W.* a Mexican or Spanish peso.
1898 Bowe *13th Minn.* 44: The American soldier did not exchange special favors for dobie dollars. 1900 McManus *Soldier Life* 28: "Un peso" or a "dobe" dollar...is equivalent in value to 50 cents, American coin. 1901 Williams *Odyssey* (June 14) 265: They gladly bartered for a couple of "dhobie" dollars. 1909 Warner *Lifer* 63: Two of the sacks contained "dobe" dollars. 1934–43 F. Collinson *Life in Saddle* 209 [ref. to 1880's]: Silver "dobe" dollars [were] worth fifty cents in United States money.

dobe-wall *v.* [aph. form of *adobe wall*] *Army & S.W.* to stand against an adobe wall and execute by firing squad.
1928 Dobie *Vaquero* 70 [ref. to *ca*1875]: His idea of inspiring respect for law was to "dobe-wall" the lawless—stand them up against an adobe wall and shoot them. 1932 Halyburton & Goll *Shoot & Be Damned* 206 [ref. to 1916]: "Let 'em shoot him, of course," said Geoghegan. "But we can't do that. He's an American. If we allowed the Germans to dobe wall him, they'd soon try it on some of us." *Ibid.* 21: You can dobe wall us [deserters] if you want to. We've seen Paris.

Dobie *n.* a Doberman pinscher.
1981 C. Nelson *Picked Bullets Up* 12: I examined the Dobies for ticks. 1982–84 Chapple *Outlaws in Babylon* 24: I...should get a couple of Dobies for this operation.

dobie *n. Army.* an infantryman; DOUGHBOY.
1911 D. Runyon *Tents* 123: Late o' the sixteenth 'dobies, sergeant and nine years in;/Now I'm a cavalry captain, hangin' around Tien Tsin.

do-boy var. DOUGHBOY.

doc[1] *n.* **1.** a doctor; (*specif.*) a physician; (*Mil.*) a medical corpsman.
1840 *Spirit of Times* (May 30) 152: But chiefly thee, Dear Doc, did Anacreon fill full of inspiration. 1854 in Glisan *Journ.* 149: Don't you think, Doc, ague makes a fellow powerful weak? 1854 in *Ark. Hist. Qly.* XVIII (1959) 9: Am seated in the Doc's office. 1865 in O.J. Hopkins *Under the Flag* 268: Haven't seen Doc yet. 1882 W.E. Youngman *Gleanings* 107: *Doc.* Abbreviation of Doctor, commonly in use in the Western States. 1953 Paley *Rumble* 121: Get a doc quick for Della. 1954 G. Kersh, in Pohl *Star of Stars* 26: The doc was looking over the battlefield. 1962 E. Stephens *Blow Negative* 47: I'll send the doc aroun' to doublecheck your ears. 1976 Haseltine & Yaw *Woman Doctor* 111: All the other docs do. 1985 Dye *Between Raindrops* 80: You Docs...get those two as soon as I shoot.

2. fellow.—used in direct address.—now esp. in phr. **What's up, Doc?** popularized as the signature line of the Warner Bros. animated character Bugs Bunny, orig. in the theatrical cartoon *A Wild Hare* (1940); see 1972 quot.
1869 Logan *Foot Lights* 370: He is talking to a big fellow, a manager like himself, whom he calls "Doctor." "Well, Doc, I had the poorest show on the road last season, but I made stacks of money." 1875 in *DA*: "Doc"—which is Chinese for Aaron—Torrence got his baggage all ready and started for California. 1907 in "O. Henry" *Works* 1512: "Say, doc," he said resentfully, "that's a hot bird you keep on tap." 1923 H.L. Foster *Beachcomber* 321: "That's right, isn't it, doc?" he demanded, having already awarded me the new title. *Ibid.*: That's the spirit, doc! 1937 in *AS* (1938) 46: *Doc.* General name applied to any male patron of a dance hall, especially at summer resorts. 1939 Appel *People Talk* 168: What can I do for you, Doc? 1953 Manchester *City of Anger* 275: Keep your shirt on, doc. 1972 T. Avery, in Bogdanovich *Pieces of Time* 210: "What's up, Doc?"...I brought this line out of Texas in 1929. In Dallas High Schools and with S.M.U. freshmen it was always the opening line when two friends met....All I did was put it in [Bugs Bunny's] mouth. 1979 N. Meyer *Time After Time* (film): What's up, Doc? Where to? 1988 "Boogie Down Productions" in L. Stanley *Rap* 43: What's up, Doc?

doc[2] *n.* a document.
1868 Williams *Black-Eyed Beauty* 47: We'll go round to my lawyer friend and get the "doc's" fixed. *1943 (cited in Partridge *DSUE* (ed. 8)).

dock *n.* ¶ In phrase: **in dock** *Naut.* confined by illness or injury; (*specif.*) in the hospital.

*1785 Grose *Vulgar Tongue: Dock,* He must go into dock, a sea phrase, signifying that the person spoken of, must undergo a salivation. **1848** in *AS* X (1935) 40: *Hauled into dock,* sick at home. ***1918** in Dunham *Long Carry* 138: "Jenny" was not sorry to "go into dock," as we termed the hospital. ***1919** *Athenaeum* (July 11) 582 [ref. to WWI]: While "in dock"…one lay upon "biscuits." ***ca1925** in Hugill *Sea Songs:* And now I'm in dock, boys, in safety at last. **1941** Kendall *Army & Navy Slang* 5: *In dock*…hospital—also sick bay. **1961** Burgess *Dict. Sailing* 73: *Dock, be in.* Be in hospital or sick bay, confined to bed.

dock monkey *n. Transport.* a worker who loads and unloads freight at a loading dock.

1939 *Chi. Tribune* (Jan. 22) (Graphics Sec.) 9: *Dock monkey*—a warehouse worker; dockman. **1942** *AS* (Apr.) 103: *Dock Monkey.* Freight handler at loading dock. **1971** Tak *Truck Talk* 45: *Dock monkey:* a helper who assists the loading and unloading of trucks at a dock [*sc.* truck-loading platform], and the movement of freight from one part of a dock to another. Syn: *dock walloper.*

dock rat *n.* WHARF RAT.

1864 *Harper's Mag.* (Feb.) 341: River-border citizens of the town…"dock rats." **1870** *Scribner's Mo.* (Nov.) 41: Many of the inmates are…"dock rats." **1873** *Overland Mo.* (Mar.) 280: A "roustabout" for eighteen years—a "dock rat"…—his only world was bounded by the wharf. **1908** *Independent* (Apr. 23) 908: No dock rats, ner deck swabs, ner turnpike sailors'll suit here. **1915** Lind *Androgyne* 64: A gang of youthful dockrats surprised us. **1930** Lavine *3d Degree* 179: At the North River he found a dock rat asleep. **1963** in Cannon *Nobody Asked* 200: There are yellow-eyed tramps who were referred to as dock rats in my neighborhood because they found sanctuary in the eaves of piers.

dock-walloper *n.* **1.** a laborer who works on docks or wharves, esp. a longshoreman.

1838, 1877, 1879 in *DAE.* **1891** Maitland *Slang Dict.* 94: *Dock-walloper* (Am.), a laborer on the wharves or docks. **1898** *Story of a Strange Career* 178: "Dock-wallopers" had to be hired in our stead to dock the ship. **1911** A.H. Lewis *Apaches of N.Y.* 165: A lad…named Brady…an' a dock-walloper from Williamsburg. **1915** Braley *Songs* 55: Deckhands we be,/An' dock wallopers, too. **1931** Adamic *Laughing* 246: And some of the lumber-jacks and dock-wallopers looked as if they could eat five cops apiece for breakfast. **1942** Casey *Torpedo Junction* 24: But there was nothing imaginary about the looks you saw on the faces of the dock wallopers. **1953** Paley *Rumble* 27: No other dockwalloper'll be seen with us dead—today! **1959** Lederer *Never Steal Anything Small* (film): I been a dockwalloper ever since I was old enough to ride a lift. **1977** Hamill *Flesh & Blood* 84: Saloons where the iron workers and dock-wallopers drank.

2. a waterfront loafer.

1859 Bartlett *Amer.* (ed. 2) 124: *Dock walloper.* A loafer that hangs about the wharves. New York. **1903** A.H. Lewis *Boss* 119: You don't think that these dock-wallopers an' river pirates are stuck on you personally, do you?

3. DOCK MONKEY.

1971 (quot. at DOCK MONKEY). **1976** Dills *CB 1977* 31: *Dock-Walloper:* dock worker who unloads freight from vehicles.

doctor *n.* **1.** usu. *pl. Gamb.* a false or loaded die or (*later*) a marked or otherwise altered playing card.

*1688 Shadwell *Squire of Alsatia* (gloss.): *The Doctor.* A particular false Die, which will run but two or three Chances. *Ibid.* I i: I believe they put the *Doctor* upon me. ***1709** in *F & H* II 298: Now, sir, here is your true dice…here is your false, sir; hey, how they run! Now, sir, those we generally call *doctors.* ***1749** H. Fielding, in *F & H* II 298: Here, said he, taking some dice out of his pockets, here are the little doctors which cure the distempers of the purse. ***1785** Grose *Vulgar Tongue: Doctors.* Loaded dice that will run but two or three chances. ***1823** Sir W. Scott, in *F & H* II 298: The dicers with their *doctors* in their pockets, I presume. **1859** Matsell *Vocab.* 26: *Doctors.* False cards or dice.

2. [cf. SAfrE *Cape Doctor* and Austral.E *Albany Doctor* and *Fremantle Doctor,* all ref. to types of sea breezes] *Naut.* a pleasant sea breeze.

*1740 in *OEDS.* **1844** in *DAE:* [In St. Augustine] we were beginning the summer custom of gathering every morning to meet the "doctor" (sea-breeze) on the square. **1945** Hamann *Air Words: Doctor.* A colloquial name for a sea breeze in tropical climates. The term is sometimes applied to other invigorating breezes.

3. [orig., alcohol that has been "doctored"; in recent use,

prob. ref. to the supposed restorative powers of alcohol] a mixed drink of milk, water, rum, and nutmeg (*obs.*); (*also*) an alcoholic beverage.

1770 in *OED2:* He drank his Doctor. ***1785** Grose *Vulgar Tongue: Doctor* Milk and water, with a little rum, and some nutmeg. **1821** Waln *Hermit* 24: What say you to a *whet,* Dashall?—a little *cup of the creetur?*—some of the *doctor?*—a stiff *flip? *a1890–91 F & H* II 298: *Doctor*…(licensed victuallers').—Brown sherry. **1989** P. Munro *U.C.L.A. Slang* 34: *Doctor* alcoholic beverage/Hand me the doctor.

4. Orig. *Naut.* a cook, esp. on shipboard.

1821 in *OEDS:* The cook, at sea, is generally called doctor. **1835** [Ingraham] *South-West* I 26: One of "the Doctor's" plumpest…pullets. *a1868* N.H. Bishop *Across So. Amer.* 14: From the old man (the captain) in the cabin to the doctor (cook) in the galley. **1884** Bruell *Sea Memories* 7 [ref. to 1845]: Which call was obeyed by the "doctor's" opening the door [of the galley]. **1913** in R.C. Murphy *Logbook* 254: On most ships these are led by the "doctor" (meaning the cook). **1936** Mulholland *Splinter Fleet* 181: "Doctor," as we called our cook on the *IX4,* was a lean, slick-skinned individual.

5. a pump that supplies water to the boilers on a steamboat.

1848 in *DA.* **1875, 1882, 1889, 1907** in *DAE.*

6. *Und.* (see quot.).

1909 Chrysler *White Slavery* 40: Concealed between his fingers he has a "doctor," a little rubber…tube or pouch which when squeezed would allow the drug to flow into the glass with a quick squirt.

doctor *v.* **1.** to alter so as to deceive; tamper with; adulterate; drug; falsify. Now *S.E.*

*1774 in *OED:* I wish we had time though to doctor his face. ***1820** in *OED:* Directions for…doctoring all sorts of wines. ***1837** in *F & H* II 298: She *doctor'd* the punch and she *doctor'd* the negus, taking care not to put in sufficient to flavor it. ***1847** in *OED:* Modes of doctoring dice. **1867** A.D. Richardson *Beyond Miss.* 279: Nearly all liquors were "doctored" and excited far more recklessness and malignity than pure whisky or brandy would have done. ***1873** Hotten *Slang Dict.* (ed. 4): *Doctor,* to adulterate or drug liquor; to poison, to hocus; also to falsify accounts. **1881** Trumble *Man Traps* 36: Once in their hands, [the horses] are "doctored," groomed and made to appear young and healthy, their defects screened. **1885** S.S. Hall *Gold Buttons* 8: I…doctored his whiskey. **1905** Phillips *Plum Tree* 49: Never before had Dominick "doctored" the tally sheets so recklessly. **1912** Mathewson *Pitching* 290: The Orioles did not stop at doctoring the infield. **1953** Gresham *Midway* 137: The snake was not "doctored" in any way—he had both his fangs in good condition and the poison sacs behind his eyes were full.

2. to kill (a person). *Joc.*

1830 "Socio" *Post-Chaise* 20: He would *doctor 'em*…Why, kill 'em to be sure.

Doctor Feelgood *n.* an unscrupulous physician who prescribes mood-altering drugs, esp. amphetamines, on demand.

[**1967** J. Kramer *Instant Replay* 40: Ever since then, we've called him "Doctor Feelgood."] **1973** *Oui* (Apr.) 55: Dr. Feelgood used to shoot Duke What's-His-Name in the ass every week or so with a nice rich mixture of speed and vitamins. **1977** *L.A. Times* (Mar. 1) II 4: He bought…the Quaaludes on the street, or…through a "Dr. Feelgood" type of physician who serves the stars. **1981** *N.Y. Daily News* (Aug. 5) 39: A speed merchant…is likely to mean a doctor who specializes in prescribing amphetamines, usually in the guise of diet pills, to patients who have acquired the "speed" habit. Fortunately, the Legislature enacted a bill this session…cracking down on these Dr. Feelgoods. **1983** WINS Radio (Dec. 14): Irresponsible prescribing by Dr. Feelgoods who run so-called stress centers. **1985** Dye *Between Raindrops* 1: Dr. Feelgood peering at his patient through his head mirror.

Doctor Green *n.* [pun on *green* 'gullible; unsophisticated'] *Und.* (see quot.).

1859 Matsell *Vocab.* 26: *Doctor Green.* A young inexperienced fellow.

Doctor Hall *n.* (esp. among tramps) grain alcohol.

1925–26 J. Black *Can't Win* 66 [ref. to *ca*1890]: A fifty-cent bottle of alcohol—Dr. Hall, white line. **1934** in Partridge *Dict. Und.:* "Dr. Hall" (alcohol and water).

document *n.* **1.** usu. *pl. Gamb.* a playing card. [The 1849 quot. may poss. belong with **(2)**, below.]

1840 *Spirit of Times* (Nov. 14) 484: They would throw down their "documents" on the barrel head which served them for a table. **1845** Hooper *Simon Suggs* ch. 45: Let me git one o' these book-larnt fellers over a bottle of "old corn," and a handful of the dokkyments, and I'm d—d apt to git what he knows. **1849** "N. Buntline" *B'hoys of N.Y.* 39: I'll take that bet—down with the documents!

2. exactly what is required.—constr. with *the*.

1850 Garrard *Wah-to-Yah* 191: We walked with the sheriff to the jail, taking the halters—the significant loops, conspicuous, drawing the attention of both soldier and native, eliciting from the former familiar exclamations, such as—"Go it, my boys," "them's the *dokyments*"—"Sarve 'em up brown."

dod *interj. & prefix.* [euphem.] God.—used in various mild oaths.

*1676 in *OED:* A Dod, she's too serious. **1835** in *OED:* I'll be dod blamed if I do! **1840** *Spirit of Times* (Dec. 19) 499: Dodblasted. **1843** in G.W. Harris *High Times* 21: *Dod rot* his skin, I told him he'd lose me! **1884** in Lummis *Letters* 121: These dodgasted sandhills. *a*1889 in Barrère & Leland *Dict. Slang* I 315: It was one of those *dodgasted* electrical machines! **1898** Bellamy *Blindman* 285: It's a dodrotted shame to 'em.

dode *n.* [shortening of *dodo*] a fool.

1989 *21 Jump St.* (Fox-TV): 'Cause it's far away from you dodes. …Later, *dode!* **1990** *21 Jump St.* (Fox-TV): Other bulletheaded bourgeois college dodes. **1992** D. Burke *Street Talk* II 230: Our new teacher is the biggest dode!

dodgast var. DADGAST.

dodge *n.* **1.** a cunning trick, esp. an artifice by which to evade, cheat, or rob; a fraudulent scheme. Orig. *S.E.*

*1638 in *OED:* I have beate the Iesuit heretofore out of this dodge. **1681* in *OED:* To put a dodge upon the Protestants to weaken their faith. **1837* Dickens *Pickwick Papers* ch. xvi: "It was all false of course?" "All, sir…reg'lar do, sir; artful dodge." **1851** M. Reid *Scalp-Hunters* 90: I tried that dodge once afore. **1853** "P. Paxton" *In Texas* 126: I'd been expectin' another dodge. **1858** [S. Hammett] *Piney Woods* 50: One of the cutest dodges that I ever heern tell on. **1858* A. Mayhew *Paved with Gold* 2: "Ain't you got no lodgings, my good woman?"…"I was turned out of them two days ago."…"Oh, come on, Bill, it's only a dodge." **1866** *Nat. Police Gaz.* (Nov. 17) 2: It is said that several "green 'uns" have been bled lately, by means of the old familiar panel dodge. **1868** "W.J. Hamilton" *Maid of Mtn.* 12: That's a dodge these fellows are all up to. **1872** Burnham *Secret Service* v: *Dodge*. A quick artful trick, device or manipulation. **1873** *Overland Mo.* (Feb.) 113: Smith…tried to coax him, but the soft-soap dodge wouldn't work. **1876** Cody & Arlington *Life on Border* 27: That's a good dodge. I'll folly suit. **1885** "Lykkejaeger" *Dane* 47: Finding that the "land-wrecked sailor" was the most "taking dodge," I "worked the racket" of a man-of-war's-man trying to get back to his ship, for all it was worth. **1887** W.P. Lane *Advent.* 6 [ref. to 1830's]: The old man said to me at supper, "Sonny, never try that *dodge agin* in Texas." I did not. **1928** in Tuthill *Bungle Family* 48: An advertising dodge of some sort. **1948** Seward & Ryan *Angel's Alley* (film): Think I'm gonna fall for that corny dodge? **1962** Perry *Young Man* 44: I'm gonna hustle—get me a dodge. **1963** *Car 54* (NBC-TV): Oh, you're using the reverend dodge again, are you?…Well, you better start passing that counterfeit money.

2. a business, profession, or occupation.

*1863 in T. Taylor *Plays* 208: I've tried the honest dodge, too.…Whatever I tried, I was blown as a convict and hunted out from honest men. **1929–31** D. Runyon *Guys & Dolls* 89: An accident…puts her out of the dancing game. **1934** D. Runyon, in *Collier's* (Nov. 24) 8: She is working for a guy in the real estate dodge. **1981** W. Safire, in *N.Y. Times Mag.* (Sept. 13) 16: Part of the gruntwork of people in the language dodge is to keep track of neologisms. **1983** *Morning Edition* (Nat. Public Radio) (Oct. 31): That's when I discovered that this lovely dodge has its ugly side.

¶ In phrases:

¶ **get [the hell] out of Dodge [City]** [alluding to Dodge City, Kans., the locale of innumerable Wild-West films and novels and, notably, the CBS-TV series *Gunsmoke* (1955–75); badmen might stereotypically be instructed to "get the hell out of Dodge." Transf. use of the phr. app. arose in the 1960's] to leave or get out at once.

1965 in *AS* XLI (1966) 72: Teen-Gang Talk in Philadelphia…*Get out of Dodge*…To lie low. **1970–72** in *AS* L (1970) 58: If you don't want to stay here, then get the hell out of Dodge. **1974** *UTSQ:* Let's get the hell out of Dodge. **1978** *UTSQ:* [Leave] Let's *hit the road, split, get the hell out of Dodge.* **1980** M. Baker *Nam* 154: Time to get the hell out of Dodge. **1981** *Rod Serling's TZ Mag.* (July) 72: Ain't never seen nothin' like it…Listen, boy, we got to get the hell out of Dodge. **1984** J.R.

Reeves *Mekong* 180: Okay, let's get the hell outta Dodge! **1984** Bane *Willie* 168: The idea being to play one day and get the hell out of Dodge. **1985** Dye *Between Raindrops* 268: Just barrel this [truck] up the street…and get the fuck out of Dodge. **1986** Thacker *Pawn* 250: Split the scene. Get the hell out of Dodge City. *a*1989 R. Herman, Jr. *Warbirds* 238: I was busy getting the flight together and getting the hell out of Dodge.

¶ **on the dodge** Esp. *West.* evading or hiding from the law; dodging.

1885 Siringo *Texas Cowboy* 148: I…told them that I was on the "dodge" for a crime committed in Southern Texas. **1902** "O. Henry" *Sixes & Sevens* 838: I don't think I ought to close without giving some deductions from my experience of eight years "on the dodge." **1903** Benton *Cowboy Life on a Sidetrack* 112: He was still on the dodge, and I made several passes at [his head] and missed. The bull was getting mad by this time, and lowering his head and elevating his tail he soon had me on the dodge. Whenever I wasn't chasing the bull, he was chasing me. **1922** Murphy *Black Candle* 340: He is always looking for "shadows." To use the colloquialism of the profession "he is on the dodge." **1929** *AS* (June) 343: On the dodge—A fugitive from justice. **1932** Z. Grey *Robbers' Roost* 11: "On the dodge?" queried Lincoln, after a pause. **1935** Coburn *Law Rides Range* 9: Many is the poor devil on the dodge that Bob Burch has helped. **1939** "L. Short" *Rimrock* 113: St. Cloud was an outlaw on the dodge. **1947** Overholser *Buckaroo's Code* 113: Your job is to stay on the dodge till Abernethy's game develops. **1958** J. Ward *Buchanan* 8: You on the dodge, son,…or just driftin'? **1958** Constiner *Gunman* 5: He says he's not on the dodge, and I believe him. **1959** L'Amour *Fast Draw* 12: If a man like Bob Lee could be on the dodge…how could I hope to stick it out?

¶ **up to the dodge** shrewd; knowledgeable; alert.

1846 in G.W. Harris *High Times* 66: I had ridden a few quarter races in my time, and was pretty well up to the dodge.

Dodge City *n. Mil. Av.* heavily defended air space over and around Hanoi, North Vietnam. Now *hist.*

1969 in J.T. Ward *Dear Mom* 92: "Dodge City" is close to An Hoa. **1987** Nichols & Tillman *Yankee Sta.* 121: A hilly jungle area southwest of "Dodge City"—Hanoi.

¶ In phrase:

¶ **get [the hell] out of Dodge City** see s.v. DODGE.

dodger *n.* **1.** a handbill or flyer.

1879 in *DA.* **1890** Roe *Police* 299: That corresponded to the time the dodger…might have been printed. **1895** *Billboard* (Aug. 1) 5: A miserable little circular, 6 x 9 inches, printed in the "dodger" style. **1933** Ersine *Prison Slang* 33: *Dodger, n.* A paper carrying a wanted man's picture and description. It is sent to police chiefs and sheriffs. **1937** "L. Short" *Brand of Empire* 88: There was no picture on that reward dodger. **1971** "L. Short" *Man from Desert* 170: No reward dodgers out and the sheriff's satisfied. **1982** Braun *Judas Tree* 220: The reward dodger says dead or alive.

2. the penis.

1888 *Stag Party* 41: Esculapius said he'd examine his dodger. *Ibid.* 70: He pulled out his dodger and shoved it in very gently. **1888** *Field Socratic Love* st. 1: The story goes that Socrates…/Carried…a rara avis dodger,/Wherewith he used…/To ransack holes that did not appertain to his Xantippe. **1889** Barrère & Leland *Dict. Slang* 316: *Dodger*…(American)…in vulgar slang, the *penis.*

dodo *n.* **1.a.** a stodgy person holding antiquated beliefs.

1877 *Puck* (June) 13: I have been called an ignorant old dodo. **1891* *F & H* II 300: *Dodo*…A stupid, old man. **1923** in Cornebise *Amaroc News* 222: Country fullup with dodos now. **1926** Wood & Goddard *Amer. Slang* 15: *Dodo*. Fossil; antiquated specimen.

b. a fool. Now *colloq.*

1898 Norris *Moran* 55: Shut up, you crazy do-do, ain't we coming fast as we can? **1922** F.S. Fitzgerald *Letters* 164: Bridges had been a dodo about some Y.M.C.A. man. **1924** *N.Y. Eve. Graphic* (Sept. 16) 21: I've seen some awful hams in my day but this dodo…is the worst yet! **1928** Carr *Rampant Age* 104: The dumb dodos gave you lunch the fifth, didn't they. **1930** *AS* V (Feb.) 238: *Dodo.* An unintelligent person…"That freshman is a dodo." **1968** Tauber *Sunshine Soldiers* 194: Last week some dodo got orders not to let anyone leave his post with anything and arrested the garbage man. **1968** Baker et al. *CUSS* 106: *Do-do.* A person without much academic ability. **1974** Strasburger *Rounding Third* 239: *Sure* I'm persecuted. Any dodo could see that. **1980** Gould *Ft. Apache* 162: I forgot you were a nuclear physicist in your spare time. For the rest of us dodos the technique is perfect. **1989** "Capt. X" & Dodson *Unfriendly Skies* 147: He had become completely unhinged, the dodo!

2. *USAF.* a flight cadet who has yet to make a solo flight.

1933 Stewart *Airman Speech* 59. **1937** Lay *I Wanted Wings* 48 [ref. to 1932]: *Dodo.* A bird that can't fly. When he does, he flies backwards to keep his tailfeathers cool. New Flying Cadets are Dodos during Hell Month. **1941** *Nat. Geo.* (July) 36: A "dodo" is a flying cadet who has not yet soloed. **1942** *Life* (May 11) 53: At lunch formation, Jim and the other "dodos" (Air Force rookies) must fall into ranks five minutes earlier than the upperclassmen. **1955** Klaas *Maybe I'm Dead* 62: I was still a dodo flying cadet in the Class of 41G. **1960** Archibald *Jet Flier* 37: Tomorrow you dodoes will be taking your introductory rides, and shown starting procedure. **1965** LeMay & Kantor *Mission* 55 [ref. to 1929]: As I pointed out, a dodo was merely a kind of probationary cadet; technically a cadet, but actually a dodo. **1965–66** *Air Officer's Guide* 437: *Dodo.* Student pilot who hasn't soloed. **1978** Ardery *Bomber Pilot* 19 [ref. to WWII]: I learned from the upperclass that here I was "just another lousy dodo, lower than whaleshit."

3. money; DOUGH.

1941 Macaulay & Wald *Manpower* (film): I don't know how you're fixed for dodo.

4. *Bowling.* a 1–10 or 1–7 leave. Also **dodo split.**

1949 Cummings *Dict. Sports* 109. **1979** Cuddon *Dict. Sports & Games* 287.

dodo ball *n. Bowling.* an illegally weighted ball.

1961 *WNID3.* *a***1986** in *World Bk. Dict.*: Balls that have been craftily hollowed out or packed with lead can be made to roll in tricky curves— "dodo balls," they are called.

dodrabbit *v.* to damn; darn.

1866 in G.W. Harris *High Times* 164: I'l agree to be doddrabited, if my bristils ain't sot this morning. **1867** in *ibid.* 188: Dod rabbit me, if I ever try. **1977** Coover *Public Burning* 618: Come on, you dodrabited whey-faced no-good varmints!

dodsey *n.* [orig. unkn.] *Und.* a woman.

***1708** (cited in Partridge *Dict. Und.* 195). ***1796** Grose *Vulgar Tongue* (ed. 3): *Dodsey.* A woman; perhaps a corruption of Doxey. *Cant.* **1845** *Nat. Police Gaz.* (Nov. 8) 91: War Among the "Dodseys."—Quite an eruption has broken out among the domestic partners of George Potter, Bob Pinkerton, and Jack Gibson.

dodunk *n.* [orig. unkn.; perh. infl. by PODUNK] a blockhead.

1894 *DN* I 387: *Dodunk,* n. A stupid, simple person. **1959** in *DARE: Dodunk*...Someone not very bright. Occasional [in Vermont].

doe *n.* **1.** *Und.* a baby; child.

1904 *Life in Sing Sing* 247: *Doe.*—An infant. **1931** (cited in Partridge *Dict. Und.* 195).

2. a woman. *Joc.*

1909 Ware *Passing Eng.* 52: *Buck or a doe* (Anglo-Amer.). A man or woman. **1948** Lait & Mortimer *New York* 155: Census bureau says there will be more than 750,000 more does than stags in this postwar world. **1954–60** *DAS: Doe*....a woman unaccompanied by a male escort.

3. (see quot.).

1961 Himes *Pinktoes* 51: In Harlem idiom a square is a lain, a doe, a John, a mark—in other parlance a fool, a chump, a sucker, a simpleton.

doe-boy var. DOUGHBOY.

doeskin *n.* money.

1969 Whittemore *Cop!* 136: Now there's some doeskin in this kind of thing, so I want you to keep your ears open, okay? I mean, we'll put a little something in your pocket.

dofunny *n.* a thing the name of which is unknown or forgotten; DOODAD.

1886 Nye *Remarks* 207: A Frenchman invented a flying machine, or dofunny, as we scientists would term it, in 1600 and something. **1915** in *DA.* **1922** Rollins *Cowboy* 153 [ref. to 1890's]: Each of such useless objects and of such luxuries, particularly if it were small in size or novel in construction, was apt to be called a "dofunny." **1927–30** Rollins *Jinglebob* 20 [ref. to 1880's]: It's a dofunny for your sombrero. **1931** in *DAE.*

dog *n.* **1.a.** the penis; in phrs. of the sort **beat the dog** to masturbate.

1600** in Wardroper *Love & Drollery* 162: Will you buy a fine dog with a hole in his head?/ With a dildo, With a dildo, dildo [etc.]. [ca***1730** *Country Spy* 21: Exposing in the most undecent Manner those *Parts* which ought to have remain'd concealed, he cried out...*To her, Towzer; To her, Towzer.*] **1916–22** Cary *Sexual Vocab.* III s.v. *masturbation:* English synonyms...beating the dog, beating the pup. *ca***1930** in *F & H*

I (rev.) (1966 ed.) lxxi: One's Dog was kenneled in her cosy Manger. **1974** Lahr *Trot* 20: She puts his old dog deep into her mouth. **1985** *Maledicta* VIII 106: To masturbate (of males)...*flog your dog.* **1989** *Maledicta* X 54: Penis...*dog...dork* [etc.].

b. (see quot.).

1975 Univ. Tenn. grad. student: My granddaddy [born in Ga., 1894] calls a girl's whole pubic area her *dog.* He talks about "going *dog-hunting,*" "getting some *dog.*"

2. a pistol. Cf. syns. BARKER and BULLDOG.

1833 A. Greene *Travels* 135: "Besides, I've got a couple of little dogs here"—showing a pair of pistols—"that...'re tarnal apt to bark when anything don't go to please 'em." **1855** W.G. Simms *Forayers* 170: The pistols, Carrie, the old dogs!

3. a bond or promissory note.

1833 [M. St.C. Clark] *Sks. D. Crockett* 121: I found out that bonds, or promissory notes were termed dogs—and that they were said to be of a good or bad breed, according to the ability and punctuality of the obligor.

4.a. meanness; treachery.

1845 J. Hooper *Simon Suggs* 170: Strip, and I'll whip as much *dog* out of you as'll make a full pack of hounds! You swindlin' robber! **1972** P. Hamill, in *N.Y. Post* (Dec. 20) 39: Our leaders stand exposed as men with a streak of dog in them as wide as the Mississippi.

b. *Esp. Black E.* a treacherous or brutal person.

1966 S. Harris *Hellhole* 239: The nicknames they have for them—"guttersnipes" and "dogs." **1968–70** *Current Slang* III & IV 38: *Dog*...A brutal or hard-line policeman. **1972** Wambaugh *Blue Knight* 39: She's a *dog* motherfucker. *Ibid.* 40: A righteous dog. He deserves to fall. **1967–80** Folb *Runnin' Lines* 235: *Dog*...1. any male who mistreats or demeans another (often used by females in reference to males). 2. Bad or evil-tempered male. 3. Male who aggressively pursues sexual relations with a number of women (implies infidelity).

5. *Und.* **a.** a police spy; stool pigeon.

1846 *Nat. Police Gaz.* (Feb. 21) 210: Dick White had been playing the "dog," and he and the "coppers" are now within ten minutes of the house. **1956** Resko *Reprieve* 124 [ref. to *ca*1940]: The whole place fulla dog, rat, punk!

b. a detective or police officer, esp. a plainclothesman.

1867 *Nat. Police Gaz.* (Jan. 26) 3: The "dog" who "nailed" him was specially detailed to attend the market. **1913** Kneeland *Commercialized Prostitution* 149: The "dogs" are outside. ***1942** S.J. Baker *Austral. Lang.* 137: A plainclothes railway detective is a *dog.* **1972** Carr *Bad* 203: I...downed a couple of dogs as I was coming up for air. **1979** Haas & Hunter *Over the Edge* (film): I bet he had that dog bust the Rec so it wouldn't be here when those turkeys showed up. **1980** *AS* LV 197: Bull, cop, copper,...dog...flatfoot, fuzz [etc.].

6.a. ostentation of style; airs.—usu. constr. with *put on [the].*

1865 in McKee *Throb of Drums* 216: We...go out on grand reviews occasionally [*sic*] and put on a D—D sight of Dog generally. **1871** Bagg *Yale* 44 [ref. to 1865–69]: *Dog,* style, splurge. To *put on dog* is to make a flashy display, to cut a swell. **1891** Maitland *Amer. Slang Dict.* 95: *Dog,* "too much" (Am.), is the equivalent for "too much side" or style. **1893** James *Mavrick* 180: The man...comes there merely to ventilate himself; or, in the characteristic language of the cow-boy, "to pile on dog." **1895** Foote *Coeur D'Alene* 88: The old man put on a heap o' dog. **1897** A.H. Lewis *Wolfville* 126: The Dallas sharp, puttin' on a heap of hawtoor an' dog, walks over to the tavern ag'in. **1900** *DN* II 32: *Dog,* n....style; good clothes. **1900** Ade *More Fables* 158: It is a great Satisfaction to get up in a Lodge Hall and put on a lot of Ceremonial Dog. **1902** Corrothers *Black Cat Club* 136: At's why he tried to put on so much dog, an' made Pomp tell so many lies. **1903** A. Adams *Log of a Cowboy* 243: Old Joe's putting on as much dog as though he was asking the Colonel for his daughter. **1904** Ade *True Bills* 102: The only thing that makes me sore is to think that all of this Hot Dog you're throwin' on comes out of the Pockets of poor, hard-workin' Guys, such as me. **1905** *DN* III 91: She's *putting on (raw) dog.* **1917** in Grider *War Birds* 36: A man with a lot of rank and a lot of medals and a lot of dog. **1923** in Horowitz *Campus Life* 135: They think you're throwing on the dog. **1926** Springs *Nocturne* 198: That's the way to put on dog nowadays. **1934** Jevne & Purcell *Palooka* (film): Puttin' on the dog, isn't he? **1936** in R.E. Howard *Iron Man* 161: Gentleman Jack, and isn't he putting on the dog? **1942–43** C. Jackson *Lost Weekend* 59: She puts on the dog about her wonderful wardrobe or husband's fine job or something. **1943** Holmes & Scott *Mr. Lucky* (film): Where can I get a car? I've got to put on the dog for a few days. **1945** Hartman & Grant *Naughty Nineties* (film): Now we're going in here, and put on the dog. **1983** Flaherty *Tin Wife* 52: They insisted on putting on the dog: theater tickets or dinner and sometimes both.

b. *pl.* something superlative; the CAT's.—constr. with *the.*

1932 in Farrell *Short Stories* 126: Wouldn't it be the dogs to be paged like that?

7. a sausage; (now *specif.*) a frankfurter; hot dog. Cf. DOG's PASTE.

[**1845** Corcoran *Pickings* 152: Dogs....they retails the latter, tails and all, as sassenger meat.] [**1864** in R. Jackson *Pop. Songs* 60: Un sasage ish goot, bolonie of course/...Dey makes um mit dog und dey makes um mit horse.] [**1878** Hart *Sazerac* 158: We know of no sure test to detect the presence of dog in sausage. One of the oldest expedients is to whistle to the sausage, and if it tries to wag itself, there is dog in it.] [**1883** Peck *Peck's Bad Boy* 170: Beware, you base twelve ounces to the pound huckster, you gimlet-eyed seller of dog-sausage. *Ibid.* 180: I hope to die if there wasn't a little brass padlock and a piece of...dog collar imbedded in the sausage.] **1884** Hartranft *Sidesplitter* 29: A sausage maker...is continually dunning us for a motto. The following, we hope, will suit him to a hair: "Love me, love my dog." *1890–91 F & H* II 303: Dogs...(university)...Sausages. **1900** *DN* II 32: Dog, n....Sausage. *Ibid.* 42: Hot-dog, n....A hot sausage. **1904** Miles *Breeze* 21: Oatmeal, "dogs" (frankfurters), potatoes, steak, pork chops and coffee. **1906** Beyer *Battleship* 199: Now we often has dorgs (sausages) for breakfast. **1906** M'Govern *Sarjint Larry* (gloss.): *Dog:*—Vienna Sausage. **1917** *Wadsworth Gas Attack* 23: Bull, gravy, dogs and sinkers/Are all my long suit. **1962** Houk & Dexter *Ballplayers* 104: I'd gobble the dogs, gulp the Cokes and then try to get forty winks. **1964** Gelber *On Ice* 78: Baked dog on white! Don't spare the mayo! **1972** *Life* (Nov. 17) 75: I used to eat a lot of dogs, about four a week. **1981** Alka-Seltzer radio ad: Gimme a dog, heavy on the kraut. Make that two dogs.

8.a. Esp. *Horse Racing.* a slow or worthless horse; (*hence,* in the livestock industry) a poor-grade animal; (*Army*) a horse or mule. [The sense intended in the 1840 quot. is not entirely clear.]

1840 *Spirit of Times* (June 27) 199: Asking who the "old codger on the dog horse" is, and learning that he is your informant's father. **1893** in Ade *Chi. Stories* 10: That settles it, Steve; it's the last time I'll ever play that dog. **1899** Cullen *Tales* 82: The dog ran a rank last the last time out! **1899** Ade *Horne* 206: And at that this dog only wins by a head. **1899** A.H. Lewis *Sandburrs* 206: As I'm singin' out d' last, I'm givin' me driver d' office to beat his dogs an' chase, see! **1905** Hobart *Get Next!* 24: Every dog we had mentioned to the Bookies proved to be a false alarm. **1913–15** Van Loan *Taking the Count* 337: Now on a dry track, that dawg wouldn't have been one, two, nowheres. **1920** Weaver *In American* 39: Now in the third race, they's a dog name Lucas. **1925** in Faulkner *N.O. Sks.* 94: So we worked out them dogs. Cheest, they was a terrible lot. **1935** *AS* (Dec.) 270: Dogs. Low-grade animals [i.e., livestock]. **1941** in Grayson *New Stories for Men* 127: Free Lance is just as likely to cop as any dog in it. **1944** Kendall *Service Slang* 5: Dog...affectionate term for a cavalryman's horse, also called a job. *1945* S.J. Baker *Austral. Lang.* 175: A *dog* is a horse difficult to handle. **1965** Fink, Saul & Peckinpah *Maj. Dundee* (film): They're a bunch of...spavined, swaybacked dogs! And you call yourself a horse thief? **1968** Ainslie *Racing Guide* 466: Dog...cheap horse.

b. Esp. *Sports.* a performer of little promise or ability; (*specif.*) a prizefighter or other athlete who lacks aggressiveness or spirit in competition.

1934 Weseen *Dict.* 252: Dog—An athlete who lacks enthusiasm for the game that he is in. **1942** *ATS* 554: Dog...an inferior player [of music]. **1947** Schulberg *Harder They Fall* 98: You don't mean that dog Cowboy Coombs, for Chrisake? **1968** Ainslie *Racing Guide* 466: Dog...quitter. **1976** WINS Radio (July 5): I love the language of boxing...Do you know what a *dog* is? It's a coward, also known as a *geezer.* **1976** Atlee *Domino* 62: It is almost an axiom in the American military that you dump the dogs and dullards into G2. **1981** *Richmond* (Va.) *Times-Dispatch* (Oct. 25) B-15: There are few apparent dogs among the 23 [NBA] teams and that should make for a more interesting season. **1982** Considine *Lang. Sport* 87: Dog. The lowest scoring [bowler] in a team game and/or a series.

c. Orig. *Boxing.* basic lack of competitiveness or fighting spirit in the ring; cowardice.

1958 Heinz *Professional* 227: He ain't the fighter people think he is. He got dog in him. **1981** P. Sann *Trial* 228: I didn't have to be carried off screaming and hollering like there was any dog in me.

9. dogleg tobacco.

1906 in A. Adams *Chisholm Trail* 212: I'll bet a twist of dog.

10.a. a pint bottle of liquor; **short dog** a half-pint bottle.

Cf. *kill (one's) dog,* below.

1901 *Our Naval Apprentice* (Sept.) 14: As all men-of-war men know what a "Navy dog" is, it is needless to explain here...Fishing for "dogs," do you say; do you mean to tell me that that is the way rum is getting on board? **1906** Beyer *Battleship* 82: "Dog"—a bottle of liquor. **1970** Terkel *Hard Times* 37 [ref. to 1930's]: I bought this half a dog of booze. Half a pint. **1972** Bunker *No Beast* 119: I gave him enough money for a couple of short dogs of wine. **1972** Wambaugh *Blue Knight* 143: A wino [was] staggering down Broadway sucking on a short dog...He started walking away from the short dog, which was rolling around on the sidewalk spilling sweet lucy all over the pavement. "Pick up the dog, you jerk."

b. a state of intoxication; BUN.

1924 Wilstach *Stage Slang* 26: An intoxicated person has a "bun" or a "dog."

11.a. usu. *pl.* a person's foot; in phrs. **shake (one's) dogs** to dance; **barking dogs** aching or sore feet.

1913 T.A. Dorgan, in *N.Y. Eve. Jour.* (July 7) 13: Waitin for my sore dog to heal up. **1915–16** Lait *Beef, Iron & Wine* 118: Many a night I carries the banner, keepin' on my dogs so I won' freeze to death. **1917** in Runyon *Poems for Men* 115: A couple o' yanks to cover my shanks,/And then my dogs'd freeze! **1918** *Variety* (Aug. 16) 7: Yesterday one of my men had his "dogs" go bad and I had to carry his pack as well. **1919** *Ladies' Home Jour.* (Sept.) 27: A Marine never calls a foot anything but a dog. **1919** Piesbergen *Overseas* 58: "Me dogs are hurtin', I think I'll fix de lay," which means in English, "My feet ache, I think I'll go to bed." **1922** S. Lewis *Babbitt* 172: Shake the Old Dogs to the WROL-LICKING WRENS. **1925** Van Vechten *Nigger Heaven* 244: How you can shake your dogs! **1925** Weaver *Poems* 125: Now, girlie, about this dance:/You sure do shake your dogs the way you oughta. **1942** *ATS* 146: Barking dogs. **1954** Schulberg *Waterfront* 247: I was just resting my dogs a minute. **1954** Marx *Groucho Letters* 97: I lay there in bed with a hot-water bottle on my dogs. **1958** Rumaker *Stories* 30: All this shoe leather burnt for nothing, and're my dogs in heat! **1966** "T. Pendleton" *Iron Orchard* 264: "My dogs are barking," he said. **1973** Wideman *Lynchers* 39: The cat have some funky dogs. **1977** P. Rizzuto, on N.Y. Yankees Baseball (WPIX-TV): He slammed that dog down just before Rupert Jones got there. **1977** Stallone *Paradise Alley* 61: I know ya dogs are tired. **1988** *Sonny Spoon* (NBC-TV): Hey, man, my dogs are barking, man.

b. usu. *pl.* a shoe.

1914 T.A. Dorgan, in *N.Y. Eve. Jour.* (Oct. 26) 12: He's been [shining] those old dogs for an hour now. **1918** Rowse *Doughboy* 89: Orders for the day call for shoes marching, instead of the field dog he wears. **1919** Farrell *1st U.S. Engrs.* 120: He wears a good old campaign hat/ And a pair of russet dogs. **1919** Whittemore *B Co.* 78: The shock of hobnailed "dogs" on stone pavements is wearing on the nerves and muscles. **1926** Boughton *11th Engrs.* 93: British "Dogs" and Wrapped Puttees. **1926** in E. Wilson *Twenties* 270: Got a new pair of dogs? **1942** Davis & Wolsey *Call House Madam* 296: The sport suit...doesn't fit the Forty-second Street dogs I brought out from New York.

12. [ref. to dogs barking at the full moon] *Und.* the moon.

1919 *Am. Leg. Wkly.* (Sept. 12) 9: "The town is dead after eleven o'clock. There won't be any 'dog' out, Charles." "Dog," in the argot of the underworld, was the moon. **1925** (cited in Partridge *Dict. Und.* 196).

13. *Stu.* (at some Southern colleges) a new freshman.

1931 Uhler *Cane Juice* 24: Six bits, dog—and now for kennel formation...Mush! *Ibid.* 222: You stay a dog till you join [a] fraternity. **1929–32** in *AS* (Dec. 1934) 288: Dog (also *canine, hound, pup,* and *puppy*). The usual commonly applied term for a freshman.

14. *Black E.* something extraordinary, esp. something difficult or unpleasant; BITCH.

1928 R. Fisher *Jericho* 206: "Ain't this a dog?" "Salty dog, I mean." *Ibid.* 299: Dog. Any extraordinary person, thing, or event. "Ain't this a dog?" is a comment on anything unusual. **1956** Childress *Like One of Family* 34: Honey, it was a dog!...Oh, yes, it was a real snazzy affair. **1973** *TULIPQ* (coll. B.K. Dumas): That exam was a real dog.

15.a. *Jazz.* an inferior piece of music. Also **dog tune.**

1929 T. Gordon *Born to Be* 170: He insisted upon me singing it....During rehearsal, we tried to show him it was a dog. **1941** *Slanguage Dict.* 13: Dog...a popular song of mediocre quality. **1942** *ATS* 560: Dog tune, an inferior one, an unpopular piece. **1959–60** Bloch *Dead Beat* 44: "Clair de Lune"..."Malaguena" and "Jalousie"...all dogs. **1964** *Down Beat* (Jan. 30) 32: "Bésame Mucho," something of a dog tune, became more fascinating...the way he played it. **1974** *N.Y. Times* (June 9) Sec. 3 II 24: Everything moves, even the dog tunes.

b. an inferior, unsatisfactory, or defective manufactured item or product; (*specif.*) an item or product that is unprofitable or difficult to sell. [The 1936 ex. adduced by *OED2* properly belongs to **(15.a.)**, above.]

1938 *AS* (Apr.) 150: *Dog.* [Among shoe salesmen] A shoe which is difficult to dispose of owing to its style, fit, off size, discoloration, or any similar reason. *ca*1940 in Mencken *Amer. Lang. Supp. II* 753: *Dog.* A dress that does not sell well. **1952** *N.Y. Times Bk. Review* (Aug. 10) 8: Unless of course the book turns out to be a dog. **1955** Salter *Hunters* 62: I'll be surprised if we just make it up there and back in these dogs [airplanes]. **1961** *N.Y. Post* (Aug. 14): It's horrible, and you think to yourself who'd buy that dog? **1971** Tak *Truck Talk* 45: *Dog:* a truck with little power or a poor appearance. **1973** "J. Godey" *Pelham* 23: It was just a train that bucked, one of those dogs that motormen hated to be stuck with. **1982** A. Shaw *Dict. Pop/Rock* 109: "Dog." A music-biz colloquialism for a song or disk that does not make it. **1987** *NewsWatch* (CNN-TV) (Aug. 21): It's been a bit of a dog in terms of sales.

c. *Entertainment.* an extremely poor act, show, production, etc.

1955 Kurtzman *Inside Mad* 106: It was wonderful to get out of the theater. I was dying looking at this dog and it felt so good to leave when it finally ended. **1956** in J. O'Hara *Sel. Letters* 249: If it turns out to be a dog, the script is blamed. **1961** in R.S. Gold *Jazz Talk* 71: The *ABC* [album] is a dog, the *Impulse!* a mild winner. **1966** Susann *Valley of Dolls* 298: Why I ever let myself be talked into doing this dog… **1969** H.A. Smith *Buskin'* 36: Toward the end of his life John Barrymore was on tour in a dog of a play. **1982** *Good Morning America* (ABC-TV) (May 10): Some of the acts *were* dogs. **1993** *Newsweek* (Jan. 18) 65: Shooting up another dog on MST3K [a TV show spoofing notably bad movies].

16. (among men) a very homely young woman; (later, among women) a very homely young man.

1937 Weidman *Wholesale* 170: I don't like to have a bunch of dogs floating around. While I'm at it, I might as well hire something with a well-turned ass and a decently uplifted tit. **1948** I. Shaw *Young Lions* 304: She had fat legs and the seams of her stockings were crooked, as always. Why is it, Lewis thought automatically, why is it the dogs are the ones who join up? **1952** in Yates *Loneliness* 31: You don't want the roommate, Eddie. The roommate's a dog. A snob, too. **1954** Chayefsky *Marty* (film): I got stuck on a blind date with a dog. **1955–57** Felder *Collegiate Slang* 2: *Dog*—a very unattractive girl. **1957** Margulies *Punks* 53: A couple are real dogs, some are pretty. **1968** Baker et al. *CUSS* 106: *Dog.* An ugly person, male. An ugly person, female. **1978** *Penthouse* (Apr.) 126: I'm no Marty. I'm no dog. **1989** *Geraldo* (synd. TV series) (May 19): He was not good-looking….He was a dog, in fact.

17. dog-wagon.

1950 in *DAS* 153: Half a century ago, your historian took his meals at Hank Norwood's dog.

18. (*cap.*) *Miss.* the Yazoo and Mississippi Valley (Yazoo Delta) Railroad.—constr. with *the*.

1935 in Oliver *Meaning of Blues* 94: The Southern cross the Dawg at Moorhead, mama.

19. syphilis or gonorrhea.—usu. constr. with *the*.

1942–49 Goldin et al. *DAUL* 60: *Dog*…A venereal disease, especially syphilis….Getting a bite of the old dog (syphilis). *Ibid.* 324: Venereal disease, neglected…*Old clap; ten-year-old dog.* **1982** F. Hailey *Soldier Talk* 18: *Dog, the*…V.D.

20.a. [sugg. by *Dog,* mil. comm. alphabet for the letter *D*] *USAF.* (a nickname for) the "D" model of an aircraft, as the F-86D Sabrejet or F-100D Super Sabre.

1955 F. Harvey *Jet* 45: "We've got F-86 dogs." "You mean the ones with radar?" **1956** *AS* XXXI (Oct.) 228: *Dog, n.* An F-86D. **1961** L.G. Richards *TAC* 73: Every F-100 pilot…knows you can't crash-land a Dog and walk away from it.

b. *Stu.* an academic grade of D.

1964 in *Time* (Jan. 1, 1965) 56: D's are *dandies* or *dogs.* **1968** Baker et al. *CUSS* 106: *Dog.* The grade "D." **1974** Miami Univ. student: A "D" is a *dog.* **1980** Eble *Campus Slang* (Oct.) 2: *Dog*…the grade D: "One more dog and I won't be back next semester."

21. *Gamb.* a gambling marker.

1967 in J. Flaherty *Chez Joey* 126: "Here's the dog I owe you, and give me twenty to win on Advocator."…All [bookies] give their clients the benefit of the "dog" or "marker," inside names for credit.

22. *Gamb.* an underdog. Often attrib.

1975 Mahl *Beating Bookie* 36 (chart): 23 "Dog" Bets…Favorite wins. "Dog" wins…23 Favorite Bets…Favorite wins. "Dog" wins…He makes a higher percentage vig on the underdog. *Ibid.* 44: If you like the

"dog" opponent, your spot is Plus 1 goal. **1984** *N.Y. Post* (Sept. 3) 17: With the Eagles coming in as two-point dogs, the true Giant fan basked in the best of both worlds. **1984** D. Jenkins *Life Its Ownself* 261: Three years ago, 10 out of 12 dogs covered in the games he worked. **1990** *N.Y. Post* (Jan. 2) 33: If someone told you a year ago that Hilton would be the dog to DeWitt, you'd think they were nuts.

23. *Skiing.* a show-off; HOTDOG.

1976 *Webster's Sports Dict.* 116: *Dog*…A hot dog skier.

24. (*cap.*) a Greyhound bus.

1979 Hiler *Monkey Mt.* 160 [ref. to *ca*1971]: Always the bus. Jesus, I got tired of ridin' the Dog. **1986** Merkin *Zombie Jamboree* 194: They piled us all into a chartered Dog and shuttled us south into the darkness.

¶ In phrases:

¶ **beat the dog** see **(1)**, above.

¶ **cut loose (one's) dog** *West.* to go ahead without restraint; cut loose.

1903 A. Adams *Log of Cowboy* 81 [ref. to 1882]: Any time that you have the leisure and want to shoot me, just cut loose your dog.

¶ **dog bite (someone** or **something)** (used as a mild oath).

1864–65 G.W. Nichols *Great March* 74: Why, dog bite them, the newspapers have been lying all along. *Ibid.* 75: Dog bite their hides! **1923** in Partridge *DSUE* 57: A lower-classes' cry of astonishment…(*dog*) *bite my ear!* **1930** G. Schuyler *Black No More* 79: "Dog bite it, Doc!"

¶ **flog the dog** see **(1)**, above, and cf. similar phrs. s.v. FLOG.

¶ **fuck** [or occ. **screw** or **finger**] **the dog, 1.** to loaf on the job, esp. while pretending to be hard at work; fool around; idle; waste time.—usu. considered vulgar. [1918 and 1919 quots. presumably euphemize this expression.]

[**1918** in Sullivan *Our Times* V 328: *F.T.D.:* Feeding the dog. The supposed occupation of a soldier who is killing time.] [**1919** Warren *9th Co.* 35: The Engineer's Dictionary…*Walking the dog*—Soldiering on the job. When one is caught at it he is said to have stepped on the puppy's tail.] **1935** J. Conroy *World to Win* 201: One of the first things you gotta learn when you're f—n' the dog…is t' look like you're workin' hard enough t' make yer butt blossom like a rose. Rattle templets, beat with a hammer on a beam, but do *somethin'*. If the boss ketches you f—n' the dog while you're helpin' me, he'll eat *me* up blood raw. **1939** Bessie *Men in Battle* 331: They were "fucking the dog," spending what money they had. **1942** *ATS* 490: Fuck the dog, *to loaf on the job.* **1948** Guthrie *Born to Win* 19: I'll do all I can to stay alive and argufying, alive and kicking, alive and flurking [*sic*] the dog. **1954** *Inter. Jour. of Psychoanalysis* XXXV 351: This was followed by a four-month period of "funking," "fucking the dog," characterized by drinking, missed hours, tardiness, and "sponging" on mother. **1962** E. Stephens *Blow Negative* 54: Those apes are screwing the dog all day long up there. **1967** W. Crawford *Gresham's War* 125: "And meantime?" "Frick the dog, I reckon." **1967** Kolb *Getting Straight* 70: Until you said that, I thought you'd been screwing the dog on this project. **1977** Sayles *Union Dues* 58: You let me catch you fuckin the dog again, so help me, you'll be some sorry characters. **1978** Alibrandi *Killshot* 146: "You bet our entire stake on this one match?" "You got it, kid. No sense fucking the dog. We came to gamble, remember?" **1983** K. Weaver *Texas Crude* 93: Fuckin' the dog and sellin' the pups. Wasting time and loafing on the job. **1986** Stinson & Carabatsos *Heartbreak* 125: You hotshots are "fingering the dog" and you wind up killin' every swinging dick in this platoon.

2. to bungle; blunder.—usu. considered vulgar. Cf. *screw the pooch* s.v. POOCH.

1962 Killens *Heard the Thunder* 144 [ref. to WWII]: Saunders, I don't know what I'm going to do with you…You've gone and fucked the dog again. **1985** Heywood *Taxi Dancer* 34: But he had "screwed the dog by the numbers." He had failed to conserve fuel and he had forgotten about their bombs.

¶ **have to see a man about a dog** (used to excuse oneself, now specif. for the purpose of using the lavatory). Also vars.

ca*1867 in *OEDS*: Excuse me, Mr. Quail; I can't stop; I've got to see a man about a dog. **1895 Townsend *Fadden* 178: Well, de night me friend de barkeep give de reception at his drum I told de Duchess I had t' see a felly 'bout a bull pup…and she asks me wasn't dat pup a grandfadder yet. **1928** *AS* III (Feb.) 221: *See a man about a dog.* To go out and buy liquor. **1981** C. Nelson *Picked Bullets Up* 68: Jenkins had to see a man about a dog so we stopped by the shitter.

¶ **it shouldn't happen to a dog** (said in commiseration or complaint).

*a*1946 in W.C. Fields *By Himself* 146: Canines have become synonymous with all that is low and mean, as witness "you dirty dog," "yellow dog," "I wouldn't do that to a dog," "a dog's life," "he dogged it," "it shouldn't happen to a dog," "doggone it," etc.

¶ **kill (one's) dog** to be drunk. Cf. **(10.a.),** above.

1737 *Pa. Gaz.* (Jan. 13) 1 (syns. for *drunk*): He's kill'd his Dog.

¶ **kiss the dog** *Und.* (see quot.).

1973 *Reader's Digest* (Oct.) 203: The dip [pickpocket] hates to "kiss the dog," or face his victim.

¶ **like a big dog** to a great extent or degree.—also used as an intensive.

1976 *UTSQ*: He's lying like a big dog. **1983** Eble *Campus Slang* (Nov.) 1: *Big dog*—used in a number of expressions having to do with success: get off like a big dog, pee like a big dog. **1992** *American Detective* (ABC-TV): You got him to talk like a *big dog.*

¶ **on the dog** *on the hog* s.v. HOG.

1933 Milburn *Trumpets* 143: "The way you see me now," he says, "I'm on the dog, just a poor down-and-outer."

¶ **put on the dog** see **(6.a.),** above.

¶ **till the last dog is hung** until the end or resolution.

1863 in *Civil War History* XIV 22: I stayed until the last dog was hung and had to laugh to see how mad the Col got. **1902** in *DA*. **1937** Parsons *Escadrille* 174: No matter what happened, Didier was going to be there till the last dog was hung. **1965** LeMay & Kantor *Mission* 41: I stayed there until the last dog was hung.

¶ **walk (one's) dog** to urinate.

1968 Gover *JC* 130: The john...I went in there to "walk my dog," you know.

¶ **walk the dog** to *put on the dog* s.v. **(6.a.),** above; show off, as by going at great speed; do well.

1927 Niles *Singing Soldiers* 136 [ref. to 1919]: Did we walk de dog! Why, man, dey passed out refreshments I ain't never tasted since I been put here. **1940** *R.R. Mag.* (Apr.) 55: *Walk the dog*—Wheel a freight so fast as to make cars sway from side to side. **1976** Whelton *CB Baby* 122: That's a great big ten-four...You're wall-to-wall and really walking the dog.

¶ In sometimes vulgar similes and proverbs. See also **broke-dick.**

1943 R.L. Scott *God Is Co-Pilot* 154: As they say in the slang of fighter stations, "I took off like a scalded dog." *a***1961** J. Jones *Thin Red Line* [ref. to WWII]: Trembling like a dog shitting peach seeds. **1974** E. Thompson *Tattoo* 221: The entire ship shuddering, as someone said, "like a dog passing peach pits." **1974** Beacham & Garrett *Intro 5* 71: He just stood there...shakin' like a poor dog tryin' to shit out persimmon seeds. **1977** Bunker *Animal Factory* 149: "Snitchin', huh?" "Does a dog have fleas?" *a***1986** in E. Knight *Essential* 65: He was cleaner/Than a broke/dick dog.

dog *adv. Mil.* DOGGO.

1985 K. Miller *Lurp Dog* 4 [ref. to Vietnam War]: I aim to...find me the thickest bush I can, and lay dog for three days. **1987** "J. Hawkins" *Tunnel Warriors* 77: She would "lay dog" herself, for as long as it took. *Ibid.* 333: *Lay dog* Lie low in jungle during recon patrol.

dog *v.* **1.** Esp. *So.* to confound; darn; in phr. **dog my cats!** (used as a mild oath).

1839 *Spirit of Times* (Mar. 23) 30: Dog my cats if such an ugly set of customers can be found in the oldest settlement of the hottest region *on earth.* **1854** in G.W. Harris *Lovingood* 35: Dorg my cats, ef eny sich good luck ever cums wifin reach. **1857** in *DAE*: I'll be dogged if I could use it. **1878** Harte *Drift* 37: Why, dog my skin! that's just the contrariness o' things. **1883** "M. Twain" *Huck. Finn* 15: Dog my cats ef I didn' hear sumf'n. **1891** C.H. Smith *Farm & Fireside* 41: Dog my cat if I don't be the last one to leave this ship. **1905** *DN* III 77: Dog my cats, v. phr. Mild imprecation. **1935** Sayre & Twist *Oakley* (film): Well, dog my cats! **1944** Bontemps & Cullen *St. Louis Woman* 34: Well, dog my cats! **1947** Willingham *End As a Man* 77: I be dog if I know. **1953** Manchester *City of Anger* 252: Well, I'll be *dogged!* **1960** Bluestone *Cully* 138: So I be dogged, yo' do the best yo' can. *a***1973** in Bontemps *Old South* 120: "Well, dog my cats," King said.

2. [**a.** *Va. & Ky.* to nag or scold.—constr. with *at*. [Dialectal, but related to slang senses below.]

1896 in *DAE*: Don't cry, sis...The folks in the house'll...think I'm doggin' at you. *ca***1960** in *DARE*: Dog at...To provoke, annoy, nag, vex.]

b. to treat with contempt or disdain; haze or harass; humiliate; (hence) to beat (an opponent) soundly.—now also constr. with *out.*

1930 in M. Taft *Blues Lyric Poetry: Concordance*: I know you 'buke and

dog me. *Ibid.* Reason I'm leaving you: you dog me all the time. **1959** in Leadbitter & Slaven *Blues Records* 33: Don't Dog Your Woman. **1970** in *DARE*: I'd rather quit than be dogged around. **1971** Wells & Dance *Night People* 117: Dog, v. To...distress. **1983** Eble *Campus Slang* (Nov.) 2: *Dog*...beat badly in a sporting contest. **1984** S. Hager *Hip Hop* 109: *Dog*...to embarrass an opponent. **1985** Petit *Peacekeepers* 31: "You're going to get dogged," the...clerk warned. "He had Elroy and Dodson working...twenty-four hours a day." *Ibid.* 103: When Gunny first started dogging me...I thought it might have been because I'm black. **1987** in Thorne *Dict. Contemp. Slang* 139: Dog the dorm rules now! **1988** Lewin & Lewin *Thesaurus* 3: Abused adj. dogged,...shafted [etc.]. **1989** G.C. Wilson *Mud Soldiers* 79: He had been dogged for his offense by performing dozens of punitive push-ups...."Now tell everybody why you got dogged out." *Ibid.* 207: "They got dogged too much."...This was soldier talk for overworking and harassing the troops. **1991** Lott & Lieber *Total Impact* 266: Somebody...told him that veterans dog rookies in the NFL. The 49ers have never hazed rookies. **1992** "Fab 5 Freddy" *Fresh Fly Flavor* 20: *Dog*—To treat badly.

c. *Specif.* to taunt, tease, or ridicule.—also constr. with *around.*

1973 Ace *Stand On It* 40: "That was the first year you won that sumbitch. The prettiest piece of driving I ever did see. I was there in the stands." "With a hamper full of fried chicken?" "Don't dog me around, boy." **1984** (quot. at **(d.),** below). **1990** P. Heller *Bad Intentions* 169: I was doggin' her a little bit because she wouldn't give me any pussy all this time. **1992** *Sally Jessy Raphaël* (synd. TV series): They're just doggin' me, that's all.

d. *Specif. Stu.* to fail to keep an appointment with; stand up.

1984 Mason & Rheingold *Slanguage: (To be) dogged* To get stood up, put down, insulted or teased. Dogging usually takes place between a couple (or couple to be). **1989** P. Munro *U.C.L.A. Slang* 34: *Dog*...to fail to keep an appointment with.

e. *Specif.* to criticize unjustly; insult; belittle.—also constr. with *out, on.*

1986 Eble *Campus Slang* (Fall) 3: *Dog on*—verbally abuse: "He was dogging on her real bad." **1989** P. Munro *U.C.L.A. Slang* 35: We dogged on him (talked badly about him). *a***1990** P. Dickson *Slang!* 216: *Dog*...To criticize or bother. **1991** Lott & Lieber *Total Impact* 5: Then Burt dogged me even more, delivering the most painful [verbal] blow of all. **1991** in *Rap Masters* (Jan. 1992) 23: A rude awakening in the form of getting dogged out, then discarded. **1992** "Fab 5 Freddy" *Fresh Fly Flavor* 20: *Dog you out*—Talk about you in a negative way.

3. *West.* to bulldog (a steer). Hence **dogger,** *n.*

1922 Rollins *Cowboy* 233: The instant the dogger took hold, the seized beast began to run. *Ibid.* 245: The entire task of "spilling" a fully grown steer by roping or "dogging" it. **1976** Hanes *W. Pickett* 59: Thus it was practical to dog to the left, since horses were trained to expect such procedures.

4.a. to shirk, dodge, or avoid (work or other responsibility). Occ. intrans. See also *dog it,* below.

1930 *AS* V (Feb.) 239: *To dog:* to avoid, dodge, or evade work or studies. "He dogged his work whenever possible." **1939** Fessier *Wings of Navy* (film): Looks to me like you're just dogging. **1942** *ATS* 241: *Shirk*...dog on the job. **1955** Graziano & Barber *Somebody Up There* 144: "I hear you're dogging the fights in the amateurs"...He's scared to go fight in the amateurs.

b. to hang back in the performance or execution of.

1986 *Larry King Live* (CNN-TV) (Apr. 30): Don't dog the show, man. Don't dog it. Don't go out there like you're doing the audience a favor.

5. *Football.* RED-DOG.

1976 *Webster's Sports Dict.* 116. **1982** Considine *Lang. Sport* 136.

6. (see quot.).

1985 "Blowdryer" *Mod. Eng.* 88: *Dog*...To crumble under pressure. "He really dogged when he saw those five cholos coming."

7. to copulate or copulate with.

1988 R. Menllo & R. Rubin *Tougher Than Leather* (film): Bernie said he dogged her. *a***1990** P. Dickson *Slang!* 216: *Dog*...To have sexual intercourse.

8. to filch.

1989 Sorkin *Few Good Men* 22: I got some Spiderman's and some Batman's sittin' in my footlocker. Somebody'll dog 'em for sure if they're not secured, ma'am.

9. [fr. DOG, *n.,* 20.b.] *Stu.* to get a grade of D on (an examination) or in (a class).

1990 *Today* (NBC-TV) (May 23): Physics....I dogged it, almost flagged it.

¶ In phrase:

¶ **dog it, 1.a.** Esp. *Sports.* to hang back; do less than what is required or expected; *(specif.)* to loaf, shirk, or renege.

1905 in *OEDAS* I 93: I expected to see the youngster dog it. **1916** T.A. Dorgan, in Zwilling *TAD Lexicon* 32: Get up, don't dog it. **1920–21** Witwer *Leather Pushers* 19: He'll play safe and be satisfied to stall the rest of it and dog it. **1927** in *DAS* 153: They'll all come home if they don't dog it. **1929** Booth *Stealing* 286: Do we root—or are you going to dog it? **1930** Lait *On the Spot* 24: I thought he was gonna pull his rod an' open up right then an' there…when he didn't, I knew he was doggin' it. *Ibid.* 202: Dog it…To get cold feet, turn coward. **1942** in Stilwell *Papers* 71: Liao and Tu have dogged it again. **1950** Cleveland *Great Mgrs.* 173: His erstwhile pal and roommate "dogged it"—loafing and failing to run out hits. **1953** Paley *Rumble* 32: Stop doggin' it, Banigan. Get your men movin'. **1970** Scharff *Encyc. of Golf* 416: Dog it. To play poorly under stress. **1973** Gent *N. Dallas* 241: Anyway I overheard the coaches talkin' and they're beginning to think you're doggin' it. **1974** Scalgo *Stand on Gas* 30: Even on his favorite dirt tracks he often dogged it. Sometimes his heart just wasn't in it. **1978** Wharton *Birdy* 290: I think he might be "dogging it." **1987** *RHD2*: A sponsor who dogged it when needed most. **1992** Strawberry & Rust *Darryl* 37: Is Darryl dogging it?

b. to proceed slowly.

1925 Hemingway *Our Time* 152: He'd just be dogging it along with his eyes on my back. **1970** *Current Slang* V 6: Dog it, v. To go slowly on purpose.—We *dogged it* from Sacramento to Roseville.

2.a. to leave quickly or furtively; run away.

1931 in Partridge *Dict. Und.* 196: Paul's friends had persuaded him to dog it out of town while he was all in a piece. **1933** Ersine *Pris. Slang* 33: Dog, v. To run, flee. "Jim dogged it to Montreal." **1934** *WNID2*: Dog it…to run away. Slang. **1962** Perry *Young Man* 153: Want to dog it?…Me and Harry want to duck out.

b. [infl. by DOG, *n.*, 11.] to go on foot; walk.

1973 Andrews & Owens *Black Lang.* 69: Doggin' it—Walking.

3. to put on the DOG, *n.*, 6; show off.

1932 C. McKay *Gingertown* 42: I guess you're going to dog it some tonight, brother!…That necktie…sure does mean something. **1938** *AS* (Apr.) 152: Dog it. To show off to advantage. A smartly dressed person struts along and an admiring observer ejaculates, "Aw, dog it, now!"

dogan *n.* [prob. fr. *Dogan*, Irish family name] *No.* an Irish Catholic.—used disparagingly. [App. of Canadian orig.]

1854 in *OEDS*: I would be overly liberal if I estimated their number as a couple of Dogans! **1898–1900** Cullen *Chances* 219: Like the innocent big dogan that he was. **1933** in *OEDS*: Many a time I got a smart clout on the lug and was told to take that for a dirty little dogan. **1936** Partridge *DSUE: Dogun*…A Roman Catholic: Canadian: late C.19–20. **1966–67** in *DARE*.

dog-and-pony show *n.* an elaborate formal occasion or undertaking; *(specif.)* an official briefing or visual presentation, usu. for public-relations purposes. Hence **dog-and-pony,** *attrib.*

1957 Hecht *Charlie* 14 [ref. to 1916]: Black Jack Pershing, in charge of the hostilities, dubbed it "Colonel Foreman's Dog and Pony Show." **1974** Terkel *Working* 71: I go into my act: we call it dog and pony time, show time, tap dance…[The client] says…"How much will it cost us?" **1976** *Business Week* (Aug. 30) 60: "We had a real dog-and-pony show" for the agencies. **1978** Groom *Better Times* 326 [ref. to Vietnam War]: In this battalion there's not going to be any outward celebration of Christmas. Doesn't mean they can't recognize Christmas, but no dog-and-pony show. **1978** Maupin *Tales* 90: I have a dog-and-pony show for Fartface Siegel this morning. **1981** *Harper's* (Dec.) 38: The September 1980 decision [was] almost ignored by the press because it occurred during the quadrennial dog-and-pony show held to select the leader of the Free World. **1984** Hammel *Root* 104: Dog and pony shows were incessant and drew extremely negative reviews from the troops and junior officers. **1984** Riggan *Free Fire* 69: Despite certain dog-and-pony characteristics to many of these trips. **1985** Wells *444 Days* 409: It would be just like those sons of bitches to put us in much better circumstances and have some kind of big dog and pony show. They never missed a chance for a photo opportunity. **1989** J. Weber *Defcon One* 114: The president didn't care for officious functions. He referred to the rituals as dog-and-pony shows.

dog-ass *n.* a worthless person.—usu. considered vulgar.

1959 Griffin *Black Like Me* (Nov. 8): "Okay, dog ass, come get some food." The man bolted across the street and grabbed the pan. **1972** Jenkins *Semi-Tough* 49: Those dog-asses don't have anybody hurt.

1976 "N. Ross" *Policeman* 164: Reverend Jones loaded them up with over a hundred of the worst looking dog asses he could find. **1991** C. Fletcher *Pure Cop* 285: There are dog asses…scared shitless of their own shadow.

dog-ass or **dog-assed** *adj.* worthless; contemptible; bad.—usu. considered vulgar. Also as adv.

1953 Petry *Narrows* 266: A brokedown dogass white man if I ever see one. **1956** Holiday & Dufty *Lady Sings* 61: He would spend a fortune on arrangements for a little dog-assed vocalist. **1962** Killens *Heard the Thunder* 29 [ref. to WWII]: Corporal Crute, you don't suppose to be in no dog-assed Quartermaster outfit. **1964** Rhodes *Chosen Few* 5 [ref. to *ca*1950]: Thinks his dog-ass daughter is too good for me. **1967** Mailer *Vietnam* 7: A dog ass trail which gets dull and then monotonous. **1972** Jenkins *Semi-Tough* 21: The dog-ass New York Jets. *Ibid.* 161: They're more dog-ass dumb than I ever thought. **1976** "N. Ross" *Policeman* 31: He sounds more Black than the worst dog-assed nigger. **1990** Thorne *Dict. Contemp. Slang* 140: Dog-ass…American…worthless, inferior, bad.

dog basket *n.* [cf. colloq. *doggie bag*] *Naut.* a basket containing leftovers from the cabin to be eaten by sailors in the forecastle. Now *hist.*

1833 Ames *Old Sailor's Yarns* 206: The steward…came up with the breakfast dishes, &c. or "dog basket," as it is called by them of the forecastle. **1884** Symondson *Abaft Mast* 57: If "chummy" with the steward, the latter brings him for'ard every evening in the "dog-basket" such snacks and scraps as have come off the cabin table. **1929* Bowen *Sea Slang* 38: Dog basket—The receptacle in which the remains of the cabin meals were taken—or smuggled—forward.

dog biscuit *n.* **1.** *Mil. & Naut.* a hardtack biscuit or plain cracker.

1908 in "O. Henry" *Works* 270: On weak tea and dog biscuits. [**1916** in Roy *Pvt. Fraser* 79: The difference is made up of huge hard biscuits, not unlike dog biscuits.] **1917** Imbrie *War Ambulance* 215: We had "dog biscuits"—hardtack—too. **1919** Cober *Bttry. D* 122: Bully beef, dog biscuit, spuds unboiled with the jackets on. **1931** Ellsberg *Pigboats* 272 [ref. to 1918]: Two hours solitary, on dog biscuit and water. **1936** *AS* (Feb.) 43: *Dog biscuit.* Cracker. **1948** A. Murphy *Hell & Back* 22: For sixty bucks a month and a few dog biscuits. **1960** Matheson *Beardless Warriors* 191: "Who needs cake when there's dog biscuits?" said Guthrie, biting into one of his ration crackers. **1971** Waters *Smugglers* 85 [ref. to *ca*1920]: Weevil-ridden "dog biscuits," the latter being ships' biscuits.

2. *Stu.* (see quot.).

1945 *Amer. N & Q* (Aug.) 70: The unattractive girl is a "rusty hen," a "dog biscuit," a "seaweed."

dogbody *n.* DOG'S BODY.

dogbone *n.* *Mil. Av.* (see quot.).

1984 Trotti *Phantom* 228 [ref. to 1960's]: *Dogbone.* Weapon select panel in the F-4 cockpit, so named for its shape.

dogbox *n.* (see quots.).

1971 Tak *Truck Talk* 45: *Dog box*: the high covering over the engine in the center of the driver's area of a cabover…Syn: dog house. **1977** M. Franklin *Last of Cowboys* 104: That's the dogbox. The transmission mount is underneath. **1978** Lieberman & Rhodes *CB* (ed. 2) 297: Dog box—Gear box.

dog-breath *n.* offensive breath; *(hence)* a person having offensive breath.—used as a contemptuous term of address.

*ca*1944 in Kaplan & Smith *One Last Look* 89: Dog Breath [B-17 of Eighth Air Force]. **1981** *Daily Beacon* (Univ. Tenn.) 2: Listen very carefully, dog-breath. **1981** *Hill St. Blues* (NBC-TV): You forgot to pay your fare, dog breath! **1992** *Beverly Hills 90210* (Fox-TV): I mean, who's singing it, dogbreath?

dogcatcher *n.* *R.R.* a member of a train crew sent out to relieve another crew that has already worked the maximum number of hours allowed by law.

1931 *Writer's Dig.* (May) 41: Dog Catchers—A crew sent to relieve a crew that has become outlawed. **1945** Hubbard *R.R. Ave.* 340: Dogcatchers—Crew sent out to relieve another that has been *outlawed*—that is, overtaken on the road by the sixteen-hour law, which is variously known as *dog law, hog law,* and *pure-food law.*

dog-chaser *n.* *R.R.* DOGCATCHER.—occ. in extended use.

1934 Weseen *Dict. Slang* 70: Dog chasers—A train crew sent out to relieve another crew. **1940–43** (cited in *DAS*). **1967** *Lit Dictionary* 48: Dog Chaser—Your replacement or relief man; a substitute while you take a break.

dog collar *n.* **1.** a clergyman's collar; (*broadly*) any high, stiff collar.

*1861 in *OEDS*. **1883** in *F & H* II 302: The dog-collar which rose above the black cloth was of spotless purity. **1913** Meyer *10 Yrs.* 9 [ref. to 1854]: The most objectionable part of the whole uniform was the leather stock or "dog collar," as we called it, intended to serve as a cravat and keep the soldier's chin elevated. *1934 Yeates *Winged Victory* 129: The padre…[should] take off his dog collar and come over the lines.

2. a choker necklace.

1915–16 Lait *Beef, Iron & Wine* 186: She sees a pearl dog-collar on a society woman's neck. *1937 (cited in Partridge *DSUE* (ed. 8)). **1969** L. Sanders *Anderson Tapes* 273: Things like Victorian tiaras, bracelets, "dog collars."

dog days *n.pl.* the days of a woman's menstrual period.

1954–60 *DAS*. **1971** Dahlskog *Dict.* 19: *Dog days*…A woman's menstrual period.

dog-drunk *adj.* thoroughly or exceedingly drunk. [*OEDS* offers several *adj. dog-* compounds of this sort, the earliest (colloq. *dog-cheap*) being attested for 1526.]

*a1625 in *OED*: Would I were dog-drunk, I might not feel this. **1859** "Skitt" *Fisher's River* 254: So ongentlemanly dog drunk. **1942** *ATS* 122. **1984** *UTSQ*: Smashed, blitzed,…dog drunk, one step beyond.

dogear *v. Army.* to select by marking the records file of.

1956 Hargrove *Girl He Left* 34: The following men have been dog-eared for Fort Burnside, California.

dogee var. DUJI.

dog-eye *n.* Esp. *Pris.* a sidelong or unfriendly glance.—usu. constr. with *the*.

1912 Lowrie *Prison* 148: This guy is altogether too fresh and keeps giving me the dog eye. **1924** Henderson *Crookdom* 403: *Dog's eye*—Sidelong glance. *Give him the dogeye*—To glare at him. **1937** Johnston *Prison Life* 69: The men won't work with me and they all gimme the dog-eye. **1944** *AS* XIX 106: [Among merchant seamen, a] reproachful or supplicatory stare is the *dog-eye*.

dog-eye *v.* Esp. *Pris.* to eye, esp. with a sidelong or unfriendly glance.

1912 Lowrie *Prison* 189: This stiff is trying to stir up trouble all the time, and he keeps dog-eyeing me. **1937** Johnston *Prison Life* 11: There was some dog-eyeing and some out-of-the-corner-of-the-mouth confabs. **1954** Gaddis *Birdman* 34: He ain't my con. But he was dog-eyeing me the other day. **1962–68** B. Jackson *In the Life* 332: And he's trying to dog-eye that thing. He ain't sure, he can't see too good anyway, and he's not sure what he's seeing. And they'd accuse him of being crazy anyway. **1977** Caron *Go-Boy* 5: Standing off to both walls were five guards dog-eyeing our every move.

dogface *n.* **1.** an ugly individual.—usu. used as a derisive nickname.

1849 J.J. Hooper, in Chittick *Roarers* 246: Dog-face Billy Towns is here, and he'll go your security. **1906** Tomlin *H. Tomlin* 228: The boys called him "Dog-face Williams"…"Dog-face" and I had some words about the matter. **1919** *Camp Pike Carry-On* (Mar. 13) 8: "Dog Face" Francis is our company clerk for 20 days. Gold-bricking again, eh, Dog Face? **1928** Bodenheim *Georgie May* 122: Two of [the turnkeys]…were dubbed Slimy Pete and Dog-Face by the prisoners. **1945** *Amer. N & Q* 70: The unattractive boy is a "dog face," a "void coupon," a "stupor man." **1945** House *Texas* 50: Old Dog Face is one of the best trail men that ever drove a cow. **1950** Bissell *Stretch on R.* 54: Hey, Dogface, how you like that fuel man? **1963** T.I. Rubin *Sweet Daddy* 8: I invited only the local dog faces. **1977** Bredes *Hard Feelings* 302: What kinda jive trick you draggin' in now, you dogface nigger?

2.a. *Mil.* a soldier, esp. a low-ranking enlisted man; **dog-face[d] soldier** a common soldier. [Assertions, occ. met with during and after WWII (e.g., in 1945 and 1967 quots. below), that *dogface* in this sense was in use during the Plains Indians Wars or WWI cannot be confirmed and may simply reflect memories of the earlier usage in (**1**), above; cf. DOG SOLDIER.]

1930 *Our Army* (Dec.) 27: The Provost say to "ride 'em"/But, Hell, it's hard to do./These guys are dawg faced soldiers/The same as me an' you. **1932** *Our Army* (Dec.) 32: So this Cpl Harrison he looks at me and then he says, kine of slow like, you see, Hill, they call a soldier a dog-face down hear. So…we say they're trying it out on the *dog-faces*, see?

1934 *Our Army* (Jan.) 33: *Dogface*: "That guy's certainly a wit." *Dogrobber*: "Yep—nit-witt." **1934** *Our Army* (Nov.) 6 (cartoon caption): Believe It or Not, Dogface, This Isn't a Bucket Brigade. **1935** *Our Army* (Mar.) 12: Outside of that, just check up on how many men under those noncoms above mentioned who also can't speak plain English have ratings which a good American-speaking dog-face can't have because he isn't in their clique. **1941** *AS* (Oct.) 165: *Dogface.* Enlisted man. **1942** *Leatherneck* (Nov.) 144: *Dog-face*—A soldier. **1945** *N.Y. Times Mag.* (Jan. 7) 2: As to the term Dogface in the article "Doughfoot or Doggie." In World War I the name Dogface was applied to any soldier regardless of the branch of service he served in. **1946** S. Wilson *Voyage* 177: "I made a deal with a Filipino dogface," Wortly replied. **1948** Lay & Bartlett *12 O'Clock High!* 75: I can't have a plain dogface private driving me around. Put those three stripes back on in the morning. **1954** Crockett *Magnificent Bastards* 11: It was a foolish girl who let a Marine and a Dogface make a play for her at the same time! **1955** Archibald *Aviation Cadet* 14: Maybe I should have joined the dogfaces and found a soft desk job. **1965** Hersey *Too Far to Walk* 185: John hung back at the outer rim of the half circle of dogfaces. **1966** Adler *Vietnam Letters* 20: Boy, Pop, I never thought a dirty, dog-faced soldier could look so good. **1967** Morris & Morris *Word & Phrase Origins* II: *Dogface* was not common until World War II. But…I heard it used by soldiers as early as my first enlistment in 1907. It was also used by Indian War veterans. **1970** *Playboy* (Aug.) 108: You coming, dogface? **1976** Braly *False Starts* 32: No one wanted to be a dogface…Nice girls didn't want to go out with soldiers. **1966–80** McAleer & Dickson *Unit Pride* 273: We'll show these dogfaces. **1980** *N.Y. Times* (June 29) II 14: On June sixth, 1944, Corporal Sam Fuller was just another dogface soldier piling onto Omaha Beach…For 35 years he wanted to make a film about what war looks like and feels like when you are a dogface soldier. **1983** Eilert *Self & Country* 175 [ref. to 1968]: The guy's an Army dog face, a doggy. **1987** Norst & Black *Lethal Weapon* 153: The…[Army Special Forces] green beret meant only that a dog face was field-qualified to serve as a PFC in [the Marines].

b. *Army.* an infantryman, esp. a rifleman.

1942 Kahn *Army Life* 117: "Keep fifty feet clear of them [paratroopers]," the sergeant said. "They are tough babies and do not like you dogfaces." **1959** "D. Stagg" *Glory Jumpers* 110: [A paratrooper speaking]: Maybe bluff the Krauts off till the dogfaces show. **1963** Ross *Dead Are Mine* 5: With such a brain, how did you end up being a dog face, Martinelli? You should be in G-2.

dog-fashion *adv.* with one partner entering the other from behind, esp. anally. Also **doggie-fashion**.

*1900 *Horn Book* 68: The man stands behind her, fucking her dog-fashion. **1916** Cary *Venery* I 70: *Dog fashion*—To copulate with the woman on her knees; the man entering either the podex or the vagina from behind. **1927** [Fliesler] *Anecdota* 76: He hates to screw dog-fashion. **1954–60** *DAS*: *Dog fashion*…Heterosexual anal intercourse. **1961** R.E.L. Masters *Forbidden* 173: There is reason to believe…that early man copulated "dog fashion," with the woman kneeling and the man penetrating her from behind. **1964** Rhodes *Chosen Few* 174.

dog fat *n.* butter.

*1931 Brophy & Partridge *Songs & Slang* 302 [ref. to 1918]: *Dog Fat.*—Butter. **1941** Hargrove *Pvt. Hargrove* 83: Milk is *cat beer*; butter, *dog fat*.

dog food *n.* food, esp. canned corned-beef hash, thought to resemble dog food.

1945 in *Calif. Folk. Qly.* V (1946) 381: *Dog Food.* Corned beef hash. **1965** Friedman *Totempole* 270: Dog food. **1969** Sidney *Love of Dying* 37: Meat and beans, meat and noodles, corned beef hash. Couldn't eat 'em. Dog food.

dogfuck *n.* trouble.—constr. with *the*.—usu. considered vulgar.

1978 Groom *Better Times* 30: We're really in the dogfuck now.

dogfuck *v.* to engage in copulation dog-fashion.—usu. considered vulgar.

1967–80 Folb *Runnin' Lines* 235: *Dog fuck.* Engage in anal intercourse. **1981** in L. Bangs *Psychotic Reactions* 348: When they were done dog-fucking they sprawled back awhile to rest and pant. *a1986 in Chapman *NDAS*: Including how to 69 and dogfuck.

dogged *adj.* utterly fatigued; dog-tired.—occ. constr. with *out*.

1942 *ATS* 262: Tired out…*dogged (out), dog-tired.* **1968** Baker et al. *CUSS* 106: *Dogged.* Very tired.

dogged up *adj.* dressed up. Also **dogged out**.

1912 Lowrie *Prison* 126: They thought they could…go back all dogged up an' "cut a figger." **1929–33** Farrell *Manhood of Lonigan* 247: He was…dogged out in classy clothes. **1941** Kendall *Army & Navy Slang* 5: *Dogged up*…dressed up. ***1984** Partridge *DSUE* (ed. 8): *(All) dogged-up*. In one's smartest clothes.

dogger *n.* **1.** Esp. *Sports.* a slack player or performer.

1960 Garagiola *Funny Game* 2: My advice to kids who have the dream of someday walking through those clubhouse doors is never be a dogger.

2. *pl. Surfing.* multicolored canvas swim trunks.

***1963** in Partridge *DSUE* (ed. 7) 1104. **1968** Kirk & Hanle *Surfer's Hndbk.* 138: *Doggers:* multicolor canvas swim trunks.

3. *Skiing.* a show-off; hotdogger.

1976 *Webster's Sports Dict.* 116. ***1984** Partridge *DSUE* (ed. 8).

doggery *n.* a low drinking saloon or groggery.

1821 in Royall *Letters from Ala.* 228: A *Doggery* is a place where spirituous liquors are sold, and where men get drunk, quarrel, and fight, as often as they choose, but where there is nothing to eat. **1837** *Spirit of Times* (June 10) 132: I'll catch the lawyer at the doggery next Saturday. **1841** Porter *Big Bear of Ark.* 89: Jerry…invited Quashey "to go up to the doggery and liquor." **1847** in H.C. Lewis *Works* 130: I mounted Chaos and started at a speed that beplastered the skeleton houses on each side of the way with mud, heaving a delectable morsel as I passed the "doggery" full in the mouth of a picayune demagogue. **1850** Finley *Prison Life* 75: I became a bar-keeper in a little, filthy, "doggery." *a*1867 G.W. Harris *Lovingood* 51: I found Sut in a good crowd in front of Capehart's Doggery. **1884** "M. Twain" *Huck. Finn* 206: We found him in the back room of a little low doggery, very tight, and a lot of loafers bullyragging him for sport. **1893** Hampton *Maj. in Washington* 51: He was inveigled into a game of cards at that wretched doggery called the Burnt Rag. **1897** Ade *Horne* 97: Well, I wouldn't transact any business with a saloon-keeper if I had to sit around a doggery and drink liquor. **1901** *Puck* (Mar. 13) (unp.): Now the doggeries are all closed. **1911–12** Ade *Knocking the Neighbors* 156: Doggeries with swinging Doors.

doggie *n.* **1.** *Army.* an officer's orderly; DOG-ROBBER. [Quots. ref. to WWI.]

1919 Wilkins *Co. Fund* 22: "I'm not the Dog-robber but the Doggie's assistant," but "I'll be the Doggie while he's on pass." [***1925** Fraser & Gibbons *Soldier & Sailor Words: Skipper's Doggie:* Midshipman acting as captain's A.D.C.]

2. a person's foot; DOG, *n.,* 11.a.

1920 Ade *Hand-Made Fables* 281: The poor overheated Doggies…threatened to explode like Shrapnel. **1922** in Leadbitter & Slaven *Blues Records* 314: I've Got To Cool My Doggies Now. **1928** Bodenheim *Georgie May* 23: Come on, we'll take a load off ouah doggies. **1949** Robbins *Dream Merchants* 200: Joe held his feet up and looked at them. "Do you hear that, doggies?…Now we know where we're goin'. **1957** Myrer *Big War* 4: Man, just listen to these doggies bark. **1984** N. Bell *Raw Youth* 42: Massage my doggies?

3.a. *Army.* an infantry soldier; DOGFACE, *n.* 2.b.

1937 *Our Army* (Jan.) 20: Right after lunch, consisting of the lousiest G.I. mule ever foisted upon defenseless doggies, I'm picking the harness out of my teeth as I walk into the orderly room. **1944** *N.Y. Times Mag.* (Dec. 10) 36: "Dogface" is usually cut down to just plain "doggie."…There is no doubt that more infantrymen call other infantrymen and themselves "doggies" than anything else this correspondent has heard. **1957** E. Brown *Locust Fire* 20 [ref. to 1944]: You know how Bill Mauldin draws those E.T.O. doggies? **1957** Hall *Cloak & Dagger* 20: You ain't got a thing to worry about, doggie. We fired over your heads. **1959** Brosnan *Long Season* 20: Baseball's infantrymen we'd be. Doggies!

b. Esp. *USMC.* a member of the U.S. Army.—used derisively. [Early quots. ref. to WWII.]

1945 *Am. N & Q* (Apr.) 7: *Doggies:* Marines' name for Army men. **1952** Lamott *Stockade* 68: A doggie…What's this gook doing in a doggie uniform? **1954** Crockett *Magnificent Bastards* 11: Sure the Doggies are okay—for pushin' a broom! **1957** Leckie *Helmet* 74: It didn't hit the doggies, but it sure scared hell out of them. **1959** Cochrell *Barren Beaches* 13: "Get outa here, doggies," the blonde said. **1961** R. Davis *Marine at War* 178: They ain't doggies…They're Marines from some other division. **1968** Mares *Marine Machine* 54: The doggies don't have any history classes in basic training because they don't have any history. **1973** Huggett *Body Count* 161: Let's go see what we can steal from the doggies.

4. a sausage, esp. a hot dog.

1900 *DN* II 32: *Doggie*…A sausage [College slang]. ***1950** (cited in Partridge *DSUE* (ed. 8)). **1986** Boar's Head Provisions ad (WINS Radio) (July 3): Gimme a doggie wit' the works.

doggie-style *adj. & adv.* DOG-FASHION.

1966–71 Karlen *Sex. & Homosex.* 415: Coitus a tergo—"doggy style." **1983** Thickett *Outrageously Offensive* 49: How does a Jewish couple perform "doggie style" sex? **1986** X. Hollander, in *Penthouse* (Aug.) 32: His favorite position is to take me doggy-style. **1987** *Penthouse Letters* (Oct.) 77: Jackie rolled over onto her elbows and knees and I fucked her doggie-style. **1990** *Cosmopolitan* (July) 166: The scene in which their characters make love "doggie-style."

doggo *n.* [*dog* + *-o*] fellow.

1922 S. Lewis *Babbitt* 79: Say, old doggo, what do you think they're paying me now?

doggo *adv.* [perh. orig. alluding to a trained dog's playing dead] quietly or prone, as in concealment; hidden; hiding; under cover.—often constr. with *lie*, *lay*.

***1893** R. Kipling *Many Inventions* 259: I wud lie most powerful doggo whin I heard a shot. **1933** Raine *Honor & Life* 24: If I can reach the border, there are mountain ranges in Mexico where I can lie doggo. **1942** Casey *Torpedo Junction* 275: The scouts…have been lying doggo out there with orders not to attack. **1944** Huie *Can Do!* 35: By lying doggo for forty-eight hours, the group eluded the Japs. **1952** Geer *New Breed* 303: If you get fired on hit the deck and stay doggo. **1956** in J. O'Hara *Sel. Letters* 253: Adlai momentarily lies doggo. **1958** Frankel *Band of Bros.* 95: We'll try to play doggo. **1963** Cameron *Black Camp* 56: Duck over the wall and play doggo until the rest of us are out of sight. **1966** Derrig *Pride of Green Berets* 202: But it just isn't like the VC to stay completely doggo, not to stir up anything at all, give us some troubles. **1975** McCaig *Danger Trail* 157: They might lie doggo until sundown, then hit us with a night raid. **1977** T. Berger *Villanova* 18: Had Bakewell lain doggo in the third-floor toilet and, only now, the coast cleared, taken the descent to the street?

doggone *n.* a darn.

1947 Overholser *Buckaroo's Code* 25: I don't give a doggone how long it would last. **1970** E. Thompson *Garden of Sand* 71: I don't give a good doggone.

doggone *v.* to darn; confound. Also as interj., adj., adv. Also vars. [Often regarded simply as a euphem. for *God damn*.]

***1826** in *SND* s.v. *dag:* Dog on it, if I don't believe you are the author…yourself. ***1828** in *SND:* Dog on it, I aye wonder yet how I got through with it. **1851** Glisan *Army Life* 91: Dog gone you, Galen, where did you get those turkeys? **1851** M. Reid *Scalp-Hunters* 30: I'm dog-gone,Jim, if I don't feel queery about hyar. *Ibid.* 107: It's dog-gone good eatin', I say. **1853** "P. Paxton" *In Tex.* 27: Dog gone de fool! *Ibid.* 231: Shut up,…you dog-on, no-account critter. **1858** [S. Hammett] *Piney Woods* 41: I'm "dog on" ef I hadn't half a mind to try campin' out. **1871** Crofutt *Tourist's Guide* 164: Dog on my skin if it ain't. ***1873** Hotten *Slang Dict.: Dog gone,* a mild form of swearing used by boys. **1887** "Bunny" *Cow Boy* 98: They were profuse in their praises of my "grit," and from that day I ranked as a "dog on cow boy." **1900** Flandrau *Freshman* 248: They're so dog-gonned *right*. **1917** in Truman *Dear Bess* 227: You doggone bettya. **1926** W. James *Smoky* 134: Well, I'll be daggoned. **1929** "M. Brand" *Beacon Creek* 66: Dog-gone me if you don't talk like a scholar. **1935** Coburn *Law Rides Range* 6: Dog-gone. I shore made a mistake. *ca*1938 in D. Runyon *More Guys* 179: Oh, dag-gone her son! **1939** in A. Banks *First-Person* 259: The doggone thing moved its head and wagged its tail. **1940** F. Hunt *Trail fr. Tex.* 110: Daggone! George Ray! **1958** S.H. Adams *Tenderloin* 86: I don't think that's so doggone funny. **1962** G. Olson *Roaring Road* 85: You doggone right we will! *a*1973 in Bontemps *Old South* 97: You daggone right it didn't. **1984** Tiburzi *Takeoff?* 5: Did I really know my stuff? Well, doggone. **1986** Ciardi *Good Words* 93: We had a doggone good time!

doggy *adj.* **1.** attractively stylish; fancy.

1885 *Puck* (July 29) 343: "Oh, that's just too doggy for anything," approvingly remarked a radiant maiden. ***1889** in *OEDS.* ***1891** *F & H* II 303: *Doggy*…(colloquial). Stylish. **1894** *Lucky Bag* (No. 1) 66: *Doggy*…Swell. **1897** in *DARE:* Twenty years ago the college man had a most picturesque…vocabulary…"banger," "snab,"…"doggy," "mucker." **1906** *Army & Navy Life* (Nov.): *Doggy* is interpreted to mean *swell*. **1923** *Bomb* (Iowa State Coll.) 418: The boys are all neat and doggy dressers. **1929** Burnett *Iron Man* 162: "Take a look at this"…"Doggy." **1930** in D.O. Smith *Cradle* 14: We were issued doggy looking grey raincoats with a cape. **1936** Levin *Old Bunch* 245: Y'know a name I like? Clarence…Clarence is a doggy name. **1945** in *DARE:* It was no doggy place with tables.

2. *Av.* slow.

1978 in Higham & Williams *Combat Aircraft* 154: The range increased a bit, but the bird really got "doggy" with [pylon fuel tanks].

doggy *interj.* gosh!

1930 Sage *Last Rustler* 9: Doggie! I wisht I'd follered that yeller hound. **1948** J. Stevens *Jim Turner* 59 [ref. to *ca*1910]: Well, by doggy! That's news to me!

dog hair *n.* [sugg. by phr. *hair of the dog [that bit one]*] an alcoholic drink, usu. whiskey, taken as a supposed remedy for a hangover.

*ca***1940** in Botkin *Treas. Amer. Folk.* 544: No dog hair!…No booze-hister! Git out! **1963** D. Tracy *Brass Ring* 272: Tomlinson had come into this dump for some dog hair, himself.

dog-hanged *adj.* confounded; doggoned.

1893 in S. Crane *Complete Stories* 128: "Well, I be dog-hanged," he frequently said. **1894** S. Crane *Red Badge* 78: You always talk like a dog-hanged parson.

doghole *n.* **1.a.** a place supposedly fit only for dogs.

*****1579** in *OED:* The Schoole which I builde is narrowe, and at the first blushe appeareth but a doggehole. *****1601** Shakespeare *All's Well* II iii: France is a dog-hole. *ca***1624** Fletcher *Rule a Wife* III ii: Shall I never return to mine own house again? We are lodg'd here in the miserablest dog-hole. *****1726** J. Swift, in *OED:* You all live in a wretched dirty doghole and prison. **1830** W. Dunlap *Trip to Niagara* 28: So…here we must stay, in this wretched dog-hole. **1841** [Mercier] *Man-of-War* 193: Thank God we have bid a last adieu to Talcahuana; and my curses light on it, I say; I hope these eyes of mine will never behold that infernal *dog-hole* again.

b. *Naut.* a forecastle. Now *hist.*

*a***1947** in W.M. Camp *S.F.* 250: These "dogholes" were generally forward, below deck, ill-ventilated and unprotected against heat, cold, dampness, and fumes from the bilge and engine.

2. a low drinking den; DOGGERY; (*also*) a jail.

1818 in *DARE:* "The Fountain Inn" is…what you would call a doghole. **1859** Bartlett *Amer.* 181: Groggery…In the West, often called a Doggery or Dog-hole. **1860–61** R.F. Burton *City of Saints* 554: At every few miles was a drinking "calaboose"…In the Hispano-American countries it is used as a "common jail" or a "dog hole."

3. (see 1961 quot.).

1919 in *DARE:* And there's a dog-hole down on the Gold Coast where I intend to land this cargo. **1961** *WNID3: Doghole*…*West:* a small inlet on the coast where ships tie up in order to load lumber.

4. a small coal mine.

1943 Korson *Coal Dust on Fiddle* 4: Small mines…called…"dog holes." **1965** *World Bk. Dict.: Doghole*…*U.S. Slang.* a small coal mine.

doghouse *n.* **1.** a saloon; DOGGERY.

1821 in Royall *Letters from Ala.* 229: I ben't a dog to go into that are dog house.

2. Orig. *Army.* a pup tent.

1862 in Wightman *To Ft. Fisher* 42: "Dog houses" as the boys call our little shelter tents. **1863** in Heartsill *1491 Days* 167: We are all busy erecting our blanket tents, alias "Dog houses." **1864** in *Civil War Hist.* XXVIII (1982) 327: We reached…our dog houses shortly after dark. **1865** Springer *Sioux Country* 24: What would some of those…counter-hoppers think if they had to crawl into our dog-houses in such weather? **1899** Elmendorf *71st N.Y.* 38: It was in this storm that a head protruded from one of the wettest looking dog houses…"Sir, I have to report that this tent has sprung a leak and is sinking." **1917** McCann *Nat. Guard* 124: Some of the cooks…insisted on brewing coffee for the boys before they crawled into their dog houses for rest. **1921** Floyd *Co. F* 29 [ref. to 1918]: At night we could see the flash on the sides of our Dog House Tents, and a moment later we would hear a roar that would raise a sleeping man about two inches.

3. a place of confinement; jail.

1877 in Miller & Snell *Why West* 13: Miss Frankie Bell and one of her associates were deposited in the dog house this afternoon. *Ibid.* 278: She was finally landed in the dog house with him. *Ibid.* 323: Marshal Deger…started for the dog house with him. **1937** Herndon *Let Me Live* 110: For eleven days they kept me in jail and most of the time in the "dog house." The "dog house" is the place where they keep the insane prisoners…All night long the insane people raised an unearthly howl. **1941** Kendall *Army & Navy Slang* 5: Dog house…the guardhouse. **1987** *Miami Vice* (NBC-TV): There might be some fun in the old doghouse tonight.

4. *R.R.* a caboose.

1897 Hamblen *General Mgr.* 43: You go back in the doghouse an'…watch out good an' sharp that yer train don't break in two. **1900** in Botkin & Harlow *R.R. Folklore* 314: The "con" was…in the dog-

house. **1926** *AS* I (Jan.) 250: Doghouse. Freight caboose. **1937** *AS* (Apr.) 154: *Dog house.* Caboose. **1945** Hubbard *R.R. Ave.* 340: Doghouse—Caboose or its cupola.

5. *Baseball.* a dugout.

1908 in Fleming *Unforget. Season* 127: What happened in the doghouse, screened by red awnings, no one knows.

6. a more or less kennel-shaped shed, shack, or other shelter.

1918 *DN* V 24: *Doghouse man,* n. The man who sews sacks under a weather shelter on a combine. Farmers. **1929** *AS* IV 236: *Doghouse.* A small garage rented from a householder in a residence district, used for the safe storing of a stolen car for a few days until it can be disposed of. **1944** Boatright & Day *Hell to Breakfast* 147: A pumper's office is his "dog house" and the territory he covers is his "beat." **1951** Pryor *The Big Play* 150: Tom thought he must have wanted to get something from the pocket of his extra coat hanging in the doghouse. **1965** O'Neill *High Steel* 270: *Doghouse.* A shanty in which workmen change to work clothes.

7. *Jazz.* a double bass.

1920 *Atlantic Mo.* (Feb.) 180 [ref. to 1918]: An icy wind blew full upon the ill-starred doghouse that I clutched between my knees. **1923** McKnight *Eng. Words* 45: Dog-house, dog-kennel (bass violin). **1933** *Fortune* (Aug.) 47: *A couple of jigs got on the bus with a doghouse…*two Negroes got on the bus with a bass viol. **1936** Parker *Battling Hoofer* (film): Suppose you had to carry a doghouse around all your life. **1937** *AS* (Oct.) 181: *Doghouse.* Bass Fiddle (slapped, not bowed). **1947** Goffin *Horn* 114: Here a drummer carried the big drum on his head, there a bull-fiddler had not abandoned his bulky "dog-house." **1948** Manone & Vandervoort *Trumpet* 115: I had Carmen Mastren on guitar, and Sid Weiss on the doghouse. **1987** *CBS Sunday Morning* (CBS-TV) (Aug. 2): The double bass has been called a "doghouse,"…the "bullfrog of the orchestral lily pond."

8.a. a more or kess kennel-shaped housing or cover for a machine part or parts; (see also 1959 quot.).

1934 *WNID2: Doghouse*…any small kennel-shaped…part of a machine. **1951** Shidle *Clear Writing* 94: *Doghouse*…Covering of engine in cab-over-engine truck. **1959** Heflin *Aerospace Glossary: Doghouse,* n. A protuberance or blister that houses an instrument or instruments on an otherwise smooth skin of a rocket. **1972** *N.Y. Times Mag.* (Nov. 12) 95: On the "doghouse" over the engine between the two seats…he keeps a stack of paper towels. **1976** Bibb & Marcus *CB Bible* 92: *Dog house.* Motor cover.

b. *USAF.* (see quot.).

1945 Hamann *Air Words: Doghouse.* Stinger turret or tail turret of a bomber, particularly the B-29 Superfortress. In other type planes, the "doghouse" was an exposed cabin projecting from the main line or contour of the plane.

9. *Naut.* (see quots.).

1948 McHenry & Myers *Home Is Sailor* 69: The big Seamen's House on South Street, more familiarly known as the "Doghouse." **1972** Pearce *Pier Head Jump* 111: The Dog House is what everybody calls the Seaman's Church Institute over on South Street in Manhattan. It's this great big monstrous flophouse especially reserved for nothin' but us merchant seamen.

10. *Printing.* a circumflex; (*also*) a caretlike mark placed over a comma that is to be inserted into a text.

1961 *WNID3: Doghouse*…circumflex. **1982** *Chicago Manual* (ed. 13) 55.

¶ In phrase:

¶ **in the doghouse** in disfavor.

1926 Finerty *Criminalese* 31: *In doghouse*—In disfavor. **1936** Miller *Battling Bellhop* (film): Am I in the doghouse again? *Ibid.:* Am I out of the doghouse? **1936** Connell & Adler *Our Relations* (film): You know, that's funny. I'm in the doghouse, too. **1936** Monks & Finklehoffe *Brother Rat* 121: Then, when the game is over…Where will we be?…In the dog-house. **1942** Hollingshead *Elmtown's Youth* 234: Joan soon realized she was "in the dog house" with her clique mates and the acceptable boys. **1945** Wolfert *Guerrilla* 127: You're in the doghouse as far as the Navy is concerned. **1948** J.H. Burns *Lucifer* 275: I don't want to get anybody in the doghouse. **1957** MacDonald *Price of Murder* 91: Danny was responsible for the way Lee was acting. Danny had put her in the dog house…had really made her unfaithful to Lee. **1958** J. King *Pro Football* 90: Say, I'd have been in the doghouse if it had failed. **1960** Hurst *Family!* 113: Are we in the doghouse, and if so, why? **1969** L. Hughes *Under a Flare* 187: The three of them were in the doghouse with Captain Lyons. **1990** *U.S. News & W.R.* (Nov. 26) 17: After more than a decade in the doghouse…nuclear power is beginning to look viable once again.

dogie[1] *n.* [prob. alter. DOUGHGUT; poss. < Afr creole *dogi* 'small'] (esp. among cowboys) a runtish usu. motherless calf; (*broadly*) a usu. small or inferior adult animal, esp. a steer in a range herd. Now *S.E.*

1888 T. Roosevelt *Ranch Life* 89: A bunch of steers had been seen traveling…to the head of Elk Creek; they were mostly Texan *doughgies* (a name I have never seen written; it applies to young immigrant cattle). **1891** in J.I. White *Git Along* 96: We range-herded dogies/Out on the Little Dry. **1893** in J.I. White *Git Along* 17: Sing hooplio get along my little dogies,/For Wyoming shall be your new home. **1914** Callison *Bill Jones* 120: "What's a dogie?" one of the tenderfeet wanted to know. **1922** Knibbs *Saddle Songs* 42: When you're hazin' the dogies. **1929** "M. Brand" *Beacon Creek* 98: Rounded up a bunch of the Montague dogies. **1931** Larkin *Singing Cowboy* 18: Git along there you little dogies, git along there slow. **1933** J.V. Allen *Cowboy Lore* 51: Definition of *dogie*: A pore little calf who has no maw and whose papa ran off with another cow. **1935** *AS* (Dec.) 270: *Dogey* or *dogie*. Small common-bred cattle native to the southern states…The popularity of the term has caused it to be widely and indiscriminately used. **1940** Jones & Houser *Dark Command* (film): Them dogies are the bawlin'est critters I ever laid eyes on. **1942** *Calif. Folk. Qly.* I 208: Thus *dogie* occurs as merely a synonym of cattle, in *New Mexico* as "a motherless calf," and in *South Dakota* as "a young steer two or three years old." **1965** D. Moore *Cowboy* 210: *Dogie*—Motherless calf.

dogie[2] var. DUJI.

dog in a blanket *n.* (see *1891 quot.).

*1887 in *F & H* II 303: Bubble and squeak…is no more slangy than…dog in a blanket. *1891 in *F & H*: *Dog in a Blanket*…A pudding of preserved fruit spread on thin dough, rolled up, and boiled. **1893** "M. Twain" in *Sks. & Tales* 544 [ref. to *ca*1875]: In those old times the dinner bill of fare was always the same: a pint of some…homely soup, boiled codfish and potatoes, slab of boiled beef, stewed prunes for dessert—on Sundays "dog in a blanket," on Thursdays "plum duff."

dog it see s.v. DOG, *v.*

dog joint *n.* a cheap restaurant or a hot-dog stand.

1926 Finerty *Criminalese* 16: *Dog joint*—Place where sausages and sandwiches are sold.

dog kennel *n.* **1.** *Army.* DOG TENT.

1894 in J.I. Robertson *Blue & Gray* 45 [ref. to Civil War]: To enter one of these "dog-kennels," as they were called, you had to get down on your knees.

2. *Jazz.* a double bass.

1923 (quot. at DOGHOUSE, 7.).

3. *Baseball.* a dugout.

1926 *AS* I (Apr.) 369.

dog-kickers *n.pl.* the feet. *Joc.*

*ca*1851 in J.Q. Anderson *With the Bark On* 135: He had got a *ramfoozleifycation* in one of his dog-kickers so he couldn't walk no way it could be fixed.

dog meat *n.* **1.** a worthless or unattractive person or persons.

1908 in Fleming *Unforget. Season* 216: [They] look like dog meat when arrayed against other clubs. **1925–26** Black *You Can't Win* 200: You was a good bum, but you're dog's meat now. **1932** Hecht & Fowler *Great Magoo* 31: He's just a lot of dog-meat. **1944** W. Duff *Marine Raiders* (film): Come on, ya dirty buncha dog meat! **1965** Hardman *Chaplains* 14: Here, you in there…you, dog meat! You with the two left feet…fall out and get back to the ass end. **1987** Univ. Tenn. student theme: "Dog meat" refers to a female who resembles a canine. **1989** "Capt. X" & Dodson *Unfriendly Skies* 161: You can't imagine how stewardesses love to fly into Moslem country…They're treated like dog meat.

2. a person who is doomed, thoroughly defeated, or dead.

1977 J. Wylie *Homestead Grays* 304: You'll be dogmeat like the rest of us! **1985** *Miami Vice* (NBC-TV): In protective custody you walk, talk, and breathe. On the streets you're dog meat. **1986** Gilmour *Pretty in Pink* 120: When Bill and Joyce get through with you, you'll be dogmeat.

dog-nipper *n. Und.* (see quot.).

1859 Matsell *Vocab.* 26: *Dog-Nippers.* Rogues who steal dogs, and restore them to their owners after a reward has been offered.

Dog Patch *n.* [the name of the impoverished rural community in Al Capp's comic strip *Li'l Abner*] (see quots.). [Quots. ref. to Vietnam War.]

1988 C. Roberts & C. Sasser *Walking Dead* 77: Trucking through the slums of Da Nang we called "Dog Patch." **1989** *Care Viet. Spook Show* 104: Beyond the compound was the tar-paper-shack village known as Dogpatch…home to refugees and orphans and urchins and thieves and…VC. **1990** G.R. Clark *Words of Vietnam War* 149: Dogpatch GI nickname for the Vietnamese shanty towns that sprung up outside the gates of many U.S. base camps. *a*1991 J.R. Wilson *Landing Zones* 29: Dogpatch [was] two miles of whorehouses outside the [Danang] base.

dog pen *n. Army.* DOG TENT.

1863 Beatty *Volunteer* 173: Last fall the shelter tents were used for a time by the Pioneer Brigade. They are so small that a man cannot stand up in them. The boys…called them dog tents and dog pens.

dogpile *v.* (of groups of people) to leap on top of (someone). Also intrans. Also as *n.*

1945 in Shibutani *Co. K* 273: He can either take a beating from one man or…be dogpiled by a dozen men. **1947** *Merrie Melodies* (animated cartoon): It's a rabbit! Dog-pile on the rabbit! **1990** *Jim Henson's Muppet Babies* (CBS-TV): Dogpile on the kid with the glasses! **1992** *Donahue* (NBC-TV): *Dogpiling*—many wrestlers piling on one. **1993** "J.B. Briggs" in *Knoxville News-Sentinel* (Detours) (Nov. 11) 10: One guy actually crushed to death by a bimbo dogpile.

dog-raper *n. Army.* DOG-ROBBER.—used derisively.

1971 Sgt. E-7, U.S. Army, age *ca*40 (coll. J. Ball): The only one of you I can't get for KP is the dog-rapers. **1973** MSgt., U.S. Army, age *ca*50 (coll. J. Ball): You're turnin' into a regular dog-raper, aren't you, Private?

dog-rob *v. Army.* **1.** to work as an officer's orderly; be a DOG-ROBBER; (*hence*) to perform menial tasks for someone.

1878 Mulford *Fighting Indians* 45: An Orderly did not have to stand guard nor do much of anything but buzz the hired girl in the kitchen and eat up all the cold victuals he could find. This was called "dog robbing"—a very suitable name! **1898–1900** Cullen *Chances* 63: Necessitated the turning of his dog-robbing work over to another man. **1900** Baker *30th Inf.* 68: I took up my duty as orderly for the officers…This work is known as "dog robbing" by the enlisted men. **1900** Reeves *Bamboo Tales* 23: Daly [was] now "dog-robbing" for "Bues." **1918** *Sat. Eve. Post* (Nov. 2) 21: We were dog-robbing for the engineers all last winter—building railroads, unloading supply trains, putting up barracks. **1920** *Am. Leg. Wkly.* (May 14) 9: I took the sacred vow to dog rob until the hounds of war overran the field kitchens and cleaned up the very mess gear. **1936** *Our Army* (Aug.) 20: You may have had it too easy, had "gugus" dog-rob for you. **1942** *Yank* (Nov. 4) 16: We [telegraphers]…dog rob for the ATC.

2. to appropriate nonregulation material or other luxuries; pilfer; scrounge.

1919 Haterius *Remin.* 38 [ref. to WWI]: Another "commendable" feature of army life…was…"dog-robbing"…You take what the other fellow thought he had while this other fellow is looking the other way. **1975** Stanley *WWIII* 41: Sarge can go dogrobbing for his own damn rations. **1978** Diehl *Sharky's Machine* 69: I give you…anybody you can dog-rob outa some other department. *a*1990 R. Herman, Jr. *Force of Eagles* 106: The chief had been out dog-robbing.

3. *Army.* to idle; loaf. Now *hist.*

*ca*1930–73 E. Mackin *Suddenly Didn't Want to Die* 135 [ref. to 1918]: Moore and me were dog robbing a bit, keeping away from the drill and killing time.

dog-robber *n.* **1.** *Army.* a soldier or other person who pilfers scraps of usu. leftover food; scavenger; (*hence*) (*obs.*) a forager; scrounger.

*1832 B. Hall *Voyages* (Ser. 2) I 126: The dandified, shore-going, long-coated gentry…whom the sailors, in their coarse but graphic vocabulary, call "dog robbers," from their intercepting the broken meat on its way to the kennel from their master's table. **1862** Galwey *Valiant Hours* 66: On Tuesday the 16th we returned to our old quarters; but in our absence the camp followers—dog-robbers and pot-whollopers they are called—had pillaged our comfortable huts, leaving nothing but mere shells. **1864** in Gould *Maine Regt.* 485: A large gang of hostlers and men that we call "bummers" and "dog-robbers" came rushing in from the front where they had been foraging. **1913** Meyers *Ten Years in the Ranks* 210 [ref. to 1862]: The camp-followers, or "dog-robbers," as we called them, kept up close with the command to which they belonged, except when they heard any firing going on in front, in which case they did not show up until all was quiet again. **1919** Haterius *Remin.* 38: An efficient dog-robber can upon request obtain anything from a can of "corn willie" to a colonel's uniform, and no one is any the wiser. **1923**

Platt *Mr. Archer* 81: Come on, you dog-robbers, here's a bath offered to us. **1926** *Marine Gaz.* (Dec.) 241: You old dog robber, how in the H—l did yuh ever check in at this hotel? **1928** Scanlon *Have Mercy* 253 [ref. to 1918]: It was always customary to curse out the chow detail…We would call them all kinds of dog-robbers, accuse them of eating our food on the way, or of selling part of it to some other outfit. **1952** Wiley *Billy Yank* 244 [ref. to Civil War]: Each…took his turn in serving as cook—or "dogrobber" as some Yanks put it. **1966–67** W. Stevens *Gunner* 61 [ref. to WWII]: You do a big business…with the dog-robbers. **1975** Stanley *WWIII* 87: "Every outfit has a scrounger." "A dogrobber, huh?"

2. *Army.* an officer's orderly.—often used contemptuously. **1863** Hollister *Colo. Vols.* 149: Driven by (Gen.) Canby's "dogrobber" (private servant). **1865** in Horrocks *Dear Parents* 136: He is what the fellows here call my *dog-robber*…I believe the origin of it is this: If an officer has such a man, he generally allows him to dine from the leavings on the table, so as the man gets what is the dog's share, he is called a dog-robber. **1868** *Harper's Mo.* (Feb.) 300: From that time there was not a more energetic snake-hunter in camp than our "dog-robber" "Schleswig." **1888** McConnell *Cavalryman* 107: Every officer in the army has (or had twenty years ago) one or more of the enlisted men hanging around his quarters, who perform service part military and part menial, who fall heir to his cast off clothing, drink his whiskey, run errands for his wife, build chicken coops, draw rations, attend his horses, and, in short, gobble up all the "crumbs" of whatever kind that "fall from his table;" hence the very expressive term *dog-robber.* **1890** Finerty *War-Path* 304: I know that many soldiers employ the offensive name "dog robbers" to comrades who do what is called menial work for their officers. **1893** C.C. King *Waring's Peril* 79: He's gone to get square with the lieutenant and his cockney dog-robber. **1900** Reeves *Bamboo Tales* 19: "Cougar" Daly's connection with the company had not extended two days till he was duly installed as "dog-robber" for Lieutenant John Buestom. **1906** M'Govern *Sarjint Larry* (gloss.): *Dog-Robber:*—A soldier who does work for an officer. **1913** Meyers *Ten Years in the Ranks* 149 [ref. to 1857]: Our corpulent commander did not leave the sleigh, and had his breakfast cooked and brought to him by his "dog-robber," as the men called an officer's soldier-servant. **1919** Cober *Btty. D* 80: He was a "dog robber" for several officers, but popular nevertheless. **1922** Paul *Impromptu* 157: The "dog robber" from the officer's mess approached with a paper. **1930** Barkley *No Hard Feelings!* 97 [ref. to 1918]: The battalion commander came along followed by a bunch of "dog-robbers"—our name for orderlies. **1941** Hargrove *Pvt. Hargrove* 84: *Dog robber*—an orderly. **1949** J. Jones, in *Harper's* (June) 97: You could even have a bed-roll and a dog-robber. **1965** Beech *Make War in Madness* 193: "I'm an aide."…"How do you like being a dog-robber?"…"I don't think of it that way." **1973** Gwaltney *Destiny's Chickens* 5: He had been Major Tay Hogg's dog robber. **1984** in Terkel *Good War* 162 [ref. to WWII]: A dog robber is a guy that cleans the officer's quarters, shines his shoes, takes this, drives a jeep and everything.

3. *Esp. Army.* a flunky; lackey. **1892** Cox *5 Yrs. in Army* 107 [ref. to 1875]: A big surly savage scowled at our scout and said something about "dog robbers." That was insult enough to precipitate a fight. **1898–1900** Cullen *Chances* 60: He had been holding down the job of dog-robber for the bookmakers for two seasons. **1903** Benton *Cowboy Life on Sidetrack* 50: Milord's dogrobber speaks up. **1908** in Weaver *Brownsville Raid* 221: The few soldiers who conscientiously tried to help their white officers investigate the shooting "were called 'dog robbers,' and made to feel the displeasure of their fellows," Browne and Baldwin reported. **1921** Benet *Wisdom* 287: There was the battery dog-robber…who licked non-commissioned boots and greased non-commissioned palms and applied for a three-day pass every fortnight. **1926** *Amer. Leg. Mo.* (Sept.) 9 [ref. to 1918]: He's a bootlicker, a handshaker, a natural-born dog-robber, and if you don't do something about him, Grasby, you and I are going to have a falling out. **1930** "D. Stiff" *Milk & Honey* 204: *Dog robber*…a flunky. **1972** *Banyon* (NBC-TV): Get yourself another dog-robber.

dog-robbing *adj.* lazy. Now *hist.* **1925** Thomason *Fix Bayonets!* 203 [ref. to 1918]: Hey, yuh dog-robbin' battalion runner, you—what's up? *ca*1930–73 E. Mackin *Suddenly Didn't Want to Die* 133 [ref. to 1918]: We guys of the battalion headquarters group sure had a dog-robbin' time through those days…free men.

dog's age *n. No.* a very long time. Cf. DOG'S YEARS. **1836** *Knickerbocker Mag.* VII 17: That blamed line gale has kept me in bilboes such a dog's age. **1916** in *OEDS*. **1959** E. Hunter *Killer's Wedge* 69: The Puerto Rican girl was the most delicious-looking female he had seen in a dog's age. **1992** Strawberry & Rust *Darryl* 209: This guy

hasn't pitched in a dog's age.

dog's body *n.* **1.** *Naut.* pease pudding. *1818 in *OEDS*: I'll get you the Dog's-body Squeezer. **1849** Melville *White Jacket* 134 [ref. to 1843]: Scouse, Lob-scouse…Lob-Dominion, Dog's Body, [etc.]. *1851 in *F & H* II 303. *1883 Russell *Sailors' Lang.* 42: *Dogs-body.*—A mess made of pea-soup, powdered biscuit, and slush. **1901** (quot. at STRIKE-ME-BLIND). **1945** Colcord *Sea Language* 67: *Dog's-body.* A sea dish of peas boiled in a cloth like pudding. **2.** an inconsequential person, esp. a menial or drudge. Also **dogbody.** [The term app. arose in the Royal Navy, where it was applied esp. to junior midshipmen; see *OEDS*.] *1922 T.E. Lawrence, in *OEDS*: I'll have got used to being a dog's body. *1925 Fraser & Gibbons *Soldier & Sailor Wds.* 80 [ref. to WWI]: He's only a dogsbody sub. **1952** Brossard *Darkness* 153: Where is that dog's body Porter? **1966** Terry *Viet Rock* 43: That's a protestor, you dogbody, you piss-headed lassie! *Ibid.* 53: Goddammit you dogbodies! **1974** E. Thompson *Tattoo* 242: That tall, dark sailor…had appointed himself her unofficial dogsbody, *happy* for any errand or mundane word. **1982** *California* (Feb.) 72: The center's clout comes from the dogsbody work of taking part in public hearings, alerting the troops to important developments, and filing legal challenges when necessary.

dog's breakfast *n.* a mess; confused mixture. *1934 (cited in Partridge *DSUE* 231). *1936 in Partridge *DSUE*: *Dog's breakfast.* A mess: low Glasgow. *1959, *1963 in *OEDS*. **1970** Thackrey *Thief* 110: But, man! Didn't I feel like a dog's breakfast! **1978** *Business Week* (Apr. 24) 79: For all of these reasons [*sc.* regulatory and competitive difficulties]…"coal is a dog's breakfast." *a*1986 in *NDAS*: The plot is a dog's breakfast of half-baked ideas. **1987** R.M. Brown *Starting* 88: We're mixed up worse than a dog's breakfast. **1993** W. Safire, in *N.Y. Times* (Feb. 22) A 17: A dog's breakfast of a budget proposal.

dog's chance *n.* the least chance. Now *rare* in U.S. **1842** *Spirit of Times* (Aug. 27) 301: Wagner [a racehorse]…never had a decent dog's chance. *1902 in *OEDS*: They all felt that Adderman's wouldn't have a dog's chance when Ardenwood College had got fairly going. *1939 in *OEDS*. **1942** in *ATS* 188. **1987** *RHD2*: That product didn't have a dog's chance of succeeding.

dog's duty *n. Army.* dull or unpleasant military duty. **1878** Mulford *Fighting Indians* 151: Old man, I wish that I was you. You are now your own boss; and will not have to do dog's duty any more!

dog's head *n.* a kind of beer. **1897** Norris *Vandover* 361: "Bring me a stringy rabbit and a pint of dog's-head."…They…settled down to their beer and rabbits. **1899** (quot. at WHIZZ).

dog shift *n.* DOG WATCH. **1977** S. Foote *September September* 71: I was working the dog shift at U.S. Gypsum. **1980** *Harper's* (Oct.) 57: The foreman from last night's dog shift had set the machines, as usual. **1990** G.R. Clark *Words of Vietnam War* 148: *Dog Shift* Slang for the work shift from 1800…to 0600 hours.

dogshit *n.* **1.** daylights; hell.—usu. considered vulgar. **1967** W. Crawford *Gresham's War* 116 [ref. to 1950's]: He just knocked the dogshit out of one M.P. **1962–68** in B. Jackson *In the Life* 434: Your old man…ought to kick the dog shit out of you. **1972** Jenkins *Semi-Tough* 288: Winnin' ain't the only good thing in life but it beats the dog shit out of whatever's next. **1976** Univ. Akron student: I'll beat the dogshit out of him. **1977** Univ. Tenn. student: He could play the dogshit out of that fiddle! It was beautiful! **1984** Sample *Racehoss* 85: He'd beat the dogshit out of her.

2. something that is thoroughly unsatisfactory, worthless, or contemptible; (*specif.*) nonsense; HORSESHIT.—usu. considered vulgar. **1965–68** E.R. Johnson *Silver St.* 58: Telling you not to hand them that…dogshit. **1971** H.S. Thompson *Las Vegas* 107: I'm tired of listening to this dogshit. **1972** C. Gaines *Stay Hungry* 196: "These people stand for a quality of life, a kind of dignity and grace…" "Dogshit," said Mary Tate. *a*1986 in *NDAS*: None of this fancy-pants bullshit, poodle-top haircuts and fancy clothes. None of that dogshit. **1986** Jarmusch *Down by Law* (film): Whatchoo lookin' at, dogshit? **1992** Mowry *Way Past Cool* 6: That ain't nuthin but TV dogshit, sucker!

3. anything; SHIT.—usu. considered vulgar. **1976** Akron Univ. student: So I wasn't looking up for dogshit. **1992** Mowry *Way Past Cool* 89: Lots of word go round don't mean dogshit.

4. (used as a standard of comparison).—usu. considered

vulgar. [1926 quot., ref. to WWI, is almost certainly euphem.]

[**1926** Nason *Chevrons* 29: He must have been mean as dogwood and twice as nasty.] **1969** Beck *Black Widow* 118: Ain't worth a pint of dog shit. **1973** Overgard *Hero* 82: It's been a good berth, the kind every retired sailor dreams about, but dull as dog shit. **1976** Rosen *Above Rim* 13: You ain't worth dog shit in the street. **1978** Schrader *Hardcore* 45: Those Mexican phones ain't worth dogshit, so I thought I better call from here. **1985** Dye *Between Raindrops* 118: The...ricochets [will] kill you dead as dog shit. **1989** G.C. Wilson *Mud Soldiers* 132: I was drunker than dogshit.

dogshit *adj.* **1.** worthless; contemptible; thoroughly unsatisfactory.—usu. considered vulgar.

*ca*1967 in Tuso *Vietnam Blues* 133: Always in dogshit weather. **1970–71** Rubinstein *City Police* 390: I guess he's never seen that dog-shit numbers slip you got. **1974** Univ. Wisc. student: So just turn in a dogshit notebook. **1987** Robbins *Ravens* 202: The weather was dogshit and we...were really on the retreat.

2. crazy.—usu. considered vulgar. Cf. APESHIT, BATSHIT.

1981–85 S. King *It* 66: Stuttering so badly that it almost drove you dogshit. **1986** Merkin *Zombie Jamboree* 159: The dog...instantly started going ape-shit or dog-shit.

dogskin *n.* a person's own skin. *Joc.*

1845 in *DAE*: Dern my everlastin' dog-skin er I'll stand it! **1850** Garrard *Wah-to-Yah* ch. xxiv: Feel if you haven't got a hole in your dogskin. **1876** J.M. Reid *Old Settlers* 111: Hugh W. Sample "tanned their dog skins," and was made President of the Public Works.

dog's nose *n.* (see 1909 quot.); (*also*) a mixture of the residue of various alcoholic drinks.

*1812 (cited in Partridge *DSUE* (ed. 8)). **1836* Dickens *Pickwick* ch. xxxiii: Dog's nose...[is] compounded of warm porter, moist sugar, gin, and nutmeg. **1890–91* *F & H* II 303: Dog's-nose...(common).—A mixture of gin and beer. **1891** Campbell, Knox & Byrnes *Darkness & Daylight* 496: This liquid [remains of drinks, ladled from a tub] is known by fancy names such as "dog's nose," "all-sorts," "swipes," and other terms. **1909** *WNID*: Dog's nose. A mixed drink of beer or ale and gin or rum. **1975** (cited in Partridge *DSUE* (ed. 8)).

dog soldier *n. Army.* **1.** DOG-ROBBER, 2.

1900 in Remington *With the Bark On* 156: Saw the "old man" in a nipa hut with a doctor, and between them old Oestreicher, shot through the head and dying. There was the colonel sitting around doing what he could for his old dog soldier. I tell you it was a mighty touching sight.

2. a common soldier; DOGFACE, 2.a.

1946–50 J. Jones *Here to Eternity* ch. xxxiii [ref. to 1941]: Got paid out on Monday/Not a dog soljer no more. **1958** Frankel *Band of Bros.* 48: Man,...you are the luckiest dog soldiers! **1977** *N.Y. Times Bk. Review* (July 24) 18: His ear for dialog, the rhythmic profanity of the dog soldier, is especially sensitive. **1983** Goldman & Fuller *Charlie Co.* 12: The doughboys of World War I and the dog soldiers of World War II commonly served longer tours under more sustained fire. **1987** *Daily Beacon* (Univ. Tenn.) (May 8): No one bothered to debrief the average dog-soldier after they got home [from Vietnam].

dog's paste *n.* (see quot.).

1859 Matsell *Vocab.* 26: Dogs-Paste. Sausage-meat; mince-meat.

dog's soup *n.* water, usu. as opposed to alcohol. Also **dog soup**. *Joc.*

*1785 Grose *Vulgar Tongue*: Dog's Soup. Rain water. **1836* in *F & H* II 304: For she never lushes *dog's-soup* or lap. **1890–91* in *F & H* II 304: Dog's soup...(common).—Water. **1936** *AS* (Feb.) 43: Dog soup. Water.

dog-style *adj. & adv.* DOG-FASHION. Occ. as *n.*

1954–60 in *DAS*. **1967** M. Howard *Call Me Brick* 53: What's dog-style? **1970** *Nat. Lampoon* (Apr.) 56: Doin' It Dog-Style or "Lass but Not Leash." **1971** Simon *Sign of Fool* 145: "Spyder, ya wanna do it dog style?"...Lacking vaseline, I found an old tube of...hair cream and lubricated her...ass. **1971** Wilson *Bent* (unp.): Some nice dog-style while whizzin' through space. **1985** J. Dillinger *Adrenaline* 18: Down on all fours...beckoning all...dog-style devotees.

dog's years *n.pl.* [cf. possibly related syn. Northeastern Yid *hunts yorn*, lit. 'dog's years'] a very long time; DOG'S AGE; DONKEY'S YEARS.

1956 M. Wolff *Big Nick.* 62: Once in dog's years we go out together.

dogtag *n. Mil.* an identification tag worn by military personnel. Now *S.E.*

1918 in K. Morse *Letters* 68: He took their names and then was inspired to look at their "dog tags" in confirmation and found that not one of the names agreed! **1918** Straub *Diary* (entry for July 24): After evening mess we had dog-tag inspection. **1921** Dos Passos *Three Soldiers* 354: Look at his dawg-tag, Handsome. **1922** Colonna *Co. B* 77: The next man took the "dog tags" and asked your name and number and compared your answer with the tags. **1926** Nason *Chevrons* 253: What's the name on that dog-tag? **1944** H. Brown *Walk In the Sun* 41: Let the bombardier up there...be a fraction of an inch off, and they might not even find your dog-tags. **1945** Monks *Ribbon & Star* 48: If he hits that ammo dump, they won't even find our dog tags. **1961** L.G. Richards *TAC* 37: Each...had his dog tags rechecked. **1965** C.D.B. Bryan *Wilkinson* 356: I got a new set of dog tags which were different from the ones I had in Korea. **1977** Caputo *Rumor of War* 269: Sergeant Bittner, get me the dog tags of the evacs, and hustle. **1982** R.A. Anderson *Cooks & Bakers* 204: Check his dog tag. What's his religion? **1984** T. Clancy *Red October* 201: Don't your guys wear dogtags?

dog tent *n.* Orig. *Army.* a PUP TENT.

1862 in Andrus *Letters* 25: We have tents called Dog tents. Just large enough for 2! 5 feet square. **1862** in Bear *Letters* 12: He soon saw enough of our little dog tents. **1863** McIntyre *Federals* 197: There is a regular little city of dog tents. **1870** Keim *Sheridan's Troopers* 165: The men...began to exercise their ingenuity in contriving...additions to the limited space allowed by their "dog" tents. **1891** Bourke *On the Border* 251: A minimum supply of "A" and "dog" tents. **1898** King *Warrior Gap* 17: Two companies...pitched their "dog tents." **1916** *Army & Navy Jour.* (Sept. 2) 31: "Charley, dear," said young Mrs. Tomkins, "they have dog tents in the army, don't they?" **1919** Amerine *Alabama's Own* 42: The nights spent in the little "dog" tents while on the march were bitterly cold. **1919** Gilder *Defending Democracy* 268: We put up our "dog-tents" after a six-mile hike through mud and rain. **1955** Post *Little War* 15 [ref. to 1898]: He and Jack O'Brien bunked together in their dog tent.

dog town *n.* [sugg. by phr. *try it out on the dog*] *Theat.* a town or city where a theatrical production is tried out before it appears in a major metropolitan theater. [Cf. entry in *DARE*, which cites towns actually named "Dog Town."]

1901 *Chi. Tribune* (July 28) 36: The "dog" towns, such as Elizabeth, N.J., New Haven, and also Baltimore and Washington, can count up most all the successes—and failures. **1923** *N.Y. Times* (Sept. 9) VII 2: Dog towns: Where plays are tested before being brought to New York. **1924** Isman *Weber & Fields* 249 [ref. to *ca*1900]: It was a prevalent custom...not to bring a show to Broadway until it had been smoothed and polished in try-out performances at Wilmington, Atlantic City, Bridgeport or some such "dog" town. **1961** *WNID3*.

dog tune *n.* see DOG, *n.*, 15.a.

dog-wagon *n.* a lunch wagon.

1900 *DN* II 32: Dog-wagon...Night lunch-wagon. [In use at Harvard Univ.]. **1928** *New Yorker* (Dec. 8) 24: The food...is fairly good in dog wagons. **1936** Dos Passos *Big Money* 358: Let's go to the dogwagon and tell Tony. **1941** in Stilwell *Papers* 23: Had chow at dog-wagon. **1946** *New Directions* 205: He's down in that dogwagon middle the block. **1952** *New Yorker* (Feb. 16) 53: He preferred dog wagons to Le Pavillon. **1966** Longstreet & Godoff *Wm. Kite* 93: The depot dog wagon called The Beanpot, for deadly hamburgers.

dog watch *n.* a night shift; (*specif.*) (see 1942, 1966 quots.).

1901 in *OEDAS* I 93: The building shakes with the rumble of the presses; the "dog watch," detailed to duty in the event of news demanding an extra, opens its game of poker. **1902** Clapin *Amer.* 162: Dog watch. Among reporters attached to an evening paper, said of being on duty from nine until midnight. **1935** Pollock *Und. Speaks*: Dog watch, employees of gambling house who begin work at midnight. **1942** *ATS* 495: Dogwatch...the shift of newspapermen after the regular editions have gone to press. **1954** *AS* XXIX 274: Dogwatch. The third or last watch detail (6 p.m. to 9 a.m.) [in a firehouse]. **1962** in *AS* XL (1965) 255: Dog watch. After-midnight broadcasting. **1966** *RHD*: Dog watch...Journalism slang. The period, after the regular editions have gone to press, during which staff personnel remain on duty to await any new developments that may warrant an extra issue.

dog water *n.* clear drops of seminal fluid.

1965 C. Brown *Manchild* 80 [ref. to 1940's]: "Man, that's the real stuff."..."Man, that ain't nothin' but dog water." **1976** *Esquire* (Sept.) 136: Also, a spot of "dog water" there, pre-coital seepage, as if a puppy had peed in my lap. **1986** J.A. Friedman *Times Sq.* 103: No dry spasms, piss or clear drops of dog water!

dog work *n.* tedious, esp. menial, work; drudgery; DONKEY WORK.

1985 Boyne & Thompson *Wild Blue* 256: Eatherton…gave her most of the office dog work to do. **1987** *RHD2.* **1990** Julia Child, in *Cosmopolitan* (May) 246: It's important to learn all the dog work so you can do it very fast.

do-hickey var. DOOHICKEY.

do in *v.* to kill, beat up, tire out, destroy, injure, cheat, betray, etc.; in phr. **do (oneself) in** to commit suicide. Now *S.E.*

*1905 in *OEDS* I 829: I heard people tell her to do me an injury, throw glasses at me, and "do me in." ***1917** in *OEDS:* I feel absolutely done in. **1919* *Athenaeum* (July 25) 664: "To be done in," to get killed. **1927** in E. Wilson *Twenties* 432: Franz has done himself in. **1934** *WNID2.* **1939* *New Directions* 75: He doesn't make any bones about doing Tom in. **1952** Ellson *Golden Spike* 3: His best friend doing him in? **1965** C. Brown *Manchild* 113: Johnny used to be always on the verge of getting done in. **1966** Thompson *Hell's Angels* 11: The Angels hunted them down one by one and did them in. **1971** Dahlskog *Dict.* 19: *Do in*…to exhaust, as: It *does* me *in* to stay up late. **1963–78** J. Carroll *B. Diaries* 9: A giant fire…did in three buildings on the corner of 25th Street. **1978** Wharton *Birdy* 53: How many people in my family have done themselves in?

doink *n. Stu.* a clumsy, obnoxious, or overly studious person.

1968 Baker et al. *CUSS* 106: *Doink.* A person who always does the wrong thing. **1969** *Current Slang* I & II 28: *Doink*, n. A bookworm, a grind.—Air Force Academy cadets. **1989** *New Yorker* (Nov. 13) 53: He's not a dork. He's a dufus. Maybe. Maybe a doink.

do-it fluid *n. Black E.* alcoholic liquor. *Joc.*

1968 in *DARE.* **1978** C. Miller *Animal House* 69: Hey, we ready to play, man. We need some do-it fluid. **1967–80** Folb *Runnin' Lines* 235: *Do-it fluid* Liquor.

dojee var. DUJI.

dojigger var. DOOJIGGER.

dokus *n.* TOKUS.

1949 H.L. Mencken, in *New Yorker* (Oct. 1) 56: Woodrow Wilson…landed on his *dokus* like the humblest of the common…professors.

dol or **doll** *n.* a dollar.

1850 in *DA:* The steemers "Noo World" & "Hartford" were going to run to Frisky at from 3 to 5 dols a tikket. **1857** in *Calif. Hist. Soc. Qly.* IX (1930) 161: Win about twenty doll's. **1871** *Yale Naught-Ical Alm.* 24: Fine 5000 Dolls. **1883** in F. Remington *Sel. Letters* 32: One thousand dol's…for expenses. **1885** *Puck* (Apr. 8) 83: Here, Mike, take a couple of dols for drinks.

doll *n.* **1.a.** [cf. earlier literary sense, 'mistress'] a woman, esp. if young and attractive.

1840 *Spirit of Times* (Nov. 21) 447: Oh, she was a rael [*sic*] doll! she was a dandy, that's a fact. **1846* in Partridge *DSUE* (ed. 7) 1105: Soldiers and their Dolls…another resort for soldiers and their girls. **1858* Mayhew *Paved with Gold* 101: The insulting epithet of "doll" was applied to every aged female, the younger members of the gentler sex being known by the peculiar title of "doxy." *Ibid.* 102: A doll and a kiddy! **1900** Ade *More Fables* 153: It's a good thing for a Strong Josher to come along now and then, just to show you Proud Dolls how to take a Joke. **1903** McCardell *Chorus Girl* 53: I'm getting my education among a bunch of society dolls. **1908** H. Green *Maison* 8: You had only to take one peek at that old doll's face. **1911** *Adventure* (Jan.) 442: Agnes…has the English dolls aboard looking like a row of lead nickels. **1911** A.H. Lewis *Apaches of N.Y.* 80: "He never made no money off a woman." "Never in all his life took a dollar off a doll!" **1918** *Bugler* (Mar. 9) 3: "Now he is talking about that doll again." "Sure she is a dream—not." **1921** *Variety* (Apr. 1) 7: A swell lookin' doll trips down one of the aisles and climbs up on the stage. **1926** Donahue *What Price Glory?* (film): I warned the men about these French dolls. **1930** D. Runyon, in *Collier's* (Jan. 20) 12: A big fat old doll who does not talk English comes in. **1970** Wakefield *All the Way* 20: He didn't know what the hell the old doll was talking about. **1991** *Beetlejuice* (ABC-TV): It's Mr. Monitor and his new doll.

b. *Homosex.* a catamite; (*also*) a passive female homosexual.

1949 *Gay Girl's Gde.* 8: *Doll*…a beautiful kid. **1963** Stearn *Grapevine* 3: For every butch, of course, there was a feminine counterpart—the "femme" or "doll." **1970** L.D. Johnson *Devil's Front Porch* 109 [ref. to 1920]: He cannot let another man take his "doll" without retaliating.

2. see DOL.

3.a. (used as an endearment).

1866 in *Iowa Jour. of Hist.* LVII (1959) 201: He said she was his idol, ideal, doll,…duck, [etc.]. **1942** *ATS* 216: Child Pet Names…*doll.* **1949** *Gay Girl's Gde.* 8: *Doll:* As a vocative, synonymous with *darling.* **1954** Matheson *Born of Man & Woman* 21: "Help your mother, doll," he told his daughter.

b. an attractive or pleasant person of the opposite sex.

1920 Fitzgerald *Paradise* 129: If a blond girl doesn't talk we call her a "doll," if a light-haired man is silent he's considered stupid. **1933** Hammett *Thin Man* 239: That guy's so handsome…Just a big doll. **1953** Hackett & Goodrich *Give Girl a Break* (film): Ted! You're a doll! **1961** *Dick Van Dyke Show* (CBS-TV): Rob is a doll. **1967** Hinton *Outsiders* 23: Man, your brother is one doll. **1983** W. Walker *Dime to Dance* 53: This is my ex-husband. Isn't he a doll?

c. a superlative example.

1836 in Haliburton *Sam Slick* 48: I raised a four-year-old colt once…could gallop like the wind; a rael [*sic*] daisy, a perfect doll. **1972** Halberstam *Best & Brightest* 236: We have a doll of a car and people will buy it.

4. [said to have been coined by Jacqueline Susann in her novel *Valley of the Dolls* (1966); but cf. DOLLY, 2.a] a tablet or capsule containing a barbiturate or occ. an amphetamine.

1966 Susann *Valley of Dolls* 421: I think tonight I may take my first doll. **1974** Hyde *Mind Drugs* 152: *Blue Dolls*…Amytal Sodium. *Ibid.* 156: *Red Dolls*…Seconal Sodium. *Ibid.* 159: *Yellow Dolls*…Nembutal Sodium. **1986** *NDAS.*

dollar *n.* one hundred dollars.

1972 Smith & Gay *Don't Try It* 200: *Dollar.* One hundred dollars. **1974** Hyde *Mind Drugs* 153: *Dollar*…One hundred dollars. **1993** *L.A. Times Mag.* (May 23) 11: Gambler gab…*dollar n.* $100.

¶ In phrase:

¶ **another day, another dollar** (used ironically to indicate the tedium of one's occupation).

1920 Skillman *A.E.F.* 173: Familiar Expressions of the A.E.F.: Another day, another dollar; a million days, a million dollars.

dollar boat *n. U.S. Coast Guard.* (see quot.). Now *hist.*

1971 Waters *Smugglers* 60 [ref. to ca1920]: The 100- and 125-footers, which we called "dollar" and "dollar-and-a-quarter boats"…, were steel-hulled, with twin diesels.

Dollar-Four *n. USAF.* the Lockheed F-104 Starfighter aircraft.

1963 E.M. Miller *Exile* 132: Just made it in for the happy hour in my burnin' churnin' fireball Dollar-Four. *Ibid.:* Incidentally, you don't fly this Dollar-Four, man, you just aim it.

dollar hole *n.* (see quot.).

1958 McCulloch *Woods Words* 49: *Dollar hole*—Compound low gear on a truck.

dollar ride *n.* [fr. the informal custom of paying a flight instructor one dollar for the privilege of flying] *Mil. Av.* **1.** a flight cadet's initial training flight.

1975 in Higham & Siddal *Combat Aircraft* 5: The initial "dollar" ride was truly a joy! **1987** Fleisher *Top Flight* (CBS-TV). **1989** *Comments on Ety.* (Jan.) 5 [ref. to 1956]: The "dollar ride," the first assay aloft in the aircraft (a T-33, or "T-bird").

2. a pilot's first combat flight.

1987 Robbins *Ravens* 13 [ref. to Vietnam War]: After a few dummy tree-busting runs a FAC was supposed to be ready for the real thing, known in the trade as the "dollar ride." *a*1991 Kross *Splash One* 245: So the new GIB flew his "dollar ride," his first introduction to the easiest part of the combat zone.

doll down *v.* DOLL UP.

1987 in *N.O. Review* (Spring, 1988) 50: Some high-classed looking female all dolled down.

dollface *n.* an attractive person of the opposite sex.—usu. used as an endearment.

1905 J. London *Game* 49: That stuck-up doll-face. **1951** M. Shulman *Many Loves* 69: Hello, dollface. **1990** Thorne *Dict. Contemp. Sl.* 142: *Dollface n. American* an attractive or cute person.

doll out *v.* DOLL UP.

1928 Santee *Cowboy* 124: Joe put on a pretty shirt, an' dolled himself all out.

doll up *v.* to make or become neat, attractive, fancy, or elegant, esp. in dress or grooming; dress up. Now *colloq.*

*1906 in *OEDS.* 1908 in H.C. Fisher *A. Mutt* 110: I'll show 'em I can keep dolled up. 1910 *N.Y. Eve. Jour.* (Apr. 6) 16: Run on in...and get dolled up. 1912 Stringer *Shadow* 253: You're all dolled up...like a lobster palace floater. 1915 H.L. Wilson *Ruggles* 97: Does he doll Sourdough up like that all the time? 1917 in Grider *War Birds* 35: The Colonel wants to doll us up like Englishmen. 1920 Cheley *Fifty-Minus* 17: I didn't see any use anyway in "dolling up." 1920 O'Neill *Diff'rent* 226: He'll be busy as a bird dog for an hour getting himself dolled up to pay you a call. 1924 Howard *What They Wanted* 136: In there, gettin' dolled up. 1925 W. James *Drifting Cowboy* 42: I'm all dolled up. 1927 *AS* II (May) 352: *Dolled up.* Dressed well. "She is all dolled up in her best clothes." 1928 W.C. Williams *Pagany* 73: A few dolled-up old women on the raised hotel emplacements looked curiously at them.

dolly *n.* **1.** an attractive young woman.
[*1891 *F & H* II 304: *Dolly*...A mistress.] *1906 in *OEDS.* 1913 *Sat. Eve. Post* (July 5) 4: Myrtle is certainly some dolly! 1914 Knibbs *Outlands* 57: And he winks at some pink dollie what lays down her cigarette,/Waddles on the stage and sings, "The Boys in Blue." 1917–20 Dreiser *Newspaper Days* 141 [ref. to 1890's]: A girl or two...—friends of...these newspaper men, their "dollies." 1926–35 Watters & Hopkins *Burlesque* 25: What a dumb dolly you are. 1945 in Kluger *Yank* 273: We need some real live dollies. 1951 [VMF-323] *Old Ballads* 37: I would rather lay a dollie than be shot up in Mig Alley. 1952 J.D. MacDonald *Damned* 36: He stared at the old dollie in the back seat. 1956 H. Ellison *Deadly Streets* 192: He's got plenty to take his dollie out. 1961 Terry *Old Liberty* 10: It was where the Liberty boys went to drink beer and pick up the dollies. 1963 Braly *Shake Him* 64: You're a bold dolly. 1969–71 Kahn *Boys of Summer* 289: You got caught with a dolly. Run and you make yourself look worse. 1973 Gent *N. Dallas* 18: Don't forget to call, we'll get some dollies. 1974 *N.Y. Times Bk. Review* (Apr. 14) 19: Persons of my gender are also regularly referred to by Rolling Stone as chickies, broads, dollies, foxes, and so-and-so's old lady. 1984 Holland *Let Soldier* 213: He's hardly met a dollie, and he's off into the night with her.

2.a. *Narc.* Dolophine, a trademark for a brand of methadone; a capsule containing Dolophine or an equivalent product.
1954 in W.S. Burroughs *Letters* 198: Both ex-junkies...chippying with dollies. 1957 in Rosset *Evergreen Reader* 116: Even without dollies...I could kick it in three days. 1962 Larner & Tefferteller *Addict In Street* 69: He was giving out dollies and goof-balls to everyone. 1965 in Sanchez *Word Sorcerers* 193: He...sed he wud git her a coupla sleeping pills. He wud also pick up some dollies fo himself cuz Saturday wuz kicking time fo him. 1966 Schaap *Turned On* 149: Dollies. Dolophine (brand of) methadone. 1962–68 B. Jackson *In the Life* 88: I had one little bitty piece of dolly in my aspirin box. *a*1979 Pepper & Pepper *Straight Life* 167: Some dollies, some Dolophines.

b. DOLL, 4.
1970 Landy *Underground Dict.* 68: *Dolly*...Any drug in pill form.

3. a thing; item. *Joc.*
1961 Brosnan *Pennant Race* 44: We'll win this little dolly [a baseball game] four to one. *Ibid.* 63: We're tryin' to find out what makes this dolly jump, Broz.

dollybird *n.* an attractive young woman. *Rare* in U.S.
*1984 Partridge *DSUE* (ed. 8): *Dolly-bird*...since early 1960's, but not gen. before *ca*1967...The term belongs particularly to the brief era of the mini-skirt. 1985 Boyne & Thompson *Wild Blue* 459 [ref. to 1970's]: So the white dudes get mad when they see us steppin' out with some dolly birds.

dolly mop *n.* a sexually promiscuous young woman, esp. a prostitute; FLOOZIE.
*1833 Marryat *Peter Simple* ch. iv: His liberty's stopped for getting drunk and running after the Dolly-Mops! *1851 H. Mayhew *London Labour* IV 234: Those women who, for the sake of distinguishing them from the professionals, I must call amateurs, are generally spoken of as *Dolly-mops.* 1866 *Night Side of N.Y.* 30: They represent the lowest type of the "dolly-mop," or sailor's courtesan.

dolphin *n.* ¶ In phrase: **flog (one's) dolphin** *Orig. Naut.* (of a man) to masturbate; (*also*, as in 1981 quot., used as an exclam. of surprise).
[*1922 T.E. Lawrence *Mint* 63: Lofty was being charged with blanket drill. "Swinging the dolphin," Sailor called it, with a lapse into seafaring.] 1970 *Nat. Lampoon* (Apr.) 48: 27 privates flogging their dolphins in quiet cadence. 1971 *Nat. Lampoon* (Dec.) 37: I mean, just leave me

alone for a minute and I've got to flog my dolphin. 1972 R. Wilson *Forbidden Words* 119: To masturbate...*flog the dolphin.* 1975 in *West. Folk.* XXXVI (1977) 359: Flog my dolphin. 1981 *Hill St. Blues* (NBC-TV): Well, flog my dolphin! Just look at that woman!

Dolphs *n.pl. Football.* the Miami Dolphins of the American Football League.
1983 *N.Y. Post* (Sept. 2) 72: Dolphs vs Vikes.

D.O.M. *n.* [*d*irty *o*ld *m*an] a lecherous man, esp. if elderly.
1966 "Petronius" *N.Y. Unexp.* 116: New York's *dirty old man* is the...sharpest D.O.M. in the world! 1972 in *Penthouse* (Jan. 1973) 78: How To Be A Dirty Old Man...There is absolutely no point to becoming a d.o.m. if you're going to be coughing all the time. 1978 Asimov, Greenberg & Olander *Sci. Fiction Shorts* 245: His next desire arose naturally from the lecherous D.O.M. deep within all of us. 1984 in *Maledicta* VI (1985) 24: D.O.M....dirty old man.

dome *n.* **1.** the head.
[1843 [W.T. Thompson] *Scenes in Ga.* 27: [A hat] designed for the covering of the "dome of thought."] [1863 in Swisshelm *Crusader* 244: A head which realizes the idea of "a dome of thought," with the great, broad, high forehead, the brown hair thinly sprinkled over the top, [etc.].] 1881 Nye *Forty Liars* 153: The sun...lights up the shellac polish on our intellectual dome. *1890–91 *F & H* II 305: *Dome*...(common).—The head. 1902 Ade *Girl Prop.* 50: The Sister with the busy Dome was in two or three Philadelphia Library Clubs. 1907 in H.C. Fisher *A. Mutt* 6: Get wise to yourself. You're dotty in the dome. 1910 *N.Y. Eve. Jour.* (Feb. 3) 14: He copped Tommy with a fast right in the second round that shook the Harlemite from toes to dome. 1914 Graham *Poor Immigrants* 248: Him with the polished dome. 1914 Elliott *Animated Slang* 4: I knew that his DOME WAS SOLID IVORY and that a FEW WHEELS WERE LOOSE. 1921 *Variety* (Apr. 1) 7: I stuck Tomato's dome right in the bucket. 1931 in Woods *Horse-Racing* 68: So put it away in your dome and forget it till the day of the race. 1932 Binyon & Bolton *If I Had a Million* (film): I can't get it through my dome. 1934 Lomax & Lomax *Amer. Ballads & Folk Songs* 349: I...broke a Pilsner bottle on his dome. 1952 Bellow *Augie March* 77: March got knocked on the dome. 1970 A. Young *Snakes* 39: I be's groovin behind what's swishin round up in my dome, dig it? 1984 W. Murray *Dead Crab* 13: A battered porkpie hat...on his balding dome. 1991 "De La Soul" in L. Stanley *Rap* 69: I'd pop their dome like bubbles.
2. a hat.
1907 in H.C. Fisher *A. Mutt* 16: I might as well show a flash of class and grab one of these domes.

dome doctor *n.* a psychotherapist.
1955 Reifer *New Words* 66: *Dome doctor.* *Slang.* Psychiatrist. 1957 Townley *Up in Smoke* (film): You mean one of them dome doctors?

dome piece *n.* the head.
1977 *N.Y. Times Mag.* (Aug. 28) 64: I just been hit across the dome piece with a baseball bat.

domino *n.* **1.** usu. *pl.* a tooth.
*1828 Moncrieff *Tom & Jerry* II 53: Sluice your dominos—vill you?...Drink, vill you? don't you understand Hinglish? 1832 *Spirit of Times* (Mar. 31) 2: The *Reverend* gentleman, highly pleased with the result of the battle, showed his dominoes and chaffed very strongly. 1859 *Spirit of Times* (Apr. 9) 104: Holmes's frontispiece and "dominoes" were...damaged. *1917 (quot. at KISSER).
2. *pl.* [cf. GALLOPING DOMINOES] dice. [Quots. ref. to WWI.]
1924 *Amer. Leg. Wkly.* (June 13) 19: The kid draws back his hand and gets ready to roll the dominoes. 1928 Nason *Sgt. Eadie* 196: No dominoes galloping across the floor all night.
3. *Narc.* (see quot.).
1970 Landy *Underground Dict.* 64: *Domino*...12.5 mg. capsule of combined amphetamine and sedative.

dommy *n. Jazz.* a domicile. Also vars.
1943 *Yank* (Jan. 13) 20: Back to our dommie. 1944 in R.S. Gold *Jazz Talk* 72: I live in a righteous domi. 1946 Mezzrow & Wolfe *Really Blues* 52: We headed straight for his dommy. 1959 in R.S. Gold *Jazz Talk* 72: She cut into his dommy and helped kill the fifth.

Don *n.* [< Sp *don*, a title of respect preceding the given name of a male, as in *Don Juan*] **1.** *Mil. & Naut.* a Spaniard or (*occ.*) a Portuguese; (*also*) a person of Spanish or Portuguese descent.
*1779–83 in McGuffie *Rank & File* 408: D—n me, if I don't like fighting: I'd like to be ever tanning the Dons. 1795 in *DA.* 1806 in *DAE:* Found the Dons in some confusion. 1827 J.F. Cooper *Rover* 347: I may

have tired of chasing your indolent Don, and of driving *guarda costas* into port. *1833 Marryat *Peter Simple* 289: There's no want of courage in the Dons, Mr. Simple, but they did not support each other. **1839–40** Cobb *Green Hand* II 78: What a scampering the Dons made when boarded. **1848** *Rough & Ready Songster* 61: Heigh ho united go/To crush the Dons of Mexico. **1855** Wise *Tales* 271: Ask them dons [Portuguese] theer. *ca*1875 Williams *Black Cruiser* 52: We shall have a scrimmage may be, after all, with them here strange Dons. **1880** *United Service* (June) 287: In the popular language during the Cuban troubles, "our mosquito fleet of torpedo craft would attack the ironclad dons in swarms." **1899** Abbot *Blue Jackets of '98* 128: Why can't we finish off the Dons, now we've got them going? **1899** Pierce *Co. L* 53: Oh, you bet, we're not the men to crawl,/From the Dons we're going to take a fall. *a*1917 Hard *Banners* 18 [ref. to 1898]: 'Nother great victory! The Boys in Blue! They licked the Dons again! **1918** Griffin *Ballads of the Reg't.* 44: Twas Roosevelt's bold Rough Riders put the "Dons" upon the "bum." **1939** Howsley *Argot* 56: Mexican: *Spig, Don, Spiggity*.
2. *Naut.* a Spanish vessel.
*1794 in Holloway & Black *Broadside Ballads* 29: Our vessel blew up,/ A fighting that there Don. **1823** J.F. Cooper *Pilot* 86: The Alacrity is kept at coast duty and is not of a size to lay herself alongside a Don, or a Frenchman with a double row of teeth.

dona *n.* [< Polari < It *donna*] *Und. & Circus.* a woman, esp. of the demimonde. Also vars.
*1859 Hotten *Slang Dict.*: *Dona*…a woman. **1871** in Asbury *Gem of Prairie* 99: The oldest dones in the world. *1873 T. Frost *Circus Life* 277: *Dona* (lady) is so constantly used that I have seldom heard a circus man mention a woman by any other name. *1875 in *F & H* III 307: A circus man almost always speaks of a circus woman, not as a woman, but a dona. **1877** in Asbury *Gem of Prairie* (opp. p. 144): That was a poor stiff that done gave Lieutenant Bell…on Monday night. *a*1890–93 *F & H* III 307: *Dona, Donna, Donny,* or *Doner*…(vulgar).—A woman. (From the Italian). **1905** in *JAF* XXVIII (1915) 184: If yer don't quit a-foolin' with my dony…I'll cut yer goozle in two. **1908** *DN* III 306: *Dony,* n. Girl, sweetheart…."My *dony* don' wear no drawers,"—a line from a popular negro song. **1917** *DN* IV 411: *Doney*…Sweetheart. Also *doney gal.* **1946** *PADS* (No. 5) 20: [Virginia Words]…*doney:* Girl friend; not common.

Donald Duck *n. Navy.* **1.** a loudspeaker.
1942 Casey *Torpedo Junction* 10: *Donald Duck.* The loud-speaker aboard ship, so-called because of its accent. *Ibid.* 109: Donald Duck set us at rest almost immediately. *Ibid.* 114: Donald Duck sounded the routine call, all hands to battle stations.
2. (see quot.).
1945 in *Calif. Folk. Qly.* V (1946) 386: Many sailors…call the flat-topped, beribboned winter dress cap a *Donald Duck.*

Donald Duck Navy *n. Navy.* submarine chasers and antisubmarine patrol boats. Now *hist.*
1947 Morison *Naval Ops. in WWII* I 231: The Subchaser Training Center at Miami was especially set up to train young officers for this "Donald Duck Navy," as the SCs and PCs were nicknamed. **1962** Farago *10th Fleet* 143: Swasey again became responsible for the…build-up of a great number of improved craft for what became known as the "Donald Duck Navy."

Donald Duck suit *n.* [ref. to the sailor suit worn by the Disney cartoon character *Donald Duck*] *Navy.* the blue U.S. Navy uniform. *Joc.*
1972 Ponicsan *Cinderella Liberty* 169: Well, your Donald Duck suit is jake. **1973** Former USN QM, age 27: Your *Donald Duck suit* is your blue uniform. [Heard in 1968.].

donation station *n. CB.* a toll station.
1976 Whelton *CB Baby* 15: Get yourselves ready to back it on down about one mile east of the donation station. *Ibid.* 16: I slowed down for the donation station [and] picked up my toll ticket from a machine.

Don Diego *n. Naut.* DON, 1. Also **Don Dego.**
1666 Alsop *Maryland* 72: Like so many *Don Diegos* that becackt *Pauls.* **1833** Ames *Yarns* 264: Their hopes of a brush with the "Don Degos" were most keenly excited.

donegan *n.* [prob. < obs. E cant *danna* 'excrement' + KEN] **1.** Esp. *Und.* a slop pail or privy; lavatory. Also (*obs.*) **dunnakin** and vars. Cf. DONNICKER.
*1797 in Partridge *Dict. Und.* 216: *Dunnakin,* a necessary. *1811 *Lexicon Balatron.*: *Dunegan.* A privy. A water closet. *1820–21 P. Egan *Life in London* 220: It would have been *dinged* into the *dunagan.* *1821 *Real*

Life in Ireland 143: What is in London gaols termed a *dunniken,* was fixed behind the door. **1908** Sullivan *Criminal Slang* 8: *Donegan*—The toilet room, gent's walk. **1914** Jackson & Hellyer *Vocab.* 41: I must step into the hotel donegan (lavatory). **1926** Finerty *Criminalese* 17: *Donigan*—The toilet room. **1930** Irwin *Tramp & Und. Sl.*: *Donegan.* A toilet or wash-room. **1965** O'Neill *High Steel* 270: *Donegan.* A portable toilet, on a construction site.
2. *R.R.* (see quot.).
1940 *R.R. Mag.* (Apr.) 42: *Donegan*—Old car, with wheels removed, used as residence or office.

doney var. DONA.

dong *n.* [cf. DINGDONG] **1.** the penis. Usu. *Joc.*
*a*1900 in H.P. Beck, Jr. *Down-East Ballads* 409: With a sharp lance in one hand,/The other my dong. **1918** in *Lyra Ebriosa* 10: Hurrah for the Colonel with his hand upon his dong! **1927** *Immortalia* 46: His terrible dong to his knees hung down. **1938** Steinbeck *Grapes of Wrath* 198: Tell 'em ya dong's growed sence you los' your eye. **1942** H. Miller *Roofs of Paris* 12: She plays with his dong. **1952** Bellow *Augie March* 440: His walk was…as if he had to remind himself not to step on his dong. **1959** Morrill *Dark Sea* 22: Ordinary store pants are all left-dress…Better tell the tailor to switch yours or your dong will always be in your way. **1967** Mailer *Vietnam* 1: Let go of my dong, Shakespeare. **1968** P. Roth *Portnoy* 18: I was wholly incapable of keeping my paws from my dong. **1971** Cole *Rook* 57: Them days the man with the biggest bull dong had the longest cortege of women at his funeral. **1973** Karlin, Paquet, & Rottmann *Free Fire Zone* 132: They…start flongin' [*sic*] their dongs again. **1987** R. Miller *Slob* 12: Even the affluent yuppie suburbs had their fair share of raincoat flashers, hugger-muggers, dong danglers, and wienie waggers.
2. a dolt.
1958 Berger *Crazy in Berlin* 302 [ref. to WWII]: I take pneumonia with no shirt on, you dumb dong.
¶ In phrase:
¶ **put the slippery dong to** to betray.
1946–51 J. Jones *Here to Eternity* ch. xii: Benedict Arnold put the slippery dong to the Point—and got reamed for his pains.

donger *n.* DONG, 1.
1975 *Nat. Lampoon* (Apr.) 84: Dat's what I get for buyin' rubbers too small for my big donger. **1982** Downey *Losing the War* 103 [ref. to WWII]: Slammed the book shut on my swollen donger! **1992** *AS* LXVII 410: Or families may have private code words for taboo terms (e.g. *donger* for "penis"…in one of the co-author's family units).

donick *n.* [fr. DONNICKER] excrement.
1935 Algren *Boots* 105: Do a man have to wait all mornin' in line to git a tin plate o' cow-donick? I kin get garbage out o' any old can.

donicker var. DONNICKER.

donk *n.* **1.** a donkey.
1868 *Galaxy* (Mar.) 329: By the donks' support…a huge bull-fiddle did show. **1886** in S. Hale *Letters* 164: We were all very happy on our "donks." **1899** Hamblen *Bucko Mate* 123: Do you want one of these donks or not?
2. (see quot.).
1929 *AS* IV (June) 386: Whiskey is sometimes called *donk* or *mule* because of its powerful "kick."
3. a donkey engine.
1942 *ATS* 728. **1963–64** Kesey *Great Notion* 222: Let me tell you, me an' the donk.

donkey *n.* **1.** *Stu.* (see quot.).
1851 B. Hall *College Wds.* 178: At Washington College, Penn., students of a religious character are called *lap-ears* or *donkeys.*
2. a black man.—used contemptuously.—usu. considered offensive. Cf. MOKE.
1857 J.D. Long *Pict. of Slavery* 381: If you wish to plant a thorn in the heart of a colored man, call him "Nigger" in derision…"Darkey" and "Donkey" are felt as still more degrading epithets.
3. *Naut.* a sea chest.
1859 in C.A. Abbey *Before the Mast* 216: Another hand is…overhauling his "*Donkey*," (chest). **1868** Macy *There She Blows!* 31: I fix up a bed on dese two donkeys. **1871** *Overland Mo.* (Feb.) 171: When you send to the schooner for your donkey, you had better get the skipper to throw some of the old duds out of it. **1883** Russell *Sailors' Lang.* 42: *Donkey.*—A sailor's chest.
4.a. a lower-class Irish person.—used disparagingly.
1927–28 in R. Nelson *Dishonorable* 179: Sullivan: Those donkeys're too

busy fightin' among 'emselves to vote. **1934** Appel *Brain Guy* 93: "That's donkey's watching us." "I can lick any mick alive." **1940** Raine & Niblo *Fighting 69th* (film): Aah, ya big thick donkey. **1956** "T. Betts" *Across the Board* 96: Mara called me a crazy wop, and I called him a thick donkey. **1971** D. Smith *Engine Co.* 72: Guinea, spic, hebe,…nigger, donkey, mick, fishhead…When I was a kid [1950's]…if someone called one of us a donkey he'd get his lumps. **1973** "J. Godey" *Pelham* 25: The reporter, a sharp enough young donkey, had asked enough questions. **1976** Selby *Demon* 284: He stared at the dumb fucking donkeys with their goddamn pope-loving bullshit.

b. a manual laborer.

1932 in *DARE: Donkeys*—Section men. **1940** *R.R. Mag.* (Apr.) 42: *Donkey*—Derisive term for section man. **1968** *N.Y.P.D.* (ABC-TV): I'm an engine-room donkey. **1977** Schrader *Blue Collar* 93: Any more lip from you and you'll be another donkey in the street.

c. *Baseball.* (see quot.).

1960 Garagiola *Funny Game* 6: It is called the donkey's room, because all workout and tryout boys are called donkeys.

5. (see quot.).

1937 *Rev. of Reviews* (June) 43: Truckman Talk…*Donkey*—A tractor.

6. [sugg. by ASS] *Trucking.* the human rump; the rear, as of a truck.

1976 Bibb & Marcus *CB Bible* 92: Donkey. Rear. **1977** Corder *Citizens Band* 101: "What's your twenty?"…"Right on your donkey, partner!" **1990** Rukuza *W. Coast Turnaround* 205: Wild Card, what's it look like over yer donkey?

donkey dick *n.* **1.** Esp. *Mil.* a frankfurter, salami, or bologna.—usu. considered vulgar.

1971 Former Cpl., U.S. Army, age 29 [ref. to 1962]: Food words. "Cow juice," milk. And "donkey dicks" were hot dogs. **1975** Wambaugh *Choirboys* 159: We wake our prisoners up at five A.M. and serve them meals of red death, Gainesburgers, and donkey dicks. **1980** Cragg *Lex. Milit.* 130: *Donkey Dicks*…Army slang for sliced salami or bologna. **1986** *NDAS: Donkey dick*…WW2 armed forces. Salami and other coldcut sausages. *a*1990 Poyer *Gulf* 187: "What's for lunch?"…"Donkey dicks an' fries."

2. a dolt.—usu. considered vulgar.

1985 J. Hughes *Weird Science* (film): You two donkey dicks couldn't get laid in a morgue!

donkey doctor *n.* a mechanic who maintains and repairs donkey engines.

1919 *DN* V 55: *Donkey doctor.* One who repairs the donkey engine. **1942** *AS* (Dec.) 221: *Donkey Doctor.* Donkey-engine mechanic. **1956** *AS* (May) 150: *Donkey doctor*…A person who makes mechanical repairs on logging equipment. **1958** McCulloch *Woods Words* 50: *Donkey doctor.* A machinist who repairs donkeys. **1965** O'Neill *High Steel* 270: *Donkey Doctor.* A mechanic for power equipment.

donkey-puncher *n. Labor.* an operator of a donkey engine. Also **donkey jammer, donkey pounder.**

1920 *DN* V 81: *Donkey puncher.* Engineer on donkey engine. **1925** *AS* (Dec.) 136: The donkey-puncher, the loader, and the mechanic…are under his authority. **1930** in *Dict. Canad.* 216: Bull-cooks and donkey-punchers. **1941** *AS* (Oct.) 233: *Donkey Puncher.* One who operates a donkey engine. *a*1944 Binns *Timber Beast* 15: I was a donkey puncher at a haywire logging camp. **1953** in *Dict. Canad.* 216: I'm a donkey jammer from hell and back. **1958** McCulloch *Woods Words* 50: *Donkey pounder*—A donkey engineer. *Ibid.: Donkey jammer*…donkey engineer.

donkey roast *n.* an elaborate social affair; banquet.

1964 in *DAS* (1975 ed.) 693: The…benefit party at $100 a ticket…promises to be a real fine donkey roast.

donkey's breakfast *n.* Esp. *Naut.* a straw mattress.

1898 Norris *Moran* 41: Kitchell showed him his bunk with its "donkey's breakfast" and single ill-smelling blanket. *Ibid.* 84: Hide 'em under the donkey's breakfast. **1901** King *Dog-Watchers* 57: The sailors were busy…getting their donkeys' breakfasts (straw beds) spread out in their bunks. **1903** *Independent* (Dec. 31) 3107: One straw mattress, or "donkey's breakfast." **1923** in O'Brien *Best Stories of 1923* 14: The watch below rolled into their bunks onto "donkey breakfast" straw mattresses. **1923** Riesenberg *Under Sail* 12 [ref. to 1897]: Some of the shore crowd…helped to pass up the chests and bags of dunnage, and the bundles of "donkey's breakfast." **1929** in W. Williams *Whaling Family* 254 [ref. to *ca*1870]: A boarding house keeper…was supposed to provide…an outfit, including a chest and a mattress, always referred to as a "donkey's breakfast." **1947** W.M. Camp *S.F.* 249 [ref. to *ca*1900]: The sailor carried aboard with him…his "donkey breakfast," bedding,

blankets, and clothing bag for a pillow. **1948** McHenry & Myers *Home Is Sailor* 198: The "donkeys' breakfasts," as the seamen called the bedding, had not been replaced.

donkey-skinner *n.* an operator of a donkey engine.

1934 Weseen *Dict. Slang* 79.

donkey's years *n.pl.* [a punning allusion to the length of a donkey's ears] a very long time.

*1916, *1927, *1928 in *OEDS.* **1951** *New Yorker* (Mar. 17) 27: You won't have them in your class for donkey's years. **1952** in *DAS:* I got interested in his apprenticeship donkey's years back. **1957** in S.J. Perelman *Don't Tread on Me* 203: We haven't been south of the Amboys in donkey's years. **1978** *Harper's* (Dec.) 59: Helen and I bought it donkey's years ago. **1992** *N.Y. Observer* (May 25) 15: It must be donkey's years since I saw two players…shake hands as if they really meant it.

donkey work *n.* drudgery done at the behest of a superior.

*1920, *1928, *1940 in *OEDS.* **1968** J.D. Houston *Between Battles* 66: Always looking for volunteers to do the donkey work. **1974** *Business Week* (Dec. 14) 55: What Greenhill calls "donkey work." **1979** *Atlantic* (Sept.) 75: The donkey work was done by head girls. **1982** "W.T. Tyler" *Rogue's March* 199: I'm fucking tired of doing their goddamn donkey work. **1985** Sawislak *Dwarf* 89: She was willing to do the donkey work in the lab. **1986** Dye & Stone *Platoon* 78: They were mostly excused from the tedious donkey-work.

Donnelly *n.* [fr. Daniel *Donnelly* (1788–1820), celebrated Irish pugilist] a heavy blow with the fist.

1845 Corcoran *Pickings* 125: Ye gave me this Donnelly (a thump) under the eye.

donnicker *n.* [alter. of DONEGAN] **1.a.** Esp. *Circus & Carnival.* a lavatory; latrine. Also vars.

1931 *AS* VI (June) 330: *Donnicker*, n. A toilet or water-closet. **1935** *Amer. Mercury* (June) 229: *Doniker*: toilet. **1935** Pollock *Und. Speaks: Doniker*, a rest room. **1939** *AS* (Oct.) 239: *Donnicker*, Public lavatory. **1942** Sanders & Blackwell *Forces* 118: *Donagher*…A wash-room; a latrine. **1948** McHenry & Myers *Home Is Sailor* 166: Don't quote the Hearst press to me,…I wouldn't even hang those papers in the donicker. **1951** Mannix *Sword-Swallower* 102: On a city lot, the canvasmen can't dig donikers (as the carnies call latrines). **1952** Randolph & Wilson *Holler* 240. **1961** Clausen *Season's Over* 64: The doniker? It's outside the car, on the platform. **1964** *AS* (Oct.) 281: *Doniker*, n. An outdoor toilet. **1970** A. Lewis *Carnival* 186: No one in this division of carnival or circus show biz ever calls these comfort stations anything but "donnikers." **1978** Ponicsan *Ringmaster* 38: Where are the donnikers? **1981** O'Day & Eells *High Times* 199: I got the donicker detail…somebody always has to clean the toilets.

b. a filthy or vile place.

1970 A. Lewis *Carnival* 187: This location really is a donnicker.

2. *R.R.* a freight brakeman.

1932 in *DARE: Doniker*—Freight brakeman. **1939** *Sat. Eve. Post* (Apr. 15) 26: They didn't use any breeze those days, so the donikers on the reefers didn't have to look out for a dynamiter. **1976** R. Adams *Railroader* 46: Donniker: A freight brakeman.

3. the buttocks; (*also*) the penis.

1951 *Erotic Verse to 1955* 52: His donnicker found the mark. **1953** in Russ *Last Parallel* 120: *Whereupon* I--will execute--a--half-gainer--thereby--positioning--*my*--glorious tessatura--*directly*--adjacent--to--*your*--stately--donicker. **1962** Quirk *Red Ribbons* 28 [ref. to WWII]: I shaved and showered and got myself clean as a Yale man's doniker so I wouldn't catch infection on the operating table. **1974** Millard *Thunderbolt* 84: [Women are] wetting their panties for a crack at his donnicker. *a*1986 in Logsdon *Whorehouse Bells* 96: I…landed my donneker right square in her ass.

do-nothing stool *n. Black E.* the rump. *Joc.*

*ca*1974 in J.L. Gwaltney *Drylongso* 16: Some folks…would kick this Tom dead in his do-nothing stool.

don't-speak-of-ems *n.pl.* [sugg. by *unmentionables*] trousers. *Joc.*

1864 Norton *Army Letters* 216: Who should I see but Mr. Johnny just getting into his don't-speak-of-'ems.

donut hole *n.* [sugg. by *Donut Dolly*, the official American Red Cross designation for female volunteers; *hole* alluding to the vagina] *Army.* a female volunteer worker with the American Red Cross.

1985 Bodey *F.N.G.* 265 [ref. to Vietnam War]: We are Red Cross volunteers. And the Red Cross designates us as Red Cross Donut Dollies.

And, as we all know, you guys...call us Donut Holes. *Ibid.* 266: They're dancing with the Donut Holes.

dony var. DONA.

doo var. DO, *n.*, 2.

doob *n.* DOOBIE, 2.
> **1986** Eble *Campus Slang* (Nov.) 3: Better not light up a *doob* here. **1991** *Mystery Sci. Theater* (Comedy Central TV): I'll roll us a doob.

doobage *n.* [DOOBIE, 2 + -AGE] *Stu.* marijuana.
> **1985** J. Hughes *Breakfast Club* (film): Can I have my doobage? **1990** P. Munro *Slang U.* 71: *Doobage* marijuana. **1993** *Daily Beacon* (Univ. Tenn.) (Mar. 12) 4: The Jamaican character Marley Doobage is clearly a stereotype....''Doobage'' is slang for marijuana.

doober *n.* [orig. unkn.] **1.** a piece of excrement; (*also*) a stupid or objectionable person.
> **1975** Cosby, Tenn., man, age *ca*35: Don't step in the horse doobers. **1977** Univ. Tenn. student: I knew this person from Winston-Salem, North Carolina, who called fools *doobers*. That was in 1973.

2. [cf. DOOBIE] a marijuana cigarette.
> **1973** Univ. Mich. student: A *joint* is also a *doober* or a *dooby.*

doobie *n.* [var. Scots *dobie* < *Dobbie*, hypocoristic form of *Robert*] **1.** a foolish or inconsequential person; individual.
> ***1825** Jamieson *Ety. Dict. Scot.* II 79: *Doobie*...A dull stupid fellow. **1980** Garrison *Snakedoctor* 34: Be a good doobie and don't ask too many questions.

2. [perh. of independent orig.] a marijuana cigarette; (*also*) marijuana. Also vars.
> **1967** J.B. Williams *Narc. & Halluc.* 111: *Dubbe*—Negro slang for a marijuana roach. **1967** Rosevear *Pot* 158: *Duby:* Marihuana. **1970** Landy *Underground Dict.* 72: *Dubee*...Marijuana cigarette. **1972** Smith & Gay *Don't Try It* 201: *Dubie.* A joint, or marijuana cigarette. **1976–77** Kernochan *Dry Hustle* 67: And we saved a whole big doobie of Colombian for you. **1979** *Easyriders* (Dec.) 28: While you down your fifth beer or smoke another doobie. **1986** *Lang. in Soc.* XV 155: We were tokin' away on this doobie.

doodad *n.* [orig. unkn.] a small item or ornament, esp. one whose correct name is not known; (*specif.*, in 1877 quot.) a small valuable.
> **1877** E. Wheeler *Prince of Rd.* 82: There is need o' yer dutchin' out yer dudads right liberal. **1905** in Wentworth *ADD* 173. **1908** McGaffey *Show Girl* 187: This machine has got a dudead on it that prevents it from going more than ten. **1932** in Fitzgerald *Corres.* 286: The baubles and tawdry doo-dads of life. **1938** Chandler *Big Sleep* 11: There were full-length mirrors and crystal doodads all over the place. **1939** Hartney *Up & At 'Em* 20: To them flying was still in the ''doodad'' stage, a passing fad. **1942** ''E. Queen'' *Calamity Town* 22: I don't like these doo-dads. **1947** Mailer *Naked & Dead* 295: Ah'm gonna learn all the little doodads in that brake. **1949** in Truman *Dear Bess* 558: Glad you liked the ''doodads.'' **1963** Horwitz *Candlelight* 51: It was an edifice, burdened with the doodads of the nineteenth century. **1989** *U.S. News & W.R.* (Dec. 4) 82: Get a sense of what the doodads you covet are worth.

doodah *n.* **1.** DOODAD.
> **1924** in D. Hammett *Continental Op* 121: To bring out books of verse and buy doo-daws for his rooms. **1988** *NewsWatch* (CNN-TV) (Oct. 1): He has it fixed up with all his little doodahs. **1992** *CBS This Morning* (CBS-TV) (June 23): Robert asked me about these doodahs I have in my mind.

2. [cf. Brit. *all of a doodah* 'in a state of excitement'; perh. ult. sugg. by the refrain *Doodah! Doodah!* in Stephen Foster's minstrel song ''Camptown Races''] foolishness; nonsense.
> **1986** *Miami Vice* (NBC-TV): This is America. Freedom of speech and all that doodah! *a*1990 Poyer *Gulf* 47: That's enough doo-dah for the fucking XO.

doodle *n.* [orig. unkn.] **1.a.** a silly fool; dolt.
> ***1628** in *OED*: Vanish, doodles, vanish! ***1764** in *OED*: Why, doodle, jackanapes harkee, who am I? **1767** in *DA*: Yankee Doodle. ***1785** Grose *Vulgar Tongue: Doodle.* A silly fellow, or noodle...Also a child's penis. ***1830** in *F & H* II 309: That abominable old addlehead, Dr. —, a doodle that he is!

b. (*cap.*) [sugg. by *Yankee Doodle*] (during the Civil War) a Unionist, esp. a Union soldier; Yankee.—used derisively.
> **1861** in *DA*: He'll may-be change his mind, and stay/Where the good Doodles do! **1862** *N.Y. Tribune* (May 13): Whoop! the Doodles have broken loose/Roaring round like the very deuce!

2. the penis.
> ***1785** (quot. at **(1.a.)**, above). ******ca*1866 *Romance of Lust* 39: How your doodle has grown. **1952** Randolph & Wilson *Holler* 101: In Barry County, Missouri, one often hears *doodle* used in the same meaning (i.e., penis). **1970** in L. Bangs *Psychotic Reactions* 33: Whack your doodle at home at night. **1974** *Coq* (Apr.) 46: I mean is your doodle over ten inches in length? **1993** *Simpsons* (Fox-TV): Hey, Homey! I can see your doodle!

3. DOOZY.
> **1913** *DN* IV 16: Used by Nebraska students. ''The hat is just a *doodle.*'' ''Isn't that book a *doodle*?'' ''He's a *doodle.*''

4. *pl.* something that is superlative.—constr. with *the.*
> **1932** Hecht & Fowler *Great Magoo* 151: She's the doodles.

doodle *v.* **1.** to befool; cheat; DIDDLE. *Rare* in U.S.
> ***1821** *Real Life in London* I 270: Who doodle John Bull of his *gold, silver,* and *brass.* ***1823** in *F & H* II 309: I have been dished and doodled out of forty pounds to-day. ***1834** in *OED*: It might have doodled our whole party. ***1880** in *OED*: Doodle, to cheat; to deceive; to trifle. **1954–60** *DAS: Doodle*...To deceive or trick someone; to trick someone. *Archaic.*

2. (of a man) to copulate with; DIDDLE.
> **1958** W. Burroughs *Naked Lunch* 177: All [he] wants to do is doodle a Christian girl. **1963–64** Kesey *Great Notion* 77: Ride a motorcycle and doodle a cousin an' all that sorta thing. **1970** *Nat. Lampoon* (Apr.) 62: And he didn't know doodling your mommy's not right.

doodlebug *n.* **1.a.** Esp. *Petroleum Industry.* a divining rod or other device that allegedly can locate underground wells or deposits of oil, gas, or minerals; (*hence*) a seismograph, gravitometer, or the like used in locating such deposits.
> **1924** Henderson *Crookdom* 157: One old fraud...had a ''chemical battery'' or ''doodlebug,''...which he said would spot oil-producing ground at once. **1932** *AS* (Apr.) 266: *Doodlebug, n.* A divining rod (used to find oil). **1942** *Calif. Folk. Qly.* I 35: To many of these contraptions the somewhat opprobrious term ''doodlebug'' has been assigned, although this term may likewise refer to certain kinds of gold-dredging machinery. **1944** *Calif. Folk. Qly.* III 53: ''Doodlebug'' is a term of somewhat jocular contempt in oil parlance used to denote any bogus mechanical instrument (and even the operator thereof) employed to divine the location of oil. The term is also widely used by prospectors and miners generally with reference to mechanical contraptions used in locating mineral deposits. **1948** *Sat. Eve. Post* (Dec. 11) 122: For example, those regulations laid down by the California fish-and-game commissioners, who have the final say-so about where the doodlebug boys can shoot and when. *Ibid.* 126: A doodlebug fleet is a busy little armada. **1951** *PADS* (No. 15) 74: The term *doodlebug* was first applied to the divining rods and quack devices for hunting oil and locating wells—and later to the persons using them. It has been extended...to mean the seismograph crew and the strictly scientific machinery used by it. **1965** *World Bk. Dict.*

b. a person who employs such a device; DOODLEBUGGER.
> **1943** in *Calif. Folk. Qly.* III (1944) 55: The doodle bug must have technique,/Must know his racket, so to speak. **1951** (quot. at **(1.a.)**, above). **1951** Pryor *The Big Play* 74: In spite of startling successes scored by geologists...they still considered them at best as only a kind of glorified doodlebug.

2. a small vehicle.
> **1935** Pollock *Und. Speaks: Dudle bug*, a small aeroplane. **1940** *R.R. Mag.* (Apr.) 42: Gas or gas-electric coach...*doodlebug.* Another meaning for *doodlebug* is rail-motor car used by section foreman, line-men, etc. **1941** *Army Ordnance* (July) 79: *Doodlebug*....Tank. **1941** *AS* (Oct.) 165: *Doodle Bug.* Reconnaissance car or tank. **1945** *Yank* (Mar. 2) 4: The Army's M29 weasel or ''Doodle Bug'' is the most effective snow vehicle. **1961** *WNID3.* **1971** Tak *Truck Talk* 47: *Doodle-bug:* a small tractor used to pull two-axle dollies in a warehouse. **1978** Lieberman & Rhodes *CB* (ed. 2) 298: *Doodlebug*—Small warehouse truck used to transport skids of cargo...Forklift.

3. *Mil.* a German V-1 flying bomb. Now *hist.*
> ***1944** in *OEDS.* **1944** *Time* (July 24) 26: ''Doodlebug'' was frowned on as too flippant. Most Londoners called the bombs ''those things.'' **1945** in Giles *G.I. Journal* 222: He laughs at us for freezing when the doodlebugs go over. **1946** Nason *Contact Mercury* 35: The V-1, the buzz-bomb, the doodlebug. **1950** Calmer *Strange Land* 39: When the heinies were here there was no doodle-bug trouble. **1963** Horwitz *Candlelight* 127: We saw a doodlebug hurtling across the sky for no target except the earth where it would fall.

doodlebugger *n. Petroleum Industry.* a person who employs a

DOODLEBUG to locate mineral deposits.

1936 in Pyle *Ernie's Amer.* 211: Doodle-buggers are the guys who say they know how to find oil. **1943** in *Calif. Folk. Qly.* (1944) III 54: The water witch is the parent of the doodlebugger. **1948** *Sat. Eve. Post* (Dec. 11) 122: The doodlebugger's chore consists of touching off little earthquakes near the earth's surface [to detect potential drilling sites]. **1966** "T. Pendleton" *Iron Orchard* 62: An even more sophisticated sub-breed was born, a mixture of practical geologists and engineers and earthquake seismologists, who came to be called "doodle-buggers," and, more properly, geophysicists.

doodle-doo *n.* the least bit. Also **doodly-doo.**

1969 Broughton *Thud Ridge* 92: The bomb can't do doodle-doo about it. **1979** McGivern *Soldier's* 315: That don't make a doodly-do bit of difference.

doodly *n.* DOODLY-SQUAT.

1939 *Pittsburgh Courier* (July 15) 12: Your company ain't worth doodley now. **1974** E. Thompson *Tattoo* 361: This college shit don't mean doodley if you lose your friends. **1984** *The Fall Guy* (ABC-TV): Take off them glasses. You can't see doodly as it is.

doodly-crap *n.* DOODLY-SQUAT.

1972 Sherburne *Fort Pillow* 53: We're a new regiment, and we don't have a doodly-crap of any tradition.

doodly-drop *n.* DOODLY-CRAP.

1957 E. Brown *Locust Fire* 95 [ref. to 1944]: Had got to where a white man wasn't worth a doodly-drop no more.

doodly-shit *n.* DOODLY-SQUAT.—usu. considered vulgar.

1966 Fariña *Down So Long* 87: A lot of doodley-shit. **1971** Cameron *First Blood* 13: Any time you say doodlely shit...I'll whip your ass.

doodly-squat *n.* So. **1.** the least bit; emphatically nothing. Cf. DIDDLY-SQUAT.

1934 Hurston *Jonah's Vine* 217: She ain't never had nothin'—not eben [*sic*] doodly-squat. **1935** *Amer. Mercury* (June) 229: *Doodle-e-squat:* broke. "I haven't got *doodle-e-squat.*" **1935** Hurston *Mules & Men* 90: "Oh, Ah ain't got doodly-squat," I countered. **1946** Mezzrow & Wolfe *Really Blues* 97: These cats weren't from doodly-squat. **1954** Killens *Youngblood* 49: White folks got everything. Niggers ain't from doodly-squat. **1958** Frankel *Band of Bros.* 232 [ref. to 1950]: One less guy in Korea won't mean doodly-squat to the marines. **1958** Frede *Entry E* 46: I hate this doodly-squat betting that goes on around here. First Gordy gets a buck ahead, then Stew...doodly-squat! **1961** O. Davis *Purlie* 310: Purlie ain't done doodley squat! **1961** Forbes *Goodbye to Some* 246: You haven't lost doodley squat. **1970** A. Young *Snakes* 18: These other dudes...aint hittin on doodleysquat when it come to talkin trash. **1972** Meade & Rutledge *Belle* 116: Not doing doodly-squat in school.

2. a damn.

1958 Hughes & Bontemps *Negro Folklore* 483: I don't give a doodley-squat.

doo-doo *n.* **1.** [redup. of DO, *n.,* 3] **a.** excrement. [Orig. a nursery euphem.; adult slang uses are more recent.]

1948 (cited in *W10*). **1962** T. Berger *Reinhart* 304: Doo-doo floating in plain sight and suchlike. **1970** Baraka *Jello* 18: A pile of rat doodoo. **1976** Knapp & Knapp *One Potato* 62: Nanny, Nanny boo-boo,/Stick your head in doo-doo. **1978** S. King *Stand* 14: Any gull...dropping a splat of white doodoo. **1980** Syatt *Country Talk* 52: That's slicker than owl doodoo on a hickory limb. **1982** Rucker *57th Kafka* 125: Bodily wastes...doo-doo. **1983** *All Things Considered* (Nat. Pub. Radio) (Jan. 13): I'm talking about pigeon doo-doo, Mr. Ross! **1992** N.Y.C. woman, age *ca*60: I can remember when I was really little [*ca*1937] being at this lake house, and there was another little kid there and his mother was always chasing after him screaming "Do you have to make doodoo?"

b. nonsense.

1958 T. Berger *Crazy in Berlin* 60: Is Pound going to start that awful Cook's Tour doodoo again? **1973** *Atlantic* (Sept.) 107: Their male secretaries...snicker at the pomposities they must type: "What doo-doo." **1986** *L.A. Law* (NBC-TV): You expect them to believe this doodoo? *a***1988** C. Adams *More Straight Dope* 164: The part about the czars and the craftsmen is apocryphal doodoo.

c. daylights; stuffing.

1970 A. Young *Snakes* 25: I'll whip the dudu outta you. **1973** I. Reed *La. Red* 25: I'll stomp the do-do out of it.

d. [euphem. for *deep shit* s.v. SHIT] trouble.—constr. with *deep.* [Popularized in a speech by President-elect George Bush in January, 1989.]

1989 *CBS This Morning* (CBS-TV) (Jan. 17): *Real* Texans do not describe trouble as "deep doodoo." **1989** *New Republic* (Dec. 4) 10: If your position is to the right of Bush, you're in deep doo-doo. **1990** *N.Y. Times* (Mar. 26) A 17: If he tries to raise taxes, he's in deep doo-doo. **1990** G. Vidal, in *Nation* (Aug. 27) 185: Today the poor...are in deep doo-doo. **1994** N. McCall *Wanna Holler* 301: I got myself into deeper doo-doo while trying to clean up my act.

2. [a nursery euphem.] the penis.

1972 Hannah *Geronimo Rex* 117: They let me crawl off with a book and play with my doo-doo in the corner.

3. *Black E.* the rump.

1973 Andrews & Owens *Black Lang.* 95: Got knocked right on his doo-doo.

doody var. DOOTY.

doof *n.* [of Scots orig.; prob. related to G *doof* 'dense, stupid, dull-witted'; not, as sometimes claimed, of Yid orig.] **1.** a dolt; DOOFUS.

*****1728** in *SND:* He get her! slaverin Doof. *****1788** in *SND:* A bigger doof was never seen. *****1825** Jamieson *Ety. Dict. Scot.* II 80: *Doof. n.* A dull, stupid fellow. **1971** *Current Slang* V 10: *Doof, n.* A bumbling fool; idiot. **1975** in G.A. Fine *With the Boys* 169: *Doof, n.* Foolish, awkward boy. **1987** *21 Jump St.* (Fox-TV): Hey, check this doof out.

2. (see quot.).

1955 *AS* (Dec.) 303: *Doof, n.* Practical joke [at Wayne State Univ.].

doofball *n.* [prob. *doofus* + *goofball*] *Juve.* (see 1977 quot.).

1977 Univ. Tenn. student [ref. to 1962]: A *doofball* is a pejorative term for a person. It refers to those little bits of lint and fecal matter that cling in the same area as *dingleberries,* which mean the same thing. **1979** Univ. Tenn. student: A *doofball* is like a nerd or a moron. We always used to call people *doofballs* when we were kids [*ca*1968].

doofless *adj.* [alter. DOOFUS] stupid; doltish.

1979 J. Morris *War Story* 198: Not the doofless types you usually see, but really mean looking motherfuckers.

doofus or **dufus** *n.* [prob. alter. of GOOFUS but cf. DOOF; not, as sometimes claimed, of Yid orig.] **1.** a fool; dolt; oaf.—often attrib.

1960 N.Y.C. schoolboy: You doofus! **1964** N.Y.C. high-school student: Man, you're such a doofus!...Hey, doofus! **1966** C. Cooper *Farm* 27: Smiling a great big stupid doofus grin. **1976–77** Kernochan *Dry Hustle* 39: They'd have a new volunteer, a real doofus. **1978** Truscott *Dress Gray* 99: Feeling like some kind of dufus fool. **1979** Sagendorf *Popeye* 113: The name Dufus was brought home from Vietnam [in the mid-sixties] by my oldest son. Used to describe a slow-witted airman, it is an apt name for Popeye's lovable nephew. **1980** Rimmer *Album* 8 [ref. to 1963]: You *are* home...Dufus. **1981** Hathaway *World of Hurt* 55: Damned doofus trainee. **1983** Eilert *Self & Country* 17: After a while, duffus, you just know it's coming. **1985** *Campus Voice* (Apr.) 22: He speaks in his best dufus voice. **1989** *New Yorker* (Nov. 13) 53: He's not a dork. He's a dufus. **1990** *New Republic* (Dec. 31) 42: We too are a doofus. **1991** B.E. Ellis *Amer. Psycho* 100: What a complete and total *dufus.*

2. the penis.

1984 N. Bell *Raw Youth* 21: In his birthday suit with his doofus cocked.

doofy *adj. Juve.* being or typical of a DOOFUS; GOOFY.

1972 N.Y.C. schoolboy: That was pretty doofy. You're really doofy, Cornelius. **1976** in G.A. Fine *With the Boys* 105: If anyone acts doofy, Laurel acts doofy.

doogy var. DUJI.

doohickey *n.* [perh. *doodad* + *hickey*] any small object or device; contrivance; thingamabob.

1914 *Our Navy* (Nov.) 12: We [sailors] were compelled to christen articles beyond our ken with such names as "dohickeys," "gadgets," and "gilguys." **1926** *AS* II (Oct.) 62: Every snipe endeavors to impress the poor swabbos with his talk of gillguys, gadgetts [*sic*] and gimmicks, to say nothing of other doohickies. **1952** Steinbeck *E. of Eden* 365: What's this do-hickey, Father? **1970** *Nat. Lampoon* (Apr.) 5: Insert little do-hickey on side of can into slot in key. **1992** *Newsweek* (Dec. 7) 71: The Digital Book System...a doohickey slightly bigger than a cassette box—that stores the equivalent of 10 Bibles.

doojee, doojer vars. DUJI.

doojigger *n.* DOOHICKEY.

1927 *AS* II: *Doojigger.* Mechanical contrivance. **1956** M. Wolff *Big Nick.* 24: I knew I'd seen this ribbon doojigger around the house some place. **1976** W. Johnston *Super Sweathogs* 40: Jiggle that doo-jigger.

dookey var. DUKEY.

dookie *n. So.* excrement; (*hence*) rubbish; (*also*) "daylights." Also as *v.* Also **dukey.**

1969 Bullock *Watts* 47: Like we get dog dukey, put it in a bottle, throw it on them. **1970** Conaway *Big Easy* 94: Fowl droppings...Little bitty balls of dookie. **1973** Andrews & Owens *Black Lang.* 105: *Dukey*—A nice way for calling it shit. **1974** R. Carter *16th Round* 325: I would gladly have stepped into my hip boots just to keep the dukey out of my pockets. The shit was really getting deep! **1983** K. Weaver *Texas Crude* 40: He can't run fast enough to scatter his dookie. **1990** *New Yorker* (Sept. 10) 84: Terry was scared. "I almost dookied myself." **1990** *New Yorker* (Sept. 17) 73: I would have stomped the *dooky* out of him. **1991** *Bill & Ted's Exc. Adven.* (Fox-TV): Good music instead of that dooky you used to play.

dooley *n.* [perh. fr. the family name *Dooley;* the reason for its application is unkn.] dynamite.

1919 *Bookman* (Apr.): Would he make use of soup or of dooley, and why? **1925** (cited in Partridge *Dict. Und.* 198).

doolie[1] *n.* [prob. < Gk *doûlos* 'slave' + E dim. suff. *-ie*] a first-year cadet at the U.S. Air Force Academy.

1961 *AS* (May) 149: A *doolie*...is...a Fourth Classman, a cadet in his first year at the Air Force Academy. **1961** *Sat. Eve. Post* (Oct. 14) 76: For the "doolie" (first-year man) this is a brutal baptism, a day which keeps him on the edge of exhaustion. **1963** *Sat. Eve. Post* (Nov. 23) 91: "Fourth-class knowledge"...must be memorized by every doolie (freshman) at the U.S. Air Force Academy. **1965** *Newsweek* (Feb. 8) 84: Life at the Academy seemed to keep its old cadences—doolies double-timed to classes. **1977** in Stiehm *Bring Men & Women* 54: Remember When...Doolies buffed upper class floors for stereo privileges? **1979** Lovell *Athens nor Sparta* 69 [ref. to 1950's]: He was unable to make the reforms he thought were essential in the indoctrination of "doolies" (freshmen). **1986** R. Walker *AF Wives* 35: One giant step for a doolie—a freshman, he explained. **1990** *CBS This Morning* (CBS-TV) (Apr. 3): You are a freshman, or a *doolie* as they're called.

doolie[2] *n.* [perh. related to DOOLIE[1]] (see quots.).

1976 Univ. Tenn. student: He's one of the head doolies down there....A *doolie's* a big shot. **1980** *N.Y. Times* (Dec. 28) V 8: "We're all a bunch of big doolies now," the...captain [of the U.S. Olympic hockey team] Mike Eruzione, would say later. "Big doolie," Phil Verchota explained, "just means big wheel, big gun, big shot."

doomsday mission *n. USAF.* a large-scale bombing mission that is unusually critical and dangerous.

1966–67 Harvey *Air War* 144: You know what happened on that first Doomsday Mission (as the boys call a big balls-to-the-wall raid) against Hanoi oil.

door *n.* ¶ In phrase: **blow** [or **tear**] **the doors off** to pass (an automobile) at great speed; (*hence*) to be very successful at (something); surpass (someone or something).

1971 Wurlitzer & Corry *Two-Lane Blacktop* (film): Probably blow her doors right off. **1973** Ace *Stand On It* 38: Stock sedan class. Small purse, but I blew their goddamn doors off. **1974** Univ. Tenn. student: Well, did you blow the doors off that test? **1977** Univ. Tenn. student: I blew the doors off of that exam. **1983** *Good Morning America* (ABC-TV) (May 13): This car can tear the doors off the competition. **1988** *Friday the 13th* (Fox-TV): You blew his doors off. Isn't that enough?

doorknocker *n. FBI.* (see quot.).

1986 "H.S.A. Becket" *Dict. Espionage* 63: *Doorknocker.* An agent assigned to do personnel security interviews, to ascertain whether persons needing a security clearance have no nefarious activities in their past.

doormat *n.* a weak-willed person who is frequently exploited or dominated by others.

[*1861** C. Dickens in *OED2:* She asked me and Joe whether we supposed she was door-mats under our feet, and how we dared to use her so.] *1883** in *Passing Eng.* 115: I made a doormat of him. **1908** in H.C. Fisher *A. Mutt* 68: Citizen Pickels [is] impersonating a doormat for the comfort of his boss. *a***1904–11** Phillips *Susan Lenox* II 313: Me—...a doormat for a lot of cheap people that are tryin' to make out they ain't human like the rest of us. *Me!* **1911–12** Ade *Knocking the Neighbors* 119: Edgar...was one of the most popular Door-Mats that ever had "Welcome" marked up and down his Spinal Column. **1914** Ellis *Billy Sunday* 204: A wishy-washy, sissified sort of a galoot that lets everybody make a doormat out of him. **1926** Maines & Grant *Wise-Crack Dict.* 7: Door-

mat—A coward. **1926** in Paxton *Sport* 140: Philadelphia had been the doormat of the National League for five successive seasons. **1980** Freudenberger & Richelson *Burn Out* 37: She saw him as a doormat and a patsy. **1990** *Cosmopolitan* (Dec.) 208: She no longer felt like a doormat, "some little nothing who could be avoided and made a fool of."

doormat thief *n. Und.* a petty or incompetent thief. Also **doormat grafter.**

1848 (quot. at IN). **1902** Hapgood *Thief* 335 [ref. to 1898]: You doormat thief. You couldn't get away with a coal-scuttle. **1910** Hapgood *City Streets* 318: Now I'm little better than a door-mat grafter. **1934** W. Smith *Bessie Cotter* 264: Not that doormat grafter. **1959** Lederer *Never Steal Anything Small* (film): I ain't doin' this for you, you doormat thief.

doorshaker *n. Police & Und.* a watchman or guard who inspects buildings at night.

1942 *ATS* 460. **1944** *Pap. Mich. Acad.* XXX 598: *Doorshakers,* merchant patrol or special police. **1960** C. Cooper *Scene* 308: *Doorshaker:* a private policeman usually hired by a business establishment for extra security. **1975** Wambaugh *Choirboys* 149: I know it's him because the noises the doorshaker said he made.

door-slinger *n. R.R.* a freight brakeman.

*a***1946** in W.C. Fields *By Himself* 8: As we came upon the bridge, the fireman, the engineer, or the door slinger dropped the scoop into the trough and we took "water on the fly."

dooteroomus *n.* [of fanciful orig., perh. a joc. elaboration of DUTY infl. by unrelated *Deuteronomy*] money. Also **doot.**

1871 Schele de Vere *Amer.* 296: Among the less generally known terms [for money] are...*spondulics, dooteroomus,...dirt.*

dooty *n.* [prob. resp. of *duty,* sugg. by *do (one's) duty,* s.v. DUTY] *Juve.* excrement. Also **doody.**

1969 Jessup *Sailor* 36: Dried chicken dooty. **1972** Meade & Rutledge *Belle* 18: Oh...chicken doody! **1987** *Wkly. World News* (May 12) 30: I'd had it with dog doody. **1987** *Nat. Lampoon* (Oct.) 103 (ad): Shit in a Can. Can sprays any size doodie! Make your own shapes...Hilarious! From England...Order with Stench Spray in this ad. **1993** N.Y.C. woman, age *ca*60: I can remember people saying "I stepped in dog dooty" before 1940. That was pretty much the standard term for dog shit.

doo-whanger *n.* DOOHICKEY.

1927 Ranlett *Let's Go* 109: Whoever fired that doo-whanger at him's a poor shot.

doo-wop *n.* [imit. of the nonsense syllables sung in such music] **1.** *Music.* a style of rhythm and blues in which a lead vocalist sings over a rhythmically chanted background of nonsense syllables: a style popular esp. in the 1950's. Now *S.E.*

1969 in *OED2:* They knew the doo-waps, rock and roll, rhythm and blues. **1976** *6,000 Words.* **1981** D.E. Miller *Jargon* 127: *Doo-wop:* Type of fifties rock or R and B in which the backup vocals involved the repetition of such phrases as "doo-wop," "Sh-bop," "Sh-boom," "doo-lang," and the like. **1987** *Newsweek* (Mar. 23) 60: Play ball, drink wine, sing doo-wop, jive with girls.

2. a foolish, inconsequential person.

1971 D.L. Lee *Directionscore* 207: Young lovers of current doo-wops. **1974** Beacham & Garrett *Intro 5* 65: You would have to be classified as a "do-wop" or...a "dufus."

dooze *n.* DOOZY.

1977 Olsen *Fire Five* 11: They say our new battalion chief's a dooze.

doozer *n. No.* DOOZY. [Def. in 1942 quot. is prob. local or erroneous.]

1930 (cited in *Oxford Dict. Mod. Sl.*). **1942** *ATS* 400: Ladies' man...*doozer.* **1949** in *Dict. Canad.* 216: Paying for three World Wars now. Next one'll really be a doozer, and expensive. **1956** Hargrove *Girl He Left* 164: That's a thigh-slapping doozer. **1960–61** Steinbeck *Discontent* 113: Well, there was a big military tea, a real doozer, maybe five-hundred guests. **1963–64** Kesey *Great Notion* 112: And there was some doozers. **1976** *L.A. Times* (Oct. 9) I 7: The candidate who makes the biggest mistake will lose it. And Ford made a doozer last night.

doozy *n.* [prob. fr. the adj.] something that is a remarkable example of its kind. Also vars.

1916 *DN* IV 274: *Dozy* [*sic*], *adj.* Term of praise. "Isn't that fish a *dozy*?" Brought...from eastern Ohio. **1951** in *DAS:* The first orchestra I had was really a doozie. **1955** Shapiro *Sixth of June* 58 [ref. to WWII]: But you've certainly got a couple of doozies—Bradford Gamaliel. **1966** R.E. Alter *Carny Kill* 11: I'll bet that first initial covers up a doozy [of a name]. **1971** *Playboy* (Mar.) 21: Hell, I ain't hoid dat woid in years. It's a doozy. **1984** *New Yorker* (Oct. 1) 79: Now we've got ourselves in a doozie of a spot. **1986** Ciardi *Good Wds.* 97: That guy is a real dusie.

doozy *adj.* [perh. alter. DAISY, infl. by Italian actress Eleonora *Duse* (1859–1924), discussed by G. Cohen in *Comments on Etymology* XXI 5 (Feb. 1992) pp. 3–5 and XXI 8 (May 1992) pp. 30–31] fancy; splendid.
  1903 Kleberg *Slang Fables* 83: He began to evolve schemes—one Doozy Scheme followed the other. **1911** *DN* III 543: *Doozy, adj.* "Sporty" or "flossy." **1929** Milburn *Hobo's Hornbook* 72: We are four bums, four doozy old bums,/We live like dukes and oils.

dope *n.* [< Du *doop* 'sauce'] **1.a.** a sauce or gravy.
  1807 W. Irving, in *DA*: Philo Dripping-pan was remarkable for his...love of what the learned Dutch call *doup*. **1809** in *DA*: Swimming in doup or gravy. **1923** *DN* V 205: *Dope*...Meat gravy. **1938** *AS* (Oct.) 237 [ref. to *ca*1860]: Dope was sowbelly gravy. **1950** in *DARE*. **1968** in *DARE*.
  b. a thick or sweet syrup; (*also*) molasses.
  1904 in *DA*: The [pancake] batter is rather thin,..."flipped" when brown on one side, and eaten with larrupy dope or brown gravy. **1916** Thompson *Round Levee* 45: "Dope" is molasses. **1929** *AS* (June) 420: *Dope*—Any sauce which is put over ice cream as, "All dopes 5 cents extra."...Oberlin, Ohio. **1934** Weseen *Dict.* 179: *Dope*...sauce or flavoring put on ice cream. **1965–70** in *DARE*. **1987** *RHD2*.
  c. *So.* any sweet carbonated soft drink, esp. a cola drink.
  1914 Graham *Immigrants* 77: Couples sit on high stools in the soda-bars and suck various kinds of "dope." **1915** *Printer's Ink* (Sept. 23) 46: Finally, there is the problem with which we are immediately concerned, the propensity of a large proportion of those who regularly drink Coca-Cola to call for their favorite drink as "dope" or "coke" or "koke." **1918** *Grindstone* (Baldwin-Wallace Coll.) 185: Mr. Simpson, seller of "dopes" and sodas. **1930** Caldwell *Swell-Looking Girl* 17: When they were gone the boy would put the other three cases in the tub and give the dopes a chance to cool. **1932** Burns *I Am a Fugitive* 76: I stopped at this stand and got a "dope" (as they call Coca Cola in Georgia). **1942** Wilder *Flamingo Road* 84: Give me a dope with a little lime, Roy. **1944** L. Smith *Strange Fruit* 23: Like a Coca-Cola?...Like a dope? **1972** N.Y.U. student: Down South they call Coca-Cola *dope*. **1977** Univ. Tenn. student: When I was a kid [*ca*1964], we called Coca-Cola *dope*. But we had to quit when we got to high school because it sounded too much like, you know, drugs.
  d. *Ohio.* an ice-cream sundae.
  1949 *PADS* (No. 11) 6: *Dope: n.* A sundae. Columbus, Ohio.
  2.a. a stupid person. [The English quots., app. synonymous with later U.S. usage, seem to derive from a different source, perh. dial. *daup* 'a carrion crow,' or even *dupe*, as sugg. by Barrère & Leland; the sense is exceedingly rare in the U.S. before 1900, and appears to derive from **(b)**, below.]
  *1851 in *OEDS*: *Dope*, a simpleton. **1862** in *Jour. Ill. Hist. Soc.* XVIII (1926) 824: Kersting came in his stead, a nice well educated man, but a dope. *1866 in *OEDS*: She was...a "dozened lile dope." *1889 Barrère & Leland *Dict. Slang* 322: Old cant *dope*, a simpleton, dupe. **1900** Patten *Merriwell's Power* 51: "Footless freshmen!" "Rotten!" "Pie-eyed!" "Dopes!" **1904** Hobart *I'm from Missouri* 27: I don't know who the Dope is that cooked this up...but he knows how to play ball. **1906** H. Green *Boarding House* 30: Aw, them skoits is dopes, on the dead level. **1918** *N.Y. Eve. Jour.* (Aug. 8) 18: He's a nice dope. *1919 Downing *Digger Dialects* 20: *Dope.* (n.)—(1) An unintelligent person. **1920** O'Neill *Emperor Jones* 34: What yo' whistlin' for, you po' dope! Want all de worl' to heah you? **1921** *Variety* (Nov. 18) 10: This came in handy when figuring out the dope character, probably with Lew Kelly taken as a model for style. **1923** Ornitz *Haunch, Paunch & Jowl* 22: G'wan up, you dope. **1929** *Variety* (Oct. 30) 70: Other naive dopes laugh like gloating hyenas. **1929** E. Wilson *Daisy* 103: Come on, yuh dope! **1932** Binyon & Bolton *If I Had a Million* (film): I suppose you dopes thought I was dumb enough to fall for a gag like that. **1933** in Ruhm *Detective* 71: Listen, dope, you can't sign any contracts, so she wouldn't be interested in you. **1934** H. Roth *Call It Sleep* 89: Yuh big dope, yuh can' even do nuttin'. **1938** Bezzerides *Long Haul* 35: How are you, you dope? **1939–40** O'Hara *Pal Joey* 12: I was sorry if it embarrassed her me calling attention to her dope boyfriend. **1941** Schulberg *Sammy* 232: Mr. Glickstein, don't be a dope. **1947** Hart *Gentleman's Agreement* (film): Go on and call her, you big dope! **1951** Styron *Lie Down* 77: Mother,

don't be a dope. **1955** Post *Little War* 21 [ref. to 1898]: Another were two men, brothers, good soldiers but quiet, who were promptly nicknamed Dope No. 1 and Dope No. 2. **1964** "H. Green" *Rose Garden* 249: I'm more than just a careless and brainless dope! **1970** N.Y.U. student: You really gotta be a dope to do that. **1985** Univ. Tenn. instructor: Don't you find that your students are, by and large, dopes? **1992** *Mystery Sci. Theater* (Comedy Central TV): Think *real* hard, you poor dope!
  b. [sugg. by **(4)**, below] a drug addict.
  1899 A.H. Lewis *Sandburrs* 10: It's then det quits callin' her Mulberry Mary, an' she goes be d' name of Mollie d' Dope. *Ibid.* 11: I'm only Mollie d' Dope—Mollie d' hop fiend. **1902** Hapgood *Thief* 298 [ref. to 1898]: They would have a good story against a dope copper who smoked too much. **1909** *Century Dict.* (Supp.): *Dope*...A person under the influence of, or addicted to the use of, some dope. **1918** *Camp Meade Herald* (Aug. 16) 2: Among the "dopes" was a lad who had been addicted to the use of morphine for nearly fifteen years. **1922** N. Anderson *Hobo* 68: He denied being a "dope" then and it was not until three days later...that he admitted the fact. He came to Chicago because he...was certain of getting morphine. **1922** *Variety* (July 7) 11: Steer clear of the "dopes." For...these drug addicts...will lead their associates into trouble. **1923** O'Hara *In Prison* 83: The others were "dopes"—drug addicts...convicted of violations of the Harrison Drug Act. **1923** in Lardner *Best Stories* 297: I was sure he wasn't no stew...And if he'd been a dope I'd knew about it—roomin' with him. **1932** Berg *Prison Doctor* 4: Freddie Winkler, called Freddie the Dope! He had...become a "cokie." **1936** Dai *Opium Add.* 140: And around the neighborhood he saw plenty of "dopes"—addicts—begging from the "sports" the price of a "shot." **1937** Reitman *Box-Car Bertha* 93: Oh, booze...jazz...and stealin'. Some of them are dopes. **1944** C.B. Davis *Leo McGuire* 172: He had been pinched on a very silly caper in Denver that nobody except a goof or a marihuana dope or possibly a jake-hound would have done. **1970** E. Thompson *Garden of Sand* 385: Dopes can't stop. Once they start, they can't stop it.
  3.a. grease; (*hence*) a lubricant, coolant, salve, additive, or emulsion. [Now S.E. in technical senses.]
  1876, 1890 in *DA*. **1897** Hamblen *Gen. Mgr.* 14: An' then I have to cart a carload of dope round the yard every day. **1902** *DN* II 233: *Dope, n.*...Any kind of lubricator, emulsion, or salve. **1904** F. Lynde *Grafters* 287: An oil-begrimed wiper crawled from under the 1031 [and] spat at the dope-bucket. **1909** *WNID*: *Dope*...Any thick liquid or pasty preparation, as of...grease for a lubricant. *1912 in *OEDS*: Cellon...The Fabric Dope used by the leading British and Continental Aeroplane and Hydro-aeroplane builders. **1923** *DN* V 205: *Dope*...Axle grease. **1930** *AS* (Apr.) 290: *Dope, n.* Liquid for shrinking and making fabric of the wings air tight. **1933** J. Conroy *Disinherited* 73: He...began pulling the lubricating waste known to railroaders as "dope" out of a journal box. **1934** *WNID2* (in various technical senses). **1976** R. Adams *Lang. Railroader* 47: *Dope*...A heavy, black semiliquid cooling compound for hot journals...*dope bucket*: A container for *dope*...*dope puller*: One who pulls lubricating waste out of journal boxes. **1976** Univ. Tenn. student: I worked one summer on the pipeline in Texas. The worst job in the world was working with what they called *hot dope*. There was *cold dope* too. It was this thick stuff that had to be smeared on the pipes.
  b. butter.
  1889 in *Dict. Canad.* 217: Some of the old-timers feast on hard tack covered with dope—butter.
  c. *Hobo.* the Baltimore & Ohio Railroad.—constr. with *the*.
  1893 *Century* (Nov.) 99: I was sitting one spring afternoon on a railway-tie on "The Dope"*...*The Baltimore and Ohio Railroad—called "The Dope" because it is so greasy. **1927** *DN* V 444: *Dope, the, n.* The Baltimore and Ohio Ry.
  4.a. an unidentified unwholesome or poisonous liquid. [Cf. 1862 quot. at DOPE, *v.*, 1.]
  1872 in *DAE*: He...bids us beware of the sugar, for it is full of flour and sand;...of the milk, for it is compounded of dope. **1918** in Fraser & Gibbons *Soldier & Sailor Wds.* 81: *Dope.* Medicine. Poison.
  b. a usu. illegal stupefying or stimulating drug. Now *colloq.* [Orig. as administered illicitly to a racehorse to improve or impair its performance; cf. 1875 quot. at DOPE, *v.*, 3.]
  1898–1900 Cullen *Chances* 39: Dope makes a horse about as frisky as three drinks of whisky makes a man who's been off the booze for a long while. **1900** Willard & Hodler *Powers* 186: "Give me some more o' that dope there—"...The stimulant revived him for a moment. **1902** Cullen *More Tales* 89: It all went through like a pony with the dope. **1902** Dunne *Observations* 25: Pass th' dope, Watson. **1909** *Century Dict.* (Supp.): *Dope*...Any drug, such as opium, laudanum, morphine,

cocaine, hydrate of chloral, hashish, etc., which has the property of inducing sleep or stupefying; a narcotic. (Slang.). **1924** Henderson *Keys to Crookdom* 403: Dope. Narcotic drug, opium, morphine, cocaine, heroin, yen shee. **1936** Tully *Bruiser* 207: We'll take no chances on anyone slippin' dope in the [fighter's] food. **1950** A. Lomax *Mr. Jelly Roll* 50: Hop...or coke. In fact those days you could buy all the dope you wanted in the drugstore. **1974** *Harper's* (June) 75: I would estimate 60–70 percent of the guys do some kind of dope. **1979** D. Glasgow *Black Underclass* 95: Barbiturates and amphetamines...[were] also sometimes referred to as dope. **1988** *CBS Morning News* (CBS-TV) (Nov. 3): A way to beat athletes who use dope [steroids] to train and then clean out in time for competition. **1990** Rukuza *W. Coast Turnaround* 180: Nobody pestered them to buy "smokin' dope."

c. *Specif.*, opium or an opium derivative such as morphine or heroin. Now *colloq.* or *S.E.*
1891 Campbell, Knox & Byrnes *Darkness & Daylight* 570: The opium used for smoking—called by the smokers "dope"—is an aqueous extract of the ordinary commercial gum. **1891** in Dobie *Rainbow* 172: Went to the hop-point [*sic*], went in a lope;/Sign on the 'scription case, "NO MORE DOPE." **1892** Norr *China Town* 36: Bring's a shell of dope, will you? **1896** Ade *Artie* 44: I would advise you to stop smokin' that double-X brand of dope, because it gives you funny dreams. **1922** E. Murphy *Black Candle* 20: In 1910, heroin began to be used and by 1916 it was the daily "dope" of 81 per cent. of the addicts. **1925** in Moriarty *True Confessions* 27: I had to have dope, that's all there was to it, if I had to kill to get it...Lady Morphia. **1958** S.H. Adams *Tenderloin* 9 [ref. to 1890's]: From the powerful presidents of railway and shipping lines to the dope-joint proprietors of Mott Street. **1971** P.E. Lehman, in *Drug Forum I* 178: According to the 1933 edition [of the *OED*] the word "dope" comes from the French [*sic*] term *doop* referring to a dripping or sauce. Thus "dope" originally meant some type of thick liquid. In all probability the term was the name given to the thick gooey mass of cooked opium that the smoker prepared for his pipe. **1971** Woodley *Dealer* 18: My partner's thing is dope...You know, duji, smack, scag, tragic-magic. **1979** D. Thoreau *City at Bay* 271: A dope dog sniffed out eighty-two pounds of heroin. **1984** J.R. Reeves *Mekong* 173: A lot of them used dope—heroin, that kind of stuff.

d. *Specif.*, marijuana or hashish. [*1946 quot. is from South Africa; this sense gained wide currency in the U.S. in the late 1960's. As shown by 1909 quot. at (b), cannabis has long been regarded as *dope* in a general way.]
*1946 (cited in Partridge *DSUE* (ed. 8)). **1950** Riesenberg *Reporter* 118: They have to find the dope, or reefers, on the person. **1962** H. Simmons *On Eggshells* 207: Man, this cat's been smoking too much of that dope. **1973** *Oui* (Feb.) 7: It's *grass*, Karpel, or better yet, *dope*—today, only the outsiders...[say] *pot*. **1991** Lott & Lieber *Total Impact* 145: The moxa stick...smells like dope.

e. a drugged state; (*hence*) a stupor; torpor.
1919 in *Marine Corps Gazette* (Dec. 1925) 187 [ref. to 1918]: Snap out of your dope and fall in column of fours! **1922** *Sat. Eve. Post* (June 3) 10: Walks around in a kind of dope.

5. medicine or medication of any kind.
1877 Burdette *Mustache* 115: Bolus' Anti-bilious Dope. **1902** *DN* II 233: *Dope*, n...Facetiously for medicine. **1903** Ade *Society* 55: He had been blistered in so many different Places and handed so many kinds of Dope that he became Leery, in time, and always claimed to be feeling Immense, even though he did not think he would live through the Day. **1915** Poole *Harbor* 53: The "dope" he used was mailed to him by a drug firm in Chicago. **1954** Gaddis *Birdman* 138: "You must be sousing up on your bird dope," the guard said.

6. any absorbent or adsorbent solid material used in the manufacture of high explosives (now *S.E.*); (*also*) (see 1942 quot.).
1880, 1881 in *OED*. **1909** *WNID*. **1942** *ATS* 35: *Dope*, a mixture of sawdust and kerosene used in building fires.

7. an alcoholic drink, esp. whiskey; alcohol.
1889 in *OEDS*: The oldest of the trio, an Irishman from County Cork, was very hilarious....The "dope" made him 20 years younger and very pugnacious. **1893** F.P. Dunne, in Schaaf *Dooley* 189: Mr. Dooley...was mixing a Tom-and-Jerry dope on the end of the bar. **1919–31** in *AS* (Oct. 1933) 34: Jargon of Fistiana...Dope...alcohol.

8. [sugg. by (**4.b.**), above] coffee.
1899 Munroe *Forward March* 28: Had breakfast hours ago, you know, and a prime one it was. Scouse, slumgullion, hush puppy, dope without milk, and all sorts of things. **1905** (quot. at DUFFER). **1942–44** in *AS* (Feb. 1946) 32: *Dope*, n. Coffee.

9. [app. sugg. by (**4.b.**), above] **a.** *Horse Racing.* information about a racehorse's record, condition, etc., for use by a bettor; (*hence*) advance information or predictions of any kind.
1899 A.H. Lewis *Sandburrs* 243: Mike is an oldtime tout...an' we're runnin' over d' dope in d' papers seein' what d' horses has done. **1905** *Nat. Police Gaz.* (Nov. 18) 3: The bunch begin figuring dope for the next race. **1906** H. Green *Boarding House* 17: It showed Shy Ellen to be a rank outsider. There was no dope on her, because she couldn't run in the mud. **1906** *DN* III 134: "Base-ball dope" and "foot-ball dope." **1907** in H.C. Fisher *A. Mutt* 3: Mr. A. Mutt...after wising himself on the dope...invests thusly. **1908** in Fleming *Unforget. Season* 274: It's in the dope that Covaleski...will prove the undoing of the Giants. **1911** Runyon *Tents* 37: The players no longer followed dope, but only the hosses I rode. **1913** in M. Gardner *Casey* 90: Again the Frogtown twirler figures dope on Mudville's Pride. **1927** Benchley *Early Worm* 27: Thus far, the football season of 1927 has been one of upsets. Nothing has turned out according to the dope. **1934** Faulkner *Pylon* 32: It looks like Roger Shumann is going to try to upset the boys' dope.

b. full, esp. inside, information of any kind; news; data.
1902 *Sporting News* (Sept. 20) 4 (cited in Nichols *Baseball Term.*). **1906** London *Moon-Face* 48: I thanked him, and asked the pay for my copy—*dope*, he called it. **1908** in H.C. Fisher *A. Mutt* 34: Count Igot the Dopesky, Chiefsky of the Russian Secret Servicovitch. **1908** in Fleming *Unforget. Season* 144: A statistician could have secured some very interesting dope in connection with the great battle. **1911** Howard *Enemy to Society* 134: I put in two weeks getting the dope on that place. **1912** *Lucky Bag* (No. 19) 340: "Charles," said he, "got the latest dope?" **1914** Lardner *Al* 117: Al that peace in the paper was all O.K. and the right dope just like you said. **1916** S. Lewis *Job* 55: Now read me the dope. **1917** Empey *Over the Top* 66: Well, if this happened, I was to send the dope to Cassell and he would transmit it to the Battery Commander as officially coming through the observation post. **1918** McNutt *Yanks* 119: Say, mister, have you got any dope on whether this division's goin' to France or not? **1918** E. O'Neill *Moon* 33: Yuh know what we said yuh'd get if yuh sprung any of that lyin' New Guinea dope on us again, don't yuh? **1919** *5th Div. Diamond* (Apr. 16) 2: There's dope galore, and something more, you hear it every day... **1929** Hammett *Falcon* 27: Can you give me some dope on an ex-guest, and then forget that I asked for it? **1940** R. Wright *Native Son* 135: Listen, here's the dope, see? **1944** H. Brown *Walk in the Sun* 32: "What's the dope?" Sergeant Porter said. **1956** E.S. Gardner *Curves* 49: Give me some more dope. **1973** W. Crawford *Gunship Cmndr.* 60: Give Colonel Brown the deep dope and inside-skinny. **1980** Manchester *Darkness* 191: They gave us bad dope, as usual. **1987** G. Trudeau *Doonesbury* (synd. comic strip) (Mar. 6): Listen, I got some solid dope on Blipco.

c. *Shooting.* (see quot.).
1987 D. da Cruz *Boot* 135: When the actual shooting begins, he will be able to tell...whether his dope—sight adjustment—is correct. *Ibid.* 298: *Dope* adjustment of rifle sights for various ranges and wind conditions.

10. stuff (in the broadest sense).
1899 A.H. Lewis *Sandburrs* 95: An' bein' off me guard, I takes d' soup for tea or some such dope, an' is layin' out to sugar it. **1901** Hobart *John Henry* 77: I've known Tommy for a long time, so he feels free to read his dope to me. **1906** Tomlin *H. Tomlin* 263: They are the real dope for vacation wear, take it from me. **1907** "Clivette" *Red Rag* 4: He's got the right dope [i.e. abilities]—he smokes the right "hop." **1908** in H.C. Fisher *A. Mutt* 27: "That's a good idea of yours, kid,...to get ma in a good humor."..."It's the only dope." *Ibid.* 109: "Is this [tuxedo] the dope?" "Fine, all but that turndown collar." **1909** *DN* III 395: Swell *dope* is anything and everything mental, oratorical, musical, artistic, or gastronomic that the speaker approves of. *ca***1912** in Kornbluh *Rebel Voices* 134: By gee! The Industrial Workers is the dope for me. **1912** Lowrie *Prison* 45: Dey makes too much of dat high-toned dope. It rags an' waltzes. **1913** *Nation* (Aug. 21) 161: Can the highbrow stuff. It isn't baseball...Come across with the real dope. **1913** T.M. Osborne *Pris. Walls* 309: This Osborne guy is no novice in prison dope. **1915** Poole *Harbor* 55: This darned library shut its doors...just as the real dope was coming along. **1915** Braley *Workaday World* 61: My grub is all tastin' of su'ge,/My pipe smells all day of the dope. **1917** in Truman *Lttrs. Home* 34: Some of those letters were works of art at the time of their composition but are stale dope now. **1918** Lardner *Treat 'em Rough* 87: I figure it's bad dope for the officers to mix up with the men. **1921** O'Neill *Hairy Ape* 199: Care for nobody, dat's de dope! **1927** S. Lewis *Elmer Gantry* 50: You certainly can make that hymn dope sound as if it meant something. **1927** Saunders *Wings* 87: Bombing is the real dope. I want to drop eggs on Berlin. **1929** A.C. Doyle *Maricot* ch. ii: That's the dope...Cut loose and have done with it. *Ibid.* ch. iii: We don't want them to pull no such dope on us. **1940** E. O'Neill *Long Day's*

Journey II i: It would be wrong dope to kid yourself. **1942** Garcia *Tough Trip* 154: Strictly cash business was slow, but it was the right dope. **1964** Howe *Valley of Fire* 95: "You a corpsman?"..."I am." "Good dope."

11. flattery; cajolery; foolishness; nonsense.

1906 *DN* III 134: *Dope*, n. Cajolery; optimistic talk; humbug. "He's just givin' you *dope*." "He gave him some *dope* about the investment." **1909** "O. Henry" *Options* 782: Say,...tell me one thing. Can you hand out the dope to other girls? *a***1904–11** Phillips *Susan Lenox* II 119: He says he talks the other sort of thing—the dope—the fake stuff—just as the rest of the hustlers do. He says it's necessary in order to keep the people fooled. **1917** in Truman *Dear Bess* 215: When I was a kid...I believed all the Sunday school books and idealist dope we were taught. **1919** in *OEDS*: I suggested it to a detective, but he laughed at me and said the article was nothing but "*dope*." **1921** in *OEDS*: He does not quite believe that the Bolshevik leaders themselves believe in their doctrines. He strongly suspects that on their part it is mainly "dope."

12. [sugg. by **(4.b., c.),** above] a cigarette.

1918 Wadsworth *Gas Attack* 37: He'd haul out one of his iodine-dipped dopes and light one up. **1921** *Am. Leg. Wkly.* (Mar. 25) 16: The soothing benediction of a "dope" or a "chew."

13. *Baseball.* a slow pitch.

1929 *N.Y. Times* (June 2) IX 2: A slow ball is sometimes referred to as a "dope." A half-speed ball is a "mixer."

dope *adj.* *Rap Music.* excellent; wonderful; superb; very attractive or enjoyable.

1981 J. Spicer, in Stanley *Rap* 301: Yo, man, them boys is dope....This record is dope. **1988** *N.Y. Times* (Aug. 29) C 15: Dope...superb, outstanding...That's a dope Porsche. **1988** *Spin* (Oct.) 47: Dope, *adj.*, the ultimate...fresh, incredible. *Ibid.* 48: Gucci may be good, but fake Gucci is what's really dope. *Ibid.* 58: This is a dope jam. **1989** *Harper's* (Mar.) 23: That studded bra is kinda dope—I could go for that. **1989** *Village Voice* (N.Y.C) (Apr. 11) 21: "I'm proving you can rap in Spanish and still be dope." Just how dope was soon demonstrated. **1990** *CBS This Morning* (Apr. 26): It's the stupidest, freshest, dopest thing on TV. **1991** *Fresh Prince of Bel-Air* (NBC-TV): Come on, baby, that sounds dope. Let's go.

dope *v.* **1.** to poison; (*hence*) to drug (food or drink).

1862 in Bensill *Yamhill* 12: Our scanty and coarse fare caused a deal of Mirth...Some of the Boys fall down, kick and struggle in sham death throes. When he is conscienceous [*sic*] the "Doped" victim swears its all owing to the want of nutriment. **1891** Maitland *Slang Dict.* 96: Dope, to dose, to poison. **1911** in Mager *Sherlocko* 89: Somebody's trying to poison me! All my food is doped. **1912** Lowrie *Prison* 198: I'll dope a certain guard's coffee. **1950** Riesenberg *Reporter* 178: It's a cinch the chili is doped. **1988** Barrow & Munder *Joe Louis* 74: "They done doped him or something. I believed he was doped for that fight."..."Hitler had someone poison Joe's food."

2. to apply a lubricant, salve, or varnish to.—also constr. with *up.*

1868 *Putnam's Mag.* II 363: With their snow-shoes thoroughly "doped." **1902** *DN* II 233: Dope, *v.tr.* 1. To smear, or lubricate. 2. To put salve on a wound. **1906** *DN* III 117: He *doped* the wagon wheels. **1918** Straub *Diary* (entry for July 27): I found some German shoe grease lying on the floor, so I doped up my shoes then took a good wash and shave, repacked my saddle bags and cleaned up the room.

3. to administer a stupefying or stimulating drug to (orig. a racehorse), esp. illicitly; to stupefy or stimulate, esp. with an addictive or illicit drug; to drug (a person).—used esp. in past ppl.—often constr. with *up,* now also with *out.*

1875 in Tamony *Americanisms* (No. 29) 5: Mr. Short...caused his hostler...to be arrested on the charge of maliciously injuring his horse by "doping" it with some deleterious substance. During the trial...it transpired that $35...had been given to "dope" the horse. **1889** Barrère & Leland *Dict. Slang* I 322: Dope, to (American). Doping is the stupifying men (sic) with tobacco prepared in a peculiar way..."Nine out of ten saloons in the slums employ doping as a means to increase their illicit revenue."—*American Newspaper.* **1896** C.C. King *Garrison Tangle* 245: 'Twas them that persuaded her...to "dope" both Mrs. Barry and Mary. **1898–1900** Cullen *Chances* 137: He had given his horse a half pint of whisky before the race...Doping horses was all right at Alexander. **1899–1900** Cullen *Tales* 241: That cigarette doped me up a little and kept me from having 'em [i.e., d.t.'s] right there, and bad. *****1900** in *OEDS*: They urge a liberal investment on the American horse, and confidentially impart the information that the animal is "doped." **1905** Sinclair *Jungle* 307: A horse could be "doped" or doctored, under-

trained or overtrained. **1906** *Nat. Police Gaz.* (Dec. 8) 3: I'll bet a hundred to one he's doped the girl. **1908** in H.C. Fisher *A. Mutt* 25: Dope the horses...shoot a jolt of hop into Nappa. **1911** *Hampton's Mag.* (Mar.) 285: Turk McMeekin doped him up. **1913–15** Van Loan *Taking the Count* 14: "What's wrong with him? Can he be doped or something?" "Yes...Doped with alcohol and nicotine. The stamina isn't there." **1921** in *Englische Studien* LX 284: I can recall exactly when I first became acquainted with [the word *dope*]. In 1893, at the Chicago Exhibition, I was told that the trained animals in the Hagenbach show were not doped. **1922** E. Murphy *Black Candle* 62: A horse is frequently "doped" or "doctored" before a race in order that it may be capable of extra effort. **1936** Tully *Bruiser* 96: "Wilson couldn't of doped him?" "Nope—I watched his food and drink." **1966** H.S. Thompson *Hell's Angels* 38: An army of vicious, doped-up Caucasian hoodlums. **1974** A. Bergman *Big Kiss-Off* 11: Maybe he was doped up. **1987** S. King *Misery* 48: Counterparts had visited Annie while he was doped out.

4. to adulterate; (*hence*) to alter unfairly or deceptively; tamper with; DOCTOR.

1898 in *OEDS*: They will...dope the flour to suit themselves. **1906** in *OEDS*: Before you "dope" that kind of stock with a strange mixture. **1912** Mathewson *Pitching* 288: Another method which has upset...many visiting teams is "doping" the grounds...The groundkeeper sank the pitcher's box...below the level of all the bases instead of slightly elevated as it should be. *Ibid.* 289: Sure. They "doped" the grounds for you. **1931** in *DA.* **1934** *WNID2*: Dope...To treat or impregnate with a foreign substance in order to impart a deceptive appearance or weight; to load.

5.a. Orig. *Horse Racing.* to study and make predictions from the records and performance of; predict.

1901 *Chi. Tribune* (July 28) 18: Baseball is the most uncertain of all sports and therefore the most difficult to "dope" in advance. **1904** *Life in Sing Sing* 247: Dope...picking winners from past performances. **1905** *Nat. Police Gaz.* (Nov. 18) 3: I've been doping the ponies for five years now, and so some of the wise ones get their tips from me. **1908** in H.C. Fisher *A. Mutt* 50: Mutt Gets A Few Interruptions From the Boobs While Trying to Dope the Entries..."After dinner, Rockefeller. I'm doping the entries now." **1910** T.A. Dorgan, in *N.Y. Eve. Jour.* (Jan. 22) 5: Of course Willus was spreading a press story, but he doped it almost right. **1937** *Atlanta Constitution* (Oct. 1) 21: He is doped to beat the South Carolinians rather definitely. **1957** E. Lacy *Room to Swing* 27: I spend hours at night doping the races.

b. DOPE OUT.

1898–1900 Cullen *Chances* 20: He dopes it that she can beat the lot. **1901** Hobart *Down the Line* 14: I doped a turtle [slow horse] named "Pink Toes" to win the next day. **1902** Cullen *More Tales* 46: I doped it that when he wanted to tip me off as to his lay he'd do it. **1908** H. Green *Maison* 1: I'm wore out by dopin' these here problems. **1915** Lardner *Gullible's Travels* 96: I had it doped that Bishop was afraid o' water or else he wouldn't of turned down all our swimmin' parties. **1918** Rowse *Doughboy Dope* 89: He gasses you into insensibility with his talk...about someone having doped the "tariff" wrong. **1921** "M. Brand" *Black Jack* 224: You dope it that he'll cut for the house of Pollard? **1926** Nason *Chevrons* 105: I right off doped I'd give it to the "Y" guy. **1958** Eyster *Customary Skies* 165: Swing her east. If we find a barrel, we can dope the rest. **1960** Carpenter *Youngest Harlot* 132: I'd had you doped all wrong, that you wasn't anything at all like that I cracked you up to be.

c. to train or study. Also trans.

1916 D. Runyon, in Paxton *Sports* 96: At a boat race,...the crew that had "doped" best is showing a wide gap of open water. **1918** Palmer *Amer. in France* 152: "Doping the black stripe," it was called; for one day the reserve officer students might wear the black stripe of the General Staff on their arms.

d. to explain.

1920 *Am. Leg. Wkly.* (Jan. 30) 34: What show have we got to dope the whole proposition to you?

6.a. to take medication or administer medication to.

1902 *DN* II 233: "To dope yourself," to take medicine in excessive quantities. **1906** *DN* III 117: He's dopin' for the chills.

b. to use narcotic or psychotropic drugs.—also constr. with *up* or (later) *out.*

1909 *Century Dict.* (Supp.): Dope...intrans. To indulge habitually in the use of opium or other drugs either for the pleasurable sensations produced or as anesthetics. **1909** J. Addams *Spirit of Youth* 66: At least three of the boys could have stood but little of the irregular living and doping. **1917** in H.W. Morgan *Addicts* 138: Thinking I had not taken enough, I would dope up more. **1936** Dos Passos *Big Money* 247: I bet you that boy dopes. **1970** in L. Bangs *Psychotic Reactions* 33: Go back and dope out with the gang. **1976–77** McFadden *Serial* 110: She still had this puritanical *thing* about driving and doping. **1985** J. Dillinger *Adrenaline* 20: Jeff went berserk...doping heavily.

7. to loaf, idle, or move slowly.—usu. constr. with *around* or *along*. Cf. DOPE OFF.

1905 *Independent* (June 22) 1398: The man of the tenement? Oh, he broods and "dopes" his life away and would crack many a joke at the expense of his brother, the ox, did he but know of him. **1910** *Our Navy* (Aug.) 32: Civilians could go down the street...throwing firecrackers on the sidewalk...and the police could always manage to be doping off on some street corner at a distance. **1929–33** Farrell *Manhood of Lonigan* 245: A middle-aged guy with a paunch doped along. **1942** Faulkner *Go Down, Moses* 61: I would like to see your south creek piece planted by tomorrow night. You doped around in it today like you hadn't been to bed for a week. **1948** J. Stevens *Jim Turner* 9: Even while I doped around and stuffed myself I felt sore guilt. **1972** West *Village* 160: No Cong would dope along the way those guys did. They're too smart to do that.

dope book *n. Horse Racing.* a small book or pamphlet containing racing statistics and other information about horses, jockeys, etc.

1899–1900 Cullen *Tales* 235: I didn't pack around any dope book or handicapping outfit. **1904** T.A. Dorgan, in Zwilling *TAD Lexicon* 33: Excess baggage such as dope books, form sheets, overnight entries, etc. **1909** *Century Dict.* (Supp.): *Dope-book*, a miscellaneous collection of racing information (Racing Slang.). **1919** Witwer *Alex the Great* 90: This bird is...readin' a dope book on the races!

dope daddy *n. Narc.* a man who supplies narcotics to an addict.

1936 Duncan *Over the Wall* 145: Gwen...had wrecked Tom Murray's future by bargaining for her "dope daddy's" freedom. **1955** *AS* (May) 87: *Dope daddy, n.* A [drug] peddler.

dope fiend *n.* a person addicted to an opiate; drug addict.

1895 (quot. at FIEND). **1896** *DAE*: A "dope fiend."...A victim of the opium habit. **1909** *Century Dict.* (Supp.): *Dope-fiend*...A habitual user of drugs, such as opium or cocaine. (Slang.). **1910** *Variety* (June 18) 10: The Dope Fiend. **1913** in Tyler *Org. Crime* 373: The saloon of the old pickpockets...kept by the "dope fiend" and banker of criminals. **1921** *Variety* (Apr. 8) 1: The censors ruled no for any show in which a dope fiend was characterized on the stage. **1927** in Truman *Dear Bess* 331: He said he was a dope fiend...and that he was either going to quit or die in the attempt. **1938** in A. Lomax *Mr. Jelly Roll* 43: He finally came to be a dope fiend and smoked so much dope till he died. **1956** E. Hunter *Second Ending* 21: That's because the newspapers run articles on dope fiends—*fiends*, that's a laugh. **1963** Williamson *Hustler!* 107: You don't find many dope fiends that're afraid of a pistol. **1965** in Wilner & Kassebaum *Narcotics* 200: I didn't want to stop being a dope fiend. First, I began to look for the connection in the joint. **1979** in Terkel *Amer. Dreams* 218: So I became the first dope fiend in the neighborhood.

dopehead *n.* **1.** a drug addict.

1903 (cited in *W10*). **1924** Henderson *Keys to Crookdom* 403: *Dope fiend.* Drug user, dope head. **1925** Dos Passos *Manhattan Trans.* 387: Well you sure have dished your gravy this time kid, cap'n 's a dopehead, first officer's the damnedest crook out o Sing Sing, crew's a lot o bohunks. **1927** *Dopehead Blues* (record title). **1930** in Hemingway *Sel. Letters* 336: If dope didn't constipate you I would most certainly become a dope head. **1934** Lomax & Lomax *Amer. Ballads & Folk Songs* 186: The origin of this cheerful ditty of the dope-heads is doubtful. **1958** Motley *Epitaph* 143: The heat is on all the dopeheads. **1964** Harris *Junkie Priest* 98: We don't want any New York dopeheads in this town.

2. a blockhead.

1940 Raine & Niblo *Fighting 69th* (film): Roust outa there, dopeheads! *a***1961** J. Jones *Thin Red Line* 61: And where do you find germs? In dirt, dopehead.

dope house *n.* a house or apartment where illicit, esp. addictive, drugs are bought, sold, and used.

1967–68 von Hoffman *Parents Warned Us* 157: Mona had run one of the wildest, widest-open dope houses in San Francisco, until she was busted.

dope in *v.* to inform; tell.

1963 Rubin *Sweet Daddy* 72: Doc Smith has doped me into plenty. **1968** Sackler *Great White Hope* 978: Well, the boys'll dope me in.

dope monkey *n. R.R.* a car inspector.

1940 *R.R. Mag.* (Apr.) 42: *Dope monkey*—Car inspector. **1976** R. Adams Lang. *Railroader* 47: *Dope monkey.* A car inspector who sees that there is *dope* in the journals.

dope-off *n. Mil.* a lazy or inattentive person.

1945 *Amer. N & Q* (Apr.) 8: *Feather Merchant:* Army-Navy expression meaning a "dope-off," a lazy person. *a***1949** D. Levin *Mask of Glory* 143: He was just a dope-off, and he was yellow. **1957** Myrer *Big War* 333: Did they all have to turn into...rummies and dope-offs and everything else. **1965** Hardman *Chaplains* 14: I'll send a road-scraper through to cover the goof balls and ass-draggin' dope-offs that don't make it.

dope off *v.* **1.** to fall asleep; doze; in phr. **doped off** asleep.

1918 "Commander" *Clear the Decks!* 204: They dope off down here and then wonder why their bellies go back on them. **1918** Poague *Diary* (entry for Aug. 2): It is a common saying here, "Snap out of the hop, old man." Instead of sleeping, we term it "doping off." **1942** Anderson & Stallings *What Price Glory?* 103 [ref. to 1918]: And dope off for a little while...that's it, give him a blanket. **1945** J. Bryan *Carrier* 115: I was doped off. **1952** "Dr. Seuss" *5,000 Fingers* (film): Holy gosh, I must have doped off! **1978** E. Thompson *Devil to Pay* 31: I fill my stomach...and I'll start to dope off and yawn. **1966–80** McAleer & Dickson *Unit Pride* 153: The sun felt nice...I was doping off when I heard Dewey.

2. Esp. *USMC.* to be inattentive; loaf or (*occ.*) malinger. Cf. 1910 quot. at DOPE, *v.,* 7.

1922 *Leatherneck* (Apr. 22) 5: *Dope Off:* To be sleepy or inattentive. **1945** in *Calif. Folk. Qly.* V (1946) 387: A man who is not alert or attentive on watch *dopes off,* but whoever *knocks off* work in order to rest or sleep...*caulks off.* **1946** *Am. Leg. Mag.* (Apr.): *Doping off:* Half asleep, inattentive while on duty. **1949** Brown & Grant *Iwo Jima* (film): You doped off and got one of my men killed and one bayoneted. **1951** Morris *China Station* 258: Stand alert watches, don't dope off. **1952** Uris *Battle Cry* 104: Maybe I'd better tell him about the way you doped off on that ditch digging detail yesterday. **1958** Frankel *Band of Bros.* 212: The medics looked me over and decided I was dopin' off. **1962** Gallant *Valor's Side* 182: You're right about that. He dopes off. **1965** Gallery *Eight Bells* 104: However, I doped off on that opportunity and simply admitted that I was an American naval officer. **1967** Dibner *Admiral* 51: The brig guard left the key where Stick could get it. Then he doped off and Stick jumped ship. **1967** Flood *More Lives* 15: Don't go doping off on the firing range because you start thinking you're gonna end up guarding the Panama Canal. *a***1981** "K. Rollins" *Fighter Pilots* 188: You doped off.

dope out *v.* **1.** to work or figure out; DOPE, *v.,* 5.b.

1902 Cullen *More Tales* 39: I'd...try to dope it out where I'd stacked up against him before. **1903** Townsend *Sure* 99: Say, wouldn't it take a forn French mug to dope out a game like that. **1906** *Nat. Police Gaz.* (Sept. 22) 6: Well, you can dope it out. **1906** H. Green *Boarding House* 250: He doped out a cautious play. **1908** in H.C. Fisher *A. Mutt* 51: I'll get you a match as soon as I dope out a winner. *a***1904–11** Phillips *Susan Lenox* I 250: Anstruther can dope out the accompaniments on that wheezer. **1912** in Truman *Dear Bess* 104: I had it all doped out to write you as much as (I could). **1914** in Kornbluh *Rebel Voices* 150: I might try to dope something out about that Frisco Fair. **1918** Streeter *Dere Mable* 14: The fello who doped it out had some bean. **1918** *Stars & Stripes* (Apr. 19) 7: It ain't so easy to dope out fake calls. **1919** Bliss *805th Inf.* 107: I was...still trying to dope out about those postal cards. **1925** Weaver *Collected Poems* 162: I had it all doped out. **1931** Armour *Little Caesar* (film): Here's the way I doped this thing out. **1934** Appel *Brain Guy* 207: I'm the brain guy, but I didn't dope out your pounding. **1935** Lindsay *She Loves Me Not* 39: I've got to dope out a telegram. **1958** "R. Traver" *Murder* 25: Only Parnell could have doped it out this way. **1961** Sullivan *Shortest Yrs.*: Still trying to dope out that old moral dilemma. **1966** in Asimov, Greenberg, & Olander *Sci. Fiction Shorts* 232: I got to think about it, dope it out. **1975** *Sing Out!* (July) 2: I try to dope it out myself. **1985** N.Y.C. woman, age 52: I'll see what I can dope out. **1987** *Crossfire* (CNN-TV) (Apr. 30): I'm always interested in trying to dope out what you're up to.

2. see DOPE, *v.,* 3, 6.b.

doper *n.* **1.** *Sports.* DOPESTER, 1.

1906 *Nat. Police Gaz.* (June 9) 10: Prize Ring "Dopers" Find it Difficult to Place Blame for Recent Nelson-Herrera Fiasco in Los Angeles.

2. *Narc.* **a.** a habitual user of illicit drugs.

1922 Murphy *Black Candle* 32: To force an entry to a drug den at two o'clock in the morning when the "dopers" are irresponsible either wholly or in part, is an unpleasant and often a dangerous task. **1925** *Amer. Mercury* (Feb.) 196: Who look no more like "dopers" than criminals resemble the so-called criminal type. **1935** Macdonnell *Visit* 59: Say, listen, do you know how dopers inject themselves? **1971** *Newsweek* (Sept. 13) 41: The air is cleaner out here and there's not so many crazy dopers around. **1972** *Nat. Lampoon* (July) 6: He isn't a doper.

b. a person involved in the manufacture, transport, or sale of illicit narcotics.

1934 *WNID2: Doper*…One engaged in illicit distribution of narcotics. *Cant.* **1986** Philbin *Under Cover* 112: I haven't really done enough against these dopers. **1986** *Newsweek* (July 28) 27: It's gonna be a tremendous morale crusher for the dopers.

dope sheet *n.* **1.** *Horse Racing.* a sheet of paper containing information on entries in a horse race.

1899–1900 Cullen *Tales* 293: You must've spent the night over the dope sheets. **1902–03** Ade *People You Know* 111: When he arrived at the Track he gave up for a Badge and a Dope-Sheet. **1909** *Century Dict.* (Supp.): *Dope-sheet*…A list of race-horses, giving the record of their performances in previous races. (Racing slang.). **1940** E. O'Neill *Long Day's Journey* I: Instead of the dope sheet on the ponies. **1942** Liebling *Telephone* 73: They are reaching for a communal dope sheet, a ten-cent racing paper giving the entries at all tracks.

2. a sheet providing information or instructions of any kind.

1918 *Stars & Stripes* (May 10) 3: You'll find your dope sheet is a gem. **1921** *15th Inf. Sentinel* (Jan. 14) 10: "C," Co. Dope Sheet. **1936** Cain *Double Indemnity* 366: Once you're in, they've got to listen to you, and you can pretty near rate an agent by how quick he gets to the family sofa, with his hat on one side of him and his dope sheets on the other. **1956** Heflin *USAF Dict.* 174: *Dope sheet.* A last-minute bulletin or information sheet giving details overlooked or not available earlier. *Slang.* **1980** Pearl *Pop. Slang* 40: *Dope sheet*…2. (Broadcasting) detailed written instructions for filming an animated sequence. **1981** O'Day & Eells *High Times* 39: The publicity man put out a dope sheet, dishing out Walkathon gossip. **1984** J. Green *Newspeak* 73: *Dope sheet* (TV) the breakdown of instructions for shooting each scene.

dopester *n.* **1.** *Sports.* a person who compiles and analyzes the records of racehorses, athletes, or sports teams and predicts their future performance; (*broadly*) a political or other forecaster or analyst.

1907 in *OEDS:* As we talked on a corner not long ago, a Dopester…stepped up to us. **1910** T.A. Dorgan, in *N.Y. Eve. Jour.* (Feb. 16) 14: Figuring up the Jeffries-Johnson fight, the way the dopesters get at the ponies, is a very interesting thing. **1921** in Cornebise *Amaroc News* 90: Dopesters say his argument will be full of force. **1942** Liebling *Telephone* 237: Some of the dopesters he has listened to…have a high opinion of German prowess. **1948** L. Allen *Reds* 191: Most fans recall the great Philadelphia Athletics of 1914, who were upset by the Boston Braves in the World Series, much to the chagrin of the game's dopesters. **1965** *World Bk. Dict.: Dopester*…an analyst.

2. a poisoner; (*also*) a drug addict.

1913 J. London *J. Barleycorn* 115: Oh! John Barleycorn is a wizard dopester. **1938** (cited in *Oxford Dict. Mod. Sl.*). **1942** *ATS* 476. **1946** Petry *Street* 266: He hated the sight of the drunks and dopesters who frequented the places where he played.

dope-stick *n.* a cigarette.

1904 T.A. Dorgan, in Zwilling *TAD Lexicon* 33: The old sport took another drag on the dope stick and faded away in the darkness. **1918 in OEDS:* Cigarettes! smokes, fags, weeds, dope-sticks—they are known by many strange names. **1930** in *OEDS.* **1942** *ATS* 127. **1954– 60** *DAS: Dope stick* n. A cigarette. *c1915.*

dope story *n. Journ.* (see 1968 quot.).

1943 in J. Gunther *D Day* 54: Gilling and I had been informed…that we might write "dope" stories when the campaign began but that we could not touch actual operations. **1968** Safire *New Lang.* 120: *Dope story.* Information leaked to a reporter and published as his own analysis; useful method of launching "trial balloons" or conditioning public opinion.

dope trap *n. Narc.* DOPE HOUSE.

1962–68 B. Jackson *In the Life* 227: So every time I went down to the dope trap, it's known. The law knows where those dope traps are, they know what's going on, nobody's a fool.

dope up *v.* see DOPE, *v.*, 2, 3, 6.b.

dopey or **dopie** *n.* DOPER, 2.a.

1929 Zombaugh *Gold Coast* 96: [She]…holds the international suicide-attempt record, [and is] a "dopey." **1936** Dai *Opium Add.* 198: *Dope-fiend.* A hypodermic needle user. Also called *hypos, byps, dopey,* and *old*

dopey. **1958** A. King *Mine Enemy* 98: Dr. Moreno…told me right off the bat that he didn't generally tackle dopeys. **1967** C. Cooper *Farm* 23: All the new dopie entries were standing around waiting for the unit physician. **1971** J. Brown & A. Groff *Monkey* 58: It was thought that a dopie could be switched from opium to coal tar. **1971–73** Sheehy *Hustling* 49: I'm not a dopie. I'm a model with a daughter to support. **1976** "N. Ross" *Policeman* 78: First of all you have to rely on a dope addict's truthfulness. Many times a dopey will give you bullshit.

dopey *adj.* **1.** drugged or as if drugged; (*hence*) groggy; sleepy.

1896 in *OEDS:* A man who acts as if under the influence of the poppy drug is said to be dopy. **1897** Townsend *Whole City Full* 183: I wouldn't smoke [the opium], then,…until after the church. It's terrible unlucky to be dopey in church. **1897** Ade *Pink* 191: Don' say no mo'! I'm so dopey now I can't finish yo' shoe. **1899** A.H. Lewis *Sandburrs* 60: Mike is settin' on a stool keepin' mum an' lookin' w'ite and dopey. **1899** Cullen *Tales* 46: The tall man was so dopey that he could barely raise his arms, and he ran around the ring in a dazed kind of way. **1900** Ade *More Fables* 172: He was so wrapped up in his Art that he acted Dopey most of the time, and often forgot to send out the Laundry so as to get it back the same Week. **1905** Bowe *13th Minn.* 71: The other side were a little dopy, and…our boys got the best of it. **1906** M'Govern *Sarjint Larry* 65: Old Dad's sorry his fiddlin' made you dopey, though. **1906** "O. Henry" *Four Million* 81: It's Dopy Mike…He hits the pipe every night. **1909** *Century Dict.* (Supp.): *Dopy*…Stupid, as if under the influence of some drug; dull; heavy. Also *dopey.* (Slang.). **1919* Downing *Digger Dialects* 20: *Dopey* (adj.)—…(2) Dazed, bemused. **1929** Hemingway *Farewell* 198: "I was dopey," I said. **1930** Weaver *Collected Poems* 233: And then they called him Dopey,/Because he acted like he was full of hop. **1957** Thornton *Werewolf* (film): It won't make me dopey or anything? I have to drive home.

2. dull; stupid; silly.

1903 McCardell *Chorus Girl* 43: Like as if it made any difference to Dopey McKnight. **1904** McCardell *Show Girl* 137: As for Dopey, he's more "dopey" than ever. **1906** Ford *Shorty McCabe* 264: Say, if I hadn't been havin' a dopey streak I'd a known something was about due. **1919* Downing *Digger Dialects* 20: *Dopey* (adj.)—(1) Unintelligent. **1923** Ornitz *Haunch* 161: Low grade imbeciles like Dopie Ike. **1925** Gross *Nize Baby* 180: You shouldn't esk dopey questions. **1926** Furfey *Gang Age* 54: He was a dopey-looking guy. **1933** "W. March" *Co. K* 112: Listen to me, you dopey old son of a bitch! **1934** H. Roth *Call It Sleep* 301: Dopy mutts! **1950** Calmer *Strange Land* 101: He's the only one that doesn't treat me like a dopey kid. **1961** *Twilight Zone* (CBS-TV): You let that dopey red suit go to your head. **1963** D. Tracy *Brass Ring* 17: He stood there with the dopey cloth hat in his hand. **1977** L. Jordan *Hype* 125: Too many dopey young girls to cope with. **1993** *TV Guide* (Feb. 6) 47: Clips from their dear if sometimes dopey series.

do-re-mi *n.* [pun on syn. DOUGH] money.

1926 Dunning & Abbott *Broadway* 218: She needs the do-ray-me pretty bad. **1929** in Runyon *Guys & Dolls* 72: It must cost him plenty of the do-re-mi. **1932** V. Nelson *Prison Days & Nights* 23: They're all out for the old do-ray-me. **1934** Berg *Prison Nurse* 81: I ain't never seen a one where you couldn't get the stuff if you had the do-re-mi. **1936** Levin *Old Bunch* 130: One of them gets into that pot of dough-re-me. **1936** West *Cool Million* 162: He got off at the last station and your dough-re-me went with him. **1942** Davis & Beverley *Call House Madam* 76: Jim Hanford he picked out to stake the joint, furnish the do-re-mi. **1946** Gordon *Years Ago* 91: I ain't got the do-re-mi to give you. **1946** Gresham *Nightmare Alley* 29: Any place is grand, long as you got the old do-re-mi in the grouch bag. **1953** Manchester *City of Anger* 6: They sure love that do-re-mi. **1962** Plath *Bell Jar* 170: When I collect enough do-re-mi to buy a car, I'm clearing out. **1968** Swarthout *Loveland* 64: All you needed to buy beer was long trousers or a skirt, an adult expression and the dough-re-mi. **1970** *Playboy* (Aug.) 108: I'm a little short of do-re-mi.

dorf *n.* [perh. alter. of DORK, infl. by DOOF] *Stu.* a stupid or annoying person.

1975 *Univ. Tenn. student: Dork* and *dorf* mean the same thing, like a stupid person. **1989** Spears *NTC Dict.* 104: You are a prize-winning dorf.

do-right *adj. Und.* law-abiding; (*also*) honest; right-acting. Also as n.

1936 D.W. Maurer, in *AS* (Apr.) 120: *Do-right people* 1. Nonaddicts. Also, *square John.* 2. Legitimate people or those with no criminal connections. 3. The tax-payers (prison argot). **1949** Monteleone *Crim. Sl.* 71: *Do-right Johns…Do-right People*…Non-addicts. **1961** *Social Problems* X 152: The thief…[will] confine [his] exploitations to the "do rights." **1966–67** P. Thomas *Mean Streets* 234: I was sent to the Tombs, the House of Do-Right, on 125 White Street. **1968** in Giallombardo *Impris. Girls* 163: I'll be a "Do right all *day* woman, If you will be a do right all *night* man." **1980** *AS* (Fall) 197: Cop, copper,...Dick, do-right boy...Mr. Do-Right.

dork *n.* [perh. joc. alter. of DICK] **1.** the penis.
   1961 Peacock *Valhalla* 339 [ref. to 1953]: You satisfy many women with that dorque? **1964** *AS* (May) 118: Two variants [of *dick*] which are probably Midwestern, *dirk* and *dork*, also meaning "penis." **1966** H.S. Thompson *Hell's Angels* 14: They scurry about...with their dorks carried low like water wands. **1968** P. Roth *Portnoy* 219: The glorious acrobatics she can perform while dangling from the end of my dork! **1969** Cray *Erotic Muse* 38: My dork is short. **1970** Byrne *Memories* 83 [ref. to *ca*1945]: When you had a dork you were never safe, as it was an involuntary muscle. **1970** *Playboy* (Dec.) 282: You know that dope doesn't zap your brain...leaving you with three eyes and a dork the size of a pineapple. **1970** Wambaugh *New Centurions* 186 [ref. to 1962]: But some faggots are real aggressive. You say hello and bang, they got you by the dork. **1972** *Playboy* (Dec.) 148: What if my dork, regulation-sized by New York locker-room standards, is dwarfed by acrobatic, hyperactive Valley orgiasts?
   2. *Stu.* a stupid or obnoxious person.
   1967 Moser & Cohen *Pied Piper* 32 [ref. to 1963]: I didn't have any clothes and I had short hair and looked like a dork. Girls wouldn't go out with me. **1974** Strasburger *Rounding Third* 1: I'd be a king-sized dork if...I didn't offer to take it off your hands for you. **1972–76** Durden *No Bugles* 226: I got to go huntin' slopes with you dorks tomorrow. **1983** K. Miller *Lurp Dog* 8: Giggle away, you goofy dork. **1991** B.E. Ellis *Amer. Psycho* 127: What a dork. **1992** *N.Y. Observer* (Apr. 20) 20: A number of parents...put on bright orange jackets...."You kind of feel like a dork."

dork *v.* to copulate with (a woman).
   1971 B. Rodgers *Queens' Vernacular* 88: *Dork* (teen sl[ang], '60's)..."Somebody would even dorkin' me in the ear!" **1976** Whelton *CB Baby* 136: Junior would be dorking another woman. **1987** *Nat. Lampoon* (June) 82: How'd you like to dork Miss Goldbudner...before a capacity crowd at Yankee Stadium?

dork around *v.* to fool around.
   1983 S. King *Christine* 120: A sleazy-looking guy...was dorking around with an old BSA bike.

dorkbrain *n. Juve.* a blockhead.
   1974 Univ. Tenn. instructor: *Dorkbrain*—I haven't heard that one in years. **1976** Univ. Tenn.: I've never seen so many dorkbrains living in one dormitory. **1984** J. Green *Dict. Contemp. Slang.*

dorkbreath *n.* Esp. *Stu.* a stupid or contemptible person.
   1974 *Nat. Lampoon* (Oct.) 36: Indicates some dorkbreath still reading this tiny type. **1974** Univ. Tenn. student: Dickbreath, dorkbreath, cuntbreath—all mean *asshole*. **1978** C. Miller *Animal House* 62: Thanks to the dorkbreath twins here. **1985** Univ. Tenn. student theme: "Dork-breath" and "dork-head"...mean the same as "dork." **1991** *Daily Beacon* (Univ. Tenn.) (Jan. 31) 6: Eat my boots, dork breath!

dorked *adj.* fatigued.
   1956 Hargrove *Girl He Left* 77: I am dorked. Bugged. Bushed. Beat.

dorkface *n. Juve.* a stupid-looking, stupid, or contemptible person.
   1976 Univ. Tenn. student: I hate that dorkface. **1992** *Caroline's Comedy Hour* (A&E-TV): You could call me...dorkface.

dorkhead *n.* DORKBRAIN.
   1984 Holland *Better Off Dead* (film): That dorkhead. **1985** (quot. at DORKBREATH).

dorkus *n. Juve.* DORK, 2.
   1979 *Nat. Lampoon* (Dec.) 58: The ordinary dorkus makes cigar money compared to what I make. **1984** Algeo *Stud Buds* 3: A rather stupid person...*dorkus.*

dorky *adj. Juve.* clumsy; stupid; JERKY.
   1968–70 *Current Slang* III & IV 39: *Dorky,*...Ridiculous; unfair. **1972** B. Rodgers *Queens' Vernacular* 66: *Dorky* absurd, peculiar, strange. **1980** Birnbach *Preppy Hndbk.* 219: *Dorky adj.*...characterized by clumsiness. **1982** S. Black *Totally Awesome* 12: There are these dorky little theories about it. **1983** S. King *Christine* 62: Her dorky-looking boyfriend. **1983** K. Miller *Lurp Dog* 175: This dorky bullshit. **1985** J. Dillinger *Adrenaline* 253: Looking even dorkier. **1987** G. Matthews *Rooster* 65: Nine-to-five factory bozos with...those dorky little lunch pails. **1993** *TV Guide* (Jan. 23) 9: Every TV cop has to have a gimmick, no matter how dorky.

dorm *n. Stu.* a dormitory. Now *S.E.*
   1900 *DN* II 17: The student...lives in the *dorm* (dormitory).

dormie *n. Stu.* a student who resides in a campus dormitory.
   1966 Goldstein *1 in 7* 146: Even when the "dormies" are not straight...they are uncool. **1966** in IUFA *Folk Speech: Dormy:* person who lives in the dorm. **1988** *Campus Voice* (Spring) 48: I...brought home an obese dormie named "Velveeta."

dorm rat *n. Stu.* DORMIE.
   1963 in IUFA *Folk Speech: Dorm rat*—Someone who lives in the dormitory. **1975** Graffito, Univ. Tenn.: Frat Rat Dorm Rat. **1980** Eble *Campus Slang* (Oct.) 5: How long have you been a dorm rat? **1984** Algeo *Stud Buds.*

dornick *n.* [extension of earlier sense 'pebble; stone' < Ir *dornóg*] a coin.
   1844 *Spirit of Times* (Sept. 21) 349: "In town with a pocketfull of dornicks," said Barbecue..."Plenty of whiskey, I hopes, dancin and wimmin."

dorse var. DOSS.

dose *n.* **1.** a bracing drink of liquor.
   *****1676** in D'Urfey *Two Comedies* 122: I'll take another dose of sack here. **1862** C.F. Browne *A. Ward* 171: Took a grown person's dose of licker with a member of the Injianny legislater. **1866** in Hilleary *Webfoot* 211: If he had stopped at one "dose" he would not have got "So Sick." **1927** Rollins *Jinglebob* 75 [ref. to 1880's]: Better take a dose. It'll be the last you get.
   2.a. a beating; (*hence*) a finishing or killing blow or wound.
   *****1819** [Moore] *Tom Crib* 17: Sandy tipp'd him a *dose* of that kind. **1832** *Spirit of Times* (Feb. 4) 1: Pound the dog—bleed him—give him a dose. **1871** "M. Twain" *Roughing It* 31: I was armed...with a pitiful little Smith & Wesson's seven-shooter, which carried a ball like a homeopathic pill, and it took the whole seven to make a dose for an adult. **1873** Scammon *Marine Mammals* 267: I'll give old Rip-sack a dose he can't give to the 'pothecary's. **1874** Alger *Julius* 70: Just let me get a stick. I'll give her a dose. **1879** Burt *Prof. Smith* 66: I'se done got my dose, massa. I'se done got my dose! **1886** Lozier *Forty Rounds* 40: I've got a feelin'/That I'm goin' to get a dose to-day. *Ibid.* 56: He got his dose at last. **1889** "M. Twain" *Conn. Yankee* 20: At last I met my match, and I got my dose. **1904** in "O. Henry" *Works* 1437: I wouldn't have a man...that didn't beat me up at least once a week....Say! but that last dose Jack gave me wasn't no homeopathic one. **1927** in Hammett *Knockover* 312: Why didn't you let the bum die where he got his dose? **1939** Lomax & Lomax *Singing Country* 225: I will learn a damn Yankee to face the bold Scot/I'll cook you a dose and you'll get it red-hot.
   b. *Pris.* a prison sentence.
   *****1860** Hotten *Slang Dict.* (ed. 2): *Dose,* three months' imprisonment, with hard labour. *****1871** (cited in Partridge *Dict. Und.* 199). *****1877** in Partridge *Dict. Und.:* What's yer dose?...Five, oh, you can do that...on yer 'ed easy. **1902** "J. Flynt" *Little Bro.* 144: The "old man" was prepared to give the men their "doses." **1928** O'Connor *B'way Racketeers* 71: They had us dead to rights. I got twenty flat and the Dutchman and Curly took the same dose.
   3.a. an infection.
   1864 in C.H. Moulton *Ft. Lyon* 170: Lieut. Platt...was afraid that he would have a "dose" sure, as he laid on my bed when I was "breeding" the disease [smallpox].
   b. *Specif.* a venereal disease, esp. gonorrhea.
   1877–1914 in *DN* IV (1914) 102: *Dose. n.* venereal disease. **1918** *Social Hygiene* (Apr.) 268: Mr. Worldly Wise Guy. He had his first dose when only sixteen. A few years later, he developed gonorrheal rheumatism. **1918** in *V.D. Blues* (Sept. 1972) (WNET-TV): A dose of clap can ruin any man. **1918** in Carey *Mlle. From Armentières* I (unp.): Mademoiselle from gay Paree/Had a dose and gave it to me. *****1914–22** Joyce *Ulysses* 151 [ref. to 1904]: Some chap with a dose burning him. **1923** McAlmon *Companion Volume* 246: It's a wonder you haven't had a dose before this, the chances you take. **1927** Hemingway *Men Without Women* 205: If you love women, you'll get a dose. **1929–30** Dos Passos *42d Parallel* 62: Aw, hell, a man's not a man until he's had his three doses. **1934** H. Miller *Tropic of Cancer* 267: Of course, he had a dose...So far as they could see, he didn't have syphilis. **1938** Wolfe *Web & Rock* 58: Reese McMurdie...said you couldn't call yourself a man until you'd caught a dose. **1941** Schulberg *Sammy* 256: All he got for his troubles were a Heidelberg scar, a dose, and a couple of years on the Island. **1942** McAtee *Supp. to Grant Co. Dial.* 4 [ref. to 1890's]: *Dose,* n., attack of venereal disease, usually the clap or gonorrhea. **1959** Farris *Harrison High* 360: There was some talk about her giving a boy a dose. **1963** Coon *Short End* 34: But in town, man, you can get doses they haven't even thought

up names for yet. **1971** Faust *Willy* 115: Churchill's old man had a dose. **1990** Murano & Hoffer *Cop Hunter* 84: You got a dose?

dose *v.* to infect with a venereal disease.—also constr. with *up*.
1918 in Carey *Mlle. from Armentières* II (unp.): She dosed the Colonel and dosed him again. **1929–33** Farrell *Manhood of Lonigan* 194: What does he do but knock her up, and I suppose dose her. **1944** Stiles *Big Bird* 94: In the movie there were a lot of ugly things about sex that people never think about until they get dosed up. **1953** Paley *Rumble* 182: The girls couldn't be sick—there ain't been any business to dose them up. **1982** Downey *Losing the War* 207: The first punk…felt betrayed by the man who had "dosed" him.

dosh *n.* [orig. unkn.] money. *Obs.* in U.S.
1854 St. Clair *Metropolis* 16: I mean for you to fork over to me twenty-five dollars as my share of the dosh. **1871** Thomes *Whaleman* 168: I wants the dosh now, to carry on my house and meet my payments…He leaves me minus the dosh for his grub and drinks. *1953, *1959, *1970 in *OEDS.* *1990 T. Thorne *Dict. Slang: Dosh*…money….Revived in the money-conscious late 1980's.

doss *n.* [ult. < L *dorsum* 'back'] Orig. *Und.* **1.** a bed; place to sleep. Also **dorse.**
*1744 (cited in Partridge *Dict. Und.* 199). *1789 G. Parker *Life's Painter* 174: Dorsed [*sic*]. The place where a person sleeps, or a bed. **1791** [W. Smith] *Confess. T. Mount* 19: A bed, *a dause.* *1839 Brandon *Poverty, Mendicity, & Crime* (gloss.): *Doss*—a bed [in Scots cant]. *1846 in *OEDS:* She stalled a lushy swaddy to a doss t'other darky. **1859** Matsell *Vocab.* 27: *Doss.* A bed. **1871** Banka *Prison Life* 492: Bed….*Doss.* **1894** *Century* (Mar.) 708: This district supports a queer kind of lodging-house called by the men who use it "the two-cent doss." **1901** King *Dog-Watches* 38: There were seven beds in this room, not including the canvas cot which the boy said was my "dos." *a*1909 Tillotson *Detective* 91: *Dos*—A bed. **1914** Jackson & Hellyer *Vocab.* 29: *Doss,* Noun. General currency. A place to sleep; a bed. *a*1930 in Tomlinson *Sea Stories* 551: Know any place I kin get a doss?
2. sleep; rest.
1894 *Century* (Feb.) 520: Find good barns for a doss at night. *Ibid.* (Mar.) 706: They can curl up and have a "doss." (sleep) **1899–1900** Cullen *Tales* 243: They had…some kind of a shakedown to have a doss on. **1913** *Sat. Eve. Post* (Mar. 15) 37: Cut loose from yer doss! **1930** Irwin *Tramp & Und. Sl.: Doss*—A sleep; not, as in English slang, a place to sleep. **1967** [Beck] *Pimp* 116: Sugar, let's cop some "doss."

doss *v.* [cf. the *n.*] Orig. *Und.* to sleep; lodge for the night.—also constr. with *it.* Now *rare* in U.S. Also **dorse.** [The "1785" ex. adduced by *OED2* is not found in the work cited; it is almost certainly interpolated from *F & H,* which erroneously attributes *1812 Vaux ex. (quoted below) to 1785 Grose *Dict. Vulgar Tongue.*]
*1789 in J. Farmer *Musa Pedestris* 65: Ere we dorse this night. *1789 G. Parker *Life's Painter* 174: I dorsed there last night. *1812 Vaux *Vocab.:* To *dorse* with a woman, signifies to sleep with her. **1866** *Nat. Police Gaz.* (Nov. 24) 3: They "doss" in the "Burg." **1871** Banka *Prison Life* 492: Sleeping…*Dossing.* **1879** *Snares of N.Y.* 81: Say, boss, can I doss in here to-night? **1897** in J. London *Reports* 320: *Dorse* or *kip,* to sleep. **1899** "J. Flynt" *Tramping* 393: *Doss:*…verb, to sleep. **1899** Cullen *Tales* 116: Stop dossin' agin the post. **1902** Cullen *More Tales* 80: I'll just doss it out [in the open air] to-night. **1907** J. London *Road* 107 [ref. to *ca*1893]: "Kip," "doss," "flop," "pound your ear," all mean the same thing; namely, to sleep. **1967** [Beck] *Pimp* 130: Hell no she ain't "dossing."

doss down *v.* to bed or lie down. Now *rare* in U.S.
*1896 in *OEDS:* Hodgkins and I "dossed down" by the side of it. **1899** Boyd *Shellback* 240: Waal, you b— lot of sojers. Was yer concludin' to doss down up there? **1980** (quot. at CRUMB-ROLL).

doss-house *n.* a cheap rooming house; FLOPHOUSE. Now *rare* in U.S.
*1889 Barrère & Leland *Dict. Slang* I. *1889 in *F & H* II 311: People who are at present residing in the doss-houses of London. *1890 in *F & H:* Equally bad doss-houses exist in Notting Hill near Drury Lane. **1899** "J. Flynt" *Tramping* 393: *Doss-House:* A lodging house. **1918** Livingston *Delcassee* 16: Nor did the interior layout of the dosshouse vary…from those of the other dumps catering to the custom of the roving vagrants. **1926** Tully *Jarnegan* 208: Ethel's mother ran a doss-house in Seattle. **1977** T. Berger *Villanova* 153: You look as if you spent the night in a doss house. **1993** *N.Y. Times Bk. Review* (Oct. 10) 1 [ref. to 1905]: A squad of Fleet Street feature writers made their way down to the South London doss house where [W.H.] Davies was quartered.

dossing ken *n. Und.* DOSS-HOUSE.
*1838 in *F & H* 311: The hulks is now my bowsing-crib, the hold my dossing-ken. **1866** *Nat. Police Gaz.* (Nov. 24) 3: Curly was coming up the street from a "dossing ken."

doss-ken *n. Und.* DOSS-HOUSE.
1872 Burnham *Secret Service* v: *Doss ken,* a lodging house, of a low character.

dossy *n.* [prob. alter. of DOXY] a girl or woman.
*1895 in Partridge *Dict. Und.* 200: The travelling tinker…and with him his "dossy" (woman). **1923** O'Hare *In Prison* 55: Lelia and Esther were two little coloured girls from Kansas City, both under sixteen. They were typical little negro "dossies" of the coloured slum sections of our Southern cities.

dot-and-go-one *n.* a person who limps or has a wooden leg.—used derisively. [Farmer & Henley also give syn. *dot-and-carry-one* from Sir Walter Scott, 1822, a form not recorded in U.S.]
*1785 Grose *Vulgar Tongue: Dot and Go One*…generally applied to persons who have one leg shorter than the other. *1837 in *F & H* II 311: How he rose with the sun, limping Dot and Go One. **1895** Coup *Sawdust* 217: He described the jailer, whom he disliked, as "Dot-and-Go-One," from the fact of his having a wooden leg.

dot head *n.* [fr. the caste mark worn by some Hindu women] an inhabitant or native of India.—usu. considered offensive.
1988 Univ. Chicago student (coll. J. Sheidlower): She's pretty, but my parents would kill me if I went out with a dot head. **1989** in Random House files. **1993** *N.Y. Times* (Feb. 11) B 14: As Dr. Sharan…left a downtown office the defendants yelled: "There's a dot head! Let's get him!"

dots *n.pl. Jazz.* musical notation; *(also)* sheet music.
1927 in R.S. Gold *Jazz Talk:* I will give you the "dots" for them. **1958** in *ibid.* 73: Firstly, most St. Louis musicians could read music, and were seen carrying their "dots" about with them.

dotty *adj.* **1.** peculiar or crazy; *(often)* eccentric from age. [The survival of this term from ME, without a trace for more than four centuries, would be virtually unparalleled.]
[*ca*1400 in *OEDS:* Ale mak many a mane to have a doty poll.] *1885 in *OED:* I am not mad, drunk, or dotty. *1888 in *OEDS: Dotty,* silly from age; senile. **1899** in Ade *Chicago Stories* 249: I think I'm dotty the minute I begin to feed myself the quinine. **1901** Irwin *Sonnets* (unp.): Last night I dreamed a passing dotty dream. **1901** Hobart *Down the Line* 35: "She's such a happy wappy 'ittle fing," giggled the dotty dame. *1902 Masefield *Salt-Water Ballads* 9: 'N' the stooard he goes dotty. **1906** *Nat. Police Gaz.* (Apr. 28) 3: What's the matter, are you dotty? **1907** in H.C. Fisher *A. Mutt* 6: You're dotty in the dome. **1911–12** Ade *Knocking the Neighbors* 70: Ophelia goes Dotty and picks the imaginary Dandelions. **1921** Z. Grey *Mysterious Rider* 197: Say, Wade, are you growing dotty? **1927** Behrman *Second Man* 337: And here's Austin Lowe absolutely dotty about her. **1943** Wendt & Kogan *Bosses* 229: John isn't dotty and he ain't full of dope. **1968** Van Dyke *Strawberries* 59: He thinks I'm dotty. You think I'm off my head? **1979** Whipple *Whalers* 170: A dotty old man stomping through his fields in Eskimo boots and a sombrero. **1979** Gutcheon *New Girls* 57: I really think I am getting a bit dotty after all.
2. wildly enthusiastic.
1899 Thomas *Arizona* 10: He's pretty sure to be a little "dotty" about her. Can't you see, the lad's dotty with the gas?—Norris, Moran, 1898, p. 67. **1899** Ade *Fables* 23: He smoked Heny Cigarettes until he was Dotty. **1901** Ade *Modern Fables* 74: The whole Crowd was Dotty about her.

double *n.* a duplicitous action; doublecross.—constr. with *the.*
*1821 *Real Life in London* I 139: Tipp'd us the double, has he? **1868** Williams *Black-Eyed Beauty* 13: I think you're coming the double over me, Bill…You must have got more'n sixteen dollars for that watch! *1873 (quot. at DOUBLECROSS, *n.,* 1.). **1914** Jackson & Hellyer *Crim. Slang* 29: *Double,* Noun. General usage…the "double-cross." Example: "He got the double."

double *adv.* exceedingly or especially. Cf. S.E. sense, 'to twice the amount or extent; doubly'.
[*1726 A. Smith *Mems. of J. Wild* 128: May I be double-d—mn'd if I do not.] **1846** *Crockett's Almanac* (unp.): We…war double ready for a fight. **1923** Witwer *Fighting Blood* 5: I'm double cuckoo! I don't know what it's all about. **1940** Baldwin *Brother Orchid* (film): That's double jake by me. **1943** Holmes & Scott *Mr. Lucky* (film): And brother, you got to

understand he wasn't just ordinary tough—he was double tough. **1953** T. Runyon *In For Life* 117: At least one convict played a double-tough brand of football. **1963** Braly *Shake Him* 56: This is double wild. **1966** Elli *Riot* 46: A double-tough twenty-three-year-old lifer. **1966** H.S. Thompson *Hell's Angels* 119: Man, those mothers up there are double-shook. **1970** Thackrey *Thief* 397: Lew was really, for sure, one double-rough son of a bitch. **1970** Boatright & Owens *Derrick Floor* 70: They was double-tough. **1979** Decker *Holdouts* 43: I used to like the idea of being a double-tough bronc rider. **1981** O'Day & Eells *High Times* 111: What was she? Double-dumb? **1987** *Tour of Duty* (CBS-TV): You're gonna have to deal with double-bad Aubrey Decker.

¶ In phrase:

¶ **play (someone) double** to treat with duplicity.
*__**1868** G. Eliot, in *OED:* Thought played him double. **1901** Irwin *Sonnets* (unp.): You played me double and you knew it, too.

double *v.* to DOUBLECROSS.—constr. with *on*.
*__**1863** in T. Taylor *Plays* 221: [No] man...tries to double on me. *__**1873** (quot. at DOUBLECROSS, *n.*, 1.). **1941** in Inman *Diary* 1039: I never double on a customer.

double-bagger *n.* [see quots.] *Stu.* an extremely ugly person.
1982 M. Pond *Valley Girl's Guide* 55: *Double-Bagger*—Someone who looks skanky or grody—like they're *so* ugly you need *two* bags, one for them and one for you. **1986** *NDAS: Double-bagger*...A very ugly person. **1989** P. Munro *U.C.L.A. Slang* 87: *Double bagger* ugly person (so ugly you need to put one bag over his/her head and one over yours just in case his/hers rips). **1990** P. Dickson *Slang!* 216: *Double bagger.* Person so ugly he or she needs two bags over his or her head instead of just one.

double-bang *n.* DOUBLECROSS.
1988 H. Gould *Double Bang* 33: It was a double bang.

double-bang *v.* **1.** (see quot.).
1980 Pearl *Pop. Slang* 41: *Double-bang v.* (Crime) to burglarize the same place twice.
2. DOUBLEBANK, 1.
1988 H. Gould *Double Bang* 81: They...frisked him for a wire—you never knew who was double-banging who anymore. *Ibid.* 145: I don't double bang my own blood.

double-bank *v.* **1.** *Und.* to treat with duplicity; DOUBLECROSS.
1867 *Nat. Police Gaz.* (Mar. 30) 2: But they deceived him, and in turn were themselves "double-banked." **1867** *Nat. Police Gaz.* (Oct. 26) 2: No "double-banking" of a "cove"...The "knucks" and "molls" were true as steel. **1942** Goldin et al. *DAUL* 61: *Double-bank, v.* To doublecross.
2. to attack with more than one assailant or from more than one direction at once; DOUBLE-TEAM.
1882 A.W. Aiken *Joe Buck* 5: Hyer is whar you double-banked my pard....You double-banked him, or else you never could have downed him. He's more than a match for any five [of you]. **1883–84** Whittaker L. Locke 282: They double-banked me, at last, didn't they?...I'll not deny they double-banked me...for they took me off my guard...I knocked two of 'em stiff afore I went down. **1942** Goldin et al. *DAUL* 61: Three strange weeds...double-banked me and kicked my lemon...in. **1994** N. McCall *Wanna Holler* 55: The best way to guarantee winning a rumble was to double-bank someone, get several guys and gang up on him.

double-barreled *adj.* **1.** extreme; absolute.
*a*__**1867** G.W. Harris *Lovingood* 77: Ole Bullen's pint is a durn'ed fust rate, three bladed, dubbil barril'd, warter-proof, hypockracy. **1882** Sweet *Sketches* 162: You are a kind of double-barrelled fool. **1915–17** Lait *Gus* 63: You are the double-barrelled bearcat o' the flock. **1956** W. Taylor *Roll Back Sky* 172: Well I'll be a goddamned, double-barreled son of a bitch! **1959** Farris *Harrison High* 18: He was a double-barreled sensation.
2. *Prost.* habitually engaging in passive anal as well as genital copulation; (*also*) bisexual.
*__**1890–91** *F & H* II 313: *Double-barrelled*...Said of a harlot working both before and behind. *__**1903–09** *F & H* I (rev.) 93: *To give back-and-belly* (venery) = to work both ends: said of a *double-barrelled* harlot. *__**1936** Partridge *DSUE: Double-barrelled* Applied...to any person both normal and abnormal in sex: from *ca*1900. **1942** Goldin et al. *DAUL* 61: *Double-barreled.* Skilled in degeneracy, especially applied to loose women. **1967** Colebrook *Lassitude* 155: Beppo is a "bull-dagger," a "low dyke," a "lady-lover," a "Les-wolf," and a "double-barreled broad."

double C *n. Music.* the C above middle C.

1956 E. Hunter *Second Ending* 221: Was it any harder than busting double C?

double-clutcher *n.* (esp. among truck drivers) a usu. joc. euphem. for MOTHERFUCKER.
1967 *DAS* (Supp.) 681: *Double-clutcher*... = mother fucker. Orig. Negro use; pop. by Negro construction workers during the Korean War. [*double-clutch*]*ing*... = mother fucking.

double-clutch hat *n. Trucking.* (see quot.).
1950 *West. Folk.* IX 381: *Double-clutch hat.* A cap with a visor, usually worn by truck drivers.

double-clutching *adj.* **1.** (esp. among truck drivers) a usu. joc. euphem. for MOTHERFUCKING.
1964 Walnut Ridge, Ark., service-station attendant (coll. J. Ball): That double-clutching son of a bitch. **1967** (quot. at DOUBLE-CLUTCHER). **1973** *Roll Out!* (CBS-TV series): We been driving them double-clutching buckets all the way to the front.
2. (among truck drivers) pertaining to, involved with, or typical of truck driving. *Joc.*
1968 in *DARE:* Double-clutching boot. **1971** Tak *Truck Talk* 48: *Double-clutchin' boots:* a trucker's boots...*double-clutchin' man:* a trucker.

doublecross *n.* **1.** Esp. *Und. & Gamb.* an act or instance of double duplicity, as when a boxer or jockey who has illicitly engaged to lose a contest decides to break his word without warning. [Orig. as two words.]
*__**1826** "Blackmantle" *English Spy* II 208: A good bit of *blunt* I'd have netted;/But a *double X* spoilt it, and Bob won the fight. *__**1834** Ainsworth *Rookwood* 258: The Double Cross...Two *milling coves*, each vide avake,/Vere backed to fight for heavy stake:/But.../Both *kids* agreed to *play a cross*. *__**1848** in *OEDS:* All bets are off. It has...been "rumoured," that a double cross was intended. *__**1873** Hotten *Slang Dict.* (ed. 4): *Double cross*, a *cross* in which a man who has engaged to lose breaks his engagement, and "goes straight" at the last moment. This proceeding is called "doubling" or "putting the double on," and is often productive of much excitement in athletic circles. **1880** *N.Y. Clipper Almanac* 44: It is a double cross where the party who agrees to lose either wins or tries to win without giving warning to his confederates. *__**1887** in *F & H* II 313: When the pair raced before...a double cross was brought off. Teemer promised to sell the match, and finished by selling those who calculated on his losing.
2. an act or instance of treachery, esp. by violating one's promise or obligation; a deliberate betrayal. Now *colloq.*
1894 in Ade *Chicago Stories* 46: Tommy, they're givin' y' the double-cross. **1895** *Harper's* (Sept.) 620: If you git de double cross put on you, yer'll take it like it was medicine. **1902** Townsend *Fadden & Mr. Paul* 226: "How," he says, "shall I give de double-cross to Uncle Ned?" meaning King Edward. **1902** in Blackbeard & Williams *Smithsonian Comics* 23: Johnny Wise Gets The "Double Cross." **1906–07** Ade *Slim Princess* 46: The Pike family...gave the double cross to the common people. **1926** "M. Brand" *Black Jack* 68: Are you handing me a double cross like this? **1932** in E. O'Neill *Letters* 395: The old P.P. group gave me the double-cross. **1936** Benton & Ballou *Where Do I Go?* 207: Either stupidity or some subtle double cross. **1953** Manchester *City of Anger* 145: That's what makes his double-cross so dirty. **1955** Harrington *Dr. Modesto* 120: Somebody pulled a double-cross. **1960** C.L. Cooper *Scene* 220: It's a dirty doublecross! **1972** Madden *Bros.* 144: Jack had a double-cross worked out in advance. **1984** "W.T. Tyler" *Shadow Cabinet* 308: That was the double cross I told you about.

doublecross *v.* to treat with double-dealing or duplicity; betray. Now *colloq.*
1901 (quot. at QUEER, *adj.*). **1903** Ade *People You Know* 153: Although he had been double-crossed and put through the Ropes, he still had a Punch left. **1903** A.H. Lewis *Black Lion* 306: He's out to double-cross me. *a*__**1904–11** Phillips *Susan Lenox* I 251: Some sly trickery of prompting from an old expert of theatrical "double-crossing." **1913** *Sat. Eve. Post* (Jan. 4) 25: Dem double-crossers will take care of de bill, dey says. **1913** J. London *Valley of Moon* 88: They've learned...to double-cross an' lay down to the bettin' odds an' the fight fans. **1919** *Lit. Digest* (May 10) 66: Are we that got the War Cross over there to be double-crossed over here? **1921** in E. O'Neill *Hairy Ape* 191: Dey'd double-cross yuh for a nickel. **1924** in Oliver *Blues Tradition* 64: She'll two-time you like she double-crossed me. **1938** "E. Queen" *4 Hearts* 161: You'd double-cross your own father. **1940** W.C. Williams *In the Money* 44: Just another double-crossing son of a bitch of a sneakin' stool pigeon. *ca*__**1943** in L'Amour *Over Solomons* 37: He'd doublecross his own mother. **1960** J. Mitford *Daughters* 218: But it seems we were double-

crossed in the sixth race. **1988** Kienzle *Marked for Murder* 57: Looking for someone who had double-crossed them.

double-decker *n.* (see quot.).
    1891 Maitland *Slang Dict.* 96: *Double-decker* (Am.), two "cocktails," or other morning refreshers in one; a drink for a thirsty man.

double-digit days *n.pl. Mil.* the final ninety-nine days of a tour of duty.
    1969 Sgt., U.S. Army, age *ca*22: *Double-digit days* are your last ninety-nine days in Vietnam before your tour is up.

double-digit midget *n.* [sugg. by SHORT, *adj.*] *Mil.* a person in military service having fewer than one hundred days remaining in a tour of duty. Cf. SINGLE DIGIT MIDGET. [Quots. ref. to Vietnam War.]
    1969 *Life* (Aug. 8) 51: The obsession with passing time increases when a man begins his last 100 days [in Vietnam] (he is then a "double-digit midget"). **1985** Bodey *F.N.G.* 37: Me, I'm a double-digit midget, ninety-seven days. **1987** Pelfrey & Carabatsos *Hamburger Hill* 102: "Double-digit midget," announced Bienstock as he marked the milestone 99 on his cardboard calendar.

double dime *n.* twenty dollars.
    1969 Beck *Black Widow* 226: I got Hickey Freemans your size…that you ain't gonna believe at a double dime.

double-dip *n. Baseball.* a doubleheader.
    1984 *N.Y. Post* (Aug. 11) 37: Ray Fontenot…closed out the double-dip with his third straight victory.

doubledome *n. Journ. & Pol.* a scholar or intellectual, esp. a highly educated person who holds impractical or unrealistic views.
    1943 H.A. Smith *Putty Knife Factory* 207: Arthur Brisbane [†1936]…was known among fellow newspapermen as Old Double Dome. **1953** Michener *Sayonara* 11: Then the doubledomes in Washington set a deadline. **1966** Longstreet & Godoff *Wm. Kite* 173: She got next to this double-dome from Columbia, a molecular physicist.

double-ender *n. Riverboating.* a ship's officer holding both a pilot's and an engineer's license.
    1977 in Curry *River's in My Blood* 29 [ref. to *ca*1930]: Cap'n Wethern had an engineer's license also. He was what we call a "double-ender."…Engineer and pilot license.

double fin *n.* [*double* + FIN] **1.** Esp. *Und.* a British ten-pound note; (*hence,* in U.S.) a ten-dollar banknote.
    *1879 *Macmillan's Mag.* (Oct.) 505: Yes, there it was, fifty quid in double finns (£10 notes). **1942** *ATS* 537: Ten-dollar bill…*double finn.* **1965** *Mad* (June) 28: A double fin.
    2. *Pris.* (see quot.).
    1942 *ATS* 465: *Double fin*…a ten-year sentence.

double-fucking *adj.* FUCKING.—used as an intensive.—usu. considered vulgar.
    *1929 Graves *Good-Bye to All That* 79 [ref. to 1917]: The Bandmaster, who was squeamish, reported it as: "Sir, he called me a double-effing c—." **1991** Tolkin *Rapture* (film): No double-fuckin' *way* would I stop.

double-gaited *adj.* bisexual.
    a1927 in P. Smith *Letter from Father* 144: Helen…was fairly promiscuous as well as being double-gaited and preferring girls to men. **1940** O'Hara *Pal Joey* 176: Duilio is not double gaited as far as I knew. **1956** M. Wolff *Big Nick.* 168: This dubious double-gaited bastard of yours. **1962** in J. Blake *Joint* 319: This time it was a black pappagallo, a double-gaited male courtesan. **1963** in Bruce *Essent. Bruce* 217: I never did meet any cat who was double gaited. **1966** Jarrett *Sex Is a Private Affair* 64: She was also double-gaited—that is, she went for women as well as men. **1966** Susann *Valley of Dolls* 256: Probably cruising, the double-gaited sonofabitch.

double-geared lightning *n.* (used as a figurative standard of comparison for quickness or dexterity).
    1894 C.C. King *Initial Experience* 109: Tonto air double-geared lightenin' on pullin' trigger. **1915** [Swartwood] *Choice Slang* 46: *Double-geared light[n]ing*—Very fast or exceedingly quick. **1930** Sage *Last Rustler* 4: He could handle a rope like double-geared lightning.

double harness *n.* marriage.
    1885 Siringo *Texas Cowboy* 81: I asked her how she would like to jump into double harness and trot through life with me. **1910** T.A. Dorgan, in *N.Y. Eve. Jour.* (May 2) 18: They haven't landed us for that double harness stunt…—not us—nitsky.

double nickel *n. Trucking.* a highway speed limit of 55 m.p.h.—constr. with *the.* [This limit was set nationally in 1974.]
    1976 Whelton *CB Baby* 16: I didn't want to break that double nickel until I had an eyeball on those Smokeys. **1976** Lieberman & Rhodes *CB* 127: *Double Nickels*—55 mph speed limit. **1983** S. King *Christine* 33: The double-nickel speed limit had still been fifteen years away. **1990** Rukuza *W. Coast Turnaround* 205: Even during the height of the "double nickel" madness, no speed-limit signs ever marred the roadsides.

double nuts *n.pl. Mil. Av.* double zero, esp. as a radio frequency or identifying number.
    1981 Mersky & Polmar *Naval Air War in Viet.* 43: The "00" or "double nut" marking indicates that it is flown by the air wing commander. **1983** M. Skinner *USAFE* 41: Double zeroes, called "double nuts" in the Navy. **1986** Coonts *Intruder* 287 [ref. to Vietnam War]: "Devil Five Oh Oh, strangling parrot." "Black Eagle copies, Five Double-nuts." **1988** Poyer *Med* 197: Double-nuts wants the ops type to have the traffic memorized when he gets up.

double-o *n.* **1.** [prob. fr. ONCE-OVER] a close and searching look; scrutiny; inspection.—usu. constr. with *the.*
    1913 T.A. Dorgan, in Zwilling *TAD Lexicon* 33: You go to the cooler for 30 days and give that the double o awhile. **1919** Cowing *Dear Folks* 17: And from what was left the lieutenant picked out twelve to go over to the colonel and have him give us the double O. **1929–31** J.T. Farrell *Young Lonigan* 59: He took his pajama top off and gave his chest the double-o. **1940** Baldwin *Brother Orchid* (film): You know, I been givin' this joint the double-o…and you're all OK guys. **1948** I. Shulman *Cry Tough!* 182: Andy didn't like strangers giving him the double-o while he ate. **1951** Robbins *Danny Fisher* 275: I gave them the expected, appreciative double-O. **1960** Barber *Minsky's* 230: This broad gives us the double-o. **1971** *Newsweek* (Nov. 7) 54: Ed Boynton…patrols the perimeter with a vigilance that has earned him the nickname "Double-O." **1972** *All in the Family* (CBS-TV): Lookit dese two, givin' me de big double O here. **1983** *Daily Beacon* (Univ. Tenn.) (Nov. 14) 10 (crossword puzzle): Give the double-O…*Eye.*
    2. DOUBLECROSS.
    1929 in Partridge *Dict. Und.* 201: I guess you guys know what it is to get the double-o, don't you? **1936** Tully *Bruiser* 35: "I'd like to fight Barney McCoy…I licked him once and he licked me."…"Are them the only reasons?" "No—he put the double-O on me."
    3. *Gamb.* nothing; zero.
    1947 Schulberg *Harder They Fall* 165: All them fancy words of yours add up to double-o.

double-o *v.* **1.** to look at or examine carefully; inspect.
    1918 *Stars & Stripes* (June 28): Have yuh double-o-ed a dame? **1934** Weseen *Dict. Slang* 11: *Double O*—To examine; to spy. **1952** *Esquire* (June) 131: I stop for a second to double-o the frame.
    2. to DOUBLECROSS.
    1929 in Partridge *Dict. Und.* 201.

double out *v.* to go into partnership.
    1927 Murphy *Gray Walls* 55: I next went to Alaska, where I doubled out with an old miner.

double saw *n.* DOUBLE SAWBUCK.

double sawbuck *n.* **1.** a twenty-dollar banknote. Also **double saw.**
    1850 in *OEDS*: Send me the two double "saw-bucks." **1926** Maines & Grant *Wise-Crack Dict.* 7: *Double saw*—twenty-dollar bill. **1931** *AS* (June) 330: *Double-saw buck,* n. A twenty-dollar bill. *Double-saw,* n. A twenty-dollar bill. **1935** *Amer. Mercury* (June) 230: *Double saw,* 20 dollars. **1936** Duncan *Over the Wall* 21 [ref. to 1918]: A twenty [was] a double-saw. **1949** *Set-Up* (film): How bout puttin' up a double sawbuck for me? **1953** in Cannon *Like 'Em Tough* 103: I bought a jug of rye with four bucks out of Semmler's double sawbuck. **1955** Q. Reynolds *HQ* 135: That ought to be worth a double saw. **1961** Sullivan *Gladdest Years* 181: I pushed a double-sawbuck at Frank. **1970** Thackrey *Thief* 158: A double sawbuck to the dude in charge of the training fixed that.
    2. *Pris.* (see quots.). Also **double saw.**
    1930 Irwin *Tramp & Und. Sl.: Double Sawbuck*…a twenty years sentence in gaol. **1941** *Slanguage Dict.* 13: *Double sawbuck*…a twenty-year penitentiary sentence. **1942** Goldin et al. *DAUL* 61: Wants him to cop out…and settle for a double saw. **1945** in *OEDS: Double sawbuck,* a twenty-year jail sentence.

double sawski *n.* DOUBLE SAWBUCK.
    1980 Lorenz *Guys Like Us* 23: A double sawski says you won't.

double shuffle *n.* duplicitous treatment; doublecross.—constr. with *the*.
> **1890–91* F & H II 314: *Double-shuffle*…(common).—A trick or fakement. *1949* W.R. Burnett *Asphalt Jungle* 145: Cully found himself in the corridor. The double shuffle? But why? *1952* Bruce & Essex *Kansas City Confidential* (film): You gave Harris the double shuffle.

Double Sing *n.* Sing Sing Prison, in Ossining, New York.—constr. with *the*.
> *1867* Nat. Police Gaz. (Oct. 19) 3: They will have time to…[reflect] in the walls of the Double Sing.

double-team *v.* to set upon, assail, or set to work on as or in a pair; (now *specif.*, in football and basketball) to defend against or block (an opponent) with two players simultaneously. Also (*obs.*) intrans.
> *1860* in *DA:* In respect to the Senator's allusion to "double-teaming" upon him…I do not exactly agree with my friend from Mississippi. *1866* Williams *Gay Life in N.Y.* 88: I'll bet…he can take any of the crowd agin him, if they don't double-team him. *1930* Lait *On the Spot* 26: Maybe it'd be better to double-team the kid downtown. *Ibid.* 202: *Double team*…To close in on a victim, two enemies coming at him from two sides simultaneously. *1933* Ersine *Prison Slang* 33: *Double Team.* To gang up on a mark. *1949* Leahy *Notre Dame* 32: Therefore, we "double-team" him, which means we assign both our center and our right guard to insure that he does not stop the ball carrier's forward progress. *1954* McGraw *Prison Riots* 47: Another time two screws double-teamed me. *1962* H. Simmons *On Eggshells* 30: He could get double-teamed and knocked flat on his back. *1974* Blount *3 Bricks Shy* 110: For thirteen years guys had just been double-teaming his ass. *1976* Crews *Feast of Snakes* 108: He was wishing he and Joe Lon could double-team her little ass. *1980* *AS* (Fall) 202: I was a boy, and they all kind of double-team[ed] me….All them hillbillies. *1981* Pietropinto & Congress *Clinic* 67: "And did I detect a note of snobbery…?" I added, double-teaming him with Connie. *1987* *RHD2:* The company is double-teaming the more complicated jobs with both a scientist and a group manager.

double trouble *n. Narc.* a Tuinal capsule.
> *1970* Landy *Underground Dict.* 70: *Double trouble*…Tuinal. *1970* Horman & Fox *Drug Awareness* 466: *Double trouble*—"Tuinal"…capsules. *1972* Nat. Lampoon (Oct.) 38: *Tuinal* 100 mg. (double trouble).

Double Ugly *n. Mil. Av.* the McDonnell-Douglas F-4 Phantom II fighter-bomber. *Joc.*
> *1984* M. Meyer *Wings* 129: F-4 Phantom II. Nicknames: Double Ugly,…Rhino. *1987* G. Hall *Top Gun* 31: Even the Navy Reserve is giving up on "Old Double-Ugly." *1988* M. Maloney *Thunder Alley* 111: The Indian…was riding backseat in the lovable "Double Ugly."

double up *v.* Orig. *Und.* to enter into partnership, esp. to live together as man and wife.
> *1886* N.O. Lantern (Nov. 10) 2: Isaac…and Grace…concluded, in the parlance of the fancy, to double-up. *1904* Life in Sing Sing 255: *Doubled up*—Married; paired. *1906* Nat. Police Gaz. (Feb. 3) 3: Suppose you and I double up, and then I'll show you how to get the money. *1915* Howard *God's Man* 282: I never let any girl I was doubled up with have more'n half a dollar at a time. *1922* Variety (Oct. 13) 7: With the girls who live on the show train there is little to worry about, as most are either married or "doubled up." *1933–35* D. Lamson *About to Die* 198: You gotta work alone; it's doublin' up that gets you grief. *1936* Duncan *Over the Wall* 158: I believe we'll double up, Helen, and you ought to make a good partner.

double X *n.* **1.** [fr. *X* 'the Roman numeral the value of which is ten'] a twenty-dollar bill; twenty dollars.
> *1841* Spirit of Times (Mar. 20) 25: Enclosed I transmit a "double X," turned out from one of the Currency Manufactories here. *1852* in *DA:* Dashing young fellows sporting their double X's in careless profusion. *1902* Townsend *Fadden & Mr. Paul* 294: He looks at de double X like he was tired and says, "What is dis for?" *1915–16* Lait *Beef, Iron & Wine* 35: Here's a dubble X for you.

2. an instance of doublecrossing.
> *1930* M. West *Babe Gordon* 189: Lou an' Harry gives me the double-X. Goddam 'em. *1978* Shaner, Ramrus et al. *Goin' South* (film): You're gonna put the ol' double X to Henry Moon?

douche *n.* **1.** DOUCHEBAG, 2.
> *1968* Baker et al. *CUSS* 107: *Douche.* A person who always does the wrong thing. *1970* N.Y.U. student: Man, this guy was a real douche. If you just started talkin' about smoking dope he'd give you a lecture. If

ever anybody was a douche it was this guy. *1970* Current Slang V 15: Lt. Jones is a real douche. *1983* Flaherty *Tin Wife* 200: That douche…is a bearded Robin Hood.

2. a cleaning; (*also*) a bath; "dip." Cf. DOUCHE JOB.
> *1972* T.C. Bambara *Gorilla* 164: Look, just give the floor a quick douche. *1988* C. Roberts & C. Sasser *Walking Dead* 43 [ref. to ca1966]: Feel like a douche?

¶ In phrase:

¶ **take a douche** to go away quickly.—usu. in imper.
> *1969* Current Slang I & II 87: *Take a douche*…to "get lost."—College males, Arizona. *1971* Dahlskog *Dict.* 19: *Douche, take a. Vulgar.* A command to leave one alone; to get lost. *1986* NDAS.

douche *v.* **1.** to reject or dismiss.
> *1968* Baker et al. *CUSS* 107: *Douche.* Reject someone for membership in a club, frat., etc. *1976* Price *Bloodbrothers* 245: She told me…how you douched her almost right away after that night.

2. to ruin or victimize; CLEAN OUT.—also constr. with *out*.
> *1968* Baker et al. *CUSS* 108: *Douched, get.* Do poorly on an exam. *1978* Lieberman & Rhodes *CB* (ed. 2) 298: *Douched out*—Robbing someone or someone who was robbed.

3. to shower; bathe.
> *1984* Glick *Winters Coming* 107: "I'm gonna douche." …Mingo…tipped the water can over Haney's head.

douchebag *n.* **1.** a despicable or offensive woman; BAG. [Prob. the original sense.]
> *1942–49* Goldin et al. *DAUL* 61: *Douche-bag.* A term of utmost contempt for a woman. *1960* H. Selby, Jr., in *Provincetown Rev.* III 79: You shouldn't talk to my girlfriend like that. That Douchebag! *1966* Bogner *7th Ave.* 173: "Vince," Jay said, "throw this douchebag out." *1969* Maitland *Only War We've Got* 192: Why, you silly old douche-bag! *1971* Selby *Room* 39: The dried up old douche bags. Why in the hell do they teach school if they hate kids so much. *1972* R. Wilson *Forbidden Words* 92: *Douche Bag.* An unattractive woman. *1978* Nat. Lampoon (Oct.) 8: I walk over to the old douchebag and give her a proposition. *1966–80* McAleer & Dickson *Unit Pride* 273: "Listen, you…douche bag," I told her. *1987* W. Allen *Radio Days* (film) [ref. to ca1940]: You're lucky I love you, you douchebag.

2. a stupid, contemptible, or despicable person of either sex. Also attrib.
> *1945* in *AS* (Oct. 1946) 238: *Douche bag.* A military misfit. *1946–51* J. Jones *Here to Eternity* 311 [ref. to 1941]: You cant see any further than that douchebag nose of yours. *1967* AS XLII 228: *Douche bag*…any individual whom the speaker desires to deprecate. *1973* TULIPQ (coll. B.K. Dumas): He's a real douchebag. *1974* Nat. Lampoon (Aug.) 17: I ran into this big bully named Vince and his douchebag pals. *1978* S. King *Stand* 171: Even scummy douchebags like you. *1983* Stapleton *30 Yrs.* 159: He used to call one…a dildo and the other one a douche bag. *1986* Thacker *Pawn* 69: That REMF douche bag. *1990* Murano & Hoffer *Cop Hunter* 177: You're dealing with…douche bags.

3. any sort of small bag used in washing or cleaning.
> *1971* Tak *Truck Talk* 50: *Douche bag:* a container that holds water…to clean the windshields. *1971* N.Y.U. student: My father's a draftsman. They use these plastic bags to hold the little bits of paper and eraser that they've cleaned off a diagram. He always calls those *douchebags.*

douched *adj.* tired out.
> *1968* Baker et al. *CUSS* 108: *Douched.* Very tired.

douche down *v. Mil.* to direct machine gun or rocket fire against; HOSE.
> *1971* Mayer *Weary Falcon* 38: If you see tracers coming up from somewhere it is easy to douche the area down.

douche job *n.* a washing.
> *1971* Tak *Truck Talk* 73: *Give it a douche job:*….to wash a truck…to steam-clean a trailer. *1976* Lieberman & Rhodes *CB* 127: *Douche Job*—Cleaning a car or truck.

douche kit *n. Mil.* a man's shaving kit.
> *1970* Ponicsan *Last Detail* 130: Billy rinses out his razor and drops it into his douche kit. *1989* Leib *Fire Dream* 95 [ref. to Vietnam War]: He…picked up his GI douche kit from the bureau.

dough *n.* **1.** money; in phr. **in the dough** having money; wealthy.
> *1851* in Thornton *Amer. Gloss.:* He thinks he will pick his way out of the Society's embarrassments, provided he can get sufficient dough. *1851* Spirit of Times (July 19) 253: "What will you take for that horse?" eagerly asked Valentine, as he forked over the dough. *1856* Ballou's

Dollar Mo. Mag. (Sept.) 300: Mrs. Fly was asked if she kneaded her dough or beat it up with a stick. "If you can find anybody that 'needs the dough' more than I do," said she, "pity take mercy on 'em!" **1865** Williams *Joaquin* 21: I'm dry...and I've got to raise some "dough" afore long. **1868** Williams *Black-Eyed Beauty* 22: Where the blazes is the "dough" to come from?...You gals spend enough to know something about earning cash. **1894** C. Lawlor & J. Blake *Sidewalks of N.Y.* (pop. song) st. 2: With Jakey Krause, the baker, who always had the dough. **1895** in J.I. White *Git Along Dogies* 66: Look at pay-day; we get our dough and where is it? **1896** Ade *Artie* 10: I pulled in the dough and picked up the cards. **1898** F.P. Dunne *Dooley in Peace & War* 221: Will-lum J. O'Brien wint on handin' out th' dough that he got fr'm th' gas company an' con-ciliatin' th' masses. **1903** Merriman *Letters from Son* 15: He has got more dough than this whole blamed college is worth. **1903** Benton *Cowboy Life on Sidetrack* 162: To make mon out of cattle or get any dough. **1903** Sonnichsen *Deep Sea Vagabonds* 54: Bob was pretty well fixed an' 'ad lots o' dough. **1905** W.S. Kelly *Lariats* 180: I'll send the dough. **1911** *N.Y. Eve. Jour.* (Jan. 10) 14: Don't forget to bring some dough along. **1928** in J. O'Hara *Sel. Letters* 37: I was making dough on the market. **1930** in Johnson & Williamson *Whatta-Gal* 72: This is just to make them break loose and pay me a little more dough. **1929–33** Farrell *Manhood of Lonigan* 244: Clayburn...was in the dough. **1937** Wexley & Duff *Angels With Dirty Faces* (film): You got any dough? **1940** R. Wright *Native Son* 135: Look, Bessie, if I had to leave town and wanted dough, would you help me if I split with you? **1944** C.B. Davis *Leo McGuire* 146: Leo and I are in the dough. **1951** Styron *Lie Down in Darkness* 194: I'm glad to hear you're going to make big dough, Pookie. **1958** Fields *Tunnel of Love* (film): You could make some real dough. **1974** Millard *Thunderbolt* 125: You mean that's all the dough they've got in here? **1979** Gillespie & Fraser *To Be* 42: Young kids [were] coming in because of the dough, man. We were making dough.

2. [fr. DOUGH(BOY)] *Army.* an infantryman. Now *hist.* Also **doughie.** [This term remained current particularly in armored units through the end of the Korean War.]
1909 Brown *9th Inf.* 114 [ref. to *ca*1885]: His gallant cavalry Captain...remonstrated in no mild terms with this soldier for leaving his troop and "taking on" with the "doughs." **1911** Runyon *Tents* 92: Once with the doughies an' field guns,/Once with the coast guns, too. **1918** Sherwood *Diary* 60: At 12:30 we put over a big barrage and at 4:30 the "doughs" stormed and captured the village of Bazoches on our immediate front. **1926** Nason *Three Lights* 144 [ref. to 1918]: Yes, an' all you done with us is...get us beat up by our own doughs. **1931** *Our Army* (Dec.) 12: A lot of doughs'd rather pull a three-bit in the mill than do squads east and west on the parade ground. **1942–45** Caniff *Male Call* (unp.): I've seen this new doughie work. **1945** *Stars & Stripes* (May 27): Doughs drink watery beer and jitterbug with the girls of the town. **1952** Kahn *Able One Four* 28: The doughs were glad to have some armor around, but there was an uneasy air throughout. **1958** Davis *Spearhead* 65 [ref. to 1945]: Take a quick police of the airfield so we're sure it's cleared behind us and then we'll marry up the tanks and doughs and start clearing our zone. **1962** W. Robinson *Barbara* 331 [ref. to WWII]: We're getting small arms from enemy doughs in those houses ahead. **1982** D.J. Williams *Hit Hard* 175 [ref. to WWII]: Doughs in the ditches getting shelled. Out.

¶ In phrase:

¶ **spoil (someone's) dough** to ruin (someone's) plans.
1891 Lummis *David* 88: But I'll spile *his* dough!

doughball *n.* (see quot.).
1851 B. Hall *College Wds.* 104: *Dough-Ball.* At the Anderson Collegiate Institute, Indiana, a name given by the town's people to a student.

dough bat *n.* a heavy blow.
1833 in *DAE.*

dough-beater *n.* *So.* a wife. Also **dough-baker.**
1911 *DN* III 538: *Dough-beater, n.* Wife. **1940** in *DARE:* A feller who's got a doughbeater promised is square in luck. **1941** Nixon *Possum Trot* 38 [ref. to early 1900's]: But that style of courting was one way to win a "dough-baker." **1967–69** in *DARE:* Dough beater.

doughbelly *n.* a grossly fat person. Hence **dough-bellied,** *adj.*
1942 *Calif. Folk. Qly.* I 220 [ref. to 1890's]: Get away from me, you little doughbelly! *ca*1969 *Gunsmoke* (CBS-TV): You ain't got the guts *or* the caliber, doughbelly! **1975** S.P. Smith *Amer. Boys* 143: Chase was young, competent, and not a dough-bellied alcoholic like most of the lifers.

doughboy *n.* **1.** a man who is a baker; a boy who assists a baker.
[**1838** Crockett *Almanac 1839* 3: I went...with my nigger b'y Dough-boy.] **1917** Appleton *With Colors* 24: He's jest a "dough-boy," of a sort;

it's Jimmy's job to cook. **1918** Ruggles *Navy Explained* 20: The bakers are called the "dough-boys." **1942** *Yank* (Dec. 2) 8: Neither bombs nor bullets can stay this "dough"-boy from the...pursuit of his baker's art. **1947** *AS* (Apr.) 121: *Dough boy.* Bake shop boy.

2.a. *Army.* an infantryman.—orig. used derisively. Now *hist.* [Despite much speculation, the reason for the orig. application of the term remains obscure.]
1847 N.J.T. Dana *Monterrey* 166: We "doughboys" had to wait for the artillery to get their carriages over. **1847–***ca***1860** S. Chamberlain *Confession* 63: If twenty Dragoons can't whip a hundred greasers with the Sabre, I'll join the Doughboys and carry a fence rail all my life. *Ibid.* 68: No man of any spirit and ambition would join the "Doughboys" and go afoot. **1863** Hollister *Colo. Vols.* 30 [ref. to 1861]: Our [cavalry] officers would not accept promotion that transformed them into "doboys." **1863** Lyman *Meade's HQ* 58: A lovely moon...seemed to me to be laughing derisively at our poor doughboys, tramping slowly along the road. **1865** in *PADS* (No. 70) 30: We left them behind to go with the "Dough Boys" (otherwise "Infantry."). **1867** *Beadle's Mo.* (May) 415 [ref. to Civil War]: To us "dough-boys" (the origin of the name is one of the inscrutable mysteries of slang)...the constant marching...became a wearisome iteration. **1867** G.A. Custer, in E. Custer *Tenting* (ed. 1) 516: We passed the infantry about five miles out. Wasn't I glad I was not a doughboy. **1873** *Custer's Yellowstone Exped.* 26: Here come the dough boys. They'll give the reds the devil if they get a chance. **1880** *United Service* (Oct.) 459: It was d—d doughboy work, and they hadn't 'listed in the cavalry for such. **1887** Hinman *Si Klegg* 694 [ref. to Civil War]: The "walk soldiers"—or "doughboys," as the cavalrymen called them—thought that those who rode horses had a "soft thing." **1887** E. Custer *Tenting* 230: "Joined the doe-boys, eh?" "How do you like hoofing it?" **1887** E. Custer *Tenting* (ed. 1) 516: A "doughboy" is a small, round doughnut served to sailors on shipboard, generally with hash. Early in the Civil War the term was applied to the large globular brass buttons of the infantry uniform, from which it passed, by a natural transition, to the infantrymen themselves. **1889** C.C. King *Marion's Faith* 300: There's a doughboy sergeant out there, sir. **1899** Bonsal *Gold. Horseshoe* 247: The jackies dressed ship and the "dough-boys" presented arms. **1906** Stewart *N'th Foot* 77: The cavalry was hotly engaged with the enemy, and the "doughboys" fell in to go to their support. **1909** M'Govern *Krag Is Laid Away* 1: The horns of the artillery, the trumpets of the cavalry, and the bugles of the "doughboys" broke loose upon the still air of the Mindanao mountains. **1914** Giles *Rags & Hope* 95: Then they wrapped the dough around their ramrods and cooked it before the fire and broiled their bacon on the coals. Maybe that's why Confederate soldiers were called "doughboys." **1918** *Stars & Stripes* (Apr. 19) 3: Doughboy...Time was when there was a suggestion of good-natured derision in it. **1919** T. Kelly *What Outfit?* 109: The Boches...was makin' a stab at gettin' their yellow doughboys over the scare that we threw in 'em. **1921** *N & Q* (Dec. 31) 538: *Doughboy*...was in use in the Regular U.S. Army (in which I served) during the Civil War...As far as I could learn from veterans of the Mexican War (1846–47), of whom we had quite a number yet in the service, the phrase originated in Mexico..."Adobes"...was quickly corrupted into "Dough-boys." **1926** Nason *Chevrons* 55 [ref. to 1918]: A doughboy officer, Eadie knew at once. The infantry officers...do not go in very strongly for an officer-like appearance. **1928** Scanlon *God Have Mercy* 95 [ref. to 1918]: Some damned doughboy outfit! **1943** Pyle *Here Is Your War* 19: One touchy doughboy heaved a hand grenade out the window at an imagined shadow. **1944** in Stilwell *Papers* 234: They won't give me any doughboys. **1955** Goethals *Chains* 85 [ref. to WWII]: His life had been back there at the guns, only a few thousand yards behind this thin screen of doughboys. **1963** Marshall *Battle* 169: The Doughboys...kept the perimeter unbroken without losing a weapon to the Japanese. **1963** Stallings *Doughboys* 4: In Texas, U.S. Infantry along the Rio Grande were powdered white with the dust of adobe soil, and hence were called "adobes" by mounted troops. It was a short step to "dobies," and then...Doughboys.

b. *Broadly,* an army soldier; (now *specif.*) *Journ.* a U.S. soldier in World War I. Now *hist.* and *S.E.*
1919 *Lit. Digest* (Jan. 11) 49: This great hospital at Lakewood, N.J., where doughboys and marines, veterans all, are...healing. **1920** *Infantry Jour.* (Sept.) 292: It has been the fashion these days in certain circles to call any uniformed Tom, Dick and Harry a doughboy. **1920** *Amer. Leg. Mo.* (Oct. 15) 17: Doughboy, gob and leatherneck. **1924** *Our Navy* (Dec. 1) 27: Marines Whip Doughboys. **1931** Dos Passos *1919* 393: It won't make the doughboys forget about K.P. **1963** Stallings *Doughboys* 1: The gulf between the Doughboys and their sons who fought in a far more complex war is simply unfathomable. **1970** *Playboy* (Aug.) 108: I mean, here we are...a doughboy, a gob and a leatherneck. **1980**

Manchester *Darkness* 25: A huge wedge of fifty-six thousand doughboys to break the back of…Ludendorff's last-ditch defenses. *a*1993 Millett *In Many a Strife* 51: The soldiers and Marines exchanged insults…as the Doughboys marched by.

3. see DOUGHBOY DRILL.

doughboy drill *n. Army.* infantry close-order drill. Also **doughboy.**

1911 *Howitzer* 202: You keep on boning doughboy the whole soirée through. **1918** Straub *Diary* (entry for July 3): We also received orders to line up at 1:30 with side-arms and we all thought that we were going to have some "doughboy" drill un until 3:30. **1919** McKenna *Bttry. A* 24: Much close order drilling was done, but this was easily abandoned at the slightest excuse, neither officers nor men putting any interest into the drudgery of "doughboy drill."

doughboy kit *n. Army.* PRO KIT. Now *hist.*

1982 D.J. Williams *Hit Hard* [ref. to WWII]: Every man who goes on pass…[should] be furnished with a pack of rubbers and a doughboy kit.

doughbrain *n.* DOUGH-HEAD.

1982 Eble *Campus Slang* (Nov.) 2: *Dough brain*—space cadet, dumby: I'm such a *dough-brain.* I forgot all about the assignment. You *dough-brain!*

doughby *n.* [prob. resp. DOBE, infl. by syn. DOUGH] money.

1944 in W.C. Fields *By Himself* 494: I have enough of their doughby left to take care of you and I in a moderate way until Gabriel gives his last toot.

dough-dish *n.* a sailing vessel.—used derisively.

1898 Norris *Moran* 46: Strike me, if I haven't thought of scuttling the dough-dish for her insurance. *Ibid.* 99: And we're to stop on board your dough-dish and navigate her for you? **1899** Norris *Blix* 14: You should have seen Billy Isham on that Panama dough-dish; a passenger ship, she was.

doughface *n.* **1.** *Pol.* a northern congressman who did not oppose slavery or its extension; (*hence*) a northerner who favored the Confederacy. Now *hist.*

1830 in *DA:* The protecting duty will be repealed, if the anti-tariff party can get enough dough faces to join them. **1859** J. Brown, in *Mo. Hist. Rev.* XVII (1923) 278: All pro-slavery, conservative, Free-state, and dough-face men and Administration tools are filled with holy horror. **1879, 1941** in *DA.* **1956** P. Murray *Proud Shoes* 116: You must be a damned doughface or a secesh!

2. [DOUGHFOOT (or DOUGHBOY) + DOGFACE] *Army.* DOUGHBOY, 2.a.

1945 *Yank* (May 11) 18: Ask a tanker or a TD man…whether he's willing to shoulder a part of the doughface's income tax. You're damn right he is. **1987** in Safire *Coming to Terms* 21: A doughface…asks [the officer] [etc.].

doughfoot *n.* [sugg. by DOUGHBOY; the word gained currency during WWII] an infantry soldier.

1943 *N.Y. Times Mag.* (Dec. 26) 6: Nobody can deny it is the ordinary "doughfoot" who consistently takes the greatest punishment in every way and gets least credit individually. **1944** H. Brown *Walk in the Sun* 109: How's your gun, doughfoot? **1946** J.H. Burns *Gallery* 2: The other doughfeet yelled at the Neapolitans and called them paesan. **1950** *Time* (Nov. 27) 27: The U.S. tanks splashed across the stream while doughfeet swarmed across the bridge's torn girders. **1954** Faulkner *Fable* 332: Maybe because an American doughfoot is the only bastard they could bribe with a trip to Paris. **1954** Crockett *Bastards* 320: Thousands of Navy guys and a couple of divisions of doughfeet. **1964** Webb *Cheyenne Autumn* (film): Captain What's-his-name's an infantry officer—a doughfoot. **1964** Crane *Sergeant & Queen* 91: And right then, Ben Corbin would have swapped places with any grimy doughfoot along the DMZ. **1984–88** Hackworth & Sherman *About Face* 79: A change of socks…—and lots of ammo—were the real essentials in a doughfoot's kit.

dough god *n. No. & West.* a usu. fried biscuit. Cf. DOUGH JEHOVAH.

1899 in *DA:* The hay boy…ate his dinner of dough-god and bacon with hearty relish. **1913** *DN* IV 26: *Dough god, n.phr.* Flour and water cooked in a frying-pan like biscuit. **1915** *DN* IV 244: *Dough god, n.phr.* Biscuit. "I don't care for *dough gods.*" **1918** *DN* V 24: *Dough-god, n.* A loaf of baking powder bread baked in a pan by an open fire; not always "done." Woodsmen, prospectors, etc. **1920** *DN* V 81: *Dough god.* Camp bread. **1950** *Western Folklore* IX 139 [ref. to *ca*1850]: Biscuits were sometimes called *sinkers* or *doughgods.*

doughgut *n. West.* DOGIE[1].

1947 Lomax & Lomax *Folk Song U.S.A.* 248: George W. Sanders of the San Antonio stockyards said that a motherless calf, forced to eat grass before it was old enough to digest it, developed a big stomach…These calves came to be called "doughguts,"…[which] was shortened…to "dogies." **1960** A. Lomax *Folk Songs N. Amer.* 357: Sick and feeble, their young bellies swollen by a too early diet of grass, these little "dough-guts" trailed along in the drag of the herd.

doughguts *n.* a grossly fat individual.

1862 Patrick *Rebel* 42: You infernal old doughguts, you expect to poke your finger in my eye, don't you?

dough-head *n.* **1.** a blockhead. Hence **dough-headed** stupid.

1838 in *DARE:* You silly dough-head. **1854** Avery *Laughing Gas* 61: A Dough-head. **1864** in C.H. Moulton *Ft. Lyon* 204: An officer who is just about as much of a "dough-head" as Joy used to be. **1866** Dallas *Grinder Papers* 245: You're such a pack o' dough heads. **1914** Patten *Lefty o' the Bush* 188: It made me sore to think that old doughhead, Cope, should beat me to it. **1915** in Lardner *Haircut* 143: And that's just what you might expect from one o' them doughheaded reporters. **1934** *WNID2.* **1989** P. Munro *U.C.L.A. Slang* 35: That guy…always gets lost on his way to class—what a dough head.

2. a baker.

1926 *AS* I (Dec.) 651: *Dough-head*—a baker. **1937** *Lit. Digest* (Apr. 10) 12: *Doughhead.* Baker.

dough jehovah *n. Naut.* DOUGH GOD.

1883 Russell *Sailors' Language* xii: Dough jehovahs are a Yankee pudding, and worthy of the people who first taught the British sailor to eat pork with treacle.

doughnut *n.* **1.a.** *Naut.* a ring-shaped life preserver.

1895 Tisdale *Guns* 23: We have tested the patent life preservers—those great sugar doughnuts that hang at quarters. **1918 Fraser & Gibbon Soldier & Sailor Wds.* 82: *Dough Nuts.*—A Navy name for the "Carley Floats," life-saving rafts of circular shape, carried on board ships of war. **1928** Nason *Sgt. Eadie* 61 [ref. to 1918]: He mounted the crest of a long roller and here he could view the many swimmers, a great multitude of empty rafts, "dough-nuts" clustered thickly with soldiers like gulls on a log, a few boats.

b. a rubber tire.

1922 T.A. Dorgan, in Zwilling *TAD Lexicon* 33: [Sign on garage over stack of used tires:] Try our second hand doughnuts. **1930** *Amer. Mercury* (Dec.) 455: *Doughnut, n.:* An automobile tire. "We clout ten doughnuts an' call it a day." **1971** Tak *Truck Talk* 50: *Doughnuts:* small tires used on drop-bottom trailers. **1975** Ellison *Gentleman Junkie* 179: Underneath me twelve big overweight doughnuts out of Goodyear. **1976** Lieberman & Rhodes *CB* 127: *Doughnut*—A tire.

c. any of various usu. small ring-shaped contrivances.

1969 Cagle *Naval Av. Guide* 392: *Doughnut.* An apparent speed indicator. **1972** Haslam *Oil Fields* 100: *Doughnut, n.* A steel ring used to hold tubing in place. **1980** Wielgus & Wolff *Basketball* 106: There are also "donuts"—disks of thick gauze with the center snipped out—that can be taped over the wounded area to prevent the blister from spreading its irritation.

d. *Sports.* a zero. Cf. BAGEL.

1979 Frommer *Sports Lingo* 174.

e. (of a woman) a state of sexual excitement.—usu. considered vulgar. *Joc.*

1981 Jenkins *Baja Okla.* 213: Women don't get hard-ons….We get doughnuts.

2. a dollar. *Joc.*

1979 S. Martin *Jerk* (film): 250 dollareenies—250 doughnuts.

3. (see quots.).

1992 *N.Y. Times* (June 14) Metro 51: The black Camaro drove into sight…then turned in several squealing, tight circles—"doughnuts"—that left black tire smudges on the asphalt. **1992** *CBS This Morning* (CBS-TV) (Sept. 17): A *doughnut* is where they spin the car in a tight turn.

¶ In phrase:

¶ **dollars to doughnuts** [fr. the expression *bet dollars to doughnuts [that];* see 1929 quot.] most certain; most assuredly.

1893 *Chi. Daily Tribune* (Sept. 1) 7: The best he could do was to make a dead heat of it after it had looked dollars to doughnuts that he would be beaten. **1895** *Harper's* (Nov.) 856: Dollars to doughnuts Uncle Sam never sees a cent of that money again. [**1901** Ade *Modern Fables* 33: It was Dollars to Dumplings that many a Moon would Wax and Wane ere

George went against that Combination once more.] **1910** T.A. Dorgan, in *N.Y. Eve. Jour.* (Jan. 18) 12: It's dollars to doughnuts that if ever Steve's wallop lands first they'll be picking Mr. Thomas up in a dustpan piece by piece. **1929** "E. Queen" *Roman Hat* ch. x 113: I'll bet dollars to doughnuts Field played the stock market or the horses. **1945** Dos Passos *Tour* 224: Dollars to doughnuts I shan't get to go. **1948** J.H. Burns *Lucifer* 196: Dollars to doughnuts they're happy to be getting back. **1966** Shepard *Doom Pussy* 55: I bet a dollar to a doughnut we can make some wicked music together. **1977** A. Patrick *Beyond Law* 4: When Tony Baretta couldn't concentrate, you could bet dollars to doughnuts that it involved his work. **1979** in J.L. Gwaltney *Drylongso* 210: I'll bet you dollars to doughnuts they out-know it.

doughnut foundry *n.* (see quot.). *Joc.*
   1927 *AS* (June) 392: The cheapest of eating-houses are known as *doughnut-foundries*.

doughnut head *n.* a dolt.
   1977 in C.G. Fuller *UFO Cong.* 273: Excluding those doughnut heads eager to book passage on the next flying saucer to Venus.

dough over *v.* to hand over money.
   1874 in Miller & Snell *Why the West Was Wild* 147: They just levelled a shotgun and six-shooter upon the scalawags...and told them to "dough over," which they did, to the amount of $146.

dough-pop *v. Tex.* **1.** to strike hard. Cf. DOUGH BAT.
   1972 Jenkins *Semi-Tough* 23: I'll dough-pop him on his black ass. *Ibid.* 183: I may have to dough-pop Cissy Walford before I ever get around to the dog-ass Jets.
   2. to defeat; CLOBBER.
   1972 Jenkins *Semi-Tough* 37: We...dough-popped Arkansas thirty-seven to twenty-one.

dough-pounder *n.* a baker.
   1956 Sorden & Ebert *Logger's* 12 [ref. to *a*1925]: *Dough-pounder*, A baker.

dough-puncher *n. Mil.* a baker.
   1909 Moss *Officers' Manual* 283: *Dough-Puncher*—the baker. **1914** *DN* IV [Navy]: *Dough Puncher*. Baker. **1944** Kendall *Service Slang* 21: *Dough puncher*...a baker, also known as "Dough-head." **1945** (quot. at DYNAMO-BUSTER).

dough-roller *n.* **1.** a baker or cook.
   1920 J. Hunter *Trail Drivers* 299: The cook...is called..."dough roller." **1925** *AS* I (Dec.) 137: A camp cook is simply a cook until the loggers have graded him; and for each grade of cook they have a name full of meaning..."stomach-robber," "stewbum," "sizzler," "dough-roller," and "star chef." **1933** *AS* (Feb.) 27: *Dough-Roller*. Cook. **1962** in *AS* (Dec. 1963) 271: Baker...*dough roller*.
   2. *Black E.* a wife or female lover. Also **dough-roll.**
   1929 in Oliver *Blues Tradition* 119: Did you ever wake up and find your dough-roller gone? **1960** in Leadbitter & Slaven *Blues Records* 237: When Your Dough Roller Is Gone. **1962** B. Jackson *In the Life* 162: I got a dough-roll (wife) and two crumb-catchers (children), you know.

do under *v. Black E.* to do in; defeat, destroy, ruin, or kill.
   1962–68 (quot. at SNAP). **1971** N.Y.U. professor: He *knew* they were gonna do him under. **1980** Kotzwinkle *Jack* 254: Hey, but you guys did us under in baseball.

do up *v.* **1.a.** to injure; (*hence*) to thrash; beat up; vanquish. Cf. similar uses of DO.
   1821 Waln *Hermit in Phila.* 25: Beat you before you can *say Jack Robinson; done up* in a *jiffy*. **1839–40** Cobb *Green Hand* I 125: 'Twas after the chase, that my leg was done up. **1887** *N.O. Lantern* (Apr. 30) 2: The idea of this gang jumping on J. C. Matthews and doing him up. **1891** Maitland *Slang Dict.* 94: To "do one up" means to thrash him. **1891** Riis *Other Half* 164: A successful raid on the grocer's till is a good mark, "doing up" a policeman cause for promotion. **1896** F.H. Smith *Tom Grogan* 97: There was five men 'p'inted to-day to do up the scabs an' the kickers who won't go out. **1897** Ade *Pink* 139: Uni'd States could do [England] up if it eveh come to [a] case o' scrap. **1904** in "O. Henry" *Works* 1438: He just lushes till he remembers he's married, and then he makes for home and does me up. **1972** P. Thomas *Savior* 55: He was gonna do me up, but you got in between us. **1972–76** Durden *No Bugles* 223: Suchow's com'ny got did up in a ambush...Six got out.
   b. to bring about the ruin of.
   1839 *Amer. Joe Miller* 114: This here coal is doing us up.
   c. to tire to exhaustion.
   1844 Carleton *Logbooks* 38: The Black Hussars (our servants) are the most "done up"...of all.

d. to kill.
   1864 "E. Kirke" *Down in Tenn.* 51: Our boys fit like fien's...I'd done up two myself, when the Capt'n come onter me. **1889** O'Reilly & Nelson *Fifty Years on Trail* 83: Take good aim and do him up in shape. **1891** Clurman *Nick Carter* 24: That's him, and he's got to be done up. **1900** Hammond *Whaler* 287: This devil's—been tryin'—to do up—Tom—with a knife, sir. **1921** A. Jennings *Through Shadows* 32: "Ed's done up."...Ed was dead....He had been shot through the head. **1931** Bontemps *Sends Sunday* 33: Niggers is crazy to shoot up one anuther dat-a-way...Meantime [white folks]...do up niggers right an' lef' an' nobody says boo. **1942** Garcia *Tough Trip* 154: I thought it must have been one of the Pend d'Oreille warriors who was trailing me, and was going to do me up on the quiet.
   e. to swindle or rob.
   1887 Peck *Pvt. Peck* 45: I must keep it until a new recruit came that was green enough to allow the boys to do him up. **1889** Bailey *Ups & Downs* 47 [ref. to *ca*1870]: He informed me, in no gentle tones, that he had been "done up" in my rooms to the tune of $1,650 and he had just about made up his mind that he would not wait much longer to get the boodle back, either.
   2. *Narc.* to take (an illicit drug). Also intrans.
   1952 Ellson *Golden Spike* 43: I didn't see you on the scene so I did it up myself. *ca*1953 Hughes *Fantastic Lodge* 66: I was doing up six and ten joints a day. **1954** in *Social Problems* III (1955) 36: They were doing up a couple of [marijuana] cigarettes. **1958–59** Lipton *Barbarians* 24: He offered me a fix—did I want to do up? **1963** Braly *Shake Him* 10: This is a good place to do up a joint. **1967** Kornbluth *New Underground* 118: He is sitting in the streets, doing-up smack doing your death trip super. **1967–68** von Hoffman *Parents Warned Us* 152: They were doing up heavily. **1969** *Current Slang* I & II 28: *Do up*, v. To become intoxicated on a drug.—College males, Arizona.—I'm going to do up before the party tonight. **1970** Landy *Underground Dict.* 68: *Do up*...Inject or smoke a drug. **1986** R. Stone, in *Harper's* (Dec.) 51: After he'd done up, his nose started to bleed.
   3. to copulate with.
   1971 N.Y.U. student: It's real hip to say, like, "I'm gonna do up my chick," when you mean you're gonna ball her.

douse *v.* **1.a.** to extinguish (a light). Now *S.E.*
   1785 Grose *Vulgar Tongue: Dowse the glim;* put out the candle. **1807** Tufts *Autobiog.* 293 [ref. to 1794]: *Douse the glin* [*sic*]...put out the light. **1815* Sir W. Scott, in *F & H* II 319: Dowse the glim! **1824** W. Irving, in *OED*: "Dowse the light!" roared the hoarse voice from the water. **1843** *Spirit of Times* (July 29) 253: Douse the glim. **1874** (quot. at GLIM, *n.*). **1912** Stringer *Shadow* 180: We're goin' with our lights doused!
   b. to put out or injure (an eye); blind.
   1821–26 Stewart *Man-of-War's-Man* I 134: A great horse of a chap, as I've heard say, who had his starboard eye doused, and wore large red whiskers. **1845** Corcoran *Pickings* 175: I'll douse your glims. **1924** in Partridge *Dict. Und.*: Doused glim (= blackeye).
   2. to remove; doff.
   1785 Grose *Vulgar Tongue: Dowse your dog vane;* take the cockade out of your hat. **1828* in *OED*: The latter have doused their butter-churn boots. **1841* W.M. Thackeray, in *OED*: I...doused my cap on entering the porch. **1910** T.A. Dorgan, in *N.Y. Eve. Jour.* (Apr. 18) 14: Don't forget to douse the Kelly on entering. **1966** *RHD*.
   3. to be done with; finish; quit.
   1883 Russell *Sailors' Lang.* xiii: Douse that, now, is a sailor's way of saying "Hold your Tongue." **1971** Sorrentino *Up from Never* 61: Hurry up and douse them eggs, San Diego.

dove *n. Pol.* a person, esp. in public office, who advocates peace or a conciliatory national attitude. Now *S.E.* [Given wide currency in journalistic accounts of the Cuban missile crisis of Oct., 1962; 1930 quot. is atypical of its period. Usu. contrasted with HAWK.]
   1930 Nason *Corporal* 189: If this is war,...then give me peace at any price. Man, I'm a dove from now on! **1962** *Sat. Eve. Post* (Dec. 8) 20: The hawks favored an air strike to eliminate the Cuban missile bases...The doves opposed the air strikes and favored a blockade. **1964** J. Lucas *Dateline* 43: The 15,500 U.S. military personnel in Viet Nam are divided into two camps—the "Hawks" and the "Doves." The Hawks believe...[the] solution...is to kill the Viet Cong. The Doves...believe in something called "civic action." **1967** "M.T. Knight" *Terrible Ten* 52: A reporter...had facetiously inquired if she was a hawk or a dove.

dovetail *n.* [sugg. by SHAVETAIL] *Army.* **1.** a soldier who has completed officer's training but has not yet received a commission. *Joc.*

1919 Davis *Bttry. C* 157: Sergt. Choate came back a "dovetail" from the Officer's Training School. **1919** Ellington *Co. A* 45: Frost and Ament return from the R.O.T.C. 3rd Looeys or Dovetails. **1919** Law *Second Army Air Service Book* (unp.): Us dovetails all are sorry now/Sorry la guerre est fini. **1919** *Lit. Digest* (Apr. 19) 107: But between graduation in France and discharge in the States, we have no standing. We are supposed to fit in some place between a buck private and a "Shavetail," so some bright bird christened us "Dovetails" or "Third Lieutenants," and the name has stuck. **1930** *AS* V (June) 383 [ref. to 1918].

2. (see quot.). *Joc.*

1948 Taylor *Lang. of WWII* 70: *Dovetails:* Nickname for WAC 2nd Lieutenants—*Democrat & Chronicle.* Rochester, N.Y., October 9, 1943, p. 1.

down *n.* **1.** a heavily diluted or nonalcoholic drink, esp. one sold fraudulently to a male customer to be drunk by a B-GIRL.

*a*1890–91 *F & H* II 316: *Down*, subs.…(American) Small beer. **1930** *Variety* (Jan. 8) 106: Only the take joints pass out downs to the gals. **1954–60** *DAS.* **1970** Winick & Kinsie *Lively Commerce* 171: She usually has an arrangement with the bartender whereby he will serve her "downs," or diluted drinks with a minimum of alcohol. *a*1989 in Kisseloff *Must Remember This* 595 [ref. to 1920's]: Sometimes when we were drinking with the customers, they gave us "downs," which were ginger ale or something like that. Then you had to pretend it was real.

2.a. Orig. *Narc.* a feeling or period of depression, as that following drug intoxication.

1950 *AS* XXV 173: *Down*, a low condition. **1967** McNeill *Moving Through Here* 85: I was feeling down Thursday night—one of those downs when even spending money seemed futile. **1971** Curtis *Banjo* 214: But what a come-down. Oh my, what a down! **1976** Braly *False Starts* 136: However, the downs were ferocious. For every golden moment there was one of leaden aftermath.

b. *Narc.* a depressant drug, esp. a barbiturate.

1967 *Esquire* (Sept.) 193: *Downs*—codeine or fake codeine cough syrups. **1967** Bronsteen *Hippy's Handbook* 13: *Downs* n. barbiturates. **1969** *N.Y. Post* (Nov. 19) 5: Downs (barbiturates) opened at three for a dollar. **1969** *Playboy* (Dec.) 73: "Downs" (barbiturates or tranquilizers). **1968–77** Herr *Dispatches* 5: I knew one 4th Division Lurp who took his pills by the fistful, downs from the left pocket of his tiger suit and ups from the right. **1984** W.M. Henderson *Elvis* 84: No heavy downs, just a Valium or two. **1990** Rukuza *W. Coast Turnaround* 13: The maze of painkillers and downs remapping his brain patterns.

c. something that is discouraging or depressing; DRAG.

1969 Mitchell *Thumb Tripping* 178: You're really a down tonight, Gary…Man, don't be a drag this way. **1968–71** Cole & Black *Checking* 104: Chicago was such a down no one felt anything. **1971** Sonzski *Punch Goes Judy* 10: It was a down.

d. *pl.* low spirits.—constr. with *the.*

1966–72 Winchell *Exclusive* 10: She nursed my black eyes after a fight and comforted me when I had the downs.

3. [ref. to pressing down the lever on a toaster] *Restaurant.* an order of toast. Cf. DOWN, *adv.*, 3.b.

1954–60 *DAS:* An order of down.

down *adj.* **1.** *Und.* aware; WISE.—often constr. with *on, upon,* or *to;* in phr. **down as a nail** [or **hammer**] exceedingly aware or astute.

*1760 in J. Farmer *Musa Pedestris* 53: For if the cull should be down/ And catch you a fileing [*sic*] his bag,/Then at the Old Bailey you're found. **1774* in Partridge *Dict. Und.* 202: Then he said to the man who had the bag *d—n your eyes he is down!* meaning as I am told that I was watching him. **1793* in *OED*: Egad, the Baronet was down upon it. **1810* in Partridge *Dict. Und.* 202: Asked me if I was down to the queer. **1812* Vaux *Vocab.:* *Down*, sometimes synonymous with *awake*, as when the party you are about to rob, sees or suspects your intention, it is then said that the *cove is down* (had knowledge of it). *Down as a hammer*,…*down*…to any matter, meaning, or design. **1817* in *OED*: Down as a nail. **1825* "Blackmantle" *English Spy* I 145: Dick's a *trump*…and *down* to every *move* of the domini. **1839* in *F & H* II 317: I am, my flash cove…I'm down as a hammer. **1848** *Ladies' Repository* VIII (Oct.) 315: *Down On*, To suspect. **1850* in *F & H* II 317: You're down to every move, I see, as usual. **1859** Matsell *Vocab.* 27: "The copper…is down on the job," the officer…suspects what we are about. **1865* in *F & H* II 317: I'm down on it all; the monkey never bit your dog.

2. depressed; sad; in low spirits.

1862 in *DARE:* The captain was rather down about it. **1865** in Hafen & Hafen *Reports from Colo.* 319: The secessionists…were awfully down. **1889** *Harper's Mag.* (Sept.) 580: He went off, and Jane's been reel kinder down ever since [*sic*]. **1939** Appel *People Talk* 327: They get me so down I started locking the chain. **1949** D. Cooper & J. Davis *Duchess of Idaho* (film): Sorry, Deacon, but I'm feelin' down.

3. *Gamb.* **a.** having placed a bet.

1907 in H.C. Fisher *A. Mutt* 4: He would have breezed in and I was down strong.

b. having lost a specified amount; behind.

1981 D.E. Miller *Jargon* 292: I'm *down* five bucks. **1987** *ALF* (NBC-TV): How much am I up?…Well, how much am I down?

4. *Und.* in prison.

1927–28 in R. Nelson *Dishonorable* 189: I thought Enright was down for some bank job. **1972** Bunker *No Beast* 47: I was down two years. **1974** Andrews & Dickens *Over the Wall* 181: He is twenty-five years old and has been "down" eight years. **1977** Bunker *Animal Factory* 12: You'll look like Gina Lollobrigida to some of those animals who've been down for eight or nine years.

5. behind schedule.

1938 in *AS* XVII (1942) 103: *Down.* Behind schedule. **1972** *Urban Life & Culture* I 343: If the [bus] driver should be operating behind schedule ("down").

6. *Black E.* **a.** ready and eager for action; (*also*) formidable in a fight; tough.

1944 Burley *Hndbk. Jive* 137: *Down with It*…to be ready for action. **1952** Ellson *Golden Spike* 15: Are you still down for it? *Ibid.* 69: Let's jump them now…Is everybody down? **1955** Yablonsky *Violent Gang* 44: Having a [social] worker makes you a real "down" club. All "bad" clubs have a "man" trying to change them. **1957** *New Yorker* (Sept. 21) 142: "Let's cut out." "I'm down for that," Johnny Meatball said. **1964–66** R. Stone *Hall of Mirrors* 181: They jus' lookin' for a excuse to look like they real *down* M.P.'s. **1966–67** P. Thomas *Mean Streets* 59 [ref. to 1940's]: We're down…an' the shit's on. **1968–71** Cole & Black *Checking* 98: *Hector*…: Ah bullshit, you just wanna fight. *Lolo*…: Yeah, you down? *Hector:* Fuckin' right. **1974** Gober *Black Cop* 105: I'm gonna go out like a down dude is 'sposed to. I'm gonna go cool. **1978** Selby *Requiem* 16: Anyway, lets go where theres some life. Whattaya say? Hey baby, Im down. **1987** *Newsweek* (Mar. 23) 72: But Ronnie was a down dude just like Honk, and when he said…"Get the pistols!"—Honk slid off his stool. **1992** *Martin* (Fox-TV): No, no. Me an' the fellas are down. What's up, we down.

b. knowledgeable or conversant, esp. thoroughly.—constr. with *with;* (*hence*) smart; canny; sophisticated; HIP. Cf. **(1),** above.

1944 Burley *Hndbk. Jive* 15: I'm with it.…I'm down with the action to my own satisfaction. Do you dig? *Ibid.* 47: That square, Iago, is down with the action. *Ibid.* 137: *Down with it*—To understand, know. **1955** in R.S. Gold *Jazz Talk* 75: I don't know who the singer is, 'cause I'm not down with all the singers now. **1959–60** R. Reisner *Jazz Titans* 154: *Down With Something, To Be:* to know something thoroughly. **1964** Redfield *Let. from Actor* 38: Brando laughed. "See what I mean?" he said. "That cat is *down*." **1965** C. Brown *Manchild* 159 [ref. to 1950's]: He didn't want to make any money, or he didn't know how. He just wasn't *down* enough. *Ibid.* 166: The first thing they usually did was…start using drugs to be hip, to be accepted into the street life, to be down. **1966** Braly *On Yard* 136: He's supposed to be a schooled hustler, down with all games. **1966–67** P. Thomas *Mean Streets* 39 [ref. to 1940's]: Those cats were so down and cool that just walking made a way-out sound. **1968** Heard *Howard St.* 155: To be *down* is to be hip, with it. **1982** *Special Assignment* (AP Radio Network) (Oct. 17): Hey, man, you gotta get with it! All the down guys use it. **1989** *Rolling Stone* (Oct. 19) 54: The whites want to be down…they want an insight on black culture. **1993** *Newsweek* (July 26) 46: I associate myself with all the bad motherf----- in the world. Gary Oldman, De Niro, Pacino [etc.]…I'm *down* with them. I've been working with them since I was 14.

c. eliciting a strong emotional response; most enjoyable; excellent.—also constr. with *with it.*

1946 Mezzrow & Wolfe *Really Blues* (gloss.): *Down with it:* Top-notch, superlative. **1957** Simmons *Corner Boy* 209: She had the downest juke-box in town. **1964** *N.Y. Times Mag.* (Aug. 23) 64: *Down:* hip, just right and true, as in "That was a down movie." **1966–67** P. Thomas *Mean Streets* 113 [ref. to 1940's]: She was a beautiful girl—dark, curly hair,…and a real down figure. **1971** Dahlskog *Dict.* 19: *Down, a.* Good; the best ever, as: That music is really *down*. **1972** *Down Beat* (June 8) 26:

Dupree is as down a guitar player as there is out there. **1987** Univ. Tenn. student theme: I soon realized that *down* meant "good" and *wack* meant "fake."

d. admirable; loyal; steadfast.

1952 Ellson *Golden Spike* 244: *Down cat*—a good guy. **1953** W. Brown *Monkey On My Back* 36: Dave was a down cat (nice guy). **1958** *Life* (Apr. 28) 70 [ref. to *ca*1950]: You never met a cat so down as Little Al Cohen [the training school superintendent]. **1959** E. Hunter *Conviction* 75: He's okay, though. A down cat. **1966** Samuels *Baby* 243: The leaders were "down kids with heart." **1967** Gonzales *Paid My Dues* 79: A friend…had told me I was "down people" and to turn me on when I arrived. **1972** P. Thomas *Savior* 73: Trying to keep your down rep on the street while trying to be a down Christian. **1977** *Watch Your Mouth* (WNET-TV): "He's really a sharp little dude." "Yeah. He's down." **1980** Gould *Ft. Apache* 113: Toni was a real down *Latina*, all right, standing out there in the cold taking care of her man. **1984** Sample *Raceboss* 238 [ref. to 1960's]: A squad of "stone down gorillas," the highest compliment one con gives another. **1988** *Harper's* (Aug.) 28: You ain't really down for your set [gang] if you ain't ready to *die* for the set.

e. stylishly dressed; fashionable.

1954 in Wepman et al. *The Life* 36: I wore solid gold cufflinks—I knew I was down. **1968** in Andrews & Dickens *Big House* 13: He was choked up tight in a white-on-white/And his cocoa-brown suit was down.

7. *Black E.* current and of interest.

1966–67 P. Thomas *Mean Streets* 243 [ref. to 1940's]: You've been here before and are hep to what's down.

8. DOWNBEAT.

1968 *Mike Douglas Show* (WCBS-TV) (Dec. 27): We'll have to make this a down show. **1973** Hollander *Xaviera* 401: I don't see the point of making such a "down" picture.

¶ In phrases:

¶ **down and out** vanquished; finished; (*specif.*) (now *S.E.*) destitute.

1899 Cullen *Tales* 17: I never hit St. Louis that it didn't get me down and out before I so much as had a chance to take a look at Shaw's Gardens. **1901** "H. McHugh" *John Henry* 31: Say! I was down and out—no kidding! **1903** A.H. Lewis *Boss* 78: You're down and out…your reputation is gone too; you were a fool. *Ibid.* 207: I'm down an' out, done for an' as good as dead right now. **1905** Riordan *Plunkitt* 35: And poor Platt! He's down and out now and Odell is in the saddle. **1906** *Nat. Police Gaz.* (Oct. 20) 10: The fighting game is down and out in England. **1910** Solenberger *Homeless Men* 130: He began to drink heavily and…was completely "down and out." *a*1904–11 Phillips *Susan Lenox* II 157: You get caught sooner or later, and then you're down and out. *Ibid.* 298: "Oh—he's down and out—eh? Why?" "Drink—and hard luck." **1913–15** Van Loan *Taking the Count* 21: Here's all the papers hollering that I'm through—down and out. **1962** in Wepman et al. *The Life* 103: And his pants was down and out for the count—/Each leg was going for broke.

¶ **down on** having a poor opinion of; opposed or hostile to. Now *colloq.*

1848 *Ladies' Repository* VIII (Oct.) 315: *Down On.* To…dislike. **1851** in *OEDS:* Here the factory girls appear to be down on the style. **1856** *Ballou's Dollar Mo. Mag.* (Oct.) 324: You all know the fate of a man, when the officers are "down on him." **1862** in C.W. Wills *Army Life* 135: Confound this railroad guarding; I'm down on it. **1874** "M. Twain," in *OEDS:* I was down on sich doin's. **1902** W. James *Var. Religious Exper.* ch. xiv: Some persons…glory in saying that they are "down" on religion altogether.

down *adv.* **1.** [fr. *downright*] exceedingly.

1893 in *DARE.* **1910** Hapgood *City Streets* 38: But a junk is a down bad man, real bad, yer know, wid a fence around his neck. **1912–43** *Frank Brown Collection* I 534: *Down. adv.*…Very, exceedingly. He's a *down* good hoehand.

2. Orig. *Black E.* to the limit.

1928 R. Fisher *Jericho* 299: *Drunk down:* the nadir of inebriation. **1942** *Amer. Mercury* (July) 94: *Draped down:* dressed in the height of Harlem fashion; also *togged down.* **1971** Thigpen *Streets* 9: He…gets cocained down. **1978** S. King *Stand* 397: Two disco dancers and the words Boogie Down! on its hot pink cover. **1979** Gram *Foxes* 47: Hey, you wanta cruise with us, esa? Party down a little? **1985** *MacGyver* (ABC-TV): I'd like to spend some time with friends, party down.

3. *Restaurant.* **a.** (of eggs) fried on both sides.

1942 *ATS* 99: *Two down*…two eggs fried on both sides.

b. (of a sandwich) on toast.—used postpositively. Cf. DOWN, *n.*, 3.

1954–60 *DAS.* **1972** Rossner *Any Minute* 54: As if he'd just ordered a BLT down. **1987** *RHD2:* Give me a tuna down.

¶ In phrases:

¶ **down and dirty, 1.** not governed by notions of fairness or decency; vicious.

1984 in *NDAS:* Mississippi: A Down And Dirty Campaign. *a*1988 D. Smith *Firefighters* 88: It was a real hot, down-and-dirty, nasty kind of fire. **1988** *Time* (Nov. 21) 23: The to-and-fro of politics fascinates him even when the exchanges are as down and dirty as they were this year. **1990** *Inside Edition* (synd. TV series): Down and dirty. Mexico is more deeply involved in drugs than ever.

2. intensely earthy or sexual; sexually uninhibited.

1988 W. Goldman & J. Toll *Casual Sex* (film): Didn't you guys have some down-and-dirty sex? **1989** *Time* (June 26) 86: A growling, down-and-dirty setting of Jimi Hendrix's *Purple Haze.* **1990** *New Yorker* (May 21) 12: L.A. club people rarely get down and dirty on a dance floor. **1991** *Newsweek* (May 13) 66: [Madonna's] dishy, down-and-dirty new documentary. **1992** *Bold & Beautiful* (CBS-TV): An honest-to-God, down-and-dirty, nitty-gritty woman who knows how to make a man feel like a man!

¶ **down for the count** [fr. the boxing sense] virtually defeated or finished; doomed.

1929–33 Farrell *Young Manhood* 233: "I hope he pulls through." …"He's down for the count."

¶ **down to the ground** through and through; perfectly. Also as adj.

1867 in *OED:* Suited me down to the ground. **1936 N. West *Cool Million* 168: Betty suited him down to the ground. **1958** Gardner *Piece of the Action* 41: She's a bitch, a professional down-to-the-ground, flesh-and-blood bitch. **1976** Hayden *Voyage* 176: It would suit me right down to the ground. **1987** *N.Y. Daily News* (July 2) 48: Moreover, Bork's judicial philosophy suits Reagan right down to the ground.

¶ **get down, 1.** *Gamb.* to place a bet; wager. Cf. DOWN, *adj.*, 3.a.

1901 H. Robertson *Inlander* 115: You and Rod get down strong on *Doublequick* in handicap to-morrow. **1910** T. A. Dorgan, in *N.Y. Eve. Jour.* (Jan. 19) 12: Get down on Kaufman, hook, line, and sinker. **1946** G.W. Henderson *Jule* 114: Hold them dice!…Let's get down, boys. Let's get down hard. Let's get down with all we's got. **1950** Lomax *Mr. Jelly Roll* 107: All right, get down on this card. **1964** in Wepman et al. *The Life* 132: They were getting down heavy and letting the pots ride. **1975** Mahl *Beating Bookie* 16: The sports book has a gimmick which allows the pundit to get down on two teams in a so-called parlay situation. **1981** Jenkins *Baja Okla.* 31: Everybody better get down on Baylor Saturday.

2. GO DOWN.

1930 in H. Miller *Letters to Emil* 51: Start off by letting her get down on me.

3. *Narc.* to take an addictive or psychotropic drug, esp. heroin.

1952 Ellson *Golden Spike* 92: "Where're you going?"…"To get down again." "What with?" "Whatever I can get, and I can't spare a taste this time, not even the cotton." **1969** Smith & Gay *Don't Try It* 100 [ref. to *ca*1947]: Commonly, four persons would contribute one quarter each and *get down on a cap.* **1970** Cain *Blueschild Baby* 52: You want to get down, baby? I got works and a place to get off right around the corner. **1970** in Thigpen *Streets* 18: Cool man, let's get down. **1972** Smith & Gay *Don't Try It* 202: Get down. Shoot heroin. **1980** Gould *Ft. Apache* 147: Maybe she got down every day, snorting sometimes, skin-popping when she had a little more time, even hitting the mainline once in a while. **1980** DiFusco et al. *Tracers* 47: We're just gonna get down a little bit. No big fuckin' deal. **1992** *Amer. Detective* (ABC-TV): Lemme see your arms. When's the last time you got down?

4. to engage in copulation.

1966 Braly *On the Yard* 165: It was one of the places…where you could get down. **1962–68** B. Jackson *In the Life* 383: We used to get down some (manage sexual encounters). **1978** *N.Y. Post* (Dec. 9) 14: You told me that the girl who gets married in certain cliques [i.e., gangs] has to get down with all the guys in the clique. Do the girls feel like that is being raped? **1981** in Safire *Good Word* 87: I get down with my girlfriend because I love her. **1981** Crowe *Fast Times* 146: It had all these drawings of men and women getting down, in all kinds of positions.

5. to get down to business; apply oneself in earnest; get busy.

1967 [Beck] *Pimp* 65: Forget her and get down on a fresh bitch. **1970** Landy *Underground Dict.* 87: *Get down with it*…Start to do something;

be serious about doing something. **1970** M. Thomas *Total Beast* 117: A man's in bad shape if he gets in here and nobody to get down for him and stick by him. **1980** Gould *Ft. Apache* 251: Then talk to him, don't be wastin' my time. I wanna get down. **1990** *New Yorker* (Sept. 10) 63: Yo, man, you should get down, you should get down...start dealing drugs.

6. *Black E.* (see 1970 quot.).

1970 Landy *Underground Dict.* 87: Get down....Fight. **1992** *Jerry Springer Show* (synd. TV series): If I seen you and you seen me, we got down.

7. to be uninhibited, esp. in dancing or performing music; enjoy oneself intensely.

1971 H. Roberts *Third Ear* (s.v. get): *Get down, v.* to do something in a bigger way; to put the intensity of "soul" into dance movements; e.g. He *got down* last night at the party. **1972–74** Hawes & Asher *Raise Up* 31: I'm gonna get down*...*Soulful (in playing jazz). **1976** Univ. Tenn. student: Like at discos you say, "Get down!" It means really *go.* **1977** *Sanford & Son* (NBC-TV): What are we standing around for? Why don't we get down? **1981** *Nat. Lampoon* (Sept.) 36: I really get down on that poetry. **1987** *Time* (Aug. 17) 10: They samba, mambo, rhumba, tango, fox-trot, lindy, peabody and what can only be called, in street language, *get down!* **1987** *RHD2*: Getting down with a bunch of old friends.

¶ **go down** see GO DOWN.

down *v.* **1.** to pass (food) at a mess table.

1942 *Leatherneck* (Nov.) 145: *Down*—To pass. "Down the meat."

2. *Und.* to sell (stolen goods) at wholesale; FENCE.

1971 *N.Y. Mag.* (Nov. 22) 35: For example, a man's leather coat selling for $120 in a retail store can be downed (sold) on the swag market for $50. *Ibid.* 36: They can turn you on to a lot of customers and they down a lot of stuff for you, too. **1973** *N.Y. Times Mag.* (Dec. 16) 22: Junkies...used the vacant apartments to stash their loot until they could "down it." **1975** *N.Y. Post* (July 22) 71: I stole it. You guys down it.

3. to disparage; criticize adversely.—occ. constr. with *on.*

1970 in *Rolling Stone Interviews* 390: My friends downed me for listening to country music. **1970** Eckels *Business* 24: Yes they had you/downing you. **1990** *CBS This Morning* (CBS-TV) (Mar. 22): I used to down drug users as well as drug dealers. **1992** *Donahue* (NBC-TV): I was an outcast. I can remember kids downin' on me.

down-and-out *n.* a person who is down and out. Now *colloq.* Also **down-and-outer.**

1889 in *OEDS.* **1911–12** Ade *Knocking the Neighbors* 13: He would read...about the Down-and-Outs of the City hiking back to the Soil. **1913** A. Palmer *Salvage* 150: Among the "down-and-outs." **1913** Brown *Broke* 120: With two or three other "down and outs," I lay down on the grass in Jefferson Park. **1914** Ellis *Billy Sunday* 21: The "down and outs," the millionaires, the society women, [etc.]. **1924** Henderson *Keys to Crookdom* 403: *Down and outer*—One physically or financially at low ebb. **1949** W.R. Burnett *Asphalt Jungle* 39: Well, he was a struggling down-and-outer. *****1970** Moorcock *Warlord of Air* 13: The down-and-out hardly seemed to hear. **1973** Schiano & Burton *Solo* 126: They're sure I'm a down-and-out on a shoplifting expedition. **1982** *N.Y. Review of Books* (Apr. 1) 37: A drunk and down-and-outer.

downbeat *n.* ¶ In phrase: **on the downbeat** Esp. *Jazz.* in decline.

1943 in W.C. Fields *By Himself* 482: It is very difficult to make facetious cracks about the deceased, those on the down beat or those that the Grim Reaper is taking his last swing at. **1946** Boulware *Jive & Slang* 6: *On The Down Beat*...Losing popularity.

downbeat *adj.* gloomy; subdued; pessimistic. Now *S.E.*

[**1947** *ATS* (Supp.) 2: Unpopular person...*downbeat.*] **1950** (cited in *W9*). **1952** *N.Y. Times Mag.* (Jan. 6) 10: Distressed by the down-beat mood of the people [in Europe]. **1952** in *DAS:* It looks like a triumph of upbeat pictures over the downbeat. **1956** in Cheever *Letters* 193: It may be that I'm such a downbeat type that I'm not fit to comment on anything. **1974** *U.S. News & W.R.* (June 24) 53: America is going through a very downbeat and dangerous period.

Down Easter *n.* **1.** Esp. *Naut.* a native of Maine, esp. a seaman. Also (*obs.*) **Down East.** Now *S.E.*

*a***1828** in *OEDS:* This curious class of mammalia, the "Down Easter" as it is often called. **1845** Ingraham *Harefoot* 15: I say, Down East, who made your coat? **1849** in Dorson *Long Bow* 79: "Mornin', Squire!" said "down east." **1849** Melville *White Jacket* 133: A raw-boned, crack-pated Down Easter. *ca***1862** Dodge's *Sketches* 30: "Say, yeou," observed one of the "down Easts,"..."that yeour'n, eh?" **1935** in Paulding *Bulls*

& Jons. 67: Came at last to consider the Down-Easters no better than they should be. **1945** Colcord *Sea Language* 68: *Down East.* A general term for Maine and the Maritime Provinces of Canada...A "down-easter" may be either a person or a vessel hailing from that region. **1984** T. Clancy *Red October* 39: Greer [was] a down-easter from Maine.

2. *Naut.* a vessel from a Maine port. Now *S.E.*

1835 in *OEDS.* **1945** (quot. at (1.), above). **1961** Hugill *Shanties* 80 [ref. to 1920's]: So I shipped away across the sea,/In a hard-case Down-Easter to Mirramashee. **1976** Hayden *Voyage* 89: In command of a crack new Down Easter.

downer *n.* **1.** *Und.* a nickel. [In somewhat earlier Brit. use, a sixpence; see Partridge *Dict. Und.* 202.]

1859 Matsell *Vocab.* 27: *Downer.* A five cent piece.

2. *Baseball.* (see quot.).

1964 Thompson & Rice *Every Diamond* 140: *Downer:* Good overhand curve.

3.a. *Narc.* a depressant drug; (*specif.*) a barbiturate.

1965 J. Carroll, in *Paris Rev.* (No. 50) 110: I got about eight ups and a lot of downers. **1967** Wolf *Love Generation* 277: *Downer.* A drug which slows perception: heroin, barbiturates, tranquilizers. **1967–68** von Hoffman *Parents Warned Us* 223: Smoke some grass or take downers. **1970** R. Ebert *Beyond Valley of Dolls* (film): What you need is grass or a downer or something.

b. *Narc.* a somnolent drug-induced state.

1967 Wolf *Love Generation* 49: If what you want from a drug is a downer that is total and complete, has dream state...antisocial function...heroin is complete.

c. something depressing or unpleasant; often in phr. **on a downer** in a dejected mood.

1967–68 von Hoffman *Parents Warned Us* 81: War's a downer. It's a bum trip for everybody, Mike. **1970** *Playboy* (Dec.) 287: I'll tell you what else is a drag...A real downer this is, too. **1971** *All in the Family* (CBS-TV): Isn't that a downer? **1972** Gover *Mr. Big* 13: When I'm on a Downer, as I've been lately, I get filled with the idea that I'm nothing to nobody. **1972** Kerr *Dinky Hocker* 82: While your imagination blows our minds, your philosophy is often a downer. **1973** *N.Y. Times* (Jan. 7) 17: It's a downer day, man—let's lift it up! **1976** W. Johnston *Sweathog Trail* 65: This whole idea is a downer. **1976** T. Walker *Ft. Apache* 96: But the series of events...had depleted that goodwill he felt toward the residents of Fort Apache. Which put me on a downer. **1978** Maupin *Tales* 132: I get on downers...Depressed. Bummed out. **1982** in "J.B. Briggs" *Drive-In* 31: So in my opinion it ended on a downer. **1990** *Evans & Novak* (CNN-TV) (Mar. 31): There's a tremendous downer in this town,...a sense of dismay. **1992** G. Wolff *Day at Beach* 127: Gee, downer, you must be depressed.

down freak *n.* *Narc.* DOWN HEAD.—sometimes attrib.

1980 Whalen *Takes a Man* 272: A pain-killer some of his down freak customers bought by the hundreds.

down front *adv. & adj.* *Black E.* UPFRONT.

1955 in Wepman et al. *The Life* 78: I've come down front 'cause there's something I want. **1972–74** Hawes & Asher *Raise Up* 119: That's the big mistake down front, because there is no way he can possibly conceive of where I'm coming from.

down head *n.* *Narc.* a person addicted to depressant drugs, esp. barbiturates.

1973 *N.Y. Times Bk. Review* (Mar. 4) 43: Is it because speed freaks and down heads aren't quite so prone to violent crime?

downhills *n.pl.* *Gamb.* dice that are loaded so as to roll a low number. Cf. UPHILLS.

*****1662** in Partridge *Dict. Und.* 202: Taught yow the use of up hills,/ downe hills, and petarrs. *****1785** Grose *Vulgar Tongue: Down Hills.* Dice that run low. **1980** in Safire *Good Word* 132: "Downhills" is when dice are loaded to bring out a low, or down, number.

downie *n.* *Narc.* a barbiturate or other depressant drug.

1966 (quot. at UPPIE). **1967** Bronsteen *Hippy's Handbook* 13: The beautiful thing about downies is...you just go to sleep.

downmouth *v.* [prob. fr. *down*grade + (BAD)MOUTH] to derogate.

1981 in Safire *Good Word* 53: It's fashionable these days to downmouth economists.

down out *v.* to stupefy with or as if with a barbiturate or tranquilizer.

1976 Univ. Tenn. student: I took Valiums till I was completely downed out. **1976** Univ. Tenn. student: It's not enough to down you out. **1984** Glick *Winters Coming* 245: He'd be drunk or downed out. **1987** *Campus Voice* (Winter) 13: One afternoon I came home downed out on Quaaludes.

downside *n.* a discouraging or negative aspect.

1977 *Wash. Post*, in *OEDAS* II 13: The downside…is that there would be consequences for the administration as well as Congress. **1978** *Project U.F.O.* (NBC-TV): That's the downside. Here's the upside. They caught the guy. **1978** *Business Week* (Dec. 11) 56: There are no legal downsides. **1980** *Business Week* (Sept. 15) 103: We have so many more strengths than downsides. **1983** *L.A. Times* (July 25) I 14: Little diversity…that's the downside of living in Hacienda Heights. **1990** *U.S. News & W.R.* (Dec. 17) 38: The downside could be further shrinkage in the airline industry.

downstairs *adv.* **1.** in hell. *Joc.*

***a1845** in *OED.* **1977** Dunne *Confessions* 331: You're not going to lie [in confession]. Not if it's going to put you in the shithouse downstairs. **2.** *Boxing.* in the belly.

1913–15 Van Loan *Taking the Count* 167: A glove thudded into the…pit of the stomach. "Thatta boy!…Downstairs!" **1981** Univ. Tenn. instructor, age 40: A [prize]fighter who's *soft downstairs* is weak in the midsection. **1986** Ciardi *Good Words* 95: *Downstairs*…The belly, esp. as a target for a boxer's punching. **3.** *Av.* at or to a lower altitude; below.

1942 *ATS* 69: Land; ground…*downstairs* (aviation sl.). **1944** E.H. Hunt *Limit* 98: Twenty Bogies going downstairs for run at cruisers. **1951** *Air Cadet* (film): Let's go downstairs. **1956** Heflin *USAF Dict.* 175: *Downstairs, adv.* In the lower atmosphere, near the ground or water. *Slang.* **1958** Johnson & Caidin *Thunderbolt* 175: I rolled the Jug and went downstairs. **4.** *Baseball.* low in the strike zone.

1978 Tommy Holmes, former major-leaguer (WINS Radio) (July 26): The ball came in downstairs and he hit it to left field. **5.** in the genital or pubic area. Cf. *go downtown,* 1 s.v. DOWNTOWN.

1963 Rubin *Sweet Daddy* 83: June was shaving off my hair, Doc, all of it; downstairs also. ***1990** Thorne *Dict. Contemp. Sl.* 149: *Downstairs*…(in) the genital area.

downtown *n.* **1.** *Mil. Av.* the Vietnamese cities of Hanoi and Haiphong and the area immediately surrounding as targets of bombing attacks and locations of intense antiaircraft fire. Also as adv. Now *hist.*

1966–67 in Tuso *Vietnam Blues* 76: To go Downtown, tried flying fast and slow. **1970** *Current Slang* V 15: *Downtown,* n. Airspace over Hanoi, North Vietnam, or generally any airspace in the area of Hanoi.—He flew 20 missions in the *downtown* area. **1986** Coonts *Intruder* 209: We're going right downtown. It won't be any piece of cake. **2.** *Basketball.* (see quot.).

1980 Wielgus & Wolff *Basketball* 43: *Downtown*…Way outside; roughly, the three-point field goal region.

¶ In phrases:

¶ **go** [or **have lunch**] **downtown, 1.** to engage in active oral copulation.

1928 Panzram *Killer* 157: A face artist is one who goes downtown for lunch and nose-dives into the bushes when he's hungry. **1947** Willingham *End as a Man* 178: "It seems to me that a lot of your friends…look as if they have their lunch downtown." "Sir, I swear none of my friends are like that." **1966** (quot. at SWITCH-HITTER). [**1970** Winick & Kinsie *Lively Commerce* 207: Anal intercourse ("Greek") is popular, as is cunnilingus ("going below 14th Street") and fellatio before coitus ("half and half").]

2. *var.* **hit it downtown,** below.

¶ **hit it** [or **take it** or **go**] **downtown** *Baseball.* to hit a long home run.

1977 L. Nelson, on N.Y. Mets Baseball (WOR-TV) (Aug. 20): Mike Vail takes a 3-2 fastball downtown and Fred Norman loses his shutout. **1977** F. Messer, on N.Y. Yankees Baseball (WPIX-TV) (Aug. 21): And Horton was trying to go downtown! **1983** L. Frank *Hardball* 94: To hit a home run is to "hit it downtown," because in some of the ballparks, such as Wrigley Field in Chicago, a ball hit over the outfield fence will very often land on the city streets. **1987** *Daybreak* (CNN-TV) (July 5): Ossie Virgil goes downtown in the eighth inning. **1990** *Sciences* (May) 14: To hit a home run is to "go downtown."

¶ **take downtown** *Baseball.* to hit a home run off (a pitcher).

1978 F. Messer, on N.Y. Yankees Baseball (WPIX-TV) (Sept. 14):

Slayton's been taken downtown 26 times this year, counting the two home runs this game.

downtown *v. Baseball.* to hit (a long home run).

1971 Coffin *Old Ball Game* 55: "Downtown one" (hit a homer). **1978** K. Jackson, on *ABC-TV Monday Night Baseball* (June 26): And Graig, trying to downtown it, misses.

down trip *n.* **1.** *Narc.* a frightening, dismaying, or unpleasant hallucinatory experience induced by LSD or a similar drug.

1968 "J. Hudson" *Case of Need* 184: She took a couple of down-trips, real freaks, and it shook her up. **1968** J.D. MacDonald *Pale Grey* 152: They had some new short acid…that never gives you a down trip. **1971** B.B. Johnson *Blues for Sister* 21: I would have tabbed it immediately as a down trip, the kind that leaves you hating the world.

2. (see quot.).

1968 N.Y.U. student: A *down trip* means anything boring, unpleasant, or uninspiring.

downy *n.* a bed.—constr. with *the.*

1843 Field *Pokerville* 158: The candidate yawned, looked at his bed,…finally…seating himself upon "the downy." ***1846** in *OEDS: Dab,* a letter, doss, downey, bed. **1914** S. Lewis *Our Mr. Wrenn* 10: Well-l-l, Willum, guess it's time to crawl into the downy. **1918** in *St. Lawrence U. in the War* 149: Hit the downy and had bed for 2 francs—first time I have slept in white sheets for 7 months. **1918** in Rossano *Price of Honor* 214: I…put in another three-hour workout on the "downy."

downy *adj.* [prob. DOWN, *adj.,* 1., + *-y*] knowing; artful; shrewd. *Rare in U.S.*

***1821** in Partridge *DSUE* (ed. 8) 337: Downy as a hammer. ***1823** in *ibid.*: You're a downy von. ***1823** "J. Bee" *Slang Dict.* (s.v. *down*): *Downy cove,* a shrewd or very alert fellow. ***1841** in *F & H* II 319: Tom Bullock, the downiest cove, the leary one that never goes to sleep. **1851** W. Kelly *Ex. to Calif.* II 173: Leaving the dupe to be laughed at and the "downy cove" to be patted on the back. **1859** Matsell *Vocab.* 27: *Downey.* A smooth, pleasant talker; a knowing fellow.

doxology works *n.* a church. *Joc.*

1871 "M. Twain" *Roughing It* 249: That is, if I've got the rights of it and you are the head clerk of the doxology works next door. **1887** Walling *N.Y. Chief of Police* 316: By G-d, it makes me sick to think of you standing up in your old doxology works every Sunday and ladling out religion.

doxy *n.* [perh. fr. obs. *docke* 'rump' or arch. Du *docke* 'doll'] a girlfriend; woman. Now *S.E.* [In earlier cant use, 'the mistress of a beggar or thief'; see *OED2* and *F & H.*]

***1818** in *EDD:* Dick Delver the charmer…journey'd, like folks more refined,/To search for a doxy again. ***1825** in *OED2: Doxy,* a sweetheart; but not in the equivocal sense used by Shak. and other play writers. ***1827** in *OED2:* Surrounded by plough-boys and their doxeys. **1836** D. Crockett's *Almanack* (1837) 17: I determined to make a call on my doxy. **1847** in Oehlschlaeger *Reveille* 74: He donned his best suit to visit his *doxy.* **1859** Matsell *Vocab.* 27: *Doxy.* A girl. **1950** *New Yorker* (Feb. 18) 75: The middle-aged man who shatters a long-standing and happy marriage by going off the deep end over a stylish doxy. **1970** Rudensky & Riley *Gonif* 185: *Doxy*…a girlfriend or woman. **1983** W. Safire, in *N.Y. Times Mag.* (June 12) 20: She would warn him not to *get fresh,*…lest she be considered his *doxy,* now armpiece.

doze *v.* to clear or excavate with a bulldozer. Now *S.E.*

1945 (cited in *W9*). **1979** *TriQuarterly* (Spring) 193: Like walking through a dump after it had been 'dozed for the day. **1985** Boyne & Thompson *Wild Blue* 103: Next day there'd be two or three runways dozed.

dozens *n.pl. Black E.* a provocative exchange of obscene, often rhymed insults concerning esp. the mothers of those participating. Also **dozen, dirty dozen(s).**

1915 in White *Amer. Negro Folk-Songs* 365: I don't play the dozen/And don't you ease me in. **1926** Odum & Johnson *Negro Workaday Songs* 7: Plaintive blues, jolly blues, reckless blues, dirty dozen blues, mama blues, papa blues… **1928** Fisher *Jericho* 9: It is the gravest of insults, this so-called "slipping in the dozens." To disparage a man himself is one thing; to disparage his family is another. **1929** T. Gordon *Born to Be* 26 [ref. to Montana, *ca*1905]: Jewell had hardly gotten out of the door before Maude began playing the dozens with Billy. He tried to defend himself. **1933** E. Caldwell *God's Little Acre* 76: If you want to play the dozens, you're at the right homestead. **1931–34** in Clemmer *Pris. Community* 90: "Playing the Dozens" is the most common way a convict has of using profanity. **1945** Himes *If He Hollers* 96: I don't play no dozens, boy. **1950** *Commentary* X 60: "Playing the dozens" was a fad current among New York City Negroes some fifteen years ago. **1971** Guffy & Ledner *Ossie* 50 [ref. to *ca*1940]: Maybe they shouldn't use bad words, but that "doin' the dozen"—there's nothing wrong with that game. My brothers…said it taught them to hold their temper. **1971** Contini *Beast Within* 110: They were putting Leroy through the dirty dozen again but there was nothing I could do about it. **1972** Burkhart *Women in Pris.* 449: Playing the dozens. **1982** D. Williams *Hit Hard* 22 [ref. to WWII]: Just playin' the dozens…Call names back and forth about your Mama. *Ibid.* 98: I was probably being put in the dozens silently. **1990** *Nation* (June 25) 902: A singsong, usually macho, deep-voiced, street-style poetry that descends from the dozens.

dozer *n.* BULLDOZER.
    1942 in *OEDS.* **1944** Huie *Can Do!* 29: We…dragged the trucks clear with the 'dozer's winch. **1953** Cain *Galatea* 3: The order was to get out trees, and the right way was to hire a dozer. **1971** *Playboy* (Aug.) 112: Steel dozer blades churn through forests or jungle, leveling the land. **1979** G. Wolff *Duke of Deception* 161: You might…find a 'dozer middle of the road.

D.Ph. *n.* a damned fool.
    1917 *DN* IV 357: *D.f.* Damn(ed) fool…Also *d.ph.* **1962** N.Y.C. high-school teacher, age *ca*45: There's not much difference between a Ph.D. and a D.Ph.—a damned fool.

D.Q. ¶ In phrase: **on the D.Q.** on the "dead quiet"; in strict confidence; on the q.t.
    *a*1890–91 *F & H* II 320: On the D.Q.…(American).—On the dead quiet. **1895** *Harper's* (Sept.) 620: And she won't never get no divorce—she told me so on the d.q.

D.R. *n. Mil.* the Dominican Republic.—constr. with *the*.
    1982 Leonard *Cat Chaser* 25: You been back to the D.R. since?

Dracula *n. Hosp.* a hematologist.—used esp. as a nickname.
    1943 Horan & Frank *Boondocks* 191: He was the fellow in the hospital who was always fixing me up for a blood transfusion…Hell, I was always calling him "Dracula." **1968** W.C. Anderson *Gooney Bird* 34: You're going to have your blood drawn and your system pumped full of serum by the Dracula boys. **1971** N.Y.C. draftsman [ref. to WWII]: We called those guys who took blood samples "Dracula," "Bela Lugosi," "vampire," "bloodsucker." **1983** Eilert *Self & Country* 134: To awaken to Dracula was becoming routine.

draft *n.* ¶ In phrase: **feel a draft** to detect unfriendliness or hostility.
    [*1925 in *OEDS* s.v. *feel*: When the wind changed it might be the Conservative Party which would be feeling the draught.] **1957** in R.S. Gold *Jazz Talk* 91. **1963** H. Ellison *Sex Misspelled* 41: A couple of black dudes…"felt a draft" and old Rog was about to get frozen out. **1965** Hentoff *Jazz Country* 27: If you want to be any part of the jazz scene, you're going to have to be able to feel a draft sometimes without catching cold. **1972–74** Hawes & Asher *Raise Up* 93: I sat beside a sucker in silk vines from Georgia. Feeling a draft, you understand.

drafty *n.* a draft beer.
    1968–70 *Current Slang* III & IV 41: *Drafty,* n. Draft beer.—College males, New Hampshire.

drafty *adj. Black E.* (of an establishment) unfriendly to blacks. Cf. *feel a draft* s.v. DRAFT.
    1961 J.A. Williams *Night Song* 75: Hillary knew that "drafty" meant the suspected or real presence of discrimination.

drag *n.* **1.a.** *Orig. Und.* a horse-drawn vehicle such as a cart, wagon, carriage, or coach. [The "carriage or coach" sense seems to have become S.E. by *ca*1840.]
    [*1785 Grose *Vulgar Tongue: Go on the drag,* to follow a cart or waggon in order to rob it.] *1797 in Partridge *Dict. Und.* 204: *Drag,* a waggon, or cart. *1812 Vaux *Memoirs* (gloss.): *Drag:* a cart. *1819 [T. Moore] *Tom Crib* 11: While Eldon, long doubting between a *grey* nag/And a *white* one to mount, took his stand in a *drag.* **1836** *Spirit of Times* (July 16) 170: Their *drags*…ought to have been framed and glazed for the honor of the coachmakers. *1839 in *F & H* II 321: He turned out what he calls a four-in-hand *drag* which dragged nine hundred pounds out of my pocket. *1855 W.M. Thackeray, in *F & H* II 321: Lord Kew's drag took the young men to London. **1859** Matsell *Vocab.* 27: *Drag.* A cart or wagon. **1866** Meline *On Horseback* 60: Oh! here comes a pair of handsome grays before a neat but modest drag. **1876** in Manchester *Sport in America* 172: Mr. F. B.'s drag.—A very dashing affair; every thing in the best style. **1886** Harbaugh *Coldgrip in N.Y.* 5: Mebbe we'll

sport a drag on the Avenue one of these days. **1904** *Life in Sing Sing* 247: *Drag*—Horse and wagon.
    b. *Und.* DRAGSMAN, 1.
    1791 [W. Smith] *Confess. T. Mount* 19: *A drag,* one that robs a waggon on the highway.

2.a. a street, esp. a main street; thoroughfare.
    *1851 Mayhew *London Labour* I 248: Another woman…whose husband has got a month for "griddling in the main drag" (singing in the high street). *1859 Hotten *Slang Dict.: Drag,* a street or road; *back-drag,* back street. **1897** in J. London *Reports* 320: *Main-drag*…main street. **1906** London *Moon-Face* 36: I hit the *drag* (the drag, my dear fellow, is merely the street)…for a newspaper office. **1933** Ersine *Prison Slang* 33: *Drag*…A street, usually a busy one. **1937** *Lit. Digest* (Apr. 10) 12: *On the drag.* On the road. **1948** in *DAS*: A block down the drag. **1992** G. Wolff *Day at Beach* 128: At the other end of Philipsburg's main drag.
    b. *Hot Rodding.* a drag race.
    1954 *AS* XXIX 95: *Drag.* A race between two cars to determine which can accelerate faster. **1959** Gault *Drag Strip* 50: There was a private beach for those who didn't come to watch the drags. **1961** Ellison *Gentleman Junkie* 130: He hadn't spilled the beans to Pop about that drag on the Bluffs Road.
    c. *Hot Rodding.* a car used in drag racing; dragster.
    1965 Lurie *Nowhere City* 125: A 1932 Ford with a '45 Ford flathead V-8 engine. It was a "street drag" (the term "hot rod," he had learned, was obsolete) equipped and tuned for riding around town in, rather than a "competition drag" intended for racing.

3. something that is exceedingly tiresome or unpleasant; bore. *Orig. colloq.* [Esp. typical of the period *ca*1950–70 and not often applied to persons before the 1950's.]
    1863 in L.F. Browne *J.R. Browne* 270: My autograph is in great demand.…Still it is a dreary drag….I really have no taste for personal notoriety. **1863** [Fitch] *Annals of Army* 618: "General, you are leading a hard life," we remarked. He answered, gently,—"Yes, rather hard; and if this life were *all,* it would be a wretched drag." **1863** in Heartsill *1491 Days* 139: Drilling commences again and it is a perfect "drag"; the less a soldier has to do, the less he wants to do. **1867** S. Clemens in *Twain's Letters* II 57: Corresponding has been a perfect drag ever since I got to the States. **1880** Nye *Boomerang* 168: Until woman's suffrage came along, life was a drag—a monotonous sameness, and simultaneous continuousness. Now it is not that way. **1900** *DN* II 32: *Drag,* n.…2. A bore. **1901** *Broad Axe* (Chicago) (Jan. 26) 3: Life is a drag to me. **1943** in Himes *Black on Black* 195: They do not want to go to heaven because from all they have heard of it, it must really be a drag. **1946** Mezzrow & Wolfe *Really Blues* 36: I woke up to find myself in jail again. It was getting to be a drag. **1946** Boulware *Jive & Slang* 3: *Drag*…Old-fashioned person. **1949** Ellson *Tomboy* 130: I know, but this is just a drag. **1951** *Neurotica* (Spring) 74: Life's a drag. **1951** *Amer. Journ. Sociol.* XXXVII 141: I was playing solo for one night…What a drag! **1952** Mandel *Angry Strangers* 206: "Edna's been sick, Lukey."…"Oh, that's a drag, it's bad to hear." **1958** A. King *Mine Enemy* 87: It was a real drag! **1958** in C. Beaumont *Best* 108: It was getting to be a drag. So they experimented with strip poker one night. **1958–59** Lipton *Barbarians* 316: *Drag*—A bore, disappointment. A political convention is a big drag. An evening with squares is a sad drag. **1959** Zugsmith *Beat Generation* 27: College…It's too much of a drag…A drag was a bore in the language of the bums who were Stan's buddies. **1960** R. Reisner *Jazz Titans* 154: *Drag:* an annoying person. **1965** C. Brown *Manchild* 105: It would be a drag for someone to come up to you and say, "Man, you ever snort any horse?" and you would have to say, "No." **1982** G. Larson *Far Side* (unp.): Listen!…This party's a drag. **1992** *Middle Ages* (CBS-TV): It's a big drag. It's inconvenient. But we're in no danger. **1993** *New Yorker* (Jan. 11) 65: Shakespeare….That language was too much of a drag,…too many complications.

4.a. *Orig. Theat.* women's clothing worn on the stage by a male actor; (hence) *Homosex.* transvestite apparel. Now *colloq.* or *S.E.* See also **(4.e.),** below.
    *1870 *Reynolds Mag.* (May 29): We shall come in drag, which means men wearing women's costumes. *1873 Hotten *Slang Dict.* (ed. 4): *Drag,* feminine attire worn by men. A recent notorious impersonation case led to the publication of the word in that sense. **1891** Maitland *Slang Dict.* 98: *Drag* (Eng.), feminine apparel worn by men. *1909 Ware *Passing Eng.* 117: *Drag*…[a name] also given to feminine clothing by eccentric youths when dressing up in skirts. **1914** Jackson & Hellyer *Vocab.* 30: Amongst female impersonators on the stage and men of dual sex instincts "drag" denotes female attire donned by a male. **1925** McAlmon *Stockings* 62: I wuz at the Y.M.C.A.—in drag you know—

some outfit I had too, stars and spangles and jewels all over me, Mary. *Ibid.* 77: You could pass off as a girl in drag—men's clothes you know. **1928** J. Conway, in *Variety* (Sept. 19) 47: Lester Sheehan will kill you in drag in the last act. **1933** Ford & Tyler *Young & Evil* 11: We thought you were a Lesbian in drag when we first saw you. **1946** J.H. Burns *Gallery* 151: Why, you've all got as much allure as Gracie Fields in drag. **1948** Lait & Mortimer *New York* 74: It is a law violation for entertainers to appear in "drag" (clothes of the opposite sex). **1959** J. Rechy in *Big Table* I (No. 3) 36: In the most lavish drag…heels! and gown! and beads!

b. *Homosex.* a party held for transvestites and male homosexuals. Cf. **(12.a.)**, below.

1927 *Variety* (Feb. 2) 49: Outside the "drag," the play is utterly without merit as a dramatic performance. **1927** Rosanoff *Manual of Psych.* (ed. 6) 208: *A drag,* a social gathering of homosexuals at which some are in female dress. **1930** "D. Stiff" *Milk & Honey* 204: A *drag* is also a homosexuals' party. **1933** Ersine *Prison Slang* 33: *Drag*…a dance held by sexual perverts. **1940** in T. Williams *Letters* 11: They had a "drag" at the "White Whale" night club last night. Most of the boys went as girls but Froufrou thought it would be more of a masquerade if she went as a man, so she *did.* Woo! **1947** *Tomorrow* (Aug.) 29: *Drag,* a fancy-dress ball for men masquerading as women. **1955** Lindner *Must You Conform?* 49: He has frequented gay bars, attended "drags," and invaded so-called "circles" where inverts gather.

c. *Homosex.* a transvestite; DRAG QUEEN.

1929 T. Gordon *Born to Be* 218: "Don't bother the women. You are in America now."…"Must I turn drag, eh?" **1931** B. Niles *Strange Bro.* 210: The men, so dressed, were called "drags." **1959** Burroughs *Naked Lunch* 6: A fat queen drag walking his Afghan hound through the East Fifties. **1966** "Petronius" *N.Y. Unexp.* 107: The gay motorcyclists, the drags, the very young fags, young dykes [etc.]. **1967–68** von Hoffman *Parents Warned Us* 95: I was almost a butch drag, but I got straight when I dropped acid. **1972** Wambaugh *Blue Knight* 53: The two in dresses were drags. **1981** Eells & Musgrove *Mae West* 87: The police…wouldn't let the drags change into male clothing.

d. *Homosex.* a bar that caters primarily or exclusively to transvestites.

1931 *New B'way Brevities* (Oct. 5) 10 (cited in Tamony *Amer.* (No. 9) 1): Up to that time his greatest triumph had been the management of a drag of his own at Bryant Hall, overlooking Bryant Park, so that most of the customers merely crossed the street to camp in a hall instead of a park.

e. *pl. Homosex.* transvestite attire. See also **(4.a.)**, above. *Joc.*

1933 Ford & Tyler *Young & Evil* 114: Take off your drags, dear. **1972** B. Rodgers *Queens' Vernacular.* **1973–76** J. Allen *Assault* 125: He setting there in the bull pen with drags on…He look pretty good, got a wig all fixed, and looking hip.

f. costume; disguise.

*1959 in *OEDS:* My Spartan hair-do and my teenage drag and all. **1966** *Time* (Feb. 11) 87: White has written a mystery play in drag. **1968** I. Reed *Yellow Back Radio* 11: That angel in drag like a john, he gave her the news and showed her her notices. **1971** Merrick *One for Gods* 186: You'll soon be back in civilian drag. **1976** *N.Y. Post* (June 19) 21: It's the same role he's played in…previous Universal epics…only this time he's doing it in military drag. **1977** Langone *Life at Bottom* 84: Is it true that all glaciologists and geologists in Antarctica are really prospectors in drag? **1978** *L.A. Times* (Feb. 5) V 11: He had changed into jock drag—Yankees hat, tennis shoes. **1984** *All Things Considered* (Nat. Pub. Radio) (Mar. 14): This is really an adult comedy in teenage drag.

5. *Und.* a crowbar or similar tool used by burglars to force entrance.

*1890, 1897 (cited in Partridge *Dict. Und.*). **1904** *Life in Sing Sing: Drag*…burglar's tool. **1935** D.W. Maurer, in *AS* (Feb.) 15 [ref. to a1910]: *Drag*…A jimmy-bar or tool for forcing entrance. *Obs.*

6. [cf. *pull*] influence, esp. political influence.

1896 Ade *Artie* 60: He knows I've got a drag in the precinct. **1898** Dunne *Peace & War* 203: I have a dhrag at th' station. **1912–14** in E. O'Neill *Lost Plays* 44: Oh, he's got a drag somewhere. He squares it with the cops so they don't hold me for walkin' the streets. **1914** Ellis *Billy Sunday* 29: Well, he had some drag with me and influenced me. **1924** in Nason *Three Lights* 23: You go ask him, Simmons. You got a drag with him. **1928** *AS* III (Feb.) 219: *Drag.* Influence, pull. "She must have a drag with Agnes, to get away with that stuff." **1932** Lorimer *Streetcars* 26: You'll have an eternal drag with me if you'll dance with her. **1951** Bowers *Mob* (film): What's your angle, Flynn? Where do you get your drag? **1957** E. Brown *Locust Fire* 19 [ref. to 1944]: They can't ground Pappy. He has a big drag with Colonel Rogers.

7. *Stu.* a jest.

1900 *DN* II 32: *Drag,* n.…5. Personal but good-humored joke.

8. *Stu.* (see quot.).

1900 *DN* II 32: *Drag,* n. 1. One who tries to curry favor.

9.a. a usu. deep inhalation of smoke from a pipe, cigar, or cigarette. Now *S.E.*

1904 T.A. Dorgan, in Zwilling *TAD Lexicon* 33: The old sport took another drag on the dope stick. **1914** Jackson & Hellyer *Vocab.* 30: *Drag*…An inhalation of smoke, tobacco or opium. **1920** in *DAS.* **1926** Eadie *Chevrons* 305: A long drag and a cloud of smoke rolled out into the aisle. **1950** *New Yorker* (Aug. 26) 27: The cigarette tasted tinny, and after one drag he crunched it out. **a1961** in *WNID3:* The professor took a long, deliberate drag on his five-cent cigar.

b. a cigarette.

1942 *ATS* 127: Cigarette…*drag.* **1956** Longstreet *Real Jazz* 128: With a glass in your hand and a drag smoking on your lip. **1966–70** in *DARE.* ***1984** Partridge *DSUE* (ed. 8): *Drag*…a cigarette…since ca1925.

10.a. an often illicit share or percentage, as of profits; rake-off.

1907 J. London, in *DAS* [ref. to ca1892]: I had a sneaking idea that [the brakeman] got a "drag" out of the constable fees. **1940** in A. Banks *First-Person* 107: All I do is run a poker game and sell…beer. I get a drag on every pot, sure.

b. [cf. *pull* 'to earn'] wages.

1915 T.A. Dorgan, in *N.Y. Eve. Jour.* (Aug. 2) 11: Their drag was five bucks apiece. **1918** T.A. Dorgan, in *N.Y. Eve. Jour.* (Aug. 6) 10: His wiff wants 30 per cent of his weekly drag.

11. *R.R.* a freight train; (*hence*) *Trucking.* a freight truck.

1925 Tully *Beggars:* We caught a slow freight, commonly called a "drag." **1927** *AS* (June) 388: A freight is called a *drag. Dise-drag* (merchandise), *silk-drag, coal-drag, fruit-drag* and *slow drag* result from this word. **1929** Barr *Let Tomorrow Come* 266: *Drag*—a freight train. **1929** *Bookman* (July) 525: A B. & A. drag is snakin' its way to the crossin'. **1938** in N. Cohen *Long Steel Rail* 435: Now, they wouldn't let me ride no fast train, they put me off on a doggone drag. **1939** Attaway *Breathe Thunder* 216: There was a "drag" on the right-of-way. **1952** in Fenner *Throttle* 16: He hooked her up neatly, getting our short but heavy freight drag wheeling without the drivers spinning away from him. *Ibid.* 17: Keep this drag up to schedule. **1970** *Business Week* (Apr. 18) 55: Once upon a time they called freight trains "drags." **1971** Tak *Truck Talk* 50: *Drag:* a slow freighter [truck].

12.a. a dancing party.

1925 *Lit. Digest* (Mar. 14) 65: College dances are often called "drags." **1952** in *OEDS:* The cotillion orchestra and polite quartet that accompanied high society drags. ***1970** Partridge *DSUE* (ed. 7) 1110: *Drag*…A dance or ball: Canadian: ca1925–30. Also Australian teenagers: since ca1950.

b. *Stu.* a young woman who is being escorted to a social gathering.

1928 *AS* (Aug.) 453: *Drag*…the girl being escorted. **1950** Monks et al. *West Point Story* (film): I'm his drag. **1962** Quirk *Red Ribbons* 21: A sharp-looking girl…was his drag on those rare occasions when he entered into the Academy social life. **1986** R. Walker *AF Wives* 241: The drags are all gussied up in formals and spike-heeled shoes.

c. a girlfriend or a young woman.

1956 H. Ellison *Deadly Streets* 42: When you've won the bet I'll be your drag. *Ibid.* 181: In the Poppers, when a drag ties up with a stud, she carves her initials in her…arm.

13. *Police.* a police dragnet.

1931 Wilstach *Under Cover Man* 34: Send out a drag for them before they start to work. **1949** W.R. Burnett *Asphalt Jungle* 177: You mean they got the drag out again? **1969** Pendleton *Death Squad* 108: He had over reacted to Braddock's decision for a Mafia drag.

14. a distance to be traversed; HAUL.

1953 Chandler *Goodbye* 30: It's a long drag back from Tijuana and one of the dullest drives in the state.

15. *Circus.* a street parade.

1980 D.W. Maurer, in *AS* 55: 191: *Drag*…persisted in circus argot also as a term for "street parade."

drag *adj.* **[1.** *Theat.* being a female theatrical role, esp. a comic role, played by a male actor. [Unattested in AmE, but related to **(2)**, below and to related senses of DRAG, *n.,* 4.]

*1887 in Ware *Passing Eng.* 117: Mrs. Sheppard is now played by a man…I don't like to see low [comedians] in drag parts, but…Mr. Steyne is really droll.]

2. *Homosex.* transvestite; of or involving transvestites.

1925 McAlmon *Stockings* 62: I'd been to a drag dance with earrings on. *Ibid.* 63: You shudda seen some of the drag costumes them bitches wore. **1929** T. Gordon *Born to Be* 228: The drag dances are staged by men from Kansas City to New York…and really some of them would fool many a fly shiek if they were permitted to walk Broadway the way they look at the ball. They pay as high as $500 for their gowns to wear in the famous Harlem Drag Balls. **1931** B. Niles *Strange Bro.* 99: I go to the Drag Balls. **1958** Talsman *Gaudy Image* 81: I thought you said it wasn't drag…Here you clank jewelry while I'm caught respectable. **1967** Humphreys *Tearoom Trade* 25: He then got me invited to cocktail parties before the annual "drag ball," and my survey of the subculture neared completion. **1966–71** Karlen *Sex. & Homosex.* 556: Only one butch in three…was a "drag butch." The drag butches cropped their hair in DA…style. **1971** *Playboy* (Jan.) 76: At a drag ball here recently, there were 16 Mae Wests. **1973** *Oui* (July) 75: The buddy…preferred the drag bars of Canal Street. **1978** Maupin *Tales* 197: Tripping through Golden Gate Park with drag bridesmaids and quotations from "Song of the Loon." **1985** D.K. Weisberg *Children of Night* 26: John started hustling in New Orleans, where…he learned about "drag" prostitution.

drag *v.* **1.** to search, esp. for contraband; frisk.

1895 Townsend *Fadden* 67: I taut de mug would slug me an' drag me jeans fer de boodle.

2. *Stu.* to escort (someone), as to a dance; (*also*) to date. Also absol.

1897 *Lucky Bag* (No. 3) 107: *Drag*—To drag a femme to a hop is to escort her. **1900** *Howitzer* (No. 1) 119: *Drag.*—To escort or accompany. **1906** in *Army & Navy Life* (Nov.): To "drag a femme to a hop." *ca*1909 in Warren & Warren *Everybody Works* 109: You "drag a queen (or a brick)" to the hop. **1922** *DN* IV 189: Instead of taking a girl to a dance, the young man drags her there. **1924** Marks *Plastic Age* 136: Along with the other men who weren't "dragging women" Hugh walked the streets and watched the girls. **1930** in D.O. Smith *Cradle* 137: I'm dragging blind—the femmes from York won't be up until later. **1935** F.H. Lea *Anchor Man* 15: He was in hot water and couldn't drag her. **1950** *Sat. Eve. Post* (July 22) 6: The girl I dragged for two years at the academy. **1962** in *Harper's* (Jan. 1963) 50: Fourth Classmen may not "drag" during their first year. **1970** Landy *Underground Dict.* 70: *Draggin'.*…Be with a date—eg. *Are you draggin' tonight?* **1986** R. Walker *AF Wives* 128: How come you never drag anyone to the hops?

3. *Stu.* (see quot.).

1900 *DN* II 33: *Drag*, v.i. 1. To curry favor with an instructor.

4. *Stu.* (see quot.).

1900 *DN* II 33: *Drag*, v.i.…3. To tease. 4. To joke.

5. *Stu.* (see quot.).

1900 *DN* II 33: *Drag*, v.i.…2. To understand.

6. Esp. *S.W.* **a.** to go; come; depart. Also (vulgar) **drag ass**, **drag it.** Cf. *drag* [(one's)] *ass*, below, and DRAG-ASS.

1900 *DN* II 33: *Drag in*, v.i. To arrive. **1919** Emmett *Give 'Way* 78: Thanks. If that's the cathedral we hear so much about, let's be dragging it. **1926** Nason *Chevrons* 177 [ref. to 1918]: "Let's drag," said Eadie. **1927** Tully *Circus Parade* 3: I had, as the hoboes say, dragged a long haul from Hot Springs, Arkansas, to McComb City, Mississippi, some hundreds of miles. **1934** Berg *Prison Nurse* 28: But the minute things start getting tough you want to "drag arse" out. *a*1940 in Lanning & Lanning *Texas Cowboys* 56: The kid never dragged to the farm again. **1958** *Life* (Apr. 14) 137: Drag outa here with that stick! **1954–60** *DAS*: *Drag ass*…to depart. **1960** MacCuish *Do Not Go Gentle* 73 [ref. to 1940]: Time to drag ass back, Isolde. **1963** Coon *Short End* 209: He told them to drag ass, and you know they dragged? **1965** Daniels *Moments* 266: We're gonna drag-ass outa here.

b. to quit one's job; (*hence*) to stop what one is doing. Also **drag it.** Cf. syn. DRAG UP.

1927 (quot. at BUNCH). **1958** McCulloch *Woods Words* 52: *Drag 'er*—To quit the job. **1965** O'Neill *High Steel* 271: *Drag.* To quit work just to draw pay; a man who "drags" usually tries to return to work after he has gotten his money. **1974** Former Texas oil pipeliner, age 24: *Let's drag up* or *let's drag* means "let's quit," especially a job you're working on at that moment.

7. to bore; dispirit; (*hence*) to annoy.

1944 L. Armstrong, in Hodes & Hansen *Sel. From Gutter* 80: He didn't say he wanted to drag me, but I mean, he said…it jus' look so *bad*. **1947** *Tomorrow* (Aug.) 28: "That's a drag," or "That drags me." **1951** *Amer. Jour. Sociol.* XXXVII 143: I can't stand to be around squares. They drag me so much I just can't stand them. **1952** J.C. Holmes *Go* 121: I was

real hungup on it two years ago…but it drags me now. **1952** Brossard *Darkness* 107: Jokes drag me. **1955** *Down Beat* (Sept. 21) 33: If there's anything that drags me, it's when they put the piano up too loud in the control room. **1956** Holiday & Dufty *Lady* 53: He didn't let his money drag him like some people do. **1959** L. Hughes *Simply Heavenly* 141: You come back to bug me/Like you drug me yesterday? **1961** Terry *Old Liberty* 103: I had always thought he was a real dragger. **1971** T.C. Bambara *Gorilla* 14: The "my love" part kinda drag Big Brood some.

8.a. *Hot Rodding.* to take part in a drag race; (*trans.*) to compete against in a drag race. Now *S.E.*

1950 in *OEDAS* II 15: There ought to be a place to drag in every city.…There would be no excuse to drag on the streets. **1953** Paxton *Wild One* (film): You wanna drag Johnny a hundred yards for a beer? **1953** Felsen *Street Rod* 48: You'll have to go some to drag with him. **1954–60** *DAS*.

b. to drive up and down (a street); CRUISE.

1969 *Current Slang* I & II 29: *Drag the gut, v.* To drive up and down main street.—High school males, Minnesota. **1971** Sorrentino *Up from Never* 250: My hangout in the city was the poolroom. He said he spent a lot of his time dragging Main.

¶ In phrases:

¶ **drag [(one's)] ass, 1.** to depart; go; proceed.—usu. considered vulgar. Also euphem. vars. Cf. **(6.a.),** above and DRAG-ASS.

1926 *Sat. Eve. Post* (Mar. 6) 158 [ref. to 1918]: Here you men, drag your tails out of here. **1926** Nason *Chevrons* 32 [ref. to 1918]: Drag your tail down the main stem and across the railroad bridge and you'll see the town gate. **1966** IUFA *Folk Speech:* Make like a crocodile and drag your ass out of here.

2. to move or work slowly, half-heartedly, or dejectedly.—usu. considered vulgar. Also euphem. vars. Cf. DRAG-ASS.

1930 Caldwell *Poor Fool* 125: Why in hell do you want to walk around dragging your butt on the ground because of her? **1937** Di Donato *Christ in Concrete* 18: Goddammit, Geremio, if you're givin' the men two hours off today with pay, why the hell are they draggin' their tails? **1950** Stuart *Objector* 8: If I find my orders being disregarded I'll have the guilty man or men dragging their asses from sunup to sundown. **1953** R. Wright *Outsider* 111: "How you, guy?"…"Just dragging my black ass, serving these white sons of bitches." **1944–57** Atwell *Private* 248: On a twenty-five mile hike he keeps right on goin' when everyone else is draggin' ass. **1968** Spooner *War in General* 277: Everyone else…cursed and laughed and coughed and dragged their ass, unwilling to do more than anyone else. **1971** Polner *No Victory Paradise* 15: I still think we could win over there and that dragging our asses caused more deaths than it prevented. **1974** Millard *Thunderbolt* 80: He must have had a hard day. He's sure draggin' his ass. **1975** S.C. Smith *Amer. Boys* 93: No one was up for it anymore, and the whole platoon dragged ass.

¶ **drag (one's) time** *Mining.* to collect (one's) wages and leave a job.

1916 in *Calif. Folk. Qly.* I 228: So I worked six months/And I dragged my time,/Farewell to Kerry/And his big Scotia Mine.

drag-ass *n.* a slow worker; slowpoke.—usu. considered vulgar.

1984 Sample *Raceboss* 185: Boss, git them Gotdam drag-asses outta the way.

drag-ass *adj.* **1.** tired.—usu. considered vulgar.

1952 in Hemingway *Sel. Letters* 753: Then if I start to feel low, or tired or drag ass I start them again. **1968** D. Stahl *Hokey* 80: I didn't feel spongy or drag-ass any more. My body was springy and quick and alive. **1986** Ciardi *Good Words* 229: "I'm worn out/exhausted." In slang, "I'm drag-ass."

2. slow-moving; (*hence*) tedious; lazy.—usu. considered vulgar.

1955 T. Anderson *Your Own Beloved Sons* 64: Makes me sick, digging in all the time. Guarding them drag-ass howitzers. *a*1961 Longman *Power of Black* 266: Long before us dragass Americans got the…habit. **1976** Price *Bloodbrothers* 113: After a drag-ass week and weekend made even more drag-ass by Stony's hunger to get started at the hospital, Monday came as a total shock. **1984–88** Hackworth & Sherman *About Face* 297: Now the guys' drag-ass defensive attitude was being replaced with a keen offensive spirit.

3. annoying; damned.—usu. considered vulgar.

1954 Hunter *Jungle Kids* 60: I forgot all about the dragass pusher. **1962** Mandel *Wax Boom* 143: We'll have to use those drag-ass overcoats.

drag-ass *v.* to move or work slowly, half-heartedly, or dejectedly.—usu. considered vulgar. Cf. DRAG, *v.*, 6.a. and *drag* *[(one's)] ass* s.v. DRAG, *v.* [The 1949 and 1959 quots. might just as easily go with *drag [(one's)] ass*, 2., s.v. DRAG, *v.*, from which this verb developed; this verb is distinguished from the verbal compounds with DRAG by the attachment of inflectional endings to *-ass* rather than to *drag.*]

1949 Bezzerides *Thieves' Market* 106: Drive slow, you bastards, drag ass, drive slow for about five miles. **1959** Morrill *Dark Sea* 92: If you drag ass on this job the lines will bury you. **1963–64** Kesey *Great Notion* 183: He drag-assed right on upstairs. **1972** DeLillo *End Zone* 11: Anything I have no use for, it's a football player who consistently drag-asses. **1978** Selby *Requiem* 82: She opened the door and Tyrone drag-assed in. **1983** K. Miller *Lurp Dog* 156: Dragassing into my...bunker...in the morning. **1984** Sample *Raceboss* 208: But I heard you nigguhs jes been drag-assin.

drag down *v.* to draw or earn as wages.

1904 T.A. Dorgan, in Zwilling *TAD Lexicon* 33: What did you drag down. [**1908** in Butterfield *Post Treasury* 93: The first day of the month was "drag day," when a man might draw his time-slip, which was negotiable.] **1915** in Lardner *Haircut* 153: I'll be draggin' down about seventy-five bucks a month next year. **1918** Witwer *Baseball to Boches* 95: The French doughboy...drags down the sensational sum of a nickel a day for fightin', and it ain't no wonder they're such boss scrappers. **1920** Weaver *In American* 18: Miss Cole she gets a salary that's easy/ Ten times what this Miss Ames drags down per week. **1922** S. Lewis *Babbitt* 182: I, for one, am only too glad that the man...has a chance to drag down his fifty thousand bucks a year. **1944** H. Brown *Walk in the Sun* 62: That's the life, the war plants. Two hundred bucks a week they drag down.

dragged *adj.* **1.** tired out.—usu. constr. with *out.*

1831 in *DA:* The poor Huntonites seemed to be a most dragged out. **1848** Bartlett *Amer.* 121: *Dragged out.* Fatigued; exhausted; worn out with labor. **1873** *Slang & Vulgar Forms* 11: *Dragged out* for *fatigued, exhausted.* **1879** Shippen *30 Yrs.* 125: But the whole ship's company looked "dragged out" and bilious. **1895** Wood *Yale Yarns* 175: This making a night of it is a little wearisome. I feel quite dragged. **1905** *DN* II 8: *Dragged out*, adj. phr. Fatigued. **1948** Wolfert *Act of Love* 159: I'll be...dragged out by the time we get there.

2. Esp. *Black E.* sad; dejected; bored; annoyed; fed up.

1952 Brossard *Darkness* 8: "What's new, man?"..."Nothing."..."Everything is pretty dragged right now." *a*1953 in *Amer. Jour. Soc.* LIX 240: She's dragged. **1960** L. Jones, in *Blues People:* She was extremely dragged when she found out I was just an American G.I. without even money enough to buy a box of prophylactics. **1960** R. Reisner *Jazz Titans* 154: *Dragged:* Depressed. **1972** T.C. Bambara *Gorilla* 174: Hey I'm dragged...Rudi's rap is such a drag. **1975** C.W. Smith *Country Music* 104: They had to reschedule my recital three times—boy, were they dragged! **1979** Gram *Foxes* 19: You guys are so dragged with me.

draggin' wagon *n.* **1.** a tow truck; *(Mil.)* a tank recovery vehicle. Also **dragon wagon.**

1945 *Sat. Rev. of Lit.* (Nov. 3) 7: The Dragon Wagon is a tank recovery vehicle. **1976** *Sci. Mech. CB Gde.* 165: Do you need the draggin' wagon? **1976** Lieberman & Rhodes *CB* 127: *Draggin' Wagon...Dragon Wagon*—A wrecker. **1976** Whelton *CB Baby* 71: The Dragon Wagon was [the CB handle of] Roy Stover, down at the Gulf Station. **1980** Pearl *Pop. Slang* 42: *Draggin' wagon n.* a tow truck.

2. an automobile, as a dragster, capable of quick acceleration and high speed.

1971 Jacobs & Casey *Grease* 25: Ya know that I ain't braggin', she's a real draggin' wagon.

draggy *adj.* **1.** dull; tedious.

1860 in Mohr *Cormany Diaries* 88: Work on my House goes slowly— a little draggy. **1922** in *OEDS:* We were both prepared to be thrilled, I expect, but we soon found that an early rehearsal is rather a draggy affair. **1959** E. Hunter *Matter of Conviction* 211: That was the draggiest party I've been to in years. **1963** Braly *Shake Him* 42: I know it sounds draggy.

2. bedraggled or fatigued.

1880 Bailey *Danbury Boom* 49: She was coming out the door with a pail, and was looking very much heated and upset,—"draggy," she would call it.

drag king *n.* [patterned on DRAG QUEEN] a female transvestite.

1991 *Donahue* (NBC-TV): So I dressed as a drag king. **1993** *Jerry Springer Show* (synd. TV series): These women...call themselves *drag kings.*

dragon *n. Army.* DRAGON SHIP.

1966–67 Harvey *Air War* 46: The defenders have called for Dragon fire right into the fort itself. **1970** Whitmore *Memphis-Nam-Sweden* 50 [ref. to 1967]: They call it a dragon because it looks like it's always spitting fire. Every fourth round is a tracer round. But these guns fire so fast that only red lines of fire can be seen coming out of about ten different holes in it. **1981** C. Nelson *Picked Bullets Up* 327: That old dragon never got all them suckers. There's...ten still coming.

¶ In phrases:

¶ **chase the dragon** *Narc.* to inhale the fumes of burning heroin or a similar drug.

1961 in Partridge *Dict. Und.* (ed. 2) 805. **1965 in Wilner & Kassebaum *Narcotics* 278: Dragon-chasing...often ends when the addict shifts to heroin injection to sustain his cravings. **1971** Guggenheimer *Narc. & Drug Add.* 9: *Chasing the dragon.* Chinese way of using opium. Heating heroin for injection. Inhaling H or barbiturates through a straw. **1978** *N.Y. Times* (July 30) IV 4: Aboard [U.S. Navy] ships, opiate use is referred to as "chasing the dragon." **1991** *Mother Jones* (July) 41: They...duck into a phone booth with a bit of [heroin] on a scrap of folded foil, lighting it and sucking the smoke through a straw, a procedure known as "chasing the dragon."

¶ **drain the dragon** (of a man) to urinate. *Joc.* Cf. syn. *bleed the lizard* s.v. LIZARD; *drain the [main] vein* s.v. DRAIN, *v.*

[**1890–91* F & H II 322: To water the dragon...(common).—To urinate.] **1983** K. Miller *Lurp Dog* 175 [ref. to Vietnam War]: I gotta go drain the dragon. **1985** *Maledicta* VIII 106: To urinate...*drain the dragon.*

dragon breath *n.* very bad breath.

1977 Shryack, Butler & Slade *The Car* (film): Ugh—you've got dragon breath! **1984** Columbus *Gremlins* (film): You've got dragon breath. Bad breath. **1984** Amer. Cancer Society ad (WUTK Radio) (July 28): Where you goin' with that dragon breath [from smoking]?

dragon lady *n.* [orig. the name of a villainous Asian character in the comic strip "Terry and the Pirates," by Milton Caniff] a woman who is domineering, belligerent, or the like.

1952 "R. Marsten" *So Nude* 126: I met the dragon lady. Is she the reason Eileen took a fast powder? **1971** *Playboy* (Aug.) 118: Some of the fire-breathing dragon ladies...have given women's lib an undeserved bad name. **1975** V.B. Miller *Deadly Game* 126: Okay, Ernie, we got the dragon lady in the Mercedes. **1978** Maupin *Tales* 48: The rest belongs to Dragon lady. **1985** D. Steel *Secrets* 151: Now get some sleep, beautiful, or the Dragon Lady will eat you up tomorrow. **1989** *TV Guide* (Oct. 21) 4: Dragon Lady—or Battler with a Cause?

dragonologist *n. Pol.* (see quot.). *Joc.*

1966 *New Yorker* (Feb. 12) 44: Professional China Watchers—often referred to as Pekingologists, or, more flippantly, as dragonologists.

dragon ship *n. Army.* an AC-47 ground-attack airplane; PUFF THE MAGIC DRAGON.

1966–67 Harvey *Air War* 29: Larrieux said [it] was a Dragon Ship firing its guns at the Vietcong. *Ibid.* 44: Dragon Ships—old...DC-3s...with...miniguns. **1968** W.C. Anderson *Gooney Bird* 103: One of the dragon ships came galloping to the rescue. **1969** Eastlake *Bamboo Bed* 191: A dragon ship is a C-47 converted to a gun ship. **1975** in Higham & Siddall *Combat Aircraft* 51: A thorny complication to our Dragonship's on-target operations. **1987** Robbins *Ravens* 14: The AC-47...The Dragonship...was equipped with three rapid-fire Gatling guns.

dragon wagon var. DRAGGIN' WAGON.

drag-out *n.* **1.** a brawler.

*a*1859 in Bartlett *Amer.* (ed. 2): He's a rael stormer, ring clipper, snow belcher, and drag out.

2.a. a brawl.

1870 in *DA:* We have been forcibly struck by the number of encounters...knock-downs, drag-outs, [etc.,]...in which the Representative...has been engaged.

b. a rough party.

1887 *N.O. Lantern* (Aug. 6) 3: Drag-outs, what is called dances, given by street loafers an' sich.

drag queen *n.* a male homosexual transvestite; *(also)* a female impersonator.

1941 G. Legman, in Henry *Sex. Vars.* II 1164: *Drag-queen.* A professional female impersonator; the term being transferentially used of a male homosexual who frequently...wears women's clothing. **1949** *Gay Girl's Guide* 8: *Drag-Queen:* One who makes a living doing female impersonations in a *drag-show*, or otherwise appears frequently in *drag*. **1965** *Fact* (Jan.) 26: Drag queen—A homosexual accustomed to wearing female attire. **1978** Schrader *Hardcore* 81: Drag queens and leather boys strutted the…sidewalks like hungry packs of jackals. **1981** *Penthouse* (Mar.) 172: One day I scored from this drag queen and her boyfriend on West Seventeenth Street. **1981** Wolf *Roger Rabbit* 173: I had an amorous drag queen too. **1993** Styron *Tidewater Morning* 36: "It wasn't a *she*,…but a *he*."…"A drag queen…a transvestite?"

dragsman *n.* **1.** *Und.* a thief who steals from carts, wagons, or coaches.

    *1812 Vaux *Memoirs* (gloss.): *Dragsman*: a thief who follows the *game* of *dragging*. **1859** Matsell *Vocab.* 27: *Dragsman*. A thief that steals from express wagons and carts; also trunks from the back of coaches. They sometimes have a fast horse and light wagon. ***1862** Mayhew *London Labour* IV 332: *Dragsmen*…those persons who steal goods and luggage from carts and coaches.

    2. a coachman or wagoner. Also **dragman.**

    *1823 "J. Bee" *Slang Dict.*: *Dragsman*. ***1832** in *F & H* II 322: The Swell Dragsman or in plain English a well-dressed stage coachman. **1836** *Spirit of Times* (Feb. 27) 1: Tolly, A Baltimore Dragman.

drag up *v.* [cf. DRAG, *v.*, 6.b.] Esp. *S.W.* to quit one's job; (*occ.*) to leave.

    1930 Botkin *Folk-Say* 105: To hell with the pipeline. Somebody's going to drag up. **1940** *AS* (Apr.) 221: He may be instructed either to "angle in" (enter) or "drag up" (leave). **1944** Boatright & Day *Hell to Breakfast* 139: He may say, "I'm ready to drag up (quit), I've got money in the bank and cattle out west." **1974** Cherry *High Steel* 202: "Tommy's draggin' up."…"When did he decide to leave?"

drain *n.* a drink of liquor.

    *1836–39 C. Dickens, in *F & H* II 322: Those two old men who came in just to have a drain, finished their third quartern just a few seconds ago. **1849** Mackay *Western World* II 152: "You'll be better, p'r'aps, of a drain," he continued,…offering him a small flask. *Ibid.* 274: He expressed a desire to have "another drain." ***1852** C. Dickens *Bleak House* ch. xix: He stood drains round. **1865** *Harper's Mo.* XXX 607: In Australia…what is…here a "drain" or "drink," is spoken of as a "nobbler."

drain *v.* ¶ In phrases:

    ¶ **circle the drain** *Hosp.* to be nearly dead; be dying.

    *a*1982 Medved *Hospital* 175: He'll just shrug and say, "I guess that's another one for the coroner," or "He's circling the drain." **1988** *Maledicta* IX 198: Patients…*circle the drain*, cool, etc.

    ¶ **drain the dragon** see s.v. DRAGON.

    ¶ **drain the lizard** see s.v. LIZARD.

    ¶ **drain the [main] vein** (of a man) to urinate. *Joc.*

    1968 Baker et al. *CUSS* 218: *Vein, drain the.* Urinate. **1990** P. Dickson *Slang!* 216: *Drain the main vein* For a male to urinate. **1992** N.Y.C. man, age *ca*25 (coll. J. Sheidlower): Gotta go drain the main vein.

drama queen *n.* a histrionic woman or (in homosexual use) man. [Despite the plausibility of Thorne's remarks, no earlier citations are known and the term need not have arisen in homosexual circles.]

    *1990 T. Thorne *Dict. Contemp. Slang* 151: *Drama queen*…a self-dramatizing or hysterical person.…originally (in the 1960s) applied by male homosexuals to their fellows. In the 1970s the phrase was adopted by heterosexuals and applied to women. **1993** *Real World* (MTV): "The words *drama queen* did not come from my lips."…"All my friends say I'm a drama queen."

dram-crit *n.* *Journ.* a drama critic.

    1868 Williams *Black-Eyed Beauty* 62: Got in with the *dram-crits* and they mumble of "descended from Duke of York, royal blood," all my eye, *et cet.*

drape *n.* **1.a.** Orig. *Jazz.* a suit of clothes; (*pl.*) clothing, esp. a ZOOT SUIT.

    1938 Calloway *Hi De Ho* 16: *Drape:* suit of clothes, dress, costume. **1939** Calloway *Swingformation Bur.*: That drape is a killer-diller. **1942** in Himes *Black on Black* 176: Sharp-cat Mexican youths in their ultra drapes. **1946** Mezzrow & Wolfe *Really Blues* 38: The drapes they handed me a jungle bum wouldn't wear on weekdays. **1947** *Tomorrow* (Aug.) 29: A friend with a new *drape* or suit of clothes. **1949** in Duran *Chicano Studies* 423: Mexican-American boys never use the term "zoot-suit," preferring the word "drapes" in speaking of their clothes. **1967** Salas *Tattoo* 214: You wear drapes, don't you? **1970** Sorrentino *Steelwork* 63 [ref. to 1945]: Any kid with drapes and a duck's ass haircut on

the street got his lumps right away. **1967–80** Folb *Runnin' Lines* 235: *Drapes.* Clothes. **1985** "Blowdryer" *Mod. Eng.* 60: *Drapes*…Pachuco clothing in general, wardrobe or clothes. **1990** *All Things Considered* (Nat. Pub. Radio) (Apr. 19): The term *drape* as used in Baltimore in the 1940's and '50's referred to…the zoot-suits then in vogue with young hepcats.

    b. (among schoolgirls) a dress.

    1946 in Partridge *DSUE* (ed. 7) 1048: *Dig the drape*, buy a new dress. **1947** in *DAS*: Dresses are drapes, and with belts they are shaped drapes.

    2. a tough; hood.

    1990 J. Waters, on *CBS This Morning* (CBS-TV) (Apr. 19): A *drape* was Baltimore slang in 1954 for a *hood*. Then there were the *squares*…and a *nerd* was neither one.

drape *v.* *Black E.* to clothe; attire.—usu. constr. with *down* or *out*.

    1942 *Amer. Mercury* (July) 94: *Draped down:* dressed in the height of Harlem fashion. **1948** Manone & Vandervoort *Trumpet* 161: If you don't drape me out like I want you to, you ain't gonna get this first mess [of money] down. **1950** L. Brown *Iron City* 39: I'm all draped down in new togs. **1952** Landon *Angle of Attack* 11: I say he'll be draped out like a New Orleans pimp. **1967** [Beck] *Pimp* 101: I was draped in my P.J.'s.

drape ape *n.* a small child; toddler.

    1976 Univ. Tenn. student: *Rug rat* and *drape ape* mean "small child." I heard those in Seattle in 1968. **1986** *NDAS.*

draped *adj.* drunk.

    *1943 in *OEDS: Draped*, the worse for drink. **1943** Hersey *G.I. Laughs* 171: *Slightly draped*, a couple of sheets in the wind. **1945** Hamann *Air Words: Draped.* Intoxicated.

drat *v.* [fr. *'d rot* < *God rot*] to darn; confound.—usu. used optatively.

    *1815 in *OED*: "Now drat that Betty," says one of the washer-women. **1844** *Spirit of Times* (Feb. 10) 590. **1845** in G.W. Harris *High Times* 49: If he comes a near me I'll unjint his dratted neck. ***1852** C. Dickens *Bleak House* ch. xxi: Drat you, be quiet! **1858** J.C. Reid *Tramp* 47: Them dratted Mexicans. ***1869** in *F & H* II 322: If that dratted girl had been at her post indoors…it might never have happened. **1945** Fay *Be Poor* 30: You will "*save*" (drat the word!) your cake.

drathers var. DRUTHERS.

draw *v.* ¶ In phrases:

    ¶ **draw flies** to attract a minimal number of patrons.

    1957 *Looney Tunes* (animated cartoon): "But Daffy, our billing is based on drawing power." "Oh yeah? That rabbit couldn't draw flies if he was covered with syrup!" **1959** Brosnan *Long Season* 13: Even when the Giants were drawing flies in 1956, Louie was there in the bleachers every day.

    ¶ **draw it easy** *draw it mild*, below.

    1856 *Spirit of Times* (Apr. 5) 87: Don't be hard on a poor ole man. Draw it easy.

    ¶ **draw it mild** [lit., in reference to beer] to be moderate in word or action; refrain from exaggeration; go easy.

    *1837 W.M. Thackeray, in *OED*: Dress quiet, sir: draw it mild. ***1841** in *F & H* II 324: Draw it mild! as the boy with the decayed tooth said to the dentist. ***1850** in *F & H*: Draw it mild, old fellow! interrupted the young gentleman in question. ***1851** in *F & H*: This caused angry words, and Nancy was solemnly requested to draw it mild, like a good soul. **1871** "M. Twain" *Roughing It* 251: Beg your pardon, friend, for coming so near saying a cuss word—but you see I'm on an awful strain, in this palaver, on account of having to cramp down and draw everything so mild.

    ¶ **draw it strong** to exaggerate.

    1871 "M. Twain" *Roughing It* 251: He was one of the whitest men that was ever in the mines. You can't draw it too strong. **1876** Small *Centennial* 55: I think you are drawing it strong now.

    ¶ **draw to** [sugg. by the poker sense] to try for.

    1893 James *Mavrick* 92: This I am guessing at and will leave it to the reader to draw to.

draw down *v.* to earn as wages.

    1897 Norris *Vandover* 571: I drew down twenty dollars a week there. **1920** Weaver *In American* 39: You draw down what you need, six hundred frogskins. **1922** Paul *Impromptu* 70: How much dough do we draw down?

draw-one *n.* [fr. the phr. *draw one!* used in relaying the order] a cup of coffee ordered at a lunch counter.

1896 (quot. at SINKER). **1900** O. Wister, in *Harper's* (May) 885: "Coffee an' no milk," said the Virginian. "Draw one in the dark!" the Colonel roared. **1934** Weseen *Dict. Slang* 289: *Draw one in the dark*—Black coffee.

dreads *n.pl.* dreadlocks; (*hence, sing.*) a person having dreadlocks.

1977 *N.Y. Times* (June 21) 35: The men therefore let their hair grow into long ropelike strands…referred to as the dreadlocks…or "dreads." **1983** *Penthouse* (June) 187: Marley was hustled away under police escort…accompanied by various dreads. **1989** *Village Voice* (N.Y.C.) (June 20) 39: Braids, dreads, and skinheads are all acceptable. **1990** *Puncture* XIX (Summer) 45: The dreads present match the scene well—you turn around and they're standing on a chair flashing locks. **1991** *Source* (Oct.) 44: They wanted to make him have dreds [*sic*].

dream *n.* **1.** an attractive person of the opposite sex, esp. a beautiful young woman.

1895 Townsend *Fadden* 165: Chimmie, yer a dream. **1896** Ade *Artie* 19: Say, she's a dream.…If she had the clothes she'd make the best of 'em look foolish. **1899** Kountz *Baxter's Letters* 81: Hear the women say, "She isn't so much,"…and hear the men say, "Gee! a dream!" **1903** Townsend *Sure* 61: Well, say, Duchess and Maggie was dreams! **1906** H. Green *Boarding House* 12: She's a peach—a dream. **1911** Van Loan *Big League* 57: Ain't she a dream?

2. an expert; master.

1911 A.H. Lewis *Apaches of N.Y.* 219: It'll be a gun-fight, an' he's a dream wit' a gatt.

3. a cigarette.

1928 MacArthur *War Bugs* 208 [ref. to 1918]: It was grand to shed iron hats and…twirl a dream, as the handmade construction of cigarettes was called.

4. *Narc.* an opium pellet; (*hence*) addictive psychotropic drugs. Also **dreams.**

1929 *Sat. Eve. Post* (Apr. 13) 54: Opium is…simply *dreams.* **1942** Goldin et al. *DAUL* 62: *Dreams.* Opium pellets for opium eating. **1965** Yurick *Warriors* 166: And he could see the pushers passing around all kinds of dream, back and forth, and he knew you could buy any kind of kick here. **1970** Landy *Underground Dict.* 70: *Dream*…Opium…Morphine.

¶ In phrase:

¶ **in your dreams!** No, in spite of your wishes! Not at all!

1988 *Golden Girls* (NBC-TV): "You'll have to deliver these on your break." "In your dreams!" **1990** *Get a Life* (Fox-TV): Yeah! In your *dreams*! **1991** N.Y.C. construction workers: "The Giants are gonna lose." "In your fuckin' *dreams*!"

dreambag *n. Navy.* a hammock; DREAM SACK.

1847 Downey *Portsmouth* 61: After a moments delay, "Jimmy-Legs" appears, dodging under the hammocks, singing out in his peculiarly musical voice, "Come, come, rouse out here, lash and carry, fore and aft." The deck is now cleared of dream bags, and Holy-Stones and Sand comes next in order. **1856** *Ballou's Dollar Mo. Mag.* (Oct.) 323: I began to…have longing thoughts of my hammock, and to wish that I was snugly coiled away in the comfortable old dream-bag. **1898** Doubleday *Gunner* 186: We slipped out of our "dream bags" with the best grace we could muster.

dreamboat *n.* **1.** an especially attractive member of the opposite sex. Also attrib.

1944 *Slanguage Dict.* 61: *Somebody's rocking my dream boat*—another fellow is dating my girl. **1948** A. Murphy *Hell & Back* 70: He had a nice old lady and a dreamboat of a sister. **1949** Gresham *Limbo Tower* 122: Honestly, Anne, you could be such a dreamboat if you only took a little trouble. **1949** Chandler *Little Sister* 81: On your way, dreamboat. Make with the feet. **1953** Brossard *Bold Saboteurs* 8: The dumb ones went for him, he was their dream boat. **1959** Hecht *Sensualists* 82: She searched her college days for a proper phrasing. "He's a real dream-boat." **1962** L'Engle *Wrinkle in Time* 53: You've got dream-boat eyes. **1963** D. Tracy *Brass Ring* 202: She was a dreamboat when you talked me into blind-dating her. **1967** Talbot *Chatty Jones* 96: You're everybody's dreamboat. **1976** Knapp & Knapp *One Potato* 93: Hey, dreamboat. Not you, shipwreck. **1987** *'Teen Mag.* (Jan. 1988) 44: He's blue-eyed, brown-haired and a dreamboat.

2. a luxurious or perfectly designed automobile or aircraft.

1945 Hamann *Air Words*: *Dreamboat.* (1) B-29 Superfortress. (2) Luxury liner. **1948** J.H. Burns *Lucifer* 224: Each tenderly described his Dreamboat: its white-walled tires, its motor, its accouterments. **1959**

Gault Drag Strip 24: The car…That dreamboat. **1960** Hamilton *Death of a Citizen* 72: We'll go back to Mr. Blackhat and his Plymouth dreamboat. **1965** *Strange Tales* (Aug.) 6: I wonder where you buy one of *those* dreamboats. **1973** *Oui* (Mar.) 75: You still see these dreamboats cruising around Uptown. **1978** in Higham & Williams *Combat Aircraft* 28: The B-10s were real dreamboats. **1980** Millard *Thunderbolt* 15: Girls would be clawing at the doors on both sides to win the coveted prize—a night with the owner of such a dreamboat. **1982** R. Sutton *Don't Get Taken* 58: Only to return the next day and find your dreamboat gone.

dreambox *n.* the head.

1915 *DN* IV 223: He is dippy in the dream-box. **1946** Mezzrow & Wolfe *Really Blues* 163: My dreambox kept spinning in circles.

dream dust *n.* any narcotic in powdered form.

1957 H. Ellison *Deadly Streets* 159: You still on the dream dust, Leon? **1987** *Newsweek* (Mar. 23) 81: That one golden score that could keep you in bread and dream dust forever.

dream girl *n.* an especially ideal young woman.

1924 F.P. Adams *Velvet* 50: To a Dream Girl. **1928** Carr *Rampant Age* 324: Doris, his dream-girl, was…waiting. **1944** N. Johnson *Womin* [*sic*] *in Window* (film): We've decided she's our dream girl—just from her picture! **1945** in Mencken *Amer. Lang.* (Supp. II) 781: Such commonplaces as *dream girl*. **1955** L. Shapiro *Sixth of June* 99: Others called her "dream girl," "baby," and "cutie." **1972** N.Y.U. student: I'm just looking for my dream girl.

dream guy *n.* an especially ideal young man.

1987 *'Teen Mag.* (Jan. 1988) 50: The Dream Guy Contest 1987.

dreamland *n.* a state of unconsciousness.

1908 in Fleming *Unforget. Season* 280: [He] delivered many telling punches before he was finally knocked into dreamland. **1910** T.A. Dorgan, in *N.Y. Eve. Jour.* (Jan. 19) 12: Pepke will be the one that will be handed the ticket to dreamland. **1920–21** Witwer *Leather Pushers* 66: You ain't never…[been] socked to dreamland. **1946** Gresham *Nightmare Alley* 244: I'll play with you that long and then send you off to dreamland. **1981** Ballenger *Terror* 155: I had to put him in dreamland with just one lick. **1988** M. Maloney *Thunder Alley* 182: Someone…sprayed some gas up my nose, and, next thing I knew, I'm in dreamland.

dream off *v.* (see 1942 quot.); (*also*) to sleep or loaf on the job.

1935 J. Conroy *World to Win* 201: Come on!…Layin' up there and dreamin' off. **1942** McAtee *Supp. to Grant Co.* 4 [ref. to 1890's]: *Dream off, v. phr.,* have an emission of semen while asleep.

dream puss *n.* [*dream* + PUSS] *Stu.* (see quot.).

1945 *Amer. N & Q* (Aug.) 70: The attractive girl is a "slick chick," a "rare dish," a "dream puss."

dream sack *n. Navy.* a hammock. Now *hist.*

1918 Noyes *MS.* (unp.): *Dream Sack* = hammock. **1918** Ruggles *Navy Explained* 50: *Dream Sack.* The hammock is universally known as the dream sack. **1969** Bosworth *Love Affair* 61 [ref. to *ca*1920]: I remember the hammock fondly. It was called a "dream sack," and worse, but I was young and supple, and sleep in a hammock came easily to me.

dream sheet *n. Mil.* a printed form on which an individual can indicate his or her preferred assignment.

1971 S/Sgt., U.S. Army, Ft. Campbell, Ky. (coll. J. Ball): Put it on your dream sheet and see what happens. **1973** N.Y.U. student [ref. to 1971]: My husband's friend uses *dreamsheet* all the time. When he was in the Army he had to fill out a form showing where he wanted to be stationed. **1986** Thacker *Pawn* 266 [ref. to 1970]: Fill in spaces on the dream sheet. **1986** L. Johnson *Waves* 153 [ref. to 1971]: Each student had filled out a "dream sheet," listing his or her first three choices of duty station.

dream-stick *n.* **1.** *Narc.* an opium pipe.

1936 D.W. Maurer, in *AS* (Apr.) 121: *Dream-stick.* An opium pipe.

2. a cigarette.

1943 *AS* (Apr.) 153: *Dream stick.* Cigarette.

dreamsville [*dream* + -SVILLE] **1.** *n.* a state of sleep or unconsciousness.

1959 *Swinging Syllables*: *Dreamsville*—Sleeping. **1968** (quot. at SKIN-GRAFT).

2. *adj.* DREAMY.

1957 M. Shulman *Rally* 202: But where was such a dreamsville boy?

dreamy *adj.* (esp. among young women) enchanting; delightful.

1926 in E. Wilson *Twenties* 258: The dreamiest bed—dreamiest mirror. **1944** Busch *Dream of Home* 134: They're all dreamy kids, really a keen crowd. **1950** Solt *In Lonely Place* (film): I think it'll make a dreamy picture, Mr. Steele. **1954** *I Love Lucy* (CBS-TV): Oh, he's dreamy! Oh, William *Holden*! **1963** in S. Lee *Son of Origins* 52: He's the dreamiest thing this side of Rock Hudson. **1966** van Itallie *Really Here* 40: *Elevator Man:* Did you have a good afternoon, Miss Prettyasabutton? *Doris:* Dreamy. Just dreamy. **1972** Parker *Emotional Common Sense* 6: There was this dreamiest guy, but when I found out he was a Taurus—I'm a Leo—that really turned me off. **1989** *TV Guide* (Mar. 4) 34: Oh my god....He is so cute and dreamy. **1993** *Beyond Reality* (USA-TV): Isn't he the absolute dreamiest?

dreck *n.* [< Yid *drek* 'shit'] rubbish; junk; nonsense. Hence **drecky,** *adj.*

    *1914–22 Joyce *Ulysses* 511 [ref. to 1904]: Farewell. Fare thee well. *Dreck!* **1945** in Norse *Memoirs* 146: Dreck, Henry, dreck. **1950** Bissell *Stretch on the River* 132: Broken glass, defiled sidewalks, and all the "beautiful dreck" of the big city. **1957** in S.J. Perelman *Don't Tread on Me* 199: His drecky novel. **1967–68** von Hoffman *Parents Warned Us* 46: Casually examining the dreck on the floor. **1968** P. Roth *Portnoy* 12: I'm not talking *dreck*, either. **1971** *Playboy* (Mar.) 76: Instead of "Where will tomorrow's talent come from?," its motto would be, "Let's tell today's dreck where to go!" **1981** *Rod Serling's Mag.* (Sept.) 80: This...this *dreck!* Cardboard people, hackneyed plot, dialogue out of comic books. **1983** S. King *Christine* 50: Auto-parts, wreckage, and general all-around dreck. **1986** E. Weiner *Howard the Duck* 18: Humans...are cheapskates, who buy dreck. **1987** Blankenship *Blood Stripe* 58: I've given up sushi...No one eats that dreck anymore.

dreep *n. Stu.* an obnoxious person; DRIP.

    1948 J.H. Burns *Lucifer* 225: Everyone in school knew he'd become intimate with the Dreeps, the Fruits, the Awfuls.

drelb *n.* [humorous coinage introduced in 1968 quot. as the name of a fanciful creature] an inconsequential person.

    [**1968** *Rowan & Martin's Laugh-In* (NBC-TV): And introducing Morgul as the friendly drelb!] **1978** Univ. Tenn. grad. student: Get some drelb in here to clean up....A drelb is a janitor-type, a lackey by heredity. They used the word at Maryville College in 1973.

drenched *adj.* very drunk. Cf. DAMP.

    1926 Traven *Death Ship* ch. ix: The bos'n was so well drenched that it lasted until Boulogne. **1941** Kendall *Army & Navy Slang* 26: *Drenched*...Swacked...croched, binged, boiled, goofed up...or even intoxicated. **1966** in IUFA *Folk Speech: Drenched*—drunk.

dresser *n. Homosex.* a cross-dresser; transvestite.

    1992 N. Cohn *Heart of World* 226: Transvestites, *dressers,* [were] its prime targets.

Dr. Feelgood see DOCTOR FEELGOOD.

dribble-puss *n.* [*dribble* + PUSS] a person, usu. a small child, having a running nose or drooling mouth.

    1942 *ATS* 387: *Dribble-puss*...a person with a running nose. **1985** Northport, N.Y., woman, age *ca*33: You're such a dribble-puss.

dribbles *n.pl.* diarrhea.—constr. with *the.* Also **dribble-shits.**

    1973 SFC, U.S. Army, age *ca*35 (coll. J. Ball): Everybody got the dribbles [in Vietnam]. **1981** Hathaway *World of Hurt* 171: Slouching along with the dribble-shits.

drift *v. Esp. West.* to leave; go.

    1853 "Tally Rhand" *Guttle* 15: Come, Tom, let's be drifting. **1902** in "O. Henry" *Works* 832: We had to drift, which we did, and rounded up in Oklahoma. **1910** Raine *O'Connor* 20: Drift, you red-haired son of a Mexican. **1915** in J.I. White *Git Along Dogies* 144: So I gits in his buckboard and drifts tuh his ranch. **1925** McAlmon *Silk Stockings* 61: Tell them elegant bitches...that I'm drifting right now. **1926** C.M. Russell *Trails* 5: I begin longin' for bigger burgs, so I drift for Chicago. **1927** *Amer. Leg. Mo.* (Sept.) 87: So drift. **1930** *AS* V (Feb.) 238: *Drift:* get out. "Drift, brother, and close that door behind you." **1939** "L. Short" *Rimrock* 57: Then saddle up your pony and drift, mister. **1942** Chandler *High Window* 361: Beat it...Drift....Take the air. Scram. Push off. **1949** Brown & Grant *Sands of Iwo Jima* (film): Drift! **1954** Overholser *Violent Land* 64: Now drift, the whole kaboodle of you. **1957** Simmons *Corner Boy* 11: Say, man, they got a crowd over at Zodie's, let's drift. **1958** Constiner *Gunman* 39: Kruger thought he'd better drift. **1986** Merkin *Zombie Jamboree* 111: Let's drift, Uncle.

drill *n.* **1.** *Army.* a drillmaster; drill sergeant.

    1891 *United Service* (Jan.) 121: Major Snaffle...was universally popular, and recognized as the best poker-player and the worst "drill" in the army. **1981** Rogan *Mixed Co.* 45: "Knock 'em out, Sonny," the drill

would say cheerily. **1989** G.C. Wilson *Mud Soldiers* 66: "The drills" took over the training of these...determined teenagers.

2. the penis.

    1916–22 Cary *Sex. Vocab.* I: *Drill.* The penis.

3.a. Orig. *Mil.* a correct, recognized, or customary procedure or method; routine.—usu. constr. with *the.* [Rare in U.S. before *ca*1965.]

    *1940 in *OEDS.* **1941* in Wiener *Flyers* 45: The right drill. Correct method. **1958* in Stern *Other Side of Clock* 206: I'll go over the drill again. **1964** R. Moore *Green Berets* 234: They're civilians, Binney. You know the drill. **1966** B. Cassiday *Angels Ten* 199 [ref. to WWII]: Here's the drill. Fly in formation to the Adriatic. **1966** C. Ross *N.Y. After Dark* 18: Dark girls go in twos—for more of the orgy type of drill. **1972** J. Mills *Report* 64: He'd been mugged so often he knew the whole drill. **1975** De Mille *Smack Man* 25: Benny shook his head...He knew the drill. **1977** T. Berger *Villanova* 218: Alas,...I don't know the drill for getting hold of our sky arm. **1978** Strieber *Wolfen* 160: "You used this before?" "You know I have." "Well I'm gonna go through the drill anyway....You open the control panel like this." **1981** Wolf *Roger Rabbit* 47: You know the drill as well as I do. **1987** B. Ford & Chase *Awakening* 108: We went through the whole drill, let the admissions people take our histories, signed a dozen different forms.

b. a course of action; *(also)* a state of affairs.

    1973 Overgard *Hero* 152: "What's the drill?" said Hero, not unlike a drunk just staggering out of a bar. **1981** E. Keyes *Double Dare* 22: So what's the drill?

4. *Black E.* a walk.

    1944 Burley *Orig. Hndbk. Harlem Jive* 12: But I cops a drill right after him, ole man.

drill *v.* **1.** to shoot a bullet through; *(hence)* to shoot dead.

    [**a1720* in D'Urfey *Pills* I 24: A damn'd bit of Lead,/Drills me quite thro' the Head.] **1808* in *OEDS:* It would be a terrible affair to *us*...if we should be drilled with a bullet. [**1858** [S. Hammett] *Piney Woods* 70: I'll drill a hole through him afore he can say Jack Robinson!] **1871** *Overland Mo.* (Dec.) 576: He chanced to drill a stranger's head. **1897** A.H. Lewis *Wolfville* 160: Hands up!...or I'll drill you. **1901** R.W. Chambers *Cardigan* 129: Swing that canoe, I say!...—or I'll drill you both with one ball! **1926** "M. Brand" *Iron Trail* 27: Why not drill the skunk clean, while I got the chance? **1929** Ferber *Cimarron* 185: I'll drill the first son of a bitch that fires another shot. **1948** Cozzens *Guard* 160: Benny...must have drilled thirty, forty Krauts. **1958** "R. Traver" *Murder* 10: Some soldier up there blew his top and drilled Barney Quill five times with a .38. **1958** Chandler *Playback* 30: I could drill you and get away with it. **1971** Glasser *365 Days* 16: Got drilled right through the head.

2. *Esp. Hobo.* to step or walk, esp. deliberately as opposed to under orders; *(also)* to leave.

    1893 *Century* (Nov.) 106: The blanket-stiffs are men (or sometimes women) who walk, or "drill," as they say, from Salt Lake City to San Francisco about twice a year. **1894** *Atlantic* (Sept.) 323: I wuz drillin' one day...on the Boston 'n' Albany road. **1894** in Ade *Chicago Stories* 94: No more drillin' in the snow; no soup houses; never again in a bucket. *ca*1894 in *Independent* (Jan. 2, 1902) 28: This class never walk, or "drille" [*sic*] as they call it. **1896** Ade *Artie* 84: Gee, I went drillin' way back to the barn through the hot sun, and when I sprung the left-handed monkey wrench on the uncle it made a horrible hit with him. **1899** Cullen *Tales* 165: I ain't takin' chances, and I got t' drill. **1907** *McClure's Mag.* (Feb.) 380: Another big gang is standing around rubbering at us as we drills into camp. **1919** I. Cobb *Life of Party* 22: Say, wotcher mean drillin' round dis town in some kinder funny riggin' wit'out no plunder on you? **1920–21** Witwer *Leather Pushers* 44: I drilled back to the hotel. **1921** Casey & Casey *Gay-Cat* 40: Git some coin, and...yuh can drill right by them hayseed coppers and buy a square. **1927** *AS* II (June) 385: The word *drill,* a relic of the Civil War, is still in use; it means "to hike."

3. to copulate with (a woman).

    1960 *Esquire* (June) 137: I'd like to make her right on the floor while she's singing. I'd like to drill her. **1965** Eastlake *Castle Keep* 21: After chow we were going to have drill—drilling the girls. I mean we all went into Saint-Croix to the whorehouse. **1967** Mailer *Vietnam* 43: Dallas debutantes...lucky enough to get drilled by him and Tex. **1967** "M.T. Knight" *Terrible Ten* 6: "I thought you were going to drill me in Italian now?" "You drill me first, darling." **1975** Univ. Tenn. student: I'd like to drill her eyes out. **1990* Thorne *Dict. Contemp. Sl.* 152: *Drill*...to have sex with. A rare usage.

4. to stare.

    1965 Gary *Ski Bum* 36: That guy at the bar is sure interested in your behind. Keeps drilling. In America it's breasts, but in Europe it's always your ass that really matters.

5.a. *Surfing.* (of a breaking wave) to slam (a surfer) under the surface of the water.

1981 in Safire *Good Word* 111: You were drilled so hard and for so long you were going numb from lack of oxygen.

b. *Football.* to block and knock down.

1984 *N.Y. Post* (Sept. 3) 17: I was running downfield and the guy drilled me.

6. *Av.* to fly, esp. aimlessly.

1984 Trotti *Phantom* 5 [ref. to Vietnam War]: If there was no activity other than drilling around the orbit point, we could stay on station for up to two hours before returning to the barn.

drillion *n.* [alter. of *trillion*] an indeterminately large number.

1948 Manone & Vandervoort *Trumpet* 115: But, man, that record sold over a drillion copies. **1971** *Time* (Jan. 11) 24: Plus about a drillion dollars.

drink *n.* **1.** a river or other body of water; (now *esp.*) an ocean.—constr. with *the*.

1832 in *DA*. **1838** *Crockett Almanac* (1839) 35: He led her up to the neck into the drink. **1845** in Robb *Squatter Life* 65: She struck a snag, and made a lurch, throwing me about six feet into the *drink*. **1851** Burke *Peablossom's Wedding* 152: I went kerwash into the drink! **1856** *Ballou's Dollar Mo. Mag.* (Oct.) 322: There never was that amphibious yet that ever twirled a marline-spike, or had been on the drink...three long days come day after tomorrow, but would swear...that he had been shipmates with that craft. **1867** *Nat. Police Gaz.* (Mar. 16) 2: How is it that Wes Allen has been brought to trial across the Drink? **1873** Badger *Little Thunderbolt* 19: Ketch holt, boys. Take 'em to the drink. **1875** *Funny Fatherland* 23: He cannot set out the Glass without letting in the "drink." **1890** *United Service* (Dec.) 580: Our sailors say, when a man falls overboard, "he has tumbled into the drink." **1899** Boyd *Shellback* 171: If he don't clear out of this in quick sticks I'll chuck him in the drink. **1903** Harriman *Homebuilders* 43: Git a shampoo, fall in th' drink and bury them clothes! **1908** in H.C. Fisher *A. Mutt* 87: This afternoon we all went out to the beach and took a splash in the drink. **1927** Shay *Pious Friends* 97: Now all McGee and me could think/Was how we'd like to cross the drink. **1942** Casey *Torpedo Junction* 382: I guess most of their planes are in the drink too. **1943** in Loosbrock & Skinner *Wild Blue* 215: One of the bogies is down in the drink. **1944** *AAF* 369: *Drink, in the.*—forced down at sea. **1961** L.G. Richards *TAC* 78: At Myrtle Beach, just before taking off across the drink. **1963–64** Kesey *Great Notion* 6: Somebody drive off into the drink? **1964** Hunt *Ship with Flat Tire* 7: Anywhere else they'd be a little bit disturbed about an ensign dropping everything in the drink. **1964** Newhafer *Last Tallyho* 90: What happened to the pilot in the drink? **1981** Mersky & Polmar *Nav. Air War in Viet.* 28: Steaming in the carrier's wake to pick up the crew of any aircraft that "goes into the drink" during flight operations.

2.a. *R.R.* an act or instance of watering a locomotive.

1940 *Railroad Mag.* (Apr.) 43: *Drink*—Water for locomotive.

b. *USAF.* an act or instance of inflight refueling.

1966–67 Harvey *Air War* 5: They can plug in and get a drink.

drinkage *n.* [*drink* + -AGE] alcoholic beverages. *Joc.*

1987 Univ. Tenn. student theme: *Cool ones, brews*...and *drinkage* all refer to beer.

drinkery *n.* a place where liquor is sold; groggery. Now *hist.*

1840 Kennedy *Quodlibet* 222: The sergeant took a small frame house next door to Sim Traver's Refectory,—or, rather, as Sim called it, his Drinkery. **1843–45** T.J. Green *Tex. Exped.* 368: We...called into the first open "drinkery." **1948** McIlwaine *Memphis* 223: Their grocery...was also a "drinkerie," or liquor store.

drink of water *n.* a tall man.—often constr. with *long*.

1936 in Weinberg et al. *Tough Guys* 1: Damned if you ain't a long drink of water. **1939** M. McCall *Maisie* (film): That's for you, you big, long, lanky drink of water! **1940** J.T. Farrell *Father & Son* 73: He talks too much. Give it to the drink-of-water. **1947** Overholser *Buckaroo's Code* 156: He's a long drink of water that used to buckaroo for Malloy. **1963–64** Kesey *Great Notion* 28: His oldest boy, a thin, pale drink of water. **1974** Millard *Thunderbolt* 50: He took Red to meet Dunlop, the long drink-of-water you clobbered back in the cornfield. **1977** Blackbeard *Google XIII*: But the husband-character of the strip [was] a long drink of water named Aleck. **1979** Decker *Holdouts* 163: You get that long drink of water out of here, Sam. **1987** *Sable* (ABC-TV): My favorite one of your characters is that funny tall drink of water.

drinky-poo *n.* a drink of liquor.—used facetiously.

1983 *Magnum, P.I.* (CBS-TV): I just want to go back to my nice big house and have a drinky-poo. **1990** *Simpsons* (Fox-TV): What do you say we freshen up our drinky-poos?

drip *n.* **1.** drivel.

1919 O'Brien *Wine, Women & War* 306: Drool about duties by Navy egg...Usual R.O.T.C. drip. **1924** Marks *Plastic Age* 297: It was full of errors that weren't marked, and it was nothing in the world but drip. **1934** Weseen *Dict. Slang* 53: *Drip*—useless talk; nonsense; foolish advice. **1942** Hertz & Ludwig *Journey for Margaret* (film): Do I have to do some sentimental drip about kids?

2. an obnoxious, esp. a tedious, person.

1932 Lorimer *Streetcars* 113: I was just thinking over the drips she goes with. *Ibid.* 114: He's no drip...Ted's a darn good egg. *Ibid.* 148: "I feel like a drip," Bob muttered, walking around in a circle. **1938** *Amer. Mercury* (Sept.) 123: Mr. Bell...is a *drip!* **1941** Macauley & Wald *Manpower* (film): Watch yourself, you Yankee drip! **1941** Hargrove *Pvt. Hargrove* 132: "Come in, drip," said Bushemi. **1942** Wylie *Vipers* 81: This is not the stuff to give drips, because it compounds drippery. **1944** Chase *Harvey* 596: I saw you Saturday night—dancing with that drip in the Rose Room down at the Frontier Hotel. **1945** S.J. Baker *Australian Lang.* 130: Fools of one kind and another have carved a considerable niche for themselves in Australian speech...*hoon, tonk, twit,...drip, flathead,* [etc.]. **1946** G.C. Hall, Jr. *1000 Destroyed* 380: What kind of drip would my boys think I was if I didn't make a tough show like this one? **1947** Hart *Gentleman's Agreement* (film): He's just a drip, let's face it. **1952** Chase *McThing* 66: The Loomis girls—those drips! **1953** Rodgers & Hammerstein *Me & Juliet* 514: What's the matter with you, you big drip? **1958** Johnson *Henry Orient* 42: I had previously been a sort of a drip. **1965** *Dick Van Dyke Show* (CBS-TV): What's the difference? Rain, Rob, they're both big drips. **1978** Pilcer *Teen Angel* 29: Shut up, postnasal drip!

3. urethritis or gonorrhea.—often constr. with *the*.—often pl.

1962 Mandel *Wax Boom* 6: The one who caught a drip in Tongres. **1970** E.W. Johnson *Sex* 86: *Gonorrhea* the clap, the drip. **1976** Floyd *Long War Dead* 23: Besides, a man with the drips/Couldn't be sent back into combat. **1986** Stinson & Carabatsos *Heartbreak* 3: To develop the clap, the drip, and the crabs. **1987** Zeybel *Gunship* 211: At least I didn't catch the drip the last time I was with her.

dripping *adj.* abundantly supplied.—constr. with *with*.

1922–24 McIntyre *White Light Nights* 212: Les...was dripping with wise-cracks. **1940** Raine & Niblo *Fighting 69th* (film): Come back drippin' with medals. The world's yer oyster. **1943** Chandler *High Window* 416: "Do you regard yourself as a clever man, Mr. Marlowe?" "Well, I'm not dripping with it." **1974** *N.Y. Times Bk. Review* (Mar. 10) 23: Bolan, in commando outfit and dripping with guns and explosives, raids a gang training-center and kills an estimated "twenty or thirty" more men. **1990** *New Leader* (Sept. 17) 23: That wandering woman dripping with rhinestones and wearing a silver dress.

drippy *adj. Stu.* being or resembling a DRIP, 2; foolish or driveling. Also as n.

1947 *ATS* (Supp.) 5: *Drippy*...descriptive of a "drip" or "jerk." **1959** C.W. Gordon *High School* 112: Therefore, she's "drippy too." **1987** Univ. Tenn. instructor: His friends are pretty drippy. **1992** *Married with Children* (Fox-TV): Now listen to me, drippy.

drippy tummy *n.* diarrhea. Cf. GYPPY TUMMY.

1962 Tregaskis *Vietnam Diary* 23: He's been battling a severe case of the drippy tummy but insisted on flying. *Ibid.* 36: He had the drippy tummy.

drive *n.* a thrill of intense pleasure; KICK.

1921 *DN* V 111: *To get a drive out of*, vb. phr. To be deeply stirred. By analogy with "to get a kick out of." **1927** *AS* (June) 390: To get a *drive* out of anything is to get a thrill or "kick." **1934** Weseen *Dict. Slang* 330: *Drive*—A thrill. **1949** in *OEDS*. **1966** Brunner *Face of Night* 141: It don't give you any drive like the old days. *Ibid.* 232: *Drive*—the sensation produced by taking drugs. **1989** *Donahue* (NBC-TV): I had heard that chocolate is a love drive.

¶ In phrase:

¶ **the long drive** (among cowboys) death.

1887 [C.C. Post] *10 Yrs. a Cowboy* 55: That was a close call, Phil....I thought you and Bob had both gone on the long drive.

drive *v.* **1.** to pass (food at a table).

1901 Calkins *My Host* 54: Drive them biscuit down the line, Cookee.

2. to come or go; proceed.—usu. constr. with a prep.

1912 Lowrie *Prison* 145: Th' next green one what drives up an' don't get his sheets'll have t' do without 'em. **1930** in D.O. Smith *Cradle* 62: He said to be sure to "drive over" as soon as academics start. **1936** Monks & Finklehoffe *Brother Rat* 70: Drive on to your room. *Ibid.* 193: Drive on away from that window. **1939** *AS* XIV (Feb.) 26: *Drive on,* v., usually in imperative. To continue about one's business (also at V.M.I.). **1941** *AS* (Oct.) 165: *Drive Up.* Come here. **1941** Boardman, Perrin & Grant *Keep 'Em Flying* (film): Drive out! Get on the ball, Jackpot! **1947** Willingham *End As a Man* 11: Drive by my room after the meal. **1969** *Current Slang* I & II 29: *Drive out here,* v. To step out of file, face the speaker, and halt.—Air Force Academy cadets. **1970** Landy *Underground Dict.* 70: *Drive on*...continue doing what one is presently occupied with; don't be distracted. **1973** Norris & Springer *Men in Exile* 143: Now he don't know any more than I do what the young broad's gonna do when I drive up on her. **1978** Truscott *Dress Gray* 164: Tell them to *drive around,* ancient academy slang for come around to my room. **1980** Conroy *Lords of Discipline* 471: Drive in, Bubba.

¶ In phrase:

¶ **drive on** *Black E.* to approach in a bullying manner; hit unexpectedly.

1971 Hilaire *Thanatos* 189: Three of them drove on me yesterday and said I had to be their kid. **1967–80** Folb *Runnin' Lines* 236: *Drive on (one)* Hit one quickly or unexpectedly.

driver *n.* **1.** usu. *pl. R.R.* a person's legs.

1900 in Botkin *R.R. Folklore* 293: His hat was always referred to as his "dome-casing";...his legs, the "drivers." **1942** *ATS* 733.

2. *Av.* the pilot of an aircraft.

1942 (cited in Partridge *DSUE* (ed. 7) 1111). **1945 *New Yorker* (Mar. 31) 74: "Big-Time Driver"...What a 10,000-hour pilot can tell you about the world of the air. **1945** Hamann *Air Words: Driver.* Pilot. **1946** J.H. Burns *Gallery* 120: Most were American airplane drivers. **1948** Cozzens *Guard* 24: Get a load of that aircraft driver! **1963** E.M. Miller *Exile* 30: You could always tell an airline driver. They used the airline term "go ahead" instead of the "over" used by military pilots. **1968** W.C. Anderson *Gooney Bird* 155: Larry! My favorite airplane driver. **1969** Coppel *Time for Laughter* 180: "Loot," Blunden said, "for an airplane driver you are remarkably well-educated." **1980** *Air Classics: Air War Over Korea* 47: The MiG driver didn't have long to reflect on his newly acquired knowledge. **1986** Coonts *Intruder* 190: Grafton is one shit-hot driver. *a*1990 R. Herman, Jr. *Force of Eagles* 180: Our drivers will beat the shit out of those assholes. **1992** Cornum & Copeland *She Went* 8: I recognized the...Apache [helicopter] drivers.

3. *Navy.* the commander of a vessel.

1984 T. Clancy *Red October* 42: You're the sub driver, James.

drizzle *n.* **1.** silly talk; drivel.

1928 Sharpe *Chicago May* 108: The dicks gave me the usual drizzle about my landlady squawking.

2. *Stu.* DRIP.

1932 Lorimer *Streetcars* 26: The drizzle hadn't had one cut back. **1943** *School & Soc.* LVIII 169: *Drizzle:* a drip going steady.

3. *pl.* diarrhea.—constr. with *the.* Also **drizzlies.**

1943 in J. Gunther *D Day* 83: One of our American friends is sick. "It's just the drizzles," he apologized. **1962** Tregaskis *Viet. Diary* 155: I only got the drizzlies when I got back because the food seemed rich. **1966** King *Brave & Damned* 142: "The beer will probably kill him, you know." "He'll be more comfortable with the drizzlies than with tearing himself raw for nothing." **1973** C. Cussler *Mediterranean Caper* 188: Ever since breakfast I've had the worst case of bowel drizzlies in my life.

drizzlepuss *n.* [*drizzle* + PUSS] *Stu.* SOURPUSS.

1938 "E. Queen" *4 Hearts* 126: Listen, drizzlepuss, I'm sittin' around here for a lot less than fifteen hundred bucks a week. **1941** *Slanguage Dict.* 13: *Drizzlepuss*...a melancholy, sour-faced person; a person disliked. **1942** Breslow *Blondie Goes to College* (film): You ain't hummin', drizzle-puss! **1943** *AS* (Apr.) 154: *Drizzle Puss*....anyone not up to par socially, or of a more disgusting appearance than the speaker. **1949** Ellson *Tomboy* 70: Not drizzle-puss Mary.

droid *n.* [shortening of *android*] a person who performs menial tasks; (*hence*) a dull, unimaginative, or spiritless person; ZOMBIE.

1980 in *Barnhart Dict. Comp.* I (1982) 59: The Nader droids are reading through the real-life Nader's Raiders files looking for "anything of social significance." **1986** E. Weiner *Howard the Duck* 28: I mean, I'm not some funky job-droid, you know...I'm an artist, too. **1986** *NDAS.* **1990** Thorne *Dict. Contemp. Sl.* 153: *Droid n. American* a stupid, slow or completely unimaginative person.

droll *adv.* vigorously; effectively.

1831 in Mathews *Begin. Amer. Eng.* 117: I put it to him mighty droll— in ten minutes he yelled Enough! and swore I was a rip-staver!

drome *n. Av.* an aerodrome.

1913 in *WNID* (Addenda). *Drome.* Short for aërodrome. *Slang.* **1918** *N.Y. Times* (July 21) 3: Soon the landing lights of the Hun drome flashed on. **1943** Arnold & Eaker *Flying Game* 163: A squadron [is] based on the floating 'drome. **1946** G.C. Hall, Jr. *1000 Destroyed* 187: Nobody said anything about low flying over Jerry dromes. *a*1990 Cundiff *Ten Knights* 61: The dromes...stretched out along the coastal plain near Port Moresby.

drone *n.* **1.** *Stu.* a tedious, spiritless, or obnoxious person.

1943 *AS* (Apr.) 154: *Drone*...anyone not up to par socially, or of a more disgusting appearance than the speaker. **1966–69** in *DARE.* **1977** in Rice *Adolescent* 272: *Drone*—one who is boring, dull, a drag.

2. *Homosex.* (see quot.).

1987 Luria et al. *Human Sexuality* (gloss.): *Drones* Slang term for gay men who dress in leather and other very masculine fashions and who may favor sadomasochism.

drool *n.* **1.** drivel; an example of drivel.

1900 *DN* II 33: *Drool, n.* Nonsense. **1911** H.S. Harrison *Queed* 84: Thim damfool tax-drools. **1915** Poole *Harbor* 54: We stand for their line of drool. **1916** S. Lewis *Job* 69: Gimme a copy of the drool. **1918** in Fitzgerald *Corres.* 26: That last section has a good deal of drule. **1919** (quot. at DRIP, *n.,* 1.). **1942** in Stilwell *Papers* 108: Chiang Kai-shek went on with a long drool about how I could not be in a dual status. **1954** Schulberg *Waterfront* 191: And the funny part is, you really believe that drool. **1971** in L. Bangs *Psychotic Reactions* 5: Ah, cut the...drool an' get on with the fuckin' archaeology. **1988** *Mad* (Oct.) 3: At least *we* think it's drool!

2. *Stu.* DRIP, 2.

1943 *AS* (Apr.) 154: *Drool*....applied to anyone not up to par socially, or of a more disgusting appearance than the speaker.

drool *v.* to speak drivel.

1900 Flandrau *Freshman* 130: You don't mean to say you got me away over here...to hear Duggie Sherwin drool about football. **1909** Krapp *Mod. Eng.* 208: When he or his professor talks vaguely and beside the point, he *drools.* **1915** Poole *Harbor* 54: Our school history gave it five pages and then drooled on about courts and kings. **1941** Foreman *Spooks Run Wild* (film): Aah, quit droolin', ya gettin' me wet.

¶ In phrase:

¶ **droolin' with schoolin'** *Stu.* offensively learned. *Joc.*

1944 *Slanguage Dict.* 59: *Droolin' with schoolin'*—too much with the books. **1946** in Partridge *DSUE* (ed. 7) 1048: *Droolin' with schoolin',* a grind [*sic*]. **1965** N.Y.C. high-school student: He's droolin' with schoolin'. Got a burning yearning for learning.

drooler *n. Hosp.* a drooling, esp. a catatonic, patient.

1911 in J. London *Short Stories* 494: There are fifty-five low-grade droolers in this ward. **1972** *Nat. Lampoon* (July) 76: *Drooler* A catatonic patient.

drooly *n.* **1.** DRIP.

1946 Rivkin *Till End of Time* (film): You make the rest of them look like droolies. **1947** *ATS* (Supp.) 2: Unpopular person; "drip."...*droolie* [etc.].

2. (see quot.).

1954–60 *DAS: Drooly n.* An attractive and popular boy. *Very popular teenage use c1940.*

drooly *adj. Stu.* **1.** stupid or offensive.

1947 *ATS* (Supp.) 5: *Drooly*...descriptive of a "drip" or "jerk."

2. exceptionally attractive or pleasing.

1952 *N.Y. Daily News* (Aug. 26) 11c: Rain can turn the sharpest dressed drooly dream boat into a drizzly drip from the knees down.

droop *n. Stu.* an obnoxious, esp. a tedious, person; DRIP, *n.,* 2.

1929–32 Farrell *Young Lonigan* ch. iv: He was afraid that he might be acting like a droop. **1932** Lorimer *Streetcars* 28: I tried to keep her from inviting the droop in the first place. **1940** in *AS* XVII (1942) 205: Don't be a droop. **1942** A.C. Johnston *Courtship of A. Hardy* (film): That's why Melody Nesbit is something of a droop. **1965–70** in *DARE.*

droop-snoot *n. Av.* an aircraft having a down-pointing nose section; (*also*) this section itself; (see also 1984 quot.). [The name was orig. applied specif. to the Lockheed Lightning.]

1945 *N.Y. Times* (Apr. 5) 1: America's "droop-snoot" bomber, a P-38 Lightning modified to lead standard P-38 formations in precision bombings. **1953** *ATS* (ed. 2) 709: *Droop Snoot,* the British SB3 anti-sub stalker. **1956** in Harvey *Air Force* 66: The...F-100 Super Sabre: barrel belly, droop-snoot air intake. **1961** Joswick & Keating *Combat Camera-man* 155: Ours had a sharp plexiglass nose, called a "droop snoot," where the navigator-bombardier sat in front of the pilot and a little lower. **1972** Carpentier *Flight One* 12: Were you getting a cocquyt effect in spite of the droop snoot? **1984** J. Green *Newspeak* 75: *Droop snoot*...any aircraft with an adjustable nose or with an adjustable flap on the leading edge of a wing.

droopy-drawers *n.* a person, esp. a child, whose drawers or pants are comically too large.

1929–31 J.T. Farrell *Young Lonigan* 97: Studs Lonigan hadn't even begun to pay that little droopy-drawers back yet. **1935** Algren *Boots* 171: We won't be back tomorrer, Droopy-Drawers. **1939** in *OEDS*: That droopy drawers...looks like something whose mother was scared by a moose! **1948** A. Murphy *Hell & Back* 114: Can you guess what the kids called me?...Droopy drawers. **1949** Rodgers & Hammerstein *South Pacific* 283: Come back!...Droopy-drawers! **1953** Michener *Sayonara* 156: Old Droopy Drawers lives by the book.

drop *n.* **1.** *Und.* a pocket.

1798 in Greene *Secret Band* 113: The word CONEY means Counterfeit paper money...The word DROP means Pocket, &c.

2.a. Esp. *West.* the advantage of covering someone with a firearm or other weapon.—constr. with *the.* Now *S.E.*

1836 W.G. Simms *Mellichampe* 14: More than once I had the drop on both of 'em, and could easy enough have brought down one or t'other with a wink. **1866** Dimsdale *Vigilantes* 42: Not being able "to get the drop on him" (in mountain phrase), and finding that he could not intimidate him, he turned and went off. **1869** McClure *Rocky Mts.* 233: So expert is he with his faithful pistol that the most scientific of rogues have repeatedly attempted in vain to get "the drop" on him. **1883** in Rosa *Wild Bill* 58: Waiting to "get the drop" on a "rebel!" **1884** Triplett *American Crimes* 532: Jack McCall "took the drop" on him and killed him. **1887** "Bunny" *Cow Boy* 82: Resistance was useless: he had "the drop on me," and approaching with the gun still at me, he demanded me to dismount. **1890** Roe *Police* 241: They attempted to "get the drop on the officer." **1893** Corby *Chaplain* 202 [ref. to Civil War]: Pettit wheeled his battery into position, with his usual skill, "got the drop on them," and soon put a stop to the intrusion. **1918** in Loosbrock & Skinner *Wild Blue* 77: The squadron loses its close formation if the enemy gets the drop on us. **1951** Pryor *The Big Play* 30: It's allus a question of who gets the drop first. **1974** Radano *Cop Stories* 100: Red pulls out his revolver...If the thieves try to come out the front door he'll have the drop on them. **1979** *Young Maverick* (CBS-TV): I tell you that stranger got the drop on me.

b. advantage or superiority gained esp. through quick or advance action.—constr. with *the.*

1867 in A.K. McClure *Rocky Mts.* 211: When one gets the decided advantage of another, whether in deadly conflict or in business, he "has the drop on him." **1889** "M. Twain" *Conn. Yankee* 504: I should never be able to dodge his sword...If he got the drop on me, I could name the corpse. **1908** Raine *Wyoming* 121: That's where y'u've ce'tainly got the drop on me, ma'am. **1909** Munro *N.Y. Tombs* 79: The police could not get "the drop on me," but were pleased to call me a "Twentieth Century up-to-date Second Story Man." **1929–30** Dos Passos *42d Parallel* 175: He had the drop on her now. He kissed her. **1972** in Kimball & Balcolm *Sissle & Blake* 239: You both had the drop on most of the white writers. You could write for the white and the black stage equally well.

3. *Und.* an arrest.

1914 Jackson & Hellyer *Crim. Slang* 31: *Drop*, Noun. General currency. An apprehension in criminal action. **1928** *AS* III (Feb.) 254: *Drop, fall*—Arrest.

4.a. *Und. & Police.* a receiver of stolen goods; FENCE.

***1915** in *OEDS*: I thought that they called these men "fences."...Perhaps the fashion has changed. One usually associates a "drop" with a more serious offense. **1958** *N.Y. Times* (July 13) VII 22: An assignment as a drop in a heroin-smuggling operation. **1963** *Time* (May 17) 117: An international jewel thief who had been using her as a diamond drop. **1967** Maurer & Vogel *Narc. & Narc. Add.* (ed. 3) 354: Joe was a good drop until the heat was put on him.

b. *Und. & Police.* a place where stolen or illegal goods are delivered, purchased, or stored.

1922 *N.Y. Times* (June 4) VI 7: "Drop"—The place where the plunder is stored temporarily. **1937** Hoover *Persons in Hiding* 237: He knew every thief, every "drop owner," every number changer and fence. **1939** Howsley *Argot* 5: A *Drop*—A place to conceal a victim (kidnapping) or loot. **1948** *N.Y. Times* (Oct. 21): A suspected "dope drop" on East Tenth Street. **1960** Roeburt *Mobster* 66: The getaway car's stored

in a drop in Bay Ridge. **1962** Perry *Young Man* 100: The drop is where we stash the hot car until it's needed, or where you work it over, or change the plates. **1962** Fraley & Robsky *Last Untouchables* 29 [ref. to 1920's]: I'm gonna tell you where there's a drop, a spot where they leave the stuff for local delivery. **1970–71** J. Rubenstein *City Police* 143: [Abandoned cars] are used as storage places for contraband, "drops" for illicit sales. **1977** Wood *Salt Bk.* 147 [ref. to ca1930]: They'd have three or four places where they would land this liquor. And those were called drops. **1978** Diehl *Sharky's Machine* 22: I figure, you used the Pittsburgh drop, it had to be something serious.

c. *Und. & Police.* a place where bets on an illegal lottery are delivered, made, or paid off.

1943 Ottley *New World* 155: In every street either a candy store, barber shop, beauty parlor, or tavern is a collection headquarters [for policy gambling]—called a "drop." **1949** *N.Y. Times* (July 31) IV 2 E: A bettor goes to a "drop"...where he knows he can place a wager. **1953** Manchester *City of Anger* 205: Policy slips were in the drops for only a brief period. *Ibid.* 310: I'm gonna hold 'em at the drop while the papers come. **1954** Hunter *Runaway Black* 1: He went past the candy store on the corner where Freddie ran a drop. **1965** Horan *Seat of Power* 17: He wanted me to organize the operation. I was to locate the drops. *Ibid.* 53: It was a typical Harlem numbers drop.

d. *Police.* an underworld hideout or hangout.

1955 Q. Reynolds *HQ* 74: Malone tells me there's a back entrance to this drop. He'll knock on the door and I'll grab them when they try to get out the back. **1959** Zugsmith *Beat Generation* 121: I'm beginning to think you have a new drop, sonny-boy.

e. *Espionage.* a place used by spies for the dropping off of information.

1950 *Sat. Eve. Post* (July 29) 30: The FBI instructed me to use a "drop" instead of bringing my reports to the FBI headquarters. **1957** *N.Y. Times* (Oct. 20) IV 2 E: Hayhanen traveled about the country making contact with various agents and exchanging messages with them at the "drops." **1968** *New Yorker* (Apr. 6) 138: A combination tobacconist's shop and foreign-agents' "drop."

5. *pl.* KNOCKOUT DROPS.

1932 Riesenberg *Log of the Sea* 36: They also had brass "knuckle dusters" in their trousers pockets, and in their elegant vest pockets they carried vials of "drops."

6. [fr. DROP, *v.,* 3.b.] *Gamb.* (in a casino) income from bettors; (*specif.*) income from the sale of chips.

1935 Pollock *Und. Speaks*: The drop, kitty or rake-off in a gambling house. **1961** Scarne *Comp. Guide to Gambling* 678: *Drop*...Money used to purchase chips in a casino game. **1987** *RHD2*.

7. *Und. & Police.* a clandestine dropping off or delivery of stolen or illegal goods.

1976 R. Daley *To Kill* 195: When is the drop and where? **1977** P. Wood *Salt Bk.* 152 [ref. to 1920's]: Some of these thugs would find out about a drop being made. **1986** *Time* (Sept. 15) 69: The smugglers...can afford to lease an entire ranch for one drop.

¶ In phrases:

¶ **have a drop in (one's) eye** to be drunk or tipsy.

***1698–99** "B.E." *Dict. Cant. Crew: Drop-in-his-eye*, almost drunk. ***1738** J. Swift, in *OED*: You must own you had a drop in your eye; When I left you, you were half seas over. **1813–18** Weems *Drunk. Look. Glass* 60: Half shaved—swipy—has got a drop in his eye. **1821** Waln *Hermit in Phila.* 27: Always *a drop in his eye.* **1866** (quot. at *have a brick in (one's) hat* s.v. BRICK).

¶ **take a drop** to get out; scram.

1875 in R.L. Wright *Irish Emigrant Ballads* 595: He told the old woman for take a drop,/And to shut up her giving him her slang.

¶ **take a drop to** to realize; understand. Cf. *take a tumble to* s.v. TUMBLE.

1899 Cullen *Tales* 72: Take a drop to the pulp-headedness of this.

drop *v.* **1.** to give birth to (a child). [In S.E. used only of livestock; see *OED*.]

***1662** S. Pepys, in *OED*: A Portugall lady...that hath dropped a child already since the Queen's coming. **1927** *Immortalia* 145: Nell dropped twins. **1930** Botkin *Folk-Say* 105: Hell no, got to stay with the old woman, got to drop one. **1934** H. Miller *Tropic of Cancer* 271: Meanwhile she'll be dropping a kid. **1945** Peeples *Swing Low* 99: "It ain't somethin' you'n' Amy done invented," said Al. "Womenfolks always dropping kids around here." **1953** Eyster *Customary Skies* 4: The Lord sure musta frowned on his ma to make her drop one that size. **1976** Chinn *Dig the Nigger Up* 83: I hope she don't start droppin' 'em here!

2.a. to shoot down; (*broadly*) to kill.

*1726 in *OED*: I…dispatch'd two of 'em immediately, and I had made a shift to drop a third. **1836** W.G. Simms *Mellichampe* 15: I could ha' dropped one or t'other for certain. **1858** [S. Hammett] *Piney Woods* 69: With a shootin' iron in his hand, [he] looked round the crowd to see which one he'd best drap first. **1869** J.R. Browne *Apache Country* 462: The first man that lays a hand on that flag I'll drop him sure! **1877** Pinkerton *Maguires* 310: Bill…can be dropped, an' the men make sure their escape. **1878** [P.S. Warne] *Hard Crowd* 8: Take the back door!…an' drop everybody that stands in the way! **1911** Howard *Enemy to Society* 154: Those fellows'd drop you jest t'see which way you fell. **1911** A.H. Lewis *Apaches of N.Y.* 86: Ike dropped one…It's Ledwich. **1922** Hough *Covered Wagon* 47: Make one move an' I drop ye! **1972** Carr *Bad* 145: I'm gonna drop him right. **1977** Caputo *Rumor of War* 230: Tell 'em to drop anything that moves on that road. **1991** in *N.Y. Times* (Nov. 2, 1993) A 16: Drop them or let them drop you? I choose droppin' the cop!

b. to knock down, as in a fight; (*Boxing*) to knock out.

*1812 in *OED*: The coachman dropped his man the first round. *1834 in *OED*: I…planted my fist…under his jaw-bone, and dropped him at once. **1907** Siler *Pugilism* 131: Dey are bot' clever an' can show yer how t' drop a bloke. **1913** J. London *J. Barleycorn* 122: One…dropped me, and started the fight. **1913–15** Van Loan *Taking the Count* 278: I'm going to drop this greaser in three rounds, sure. **1922** Tully *Emmett Lawler* 289: But I made you listen to birds, and you couldn't drop me. *Ibid.* 303: Ryan couldn't drop Conway in six rounds. **1955** Graziano & Barber *Somebody Up There* 220: They are yelling like madmen when I drop the guy. **1970** La Motta, Carter & Savage *R. Bull* 98: I dropped him five or six times, the last time at the end of the tenth round. **1971** Torres *Sting Like a Bee* 72: Bonavena…has been the only man to drop the Canadian. **1975** Brownmiller *Against Our Will* 205: When he started boxing in the Army he astounded himself by his ability to "drop" bigger men. **1989** *21 Jump St.* (Fox-TV): My dad tried givin' me boxing lessons. He wanted me to just drop the guy.

3.a. Orig. *Und.* to give or pay (money); spend. Also absol.

[*1676 Wycherley *Plain Dealer* III i: They drop away all their money on both sides.] *1780 *Town & Country Jester* 35: It is I that have *dropt* a Guinea. *1789 G. Parker *Life's Painter* 177: They *drop* him, as they call it, from a crown to a guinea. *1812 in Vaux *Memoirs* 237: *Drop*: to give or present a person with money, as he *dropp'd me a quid*, he gave me a guinea. *ca*1835 in Holloway & Black *Broadsides* II 61: She told me five shillings was the lowest price,/Five shillings, said I, and thus did begin./I told her in plain I would drop but six win. *Ibid.*: I have dropt the bit for another odd pot. **1885** in Lummis *Letters* 282: So the deluded victims…drop their last dollar for grub. **1938** in Partridge *Dict. Und.* 208: How much a priest was likely to "drop."

b. to lose (money) in gambling or business.

1836 *Spirit of Times* (July 16) 170: Every body is on the *qui vive*—some to look after the blunt—others to "*drop it*," as the sporting folks say. **1845** Hooper *Simon Suggs* 40: Ask him if he didn't drop a couple of hundreds at the Big Council! *1849 W.M. Thackeray, in *F & H* II 329: We played hazard on the dining table. And I dropped all the money I had from you in the morning. *a*1889 Barrère & Leland *Dict.* I 331: It is estimated that the Minnesota men dropped $8000 on the fight. **1890** Quinn *Fools of Fortune* 277: He dropped $10 to the "crap" roller. **1898** in J. London *Short Stories* 24: He goes into [the casino]…and drops the whole sack. **1908** in H.C. Fisher *A. Mutt* 35: He dropped 300 bucks yesterday and desired to recoup. **1922** in Ruhm *Detective* 3: Why, the best safe cracker in the country…will drop all his hard-earned money in three weeks on the race track. **1933–35** D. Lamson *About to Die* 187: He dropped the fifty in a crap game.

c. *Und.* to pass (worthless checks, counterfeit money, or the like).

1926 Finerty *Criminalese* 18: *Dropped a map*—Passed a worthless check. *1938 in *OEDS*: "Dropping" the forgers' cheques. *1962, *1968 in *OEDS*. **1972** B. Jackson *In Life* 24: His present sentence is for bad checks he dropped at a gas station.

d. to wager. *Joc.*

1962 Quirk *Red Ribbons* 194: A…working stiff can drop a nickel on the numbers when he feels like it.

4.a. Orig. *Und.* to become aware of; discover.—constr. with *to* or *on* [*to*].

*1812 in Vaux *Memoirs* 237: To *drop down to* a person is to discover or be aware of his character or designs. **1846** *Nat. Police Gaz.* (June 20) 347: Should it any time drop out that they come from him, and if none but *Bony* and you and myself know where they come from, they [the authorities] cannot drop on it. **1859** Matsell *Vocab.* 54: The cop-

per…could not drop to my chant or mug,…the officer could not recollect my name or face. **1876** in *DAE*: Drop on yourself, Lent, you are out of season. **1880** Small *Mother-In-Law* 66: He came twice to the house, pretending that he felt anxious regarding my health, before I "dropped" to his little game. **1882** in Botkin *Folk-Say* 94: I [stole] his coat, but he dropped to the racket, and went out and had me arrested. **1886** *N.O. Lantern* (Oct. 6) 2: The crowd dropped to his little game. **1887** *N.O. Lantern* (Sept. 17) 2: The boys…ain't never dropped onto the way of Ed Vaz. **1928** Sharpe *Chicago May* 103: The plan was simple enough, but, like most simple plans, it was a wonder no one had dropped to it before.

b. to understand.

1877 in Asbury *Gem of Prairie* [opp. 136]: That Sheeney…never will tumble.…Why can't you drop? **1885** *Puck* (Apr. 22) 115: And they will not smash the old Mahdi worth a cent. Do you drop? **1887** DeVol *Gambler* 50: He caught sight of me, and then he "dropped," and said to me, "George, *you* gave that picture to the Chief." **1900** *DN* II 33: *Drop, v.i.* To understand. **1900** Ade *More Fables* 136: Give him a little Time, and then he Drops. *1909 Ware *Passing Eng.* 118: "Ah!" sobbed the girl, "you do not drop."

c. *Und.* to recognize.

1928 Hammett *Harvest* 31: And will you look at the sap he's toting?…Big enough to sink a battleship. You drop him?

5.a. *Und.* to allow (a confederate) to be arrested.

1902 Hapgood *Autobiog. of a Thief* 204 [ref. to *ca*1890]: By giving up a certain amount of stuff and dropping a stall or two to keep up the flyman's reputation, they are able to have a bank account and never go to stir.

b. *Police & Und.* to place under arrest.

1904 *Life in Sing Sing* 247: Dropped.—Arrested. **1926** Finerty *Criminalese* 16: *Dropped*—Arrested. **1948** Kingsley *Detective Story* 328: Getting dropped today was the luckiest thing that ever happened to you, Lewis. **1970** Horman & Fox *Drug Awareness* 466: *Dropped*—arrested.

c. *Pris.* to be arrested.

1933 Ersine *Prison Slang* 33: *Drop*…To fall, be arrested.

d. to convict of a crime.

1978 Diehl *Sharky's Machine* 237: He was dropped twice in New York State, both felonies.

6. (esp. among pitchmen) to sell.

1925–26 Black *You Can't Win* 128 [ref. to 1890's]: "Brass peddlers"…with their ninety-cents-a-dozen gold "hoops"…"dropped" them to the Indian squaws and railroad laborers for any price from one dollar up. **1928** *AS* II (June) 375: *Drop*—To sell. **1930** *Variety* (Jan. 8) 123: Other…[con] men "hustle slum" (sell junk jewelry) or "drop a hoop" (peddle a cheap ring). **1985** *Time* (Apr. 15) 57: If Jane Fonda can drop 250,000 how-to exercise videos, why can't Bobby Seale drop a half-million of these [cookbooks] every barbecue season?

7. Orig. *Narc.* to swallow (a pill or capsule, esp. one containing LSD). Occ. absol.

1963 in Bruce *Essen. Bruce* 149: So don't smoke—drop a few pills, but don't smoke. **1965** Cleaver *Soul* 38: Dropping Reds and busting heads. **1965** Bonham *Durango St.* 59: When you drops a couple of yellajackets and washes them down with a can of beer—you clear out of this world. **1966** Braly *On Yard* 190: A world ready to…drop an overdose of sleepers. **1967** *Zap Comics* (Oct.) 16: Dropped acid for three weeks! **1967–68** von Hoffman *Parents Warned Us* 96: If someone's under eighteen, they should tell their parents if they're dropping. **1970** *N.Y. Times* (Dec. 20) 17: I took speed a long time ago…I dropped it. I didn't shoot it up. I dig it. **1972** Morris *Strawberry Soldier* 81: How many times have you dropped? **1979** Crews *Blood & Grits* 39: I don't know why people who drop acid are always trying to get everybody else to do it too. **1983** Flaherty *Tin Wife* 326: Find a water fountain and drop a pill. **1987** *Newsweek* (Mar. 23) 81: Snorting coke and heroin, and dropping diet pills. **1992** *Middle Ages* (CBS-TV): She dropped acid and jumped off a roof.

8. *Police.* to plant (evidence).

1976 "N. Ross" *Policeman* 54: Narcotics dicks, for the most part, don't drop (or plant) dope on wrongdoers.

9. *Rap Music.* **a.** to tell; impart; in phr. **drop science** to tell the real truth, usu. about social or political issues; to speak interestingly.

1989 *CBS This Morning* (CBS-TV) (Aug. 30): *Droppin' science* is when she's really explainin' what's goin' on. **1989** "Big Daddy Kane," in L. Stanley *Rap* 16: They don't drop rhymes like these. **1990** "Ice-T" in B. Adler *Rap!* 75: The knowledge I drop will be heard by millions. **1991** *Source* (Oct.) 32: More rappers became political and started dropping science on wax. **1991** *Fresh Prince of Bel-Air* (NBC-TV): That dude be droppin' science! **1991** Nelson & Gonzales *Bring Noise* 244: Pete was dropping shit. **1991** in *Rap Masters* (Jan. 1992) 59: Maestro Fresh-Wes &…Farley Flex are dropping a strictly atomic piece of science. **1992** "Fab 5 Freddy" *Fresh Fly Flavor* 24: Drop science…The phrase was popularized by the Five Percenters [a Black Islamic organization].

b. to issue (a recording); produce. Cf. **(1)**, above.

1991 in *Rap Masters* (Jan. 1992) 5: Queen Mother Rage has dropped her debut LP. *Ibid.* 58: In 1979…the Sugarhill Gang dropped their first rap album.

¶ In phrases:

¶ **drop dead** (used to express rejection and contempt).

[**1908** in Fleming *Unforget. Season* 227: I tell you the Giants can't lose out unless they all drop dead.] **1925** *Sat. Eve. Post* (Jan. 3) 14: My wife and children should drop dead [if that happens]. [**1926** Dunning & Abbott *Broadway* 217: Oh, lay dead.] **1931** Lorimer *Streetcars* 12: I quietly wished he would go drop dead somewhere. **1934** O'Hara *Appt. in Samarra* ch. vi: "Let's put snow on his face." "Oh, drop dead." **1946** J. Adams *Gags* 65: "Who do you think you are?" "Drop dead, that's who I am." **1949** Mende *Spit & Stars* 5: She told him plain…"drop dead." **1954** Matheson *Born of Man & Woman* 127: Those dumb dopes across the way—jabber, jabber!…—they should all drop dead! **1968–71** Cole & Black *Checking* 8: Go fuck yourself. Drop dead. Your mother's a whore. **1978** Reynolds *Geniuses* 17: Drop dead, mister. **1983** Van Devanter & Morgan *Before Morning* 74: When Kirk called later to ask Barbara for a date, he got a two-word answer: "Drop dead."

¶ **drop hairpins** *Homosex.* to hint about homosexuality, usu. about one's own. Also vars.

1943 in T. Williams *Letters* 77: All the local girls [male homosexuals] have gone underground for the duration, speaking in whispers and dropping never a pin in public places. **1965** Trimble *Sex Words* 67: *Drop hairpins* or *drop pins*…To hint around suggestively with a person to determine if they are homosexual. **1972** *Anthro. Linguistics* (Mar.) 101: *Drop one's beads, pearls,* or *hairpins,* etc.…To hint about one's homosexuality to another person.

¶ **drop it** to change the subject; stop talking.—usu. imper.

*1847 in Partridge *DSUE* (ed. 7) 1112: I told them several times to *drop it.* **1872* in *OED*: He looked at me angrily, and briefly answered, "drop it." **1896** Ade *Artie* 25: Drop it! Don't try to con me with no such talk.

¶ **drop off** to die.

1804 Brackenridge *Mod. Chiv.* 442: When we are gone…when they drop off. **1881** C.M. Chase *Editor's Run* 209: Prosecuting attorneys…[in New Mexico] are apt to drop off in the bloom of health…with…a disease of holes peculiar to this locality.

¶ **drop on** to give or tell.

1964 in Gover *Trilogy* 211: If you droppin gratooidies on these bartenders, it gotta be [at least] a fiver. **1970** Landy *Underground Dict.* 71: Drop it on me. **1972** Pendleton *Boston Blitz* 147: I'm going to drop a name on you, Leo, just a name. **1980** P. Rizzuto, on N.Y. Yankees vs. Mil. Brewers (WINS Radio) (July 21): And now Fran Healey has some words of wisdom to drop on us. **1985** M. Baker *Cops* 100: The owner drops a name of a guy on us that carries a .22. *a*1990 Westcott *Half a Klick* 235: Didn't mean ta be droppin' bad news on your buddy.

¶ **drop (one's) load** see s.v. LOAD, *n.*

¶ **drop science** see **(9)**, above.

¶ **drop trou** [or **trowel**] *Stu.* to expose oneself by suddenly dropping one's trousers or undergarments.

1971 N.Y.U. student: *Dropping trou* is dropping your pants. **1974** Strasburger *Rounding Third* 44: Years of not going to burlesque shows to see Blaze Starr drop trowel. **1980** Birnbach *Preppy Hndbk.* 219: *Drop trou.*…Let down one's pants. What Preppy guys do to break the ice at parties. **1988** *Nat. Lampoon* (Feb.) 14: A few drinks and I'll be…throwing up on your tie or dropping trou'. **1993** *Entertainment Wkly.* (Oct. 29) 16: Not since Mariel Hemingway dropped trou for an episode of Bochco's *Civil Wars* has a smidgen of bare skin…stirred up so much trouble.

¶ **drop wise** *Und.* to become aware.

1929 Hotstetter & Beesley *Racket* 223: *Drop wise*—To become aware of what is going on. **1936** Steel *College* 333: Finally…I dropped wise.

drop case *n.* an idiot.

1972 Jenkins *Semi-Tough* 89: Everybody in real-life business is a dunce…Every time I'm introduced to somebody who's supposed to know all about television or politics or Wall Street, he's a goddamn drop case.

drop-dead *adj.* Orig. *Journ.* dazzling; inspiring awe, astonish-

ment, or the like. Also as adv.

1970 (cited in *W9*). **1979** *N.Y. Times Mag.* (Aug. 26) 18: Debbie's drop-dead brand of glamour coolly evokes…hallowed images of Hollywood sex queens. **1979** *Nat. Lampoon* (Dec.) 55: Drop-Dead Reception Area. Super slick. Looks like a *Star-Wars* set. **1981** *N.Y. Times Mag.* (June 21) 22: Frank Sinatra is the drop-dead king of the world. Translation: When Blue Eyes walks into a room, the room drops dead at his feet. **1981** *Larry King Show* (Mutual Radio Network) (May 23): I was going to wear this really knock-out dress for the show. **1986** *Time* (Nov. 17) 100: Garr's drop-dead wardrobe…[is] straight out of *Dynasty.* **1988** *Fortune* (May 23) 83: Its graphics are drop-dead. **1990** *Live! with Regis & Kathie Lee* (synd. TV series) (Dec. 20): The gown was *drop-dead!* **1993** *N.Y. Times* (Jan. 4) C 16: That's the other way of succeeding, to be drop-dead gorgeous.

drop-dead button *n.* a channel-selector button on a television remote-control device. *Joc.*

1986 *N.Y. Times* (Dec. 31) A 19: Normally I turn off televised adolescents immediately…but as I reached for the drop-dead button the words "obsessed with Michael Jackson" appeared on the screen, and I was hooked.

drop game *n. Und.* PIGEON-DROP.

1848 Pry *Life in Baltimore* 12: Should a chance offer to play the "drop game" on an unsuspecting countryman, he is "about" with a pocket book filled with…worthless bills.

drop-in *n. Gamb.* an easy opportunity; (*also*) a gullible bettor.

1937 D. Runyon, in *Collier's* (Jan. 16) 9: This is about as soft a drop-in as anybody can wish. **1940** *AS* XV 117: *Drop-in.* Something which is easy; easy money. So-called because a fat *mark* may sometimes "drop in" to a confidence game without being steered. **1949** Cummings *Dict. Sports* 119.

drop-man *n. Und.* (see quot.).

1969 Smith & Gay *Don't Try It* 107: *Drop-man:* This person, often a young, dependable nonuser, is used by sellers to make deliveries.

drop money *n. Und.* (see quot.).

1966 Brunner *Face of Night* 232: *Drop money*—bribe money, especially bribes to the police.

dropper *n.* **1.** *Und.* a practitioner of the PIGEON-DROP.

1845 in *DAE*: It consisted of gamblers, pickpockets, droppers, burners, thimble-riggers, and the like.

2. a gun.

1882 Harbaugh *Bill Bravo* 2: That b'ar belongs to me, stranger, an' I'll trouble you by askin' you to lower yer dropper. **1886** Harbaugh *Coldgrip in N.Y.* 14: Move a hand toward [your] dropper…and I'll toss you to the coroner!

3. *Und.* a professional killer; assassin.

1926 Finerty *Criminalese* 18: *Dropper*—Professional killer. **1930** *Amer. Mercury* (Dec.) 455: *Dropper, n.:* A paid killer. "We got to send East for a couple of droppers." **1933** Ersine *Prison Slang* 33: *Dropper, n.* A gunman. "The dropper cools the hot squat today." **1967** "M.T. Knight" *Terrible Ten* 76: "Man, what a dropper!" Cosmo Nostra exclaimed with awe.

4. *Surfing.* (see quot.).

1968 Kirk & Hanle *Surfer's Hndbk.* 138: *Droppers:* big waves; very steep and fast-riding waves.

drop quiz *n. Stu.* a surprise quiz.

[**1900** *DN* II 33: *Drop,* n. An unexpected examination.] **1977** Harnack *Under Wings* 48: I usually failed the inevitable drop quizzes.

dropsy *n.* a tendency to drop things.—often constr. with *the.*—also pl.

1933 Odets *Awake & Sing!* 43: (HENNIE drops a knife and picks it up *again.*) BESSIE: You got dropsy tonight. **1966** Farrar *N.Y. Times Crosswords* XIV 43: Butterfingers habit…*dropsy.* **1983** Univ. Tenn. student: I was opening a bag of corn chips the other day and I got the dropsies and they went flying all over the place.

drop-top *n.* an automobile with a convertible top.—also attrib.

1973 Goines *Players* 43: The stars were bright overhead, and he was tempted to let the top down on his drop-top. **1990** C.P. McDonald *Blue Truth* 91: A very Palm Beachy lady in her drop-top "beamer."

drove up *adj. Black E.* excited.

1972 Carr *Bad* 176: You're pretty drove up, aren't you, boy?

drudge *n.* [orig. unkn.] (see quot.).

1871 Schele de Vere *Americanisms* 600: *Drudge,* another name for raw whiskey, originating in the Eastern States. "I doubt whether the word *drudge* is thirty years old." (S.S. Haldeman.).

drug *n.* ¶ In phrase: **on drugs** crazy.
1974 Univ. Tenn. student: Those people [bureaucrats] are all on drugs.…He's on drugs. **1982–84** in Safire *Take My Word* 241: *On drugs* is a phrase which signifies craziness, as in "My mom won't let me stay out all night. She thinks I'll get drunk. She's on drugs." **1989** *21 Jump St.* (Fox-TV): You're on drugs if you think you're going to destroy the Fibonacci sequence.

drug *adj.* [dial. var. DRAGGED] *Black E.* unhappy; DRAGGED. Also **drugg, drugged.**
1946 Mezzrow & Wolfe *Really Blues* 22: Somebody would start chanting a weary melody…until the whole block was drugg. *Ibid.* 305: *Drugg*: Brought down, depressed. **1951** *Amer. Jour. Sociol.* 37: 141: "You'll always be drug with yourself*…There'll never be any kind of a really great job for a musician."…*Unhappy. *ca*1953 Hughes *Lodge* 79: I was very disappointed and drug with life in general. **1958–59** Lipton *Barbarians* 76: I felt very drug, like I thought of killing myself. *Ibid.* 316: *Drugg*—Brought down from a high.…Depressed, bored, frustrated, blah. *Ibid.* 100: I was real drugged about it. **1960** C. Cooper *Scene* 59: Drugged…mad at somebody. **1962** in Bruce *Essent. Bruce* 264: Then I git really drug. **1963** Braly *Shake Him* 15: They'd left the gig early because they'd grown drug with blowing for one drunk. **1966** C. Cooper *Farm* 117: I'm drugged with a system that requires you to ask me a question like that. **1970** A. Young *Snakes* 42: Them silly bitches can get me drugger than a motherfucker. **1972–74** Hawes & Asher *Raise Up* 147: I was getting more and more drugged, wondering how much longer I could last [working] at Dave's. **1974** V.E. Smith *Jones Men* 186: He got really drugged when I told him that. *a*1979 Pepper & Pepper *Straight Life* 98: Ordinarily we would have been drug [because of the bad weather].

drugged *adj.* var. DRUG, *adj.*

drugger *n.* a drug abuser; DRUGGIE.
1987 Univ. Tenn. student theme: Those describe drunks or druggers. **1988** Univ. Tenn. student theme: Those who participate in drugs are known as "druggers."

druggie *n.* **1.** a user of illicit drugs; drug abuser.
1966 Young & Hixson *LSD* 63: Harvard "druggies"—that label being preferred in Cambridge to the Western term "hippies." **1967** in H.S. Thompson *Shark Hunt* 456: The press dismissed them as…a frivolous band of druggies and sex kooks. **1967–68** von Hoffman *Parents Warned Us* 224: Most experienced druggies put it down as the worst sort of junk. **1970** *Playboy* (Dec.) 122: Working as a narc…trying to bust a few druggies. **1971** Trudeau *A Lot Smarter* (unp.): This looks like a good place to nab druggies. **1987** S. King *Misery* 151: The world's only monastic druggie. Up at seven. Down two Novril with juice.
2. *Navy & Coast Guard.* a drug smuggler.
*a*1990 Poyer *Gulf* 89: "Not fishermen."…"What are they?"…"Druggies?"

drughead *n.* DOPEHEAD; DRUGGIE.
1968 *Look* (Feb. 6) 76: Violence by some freaked-out drughead. **1990** Thorne *Dict. Contemp. Sl.* 155: *Drughead* n. *American* a user of illicit drugs.

drugola *n.* [*drug* + pay*ola*] bribery in the form of illicit drugs; (*also*) (see 1989 quot.).
1973 *Newsweek* (July 30) 62: Federal investigators…are looking for friendly witnesses who will be granted immunity for telling what they know about payola and drugola. **1983** *9,000 Words*. **1989** Spears *NTC Dict.* 109: *Drugola*…a bribe paid to police for protection by drug dealers.

drugstore cowboy *n.* **1.** an idle young man who lounges at or near a drugstore soda fountain, esp. for the purpose of socializing with young women; (*broadly*) a soft or callow fellow.
1923 T.A. Dorgan, in Zwilling *TAD Lexicon* 33 [July 26]: Hangin' around that gang of drugstore cowboys. **1923** *Chi. Sun.-Trib.* (comics) (Oct. 14) (unp.): Ain't that one o' them drug store cowboys I heerd so much about? **1922–24** McIntyre *White Light Nights* 212: Les was a drugstore cowboy. His coat was belted at the back and he was dripping with wise-cracks. **1926** Maines & Grant *Wise-Crack Dict.* 7: *Drug store cowboy*—Fellow who spends nothing but time. **1928** Dahlberg *Bottom Dogs* 219: Drugstore cowboys and the corner cigar joint. **1940** S. Lewis *Bethel Merriday* 15: The…knots of young loafers who…were called "drugstore cowboys." **1945** Seaton *Junior Miss* (film): We always had at

least one of those drugstore cowboys hanging around the place. **1950** Duffy *S. Quentin* 165: He is also wearing his hair thick and long at the back of his neck, in the "drugstore cowboy" style. **1958** Plagemann *Steel Cocoon* 82: They're scraping so near the bottom of the barrel now that they may send you some drugstore cowboy all dressed up to look like a chief pharmacist's mate. **1986** N.Y.C. woman, age *ca*50: A *drugstore cowboy* is a '40's word meaning a kind of useless guy who talks big but just hangs around the soda fountain in a drugstore. Like a soda-fountain barfly.
2. a man who dresses like but has never worked as a cowboy; a would-be or ineffectual cowboy; an actor who plays the role of a cowboy.
1928 *AS* III (June) 367: *Drug Store Cowboys.* "Extras" in "horse-operas," called so because they loaf in front of drug stores when "between the pictures." **1928** Hecht & MacArthur *Front Page* 486: Jesse James, huh! The drugstore cowboy! **1981** Cody & Perry *Iron Eyes* 58 [ref. to 1925]: The corner of Sunset and Gower [in Hollywood] where…you found a drugstore with benches lined up out front. Perfect for lounging in the sun. The [movie] cowboys that hung out were called, not surprisingly, "drugstore cowboys." **1989** Zumbro & Walker *Jungletracks* 18: Them goddamn drugstore cowboys from Texas—all mouth and no guts.

drugstore handicap *n. Horse Racing.* a horse race in which one of the horses has been illicitly stimulated or treated with a drug. Also **drugstore race.**
1948 in *DAS*: What racketeers call a "drugstore race." *a*1951 in Maurer *Lang. Und.* 209: Drugstore handicap. **1973** Haney *Jock* 176: *Drugstore handicap*: Drugs used in a race.

drum *n.* [< Romani *drom* 'road'] **1.** *Und.* a place, house, or establishment; JOINT.
*1851 Mayhew *London Labour* I 418: Have a touch of the *broads* with me and the other heaps of *coke* at my *drum*. *1855 (cited in Partridge *Dict. Und.* 209). **1865** (cited in *ibid.*). *1867 in *F & H* II 332: "Where shall we go?" "Oh, to the old *drum*, I suppose." **1872** (quot. at **2.**, below). *1890 in *F & H* II 332: The two chums were footing it to the "ancient *drum*," as they called the Norwich theatre. *1899 Whiteing *John St.* 12: "That's my drum, two doors beyond."…This house…was three floors high, had three windows to a floor, and the promise of large front rooms. **1908** McGaffey *Show Girl* 115: Say, the drum was so crowded that some of the couples had to [go onto] the fire escape. **1923** *N.Y. Times* (Sept. 9) VIII 2: Nifty Drum: A petite playhouse. **1925** *Collier's* (Sept. 19) 8: This drum must set you back plenty. **1939** *AS* (Oct.) 239: *Drum.* Hotel; saloon; cabaret. **1947** Brooks *Brute Force* (film): There are ears all over this drum, and they all belong to one guy. *1959 Behan *Borstal Boy* 32: We're getting out of this drum in the morning anyway, Paddy. *1971 in Thorne *Dict. Contemp. Sl.* 155: Go and turn over his drum while we keep him locked up here.
2. *Specif.*, a tavern or saloon, esp. if shabby or disreputable.
1859 Matsell *Vocab.* 28: *Drum.* A drinking-place. **1866** *Night Side of N.Y.* 80: It is not easy to guess why the tavern to which the stern pugilist resorts, should be called a "drum," in his *lingua franca*. **1866** (quot. at LUSHING KEN). **1871** Banka *Pris. Life* 493: Saloon…*Drum* or *Lush-ken.* **1872** Burnham *Secret Service* V: *Drum*, a bad house, boarding-place, or small tavern. *Ibid.* 80: Come to the "break o' day drum" in B— Street to-morrow night…and…I'll p'int him out to yer. **1895** Townsend *Fadden* 166: "Has dey broke your drum?" says I, "'cause me friend (the bar-keep) runs his own drum, where me and Mr. Paul was to de opening what I was telling you 'bout." **1903** Townsend *Sure* 62: Why, a drum is a place, a saloon. **1903** A.H. Lewis *Boss* 32: But he said the Dead Rabbit was a drum for crooks! **1912** Runyon *Rhymes* 105: Down in a drum on Sidewise street, where the red lights burn with a wicked leer. **1927** in Hammett *Knockover* 278: Larrouy's—just one drum in a city that had a number—had been heavy with grifters who were threats against life and property. **1937** in D. Runyon *More Guys* 205: All you are liable to get around this drum is fleas.
3. *Pris.* a cell.
*1909 Ware *Passing Eng.* 118: *Drum*…A cell. **1924** Henderson *Keys to Crookdom* 403: *Drum.* A prison cell. **1936** Duncan *Over the Wall* 57: I was assigned to a drum which was also shared by an old fellow. **1976** Schroeder *Shaking It* 24: They call the man in Drum Number Eleven Coyote; my cell mate tells me he's an habitch. **1977** Caron *Go-Boy* 109: By 4 p.m. we would again be in our drums with our supper tray—deadlocked until morning.
4. *Und.* a safe or vault.
1912 (quot. at DRUM SNUFFER). **1927** *DN* V 445: *Drum*, n. A safe. **1931–34** in Clemmer *Pris. Community* 331: *Drum*…An old fashioned vault with the safe (keyster) within.

drum *v.* to sell (goods) as a traveling sales representative.

1949 A. Miller *Death of Salesman* 81: A salesman eighty-four years old, and he'd drummed merchandise in thirty-one states.

drummer *n.* a traveling sales representative; *(broadly)* anyone who publicizes a product or event.

1839 Briggs *H. Franco* I 77: Mr. Lummocks…was a drummer…sent out to drum up customers for his employers. **1848** Judson *Myst. of N.Y.* 57: Our readers may have noticed the almost professional look…of some of our city merchant "drummers." **1859** in Hafen & Hafen *Reports from Colo.* 178: Sent out "drummers" all over the town to remind…people…to [vote]. **1876** J.M. Reid *Old Settlers* 157: The Two Fancy New York Drummers. **1882** Peck *Peck's Sunshine* 103: The drummer…put his satchel on the counter. **1906** *Nat. Police Gaz.* (Apr. 21) 3: A drummer's existence is a cinch, especially if he has samples that he can afford to get away. **1943** G. Fowler *Sweet Prince* 66: A corps of salesmen known as "drummers." **1950** *Sat. Eve. Post* (Apr.) 17: "You wouldn't believe it, Ned," one storekeeper lamented to a drummer…last November. **1952** Steinbeck *E. of Eden* 452: Six or eight drummers…fell into the police net. **1957** Rowan *Go South* 69: He was a drummer from a wholesale house in Jackson. **1984** T. Kay *Dark Thirty* 35: Maybe there's some candles somewhere. Don't ever know what some drummer's pushing off on me.

drummer-boy *n.* a traveling salesman. *Joc.*

1887 in *DAE*.

drum snuffer *n. Und.* a safecracker.

1912 Stringer *Shadow* 91: The drum snuffer…would be amenable to persuasion.

drumstick *n.* a person's leg, esp. the leg of an attractive young woman. *Joc.*

*1770 in *F & H* III 333: What, d'ye think I would change with Bill Spindle for one of his drumsticks? **1873* Hotten *Slang Dict.* 151: *Drumsticks*, legs. **1889** Barrère & Leland *Dict. Slang* I 332: *Drumstick* (popular), the leg. **1942** *ATS* 149. **1986** L. Johnson *Waves* 87: Look at those delectable drumsticks. **1986** G. Brach *Pirates* (film): I've lost a drumstick, 'tis true.

drunk *n.* **1.** a drunken spree. Now *S.E.*

1839 Briggs *Franco* II 79: I have kept money enough to have a good drunk. **1847** in Peskin *Vols.* 130: Many put on, what is called here, the "big drunk." **1855** G. Thompson *Locket* 59: Iago…had not yet recovered from the memorable "drunk." **1865** Sala *Diary* II 374: The "bhoy" who has been having a "big drunk" on the previous night. *a1867* in G.W. Harris *Lovingood* 39: He…was just getting on his legs again, from a "big drunk." **1869** Peyton *Over Alleghanies* 299: Prairie-farmers, pig-drivers, huntsmen [etc.]…were assembled…to indulge in a preliminary glass previous to the "big drunk," as the Indians call it, with which so large a population out West close the…Presidential election. **1871** Schele de Vere *Americanisms* 600: *Drunk*, used as a noun, takes in the West frequently the place of *spree* or *debauch*. **1878** [P.S. Warne] *Hard Crowd* 10: Like a whirlwind on a big drunk. **1894** DeBarthe *Grouard* 20: It was a sure thing to have a big spree or drunk whenever the wagons got stuck in the mud. **1902** "J. Flynt" *Little Bro.* 87: They…kept mighty quiet after a big drunk they hed up in Haines Woods. **1918** in Truman *Lttrs. Home* 50: I look like Siam's King on a drunk. **1936** in R.E. Howard *Iron Man* 160: You look like a mildly insane college professor on a drunk. **1942–43** C. Jackson *Lost Weekend* 41: Before he had recovered from the previous drunk. **1963** Horwitz *Candlelight* 6: He loved…the booze, the drunks that sprawled him out on his cot. **1976** Whelton *CB Baby* 50: It must have been high-school kids on a drunk.

2. *Police.* a charge of being drunk and disorderly; public drunkenness.

[**1883* in *F & H* II 333: Of the twenty-nine night charges, by far the greater number were of drunks.] **1925–26** Black *You Can't Win* 156 [ref. to 1890's]: We'll vag the chronics and charge the new ones with drunk. **1975** Wambaugh *Choirboys* 153: You shouldn't be put away for ninety days for drunk…because you're a dingaling.

¶ In phrase:

¶ **have (one's) drunk out** to get drunk.

1879 Shippen *30 Yrs.* 27: He would…then go on shore again, for the rest of his forty-eight hours' liberty, and "have his drunk out."

drunk *adj. Baseball.* (of bases) loaded. *Joc.*

1959 Brosnan *Long Season* 222: Your roomie just hit one with the bases drunk, Willard. **1969** Bouton *Ball Four* 272: When the bases are loaded they're *drunk*.

drunked up *adj.* drunk. Also **drunked out.**

1945 in Litoff et al. *Miss You* 265: Nor do I go to the town bars and get

myself all drunked up. **1964–70** in *Qly. Jour. Stud. Alcohol* XXXII (1971) 731: *Drunked up*. Intoxicated. **1970–71** Rubinstein *City Police* 318: There's some shad all drunked up. **1982** C.R. Anderson *Other War* 16: They got…drunked-up one night. **1984** Ark. man, age *ca*35: I've heard "drunked up" *and* "drunked out." Which are pretty stupid. **1988** *Crossfire* (CNN-TV) (May 21): The guy gets drunked up on Saturday night and goes on a rampage.

drunkery *n.* DRINKERY. [1975 quot. is Canadian.]

1827, 1837 in *DAE*. **1889** Barrère & Leland *Dict. Slang* 317: A "dive," a "gin-mill,"…a "drunkery." **1975** (in Partridge *DSUE* (ed. 8)).

drunkie *n.* a drunkard.

*1861 in W.H. Russell *Russell's Civil War* 166: Drunkies…predominated. **1957** H. Ellison *Deadly Streets* 148: The bartender had tossed her out, yelling *drunkie* after her.

drunk-on *n.* a spell of drunkenness.

1841 in Angle *Prairie State* 199: The married man will give them money enough to have a *drunk* on. **1923** McAlmon *Village* 124: Ike…wasn't good enough a customer with his periodic drunk-ons. *Ibid.* 233: We'll have to stage some intimate drunk-on parties. **1925** McAlmon *Silk Stockings* 113: In all their various types of drunk-ons.

Drut *n. USMC Av.* the Douglas F3D-2 (later EF-10B) Sky-knight jet fighter.

1990 G.R. Clark *Words of Vietnam War* 168: The Marines nicknamed the EF-10 the "DRUT," which is "turd" backwards. **1991** Linnekin *80 Knots* 230: Beast, Hog….Drut (that's *turd* spelled backwards).

druthers *n.pl.* [contr. and alter. of *(I, you, etc.) would rather*] ¶ In phrase: **have (one's) druthers** [or **drathers**] to have (one's) preference.

1870 *Overland Mo.* (Jan.) 84: A man can't always have his 'drathers. **1936** in Botkin *Treas. Amer. Folklore* 217: Now, Paul knows wildcats, and he's never heard of one that'll come within a hundred yards of a logger if it has its 'druthers. **1956** Algren *Wild Side* 114 [ref. to *ca*1930]: You mean if I had my druthers? Why, if I had my druthers, I'd druther eat speckledly gravy. **1968** J.P. Miller *Race for Home* 284 [ref. to *ca*1930]: Well, boy, this ain't yo' party, so you don't git yo' druthers here. **1968** WINS Radio editorial: If we had our druthers, we'd druther see the Mets win the pennant. **1975** Julien *Cogburn* 40: But if I had my 'druthers, I would…jaw with you all night. **1979** *N.Y. Post* (Dec. 13) 28: Given my druthers, I'd have preferred some alternative activity. **1982** Heat Moon *Blue Hwys.* 8: If I'da got my rightful druthers, I'da took oil.

dry *n. Pol.* a supporter of alcohol prohibition. Now *S.E.*

1889 *Century Dict.*: *Dry*…a member of the Prohibition party. **1910** *N.Y. Eve. Jour.* (Feb. 5) 3: Chicago "Drys" March to File Grant Petition. **1920** in *Dict. Canad.* 225: The drys cannot pretend much longer that Alberta is "prohibition." **1948** in *DA*. **1977** P. Wood *Salt Bk.* 161: You'd get calls from people that were on the side of the dries.

¶ In phrase:

¶ **have a dry on** to be thirsty.

1864 Armstrong *Generals* 268: He'll seem as far off as the first old Father Abraham did to that rich old Cockey that had big dry on in a hot place.

dry *adj.* **1.** *Pol.* opposed to or free from the sale of alcoholic beverages. Now *S.E.*

1853 W.W. Brown *Clotel* 196: I suppose you have told 'em we are a dry set up here? **1870** in *DA*. **1887** in *OEDS*: Athens…is a dry town. **1888** in Farmer *Amer.*: If a county has voted…and gone dry. **1910** W. Archer *Afro-Amer.* 147: Between "wet" counties and "dry." **1948** *Time* (Apr. 26) 14: The natives voted…to keep the town dry. **1984** Cunningham & Ethell *Fox Two* 48: Navy ships are dry, so we tipped our soda pops and commenced celebrating. **1987** *Time* (July 13) 33: Kansas [was] the first state to go dry (in 1881).

2. *Und.* being without money; *(also)* empty-handed.

1942 *ATS* 354: "Broke."…*busted…dry*. **1942–49** Goldin et al. *DAUL* 63: *Dry*,…Without money. **1950** in Maurer *Lang. Und.* 185: *Dry*: Broke. **1962–68** B. Jackson *In the Life* 88: Wait till he comes back with the dope. Let's don't leave dry, man, 'cause we've got this habit. **1968** F. Wallace *Poker* 214: *Dry*…Broke.

dry *v.* ¶ In phrase: **hang** [or **leave**] **out to dry** to abandon to danger; leave in the lurch.

1971 Turque *Viet Vet* (WNBC-TV): The South Vietnamese fell back and just left us…out to dry, as they say. **1985** O'Neil *Lady Blue* (film): If I think they're going to hang you out to dry, I'll make my move.

dryball *n.* (see quot.).

1927 *AS* II (Mar.) 276: *Dryball*. A student devoting all his time to study.

dryballs *n.* an impotent man.—usu. considered vulgar. Also **dry-nuts.**

    1936 Le Clercq *Rabelais* 115: By the body of God, that dryballs prefers a yoke of oxen. **1938** "Justinian" *Amer. Sexualis* 21: Dry-Nuts. n. An impotent male…U.S., low coll., C. 20. **1942** Algren *Morning* 125: Run along, Dryballs.

dry beef *n. Pris.* a false or unsupported charge.

    1967 Colebrook *Lassitude* 175: You mean that time the Feds booked her on that dry beef?

dry-bob *v.* DRY-FUCK. Also as *n.*

    *1680 in J. Thorpe *Rochester's Poems* 37: Yet these Two partial *Dames*, a dry Bob, cry. ***ca1685** in Barrère & Leland *Dict. Slang* I 151: The cheating jilt, at the twelfth, a *dry bob* cries. ***a1720** in D'Urfey *Pills* II 27: And some dry Bobs. ***1785** Grose *Vulgar Tongue: Dry Bob*….copulation without emission. ***1889** Barrère & Leland *Dict. Slang* I 151: "Dry bob"…refers to fruitless coition. **1918** in Carey *Mlle. From Armentières* II (unp.): One of the boys on the "narrow gauge"/Dry-bobbed a girl with a basket of eggs.

dry fuck *n.* **1.** a simulated act of copulation, usu. while fully clothed.—usu. considered vulgar.

    1938 H. Miller *Trop. Capricorn* 104: Maybe you'll…get a dry fuck. **1965** Trimble *Sex Words* 68: Dry Fuck…The act of two lovers rubbing up against each other while clothed and in public, as while dancing, etc., which results in great excitation and, in some cases, orgasm. **1970** Landy *Underground Dict.* 71: Dry Fuck…n. The simulated act of sexual intercourse with clothes on. **1971** B.B. Johnson *Blues for Sister* 101: A professional virgin…The kind that always denied you penetration. A dry fuck.

    2. something that is exceedingly tedious or disappointing.—usu. considered vulgar.

    1945 in T. Williams *Letters* 177: If only Margo could get something of this quality into "The Project."…It is a dry fuck, really!

dry-fuck *v.* [cf. earlier syn. DRY-BOB] to simulate sexual intercourse without penetration; (*trans.*) to engage in a dry fuck with.—usu. considered vulgar.

    [**1935** in J. O'Hara *Sel. Letters* 106: Write something…that will help you get rid of the bitterness you must have stored up against all those patronizing cheap bastards in that dry-fucked excrescence on Sharp Mountain.] **ca1937** in Atkinson *Dirty Comics* 106: Try to dry-fuck the hostess who is the big shot's sweetie. **1938** "Justinian" *Amer. Sexualis* 20: Dry-Fuck. v. To rub stomach, thighs, and genitals together in an erotic manner while dancing. Popular in collegiate circles…U.S., 1925—. **1954** Himes *Third Generation* 243: Now seeing him in the arms of a sweet young girl she was scalded with jealousy. "What kind of dryfucking shit is this?" she screamed. **1958–59** Lipton *Barbarians* 156: As long ago as the twenties dancing was considered "dry fucking" by the *cognoscenti* who regarded it as something for sub-teenagers only. **1965** Ward & Kassebaum *Women's Pris.* 99: That's more or less a *bull-dagger's*…kick, this dry fucking. **1969** Briley *Traitors* 133: They had had a spell of intense sessions holding hands in the library and dry-fucking against the back wall of her sorority. **1970** Landy *Underground Dict.* 71: Dry fuck…Go through the motions of sexual intercourse without entering the vagina, usually with clothes on. **1983** E. Dodge *Dau* 110: They dry-fucked in the pre-dawn darkness.

dry goods *n.pl.* **1.** clothing.

    1851 in *DAE:* A ride over a dusty road is apt to soil a gentleman's dry goods. **1887** G. Davis *Sea-Wanderer* 177. **1920** *Red Guidon* 55: It was awful how the fellows' dry goods looked. **1946** Boulware *Jive & Slang* 4: Fine Drygoods…Good clothes. **1962** Crump *Killer* 324: Hey, what gives? Release the dry goods.

    2. a woman.—also constr. with *piece of.*

    1869 in *DA:* [The nurse is] the trimmest piece of dry-goods I have seen in many a day. **1875** in Blockson *Underground Railroad* 37 [ref. to *a*1860]: Whenever a slave succeeded in making his or her escape I was to send…the information…to be on the lookout for "packages of hardware" (men) or "dry-goods" (females). **1900** *DN* II 33: Dry goods, n. A woman. **1901** in "O. Henry" *Cabbages & Kings* 15: The main guy and the dry goods are headed for the briny.

¶ In phrase:

¶ **hold on to (one's) dry goods** to be patient.

    1861 Guerin *Mountain Charley* 26: Boys just hold on to your Dry Goods a half a second and I'll be with you.

dry-gulch *v.* **1.** *West.* to attack or kill from ambush in a deserted spot, orig. a dry gulch. Hence **drygulcher.**

    1930 in *DA.* **1933** W.C. MacDonald *Law of .45's* 11: I hate to see Hayden dry-gulched. **1934** Cunningham *Triggernometry* 23: For Longley "dry gulched him." **1938** Burt *Powder River* 353: Plenty of cowboys were "dry-gulched." **1947** Overholser *Buckaroo's Code* 31: I wonder who it was that cut loose at the damned drygulcher. **1969** L'Amour *Conagher* 84: The outfit you tied up with are a bunch of dry-gulchin' thieves. **1971** "L. Short" *Man from Desert* 95: You was trying to make sure he wouldn't do it when you drygulched him, wasn't you? **1978** Groom *Better Times* 202: The secret was not to get dry-gulched in the process.

    2. to betray in a calculated manner.

    1979 in Terkel *Amer. Dreams* 336: When he ran for the Senate, he was dry-gulched by the right-wing Republicans.

dry haul *n.* a fruitless attempt.

    1879 Shippen *30 Yrs.* 35: Shouts of laughter greet him if it is found that he has "made a dry haul."

dry house *n. Pris.* (see quot.).

    1848 *Ladies' Repository* VIII (Oct.) 315: Dry House, A dungeon.

dry-hump *v.* DRY-FUCK.—usu. considered vulgar. Also as *n.*

    1964 Pearl *Stockade* 40: Think of all…the horny bastards who have dry-humped [the mattress]. **1970** Wakefield *All the Way* 143: It rated right along with dry-humping. **1972** A.K. Shulman *Ex-Prom Queen* 86: I would neither submit to being dry-humped nor pretend to virginity. **1972** *Nat. Lampoon* (Apr.) 33: Oh, I figure to get dry humps about half the time. You gotta have space, though, like a sofa or on the beach. You can't dry hump good in the car. ***1975** (cited in Partridge *DSUE* (ed. 8)). **1976** *Nat. Lampoon* (June) 27: Very few of our jokes…are founded on the dryhump. **1977** L. Jordan *Hype* 47: Against the refrigerator a black man was dry-humping a blonde. **1980** in *Penthouse* (Jan. 1981) 174: He feverishly pawed and dry-humped them. **1983** Ehrhart *VN-Perkasie* 127: [She] dry humps the hell out of me. **1985** *Nat. Lampoon* (Sept.) 20: Close dancing where you dry-humped your partner. **1992** *Donahue* (NBC-TV): They were doing everything from dry-humping to oral sex!

dry jag *n.* a temporary sense of excitement or exhilaration not induced by alcohol.

    1900 Flandrau *Freshman* 250: Bertie gabbled…[all] afternoon. He had what he calls a "dry jag," and hardly ever stopped talking.

dry Mike *n.* (see quot.).

    1869 *Overland Mo.* (Aug.) 129 [ref. to Civil War]: Many a Rebel cavalryman has told me that…when he munched a piece of crust, or any unmoistened provisions, as he sat in his saddle, he was eating his "dry Mike."

dry murder *n.* a dry martini. *Joc.*

    1958 Heinz *Professional* 258: He makes a good dry murder.

dry out *v.* to recover or cause to recover from a drinking spree; become or make sober after extended indulgence in alcohol or drugs. Now *S.E.*

    1908 Whittles *Lumberjack* 154: The jacks work until their hides begin to crack, then follow their tongues to the nearest irrigation plant, tank up…then mosey to a camp to dry out again. **a1967** Bombeck *Wit's End* 149: And there's a strong possibility Santa Claus may not "dry out" in time to make the scene for the kiddies. **1971** J. Brown & A. Groff *Monkey* 32: I would get on a kick with drugs and spend days or weeks…"drying out." **1981** Ehrlichman *Witness* 57: But Martha Mitchell was in a sanitorium, drying out. **1986** G. Trudeau, in *Daily Beacon* (Univ. Tenn.) (Apr. 23) 4: You've been under the influence of a zombie compound. We're going to dry you out. **1988** *Newsweek* (Apr. 25) 67: Hey, Bill, you really want to dry out? I can call a place that may take you right away.

dry polish *n. West.* (see quot.).

    1873 *Custer's Yellowstone Exped.* 27: Washing is no defense [against alkali dust]. There is no recourse but a "dry polish," an army phrase for a constrained toilet made in the absence of water.

dry ride *n. Army.* a form of punishment in which an offender is made to straddle a wooden beam for a long period.

    1868 *Galaxy* (Dec.) 795 [ref. to Civil War]: There were one or two men on the horse above me, indulging in a "dry-ride," one ridden into penitence, the other still holding out in his obduracy.

dry rub *n. Homosex.* (see quots.).

    1942–49 Goldin et al. *DAUL* 63: Dry rub…Body contact, in wrestling or "horseplay," patently homosexual. **a1972** B. Rodgers *Queens' Vernacular* 69: Dry rub wrestling with strong erotic undercurrents.

dry-screw *n. & v.* DRY-FUCK.—usu. considered vulgar.

    1923 McAlmon *Comp. Vol.* 236: The girl who'll give a guy a dry screw but won't take the pin. *Ibid.* 237: This type of woman...finds...dry screwing safer, and fairly satisfactory.

dry stick *n.* an unpleasant, tedious, unsociable person.

    1905 W.S. Kelly *Lariats* 261: You'll soon get tired of dat dry stick; she ain't no company fer nobody.

dry up *v.* **1.** to stop talking; shut up; *(trans.)* to cause to stop talking.

    1853 F.A. Buck *Yankee Trader in Gold Rush* 118, in *AS* XLIII 94: I think if I were talking to you you would say "dry up." **1855** Derby *Phoenixiana* 203: Mac...requested me to "dry up," when I questioned him on the subject. **1857** Rivors *Murders* 63: G-d d-n it, dry up! What's the use talking to them? **1857** in "M. Twain" *Selected Shorter Writings* 7: Oh, *dern* yer everlastin yaller skin, won't you never dry up? **1860** in *DAE*: Mr. Bell...advised those fathers of the democracy who felt grieved about the country...to "dry up their tears." This is supposed to have been the origin of the familiar term used among the New York b'hoys, "Dry up!" **1861** in W.H. Russell *My Diary* 133: And so "the Britisher was dried up." **1862** in Bear *Letters* 19: They will buck and gag him pretty soon if he don't dry up...The Lieut. had dried Reason up just now. **1863** C.H. Smith *Bill Arp* 48: Look here, John, you've said enough about potash, just dry that up! **1864** Armstrong *Generals* 248: "Dry up on that, Captain," interrupted a brother officer. **1865** *Rogues & Rogueries of N.Y.* 56: To this officious personage my friend replied, "that if he did not want a stye raised" over his eye, he had better dry up. **1865** Blake *Army of the Potomac* 110: Dry up, you old fool. **1868** "W.J. Hamilton" *Maid of Mtn.* 19: Dry up...or I'll break your head. **1871** Banka *Prison Life* 99: Dry up, yer d—d son of a b—h! **1875** Sheppard *Love Afloat* 144: "Dry, up, Porp!" shouted Munson. **1883** Peck *Bad Boy* 128: For Heaven's sake dry up that whistling. **1914** Tarkington *Penrod* 252: Penrod, quite beside himself, danced eccentrically. "Dry up!" he howled. "Dry up, dry up, dry up, dry *up*!" **1927** Rollins *Jinglebob* 147: It near busted me buyin' liquor to dry 'em up. **1958** Frankel *Band of Bros.* 52: Aw, dry up. I had more by accident than you ever got on purpose.

    2. *Theat.* (of an actor) to forget lines during a performance; *(trans.)* to cause (an actor) to forget lines during a performance.

    *1889 Barrère & Leland *Dict. Slang* I 333: To *dry up*, to stick, *i.e.*, to forget the words of a part and break down. **1923** *N.Y. Times* (Sept. 9) VIII 2: *Dry a man up*: To give the wrong cue, or to say something aside to disconcert a fellow-actor, and so cause him to dry up. **1933** in *OEDS*: When an actor fails to remember his lines...he "dries up." **1934** Rose *Thes. Slang* 83: What's the idea of trying to dry me up in the last number?

DT *n.* **1.** a detective.

    1928 Dahlberg *Bottom Dogs* 73: Two days later a d.t. brought back Mush Tate. **1982** *N.Y. Times Mag.* (Jan. 31) 74: Then some days, kids recognize you..."Here come the D.T.'s"—that's what they call us. **1988** "Slick Rick" in B. Adler *Rap!* 39: Tried to rob a man who was a DT undercover.

    2. a person suffering from delirium tremens.

    1966 R.E. Alter *Carny Kill* 104: Like snakes in the bottom of a DT's empty glass.

DT *v. Med.* to experience delirium tremens.

    1985 Frede *Nurses* 7: And last night she starts actively DTing. *Ibid.* 8: Mr. Shaughnessy has somehow learned that his wife is DTing.

D.T.'s *n.pl.* delirium tremens. Now *colloq.*

    1857 Borthwick *3 Yrs. in Calif.* 69: D.t.s is a very common disease in California. **1935** Algren *Boots* 237: Fin's old man started throwing D.T.s. **1967–68** von Hoffman *Parents Warned Us* 73: Can you get the DTs from acid?

dub[1] *n.* [fr. earlier E cant *dup*, *dub* 'to open'] *Und.* a key, esp. as employed by a burglar. [1791 quot. is prob. a poor definition rather than a different sense.]

    *1698–99 "B.E." *Dict. Cant. Crew: Dub...A Pick-lock key. *1785 Grose *Vulgar Tongue: Dub. A picklock or master-key. *1789 in *F & H* II 335: A bunch of young *dubs* by her side, which are a bunch of small keys. **1791** [W. Smith] *Confess. T. Mount* 19: *A dub*, opening a door with a false key. **1807** Tufts *Autobiog.* 292 [ref. to 1794]: *Dub*...a false key. *1812 in Vaux *Memoirs* 238: *Dub*: a key. *Ibid.* 527: "*Dub.*" A pick-lock or master-key. To go "on the dub," is to go on a thieving expedition. **1848** [G. Thompson] *House Breaker* 8: False and skeleton keys, (in flash called *dubs*).

dub[2] *n.* [orig. unkn.] **1.** a foolish, oafish, incompetent, or unskillful person.

    1887 in *DAE*: Dem dubs is goin' to git it in de neck in a minit. **1896** Ade *Artie* 4: What kills me off is how all these dubs make their star winnin's. **1899** Kountz *Baxter's Letters* 35: I hung around...like a big dub. **1899** Cullen *Tales* 45: There were two or three preliminary bouts between dubs. **1901** A.H. Lewis *Croker* 61: He's a pretty decent kind of a dub. **1904** in Opper *Happy Hooligan* 45: There's many a slip twixt the dub and the ship. **1907** in "O. Henry" *Works* 1386: "I'm a double-dyed dub," mused John Perkins. **1912** Ade *Babel* 134: "My name's not Bubley, but Dubley." A voice: "With the accent on the 'Dub.'" **1915** Braley *Workaday World* 61: An' when you get through—gee!/The mate says, "You dub!" **1922** Rice *Adding Machine* 125: Back to earth, you dub. Where do you think? **1929** Burnett *Iron Man* 18: You're all wrong if you think that Jeff Davis is any dub. He fought ten rounds with Mike Shay before he was champion. **1930** in R.E. Howard *Iron Man* 10: Mulcahy, though strong and tough, was a mere dub, yet he clearly outboxed Brennon for nearly two rounds. **1949** Cummings *Dict. Sports* 120: *Dub*...An inept performer. Most commonly used in racket games. **1968** Baker et al. *CUSS* 110: *Dub*. A person who always fools around.

    2. *Golf.* (see quot.).

    1970 Scharff *Encyc. of Golf* 417: *Dub*. A poorly executed shot; a missed shot. Same as a *foozle*.

    ¶ In phrase:

    ¶ **flub the dub** see s.v. FLUB, *v.*

dub along *v.* to move slowly; loaf.

    1920–21 Witwer *Leather Pushers* 290: He's just dubbin' along here and there.

dub around *v.* to fool around; waste time; loaf.

    1896 (quot. at CON). **1906** H. Green *Boarding House* 355: You go dubbing around doing common work. **1908** McGaffey *Show Girl* 105: Down at Manhattan Beach dubbing around in a bathing suit. **1915** Howard *God's Man* 212: She was dubbing around with wine-agents and young stock-brokers. **1942** in Stilwell *Papers* 78: Dubbed around all day playing rummy. **1968** Baker et al. *CUSS* 110: *Dub around.* Waste time, not study.

dubbies *n.pl.* [app. alter. BUBBIES] a woman's breasts.

    1966 Fariña *Down So Long* 80: Christ, the dubbies on Lumper. *1991 Spears *Slang & Euphem.* (ed. 2) 135: *Dubbies* the female breasts...British slang.

dubby *adj.* dull; worthless.

    1941 in Stilwell *Papers* 18: Dubby day—no scares.

dub off *v.* (see quot.).

    1916 Cary *Venery* I 75: *Dub Off*—To masturbate.

dubs *n.* DUB[2], 1.

    1902 "J. Flynt" *Little Bro.* 148: Tell him 't he's an old dubs.

dub up *v.* to pay up; hand over. *Obs.* in U.S.

    *1821 *Real Life in London* I 362: Dub up the possibles. *1823 "J. Bee" *Slang Dict.* 72: *Dub up*, to pay at once. *1839 in *OEDS*: "Come, dub up!" roars a third. **1843** *Spirit of Times* (Sept. 23) 356: All this he regularly "dubbed up." *1845, *1846, *1852, *1923, *1959 in *OEDS*.

ducat *n.* **1.** a dollar; *(pl.)* money. [In 1775 quot., simply 'a piece of money'.]

    [*1775 R.B. Sheridan, in *OED*: I shall be entitled to the girl's fortune, without settling a ducat on her.] **1866** Williams *Gay Life in N.Y.* 88: My money is good and I'll bet my "ducats" he can take any of the crowd agin him, if they don't double-team him. *1873 Hotten *Slang Dict.* 152: *Ducats*, money.—*Theatrical slang*. **1878** *Nat. Police Gaz.* (Apr. 24) 6: I fight you for fun or ducats. **1882** in Miller & Snell *Why West Was Wild* 214: It goes against the old timer's grain to part with his ducats even when gambling on chance. **1889** *United Service* (Aug.) 161: But after expending about five thousand ducats for preliminary tuition I began to perceive that the feat was possible. *1889 Barrère & Leland *Dict. Slang* I 334: *Ducats* (theatrical)...cash of any description. *ca*1900 *Buffalo Bill* 204: They say he's making ducats now from shows and not from "steers." **1906** London *Moon-Face* 47: Wire me and Ill send the ducats to come on at once. **1919** *Our Navy* (Dec.) 31: You need a suit to get a job in, but the sixty ducats just about buys a collar button these days. **1947** in Botkin *Sidewalks* 430: *Oodles of ducats*: money. **1976** Eble *Campus Slang* (Nov.) 2: *Ducats*—dollar bills; How about lending me a few ducats until tomorrow? **1984** Algeo *Stud Buds & Dorks*: To be low in funds...no dinero, no duckets, [etc.]. **1987** *21 Jump Street* (Fox-TV): You got the ducats? **1993** *N.Y. Times* (Dec. 6) B 8: When you gonna come back and get some duckets?

2. a ticket, esp. for transportation or admission.

1871 Banka *Prison Life* 493: Railroad Ticket…*Ducket*. ***1873** Hotten *Slang Dict.*: *Ducket*, a ticket of any kind. Usually applied to pawnbroker's duplicates and raffle-cards. ***1879** *Macmillan's Mag.* (Oct.) 501: I took a ducat…for Sutton in Surrey. **1910** *N.Y. Eve. Jour.* (May 28) 11: I've got two ducats for th' fight. **1910** *Variety* (June 25) 13: Cutting Out "Ducats"…the elimination of gift tickets to the local councilmen. ***1911** O'Brien & Stephens *Australian Sl.* 58: *Dukets*: Aust. thieves—tickets. **1919** Darling *Jargon Book* 11: *Ducket*—Railroad ticket. **1922** J. Conway, in *Variety* (Jan. 6) 7: I rushed him a ducket to this burg. **1928** Hammett *Harvest* 50: I didn't think there was anything in it except maybe a ducat back to Philly. **1929** Barr *Let Tomorrow Come* 266: *Ducket*—A ticket. **1931** D. Runyon, in *Collier's* (Nov. 14) 7: Several duckets to the large football game. **1941** Schulberg *Sammy* 11: Now that we've got that settled, do you still want the ducats? Take 'em home and surprise your mother. **1952** Bellow *Augie March* 132: Augie and I have a pair of duckets it would be a shame to waste altogether. **1974** A. Bergman *Big Kiss-Off* 30: The ducats were row C, center. **1988** *N.Y. Daily News* (June 8) 11: For us ordinary folk, there's a nine-month wait for ducats.

3.a. (among beggars) a card, placard, letter, or certificate used in begging; (*also*) a union card.

1925–26 Black *You Can't Win* 69 [ref. to 1890's]:You slip her your ducat and she reads: "I am deaf and dumb." **1927** *AS* (June) 391: [A beggar] who uses a begging-letter *begs on a ducket*…A union card is also called a ducket. **1928** Callahan *Man's Grim Justice* 38: I slipped him a ducat (card) with the the 'phone number on it. **1930** "D. Stiff" *Milk & Honey* 204: *Ducket*—A ticket, or a card good for a feed or a flop. **1933** Ersine *Prison Slang* 34: *Ducat*, n. 1. A doctor's certificate which states that the bearer is deaf, dumb, or blind, or that he is physically unable to work. It is often used by professional beggars.

b. *Pris.* a pass or other official document relating to a convict.

1926 *Writer's Mo.* (Dec.) 541: *Ducket*—Letter from the prison board advising term of parole. **1942** *ATS* 444: *Ducat*…a warrant for arrest. **1966** Braly *On Yard* 200: He was sitting sideways at his desk typing ducats. **1971** J. Brown & A. Groff *Monkey* 51: This ducat directs me to report to the barber shop for work. **1972** Carr *Bad* 152: I got a ducat to report to Dr. Schultz's office. **1976** Braly *False Starts* 229: Sometimes he would cause a ducat to be sent me and I would pass through to the hospital to visit him in his office.

ducat *v.* to ticket.

1976 Braly *False Starts* 231: I was ducated to Identification to have a new mug taken.

ducat-snatcher *n. Circus.* a ticket-taker.

1926 Finerty *Criminalese* 17: *Ducat snatcher*—Ticket taker. **1937** *Lit. Digest* (Apr. 3) 22: *Ducat snatcher*—the ticket taker.

duck[1] *n.* **1.** a lovely or fine example.—constr. with *of a. Obs.* in U.S.

*1819 in *OEDS*: I shall presently throw my letter into *the long drawer* at the top of my *duck of a* secretaire. ***1841** in *F & H* II 336: Oh, isn't he a duck of a fellow? **1863** Norton *Army Letters* 138: A little ducksie with a duck of a bonnet. **1880** Pinkerton *Prof. Thieves & Detective* 473: The ducks which Root had shot furnished an excellent breakfast…some one cruelly remarked that Root was "a duck of a fellow." ***1890–91** *F & H* II 336: A duck of a bonnet.

2.a. a foolish, odd, or eccentric person; (*broadly*) a person.—now usu. constr. with a prec. adj.

1848 *Ladies' Repository* VIII (Oct.) 315: Duck, A simple man who is easily imposed on. **1850** "N. Buntline" *G'hals of N.Y.* 18: I aint one o' them 'ere ducks. **1855** G.G. Foster *N.Y. Naked* 64: The hope and heir of the house is a…"duck." He is a…cadaverous-looking young man, whom incessant attempts to smoke segars…and gulp down whiskey-skins…have bleached to the faintest…shadow of fresh and vigorous youth. **1871** "M. Twain" *Roughing It* 246: We'll have to barricade our doors tonight, or some of these ducks will be trying to sleep with us. **1876** Cody & Arlington *Life on Border* 51: Now, you're a nice duck, ain't you? **1878** Hart *Sazerac* 152: I aint one of them ducks what wants editors to puff their mines for *nothin'*. **1885** in S. Crane *Complete Stories* 50: The gentlemen nearly swallowed their tobacco in their amazement at the white-haired old "duck." **1893** F.P. Dunne, in Schaaf *Dooley* 55: "An' who's th' duck next to him?"…"That…is Charles Dudley Warner, th' famous novelist." **1899** Norris *McTeague* 10: I promised a duck up here on the avenue I'd call for his dog at four this afternoon. **1899** Cullen *Tales* 22: I had to wait for the auctioneer duck to come to my ring and pin. **1902** Townsend *Fadden & Mr. Paul* 160: I've piped

whole bunches of mugs in me time; wise guys and gillies; fly ducks and gazeaboos. **1904** Dunbar *Happy Hollow* 27: Bingo…laughed. "I'm a slick duck," he said. **1904** Ade *True Bills* 110: You Society Ducks don't care who you invite. **1913** in Truman *Dear Bess* 144: Some duck who thought he had a voice got her to play "The Rosary." **1914** Ellis *Billy Sunday* 141: He's a queer old duck. **1924** Marks *Plastic Age* 158: You've been reading Havelock Ellis and a lot of ducks like that. **1950** P. Green *Peer Gynt* 132: He's a funny old duck. **1965** Cleaver *Soul* 55: I have no respect for a duck who runs up to me on the yard all buddy-buddy, and then feels obliged not to sit down with me. **1973** O'Neill & O'Neill *Shifting Gears* 230: We think the guy who goes to the beach alone…is a queer duck. **1973** Haney *Jock* 58: Any female jockey worth her stirrups is an odd duck. **1978** Pici *Tennis Hustler* 74: There's more than one way to hustle a duck, kid. **1982** "J. Cain" *Commandos* 370: I never seen that duck before in my life, sir. **1984** L.I. woman, age *ca*31: You lucky duck! **1992** *Mystery Sci. Theater* (Comedy Central TV): He's a queer duck.

b. a sweetheart. Also **ducky.**

1851 [G. Thompson] *Jack Harold* 96: A present to your own *duckey*. **1855** in Meserve & Reardon *Satiric Comedies* 137: "You walk just like a duck…" "Being a *duck*, I can't help that!" **1858** in *Ind. Mag. of Hist.* XLVII (1951) 278: Spent an hour very pleasantly with my "duck." **1864** in H. Johnson *Talking Wire* 131: Al showed me his duck's *ghost* [photograph]. **1864** in *Ala. Review* X (1957) 230: I wish my "duck" could see me. **1864** in Stanard *Letters* 47: The Capt's. *duck* was there.

c. an effeminate, weak, or contemptible fellow. Also attrib.

1961 Braly *Felony Tank* 180: How much of a duck do you think I am? **1971** Torres *Sting Like a Bee* 118: "I'm embarrassed to get in the ring with this unrated duck," Clay said in a Louisville television program. *a*1972 B. Rodgers *Queens' Vernacular* 73: Effeminate homosexual…*duck* [known in Las Vegas] teen sl[ang], mid '60s: taken fr[om] limp-wristed afternoon TV cartoon character. **1983** Sturz *Wid. Circles* 38: "You called me a duck!" he yelled. "You called me a fuckin' duck!" (A duck is a wimp or an inferior or an incompetent person. The term has sexual overtones.) *Ibid.* 38: What I said was, there's some duck dudes round here. **1985** *All-Star Blitz* (ABC-TV): In the language of today's teenager…a *duck* is a *loser*. **1990** P. Munro *Slang U.* 74: *Duck* unappealing person, misfit, nerd, geek. Randy is…such a duck. **1990** "Urban Dance Squad" *Living in the Fast Lane* (rap song): Ducks stay lame while you're livin'.

3. *Sports.* a zero; DUCK EGG. *Obs.* in U.S.

*1868 in *F & H* II 337: His fear of a *duck*—as, by a pardonable contraction from "duck's-egg,"—a nought is called in cricket play. ***1883** in *F & H*: He took six wickets, and all of them for *ducks*. ***a1889** in Barrère & Leland *Dict. Slang* I 334: He won the match, for the remaining man was good for nothing else but a *duck*. **1900** *DN* II 33: *Duck*, n…Cipher in a game.

4.a. a pail used for beer; GROWLER.—often in phr. of the sort **chase the duck** to fetch beer in a pail.

1901 Ade *Modern Fables* 141: After Mr. Monnyhan and his Neighbors had Rolled the Rock and Chased the Duck and Hurried the Can for several Pints of the White Suds they would feel almost as well off as the Rich. **1904** *Life in Sing Sing* 247: *Duck*. A tin pail in which beer is carried. **1905** in "O. Henry" *Stories* 1319: How happy them folks was who could chase the duck and smoke their pipes at their windows. **1906** H. Green *Boarding House* 2: I told yuh boys onct [*sic*] yuh couldn't rush no duck in this house! *a*1909 Tillotson *Detective* 91: *Duck*—A can of beer. **1917–20** Dreiser *Newspaper Days* 232 [ref. to 1893]: The "growler" or "duck"—a tin bucket of good size—was "rushed" for beer and cheese and crackers.

b. *Hosp.* a bedpan or portable urinal; (*also*) a urine bottle.

1918 in *AS* (Oct. 1933) 26 [Ft. Leavenworth]: *Duck*. n. In the hospital, bed-urinal. **1925** *AS* VII (Oct.) 22: *Duck*—slop jar…*shooting ducks*—emptying slop jars. **1928** *Papers of Mich. Acad.* 291 [ref. to WWI]: *Ducks*, urinals; "submarines." **1963** Williamson *Hustler!* 56: He brought one of those little old piss ducks. **1966** Kenney *Caste* 124: Urine…dripped from his catheter into the "duck" strapped to his left leg. **1973–77** J. Jones *Whistle* 240: They did not even let him get out of bed, but passed him a glass duck to use. **1980** *AS* (Spring) 48. **1981** C. Nelson *Picked Bullets Up* 87: *Ducks* (portable metal urinals). **1983** Eilert *Self & Country* 69: I'll get you a duck.

5. the end of a smoked cigarette.

1908 *DN* III 308: *Duck*…A cigarette stub. **1919** Johnson *321st Inf.* 5: We were naturally very slow in understanding what digging stumps and "policing up" cigarette "ducks" and match sticks had to do with winning the war. **1938** in *AS* (Apr. 1939) 90: *Ducks*. A lighted cigarette stub. "Give me your ducks." **1939** in *AS* XIV (Feb.) 26: *Duck*, n. Par tially consumed cigarette. **1947** Willingham *End As a Man* 115: As he smoked he took out the five or six ducks accumulated during morning classes. **1975** in *Tenn. Folklore Soc. Bull.* XLIV 137: *Duck*…(1) A cigarette butt (2) A claim on a still-burning cigarette butt lit by someone else: "I've got ducks on that butt."…The phrase "shooting ducks" is used to indicate the action of relighting and smoking a previously extinguished cigarette butt.

6. *Gamb.* a two; *Cards.* a deuce. *Joc.*
1913 T.A. Dorgan, in Zwilling *TAD Lexicon* 102: Poker dice—well that's my dish. Three ducks. That don't beat sixes however. **1968** F. Wallace *Poker* 214: *Duck*—A deuce.

7. *Av.* **a.** an amphibious aircraft.
1931 *Writer's Digest* (May) 40: *Duck*—An amphibian plane. **1933** *Leatherneck* (Jan.) 23: [They] flew to San Lorenzo, Honduras, in a Sikorsky and a "duck" to assist the crew of a wrecked PAA plane near there. **1933** *USN Inst. Proc.* (Dec.) 1727: At 11,000 feet the clouds were still going up and the "ducks" couldn't go much higher with the heavy load they were carrying. **1937** Lay *I Wanted Wings* 327: *Duck. Amphibion* [sic]. A seaplane with retractable wheels capable of operating from land or water. **1944** Merillat *Island* 211: Major Joseph Renner…volunteered to take up the "duck" (Grumman amphibian) to rescue Bauer.
b. an airplane that is old, unreliable, or dangerous.
*a***1984** in M.W. Bowman *Castles* 155 [ref. to 1944]: This duck I'm riding is about to fall apart! **1988** *World News Sunday* (ABC-TV) (July 3): The Airbus was a lumbering duck.

8. [sugg. by official designation DUKW; see *1945 quot.] *Mil.* a kind of amphibious cargo-carrying vehicle. Also **duck wagon.**
1943 G. Biddle *Artist at War* 65: Enormous, sea-going "ducks." **1943** in Kluger *Yank* 105: All-purpose…"duck" trucks that will go anywhere and carry anything. **1942–45** Caniff *Male Call* (unp.): It's swell of you duck jockeys. *1945 in *OEDS:* Officially known as "Dukws"—a combination of the factory serial letters D for boat, U for lorry body, and KW for lorry chassis—they quickly became known in the Army and Navy as "Ducks." **1961** Ageton *Hit Beach* 70 [ref. to WWII]: Tractors and duck wagons to unload our ships.

9. DUCK'S ASS.
1954–60 *DAS.* **1962–68** B. Jackson *In the Life* 434: She was wearing a duck, she was out there on stud row.

10. [prob. sugg. by colloq. *sitting duck*] *Und.* (see quot.).
1963 Williamson *Hustler!* 155: It was considered by hustlers a duck* 'cause it was on a dark corner…*Duck*—a place that's extremely easy to rob.

11. *Pool.* an object ball that hangs at the edge of a pocket; (*hence*) an easily made shot.
1980 *AS* (Summer) 98.

12. *Mil.* a sailor.—used derisively.
1973 Former Q.M., USN [ref. to 1968]: A sailor is called a *squid*, a *swabbie*, or a *duck*…Like you could say, "There were some ducks in the bar."

13. *Mil.* (see quot.).
*a***1982** Dunstan *Viet. Tracks* 118 [ref. to 1967]: The Cadillac Gage V-100 Commando Armored Car. Nicknamed "the Duck" or simply the "V."

¶ In phrases:

¶ **can a duck swim?** emphatically yes. Also vars.
1892 in F. Remington *Sel. Letters* 136: Do I want the Indian photos— does a duck swim? **1893** Wawn *South Sea Islanders* 392: "Would you like a glass of whiskey, Pilot?" said he. "Will a duck swim?" rejoined I. **1907** in H.C. Fisher *A. Mutt* 11: Will he be there Monday? Can a duck swim? **1929** Sullivan *Look at Chicago* 77: Did he get it? Can a duck swim? **1932** Tully *Laughter* 137: "You don't wanta be goin' outen the world at your age, do you?"…"Does a duck wanta swim?" **1942** "D. Ormsbee" *Sound of American* 309: "Can you handle it?" "Can a duck swim?"

¶ **column of ducks** *Army.* a column of soldiers.
1980 D. Cragg (letter to J.E.L., Aug. 10) 3 [ref. to Ft. Dix, NJ, 1958]: Awright, men, fall in and line up in a column of ducks! **1982** Cox & Frazier *Buck* 26 [ref. to 1951]: Get your tails off the truck and fall in a column of ducks.

¶ **drink with the ducks** *Naut.* to have fallen or been thrown into the sea; (*hence*) to be drowned.
1830 Ames *Mariner's Sketches* 201: Wearing a Scotch bonnet…or a checked or red flannel shirt, would in our service, subject the wearer to "drinking with the ducks" or getting "his *back* rations" in the gangway. **1847** Downey *Portsmouth* 6: The Old Salts…ended by prophecying that a goodly number of poor fellows would drink their Grog with the Ducks tomorrow morning.

¶ **drunk as a duck** quite drunk.
1968 E.M. Parsons *Fargo* 48: Drunk as the Governor's duck, d'you see. **1972** Ind. man, age 21: My father says, "He's drunk as a duck and don't give a quack." **1987** Univ. Tenn. instructor, age 38: I'm drunk as a duck and don't give a fuck.

¶ **for ducks** for no particular reason; for fun.
1900 Fisher *Job* 13: "Gracious sakes, boy! what did you scare me for?" "Oh, just for ducks!" **1931** Steffens *Autobiog.* 276 [ref. to 1890's]: "But what are you doing it for?" "Oh, just for ducks." **1938** Steinbeck *Grapes of Wrath* 10: He just done it for ducks. He wasn't puttin' on no dog. **1962** Shepard *Press Passes* 219: They're never happier than when pounding newsmen with their rifle butts, just for the ducks of it.

¶ **fuck a duck** see s.v. FUCK, v.

¶ **have (one's) ducks in a row** to have (one's) business planned or arranged in an efficient manner.
1979 S. King *Stand* 396: I'll bet *he's* got…all his ducks in a row. **1980** Rodeway Inn ad (WINS Radio): Well, when I'm on the go I like my ducks in a row. **1983** S. King *Christine* 303: He had a call to make, but it might be better to finish thinking this through first—have all his ducks in a row. **1992** Hosansky & Sparling *Working Vice* 222: You really have to have all your ducks in a row. You have to be thinking all the time.

¶ **line up (one's) ducks** to prepare by setting (one's) business in order.
1978 Truscott *Dress Gray* 22: And so Hedges was already lining up his ducks for his next move. **1985** Sawislak *Dwarf* 41: I'd guess he was lining up the ducks for a campaign. **1987** Averill *Mustang* 14: We should not have had any doubts. He had his ducks lined up.

¶ **Lord love a duck!** good heavens!
*1917** (cited in Partridge *DSUE* (ed. 8)). *a***1961** Longman *Power of Black* 252: Lord love a duck—what a holiday season! **1975** C.W. Smith *Country Music* 28: Lord love a duck!…the whole town's in an uproar! **1986** E. Weiner *Howard the Duck* 135: Lord love a duck!…Is this the end of Howard?

¶ **stick (one's) duck in the mud** (of a man) to engage in copulation.
1974 N.C. man, age 23: "Think I'll go stick my duck in the mud." Means I think I'll go fuck some bitch.

duck² *n. Theat.* a bow, as at the end of a performance.
1923 *N.Y. Times* (Sept. 9) VIII 2: *Duck*: A bow.

¶ In phrases:

¶ **cop a duck** *Und.* to lie low; stay out of sight.
1970 Rudensky & Riley *Gonif* 85: I copped a duck until mess.

¶ **do a duck** to keep out of sight; (*also*) to leave.
*1889** Barrère & Leland *Dict. Slang.* I 334: *Duck, doing a* (thieves), getting under the seat of a railway carriage when the ticket-collector comes round, so as to avoid paying the fare. **1902–03** Ade *People You Know* 109: The Victim did the tall Duck. **1908** McGaffey *Show Girl* 59: They all did the grand duck for the theatre.

¶ **play the duck** to keep out of sight; avoid notice; (*also*) to avoid.
1932 D. Runyon, in *Collier's* (Mar. 26) 8: Many citizens are…playing the duck for her and Sorrowful. **1942** Liebling *Telephone* 80: So after that he had to play the duck for Johnny for a couple of years. **1942** Pegler *Spelvin* 183: It does no good to play the duck for [describing] the beautiful oval of her face and start in on her finely chiseled throat. **1977** Caron *Go-Boy* 63: I played the duck to her for the rest of the day.

duck *v.* **1.a.** to get away or part from (a person).
1864 in J.W. Haley *Rebel Yell* 163: They could have…rushed us before we could duck them. **1896** Ade *Artie* 34: Purty soon he ducks 'em and comes over.
b. to avoid, evade, or absent oneself from (a responsibility).
1918 Rowse *Doughboy Dope* 25: The scared individuals in the picture think they are ducking Fatigue. **1922** *Leatherneck* (Apr. 22) 5: *Duck a Detail:* To avoid work. **1928** Santee *Cowboy* 8: But we usually made some good excuse for duckin' church. **1950** Lomax *Mr. Jelly Roll* 5: They always had it in their minds that a musician was a tramp, trying to duck work.

2.a. to depart hurriedly or surreptitiously; leave; go.—often constr. with *out.* Also trans.
1892 F.P. Dunne, in Schaaf *Dooley* 43: Oi think Oi'll put on the rollers an' duck. **1896** Ade *Artie* 4: I say, "You're all right, Percy, and you can take the car to yourself," and then I duck. **1899** Ade *Fables* 16: Having delivered herself of these Helpful Remarks she would Duck. **1903** McCardell *Chorus Girl* 98: We meets Charlie ducking into a beanery.

1908 McGaffey *Show Girl* 121: The dame tried to...duck the dump. **1914** Jackson & Hellyer *Vocab.* 29: *Duck*...To retire, to leave, to flee, to disappear. **1912** *Hampton's Mag.* (Jan.) 847: Fat had probably figured I wouldn't duck without them. **1919** S. Lewis *Free Air* 362: Come on! Let's duck! Drive back with me! **1922** S. Lewis *Babbitt* 87: I'll have to duck! **1928** Hecht & MacArthur *Front Page* 483: It don't have to rhyme! Now duck! **1934** *WNID2*: *Duck out.* To escape; to leave surreptitiously. *Slang.* **1934** Hackett & Goodrich *Thin Man* (film): Now *wait* a minute, I ducked out on him.

b. to extinguish (a cigarette), esp. for use later.

1947 Willingham *End As a Man* 114: There was never time to finish a cigaret. It was his habit to duck an unfinished end. **1958** Frankel *Band of Bros.* 7: And duck that butt. You hear anybody say the smoking lamp was lit? **1961** Clausen *Season's Over* 14: Hey, Anne, duck that cigarette. Here comes Barbette.

c. to get rid of; put out of sight.

1942–49 Goldin et al. *DAUL* 63: Duck that gat!

duck-ass see DUCK'S ASS.

duckboy *n. Army.* a marine.—used derisively.

1958 in Rumaker *Stories* 33: "That settles the big-mouthed duckboy!" hooted one [soldier], panting for breath. *Ibid.* 31: "Who you shouting orders at, duckboy?" said one of the soldiers.

duck buddy *n.* (see quot.).

1919 Amerine *Alabama's Own* 303: Brownie and me are "Duck Buddies," have been from the first. Don't know what a "Duck Buddie" is? Well, you see, if a man has some "makin's" and his buddie hasn't, the buddie always gets the "ducks"—the last half inch or so of the cigarette, I mean.

ducket var. DUCAT.

duckbutt *n.* a runt.

1939 *AS* XIV (Feb.) 26: *Duck-Butt*...A short person. **1980** Conroy *Lords of Discipline* 184: I'll also beat the living shit out of every one of you duckbutts.

duck butter *n. So.* smegma or semen; (*also*) sweat that gathers on or near the genitals.

1933 *AS* (Feb.) 48: *Duck butter*, n. Sperm, seminal fluid. **1944** *PADS* (No. 2) 19: *Duck butter: n.* Smegma. ((In s. Va.: *gnat-bread*)). **1950** in Randolph *Pissing in Snow* 138: He smeared a handful of duckbutter right under the town girl's nose. **1952** Randolph & Wilson *Holler* 114: The common term *duck-butter*...means semen or seminal fluid. **1964** Rhodes *Chosen Few* 27: Th' las' cat...went up for havin' duck butter on his joint. The doc reported it after short-arm inspection. **1974** Univ. Tenn. student: Another term for semen is *duck butter.* **1977** Univ. Tenn. grad. student, age 25: *Duck butter* refers to the guck, the glop, the yuck that gathers...between the legs near the genitalia on hot days. Or gathers on the penis itself. **1981** *AS* (Spring) 16: In...the Gulf coastal plain of Texas *duck butter* means "smegma."...The synonyms *gnat butter* and *nut butter* also turned up [in the South].

duck egg *n. Sports.* a zero; GOOSE EGG.

***1868** (quot. at DUCK, *n.*, 3). **1885** *Puck* (Oct. 7) 90: The ball went flying at a wondrous rate/...But after that were duck-eggs all around. **1900** *DN* II 33: *Duck egg,* n. Cipher in a [cricket] game. **1934** *WNID2*: *Duck egg.*

duck fit *n.* a fit of temper.

1901 Irwin *Sonnets* (unp.): Still I might throw a duck-fit. **1902–03** Ade *People You Know* 127: They would have 37 different kinds of Duck Fits and say that...her Taste was faultless. **1928–29** in *DAS.*

duck-fucker *n. Esp. Mil.* a loafer; lout.—usu. considered vulgar.

[***1785** Grose *Vulgar Tongue: Duck f-ck-r.* The man who has care of the poultry on board a ship of war.] [**1976** Lieberman & Rhodes *CB Hndbk.* 313: *Duck-plucker*—Obscene term.] *a***1986** D. Tate *Bravo Burning* 119 [ref. to Vietnam War]: Dinks got that hill now, those duck-fuckers. **1988** Poyer *The Med* 258: The XO, a notorious duck-fucker and nose-picker.

ducks *interj.* (see quot.); DIBS.

1939 *AS* XIV (Feb.) 26: *Ducks,* n., with verbal force. 1. Request for a portion of a cigarette, candy bar, etc., after the owner has had enough. 2. Request for the use of an article after the owner is through, as "Ducks on your electric razor." **1975** (quot. at DUCK, *n.*, 5).

duck's ass *n.* a ducktail haircut.—usu. considered vulgar. Also quasi-adv. Also **duck ass.**

[**1946** I. Shulman *Amboy Dukes* 2: The boys sported ducktail haircuts:

long, shaggy, and clipped to form a point at the backs of their heads.] ***1951** (cited in *Oxf. Dict. Mod. Slang*). **1958** in R. Russell *Permanent Playboy* 360: Leather, silver trim, sideburns, and duck-ass haircuts. **1959** O'Connor *Talked to a Stranger* 3: A tall, thin, zooty boy with thick black hair folded over at the back of the head (in a style that the police call "duck's ass"). **1959** Groninger *Run from Mt.* 5: None of the guys I knew owned motorcycles or wore their hair in a duck's ass, either. **1961** H. Ellison *Gentleman Junkie* 122: He had brown hair that he wore duck-ass. **1964** Peacock *Drill & Die* 142: I worn a duck's ass since I been in this goddam country. And my sideburns ain't too long. **1965** S. Harris *Hellhole* 234: Doubtless the greatest single affection among the "stud broads" in the House of Detention is the close-cropped men's haircut, ranging from a practical crew to the popular "Duck's Ass." **1967** Salas *Tattoo* 16 [ref. to *ca*1951]: You'll stay here until the doctor's examined you, until that duck's ass haircut has been clipped. **1978** T. Sanchez *Zoot-Suit* 118 [ref. to 1944]: You'll notice we gave him a white man's haircut, cut the duck's ass right off him. **1984** W.M. Henderson *Elvis* 26: A shaggy, sweeping duck's-ass.

duck shoot *n. Mil. Av.* TURKEY SHOOT.

1972–79 T. Wolfe *Right Stuff* 93: During that great duck shoot over Korea...he had never succeeded in downing an enemy plane.

duck soup *n.* **1.a.** something that offers no difficulty or challenge; that which is easily overcome; a cinch; (*hence*) an easy victim.

1902 T.A. Dorgan, in Zwilling *TAD Lexicon* 34: [Picture of man juggling a bottle, pitcher, plate and salt shaker:] Duck soup. **1908** in H.C. Fisher *A. Mutt* 35: Attorney Shortribs announced that it would be duck soup to clear their client. **1911** A.H. Lewis *Apaches of N.Y.* 84: Tough nothin'!...They'll be duck soup to Ike. **1918** Lardner *Treat 'Em Rough* 23: Then they gave us an hour of drilling and that was duck soup for me. **1923** in Kornbluh *Rebel Voices* 89: French windows are duck soup to the heroic burglar. **1926** Dunning & Abbott *Broadway* 234: That's duck soup for me, you know. **1927** Saunders *Wings* 70: "Duck soup," said Johnny briefly. **1928** MacArthur *War Bugs* 31: The Heinies were duck soup for freeborn Americans. **1944** C.B. Davis *Leo McGuire* 32: When you're beating up close to shore you're just duck soup for any Fed who's laying for us. **1957** Gurney & Martin *Saucer Men* (film): This was duck soup. **1969** Eastlake *Bamboo Bed* 25: When they force you in the valley you are duck soup. **1979** in Terkel *Amer. Dreams* 292: For us, it was duck soup. **1990** Rukuza *West Coast Turnaround* 148: It should be duck soup.

b. that which is certain of success.

1907 in H.C. Fisher *A. Mutt* 10: Now I got a hunch that "Como" is duck soup for the 6th [race]. **1933** MacDonald *Law of .45's* 186: This raidin' idea looks like duck soup.

2. something that is ideally suited.

1907 *McClure's Mag.* (Feb.) 380: Why, this is duck soup for us all. Think of two cases a shift for snoljering! **1915–16** Lait *Beef, Iron & Wine* 278: I...nominate one who...is...duck soup for this situation. **1929** Perelman *Ginsbergh* 195: "Frances, you fascinating little witch." This is just plain duck soup to Frances. **1931** D. Runyon, in *Collier's* (May 16) 12: It...will be duck soup for the newspapers...as they do not have a good shooting mystery for several days. **1941** in W.C. Fields *By Himself* 401: This is a duck soup situation for Fields, especially when she adds she thinks *he* is beautiful.

duck's quack *n.* CAT'S MEOW.

1923 Witwer *Fighting Blood* 13: His old man owned the carpet factory here, which seems to make this fathead think he's the duck's quack. **1927** Mayer *Between Us Girls* 57: I mean they were actually the duck's quack and I mean she simply adored them.

ducky *n.* see DUCK, *n.*, 2.b.

ducky *adj.* (esp. among young women) lovely; fine; cute.—now ironic.

1901 Atherton *Aristocrats* 45: Occasionally—I should have put it first—a ducky little cutlet. **1929** McEvoy *Hollywood Girl* 12: He's ducky, too. **1929** Perelman *Ginsbergh* 151: Hannah's flannel-cakes were just too ducky for words. **1930** Farrell *Calico Shoes* 29: Carrie, dear, you look just ducky. **1935** Odets *Waiting for Lefty* 9: Everything was gonna be so ducky! **1938** H. Gray *Arf* (unp.): So she paid yuh in full, eh? Now ain't that ducky? **1939** N. West *Locust* 279: That sounds ducky. **1939** Willoughby *Sondra* 37: Anyway, it's a ducky suite. **1943** Bodeen *Cat People* (film): Isn't he a ducky little angel? **1956** Lee & Bradley *Passed for White* 188: Isn't that just ducky? **1987** N.Y.C. woman, age 54: Now they've got some ducky machine that sucks out three drops of your blood and tells you how long you've got. **1983–88** J.T. McLeod *Crew Chief* 173: He and Halsey should get along just ducky.

ducrot /'duk,rou/ *n.* [orig. unkn.] Esp. *U.S. Mil. Acad.* an inconsequential thing or person, esp. a cadet.

1900 *Howitzer* (No. 1) 119: *Ducrot, Du John* [*sic*], *Dumflicket.*—Names applicable to things, as fourth classmen, etc. **1904** *Howitzer* (No. 5) 220: *Ducrot*—an inanimate object or person whose name is unknown or too difficult to use. **1905** *Howitzer* (No. 6) 293: *Ducrot*—Nom de plume for an object or person whose name is either unknown or of no importance. **1916** *Army & Navy Jour.* (Nov. 25) 392: Lieutenant Ducrot. **1947** Willingham *End As a Man* 7: Ducrow, bear up on that pile of guts.

dud *n.* [ME *dudde* 'a coarse cloak'; prob. of Gmc orig.] **1.a.** an article of clothing (*obs.*); (*pl.*) (now *colloq.*) clothes. [See *MED* for earlier evidence.]

*ca***1440** in *OED*: Dudde, clothe, *amphibulus.* ****1567** in *OED*: We will fylche some duddes. **a***1605** in *OED*: When thy duddes are bedirtten. ****1610** in *F & H* II 339: *Dudes*, clothes. ****1651** in *OED*: Upper and nether duds. ****1698–99** "B.E." *Dict. Canting Crew*: *Dudds*…Cloaths or Goods. *Rum dudds*…fine or rich cloaths or Goods. ****1698–1720** in D'Urfey *Pills* V 243: Off wi' your Duds. ****1785** Grose *Vulgar Tongue*: *Duds.* Clothes. **1793** Brackenridge *Mod. Chiv.* 199: There might not have been time to have washed his duds. **1815** in M. Mathews *Beginnings of Amer. Eng.* 58: *Duds*, old clothes. ****1822** in *F & H* II 339: A ragged rascal, every dud upon whose back was bidding good-day to the other. **1823** J.F. Cooper *Pioneers* 55: She has got on her woman's duds. **1839–40** Cobb *Green Hand* I 36: He…inquired where he should deposit his "duds." **1861** in W.R. Howell *Westward* 69: Wash and put on "clean duds." **1863** in Upson *With Sherman* 53: We got our duds on as best we could. **1867** Browne *Ward: London* 153: Put on your duds and go right straight home. **1889** Harte *Dedlow Marsh* 60: He must hev got some other duds near by in some underhand way. **1912** Field *Watch Yourself Go By* 410 [ref. to 1870's]: Thar hain't a durned dud of yers in this house. Air yu fixin' to fly the coop?

b. (*pl.*) belongings; personal effects.

****1662** in *F & H* II 339: All your duds are binged avast. ****1698–99** (quot. at **(a)**, above). **ca***1811** in *F & H* VII 41: They sweated their duds till they riz it. ****1829** Marryat *Frank Mildmay* 247: Tired of kicking about at sea, he should take all his *duds* with him, and bring himself to an anchor on shore. **1853** in Clemens *Twain's Letters* I 3: I packed up my "duds" and left for this village. **1855** W. Whitman *Leaves of Grass* 80: Shoulder your duds, and I will mine, and let us hasten forth. *ca***1880** Bellard *Gone for a Soldier* 151: We packed up our duds, and marched down to the depot under command of Captain Gamble. **1887** (quot. at HOOK). **1948** Robinson & Smith *J. Robinson* 71: Pack your duds, fellows. We're blowin'.

2. a useless, dull-witted, inept, tedious, or socially unsuccessful person. [After *ca*1918, widely associated with **(3.b. & c.)**, below]

****1825** Jamieson *Scots. Dict.*: *Dud*…Applied to a thowless fellow…"He's a soft dud." ****1840** T. Carlyle, in *OEDS*: A wretched Dud called —, member for — called one day. **1870** in *OED*: I think she is dressed like a dud; can't say how she would look in the costume of the present century. **1880** Nye *Boomerang* 53: They wouldn't dance with me all the evening, and I would be a wall-flower, and they would call me a perfect dud. **1881** in Nye *Western Humor* 18: After we have spent so much time constructing an elaborate wardrobe, we do not wish the journals of the territory to come out the next day, and make each one of us appear like "a perfect dud." ****1908** in *OEDS*: We want talent, not duds. **1917** Empey *Over the Top* 65: You blankety blank dud, I have been trying to raise you for fifteen minutes. What's the matter, are you asleep? **1918** *Stars & Stripes* (Aug. 30) 3: Dud At West Point Is Hero At Fismes. **1931** Hellinger *Moon* 159: The girl…was a terrific dud. Didn't wear nice clothes either. **1963** Doulis *Path* 55: I wonder what those duds see in parachuting…Those duds can't think for one minute without getting a headache. **1971** Barnes *Pawns* 120: A lot of the soldiers who go AWOL would stick around if the army weren't quite so hard to take—if their sergeants didn't razz them for being "duds." **1986** R. Walker *AF Wives* 73: The man was a dud—I told him I had a headache. **1993** *Village Voice* (N.Y.C.) (June 22) 34: Crack "slangin'," ya duds, is…wack.

3.a. a worthless or (*rare* in U.S.) counterfeit item.—often attrib.

****1897** in *OEDS*: He admitted that he knew that he ought not to have sold the piracies, and that such works were known as "Duds." ****1903** in *OEDS*: I…got him to give me half a crown for a dud ring. ****1908** in *OEDS*: Gambling with "Duds."…A "dud" car is a worthless contraption, which…has arrived at a stage when it would be dear at any price. **1917** *Everybody's* (May) 517: He called the broken machine a "dud." **1928** Sharpe *Chicago May* 287: *Dud*—substitute or fake. **1957** *Sing Out!*

(Winter) 21: It…includes a raft of…highly singable songs. Some duds slipped in, too, but every man to his taste. **1966** Noel & Bush *Naval Terms* 155: *Flyable dud*: An aircraft that can be flown but is not in shape for combat.

b. *Specif.* (*Mil.*) a bomb, shell, etc., that fails to explode. Now *S.E.*

****1915** in *OEDS*: Our weary hearts rejoice/When Silent Susan sends us down a dud! **1917** Eddy *In France* 54: During the morning there were only four "duds," or bombs that would not go off. **1918** Straub *Diary* (entry for June 2): I have noticed too that about four out of ten of them are "Duds" or, shells that do not explode. **1918** Swan *My Company* 232: Then we would know a "dud" (unexploded shell) had landed. **1964** Gallant *Friendly Dead* 106: "Fourteen-inch dud," the sergeant agreed. **1968** in Holley *Vietnam* 53: Another round…embedded itself in the soft dirt—a dud! **1985** Dye *Between Raindrops* 101: Still no explosion…Must have been a dud. **1987** *U.S.A. Today* (May 21) 1: [USS] Stark hit twice; second a "dud."

c. something that is a failure; FLOP; something unsatisfactory or unexciting.

1920 Lee *Artilleryman* 19: Alas, it soon developed that our first night was merely a "dud." Wind, wind, and still more wind. **1929** "E. Queen" *Roman Hat* ch. xxii 219: You act as if you'd pulled a dud rather than succeeded. **1932** Lawes *Sing Sing* 216: I told a story about the necessity for mutual understanding. It was a dud, went flat—no laughs, no comments—still silence. **1934** *WNID2*: *Dud*…a flat failure. *Slang.*

d. something tedious or disappointing.

1971 Keith *Long Line Rider* 7: Forrest City was a dud. **1983** Pond *Valley Girls' Gde.* 55: What a dud, you know, like a bummer only more boring. **1993** *N.Y. Times* (Aug. 31) C 1: The date is a dud and both parties know it.

dud *adj.* [orig. attrib. use of n.] worthless; unsatisfactory; poor; (now *usu.*) tedious; unexciting; spiritless; disappointing.

****1903** (quot. at DUD, *n.*, 3.a.). ****1904** in *OEDS*: Wanted comedy and dramatic sketches. Something with life and go in it. No Dud stuff required. ****1914** Rosher *Flying Squadron* 32: I…found my air-speed indicator was not working and my compass dud. ****1917** Lee *No Parachute* 48: The weather has been dud all day, with no patrols, and we've had an easy time, loafing around. **1918** Paine *Fighting Fleets* 288: It's a dud bus. Too much stagger and prop stops in a spin. **1918** *Stars & Stripes* (Feb. 15) 3: *Dud*, adj.: totally defective; zero in degree; of no account; worthless. **1918** in Rossano *Price of Honor* 85: Flying yesterday was what they call "dud" [with several crash landings]. **1919** Law *Air Service* (unp.): Wylie "failed to return," but was located all O.K. that night, having landed just back of our lines with a "dud" engine. **1919** Rickenbacker *Flying Circus* 35: "Rain and Mud!" "Dud weather!" "No flying today!" *Ibid.* 1: *Dud.* Dead, or bad. **1920** Clapp *17th Aero Squadron* 42 [ref. to 1918]: On "dud" days we sent to Abbeville and Boulogne for a little luxuries for the mess. **1934** *WNID2*: *Dud*, *adj.* Without energy. *Slang.* **1977** Univ. Tenn. grad. student: So it's another dud evening at home.

dud *v.* to fail to explode.

1991 C. Fletcher *Pure Cop* 26: Military ordnance that hadn't detonated; in other words, they had dudded.

dude *n.* [orig. unkn.] **1.a.** a usu. over-refined or effete man or boy who is pretentiously concerned with his clothes, grooming, manners, etc.; dandy; (*broadly*) *West.* a city person, esp. if new to the West; a guest at a DUDE RANCH. Now *S.E.* [1913 quot. recalls personal experience fr. 1854; term's currency at such an early date is uncertain.]

1877 in F. Remington *Sel. Letters* 15: Don't send me any more [drawings of] women or any more dudes. **1878** Mulford *Fighting Indians* 16: Company C, 20th Infantry, was at that time composed of dude soldiers, pets of dress parade officers. **1881** in Aswell *Humor* 359: Compare…the feeble arm of a New York dude to the muscles of a Roman gladiator! But *never* change the name of Arkansas! Hell, *no!* **1883** *Life* (Mar. 22) 143: Second Dude (*languidly*): Rather (*relapses into silence*). **1883** Bunner *Letters* 90: Brander Mathews…is not enough of a dude to be ashamed of feeling a thrill up his backbone when the old flag goes by? **1883** Peck *Bad Boy* 259: It was said she was going to get married to a fellow who is now in the dude business…she had been so kind to me at school just 'cause the dude wouldn't marry her. **1886** Wilkins *Cruise* 13: Oh, Johnnie, come and see the dude sailor. **1887** Gunter *Mr. Barnes* 40: An American dude…even in his agony does not forget his beloved English accent and pointed varnished gaiters. **1887** Francis *Saddle & Moccasin* 156: 'Sides, ain't you one of these dudes as the Colonel brings down sometimes from El Paso and Silver, that wants kettles o' hot water to twelve o'clock. **1888** *Stag Party* 26: A base-ball dude and would-be masher leaned over the seat. **1889** "M. Twain" *Conn. Yankee* 143: Of course these iron dudes of the Round Table would think it was scandalous. **1894** *Harper's* (Feb.) 356: I may be tempted to ask him if he will not wash his hands, whereat the boys may indicate that I am a "dude," and will look down on me. **1894** in F. Remington *Sel. Letters* 260: It's pretty fine for a dude who has never been in A[rizona]. **1895** Townsend *Fadden* 123: Den dose dudes dey laughed too, and kept sayin' "Bah Jove," and "I say, you know." **1896** F.P. Dunne, in Schaaf *Dooley* 239: It'll go hard with some iv thim Wall sthreet joods. **1902** *N.Y. Eve. Jour.* (Dec. 6) 12: Say! Dat dude said I wus one of de great unwashed! **1913** Meyers *Ranks* 19 [ref. to 1854]: He spent much time in "priming" himself and the boys called him "the dude." **1927** H. Miller *Moloch* 144: A couple of dudes in spats and butter-colored gloves. **1929** Ferber *Cimarron* 15: In the back seat was a dude in a light tan coat and a cigar in his mouth and a diamond in his shirtfront. **1938** Burt *Powder River* 49: Hunt was undoubtedly the first perfect tenderfoot ever to come west, the first simon-pure "dude" ever to enter Wyoming. **1944** Botkin *Treas. Amer. Folk.* 360: The hazing of "dudes" and tenderfeet has produced many classics among sells. **1958** Bard & Spring *Horse Wrangler* 132: Then we met up with the real dudes [i.e. Western tourists], some of the nicest people to be found anywhere. **1965** D.G. Moore *20th C. Cowboy* 181: A dude girl from Indiana. **1974** Blount *3 Bricks Shy* 53: He was a real dude. And he had on a camel's hair coat.

b. *Mil.* a soldier newly inducted or arrived.

1936 *Our Army* (Oct.) 36: All right, you dudes! Fall out! **1947** *ATS* (Supp.) 15: Recruit...*dude.* **1956** Hess *Battle Hymn* 53 [ref. to WWII]: Hailing from Denver, Colorado, he called his plane "Poco Loco," always carried a hunting knife in his belt, and got a special kick out of calling our new pilots "dudes."

c. a foolish or obnoxious fellow.

1967 Fiddle *Shooting Gallery* 318: I shouldna tipped that old dude off like that. **1970** N.Y.U. student: There were a lot of good kids in that school. Also, a lot of dudes, but a lot of good kids, too. **1971** N.Y.U. student: Man, what a dude he is! **1971** N.Y.U. student: What a bunch of dudes! He is a *dude!*

2.a. a male person; fellow. [Esp. common since late 1960's; Straub 1918 quot. extends the sense to horses and mules.]

1883 Peck *Bad Boy* 284: I get to thinking about Adam and Eve in the garden of Eden, and of the Dude with the cloven hoof that flirted with Eve. *Ibid.* 333: Eve...got mashed on the old original dude, and it stands to reason that Solomon's wives were no better. **1895** Townsend *Fadden* 21: Say, I was kinder layin' fer dat dude, anyhow, cause 'e is allus roastin' me. **1912** *Chi. Defender* (Oct. 26) 3: The dudes...worked on the S.S. Minnesota this summer. **1916** *Chi. Defender* (July 15) 6: Guess Who...the doll...is who is fast becoming popular with all the dudes. *Ibid.* You sure made more than one dude look twice at you, girlies. **1918** Ruggles *Navy Explained* 139: In a gang of snipes below there is generally one dude who is known as the "king snipe." He is considered the leading snipe of the watch. **1918** Straub *Diary* [entry for June 23]: Armstrong and I helped some of the Battalion men load some of their horses and mules because it is certainly a job to get the old "dudes" into a car without fighting some of them. **1918–19** MacArthur *Bug's-Eye View* 93: Listen to this guy!...Here they're pegging shells at us like confetti, and this dude is trying to sell me a helmet. **1919** Johnson *Heaven, Hell, or Hoboken* 21: Things We Hated..."Gimme a cigarette" (twenty times a day from the same dude). *Ibid.* 119: The new men from the 86th Division came to us at the Gully. Remember how we felt for the poor dudes? **1921** *Pirate Piece* (Apr.) 3: Now you here dudes have got to give me a lift on this thing. **1923** McKnight *Eng. Words* 62: The girls' list of names for members of the other sex is nearly as rich. Noncommittal in general are: *dude, goof, john...guy, kid.* **1933–35** D. Lamson *About to Die* 37: I been watching them dudes [convict workmen] up there for the last fifteen minutes. *Ibid.* 200: And suppose some other dude starts another shop across the street. **1940** Lawes *Murderer* 271 [ref. to 1933]: Maybe that'll give 'em a chance to grab some other dude before he's in a spot like me. **1963** Braly *Shake Him* 53: Just you dudes in this? **1965** Wade & Kassebaum *Women's Pris.* 122: They can't wait to get with a dude [man] again. **1967** Taggart *Reunion* 63: Now who the hell was *that* dude? **1967** Yablonsky *Hippie Trip* 76: This cat, a beautiful dude, gave drugs to anybody who wanted it. **1968** Carey *College Drug Scene* 16: And I got into symbolic logic and semantics with a cat who had studied with Korzybski and electronics from a dude who had an Associate of Arts degree in anthropology from 1941. **1968** *N.Y. Post* (Aug. 14) 5: I shot two dudes (policemen). **1970** A. Young *Snakes* 91: Dudes, chicks, little children. **1970** M. Thomas *Beast* 245: What kind of a dude was he? **1974** Strasburger *Rounding Third* 2: So let's us shrewd dudes not go fooling anyone, all right?

b. (used in direct address to a male person; MAN).

1877–88 in J.W. Crawford *Plays* 113: Why redskin dude, is there any other little thing you'd like? **1945** Trumbull *Silversides* 25: Hey, dude, there's a ship out here! **1951** *Popeye the Sailor* (animated cartoon): Don't you *dare* to reproach me, you rude dude! **1977** Dillard *Lexicon of Black Eng.* 16: *Man* or *dude* (as terms of address)...obviously came to white America from the Black community. **1967–80** Folb *Runnin' Lines* 236: *Dude.* Term of address for a male. **1984** Univ. Tenn. instructor, age 34: What's goin' on, dude?

c. *usu. pl.* a person of either sex. Cf. sim. sense development of CAT, GUY.

1974 Eble *Campus Slang* (Mar.) 2: Dude—any person, usually a male. **1981** Jenkins *Baja Okla.* 269: We're not talking about a lame chick and a gnarly guy. We're talking about a couple of far-out dudes! **1985** B.E. Ellis *Less Than Zero* 116: Mom asked me, and I said, "No way, dude." **1986** Female Univ. Tenn. student [to mixed group]: See you dudes later. **1992** D. Burke *Street Talk* I 245: It is actually common to hear a teenager say, "Hey, dudes," when addressing a group of young women. **1993** *Funny Times* (Apr.) 16: A dude can be a dude [man] and a dude can be a lady.

d. *Army.* a German soldier.

1918 *Lit. Digest* (Sept. 7) 50: Ah took ma rifle, a French gun, just like dis, and hit a Dude right on de haid and broke the rifle right here. Ah went after de Dudes carryin' way ma pardner...Den one of de Dudes comes at ma hollering "Kumrad."..."Look, youse all bloody." "Oh," I says, "dat's from de Dudes."

3. a fancy or excellent example.

1919 T.A. Dorgan, in Zwilling *TAD Lexicon* 102: Ain't that a dude of an idea? I'll say it is. **1920–21** Witwer *Leather Pushers* 70: The fight was a dude while it lasted, both men bein' seasoned campaigners. *Ibid.* 331: A dude of a cave, kid. **1923** Witwer *Fighting Blood* 80: Mark Twain...tells a dude of a yarn.

4. item; thing.

1960 Peacock *Valhalla* ch. 9 [ref. to 1953]: "You go on back and get a booth," he said. "I'll go pick up the first case." "I'll go with you, old friend," Poke Turner suggested. "I wouldn't want you to get lost with all them cold dudes." **1968** W.C. Anderson *Gooney Bird* 76: "When the FAC pilot gets the green light to go in, he fires one of these dudes to mark the target." He patted a long, lethal-looking rocket hung under the wing. **1969** in Tuso *Vietnam Blues* 126: Those dudes are mighty fine ships. **1971** N.Y.U. student: Man, I gotta quit this! I'm callin' everythin' "dudes"! This morning, I'm lookin' at my shoes and I'm thinkin', "I gotta get me a new pair of these dudes"! **1972** W.C. Anderson *Hurricane* 153: She [a hurricane]'s a frisky little dude. **1979** Gram *Blvd. Nights* 26: We're gonna make this Ventura dude one fine foxy ride. **1985** Boyne & Thompson *Wild Blue* 185: I've had two engine fires in the last four flights, and there is no way to get out of that dude.

5. *pl.* fancy clothing; DUDS, 2.

1970 *Nat. Lampoon* (Apr.) 12.

dude *adj.* being or typical of a DUDE, 1.a. Also adv.

1878 (quot. at DUDE, *n.*, 1.a.). **1886** Nye *Remarks* 397: A red-headed horse-physician with dude shoes. **1895** Townsend *Fadden* 135: His Whiskers is a real gent, not because he dresses dude, but because he was borned so.

dude *v.* to behave in the manner of a DUDE, 1.a.

1899 in Ownby *Subduing Satan* 83: I know...young men who "dude" around our streets all the week,...play cards, [etc.].

dude ranch *n. West.* a ranch operated as a vacation resort for paying guests and tourists. Now *S.E.*

1921 *Scribner's Mag.* (Mar.) 343: Is this Scott Lawson's dude ranch? **1928** W.H. Dixon *West. Hoboes* 82: Tucson...[is] apparently devoid of "dude" ranches. **1934** *WNID2: Dude ranch...slang.* **1941, 1948** in *DA.*

dudester *n.* fellow; DUDE, 2.

1986 *New Leave It to Beaver* (synd. TV series): See ya, dudester.

dudette *n.* a girl or woman. *Joc.*

1984 Mason & Rheingold *Slanguage: Dudette sup* [i.e. *what's up*]...A greeting...."Hello...mademoiselle, what is new at present?" **1987** *ALF* (NBC-TV): Later, dude! Dudettes! **1988** *Daily Beacon* (Univ. Tenn.) (Aug. 24) 2: Welcome Back...Dudes and Dudettes. **1989** *Beachin' Times* 13: Hey Dude-ettes...How to Find the Ultimate Babe! **1991** *Bill & Ted's Adventures* (CBS-TV): Go get 'em, dudette. **1993** *Newsweek* (July 26) 8: Sex is grafted onto their *real* consuming passion—to be the most radical dude or dudette in their crowd.

dude up *v.* to dress up; DOLL UP.

1899 in *DA.* **1916** O'Brien *Best Stories of 1916* 42: She..."duded up" her hair a bit. **1948** in *DA*. **1949** Bezzerides *Thieves' Market* 174: I guess that dudes you up. **1962** Bonham *War Beneath Sea* 138: The…[ship's] all duded up with bunting. **1963** D. Tracy *Brass Ring* 116: Don't get all duded up. This isn't the Country Club you know. **1975** Julien *Cogburn* 25: Duded-up Yankee lawyers who won spelling bees back home.

dude wrangler *n. West.* a dude-ranch employee who entertains tourists.

1928 W.H. Dixon *West. Hoboes* 339: All the "dood-wranglers" in the Park. **1934** *WNID2*. **1986** *CNN World News* (Apr. 26): And once a dude wrangler, always a dude wrangler.

dudish *adj.* being or typical of a DUDE, 1.a. Now *S.E.*

1908 Fletcher *Rebel Private* 132 [ref. to Civil War]: When I had gotten them on and hair combed, I felt "dudish," and when I smiled before a glass, I had the vain thought of How handsome.

dudhead *n.* a dolt.

1963 Horwitz *Candlelight* 171: "I need some truth, some truth," he was saying to a magnificent dudhead blonde.

due *n.* ¶ In phrase: **pay dues, 1.** Orig. *Jazz.* to endure a period of apprenticeship or preparation.

1942 in Gold *Jazz Lexicon* 92. **1957** Gelber *Connection* 91: We all pay our dues whatever we do. **1957** Guttwillig *Long Silence* 51 [ref. to 1951]: Lester Young and James Joyce…had "paid their dues." **1958–59** Lipton *Barbarians* 40: You got to pay your dues, man, like everybody else. **1963** Braly *Shake Him* 105: He thought of it as paying dues, the musician's expression for any debt or obligation. It covered the hours of practice and study required to perfect technique, or any tedious preliminary to a desired end. **1973** Wagenheim *Clemente!* 65: He had "paid his dues" with thousands of hours of arduous labor. **1993** Fidelity Investments TV ad (CNN-TV): I always thought if I paid my dues, one day I'd have a business of my own.

2. Esp. *Black E.* to take consequences; endure hardship.

1956 Childress *Like One of Family* 149: If they wasn't afraid of payin' them heavy dues by ruinin' their health. **1960** C.L. Cooper *Scene* 262: If you can't pay the dues, don't play. **1966** I. Reed *Pall-Bearers* 2: I have paid a lot of dues, son, and now I'm gonna pop off. **1970** Quammen *Walk the Line* 49: The cat who had helped him…had paid the dues: he was dead. **1967–80** Folb *Runnin' Down Lines* 249: *Pay dues.* 1. Suffer. 2. Go through hard times.

duff[1] *n.* [orig. unkn.] the human rump; BUTT. Also in fig. senses.

ca*1835–40** in Speaight *Bawdy Songs of Music Hall* 35: Your lilly duff. *Ibid.* 60: Lay her on her duff, then,…her belly white to kiss. **ca***1844** in L. James *English Pop. Lit.* 322: Her duff she up and down did jerk,/Did frisky Nancy Dawson. **1939** Polsky *Curtains for Editor* 99: "Go powder your duff," says he to her. She went. **1942** in Legman *No Laughing Matter* 407: Otherwise she'd fall on her duff. **1958** Frankel *Band of Bros.* 116: Knock him on his duff. **1959** Sterling *Wake of Wahoo* 76: I wouldn't be just sitting on my duff. **1962** Davis *Marine* 62: All right, then, if you think so, why don't you waltz your duff down to Division and get 'em back in here? **1970** Gattzden *Black Vendetta* 153: I…worked my duff off. **1971** *All in the Family* (CBS-TV): Sitting around on his duff. **1974** Foster *Star Trek Log One* 11: Davis, Gardner, get off your duffs! **1979** *Buck Rogers* (NBC-TV): Come on, you turkeys, get off your duffs and give me some instructions. **1981** D. Burns *Feeling Good* 108: Her mother…kept telling her to get off her duff and do something. **1988** *Newsweek* (Feb. 8) 60: Couch potatoes: off your duffs.

duff[2] *n.* a duffel bag.

1956 Gold *Not With It* 100: Smoke nothing but big two-for-thirty-five cigars now…Got a boxful in my duff.

duff[1] *v.* [back formation fr. DUFFER] *Golf.* to execute (a shot) badly; (*hence*) to bungle; muff.

*****1897** in *OEDS*: The verb "to duff"…[means] simply to hit the ground first, behind the ball, so that the ball is…sent only a short way into the air. *****1909** Ware *Passing Eng.* 119: He duffs everything he touches. **1948** Cozzens *Guard of Honor* 390: Now, suppose he gets down and it looks bad; the terrain, or enemy dispositions make it dangerous to land, and he sees he'll probably duff it.

duff[2] *v.* [orig. unkn.] to copulate with.

1963–64 Kesey *Great Notion* 235: Tell me which one them varmints been duffin' my wife. **1987** Univ. Tenn. prof., age *ca*42: I can recall the verb *duff* in a sexual sense from my days as a street kid in the Bronx. Early 1960's.

duff[3] *v.* [perh. fr. ARTHUR DUFFY] Esp. *Pris.* to run away or escape; leave.—sometimes constr. with *out.*

[**1942–49** Goldin et al. *DAUL* 63: *Duff, on the.* In flight; in the act of moving farther away from any source of danger.] **1963** J.A. Williams, in *Provincetown Rev.* VI 12: I duff out. **1972** Bunker *No Beast* 152: He's up at a road camp and wants to duff.

duffer[1] *n.* [orig. unkn.] **1.a.** a foolish, inept, or objectionable person; (now *esp.*) a foolish or objectionable old man; (*rarely*) a fellow. [The British sense, 'a worthless, esp. counterfeit item', app. the immed. source of the present sense, is unrecorded in the U.S. The 1918 quot. has neutral force.]

ca*1730** Haddington *Sel. Poems* 214: Ye doited, donnart, duffar! *****1842** in *OED*: I do not think him the mere duffer that most people make him out. **1859** *Spirit of Times* (Feb. 12) 7: He was by…the Israel-ite female, designated a "duffer," as she continued to drive a carving-fork…in his…fleshy parts. *****1873** Hotten *Slang Dict.* (ed. 5): *Duffer*…is now general in its application to a worthless fellow. **1875** Daly *Pique* 312: The psalm-singing duffers haven't spoiled you, Sally. **1876** in Rosa *Wild Bill* 298: The old duffer—he broke me on the hand. **1876** Cody & Arlington *Life on Border* 43: You're a nice old duffer, ain't you. **1877** *Puck* (Aug. 22) 2: As an Indian fighter General O.O. Howard is what the theatrical people would call a "duffer." *ca***1880** in *Calif. Folk. Qly.* II (1943) 98: We drank at Ed Dyart's, the solid old duffer. **1882** *Judge* (Oct. 28) 7: An then a sanktimonyus duffer…sed Sunday-scool boys Hadn't ought ter talk that Way. **1882** "M. Twain" *Life on Miss.* 225: I'm a professional gambler myself, and I've been laying for you duffers all this voyage! *****1881–84** Davitt *Prison Diary* I 201: Get along, you duffer! He has only one duke (arm). **1892** Crane *Maggie* 25: "Gawd," he said, "I wonner if I've been played fer a duffer?" **1898** *Sat. Eve. Post* (July 30) 70: I suppose I am an awful duffer not to be able to call the trick. **1900** Patten *Merriwell's Power* 5: Wrap me up in my tarpaulin jacket/And say, "A poor duffer lies low!" *Ibid.* 70: I think there are a lot of duffers in this college. **1902** "J. Flynt" *Little Bro.* 190: Take that, you duffer! **1904** *Life in Sing Sing* 247: *Duffer.* A name applied in contempt. **1912** Field *Watch Yourself Go By* 284: This kid finds me skinning a couple of old duffers and forthwith he sets about to skin me. **1918** E.E. Rose *Cappy Ricks* 118: A husky, good-looking duffer. **1930** Sage *Last Rustler* 215: Young duffer, I hear yer lookin' for work.

b. *Horse Racing.* (see quot.).

1880 *N.Y. Clipper Almanac* 44: *Duffer.*—A horse which loses heart or refuses to exert himself during a race.

c. *Golf.* an unskillful player.

1942 *ATS* 676: Golf…*duffer*, a poor player. **1949** Cummings *Dict. Sports* 120: *Duffer*…An inept performer. Most commonly used in golf. **1958** Frankel *Band of Bros.* 254: Hope you're not practicing [your golf game] too much, duffer. **1970** Scharff *Encyc. of Golf* 4: *Duffer.* An unskilled golfer. **1993** *CBS This Morning* (CBS-TV) (June 4): And now, for the discouraged duffer—[a laser-equipped putter].

2.a. *Und.* a swindler who sells merchandise that is alleged to be contraband.

*****1742** (cited in Partridge *Dict. Und.* 214). *****1785** Grose *Vulgar Tongue*: *Duffers.* Cheats who…pretend to deal in smuggled goods,…selling…Spitalfield goods at double their current price. *****1796**, *****1823**, *****1828**, etc. (cited in Partridge *Dict. Und.* 214.). **1859** Matsell *Vocab.* **1873** Lening *N.Y. Life* 602: Another class of cheats are…"Duffers." These "duffers" carry on their business in the garb of sailors…They say that they have just arrived from a trip to France, and that they have smuggled…goods through the custom-house…His bundles are bought, and the buyer finds to her mortification…that her purchase is…not worth half the money paid for it.

b. *Police.* (see quot.).

1872 Crapsey *Nether Side* 185: The intruder…was a "duffer," by which name the police mean one who, following some honest pursuit during the day, occasionally sallies forth at night to commit some house robbery.

duffer[2] *n.* [prob. alter. of *duff*, dial. pronun. of *dough*; cf. S.E. *duff* 'boiled or steamed flour pudding'] *Hobo.* a piece of bread; bread; (*occ.*) bread and coffee.

1905 Sinclair *Jungle* 184: His supper…was "duffers and dope"—being hunks of dry bread on a tin plate, and coffee, called "dope" because it was drugged to keep the prisoners quiet. **1925** Mullin *Scholar Tramp* 34 [ref. to *ca*1912]: I received punk (bread) and a cup of mud (black coffee) or—to use the familiar hobo expression for the combination—duffer. **1926** in *AS* LVII (1982) 261: *Duffer.* Bread. **1935** Pollock *Und. Speaks*: *Duffer*, bread. **1948** Mencken *Amer. Lang.* (Supp. II) 674: Bread [is called] *duffer*, or *punk*.

duff-maker *n. Naut.* a cook.

1836 *Naval Mag.* (Sept.) 433: I hallooed, at the top of my lungs, for the vile "*duff-maker*" to come and extricate me from the mazes of vegetable lumber in which I was cast.

duffus[1] *n.* the rump; DUFF.
  1948 Wolfert *Act of Love* 432: He wouldn't…sit out the war on his duffus.

duffus[2] var. DOOFUS.

duffy[1] *n. Hobo.* a loaf of bread; DUFFER.
  1906 Tomlin *H. Tomlin* 235: I reached and got a "duffy" (loaf of bread) and cut it in two.

duffy[2] *n.* [perh. fr. *Duffy*, family name] a derby hat.
  1930 "D. Stiff" *Milk & Honey* 138: Neither does the hobo wear a hard hat or "duffy," known by many an uncomplimentary name, the least of which is "pimp's turban."

duffy[3] *n.* ¶ In phrase: **take it on the Arthur Duffy** see ARTHUR DUFFY.

duflicket *n. U.S. Mil. Acad.* an inconsequential person, esp. a cadet.
  1878 Flipper *Colored Cadet* 75 [ref. to 1875]: *Second Marcher.*—Bejay! Barnes! Du Furing! Swikeheimer! Du Flicket [etc.]. **1916** *Army & Navy Jour.* (Nov. 25) 392: Lieutenant Duflicket.

dufus var. DOOFUS.

dugee var. DUJI.

dugout *n.* (see quot.).
  1916 in Roy *Pvt. Fraser* 145: "Dug-outs," an epithet commonly applied to those officers whose chief concern is the depth of their trench abode.

dugout-ducker *n. Army.* a soldier who clings to the safety of a dugout when others are under fire. [Quots. ref. to WWI.]
  1928 Nason *Sgt. Eadie* 295: Maybe I ain't got no brains, but I ain't no dugout ducker. **1928–29** Nason *White Slicker* 42: It'll be the sorriest day you've had since you joined the diarrhoea corps, you dugout ducker!

dugout-hound *n. Army.* DUGOUT-DUCKER. [Quots. ref. to WWI.]
  1920 *Hicoxy's Army* 47: Big John…yelled at two dugout-hounds. **1932** Ward *Big Parades* 77: The answer is, he's a dug-out hound. **1942** *Inf. Jour., Amer. vs. Germans* 172: Come outa there, you dugout hounds, and let's git goin'!

dugout king *n. Army.* DUGOUT-DUCKER. [Quots. ref. to WWI.]
  1922 *Amer. Legion Wkly.* (Jan. 20) 23: Remember how it was in a dug-out, you dugout kings, where all hands were ordered not to drop off to sleep? *1930 Brophy & Partridge *Songs & Slang* 120: *Dug-Out King.*

duh *interj.* [fr. *duh*, inarticulate exclamation of a blockhead pausing in thought, as in 1943 quot.] (used to express annoyance at the stupidity of a previous comment); "that is exceedingly obvious." Also as *adj., n.*
  [**1943** *Merrie Melodies* (animated cartoon): Duh…Well, he can't outsmart me, 'cause I'm a moron!] **1963** *N.Y. Times Mag.* (Nov. 24) 52: A favorite expression is "duh."…This is the standard retort used when someone makes a conversational contribution bordering on the banal. For example, the first child says, "The Russians were first in space." Unimpressed, the second child replies (or rather grunts), "Duh." **1969** *Esquire* (Aug.) 70: As They Used to Say in the 1950's…*How's that grab you? Duhhh!* **1975** in G.A. Fine *With the Boys* 169: *Duh*, interj. That's stupid. **1988** Groening *Childhood* (unp.): Is TV the coolest invention ever invented? Well, *duh.* **1988** *Atlantic* (May) 98: That's so *duh* that you've got to smile. *Ibid.* 98: He's a real *duh.* **1992** *Mystery Sci. Theater* (Comedy Central TV): "Sounds like he's in trouble." "No, duh!"

duji *n.* [orig. unkn.] *Narc.* heroin. Also vars. [The sense intended in the 1939 quots. (titles of swing tunes) is not clear]
  [**1939** in Ellington *Music My Mistress* 498: Dooji Wooji. *Ibid.* 499: King Dooji.] **1959–60** R. Reisner *Jazz Titans* 154: *Dugie:* heroin. **1965** C. Brown *Manchild* 189: About 1955, duji became the thing. **1966** S. Harris *Hellhole* 135: For, by 1961, Harlem had been hit by what is coming to be known as the "plague"—heroin—nicknamed "shit" and "poison" and "duji" and "stuff". **1966** Neugeboren *Big Man* 104: The bongo player…just leans forward chewing gum, looks like he's on dujie. **1966–67** P. Thomas *Mean Streets* 195 [ref. to ca1950]: Yet there is something about dogie—heroin. **1968** Heard *Howard St.* 174: He marveled at the New Yorker's good, good doogie. **1970** Landy *Underground Dict.* 68: *Dojee…dojie…*Heroin. *Ibid.* 69: *Doojer…Dooji…*Heroin.

1970 Horman & Fox *Drug Awareness* 465: *Doojee*—heroin. **1972** Smith & Gay *Don't Try It* 201: *Dugee.* Heroin. **1976** Chinn *Dig the Nigger Up* 82: When I was introduced to heroin in 1948, it was called "junk" and "horse." About 1950, it took on the name "doogy." **1978** Selby *Requiem* 245: There be one place you can stash ol doogie without you worryin about it. **1985** D. Killerman *Hellrider* 127: Half…had been out of their skulls on Doo-Gee, pot, or Ludes. **1987** Santiago *Undercover* 90: The air around them was smoky with dujie.

duke *n.* **1.a.** a hand or (usu. *pl.*) fist; (*pl.*, in 1974 quot.) fisticuffs.
  [*1839 Brandon *Poverty* (gloss): *Dookin*—fortune-telling.] [**1859** Matsell *Vocab.* 27: *Dookin cove.* A fortune-teller.] **1859** Matsell *Vocab.* 28: *Dukes.* The hands. *Ibid.* 126: [Pugilists' slang] *Dukes.* The hands. *ca1859* Chamberlain *My Confession* 8: I…landed a stinger on his "potatoe trap" with my left "duke," drawing the "Claret" and "sending him to grass." **1866** *Nat. Police Gaz.* (Nov. 10) 3: The watch and chain…are in the "dukes" of…Robert White. *1874 Hotten *Slang Dict.* (ed. 5): *Dukes, or dooks,* the hands, originally modification of the rhyming slang, "Duke of Yorks," forks = fingers, hands…The word is in very common use among low folk. "Put up your dooks" is a kind invitation to fight. **1884** *Life* (June 12) 324: Put up your dukes! **1886** Nye *Remarks* 171: He pointed the gun…with his left and manipulated the gad with his right duke. **1887** DeVol *Gambler* 87: He did not use that duke any more. *1889 Barrère & Leland *Dict. Slang* I 338: *Dukes* or *dooks*…the hands, from the gypsy *dūk, dook,* which refers to palmistry. **1890** *United Service* (Mar.) 335: He could "put up his dukes" in first-rate style. **1891** Maitland *Slang Dict.* 100: "Put up your dukes" is an invitation to fight or spar. **1892** S. Crane *Maggie* 18: Den deh mug he squared off an' said he was fine as silk wid his dukes (See?) an he wanned a drink damn-quick. **1893** F.P. Dunne, in Schaaf *Dooley* 53: Th' ghost accused O'Connor's uncle iv pickin' up th' mit he thrun away an' demanded him to give it back because th' poor ghost couldn't cut his meat with only wan dook. **1901** A.H. Lewis *Croker* 61: I go ag'inst Quincy an' extends me duke. **1905** Riordon *Plunkitt* 26: The young Feller that's handy with his dukes. **1922** Tully *Emmett Lawler* 299: I want you to swear with your right duke on this book. **1926** Norwood *Other Side of Circus* 58: A shine with three fingers off his left duke joined out the other day, and they were calling him "Seven Spot" before he'd been on the job an hour. **1929** Booth *Stealing* 98: He was then working with a "mob" of pickpockets—"putting his duke down." **1930** Farrell *Grandeur* 213: When he sez put up your dooks…It's curtains. **1930** Conwell *Thief* 45: The third operation is to put the duke (hand) down and extract the poke (pocketbook). **1935** in Oliver *Blues Tradition* 153: If he hits with that left duke,/Tha's a kick from a Texas mule. **1949** Ellison *Tomboy* 36: He's supposed to be good with his dukes. **1971** Torres *Sting Like a Bee* 99: Clay…began taking punishment…for carrying his dukes too low. **1974** E. Thompson *Tattoo* 199: But you guys ever let *that* get out and we'll go to dukes. **1980** Lorenz *Guys Like Us* 150: When you come out,…make sure you got your dukes on top of your head. **1992** Majors & Billson *Cool Pose* 29: Keep up your dukes.
  b. *Gamb.* a hand of cards.
  1942–49 Goldin et al. *DAUL* 63: I…gave everyone a duzey…of a duke.
  c. *Und.* a method of swindling at cards.—constr. with *the.*
  1930 *Variety* (Jan. 8) 123: Some racketeers…ride trains to…"play the duke," which means getting an easy mark into a card game with a cold deck. The sucker himself deals the hand and has no chance to squawk. **1930** Conwell *Pro. Thief* 236: *Duke,* n.—A confidence game involving fraud at cards.
  d. *Boxing.* a fight decision.—usu. in phr. **get the duke.**
  1934 D. Runyon, in *Collier's* (Nov. 24) 8: Ledoux gets the duke by unanimous vote of the officials. **1936** Tully *Bruiser* 22: Even if I lose the duke I got forty percent of five hundred, ain't I? **1942** Algren *Morning* 223: I switched the whammy to the judges…'n then switched it on the ref 'n sure enough…Lefty got the duke. **1949** Cummings *Dict. Sports* 120: The winner of a [boxing match] "gets the duke" because the referee holds up the boxer's fist as a symbol of victory. **1949** in J. O'Hara *Sel. Letters* 225: I can't run the 100 in 10 or get the duke off Joe Louis, either. **1959** in Cannon *Nobody Asked* 148: They sang the blues as men alone knew them and how luck maimed them or the law tripped them or how they were hooked on junk or horses or dropped a duke to rum. **1972** in P. Heller *In This Corner* 177 [ref. to 1930's]: The last 3 rounds…he never got near me so they gave me the duke.

2. Esp. *Pris.* a prominent or consequential fellow; boss; (*also*) a tough or pugnacious fellow.—usu. constr. with prec. adj. [The appositeness of the early bracketed quots. is uncertain.]
  [*1698–99 "B.E." *Dict. Canting Crew:* *Rum-duke*…a jolly handsom

Man....*Rum-dukes*...the boldest or stoutest Fellows (lately)...Sent to remove and guard the Goods of...Bankrupts.] [**1785** Grose *Vulgar Tongue: Duke*, or *Rum Duke*. A queer unaccountable fellow.] **1939** in A. Banks *First-Person* 179: Even when some duke tells you about some job in a big office, you don't try for it. **1949** Monteleone *Crim. Slang* 76: *Duke*...The keeper of a jail; the warden of a prison; the first. **1954** Chessman *Cell 2455* 91 [ref. to *ca*1937]: There were those who wanted his job, who wanted to make a reputation as tough guys, bad dukes, at his expense. **1966** Braly *On Yard* 135: Two little punks and a duke, who could probably cause some trouble if he wasn't a stone nut. **1974** R. Carter *16th Round* 79 [ref. to early 1950's]: Each cottage had its own dukes, fellows who could outfight anybody else in their respective houses. **1976** Braly *False Starts* 45: A big duke from L.A. or Frisco, who knew he was bad and ready to get it on with anyone who pushed. *Ibid.* 52: The baddest duke on the hill had been caught. **1986** J.A. Friedman *Times Sq.* 25: "You'll be the first I'll tell, if I need help," she tells her dukes, who are eager to defend her. **1990** Vachss *Blossom* 108: The duke. The head man.

3. [perh. sugg. by DUCAT] a restaurant check.

1952 *Park East* (Sept.) 20: When it comes to pickin' up the duke, he's a fast man on the draw.

¶ In phrases:

¶ **blow the duke** *Und.* to bungle or botch something completely.

1966 H.S. Thompson *Hell's Angels* 36: Yet the editors make no claims to infallibility, and now and then they will blow the whole duke. **1970** Thackrey *Thief* 191: Yeah, that's so—though if I'd figured you were going to be such a horse's can...maybe I would have blown the duke for you last night, at that.

¶ **tip (one's) duke** *Gamb.* to tip (one's) hand.

1933 in D. Runyon *More Guys* 29: He tipped his duke to Robare.

duke *v.* **1.a.** to shake hands with in welcome or congratulation.

***1865** in *OEDAS* II 21: The foremost to "duke" me upon entering was Squib Dixon. **1895** Tisdale *Behind the Guns* 8: A fellow walked up with extended hand and said, "Duke me, kid!" From this gesture I knew it was a handshake and responded. **1908** in H.C. Fisher *A. Mutt* 48: Duke me, Sis, duke me. ***1911** O'Brien & Stephens *Australian Slang* 55: *Dook-me*/ Aust. thieves and push/ shake hands with me. **1911** Howard *Enemy to Society* 342: Duke me, Steve! You're a regular fella! **1913–15** Van Loan *Taking the Count* 309: Duke me, kid! **1929–31** Runyon *Guys & Dolls* 96: Duking the proud old Spanish nobleman...and giving Madame La Gimp's sister a good strong hug.

b. to hand something over to; give; pay; (*also*) to tell about.—also constr. with *on* or *to*.

1926 Maines & Grant *Wise-Crack Dict.* 8: *Duke me*—Hand it to me. **1943** in Botkin *Sidewalks* 267: You...duke him, that is, you hand him the article and say thanks. **1966** Braly *On Yard* 173: I figured when I got it done, I'd duke it on the gov'nor. **1969** Salerno & Tompkins *Crime Confed.* 154: I always duke the guy a few so he tells me if anyone's around. **1977** B. Davidson *Collura* 92: Collura would pleadingly ask the dealer if he'd "duke us a couple of nickel bags." **1984** *Miami Vice* (NBC-TV): I'm gonna duke you to a warehouse full of speed, man.

2. Esp. *Black E.* to fight with the fists; (see also 1966 quot.).—often in phr. **duke [it] out.**

1935 L. Hughes *Little Ham* 66 [ref. to *ca*1927]: *Tall Guy (Raising his fists)* I don't duel, I duke, and I'll choose you out. **1945** Himes *If He Hollers* 99: I was in Chicago, man,...learning how to duke. **1961** J.A. Williams *Night Song* 66: He could duke too, and Eagle smiled seeing again how the drummer had moved into the path of that waiting right. **1964** in Bruce *Essential Bruce* 48: The reason I had the hostility is that I had no balls for fighting, and *they* could duke. **1965** *Esquire* (July) 45: *Duking it out* in an alley or *going down* on a rival gang. **1966** in *Trans-action* IV (Apr. 1967) 5: Street people are known also by their activities—"duking" (fighting or at least looking tough). **1970** A. Young *Snakes* 34: I'll duke a few rounds with anybody here. **1973** Huggett *Body Count* 318: Watch and be ready to duke it out. **1986** *TV Guide* (Nov. 8) A-125: A street punk dukes it out with Doyle. **1987** *Frank's Place* (CBS-TV): Hey, you guys wanna duke out, duke out with gloves on.

3. [cf. DUKED OUT] to dress.

1981 Graziano & Corsel *Somebody Down Here* 21: So we start duking ourselves in fancy clothes.

duked out *adj.* dressed up. Also **duked up.**

1938 O'Hara *Hope of Heaven* 99: You're all duked out. What's it, a party? **1942** in J. O'Hara *Sel. Letters* 168: All duked out in their zoot suits. **1956** Ross *Hustlers* 16: I watched a big guy getting all duked up for the night. **1967–69** in *DARE.*

duke-in *n.* *Und.* an introduction; (*hence*) a person introduced or referred.

1942 *ATS* 445: *Duke-in*, an initial confidence talk. **1942–49** Goldin et al. *DAUL* 63: *Duke-in.* An introduction; a come-on. **1975** Wambaugh *Choirboys* 302: Baxter Slate...was given a duke-in name of Gaylord Bottomley. **1975** Harrell & Bishop *Orderly House* 72: I depended largely on referral business. Known in the trade as "Duke-ins"—why, I don't know—these friends of friends often turn out to be smart-ass vice cops.

duke in *v.* **1.** *Und.* to introduce for the purpose of participation in a group or undertaking; deal in.

1930 *Variety* (Jan. 8) 123: My sticks duked him in and he went for about 3C's on a set joint when he got hip to the squeeze. **1934** in Partridge *Dict. Und.* 214: When the criminal asks to be introduced to another person he says he wants to be duked in. **1964** in Bruce *Essential Bruce* 188: First of all, like, you gonna duke me in on the insurance bread? **1975** Wambaugh *Choirboys* 92: Yeah, but...Lieutenant Finque ain't trying to duke you into the Oriental community by using you as a part time community relations officer at Japanese luncheons. **1976** *Deadly Game* (ABC-TV movie): Duke in one of our people to Alec. Introduce him as a righteous criminal and we'll do the rest. **1986** *Miami Vice* (NBC-TV police series): That's where I duked myself in.

2. *Und.* to enter as a participant.

1976 *Deadly Game* (ABC-TV movie): We need $1000 to duke into a very special deal.

duke-out *n.* a brawl; altercation.

1975 *Atlantic* (Mar.) 48, in *BDNE3*: The last all-House duke-out...over ten years ago....there have been a fair number of fistfights in the capitol since. **1978** *Rolling Stone* (Feb. 23) 28: One of last summer's livelier duke-outs involved three of Bill Graham's security guards in various scuffles. **1984** *Post N.Y. Post Parody* 18: Reagan...blamed the nuke duke-out totally on the Soviet Union. **1986** Merkin *Zombie Jamboree* 260: Finally one night we had a big duke-out about...*Hogan's Heroes*. *a*1990 Westcott *Half a Klick* 94: The captain...challenged him to a duke-out.

duke out *v.* **1.** see s.v. DUKE, *v.*, 2.

2. *Boxing.* to knock out.

1977 *Nat. Lampoon* (Aug.) 45: We can't take a chance on the Kosher Butcher getting duked out...by a Costa Rican. *a*1986 in *NDAS.*

duke player *n.* *Und.* (see quot.).

1937 Reitman *Box-Car Bertha* 308: The...Crooked Gambler. The most common is the "duke player," the person who cheats at cards or checkers.

dukey var. DOOKIE.

dukie *n.* [perh. alter. DUKE 'hand'] (esp. among tramps and hobos) a handout of food; (*Circus.*) a box lunch; lunch.

1914 Jackson & Hellyer *Vocab.* 30: *Dukie*...A hand-out, or donation of cold victuals to a beggar. **1925** Mullins *Scholar Tramp* 14 [ref. to *ca*1912]: She may prepare a lunch and wrap it in an old newspaper or paper bag. Her parcel is known in Hoboland as a "lump," a "hand-out," a "poke-out," or a "dukee." **1926** Norwood *Other Side of Circus* 74: Here comes John bringing his "dukie" with him...That's circus slang for a lunch...Ollie Webb puts up box lunches. We call them "dukies."..."Most any elephant will grab a dukie of hay." **1936** Fellows & Freeman *Big Show* 259: Hundreds of boxes of food, called "dukies," are put up in the cook tent on Saturday night and distributed on the train. **1940** in D. Runyon *More Guys* 363: Sometimes I mooch a dookey at a kitchen door. **1961** Clausen *Season's Over* 64 [ref. to *a*1945]: "Dukey run"...was the expression for any trip longer than an overnight haul; dukeys were box lunches given out by the circus. **1972** in *DARE: Dukey*...a lunch box; a steel mill term.

dulcy *n.* [< Sp *dulce* 'sweet'] Esp. *S.W.* a female sweetheart.

1875 Sheppard *Love Afloat* 291: He was writing to his dulcy, doctor. **1897** in *DARE:* It [*sc.* a letter] may be from his "girl," as he calls it (his "*dulce*," it would be in the South). **1912** in *DA.* **1932, 1934** in *DARE.*

dullhead *n.* a dull or conventional person.

1971–73 Sheehy *Hustling* 179: I'm very nice, a dullhead.

dullsville *n.* [*dull* + -SVILLE] a place, situation, etc., that is extremely dull. Also *adj.*

1960 *N.Y. Times Mag.*, in *OED2:* He's from Dullsville. **1966** *Time*, in *OED2:* Johnson is square, folksy and dullsville, sounding...like dozens of boring politicians from the past. **1970** *U.S. News & W.R.* (Aug. 3) 17: When the lights went out in the office buildings and workers headed for their homes in the suburbs, downtown was truly Dullsville. **1973** "J. Godey" *Pelham* 95: But it turned out to be dullsville. **1974** Leggett,

Mead & Charvat *Prentice-Hall Handbook* 353: The movie was like dullsville. **1983** D. Young, in *N.Y. Post* (Sept. 5) 37: The Giants...were blanked from then on. It was Dullsville. **1985** *Daily Beacon* (Univ. Tenn.) (Nov. 27) 2: Haig slams "dullsville" 1984 election...Alexander Haig, former Secretary of State and presidential adviser, said the last presidential campaign was "dullsville."

du-ma *n.* [pidgin, < Vietnamese *đù* 'fuck' + *mâu* (bound form of *mè*) 'mother'] *Mil.* MOTHERFUCKER. [Quots. ref. to Vietnam War.]

1983 C. Rich *Advisors* 440: Du-ma—Vietnamese for motherfucker. [**1985** J.M.G. Brown *Rice Paddy Grunt* 122: The gook tells him, "*Du Mau, Du Mau*" (to fuck his mother, in Vietnamese).] **1985** "J. Cain" *You Die, Du-Ma!* (title). **1990** G.R. Clark *Wds. of Viet. War* 147: Du Ma...Colloquial Vietnamese phrase loosely translated as "motherfucker." GIs were quick to pick up the phrase.

dumb *adj.* [sugg. by SMART, *adj.*] (of a bomb or similar weapon) unguided; (*broadly*, of any equipment) lacking the capacity to process data.

1977 in *OED2*: The totally nonintelligent, or dumb, or basic terminal is one thing that can be defined nonsubjectively. **1983** M. Skinner *USAFE* 120: They're still interested in "dumb bombs." **1984** Doleman *Tools of War* 130: Conventional "dumb" bombs in Vietnam averaged a 420-foot circular area probability. *Ibid.* 157: Sensors and other electronic detectors were "dumb"—they only collected data without processing them or responding to them. **1986** in Safire *Lang. Maven* 267: For a brief period, bombs that were not smartened with homing devices were called *dumb bombs.* **1987** Zeybel *Gunship* 170 [ref. to Vietnam War]: Use of the terms "smart" and "dumb" was forbidden in reference to bombs [for public relations reasons]. **1987** G. Hall *Top Gun* 35: Either "smart" or iron "dumb" ordnance. **1991** Dunnigan & Bay *From Shield to Storm* 146: Iron "dumb bombs" dropped by coalition air forces. *Ibid.* 165: "Dumb" (unguided) bombs and rockets.

dumb-ass *n.* **1.** a dolt.—usu. considered vulgar.

1958 J. Davis *College Vocab.* 7: Dumb-ass—One who acts stupid. **1961** J. Jones *Thin Red Line* 389 [ref. to WWII]: I don't know what these dumbasses would do. **1966–67** W. Stevens *Gunner* 35 [ref. to WWII]: Clark's up front, you dumb ass. **1973** Herbert & Wooten *Soldier* 37: The rest of the dumbasses they made enlisted men. **1987** Univ. Tenn. prof., age *ca*65: Dumbass was in use in Albany, N.Y., by 1930 at the latest. **1992** L. Johnson *My Posse* 4: Everybody thinks I'm a dum ass.

2. stupidity.—constr. with *the.*—usu. considered vulgar.

1972 Jenkins *Semi-Tough* 10: I'm what a lot of you spooks might think of as a red neck with a terminal case of the dumb-ass. **1984** Univ. Tenn. student: He just woke up this morning with a bad case of the dumb-ass. **1988** T. Harris *Silence of Lambs* 37: You eat up with the dumb-ass, girl.

dumb-ass or **-assed** *adj.* stupid.—usu. considered vulgar.

1957 H. Simmons *Corner Boy* 198: You're nothing but a dumb-assed nigger. **1963–64** Kesey *Great Notion* 79: A dumb-ass thing, keeping a cow. **1967** J. Kramer *Instant Replay* 70: I got caught offside, a real dumb-ass play. **1967** Styron *Nat Turner* 30: Them other niggers didn't know. Either that or they were too dumb. Dumb-assed! Dumb! *Dumb!* **1973** Childress *Hero* 24: Everybody don't dig bein told how dumb-ass they actin. **1978** Schrader *Hardcore* 17: Rather work in a dumb-ass car wash. *a*1981 H.A. Applebaum *Royal Blue* 84: They kept asking him when he was going to stop smoking his "dumb-ass" cigars. **1989** *Booker* (Fox-TV): That dumb-ass juror wanted to change her vote.

dumbbell *n.* a stupid person; a blockhead.

[**1857** *Spirit of Times* (Dec. 19) 529: He...personated O'Smirk in the "Dumb Belle."] [**1898** Allen *Navy Blue* 124: The two brothers Whittaker, who were constantly together, were tagged "Dumb" and "Bell."] **1918** *N.Y. Eve. Jour.* (Aug. 18) 11: He's the last person in the world I wanted to see. Oh, what a dumbbell. **1918** in Hall & Niles *One Man's War* 306: Poor dumb-bell! **1919** *Camp Knox News* (July 26) 1: If the dumbell was a general he would be wearing star-fish on each shoulder. **1920** Weaver *In American* 53: I s'pose I was a dumb-bell. That's what Mame said. **1920–21** Witwer *Leather Pushers* 6: Shut up, you dumbbell! **1921** *Variety* (July 22) 7: My dumbell was flattered to death to think they had picked him out as a wise guy. **1923** Bellah *Sketchbook* 58: "Dumb-bell!" he hissed. **1924** Boyd, in *Points of Honor* 246: My wife's just had a baby, you dumbbell; it's a boy. **1927** Behrman *Second Man* 344: You're an awful dumb-bell, Monica. **1928** Nason *Sgt. Eadie* 184: We'll never get anywhere talking to these dumbbells. **1932** Binyon & Bolton *If I Had a Million* (film): Dumbbell! Shut up! **1938** Bezzerides *Long Haul* 174: All right, you big dumb-bell. **1949** Robbins *Dream Merchants* 147: What a dumbbell I am not to think of it before. **1982** R.M. Brown *So. Discomfort* 218: Adam was a dumbbell.

dumb bunny see s.v. BUNNY, *n.*, 1.

dumbbutt *n.* a stupid person. Also attrib.

[**1971** Giovanni *Gemini* 19 [ref. to 1950's]: You dumbbumbs!] **1973** *TULIPQ* (coll. B. K. Dumas): What term would you use for a naive person? [Ans.] Stupid, dumb-butt. **1973** W. Crawford *Gunship Cmndr.* 40: Go ahead, dumbutt, turn up the flame under that ulcer! **1984** Algeo *Stud Buds* 3: A rather stupid person...*dumb-butt.* **1987** Eyre *What Price Victory* (film): Pull your head out and try to learn somethin', dumbutt.

dumb cluck see s.v. CLUCK, *n.*

Dumb Dora *n.* a stupid or silly woman.

1922 in *DN* V 147: Dumbdora—a stupid girl. **1923** Wilstach *Stage Slang* 15: Dumb-Dora—See tomato. **1922–24** McIntyre *White Light Nights* 184: Hardened habitués of...the Tenderloin call them "Dumb Doras." **1925** *Collier's* (Feb. 14) 12: I can get $1,000 a week on the stage as a reputed beauty, a Dumb Dora. **1936** Levin *Old Bunch* 81: She was just a Dumb Dora. **1939** M. Levin *Citizens* 4: A dumb dora injected horse blood serum into the wrong rabbit. **1951** J. Reach *My Friend Irma* 29: A cartoon...about her and her dumb-Dora cracks. **1964** Faust *Steagle* 73: Dumb Dora the kids useta call me. **1972** N.Y.U. student: A *Dumb Dora* is a dummy.

dumb down *v.* to revise to appeal to persons of lesser intelligence.

1933 H.T. Webster, in *Forum* (Dec.) 372: I can cheer, too, for the Hollywood gag men in conference on a comedy which has been revealed as too subtle, when they determine they must dumb it down. That phrase saves time and wearying gestures. **1951** in S.J. Perelman *Don't Tread On Me* 119: The bulk of the changes was an effort to dumb the piece down for the *Redbook* reader. **1980** J. Michener, in *U.S. News & W.R.* (Feb. 4) 42: Education has taken several very backward steps in the last 20 years—for example, the so-called dumbing down of the textbooks. **1983** *Atlantic* (June) 29: People who...read only simplified—"dumbed down"—material. **1985** *Knoxville Jour.* (Mar. 12) 1 (headline): Are we "dumbing down" texts and minds? **1993** *New Yorker* (Nov. 8) 122: He dumbed down his style...abandoning the complicated, cursive...style...and returning to a squared-off, bluntly outlined manner.

dumbfuck *n.* a contemptibly stupid person.—usu. considered vulgar. Also attrib., adv.

1946–50 J. Jones *Here to Eternity* 531 [ref. to 1941]: Shut you dumb fuck Turniphead you. **1966** in IUFA *Folk Speech*: Denoting someone's stupidity. *Dumb fuck.* **1970–71** Rubinstein *City Police* 427: You know why that dumb-fuck sergeant has Smith drive him? **1973** *TULIPQ* (coll. B.K. Dumas): Dingbat; super dumbfuck. **1980** Conroy *Lords of Discipline* 150: I want you to rack that chin into your beady, ugly neck, dumbfuck. *a*1987 Bunch & Cole *Reckonings* 151: Of all the dumb-fuck things to do. **1989** Cáre *Viet. Spook Show* 22: Why'd you do something as dumbfuck crazy as that?

dumbguard *n.* *U.S. Mil. Acad.* a dolt.

1900 *Howitzer* (No. 1) 123: Now it came to pass in the days of Dumguard, the son of Duflicket, that great dissensions arose even in the Academy of Uncle Samuel. *ca*1918 in Fitzgerald *Notebooks* 275: Those dumguards. **1934** "J.M. Hall" *Anecdota* 162: I'm attending a dinner given by General Dumbguard.

dumbhead *n.* [cf. G *Dummkopf*] a simpleton.

1887 in *DA*. **1898** Westcott *D. Harum* 173: He was the biggest dumbhead I ever see. **1918** *N.Y. Eve. Jour.* (Aug. 13) 13: Only a dumb head like "Blubber" would ask such a question. **1919** *DN* V 61: *Dumb-head*, a dullard. "Miss D. put all the *dumb-heads* out of her class." **1925** Weaver *Coll. Poems* 115: You're such a dumb-head! **1928** Harlow *Sailor* 24: You little dumb-head! **1937** in Sagendorf *Popeye* 29: You dumbhead. **1938** E.S. Gardner, in Ruhm *Detective* 228: Of all the dumbhead plays you've made, that's the worst. **1965** C. Brown *Manchild* 170: They had an old, dumbhead waiter who was a real Tom. **1968** Kirkwood *Good Times/Bad Times* 176: "Dumb-head!" he said. **1988** *Wkly. World News* (May 31) 23: The 3 Stooges are NOT dumb-heads!

dumb Isaac *n.* a stupid man. Cf. SMART-ALECK.

1906 T.A. Dorgan, in *N.Y. Eve Jour.* (Feb. 17) 6: He had a line of bull that would make the book agent look like a dumb Isaac. **1915** T.A. Dorgan, in *N.Y. Eve. Jour.* (Aug. 2) 10: I'm a dumb Isaac if you say so. **1920** in De Beck *Google* 99: You dumb Isaac.

dumbjohn *n.* Orig. & Esp. *U.S. Mil. Acad.* DUCROT.

1882 "Dum John" *Autobituary* (title): The Autobituary of a West Pointer. Written at the request of George Washington, General Chewflicket [etc.]...by Captain Dum John. [**1900** *Howitzer* (No. 1)

119: *Ducrot, Du John, Dumflicket.*—Names applicable to things, as fourth classmen, etc.] [**1908** *Howitzer* 325: Ducrot, *n.* A generic term for plebes. Syn. Dumguard, Dujohn, etc.] **1911** *Howitzer* 225: *Dumjohn, n.* See *Ducrot.* **1930** in D.O. Smith *Cradle* 20: The hell you do, Mr. Dumbjohn. **1930** *Our Army* (Feb.) 21. **1934** Wohlforth *Tin Soldiers* 15: Well, Mister Dumbjohn…Who gave you permission to talk? **1935** *Our Army* (July) 7: Private Dumbjohn had took his C. C. pills. **1936** Mencken *Amer. Lang.* 573: [For *rookie*] the Regular Army…prefers *John* or *dumb John.* **1946–51** J. Jones *Eternity* ch. 9: We could play like back at the point, upper-classmen hazing the Dumb-johns. **1974** Stevens *More There I Was* 43: This is Cadet Dumbjohn. I've lost my headset…Landing instructions please. **1978** Ardery *Bomber Pilot* 29 [ref. to 1941]: I would never again…be a lousy dodo, or a dumbjohn, or a gadget.

dumb-nuts *n.* NUMB-NUTS.—usu. considered vulgar.
   1977 Coover *Public Burning* 167: Greenglass was just some dumb-nuts…kid. *a*1986 D. Tate *Bravo Burning* 3: He asked for and got…straightleg dumb-nuts infantry.

dumbo /ˈdʌmboʊ/ *n.* **1.a.** a dolt.
   1932 R. Fisher *Conjure-Man* 13: All right, dumbo…wouldn't that be a bright move? **1941** Walt Disney Prods. *Dumbo* (film): "Who cares about her precious little Jumbo?" "Jumbo? You mean—Dumbo!" **1950** C.W. Gordon *High School* 58: One member was the "dumbo" of our group. **1964** Thompson & Rice *Every Diamond* 38: "Knucklehead," "Dumbo," and "Creep" were his choice names. **1966** Elli *Riot* 81: This is the only place in the world the dumbo can earn a livin'. **1971** Curtis *Banjo* 160: I know these dumbos. **1978** Maggin *Superman* 118: You screaming dumbo, Kent. **1980** *Time* ad (WINS Radio) (Aug. 26): Law was always mumbo-jumbo. Made me feel like such a dumbo! Till I got *Time* on my side.
   b. a foolish mistake.
   1952 *Sat. Eve. Post* (Sept. 20) 40: If you think you've seen dumbos pulled on the highways, you haven't seen anything.
   2. [see 1949 Morison quot.] (*cap.*) *Mil. Av.* a multiengine search and rescue aircraft. Now *hist.*
   1945 Dos Passos *Tour* 38: If the sea was smooth enough, the Dumbos came down to pick up the survivors. If not, they kept their location spotted for the crash boats. **1945** Hamann *Air Words:* Dumbo. C-46 Commando in the Army; A PB4 Catalina in the Navy. **1945** in *AS* XXI 140: In Navy parlance, a "Dumbo" is any air-sea rescue plane. **1949** Quigley *Corsica* 148: He had felt let down to be set to work flying mathematical zigzags for a Dumbo. **1949** Morison *Naval Ops. in WWII* V 332: First cousin to the Black Cat was "Dumbo," the rescue PBY…These successful though incidental rescues led to the creation of a specially equipped PBY known throughout the Navy as "Dumbo" after Walt Disney's cartoon character, the flying elephant. The beginning of 1943 saw the first regularly assigned Dumbo. **1954** Crockett *Bastards* 16: The big clumsy Dumbos warming up to start their rescue search for figures bobbing in the drink. **1955** Scott *Look of Eagle* 113: The Dumbos were B-29s with drop gear such as power lifeboats, rafts, provisions, emergency radios, and visual signal paraphernalia. **1958** Craven & Cate *AAF in WWII* VII 124: Nicknamed "Dumbo"…the C-46 had but one decided advantage. **1962** Mahurin *Honest John* 164 [ref. to WWII]: It was a Dumbo, an aircraft especially designed for air-sea rescue. Although appearing to be a standard B-17, it carried a 40-foot lifeboat attached to the underside of the fuselage.

dumbo sub *n.* [sugg. by DUMBO, 2] *Navy.* a submarine available to rescue aviators downed at sea. Now *hist.*
   1961 Forbes *Goodbye to Some* 162 [ref. to WWII]: They tell us to try to raise that dumbo sub…and when I heard the talk I figured it might be her. *Ibid.* 163: The dumbo sub is looking for him.

dumbshit *n.* a blockhead; DUMBBELL.—usu. considered vulgar.
   1961 N. Ford *Black, Gray & Gold* 21: If you can talk, your neck's not in, Dumbshit! **1962** in *AS* (Oct. 1963) 170: A rather stupid student…*dumb shit.* **1968** Baker et al. *CUSS* 110: *Dumb shit.* A person without much social or academic ability. **1970** Calley & Sack *Lt. Calley* 122: Oh, dumb shit here. He blew it. **1971** *Playboy* (Aug.) 203: No, ya dumshit, it's the peace symbol. **1978** B. Johnson *What's Happenin'* 221: We wanna go west, dumbshit. **1984** Riggan *Free Fire* 119: Isn't that dumbshit going to slow down? **1985** B.E. Ellis *Less Than Zero* 193: You fucking dumb-shits. **1986–91** Hamper *Rivethead* 42: The dumbshit's on some crazy drug trip.

dumbshit *adj.* stupid.—usu. considered vulgar.
   1967 in H. Ellison *Dangerous Visions* I 80: Would I be dumbshit enough to tell you? **1972** T.C. Bambara *Gorilla* 88: Some old dumb shit foolishness. **1972** *Playboy* (Sept.) 150: It was a dumb-shit move…When

I came back ten minutes later, everything was gone. **1974** U. Wisc. student: He's pretty dumbshit. **1979** Gram *Blvd. Nights* 65: Is that dumb-shit or what? **1979** Hiler *Monkey Mt.* 145: How come I gotta go to this dumb-shit meeting? *a*1984 in Terry *Bloods* 164: We did a lot of dumb-shit things over there. **1984** L. Heinemann, in *TriQuarterly* (Spring) 382: The funny, dumb-shit look that came over the guy's face. **1991** Marcinko & Weisman *Rogue Warrior* 208: That kind of dumb-shit thinking.

dumbsmack *n.* a dolt.
   1942 *ATS* 367: Terms of disparagement…*dumb smack.* **1977** Lyon *Tenderness* 17 [ref. to 1950's]: Wipe that smile off your face, Dumb Smack!

dumbsock *n.* a dolt.
   1930 *AS* V (Feb.) 238: *Dumb sock:* a person who is not very bright. "That farmer is a dumb sock." **1929–31** Farrell *Young Lonigan* 142: He's the biggest dumbsock I ever saw. **1935** *AS* X 52: Epithets disparaging mentality: The dumb sok [*sic*]. **1950, 1964** in *DARE.*

dumbsquat *n.* a dolt.
   1980 Conroy *Lords of Discipline* 131: Pop off, dumb squat.

dumb up *v.* DUMB DOWN.
   1928 Wilstach *Motion Picture Sl.* (unp.): Dumb it up!…Every thinker from Pythagoras to Nietzsche is rewritten in subway prose.

dumbwad *n. Stu.* a blockhead.
   1978 *UTSQ:* (Idiot)…*dumbwad.* **1980** Conroy *Lords of Discipline* 152: Clean your loathsome bodies, dumbwads.

dumbwaiter count *n. Boxing.* an unfair referee's count that takes longer than ten seconds.
   1921 J. Conway, in *Variety* (Nov. 18) 29: The ref. gave Tomato the dumbwaiter count that all the hometowners get when their battlin in their own back yard.

dumbwit *n.* DIMWIT.
   1933 in Goodstone *Pulps* 105: Any dumbwit you drag to the altar will be going for a cleaning instead of a honeymoon.

dum-dum *n.* [sugg. by *dumb*] **1.** simpleton.
   1937 Steinbeck *Mice & Men* 86: A nigger an' a dum-dum and a lousy ol' sheep. **1942** *Randolph Field* 56: He…may be the owner of a Phi Beta Kappa key…but to the processors he is just another "dum-dum." **1961** Pirosh & Carr *Hell Is for Heroes* (film): Look, dumdum. Up here, your gun is your life. *a*1967 Bombeck *Wit's End* 44: Face it, Luvie, you're a dum dum. **1969** *Current Slang* I & II 30: *Dum dum,…n.* One lacking intellectual prowess.—Air Force Academy cadets. **1973** Haring *Stranger* 81: That's the point, dumdum. **1983** Stapleton *30 Yrs.* 164: You see all the dum-dums running around with degrees nowadays.
   2. a deaf mute.
   1943 Guthrie *Glory* 284: What's wrong? Buncha dam dumb-dumbs? Can't none of you men say nothin'? **1969** L. Sanders *Anderson Tapes* 133: Two are drivers, one of them a dumdum.

dumfoozled *adj.* quite dumbfounded.
   1843 [W.T. Thompson] *Scenes in Ga.* 172: I…[was] completely dum-foozled. *ca*1845 in *DAE.* **1888** in *DARE.*

dummied up *adj. Esp. Und.* silent, esp. when under pressure to talk.
   1943 Chandler *High Window* 389: How long you expect to stay dum-mied up? **1966** Braly *On Yard* 39: Keep dummied up until you learn your way around.

dummo *n.* DUMBO, 1.
   1971 D. Smith *Engine Co.* 8: I don't mean it that way, dummo, I mean about the investigation.

dummox *n.* [blend of *dumb* + *lummox*] an oaf; lout.
   1958 S.H. Adams *Tenderloin* 18 [ref. to 1890's]: Can you see that big dummox's manager let him come into court and be questioned about getting knocked cold by a kid? **1976** Haseltine & Yaw *Woman Doctor* 99: I didn't take you for a dummox.

dummy *n.* [*dumb* + *-ie*; orig. in Scots dial.] **1.a.** a mute person, esp. a deaf mute.—usu. (now esp.) used derisively.
   ***1598** in *OED:* Dummie canna lie. ***1681** in *OED:* Like to dumbies making signs. ***1823** in *OED:* The wise men of Egypt were secret as dummies. **1862** Duganne *King's Man* 57: Is dat yar dummy Mauss' Bob's darter? **1912** Mathewson *Pitching* 92: Many New York fans will remember "Dummy" Taylor, the deaf and dumb pitcher of the Giants.
   b. a representation of a human figure on which clothes may be designed, modeled, or displayed; mannequin. Now *S.E.*

*a1845 in *OED*: She was deaf as any tradesman's dummy. *1850 in *OED*: A dark green suit...off the dummy at the door.

c. *Theat.* a non-speaking role in a theatrical production.

1846 Durivage & Burnham *Stray Subjects* 148: The theatre-going man will...believe, if he be sufficiently credulous, that all the characters down to the "dummies," are supported by gentlemen from the Royal Theatres of London.

2. a blockhead; fool. Now *colloq.*

*1796 in *OED*: Those who take you for a dummy will be out of their reckoning. *1812 in Vaux *Memoirs* 238: *Dummy*...a silly, half-witted person. **1833** A. Greene *Duckworth* I 93: He's not such a simpleton as that comes to—he's not a mere dummy. **1844** "F." *Working a Passage* 95 [ref. to 1832]: "Don't fall, dummy," the mate would call out to him when he was aloft, in a sneering voice. **1865** in "M. Twain" *Sks. & Tales* 61: So they put it up that the simple old dummy was to keep his eye on the panorama after that. **1884** "M. Twain" *Huck. Finn* 193: So him and the new dummy started off. **1903** Ade *Into Society* 144: You act like a Dummy. *Ibid.* 149: As a rule, the pink-faced Collegian is...more or less of a Dummy on any Topic except Himself. **1938** Haines *Tension* 143: Listen, dummy; this thing is worth dough. **1950** Van Ronkel, Heinlein & O'Hanlon *Destination Moon* (film): You're all gonna look like a bunch of dummies. **1951–52** Frank *Hold Back Night* 46: Mao knows that. He's no dummy. **1958** Lasky & Berenice *Buccaneer* (film): Drop that loot and jump, you blasted dummy!

3. *Und.* a pocketbook or wallet. [*F & H* and *OED* (quoting *F & H*) adduce a spurious reference to Grose *Dict. Vulgar Tongue* (1785); the word is not found there.]

1798 in Greene *Secret Band* 113: The word *coney* means Counterfeit paper money...[The word] *dumby* [means] Pocket-book, purse, &c. *1811 *Lexicon Balatron*: Dummee. A pocket book. A dummee hunter. A pickpocket...Frisk the dummee of the screens; take all the bank notes out of the pocket book. *1812 in Vaux *Memoirs* 238: *Dummy*: a pocketbook; a silly half-witted person. *1834 Ainsworth *Rookwood* 187: Then out with the dummy...and off with the bit,.../Oh! the game of high toby for ever! **1845** *Nat. Police Gaz.* (Oct. 16) 52: *Frisking a dummy*...stealing a pocket-book. **1848** Judson *Mysteries* 34: As daring a cove as ever...touched a dummy. *Ibid.* 527: "*Dummy*." A pocketbook. **1849** "N. Buntline" *B'hoys of N.Y.* 33: By dam, I no touch his dummy. **1866** *Nat. Police Gaz.* (Nov. 3) 2: Poll...went through him for his "dummy." **1871** Banka *Prison Life* 492: Pocket Book,...Leather or *Dummy*.

4. dumbwaiter.

1864 in *OED*: *Dummy*...A dumb-waiter.

5. the penis.—used esp. in var. phrs. ref. to masturbation.

*ca1866 *Romance of Lust* 127: Patting it with her hand, she said—"Ah! my dear little dummy, I am glad to see you are of my opinion." *a1890–91 *F & H* II 381: *To feed the dummy*...(venery).—To have connection. **1916–22** Cary *Sexual Vocab.* III s.v. *masturbation*: Flogging one's dummy. Flogging the pup. Flubbing the dummy. **1930** Farrell *Calico Shoes* 151: So he goes along whipping the dummy, until he went plumb crazy. **1935** J. Conroy *World to Win* 40: If you don't quit floggin' yer dummy, the undertaker's gonna have a job. **1940** Farrell *Father & Son* 115: Haven't you ever heard talk about whipping the dummy? *Ibid.* 563: He better quit flogging the dummy. **1947–51** Motley *We Fished* 246: So you flogged your dummy. Is that anything to be ashamed of? **1952** Bellow *Augie March* 86: So take my advice and don't play with your dummy. **1965** Trimble *Sex Words* 24: *Beat the Dummy*...Masturbation of the male Member. **1971** Cole *Rook* 178: Brother bores, we share the whores and flog our dummies black and blue. **1972** *Anthro. Linguistics* (Mar.) 99: *Beating The Dummy* (n.): Same as Beating The Meat. **1975** T. Berger *Sneaky People* 230: The head of his little dummy was chafed. **1988** Southeastern La. Univ. prof., age 41: To *cuff the dummy* means to masturbate. I heard that in the mid-'70's from a guy from New Jersey.

6.a. *R.R.* (see quots.).

1864 in *OED*: *Dummy*...A locomotive with condensing engines, and, hence, without the noise of escaping steam. **1961** Kalisher *R. R. Men* 54: Back in them days...they had them cars didn't have air brakes on 'em. Dummies we call 'em. Well, five of 'em was the most you was allowed to have on your train. **1977** R. Adams *Lang. Railroader* 50: *Dummy*...a type of switch engine on which the boiler and running gear are housed.

b. a streetcar; (*also*) a railway car.

1865 J. Pike *Scout and Ranger* 337: We went to Chattanooga by railroad, riding on the General's "dummy" car. **1878–81** W.G. Marshall *Through Amer.* 264: The dummy cable car...[is] peculiar to the Golden City. **1881** Duffus-Hardy *Cities & Prairie Lands* 83: Bleak windy space yawned behind [our passenger car] and the car yclept "the Dummy!"

which was to carry us to Omaha. **1885** in N. Cohen *Long Steel Rail* 486: Riding on the dummy, glad to get a seat. **1946** Atherton *My S.F.* 231: Men and women standing precariously on the running boards of the "dummies." **1977** R. Adams *Lang. Railroader* 50: *Dummy*...A car running on its own power.

c. *R.R.* a short branch line or short train, as one that transports loggers or other work crews.

1894 in *DARE*. **1905** *DN* III 78: *Dummy*, *n.* Short branch railway...Rare. **1908** *DN* III 308: *Dummy*...A small-sized locomotive engine; also the train pulled by such an engine. "Are you going to Opelika on the *dummy*?" **1912** in Truman *Dear Bess* 98: The dummy that brought me here was exactly on the tick but it ran so fast I didn't get much sleep. **1940** *R.R. Mag.* (Apr.) 43: *Dummy*—Employees' train. **1948** McIlwaine *Memphis* 19: Some folks say de Dummy don' run.../ An' she rolled into Memphis at de settin' of the sun. *Ibid.* 252 [ref. to ca1910]: After breakfast the flatheads piled on the cars of the log train on the spur railroad ("dummy line") and rode deep into the woods...to work. **1966–68** in *DARE*.

7. *Hobo.* bread. Cf. TOMMY.

1897 in J. London *Reports* 320: *Punk* or *dummy*, bread. *a1909 Tillotson *Detective* 91: *Dummy*—Bread. *1909 Ware *Passing Eng.* **1914** Jackson & Hellyer *Vocab.* 30: *Dummy*, Noun. Current amongst yeggmen, hobos and prison habitués. Bread. **1927** *AS* (June) 389: Bread is also called *dummy*. **1977** Caron *Go-Boy* 109: One dry piece of toast with a small pat of margarine, three slices of homemade dummy, and a scoop of C.N.R. strawberries.

8. a dumdum bullet.

1986 Former SP4, U.S. Army, age 35: Real assassins like to fire dummies.

¶ In phrases:

¶ **catch a dummy** *Pris.* to be silent.

1970 M. Thomas *Total Beast* 69: "Knock it off in here!" "Dummy up!" "Catch a dummy!"

¶ **chuck a dummy** *Hobo.* to feign convulsions or a fainting fit in order to elicit sympathy. Cf. DUMMY-CHUCKER.

*1885 Davitt *Pris. Diary* ch. xii [I saw a fellow prisoner] fall upon his back, and go through the most horrible writhings I had ever witnessed. His eyes appeared as if bursting from their sockets, blood and foam issued from his mouth, while other prisoners could scarcely hold his arms...What we call "chucking a dummy," or..."counterfeiting a fit." *1889 Barrère & Leland *Dict. Slang* I 251: *Chuck the dummy*, to (thieves), to feign an epileptic attack or a fit. **1906** *McClure's Mag.* (Mar.) 486: You chuck a dummy (*i.e.*, feign epilepsy or unconsciousness) like a hospital grafter. *1909 Ware *Passing English* 75: I chucked a dummy this mornin', an' 'ad to be brought to with o-der-wee! **1920** O'Brien *Best Stories 1920* 201: He's chuckin' a dummy...He t'rows phony fits. **1926** *AS* I (Sept.) 650: *Dummy, chuck a*: To feign a fainting fit in order to get sympathy. **1930** "D. Stiff" *Milk & Honey* 202: *Chuck a dummy*—To pretend a fainting fit.

¶ **on the dummy** *Pris.* DUMMIED UP.

1967 [Beck] *Pimp* 51: That screw was making the rounds again, so the repeater got on the "dummy."

dummy-chucker *n.* a beggar who feigns muteness or fainting. Cf. *chuck a dummy* s.v. DUMMY, *n.*

1911 *Hampton's Mag.* (Oct.) 432: Drinking-places where pocket-slashers and till-tappers and dummy-chuckers and dips forgot their more arduous hours. **1912** Stringer *Shadow* 53: A police surgeon hit on the idea of etherizing an obdurate "dummy chucker" to determine if the prisoner could talk or not. **1922–24** McIntyre *White Light* 17: "Dummy chuckers" are no longer throwing their fake fits in front of Beefsteak John's. **1934** Kromer *Waiting* 93: One more dummy-chucker. **1944** C.B. Davis *Leo McGuire* 117: They're no better than dummy-chuckers or moll-buzzers pulling their cheap little sympathy gags on women.

dummy up *v.* **1.** (among beggars) to feign being a deaf mute.

1925–26 J. Black *You Can't Win* 69: I was dummyin' up, see? Imitatin' a deaf an' dumb man.

2.a. Orig. *Und.* to hold one's tongue; shut up. Also **dummy**.

1925–26 J. Black *You Can't Win* 282: Red...dummies up on the natives an' in a couple of days they let him go. **1927–28** Tasker *Grimhaven* 41: The biggest thing I learned in all that time was—to dummy up. It's murder just to breathe to anybody that your thinking about [escape]. **1929** in Hammett *Knockover* 37: "This a swell time to be dummying up," she spit at him. **1936** Duncan *Over the Wall* 233: Dummy up, you. I'll tell you when to open your damned trap. **1937** Johnston *Prison Life* 33: He better dummy if he don't want somethin' bounced on his bean.

1941 Horman *Buck Privates* (film): Don't you recruits dummy up on me! **1948** Cozzens *Guard* 455: Oh, dummy up, Jones! **1956** Chamales *Never So Few* 238: She ain't dead. She's dummying up. **1961** Braly *Felony Tank* 21: You better dummy on *anything* you hear in this cell. **1971** *All in the Family* (CBS-TV): Dummy up, will ya? Dummy up!

b. to keep (something) secret.

1966 Elli *Riot* 160: It's up to you to dummy 'em up. **1979** Charyn *7th Babe* 56: They can't hide a signal from you, Scarborough…They can dummy things up for a while. It won't do them any good.

3. to concoct fraudulently.—used trans.

1968 C. Victor *Sky Burned* 32: They dummy up a realistic background for them. **1984** P.J. Buchanan, in *N.Y. Post* (Aug. 23) 39: A perhaps bogus transaction [which was] dummied up to hoodwink the Federal Election Commission.

dump[1] *n.* [prob. back-formation fr. *dumpy*] **1.** a small coin of little value.

[*1785 Grose *Vulgar Tongue*: Dumps are…small pieces of lead, cast by schoolboys in the shape of money.] *1821 in *OED*: Dollars and Dumps that are not Silver. *1827 in *ibid.*: My dumps are made of more than lead. **1868** *Overland Mo.* (July) 81: I had given him a quarter of a dollar by mistake for a copper "dump" or two-cent piece. *Ibid.* 82: Usually each of us gave him a "dump."

2. a fat or dumpy person.

*1840 in *OED*: Her dump of a daughter. *1867 in *ibid.*: A puffy, thickset, vulgar little dump of an old man. *1887 in *ibid.* **1968** Baker et al. *CUSS*: Dump…a fat or ugly girl.

dump[2] *n.* **1.** *Restaurant.* an egg.

1885 *Puck* (Mar. 11) 19: Mr. Boru has no equal in his noble profession [waiter] and his "Wan!" "Two doomps wid hard on the side!" and "Coffee in the dark!" are familiar as household words in the ears of our best citizens.

2.a. a low lodging-house or cheap business establishment; (now *usu.*) any house or place that is dirty, shabby, or disreputable.

1899 "J. Flynt" *Tramping* 393: Dump: a lodging-house or restaurant; synonymous with "hang-out." **1904** Ade *True Bills* 109: My Children…tell me every Day…how to back over the Dump. **1905** *Nat. Police Gaz.* (Dec. 9) 9: In A Bowery "Dump"…Where the Mixed-Alers Meet. **1906** H. Green *Boarding House* 59: Pugnose…conducted a "dump" within…Chinatown. **1908** *Hampton's Mag.* (Oct.) 462: It is played and sung in the cheap dance halls, and beer gardens, and all such places, known technically as "dumps." **1910** Roe *Panders* 128: They told him over at the "dump" that these girls were dope fiends. **1911** A.H. Lewis *Apaches of N.Y.* 21: W'en I'm bounced out of a dump like this, the bouncin'll come off in th' smoke. **1911–12** Ade *Knocking the Neighbors* 116: In a sequestered Dump lived two Urchins. **1912** *Hampton's Mag.* (Jan.) 846: I find myself in a dump the size of a hat. **1914** Spencer *Jailer* 138: Prison is heaven compared to what this dump is. **1915** O'Brien *Best Stories of 1915* 100: Come on; let's get out of this dump. **1917** *Forum* (Dec.) 686: Suicide Annie's gang swore they wuz goin' t' clean out th' dump. **1919** Janis *Big Show* 48: Such a dump. Even the officers still sleeping in tents. **1924** P. Marks *Plastic Age* 10: Say, I'll tell you how we'll fix this dump. **1936** "E. Queen" *Halfway House* 22: Who owns this dump? **1936** H. Gray *Arf* (unp.): I'm sick o' livin' in dumps. **1964** R. Kendall *Black School* 24: This dump is better than some dumps cause it got much nicer things in it. **1985** Wells *444 Days* 288: The room they put us in was a dump. I mean, a real mess. Absolutely filthy. **1991** Sachar *Let Lady Teach* 24: I hear…[the school is] a good-for-nothing dump.

b. *Specif.* (*Und.*) a prison.

1902 Hapgood *Thief* 118 [ref. to *ca*1890]: I am determined to make my elegant, (escape) come what will. Do you know the weak spots of this dump? **1904** *Life in Sing Sing* 247: Dump.—A prison. **1908** Kelley *Oregon Pen.* 71: The "frame-up" is a prisoner who tries to get his work in by playing a job.…The officers know he will…boost the dump and do any lying they want him to. **1912** Berkman *Prison* 164 [ref. to 1893]: Columbus is a pretty tough dump. *Ibid.* 172: Man alive, the dump's chuckful of punks. **1912** Lowrie *Prison* 58: He's the oldest dumnie in the dump. **1914** London *Jacket* 69: Unless, maybe, it will be on us for sticking round this old dump when we could get away that easy. **1935** D.W. Maurer, in *AS* (Feb.) 15: Dump. A penitentiary. Giving way to *big house, stir*.

c. a place of business or residence irrespective of quality or state of repair; place.

1908 in H.C. Fisher *A. Mutt* 29: Ha! There's the dump. I shall…make the pinch alone. **1914** Jackson & Hellyer *Vocab.* 30: Dump…an estab-

lishment of any kind. **1914** in C.M. Russell *Paper Talk* 107: This was the piece maker hired by the owner of the dump to quiet the noisy ones. **1915** Braley *Songs of Workaday World* 77: Out av that dump came the clan, Smilin' as whin they came in. **1919** in De Beck *Barney Google* 22: Gosh—who couldn't sing if they lived in a swell dump like this? **1920** *Variety* (Sept. 3) 5: Hotel Plaza…It's a great dump. **1920** in O'Brien *Best Stories 1920* 203: His eyes wandered around the room. "*Some dump," he stated. **1922** S. Lewis *Babbitt* 156: Well, by golly!…You got to go some to beat this dump! **1923** McAlmon *Companion Volume* 250: It's a pretty good dump on the third floor of the boarding house. **1923** in Kornbluh *Rebel Voices* 90: [Heaven] was a funny lookin' dump. **1925–26** J. Black *You Can't Win* 138: The guns…are probably stolen from some pig-iron dump (hardware store). **1929** Burnett *Iron Man* 284: The estates of the rich began to appear…"Some day I'm gonna have me a dump like that." **1929** Hammett *Falcon* 16: Turn the dump upside down if you want. I won't squawk—if you've got a search-warrant. **1932** Berg *Prison Doctor* 211: Shows and swell dumps to eat in, night clubs—you know, the works. **1936** Gaddis *Courtesan* 95: Swell duds, swell dumps to live in, a bank full of money to spend. **1984** Kagan & Summers *Mute Evidence* 458: Not many other schools can afford the expertise we've got in this dump…We have the bucks. **1993** *New Yorker* (Oct. 6) 218: Two righteous cops…who act as if they owned the dump.

3. *Und.* (see quots.).

1904 *Life in Sing Sing* 247: Dump…railroad transfer or terminals. **1942–49** Goldin et al. *DAUL* 64: Dump…A railroad or subway station, or any place where crowds leave a common carrier.

4. an act or instance of ejection, abandonment, or dismissal.—constr. with *the*.

1907 *American Mag.* (Sept.) 580: What siding's that? We nearly got the dump.

5.a. an act of defecation.—constr. with *take a*.

1942 *ATS* 152: Defecation.—*n.*…call of nature, crap, dump. *Ibid.* 153: Defecate…take a crap, -a dump, &c. **1958** Frankel *Band of Bros.* 6 [ref. to 1950]: As good a marine as ever took a dump behind a pair of boondockers. **1959** Groninger *Run from Mtn.* 10: The day the war ended, I took a big dump. **1962** T. Berger *Reinhart* 402: I had been reading while taking a dump during my lunch ar. **1971** Flanagan *Maggot* 49: I want that head so sanitary and sparkling that my own grandmother…would be proud to go in there and take a dump. **1972** Jenkins *Semi-Tough* 7: Instead of going down the hall to the toilet T.J. had a habit of taking a dump in his closet. **1978** Lyle & Golenbock *Bronx Zoo* 83: The damn mule…would always take a dump right in front of our bullpen.

b. feces.

1972 Jenkins *Semi-Tough* 7: A man who can live with a mad dog and a closet load of dump.

6. *Sports.* a thrown contest; (*specif.*, *Boxing.*) a feigned knockout.

1951 *Time* (Mar. 4) 50: "Dumps" and fixes. **1955** Graziano & Barber *Somebody Up There* 269: So get in there tonight and take a dump, go in the tank. **1967** in J. Flaherty *Chez Joey* 129: Those [players] are so hungry they're easy pickings for any sharpie who waves a couple of hundred under their noses for a dump. **1974** *Everett* (Wash.) *Herald* (Nov. 6) 12C: "It was a dump—it had to be a dump."…"Foreman threw it, he didn't try." **1981** Brenner & Nagler *Only the Ring* 28.

7. *Hosp.* (see quot.).

1976 Haseltine & Yaw *Woman Doctor* 90: "Dumps" were people disabled by age, disease, or injury whose families could not or would not care for them anymore and who had nowhere else to go but the wards.

dump *v.* **1.a.** to knock to the ground; knock down; (*also*) to bring down with a bullet; kill or injure by shooting.

1883 Sowell *Rangers and Pioneers* 115: Once more he hastily primed his gun, and before the Indian could get to cover, "dumped his carcass" with a large rifle ball in the back. [**1894** *Harper's* (Oct.) 696: I'm willin' to tear de clo'se off his back if youse fellers'll jump in an' t'ump him.] [**1895** Townsend *Fadden* 197: I says he lies, an' he tries to tump me an'—.] **1942** *Americans vs. Germans* 94 [ref. to 1918]: I saw them dump a couple of Dutchmen, but most of the time I couldn't even see what they were shooting at. **1948** Chaplin *Wobbly* 42 [ref. to *ca*1897]: Gang warfare broke out occasionally. To be caught alone at such times meant anything from a "dumping" to a volley of stones or a peppering with pellets from slingshot and air rifle. *Ibid.* 43: On more than one occasion we were dumped and our papers destroyed. **1955** Graziano & Barber *Somebody Up There* 270: Who…brought her here to see me dumped? **1957** Murtagh & Harris *First Stone* 304: Dump (prison slang) to knock down. **1961** *WNID3*: Dumped their attackers, who scrambled to their feet and fled. **1962** Perry *Young Man* 93: Aw, knock it off or I'll dump you! **1963** J. Ross *Dead Are Mine* 58: Blair, there's a pick lying around the corner of the house. Pick it up on your way around. If I get dumped, knock a hole in the back of the house with it. **1987** *RHD2*: The champion was dumped twice but won the fight.

b. *Football.* to tackle (a quarterback) before he can throw a pass; sack.

1970 *Time* (Nov. 19) 140: He who would describe a quarterback caught behind the line of scrimmage as having been "dumped" rather than "sacked" reveals his status as a postulant before the mysteries. **1976** *Webster's Sports Dict.* 128. **1982** Considine *Lang. Sports* 137.

2.a. to abandon, discard, get rid of, dismiss, jilt, etc.

1897 Hamblen *General Mgr.* 79: That's better than to start in somewhere bran new and git dumped agin, ain't it? **1898–1900** Cullen *Chances* 13: I knew that my two pals hadn't dumped me, because hadn't I played $2000 of their money? **1899–1900** Cullen *Tales* 344: He didn't know that he had any cause for dumping you. **1901** S.E. Griggs *Overshadowed* 64: That blue-veined crowd dumped me. *1919* *Athenaeum* (Aug. 15) 759: To "dump" a thing that is a nuisance to carry means to get rid of it. **1936** Miller *Battling Bellhop* (film): You're crazy to dump him after taking him this far. **1942** *ATS* 338: Jilt...*dump.* **1987–91** D. Gaines *Teenage Wasteland* 68: His girlfriend dumped him last year.

b. to leave (a place).

1969 B. Beckham *Main Mother* 120: We dump this place for the Apple.

c. to overthrow or ruin.

1975 V.B. Miller *Deadly Game* 11: That was the only way we were going to dump the joy-boys who were dealing the big dope.

3.a. to administer a beating to.

1934 in Partridge *Dict. Und.* 216. **1935** Pollock *Und. Speaks: Dumped*, compelled to talk by police from the effects of a brutal beating (3rd degree). *Dumping*, administering a brutal beating. **1943** in *AS* XIX (1944) 108: To dump...means to beat the Jesus out of. **1946** in M. Crane *Roosevelt* 312: The longshoremen specialized in finding lone strikers and, in the waterfront term for beating a man up, "dumping" them. **1947** Boyer *Dark Ship* 153: When they speak of being assaulted, they say they were "dumped." **1953** Paley *Rumble* 14: It was too early to dump a squarehead. **1957** Murtagh & Harris *First Stone* 183: You got no idea how many tricks want to dump you. Sometimes they do it so hard you land in the hospital...Tricks pay a hundred dollars to dump girls. **1971** Sorrentino *Up from Never* 77: Hey, Rocky, I hoid ya dumped four guys and were in the Yout' House. **1977** Caron *Go-Boy* 205: Punchy was roaring like a tiger and bragging that he was going to dump me first chance he got. **1984** D. Smith *Steely Blue* 52: Don't cause no trouble, Jack,...because me and Joey can dump you together.

b. *Und.* to murder.

1942 *ATS* 135: Kill; murder...*dump.* **1973** W. Crawford *Stryker* 11: You call dumping a teen-age girl OK? **1976** Hayden *Voyage* 416: You ever dumped a man? **1977** *L.A. Times* (July 28) III 1: I was told I was gonna get dumped (killed) or stabbed.

4. *Sports.* to defeat.

1942 *ATS* 634. **1954** Schulberg *Waterfront* (film): I thought you were gonna take him that night, but he really dumped you. **1984** *N.Y. Post* (Aug. 13) 29: Cubbies dump Expos to stay 4½ games up.

5. *Av.* to lower (flaps or landing gear).

1946 G.C. Hall, Jr. *1000 Destroyed* 290: Red Dog dumped his flaps 20° to brake his speed. **1950–53** W. Grove *Down* 216: Cole dumped the flaps. **1966–67** Harvey *Air War* 37: Clear the trees by dumping full flaps on the C-123. **1985** Boyne & Thompson *Wild Blue* 104: I dumped the gear and nothing happened.

6.a. to defecate.

[**1929–31** Farrell *Young Lonigan* 139: Fire, fire, false alarm,/Baby da-dumped in papa's arm.] **1958** T. Berger *Crazy in Berlin* 187: I was dumping in my pants for fear. **1968** Baker et al. *CUSS* 111: *Dump* (verb)...To defecate. **1970** Landy *Underground Dict.* 72: *Dump*...Have a bowel movement; shit. **1976–77** C. McFadden *Serial* 22: A gull had dumped on her shrimp Louie.

b. to vomit.

1953 Freeman *Gobi* (film): Dump it over the side. **1968–70** *Current Slang* III & IV 42: *Dump*, v. To vomit under the influence of a drug. **1970** Landy *Underground Dict.* 72: *Dump v.*...Vomit.

7. *Sports.* to throw a match; lose deliberately. Also trans.

1951 *N.Y. Times* (Jan. 21) IV 2 E: A bribed player...can "dump" (throw) a game for gamblers without having his team lose. **1951** in *DAS*: Players accepting bribes to "dump" games. **1966** Neugeboren *Big Man* 41: I didn't have to play bad to dump, see? **1972** in J. Flaherty *Chez Joey* 179: A radical sportswriter who is going to smear you for dumping the Patriots game. **1981** Brenner & Nagler *Only the Ring* 128:

He dumped to Blackjack Billy Fox in the old Garden. **1981** *N.Y. Post* (Aug. 15) 42: At least seven Chicago White Sox players have said...that if they needed to lose a key series with Oakland in order to make the...Playoffs, they would dump the games. **1982** D. Young in *N.Y. Post* (Aug. 17) 60: The Black Sox had dumped the 1919 World Series. **1984** *N.Y. Post* (Aug. 9) 76: I'm not saying the USA dumped the game.

8. *Und.* to sell (stolen goods).

1951 *Sat. Eve. Post* (Aug. 18) 21: The hijackers no longer limit themselves to finished products easy to "dump"—the trade's word for "sell." **1968** "H. King" *Box-Man* 90: I'd go to a fence...and try to dump it.

9. to swallow (a drink); guzzle.

1953 Paley *Rumble* 156: He was with Brindo dumping a few drinks in an East New York joint.

10. *Mil Av.* to bail out of (a crippled aircraft).

1968 J.D. Houston *Between Battles* 59: Mize already dumped two birds in the last two years.

11. to complain or criticize in a whining or unjustified manner. Cf. *dump on*, below.

1970 J. Howard *Please Touch* 84: Only in Games and Stews [at Synanon] may people "dump" or vent...grievances and grudges. **1980** *L.A. Times* (July 1) V 4: They call just to dump but we're a service with a heart and an ear so we listen. **1980** *L.A. Times* (Nov. 10) V 7: We want candor, not dumping. **1987** *RHD2*: He calls me up just to dump.

12. *Skydiving.* to pull the ripcord.

1976 *Webster's Sports Dict.* 128.

¶ In phrase:

¶ **dump on** [or **all over**] to treat unfairly or with contempt; (now *esp.*) to disparage unjustly; pick on. [Widely current in the 1970's.]

1942 in Craven & Cate *AAF in WWII* VII 467: Colonel, we are being dumped on. **1961** N. Ford *Black, Gray & Gold* 21: Do you feel dumped on, mister? **1964** in Reuss *Field Collection* 74: "Dumped-on" (for girls who have been let down by supposed "boy friends"). **1966** in *Amer. Jour. Soc.* LXXII (1967) 467: Like when Jim and I first started dating, we got along just fine. Then I started to dump on him, being a little snotty once in a while and stuff like this. **1966** Neugeboren *Big Man* 47: I figure he likes being dumped on, so I dump, make him pay to get his car washed again. **1969** *Current Slang* I & II 30: *Dump on, v.* To treat meanly or unfairly.—College females, New York. **1970** Waterhouse & Wizard *Turning the Guns* 94: To the lifer mentality, this marks him as a "fuck up" and means he should be dumped on any time he steps out of line. **1971** Dahlskog *Dict.* 20: *Dump on (someone)*...Figuratively, to defecate on someone; hence, to give someone a hard time; to criticize someone severely; to put someone down. **1971** *Playboy* (Mar.) 45: Man Finds True Love But Gets Dumped On. **1972** Parker *Common Sense* 3: Your boss abuses you, your mate dumps on you, your friends kid you. **1972** Meade & Rutledge *Belle* 41: If a nigger's got a vote, I don't dump on him. **1973** Lucas, Katz & Huyck *Amer. Graffiti* 18: He didn't dump on me, you little dip! **1978** J. Reynolds *Geniuses* 42: I give you a sincere, honest answer, and you just dump all over me! **1967–80** Folb *Runnin' Lines* 236: *Dump on.* Disparage or ridicule with particular force. **1984** Univ. Tenn. student: People are always dumping on freshmen! **1993** Sen. R. Dole (R.–Kansas) on *CBS This Morning* (CBS-TV) (Feb. 18): I think there'll be some Republicans and some Democrats dumping all over...[Pres. Clinton's economic] package.

dumper *n.* **1.** *Surfing.* a heavy plunging wave that can knock a surfer down. [Orig. Australian usage.]

1933 in *OEDS*: Done them in in a dumper yesterday at the surf. *1956*, *1963* in *OEDS*. **1968** Kirk & Hanle *Surfer's Hndbk.* 138: *Dumper*: crashing, plunging wave; a wave that curls steeply and crashes into shallow water.

2. a toilet. See also *in the dumper*, below.

*ca*1944 in M. O'Leary *Warbirds* 164: The Denver Dumper [name painted on nose of B-25J bomber, with illustration of toilet commode].

3. *Prost.* a sexual sadist.

1957 Murtagh & Harris *First Stone* 183: Because how are you going to believe anything a dumper tells you? *Ibid.* 304: *Dumper* A man who gets sexual excitement from beating a girl. **1961** Rubin *In the Life* 24: Leave it to those other babes who don't care about taking on the dumpers and nuts. *Ibid.* 157: *Dumper.* sexual sadist.

4. *Prost.* (see quot.).

1973 Schulz *Pimp* 16: So the girls working 14th Street...almost all of them are drug addicts, and quite a few of them are dumpers, old women over forty.

¶ In phrase:

¶ **in the dumper, 1.** in disfavor or disgrace.
1981 *Nat. Lampoon* (Aug.) 20: Johnny is really in the dumper…He's a forgotten person.
2. lost; ruined; "down the tubes."
1982 in *Nat. Lampoon* (Feb. 1983) 16: Forget it. Gone. Forgotten. Nowhere. In the dumper. **1986** Stinson & Carabatsos *Heartbreak* 13: The day was already in the goddamned dumper. **1991** *CBS This Morning* (CBS-TV) (Apr. 16): A lot of those [TV series] went in the dumper.

dunced out *adj.* dumbfounded; stumped; (*hence*) stupid.
1964 in Bruce *Essential Bruce* 113: Completely dunced out, you know?
1973 in L. Bangs *Psychotic Reactions* 114: Totally meaningless, dunced-out trash.

duncehead *n.* a dunce.
1979 Homer *Jargon* 142: Go stand in the corner, duncehead!

dunderfunk *n.* [orig. unkn.] *Naut.* a sailor's dish made of bits of hardtack soaked in water and baked with fat and molasses. Now *hist.*
1841 [Mercier] *Man-of-War* 178: Why, *dunderfunk*, sir a cruel nice dish as ever man put inside of him, I swear…Nothing but molasses and bread, and a little *dab* of slush, to give it a *flavourality* like; then shove it in the oven, and 'tis fit for *scoffin* in less than no time. **1849** Melville *White Jacket* 134: *Dunderfunk* is made of hard biscuit, hashed and pounded, mixed with beef fat, molasses, and water, and baked brown in a pan. **1900** Benjamin *Naval Acad.* 62 [ref. to *ca*1860]: "Dunderfunk"…was made of pounded hard-tack…mixed with beef, fat, and plenty of molasses and then baked.

dune coon *n.* [*dune* + COON, 2] an Arab.—used contemptuously.—usu. considered offensive.
1984 D. Jenkins *Life Its Ownself* 92: We got to deal with Dune Coons. **1988** Dye *Outrage* 9 [ref. to 1967]: Every dune coon in the goddamn world is runnin' around this AO.

duner *n.* a dune-buggy enthusiast.
1974 *New Yorker* (Mar. 11) 106: Duners go out on runs—trips by a half-dozen dune buggies.

dungaree navy *n. Navy.* crews of submarines and destroyers.—constr. with *the.*
1917 Battey, in *Sub. Destroyer* 266: A submarine destroyer of the so-called "Dungaree Navy." *Ibid.* 106: Some folks think the Dungaree Navy is not very regulation. **1918** Commander *Clear the Decks!* 241: Migg's command in the "Dungaree Navy"—(subs and torpedo boats) was his immediate reward for persistent energy and efficiency over an extended period of time. **1943** Fetridge *2nd Navy Reader* 106: They call destroyer duty the "Dungaree Navy."

dunghill *n.* [abbr. *dunghill* cock 'a barnyard rooster (as distinguished from a gamecock)']
1. *Cockfighting.* a gamecock of poor fighting spirit; (*hence*) a coward.
*1761 in *OED*: There would be no sport, as the combatants were both reckoned dunghills. **1785** Grose *Vulgar Tongue*: *Dunghill*, a coward; a cockpit phrase. **1820** Sir W. Scott *Ivanhoe* ch. xliii: To see…whether the heroes of the day are, in the heroic language of insurgent tailors, flints or dunghills. **1936–39** in Mencken *Amer. Lang.* Supp. II 746: *Dunghill*. A cock which runs from a fight.
2. *Horse Racing.* (see quot.).
1843 *Spirit of Times* (Sept. 16) 342: I said that, at the South, horses that could run but one heat were called "dunghills."

dunk *v.* **1.** *Navy.* to sink.
1942 Casey *Torpedo Junction* 21: Draw everything you've got coming from the paymaster. If we get dunked the records all get dunked too.
2. *Naval Av.* DITCH.
1945 Jensen *Carrier War* 153: Aviators who had "dunked" signalled for rescue.
3. *Golf.* (see quot.).
1970 Scharff *Encyc. of Golf* 417: *Dunk.* To hit a ball into a water hazard.

dunker *n. Baseball.* a weakly hit fly ball that falls for a base hit.
1937 *Sporting News Record Book* 64 (cited in Nichols *Baseball Term.*). **1977** F. Messer, on N.Y. Yankees baseball (WPIX-TV): A couple of dunkers have fallen in.

dunnage *n. Naut.* personal equipment; possessions.
*1803 Wetherell *Adventures* 33: Obrian dragged me and my dunnage aft. **1841** [Mercier] *Man-of-War* 42: All the *donnage* [*sic*] that I owned was on my back. **1847** Downey *Portsmouth* 80: When the word is passed

to clean, out come the Bags, and one and all give their dunnage a thorough overhaul. **1857** in *F & H.* **1864** Fosdick *Frank on a Gun-Boat* 68: You need not take your donnage. **1868** *Overland Mo.* (Nov.) 399: Send your dunnage aboard now, and go with me. **1871** Thomes *Whaleman* 314: He has made a will, and left you all his dunnage. **1888** Spear *Old Sailor* 25 [ref. to 1820's]: Then he told Ben Blackford to tumble my "dunnage" on to the wharf. **1931** Dos Passos *1919* 8: Get your dunnage and be back here in an hour.

dunnage barge *n. Naut.* a sea chest.
1893 Hill *20 Yrs at Sea* 16 [ref. to 1840's]: "What in thunderation have you got in this dunnage barge?" said Jim, as he looked at my beloved chest.

dunnigan *n.* [var. DONEGAN] Esp. *Naut.* a low or contemptible person.
1926 *AS* I (Oct.): Lookit, see that fella all rigged out in a harbor gasket and everything, like a parlor dunnigan. **1961** McKenna *Sons of Martha* 75 [ref. to *ca*1935]: "Go clean bilges, you dunnigan!" he'd beller. **1982** in Ciardi *Good Words* 217: Sam is not like the sleazy dunnigans who work toilets, or the dips who grift with squealers.

dupe *n.* a duplicate. Also attrib.
1891 Maitland *Slang Dict.* 101: *Dupe* (Am.), in printing office parlance, means the duplicate proofs. **1916** in *OEDS.* **1929–33** J. Lowell *Gal Reporter* 6: Mr. Gray wants two dupes on your copy. **1983** S. King *Christine* 305: Will knew damned well Cunningham had never given him a dupe set of keys. **1986** R. Campbell *In La-La Land* 228: It's reserved for Mr. Cope, but I can run you a dupe.

dupe *v.* to make a duplicate of.
1912 in *OEDS.* **1929–33** J. Lowell *Gal Reporter* 5: Miss Lowell, didn't you dupe your copy? **1949** Robbins *Dream Merchants* 194: Then we can start duping prints and rush 'em out into the theaters. **1980** *Psychology Today* (Sept.) 84: [He] had asked Saul to dupe a few copies.

dusie var. DOOZY.

dust *n.* **1.** Orig. *Gamb.* money; cash. Now esp. *Black E.*
*1607 in *OED*: Come, down with your dust. *1655 in Dryden *Dramatic Works* IV 545: The abbot down with his dust. *1677–78 in Dryden *Dramatic Works* IV 291: Come, down with your dust, man. *1748 in *F & H* II: *Dust*…a cant name for money. *1753 T. Smollett, in *OED*: I have more dust in my fob than all these powdered sparks put together. *1785 Grose *Vulgar Tongue*: *Dust.* Money. Down with your dust; deposit the ready. **1821** Waln *Hermit in Phila.* 26: Down with *the* dust…out with *the* shiners. **1834** *Mil. & Nav. Mag. of U.S.* (Apr.) 145: The appeal was, however, too emphatic to resist and every plebe "down with his dust." **1839** (quot. at COLE). **1848** *Life in Rochester* 53: Old fool of an adopted daddy, will, of course, have to come down with the dust, and back the concern. **1848** Judson *Mysteries* 36: I was short of the dust, and had to do it to pay expenses. *Ibid.* 527: "Dust." Slang term for money. "Out of dust," is to be lacking change. *Ibid.* 122: Fifty thousand, hard dust. **1850** J. Greene *12 Days in Tombs* 148: Down with your dust and I will cover it. **1858** in Dwyer & Lingenfelter *Gold Rush* 154: It's "Starve or pay the dust,"/for merchants will not trust. **1862** C.F. Browne *A. Ward* 107: They sed ef I didn't down with the dust thay'd wipe my show from the face of the earth! **1889** S.A. Bailey *Ups & Downs* 19: I counted up the dust and found $300. **1889** Field *Western Verse* 5: Casey kept on sawin' wood 'nd layin' in the dust. **1890** Quinn *Fools of Fortune* 365: Here's the dust you loaned me some time ago. **1897** A.H. Lewis *Wolfville* 37: Thar's nothin' for us to do but settle up an' fork over some dust we owes your paw. **1899** *Tip Top Wkly.* (Apr. 22) 24: They are playing for big dust. **1900** Willard & Hodler *Powers That Prey* 87: She made him "hustle for the dust." **1903** Jarrold *Bowery* 176: Oh, you'll get your dust all right—$10 a week. **1905** White *Boniface* 27 [ref. to 1865]: Jim said he'd go on the dust in case there was no conviction. **1906** A.H. Lewis *Confessions* 72: I was out for the dust and made every dollar I could. **1909** *DN* III 395: *Dust, the*…Money. **1919** Darling *Jargon Bk.* 11: *Dust*—Money. **1923** *N.Y. Times* (Sept. 9) VIII 2: *Dust*: Money. *a*1972 *Urban Life & Culture* I 88: A dude can make big money, "top dust." **1972** Casey *Obscenities* 12: The dude found his dust: the soldier found his money. **1974** V.E. Smith *Jones Men* 123: They get big dust for what they do. **1977** Sayles *Union Dues* 313: Fuckin-A it's nice. Put me out some heavy dust. **1978** Wheeler & Kerby *Steel Cowboy* (film): Got just enough dust for a call home.
2. a fight; disturbance; row.
*1753 in *OED*: Mr. Buck…will…then adjourn to kick up a Dust. *ca*1778 in B.I. Granger *Pol. Satire* 179: [He] kick'd up a dust, for his favorite wrangle. **1787–89** Tyler *Contrast* 56: Kicking up a…dust against [the] government. *1805 in *OED*. This dust has cut me up. **1806–08** in *DAE*: My men…wished to have a little *dust* (as they

expressed it) and were likewise fearful of treachery. **1819** Clopper *Bawlfredonia* 101: The Spaniards may kick up a dust in the south. **1821** Waln *Hermit in Phila.* 30: Who'll *raise a breeze? kick up a dust?* and *play the d—l?* **1831** in [S. Smith] *Letters of Downing* 52: But that...has kicked up a monstrous dust...all over the world almost. **1838** *Crockett Almanac* (1839) 10: An old injun...axed me if it were the way in Kentuck to hinder the children from having a little dust of diversion. **1850** in *Mo. Hist. Soc. Bull.* VI (1949) 14: It made Booker mad and he was about to kick up an awful dust about it.

3. a pretender; FOURFLUSHER.

1844 in *DA* 113: "Well, you're a big dust of a doorkeeper!" said the rowdy as he went in.

4. a taste; a drink. Cf. *dampen the dust*, below.

1853 W.W. Brown *Clotel* 195: I keep a little brandy...for the rheumatics, and being it's you, I'll give you a little dust.

5. *Narc.* **a.** any narcotic or stimulating drug in powdered form, esp. heroin or cocaine.

1916 *New Republic* (Apr. 22) 315: He will, as he expresses it, "do almost anything to get the 'dust' [heroin]." **1942** *ATS* 474: Powdered narcotic...*dust.* **1953** Anslinger & Tompkins *Traf. in Narc.* 308: Dust. Marijuana, heroin, morphine, or cocaine. **1970** Horman & Fox *Drug Awareness* 466: *Dust*—cocaine. **1971** Guggenheimer *Narc. & Drug Abuse* 19: *Dust.* Cocaine. **1975** S.P. Smith *Amer. Boys* 99: Some of the cats on the block were fuckin' up gang warrin' and tippling and smokin' shit and snortin' dust.

b. ANGEL DUST.

1978 *Channel 2 Eye On: Angel Dust* (WCBS-TV): I was introduced to it as *dust*—that's the street code, just *dust.* "You want to smoke some dust?" **1979** Gram *Blvd. Nights* 93: Got fucked up on some dust. **1981** Wambaugh *Glitter Dome* 129: Rainbows, dexis, bennies, ludes, speed, even some dust. **1983** Sturz *Wid. Circles* 6: It's no wonder you can't remember anything with all the dust you smoke. **1984** *All Things Considered* (Nat. Pub. Radio) (June 13): I get two or three bundles of dust and I sell it. **1986** *Community* (WCBS-TV news series) (Sept. 21): Dust, coke, pills...that was my life. **1993** *New Yorker* (Jan. 11) 68: They both smoked dust.

6. Esp. *Pris.* finely flaked tobacco for rolling handmade cigarettes.

1933 (cited in Spears *Drugs & Drink*). **1934** Weseen *Dict. Slang* 11: *Dust*—Smoking tobacco. **1966** Braly *On Yard* 45: A fine, powdery rolling tobacco, called "dust." **1972** P. Thomas *Savior* 88: Don't smoke that dust, here's some tailormades. **1984** Sample *Raceboss* 235: A fresh bag of "dust" (Bull Durham).

¶ **In phrases:**

¶ **bite the dust** to die; (*hence*) to suffer defeat; be ruined. [Orig. literary S.E., specifically 'to fall to the ground wounded, esp. fatally', as in 1750 quot.]

[*1750 T. Smollett, in *OEDS*: We made two of them bite the dust, and the others betake themselves to flight.] **1846** Thorpe *Rio Grande* 133: His days will be numbered, and his father's son will bite the dust for his rascality. **1857** in Walser *Tar Heel Laughter* 57: Divers youngsters...have bit the dust in these diggins. **1864** in W. Wilkinson *Mother* 300: The order to *Charge* was *Counter Manded.*...Many of us would have *bitten* the *dust.* **1881** C.M. Chase *Editor's Run* 110: Billy the Kid was the last prominent desperado to bite the dust. **1950** *New Yorker* (June 10) 96: A gang of terrible old dope smugglers, many of whom bite the dust. **1950** *N.Y. Times* (Aug. 20) I 69: The four Senators have bit the political dust in primaries. **1978** De Christoforo *Grease* 172: You never know who'll bite the dust or live to tell about it. **1981–85** S. King *It* 70: Every man's got a fambly, and someone in his just bit the dust. **1985** MacLaine *Dancing* 37: I saw the police say another drunk driver had bitten the dust.

¶ **dampen the dust** to take a drink. Cf. **(4),** above.

1851 [G. Thompson] *Jack Harold* 57: Bill "dampened his dust" and renewed his quid.

¶ **eat dust** to be killed.

1890 E. Custer *Guidon* 32 [ref. to *ca*1870]: The bouncer placed his pistol on the table and quietly remarked, "Any man as calls sop gravy has got to eat dust or 'pologize."

¶ **hit the dust** to start on one's way.

1918 *N.Y. Sun* (Aug. 25) 5: 7: Hit the dust down to the Battery.

¶ **no dust on** nothing old-fashioned or stodgy about.

1890 Howells *Hazard* 115: "But what's the matter with the young lady in young lady's clothes? Any dust on *her?*" "What expressions!...Really, Alma, for a refined girl you *are* the most unrefined!"

¶ **take the dust** to be surpassed in speed.

1871 Small *Parson Beecher* 7: Why he takes no dust from anybody. **1904** in "O. Henry" *Works* 571: The *Rambler*—that's her name—don't take the dust of anything afloat.

¶ **watch my dust!** watch me go!

1962 Killen *Heard the Thunder* 19: Just watch my dust. Section 8, here I come.

dust *v.* **1.a.** to strike hard; thrash; beat up; knock to the ground.—in mod. use also constr. with *off.* [The absence of exx. between 1612 and 1803 suggests reinvention rather than survival.]

*1612 in *F & H* II 346: To dust her often hath in it a singular...vertue to make her much better. **1803* in J. Ashton *Eng. Satires on Napoleon* 161: Says the Dust-man, I'll *dust* him—you know what I mean,/I'll give him a hide all black, blue, and green. **a1890–91 F & H* II 346: Dusted...(colloquial).—Drubbed; severely criticised. **1928** C. McKay *Banjo* 262: And they dusted us, pardner. Fist and feet they dusted us good and proper and didn't miss no part but the bottom of our feets. **1928–30** Fiaschetti *Gotta Be Rough* 66: Crooks open up to their broads as no third degree or dusting off in the back room of a station house can make them. **1941** *Slanguage Dict.* 14: *Dust off*...to administer a thorough beating to. **1963** E.M. Miller *Exile* 11: He fought back the urge to dust Cyril off as he swung the Super Sabre out of the line of parked planes. **1971** Dahlskog *Dict.* 20: *Dust, v.* To beat up; to defeat; to strike, as in a fight. **1972** R. Wilson *Forbidden Words* 73: The classic method is to dust his cranium with the barrel of a gun. **1967–80** Folb *Runnin' Lines* 236: *Dust (one)*...Knock one down or out cold. **1982** "J. Cain" *Commandos* 394: Maybe you should go over and dust that punk. **1985** *Jeffersons* (ABC-TV): If this wasn't a church I'd dust you!

b. *Rodeo.* (see quot.).

1949 Cummings *Dict. Sports* 121: *Dust*...Rodeos. Slang. To fan a bucking bronco with the hat...to make it buck harder.

c. *Baseball.* DUST OFF; (*hence*) to hit in the head. Cf. DUSTER.

1950 *Time* (Jan. 30) 14: Dusted one of the lieutenants with an old shoe for trying to talk them back to work. **1952** Malamud *Natural* 23: If he tries to dust me, so help me I will smash his skull.

d. Esp. *Und.* to kill; DUST OFF.

1972 Bunker *No Beast* 249: You eat and shit and breathe even when you've dusted a copper. **1978** Kopp *Innocence* 107 [ref. to 1940's]: The dude he was gonna dust turned out to be you! **1981** Wambaugh *Glitter Dome* 162: The guy...that got dusted in the parking lot. **1986** Thacker *Finally the Pawn* 66 [ref. to 1970]: A fine fellow who got dusted. **1988** North Fork, Calif., man, age *ca*50, on *Newswatch* (CNN-TV) (Jan. 7): He's a bad case. He's been bad news around here forever, and if he comes near my place I'm gonna dust him. **1989** L. Roberts *Full Cleveland* 94: Maybe whoever killed Mulkey dusted Shane too.

e. to destroy.

1979 Alibrandi *Custody* 226: They'd been shredded...."Sorry we had to dust your boots."

2.a. to hasten away; clear out; depart; hurry.

1863 in J.W. Haley *Rebel Yell* 118: After dinner we were ordered to "dust out of this." **1863** in *La. Hist.* VIII (1967) 375: They were obliged to "dust." **1864** *Battle-Fields of So.* 93: We had better "up stakes and dust" out of the neighborhood "in a mighty big hurry." **1866** Dimsdale *Vigilantes* 127: On inquiry it was found that a message had arrived from Virginia, warning the robbers to "Get up and dust, and lie loe for black ducks." **1867** in G.W. Harris *High Times* 176: All the men folks am run plum off but me, an' I speck I'd a dusted too but fur bein'...a natral born'd durn'd fool. **1870** Keim *Sheridan's Troopers* 111: I've just made that ole critter of mine out thar get up and dust, for the last thirty-six hours. **1880** in M. Lewis *Mining Frontier* 96: And the waiters was jist a gettin' up an' dustin'. **1881** Ingraham *Buffalo Bill from Boyhood* 92: They are some of the horse-thieves, Davie, that have been playing the mischief of late about here, and we'd better dust. **1882** D.J. Cook *Hands Up* 235: He felt that his safety depended on the celerity of his movements, and he decided to "get up and dust." **1883** *Life* (Aug. 2) 68: Now look a here, you, I want you to dust! **1883** Peck *Peck's Bad Boy* 224: They all yelled "Hang him"...Pa got up and dusted. **1889** Cox *Frontier Humor* 159: What on earth could have turned up to make Jim dust out of town so all-fired sudden. **1889** Farmer *Americanisms* 546: UP AND DUST!—Look alive! be quick! make the dust fly! **1889** in Remington *Own West* 23: Ef dat lieutenant warn't a right brave man, he'd 'a' done dusted out and lef' me as I tole him to. **1891** in Evans *Sailor's Log* 254: The Errazuria [a Chilean warship]...may make an effort to beat us to Valparaiso; but she will have to "dust" if she does it, for we have averaged twelve knots since leaving the river. **1913** Light *Hobo* 43: We figured it was time to "dust." **1927** *DN* V 445: *Dust, v.* To escape; to decamp. **1936** Gaddis *Courtesan* 43: What became of...Lulie, when she dusted out of Dave's hotel? **1959** A. Anderson *Lover Man* 46: He'd grabbed up all the loot and dusted. **1988** *Knightwatch* (ABC-TV): It's no good. Go on! Dust!

b. to depart or escape from; (*also*) jilt.—used trans.

1942–49 Goldin et al. *DAUL* 64: Three lifers dusted that can…yesterday. **1962** Crump *Killer* 245: After today, I'm dusting this park. **1963–64** Kesey *Great Notion* 207: Leave these squares. Dust 'em all. **1984** Eble *Campus Slang* (Mar.) 2: *Dust*—get rid of someone: Those guys…dusted her for some other girl. **1987** *Growing Pains* (ABC-TV): Why don't you dust that shrink?

3.a. to pass on a road, so as to expose to the dust raised by one's horse or vehicle; outrace or outspeed.—also constr. with *off*.

*****1890** in *OED*: I could have dusted any of 'em with Ben. **1961** Gover *$100 Misunderstanding* 157: You can dust just about anything moving with that Imperial. **1971** Tak *Truck Talk* 54: *Dust 'em off:* to pass another truck at high speed. **1987** Kent *Phr. Book* 117: In the race for excellence, we dust the competition.

b. to defeat or surpass.

1968–70 *Current Slang* III & IV 42: *Dusted…*beaten in a gambling game. **1987** *Campus Voice* (Winter) 38: You know that your work is going to be put right next to Joe Blow's work, and you just don't want to look dusted by it. **1991** D. Anderson *In Corner* 157: Kenny dusts him in eight rounds.

4. to tease or hoax. [The sense in 1814 quot. is 'to deceive or mislead'.]

[*****1814** in *OED*: This is termed "Dusting the public."] **1956** E. Hunter *Second Ending* 277: "Oh, come on, man, you're dusting me." "I kid you not.…What's mootah?"

¶ In phrases.

¶ **dust (one's) throat** to slake (one's) thirst.

1873 Small *Joining the Grangers* 48: The nicest old Granger rye that you ever saw or dusted your throat with.

¶ **dust (someone's) coat** [or **jacket**] to thrash; beat up.

*****1690** in *OED*: I'll dust your coat for you. *****1698** in *ibid*.: Or I'll dust the secret out of your jacket. **1807** in *OEDS*: Go in peace, or I will dust thy jacket with this horse-whip. **1828** Bird *Looking Glass* 18: "Can you do anything besides joking and railing?" "I can thrash your jacket, and dust your coat." **1864** in J.W. Haley *Rebel Yell* 220: The Rebs dusted his coat for him in good shape. **1869** Gough *Autobiog.* 40: My father declared he would "dust my jacket for me."

¶ **dust the sidewalk with** to trounce; to beat up.

1887 Francis *Saddle & Moccasin* 308: Couldn't you…dust the sidewalk, and knock a few flies off the wall with him?

dust beater *n. Army.* an infantryman. Now *hist.*

ca**1915** in Wiley & Milhollen *They Who Fought* 19 [ref. to Civil War]: The men who we as Cavalry or Artillery dubbed "flat feet" and "dust beaters" and often ridiculed on the march.

dustbin *n. Mil. Av.* (see 1945 quot.). Now *hist.*

1941 in C.R. Bond & T. Anderson *Flying T. Diary* 61: They lowered their "dustbin" rear fighting guns to defend against us. *Ibid.* 62: Their "dustbin" gunners…kept up their fire. **1945** Hamann *Air Words*: *Dustbin.* Underside gun turret of a bomber; also a projecting cabin provided for the protection of a gunner. **1956** Heflin *USAF Dict.* 178: *Dustbin, n.* A gun turret on the underside of the fuselage. *Slang.* **1959** Scott *Flying Tiger* 179 [ref. to WWII]: We hadn't flown "up the tails" and into the fire of their "dust-bin" guns and thereby put their tail gunners at a disadvantage.

dust bunny *n.* a loose tangle of dust and lint, as found under furniture.

1966, 1969, 1965–70 in *DARE*. **1980** *New Yorker* (Feb. 18) 31: Her grandmother always told her to dust under her bed, so the dust bunnies would not multiply and take over. **1984** Wilder *You All* 28: *Dust bunnies…*Piles of dust and lint. **1990** *Cosmopolitan* (May) 256: He'd exhausted himself snapping up dust bunnies from under the bed.

dust-cutter *n.* a bracing drink of liquor.

1908 Raine *Wyoming* 111: Have a dust-cutter, Mac, before she grows warm. **1958** J. Ward *Buchanan* 8: Then maybe a dust cutter.

dust-eater *n. Mil.* the vehicle at the tail end of a line of moving vehicles.

1986 R. Zumbro *Tank Sgt.* 88 [ref. to 1967–68]: After the last truck had passed, the second tank, the "dust eater," would tag along as far back as possible. *Ibid.* 118: We tagged onto the end of the string, cursing the dumb ass who had forced us into the dust-eaters' position.

dusted *adj. Narc.* high, esp. on ANGEL DUST.—also constr. with *out*.

1959 (cited in Spears *Drugs & Drink*). **1970** Landy *Underground Dict.* 72: *Dusted…*Completely fucked-up on hog. **1979** *Nat. Lampoon* (Sept.) 46: Must'a really been, like, dusted! Really, I mean, like, really gone. **1983** Wambaugh *Delta Star* 10: The trucker was dusted out on PCP. **1984** in *Rolling Stone* (June 11, 1992) 129: Ricky was totally dusted out and went unconscious for a while. **1985** J. Dillinger *Adrenaline* 154: Dusted Chicanos, junkies with gray ponytails. **1992** *DayWatch* (CNN-TV) (Mar. 31): I said…"Watch out! I think he's dusted!"

duster *n.* **1.** *Petroleum Industry.* (see 1944 quot.).

1898 in *DN* II 340: There are thirteen producing wells and fifteen *dusters* in the pool. **1944** Boatright & Day *Hell to Breakfast* 141: A well which fails to produce oil or gas is a "duster" or "dry hole." **1951** Pryor *The Big Play* 74: This one would be a dry hole, a duster. **1978** *U.S. News & W.R.* (Mar. 6) 35: American oil companies have drilled a series of "dusters" in once-promising waters off Southern California.

2. *Naut.* the red ensign of the British merchant service. In full, **red duster.**

*****1904** in *OEDS*. *****1929** Bowen *Sea Slang* 111: *Red Duster*, the Red Ensign. **1939** in Murrow *Search of Light* 34: Many of them still flew that familiar red duster—the flag of the British merchant navy. **1975** Mostert *Supership* 151: The normal flag of the British merchant service is the "red duster."

3.a. *Baseball.* BEAN BALL.

1929 *N.Y. Times* (June 2) IX 2: The deliberate aiming of a ball at the batsman is, of course, strictly forbidden, but "dusters" are often used in the first two or three innings. **1939–40** Tunis *Kid from Tomkinsville* 194: Nowadays hurlers who take nicely calculated dusters at his noggin live to regret it. **1950** Taylor & Mann *Jackie Robinson* (film): What are you gonna do if a pitcher throws a duster at your head? **1969** Bouton *Ball Four* 68: Only once in the years I've been pitching had anybody ever ordered me to throw a duster…I came into a game in relief and John Olerud, the catcher, came out and said, "Joe wants you to knock this guy on his ass." **1973** Wagenheim *Clemente!* 87: I was famous for my dusters, especially when I pitched for the Giants with Sal Maglie, who was a master at it.

b. *Tennis.* a shot which strikes a chalkline and sprays dust.

1976 *AS* LI 293.

4. *Und.* a fugitive.

1935 D.W. Maurer, in *AS* (Feb.) 15 [ref. to a1910]: *Duster.* A lamster; sometimes applied to a criminal who jumps bail to escape trial.

5. the human rump; in phr. **on (someone's) duster** harassing (someone).

[**1898** W.H. Krell *Shake Yo' Dusters or Picaninny Rag* (ragtime song)]. **1946** Mezzrow & Wolfe *Really Blues* 171: Keep on wriggling your saucy duster and smelling sweet. **1964** Gold *Jazz Lexicon* 93. **1972** Radio ad for Plymouth Duster (Apr.): But we didn't outsell Ford and GM's compacts by—sitting on our dusters. **1978** Diehl *Sharky's Machine* 114: I sit here on my duster all day. **1978** in Curry *River's in Blood* 166: He was really on my duster from then on.

6. *Army & USMC.* a kind of armored fighting vehicle mounting twin 40mm guns.

1969 in Lanning *Only War* 88: Blew one 40mm duster round. **1972** Haldeman *War Year* 118: It wasn't a regular "tank," but rather a "duster," an armored vehicle with twin repeating cannons. **1978** Hasford *Short-Timers* 76 [ref. to Vietnam War]: Two Dusters, light tanks with twin 40mm guns, grind by. **1980** Cragg *L. Militaris* 144: *Dusters.* Forty millimeter antiaircraft guns modified for use as anti-personnel weapons during the Vietnam War. **1980** Santoli *Everything* 84 [ref. to 1968]: A duster (truck with multiple cannons mounted) tried to pull up and…they blew that son of a bitch up. **1986** Thacker *Pawn* 278: Lotta firepower…dusters, fifty cals, canister rounds.

7. *Narc.* (see quot.).

1969 (cited in Spears *Drugs & Drink*). **1972** Smith & Gay *Don't Try It* 201: *Duster.* Heroin cigarette (prevalent now in Vietnam).

8. *Narc.* a user of ANGEL DUST.

1979 (cited in Spears *Drugs & Drink*). **1980** *L.A. Times* (Aug. 17) I 32: "Dusters" are not predictable. Violence is a nature of the drug. **1983** Wambaugh *Delta Star* 10: A…cop…was nearly beaten to death with his own stick by a duster. *Ibid.* 205: A duster is what I think. **1992** *CBS Morning News* (CBS-TV) (Mar. 5): The police…had a duster on their hands.

dust express *n.* (see quot.).

1888 *Scribners Mag.* (Nov.) 548: The brakeman…calls a grand train a "dust express," and refers to the pump for compressing air for the power-brakes as a "wind-jammer."

dustie *n.* a person addicted to the inhalation of powdered narcotics.

1957 Ellison *Web of the City* 90: Talk, you dustie, talk!

dust-inspector *n. Army.* (see quot.).

1930 *Our Army* (Jan.) 21: *Dust Inspector.* Any inspecting officer who is exceptionally careful and will find fault, for lack of anything else objectionable, in the light dust which may collect on boots or rifle stock or barrel after these have been cleaned just before inspection.

dust kitten *n.* DUST BUNNY.

1982 *AS* LVII 276: In Minnesota they are *dust kittens.*

dust monkey *n.* (see quot.).

*a***1986** Montell *Killings* 78 [ref. to *ca*1930]: Sawyers, saw filers,…lumber stackers, and dust monkeys (young boys who carted the sawdust out of the large hole below the saw blade [in the mill]).

dust-off *n. Mil.* **1.** an air ambulance unit.

1964 J. Lucas *Dateline* 94: Kelly's call sign is Dust Off. Dust Off…had a chopper-load of casualties. **1968** in B.E. Holley *Vietnam* 6: The air-ambulance team, affectionately known as the "dust-off." **1984** Riggan *Free Fire* 15: All the officers generally showed up, along with all the personnel from Dust-Off.

2. a medical-evacuation helicopter.

1967 D. Reed *Up Front* 27: Eighteen American…wounded…were taken out in "dustoff" medical evacuation choppers (so named because they stir up a lot of dust during takeoffs and landings). **1967** Sadler *Lucky One* 152: Over his radio he heard the "scramble" and "dust-off" commands there. **1969** Marshall *Ambush* 48: Still unconscious, he was picked up by the crew of a dustoff (medical evacuation) Huey and flown to hospital.

3. a medical evacuation mission.

1968 in B.E. Holley *Vietnam* 5: Air-ambulance missions, referred to as "dust-off" missions. **1969** Austin *Grunt's Little War* (WCCO-TV): The helicopter's crew starts on a dust-off, this war's equivalent of an ambulance run. **1983** T. Page *Nam* 17 [ref. to Vietnam War]: Missions all over the Corps: eagle lifts,…resupply runs and dustoffs.

dust off *v.* **1.** DUST, *v.*, 1.a.

2. *Baseball.* to pitch at the head of (a batter).

1928 Ruth *Baseball* 34: The next time he comes up to hit dust him off! Drop him in the dirt! **1929** *N.Y. Times* (June 2) IX 2: "Dusting them off" is a phrase used to describe balls aimed at or close to the batsman's head. **1939–40** Tunis *Kid from Tomkinsville* 113: The pitcher [was] dusting off the hitters as if they were there for that one purpose. *Ibid.*: Why, Buzzy, you haven't got guts enough to dust me off. **1941** *Sat. Eve. Post* (May 17) 86: Smart pitchers never dust off a good hitter.

3. (see quot.).

1938 *AS* (Apr.) 156: *Dust 'em off.* To sand blast.

4. *Mil. Av.* to fly low over (another plane); BUZZ.

1939 R.A. Winston *Dive Bomber* 160: Took time out to "dust off" an Army A-17 attack plane that was cruising peacefully towards Langley Field. **1989** T. Blackburn *Jolly Rogers* 50: An "F4U appeared from nowhere" to dust off a patrol plane or some such.

5.a. to finish off.

1940 *Whiz Comics* (Feb.) (unp.): About ten seconds of this'll dust the old guy off for keeps. **1948** Cozzen *Guard* 160: Red flight of this squadron of Benny's came down to dust off the park and never saw these Krauts. **1953** "L. Padgett" *Mutant* 137: The tribes that unified got dusted off…We ain't unifying, brother. **1968** Lockridge *Hartspring* 97: If you two don't get the hell out of here right now, I'll have Charley dust you off good.

b. to kill; DUST, *v.*, 1.d.

1940 Thompson & Raymond *Gang Rule in N.Y.* 33: Owney found himself looking at a ring of eleven Dusters who had come to dust him off. **1940** Zinberg *Walk Hard* 30: I had a brother that was a plumber till he got dusted off in the war. **1942** *ATS* 135.

c. *Sports.* to defeat easily.

1962 Houk & Dexter *Ballplayers* 103: Frank Lary dusted us off in the opener.

d. DUST, *v.*, 3.

6. to reject or dismiss casually; BRUSH OFF.

1942 *ATS* 338: Jilt…ditch, dump, dust off. **1957** Kohner *Gidget* 97: [Parents] can be trying. I dusted mine off a long time ago. **1961** Forbes *Goodbye to Some* 100: About three months ago he got dusted off. They weren't married but they had gone together since high school. **1983** Ehrhart *VN-Perkasie* 397: You sucker me in; then when things get

tough, you dust me off! **1991** *Eerie, Indiana* (NBC-TV): I just dusted off my best buddy.

7. *Mil.* to evacuate (a wounded soldier), esp. by helicopter, for medical treatment.

1968 in B.E. Holley *Vietnam* 72: We had to dust-off another case of malaria with a temperature in excess of 105 degrees. **1971** Hammer *Calley Court-Martial* 243 [ref. to 1968]: I lost my RTO…and by the time I could get him dusted off, I had a couple of other men go into shock on me. **1971** Polner *Victory Parades* 67: I hoped I'd get wounded and be dusted-off for good. **1984–87** Ferrandino *Firefight* 77: I got dusted off 'bout a week after you did.

dust-up *n.* a fracas; fight; altercation; argument.

*****1897** in *OEDS*. **1935** S. Lewis *Can't Happen* 214: I'm having a little dust-up with that snipe Nipper. **1939** (cited in *AS* (Feb. 1954) 72). **1942** Casey *Torpedo Junction* 49: Just before the present dustup the foreign office relented a bit further. **1948** *New Yorker* (Mar. 27) 23: He has been making a considerable dustup over the matter. **1955** Shapiro *6th of June* 153: We get sent out on patrol just to make sure they're gone and we have a dust-up with a few who were left behind. **1967** Michaels *Berets* 121: You expected an easy patrol, but you might get shafted instead. More personnel and maybe a few real dust-ups with Charlie. **1971** Dahlskog *Dict.* 20: *Dust-up, n.* A brawl; an uproar; a big fuss, as: a big *dustup* in the locker room over some missing gear. **1973** P. Benchley *Jaws* 98: Another dustup took place on the public beach, when a New York lawyer started reading the United States Constitution to a policeman and a multitude of cheering youths. **1979** Cassidy *Delta* 267: Except for that dust-up you guys had with the ambush, things have been awfully quiet all over the Delta. **1982** I.M. Hunter *Blue & Gray* (NBC-TV): It'll be a fine old dust-up. **1985** Sawislak *Dwarf* 78: She covered some dustups between right- and left-wing students at the college. **1987** Kent *Phr. Book* 13: She gave him a most unladylike dustup.

dusty *adj.* dangerous; tough; BAD.

1859 Matsell *Vocab.* 29: *Dusty.* Dangerous. "Two fly-cops and a beak tumbled to us, and Bill thought as how it was rather dusty, and so, shady was the word," two detectives and a magistrate came upon us suddenly; Bill said it was rather dangerous, and so we got out of sight. **1866** (quot. at SKULL, *n.*). *****1868** in Partridge *DSUE* (ed. 8): The passage is what the Captain has already prophesied it would be—"dusty." **1868** Willams *Black-Eyed Beauty* 30: Now Lon, in earlier days, had fallen in with a rough crowd up town around Mackerelville, and when he liked he could be the "dusty boy, you just bet high."

¶ In phrase:

¶ **not so dusty** not bad.

*****1854** in *F & H* II 347: "Why is the fact of the contents of a backgammon board having been thrown out the window like Milton's *chef d'oeuvre?* …Because it's a *pair o' dice lost.*" None so dusty that—eh? for a commoner like me? *****1864** Hotten *Slang Dict.* (ed. 3): "Well, it's not so dusty," *i.e.*, not so bad. *****1884** in *F & H*: I'm not so dusty, and if it wasn't for my disgusting weight I'd…let 'em see…what I can do. **1922** F.L. Packard *Doors of Night* 55: An' dat ain't so dusty a place to hide it, neither! **1933–34** Lorimer & Lorimer *Stag Line* 110: "You're not so dusty" is better than "You're too wonderful."

dusty-butt *n.* **1.** *So.* a short person.—used derisively.

1941 Attaway *Blood on the Forge* 75: One of the old hands, Dusty-butt Jones, he was called, waved his bottle and shouted…He got his name because of his shortness. Men said that the seat of his pants dusted the ground. **1942–44** in *AS* (Feb. 1946) 31: *Dusty, n.* [A nickname for] an Aggie short in stature, built too close to the ground. From *dusty butt.* **1947–52** Ellison *Invisible Man* 156: Did old…dusty-butt, love her or hate her?

2. *Black E.* a cheap prostitute; slut.

1942 *Amer. Mercury* (July) 94: *Dusty butt:* cheap prostitute. **1977** Miss. man, age *ca*25: Voncille, she a regular dusty-butt.

Dutch *n.* **1.** the German or (*rarely*) a Scandinavian language.—usu. used contemptuously. [Orig. S.E.; see *OED*.]

ca*1380**, *****1485**, *****1547**, *****1548**, *****1578**, **a***1634**, *****1682**, *****1721**, *****1756–57** in *OED*. **1843** Field *Pokerville* 134: Ole Bull speaks English very well, but still there is something of "the Dutch" about it. **1858** in G.W. Harris *High Times* 148: When he sot in tu cussin, he did hit in Dutch mostly. **1900** *DN* II 33: *Dutch, n.* German language. **1906** *DN* III 134: *Dutch, n.* The German language.

2. Germans; a German.—usu. used contemptuously. [Orig. S.E.; see *OED. Pennsylvania Dutch* is a dignified survival of this term, now regarded as a simple "misnomer."]

*****1601** in *OED*. **1918** in Truman *Ltrs. Home* 51: I am…scared…the

Dutch will get...licked before D Battery gets to unload a volley at them. **1939** Appel *Power-House* 381: And you're a dumb Dutch, Schneck.

3. DUTCH ACT.

[***1889** Barrère & Leland *Dict. Slang* I 341: *Dutch* (milit.), to *"do a Dutch,"* to run away, to desert.] **1915** Howard *God's Man* 391: "Doing the Dutch"—Archie's favorite topic during the past few months. **1943** in Ruhm *Detective* 361: She did the Dutch after they found him in the river. **1946** Gresham *Nightmare Alley* 185: Doree Evarts...did the Dutch night before last. **1947** Spillane *I, the Jury* 8: Four years ago, when Jack was on the force, he had grabbed her as she was about to do a Dutch over the Brooklyn Bridge. **1977** Caron *Go-Boy* 263: *Doing the dutch*—committing suicide.

¶ In phrases:

¶ **beat the Dutch** see S.V. BEAT, *v.*

¶ **get (someone's) Dutch up** to anger (someone).

1848 in Peskin *Vols.* 272: Mechling...got his Dutch up. **1891** Maitland *Amer. Slang Dict.* 150: *"To get one's Irish up,"* to become angry. *To get one's Dutch up* means the same thing. **1915** Raine *Highgrader* 155: What's the use of gettin' your Dutch up? **1949** Robbins *Dream Merchants* 491: The stubborn old fool! This is a hell of a time for him to get his Dutch up. **1971** Dahlskog *Dict.* 21: *Dutch up, get (one's),* to be or to make angry or wrathful, as: Don't *get his Dutch up,* or you'll be sorry.

¶ **in Dutch, 1.** in trouble or disfavor.

1851 [Byrn] *Ark. Doctor* 152: It had to come off or I would have been mobbed, or shot; just the same in Dutch, you see. **1910** *N.Y. Eve. Jour.* (Apr. 16) 11: I'm in dutch, Psycho—they're goin' t' pinch me if I don't pay my board bill to-day. **1912** *Adventure* (May) 137: I'm sorry...if I've got you in Dutch with the administration. **1913–15** Van Loan *Taking the Count* 75: He'll snatch our appearance money and put us in Dutch all over the country. **1917** Sterling, Costello & Lange *Der Kaiser* [cover]: Raus Mit Der Kaiser (He's in Dutch). **1917** *Forum* (Dec.) 686: They wuz in Dutch wit' th' Big Feller. **1919** *Lit. Digest* (May 10) 66: I'll get "in Dutch" if I criticize. **1926** in Fitzgerald *Stories* I 294: I suppose I'm in Dutch down there. **1934** Cain *Postman* 49: I'm in dutch all right, but I guess lying about it won't do any good. **1936** Farrell *World I Never Made* 219: I've been in enough dutch, as it is. **1948** in Himes *Black on Black* 268: Now don't go out there singing and get in Dutch again. **1982** Braun *Judas Tree* 69: He'd got himself in Dutch with the law. **1989** "Capt. X" & Dodson *Unfriendly Skies* 58: Now you're in dutch. You've got two engines missing.

2. *Gamb.* having made a DUTCH BOOK; (*hence*) having wagered wrongly; mistaken.

1911 *N.Y. Eve. Jour.* (Jan. 10) 14: Those that had [bet upon] Attell...saw that they were "in Dutch" before the bout had gone three rounds; for Abe hardly made an attempt to fight in his old form. **1914** Jackson & Hellyer *Vocab.* 47: *In Dutch,* Adverb...Mistaken; in trouble.

3. *Specif.* (of a girl) pregnant and unmarried.

1951 Elgart *Over Sixteen* 24: Guess what, Mom? I got a girl in Dutch! **1956** Metalious *Peyton Place* 166: "A girl in trouble." "She got in Dutch." "She's knocked up."

Dutch *adj.* German.—usu. used contemptuously. [Orig. S.E.; see *OED.*]

ca*1460,** ***1480,** ***1530,** ***1563,** ***1570,** ***1599,** ***1601,** ***1611,** ***1788** in *OED.* **1861** Wilkie *Iowa First* 87: You G—d d—d Dutch sons of b—s, what are you doing here? **1915** in Butterfield *Post Treasury* 136: And all the time he had the balls actin' like they was Dutch soldiers and him Kaiser William. **1938** Johnson & Pratt *Lost Bttn.* 144 [ref. to 1918]: Try and make us, you Dutch bastards! **1969** Turner *Mayberly* 29: That was Shultz's force, rest his stupid Dutch soul.

dutch *adv.* [sugg. by *Dutch treat*] with each person paying his own way. Now *S.E.*

1914 S. Lewis *Mr. Wrenn* 63: We'll go Dutch. **1930** *Amer. Mercury* (May) 13: You'd be surprised how straight chorus girls are on squaring up liquor bills when they're running Dutch. **1978** S. King *Stand* 111: If you ask me to go somewhere dutch, I'll brain you.

Dutch *v.* Euchre. (see quots.).

1864 in *West. Folk.* XI (1952) 31: *Dutch It*—To make trump of the color that is turned down in the game of euchre. **1934** *WNID2*: *Dutch it.* Euchre. To cross the suit.

¶ In phrase:

¶ **Dutch a book** *Gamb.* to botch or eliminate a bookmaker's certainty of making a profit in accepting bets; (of a bookmaker) to cheat oneself in this way.

1911 Howard *Enemy to Society* 300: You never thought of yerself in yer life. If yuh had, yuh might'a' bin somethin' instead a jest Dutchin' yer book fer a lot of no good, ungrateful rats. **1911–12** Ade *Knocking the Neighbors* 127: She had Dutched her Book and backed the wrong Paddock. *a***1951** in D.W. Maurer *Lang. Und.* 209: *Dutch a book*...to accept bets in such a proportion that [the bookmaker] will lose, no matter which horse wins the race.

Dutch act *n. Und.* suicide.—constr. with *the.*

1902 Hapgood *Autobiog. of Thief* 112 [ref. to *ca*1890]: A week later Del was found dead in his cell, and I believe he did the Dutch act (suicide). **1911** A.H. Lewis *Apaches of N.Y.* 31: Spanish...did not croak Dribben and Blum, and do the Dutch act for himself. **1922** *In the Clutch of Circumstance* 235: He was a "lifer," and not being able to endure the system longer he did the "Dutch act" in order to shorten his sentence. **1928** Burnett *Little Caesar* 74: You got the Old Man on the run and Flaherty's about ready to do the Dutch Act. **1935** J. O'Hara *Butterfield 8* 295: "She only come aboard to do the Dutch act," said Captain Parker...The thought never crossed his mind that it was anything but suicide. **1962** T. Berger *Reinhart* 19: Reinhart derived nothing but an urge to escape, by any means less final than the Dutch act. **1972** *Banyon* (NBC-TV): The Dutch act—or suicide, to the masses. **1972** in J. Mills *On Edge* 127: "I really started thinking about the Dutch act." The Dutch act is suicide.

Dutch blessing *n.* a scolding.

1856 *Ballou's Dollar Mo. Mag.* (Apr.) 329: He then called for the Spaniard, and after giving him a genuine "Dutch blessing," sent him aloft in my stead.

Dutch book *n. Gamb.* a botched method of accounting or odds-making that allows no percentage in favor of the bookmaker.

1912 *Hampton's Mag.* (Jan.) 844: I'm on for anything, but I'm making a Dutch book that I'm staying somewhere. **1942** *ATS* 691: *Dutch book,* a book with no house percentage. **1949** Cummings *Dict. Sports* 121: *Dutch book*...A bookmaker's error in which he offers odds with the percentage against himself. **1961** Scarne *Complete Gde. to Gamb.* 45: Rival bookies sent scouts to other books, looking for one who would...post an odds line that totaled up to a *Dutch book* (an odds line which totaled less than 100%). If he found a Dutch book, the smart bettor or rival bookie would win money by betting each horse in the race. The bookie with the Dutch book very quickly became an ex-bookie. **1968** M.B. Scott *Racing Game* 99: This is known as a "dutch" book.

Dutch cap *n.* a contraceptive diaphragm.

1950 in *West. Folk.* XXIV (1965) 197: *Dutch cap*—the contraceptive diaphragm. ***1981** *Macquarie Dict.* ***1984** Partridge *DSUE* (ed. 8): *Dutch cap.* A type of female pessary...since ca. 1925; by ca. 1950...widespread.

Dutch courage *n.* false courage instilled by liquor; (*hence*) liquor.

1809 (cited in *W10*). **1812** in *DAE*. **1833** Ames *Old Sailor's Yarns* 298: Although he knew that the Albatrosses didn't require any Dutch courage, the sun was over the foreyard, and it was grog time in all Christian countries. ***1833** Marryat *Peter Simple* 422: Dutch courage is a term for courage screwed up by drinking freely. **1852** in *West. Folk.* XI (1952) 29: A bottle of true Dutch courage—genuine Knickerbocker Madeira. ***1872** in *F & H* II 348: A dose of brandy...produces Dutch courage. **1883** *Life* (Mar. 22) 143: Let's go out and take a nip of Dutch courage, will you? **1940** E. O'Neill *Iceman* 145: I'll show that cheap drummer I don't have to have any Dutch courage. **1942** Garcia *Tough Trip* 229: I got my Dutch courage up enough to visit the Injun camp. **1966** *West. Folk.* (Jan.) 38: *Dutch courage*...gin. **1990** *New Republic* (Sept. 10) 48: Shy man has to give speech, tries some dutch courage, gets hopelessly drunk.

Dutch fuck *n.* (see 1948 quot.).—usu. considered vulgar.

*1948 Partridge *DSUE* (ed. 3) 1039: *Dutch f**k.* Lighting one cigarette from another. Forces': 1940+. **1974** N.Y.C. man, age 23: A *Dutch fuck* is when you light someone's cigarette with your own.

Dutch-head *n.* a German.—used derisively.

1928 MacArthur *War Bugs* 183: Who said them Dutch heads could fight?

Dutch leave *n.* FRENCH LEAVE.

1898 in *West. Folk.* XI (1952) 30: You've gone and broke the rules and articles of war...You took Dutch leave.

Dutchman *n.* **1.a.** a German man.—usu. used contemptuously. [Orig. S.E.; see *OED.*]

*1387, ***1413,** ***1538,** ***1570,** ***1599,** ***1617,** ***1788** in *OED.* **1850** Garrard *Wah-to-Yah* 118: The sojers—a lot of greenhorns and Dutchmen—came to Purgatoire, this side of Raton. **1910** Hapgood *City Streets* 118: One gradually leaves off calling the Italian a "dago" and the German a "Dutchman." **1928** Wharton *Squad* 34 [ref. to 1918]: Every night the Dutchmen drench this area with gas shells. **1933** H. Stephenson *Glass* 246: You damn lazy Dutchman. **1936** Sayre & Faulkner *Road to Glory* (film): I've got to laugh when I think of them Dutchmen down there. **1965** Spillane *Killer Mine* 25: You're a big one now who doesn't give a yell for the cloak-and-suiters or the guinea mafia or ignorant spics or the dutchmen or the micks or S.N.C.C. or any of them. **1977** T. Berger *Villanova* 20: If he was not as dead as...cold lasagna...I was a Dutchman.

b. *Naut.* a German vessel. [*OED* offers cites from 1657 in the S.E. sense 'Dutch ship'.]

*1949 W. Granville *Sea Slang* 87: *Dutchman.* Dutch or German merchant ship.

2. Esp. *Naut.* a usu. northern European man other than a Britisher; foreigner.—usu. used contemptuously.

1857 in *OEDS*: Europeans...save French, English, and "Eyetalians" are in California classed...[as] Dutchmen, or more frequently "d—d Dutchmen," merely for the sake of euphony. **1884** Symondson *Abaft the Mast* 66: Germans, Swedes, Dutchmen, and Russian Fins. All foreigners are called "Dutchmen" at sea. *1892 in *OEDS*: In sea-lingo (Pacific) *Dutchman* includes all Teutons and folk from the basin of the Baltic. **1894** *DN* I 341: *Dutchman:* any foreigner who speaks English brokenly or not at all. (Going out of use.) **1898** Westcott *David Harum* 228: He "was some kind of a Dutchman I guess" ("Dutchman" was Mr. Harum's generic name for all people native to the Continent of Europe). **1899** Boyd *Shellback* 28: Americans call sailors of every nation except themselves and the English "Dutchmen." A Frenchman or a German is a Dutchman, so is an Italian or a Greek. As a rule, a crew of Dutchmen is a difficult nut to crack. **1910** in *OEDS*: To us in the West...all foreigners whose mother tongue was other than English were "Dutchmen." *1928 in *Ibid.*

3.a. (in various trades) a small flaw or gap that requires a plug or insertion.

1859 Bartlett *Amer.* 134: *Dutchman.* A flaw in a stone or marble slab, filled up by an insertion. *ca*1940 in Botkin *Treas. Amer. Folk.* 550: Most of the smaller [print] shops never had enough leads, quads or spaces, we'd be told to "plug the Dutchman" when we complained. That meant you simply had to make out with pasteboard, toothpick sliver, tin or anything else to be found.

b. (in various trades) an often makeshift plug, filler, or piece used to fill or cover a gap or flaw.

*1874 in *OED*: *Dutchman*...a playful name for a block or wedge of wood driven into a gap to hide the fault in a badly made joint. **1894** *DN* I 341: *Dutchman*...[In carpentry] a piece of wood inserted to fill a space left or made by mistake or careless work. **1909** *WNID* 686: *Dutchman*...In mechanics, carpentry, etc., an odd piece inserted to fill an opening, hide a defect, or strengthen a weak part. **1938** *AS* (Dec.) 271: If some of the type are loose...a toothpick or a match stick is sometimes driven in as a wedge. This slipshod procedure...is called putting in a *dutchman*. **1939** in *West. Folk.* XI (1952) 30: When a form fails to fit, the stoneman should not drive in a "dutchman." **1943** in *DA*: A hole was bored and corked tight with a small steel plug known as a "dutchman." **1947** Mencken *Amer. Lang.* Supp. II 774: *Dutchman.* A cemented repair on a finished stone. **1949** Cummings *Dict. Sports* 121. **1960** *New Yorker* (Sept. 3) 20: He mended the lion by cutting recesses several inches deep wherever the stone was damaged, and fitting new pieces of stone therein. These pieces are known in the trade as dutchmen. **1961** *WNID3*: *Dutchman*...a strip of cloth used in the theater to conceal the crack between two scenery flats. *1961 Burgess *Dict. Sailing* 79: *Dutchman.* A piece of wood or metal that covers any defective joint. *1981 *Macquarie Dict.* 564: *Dutchman*...a piece or wedge inserted to hide the fault in a badly made joint, stop an opening, etc.

c. *Logging.* a stick, wedge, block, or the like used as a prop or support.

1905 in *DA*: *Dutchman*, a short stick placed transversely between the outer logs of a load to...keep any logs from falling off. **1956** Sorden & Ebert *Logger's* 13 [ref. to *a*1925]: *Dutchman*, 1. A splinter or slab of wood to be put under a wrapper chain to keep it tight, or to level up the load on a sleigh. 2. Wood left in undercut to support the heavy side of a tree when it was falling on a swing. 3. A short stick placed traversely between the outer logs of a load to keep any logs from falling off. **1958** in *AS* (Feb. 1959) 77: *Dutchman*...A prop put under a log to keep it from pinching a saw during bucking...A prop used for any similar purpose. **1963–64** Kesey *Great Notion* 468: How to place a dutchman block in an undercut.

d. (see quot.).

1909 *Century Dict.* (Supp.): *Dutchman*, a layer of suet fastened with skewers into a roast of lean beef or mutton.

e. *Logging.* (see quot.).

1958 in *AS* (Feb. 1959) 77: *Dutchman*...A certain type of block that is put around a tree to haul up the rigging. This the rigger will say, "We hung the Dutchman."

f. (see quot.).

1961 *WNID3*: *Dutchman*...a piece of pipe or duct used to replace temporarily a piece of equipment (as a heating unit in a ventilation duct).

4. *Naut.* a fraction of a knot of speed.

1897 Kelley *Ship's Company* 26: "How fast are you going, my man?" was an invariable question of the inevitable, curious passenger to the Jackie walking away with the dripping log-line. "Fourteen and a Dutchman, sir," would be his answer, or, if again pressed, "Thirteen and a marine,"...to the joy of his grinning shipmates and to the mystification of the questioner.

5. *Mining.* any condition of a drill hole that makes extraction of the bit difficult.

1929 *AS* (Dec.) 145: *Dutchman*, a ridge in the center of a drill hole causing the steel to stick. **1946** *Calif. Folk. Qly.* (Oct.) 167: Whenever a drill lurches suddenly from hard rock to soft, or into a...small cavity of some sort, without drilling a hole large enough to release the drill, old miners acquainted with the Cornish terminology say, "There's a Dutchman in the hole."

6. (see quot.).

*ca*1940 in Mencken *Amer. Lang.* Supp. II 774: *Dutchman.* A small derrick, operated by hand [among structural iron workers].

Dutchman's breeches *n.pl. Naut.* a patch of blue sky visible through clouds.

*1867 Smyth *Sailor's Wd.-Bk.*: *Dutchman's breeches*, the patch of blue sky often seen when a gale is breaking is said to be, however small, "enough to make a pair of breeches for a Dutchman." **1889** *United Service* (Sept.) 273: "Dutchman's breeches" are faint gleams of blue in a cloudy sky. **1942** Casey *Torpedo Junction* 332: Not enough cloud to make a Dutchman's breeches.

Dutchman's hurricane *n. Naut.* a calm at sea. Cf. IRISHMAN'S HURRICANE.

1905 *Bluejacket* (Apr.) 196: I have known her to roll off three and four knots in a Dutchman's hurricane, or, as you youngsters would call it, a dead calm.

Dutch milk *n.* beer. *Joc.*

1905 *DN* III 78: *Dutch milk*, *n.* Beer.

Dutch ride *n. West.* (see quot.). Now *hist.*

1966 Olsen *Hard Men* 50: It was a Dutch ride. He got dragged on a rope. *Ibid.* 64: I never ordered Sears to give him a Dutch ride.

Dutch route *n. Pris.* suicide.—constr. with *the.* Cf. DUTCH ACT.

1912 Lowrie *Prison* 105: I never thought he'd go th' Dutch route. *Ibid.*: They would cheat the gallows by going the "Dutch route" if not closely watched during the night. **1927–28** Tasker *Grimhaven* 117: I wish I'd gone the Dutch route at the beginning. I've got too much on the books now to be slitting my throat. **1938** *Amer. Mercury* (Oct.) 148: Scarcely a week passes that some man or woman does not go the Dutch route by "jumping or falling",...beneath the wheels of a [subway] train. **1953** T. Runyon *In for Life* 98: Aw, he tried the Dutch route.

Dutch rub *n. Juve.* (see 1966 quot.).

1930 Riggs *Lilacs* 148 [ref. to *ca*1905]: Ort to give you a good Dutch rub and arn some of the craziness out of you! **1938** in *DARE*. **1954–60** *DAS*. **1966** *West. Folk.* (Jan.) 38: *Dutch rub.* Mild torture practised by youthful teenagers, inflicted by applying the knuckles to the back of a smaller boy's head or neck, particularly when the victim's hair had just been cut short. Central Kansas, 1910–1918. **1980** *Nat. Lampoon* (Oct.) 46: A cop...gave me a Dutch rub and a kick in the butt. **1987** *Nat. Lampoon* (Oct.) 87: Throwing ice cream, breaking windows, giving each other Dutch rubs. **1990** G. Larson *Wiener Dog Art* 16: Maybe I'll just...give you a good Dutch rub.

Dutchy *n.* a Dutch or German person.—often used contemptuously.

1834 in Hoffman *Winter in West* II 198: Come along, Dutchee, my boy. **1858** in G.W. Harris *High Times* 151: I give Dutchy a punch. **1878** Cutler *Hans* 5: Well that's all right, dutchey. **1882** "M. Twain" *Life on Miss.* 308: Dutchy...was a German lad who did not know enough to come in out of the rain. **1909** F. Harris *Bomb* 12: Ah, go scratch your head, Dutchy. **1918** *Lit. Digest* (Apr. 20) 78: Those dutchies know we're comin'. **1918** *Outlook* (Sept. 18) 95: I'll projec' round an' bring you in one o' them Dutchies afore sundown. **1929** Brecht *Downfall* 72: Du bist dumm, like the Dutchies say. **1948** McIlwaine *Memphis* 240: Those Dutchies…are good folks. *****1949**, *****1959** in *OEDS*.

duty *n. Navy & USMC.* an experience, thing, or person (esp. a young woman) evaluated as being pleasant or unpleasant.— usu. constr. with *good* or *bad.* [Quots. ref. to WWII.]
   1948 *AS* (Oct.) 249: Rugged duty…anything difficult to accomplish. **1949** McMillan *Old Breed* 430: A Marine will say of a girl he has enjoyed being with, "She's good duty." Oppositely, if he tells a friend that a girl is "bad duty," then she's to be avoided, given a wide berth…To a Marine overseas in World War II anything superlatively good might be described as "Stateside duty." **1951** W. Williams *Enemy* 60: Maybe you're not so hot about being out of Norfolk. Maybe that tender little flier's wife was good duty.
   ¶ In phrase:
   ¶ **do (one's) duty** (a euphem. for) to defecate or urinate.
   *a*1916 in *Immortalia* 6: The Passing of the Backhouse…We did our duties promptly. **1934** Roth *Call It Sleep* 101: "Step up close an' do yer dooty, sonny me boy." He propelled the reluctant David toward the urinal. *****1935**, *****1938** in *OEDS*. **1986** Kubicki *Breaker Boys* 38: If there's a dog that's done his duty…near my house, my boys'd find some way to step in it.

duty-dodger *n. Army.* a soldier who evades duty. Hence **duty-dodging,** *n.*
   [**1918** O'Reilly *Roving & Fighting* 80 [ref. to 1899]: He was…always in trouble and always dodging duty.] **1919** Emmett *Give 'Way* 51: "Duty-dodging," therefore, became an acquired art. **1919** Small *Story of 47th* 64: We're not all "duty-dodgers." **1931** *Our Army* (Dec.) 12: He's just a gold-bricking duty-dodger. **1959** Downey *Clash of Cavalry* 26: The sorry state of "Company Q" was aggravated when it deteriorated into a refuge for a number of riffraff, malingerers, and assorted duty dodgers, well content to sit out the war in a safe place. **1979** in Fierstein *Torch Song* 143: Deserter! Defector! Duty-dodger! Ditching your post at the first sign of battle.

duty-struck *adj. Mil.* intent on the performance of one's duties to the letter, esp. as a means of self-aggrandizement.
   1923 *Amer. Leg. Wkly.* (Dec. 14) 11 [ref. to 1918]: I'd take a smoke, but that four-eyed two-striper's duty-struck 'n' I get all the guard house I want off the duty roster. **1927** J. Stevens *Mattock* 8 [ref. to 1918]: I wasn't wanted because they called trying to be a good soldier "duty-struck." **1937** Thompson *Take Her Down* 210 [ref. to 1918]: A rather poisonous, duty-struck young Bluenose (Nova Scotian) reservist for skipper. **1957** Campbell *Cry for Happy* 51: Our orders put duty-struck young officers in their place. **1958** F. Davis *Spearhead* 105 [ref. to 1945]: Forget it. Don't be so duty-struck. **1969** Bosworth *Love Affair* 37: He remembers a recruit from Fall River, named Barbarou, who was handed an ancient and empty Springfield and ordered to guard the clotheslines. Barbarou was what the Navy calls "duty-struck," and marched up and down as militarily as if he had been guarding the U.S. Mint, challenging anyone who came near.

dweeb *n.* [orig. unkn.] Esp. *Stu.* an obnoxious person; an overdiligent student. Also **tweeb.**
   1968 Baker et al. *CUSS* 111: Dweeb. A person without much social or academic ability. **1977** Univ. Tenn. student: What a bunch of dweebs! **1982** *L.A. Times* (Oct. 25) V 1: We all know a "telephone dweeb."…It's the person who is exasperating, impolite, inefficient and annoying on the telephone. **1984** Algeo *Stud Buds* 3: A studious classmate…dweeb….dud….fag [etc.] **1986** *Daily Beacon* (Univ. Tenn.) (May 2) 7: Pulverize the tweebs that forced me into this! **1987** *21 Jump St.* (Fox-TV): I can't look like a dweeb at my first inspection. **1988** Univ. Tenn. student theme: When one sees a *nerd* he has a tendency to feel sorry for him, but one always avoids a *dweeb* at any cost. **1990** *Newsweek* (Nov. 20) 54: Approached by "some dweeb" from the White House who suggested Bush would sign a congressional pay raise. **1991** B.E. Ellis *Amer. Psycho* 49: Why is he sitting with those dweebs?

dweebie *n.* DWEEB.
   1986 J. Hughes *Ferris Beuller* (film): Geeks…dweebies, wastoids—they all think he's great. **1987** N.Y.C. schoolboy, age 7: You maxi-zoom *dweebie!*

dwid *n.* [perh. var. of TWIT] DWEEB.
   1987 *Rage* (Univ. Tenn.) (No. 3) 34: You are a dwid. **1992** Thatcher & Bannon *Thrasher* 64: *Dwid*…One who is not happening.

dwindles *n.pl. Med.* a rapid decline in a patient's strength and

faculties as the result either of old age or of an acute terminal condition.—constr. with *the.*
   1981 in Safire *Good Word* 152: "The dwindles" is medical jargon for advancing years leading to death from old age. *Ibid.* 156: "The dwindles" implies a patient is dwindling in front of your eyes despite your efforts and is about to expire.

dye stuffs *n.pl.* money.
   1871 (quot. at JOHN). **1889** Farmer *Amer.*

dying quail *n. Sports.* a ball that has been thrown or hit in the air weakly or with poor control.
   [**1974** Perry & Sudyk *Me & Spitter* 18: [The ball] dipped into the dirt like a shot quail.] **1982** *Chi. Sun-Times* (Nov. 9): Ken Singleton hit a dying quail six inches in front of [the] second baseman. **1982** Considine *Lang. Sport* 17: *Dying quail.* an apparently playable routine fly ball that unexpectedly drops in for a base hit, often due to wind. **1984** *N.Y. Post* (Sept. 3) 17: Wilson mysteriously broke to the outside, away from the dying quail. **1984** Univ. Tenn. prof., age *ca*37: My brother and I have been referring to a weak pass as a *dying quail* for at least a couple of years—possibly since the '70's.

dyke[1] or **dike** *n.* [prob. fr. *morphadike,* dial. var. *hermaphrodite;* cf. BULLDYKE and BULLDYKER] a female homosexual, esp. if aggressive or masculine in appearance and mannerisms.— usu. used disparagingly; in recent use occ. non-disparaging in self-reference.
   1931 in Tamony *Americanisms* (No. 31) 8: Benches in the more obscure parts are used continually by couples, pansies and dykes. **1935** Pollock *Und. Speaks:* Dike, a lesbian; a female sexual pervert. [**1937** *AS* (Apr.) 161: *Morphadyte, morphadyke,* sb., the folk-term for *hermaphrodite,* usually applied to a horse, but sometimes to a human being. Nebraska and North Carolina.] **1941** G. Legman, in Henry *Sex Vars.* II 1163: Dike. A female homosexual, especially if aggressive and masculine. Also: *dyke.* **1942–43** C. Jackson *Lost Weekend* 31: There were [double-entendre] songs called "The 23rd Street Ferry" and "Peter and the Dyke." **1944** in J. Costello *Love, Sex & War* 94: *Q* What is a "dike"? *A* Well it is…a woman who "goes down" on other women. **1949** *Gay Girl's Guide* 7: Dike—Lesbian, female homosexual. **1949** "J. Evans" *Halo in Blood* 51: There's a dike…who runs a poor man's bordello. **1956** Holiday & Dufty *Lady Sings* 27 [ref. to *ca*1927]: One night a big dike went after me. They call them lesbians now, but we just called them dikes. **1957** J. Jones *Some Came Running* 34: But that gal's no dyke, boys. **1960** Wohl *Cold Wind* 72: Dykes, she reflected, yawning, they're worse than men. **1962** Dougherty *Commissioner* 109: That kid—the little blonde—she's a dike. Isn't that something? **1966** S. Harris *Hellhole* 196: Two dykes had me against the wall and the third burned me with a cigarette. **1987** *Campus Voice* (Spr.) 7: The fact remains that faggots and dykes are unnatural and disgusting creatures who are getting what they deserve. **1991** *Village Voice* (N.Y.C.) (Aug. 13) 11: Abzug's "Dear Sisters" leaflet makes a big pitch for the dyke vote—"*Two gay candidates* are running. *But only one of us is a woman.*" **1992** *Newsweek* (Nov. 23) 32: I'm not a fag.…I'm a dyke. **1993** *Wall St. Journal* (May 3) A1: Some lesbians prefer "dyke."…Lesbians who call themselves dykes "don't care whether someone is offended with who they are. Dykes are rebellious, strong."

dyke[2] *n.* (at Virginia Military Institute) an underclassman who is made to do tasks for an upperclassman.
   1951 *Time* (May 28) 50: In the barracks, they must…race up the stairways to their fourth "stoop" (upper-classmen live below according to class). They serve as "dykes" (fags) for their seniors, run errands, polish shoes and stack cots. **1982** *Maledicta* VI 127: At Virginia Military Institute what West Point would call *plebs* are called *dykes.*

dyke *v.* to engage in lesbian activity.
   1941 G. Legman, in Henry *Sex. Vars.* 1163: The verbal noun, *diking,* is often used to refer to Lesbian intercourse, especially tribady. **1968** Vidal *Breckinridge* 258: [She] gave up diking on the spot. **1966–71** Karlen *Sex & Homosex.* 379: She…settles for tribadism—"dyking."

dykey *adj.* being or resembling a female homosexual.
   1964 S. Bellow, in *OEDS* I 801: Lucas warned me to look out for something dikey. *****1966** in *Ibid.* **1967** *Playboy* (Jan.) 30: Dykey June turns into Sister George. **1973** *Atlantic* (Apr.) 102: You don't think it's dykey, the way you sleep around?

dynamite *n.* **1.a.** something or someone that is especially powerful or effective. See also DYNAMITE, *adj.,* 2.
   1904 in "O. Henry" *Works* 655: It's a can of dynamite. It's a gold mine. **1922** in H. Crane *Letters* 78: Another small magazine, full of compressed dynamite. **1923** "King Zany" & Billy Duval *I've Got a Cross-*

Eyed Papa (sheet music): He's got a way that spells dynamite.

b. *Specif.* strong liquor or (*Narc.*) a powerful narcotic or psychotropic drug; (*occ.*) powerful snuff.

1919 *Century* (Dec.) 293: Did you take notice to those old birds about the tents…blue with dynamite rum and ready to drool for a hand-out. **1920** *Hicoxy's Army* 132: Little did he dream…of the opportunities…to stop here and there for that mug of "Dynamite." **1924** Tully *Beggars of Life* 28: That dynamite Hinky Dink sells 'ud make a hummin' bird fly slow. **1924** Henderson *Keys to Crookdom* 403: *Dynamite.* Heroin, a synthetic drug made from morphine. **1930** Lait *On the Spot* 202: *Dynamite*…cocaine. **1933** Ersine *Pris. Slang* 34: *Dynamite, n.* Snuff made and used by convicts. It consists of tobacco, soda, salt, and sugar. **1948** T. Williams *Summer & Smoke* 27: Applejack brandy…Liquid dynamite. **1952** Ellson *Golden Spike* 92: I just got off, the three of us had a sixteenth and it was dynamite. **1952** Mandel *Angry Strangers* 162: I got some dynamite, it's from India. Real Gunja. **1953** Anslinger & Tompkins *Traf. in Narc.* 308: *Dynamite.* Heroin or cocaine. *Also* a combination of cocaine and morphine. **1958** McCulloch *Woods Wds.* 56: *Dynamite*…snuff. **1958** J.B. West *Eye* 11: She kept sipping away at that dynamite she had just distilled. **1968** Heard *Howard St.* 161: That stud…came over with that dynamite every now and then.

c. something or someone that is especially dangerous.—occ. attrib.

1927 in Hammett *Knockover* 349: Don't take any chances with them—Flora and Papadopoulos are dynamite. **1927–28** in R. Nelson *Dishonorable* 147: *Pratt:*…You know, women are poison to Nick. *McQuigg:* Maybe this one'll be dynamite. **1930** *Our Army* (Jan.) 20: *Dynamite.* A very common name given to army mules or horses of bad disposition. The title indicates the dangerous character of the animal. **1930** Lait *On the Spot* 202: *Dynamite*…Anything dangerous. **1933** Ersine *Pris. Slang* 34: *Dynamite*…Hot, dangerous. "They pulled a dynamite job right across from the window." **1934** Burns *Female Convict* 129: Be careful of O'Gorman—she's dynamite! **1940** W.C. Williams *In the Money* 39: He didn't have to butt in on J.W. Why that's dynamite. **1944** Bellow *Dangling Man* 99: He didn't have to tell me. I could tell from the beginning she was dynamite. **1958** Constiner *Gunman* 11: Respectable stockmen knew it for what it was—dynamite—and gave it a wide berth.

d. *Gamb.* (see quot.).

*a***1951** in D.W. Maurer *Lang. Und.* 209: *Dynamite*…Money that one book bets with another to cover bets he does not wish to keep.

2. Esp. *Mil.* a strong laxative. *Joc.*

1919 Warren *Ninth Co.* 34 [ref. to WWII]: The Engineer's Dictionary…*Dynamite*—What you take in case c.c.'s fail. **1944** Kendall *Service Slang* 6: *Dynamite pills*…urge nature. **1958** McCulloch *Woods Wds.* 56: *Dynamite*…A double or triple dose of a laxative.

3. (see quot.).

1935–40 in Mencken *Amer. Lang.* Supp. II 773: [Slang of] *Steel Workers*…*Dynamite.* Limestone…From *dolomite.*

dynamite *adj.* **1.** politically radical; violently anarchistic.—used attrib. Cf. DYNAMITER, 1.

1890 Howells *Hazard* 355: I don't like that dynamite talk of his.

2. stunning; exciting; absolutely superlative.—also interj. [Essentially a predicative, interjectional and attrib. use of DYNAMITE, *n.*, 1.a., but increasingly common with clearly adjectival force after *ca*1945, and esp. after *ca*1965.]

1922 Tully *Emmett Lawler* 287: I'd rather fight a hyena than that Wop; he's dynamite. **1925–26** J. Black *Can't Win* 199: I'm dynamite with them old brums in the cribs. **1935** Spewack *Boy Meets Girl* 380: And not the one with the buck teeth either. She's dynamite. **1936** Miller *Battling Bellhop* (film): That kid's dynamite! He's got the makings of a champion! **1944** Solomon & Buchman *Snafu* 31: He has *one* reaction to everything: Dynamite!…We don't exactly know what that means yet. **1945** Hartman & Shavelson *Wonder Man* (film): You're dynamite, Mac, dynamite! **1947** in *DAS* s.v. *dreamboat:* She is a dynamite dreamboat. **1948** Hargrove *Got to Give* 97: You're dynamite. You're the most masterful salesman I ever saw. **1949** *Always Leave Them Laughing* (film): What an agent! What an agent! You're dynamite! Dynamite! **1967** C. Cooper *Farm* 53: There were also some nice *Playboy* shots that I kept (1 dynamite fleshy configuration from Europe that gave me an erection). **1971** N.Y.U. student: Kim Novak could've been a dynamite star if they'd let her do some decent flicks. **1972** Kopp *Buddha* 202: Really *dynamite* grass. **1972** Grogan *Ringolevio* 142: Anna Marie gave birth to a dynamite baby girl. **1974** in Mack *Real Life* (unp.): "I work for RCA now." "Dynamite!" **1978** Maupin *Tales* 68: She was probably *dynamite* in the sack. **1979** Gutcheon *New Girls* 346: What a dynamite job you did on the reunion. **1981** *Nat. Lampoon* (Aug.) 18: Marty, I got

an idea yesterday that is so dynamite, I am trembling as I write it. **1987** WINS Radio News (Mar. 25): Said a dynamite undercover operation helped crack the case.

3. Orig. *Boxing.* (esp. of a blow) powerful.

1920–21 Witwer *Leather Pushers* 25: Usin' that dynamite left for blockin' and feintin' purposes only. **1930** Farrell *Calico Shoes* 193: Christ, what a wallop! Dynamite! **1933** Ersine *Pris. Slang* 34: *Dynamite, adj.* Powerful. **1934** Weseen *Dict. Slang* 208: The wielder of a dynamite bat is a hard hitter.

dynamite *v.* **1.a.** to talk loudly, complainingly, or out of turn. Cf. DYNAMITER, 1.b.

1929–30 Farrell *Young Lonigan* 105: Come on and quit dynamitin'.

b. to speak aggressively and insistently in an attempt to sell, persuade, impress, or seduce. Also intrans. Cf. DYNAMITER, 2.

1929 Hammett *Maltese Falcon* 9: "Well, don't dynamite her too much. What do you think of her?" "Sweet! And you telling me not to dynamite her!" **1956** "T. Betts" *Across Board* 240: Touts were allowed to advertise winners they did not have. This was called "blasting," "dynamiting," or "bulldogging." **1959** Ellison *Gentleman Junkie* 208: So I took the Tiger down to see Frankie Sullivan, who owned the joint, and in a burst of fantastic dynamiting, sold him on the kid.

2.a. *R.R.* (of a train) to suddenly come to an emergency full stop.

1934 in Fenner *Throttle* 53: And then, in spite of it, she dynamited…The fireman yelled, "Did she break in two?"

b. *R.R.* (hence also among truckers) to apply (an emergency brake) suddenly.

1958 McCulloch *Woods Wds.* 56: *Dynamite*…To slam on the emergency brake. **1971** Tak *Truck Talk* 54: *Dynamite the brakes:* to make an emergency stop. **1978** Lieberman & Rhodes *CB* (ed. 2) 298: *Dynamite the brakes*—Stop quickly.

3. expedite.

1938 *AS* (Apr.) 156: *Dynamite an order.* To rush an order through as quickly as possible.

dynamiter *n.* **1.a.** a violent anarchist or communist. Now *hist.*

1877 in *Mo. Hist. Rev.* XVIII (1924) 205: In the United States they are "dynamiters;" in Canada they are "dynamiteurs;" in England they are "dynamitards." They are cowardly scoundrels everywhere. **1884** in Lummis *Letters* 10: A friendly confab of politics. Thank heaven, there are no dynamiters this far West. **1890** Howells *Hazard* 158: "By-the-bye, March, I saw that old dynamiter of yours round at Beaton's room yesterday." "What old dynamiter of mine?" "That old one-handed Dutchman." **1905** in Blackbeard & Williams *Smithsonian Comics* 30: "I move that we declare war against America." "Dynamiter." *****1908** Chesterton *Man Who Was Thursday* 54: This…was the secret enclave of the European Dynamiters. *Ibid.* 86: You are an anarchist, you are a dynamiter! **1915** *Report on Colo. Strike* 26: A bunch of Democrats—a bunch of dynamiters, Jeff called them. **1947** W.M. Camp *S.F.* 304: Haskell…was among the first of the "dynamiters" and…did not hesitate to advocate the most violent methods for achieving a worker's revolution.

b. a chronic complainer.

1918 *Stars & Stripes* (Apr. 12) 7: A "dynamiter" in engineer parlance, is the nth degree of knocker, crabber, kicker, sourball. A "poison oaker" is about the same thing again.

c. (among tramps) an ineffectual character; sponger.

1916 *Lit. Digest* (Aug.): *Dynamiter,* some harmless blanket stiff who has specialized in chicken coops and in back doors for "hand outs." **1918** Livingston *Mother Delcassee: Dino* or *dynamiter*…Sponged food off fellow hoboes. **1930** Irwin *Tramp & Und. Sl.: Dynamiter*…A tramp who begs from his fellows in preference to begging for his own food from the public.

2.a. a high-pressure salesman.

1927 (cited in Partridge *Dict. Und.* 218). **1932** *Writer's Digest* (Aug.) 48: *Dynamiter,* a high-powered bootleg salesman. **1931–47** in Mencken *Amer. Lang.* Supp. II 773: *Dynamiter.* A stock salesman of extraordinary virulence.

b. a recklessly ambitious or aggressive person; troublemaker.

1934 Weseen *Dict. Slang* 331: *Dynamiter*—An aggressive and ambitious person. *a***1951** in D.W. Maurer *Lang. Und.* 209: *Dynamiter*…A gambler who is engineering a *coup*. *a***1955** in *Ibid.* 240: *Dynamiter*…A [pickpocket] who likes *rip and tear* techniques. Sometimes a strong-arm man. **1971** *PADS* (No. 52) 28: *Dynamiter, n. Rare.* A trouble-making

fire fighter. "An officer is very cautious of a dynamiter in his company."
3. *R.R.* (see 1932 quot.).

1930 Irwin *Tramp & Und. Sl.* 68: *Dynamiter*...A railroad car with faulty brake mechanism. **1932** *Railroad Stories* (Oct.) 366: *Dynamiter*—A car on which a defective air mechanism that sends the brakes into full emergency when only a service application is made by the engineer. **1939** *Sat. Eve. Post* (Apr.) 26: They didn't use any breeze those days, so the donikers on the reefers didn't have to look out for a dynamiter. **1962** *AS* XXXVII 132: *Dynamiter, n.* A...[defective railroad] car that has something wrong with the air.

4. (among truckers) (see quot.).

1942 *AS* (Apr.) 103: *Dynamiter.* Driver who abuses truck severely.

dynamo *adj.* DYNAMITE, *adj.*, 2.

1933 C. Wilson & J. Cluett *What—No Beer?* (film): It's terrific! It's dynamo! **1972** N.Y.U. student: We used to say *dynamo!* instead of *dynamite!* That was common usage in 1967.

dynamo-buster *n. Navy.* an electrician. *Joc.*

1914 *DN* IV 150: *Dynamo Buster.* Electrician. **1941** Kendall *Army & Navy Sl.* 18: *Dynamo buster*...electrician. **1945** in *Calif. Folk. Qly.* V (1946) 383: Humorous too are *tinbender, dough-puncher,* and *dynamo-buster* for the metalsmith, baker, and electrician.

dyno¹ or **dino** *n.* [DYN(AMITER) + -O] **1.a.** *Construction.* a member of a dynamiting crew.

1922 N. Anderson *Hobo* 93: A "dino" is a man who works with and handles dynamite. **1927** *AS* (June) 386: *Dino* is a synonym for *dingbat* [old beggar], but it originally referred to a workman who handled dynamite. **1930** "D. Stiff" *Milk & Honey* 204: *Dyno* or *dino*—A rock man who handles dynamite. **1948** J. Stevens *Jim Turner* 122 [ref. to *ca*1910]: Dynos...lived by drilling and blasting in the hard rock.

b. *Und.* a burglar who employs explosives to break into vaults or safes.

1929 Barr *Let Tomorrow Come* 3: The lowliest doormat thief will name himself a dino of surpassing ability.

2. *Hobo.* an old or drunken derelict; an old beggar or tramp.

1918 (quot. at DYNAMITER, *n.*, 1.c.). **1925** Mullin *Scholar Tramp* 258 [ref. to *ca*1912]: One was a hoary old dyno named Whale-oil Pete. **1927**

Thrasher *Gang* 267: Rolling the bums or the "dinos," jack-rolling—robbing drunken men. **1929** *AS* IV 339: The Vocabulary of Bums...*dino*—An old beggar. **1930** "D. Stiff" *Milk & Honey* 101: The dyno is a selfish and solitary fellow...He is full ready to pick up anything that you leave. **1942** Algren *Morning* 12: That dino'll find out I just been too shrewd for him. **1949** Algren *Golden Arm* 26: Someday he'll shake down the wrong dino. **1968** Spradley *Owe Yourself a Drunk* 38: We get...unsavory provender as befits bumptious, abominable winos, dinos, dingbats.

dyno² *n.* a dynamometer.

1951–53 in *AS* XXIX (1954) 96: What will your mill turn on the dyno?

dyno *adj.* DYNAMITE, *adj.*, 2.

1960 C. Cooper *Scene* 12: Crazy...It's dyno, baby. **1962** Crump *Killer* 105: That stuff is sure dyno. **1966** *Time* (July 1) 73A: It might be disastrous for advertisers...to try to get chummy with teen-agers by telling them that their products are boss, tough, out of sight, fab or dyno. **1970** Cain *Blueschild Baby* 25: "How's the stuff?" "Dyno." **1973** N.Y.U. student: It's dyno! **1980** Knoxville, Tenn., man, age *ca*35: I thought your playing was dyno. **1980** in *Penthouse* (Jan. 1981) 128: I wanted three sticks of dyno weed and a rock album of my choice. **1989** P. Munro *U.C.L.A. Slang* 36: That chick is dyno. Marcie, that dinner you made was way dyno.

dyn-o-mite /'dai'nou'mait/ *adj.* [alter. DYNAMITE, *adj.*, 2] stunning; absolutely superlative. [Introduced or popularized by the character J.J. on the situation comedy *Good Times* (CBS-TV, 1974–79).]

1976 Rosen *Above Rim* 111: How's your new pad comin'? I'll bet it's dyn-o-mite! **1977** *Nat. Lampoon* (Aug.) 35: Vocals by Peter Baldspot are dyn-o-mite. **1978** Selby *Requiem* 91: Ah got some boss shit, man. Ah mean its dyn o mite. **1981** *Nat. Lampoon* (Nov.) 60: So you're a detective now, huh? Dy-no-mite!

dyno-rouster *n. Hobo.* (see quots.).

1925 Mullin *Scholar Tramp* 283 [ref. to *ca*1912]: They were petty pilferers and dyno-rousters (thieves who specialize in robbing, or rolling, drunken men). **1927** *DN* V 445: *Dyno-rousters, n.* Thieves who rob drunken men.

eager *adj. Mil. Av.* ambitious or zealous, esp. in seeking promotion or distinction; (*specif.*) keen to distinguish oneself in combat; (*broadly*) enthusiastic.

1937 Lay *I Wanted Wings* 49 [ref. to 1932]: *Eager.* An eager Mister is the model Dodo who was probably never late to Sunday school when he was a kid. Overconscientious. Boot-licking. *Ibid.* 56: You'd better get eager in a hurry, Mister! About face! **1941** *AS* (Oct.) 165: *Get Eager.* To strive to the utmost. **1944** in Rea *Wings of Gold* 181: The lecturing officer was awfully eager for gas warfare. **1944** Stiles *Big Bird* 90: I wanted to get in the big bird and go over there. I hadn't been eager since I left Preflight, but I was eager then. **1946** G.C. Hall, Jr. *1000 Destroyed* 420: A pilot who wanted to fly every rough mission was eager. **1947** *ATS* (Supp.) 35: *Eager...*ambitious. **1955** Klaas *Maybe I'm Dead* 79: What got you eager, Tom? You had a good set-up. **1957** Anders *Price of Courage* 123: "I'm tired of eager people...." "What do you mean, 'eager'?" "Well, all the time showing off. Trying to be a big hero when some general's around. Trying to get ahead no matter what he has to do or who gets killed." **1961** Foster *Hell in Heavens* 238 [ref. to WWII]: I was becoming more "eager" all the time. Every hour of flying that I lost to bad weather or canceled hops brought a multitude of gripes from me.

eager beaver *n.* Esp. *Mil. & Stu.* an exceedingly or excessively zealous, diligent, or ambitious worker. Occ. as adj.

1943 *Yank* (May 21) 6: The Eager Beavers. **1943** (Nov. 7) in *OEDS.* **1944** *New Yorker* (June 3) 25: I'm going to be an eager beaver if it kills me. **1944** Kendall *Service Slang* 21: *Eager beaver...*lad in classroom who knows right answer first....Cordially unpopular...a compliment when meaning a WAVE. They command admiration for their alertness. **1944** Stiles *Big Bird* 125: We were a hot outfit all right...two teachers and forty eager beavers on our way to the moon. **1944** in *AS* XX 148: *Eager Beaver.* A soldier who is so anxious to impress his superiors that he volunteers for every job that offers, or otherwise displays unusual diligence. **1946** Plagemann *All for Best* 195: I know I'm being too eager-beaver about the whole thing. **1949** Lowry *Wolf That Fed Us* 114: I'll get the eager beaver busy with that printing press of his tomorrow night. **1956** Heflin *USAF Dict.* 181: *Eager beaver.* An unusually busy or diligent person. Used opprobriously. **1956** J.D. Brown *Kings Go Forth* 13: As long as we get healthy, eager beaver kids we don't have to worry. **1957** Myrer *Big War* 301 [ref. to WWII]: You've been eager-beaver enough before. **1957** *Phil Silvers Show* (CBS-TV): I don't want an eager beaver on my hands. **1959** Cochrell *Barren Beaches* 40: I mean I don't want to be an eager beaver. **1961** Baldwin *Another Country* 220: What an eager beaver you are. **1968** Westheimer *Young Sentry* 289: You're a real eager beaver, aren't you, Lieutenant? **1971** N.Y.C. man, age *ca*50: You're afraid of being thought an eager beaver. **1980** Berlitz & Moore *Roswell* 67: We had an eager-beaver PIO on the base who had taken it upon himself to call the AP on this thing. **1980** Carroll *Land of Laughs* 27: An eager-beaver grad student from Princeton.

eagers *n.pl.* excessive eagerness or apprehension.—constr. with *the.*

1928 *AS* III (Feb.) 219: *Eagers.* Anxiety or haste. "Don't get the eagers now—just take it easy." **1934** Weseen *Dict. Slang* 180: *Eagers*—Anxiety, as "He has the eagers." **1947** J.C. Higgins *Railroaded* (film): You always got the eagers, ain't ya? **1954–60** *DAS.*

eager up *v.* to make eager; excite.

1967 Hamma *Mommas* 150: The bit is for me to eager-up a couple of Joes and then have them take me out where the guys are waiting.

eagle *n.* **1.** *Mil.* a discharge certificate.

1864 in D. Chisholm *Civil War Notebook* 44: Learn to labor and to wait until you *get your eagle.* **1866** in Hilleary *Webfoot* 155: Two more soldiers...expect to get their "eagle birds" (discharge). *Ibid.* 213: After receiving their "eagles" and greenbacks the majority left...for Portland.

2. a dollar.

1891 C. King *By Land & Sea* 123: Tell him it's two eagles a quart, a bird an' a bit pint an' six-bits a half-pint. **1928** Dahlberg *Bottom Dogs* 155: Four hundred and fifty greenbacks....Four hundred and fifty eagles was no more than a day's take-in. **1950, 1966–70** in *DARE.*

3. *Golf.* a score of two under par on a hole. Now *S.E.*

1922 in *DA.* **1934** *WNID2.* **1964** in H.W. Wind *Following Through* 53: He took three of the next five holes (one with a birdie and another with an eagle).

4. *Stu.* the academic grade E.

1967 *DAS* (Supp.). **1968** Baker et al. *CUSS* 111: *Eagle.* The grade "E."

¶ In phrase:

¶ **when the eagle flies** [sugg. by the American eagle that appears on some U.S. currency] Esp. *Mil.* when pay is disbursed; on payday. Also vars.

[**1864** *Battle-Fields of So.* 251: They would squeeze a dollar until the eagle howled.] **1918** Ruggles *Navy Explained* 83: *Jawbone*—To stand a fellow off for articles ashore. To get clothes or eats on credit with a promise to pay "when the eagle walks." **1919** *Twelth Inf.* 89: The pay rolls are all in, and they say the eagle's going to squawk tomorrow. **1922 Lawrence *Mint* 247: Tomorrow the golden eagle moults on us. **1926** Nason *Chevrons* 238 [ref. to 1918]: We aren't dead yet and we may live to see another pay-day. The eagle hasn't done his bit for me for a long time and I'd like to spend a little money before I do my part to make Flanders fields fertile. **1929** Thomas *Woodfill* 25 [ref. to 1898]: Pretty nigh from the first I qualified as an expert rifleman, and that meant an extra dollar a month when the eagle screamed. **1941** Hargrove *Private Hargrove* 84: The eagle—money. On payday, the eagle flies. **1942** in *Black Scholar* (Jan. 1971) 42: The Eagle flies on Friday, and Saturday I go out to play. **1953** *ATS* (ed. 2) 816: *When the eagle flies* or *shits*, payday. **1958** Cope & Dyer *Petty Officer's Guide* (ed. 2) 342: *Eagle Screams, The.* (Slang.) Pay day. **1964** Rhodes *Chosen Few* 117 [ref. to *ca*1950]: Don't forget th' eagle flies today. **1965** Linakis *In Spring* 320 [ref. to WWII]: What if he doesn't want to pay Bello until the eagle shits? **1966** in IUFA *Folk Speech*: Military slang for payday: *When the eagle shits.* **1968** I. Reed *Yellow Back Radio* 99: Be cool till the eagle flies, that way we won't get in Dutch. **1971** Cole *Rook* 296: It's the Army Way, and whatever else happens the Eagle shits once a month. **1974** *Playboy* (Mar.) 126: It was what Ryan called The Day the Eagle Shits, the day his monthly GI Bill check came in. **1974** Beacham & Garrett *Intro 5* 76: The eagle don't fly round here till Friday. **1974** Former L/Cpl, USMC, age 25: Pay-day was *When the eagle flies* or *When the eagle shits.* **1978** *Black Clonemaster* (NBC-TV): The eagle has flown over us again, Dr. Shane. **1981** *Hill St. Blues* (NBC-TV police series): Be advised that the welfare eagle flies on Monday.

eagle-beak *n.* a person having a large hooked nose; (*broadly* and *contemptuously*) a Jew.

1920 McKenna *315th Inf.* 152 [ref. to 1917]: Jack Fields, better known as "Old Eagle Beak" and "Banana Nose." **1939** J.T. Farrell *To Whom It May Concern* 168: Read it and see what the Reds and the eagle-beaks are doin'. **1942–45** in Campbell & Campbell *War Paint* 206: Eaglebeak. **1955** Ullman & Lawrence *Dig That Uranium* (film): By the way, eaglebeak, how'd you ever get to be maitre d' chef of this outfit? **1979** in R. Carson *Waterfront* 56: Gino was nicknamed "Becco d'Aquila"—"Eaglebeak."

eagle colonel *n. Mil.* BIRD COLONEL.

1978 Diehl *Sharky's Machine* 25: An eagle colonel, U.S. Army.

eagle day *n.* [sugg. by *when the eagle flies* s.v. EAGLE] payday. Also cap.

1941 Kendall *Army & Navy Sl.* 5: *Eagle day...*pay day. **1942** *Yank* (Nov. 18) 9: Post-Eagle Day crap games. **1944–46** in *AS* XXII 55 [Army]: *Eagle's Day* Pay day (the day on which the eagle screams.) **1967** Lit *Dictionary* 13: *Eagle Day*—Pay day! **1983** *Morning Contact* (WKGN radio) (May 27): Friday morning is eagle day around WKGN. The eagle is flying high and making everybody happy.

eagle-eye *n.* **1.** *R.R.* a locomotive engineer. *Joc.*

1900 in Botkin & Harlow *R.R. Folklore* 314: "Eagle Eye" was down greasing the pig. *a*1911 in *West. Folk.* XXXII (1973) 90: James A. Michaels was the eagle eye's name. **1912** Livingston *Curse* 20: These flattering words [were]...spoken in the vernacular of the "eagle-eyes" of the rails. **1926** *AS* I (Jan.) 250: The railroad engineer is known variously as "eagle eye," "hog-head," and "throttle puller." **1927** *DN* V 445: *Eagle* *eye*, n. The engineer of a locomotive. **1945** Hubbard *R.R. Ave.* 174: Your train would have gone by the little frame station if the eagle-eye had not reversed the engine. **1958** McCulloch *Woods Words* 57.

2. *Und.* a detective.

1919 Darling *Jargon Book* 11: Eagle Eye—A detective. **1926** Clark & Eubank *Lockstep* 173: Eagle-eye—detective.

3. a lookout or observer. *Joc.*

1945 Hamann *Air Words*: Eagle eye. The observer of a military plane. **1958** McCulloch *Woods Words* 57: Eagle eye...A lookout.

eagle-eye *v.* to observe and evaluate closely; scrutinize.

1964 Thompson & Rice *Every Diamond* 3: I took batting practice with McGraw eagle-eyeing us.

eagle shit *n.* **1.** [sugg. by *when the eagle shits*, var. of *when the eagle flies* s.v. EAGLE] *Mil.* government wages.—usu. considered vulgar.

1980 Ciardi *Browser's Dict.* 117: Eagle shit, G.I. pay.

2. *Mil.* the gold ornamentation on the visor of a senior officer's cap.—usu. considered vulgar.

1986 Univ. Tenn. instructor, age *ca*30: My father calls that [gold ornamentation on a visor] eagle shit. He was in the Air Force in the '50's.

ear *n.* **1.** *Journ.* one of the small boxes at either side of a newspaper's title that usually contain weather forecasts and other printed matter.

1901 in Partridge *DSUE* (ed. 8): Those little frames on either side of the title of the paper which journalists call "ears" or "ear-tabs." **1934** *WNID2.* **1974** Pine Plains, N.Y., reporter, age 24: The ears of the newspaper are the two upper corners of the front page where they usually print the weather report or the paper's motto.

2. *pl.* (used as an intensive, euphem. for) ASS.

1929 Brecht *Downfall* 140: Oh, I kidded the ears off her. **1938** Baldwin & Schrank *Case of Murder* (film): You've been screaming your ears off for six weeks. *Ibid.*: They'll shoot your ears off.

3.a. *Mil.* a listening device; BUG; (*also*) interception radar or sonar.

1934 *WNID2*: Ear...One of the listening devices of a submarine. Slang. **1947** *ATS* (Supp.) 41: Ears, the original popular misnomer for interception radar. **1961** J. Flynn *Action Man* 71: Walked in just in time to watch a guy put an ear in it. **1962** Bonham *War Beneath Sea* 30 [ref. to WWII]: He liked sonar...picked up on the sub's sensitive sound gear—her "ears."

b. *pl.* radio headphones.

1942 *ATS* 755: Headphones...ears. **1985** (quot. at EARMUFFS).

c. *CB.* a CB radio; CB equipment.—usu. constr. with *have on*, *put on*, etc.

1976 Lieberman and Rhodes *CB* 127: Ears—Citizens Band or two-way radio. *Ibid.* 129: Got Your Ears On?—Are you listening to your CB? **1976** Bibb et al. *CB Bible* 30: One sight of those ears scares [hijackers] away. **1976** Whelton *CB Baby* 7: Break, break, break, breaker-by one-nine. Who's got ears for this Jack O'Diamonds, how about it? **1977** Corder *Citizens Band* 51: Hey, all you lonesome cowboys with ears. **1979–82** Gwin *Overboard* 152: Cherry Picker was hooked on his CB. "I allys got my ears on," he said.

4. *Black E.* a tuning peg, as on a fiddle or guitar.

*ca*1938 in Rawick *Amer. Slave* II (pt. 1) 76 [ref. to 1860's]: I see Marse Thomas a twistin' de ears on a fiddle and rosinin' de bow.

¶ In phrases:

¶ **bang ears** *Navy & USMC.* to ingratiate oneself with someone by means of flattery or the like. [Quots. ref. to WWII.]

1946 Heggen *Mr. Roberts* 88: And not only that...but the other day he was up banging ears with the Old Man again. He tells us he hates him and every chance he gets he sneaks up there and bangs ears. "That's a nice guy to have around!" **1942–48** in *So. Folk. Qly.* XII (1949) 203: The eager beaver may usually be found *banging ears* (currying favor, boot-licking) with some senior rate or officer. **1952** Uris *Battle Cry* 114: If we got to do mules' work, they could at least give us mules' rating....I think I'll bang ears for a transfer. **1954** Crockett *Bastards* 50: Beating his gums one minute 'bout the chow, bangin' ears the next with the belly-robber himself. **1959** Sterling *Wahoo* 237: Who'd you bang ears with this time?

¶ **bang (someone's) ear** to talk or complain at length to. Cf. EAR-BANGER, EAR-BANGING.

1965 W. Hoffman *Yancey's War* 55: I've been banging the lieutenant's ears about what a great guy you are. **1978** Diehl *Sharky's Machine* 103:

She ever bang your ear about what's happening with her? **1992** G. Wolff *Day at Beach* 80: I'd phone Andrew...to bang his ears with my beefs.

¶ **bend an ear** to pay attention.

1935 Wead *Ceiling Zero* (film): Stop gabbing and bend an ear. **1942** *ATS* 165: Listen:...*bend an ear.* **1962–68** B. Jackson *In the Life* 304: He told his story to...everybody that'd bend an ear. *1970 Partridge *DSUE* (ed. 7) 1003: *Bend an ear!* Listen to this!...Air Force: 1939+. **1986** G. Brach *Pirates* (film): Now bend an ear to this.

¶ **bend (someone's) ear** to talk at tedious length to (someone); (*also*) to have (someone's) attention. Cf. EAR-BENDER, EAR-BENDING.

1942 B. Morgan & B. Orkow *Wings for Eagle* (film): How could I hear a horn with this guy bending my ear in his best style? **1942** in C.R. Bond & T. Anderson *Flying T. Diary* 98: Fritz Wolf, in his drunken drawl, bent my ear about "rank" in the AVG. **1952** in *DAS* 31: MacArthur is supposed to have bent...Eisenhower's ear with a new plan...[concerning] Korea. **1953** Dibner *Deep Six* 25: You are not bending my ear or...beating your gums. **1962** E. Stephens *Blow Negative* 432: Army's been bending his ear again. **1980** *U.S. News & W.R.* (Apr. 7) 54: With so many parties bending the ear of the royal family, dealings with the Saudi government can be frustrating. **1984** N. Bell *Raw Youth* 33: Can I bend your ear in the hall a minute?

¶ **blow (someone's) ears down** to scold severely.

1933 March Co. *K* 145: I guess I got that bastard told!...I guess I blew his ears down for him!

¶ **burn (someone's) ears** to scold severely.

1952 Malamud *Natural* 53: He didn't like having his ears burned by Pop. **1961** *WNID3.* **1974** Beacham & Garrett *Intro 5* 65: Maybe I was really making a statement to more or less justify my actions to the woman—and burn her ol' man's ears.

¶ **coming out of (one's) ears** in superabundant supply.

1965 Linakis *In Spring* 316: Shipping orders [are] coming out of our ears. **1970** Della Femina *Wonderful Folks* 15: Boy, day in day out—[fashion] models coming out of your ears. **1971** Rhinehart *Dice Man* 32: She knew everything, brains coming out of her ears. **1980** in McCauley *Dark Forces* 442: Carlos has money coming out of his ears.

¶ **dry behind the ears** experienced; mature; **wet behind the ears** inexperienced; raw.

1911–12 J. London *Smoke Bellew* 78: An' him not dry behind the ears yet. **1914** *DN* IV 105: *Dry back of the ears*, mature; of persons. *1931 Brophy & Partridge *Songs & Slang* (ed. 3) 375 [ref. to WWI]: *Wet behind the ears*, a term of reproach imputing ignorance or youth. **1938** Steinbeck *Grapes of Wrath* ch. ix: When you bastards get dry behin' the ears, you'll maybe learn to let an ol' fella sleep. **1959** Montgomery & Heiman *Jet Nav.* 101: He's seen a lot of wet-behind-the-ears second looeys. **1982** Cox & Frazier *Buck* 123: This guy is a recruit, still wet behind the ears.

¶ **get [or lay] (one's) ears back, 1.** to exert (oneself) to the limit.

1883 Keane *Blue-Water* 25: He had to "lay his ears back" pretty close before he succeeded in doing that. **1891** *Outing* (Oct.) 49: Get your ears back now, girls, and get a gait on you.

2. to become intoxicated.

1968 in *DARE*: When a drinker is just beginning to show the effects of the liquor, you say he's...*Getting his ears back.*

¶ **in your ear** see *stick it in your ear*, below.

¶ **on (one's) ear, 1.** indignant or angry; in a huff; (*broadly*) in an uproar.

1871 Bagg *Yale* 44 [ref. to 1865-69]: *Ear*, dignity, hauteur, self-importance. A man somewhat offended or indignant is said to be *on his ear*, or *eary*. **1871** in Schele de Vere *Amer.* 479: They...said that I was lightning when I got up on my ear. **1878** Harte *Drift* 249: And I told him, if he didn't like it, he might lump it, and he traveled off on his left ear, you bet. **1879** Rooney *Conundrums* 80: Instead of saying, "go to the devil,"/They tell you "walk off on your ear." **1881** A.A. Hayes *New Colo.* 77: Wouldn't that just get some of his high-toned relations up on their ear? **1881–82** Howells *Modern Instance* 367: But I can cut your acquaintance fast enough, or any man's, if you're really on your ear! **1882** in *N.Y. Folk. Qly.* XXIV (1968) 169: It is all nerve,/And if you will observe,/We have got the knack of standing on our ear. **1882** Sweet *Sketches* 42: I know Jay will get on his ear and make some railroad changes if he hears of it. **1883** Peck *Peck's Bad Boy* 90: I gave my hickory nuts away to the children...but my chum, who ain't no bigger'n me, got on his ear and wanted to kick the socks off a little girl who was going home from school. **1886** Lozier *Forty Rounds* 28 [ref. to 1863]: Bast der zaloons all filt mit beer,/Der rebel vellers walkt on deir ear. **1887** Peck *Pvt. Peck* 88: I was so disgusted…that I got on my ear, as it were. **1887** Francis *Saddle & Moccasin* 125: Matt Campbell slid out on his ear, and got on his horse, and went off without saying a word. **1890** *DN* I 64: *To spin round on one's ear* means to get violently angry. **1903** *Pedagog. Sem.* X 371: Don't get up on your ear. **1913** in Truman *Dear Bess* 114: Mamma said he was on his ear in proper fashion when I wasn't there to meet him. **1918** in Bowerman *Compensations* 99: The médecin was "getting on his ear" and I dreaded the consequences. **1933** in R.E. Howard *Iron Man* 90: I'd have every reporter in town on his ear if I showed up in bloody rags like these. **1934** W. Smith *B. Cotter* 25: Don't get up on your ear because I made that crack about Carfare Bennie. **1952** Nugent *Quiet Man* (film): I don't blame Mr. Dannaher for getting on his ear. **1978** *Business Week* (June 12) 91: This campaign has set Coke on its ear, and the company charged that the tests were rigged in Pepsi's favor. **1987** *Evans & Novak* (CNN-TV) (May 3): That shows why Bill Bennett has this town on its ear! **1993** *New Yorker* (Mar. 15) 89: He has stood traditional Hong Kong policy on its ear and thereby created a huge row with China.

2. on (one's) side after having fallen or been knocked down; (*hence*) destitute; in phr. **stand (someone) on (one's) ear** to knock down; (*hence*) to defeat or overwhelm. Also fig. [The sense illus. by the 1877 quot. is not clear.]

[**1877** Lee *Fag-Ends from Academy* 24: His foot quickly slips,/And the plebe "waltzes off on his ear."] **1910** T.A. Dorgan, in *N.Y. Eve. Jour.* (Feb. 2) 12: He knocked Jim Flynn cold at Frisco with the same punch, and stood Peter Felix on his ear with one of the same kind in Australia. **1918** Witwer *Baseball to Boches* 226. **1918** in Hemingway *Sel. Letters* 9: However we had two days of regular storm when she pitched, rolled, stood on her ear and swung in wide lugubrious circles and I heaved but four times. **1919** Witwer *Alex* 9: There's guys which can sing as well as Caruso,…stand Dempsey on his ear. **1924** Anderson & Stallings *What Price Glory?* I i: This God damn army's going to run right from now on or get off on its ear. **1935** in Paxton *Sport* 205: Then Dizzy stood the Pirates on their ears with three hits. **1939** in Farrell *Short Stories* 189: His hat store went kerflooie, and he's on his ear now. **1964** "Doctor X" *Intern* 245: He's had a very bizarre story since, and now has everybody in a big flap, especially Cal Cornell and the radiologist, who is really standing on his ear. **1965** Eastlake *Castle Keep* 129: Did I tell you about Beckman and his lecture? Beckman was very good. He stood us all on our ear.

3. Esp. *Pris.* with little inconvenience or effort, as if asleep. [Quots. ref. to the serving out of prison sentences.]

1930 Shaw *Jack-Roller* 100: I told them and one guy who had done time said, "A year wasn't so much, he could do that on his ear." **1935** Pollock *Und. Speaks: On his ear*, serving a prison sentence contentedly (prison). **1942** Algren *Morning* 125: Six months in the Workie—"I'll do it on my ear." **1956** Kubrick & Thompson *Killing* (film): He's fine. He's doin' it on his ear.

¶ **on (someone's) ear** engaged in nagging.
1974 S. Stevens *Rat Pack* 144: Get off my ear, man. **1966–80** McAleer & Dickson *Unit Pride* 185: Coggins has been on our ear all day long tryin' to get you.

¶ **out on (one's) ear** ejected or dismissed ignominiously.
1919 S. Lewis *Free Air* 329: Turn the roughneck out on his ear. **1941** Smith *Gang's All Here* 128: Out on his ear. **1942** *ATS* 68: Ousted; discharged. *Out on one's ear.* *1951, *1953 in *OEDS*. **1954** Matheson *Born of Man & Woman* 213: He's a jerk. Kick him out on his ear.

¶ **pin (someone's) ears back** to defeat or chastise soundly.
1941 in *OEDS* s.v. *pin:* It certainly was intended to pin my ears back. **1942** *ATS* 657: Pin his ears back. **1943** in Inman *Diary* 1176: I'd pin your ears back if I thot that. **1947** Schulberg *Harder They Fall* 118: The Boss is pinnin' Copper's ears back. **1966** *RHD:* If he doesn't behave himself, I'll pin his ears back. **1966–80** McAleer & Dickson *Unit Pride* 101: "Now," said the captain, satisfied he'd pinned back my ears a little.

¶ **pound (one's) ear** to sleep.
1894 *Atlantic* (Sept.) 322: The most of the men…said "Pound your ear well," to their nearest neighbors, and then the candle was put out. **1895** *Harper's* (Oct.) 776: Pounds his ear* like a baby, don't he?…*Sleeps. **1899** A.H. Lewis *Sandburrs* 59: He rolls in to pound his ear. **1906** Ford *Shorty McCabe* 267: I was poundin' my ear like a circus hand on a Sunday lay-over. **1907** Bush *Enlisted Man* 28: We "pounded our ears" until the cooks woke us up. **1914** J. London *Jacket* 58: Pound your ear and forget it. **1918** Ruggles *Navy Explained* 114. **1926** Nason *Chevrons* 31: Ah, he's poundin' his ear already. **1926** *AS* (Dec.) 652: *Pounding one's ear*—sleeping in a bed.

¶ **pound (someone's) ear** to talk at tedious length to.

1972 Pearce *Pier Head* 121: Look. Don't pound my ear about this.…Call a ship's meeting if you want.

¶ **pull in (one's) ears** to duck (one's) head; mind (one's) own business; (*hence*) be quiet.
1917 in Rendinell *One Man's War* 10: Pull in your ears, low bridge. **1928** MacArthur *War Bugs* 184: By day a searching, nerve-racking fire—and good-bye to all who didn't pull in their ears. **1930** Farrell *Calico Shoes* 5: Why don't you pull in your ears? Huh? **1932** Berg *Prison Doctor* 225: Aw, pull in your ears, old-timer; you're passing through a tunnel!

¶ **[stick it] in your ear!** (used to express strong rejection or derision).
1966 in IUFA *Folk Speech: Stick it in your ear:* a reply to someone that makes a comment one does not like. **1969–71** Kahn *Boys of Summer* 312: "Go fuck yourself."…"In your ear." **1972** R. Wilson *Forbidden Words* 235: Stick it in your ear. **1973** Ace *Stand On It* 107: I hummed a few bars of "Stick It in Your Ear, Missus Murphy." **1979** in Terkel *Amer. Dreams* 141: In your ear, turkey. **1983** *Night Court* (NBC-TV): In your ear! **1983** Flaherty *Tin Wife* 200: It's their way of sticking it straight in society's ear. **1987** Kent *Phr. Book* 158: Hang it in your ear. **1987** Gill & Israel *Mayflower* (CBS-TV): In your ear, Gullet!

¶ **take it in the ear** Esp. *Stu.* to be severely victimized or defeated.
1965 in IUFA *Folk Speech:* Another saying of the modern college student when he does poorly on an exam is, "Boy, I really took it in the ear." **1968–70** *Current Slang* III & IV 124: *Take it in the ear*, v. To be treated unfairly (from an extreme form of sexual aberration).—College students, both sexes, Kentucky. [**1970** Woods *Killing Zone* 64: I said, "Why don't you take it in the left ear, Lieutenant?"] **1975** *Nat. Lampoon Birthday Bk.* 6: And if you still take it in the ear at exam time, don't blame Uncle Sam.

¶ **to the ears** completely; thoroughly.
1877 Wheeler *Deadwood Dick, Prince of Road* 80: "Are you with me?" "To the ears." **1929–30** Dos Passos *42d Parallel* 9: They're…stewed to the ears most of 'em already. **1959** J. Lee *Career* (film): Marjorie [was] dressed up to the ears.

¶ **up to (one's)** [or **the**] **ears** deeply involved; (*hence*) superabundantly supplied.
1839 W. Irving, in *OED:* I…was up to my ears in law. *1889* W.B. Yeats, in *OEDS:* I am up to the ears in Irish novelists. **1909** *WNID: Up to the ears*, deeply submerged; almost overwhelmed; as, to be in trouble up to one's ears. *Colloq.* **1932** in Mencken *New Lttrs.* 267: I have been up to my ears in the book on moral science. **1960** Bannon *Journey* 54: I'm up to my ears in this. *1966* in *OEDS:* Up to his ears in work. **1977** Sayles *Union Dues* 314: State is up to its fuckin *ears* in lumber…it grows on *trees*, lumber.

¶ **wet behind the ears** see *dry behind the ears*, above.

¶ **with ears** [or **earflaps** or **earlaps**] to an extreme degree; of an insufferable kind.
1933 Saunders & Hanemann *Ace of Aces* (film): The Big Push is here—with ears on it. **1952** H. Grey *Hoods* 78: Boy, am I lying here thinking like a shmuck, a shmuck with earlaps yet. **1970** *Current Slang* V 13: *With ears*, adv. To the last or final degree.—College students, both sexes, California.—"He is a real bastard, *with ears!*" **1976** Price *Bloodbrothers* 195: Stony stood there like a schmuck with earflaps. **1987** Blankenship *Blood Stripe* 23: Oh, he's gonna be a proper bastard, Ansel. A prick with ears.

¶ **your ear!** not at all. Cf. syn. *your ass* s.v. ASS, *n.*
1934 Appel *Brain Guy* 48: "But watching Wiberg for days?" "Watchin' your ear." "Thanks, Paddy. Thanks for nothing."

ear-banger *n. Mil.* a servile flatterer. Cf. Australian mil. slang *ear-basher* 'a chatterer; bore'. [Quots. ref. to WWII.]
1942 *Leatherneck* (Nov.) 145: *Ear-banger*—A "yes" man. Man who goes out of his way to put himself in a good light with higher-ups. **1943** *Sat. Eve. Post* (Mar. 20) 86: *Ear banger:* A handshaker or yes man. **1944** Brooks *Brick Foxhole* 6: The general's an ear-banger. **1944** Kendall *Service Slang* 6: *Ear-banger*…extols merits to officers. **1953** Eyster *Customary Skies* 248: Average walked past and Terry tried to get his foot out far enough to trip that ear-banger. **1984** in Terkel *Good War* 395: We had black petty officers, but all the men considered them air-bangers [*sic*]. Brownnoses.

ear-banging *n.* Esp. *Mil.* flattery or empty talk.
1942 Sanders & Blackwell *Forces* 128: *Ear-banging*. Gossiping. (U.S.N.). **1961** Bendiner *Bowery Man* 39: The "ear banging" of the minister's sermon is often thought too high a price to pay. **1964** *Alman.*

Naval Facts (gloss.): *Ear-banging.* Flattery, currying favor. **1966** *Gallery Start Engines* 96: All the earbanging that movie operator's been doing ain't gonna pull him out of this jam. **1993** *Nation* (Aug. 9) 165 [ref. to hoboes, mid-20th C.]: Bad missions, where "earbanging" is mandatory before being fed.

ear-bend *v.* to *bend (someone's) ear* s.v. EAR.
   1978 *Rolling Stone* (Nov. 30) 51: These record-company people were always ear-bending with their line: "He never works."

ear-bender *n.* a garrulous bore.
   1934 in *Jour. Abnor. Psych.* XXX (1935) 362: *Ear bender*—one who talks too much. **1954–60** *DAS*: *Ear-bender...*An overtalkative person. **1973** *Oui* (Feb.) 85: Dias is the proprietor and he's a real earbender.

ear-bending *n.* a long-winded talk.
   1966 Braly *Cold* 62: The only thing he's ever given me is a picture of a sailboat and an ear-bending.

ear-biter *n.* [ref. to a story that one had chewed the ear off an opponent in a fight, *ca*1845] *Post Office.* a special agent of the U.S. Post Office Department.
   1855 in *DAE*: How much the result of this first investigation, after the restoration of the "ear-biters" (as they were then sometimes facetiously called,) had to do with the radical change in opinion and action,...may not be advisable to inquire.

ear candy *n.* light, undemanding pop music. Cf. EYE-CANDY.
   1984 *Time* (Feb. 27) 96: Synthesizers are enjoying a particular vogue...because, in the words of one composer-arranger, "they fulfill pop music's never-ending quest for fresh ear candy." **1984** in *Barnhart Dict. Companion* V (1986) 13: Some fairly highbrow synthesized ear candy. **1986** in *Atlantic* (Mar. 1987) 100: Cuts like the title track...are the sure-fire ear candy he's grown adept at churning out. **1991** Nelson & Gonzales *Bring Noise* 163: Bits of ear candy and some haunting chords.

ear-flap *n.* a person's ear. *Joc.*
   1859 O.W. Holmes, in *OED*: Pretermit thy whittling, wheel thine ear-flap toward me. **1939** Appel *Power-House* 386: This time I didn't keep my ear-flaps open.
   ¶ In phrase:
   ¶ **with earflaps** see *with ears* s.v. EAR.

earful *n.* a full or clear hearing of what is being said; (*hence*) a voluble expression of opinion, esp. a sharp verbal rebuke. Now *colloq.* or *S.E.*
   1911 T.A. Dorgan, in Zwilling *TAD Lexicon* 34: The phone bell rang and Cyril rushed over to get an earful. **1911** T.A. Dorgan, in Zwilling *TAD Lexicon* 34: How about the kidnapping. Wise us up. Sure give us an earful. **1915** T.A. Dorgan, in *N.Y. Eve. Jour.* (Aug. 6) 11: Just An Earful. **1917** in Mills *War Letters* 216: Company 8 stood on the sidelines and got an earful. **1920** Ade *Hand-Made Fables* 297: They could hand you an Earful regarding certain Gentlemen who have been Wronged. **1920** Witwer *Kid Scanlan* 131: "By Jove!" he sneers, just loud enough so's we can all get an earful. **1930** Lait *On the Spot* 17: Now take an earful o' this. **1934** H. Miller *Tropic of Cancer* 21: Elsa was giving me an earful about Berlin. **1982** Braun *Judas Tree* 53: One...gave me an earful. I mean the lowdown!

ear job *n.* **1.** an act of caressing someone's ear with the mouth and tongue.
   1963 Coon *Short End* 192: But I should have been in the Big House or the Paradise or someplace, stoned and getting stonier, getting an ear job or maybe in a fight.
   2. a sexually stimulating telephone conversation, as with an employee of a sexual phone service. Cf. EAR SEX.
   1978 Diehl *Sharky's Machine* 100: It's what we call an ear job....Probably the neatest phone-and-fuck operation I've ever run into.

earl *v. & n.* [prob. imit.; cf. syn. RALPH] *Stu.* to vomit; as n. **Earl** (used in var. phr. meaning 'to vomit').
   1968 Baker et al. *CUSS* 93: Call earl. Vomit. **1984** Eble *Campus Slang* (Sept.) 3: *Earl*—vomit: After having too much to drink he earled. **1986–87** in *DARE*: You had to "earl." We also would say that "Earl's knocking at the door....We'd also say "going to see Earl." **1989** Eble *College Slang 101* 78: Vomiting...call *Earl*...talk to *Earl.* **1990** Munro *Slang U.* 75: She earled all over the carpet.

earlap *n.* ¶ In phrase: **with earlaps** see *with ears* s.v. EAR.

early bright see s.v. BRIGHT.

earmuffs *n.pl. Radio.* headphones.
   1942 *ATS* 755: Headphones...*ear muffs.* ***1974** P. Wright *Lang. Brit. Industry* 84: Headphones are *cans* or *ear-muffs.* **1985** Ark. man, age 35: When I worked with headphones in the mid-'70's we called them *phones, ears,* or *earmuffs. Ears* was very common.

ear of corn *n.* a country person.—used derisively.
   1912 Lowrie *Prison* 143: I hate t' run that ear o' corn up agin a play like that, but he was so green I couldn't help it.

ear sex *n.* (see quot.). Cf. EAR JOB, 2.
   *a***1988** C. Adams *More Straight Dope* 214: We're also not discussing "ear sex," in which someone talks dirty to you on the phone.

earth *n.* ¶ In phrase: **earth to ——** [sugg. by radio transmissions to space explorers in science fiction] (used to deride someone's foolish ideas or to get someone's attention). *Joc.*
   1977 Univ. Tenn. student: Earth to Julie! Earth to Julie! Come in, please, Julie! **1979** Eble *Campus Slang* (Mar.) 3: *Earth to ——*Please pay attention. Often preceded by noise such as static on a radio: Earth to Joe! **1980** Rimmer *Album* 8 [ref. to 1963]: Earth to Trish, Earth to Trish.... **1984** *Miami Vice* (NBC-TV): Earth to Linus! Come in, Linus! **1987** N. Bell *Cold Sweat* 42: Alice? Earth to Alice, earth to Alice, Alice—come in. **1992** Strawberry & Rust *Darryl* 40: Earth to Strawberry. Frank's made his decision.

earthpads *n.pl.* shoes.
   1946 Boulware *Jive & Slang* 3: *Earth Pads...*Feet, shoes. **1969** *Current Slang* I & II 30: *Earth pads,* n. Sneakers.—College females, New York State.

earthquake *n.* **1.** a powerful or invincible fighter.
   [**1821** Wetmore *Pedlar* 27: That dog Planter's an earth quake!] **1845** Thorpe *Backwoods* 182: I am a roaring earthquake in a fight. **1848** in Blair & Meine *Half Horse* 180: "I'm an arthquake!" roared Mike.
   2. a kind of mixed drink.
   1869 "M. Twain" *Innocents* I 145: The uneducated foreigner could not even furnish a Santa Cruz Punch, an Eye-Opener, a Stone-Fence, or an Earthquake. *a***1891** *F & H* II 351: *Bottled earthquake...*(American).—Intoxicating drinks.

earwig *v.* to eavesdrop.
   1927 *DN* V 445: *Ear wigging,* v.n. Listening; eavesdropping. ***1942** (cited in Partridge *DSUE* (ed. 3) 1040).

easeman var. EASTMAN.

Eastie *n. Boston Area.* East Boston, Mass.
   1983 Stapleton *30 Yrs.* 203: The Callahan Tunnel...connects Downtown to Eastie.

East Jesus *n.* a remote or provincial town or place.
   1961 Forbes *Goodbye to Some* 246 [ref. to WWII]: We been out seventeen years...and sailed through nine typhoons and been to East Jesus and back five hundred and fifty times. **1972** B. Rodgers *Queens' Vernacular* 150: *East Jesus* any small hole in the mud town; blink your eyes and you miss it. **1974** N.Y.C. man, age 25: *East Jesus* means way out in the boondocks. **1979** J. Morris *War Story* 224: Advising the Igluks in East Jesus. **1988** *21 Jump St.* (Fox-TV): Some guy in East Jesus...has lived with AIDS for seven years. **1992** *Harper's* (Sept.) 32: The minors are all those 170 or so teams scattered...from Edmonton to El Paso to East Jesus.

eastman or **easeman** *n. Black E.* a parasitical man who is supported by a woman or women.
   1911 *JAF* (Oct.) 354: The "Eastman" is kept fat by the women among whom he is universally the favorite. **1915** White *Negro Amer. Folk-Songs* 375: I'm a natchel-born eastman/An' it ain't no joke. **1925** Van Vechten *Nigger Heaven* 285: *Eastman:* a man who lives on women. **1934** Lomax & Lomax *Amer. Ballads & Folk Songs* 34: An "easman" [*sic*] is a "hustler," that is, a man who wanders from town to town living off women, often other men's wives. **1948** McIlwaine *Memphis* 333: *That* is a pimp; Beale [Street] calls him an easy rider, an ease man, or a sweet man.

easy *n.* **1.** a soft or gullible person; easy mark.
   1903 Kildare *Mamie Rose* 137 [ref. to *ca*1895]: I...was ceremoniously introduced by Mulvihill to the "easies," who had traveled quite a distance to bask in the radiance of a real fighter.
   2. (*cap.*) (short for) BIG EASY.—constr. with *the.*
   1970 Conaway *Big Easy* 204: He wasn't feeding the Easy any longer.

easy *adj.* **1.** easily taken advantage of or imposed upon; gullible. [In 17th C. S.E. or colloq.; see *OED*.]
   ***1698–99** "B.E." *Dict. Canting Crew:* He is an easy fellow, very silly or soft. **1896** *DN* I 416: *Easy:* easily hoodwinked. **1907** *American Mag.* (Sept.) 453: And the Devil laughs. "Say," he says, "I'm not so easy as all

that! I'm from Missouri: You've got to *show* me!" **1926** C.M. Russell *Trails* 5: The way they trim that roll [of money], it looks like somebody's pinned a card on my back with the word "EASY" in big letters. **1930** Irwin *Tramp & Und. Sl.*: *Easy.*—Soft-hearted; charitable; easy to influence. **1959** *Encyc. Brit.* XX 768: *Easy*—gullible; easily duped.

2. (of a woman) sexually forward; (*hence*) sexually promiscuous.

1698–99 "B.E." *Dict. Canting Crew: An easy mort*…a forward or coming wench. *1914* (cited in Partridge *DSUE* (ed. 8)). **1936** B. Traven *Sierra Madre* 104. **1942** *ATS* 311: Of easy morals; wanton…*easy.* **1961** *WNID3.*

3. *Und.* seeking or willing to accept bribes.

1872 Burnham *Secret Service* (gloss.): *Easy.*—Pliable; approachable; bribeable; purchasable.

easy digging *n.* granulated sugar. *Joc.*

1938 *AS* (Feb.) 70 [R.R. linemen]: *Easy digging.* Sugar.

easy mark *n.* see s.v. MARK, *n.*

easy meat *n.* see s.v. MEAT, *n.*

easy rider *n. Black E.* **1.** a parasitical man usu. without a steady job who lives by gambling or sponging, (*specif.*) a man who is supported by a woman, esp. a prostitute.

1914 in Handy *Blues Treasury* 77: Dear Sue, your Easy Rider struck this burg today. **1919** Wiley *Wildcat* 53: Where at is my li'l easy rider gone? **1934** G.W. Lee *Beale St.* 76: The "sweet men" and "easy riders" hung out on the second floor. **1935** Pollock *Und. Speaks: Easy rider*, a person who attempts to make a living by betting on horse races. **1944** Bontemps & Cullen *St. Louis Woman* 22: Easy rider left me high and dry/I had some Macks that satisfied my soul/But there ain't nobody else who can rock me/With a steady roll. **1948** McIlwaine *Memphis* 346 [ref. to 1909–14]: To Beale [Street], *easyriders* meant pimps; to Main Street, political grafters and protected vice lords. **1968–70** *Current Slang* III & IV 43: *Easy rider*, n. A man who lives off what his wife makes as a prostitute.—New Mexico State. **1975** De Mille *Smack Man* 40: Women have been whoring since long before the first easy rider saw a chance to make an easy buck. **1976** *Esquire* (Sept.) 69: And all your Easy Riders just snuck in all *over* the place. **1977** S. Foote *September September* 57: Pimps and whores and gamblers, easy riders and their marks.

2.a. a sexually satisfying lover.

1927 *Jour. Abnor. & Soc. Psych.* XXII 16: *Easy rider*…a man whose movements in coitus are easy and satisfying. **1946** Blesh *Trumpets* 128: In Negro "city talk," the term *easy rider* has come to mean either a sexually satisfying woman or a male lover who lives off a woman's earnings. **1961** in Oster *Country Blues* 228: An' he wants some one to tell him where his easy rider gone.

b. a young woman who is sexually promiscuous or easily seduced. Also **easy ride.**

1952 Mandel *Angry Strangers* 116: I'm an easy-rider woman, never/Do no one man no good. **1971** *Current Slang* V 10: *Easy rider*, n. Girl who "gives everything" on a first date. **1967–80** Folb *Runnin' Lines* 236: *Easy ride.* Sexually promiscuous female. **1985** *Univ. Tenn.* student theme: Girls who have a reputation for being easy are called "easy riders."

3. a guitar.

1946 Blesh *Trumpets* 128: In rural Negro parlance…*easy rider* meant the guitar…carried suspended by its cord. **1958** in *OEDS.*

4. a person who is not easily ruffled or provoked.

1971 S. Stevens *Way Uptown* 45: If you show mad, someone goin' beat you all the time. You gotta be an easy rider.

easy street *n.* a condition of ease and comfort, esp. financial success. Also cap. Now *colloq.*

1897 Hamblen *General Mgr.* 215: He has arrived at the railroad man's "easy street." **1901** in *OEDS:* Until he has got a million and is residing on easy street. **1902** Mead *Word-Coinage* 165: To walk down Easy street is to do anything easily. **1903** A.H. Lewis *Boss* 205: Just as a sport finds himself on easy street, along comes a scientist an' tells him it's all off. **1905** *McClure's Mag.* (Sept.) 452: Why, we're on easy street, my girl! I get my board and lodging free. **1906** London *Moon-Face* 81: On Easy Street, eh? Everything slidin' your way. *a1904–11* Phillips *Susan Lenox* I 251: We've hit on something that'll land us in Easy Street. **1914** in Handy *Blues Treasury* 86: On Easy Street I felt no pain. **1925** in Moriarty *True Confessions* 28: Sell my house and land, and I would again be on Easy Street. **1928** Sharpe *Chicago May* 43: It was to bring enough interest to keep him on Easy Street. **1936** Dos Passos *Big Money* 329: We'll be on easystreet from now on. **1976** Hayden *Voyage* 99: Whoever inherits it will be on easy street for life.

eat *n.* **1.** a meal. [Extant in OE and ME; in modern use prob. a reinvention rather than a survival.]

1782 in *OED2:* I was too much tired to choose appearing at dinner, and therefore eat my eat upstairs. *1844* in *OEDS:* What was he to do "between the eats?" **1868** in T. Whitman *Dear Walt* 127: The speeches were sickening—and the "eat" jolly—the sail splendid. **1899–1900** Cullen *Tales* 314: We'll take a mild eat, [and] get some sleep. **1904** in *OEDS:* One Tennessee innkeeper described his establishment as…25 cents a sleep, 25 cents an eat. *1951* in *OEDS.* **1969–70** in *DARE.*

2. *pl.* things to eat; food. [Note at **(1)**, above, applies here as well.]

1841 in Blassingame *Slave Testimony* 41: They love us and Comforted our apretites gave plenty eats. **1889** in *OEDS:* A majority…adjourned to the Coates House for "eats" and refreshment. **1889** (quot. at PIKER). **1903** Hobart *Out for the Coin* 40: Nominate your eats! **1903** Ade *Society* 50: After the Eats we are going over and sit in all of the Boxes at that Rough-House Show that I've been reading about. **1928** Dahlberg *Bottom Dogs* 179: The others took their eats out of papersacks. **1929** Tully *Shadows of Men* 81: You'd git good eats and java. **1930** Rogers & Adler *Chump at Oxford* (film): Take your eats with you, now. **1937** in Rawick *Amer. Slave* II (pt. 1) 329 [ref. to 1865]: De Yankees…stole all the cattle and all the eats. **1938** in W. Burnett *Best* 493: I parked near the least pretentious of the restaurants—the sign over it was merely "EATS." **1954** Schulz *More Peanuts* (unp.): Tricks or treats, money or eats. **1959** M. Harris *Wake Up* 36: You always want the basic eats and flop. **1973** Gwaltney *Destiny's Chickens* 2: We'll be needing eats, Momma. **1977** Stinnett *Pleasures* 157: A restaurant whose only sign outside reads EATS. **1993** *New Yorker* (June 14) 23: Pack your best eats.

eat *v.* **1.** to annoy, bother, or vex.—occ. constr. with *on.*

1892 S. Crane *Maggie* 36: "Well," he growled, "what's eatin' yehs?" **1894** F.P. Dunne, in Schaaf *Dooley* 158: What's atin' ye?…What ails ye, man alive? **1896** Ade *Artie* 66: Aw, what's eatin' you? **1899** *Sat. Eve. Post* (July 1) 3: The head brakeman asked him, in the language of the caboose, "what was eatin' him." **1907** *Lippincott's Mag.* (Apr.) 552: What's eating you, pal? **1918** Gibbons *Thought Wouldn't Fight* 99: What's eating on you, kid? **1933** Milburn *No More Trumpets* 145: What's eatin' yuh, kid? **1937** Steinbeck *Mice & Men* 59: What's eatin' on Curley? **1939** O'Brien *One Way Ticket* 8: What the hell's eatin' on you, fella? **1949** Van Praag *Day Without End* 33: What's eating his ass? **1952** Sandburg *Young Strangers* 143 [ref. to 1880's]: Anything eatin' you today, you old galoot? **1961** Terry *Old Liberty* 31: I listened and tried not to let their talk eat on me too bad. **1967** W. Crawford *Gresham's War* 134: What's eating out your bum?

2. to defeat decisively; trounce; destroy.—also constr. with *alive.*

1803 in J. Ashton *Eng. Satires on Napoleon* 178: I'll eat him. **1914** S.H. Adams *Clarion* 29: She eats 'em alive. **1960** Sire *Deathmakers* 94: We'll get a spoon and eat those bastards alive. **1961** *WNID3:* Our team can eat those chumps. **1974** L.D. Miller *Valiant* 67 [ref. to WWII]: His huge fist gathered Harmon right up to his face, and he hissed, "I'll eat your goddamned tough ass, boy!" **1989** Hynes & Drury *Howard Beach* 227: He "ate young assistant DAs for breakfast."

3. to provide a meal or meals for. *Joc.*

1837 in *DA:* Well, Capting, do you ate us, or do we ourselves? **1842** in Thornton *Amer. Gloss.:* [Mr. Dickens] has declined the invitation of the Philadelphians to eat him. **1855** Thomson *Doesticks* 53: I resolved…to quit the premises of the Emerald Islander who agreed to "lodge and eat" us. **1888** Farmer *Amer.:* A steamer is alleged to be able to eat 400 passengers and sleep about half that number. **1928** Benét *John Brown's Body* 367: You ought to be et. We'll eat you up to the house when it's mealin' time. **1939, 1954** in *DARE.*

4. to perform cunnilingus or fellatio on (a person).—rarely constr. with *up.*—usu. considered vulgar.

1916 Cary *Venery* I 77: *Eat up*—To tongue a woman, or suck a man. **1927** *Immortalia* 168: He got down on his knees and he ate 'er! *ca1938* in Maurer *Lang. Und.* 116: To eat pussy. Cunnilingus. **1941** G. Legman, in Henry *Sex Vars.* II 1164: To perform cunnilinctus…*eat cunt; eat fish; eat pussy;* and eat *hair-pie.* **1942** H. Miller *Roofs of Paris* 255: She acts nuts enough to eat him. **1947** Willingham *End As a Man* 174: He began to eat the old mammy. **1952** Viereck *Men Into Beasts* 36 [ref. to 1918]: "Molly,…I wish you were here! I could eat you!" "That's about all you can do," shouted another voice. **1955** McGovern *Fräulein* 199: You wanna eat, I got somethin yuh kin eat. **1963** Blechman *Camp Omongo* 4: "Fuck you" [was] carved in the plywood door. "Mike eats cunt." "Fatso takes it up the ass." **1964** Reuss *Field Collection* 220: So sing me a chorus,/While I eat your clitoris. **1967** Rechy *Numbers* 188: I want to eat your ass. **1968** P. Roth *Portnoy* 206: Bubbles will be down eating cock on her knees. **1970** Sorrentino *Steelwork* 48: If you eat pussy you're a maniac....If you eat pussy you're a moron. **1976** Arble *Long Tunnel* 174: They kidded him about his lack of practice in eating pussy. **1978** Schrader *Hardcore* 137: Hell, in five minutes I can make more money eating some guy's asshole than I can all week at the Copper Penny. **1983** R. Thomas *Missionary* 7: A white T-shirt that posed the suspect question "Have You Eaten Your Honey Today?"

5. EAT UP, *v.*, 2.a.

6. *Business.* to absorb (a financial loss, expenses, etc.).

1955 *New Yorker* (Oct. 1) 49: Jackson found himself "eating" Canso stock—holding a great many shares of little value or promise and in no demand. **1983** *L.A. Times* (Oct. 5) V 1: Sometimes, he has to "eat" tickets; that is, the demand isn't there and they go unsold. **1984** *Business Week* (May 7) 78: Stations pay high sums for an entire set of reruns...If [series] fail, he says, "stations have to eat it." **1987** J. Thompson *Gumshoe* 35: I might end up having to eat those six hours. **1988** *Headline News Network* (June 17): Still others are selling at cost—and eating the loss. **1990** *Newsweek* (July 9) 7: *Eating the bill:* Providing care for indigent patients who are not covered by insurance...."We ate the bill on that guy." **1990** Rukuza *West Coast Turnaround* 9: He was perfectly willing to eat the fine.

7. to strike face-first; (*also*) to be struck by (as a bullet).

1975 Wambaugh *Choirboys* 49: Hit him on the inner rear fender and he'll eat the windshield. **1984** Trotti *Phantom* 28: One of our planes was a write-off, three others ate bomb fragments. *Ibid.* 203: Tom...had eaten some flak over the Ho Chi Minh Trail...and had ejected into the forest. **1985** Bodey *F.N.G.* 160: "Our Eltee ate an eighty-two round." "Dead?" "Fuckin'-A dead." **1987** E. Spencer *Macho Man* 137: Our sergeant major ate a rocket in a command bunker. **1988** Chetwynd *To Heal a Nation* (film): The guy...got off a chopper and ate one right in the back of the head.

¶ In phrases:

¶ **eat concrete** (among truckers) to drive rapidly down a major highway.

1971 Tak *Truck Talk* 55: *Eatin' concrete:* to drive a truck down a highway. **1976** *Nat. Lampoon* (July) 55: The rolling house of ill-repute is eatin' concrete on Mississippi Rt. 8.

¶ **eat crap** see *eat shit*, below.

¶ **eat dirt** [or **gravel**] to be thrown on one's face.

1933 J.V. Allen *Cowboy Lore* 60: *Eating gravel.* Being thrown from a bucking bronc or wild steer. **1974** Price *Wanderers* 57: The football went flying; the midget ate dirt.

¶ **eat face** *Stu.* to engage in passionate kissing of the mouth and face.

1968 Baker et al. *CUSS* 112: *Eat face.* To neck. **1978** Eble *Campus Slang* (Apr.) 2: *Eat face*—kiss, cuddle: Boy, I wouldn't mind eating face with him. He's cute. **1981** Eble *Campus Slang* (Mar.) 3: *Eat face*—kiss: "I saw a picture of you eating face with Bill." **1988** Univ. Tenn. student theme: Kissing..."eating face."

¶ **eat it, 1.a.** to perform cunnilingus or fellatio.—also constr. with *raw.*—usu. considered vulgar.

1916–22 Cary *Sexual Vocab.* I: *To eat it.* To "suck a prick or lap a cunt." **1927** [Fliesler] *Anecdota* 75: He's so old he'll have to eat it with a spoon! *Ibid.* 84: If she'd put out the light he'd eat it. **1928** Panzram *Killer* 157: A gunsel is a poofter and a poofter is a pratter and pratter is similar to a fruiter. The only difference between the two is that one likes to "sit" on it, and the other likes to "eat" it. **1933** Ford & Tyler *Young & Evil* 157: He eats it. **1941** G. Legman, in Henry *Sex Vars.* II 1164: *Eat it.* To perform cunnilinctus. **1960** Sire *Deathmakers* 44: Man, I bet he eats it! Hey, Allen, you got any hair on your teeth? **1965** Linakis *In Spring* 121: She is the loveliest girl....Don't you eat it? **1972** *Nat. Lampoon* (July) 82: And remember that a Masculine He-Man must also be able to excel at Eating It Raw.

b. (used as a vulgar taunt or retort).

1952 Uris *Battle Cry* 311 [ref. to 1943]: "Eat it," Levin spat. **1957** Kohner *Gidget* 56: "Cut the bull." "Aw—eat it raw." **1974–77** A. Hoffman *Property Of* 212: "Eat it," Tony said quietly. **1980** Rimmer *Album* 39 [ref. to 1965]: Hey, eat it!...Eat me!...Your mother! **1980** Kotzwinkle *Jack* 115: But he'd only learned how to signal *Fuck You* and *Eat It, Mac.* **1985** *Call to Glory* (NBC-TV): "So, Patrick, get any action lately?" "Eat it." **1988** Poyer *The Med* 429: Ah, eat it.

c. to be extremely objectionable, offensive, or unsatisfactory; SUCK.—usu. considered vulgar.

1940 Del Torto: The Greek eats horseshit. The Greek eats it. **1955** Yablonsky *Violent Gang* 60: Frenchie's favorite and repeated pattern was to point to another boy (any other boy), and comment. "That fag-

got eats it." **1961** Terry *Old Liberty* 17: Here's to Brother Walker....He eats it! **1965** W. Crawford *Bronc Rider* 234: You eat it; your mother runs rabbits and howls at the moon, Dandy. You're cheap, you're yellow. *Stand up you fuckin coward!* **1972** *Nat. Lampoon* (July) 6: Well, this "Surprise" issue really eats it, and so do you. **1973** Browne *Body Shop* 55: This place really eats it.

2.a. to submit to degrading treatment.

1928 in Paxton *Sport* 127: The idea is to beat hell out of 'em and make 'em eat it. **1953** Dibner *Deep Six* 138: Eat it, Alec Austen, he thought to himself. Dutch eats it. Dooley eats it. In the Navy everybody eats it.

b. *Stu.* to do very poorly.

1968 Baker et al. *CUSS* 111: *Eat [it].* Do poorly on something. Do poorly on an exam. **1969** *Current Slang* I & II 31: I ate it on the final. **1971** Dahlskog *Dict.* 21: I really ate it on that exam.

3. Orig. *Surfing.* to be thrown from a surfboard or skateboard.

1976 *N.Y. Times Mag.* (Sept. 12) 85: Rip-offs being considered much more serious than possible injuries from "eating it" (falling on your face). **1977** Filso *Surf. Almanac* 181. **1987** J. Thompson *Gumshoe* 157 [ref. to 1978]: I heard the race of skateboard wheels and laughter. "You ate it, Ev," a boy yelled, laughing.

4. *Mil.* to be killed; die.

1982 Del Vecchio *13th Valley* 548 [ref. to ca1968]: Everybody's got a life wish and a death wish. When the second's stronger...then a dude eats it. **1985** *A-Team* (NBC-TV): OK—nobody move or Fulbright eats it! **1987** E. Spencer *Macho Man* 136: J.B. hurts...when his guys eat it.

¶ **eat lead** see s.v. LEAD, *n.*

¶ **eat me** [**raw**] (used as a vulgar taunt or retort, in ref. to (4), above).

1957–62 Higginbotham *U.S.M.C. Folklore* 24: Eat me like an onion, raw. **1970** Standish *Non-Stand. Terms* 11: It was also, during the Fifties, an expression of male challenge or disgust, as in "Eat me, you chicken!" **1971** N.Y.U. student: We used to say "Eat me!" which is the same as "Fuck you!" **1980** Men's room graffito, Knoxville, TN: Eat me raw. **1990** Rukuza *West Coast Turnaround* 209: Eat me, fuckhead! *a*1991 Kross *Splash One* 87: Eat me, you big Swede. At least *I* was trolling.

¶ **eat my shorts!** (used as a semi-joc. imprecation).

1979 *Nat. Lampoon* (Dec.) 17: Eat my shorts. **1980** Birnbach *Preppy Hndbk.* 219: *Eat my shorts*...Drop dead, go jump in the lake. **1984** Riggan *Free Fire* 84 [ref. to Vietnam War]: Why don't you eat my shorts, lifer? **1986** L. Johnson *Waves* 128 [ref. to ca1970]: Eat my shorts, jarhead! **1990** *Simpsons* (Fox-TV): Eat my shorts!

¶ **eat (one's)** [or **the**] **gun** *Police.* to commit suicide by shooting (oneself) with the barrel of the gun inserted in the mouth.

1975 Wambaugh *Choirboys* 207: Yeah, it's usually the workin cop who eats his gun. **1981–85** S. King *It* 135: Unless you're willing to take the pipe or eat the gun. **1986** *Miami Vice* (NBC-TV): Finally I just wanted to eat my gun. **1986** Philbin *Under Cover* 22: She was afraid I was going to eat my .38 in the house and dirty her wallpaper. **1987** Tapply *Marine Corpse* 153: "You're sure it was suicide though?"..."He ate his gun." **1989** Leib *Fire Dream* 463: He might eat his gun.

¶ **eat (one's) lunch** *Surfing.* to be thrown from a surfboard.

1981 in Safire *Good Word* 111: You wiped out. You took gas. You ate your lunch.

¶ **eat shit** [or **crap**], **1.a.** to submit to degrading treatment.—usu. considered vulgar.

[***1660** Pepys *Diary* I (Feb. 7) 45: Mr. Moore told me of a picture hung up at the Exchange, of a great pair of buttocks shitting of a turd into Lawson's mouth, and over it was writ "The thanks of the House."] [**1858** in *N. Dak. Hist.* XXXIII (1966) 151: Among old trappers and mountaineers, this country goes by the name of "The country where a man eats s—t & goes naked."] **1930** J.T. Farrell *Grandeur* 215: "They don't eat nobody's crap," Weary said challengingly. **1934** Faulkner *Pylon* 119: Even if I am a bum there is some crap I will not eat. *a*1949 D. Levin *Mask of Glory* 185: Why do I always want to make him eat crap? **1953** Harris *Southpaw* 170: It is a stupid f—ing way to make a living but it is better than eating somebody's crap in a mine or a mill or a farm or an office. **1955** Puzo *Dark Arena* 220 [ref. to WWII]: He'd eaten shit all week. **1962** Larner & Tefferteller *Addict in Street* 78: I said to myself, I don't want to get in bad with him, I can't afford to. I have to eat shit, in other words, off of him. [**1970** Woods *Killing Zone* 64: I eat a yard of her shit just to see where it came from.] **1971** Cole *Rook* 203: *He* wouldn't of eat shit like that for no colonel. Yes, sir. No, sir. Oh gee golly whiz, sir! **1974** Blount *3 Bricks Shy* 105: Football players have to eat so much shit. **1986** *NDAS*. **1989** *21 Jump St.* (Fox-TV): I wasn't gonna eat his crap.

b. (used as a vulgar taunt or retort).
[**1838** *Crockett Almanac 1839* 11: Do you see what that cow has just let drop?…eat every atom of it.] **1961** McMurtry *Horseman* 109: "Eat shit," he said. **1972** N.Y.U. student: When somebody says, "Eat shit!" the comeback line is "Hop on a spoon!" Then, "Shove over, no room!" and "Tell your mother to get off!" **1984–87** Ferrandino *Firefight* 25: Eat shit and die! **1992** Mowry *Way Past Cool* 9: Eat shit and die, suckers!
2. to be utterly contemptible.—usu. considered vulgar.
1942 in Morison *Naval Ops. in WWII* V 193: GI: "Tojo eats s—!" **1957** H. Danforth & J. Horan *D.A.'s Man* 13 [ref. to *ca*1928]: "All Irish eat ——," he said coolly. **1966** Graffito, N.Y.C. high school: You eat shit. **1971** Mayer *Weary Falcon* 156: This fucking operation eats shit….It sucks. **1983** *N.Y. Daily News* (Aug. 31) 36: All you guys eat ——! **1986** *NDAS.*

¶ **eat (someone's) ass [out]** [or **off**] Esp. *Mil.* to rebuke or scold sharply or severely; CHEW OUT.—usu. considered vulgar. [1927, 1934, 1953 quots. offer clearly euphem. forms.]
1927 Stevens *Mattock* 116 [ref. to 1918]: All you'd get would be your leg in a sling. [Lieut.] Pickle would simply eat your liver out, like he did sarge. **1934** in Fenner *Throttle* 63: He was up all night, eating the pants out of everybody. **1943** Chandler *High Window* 425: Too late to mention it now. They'd eat my ass off. **1946** Heggen *Mr. Roberts* 83 [ref. to WWII]: Then the Captain called him up and ate his ass out for the way the signalmen were keeping the flying bridge. **1948** Shaw *Young Lions* 310 [ref. to WWII]: You should have seen Colclough's face the day you went over the hill!…And did he eat Rickett's ass out! **1951** Robbins *Danny Fisher* 102: The boss is got his tail up and he's been eatin' my ass off all day. **1952** Lamott *Stockade* 91 [ref. to WWII]: He ate my ass out last night. **1953** Freeman *Gobi* (film): He's been eating my tail out to raise Chungking. **1953** Chandler *Goodbye* 48: Had a guy break from me once. They ate my ass off. **1954** Lindner *50-Min. Hour* 56: "I'd have my ass eaten out but good if anyone knew about it," Mac agreed. **1959** Brosnan *Long Season* 221: He says it was a good pitch…but Scheffing really ate his ass out. **1962** Killens *Heard the Thunder* 65: The CO must have gotten his ass eaten out up at regimental. **1967** *Playboy* (July) 60: The Old Man's on the warpath. He's eatin' ass like it was steak. **1984** D. Smith *Steely Blue* 30: The lieutenant sees you parked there, he'll eat your ass….The lieutenant will eat your ass out. **1987** E. Spencer *Macho Man* 19: I'd get right in a guy's face when I'd eat his ass.

¶ **eat (someone's) cookies** to vanquish (someone).
1974 Blount *3 Bricks Shy* 103: I went up against this big kid who was a senior. He ate my cookies.

¶ **eat (someone's) lunch** to defeat, drub, outdo, injure, etc.; make short work of.
1959 Maier *College Terms* 4: *That ate my lunch*—a tough test or clutch situation. **1969** *Current Slang* I & II 31: *Eat…lunch.* v. To get revenge.—College students, both sexes, Kansas.—"I'm going to eat your lunch." **1972** Haslam *Oil Fields* 101: *Eat Your Lunch,* v. To beat physically. (Example: That feller's gonna eat your lunch.) **1975** Univ. Tenn. student: She really ate that woman's lunch. **1976** Rosen *Above Rim* 169: From 1957 to 1966 a flabby ex-Globetrotter named Woody Sauldsberry made a career out of eating Elgin Baylor's lunch. **1981** in Safire *Good Word* 26: "If we don't improve our product distribution, our competitors will eat our lunch."…"We're really gonna eat their lunch this time!" **1984** *Prairie Home Companion* (Nat. Pub. Radio) (Oct. 22): I thought the Buckeyes come out and eat our lunch! **1984** Holland *Let Soldier* 189: Without tracers, that guy could eat our lunch before we find him. **1987** Zeybel *Gunship* 186: But a lot of [pilots] had also watched the goddamn SAMs eat their lunch. **1988** *Tour of Duty* (CBS-TV) [ref. to Vietnam War]: Now I don't have to worry about anybody getting upset if Charlie eats my lunch! Ain't life grand! **1993** *CBS This Morning* (CBS-TV) (Nov. 10): I thought the Vice President ate Ross Perot's lunch. It was a decisive victory.

¶ **eat the ball** *Football.* to be tackled while holding the ball rather than throw a bad pass.
1950 *Sat. Eve. Post* (Oct. 7) 159: He threw the ball when he was pressed and off-balance, instead of eating it. **1958** J. King *Pro Football* 124: Layne had been booed…because he had to "eat" the ball without adequate protection. **1976** *Webster's Sports Dict.* 130. **1979** Cuddon *Dict. Sports & Games* 299. **1980** Pearl *Pop. Slang* 45: *Eat the ball*…of a football quarter back, to avoid throwing an unsuccessful pass and thus be tackled carrying the ball.

¶ **eat the big one!** to hell with you!—usu. considered vulgar.
1983 Breathed *Bloom Co.* (2): Perspicuously speaking, eat the big one, boys!

¶ **eat wool** *Tennis.* to be hit or, esp., nearly hit in the face by a volley.
1976 *AS* LI 293.

eat-'em-up *n. CB.* a roadside restaurant.
1976 Lieberman & Rhodes *CB* 127: *Eat 'Em Up*—Truckstop restaurant or roadway restaurant. **1976** *Sci. Mech. CB Gde.* 165: That eatum up is a negatory.

eatery *n.* a restaurant. Now *S.E.*
1901 "H. McHugh" *Down Line* 52: One of those eateries where the waiters look wise. **1958** S.H. Adams *Tenderloin* 135: Picked him up in a Sixth Avenue eatery. **1970** *Business Week* (June 20) 122: Eateries…use microwave ovens to speed service. **1983** *N.Y. Post* (Sept. 5) 9: 2 cops wounded in eatery shootout.

eatings *n.pl.* food; EATS.
1876 McKay *Hosp. & Camp* 220: He would buy his "eatings" by the way. **1902** Carrothers *Black Cat* 30: His ability to consume large quantities of liquor and "good eatin's." *ca*1938 in *DARE.* **1960** Bluestone *Cully* 28: Don' bitch 'bout the eatins. We all eats it, too.

eating tobacco *n.* chewing tobacco.
[**1865** in H. Johnson *Talking Wire* 210: All I have to do is eat some tobacco and the toothache is no longer remembered.] **1901** *Chi. Sunday Trib. Mag.* (July 21) (unp.): Will you have some of the eating tobacco? **1928** MacArthur *War Bugs* 223 [ref. to 1918]: The drivers dismounted to mooch eating tobacco off the cannoneers. **1944, 1948** in *DA.* **1963** in *DARE.*

eating tool *n.* an eating utensil.
1927 Rollins *Jinglebob* 180 [ref. to 1880's]: Also we stocks up with grub, eatin' tools, cookin' ware, an' blankets. **1956** Resko *Reprieve* 76: Sneakin the eatin tools outa the mess hall. **1966** in *DARE*: Knives, forks, etc., called "weapons" or "eating tools."

eat out *v.* **1.** [orig. a euphem. for *eat (someone's) ass out* s.v. EAT] Esp. *Mil.* to rebuke or scold sharply or severely; CHEW OUT.
1944 Boatright & Day *Hell to Breakfast* 139: If this man is really a trouble maker, he may get "run off" (fired). He might just get "eat out" or a "reaming" from his boss, the driller. **1944** Liebling *Back to Paris* 285: The divisional chief of staff…let off a bit of steam by "eating out" the headquarters mess officer for serving C-rations. **1948** *N.Y. Folk. Qly.* (Spring): I just got eaten out. **1950** Felsen *Hot Rod* 24: Highway patrol was in tonight eating me out for going so fast they couldn't catch me to give me a ticket. **1951** Wouk *Caine Mutiny* 165: Did the old man eat you out? **1951–52** Frank *Hold Back Night* 9: It was ridiculous for him to be eating out Beany Smith at this time, when he had accepted destruction and dissolution for himself and for all of them. **1961** *N.Y. Times* (Sept. 1) VII 6: Mr. O'Connor also takes him to task for "eating out" the 42d (Rainbow) Division for slack discipline. **1966** King *Brave & Damned* 36: Who ate you out? **1968** Westheimer *Young Sentry* 97: He'd eat me out if he knew I was in here. **1969** Searls *Hero Ship* 15: It was as close as he ever came to eating out a man in public. **1971** Waterhouse & Wizard *Turning Guns Around* 106: Better send him up before the man 'n' get him all et out/For havin too much fun. **1983** Stapleton *30 Yrs.* 34: They'll love seeing that snotty little gal get eaten out.
2. EAT, *v.*, 4.—usu. considered vulgar.
1966 Reynolds & McClure *Freewheelin Frank* 28: I'll eat your box out right here! **1972** *Penthouse* (Aug.) 68: He thought of Tina and how she raved about how he ate her out. **1967–80** Folb *Runnin' Lines* 236: *Eat out.* Engage in cunnilingus. **1981–85** S. King *It* 98: If it's that bull dyke Lesley, tell her to go eat out some model and let us sleep.

eats *n.pl.* see s.v. EAT, *n.*, 2.

eat up *v.* **1.a.** to administer a decisive or ruinous defeat to; make short work of.
1830 in [S. Smith] *Letters of Downing* 32: And the Augus has eaten up the Huntonites in Newfield. **1831** in *Ibid.* 53: Mr. Van Buren would eat up the whole toat of 'em. **1833** S. Smith *Pres. Tour* 16: The President rared right up…and looked at me in the face as if he'd eat me up as quick as your old grey hound will swallow a junk of fresh meat. **1838** [Haliburton] *Clockmaker* (Ser. 2) 195: They'd fairly eat the minister up without salt. **1845** Hooper *Simon Suggs* 139: Well, ses I, ef you don't want to be eet up boddaciously, ses I, you'd better git a-top of him and slope. **1864** Galway *Val. Hours* 215: We have men enough, and good men too, to "eat up" the Johnnies. **1867** Dixon *New America* I 25: Captain Clay Pate…put himself at the head of fifty-six Sons of the South, and threatened to eat up old John Brown, of Osa watomie. **1874** Carter *Rollingpin* 43: He seemed determined to draw…[him] into a fight, and, to use his own language, "Eat him up without salt." *Ibid.* 44: There's a man in this house can eat you up in a minute. **1887** DeVol *Gambler* 92:

I told him that he might be a good man down in Texas, where he came from, but he was a sucker up in this country, and I could eat him up. **1892** M.O. Frost *10th Mo.* 126: Dar were Rebels enought just ahead to eat us all up. **1904** in "O. Henry" *Works* 1428: Eat 'em up! *a***1911** in Spalding *Base Ball* 167: When we marched on a field with our big six-footers out in front it used to be a case of "eat 'em up, Jake." **1973** R. Jackson *World Series* (NBC-TV) (Oct. 20): He ate me up at the plate in New York. **1976** Woodley *Bears* 139: Wow, we're just eating people UP, Dad. **1984** Trotti *Phantom* 50: The [MiG] 21 is in its element at high mach above 25,000 feet, but get him down to 10,000 and the Phantom...will eat him up. **1989** *Headline News Network* (Mar. 5): San Antonio ate up the Nuggets.

b. to rebuke or scold sharply or severely.

1843 in Barnum *Letters* 16: But *don't* eat a fellow up now without giving him a chance for his life. **1878** Flipper *Colored Cadet* 52: *To eat up*—See "to crawl over." *Ibid.* 69: He "eats" that plebe up entirely, and then sends a corporal around to instruct him in his orders. **1933** J. Conroy *Disinherited* 109: "Why the hell you eatin' me up blood-raw all the time?" Ed demanded...after a particularly vitriolic bawling-out. **1950** Girard & Sherdeman *Breakthrough* (film): I guarantee Regimental'll eat me up proper for doing it.

c. to get the better of; baffle; foil.

1944 Boatright & Day *Hell to Breakfast* 140: If you cannot handle your job, it "eats you up." **1983** L. Frank *Hardball* 81: A ground ball that a fielder cannot handle is said to "eat him up."

2.a. to take in greedily with the mind or senses; (hence, usu.) to enjoy avidly. Also (*occ.*) **eat.**

***1873** R. Browning, in *OED*: Monsieur Leonci Miranda ate her up with eye-devouring. **1911** in *OEDS*: They ate the piece—it was only Galbraith they were guying. **1913** J. London *Valley of Moon* 5: You're sure a fierce hustler—just eat it up. **1914** Atherton *Perch* 176: To use her own phrase, she "ate up" the Latin languages [*sic*] and her diction was remarkably good. **1915–16** Lait *Beef, Iron & Wine* 45: Maybe Roger won't eat up that green sled wit' the steerin' bars, huh? **1919** Hurst *Humoresque* 195: You wait until you see the way they're going to eat me up in the court scene in "Saint Elba." **1921** *Variety* (Feb. 4) 7: Over in Smack's corner they ate it up and hollered for us to put on the gloves and stop beefin'. **1926** Dunning & Abbott *Broadway* 229: Well, Boss, they're eating it up out there. **1929** Millay *Agst. the Wall* 346: They'd eat it up! **1929** E. Wilson *Daisy* 6: More! I eat that stuff up! **1930** Graham & Graham *Queer People* 63: The old man eats 'em up [*sc.* banquets]. **1958** Feiffer *Sick Sick Sick* (unp.): I kid the office staff. Tell 'em gags on the boss. They eat it up. **1986** Coonts *Intruder* 282: "So how do you like the fleet, Ferd?"..."I'm eating this shit with a spoon."

b. to believe eagerly; accept unquestioningly.

1908 in H.C. Fisher *A. Mutt* 78: Judging from the native's facial expression I deduce that he is eating up Tobasco's line of bull. **1919** Darling *Jargon Bk.* 41: *Eat It Up*—To believe a story or thing with eagerness. **1967** W. Crawford *Gresham's War* 9: "Guy back there said we'd be in soon, less'n an hour." "You eat it up, don't you, Goat?" James needled Lee worse than I did. **1978** Wharton *Birdy* 13: Birdy eats it up;...he'll believe anything.

Ebenezer *n.* (one's) passions, esp. ire.

1836 in Haliburton *Sam Slick* 61: He must have had a tempestical time of it; for she had got her Ebenezer up. **1836** in Thornton *Amer. Gloss.*: That ris Deb's ebenezer. **1838** in *DAE*: His Ebenezer is up in a minit. **1839–40** Cobb *Green Hand* I 88: Once get up my ebenezer, some of you will call out "enough." **1842** in *DAE*: It's enough to put one's Ebenezer up, and make the blood bile. **1843** "J. Slick" *High Life in N.Y.* 5: I felt my ebenezer a gitting up to hear her call her husband's own uncle...such stuck up names. **1847** Downey *Cruise* 121: Even the "Mokes" in the "black sea"...laughed so long and strong at thee as to raise thy Ebenezer, and almost provoke thee to go forward and chastise them. **1861** in Silber *Songs of Civil War*: How are you, boys, I'm just from camp,/And feel as brave as Caesar;/The sound of bugle, drum, and fife/Has raised my Ebenezer.

eccy *n. Stu.* the study of economics; economics.

1924 Marks *Plastic Age* 232: I've got a quiz in eccy to-morrow. **1980** *N.Y. Times Mag.* (Sept. 7) 130: So we wouldn't fry our eccy midterm.

echelon hound or **echelon king** *n. Army.* a holder of a soft job in a rear echelon. [Quots. ref. to WWI.]

1922 Jordan *Btry. B* 35: After becoming acquainted with it there was not a day passed that the "echelon hounds" weren't lined up to buy chocolate, condensed milk, canned fruit, jam, eggs, champagne, and many other things. The canteen...made it a great war. **1922** *Pirate Piece* (Oct.) 3: And if I guide the relief thro' Hell's shellin' pot/I'm

pelted with "Esch'lon King" gags.

ecofreak *n.* [ecology + FREAK] an environmental activist.—used derisively.

1970 (cited in *W9*). **1972** *U.S. News & W.R.* (Apr. 10) 92: Convince inner-city residents that conservationists "are not 'eco-freaks'—middle-class whites interested only in stopping things like power plants which will provide heat and jobs for the ghetto." **1977** *Time* (June 6) 63: Ecofreaks. **1982** *Time* (May 24) 86: People with only limited commitments to environmental preservation will tend similarly to allude not to environmentalists but to eco-freaks. **1986** *NDAS.*

eco-nut *n.* an environmental activist.—used derisively.

1972 (cited in *BDNE3*). **1979** Homer *Jargon* 34. **1986** *NDAS.*

ecstasy *n.* MDMA (3, 4-methylene dioxymethamphetamine), an amphetamine derivative used as a psychotropic drug.

1985 *L.A. Times* (Mar. 29), in *OEDAS* II 29: Yet another new drug...MDMA...On the street, its name is "ecstasy" or "Adam." **1985** *Psych. Today* (May) 68: MDMA...a psychedelic drug sold on the street as "Adam" or "Ecstasy." **1987** *Miami Vice* (NBC-TV): Have you been taking any psychoactive drugs? LSD? Ecstasy? **1987** *Headline Network News* (Dec. 21): More than a third of college students polled have tried ecstasy. **1989** *U.* (Sept.) 10: A great deal of the movement involves consumption of...Ecstasy, a pill-based drug similar to LSD. **1992** *International Hour* (CNN-TV) (Feb. 11): A new designer drug called *ecstasy*.

ECU *n. Hosp.* the condition of death.—constr. with *the. Joc.*

1981 in Safire *Good Word* 154: A patient that expires...is "transferred to the ECU" (Eternal Care Unit).

edge *n.* a state of mild intoxication; usu. in phr. **have an edge on** to be somewhat drunk.

1897 Norris *Vandover* 362: All the men were trying to get a dance with her. She had an edge on. **1899** Thayer *Co. K* 146: Both men had a slight "edge on." **1906** *Nat. Police Gaz.* (Dec. 8) 6: I can git kind o' a edge on, but as f'r goin' down an' out, nix. **1920** F.S. Fitzgerald, in *OEDS*: We'll drink to Fred Sloane, who has a fine, distinguished edge. **1925** Hemingway *In Our Time* 60: I've just got a good edge on. **1934** H. Miller *Tropic of Cancer* 13: Seems to me she has a slight edge on already. **1934** O'Hara *Appt. in Samarra* ch. vi: I'm getting an edge on myself. **1938** "R. Hallas" *You Play the Black* 159: We...did some...drinking and got a real edge on. **1966** Jurgensen & Schenkkan *Peer Gynt* 25: I *have* got a bit of an edge on.

¶ In phrase:

¶ **over the edge** insane.

***1929** in *OEDS*: He would go over the edge, quite mad. **1978** Wharton *Birdy* 184: I've got to do something before she goes over the edge.

Edge City *n.* a place or condition characterized by tension, desperation, or alienation. [Cf. later S.E. *edge city* 'a suburb existing independently of a city'.]

1971 *Current Slang* V 10: Edge city, n. The drug users' world. **1976** Calif. man, age 32: This is Edge City, man. Right here. We're all living in Edge City.

edged *adj.* **1.** tipsy; intoxicated. Cf. EDGE.

1894 *Yale Wit & Humor* 21 (cited in Weingarten *Dict. Slang*). **1927** (quot. at SQUIFFY). **1934** in Chandler *Simple Art*: When he was nicely edged he was a pretty good sort of guy, besides being the best smut director in Hollywood.

2. angry.

1982 Corey & Westermark *Fer Shurr!*: Edged...incensed, angry, mad as hell...I'm *edged*, fer shurr! **1985** "Blowdryer" *Mod. Eng.* 10: Edged...Mad, angry. **1991** *Houston Chronicle* (Nov. 13) 5D: *Fully edged*: Really angry.

Edison *n.* [alluding to Thomas A. *Edison*, pioneer in electrical research] *Horse Racing.* a hand battery used illicitly by a jockey to goad a horse into running faster.

1949 Cummings *Dict. Sports* 122. **1979** Cuddon *Dict. Sports & Games* 299.

Edison Special *n. Pris.* death in the electric chair.—constr. with *the. Joc.*

1974 Andrews & Dickens *Over the Wall* 151: Okay, gang, I've got to cut out. Going to take the Edison Special!

Edsel *n.* [alluding to the Ford *Edsel*, popularly regarded as a poorly designed automobile] *USAF.* the General Dynamics F-111 Switchblade fighter-bomber.—used derisively.

1972 *N.Y. Times Mag.* (Oct. 29) 106: The F-111...was first introduced into the air war in 1968. Within a few days...one had disappeared and another had crashed....Another crashed a few weeks later, prompting another hunt for the wreckage. "We used to call them Edsel searches," Brown recalled. **1973** *Nat. Lampoon* (Sept.) 48: F-111, "The Flying Edsel." **1984** Trotti *Phantom* 244 [ref. to Vietnam War]: *F-111.* Aardvark (TFX, Edsel).

eel *n.* the penis.—used in var. phrs. meaning 'copulate' or 'fellate'.

1968 Coppel *Order of Battle* 112 [ref. to WWII]: Maybe a few practice sessions in the air instead of all your free time in Bourneham dipping the eel, okay? **1977** Olsen *Fire Five* 78: Says she'd like to chew the eel first chance we get.

¶ In phrase:

¶ **skin (one's) own eels** to tend to (one's) own affairs.

*ca*1840 in *DA:* Let every body skin their own eels. **1843** *Spirit of Times* (Feb. 11) 595: Let every man skin his own eels. **1879** Thayer *Jewett* 36: Let every man skin his own eels.

eel's ankle *n.* CAT'S PAJAMAS. Also **eel's hips.** *Joc.*

1923 Witwer *Fighting Blood* 103: It was the eel's ankle, no fooling! **1926** *AS* (Dec.) 145: The eel's hips.

eelskin *n.* **1.** a banknote; paper dollar.

1834 Caruthers *Kentuck. in N.Y.* I 96: I had an order on them for some of the eel-skins. *Ibid.* 98: He gave me an order on the bank for the eel-skins. **1840** *Spirit of Times* (Mar. 7) 8: Well, I'll draw out the old eelskin for better luck.

2. a New Englander.—used derisively. Also **eel.**

1836 *Crockett Almanac* (1837) 16: Encounter between a Corncracker and an Eelskin. **1838** [Haliburton] *Clockmaker* (Ser. 2) 264: There's the hoosiers of Indiana,...the wolverines of Michigan, the eels of New England.

3. *Pol.* (see quot.).

1877 Bartlett *Amer.* (ed. 4)·199: *Eel-Skin.* A thin, narrow slip of paper, with the name of a candidate on one side, and coated with mucilage on the other, so as to be quickly and secretly placed over the name of an opponent, on a printed ballot.

eff or **F** (a partial euphem. for) FUCK in var. senses and parts of speech; esp. **effing** FUCKING.

*1929 Graves *Good-Bye to All That* 79 [ref. to 1917]: The Bandmaster, who was squeamish, reported it as: "Sir, he called me a double-effing c—." **1931** E.E. Cummings *I Sing of Olaf Glad and Big* l. 19: I will not kiss your f.ing flag. **1931* J. Hanley *Boy* 252: Tell the effin bosun there's only the crew's stuff here now. **1943, *1944** in *OEDS.* **1945** in Hemingway *Sel. Letters* 579: You'll hear I'm a phony, a liar, a coward, maybe even a Man of Honor. Just tell them to Eff off. **1950** Hemingway *Across River* 78: "Eff Florence," the Colonel said. *Ibid.* 173: You would eff-off, discreetly. **1959** Cochrell *Barren Beaches* 130: They've come closer to solving the recreation problem than anyone else in this effing division. **1961** J.A. Williams *Night Song* 152: "Eff you, man," Yards said. **1961** Ellison *Memos* 43: Turn that effin' thing off before I put a fist through it. **1965** Hardman *Chaplains* 34: An effing chaplain's assistant! **1967** Taggart *Reunion* 189: You effin well know it. **1970** Landy *Underground Dict.* 76: *F. you*—Fuck you. *Ibid.* 77: *F-ing v.* Fucking; having sexual intercourse. *Ibid.* 78: *F-ing around*...Goofing off. **1973** Overgard *Hero* 61: Where in the effin hell have you been? **1977** *N.Y. Post* (Mar. 18) 37: With the language sensitivity of one who knows what will and will not get on TV she later asked: "Am I being effed around, or not?" He actually said "effed." *a*1984 in Terry *Bloods* 127: What the F was I there for? **1987** *Newsweek* (Mar. 23) 58: Don't F with him. *Ibid.* 63: He says he F'd you up. *Ibid.* 65: Stay the F out of the way. *Ibid.* 73: He said *F* the doctors. **1993** *Wash. Post* (Sept. 3) A 8: What the f are you doing here?

egg *n.* **1.a.** a person, esp. a man.—in earliest use constr. with *bad* or *good.* [The phr. in 1848 quot. is presumably a proverb rather than an ex. of this specific sense.]

[**1848** Judson *Mysteries* 350: "You'll ruin me!" "It's cussed hard to spile a rotten egg!"] **1855** "P. Paxton" *Capt. Priest* 319: In the language of his class, the Perfect Bird generally turns out to be "a bad egg." **1864* in *OED:* "A bad egg,"...a fellow who had not proved to be as good as his promise. **1866* in *F & H* (rev.) 102: The man in black...looked from head to heel a bad egg. **1871** *Overland Mo.* (July) 91: Dammum! She wus a good eg. **1883** Hay *Bread-Winners* 187: A lot of bad eggs among the strikers...intend to go through some of the principal houses on Algonquin Avenue. **1891** Maitland *Amer. Slang* 22: Bad egg, a rascal. **1891** Garland *Main-Travelled Roads* 29: Oh! he's a bad aig—he lit out f'r the West somewhere. He was a hard boy. **1902** Hapgood *Thief* 323:

Allison, chain her up. She is a bad egg. **1914** Lardner *Al* 92: Her other sister...had a bad egg for a husband. **1917** Oemler *Slippy McGee* 99: You *could* be a bad egg instead of a good nut, you know. **1921** *Variety* (Feb. 18) 8: But them two eggs sure love to play ball. **1922** Fitzgerald *Beautiful & Damned* 368: A Scroll and Keys man at Yale, he possessed the correct reticences of a "good egg." **1923** Witwer *Fighting Blood* 24: Knocking around since I been a kid has made me a pretty hard-boiled egg. *Ibid.* 359: This egg stopped Kid Christopher at Philly...in one round. **1929** Hammett *Dain Curse* 151: Might have been a friend of her father's. Did you ask him? He goes in for old eggs. **1933** Creelman & Rose *King Kong* (film): He's a tough egg, all right. **1934** Cain *Postman* 97: Christ no. That egg will want to pump your legs up and down. **1936** Gaddis *Courtesan* 42: He ain't that kind of an egg. **1948** Ives *Stranger* 38: They were not well liked; they were considered bad eggs. **1951** Spillane *Lonely Night* 104: Maybe those two eggs were holed up in there when they got caught up with. **1958** Johnson *Henry Orient* 40: Oh, she's a good egg, underneath it all. **1968** Cuomo *Thieves* 227: He was kind of a funny egg. **1987** D. da Cruz *Boot* 23: They're genuine tough eggs.

b. a foolish, ineffectual, or obnoxious person.

1918 Casey *Cannoneers* 130: Wonder what's going to happen to the poor egg. **1926** Anderson *Saturday's Children* 376: If only she wasn't such an egg!...she's so unhatched, somehow—she doesn't know her way around the block—she never did. **1931** *AS* VI 204: *Egg:* person of unpolished manners. **1932** Lorimer *Streetcars* 35: She slapped him and called him an egg.

c. an item; thing.

1931 Wilstach *Under Cover Man* 13: That's the last we'll see of those bad eggs [stolen cars].

2.a. *Mil.* an artillery shell or aerial bomb.

1863 in J.W. Haley *Rebel Yell* 58: "See dar. Hell has laid an egg." We were soon the recipients of as many of these favors, or "eggs," as we could attend to. **1864** in Wightman *To Ft. Fisher* 224: I'd rather Johnny'd be where them eggs is breaking than me. **1916* (cited in Partridge *DSUE* (ed. 8)). **1917* in *OEDS.* **1918** Sherwood *Diary* 46: Often they lay eggs (bombs) on us; and again have the audacity to zoom toward the ground and open their machine guns on us. **1918** *N.Y. Times* (July 21) 3: I felt Roy make a steep bank and stood by to let the "egg" go when the time came. **1919** Rickenbacker *Flying Circus* 129: Nightly these squadrons flew over to the Rhine cities and laid their eggs in and about these railroad centers and factory localities. **1928** Scanlon *God Have Mercy!* 335 [ref. to 1918]: The plane soon flew away without flipping off any eggs. **1948** Lay & Bartlett *12 O'Clock High!* 43: The target was pouring up smoke and we clobbered it with a few more eggs right down the middle. **1957** Anders *Price of Courage* 126: The artillery's been laying eggs out there all night. A few of 'em have been damned close, too. **1969** Eastlake *Bamboo Bed* 280: The obstacle in front, the instant swimming pools, were caused by our B52 eggs.

b. *Navy.* a naval mine; (also) a depth charge.

1918 *Texas Rev.* IV 86: [Naval] Mines are "eggs" and depth charges are "ash-cans." **1918** *Sat. Eve. Post* (Oct. 12) 89: The depth charge is known in the Navy as the "egg" or the "ash can." **1931** Ellsberg *Pigboats* 49 [ref. to 1918]: The Huns got wind you're going out and laid a few eggs there. **1936** Mulholland *Splinter Fleet* 167 [ref. to 1918]: It must be a mine-laying sub, surprised while laying her eggs off the entrance to Corfu. **1944** in Inman *Diary* 1209: I was on a fleet escort mine-sweeper, only we spent most of our days laying eggs and fighting off enemy aircraft. **1947** in Morison *Naval Ops. in WWII* I 137: Two of the minelaying submarines, *U-701* and *U-166,* were sunk by aircraft shortly after "laying eggs." **1968** Maule *Rub-A-Dub* 161 [ref. to WWII]: The destroyers did not lay any eggs.

c. *Mil.* a hand grenade.

1919 Haterius *137th U.S. Inf.* 104: A grenade was thrown out from our trench, and following the explosion the object was seen no more. Quick work with a few more "eggs" and steadily held rifles seemed to clear the field of any lurking enemy. **1919** Hinman *Ranging in France* 141: The grenade throwers wore their aprons, filled with the deadly "eggs" so greatly feared by the Germans. **1943** R.D. Andrews *Bataan* (film): When we start layin' these eggs, fire at will to cover us. **1949** Murphy *Hell & Back* 13 [ref. to 1943]: Here...Take my two aigs, and don't say I never give you nothing. **1982** Goff, Sanders, & Smith *Bros.* 9: I...tossed my first egg, and it was all over.

3. *Football.* a football.

1900 Patten *Merriwell's Power* 111: Again Columbia's big center kicked the yellow egg. **1974** Blount *3 Bricks Shy* 55: Hold *on* to that egg, guv'nor.

4. a dollar.

1911–12 Ade *Knocking the Neighbors* 71: Papa…began to sign Checks. It took many an egg to have Lila properly Conservatoried.

5.a. *pl.* testicles. [**1855** quot., in poetry, may not reflect slang usage of the day.]

[**1855** Whitman *Leaves of Grass* (comp. ed.) 53: Nest of guarded duplicate eggs! it shall be you!] **1916** Cary *Venery* I 77: *Eggs*—the testicles. **1952** Larson *Barnyard Folklore* 83: Testicles…bolls, eggs, stones, nuts, bollicks, oysters (mountain oysters: sheep nuts eaten by sheepherders). **1969** Hamill *Doc* 165: I seen your kind in a dozen towns, marshal. Walkin' around, swingin' your eggs like you wanted to use 'em. **1978** in *Maledicta* VI (1982) 23: Testicles…*balls*,…*eggs, family jewels*.

b. virile courage; guts; BALLS, 4.a.

[**1959** Searls *Big X* 213: They got an expression down there—the Mexicans—*no tiene huevos*. No eggs. They use it on a bull that's yellow. Or a matador.] *ca***1965** in Schwendinger & Schwendinger *Adolescent Subcult.* 194: They really got their eggs (testicles or "balls") to fight.

6. the skull; head.

1927 *Amer. Leg. Mo.* (June) 73 [ref. to 1918]: Make a pass at me an' I'll chip your egg with this entrenchin' tool. ***1933** (cited in Partridge *DSUE* (ed. 8)). **1935** *AS* (Feb.) 53: Put this hat on your egg.

7. *Narc.* a capsule of a drug.

1973–76 J. Allen *Assault* 161: Most of the time people call the cap an egg: "Give me twenty eggs." *Ibid.* 198: I shoot three eggs tonight, then three in the morning before I leave. **1981** (cited in Spears *Drugs & Drink*).

8. (see quot.).

1983 *N.Y. Times* (Sept. 6) B 6: An "egg" is a male mark [for pickpockets] under 30.

¶ In phrases:

¶ **bad egg!** (used to express disappointment). [Cf. corresponding use in England of *good egg!*, in *OEDS* from 1903.]

1862 in Stuart *40 Yrs.* 210: They…found bed rock at nine feet with one inch of gravel that prospects one cent per pan of dirt. "BAD EGG." **1890** *F & H* I 94: *Bad egg*…In the States the term is also applied to a worthless speculation.

¶ **bust (someone's) eggs** to make short work of; fix.

1977 M. Franklin *Last of Cowboys* 92: They're gonna bust your eggs, man.

¶ **egg in your beer** a bonus; something for nothing; the good life.—usu. in phr. **What do you want—egg in your beer?** Stop complaining; are you never satisfied?—usu. ironic. [Esp. common during WWII.]

1938 *AS* (Apr.) 156: *Egg in your beer*. An easy job; something for nothing. **1941** *AS* (Oct.) 165: *Egg in Your Beer*. Too much of a good thing. **1945** Bowman *Beach Red* 60: What else do you want—egg in your beer? **1949** Pirosh *Battleground* (film): What do you want, egg in your beer? **1950** Calmer *Strange Land* 124: Whaddya want, an egg in your beer? **1952** Uris *Battle Cry* 5 [ref. to 1942]: "What you want, chief, eggs in your beer?" The Injun laughed. **1957** Leckie *Helmet* 44 [ref. to 1942]: What's eating you? You never had it so good.…Whaddya want—egg in your beer? **1960** Hoagland *Circle Home* 12: And all the food. And Margaret every night for egg in his beer. **1966–80** McAleer & Dickson *Unit Pride* 84: You really want egg in your beer, don'tcha?

¶ **go lay** [or **fry**] **an egg!** (used as a rejective retort).

1928 Hecht & MacArthur *Front Page* 449: Lay an egg. **1932** *AS* VII (June) 332: Go lay an egg—"mind your own business." **1935** Clarke *Broadway* 79 [ref. to *ca*1910]: "Go lay an egg," Lefty snarled, drawing back his fist. **1943** P. Harkins *Coast Guard* 20: Oh, go lay an egg. **1985** D. Steel *Secrets* 265: Oh, go fry an egg, Sabina. **1985** C. Busch *Times Sq. Angel* 21: Aw, go suck an egg.

¶ **have an egg in the nest** to be pregnant.

1916 Cary *Venery* I 77: *Egg in the Nest*—The condition of pregnancy. ****1986** J. Green *Slang Thesaurus* 29: Pregnant: *a bun in the oven,…egg in the nest*, [etc.].

¶ **have egg on (one's) face** to look foolish or be embarrassed. Now *colloq.*

1951–53 *Front Page Detective* (syndic. TV series): I can see egg all over my face. **1972** B. Harrison *Hospital* 132: If you idiots did what you were supposed to do in the first place you wouldn't have to stand around with egg on your face being sorry. **1977** *L.A. Times* (Apr. 2) I 6: Anyone who tries to relate this decision to any future decision is making a mistake and will wind up with egg on his face. **1981** *Magnum, P.I.* (CBS-TV): Remember I told you I don't like getting egg on my face? I feel like I'm wearing a whole omelet!

¶ **lay an egg** Orig. *Theat.* [poss. sugg. by TURKEY, *n.*; in 1861

quot., the sense is 'to score a zero (in the game of cricket)'] to fail; fall flat; FLOP.

[****1861** in *OEDS*: Dowson "laid an egg."] **1929** McEvoy *Hollywood Girl* 201: Boys, it looks like we laid an egg. **1929** *Variety* (Oct. 30) 1: Wall Street Lays An Egg.…The most dramatic event in the financial history of America is the collapse of the New York Stock Market. **1931** Barry *Animal Kingdom* 350: I suppose he was full of explanations about those choice eggs the Bantam Press has been laying lately. **1939** Goodman & Kolodin *Swing* 184: The Goodman band, on its first booking in a hotel, laid an egg. **1940** in *AS* (Feb. 1941) 147: "Pinocchio," I hear, is laying a financial egg. **1948** Ives *Wayfaring Stranger* 207: "How can I sing ballads here?" I wondered. "I will lay the biggest ostrich egg in history tonight." **1958** A. King *Mine Enemy* 66: The book had…obviously already laid an egg. **1961** Baar & Howard *Missileman* 119: And there is where [the idea] laid an egg? **1982** *All Things Considered* (Nat. Public Radio) (July 8): If that [joke] lays an egg it's on your face.

¶ **make (someone) lay eggs** to succeed in copulating with (a woman).

1929–31 Farrell *Young Lonigan* 111: I was jus' tellin' myself about the chicken I made lay eggs today.…This chicken was the maid. See! **1933** Farrell *Guillotine Party* 211: Nate…told him about a chicken he had made lay eggs, and she had been a real hot one, too.

egg *v.* **1.** to deride; provoke; make fun of.

1933 Farrell *McGinty* 63: Don't let 'em egg you, John. *Ibid.* 90: She's always egging me like this when she's got something on me. **1965** Yurick *Warriors* 94: "All right," the little leader said. "Stop egging me."

2. *Rodeo.* to award a score of zero to. Cf. BAGEL.

1965 W. Crawford *Bronc Rider* 21: "Judges egged me," Del said. "Claimed I slapped my bull."

egg-bag *n. So.* (see quots.).

1898 Green *Va. Folk-Speech* 130: Egg-bag, *n.* Some intimate part of the anatomy supposed to be affected by intense desire for something. "I hope his *egg-bag* is easy at last." **1984** Wilder *You All* 22: *Don't strain your egg bag*: Don't try to kid me.

eggbeater *n.* **1.** an autogiro or helicopter.

1936 in *Atlantic Mo.* (Jan. 1937) 26: Pilots of airplanes contemptuously term autogiros "egg beaters," and the whole idea appeared to be a colossal flop. **1945** Hamann *Air Words.* **1951** *Sat. Eve. Post* (Dec. 16) 27: Lt. William Evans…grounded his egg-beater within a dozen feet of Dorris.…The helicopter took off as soon as Dorris had a firm grip. **1955** *I Love Lucy* (CBS-TV): You turn this eggbeater around and head back to the airport. **1955** in Loosbrock & Skinner *Wild Blue* 497: The eggbeater crew was quickly briefed. **1961** in Algren *Lonesome Monsters* 105: No, it's just an ol' egg beater. **1969** Briley *Traitors* 284: There were moments when he was fluttering some eggbeater across the treetops when his whole being exulted at the thrill of it. **1970** Gattzden *Black Vendetta* 96: The…pilot banking the eggbeater into an arc. **1977** T. Berger *Villanova* 214: He's just a lousy crook in an egg beater. **1988** Coonts *Final Flight* 337: No naval aviator in his right mind would set one of those eggbeaters down on top a JBD.

2. an outboard motor.

1942 *ATS* 83. **1956** in *Dict. Canadianisms* 234: They called it an eggbeater and burst into laughter at the sight of it. **1964** in *Yachting* (Jan. 1965) 77: There are the purists who wouldn't be caught dead with an eggbeater on their boat.

egg crate *n.* an old or clumsy airplane or automobile; CRATE.

1922 T.A. Dorgan, in Zwilling *TAD Lexicon* 35: If he can make that egg crate go I'll suggest his name for a medal. **1937** Lay *I Wanted Wings* 108: I stopped to think that this was a sluggish old "egg crate" with no performance at all. **1942** *ATS* 81: Automobile…*egg-crate*. **1945** Hamann *Air Words*: Egg crate…Any poorly constructed plane. **1952** Uris *Battle Cry* 105: Where the hell did they dig up this crap detail, guarding them goddam egg crates. **1952** in *DAS*: I know the home port of that egg-crate they were driving!

egghead *n.* **1.** a bald person.—used derisively.

1907 in Butterfield *Post Treasury* 77: His genius lived in the nicknames of the Egghead, Beauty Sawtelle, Morning Glory, Red Dog, Wash Simmons and the Coffee Cooler, which he had bestowed on his comrades with unfailing felicity. **1942** Tregaskis *Guadalcanal Diary* (entry for Aug. 2): "Don't take any chances," said the major, "it's better to shoot a few cocoanuts than miss a Jap egg-head." **1951** Elgart *Over Sexteen* 85: A fellow we call Egghead enticed me into a bar where he proceeded to get himself a snootful. **1987** *Frank's Place* (CBS-TV): How you doin', Egghead?

2. Orig. *Journ.* a usu. vapid or unrealistic intellectual. [Pop.

during the presidential election campaign of 1952.]

1918 Carl Sandburg, in *N.Y. Times Mag.* (Dec. 20, 1981) 12: "Egg heads" is the slang here [office of *Chicago Daybook*] for editorial writers.…At that it isn't so much the policies of the papers as the bigotry and superstition and flunkeyism of the Egg Heads. **1919** in Sandburg *Letters* 159: Of course, this makes no immediate enthusiasm among the egg-head editors. **1920** in Cornebise *Amaroc News* 87: Eggheads… [and] chinless chappies…who hid behind petticoats to avoid French mud…and German machine guns. **1936** Washburn *Parlor* 72: She doesn't "sell herself" as these egg-heads keep shouting. Such statements are unfair and unjust. As for the moral and aesthetic standpoint—who knows! They write books about it but get nowhere. **1952** in *OEDS*: A good many intelligent people…obviously admired Stevenson. "Sure," was the reply, "all the egg heads love Stevenson." **1957** *Esquire* (Nov.) 66: Eggheads Make the Best Lovers. **1959** Farris *Harrison High* 311: Learning is for eggheads. **1959** Searls *Big X* 192: They never ought to let a piece of gear go into production until the egghead that designed it tests it out. **1961** R.L. Scott *Boring Holes* 250: Mr. Quarles was a brilliant engineer, a type referred to now as an "egg head." **1968** Safire *New Language* 126: Egg-head. An intellectual, a highbrow. When used derogatively, an effete, bookish person with intellectual pretensions; when used affirmatively, a man with brains. **1973** C. Cussler *Mediterranean Caper* 100: Just what are these seagoing eggheads looking for? **1990** *New Republic* (Apr. 23) 36: A certain professor who typifies a modern egghead trying to make sense of the historical process.

3. a dolt.

1941 Riskin *Meet John Doe* (film): Quiet down, egghead. **1956** Lockwood & Adamson *Zoomies* 108: And you, you…egg-head, try to scuttle them. And us too! **1959** Trocchi *Cain's Book* 145: Fuck you, egghead! **1978** *UTSQ*: [Syns. for *idiot*:] dumb-ass, dork, egghead, retard.

eggheaded *adj.* **1.** having a bald head.

1920 in Safire *Stand Corrected* 142: A little eggheaded pedant. **1974** R. Carter *16th Round* 109: You stupid egg-headed bastard! **1986** E. Weiner *Howard the Duck* 37: He…swung, just as the eggheaded guy reached him.

2. vapidly intellectual; being an EGGHEAD, 2.

1956 *N.Y. Times* (July 8) 7 24: For the sophisticated or even the eggheaded reader, [etc.]. **1958** *Time* (Sept. 15) 84: Thornton was just an eggheaded visionary. **1965** *Harper's* (Oct.) 66: A short animated cartoon…about a little eggheaded boy. **1973** *Seattle Times* (Apr. 22) F1: "Maud" did get bogged down occasionally in literary discussions, and "Chloe" is free of its eggheadedness. **1975** Univ. Tenn. prof.: Talking about eggheaded intellectuals in their ivory towers.

egg jockey *n. Mil. Av.* a bomber pilot.

1943 *Life* (Aug. 9) 48: The bomber pilots, or egg jockeys as Cochran calls them, had a go at it without success. **1944** E.H. Hunt *Limit* 114: I'm playing egg-jockey again. *Ibid.* 202: Egg-jockies from Flint.

egg-layer *n. Navy.* a mine-laying vessel.

1948 in Morison *Naval Ops. in WWII* V 117: Little *Oglala*, the "egg-layer" alongside, was not so lucky.

eggnog *n.* a foolish or obnoxious person.

*ca***1921** in W.C. Fields *By Himself* 117: What an awful egg-nog he is.…You say the word and I'll throw him off the back platform.

eggplant *n.* a black person.—used derisively.

1973–74 M. Smith *Death of Detective* 190: "Which black man?"…"The blackest. Blue-black. Eggplant." **1979** S. Martin *Jerk* (film): We'll keep out the eggplants…the jungle bunnies…the niggers.

egg roll *n.* an East Asian.—used derisively.

1983 *Maledicta* VII 23: In New York in 1983 the new Korean immigrants and probably other Asian groups are sometimes called *egg roll.*

egg-suck *v.* to curry favor.

1980 *Magnum, P.I.* (CBS-TV): You can kiss those gold bars goodbye that you spent thirty years eggsuckin' for!

eggsucker *n.* a sneaking or contemptible person, now esp. a toady or flatterer.

1838 *Crockett Almanac* (1839) 30: You thin-gutted egg-sucker. **1853** in *DARE*: They [*sc.* sheriffs] are bloodsuckers, and egg-suckers, and throat-cutters. **1924** Garahan *Stiffs* 59: What sort of work do you call that, you…you…egg-sucker? **1945** in *Calif. Folk. Qly.* V (1946) 385: A seaman, first-class, who is studying toward a third-class rate…is known as a *striker.* This term also applies to the smooth operator who strives to win advancement through politics, ingratiation, and flattery, rather than by honest work and service. [Note] This specimen is also called *egg-sucker.* **1972** Poniscan *Cinderella Liberty* 39: Eggsucker! **1972** C.

Gaines *Stay Hungry* 39: You're a liar, eggsucker, cause I watch every game they play. **1990** *Simpsons* (Fox-TV): Back-scratcher! Bootlicker! Egg-sucker!

egg-sucking *adj.* sneaking or contemptible.—used prenominally. Cf. SUCK-EGG.

1845 Hooper *Simon Suggs* 24: You sassy, aig-sukkin', roguish, gnatty, flop-eared varmint! **1875** "M. Twain" *Old Times* 73 [ref. to *ca*1860]: Cain't you see nothin', you dash-dashed aig-suckin', sheep-stealin', one-eyed son of a stuffed monkey! **1935** Algren *Boots* 25: Sly black egg-suckin' son a bitch. **1941** Hargrove *Pvt. Hargrove* 52: What's eating you, Walter…besides that egg-sucking grin? *ca***1969** *Gunsmoke* (CBS-TV): Come on out, you egg-suckin' pigs! **1977** *Daily Beacon* (Univ. Tenn.) (Apr. 1) 7: [You] egg-sucking offspring of a Paris w—. You'll pay for this treason, you filthy little scumbag.

egg wagon *n. Army.* a bombing plane.

1919 Amerine *Alabama's Own in France* 303: We used to have some pretty exciting times when the "egg wagons" came over. "Egg wagons" are German aeroplanes, you know. They'd come over every now and then and lay an egg—a big high explosive bomb.

ego trip *n.* [*ego* + TRIP] **1.** an act or course of action undertaken primarily to satisfy one's own vanity or for self-gratification.

1967 (cited in *W9*). **1967–68** von Hoffman *Parents Warned Us* 97: All these people on power trips and ego trips! **1968** in *Maledicta* X (1990) 17: Sainthood Is All Ego Trip. ***1969** in *OEDS*. **1970** *New Yorker* (Feb. 21) 29: We think John Lennon is…on a super ego trip. **1971** Simon *Sign of Fool* 15: The elite of Park Station, that was his ego trip. **1972** Singer *Boundaries* 14: This is, of course, an ego trip. **1982** *L.A. Times* (Jan. 17) V 3: The big company…"will have to get rid of some of those…interminable staffs of flacks (public relations people) for corporate ego trips."

2. an arrogant sense of one's own superiority.

1985 M. Baker *Cops* 24: There's a whole ego trip that goes with the job.

ego-trip *v.* to behave in a self-serving manner.

1967 (cited in *W9*). **1970** *Atlantic* (Nov.) 118: They are not for profit or ego-tripping, but all and only for the good of the movement. **1973** *Penthouse* (July) 59: I see too many people start ego-tripping and run off on a tangent. **1976–77** C. McFadden *Serial* 64: Relate to the other person's feelings instead of just ego-tripping.

Egypt *n. Stu.* (see quots.).

1900 *DN* II 33: *Egypt,* n. 1. Privy, water-closet. [Reported from eight widely scattered colleges] **1984** in *DARE* [ref. to 1906]: He didn't mind going to Egypt, which was what everybody in town called privies.

¶ In phrase:

¶ **holy Egypt!** (used to express surprise).

1843 Field *Pokerville* 101: Holy Egypt! out I came again, howling!

Egyptian flu *n.* (see quot.). *Joc.*

1987 Lanning *Only War* 47 [ref. to 1969]: She wrote that the doctor said that she had the "Egyptian flu"—she was going to "be a mummie."

eight *n.* ¶ In phrase: **one over the eight** enough drinks to become intoxicated.

1954 Collans & Sterling *House Detect.* 49: People who've had "one over the eight," as the bartenders say, often neglect to lock their doors.

eight ball *n.* **1.** [the eight ball in the game of pool is black] a black person.—used contemptuously.

1919 *Fifth Div. Diamond* (June 13) 8: Eight Ball, did you remark that strange cemetery with all them toomstones we passed? Ah ain't seen it afore. **1921** *Variety* (July 29) 4: An old negro convict, known as "Eight Ball," shouted to the runner. **1928** R. Fisher *Jericho* 297: Boogy…cloud, crow, darky, dinge, dinky, eight-ball. **1929–30** Farrell *Young Lonigan* 24: He'd have to get away from the eight balls and tin-horn kikes. **1946** Michener *South Pacific* 367: One morning I tell him twice we doan' have no eggs. He git very mad. "Won't have no goddam eight ball tellin' me what to do and what not to do!" **1951** Pryor *The Big Play* 384: Billie's brother…had called him an eight-ball, a jigaboo, and a…coon. **1958** Motley *Epitaph* 294: Hello, eight-ball. **1959** F.L. London *Trumbull Pk.* 42: "Nigger!" "Jungle bunny!" "Eight balls!" **1965** Himes *Imabelle* 122: An eight-ball like him sweet on a high-yaller gal out where Hitler is buried at. **1977** T. Berger *Villanova* 135: I never could tell one eight ball from another.

2. Esp. *USMC.* a bungler; troublemaker; misfit.

1933 *Leatherneck* (Dec.) 19: That's typical of the eight-ball squad! **1941** *Amer. N & Q* (Dec.) 140: 8-balls: useless soldiers. **1942** Tregaskis *Guadalcanal Diary* (entry July 31): I heard a group of them, today, talking about an "eight ball," which is marine slang for a soldier who disgraces his fellows…. **1942** *Leatherneck* (Nov.) 145: *Eightball*—Man who is slow on the pick-up. **1949** McMillan *Old Breed:* There was not a single 8-ball among the party organized to make the trip. **1957** Leckie *Helmet* 113 [ref. to 1943]: This company has been goofing off long enough—and it's all because of a few eight-balls and yardbirds. So today we're getting rid of them. **1963** *Sat. Eve. Post* (July 27) 25: The first GI to go across [i.e. defect] was Pvt. Larry A. Abshier, an "eight-ball" soldier who had just been busted from PFC for getting too drunk to stand guard. **1968** "R. Hooker" *MASH* 164: I've got orders for you two eight-balls to ship out of here a week from today. **1978** S. King *Stand* 38: This eight-ball…wanted to run him down.

3. *USAF.* (see quot.). Now *hist.*

1980 *Air Classics—Air War Over Korea* 50 [ref. to 1949]: One permanent bug in the new [F-82] aircraft was the tumble-proof attitude indicator: the "eight ball."…It indicated backwards! Down was up and up was down. That bugged us all in the beginning.

4. *Narc.* an eighth of an ounce of a drug.

1989 Radford & Crowley *Drug Agent* 51: An eightball is an eighth of an ounce [of cocaine]. **1989** *New York* (Feb. 20) 44: An eight ball (three and a half grams of coke) barely lasts him several days. *a***1990** E. Currie *Dope & Trouble* 30: Like one of my friends had an eight-ball and was supposed to sell it for three-hundred-some dollars. **1990** *Cops* (Fox-TV): An eightball of crank.

¶ In phrase:

¶ **behind the eight ball** at a serious disadvantage; in or into trouble.

[**1926** Finerty *Criminalese* 19: *Eight balls*—Bad luck.] **1932** *World's Work* (Feb.) 26: Mr. Ells, the wizard of the cue, in a position he expertly diagnosed as squarely behind the 8-ball. **1929–33** J.T. Farrell *Young Manhood* 233: He's one poor bastard who ended up behind the eight-ball. **1936** "E. Queen" *Halfway House* 9: I'll probably finish behind the eight-ball, pleading small claims cases. **1937** *Our Army* (Mar.) 3: Here I am, gentlemen—over here behind the eight ball as usual. **1941** Cain *Mildred Pierce* 249: It's you that's behind the eight ball, not us. **1941** Macauley & Wald *Manpower* (film): Because you and Hank were friends, I was setting myself up behind the eightball again. **1941** Schulberg *Sammy* 16: Since Sammy burst into the office over a year before, I had tried every method I could think of to overcome him….And after twelve months of Sammy Glick I was still behind the eight-ball. **1946** Haines *Command Decision* 3: Eddie was always behind the eight ball with girls. **1949** E.S. Gardner *Negligent Nymph* 35: "Just where does that leave you, Chief?" "Right behind the eight ball." **1959** *N.Y. Times* (Mar. 22) 1 63: Ike has spent so much time standing behind a golf ball that he has got the American people standing behind the eight ball. **1963** Ross *Dead Are Mine* 206: One of these days you're going to end up so far behind the eight ball they'll have to pipe daylight to you. **1992** *CBS This Morning* (CBS-TV) (Sept. 1): They're a little bit behind the eightball on this one.

eight-ball *v.* **1.** *USMC.* to transfer (a marine) for being a misfit or troublemaker.

1945 Monks *Ribbon & Star* 80: Any officer who fails to give his men the proper training is a no-good eight-ball….I'll eight-ball that no-good lazy guy back to the States.

2. to thwart or ruin, esp. by cheating or trickery. [Perh. the orig. sense.]

1947 Helseth *Martin Rome* 122: I'll give you a chance to eight-ball him, and at the same time get half the de Grazia stuff. **1956** Hargrove *Girl He Left* 171: You've done your damnedest to eight-ball me for eight weeks. **1976** *Kojak* (CBS-TV): We been eightballed, baby! **1981** Ballenger *Terror* 147: We're eight-balled now.

eighteen-carat *adj.* first-class; utter; absolute.

1880 Nye *Boomerang* 286: The gorgeous eighteen-karat-stem-winding profanity of the present day. **1893** Bangs *Coffee & Repartee* 49: He informed me that I was an 18-karat sciolist. **1900** Willard & Hodler *Powers That Prey* 38: Eighteen-carat place you got here, Buck, old sport. **1920** Witwer *Kid Scanlan* 246: She had him figured as a eighteen-carat simp. **1929** Booth *Stealing* 133 [ref. to *ca*1916]: What an eighteen-carat sap I was! **1942** (quot. at WHACK, *n.*).

eight-miler *n. Trucking.* (see quot.).

1971 Tak *Truck Talk* 55: *Eight-miler:* a careless tourist or trucker who runs down the road with a signal light on for several miles.

eight-rock *n.* **1.** *Pool.* the eight ball.

1940 Sturges *McGinty* (film): Look right over behind the eight-rock.

2. EIGHTBALL, *n.*, 1.

1935 Pollock *Und. Speaks: Eight rock,* a negro. **1954–60** *DAS.*

eighty days *n. Craps.* the point 8.

1908 Stell & Null *Convict Verse* 18: Eighty days an-ah great Big Dick! **1919** Wilkins *Co. Fund* 45: Little Jo. Eighty days. Half of it. Shoes for the baby.

eighty-eight *n.* **1.** [sugg. by the eighty-eight keys of the keyboard] *Music.* a piano. Also as *v.*

1942 *ATS* 559. **1949** *Sat. Eve. Post* (Dec. 17) 45: A bit of jive talk—"88" for the piano. **1952** Felton & Essex *Las Vegas Story* (film): My business is sittin' here just poundin' the eighty-eight. **1957** *Sat. Eve. Post* (Mar. 9) 55: The player took a fast walk on the piano. "That's real eighty-eighting." **1958** Hughes & Bontemps *Negro Folklore* 483. **1971** Curtis *Banjo* 233: Basie's one finger on the eighty-eight. **1972** Winchell *Exclusive* 18: Harry played the "88" while I tenored the tunes. **1992** D. Burke *Street Talk* I 228: Playing the ol' eighty-eight sure put me on cloud nine.

2. *pl.* [sugg. by *.88,* a German .88-mm. shell] *Army.* barbiturate capsules. [Quots. ref. to WWII.]

1949 Van Praag *Day Without End* 72: "We'll take him to the aid station," said Saunders. "Give him some blue eighty-eights." **1965** Linakis *In Spring* 58: You'd better not take the eighty-eights….The goof balls, yellow jackets, sleeping pills, they're eighty-eights. The red are minis. **1991** Standifer *Not in Vain* 214: A glass of water and a blue 88….A blue 88 was amobarbital, used as a strong sedative for men with combat fatigue.

3. *pl.* "love and kisses." Cf. SEVENTY-THREE.

1934 Weseen *Dict. Slang* 166: Love and kisses, in the lingo of telegraph operators….88's. **1977** P. Wood *Salt Bk.* 175: 73's [&] 88's [on a business card, without further explanation].

eighty-eighter *n. Music.* a pianist.

1949 in Gold *Jazz Lexicon.* **1982** A. Shaw *Dict. Pop/Rock* 117: *Eighty-eighter.* Swing term for a pianist.

eighty miles *n. Craps.* the point 8.

1911 *Howitzer* 177: Big Dick from Boston—eighty miles from home—Phoebe—Little Joe—four's my point…!

eighty-six 1. *interj. & adj.* (among waiters and bartenders) out of stock; out (of an item ordered by a customer).

[**1926–35** Watters & Hopkins *Burlesque* 47: *Waiter*…If you need any Scotch or gin, sir—…My number is Eighty-Six….Skid….Yeah. Eighty-Six. I know. (*Waiter exits R. Skid* draws enormous flask from pocket.)] **1936** *AS* (Feb.) 43: *Eighty-six.* Item on the menu not on hand. **1945** *Calif. Folk. Qly.* IV 55: *Eighty-six*…We do not have the item ordered. **1953** A. Kahn *Brownstone* 214: "Eighty-six on the Danish," he proclaimed as he removed the last glossy brown pastry from under the glass cover. **1976** *Nat. Lampoon* (July) 76: My Order Is Always Eighty-Six in the Restaurant of Love. **1981** Eble *Campus Slang* (Oct.) 3: *Eighty-six*—no, nix: Eighty-six the baked potatoes—we ran out of them two hours ago.

2. *n.* **a.** an unwelcome customer who is to be denied service.

1943 G. Fowler *Sweet Prince* 227 [ref. to 1920's]: There was a bar in the Belasco building…but Barrymore was known in that cubby as an "eighty-six." An "eighty-six" in the patois of western dispensers means, "Don't serve him!" **1954** *N.Y. Times* (May 16) VI 39: Pages…are alert against "eighty-sixes"…meaning regulars who have made pests of themselves. **1976** *Dallas Times Herald* (Nov. 21) 2A: How did the term "86" in the restaurant business come to apply to deadbeat customers?

b. *Sales.* a remaindered item.

1987 Eble *Campus Slang* (Oct.) 9: *86*—a piece of clothing that nobody wants: "There's a lot of 86's over in the corner."

3. *adj.* unwelcome, as at a bar.

1963 Braly *Shake Him* 98: And even if Carver did street him Bear would be eighty-six all over town.

eighty-six *v.* [fr. the *interj.*] **1.a.** to end; stop; quash; discard or get rid of.

1955 Woods & Gordon *Bride of Monster* (film): The police want those monster stories eighty-sixed. **1973** *Sanford & Son* (NBC-TV): OK. OK. Eighty-six the trees [from the set of a TV commercial]. **1974** (cited in *Barnhart Dict. Comp.* I (1982) 37). **1978** De Christoforo *Grease* 102: "Junk it."…"It's a major piece of machinery! We can't eighty-six it." **1979** *Stripper* (CBS-TV movie): Come on, eighty-six that [costume]. **1981** *Nat. Lampoon* (Sept.) 47: I was sadistically pleased and proud that the college had decided to eighty-six their executive refresher course. **1987** Eble *Campus Slang* (Oct.) 9: *86*—Negate, eliminate, forget: "86 that idea." From the jargon of restaurant servers in which the number 86 means "leave off," e.g. "86 the fries." **1989** *News-*

week (July 31) 6: *86.* Remove a dish from the menu...."Eighty-six the liver and onions."

b. to eliminate by killing; murder.

1978 *L.A. Times* (Mar. 15) I 26: At least it suggests that the police haven't 86ed (murdered) him. **1980** L.N. Smith *Venus Belt* 125: Take those attacks: somebody'd tried to eighty-six me with a tampered Webley. **1984** *Buckaroo Banzai* (film): Your job is to eighty-six John Whorfin. **1987** A. Parker *Angel Heart* (film): He was into Voodoo—they eighty-six one another two a week.

2.a. to eject; put out; dismiss; send packing.

1958 *Sat. Eve. Post* (July 26) 54: Mr. Hamish became a little boisterous and uncertain on his feet, but Tom didn't very well see how he could eighty-six the president of a large bank, particularly at a wedding reception. **1959** in Russell *Perm. Playboy* 370: When I go into a jazz joint I still feel like yelling "Blow baby blow!" to the musicians though nowadays I'd get 86d for this. **1959** A. Anderson *Lover Man* 118: If she gets salty then I'll be eighty-sixed too. **1963** Rechy *City of Night* 173: I'll have you eighty-sixed out of this bar so fast. **1966** H.S. Thompson *Hell's Angels* 201: Another journalist was eighty-sixed for being too sympathetic. **1967** Taggart *Reunion* 101: "I think we better call it a night, Nola." "You eighty-sixin' me, Angelo?" **1973** in J. Flaherty *Chez Joey* 112: Madalyn Murray had God 86ed in public school classrooms. **1974** *Playboy* (Feb.) 62: Why did you leave Universal at the end of a year and a half? [Clint] Eastwood: They 86'd me....They called me in and said they didn't feel I was of any value to them. **1976** Price *Bloodbrothers* 246: 'Cause that's what you were that night when you eighty-sixed Annette. **1981** *Hill St. Blues* (NBC-TV police series): He'll eighty-six your kiester. **1984** D. Smith *Steely Blue* 52: They were caught smoking in the bathroom of the Kip's Bay Boys' Club and were eighty-sixed there for the day. *Ibid.* 300: If somebody made a mistake, why don't you just eighty-six him?

b. to get out.—used imper.

1967 Gelber *On Ice* 7: It's 86. Get out of here! 86! Just go. **1969** Gordone *No Place* 426: Eighty-six, ol' timer! We ain't hirin'. **1975** *Welfare* (WNET-TV): Just get your black power together and eighty-six out. **1983** *Nat. Lampoon* (Aug.) 91: Eighty-six, Jack.

el see EL —— O.

elakazoo *n.* [orig. unkn.] money.

1960 Jordan & Marberry *Fool's Gold* 221 [ref. to 1900]: He tried to sue for his elakazoo.

elbow *n.* [perh. fr. ELBOW, *v.*] **1.** *Und.* a police officer or detective.

1899 "J. Flynt" *Tramping* 385: The word "elbow," meaning detective, is one of the slang terms common among both hoboes and criminals. It comes from the detective's habit of elbowing his way through a crowd. **1900** Willard & Hodler *Powers That Prey* 179: I'd rather take my chanst with ten o' these Rube coppers here in Paris 'n with one o' the fly elbows in York. **1901** "J. Flynt" *World of Graft* 23: "No up-to-date elbows*...would let as many touches come off as these Chicago guys do."...*Detectives. **1902** F.P. Dunne *Observs.* 125: They aint lot iv diff'rence between th' mos' ordhinry flat-footed elbow...an' th' gr-reatest gin'ral. **1906** H. Green *Boarding H.* 59: He puts up a beef about the elbows shakin' him down ag'in an' cleanin' him out. **1912** Stringer *Shadow* 90: He closeted himself with two dependable "elbows." **1914** Jackson & Hellyer *Vocab.* 31: *Elbow,* Noun. General usage in cosmopolitan centers. A detective. **1916** *Lit. Digest* (Aug. 19) 424: In the West, Central Office men are known as "C.O. dicks" or "elbows," from a habit they have of elbowing into crowds after their prey. **1923** in Hammett *Knockover* 141: If everything's all right, and there's no elbows tagging along, somebody'll come up to you between your house and the waterfront. **1925** Mullin *Scholar Tramp* 26: The yard dick is the one constant...fear of the railroad vagrant. He is known...not only as a "dick" but...[also] as "bull," "soft-shoe," "gumpshoe," an "elbow," a "flatty," or a "mug." **1927** *AS* II 385: A plainclothesman, now called a *fly-dick,* was an *elbow,* from his way of elbowing through a crowd when he saw someone he wished to keep in sight. **1948** in *DAS.*

2. *Und.* a pickpocket's assistant.

1925 (cited in Partridge *Dict. Und.* 221). **1934** W. Smith *Bessie Cotter* 21: He's a shine pickpocket....He ain't even a good elbow for that dip mob he trails with.

¶ In phrases:

¶ **crook** [or **bend**] **(one's) elbow** to drink liquor, esp. immoderately.

1821 Waln *Hermit in Phila.* 23: I warrant the bang-ups have crooked their elbows...all been in for a dinner-party; blue as razors, no doubt.

*1825 Jamieson *Scot. Dict. Supp.* I 271: She *crooks* her *elbow,* a phrase used of a woman who uses too much freedom with the bottle...bending her elbow in reaching the drink to her mouth. **1859** Bartlett *Amer.* (ed. 2): To crook one's elbow or one's little finger is to tipple. **1868** Macy *There She Blows!* 76: It isn't every shipmaster that can have charge of it without crooking his own elbow too often. **1888** in *F & H* II 216: I'll...ask him to take a drink, chat with him while he crooks his elbow. **1901** in *AS* LXIII (Summer 1988) 114: In Devery's vivid vocabulary, *bendin' the elbow* means "drinking." **1938** D. Runyon *Take It Easy* 247: He stops bending his elbow and helps Hattie cook and wash the dishes. **1944** *Calif. Folk. Qly.* III 244: There was a San Francisco woman...who had a habit of "crooking her elbow" too much. ***1967** in *OEDS:* Too fond of bending the elbow.

¶ **on (one's) elbows** *Black E.* indignant.

1944 in Himes *Black on Black* 203: Well all root, man....Don't get on your elbows.

elbow *v.* *Und.* (see quots.).

1859 Matsell *Vocab.* 30: *Elbow.* Turn the corner; get out of sight. [**1930** Irwin *Tramp & Und. Sl.: Elbow*...often used as a word of warning from one crook to another when a detective is about.]

elbow-bender *n.* [fr. earlier *bend (one's) elbow* s.v. ELBOW] an immoderate drinker.

1942 Davis & Wolsey *Call House* 20: Like a hint to the elbow-benders. **1944** Kober & Uris *In Meantime, Darling* (film): I got a mob of elbow-benders in my room. **1958** McCulloch *Woods Words* 57: *Elbow bender.* A drinking man. **1975** DeMille *Smack Man* 104: The mostly working class elbow benders looked...serious.

elbow-bending *n.* [fr. earlier *bend (one's) elbow* s.v. ELBOW] immoderate drinking.

[**1912** T.A. Dorgan, in Zwilling *TAD Lexicon* 35: Later on I hoist a few dark brews—elbow exercise.] **1934** *Esquire* (Apr.) 36: The gentlemanly art of refined elbow-bending. **1957** *Playboy* (May) 14: Swimming, dancing and elbow bending. **1975** Morehouse & Gross *Total Fitness* 71: The only exercise they took was elbow bending at the officers' club.

elbow grease *n.* **1.** effort or exertion in physical labor. Now *colloq.*

*1672 A. Marvell, in *OED2.* ***1698–99** "B.E." *Dict. Canting Crew: Elbow grease*...A derisory Term for Sweat. ***1785** Grose *Vulgar Tongue: Elbow grease.* Labour. Elbow grease will make an oak table shine. **1807** J.R. Shaw *Autobiog.* 128: By the dint of assiduity and elbow grease, I soon earned my shirt and shoes. **1821** Waln *Hermit in Phila.* 25: "Any man that holes such a ball would rob a church!"—"You want more elbow-grease." **1841** [Mercier] *Man-of-War* 32: Use them with a little *elbow-grease.* ***1870** in *F & H* II 356: Often have I been...admonished to put some elbow-grease into my work. **1923** in Glasgow *Stories* 201: It takes what Mammy Rhody calls elbow grease to put it over, and I did put it over. **1928** Bodenheim *Georgie May* 88: Ah make 'em use elbow grease all raght but ah ain no Simon Legree, no siree! **1930** Sage *Last Rustler* 283: I found out there was no sale for honest elbow grease. *ca*1940 in Botkin *Treas. Amer. Folk.* 535: He didn't stint the elbow grease. **1986–91** Hamper *Rivethead* 130: It was our labor, our...elbow-grease.

2. fiddle-playing. *Joc.*

1834 Caruthers *Kentuck. in N.Y.* 217: What jaunty heels they would have to sling after such elbow-greese as that?

elbow-shaker *n.* a dice gambler.

*1748 in *F & H* II 356: *Elbow-shaker*...a gamester, one that practices dice playing. ***1796** Grose *Vulgar Tongue: Elbow shaker.* A gamester, one who rattles Saint Hugh's bones, i.e. the dice. **1859** Matsell *Vocab.* 30: *Elbow-shaker.* A man that gambles with dice.

el cheapo *adj.* cheap.—used prenominally. Cf. CHEAPO.

1967 (cited in *Oxf. Dict. Mod. Slang*). **1969** (cited in *W10*). **1976** Conroy *Santini* 476: The El Cheapo Marines use this candlelight because they hate spending a dollar or two on electric light. **1981** G. Wolf *Roger Rabbit* 38: In any el cheapo second-hand store in town. **1983** *Morning Contact* (WKGN radio) (Apr. 1): And it's not an el cheapo cake—it's a big two-layer.

El D *n.* a Cadillac El Dorado automobile.

1972 *Newsweek* (Feb. 28) 19: Their swanky El D's lined the street for blocks. **1974** Andrews & Dickens *Over the Wall* 241: The black El D zipped along the desert floor. **1976** Price *Bloodbrothers* 143: What kinda car you got, a LD? **1967–80** Folb *Runnin' Lines* 236: *El D*...Cadillac El Dorado.

el dingo *adj.* [pseudo-Sp form of DINGY] DINGY.

1981 O'Day & Eells *High Times* 40: [The Walkathon] was a flop and I was a little el dingo.

Eldo *n.* EL D.

    1976 Braly *False Starts* 301: A big dark-blue Eldo.

election *n.* ¶ In phrase: **hell bent** [or **full bent**] **for election** at reckless speed.

    1880 in Rosa *Gunfighter* 41: I'll turn loose and scatter death and destruction full bent for the next election. **1913** J. London *Valley of Moon* 425: Does a Chink ever want to ride a horse hell-bent for election?

electric *adj. Mil. Av.* (of an aircraft) modified for operations requiring electronic countermeasures.—used prenominally.

    1984 Cunningham & Ethell *Fox Two* 60 [ref. to Vietnam War]: The Electric Whales (EA-3s) and EA-6s jammed enemy radar effectively. *Ibid.* 151: The A-3's size earned it the affectionate nickname "Whale," and EA-3s were sometimes called "Electric Whales." **1987** Nichols & Tillman *Yankee Sta.* 88: The "Electric Spads" (EA-IFs) flew with…two enlisted men as ECM operators [in 1965].

elegant *n.* ¶ In phrase: **make (one's) elegant** *Und.* to make (one's) escape.

    1902 Hapgood *Autobiog. of a Thief* 118 [ref. to ca1890]: I am determined to make my elegant, (escape) come what will. *Ibid.* 168: He was discovered trying to make his elegant (escape).

elegantifferously *adv.* exceedingly; remarkably. *Joc.*

    1846 in Botkin *Treas. Amer. Folk.* 25: The way he…wiped his red tongue about was elegantifferously greedy.

element *n.* alcoholic liquor; in phr. **in (one's) element** intoxicated.—constr. with *the*.

    1737 *Penn. Gaz.* (Jan. 6) 1: He's…In his Element. **1855** Simms *Forayers* 241: At that time [I] hadn't drank a thimbleful of the element.

elephant *n.* **1.** a remarkable or astonishing sight or sights; worldly practices, experiences, or the like.—usu. constr. with *the* and alluding to *see the elephant*, below.

    1848 Baker *Glance at N.Y.* 9: His business was to show up the Elephant to country people, or in other words, take them about town to see the sights. **1851** M. Reid *Scalp-Hunters* 182: We, too, came in for a share of their curiosity; but O'Cork was "the elephant." **1855** Brougham *Chips* 336: Stay a minute or two longer, and you'll see the Helephant. **1861** Guerin *Mountain Charley* 26: I know who's got a nelephant up town, tail, trunk and horns. I want to visit that animal, I do! **1881** Ingraham *Buffalo Bill from Boyhood* 104: I proceeded to New York, where I was shown the "elephant." **1958** S.H. Adams *Tenderloin* 242 [ref. to 1890's]: A virgin…Ain't it straight that you was showin' him the elephant? **1968** Myrer *Eagle* 15: *That* was the elephant and no mistake.

    2. *Army.* an observation balloon.

    1918 *World's Work* (Nov.) 719: The "Eyes of the Artillery" are the captive balloons, familiarly known to the members of the A.E.F. as "elephants."…The standard crew of an "elephant" consists of a pilot and one artillery observer.

    3. *Navy. Av.* a large tanker aircraft.

    1969 Cagle *Naval Av. Guide* 400: Big tanker (Elephant Whale)—KA-3, EKA-3, or KA-6.

    4. (in joc. expressions).

    1975 C.W. Smith *Country Music* 247: Too bad it was as useless as a flea crawling up an elephant's hind leg with rape in its mind! **1984** N.Y.C. elevator operator, age ca48: What is the quietest thing in the world?…A flea wearing sneakers walking on an elephant's balls.

¶ In phrase:

¶ **see the elephant, 1.** to see or experience all that one can endure.

    1835 Longstreet *Georgia Scenes* 2: That's sufficient, as Tom Haynes said when he saw the Elephant. **1842–44** Kendall *Santa Fé Exped.* I 108: There is a cant expression, *"I've seen the elephant,"* in very common use in Texas. *Ibid.* 109: When a man is disappointed in anything he undertakes, when he has seen enough, when he gets sick and tired of any job he may have set himself about, he has "seen the elephant." **1844** Carleton *Logbooks* 33: No body has seen the "Elephant" yet, although sometimes several were on the point of doing so.…When one gets tired of the journey, and wishes to turn back, he has "seen the Elephant"—a cant phrase used by all voyageurs of Western Prairies. **1843–45** T.J. Green *Tex. Exped.* 53: Some would conclude that "they had seen enough," while others would say that "they had seen the elephant," and some, "if they ever got out of that place they would go home." **1845** in G.W. Harris *High Times* 45: I think if he was to occur in this rootin…he would *"See the Elephant,"* sure! **1847** Buhoup *Narrative* 140: These men

looked as though they had not only seen the elephant but the kangaroo also. Their sufferings must have been very great. **1853** Ballantine *Autobiography* 139 [ref. to Mexican War]: A few months afterward, when their time expired, great exertions were used to influence them to remain, but with no effect; the poor fellows had "seen the elephant," and were perfectly satisfied with the exhibition.

    2.a. to gain worldly experience or to learn a hard lesson from experience; lose one's innocence; (*hence*) to see remarkable sights.

    1842 *Spirit of Times* (Sept. 3) 324: But, Squire, I'll say no more, *I've seen the elephant.* **1845** Durivage & Burnham *Stray Subjects* 63: This mornin' I see the elephant, and naow I'm bound to see *this* crittur. **1845** in G.W. Harris *High Times* 50: I felt my bristles a raisin my jacket-back up like a tent cloth, so I axed him if he'd *"ever seen the Elephant?"* He said no, but he had seen a *grocery walk.* **1850** Garrard *Wah-to-Yah* 268: He…was seized with a desire to see the oft-vaunted "elephant," so he started out as a teamster. **1854** in M. Lewis *Mining Frontier* 38: I am a man who wandered "from away down east," and came to sojourn in a strange land and "see the elephant." **1872** Burnham *Secret Service* viii: *Seeing the elephant*, up to the latest dodge; knowing; not "green." **1880** Sprague *Campus Melodies* 31: So, to college I was sent, sir,/To see the Elephant. **1893** James *Mavrick* 29: We once had a character in our range who clearly wished to appear as a great and wealthy man, one who had seen the elephant and heard the owl. **1906** in "O. Henry" *Works* 176: No doubt the drivers of those wagons were scattered about the town "seeing the elephant and hearing the owl." **1916** Cary *Venery* I 77: *To see the elephant*—To be seduced. **1947** W.M. Camp *S.F.* viii: I had read somewhere that the first thing visitors did upon arriving in the place was to "see the elephant," a term which meant seeing the sights. **1968** S.O. Barker *Rawhide Rhymes* 25: I'm just a pore ol' country boy…/ Ain't never seen the elephant nor spun the world, like Buck! **1968** Kirkwood *Good Times/Bad Times* 130: Oh, he's seen the elephant and heard the hooty owl, this one has. **1974** *Gunsmoke* (CBS-TV): I've had a checkered life. You might say I've seen the elephant. I've had a good look at him, from all sides. **1976** Univ. Tenn. student: You seem to know a lot about life. You've seen the elephant, as you might say. **1979** Decker *Holdouts* 12: As old Jake would say, I've seen the elephant and heard the owl. **1985** Dye *Between Raindrops* 265: He better not try to shit those guys. They've seen the elephant.

    b. *Specif.* (*Mil.*) to see combat, esp. for the first time.

    1847 in J.M. McCaffrey *Manifest Destiny* 186: I came to Mexico to see the "Elephant." I have seen him & am perfectly willing now to see him again. **1862** in Frank & Reaves *Seeing Elephant* 130: All were anxious for to get a shot or two at the rebels and we had the satisfaction of seeing the elephant. **1863** [Fitch] *Annals of Army* 650: And now whene'er we hear a man…tell how many foes he'd whip and make them run and pant,/We simply say, "You ne'er have seen the famous 'Elephant.'" **1864** in Allan *Lone Star Ballads* 151: They faced about, at "double-quick," and run with all their might,/For they had seen the "elephant," and did not like the sight. **1887** Hinman *Corporal Si Klegg* 57 [ref. to Civil War]: The fledglings were panting to "see the elephant," and there was good prospect that they would soon gaze upon him in all his glory and magnitude. **1968** Cameron *Dragon's Spine* 150: He wondered if, maybe, some of them had "seen the elephant." **1982** I.M. Hunter *Blue & Gray* (NBC-TV movie) [ref. to Civil War]: "Before you get there you can expect to see the elephant." "What elephant?" "To see the elephant means to be in a battle." "Have *you* seen the elephant?" "Once. Over my shoulder." **1985** J.M.G. Brown *Rice Paddy Grunt* 242: Those of us who were there and "saw the elephant" know what America is.

elephant business *n.* sightseeing. *Joc.*

    1888 *Stag Party* (unp.): He thought he would try a little elephant business in the city.

elephant ear *n. Rocketry.* (see quot.).

    1959 Heflin *Aerospace Gloss.*: *Elephant ear.* A thick plate on a missile's skin that reinforces a hatch or hole. *Slang.*

elephant gun *n.* **1.a.** a long heavy-caliber firearm; (*Army, obs.*) an antitank rifle.

    1918 in Woollcott *Command is Forward* 161: The anti-tank rifle [is] a villainous affair, an elephant gun, really, nearly six feet long and firing a five-and-a-half-inch long armor piercing shell. **1920** *Inf. Jour.* (Jan.) 533 [ref. to 1918]: The "Elephant Guns" firing an armor-piercing bullet of 53 caliber, which were made in large numbers especially for tanks, did not stop them. **1931** Bullard *Amer. Soldiers* 100 [ref. to 1918]: Also those new "elephant guns," rifles of large bore and power, which no one man can handle, whose bullets will penetrate tank armor. **1962** G. Ross *Last Campaign* 112 [ref. to 1950]: That's a Goddamn fifty-one. Long-range sonovabitch. They call it a elephant gun. And the fucking

things'll shoot through a truck motor. **1963** Fehrenbach *This Kind of War* 721: Each NKPA division carried 36 of these, called by Americans the "elephant" or "buffalo" gun. **1986** "J. Cain" *Suicide Squad* 134: Back off! Take that elephant gun with you, too.
b. *Army.* a grenade launcher.
1964 R. Moore *Green Berets* 160: Carrying elephant guns, as the M-79 grenade launchers had been dubbed. **1969** Maitland *Only War We've Got* 22: Two Platoon let go with their "Elephant Guns"—wide-barrelled weapons that fired two-point-eight-inch grenades. **1987** "J. Hawkins" *Tunnel Warriors* 221: Some GIs call bloopers elephant guns, or thumpers.
2. *Surfing.* a large surfboard; BIG GUN.
1963 in Filosa *Surf. Almanac* 25: The "elephant gun" boards are not needed in this instance. **1968** Kirk & Hanle *Surfer's Hndbk.* 139: *Elephant gun:* heavy board for big waves.

elephant hunter *n.* (see quot.). Hence **elephant hunting.**
1884 Costello *Police Protectors* 319: *Elephant hunters,* as "slummers" are termed by the Central Office Detectives—who act as cicerones now-a-days—are treated to a sight of an opium den. **1928** Asbury *Gangs* 188: A writer for the *Cincinnati Enquirer*…went slumming, or as it was then called, elephant hunting, among the dives of New York in the early eighties.

elephant pill *n.* (see quot.).
1980 Cragg *L. Militaris* 334: The anti-malarial chloroquine-primiquine tablet.…Also known as the *elephant pill* (because of its size).

elephant rubber *n. Army.* a large plastic bladder used for water or fuel in air resupply operations.
1970 Calley & Sack *Lt. Calley* 123 [ref. to 1968]: The man needed water, and it was hours before the choppers would come and "elephant rubbers" or five-gallon cylinders would be crashing through: and busting apart.

elephant trunk *adj.* [rhyming slang] drunk. Also **elephant's trunk.** *Rare* in U.S.
***1859** Hotten *Slang Dict.*: *Elephant's trunk*…drunk. ***1909** Ware *Passing Eng.* 123: Get out—You're drunk.…Elephant's Trunk. **1928** Sharpe *Chicago May* 288 [ref. to 1890's]: *Elephant trunk*—drunk. ***1979** in J. Green *Dict. Contemp. Slang.* Elephant's trunk.

elevate *v.* **1.** *Poker.* to raise (an opponent).
1883 *Life* (Feb. 8) 80: The Drum-mer said that as he had Got his other Tray, he would just El-e-vate him about Fif-ty.
2. *Und.* **a.** to rob at gunpoint; hold up. Cf. ELEVATOR.
1925–26 Black *You Can't Win* 181: Sanc was a hard loser and followed "Soapy" around town for a week trying to "elevate" him.…[Finally] Sanc gave up the notion of sticking him up. **1928** Callahan *Man's Grim Justice* 72: If they met the coon they were to "elevate" him (hold him up).
b. to put up one's hands.
1928 in *DAS*: The clerk…stubbornly refused to elevate at Slim's command. **1932** in *AS* (Feb. 1934) 26: *Elevate.* Stick up your hands.

elevated *adj.* exhilarated by liquor; tipsy. *Joc.*
***1748** T. Smollett *Rod. Random* ch. xvii: The liquor mounted up to our heads.…I, in particular, was much elevated. ***1748** in *F & H* II 357: *Elevated*…sometime spoke of a person that has drank a little too freely. ***1827** in *OEDS*: A *leetle* elevated in liquor. ***1837** C. Dickens *Pickwick* ch. 1: Except when he's elevated, Bob's the quietest creature breathing. **1853** Doten *Journals* I 145: Two of them…were somewhat "elevated." **1861** Guerin *Mountain Charley* 24: Result, he or she gets a little elevated. **1930** Irwin *Tramp & Und. Sl.*: *Elevated.*—Under the influence of liquor or drugs.

elevator *n. Und.* a hold-up man; thief.
1914 Jackson & Hellyer *Vocab.* 31: *Elevator*…A lifter; a booster; a hoister; a "stick-up man." **1926** in *AS* LVII (1982) 261: *Elevator.* Hold-up man.
¶ In phrase:
¶ **(one's) elevator doesn't go all the way to the top** (one) is eccentric, simple-minded, or foolish.
1984 Univ. Tenn. student: The way I see it, his elevator don't go all the way to the top. **1989** *21 Jump St.* (Fox-TV): His elevator doesn't go all the way to the top, if you know what I mean. **1993** *Sally Jessy Raphaël* (synd. TV series): I think your elevator doesn't go to the top.

elevator jockey *n.* an elevator operator.
1960, 1974 (quots. at JOCKEY, *n.*).

eleven bang-bang *n. Army.* ELEVEN BUSH.
1980 Cragg *Lex. Militaris* 150: *Eleven Bang-Bang.* An infantryman in MOS 11B.

eleven bravo *n. Army.* ELEVEN BUSH.
1970 Vietnam veteran, age 22: An eleven bravo is an infantryman. **1984** J. Fuller *Fragments* 171: You have any listings for Eleven Bravos? **1986** Merkin *Zombie Jamboree* 120: Becker says you're eleven-bravo. **1987** (quot. at ELEVEN BUSH).

eleven bush *n. Army.* infantry specialization; (*hence*) an infantryman.
1970 *N.Y. Times Mag.* (Feb. 8) 92: That's all they seem to do any more with college guys is make them 11 bushes. **1984** J. Fuller *Fragments* 40 [ref. to Vietnam War]: He moved from man to man…bucking up the other Eleven Bushes. **1987** Lanning *Only War* 86 [ref. to Vietnam War]: The Infantry MOS was 11B, officially pronounced "11 Bravo." Soldiers referred to it as 11 Bush because that is where the grunt was found.

el foldo *n.* Esp. *Sports.* a collapse, failure; (*Boxing.*) a feigned knockout.
1943 *AS* XVIII 154: *El foldo.* Failure to make the grade. **1947** Schulberg *Harder They Fall* 10: Picking up a quiet C by arranging for one of his dive-artists to do an el foldo. **1977** *L.A. Times* (Dec. 31) III 3: The Rams have performed their annual el foldo. *a*1986 in *NDAS*: The Saints chose that time to pull an el foldo.

Eli *n.* [after Elihu Yale (1648–1721), early benefactor of Yale College] **1.** *Stu.* a Yale student.
1879 *DA*: They…were exceeding glad to get away for the fun,—as we Elis all are. **1893** W.K. Post *Harvard* 25: How those Elis do fight. **1949** *Time* (Mar. 14) 51: He was the first non-Eli since 1766 to be elected president of Yale. **1966** Farrar *N.Y. Times Crosswords* XIV 38: *Elis*…Yalemen. *Ibid.* 40: Student on High Street…*Eli.*
2. Yale University; (*hence*) a sports team, esp. the football team, of Yale University.
1890 in F. Remington *Sel. Letters* 96: Whats the matter of that Eli. [**1899** in *DA*: Trod by the sons of Eli from time immemorial.] **1980** Birnbach *Preppy Hndbk.* 219: *Eli* n. Yale University. **1993** *Cornell Daily Sun* (Nov. 5) 32: Eli quarterback Chris Mills…has been there all along. *Ibid.*: The Eli attack presents no unusual problems for the Red.
¶ In phrase:
¶ **get there, Eli!** (used as a cry of encouragement).
1887 Hinman *Si Klegg* 581 [ref. to Civil War]: Among scores of expressions used by the soldiers…were "Grab a root;"…"Git thar, Eli." **1887** Peck *Pvt. Peck* 52 [ref. to Civil War]: He said the horse I rode, from its friskiness, and natural desire to "get there, Eli!" would eventually get me killed. **1889** E. Field *Western Verse* 155: An', though I ain't no Frenchie, nor kin unto the same,/I kin parley voo, an' git there, too, like Eli, toot le mame. **1897** A.H. Lewis *Wolfville* 141: Great big taters in sandy land,/Git thar, Eli, if you can.

ellick *n.* [perh. dial. var. of *Alec,* male given name] the penis.
*ca*1900 in Logsdon *Whorehouse Bells* 76: My "ellick" grew hard; it did, I declare. *a*1920 in Logsdon *Whorehouse Bells* 185: I introduced her to my ellick, and I shoved it up her ass.

Elmer *n.* [considered to be a typical rustic name; cf. ALVIN, HICK, RUBE] an unsophisticated, esp. rustic, man or boy.
1926 Finerty *Criminalese* 19: *Elmer*—a sucker for confidence men. **1954–60** *DAS*: *Elmer*…An inexperienced, stupid boy. **1963** D. Tracy *Brass Ring* 92 [ref. to 1930's]: A Dorset man…who did not pet with his date was an elmer.

el ——o [< Sp *el* 'the' + *-o* nominal suffix] (used to create *joc.* nominal constructions in imitation of Spanish). See also EL CHEAPO, EL DINGO, EL FOLDO, EL-PRIMO.
1940 in W.C. Fields *By Himself* 173: After doing an el floppo as a writer, you are back in dear old Kansas City telling what is wrong with pictures. **1943** in Kaplan & Smith *One Last Look* 12: El Rauncho [nickname of B-17 of 384th Bomb Group, USAAF]. **1961** Forbes *Goodbye to Some* 158: El cheato grande! *Ibid.* 180: Somebody pass El Juggo up here, please. **1974** *Odd Couple* (ABC-TV): Boy, are you crude! El crudo! La creme de la crude! **1983** S. King *Christine* 49: I flipped Ralph the old El Birdo. **1984** Hindle *Dragon Fall* 80: She was nothing, El Zilcho.

el-primo *adj.* prime; first-rate.
1983 Goldman & Fuller *Charlie Co.* 65: Stashes of el-primo no-seed, no-stem marijuana.

El Ropo *n.* [pseudo-Sp, 'the rope'] a cheap cigar. *Joc.*
[**1911** in Mager *Sherlocko* 24: He was smoking a "Ropo."—They are 6 for 5.] *ca*1960 in *DARE*: Rope…Nickname for a strong cigar. Sometimes *El Ropo.* **1962** T. Berger *Reinhart* 44: Reinhart [was] choking on

the El Ropo. **1965–70** in *DARE*. **1986** *NDAS*.

el-tee *n.* [pron. spelling of *Lt*, official abbr.] *Army & USMC.* a lieutenant.
  1978 Truscott *Dress Gray* 17: He told the sergeant to tell the eltee he was finished. **1987** Pelfrey & Carabatsos *Hamburger Hill* 84 [ref. to Vietnam War]: You're doing fine, El-tee. **1990** Ruggero *38 N. Yankee* 148: We got it under control, el-tee.

embalmed *adj.* extremely drunk.
  1934 Weseen *Dict. Slang* 275: *Embalmed*—Highly intoxicated. **1965** LeMay & Kantor *Mission* 120: I don't mean just in a slightly singing or slightly bellicose mood...What I'm talking about is ossified, pickled, embalmed.

embalmed beef *n. Mil.* canned beef. Also vars.
  1898 Bowe *13th Minn.* (July 24) 25: What some people call embalmed beef and others call canned beef is very unlike the article that is sold in America. **1899** Johnson *Negro Soldiers* 110: The beef was fresh and sweet, for it had not been "embalmed." **1906** M'Govern *Bolo & Krag* 111: I sat down to some of Bill's "embalmed horse," coffee and Highland cream. **1918** O'Reilly *Roving & Fighting* 12 [ref. to 1898]: "Embalmed beef"...was a slimy, ill-smelling mess, disgusting in appearance and fatal in effect. **1919** T. Kelly *What Outfit?* 13: Just a little of that embalmed mule will kill any good man. **1935** *Our Army* (Apr.) 10: No diet of "embalmed beef" is thrust on you. **1955** Post *Little War* 213 [ref. to 1898]: Shafter gave Mary Hanna and President McKinley a brilliant military victory despite the Secretary of War's embalmed beef and shoddy shoes and ponchos. **1961** L.G. Richards *TAC* 51: This is the usual embalmed beef sandwich.

embalming fluid *n.* vile whiskey.
  1894 Gardner *Doctor & Devil* 22: The embalming fluid he sells as whiskey. **1922** S. Lewis *Babbitt* 170: They were finishing a bottle of corrosive boot-legged whiskey and imploring the bell-boy, "Say, son, can you get us some more of this embalming fluid?" **1949** Taradash & Monks *Knock on Any Door* (film): Get yourself some chow instead of that embalming fluid you drink. **1981** C. Nelson *Picked Bullets Up* 222: We ended up drinking embalming fluid at a little redneck joint.

emigrate *v.* to leave; be off.
  1837 Neal *Charcoal Sketches* 97: You'd better emigrate—the old man's coming.

empty *adj.* having no money; broke.
  1975 Durocher & Linn *Nice Guys* 315 [ref. to 1950's]: "Man...I'm empty." He'd pull out his pockets. "I'm empty."

empty suit *n.* a useless, inconsequential, or insincere person.
  1980 Gould *Ft. Apache* 82: He's an empty suit, don't even think about him. **1984** C. Francis *Who's Sorry?* 16: If...I discover that someone I trusted turns out to be an empty suit (a fake person) or worse, a phony or a cheat.... *Ibid.* 188: He was a fake guy, Pidge—a real empty suit! **1987** Taubman *Lady Cop* 92: So you got stuck with another empty suit?...When're you going to work with a real cop again, Randall? *Ibid.* 268: *Empty suit:* Derogatory term for a cop who doesn't work, often used by men who dislike the idea of women on patrol to describe any woman officer. **1990** *TV Guide* (Oct. 6) 39: What were those empty suits at NBC thinking of when they allowed Pauley...to...quit the *Today* show? **1993** *CNN & Co.* (CNN-TV) (May 12): [Pres. Clinton] is an empty suit, a man with no backbone.

enchilada *n.* the penis.
  1978 T. Sanchez *Zoot-Suit* 71: Look at that big black enchilada on that [donkey].
  ¶ In phrases:
  ¶ **big enchilada** see BIG ENCHILADA.
  ¶ **the whole enchilada** everything; all there is.
  1966 B. Garfield *Last Bridge* 6: The Air Force is murdering them. Napalm, the whole enchilada. **1972** R. Barrett *Lovomaniacs* 194: About the whole enchilada. Everything. His family. The world. **1972** DeLillo *End Zone* 151: We release to newspapers, to sports pubs, to local radio and TV, to the networks. The whole enchilada. **1973** I. Reed *La. Red* 103: He...wanted to wipe out "the whole enchilada," as high-class lawyers from Orange County say. **1974** *N.Y. Post* (June 3) 31: A place where literally anything goes: prostitution, sex movies, sex shops, pornography shops, the whole enchilada, as our leaders used to say. **1975** V. Miller *Trade-Off* 99: I wanna know who put up his bail. When, where—the whole enchilada. **1977** A. Patrick *Beyond Law* 131: What do ya say, creep? Give us the whole enchilada. **1987** *Sports Update* (CNN-TV) (Sept. 12): My personal choice as to who will win the whole enchilada is the Cincinnati Bengals.

end *n.* **1.a.** a share (of profits or responsibility).
  1887 Walling *N.Y. Chief of Police* 460: Mr. Pettingill had "done his end of the job." **1898–1900** Cullen *Chances* 22: She's got a show for the big end of it. **1903** Ade *Society* 2: The Large End of all the Scads mentioned in the last Will and Testament went to a son named William H. Jimpson. **1903** A.H. Lewis *Boss* 201: There's two hundred thousand dollars' worth of Uncle Sam's bonds....That's your end of Mulberry Traction. **1913–15** Van Loan *Taking the Count* 65: The loser's end ought to be eight thousand, at least. **1915** T.A. Dorgan, in *N.Y. Eve. Jour.* (Aug. 2) 11: Well, Lew usually slips the main eventer fifty bucks for his end. **1920–21** Witwer *Leather Pushers* 5: You oughta grab about three hundred men for your end. **1931** Z. Grey *Sunset Pass* 35: They own the Bar X outfit....Dabb has the big end of it. **1940** Dempsey & Stearns *Round by Round* 106: That's all your end came to. **1942** Maltz & Burnett *This Gun for Hire* (film): Here's your end. **1950** in Cannon *Nobody Asked* 127: All he took for his end was a dollar. **1961** Considine *Ripley* 33: I gave the whole hundred and fifty to Baer. He said he'd handle your end for you.

  b. *pl.* money.
  1960 C.L. Cooper *Scene* 62: His woman is making *some* ends for him. **1964** in B. Jackson *Swim Like Me* 106: My ends was pretty low. **1968** in Andrews & Dickens *Big House* 15: I'll get you a piece, on a short-term lease/And you don't have to put up no ends. **1970** Horman & Fox *Drug Awareness* 466: *Ends*—money. **1971** Goines *Dopefiend* 143: If Porky can support that oilburner Smokey got, we should have no problem taking care of ours, plus making a few ends.

  2. *Esp. Jazz.* the extreme, the ultimate; that which is extraordinary, usu. in a favorable sense.—constr. with *the [living]*.
  *****1938** in *OEDS*: The sort of people who go there are just simply The End...the most unspeakable curiosities. **1948** Manone & Vandervoort *Trumpet* 68: When I played that for Jack he thought it was the end. He decided nobody else could ever top that. **1950** *Neurotica* (Autumn) 45: This shit is the end! **1952** J.C. Holmes *Go* 173: Everything...last year was "crazy," "frantic," "gone."...What can one designate the moment that comes after "the end," after all? **1953** in Russ *Last Parallel* 290: The ride down here was the end. Spring is here for real. **1956** E. Hunter *Second Ending* 155: I really could blow in those days....I could blow the end, the very end. **1959** Farris *Harrison High* 361: Brother, that was really the end. **1959–60** R. Reisner *Jazz Titans* 154: *End, The:* the best, the utmost. **1960** MacCuish *Do Not Go Gentle* 328 [ref. to WWII]: "*That's* the livin' end," Hudge said. **1960** *Donna Reed Show* (ABC-TV): I think he's the bitter, burning *end!* **1965** Karp *Doobie Doo* 146: Jeezus, that's the living *end*. *****1966** G.M. Williams *Camp* 7: To have it away with her would be the ultimate *end*. **1968** Kirkwood *Good Times* 100: Christ, she was the end! I mean, she was— (Whistles).

  3. (see quot.).
  1961 *N.Y. Times Mag.* (June 25) 39: When a hipster buys clothes, he begins with "ends" or shoes.

  ¶ In phrases:
  ¶ **get (one's) end in** [or **wet**] to effect intromission of the penis; (of a man) to engage in copulation.—usu. considered vulgar.
  *ca***1935** in Holt *Dirty Comics* 86: Snuffy...comes upon a love-sick swain...who is doing his best to get his end in. **1938** H. Miller *Trop. Capricorn* 86: How was it yesterday? Did you get your end in? **1957** M. Shulman *Rally* 191: You wanna get your end wet, call me. I got...any kind of broads you want. **1971** Horan *Blue Messiah* 45: You gonna get your end wet tonight, Sully? **1980** Manchester *Darkness* 186: Now I guess you want to get your end wet.

  ¶ **go off the deep end, 1.** to become unduly excited; become hysterical.
  *****1921** *N & Q* (Dec. 24) 503 [ref. to WWI]: *Deep end (to go off the).* To get excited or angry. *****1923** in *OEDS* I 756: He goes off the deep end a trifle too explosively. **1936** Steel *College* 337: I hope you'll forgive me, Hank, for going off the deep end. **1982** P. Michaels *Grail* 146: The girl had gone off the deep end when she heard the victim was female.

  2. to be carried away by one's enthusiasms or unrealistic beliefs; (*specif.*) to lose one's sense or sanity.
  *****1921** in *OEDS* I 756: Saint-Saëns rarely, if ever, takes any risks; he never, to use the slang of the moment, "went in off the deep end." **1942** *ATS* 180: Go insane; crazy...*go off the deep end*. **1947** Overholser *Buckaroo's Code* 35: Now for some reason you go off the deep end, and you've got yourself into a fix. **1954** Chessman *Cell 2455* 100: He's about to go off the deep end again. **1966** N.Y.C. high school student: Sounds like he's going off the deep end. **1967** Head *Mr. & Mrs.* 11: Just because we fell off the deep end once...it doesn't mean it will happen

again. **1968** Hawley *Hurricane Yrs.* 66: All the men who've suddenly gone off the deep end. **1987** *N.Y. Times* (July 7) A 26: How can anyone as bright and realistic as William Safire go so far off the deep end?

¶ **the dirty** [or **short**] **end** [**of the stick**] unfair treatment, esp. a disadvantageous position. Also vars. [The frankly scatological variants are usu. considered vulgar.]

*1846 *Swell's Night Guide* 49, in *OEDS*: Which of us had hold of the crappy...end of the stick? **1890* in *OED*: The apparently impassive countryman has "got the wrong end of the stick." **1907** *Reader* (Sept.) 346: I knew I was getting the dirty end, but I couldn't holler. **1918** *Sat. Eve. Post* (Jan. 19) 62: It's funny how soldiers always figure they're getting the short end of the stick. **1918** *Lit. Digest* (Aug. 31) 42: The gang just got tired of having the short end slipt to them. **1924** in Hemingway *Sel. Letters* 130: Yen as usual [is] being presented with the soiled end of the stick with no additional compensation. **1924* in *OEDS* I 812: Somehow or other they've handed us the dirty end. **1926** Nason *Chevrons* 112 [ref. to 1918]: You go out of your way to do a favor for someone and all yuh get out of it is a stick with the dirty end towards yuh. **1930** Dos Passos *42d Parallel* 58: I guess I always get the dirty end of the stick, all right. **1934** O'Hara *Samarra* ch. 6: Al almost but not quite reached the opinion that all women are so used to getting the dirty end of the stick that they took it for granted when they did get it, and took it for granted they were going to get it when they didn't. **1935** Spewack *Boy Meets Girl* 385: Susie, nature meant you for a sucker. You were designed to get the short end of the stick. **1935** J. Conroy *World to Win* 66: I'm of the kind that always gets the dirty end of the stick. **1951** in Elliott *Among the Dangs* 172: I've always got the short end of the stick and I'm sick and tired of it. **1960** *Twilight Zone* (CBS-TV): You got the crummy end of the stick. **1961** J.A. Williams *Night Song* 78: It's the only way you can go on; you count on someone else getting the messy end of the stick. **1967** Breen *Tony Rome* (film): I'd never leave you holding the greasy end of the stick, would I? **1967** M. Howard *Call Me Brick* 113: Wound up with the shitty end of the stick in their own hands. **1974** Gober *Black Cop* 21: Black people had been getting the shit out of the stick too damn long. **1974** Millard *Thunderbolt* 50: That's the team that handed Brinks and the cops the brown end of the stick. **1985** Univ. Tenn. instructor: So you wind up with the shitty end of the stick.

¶ **swap** [or **change**] **ends** *West.* (of a bucking horse) to turn around violently and esp. repeatedly.

1882 Baillie-Grohman *Rockies* 99: The mare "swapped ends," i.e. turned a clean somersault. **1885** Roosevelt *Ranchman* 6: The horse puts his head down between his forefeet, arches his back, and with stiff legs gives a succession of jarring jumps, often "changing ends" as he does so.

end *adj.* *Jazz.* wonderful; (*also*) absolute or total.—used prenominally.

*ca*1953 Hughes *Lodge* 176: She was an end junkie and hard as tacks. **1963** in R.S. Gold *Jazz Talk* 83: I was blowing some jazz in the student lounge on this end Steinway.

endo *n.* *Motor Racing.* a crash in which one vehicle is thrown end over end.

1976 *Webster's Sports Dict.* 133. **1979** Frommer *Sports Lingo* 165: *Endo.* The accidental going end-over-end of a bike and rider.

endo *v.* *Motor Racing.* to be hurled end over end in a collision.

1979 Frommer *Sports Lingo* 165.

endsville *adj. & n.* **1.** END, *n.*, 2 & *adj.*

1957 M. Shulman *Rally* 217: This is the endsville! **1957** *N.Y. Times Mag.* (Aug. 18) 26: Scrambled eggs from endsville. **1959–60** Reisner *Jazz Titans* 154: *Endsville:* The greatest. **1962** Reiter *Night in Sodom* 119: Crazy...Endsville. **1962** F. Harvey *Strike Command* 101: Most GI's said it was Endsville with flies.

2. the end; a depressing or finishing situation; (*specif.*) death.

1961 *Time* (Apr. 21) 45: The East River Park—to chauvinistic Villagers the equivalent of a one-way ticket to Endsville. **1961** Kohner *Gidget Goes Hawaiian* 18: It's grim enough if you yourself feel like Endsville. **1962** *Time* (Oct. 19) 34: Endsville....There was no football team...and, worse yet, no girls. **1972** R. Barrett *Lovomaniacs* 140: As soon as that...judge made it legal—endsville! **1981** Sann *Trial* 11: Destination: Endsville [i.e. death].

enforcer *n.* *Und. & Police.* a strong-arm man or professional killer; TORPEDO.

1929–31 in Partridge *Dict. Und.* 222: *Enforcer.* Hard-boiled member of a mob, who works on the outside to keep saloon keepers and other tribute payers in line. **1950** Rackin *The Enforcer* (film title). **1957** H. Danforth & J. Horan *D.A.'s Man* 29 [ref. to 1935]: Luciano bossed with gun and club a small army of "enforcers" who milked millions of dollars into

their own greasy pockets. **1960** Roeburt *Mobster* 28: A man famous locally as Dudu the Enforcer. **1969** Salerno & Tompkins *Crime Confed.* 102: The enforcer maintains internal security and discipline. **1979** F. Thomas *Golden Bird* 86: The large one was, as you might say, the enforcer. **1988** *TV Guide* (Mar. 19) A-121: Violent melodrama about a Chicago enforcer...sent to eliminate a swinish Missouri mobster. **1993** *Early Prime* (CNN-TV) (Mar. 24): The [hockey] team's tough guy—the enforcer.

engine room *n.* *Rowing.* the midsection of an eight-oared racing shell, typically occupied by the strongest oarsmen.

1949 Cummings *Dict. Sports* 125. **1982** Kiesling *Shell Game* 33: The three of us battled for seats in the middle of the boat, the engine room....The boat was arranged with the largest men in the middle.

English *adj.* *Prost.* sadomasochistic. Also quasi-n.

1969 Bartell *Group Sex* 82: "English culture" usually refers to discipline or sado-masochism. **1976–77** Kernochan *Dry Hustle* 130: English is pure gravy....Then when they get hard, you just "command" them to jerk themselves off.

enlisted dog *n.* *Mil.* an enlisted person.

1982 T.C. Mason *Battleship* 182 [ref. to 1941]: Around his neck the striker had hung a crudely lettered sign that summed up all of his despair: "I'm just an enlisted dog."

enlisted swine *n.* *Mil.* an enlisted person or persons. [Quots. ref. to Vietnam War.]

1986 Merkin *Zombie Jamboree* 206: An...officerly chat with the enlisted swine. **1987** Zeybel *Gunship* 94: Back in the States we're just more enlisted swine. **1989** P.H.C. Mason *Recovering* 92: None of those enlisted swine would throw a grenade in this room.

enormous *adj.* splendid; IMMENSE.

1887 *Lantern* (N.O.) (Jan. 29) 3: Ed Connelly as B. Wiley Dodge is simply enormous.

entered *adj.* intoxicated.

1722 B. Franklin, in *AS* XV (Feb. 1940) 103: [Drunkards] are Almost froze, Feavourish, In their Altitudes, Pretty well entered, &c.

ep *n.* *Film.* a filmed episode.

1915 *Variety* (Oct. 29): In this "ep" their delivery is shown accompanied by a semi-sensational escape.

epar *interj.* *Stu.* (see quots.). *Joc.*

1958 J. Davis *College Vocab.* 11: *Epar*—Rape spelled backwards; a popular cry at parties when gentlemen get too fresh. **1968–70** *Current Slang* III & IV 43: *Epar, n.* (Rape spelled backwards—used as a cry of distress when one doesn't really want help.)—University of Kentucky.

epaulet *n.* *Navy.* a commissioned officer.

*1829 Marryat *Mildmay* ch. xvi: My captain elect...herded not with his brother epaulettes. **1849** Melville *White Jacket* 21: He...will stay there till grim death or an epaulet orders him away.

ephus /'ifəs/ *n.* [orig. unkn.] truth; (*also*) a trick or gimmick.—constr. with *the.*

1935 Pollock *Und. Speaks: Ephus,* dependable information; the low down. **1958** Cooley *Run for Home* 15: There's something about those Russians. They got the ephus on everybody. I don't know what it is. They cut and bleed and die just like anyone else, but they've got everybody believing they're tough as shark hide. **1959** Lederer *Never Steal Anything Small* (film): The gimmick, the gizmo, the gadget, the ephus. If I could just think of the ephus.

ephus ball *n.* *Baseball.* an especially deceptive slow pitch. Also **ephus pitch.**

1943 *Yank* (Sept. 10) 23: Rip Sewell's ephus ball...soars 25 feet in the air and then dips suddenly, crossing the plate between the batter's knees and shoulders for a strike....It was catcher Al Lopez who named the pitch the ephus. Lopez had once heard the word ephus and didn't know what it meant, and he figured quite logically that "the hitters can't figure out what to do with it any more than I can figure out the meaning of ephus." **1946** *N.Y. Times* (July 10) 26: Sewell's "Ephus" Ball Belted for Homer for First Time....Sewell was surprised to have his "ephus" throw belted out of the park. "I've been using it since 1941 and the longest previous hit was a triple by Stan Musial," Sewell declared. **1973** Karst & Jones *Pro. Baseball* 820: [Sewell was] Noted for throwing a high, arching, change of pace, or eephus, pitch which baffled batters. **1973** Boyd & Harris *Baseball Card* 108: Stick that in your old ephus ball Stu. **1981** N.Y.C. man: Did you see the guy with the ephus pitch last night? Dave LaRoche. **1982** T. Considine *Lang. Sport* 10: Originated...by...Rip Sewell (the "ephus pitch"), the blooper was revived in the mid to late 1960s by New York Yankees relief pitcher Steve Hamilton ([as] the "Folly Floater"), and in the 1980s by Yankees reliever Dave LaRoche (the "La Lob"). **1982** *All Things Considered* (Nat. Public Radio) (June 9): Satchel Page came up with all sorts of pitches—the ephus ball, the trouble ball, the V ball.

equalizer *n.* a deadly weapon, esp. a pistol. Cf. DIFFERENCE.
1899 Gunter *M.S. Bradford* 281: I haf der Equalizer in my hand....Fifty t'ousand dollars, or I throws dis Equalizer at your foots, and blow you to nottingness! **1929** in D. Runyon *Guys & Dolls* 73: He has the old equalizer in his duke. **1940** Thompson & Raymond *Gang Rule in N.Y.* 32: He preferred an "equalizer," or pistol, a weapon that would make all men his own size. **1943** Crowley & Sachs *Follow the Leader* (film): Oh, that's the old equalizer [a blackjack]. **1946** Gresham *Nightmare Alley* 9: Some day I'll blast 'em. I don't keep that equalizer in my trunk to play Boy Scout with. **1955** Q. Reynolds *HQ* 35: Use the wits God gave you and you won't have to be going for your equalizer. **1968** Heard *Howard St.* 86: I got my equalizer. **1973** Mathers *Riding the Rails* 50: Blackey quickly pulled his "equalizer" (knife) from his boot and stabbed the guy in the heart. **1986** Sliwa *Attitude* 25: Many of them...pack at least one .45-caliber "equalizer. **1994** N. McCall *Wanna Holler* 68: I had the loaded .25 tucked into my coat. I had the equalizer, and I wasn't scared.

equipment *n.* **1.** the genitals, esp. of a man.
1877 in J.M. Carroll *Camp Talk* 111: The "black spot" fold in the crease of her drawers is...suggestive....I might...[pencil] in equipment complete, but refrain. **1942** *ATS* 147. **1973–74** M. Smith *Death of Detective* 86: Your equipment...you know, your organs. **1979** J. Morris *War Story* 16: [In the dream] I had been shot in the groin, and lost all my equipment. **1983** Eilert *Self & Country* 21: Doc investigated quickly. "Yep, equipment's still there."
2. a woman's breasts.
1940 Wald & Macauley *They Drive By Night* (film): I was there with these two beautiful dames. What equipment! **1953** Wicker *Kingpin* 74: I've seen 'em prettier, but she's okay. All the standard equipment and a bit to boot. **1965** Pollini *Glover* 197: What equipment! She's got *all* the equipment. **1975** Univ. Tenn. student: Oh yeah, she's got the right equipment. **1983** in "J.B. Briggs" *Drive-In* 131: Some bimbos...jump around on the beach and jiggle their equipment.

-erama var. -ORAMA.

Erie *n.* ¶ In phrase: **on the Erie** [punning on *on (one's) ear* s.v. EAR, *n.*, and the *Erie* Lackawanna Railroad] **1.** indignant, indignantly.
1888 in *F & H* II 350: A man who walked on his ear out of a store said "he came out on the Erie route."
2. Esp. *Und.* eavesdropping; listening; (*hence*) being overheard; (*interj.*) someone is eavesdropping.
1930 Lait *On the Spot* 208: On the Erie...A stool-pigeon. **1930** *Amer. Mercury* (Dec.) 457: On the Erie: Shut up; someone is listening. "The best way is to go on the Erie." **1937** in D. Runyon *More Guys* 123: But Horsey is there on the old Earie, and very much interested in their conversation. **1941** "G.R. Lee" *G-String* 98: "Thought maybe we were on the Erie."..."Who'd want to listen?" **1948** McHenry & Myers *Home Is Sailor* 123: Some people here are what you Americans call "on the earie." **1961** Clausen *Season's Over* 153: Mary Louise was on the Erie....If you suddenly bring up Erie, Pennsylvania, that means someone's listening. **1961** Braly *Felony Tank* 20: That sonofabitch was on the Erie!...I tell you, the sonofabitch was listening. **1974** *Time* (June 17) 59 [prison]: *On the erie:* eavesdropping.

Erie *v. Und.* to overhear.
1940 *AS* (Apr.) 114: Make it your business to drop any lingo that he might erie.

-erine *suffix.* -ERINO.
1899 Creager *14th Ohio* 87: The "soldierines" as they sometimes called themselves, began to realize that the life of a soldier is attended with some labor. **1900** *DN* II 48: *Peacherine*, n. Synonym for peach. **1902** Hobart *Back to the Woods* 42: Oh, you mark! You Cincherine! **1902–03** Ade *People You Know* 140: Some 80 Buckerines. **1906** H. Green *Actors' Boarding House* 51: They put a dressin' room...on the fritzerine last week. *Ibid.* 256: If it's too much on the cheeserine, we can vamp out easy.

-erino *suffix.* (used to create joc. forms of various nouns and adjectives). Also **-erina.** See also PEACHERINO.
1896 Ade *Artie* 39: Hello, girlerino! How's everything stackin'? **1898–1900** Cullen *Chances* 226: Would point the swellerino buck out to young strangers. **1902** Cullen *More Tales* 43: The cabman took us over

to a swaggerino road house on the South Side. **1902–03** Ade *People You Know* 158: There [he] met a Corkerina who had come to visit a School Friend. **1906** *Nat. Police Gaz.* (July 21) 6: Deemed a punkerina not worth considering. **1911** *N.Y. Eve. Jour.* (Feb. 11) 12: So Ma thinks Bennie's going back on the 10 o'clock train to college, hey? Nixerino! **1924** Tully *Beggars of Life* 14: Forget all that stuff. It's bunkerino. **1934** in Ruhm *Detective* 118: There's your man, skipperino. **1943** Wendt & Kogan *Bosses* 247 [ref. to 1904]: A bedtime story. The bunkerino.

-eroo *suffix.* [prob. by reanalysis of BUCKAROO or *kangaroo* on pattern of -ERINO; pop. by newspaper columnist Walter Winchell] -ERINO. Also **-aroo.**
[**1919** N. Helvey & D. Peyton *Jazzero Rag* (musical composition) (South Jacksonville, Fla.: Neal Helvey, 1919).] **1931** *AS* VII 45: Walter Winchell loves to...[see] *terpsichorines*...in *revusicals* which might even turn out *floperoos*. **1933** D. Runyon, in *Collier's* (Dec. 23) 8: The baby is a darberoo. **1936** R. Riskin *Mr. Deeds Goes to Town* (film): I've gotten the sackeroo in many ways, but never in rhyme. **1938** in J. O'Hara *Sel. Letters* 140: At least our mob knows that the fixeroo is in. **1939** M. Berle, in *AS* XVII (1942) 13: We must go on to the next jokeroo. **1940** J. O'Hara *Pal Joey* 194: Methinks the bageroo is got her finger wedged in my doorbell. **1940** J.H. Lay et al. *Slightly Honorable* (film): It looks to me like the old frameroo. **1942** Swerling & Mankiewicz *Pride of the Yankee* (film): It's a pipperoo! **1943** Halliday *Murder Wears Mummer's Mask* 48: Lots of floss outside and the same old jipperoo when you lay your money on the line. **1955** O'Connor *Last Hurrah* 189: What he'd do, he used to walk around the lobby with his tie pulled up tight around his neck, giving himself the old chokeroo. **1955** L. Shapiro *Sixth of June* 153: Between us, boy, it's a fakeroo. **1957** Myrer *Big War* 6: Give us the old pooperoo. **1960** in Rosset *Evergreen Reader* 327: Look at that chest, look at that asseroo. **1961** Hemingway *Islands* 45: So then, after he's back on the job, I get the real frameroo. **1962** Serling *New Stories* 22: They're the old busteroos! **1970** E. Thompson *Garden of Sand* 269: A charming conneroo of your own was preferable. **1972** *Maude* (CBS-TV): Arthur, you mean the old fixeroo! **1973** Turbeville *Buster & Billie* (film): I do believe I detect a couple of gorgeous babe-eroos. **1978** Pilcer *Teen Angel* 111: Her mother posed for another old smoocheroo. **1980** Gould *Ft. Apache* 235: The old tosseroo. **1982** in *Nat. Lampoon* (Feb. 1983) 16: Let's...have a few drinkaroos. **1988** *Wkly. World News* (May 3) 12: In a new royal shockeroo, sources...report that stuffy Queen Elizabeth is paying her spoiled daughter-in-law Princess Di $500,000 to...[stay with] Prince Charles. **1992** *New York* (June 8) 41: Sex in public?..."I'm sure that's a big shockeroo."

-eroonie *suffix.* -ERINO. Also **-aroonie, -oroonie.**
[**1902** Townsend *Fadden & Mr. Paul* 70: Mr. Paul and Whiskers was having a hot-air conversatserony on police blackmail.] **1966** K. Hunter *Landlord* 158: One hundred and twenty-five smackeroonies a week. **1968** Bullins *In Wine Time* 383: It's eighty-two degrees...maaan, that's hot-oh-rooney! **1970** Southern *Blue Movie* 56: Ten percent of the box-oroonie. **1972** *Nat. Lampoon* (Feb.) 15: There's...a lot of lunks who need a size eight hushpuppy in the old crotcheroonie. **1972** R. Barrett *Lovomaniacs* 10: Six million smackeroonies. **1986** Stroud *Close Pursuit* 315: Nunzio is not all that healthy in the old beaneroonie.

Ese /ˈɛseɪ/ *n.* (see 1985 quot.).
*ca*1960 in Schwendinger & Schwendinger *Adolescent Sub.* 75: An Ese is not a guy looking for trouble or trying to pick a fight. An Ese is a cool guy. **1985** Schwendinger & Schwendinger *Adolescent Sub.* 61: Ese—derived from *Ese Vato*—is the classic name for Mexican-American streetcorner youth in southern California. **1990** Bing *Do or Die* 19: Had an Essay* fix it up for me....*anyone of Hispanic origin, usually a gang member.

Esky *n.* [fr. *Eskimo*] *Alaska.* an Inuit.—used derisively.
1907 *N & Q* (Jan. 12) 36: They are Eskimo dogs, Eskimos, shortened to Eskies, and corrupted to Huskies. [**1942** *ATS* 932: *Esquimama* [joc. for "Eskimo woman"].] **1974** *Coq.* (Apr.) 43: Polock, Frog, Spic, Wop,...Towel-head, Esky. **1983** in Random House files: *Esky* for Eskimo.

essence *n.* whiskey.—constr. with *the. Joc.*
1865 in Woodruff *Union Soldier* 45: More or less of the "Esence" passes his black throat evry day. He is never empty & never draws a sober breath.

essence of hickory *n.* a whipping with a hickory switch.
1917 Kuykendall *Frontier Days* 2 [ref. to 1840's]: A little "essence of hickory" would work wonders.

essence-peddler *n.* a skunk. *Joc.*
1849 Lowell, in *DARE*: A skunk was shot in our back-kitchen this

morning. There were two of these "essence-peddlers," as the Yankees call them. **1862** in Lowell *Poetical Works* 247: Essence peddlers…A rustic euphemism for the American variety of the *Mephitis.* **1882** Baillie-Grohman *Rockies* 108: The Plainsman is generally brimful of tales of the "Essence pedlar." **1890** E. Custer *Guidon* 200 [ref. to 1868]: The passage was disputed by a small but well-armed foe….As soon as that essence-peddler saw fit to move on, the major-general commanding would issue his order to march. **1899, 1923, 1946, 1969, 1975** in *DARE.*

ether tickler *n.* a radio telephone.
  1958 Whitcomb *Corregidor* 44 [ref. to 1941]: You're going to keep your ether tickler up here and keep in contact with us Air Corps boys.

Ethiopian paradise *n.* [sugg. by NIGGER HEAVEN] (see quot.).— usu. considered offensive. *Joc.*
  1900 *DN* II 33: *Ethiopian paradise.* Top gallery in a theatre.

ETKM *Hosp.* (see quot.).
  1964 "Dr. X" *Intern* 29: The more tests I took, the more baffled I was at just *what* was wrong with her. At Hopkins they used to call cases like this "ETKM"—Every Test Known to Man.

euchre *n.* a swindle.
  1872 *Galaxy* (Mar. 29): I'd much rather settle squarely with *you* than have you come this ecclesiastical euchre on me.

euchre *v.* to get the better of; cheat; swindle; trick.
  1853 in *AS* (Oct. 1951) 225: Watkins your [*sic*] a trump! and may you never get *euchered!* **1855** in *DA:* Smith…got "one-eye" Brown to play cards with him, slipped upon the blind side of him and euchred him! **1858** [S. Hammett] *Piney Woods* 83: All hands is mighty apt to get ukered in the eend. **1861** in G.W. Harris *High Times* 270: Next time I see you…Il tell you how we eucherd all Bald-timore. **1862** in Patrick *Reluctant Rebel* 42: I said half aloud "If you ain't a euchred General *one time,* I'll be damned." **1864** Hill *Our Boys* 171: "Euchered!" exclaimed General Reynolds. **1864** in Gould *Maine Regt.* 486: We heard of one regiment whose colonel was bound not be "euchred," as he said, and so he selected the 2d, 3d and 4th Articles of War as being the most pious things he could find, and made his adjutant read them [as a Thanksgiving service]. **1889** *Harper's Mo.* (Mar.) 633: I seen how I cud euchre the old cat. **1906** Ford *Shorty McCabe* 81: They euchered him out of his castle and building lots. **1957** Campbell *Cry for Happy* 52: Writing down my name and number to euchre me into givin' you a lift? **1962** *Time* (Dec. 14) 20: We have now been euchred into the position of baby-sitting for Castro. **1965** Borowik *Lions* 50: He euchres professional athletes out of their dignity. **1985** Roskey *Muffled Shots* 36: I wasn't about to be euchred out of an extra $55 a month.

evac *v. & n. Mil.* to evacuate; an evacuation.
  1944 in Kluger *Yank* 174: Ransack it and sack it,/Evac to Iraq it. **1954** K. Beech *Tokyo* 107 [ref. to 1950]: This was, the pilot said, the last "evac" flight into Kimpo. **1977** Caputo *Rumor of War* 266 [ref. to Vietnam War]: We'll have you evacked in no time.

eval *n.* an evaluation.
  1986 Coonts *Intruder* 101 [ref. to Vietnam War]: Now go work on those evals.

evaporate *v.* to leave; get out; take off. *Joc.*
  *1829 in Partridge *DSUE* (ed. 8): I suppose she put him in mind of his wife, that he evaporated with such alacrity. ***1852** Dickens *Bleak House* ch. xxii: Upon which the young man, looking round, instantly evaporates. ***1857** in *F & H* II 359: Mr. Bouncer evaporates with a low bow. **1871** (quot. at MIGRATE). **1930** Sage *Last Rustler* 38: Well, Dutch gettin' killed and Roxie evaporatin' leaves it a fifty-fifty split between me and you.

Eve *n.* ¶ In phrase: **Eve with the lid on** *Restaurant.* an order of apple pie.—used in relaying orders.
  1923 McKnight *Eng. Words* 45: *Eve with the lid on* (apple pie). **1935** in *AS* (Feb. 1936) 43: *Eve with the lid on.* Apple pie.

even *adv.* at all; in fact.—used for negative emphasis. [As in S.E., used after a negative verb to emphasize the following clause; yet in the present examples the emphasized clause conveys no notion of contrast with some other, less extreme possibility or circumstance. A second distinction is that unlike S.E. usage, which stresses a following verb, the present examples stress and prolong the initial syllable of *even* and give ordinary stress to following elements.]
  1982 Univ. Tenn. student: Don't *even* forget to give that book back. I need it to study. **1984** J. Fuller *Fragments* 159: And now they're sending

me back to the Place, and I won't *even* have to see that filthy bitch again. **1986** *New Image Teens* (KPBS-TV): You cannot *even* get pregnant in the back seat of a convertible car. **1989** P. Munro *U.C.L.A. Slang* 62: *Not even* not at all. That is not *even* funny. **1990** P. Munro *Slang U.* 139: My bio professor…is going to give everyone an A.—You're not even serious! I just dropped that class.

even-steven *adj.* even in settling of accounts; (*hence*) equal, as in score. Now *colloq.* [C.F. Hahn ("Origins of Even-Steven," *AS* LVIII, 319-24) posits, on circumstantial but questionable evidence, an origin in ME.]
  [***1710–11** J. Swift *Jour. to Stella* I 171: Now we are even, quoth Stephen, when he gave his wife six blows for one.] **1866** C.H. Smith *Bill Arp* 64: You allowed the members to exchange two hundred dollars for two hundred dollars of State money, even steven. **1906** *DN* III 135: *Even-Stephen*…An even game. "It's even Stephen. I believe they'll tie." **1927** D. Hammett, in *DAS:* Give me the hundred and fifty and we'll call it even-steven. **1949** H. Robbins *Dream Merchants* 454: After that I collect even-steven with you until the cost comes back. **1956** M. Wolff *Big Nick.* 84: That makes us even-steven, and you don't owe me anything, Grandpa. **1968** Swarthout *Loveland* 188: Do something for me and we're even-Steven. **1971** T.C. Bambara *Gorilla* 17: I figured it was even-steven.

evergreen *n.* money.
  1908 McGaffey *Show Girl* 237: These two boobs are dirty with the evergreen.

ever-loving *n.* **1.** (one's) spouse or sweetheart.
  1937 in D. Runyon *More Guys* 109: I hear Willie the Worrier and his ever-loving make up again. **1942** Pegler *Spelvin* 132: The ever-loving…spread the table for dinner. **1945** Atlas, Endure & Stevenson *GI Joe* (film): Did you hear that? My ever-lovin' comin' to town. **1949** Gordon & Kanin *Adam's Rib* 18: Woman popped her ever-lovin'. You see that? **1962** Serling *New Stories* 11: "Honey," he said into the phone, "it's your ever-lovin'!" **1972** Parker *Emotional Common Sense* 4: You or your ever-loving are spending your most productive hours…earning it. **2.** (one's) mind.
  1965 Linakis *In Spring* 20: "She must have been out of her mind." "Her ever-lovin'." **1975** S.P. Smith *Amer. Boys* 189: Blowed out of his ever-lovin' every night….He stayin' fucked up.

ever-loving *adj. & adv.* (used as an intensive).
  1919 McKenna *Btry. A* 188: Your ever-lovin' gas mask. **1926** in N. Cohen *Long Steel Rail* 478: Let the Midnight Special shine her ever-loving light on me. **1950** in Galewitz *Great Comics* 281: Be ready for that ever-lovin' pay-off. **1951** in Matheson *Born of Man & Woman* 63: Davey Jones has not seen fit to stash [it] away in his everloving locker. **1960** *Twilight Zone* (CBS-TV): Professor, I am going out of my ever-lovin' mind! **1974** R. Carter *16th Round* 94: That meant tangling with…some farmer's ever-loving shotgun. **1982** Cox & Frazier *Buck* 1: Boy, she was ever-lovin' sweet. **1982** Heat Moon *Blue Hwys.* 97: Right here….Selma, ever-lovin' Alagoddamnbama. **1993** *Mystery Sci. Theater* (Comedy Central TV): I hate his ever-lovin' guts.

everybody *pron.* ¶ In phrase: **everybody and his cousin** [or **dog**] absolutely everyone.
  1865 in J. Miller *Va. City* (June 6): Everybody and his cousin. **1937** E. Anderson *Thieves Like Us* 94: Everybody and his dog is coming. **1960–61** Steinbeck *Discontent* 8: Everybody and his dog cashing checks. **1967** N.Y.C. high school student: Now everybody and his dog is doing it.

evil *adj. Black E.* in an evil temper; evil-tempered.
  1939 in R.S. Gold *Jazz Talk* 84: *Evil:* in bad humor. **1944** Burley *Jive Hndbk.* 137: *Evil*—In a bad mood. **1956** Condon & Gehman *Treas. Jazz* 239: They forgave him…when Bird felt evil. **1973** Wideman *Lynchers* 35: Go on, nigger, I'm tired and evil today. **1986** Clayton & Elliott *Jazz World* 115: The doctors were evil at having to get up so early.

ewie /'iwi/ *n. USAF.* electronics warfare officer (EWO).
  1970 SAC navigator, age *ca*28: The electronics warfare officer is called the *EWO* or the *ewie.*

ewscray *v.* [pig Latin form of syn. SCREW] to get out; SCRAM.— used imperatively.
  1930 Franklyn *Kts. of Cockpit* 48: I say to you, pal, "ewscray!" **1931** C. Ford *Coconut Oil* 95: Blow. Ewscray….Scram. **1942** *ATS* 60.

ex[1] *n.* **1.** a person who formerly held a position made clear by the context.
  *1827 in *OEDS:* You're one of the people called *Ex's* at present. **1902** Cullen *More Ex-Tank Tales* 27: It's going to form a part of my mem-

oirs...to be published after I've become a total Ex. **1987** *Daywatch* (CNN-TV) (May 3): Supporters of the Philippines' ex, Ferdinand Marcos.

2. a former spouse or (in recent use) lover.

1929 E. Wilson *Daisy* 67: "Phil was your first husband, was he?" "Yes: he's my ex," she said. **1957** N.Y.C. woman, age *ca*45: When was the last time you heard from the ex? **1963** in Marx *Groucho Letters* 63: Dee (that's Howard Hawks's ex). **1963** J.A. Williams *Sissie* 14: Eve's ex is the lead in the play. **1965** Matthiessen *Fields of Lord* 381: Richard, writes my Ex, jams all his toys down toilets. **1987** pop. song: All my exes are in Texas.

3. *Pris.* an ex-convict.

1908 Kelley *Oregon Pen.* 56: When he comes out he is...an "ex." **1938** (cited in Partridge *Dict. Und.* 223).

ex² *n.* [fr. *exclusive privilege*] *Circus & Carnival.* (see quots.).— constr. with *the.*

1930 Irwin *Tramp & Und. Slang: Ex, the.* Any exclusive privilege granted by a carnival or circus; the right to sell sandwiches, soft drinks or tobacco, to gamble or even, with a crooked show, to pick pockets. **1946** Dadswell *Hey, Sucker* 99: *The X*...this expression means "exclusive" and conveys the knowledge that in the purchase of a concession privilege there will be no competition from similar attractions or joints.

exam *n.* an examination. Now *colloq.* or *S.E.*

1848 (cited in Weingarten *Slang*). ***1883** in *F & H* I 360: I read all about it for my exam. ***1889** Barrère & Leland *Dict. Slang* I 346: *Exam.* (schools), short for examination. **1900** Flandrau *Freshman* 32: My entrance exams divulged this.

excellent *adj. Stu.* exceptionally good; wonderful; stunning; exciting; AWESOME.

1982 M. Pond *Valley Girl's Guide* 55: *Excellent*—What dudes say instead of mega major maximum brilliant, they just go, "Excellent, man." **1982** Mathison *ET* (film): I want you to make me the most excellent promise. **1989** C. Matheson & E. Solomon *Bill & Ted's Excellent Adven.* (film): That is why we need a triumphant video....Excellent! *Ibid.*: Be excellent to each other. **1989** *ALF Tales* (NBC-TV): *Excellent* pad, dude! **1990** *Teenage Mutant Ninja Turtles* (CBS-TV): Whoa! Scope out the excellent light show! **1993** *New Yorker* (Nov. 15) 67: You know what? He's an *excellent* guy.

ex-con *n.* an ex-convict.

1906 *Nat. Police Gaz.* (Sept. 1) 3: I know that it is hard for an ex-con to get a chance. **1907** London *The Road* 146 [ref. to 1890's]: An "ex-con" who had done five years in Sing Sing. **1913** T.M. Osborne *Pris. Walls* 166: People will spot you as an ex-con at once. **1933–35** D. Lamson *About to Die* 303: An outcast, a jailbird, an ex-con. **1962** Ragan & Finston *Toughest Pris.* 798: *Ex-con*—An Ex-convict. **1978** in Partridge *DSUE* (ed. 8).

exec *n.* **1.** a business executive. Now *colloq.*

***1896** G.B. Shaw, in *OEDS*: The Execs will be safe, I should think, to sanction the expenditure. **1934** Weseen *Dict. Slang* 332: *Exec*—an executive. **1979** Terkel *Amer. Dreams* 4: One of the big execs from General Motors asked me to do a speech in Washington, D.C.

2. *Mil.* an executive officer.

1898 Allen *Navy Blue* 212: Ask the exec. for leave. **1918** in York *Mud & Stars* 41: Our young "Exec" with anxious brow,/Walks the deck and says as how.... **1922** *Am. Leg. Wkly.* (June 30) 16: The Exec placed a small megaphone to his lips. **1938** Connolly *Navy Men* 42 [ref. to 1903]: The "exec." said he guessed he had enough. **1962** Bonham *War Beneath Sea* 59: "O.K.," the exec said. "You're relieved."

exflunct *v.* [of fanciful orig.] *So.* to overcome, overwhelm, destroy; (in 1969 quot.) to make drunk. Also in elaborated vars.

1831 in Mathews *Begin. Amer. Eng.* 117: If I a'nt, I wish I may be tetotaciously exfluncted! **1833** Paulding *Lion* 21: If I hadn't I wish I may be te-to-taciously ex-flunctified. **1835** in Meine & Owens *Crockett Alms.* 49: My throat and jaws were so exflunctoficated with the influenza that I even snored hoarse. **1838** *Crockett Almanac* (1839) 17: I was completely exflunctificated when I red this. **1839** in Thornton *Amer. Gloss.*: The mongrel armies are prostrate-used up-exfluncticated. **1844** Featherstonhaugh *Slave States* 71: Stranger, if that ar hoss don't go like a screamer, I'll give you leave to ex-flunctify me into no time at all. **1853** in *DARE*: You exflunctified, perditioned rascal. **1969** Turner *Mayberly* 74: Only thing to do is get him exflunctied. **1977** Coover *Public Burning* 112: Those squonks can haul off and exflunctificate...the whole durn shootin' match!

ex-o *adj.* excellent.

1983 *N.Y. Daily News* (Mar. 25): Teentalk Glossary...*ex-o:* short for excellent. **1987** TV commercial: "Awesome!" "Ex-o, man!"

expat *n.* an expatriate.

1961 *N.Y. Times* (May 21) I 3: The easygoing Malays still retain many Britons, whom they call expatriates, or "expats," in key positions. ***1962, *1968** in *OED2.* ***1968** (cited in Partridge *DSUE* (ed. 8)). **1974** *Business Week* (Mar. 9) 40: The U.S. expatriate population in Buenos Aires has already plunged....Esso is moving 18 of its 22 expats. And Ford...pulled its expats out in December. **1978** *Atlantic* (Aug.) 20: Many "expats" are British subjects who have leapfrogged down the continent. **1983** *L.A. Times* (July 31) I 13: The total number of expats here really hasn't fallen much.

explore *v.* ¶ In phrase: **explore me!** *search me* s.v. SEARCH.

1913 Brown *Broke* 245: "Where can a fellow that's broke find a 'flop'?" "Explore me!"

express *n.* **1.** *Army.* a heavy artillery shell in flight, esp. as part of a regular enemy bombardment.—usu. constr. with *the.*

1864 in R.G. Carter *4 Bros.* 463: The Petersburg Express (now called the "Seven Sisters," 30 pdr. Rodmans) is close to us, and the iron messengers are being sent into the city at regular intervals. **1865** Sala *Diary* I 393: They christened one of the guns down at the Appomattox the "Petersburg Express." **1919** Kuhn *Co. A* 33: Of course we christened the episode and the repeated shelling of Steenvoorde was referred to as the "Mary Steenvoorde Express." **1920** Baker *Co. History* 24: At about midnight...the first "Steenvoorde Express" went by.

2. *Baseball.* a fastball.—constr. with *the.*

1964 Thompson & Rice *Every Diamond* 215: When I signal for the express you throws me the local.

exterminator *n. FBI.* (see quot.). *Joc.*

1986 "H.S.A. Becket" *Dict. Espionage* 29: Counterintelligence specialists responsible for finding and dismantling bugs are aptly called "exterminators."

extortion *n.* price; cost. *Joc.*

1891 Maitland *Slang Dict.* 87: "What's the damage?" how much is to pay? Sometimes varied to "What is the extortion?"

extra *n.* a mistress.

1893 Macdonald *Prison Secrets* 68: That ar campound av sin an' vanity is the new post-affice thafe's hextra.

eye *n.* **1.a.** [sugg. by the watchful eye emblem of the Pinkerton Agency and its accompanying slogan, "The Eye That Never Sleeps"] *(cap.) Und.* the Pinkerton Detective Agency.—constr. with *the.*

[**1892** L. Moore *Own Story* 281: Pinkerton's "all-seeing-eye" office. *Ibid.* 289: I was being kept under the "eye-that-never-sleeps" from the time I left the hotel in the morning until I returned at night.] **1900** Willard & Hodler *Powers* 21: Old 'Frisco Slim touched up one o' the big joolry places not knowin' that it was in the Eye's dead-line. **1914** Jackson & Hellyer *Vocab.* 31: Eye, the,....The Pinkerton Detective Agency; an operative of the Pinkerton Agency. **1919** *Amer. Leg. Wkly.* (Sept. 12) 8: The "Eye" was the underworld name of a famous detective agency. **1930** Conwell *Thief* 128: When the Eye (Pinkertons) are brought in to protect a race track or exposition, that is bad. *Ibid.* 237: *Eye*, n. Pinkerton Detective Agency. *ca*1935 in Dunne *Dooley Remembers* 61: The seasoned robber knew that "the eye" was on him. The eye that never slept. **1955** in *OEDS*.

b. *Und.* a detective or armed guard employed by the Pinkerton Agency.

1914 (quot. at (a), above). **1928** O'Connor *B'way Racketeers* 182: He imagined he was getting a tail from the Burns men, the "Eyes" and a half dozen headquarters dicks. **1931** in D.W. Maurer *Lang. Und.* 46: *Eye*, n. A Pinkerton detective, sometimes called a "pink." "He's an eye." **1929–31** in Partridge *Dict. Und.* 224: *Eye man.* A Pinkerton detective. **1931–34** in Clemmer *Pris. Comm.* 331: *Eye*...A watchman.

c. *Orig. Und.* a private detective. [As *private eye*, now *colloq.* or *S.E.*]

1930 (quot. at PINK, *n.*). **1933** Ersine *Prison Slang* 33: *Eye*, n. A private detective. **1941** *Slanguage Dict.* 14: *Eye*...a detective; a private detective. **1944** Paxton *Murder, My Sweet* (film): You're a private eye, huh? I want you to look for somebody. **1949** Chandler *Little Sister* 181: I can see that you are just another dumb private eye. **1952** Chase *McThing* 62: That...would make any cop—even a private eye—fly into a rage, see? **1952** "M. Roscoe" *Black Ball* 12: When a private eye walks in everybody gets nervous. They know an eye might be checking anybody, and for any reason. **1953** in Cannon *Like 'Em Tough* 14: What makes a private eye think he's got rights an ordinary citizen hasn't? **1955** *Western Folk.* XIV 135: *Eye.* A detective. **1956** I. Fleming *Diamonds* 128: What's his racket? Is he an eye? **1968** M.H. Albert & J. Guss *Lady in Cement* (film): I got a right to talk to my eye alone. **1981** G. Wolf *Roger Rabbit* 2: All the cash in the world wouldn't persuade a private eye to take on an unjust cause. **1986** R. Campbell *In La-La Land* 21: "I'm a private investigator." "An eye?"

2. *pl.* a woman's breasts. *Joc.*

1932 *AS* VII (June) 329: *Big brown eyes*—breasts. **1948** Lowry *Wolf* 56: "Did you ever see such big eyes, Bill?" "*Vieni con me*, hot pants." **1960** MacCuish *Do Not Go Gentle* 328 [ref. to WWII]: You know, you have the loveliest eyes—all thirty-six inches of them! **1963** Lundgren *Primary Cause* 128: And there sits this red-haired WAF with great, big bouncing eyes. **1971–73** Sheehy *Hustling* 188: Will you look at the pair of eyes on this girl? **1989** P. Munro *U.C.L.A. Slang* 37: *Eyes* breasts. She's got some big eyes.

3. *pl.* esp. *Jazz.* a desire.—usu. constr. with *for.*

1933–34 Lorimer & Lorimer *Stag Line* 7: He had eyes for none other than she. **1948** *New Yorker* (July 3) 28: Have you eyes for a sandwich? *ca*1953 Hughes *Fantastic Lodge* 26: He developed a certain amount of eyes for me. *Ibid.* 72: I had big eyes for the drummer. *Ibid.* 90: He took me in his arms and told me that he had eyes. **1956** E. Hunter *Second Ending* 350: That chick has eyes that are the biggest, you know that, don't you? **1956** Holiday & Dufty *Lady* 12: I had no eyes for sex. **1958** Ferlinghetti *Coney Island* 46: Maybe she has no eyes for him or him no eyes for her. **1960** *Mad* (Sept.): I got big eyes for this chick, see?…Should I marry the broad? **1961** Russell *Sound* 13: Think you'd have eyes to work for him? **1964** R.S. Gold *Jazz Lexicon* 98: *Eyes.* A desire or inclination (for something)….probably suggested by *I Only Have Eyes For You*, 1934 song which became a jazz standard; according to jazzmen, Lester Young was the first to use the term in a special jazz slang sense c. 1940. **1967** Taggart *Reunion* 63: He looked like he's got eyes. **1970** *N.Y. Times* (Dec. 27) 19: Now, one of those crumcrushers was named Little Red Riding Hood. One day, she told the old lady she had fat eyes to make her Grandma's scene at the other end of the woods. **1970** Southern *Blue Movie* 171: "I was wondering…if you'd fucked Angie yet."…"No, man,…I'm not sure I've got eyes." **1986** Pietsch *Cab Driver's Joke Bk.* 133: A jazz musician's…son is plucking the petals from a daisy….saying "She digs me; got no eyes; digs me, got no eyes…."

4. *Stu.* television.—constr. with *the.*

1954–60 *DAS: Eye…*A television set; a television screen. Teenage use, common since c1955. **1968** Baker et al. *CUSS* 113: *Eye.* Television. **1974** N.Y.U. student: As soon as I get home I turn on the eye for about two hours.

¶ In phrases:

¶ **cut in the eye** see s.v. CUT, *adj.*

¶ **damn your eyes!** goddamn you! Also vars.

1751 in Breslaw *Tues. Club* 304: Sweet honey dear! and damn my eyes! **1761* Sterne *Trist. Shandy* Bk. III ch. xii: The lowest oath of a scavenger, (Damn your eyes). **1838** [Haliburton] *Clockmaker* (Ser. 2) 219: Here, waiter, d—n your eyes! **1845** *Nat. Police Gaz.* (Nov. 15) 98: G-d d—n their eyes…they think they've got me fast. **1854** G.G. Foster *15 Mins.* 35: The gentleman with the button d—s its eyes. **1904** *Independent* (June 23) 1432: And blast my eyes if it wasn't Spike Riley. **1931** Harlow *Old Bowery* 204: Stand aside, damn your eyes, or we'll run you down! **1935** Coburn *Law Rides Range* 44: Damn your damn eyes, wait! **1942–43** C. Jackson *Lost Weekend* 111: Damn his eyes. **1959** "D. Stagg" *Glory Jumpers* 11: They're even sending me a pigeoneer…in case the radios break down as usual….A pigeoneer, damn their eyes! **1962** Kesey *Cuckoo's Nest* 207: Here, George, damn your eyes! **1963** Morgan *Six-Eleven* 163: But God damn my eyes, boy,…a man could get killed. **1971** Cameron *First Blood* 93: I'm an *officer*, God damn your eyes! **1974** Dawson & Peckinpah *Garcia* (film): God damn your fuckin' eyes! **1974–77** Heinemann *Close Quarters* 34: Haskins, damn your eyes, what's for breakfast?

¶ **have a brass eye** to be drunk.

1737 *Penn. Gaz.* (Jan. 6) 1: He's…Cock-Ey'd…Got a brass Eye.

¶ **in (one's) eye** (of liquor consumed) sufficient to cause intoxication.

*1738 J. Swift, in *OED:* You must own you had a Drop in your Eye…you were half Seas over. **1918–19** MacArthur *Bug's-Eye View* 17: Mr. MacFarland…got some Triple Sec in his eye, a circumstance which prevented him from reading Schopenhauer for nearly three days.

¶ **in your eye!, 1.** indeed not! like hell! (*hence*) (used as an abusive retort).

1894 Crane *Red Badge* 109: Lickin'—in yer eye! We ain't licked, sonny.

1929 McEvoy *Hollywood Girl* 91: In your eye. In your hat. **1972** R. Wilson *Forbidden Words* 99: The army oath, *in your eye, all six inches of it.* **1980** Birnbach *Preppy Hndbk.* 220: *In your eye*…"you're mistaken, know-it-all."

2. [abbr. "Here's mud in your eye!"] (used as a toast).

1948 *Neurotica* (Spring) 29: Well in your eye i said/and down the hatch she said.

¶ **keep a red eye out** to keep alert.

1828 J. Hall *Letters* 290: The new settler had to…"keep a red eye out" for Indians.

¶ **my eye, 1.a.** arrant nonsense.—usu. constr. with *all.*—also constr. with *Betty Martin. Obs.* in U.S. [The Betty Martin element remains unexplained.]

*1768 O. Goldsmith, in *OED:* That's all my eye—the king only can pardon. **1778** in F. Moore *Songs & Ballads of Revolution* 233: They swore they'd make bold Pigot squeak,…/But that was all my eye, sir. **1782* in *OED:* That's all my eye, and my elbow, as the saying is. **1785* Grose *Vulgar Tongue: That's my eye, Betty Martin;* an answer to anyone that attempts to impose or humbug. **1805** *Port Folio* (Aug. 24) 261: 'Tis all my eye. **1808** in Nevins & Weitenkampf *Cartoons* 25: Why, 'tis all in my eye, Jack. **1819* T. Moore *Tom Crib* 2: All my eye, Betty Martin. **1821** Waln *Hermit* 24: "Jumped out of the pocket, by heavens!—" "Boh! that's my eye, Betty Martin." **1821* Stewart *Man-of-War's-Man* I 141: But the whole of this flummery was all in my eye and Betty. **1829** Marryat *Frank Mildmay* 292: "Yes," said the man, "I knew that, but that's what we call in our country [America] 'all my eye.'" **1833** in [S. Smith] *Letters of Downing* 175: And old laws are "all my eye." **1835** in Paulding *Bulls & Jons.* 54: Though they do make such a fuss about their great riches, and all that, it's all my eye Betty Martin. **1838** [Haliburton] *Clockmaker* (Ser. 2) 66: You thought it all "in my eye." **1842* T. Hood, in *OED:* The tenderness of spring is all my eye. **1867** Clark *Sailor's Life* 49: That's all in my eye; don't you 'spose the old man knows the road? **1920* in D.H. Lawrence *Letters* I 617: One becomes indifferent to all political fates—Fiumes, Jugo-Slavakis and such like my-eye.

b. indeed; "like hell."—used to indicate disbelief.

*1842 in *OED:* Church, my eye, woman! church indeed! **1905** in "O. Henry" *Works* 1676: "Tragic, my eye!" said my friend, irreverently. **1928** in Paxton *Sport* 128: Gentlemen, me eye! You've got to get over being gentlemen if you're going to play football on my team! **1929** Faulkner *Sound & Fury* 138: "How about Bigelow's Mill…that's a factory." "Factory my eye." **1965** N.Y.C. woman, age 77: Too busy, my eye! What's he busy at? **1992** *Guiding Light* (CBS-TV): A coincidence? My eye! **1992** *Simpsons* (Fox-TV): Oral thermometer, my eye!

2. (used to indicate surprise). Also *pl.*

*1806 in Partridge *DSUE* (ed. 8): My eyes, how he mauled her! **1826* in *OEDS:* My eye, what a spot for a "walky, walky." **1834** *Davy Crockett's Almanack* (1835) 8: My eyes! here was a pretty predickyment! **1837* Dickens *O. Twist* ch. viii: "My eyes, how green!" exclaimed the young gentleman. "Why, a beak's a madg'strate." **1840** *Crockett's Comic Alm.* (unp.): My eyes! How dry I and my pockets are. **1876* in *OED* (s.v. fit, adj. def. 6): My eye, ain't she fit! **1905** Brainerd *Belinda* 16: My eye! and who's chaperoning the pretty chaperon? **1934** H. Miller *Tropic of Cancer* 45: My eye, but I've been all over that ground.

¶ **open an** [or **(one's)**] **eye** to take a drink of liquor. Cf. EYE-OPENER.

1848 in Oehlschlaeger *Reveille* 202: "Opening his eye" with a tumbler full of whisky. **1859** *Spirit of Times* (Apr. 2) 86: After dining, "opening both eyes," &c.

¶ **out like Lottie's eye** unconscious.

1970 Thackrey *Thief* 42: I must have hit the ground, but damn if I can remember doing that….I was out like Lottie's eye.

¶ **pipe (one's)** [or **the**] **eye** Esp. *Naut.* to shed a tear; weep.

*1789 C. Dibdin (cited in Partridge *DSUE* (ed. 1)). **1798** *Amer. Musical Misc.* 60: What argufies sniv'ling and piping your eye? **1856** in C.A. Abbey *Before the Mast* 59: He spits & pipes his eye. **1883* R.L. Stevenson *Treasure I.* ch. xix: The smoke…kept us coughing and piping the eye.

¶ **[with their] eyes [wide] open** *Rest.* (of eggs) fried on one side only.—used in relaying orders.

1923 McKnight *Eng. Words* 45: Two with their eyes open. **1942** *Sat. Eve. Post* (Nov. 28) 65: Eyes wide open. **1944** Kendall *Service Slang* 6: *Eyes wide open*…eggs straight up.

¶ **your eye** *my eye,* 1, above.

1899 Norris *Blix* 163: *Barkentine* your eye! **1901** Wister *Philosophy* 12 [ref. to 1880's]: So he says color is all your eye, and shape isn't? and substance isn't?

eyeball *n.* **1.** a look; glance; in phr. of the sort **give the eyeball** or **put the eyeball on** to inspect; EYEBALL, *v.* Cf. HAIRY EYE-BALL.

1951 (quot. at REETY). **1972** Grogan *Ringolevio* 140: He was...best at what was known as the Viminal Eyeball, which was the look that everyone got when someone returned a rented car or scooter. **1976** Lieberman & Rhodes *CB* 132: *Mobile Eyeball*—One truck checking another truck's rig while moving. **1976** Whelton *CB Baby* 8: I'm about to put the eyeball on a street sign right now. **1978** Truscott *Dress Gray* 152: Any chick catch an eyeball on you like this, man, she gonna figure you for some kinda faggot or somethin'. *Ibid.* 389: Put an eyeball on this, guys. *a*1988 C. Adams *More Straight Dope* 478: Give each card the old eyeball one at a time. **1989** *48 Hours* (CBS-TV) (May 4): We got an eyeball on him [*sc.* a suspect]. **1992** *Amer. Detective* (ABC-TV): I'm trying to get an eyeball on the house.

2. *CB.* a face-to-face meeting of CB operators.

1976 Adcock *Not for Truckers Only* 43: How about some coffee and an eyeball at that Union 76 up at the next exit?

¶ In phrases:

¶ **eyeball to eyeball** face-to-face, esp. as on the brink of decisive conflict. Now *colloq.*

1953 in Loosbrock & Skinner *Wild Blue* 464: The pilot dives down on the deck to view the face of the enemy "eyeball to eyeball." **1959** Webb *Pork Chop* (film): The Chinese love this eyeball-to-eyeball stuff. **1962** D. Rusk, in *Sat. Eve. Post* (Dec. 8) 16: We're eyeball to eyeball [with the Soviet Union], and I think the other fellow just blinked. **1979** *N.Y. Times Mag.* (Oct. 21) 19: According to Gen. Harold Johnson, Army Chief of Staff in the mid-60's...When General MacArthur's headquarters sent an inquiry to the 24th [Inf.] regiment [in Korea, November, 1950]—"Do you have contact with the enemy?"—the reply, widely reported at the time, was "We is eyeball to eyeball."

¶ **play eyeball** to exchange flirtatious glances.

1976 C. Keane *Hunter* 24: Tommy played eye ball with a woman officer across the room.

¶ **shoot** [or **make**] **an eyeball at** to see or look at.

1976 Adcock *Not for Truckers Only* 47: Maybe never even shoot an eyeball at a [cop]. **1977** Langone *Life at Bottom* 201: And if you make a eyeball at 'em—it's the least we can get after the work we do for them broads—Christ, you'll get your ass up to mast.

¶ **to the** [or **one's**] **eyeballs** to the limit; to an extreme degree. Cf. colloq. *to the eyes*, in *OED2* fr. 18th C.

1911–12 Ade *Knocking the Neighbors* 138: They had covertly planned to get him Saturated to the Eye-Balls. **1925** McAlmon *Silk Stockings* 39: She was "coked to the eyeballs." **1955** E. Hunter *Jungle Kids* 103: I could tell them Django was not only heeled but that he was probably heeled to his eyeballs. **1963** Boyle *Yanks* 202: He was in hock up to his sunken eyeballs. **1975** C.W. Smith *Country Music* 219: You got me in hock up to my eyeballs. **1982** R. Baker, in *N.Y. Times Mag.* (Aug. 29) 10: I can be sued to the eyeballs by the man whose real name is not Biff. **1990** *New Yorker* (Oct. 29) 114: Under the obtrusive direction of Michael Greif, the production is expressionist to its eyeballs.

eyeball *adj.* **1.** (of an inspection or the like) done personally by the responsible individual or individuals.—used prenominally.

1960 Rankin *Rode Thunder* 97: He runs a tough outfit. He holds eyeball inspection every morning.

2. eyewitness.—used prenominally. Also as adv., visually.

1959 Brosnan *Long Season* 16: Anxious for the eyeball report of the student technician with...the high bust. **1971** *60 Minutes* (CBS-TV): We did have eyeball witnesses on the *Turner Joy.* **1977** Hynek *UFO Report* 72: What is to be believed here—the lack of a radar observation or the eyeball testimony of many independent witnesses over a considerable geographical stretch? **1979** Cassidy *Delta* 118: We've got rumors and some eyeball reports that are pretty definite. *a*1986 K.W. Nolan *Into Laos* 140: He never missed a day commanding it "eyeball" from his own chopper over the scene of action in Laos. **1991** C. Fletcher *Pure Cop* 177: And you have no eyeball witness.

eyeball *v.* **1.** to catch sight of; see; stare at; watch; (*intrans.*) look.

*1846 in Wilkes *Dict. Austral. Colloq.* 326: This day's work [climbing a tree to look around] is what is generally though not elegantly termed "eye-balling." **1901** *Harper's Mo.* (Feb.) 442: "God!" burst from the lips of the man as he eyeballed his attendant. **1933** J.V. Allen *Cowboy Lore* 60: *Eyeballer*, Anyone poking his nose into the affairs of others. **1942** *Amer. Mercury* (July) 85: He would eye-ball the idol-breaker. **1943** Pyle

Brave Men 146: Another term was "eyeballing," which meant viewing and gandering around, such as "eyeballing into Naples." **1944** Bontemps & Cullen *St. Louis Woman* 15: Don't eye-ball me/City Hall me. **1944** *Slanguage Dictionary* 50: *Eyeballing*—looking over the immediate area. **1946** Mezzrow & Wolfe *Really Blues* 22: Just lying in my bunk, eyeballing the whitewashed ceiling. **1959** *Swinging Syllables* s.v.: *Eye ball*—To see. **1965** Hernton *Sex & Racism* 27: Several years ago in Mississippi there occurred the infamous case of rape by "reckless eyeballing." **1966** Braly *On Yard* 73: We could...eyeball them fine broads. **1968** Mares *Marine Machine* 25: They punish just those actions which in civilian society seem the most automatic and innocent: "running your mouth," "scratching," "eyeballing." **1968** Spradley *Drunk* 55: Eye-ball the sign in the courtroom: "Equal Justice for All under the Law." **1971** Contini *Beast* 80: Bad enough we're being eyeballed as it is. **1985** J.G. Hirsch *Richard Beck* (film): We got a witness who eyeballed the whole thing.

2.a. to examine or estimate by sight; inspect.

1946 Mezzrow & Wolfe *Really Blues* 29: When a john had eyeballed the parade and made his choice he would follow her upstairs. **1958** McCulloch *Woods Words* 58: *Eyeballing a line*—Making a preliminary survey by eye, mostly by guess, not by instrument. **1961** L.G. Richards *TAC* 67: In tactical formation your position isn't flown by the book. You "eyeball" it, pretty much. **1971** Tak *Truck Talk* 57: *Eyeball it:* to measure the height, width or length of a trailer's cargo by sight. **1975** V.B. Miller *Trade-Off* 71: I start eyeballing the place in detail.

b. to accomplish by direct observation rather than through the use of instruments.

1985 Boyne & Thompson *Wild Blue* 563: I'm going to eyeball this [shot], Lieutenant.

3. *CB.* to meet in person.

1976 *N.Y. Post* (June 19) 27: Breaker One-Eight. This is Teddy Bear for the Foxy Lady. Can we eyeball at the coffee break?

eyebrow *n.* ¶ In phrase: **to the** [or **(one's)**] **eyebrows** to the limit.

1905 Brainerd *Belinda* 31: She was up to her eyebrows in romance. **1925* in *OEDS.* **1973** Schiano & Burton *Solo* 94: In comes a tall young man, stoned to the eyebrows. **1973** Droge *Patrolman* 75: The sergeant...had had it up to his eyebrows and decided to wait no longer.

eye-candy *n. Adver.* (see quot.). Cf. EAR CANDY.

1984 in Seyler & Boltz *Lang. Power* 211: This ad also features an elegantly dressed woman with conspicuous cleavage, which advertising executives reportedly refer to as "eye-candy."

eye-fake *v. Football.* to mislead an opponent by glancing in a direction opposite to that in which a play is to be made.

1974 Blount *3 Bricks Shy* 108: I eye-fake. If I'm going to block a guy straight ahead I'll look down the line.

eye-fuck *v.* to gaze or stare at lecherously; (hence, esp. *Mil.*) to stare at.—usu. considered vulgar.

1916 Cary *Slang of Venery* I 79: *Eye Fuck*—To stare and leer at a woman. **1971** Barnes *Pawns* 69: The DI's have picked out the recruits who don't look sharp, who fall behind in the runs, or are caught "eye-fucking." ("Eye-fucking" is a heinous crime in Marine Corps boot camp. It consists of moving one's eyeballs to the side while standing at attention.) **1972** B. Rodgers *Queens' Vernacular* 77: *Eye fuck* (late '60s)...to stare holes through someone. **1980** M. Baker *Nam* 36: Smokey catches the dude looking at him out of the corner of his eye. He says, "Are you eye-fucking me, boy? I don't want your scuzzy eyes looking at me." **1980** Di Fusco et al. *Tracers* 12: While maggots are at attention, they will not talk, they will not eye-fuck the area, they will listen to me and only me! **1983** Ehrhart *VN-Perkasie* 30 [ref. to 1966]: You will not talk. You will not eye-fuck the area. *Ibid.* 32: You eye-fuckin' me, sweetpea? You wanna fuck me, scum? **1988** Norst *Colors* 17: Killer Bee...was...eye-fucking McGavin. **1991** J.T. Ward *Dear Mom* 5 [ref. to 1968]: You will stand at attention, eyes forward. I don't want you eyefucking me or the area.

eyeful *n.* a good look. Now *colloq.*

*1899 in *OEDS:* She took an eyeful out of Jack, an' right well plaised she was with his appearance. **1912** T.A. Dorgan, in Zwilling *TAD Lexicon* 35: Ladies tailors getting an eyeful of fashion. **1914** Jackson & Hellyer *Vocab.* 31: The mark on your left is getting an eye full. **1915** Howard *God's Man* 198: They'll always fall for...the clothes and the lights and people gettin' an eyeful of their new hat. **1918** Witwer *Baseball* 182: The next mornin' I stuck my dome up over the edge of the trench for an eyeful. **1919* Downing *Digger Dial.* 26: *Get an eye-full,* see. **1920** Witwer *Kid Scanlan* 19: [The horse] took a good eyeful and

kinda curled up its lip. *1914–22 J. Joyce *Ulysses* 765 [ref. to 1904]: Ill put on my shift and drawers let him have a good eyeful out of that. **1924** Hecht & Bodenheim *Cutie* 7: She offered an eyeful which would make a brass monkey run a temperature of 209 degrees. **1938** Baldwin & Schrenk *Murder* (film): Get an eyeful of that.

eye in the sky *n.* **1.** *Casino Gamb.* a two-way mirror concealing a security guard or camera.

1961 Scarne *Comp. Guide to Gambling* 224: Some of the larger Nevada casinos have observation posts concealed behind one-way glass in the walls and in the ceilings above each gaming table, known as "eyes in the sky." **1963** (cited in T.L. Clark *Dict. Gamb.* 74). **1985** E. Leonard *Glitz* 229: Look down through one-way smoked glass at the casino floor...."The Eye in the Sky," Nancy said.

2. a reconnaissance satellite or aircraft, now esp. a traffic or observation helicopter.

1975 Dills *CB Slanguage: Eye in the Sky:* Police helicopter. **1976** Lieberman & Rhodes *CB* 128: *Eye In The Sky*—Police aircraft. **1980** W.C. Anderson *Bat-21* 26: Your report confirms big eye in the sky. **1983** Van Devanter & Morgan *Before Morning* 264: Bill was...a traffic reporter for the radio station's "eye in the sky." **1985** Univ. Tenn. instructor, age 36: The [Space] Shuttle's planting another eye in the sky.

eyelid movies *n.pl.* reveries experienced with one's eyes closed. *Joc.*

1971 *Current Slang* V 11: *Eyelid movies,* n. Hallucinations. **1985** *Maledicta* VIII 106: To masturbate...*watch the eyelid movies.*

eye-opener *n.* **1.** a bracing drink, usu. of liquor; (now *usu.*) such a drink taken early in the day, as immediately after arising. Now *colloq.*

1817 Fearon *Sketches of America* 249: The latter is effected by individuals taking their solitary "eye openers," "toddy," and "phlegm dispensers," at the bar. **1839** *Spirit of Times* (July 27) 247: He should take an eye-opener, in about an hour, a fleme cutter, and jist as he sits down to breakfast, a gall-buster. **1839** in Blair & Meine *Half Horse* 66: As we've had our eye-openers a-ready, we'll now take a flem-cutter, by way of an antifogmatic. **1865** Sala *Diary* II 313: Jersey lightning...eye-opener ...gin sling. **1873** Beadle *Undeveloped West* 270: We took the invariable [3 A.M.] "eye-opener" of California white wine. **1925** Mullin *Scholar Tramp* 112: Then when I was asleep this morning, he stole another bottle off 'n me that I was savin' fer an eye-opener. **1937** Reitman *Box-Car Bertha* 136: You've had an eye opener. Go out and get some money if you want to have anything more to drink. **1941** in Botkin *Treas. Amer. Folk.* 125: He was out lookin for...an eye opener to cool the burnin thirst in his throat. **1943** J. Mitchell *McSorley's* 29: Few of the men to whom Mazie gives money for eye-openers are companionable. **1967** in J. Flaherty *Chez Joey* 126: Hey, Frankie, how about an eye-opener? **1987** *Tour of Duty* (CBS-TV): Just lemme get an eye opener.

2. (*Specif.*) *Narc.* a dose of a drug taken early in the day, as immediately after arising.

1938 in D.W. Maurer *Lang. Und.* 101: *Eye-opener.* The first injection of the day, often taken in bed. **1971** Goines *Dopefiend* 89: Man, we damn near got enough stuff to go and buy us an eye-opener now.

eye-popper *n.* a sensational or astonishing sight.

1942 *ATS* 199: Something surprising; astonishing...*eye-popper.* **1981** *Natural History* (July) 89 (ad): This magnificent mural map is a real eye-popper, ideal for an office, reception area, classroom, den or child's room.

Eyetie /ˈaɪˌtaɪ/ *n. & adj.* **1.** Esp. *Mil.* an Italian; as adj., Italian.—used derisively.

*1919 *Athenaeum* (Aug. 22) 791: Our army in Italy always spoke of the Italians as the "Itis" (pronounced "Eye-ties"). *1921 *N & Q* (Nov. 21) 424 [ref. to 1918]: *Itis.* (Pronounced "eye-ties") Italians. *1925 Fraser & Gibbons *Soldier & Sailor Words* 90: *Eyeties:* Italians. *1941 *Saturday Review* (Oct. 4) 11: *Eye Tie.* An Italian plane to English aviators. **1943** Hersey *Bell for Adano* 75: But boy, those Eyeties sure did a lot of paper work. **1943** Pyle *Your War* 166: We hardly ever heard Italian soldiers referred to as Italians. It was either "Eyeties" or "Wops" or "Guineas." **1944** in *Best from Yank* 25: I've been fighting with the Eyetie Partisans up in the hills. **1945** Bellah *Ward 20* 57: I was wore out all the time...running after Eyties all over Africa. **1950** *New Directions* 385: Weren't any of the Eye-ties out celebratin even then? **1955** Klaas *Maybe I'm Dead* 96: Mortay. That's Eytie for dead. **1956** Metalious *Peyton Place* 356: That Eye-tie over on the Pond Road. **1956** Lee & Bradley *Passed for White* 66: Her brothers had been in Italy during the war and she told me they had had "Eyetie" girls. **1956** I. Shulman *Good Deeds* 62: Don't cry to anyone who wasn't one of us about how tough it was for the Eyties. **1958** Camerer *Damned Wear Wings* 46: A dog-eared Eyetie art magazine. **1959** Duffy & Lane *Warden's Wife* 77 [ref. to *ca*1915]: I was...advised to try North Beach because, "Them Eyeties like 'em plump." **1971** Cole *Rook* 66: Negroes, Eyeties, Heebs and Poor White Trash. **1985** Heywood *Taxi Dancer* 120: A NATO exercise—with the goddamned Froggies and Eye-ties.

2. the Italian language.

1945 *Yank* (July 27) 22: I...still can't speak a word of Eyetie.

eyewash *n.* **1.** Esp. *Mil.* outward show intended to forestall criticism from superiors; sham.

1917 in Cushing *Surgeon's Jour.* 205: They could do nothing more than send in a whitewashing report—"eye wash," in short. *1924 Blunden *Undertones* 39 [ref. to WWI]: The artificial parts of army life—"eyewash," in the term then universal. *1925 Fraser & Gibbons *Soldier & Sailor Wds.* 90: *Eyewash:* Humbug. Sham. Deceit. Flattery. Any merely complimentary outward show. **1933** A.B. Leonard *Judson Case* 156: Forget the eyewash about cigarettes an' pine needles. There's no more sense in one than in the other. **1942** in Cheever *Letters* 67: Some eyewash by Saint Eupery [*sic*]. "There is no despair in defeat....the vast brotherhood of death, etc." **1942–43** C. Jackson *Lost Weekend* 22: The whole thing was so much eyewash. **1954** Wertham *Innocent* 22: If they read such signs at all they know that they are only "eyewash" intended to influence parents and teachers who have no time to read the whole comic book. **1955** Scott *Look of the Eagle* 19: I don't need the rest of the eyewash and the crap. **1958** Camerer *Damned Wear Wings* 138: What had seemed urgent...now seemed...so much eyewash. **1968** Corson *Betrayal* 265: Crocodile tears over the plight of ground forces are eyewash to cover up a vain desire to get more planes, more pilots, and more appropriations. **1970** *N.Y. Times Mag.* (Apr. 12) 133: The grunts, the combat troops, don't like to see their hard fights reduced to public-relations eyewash. **1977** Stone *Blizzard* 28: Because it's been eyewash from the start....Just going through the motions to avoid charges of cover-up. **1979** Lovell *Athens nor Sparta* 169: Some found even the appointment of a civilian dean to be largely "eyewash." **1993** *N.Y. Times* (Oct. 12) B 6: Is this governmental eyewash?

2. cheap liquor.

1925 (quot. at RUM HOUND). **1972** B. Rodgers *Queens' Vernacular* 77: *Eyewash* cheap champagne; by extension, any cheap liquor.

eye-water *n.* gin or whiskey.

*1823 P. Egan *Vulgar Tongue: Eye-water.* Gin. *1869 in *F & H* II 362: And a three of eye-water. *1886 in *F & H* II 362: He imbibed stupendous quantities of jiggered gin, dog's nose, and Paddy's eye-water. **1940** *AS* (Dec.) 447: *Eye Water.* Liquor. "Eye water's more plentiful in Jackson County now than common."

F var. EFF.

fab *adj.* [clipping fr. *fabulous*] Esp. *Stu.* delightful; wonderful; fine. [Popularized in U.S. by the Beatles, 1964.]

1957 Kohner *Gidget* 65: And the great Kahoona. He's absolute fab. **1961** Kohner *Gidget Goes Hawaiian* 26: I had my eyes glued on that fab sight. *****1961** Partridge *DSUE* (ed. 5) 1082: *Fab*...Very good...teenagers' (esp. the coffee-bar set): 1957–58. *****1963** in *OEDS:* Daddy, this fire's simply fab. **1965** *N.Y. Times* (Dec. 27) 20: "Groovy" is a superlative like "cool," "fab," or "great." **1967** P. Roth *When She Was Good* 247: He's wonderful. He's fab, really. **1967** Ragni & Rado *Hair* 165: Sheila, how come you're so groovy looking tonight? You've got fab eyes. **1974** Lahr *Trot* 115: I had a fab time. **1976** Angelou *Singin' & Swingin'* 94: Darling, you're going to be fab. **1976** Rosten *To Anywhere* 27: "Okay?" "Fab!" **1985** B.E. Ellis *Less Than Zero* 171: You're terrific, you kids. Just fab. **1986** *Show Biz This Week* (CNN-TV) (Oct. 11): Get ready for the second U.S. invasion of some of those fab British groups from the '60's. **1987** *Campus Voice* (Winter) 30: Fab Fanzines. **1988** *Nat. Lampoon* (Feb.) 8: And I just think it's fab! **1992** Watterson *Calvin & Hobbes* (synd. cartoon strip) (Sept. 1): "Two generations can be divided by the same language!"..."Marvy. Fab. Far out." **1993** *TV Guide* (June 12) 3: Guess those jobs explain where their fab apartments come from.

face *n.* **1.a.** the mouth regarded as a source of usu. insolent or otherwise offensive speech.—usu. in phr. **shut** [or **open**] **(one's) face.** See also *shoot off (one's) face,* below.

1834 Caruthers *Kentuck.* I 99: They shut up their faces like steel-traps. **1894** in Ade *Chicago Stories* 46: Keep your face closed. **1896** Ade *Artie* 20: If you open your face to this lady again to-night I'll separate you from your breath. **1896** F.P. Dunne, in Schaaf *Dooley* 244: Who's th' greatest orator that ever opened his face? Bill Bryan. **1896** Crane *George's Mother* 173: Close yer face! **1904** J. London *Sea Wolf* ch. xv: Shut yer faces. **1915** Garrett *Army Ballads* 34: Close y' face. **1925** Kearney *Man's Man* 70: Shut your face, you poor boob. **1927** "M. Brand" *Pleasant Jim* 35: You, Chuck, shut your face...If it ain't a shame the way all these kids will shoot off their faces! **1930** Fredenburgh *Soldiers March!* 48: Hey, shut your face and let a guy sleep. **1960** Hall *Linguistics & Your Language* 51: Were the noises that the Elizabethans made with their faces...any better...than those that we make with our faces? **1969** Gardner *Fat City* 10: Oh, no, you just sit there with your sad-ass face shut until the minute I start having a good time. **1980** McAleer & Dickson *Unit Pride* 43: Don't let me catch any of you guys openin' your face to anythin' different, get me? **1992** L. Johnson *My Posse* 23: Shut your face.

b. the mouth, as used for eating or drinking. See also *feed (one's) face,* below.

1895 Townsend *Fadden Explains* 34: He trowed schooners down his face, till de gang was all stuck on his style. **1910** *Adventure* (Nov.) 155: I was goin' to take a face-full o' the stuff.

2. effrontery; nerve; influence.

1851 in *DARE:* How can you have the face to talk to me, arter saying what you sed? **1865** in Dunkelman & Winey *Hardtack Regt.* 135: I never had face enough on me to...step up to a young girl and demand her rings. **1895** Gore *Stu. Slang* 16: *Face* n. Audacity, impudence. **1926** *AS* II 10: The copy reader hasn't the "face" to correct a reporter for using a word which he himself has sponsored. **1968** in *DARE: When someone does something unexpectedly bold or forward, you might say: "Well, she certainly has a lot of"...Face.*

3. credit granted esp. on the strength of one's trustworthy appearance or (following **(2)**, above) sheer impudence. Cf. *run (one's) face,* below.

1856 in *DAE:* [I] must travel on my face after this. **1859** in Thornton *Amer. Gloss.:* If you have not a ready tongue and cannot travel on your face. **1873** *Overland Mo.* (Feb.) 105: Every old miner knew that his face was good for a week at Robinson's bar. **1899** Cullen *Tales* 56: I can't do the Continent, if that's where I'm bound, on my face. **1919** *Twelfth Inf.* 170: His face is good for a flop and a feed. **1965–70** in *DARE:* Bought it on my face.

4. one's face as a symbol of meddling or interference; "nose."

1896 (quot. at IT). **1940** Chandler *Farewell* 9: Who the hell asked you to stick your face in? **1946** Miller & Bruce *Two Years Before Mast* (film): Keep your face outa this. **1950** Calmer *Strange Land* 231: Pull in your face, Boyce. Nobody wants to go to school just to go to school.

5.a. (in U.S. esp. *Black E.*) fellow.—used in direct address.

*****1890–91** *F & H* II 363: *Face*...(common).—A qualification of contempt: e.g., "Now face! where are you a-shoving of?" *****1923** P.G. Wodehouse, in *OEDS:* I ran into young Bingo Little..."Hello, face," I said. "Cheerio, ugly," said young Bingo. **1938** in *OEDS:* Come on, face—don't get mopey. **1946** Mezzrow & Wolfe *Really Blues* (glossary): *Face:* a form of greeting. **1948** Manone & Vandervoort *Trumpet* 172: Do you collar, Face? **1981** Safire *Good Word* 80: Hey, Face, what's goin' down?

b. *Black E.* a person; fellow, esp. if white.

1944 Burley *Hndbk. Jive* 138: *Face*—white person. **1945** L. Shelly *Jive Talk* 11: *Face*—a white man. **1955** in R.S. Gold *Jazz Talk* 86: "Real cool tonight!" said one face. **1959–60** Reisner *Jazz Titans* 155: *Face:* person, man. **1961** *N.Y. Times Mag.* (June 25) 39: *Bad face*...a surly, mean, no-good cat. **1969** in R.S. Gold *Jazz Talk* 86: He's a West Coast face. **1974** Piñero *Short Eyes* 79: This fucking face [and] a white woman. **1978** Kopp *Innocence* 107: Saturday night I was partying with some bad faces over in the East Bronx.

6. (see 1986 quot.). Now *colloq.*

*****1946** in *OEDS.* **1986** Ciardi *Good Words* 111: The cosmetic kit is a standard article of ladies' luggage, and it is now common for an American woman to refer to her kit as "my face."

7. fellatio or cunnilingus.—usu. constr. with *give* or *get.* Cf. earlier FACE ARTIST.

1968 *Trans-action* VI (Dec.) 16: "You'll have to give up some face."..."We're gonna make a girl out of you." **1970** N.Y.U. student: I bet she gives good face. **1970** in Brownmiller *Against Our Will* 266: You'll have to give up some face. **1976** *Nat. Lampoon Book of Funnies* 8: Who gets chicks to give them face? **1981** *Easyriders* (Oct.) 83: [T-shirt:] I'm His Because He Gives Good Face. **1985** *Nat. Lampoon* (Sept.) 39: Duvall gives face. *Ibid.* 40: I go for givin' face.

8. *Stu.* an instance of successfully humbling or embarrassing someone. [Corresponds to FACE, *v.*]

1979 *S.F. Examiner & Chronicle* (Apr. 1) 1: We booked on past the Impala, and it was a total face. **1989** P. Munro *U.C.L.A. Slang* 37: *Face* insult, burn/What a face!

¶ In phrases:

¶ **catch** [or **throw on**] **a face** to get intoxicated on alcohol or drugs.

1974 N.Y.C. barmaid, age 22: Last year people were saying, "Let's throw on a face" for get drunk. It means "Let's get shitfaced." **1974** Syracuse Univ. student: At school they say, "You want to catch a face?" for "You want to get high?" When you smoke it's called catching a face.

¶ **change** [or **break**] **(someone's) face** to beat and disfigure (someone's) face.

1896 Ade *Artie* 32: If you come into the same part o' town with me I'll change your face. **1910** in McCay *Little Nemo* 242: I'm going to break that fellow's face when I get out. **1948** I. Shulman *Cry Tough!* 15: I'd like a...chance to change your face. **1983** Eilert *Self & Country* 152: I'll come over there and break your face. **1987** Bombeck *Family* 52: You leave this table...and I'll break your face.

¶ **eat face** see s.v. EAT, *v.*

¶ **feed (one's) face** to eat greedily. Also vars.

1894 *Yale Wit & Humor* 66. **1895** J.L. Williams *Princeton* 39: In freshman year they say, "Are you ready to feed your face?" instead of "Are you going to dinner?" **1895** *Harper's Mo.* (Apr.) 786: Say, Tilly, what kind er cream is dat you're feedin' your face wid? **1895** Townsend *Fadden* 179: Before I was tru feeding me face Mr. Paul had done de handshake wid every mug in de drum. **1897** Siler & Houseman *Fight of the Century* 27: He is to cook the toothsome and muscle-building dishes Fitz is to "feed his face with." **1905** *Howitzer* (U.S.M.A.) VI 294: Post

Spoonoid. One who attends five o'clocks for the purpose of feeding his face. **1916** Thompson *Round Levee* 44: Beans means dinner, and the bean bell, or bean time, is the time to feed your face. *ca***1920** *Hobo Songs* (unp.): No chance for a bo to feed his face. **1927** H. Miller *Moloch* 151: I wanta feed my face. **1936** Reddan *Other Men's Lives* 236: Everybody was busy, if I am permitted to quote slang, "filling his face." **1971** N.Y.U. student: Will you stop feeding your face long enough to answer a question? **1986** N.Y.C. woman, age 52: Let's go stuff our faces.

¶ **get out of (one's) face** Esp. *Black E.* to leave alone; stop bothering or pestering.

1928 in P. Oliver *Songsters & Saints* 33: Take those scroungers out of my face. **1931** in *DARE:* Git out o' my face, or I'll slap ye into the middle of next week! **1942** Z.N. Hurston, in *Amer. Mercury* (July) 87: Git out of my face, Jelly! **1946** Mezzrow & Wolfe *Really Blues* 14: Jim Crow just wouldn't get out of my face. **1952** Ellson *Golden Spike* 41: Get out of my face before I stretch you! **1954** Killens *Youngblood* 33: Man, get outa my face. **1954** McGraw *Prison Riots* 268: Get out of my face! "Go away!" **1957** E. Lacy *Room to Swing* 8: Get out of my face! **1964** in A. Chapman *New Black Voices* 70: You git outa my face. **1970** Baraka *Jello* 17: Get outta my face! **1972** Wambaugh *Blue Knight* 64: Why don't you go back over to your beat, and get outta my face? **1973** Childress *Hero* 71: Get outta my face! **1973** Wideman *Lynchers* 39: Get out my face with that…shit. **1985** Univ. Tenn. instructor, age *ca*30: She better get off my case and out of my face!

¶ **in** [or **on**] **(one's) face** Orig. *Black E.* annoying or pestering (one).

[**1930** in P. Oliver *Songsters & Saints* 121: The rabbit and the terrapin had a race,/The terrapin put it in the rabbit's face.] **1953** W. Fisher *Waiters* 125: Not for nothing…was Asher forever "in the Kingfish's face." **1963** Braly *Shake Him* 11: But…he made the mistake of getting in their faces, rubbing it in their chests about how they couldn't get anything on him. **1970** Eisen *Altamont* 128: But if…he's gonna get on my face I'm gonna hurt him. *ca***1974** in J.L. Gwaltney *Drylongso* 20: The Italians and Irish are always up in my face talking about the Jew. **1989** G. Trudeau *Doonesbury* (synd. cartoon strip) (Sept. 12): "You're the one who asked Zonker to live with us, Mike." "Well, I blew it, okay? The guy's really starting to get in my face." **1993** *Newsweek* (June 21) 54: Lesbians suddenly seem to be out of the closet and in your face.

¶ **in your face!** Orig. *Basketball.* (used as a phrase of contempt or derision); (*hence,* as adj. phr. **in-your-face**) confrontational; defiant; provocative.

1976 Rosen *Above Rim* 140: In yo' face, Doobie! **1978** *Washington Post* (June 8) A1: A dozen people…leaped to their feet and yelled in unison, "In your face!" **1978** B. Johnson *What's Happenin'* 141: In your face, mother-fucker. It ain't who wins. It's whose move is the coolest. **1980** Wielgus & Wolff *Basketball* 46: *In your face* (prep) The taunt uttered after the execution of a *face job.* You're entitled to say this after scoring a shot despite tight defense, or after returning a shot in an opponent's face. Syn. *in your eye, in your mug.* **1982** Considine *Lang. Sport* 69: [Basketball terms] *In-your-face:* Aggressively challenging, disrespectful, or disdainful. **1988** *Newsweek on Campus* (Apr.) 20: And once fans witness the Longhorns' "in your face" style, they come back for more. **1988** *Comments on Ety.* XVII (No. 11-12) 5: Just listen as the basketball is slam-dunked: "In yo' face!" **1990** *Cosmopolitan* (Nov.): The drugs had preyed upon his natural predisposition to shyness, leading him to cultivate a facade of in-your-face arrogance. **1991** *N.Y. Times* (July 21) H 5: Wondering aloud if the frenetic "in-your-face" approach might have turned people off. **1992** *Time* (May 4) 69: Artists whose speech, dress and demeanor reflect the in-your-face bravado of black urban adolescents. **1993** *Court TV* (Nov. 15): In your face! I will not apologize.

¶ **out of (one's) face** out of (one's) right mind, esp. as a result of drug or alcohol intoxication. See also *get out of (one's) face,* above.

1972 Grogan *Ringolevio* 46: Both of them were goofballed out of their faces and were hardly able to see straight. **1973** Mt. Vernon, N.Y., telephone technician: Man, I was stoned out of my face.

¶ **put a face on** *Boxing.* to batter and injure the face of.

1971 in P. Heller *In This Corner* 223 [ref. to 1930's]: He put an awful face on me, busted me all up with everything.

¶ **run (one's) face** to get credit on the strength of (one's) appearance or impudence.

1839 *Spirit of Times* (Oct. 5) 368: The Picayune says there is a chap in New Orleans who has "run his face so often for drinks, that it is completely worn off." **1845** Hooper *Simon Suggs* 63: It was, therefore, time to "run his face." **1848** Bartlett *Amer.* 281: Any one who can run his face for a card of pens [etc.]…may set up for an editor. **1856** in Dwyer

& Lingenfelter *Songs of Gold Rush* 120: A for a glass of "whiskey straight"/He tries to "run his face." **1862** Gilbert *Confed. Letters* 19: It has injured the credit of the regiment by going on "tick" wherever it could run its "face." **1862** J.R. Lowell, in *OED:* Men that can run their face for drinks. **1865** in *F & H* II 363: *To run one's face,* to make use of one's credit; *to run one's face* for a thing is to get it "on tick." **1870** W.W. Fowler *Wall St.* 237: I…"ran my face" for a dinner that day. **1871** Schele de Vere *Americanisms* 325: In the same manner people *run a bank,* a store, and anything they undertake—even their own *face,* when they obtain credit solely on account of their respectable appearance. **1882** Baillie-Rohman *Rockies* 2: As ragged, unkempt, and disreputable-looking a being as ever "ran his face" among a civilized community, and got "policed" as a cut-throat. **1905** *DN* III 17: *Run one's face, v. phr.* To make use of one's credit. **1942** McAtee *Dial. Grant Co.* 53 [ref. to 1890's]: *Run one's face*…use one's credit, buy on tick. **1965–70** in *DARE.*

¶ **shoot off (one's) face** to speak offensively or out of turn; shoot (one's) mouth off.

1894 in S. Crane *Complete Stories* 206: Say, young feller, if yeh go shootin' off yer face at me, I'll wipe d' joint wid yeh. **1906** M'Govern *Sarjint Larry* 131: It's a swift, sweet pain in me gizzard Oi'm afther gettin' every toime Oi comes to Manily an' hears Americans shootin' off deir faces about wot's to become of de Philipeens and de Filipeeners. **1928** Rice *Street Scene* 576: He's shootin' off his face again. **1939–40** O'Hara *Pal Joey* 22: You shoot off your face about I wrote you and told you to look her up. **1943** Daves & Maltz *Destination Tokyo* (film): You're always shootin' off your face about women. **1948** Cozzen *Guard* 342: And one or two of them were shooting their faces off—saying they came from hot outfits that had overseas orders.

¶ **suck face** *Stu.* to kiss or exchange kisses in a passionate manner.

1980 L. Birnbach *Preppy Hndbk.* 222: Suck face v.…Get to first base. **1982** *Nat. Lampoon* (Sept.) 59: Smooching, Snuggling, Spooning, Sucking Face. **1983** Eble *Campus Slang* (Spring) 5: *Suck face*—kiss. **1988** Univ. Tenn. student theme: Kissing has…become "sucking face." **1989** *Roseanne* (ABC-TV): Becky spent the whole night sucking face with some guy.

face *v.* to humble; embarrass; humiliate. Cf. FACE JOB; *in your face!* s.v. FACE, *n.*

1979 *S.F. Examiner & Chronicle* (Apr. 1) 12: As for "face!" and "faced," the expression came west from the playgrounds of New York City…."In your face!" **1981** in Safire *Good Word* 83: You sure "faced" her "old man." **1984** Mason & Rheingold *Slanguage* (unp.): *(To) face…*To embarrass or humiliate someone. Also to be beaten miserably in any competition. **1987** Eble *Campus Slang* (Spring) 3: She faced Bill by going to the dance with Steve. **1988** *Comments on Ety.* XVII (No. 11-12) 4: "When you cut left, you really faced that dude." "The teacher thought I didn't know the answer. I faced her."…What does "face" mean? "Uh, it's like, well, like to show up somebody." **1990** *Mystery Sci. Theater* (Comedy Central TV): We really faced him! What a maroon!

¶ In phrase:

¶ **face the music** see s.v. MUSIC, *n.*

face *interj.* [fr. *in your face!* s.v. FACE, *n.;* cf. FACE, *n.,* 8 and FACE, *v.*] *Stu.* (used to express satisfaction at humbling or outdoing someone). Cf. PSYCH, *interj.*

1979 (quot. at FACE, *v.*). **1989** P. Munro *U.C.L.A. Slang* 37: *Face!…* (exclamation used after an insult or burn). **1992** *Mystery Sci. Theater* (Comedy Central TV): Face! [in a ball game].

face artist *n. Prost. & Homosex.* a fellator.

1927 C. McKay *Home to Harlem* 148: "You lowest-down face-artist!" the girl shrieked at Yaller Prince. "I'll bawl it out so all a Harlem kain know what you is." **1928** in Panzram *Killer* 157: A fruiter…likes to "eat" it. A face artist is an exceptionally well-experienced fruiter. One who knows his bananas better than an amateur. **1933** Ford & Tyler *Young & Evil* 165: Do you have to go into a song and dance about a face artist? **1935** Pollock *Und. Speaks: Face artist,* a sexual pervert.

faced *adj.* [fr. SHITFACED] Esp. *Stu.* intoxicated.

1968 Baker et al. *CUSS* 113: *Faced.* Drunk. **1968–70** *Current Slang* III & IV 44: *Faced,* adj. Intoxicated (from *shit faced*).—College students, both sexes, New Hampshire. **1980** Birnbach et al. *Preppy Hndbk.* 108: Drunk…*Blasted. Bombed. Faced.* **1980** Eble *Campus Slang* (Oct.) 3: *Faced*—Very drunk (clipped from *shit-faced*): "George got faced Thursday night." **1981** Univ. Tenn. student: I was *faced* last night! **1981–85** S. King *It* 29: I know that's a bad sign but I was pretty 'faced, you know? **1988** Univ. Tenn. student theme: A common word for drunk is *faced.*

1988 M. Maloney *Thunder Alley* 27: *I'm* going out and get 'faced. **1991** *Get a Life* (Fox-TV): I got sort of faced last night.

face job *n.* [sugg. by taunt *in your face!* s.v. FACE, *n.*] *Basketball.* a play or game which humiliates the opposition; a one-sided victory.

1980 Wielgus & Wolff *Basketball* 43: Face job (*n*) A [*sic*] individual offensive or defensive move so captivating that it wins, for one player for one moment, the kharma of *face.* Syn. *facial.* **1981** in Safire *Good Word* 83: First you "burn" someone with a nice move; then swish; then you say "face job." **1984** *N.Y. Post* (Aug. 3) 85: It was a typical U.S. face-job. The Americans led…40–20 [at half-time].…Asked if the lopsided victories were becoming boring, forward Janice Laurence…said, "No, we enjoy basketball." **1984** Eble *Campus Slang* (Sept.) 3: *Face job*—in basketball, a jump shot when guarded closely by an opponent. Sam Perkins gave Ralph Sampson a face job.

face lace *n.* a beard. *Joc.*

1927 *DN* V 445: *Face lace*, n. Whiskers. *a*1984 Safire *Stand Corrected* 200: "Face lace"…was never more desirable than in the 1960s.

faceless *adj. Stu.* FACED.

1985 Univ. Tenn. student theme: The student may "catch a buzz" [or]…reach the state of "being faceless."

face man *n.* **1.** a person, usu. a man, who influences or beguiles others through his appearance or demeanor.

1958 in Reuss & Legman *Songs Mother Never Taught Me* (unp.): Face men of the world unite! **1963** *Ibid.*: Face Men (= smoothies). **1968** Baker et al. *CUSS* 113: Face man.…A socially adept person. **1974** Terkel *Working* 66: [Woman speaking:] The clients figured that I'm just a face-man. A face-man is a person who looks good, speaks well, and presents the work. **1980** Wielgus & Wolff *Basketball* 68: But for most of us, being a "face man" before a game begins is the best way to get a chance to be an in-your-face man once it starts…The key is being street-smart and making a good impression. **1984** Eble *Campus Slang* (Mar.) 3: *Faceman*—goodlooking male with an exceptionally handsome face: There's really nothing to Keith—he's just a faceman. **1984** Heath *A-Team* 26: They call him the Face Man, in case you hadn't guessed.…A con man, a real operator. **1987** E. White *Beautiful Room* 66: This strangely objective term they'd invented, "face man."

2. (see quot.).

1970 Winick & Kinsie *Lively Commerce* 207: Increasingly, and especially in the last decade, prostitutes and madams report substantially more customers who are seeking oral satisfaction ("muff diver" or "face man").

face out *v.* to overcome (someone) with coolness, effrontery, or impudence; face down. Orig. *S.E.*

*1533 T. More, in *OED*: He…scoffeth that I face out the trouth with lies. *1580 in *OED*: And so faced out thy poore Father before our face. **1821** Martin & Waldo *Lightfoot* 11: He…actually sent for a sheriff to arrest me; but I insisted so much upon my innocence, and *faced him out* so well, that he said no more about the subject.

face prop *n.* a tooth. *Joc.*

1920 in C.M. Russell *Paper Talk* 177: That tooth hunter tore my face props out.

face queen *n. Homosex.* (see quot.).

1972 *Anthro. Linguistics* (Mar.) 101: Face Queen. (n): A male homosexual who is extremely attracted to the face.

facer *n.* **1.** *Boxing.* a usu. direct blow to the face. [Farmer & Henley erroneously attribute a 1785 date to the present 1811 quot.]

*1810 in *OED*: Each of the pugilists exchanged…half a dozen facers. *1811 *Lexicon Balatron.*: *Facer*…a violent blow on the face. *1819 T. Moore *Tom Crib* 24: In short, not to dwell on each *facer* and fall,/Poor Georgy was done up in no time at all. **1823** J.F. Cooper *Pioneers* 366: Howsomnever, they didn't come to facers, only passed a little jaw fore and aft. *1834 Ainsworth *Rookwood* 258: No *facers* sound—no smashing blows—/Five minutes pass, yet not a *hit*. **1837** Neal *Charcoal Sketches* 41-42: Rocky Smalt is a very little man…If he "squares off" at a big fellow, he is obliged, in dealing a facer, to hit his antagonist on the knee. **1865–67** De Forest *Miss Ravenel* 171: He would permit any man to give him a facer for a shilling a crack. **1893** W.K. Post *Harvard* 281: He fell in love with some girl and got a facer. *ca*1895 McCloskey *Across Continent* 89: Gets a facer from seltzer bottle, and retires. **1905** *Nat. Police Gaz.* (Dec. 30) 7: O'Brien forced Fitz to the ropes with a straight left facer. *a*1924 A. Hunter *Yr. on Monitor* 114: His blow simply swept my cap off instead of giving me the "facer" that he intended.

2. *Und.* (see quot.).

1859 Matsell *Vocab.* 30: *Facer*…a staller, or one who places himself in the way of persons who are in hot pursuit of his accomplices.

face-to-face *n.* a face-to-face meeting, esp. a frank private conversation between two persons.

1986 *Miami Vice* (NBC-TV): I need a face-to-face with you.

facial *n.* an instance of humiliation; FACE JOB.

1978 Eble *Campus Slang* (Apr.) 2: Ben got turned down by that girl again—what a facial! **1980** Wielgus & Wolff *Basketball* 25: Work on developing your game with an eye toward that moment when you'll pull a facial in a full-court affair.

fact *v. Black E.* to speak frankly and truthfully.

1942 *Amer. Mercury*, in *DARE*: *I'm cracking but I'm facking*—"I'm wise-cracking, but I'm telling the truth." **1957** Simmons *Corner Boy* 121: Yeh, I'm cracking, and I'm facting. **1974** Lacy *Native Daughter* 8: Factin' is factin'.

fade *n.* **1.** a worthless fellow.

*ca*1893 in Ware *Passing Eng.* 126: A young lady employed at one of the Exposition displays rather took the shine off of a fade the other day. The fade, recently a dude, walked up to the place where she was stationed, etc.

2. FADE-OUT, *n.*

1942 *ATS* 241: Flee; escape…*do a fade* or *fade-out.* **1952** Sandburg *Strangers* 170 [ref. to *ca*1890]: Do a fade now, do a fade, Bo. **1963** Hayden *Wanderer* 341: Then I'm doing a fast fade and you and Huston can get to know each other. **1972** Grogan *Ringolevio* 264: He also pulled the same kind of a fade back in the seventeenth century, leaving the historians puzzled as to what kind of a man he had been. **1972** Pendleton *Boston Blitz* 29: You understand the shape the Boston territory has been in since BoBo Binaca took the fade.

3. Esp. *Black E.* a hairstyle in which the sides of the head are close-cropped and the top hair is shaped into an upright block.

1989 *Village Voice* (N.Y.C.) (June 20) 39: The fade is the current common denominator.…At…Afrocentric barbershops the fade flattop became a sculpture. **1989** *Jet* (Nov. 13): U.S. Olympic champion sprinter Carl Lewis…popularized the fade haircut (cropped sides and a high top) during the 1984 Olympics. **1990** *New Yorker* (Sept. 17) 61: A slim, strikingly good-looking boy, he has his hair cut in a flashy high-low fade. **1991** *New York* (Oct. 21) 41: A drug-dealer's description comes over the radio: "Red-and-white jacket, dark pants, high-top fade." **1994** *Newsweek* (Jan. 10) 49: The…baggy jeans, sweat shirts and footgear that go with Marc's earrings and Shawn's modified fade.

fade *v.* **1.a.** to surpass, defeat, overcome, outdo, overshadow, etc.—usu. used in passive.

1894 in Ade *Chicago Stories* 32: He went up agin it and was faded; now he wants to beef. **1897** Ade *Pink Marsh* 135: Gawge Lippincott had me done easy—had me faded. **1899** Kountz *Baxter's Letters* 39: The opera had Thornton's faded for noise. **1903** A.H. Lewis *Boss* 119: We've got to break even with 'em, or they'll have us faded from th' jump. **1905** Hobart *Search Me* 19: This Skinski has them all faded to a whisper. **1908** *Atlantic* (Aug.) 227: The uproar [of angry baseball fans] "has feeding time at the zoo faded to a whisper." **1914** in J. London *Reports* 200: Jack, this ain't no Klondike. It's got Klondike faded to a fare you well. **1915** Howard *God's Man* 439: Help hold this rudder straight. It's got me faded. **1942** Chandler *High Window* 364: "Look out—gun." "I can fade that too," the carroty man said [reaching for his own gun]. **1973** J.E. Martin *95 File* 40: You're faded. That knife isn't going to stop a thirty-eight. **1991** Eble *Campus Slang* (Spring) 4: *Fade*—take advantage of.…"No girl is ever going to fade me."

b. *Gamb.* to bet against (another gambler, usu. the shooter in craps); (*also*) to match (another's wager) in full or in part.—usu. in passive. Now jargon.

1890 *DN* I 61: *To fade*…to bet against the player shooting. **1919** in De Beck *Google* 5: I say this town is full of pikers—I wanna bet a hundred to one that Willard won't last two rounds and nobody will fade me. **1923** *Chi. Daily Trib.* (Oct. 2) 24: Shoot rattle an' roll boy, yo' faded fo' one dollah. **1929–33** J.T. Farrell *Young Manhood* ch. xvii: Weary…faded ten of the fifteen. **1941** Wald, Macauley et al. *Navy Blues* (film): OK, you mugs. Fade that. **1947** Schulberg *Harder They Fall* 268: I was tempted to go in and fade that guy.

c. *Und.* (see quot.).

1929 *N.Y. Times* (Aug. 22) 25: "A cannon fades a mark." A gunman holds up a citizen.

d. *Gamb.* to deal with; put up with.

1962–68 in B. Jackson *In the Life* 289: But, he said, he just couldn't fade it (handle it), looking at that head. *a***1969** B. Jackson *Thief's Primer* 69: "If the Rangers get you, they're going to get a confession."..."I can fade 'em."..."You want to stay here and fade the beef." **1970** M. Thomas *Total Beast* 43: But then you got to fade them dogs. There's been one or two beat the shotgun mulligans and the highriders and everything, but the dogs get them.

2.a. to depart; run away.—also constr. with *away* or *out*.
1898–1900 Cullen *Chances* 109: Fade away—fade away...Do a disappearing stunt. **1900** Ade *More Fables* 101: The Bookie told him to Back Up and Fade and do a Disappearing Specialty. **1903** *Pedagog. Sem.* X 371: *Rebuke to Pride...Fade away.* **1906** Ford *Shorty McCabe* 175: Hully chee!...Here's where I ought to fade! **1911** A. H. Lewis *Apaches of N.Y.* 131: Fade's the woid! I'll meet youse over in Hoboken. **1912** *Pedagog. Sem.* (Mar.) 96: Get out...fade away...beat it while the beating is good...Go jump in the lake. **1915–16** Lait *Beef, Iron & Wine* 235: She wants to know are you gonna fade away to-morrow, 'cause there's another ham wants to move in here. **1919** Witwer *Alex the Great* 94: "Fade!" I warns him. **1921** Casey & Casey *Gay-Cat* 77: Thet was my cue. I faded. **1926** Nason *Chevrons* 215: Come on, we got orders to fade to hell away out of here. **1927** *Sat. Eve. Post* (Mar. 26) 11: Go on now, fade! **1927** Rollins *Jinglebob* 116 [ref. to 1880's]: Fade out o' here. Fade quick....Git to hell out o' here. **1929** Segar *Thimble Th.* 108: Now fade out. I want to talk to the professor. **1949** Rodgers & Hammerstein *South Pacific* 302: Fade. Here he comes. **1951** Sheldon *Troubling of a Star* 95: Well, in that case, Braith, I'll fade out. **1959** W. Miller *Cool World* 78: An I say to the guys, "All right. Fade. And stay off the streets." **1986** Stinson & Carabatsos *Heartbreak* 162: Fade, numb-nuts. **1988** Norst *Colors* 196: I faded, man.

b. to die.—constr. with *out*.
[**1911** H.S. Harrison *Queed* 86: You're fadin' out fast for the need of [exercise].] **1942** *ATS* 132: Die...*fade out.* **1942** Davis & Wolsey *Call House Madam* 120: You'll fade out if your tired heart don't get something to fasten on.

3. to make unhappy.
1915 H.L. Wilson *Ruggles* 99: Ain't that right? Don't it fade you?

fadeaway *n.* a departure or escape.
1900 in F. Remington *Sel. Letters* 296: That's my sad fade-away now. **1911** H.S. Harrison *Queed* 56: She had only pretended to die in order to make a fade-away with the gate receipts. **1919** Stringer *House of Intrigue* 29: Bud...would hop the fence for a fade-away. **1926** *Marine Corps Gazette* (Dec.) 241: Jim, b'lieve me I did a fade-away. **1934** Wohlforth *Tin Soldiers* 113: The son of a bitch did a fadeaway. **1965** C. Brown *Manchild* 176: The cat pulled a fadeaway. *a***1968** in D. McKay *Wild Wheels* 170: You have to do a fadeaway from ye old abode.

fade-out *n.* **1.** a disappearance, departure, or escape.—usu. constr. with *do* or *pull*.
1918 in Gelman *Photoplay* 11: Sergeant Shields beginning a "fade out" in his mosquito proof apartment. **1924** in Galewitz *Great Comics* 138: I'll give you hoodlums just two seconds to do a fade-out. **1926** Tully *Jarnegan* 249: That little broad thought I'd go kerfluey when she took the fade-out with the kid. **1932** in Fortune *Fugitives* 84: So I "staged" a "big fade out" beside him/And knocked the forty-five out of his hand. **1933** Ersine *Prison Slang* 35: The boys all did a fadeout. **1946** Mezzrow & Wolfe *Really Blues* 59: We would have made Miss Peacock pull a fade-out. **1962** Tregaskis *Viet. Diary* 128: They're pretty good at the fast fade-out. **1965** Donlon *Outpost* 102: Soon he would do a fade-out.
2. Esp. *Film.* the point of finish; end; death; CURTAINS.
1926 Tully *Jarnegan* 224: It's the kind of thing that leaks if you don't stop it. It'll be your fade-out. **1927** in Gelman *Photoplay* 114: The producers' only hope is an untiring search for talent that can constantly be brought forward in the place of those who have reached the fade-out. *****1930** in *OEDS*: Personally I don't want a sticky fade-out yet. **1951** G. Fowler *Schnozzola* 131: Madden...had been made a scapegoat for Little Patsy's fadeout.

fag[1] *n.* [Brit. colloq. *fag* 'to work hard; labor'] **1.** *Stu.* a lower-classman, typically a freshman, who is compelled to perform various duties for an upperclassman. Now *S.E.* [The practice—hence the word—died out in American colleges early in the nineteenth century, and the term is now understood solely as a Briticism.]
*****1785** in *OED*: I had the character at school of being the very best *fag* that ever came into it. *****1785** Grose *Vulgar Tongue*: A fag also means a boy of an inferior form or class, who acts as a servant to one of a superior, who is said to fag him. **1836** *Harvardiana* II 106: They are *fags*,—Freshmen, poor fellows, called out of their beds...to wait upon their

lords the Sophomores in their midnight revellings. **1856** B. Hall *College Wds.* (ed. 2) 188: *Fag.* A laborious drudge; a drudge for another. In colleges and schools, this term is applied to a boy of a lower form who is forced to do menial services for another boy of a higher form or class. *****1857** in *F & H* II 366: Is still enumerated among the feats of the brave days of old, by the *fags* over their evening small beer.
2.a. a drudge; an errand boy or clerk.
*****1813** in *OEDS*: Mr. Macintosh...a good fag. *****a***1839** in *OED*: William Tag, Thalia's most industrious fag. *****1855** W.M. Thackeray, in *F & H* II 366: Bob Trotter, the diminutive *fag* of the studio, who ran all the young men's errands. **1856** (quot. at **(1)**, above). **1859** Matsell *Vocab.* 30: *Fag.* A lawyer's clerk.
b. *Stu.* an overdiligent student.
1856 B. Hall *College Wds.* (ed. 2) 188: *Fag*...A diligent student, i.e. a dig.

fag[2] *n.* [fr. Brit. colloq. *fag* 'that which causes weariness; hard work, toil'] ¶ In phrase: **stand [(someone)] a fag** to put up a good fight against (someone); compete on equal terms.
[*****1785** Grose *Vulgar Tongue: To stand a good fag*; not to be soon tired.] **1801** in *DAE*: In boxing, no Yankee can stand me a fag. **1825** in *DAE*: I'll stan' him a pooty good fag, myself. **1832** S. Smith *Maj. Downing* 80: If I should lose my feet, I shouldn't stand much of a fag with the British down there. **1840** D.P. Thompson *Green Mt. Boys* 139: They...will stand no fag at all with a regular York army.

fag[3] *n.* [prob. fr. *fag-end*; cf. sim. sense development of syn. BUTT] a cigarette. Now *rare* in U.S. and generally regarded as a Briticism.
*****1888** in *EDD*: They...burn their throats with the abominable "fag," with its acrid paper and vile tobacco. *****1893** in *OEDS*: Stimulants he calls "booze" and a cigarette a "fag." *****1898** in *EDD*: Here we are often asked by youngsters to "chuck" them "a fag"—and whole cheap cigarettes are also often called fags. *****1911** O'Brien & Stephens *Australian Sl.* 63: *Fag*: a cigarette. **1919** *Lit. Digest* (Mar. 15) 50: A square in Seville...a fag factory on the right. **1936** Duncan *Over the Wall* 150: I squatted down on a wet boulder to light a fag and rest. **1939** Stegner *Darkling* 62: Fag? **1958** J.B. West *Eye* 15: I reached in my pocket for a fag. **1961** Sullivan *Gladdest Years* 251: She was lighting one fag from another. **1973** N.Y.U. student: I was looking for a fag. **1981–89** J. Goodwin *More Man* 14: [Among homosexual men] *fag* can mean "cigarette." **1994** B. Ehrenreich, in *Nation* (Jan. 31) 114: As for smoking: You might as well snatch an infant from its carriage and publicly strangle it as reach into your maternity smock and pull out a fag.

fag[4] *n.* [short for FAGGOT, *n.*] **1.** a male homosexual; (*also*) an effeminate fellow.—usu. used derisively.
1921 Lind *Impersonators* 89: Androgynes [are] known as "fairies", "fags", or "brownies". **1921** in J. Katz *Gay/Lesbian Almanac* 401: Does the "fairy" or "fag" really exist?...There is no doubt but that this type of degenerate is a reality. **1922** N. Anderson *Hobo* 103: Fairies or Fags are men or boys who exploit sex for profit. **1927** [Fliesler] *Anecdota* 122: A fag was complaining to his friend. **1932** *AS* VII (June) 331: *Fag*—an effeminate man; a pervert. **1933** N. West *Miss Lonelyhearts* 87: The old fag is going to cry. **1934** Fishman *Sex in Prison* 59: They are of the passive type known variously as "punks," "girls," "fags," "pansies," or "fairies." **1934** Appel *Brain Guy* 131: Three fags sat discreetly in an ambush of palm trees. **1935** Algren *Boots* 97: He was half an inch taller than this fag, and *twice* as tough. **1937** Weidman *Wholesale* 185: Here I was in the dress business only a couple of months and already I was beginning to talk like Phil the Fag. **1941** Schulberg *Sammy* 70: He had the body of a wrestler and the face of a fag. **1948** J.H. Burns *Lucifer* 146: Shakespeare was a fag, for Chrisake. **1950** Spillane *Vengeance* 56: It used to be a fag joint. **1952** J.C. Holmes *Go* 239: So you're a big fag, eh? So you like little boys, eh? **1960** Wohl *Cold Wind* 28: The long eyelashes. God! He almost looked like a fag. **1967** Wolf *Love Generation* 126: I don't want to be another fag sucking the economic cock of the country. **1968** Radano *Walking the Beat* 31: "Know what they call a Jewish fag? A He-Blew." "Know what they call an *Irish* fag? A Gay-Lick." **1975** UCLA *Daily Bruin* (Jan. 8) 11: Ever get labeled a fag simply because you chose not to hide your emotions? **1992** *Newsweek* (Nov. 23) 32: At the gay and lesbian community center...the caller ranted about "fags." *Ibid.* I'm not a fag...I'm a dyke.
2. *Juve. & Stu.* an offensive person.
1963 *N.Y. Times Mag.* (Nov. 24) 50: "Fag" is another favorite grammar-school term of opprobrium but again the youngsters seem quite unconcerned about usual definitions. **1979** W. Cross *Kids & Booze* 88: Abstainers [from alcohol] are often referred to with scorn by upper classmen as "squares"...[and] "fags." **1983** *N.Y. Daily News* (Mar. 25): Teentalk glossary...*fag*—someone who behaves offensively. **1984**

Univ. Tenn. student: "You fag!"—when anybody cuts me down I call them that. **1987** Univ. Tenn. student theme: In high school we used to call people we didn't like *fags*. It is only since I am in college that I have learned that this word means homosexual. **1988** Univ. Tenn. student theme: If a guy is really gross and thinks he is God's gift to women, we [girls] usually say "what a fag!" and leave him to drown in his ego. **1989** *Life* (July) 29: "Fag" is used as an all-purpose disparagement.

fag¹ *v.* [general Brit. colloq. *fag* 'to toil; labor'] **1.** *Stu.* to toil diligently at one's studies.

*1795 *Gentleman's Mag.* LXXVII 20: How did ye toil and *fagg*, and fume, and fret. *1795 in *OEDS:* He is the most fagging student I ever knew and this to the exclusion of all other enjoyments. *1803 *Gradus ad Cantab.* 8: A helpless undergraduate still,/To *fag* at mathematics dire. *Ibid.* 48: Dee, the famous mathematician, appears to have *fagged* as intensely as any man at Cambridge. **1856** B. Hall *College Wds.* (ed. 2) 187: *Fag*...To study hard; to persevere in study.

2. *Stu.* to be a FAG¹, *n. Obs.* in U.S.

*1806 in *OED:* Fagging for a niggardly glutton. **1840** in *DAE:* The system of "fagging" (as it was called) was just then dying out [at Harvard], and I believe that my own class was the first that was not compelled to perform this drudgery at the command of the Senior class in the most humble services. **1856** B. Hall *College Wds.* (ed. 2) 189: *Fagging*. Laborious drudgery; the acting as a drudge for another at a college or school. *1884 in *F & H* II 366: He refused to fag.

fag² *v.* [fr. FAG³, *n.*] **1.** to supply with a cigarette. Cf. BUTT, *v.*, 1.

1926 Maines & Grant *Wise-Crack Dict.* 8: *Fag me*—Give me a cigarette. **1954** Faulkner *Fable* 324 [ref. to WWI]: "Fag me again." The corporal gave him another cigarette.

2. to smoke a cigarette.

1940 *AS* XV 335: To smoke is...*to fag*.

fag³ *v.* [fr. FAG⁴, *n.*] to behave in a manner reminiscent of a homosexual; (*trans.*) to subject to homosexual copulation or make a homosexual of.—used derisively.

1968 Duay *Fruit Salad* 122: All their free time is spent *faggin'* around...Who cares if he's *faggin'* the boys? **1968** Cuomo *Thieves* 216: It was to your benefit that someone like Penney tried to fag you early, as long as you could cut him down.

fag-bagging *n.* robbing or extorting money from homosexuals.

1977 Sayles *Union Dues* 290: There's a couple dudes around making a living from fag-bagging but you don't last long. The word gets around and the fruits protect their own.

fag-bait *n.* an effeminate boy or man.—used derisively.

1974 Lahr *Trot* 17: He wears no underwear under those hip huggers. Bum-boy. Fag-bait. **1987** *Nat. Lampoon* (Dec.) 26: Is there anyone who doesn't think Ralph...is fag bait?

fag-bashing see S.V. BASH.

faggot *n.* **1.a.** a shrewish, bad-tempered, or offensive woman; BATTLEAXE.—used as a general term of abuse.

*1591 in *OED:* A filbert is better than a faggot, except it be an Athenian she handfull. *1820 in *F & H* II 367: I have got a faggot here,/ Aye, and quite a bad one;/Were I married, p'rhaps my dear/Might think that *he* too had one. *1833 Marryat *Peter Simple* 30: "So, Master Simple, old Trotter and his faggot of a wife have got hold of you—have they?" I replied, that I did not know the meaning of faggot, but that I considered Mrs. Trotter a very charming woman. At which he burst into a loud laugh... *1840 in *OED:* What's that you say, old faggot? **1840** *New-Yorker* (Mar. 21) 8: "So—you infernal faggot. I'll down with you if you don't let me pass." "She's dying, you brute, she is," returned the woman. *1843 in *SND:* A band of horrible women,—real Glasgow faggots,—incorrigible devils were sent to Botany in a batch. *1862 in *OED:* She...struck at me, she did, that good-for-nothing faggot! **1889** *Century Dict.: Faggot*...Applied, as a term of abuse, to a woman. *1890 in *SND:* I kent fine 'at the auld faggot was carryin' on wi' that kind o' tamfoolery. *1914–22 J. Joyce *Ulysses* 723: That old faggot Mrs. Riordan.

b. (a term of reproof or abuse directed at a child).

*1873 Hotten *Slang Dict.* (ed. 4): *Faggot*, a term of opprobrium used by low people to children and women; "you little *faggot*, you!" *1876–81 in *EDD:* You little *faggot*, you. *1892 in *OEDS: Faggot*, a term of reproach used to children. **1920–22** in *DN* V 330: *Faggot*...A naughty child;—in mild reproof.

2.a. a male homosexual; (*also*) an effeminate, weak, or cowardly fellow.—usu. used contemptuously.

1914 Jackson & Hellyer *Vocab.* 30: All the fagots (sissies) will be dressed in drag at the ball tonight. **1926** Hemingway *Sun Also Rises* 116: You're a hell of a good guy, and I'm fonder of you than anybody on earth. I couldn't tell you that in New York. It'd mean I was a faggot. That was what the Civil War was about. Abraham Lincoln was a faggot. He was in love with General Grant. **1926** Wood & Goddard *Amer. Slang* 16: *Fagot*. A chorus man; an effeminate man. **1927** McIntyre *Slag* 10: The dirty fagots! What-a they know? **1932** V. Nelson *Pris. Days & Nights* 29: He hands you a set of rules that not even a Y.M.C.A. faggot could live up to. **1933** Ford & Tyler *Young & Evil* 46: They saw me and called out hey faggot! as they passed. **1936** Dos Passos *Big Money* 244: The first thing Margo thought was how on earth she could ever have liked that fagot. **1949** Ellson *Tomboy* 50: I got an old faggot spotted. **1952** in Russ *Last Parallel* 17: Sallie's three dogs are all faggots. **1953** in Wepman et al. *The Life* 117: He was the dude who wasn't afraid to die,/But we all heard that big faggot cry. **1954** Yablonsky *Gang* 64: You guys are nothing but a bunch of mother-fuckin' faggots; I think we ought to beat your heads in, have it out right here and now, once and for all. **1956** P. Moore *Chocolates* 9: It would be an awful mess to be a faggot. **1956** M. Wolff *Big Nick*. 154: I've been gay all my life, but I always felt clean and decent. You make me feel like a faggot. **1959** A. King *Mine Enemy* 221: I was quite sure that any friend of his was bound to be a leaping faggot. **1965** C. Brown *Manchild* 146: I met some faggots who were pretty nice guys. **1966–67** P. Thomas *Mean Streets* 120: Enough for you and them two faggots you got with you. **1968** L.J. Davis *Whence All Had Fled* 142: It wasn't fair for a faggot to have more money than an artist. **1969** Hannerz *Soulside* 136: "Faggot" is in frequent use as a term of abuse among [black] men. **1970** in J. Flaherty *Chez Joey* 18: So the word most frequently heard during the demonstrations (except U.S.A.) was faggot—[Mayor] Lindsay was one, the [war] protestors...were all faggots, [etc.]. **1972** Wurlitzer *Quake* 104: You spicks get undressed and line up with the rest of them faggots. **1972** Bunker *No Beast* 40: The bar was swarming with flaming faggots. **1978** *N.Y. Times Mag.* (Mar. 12) 16: A heterosexual freshman at Stanford complained that he always had been called "faggot"...because he liked to dress well and to iron his shirts. *a1984 in Terry *Bloods* 41: You cryin' because you a big faggot, and you gettin' ready to die. **1987** *Sonya Live in L.A.* (CNN-TV) (July 2): "Now, you have described yourself as 'a human being in a gay body'..." "What I actually said was, '...in a *faggot*'s body.'" **1993** *N.Y. Times* (Dec. 8) A 18: They spit on me and threw things at me and called me faggot, homo.

b. a homosexual of either sex.—usu. used contemptuously.

*ca1953 Hughes *Lodge* 121: The newspapers described..."two young attractive office workers." One, a faggot, a chick dressed like a man, and one old bum in seaman's clothes! *Ibid.* 183: These chicks...were homos and faggots.

c. a very unattractive young woman. Cf. (**1.a.**), above.

1968–70 *Current Slang* III & IV 44: *Faggot*, *n*. An unattractive girl.—College males, South Dakota. **1985** *Maledicta* VIII 281: Bruce Rodgers recently heard teens use *faggot* for "ugly girl."

3. a cigarette; FAG³.

1929 Tully *Shadows* 201: I tried to light a faggot—then I watched the match burn up. **1933** Ersine *Pris. Slang* 35: *Faggot*, *n*. A cigarette.

faggot moll *n.* FAG MOLL. Also **faggot's moll**.

1969 in *DAS* (ed. 3): I'd hazard a guess that you're simply a Faggot's Moll, Fag Hag, or Fruit Fly. **1971** N.Y.U. student: A *faggot moll* is some girl who likes hanging around gay guys and gay bars.

faggotry *n.* male homosexual practices; homosexuality.—usu. considered offensive.

1970 *Harper's* (Feb.) 64: A wave of faggotry was upsetting the balance. **1973** *Esquire* (Nov.) 42: To a Midwestern boy faggotry was at the very least a terrible embarrassment. *a1990 Westcott *Half a Klick* 30: Drugs and faggotry.

faggoty *adj.* effeminate; homosexual.—used derisively.

1927 C. McKay *Harlem* 20: And there is two things in Harlem I don't understan'/It is a bulldyking woman and a faggoty man. **1930** Graham & Graham *Queer People* 116: I caught that faggoty ham, Bill Holmes, passing a fly crack about "Mr. Bagshaw" one day. **1955** Graziano & Barber *Somebody Up There* 51: Not being yellow or faggoty. **1966** K. Hunter *Landlord* 173: Them faggoty City Hall men been all over this block for months. **1972** Pfister *Beer Cans* 5: Cryin' their faggoty hearts out. **1977** B. Davidson *Collura* 31: Acting is a faggoty thing to do. **1982–84** Chapple *Outlaws in Babylon* 170: That faggoty guy.

faggy *adj.* effeminate; homosexual.—used derisively.

1951 J.D. Salinger, in *DARE:* You could hear them [*sc.* football fans] all yelling, deep and terrific on the Pencey side,...and scrawny and faggy on the Saxon Hall side. **1952** Brossard *Darkness* 4: He…said they were overmannered and inclined to be faggy. **1963** Cameron *Black Camp* 14: A faggy English accent. **1972** R. Barrett *Lovomaniacs* 352: That faggy ex-husband of yours. **1973** Ace *Stand On It* 44: Boy, that is a very faggy costume you have got on, there. **1991** B.E. Ellis *Amer. Psycho* 205: "I think you'd look adorable in, oh, a Geoffrey Beene, Taylor," I whine in a high, faggy voice.

fag hag *n.* **1.** *Stu.* a young woman who is a smoker. *Joc.*

1944 *Slanguage Dict.* 59: Fag hag—girl who smokes. **1945** Shelly *Jive Talk* 24: Fag hag, girl chain smoker. **1955** *AS* (Dec.) 303: *Fag hag, n.* Female cigarette smoker [at Wayne State Univ.]

2. *Homosex.* a woman who regularly seeks the company of homosexual men.—used derisively.

1969 in Girodias *New Olympia Reader* 629: And it's unfortunate that most of the "easy" girls, the fag-hags and such, are such skanks. **1969** in *DAS* (ed. 3): I'd hazard a guess that you're simply a Faggot's Moll, Fag Hag, or Fruit Fly. **1970** G. Walker *Cruising* 45: He wondered if she was one of these fag hags he'd heard about. **1972** *Anthro. Linguistics* (Mar.) 101: *Fag Hag* (n): A female, usually heterosexual, who regularly associates with homosexual males. **1973** *Oui* (Oct.) 116: Do they actually believe that she is such a peripatetic fag hag that she is familiar with the ins and outs of every Turkish bath, Gay bar, and cruisy park in North America? **1975** Legman *No Laughing Matter* 61: Guaranteed unfuckable "fag-hags" and lesbians. **1978** Maupin *Tales* 85: Do you think I'm a fag hag?…I'm practically a fixture at The Palms. **1985** J. Dillinger *Adrenaline* 30: She was a fag hag with ulterior designs. **1986–89** Norse *Memoirs* 115: A few older women known as "fag hags"…frequented the place. Fag hags ran to type then [1943] as now. **1991** B.E. Ellis *Amer. Psycho* 37: Meredith's a *fag hag*…that's why I'm dumping her.

Fagin *n.* [after a character in Dickens' novel *Oliver Twist* (1837–39), who leads a gang of young thieves] a person who trains young boys to be thieves.

*1905 in *OED2*: This school of crime bore outwardly the innocent semblance of a greengrocer and ice-cream shop.…The two Fagins who conducted it [etc.]. **1913** *Chi. Daily Trib.* (May 1) 9: He is described as a "Fagin"—a teacher of young criminals. **1921** in H.W. Morgan *Addicts* 211: The power of dispensing the much prized drug is one of the surest ways for a "Fagin" to hold his pupils. **1928** *Amer. Mercury* (Aug.) 478: Her mother [was] a Fagin and tipster for…racketeers. ***1965, *1970** in *OED2*. **1993** in *Harper's* (Jan. 1994) 38: He was a fagin. Many of his friendships were with adolescent boys. He gave them money to help him…steal things.

fag moll *n.* Esp. *Homosex.* **FAG HAG, 2.**

1966 "Petronius" *N.Y. Unexp.* 97: No. 1 foxes with minor hangups, who are known as "fag-molls."…Very few fag-molls can resist the temptation of a tryst with a genuine fag. **1973** N.Y.C. man, age 24: A *fag moll* is one of these crazy bitches who thinks it's cool to hang out with queers. **1993** *Jerry Springer Show* (synd. TV series): There are fag molls.

fagola *n.* [FAG⁴ + -OLA, infl. by Yid *fegele*] FAG⁴, 1.—used derisively.

1977 Hamill *Flesh & Blood* 30: They gonna come on strong, the Fagola Army, and try and make you a jailhouse punk. **1981–85** S. King *It* 19: He would probably call Springsteen a wimp or a fagola. **1988** *Wkly. World News* (July 5) 23: It produced your fagola hubby and his boyfriend.

fag-roller *n.* *Und.* (see quot.).

1962 Riccio & Slocum *All the Way Down* 91: Some were "fag rollers"—they completed their connection with homosexuals by robbing them.

fag tag *n.* a locker loop on the back of a man's shirt. Cf. earlier syn. **FAIRY LOOP.**

1980 Birnbach *Preppy Hndbk.* 219: *Fag tag n.* The loop on top of the back pleat on button-down shirts. **1993** N.Y.C. man, age 40 (coll. J. Sheidlower): There are two names for a shirt's locker loop: *fruit loop* and *fag tag.* I'm familiar with both terms at least since junior high.

fairy *n.* **1.** a woman or girl. [In 1856 quot., specif. a prostitute.]

1856 in *Ark. Hist. Qly.* XVIII (1959) 11: I met eight men on their way to Kansas…a hard, & rough looking set of fellows.…they told me they stopped the night before at Bangor in a house of the "Farries" [sic], & one [persuaded one of them] to accompany him to the Territory.…She goes for the especial accommodation of the company, though under the name of the wife of one: I…mention this…just to show you, what iniquity is carried on here. **1862** J.S. Warner *Albion* 80: And the fairy is Miss St. John! **1866** H.J. Harris *So. Sketches* 13: You will tell us no more

of the "fairy." I dare say she has you irrevocably charmed. **1866** in *Iowa Jour. of Hist.* LVII (1959) 202: He said she was his…nymph, duck, dearest, seraph, fairy,…his maiden, young lady, youthful female [etc.]. **1886** *Lantern* (N.O.) (Oct. 13) 3: Oliviera…asked a fairy if he was pretty. The girl…told him yes. **1890** Atherton *Los Cerritos* 223: A large Mexican woman waddled to the door…Acres of fat quivered…as she walked. "Scott! What a fairy!" observed the sheriff. "But she won't cuss, that's one comfort." **1891** McCann & Jarrold *Odds & Ends* 83: I did say Wilk was stuck on a girl, an' that's what galls me, for I'm kind o' gone on the same fairy myself. *Ibid.* 85: It's about time for the fairy to come. **1892** Norr *China Town* 21: Well, I'm hanged if here isn't another fairy stuck on [a] Chink. The Irish are not in it. *Ibid.* 32: Come here, me fairy, and give's a kiss. **1895** Townsend *Fadden* 58: An' dere was 'is Wiskers with a fairy in de box! *Ibid.* 73: I had t' tump a gang er kids de first ting fer yellin' "Pipe de dago fairy!" when dey got onto de Duchess. **1896** Ade *Artie* 50: If she'd ever saw me with that fairy I wouldn't be deuce-high with her now. **1897** Ade *Pink* 193: 'At's what 'at long-waisted fai'y done to Hen'y Clahk. **1897** Ade *Horne* 171: I've got a brother that don't know a thing about them fairies. **1899** Kountz *Baxter's Letters* 54: Now, what do you think of that frosty-hearted fairy? **1900** *DN* II 34: *Fairy, n.* A pretty girl. **1902** F. Remington *John Ermine* 190: Faith, who'd roon away from a fairy? **1904** Ade *True Bills* 108: You can't tell by lookin' at one of these Fairies nowadays what kind of Clothes her Father wears. **1906** Ford *Shorty McCabe* 46: This fairy might have seen seventeen summers, or maybe eighteen, but she was no antique. *Ibid.* 213: Ever see a hundred-and-eighty pound fairy with a double chin turn kittenish? **1908** in H.C. Fisher *A. Mutt* 84: The swell Eastern fairies may tie her but they'll never beat her. **1911** A.H. Lewis *Apaches of N.Y.* 147: It's somethin' fierce th' way them high s'ciety fairies comes buttin' in on us. **1927** *Immortalia* 77: Madame Du Barry/Was a lively old fairy/Who sold herself to a king. **1934** Burns *Female Convict* 40: "Ha-Ha!" they greeted me with coarse laughter, "welcome to our hotel, little fairy!"

2. an effeminate man who is a homosexual.—usu. used contemptuously.

1895 *Amer. Jour. Psych.* VII 216: "The Fairies" of New York are said to be a similar secret organization. The avocations which inverts follow are frequently feminine in their nature. They are fond of the actor's life, and particularly that of the comedian requiring the dressing in female attire, and the singing in imitation of a female voice, in which they often excel. **1899** (quot. at NANCY). **1908** Sullivan *Criminal Slang* 2: *A fairy*—An effeminate man. **1912** *Phila. Vice Comm. Report* 81: There are a lot of "faries" [sic] (sexual perverts) hanging around the tenderloin. **1914** Jackson & Hellyer *Vocab.* 46: Hoop…A finger ring, not to be confounded with the jovial exclamation, "Whoops! my dear," of fairies and theatrical characters. **1919** Lind *Androgyne* 64 [ref. to 1892]: I've got a fairie here!…Hand out your money! **1922** Paul *Impromptu* 240: Damned if Reed hadn't had a good time, but he thought the male dancers must all be fairies. **1923** Ornitz *Haunch* 94: Flitting, temperamental fairies, the queer effeminate men. **1923** McAlmon *Companion Volume* 168: You'll omit the name of one or two fairies and waitresses that you know. **1927** Aiken *Blue Voyage* 201: Have you a little fairy in your home? Well, we had, but he joined the navy.…That town's so tough it kicked us fairies out. **1928** Hecht & MacArthur *Front Page* 453: Ooh! Lookit the cane! What are you doing? Turning fairy? **1929** Tully *Shadows* 168: He was precise and effeminate in manner. As a result, he was called "the old fairy." **1931** Steffens *Autobiog.* 223 [ref. to ca1894]: Max…was reporting a police raid on a nest of fairies. "Fairies!" Riis shouted, suspicious. "What are fairies?" And when Max began to define the word Riis rose up in a rage. "Not so," he cried. "There are no such creatures in this world." **1935** D.H. Clarke *Regards* 37 [ref. to ca1910]: So you're a hairdresser, too? I thought only fairies were. **1939** T. Wolfe *Web & Rock* 556: Your jokes about the fairies and the lesbians. **1943** Wakeman *Shore Leave* 114: There's so many fairies and lesbians down there now they'd drive a normal guy clear out into the Jersey swamps. **1959** Knowles *Separate Peace* 16: Pink! It makes you look like a *fairy!* **1963** Boyle *Yanks* 61: Mabel had a lot of other characteristics that stamped him as a bona-fide fairy—his voice, his little mincing steps, his girlish giggles, and the way he would bite his lip and nervously wring his hands when he got agitated with us. **1978** Maupin *Tales* 97: Lotta guys get sick of the glitter fairies in this town. **1987** *Wkly. World News* (July 21) 32: What your "man" wants is a wife to show off and cover the fact that he's a fairy.

fairy-killer detail *n.* *Police.* the antihomosexual detail of a vice squad.

1965–68 E.R. Johnson *Silver St.* 25: On the fairy killer detail of the vice squad…all you did was stand around the toilet at the bus station…waiting for someone to grab your jock. *Ibid.* 50: He's too good to waste on the fairy killer detail.

fairy loop *n.* FAG TAG.

*ca*1970 in *DARE*: "Fairy loops" (hanging loops on the back of men's shirts). **1993** N.Y.C. man, age 36 (coll. J. Sheidlower): I heard *fairy loop* for the first time in the sixth grade, in 1969–70.

fake *n.* **1.a.** *Und.* a dishonest stratagem or action, esp. a method of swindling; (*hence*, as in 1904 quot.) a criminal specialty.

*1829 in Partridge *Dict. Und.* 226: And the fogle-hunters doing...Their morning fake in the prigging lay. *1851–61 H. Mayhew *London Labour* I 352: I tried the same caper; but my pal cut with the gold ring the first day, and I've never had another go at that *fake* since. **1886** F. Whittaker *Pop Hicks* 23: It had seemed to him at first like a hoax, what he called "a fake," to put him in a passion. **1889** *Century Dict.*: *Fake...n....*A swindle; a trick. *1889 in Barrère & Leland *Dict. Slang* I 351: That was one of the best *fakes* of the time, and there was lots of money in it too...Now to learn some new fakes with the broads [cards]. **1902** Clapin *Amer.* 176: *Fake...*A falsity, or swindling of any kind. **1904** in "O. Henry" *Works* 328: Take my advice and go into some decent fake. **1928** in Grayson *New Stories* 215: He would either lose his twenty dollars, or we would have to pull a fake.

b. *Orig. Und.* a spurious or counterfeit document; (*hence*, in later use) anything of a spurious, counterfeit, or fraudulent nature. Now *S.E.*

*1851–61 H. Mayhew *London Labour* I 312: I have already hinted at the character and description of the persons by whom these forgeries are framed...All the "regular bang-up fakes" are manufactured in the "Start" (metropolis), and sent into the country to order. **1886** *Sci. Amer.* (Mar. 13) 165: A man...has derived a large revenue from this and similar "fakes" gotten up for the use of street venders...They paid this man fifty dollars each for the secret of this "fake" [an imitation microscope]. **1889** Alger *Snobden's Office Boy* 66: It was a fake, then! **1895** Coup *Sawdust* 46: Strange to relate, the success of this "fake" was the means of bringing from Europe the original dog-faced boy, "Jo-jo." **1905** Sinclair *Jungle* 235: The newspaper advertisements...were "fakes," put in by...establishments which preyed upon the helpless ignorance of the unemployed. **1905** Riordan *Plunkitt* 12: What is representative government, anyhow? Is it all a fake that this is a government of the people, by the people and for the people? **1906** *Nat. Police Gaz.* (Mar. 10) 10: [Boxer Joe Gans] has declared that his battle with Britt in 1904 was a fake pure and simple. **1906** *Independent* (Nov. 29) 1269: That letter's a fake...an' yur a fraud. **1914** Ellis *Billy Sunday* 214: It's all a fake. **1942** Pegler *Spelvin* 115: It has been a long time since I saw a good, old-fashioned fake in the ring. **1947** Kuttner *Fury* 192: Those treatments...are fakes. **1987** N.Y.C. man, age 39: That innocent pose is all a fake.

c. *Sports.* a feint. Now *colloq.*

1941 in *OEDAS* II 77: A head fake...will often provide an uninterrupted course to the basket. **1949** Leahy *Notre Dame* 15: If the back makes a good fake, the defensive lineman will take a step. **1958** J. King *Pro Football* 131: When he fell for our inside fakes he was set up for long ones over his head.

2.a. an invented or spurious report, story, or account prepared for sale, as on a broadsheet or in a newspaper.

*1851–61 H. Mayhew *London Labour* I 223: After that we had a fine "fake" [an invented news story to be hawked by a vendor]—that was the fire of the Tower of London—it sold rattling...First we said two soldiers were taken up...and then we declared it was a well-known sporting nobleman who did it for a spree. **1888** in Farmer *Amer.*: The telegraph man...has edited Mulhatton's yarns before, and knows a fake from a barn-door. **1889** in Barrère & Leland *Dict. Slang* I 351: The report sent out...does not bear investigation. It is a *fake* and nothing else. **1891** in *DAE*: Leads us to believe that the report that Johnson was taken sick was a "fake." **1892** *DN* I 206: A [newspaper] story is called a *fake* when a writer has evidently been at no pains...to gather his material; when he has depended on a too fertile imagination for his details; or when he has invented the whole thing and some delicacy is felt about calling him point-blank a liar. *Fakes* are the natural and habitual product of...*space-grabbers*...To *fake* and *faker* are obvious cognates of the noun...The opposite of a *fake* is a *straight story.* **1893** in B. Matthews *Parts of Speech* 209: From the stage the word passed to the newspapers, and a *fake* is a story invented...."made out of whole cloth." **1893** M. Philips *Newspaper* 63: To the other newspapers, you are a "daily fake" or a "mendacious contemporary." **1894** in *DAE*: The reporter who thinks it is smarter to write a "fake" than to shag around and get the facts is a fool.

b. a false rumor or false story of any kind. Now *S.E.*

*1851 H. Mayhew *London Labour* I 229: His hanging hisself in prison

was a fake, I know. **1889** in Barrère & Leland *Dict. Slang* I 351: "I heard your brother had gone to New York." "Oh, that was a *fake.* He was badly punished at football, and is lying low to fetch up." **1902** Clapin *Amer.* 176: *Fake...*a story without foundation. **1906** *Nat. Police Gaz.* (Aug. 11) 6: There [never]...was anything in this "honor among thieves" fake.

3.a. (among peddlers and street hawkers) any odd item to be sold on the street or door to door, esp. if worthless or deceptive; (*also*) *Theat. & Und.* an object, device, or contrivance of any kind; gimcrack; GIZMO.

1889 *Century Dict.*: *Fake...n....*any odd bit of merchandise sold by street-venders...*slang.* **1897** in J. London *Reports* 316: Some sell trinkets and gew gaws and others, "fakes." These "fakes" are as curious and interesting as they are innumerable....Next day the young man reappears and puts his little "fake" on every burner in the house. *1899 C. Rook *Hooligan Nights* (cited in Partridge *DSUE* (ed. 8)). **1926** in *AS* LVII (1982) 261: *Fake.* Term used when the true object or name is best not mentioned. **1935** Horwill *Mod. Amer. Usage* 126: The word [*fakir*] is applied esp. to a street pedlar, who goes about selling *fakes*, or odds and ends, largely sham or worthless. **1938** in D.W. Maurer *Lang. Und.* 102: *Fake* or *fake-a-loo.* The [drug addict's] medicine dropper. **1941** in *Lang. Und.* 126: *Fake...*synonymous with "thingamajig" in legitimate usage.

b. (among performing magicians) any contrivance or device used to impart the illusion of magic.

*1889 Barrère & Leland *Dict. Slang* I 351: *Fake...*In conjuring, any mechanical contrivance for the performance of a trick. **1961** *WNID3.*

c. *Theat.* (see quots.).

*1889 Barrère & Leland *Dict. Slang* I 352: *Fakes and slumboes* (theatrical), one of the numerous synonyms used by pantomimists to describe properties. **1889** *Century Dict.*: *Fake...Theat.*, any unused or worn-out and worthless piece of property.

d. *Carnival & Theat.* a performance.

1885 *Puck* (Mar. 11) 22: An Actor's Lament...I...swear I'll...no more engagements make with a "one-night fake"/So far away from home. **1912** Field *Watch Yourself* 269: I'll have hell with that gilly kid, he thinks its a minstrel show; I got to hold him down or he'll queer the fake.

e. a patent medicine.

1923 G. McKnight *Eng. Words* 44: The drug store contributes...*fakes* for patent medicines.

4.a. *Orig. Und.* a thief (*obs.*), swindler, or charlatan; (*specif.*) a confidence swindler.

*1881–84 Davitt *Prison Diary* I 118: They are always taken in hand by the old "faikes" (experienced criminals), trained in all the ways of theft, and fixed for life in a circle of reproductive crime. **1888** in *F & H* II 368: Both ladies then came to the conclusion that the fortune-teller was a fake, and they decided to notify the police. **1889** *Century Dict.*: *Fake...n....* A swindler; a trickster. **1965** in B. Jackson *Swim Like Me* 125: They's all alike the whole world round,/they'll love a fake when he's up and hate him when he's down.

b. an impostor; (*broadly*) an affected or insincere person; poseur; PHONY.

1886 in *Century Dict.*: To call such social lepers actors is as illogical and unfair as it would be to call Uriah Heep a man of honor...Professionally considered your *fake* is as unworthy as he is socially. **1893** in Dreiser *Journals* I 154: You fake, let her speak! *1899 Whiteing *John St.* 214: She went so far as to affirm her conviction that I was a "fake." She has questioned me as to what I am, where I came from, how I came to be here. *a*1904–11 Phillips *Susan Lenox* II 185: Well, you Irish fake—so the kid's dead, eh? *ca*1912 in Kornbluh *Rebel Voices* 74: While a fat grafter, sky pilot, or fake,/Laughs at our troubles and gives us the shake. *1927 in *OEDS*: You Fake! **1929–33** Farrell *Young Manhood* 371: He's the biggest fake in the joint. He's got dough and his old man lets him have a Lincoln so he thinks he's the reincarnation of Jesus Christ.

fake *adj.* **1.a.** fraudulent; spurious; counterfeit; false; pretended. Now *S.E.* [The lack of any exx. in the century and more after 1775 is remarkable; though not published until 1904, the initial quot. is presumably authentic.]

*1775 in *OEDS*: So many artifices have been practiced upon Strangers under the appearance of Friendship, fake Pilots &c., that those coming out with Stores cannot be put too much on their guard. **1886** *Lantern* (N.O.) (Sept. 15) 4: Did Alderman Carey whack up with brother members on this fake contract? **1890** Quinn *Fools of Fortune* 198: Still another resource...remains to the dealer of a "fake" game. **1890–91** *F*

& H I 289: *Fake-boodle*…(American thieves').—A roll of paper over which…a dollar bill is pasted, and another bill being loosely wrapped round this it looks as if the whole roll is made up of a large sum of money in bills. **1893** in *DAE:* A runner was placed behind the heavier mass, a pretending, or "fake," runner nearer the middle, and a man at the ball to put it in play. **1897** in *DN* VI 260: The P.O. Department is powerless to stem the growth of the tide of "fake" newspapers. **1901** *Chi. Tribune* (Aug. 25) 3: Compelled to put up money for "fake" expenses. **1910** Solenberger *Homeless Men* 35: There were other "fake" or "phoney" cripples (to use the men's own terms) as well as a number of "hospital rounders." **1910** W. Raine *O'Connor* 42: Fake medical remedies. **1912** Mathewson *Pitching* 222: Sending out fake stories of new and wonderful curves for several years. **1915** *Lit. Digest* (Aug. 21) 340: Fake foods for fighters. *a*1916 Sandburg *Chi. Poems* 61: He never made any fake passes and what he said went. **1921** U. Sinclair *K. Coal* 234: I know it's all fake, but just the same, it makes my little heart go pit-a-pat. **1949** Monteleone *Crim. Slang* 80: *Fake crip.* A beggar who pretends to be crippled.

b. (in a weakened sense, esp. in current use) made in imitation without fraudulent intent; artificial. Now *S.E.*

*1909 Ware *Passing Eng.* 127 [ref. to 1880]: *Fake pie*…a towards-the-end-of-the-week effort at pastry, into which go all the "'orts," "overs," and "ends" of the week. **1970** N.Y.U. student: Is that real fur or is it fake? **1972** R. Barrett *Lovomaniacs* 211: A fake cigarette—one of those pacifiers for people trying to break the smoking habit. **1988** Univ. Tenn. grad. student: First they had fake sweetener, now they're developing fake fat.

2. worthless; useless. [Without further context, the 1890 quot. is somewhat ambiguous; it may illustrate **(1.a.)**, above.]

1890 in *DAE:* The Rio Grande C. & I. company…still continues the farce of surveying for their fake ditch. **1913** London *Valley of Moon* 5: Twelve and a quarter…And I'd a-made more if it wasn't for that fake bunch of starchers.

fake *v.* [prob. dial. var. of obs. S.E. *feague, feak* 'to whip, beat' in unrecorded sense; cf. *OED*, and see early quots. at FAKER]

1. *Und. & Theat.* to dress (the hair); make up or dress up.—also constr. with *up*.

*1797 in Partridge *Dict. Und.* 698: Strummer feker [a hairdresser]. *1885 in *F & H* II 369: The landlady left, and the chorister fair/Faked herself up, and frizzed her hair. *1909 Ware *Passing Eng.* 266: *Wig-faker* (low London, 18 cent. on). Hair dresser. **1912** Ade *Babel* 181: Next night he was faked up just about right, an' he sent up his card before she had time to come down.

2.a. Orig. *Und.* to counterfeit or forge; (*hence*) to make or shape for a fraudulent or deceptive purpose.—also constr. with *up*. See also earlier FAKER, *n.*, 1.

*1812 Vaux *Vocab.:* *Bit.* money in general. *Bit-Faker:* A coiner. *See* Fake. *Bit-Faking.* coining base money. *1812 *Ibid.* s.v. *fake:* [Among thieves] to *fake a screeve* is to write any letter or other paper; to *fake a screw*, is to shape a skeleton or false key. *1851–61* H. Mayhew *London Labour* I 352: The ring is made out of brass gilt buttons [not gold], and stunning well: it's faked up to rights, and takes a good judge even at this day to detect it without a test. **1888** Bidwell *Forging His Chains* 466: He had managed to "fake" a sore on his left knee-joint, and to keep it open until the leg had become permanently crooked and stiff. **1897** *Harper's Wkly.* (Jan. 23) 86: This bravery was a little faked. **1908** Train *Crime Stories* 88: Of course it would have been comparatively easy to "fake" a violin. *Ibid.* 93: He was…guilty of having "faked" a cheap Nicholas violin into a Strad. **1935** Lindsay *She Loves Me Not* 109: *That* picture is faked! **1942** *ATS* 460: *Fake*…to forge. **1942** in Mencken *Amer. Lang.* (Supp. I) 508: On the claim of having discovered a papist plot (which they faked). **1988** *Headline News Network* (cable TV) (June 17): Next, jail sentences for two men accused of faking apple juice.

b. to concoct or devise, esp. for a deceptive purpose.—usu. constr. with *up*.

*1889 in *F & H* II 369: In order to prevent any chance of a dishonest person winning by means of a faked puzzle we shall provide a number of puzzles ourselves, and these will be used by all competitors. **1896** Bangs *Bicyclers* 93: Fake up. **1902–03** Ade *People You Know* 86: So I want you to fake something up that'll kill 'em right in their seats. **1903** A.H. Lewis *Boss* 209: Have as many lieutenants as you can…Two might fake up a deal with each other to throw you down. **1919–21** Chi. Comm. on Race Relations *Negro in Chicago* 491: Time and again these charges…have been shown to be "faked." **1930** E. Pound, in Ahearn *Pound/Zukofsky* 73: What some Roman perfessor faked up to prevent

his students understanding Sappho better than he did.

3.a. *Und.* to tamper with, alter, or arrange in any manner for advantage or profit; (*hence*) to rig.—also constr. with *up*.

[*1785 Grose *Vulgar Tongue: Feague.* To feague a horse, to put ginger up a horse's fundament, and formerly, as it is said, a live eel, to make him lively and carry his tail well; it is said, a forfeit is incurred by any horse-dealer's servant who shall shew a horse without first feaguing him.] *1812 Vaux *Vocab.:* A man who inflicts wounds upon, or otherwise disfigures, himself, for any sinister purpose, is said to have *faked* himself…to *fake your pin*, is to create a sore leg, or to cut it, as if accidentally, with an axe, *&c.*, in hopes to obtain a discharge from the army or navy, to get into the doctor's list, *&c.* **1859** Matsell *Vocab.* 30: *Faking.* Cutting out the wards of a key. *1872 in *F & H* II 369: Since the *faking* of the scales in Catch-'em-alive's year the oldest habitué of Newmarket so sensational a Cambridgeshire week as the last one. *1873 T. Frost *Circus Life* 279: "Faked up" meaning "fixed." *1883 in *OEDS: Faking*, dying, staining, clipping, or otherwise interfering with the dog's coat or appearance, to hide defects and deceive the judges or public. **1886** in *Century Dict.:* He supposed it was an old one *faked* over to last until the end of Lent. *1886 in *OED:* What has been termed a "faked" machine. **1886** in Partridge *Dict. Und.* 226: When the thief has properly "faked" the room, as he calls it—that is, "fixed" it for his entrance in the evening. *1888 in *OED:* The horse-brand…had been "faked" or cleverly altered. **1889** *Century Dict.:* To *fake* a dog or a fowl by coloring the hair or feathers. **1890** Quinn *Fools of Fortune* 245: A "faked" box [used to cheat in the game of faro]. **1893** in B. Matthews *Parts of Speech* 209: "Are you going to get up new scenery for the new play?" might be asked; and the answer would be, "No; we shall *fake* it," meaning…that old scenery would be retouched and readjusted so as to have the appearance of new. **1906** *Nat. Police Gaz.* (Mar. 10) 10: On account of his self-confessed participation in faked fights. **1942** Pegler *Spelvin* 117: I don't know whether they go in for faking [i.e. setting up fake prizefights] any more, but…if [not], then pugilism will have lost much of its charm and beauty.

b. to misrepresent.—occ. constr. with *it*. Now *colloq.*

1892 (quot. at FAKE, *n.*, 2.a.). **1902** Clapin *Amer.* 177: *Fake*…To commit a swindling. **1906** *Nat. Police Gaz.* (Mar. 10) 10: Joe Gans Cries Fraud…But Admits He Faked. **1911** in Sinclair *Plays* iii: "If you want to deal with politics and high finance, you must treat it sentimentally, you must 'fake' it."…I do not intend to deal with American capitalism "sentimentally," I do not intend to "fake" my portrayal of it. **1921** *Am. Leg. Wkly.* (Jan. 28) 19: Faking it for a furlough was a piece of skull work which even the framers of the Articles of War could not properly reckon with. **1971** Capon *3d Peacock* 21: There will never be a solution until we stop faking the facts.

4. *Und.* to steal. *Rare* in U.S.

*1812 Vaux *Vocab.:* *Fake away, there's no down:* an intimation from a thief to his *pall*, during the commission of a robbery, or other act, meaning, go on with your operations, there is no sign of any alarm or detection. *1841 in Partridge *Dict. Und.* 227: The Faking Boy. *1859 Hotten *Slang Dict.: Fake*…to steal or rob. *1859 in Partridge *Dict. Und.* 226: Whether he had faked the swag or not, he was a tip-top mob. **1867** *Galaxy* (Aug.) 442: Jack Sheppard and his jolly pals who "fake away" so obstreperously in the burden of the chorus and the pockets of the unwary. *1873 T. Frost *Circus Life* 279: "To fake" means, in the thieves' vocabulary, to steal. **1895** Gore *Stu. Slang* 5: *Fake*…1. *v.* To steal. **1901** J. London *God of His Fathers* 75: I never had half a chance.…I was faked in my birth and flim-flammed with my mother's milk. **1906** *DN* III 135: *Fake, v. tr.* To steal. "We *fake* eggs every night and then roast 'em."

5.a. to trick; fool.

*1859 Hotten *Slang Dict.: Fake*, to cheat, or swindle. **1889** in Barrère & Leland *Dict. Slang* I 350: Having set his mind upon shirking all work, he announces his attention to *fake* the doctor and "work" the person. **1895** Gore *Stu. Slang* 5: *Fake*…to deceive; to trick. **1934** Appel *Brain Guy* 10: Tony is a fool if he can't see how she's faking him. **1951** Thacher *Captain* 98: Capt'n, you sayin' I'm fakin' you? **1974** "A.C. Clark" *Revenge* 91: That should fake the motherfuckers out of their socks.

b. (among peddlers and street hawkers) to sell.

1903 *Independent* (July 23) 1722: I think that, for straight faking, aluminum gas tips were the most profitable thing I ever handled.

6.a. *Specif.*, to feign illness, injury, or disability; malinger.

*1881–84 Davitt *Prison Diary* I 145: "Faiking" (malingering)…is practiced only by the lowest type of criminal [in prison]…As these are all more or less inoculated with the worst forms of bodily disease, it becomes an easy task for such prisoners to so tamper with themselves as to compel medical treatment to be given them. **1889** Barrère & Leland *Dict. Slang* I 351: *Fake*...To...malinger or counterfeit illness or sores. **1903** in "O. Henry" *Works* 162: The croaker...said I was fakin', did he? **1939** M. Levin *Citizens* 70: Doc, a lot of these guys are faking. **1974** L.D. Miller *Valiant* 158: "You can just suffer until sick call—tomorrow!" "Have a damned heart!... Can't you see we ain't faking?" **1986** *World Book Dict.*: He isn't really hurt; he's only faking. **1989** *21 Jump St.* (Fox-TV): No! I'm not fakin'!

b. to feign or simulate; pretend.—often constr. with *it.* Now *S.E.*

***1889** in Barrère & Leland *Dict. Slang* I 351: Or ask what their age is, they'll scornfully say—/"I do not *fake* (and smiling), I'm twenty to-day." **1896** Hamblen *Many Seas*: Riley...said the Dutchman was only "faking" to avoid punishment. **1897** *Forum* (Feb.) 748: They have judged of his moral status simply from his "faked" attitude toward the world at large. **1901** "J. Flynt" *Graft* 69: He frankly confessed to me that he wasn't living his own real life when he was wearing red neckties; he was trying to "fake the feathers of the main guys" in the Upper World. **1912** Mathewson *Pitching* 223: It's all right to "fake" about new curves, but when it comes to being vulgar about it, that's going too far. **1921** Casey & Casey *Gay-Cat* 88: He was a professional stool-pigeon who faked he was a yegg. **1934** Burns *Female Convict* 141: Let's fake it, and make believe we're from an insane asylum. **1935** O'Hara *Dr.'s Son* 40: She's faking sick. ***1941** in *OEDS*: Faking an interest in the goods displayed. **1950** Cleveland *Great Mgrs.* 28: The tip-off as to when Grimes was throwing his spitter and when he was only faking. **1953** Gresham *Midway* 15: I got to get me a real geek. You can't draw no crowd, faking it that way. **1954** Dodd *On Football* 31: Offensive line play can't be faked. *a*1967 Bombeck *Wit's End* 14: By taking my pulse they will be able to figure out...if I am faking or not. **1971** Torres *Sting Like Bee* 19: Then I react by faking that I was not him (when, in fact, I was). **1974** Radano *Cop Stories* 63: I'll fake being nuts. **1976** Dyer *Erroneous Zones* 74: Trying to impress others with your knowledge of something that you know nothing about by "faking it." **1978** Alibrandi *Killshot* 87: Guys would fake injuries when it was obvious they had no chance of winning. **1984** J. McCorkle *Cheer Leader* 37: Cindy told me later that she was faking. **1986** Cosby *Fatherhood* 66: How to fake being asleep.

c. *Sports.* to feint.

1939 in Paxton *Sports* 324: Sometimes the receivers will fake out and cut in sharply...The faking is done with eyes, head and body. **1949** Leahy *Notre Dame* 15: It is much easier to fake a man out of position than to block him out. **1983** Helprin *Winter's Tale* 356: He would fake to his left, and...bound to the right.

7.a. Orig. *Theat.*, now esp. *Music.* to improvise (words or music); ad-lib.—often constr. with *it.*

***1889** Barrère & Leland *Dict. Slang* I 351: Bustling through a show of any kind under difficulties artfully concealed from the spectators is *faking* it. **1896** Ade *Artie* 19: He took me over and says: "Miss Lumyum and so-and-so," fakin' it as he went, "I want you to shake hands with my friend, Mr. Ta-ra-m-m-m," and then he ducked. **1899** Ade *Fables* 32: When he would get tired of faking Philosophy he would quote from a Celebrated Poet of Ecuador or Tasmania. **1906** H. Green *Actors' Boarding House* 36: She faked on the cornet in their musical finish. **1915** *DN* IV 233: College Slang...*fake, v.t.* To attempt to recite as if prepared. **1923** *N.Y. Times* VIII (Sept. 9) 2: *Fake:* To improvise speeches in place of forgotten ones. **1924** in *AS* I (1926) 516: "Chaz" could not read music, but he had a gift for "faking" and a marvelous sense of syncopated rhythm. **1933** *Fortune* (Aug.) 92: His band of fourteen can *fake* (improvise) as adroitly as the early five-piece combinations. **1939** C.R. Cooper *Scarlet* 292: This was especially true of piano-players, who often were required to "fake" for hours. **1956** E. Hunter *Second Ending* 182: He was hitting the notes sloppily, faking a lot of notes. **1959** Bechet *Treat It Gentle* 107: Well, it would be easy for me to tell you some lyrics, make up others, just fill it in and fake it for you.

b. *Art.* (*specif.*) to delineate with minimal detail.

***1909** Ware *Passing Eng.* 126: *Fake a picture* (Artistic, 1860 on). To obtain an effect by some adroit, unorthodox means...it is much used by inferior artists. **1914** S. Lewis *Mr. Wrenn* 100: And see how I've faked this figure [in a sketch]? It isn't a real person at all.

fakeloo /ˌfeikəˈlu/ *n.* [FAKE, *n.* + -*eloo* prob. of expressive origin; cf. -EROO] FAKE, *n.*, 2.b., 3.a.

1926 Finerty *Criminalese* 22: *Fakealoo*—Fictitious story; yarn intended to deceive. **1938** in D.W. Maurer *Lang. Und.* 102: *Fake* or *fake-a-loo.* The [drug addict's] medicine dropper. **1940** R. Chandler *My Lovely* 81: A fakeloo artist, a hoopla spreader, and a lad who had his card rolled up inside sticks of tea, found on a dead man. **1958** McCulloch *Woods*

Words 59: *Fakealoo*—Any thing or scheme for which a better name is lacking.

fake-out *n.* a feint or bluff; deception; (*broadly*) an unpleasant surprise.

1959 N.Y.C. schoolboys: What a fake-out!...School's just a fake-out to get you to do what you're told....The Coke machine was empty! What a fake-out! **1967** Hinton *Outsiders* 128: I groaned, and it wasn't all fake-out. **1984** *A Note to You* (WGBH radio) (June 30): Beethoven would not write a lavish quartet such as this as a fake-out.

fake out *v.* **1.** Orig. *Football & Basketball.* to fool (an opponent) with a feint; (*hence*, in gen. use) to bluff; fool; get the better of.

1949 Leahy *Notre Dame* 69: If they are faked out they are lost temporarily. **1956** *AS* XXXI 238: Someone who gets into the traffic pattern before you, or taxies out in front of you, has "faked you out," or "beaten you to the draw." **1959** N.Y.C. schoolboy: Man, he really faked *you* out! **1961** Forbes *Goodbye to Some* 149 [ref. to WWII]: The first Jap tried to fake him out by pretending to bang a mortar shell on the catwalk. **1966** Neugeboren *Big Man* 59: You listen to the older guys gas with each other about...who can fake who out of whose jock. **1966** Shepard *Doom Pussy* 142: We had been faked out before, and took it with a grain of salt. **1967** P. Roth *When She Was Good* 54: Wild Bill had spent three years faking the opposition out of their pants. **1967** in Briscoe *Short-Timer* 28: It was rumored that the Marines did kill 300 V.C., who were faked out by the simulated attack. **1970** Segal *Love Story* 11: I faked out one defenseman. **1970** in Sanchez *Word Sorcerers* 103: Sonny asked his mother how come the robins get faked out like that and she told him Chicago weather could fake out anybody. **1972** T. O'Brien *Combat Zone* 6: Surprised them...Faked them right out of their shoes. **1974** Nims *Western Wind* 48: Robert Frost can be a tricky writer, faking out a hasty reader in poem after poem. **1976** Atlee *Domino* 57: Man, I could fake them out of their shoes with that kind of ball-handling. **1977** Corder *Citizens Band* 126: "I'll bet he had you faked out real good." "Right out of my socks." **1978** De Christoforo *Grease* 40: Finn left the jocks faked out of their straps when he was on the field or court. **1982** Braun *Judas Tree* 33: You could always fake 'em out. **1983** *N.Y. Times* V 53: That is what has faked me out so badly, I think. There hasn't been anything hurting, but something's obviously been wrong.

2. *Stu.* to sneak away.

1956 P. Moore *Chocolates* 109: Sorry we faked out...You drank us under the table. *Ibid.* 152: But if she had had a date he had either passed out or faked out.

faker *n.* one who fakes; *specif.*:

[**1.** *Und.* a counterfeiter; forger. Cf. FAKE, *v.*, 2.a. [Not attested in Am E, but related to senses below and to FAKE, *v.*] [***1610** in *OED*: A Feager of Loges, one that beggeth with false passes or counterfeit writings.] ***1612** in Partridge *Dict. Und.* 32: *Ben-feakers of Jybes,* (that is to say) Counterfeiters of Passports....They who are Counterfeiters of Passports are called *Ben-feakers,* that is to say, Good-Makers. ***1688** in Partridge *Dict. Und.*: *Ben-fakers.* ***1785** Grose *Vulgar Tongue: Bene feakers,* (*cant*) counterfeiters of bills. ***1812** Vaux *Vocab.*: *Bit-faker:* A coiner.]

2. *Und.* a thief. Cf. FAKE, *v.*, 4.

***1841** (cited in Partridge *Dict. Und.* 227). ***1851** in *F & H* II 370: We never calls them thieves here, but *prigs* and *fakers.* ***1869** in *F & H*: Them pusses is mannyfactered express for the convenience o' the *fakers.* **1915** *DN* IV 201: *Faker,* a thief. "Two *fakers* are sleeping in the cooler tonight."

3. [orig. among itinerants] an itinerant artisan, mechanic, or tradesman; (*hence*) a peddler, pitchman, or traveling showman.—usu. used in comb. Also **fakir.** [The spelling *fakir* reflects the erroneous assumption that the word is the same as S.E. *fakir,* popularly pronounced /ˈfeikər/ in U.S.]

***1839** in Partridge *Dict. Und.* 458: Itinerant umbrella makers and repairers...are called *mushroom fakers.* **1859** Matsell *Vocab.* 31: *Faker.* A jeweller. *Ibid.* 57: *Mushroom fakers.* Umbrella hawkers. **1865** C.F. Browne *Ward: Travels* 23: Tip us yer bunch of fives, old faker! **1889** *Century Dict.*: *Faker...n.*...a street-vender...slang. **1893** in *Independent* (Dec. 19, 1901) 3012: Fakers and Mush Fakers, Mechanics and others [are] on the Tramp hunting work, and some of the finest mechanicks in the country, comprising all trades, get on the road...Partly from drink. **1897** in J. London *Reports* 316: "Fakirs"...are tinkers, umbrella menders, locksmiths, tattooers, tooth-pullers, quack doctors, corn doctors, horse doctors [etc.]. **1899** Cullen *Tales* 140: I got a lift from a medicine fakir who was just driving into Peoria in his perambulating pharmacy. **1902** Clapin *Amer.* 177: *Fakir*…An itinerant merchant. **1903** *N.Y. Eve. Post* (Oct. 5) 31: One may see at almost any of the downtown corners a street fakir selling shoestrings. **1927** *DN* V 445: *Faker, n.* A peddler who attracts a crowd by a speech, song, or acrobatic performance and then proceeds to sell them some wonderful article. **1932** E. Wilson *Amer. Jitters* 95: Outside, in front of the courthouse, they find the patent-medicine fakir on his motor-truck still holding a considerable crowd. **1949** *AS* XXIV 261: The business of the old medicine-show *fakers* was to…defraud the public. **1968–69** in *DARE: A person who sets out to cheat others while pretending to be honest…Faker* [11 or 12 Inf[ormant]s old].

4.a. Orig. *Und.* a swindler; charlatan; *(broadly) (obs.)* crook. Now *S.E.* [See spelling note at **(3)**, above.]

1881 in Partridge *Dict. Und.* 227: New York…celebrated for its large army of petty swindlers, or, as they style themselves, "fakers." **1882** in Horan & Sann *Wild West* (frontis.): Notice! To Thieves, Thugs, Fakirs And Bunko-steerers.…If Found within the Limits of this City after Ten O'Clock P.M., this Night, you will be invited to attend a Grand Neck-Tie Party. **1895** Coup *Sawdust* 55: The fakirs are…the camp-followers who hang on the heels of a circus for the purpose of swindling the public by every variety of device known to the "blackleg fraternity." *Ibid.* 56: Lottery schemes, gambling games…, pocket-picking and robbing are among the methods by which these fakirs reap their harvest. **1898** in Sampson *Ghost Walks* 146: Fakirs, Three Card and Thimble Riggers. **1906** *Nat. Police Gaz.* (Mar. 10) 10: There should be a way to finish fakers in pugilism. **1911** Roe *Prodigal Daughter* 166: Pickpockets and sneak thieves, fakirs and confidence men were all out in full force.

b. a hoaxer. Now *S.E.*

1892 (quot. at FAKE, *n.*, 2.a.). **1902** Clapin *Amer.* 177: *Fakir*.…In newspaper parlance, a reporter who draws upon his imagination for his facts. **1920** S. Lewis *Main St.* ch. xi: Papa says these folks are fakers. Especially all these tenant farmers that pretend they have so much trouble getting seed and machinery. Papa says they simply won't pay their debts.

c. a person who feigns illness, injury, or disability; malingerer. Now *colloq.*

1910 *Adventure* (Nov.) 158: I know that half of them are probably malingerers—"fakers"—come to try out the new doctor. **1917** Fornaro *Purgatory* 67: I'll cure you!…You're a faker, that's what you are! **1918** Ruggles *Navy Explained* 59: *Faker's Palace.* The ship's sick bay.…If there is a hard day's work ahead some of the lazy men might try to evade it by going to the sick bay and "faking the list." **1930** *Our Army* (Aug.) 15: God pity the gold-brick and faker when the Top had him up on the mat. **1956** N.Y.C. man, age *ca*70: He's a faker. He doesn't have any stomachache.

fakir *n.* see FAKER, 3, 4.

fakus *n.* [FAK(E) + (DING)US] *Und.* a thingamabob, esp. if used for cheating; FAKE, *n.*, 3.

1905 *DN* III 66: Indefinite expression applied to something, the name of which is not readily recalled…*fakus*. **1929** Milburn *Hornbook* 157: He took me by the facus [*sic*] and tossed me in the cage. **1940** *AS* (Apr.) 118: *Fakus* or *Mr. Fakus.* Any cheating mechanism used in *short-con* games, especially on gambling devices and *flat-joints.* **1942** *ATS* 74: Contrivance; indefinite objects; "gadget"…*fakus.*

fall *n.***1.a.** *Und.* an arrest or conviction; esp. in phr. **take a fall** to be arrested or convicted.

1893 (quot. at FALL MONEY). **1894** in *OEDS*: This man…is now in prison on the Continent. The story of his last "fall" is interesting. **1902** Hapgood *Thief* 39 [ref. to 1880]: But I always had great difficulty in saving "fall money," (the same as spring-money; that is money to be used in case of a "fall," or arrest. **1912** *Hampton's Mag.* (Jan.) 846: "It's a fall," I says to the gang. **1912** Stringer *Shadow* 34: Blake…decided he would gain most by a "fall." **1928** O'Connor *B'way Racketeers* 31: When a cannon took a fall, the term used for those arrested, Barry was entrusted with the so-called fall money. **1960** C.L. Cooper *Scene* 226: Beeker called to say Ace has taken a fall. **1965** Cleaver *Soul* 54: He says that at home he has every copy of the *Realist* published up to the time of his fall. **1971** Woodley *Dealer* 30: My partner took a fall…got busted. **1976** *S.W.A.T.* (NBC-TV police series): Barnes has a couple of robbery falls. Nothing big. **1984** Caunitz *Police Plaza* 6: I'm not going to take a fall. I have no intention of going inside.

b. *Pris.* a prison term.

1933 Ersine *Pris. Slang* 35: *Fall* 1. An arrest. 2. An imprisonment. **1934** *AS* IX 26: *Fall n.* a term in prison. **1963** *Time* (Aug. 2) 14: *Fall.* Prison term. **1974** R. Novak *Concrete Cage* 36: Did a fall for armed robbery.

2. Orig. *Pris.* consequences, esp. blame taken for another person.—usu. constr. with *the.*

[**1929** Hammett *Dain Curse* 180: You…killed your sister Lily, his first wife, and let him take the fall for you.] **1932** L. Berg *Pris. Doctor* 122: This guy took one fall for you. Now see if you can wiggle out of this one, you eel! *Ibid.* 274: [Death is] one fall—I got to take—whether I—I like it or not. **1970** Landy *Underground Dict.* 181: *Take the fall…*Accept the inevitable. **1987** Iran-Contra Hearings (CBS-TV) (July 13): You proposed to take the fall in terms of any political damage. **1989** *Studio 5B* (ABC-TV): [Your boss] needed someone to take the fall, and you were an easy target.

¶ In phrases:

¶ **go over the falls** *Surfing.* to be thrown over by the curl of a wave.

***1977** Filosa *Surf. Almanac* 191: *Over the falls.* (South African) Caught in the curl of a wave and sucked over with the wave as it crashes. **1981** (quot. at ROPEY).

¶ **take a fall** see **(1.a.)**, above.

¶ **take** [occ. **get**] **a fall out of, 1.** to knock down.

1892 Norr *China Town* 18: I'd like to take a fall out of that red-nosed bum there.

2. to get the better of; *(joc.)* to involve oneself with (something).

1889 in *DA*: You just see me take a fall out of my "Universal History." **1896** Ade *Artie* 91: There was…Mame's old man takin' a fall out of a wheel [bicycle]. **1899** Dunne *Hearts of Countrymen* 126: I've brought me frinds…f'r to hear Molly take a fall out iv th' music-box. **1902** Hobart *Up to You* 46: We all went…to take a fall out of…the…wedding breakfast. **1908** in H.C. Fisher *A. Mutt* 22: Old Kid Cupid took a fall out of A. Mutt. **1913** London *Valley of Moon* 325: I'll get a fall outa whatever it is. **1914** Patten *Lefty o' the Bush* 12: See you took a fall outer Fryeburg yestiddy.

fall *v.* **1.** Esp. *Black E. & Jazz.* to come or go.—constr. with following prep. [Rare before the 1940's.]

***1789** G. Parker *Life's Painter* 178: The gentry begin to fall in one after another, some call for punch, some call for porter, &c. **1899** Cullen *Tales* 132: I was…going from Chicago to St. Louis without money…when I fell into Minonk. **1943** *Yank* (Jan. 13) 20: To…"fall back to our dommie." **1946** Mezzrow & Wolfe *Really Blues* 25: We fell into a lunch-counter to knock out some vittles. *Ibid.* 57: Pimps and simps would fall in from here, there and everywhere. **1948** Manone & Vandervoort *Trumpet* 92: On one of my trips out of town I fell into Detroit. **1952** Mandel *Angry Strangers* 337: I'm hip you gonna like—fall up to the loft now'n then. **1953** in R.S. Gold *Jazz Talk* 88: You'll have to fall over to the apartment sometime. **1956** H. Ellison *Deadly Streets* 179: Maybe I'll fall over to the club room. **1957** H. Ellison *Web of the City* 70: Just fell down to find my kid sis—. **1958–59** Lipton *Barbarians* 86: If you fell into the pad after six o'clock…you had to come in by way of a basement door. *Ibid.* 316: *Fall In*—Arrive, show up, make the scene. **1959** in Russell *Playboy* 248: Glad you could fall up to my pad, Dad. **1959–60** R. Reisner *Jazz Titans* 155: *Fall By:* to visit. **1965** Lurie *Nowhere City* 112: And then later…Walter fell in. **1970** Quammen *Walk the Line* 52: So le's me and you fall on up there and cop what they're saying. *Ibid.* 156: We fall around together, and that's cool. **1970** A. Young *Snakes* 20: We'd fall in J. L. Hudson's, the big department store. **1970** Grissim *Country Music* 91: On one occasion Cash, Perkins, Presley and Lewis just happened to fall by the studios at one time for several hours of rapping, jamming, singing, joking and fooling around. **1978** Rascoe & Stone *Who'll Stop Rain?* (film): I'll fall by your place tomorrow. **1994** N. McCall *Wanna Holler* 106: I fell into the football stadium looking like Superfly in the flesh.

2. *Und.* to be arrested or convicted.

1873 Sutton *N.Y. Tombs* 477: Riley…has just been sent to Sing Sing, and his three pals…"fell" on another racket. ***1879** *Macmillan's Mag.* (Oct.) 502: I fell (was taken up) again at St. Mary Cray for being found at the back of a house. **1893** L. Moore *Own Story* 447: I want you to follow my instructions when the case is tried, and if I fall I will find no fault with you. **1902** Hapgood *Thief* 95 [ref. to *ca*1880]: Johnny "fell," that is to say, was arrested. **1911** A.H. Lewis *Apaches of N.Y.* 140: Mack's fell for something.…You can gamble he's in hock somewheres. **1925–26** J. Black *Can't Win* 108: If you do fall, the government don't hang a lot of prior convictions on you. **1937** Johnston *Prison Life* 34: "Where they fall from?"…"Where they all from—good old L.A." **1942** Algren *Morning* 93: Where'd you fall from? **1950** Maddow & Huston *Asphalt Jungle* 15: I'm getting tired of you guys that fell putting the bite on me. **1965** Cleaver *Soul* 54: There's this one Jewish stud out of New York who fell out of Frisco. **1972** A. Kemp *Savior* 195: Don't surprise me so many guys fall again—what does surprise me is that any at all stay out.

¶ In phrases:

¶ **fall for, 1.** to be deceived or taken in by (something or someone); (*also*) to naively accept as true. Now *colloq.*

1903 McCardell *Chorus Girl* 28: Well, the mayor fell for it. **1906** H. Green *Boarding House* 81: I don't fall for that old gag. **1906** *Nat. Police Gaz.* (Sept. 22) 6: I don't fall much for the sob-music stuff. **1907** in H.C. Fisher *A. Mutt* 20: That old "sure thing" bull works wonders. They all fall for it. **1910** *N.Y. Eve. Jour.* (Mar. 8) 14: It was fixed, of course, but the rum fell for it. **1912** Lowrie *Prison* 152: Some mutt'll fall f'r that, sure's y'r born. **1914** Jackson & Hellyer *Vocab.* 32: "To fall for" is to be deceived by, to be taken in, to be influenced. **1915** T.A. Dorgan, in *N.Y. Eve. Jour.* (Aug. 5) 12: How can anyone fall for that stuff? **1917** Oemler *Slippy McGee* 129: Their beans would have to turn inside out before they fell for it that *I'd* come back. **1918** *Vanity Fair* (Sept. 9) 52: You don't mean to tell me that you fall for that stuff, do you? **1930** E. Goldman *Living My Life* 179: The American liberals...so easily fall for every new political scheme.

2. to become charmed or captivated by, esp. (now *solely* and *colloquially*) to fall in love with; (*broadly*) (*obs.*) to like or enjoy.

1906 *Nat. Police Gaz.* (July 21) 6: The race-player..."falls for" one favorite after another. **1911** Van Loan *Big League* 64: Biff had "fell for a skirt," as they phrased it. **1911** A.H. Lewis *Apaches of N.Y.* 239: Them rich frails would fall for me in a hully second. **1912** Mathewson *Pitching* 242: You are such a Romeo...that even the cross-eyed ones fall for you. **1914** Elliott *Animated Slang* 4: As soon as he saw me he FELL HARD FOR ME. **1918** Griffin *Ballads of Reg't* 16: I "fell for his tin type," yet never knew why. **1920** E. O'Neill *Diff'rent* 224: And if you fall for that jazz stuff, all you got to do now is learn to dance it. **1927** "M. Brand" *Pleasant Jim* 17: I fall for this job. **1927** Mayer *Us Girls* 233: He honestly fell for me like a ton of bricks. **1929** T. Gordon *Born to Be* 24: Old Billy fell for her, hook, line and sinker. **1936** Tully *Bruiser* 40: Don't fall too hard for a dame in a railroad restaurant. **1940** Fitzgerald *Last Tycoon* 75: You've fallen for me—completely. You've got me in your dreams. **1962** McElfresh *Jill Nolan* 91: You wouldn't be falling for the doc, would you?

¶ **fall off the roof** to begin a menstrual period.

1936 Levin *Old Bunch* 90: He thought maybe she was falling off the roof, maybe that had something to do with it. *a***1948** in *Word* IV (1948) 184: One [euphemism]...commonly used by high school and college girls is *to fall off the roof* (variants, *to fall off, to be off*). **1959** Russell *Perm. Playboy* 352: "I'm sorry," she said. "I think I'm due to fall off the roof today." **1962** B. Davis *Lonely Life* 40 [ref. to 1920's]: Every generation has its own expression for the "monthly it"—in my day, it was "falling off the roof." **1967** *DAS* (Supp.) 683: *Fall off the roof*—To begin a menstrual period. *Common since c.1925.* **1973** Eble *Campus Slang* (Mar.) 2: *Fall off the roof*—to begin one's menstrual period.

¶ **fall to** *Und.* *fall for*, 1, above.

1904 *Life in Sing Sing* 260: The conny fell to the graft and tipped the sucker to the lay. **1905** *McClure's Mag.* (Sept.) 516: And when he throws the game into you, just pretend you fall to it an' hand him your box.

¶ **go fall on yourself!** go away! get out!

1892 S. Crane *Maggie* 37: "Oh, hell," said Pete, easily. "Go fall on yer-self."

fall guy *n.* **1.** Orig. *Und.* a person who must take the blame for the actions of confederates; (*broadly*, now commonly) a scapegoat.

1904 A.H. Lewis *President* 420: Dan used to be a strong-arm man himself, but since he's got this joint, he...has turned fall-guy for a fleet [of pickpockets] that operates along the Bowery. **1908** in H.C. Fisher *A. Mutt* 44: Mutt is merely the fall guy. We are after the "higher ups." **1910** Roe *Panders* 65: When I did get into trouble they tried to make a "fall guy" out of me. **1911** Howard *Enemy to Soc.* 293: We ain't goin' to be th' "fall guys" for Steve....If we've got to do time, so has he! **1913** W. Wilson *Hell in Nebr.* 99: Andy is innocent and was just made the "fall guy" for the real murderers. **1919** Darling *Jargon Book* 12: *Fall guy*—One who takes the blame. **1923** Ornitz *Haunch* 163: He would be the "fall guy," assume all the blame and exonerate the other two. **1948** Lay & Bartlett *12 O'Clock High!* 80: Why should *you* be the fall guys, you're asking yourselves. **1961** Grau *Coliseum St.* 124: It's not anybody else, with me for the fall guy? **1970** E.S. Gardner *Cops* 38: We were thoroughly convinced that Louis Gross was innocent and that he had been framed as a fall guy. **1987** T.C. Clark *Dict. Gamb.* 76: The *fall guy* carries incriminating evidence or otherwise puts himself in a position to be arrested in place of any other mob member. He is then bailed out

of jail by his confederates, and the rest of the mob goes free. **1987** *N.Y. Times* (July 10) A 1: [Col. Oliver North] would play the "fall guy," as he put it in his tough-guy lingo, allowing his superiors to finger him on a scheme that was going down the tubes.

2. a person who is easily duped; easy victim; SUCKER.

1906 H. Green *Boarding House* 226: I never thought I'd be the fall guy for such raw work as this. **1908** in H.C. Fisher *A. Mutt* 51: Poor Little Jeffries! He's the Fall Guy for Everything in the Bughouse. **1911** A.H. Lewis *Apaches of N.Y.* 43: In th' old days...th' Paynims was th' fall guys. **1914** Jackson & Hellyer *Vocab.* 32: *Fall Guy,* Noun. General currency....a victim. **1916** Livingston *Snare* 120: "Here comes my fall-guy!" I mused,...[knowing] that a citizen of prosperous appearance when in company with a lady will rarely ever refuse a plea for financial aid. **1924** Henderson *Keys to Crookdom* 403: Easy mark...*sucker, fall guy, sap, gull, dupe.* **1925** in Moriarty *True Confessions* 27: He's the greatest fall guy in the world when it comes to pretty women. **1929** *AS* IV (June) 340: *Fall guy.* An easy victim; the loser. **1945** in Hodes & Hansen *Sel. from Gutter* 19: First one guy sidles up to this fall guy. **1981** G. Wolf *Roger Rabbit* 5: Roger makes a perfect fall guy and his fans love him for it.

3. *Film.* a stuntman. *Joc.*

1929 *Sat. Eve. Post* (Apr. 6) 8: *Fall Guys*—By Dick Grace. **1984** *The Fall Guy* (ABC-TV series title).

fall-guy *v. Und.* to exploit as a FALL GUY, 1.

1930 Lait *On the Spot* 51: There ain't no use fall-guyin' a girl like Polack Annie.

falling den *n. Black E.* a bed.

1911 *JAF* (July) 284: The singer uses the common slang "fallin' den" for his bed...Somebody in my fallin' den.

fall money *n. Und.* money to be used in case of arrest for bail, bribery, or legal fees. Also vars.

1893 L.W. Moore *Own Story* 197: If any accident happened to us, Hall was to stand his part of the "fall" money. **1900** Willard & Hodler *Powers That Prey* 97: The probable amount of "fall money"...he had at his disposal. **1901** "J. Flynt" *Graft* 219: *Fall money,* funds saved by criminals to pay lawyers, secure cash bail, and to bribe officials. **1906** H. Green *Actors' Boarding House* 62: The "fall money" of two pals. **1912** Berkman *Prison* 198 [ref. to 1893]: A real good gun's always got his fall money planted,—I mean some ready coin in case of trouble. **1915** Howard *God's Man* 129: She had a mouthpiece there with the fall money. **1930** Conwell *Pro. Thief* 29: These three grifted together for years with no thought of anyone being boss or having fall-dough (money to be used in case of arrest). **1937** Reitman *Box-Car Bertha* 297: Friends. "Fall jack," "mouth pieces." **1942–49** Goldin et al. *DAUL* 286: Fall dough. **1965** in IUFA *Folk Speech: Fall doe* [sic]—Money to be used if one member of a gang is arrested. **1969** Salerno & Tompkins *Crime Confed.* 172: Some criminals carry $5000...at all times as "fall" money.

fall out *v.* **1.** Esp. *Black E.* to collapse; pass out; (*hence*) to go to sleep.

1941 Attaway *Blood on the Forge* 41: Gonna drink red pop till I falls out. **1947** *Time* (Oct. 6): To scarf (to eat), "to fall out" (to sleep), "gassed" (tickled pink). **1950** Roeder *J. Robinson* 54: I was worried sick Mack would fall out dead. **1950** *Neurotica* (Autumn) 41: One jolt now, then fall out for a few hours. **1952** Himes *Stone* 217: "Walks like a hobbled horse."..."He's got it bad, ain't he?"..."He's about to fall out with it." **1952** E. Brown *Trespass* 19: I'm going to say a toast...before I fall out. *ca***1953** Hughes *Lodge* 68: I have big eyes to fall out. **1962** in Rosset *Evergreen Reader* 456: I'm gonna go fall out in the fall-out shelter. **1966** Armstrong *Self-Portrait* 39: And the minute you come off the stage, you just fell out. **1966** Brunner *Face of Night* 232: *Fall out*—to become unconscious from an overdose of drugs. **1968** Wojciechowska *Tuned Out* 69: He was on speed and he's fallen out. **1969** Geller & Boas *Drug Beat* 247: They pay little attention to dosage and some munch enough of the pills to stagger through the days as mindless zombies, "falling out" (sleeping) here and there for short periods, eating little. **1972** N.Y.U. student: Yeah, *fall out* and *crash* mean the same thing, go to sleep.

2. *Black E.* to be overcome, as with shock or laughter.

1938 Calloway *Hi De Ho* 16: *Fall out*—To be overcome with emotion...."The cats fell out when he took that solo." **1946** Mezzrow & Wolfe *Really Blues* 90: They all fell out at this funny gag. **1958** R. Russell *Playboy* 74: [The notes] danced out of the horn strop-razor sharp and sliced up high and blasted low and the cats all fell out. "Do it! Go, man! Oooo, I'm out of the boat, don't pull me back!" **1959–60** R. Reisner *Jazz Titans* 155: *Fall Out Laughing, To:* to break up with mirth. **1966–67** P. Thomas *Mean Streets* 27: Everybody fell out with a laugh kick. **1970** Cain *Blueschild Baby* 38: You know how that killed them crackers, man, they fell out, the whole fucken company. **1974** R. Carter *16th Round* 307: My wife…fell out in the courtroom when the verdict was announced.

3. *Army.* (see quot.).

1956 Boatner *Military Customs* 116: *Fall out.* Colloquially, the expression means to relax when associating in an off-duty status with one's military superiors.…An old soldier knows when and how much to "fall out" around officers.

4. *Und.* to be arrested; FALL, *v.*, 2. [The *out* in 1934 quot. is prob. merely a directional reference.]

[**1934** Rose *Thes.*: Duke fell out in Chi last week.] **1962** B. Jackson *In the Life* 160: That was St. Louis where I fell out.

fall partner *n. Pris.* one of two or more persons arrested at the same time for the same offense; (*broadly*) a criminal's partner.

*a***1969** B. Jackson *Thief's Primer* 57: *Fall partner*, a person with whom one has been arrested. *Ibid.* 69: So we got in to the place and I told my fall partner, "Let's go, man, everything's packed." **1985** *N.Y. Times* (Aug. 21) A 23: He calls everybody arrested with him his "fall partners."

fall togs *n.pl. Und.* (see 1962 quot.).

1927 *DN* V 445: *Fall togs*, n. Good clothes to be worn when on trial so as to create a favorable impression. **1930** Irwin *Tramp & Und. Sl.*: *Fall Togs*…Clothing especially selected by a criminal…to give him a good appearance on trial. **1962** Regan & Finston *Toughest Pris.* 798: *Fall togs*—Clothing especially selected by a criminal or his lawyer to give him a good appearance on trial and thus possibly influence the jury or judge in his favor.

false alarm *n.* a person who bluffs or exaggerates or who does not fulfill expectations; (*hence*, commonly) a worthless person.

1900 Ade *More Fables* 170: The Fable of Lutie, the False Alarm, and How She Finished about the Time that she Started. **1902** Wister *Virginian* 4: Shucks! You're a false alarm. **1904** Hobart *Jim Hickey* 18: How'd a real woman like his wife ever come to marry a false-alarm like Sam? **1906** A.H. Lewis *Confessions* 207: Say, I'm wise to that mut! Say, he's a false alarm; he don't know he's alive! **1906** H. Green *Boarding House* 50: I'm in vodeville…an' no two false alarms from the legit can stick up their noses at me. **1909** Raine *Ridgway* 119: Don't try to bully *me*, you false alarm. You're a shallow, scurvy imposter. **1927** Hemingway *Men Without Women* 208: That false alarm! **1930** in R.E. Howard *Iron Man* 18: Mike, I hate to say it, but as a fighter you're a false alarm. **1932** Behrman *Biog.* 270: *Marion.* …Young man, you're insufferable! *Kurt.* And you're a false alarm! **1937** in J.P. Cannon *Notebook* 119: One of the tricks…for putting this four-flushing false alarm across is to represent him as super-human.

falsie *n.* **1.** usu. *pl.* a pad worn inside a brassiere to enhance the appearance of the breasts.

1943 in *OEDS*: "Falsies"…the term for the pads that convert [nightclub chorus girls]…from 32s to 34s. **1949** Gresham *Limbo Tower* 92: I'll take you and get ya fitted for a custom-made set of falsies. **1950** Spillane *Vengeance* 31: They can't let their breaths out all the way without losing their falsies. **1954** in Yates *Loneliness* 138: I can spot a paira falsies a mile away. **1957** Simmons *Corner Boy* 74: She's got a fine shape, too, honey and she don't have to go downtown and buy falsies like some people I know. **1957** Kohner *Gidget* 16: Those damn falsies stick out all over the place. **1963** D. Tracy *Brass Ring* 392: That terrible woman with the red wig and the falsies that anybody could spot. **1978** De Christoforo *Grease* 92: "I happen to know she wears falsies."…"You oughta know, Foam-Domes!" **1992** Hosansky & Sparling *Working Vice* 59: It was a large…envelope.…Lucie opened it, and out fell a pair of falsies.

2. *pl.* false teeth.

1983 K. Miller *Lurp Dog* 45: Never wear my falsies in the field…Too shiny.

fam[1] *n.* [fr. earlier Brit. cant *famble*, of unkn. orig.] *Und.* a hand.

*****1698–99** "B.E." *Dict. Canting Crew: Famms*…Hands. *****1819** [T. Moore] *Tom Crib* 28: *Fams* or *fambles*, hands. *****1826** in J. Farmer *Musa Pedestris* 99: The flask…in her fam appeared. **1859** Matsell *Vocab.* 31: *Fams.* Hands.

fam[2] *n. USAF.* a familiarization flight. Also as *v.*, to familiarize, as with an aircraft.

1984 Trotti *Phantom* 196 [ref. to Vietnam War]: Another Phan-

tom…flown by a new pilot on his area fam, bull's-eyed the tanker head on. **1989** T. Blackburn *Jolly Rogers* xii [ref. to WWII]: *Fam, fammed* familiarize(d). *Ibid.* 78: It won't take me long to get refammed.

family *n.* **1.** *Und.* professional criminals, esp. thieves and swindlers, and their associates.—constr. with *the.* Hence **family man** [or **woman**] a man or woman who is a professional criminal or a trusted associate of criminals.

*****1749** in *F & H* II 371: "Oath of the Canting Crew": No dummerar, or romany; No member of the family. *****1753** in Partridge *Dict. Und.* 230: They had been out together on the Sneak: He is an old Family Man. *****1788** in *F & H* II 371: Let the people say what they will against gamesters, gamblers, or *family-men*. *****1812** Vaux *Vocab.*: *Family*: Thieves, sharpers and all others who get their living *upon the cross*, are comprehended under the title of "The Family." *Family-Man*, or *Woman*: any person known or recognized as belonging to the *family*; all such are termed *family people*. *****1838** Glascock *Land Sharks* I 193: The house…was a favourite resort of "the *family*," or, to speak with less reserve, it was a thieves' house, where many a burglary was planned. **1845** *Nat. Police Gaz.* (Oct. 16) 51: The above party…admired a "*family man*" (a first class man), with all the professional ardor of their souls. **1846** *Nat. Police Gaz.* (June 20) 349: A cluster of the English "*family*" may be seen hovering around the corner of Courtlandt street, to "wing" every stranger that comes along. *****1857** in *F & H* II 371: Thieves: *Family-men.* **1899** A.H. Lewis *Sandburrs* 155: As I states, Joe skips into this lawyer's office, d' same bein' open for d' poipose, an' one of d' "fambly" holdin' it down.

2. *Und.* a unit of an organized crime syndicate, esp. the Mafia, operating in a usu. well-defined geographical area. Now *S.E.*

1963 in Salerno & Tompkins *Crime Confed.* 143: They are going to make Nick or Chick a member of the "family" Wednesday night. **1966** C. Ross *N.Y.* 48: Control and sale belongs to the Mafia's many families. **1967** *N.Y. Times* (May 9) 38: A Mafia family is a group of individuals who are not necessarily blood relatives. **1978** Diehl *Sharky's Machine* 133: It ain't gonna be easy now, keepin' the Feds *and* the Family from tumblin' on to me. **1985** WINS Radio News (Dec. 17): The largest, most powerful organized crime family in the country. **1980–86** Steffensmeier *Fence* 19: Maybe somebody that's connected with the family (Mafia).

family disturbance *n.* (see quot.). *Joc.*

1942 *AS* (Feb.) 75: Hard liquor is *family disturbance.*

family jewels *n.pl.* the male genitals; (*specif.*) the testicles.—constr. with *the.*—usu. considered vulgar. *Joc.*

1916–22 Cary *Sexual Vocab.* II: *Family jewels.* The penis and testes. **1942–44** in *AS* (Feb. 1946) 33: *Family jewels*, n. Testicles. **1949** McMillan *Old Breed* 62: I hope the family jewels are safe. **1978** W. Brown *Tragic Magic* 8: I almost kicked that dude in his family jewels. **1987** *Daily Beacon* (Univ. Tenn.) (May 4) 4: All that Van Allen radiation and other substances have atrophied Carl's family jewels.

fan[1] *n. Und.* a vest.

*****1839**, *****1847**, *****1859** (cited in Partridge *Dict. Und.*). **1859** Matsell *Vocab.* 31: *Fan.* A waistcoat. **1866** *Nat. Police Gaz.* (Nov. 24) 3: A "fan" of an unexceptional cut, "real super and slang" to match, and a shiney black "cady." *****1889** (in Partridge *Dict. Und.*).

fan[2] *n.* [shortening of *fanatic*] *Orig. Baseball.* a spectator or enthusiastic devotee of a sport; (*broadly*) an aficionado, esp. of motion pictures; (*hence*) an admirer. Now *S.E.*

1889 in *OEDS*: Kansas City baseball fans are glad they're through with Dave Rowe as a ball club manager. **1896** Ade *Artie* ch. xvii: I'm goin' to be the worst fan in the whole bunch. **1901** *DN* II 139: *Fan*, a base ball enthusiast; common among reporters. **1907** Siler *Pugilism* 27: Fight fans delight in witnessing a knockout. **1908** in Fleming *Unforget. Season* 14: New York baseball "fans" missed one treat last fall. **1908** *Atlantic* (Aug.) 221: The child is father of the "fan", and the middle-aged—the aged, even—renew their youth while "rooting" on the bleachers. **1913** *Lit. Digest* (Sept. 6) 380: Wouldn't that make the fans sit up and take notice? **1913** in *DAS*: A good…movie…turns up for the faithful "fan." **1914** Ellis *Billy Sunday* 34: His slides and stolen bases were…beloved of the "fans".

fan[3] *n. Av.* an aircraft propeller.

1918 in Hall & Nordhoff *Escadrille* II 184: How could I shoot through the fan without hitting it? **1920** Bingham *Air Service* 104: Stop those fans! Don't you see they scare my horse? **1943** Tregaskis *Invasion Diary* 88: It had the big tail and the three fans, overlapping. It was all shiny, just like new. **1944** in Inks *Eight Bailed Out* 9: The ship's got a couple of wings and four fans. **1955** Scott *Look of Eagle* 190: He hated Gooney Birds and old fan jobs. **1959** *Sat. Eve. Post* (May 2) 26: Not with those big eighteen-foot fans putting out 24,000 horsepower. **1961** L.G. Richards *TAC* 122: By the time we had the fans turning she was kicking up thirty-five knots. **1965–66** *Air Officer's Guide* 437: *Fan*—propeller. **1990* T. Thorne *Dict. Contemp. Sl.* 172.

¶ In phrases:

¶ **hit the fan** see s.v. HIT.

¶ **turn on the fan** Esp. *Pris.* to run away; escape.

1935 Pollock *Und. Speaks: Turned on the fan,* escaped from prison or the police (gave them the air). **1970** L.D. Johnson *Devil's Front Porch* 130 [ref. to *ca*1930]: I don't mind confessing that I stepped aside and was all set to "turn on the fan"* at a moment's notice….(*Run away very fast). **1973** Ellington *Music My Mistress* 234: There was no fighting back. Step and his bodyguard turned on the fan.

fan *v.* **1.a.** to beat or strike, esp. repeatedly or soundly; deliver a blow to, esp. with a club.

*1785 Grose *Vulgar Tongue: To Fan.* To beat any one. *I fanned him sweetly;* I beat him heartily. **1839–40** Cobb *Green Hand* I 61: Let the loblolly boy be in readiness with the bite of a rope, to fan him to sleep. **1905** in "O. Henry" *Works* 1671: Out of th' park, now, for yours, or I'll fan yez. **1913** in J. Reed *Young Man* 31: "Chop it!" rumbled the cop, waving his club suggestively at me, "Now git along, or I'll fan ye!" **1917** Fornaro *Purgatory* 43: A guard "fans" him over the back with a club. **1928** Sharpe *Chicago May* 65: Go along with you, or I'll fan ye with my club. *Ibid.* 69: They had already fanned the kid; but they could get nothing out of him. **1934** L. Berg *Prison Nurse* 57: He put up a battle but when I got through fanning that rat, it was all he could do to make a No. 2 cell on his own. **1942** McAtee *Supp. to Grant Co.* 4 [ref. to 1890's]: *Fan with a brick*…strike with a thrown brick. **1953** Paley *Rumble* 108: You guys are gonna be chased off every street corner and you're gonna get fanned every time we see you. We're gonna get you guys in a hallway and dump you. **1956** I. Shulman *Good Deeds* 251: I've a good mind to fan your rear. **1968** in *DARE:* My father, he fanned me one time, and I remember it till now. **1987** in *DARE: Fan* = spank.

b. *Specif.* to strike (a horse or team) to urge it on, as with a whip or quirt.

1887 in *OED:* Fanning them, which in the tongue of coachmen, is whipping them. **1915** in J.I. White *Git Along Dogies* 144: The bronk never lived that I couldn't fan. **1916** in *OEDS:* His quirt fell….He fanned his pony again. **1937** *DN* VI 619: A skilful cowboy who rides the horse and *fans* him by whipping the pony with his hat. **1961** in *DARE:* Modern rodeos forbid quirtin', fannin', or even touchin' the animal with the hand.

c. *Specif.* to strike (the hammer of a revolver) repeatedly and rapidly with the side of the free hand so as to fire several shots quickly; to fire (a pistol) in this manner. Now *S.E.*

1891 *Outing* (Oct.) 22: A cowboy outfit…amuse themselves by rapidly firing their triggerless six shooters in the manner technically termed "fanning the hammer." **1901** F. Norris, in *DA:* He "fanned" his revolver. **1924** G. Henderson *Crookdom* 404: Fanning a revolver hammer. **1961** in *DARE:* Fannin' was done by holdin' the gun in one hand in the usual way and strikin' the hammer back repeatedly with the heel of the other hand. **1979** Edson *Gentle Giant* 50: By continuing to "fan" the hammer with his left hand, the youngster was able to discharge the remaining four bullets…in extremely rapid succession.

d. to defeat.—constr. with *out.*

1879 Tourgee *Fool's Errand* 261: When…we met them in battle, there was always one satisfaction, whoever got "fanned out,"—it was always our own folks that did it, and one couldn't well help being proud of the job. **1895** J.C. Harris *Rabbit at Home* 187: He had met the great Brindle Dog…and had fanned him out in a fair fight. *ca***1960** in *DARE: Fan out*…Whip or overcome.

2. *Stu.* to make a perfect recitation or do well in an examination.—also constr. with *out.*

1834 *Mil. & Nav. Mag. U.S.* (Mar.) 25: The Blackboard…that abomination of him who has to "'fess"—that delight of him who hopes to "fan." **1859** Bartlett *Amer.* 141: *To Fan Out,* to make a show at an examination….The term originated at the United States Military Academy at West Point, where for years it was local; but it is now gradually finding its way through the country.

3.a. [perh. alter. of earlier BrE criminal slang *fam,* with similar meaning; for exx. see Partridge *Dict. Und.*] *Und.* to feel or touch (the pocket of a victim) for the presence of money or valuables; (*broadly*) to rob in this manner. Also as *n.*

1847 *Nat. Police Gaz.* (Jan. 16) 149: They'll have you *fanned out of your dimmy and your thimble. *1851–61* H. Mayhew *London Labour* IV 319: Joe…had fanned the gentleman's pocket, i.e., had felt the pocket and knew there was a handkerchief. **1889** in Barrère & Leland *Dict. Slang* I 353: Pete *fanned* the countryman's pocket where he had seen him put the roll. **1904** *Life in Sing Sing* 255: *Fanning*—Locating purse. **1914** Jackson & Hellyer *Vocab.* 32: Fan the pratt for a poke. **1930** Conwell *Pro. Thief* 45: Also the sign, "Beware of Pickpockets," is helpful, for whenever a sucker sees this sign he feels the pocket in which his money is located to discover whether his pocketbook is still there, thus relieving the mob of the necessity of fanning him. **1931–34** in Clemmer *Pris. Comm.* 332: *Fan,* v.t. Frisking by a pickpocket in an effort to locate the pocketbook. **1958** *N.Y. Times Mag.* (Mar. 16) 88: *Fan*—The brush or feel a pickpocket gives a potential victim.

b. *Und. & Police.* to search (a person), as for the presence of weapons or contraband; frisk.

1923 Fishman & Perlman *Crucibles* 128: Frequent "fanning" or "frisking" (as the prisoner designates searching of the trusties…is necessary. **1927** Coe *Me—Gangster* 90: He ordered a cop to fan them. **1927, 1946** in *OEDS.* **1962** Regan & Finston *Toughest Pris.* 798: *Fan*—To search, esp. a person or his clothes.

c. *Police.* to search (a place).

1929 in Partridge *Dict. Und.* 230: We'll fan the place. **1930** in Partridge *Dict. Und.* 231: We began fannin' the joints on South Halstead and Clark, but Pinky had flitted. **1948** Wilder & Monroe *Song Is Born* (film): They'll fan every hotel in town.

4.a. *Baseball.* (of a batter) to strike out; (*trans.*) to strike out (a batter). Also constr. with *out.* Now *colloq.*

1886 in *DA:* The man who…"fans out" or "pops one up." **1888** *N.Y. Press* (Apr. 21) (cited in Nichols *Baseball Term.*). **1901** *Chi. Tribune* (Aug. 25) 19: Pitcher Hughes…fanned eleven. **1905** in Paxton *Sport USA* 24: The unfortunate player…had just "fanned" for the third time. **1908** in Fleming *Unforget. Season* 41: Mathewson…fanned some Quakers with ridiculous ease. *Ibid.* 77: The ump said Slagle walked. The Giants said he fanned. **1912** Mathewson *Pitching* 10: Then I fanned the next two batters. **1914** Patten *Lefty* 128: Every time a man fanned…those Kingsbridgers howled. **1915** Lardner *Haircut* 154: He fanned me on three pitched balls again in the third. **1918** Witwer *Baseball* 14: He has lived up to his name by fannin' four times in four times at bat. **1948** L. Allen *Reds* 120: Vaughn fanned ten batters and Toney only three.

b. (in various sports) to fail to hit the ball, puck, etc.

1970 Scharff *Encyc. of Golf* 417: *Fan.* To miss the ball completely. Same as *whiff.* **1976** *Webster's Sports Dict.* 142 [ice hockey].

5. [cf. **(1.b.),** above] Esp. *West.* to ride or go fast, esp. on horseback.—also constr. with *it.*

1899 Green *Va. Folk-Speech* 169: *Fan*…To stir about briskly: as, "She goes fanning about." **1900** *Harper's* (May) 892: This hyeh train?…Why, it's been fanning it a right smart little while. *Ibid.* 904: Out he comes a fannin' and a foggin' over the Southern Pacific. **1914** Knibbs *Songs of Outlands* 14: Oh, it's Heaven, but it's lonely, and we've had our little airin',/So we'll fan it back to Arizona now. **1933–35** D. Lamson *About to Die* 63: He…takes off…with the bulls fannin' along behind him hollerin' for him to stop. **1967** Schaefer *Mavericks* 100: They'll…come afannin' behind me.

6. to converse; chat.

1905 in Paxton *Sport USA* 23: Toward others of the team he has so much reserve that he would rather sit reading advertisements on the hotel-blotters than "fan" with them. **1928** O'Connor *B'way Racketeers* 251: *Fanning Bee*—A discussion. **1949** Cummings *Dict. Sports* 132: *Fan*…*Slang.* To discuss a sport, thus playing the part of a fan. **1952** *New Yorker* (Jan. 19) 20: All the other chauffeurs I'd stand around fanning with…called me Moore.

7. (see quots.). Cf. syns. COOL OUT, COOL OFF.

1971 Wells & Dance *Night People* 51 [ref. to 1930]: If we had been on good terms with the rooming house and restaurant the last time, he wouldn't be gone long, but if he had to rub them down (or "fan" them, as Buddy Tate would say), he would be gone just about all day. *Ibid.* 117: *Fan,* v. mollify.

8. *Stu.* to absent oneself from (a class); BLOW OFF.

1989 P. Munro *U.C.L.A. Slang* 37: Let's fan chemistry, I'd rather hit the beach.

fancy *n.* **1.** *Stock Market.* a fraudulent or worthless security.

1841 in *DA:* A very large portion of the stocks termed "fancies", are entirely worthless in themselves. **1854** G.G. Foster *15 Mins.:* "Fancy stocks", by which is meant those stocks, and only those which are…intrinsically worthless….The stock sinks into the unfathomable abyss of ill-considered and fraudulent speculations, and thereafter is known as a "fancy"…."The fancies were somewhat depressed today." **1882** in *DA*.

2. Orig. *Boxing.* followers of prizefighting; (*hence*) rowdies or sporting and gaming enthusiasts collectively.—constr. with *the*. Also attrib. [Still in occ. Brit. use as a deliberate archaism.]

*1807 R. Southey, in *OED2:* The Amateurs of Boxing, who call themselves *the Fancy*. *1818 P. Egan, in *F & H* III 372: The various gradations of *the Fancy* hither resort, to discuss matters incidental to pugilism. *1820–21 P. Egan *Life in London* 34: Although "one of the Fancy," he was not a *fancy-man*. *1848 W. Thackeray, in *F & H* III 373: Mr. William Ramm, known to the Fancy as the Tutbury Pet. **1858** in A. Cook *Armies of Streets* 20: Crowds of the "fancy"…rushed in from neighboring streets. Clubs and stones were freely used. **1872** in *DAE:* A great number of fancy gentry are present, and it is thought the town was set on fire for the purpose of plunder.

fancy Dan *n.* **1.** a dandy; an affected or pretentious fellow; a show-off.

1943 *AS* XVIII 107: *Fancy Dan*…a dressy player. **1949** Robbins *Dream Merchants* 8: Did Janey think I was this fancy a Dan? **1950** A. Lomax *Mr. Jelly Roll* 49: Then you could observe the fancy Dans, dressed fit to kill, wearing their big diamonds. **1962** E. Stephens *Blow Negative* 479: Some undercover hanky-panky among you fancy dans? **1970** Terkel *Hard Times* 95: My father was sort of a fancy Dan….He had a lot of pretentions.

2. *Specif.* a showy, usu. ineffective, athlete.

1927 *Sporting News Record Bk.* 64 (cited in Nichols *Baseball Term.*). **1939–40** Tunis *Kid from Tomkinsville* 53: Say, that guy's one swell ballplayer; he's a Fancy Dan out there in the field. **1942** *ATS* 627: Athlete…Poser. *Fancy Dan*. **1947** Schulberg *Harder They Fall* 264: The new light-heavy…a regular Fancy Dan. **1949** Cummings *Dict. Sports* 132: *Fancy Dan. Slang.* A clever athlete sometimes noted for spectacular "grandstand" playing. In boxing the term denotes a boxer noted for cleverness rather than hitting ability. **1972** in P. Heller *In This Corner* 119 [ref. to 1920's]: I always thought you were a Fancy Dan, but now you're on your way to the title.

fancy-Dan *adj.* fancy; pretentious; affected.

1938 (cited in *W10*). **1942** Pegler *Spelvin* 70: Those main-event ideology blokes and Fancy-Dan economists. **1951** Haines & Burnett *Racket* (film): So this is the fancy-Dan operation, is it? **1956** Lay *Toward Unknown* (film): How 'bout all this fancy-dan flying? **1966** Susann *Valley of Dolls* 295: I know this is one of those fancy-Dan rooms that don't serve booze while the act is on. **1972** Newman & Benton *Bad Company* (film): A fancy-Dan watch like that! **1982** "J.R. Roberts" *N.O. Fire* 59: I don't think that fancy-Dan desk clerk liked me smelling up his hotel.

fancy-Dan *v.* Esp. *Sports.* to show off.

1955 L. Shapiro *6th of June* 69: It's all right for you fellows to go fancy-danning around London where they're civilized. **1980** McDowell *Our Honor* 229: The boxers were to fight fair…and…there was to be no "fancy Danning or showboating."

fancy-girl *n.* **1.** Esp. *Und.* a man's sweetheart or mistress. Also **fancy-woman.** Now mainly *hist.*

*1812 Vaux *Vocab.*: A woman who is the particular favorite of any man, is termed his *fancy woman*, and vice versa. *1822 in Partridge *DSUE* (ed. 8): Fancy-girl. *1821–26 Stewart *Man-of-War's-Man* II 196: You'll have but a paltry account of your fancy girls before all these fellows are gone. **1892, 1930, 1969** in *OEDS* [all for the form *fancy-girl*].

2. a demimondaine, esp. a prostitute. Also **fancy-woman.** Now mainly *hist.*

1824 in McWhiney *Cracker Culture* 173: A party in the public-room [was] discussing the merits of the different dealers in "fancy-girls"…and their respective stocks. **1852–55** C.G. Parsons *Inside View* 135: She is a high priced *fancy* girl. **1863** Massett *Troubadour* 68: Omnibus drivers,…saloon proprietors,…"fancy women." **1874** Pinkerton *Expressman* 202 [ref. to 1859]: Does he ever go to see the fancy girls? **1907** *DN* III 187: *Fancy woman*, n. A kept woman; a harlot. **1931** Bontemps *Sends Sunday* 65: One of the…best-looking fancy girls on Targee street. *Ibid.* 74: The black sports and fancy women of St. Louis. *a*1973 in Bontemps *Old South* 50: If you was out riding with a sure 'nough fancy gal, Norman, it wouldn't be like courting somebody you aimed to marry. **1982** R.M. Brown *So. Discomfort* 33: You can't be taking fancy women out in public. **1988** Kinoy *Vidal's Lincoln* (NBC-TV) [ref. to 1860's]: You look like a fancy woman, Molly.

fancy house *n.* a brothel. Now mainly *hist.*

1864 in Gordon *Exp. in Civil War* 45: Some of the "Shoulder Strap" men…in my opinion have brought on a few of those estimable Ladies who reside in the "fancy" houses in Baltimore and other Cities. **1871** Still *Underground R.R.* 134: This whipping was at the *"Fancy House"* [in New Or.]. **1889** Barrère & Leland *Dict. Slang* I 353: *Fancy house* (prostitutes), a house of ill repute. **1907** *DN* III 187: *Fancy house*, n. A house of bad repute. **1930** K.A. Porter *Flowering Judas:* I worked for a long time in a fancy house—maybe you don't know what is a fancy house? Naturally…everyone must have heard some time or other. **1931** Bontemps *Sends Sunday* 60: A savage bearing that was the rage of the fancy-houses. **1938** Holbrook *Mackinaw* 109: A number of saloons and two monstrous fancy-houses. **1951** Pryor *The Big Play* 37: The thing to do now was…go to a fancy house and have themselves a time. **1961** R.E. Pike *Spiked Boots* 46: "Git your rosin, girls! The drive's coming" is the cry that used to go through the fancy-houses. **1973** Tidyman *High Plains Drifter* (film): I can do better than you in a four-bit fancy house.

fancy-man *n.* **1.** the lover of a woman, esp. a man who lives on the earnings of a woman, usu. a prostitute; (*broadly*) a pimp. Now mainly *hist.* in U.S.

*1811 *Lexicon Balatron.:* *Fancy man.* A man kept by a lady for secret services. *1820–21 P. Egan *Life in London* 34: Although "one of the Fancy," he was not a *fancy-man*. **1836** *Spirit of Times* (Feb. 20) 3: The "sporting" character has ceased to be a mixture of the pugilist, the bully, the fancyman, and the blackleg. **1848** G.G. Foster *N.Y. in Slices* 48: Lawless boys and lazy "fancy-men", supported by their mistresses. **1850** G.G. Foster *Gas-Light* 39: A prostitute…The rooms…are…kept by her "fancy man." *1851 H. Mayhew *London Labour* I 178: The women of the town buy [sandwiches] of me, when it gets late, for themselves and their fancy men. They're liberal enough when they've the money. **1855** Whitman *Leaves of Grass* 41: A farmer, mechanic, or artist…a gentleman, sailor, lover or quaker,/A prisoner, fancy-man, rowdy, lawyer, physician or priest. **1868** Williams *Black-Eyed Beauty* 12: He might have seen her "fancy" man pawn a timepiece at Moneypenny's. *a*1900 in Doerflinger *Shantymen* 38: If ever I get my foot on the land/I will be some lady's fancy man! **1956** Resko *Reprieve* 234: A single-o fancy man: "One chick on the turf at a time." **1967** Talbot *Chatty Jones* 30: Stan! Who's he? That fancy man of Mabel's? **1981** M.S. Goldman *Gold Diggers* 103: Pimping involved few concrete obligations, and fancy men rarely assisted prostitutes with business. **1982** Rosen *Lost Sisterhood* 89: Lulu…permitted herself to become involved with a "fancy man" who disappeared to Hollywood with her savings of $150,000.

2. *Naut.* a member of a warship's crew who does not stand watch; idler; (*broadly*) a person lacking practical experience.

*1818 in *OEDS:* The Sweepers e'en, were *fancy men!* *1821–26 Stewart *Man-of-War's-Man* I 158: The idlers, fancy men, and other loblollies, not forgetting Jack in the dust, may either wash in the first or middle watches. **1869** in *DAE:* The reason English marine engines are superior to ours is not because our workmen are inefficient, but because they are mere cloister engineers, as we call them, or fancy men.

3. Esp. *Naut.* a favorite or favored fellow; best friend; (*hence*, contemptuously) a sycophantic fellow who acts as an informer. Now *hist.*

[*1812 (quot. at FANCY-GIRL, 1).] *1821–26 Stewart *Man-of-War's-Man* II 193: Jack Adams, come, you're my fancy man, you know. *1838 Glascock *Land Sharks* II 101: Why, you must be a fancy man with the women. **1849** Melville *White-Jacket* ch. lxxiii: On board of most men of war there is a set of sly, knavish foxes among the crew, destitute of every principle of honor. In man of war parlance they…are called *fancy men*, because, from their zeal in craftily reporting offenders, they are presumed to be regarded in high favor by some of the officers. *1902 Masefield *Salt-Water Ballads* 37: So long, my fancy man! **1980** Valle *Rocks & Shoals* 328 [ref. to *a*1860]: *Fancy man.* Slang. An informer. Especially a regular source of information for the master-at-arms.

4. [sugg. by FANCY, 2] a man who is a patron of gambling, boxing, horse racing, etc.

1852 in *DAE:* A Long Island fancy man: lots of money and no end of fast horses. **1853** in *DAE*. **1938** Holbrook *Mackinaw* 192: No woman was allowed in the place, nor were gamblers or any sort of fancy-men.

5. a male homosexual.

1975 in *Tenn. Folklore Soc. Bull.* XLIV 137: *Fancy-men*…Male homosexuals or transvestites; "Seen any more fancy-men lately?" **1985** *Golden Girls* (NBC-TV): Is the fancy man in there?

fancy-pants *n.* a dandy; snob. Also as *v.*

1934 Peters & Sklar *Stevedore* 31: All right, fancy pants. **1936** in Botkin

Treas. Amer. Folk 219: He gives old Chief Fancypants a broken jackknife. **1936** in Weinberg et al. *Tough Guys* 21: If you hadn't tried to fancy pants around last night. **1939** A. Johnson et al. *Hardys Ride High* (film): Me and my girl, we split up over a fancy-pants. **1941–42** Gach *In Army Now* 158: Please show this bum outside, Miss Fancypants. **1950** Hartmann & O'Brien *Fancy Pants* (film): Hey, fancy-pants! **1960** Hoagland *Circle Home* 189: Same hills as Boston,…same fancy-pants as New York. **1975** McCaig *Danger Trail* 93: Never mind bitching, fancy-pants.

fancy-pants *adj.* fancy or snobbish.—used derisively.
    1949 "R. MacDonald" *Target* 114: You're getting awful fancy-pants since he took you off the street. **1952** Lamott *Stockade* 40: My God, Charley, the army's getting fancy-pants these days. **1960–61** Steinbeck *Discontent* 36: You could climb out of it if you didn't have your old-fashioned fancy-pants idea. **1965** Linakis *In Spring* 122: I became a fancy-pants paratroop major.

fancy-woman var. FANCY-GIRL.

fandango *n.* **1.a.** a dancing party or celebration of any kind; (*hence*) any boisterous assembly or occasion; a fight. Now mainly *hist.* [1780 quot. prob. illus. S.E. sense.]
    [**1780** in *DAE:* They were found at a *fandango,* or merry-meeting, with a party of lasses.] **1847** J.R. Lowell, in *DAE:* I started out to go to a fandango. **1850** Garrard *Wah-to-Yah* 168: Fandango—dance, fight—any occupation giving excitement. **1871** Schele de Vere *Amer.* 132: Miners and hunters delight in getting up an occasional *fandango* when they happen to be in town. *Ibid.* 133: In the Eastern States…any very boisterous assembly, even a row, is familiarly called a *fandango.* **1882** A.W. Aiken *Joe Buck* 5: Let 'em…draw their we'pons an' the fandango will begin to onest [*sic*]! **1898** Bellamy *Blindman* 287: Ef you'll ask her to your fandango to-morrer…I'll let ye go. **1942** Garcia *Tough Trip* 82: Some of the bucks crowded their horses around us in a threatening way; I thought that the fandango was due to start. **1957** O'Connor *Co. Q* 89: I must say you're a welcome change from men who shot themselves in the foot to avoid joining the fandango at Rocky Face Ridge. **1962** G. Olson *Roaring Road* 12: A short race…can be a very happy fandango. **1978** L'Amour *Proving Trail* 77: There was some sort of a fandango down in Mexico…getting somebody out of jail down there and back across the border.
    b. a confused or foolish action or undertaking; foolishness.
    1841 in *OEDS:* All the fool Federal fandangoes that disgraced the country. **1892** Bierce *Beetles* 248: I'm cussed ef I can sarvy…/What good this dern fandango does the State. **1894** in *OEDS:* The hippopotamus does not indulge in these fandangos. **1934** in Mencken *New Ltrs.* 328: Nothing even remotely approaching the Brain Trust fandango has ever been witnessed in Christendom. **1974** *Odd Couple* (ABC-TV): The deceit…you used in tricking me into this entire fandango.
    2. a contrivance or item; doodad.
    1797 in *DAE:* [At Bunker's Hill] a Fandango is erected, which was invented at Haverhill. On two ropes a chain slides down hill to a place accomodated to receive it, with the person who dismounts below. **1856** in *OED:* No fripperies or fandangos of any sort.
    ¶ In phrase:
    ¶ **the whole fandango** the entire lot.
    1870 *Overland Mo.* (Dec.) 581: Gray's was the highest peak in the whole fandango.

fan-fucking-tastic *adj.* wonderful; fantastic.—usu. considered vulgar. Cf. -FUCKING-, *infix,* for related forms.
    1970 Southern *Blue Movie* 108: Tony was delighted. "Fan-fucking-tastic!" **1971** *Nat. Lampoon* (Aug.) 26: Just groove on those colors! Fan-fucking-tastic! **1976** Schroeder *Shaking It* 78: "Fan-fucking-tastic!" Corso whistles in astonishment. **1977** Bredes *Hard Feelings* 42: He said "Fan-fucking-tastic!" over and over. **1981** Graziano & Corsel *Somebody Down Here* 156: Frankie…is fanfuckintastic! *a***1988** M. Atwood *Cat's Eye* 298: Fan-fuckin'-tastic.

fang *n.* **1.** usu. *pl.* a human tooth. *Joc.*
    *****1840** C. Dickens, in *OED:* The few discolored fangs gave him the aspect of a panting dog. **a***1890–91** *F & H* II 374: *Fang-faker*…a dentist…*fang-chovey,* a dental establishment. **1922** in Hemingway *Sel. Letters* 64: Picture the Duke honeymooning with that mouthful of false fangs. **1942** in *Jour. Gen. Psych.* LXVI (1945) 132: Shut up, or I'll knock your fangs out. **1959** *Swinging Syllables: Fangs*—Teeth. **1983** in "J.B. Briggs" *Drive-In* 148: Wanda Bodine…is lying through her fangs.
    2. *Jazz.* (among brass players) lips; embouchure.
    1958 in R.S. Gold *Jazz Talk* 89: To use the hip vernacular—they're saying "fangs" now instead of chops. **1959–60** R. Reisner *Jazz Titans* 155: *Fangs:* Lips.

fanger *n. Med.* a dentist or oral surgeon.
    1981 in Safire *Good Word* 154.

fangs-out *adj. Mil. Av.* all-out; at full speed.
    1983 M. Skinner *USAFE* 50: *Fangs Out:* Going for an air-to-air victory to the exclusion of all other considerations. **1987** G. Hall *Top Gun* 48: I'm squashed into the seat by a "fangs out" 6-G bat turn to the left. **1989** J. Weber *Defcon One* 20: Each succeeding F-14 snapped into a "fangs-out" knife-edge break.

fanner *n. Hobo.* a slapping with a policeman's nightstick as a signal to quit loitering. Also **fanning.**
    1927 H. Miller *Moloch* 16: I'll be minded to give yuh a polite fannin'. **1930** "D. Stiff" *Milk & Honey* 205: To *get a fanner* is to be moved on by the police.

Fannie Mae *n.* [vocalization of the initialism *FNMA*] *Finance.* the Federal National Mortgage Association.
    1948 in *OEDAS* II 79. **1953** (cited in *BDNE3* s.v. *Ginnie Mae*). **1969** *N.Y. Post* (Dec. 12) 89: *Fannie Mae*—the Federal National Mortgage Association. **1980** *N.Y. Times* (June 22) IV 5: Fannie Mae, the Federal National Mortgage Association, is a shareholder-owned corporation which helps meet people's housing needs by supplying money to the home mortgage industry. **1982** WINS Radio News (Aug. 24): The Federal National Mortgage Association—or *Fannie Mae,* as it's called.

fanny *n.* [orig. unkn., but perh. cf. *Fanny Hill* (1748–49), erotic novel by John Cleland]
    1. the vulva or vagina.—usu. considered vulgar. [Chiefly BrE and always rare in U.S. The **1882 quot. could possibly belong at (2), below.]
    ca*1835–40** in Speaight *Bawdy Songs of Music Hall* 76: I've got a little Fanny,/That with hair is overspread. *Ibid.* 39: Johnny touched her Fanny up. *****1882** *Boudoir* 88: Come…feel our soft little fannys. *****1889** Barrère & Leland *Dict. Slang* I 354: *Fanny* (common), the fem. pud. **1933** Rogers & Miller *Eagle & Hawk* (film): Well, you may be Fifi to the rest of the world but you're nothing but Fanny to me! **1957** *College Songs, Bawdy Parodies* in IUFA: While the bees are makin' honey,/Let your fanny make some money. **1980** E. Jong, in *OED2:* "Madam Fanny….D'ye know what that means in the Vulgar Tongue?"…"The Divine Monosyllable, the Precious Pudendum, [etc.]."
    2. the backside; buttocks.—also used in substitution for ASS in various senses.
    1919 *12th U.S. Inf.* 73: They made us all get in a circle and stoop over while a guy ran around and hit us on the—never mind where—with a strap—I believe they call the game "Bat the Fanny" and they sure did bat me. **1925** McAlmon *Silk Stockings* 76: He gives me an ache in my fanny. **1925** Dos Passos *Transfer* 273: They can…hang them on the Commanding General's fanny for all I care. **1928** Hecht & MacArthur *Front Page* 474: Yeah, parking her fanny in here like it was a cathouse. **1929** E. Wilson *Daisy* 69: They all had to sit there at the table with their fannies freezing and not knowing what was the trouble. **1934** Kromer *Waiting* 19: Me spend five bucks…? Not on your fanny. **1938** Bezzerides *Long Haul* 20: We'd still be there, sitting on our fannies. **1939** in A. Banks *First-Person* 65: Alright, shake your fannies, it's eleven o'clock! **1946** Dadswell *Hey, Sucker* 40: Strippers, G-stringers and fanny-dancers. **1948** Cozzens *Guard* 192: "Oh, my poor fanny," she said, squirming. "These damn chairs!" **1983** *Hour Magazine* (ABC-TV) (May 10): A couple of whacks on the fanny would do it. **1987** *Night Court* (NBC-TV): You are such a *fanny!*
    3. one's self. *Joc.* Cf. identical use of ASS, BUTT, etc.
    1925 Mullin *Scholar Tramp* 114 [ref. to *ca*1912]: Say, you fellas…if you don't fly your flannies [*sic*] out o' town pretty quick on the next freight, I'll throw you all in the jug. **1947–53** Guthrie *Seeds* 278: Le's jump up an' scoot our fannies outta here. **1956** Lasly *Turn Tiger Loose* 136: His fanny belongs to us. We'll have him boxed in. **1978** Truscott *Dress Gray* 243: Get your fannies ready for bed.

fanny-dunker *n. Surfing.* a wader or swimmer. *Joc.*
    1968 Kirk & Hanle *Surfer's Hndbk.* 20: The air or the water or both are too cold for gremlins, fanny dunkers, doggy paddlers and other forms of beach traffic.

fan out see var. senses s.v. FAN, *v.*

fantabulous *adj.* [blend *fanta*stic + *fabulous*] wonderful; marvelous.
    1958 J. Davis *College Vocab.* 8: *Fantabulous*—Really great. **1961** Partridge *DSUE* (ed. 5) s.v. *fab:* An ephemerid of 1958 was *fantabulous.* **1962** in Clarke *Amer. Negro Stories* 259: And the English this man spoke was fantabulous! **1973** N.Y.U. student: Here's a word I use all

the time: *fantabulous*. It means *fantastic* and *fabulous*. **1978** Maupin *Tales* 3: "Fantabulous!" squealed Connie. **1984** Blumenthal *Hollywood* 103: It's brilliant, Murray! Fantabulous! **1988** *N.Y. Daily News* (June 18): Petey, he's fantabulous! **1993** *Beyond Reality* (USA-TV): That coffee smells fantabulous!

fantail express *n. Navy.* (see quot.). *Joc.*

1969 Cagle *Nav. Av. Guide* 393: *Fantail express.* The boatswain's chair used for at-sea, high line transfer.

fantastic *adj.* amazing; extraordinarily good or pleasing; exciting. Now *colloq.*

1929 J.M. Saunders *Single Lady* 81: Wasn't that fantastic?...Did you ever see anything so fast in your life? **1938** in Hammerstein *Kern Song Bk.* 189: Your pose! That cute fantastic nose! **1956** Kitt *Thursday's Child* 145: Opening night in Paris was fantastic. **1969** McGinniss *Selling of Pres.* 147: "You like that?"..."Fantastic. Just fantastic." **1978** W. Craven *Stranger in Our House* (film): "Let me help. Lean back and relax." "Oh, yes, that's fantastic." **1986** Hodges & Whitten *Harbrace* (ed. 10) 209: *Fantastic.* Informal—overworked for "extraordinarily good" or "wonderful, remarkable."

fantods *n.pl.* [perh. alter. of earlier BrE *fantique, fantigue*] a state of anxiety or uneasiness; fidgets; jitters; nervous hysteria.—usu. constr. with *the.*

1839 Briggs *Harry Franco* I 249: You have got strong symptoms of the fantods; your skin is so tight you can't shut your eyes without opening your mouth. **1867** Smyth *Sailor's Word-Bk.*: *Fantods*, a name given to the fidgets of officers. **1869** in "M. Twain" *Stories* 29: Mush-and-milk journalism gives me the fan-tods. **1884** in "M. Twain" *Huck. Finn* 105: These was all nice pictures, I reckon, but I didn't somehow seem to take to them, because if ever I was down a little they always give me the fantods. **1919** S. Anderson, in Woods *Horse-Racing* 33: It's what give me the fantods. I can't make it out. **1940** O'Neill *Iceman* 114: You and the other bums have begun to give me the graveyard fantods. **1977** *N.Y. Times* (May 1) X 1: Heebie-jeebies. Butterflies in the stomach. Fantods. **1979** Cassidy *Delta* 222: *That* kind of a woman would just give a man like you a case of the fantods.

far away *adj. & interj. Stu.* FAR OUT. *Joc.*

1972 N.Y.U. student: *Farm out! far away! right arm!* That's *far out! right on!* when you're making fun of somebody. **1974** *Nat. Lampoon* (Dec.) 55: I've got some real "far-away" stuff here.

far darter *n. USAF.* (see quot.). *Joc.*

1955 *AS* XXX 116: *Charger: Big Spender From* (home town); *Far Darter*, n.; *n. phr.* Man who talks a good game and exudes self-confidence but always loses bets, card games, etc., always gets stuck with the check, and always gets outfumbled and has to pay for the drinks.

Far East *interj. Mil.* in East Asia. FAR OUT. *Joc.*

1983 Eilert *Self & Country* 265 [ref. to 1968]: He took off your casts. The doctor took them off. Far *East!* **1985** Former U.S. Army SP4: I was in the China Night Club in Taipei, Taiwan, shortly after I went into the service [in 1971] and a guy was saying, "Far fuckin' East, man! Far fuckin' *East!*" He meant *far out.*

Far East two-step *n.* diarrhea contracted in the Far East. Cf. TWO-STEP, AZTEC TWO-STEP.

1966 E. Shepard *Doom Pussy* 227: Members suffering from the Far East Two-step, known in Egypt as the Pharaoh's Revenge, may leave any formal or informal gathering at a brisk trot at any time...

farm *n.* **1.** *Navy.* sand, gravel, or dirt on a ship's deck.

1878 Shippen *30 Yrs.* 376 [ref. to 1865]: On board the Ironsides we found "Jack" at work with hose and buckets, brooms and squillgees, washing down the spar-deck, and getting rid of our "farm," as the men called the sand.

2.a. *R.R.* a sidetrack or sidetracks.—constr. with *the.* [In later S.E. 'a storage installation, esp. for fuel; see *OEDS.*]

1926 *AS* I (Dec.) 651: *Going on the farm*—put on a side track. **1930** "D. Stiff" *Milk & Honey* 206: *Going on the farm*—When a train goes on the sidetrack.

b. *Av.* an airfield.

1985 Heywood *Taxi Dancer* 147 [ref. to Vietnam War]: Phuc Yen, the NVA's primary MiG farm in the Hanoi area.

3. *CIA.* the CIA training facility at Camp Peary, Va.—constr. with *the.*

1981 D.E. Miller *Jargon* 220: *Farm, the.* A major CIA training base, located at Camp Peary, near Williamsburg, Virginia. **1986** "H.S.A. Becket" *Dict. Esp.* 31: Agency people called Peary "The Farm".

4. FUNNY FARM.—constr. with *the.*

1977 Dunne *Confessions* 156: She's ready for the farm, but she won't file charges. **1978** Univ. Tenn. student questionnaire: Insane asylum...*madhouse, farm.*

¶ In phrase:

¶ **buy the farm** see s.v. BUY, *v.*

farmer *n.* **1.** an ignorant rustic; (*hence,* commonly) a naive or foolish fellow; SAP.

*1864 Hotten *Slang Dict.* (ed. 3): *Farmer*...In London...is used derisively of a countryman, and denotes a farm-labourer, clodpole. **1892** S. Crane *Maggie* 18: Mos' ev'ry day some farmer comes in an' tries teh run deh shop. **1894** *Harper's* (Dec.) 106: You see, I'm no farmer, trying to write a song for *you.* **1894** Henderson *Sea Yarns* 2: You may call me a farmer if this wasn't the way of it. **1896** Ade *Artie* 26: I may be a farmer, but it takes better people than you to sling the bull con into me. **1902** Greenough & Kittredge *Words & Ways* 285: In this country..."farmer" is sometimes jocosely applied to a greenhorn, or to a person who has made himself ridiculous, particularly by awkwardness or stupidity. **1911** A.H. Lewis *Apaches of N.Y.* 104: That doll's makin' a farmer of Louie. **1920–22** in *DN* V 330: *Farmer, n.* A poor sailor;—term of contempt. **1925** Faulkner *N.O. Sketches* 95: "Cheest," I says, "it gives me a pain to see a good horse butchered like that farmer done that one." **1936** in Thomason *Stories* 302: Yeh, it was your second platoon—a bunch of farmers with two left feet, as ever was. **1951** W. Williams *Enemy* 180: Come on, you farmers, you ain't at the general store. Turn to. Get on those decks. **1959** Tevis *Hustler* 37: I bet you already beat every nine-ball shooting farmer from here to the West Coast. **1962** Dougherty *Commissioner* 22: "What was that about the farmers in Brooklyn?" Madigan muttered. **1965** C. Brown *Manchild* 161: There were farmers everywhere who wouldn't listen, who were dreaming. **1967** *Lit Dictionary* 14: *Farmer*—A square. **1972** Carr *Bad* 149: You're a young fool for lettin' this farmer watch it. **1983** N.Y.C. man, age *ca*32: Catch the ball, farmer!

2. *Naut.* (see 1896 quot.).

1886 in *OEDS*: I'm a farmer to-night, and means to have a quiet and peaceful night's rest. **1896** Hamblen *Many Seas* 40: A "farmer" on shipboard is a man who has neither a wheel nor a lookout to take during a given night watch, so that...he may hope to get quite a good bit of sleep in his watch on deck. **1925** Farmer *Shellback* 71: A "farmer" is any one of the watch who has neither wheel nor look-out during the night watches on deck.

farm hand *n. Baseball.* a minor-league player belonging to a major-league club's farm team.

1934 Weseen *Dict. Slang* 209: *Farm hand*—An inexperienced baseball player recently added to a team. **1938** Nichols *Baseball Term.* 24: *Farm-hand:* A minor-league player belonging to one of the major league clubs. **1939–40** Tunis *Kid From Tomkinsville* 212: The Dodgers...are so far behind these days they're calling in their farm hands. **1982** WINS Radio News (Aug. 28): The winning hit was a homerun by...a former Yankee farmhand.

far out *adj.* **1.** Orig. *Jazz.* daringly creative; avant-garde; (*also*) extremely unusual or eccentric. Now *colloq.*

1954 *Time* (Nov. 8) 70: A daring [jazz] performance was "hot," then "cool," and now is "far out." **1956** Stearns *Story of Jazz* ch. xviii: There were too many choices in "far-out" harmony. **1958** in R.S. Gold *Jazz Talk* 89: Mike wondered what he would play. Nothing too far out, but a real old tune wouldn't get it either. **1959** in R.S. Gold *Jazz Talk*: It's too far out for the average gin-mill owner. **1960** Swarthout *Where Boys Are* 48: Most human beings poop away their years waiting for some shimmering, mystic, way-far-out thing to happen. **1960** R. Reisner *Jazz Titans* 155: *Far Out:* very advanced; something intricate or involved, musically or otherwise. Jackson Pollock is far out. **1968** in *Rolling Stone Interviews* 50: I played further out riffs. **1976** Dyer *Erroneous Zones* 14: I am just "far out" enough to believe that...you can be anything you choose.

2. extraordinarily good or pleasing. Also as interj.

1954 *Time* (Nov. 8) 70: Far-Out Words for Cats. **1955** *Science Digest* (Aug.) 33: What was originally "hot" suddenly becomes "cool" and is now "far out." **1956** *Esquire* (Sept.) 79: "Far out" is the new *hip*, not *hep*, term of critical approval. **1958–59** Lipton *Barbarians* 72: You know, *far out*—but, like, man you got to come *back. Ibid.* 80: We've been making a swinging scene every night. *Far out!* **1959** Zugsmith *Beat Generation* 137: We're going to have a real beat hootenanny...One that's far out! **1969** Mitchell *Thumb Tripping* 9: "Far out!" laughed Gary, digging it. **1972** R. Barrett *Lovomaniacs* 49: Those far-out legs of hers. **1977** Sayles *Union Dues* 371: Far out! Far-fucking-out! **1984** Heath *A-Team* 77: Wow!...Far out!...Bitchin'! **1988** *N.Y. Times Mag.* (Dec. 11) 24: Far *out*, for *astonishing* or *wondrous*, was another common term of 20 years ago that seems to have completely disappeared. **1990** *Garfield & Friends* (CBS-TV): Doin' a play sounds far out, man!

fart *n.* **1.a.** an expulsion of gas through the anus.—usu. considered vulgar. Also *fig.* Orig. *S.E.*

ca*1386** Chaucer *Miller's Tale*, in *OED*: This Nicholas anon let flee a fart. **1562 in *OED*: I shall geat a fart of a dead man as soone As a farthyng of him. **1645 in Wardroper *Love & Drollery* 203: Music is but a fart that's sent/From the guts of an intstrument. **1650 in *OED*: The Guineans are careful not to let a fart. **1728 J. Swift, in *OED*: Punch comes, like you, and lets a f—t. **1775** in Silber *Songs of Independence* 72: Dolly Bushel let a fart,/Jenny Jones she found it. **1888** *Stag Party* 42: He...let a most diabolical fart. **1928** in Read *Lexical Evidence* 50: Now and then a fart is heard. **1935** J. Conroy *World to Win* 40: I'll knock a string o' farts out o' you as long as a grapevine. **1948** Wolfert *Act of Love* 223: Blew a fart back at you, eh? **1958** Camerer *Damned Wear Wings* 173: No bigger'n a baby's fart. **1961** Gover *$100 Misunderstanding* 38: Francine pop in. Yeah! Loud's a fart in a empty tin can. **1966–67** P. Thomas *Mean Streets* 31: When you're in the bathtub and you lay a fart, little bubbles come up. **1974** *Penthouse* (Feb.) 90: You're as funny as a fart in a spacesuit. **1975** in *Tenn. Folklore Soc. Bull.* XLIV 137: That's like a Friday fart at a Saturday market.

b. (used—now often with elaboration—as a symbol of worthlessness and contempt); a damn.—usu. considered vulgar.

ca*1400** in *MED* s.v. *fert*: Elles it nere nauȝt worþ a fart. **ca***1425** in *MED*: Thy speach is not worth a fart. **ca***1460** in *OED*: Bi alle men set I not a farte. **1535** Sir D. Lyndsay *Thrie Estaites* (unp.): I will give for your play not a sow's fart. **1645 in Wardroper *Love & Drollery* 203: What's he get by it? Not a fart....I cannot write/Rimes that are worth the thing I praise. I do not care a fart. **ca***1650** in Child *Eng. & Scot. Pop. Ballads* III 141: Your news is not worth a fart. **1661** in Burford *Bawdy Verse* 146: And all not worth a fart. **1698** Ward *London-Spy* 2: A Fig for St. *Austin* and his Doctrines, a Fart for *Virgil* and his Elegancy, and a T—d for *Descarts* and his *Philosophy*. *Ibid.* 27: They found their Project would not signifie a Fart. **1734** in Whiting *Early Amer. Proverbs* 145: As for his protest, if he should set a f—t against a N.W. wind, how then? **1749** H. Fielding *Tom Jones*, in *F & H* II 375: "I don't give a fart for 'n," says the squire, suiting the action to the word. **1785** R. Burns, in *F & H*: But Dr. Hornbook with his art...Has made them baith no worth a f—t. **1826** in Audubon *Journal* 50: Without caring a f—. **1914–21** Joyce *Ulysses* 330: They were never worth a roasted fart to Ireland. **1927** *Immortalia* 7: He don't care a fart. **1933** J. Conroy *Disinherited* 38: Ye'll last about as long as a fart in a whirlwind. **1936** J.T. Farrell *World I Never Made* 342: And, yes, a great big fart out of my ass for you, you drunken streetwalker. **1937** Weidman *I Can Get It For You Wholesale* 44: Because before you know it the whole goddam strike won't be worth a fart. **1942** McAtee *Supp. to Grant Co.* 4 [ref. to 1890's]: *Fart in hell*, n. phr., very little; I wouldn't give a —— for his chances. **1920–54** Randolph *Bawdy Elements* 107: He don't amount to a fart in a whirlwind. **1961** Peacock *Valhalla* 15: I don't give two farts in hell for no...Charley. **1961** Garrett *Which Ones* 44 [ref. to *ca*1952]: You can say that again. They weren't worth a country fart. **1962** Quirk *Red Ribbons* 89: He hasn't got the chance of a fart in a windstorm. **1964–66** R. Stone *Hall of Mirrors* 53: Nobody here gives a cold fart what you can't stand. **1966** King *Brave & Damned* 41: They'll last about as long as a fart in the wind. **1971** Gallery *Away Boarders* 93: The U.N. don't amount to a fart in a piss pot. **1977** *Nat. Lampoon* (July) 46: Foreign policy during his administration wasn't worth a roasted fart. **1973** Beck *Folklore & the Sea* 67: One who is generally ineffectual is said to be about as much good as a spare boiler or not to amount to anything "more than a hen fart in a gale." **1976** Hayden *Voyage* 541: Not worth...so much as a "fart in a gale of wind." **1983** K. Miller *Lurp Dog* 165: Wouldn't have cared two farts in a shitstorm. **1986** Stinson & Carabatsos *Heartbreak* 3: Asshole to asshole [they] ain't worth a beer fart in a windstorm. **1989** Wittliff *Lonesome Dove* (CBS-TV): A little fart of a town in South Texas.

2. a contemptible person.—now esp. constr. with *old*.—usu. considered vulgar.

a*1890–91** *F & H* II 375: *Fart*...By implication, a contemptible person. **1931** J.T. Farrell *Gas-House McGinty* 39: He's a fart as noisy as a Kansas cyclone. **1934** Halper *Foundry* 239: Which one is it going to be this time, you old fart? **1936** Levin *Old Bunch* 121: There's an old fart of a hotel. *Ibid.* 330: That fart would always have a tricky excuse. **1946** Heggen *Mr. Roberts* xiv: Captain Morton is an old fart. **1946** Saroyan *Wesley Jackson* 50: Old fart. **1961** C. Cooper *Weed* 101: I'm gonna tell Grandmommie what you did, you fart you! **1961** Sullivan *Gladdest Yrs.*

15: The three guys...were all "nuclear physics farts and about thirteen years old." **1963** Boyle *Yanks* 9: Christ, that little fart isn't big enough to whip a sick whore with a beer bottle! **1968** Tiede *Coward* 333: A yellow-bellied fart like you...can't even take care of paper work. **1969** Gardner *Fat City* 71: Well, you old fart, are they hiring or not? **1972** *N.Y. Post* (Apr. 15) 52: You may think of me as a sentimental old fart. **1979** Crews *Blood & Grits* 21: You gone let that skinny fart talk to you like that, Edsel? **1992** *Donahue* (NBC-TV): I didn't always look like an old fart like this.

3. (used interjectionally to express astonishment, exasperation, etc.).—usu. considered vulgar.

1936 Farrell *World I Never Made* 342: Fart on you! **1962** Crump *Killer* 300: Holy pink fart, what a dumb question!

fart *v.* **1.** to expel gas through the anus.—usu. considered vulgar. Also *fig.* Orig. *S.E.*

ca*1250** in *OED*: Bulluc sterteþ, bucke uerteþ. **ca***1386** G. Chaucer, in *OED*: He was somdel squaymous of farting. **ca***1532** in *OED*: To farte or to burste, *crepiter*. **ca***1580** in *OED*: A great farter. **1610** B. Jonson *Alchemist* I i: Thy worst! I fart at thee! **1632** in *OED*: Tho' the devil fart fire, have at him! **1740** T. Gray, in *OED*: They...never speak, but they f—t. **1888** *Stag Party* 32: And the folks heard him f—t/Just a mile and a half from Toledo. **1919** in Mencken *New Ltrs.* 118: Eating beans causes one to fart. **1928** in Read *Lexical Evidence* 50: Here I sit all broken hearted/Came to shit and only farted. **1970** E. Thompson *Garden of Sand* 187: His hollerin ain't no more than fartin in the breeze. **1974** Knoxville, Tenn., truckdriver, age *ca*30: Now if a girl's real good-lookin' you say, "I'd crawl on my belly through a mile of broken glass and drunkard's puke just to hear her fart over a field telephone." **1975** C.W. Smith *Country Music* 228: Holy Moley!...I'd crawl through forty miles of barbed wire and mortar fire just to hear her fart through a field phone! **1978** Gann *Hostage* 445: That little runt would as soon kill you as fart. **1982** Downey *Losing War* 43: Farted like a work horse. **1983** Eilert *Self & Country* 17: It's so quiet you could hear a popcorn fart. **1985** Ark. man, age 35: I've heard "so quiet you could hear a *pen* fart," "a *pencil* fart," "a *roach* fart," anything small and unlikely to fart. **1983** K. Miller *Lurp Dog* 5 [ref. to Vietnam War]: I'd eat a mile of commo wire just to hear her fart over a field phone! **1986–91** Hamper *Rivethead* 55: *No wonder* my new vehicle farts like a moose full of chickpeas! **1992** *Donahue* (NBC-TV): "Do you mind if I smoke?" "No. Do you mind if I fart?"

2. to meddle; interfere; trifle.—usu. considered vulgar.

1971 Keith *Long Line Rider* 215: Now y'all get out'n heah an' leave me alone. Y'all take up nine tenths o' my time an' ah'm tard o' fartin' with ya! **1974** *Playboy* (Apr.) 219: Son, you got to learn that some folks won't do to fart with.

¶ In phrases:

¶ **fart fire** to be in a rage; show or feel fury.—usu. considered vulgar.

1632 (quot. at (1), above). **1920–54** Randolph *Bawdy Elements* 106: Polly has been a-farting fire all evening...I ain't going home till her ass cools off.

¶ **fart through silk** (orig. of women) to live a life of luxury.—usu. considered vulgar. *Joc.*

1927 [Fliesler] *Anecdota* 181: She never farted through silk all her life. *ca***1953** in Hammett *Knockover* 242: As a matter of fact, I'm pretty well fixed right now, sweating against silk, as the boys used to say, only that isn't exactly what they said. **1920–54** Randolph *Bawdy Elements* 106: Mabel's a-fartin' through silk nowadays. **1974** *Nat. Lampoon* (Apr.) 53: The pimps got a payroll in New York bigger than General Motors. Fucking cops are farting through silk in this city. **1979** G. Wolff *Duke of Deception* 140 [ref. to 1950's]: The bosses always screw the working stiff...I sleep in a trailer, his wife farts through silk. **1984** Wilder *You All* 25: Stick with Terry and you'll fart through silk. Terry Sanford's cheerful admonition to spirit up the troops—in the 517th Parachute Combat Team in World War II and in his political campaigns. **1985** Yeager & Janos *Yeager* 54 [ref. to 1944]: "Honey...you stick with me and you'll be fartin' through silk." That line became famous throughout the entire Eighth Air Force.

¶ **feathers and farting** commotion.—usu. considered vulgar.

1970 Thackrey *Thief* 126: Well, when all the feathers and farting was done, there in the house, my sister went to cook up a meal.

fart around *v.* to fool around; waste time.—usu. considered vulgar. [*Fart about*, as in the **1900 quot., is the usu. BrE form.]

[**1900** in *EDD*: Thoo's allus farten aboot.] **1931** Dos Passos *1919* 19 [ref. to *ca*1918]: What the hell do they want to be fartin' around here for? **1932** in H. Miller *Letter to Emil* 94: I did a lot of farting around, I wrote junk. **1936** Levin *Old Bunch* 121: A fellow farts around the Loop all morning. **1938** H. Miller *Trop. Capricorn* 94: What's the use of farting around in this place? **1938** Steinbeck *Grapes of Wrath* 110: I was a squirt jus' like you, a-fartin' aroun' like a dog-wolf. But when they was a job, I done it. **1943** *AS* (Feb.) 43: Now, the American expression "to fart around" has the same connotation and denotation as the Yiddish *arumfartzen*, from which, I take it, the expression stems. **1946** Lea *Peleliu Landing* 90: Let's quit this farting around. Tell him to take us in! **1952** Uris *Battle Cry* 229: If the Army wants to fart around for six weeks, it's their business. **1958** Plagemann *Steel Cocoon* 64: "You have to fart around so much with women," he said uncomfortably. "You have to buy beers and sit around, and—oh, you know, even talk to them. And then you never know until the last minute whether you're going to get in or not." **1961** Garrett *Which Ones* 65: "I'm asking you a serious question." "Oh…excuse me, I thought you were just farting around." **1966–67** P. Thomas *Mean Streets* 30: Come on, man….Hey, Moms, tell James to stop farting around. **1984** H. Searls *Blood Song* 288: If your daddy don't quit fartin' around, I'll never get past here.

fart away *v.* to squander.—usu. considered vulgar.
    1928 Dahlberg *Bottom Dogs* 269: What he could have done with the ninety cents he had farted away to those bums. **1976** *Esquire* (Sept.) 61: You can…fart away Sunday in a fun house.

fart-blossom *n.* a worthless or despicable person.—usu. considered vulgar.
    1938 "Justinian" *Amer. Sexualis* 21: *Fart. n.*….Also, a symbol of contempt; a person of little significance. Also, in latter sense, *fart-blossom, fart-face*, et al. **1952** Bellow *Augie March* 493: You listen here to me, fart-blossom, you chiseler. **1968–70** *Current Slang* III & IV 45: *Fart blossom, n.* A person inclined to stupid behavior.—College males, South Dakota. **1976** Conroy *Santini* 219: So I look upon it as my sacred duty to run as many of you fart blossoms out of the Marine Corps as I can. **1977** Univ. Tenn. student: I have an aunt who's 75 who's used that term as long as I can remember. But it's mostly as an endearment for a little child: "you little fart blossom." **1984** Israel & Wilson *Police Academy* (film): Listen up, fart-blossom. *a*1986 D. Tate *Bravo Burning* 52: All you fartblossoms.

fart-box *n.* the anus or rectum; the buttocks.—usu. considered vulgar. *Joc.*
    1966 in IUFA *Folk Speech*: *Fart box* anus or rectum. **1968** in *DARE*: *Joking words for the part of the body that you sit on*…Fart-box. **1966–70** in *DARE* s.v. *box, n.*, 5.b. **1974** Univ. Tenn. student: A fart box is a damn asshole.

fartbreath *n.* (used as a term of contempt).—usu. considered vulgar.
    1974 *Nat. Lampoon* (Oct.) 20: Anyway, fartbreaths,…you'd better fork over. **1976** Univ. Tenn. student: Shut up, fartbreath.

fart-buster *n.* FART-KNOCKER.—usu. considered vulgar.
    1959 F.L. Brown *Trumbull Pk.* 321: But, listen, you little fart buster….You got guts.

fart-catcher *n.* (see quots.).—usu. considered vulgar.
    *1785 Grose *Vulgar Tongue*: *Fart Catcher.* A valet or footman, from his walking behind his master or mistress. **1977** Stallone *Paradise Alley* 26: I ain't walkin' behind nobody—I ain't nobody's fart catcher!

fart-face *n.* an ugly or contemptible person.—usu. considered vulgar. Hence **fart-faced**, *adj.*
    1938 (quot. at FART-BLOSSOM). **1943** Hersey *Bell for Adano* 112: It's surer'n hell goin' to get the Major busted when old fart-face sees it. **1961** Gover *$100 Misunderstanding* 186: That fart face done flipflop his Whiteass lid for sure! **1972** R. Wilson *Forbidden Words* 102: *Fart-face*, anybody the speaker wishes to insult. **1974** Kurtzman *Bobby* 35: Shut your damn mouth you old fart face. **1977** *Maledicta* 7: Some day, we may be able to freak out our fartfaced colleagues. **1978** Wharton *Birdy* 180: No fartface…miner's going to outdo Al. **1978** Pilcer *Teen Angel* 46: Those yellow-livered fartfaces. **1985** in M. Groening *School Is Hell* (unp.): Melvin and Fartface got hit.

fart-hammer *n.* FART-KNOCKER.—usu. considered vulgar.
    1970 E. Thompson *Garden of Sand* 326: Old farthammer over there got fresh with her.

farthead *n.* a stupid or despicable person; SHITHEAD.—usu. considered vulgar.
    1962 H. Simmons *On Eggshells* 118: You little farthead. **1963** Parks *Learning Tree* 78: You bunch of fart-heads hit the floor! **1973** Browne

Body Shop 155: Keep it down, old farthead'll hear. **1973** *Nat. Lampoon* (June) 8: You fartheads haven't sent me a check yet. **1975** Univ. Wisc. student: Tell that farthead to get on the stick.

farthole *n.* **1.** the anus; SHITHOLE.—usu. considered vulgar.
    1986 Stinson & Carabatsos *Heartbreak* 40: Our operations officer's fart hole is sewed so tight he shits out of his mouth.
    2. (see quots.).—usu. considered vulgar.
    1970–72 in *AS* L (1975) 58: *Fart hole* n. Person considered contemptible. **1980** Pearl *Pop. Slang* 48: *Farthole* n. an obnoxious or foolish person.

fart hook *n.* a stupid or useless person; SHITHOOK.—usu. considered vulgar.
    1972 Hannah *Geronimo Rex* 194: What does that big farthook Silas *do*, by the way? [*Ibid.* 118: You think men of ideas are going around trying to catch farts with a hook, don't you?]

fart-knocker *n.* (used as a term of contempt).—usu. considered vulgar. Hence **fart-knocking**, *adj.*
    1952 Uris *Battle Cry* 255 [ref. to 1942]: Seabags, you old fart knocker— we thought you was dead. **1963–64** Kesey *Great Notion* 128: Cocksuckin', *ass*lickin', *fart*knockin', *shit*eatin' (bastard). **1983** K. Weaver *Texas Crude* 44: *Fartknocker.* Any obscure person. **1993** *Beavis & Butthead* (MTV): Shut up, fartknocker.

fartleberries *n.pl.* (see quots.).—usu. considered vulgar. Cf. DILLBERRY, DINGLEBERRY.
    *1785 Grose *Vulgar Tongue*: *Fartleberries.* Excrement hanging about the anus. **1984** Wilder *You All* 38: *Fartleberries*: Small wads of fecal and seminal deposits in the hair of the anus and the female pudendum.

fartnose *n.* a contemptible person; SHITNOSE.—usu. considered vulgar.—also attrib.
    1974 *Nat. Lampoon* (Oct.) 84: So get on the stick, fartnoses. **1981** Hathaway *World of Hurt* 182: Old fart-nose mama-sans.

fart-off *n.* a person who shirks responsibilities; loafer.—usu. considered vulgar.
    1942–44 (quot. at FART OFF, *v.*, 1.b.). **1968** Baker et al. *CUSS* 115: *Fart off.* A person who always fools around. **1971** Dahlskog *Dict.* 22: *Fart-off, n. Vulgar.* One who shirks or neglects his work; a gold-bricker.

fart off *v.* **1.a.** to fool around; neglect one's duties; blunder through inattention.—usu. considered vulgar.
    1968 Baker et al. *CUSS* 115: *Fart off.* Waste time, not study. **1971** Dahlskog *Dict.* 22: *Fart off, v. Vulgar.* To goof off; neglect one's work; to procrastinate. **1972** Hannah *Geronimo Rex* 197: I was sounding like the mother of music, then you fart off!
    b. to slight; neglect; ignore.—usu. considered vulgar.
    1942–44 in *AS* (Feb. 1946) 33: *Fart-off, n.* An insult. *v.t.* To insult. **1969** *Current Slang* I & II 32: *Fart it off, v.* To show a lack of concern.— College males, South Dakota.—"You flunked the test. Fart it off." **1970–72** in *AS* L (1975) 59: I decided to fart off studying for the test. **1974** Univ. Tenn. student: I can't keep just farting it off.
    2. (see quots.).—usu. considered vulgar.
    1971 Dahlskog *Dict.* 22: *Fart off*…Shove off; get lost; flake off. **1972** N.Y.U. student: *Fart off* means bug off, *fuck off*.

fartsack *n.* Esp. *Mil.* a sleeping bag, bedroll, bunk, cot, or bed; SACK.—usu. considered vulgar. [Early quots. ref. to WWII.]
    1943 in M.W. Bowman *Castles* 80: *Phartzac* [B-17 of 100th Bomb Group, USAAF]. **1946** T.H. Burns *Gallery* 319: Get out of that fartsack. **1944–48** A. Lyon *Unknown Station* 94: He untied the string and opened the roll. "It's okay, it's a fart-sack all right." **1950** Stuart *Objector* 72: What the hell are you doing in that fart sack? **1953** Dibner *Deep Six* 147: Just in my fahrt sack. Can't a guy sleep? **1960** Leckie *Marines!* 45: I ain't sleeping for nobody. I'm sitting right here on my fartsack with my eyes wide open until they catch The Ghoul. **1960** MacCuish *Do Not Go Gentle* 115: You ape asses gonna make those fart-sacks right, understand? **1962** Killens *Heard The Thunder* 48: Just sit on your dead ass on your fart-sack all the time, looking at the floor or up at the ceiling. **1972** Pearce *Pier Head Jump* 156: What a stupid time to get out of the fart sack. **1979** McGivern *Soldiers* 11: He's in the truck in his fart sack with a lot of blankets on top of him.

fartsnatcher *n.* a contemptible person.—usu. considered vulgar.
    1935 Algren *Boots* 49: The fartsnatcher ain't give me a dime yet, Jackie, an' he tried to heel out with mah ring on top of it.

fart-sucker *n.* (see *a*1890-91 quot.).—usu. considered vulgar.
    *a*1890–91 *F & H* II 375: *Fart-sucker*…(common).—A vile parasite; an

"arsehole creeper." **1975** Wambaugh *Choirboys* 32: "How about fart-suckers [as an epithet]?" "Not rotten enough."

fascinoma *n.* [*fascin*ating + *-oma*, suff. used to form names of tumors] *Med.* a serious illness that is hard to diagnose or is otherwise interesting or unusual; (*also*) a patient having such an illness.

    1978 Shem *House of God* 407: Olive, a real "fascinoma," seemed to perk him up. **1981** in Safire *Good Word* 152. **1985** *Discover* (May) 82: For the resident and attending physician, being able to identify a fascinoma means something different.

fash *n. Stu.* fashion.

    1895 Gore *Stu. Slang* 6: *Fash* n. Fashion. **1986** in *OEDAS* II 79: Two heaps on the floor afforded a primer on kiddie fash ins and outs.

fast buck *n.* an amount of money made easily or quickly and often unscrupulously; in phr. **fast-buck artist** a person, esp. a swindler, intent on making a fast buck.

    1949 *Time* (Sept. 5) 13: All his years of pursuing the fast buck around the national capital. **1949** *New Yorker* (Nov. 5) 82: Goin' from this studio to that studio tryin' to hustle me a fast buck. **1955** *Popular Science* (Oct.) 20: Many dealers are just out for the fast buck. **1970** Rudensky & Riley *Gonif* 98: Kenneally was a fast-buck guy who had a reputation for hot loads. **1974** in Asimov, Greenberg, & Olander *Sci. Fiction Shorts* 268: Now there was not…any way to identify…Mills as a fastbuck artist. **1977** WINS Radio (Aug. 3): Then the fast-buck artists jumped in. **1981** O'Day & Eells *High Times* 121: All the fast-buck artists had opened up, giving the place the worst characteristics of a boomtown. **1984** J. McNamara *First Directive* 27: New condominiums put up by fast-buck artists. *a***1990** E. Currie *Dope & Trouble* 8: If I see a fast buck, I'ma go for it.

fast-burner *n. Mil.* an energetic, ambitious person; BALL OF FIRE.

    1986 R. Walker *AF Wives* 63: Why not simply latch on to a fast burner and ride his coattails to the top? *a***1989** R. Herman, Jr. *Warbirds* 132: He's made early promotion on every rank since captain. He's a fast burner, uses people for fuel.

fast house *n.* a brothel.

    1869 "G. Ellington" *Women of N.Y.* 206: Can you tell me where there are any "fast" houses around here? *a***1904–11** Phillips *Susan Lenox* II 209: On the chair beside the bed, a fast-house parlor dress of pink cotton silk, and a kind of abbreviated chemise. **1916** in Duis *Saloon* 286: It is as big as any twenty fast houses that we have ever had in the City of Boston. **1942** Davis & Wolsey *Call House Madam* 7: Hers is the story of a "madam" of fast houses. **1942** in Inman *Diary* 1085: Mrs. Cash has always had a hankering to run a "fast house."

fastie *n.* **1.** FAST ONE, 1.

    1934 Jack Yellen, Irving Caesar, & Ray Henderson *Nasty Man* (sheet music): I know what's on your mind;/You'll pull a "fasty." **1941** Wald, Macauley, et al. *Navy Blues* (film): You guys are tryin' to pull a fastie on me.

    2. *Baseball.* a fastball.

    1984 *N.Y. Post* (Aug. 2) 84: The USA batters were a bit skeptical about the clockings on Kauo's fastie.

fast lane *n.* **1.** a style of living characterized by recklessness or dissipation.—usu. constr. with *[life] in the.*

    1976 G. Frey et al. *Life in the Fast Lane* (rock song): They knew all the right people/They took all the right pills/They threw outrageous parties/They paid heavenly bills./Life in the fast lane, surely make you lose your mind. **1977** *L.A. Times* (Dec. 5) III 1: Stabler…has been receiving much publicity lately for living life in the fast lane. **1983** *Time* (May 30) 23: He has been ambivalent about these values and regularly swerved into the fast lane. **1985** D.K. Weisberg *Children of Night* 31: Gene felt the life he was leading was too much "in the fast lane." **1988** *Wonder Years* (ABC-TV): Our relationship was entering the fast lane of the seventh-grade social scene.

    2. FAST TRACK.

    1982 *Maclean's* (Oct. 20) 17: One in the fast lane…has been with the company 17 years and is now a Drake area manager for Calgary, Toronto and Edmonton. **1992** *Middle Ages* (CBS-TV): She's grooming me for the fast lane.

fast mover *n. Mil.* a jet fighter-bomber. [Quots. (except for the *a*1990 quot.) ref. to Vietnam War.]

    1972 in Lavalle *Airpower* 44: Funny little black missiles following some of the fast-movers off the target. **1982** Del Vecchio *13th Valley* 194: Chas don't like them fast movers. *Ibid.* 651: *Fast mover.* An F-4. **1985**

L. Scott *Charlie Mike* 436: *Fast movers* [*sic*]. An Air Force F-4 Phantom Jet. **1987** Zeybel *Gunship* 3: F-4 Phantom jet fighters, "fast movers" in air force talk, had a limited appeal for me. **1987** Nichols & Tillman *Yankee Sta.* 53: But let's not let anyone ever tell us again that guns can't knock down fast-movers. *a***1990** Poyer *Gulf* 89: What kind of bogeys? Fast movers?

fast one *n.* [**1.** a tall tale. [Referring to a horse race, this is perh. a literal nonce term, but the use of quotation marks may imply that it is punning on an existing idiomatic sense, which may be the origin of (2), below.]

    1851 in Dorson *Long Bow* 129: Allow me to present to you and the readers…a "fast one," and which I will tell on my own responsibility.]

    2. [perh. orig. alluding to a fastball in baseball] a quickly accomplished and unscrupulous deception.—usu. constr. with *pull* or *put over.*

    1923 *Cosmopolitan* (Nov.) 98: He's trying to put over a fast one! **1928** in Tuthill *Bungle Family* 61: We Browns had a fast one put over on us. **1929** Hammett *Maltese Falcon* 159: But the next time I tried to put over a fast one they'd stop me…fast. **1930** Bodenheim *Roller Skates* 127: Don' pull a fast one on me. **1931** J.T. Farrell *McGinty* 42: I think that goddamn Bohunk slipped a fast one over on you. **1939** Appel *Power-House* 298: Bill's always pulling fast ones on me! **1948** Lay & Bartlett *Twelve O' Clock High!* 120: I hope the brass upstairs don't pull any fast ones. **1961** Kanter & Tugend *Pocketful of Miracles* (film): You ain't pullin' a fast one on me, are you?

    3. a quickly accomplished act of sexual intercourse; QUICKIE.

    1934 H. Miller *Tropic of Cancer* 155: He pretends to run a little errand so that we can pull off a fast one.

fast pill *n. Horse Racing.* a stimulant illicitly administered to a racehorse before a race.

    1949 Cummings *Dict. Sports* 133. **1976** *Webster's Sports Dict.* 142.

fast shuffle *n.* a deception or other unfair treatment; swindle. Also as v., to trick or swindle.

    1930 Graham & Graham *Queer People* 202: Do you think that you're the only blonde cutie that ever tried to fast-shuffle him? **1954–60** *DAS.* **1966–70** in *DARE.* **1975** *Kojak* (CBS-TV): Some of the men think Daley is getting a fast shuffle. **1981** Sann *Trial* 16: In my time I had gone against some fast shuffles but this was the living end. **1982** Braun *Judas Tree* 81: Tomorrow he'll give me the fast shuffle—so long and goodbye!

fast track *n.* a realm of work or activity characterized by quick success and intense competition.

    1965 in J. Mills *On the Edge* 3: [The Times Square precinct] is a fast track, and if you can't stay in the ball game, you get farmed out. **1965** in *BDNE3.* **1972** Kochman *Rappin'* 386: The years he spent on the "fast track" of Chicago's South Side. **1977** Coover *Public Burning* 171: New York…A fast track, faster even than Los Angeles. *Ibid.* 658: You hanker for the fast track…the big leagues. **1981** *N.Y. Times* (Feb. 14) 32: At Morgan Stanley, he moved ahead on a fast track, becoming a vice president in 1977. **1985** Boyne & Thompson *Wild Blue* 408: I hate all these fast-track bastards. **1987** Thom *Letters to Ms.* 119: But like many other women headed for the "fast track," she stopped to reconsider her life-choices in the mid-eighties. **1993** *N.Y. Times* (Jan. 19) D 1: An episode that might have thrown the company off its fast track.

Fat *n.* a Fatima cigarette. [*Fatima* was once a popular brand name.]

    1927 Wylie *Heavy Laden* 82: Luckies, Fats, Camels—what do you smoke?

fat *adj.* **1.** Esp. *Und. & Gamb.* (usu. of a victim or gambler) having money; flush. [The earliest quot. may merely illus. the related S.E. sense 'affluent; prosperous'.]

    ***1698–99** "B.E." *Dict. Canting Crew: Fat Cull*…a rich fellow. **1821** Martin & Waldo *Lightfoot* 124: There might be some *fat ones* among them. **1851** (cited in Partridge *Dict. Und.* 232). **1961** Scarne *Guide to Gambling* 678: *Fat.* Said of a person with plenty of money. "He's fat." Same as *loaded.* **1979** Homer *Jargon* 39: I've got some *fat* people behind me. **1991** *Houston Chronicle* (Nov. 13) 5D: *Fat:* Has money.

    2.a. Esp. *Black E. & USAF.* comfortable; advantageous; fine; pleasant; OK. Also as adv. Also (in recent use) **phat.**

    1902 Dunbar *Sport* 121: As she would have expressed it, "everything was going fat." **1915** T.A. Dorgan, in Zwilling *TAD Lexicon* 103: There's a guy back there with a fat hand and this is his station. **1947** J.C. Higgins *Railroaded* (film): We're fat if you keep your head and stick to your identification. **1950** *Western Folklore* (May) 158: Current

Mountaineering...Vocabulary...*You're fat*...."You're in," or "You've got it made." **1951** Sheldon *Troubling of Star* 51: If you played your cards right, you had it fat; you had it made brother, and, in fact, you never had it so good. **1955** *AS* XXX 117: *Fat; Fat and happy, adj.; adj. phr.* All set; in an excellent situation. **1958** Camerer *Damned Wear Wings* 132 [ref. to WWII]: Looks like he made it, fat! **1961** L.G. Richards *TAC* 237: With reliable auto pilots and airborne radar the fighter pilots would be "fat." **1962** Harvey *Strike Command* 8: The 614th, in Air Force language, was "fat" on a mission of this kind. *Ibid.* 13: The skies were clear. Everybody was "fat." **1963** *Time* (Aug. 2) 14: *Mellow, phat,...boss.* General adjectives of approval. **1967** *Lit Dict.* 14: *Fat*— great; cool; you dig it. **1968** Baker et al. *CUSS* 115: *Fat*...a general complimentary adjective....A fat pad is a great place to live. **1971** Glasser *365 Days* 206: Fat. That's real fat. **1986** *Life* (Mar.) 46: In...[a] Washington, D.C., high school, a girl with a good figure is "fat to death." **1991** in *Rap Masters* (Jan. 1992) 49: The phat new single and video. **1992** Eble *Campus Slang* (Fall) 3: *Fat*—good, cool. "That's a fat car." **1992** *Yo! MTV Raps* (MTV): This is kinda *fat!*...This is where it's *at!* **1992** *N.Y. Newsday* (Dec. 31) 47: What's In and Out for '93...[In] "Phat" [Out] "Fierce." **1993** *Crain's* (Mar. 15) 6: The boutique will offer all manner of *phat* fashions. That means nothing too trendy, but oversized, quirky takes on contemporary classics.

b. *Av.* plentifully supplied, esp. with fuel.—sometimes constr. with *on*.

1955 R. Scott *Look of Eagle* 93: He called for another fuel count. But everybody was fat, and the second leg of the flight was in the final stage. **1974** Former SAC navigator, age 33: When you have lots of fuel, you're *fat on fuel.* **1978** Gann *Hostage* 279 [ref. to WWII]: "How are we doing on fuel?" "We're fat. I figure we'll have better than two hours reserve when we get there."

¶ In phrases:

¶ **fat, dumb, and happy** blissfully and stupidly contented. **1944** Hart *Winged Victory* (film): You were sittin back there, fat, dumb, and happy, and nearly flew right into the ground. **1986** *NDAS.*

¶ **shoot the fat** *chew the fat* s.v. CHEW.
1958 Gilbert *Vice Trap* 67: The World driver likes to shoot a little fat.

Fat Albert *n.* [the name of a character featured on the CBS-TV Saturday-morning cartoon show *Fat Albert and the Cosby Kids* (premiered Sept. 9, 1972)] *USAF.* a Lockheed C-5 Galaxy jet transport aircraft; (*also*) a Boeing 747 jet liner. **1984** M. Meyers *Wings* 137: C-5 Galaxy. Nickname...Fat Albert. *a*1988 Lewin & Lewin *Thes. of Slang* 13: Fat Albert (jumbo jet).

fat-ass *n.* a grossly fat person.—used derisively.—usu. considered vulgar.

1931 J.T. Farrell *Guillotine Party* 46: Jeff the fatass of Fifty-eighth Street. **1936** J.T. Farrell *World I Never Made* 334: Ah, the woman in the picture was just a big fatass. **1938** "Justinian" *Amer. Sexualis* 21: *Fatass, n.* A broad-buttocked person, generally a woman....U.S. vulgarism, C. 20. **1974** Kurtzman *Bobby* 7: They push me, one fat ass's got his grip squeezed into my arm. **1974** Millard *Thunderbolt* 87: I asked the boss to loan me a pair that would fit the biggest fat-ass in Montana, but I didn't give him your name.

fat-ass *v.* to loaf; idle.—constr. with *it*.—usu. considered vulgar.

1971 *Playboy* (June) 60: Man is going to need bigger and better weekend stimulation than fat-assing it in front of his TV set.

fatback *adj.* rural; rustic.

1934 in Wentworth *ADD*: That'll be ol' fat-back Shelton. **1972–74** Hawes & Asher *Raise Up* 67: Even the old fatback career sergeants started to dig it. **1977** in E.C. Fine *Folklore Text* 189: Down there in Fatback Georgia. **1984** Toop *Rap Attack* 114: New Orleans fatback funk was one of the main roots of hip-hop beats.

fatbelly *n.* a fat person.—used derisively.

1933 J. Conroy *Disinherited* 238: As many as the fatbellies want.

fatbody *n.* a fat person.—used derisively.

1974 Former L/Cpl., USMC, age *ca*27 [ref. to 1967]: A *fatbody* was a fat guy. At Parris Island they had what they called the *fatbody platoon* where they put all the fat guys. And they had all kinds of ways to *make* you lose weight. **1977** Univ. Tenn. student: There's a fatbody on all of those motorcycles. **1987** Kubrick et al. *Full Metal Jacket* (film): Because you are a disgusting *fatbody!*

fatboy *n. Army.* an 81mm mortar.

1960 Bonham *Burma Rifles* 147 [ref. to Burma, WWII]: A little hilltop near the village...had hidden a nest of "fatboys"—eighty-one millime-

ter mortars. *Ibid.* 157: Mad Mike frowned at the "fatboys."

fatbrain *n.* FATHEAD.

1853 *Full & True Report* 10: A gull, a dizzard, an illiterate idiot,...a fat brain.

fat cat *n.* **1.a.** *Pol.* a wealthy and privileged individual, esp. a financial backer of a political campaign.

1928 F.R. Kent *Pol. Behavior* 59: These capitalists have...money to finance the campaign. Such men are known in political circles as "Fat Cats"...any "Fat Cat" able and willing to spend as much as is necessary can get whatever he wants in state politics. **1930** *Time* (May 19) 15. **1950** in Truman *Dear Bess* 561: I had the pleasure of telling off a lot of "fat cats" last night. **1953** Manchester *City of Anger* 58: "I'm a cinch in the primary if I can get city support." "And a fat cat to pay the bill." **1958** Drury *Advise and Consent* 56: He'll get it yet, you wait and see, even if he does have General Motors and half the fat cats in Michigan in his corner. **1963** Behan *N.Y.* 97: "Fat cats"...people who have got a lot of money. **1968** Longstreet *Wilder Shore* 31: Not until 1855 were they licensed by the city with a bit extra for graft to the political fat cats. **1968** Tiede *Coward* 45: Thousands of people just like me need you in this struggle against the power bloc, the fat cats of this goddam country. **1981** Raban *Old Glory* 233: Like a gang of bland corporate fat cats. **1984** WINS Radio News (Aug. 19): The [Republican] party doesn't like to say no to wealthy contributors, affectionately known as fat cats. **1992** Sen. Albert Gore, Jr. (D–Tenn.), in *N.Y. Times* (July 27) A 11: They couldn't care less about the people who live downwind of pollution. They only care about the fat cat who owns the smokestack.

b. a smug self-satisfied individual.

1955–57 Felder *Collegiate Slang* 2: *Fat cat*—one who was oversatisfied with himself or herself.

2.a. *Av.* a luxury airplane.

1945 Hamann *Air Words*: *Fat cat.* Luxury liner, that is, a plane with plush covered, overstuffed seats.

b. *Naval Av.* a resupply plane.

1958 Craven & Cate *AAF in WWII* VII 451 [ref. to WWII]: "Fat-cat" shipments of extra supplies to forward areas. **1961** Forbes *Goodbye to Some* 62 [ref. to WWII]: I shake hands with the new ensign....He arrived two nights ago in the Fat Cat. *Ibid.* 229: Every fourth day the Fat Cat comes with mail and supplies.

fat-cat *adj.* suggestive of wealth, ease, or privilege; luxurious; cushy.

1959 Scott *Flying Tiger* 146: One of these "fair-haired boys" had come out on a plush, fat-cat airplane to command Chennault's Flying Tigers. **1972** W.C. Anderson *Hurricane* 41: Lou could be given a fat-cat job...flying transports. **1980** Grizzard *Billy Bob Bailey* 119: I would have all those fat-cat jobs to hand out.

fat chance *n.* little or no chance.—used sarcastically.—often as *interj.*

1905 T.A. Dorgan, in Zwilling *TAD Lexicon* 35: The sports outside the ropes had a fat chance of seeing anything. **1906** in *OEDS*: A fat chance I'd stand of having it printed. **1908** in Fleming *Unforget. Season* 250: He will have a good, fat chance! **1909** Chrysler *White Slavery* 32: What? That nasty little hussy trying to...have some one arrested? Well, she has a fat chance! **1911** *Hampton's Mag.* (June) 744: Fat chance we'll have to vote for anyone. **1915** T.A. Dorgan, in *N.Y. Eve. Jour.* (Dec. 10) 26: He's gotta fat chance with me. **1918** McNutt *The Yanks Are Coming* 143: Why, we've got a fat chance of getting to be noncoms with this outfit. **1922** S. Lewis *Babbitt* 63: Fat chance! **1934** O'Hara *Samarra* ch. iii: "I think the best thing is for you to take me home and then go to his house and apologize in person." "Fat chance." **1944** A. Scott et al. *Here Come WAVES* (film): "We've come to take you back." "Fat chance." **1953** Wicker *Kingpin* 30: "We're in." "Fat chance." **1960** Roeburt *Mobster* 19: Fat chance I've got ever being accepted to the Force. **1986** Hillerman *Skinwalkers* 271: "Then I need to make a call."..."Fat chance."

fat city *n.* **1.** the condition of being extremely well off or having a superior advantage; EASY STREET. Also as *adj.*

1964 in *AS* XL (1965) 194: "You're in *fat city*" = "You've got it made." **1965** *N.Y. Times* (Dec. 27) L 20: Johnny came...home from college this Christmas and announced he was in "fat city" and everything was "swave." **1966** H.S. Thompson *Hell's Angels* 158: And then came the war—fat city, big money. **1967** *Time* (June 23) 16: [Pres. Lyndon Johnson said] "I have kept my cool. I haven't bugged out. I am still in Fat City." **1969** *Current Slang* I & II 32: *Fat city, adj.* Superior.—*College males, Utah.* **1970** *Playboy* (Dec.) 122: If he decided to check..., well, that'd be Fat City for the narcs. **1971** Sonzski *Punch Goes Judy* 161: Back in Fat City, U.S.A. [Easy Street]. **1972** in *Playboy* (Feb. 1973) 184:

He's gonna run about five K, expenses, on ninety, he's Fat City and everybody else's full of shit. **1975** V.B. Miller *Deadly Game* 29: The Hotel Athdara isn't exactly doing "Fat City" business. **1983** Van Devanter & Morgan *Before Morning* 63: But when we got to our suite, we realized that we were in Fat City. **1984** Ehrlich *Marking Time* 193: The power brokers give most of the rest of us enough to think we're in Fat City. **1985** Heywood *Taxi Dancers* 119: With F4-Es Da Nang would be in fat city. **1985** Wells *444 Days* 211: It was obvious that they wanted the world to see that the hostages were living in Fat City.

2. the condition of being overweight.

1970–72 in *AS* L (1975) 58: *Fat city*…State of being overweight. **1976–77** McFadden *Serial* 138: Harvey watched the needle on the scale swing slowly to the right.…"Wow…Fat City." **1980** *Mork & Mindy* (ABC-TV): Oh! Fat City! *a*1986 in *NDAS*: Its principal characters wind up in "fat city" (argot for "out of condition").

fat farm *n.* a resort or camp where overweight people go to lose weight.—used derisively.

1969 (cited in *W10*). **1970** *Time* (Mar. 2) 64: The places that thin people like to call fat farms. **1971** Barnes *Pawns* 69: There is the two-section Physical Proficiency Platoon, filled with weak bodies that can't take the strenuous pace—one section, the "fat farm," for overweight recruits, the other for skinny ones. **1971** *Odd Couple* (ABC-TV): If you're not fat, it's a health farm; if you're fat, it's a fat farm. **1974** *Playboy* (Feb.) 127: Terror Stalks The Fat Farm. Those twenty pounds were gone, perhaps forever—but at what terrible cost? **1978** Maupin *Tales* 155: At the fat farm. **1987** *21 Jump St.* (Fox-TV): My girlfriend, she went to a fat farm.…She's always dieting. **1992** *Golden Girls* (NBC-TV): She's at a fat farm in Sarasota.

fat friend *n.* **1.** *Mil.* a kite balloon. Cf. BIG FRIEND, LITTLE FRIEND.

1941 *AS* (Oct.) 165 (Army): *Fat Friends*. Balloons.

2. *Mil. Av.* a tanker aircraft.

1959 Montgomery & Heiman *Jet Nav.* 197: Wouldn't be any need to go down and have a drink from our fat friend.

fatgut *n.* a grossly fat individual.—used derisively.

1954 Schulberg *Waterfront* 39: Foley, a fatgut who had started out doing a job on these waterfront cases until his captain had straightened him out.

fat handles *n.pl.* LOVE HANDLES.

1983 Wambaugh *Delta Star* 8: With fat-handles hanging over her panty girdle.

fathead *n.* a stupid person; idiot. Now *colloq.*

1842 in *OED*: You little Fat-head. ***1851** H. Mayhew *London Labour* I 228: Why look at it, says I, fat-head—I knew I was safe. **1898** in S. Crane *Complete Stories* 520: Grierson, you fathead. **1904** Hobart *I'm from Mo.* 16: What else are you here for, you fathead? **1907** Hobart *Beat It!* 66: Why do these fat-heads come over here? **1911** T.A. Dorgan, in *N.Y. Eve. Jour.* (Jan. 6) 16: Oh you fat head. **1915** Braley *Workaday World* 121: An' he calls the minor a fat-head chump. **1919** Witwer *Alex* 145: The poor fathead went and fell for that bunk. **1932** Sweet *Loops* (film): That little fathead. **1938** "E. Queen" *4 Hearts* 12: I've phoned your office twice a day, six days a week, fathead.

fatheaded *adj.* stupid.

***1748** in *OED*: This I leave to thy own fat-headed prudence. ***1768** in *OED*: The fat-headed majority, intoxicated by the fumes of excess. *ca*1867 in G.W. Harris *Lovingood* 62: While Sut was telling this story, a fat-headed young man listened throughout without moving a muscle of his face. **1893** Frye *Staff* 170: Say, d'youse know Hickey, dat big, fat-headed corp'ral in K?

father-grabbing *adj.* MOTHER-GRABBING.

1948 Manone & Vandervoort *Trumpet* 72: I couldn't get a note out of that father-grabbin' cornet.…Those father-grabbin' sheriffs…sure liked to catch us guys from New Orleans. *Ibid.* 161: Let your conscience be your father-grabbin' guide. **1971** *Black World* (Apr.) 59: The civil rights don't mean a father-grabbin' thing to us.

fatigews *n.pl. Mil.* fatigues. *Joc.*

1980 Cragg *L. Militaris* 159: *Fatty gews*. The fatigue or utility uniform.

fat lady *n. USAF.* a large high-explosive bomb.

1966–67 Harvey *Air War* 58: The staple demolition bombs used in Vietnam…came in "fat lady" or "Slim Jim" shapes, depending on how much air drag you were trying to eliminate from the airplane that carried them.

fat lip *n.* a lip swollen by a blow; (*also*) a punch or blow to the mouth.

1944 Kendall *Service Slang* 22: *A fat lip*.…a sock in the puss. **1947** Motley *Knock On Any Door* 208: Say, are you looking for a fat lip? I told you to beat it! **1950** Stuart *Objector* 91: You're looking for a fat lip. **1951** D. Wilson *My Six Convicts* 91 [ref. to *ca*1933]: Some smart bastard's beggin' for a fat lip! **1953** Manchester *City of Anger* 355: She saw his fat lip and glanced away. **1961** *Dick Van Dyke* (CBS-TV): Some day he's gonna get a big fat lip to go with that fat head. **1967** J. Kramer *Instant Replay* 135: Flakey was going around with a fat lip. **1968** Swarthout *Loveland* 168 [ref. to 1930's]: You're overdue for a fat lip. **1969** Joseph *The Me Nobody Knows* 63: You're looking for a fat lip. **1973** *Sanford & Son* (NBC-TV): How would you like a fat lip? **1966–80** McAleer & Dickson *Unit Pride* 344: Get outa here before you get a fat lip.

fat lot *n.* a small or nearly nonexistent amount.

***1892** in *OEDS*: A fat lot I care. **1911** Howard *Enemy to Society* 6: An' a fat lot I care. **1928** E. Rice *Street Scene* 1: A fat lot he cares whether his wife has ginger-ale! **1933** Hammett *Thin Man* 226: A fat lot of good that's doing me. **1958** N.Y.C. woman, age 70: A fat lot of good it'll do you! **1972** M. Rodgers *Freaky Fri.* 75: A fat lot you know about it, Silky Dilky!

fat mama *n.* a Fatima brand cigarette.

1919 Emmett *Give 'Way to the Right* 44 [ref. to WWI]: Ashes to ashes,/ Dust to dust;/If the camel's don't get you,/The "fat-mammas"* must.…*The Soldier's term for "Fatimas."

fat man *n.* ¶ In phrase: **bet a fat man** *Black E.* to assure or believe with supreme confidence. Also in extended vars.

1952 Himes *Stone* 159: But you can bet a big fat man they ain't going to dump no whole lot of convicts out of here at one time. **1954** Killens *Youngblood* 48: Bet a great big fat man. **1958** R. Wright *Long Dream* 53: I bet a fat man she scared to death awready. **1962** Killens *Heard the Thunder* 171 [ref. to 1943]: When my namesake freed the slaves, he didn't know about Rutherford's plantation, I bet a great big fat man. **1965** C. Brown *Manchild* 41: I bet you a fat man. **1969** Gordone *No Place to be Somebody* 414: An' they ain't no whiter, ha'f-white house Nigger in New Yawk than Gabe is, I'll bet a fat man. *a*1973–87 F.M. Davis *Livin' the Blues* 44 [ref. to *ca*1920]: I bet a fat man I can sho break you of the habit.

fat mouth *n.* **1.** Esp. *Black E. & So.* a loudmouth; (*hence*) a fool.

1926 in Leadbitter & Slaven *Blues Records* 356: Fat Mouth Blues. **1952** Mandel *Angry Strangers* 74: Diane…began to ramble, and called herself a fatmouth, a word Joe recognized as Dixieland jargon. **1956** McGuire *Delicate Delinquent* (film): OK, fatmouth! **1968** I. Reed *Yellow Back Radio* 36: O.K., fat mouth, you asked for it. **1974** Radano *Cop Stories* 80: If that fatmouth hadn't made these wise-ass remarks it would never have happened. *a*1973–87 F.M. Davis *Livin' the Blues* 33 [ref. to *ca*1918]: Don't let no yelluh woman make a fatmouth outta you.

2. a propensity for loud or offensive talk.

1960 Matheson *Beardless Warriors* 32: He's got a fat mouth.

fatmouth *v.* Esp. *Black E.* **1.** to talk foolishly or at length; (*also*) to boast.

1962 Crump *Killer* 55: That beanpole fatmouthing to me about being a star. **1967** Colebrook *Cross of Lassitude* 37: Why you standin' there fatmouthin'? **1969** E. Cleaver, in *Ramparts* (Sept.): They have never forgiven the fat-mouthing you did…when you presumed to tell them how to conduct their business. **1972** Carr *Bad* 61: I started fatmouthing, saying "Whatchyou talkin' about?" **1978** Selby *Requiem* 176: He sittin back fat mouthin while he gettin ready to do some more time. **1983** Goldman & Fuller *Charlie Co.* 177: If my wife suffers complications while you're sitting here fat-mouthing, I'm gonna fuck you up. **1987** *Tour of Duty* (CBS-TV): I got no time to be fatmouthin' with no honky.

2. to speak badly of; insult.

1978 Knoxville, Tenn., maintenance man, age *ca*30: Are y'all standin' around fatmouthin' me? **1978** Selby *Requiem* 38: Ah doan mind him fat mouthin that [TV] set.

fat-mouthed *adj.* Esp. *Black E.* loudmouthed.

1960 C.L. Cooper *Scene* 207: Why, you fat-mouthed preacher! Do you think he's actually doing these young punks any good? **1974** Radano *Cop Stories* 79: It all started when one of our guys tried to lock up some fat-mouthed neighborhood punk.

fat one *n. Black E.* one hundred dollars; (*also*) one dollar. Cf. BIG ONE, *n.*

1967 Beck *Pimp* 71: I was going to collect five fat ones for my pleasant night's work. **1971** Goines *Dopefiend* 155: Four hundred fat ones for some cut stuff.

fat-rat *adj.* FAT-CAT.

1983 Goldman & Fuller *Charlie Co.* 317: He negotiated a fat-rat job off the line as a jeep driver.

Fats *n.* (used as a nickname for a fat person).
  1933 in D. Runyon *More Guys* 20: Hello, Fats. **1938** in W.C. Fields *By Himself* 309: Glad to know you, Fats. **1955** Mankiewicz *Trial* (film): If Angel is acquitted, the town won't reelect Fats.

fatso *n.* a very fat person.—usu. used as a nickname.
  1933 in D. Runyon *More Guys* 3: Fatso Kling was a big Heeb from up in the Bronx. **1937** Hoover *Persons in Hiding* 105: I'm going away, Fatso. **1958** Chandler *Goodbye* 120: Out of my way, fatso. **1974** Radano *Cop Stories* 81: They tell Fatso to shut up. **1977** L. Jordan *Hype* 41: A fatso with a handlebar mustache. **1985** E. Leonard *Glitz* 257: That fatso told me.

fat stuff *n.* a very fat person.—used derisively.
  1926 in Blackbeard & Williams *Smithsonian Comics* 103: Der Captain iss a fat stuff! **1937** in Galewitz *Great Comics* 39: Put up yer dukes, fat stuff! **1939–40** Tunis *Kid from Tomkinsville* 5: "Fat Stuff" Foster and Razzle Nugent. **1940** *Time* (Jan. 29) 46: Decided to nickname him Fat Stuff. **1948** *Neurotica* (Spring) 33: Myrtle hates Joe; Fatstuff hates Beulah. **1955** Ellson *Rock* 116: Don't sonny boy me, fat-stuff. **1963** Blechman *Camp Omongo* 23: "What's the difference?" said Fat Stuff. **1976** *Muppet Show* (CBS-TV): You weren't thinking of doing anything with that cake, were you, fat stuff?

faunch *v.* [orig. unkn.] to be angry or impatient; storm; rage; rave.
  1911, 1923, 1928, 1929 in Wentworth *ADD* 209. **1942** *ATS* 293: *Angry…faunching.* **1948** J. Stevens *Jim Turner* 100 [ref. to *ca*1910]: Then old Ellis Coot faunched out, yelling…"You run these minors in, Marshal, and see to it they stop pesterin' me!" **1961** *WNID3*: It was enough to make anybody faunch. **1973** Hogan *Guns of Stingaree* 76: Seen him come faunchin' out of there madder'n a tromped-on rattler. **1982** in *DARE*: She was describing how upset and agitated and downright angry she was at her grandmother….she again said that she "was faunched."

fave *n. & adj.* favorite. Also **fav.**
  1921 *Variety* (Apr. 8) 7: Meanwhile the eggs in the know would bet on their fav to cop. **1940** *AS* (Apr.) 204: *Fave.* Favorite. **1952** Lait & Mortimer *USA* 163: The fan club fave needed the money to pay her income tax. **1956** "T. Betts" *Across the Board* 190: When da jock on da fave he's a gonna fall? **1970–72** in *AS* L (1975) 59: *Fave…*Favorite person. **1983** *N.Y. Post* (Sept. 5) 30: *Master Digby…*2-1 fave, finished seventh of eight. **1989** *TV Guide* (Mar. 4) 34: Does she have a fave?

fawney[1] *n.* [< Ir *fáine* 'a ring'] Esp. *Und.* a finger ring. Also **fawny.**
  ***1781** G. Parker *View of Society* II 166: The Fawney Rig [*i.e.* trick]. ***1789** in *F & H* II 378: *Fawny.* An old, stale trick called ring-dropping. ***1796** Grose *Vulgar Tongue* (ed. 3): *Fawney.* A ring. *Fawney Rig.* A common fraud, thus practised: A fellow drops a brass ring, double gilt, which he picks up before the party meant to be cheated, and to whom he disposes of it for less than it is supposed, and ten times more than its real, value. ***1812** Vaux *Vocab.*: *Fawney:* a finger-ring. ***1834** Ainsworth *Rookwood* 178: Fogles and fawnies soon went their way/…To the spout with the sneezers in grand array. ***1851** H. Mayhew *London Labour* I 423: He wears a stunning fawny (ring) on his finger. ***1857** "Ducange" *Vulgar Tongue* 39: Fawney-droppers gammon the flats and take the yokels in. **1859** Matsell *Vocab.* 124: The fawneys…and well-filled readers. ***1864** in *Comments on Ety.* XVII (No. 11) 22: As for the "fawney" that had been "sided," that was turned up,…it being of considerable value. **1906** A.H. Lewis *Confessions* 202: I fenced the fawney for fifty.

fawney[2] *n.* see PHONY.

fawney man *n.* (among tramps and pitchmen) a man who sells cheap or fake jewelry.
  1891 *Contemporary Rev.* (Aug.) 259: The man who comes nighest criminal success is called among tramps "The Fawny Man." This man's business is to sell bogus jewellery. **1893** *Century* (Nov.) 103: I tramped through Connecticut and Rhode Island once with a "fawny man."*…*A peddler of bogus jewellery. **1899** "J. Flynt" *Tramping* 393: *Fawny Man:* a peddler of bogus jewelry.

fawney shop *n. Und.* a shop that sells cheap or fake jewelry.
  1902 Hapgood *Thief* 57 [ref. to 1885]: He then goes to a fauny shop (imitation jewelry) and buys a few diamonds which match the real ones he has noted.

fay *n.* [aph. fr. OFAY] *Black E.* a white person.—usu. used contemptuously.

1927 R. Fisher, in *Amer. Mercury* (Aug.) 393: "What a lot of 'fays'!" I thought, as I noticed the number of white guests. **1928** R. Fisher *Jericho* 8: Fays don' see no difference 'tween dickty shines and any other kind o' shines. **1932** Daly *Not Only War* 42 [ref. to 1917]: Those were fays,* you poor sap….*white people. *ca*1953 Hughes *Lodge* 74: I was a fay and he was not. **1971** Goines *Dopefiend* 157: She's the only cool fay down there, too. **1974** A. Bergman *Big Kiss-Off* 90: Everybody givin' this fay the shuffle.

fay *adj. Black E.* Caucasian.—sometimes used contemptuously.
  1928 Fisher *Jericho* 8: Hyeh's s dickty tryin' his damnedest to be fay—like all de other dickties. **1929** Larsen *Passing* 141: Fay—adj.: Caucasian, white. In less than five minutes, I knew she was "fay." **1946** Mezzrow & Wolfe *Really Blues* 59: He was the first fay boy I ever heard who mastered this vital foundation of jazz music. **1952** E. Brown *Trespass* 17: Just like a goddam 'fay landlord. *ca*1953 Hughes *Lodge* 119: In spade areas, much more so than in fay. **1960** in T.C. Bambara *Gorilla* 49: This same fay cat? **1961** in H. Ellison *Sex Misspelled* 309: How many lives I gotta lead, steppin' down into the gutter for some 'fay cat? **1969** Pharr *Book of Numbers* 70: Now tell me about that fay boy. **1970** Knight *Black Voices from Prison* 99: I happened to see this fay chick I knew, walking down the street with a fay sailor.

f-ball *n. Sports.* the game of football. Cf. B-BALL.
  1981 Crowe *Fast Times* 79: That fabled high school f-ball glory.

FBI *n. & adj.* (interpreted in various facetious ways; see quots.).
  1943 *Newsweek* (July 26) 32: The [airmen] he met in Iceland, he said, called themselves the FBI's (Forgotten Bastards of Iceland—which the Secretary softened to "Boys"). **1961** *Dick Van Dyke Show* (CBS-TV): I'm from the F.B.I.…The F.B.I.—that's you: fat, bald, and ignorant! **1963** Behan *N.Y.* 54: An F.B.I. man…You are F.B.I.…Foreign-born Irish. **1965** Gallery *Eight Bells* 116: We called ourselves the F.B.I.'s and after you had been up there one hundred days you got a handsome certificate of membership in this exclusive club. "Forgotten Bastards of Iceland" is what the initials meant. **1974** S. Stevens *Rat Pack* 150: "Easy, man. His mama in the F.B.I." "Yeah, she Fat, Black, and Ignorant." **1978** Lieberman & Rhodes *CB* (ed. 2) 301: Funny Bunch of Idiots—FBI.

feather *n.* **1.** *pl.* fancy clothing.
  1864 in J.H. Gooding *Altar of Freedom* 109: These 'ere fellers, with their bands and fine feathers. **1893** W.K. Post *Harvard* 180: Your clothes…feathers. **1901** "J. Flynt" *Graft* 69: He was trying to "fake the feathers of the main guys." **1927** [Fliesler] *Anecdota* 92: Sich gay feathers, and your Sammy's been only dead a week. **1965–70** in *DARE*: Joking ways of referring to person's best clothes…*Fine feathers.*
  2. [alludes to a *feather* mattress] *pl.* a bed.—constr. with *the*; in phr. **hit the feathers** to go to bed.
  [**1893** Corby *Chaplain Life* 235 [ref. to 1864]: The ground was…covered with the "pine-needles."…These pine-needles we used to call "Virginia feathers." We…could spend at least a part of the night in sweet repose.] **1899** in Ade *Chicago Stories* 247: They had me in the feathers with about seven kinds o' dope shot into me. **1904** *Life in Sing Sing* 248: *Feathers.* Bed. **1905** *Nat. Police Gaz.* (Dec. 16) 3: I think I'll hit the feathers early to-night. **1908** in H.C. Fisher *A. Mutt* 112: I'm beating it for the feathers. **1915** Lardner *Gullible* 98: And I buried my good ear in the feathers. **1918** Griffin *Ballads of Reg't.* 4: Well, it's time to hit the feathers. **1961** Russell *Sound* 21: It's not like just a stick of pot…or making it in the feathers with me. **1966** Susann *Valley of Dolls* 97: If a guy digs you he wants to jump in the feathers with you.
  3. *Boxing.* a featherweight.
  1920 T.A. Dorgan, in Zwilling *TAD Lexicon* 35: [He] suggests holding a featherweight tourney with eight of the best feathers entered. **1940** Zinberg *Walk Hard* 49: The feathers left the ring and two lumbering heavyweights stepped in. **1960** Hoagland *Circle Home* 92: The feathers, like the welters, at their top, had a few fine admirable fighters. **1981** *N.Y. Post* (Dec. 14) 42: Sanchez keeps feather title.

featherbed *n.* **1.** *Army.* a FEATHERBED soldier.
  *ca*1900 Strong *Yankee Pvt.* 208 [ref. to 1865]: The Feather Beds.
  2. *Labor.* a FEATHERBED job.
  1984 Kagan & Summers *Mute Evidence* 387: I could have come up with indeterminate findings, demanded more staff, more funding, and really played it up into a nice featherbed.

featherbed *adj.* **1.** *Mil.* (of a soldier or military organization) soft; noncombatant; holding a position of ease or comfort.—used prenominally.—usu. used contemptuously. Also quasi-adv.
  [***1692** in *OED*: Is it because some Feather-bed Captains sell such Ware?] ***1837** in *OED*: Our position…has certainly not been that of

feather-bed soldiers. **1848** W. Irving *Hist. of N.Y.* 188: The sturdy Peter...determined to give his feather bed soldiers a seasoning. **1862** in C.H. Moulton *Ft. Lyon* 50: These "feather bed" 9 months men will never receive the welcome that the 3 years soldiers will. **1862** in *DAE*: Feather-bed soldiers in Congress. **1882** in Sweet *Texas* 31: I'm no feather-bed soldier. I'm old pie, I am. **1887** E. Custer *Tenting* 127 [ref. to 1866]: "The officers will think you a 'feather-bed soldier,'" which term of derision was applied to a man who sought soft places for duty and avoided hardships, driving when he ought to ride. **1892** Cox *5 Yrs.* 163 [ref. to 1875]: "Feather bed" soldiers could never perform such duties. *ca*1900 Strong *Yankee Pvt.* 208 [ref. to 1865]: [Sherman's troops referred to the Army of the Potomac as] Feather Bed Soldiers...Feather Bed Army. **1912** Tilney *My Life* 45 [ref. to Civil War]: The men from the cities, "featherbed soldiers" the army dubbed them, were inclined to sneer at us from the shabby appearance we made. **1927** *Amer. Legion Mo.* (Jan.) 19 [ref. to 1898]: I've been 13 years a soger an' divil a day of it featherbed sogerin'. **1932** Harvey *Me and Bad Eye* [ref. to 1918]: You're in the army now, the Coast Artillery is a feather bed outfit no longer, captain.

2. *Labor.* (of a job) soft or easy, esp. as a result of featherbedding.—used prenominally. Now *S.E.*

1922 in *OEDS*: The annual cost of these so-called "feather-bed practices." **1938** in *OEDS*: But he does feel that "featherbed jobs" should be abolished. **1951** Bowers *Mob* (film): Bingo. I'm in a featherbed job.

featherbed *v. Labor.* to be employed at a superfluous job; (*hence*) to provide for or require such jobs.—usu. constr. in ppl. or gerund. Now *S.E.*

1921 in Mencken *Amer. Lang.* (Supp. II) 776: *Featherbedding.* Getting pay for work not done. **1943** *Reader's Digest* (Mar.) 26: For the unions, featherbedding has become an established business procedure. **1952** M. McCarthy *Academe* 84: Plus a certain number of seasoned non-conformists and dissenters, sexual deviants, featherbedders, alcoholics, impostors. **1955** O'Connor *Last Hurrah* 108: Oh yes. All kinds of public featherbedding and thievery began and continued. **1962** E. Stephens *Blow Negative* 438: Waste...sloth...feather-bedding. **1963–64** Kesey *Great Notion* 469: That bunch of...featherbeddin' *so-slists.* **1973** *AS* XLVI 82: Nonworking city employees...*boondogglers, featherbedders.* **1974** Terkel *Working* 190: He's long overdue for extra work. He's featherbedding. **1977** R. Adams *Lang. R.R.* 58: *Feather-bed:* To require an employer under a union rule or safety status to use and pay more employees than are needed. **1987** *U.S. News & W.R.* (Apr. 6) 7: We did not strike for big pay raises or to keep expensive, featherbedding work rules.

featherbed lane *n.* a bad road. *Joc.* [It is doubtful that the folk ety. related in the second 1968 quot. was ever taken seriously.]

*1698–99 "B.E." *Dict. Canting Crew: Feather-bed-lane,* any bad Road. **1773* Goldsmith *She Stoops to Conquer* V: I first took them down Feather-bed-lane, where we stuck fast in the mud. [**1968** in *DARE: When unpaved roads get very rough, you call them...*Feather beds.] **1968** N.Y.C. dentist: I was told as a child that Featherbed Lane got its name in the Revolution. The story was that Washington was afraid his troops would make too much noise marching through town at night, so to fool the redcoats he got all the housewives to pave the road with their featherbeds so the army could move silently. It's a foolish story, but that was the explanation.

feather duster *n.* **1.** *pl.* heavy side whiskers.

1919 Sandburg *Smoke & Steel* 20: And another manner of beard assumed in their chatter a verbal guise/Of "mutton chops," "galways," "feather dusters."

2. *U.S. Mil. Acad.* the upright brushlike ornament on a cadet's full-dress cap.

1936 (quot. at FRIED EGG).

featherhead *n.* **1.** *West.* an American Indian.—used derisively.—usu. considered offensive.

1859 Avery *Comical Stories* 57: Look at me, old featherhead! I'm one of 'em. **1966** Herbert *Fortune & Men's Eyes* 15: He was one o' them featherheads from Matachewan Reservation, tryin' t' get a job in the mines.

2. a scatterbrain; featherbrain. Also attrib.

1868 J. Chisholm *So. Pass* 151: Are you some city feather head, coming round here to put on airs, or a man? **1955** O'Connor *Last Hurrah* 17: I've sired a featherhead...a waltzing featherhead. Or am I doing the boy an injustice? Perhaps he fox-trots as well. **1962** Bonham *War Beneath Sea* 122: Start a featherhead rumor like this and there's grief within twenty-four hours. **1979** *New Fred & Barney Show* (NBC-TV): Bring it here, featherhead.

feather merchant *n.* [sugg. by S.E. sense 'a dealer in feathers'; see *DAE*] **1.a.** Esp. *USMC.* a small man, esp. a recruit; featherweight.—used derisively.

1939 *S.F. News* (Nov. 22) 17 (Tamony Coll.): Offensively, the Mechanics could be tougher....The problem seems to be springing loose Tom Ellis and Mert Dilly, a pair of "Feather Merchant" left halfs. **1942** *Leatherneck* (Nov.) 145: *Feather Merchant*—A little man who goes around saying: "The bigger they are, the harder they fall." **1944** Kendall *Service Slang* 36: *Feather merchant*...an undersized Marine. **1952** Uris *Battle Cry* 5: This customer couldn't weigh over a hundred and twenty-five pounds with a mortar on his back. A real feather merchant. **1958** McCulloch *Woods Words* 60: *Feather merchant*—A small logger. **1962** Gallant *On Valor's Side* 21 [ref. to 1941]: I was among the taller men, though I don't think anyone was lighter in weight, with the exception of the shorter boots, who were called "feather merchants" by the drill instructor. We never did fully understand what this term meant, though it was used with contempt and utter disdain. **1963** Coon *Short End* 26: Right then and there I decided that this company needed some midgets so feather merchants like me could have somebody to push around. **1981** Sledge *Old Breed* 11 [ref. to 1943]: Every platoon had its "feather merchants"—short men struggling along with great strides at the tail end of the formation.

b. *Mil.* a weak, lazy, or incompetent fellow; (*hence*) a civilian employed by the military.—used derisively.

1941 Kendall *Army & Navy Sl.* 5: *Feather merchants*...civilian workers on army cantonments. **1944** M. Shulman *Feather Merchants* i: Every soldier knows that "feather merchants" means civilians, but few know why it does. **1945** in *Calif. Folk Qly.* (1946) 384: As *feather-merchant* is a general...term for civilians, the inference here is that...Naval Reserve officers are merely civilians. **1946** Bowker *Out of Uniform* 124: Another popular phrase borrowed from comic strips was "feather merchant," which in the services assumed the special meaning of a civilian doing similar work to that of men in uniform, but receiving higher pay. **1942–48** in *So. Folk Qly.* XIII (1949) 205: *Feather-merchant*...is from the civilian, having become widespread in the late 'thirties by...Billy de Beck's comic strip, "Barney Google and Snuffy Smith." **1956** Taylor *Roll Back Sky* 210: A bunch of fat-ass civilians sitting around at home...the feather merchants. **1956** *AS* (Oct.) 228: *Feather merchant,* n. A Civil Service employee of the Air Force. **1966** Little *Bold & Lonely* 180: Major, I thought you were a combat officer, not a goddamn feather merchant. **1969** Coppel *Little Time for Laughter* 174 [ref. to 1943]: That goddamn 4-F feather merchant.

c. *Navy.* a member of the U.S. Naval Reserve.—used derisively.

1944 Kendall *Service Slang* 22: *Feather merchant*...a Naval Reservist, sometimes called a "Reverse." **1953** Dibner *Deep Six* 205: I'm gonna kill you, you feather-merchant son of a bitch. **1966** Noel & Bush *Naval Terms* 144: *Feather merchant:* Slang: Uncomplimentary term...applied to men (especially reserves) new to the service. **1967** Dibner *Admiral* 23: He tried to drill that idea into the thick skulls of everyone aboard, and he gave not a hoot in hell if they were Academy-trained or mustangs or Feather merchants or Asiatics. **1982** T.C. Mason *Battleship* 163 [ref. to 1943]: How do you "feather merchants" like active duty now? **1992** Jernigan *Tin Can Man* 53 [ref. to 1941]: We also had a name for the Navy reserves. They were "feather merchants."

2. *Navy.* a yeoman.

1945 Dos Passos *Tour* 109: It would take the *Normandie* to house all the feather merchants in the Service Squadron....feather merchants in the Navy are the people who do the paperwork. **1945** in *Calif. Folk Qly.* (1946) 384: *Feather merchant*...further applies to Navy yeomen (stenographers and office personnel) whose insignia are crossed quills.

Fed *n.* **1.** a Federalist. Now *hist.*

1788 in *DAE*: Antis, and Feds, usurp the glory,/So long enjoy'd by Whig and Tory. **1789** in *DAE*: Then forgive us, ye Feds. **1801, 1803, 1808** in *DAE*. *ca*1818 in Harlow *Old Bowery* 178: I'm ashamed to be seen, sir, among such a set of Clintonians, Tammanies, Coodies and Feds! **1830** in [S. Smith] *Letters of Downing* 4: Calling Adams a tory and a fed. **1834** in Foner *Labor Songs* 26: None but such as Hartford Feds/ Oppose the poor and—JACKSON.

2. *Confed. Mil.* a Federal soldier. Now *hist.*

1862 in McIntyre *Federals on Frontier* 85: It is the first place I have been in where the favorite southern institutions have been preserved and where the "Fed" soldier had not intruded upon the sanctity of their holy right. **1863** in Allan *Lone Star Ballads* 48: But when the Feds commence shelling/I run to my hole down the hill. **1866** Brockett *Camp, Battle Field & Hospital* 17: The Feds are coming! the Feds are coming! **1871** Schele de Vere *Amer.* 672: Federals, Feds.

3. a federal official, esp. a member of the FBI.

1916 A. Stringer *Door of Dread* 53: Seein' Kestner and yuh'd told me the Feds had ev'rything fixt, I give him the glassy eye. **1930** Irwin *Tramp & Und. Sl.*: *Feds*...Federal law enforcement officers, especially those charged with suppressing the liquor or drug traffic. **1935** Mackenzie *Been Places* 44: They had the goods on him for bumping off the three Feds. **1955** *PADS* (No. 24) 47: The Feds got the letter where I sent him $400. **1984** Kagan & Summers *Mute Evidence* 89: Many...would have found it easy to believe that the Army, Air Force, CIA, or the feds were behind it. **1991** "R. Brown" & R. Angus *A.K.A. Narc* 205: The Fed strode in, three-piece suit, sunglasses and all.

4.a. the federal government.

1965 Tavel *Godiva* 183: Chuck the fanfare, baby, I'm here on Fed business.

b. *Finance.* the Federal Reserve System or Federal Reserve Board.

1970 *Harper's* (Oct.) 16: Professor Lekachman seems to construe a go-slow policy...for the Fed as indecision. **1973** J.R. Coleman *Blue-Collar* 205: Only the time I spend at the "Fed" gives me much feeling of being a part of the economist's world. **1981** *Time* (Sept. 21) 47: The President called for "some loosening" of the money supply, while admitting that "we can't dictate to the Fed." **1988** *Knoxville* (Tenn.) *Journal* (Feb. 1): His conviction that when the Fed raises interest rates, it does so solely to protect rich creditors.

fed *adj.* **FED UP**; esp. in phr. **fed to the teeth** [or **gills**].

*1915 in Rosher *Flying Squadron* 127: We are all "fed to the teeth!" ***1921** W.S. Maugham, in *OEDS*: I should be fed to the teeth with you sometimes. **1925** Paine *First Yale* II 19 [ref. to 1918]: Dane Ingalls was very much "fed" with Hourtin. **1935** F.H. Lea *Anchor Man* 193: I'm fed to the teeth with the whole bag of tricks. **1943** in Stilwell *Papers* 191: I'm just fed to the gills with delay, pretense, inaction, dumbness. **1957** Myrer *Big War* 108: I'm fed to the teeth. *a*1960 Fedoroff *Side of Angels* 367: He's dead set against ordinary society—fed to the teeth with it.

fed up *adj.* surfeited, bored (*obs.*), or disgusted. Now *S.E.* [Pop. in U.S. speech by WWI; no earlier U.S. exx. are known.]

*1900 in *OEDS*: It may be quite true that, to use an expression often heard in South Africa just now, the men are "fed up" with the war. ***1906** in *OEDS*: I am about "fed-up" over this motor-car. ***1907** *Living Age* (July) 117: "Fed up" (French *soupé*) is perhaps our best slang legacy from South Africa. ***1915** in Graves *Good-Bye to All That* 110: Bloke in the Camerons wanted a cushy [wound], bad. Fed up and far from home, he was. **1917** in Bowerman *Compensations* 39: He declares that the infantry are completely "fed-up" and are willing to quit any time regardless of who wins. **1917** Empey *Over the Top* 154: "Fed up." Disgusted; got enough of it. **1918** *Stars & Stripes* (Apr. 12) 7: From the Tommies has come "fed up." **1919** Rickenbacker *Fighting Flying Circus* 58: At last I began to get rather fed up with the sport. **1920** in Fitzgerald *Stories* I 202: Sometimes I drive one of his taxis and pick up a little thataway. I get fed up doin' that regular though. **1927** McKay *Home to Harlem* 19: I ain't so much for the high-yallers after having been so much fed-up on the ofays. **1927** Nicholson *Barker* 47: Listen, Lou, you're fed up with this outfit, ain't you? **1929–33** Farrell *Manhood of Lonigan* 187: He saw a little girl with a flag and, fed up, he snatched it. **1940** Raine & Niblor *Fighting 69th* (film): No, we ain't dead yet. We're just musclebound, flat-footed, fed up, and far from home. **1942** Hurston *Dust Tracks* 181: No bones are made about being fed up. **1942–46** in MSU GF2.1 (Army: Jargon:) 29: Are you nervous in the service?...No, I'm just fed up with the set-up. **1946** Dadswell *Sucker* 14: Indeed, I'm "fed up" with the gummy mud of spring, the blistering summer heat, the sweltering grimy struggle through an endless series of fall fairs. **1954** Mirvish *Texana* 50: "Are you really fed up with that job in Gulfport?" "To the ears." **1959** Bechet *Treat It Gentle* 161: After a little of that, you get fed up. **1965** Conot *Rivers of Blood* 155: We the Negro people have got completely fed up! **1965–68** E.R. Johnson *Silver St.* 68: I'm fed clear up to the ass with your crap. **1972** Kopp *Buddha* 181: No wonder his brothers got fed up with him. **1981** D. Burns *Feeling Good* 110: But by now his parents were fed up trying to motivate him. **1981** Pietropinto & Congress *Clinic* 89: You damn doctors....I'm fed up with coming here. **1984** Kagan & Summers *Mute Evidence* 383: I was fed up with cities, all the noise and congestion and dirt.

¶ In phrase:

¶ **fed up, [fucked up,] and far from home** *Mil.* disgusted, helpless, and far from one's home.—usu. considered vulgar.

*1915 (quot. above). ***1936** Partridge *DSUE* 269: In the [First World War], a military [catch phrase] ran, *fed up, f**ked up, and far from home*. **1940** (quot. above). **1977** Caputo *Rumor of War* 93 [ref. to 1965]: The

Marines are all in the same state of mind as I, "fed-up, fucked-up, and far from home." ***1984** Partridge *DSUE* (ed. 8) 383: *Fed-up, fucked up, and far from home*...is still being used by the WWI Tommies' soldier-grandsons, 1970s.

fee *n. Stu.* coffee.

1971 Dahlskog *Dict.* 23: *Fee, n.* Coffee.

feeb *n.* [clipping of *feeble*] a stupid, feeble, or weak-minded person.

1911 in J. London *Short Stories* 494: That's going some for a feeb. Feeb? Oh, that's feeble-minded. I thought you knew. **1914** in *OEDS*: We're all feebs in here. **1918** Stringer *House of Intrigue* 349: Those two old feebs!...Hasn't it ever struck you that these two old ginks are a little nutty? *ca*1940 in Fitzgerald *Notebooks* 329: You Can't Organize Feebs....say, listen, we're not talking about nuts—we're talking about feebs. **1942** Algren *Morning* 40: Kodadek would be...waiting to pinch-hit for some feeb like Bibleback. **1972** DeLillo *End Zone* 59: In my considered opinion, you're a bunch of feebs. **1982** Rucker *57th Kafka* 106: A few idlers—daytripping feebs—give their advice. **1989** *Married with Children* (Fox-TV): Nerds, dips, feebs, *and* geeks.

feebee var. **PHOEBE**.

feebie *n.* [vocalization of *FBI*] a member, esp. an agent, of the FBI. Also vars.

1942 K. Burke, in Jay *Burke-Cowley Corres.* 248: A faithful phoebe had been going the rounds, presumably begging to be told that you were a [Communist]...because you didn't support Franco. **1950** *Western Folklore* (May) 160: *Feebi.* F.B.I. [used at Los Alamos, N.M.]. **1967** in *Atlantic* (Jan. 1968) 36: A cop, FeeBie, CIA, something like that. **1969** *Time* (Feb. 28) 14: Secret Service agents derisively call the FBI men "Feebies." **1969** Salerno & Tompkins *Crime Confed.* 76: Looka what the feebies did to the old man up in Providence. **1977** *N.Y. Times Book Rev.* (Dec. 18) 12: The "Feebies" are free at last to peel off their Dacron jackets and mix it in the gutter with organized crime. **1983** R. Thomas *Missionary* 104: They were all looking for him. The narcs...the feebies. **1988** DeLillo *Libra* 45: Feebees—the FBI.

feeblo *n.* [*feeble* + -o] **FEEB**.

1931 *AS* VI (Aug.) 438: *Feeblo*, n....a simple-minded person. **1946** Gresham *Nightmare Alley* 77: If I can't read a...hypocrite of a church deacon, I'm a feeblo.

feed *n.* **1.** a meal, esp. if big or lavish.

*1808 in *OED*: A feed now and then at the first tables. ***1830** in *OED*. ***1838** Glascock *Land Sharks* II 44: What *feeds* would have been given at Whitehall! **1839** Marryat *Diary*: "Will you have a feed or a check?"—A dinner, or a luncheon? **1846** in Oehlschlaeger *Reveille* 259: Let's go take our feed. **1854** G.G. Foster *15 Mins.* 82: Public dinners, trial trips of steamboats, railroad excursions, "feeds" at the trade-sale, &c. **1858** in G.W. Harris *High Times* 86: Thompson [felt] that the "feed" was not quite up to the mark. **1887** E. Custer *Tenting* 344: The officers regretted our absence at their great "feed," as they termed it. **1900** Patten *Merriwell's Power* 12: Just one of the little feeds we have up here now and then. **1904** in Opper *H. Hooligan* 53: No royal feed for us today. **1908** in H.C. Fisher *A. Mutt* 65: It's up to him to pay for the feed. **1939** "L. Short" *Rimrock* 37: Did you get a feed at Proctor's? **1968** Cuomo *Thieves* 125: Did the Governor put on a good feed?

2. victuals.

1818 in *DAE*: I guess whiskey is all the feed we have on sale. **1835** in *DAE*: Choice rounds and sirloins...I love good feed. **1861** in H.L. Abbott *Fallen Leaves* 36: They...are living on pretty rough feed. **1866** "E. Kirke" *Guerillas* 72: Freddy had toted his feed ter him in the woods. **1884** Nye *Baled Hay* 31: He will...absorb a given amount of feed. **1908** in Fleming *Unforget. Season* 19: Murphy tells me the "feed" is O.K. too. **1967** in *DARE* s.v. *gob, n.,* 2: He had a gob full of feed and nevertheless he kept right on talking.

feedback *n.* insolence; backtalk.

1970–71 Higgins *Coyle* 31: You never got a bit of feedback from me. I don't hassle you about nothing.

feedbag *n.* ¶ In phrases:

¶ **from the feedbag** see *from the feed box* s.v. **FEED BOX**.

¶ **put** [or **tie**] **on the feedbag** to eat a meal. Also vars.

1906 *Nat. Police Gaz.* (Dec. 29) 3: She had two hundred and seventy-four invitations to put on the feed bag. **1918** *N.Y. Eve. Jour.* (Aug. 10) 9: I was just blowing over to Belmore's to put on th' feedbag. **1923** *Chi. Daily Trib.* (Oct. 2) 23: Now where'll we go to put on de feed-bag, cutie? **1926** Dunning & Abbott *Broadway* 225: Say, Billie, suppose we go out after, tie on the feed bag and talk over the act, huh? **1938** Baldwin & Schrank *Case of Murder* (film): Hey, when do we put on the feedbag? **1943** Crowley & Sachs *Follow the Leader* (film): Let's go put on the feedbag. **1949** Ellson *Tomboy* 82: "I guess I'll go up and put the feedbag on," Lucky said. "I'm starved." **1981** *Taxi* (ABC-TV): All I want to do is go home, hose myself down, and put on the feedbag. **1993** G. Trudeau, in *N.Y. Times* (Apr. 9) A 27: Nick's Kitchen is where Huntington's political elite go to strap on the feed bags.

feed box *n.* ¶ In phrase: **from [or out of] the feed box [or bag]** *Horse Racing.* (of information) confidential and reliable.
1908 T.A. Dorgan, in Zwilling *TAD Lexicon* 35: Yes—I got it straight from the feed box and it's right. **1910** T.A. Dorgan, in *N.Y. Eve. Jour.* (Apr. 16) 12: I bought a tip on the races today right from the feed box and it cost me 10 bucks. **1929–34** Farrell *Judgment Day* 498: Have you got a tip out of the…feed box? **1942** *Yank* (Dec. 23) 18: We have it straight from the Navy feed box. **1952** Lait & Mortimer *USA* 396: We say Bowles got that from the feed-bag—it is still Administration policy. **1981** *N.Y. Daily News* (July 9) 78: Thanks for the word straight from the feed box. I buy it.

feeder *n.* **1.** *Und.* a fork or spoon.
***1718** (cited in Partridge *Dict. Und.* 234). ***1788** Grose *Vulgar Tongue* (ed. 2): *To nab the feeder*; to steal a spoon. **1791** [W. Smith] *Confess. T. Mount* 18: Silver spoons, *wedge feeders*. **1859** Matsell *Vocab.* 31: *Feeders.* Silver spoons or forks. "Nap the feeders," steal the spoons.
2. the mouth and throat.
1902 T.A. Dorgan, in *S.F. Bulletin Mag.* (Jan. 11) 12: And have his "feeder" wiped out with a dirty sponge. **1909, 1913** (cited in Zwilling *TAD Lexicon* 103). **1929** Caldwell *Bastard* 75: He…stuffed 'em down his feeder with the butt end of a knife damn right.

feeding-hole *n.* the mouth.
*ca***1867** G.W. Harris *Lovingood* 208: Shet up that ar snagy feedin-hole ove yurn.

feed joint *n.* an eating place.
1905 *Nat. Police Gaz.* (Dec. 30) 3: Restaurants…Chuck Connors would call them feed joints. **1909** in *DA*: We sidled into a feed-joint.

feed trough *n.* a cheap eating place.
*ca***1910** in A. Adams *Chisholm Trail* 262: I was directed to the only feed trough in town.

feed up *v.* to eat heartily; eat up.
1917 Livingston *Coast to Coast* 124: Westbound bummers lingered to "feed up" after finishing the starvation trip of twelve hundred dreary miles.

feel *n.* an act or instance of feeling up. See also **cop a feel** s.v. COP, *v.*
1929 J.M. Saunders *Single Lady* 96: You wouldn't begrudge him a few free feels, would you, Nikki? **1934** H. Roth *Call It Sleep* 327 [ref. to *ca*1915]: Give 'em a feel. **1934** O'Hara *Samarra* ch. vi: And that husband of hers, that Harvey. Trying to give me a feel under the table. **1942** Hurston *Dust Tracks* 144: Men at the old game of "stealing a feel." **1954** Chessman *Cell 2455* 77: What are you trying to do, grab a free feel? **1955–57** J. Lee *Career* 68: We could be in Times Square gettin' a free feel in the crowd.

feel-day *n.* [pun on *field day*] *Juve.* a period of feeling up.
1929–30 J.T. Farrell *Young Lonigan* 65 [ref. to *ca*1916]: I wouldn't let him fool around and have a feel-day. **1973** *Nat. Lampoon Encyc. of Humor* 138: At first, Timmy has a "feel day."

feeler *n.* **1.** *Und.* (see quot.).
1798 in J. Greene *Band of Bros.* 114: The word *thimble* means watch, crome, clock.…The word *feeler* means dirk, sword, knife, &c.
2. usu. *pl.* a finger; in phr. **put the feelers on** to feel with the fingers.
***1831** Trelawny *Adv. Younger Son* ch. lxv: Bah!…a feeler or two smashed and jammed together. **1912** T.A. Dorgan, in Zwilling *TAD Lexicon* 36: He was about to slip his feelers around the artillery. **1944** Burley *Hndbk. Jive* 138: *Feelers*—Fingers. **1950** A. Lomax *Mr. Jelly Roll* 47: Creep joints where they'd put the feelers on a guy's clothes. **1966** Kenney *Caste* 79: Your feelers are still like dead timber!

feel up *v.* to caress or fondle in a sexual manner, esp. through the clothing.—occ. constr. with *on*.
1929–30 Farrell *Young Lonigan* 95 [ref. to *ca*1916]: He again thought of feeling her up. **1929–30** Dos Passos *42d Parallel* 65: Jeez, I thought she was going to feel me up. **1957** J. Kerouac, in *OEDS*: We used to get next to pretty young daughters and feel them up in the kitchen. **1966** Fariña *Down So Long* 243: C'mere, wanna feel you up. **1978** Wharton

Birdy 33: I begin feeling her up. **1980** *Harper's* (May) 61: The class genius…really did want to get felt up. **1993** *Jerry Springer Show* (synd. TV series): Guys would feel up on me.

feem *n.* [clipping of *female*] a woman. Cf. FEMME.
1918 *Everybody's* (Nov.) 18: "Mike" was never known to "drag a feem" to any of the class hops.

feet *n.* *Mil. Av.* see s.v. FOOT.

feeze *v.* *Stu.* (see quot.).
1856 Hall *College Wds.* (ed. 2) 348: *Pheeze*, or *Feeze*. At the University of Vermont, to pledge. If a student is pledged to join any secret society he is said to be *pheezed* or *feezed*.

fel *n.* [by clipping] a fellow.
1855 in Meserve & Reardon *Satiric Comedies* 151: I mean, old "fel," [etc.]. **1856** Wilkins *Young N.Y.* 13: I say, old fel—it ain't gentlemanly for us to be trying to overhear. **1871** "M. Twain" *Roughing It* 258: How're ye, Billy, old fel? **1875** Blessington *Campaigns* 297: No you don't, old fel. **1877** *Puck* (May) 6: Whazzer mazzer, young fel'? **1884** in Lummis *Letters* 4: Say, ole fel, what nine do ye b'long to, any way? **1896** Ade *Artie* 29: Go ahead, old fel, I never said a word.

felch *v.* [orig. unkn.] *Homosex.* (see 1972 quots.).—usu. considered vulgar.
*a***1972** B. Rodgers *Queens' Vernacular* 80: *Felch* (jocular, late '60s) complicated erotic process of sucking out the come one has ejaculated into an ass and returning it orally. **1972** *Anthro. Linguistics* (Mar.) 101: *Feltch* (v.): to use one's mouth or tongue on the anus of his partner; anilingus. **1973** *Zap Comix* (No. 6) (unp.): I not only covet my neighbours ass I *felch* my neighbours ass.…Watch us…felch your yummy desirable wife. **1981** in *Maledicta* IX (1988) 152: The Vacaville, Calif., cons…[defined] *felch*…it means to *eat out* the anus. **1985** *Nat. Lampoon* (Sept.) 15: What is your definition of "kinky"?…Felching [a prominent politician].

felch queen *n.* *Homosex.* (see quots.).—usu. considered vulgar.
*a***1972** B. Rodgers *Queens' Vernacular* 80. **1972** in *AS* XLV 57: *Felch queen n.* One who obtains sexual pleasure by seeing or coming in contact with fecal matter. **1972** *Anthro. Linguistics* (Mar.) 101: *Feltch queen* (n.): a male homosexual who licks, sucks, or tongues the anus of his partner.

fellows *n.pl.* crab lice.
1964 Rhodes *Chosen Few* 75: "You act like a cat with fellas." "With what?" "Crabs."

felony powder *n.* *Police.* heroin or another illicit drug in crystalline form. *Joc.*
1985 *Miami Vice* (NBC-TV): Unloading that felony powder. **1985** *Miami Vice* (NBC-TV): A bale of felony powder.

felony shoes *n.pl.* *Police.* sneakers. Also **felony flyers.** *Joc.*
1979 *Nat. Lampoon* (Sept.) 47: And don't forget to wear yer felony shoes! **1980** Gould *Ft. Apache* 84: Skinny black kid with felony shoes and a World War I aviator's cap. **1987** Taubman *Lady Cop* 268: All wearing sneakers (known as "Felony Flyers.")

felony-stupid *adj.* *Police.* exceptionally stupid. *Joc.*
1986 "J. Cain" *Suicide Squad* 23: I plead felony-stupid.

fem var. FEMME.

fem lib *n.* [*female liberation*] *Journ.* **1.** feminism. Also attrib.
1970 in *BDNE* 164: Should the conditions of Femlib take over, the cultural fallout will be stupendous. **1972** R. Barrett *Lovomaniacs* 401: No fem-lib oration against the institution of marriage.
2. a feminist.
1970 in *Harper's* (Jan. 1971) 95: Fem Libs be damned.

fem libber *n.* *Journ.* a feminist.
1984 R. Salmaggi, on WINS Radio News (Aug. 6): Fem libbers will climb walls when they see *Purple Rain*.

femme or **fem** *n.* [prob. clipping of E *feminine* or *female*, resp. to conform to F *femme*; poss. directly fr. F] **1.** Orig. *Stu.* a girl, or young woman, or woman. Also attrib.
1871 Wood *West Point Scrapbook* 337: *Fem.*—A woman—girl—young lady. **1878** Flipper *Colored Cadet* 53: "A fem," "femme."—Any female person. **1894** *Lucky Bag* (USNA) (No. 1) 66: *Femme*…A young lady or girl. **1900** *DN* II 34: *Fem, n.* A woman, dame. **1910** *Univ. of Tenn. Volunteer* 28: Will make good if the "femmes" don't occupy his mind too much. **1918** Swan *My Co.* 47: Have a good look boys; it's the last time you'll see for beaucoup de weeks. **1919** in Hemingway *Sel. Letters* 24: However I know there are some very priceless femmes here. **1927** *Vanity Fair* (Nov.) 132: A "femme" is a girl. **1932** Nelson *Prison Days &*

Nights 29: He…expects a man who hasn't had a drink or a piece of femme for years to keep those rules. **1933** in Galewitz *Great Comics* 34: She said the cheer-leader's assistants were gonna be fems too! **1936** *Nat. Geo. Mag.* 778: [At West Point] A young lady is a "femme" or "fem." **1947** Willingham *End As a Man* 200: I have to go see…a femme. **1964** *Time* (Nov. 20) 106: [He] decides not to upset his featherheaded fem. **1980** *N.Y. Daily News* (*Tonight*) (Aug. 28) 9: Fem offered 2d green beret test…Captain Kathleen Wilder, who is trying to become the first woman to earn a green beret, should be allowed to retake a field test she failed, according to Col. Ola Mize, the director of the Special Forces School. **1991** Nelson & Gonzales *Bring Noise* xvi: Fem voices roar.

2, *Esp. Homosex.* a person who plays the feminine role in a homosexual relationship; an effeminate male homosexual or a passive lesbian. Also as adj. Also **femmie.**

1934 "J.M. Hall" *Anecdota* 181: A dozen synonyms for male homosexuality…Fairy, pansy, queen, floosie, cock-sucker, gobbler, queerie, dickie-licker, femmie, Nancy, fruit, lapper. **1947** in J. Katz *Gay/Lesbian Almanac* 625: Femme [is] common in gay parlance. **1957** Greenwald *Call Girl* 118: Among female homosexuals the "femme" acts the role of a woman, and the "butch" acts the role of a man. **1965** S. Harris *Hellhole* 217: When they needed to, femmes and butches, working together, picked up tricks and put on circuses for them. **1966** C. Ross *N.Y.* 83: They go home to their husbands after an afternoon with a butch or a femme. **1966** Tornabene *I Passed as a Teenager* 240: "Did you ever go out with a fem?" he asked me with a mouth full of cake. "What's *that?*" I responded. "A queer. A faggot. You know, a fairy." **1968** in Giallombardo *Impris. Girls* 150: It's easier to be a fem. But butches get a lot in some ways. **1972** *Sat. Review* (Feb. 12) 24: Today's homosexual can be…manly ("stud") or womanly ("fem"). **1972** *Anthro. Linguistics* (Mar.) 101: *Fem* (n.): Usually refers to a female homosexual who presents herself in a more feminine role (opposite of "butch") than her sexual role. If one wants to add sexual emphasis to the term, in order to distinguish it from the social role, it is incorporated into the phrase "fem in bed", e.g., one might remark "she's butch but she's fem in bed" and vice versa. "Fem" is also used in referring to an effeminate male homosexual, one who acts girlish; also a male homosexual who assumes the female role in sexual relations. **1976** Univ. Tenn. student: Everybody knows he's a queer. He's real femme. **1983** *Mother Jones* (Jan. 1984) 57: Playing butch and femme roles in a lesbian relationship. **1992** *Mystery Sci. Theater* (Comedy Central TV): What a femme!

femmy *adj.* effeminate.

1967–68 in *DARE*. **1980** *Nat. Lampoon* (Aug.) 17: Kind of femmy for after-shave.

fem-sem *n.* [*fem*ale *sem*inary] *Stu.* a woman's seminary; (*also*) a student at a woman's seminary.

1895 Gore *Stu. Slang* 6: *Fem sem*…Female Seminary. **1895** Wood *Yale Yarns* 63: I think we serenaded a fem. sem. **1900** *DN* II 34: *Fem-sem, n.* 1. A seminary for women. 2. A girl at college or seminary.

fence *n.* **1.** Orig. *Und.* **a.** a knowing, usu. professional, buyer and seller of stolen property. Now *S.E.*

*1698–99 "B.E." *Dict. Canting Crew*: Fence…a Receiver and Securer of Stolen-goods. *1708 in Partridge *Dict. Und.* 235: *Fence,* one that Buys Stolen Goods. *1785 Grose *Vulgar Tongue*: *Fence*…A receiver of stolen goods. **1846** (quot. at RIVER RAT). **1848** *Ladies' Repository* VIII (Oct.) 315: *Fence,* A man who buys stolen property. **1848** Judson *Mysteries* 431: What do you mean, you thieving old fence? **1872** McCabe *N.Y. Life* 539: In the thief language, a person who buys stolen goods is called a "Fence." **1875** A. Pinkerton *C. Melnotte* 72: A "fence" is…one who makes a business of buying stolen property from thieves. **1890** Roe *Police* 228: Miss Condon [was] the "fence." **1929** "E. Queen" *Roman Hat* ch. vi 75: A gigantic criminal ring, composed of "fences," crooks, lawyers, and…politicians. **1950** *New Yorker* (Feb. 25) 43: Most of the great…gamblers, bunco steerers, fences, and international crooks of his time. **1983** *Batman* (Apr.) 4: We'll have to question all the fences and illegal gunsmiths in the city. *ca*1986 in Steffensmeier *Fence* 22: I can't speak for every fence, but the fences I knew pretty much had their fingers into different things. **1990** Murano & Hoffer *Cop Hunter* 13: Burglars,…fences, arsonists, kidnappers [etc.].

b. an establishment where stolen property is bought and sold. Now *S.E.*

*1828 in Partridge *Dict. Und.* 235: Johnson kept a *fence* and a brothel. **1845** *Nat. Police Gaz.* (Dec. 6) 125: A fellow, named Markham, who keeps a "Fence" shop at No. 212 West street,…received all the "swag" of the above depredations. **1848** Judson *Mysteries* 527: *Fence:* A place where stolen goods are bought or hidden. **1850** G.G. Foster *Gas-Light* 58: The "fences," or shops for the reception and purchase of stolen

goods. **1866** G.A. Townsend *Non-Combatant* 358: Field Lane, where he kept his "fence." **1887** Flinn *Chicago Police* 209: The murdered officer…was shot…in front of Lesser Friedburg's "fence," or pawnshop, No. 494 State street. **1897** Townsend *Whole City Full* 171: Next time he'll know enough to…find out where there's a safe fence to put a watch up in. **1906** Wooldridge *Hands Up* 195: A "fence"…is a place where stolen goods are stored. **1914** Healy *Delinquent* 328: The woman who conducted the "fence" was convicted largely on information obtained from him. **1916** Marcin *Cheaters* 40: They'll be searching for the stones all over—at every fence. **1922** E. Murphy *Black Candle* 351: Many drug stores, and other stores, are "fences" for contraband drugs.

2. a man's high detachable collar.

1910 Hapgood *Types From City Streets* 36: A bloke ain't got no show wid a gal if he ain't good-lookin', wid good clothes, wid a fence (collar) round his neck.

3. *Naut. & Av.* the International Date Line.—constr. with *the.*

1937 *Life* (Apr. 26) 38: The arc of possible operations fanning out from the Hawaiian Naval base of Pearl Harbor barely crosses the International Date Line (called "The Fence").

4. *Mil.* an international boundary.

1984 Trotti *Phantom* 112 [ref. to Vietnam War]: We hightailed it back across the fence to get turned around for another strike [against North Vietnam].

fence *v.* **1.** Orig. *Und.* to sell or pawn (stolen property). Now *S.E.*

*1610 in *OED*: To fence property, to sell anything that is stolne [*sic*]. *1753 in Partridge *Dict. Und.* s.v. *buss*: Burk will show you where you may buss a couple of Prads, and fence them at Abingdon Gaff. *1789 G. Parker *Life's Painter* 136: Which I have just *fenc'd* to the Cove at that there *Ken.* *1811 *Lexicon Balatron.: To fence.* To pawn or sell to a receiver of stolen goods. The kiddey fenced his thimble for three quids; the young fellow pawned his watch for three guineas. To fence invariably means to pawn or sell goods to a receiver. **1859** Matsell *Vocab.* 31: "The bloke fenced the swag for five cases," the fellow sold the plunder for five dollars. **1902** Hapgood *Thief* 58 [ref. to 1885]: We "fenced" the overcoats and with the proceeds continued our spree.

2. *Und.* to act as a buyer and seller of stolen property; (*trans.*) to deal in (stolen property).

*1665 in Partridge *Dict. Und.* 236: *Fencing cully,* one that receives stolen goods. *1725 in Partridge *Dict. Und.*: *Fencing cull.* *1821 in Partridge *Dict. Und.* 235: With Nell he kept a lock [house], to fence, and [gamble]. *1840 in *OED*: Does old Nanny fence? *1885 in *F & H* II 383: Moreover, he was strongly suspected of fencing—that is, purchasing stolen property. **1967** Spillane *Delta* 32: Joey Jolley ran a gin mill…and dabbled in fencing jewels to keep his hand in. **1980** Lorenz *Guys Like Us* 87: Doing some…fencing and loan-sharking. *ca*1986 in Steffensmeier *Fence* 22: This was their background before they got into fencing.

3. *Und.* (of stolen property) to be sold to a fence.

1981 G. Wolf *Roger Rabbit* 67: What he did have would fence for fifty or sixty bucks.

fence-bender *n. Navy.* (see quot.).

1958 Cope & Dyer *Petty Officer's Guide* 344: *Fence bender:* (Slang). A man with a metalsmith rating.

fence-buster *n. Baseball Journ.* a power hitter.

1942 *ATS* 647. **1949** Cummings *Dict. Sports* 135.

fence-corner *v.* (of a bucking horse) to rear up in one direction and come down in another.

1922 Rollins *Cowboy* 285: "Fence-cornering." Going up headed, say, northeast, and landing headed, say, northwest. **1927** Rollins *Jinglebob* 229 [ref. to 1880's]: Next, he began to "fence-corner," or, in other words, to leave the ground while headed at one point and to land while headed at another.

fence-house *n. Und.* FENCE, *n.,* 1.b.

*1824 (cited in Partridge *Dict. Und.* 235). **1884** Triplett *American Crimes* 71: He ran rapidly toward an isolated "fence-house,"* in the upper part of the city. Here…he obtained shelter for a few days.…*A fence-house is a receptacle for stolen goods.

fencing crib *n. Und.* FENCE-HOUSE.

*1839 in *F & H* II 384: It only leads to the fencing crib. **1848** *Ladies' Repository* VIII (Oct.) 315: *Fencing crib,* The residence of a person who buys stolen property.

fencing-ken *n. Und.* FENCE-HOUSE.

*1698–99 "B.E." *Dict. Canting Crew*: Fencing-ken…the Magazine, or

Warehouse, where Stolen-goods are secured. **1848** Judson *Mysteries* 38: Many…used his house as a fencing ken, or place of deposit for their stealings.

fender-bender *n.* a minor collision between automobiles. Also (*nonce*) as v.

1961–62 in *AS* XXXVII (1962) 268: *Fender bender,* n. A minor collision; no injuries. **1962** Serling *New Stories* 1: Ever see a buggy like this?…No teenager's gonna try to fender-bender ya with this one! **1971** Dahlskog *Dict.* 23: *Fender bender,* n. A minor automobile collision. **1980** *N.Y. Post* (July 9) 3: Anderson in an Israeli fender-bender…a small car crashed into his limousine.…No one was hurt, but the car was damaged. **1980** Garrison *Snakedoctor* 27: He knew the direction he was going in would have the most traffic, the most fender-benders.

fenderhead *n.* a blockhead.

1975 Wambaugh *Choirboys* 99: Listen, you slant eyed little fenderhead. **1980** *Easyriders* (May) 6: Tell that fenderhead…he should tell it straight.

fer *n. Stu.* marijuana.

1974 Syracuse Univ. student: *Fer* is *grass,* like, "I just got some dynamite fer." It's short for *reefer,* I guess.

ferk *v.* (a partial euphemism for) FUCK. *Joc.*

*ca*1929 *Collection of Sea Songs* 43: Perkin you're shirkin your ferkin. **1946–51** J. Jones *Eternity* ch. xxi [ref. to *ca*1940]: Ah, what's the difference? They all the ferkin same. Five cents of one, a nickel of the other. **1965** in Legman *New Limerick* 4: He jerked 'em, and ferked 'em.

fern *n. Stu.* the buttocks. *Joc.*

1965 N.Y.C. high-school student: How's your fern [after a fall]? **1965** Adler *Vietnam Letters* 99: You know, the hardest part of all this is the feeling of sitting around on our ferns, doing nothing.

ferret *n.* **1.** a detective.

1886 E.I. Wheeler *N.Y. Nell* 4: Got any detective business you want executed…? If so, I'm your ferret. ***1891** in *OED*: He engaged him as a kind of ferret or detective. **1901** Ade *Modern Fables* 64: So the Main Detective called in a couple of Ferrets, who drew Twelve a Week, and they began to Shadow the Young Man at $8 a Day. **1919** Darling *Jargon Bk.* 12: *Ferret*—A detective.

2. (among USAF prisoners of war in Germany, WWII) a German security guard. Now *hist.*

1945 *N.Y. Times Mag.* (Nov. 4) 12: "Ferret" (a German security agent). ***1946** in *OEDS*: Night and day…German security guards patrolled and snooped.…These guards were known by us as "ferrets." **1960** Simmons *Kriegie* 100: All German guards and ferrets speak perfect English. *Ibid.* 106: A *ferret* is a special guard who generally moves about the camp in overalls [searching for escape tunnels, etc.]. **1968** Westheimer *Song of Young Sentry* 222: From time to time they encountered German guards with slung rifles and men in blue coveralls carrying flashlights in their pockets and long screwdrivers in their hands. "Ferrets," said Hartman. "Sometimes they crawl under the blocks and listen, so be careful what you say. The Hundfuehrers come in at night."

3. *USAF.* (see 1945 quot.).

1945 *Amer. N & Q* (Dec.) 136: Ferret (plane carrying electronic jammer tuned to wave lengths of enemy radar and flying over hostile territory). **1962** Harvey *Strike Command* 61: I've got ferrets that can pinpoint all the enemy radars in a few hours, and I've got fighter bombers that can go out and bust those sites.

ferricadouzer *n.* a thrashing; a knock-down blow. *Rare* in U.S.

*1851 H. Mayhew *London Labour* I 228: No fear of a *ferricadouzer* for the butcher. How is it spelled, sir? Well, if you can't find it in the dictionary, you must use your own judgment.…It means…a good thrashing. ***1891** *F & H* II 385: *Ferricadouzer*…(pugilist)…a knock-down blow; a thrashing. (From the Italian *fare cadere,* to cause to fall & *dosso,* back.) **1930** in Wentworth *ADD* 212 [in Pennsylvania].

ferschlugginer *adj.* [< E Yid *farshlogener,* fr. *farshlogn* 'worried, careworn'] confounded; darned. *Joc.*

1955 Kurtzman *Inside Mad* 3: And it's so hard to buy these furschlugginer *three*-fingered kinds! **1978** *L.A. Times* (June 4) VII 5: Whoever [*sic*] got the fershluginer bug, put the fershluginer bug outta my bus. **1982** Rucker *57th Kafka* 209: *Where* did you boys say you were losing that furshlugginer inertia-winder?

fess *n.* **1.** *Stu.,* esp. *U.S. Mil. Acad.* a student who habitually demonstrates an inability to answer a professor's questions.

*ca*1890 Averell *10 Yrs.* 38 [ref. to *ca*1855]: Oh, Ryders is a perfect "fess." **2.** *U.S. Mil. Acad.* (see quots.).

1900 *Howitzer* (No. 1) 119: *Fess* (noun).—A failure. **1929** Shay *Drawn*

from Wood 47: If they go wrong I'm in a hell of a fess.*…*West Point slang meaning mix-up, jam, etc.

fess *adj. Rap Music.* having the nature of an excuse.

1991 *Source* (Oct.) 29: That's the fess answer. Now the real reason.

fess *v.* **1.** [prob. fr. con*fess* ignorance] *Stu.,* esp. *U.S. Mil. Acad.* to demonstrate an inability to answer a professor's question; (*hence*) to fail.

1834 *Mil. & Nav. Mag. of U.S.* (Mar.) 25: The Blackboard…that abomination of him who has to "fess"—that delight of him who hopes to "fan." **1851** B. Hall *College Wds.* 124: *Fess.* Probably abbreviated from *confess.* In some of the Southern Colleges, to fail in reciting; to silently request the teacher not to put further queries. **1859** in Eliason *Tarheel Talk* 135: Prof. Smith was to hear Sunday lesson. The class, to a man "fessed." When they were required to make up the lesson, they refused. **1871** Wood *Scrapbook* 337: *To fess*—To make a poor recitation. *To fess perfectly frigid*—To know *nothing* about a lesson. *To fess on a clean board*—Same as the above. **1872** Marcy *Reminiscences* 317: Of course I was obliged to acknowledge my inability to perform the task, or to "fess," as the cadets have it. **1878** Flipper *Colored Cadet* 53: "Fessed," "fessed cold," "fessed frigid," "fessed out," and "fessed through."— Made a bad recitation, failed. **1900** *Howitzer* (No. 1) 119: *Fess* (verb)— To make a failure. **1930** in D.O. Smith *Cradle* 83: We had [exams] all week in Math and I fessed one. **1937** in *DA: Fes, v.* To fail completely in a recitation.

2. to confess.—usu. constr. with *up.*

1840 in *DAE*: It would be a sad thing to die here…with a lie in your mouth, so 'fess clean. **1868** Alcott *Little Women* ch. ix: I shall…"fess" to mother how silly I've been. **1895** Gore *Stu. Slang* 6: *Fess up*…confess. **1905** in Compton *Librarian* 184: And they never saw you throw a harmless cat into the washing machine…and never fess up to the deed. **1930** in *OEDS*: The joke is on him and he may as well "Fess up" to it. ***1941, 1947** in *OEDS.* **1975** Wambaugh *Choirboys* 131: Okay, fellas. Let's fess up. Who farted? **1977** M. Franklin *Last of Cowboys* 70: Come on, 'fess up, Virginia. **1980** J. Carroll *Land of Laughs* 71: She didn't want to 'fess up to owning a place where people got killed because of owner neglect. **1991** C. Fletcher *Pure Cop* 64: He finally did 'fess up.

3. *Rap Music.* to back down; back out; decline; COP OUT.

1985 "UTFO" in L.A. Stanley *Rap* 377: The educated rapper, M.D. will never fess. **1988** "Biz Markie" *Vapors* (rap song): She always fessed,/"Talkin' about, 'Nigger, please, you work for UPS.'" **1988** "EPMD" *It's My Thing* (rap song): Rod's fresh and fresh, you never heard me fess. **1989** "The D.O.C." *The Formula* (rap song): I don't fess, I mean I'm like fresh.

fetlock *n.* the human ankle. *Joc.*

1840 *Spirit of Times* (Nov. 21) 446: I guess you don't often see such fetlocks in Slickville.

fever *n.* [prob. alter. of FIVER] **1.a.** *Craps.* the point five on a pair of dice. Also vars.

1918 Witwer *Baseball to Boches* 293: Come on, little fever! **1929** Nordhoff & Hall *Falcons of France* 28 [ref. to 1915]: Some formed vociferous rings about three or four crap games that seemed to start in every moment of leisure, and I heard shouts of "Fever in the south! Big Dick from Boston! String of box cars! Fade you! Let her ride!" **1929** in Segar *Thimble Th.* 53: Fever in the south! Come on five! Five me, dice! **1962** Crump *Killer* 185: "I never miss a five." He shook the dice. "Fever in de fun house—spread whoah!" **1962** Killens *Heard the Thunder* 289: Fever, dice! Five when you stop! **1968** Swarthout *Loveland* 112: Hah! Big fever! Hah! Eighter from Decatur!

b. *Cards.* a five.

1951 *AS* (May) 98: [Poker terms] *Fever.* A five-spot. *ca*1965 IUFA *Folk Speech: Five*—Fever. **1968** F. Wallace *Poker* 215: *Fever.* A five. **1987** T.L. Clark *Dict. Gamb.* 78.

2. *Gamb.* a five-dollar bill or chip.

1961 in Himes *Black on Black* 104: The shooter throws down a five-dollar bill. STICK MAN: Five in the circle! A fever! Winner's got him. **1987** T.L. Clark *Dict. Gamb.* 78.

few *adj.* ¶ In phrase: **a few, 1.** a little; (*hence*) considerably; a good bit.

*1761 in *OED*: I…throw my eyes about a few. ***1778** in *OED*: Your letter which diverted him not a few. ***1778** in *F & H* II 387: So I trembled a few. **1807** W. Irving *Salmagundi* 199: He was determined to astonish the natives a few! **1833** J. Neal *Down-Easters* I 53: That's into yer, a few! **1844** in Haliburton *Sam Slick* 190: He made them stare a few,…I guess. **1845** in G.W. Harris *High Times* 51: When he bursted the hoops and cum out he rared a few. ***1853** C. Dickens *Bleak House* ch. xx: Mr.

Smallweed bears the concise testimony, a few. **1871** Schele de Vere *Amer.* 601: *Few, a,* in slang means *a little.* "Were you alarmed?" "No, but I was astonished a few." ***1873** Hotten *Slang Dict.* (ed. 4): "Don't you call this considerably jolly?" "I believe you, my bo-o-oy, *a few.*" **1899** Cullen *Tales* 130: I'm just throwing it into him a few to sort o' square up a personal grievance. **1911–12** J. London *Smoke Bellew* 47: Say, we went a few, didn't we? **1938** P. Crawford *Hello, Boat!* 7: "How much will it cost?" "Quite a few, I reckon."

2. formidable.

1850 in Blair & McDavid *Mirth* 104: You know he's a few in that line! **1851** Burke *Peablossom's Wedding* 146: That chap Arch Coony, was er few in that line!

fib *n. Med.* coronary fibrillation.

1985 Frede *Nurses* 48: You trying to put all our patients into fib?

fib *v.* [orig. unkn.] *Orig. Und.* to strike or beat; punch or pummel; beat up. Now *hist.*

*1665 in *OED*: *Fib,* to beat. ***1785** Grose *Vulgar Tongue:* *Fib the cove's quarron in the rumpad…*beat the fellow in the highway. ***1808** in *OED*: *Gully…*fibbed him and kept him from falling. ***1810** in Holloway & Black *Broadsides* II 251: He's come to mill our champion Cribb,/And doth declare he will him fib,/No fear that he will ever jib/On the Eighteenth of December. ***1820–21** P. Egan *Life in London* 96: Randall and Cribb/Know how to *fib.* **1842** *Spirit of Times* (Sept. 3) 322: Bill…fibbed him severely. **1866** *Nat. Police Gaz.* (Nov. 17) 3: A dozen of the "mob" went at the "cop" and "fibbed" him bad. **1870** *Putnam's Mag.* (Mar.) 301: Knocking the unfortunate knocker off his pins…to say nothing of boring, fibbing and sending him to grass. **1953–55** Kantor *Andersonville* 170: Then you can…get away before he fibs you.

fibbie *n.* FEEBIE.

1982 P. Michaels *Grail* 300: And the Fibbies…are being pressured by the State Department. **1991** Grisham *Firm* 43: Still ain't talked to the Fibbies, as far as we know.

fid[1] *n.* **1.** *Naut.* **a.** a quid of tobacco.

*1796 Grose *Vulgar Tongue* (ed. 3): *Fid of Tobacco.* A quid, from the small pieces of tow with which the vent or touch-hole of a cannon is stopped. **1848** Bartlett *Amer.*: *Fid of tobacco.* A chew, or quid of tobacco. **1891** Maitland *Slang Dict.* 109: *Fid,* a plug of tobacco. **1943** in *DARE*: *Fid* (a small piece of tobacco).
b. a drink of liquor.

1830 in *DARE*: Their breakfast consists of coffee…with a "fid" of gin that would infallibly overthrow any ordinary worshipper of Bacchus. **1866** in "M. Twain" *Letters From Hi.* 78: He'd been among his friends having a bit of a gam, and had got about one fid too much aboard. *Ibid.* 83: "Fid"—the whaleman's term for our "smile"—drink. A fid is an instrument which the sailor uses when he splices the main brace on board ship. *Ibid.* 84: Take a "fid" with him. **1891** Maitland *Slang Dict.* 109: *Fid,* a drink. The word is used by sailors and especially by whalers.
2. *Naut.* a fellow.

1853 "Tally Rhand" *Guttle & Gulpit* 9: Didn't you see I was a bamboozlin' the fid?

fid[2] *n.* a fiddle.

1899 Cullen *Tales* 24: I got the old fid out…and strung her up. **1987** Southeastern La. Univ. prof., age 40: I haven't been practicing on the fid much.

fiddle *n.* **1.** (see 1873 quot.). *Rare* in U.S.

[***1857** "Ducange" *Vulgar Tongue* 8: *Fiddler.* A sharper, or cheat. Thieves.] **1873** Hotten *Slang Dict.* (ed. 4): *Fiddle…*In America, a swindle or imposture. ***1947, *1958, *1959** in *OEDS*.
2. [fr. FIDDLE AND FLUTE] a suit of clothes.

1943 Holmes & Scott *Mr. Lucky* (film): I've got to…change my fiddle. **1952** Holmes *Boots Malone* (film): Hey, you look sharp in the new fiddle, kid. **1968** Spradley *Owe Yourself a Drunk* 47: Got $200-fiddle (suit) on.
¶ In phrase:

¶ **hang up (one's) fiddle** to stop what (one) is doing.

1833 in *OEDS*: You'll have to hang up your fiddle till another year. **1834** in Foner *Labor Songs* 30: We'll now hang up our fiddle./And leave you to Old Nick. **1840** in Haliburton *Sam Slick* 129: And when a man ain't cool, he might as well hang up his fiddle. **1855** W.G. Simms *Forayers* 100: We've lost him, I reckon,…and may as well hang up our fiddles.

fiddle and flute *n.* [rhyming slang] a suit of clothes.

1919 T.A. Dorgan, in Zwilling *TAD Lexicon* 36: Fiddle and flute that's a suit. **1928** Sharpe *Chicago May* 287 [ref. to 1890's]: *Fiddle and flute*—suit. **1943** Holmes & Scott *Mr. Lucky* (film): *Fiddle and flute:* suit.

fiddlefart *v.* to FIDDLEFUCK.—usu. considered vulgar.

1970–72 in *AS* L (1975) 59: *Fiddle fart around…*loaf, shirk responsibility. **1976** Univ. Tenn. student: By the time they're through fiddlefartin' around, three months have passed. **1984** H. Gould *Cocktail* 16: While they fiddle-fart around at triple time. **1986** in *DARE*: *Fiddle-fart around* and *fiddle-fartin'*…carry the connotation of wasting time.

fiddle-fisted *adj.* clumsy.

1982 Downey *Losing War* 27 [ref. to WWII]: You goddam knuckle-headed, fiddle-fisted son of a civilian misfit!

fiddlefuck *v.* to play or fiddle around; FUCK AROUND.—usu. constr. with *around.* Also as quasi-*n.*—usu. considered vulgar. [1954 def. prob. represents a nonce usage.]

[**1929** in Randolph & Legman *Roll Me in Your Arms* 113: An' all that he could do was to fiddle, fuck an' dance.] **1949** in W.S. Burroughs *Letters* 35: Until such time as he gets tired of fiddle fucking around N.Y. **1954** Legman *Limerick* 387: *Fiddle-fucking*: Sub-axillary (copulation) (New Jersey, 1939). **1974** R. Stone *Dog Soldiers* 321: Some of you birds think I'm down here to play fiddle fuck around. **1973–77** J. Jones *Whistle* 506 [ref. to WWII]: It was strange, all right, and he didn't fiddlefuck around. **1979** Hurling *Boomers* 84: I'm not going to fiddle-fuck around 'til those pricks come out of the office. **1985** Dye *Between Raindrops* 192: Can't fiddle-fuck around on the perimeter.
¶ In phrase:

¶ **be fiddlefucked** to be damned.—usu. considered vulgar.

1976 Atlee *Domino* 52: This is Korea's Nuclear Reactor One…and I'll be fiddle-fucked if I understand why it hasn't fallen down yet.

fiddlefucking *adj.* FUCKING, *adj.*—usu. considered vulgar.

1970–74 P. Roth *My Life* 19: I guaranfuckingtee you gentlemen, not one swingin' dick will be leavin' this fiddlefuckin' area to so much as chew on a nanny goat's tittie.

fiddler's bitch *n.* see s.v. BITCH, *n.*

fiddler's fuck *n.* a damn; in phr. **not make a fiddler's fuck** to make no difference.—usu. considered vulgar.

[**1932** Nelson *Prison Days & Nights* 25: We could all rot to death, and they wouldn't give a fiddler's so-and-so for us.] **1961** Selby *Room* 187: They ain't worth a fiddlers fuck. **1973** W. Crawford *Stryker* 91: I don't give a fiddler's fuck about jurisdictional disputes, ace. **1976** Atlee *Domino* 175: A shamed patriot…ain't worth a fiddler's fuck. **1978** Selby *Requiem* 183: Why didn't make a fiddlers fuck. **1979** G. Wolff *Duke of Deception* 236: I didn't care a fiddler's fuck where my father was. **1984** Caunitz *Police Plaza* 22: I don't give a fiddler's fuck what the Forensic boys like.

fiddler's money *n.* a small amount of money; small change. Cf. quots. in *OED.*

1821 Waln *Hermit in Phila.* 30: *Rouse out your fidler's money* and *knock off the score.* ***1873** Hotten *Slang Dict.* (ed. 4): Fiddler's money is small money; generally from the old custom of each couple at a dance paying the fiddler sixpence.

fiddlestick *n.* ¶ In phrase: **old fiddlestick** old fellow.

1855 W.G. Simms *Forayers* 140: These rights,…old fiddlestick, kin take your ears off.

fiddly-fuck *n.* FIDDLER'S FUCK.—usu. considered vulgar.

1973 N.Y.C. man, age 25: Do you think I give a fiddly-fuck?
¶ In phrase:

¶ **play fiddly-fuck** to fool around.—usu. considered vulgar.

1964–66 R. Stone *Hall of Mirrors* 305: I didn't come out to play fiddly fuck.

FIDO *interj.* (see quots.).

1983 Eble *Campus Slang* (Nov.) 2: *FIDO*—Fuck It. Drive On. An expression of anger but resignation. **1986** Stinson & Carabatsos *Heartbreak* 93: Fido, man…Fuck it, drive on!

field *n.* ¶ In phrase: **play the field** to date a number of persons during the same period of time to avoid making an exclusive romantic commitment. Now *colloq.*

1930 Lait *On Spot* 75: Every broad what ever saw him did a flop for him. But he didn' play the field. **1936** Tully *Bruiser* 37: I play the field—they're doin' me a favor when they don't marry me. **1942** A.C. Johnston *Courtship of A. Hardy* (film): Have I whittled down to one particular cookie?…No, I'm playing the field. **1947** Conrad et al. *Love & Learn* (film): That's the one Linky and Joe had the scrap over. She plays the field. **1948** Vidal *City & Pillar* Bk. II ch. ix: Well, I've come to the conclusion that the only real pleasure is in playing the field. **1964** *World Bk. Dict.*: *Play the field.* Slang. to go with many different persons of the opposite sex.

field-day *v.* [shift of *field day*, jargon term for 'a period of cleaning quarters, equipment, etc.'] *USMC.* to make ready for inspection.

1986 Stinson & Carabatsos *Heartbreak* 91: I want the barracks field-dayed and squared away. Today.

field of wheat *n.* [rhyming slang] a street.

1920 T.A. Dorgan, in Zwilling *TAD Lexicon* 36: Field of wheat, that's street. **1923** McKnight *Eng. Words* 54: *Field of wheat*, "street." **1928** Sharpe *Chicago* May 288 [ref. to 1890's]: *Fields of wheat*—street.

field-strip *v. Mil.* **1.** [**a.** to take apart. [Always jargon, this sense is undoubtedly the orig.]

1947 (cited in *W9*). **1983** Elting, Cragg, & Deal *Soldier Talk* 105: *Field strip, to*...Officially, to break a weapon down into its basic components, usually so that it can be cleaned. **1968–90** Linderer *Eyes of Eagle* 21: Overhauling a diesel engine, fieldstripping a Remington typewriter.] **b.** (see 1983 quot.).

1963 Gant *Queen St.* 109: "What happened to the first one or two butts?"..."Field-stripped them." **1971** May *Playboy* 208 [ref. to WWII]: Aw right, you guys, police up the area and field-strip them butts. **1975** S.P. Smith *Amer. Boys* 99: Any man not field-stripping cigarettes deals with me personally. *a*1981 "K. Rollins" *Fighter Pilots* 85: He...lights a cigarette....Apologetically, he field-strips it. **1983** Elting, Cragg, & Deal *Soldier Talk* 105: *Field strip, to*...To reduce cigarette or cigar butts to shreds so that they can be disposed of outdoors without leaving a noticeable residue. **2.** to undress; strip, esp. in order to plunder.

1945 Huie *Omaha to Oki.* 85: Boyd...killed the Jap, then meticulously "field stripped" the Jap for souvenirs. **1957** McGivern *Against Tomorrow* 105: Start field-stripping, Sambo...you won't get far in your birthday suit. **1984** in Terkel *Good War* 61 [ref. to WWII]: This Jap had been hit. One of my buddies was field-stripping him for souvenirs. **1992** *Mystery Sci. Theater* (Comedy Central TV): We'll just field-strip him and get out of here.

fiend *n.* [1971 quot. at (1), below, offers a plausible ety.] **1.** an addict, esp. of an opiate.

1881 H.H. Kane *Opium Smoking* 44: A man who smokes large amounts of opium daily is, in this country, called a "fiend." **1883** in Courtwright *Dark Paradise* 73: I tell you it's a great system for the fiends who travel. **1885** Farwell *Chinese* 103: The "opium fiend," as he is known [in San Francisco], may be met with everywhere. **1886** in Courtwright *Dark Paradise* 73: The joint...is considered a sacred sanctum, and to betray...any conversation between the fiends is considered an unpardonable offense. **1892** Norr *China Town* 39: Edna got to hitting it and pretty soon she was a full-fledged fiend. **1894** Gardner *Doctor & Devil* 39: He, too, was a "dope" fiend. **1895** Tisdale *Behind the Guns* 38: There was nothing in their appearance suggestive to me of anything worse than an advanced stage of consumption, or [a] "dope fiend." **1897** Siler & Houseman *Fight of Century* 57: I'm bound not to become a fiend. This will wear off, they tell me, in time. **1902** Hapgood *Thief* 78 [ref. to *ca*1885]: They were cheap guns,—pipe fiends, petty larceny thieves and shoplifters. *Ibid.* 259: He generally becomes a whiskey fiend. **1909** *NID*: An opium fiend. **1909** Warner *Lifer* 138: Drugs—morphine, cocaine, and opium—used by fiends in the prison. **1914** Jackson & Hellyer *Vocab.* 32: *Fiend*, noun. Used by narcotic habitues chiefly. One addicted to the use of drugs, as a "hop fiend," a "dope fiend." **1921** Mencken *Amer. Lang.* (ed. 2) 194: Drug-fiend...coke-fiend. **1943** G. Fowler *Sweet Prince* 55: Cigarettes were called "coffin nails," and the users known as "fiends." **1944** N. Johnson *Casanova Brown* (film): To me a liar is even lower than a cigarette fiend. **1971** P.E. Lehman, in *Drug Forum* I 178: The word *fiend*, in referring to a heavy narcotics user, appears to derive from the...American translation of the Chinese term *opium devil*. **1986** C. Freeman *Seasons of Heart* 278: All those drug fiends and hippies. **1991** Nelson & Gonzales *Bring Noise* 19: Crack fiends bumming spare change. **2.** a person having an excessive fondness or enthusiasm for a specified thing; fanatic. Now *colloq.* [*1865 quot. alludes jocularly to a desire to eat pie.]

[*1865 Sala *Diary* I 238: There the Pie fiend reigns supreme.] **1884** Costello *Police Protectors* 429: "Red" the "stage fiend"...collected fares and avoided arrest....The "false fire alarm fiends"...had driven the Fire Department distracted with their malicious mischief. **1889** Farmer *Amer.*: The free lunch fiend...makes a meal off what is really provided as a snack. **1890** Quinn *Fools of Fortune* 212: Sam Cade, a "faro bank fiend"...was buried by a fund to which I was myself a subscriber. **1900** *DN* II 34: *Fiend, n.*...An enthusiast...An instructor who makes his students work hard. **1910** in Davidson *Old West* 54: Hungry Tom, a fiend

for eatin'. **1921** Mencken *Amer. Lang.* (ed. 2) 194: Movie-fiend,...bridge-fiend, golf-fiend,...kissing-fiend. **1923** McKnight *Eng. Words* 175: Book-fiend,...chess-fiend. *1929 R. Graves *Good-bye* ch. xxviii: A letter from an autograph-fiend. **1929** "E. Queen" *Roman Hat* 109: Field was an absolute fiend when it came to clothes....Last year he bought fifteen suits and...a dozen hats. **1957** Kohner *Gidget* 17: They always meet with a bunch of other fresh-air fiends. **1987** *Time* (July 13) 30: The man of action turned into a fiend for paperwork and was often at his cluttered desk by 7 a.m. and still there after midnight. **3.** *Stu.* (see 1909 quot.).

1895 *DN* I 416: *Fiend.* One who gets high marks. **1895** Gore *Stu. Slang* 17: *Fiend*...an expert. **1900** *DN* II 34: *Fiend, n.*...A hard student....One who excels in anything. **1900** *Howitzer* (No. 1) 119: *Fiend.*—An adept. **1904** *Howitzer* (No. 5) 221: *Fiend*—a clever person. **1909** *WNID*: *Fiend*...In student slang, a student devoted to, or very clever in, some study; as, he is a *fiend* in mathematics; a botany *fiend*. *U.S.* **4.** *Stu.* (see quot.).

1900 *DN* II 34: *Fiend, n.*...A fool, a blockhead.

fiend *v.* Esp. *Rap Music.* to crave; to yearn desperately.

1988 "Eric B. & Rakim" *Follow the Leader* (rap song): Still I fiend. **1988** "Public Enemy" *Don't Believe the Hype* (rap song): I'm not an addict, fiendin' for static. *a*1990 E. Currie *Dope & Trouble* 29: Dope....I have people comin' to me every day, fiendin' for it, because my stuff is pure....They're fiendin' bad. *Ibid.* 238: I fiend for rock and roll! **1993** *Source* (July) 52: Hardrocks that fiend for hip-hop.

fiender *n. Narc.* a drug addict.

*a*1990 E. Currie *Dope & Trouble* 29: A dope fiend. A fiender.

fiendish *adj.* extraordinarily good; wonderful.—in recent Black E use also constr. with *back.*

1900 *Howitzer* (No. 1) 119: *Fiendish.*—Extraordinarily good. **1905** *Howitzer* (No. 6) 293: *Fiendish*—Clever, remarkable; also eminently O.K., as, a fiendish femme. **1968–70** *Current Slang* III & IV 45: *Fiendish, adj.* Attractive; good; more than words can explain. *Ibid.* 46: *Fiendish back, adj.* Good-looking; hard to surpass. Watts [L.A.]—"That house is fiendish back."

fierce *adj.* **1.** very bad or unpleasant; hard to endure; (*broadly*) difficult. Now *colloq.* Also as *adv.*

1903 J. London *Abyss* 150: To use a Briticism,...[the situation] was "cruel"; the corresponding Americanism was more appropriate—it was "fierce." *ca*1906 "O. Henry," in *DA*: How can you wear a waist like that, Lou?...It shows fierce taste...But it's fierce now, how cynical I am, ain't it? **1909** Krapp *Mod. English* 202: At the time of the present writing...the adjective *fierce* is much used as a general slang term of disapproval; anything which is unpleasant is *fierce*. **1914** S. Lewis *Mr. Wrenn* 205: How sorry I was for the way I spoke to you. Gee! it was fierce of me. **1917** in Bowerman *Compensations* 6: My beard is fierce. I must shave tomorrow. **1925** *Eng. Journal* (Nov.) 699: That is a fierce lesson we have today. *ca*1935 in Horwill *Mod. Amer. Usage* 130: "At any conversational melee you may learn that the weather has been fierce, that the last play was fierce, that the cradle song at yesterday's recital was fierce, that the servant problem is fierce, and that the dinner tomorrow night is likely to be fierce."..."It ached fierce." **1935** A.G. Kennedy *Current Eng.* 554: The person who possesses only a pair of adjectives like *keen* and *fierce* to express all degrees of approval and disapproval is sadly handicapped. **1954** in S.J. Perelman *Don't Tread on Me* 157: Everyone eats at home, & the only place to go...[serves] pretty fierce grub for the money. **2.** remarkable; (*hence*) splendid.

1901 W. Irwin *Sonnets* (unp.): You're fierce at [cadging drinks]. **1903** *Pedagog. Sem.* X 374: *Exaggerations....*That's fierce. Wouldn't that kill you....To beat the band. **1913** J. London *Valley of Moon* 5: You're sure a fierce hustler. **1930** in Partridge *DSUE* 273: "Such a one!" "A regular comic." "Fierce, I call him." **1988** Wendy's, Inc., TV ad: So now you don't have to clean your fierce new grill. **1992** *N.Y. Newsday* (Dec. 31) 47: What's In and Out for '93...[In] "Phat" [Out] "Fierce."

fifteen fucker *n. Army.* (see quot.).—usu. considered vulgar.

1981–89 R. Atkinson *Long Gray Line* 295: Each of them was reprimanded, fined $300, and given an Article 15—an administrative punishment known within the ranks as a Fifteen Fucker—"for conduct totally unbecoming an officer."

fifty-fifty *n. Prost.* (see 1941 quot.).

1941 G. Legman, in Henry *Sex Vars.* II 1165: *Fifty-fifty*...alternating fellation or pedication. It is a relatively new coinage. **1992** G. Hays & K. Moloney *Policewoman One* 97 [ref. to 1970's]: Words for...sex acts—straight lay, head job, "50-50," golden shower.

fifty-mission cap *n. Mil. Av.* (see 1956 quot.); (*broadly*) any similar cap, esp. as worn by a long-distance truckdriver. [The style is associated with bomber crews of WWII.]
1956 Heflin *USAF Dict.* 202: *Fifty-mission cap.* The service cap when worn without the front spring stiffener and grommet. *Jocular.* **1971** Tak *Truck Talk* 59: *Fifty-mission cap:* A trucker's hat that usually has several safety badges fastened to it...*fifty-mission crush hat:* A trucker's cap that looks like the Air Force cap of the same name. **1978** Gann *Hostage* 295 [ref. to WWII]: They still wore their 50-Mission caps jauntily.

fifty-spot *n.* a fifty-dollar bill; fifty dollars.
1868 in *DA*: He pulled out a fifty-spot, the largest bill he had, and offered to bet that on the game. **1899** Cullen *Chances* 47: The last fifty-spot I had on earth.

fifty-two-twenty *n. Labor.* unemployment compensation given to servicemen immediately after WWII; in phr. **fifty-two twenty club** the men receiving such compensation. Now *hist.* [Quots. ref. to post-WWII.]
1946 in *Britannica Book of Year* (1947) 840: *52-20 club.* The veterans of World War II who, rather than take low-salaried jobs, are accepting the $20 a week unemployment compensation the government will pay for a year (*i.e.*, 52 weeks). **1949** *N.Y. Times* (Aug. 3) 12: The state division of unemployment security said the "52-20 club" was not "a gravy train for the majority." **1957** *Sat. Eve. Post* (Jan. 12) 72: For a time he was a member of the "52-20 Club," the ex-GIs who got twenty dollars a week while they were job-hunting. **1959** J. Lee *Career* (film): I've been livin' on fifty-two twenty. **1974** Matthews & Amdur *Race Be Won* 18: My father...was collecting his "fifty-two twenty," as he liked to call it. That was the $20 a week for fifty-two weeks unemployed servicemen received from the government. **1984** in Terkel *Good War* 82: There wasn't any work at that time. I joined the 52-20 club. *Ibid.* 361: They were members of the 52-20 club: twenty bucks a week for fifty-two weeks.

fig bar *n.* (see quot.).
1935 O'Hara *Butterfield 8* 282: She all but did what they call in the movies a "fig bar." Fig bar is a term which covers the whole attitude of the very bashful child; the toes turned in, eyes lowered, and especially the finger in the mouth.

fig-fig *n.* [pidgin < G *ficken* 'to fuck'] *Mil.* sexual intercourse. Also as *v.* Also vars. [Quots. ref. to WWII.]
1948 Lowry *Wolf That Fed Us* 91: Hello, blondie, you wanta figgy-fig? **1955** McGovern *Fräulein* 158: You doan wann no fig-fig today? **1961** Heller *Catch-22* 52: Si, si, si! Hollywood star. Multi *dinero.* Multi divorces. Multi ficky-fick all day long. **1964** Faust *Steagle* 18: Fig fig, zig zig. **1967** W. Stevens *Gunner* 171: Fig-Fig. **1967** Taggart *Reunion of 108th* 104: A G.I....traded Meat-and-Beans, Meat-and-Vegetable Stew, Hash, K Rations, for a little feeki-feeki.

fight *n.* a party; BRAWL.
***a*1890–91** F & H II 393: *Fight*...A party; *e.g.*, *Tea fight, Wedding fight*, etc. **1926** Wood & Goddard *Amer. Slang* 17: *Fight.* A party; as, a tea-fight. Hence, *henfight*, woman's party. **1950** in *DAS*: The cocktail fights frequented by the old man.

fight *v.* to drink (whiskey), esp. to excess.
1844 Porter *Big Bear* 121: Well, Capting, they war mighty savagerous arter likker; they'd been fightin' the stranger* mightily comin' up, and war perfectly wolfish arter some har of the dog, and dam'd the drop did I have...*A barrel of whiskey is called a "stranger" from the fact that it is brought from a distance, there being none made in the country. **1911** in Tuchman *Stilwell* 39: The foreigners "just fight booze." **1929** in Garon *Blues* 92: Getting sick and tired of fighting that jug. **1939** in *Calif. Folk Qly.* I 229: I fight my whiskey with both hands.

fighting whiskey *n.* whiskey strong enough to make the drinker pugnacious. *Joc.*
1874 (quot. at TANGLE-LEG). **1887** J.W. Nichols *Hear My Horn* 22: I mad[e] it back with about two gallons of fighting whiskey.

FIGMO *interj. & adj. Mil.* (see quots.). Also **fuigmo.** Cf. FUJIGMO. *Joc.*
1962 F. Harvey *Strike Command* 101: Everybody in the Air Force is familiar with the expression a man about to ship out to some new duty station gives those about him who have some insane notion that they'll get some useful work out of him. It is "FIGMO!"...the expression which...[he] delivers at his new duty station...is FIGMO spelled backward, or OMGIF! **1968** J.D. Houston *Between Battles* 212: Once he knows [he is scheduled to rotate], he goes FUIGMO—Fuck U, I Got My Orders. At the PX he buys a FUIGMO button. **1969** Moskos

Enlisted Man 144: Rather, the attitude is typically, "I've done my time, let the others do their's." Or, as put in the soldier's vernacular, he is waiting to make the final entry on his "FIGMO" chart—fuck it, got my orders [to return to the United States]. **1969** *Current Slang* I & II 32: *Figmo*..."Forget it, I've got my orders."—Air Force Academy cadets. **1983** Groen & Groen *Huey* 102 [ref. to 1971]: Roger and John were among the few remaining...who were not figmo (fuck it, got my orders). *Ibid.* 105: You're figmo...I'll send them.

fig newton *n.* [pun after the trademark name for a fig cookie]
1. a figment of the imagination. *Joc.*
1959 N.Y.C. schoolboy: It's a fig newton of your imagination. **1982** Huttmann *Code Blue* 25: I'm here to see what *really* happens...what's real and what were Fig Newtons of my imagination. **1992** *CBS This Morning* (CBS-TV) (Oct. 26): That's mostly a fig newton of the media's imagination.
2. a silly, crazy, or eccentric person.
1974 Verona & Gleckler *Lords of Flatbush* (film): Pay no attention to the fig newton. He don't know what he's talkin' about.

figure *n.* ¶ In phrases: **come the big figure** to do or provide what is required.
1848 Baker *Glance at N.Y.* 16: A foo-foo...is a chap wot can't come de big figure....The big figure here, is three cents for a glass of grog and a night's lodging.
¶ **go [it on] the big figure** to do things on a large scale or in a lavish way.
1831 in *DA*: The opponents of the existing militia system...are "going it" at New York "on the big figure." **1833** Paulding *Lion of the West* 21: But, uncle, don't forget to tell Aunt Polly that I'm a full team going it on the big figure! **1836** "D. Crockett" *Exploits in Tex.* 52: When a man sets about going the big figure, halfway measures won't answer no how.
¶ **go the whole figure** to risk or do everything possible.
1833 N. Ames *Old Sailor's Yarns* 364: He was determined...to "go the whole figure." **1839** in Thornton *Amer. Gloss.*: I was determined to go the hull figure, and see all. **1841** [Mercier] *Man-of-War* 218: So go the whole figure on it if you like, I've got a shot or two left in the locker yet. **1844** Haliburton *Attaché* (Ser. 2) iii: It's ginirally allowed I go the whole figure, and do the thing genteel. **1856** in *DAE*: Darned if I don't go the hull figger, and send in my card as they do to Boston. **1914** H. James, in *DAE*: The...momentous season, or scene,...in which she goes the whole "figure."
¶ **on the big figure** lavishly or on a large scale.
1848 Bartlett *Dict. Amer.*: *Big figure*, To do things on the big figure, means to do them on a large scale.

figurehead *n.* **1.** *Naut.* the face.
***1826** "Blackmantle" *Eng. Spy* II 185: I just got a glimpse of his figure head t'other morning. **1833** J. Neal *Down-Easters* I 95: You lump of tarred rattlin with a figger-head to match. ***1833** Marryat *Peter Simple* 121: Well, Mr. Simple, I said to myself, "D—n it, if her figure-head and bows be finished off by the same builder, she's perfect." ***1835** Marryat *Midshipman Easy* 165: Once I was obliged to come up the side without my trousers, and show my bare stern to the whole ship's company, and now I am coming up, and dare not show my figure-head. **1841** [Mercier] *Man-of-War* 145: I was here when you first showed your pretty figurehead. **1846** Melville *Typee* 52: His face [was] disfigured for life, for the heathens tattooed a broad patch clean across his figurehead. **1855** Brougham *Chips* 321: "Aye, aye, Jack," says he, turnin' his jolly old figure-head full on me. **1856** *Ballou's Dollar Mo. Mag.* (Oct.) 322: He...knows what a chap is thinking about just by looking at his figure-head. **1871** *Galaxy* (Jan.) 60: Reckun they'll jest chip off all my feeturs 'fore they git done with me....Git my figgerhead smooth all round. **1878** Willis *Our Cruise* 13: By thunder!...I've seen that figger-head before. **1887** Davis *Sea-Wanderer* 105: I've writ "Joe Winrow, his mark," on your figure-head, any how. **1905** Dey *Scylla* 55: You kin jedge a woman by...the cut of her figgerhead.
2. *Naut.* the head.
1839–40 Cobb *Green Hand* I 265: He ain't agoing to unship his figurehead before company, is he? **1849** Melville *White Jacket* 228: I'll fetch you such a swat over your figurehead, you'll think a Long Wharf truck-horse kicked you. **1849–50** in Glanz *Jew in Folklore* 181: He seized the Jew by the throat, whose toplights looked as if they would start from his figurehead and carry him away his top-gallant eyebrows. ***a*1909** in Ware *Passing Eng.* 130: A cove who doesn't cloud his blooming figurehead with booze.
3. [alluding to idiom *have a good head for figures*] *Labor.* a timekeeper or bookkeeper.
1945 Hubbard *R.R. Ave.* 342: *Figurehead*—Timekeeper. **1958** McCul-

loch *Woods Words* 61: *Figure head*—To a logger, anyone who works with figures; a bookkeeper. **1977** R. Adams *Lang. R.R.* 58: *Figurehead*: the timekeeper.

¶ In phrase:

¶ **old figurehead** old fellow.

1872 *Overland Mo.* (Jan.) 98: Oh, I mean you, old figure-head.

Fiji *n.* [sugg. by *Phi Gee*] *Stu.* a member of Phi Gamma Delta fraternity; *(also)* the fraternity itself.

1963 Reuss & Legman *Songs Mother Never Taught Me* (unp.): (Phi Gamma Delta) = Fiji's. **1983** Univ. Tenn. student: My roommate pledged Fiji. **1988** *Newsweek on Campus* (Apr.) 13: It seems that 25 years ago the Fijis at Texas Tech stole the ceremonial bell of the Phi Delta Thetas. **1990** in *Texas Monthly* (Jan. 1991) 121: Phi Gamma Deltas (the Fijis).

filbert *n.* **1.** the head; NUT.

***1886** in *OEDS*: Cracked in the *filbert*,…dotty. ***1889** Barrère & Leland *Dict. Slang* II 361: Cracked in the *filbert*, slightly insane. ***1909** Ware *Passing Eng.* 130: *Filbert*…Head…Derived from prize ring. "Yere— come and look at the bloke standin' on his filbert," said the boy. **1918** (quot. at FLOOZY). **1920** Ade *Hand-Made Fables* 292: Alienists tell us that this is the first Sign of a general breakdown in the Filbert.

2. a foolish, eccentric, or crazy person; NUT.

1915–17 Lait *Gus* 208: Hello, nut…What's your name, filbert? **1951** *N.Y. Times Bk. Review* (Oct. 7) 16: A self-confessed football filbert.

file *n.* [orig. unkn.] **1.** *Und.* **a.** a pickpocket.

***1665** in Partridge *Dict. Und.* 82: *Bulk and File*, The Pickpocket and his Mate. ***1676** in Partridge *Dict. Und.* 240: A *File* is a Pickpocket. ***1698– 99** "B.E." *Dict. Canting Crew*: The *File*…a Pick-pocket. ***1728** *View of London* 36: Fourscore Files, alias *Pick-pockets*. ***1743** H. Fielding *Jon. Wild* Bk. IV ch. xii: The greatest character among them was that of a pickpocket or, in truer language, a *file*. ***1812** Vaux *Vocab.*: *File*, in the old version of cant, signified a pickpocket, but the term is now obsolete. **1848** Judson *Mysteries* 13: Warn't none of the files on the tramp? *Ibid.* 527: *File*. An assistant to a pickpocket. **1859** Matsell *Vocab.* 32: *File*. A pick-pocket. **1927** *DN* V 446: *File*, *n.* A pickpocket.

[**b.** an experienced swindler. [This sense, which may have been in use in America, may also have influenced early senses of **(2)**, below.]

***1812** Vaux *Vocab.*: *File*: a person who has had a long course of experi- ence in the arts of fraud, so as to become an adept, is termed an *old file upon the town*; so it is usual to say of a man who is extremely cunning, and not to be over-reached, that he is a *deep file*. ***1821** *Real Life in Lon- don* I 92: A person who has had a long course of experience in the arts of fraud…is termed *a deep file—a rum file, or an old file.*]

2. a sharp or cunning fellow; *(broadly)* Esp. *Mil.* a fellow, esp. a soldier. [Latter sense infl. by cliché "rank and *file*."]

***1837** C. Dickens *Pickwick Papers*, in *F & H* II 396: Wot a perverse old file it is!…always agoin' on about werdicks and alleybis, and that. ***1838** C. Dickens *Oliver Twist*, in *OED*: The Dodger…desired the jailer to communicate "the names of them two files as was on the bench." **1841** *Spirit of Times* (Oct. 30) 414: Old file. **1845** Durivage & Burnham *Stray Subjects* 67: There was a queer old file, as tart as he was ignorant. ***1876** in *F & H* II 396: If you were not such a steady old file I should think you were in love with her. **1878** Flipper *Colored Cadet* 53 [ref. to 1874]: "A file."—Any male person. **1900** *Howitzer* (No. 1) 119: *File*.—A title applied to any member of the strong sex. **1903** in *Century Dict.* (Supp.): The poor file…has to carry it, as well as his gun and various other accoutrements. **1907** Moss *Officers' Manual* 243: *Old File*—An old officer. **1922** *Marine Corps Gazette* (June) 214: Funny files they were, both among the officers as well as the enlisted men. **1925** Thomason *Fix Bayonets!* 248 [ref. to 1918]: This file is cheering his soul in the angle of the bridge at Silly-le-Long, just outside of Cognac Pete's buvette. In a little while an M.P. with no ear for music will run him in. **1956** Boat- ner *Mil. Customs* 117: *File* An Individual (He's a sloppy file."). **1990** C. Cawthon *Other Clay* 27 [ref. to WWII]: He characterized my perfor- mance as that of a "good file"—that is, a good fellow.

file *v.* to toss into a wastebasket.—usu. imper. *Joc.*

1934 Weseen *Dict. Slang* 334. **1976** Univ. Tenn. instructor: File this [a wadded piece of paper]. **1982** Eble *Campus Slang* (Nov.) 2: *File*—to throw away. *File* this can, please.

File 13 *n.* **1.** Esp. *Mil.* a wastebasket. *Joc.*

[**1941** *AS* (Oct.) 165: *File*. Waste basket.] **1942** *Yank* (Dec. 16) 18: File No. 13 is laden with protests…and dire threats. **1945** *AS* (Oct.) 226: *File 13*. The waste basket. **1952** Cope & Dyer *Petty Officer's Guide* (gloss.): *File 13*: wastebasket. **1956** Heflin *USAF Dict.* 203: *File 13*. A

waste basket. *Slang.* ***1974** (cited in Partridge *DSUE* (ed. 8)). **1979** *N.Y. Post* (Aug. 25) 47: The protest, of course, goes into File 13, because the Yanks won.

2. a private or classified file containing harmful or embar- rassing information.

1969 Graham *Violence in Amer.* 472: The Crime Commission found a secret "file 13" in one city containing a catalog of complaints that were not officially reported [in crime statistics].

fill *n.* **1.** an exaggerated or fictitious account; hoax.

1893 Putnam *Blue Uniform* 131: Don't put any faith in…their stories either. As the phrase goes, they are giving you a "fill."

2. FILL-IN, 2.

1985 Sawislak *Dwarf* 120: When he needed a quick fill on some state or local political situation.

¶ In phrase:

¶ **make a fill** *Und.* to join in association.

1914 Jackson & Hellyer *Vocab.* 32: If you know a good man who can make a fill, steer him in.

fill *v.* to hoax or mislead.—also constr. with *up*.

1880 "M. Twain" *Tramp Abroad* ch. xxv: They simply took your mea- sure and concluded to fill you up. **1890** *Overland Mo.* (Feb.) 124: Beauty,…"filled" by his pals, had come to the conviction that no com- mon wrong had been done him.

fill-in *n.* **1.a.** a substitute, esp. a person who substitutes for another. Now *colloq.* or *S.E.* [The 1918 quot. in *OEDS* does not illustrate this sense.]

***1928** in *OEDS*: I can hardly say my interest was aroused in the "new art" except as a fill-in for the stage. **1936**, **1944** in *OEDS*. **1952** *Harper's* (Apr.) 31: I've seen that happen when I was a fill-in. **1954–60** *DAS*: *Fill-in*…A substitute worker. *Colloq.*

b. duty as a fill-in.

1968 G. Kerr *Clinic* 180: He would take over as Dr. Hatch's regular assistant, with Harry available for fill-in as needed.

2. *Journ.* an account intended to fill gaps in one's knowl- edge; briefing. Now *colloq.*

1944 Liebling *Back to Paris* 9: He…had to get back to headquarters…so he could get a fill-in on the general picture. **1946** in *OEDS*: George Holmes…had given the President a fill-in on Stimson's literary back- ground. **1951** in *DAS*. **1951** *Sat. Eve. Post* (Apr. 21) 10: A friend gives me a fill-in on how Costello is running the country instead of Truman. **1975** Sepe & Telano *Cop Team* 83: That was all the fill-in D'Amico needed.

fill in *v.* **1.** *Und.* to join or take part; *(trans.)* to add or invite to join.

1904 *Life in Sing Sing* 255: *Fill In*. To become one of a party. *Ibid.* 261: I did the grand to Chicago and filled in with a yeg mob.…I purchased a first-class ticket to Chicago and met a gang of safe burglars whom I joined. **1924** in Partridge *Dict. Und.* 241: *Fill in*. Gambling term, to join in game. **1926** Clark & Eubank *Lockstep* 35: Bigfoot knew me to be O.K. and let me fill in on his mob. **1931** in Maurer *Lang. Underworld* 47: *(To) fill (him) in*…To add an extra man to a gang for a special job. "We didn't like him, but we filled him in anyway." **1949** in *Harper's* (Feb. 1950) 73: Pete filled in another man and [accomplished the robbery].

2. to take the place of another; be a substitute. Now *S.E.*

1930 (quot. at STORM-AND-STRIFE). **1934** *WNID2*: To *fill in* at bridge or for an ill employee. **1959** N.Y.C. man, age *ca*30: Who's filling in at third base? **1954–60** *DAS*.

3.a. to advise of or make conversant with, esp. recent devel- opments. Now *colloq.*

1942 in C.R. Bond & T. Anderson *Flying T. Diary* 143: I presume that he filled in the Old Man about our success at Chiang Mai. **1945** in *OEDS*: Can you fill me in on them? **1963** D. Tracy *Brass Ring* 317: What he didn't fill me in on, Larson did. **1975** V.B. Miller *Deadly Game* 83: I nod to him…indicating that Crocker has already filled me in. **1976** Conroy *Santini* 299: Well, I'll fill you in. **1966–80** McAleer & Dickson *Unit Pride* 133: One of 'em filled me in. **1980** Lorenz *Guys Like Us* 177: Fill me in. **1983** *Judge Dredd* (comic book) (Nov.) [7]: I'd better fill you in, Anderson.

b. to be filled in or advised.

1951 *Time* (Mar. 19) 46: He felt chipper enough to spend an hour…with General MacArthur, "filling in" on U.S. affairs.

filling *n.* daylights; STUFFING.

1887 Francis *Saddle & Moccasin* 83: He "scared the filling out of *them* durned quick."

filling station *n.* **1.** a small rural town. *Joc.*
  1927 *AS* (June) 389: The advent of gasoline…has brought the expression *filling-station* to take the place of *tank town* or *jerkwater*. **1941** *Slanguage Dict.* 15: *Filling station*…a small town.
  2. a place to eat or drink; (*specif.*) a nightclub.
  1933 Ersine *Pris. Slang* 36: *Filling station.* 1. A lunchroom. 2. A speakeasy. **1940** Chandler *Farewell, My Lovely* 25: Hoofers and comics from the filling station circuit. **1942** *Pittsburgh Courier* (Jan. 17) 7: *Filling station*—Eating establishment.

fill out *v.* [poss. alter. *feel out*] *Und.* (see quot.).
  1904 *Life in Sing Sing* 255: *Fill Out.* To locate valuables or places worth while to rob. Obtaining information through diplomacy.

fill-up *n.* a feast or filling meal.
  1864 in J.W. Haley *Rebel Yell* 187: Heaven knows we need the fill-up. *Ibid.* 226: A grand fill-up was the order of the day.

filly *n.* a young woman or girl.
  ***1614** B. Jonson *Bartholomew Fair* IV iii: Say'st thou so, filly? ***1616** Beaumont & Fletcher, in *OED*: A skittish filly will be your fortune, Welford. ***1668** in *OED*: Nobody will be very fond of a Hyde-Park Filly for a Wife. ***1668** in *F & H* II 397: I told you they were a couple of skittish fillies, but I never knew 'em boggle at a man before. ***1711** in *OED*: I am joined in Wedlock for my Sins to one of those Fillies who are described in the old Poet. ***1821** *Real Life in Ireland* 119: "He is one of *Ton*, keeps a *filly* and —" "He be d—d!…What dashing belle is that making love to a young officer?" **1859** Holmes *Prof.* 169: What do you think of our young Iris?…Fust-rate little filly. **1869** Carleton *Kaleidoscope* 18: And a high-stepper you'll get, too—she's a gay filly. **1871** "M. Twain" *Roughing It* 288: He lit on old Miss Jefferson's head, poor old filly. **1941** Macaulay & Wald *Manpower* (film): I feel sorry for the filly. **1951** Elgart *Over Sexteen* 106: After a few moments a good looking filly jaunts over to his table and lays down the menu. **1956** H. Gold *Not With It* 14: Now you hurt the filly's feelings. **1957** Townley *Up in Smoke* (film): Wow, get a load of that filly! **1978** B. Johnson *What's Happenin'* 157: The dude who had been standing between the two fillies at the bar was gone.

filthy *n.* [short for *filthy lucre*] money.—constr. with *the*. *Joc.*
  1925 Riesenberg *Under Sail* 346 [ref. to 1898]: I made friends among a fast bunch, spent the filthy. ***1931** P.G. Wodehouse, in *OEDS*: Just trying to make a bit of the filthy. **1945** Fay *Be Poor* 20: I put away chunks and gobs of the "filthy" for the "rainy day."

fin[1] *n.* a hand or (*obs.*) an arm.
  ***1785** Grose *Vulgar Tongue: Fin.* An arm. *A one finned fellow*; a man who has lost an arm. ***1819** [T. Moore] *Tom Crib* 45: *Fin*…Arm. **1827** J.F. Cooper *Rover* 392: A man who has been docked of his fins, and who is getting to be good for little else than to be set upon a cat-head to look out for squalls. **1836** in [Haliburton] *Sam Slick* 56: How he outs fins and flops about. **1836** *Spirit of Times* (Feb. 27) 15: He tossed a handful o' coppers into his starboard fin. **1840** *Spirit of Times* (Nov. 21) 446: H'are you boy?…Give us your fin. **1855** Brougham *Basket of Chips* 156: His hands—fins—flippers…were surrounded…with kid gloves. **1879** *Puck* (Dec. 3) 636: There's my fin and let's shake. **1891** McCann & Jarrold *Odds & Ends* 61: I'd mashed the old man in the jaw. I ain't so slow with my fins, either. Just feel of my muscle! **1896** Hamblen *Many Seas* 390: "Hello, Fred," said he, sticking out his fin. **1896** Ade *Artie* 59: Him standin' behind with one of his fins kind o' hid. **1901** Irwin *Sonnets* (unp.): Clinching fins in public, heart-to-heart. **1904** J.H. Williams, in *Independent* (June 23) 1430: "Hello, sonny," he said, cheerily, extending his fin. **1908** in H.C. Fisher *A. Mutt* 59: Choked with pleasure, General. Slip me your fin. **1923** in W.F. Nolan *Black Mask Boys* 64: I stand there, a gun in either fin. **1938** Bellem *Blue Murder* 46: Now stick out your fins.

fin[2] *n.* [clipping of FINIF] **1.a.** a five-dollar bill; five dollars. [In Brit. or Austral. quots., a five-pound note.]
  ***1868** in *OEDS*: "What are 'fins'?" "Five-pound notes." ***1911** O'Brien & Stephens *Austral. Sl.* 65: *Fin*: a five-pound note. **1916** *Railroad Man's Mag.* (Aug.) 707: The bunch shills fer him, and after some beefin' Pauline digs into th' First National an' produces th' finn. **1925** in *OEDS*: *Fin*…five dollars. **1927** *AS* (June) 390: A five-dollar note [is] a *fin*. **1929** Barr *Let Tomorrow Come* 149: What are you supposed to do with the fin—buy a new front and a new heater? **1930** Bodenheim *Roller Skates* 237: "What's he asking for?" "Ten fins." **1935** Algren *Boots* 17: You could stay on for a fin, cash down on the barrelhead. **1936** Duncan *Over the Wall* 21 [ref. to 1918]: A five was a fin. **1940** O'Hara *Pal Joey* 164: It paid I think around $18.40 and Pablo was on it for a fin. **1943** in Loosbrock & Skinner *Wild Blue* 213: I bet that noisy AA corporal a fin. **1953** E. Hunter *Jungle Kids* 27: You got a fin, Cole? **1991**

Donahue (NBC-TV): Just slip a fin in my T-bar. **1992** *Rolling Stone* (June 25) 18: The band charged its usual five-dollar admission…—for a measly fin, ticket buyers get intense, impassioned performances.
  b. *Gamb.* five hundred dollars.
  1978 Alibrandi *Killshot* 220: Side bets. A fin is five hundred bucks.
  2. *Pris.* a five-year prison sentence.
  1925 in *OEDS: Fin*…a five-year term. **1930** in Partridge *Dict. Und.* 241: I'd do a fin for auto banditry. **1934** Weseen *Dict. Slang* 13: *Fin*— A five-year sentence. **1967** [Beck] *Pimp* 101: I got a "fin"…in the State Joint. **1977** Caron *Go-Boy* 102: A fin, eh? I guess that can be a long haul for a boy of your age.

finagle *v.* [alter. dial. E *fainaigue* 'to cheat', of unkn. orig., + -*le*, freq. suff.] **1.** to scheme or intrigue.—occ. constr. with *around*. Also vars. Hence **finagler,** *n.*
  1922 in *DN* V 147: *Finagler*—one who stalls until someone else pays the check. **1924** Anderson & Stallings *What Price?* III [ref. to 1918]: I'm a weary man, and I don't want any finnaggelling from you. **1926** in Wentworth *ADD* 216: *Finagle.* U.S. political cant. **1936** in Ruhm *Detective* 178: Scheme and connive and finagle. **1936** S. Anderson *High Tor* 60: Are you two finnegling with us. Because if you are—! **1939** Willoughby *Sondra* 31: I finagled around till I learned Baranov Packers have a husky deposit in his bank. **1944** C.B. Davis *Leo McGuire* 177: Well,…I don't agree that all girls are finaglers. **1944** Wentworth *ADD* 215: Finagle, fenagle, phenagle, feniggle, faniggle, finigal [var. forms].
  2. to maneuver or manipulate by devious means; trick, swindle, or cheat.—sometimes constr. with *out of*. Also vars.
  1927 H. Miller *Moloch* 160: Before Dave had a chance to finagle, he threw his arms around the blonde. **1933–35** D. Lamson *About to Die* 106: Petty conniving, grafting, fenagling, racketeering, prison politics. **1937** in H. Gray *Arf* (unp.): Look what he phenagled Sirob and his pals into doin' for themselves. **1939** in Botkin *Sidewalks* 288: I run across a finagler last Monday…I seen him take a buck from the driver. **1942** *Time* (June 8) 64: Reporter Reilly finagled through the City Council an ordinance requiring newsboys to pay a…legal fee. **1943** Wolfert *Tucker's People* 5: He had some stocks and bonds left over from trying to get rich on Wall Street after being finagled out of his garage. **1944** C.B. Davis *Leo McGuire* 105: He certainly doesn't finagle one bunch of little guys into killing another bunch of little guys. *Ibid.* 142: Deceit and finagling are uncivilized. **1955** *PADS* (No. 24) 164: Big business is trying to…phenagle us all out of a dollar. **1986** R. Salmaggi, on WINS Radio News (June 23): Beuler even finagles his girl into the act.
  3. to trifle.—also constr. with *around*. Also vars.
  1928 *New Yorker* (Dec. 15) 55: [The car] is locked too tight to finagle with. **1932** D. Runyon, in *Collier's* (June 11) 7: Higginbottom…promises…to…blow a hole in Frank…if Frank tries any phenagling around with my friend. **1934** Appel *Brain Guy* 83: An' what's the use phenaglin' in the scum for pennies when the big dough's waitin'. **1946** Warner Bros. *Looney Tunes* (animated cartoon): I'll get dat wise guy, finaglin' around up dere!
  4. to adjust or invent for a fraudulent purpose.
  1944 C.B. Davis *Leo McGuire* 238: Now if we do not have enough evidence to stick this lug McGuire, it's our duty to finagle some evidence because the big shots…approve of finagling for a proper purpose.
  5. to secure by trickery or indirect methods; WANGLE.
  1951 Sheldon *Troubling Star* 38: I finagled the assignment as crew chief on the flight. **1961** *WNID3*: Finagle a 10-day leave. **1988** Univ. Tenn. instructor: I need to finagle about 10% more income to *live* as well as survive. **1992** *Early Prime* (CNN-TV) (Dec. 25): So we end up finagling a piece of wood, and that's how we made a pool table [in Somalia].

finale-hopper *n.* (see quots.).
  1922 T.A. Dorgan, in Zwilling *TAD Lexicon* 36: I thought they called them cake eaters. No—a finale hopper is a jobbie who never takes a twist to a dance but who horns in on the last dance as the band is playing Home Sweet Home. **1922** in *DN* V 147: *Finale hoppers*—Persons who make a business of appearing late at dances after the ticket takers have gone. **1929** *AS* IV 430: Among the terms which the daily press credits…[T.A.] Dorgan with inventing [is]…finale hopper ("cake eater"). **1964** Beaumont & O'Hanlon *For Those Who Think Young* (film): A cheap little orphan finale-hopper. **1973** N.Y.C. woman, age *ca*70 [ref. to 1920's]: *Finale-hoppers* were people who would always arrive at shows and parties at the last moment.

Finchie *n.* a student at or graduate of Finch College.
  1970 *N.Y. Times Mag.* (Dec. 27) 6: Again and again I found myself backed to the snack-bar wall by packs of furious, red-faced Finchies, as they hate to be called.

fine *adj.* *Black E.* (of a person of the opposite sex) attractive; sexy.

1944 Burley *Hndbk. Jive* 138: *Fine dinner*—An attractive female. *Fine fryers*—Pretty young girls, chicks. **1953** W. Fisher *Waiters* 36: I know where there's some fine chicks. **1959** A. Anderson *Lover Man* 115: "She was fine, wasn't she?"…"I got a gal…that's finer than that." **a***1972** B. Rodgers *Queens' Vernacular* 80: *Fine*…good-looking, shapely. **1981** Eble *Campus Slang* (Mar.) 3: *Fine*—good-looking. **1987** *21 Jump St.* (Fox-TV): Well, I believe that Jeremy Woods is totally fine…I'd let him eat crackers in my bed. **1993** *N.Y. Times* (Mar. 10) B 3: "Mmmm, that sister's fine," shouts someone else.

¶ In phrases:

¶ **fine as wine** *Black E.* extraordinarily good, attractive, or sexy.

1942 *Pittsburgh Courier* (Apr. 4) 7: She was sweet as wine, though twice as fine. **1942** *Yank* (Sept. 23) 14: A prima donna caught his eye,/Fine as wine. **1950** L. Brown *Iron City* 108: Fine as wine, Jack—really fine! **1961** Terry *Old Liberty* 24: It was fine as wine in the summertime. **1966–67** W. Stevens *Gunner* 199: Fine as wine, Joe. **1978** Wheeler & Kerby *Steel Cowboy* (film): She's my old lady—fine as wine. **1980** Univ. Tenn. freshman theme: She is fine as wine, nice tits, nice ass.

¶ **fine-feathered friend** a fine friend.—used ironically.

1937 Odets *Golden Boy* 260: What would you like to say, my fine-feathered friend? **1938** "E. Queen" *4 Hearts* 55: No dice, my fine-feathered friend. **1941** *Slanguage Dict.* 15: *Fine feathered friend*…fine friend: slightly ironic. **1946** Petry *Street* 25: This look, my fine feathered friend, should give you much food for thought. **1956** N.Y.C. schoolgirl: I'll take that, my fine-feathered friend.

fineesh *adj.* [pidgin < F *fini* + E fin*ished*] *Mil. in France.* finished; gone. [Quots. ref. to WWI.]

[**1918** in Battey *Sub Destroyer* 321: We were all a little disappointed, for we wanted that sub for a pet most awfully, and it was hard to go away and leave it without being sure it was "feenish."] **1919** Johnson *321st Inf.* 35: Some sold out entirely, and "fineesh" was the prompt reply to every would-be purchaser. **1926** Nason *Chevrons* 143: "Fineesh!" said Eadie. **1928–29** Nason *White Slicker* 55: That dressing station is *fineesh*.

fine-worker *n.* *Und.* a pickpocket.

1899 A.H. Lewis *Sandburrs* 24: His name's Mollie Matches, an' d' day was when Mollie's d' flyest fine-woiker in Byrnes's books. **1903** A.H. Lewis *Boss* 168: A mob of them Western fine-workers are likely to blow in on us.

finger *n.* **1.a.** a quantity of liquor that when poured into a glass is a fingerbreadth high.

1813–18 Weems *Drunk. Look. Glass* 67: He has but to dash up to the side board, and turn off a *four-fingered bumper* of his beloved Helicon. **1856** in *OEDS*: We each took a first mate's drink—i.e., three fingers. **1871** Hay *Pike Co. Ballads* 26: Some says three fingers, some says two. **1889** in F. Remington *Sel. Letters* 85: The receipt of your letter was like "three fingers" on me. **1914** in Truman *Dear Bess* 161: He's hankerin' for about three fingers in a small glass. **1972** W.C. Anderson *Hurricane* 21: Pour yourself about four fingers of Old Crow into a hot toddy. **1980** Whalen *Takes a Man* 82: Two fingers of rye. **1980** Birnbach et al. *Preppy Hndbk.* 168: Pour in two fingers of vodka.

b. *Narc.* (see quots.).

1936 Dai *Opium Addiction* 199: *Finger of stuff.* A quantity of drugs which is smuggled into prison in a rubber finger. **1971** Guggenheimer *Narcotics & Drug Abuse* 22: *Fingers.* hashish rolled into finger shape.

2. *Und.* a police officer; (*occ.*) a prison official.

1899 "J. Flynt" *Tramping* 385: The word "finger"…is synonymous with "bull."…The finger is in uniform…."Finger" comes from the policeman's supposed love of grabbing offenders. "They like to finger us," a hobo said to me, one night. **1904** *Life in Sing Sing* 248: *Finger.* An officer. **1912** Furlong *Detective* 168 [ref. to 1880's]: I do not care what "the big finger" (Chief of Police) says about it. **1927** *AS* II (June) 385: A uniformed officer, now termed a *harness-bull*, was called a *finger* from his itching desire to get his fingers on [yeggs]. **1928** in Panzram *Killer* 158: *Big finger*—warden; *second finger*—P.K. or deputy. **1980** *AS* (Fall) 197: Lexical Data from the Gulf States…*cop, copper*,…*finger, flat-foot, fuzz*.

3.a. *Und.* a police spy; stool pigeon; informer.

1914 Jackson & Hellyer *Vocab.* 33: *Finger*…An informer; an investigator for officers. **1931** *AS* VI (Aug.) 438: *Finger*: A police informer. **1931** in D.W. Maurer *Lang. Und.* 47: He's a finger for the Eye. **1933** Ersine *Prison Slang* 36: *Finger, n.* 1. A *rat, fink.* **1941** Algren *Neon Wilderness* 63: I guess we figure'd there'd be so many guys with heads shaved it'd

be harder to catch a finger than if we all had hair.

b. *Und.* a person in the employ of criminals who locates and identifies potential targets and victims; FINGERMAN.

1926 in *OEDS*: If th' stunt was pulled right an' the Finger does call you, you know th' getaway is in th' clear. **1931** D. Runyon, in *Collier's* (Sept. 26) 7: The finger must know these reasons. **1932** in *OEDS*: The café owner had taken me for a professional finger, one of the scouts of the underworld. **1933** in D. Runyon *More Guys* 14: Who is the finger, and is he reliable? **1944** Paxton *Murder, My Sweet* (film): Now I'm a finger for a heist mob. Also I'm Jack the Ripper. **1950** Rackin *Enforcer* (film): The finger don't speak much English. **1952** H. Grey *Hoods* 66: John, the finger, doesn't want anybody hurt. **1963** Westlake *Getaway Face* 19: Five guys cutting up a fifty-thousand dollar pie after the finger's ten per cent. *Ibid.* 38: She's the finger.

4.a. an obscene gesture of contempt made by closing the fist and extending the middle finger, often with a jab upward.—usu. constr. with *the*. [Despite the dates, this is unquestionably the orig. sense; cf. syn. L *digitus impudicus*.]

[**1938** Bezzerides *Long Haul* 93: "This to you—" and he stuck up a thick forefinger.] **1961** McMurtry *Horseman, Pass By* 81: They were too silly even to bother giving them the Finger. **1962** Shepard *Press Passes* 209: Everyone roared. It was a wooden novelty, better described as "the finger." The inscription read: "To Thine Enemies." **1965** Summers *Flunkie* 78: They was all cheering and waving goodby and shooting us the finger. [**1966** Newhafer *No More Bugles* 78: Dowdle responded with the age-old signal consisting of the middle finger of the right hand held upright, the other fingers being held close to the palm. Through several wars and elsewhere, this gesture has been rudely construed to mean, "Go screw yourself," or words to that effect.] **1970** T. Wolfe *Radical Chic* 70: He gives me the finger…and for some reason or other, this kind of got the old *anger* boiling…you know? **1975** C.W. Smith *Country Music* 229: Coolly, she shot them the finger. **1978** Strieber *Wolfen* 7: The driver shot the finger but moved the vehicle. **1984** J.R. Reeves *Mekong* 10: Brewster…flipped me a finger. *Ibid.* 16: I shot him a finger. **1987** M. Groening *School Is Hell* (unp.): When I was a little girl, we didn't give our teacher the finger when we were bored. **1988** *Newsweek* (Feb. 8) 48: Irving Azoff…, the controversial president of MCA Inc.'s Music Entertainment Group took out a full page ad in Hits magazine that showed him and his top executives smiling broadly—giving "the finger." **1991** B.E. Ellis *Amer. Psycho* 94: I wave to a beggar…, then give him the finger.

b. contemptuous or malicious treatment; mocking; betrayal.—constr. with *the*.

1890–93 *Standard Dict.* 682: *Finger, n.….To give one the f.*, to disappoint one after holding out hopes that his desires would be fulfilled; turn a cold shoulder to one. **1914** *Century Dict. & Cyclopedia* (rev. ed.) IV (Supp.): *To give one the finger* to give scanty recognition or encouragement; to act coldly or disappointingly toward one who had been led to expect assistance or friendship. **1930** Lait *On Spot* 203: *Giving the Finger*…Cheating. **1929–33** Farrell *Manhood* 233: Say, let's give the Greek the finger on this game. **1938** in *AS* (Feb. 1939) 27: I talk with the dean, and he give me the feengaire. **1939** N. West *Locust* 266: So she thinks she can give me the fingeroo, hah? **1941** Schulberg *Sammy* 93: "Let me show you how to give that guy the Finger," he said. **1948** Guthrie *Born to Win* 89: I got the screws put to me/The skids slid under me/Got the old greasy Finger. **1956** I. Shulman *Good Deeds* 97: Busy!…He's just giving you the finger. The old brush-off. **1957** Yordan *Men in War* (film): Somebody out there heard ya. He's givin' you the finger. **1963** Morgan *Six-Eleven* 169: You think you've been picked out for the finger. **1980** Gould *Ft. Apache* 12: "Sure, sure, give me the finger," Connolly said with quiet anger. "You think I'm full of shit, that I.A.D.'s full of shit, too."

c. a poke with the finger, esp. between the buttocks; GOOSE.—constr. with *the*.

1947 Schulberg *Harder They Fall* 96: He came up behind Solly…and gave him the finger…everybody knew Solly was very goosey.

5. *Police.* an identification of a suspect.

1931–34 in Clemmer *Pris. Community* 332: I caught three fingers. **1976** "N. Ross" *Policeman* 91: Out of 21 victims, we got nine fingers (identifications).

¶ In phrases:

¶ **crook (one's) little finger** to tipple.

1836 in *DAE*: William Martin was fined for, as he quaintly expressed it, crooking his little finger too often. **1859** Bartlett *Amer.* 109: To crook one's elbow or one's little finger, is to tipple.

¶ **fickle finger** an instance of mean or treacherous treatment; in phr. **fickle finger of fate** the unpredictable, usu. injurious, workings of fate.—constr. with *the*. See also *fucked by the fickle finger of fate* s.v. FUCK, *v.*

1955 Goethals *Chains of Command* 35 [ref. to WWII]: He was...castigating...Delfin for slipping him the fickle finger without any warning. **1964** Howe *Valley of Fire* 56: He that lingers is slipped the fickle finger. **1968** *Rowan & Martin's Laugh-In* (NBC-TV): And now, our Flying Fickle Finger of Fate Award. **1969** Coppel *A Little Time for Laughter* 188: We saved their asses in 1918, and now you gotta do it again, and as God made little apples, when it's over they'll give us the Fickle finger, wait and see.

¶ **get** [or **pull**] **(one's) finger out** [of **(one's) ass**] *Mil.* to get busy; get moving. [Adapted from Brit. and Austral. usage in WWII.]

*1941 in *OEDS: Pull out your finger!* Hurry up! **1942* in *OEDS*: We stooged about a bit above our target...and then we pulled our fingers out and pranged it. **1946** Haines *Command Decision* 108: Them guys on the line really got their fingers out tonight, sir. **1947** Mailer *Naked & Dead* 367: You men better get your finger out of your ass. **1977** First Sgt., U.S. Army (coll. J. Ball): Ever' time I drop by, you lazy fuckers are sittin' around with your fingers up your goddam asses. Well, get 'em out and police up this area. **1984** Partridge *DSUE* (ed. 8) 1200: I wish they'd...hurry up and get their fingers out.

¶ **put the finger on** *Und. & Police.* FINGER, *v.*, 2.a., b.
1924 Henderson *Keys to Crookdom* 414: *Put a finger on.* To point out. A dip's stall puts his finger on a prospective victim. **1925–26** J. Black *You Can't Win* 84 [ref. to *ca*1890]: If I'm grabbed with this junk I'll rot in jail before I put the finger on you. **1929** Hammett *Red Harvest* 124: You think I killed them, don't you, Dick?...Going to put the finger on me? **1931** *AS* VI (Aug.) 440: *Finger on, put the*, v.t. To point out someone to the police; a stoolo's work. **1931** Hellinger *Moon* 172: They've put the finger on me. I've got to get out of town. **1938** J. Swerling *I Am the Law* (film): They got the finger on him, and all the cops in the world can't stop it. **1942** *ATS* 462: *Put the...finger on*, to mark for death. **1955** Q. Reynolds *HQ* 106: The bartender...put the finger on Levy and his associates. **1959** Tevis *Hustler* 14-15: They whispered about me the first time I ever set foot in this poolroom and they put the finger on me for Big John from Columbus and they steered me to old Bennington himself. **1962** H. Simmons *On Eggshells* 122: Teacher put the finger on him...and the cops picked him up. **1974** A. Bergman *Big Kiss-Off* 57: Jack, I could put the finger on so many people your hair would stand on end. **1978** Strieber *Wolfen* 153: He had put the finger on Neff...didn't need Neff's silence any more. **1994** *New York* (Feb. 21) 22: I am *not* going to put the finger on anybody.

finger *v.* **1.** *Und.* to place under arrest.
1899 "J. Flynt" *Tramping* 386: "They like to finger us," a hobo said to me, one night, in a Western town where we were both doing our best to dodge the local police force. **1929** in Partridge *Dict. Und.* 242: When a single bootlegger is fingered, he can't reach us because he won't...know...where the booze comes from. **1951** Robbins *Danny Fisher* 133: Leave it! Yuh want the cops should finger you the first time yuh show with it? **1986** *Primenews* (CNN-TV) (June 3): He figures police would love to finger him for [painting] all those footprints [on the sidewalk].

2.a. *Orig. Und.* to point out or identify, esp. as a potential target or victim.
1930 (cited in Partridge *Dict. Und.* 242). **1931** D. Runyon, in *Collier's* (Sept. 26) 395: The finger guy must know the party he fingers has plenty of ready scratch. **1937** J.E. Hoover *Persons in Hiding* 153: All you'd have to do would be to finger a certain man for us. **1955** Graziano & Barber *Somebody Up There* 178: Blackie fingered the guy, then he got lost. **1966–67** Harvey *Air War* 107: The [bomb] drop is fingered by a Bird Dog or a chopper hovering in the area, so the load lands exactly where it was intended to. **1970** Conaway *Big Easy* 52: Christ, an intellect! I can always finger them. **1972** *N.Y. Times* (Nov. 12) 6: The lymphocytes finger the cancer by depositing chemical "flags" upon it; the macrophages, spotting the flags, attack and destroy the cancer. **1978** *N.Y. Post* (Mar. 24) 9: Key figure in rubout of union aide is fingered [by police]. **1984** *CNN News Network* (Nov. 13): It may enable authorities to finger potential child abusers before the fact.

b. *Orig. Und.* to inform on, implicate, or betray to authorities; identify for police.
1930 Irwin *Tramp & Und. Sl.: Finger*...To betray to the police. **1930** in *OEDS*: Frank Lee...had "fingered" many, many dealers to the Feds. **1933** Ersine *Pris. Slang* 33: He fingered his partner. **1952** Mandel *Angry Strangers* 232: He busts out sweatin for Horse 'n fingers the con-

nections. **1957** *Sing Out!* (Winter) 21: [He] fingered, like any common stool pigeon, some of his radical associates of the early 1940's. **1968** *N.Y.P.D.* (ABC-TV): Why didn't you finger Richmond when you had the chance? **1974** Terkel *Working* 79: Somebody had stolen her purse in the movie house and she fingered me. **1983** *20/20* (ABC-TV) (Jan. 20): Do you think the prosecutor wants you to finger other athletes for selling cocaine? **1984** *All Things Considered* (Nat. Pub. Radio) (June 18): Others who were on the boat fingered some of those who had come with them and called them Communists. **1987** *N.Y. Times* (July 10) A 1: [Col. Oliver North] would play the "fall guy"...allowing his superiors to finger him on a scheme that was going down the tubes. **1991** "R. Brown" & R. Angus *A.K.A. Narc* 203: The Feds would...haul the dopers off to jail as I fingered them.

c. to select; single out.
1958 J. King *Pro Football* 129: Walt Kiesling, Steeler coach, passed by the magazine-cover kids to finger little-known Glick. **1962** Mandel *Wax Boom* 12: Old Man fingers this platoon because we got Proctor. Then Enshaw fingers. Always this section. **1984* Partridge *DSUE* (ed. 8) 392: *Finger*...to nominate a person for a job:...since *ca*1965; prob. ex US.

3. to give; hand over.
1952 Sandburg *Strangers* 170 [ref. to *ca*1890]: Well, I could slide yuh out one little William the Fifth. If I could finger you more I would.

fingerbang *v.* [*finger* + BANG, *v.*] to masturbate (a woman).—usu. considered vulgar.
1970 in Giallombardo *Impris. Girls* 224: She let a girl finger-bang her. **1975** U.C.L.A. student: I think it's unbecoming to fingerbang a sixty-year-old woman. **1978** Hasford *Short-Timers* 13: Your days of finger-banging ol' Mary Jane Rottencrotch...are over.

finger bowl *n.* (see quots.). *Joc.*
1966 IUFA *Folk Speech*: Folk speech, Negro. *Finger bowl.* a drive-in movie. **1984** Partridge *DSUE* (ed. 8) 392: *Finger bowl.* An outdoor cinema: Can[adian]: since *ca*1960.

fingerbuster *n. Music.* a musical piece that requires particular dexterity to play.
1938 in A. Lomax *Mr. Jelly Roll* 173: The most difficult piece of jazz piano ever written, except for my *Fingerbuster*. **1958** in Leadbitter & Slavin *Blues Records* 89: Fingerbuster. **1983** *Prairie Home Companion* (Nat. Pub. Radio): This is kind of a fingerbuster here—a George Gershwin song called "I Got Rhythm."

finger-frig *v.* FINGERFUCK.—usu. considered vulgar.
1916 Cary *Venery* I 84: *Finger frigging.*—A form of sodomy. **1927** *Immortalia* 51: She saw her lovin' Johnnie/Finger-frigging Alice Bly.

fingerfuck *n.* an act of masturbation of the vagina or anus.—usu. considered vulgar.
1970 Landy *Underground Dict.* 77: *Finger fuck*...n. Stimulation of the female sex organs with the finger. **1978** J. Webb *Fields of Fire* 228: This bastard wants to kill me for a damn finger-fuck.

fingerfuck *v.* (see 1971 quot.).—usu. considered vulgar. Also intrans.
*a1793 R. Burns *Merry Muses* 29: She m—s like reek thro' a' the week,/ But finger f—s on Sunday, O. **ca1866* *Romance of Lust* 197: Anything but finger-fucking. **a1890–91* *F & H* II 398: *Finger-fucking*...Masturbation (said of women only). **1916** Cary *Venery* I 84: *Finger fucking*—To induce a sexual spasm in a woman by digitation. **1921** in Cray *Erotic Muse* 195: There she saw her lovin' boy/Finger-fucking Nellie Bly. **1945–48** *Marianas Coll.* (unp.): I started finger fucking myself. **1968** P. Roth *Portnoy* 143: She wants you to finger-fuck her *shikse* cunt till she faints. **1970** Byrne *Memories* 157: I get tired of finger-fucking Wanda Farney all the time. **1970** Cain *Blueschild Baby* 53: Boy and girl flirting in hall shadowkiss and finger fuck. **1971** Dahlskog *Dict.* 23: *Fingerfuck, v. Vulgar.* To arouse (someone) sexually by vaginal or rectal stimulation with the finger.

finger job *n.* FINGERFUCK. [1950 quot. elaborates FINGER, *n.*, 4.b.]
[**1950** Stuart *Objector* 217: "Up Jake's," a soldier declared angrily, "that's the old finger job, and this Army is giving it to us."] **1963** Rubin *Sweet Daddy* 139: She loved it...Finger job. **1970** Landy *Underground Dict.* 77: *Finger job n.* Use of the finger to caress and insert into the vagina and/or anus.

fingerman *n. Und.* FINGER, 3.b.
1930 in *OEDS*: Martin was knocked off...It was thought Butch Swang had brought in the finger men to put Martin on the spot. **1930** *Amer. Mercury* (Dec. 12) 455: *Finger man, n.*: A person who obtains detailed information. "He's finger man for a mob." **1931** *AS* VI (Aug.) 438: *Fin-*

ger-man, n. One who points out the victims for a kidnapping mob. **1937** Hoover *Persons in Hiding* 172: Other robbers had deemed it necessary to hire a "finger man" in every town, someone either connected with the bank or aware of its operations, so that there might be a knowledge of cash and bonds on hand. **1939** C.R. Cooper *Scarlet* 82: He was the town finger-man for this new style of crook that's on the road, the in-and-outer. **1942** *N.Y. Times Mag.* (Jan. 25) 30: *Finger-man*—one who points out the victim for a killing or kidnapping. **1952** Lait & Mortimer *USA* 16: Burglars cannot operate without "fingermen." **1969** Salerno & Tompkins *Crime Confed.* 102: A "fingerman"…will case the location and identify the victim. **1973** *Playboy* (Sept.) 213: Two guys with guns figured me for a finger man setting up to heist the crap game they were protecting.

fingernails *n.pl. Printing.* parentheses.
  1927 *AS* II (Feb.) 239:…But few outside the trade know that parentheses are "finger nails" or that exclamation points are "screamers," "astonishers," or "shouts."

fingerpaint *v. Hosp.* (of a patient) to smear feces on surfaces, as walls. *Joc.*
  1979 *AS* (Spring) 37: It also takes time to care for the patient who has been *fingerpainting* "experimenting with his feces."

fingersmith *n. Und.* a pickpocket.
  *****1823** P. Egan *Vulgar Tongue*: Finger-smith. *****1883** in *F & H* II 398: The delicate expression *fingersmith*, as descriptive of the trade which a blunt world might call that of a pickpocket. *****1884** in *OED*: A couple of "finger-smiths"—pickpockets. **1926** Finerty *Crim.* 21: *Fingersmith*—A pick pocket. **1935** Pollock *Und. Speaks*: *Fingersmith*, a dexterous pickpocket. **1979** Edson *Gentle Giant* 56: Only a "fingersmith" of exceptional ability could have done so. *Ibid.* 102: You…lousy fingersmith!

fingerwave *n.* the insertion of a finger into the rectum, esp. in order to search for drugs.
  1962 Maurer & Vogel *Narc. & Narc. Add.* (ed. 2) 302: *Get a finger wave*. The process of having the rectum searched for drugs. *a*1972 B. Rodgers *Queens' Vernacular* 81. **1990** *Newsweek* (Jan. 15) 68: X-rays can be requested instead of the manual "finger wave."

finger worker *n.* a tradesman who cheats or short-changes his customers.
  1917 Cahan *D. Levinsky* 12: Moe, a red-headed, broad-shouldered "finger worker," a specialist in "short change," yardstick frauds, and other varieties of marketplace legerdemain.

finger-wringer *n. Theat.* (see quot.).
  1928 *N.Y. Times* (Mar. 11) VIII 6: *Finger-Wringer*—an actress given to emoting.

finif /ˈfɪnɪf/ *n.* [< W Yid *finef* 'five'] **1.** a five-dollar bill; five dollars. Also vars.
  1859 Matsell *Vocab.* 30: "A deuce of finifs"…two five-dollar bills. *Ibid.* 32: *Finniff.* Five dollars. **1871** Banka *Prison Life* 492: Five dollars,…*Pheniff.* Ten dollars,…*Double Pheniff.* **1906** H. Green *Boarding House* 212: A few blank checks and a "finiph" or so are all a wallet contains. **1906** *Independent* (July 5) 142: When them ponies is runnin' I kin make me finipth [*sic*] a day on de track. **1920** S. Lewis *Main Street* 217: I raise you a finif. **1924** *N.Y. Times* (Aug. 3) VIII 16: Finif for five has become common property. **1928** Hecht & MacArthur *Front Page* 455: How about a finif till tomorrow? **1937–40** in Whyte *Street Corner Society* 134: I'll give you a finif for it ($5.00). **1944** C.B. Davis *Leo McGuire* 180: Neither Cliff nor Bill Bannister had anything except the finif the state had given them. **1955** Stout *3 Witnesses* 152: Not three hours for a finif. **1959** Lederer *Never Steal Anything Small* (film): Look, a finif. **1968** I. Reed *Yellow Back Radio* 157: I was going to give him…two tickets back East and some fast finnifs.
  2. *Pris.* a five-year prison sentence.
  1904 *Life in Sing Sing* 248: *Finif.* Five years. **1924** Henderson *Keys to Crookdom* 404: *Finif.* Five. Five years.

fink *n.* [either < G *Fink* 'student not belonging to the students' association [*Bunschenschaft*]' (lit. 'finch'), hence 'not "one of the guys"', hence 'someone poorly regarded'; or < colloq. G *Schmierfink* 'a low dirty person; a hack'. The suggestion, as in the 1925 quot. at **(2.b.),** below, that it derives fr. *Pinkerton* is phonologically improbable and unsupported by early evidence]
  1.a. a contemptible, offensive, or unreliable person. [Gained wide currency, esp. among students, in the 1950's and early 1960's.]

1894 in Ade *Chicago Stories* 33: Everybody that's on to him says he's a fink…You know what I mean; he's a stiff, a skate. He drinks and never comes up. He's always layin' to make a touch, too. **1911** *Hampton's Mag.* (June) 740: He's a fink, not because of what he did to your petition, but on general principles. **1914** Jackson & Hellyer *Vocab.* 26: This fink crabbed the play and we went on the nut for a double-sawbuck. *Ibid.* 33: *Fink*…An unreliable confederate or incompetent sympathizer. **1928** Callahan *Man's Grim Justice* 25: Dese mugs…ain't grifters,…dey're just eighteen-carat-ham-fatters, finks. **1933–34** Lorimer & Lorimer *Stag Line* 163: Yeah, couple of finks. **1938** Baldwin & Schrank *Case of Murder* (film): Lucky fink, that Little Dutch. **1956** Yordan *Harder They Fall* (film): You phoned from the stadium, you fink! **1958** Cooley *Run for Home* 161: I also caught a lousy fink who plays with a cold deck! **1961** Sullivan *Gladdest Years* 221: My music section man was a hostile, neurotic little fink who would leap at the opportunity to get me chucked. *Ibid.* 298: Some poor-grading fink. **1962** T. Berger *Reinhart in Love* 204: His little bride…proved no fink when the chips were down. **1964** Hill *Casualties* 132: I guess at makes me a fink or sumpin, but I don't wanta go fishin with my own father. **1965** Hersey *Too Far to Walk* 17: I'd to come and talk with you some time when that fink Flack isn't around. *a***1967** Bombeck *Wit's End* 31: That fink Edith had the nerve to call and ask if she could have the blouse to the gray suit. **1972** M. Rodgers *Freaky Fri.* 16: Every day he's ready ahead of time, just to show me up, the fink! **1973** Lucas, Katz, & Huyck *Amer. Graffiti* 10: You chicken fink!…You can't back out now! **1979** Fowler *UFOs* 74: My conscience was…telling me what a *fink* I was for not taking the kids to the zoo. **1980** *Vegas* (NBC-TV): You're a fink—you marry my sister, take her to Spain, and I don't see either one of you for two years. **1983** Stapleton *30 Yrs.* 121: Get lost, you fink.
  b. (see quot.).
  1947 W.M. Camp *S.F.* 450 [ref. to *a*1923]: In the sailor's vocabulary the lowest kind of a prostitute has for many years been called a "fink."
  2.a. *Specif.* a betrayer of associates, esp. an informer or stool pigeon; (with weakened force, esp. since *ca*1955) a tattletale.
  1902–03 Ade *People You Know* 60: Any one who goes against the Faculty single-handed is a fink. **1923** in Kornbluh *Rebel Voices* 93: Every gunman's hand is against me. Every scab and fink hates me and all that are like me. **1923** in Holbrook *Mackinaw* 205: The bull-bucker here…is a fink. Pretends to favor the One Big Union but when you ask him to stamp-up he turns you in. **1926** *Writer's Mo.* (Dec.) 541: *Rat, Fink, Pigeon, Cat*—One who tells on his fellow convicts. **1928** Anderson & Hickerson *Lightning* 543: You lousy fink, is this your affair? **1938** Sherman & Sherman *Crime School* (film): I ain't playin' fink for you. **1948** Webb *Four Steps* 60: "It's just something I could blab, isn't it?" "So you admit you're a fink, eh?" **1952** Himes *Stone* 12: He's a fink, Jim.…He was the one who ratted on those ten men who were digging out of the woollen mill. **1960** Barber *Minsky's* 262: Maybe you're a fink for the wives a guys shouldn't be here. **1963** D. Tracy *Brass Ring* 361: A guy asks you a question and right away you make him out a comp'ny fink or somethin'. **1968** Maule *Rub-A-Dub* 137: You some kind of company fink? **1972** P. Thomas *Savior* 152: Diggit, like in jail, *Fink* means a rat, a squealer. **1992** L. Johnson *My Posse* 105: Junior…told everybody I was a fink [for reporting a threat to a teacher].
  b. *Labor.* a strikebreaker; a nonunion worker.
  1917 in E. Levinson *Strikes* 202: The cars emptied swiftly, the "finks" scattering by way of all available streets and alleys. **1925** in *Amer. Mercury* (Jan. 1926) 63: Dating from the famous Homestead strike of 1892 is the odious *fink*.…According to one version [it] was originally *Pink*, a contraction of Pinkerton, and referred to the army of strikebreakers recruited by the detective agency. **1926** *AS* (Dec.) 651: *Fink*—A strikebreaker. **1928** Sharpe *Chicago May* 272: Later, I heard the truth from another fink (strike-breaker). **1930** "D. Stiff" *Milk & Honey* 205: *Fink*—A scab. One who takes a striker's job. **1936** Farrell *World I Never Made* 153: I'm a union man and always will be one…I don't like finks either. **1939** Saroyan *Time of Your Life* IV: Sixty strikers…want to stop the finks who are going to try to unload the *Mary Luckenbach* tonight. **1939** M. Levin *Citizens* 245: Bitchin finks ride right in past you and you got to keep your mouth shut. **1947** W.M. Camp *S.F.* 450: In 1923, when the sailors' strike was lost in San Pedro, Andrew Furuseth described the employers' new hiring hall as "Fink Hall," and thereafter the word began to be heard all up and down the Pacific Coast. **1947** Boyer *Dark Ship* 231: It became clear that the Gulf officials who had favored the strike were trying to break it by supplying finks to struck ships. **1947–52** R. Ellison *Invisible Man* 198: They ask me who I work for and when I tell them, they call me a fink. **1958** Cooley *Run for Home* 11: Ivan was well known in every fink hall on both coasts. *a***1989** in Kisseloff *Must Remember This* 536: The shipowners were goin' crazy because they couldn't recruit finks.

fink *v.* **1.** Orig. *Pris.* to turn informer; betray one's associates to authorities; (in a weakened sense) to tattle.

1925 in *OEDS: Fink*, to squeal; to inform on. **1933–35** D. Lamson *About to Die* 106: I don't think the guards expect you to fink. **1947** *AS* (Apr.) 121: *Fink.* To tell on someone. To tattle or to "rat." **1948** J. Stevens *Jim Turner* 167 [ref. to *ca*1910]: You could fink on us. **1954** Chessman *Cell 2455* 90: Snitching, finking to the man was encouraged. **1959** O'Connor *Talked to a Stranger* 78: Somebody finked on us. They told on us. Told the coppers. **1966** Samuels *People vs. Baby* 69: He didn't fink to the cops about Chip's dope habit. **1970** *Adam-12* (NBC-TV): I don't fink! **1971** *The Smith Family* (ABC-TV): They say you finked on your friend. **1971** *Room 222* (ABC-TV): Is that what you're penalizing him for? For not finking? **1976** J.W. Thomas *Heavy Number* 105: Your old man still won't know who burned him unless you fink. **1984** Ehrhart *Marking Time* 253: Those creeps that were finkin' to the FBI. **1993** *Smithsonian* (July) 69: Convincing him it was in his best interest to fink.

2. to be a **FINK**, *n.*, 2.b.

1942 *ATS* 504: To take the place of a striker, or work for less than the established wage…*fink*…*scab. a*1961 *WNID3: Fink*…*slang:* to act as a strikebreaker. *a*1989 in Kisseloff *Must Remember This* 599: So-and-so Iron Works is goin' out, and all you people that's unemployed don't fink.

fink book *n. Naut.* a book containing a seaman's work record as evaluated by former employers. Now *hist.*

1936 *ISU Pilot* (Aug. 14) 1: "Fink Books for Finks" is the slogan.…Refuse to accept a fink book! **1948** McHenry & Myers *Home Is Sailor* 164: "Every man sailing American ships should have down in black and white what vessels he has been on and how he behaved aboard them." "You mean the fink book, admiral?" **1967** Raskin *True Course* 10 [ref. to 1921]: The "fink books" (or as they were officially titled "employer grade books") came back. Copied after the British system, this was an employment record carried by each seaman in which was marked his conduct and abilities, according to the shipowner's standards. Without the fink book no man could get a ship. *a*1989 in Safire *Coming to Terms* 119: Seamen's discharge records were…compiled in a book issued by the U.S. Government which showed the names and voyages of the vessels in which the seaman had served. At one time these books contained a column in which the shipmaster could indicate the deportment of the sailor; they came to be known as "Fink books."

fink-out *n.* an act or instance of finking out.

1967 in *BDNE* 167: The cop-out is like a fink-out, only more graceful.

fink out *v.* **1.** to turn informer; **FINK**.

1962 *Mad* (Dec.) 44: A Dalmatian…who got fat on Gestapo food because he personally finked out on 374 Allied Cocker Spaniels.

2. to go back on one's word; back out; renege.

1966 in *IUFA Folk Speech: Fink out:* let someone down. **1966** in *BDNE* 167: The opposition finked out. **1969** *Current Slang* I & II 33: *Fink out,* v. To disappoint.—College students, both sexes, Kansas.—She really *finked out* on her date. **1972** N.Y.U. student: Don't fink out on me now. **1992** *Atlantic* (Sept.) 124: Administration officials had "*finked out* and did not follow through after they had a big Rose Garden show."

3. to fail miserably.

1975 *DAS* (Supp. 2) 698: *Fink out*…to fail utterly. *a*1986 in *World Bk. Dict.*: If this fellow had really been a magician he would have finked out, busted. Instead, he's a success. **1992** Strawberry & Rust *Darryl* 294: I was placed under the microscope to see whether I would fink out on the Mets.

fink sheet *n. Police.* (see quot.).

1968 Camp *Night Beat* 42: We call it a fink sheet. It's your Cadet Evaluation Report. It lets the boy scouts up at the Academy know if you've been good or not.

finky *adj.* being or resembling a **FINK**; (*broadly*) unpleasant or obnoxious.

1948 McHenry & Myers *Home Is Sailor* 88: That finky mate…wants the whole crew to line up and salute for that drunk royalty bitch. **1971** Sloan *War Games* 67: For a finky broad? **1971** Sonzski *Punch Goes Judy* 114: I felt the finkiness settle in. **1972** M. Rodgers *Freaky Fri.* 54: What's so great about a person who pulls that kind of finky trick? *a*1986 in *World Bk. Dict.*: Students…are tired of all these finky rules.

finny *n. Whaling.* a finback whale.

1900 Hammond *Whaler* 255: 'Twas about all old finny wanted to do to climb over 'em.

Finnski *n.* [*Finn* + -SKI] a Finn.—used derisively.

1919 S. Lewis *Free Air* 105: I was workin' for a Finnski back here a ways, and he did me dirt—holdin' out my wages on me till the end of the month.

finski or **finsky** *n.* [FIN² + -SKI] a five-dollar bill; five dollars; five dollars' worth.

1952 Uris *Battle Cry* 142 [ref. to WWII]: Lend me a finsky till payday. **1966** Bogner *Seventh Avenue* 16: Some idiot wants me to emcee his wedding and I get a finsky for making a public nuisance of myself. **1966** Braly *Cold* 100: I want to live—at least until I drink up this finski. **1987** J. Hughes *Ferris Beuller* (film): See what a finski can do for a guy's attitude?

F.I.O. *Stu.* (see 1971 quot.).

1968–70 *Current Slang* III & IV 45: *FIO, v.* To give up; to cast off.—College males, Kansas. **1971** Dahlskog *Dict.* 23: *FIO, vulgar.* Fart it off; to shrug something off; to avoid or get rid of something, as a duty or responsibility.

fip *n.* [abbr. *fippenny* (i.e., fivepenny) *bit*] a half real, formerly acceptable as currency in the U.S.; (*broadly*) a sixpence or half dime.

1822 in Thornton *Amer. Gloss.*: A dispute now commenced…respecting some cents and a "fip," which had fallen from his pocket. **1836** *Every Body's Album* I 143: Adieu to the "fip" and the "levy,"—/(Sad change, 'tis, this parting with you). **1837** Neal *Charcoal Sketches* 15: Even that is registered for fip-levy boobies as a sin. **1848** Bartlett *Amer.* 139: *Fippenny Bit,* or contracted *Fip.* Fivepence. In the state of Pennsylvania, the vulgar name for the Spanish half-real. **1850** in *DAE*: Not a quarter or fip fell to the floor. **1853** in S. Clemens *Twain's Letters* I 20: I…paid my sixpence, or "fip" as these heathen call it. **1891** in *DAE* [ref. to 1830's]: It was common, particularly in New England, to call a sixpence or a half dime a *fip*. **1912** Field *Watch Yourself* 144: I'll bet a fip Sammy Steele's mewel's kicked thet boy. **1949** *New Yorker* (Nov. 19) 69: Grandfather would not give a cent. He said he had paid to travel by steam and he wouldn't give a fip for any other way of travel.

fire *n.* **1.** Esp. *Und.* danger, esp. from the police; in phr. **on fire** very dangerous; **HOT**.

1859 Matsell *Vocab.* 32: *Fire.* Danger. "This place is all on fire; I must pad like a bull or the cops will nail me," everybody is after me in this place; I must run like a locomotive or the officers will arrest me. **1927** Coe *Me—Gangster* 92: They'll make plenty of fire! **1929** in Hammett *Knockover* 47: The big man was a yegg. San Francisco was on fire for him. The yegg instinct would be to use a rattler to get away from trouble. **1930** *Liberty* (Aug. 23) 31: A bank heist is full of fire at best, but there are a lot of items you can look after to hold down the risk. **1955** D.W. Maurer, in *PADS* (No. 24) 137: Things are getting warm here for strange whiz mobs. In fact, the place is on fire. *Ibid.* 175: The town's on fire, I tell you. **1974** R. Carter *16th Round* 227: Your ass is in the fire now!

2. a light for a cigarette, pipe, or cigar; match or cigarette lighter.

1959 *Swinging Syllables: Fire*—Matches, cigarette lighter. **1968–70** *Current Slang* III & IV 46: *Fire*…n. Match; a light for a cigarette.

3. *Und.* a firearm or firearms.

1992 Mowry *Way Past Cool* 210: I know you packin the fire.

¶ In phrases:

¶ **fire in the paint locker!** *Navy & USMC.* hurry up! on the double!

1945 Wead *They Were Expendable* (film): Fire in the paint locker! *a*1982 H. Berry *Semper Fi* 192 [ref. to WWII]: "Fire in the paint locker" told you to move fast.

¶ **get the fire** (see quot.).

1900 *DN* II 34: "To get the *fire,*" to be expelled.

¶ **where's the fire?** what's the reason for the hurry? [Stereotypically assoc. with traffic police officers.]

1924 in *OEDS*: A husky voice enquired of me, "Where's the fire?" **1929–31** J.T. Farrell *Young Lonigan* 110 [ref. to 1916]: Nate started to shuffle away and Studs asked him where the fire was. *Ibid.* 143: Here's your hat. What's your hurry? Where's the fire? **1963, 1971** in *OEDS*.

fire *v.* **1.a.** to hurl (a brick or similar missile); throw (a ball) forcefully. Also intrans. Now *colloq.* or *S.E.*

*1849 in *OED*: They fired styens [stones] at him. **1870** in Schele de Vere *Amer.* 471: *Fire, to,* a term very generally used for to throw. "The boys were *firing* stones at the house at a great rate, and, after a while, the negroes began *firing* back with rocks, chunks, and broken bricks." **1878** in *OED*: A boy having fired a brick at her. **1908** in Fleming

Unforget. Season 137: Wagner…fired to Swacina for the…double play. **1917** Ruggles *Navy Explained* 58: "Who fired that swab," the boatswain's mate of jimmylegs might ask if he were hit on the konk. **1980** Lorenz *Guys Like Us* 67: So far I'm firing strikes. **1992** Wimmer *Schoolyard Game* 115: He fired a baked potato at her.

b. *Gamb.* to shoot (dice).

1974 "A.C. Clark" *Revenge* 9: The guy is used to firin' the craps that way.

c. *Baseball.* to pitch (a game).

1983 WKGN Radio News (Apr. 21): He fired a no-hitter yesterday.

d. to throw (a party).

1857 in Eliason *Tarheel Talk* 270: Mrs. Robertson…says…she will be willing to fire you a little party when you come home.

2. to ejaculate (semen).—also intrans. Cf. associated sense of SHOT, *n.*

*a1890–91 F & H II 399: *To fire a shot*…(venery).—To emit. *ca*1900–10 (quot. at SHOT). **1960–69** Runkel *Law* 238: When the first guy had fired he got up off her.

3.a. to toss, throw, or drive out, esp. to eject forcibly; (*hence*) to expel, as from school.—also (*obs.*) constr. with *out.*

1871 *Overland Mo.* (Mar.) 285: The thought that I was fired by some stranger, who wasn't a-takin' no hand…is not a good thought to die on. **1877** Dacus *Great Strikes* 415: The chairman was advised to "fire her out." **1882** in *DAE*: Some of them got behind the deacon and helped the officer fire him out. **1882** *Judge* (Oct. 28) 7: Yaller got fired. We tyed Him too the dock so as we cud git him when we cum back. **1883** Peck *Peck's Bad Boy* 124: How does your Pa take your being fired out? I should think it would break him all up. **1885** "Lykkejaeger" *Dane* 26: Then he "fired me out" into the street. **1885** in *DAE*: The disgusted woman banged the vulture of crime over the head with a broom and fired him. **a1889* in Barrère & Leland *Dict. Slang* I 363: Tell him he mustn't fall asleep in a public place or he'll get fired, and ask him if you can't go to get him a cab. **1895** Wood *Yale Yarns* 87: Bounce de kite!…'E orter be fired, so 'e ort! **1900** *DN* II 34: *Fire, v.t.*….2. To order from a class-room. **1906** *Nat. Police Gaz.* (Apr. 21) 3: "Skid-doo, sir." "So I'm to be fired, eh?" **1908** in Opper *H. Hooligan* xvi: He spanked me with a club and fired me out of the school. **1912** Ade *Babel* 40: A brakeman seen us and fired us out. **1919** Tarkington *Clarence* 10: Bobby…(showing the dice.) This is what I got fired for from my last school, too. I've been fired from three schools for it. **1942** Kline & MacKenzie *Died With Their Boots On* (film): I didn't know you could get fired from the army for fighting. **1947** Willingham *End As a Man* 14: You ought to fire those kids.

b. *Specif.* to discharge or dismiss from employment.—also (*obs.*) constr. with *out.* Now *S.E.*

1882 Sweet & Knox *Texas Siftings* 42: If Gould fires you out, the only railroad in Texas that will employ you will be some street railroad. **1885** Siringo *Texas Cowboy* 61: Geo. Gifford and Tom Merril…were fired. **1885** in *DA*: They immediately suspend the cashier and fire the directors. **1886** Nye *Remarks* 92: If one of my clerks should date an egg ahead, I would fire him too quick. **1887** M. Roberts *Western Avernus* 183: "Why, I nearly fired him the first morning"…and "fired" means being discharged. **1893** F.P. Dunne, in Schaaf *Dooley* 227: Googin's big kid, Malachi, was fired fr'm th' rid bridge [job]. **1896** F.H. Smith *Tom Grogan* 97: Schwartz won't fire yer man. **1901** Dunne *Mr. Dooley's Opinions* 119: Th' millyionaire bounced him. He fired him out. **1907** *Living Age* (July) 117: "To fire out," which latterly has become simply "to fire," is more vivid than "to sack" or "to boot." **1911** Harrison *Queed* 44: Colonel Cowles is the man who hires and fires. **1914** S. Lewis *Mr. Wrenn* 143: He told Guilfogle what he thought of him, so of course Guilfogle fired him. **1955** in *Dict. Canad.* 256: Six mechanics were fired because they joined a trade union.

4. *Narc.* to inject a drug by means of a hypodermic needle. Also trans.

1936 *AS* (Apr.) 121: *To Fire.* To inject dope from a hypodermic. *a*1970 in *Social Problems* XIX 114: Both authors have been present while drug users have "fired" ("fire" means to take an injection of heroin). **1972** *Playboy* (Sept.) 176: Plus I was firing narcotics at the same time. **1973–76** J. Allen *Assault* 168: Clayton used to fire in his leg—he had a big vein in his calf.

5. [cf. FIRE UP, 1] *Black E.* to prepare; get ready.

1963 in Wepman et al. *The Life* 86: I packed my shit, firing to split.

6. [cf. FIRE UP, 2.a., b.] to light (a cigarette or the like).

1979 D. Glasgow *Black Underclass* 95: "Firing a joint" was usually a social activity.

¶ In phrases:

¶ **fire away, Flanagan!** Orig. *Naut.* go to it!

1783 in Freneau *Poems* 321: Scarce a broadside was ended 'till another began again/—By Jove! it was nothing but *Fire away Flannagan!*…*A cant phrase among privateersmen. **1839** in *DA*: Fire away, Flanagan. I'll be as grave as a jackass; or a justice of the peace when he wants his dinner.

¶ **fire on** *Black E.* to strike with the fist; to attack.

1969 D.L. Lee *Don't Cry* 30: I fired on the muthafucka & said, "I'm practicing." **1970** Landy *Underground Dict.* 78: Fire on v. Attack physically or verbally. **1973** Andrews & Owens *Black Lang.* 77: *Fire on*—To swing on somebody with your fists. "That cat called me a punk and I *fired on* him." **1975** S.P. Smith *Amer. Boys* 50: Bip! He fired on the clown. **1975** Wambaugh *Choirboys* 107: Then this honky just fired on the brother and took the box.

fire-ass *adv.* at great speed.—usu. considered vulgar.

1975 Stanley *WWIII* 238: He'd jumped out…and made fire-ass toward the British lines.

fireball *n.* **1.** an enthusiastic or energetic person. Cf. BALL OF FIRE.

1949 *Time* (Jan. 17) 13: Minnesota's brash, bustling young Senator Hubert H.…Humphrey Jr., 37, a hard-working, fast-talking fireball from the midwest. **1950** *Sat. Eve. Post* (Jan. 21) 89: He wanted young fireballs…who would work fifteen hours a day. **1957** Myrer *Big War* 118: He's a fireball. **1958** Mayes *Hunters* (film): This little stinker's a fireball. He gets Migs. **1960** Bluestone *Cully* 186: Listen, old fireball,…least you can do is look like you workin'. **1967** in Bullins *Hungered One* 104: My dad's a real fireball.

2. *Med.* a fibroid tumor.

1980 *AS* (Spring) 49.

firebox *n.* *R.R.* the stomach.

1958 McCulloch *Woods Words* 62: *Fire box*—Stomach.

fire-boy *n.* a man who is a firefighter or a locomotive fireman.

1848 Baker *Glance at N.Y.* 20: The fire-boys may be a little rough outside, but they're all right here. (Touches breast.). **1930** Irwin *Tramp & Und. Sl.: Fireboy*…A railroad fireman. **1962** *AS* XXXVII 132: *Fire boy, n.* A [locomotive] fireman. **1962** Dougherty *Commissioner* 280: Let the fireboys worry, Rock, come on.

firebug *n.* a pyromaniac or incendiary.

1872 Holmes *Poet* 3: Why, those chaps that are setting folks on to burn us all up in our beds. Political firebugs we call 'em up our way. **1891** Riis *Other Half* 101: In New York a Bohemian criminal is such a rarity that the cases of two firebugs of several years ago is remembered with damaging distinctness. **1896** F.H. Smith *Tom Grogan* 141: Say, Carl, I got de firebug. Ye kin smell de ker'sene on his clo'es. **1903** Ralph *Journalist* 56: One…confessed he was a "firebug" who had been terrifying the countryside. **1924** H.L. Wilson *Professor* 84: You little old murderer—and a firebug too! **1925** Dos Passos *Manhattan Transfer* 14: It's an incendiary done it. Some goddam firebug. **1929** Tully *Shadows* 246: Where the hell's that damn firebug—he'll be burnin' his own coffin if we don't git him buried soon. **1942** Algren *Morning* 140: You're a firebug. **1955** Q. Reynolds *HQ* 329: The men of the 68th Squad picked up a firebug during the night. **1982** WINS Radio News (Aug. 27): Lawmen have had little luck in catching the firebugs. **1990** *Flash* (CBS-TV): The firebug's headed for the waterfront. **1993** *N.Y. Times* (Aug. 25) A 6: Did a Town in Germany Pay Firebug For Attack?…Citizens joined together to hire a firebomber.

firecan *n.* *Mil. Av.* a jet airplane.

1950 *Nat. Geographic* (Sept.) 311: Some pilots call their jets "blowtorches," "firecans," or just "cans." **1951** Richards *Air Cadet* (film): We're firecan jockeys—jet pilots. **1957** Wallrich *AF Airs* 75: Get this fire-can rolling.

firecracker *n.* **1.a.** a person having an explosive temper.

1852 Stowe *Uncle Tom* ch. xxiii: The boy is generous and warm-hearted, but a perfect fire-cracker when excited. **1954** Mirvish *Texana* 14: An easy-paying, quickly served "fire-cracker." **1981** D. Burns *Feeling Good* 138: You are a true anger champion…you may have the reputation of a firecracker…among people you know.

b. a person having a sharp wit.

1884 Hedley *Marching Through Ga.* 285: [The man nicknamed] "Firecracker" [has] a sharp tongue and a ready wit…, firing his jokes and repartees at his companions [all day].

c. a brash, aggressive person; HOTSHOT.

1974 Charyn *Blue Eyes* 131: He's a regular firecracker….He takes starlets to the movies.

d. a passionate woman.

1976 Rosen *Above Rim* 205: I jus' want you to meet that lil firecracker bitch I tol' you about. **1978** Wharton *Birdy* 232: Doris is one of the hottest firecrackers in the whole school.

2. *Mil.* a bomb, grenade, or torpedo. [1898 quot. is merely metaphorical.]

[**1898** in Remington *Wister* 249: The clicking in the leaves continued and the fire-crackers rattled out in front.] **1942** *ATS* 80: Bomb...*firecracker.* **1945** in *Calif. Folk. Qly.* V (1946) 379: Bombs are *eggs* and *firecrackers;* while torpedoes are...*fish, firecrackers,* or *torps.*

3. *pl. Logging.* beans.

1956 Sorden & Ebert *Logger's* 14 [ref. to a1925]: *Fire-crackers,* Beans.

firecracker mechanic *n. Naval Av.* (see quot.).

1945 in *Calif. Folk. Qly.* V (1946) 378: Firecracker mechanics* prepare the Hellcats...for flight...*Aerial bomb-and-torpedo loaders.

firedog *n.* a firefighter, esp. a veteran.

1971 S. Stevens *Way Uptown* 269: We jap the pigs and the fire dogs. You dig? It's a battlefield. **1977** J. Olsen *Fire Five* 218: Old firedog! Last I saw him, the angels were warming up for a Requiem Mass.

fired up *adj.* intoxicated.

1843 Field *Pokerville* 50: Dr. Slunk,...tolerably "fired up" and in an evident ill humour, "paraded himself."

fire-eater *n.* **1.a.** a pugnacious, quarrelsome, or recklessly bold person.

1804 in *OED*: The Sieur W-d-m, fire-eater in ordinary to the troop. **1827** in *OED*: About the year 1777, the "Fire-Eaters" were in great repute. *1873 Hotten *Slang Dict.* (ed. 4): *Fire-eater,* a quarrelsome man, a braggadocio or turbulent person who is always ready to fight. **1885** Cannon *Where Men Only* 176: Perhaps she mistook Richardson for that very scarce individual, a "fire-eater" in the army during the last years of the War! *a1899 B.F. Sands *Reefer* 36: McClung was what is known as a "regular fire-eater." He entered the service under the impression that to make a good record in the Navy it was necessary to fight one's way through it. **1930** Sage *Last Rustler* 128: I was looking for trouble...People...looked at me as if I'd been some kinda fire-eater. **1949** Monteleone *Crim. Slang* 84: *Fire eater*...A brave person; a plucky person. **1984** J. Green *Contemp. Slang* 93: *Fire-eater n.* A noticeably courageous person.

b. *Horse Racing.* a spirited and aggressive racehorse.

1840 *Spirit of Times* (June 27) 198: *Volcano's* get are looked upon in these parts as real "fire-eaters."

2. *Pol.* an uncompromising partisan of Southern interests before and during the Civil War. Now *hist.*

1846 in *DA.* **1855** in *DAE*: I would say...to all true Georgians, whether Whigs or Democrats, Union men or Fire-Eaters, whither are you drifting? **1858, 1859, 1860, 1861, 1865, 1868** in *DAE.* **1879** [Tourgée] *Fool's Errand* 30: An original Secesh, a regular fire-eater.

3. a firefighter.

1928 L. Brown *Golden '90's* 294 (cited in Weingarten *Dict. Slang*). **1930** in Botkin *Sidewalks* 253: This old fire-eater contracted tuberculosis from exposure. **1939** Howsley *Argot* 18: *Fire Eater*—a fireman. **1980** Whalen *Takes a Man* 198: Brooklyn's Rescue Company No. 2, the fearless fire eaters from Carlton Avenue.

fire escape *n.* [cf. DEVIL-DODGER] a clergyman. *Joc.*

*a1890–91 *F & H* II 400: *Fire-escape*...(common) a clergyman. **1929** Bowen *Sea Slang* 48: *Fire Escape.* A chaplain in the U.S. Navy.

firefly *n.* a fellow.

1854 *Spirit of Times* (Feb. 5) 179: Give it to em, Judge! Go in ole firefly!

firehose *n. Mil.* (see quot.).

1980 Cragg *L. Militaris* 163: *Fire Hose*...Aiguillette, Shoulder Cord or Fourragère.

fire-iron *n.* a pistol; firearm.

1882 Baillie-Grohman *Rockies* 29: The turning worm is apt to handle his fire-irons just as dexterously as he who would...crush him. **1912** *DN* III 550: *Fire-iron,* gun. **1965** in *West. Folk.* XXVI (1967) 251: They accuse me a robbin', poor boy, with a fire iron. **1970** Benteen *Sharpshooters* 98: Ye'd better not try to run and ye'd better not touch a far-arm.

fire laddie *n.* (among firefighters) a man who is a firefighter. *Joc.*

1930 H. Asbury *Ye Olde Fire Laddies* (title). **1948** McIlwaine *Memphis* 359: Movie shorts of the Memphis fire "laddies" in action. **1980** Whalen *Takes a Man* 292: Have to leave this one to the fire laddies.

fireproofer *n. Und. & Police.* a religious swindler.

1928 O'Connor *B'way Racketeers* 129: The Fire-Proofer is so called because he makes a business of "saving souls" from the fires of Purgatory and Hell—at fifty cents a soul. *Ibid.* 251: *Fire-Proofer*—A racketeer who preys on religious people. **1942** *N.Y. Times Mag.* (Jan. 25) 30: *Fireproofer*—one who preys on religious people.

fire queen *n. Homosex.* a violent partisan of homosexual rights.

1975 Legman *No Laughing Matter* 63: The American homosexuals' tactical blunder of confronting the police recently, in "fire-queen" style. *Ibid.* 98: The "fire-queens," or sadomasochistic would-be killers and shit-bombardiers of the new and aggressive "Gay Liberation" movement in the United States.

fireship *n. Naut.* a woman, esp. a prostitute, who has a venereal disease.

*1675 in Duffett *Burlesque Plays* 68: Every...Fireship you have, shall...receive a man aboard. *1691 in R. Thompson *Unfit for Modest Ears* 87: The Female Fire-Ships. A Satyr Against Whoring. *1698–99 "B.E." *Dict. Canting Crew*: *Fire-ship,* a Pockey Whore. *1821 *Real Life in Ireland* 143: Amidst two score of fireships. *ca1900–10* in Cray *Erotic Muse* 23: She was nothing but a fire ship rigged up in a disguise. **1964** N. Algren, in *Sat. Eve. Post* (Sept. 26) 45: I saw...fireships, finks, and coneroos.

firestick *n.* a firearm.

1954–60 *DAS*: *Fire stick.* A gun. Teenage and adolescent hoodlum use since *ca1950.* **1980** L.N. Smith *Venus Belt* 182: One hell of a firestick you've got there! You should've seen the blast from *this* side.

firetrack *n. Army.* a tracked vehicle equipped with a flamethrower.

1971 Glasser *365 Days* 243: *Fire track.* Flame-thrower tank.

fire up *v.* **1.** to begin; get ready; get going.

1840 in *DAE*: Come, gentlemen, "fire up, fire up!" **1843** Field *Pokerville* 45: Doctor Slunk had not yet arrived, to ask him to "fire up." **1843** in *DAE*: At the end of the third day, we came to the unanimous decision that it was high time to "fire up" and depart. **1894** in F. Remington *Sel. Letters* 208: Fire up...let your imagination play. **1900** Dreiser *Sister Carrie* 134: Put life into it...Now go on and fire up. You can do it.

2.a. to light a cigar, pipe, or cigarette. Also trans.

1890 in *OED*: When we had fired up he grew more and more in cordial mood. **1903** in *OEDS*: Then the two statesmen fired up their cigars. **1960** Simmons *Kriegie* 71: Koebeig fired up and blew smoke about the room. **1968–70** *Current Slang* III & IV 46: *Fire me up, v.* Give me a match or give me a light. **1972** Wambaugh *Blue Kt.* 20: I fired up one of those fifty-centers which are okay when I'm out of good hand-rolled custom-mades. **1980** Whalen *Takes a Man* 13: Fire that sucker up, D.J. **1985** Dye *Between Raindrops* 50: Can I afford to fire up a smoke?

b. *Specif.,* to light a marijuana cigarette.

1962 H. Simmons *On Eggshells* 166: Jerome handed over another joint. Raymond fired up. **1968** Gover *JC* 23: An when she done rollin, she allows me t'fire up. **1970** Landy *Underground Dict.* 78: *Fire up*...Smoke marijuana. **1974** Univ. Tenn. freshman theme: Everywhere you look people was firing up everywhere. **1988** (quot. at GANGE).

3.a. to start (the ignition of an engine). Also absol.

1951–53 in *AS* (Feb. 1954) 96: *Fire up, v.t.* To start (an engine). "Jim just fired up his dragster." This is the usual expression [among hot rodders]. **1955** Scott *Tiger in Sky* 43: You didn't simply start a jet engine....You "fired up." **1965** Harvey *Hudasky's Raiders* 3: The jets began to fire up. **1986** *NDAS*: Fire up and split, dudes.

b. *Broadly,* to start or warm up (any mechanical device).

1976–77 McFadden *Serial* 135: Frank...fired up these outdoor speakers of his. **1990** G. Trudeau *Doonesbury* (synd. comic strip) (Aug. 29): Fire up the Jacuzzi, kid.

4. *Stu.* (see quot.).

1980 Birnbach *Preppy Hndbk.* 219: *Fire up v.* Engage in sexual relations, as in, "I'm going to fire her up."

5. *Mil.* to bombard or strafe; to shoot.

1982 Del Vecchio *13th Valley* 193 [ref. to 1969]: Then if he fires us up tonight maybe he'll drop em in on the same spot he missed us in the morning. **1968–90** Linderer *Eyes of Eagle* 55: The enemy soldier we fired up had probably been a Chinese...advisor. *Ibid.* 94: The gunships...might spot us and "fire us up."

firewagon *n. Army.* an armored vehicle equipped with a flamethrower.

1985 Westin *Love & Glory* 406 [ref. to 1944]: What had she heard them called?—*Schützenpanzerwagen.* Firewagon! The name held terror in it for every dogface.

firewall *v. Mil. Av.* to apply full throttle to (a jet engine). Also intrans.

1956 *AS* (Oct.) 228: *Firewall the throttle*...To give the aircraft full throttle. **1962** Quirk *Red Ribbons* 181: He rammed his nose down and firewalled to try to get out from under. **1969** (quot. at COB, *v.*).

firewater *n.* [orig. frontier pidgin] **1.** strong liquor, esp. whiskey.

1817 in *DA*: He informed me that they [*sc.* the Indian chiefs] called the whiskey fire water. **1836** Cather *Voyage* 117: "Fire water" was then...passed round in a gourd. **1844** Carleton *Logbooks* 88: The enemy was whiskey or *fire water*. **1856** Colt *Kansas* 150: Our teamster took occasion to have his tin bottle filled with "fire-water," as the Indians call whisky. **1883** G.H. Holliday *On Plains* 38: [The soldiers] thought 25 cents a very pious, honest price for a glass of Irish fire-water. **1888** Hawes *Cahaba* 233: Half crazed by the "fire water"...he became boisterous. **1901** King *Dog-Watches* 136: Although under the influence of the "firewater," [he] did his work...in a manner satisfactory to the officers. **1906** Buffum *Bear City* 60: Dutch Jake suggested that it might bring them good luck to treat us burros to the fire-water. **1913** Light *Hobo* 25: I found a jug of "fire water" in the haystack. **1929** "E. Queen" *Roman Hat* 98: I'll have the firewater analyzed. **1931** Uhler *Cane Juice* 121: She poured that fire-water down her gullet till I thought she'd choke. **1944** Inks *Eight Bailed Out* 36: He brought out some *rakija*, the local firewater. **1953** R. Wright *Outsider* 85: "Are you stingy with that firewater?" she asked, nodding toward his whisky bottle sitting on the night table. **1962** Crump *Killer* 296: Let's see what kinda firewater we can raise. **1963** Behan *N.Y.* 125: They become addicted to this particular kind of fire-water. **1984** Sample *Raceboss* 29: When that fire-water hit...she started "talking" to the dice. **1993** *N.Y. Observer* (Jan. 11) 6: The speech I delivered after the nuptials was unfortunate, mostly due to my having consumed too much firewater.

2. *Av.* fuel.

1945 Hamann *Air Words*: Fire water. Gasoline.

fireworks *n.pl.* **1.** guns.

*1831 Trelawny *Adv. of Younger Son* ch. xxvii: If you...play your fireworks off under our stern, you shall hear the roar of this brazen serpent. **1853** [S. Hammett] *Yankee in Texas* 128: The old woman said Charley didn't take his fire-works.

2. *Mil.* gunfire, bombardment, or shelling; (hence) *Und.* gunplay; shooting.

1864 in Blackett *Chester* 98: The Grand Fireworks [at Petersburg, Va.]....a display of fireworks on...[a] grand scale. *ca***1880** Bellard *Gone for a Soldier* 140: After dark the rebels opened fire on some of our men, and going into the road to see what was the matter, we saw a splendid show of fireworks. **1893** Wawn *South Sea Islanders* 423: During 1889, H.M.S. *Royalist*...shelled the island. Little damage was done, and no one hurt; the inhabitants enjoying the "fireworks" from a safe distance. **1918** I.S. Cobb *Glory* 73: Now we ought to see some real fireworks. **1918** Casey *Cannoneers* 118: The boys are still preparing for the fireworks that were to have been set off three days ago. **1922** in Ruhm *Detective* 13: And that gun is always with me...I ain't a bird to fool with and am just as likely to start the fireworks as they are. **1927** *DN* V 446: Fireworks, n. Gunplay. **1943** Perrin & Mahoney *Whistling in Brooklyn* (film): He's willing to give himself up as long as there's no fireworks. **1949** Pirosh *Battleground* (film): Start the fireworks.

3. an uproar or display of anger.

1889 Barrère & Leland *Dict. Slang* I 363: *Fire-works* (tailors), a great disturbance, a state of intense excitement. **1909** T.A. Dorgan, in Zwilling *TAD Lexicon* 36: Where's all the fireworks and the threats and the forfeits? **1919** S. Lewis *Free Air* 13: His nerve-fuse burnt out the second time, with much fireworks. **1926** Dunning & Abbott *Broadway* 228: That's what I say—that's why it looks like fireworks. **1939** Fearing *Hospital* 84: Mostly, he's harmless, but once every four or five months there's some fireworks. **1960** N.Y.C. woman, age *ca*45: There'll be fireworks when she finds out.

firing-iron *n.* a firearm; FIRE-IRON.

1888 *Outing* (Apr.) 41: Hi, boss! ef you can manage to give me a hand to cut these yere cables, I can work some of yer firin' irons to advantage.

first base *n.* see s.v. BASE.

first-cabin *adj. & adv.* Orig. *Naut.* in first-class fashion; (hence) first-class.

1921 *Variety* (Apr. 8) 7: I collected my bets under heavy guard and we went away from there first cabin. **1952** Uris *Battle Cry* 125: Cigarettes and gum!...Man,...that Army goes first-cabin. **1959** on *Golden Age of TV* (A&E Network, 1988): You're first-cabin. Come to help me break

the pizza habit for good?

first-chop *adj. & adv.* first-rate; splendid; very well.

*1805 J. Davis *Post-Captain* 200: I will take her to court. She shall be introduced to the first-chop mandarines. **1833** J. Neal *Down-Easters* I 16: Fuss chop too for yeller-fever an moths. **1836** in Haliburton *Sam Slick* 38: It is a beautiful article, a rael first chop,...superfine—but I guess I'll take it back. **1838** Crockett *Almanac* (1839) 2: The kalkulations for the sun and the moon shall be fust chop. **1838** [Haliburton] *Clockmaker* (Ser. 2) 122: A real right down, first chop genu*wine* thing. **1858** [S. Hammett] *Piney Woods* 140: I hatched [a plan] that...was first chop. **1868** "W.J. Hamilton" *Swamp Scout* 82: "How do ye like it, fur as ye've got?" "First chop," said Jack.

first john *n.* see s.v. JOHN.

first man *n. Army.* a first sergeant.

1941 *AS* (Oct.) 165: *First Man*. First Sergeant. **1944–46** in *AS* XXII 55: *First Man*. First Sergeant.

first-of-May *n. Circus & Carnival.* an inexperienced employee.—used derisively. Also **first-of-Mayer**.

1926 Norwood *Other Side of Circus* 112: Got a First-of-May for you. **1939** *N.Y. Times* (June 18) 11: A beginner at barking is known as a "first of May." **1946** Dadswell *Hey, Sucker* 15: If you do stop [traveling with the carnival], you're a "heel"—or, worse, a "First of May!" **1951** Mannix *Sword-Swallower* 111: A First-of-Mayer is a carny who never comes out until after the first of May when the cold, wet spring is over....Carnies use the expression as a term of contempt for an amateur. **1956** H. Gold *Not With It* 10: I was no First-of-Mayer staying put with the rent at home until the spring made it nice on the lot. **1961** Clausen *Season's Over* 15: She explained that a First-of-May was a new girl and added, "Everybody gives First-of-Mays a hard time." **1974** E. Thompson *Tattoo* 475: Know what they call you? "First-of-May." That's an old carnival term for someone who comes out in the spring but doesn't last through the winter. **1975** McKennon *Horse Dung Trail* 17: The "First of Mays"...had just joined on the show. **1986** Heinemann *Paco's Story* 51: Some first-of-May...rookie medic.

first pig *n. Army.* a first sergeant or sergeant major. [Quots. ref. to Vietnam War.]

1975 S.P. Smith *Amer. Boys* 165: The next day he got the first pig to put him on a pass list. *Ibid.* 178: First pig even made it out tonight. **1986** Merkin *Zombie Jamboree* 81: The First Pig sent word that my presence was required in the orderly room. **1988** Clodfelter *Mad Minutes* 55: First sergeants [were] also often called "first pigs."

first-sacker *n. Baseball.* a first baseman.

1907 in Fleming *Unforget. Season* 8: Tenney...has topped all National League first-sackers in the number of assists. **1964** Thompson & Rice *Every Diamond* 6: Stuffy McInnis [was] the first sacker.

first shirt *n. Mil.* a first sergeant or sergeant major.

1969 Crumley *One to Count Cadence* 20: 1/Sgt. Tetrick, ex-Marauder, twenty-two years service—the last twelve as a first shirt... **1971** Former U.S. Army SP4 [ref. to 1961]: We called first sergeant *first shirt* or *first sleeve*. I don't think I heard one called *topkick* more than once or twice. **1973** Karlin et al. *Free Fire Zone* 57: First Shirt, we'll have a formation and do it democratically. **1974** Eble *Campus Slang* (Mar.) 3: *First shirt*—a first sergeant in the Army. **1978** Hasford *Short-Timers* 62: The First shirt went to Da Nang for some...R & R. **1985** Bodey *F.N.G.* 251: The only other NCO's...except for the First Shirt.

first skirt *n. Army.* the ranking female noncommissioned officer of a unit, esp. a first sergeant. Cf. FIRST SHIRT.

1972 U.S. Army S/Sgt. (coll. J. Ball): That's something you'll have to take up with the first skirt. **1980** D. Cragg, letter to J.E.L. (Aug. 10) 3: I first heard this used as early as...1959 in Germany. "Who's the first skirt of this outfit anyway?"

first sleeve *n. Mil.* FIRST SHIRT.

1956 *AS* XXXI (Oct.) 226: A *first sleeve* is a first sergeant. **1971** (quot. at FIRST SHIRT). **1985** Former U.S. Army SP4, age 35: *First shirt* or *first sleeve* meant the first sergeant [during the 1970's], but I think *first sleeve* was more an Air Force term. **1988** Clodfelter *Mad Minutes* 55: First sergeants ("first sleeves").

first soldier *n. Army.* a first sergeant or sergeant major.

1944–46 in *AS* XXII 55: *First Soldier*. First sergeant. **1956** Hargrove *Girl He Left* 106: Looking into the first-soldier's peculiarly...knowing eyes. **1963** Coon *Short End* 12: These the new men, First Soldier? **1964** W. Beech *Article 92* 24: It was actually the first soldier's idea. **1980** Manchester *Darkness* 170: In 1918 he had been a First Soldier, a Top Kick.

fish[1] *n.* [< F *fiche*] **1.** *Gamb.* a counter or chip used in wagering. Orig. *S.E.*

***1728** in *OED*: I am now going to a party at Quadrille...to piddle with a little of it [*sc.* money], at poor two guineas a fish. **1751** in *OED*: She was just going to call for the cards and fishes. ***1766** in *OED*. ***1816** in *OED*: A notorious gamester...at a game of loo, accumulated a large quantity of fish. ***1825** in *OED*. **1836** in T.L. Clark *Dict. Gamb.* 80: The players put eight counters or *fish* into the pool, and dealer four additional. **1859** Matsell *Vocab.* 110: A hundred dollar chip is the highest "fish," as the gambler calls it. **1897** Work *Waifs* 186 [ref. to 1863]: "Give me a stack of thousand-dollar fish," said Timberlake.

2.a. a dollar.

1917 Ruggles *Navy Explained* 106: Three hundred fish for me at the end of this hitch. **1919** *Our Navy* (Dec. 12) 31: They set you back ten fish for a lid. **1920** Witwer *Kid Scanlan* 15: What does the Kid have to do for the twenty thousand fish? **1921** J. Conway, in *Variety* (Mar. 18) 5: But it takes a lot of smacks on the beezer to make you forget all the things you could do with 1,000 fish. **1925** *Collier's* (Sept. 19) 8: He owed me two thousand fish. **1939** Thurber & Nugent *Male Animal* 278: Remember, I've got a thousand fish on that game. **1941** H.A. Smith *Low Man* 174: I mean seven fish...seven bucks. Seven dollars. **1943** in Ruhm *Detective* 365: She writes me out a check for a hundred fish. **1949** Shane & Cooper *City Across the River* (film): Let's see, I promised you five fish apiece. **1952** Holmes *Boots Malone* (film): Here. Seven fish on account of what I owe ya. **1962** T. Berger *Reinhart in Love* 166: Twenty-five a week from Claude, ninety fish a month from the G.I. Bill. **1965** Lardner & Southern *Cincinnati Kid* (film): Cost you one hundred and ninety-four fish. **1979** Charyn *7th Babe* 208: A thousand fish....They might lift it out of my pants.

b. *Gamb.* one hundred dollars.

1978 Pici *Tennis Hustler* 16: Three hundred and fifty in side bets; one hundred and fifty from Dawkins. Five big fish.

fish[2] *n.* **1.** a peculiar fellow; character.—usu. constr. with prec. adj. See also COLD FISH.

***1750** in *OED*: They smoked him for a queer fish, as the phrase is. **1771** B. Franklin, in *OED*: He was an odd fish. **1807** W. Irving *Salmagundi* 50: All the queer fish...are pointing...empty guns at us. ***1825** "Blackmantle" *English Spy* I 69: A *right cool fish. Ibid.* 75: And odd *Fish* Bill. **1836** *Spirit of Times* (Feb. 20) 1: A queer fish promised to send us an account of the shooting down on Long Island. ***1837** in *F & H* V 88: He's a devilish odd fish. **1846** Neal *Ploddy* 149: "A werry flat sort of a fish, that chap is," said Charley. **1847** Downey *Portsmouth* 25: Next appeared an odd sort of fish nicknamed Spouter from the fact that he was always boasting about his cruises in a Whaler. **1848** in Schele de Vere *Amer.* 621: What an *odd-fish* the old man is, sure enough, but...as pious a soul as ever lived. **1849** MacKay *Western World* II 151: If there's such a fish on board, I'll hook him. **1856** Cooke *Last of Foresters* 42: An odd fish, young man;...take care not to make him your model. ***1873** Hotten *Slang Dict.* (ed. 4): *Fish*, a person; "a queer *fish*," "a loose *fish*." Term never used except in doubtful cases, as those quoted. **1875** Sheppard *Love Afloat* 55: Pshaw, you old fish! **1883** Hay *Bread-Winners* 187: A lot of...strikers—not the unionists proper, but a lot of loose fish— intend to go through some of the principal houses on Algonquin Avenue. **1889** Barrère & Leland *Dict. Slang* I 364: *Fish* (common), a person; used in such phrases as an odd, a queer, prime, shy, loose *fish*, &c. **1918** *Stars & Stripes* (Feb. 15) 7: This fish uses his helmet for a candle stand. **1926–35** Watters & Hopkins *Burlesque* 14: Bonny's a good kid, but she does mix up with some awful fish. **1950** Bissell *Stretch on the River* 8: The Country Club was quite an exclusive group of fish. **1965** Spillane *Killer Mine* 82: While he sweats out an investigation he makes big noises about getting the fish who fingered him.

2.a. *Mil.* a new recruit.—usu. constr. with *fresh*.

1871 Willis *Forecastle Echoes* 10: Ha, there's "fresh fish"—I plainly mark the guilt-betraying blush. **1887** Hinman *Cpl. Klegg* 581 [ref. to Civil War]: Raw recruits were "fresh fish." **1888** McConnell *5 Yrs. Cavalryman* 12 [ref. to 1866]: As we entered the garrison and marched past the guardhouse we were greeted with cries of "fresh fish," "greenies," etc. **1894** S. Crane *Red Badge* 11 [ref. to Civil War]: They persistently yelled "Fresh fish!" at him. *Ibid.* 13: They call the reg'ment "Fresh fish" and everything. **1898** *Cosmopolitan* 216: "Fresh fish, eh?" queried Sergeant Oakes. *Ibid.* 218: See here, fresh fish, there's no use getting all upset over this thing. **1913** Meyers *10 Yrs. in Ranks* 2 [ref. to 1854]: On my entrance into the room there were cries of "fresh fish" from the boys who were present. *a***1917** Hard *Banners* 16 [ref. to 1898]: The "rookies"...were greeted good-naturedly with cries of "fresh fish." **1975** S.P. Smith *Amer. Boys* 189: Platoon goes out at noon, and I got two green fish to look after.

b. *Pris.* a new and inexperienced inmate.—often (in early use *usu.*) constr. with *fresh*.

1864 in E. Newsome *Experiences* 98: The old...prisoners would scarcely associate with "Fresh Fish." **1864** James *Civil War Diary* 42: As "fresh fish" have been sent here from time to time, we have been obliged to give up some of our surplus room to the luckless newcomers, nearly all of whom belong to the Vermont 9th regiment. **1867** Duke *Morgan's Cav.* 465 [ref. to 1863]: It was the custom...in the various prisons for the older inmates to collect about the gates...when "Fresh fish," as every lot of prisoners just arrived were termed, were brought in, and inspect them. **1871** Banka *Prison Life* 60: "I say, Bill! Where did they put that 'fresh fish'?—Fresh fish is the name applied to all newcomers...."They didn't put him in Carson's cell?" **1888** Hawes *Cahaba* 222 [ref. to Civil War]: The cry of "fresh fish" (new prisoners) is shouted through the prison. **1912** Lowrie *Prison* 39: The new arrival, or "fish," is always an object of interest to the other prisoners. **1926** *AS* (Dec.) 651: *Fresh fish.* County jail term for newcomers. **1927–28** Tasker *Grimhaven* 14: One of you guys take this fish over to second set-up with you! **1930** Shaw *Jack-Roller* 111: Antipathy is always in a "fish" (a new prisoner). **1934** L. Berg *Pris. Nurse* 9: He does that to every "fish"— excuse me, I mean newcomer. **1954** Lindner *50-Min. Hr.* 120: During the group psychiatric examination, which he took with the other "new fish"...it was obvious that he was eager to preserve a distance from his fellows. **1954** McGraw *Prison Riots* 142: They call you "fresh fish" when you first go in there. **1963** Williamson *Hustler!* 70: *Fishes*—new inmates. **1971** Horan *Blue Messiah* 159: The fresh fish...are turned over to the old cons. **1977** Hamill *Flesh & Blood* 28: I'm a new prisoner and that means I'm a fish. All new guys are called fish.

c. a naive newcomer or beginner; novice. Also attrib.

1897 Hamblen *Gen. Mgr.* 17: Them's all fresh fish that you saw. Ain't been at the business long. *Ibid.* 26: Bill, here's a fresh fish Dawson wants to break in. **1927–28** Tasker *Grimhaven* 124: The new guards—the "fish bulls"—were shoving and poking men about in line. **1938** *AS* (Apr.) 156: *Fish.* A beginner, a new man on the job. **1953** W. Brown *Monkey on My Back* 64: "You knew what that meant?" "Of course I did. I'm no fish." **1963** Westlake *Getaway Face* 42: This Alma was a busher, a new fish, she didn't know how this kind of operation was handled. **1968–70** *Current Slang* III & IV 47: *Fish*...A person new in a situation. **1966–80** McAleer & Dickson *Unit Pride* 152: Imagine that sonofa-bitchin' officer...thinkin' he's got a fish that'd walk into somethin' like that.

d. *Stu.* a freshman.

1898 *Univ. of Tenn. Volunteer* 159: I reckon one blip apiece will do fur the kid, if he'll promise to help on the other "fish." **1900** *Univ. of Tenn. Volunteer* 26: Greeted we were by waiting Sophomores with cries of "fish, fish, fish." *Ibid.* 97: A comparison of the Seniors and the "Fish." **1900** *DN* II 35: *Fish*, n. A freshman. **1942–44** in *AS* (Feb. 1946) 33: *Fish*, n. A freshman.

e. easy prey.

1918 *Lit. Digest* (Sept. 28) 65: If the Kaiser's troops are all like these birds, they're our fish, that's all.

3. *Stu.* (see quot.).

1851 B. Hall *College Wds.* 129: *Fish, Fisher,* one who attempts to ingratiate himself with his instructor, thereby to obtain favor or advantage; one who curries favor.

4. a foolish or ineffectual person, esp. one easily cheated, beaten, or hoaxed; (*specif.*) *Gamb. & Und.* SUCKER; *Carnival, Prost., etc.* a customer; MARK. Cf. *OED.*

1876 in Dwyer & Lingenfelter *Songs of Gold Rush* 189: But they like many another fish/Have now run out their line. **1887** DeVol *Gambler* 91: Up came the big fish, and wanted to know what was the least bet I would take. **1900** *DN* II 35: *Fish*...A person easily fooled. **1903** A. Adams *Log of a Cowboy* 257 [ref. to 1880's]: My, but you fellows are easy fish! **1920** S. Lewis *Main Street* 23: This poor fish of a bum medic that we keep around here. **1924** P. Marks *Plastic Age* 53: You make me feel like a fish. **1925** Faulkner *N.O. Sketches* 164: Why, you poor fish, whatayou mean? **1927** Nicholson *The Barker* 103: *Fish*—Townspeople (as regarded by carnival workers). **1931** Cressey *Taxi-Dance Hall* 35: *Fish.*—A man whom the girls can easily exploit for personal gain. *Ibid.* 42: My "fish" might get jealous. **1933** Kingsley *Men in White* 438: I know you, you fish! **1936** Anderson *High Tor* 68: Pick your pocket, you fish? All I ask is keep your feet out of my face. **1940** in A. Banks *First-Person* 105: I worked in the stone sheds. My brother Dante is still in there. I tell him he's fish but he don't listen. **1956** Levin *Compulsion* 46: Christ, don't be a fish!...The cops can put that much together...They're not that dumb. **1957** Murtagh & Harris *Cast First Stone* 14: They open their doors around 10 p.m. when the pimps, having kissed their girls good night and sent them off to "get some fish," come in to do some early drinking. *Ibid.* 305: *Get some fish.* To solicit and get some customers. **1958** Motley *Epitaph* 357: I caught a fish. **1968** F. Wallace *Poker* 119: Besides, he's a good player....We need more fish with lots of money. **1971** *Adam-12* (NBC-TV): That's what you said yesterday when I picked Phoenix by eight points. That I was a fish. **1976** Eble *Campus Slang* (Nov.) 2: *Fish*—n. Socially unpopular male: Jane's blind date last night was such a fish. **1979** T.R. Kennedy *Gotta Deal* 51: As I walked away, I heard them laugh and say, "We got us a fish." **1988** *T and T* (synd. TV series): That woman was the wrong fish.

5.a. [orig. short for S.E. *fish torpedo,* used to distinguish the self-propelled weapon from earlier minelike torpedos] *Navy.* a self-propelled torpedo. Cf. syn. TIN FISH.

1876 in *DA*: Next to this was the "fish" torpedo, the power of propulsion of which is thirty atmospheres. **1879** *United Service* (Apr.) 253: Like the "fish"-torpedo, left to their own guidance when released. **1898** *Chicago Record's War Stories* 120: The fan is revolved by the resistance of the water as the steel fish darts ahead. **1914** *Independent* (Nov. 2) 165: In nearly all lay discussions of attack by the automobile [i.e., self-propelled] or fish torpedo...[etc.]. **1918** Beston *Full Speed Ahead* 23: In about five minutes we'll come up and take a look-see (stick up the periscope) and if we see the bird, and we're in a good position to send him a fish (torpedo), we'll let him have one. **1942** S. Johnston *Queen of Flat-tops* 180: Commander Brett, now free of the fighters was dropping his own "fish." **1944** Hubler & DeChant *Leathernecks* 129: Only one of the TBF's dropped its fish. **1945** Dos Passos *Tour* 90: It's a Jill...Torpedo plane. He's got a fish. **1958** Gay *Run Silent* (film): At fifty feet we'll give her two fish. **1967** Dibner *Admiral* 72: Maybe he's a Nazi spy and he's got us out here so one of the Nip subs can lay a fish into us. **1984** T. Clancy *Red October* 358: The "fish" would have to do some of the tracking by itself. **1989** J. Weber *Defcon One* 53: Load and arm four fish.

b. *Navy.* a submarine. Cf. syn. TIN FISH.

1918 Beston *Full Speed* 88: Well, the ocean is a pretty big place, and the fish has the tremendous advantage of being invisible. A submarine need only show *three inches* of periscope if the weather is calm. **1944** Mellor *Sank Same* 119: Have sighted a fish and am going in on it. Over.

c. *Navy.* (see quot.).

1918 in *Papers Mich. Acad.* (1928): *Fish*...a dirigible balloon.

6. *West.* a rain slicker.

1903 A. Adams *Log of a Cowboy* 47 [ref. to 1882]: On reaching the turned leaders...[I] flaunted my "fish" in their faces until they re-entered the rear guard of our string. **1905** in A. Adams *Chisholm Trail* 136: The next switch brought the yellow "fish" bumping on his heels. **1944** R. Adams *West. Wds.* 59: *Fish.* The yellow oilskin slicker that all oldtime cowboys kept neatly rolled and tied behind the cantles of their saddles took this name from the picture of its trademark, a fish.

7. [sugg. by phr. *drink like a fish*] a heavy drinker.

1914 Z. Grey *West. Stars* 102: Why, Danny was a fish fer red liquor. **1985** Eble *Campus Slang* (Oct.) 4: *Fish*—one who is able to consume massive amounts of alcohol. "That guy's a real fish!"

8.a. a prostitute; (*hence*) a woman; (among homosexuals) a heterosexual woman (now the usu. sense).

a*1890–91** *F & H* II 401: *Fish market* = a brothel. **1923** Dobie *Coffee in the Gourd* 47: When you go fishin', you tryin' to flirt,/The fish you is fishin' for is got on a skirt. **1939** *AS* (Oct.) 239: *Fish.* Prostitute. *Fish business.* Pandering. **1939** Attaway *Breathe Thunder* 232: I...brought a bunch of fish with me from the coast. Making a lot of money taking these gals around from town to town. **1949** *Gay Girl's Guide* 9: *Fish:* A woman (usually excluding Lesbians). **1963** Rechy *City of Night* 108: She's not a fish, she's a fruit. **1964** in *Fact* (Jan. 1965) 26: *Fish n.* A woman, usually a heterosexual. **1969** Girodias *New Olympia Reader* 629: I know that women are referred to as "fish" in fag-lang. But that's defamation. Clean women don't smell any more than do clean men. **1972** *Anthro. Linguistics* (Mar.) 102: *Fish* (n.): A heterosexual female. **1967–80** Folb *Runnin' Lines* 237: *Fish*...Female. **1985** "Blowdryer" *Mod. Eng.* 10: *Fish*...is what gay guys call girls. "Ewwww, I smell fish." **1987** E. White *Beautiful Room* 54: Sorry, Dearie, I thought you were a Fish for a moment.

b. the vulva or vagina; (*hence*) copulation.

a*1890–91** *F & H* II 401: *Fish*...(venery).—Generic for the female *pudendum*: e.g., *a bit of fish* = a grind. **1927** *Immortalia* 35: She hung a sign upon the door,/"Fresh fish here for sale." **1939** in Garon *Blues* 70: I want some fish...and you know just what I mean. **1941** G. Legman, in Henry *Sex Vars.* II 1165: To perform cunnilinctus...*eat fish* and *chew the fish*...A popular American song of the late 1930's, "Seafood Mama,"

with the chorus-line: "I get my favorite dish—fish!" was finally banned from the radio after being innocently allowed for several months. *a***1972** B. Rodgers *Queens' Vernacular* 81: *Fish*...the vulva...."We call it fish, darling, because it absolutely smells like one—a dead one!" **1978** Selby *Requiem* 36: Go ahead ya fuckin hound, stick ya nose up her drawers. What's the matta, donta ya like fish? **1983–86** Zausner *Streets* 37: A lot of girls [prostitutes]...don't know how to do anything but sling fish.*....*A fish is a vagina; to sling fish is to fuck.

c. (among lesbians) a lesbian whose demeanor and behavior are girlish or feminine.

1966–71 Karlen *Sex. & Homosex.* 546: The typical...butch...denied she had ever been a fish (femme) and said she wanted nothing to do with men.

9. *Petroleum Industry.* a tool or other equipment that has accidentally fallen into a drilled well.

1944 Boatright & Day *Hell to Breakfast* 144: When anything is lost in the hole, it is a "fish" and all devices used to recover material dropped in the hole are "fishing tools." **1951** Pryor *The Big Play* 11: He finished up rather mildly, "Goddammit! We've got a fish." *a***1961** *WNID3.*

10. [shortening of FISH-AND-SHRIMP] *Und.* a pimp.

1963 Braly *Shake Him* 71: "Randozza's a fish."..."Jean wouldn't waste two minutes talking to a fish." **1975** Harrell & Bishop *Orderly House* 18: The relationship between working girls and pimps, or "fish," as we call them, is the least understood part of...prostitution.

11. an emotionless person; COLD FISH.

1956 in Beaumont *Best* 220: My wife is frigid...She's a fish, that's all. **1958** in Marx *Groucho Letters* 136: The man he called "that glib son-of-a-bitch" and "that emotionless fish."

12. *Av.* (see 1966 quot.).

1966 Noel & Bush *Naval Terms* 149: *Fish:* Streamlined weight on the end of an aircraft's trailing, suspended antenna. **1978** Gann *Hostage* 258 [ref. to WWII]: Sommers...held his hand on the trailing antenna "fish."

13. a Newfoundlander.

1974 Cherry *High Steel* xiv: Evenings with the Fish (a not wholly complimentary term for men from Newfoundland).

14. (used in mild interjections).

ca*1728** in *OED*: Gods fish! When two rogues fall out, their master then is like to know the truth. **1937** in Loosbrock & Skinner *Wild Blue* 193: Great fish!...Then you did an outside loop! **1955** Salter *Hunters* 159: Holy Fish! What's going on?

¶ In phrases:

¶ **call the fishes** *Naut.* feed the fish, 1, below. *Joc.*

1936 Mulholland *Splinter Fleet* 53 [ref. to 1918]: Even Red Dorgan, our skipper, had to lean over the lee rail and "call the fishes."

¶ **feed the fish, 1.** *Naut.* to vomit over the side from seasickness.

*****1870** in *OED*: His first act was to appease the fishes...by feeding them most liberally. *****1884** in *F & H* II 381: Although I fed myself shortly before arriving abreast of Eddystone, I *fed the fish* shortly afterwards. **1907** Kohr *Uncle Sam* 90: Many of the boys were lined up along the rail with heads bent over, "feeding the fishes." **1919** Straub *Diary* 346: I went down to my bunk because we are in the open sea now, an this old tub certainly can roll and I have to watch out or I'll be feeding the fish. **1929** Williams *Whaling Family* 261 [ref. to ca1870]: I never "fed the fishes" and could enjoy the jokes played on the greenhorns while getting their sealegs. **1939** O'Brien *One-Way Ticket* 78: What do you want me to do? Feed the fish? **1940** Simonsen *Soldier Bill* 52: Several times he leaned over the railing and "fed the fish," using a sailor's expression which he had already picked up. **1980** in Safire *Good Word* 303.

2. *Naut.* to be drowned or buried at sea.

a*1890–91** *F & H* II 381: *To feed the fishes*...to be drowned. **1894** Henderson *Sea-Yarns* 5: You fellers'll all be feedin' fish afore mornin'. **1983** *Batman* (Apr.) 2: Give me one good reason you shouldn't be feeding the fishes tomorrow morning.

¶ **give (someone) the fish** (see quot.).

1963 T.I. Rubin *Sweet Daddy* 12: Some of the lousy crumbs give me the fish. You know, turn on the ice—like I'm not there.

¶ **settle (someone's) fish** settle (someone's) hash s.v. HASH.

1974 E. Thompson *Tattoo* 11: We'll soon settle the fish of Imm-perial Japan.

fish *v.* **1.** *Stu.* to curry favor with an instructor.

1774 in *DAE*: He courts me a good deal, and fishes. **1795** in B. Hall *College Wds.* (ed. 2) 200: I give to those that fish for parts,/Long, sleepless nights and aching hearts. **1800** in B. Hall *College Wds.* (ed. 2) 201:

If a scholar appeared to perform his exercises to his best ability…I would hear the whisper run round the class, *fishing*. If one…showed common civility to his instructors,…he was *fishing*. If he refused to join in some general disorder, he was insulted with *fishing*. If he did not appear to despise the…approbation of his instructors…he was suspected of *fishing*. **1819** A. Pierce *Rebelliad* 33: Did I not promise those who fish'd/And pimp'd most any part they wish'd. *Ibid.* 35: Who would fish a fine to save!/Let him turn and flee. **1851** B. Hall *College Wds.* 128: *Fish.* At Harvard College, to seek or gain the good-will of an instructor by flattery, caresses, kindness, or officious civilities; to curry favor.

2. to sucker; inveigle.

1964–78 J. Carroll *B. Diaries* 41: N.Y.C. visitors who got fished into paying five beans to sail around the island.

¶ In phrase:

¶ **go fishing** *Baseball.* (of a batter) to reach with the bat for an outside pitch.

1973 World Series (NBC-TV) (Oct. 21): Wow, Kenny went fishing that time!

fish-and-shrimp *n.* [rhyming slang] a pimp.

1935 Pollock *Und. Speaks: Fish and shrimp,* a pimp. **1942** *ATS* 472: Pimp; procurer…*fish and shrimp.* **1944** D.W. Maurer & S.J. Baker, in *AS* (Oct.) 192: *Fish and shrimp.* A pimp.

fish bait *n.* a corpse that has been drowned, lost, or disposed of at sea. Cf. SHARK BAIT.

1944 C.B. Davis *Leo McGuire* 42: I was almost fish bait. **1984** "W.T. Tyler" *Shadow Cabinet* 276: But the old woman wants to see this animal son of hers, fish bait or not.

fishbelly *n. Black E.* a white person.—used contemptuously.

1985 Ark. man, age 35: I'll never forget when I wandered into the wrong part of Hoxie, Arkansas [in 1964], and this black guy said, "We don't allow no fishbellies in this part of town." *a*1990 Westcott *Half a Klick* 167: A fish belly lieutenant.

fishbowl *n. Police.* a room in a police station where suspects can be watched or identified, usu. through one-way glass; (*broadly*) any glass-enclosed room.

1943 Chandler *High Window* 462: And with a…hope that I won't be seeing you in the fish bowl. **1949** Chandler *Little Sister* 72: Maybe I lose a job. Maybe I get tossed in the fishbowl. So what? *a*1961 Boroff *Campus U.S.A.* 46: "Let's go check the bods in the fishbowl"…means, "Let's go to the glass-enclosed reference room in Honnold Library and look over the girls." **1970** Thackrey *Thief* 192: "A friend of whose?" "Mine. And yours—because if he wasn't, you'd be in the fishbowl right now."

fish-eater *n.* **1.** [ref. to the former obligation of Roman Catholics to eat fish on Fridays] a Roman Catholic.—usu. used derisively.

1928 Hammett *Red Harvest* 130: Reno called him a lousy fish-eater and shot him four times. **1958** F. Davis *Spearhead* 118 [ref. to 1945]: Janowicz, you're a fish eater. Go see what those two clowns are up to. **1963** Boyle *Yanks Don't Cry* 89: Fish for meat anyone? Who wants the deal? Hey! How 'bout you, Lashio, you're a fisheater ain't you? **1965** Donlon *Outpost of Freedom* 90: "They're both fish-eaters, like me." "That's all right," [the Protestant chaplain] said, "I could have converted them." **1972** Hannah *Geronimo Rex* 242: He said…he saw a fish-eater crawling in the house.…Some use that as an epithet against Catholics. **1988** D.O. Smith *Cradle* 35 [ref. to 1930]: We [West Point cadets] called the Catholics "fish eaters."

2. [alluding to FISH², *n.,* 8.a.] *Homosex.* a heterosexual man.

1987 E. White *Beautiful Room* 54: Can't bear Fish or Fisheaters.

fish eggs *n.pl.* tapioca pudding.—used derisively.

1921 *DN* V 141: *Fish-eggs,* n. Tapioca or sago pudding. "Seems to me we get nothing but fish-eggs for dessert lately." **1936** *AS* (Feb.) 43: *Fish eggs.* Tapioca. **1969** in *DARE.*

fisher *n. Esp. Stu.* one who curries favor; FISH², *n.,* 3.

1804 *Monthly Antho.* I 153: You besought me to respect my teachers, and to be attentive to my studies, though it shall procure me the odious title of a "*fisher.*" **1851** (quot. at FISH², *n.,* 3). **1890–91* *F & H* II 410: *Fisher*…(common).—A lickspittle; only used contemptuously.

fisherman *n. Stu.* (see quot.). Now *hist.*

1987 Horowitz *Campus Life* 13: College men of the nineteenth and twentieth centuries…have perceived…the student seeking faculty friendship as the "fisherman" or "brownnose."

fishery *n. Hobo.* a Christian street mission.

1926 *AS* I (Dec.) 651: *Fisheries*—religious missions in working-class

neighborhoods. **1930** "D. Stiff" *Milk & Honey* 205: *Fisheries*—Missions along the *main stem.*

fish eye *n.* **1.** *pl.* tapioca pudding.—used derisively. Also **fish eyes and glue.**

1918 Kauffman *Our Navy at Work* 6: "Fish Eyes" are tapioca pudding. **1919** *Indian* (May 19) 6: *Fish eyes*—Tapioca pudding. **1922** *Leatherneck* (Apr. 22) 5: *Fish Eyes:* Tapioca pudding. **1929** Bowen *Sea Slang* 48: *Fish-Eyes.* Tapioca pudding on shipboard. **1931** Erdman *Reserve Officer's Manual* 435: *Fish eyes.* Tapioca pudding. **1942** *Leatherneck* (Nov.) 145: *Fish-Eyes*—Tapioca. **1958** McCulloch *Woods Words* 63: *Fish-eyes*—Poorly cooked tapioca. **1969** N.Y.C. schoolboy: I always call it *fish eyes and glue.* **1979** *N.Y. Times* (Dec. 23) IV 12: Children we have known do not like tapioca pudding. "Fish eyes and glue," they call it with gleeful disgust.

2. a cold unfriendly stare, as of doubt or disdain.—constr. with *the.*

1941 in W.C. Fields *By Himself* 391: The girl gives him the fish-eye. **1952** Bruce & Essex *K.C. Confidential* (film): You been givin' me the fish eye all night. **1963** Rubin *Sweet Daddy* 83: Jolly…was giving me the fish eye the other day. **1966** Westlake *Busy Body* 3: He saw Nick Rovito giving him the fish-eye. **1970–71** Higgins *Eddie Coyle* 167: So I'm sitting there and getting the fish eye from the waitress. **1975** V.B. Miller *Trade-Off* 69: He gets in and gives me the fish eye. **1982** Braun *Judas Tree* 99: Starbuck gave him the fisheye. **1986** *N.Y. Times* (Mar. 30) IV 18: At a time when countless patients are giving countless physicians the fish eye, there's one American who can't possibly complain about his medical care.

fishface *n.* a person having a face reminiscent of a fish's.—used derisively.

a*1625 in *OED:* Whether would you, fish face? **1914 in *OEDS:* O, shut up, fish-face. **1929–33** Farrell *Young Manhood* 345: "I'll arrange a nice date for you."…"Yeah. I suppose with some fishface." **1936** "E. Queen" *Halfway House* 183: Use it on Fish-Face. **1950** Gordon & Gordon *FBI Story* 128: Fishface about? **1983** *Night Court* (NBC-TV): What's the matter, fishface? The truth hurts?

fishhead *n.* **1.** a dolt; MEATHEAD.

1943 Snell & Marks *In Brooklyn* (film): Yeah, they found it, you fishhead!

2. an East Asian.—used contemptuously.

1971 (quot. at DONKEY). **1974** Univ. Wisc. student: In 1965 we had a Filipino teacher that everybody called "Fishhead." It applies only to Filipinos. **1974** Former SP4, U.S. Army, age 24 [ref. to 1970]: We called the Vietnamese gooks and *fishheads.* **1975** Stanley *WWIII* 176: Maybe this fishhead knows something. *Ibid.* 251: Fishheads. Chinks. **1977–80** F.M. Stewart *Century* 394: Bunch of slanty-eyed fishheads. **1980** Lorenz *Guys Like Us* 77: Fish head! **1981** Former Yeoman, USN [ref. to 1971–72]: A *fishhead* was a Vietnamese. **1987** *Tour of Duty* (CBS-TV): Hey, fishhead!

fish-hook *n.* **1.** *pl.* the fingers; (*sing.*) the hand.

[**1726** in *William & Mary Qly.* (Ser. 3) XXXVIII (1981) 279: He got…all the Orphans Patrimony into his Fish-hook Fingers.] **1784** in Whiting *Amer. Proverbs* 151: These fellows…are St. Peters children,—every finger a fish-hook, and their hand a grapnel. [**ca*1819 in J. Farmer *Musa Pedestris* 82: My fingers are fish-hooks, sir.] **1848* (cited in *F & H* II 401). **1851** *Harper's Mo.* (Sept.) 470: Eagerly clutching with his fishhooks of fingers the short iron crowbar…he rammed it as far as he could. **1922** *Variety* (June 30) 6: Sent the [bettors] out to the track with the fish hook around the poke. **1939** Kaufman & Hart *Man Who Came to Dinner* 32: Take your fish-hooks off me! **1944** Burley *Hndbk. Jive* 138: *Fish-hooks*—Fingers.

2. *Cards.* (see quot.).

1968 F. Wallace *Poker* 215: Fish hook—A seven or a jack.

3. *Baseball.* (see quot.).

1964 Thompson & Rice *Every Diamond* 142: Fish Hook…A real good curve ball.

4. *pl.* (used in var. mild oaths).

1868 "W.J. Hamilton" *Maid of Mtn.* 36: Gosh all fish-hooks!…What was that? **1878** [P.S. Warne] *Hard Crowd* 4: Why, gosh all fish-hooks, stranger! **1880** Bailey *Danbury Boom* 216: He said, "Holy fish-hooks!" **1892** in Thompson *Youth's Companion* 405: Gee criminy fish-hooks! **1959** in *DARE:* Oh Fishhooks!…Common. **1989** Care *Viet. Spook Show* 110: Gosh all fishhooks.…I try not to swear.

fish-horn *n.* a wind instrument; (*specif.* and *usu.*) a trumpet or bugle. *Joc.*

1856 Cozzens *Sparrowgrass* 38: Mrs. Sparrowgrass asked me who that was, "blowing a fish-horn?" **1867** in *Life* (Oct. 28) 100: *Order:* Midshipman Thompson (1st Class), who plays abominably on a fish horn, will oblige me by going outside the limits when he wants to practice or he will find himself coming out of the little end of the horn. **1895** F. Norris *Novelist* 77: The lookout in the crow's-nest sounded upon his fishhorn and the skipper, running forward, lit a huge calcium flare. **1917** in Bowerman *Compensations* 23: The…conductor used a fish horn for a signal as they do on the [French] railways. **1919** Cober *Bttry. D* 74: Owing to his modesty he refused being made regimental bugler and consequently contented himself by pestering us with his "fish horn." **1921** Lettau *In Italy* 15: We had no time to try the famous waters, for the train starter with his little "fish horn" soon sent us on our way. **1944** Burley *Hndbk. Jive* 138: Fish horn—Saxophone.

fishing expedition *n. Law & Pol.* the asking of questions without definite purpose in hopes of eliciting some significant information.

1874 *Kansas Reports* XII 453: It is also said that this permits one to go on a "fishing expedition" to ascertain his adversary's testimony. **1916** *DN* IV 423. **1921, 1940, 1941, 1946, 1951, 1958** in *AS* 48 (1973) 132–33. **1986** *Newsmakers* (CNN-TV) (May 25): To find out whether it's really relevant to the man's defense or whether it's a mere fishing expedition.

fish-pond *n.* the ocean.

1848 Judson *Mysteries* 172: That will make folks stare more than they ever have on this side of the big fish-pond.

fish queen *n. Homosex.* a man who practices cunnilingus; (*hence*, used as a contemptuous term for any heterosexual or homosexual man); (see also 1949, 1965 quots.). Occ. as *v.*

1941 G. Legman, in Henry *Sex Vars.* II 1165: *Fish-queen.* A man who enjoys cunnilinctus, or a homosexual (or heterosexual) male who practices it for pay. The term is quite derogatory. **1949** *Gay Girl's Guide* 9: *Fish-Queen:* Properly, a "cunt-sucker," but in general usage applied to any homosexual who makes a point of bringing women with him where they'll be seen by his friends, with the apparent aim of convincing himself and others he's bisexual. **1962** Crump *Killer* 389: I'm fish-queening this broad in the car, see, when [a cop]…pops up and me with my head in the muff, see? **1964** in *Fact* (Jan. 1965) 26: *Fish-queen*…A homosexual who consorts with women. **1965** Trimble *Sex Words* 78: *Fish queen.* A very effeminate male Homosexual. **1971** Cameron *First Blood* 20: Motherfucking fish queen didn't want to let me have…the fifty, either. *a*1972 B. Rodgers *Queens' Vernacular* 80: *Fish queen* (dated) 1. one who sucks cunt 2. (pej[oratively]) any heterosexual man. **1971–74** in *West. Folk.* XXXIII (1974) 214: A "fish queen" is one whose desires include heterosexual women.

fish-scale *n.* a nickel or dime.

1900 *DN* 35: *Fish-scale,* n. A five cent piece. [Reported from Brown and Tulane universities.]. **1952** in *DAS:* Without a fish scale in my purse, I gotta sit here and witness this gastronomical orgy!

fishskin *n.* **1.** a one-dollar bill.

1936 Duncan *Over the Wall* 21 [ref. to 1918]: I learned quickly that a dollar bill was a fish-skin. **1943** *AS* (Apr.) 154: *Fish skin.* A dollar bill.
2. a condom.

1936 Levin *Old Bunch* 57: Schmutz…made over a buck a dozen on fishskins. **1938** "Justinian" *Amer. Sexualis* 21: *Fishskin.* n. A cundum of especially thin and sensitive construction and composition, aesthetically preferable to the ordinary *cundum.* C. 18-20. Coll. **1942** in Legman *Limerick* 195: He pulled out a fishskin. **1975** T. Berger *Sneaky People* 40: Laverne peeled the fishskin from his member. *a*1973–87 F.M. Davis *Livin' the Blues* 37 [ref. to *ca*1920]: To avoid…a dose…you used…a Fish Skin.
3. (see quot.). Cf. FISH², *n.,* 6.

1958 McCulloch *Woods Words* 63: *Fishskin*—A waterproof slicker worn by green hands or non-loggers; it tears so easily it is no good for woods work.

fish-trap *n.* the mouth.

1853 [W.G. Simms] *Sword & Distaff* 59: Shut up your fish-trap…or I'll tear out your tongue.

fishwife *n. Homosex.* a woman who is the wife of a homosexual man.—used derisively.

1970 Landy *Underground Dict.* 78: *Fishwife*…Male homosexual's real wife. **1975** *DAS* (Supp. 2).

fish-wrapper *n.* a newspaper. Also **fishwrap.** *Joc.*

1954–60 *DAS.* **1961** Brosnan *Pennant Race* 202: The *Chronicle* and other Frisco fish-wrappers. **1976–79** Duncan & Moore *Green Side Out*

241: I read [it] in the Jacksonville, S.C., fishwrap.

fishy *adj.* **1.** drunk.

1737 *Penna. Gazette* (Jan. 13) 1: He's Fishey.
2. [sugg. or infl. by colloq. *fish story,* an exaggerated or incredible tale] suspect; questionable. Now *colloq.*

1840 [J.P. Kennedy] *Quodlibet* 75: Jesse [was]…a little amphibious in his politics, or, in Mr. Fog's expressive language, *rather fishy.* *1844 in *OED:* I thought it was all up…The most fishy thing I ever saw. *1858 in *F & H* II 401: Highly *fishy* they were. Something about breach of trust, and the embezzling his brother's money—a man in India. **1859** *Spirit of Times* (Apr. 2) 86: Stories, that to say the least were *fishy!* **1861** in *DAE:* We did not lose a man. This all sounds rather fishy; but they had no artillery. *1873 Hotten *Slang Dict.* (ed. 4): *Fishy,* doubtful, unsound, rotten; used to denote a suspicion of a "screw being loose," or "something rotten in the state of Denmark." **1889** Barrère & Leland *Dict. Slang* I 364: *Fishy* (common), doubtful, suspicious, implying dishonesty, as in a *fishy* affair or "concern." **1899** in Botkin *Sidewalks* 440: Still, the story is not at all "fishy," but true in every point. **1912** J.W. Johnson *Ex-Colored Man* 427: As I neared the grounds, the thought came across me, would not my story sound fishy? Would it not place me in the position of an imposter or beggar? **1946** Braus *Strange Triangle* (film): I never heard of anything so fishy. And I'm going to get to the bottom of it with or without you. **1958** S.H. Adams *Tenderloin* 34: I think there's something fishy somewhere. **1967** "M.T. Knight" *Terrible Ten* 82: It still sounds fishy to me. **1984** Regis *Extraterrestrials* 59: There is something awfully fishy about this line of argument.
3. *Whaling.* (of a whaleman) experienced; seasoned; capable.

1868 Macy *There She Blows!* 45: Though a good whaleman, Grafton was not what is known to the *connoisseur* as a "fishy man."…Dunham, the second officer, was a smart young fellow of two-and-twenty, active, strong, and "fishy to the backbone."

fishyback *n.* [*fish* + *piggyback*] *Transport.* the transportation of cargo by ship or barge.

*ca*1950 (cited in *W9*). **1971** Tak *Truck Talk* 60: *Fishyback:* The transportation by ship of an entire trailer intact with cargo.

fist *n.* **1.** *Cards.* a hand of cards.

1916 S. Lewis *Job* 252: A "good, canny fist of poker."
2. [sugg. by earlier S.E. or colloq. *fist* 'handwriting'] *Telegraphy.* an operator's distinctive touch on a telegraph key.

1929 *AS* III (Oct.) 48: *Fist:* Keying technique, touch. **1945** Lyndon, Booth, & Monks *House on 92d St.* (film): That's not Bill sending. I know his fist. **1952** Uris *Battle Cry* 180: Their fists were certain as they handled the keys. **1967** Lord *Incredible Victory* 18: Call letters could change, but a particular operator's "fist"—never. **1969** Crumley *One to Count Cadence* 40: He has such an odd fist, I can always tell when he's working.

fistburger *n.* a punch in the mouth; KNUCKLE SANDWICH.

1976 Conroy *Santini* 294: I'm gonna let you slip out the back door before I commence to doling out fistburgers.

fist city *n.* the occasion of a fistfight; in phr. **go to fist city** to engage in a fistfight.

1930 Botkin *Folk-Say* 190: And I sez to him, sez I, "You and me is going to Fist City." **1960** MacCuish *Do Not Go Gentle* 110 [ref. to 1941]: You make a trip to fist city with me, clown, I'll boot yer balls into a necklace. **1963** Cameron *Black Camp* 125: You looking for a trip to Fist City, Arnold? **1964** Howe *Valley of Fire* 96: Don't kick me or we'll go to Fist City. **1966** "T. Pendleton" *Iron Orchard* 121: Looked like fer a minute that you and the stud-duck was goin' to fist city. **1975** *Kojak* (CBS-TV): I can't help you that much. When I came out it was fist city. **1976** Univ. Tenn. student: He was all set to go to fist city. **1984** *All Things Considered* (Nat. Pub. Radio) (June 13): If your favorite Stooge wasn't Shemp, it was fist city.

fisterris /fɪsˈtɛrɪs/ *n.* [orig. unkn.] a thing; object; thingamabob.

1938 *AS* (Apr.) 156: *Fisterris.* A term for an indefinite object. **1962** Maurer & Vogel *Narc. & Narc. Add.* (ed. 2) 301: *Fistaris* or *Fisstaris.* Also *Phystaris.* A currently popular word meaning about anything.…"Hand me the fisstaris."…"Button up before you show your fisstaris." **1975** U.C.L.A. student: A *fisterris* is like a doojigger. Like, "Hand me the fisterris," or "There's something wrong with the fisterris."

fist fuck *n. Homosex.* (see *a*1972 quot.).—usu. considered vulgar. Also as *v.*

*a*1972 B. Rodgers *Queens' Vernacular* 81: *Fist fuck.* The extended process of inserting a fist to the elbow anally. **1978** Price *Ladies' Man* 224:

That guy's into getting fist-fucked...right up the ass. Right up to the elbow. Can you believe that? **1984** H. Gould *Cocktail* 91: He liked to put on mesh stockings...and get fist-fucked.

fist-fucker *n.* **1.** a man or boy who masturbates habitually.—usu. considered vulgar.

1962 Killens *Heard the Thunder* 168 [ref. to WWII]: Corporal Solly, you old-fashioned fist-fucker, why don't you come out of that orderly room and get some air in your ass sometimes? **1974** E. Thompson *Tattoo* 111: I feel plumb sorry for you poor Wichita fistfuckers...got nothin to fuck there but their fists. **1984** Sample *Raceboss* 266 [ref. to 1960's]: Nelly Nuthin, Proud Walker, Bow Wow, and Fistfucker were...dunces.

2. *Homosex.* a practitioner of FIST-FUCKING, 2.—usu. considered vulgar.

*a***1972** B. Rodgers *Queens' Vernacular* 81: *Fist fuckers*...those who practice fist fucking. **1973** *Oui* (July) 73: Fist Fuckers of America: Their clenched-fist gestures are often an internal expression. **1985** J. Dillinger *Adrenaline* 213: How about *Fistfucker Beach*?

3. a despicable or contemptible fellow.—usu. considered vulgar.

1977 in H.S. Thompson *Shark Hunt* 602: If that treacherous fist-fucker ever comes back to life, he'll wish we'd had the good sense to nail him up on a frozen telephone pole.

fist-fucking *n.* **1.** male masturbation.—usu. considered vulgar.

*a***1890–91** *F & H* II 402: *Fist-fucking*...Masturbation. **1916** Cary *Venery* I 85: *Fist Fucking*—Masturbation.

2. *Homosex.* insertion of the hand into the rectum for the purpose of sexual stimulation.—usu. considered vulgar.

*a***1972** (quot. at FIST-FUCKER, 2). **1973** *Oui* (July) 75: We spent some time discussing fist fucking ("it can be dangerous"). **1981** *Film Comment* (May) 21: Oriental beheadings and Occidental gay fistfuckings. **1989** Chapple & Talbot *Burning Desires* 260: Videos that did not stop at fist-fucking.

fist holler *n. Ozarks.* FIST CITY.

1936 *AS* (Dec.) 315: When two men are said to be "goin' up *Fist Holler*" it means that they are about to have a fight.

fisting *n. Homosex.* FIST-FUCKING, 2.

1981 *Psychology Today* (May) 82: Some offensively detailed pages on the technology of what is called fisting. **1983** *Rolling Stone* (Feb. 3) 20: Fifty percent of the patients...engaged in "fisting," which involves one man inserting his fist, often up to the elbow, into the rectum of another man. **1985** "Blowdryer" *Mod. Eng.* 72: *Fisting*...is anal sex with the hand. **1992** Hosansky & Sparling *Working Vice* 289: All kinds of stuff. Fisting, golden showers, girl-girl.

fist sandwich *n.* KNUCKLE SANDWICH.

1982 in "J.B. Briggs" *Drive-In* 47: Bronk offers Artie a fist sandwich.

fit[1] *n.* ¶ In phrases:

¶ **beat to fits** to beat or surpass completely.

1861 Wilkie *Iowa First* 77: Ragged and dirty enough to beat Falstaff's recruits all "to fits." *a***1890** *F & H* I 162: To *beat...to fits*...To excel; to surpass.

¶ **give (someone) fits** to administer a beating, a decisive defeat, a severe scolding, or the like, to; give hell to.

1844 in Schele de Vere *Amer.* 602: The man ran after the thievish Indian, and the corporal cried out to him to *give him fits* if he caught him; they seemed to be bent upon making an end...to the petty thefts by which we had been annoyed in camp. **1848** B.A. Baker *Glance at N.Y.* 22: He mustn't come foolin' round my gal, or I'll give him fits! **1856** G. Derby *Phoenixiana* 48: With our six-shooters—We gin 'em perticklar fits. **1865** in Springer *Sioux Country* 31: To-day a year ago we were giving the "Johnies" fits on Hurricane Creek, Miss. **1866** Marcy *Army Life* 364: War you at the Orleans fight, whar our boys gin sich particlar fits to ole Pack? **1871** Schele de Vere *Amer.* 602: *To give one fits*, or, as emphatic Yankees say, to give one *very particular fits*, suggests such severe punishment as will produce fits. **1874** in *DAE*: Suppose you feel like giving the ducks particular fits today? **1882, 1907** in *DAE*.

fit[2] *n.* [out*fit*] *Narc.* paraphernalia used by an addict to inject drugs; (*specif.*) a hypodermic syringe.

1959 (cited in Spears *Drugs & Drink* 195). **1962** Maurer & Vogel *Narc. & Narc. Add.* (ed. 2) 301: *Fit.* A hypodermic *outfit.* **1963** Braly *Shake Him* 50: "No fit," Furg explained. **1967–68** von Hoffman *Parents Warned Us* 153: I made this fit...I even sharpened the point. *a***1969** B. Jackson *Thief's Primer* 181: This guy is doing life for traces in a fit [minute quantities of narcotics detected in a hypodermic syringe]. **1972**

Wambaugh *Blue Knight* 36: They sure was making a fit...I'd a took a chance and stuck it in my arm if there was some dope in it. **1972** Bunker *No Beast* 80: What about a fit? *a***1979** Pepper & Pepper *Straight Life* 216 [ref. to 1958–60]: He came back with...a quarter of an ounce of heroin. I said "You got a 'fit, pistolo?"

fit *adj.* ¶ In phrases:

¶ **fit to be tied** extremely angry. Now *colloq.* [Undoubtedly much older than the available evidence suggests; cf. the tenor of the exx. given in *OED* s.v. *fit, adj.,* 5.b.]

1894 in *OEDS*: The old devil was fit to be tied. *****1914–22** J. Joyce *Ulysses* 754: I was fit to be tied. **1956** Simak *Strangers in Universe* 193: The boss is fit to be tied.

¶ **fit to kill** excessively; intensely; to the greatest degree. Now *colloq.*

1808 in *OED*: It made us laugh fit to kill ourselves. **1856** in *DAE:* Then she laughs fit to kill. **1896** in *DAE:* Dressed up fit to kill. **1980** Eble *Campus Slang* (Mar.) 2: *Fit to kill*—extremely dressed up. She's dressed fit to kill.

¶ **fit to split** excessively.

1852 Stowe *Uncle Tom* ch. xxxviii: I laughed fit to split, dat ar' time we cotched Molly. **1856** in *DAE.*

five *n.* **1.** *pl.* the fingers; (*hence, usu.*) the fists.

*****1837** C. Dickens *Pickwick Papers* ch. ii: Smart chap that cabman—handled his fives well. **1842** *Spirit of Times* (Oct. 29) 416: These fives shall ne'er be raised against a friend. **1848** Judson *Mysteries* 261: Save your fives for other work. *****1887** in *F & H* II 403: Both the men of sin handled their *fives* with almost professional dexterity. *****a1889** in Barrère & Leland *Dict. Slang* I 365: As yet they have not took to use their *fives.* **1915** Howard *God's Man* 432: Strapping, sizable fellows, handy with their "fives."

2. a blow with the fist.

1930 Bodenheim *Roller Skates* 112: You want five hard? *Ibid.* 179: *Five hard*...a fist, or a punch. **1966** "Petronius" *N.Y. Unexp.* 179: All-night Dentist...if someone lands you "five in the gums." **1966–67** Harvey *Air War* 163: Nobody...badmouths the Jolly Greens—unless he wants to get five propelled by an outraged right arm in his teeth. **1973** *Zap Comix* (No. 6) (unp.): Taste five in the fangs, Pappy! *a***1982** in Berry *Semper Fi* 388: He was very close to a fast five in the chops from Lieutenant Pfuhl.

¶ In phrases:

¶ **agitate fives** to shake hands.

1843 *Spirit of Times* (Sept. 23) 354: In a short time we were able to "agitate fives" with Steve Roberts, who looked as calm as if he had just "stepped out."

¶ **bunch of fives** a fist; (*hence*) a blow with the fist. *Obs.* in U.S.

*****1821** *Real Life in London* I 228: Don't throw your water here, or I'll lend you my *bunch of fives.* *****1823** "J. Bee" *Slang Dict.*: Bunch of fives. **1837** Neal *Charcoal Sks.* 33: Orson Dabbs...[shook] his "bunch of fives" sportively. **1865** C.F. Browne *Ward: Travels* 23: Tip us yer bunch of fives, old faker! **1870** *Putnam's Mag.* (Mar.) 301: The combatants struck each other with mawleys and bunches of fives upon the head. *****1873** Hotten *Slang Dict.* (ed. 4) (s.v. *fives*): "Bunch of *fives*," the fist. **1879** *United Service* (Jan.) 88: Putting up his "bunch of fives" like an Anglo-Saxon. **1882** in Miller & Snell *Why West Was Wild* 93: The Winchester and self-cocker had given place to nature's arms, good "bunches of fives." **1891** McCann & Jarrold *Odds & Ends* 35: I'd like to put a bunch of fives under that feller's horn. **1908** T.A. Dorgan, in Zwilling *TAD Lexicon* 95: This is the best bunch of fives Cross has. This blow won him all his fights in New York. **1924** *Amer. Merc.* (Feb.) 132: Want a bunch o' fives in yer kisser? **1942** *ATS* 148. *****1980** Leland *Kiwi-Yank. Dict.* 19: Now shake this fist under someone's nose and ask in a belligerent tone of voice whether he'd like a "bunch of fives."

¶ **game of fives** a blow or beating with the fists.

1848 Judson *Mysteries* 63: Better be careful of yer blarney, my cove, or you'll know the game uv fives afore ye die!

¶ **raise five** *Army.* (see quot.).

1980 Cragg *L. Militaris* 370: *Raise Five.* To salute.

¶ **slap** [or **give**] **five** to slap someone's palm or palms in greeting or congratulation.

1959 N.Y.C. high school student: Slap me five! Yeah, man! **1967** N.Y.C. high school student: Hey, man, slap me five! **1970** Cole *Street Kids* 150: The kids slapped five and laughed. **1972** *Tuesday Mag.* (May) 18: Who were the first to slap "five" after a home run in baseball? **1975** Univ. Tenn. student: "Slap me five on the white man's side"—the white man's side is the palm of your hand. It's pink. **1978** Selby *Requiem* 16: Gahd damn, give me five. Harry slapped the palms of Tyrones hands and Tyrone slapped Harrys. **1980** Kotzwinkle *Jack* 166: "Gimme five." He laid out his palm and Spider slapped him down. **1985** Bodey *F.N.G.* 122: Eltee Williams and Prophet slap a few fives.

¶ **slip** [or **give** or **lay**] **five** to shake hands.—usu. imper.
1918 in *AS* (Oct. 1933) 31: H'are yuh, buddy? Slip me five. **1926** Maines & Grant *Wise-Crack Dict.* 13: *Slip us five*—Request for a handshake. **1928** *AS* III (Feb.) 221: To shake hands. "Hello Herb! Slip me five!" **1935** in Paxton *Sport* 202: Put it there, doc....Give me five. I congratulate you, doggone it. **1959** L. Hughes *Simply Heavenly* 126: Gimme five, Miss Mamie, gimme five! **1967** *Look* (Nov. 14) 114: With "Gimme five" and "Way to go!" he incessantly congratulates and cheers teammates and friends. **1967** Ragni & Rado *Hair* 43: He put out his hand and said: "Lay me five, man, I'm free like a cockroach."

¶ **take five** see s.v. TAKE, *v.*

five-alarm chili *n. So.* chili that is very highly seasoned.
1986 *Daywatch* (CNN-TV) (Sept. 1): Five-alarm chili, I suppose.

five-and-dime *adj. Esp. Black E.* insignificant; NICKEL-AND-DIME.
1963 *Outer Limits* (ABC-TV): I'm not afraid of these five-and-dime Valentinoes down here. **1968** Heard *Howard St.* 176: His brother and a five-and-dime prostitute! **1971** in Sanchez *Word Sorcerers* 114: Cottontail wasn't no five and dime broad, her clothes and everything was the best. **1980** Folb *Runnin' Lines* 237: *Five and dime* 1. Small-time. 2. Not classy. **1988** *Right On!* (June) 45: He felt that any time you see a man wearing sneakers other than for...sports...or job-related activities, then he's a five and dime man.

five-by *adv. & adj. Radiocommunications.* FIVE-BY-FIVE, 2.a.
1971 Former SP2, U.S. Army [ref. to 1961–62]: *Five-by* is short for *five-by-five.* "I hear you five-by, Charlie." **1982** Astronaut Ken Mattingly, aboard Space Shuttle (June 28): I read you five-by. **1990** Rukuza *W. Coast Turnaround* 205: Ten-four, Gunnysack, got you five by.

five-by-five **1.** *adj. & n.* obese; an obese person. *Joc.*
1944 Busch *Dream of Home* 22: George Company had nicknamed him Five-by-Five because that was the way he was built. **1944** Kendall *Service Slang* 46: *Five by five*...overweight. **1947** *ATS* (Supp.) 1: *Five-by-five, Mr. Five-by-Five,* an obese person. **1953** Eyster *Customary Skies* 290 [ref. to WWII]: What is she, a Five-by-five?

2. *adv. & adj.* **a.** *Radiocommunications.* loud and clear, as over a radiocommunications system.
1954 E. Hunter *Blackboard Jungle* 33: "All right, testing, one-two-three-four, one-two-three-four."..."Five by five, Mr. Halloran!" **1959** Searls *Big X* 16: "Mitch, do you read me?" "Five by five, Colonel." **1956** Heflin *USAF Dict.* 205: Five-by-five, *a.* Of radio signals or reception: Loud and clear. *Colloq.* The expression "five-by-five" is derived from a scale set up for showing numerically the strength and clarity of radio reception. **1961** R. Davis *Marine at War* 92 [ref. to 1944]: I hear you five by five. **1968** W. Crawford *Gresham's War* 61 [ref. to 1953]: "You read me?" "Loud and clear, sir." "Five by five?" "Over and out." "Rodger dodger wilco." **1981** *Rod Serling's Mag.* (Sept.) 38: "Right waist loud and clear."..."You're alive and five by five."

b. *Mil.* perfect; fine.
1983 Eilert *Self & Country* 36: "I hope everything's all right." "Yeah, everything's five by five."

five-finger *n.* a thief.
1932 *AS* VII 401: *Five-finger, n.* A thief.

five-finger *v.* to pilfer.
1919 Johnson *Heaven, Hell or Hoboken* 40: Carlin "five-fingered" a "B" deck pass from the officers' mess-hall. Where there's a will there's a way!

five-finger discount *n.* **1.** an act of pilfering or petty thievery, esp. shoplifting; in phr. **put a five-finger discount on** to pilfer.
1966 in *OED2*: Five-finger discount (stealing) pays off. **1968–70** *Current Slang* III & IV 47: *Five-finger discount, n.* A theft.—College students...Kansas. **1970** Zindel *Your Mind* 24: She was simply disappointed in what the autopsy room had to offer in the way of five-finger discount. **1973** Eble *Campus Slang* (Nov.) 2: *Five-finger discount*—steal, shoplift: Someone put the five-finger discount on my I.D. **1974** *Nat. Lampoon* (Oct.) 73: Five-Fingered Discount Store. **1987** *Obara* (ABC-TV): What are we talkin' about—the five-finger discount? **1990** *Simpsons* (Fox-TV): "Where'd you get all that great stuff?" "Five-finger discount, man."

2. an article that has been obtained by shoplifting or pilfering.
1974 Eble *Campus Slang* (Mar.) 3: *Five-finger discount*—stolen: This shirt was a five-finger discount. **1976** Lieberman & Rhodes *CB* 128: *Five-Finger Discount*—Stolen merchandise.

five-finger-discount *v.* to shoplift; pilfer.
1986 Thacker *Pawn* 87: An empty commo-wire spool he had five-finger discounted from Bravo Company.

five-fingered Mary *n.* the hand as used by a man or boy in masturbation.—used derisively. Also vars.
1971 Altman & McKay *McCabe & Mrs. Miller* (film): Go home and play with...five-fingered Mary. *a*1972 B. Rodgers *Queens' Vernacular* 116: The masturbator's hand...*five-fingered Annie.* **1977** Dunne *Confessions* 102: I bet the only action he gets is from Five-Finger Mary. *a*1984 C. Adams *Straight Dope* 76: How is the sperm collected from the donor [at sperm banks]?...Meet Five-Fingers Mary, R.N.

five f's *n.pl.* see FOUR-F METHOD.

five-H man *n.* [see 1934 quot.] *Stu.* a conceited fellow.
1934 Weseen *Dict. Slang* 181: *Five H man*—Hell how he hates himself; a very conceited person. **1968** Baker et al. *CUSS* 117: *Five H man.* A person who does well academically.

Five-O *n.* [fr. *Hawaii Five-O,* CBS-TV police series, first broadcast Sept. 26, 1968] a police officer; the police.
1983 *N.Y. Times* (Aug. 29) B 2: A "Five-O" refers to a uniformed police officer. **1988** *Newsday* (N.Y.C.) (Feb. 10) 9: So I called the police and in no time Five-O was here. **1989** *Rolling Stone* (Oct. 19) 54: "Five-O" said "Freeze!" and I got numb. **1990** *Houston Post* (May 24) A3: *Five-o:* police. **1991** *Village Voice* (N.Y.C.) (July 23) 69: Shoving a 9-millimeter [pistol] in Five-O's face. **1993** *N.Y. Times* (Apr. 13) A 1: The Five-O caught me right here with the bundles of P [a type of heroin].

five o'clock follies *n.pl. Journ. in Vietnam.* a regular afternoon press briefing by the Joint United States Public Affairs Office, Saigon. Now *hist.*
1966 *Time* (June 10) 59: The daily military briefings, known as the 5 o'clock follies. **1966** Shepard *Doom Pussy* 94: The briefing more often than not disintegrates into a shouting match, especially when the military spokesman refuses to discuss a classified operation. The daily sessions soon were known as "The Five O'Clock Follies." **1969** L. Hughes *Under a Flare* 183: I'd heard the MACV briefing referred to as the "5 O'clock Follies," but I went with an open mind. **1970** Hammer *One Morning in the War* 7: In Saigon, at the "five o'clock follies," as the afternoon press briefing is called, the American Army spokesmen that Sunday gave out a few more details to questioning reporters. **1971** *CBS Reports* (CBS-TV) (Feb. 23): This scene is popularly known among newsmen as "the five o'clock follies." *a*1987 Bunch & Cole *Reckoning for Kings* 241: What batshit the Five O'Clock Follies is. **1994** *Newsweek* (Jan. 31) 50: Arnett's gritty combat reports constantly undercut the soothing messages delivered by military briefers at the "Five O'Clock Follies" in Saigon.

five-o'clock lightning *n. Baseball.* a late-inning rally in an afternoon game.
1962 Houk & Dexter *Ballplayers* 16: We weren't licked yet, not by a damn'-sight. The Babe's gang, Joe DiMaggio's, had pulled that 5 o'clock lightning stuff—why not us?

five of clubs *n.* the fist.
1947 *AS* (Apr.) 121: *Five of clubs.* One fist. **1983** K. Weaver *Texas Crude* 55: *The five of clubs*—The fist.

fiver *n.* **1.** a five-dollar bill; five dollars.
1843 *Spirit of Times* (Jan. 7) 536: But in "fivers" something was done. **1880** Pinkerton *Prof. Thieves & Detective* 492: The "fiver" will blind him to almost anything. **1882** Baillie-Grohman *Rockies* 94: We had ten minutes' higgling over the "fiver." **1884** *Life* (Feb. 21) 109: It costs a "fiver"...to get the letters done, sir. **1898** Fitch *Moth & Flame* 539: I'll bet a fiver you're not. **1898** Atherton *Californians* 39: If you've got a fiver...I'll call it square. **1901** Hobart *Down the Line* 19: Put a fiver on Pretty Boy. **1934** L. Hughes *Ways of White Folks* 55: When I did something extra, he'd throw me a fiver any time. **1972** Madden *Bros.* 12: They'd slip him a fiver, but never a job.

2. *Pris.* a five-year term of imprisonment.
1896 (cited in Partridge *Dict. Und.* 246). **1902** "J. Flynt" *Little Bro.* 147: Jack...had received "life."...Others had been given..."fivers" and "tenners."

3. *Narc.* a quantity of heroin costing five dollars.

1964–78 J. Carroll *B. Diaries* 25: I did half a fiver, and shit, what a rush.

five rules *n.pl.* the fists.—constr. with *the.*

1834 (quot. at MARROWBONE).

fives' court *n.* [sugg. by *bunch of fives* s.v. FIVE and related terms] *Boxing.* a boxing ring.—constr. with *the.*

1836 *Spirit of Times* (Feb. 20) 3: The "sporting" man was a frequenter of flash public houses...a noted *cove* at the fives'-Court,—a regular *better* at the billiard table.

five-specker *n.* FIVE-SPOT, 2.

1928 Callahan *Man's Grim Justice* 99: He'll let me off with about a "five specker." **1938** (cited in Partridge *Dict. Und.* 246).

five-spot *n.* **1.** Orig. *Gamb.* a five-dollar bill; five dollars.

1892 Norr *China Town* 63: Strike me blind, but it's a five-spot. An' I was starvin' a minute ago. **1903** McCardell *Cho. Girl* 42: Must have cost him a five spot. **1906** Kildare *Old Bailiwick* 81: There hasn't been a day in the last fifteen years when a "five-spot" wouldn't have been a good-sized fortune to me. **1913** Light *Hobo* 59: He was going to "rustle up" a five-spot. **1915** Lardner *Gullible's Travels* 8: One o' them aviators wouldn't take you more than half this height for a five-spot. **1918** "M. Brand" *Harrigan* 120: Here's a five-spot. **1925** Cobb *Many Laughs* 34: I asked you to loan me a tenner and this is only a five-spot. **1947** Motley *Knock on Any Door* 209: Butch gave him two bucks. Juan handed him a fivespot.

2. *Pris.* a five-year term of imprisonment.

1901 "J. Flynt" *World of Graft* 97: Bob Pinkerton copped me out, an' I got a five spot up in Connecticut. **1912** Lowrie *Prison* 281: The U.S. people would let me down with a five-spot. **1953** R. Chandler *Goodbye* 51: It rates up to a five-spot in Quentin. **1957** in J. Blake *Joint* 163: Trial February 19, at which time with some luck I'll get hit with a five spot. *a*1969 B. Jackson *Thief's Primer* 57: *Five-spot:* five-year sentence.

five-square *adj. & adv.* [sugg. by FIVE-BY-FIVE] *USAF.* loud and clear.

1956 in Harvey *Air Force* 67: Read you five square. **1965** Harvey *Hudasky's Raiders* 217: Read you five square. **1966** B. Cassiday *Angels Ten* 34 [ref. to WWII]: "Do you read me, DeForrest?" "Five square, Rand." **1968** W.C. Anderson *Gooney Bird* 141: Reading you five square. How me? **1980** W.C. Anderson *Bat-21* 10 [ref. to 1972]: "How do you read on Baker?" "Five square, Bat." **1985** Heywood *Taxi Dancer* 92 [ref. to Vietnam War]: "How read?" "Five-square, Corey."

fix *n.* **1.a.** *Sports.* a contest having an illicitly prearranged outcome.

1898 *Sat. Eve. Post* (July 30) 70: As I said before, it was as clear a case of "fix" as if she had given [the runner] a drug. **1947** Schulberg *Harder They Fall* 246: A fight fix. **1949** Cummings *Dict. Sports* 144. **1955** Graziano & Barber *Somebody Up There* 320: I guess they want me to make their skin crawl with inside scandal about...every fight being a fix. **1971** Torres *Sting Like a Bee* 161 [ref. to 1965]: That's right...it was a fix.

b. *Und.* the amount needed to secure bribed cooperation.

1946 Dadswell *Hey, Sucker* 38: Yet if the "fix" is high the concessionaires are forced to make the public pay the bill. **1970** A. Lewis *Carnival* 277: The "fix" to keep the girl shows in operation was a thousand dollars a day.

c. *Und. & Police.* an illicit agreement arranged esp. through payment of a bribe.

1958 S.H. Adams *Tenderloin* 27: Enormously prosperous in their practice of fixes, blackmail, and extortion. **1983** WKGN Radio News (Apr. 13): Their attorneys also hinted that the fix was in to give the contracts to their competitors.

2. *Und.* FIXER, 1.

1930 Conwell *Professional Thief* 25: Some get in bad with the fix and can no longer get protection and are therefore useless as members of a mob. **1936** in D. Runyon *More Guys* 161: The stout fellow [is] the local fix. **1937** Reitman *Box-Car Bertha* 108: We were to meet Miller, the "fix." **1951** Algren *Chicago* 79: Who's the fix on this corner? **1952** H. Grey *Hoods* 276: The "Fix" grinned. **1968** "H. King" *Box-Man* 22: My attorney was a fix in Portland.

3.a. *Narc.* FIX-UP, 2.

1936 Dai *Opium Add.* 199: To use drugs...*to take a shot, a pop, a prod, a fix,* or *to get one's yen off.* **1938** *AS* XIII 184: *Fix...*a ration of narcotics, especially one to be injected. **1952** J.C. Holmes *Go* 7: How about a fix! How about a fix, man! **1953** W. Brown *Monkey on My Back* 128: He begged and wept and screamed for "a fix." **1955** Q. Reynolds *HQ* 276: They even had spikes in case anyone needed a fix with a speedball. **1956** E. Hunter *Second Ending* 27: Hey, Andy, how about a fix? *Ibid.* 42: A fix...Oh, God, how I want a fix! **1959** Tevis *Hustler* 44: And you get

yourself a fix with the change. **1960** R. Reisner *Jazz Titans* 155: *Fix:* a shot of heroin or any other potent drug. **1970** Southern *Blue Movie* 224: He was more than half an hour into his fix. **1977** Lyon *Tenderness* 20: A junkie seeks one fix after another. **1977** T. Berger *Villanova* 95: I'm dying for a fix...an injection. **1985** D. Steel *Secrets* 43: Expecting to see Sandy nodding out after a fix. **1990** C.P. McDonald *Blue Truth* 9: He'll be screamin' for a fix in a couple of hours.

b. a compulsively sought dose or infusion of something; a thrill.

1959 on *Golden Age of TV* (A&E-TV, 1988): All night he's been getting a fix on that kooky chick. **1960** in T.C. Bambara *Gorilla* 47: I'll be here tomorrow for my early morning coffee fix. **1970** Della Femina *Wonderful Folks* 57: God knows how many people on Madison Avenue go to the shrinks....You see everybody zipping out on Wednesday afternoon, two to three, for a fix. **1978** Hasford *Short-Timers* 179: We look forward to...a fix of Coke. **1982** *N.Y. Times Bk. Review* (Jan. 3) 3: The media addict needs his fix, and what better way to guarantee coverage on the evening news than to kidnap Patricia Hearst? **1983** *Newsweek on Campus* (Dec.) 5: Glamour?...I get my fix. I get plenty. **1990** *Nat. Geographic: On Assignment* (ABC-TV): [Diving] gives me a satisfaction I can't describe to anybody. I get a fix down there.

¶ In phrases:

¶ **give (someone) the fix** to cause the defeat or ruin of; do for.

1966–67 W. Stevens *Gunner* 48 [ref. to WWII]: Those FWs really gave us the fix, though.

¶ **on the fix** *Und.* engaged in accepting bribes.

1971 Contini *Beast Within* 84: Men who had police and judges and congressmen and senators in their pocket, "on the fix."

fix *v.* **1.** *Pol. & Und.* to secure the cooperation of (someone) through the payment of a bribe.

1790 in *DA*: It is expected of us that we should fix the Governor of Pennsylvania. **1872** Burnham *Secret Service* 72: When Biebusch saw *this* man in Court, whom he fancied he had "fixed" for certain, the criminal wilted. **1872** Crapsey *Nether Side* 58: He had "fixed" the clerk at the lace shawl counter. **1890** Quinn *Fools of Fortune* 353: We found it convenient to have recourse to the scales of a Junk dealer who had been previously "fixed" for the occasion. **1902** Hapgood *Thief* 81 [ref. to *ca*1885]: The reliable attorney got a bondsman, and two friends of his "fixed" the cops, who made no complaints. **1906** Buffum *Bear City* 244: So expert had he become in "fixing juries." **1915** Poole *Harbor* 104: Our agent will be there ahead, he'll have found a customhouse man he can fix. **1921** Conklin & Root *Circus* 167 [ref. to *ca*1880]: The town was said to be "fixed" or "safe." If it was not possible to "fix" a town the gamblers and fakers usually "took a chance," perhaps being a little more cautious and careful and on the alert for trouble. **1923** Ornitz *Haunch* 56: How to "fix" (bribe) cops and judges. **1925** Faulkner *N.O. Sketches* 198: A hayseed cop that hadn't been fixed held 'em up. **1928** Burnett *Little Caesar* 72: The Federal men were dumber and harder to fix. **1951** Pryor *The Big Play* 351: Sterling stated unequivocally that Transworld had succeeded in "fixing" him. **1976** in Earp *Wyatt Earp* 126: They even had the telegraph operator "fixed" so no one could warn Ferguson. **1979** in Terkel *Amer. Dreams* 250: They set up a store, fixed a guy in Western Union.

2.a. to alter or tamper with for a dishonest purpose.

1865 in *DA*: These cards are not in the same condition as cards which are usually used in the game of faro; they are sandpapered, as it is termed, or fixed for cheating. **1880** in Partridge *Dict. Und.* 247: A horse...is fixed when...put in such a condition he cannot win—lamed, poisoned, given a pail of water before running. **1881** in *DAE*: It is true they talk of "fixing" a horse, but they also use "nobbling" in the same sense. **1886** in Tamony *Americanisms* (No. 29) 5: There are always willing tools, who will take any chance to "fix" a horse if the reward is sufficient...Lord Jersey's Middleton was "got at" as long ago as 1825, his lad being bribed to give him a pail of water. **1889** Barrère & Leland *Dict. Slang* I 365: *Fix the ballot-box, to* (American), to tamper with the returns of an election. **1901** in *DA*: "Fixed" roulette wheels,...loaded dice and marked cards.

b. to arrange the outcome of (a contest, election, or sporting event) by secret, dishonest, or unlawful means; rig. Now *colloq.*

1880 *N.Y. Clipper Almanac* 44: *Fixed.*—A race which is decided, before coming off, to go a certain way, is said to have been "fixed." **1889** in *DA*: Where the "boss" and the fixer of elections are unknown. **1958** J. King *Pro Football* 17: An attempt to "fix" the 1946 championship game was involved.

3.a. *Narc.* to inject oneself with a narcotic; take narcotics by injection; (*trans.*) to inject oneself with (a narcotic).

1936 Dai *Opium Add.* 199: *Fix.* To use drugs. **1938** in *OEDS.* **1959** Trocchi *Cain's Book* 25: We had fixed over an hour ago. We had used all the heroin. **1964** *N.Y. Times* (Oct. 18) 6 130: He was fixing five and six times a day. **1972** Wambaugh *Blue Knight* 35: Then I went and fixed the second day out. **1973** Childress *Hero* 36: A junkie nods on and off and lets you alone when he's fixed. *a***1979** Pepper & Pepper *Straight Life* 360: We fixed the methedrine. **1979** Alibrandi *Custody* 218: I don't want to fix. **1967–80** Folb *Runnin' Lines* 237: *Fix.* Inject (a drug).

b. *Narc.* to provide with an injection of a narcotic.

1951 in *AS* (Feb. 1952) 25: *Fix me*…Sell me some drugs or give me a shot of drug. **1952** Mandel *Angry Strangers* 254: *Fix me*, Dinsh! Gimme a fi-fix! **1974–77** A. Hoffman *Property Of* 113: I know you got dope with you, fix me once and I'm gone for good.

¶ In phrases:

¶ **anyhow you can fix it** no matter how you look at it. Also vars.

1835 *Mil. & Nav. Mag. of U.S.* (Nov.) 190: But poor Tom was a gone horse, any how you can fix it. **1835** in M.W. Hill *Sisters' Keepers* 262: My language fails me, I can't draw any comparison, no how you can fix it. **1836** in *DA.* **1843** [W.T. Thompson] *Scenes in Ga.* 23: This child aint to be beat, no how you can fix it!

¶ **fix (someone's) flint** to settle matters with (someone); do for.

1833 Ames *Old Sailor's Yarns* 298: We'll fix his flint for him before the cook's dinner is ready. **1837** in *DAE*: I thought I had fixed your flint yesterday. **1838** [Haliburton] *Clockmaker* (Ser. 2) 22: But the moment he marries he's up a tree; his flint is fixed then. **1841** Mercier *Man-of-War* 82: I'll fix your flint for you to your heart's content; I'll now put you from troubling me again this blessed night. **1843** Oliver *Illinois* 70: If the hunt is possessed of a rifle, poor cooney soon has his *flint fixt.* **1846** Griffin *Dr. Comes to Calif.* 46: The devils got around me and like to have fixed my flint. **1848** Ruxton *Life in Far West* 12: Some em got their flints fixed this side of Pawnee Fork, and a heap of mule-meat went wolfing. **1856** in *DAE*: That turkey roosted on my stomach and gobbled in my ear every night. At last, though, I fixed his flint for him. **1870** in *DAE.* **1958** S.H. Adams *Tenderloin* 215: Holy-boly's night with the gals sure fixed his flint with her.

¶ **get fixed** to engage in copulation.

1948 I. Shulman *Cry Tough!* 4: The first thing he'd have to do would be to get fixed. A real party with a babe who wasn't a slut. **1956** I. Shulman *Good Deeds* 100: Wanna get fixed?

fixed *adj.* armed.

1871 "M. Twain" *Roughing It* 55: He did it with the full understanding that he might have to enforce it with a navy six-shooter, and so he always went "fixed" to make things go along smoothly.

fixed bayonets *n.pl. Mil.* strong liquor.

1918 Griffin *Ballads of the Reg't.* 34: Yet he'd drink a few "Fixed By'nets" with the gang when off on pass. **1925** Fraser & Gibbons *Soldier & Sailor Words* 94: *Fixed bayonets*: An old Army name for a brand of Bermuda rum, the effects of which were often disastrous, if not deadly. *****1936** Partridge *DSUE* 280: *Fixed bayonets*…But among prisoners of war in Germany in 1914-18 it was applied to a spirit made of potatoes and apt to render one "fighting drunk."

fixer *n.* **1.** *Und.* a go-between who arranges or adjusts matters, esp. the payment of bribes for cooperation or protection; (*also*) a lawyer employed by a traveling show.

1900 "Flynt" & Walton *Powers* 64: Do you know what fixers are travelin'? **1909** Irwin *Con Man* 52: At the head of the outfit stood the "fixer", whose job it was to bribe or stall city officials so that the gamblers could proceed with reasonable security. **1914** Jackson & Hellyer *Vocab.* 33: *Fixer*,…one who acts as go-between for thieves and bribe takers…"If you get a rumble, send for Jones, the mouthpiece; he's a sure-shot fixer and can square anything short of murder." **1921** Conklin & Root *Circus* 166 [ref. to *ca*1880]: A man known as "the fixer," an employee of the show, traveled with it, and upon the skill with which he did his work depended…the…success of the crooked gentry. **1921** Woolston *Prostitution* I 85: They had three girls, Mersky acting as "fixer," or "go-between," when trouble threatened from the police. **1922** *Variety* (Aug. 18) 8: A high-salaried "fixer," known as a legal adjustor, is carried. No expense is spared to bribe local officials. **1925** Robinson *Wagon Show* 26: "Oh," responded the "fixer," who was quick-witted and saw an opening under the sheriff's cuticle. **1927** Tully *Circus Parade* 31: He was considered one of the best "fixers" in the business. **1930** *Variety* (Jan. 8) 123: Pretty soon the fixer comes down [to the jail]

and gives me the office not to open my kisser, to stand pat, that everything's set. **1930** Conwell *Pro. Thief* 7: Jake got in the can in Chicago, where he was a stranger and was broke. Eddie heard of it and approached a person who knew the fixer and asked him to find out how much it would cost to get Jake out. *a***1969** B. Jackson *Thief's Primer* 123: Lawyers, Fixers, and the Police. **1971** J. Brown & A. Groff *Monkey* 38: I could not get far by employing an ordinary lawyer. What I had was a "fixer." **1988** *N.Y. Post* (June 6) 22: Feds eye Hollywood big as union "fixer"…to determine whether he and his associates have been coercing production companies into hiring them to guarantee labor peace.

2. *Police.* a fixed post.

1985 Baker *Cops* 61: The embassy precinct…is known for a lot of…fixers. Fixers are embassies and such that they assign a cop to stand in front of…I got a fixer on Fifth Avenue.

3. *Narc.* (see quot.).

1987 *RHD2*: *Fixer*…*Slang.* a person who sells narcotics to addicts.

fixings *n.pl.* sexual intercourse.

1932 V. Nelson *Prison Days & Nights* 38: A guy can't live without 'em [women]. Not when he's had to go without his fixings for years, like we have.

fix-up *n.* **1.** an alcoholic drink.

1867 W.H. Dixon *New Amer.* I 191: Eye-opener, fix-ups, or any other Yankee deception in the shape of liquor.

2. *Narc.* an injection, as of heroin or morphine, as taken by an addict; a dose sufficient for an injection.

1934 in *OEDS*: A shot is a geezer,…or fix-up. **1935** Pollock *Und. Speaks: Fix-up*, injection of dope. **1936** *AS* (Apr.) 121: *Fix-up.* A ration of dope from a hypodermic.

fix up *v.* **1.** to furnish with an escort or date. Now *colloq.*

1930 Farrell *Calico Shoes* 167: Come on, kid. I'll fix you up. **1940** *Accent* (Autumn) 33: "How was she, Speedy?"…"Okay, okay! Want me to fix you up?" **1942** in *Best from Yank* 104: He knoweth many women….He promiseth to fix thee up, but doth *it* not. **1946** Gresham *Nightmare Alley* 9: Any of you girls would like to date him after the show, see me and I'll fix ya up. **1957** H. Danforth & J. Horan *D.A.'s Man* 206 [ref. to 1940]: Did you fix up my friend? **1970** Della Femina *Wonderful Folks* 61: This guy knew how to get anybody in town fixed up….Blondes, brunettes or redheads, he has them. **1984** C. Guisewite *Cathy* (synd. cartoon strip) (Nov. 13): Why won't you suggest a friend to fix Charlene up with, Irving?

2. *Narc.* FIX, *v.*, 3.

1931 B. Niles *Strange Bro.* 277: Won't you fix me up? I'm sick. **1958–59** Lipton *Barbarians* 180: Rock finally got something from some girl and both of them fixed up. **1963** Williamson *Hustler!* 67: Then they fixed up*. I found out later it was heroin…*Took dope.

fizog var. PHIZOG.

fizz *n.* **1.** sparkling wine. Also vars.

*****1864** in *F & H* II 405: We…ordered some fizz,/With a devilled turkey bone. **1870** *Comic Songster* 30: A bottle of "Phizz" is all my eye,/Bring me a dozen or two. *****1873** Hotten *Slang Dict.* (ed. 4) 163: *Fiz*, champagne, any sparkling wine. **1883** in Ware *Passing Eng.* 132: Pat Feeney has sworn off fiz, and will never touch a drop for the rest of his life. **1889** Barrère & Leland *Dict. Slang* I 365: *Fiz* (common), champagne. **1905** Sinclair *Jungle* 278: We'll…have some fizz, an' we'll raise hell. **1907** *Army & Navy Life* (Dec.) 762: Drinking "fizz" and eating lobster. **1909** in "O. Henry" *Works* 1021: Let's all go down and open a bottle of fizz on the Finance Committee. **1931** in Spectorsky *College Years* 72: This was *Schaumwein* (champagne) country, with the "fizz" at seventy-five cents the bottle. **1953** Eyster *Skies* 49: You know, fizz, a snazzy band, a dame that can dress. **1958** S.H. Adams *Tenderloin* 111: A bottle of fizz…would cost a St. Louis man a ten-spot.

2. FIZZLE, 2.a.

1941 in B.O. Davis, Jr. *Davis* 79: And if he's still the way he was last year or just a fizz. *a***1986** in *NDAS*: "It was a big fizz," the ambassador said.

3. *Surfing.* sea foam.

1977 Filosa *Surf. Almanac* 198.

fizzle *n.* [see the v.] **1.** *Stu.* a poor recitation.

1846 *Yale Banger* (Nov. 10): The best judges have decided, that to get just one third of the meaning right constitutes a perfect fizzle. **1849** in *F & H* II 406: Here he could *fizzles* mark, without a sigh,/And see orations unregarded die. **1850** *Yale Lit. Mag.* XV 114: Cloudy reminiscences of a morning "fizzle" and an afternoon "flunk." **1851** B. Hall *College Wds.* 130: *Fizzle*…In many colleges in the United States, this word is applied to a bad recitation. **1860** in Thornton *Amer. Gloss.*: Some cue that will enable colloquy men to save an inglorious fizzle. **1871** Bagg *Yale* 44: *Fizzle*, a partial failure on recitation. *Flunk*, an entire failure. Both these words are also used as verbs.

2.a. a failure, fiasco, or abortive effort; FLOP. Now *colloq.*

1850 P. Decker *Diaries* 219: The affair was a "fizzle." **1851** in Schele de Vere *Amer.* 197: The speech was as complete a fizzle as has ever disgraced Congress. **1862** in *Civil War Times Illus.* (Jan. 1973) 14: Proved to be a "fizzle." **1863** in *DAE*: On his return from his diplomatic fizzle. **1864** in W. Wilkinson *Mother* 307: Our last "raid" or as we call it "fizzle." **1871** Schele de Vere *Amer.* 197: *Fizzle*...any ridiculous failure after a great effort. ***1883** in *F & H* II 406: What promised at first to be a magnificent Parliamentary "row" ended in a mere unsensational fizzle. **1898** *Story of a Strange Career* 328: That expedition was probably the worst "fizzle" of the whole war. **1902, 1907** in *DAE*. *a*1909 in Ware *Passing Eng.* 132: It is a foolish...story of love, intrigue and politics. It was little better than a fizzle. **1954** Overholser *Violent Land* 38: Some fellow...tried raising the stuff and had a fizzle.

b. a failing student (*obs.*); (*hence*) a person who is a failure.

1849 in *DAE*: Not a wail was heard, or a "fizzle" [*sic*] mild sigh,/As his corps o'er the pavement we hurried. **1896** in *DAE*: Put the lazy fizzle who can't pay his debts on an altar. **1910** in *DAE*: I am by nature a sort of fizzle.

c. a withdrawal or reneging.

1868 J.R. Browne *Apache Country* 385: I...personally had no objection to the fizzle.

fizzle *v.* [fr. earlier colloq. sense 'to break wind quietly'] **1.a.** *Stu.* to make a poor, esp. a minimally acceptable, response or recitation.

1847 *Yale Banger* (Oct. 22): My dignity is outraged at beholding those who fizzle and flunk in my presence tower[ing] above me. **1849** *Yale Lit. Mag.* XIV 144: *Fizzle*. To rise with modest reluctance, to hesitate often, to decline finally; generally, to misunderstand the question. **1854** in B. Hall *College Wds.* (ed. 2) 203: I "skinned," and "fizzled" through...Fizzling is a somewhat *free* translation of an intricate sentence [or] proving a proposition in geometry from a wrong figure. **1856** B. Hall *College Wds.* (ed. 2) 203: A correspondent from Williams College says: "Flunk is the common word when some unfortunate man makes an utter failure in recitation. He *fizzles* when he stumbles through at last."

b. *Stu.* to cause to make a FIZZLE.

1848 *Yale Lit. Mag.* XIII 321: Fizzle him tenderly,/Bore him with care/ Fitted so tenderly,/Tutor beware. **1851** B. Hall *College Wds.* 131: *Fizzle*...to cause one to fail in reciting. Said of an instructor.

2.a. to fail; come to nothing.—also constr. with *out*. Now *S.E.*

*a*1848 in Bartlett *Amer.*: The factious and revolutionary action of the fifteen has...disgraced the actors, and fizzled out! **1854** in Thornton *Amer. Gloss.*: The Stellacoom gold excitement has entirely fizzled out. **1859** Matsell *Vocab.* 32: *Fizzled*. Broke up; fell through. **1866** in Schele de Vere *Amer.* 197: The enterprise fizzled out in the most contemptible manner. **1884** in *OED*: Another of Mr. Mirams' pet fads has fizzled ignominiously. **1909** Irwin *Con Man* 37: We fizzled out because neither of us knew how to handle boosters. **1985** Ferraro & Francke *Ferraro* 87: A reporter...was disappointed the ERA flap had fizzled.

b. to cause to fail; foil.—constr. with *out*.

1855 in *DAE*: Oh, she was a most a beautiful cook, but she was fizzled out by bad cookery at de last.

c. to withdraw or renege; fail to appear.

1868 J.R. Browne *Apache Country* 385: Guess they ain't eager for [a fight]. Likely as not they'll fizzle.

fizzle-out *n.* FIZZLE, 2.a.

1861 Norton *Army Letters* 23: The Erie Regiment is one grand fizzle out. **1958** in *OEDS*: A Suez-type fizzle-out.

fizz water *n.* sparkling wine.

1902–03 Ade *People You Know* 210: He wanted her to take some of the Phizz Water. **1925** Van Vechten *Nigger Heaven* 32: Well, boys, just in time for a little fizz-water. **1925** in Charters & Kunstadt *Jazz* 149: Possibly aggravated by a magnum of fizz water. **1928** Wharton *Squad* 4: An' fizz-water costs only five francs a bottle over at d'estaminet.

fizzy *n.* sparkling wine.

*1896 R. Kipling, in *OEDS*: The Captain stood a limberful of fizzy—Somethin' Brutt. **1921** Dos Passos *Three Soldiers* 75: Come over and have a drink. We're going to have some fizzy. ***1970** in *OEDS*.

flabbergast *v.* [orig. unkn.; perh. *flabby* + *aghast*] to overcome

with surprise or bewilderment; astound. Now *S.E.*

*1772 in *OED*: Now we are *flabbergasted* and *bored* from morning to night. ***1785** Grose *Vulgar Tongue*: Flabagasted. Confounded. ***1801** in *OED*: They quite flabbergasted me. ***1823** "J. Bee" *Slang* 79: His colleagues were *flabbergasted* when they heard of Castlereagh's sudden death. ***1837** in *F & H* III 1: He was quite flabbergasted to see the amount. ***1864** in *F & H*: You're sort of *flabbergasted*. It's taken all the wind out of you like, and you feel like an old screw a blowing up Highgate Hill. ***a1889** in Barrère & Leland *Slang Dict.* I 366: The magistrate...seems to have been completely *flabbergasted* and paralysed with astonishment. **1895** *Harper's* (June) 157: I'm so flabbergasted by all that's happened this afternoon, mum, that I can't get my thoughts straight, mum. **1905** *DN* III 61: *Flabbergasted, adj.* Paralyzed, overwhelmed. "He was *flabbergasted* at the news." ***1909** Ware *Passing Eng.* 132: *Flabbergast*...To astound. Rejected of most lexicographers, but accepted of all men...."The goings on of Cock-eyed Sal flabbergasted him much." **1922** in Fitzgerald *Corres.* 114: Caddy telling flabbergasted caddy-master that he won't ever caddy again. **1930** *AS* V (Feb.) 219: Another example showing the name of the agent is *flabbergaster*. I read...of an American in Mexico who...arranged a "*flabbergaster of a funeral.*" **1972** B. Harrison *Hospital* 417: I'm flabbergasted. **1978** De Christoforo *Grease* 216: We stood there flabbergasted, completely at a loss for words. **1984** Jackson & Lupica *Reggie* 163: I was stunned, flabbergasted. **1985** Baker *Cops* 237: I'm sitting there flabbergasted. He just picked her up at random on the sidewalk.

flab out *v.* to get flabby or fat.

1980 Lorenz *Guys Like Us* 24: A lot of the guys...started flabbing out a few years ago.

flack *n.* [see 1939 quot.; the Yiddish word referred to is unkn.; the closest words available are unlikely on various grounds] *Entertainment Industry.* a press agent; public-relations specialist.

1939 *Better English* (June) 28: That alert weekly, *Variety*..., is trying to coin the word "flack" as a synonym for publicity agent. The word is said to be derived from Gene Flack, a movie publicity agent....A Yiddish word similar in sound means "one who goes around talking about the other fellow's business." **1942** *Down Beat* (Feb. 15) 2 (Tamony Coll.): [The] Metro-Goldwyn-Mayer studios where the flacks (publicity men to you) are particularly sharp. **1950** *Sat. Eve. Post* (Apr. 1) 26: My friend, the movie-studio flack, came back from hoofing it through the jungle of sound stages. **1955** *Time* (Sept. 26) 45: [She] was chaperoned into Manhattan by movie flacks. **1958** in Cannon *Nobody Asks* 363: He calls press agents flacks and show business is always show biz. **1967** Dibner *Admiral* 336: He's a stinker, but he's the smartest flack on the Strip. **1969** *Playboy* (Mar.) 23: Our coveted Press Agent of the Month Award goes to the New York flack who penned the following. **1970** Grissim *Country Music* 106: His flack man would have you believe he's still just a nice kid from Delight, Arkansas...which is true. **1970** *N.Y. Times* (Mar. 22) 24: Twenty-five years ago, the Warners flacks thought up her professional name, but she is still Betty Perske of the Bronx to anybody who has known her more than an hour. **1973** Haney *Jock* 99: Hired flacks could kill a person's past and create a new one overnight.

flack *v.* **1.** *Journ.* to act as a press agent.

1963 *Maclean's* (July 27) 27 (Tamony Coll.): Maney no longer flacks for Cohen, and therefore is not bound to compose compliments. **1970** *Time* (June 15) 40: His wife was hired to flack for Martha Mitchell. **1978** B. Johnson *What's Happenin'* 250: I'm not here to flack for you.

2. to publicize aggressively; PLUG; (*intrans.*) to provide publicity.

1963 *Time* (Sept. 13) 72: They...flack for their own drawings. **1976** *Penthouse* (Nov.) 116: There was Mr. Agnew...flacking his new book. **1977** Langone *Life at Bottom* 37: A representative from the NSF press office who is really flacking hard. **1980** *N.Y. Daily News* (Manhattan) (Sept. 10) 6: The house appears to have solved the problem in pre-publication ads that flacked "No Hard Feelings" as the male answer to "Fear of Flying." **1990** G. Trudeau *Doonesbury* (synd. comic strip) (Oct. 4): Mike would *never* compromise himself to flack for an oil company!

flack artist *n.* a press agent.

1959 Ellison *Gentleman Junkie* 211: Hey, flack-artist!

flack out *v.* FLAKE OUT.

1967 *DAS* (Supp.) 684: *Flack out*...To fall asleep; to become unconscious...To be tired or despondent...To die. *Orig. cool and beat use.* **1968–70** *Current Slang* III & IV 47: *Flack out, v.* To break a date.—College students, both sexes, California. **1974** Chicago man, age *ca*33: You had to flack out on a steel-and-concrete ledge.

fladge *n.* Orig. *Prost.* sadomasochistic flagellation.—often attrib.

> *1948 Partridge *DSUE* (ed. 3) 1048: *Fladge fiend.* A masochist: low: from *ca*1920. *ca*1972 B. Rodgers *Queens' Vernacular* 184: *Fladge fiend* (*freak, queen*) one who enjoys whipping or being whipped. *Fladge party* sadomasochistic romance. *1982 Partridge *DSUE* (ed. 8) 399: "Got any fladge, guv?"—have you any works in which the emphasis is on flagellation?

Flag *n.* *S.W.* Flagstaff, Ariz.

> **1928** W.H. Dixon *West. Hoboes* 235: We reported the incident at "Flag." **1981** Crowe *Fast Times* 234: "We're from Flag." "What's Flag?" "Flagstaff, Arizona!"

flag *n.* **1.** *Whaling.* the blood spouted by a wounded whale.

> **1839** *Knickerbocker* (May) 389: "There's the flag!" I exclaimed; "there! thick as tar!"

2. *pl.* a flagman; (*Navy*) a signalman quartermaster.

> **1891** Munroe *Campmates* 77: Rodman, front and back flagmen or "flags," chainmen, and axemen. **1941** Kendall *Army & Navy Sl.* 19: *Flags*...the signal quartermaster.

3. Esp. *Und.* an assumed name; alias.

> **1930** Irwin *Tramp. & Und. Slang* s.v. *carry: Carrying a flag.* Travelling under an assumed name or with an alias. **1933** Ersine *Prison Slang* 37: *Flag, n.* An alias. **1940** *R.R. Mag.* (Apr.) 44: *Flag*—Assumed name. Many a *boomer* worked *under a flag* when his own name was blacklisted. **1945** Hubbard *R.R. Ave.* 182: Countless numbers of men...deciding it was impossible to get a rail job any other way, elected to work "under a flag," that is, using an assumed name. **1954** Collans & Sterling *House Detect.* 220: *Under a flag.* Using a phony name, an alias.

4. a dollar or five-dollar bill.

> **1930** Huston *Frankie & Johnny* 47: One flag an' six singles—an' the rest is silver. **1944** in Himes *Black on Black* 197: He keep right on an' pick 'nother ton. Make forty flags.

5. *Stu.* a grade of F.

> **1958** J. Davis *College Vocab.* 12: *Flag day*—Day when one receives an F on a paper or test. **1968** Baker et al. *CUSS* 117: *Flag.* The grade "F." **1974** Miami Univ. student [ref. to 1969]: We said [in high school] "He got the flag," he flunked. **1983** Univ. Tenn. grad. student: He used to ask such good questions in class I almost hated to give him that flag.

6. a cigarette; FAG.

> **1964** in B. Jackson *Swim Like Me* 83: I slips him a tailor-made flag (cigarette).

7. an erection of the penis. Cf. FLAGPOLE.

> **1966** C. Cooper *The Farm* 211: I saw she wasn't wearing panties, in expectation. I grew a flag.

¶ In phrases:

¶ **fly a flag, 1.** see *the flag is up*, below.

2. *Stu.* (see quot.).

> **1969** *Current Slang* I & II 35: *Fly a flag*, v. To fail a test or a course.—College males, South Dakota.—"I'm flying a flag in Lit."

¶ **hunt a flag** *Army.* to enlist.

> **1918** Griffin *Ballad of the Reg't* 35 [ref. to early 1900's]: I'll "hunt a flag" tomorrow sure—I'm "taking on again."

¶ **the flag is up** one is menstruating. Also vars.

> *1889 Barrère & Leland *Dict. Slang* I 366: "The *flag's up*" refers to menses. *a1890–93 F & H III 2: *The flag...is up*...the menstrual flux is on. **1916** Cary *Venery* I 85: *Flag flying*—The menstrual period....*Flag Up*—The menstrual period. *Ibid.* 92: *Flying the flag*...the menstrual period. **1931** Farrell *Guillotine Party* 88: "The flag's out," Nettie said. "You wouldn't kid me, would you?" said Hennessey knowingly. **1934** H. Miller *Tropic of Cancer* 6: When the flag waved, it was red all the way back to the throat. **1937** Weidman *I Can Get It For You Wholesale* 216: The first time I figured, all right, maybe the flag was up. But I'd seen her every night for almost a month. So *that* was out, too. **1938** "Justinian" *Amer. Sexualis* 22: *Fly the flag*...to be in the menstrual period. **1968** Baker et al. *CUSS* 119: *Fly the red flag.* Be menstruating. **1972** N.Y.U. student: *Flying the flag* or *the red flag* is what guys say sometimes when a girl is on her period. It means *on the rag.* **1973** *AS* XLVI 82: The flag is out. **1987** G. Matthews *Little Red Rooster* 225: She's got the flag flying.

flag *v.* **1.** [sugg. by S.E. (formerly colloq.) *flag* 'to catch the attention of, as by waving; hail'] to extend a spoken or unspoken invitation to or strike up an acquaintance with in hopes of initiating a romantic or sexual relationship; accost.

> **1896** Ade *Artie* 81: She didn't want you to think that any Reub could go up and flag her. **1903** Townsend *Sure* 4: Some of de goils...passed

me out a glad eye...but I taut dey was flagging a mug in de next county. **1927** *DN* V 446: *Flag*...To accost a prostitute. **1941** G. Legman, in Henry *Sex Var.* II 1165: *Flag.* To signal, usually with the eyes or with a gesture of the head, to encourage a stranger to speak to one, usually with a homosexual (or heterosexual) intent. **1962** Regan & Finston *Toughest Pris.* 799: *Flag*—To accost. **1967** deCoy *Nigger Bible* 30: *Cruising, v.*—The practice of extending overt or subtle invitation for intimacy with a member of the opposite or same sex....Syn: flagging, making, hitting.

2.a. to allow (a person) to pass unnoticed or unmolested; release; (*hence*) to give the go-by; avoid; (*also*) to refuse service to; bar; send packing.

> **1899** "J. Flynt" *Tramping* 386: "Flagged"...has been taken from the railroader's parlance. It is used a great deal by pickpockets, and means that they have allowed a certain person whom they intended to victimize to go unmolested. It comes from the flagging of a train, which can be either stopped or made to go on by the waving of a flag. The person "flagged" seldom knows what has taken place. **1906** *Nat. Police Gaz.* (Jan. 27) 6: "I think I'll go over and have a little conversation with her." "A hundred even that she flags you."..."On." **1906** H. Green *Boarding House* 108: I had to flag him!...I told 'em to beat it. **1906** *Nat. Police Gaz.* (Sept. 22) 6: I'd like to flag that stoneyard gang, but I guess that's where I'll get the shove. **1927** *DN* V 446: *Flag*...To allow, as of pickpockets, a prospect to pass untouched. **1929** *AS* IV (June) 340: *Flagged*—Refused, turned away. *ca*1950 in Maurer *Lang. Und.* 185: To *flag*...To bar a player from a game or establishment. **1983** P. Dexter *God's Pocket* 58: Eleanore, I'm throwing your drink out and flaggin' you for the rest of the week. **1983** M.J. Bell *Brown's Lounge* 97 [ref. to 1973]: The patron was flagged. *Flagging* was the refusal by the barmaid to continue serving the patron and a request that the patron withdraw.

b. to abstain from; keep away from.

> **1900** *DN* II 35: *Flag*...To "cut" a recitation. **1906** *Nat. Police Gaz.* (Jan. 27) 6: Ponies, hey? Better flag 'em, son....Bookmakers are the only people who get anything out of that game.

3. to identify; PEG.

> **1906** *Nat. Police Gaz.* (Apr. 28) 3: You had me flagged for Sis Hopkins.

4. *Und.* to apprehend (a suspect).—also constr. with *down.*

> **1927** *DN* V 446: *Flag*...to be arrested [*sic*]. **1964** in Wepman et al. *The Life* 59: The narco flagged me down. **1966** in Wepman et al. *The Life* 62: They...flagged me wrong. **1971** Woodley *Dealer* 86: Now they busted my reefer man, flagged him yesterday. They been watchin him.

5. *Stu.* to fail (an examination or a course.).

> **1959** Maier *College Terms* 3: *Flag a test*—Flunk a test. **1962** in *AS* (Oct. 1963) 168: To fail to pass an examination...*flag.* **1964** in *Time* (Jan. 1, 1965) 57: A flunking student has *flagged it.* **1966** in IUFA *Folk Speech*: *Flag*—Get an "F" on a test. *Ibid. Flag a test*...get an F on a test. **1968** Baker et al. *CUSS* 117: *Flag.* Do poorly on (i.e., fail) an exam. **1968–70** *Current Slang* III & IV 47: *Flag, v.* To fail.—College students, both sexes, Minnesota. **1973** Eble *Campus Slang* (Nov.) 2: *Flag*—to get an F on a test. **1984** Algeo *Stud Buds & Dorks* 8: *Flag*: To fail, as a test. **1986** *Knoxville* (Tenn.) *Jour.* C1: *Flag*: To fail, as a test.

6. to work under a FLAG, *n.*, 3.

> **1972** *Urban Life & Culture* I 377 [ref. to 1920]: Many...were blacklisted and forced to "flag" (work under an assumed name).

¶ In phrases:

¶ **flag it** to run; hurry. Also (*vulgar*) **flag ass.**

> **1923** *Atlanta Constitution* (Feb. 1) 12: What do we do—stick around or flag it for the jungle? **1935** Algren *Boots* 17: Watch 'em flag it out of Gawgia when they've done their little bump. **1954** L. Armstrong *Satchmo* 129: Now you can quit flagging that ragged ass of yours around the block. **1967** Taggart *Reunion of 108th* 8 [ref. to WWII]: Well, flag ass over to barracks and bring it back if ya wanta get outa here today!

¶ **flag (someone's) train** to catch the attention of; hail.

> **1918** in Carey *Mlle. from Armentières* II (unp.): None of the Frogs could flag her train.

flag-about *n.* a streetwalker; slut.

> **1859** Matsell *Vocab.* 32: *Flag about.* A low strumpet.

flag day *n.* [fr. *the flag is up* s.v. FLAG, *n.*, in joc. allusion to *Flag Day*, June 14] a day of the menstrual period.

> **1968** Baker et al. *CUSS* 117: *Flag day.* Be menstruating. **1970** Byrne *Memories* 82: We had a theory that you could tell which girls were having "flag day" by the way they walked. **1973** *AS* XLVI 82.

flagging *ppl.* [fr. *the flag is up* s.v. FLAG, *n.*] menstruating.

> **1973** *AS* XLVI 82: *Flagging.* **1976** *AS* LI 14 [ref. to *ca*1930].

flagpole *n.* the penis, esp. when erect. *Joc.*

1916–22 Cary *Sexual Vocab.* II: *Flag pole.* The penis. **1967** "M.T. Knight" *Terrible Ten* 157: If you think you're going to play flagpole sitter, doll, you're sadly mistaken. **1968** Gover *JC* 87: Layin side a me, flagpole steady stickin straight up. **1977** Coover *Public Burning* 395: Well, I see that the old flagpole still stands. **1978** in *Maledicta* VI (1982) 23: Erection…*flagpole*. **1981** *Penthouse* (Apr.) 26: Sandy quickly unzipped my jeans and out sprang my erect flagpole.

¶ In phrase:

¶ **run (something) up the flagpole** *Business.* to try out (an idea, suggestion, or the like) in a tentative way. Also absol.
1962 N.Y.C. man: Let's run this up the flagpole and see if anybody salutes. **1981** Ehrlichman *Witness* 239: Some of us…were convened to "run it up the flagpole," "vet it" and "bounce it off the wall." **1983–85** in Safire *Look It Up* 69: A Madison Avenue connotation…"to run it up the flagpole." **1992** Hosansky & Sparling *Working Vice* 291: I'm just running up the flag pole, this is something you might want to know.

flagpole session *n. Business.* a business discussion for the purpose of planning strategy and developing ideas.
1971 E. Sanders *Family* 45: Once during the flagpole sessions for the film.

Flag Town *n. CB.* Washington, D.C.
1977 *Sci. Mech. CB Gde.* 169: It's clear to Flag Town.

flag-waver *n.* **1.** *Mil.* a flag signaler; (*hence*) a member of the Army Signal Corps.
1920 Bissell *63rd Infantry* 54 [ref. to 1918]: The Stokes men freely accused the signal men of manufacturing fake messages to keep the "dog robbers" busy and the "flag-wavers" made no denial. [*1921 *N & Q* 383 (Nov. 12): *Flag-wagger.* Signaller.] *1942–44 in *AS* (Feb. 1946) 33: *Flag waver, n.* A member of the Signal Corps. **1946** S. Wilson *Voyage to Somewhere* 125: "Somebody's got to watch you flag wavers," Mr. Rudd replied.
2.a. an enthusiastic, demonstrative patriot.
1925 *AS* I (Oct.) 37: The "flag-waver" who flourishes the flag for applause is despised by everyone. **1942** in Huie *Can Do!* 103: All those flag wavers who just sit pretty and look cute. *1944 in *OED*: The Pretoria flag-wavers. **1982** *N.Y. Times* (Oct. 26) D 26: Herb Brooks, an old-fashioned sort who calls himself a "flag-waver," was the coach of the American [ice hockey] team.
b. a song, movie, oration, etc., that arouses or is intended to arouse esp. patriotic fervor.
1937 in R.S. Gold *Jazz Talk* 94: "A flag waver" is the last chorus in which everybody goes to town ending up like a full ensemble of Valkyries and Norse Gods. **1942** *Yank* (July 1) 21: Friendly Enemies (United Artists). Right out of the corn bin and a flag-waver to boot. **1957** in R.S. Gold *Jazz Talk*. **1975** V.B. Miller *Deadly Game* 10: I don't want to pull any flag wavers on you…but try this out. It's *my* community that's getting burned by this stuff. **1982** A. Shaw *Dict. Pop/Rock* 129: "Flag waver."…a song, an instrumental, or…chorus…that…brings an audience to its feet.

flail *n.* a confused, anxiety-provoking activity.
1974 Hejinian *Extreme Remedies* 55: It became a real flail…He was fibrillating…Then he went nodal and blocked on us. **1988** Poyer *The Med* 203: It was the bullshit that went before, the flaps and flails and paperwork.

flak *n.* **1.** *Mil. Av.* (a joc. euphem. for) FUCK. Also as *v.*
1961 Forbes *Goodbye to Some* 120 [ref. to WWII]: The 38's will get the flak out of there. **1963** E.M. Miller *Exile* 57: "Flak you, fellows," he said as the door slammed.
2. opposition or abusive criticism. Now *colloq.*
1963 *Fortune* (Apr.) 81 (Tamony Coll.): His decision would run into political flak from Capitol Hill. **1964** *Newsweek* (Aug. 10) 16 (Tamony Coll.): Congressional flak aimed at the Administration's multibillion-dollar Apollo…program. **1968** Safire *New Language of Politics* 147: *Flak:* Opposition, especially noisy opposition to a new idea or program. To "run into flak" means to encounter some unexpected but not devastating criticism. **1969** *Business Week* (Oct. 18) 134: President Nixon and his advisers…are willing to take political flak. **1970** *Newsweek* (June 8) 23: He [*sc.* Pres. Nixon] felt that events would prove him right…and he told us that we would just have to hang in there and take the flak. **1976** Haseltine & Yaw *Woman Doctor* 57: I've been getting a lot of flak recently about being a woman doctor. **1978** Strieber *Wolfen* 23: She'd have to suffer more flak from Wilson. **1990** P. Munro *Slang U.* 55: *Catch flack/get flack* to receive negative verbal feedback. **1991** in LaBarge *Desert Voices* 103: That was far more important than giving anybody flak.

flak alley *n. Mil. Av.* enemy territory heavily defended by anti-aircraft fire.
1943 Tregaskis *Invasion Diary* 66: It's the heaviest ever encountered in the Mediterranean—heavier than "flak alley" between Bizerte and Tunis. **1943** in Loosbrock & Skinner *Wild Blue* 292: Right down flak alley we flew. **1945** *Sat. Rev. of Lit.* (Nov. 3) 7: *Flak-happy* and *Flak Alley* are two of its offspring. **1952** Geer *New Breed* 187: Marine pilots were now calling Seoul "Flak Alley." **1971** *N.Y. Post* (May 24) 39: Chopper pilots…just back from Flak Alley in Laos. **1990** Safer *Flashbacks* 18: There was more than one "flak alley" in [North] Vietnam.

flak-catcher *n.* a public-relations specialist or spokesperson hired to reply to criticisms of his or her employer. Hence **flak-catching**, *n.*
1970 T. Wolfe *Radical Chic* 110: This man is the flak catcher. His job is to catch the flak for the No. 1 man. **1975** *Harper's* (July) 73: There was a *frisson* of relish, a tendency to regard flak-catching as a Learning Experience. **1987** *Wkly. World News* (July 14) 12: A public relations flak-catcher…said, "Dr. Ruth doesn't give reactions to these kinds of things."

flake *n.* **1.** *Narc.* cocaine, esp. in flaked form.
1922 Murphy *Black Candle* 52: Cocaine is sold to school-children as "coke" or "flake." **1961** (cited in Partridge *Dict. Und.* (ed. 2) 819). **1968–69** McWhirter *Dunlop Encyc.* 522: Cocaine…slang names: coke, flake, gold dust, star dust. **1971** *Inter. Jour. of Add.* VI 356: *Flake.* cocaine. **1974** *N.Y. Times Mag.* (Sept.) 14: Cocaine—in the argot of today's traffic, "coke," "snow," "blow," "leaf," or "flake." **1974** Hyde *Mind Drugs* 154: *Flake*…cocaine. **1976** *Deadly Game* (ABC-TV film): Some people in Toronto will change it for…Bolivian flake. **1981** Jenkins *Baja Oklahoma* 17: Lonnie used his nasal spray. "Is that flake?" the girl asked. **1983** Wambaugh *Delta Star* 170: Because of his flake habit and all. **1984** McInerny *Bright Lights* 74: You snorted…pink Peruvian flake. **1990** Bing *Do or Die* xv: The weekend supply of Bolivian flake.
2. a person who is conspicuously eccentric, foolish, crazy, or unpredictable; KOOK.
1959 R. Russell *Permanent Playboy* 251: What honesty! What frankness! You're no flake, Taddie. **1968** *Time* (Feb. 9) 34: He has a well-deserved representation as something of a flake. **1969** Bouton *Ball Four* 158: There is no bigger flake in organized baseball than Drabowski. Once…he picked up the phone, called a number in Hong Kong and ordered a Chinese dinner. To go. **1969** *N.Y. Times Mag.* (Nov. 2) 110: When some flakes from the Gay Liberation Front confronted Procaccino with their question—"What are you going to do about homosexuals?"—Mario laughed. **1968–70** *Current Slang* III & IV 47: *Flake, n.* A dumbbell; one who is not very bright.—College students, both sexes, New Hampshire. **1974** Blount *3 Bricks Shy* 26: The word "flake" as a sports term for eccentrics derives from the remark [in 1956] by Wally Moon…of the baseball Cardinals, to the effect that things seemed to "flake off" the mind of his roommate, Jackie Brandt, and disappear. **1975** H. Ellison *Deadly Streets* 11: But the other guy was a certified flake.
3. a disappointment or failure.
1961 Ellison *Gentleman Junkie* 174: Spoof was feeling down. The party was a flake.
4. *Police.* a deliberate false arrest made on the strength of evidence, such as narcotics, that has been planted on the person arrested.
1971 *N.Y. Times* (Oct. 20) 36: A "flake"…is the arrest, on known false evidence, of a person for something he did not do. **1979** Homer *Jargon* 77. **1980** Gould *Ft. Apache* 111: You know the prick's holdin' [i.e., armed]…And if he's not…You lay the old flake on him.

flake *v.* **1.** FLAKE OUT, 2.
1959–60 R. Reisner *Jazz Titans* 155: *Flake:* to sleep. **1968–70** *Current Slang* III & IV 48: *Flake, v.* To go to sleep.
2. FLAKE OFF, 1.a.
1964 in Gover *Trilogy* 229: Beat it, flake, fug off, vamoose, split. **1968** (Baker et al. quot. at FLAKE OFF, 1.a.).
3.a. *Police.* to plant incriminating evidence, esp. narcotics or a weapon, on (a prisoner) or in (a room, belongings, etc.).
1972 J. Mills *Report* 78: Later she said Lockley'd flaked the nigger, that he'd never had a knife. **1973** Droge *Patrolman* 179: Some men would want…to "flake" a prisoner, i.e., to place a bag or two [of heroin] on him if he was "clean." **1974** Charyn *Blue Eyes* 5: Manfred, you won't be able to flake him without me. **1977** *N.Y. Times Bk. Review* (Dec. 18) 12: I never "flaked" anybody—planted evidence on a suspect—nor did I ever lie in testimony in court. **1980** Gould *Ft. Apache* 69: A handcuffe[d]

prisoner was struggling with a burly policeman. "You flaked me, motherfucker!" **1981** P. Sann *Trial* 91: They don't flake nobody…You either done it or you didn't. **1990** Murano & Hoffer *Cop Hunter* 71: You couldn't get on that [crime], so you flaked me on this one.

b. *Police.* to plant (incriminating evidence).
1975 De Mille *Smack Man* 55: They also flaked a hot gun in your dresser.

4. FLAKE OUT, 5.a.
1984 Glick *Winters Coming* 215: If I flake a little, I'll get over it.

flake around *v.* to fool around; trifle.
1958 Meltzer & Blees *H.S. Confidential* (film): If you flake around with the weed, you're gonna end up using the hard stuff.

flaked *adj.* FLAKED OUT, 2.
1959 Farris *Harrison High* 286: Don't know if I have the strength to drive back home or not. I'm flaked. **1961** in *OEDS*: When it was over I was flaked. **1963–64** Kesey *Great Notion* 184: Fagged and flaked and wanting nothing more than sleep. **1976** J.W. Thomas *Heavy Number* 96: They're all flaked.

flaked out *adj.* **1.a.** unconscious; (*also*) asleep.
1943** in *OEDS*: There is a man flaked out at your feet. ***1953** in *OEDS* [ref. to WWII]: "Olley, where's old Drum?" "Flaked out." **1956** Hargrove *Girl He Left* 143: While you're flaked out in your crummy little sack at night…you know what I'm doing? **1968** G. Cuomo *Among Thieves* 40: She was pretty much flaked out, actually. *a1990** Poyer *Gulf* 154: He found our mechs flaked out in the hangar.

b. lying down; reclining; resting.
1944 Kendall *Service Slang* 23: *Flaked out*…reclining on back. **1979** J. Morris *War Story* 188: The guards would be flaked out…smoking a…cigarette or trying to catch a few Z's. **1980** Manchester *Darkness* 151: Flaked out before lights out…we…shot the breeze much as we would have done at home. **1979–83** W. Kennedy *Ironweed* 146: Wake up in the weeds…flaked out 'n' stiffer than a chunk of old iron.

2. tired out; exhausted.
1958 in *OEDS*: "Can we go to bed soon?" she said. "I'm absolutely flaked out." **1959** *Swinging Syllables*: Flaked out—Exhausted, worn down. **1960** Swarthout *Where Boys Are* 34: I was flaked out from no sleep and the poolathon. **1972** N.Y.U. student: *Flaked out* means like tired out.

flake off *v.* **1.a.** Esp. *Stu.* to go away; leave.—esp. in imper. [Attribution in 1960 ex. to WWII may or may not be accurate.]
1957 M. Shulman *Rally* 59: Oh, flake off, little man! **1960** Sire *Deathmakers* 96 [ref. to 1945]: So don't flake off on any personal looting missions unless you want to get massacred. **1965** Borowik *Lions* 19: Flake off and drop this whole idea. **1966** in IUFA *Folk Speech*: Flake: to leave, go. **1968** Baker et al. *CUSS* 117: Flake (off). Leave a place. **1968** Wojciechowska *Tuned Out* 59: And then the two of them flake off. **1972** N.Y.U. student: *Flake off* means "fuck off," "get lost." **1973** *Playboy* (June) 253: Flake off, you lousy mutt! **1979** Kunstler *Wampanaki Tales* 10: Flake off, fatso.

b. to spurn; brush off.
1959 R. Russell *Permanent Playboy* 248: I made a brushing gesture of my hand against my shoulder. "Orleen will flake you off," I said….She doesn't want love, she wants a hit tune.

2. to loaf.
1971 N.Y.U. student: I think I'll quit school and just flake off for a while on the Bowery or someplace. *a***1982** Medved *Hospital* 175: Now people look at us as a bunch of wealthy guys who flake off and won't make housecalls.

flake-out *n.* **1.** FREAK-OUT.
1966 Young & Hixson *LSD on Campus* 6: It was a harmless ball, a temporary flake-out into a beery mountain of foam, a quick swim across a sewer of bad whiskey, a…plunge into…sex.

2. (see quot.).
1971 Dahlskog *Dict.* 23: *Flake-out, n.* A person or thing that fails, a flop; a bomb.

3. a lunatic.
1974 N.Y.C. barmaid, age 22: What are you, some kind of a flake-out?

flake out *v.* **1.** to collapse, as from exhaustion; faint; pass out.
***1942** in *OEDS*: During the week's [P.T.] course, two of them broke their ankles; the others usually flaked out from exhaustion before the end of the afternoon. ***1945** in Baker *Austral. Lang.* (ed. 2) 170: *Flake out*, to pass out; to go to sleep. **1961** *Sat. Eve. Post* (Oct. 14) 7: Fellows all around are flaking out under the strain. **1967** in *BDNE*. **1969** in B.E.

Holley *Vietnam* 127: My reason for not writing is sheer exhaustion. Even my eighteen-, nineteen-, and twenty-year-olds are about to flake out.

2. to recline; lie down; (*hence*) to take a nap; go to sleep.
1944 *Life* (July 17) 20: Carrier crew men "flake out" on hard deck while planes are far away fighting great air battles. **1945** in *Calif. Folk. Qly.* (1946) 387: Whoever *knocks off* work in order to rest or sleep *conks out, conks off, caulks off,* or *flakes out.* **1950** Wouk *Caine Mutiny* 113: Half the time at night when I'm trying to sleep he's pacing around talking to himself. Then in the daytime he flakes out. **1951** Morris *China Station* 182: He had to come out and flake out on the table. The deck wasn't good enough in there. **1953** Dodson *Away All Boats* 158: Three more are flaked out on the fantail asleep. **1959** Morrill *Dark Sea Running* 190: Coley Fry was flaked out on a steel I-beam like he was seasick. **1961** Pirosh & Carr *Hell Is for Heroes* (film): Find somewhere to flake out, you guys. **1969** *Harper's* (May) 13 [adv.]: Flake out for a few z's.

3. to lose one's courage.
1957 Myrer *Big War* 154 [ref. to WWII]: What did they think…kept them from flaking out or cracking up under shelling when they were wounded and shaking with dysentery. **1968** Myrer *Eagle* 135: You're flaking out. And I thought you Buckeyes had guts. **1978** J. Webb *Fields of Fire* 286: Good. I knew none of you dudes would flake out on me. **1987** *21 Jump St.* (Fox-TV): Don't start flakin' out on me now.

4. to die.
1966 I. Reed *Pall-Bearers* 153: Well, as my mother used to say before she flaked out, "Hard head makes a soft ass."

5.a. to go crazy.
1969 *Current Slang* I & II 34: *Flake out, v.* To act incoherently (as from extreme fatigue, drink, etc.)—College students, both sexes, Minnesota, South Dakota. **1980** Santoli *Everything* 104: The next thing I heard, he was in a psycho ward. He had just sort of flaked out and gone over the edge.

b. to make crazy.
1977 Olsen *Fire Five* 160: But she's still *here,* and it's flaking everybody out.

6. to astound.
1972 N.Y.U. student: Just the other day my brother said, "That really flaked me out." He meant sort of like "freaked out." **1992** *Jerry Springer Show* (synd. TV series): He told me he was working for a pimp. And that flaked me out.

flak hack *n. Army.* (see 1944 quot.).
1943 *Look* (Jan. 26) 10: Flak hack. **1944** Kendall *Service Slang* 43: *Flack hack*…a mobile anti-aircraft gun.

flak-happy *adj.* [sugg. by *trigger-happy*] *Mil. Av.* afraid, eccentric, reckless, or neurotic because of exposure to flak or aerial combat.
1943 in *AS* (1944) XIX 60: Flak Happy [name of a B-17 Flying Fortress]. **1944** *New Yorker* (May 27) 24: I suppose you think I'm flak-happy. **1944** *N.Y. Times Mag.* (June 4) 12: Airmen who say they don't mind flak are termed "flak-happy" by airmen who do mind it. **1944** Stiles *Big Bird* 16: If it had kept up much longer we'd have all been so flak-happy we'd never have made it. **1948** Lay & Bartlett *Twelve O'Clock High!* 161: But any time I get flak-happy, Doc, I promise to take a rest. **1959** Scott *Flying Tigers* 125: I should have known better than to let a bunch of flak-happy flying cowboys rile me. **1960** Simmons *Kriegie* 20 [ref. to WWII]: It seemed to me I was at the bombsight controls for over an hour…I…wondered if all of us weren't getting a little flak-happy. **1969** in B. Edelman *Dear Amer.* 117: Things happen over here that you just can't keep to yourself—if you do, you brood on them, slowly go "flak happy," get careless, and eventually get zapped when your mind has strayed from the job at hand. **1983** in Kaplan & Smith *One Last Look* 135 [ref. to WWII]: They would get "flak happy." Everybody, I think,…hated the flak worse than the fighters.

flak house *n.* FLAK SHACK. Now *hist.*
1944 Stiles *Big Bird* 107: Beach went away to the Flak House for a week. **1968** Coppel *Order of Battle* 54 [ref. to 1944]: A week at the Flak House eating steaks and drinking Scotch brought back some of the bloom, but not for very long.

flak juice *n.* (in military hospitals) sodium pentothal used in the treatment of aviation combat neurosis. Now *hist.*
1944 *Newsweek* (May 29) 68: The soldiers call it [sc. sodium pentothal] "flak juice" and refer to their condition as "flak happy." **1961** Rosten *Captain Newman, M.D.* (film) [ref. to 1944]: We use them for Sodium Pentothal sessions—but never say that or the men will think you're a cornball. They call it flak juice.

flakked up *adj. Mil. Av.* FLAK-HAPPY. Now *hist.*

1958 Camerer *Damned Wear Wings* 197 [ref. to WWII]: Sure he's back. But he's…flakked up like a punch-drunk.

flakky *adj. Mil. Av.* FLAK-HAPPY.

1944 in Stevens *More There I Was* 122: You may think I'm wacky. But I'm only slightly flakky. **1963** E.M. Miller *Exile* 181: What will we call this flakky outfit?

flako *n.* a person who is FLAKY; KOOK.

1960 *Thriller* (NBC-TV): "I have to be charming to every flako who comes in here with a crystal ball?" "That *flako*, as you call him, happens to be one of the world's leading doctors."

flako *adj.* **1.** drunk; BLOTTO.

1971 in *BDNE* 169.

2. crazy; FLAKY.

1971 *Atlantic* (Feb.) 81: They greeted Harry with a fireside grudging gruffness that said, flako or otherwise, he was…welcome. **1981** *Mother Jones* (Dec.) 12: It's one thing for a flake-o environmental group to say, [etc.]. **1983** Nelkin & Brown *Workers* 139: But this guy was flako.

flak runner *n. Pol.* a spokesperson whose job is to deflect criticism from a candidate or officeholder; FLAK-CATCHER.

1977 Coover *Public Burning* 60: I was the flak runner, the wheelhorse, I had to mend the fences and bind up the wounds.

flak shack *n. Mil. Av.* a military psychiatric facility for the treatment of aircrewmen suffering from combat neurosis. Now *hist.* [Quots. ref. to WWII.]

1944 *N.Y. Times Mag.* (June 4) 12: *Flak-shack:* The rest home where men who have had much battle strain go to relax and gain their composure. **1946** G.C. Hall, Jr. *1000 Destroyed* 324: If so, he was sent to a flak shack until it could be determined if he met the requirements for a Section 8 discharge. **1983** Kaplan & Smith *One Last Look* 143: When they were beginning to get "flak happy," combat crew members were given a week's R & R…at an Air Force rest home or "Flak Shack."

flak up *v. Mil. Av.* to hit with flak.

1946 G.C. Hall, Jr. *1000 Destroyed* 286 [ref. to WWII]: Capt. Robert R. Hobert…had been flakked-up in the attacks on the drome. He had almost limped home, but was forced to bail out over the Channel.

flak-wagon *n. Mil.* a mobile German antiaircraft gun. Now *hist.* [Quots. ref. to WWII.]

1945 *Yank* (Mar. 30) 4: First a flak wagon chased them. **1948** A. Murphy *To Hell & Back* 79: From hidden positions two *flakwagon* guns churn. **1960** Loomis *Heroic Love* 147: There would be a flak wagon behind the houses, that was it, a tracked vehicle with four guns in a turret.

flaky *adj.* [cf. FLAKE, *n.*, 2, and earlier FLAKKY] crazy, eccentric, or unpredictable; erratic; (*broadly*) absent-minded. Also **flakey.**

[**1945** in Partridge *Dict. Und.* (ed. 2) 819: We couldn't help enjoying the name Flaky Lou. She was named after cocaine, which was flaky in appearance.] **1959** Brosnan *Long Season* 241: "How come Cunningham is called Flakey, Cot? When did that start?" "People that don't know him call him that. He's got an oddball sense of humor.…'Flakey' means people don't understand you." *Ibid.* 270: Any ballplayer who is considered hard to figure out is called "flakey." **1959–60** Bloch *Dead Beat* 4: That was the sax for you, full of flaky chatter from back issues of the teen-age magazines. He played a flaky tenor, too. **1960** *Leave It to Beaver* (ABC-TV): That's a sign he's goin' flaky for her. **1964** Hill *One of Casualties* 59: The world was full of flakey floozies which…were running around loose espousing the Negro uprising as their mission in life. **1966** Bullins *Goin' a Buffalo* 194: Awww, Mamma…let's not you and me start in actin' flaky. **1967** Lit *Dictionary* 15: *Flakey*—nuts; off in the head; a snap case; a flip out. **1970** *N.Y. Post* (Apr. 7) 43: Koosman had been a flaky left-hander, true to the image, and had run his car into the ground when he wired McDonald for money. **1971** *Newsweek* (Jan. 11) 29: As the grunts would put it, the Army has become distinctly "flaky." **1971** *Playboy* (Dec.) 94: I had the image of Polanski as a flaky, perhaps even macabre character. **1972** Casey *Obscenities* 13: This here sergeant's/Shit is flaky/…Seven willies from another unit/Seen him kick/ This trainee/In the balls. **1972** Wambaugh *Blue Knight* 81: I kept that flaky look, grinning and waving at any kid who gave me the peace sign. **1978** J. Webb *Fields of Fire* 290 [ref. to Vietnam War]: Come on. Let's get the hell out of here. I'm getting flaky. *Ibid.* 412: Flaky: To be in a state of mental disarray, characterized by spaciness and various forms of unreasoning fear. **1982** Gino *Nurse's Story* 18: Jesus! Am I flakey tonight.

flam *n.* [prob. fr. flim*flam*] a deception or imposture. Orig. *colloq.* or *S.E.*

*1632 in *OED*: A flam, or a flimflam tale, *riotte*. ***1637, *1655** in *OED*. ***1689** Shadwell *Bury-Fair* II: Call generous Complements, Flams. **1708** in W.H. Kenney *Laughter in Wilderness* 108: 'Tis but a Flam. ***1720** D'Urfey *Pills* VI 214: A…well invented flam. **1817** in Royall *Letters from Ala.* 106: Oh! brother, it's all a flam. **1838** [Haliburton] *Clockmaker* (Ser. 2) 60: One of the greatest flams I ever heard tell of. *a*1860 Hundley *So. States* 144: None o' your flams nor shams. **1862** H.J. Thomas *Wrong Man* 54: I tell you that's all a flam. ***1873** Hotten *Slang Dict.* (ed. 4): "A regular *flam*," a tale devoid of truth. ***1909** Ware *Passing Eng.* 133: *Flam*…Fib—rather than lie. Quite passed away from London, but still heard in the counties. **1970** Landy *Underground Dict.* 79: *Flam*…n. Deceitful façade.

flam *v.* **1.** to hoodwink; flimflam; deceive. Orig. *S.E.*

*1637 in *OED*: You do not well to jeere and flam Me. ***ca1658, *1660, *1692, *1760** in *OED*. ***1821** Stewart *Man-of-War's-Man* I 34: Now see that the old skin-flint doesn't flam you off with some of his worn-out gear. **1836** in Haliburton *Sam Slick* 73: Some 'sponcible man…that warn't given to flammin'. **1859** Matsell *Vocab.* 32: "*Flam the bloke,*" humbug the fellow. **1982** Heat Moon *Blue Hwys.* 99: Those marchers rolled their own dice, and we got flammed. Course it ain't hard to flam George Wallace. **1985** C. Busch *Times Sq. Angel* 60: I don't think you can flam the coppers that easily.

2. (see quots.).

1856 B. Hall *College Wds.* (ed. 2) 204: At the University of Vermont, in student phrase, to *flam* is to be attentive, at any time, to any lady or company of ladies. E.g., "He spends half his time *flamming*," i.e. in the society of the other sex. **1970** Landy *Underground Dict.* 79: *Flam*…Be aggressive; flirt with; come on strong to someone.

3. *Stu.* (see quot.).

1900 *DN* II: *Flam, v.i.* To fail an examination. [Reported from Maryland and Massachusetts.]

flambergast *v.* FLABBERGAST. Cf. FLUMBERGAST.

1834 Caruthers *Kentuck in N.Y.* I 161: Well! I'm flambergasted now! if that ain't what I call a *leetle* particular. **1856** in *DARE*: Well, the hoss got stuck in one o' them are [sic] flambergasted snow-banks.

flamboozled *adj.* [prob. FLA(BBERGAST) + b*amboozled*] confused and astonished.

1956 in Asimov et al. *Sci. Fi. Short Shorts* 175: They were too flamboozled to know it was an accident.

flambustious *adj.* exciting; splendid.

1868 in Schele de Vere *Amer.* 602: We will have a flambustious time. **1913** *DN* IV 18: "That dress is rather flambustious."…"We had a flambustious time."

flamdoodle *n.* FLAPDOODLE.

1888 in *F & H* III 4: We weren't goin' to have any high falutin' flamdoodle business over him. **1902** in *DA*: All the fluffy flamdoodle that gals put on when they go out. **1921** in H. Crane *Letters* 52: M. Ray will allow the Dada theories and other flamdoodle of this section to run him off the track.

flame *n. Computers.* an instance of flaming; (*also*) a subject on which people FLAME, *v.*

1983 Naiman *Computer Dict.* 58. **1991** Raymond *New Hacker's Dict.* 158: *Flame*…An instance of flaming.

flame *v.* Now *Computers.* to behave offensively; rant; (*also*) to subject to severe criticism.

1968 Baker et al. *CUSS* 118: *Flame*…To be obnoxiously loud, esp. while under the influence of alcohol. **1973** N.Y.C. man [ref. to ca1958]: If a faggot tried to make a pass at you, we'd say, "Man, he tried to flame on me," or "He tried to flame on that guy." **1983** *L.A. Times* (Sept. 21) I 23: "Flaming"—name-calling, swearing, expressing extreme positions in an extreme manner.…People "flame" more on the computer than they do in face-to-face communication. *a*1989 in Safire *Coming to Terms* 3: He is at risk of *flaming*—another Silicon Valley locution…"getting intellectually outrageous or otherwise losing it." **1991** Raymond *New Hacker's Dict.* 158: *Flame* 1. vi. To post an email message intended to insult and provoke. 2. vi. To speak incessantly and/or rabidly on some relatively uninteresting subject.…3. vt. Either of senses 1 or 2, directed with hostility at a particular person. **1993** *New Republic* (Sept. 13) 25: "Flame" is the cyberspace word for, roughly, "speak in very heated or hostile terms."

flame chair *n. Journ.* an electric chair.

1930 in Partridge *Dict. Und.* **1932** *AS* (Feb. 1934) 26: *Flame Chair:* The electric chair. **1935** Pollock *Und. Speaks:* *Flame chair*, electrocution chair (prison).

flamer *n.* **1.a.** Esp. *Stu.* an extremely clumsy, obnoxious, or embarrassing person; (see also 1980 quot.).
*1931 J. Hanley *Boy* 32: You flamer. I know why you were late. 1968 Baker et al. *CUSS* 118: *Flamer.* A person who always fools around…An obnoxious person. 1968–70 *Current Slang* III & IV 48: *Flamer,* n. A male who is not able to control his emotions; an eager beaver—College males, New Hampshire. 1972 N.Y.U. student: If somebody's really stupid, you say "He's a flamer!" "What a flamer!" Short for *flaming ass-hole.*…A *flamer* is a real jerk who hams everything up. 1974 Eble *Campus Slang* (Mar.) 3: *Flamer*—someone who behaves ostentatiously or foolishly: Richard Nixon is a flamer; [he] is a flaming fool. 1980 Birnbach *Preppy Hndbk.* 219: *Flamer,* n. He who commits a *faux pas* or obvious error. Also, the *faux pas* itself. 1981 L.I., N.Y., woman, age 28: My boss is a real flamer.…What a flaming asshole! 1985 G. Trudeau, in *Daily Beacon* (Univ. Tenn.) (Sept. 24) 6: I'm telling you, man, the guy's a world-class flamer! I can't take one more day here! 1991 Raymond *New Hacker's Dict.* 159: *Flamer*…said esp. of obnoxious USENET personalities.
b. *Stu.* an extremist.
1974 Strasburger *Rounding Third* 105: God made the universe and (assuming you're not a flamer like William Jennings Bryan or the Pope) life began developing chemically from there.
2. *Homosex.* a conspicuously effeminate homosexual man.
a1972 B. Rodgers *Queens' Vernacular* 73. 1975 Univ. Tenn. student: A *flamer* is a supereffeminate fag. It's short for *flaming faggot.* 1986 Eble *Campus Slang* (Mar.) 4: *Flamer*—overt homosexual. 1988 R. Snow *Members of Committee* 3: What words might you use to describe a gay man who is flashy, flamboyant, or loud?…*Flamer,…Nelly,* [etc.]. a1990 Westcott *Half a Klick* 155: Some faggot…Guy was a real flamer.

flamethrower *n.* **1.** *West.* a pistol.
1922 Rollins *Cowboy* 148: He "dug for" his own…"flame-thrower," and unravelled some cartridges.
2. *Av.* a jet aircraft.
1951 Richards *Air Cadet* (film): Whoever thought I'd fall in love with a flamethrower!
3. Esp. *Mil.* a cigarette lighter.
1966 in IUFA *Folk Speech: Flame thrower* or *torch*—a cigarette lighter. 1971 Kentucky man, age 17 (coll. J. Ball): Pass me that fucking flamethrower.
4. *Baseball.* a pitcher who specializes in throwing fastballs.
1978 Lyle & Golenbock *Bronx Zoo* 73: Don't be expecting too much. I'm no flamethrower. 1980 McBride *High & Inside* 131: Fireman Aurelio Lopez is known as…"The Flamethrower." 1988 *N.Y. Daily News* (June 9) 100: The Red Sox turned their flamethrowers on the Yanks last night…Roger Clemens…and reliever Lee Smith. 1989 *Newsweek* (Aug. 28) 65: Flamethrowers are supposed to break down, lose their fast ball.

flaming *adj. & adv.* **1.** (used as an intensive); damned.
*1895 in *OEDS*: Yes, by God, I'll get flaming drunk. 1901 J. London *God of His Fathers* 68: Then what the flaming hell did you take after me for? *1922 D.H. Lawrence, in *OEDS*: I've never been patient to no flaming doctor, and hope I never shall be. 1927 Coe *Me—Gangster* 105: Sure as flaming hell I would! *1936, *1944, *1946 in *OEDS*. 1951 in W.S. Burroughs *Letters* 77: Flaming bums without tie, coat or socks. *1960, *1966, *1969 in *OEDS*. 1971 Sheehan *Arnheiter* 141: Fuck that flaming nut on the bridge! 1984 C. Crowe *Wild Life* (film): At least you don't look like a flaming geek any more. 1984 J. Dailey *Silver Wings* 92: Then that flaming Frye started yelling in my ears. 1993 *New Republic* (Aug. 16) 24: A recent flaming nonsense called *Medicine Man.*
2. (of a homosexual, esp. a man) blatant or conspicuous.
1941 G. Legman, in Henry *Sex. Var.* II 1166: *Flaming queen,* a homosexual who attempts to…attract attention and drum up trade. 1958–59 Lipton *Barbarians* 316: "Flaming faggot." A male homosexual. 1969 Crumley *One to Count Cadence* 205: What a flaming queen he is, honey. 1970 *N.Y. Times Book Rev.* (Mar. 22) 33: Here, at last, is a novel that dares to be completely honest about homosexuality.…There are no stereotyped flaming faggots. 1971 *N.Y. Times Book Rev.* (Sept. 5) 23: After a lurid 10-year life as a "flaming fag," Mr. Stanhope decided to become a "closet queen" again. 1988 *Rage* (Univ. Tenn.) I (No. 11) 20: No more…flaming queers.

flaming asshole *n.* **1.** *Mil.* the rising-sun insigne of Japanese military aircraft.—usu. considered vulgar.
*1943 (cited in Partridge *DSUE* (ed. 8) 400). *1945 S.J. Baker *Austral. Lang.* 160: *Flaming a—hole.* The large red circle painted on the side of a Japanese plane. 1963 Boyle *Yanks Don't Cry* 17 [ref. to 1941]: "Holy Christ!" he shouted. "Those are Jap planes! Look at those flaming ass holes on his wings!"

2. a flagrantly stupid or offensive person.—usu. considered vulgar.
1968 Baker et al. *CUSS* 118: *Flaming asshole*…[a fool]. 1975 De Mille *Smack Man* 94: Tell that flaming asshole…that *you* don't want anything to do with me. 1983 S. Wright *Meditations* 58: We all know what a flaming asshole he really was. 1987 R.M. Brown *Starting* 48: Don't be soured by the flaming assholes of the world. 1992 *Newsweek* (Oct. 5) 44: He had to deal with a "flaming a------ they sent out from Dallas to be our state coordinator."

flaming coffin *n. Mil. Av.* the DeHavilland DH-4 bombing and observation plane. Now *hist.* [Quots. ref. to WWI.]
1919 Rickenbacker *Flying Circus* 267: Their criminally constructed fuel systems offered so easy a target to the incendiary bullets of the enemy that their unfortunate pilots called this boasted achievement of our Aviation Department "flaming coffins." 1919 D.P. Morse *50th Aero.* 26: I believe it a bit unfair to dub [the DH-4s] "flaming coffins." [1929 Niles, Moore, & Wallgren *Songs* 173: Frankie he flew in a D.H.,/'Twas just a flamin' damned hearse.] 1964 *Esquire* (Aug.) 111: DeHavilland 4's—they were two-seaters, too, made in the U.S. with U.S. Liberty engines, and we called them "flaming coffins"; they had a big gas tank, placed right between the pilot and the observer. 1968 Hudson *Hostile Skies* 135: Comments ranged from those who saw it [the DH-4] as "two wings on a hearse" and a "flaming coffin" to those who described it as the "best on the Front."

flaming feathers *n.pl. Mil. Av.* (see quot.).
1939 Hart *135th Aero Sq.* 106 [ref. to 1918]: Then you go out some fine morning, get some Boche after you and see these "flaming feathers" go shooting by, and you come home and load up with incendiaries. *Ibid.* 145: "Flaming feathers"…Incendiary bullets, leaving a trail of smoke.

flaming four *n. Mil. Av.* FLAMING COFFIN. Now *hist.* [Quots. ref. to WWI.]
1918 in Dolph *Sound Off* 114: They've got no Sops, they've got no Spads, they've got no Flaming Fours. 1918 in Niles et al. *Songs* 196: Where they've got no Sops, no Spads, no Sals,/And not a bloody Flamin' Four. *1984 in Partridge *DSUE* (ed. 8) 400.

flaming onion *n.* **1.** *Mil. Av.* a kind of incendiary antiaircraft shell. Now *hist.*
*1917 in Lee *No Parachute* 124: We were met with…flaming onions, a string of greenish phosphorous fireballs linked together. 1918 in Rossano *Price of Honor* 126: You can see the Hun star shells and flaming onions bursting over the lines. 1925 Paine *First Yale Unit* 177 [ref. to 1918]: "Flaming onions"…were designed, it is claimed, to set fire to a machine they might strike. 1927 Roosevelt *Rank & File* 20: Incendiary shells, nicknamed "flaming onions," rush up. 1937 Codman *Contact* 76 [ref. to 1918]: Sounds like Flaming Onions.…They wrap around your wings and if they are still hot enough set you on fire. 1939 Hart *135th Aero Sq.* 147 [ref. to 1918]: We got every kind of antiaircraft known—shrapnel, high explosive, pom-poms and flaming onions. 1942 Whelan *Flying Tigers* 70: They found no defense, except the anti-aircraft fire of a few British ships in the river, and the "flaming onions" that were effective only up to three thousand feet.
2. *Army.* the flaming grenade insigne of the U.S. Army Ordnance Corps.
1944 Pyle *Brave Men* 393: Ordnance personnel is usually about six or seven per cent of the total men of an army. That means we had many thousands of ordnancemen in Normandy. Their insigne is a flame coming out of a bomb—nicknamed in the Army the "Flaming Onion." 1942–44 in *AS* (Feb. 1946) 33: *Flaming onion,* n. The insignia of the Ordnance Department. 1980 Cragg *Lex. Milit.* 168: *Flaming Onion.* The insignia of the Ordnance Corps…which is a flaming bomb.

flaming pisspot *n. Army.* FLAMING ONION, 2.—usu. considered vulgar.
1980 D. Cragg *Lex. Milit.* 168: *Flaming Pisspot*…The insignia of the Ordnance Corps. 1980 D. Cragg, letter to J.E.L. (Aug. 10): *Flaming pisspot*…[I] First heard [this at] Ft. Bragg, N.C.…1964. 1986 *NDAS.*

flange up *v. Petroleum Industry.* to finish work; (*trans.*) to bring to the end of a task.
1944 Boatright & Day *Hell to Breakfast* 141: When a man said he is ready to "flange up" he is about through. This common saying comes from the necessity of using a flange union to complete nearly all pipe connection jobs. *Ibid.* 148: I believe that flanges me up. 1972 in *DARE: Flange up*—To close off, finish.

flank *v. Army.* to foil, outwit, fool, or evade; avoid; (*also*) to steal. [Quots. ref. to Civil War.]

1862 in C.H. Smith *Bill Arp* 32: They *flanked* me in double quick, and though my time was not out, I was constrained to depart those coasts prematurely for fear of being a desolated victim of extortion. **1864** Northrop *Chronicles* 50: The order was "Shoot every man that tries to get out," so Boodger and I were again flanked. **1865** in Blackett *Chester* 248: Began to devise ways…to escape to our lines, or, in their own vernacular, "to flank de pickets." **1865** in Thornton *Amer. Gloss.*: I asked the Captain if he had Mr. Toombs. "No," he replied, "Mr. Toombs flanked us." **1871** Schele de Vere *Americanisms* 286: When the men wished to escape the attention of pickets and guards by slipping past them, they said they *flanked* them; drill and detail and every irksome duty was *flanked*, when it could be avoided by some cunning trick.…The poor farmer was *flanked* out of his pig…and…the comrade out of his pipe and tobacco. The height of strategy was employed in these *flank maneuvers*…and…in the South at least…to *flank the whole bottle* was…expressive of superlative cunning and brilliant success. **1879** in Thornton *Amer. Gloss.*: The Government never made anything by employing these "rebels," as they invariably "flanked" more than they received as pay. **1891** Rodenbough *Sabre* 138: The…battle of Spotsylvania had been fought in the mean time, and I…successfully *flanked it.*

flanker *n. Army.* a shrewd and skillful soldier who knows how to circumvent regulations; (*also*) a petty thief. [Quots. ref. to the Civil War.]
  1867 Goss *Soldier's Story* 81: We arrived on the spot just in time to save the pail from the hands of the ruthless "flankers"—another term for thieves used among us. **1888** Grigsby *Smoked Yank* 102: The flanker kept for himself all that he could carry in.

flannel *n.* FLANNEL-CAKE.
  1847 in *DAE:* Take some more of the flannels?

flannel-buzzard *n.* a body louse.
  1918 (quot. at SHIRT-HOUND). **1919** MacGill *Dough-Boys* 246-7: It's the flannel-buzzard, the shirt-hound…the blackguard that's known as the cootie.

flannel-cake *n.* a pancake. Now *colloq.* and *regional.*
  1792 in *OED:* Ten thousand thousand thousand Naples biscuits, crackers, buns, and flannel-cakes. **1847, 1869** in *DAE.* **1878** Hart *Sazerac* 175: Another said he would take some flannel cakes for his feet. **1886** Nye *Remarks* 263: Butter…sleeps on the flannel cakes at night. **1915–16** Lait *Beef, Iron & Wine* 123: He was dreaming of flowers, flannel cakes, and fairies. **1929** Perelman *Ginsbergh* 151: Hannah's flannel-cakes were just too ducky for words. **1944** Sturges *Conquering Hero* (film): How 'bout a stack of your famous flannelcakes, Mama? **1949** Schaefer *Shane* 9: Eat enough of these flannel cakes and you'll grow a bigger man than your father. **1951, 1953, 1965-70, 1973** in *DARE.*

flannelmouth *n.* **1.** a glib, insincere, boastful, or ingratiating talker. Hence **flannelmouthed**, *adj.*
  1881 in Miller & Snell *Why West Was Wild* 311: The mayor is a flannel mouthed Irishman and keeps a saloon and gambling house. **1911** Van Loan *Big League* 165: You've let these knockers get you going…Show these flannel mouths what a regular outfielder looks like. **1931** in Hemingway *Sel. Letters* 344: This damned typer skips like a stammering flannel mouthed nigger. **1933** Ersine *Prison Slang* 37: *Flannelmouth, n.* A mealy-mouthed person, a liar. **1940** E. O'Neill *Long Day's Journey* II, ii: That flannel-mouth, goldbrick merchant. **1952** Sandburg *Young Strangers* 307 [ref. to *ca*1890]: He's a flannelmouth. He's against and against and what he's for is only being against. **1964** Thompson & Rice *Every Diamond* 197: Newspapermen…and flannel-mouthed citizens got some exercise for the first time in years by jumping on and off the Dodger bandwagon. **1965** *Bonanza* (NBC-TV): Don't pay no attention to that flannelmouth. He's just tryin' to get your goat. **1974** Dubinsky & Standora *Decoy Cop* 61: A bunch of flannelmouthed politicians. **1988** *Crossfire* (CNN-TV) (May 2): Some flannelmouth congressman.
  2. an Irish person.—used contemptuously. Hence **flannelmouthed**, *adj.* [*DA* and *DARE* erroneously date *ca*1870-95 quot. as "1870"; although the source was orig. written in 1870, the only surviving copy was modernized as late as the 1890's, as it includes a reference to the Panic of 1893.]
  1893 in F. Harris *Conklin* 174: The buildin' of the [railroad] has brought a lot of Irish here—they're all Democrats—and there's quite a number of Mugwumps, an' if this Professor goes about workin' them all up—what with the flannel-mouths and the rest—it might be a close finish. *ca*1870-95 McCloskey *Across Continent* 74: Say, look here, you Irish flannel-mouth mick. **1913** J. London *Valley of Moon* 35: Hey, old flannel-mouth! Watch out! **1922** Dean *Flying Cloud* 131: Say, take a brick and go hit that flannel-mouthed Mick and cave his old dicer in.

1930 "D. Stiff" *Milk & Honey* 205: *Flannelmouth*—An Irishman. **1929-33** Farrell *Manhood of Lonigan* 245: Hello, Flannel Mouth! *Ibid.* 268: Keefe, you drunken flannel-mouth. **1940** Raine & Niblor *Fighting 69th* (film) [ref. to 1917]: "Listen, flannelmouth, I'll say what I please."…"I ain't like all these flannelmouth micks goin' around singin' 'Molly Malone' all the time." **1966-67** in *DARE.*

flap *n.* **1.a.** a jade or loose woman; (see also 1914 quot.). Cf. var. senses of FLAPPER.
  ***1631** in *OED:* Fall to your flap, my Masters, kisse and clip…Come hither, you foule flappes. **1914** Jackson & Hellyer *Vocab.* 34: *Flap*, noun. Current amongst pimps and criminals who are contemptuous of female values. An opprobrious epithet for loose women. Also employed to designate the female sex organ. **1942-49** Goldin et al. *DAUL* 71: *Flap.* A loose woman.
  b. FLAPPER, 2.c.
  1930 in Mencken *Amer. Language* (ed. 4) 586: Pash Flaps [*i.e.* passionate flappers] M.C. Fan Clubs, Rated Worthless to Theatres As B.O. Gag. **1934** Weseen *Dict. Slang* 334: *Flap*—A flapper, who is according to a British interpreter, an impassioned young woman.
  2. Orig. *Mil.* a state of confusion and excitement; uproar; hysteria. Now *colloq.*
  ***1916** in *OEDS:* Sometimes our departures are more than usually sudden and unexpected. The whole proceeding then becomes what is known amongst us as "a Flap." **1919** *Atlantic* (Feb.) 287: This huge fleet was handled with such precision, with such absolute accuracy and absence of "flaps," that it might have been a huge clockwork toy. ***1925** Fraser & Gibbons *Soldier & Sailor Wds.* 95 [ref. to WWI]: *A flap*: the familiar Navy term for the sudden "liveliness" on board ship on the arrival of an emergency order involving general activity at extreme high pressure. ***1936, *1939, *1940** in *OEDS.* **1940** in *AS* XVI 76: *A flap.* A row, enquiry, excitement. **1943** in J. Gunther *D Day* 99: I've seen more "flap" (panic, disorder) in peacetime maneuvers. **1944** *Slanguage Dict.* 50: *Flap*—a scare or alarm. **1951** Sheldon *Troubling of Star* 185: That was what was behind that whole flap this afternoon. I keep telling them again and again you can't go out of channels. **1955** Klaas *Maybe I'm Dead* 19: That put the goons in a big flap. **1955** Ruppelt *Report on UFOs* 187: In Air Force terminology a "flap" is a condition…characterized by an advanced degree of confusion that has not quite reached panic proportions. It can be brought on by any number of things, including the unexpected visit of an inspecting general…or the dramatic entrance of a well-stacked female into an officer's club bar. **1964** "Doctor X" *Intern* 330: I got into a big flap with Roger Pfeiffer, the resident on duty, about him. **1965** Bryan *P.S. Wilkinson* 14: It might be interesting to find out what this flap's all about. **1972** in Flaherty *Chez Joey* 28: There has been a flap about an Irish renaissance or what-have-you. **1972** Wambaugh *Blue Kt.* 76: Lieutenant Hilliard was a cool old head and wouldn't get in a flap over fifteen peace marchers. **1978** Truscott *Dress Gray* 165: He wasn't in a state of terminal flap. **1987** *News Watch* (CNN-TV) (Apr. 11): The flap continues about security at the U.S. embassy in Moscow.
  3.a. the mouth.
  1960 Leckie *Marines!* 58: I buttoned my flap and went over to the icebox. **1965-70** in *DARE.* **1986** Stinson & Carabatsos *Heartbreak* 118: No wonder…Choozhoo kept his…flap shut. **1988** Groening *Childhood* (unp.): Shut yer flap.
  b. FLAPDOODLE, 1.
  1959-60 Bloch *Dead Beat* 71: Listening to the line of flap he'd handed out.
  4. an ear.
  1954-60 *DAS.* **1977** in Partridge *DSUE* (ed. 8) 401.
  ¶ In phrases:
  ¶ **catch with (one's) flaps down** [sugg. by syn. *catch with (one's) pants down* s.v. PANTS] *Mil. Av.* to catch unprepared or unawares. *Joc.*
  1942 *Life* (May 25) 8: Caught With His Flaps Down. **1943** Wakeman *Shore Leave* 53: Yeah. There I was, caught with my flaps down. **1951** Sheldon *Troubling of Star* 241: The Air Force was caught with its flaps down.
  ¶ **keep (one's) flaps down** [of aviation orig.] *Pol.* to keep from attracting unnecessary media attention.
  1979 Homer *Jargon* 40: Ever since he was criticized on the ERA vote, the Senator's kept his door locked, his mouth shut, and his flaps well down.

flap *v.* **1.** *Und.* to swindle.—constr. with *jay.* Cf. JAY.
  ***1885** in *F & H* III 5: He and three others…had "cut up" £70 between them, obtained by *flapping a jay*, which, rendered into intelligible

English, means plundering a simple-minded person. **1972** *Playboy* (Feb.) 182: 'N' that's the way we flap the jays!

2. to chatter.

*1912 R. Kipling, in *OEDS:* We're a nice lot to flap about governing the Planet. **1960** Sire *Deathmakers* 180 [ref. to WWII]: You can just show me that room you've been flapping about, Fraulein.

3. to get excited or confused, esp. under pressure.

*1927 in *OEDS:* It's silly to flap about things which can't be remedied. ***1943** Hunt & Pringle *Service Slang* 32: A person who can't "cope" or who is very nervous is told to stop "flapping." **1955** Klaas *Maybe I'm Dead* 12 [ref. to WWII]: Let's take it easy, huh?…We can wait a few hours without flapping. **1978** Truscott *Dress Gray* 346: I was really flapping there for a while. *a*1986 in *NDAS.*

¶ In phrase:

¶ **flap (one's) gums** [or **lips** or **jaw**] to talk to no purpose. [***1910** H.G. Wells, in *OEDS:* You go flapping your silly mouth…and I'll give you a poke in the eye.] **1944** Kendall *Service Slang* 58: Quit flapping your lips. **1955** Graziano & Barber *Somebody Up There* 264: The three sailors are still on our heels, flapping their gums and saying the same things. **1956** H. Ellison *Deadly Streets* 199: Why don't you stop flappin' your lips. **1962** Mandel *Wax Boom* 71 [ref. to WWII]: Bound to get Buffalo Bill flapping his jaw. **1982** I.M. Hunter *Blue & Gray* (NBC-TV film): He said the nigger-lovin' abolitionists up north might stop flappin' their jaws for once and march on Charlestown to free John Brown. **1984** Ehrhart *Marking Time* 142: There's Spiro T. all the time flapping his lips about…America. *ca*1985 *A-Team* (NBC-TV): You been flapping your gums to the wrong person. **1986** "J. Cain" *Suicide Squad* 249: How's he gonna spill his guts to the interrogators if he can't flap his lips? **1988** *Sonny Spoon* (NBC-TV): He starts talkin' and flappin' his lips. **1992** D. Burke *Street Talk* I 71: Stop flapping your gums!

flapdoodle *n.* [of fanciful orig.] **1.** nonsense; silliness.—also attrib. Now *colloq.*

*1833 Marryat *Peter Simple* ch. xxviii: Flapdoodle…It's the stuff they feed fools on. **1884** "M. Twain" *Huck. Finn* 163: A speech, all full of tears and flapdoodle about its being a sore trial for him and his poor brother. **1886** Nye *Remarks* 49: Conversational flapdoodle. **1886** Harte *Tasajara* 300: He…ran off with his father's waiter gal—all on account o' them flapdoodle books he read. **1897** A.H. Lewis *Wolfville* 99. **1925** in H. Miller *Letters to Emil* 14: I'd rather…pretend I'm an artist and write some more flapdoodle. **1930** Lavine *3d Degree* 21: Eloquent flapdoodle about the "crime laboratory" at Police Headquarters and its ultra-scientific methods. **1936** Le Clercq *Rabelais* 48: Their knowledge, said Don Philippe, was but rubbish, their wisdom flapdoodle. **1938** "E. Queen" *4 Hearts* 10: "You're a writer, an artist—a sensitive plant." "Flapdoodle, with onions on the side." **1944** Bellow *Dangling Man* 24: I haven't forgotten that I believed they were devoted to the service of some grand flapdoodle. **1944** C.B. Davis *Leo McGuire* 253: Now that is flapdoodle of the first water. **1948** *Ga. Review* II 159: Interlarded with flapdoodle and misteachings.

2. a fool.

1899 F. Norris *Blix* 125: That's what the doctor says. He's a flapdoodle. **1918** E.E. Rose *Cappy Ricks* 119: That big overgrown flapdoodle there says he's going to spank me!

flap-dumper *n. Av.* a copilot.

1957 E. Brown *Locust Fire* 82 [ref. to 1944]: "My name's Applebym" said the lieutenant. "I'm just a flap dumper, myself." "Don't worry. They'll have you flying in the left soon enough."

flapjaw *n.* **1.** a garrulous person.

1950 *N.Y. Times* (Aug. 10) 4: Some of the gabbiest flap-jaws in recent history. **1954–60** *DAS.* **1967** Lit *Dictionary* 15: *Flap jaw*—An overtalkative person; Chief Running-Mouth. **1981** Ballenger *Terror* 95: It was that big flap-jaw's fault.

2. idle talk.

1952 *New Yorker* (Mar. 8) 26: We caught Manone and Moore for a moment's flapjaw before we left.

flapper *n.* **1.** a hand; (*rarely*) an arm.

*1833 Marryat *Peter Simple* ch. vii: My dear Mr. Simple, extend your flapper to me for I'm delighted to see you. **1859** Matsell *Vocab.* 32: *Flappers.* Hands. **1865** Sala *Diary* II 56: His hands were flappers, and his feet fins. ***1866** in *F & H* III 6: There's my flapper on the strength of it. **1884** "M. Twain" *Huck. Finn* 168: The king he smiled eager, and shoved out his flapper. ***1873** Hotten *Slang Dict.* (ed. 4): *Flapper,* or *flipper,* the hand. **1908** Raine *Wyoming* 107: I get him in the flapper without spoiling him complete. **1971** Wells & Dance *Night People* 117: *Flappers,* n.pl. Arms.

2.a. [cf. FLAP, *n.,* 1] a young girl.

*1888 in *OEDS: Vlapper,*…applied in joke to a girl of the bread-and-butter age. ***1892** in Ware *Passing Eng.* 133: A correspondent of *Notes and Queries* has been troubling his mind about the use of the slang word "flapper" as applied to young girls. **a*1890–93 *F & H* III 6: *Flapper*…(common)—A little girl. **1903, 1905, 1906, 1909, 1915** in *OEDS.* **1917** in E. Pound *Letters* 103: I have always wanted to write "poetry" that a grown man could read without groans of ennui, or without having it cooed into his ear by a flapper. **1917** *Sat. Eve. Post* (Dec. 8) 26: Next…came…Miss Esmé Porteous, still in her teens and barely free of the thrall of flapperdom. **1918** Stringer *House of Intrigue* 25: I was only a flapper, in those days, and there was no woman to whom I could go for advice. **1919** Darling *Jargon Book* 13: *Flapper*—A young flirty girl. **1920** Ade *Hand-Made Fables* 33: Demure little Flappers who should have been dressing their Dolls. **1925** S. Lewis *Arrowsmith* 766 [ref. to *ca*1914]: He kissed her so briskly, so cheerfully, that even a flapper could perceive that she was unimportant. **1945** Mencken *Amer. Lang. Supp. I* 515: *Flapper* began to be heard in the United States not later than 1910, and it had, from the start, the perfectly unopprobrious signification of the German *backfisch.*

[**b.** (see quots.). [In origin prob. merely a narrowing, among habitués of the demimonde, of **(a),** above; U.S. citations are lacking, but this sense may explain the transition from **(a)** to **(c).**]

*1889 Barrère & Leland *Dict. Slang* I 366: *Flippers, flappers,* very young girls trained to vice. ***1909** Ware *Passing Eng.* 133: *Flapper* (Society). A very immoral girl in her early "teens."]

c. a stylish, brash, hedonistic young woman who flouts conventional behavior. Now *hist.* [Now associated almost exclusively with the 1920's.]

1915 H.L. Mencken, in Strauss & Howe *Generations* 255: [The] Flapper of 1915…has forgotten how to simper; she seldom blushes; and it is impossible to shock her. **1918** McNutt *Yanks Are Coming* 172: During the unfortunate moments of his life when it is necessary for him to walk, he teeters precariously around in boots with heels high enough to satisfy a Broadway flapper on parade. **1918** T. Smith *Biltmore Oswald* 25: He showed more genuine appreciation than many a flapper I have plied with costly viands. **1918** in Grider *War Birds* 143: The old boy was no novice, for he'd served his time in Gaul,/And he saw she was a chicken and the flapper pose a stall. **1918** Kelland *High Flyers* 7: Hildegarde, you mean? Sassy one? Swiftest flapper that ever flapped. **1921** in Mencken *New Ltrs.* 144: The people in it are absolutely alive—even the flapper. **1922** in Dos Passos *14th Chronicle* 347: I must protest at this horrible Y man drug clerk attitude to girls or flappers or whatever one calls them that must be the mode at Yale right now. **1922** in Handy *Blues Treasury* 201: And since my sweetie left me, Harlem ain't the same old place./Though a thousand flappers smile right in my face. **1923** Witwer *Fighting Blood* 11: Most of these flappers was just wild about him. **1925** Loos *Gent. Prefer Blondes* 64: His mother does not think that all of the flappers we seem to have nowaday are what a young man ought to marry when a young man is full of so many morals. **1925** C. Harris *Flapper Anne* 107: Is she or ain't she a flapper? **1929** *Variety* (Oct. 30) 65: You might call it "midnight" when the dance halls break up and the flappers run the gauntlet of curbstone Vallees. **1933** Creelman & Rose *King Kong* (film): Isn't there any romance or adventure in the world without a flapper in it? **1938** Smitter *Detroit* 140: It was changing her from a taxi-dancing flapper and was making a woman out of her. **1946** Boulware *Jive & Slang* 3: *Flapper*…Fast girl. **1954** Himes *Third Generation* 234: And this little flapper with the gleam in her eyes, boys, is Anne. **1978** Maupin *Tales* 216: Sounding as quaintly furtive as a flapper approaching a speakeasy. **1989** *Life* (July) 27: She's 82 and still thinks the flappers were too much.

3. a flapjack.

1919 McKenna *Battery A* 137: Flappers or oatmeal…made even our breakfast a success.

4. the mouth.

1937 Steinbeck *Mice & Men* 26: You was gonna leave your big flapper shut and leave me do the talkin'. **1965–70** in *DARE.*

5. usu. *pl.* an ear.

1933 Weseen *Dict. Slang* 334: *Flappers*—The ears. **1961** Wolfe *Magic of Their Singing* 77: To his thinking, what they don't know they can't buzz in the [policeman's] wide flappers. **1979** Charyn *7th Babe* 115: Did I ever bite you on the ear?…I'd have bitten them flappers off by now if I didn't have a bad heart.

flap shot *n.* [cf. 1914 quot. at FLAP, *n.,* 1.a.] BEAVER SHOT.

1984 D. Smith *Steely Blue* 32: She has to get used to seeing…flap shots in the centerfolds.

flap-trap *n.* the mouth.

   1948 A. Murphy *To Hell & Back* 136: Aw, close the flap-trap.

flare *n. Sports.* a ball that is thrown or hit a relatively short distance.

   1976 *Webster's Sports Dict.*: *Flare*...A short pass thrown to a back who is running toward the sideline. **1980** Pearl *Pop. Slang* 50: *Flare n.* (Football) a short pass. **1984** Jackson & Lupica *Reggie* 75: Throw a little flare to right....Get the guy over to third.

flare-up *n.* a dispute; altercation.

   1846 Barbour & Barbour *Journals* 39: A Mexican from Matamoros today reports a flare-up over there....Ampudia left in disgust.

flare up *v.* to get drunk; go on a spree.

   1840 *New Yorker* (Mar. 21) 7: O the coach—went to see the old un—raise the wind—get some brads—flare up, have a lark, eh? **1841** Mercier *Man-of-War* 238: But when he did *flare up* (his own peculiar term for an amiable drunk) all hands were quickly aware of the fact.

flash *n.* **1.** [orig. abbr. of *flash language, flash lingo;* cf. FLASH, *adj.*] Orig. *Und.* underworld argot and slang; the slang of thieves, gamblers, etc. Also attrib.

   *1673 [R. Head] *Canting Academy* 45: *Stam flesh* [*sic*] To Cant; As *the Cully Stams flesh rumly.* He Cants very well. [**1746* in *OED*: They...began to talk their Flash language, which I did not then understand.] **1756* in *OED*: Copper learned flash, and to blow the trumpet. **1781* in Partridge *Dict. Und.* 249: In the language of flash, *blow up* the neighbourhood. [**1785* Grose *Vulgar Tongue*: *Flash lingo.* The canting or slang language.] **1805** *Port Folio* (Aug. 24) 261: I'm up to all your knowing flash. **1811* *Lexicon Balatron.*: *Flash:* To patter flash, to speak the slang language. **1812* Vaux *Vocab.*: To speak *good flash* is to be well-versed in cant terms. **1840** *Spirit of Times* (Nov. 21) 454: It's a sort of flash, brought up by Jack Sheppard and that school. **1843** J. Greene *Exposure of Gambling* 249: For instance, should you be conversing on some subject, and should the man you are conversing with answer you in a way calculated to confuse you...then look out, for he is then talking in such a way that his partner may understand him, however mysterious or unintelligible it may appear to you. This kind of artifice is...familiarly called among gamblers, "flash." **1845** Corcoran *Pickings* 104: Mr. Bouligny...gave them on Christmas-day what is termed in flash phrase "a blow out." **1846** J. Greene *Secret Band of Brothers* 80: He gave me information about a certain "FLASH," or comprehensive language used among professional gamblers and blacklegs. **1848** *Ladies' Repository* VIII (Oct.) 315: *Flash*, A dialect of thieves. **1848** Judson *Myst. of N.Y.* 527: "Flash." The language of thieves. **1851** [G. Thompson] *Jack Harold* 22: The use of *flash* words. **1866** (quot. at PATTER).

2.a. a quick or surreptitious look; sight; glance.

   1899 Dunne *Hearts of Countrymen* 130: "Run in, an' take a flash iv it," he says. **1900** Ade *More Fables* 103: The Cold Chills went down his Spine when he caught a Flash of the Half-Morocco Prospectus. **1903** Hobart *Out for Coin* 44: Just then I got a flash of Dike Lawrence bearing down in our direction. **1904** Ade *True Bills* 66: He immediately tossed one Arm over the Back of the Seat so that she could get a Flash at the four-ounce Ring with the three Rock-Crystals in it. **1912** Beach *Net* 154: "I'm glad you took this table," he began in a low voice. "I always sit where I can get a flash." **1912–14** in O'Neill *Lost Plays* 185: Say, I just got another flash at that dame I was telling you about. **1918** Witwer *Baseball to Boches* 14: They was a big crowd lookin' at somethin' underneath, and, thinkin' it must be the first accounts of my leavin' the club, I took a flash at it. **1919** Witwer *Alex the Great* 31: Alex takes one flash and turns red, white, and blue. **1922** *Variety* (July 21) 9: I give him a flash of the little black pea. **1922** *Variety* (Aug. 11) 8: A quick flash at the village told us that...fortune favored us once more. **1926** Dunning & Abbott *Broadway* 239: I just got a flash at a guy standin' in the back that I thought was Al Jolson. **1927** "M. Brand" *Pleasant Jim* 65: They have a flash of you going by. That's big Jim Pleasant, the horseman. **1929** Booth *Stealing* 295: Stick with Buddy a moment—I'll take a flash myself. *a*1950 P. Wolff *Friend* 156: He had a flash of MP's standing in the doorways.

b. *Specif.*, esp. *Burlesque.* a teasing exposure of a woman's breasts, vulva, legs, or buttocks.

   1946 Gresham *Nightmare Alley* 161: She stripped off her stockings and warmed her feet with her hands, giving him a flash at the same time. **1971** *Current Slang* V 11: *Flash*...n. A tantalizing glimpse of a girl's anatomy or undergarments. **1980** Algren *Dev. Stocking* 122: That hikes the skirt up....A middle-aged dude at the bar caught the flash and I knew I had him pinned.

c. an act of suddenly and briefly exposing one's genitals in public.

1971 Sonzski *Punch Goes Judy* 177: Most "flashes" were made by men over forty—and none were very impressive.

3.a. *Und.* any item or items used by swindlers to attract the interest of victims, as jewelry, expensive merchandise displayed as prizes in games of chance, etc.

   1927 Nicholson *The Barker* 102: *Flash*—A concessionaire's display. **1929** *Sat. Eve. Post* (Oct. 12) 29: *Flash.* Flashy display of merchandise or setting. **1932** in *AS* (Feb. 1934) 26: *Flash.* Something that attracts attention. **1933** Ersine *Pris. Slang*: *Flash*...Anything that is meant to be impressive. **1935** *Amer. Merc.* (June) 229: *Flash*: impressive prizes used for decoration only, because they are seldom lost. **1948** F. Brown *Dead Ringer* 188: Expensive flash that the mark couldn't win. **1942–49** Goldin et al. *DAUL* 77: *Flash.* n. 1. Anything designed to attract attention, as a window display, expensive jewelry. 2. Anything used to impress an intended victim. **1968** Beck *Trick Baby* 24: The flash was in a black velvet pouch....It was like the display at Tiffany's. **1974** *Socio. Symposium* XI 31: "Flash" (showy merchandise) is displayed prominently. **1975** *Urban Life* IV 209: High-quality "flash" (showy merchandise).

b. *Und.* a suit of clothes. Cf. FLASH LAY.

   1929 *Sat. Eve. Post* (Apr. 13) 54: A suit of clothes is a *flash.* **1942–49** Goldin et al. *DAUL* 71: Alibi Al cut out...with a flash that looked like he rolled...a stiff...for it.

4. Orig. *Sports.* a fast runner, worker, or traveler.—often used as a joc. or ironic nickname.

   1929 Hotstetter & Beesley *Racket* 225: *Flash*...a speedy runner, boxer, or automobile. **1929** in Paxton *Sport* 161: Harold Abraham was also a flash, but in a different way....Besides the flashes and morning-glories, there is still a third class of record breakers. **1931** J.M. Saunders *Last Flight* (film): Bronco Bill—the Alabama Flash. **1941** in Botkin *Sidewalks* 485: *Flash.* A very slow-moving vehicle...."Look out, boys! Flash's breeze'll knock you down!" *a*1945 in Lindner *Stone Walls & Men* 463: Just leave it to a F— Street flash. **1988** Automobile vanity license plate, Knoxville, Tenn.: *Flash.*

5. a burst of inspiration, as a sudden idea or realization.

   1924 H.L. Wilson *Professor* 90: However, I have a flash. I got it when we come along in that car. **1958** Hynd *Con Man* 124: Means was slowly working his way through the bourbon when he had a hot flash....What was surprising him from *creating* status? **1963** T.I. Rubin *Sweet Daddy* 9: Well, I got this here flash—like, why don't make with something new, different, see? **1970** Landy *Underground Dict.* 79: *Flash*...Sudden thought or insight—e.g., *I just had a flash.* **1974** R. Stone *Dog Soldiers* 4: My flash was that these people are freakier than we ever could be. **1976–77** McFadden *Serial* 127: His first flash...was that Marlene was pregnant.

6. [sugg. by journalists' jargon] an important or surprising bit of news.

   1938 "E. Queen" *4 Hearts* 174: Say, what's the matter with you? I just got the flash myself. **1949** Taradash & Monks *Knock on Any Door* (film): I got a flash for you—I did a stretch in a joint like this. **1957** E. Lacy *Room to Swing* 142: I dislike being disturbed. What's the big flash? **1962** Regan & Finston *Toughest Pris.* 799: *Flash*—A rumor. **1962** T. Berger *Reinhart in Love* 125: Take my flash...and go in the back of the store.

7.a. *Narc.* a pleasurable thrill felt upon taking a drug; (*also*) a thrill of pleasure; CHARGE; RUSH.

   1946 Mezzrow & Wolfe *Really Blues* 16: It was a lot more than a mere sex flash that kept me all keyed up. *ca*1953 Hughes *Lodge* 96: After you make it, first there's a flash. That's the sudden onrush of the horse feeling. It starts usually in about the third time you jag it off. **1957** Gelber *Connection* 75: It's been ten years since I've had a flash. **1963** Braly *Shake Him* 67: You're just shooting to keep even, but you keep hoping you might get that old flash. **1967** Yablonsky *Hippie Trip* 76: I fixed some demerol and before he could say anything, I had popped him in his one little vein. He just turned around and thanked me a million times because it was the first flash he had in five years. **1969** Mitchell *Thumb Tripping* 192: Wow!!! This paper's a real flash behind acid! **1971** *Nat. Lampoon* (Apr.) 46: Listen, if you want a *real* flash, try *this*! **1973** *Drug Forum* II 133: We have particularly noted the reported phenomenon of "pure needle flash" in our population. **1981** Hathaway *World of Hurt* 34: Jumping is supposed to be a real sex flash.

b. *Narc.* a drug-induced hallucination.

   1970 Landy *Underground Dict.* 79: *Flash*...Hallucination; visual experience. **1971** *Current Slang* V II: *Flash*, n. A hallucinogenic experience. **1972** R. Barrett *Lovomaniacs* 192: *Flashes*, the people from the party had called them; *recurrent delusions* caused by the poison, according to the doctors.

c. a strong temporary interest; KICK.

*ca*1975 in *DAS* (ed. 2) 699: His current "flash," as he calls it, tends toward gaucho suits.

8. *Navy.* (see quot.).

1971 Sheehan *Arnheiter* 77: "Flash" is a Navy nickname for signalmen which is applied selectively.

¶ In phrase:

¶ **cut a flash** make a brilliant impression; make a show.

*1795 in *OED*: Some men...cut a flash without any fortune. **1841** Mercier *Man-of-War* 3: As long as they can cut a flash (as they term it) in port.

flash *adj.* **1.a.** *Und.* connected with or pertaining to the criminal underworld or the demimonde. See also FLASH, *n.,* 1. [In established idioms such as *flash ken, flash house, flash girl,* etc., perh. to be regarded as a comb. form regularly receiving primary stress.]

*1698–99 "B.E." *Dict. Canting Crew: Flash-ken,* a House where Thieves use, and are connived at. *1718 in *OED*: A Ken or House frequented by the Thieves and Thief-Takers, or, in their own dialect, thoroughly Flash. *1718 in Partridge *Dict. Und.* 249: The Cull is Flash, *alias...*he associates himself with thieves. *1753 in Partridge *Dict. Und.*: *Flash house,* a house that harbours Thieves. *1789 in *F & H* III 12: A *flashman* is one who lives on the hackneyed prostitution of an unfortunate woman of the town. **1791** [W. Smith] *Confess. T. Mount* 21: A Song Made by a Flash Cove. *Ibid.* 20: We'll all go to the Flash-ken/And have a roaring song. *1800 in *OED*: Mack and I called at a flash ken in St. Giles's. **1807** Tufts *Autobiog.* 291: The flash fraternity...Nomenclature of the Flash Language. *1812 Vaux *Vocab.: Flash-Crib, Flash-Ken,* or *Flash-Panny,* a public-house resorted to by [criminals]...*Flash-Mollisher:* a *family* [criminal]-woman....*It's a good flat that's never down,* is a proverb among *flash* people. *1825 in *F & H* III 12: *Flash-cove,* the keeper of a place for the reception of stolen goods. *1830 in *F & H* III 10: And rarely have the gentry flash,/In sprucer clothes been seen. **1846** *Lives of the Felons* 7: Sets up a "flash ken" and becomes a thief. *Ibid.* 8: A *"flash ken,"* or thieves' den. **1848** *Ladies' Repository* VIII (Oct.) 315: *Flash Blowen,* A dishonest woman. *Flash cove,* See cross cove. **1859** Matsell *Vocab.* 33: *Flash drum.* A drinking place resorted to by thieves. *Flash-House.* A house of resort for thieves. **1866** *Nat. Police Gaz.* (Nov. 10) 3: It is said to be the intention of these "guns" to open a "flash panny" in Cincinnati. **1866** Williams *Gay Life in N.Y.* 16: A low Flash Ken*...*A drinking house which is the resort of thieves and other bad characters. **1867** in "M. Twain" *Selected Shorter Writings* 32: Two flash girls of sixteen and seventeen were of our little party, and they said they had been arrested for stopping gentlemen in the street in pursuance of their profession.

b. *Und.* counterfeit. *Rare* in U.S.

*1812 in *OED*: How could'st thou be so silly,/Flash screens to ring for home-spun rope. *1821 in *OED*: Passed for the purpose of suppressing the..."flash-notes." *1828 in Partridge *Dict. Und.* 249: Flash notes. *1829, *1859, *1869, *1885, *1889, *1891 (cited in Partridge *Dict. Und.*). **1891** Maitland *Slang Dict.* 112: Flash money is counterfeit. *1897, *1898, *1905, *1923 (cited in Partridge *Dict. Und.*). **1935** Pollock *Und. Speaks: Flash note,* a counterfeit banknote.

2.a. flashy; fancy; gaudy; showy. Also as *adv.* Now *hist.* in U.S.

*1785 in *OED*: One of that numerous tribe of flash fellows, who live nobody knows where. *1836 J.H. Newman, in *OED*: If I could write a flash article on the subjunctive mood, I would, merely to show how clever I was. **1841** Mercier *Man-of-War* 234: What do you think of your flash boat now? **1852** in Somers *Sports in N.O.* 55: Flash boys from Gotham, rejoicing in the fancy titles of Lusty Joe, Dandy Jim, Cockeyed Jack, and the like...and wearing a flashy, fantastic costume, embracing red topped boots, figured cravats, and illustrated vests. **1867** Smyth *Sailor's Wd.-Bk.: Flash vessels,* all paint outside and no order within. **1873** G. Small *Douglass & Mule* 42: But the lawyer he stole cash,/And the sawyer lived too flash. **1893** in Davidson *Old West* 151: His face is hard; he dresses flash. **1898** *Harper's Wkly.* (Apr. 2) 321: A large part of the "flash" riding of Cossacks and Comanche Indians [is] done by artificial aids of either saddlery or loops of various sorts which support them. *ca*1900 in Colcord *Roll & Go* 95: It's of a flash packet, a packet of fame,/She belongs to New York and *Dom Pedro's* her name. *a*1909 Tillotson *Detective* 91: *Flash roll*—Bills wrapped around paper to make a good showing; used by confidence men. **1932** Riesenberg *Log* 274: Believe me, shipmate, she was a flash packet. **1950** A. Lomax *Jelly Roll* 108: My, my, who's this new flash-sport drop in town? *1990 T. Thorne *Dict. Contemp. Sl.: Flash...*ostentatious, showing off. Since the 1960s...this form has tended to replace the earlier "flashy."

b. Orig. *Und.* wide-awake; (*also*) smart; expert. Now *hist.*

*1781 G. Parker *View of Society* II 83: A brother-sharper who is *flash* to the *rig.* *1811 *Lexicon Balatron.: Flash.* Knowing. Understanding another's meaning. The swell was flash, so I could not draw his fogle. The gentleman saw what I was about, and therefore I could not pick his pocket of his silk handerchief. *1819 [T. Moore] *Tom Crib* 19: Another philosopher, Seneca, has shown himself equally *flash* on the subject. *1835 C. Dickens, in *F & H* III 10: Laying aside the knowing look, and flash air, with which he had repeated the previous anecdote. *1836 F. Marryat, in *F & H* III 10: He considered me as a flash pickpocket rusticating until some hue and cry was over. **1888** in *F & H* III 10: The flash riders or horse-breakers, always called "broncho busters," can perform really marvelous feats. **1914** Z. Grey *Rustlers* 27: Be a flash cowboy. **1976** Hayden *Voyage* 240: You got a man runnin' this ship that's a real flash sailorman.

flash *v.* **1.a.** Orig. *Und.* to show, show off, display, or expose, esp. ostentatiously or briefly.—in U.S. often constr. with *on.* Now *S.E.*

*1754 in Partridge *Dict. Und.* 249: He gave me that, as he said, to *flash* to the boys, to shew it to them. *1785 Grose *Vulgar Tongue* 146: To *flash.* To shew ostentatiously. To flash one's ivory; to laugh and shew one's teeth. *1812 Vaux *Vocab.: Flash:* to shew or expose any thing: as I *flash'd* him a bean, I shewed him a guinea. Don't *flash* your *sticks,* don't expose your pistols, etc. *1819 [T. Moore] *Tom Crib* 2: His Lordship, as usual,...is flashing his gab. *1823 "J. Bee" *Slang Dict.*: He *flashed the blunt,* made a show of money to dazzle the spectators. *1837 in *F & H* III 11: Don't flash your notes or your cash/Before other people. **1890** Quinn *Fools of Fortune* 335: He...displays or "flashes" a large roll of money. **1908** Train *Crime Stories* 13: Just flash a few letters on him...letters and envelopes. **1909** Irwin *Con Man* 113: Returning to the tent we flash [the money] on Harris. **1937** in *AS* (Feb. 1938) 46: *Flash,* v. To present or show. "His band can flash six brass on some tunes."

b. *Und.* to flash money ostentatiously.

1949 in *Harper's* (Feb. 1950) 72: Big Pete...does not flash, or make a show of his money.

c. *Police.* to show one's badge to identify oneself as an officer.

1978 Strieber *Wolfen* 155: The guy, he flashed on me, see?...You don't get 'em flashin' unless it's serious business.

2.a. *Specif.* (of a prostitute, striptease dancer, etc.) to expose the vulva, breasts, or buttocks, usu. in a quick, teasing manner. Also *trans.*

*a*1890–93 *F & H* III 11: *To flash a bit...*(venery)...to permit examination; to "spread"...said of women only. **1966** Braly *On Yard* 254: The...movie was a tough flick, full of boss broads who didn't mind flashing. **1970** A. Lewis *Carnival* 38: She flashed her keister, too, Duke. I know *that* game. **1970** Cain *Blueschild Baby* 73: She flashes for me, then looks to see if I've seen. **1970** Winick & Kinsie *Lively Commerce* 53: I flash (showing the genital area), accidentally like. **1971** in Boydell et al. *Deviant Behaviour* 535: Strippers were subject to arrest if they showed their pubic hair or "flashed."

b. *Specif.* (usu. of a man) to expose (one's genitals) suddenly and briefly, esp. in a public place. Occ. *absol.*

*a*1890–93 *F & H* III 11: *To flash it,* or to *flash one's meat.*—To expose the person. (Hence *meat-flasher*) (*q.v.*) Said usually of men. **1961** Kinsey Institute Graffiti MS.: Flash it hard. [Homosexual message in public lavatory.] *a*1972 B. Rodgers *Queens' Vernacular* 82: *Flash...*to briefly expose oneself. **1973** *Oui* (Oct.) 20: I flash and I'm proud. **1977** *N.Y. Post* (July 22) 23: In Westchester flashing is very serious. *ca*1978 in Partridge *DSUE* (ed. 8) 402: *Flash,...flash it...*means "to expose, suddenly and briefly, one's genitals in public."...I've known the [expression] since 1921.

c. to surprise (a person of the opposite sex) by suddenly and briefly exposing the breasts, genitals, etc., esp. in a public place.

1974 V.B. Miller *Girl in River* 10: This guy...flashed both of them before they knew what happened. **1975** Univ. Tenn. student: Some girls have been getting flashed in the main library. **1985** O'Neil *Lady Blue* (film): We got a report he flashed a group of ladies on the elevator. **1989** *Cops* (Fox-TV): Did she flash ya—the old T-shirt up over the head thing? **1989** *Harper's* (Dec.) 34: Glimpse of...breast when she flashes a co-worker.

3. to catch sight of; notice.—occ. constr. with *on.*

1920–21 Witwer *Leather Pushers* 196: The minute he flashed me he dragged me into a little room at one side. **1927** Coe *Me—Gangster* 187: When I first flashed him I thought he was a hop head. **1971** Meggyesy

Out of Their League 202: I didn't know him very well but we had flashed on each other and figured that we were like-minded about dope. **1976–77** McFadden *Serial* 133: He flashed on Sam Stein, sitting in the gloom at the bar.

4. *Carnival.* to set up a display, as of prizes, in (a concession booth).—usu. constr. with *joint*.

1935 *Amer. Merc.* (June) 229: To arrange prizes on the shelf—"to *flash* the joint." *ca***1947–52** in *AS* (Feb. 1953) 116: "To flash the joint," to display merchandise advantageously. **1970** A. Lewis *Carnival* 256: The couple had just finished "flashing their joints" (getting them ready for the marks).

5. [alluding to *news flash*] to communicate; tell.

1956 H. Gold *Not With It* 135: I don't care what you flash to the people, Stan, I just want to play you straight. **1968** O.H. Hampton *Young Runaways* (film): My draft board just flashed me and that scene is nowhere.

6.a. Orig. *Narc.* to experience a thrill from or as if from a stimulant or esp. from a hallucinogenic drug; to experience hallucinations while staring at something, listening to something, etc.—usu. constr. with *on*. Also absol.

1967 *Sat. Eve. Post* (Sept. 23) 91: When I saw her the first time on Haight Street, I flashed. I mean flashed. **1967–68** von Hoffman *Parents Warned Us* 25: There was jewelry…good enough to flash on when you're stoned and colors glow. **1969** Mitchell *Thumb Tripping* 15: Older beatniks…hippies and hitching people all making it with the straights, showing them how to groove and flash. **1970** Landy *Underground Dict.* 79: *Flash*…Feel the sudden, initial effects after taking a drug. **1970** *Time* (Aug. 17) 32: I really flashed on that song.

b. to imagine or remember vividly.—usu. constr. with *on*.

1967 Yablonsky *Hippie Trip* 367: *Flash-on:* to think about; become intensely aware of or remember. **1967–68** von Hoffman *Parents Warned Us* 85: Know what I'm flashing on? My family back in Louisiana. **1970** Landy *Underground Dict.* 79: I just flashed that I was dead. **1972–76** Durden *No Bugles* 4: I started to flash on our two months of AIT. **1978** R. Price *Ladies' Man* 104: "Remember Estelle Spatz?" I flashed on a skinny, plain, bright girl in ninth-grade Spanish. **1987** J. Thompson *Gumshoe* 28: As he'd bent over [the]…desk to deliver the letter of authorization, I'd flashed on him as a kid in the seventh grade, sitting close to the teacher.

c. to realize; think.—usu. constr. with *on*.

1967 (quot. at **(b)** above). **1969** Mitchell *Thumb Tripping* 119: Or an automatic pilot, flashed Gary. **1971** S. Stevens *Way Uptown* 100: The first thing I flashed on was the money, all seats a buck. **1971** Simon *Sign of Fool* 29: I suddenly flashed "shark" in my mind. *Ibid.* 30: I flashed how stupid it was to try outdistancing a shark. **1975** Bellak *Tenth Level* (CBS-TV film): I just flashed on why I really came here. **1972–76** Durden *No Bugles* 116: I flashed on why the Boy Ranger had brought me along. **1976–77** McFadden *Serial* 77: Right away they flashed on how much their trips were alike.

7. to vomit. Cf. *flash (one's) hash*, below.

1962 Maurer & Vogel *Narc. & Narc. Add.* (ed. 2) 301: *Flash.* To vomit. **1964** in *AS* XL (1965) 194: *Flash*…To vomit….it is probably not as common [among students] as *barf.* **1967** J.B. Williams *Narc. & Halluc.* 111: *Flash*—To throw up. **1968** Baker et al. *CUSS* 118: *Flash.* Vomit. **1969** *Current Slang* I & II 34: *Flash, v.* To vomit.—College females, New York. **1972** Smith & Gay *Don't Try It* 201: *Flash*…to regurgitate on heroin. **1978** Lieberman & Rhodes *CB* (ed. 2) 300: *Flashing*—Getting sick.

8. *West.* to break to the saddle.

1927 Rollins *Jinglebob* 235 [ref. to 1880's]: All you does is flashin' hosses, an' our outfit is cows.

¶ In phrases:

¶ **flash (one's) cookies** *Stu.* to vomit.

1980 in Safire *Good Word* 305 [ref. to 1940's].

¶ **flash (one's)** [or **the**] **hash** to vomit. Cf. **(7)**, above.

*****1788** Grose *Vulgar Tongue* (ed. 2): *To Flash the Hash*, To vomit. *Cant.* **1944** Kendall *Service Slang* 23: *Flashed his hash*—sea sickness, retching. **1960** MacCuish *Do Not Go Gentle* 136 [ref. to WWII]: You feel you're gonna flash your hash again, Mac, give us the high sign—okay? **1968** Myrer *Eagle* 442: Old Sad Sam…flashing his hash all over the command. **1968** Baker et al. *CUSS* 118: *Flash the hash.* Vomit. **1968–70** *Current Slang* III & IV 49: *Flash*…hash, v. Regurgitate (a symptom of the flu)—University health service physician, New Hampshire.

flashboy *n. Und.* FLASHMAN.

*****1852** (quot. at FLASH, *adj.*, 2.a.). **1966** R.E. Alter *Carny Kill* 114: He was the kind of cheap flashboy who begged for a cleaning.

flasher *n.* **1.** [cf. earlier MEAT-FLASHER] Esp. *Police.* a person, usu. a male, who suddenly exposes his genitals in a public place; exhibitionist.

1962 in Bruce *Essential Lenny* 209: You know those guys in the park, the flashers? "HELLO LADY!" **1972** *Nat. Lampoon* (June) 83: What do you call a Martian who tips his hat? A flasher. **1974** V.B. Miller *Girl in River* 10: I'm supposed to tie up my squad looking for a flasher? **1978** Truscott *Dress Gray* 342: I'm sure you have heard…about the cadet "flashers," the exhibitionists. **1980** Gould *Ft. Apache* 60: Oh, they're gonna love this up in the squad….Makin' 'em work on a flasher. **1984** *Night Court* (NBC-TV): You work with rapists, junkies, muggers, and flashers. **1987** *Eyewitness News* (WABC-TV) (July 1): The police say the flashers always get busy when the weather gets hot.

2. *Meteorology.* a bolt of lightning.

1988 *Ch. 10 Eyewitness News* (WTVK-TV) (July 27): You'll see some flashers here—and that signifies some pretty heavy storms.

flash lay *n. Und.* the practice of posing as a wealthy, fashionable individual for the purpose of swindling or theft.

1852 *Harper's Mo.* (Sept.) 90: The sooner you peels off them cloth kicksies the better. There ain't no wear in 'em, and they're no good, if you ain't on the flash lay.

flashman *n. Und.* a man who is a member of the underworld or demimonde, esp. a thief, pimp, or swindler.

*****ca***1773** in Partridge *Dict. Und.* 250: I was a flash man of St. Giles. *****1788** Grose *Vulgar Tongue* (ed. 2): *Flash man.* A bully to a bawdy house. *****1789** G. Parker *Life's Painter* 150: A flash-man, a fellow that lives upon the hackneyed prostitution of an unfortunate woman of the town. **1807** Tufts *Autobiog.* 291 [ref. to 1794]: A number of my fellow prisoners were flashmen, (as they termed themselves) an appellation appropriate to such rogues and sharpers, as make exclusive use of the flash lingo. *****1812** Vaux *Vocab.*: *Flash-man:* A favourite or *fancy-man*; but this term is generally applied to those dissolute characters upon the town, who subsist upon the liberality of unfortunate women; and who, in return, are generally at hand during their nocturnal perambulations, to protect them should any brawl occur, or should they be detected in robbing those whom they have *picked up.* *****1820–21** P. Egan *Life in London* 221: Her *flash man*…was now asleep on the *dab.* **1859** Matsell *Vocab.* 33: *Flash-man.* A fellow that has no visible means of living, yet goes dressed in fine clothes, exhibiting a profusion of jewelry about his person.

flat *n.* **1.a.** a foolish or unsuspecting person; SUCKER; (*Und.*) a law-abiding citizen.

*****1753** in Partridge *Dict. Und.* 251: Two Pickers up…to bring in *Flats.* *****1762** O. Goldsmith, in *OED:* If the flat has no money, the sailor cries, I have more money than any man in the fair. *****1773** H. Kelly *School for Wives* 118: He'll make a flat of himself in this Nantzick affair. *****1789** G. Parker *Life's Painter* 142: Who are continually looking out for *flats*, in order to do them upon the *broads*, that is, cards. **1791** [W. Smith] *Confess. T. Mount* 19: *Flats*, country people. **1807** W. Irving *Salmagundi* 50: The grubs, the flats, the noddies. **1807** Tufts *Autobiog.* 291 [ref. to 1794]: *Flat*…a foolish man. *****1812** Vaux *Vocab.*: *Flat.* In a general sense, any honest man, or *square cove*, in opposition to a *sharp* or *cross-cove*….A man who does any foolish or imprudent act, is called *a flat.* **1833** A. Greene *Travs. in Amer.* 127: After gulling the flats of New York long enough, he made a voyage up this river in a steamboat. **1834** *Mil. & Naval Mag. of U.S.* (Oct.) 115: Why it's a libel…to judge of him by the slightest resemblance to ordinary "*flats*, what never saw salt water." **1836** *Spirit of Times* (Feb. 20) 3: The backers would bet *with each other* heavily, so as to gull the flats to follow their example. **1836** *Every Body's Album* I 138: A Flat Between Two Sharps. **1840** *Spirit of Times* (June 6) 159: He was likely…to take in the "flats" by making bets. **1854** St. Clair *Metropolis* 16: I mean for you to fork over to me twenty-five dollars as my share of the dosh you got of that flat this morning. **1859** Matsell *Vocab.* 33: *Flat.* A man that is not acquainted with the tricks and devices of rogues. **1865** in "M. Twain" *Sketches* 63: All the solemn old flats got up in a huff to go. **1866** *Nat. Police Gaz.* (Nov. 3) 2: Why don't you "cheese" it; here is all the "flats" "piping" us, and they will "tumble" to our "lay" if you "beef" out like you are now doing. **1868** Williams *Black-Eyed Beauty* 13: I might have taken the eyelids off of him….You never set eyes on such a flat in all the days of your life. **1889** in *F & H* III 14: The flats who play faro.

b. *Specif.*, the customer of a prostitute.

1849 [G. Thompson] *City Crimes* 39: Do as other w—es do; go and parade Broadway, until you pick up a flat.

2. *Gamb.* a playing card. *Rare* in U.S.

1791 [W. Smith] *Confess. T. Mount* 19: Cards, *broads* or *flats.* *****1812** Vaux

Vocab.: *Flats*, a cant name for playing cards. *1821 in *OED*: We played at flats in a budging-crib. **1925** (cited in Partridge *Dict. Und.* 252).

3. a rejection or dismissal.

1859 Bartlett *Amer.* 155: *Flat*...A rejection, dismissal...."Miss Deborah gave Ike the *flat*." "He's got the *flat*."...Western.

4. *Und.* a policeman; FLATTY.

*ca*1910 in Partridge *Dict. Und.* 251: "What a lot of flats you have brought with you" (flats being the thieves' term for policemen in uniform). **1925** in Partridge *Dict. Und.* **1934** Traven *Death Ship* 15: How much do they pay the flats here? **1935** D.W. Maurer, in *AS* (Feb.) 15 [ref. to *ca*1910]: *Flat* or *flatfoot*. A detective or plainclothes man.

5. (see quot.).

1925 *Sat. Eve. Post* (Dec. 19) 87 [ref. to *ca*1900]: He took flats of beer— that is, beer in a whisky glass and mostly foam.

6. *pl.* Esp. *R.R.* pancakes.

1925 *AS* I (Dec.) 139: And he goes forth to eat of...a "string of flats," and "larup (pancakes and sirup)." **1926** Maines & Grant *Wise-Crack Dict.* 11: *Order of flats*—Dish of wheat cakes. **1927** *DN* V 446: *Flats*, n. Griddle cakes. **1941** *AS* (Oct.) 233: *Flats*. The name for hotcakes or griddle cakes. **1958** in *AS* (Feb. 1959) 78: *Flats*...Hotcakes.

7. *Narc.* a thin packet of heroin or another drug.

1959 O'Connor *They Talked to a Stranger* 71: The addict...wants only to retain contact with his source and buy what white powder he needs in what he calls "flats."

flat *adj.* [short for *flat broke* 'plainly and utterly BROKE'] penniless; BROKE.

1832 (quot. at ONE-EYED). **1833** *Life & Adv. of Crockett* 20: In the slang of the backwoods, one swore...he would never be...flat, without a dollar. **1845** Hooper *Simon Suggs* 59: In half an hour Suggs was "as flat as a flounder." Not a dollar remained of his winning or his original stake. **1846** *Nat. Police Gaz.* (Oct. 17) 41: So far as money was concerned, he was "*dead flat*." **1878** Hart *Sazerac* 59: I was busted flatter'n a cold slapjack. **1880** in M. Lewis *Mining Frontier* 129: But hard luck hit him a lick at last, an' left him flat. The book don't state what he went broke on, but I reckon he got steered up agin some brace game. **1901** Ade *Modern Fables* 9: The Generous Young Fellow who is Flat and the Moneyed Man who never Comes Up. **1924** Tully *Beggars of Life* 55: "Are they broke?"..."We're flatter'n feet wit' broken arches." **1929–30** Dos Passos *42d Parallel* 67: We're flat, but I feel swell. **1937** Reitman *Box-Car Bertha* 100: I was flat in Omaha. **1940** in A. Banks *First Person* 107: I been flat, I been down-and-out, but I always come back. **1943** J. Mitchell *McSorley's* 123: I hate to bother you, pal, but I'm flat. **1946** H.A. Smith *Rhubarb* 14: "I'm flat," Myra said. **1952** H. Grey *Hoods* 88: I'm as flat as a titless broad. *1990** T. Thorne *Dict. Contemp. Sl.* 180: *Flat*...A shortened form of the colloquial "flat broke," heard in raffish speech of the later 1980's.

¶ In phrase:

¶ **in a flat spin** *Av.* confused; befuddled; in a daze.

1919 Downing *Digger Dialects* [ref. to WWI]: *Flat spin*.—To be in difficulties. Only applied to an airman. "On [*sic*] a flat spin"—in a bad position. **1926** *Writer's Monthly* (Nov.) 395: *Flat spin*...Also applied to anyone who becomes confused in conversation. **1926** Springs *Nocturne Militaire* 229 [ref. to 1918]: Then we went up to some Canadian colonel's suite after dinner. By that time I was in a flat spin. **1928** *Pop. Sci. Monthly* (May) 72: A stupid pilot is said to be "in a flat spin in a fog." **1933** Stewart *Airman Speech* 63: Persons who are drunk, off on the wrong track, or are a bit touched, are said to be in a flat spin. **1941** in Wiener *Flyers* 45: *In a flat spin*. Means he doesn't know what it's all about.

flat *adv.* indeed; truly.

1972 C. Gaines *Stay Hungry* 71: She can flat ski, cain't she?

flat *v.* **1.** to reject or dismiss (a suitor).

1807 in Eliason *Tarheel Talk* 271: Widow Yarborough has flatted the little Captain, and he is now...kneeling...before Miss Haynes. **1859** Bartlett *Amer.* (ed. 4) 155: *To flat*. To reject a lover...."She flatted him." Western. **1871** Schele de Vere *Amer.* 602: *Flat*, to, in the West, means to jilt, and is probably derived from another slang phrase, to feel *flat*, denoting the depression which is apt to follow such a disappointment.

2. *Carnival.* to operate a FLAT JOINT.

1935 *Amer. Merc.* (June) 229: To *flat* means to play for money.

flat-ass *adv. & adj.* **1.** *adv.* absolutely; flatly.—usu. considered vulgar.

1964 R. Moore *Green Berets* 44: Our Cambodes flat-ass massacred everything. **1974** Millard *Thunderbolt* 62: We heard Thunderbolt tell the kid they were flat-ass broke. **1980** Tenn. high school teacher, age 27: Now I may be flat-ass dead fuckin' wrong and we all *will* go up in

smoke. **1983** K. Miller *Lurp Dog* 25: I know he didn't flat-ass lie. **1984** J.R. Reeves *Mekong* 62: Oh, shit, yeah, man. I'm flat-ass scared! **1986** Merkin *Zombie Jamboree* 132: That flat-ass goes without saying. **1992** Shryack & Blodgett *Revenge on Highway* (film): You're flat-ass broke.

2. *adj.* absolute.—usu. considered vulgar.

1973 Ace *Stand On It* 137: Nothing. God damn fucking, flat-ass NOTHING.

flatback *n.* **1.** a servile follower.

1861 in G.W. Harris *High Times* 263: He calls me...Mister LOVINGOOD when he's got his dignity on, an a passel of flat backs roun him an he feels good an safe.

2. *Prost.* an act of coition; (*also*) FLATBACKER.

1972 *Urban Life & Culture* I 415: I found that a flat-back ain't never going to get you nothing. **1977–85** Carmen & Moody *Working Women* 1: Freaks, flatbacks, and sleaze.

flatback *v.* *Prost.* (of a female prostitute) to engage in ordinary genital coition; (*hence*) to work as a prostitute; (*trans.*) to engage in coition with (a customer).

1967 [Beck] *Pimp* 105: She can "flat back." **1968** Gover *JC* 18: Sneaked in my room after I done flatback all Fridy night, took it all an turned it inta shit. *Ibid.* 19: It's some deadend hype turnin all her flat-backin money inta shit. **1972** Gover *Mr. Big* 11: Like a...speedfreak who's just flatbacked a whole football team. **1971–73** Sheehy *Hustling* 93: When push comes to shove, it is easier to rob than to flatback. **1974** R.H. Carter *16th Round* 169: I...left the flat-backing faggots strictly to their swipe-swapping pimps. **1975** De Mille *Smack Man* 106: This is where most of the hookers flatback. **1978** Sopher & McGregor *Up from Walking Dead* 264: I won't flatback for you no mo'. **1977–85** Carmen & Moody *Working Women* 207: *Flatbacking*: engaging in conventional sex.

flatbacker *n.* *Prost.* a common female prostitute.

1967 [Beck] *Pimp* 70: You gonna starve to death, Nigger, if she's a chump flat-backer. **1970** Winick & Kinsie *Lively Commerce* 207: A "flat-backer" who offers only coitus ("old-fashioned" or "straight") is likely to lose customers. **1971–73** Sheehy *Hustling* 28: The streetwalker has nothing but slurs for "those lazy flatbackers," meaning call girls. **1975** De Mille *Smack Man* 121: The dumb pimps are losing all their flatbackers to bad skag. **1978** Lieberman & Rhodes *CB* (ed. 2) 300: *Flatbackers*—Prostitutes. **1992** Hosansky & Sparling *Working Vice* 125: A flatbacker, a woman that just turned dates.

flat bloke *n.* *Und.* an ordinary law-abiding man; SQUARE JOHN.

1866 *Nat. Police Gaz.* (Nov. 24) 3: The "flat bloke" wore a look of satisfaction.

flatboat *n.* a big, clumsy foot or shoe. *Joc.*

1885 *Puck* (May 27) 203: Why, again, should the same foot be referred to in...St. Louis...as a "ham," and in...Cincinnati as a "flat-boat"? **1886** in Herdegan & Beaudot *At Gettysburg* 79 [ref. to 1861]: Gunboats, flatboats, schooners, [etc.], were derisive names for shoes]. **1889** "M. Twain" *Conn. Yankee* 134: Then you put on your shoes—flat-boats roofed over with interleaving bands of steel. **1903** in *DA*: Don't you know a switchman oughtn't t' put his feet in flatboats?

flat-broke *n.* a person who is flat broke.

1934 Cunningham *Triggernometry* 282: They were two "flat-brokes."

flatcar *n.* *R.R.* (see quot.).

1927 *AS* (June) 389: Pancakes [are called] *flat-cars*.

flatfoot *n.* **1.** *Navy.* an enlisted sailor. ["Jemmy [and Jimmy] Flatfoot" in 1835 quots. is used in personification.]

1835 *Knickerbocker* (Jan.) 23: If this does not prove that Jemmy Flatfoot had a hand in laying out the coast of Africa, you may call me a marine. **1835** *Knickerbocker* (Feb.) 104: There you see Jimmy Flatfoot again. *1897* in *OEDS*. **1900** Cullen *Tales* 371: My fo'c'sle shipmates were all old flat-feet. **1901** King *Dog-Watches* 138 [ref. to 1880's]: My boy, you have had your spell of flunkyism for us flatfoots. **1903** *Our Naval Apprentice* (Dec.) 152: Claude—I say, sailahman, have you evah seen two ships engaged in an encounter? Flatfoot—No, sir, I ain't, but I've seen a ship spar. **1906** Beyer *Amer. Battleship* 210: Some call er sailor er flat-foot. *1909* Ware *Passing Eng.* 134: *Flat-foot* (Navy). A young sailor less than twenty-one. (See Shellback.) **1910** *Everybody's Mag.* (Jan.) 116: A fine sight I'd be riding up in a Yesler Way cable with such a bunch of flat-feet. **1918** Ruggles *Navy Explained* 60: Sailors are called flatfoot on account of so many going barefooted in tropical climates. This practice was carried out in its entirety on the old ships of our navy....The name is said to have originated in the army. **1920** Bishop *Marines Have Landed* 354: "Flatfoot"—Marine Corps slang for a sailor. **1926** *AS* I (Oct.): Old sailor expressions, such as "avast" and "belay" your modern flatfoot seldom encounters. **1932** Nicholson & Robinson *Sailor Beware!* 26: Well, come on, flatfeet, give a guy the news. **1952** *Leatherneck* (Nov.) 74: *Flatfoot* n. Bluejacket, sailor.

2. *Army.* an infantryman, esp. a militiaman.—used derisively.

1862 in Wiley *Johnny Reb* 342: I wood [*sic*] rather be corporal in company F of the Texas Rangers than to be first Lieu in a flat foot company. **1864** in *War of Rebellion* (Ser. II) vii: [The rebels] have got militia in Platte County and Clay [Mo.]....They are called "Flat Foots." ***1865** Hotten *Slang Dict.* (ed. 3): *Flat-feet*, the battalion companies in the Foot Guards. ***1889** Barrère & Leland *Dict. Slang* I 369: *Flat-feet* [*sic*] (popular),—a foot soldier; applied generally to the Foot-guards. *a**1890–93** F & H III 16: *Flat-feet*...(generally with some powerful adjective), applied to militia men to differentiate them from linesmen. *ca***1915** in Wiley & Milhollen *They Who Fought* 19: The men who we as Cavalry or Artillery dubbed "flat feet" and "dust beaters" and often ridiculed on the march [during the Civil War].

3. a black person.—used contemptuously.

1867 Helper *Nojoque* 346: Sambo, Cuffey & Co; Hucksters in Hot Corn; Woolyhead, Flatfoot & Co; Melon Mongers; Blackamoor, Blobberlip, & Co.; Peddlers in Pumpkins.

4. *Pol.* (see quot.).

1887 in *DA*: An American "flatfoot" is a man who stands firmly for his party.

5. a police patrolman; police officer or detective. Cf. FLATTY.

1912 Stringer *Shadow* 48: By the time he had fought his way up to the office of Second Deputy he no longer resented being known as a "rough neck" or a "flat foot." *Ibid.* 58: Copeland was an out-and-out "office" man, anything but a "flat foot." **1919** Darling *Jargon Book* 13: *Flat Foot*—A policeman. **1924** Henderson *Keys to Crookdom* 405: *Flat foot*—A patrolman. **1929** "E. Queen" *Roman Hat* 90: Then what the hell do you mean by sending one o' your flatfoots to keep me locked up all night, hey? **1934** H. Roth *Call It Sleep* 104: Now look what yev started, ye divil of a flat-foot! **1938** Baldwin & Schrank *Murder* (film): He really is a flatfoot. **1947** Motley *Knock on Any Door* 110: The flatfoot frisked him. **1955** Deutsch *Cops* 182: If that flat-foot wants to see me, she knows where to find me. **1955** Q. Reynolds *HQ* 27: Half of New York calls a cop a "flat-foot." **1960** Carpenter *Youngest Harlot* 76: Do I look like a flatfoot? **1977** A. Patrick *Beyond Law* 4: Baretta was no ordinary flatfoot. He made it up through the ranks...from petty thief to top-notch undercover agent.

flatfoot *v.* **1.** to drink (liquor) in a single swallow; CHUGALUG.

1963 Coon *Short End* 234: Because he flatfooted all I had left in the jug, about a quarter of a pint, which might not sound like much, and might be more impressive if I told you I would just as soon flatfoot so much lighter fluid.

2. *Auto Racing.* to drive (an automobile) at top speed.

1974 Scalzo *Stand on Gas* 110: You just set your foot on the throttle and flat-foot 'er all the way round.

flat-footed *adj.* **1.** destitute; FLAT.

1853 "P. Paxton" *In Texas* 204: The quondam owner is said to be *flat broke* or *flat footed* and must beg, borrow, or steal for a *stake*. **1858** [S. Hammett] *Piney Woods* 94: And then if you are flat-footed, I'd lend you a stake to start on.

2. *Orig. Sports.* unprepared. Now *S.E.*

1908 in Fleming *Unforget. Season* 154: Frank Chance...is flatfooted against the "spit ball." **1912, 1928, 1940, 1955, 1963** in *OEDS*.

flatfooter *n. Navy.* FLATFOOT, 1.

1938 Connolly *Navy Men* 78 [ref. to 1904]: And wouldn't you like to be standing near by when a few old-time flatfooters get hold of him and start filling him up with a juicy line of stuff about Navy life.

flat hat *n.* **1.** *Navy.* **a.** [sugg. by **(b)**, below] an enlisted sailor; bluejacket.

1883 Keane *Blue-Water* 174 [ref. to *ca*1875]: I served two months in the Turkish commissariat [in Constantinople], and even fired many a shot at a "flat hat" before I took to the sea again. **1966** Gallery *Start Engines* 20: "I had to put another one of your flathats on report this afternoon," said Peabody smugly.

b. the flat-crowned cap formerly worn as part of the enlisted man's blue winter uniform.

1918 Ruggles *Navy Explained* 11: Hey, Spud, wotell's eatin' ye? Lay off'n dat wash deck bucket, y' ding-dong boot, or I'll knock y'out from under y'r ding-dong flat hat! **1958** Cope & Dyer *Petty Officer's Guide* (ed. 2) 345: *Flat hat:* (Slang). Blue cap worn by enlisted men.

c. a naval aviator. Cf. FLATHAT, *v.*

1939 Fessier *Wings of Navy* (film): What's the matter with you, flat hat?

2. [alludes to the mortarboard of academic costume] a college student.—used derisively.

1923 Weaver *Finders* 74: I look up quick, thinkin', "Gee, here's some flat-hat" (flat-hat's a college-willy) "tryin' to make me."

flathat *v. Naval Av.* to show off by flying low or recklessly; (*broadly*) to show off in any manner.

1939 R.A. Winston *Dive Bomber* 178: "Flat-hatting" around at low altitudes. **1942** Tregaskis *Guadalcanal Diary* (Aug. 30): I was flat-hatting along the beach at about fifty feet...when I saw two Zeros ahead and to the right. **1956** Heflin *USAF Dict.* 209: *Flat-hat*...To fly needlessly and dangerously low; to fly in a foolhardy, grandstanding manner. **1959** R.L. Scott *Flying Tiger* 32: It dealt with intentional low flying called "hedge-hopping" in the Air Corps and "flathatting" in the Navy air arm. **1961** Forbes *Goodbye to Some* 241 [ref. to WWII]: That restricts us to mild flat-hatting. **1963** Dwiggins *S.O. Bees* 26 [ref. to WWII]: Blackburn had done his own share of flat-hatting. **1972–79** T. Wolfe *Right Stuff* 24: So-called hot-dog stunts, such as outside loops, buzzing, flat-hatting, hedgehopping and flying under bridges. **1979** Former USN QM, age 45: *Flathatting* means showing off in an aircraft. Once in a while they used it to mean any kind of showing off: "Quit flathatting." Evidently it comes from the old Navy flat hats, but I don't know why. **1988** Hynes *Flights of Passage* 110: Flat-hatting is simply flying very low, the lower the better.

flathatter *n. Naval Av.* a pilot who engages in flathatting.

1944 *N.Y. Times* (Sept. 24) E 2. **1955** Reifer *New Words* 83: *Flat hatter n. Mil. Slang.* Irresponsible or playful aviator. **1963** Dwiggins *S.O. Bees* 39 [ref. to WWII]: I want rebels, pilots who beat up the boondocks. Flat-hatters.

flathead *n.* **1.** a dull-witted person; blockhead. Also attrib.

***1862** in *OEDS*: He hedn't t' sense 'at he wur born wi'—a big flathead. **1884** "M. Twain" *Huck. Finn* 23: I think they are a pack of flatheads for not keeping the palace themselves 'stead of fooling them away like that. **1906** *Variety* (Jan. 6) 7: I have no kick coming unless it's when some flathead sorehead backs me up against a wall and insists on telling me [etc.]. **1911** *Adventure* (Jan.) 447: Unless a fellow is a flathead he'll admit excellence when he sees it. **1911–12** Ade *Knocking the Neighbors* 202: I can raise the Temperature of every Flathead from Bangor to San Antone. **1915–17** Lait *Gus* 108: Of all the lobs, boneheads, rummies, numbskulls, fumble-footed, feeble-minded flatheads...you're the champ. **1920** Fitzgerald *Paradise* 177: They'd let any well-tutored flathead play football. **1924** Stallings *Plumes* 247: You German flatheads. **1952** "M. Roscoe" *Black Ball* 39: "April, you better level with me." "I am, you flathead..." **1953** Harris *Southpaw* 3: 100,000,000 boobs and flatheads...swallowed down whole the lies of Krazy Kress. **1955** Ellson *Rock* 86: Hey, flathead...You feel like paying for that table? **1956** in Woods *Horse-Racing* 51: No pinhead jockeys...and no flathead stewards. **1958** P. Field *Devil's R.* 23: Right there, you flathead! **1966** Kenney *Caste* 99: The flathead had been givin' us the business. **1976** Rosen *Above Rim* 113: Charge?! You flathead cocksucker! **1987** S. Martin *Roxanne* (film): You flat-nosed, flat-faced flathead.

2. *Logging.* a sawyer in a mill; (*also, contemptuously*) a black lumberjack.

1927 *AS* II (Oct.) 24: For example a man who saws logs is a "flathead," while the man who stands behind the edging machine and separates the trimmed strips from the lumber is called the "bear-fighter." **1948** McIlwaine *Memphis* 249: In 1906 Negro lumberjacks—always called flatheads—killed a seven-foot black wolf in the Arkansas woods only eight miles...from [Memphis]. *Ibid.* 251: The flatheads...laughed at the normal supply of mosquitoes.

flat-iron *n. Naut.* a vessel that lies very low in the water, esp. a monitor. Now *hist.*

1853 *Harper's Mo.* (Mar.) 436: We are much amused at our captain rallying an acquaintance, who was pulling about in a sort of three-cornered boat, upon "going to sea in a *flat-iron*." **1919** Fiske *Midshipman* 396 [ref. to *ca*1907]: The *Arkansas* was a short, broad, shallow, slow, heavily armored coast-defense monitor, sometimes irreverently called a "flat-iron." **1919** *Our Navy* (Nov.) 16: Very little has been said in print about this old flat-iron since we became identified with a group of Mexican bandits. **1937** Thompson *Take Her Down* 121: While the old flatiron steamed but twelve knots, nevertheless she could take the heavy blows. **1949** W. Granville *Sea Slang* 98: *Flatiron.* A vessel lying low in the water, specifically: (1) A Yangtse River gunboat. (2) One of the "Monitors" that bombarded the Belgian coast in the 1914–18 War. (3) The L.C.S. (Landing Craft Support) used in the 1939–45 War.

*1961 Burgess *Dict. Sailing* 90: *Flat-iron.* Any vessel of shallow draft, abnormally wide in the beam, and with low upperworks.

flat joint *n. Carnival.* a dishonest gambling place or game. Hence **flat-jointer.** Cf. FLAT, *n.,* 1.a.

1914 Jackson & Hellyer *Vocab.* 34: *Flat joint.* Noun. Current amongst open-air sure-thing men…The "shells"; "three-card monte"; the "eight die case";…are all grafting flat joints. The term is derived from the essentiality…of a counter or other flat area across…which the swindle may be conducted. **1922** *Variety* (June 30) 8: Flat Joints Must Go. *a***1935** in *Jour. Pop. Culture* VI (1973) 599: Haggerman…was a *flat jointer* around fairs. **1935** Pollock *Und. Speaks: Flat joint,* a cheating gambling house in which the public has no chance to win. **1935** *Amer. Merc.* (June) 229: *Flat joint:* a concession which plays only for money. **1951** Mannix *Sword-Swallower* 193: A "flat joint" is the carny name for a gambling wheel that can be operated on a flat counter or hung against a flat backdrop. **1963** D.W. Maurer, in Mencken *Amer. Lang.* (rev.) 731: *Strong-joint* or *flat-joint* operators.

flatline *v.* [alluding to the flat line on the screen of such a device when vital signs cease] *Med.* (of a patient) to die while being monitored by an electronic device that measures vital signs; (*hence*) to die. Also *fig.*

1981 in Safire *Good Word* 152. **1984** W. Gibson *Neuromancer* 50: [He] flatlines on his EEG.…"Boy, I was *daid.*" **1987** *Tour of Duty* (CBS-TV) [ref. to Vietnam War]: I think he's flatlined. Nothing left. **1988** *Maledicta* IX 198: Patients…*croak* [or] *flatline.* **1991** in *AS* LXVII (Winter 1992) 423: Has one of Hollywood's hottest romances finally flatlined?

flat-noggin *n.* FLATHEAD, 1.

1864 "E. Kirke" *Down in Tenn.* 110: Ye *is* a…fool, ef ye karn't outwit two sech flat-noggin sarpints as these is.

flat-out *n.* an utter failure; a fizzle.

*ca***1870** in *DAE:* "It was a complete flat-out." "He made a flat-out."— N[ew] E[ngland]. **1886** in *DAE:* I didn't know't was goin' to be s'ch a perfect flat-out.

flat-out *adj.* out-and-out; thoroughgoing. Now *colloq.*

1964 *Time* (Nov. 27) 33: Marina Oswald…was…burdened by a…husband who was a flat-out failure in every way. **1972** J.W. Wells *Come Fly* 42: I know a librarian who is such a flat-out swinger who makes me feel positively sheltered by comparison. **1973** in H.S. Thompson *Shark Hunt* 55: I…got braced for some flat-out raving. **1972–76** Durden *No Bugles* 172: He is nuts…A flat-out freak. **1977** *Indiana Folklore* X 98: I don't mean a college degree, I mean flat-out common sense. **1981** Wolf *Roger Rabbit* 93: That's a flat-out lie. **1981** Rucker *57th Kafka* 28: The power and glory of flat-out pure mathematics. **1983** *Newsweek on Campus* (Dec.) 7: He played a flat-out criminal…in "Bad Boys."

flat-out *adv.* thoroughly; plainly; outright. Now *colloq.*

1959 in Harvey *Air Force* 131: He was flat-out scared. **1968** Gover *JC* 14: I's flatout broke an down in the mind. **1973** Browne *Body Shop* 147: They tell you flat out how it is. **1973** R.M. Brown *Rubyfruit* 37: Molly, you are flat-out crazy. **1975** C.W. Smith *Country Music* 77: She flat out lied to him! **1975** S.P. Smith *Amer. Boys* 206: Chase was crazy, flat out. **1992** Strawberry & Rust *Darryl* 330: If some other team gets flat-out hot, plays .650 ball, and beats us.

flat out *v.* to fail completely; fizzle.

1839 C.M. Kirkland *New Home* 161: He can demonstrate…that the bank never would have "flatted out," if he had had a finger in the pie. **1865** in *DA:* Men…who have failed in trade…or to use an expressive Yankee phrase, have "flatted out" in a calling or profession. **1867** in *DAE:* So all that speculation of mine flatted out. **1877** Bartlett *Amer.* (ed. 4) 226: *To flat out.* To collapse; to prove a failure…"The meeting flatted out."

flat store *n. Carnival.* FLAT JOINT.

*ca***1947–52** in *AS* (Feb. 1953) 116: *Flat store,* n. A gambling concession in which the game is rigged so that the operator can win at will. **1970** A. Lewis *Carnival* 19: The other kind [of carnival concession]—flat stores—these are the gyp joints set up solely for the purpose of taking the marks as quickly as possible…E. James Strates isn't the only owner who won't allow flatties to operate. Others feel the same way. **1971** J. Brown & A. Groff *Monkey* 18: My employers operated a "flat store"— a game of chance that could be controlled with a "gaff" or a "break," thus allowing the operator to stop the spindle at any spot he desired.

flattener *n. Entertainment Industry.* a record, film, etc., that is a great commercial success; a great hit.

1981 Jenkins *Baja Okla.* 265: Lonnie's single was no pop crossover boffo platinum flattener.

flatter *n.* a police patrolman; FLATFOOT.

1928 in Wilstach *Stage Slang* (unp.): A "flatter" (policeman).

flatter-trap *n.* (see quot.).

1859 Matsell *Vocab.* 33: *Flatter-trap.* The mouth.

flat tire *n.* a dull-witted, insipid, disappointing, or unsuccessful person; (*hence*) anything boring or disappointing.

1922 *Variety* (July 21) 4: She's such a flat tire. **1925** in *OEDS:* You think you're the berries, don't you? Well, you might have been once, but you're a flat-tire these days! **1926** Hormel *Co-Ed* 198: Her world must look upon her these days as a social failure—distinctly a "flat tire." **1926** Wood & Goddard *American Slang* 17: *Flat tire.* A dud; a vimless person. **1926** Maines & Grant *Wise-Crack Dict.* 9: *Flat-tire*—Girl never to be taken to a blow-out. **1927** W. Winchell, in *Vanity Fair* (Nov.) 132: When a person is "all wet," he's a "flat tire," a "wash-out," a "dud," a "false alarm"—meaning "He's not my type" or "no good." **1927** Mayer *Just Between Us Girls* 137: I rather suspected he…would turn out to be a flat tire. **1928** *AS* III (Feb.) 219: *Flat tire*—An unattractive girl, a poor date. **1943** Twist *Bombardier* (film): Are you a flat tire? A rundown heel with no appeal? **1963** T.I. Rubin *Sweet Daddy* 14: Take the marriage bit. That's the biggest flat tire of all. *a***1990** Cundiff *Ten Knights* 24: But if you were my boyfriend, I'd think you were a flat tire.

flattop *n. Navy.* an aircraft carrier. Now *colloq.*

1942 *Time* (June 22) 26: Scratch one flat-top. **1942** Casey *Torpedo Junction* 10: *Flat-top.* A term generally applied to a carrier but sometimes applied to a tanker. **1942** S. Johnston *Queen of Flat-tops* 181: It meant that the Navy could scratch one more Japanese flat-top [carrier], off the lists of the enemy's fleet. **1943** Hubbard *Gung Ho* (film): You might have had a shot at that flattop those planes came from. **1944** Hubler & DeChant *Flying Leathernecks* 26: "Flat-tops rush in where angels might do them damage," murmured one Marine dive-bomber pilot over the air. **1945** Dos Passos *Tour* 95: We duck under the beetling bows of the tall flattops. **1972** *N.Y. Times Mag.* (Mar. 19) 11: The thrill and danger—and the power—of flying a jet from a flat-top dominate the pilots' attitude toward their mission and the war. **1981** Mersky & Polmar *Nav. Air War in Viet.* 195: The Navy's first "flattop" [was] the U.S.S. Langley. **1982** S.P. Smith *Officer & Gentleman* 11: Zack…left…to go to the harbor and look at the flattop.

flatty *n.* **1.** [cf. FLATFOOT, *n.,* 5, and FLAT, *n.,* 4] *Und.* a police patrolman (as opposed to a detective); (*broadly*) any police officer. Also (in earliest use) **flatty cop.**

1866 *Nat. Police Gaz.* (Nov. 17) 3: They were "pulled" by a "flatty cop." **1873** Sutton *N.Y. Tombs* 481: One night he fell into the hands of a "flatty cop" and was given "five stretches" for a very badly executed river job. **1892** Norr *China Town* 40: That sucker had actually followed us to California with the flatty and nailed Fitz. **1899** "J. Flynt" *Tramping* 393: *Flatty:* a policeman, synonymous with "bull." **1900** Willard & Hodler *Powers That Prey* 51: The "flatties" in uniforms surrounded the place. **1901** Willard *World of Graft* 2: The "boss," as well as the humblest "flatty,"* receives freely both his commendation and condemnation.…*Patrolman. *Ibid.* 219: *Flatty,* uniformed policeman. **1903** *Independent* (July 23) 1721: I did not propose to be buncoed by him or any other "flatty," as we termed plain clothes men. **1904** *Life in Sing Sing* 248: *Flatty.* A plain clothes officer. **1909** in "O. Henry" *Works* 1571: Take me away, flatty, and give me gas. **1911** Runyon *Tents* 18: We'd croaked a flatty in Baltimore and we beat, by a nose, the law. **1912** Stringer *Shadow* 108: He could follow…those confident-striding "flatties" with their ash night-sticks. **1933** in Ruhm *Detective* 84: Private flattie from the studio, aren't you, boy? **1931–34** in Clemmer *Pris. Commun.* 332: *Flattie*…a policeman. **1953** W. Brown *Monkey on My Back* 152: The flatties nabbed him.

2.a. *Carnival.* an operator of a FLAT JOINT.

ca*1947–52** in *AS* (Feb. 1953) 116: *Flattie,* n. Operator of a *flat store.* **1953** Gresham *Midway* 18: Many of the show people look upon the grifting "flat joints," or gambling games, as a necessary evil. Yet they will have a friendly word for a "flattie" if they sit down beside him in the cookhouse. **1961** Scarne *Comp. Guide to Gambling* 459: *Flatty, Thief* or *Grifter:* The operator of a flat, alibi, two-way or G-joint. Any crooked game operator. *Ibid.* 463: I began…getting flatties and grifters to talk about their trade secrets. *ca***1986** in *NDAS.* **1988** Gryczan *Carnival Secrets* 2: *Flatties*—carny…operators who cheat the public.

b. *Carnival.* FLAT JOINT.

1970 (quot. at FLAT STORE). **1986** *NDAS.*

flat wheel *n.* FLAT TIRE. Also **flat wheeler.** Hence **flat-wheeled,** *adj.*

1919 *DN* V 72: *Flat-wheeled,* a term of disparagement. "He is a *flat-*

wheeled old boob." New Mexico. **1922** in *DN* V 147: *Flat-wheeler*—a young man whose idea of entertaining a girl is to take her for a walk. **1924** Henderson *Keys to Crookdom* 404: *Flat wheel*. A slow fellow, stupid person, cheapskate. **1929** in S. Smith *Gumps* 55: Show 'em you're not a flat wheel in the Carr family.

flat-wheeler *n.* **1.** *R.R.* a railroad car that frequently jolts and bounces.

[**1918** in York *Mud & Stars* 54: What a noble trip, jolt and jog and jar,/ Forty we, with Equipment C, in one flat-wheeled box car.] **1943** Guthrie *Bound For Glory* 9: Our car was a rough rider, called by hoboes a "flat wheeler."

2. see FLAT WHEEL.

flavor *n.* **1.** *Black E.* an attractive young woman.

1963 *Time* (Aug. 2) 14: *Flavor*. Pretty girl. **1991** Nelson & Gonzales *Bring Noise* 291: This…flava is a long way from being a homeboy-skeezer pleezer.

2. variety; kind. [Allegedly orig. computer jargon, applied to different varieties of operating systems in 1960's.]

1983 Naiman *Computer Dict.* 58: Formatting commands come in two flavors: embedded and print-time. **1983** Wambaugh *Delta Star* 121: All flavors…Just so they were young. **1984** Heath *A-Team* 53: Thirty-one flavors of mental illness. **1987** *Miami Vice* (NBC-TV): "I've got a kid." "What flavor?" "Boy." **1991** Dunnigan & Bay *From Shield to Storm* 346: There are always at least four "flavors" of aircraft in a "mission package." **1991** *N.Y. Times Bk. Review* (Oct. 21) 21: Historical romances come in two flavors. **1992** *Time* (Sept. 7) 28: Threats come in many flavors. **1993** *CBS This Morning* (CBS-TV) (Mar. 10): PMS comes in three flavors.

3. amusement; fun.

1993 *TV Guide* (Jan. 23) 45: The Klingon language…was created for fun and flavor.

4. *Rap Music.* a hip-hop recording; rap song.

1993 *Source* (July) 50: Bad boys…in Beamers…pumping the flavaz of the week.

¶ In phrase:

¶ **kick flavor** *Rap Music.* to perform; to be entertaining.

1990 "Justice" in B. Adler *Rap!* 51: Kickin' Some Flavor [title]….Let me…catch my breath, and I'm gonna kick some more flavor. **1990** *Yo! MTV Raps* (MTV): We went back there and kicked a little flavor. **1991** *Source* (Oct.) 58: Show Biz kicks flavor and then passes the mic to Diamond D.

flavorful *adj.* *Computers.* TASTEFUL.

1983 Naiman *Computer Dict.* 58: *Flavorful*…Beautiful; aesthetically pleasing. **1983** Steele *Hacker's Dict.*

flawless *adj.* *Homosex.* physically attractive; (*broadly*) great; wonderful.

*a***1972** B. Rodgers *Queens' Vernacular* 82: *Flawless*…handsome. **1984** Mason & Rheingold *Slanguage*: *Flawless* adj. Perfect specimen. A GQ model is flawless. **1981–89** J. Goodwin *More Man* 16: *Flawless*, denoting someone who is especially attractive or something extremely well done.

flax *v.* to defeat; whip.—usu. constr. with *out.*

1839 in *DA*: The Maine boys 'll flax out them are Brunswickers like sixty. *ca***1849** in *DAE*: When you commence a pugilistic encounter,…you are ready to…either flax out your opponent, or give nature special fits in the undertaking. *ca***1855** in *DAE*: "Old Zack" flaxed the Mexicans clean out of their boots in Mexico. **1863** in Whitman *Corres.* I 176: I tell you the copperheads got flaxed out handsomely. *ca***1867** in G.W. Harris *Lovingood* 190: Yere's what kin jis' sircumstansully flax out that ar court-hous'. **1877** Wheeler *Deadwood Dick, Prince of Road* 83: "You're flaxed ag'in, pardner!" he said, with a light laugh, as he raked in the stakes. "This takes your all, eh?"

flaxed out *adj.* fatigued to exhaustion.

1894 *Harper's Mag.* (June) 144: He looks purty well flaxed out, don't he? **1903** *DN* II 351: I'm all flaxed out.

fleabag *n.* **1.** a bed or mattress; (*also*) a bedsack or sleeping bag.

***1839** in *Englische Studien* LX (1925) 293: Troth, and I think the gentleman would be better if he went off to his flea-bag himself. **1889** Barrère & Leland *Dict. Slang* I 370: *Flea-bag* (prize-fighters), a bed. **1915** Rosher *Flying Squadron* 41: I am going to invest in a Jaeger flea bag (sleeping bag). **1917** Imbrie *War Ambulance* 7: So, having aligned our cars with the others, we shouldered our "flea-bags," as sleeping sacks are known in the army, and stumbled across a muddy road and pitch dark parade ground. **1941** Kendall *Army & Navy Sl.* 5: *Flea bag*…your

mattress. **1943** Moore *Sky Is My Witness*: Rollow, sitting on the bunk near mine, began to bang his shoe on a piece of iron pipe near my pillow. "Get up out of the flea pad!…Get up! Get up! Get up!"

2.a. a verminous lodging house; (*hence*) a cheap hotel; (*broadly*) any shabby building. Also attrib.

1922–24 McIntyre *White Light* 16: Gone are the iniquitous cesspools [of the Bowery], "The Flea Bag," "The Alligator," "Nigger Mike's." **1930** D. Runyon, in *Collier's* (Feb. 1) 7: An old fleabag in Eighth Avenue that is called the Hotel de Brussels. **1931** Harlow *Old Bowery* 519 [ref. to *ca*1911]: The whole front of Tricker's putrid dive, the Fleabag, at 241 Bowery, was shot out by two carloads of Zelig gunmen who swept past it. **1939–40** O'Hara *Pal Joey* 59: The flea-bag where I was living did not permit dogs. **1943** J. Mitchell *McSorley's* 123: Say a crap game has to float from one little fleabag hotel to another. **1946** Gresham *Nightmare Alley* 62: Getting all dressed up to walk thirty feet down the hall of a fleabag like this at four in the morning. **1950** Riesenberg *Reporter* 89: The Bowsprit Hotel. Do you know that flea bag? **1951** O'Hara *Farmer's Hotel* 67: Where are the peasants that run this flea-bag? **1954** Collans & Sterling *House Detect.* 57: Hustlers…take their casual clients to cheap rooming houses or "flea-bag" hotels on side streets where the room rates should be, if they aren't, so much per hour instead of per day. **1958** A. King *Mine Enemy* 19: One flea bag in the West Forties, the Hotel Minnetonka, left a particularly lurid shadow in my memory. **1959** Lederer *Never Steal Anything Small* (film): He's hidin' out in some fleabag. **1970** Gattzden *Black Vendetta* 171: The soldier went up to his room in the fleabag. **1975** Wambaugh *Choirboys* 65: A seventy year old pensioner who lived in a Seventh Street fleabag called the Restful Arms Motel.

b. a shabby establishment of any kind.

1941 Macaulay & Wald *Manpower* (film): You ain't gettin' rich in this fleabag [night club]. **1951** S.J. Perelman, in *New Yorker* (June 30) 22: [The movie] was unveiled at an owl show in a Forty-Second Street flea bag, complementing an Italian sex thriller called "Vesuvio."

3.a. a verminous or filthy person, esp. a prostitute; bum.

1935 Pollock *Und. Sp.*: *Flea bag*, a girl who solicits (promotes) sailors on the water front. **1944** Kapelner *Lonely Boy Blues* 90: No flea bag's calling me a filthy foreigner! **1957** Murtagh & Harris *Cast the First Stone* 305: *Fleabag*. A dirty old prostitute. **1966** S. Harris *Hellhole* 169: She and they live on the Bowery…alongside…insane and feeble-minded people, cripples, blind beggars, prostitutes called "flea-bags" because they are inclined to be syphilitic, and a few elderly eccentric Hobohemians. **1966** Kenney *Caste* 99: Jerry—the fleabag from P1. **1970** Winick & Kinsie *Lively Commerce* 74: The older prostitute who continues working into her sixties and seventies may be reduced to seeking clients on the local Skid Row and end up as a "flea bag." **1978** *Adolescence* XIII 500: The fleabags resembled…hippies…in physical appearance.

b. a worthless flea-ridden animal, esp. a dog.

1938 *Merrie Melodies* (animated cartoon): And now, Fleabag McPoodle and his trained dog act. **1942** *ATS* 120: Dog…cur…flea bag. **1963** S. Rifkin *K. Fisher's Rd.* 10: Well, so long, you old flea-bag. [**1971** Wells & Dance *Night People* 117: *Flea-bed n.* A dog.] **1977** Stallone *Paradise Alley* 28: "There ain't no reason to call Bella a fleabag." "Hey, Vic, that mutt's got no class." **1983** *Taxi* (ABC-TV): Where *is* the old fleabag? **1985** Boyne & Thompson *Wild Blue* 237: Jamie needed all the love he could get, even if it was from a fleabag. **1986** *L.A. Law* (NBC-TV): "What happened to your foot?" "That fleabag bit it."

c. *Horse Racing.* an old, poorly groomed, or worthless horse.

1973 Haney *Jock* 144: Today Beverly has twelve horses, most of which are cheap, rundown fleabags. **1987** *RHD2*.

fleabox *n.* a verminous or cramped establishment; FLEABAG, 2.

1930 Irwin *Tramp & Und. Slang* 76: *Flea Box*.—A cheap lodging-house or hotel…in which vermin are certain to be abundant. **1934–46** in Mencken *Amer. Lang.* (Supp. II) 735: *Flea-box*. A very small ball-park.

flea-farm *n.* FLEABAG, 3.b.

1963–64 Kesey *Great Notion* 247: I'll hold my fleafarm back the count of fifty.

flea-flicker *n.* *Football.* (see 1982 quot.).

1927 (cited in *W10*). **1934** *AS* (Oct.) 238: One of their steps of preparation had been an effort to halt the *flea flicker*. **1958** J. King *Pro Football* 89: That's the old fleaflicker play that Bob Zuppke used years ago. **1982** T. Considine *Lang. Sport* 140: *Flea-flicker*: a trick play that usually consists of a lateral followed by a pass, or a pass followed by a lateral. Innovative 1920's Illinois coach Bob Zuppke is given credit for developing the first flea-flicker (a pass followed by a lateral). **1987** *Headline News Network* (Dec. 14): Denver fell victim to the fleaflicker in the third quarter. **1991** Lott & Lieber *Total Impact* 8: Anderson pitched the ball back...on the flea-flicker.

fleahole *n.* FLEABAG, 2.b.

1979 A. Sweeney *Up from the Depths* (film): Let's get outta this flea-hole—we don't need this crap.

flea joint *n.* a verminous hotel; FLEABAG, 2.a.

1946 J.H. Burns *Gallery* 262: Let's get the hell out of this flea joint. **1973** *AS* XLVI 77: Shabby hotel...*flea joint.*

flea-powder *n. Narc.* (see 1967 quot.).

1956 Algren *Wild Side* 239: A man would be a fool not to trade off one little flea-powder habit for a real burning-down one, wouldn't he? **1967** Maurer & Vogel *Narc. & Narc. Add.* (ed. 2) 356: *Flea powder*—Highly diluted narcotics, especially heroin.

flea-ranch *n.* FLEABAG, 2.

1964–66 R. Stone *Hall of Mirrors* 10: A flea-ranch movie house.

flea-skip *n.* a worthless or inconsequential person.

1855 W.G. Simms *Forayers* 64: Speak you eternal flea-skip before I —.

flea trap *n.* **1.** *West.* a bedroll; shakedown; FLEABAG, 1.

1936 R. Adams *Cowboy Lingo* 37: [The cowboy's makeshift bed] was called..."hot roll,"..."shakedown," "crumb incubator" or "flea trap." **1950** *Western Folklore* IX (Apr.) 137: The cowboy called his bedroll a *bunk, dream sack,* or *flea trap.*

2. FLEABAG, 2.

1942 *ATS* 423: "Flophouse"...*flea trap.* **1946** in *DAS:* The Laycroft Hotel, a flea trap on West Madison Street. **1967** W. Murray *Sweet Ride* 121: We wound up in some third-rate flea-trap on the east side of town. **1974** R. Novak *Concrete Cage* 29: How much does this flea trap go for?

fleet *n. Und. & Police.* a gang, as of pickpockets, thieves, or swindlers; *(also)* a group of persons.

1904 (quot. at FALL GUY). **1911** A.H. Lewis *Apaches of N.Y.* 64: Tail 'em...an' when the fleet gets there go in wit' your cannisters an' bump 'em off. *Ibid.* 70: I don't want to put you in Dutch with your fleet. **1923** *Atlanta Constitution* (Feb. 1) 12: A whole fleet of flatties...[is] waiting to pull the joint. **1929–31** (cited in Partridge *Dict. Und.* 252). **1975** V.B. Miller *Deadly Game* 15: The big bad guys...are running a fleet of teen-aged prostitutes.

flemish down *v.* [fr. nautical jargon *flemish* 'to coil a rope in a Flemish coil'] *Navy.* to lie down, as to sleep.—used reflexively.

1918 Ruggles *Navy Explained* 60: I think I'll flemish myself down for a little shut eye. **1937** Thompson *Take Her Down* 66 [ref. to 1918]: Boy, you better flemish yourself down...and rest up so's you can work hard when the Captain needs you.

flesh-peddler *n.* **1.a.** *Journ.* a business agent, esp. in the entertainment industry.

1935 (cited in Weingarten *Dict. Slang*). **1940** R. Chandler *Farewell, My Lovely* 120: Buildings in which the Hollywood flesh-peddlers never stop talking money. **1941** in Botkin *Sidewalks* 491: Flesh peddlers...are agents. **1966–72** Winchell *Exclusive* 22: About 15 or 20 "flesh-peddlers" (agents)—a phrase I coined as a columnist years later—were all anxious to sign us on the dotted line.

b. a personnel recruiter.

1961 *Fortune* (June) 129: McCulloch had no compunction about using these executive recruiting firms...often derisively called "body snatchers," "head hunters," "flesh peddlers," and "pirates."

2. a prostitute.

1942 *ATS* 471: Prostitute...*flesh peddler.* **1948** Lait & Mortimer *New York* 83: The cops and courtroom loungers have long called prostitutes "flesh peddlers." **1981** P. Sann *Trial* 184: Jephthah...was the son of a flesh peddler.

flexie *n.* a flextime employee.

1985 Frede *Nurses* 54: They did not get to know the patients personally, as even the flexies did.

flick *n.* **1.** a motion picture; *(broadly)* a motion-picture theater.

*<!---->**1926** in *OEDS:* We'll occupy the afternoon with a "flick." I love the movies—especially the romantic ones. ***1927,** ***1931,** ***1936** in *OEDS.* **1936** *Esquire* (Sept.) 64: The multiplicity of...mystery mellers in the flix. *Ibid.* 160: A brit flick. **1944** E.H. Hunt *Limit* 31: Going to the flick? **1952** Sandburg *Young Strangers* 279: It faded and folded with the coming of the silver screen, the photoplay, the "moom pictures," the flicks. **1952** Ellson *Golden Spike* 92: You spend all your money to take her to the cheap flicks. **1956** Chamales *Never So Few* 77: Like a Charlie Chaplin flick he had once seen. **1957** Simmons *Corner Boy* 48: "When you

meet?" "Couple nights ago at the flick." **1958** Hughes & Bontemps *Negro Folklore* 483: *Flic, Flicker:* A motion picture. **1958** Lindsay & Crouse *Tall Story* 7: Then we can go to the late flick. **1958** Simonson & Philips *The Blob* (film): We're going to the flicks. **1959** Farris *Harrison High* 380: He'll get me work in the flicks and TV. **1961** Sullivan *Shortest, Gladdest Years* 151: Coming out of *The Grapes of Wrath* at the University flick society. **1966–67** P. Thomas *Mean Streets* 120: We were coming out of the RKO flick on 86th Street. **1992** "Fab 5 Freddy" *Fresh Fly Flavor* 25: *Flick*—Movie.

2. *Esp. Black E.* a photograph; snapshot.

1962 Crump *Killer* 386: Hey, who's got a flick of Monroe? **1963** in L. Bruce *Essential Lenny Bruce* 298: Did you see those flicks in *Time* magazine? **1966** C. Cooper *The Farm* 114: He...left right away to go down to his room on the tier and bring back the flick and 2 cigaret-packsized others. **1971** Jury *Vietnam Photo Book* 42: Wow! Yould see some of the flicks I got. Really outasight. Dead gooks and people blowed away. **1972** Bunker *No Beast* 12: There's a flick of your mama in today's *Chronicle.* **1978** W. Brown *Tragic Magic* 106: Here's a flick of the broad I want to write the letter to. **1978** J. Webb *Fields of Fire* 73: We gonna take our flick together. **1985** Dye *Between Raindrops* 318: Maybe get some final flicks on the way. **1991** B. Adler *Rap!* xiii: We needed some fly new flicks of us.

flick *v. Stu.* to go to a motion picture.—constr. with *it.*

1980 in Safire *Good Word* 214: [In the 1960's] "To flick it" meant "to go to the movies."

flicker *n.* **1.a.** (among beggars) a genuine or pretended faint.

1899 "J. Flynt" *Tramping* 393: *Flicker,* noun, a faint. **1930** Irwin *Tramp & Und. Sl.: Flicker*...A faint, or pretended faint. **1932** (cited in Partridge *DSUE* (ed. 8) 406).

b. (see quot.).

1939 *New Yorker* (Mar. 11) 43: The "flickers" are beggars who throw fits or pretend to have fainted from hunger.

2. FLICK, 1. Also attrib.

1926 in Gelman *Photoplay* 94: Do you know anything about the flicker favorites' romantic doings? **1927** *Vanity Fair* (Nov.) 132: "Flicker" is a "movie." **1933** *Leatherneck* (Nov.) 27: The smokers and flickers held...weekly are certainly a God-send. **1938** Breslow & Patrick *Moto Takes a Chance* (film): We was only makin' flickers, Reverend. **1943** in W.C. Fields *By Himself* 431: You have reinstated me in the flicker racket. **1944** Burley *Hndbk. Jive* 138: *Flickers*—Moving pictures. **1949** Ellson *Tomboy* 69: The flickers caught their fancy—five-cent short movies. **1956** in Hitchcock *Skeleton Crew* 169: He's standing in front of the flicker, goggling at the young chicks who come out. **1961** Terry *Old Liberty* 16: So I said why didn't he take the T Bird and take Horsehead to a flicker in town. **1966–67** P. Thomas *Mean Streets* 25: A Johnny Mack Brown cowboy flicker. **1972** Barker & Lewin *Denver* 161: The Opera eventually decayed into a second-run flicker mill.

flicker *v.* (among beggars) to faint or pretend to faint; *(broadly)* to die.—also constr. with *out.*

1899 "J. Flynt" *Tramping* 384: "I'm starvin', father," I yapped, 'n' begun to flicker. *Ibid.* 393: *Flicker*...to faint or pretend to faint. **1924** G. Henderson *Crookdom* 405: *Flicker out*—To die. **1926** *AS* I (Dec.) 651: *Flicker.* To faint. **1930** "D. Stiff" *Milk & Honey* 205: *Flicker*—To faint or simulate fainting. **1933–34** Lorimer & Lorimer *Stag Line* 165: We don't want the little lady flickering on us. **1935** D.W. Maurer, in *AS* (Feb.) 15 [ref. to ca1910]: To *flicker.* 1. To die. 2. To pass out or faint away; to be knocked out.

flick out *v.* **1.** to die.

1928 Wharton *Squad* 184 [ref. to 1918]: Mike Mose's flicked out.

2. *Stu.* to go to a motion picture.

1977 *N.Y. Post* (Aug. 19) 18: So Elvis had to rent a movie theater when he wanted to flick out and he had to rent a rink when he wanted to skate. **1980** in Safire *Good Word* 212.

flier or **flyer** *n.* **1.a.** a wager; *(hence)* an investment or other venture presenting financial risk. Now *colloq.*

1821 Waln *Hermit in Phila.* 29: Let's have a *flyer* if your [*sic*] *flush.* **1846** *Spirit of Times* (July 11) 229: Lend me a quarter—*one* quarter—just for a flyer. **1859** Matsell *Vocab.* 123: A *flyer* is to buy some stock with a view to selling it in a few days, and either make or lose, as luck will have it. **1870** Medbery *Wall St.* 136: A "flyer" is a small side operation, not employing one's whole capital. It is nearly equivalent to...a venture. **1885** in *DA:* He...takes "a flier," or small side venture, that does not employ his entire capital. **1890** Quinn *Fools of Fortune* 585: A [stock] speculator is said to "take a flyer" when he engages in some side venture; he "flies kites" when he expands operations unjudiciously. *a*<!---->**1890–93** *F & H* III 23: *To take a flier* (American trade)....To make a venture, to invest against odds. **1902** Clapin *Amer.* 191: *Flyer*…An outsider's venture or speculation, through the regular brokers of the Stock Exchange. "To try a *flyer* in stocks." **1905** *Nat. Police Gaz.* (Nov. 18) 3: To take a flyer on the ponies. **1916** in Truman *Dear Bess* 205: I'll have to take a flyer in wheat or something. **1949** in *DA*: A Montreal lawyer…went ski-minded and "took a flyer" in building a magnificent resort "just for fun." **1959** *Phil Silvers Show* (CBS-TV): Welcome to the Hacienda Club [a casino]. We're not open officially yet, but if you want to take a flier—.

b. a whimsical escapade; lark.

*1821 *Real Life in Ireland* 280: From whim and frolic…he would go into the racket court in the Marshalsea, and have a flyer with any prisoner for a few pots of porter, hit or miss. **1869** "M. Twain" *Innocents Abroad* ch. xxxiii: In the Hellespont we saw where…Lord Byron swam across,…merely for a flyer, as Jack says. **1877** in "M. Twain" *Sketches* 312: It so happened that we stepped into the Revere House, thinking maybe we would chance the salt-house in that big dining-room for a flyer, as the boys say. **1966** Susann *Valley of Dolls* 439: I might even forgive you if you took a flier with another girl.

c. a gambit; (*also*) a try; attempt.

1865 "M. Twain," in *DAE*: My refusal of the position at $7,000 a year was not precisely meant to be final, but was intended for what the ungodly term a "flyer"—the object being to bring about an increase in the amount. **1868** H. Woodruff *Trotting Horse* 255: He determined "just for a flyer" to let her try her mettle for the purse. **1889** "M. Twain" *Conn. Yankee* 113: The boys all took a flier at the Holy Grail now and then. *Ibid.* 424: I chanced another flyer. **1923** Witwer *Fighting Blood* 123: It wasn't long before I took a flyer at this game again. **1991** "R. Brown" & R. Angus *A.K.A. Narc* 146: I took a flyer at it. "The Mexican police coming soon?"

d. a chance occurrence; fluke.

1883 Beadle *West. Wilds* 589: An expert…condemned the mine as a flyer—that is, a mere freak of nature, without sign of permanence.

2. *Pris.* a suicidal leap; (*also*) one who attempts suicide in this manner.

1942 Algren *Morning* 146: "If I was here for more 'n six months…I'd take a flier." To take a flier was to throw oneself over the rail headfirst onto the concrete below. **1971** Wynn *Glass House* (CBS-TV movie): There's a flier in C Block!

3. *Circus.* (see quots.).

1942 *ATS* 615: *Flier*, an acrobat who is thrown from one companion to another. **1978** Ponicsan *Ringmaster* 49: A trapeze artist…A flyer? That what they call 'em?

4. *Stu.* an offensive or obnoxious fool; FLAMER, 1.a.

1969 *Current Slang* I & II 35: *Flyer*, *n.* A fool.—College females, New York. **1974** *Nat. Lampoon* (Nov.) 84: One of the guys from the college humor magazine (real dork-for-brains flyer, too, but he's got the typewriter).

¶ In phrase:

¶ **take a flier** to run off.

1914 Atherton *Perch* 67: After that take a flyer if you like. You deserve it. **1984** *Miami Vice* (NBC-TV): We were protecting him. Who'd've thought he'd take a flier?

flight jockey *n.* **1.** *Av.* a flight controller.

1973 Former USN enlisted man, age 26 [ref. to 1968]: A flight controller is called a *flight jockey*.

2. an aviator.

1988 *Supercarrier* (ABC-TV): You two flight jockeys forgot the dress code again.

flight skins *n.pl.* [*flight* + SKINS 'dollars'] **1.** *Mil. Av.* flight pay.

1945 Hamann *Air Words*: *Flight skins.* Flying pay. **1942–48** in *So. Folk. Qly.* XIII (1949) 202: The non-commissioned flying personnel get *flight-skins*. **1966** Noel *Naval Terms*: *Flight skins:* Slang for flight pay. **1969** Cagle *Naval Av. Guide* 393: *Flight Skins.* Extra pay received by Naval aviators for hazardous duty.

2. *Naval Av.* flight orders.

1969 Cagle *Naval Av. Guide* 46: Flight orders, better known as "flight skins," are just what the name implies—orders to fly. They are also issued to certain qualified enlisted men for which they receive incentive pay. The origin of this term is obscure and uncertain, although it is known to go back as far as 1919. (It is almost always heard in the plural).

flim *n. Und.* FLIMFLAM, *n.*, 1.

1914 Jackson & Hellyer *Vocab.* 34: *Flim*, noun. Current in polite criminal circles. A swindle; a fraud. **1925** in Partridge *Dict. Und.* 253: The flim is a hoary trick, but generally works.

flim *v. Und.* FLIMFLAM, *v.*

1889 Barrère & Leland *Dict. Slang* I 370: *Flimming, flim-flamming* (American thieves' flash or slang), in England, "ringing the changes" [shortchanging]. **1895** Gore *Stu. Slang* 5: *Flim*…To cheat. *flimmer*…one who cheats. **1914** Jackson & Hellyer *Crim. Slang* 34: *Flim*, verb. To swindle; to defraud. **1925** in Partridge *Dict. Und.* 253: *Flim*, v. To cheat; to swindle.

flimflam *n.* **1.** [a specialization of the S.E. sense] *Und.* a short-change swindle.

1881 Trumble *Man Traps* 28: Flim-flam…He is a "flim-flammer."…The amount of money a good flim-flam operator can obtain in one day depends upon the character and condition of his victims. **1894** in *OED*: She notified the police, but the flim-flam artist was far away.…His success in the "flim-flam" game. **1890** Quinn *Fools of Fortune* 362: The "flim-flam" operator appeals, not to the avarice but to the good nature of his victim. **1902** Hapgood *Thief* 273 [ref. to *ca*1890]: From flim-flam (returning short change) to burglary is but a step. **1908** McGaffey *Show Girl* 29: I would steer no friend…of mine up against a flim flam.

2. *Midland.* the penis. *Joc.*

1975 Univ. Tenn. grad. student: *Flimflam* means the same as *dong*. I heard it in Alcoa [Tenn.] in 1957. **1975** Univ. Tenn. grad. student: I heard *flimflam* in Memphis about ten years ago. "Then he took out his *flimflam*."

flimflam *v. Und.* to swindle by shortchanging.

1881 *Nat. Police Gaz.* (Nov. 12) 10: Among the numberless small swindles of the metropolis there is none more curious than that of the flim-flammer. **1881** Trumble *Man Traps* 28: He is a flim-flammer. **1889** (quot. at FLIM, *v.*). **1890** in *OED*: Sent [to jail]…for flimflaming a…saloon-keeper out of some money. **1903** Kildare *Mamie Rose* 72: Over charging, "palming"—retaining a coin in the palm of the hand…"flim-flamming"—doubling a bill in a number of them, and counting each end of it as a separate bill—are the most common methods of cheating employed.

flimp *n.* [orig. unkn.] *Und.* to rob or steal by pickpocketing.

*1839 in *OED*: To take a man's watch is to flimp him. **1863* in T. Taylor *Plays* 166: Not worth flimping, eh? **1867** Williams *Brierly* 21: Yes, pottering about on the sneak, flimping or smashing a little when I get the sight. **1867** (quot. at PROP). **1902** in Partridge *Dict. Und.* 253: That there visitor was flimped clean, clean as a whistle. **1906** A.H. Lewis *Confessions* 202: Then I flimped his thimble—a yellow one.

flimsy *n.* **1.** a banknote.

*1811 *Lexicon Balatron.: Flymsey.* A bank note. **1824* in *OED*: Martin produced some "flimsies"; and said he would fight on Tuesday next. **1837* in *F & H* III 24: Not "kites," manufactured to cheat and inveigle,/But the right sort of flimsy, all sign'd, by Monteagle. **1842** *Spirit of Times* (July 13) 243: He planked up the tin (*veritable*) against the "flimsey," which was won in three deals by G. **1842** *Spirit of Times* (Oct. 29) 416: Put down your flimsies, and I'll furnish mine. **1845** Durivage & Burnham *Stray Subjects* 73: Ho! landlord! there's a flimsy—/…Ten dollars for your alley/And ninety for your boy! **1848** Thompson *House Breaker* 44: The…Captain…threw a ten dollar *flimsy* down on the table.…*Flimsy*—a bank-note. **1855** in *F & H* III 24: Will you take it in *flimsies*, or will you have it all in tin? **1865** Williams *Joaquin* 9: The chant he heard so frequently in the saloons, the classical "Shove her up, shove her up to the bolt,/I'd rather have an ounce than a twenty-dollar note,/For the slug it will sink and the flimsy'll float,/So I'd rather have, etc." **1867** Williams *Brierly* 9: "I dessay he'll be flash with the shiners now." "And flush of the flimsies." **1877** Pinkerton *Maguires* 122: The secret mark…"spotted the 'flimsy' as of the sort called 'queer.'"

2.a. very thin paper.

*1857 in *OEDS:* The reporters—or, rather, the penny-a-liners—who write on "flimsey." **1888* in *OEDS: Flimsy*, thin paper, such as…telegraph forms. **1893** M. Philips *Newspaper* 8: Thin, oily paper known as "flimsy." **1909** *WNID: Flimsy*…Thin or transfer paper, or manuscript on such paper…*Newspaper Cant.* **1942** *ATS* 493: *Flimsy*, thin paper on which several duplicate copies are written at once.

b. *Journ.* copy written on very thin paper.

*1859 in *OED:* Sub-editors are now hard at work cutting down "flimsy." **1861* in *F & H* III 24: His notes…are a thousand-fold clearer, fuller, and more accurate than the reporter's *flimsy*. **1865* in *F & H*: A London correspondent, who, by the aid of flimsy, misleads a vast number of provincial papers. **1909** (quot. at (c), below).

c. a document or receipt, usu. a carbon copy, on thin paper. Now *S.E.*

*1889 in Chester et al. *Cleve. St.* 46: I have strained my eyes…over you

"flimsy," and I must enter a protest against being asked to read documents so illegible. ***1909** in *OEDS*: He sent to the defendants "flimsies" of the original reports. ***1929** Bowen *Sea Slang* 50: *Flimsy*, an officer's report at the end of a commission or when leaving a man-of-war. **1931** *Writer's Dig.* (May) 41: *Flimsy*—Train order. **1942** *ATS* 497: *Flimsy*, a thin paper carbon copy. **1950** in *DAS*: He consulted a sheaf of typewritten flimsies. **1954–60** *DAS*: *Flimsy*…in offices, a carbon copy of invoices; in stores and restaurants, a duplicate of the employees' bills of sale against which the cash receipts are checked. *a***1984** in M.W. Bowman *Castles* 132 [ref. to WWII]: The radio operators…received a canvas packet with coded data in it called a "flimsy."

d. *Journ.* (see quot.).

1958 S.H. Adams *Tenderloin* 104 [ref. to 1890's]: Down to the humble twelve-dollar-a-week hacks of the "flimsies" (local news agencies serving the dailies, so called because their reports were issued on yellow tissue paper manifolded with a stylus).

flinger *n.* *Baseball.* a pitcher.

1909 (cited in Nichols *Baseball Term.*). **1913** in *DAS*: Three of Henshaw's starboard flingers had gone wrong. **1914** Patten *Lefty o' the Bush* 13: He's some green dub of a port-side flinger. **1934** Weseen *Dict. Slang* 209.

flingle *n.* [orig. unkn.] flattery; nonsense.

1947 Willingham *End As a Man* 76: The finest line of flingle you ever heard in your life.

flint in *v.* (see quot.).

1877 Bartlett *Amer.* 782: *To flint in.* To begin doing something, as to work or to eat, energetically and without ceremony.

flip *n.* **1.** a saucy, impertinent, or forward person, esp. a young woman.

1915 *DN* IV 199: *Flip*, a person loose in morals. "That little *flip* will give him a merry chase, I'm thinking." **1934** Weseen *Dict. Slang* 335: *Flip*…a forward person. **1946–51** J. Jones *Here to Eternity* ch. xli: How many times I've seen you mentally undress every young flip we pass on the street. **1961** *WNID3*: *Flip*…smart aleck.

2. *Av.* a short flight in an aircraft.

*1914 in *OEDS*. **1918** Roberts *Flying Fighter* 335: *Flip*. A flight. **1918** in Rossano *Price of Honor* 131: I'll take a couple of practise flips. **1929, 1943, 1958, 1959** in *OEDS*. **1975** R.P. Davis *Pilot* 159: How about a flip?

3. [fr. *Filipino*] (usu. *cap.*) a Filipino.—often used contemptuously.

1931 Cressey *Taxi-Dance Hall* 35 [ref. to 1925]: *Flip*.—Filipino's name for himself. Of American origin. *Ibid.* 44: The "Flips"…are all right for anybody that wants them. **1944–46** in *AS* XXII 55 (Army): *Flips.* Filipinos. **1946** Wilson *Voyage to Somewhere* 177: I came back to the ship, got the cigarettes, and went to this Flip's shack. **1951** Leveridge *Walk on Water* 179: The way you fooled around with the Flips! **1958–59** Lipton *Barbarians* 56: I'd go out by myself or with a couple of flip artists. Filipinos, you know. **1963** Keats *They Fought Alone* 415 [ref. to WWII]: The Old Army had called them gooks, and the New Americans called them Flips. **1966** Little *Bold & Lonely* 87: The ex-U.S. Navy chief…owned the place and intervened with the assistance of several Flip laborers. **1969** Crumley *One to Count Cadence* 36: Just who the hell did the APs find under that Flip's house at three in the morning? **1967–80** Folb *Runnin' Lines* 237: *Flip*. Filipino person.

4. a crazy or eccentric person.

1952 Mandel *Angry Strangers* 190: Before you were driving like a flip, and now you're creeping. **1955** Shapiro & Hentoff *Hear Me Talkin'* 347: He's not a flip as far as business is concerned. **1957** Thornton *Teenage Werewolf* (film): That's all I need! "Tony the flip."…He wants me to go to this headshrinker…like I was a flip or something. **1958** Hansberry *Raisin in the Sun* 235: BENEATHA. Brother is a flip—let's face it. MAMA (*To* RUTH, *helplessly.*) What's a flip? RUTH…She's saying he's crazy. **1959** "D. Stagg" *Glory Jumpers* 94: Only a flip would want to fly back through that. **1959** in Cannon *Nobody Asked* 161: He was the champion of Broadway until the hour of the flips and kooks when the joints closed down and the lights were turned off. **1961** Gover *$100 Misunderstanding* 94: Like, he ain no flip, he's okay in the head. **1963** in H. Ellison *Sex Misspelled* 55: Rooney was a flip when it came to babies or tiny dogs. **1964** Smith & Hoefer *Music* 1: This world is full of chirpers, belchers, and flips from the funny papers who like to go out on the town. **1965** Yurick *Warriors* 60: He knew that everyone feared the flip, and so he psyched once in a while and they gave him room. **1984** (quot. at WINGDING).

5. a state of excitement or insanity; a mental breakdown.

*ca***1953** Hughes *Lodge* 73: He went into a real flip…And he said, "I hate everybody in this damn place!" *Ibid.* 99: Along about this time, my Aunt

Joan…had her flip.

6. something delightful or extraordinary.

1950 in *DAS*: The big flip of the year is Peter Arno's book of cartoons. **1958–59** Lipton *Barbarians* 316: *Flip*—Anything from a fit of high enthusiasm to a stretch in the laughing academy. **1966** Herbert *Fortune & Men's Eyes* 71: Ain't this gown a flip? **1974** in Mack *Real Life* (unp.): Ain't dis a flip! One little stupid [toy] bicycle for $5.00.

7. a darn; a rap.

1969 *Playboy* (Dec.) 102: I couldn't play worth a flip. **1971** J. Brown & A. Groff *Monkey* 117: He…made me feel glad that people…would give a flip about someone with my past.

flip *adj.* [of dial. E orig.] saucy; flippant. Now *S.E.*

*1893 in *OED*: She was disposed to be flip with her tongue. **1903** *Pedagog. Sem.* X 371: You're getting too flip altogether. **1904** *Life in Sing Sing*: *Flip.* Too outspoken. **1905** *Nat. Police Gaz.* (Nov. 11) 3: I guess dere a bunch of pretty flip guys wid all dere glad rags. **1909** *WNID*: *Flip*,…Flippant. *Dial. Eng. & Slang, U.S.*

flip *v.* **1.** to steal a ride on (a moving vehicle, esp. a freight train).

1904 Ade *True Bills* 43: He was down flipping the Trains every Day, in defiance of the Town Marshal. **1915–16** Lait *Beef, Iron & Wine* 101: I ain't gonna be flipping rattlers nights no more. **1918–19** MacArthur *Bug's-Eye View* 81: He…finally flipped a caisson back to the hospital. **1927** *AS* II (Sept.) 506: "Flipping a rattler," I believe, is synonymous with "nailing" one. Both refer especially to the catching of a ride rather than to the riding. **1927** Thrasher *The Gang* 62: A favorite rendezvous of the gang was a large sand pile near the railroad tracks. Here they had great fun camping, flipping freights, and pestering the railroad detectives. **1929** Farrell *Calico Shoes* 214: Another trolley car passed, and an eleven-year old boy flipped it. **1929** Milburn *Hobo's Hornbook* 27 [ref. to 1890]: Some flipped freights to other states. **1937** Reitman *Box-Car Bertha* 15: I saw one flip a freight that had stopped at our switch. **1948** Chaplin *Wobbly* 122 [ref. to 1912]: The procedure was to load up with papers and leaflets, then "flip" coal cars which we knew would pass through various points in Kanawha County. **1963** Williamson *Hustler!* 41: We'd go on the "L"—flip the "L," and come back.

2. *Narc.* (see quot.).

1936 *AS* (Apr.) 121: *Flipped.* Knocked out by some kind of knock-out shot administered by an attendant or by another addict who then *makes* his victim for any narcotics he may have. *Ibid.* 122: The *hot shot* kills the addict, in contrast to *flipping him.*

3. *Black E.* to dismiss or reject.

1946 Boulware *Jive & Slang* 3: *Flip The Chick*…Quit the girl.

4.a. to lose one's mind or self-control; get excited; react enthusiastically or rage hysterically.—now usu. constr. with *out.* Cf. earlier *flip (one's) lid*, below.

1950 *Neurotica* (Autumn) 44: If I'm not right back don't flip. **1951** *N.Y. Times Bk. Review* (Dec. 2) 50: The funniest book of the lot is enough to make a reader "flip" or "flip his lid." **1952** *Life* (Sept. 29) 67: *Flip*: to react enthusiastically. *ca***1953** Hughes *Fantastic Lodge* 65: She'll get a magazine after she gets high…and just flip. **1955** Ruppelt *Report on UFOs* 11: In certain instances a pilot can "flip" for no good reason, but [no one]…had noticed any symptoms of mental crack-up. **1955** Shapiro & Hentoff *Hear Me Talkin'* 119: Everybody flipped. It was wonderful. **1955** *Science Digest* (Aug.) 33: A hipster never goofs (makes a mistake) and always flips (gets excited) at the proper things. **1958–59** Lipton *Barbarians* 87: Phil…explains why he is afraid to flip out. **1959–60** R. Reisner *Jazz Titans* 155: *Flip*:…verb, to flip means to go wild.…Flipped can also mean going insane. **1961** Gover *$100 Misunderstanding* 189: He gonna flip so far out, I ain never gonna find him. **1961** Grau *Coliseum St.* 169: How'd I know she'd flip like this? **1962** G. Olson *Roaring Rd.* 31: He'll flip! He'll run to Papa and get you fired! **1963** in Bruce *Essential* 87: In the last days…Hitler was flipping out. **1963–64** Kesey *Great Notion* 68: Constantly threatened by the fear of flipping out. **1965** Matthiessen *Fields of Lord* 379: He had flipped out on that *ayahuasca.* **1967** Flicker *President's Analyst* (film): If I don't resume my analysis pretty soon, I'm gonna flip out. **1969** *Esquire* (Aug.) 71: Krazy, man, like I nearly flipped. **1970** Landy *Underground Dict.* 80: Flip out…Lose one's temper. **1975** Kangas & Solomon *Psych. of Strength* 101: Our first reaction was to think he had flipped. **1976** *S.W.A.T.* (NBC-TV): Sounds like he's flipped. **1982** G. Larson *Far Side* (unp.): Egad!…Sounds like the farmer's wife has really flipped out this time! **1992** *Today Show* (NBC-TV) (Feb. 18): Why he flipped out and killed him, I don't know.

b. to shock, amaze, or drive insane.—now usu. constr. with *out.*

1951 Bowers *Mob* (film): Don't let it flip ya, Smoothy. *ca***1953** Hughes *Lodge* 126: She's cross-examining me. That's what was flipping me the most. **1960** Swarthout *Where Boys Are* 65: I screamed and looked down and it was a *hamster*, I am serious, which completely flipped the class. **1960** Bluestone *Cully* 182: You flip me, Hardiman, you really do. **1966** Moran *Faster Pussycat* (film): Why should a train flip him out? **1975** in Meconis *Clumsy Grace* 104: It really started to flip me out a bit.

c. Esp. *Jazz.* to delight; thrill.

1956 Holiday & Dufty *Lady Sings the Blues* 82: Meade Lux Lewis knocked them out; Ammons and Johnson flipped them; Joe Turner killed them; Newton's band sent them. **1959** "D. Stagg" *Glory Jumpers* 18: The threads man—you know how they flip the chicks. **1965** *Mr. Ed* (CBS-TV): So that big beat really flipped ya?

5.a. *Und. & Police.* to inform on (an associate); (*intrans.*) to inform or turn informer; (*hence*) to confess.

1960 C.L. Cooper *Scene* 264: They'll probably want me to flip. **1962** Maurer & Vogel *Narc. & Narc. Add.* (ed. 2) 301: *Flip.* To inform. **1963** Williamson *Hustler!* 138: They wanted me to flip on the guy who had sold the stuff to me. **1966** Brunner *Face of Night* 36: "But I never flipped anybody in my whole life," she protested. *Ibid.* 149: I won't flip nobody for you. **1972** *Newsweek* (Jan. 24) 25: Richard "flipped" (confessed) to the agents. **1976** "N. Ross" *Policeman* 179: All in all, he flipped on about twenty guys. **1985** E. Leonard *Glitz* 142: This's an inside witness agrees to flip. **1991** C. Fletcher *Pure Cop* 79: Usually you get one [suspect] flipping on the other. *Ibid.* 212: He admitted everything. He flipped.

b. *Police.* to persuade (someone) to be an informer.

1980 W. Sherman *Times Square* 99: Something tells me we can flip these two guys. **1985** Kasindorf *Brothel Wars* 89: Martin was the man Perry and Leavitt hoped to "flip" one day.

6. to make (a turn, as with a motor vehicle).

1966 Reynolds & McClure *Freewheelin Frank* 41: I started flipping lefts and rights and circling blocks.

¶ In phrase:

¶ **flip (one's) lid** to lose (one's) mind or composure; go crazy; get excited; rage hysterically. Also vars., some nonce.

1934 in M. Starks *Cocaine Fiends* 101: She's flipped her wig. **1941** in Ellington *Music My Mistress* 179: *Flip my lid*...enjoy. **1947** Mailer *Naked & Dead* 222 [ref. to WWII]: That boy's goin' to flip his lid. **1948** Miller & Rackin *Fighter Sq.* (film): Easy, Jacobs. Don't flip your lid. *a***1950** P. Wolff *Friend* 21: I'm gonna flip my lid. **1952** Mandel *Angry Strangers* 206: Where you been since that boy flipped his wig by Paddy's? **1952** Brossard *Walk in Dkness.* ch. viii: He flipped his wig...and they took him to a sanatorium. **1955** Robbins *79 Park Ave.* 315: No, he doesn't want to marry her....He just flipped his lid over her, that's all. **1959** Lederer *Never Steal Anything Small* (film): Be ready to catch his wig when it flips. **1954–60** *DAS: Flip (one's) raspberry*—to flip (one's) lid. *a***1961** *WNID3: Flip one's lid* also *flip one's stack* or *flip one's top*...to lose self control; become furiously angry. **1967** Partridge *DSUE* (ed. 6) 1123: *Flip (one's) top.* To become extremely angry or excited, almost crazy: Australian: adopted, *ca*1950, ex U.S. **1967** [Beck] *Pimp* 102: He...started laughing. I thought he had flipped his cork. *Ibid.* 286: You're flipping your top. **1970** in Estren *Underground Comics* 63: It looked to me like he just flipped his noodle. **1980** *Nat. Lampoon* (Oct.) 10: The allergist flipped his wig when he realized his wife had been breathing pollen behind his back. **1984** *Different Strokes* (ABC-TV): Have you flipped your frijoles? **1988** *Wkly. World News* (July 5) 39: But as soon as we were in the air, he really flipped his cork. **1993** *Sonya* (CNN-TV) (Mar. 2): A lunatic...somebody who's flipped his lid.

flipflop *n.* **1.** twaddle.

1922 S. Lewis *Babbitt* 17: The first thing you got to understand is that all this uplift and flipflop and settlement-work and recreation is nothing in God's world but the entering wedge for socialism.

2. *Pris.* **a.** an act of simultaneous reciprocal oral copulation; SIXTY-NINE.

1966 Braly *On Yard* 278: Whatever sissy she would pick out on queen's row to turn flipflops with. **1970** Landy *Underground Dict.* 80: *Flip flop*...Simultaneous oral copulation.

b. a bisexual person, esp. a convict.

1972 Carr *Bad* 163: Flip-flops, also called "knickknacks," are dudes that begin by making the homos but wind up playing the female roles themselves.

3. *CB.* a change of direction; (*hence*) a return trip.

1976 Lieberman & Rhodes *CB* 128: *Flipflop*—1. Change of direction. 2. Return trip. **1977** *Sci. Mech. CB Gde.* 169: I'll give you a holler on the flip-flop. **1990** Rukuza *W. Coast Turnaround* 206: See ya on th' flip-flop.

flipmagilder *n.* [orig. unkn.] a worthless or peculiar person.

1893 Coes *Badly Sold* 5: Old Griggs is a—what did you say he was?...An old flipmagilder.

flip off *v.* to deride by gesturing with a raised middle finger; *flip a bird* s.v. BIRD. Cf. FINGER, 4.

1984 *Tri Quarterly* (Spring) 313: It looks like she's just about to flip him off too. **1985** T. Wells *444 Days* 64: The Iranians...were flipping us off, and I was standing there flipping them off in return, saying, "Get out of here, you raspberries!" **1987** Univ. Tenn. student theme: His favorite gesture is grabbing himself while flipping you off. **1990** *Cops* (Fox-TV): He flips off the deputies as he's goin' by.

flip-out *n.* **1.** FLIP, *n.*, 4.

1966 Young & Hixson *LSD* 142: LSD "flip-outs" were turning up in the wards at the rate of six a month. **1966** H.S. Thompson *Hell's Angels* 86: The outlaws will nearly always give a flip-out a bad time. **1974** N.Y.U. student: That guy is such a flipout.

2. an instance of becoming insane; FLIP, *n.*, 5.

1966 Young & Hixson *LSD* 32: It is also strongly implied that panic, fright, a "flip out" are badges of insecure aggressiveness. **1967** Yablonsky *Hippie Trip* 48: Repressive laws, paranoia-producing laws are going to cause more flip-outs. Our place was as paranoia-free a place as has ever been where there is a lot of dope. **1971** *N.Y. Times Mag.* (Oct. 17) 106: When Xylocaine wears off it's not just a downer, it's a flip-out.

3. FLIP, *n.*, 6.

1975 Univ. Tenn. student: It was a flipout finding him there.

4. ready cash.

1988 J.S. Young *China Beach* (film): Make the geetus, the folding, the flipout, the filthy lucre.

flip out *v.* see FLIP, *v.*, 4.

flipped *adj.* **1.** having lost one's mind or composure; crazy; (*hence*) delighted.—now usu. constr. with *out*.

1952 Mandel *Angry Strangers* 427: Plain nuts; flipped. *a***1953** in *Amer. Jour. Socio.* LIX 240: I got real flipped. **1966** Panama et al. *Not With My Wife* (film): It's Labrador, sir. He's just a little flipped. *****1967** Partridge *DSUE* (ed. 6) 1123: *Flipped.* Crazy: Australian: since early 1950's. **1970** Landy *Underground Dict.* 80: *Flipped out*...Angry. **1970** Grissim *Country Music* 120: Now we found only one Country-Western disc jockey that didn't like it. All the other jocks were flipped out about it. **1972** Singer *Boundaries* 343: I don't want to talk. I feel too flipped-out. **1978** W. Brown *Tragic Magic* 131: No, it's just that Otis is sort of flipped out. **1984** C. Francis *Who's Sorry?* 18: They knew how totally flipped out I was over Alan Ladd.

2. excellent; CRAZY.—also constr. with *out*.

1957 J. Jones *Some Came Running* 35: We could have a real flipped time, man. **1972** Smith & Gay *Don't Try It* 201: *Flipped out.* Crazy...very good; strange or unusual.

flipper *n.* **1.** Esp. *Naut.* **a.** a hand or arm.

*****1812** in Wetherell *Adventures* 209: Where...have you sprung from with your one flipper? *****1821** Stewart *Man-of-War's-Man* I 34: Give me your flipper, my canny Scotchman. *****1832** in *OED:* I like to touch the flipper of one who has helped to shame the enemy. **1834** *Mil. & Naval Mag. of U.S.* (Oct.) 115: He feebly announces to the surgeon, "they have carried away my starboard flipper." *****1837** in *F & H* III 27: nipp'd off his *flippers,*/As the clerk, very flippantly, termed his fists. **1838** Crockett *Almanac* (1839) 23: Give us your flipper, then, old chap. **1840** *Spirit of Times* (Sept. 12) 331: When last I grasped your flipper. **1847** Downey *Portsmouth* 4: I had a chance of shaking the flipper for the last time with my old shipmates. **1852** Hazen *Five Years* 260: Give me your flipper, you old sea elephant, till I shake the kinks out of your knuckles. **1855** Wise *Tales for Marines* 47: She shook me heartily by the flipper. **1863** *Beadle's Dime Comic Speaker* 55: Tap us your flipper, old Covey. **1864** Fosdick *Frank on a Gun-Boat* 84: Give us your flipper, my boy. **1871** "M. Twain" *Roughing It* 172: Gimme that old flipper again! **1893** Barra *Two Oceans* 52: I considered myself no chicken in handling my flippers at that time, and I put on the boxing gloves with him. **1924** Colcord *Roll & Go* 14: So I tailed her my flipper and took her in tow. **1934** Lomax & Lomax *Amer. Ballads* 546: He winked at her and tipped his flipper. **1949** Davies *Every Spring* (film): Come on, kid, let's take care of that flipper. **1953** M. Harris *Southpaw* 150: How is the flipper? **1953** in Cannon *Like 'Em Tough* 39: Loosen the flipper. **1986** G. Brach *Pirates* (film): Free our guests' flippers so they may drink to our health.

b. a leg or foot.

1896 Walker *Amherst Olio* 176: With a pair of old slippers/He covered his flippers. **1900** *DN* II 69: "*Wiggle* a flipper," to hurry up. **1926** Norwood *Other Side of Circus* 80: Shake a flipper there and clear that main-falls rope! *ca*1965 in IUFA *Folk Speech: Flippers*—Legs.

2. a pancake.

1839 Olmsted *Whaling Voyage* 153: "Flippers" or "slapjacks" for break-fast. **1850, 1856** in *DA*. **1863** in R.G. Carter *4 Bros.* 224: Bob and LeRoy are frying "flippers" (flapjacks). **1882** in *DA*. *ca*1896 A.C. Stearns *Co. K* 47: Some flour was procured, and some of the boys were detailed to cook flippers.

3. an ear.

1905 *Nat. Police Gaz.* (Dec. 9) 7: "[I'll]…lead that law murderin'…gun-poker aroun'…by both o' his ears."…"I've been a-hearin' that you had some…idea o' leadin' me aroun'…by my flippers." **1944** Burley *Hndbk. Jive* 138: *Flippers*—Ears.

4. *Av.* an airplane's elevator; (*hence*) elevator control.

1918 Guttersen *Granville* 37: It's the first case on record of a man com-ing down with both flipper wires cut and being able to tell of it. **1918** Mayers *A.E.F. Hymnal* (unp.): I'll tell you how it happened—/The flip-pers fell away. **1934** Boylan & Baldwin *Devil Dogs of the Air* (film): The stick…controls the flippers and the ailerons. **1945** J. Bryan *Carrier* 37: The ribs in the flipper were sprung. **1955** R.L. Scott *Look of Eagle* 31: Okay, we're with you, boss. Our flippers are flipping. **1983** Van Riper *Glenn* 106: Finally, by sheer desperate strength, he was able to get enough "flipper" to take the plane out of the dive.

5. *Baseball.* a pitcher.

1971 Coffin *Old Ball Game* 60: The "bellwether" of the "flippers" [is] the "workhorse" of the staff.

6. *CB.* a return trip; FLIP SIDE.

1976 Whelton *CB Baby* 95: Ten-four, Jack O'Diamonds, catch you on the flipper. We gone.

flipping *adj.* **1.** BLOODY; darned. Also as adv. [Esp. common in BrE.]

1911 in *OEDS*: Ain't it flippin' 'ot? **1948 in *OEDS*: Flipping heroes, ain't we all? **1965 in *BDNE* 171. **1983** Univ. Tenn. grad. student: The good thing about teaching is that you can grade papers anywhere you flippin' want to. **1986** R. Walker *AF Wives* 68: Because that flipping war lasted so long.

2. *Stu.* splendid; great; FLIPPY, 1.

1969 *Current Slang* I & II 34: *Flippin'*, adj. Highly admirable. High school students…California. **1978** De Christoforo *Grease* 68: "So, how was the action this summer, Danny?" "Flippin'. I met one chick who was sort of cool."

flippy *adj.* **1.** delightful.

1957 Trosper *Jailhouse Rock* (film): Flippy. Real flippy.

2. crazy or eccentric; peculiar.

1965 Lurie *Nowhere City* 174: Now she thinks I'm completely flippy. **1971** N.Y.U. student: "Flippy" means the same as "weird." Like, "Man, that's flippy!" **1974** Price *Wanderers* 33: Everyone knew his mother and father were flippy. *a*1979 Pepper & Pepper *Straight Life* 177 [ref. to 1950's]: You're getting that rep of being a loner and kind of flippy, and that's a good front.

flip side *n.* **1.** the opposite (of something).

1967 Lit *Dictionary* 15: *Flip side*—The reverse of the other side. **1967** Fiddle *Portraits From Shooting Gallery* 345. **1968** Gover *JC* 178: Baby, the flip side a love is *hate!* You think the whole world gonna turn over an play on nothin but *love?* **1965–72** E. Newton *Mother Camp* 113: [Drag] is an organic part of American culture—exactly the "flip side" of many precious ideals. **1976–77** C. McFadden *Serial* 60: On the flip side, sometimes life with Marlene was incredibly mellow.

2. Esp. *CB.* a return trip, as made by a trucker or bus driver.

1976 Lieberman & Rhodes *CB* 128: *Flip Side*—On the return side. **1977** Corder *Citizens Band* 33: We'll modulate with you on the flip side. **1984** Hindle *Dragon Fall* 48: I'll catch ya on the flip side. **1990** *Bill & Ted's Adventures* (CBS-TV): Catch you on the flip side when I come back for my bowling shoes.

flipster *n.* an eccentric or crazy person; KOOK.

1981 O'Day & Eells *High Times* 45: Hipsters, Flipsters, and Finger-Poppin' Daddies.

fliptop *n.* **1.** BLOWTOP. Also attrib.

1963 Braly *Shake Him* 113: I could never push that bunch of fliptops and professional misfits into a working group. *Ibid.* 123: In a word, man, he's insane. A fliptop cop. **1967** Lit *Dictionary* 36: This flip-top cat fell out of his tree at the beginning of the first picture.

2. (see quot.).

1971 Tak *Truck Talk* 61: *Flip top:* a tilt-cab tractor.

flirt *n.* a game of cards.

1821 Waln *Hermit in Phila.* 29: "What do you say to *a flirt*?" said the first. "*Pharo?*" inquired the other. "Ay—old Flirtaway's—let's have a *flyer* if you're *flush.*"

flit *n.* **1.** *Stu.* a foolish, silly, or offensive person.

1932 Lorimer *Streetcars* 131: They probably had flits for wives, so I suppose they went and got some mistresses. **1933–34** Lorimer & Lorimer *Stag Line* 171: I'd feel like a flit…browsing around the Kid-dies' Korner. **1979** Gutcheon *New Girls* 62: I was sure that Miss Moltke would flunk me, the flit.

2. an effeminate man; a male homosexual.

1935 *AS* (Feb.) 78: *Flit.* A pervert. **1941** G. Legman, in Henry *Sex Vars.* II 1166: *Flit.* A homosexual (College slang, recorded at Harvard in 1939). **1941** in Legman *Limerick* 102: He was Queen of the Flits in Hoboken. **1952** J.D. MacDonald *Damned* 60: Down at the head of the line he found a couple of sour-looking flits. **1957** M. Shulman *Rally* 72: She had been bored silly with the flits and lushes of café society. **1961–64** Barthelme *Caligari* 120: You're flits, you guys, huh? **1965** Hersey *Too Far to Walk* 184: Awright, awright, all you little flits get over here. **1970** Dunn *Attic* 66: When the guy showed himself the flit jumped into his arms and said "Take care of me big daddy, I'm in for five years." **1972** B. Harrison *Hospital* 222: That goddamned flit. **1988** *21 Jump St.* (Fox-TV): You haven't turned into a flit, have you? **1992** N. Cohn *Heart of World* 213: Gay.…Faggot, flit.

3. high spirits induced by intoxication; (*also*) liquor.

1947 Schulberg *Harder They Fall* 141: An undertone the woman should have been able to hear if the flit hadn't stopped up her ears. **1973–78** D. Ford *Pappy* 31: But the Irish, they were something else. All single, all drunks…Full of flit all the time, and fight? They'd fight a buzz saw!

flit *v.* to go; depart. *Obs.* in U.S.

1899 *Century* (June) 263: Multiply this figure by a hundred, which is about the number of days in a year when all trampdom "flits." **1900** Willard & Hodler *Powers That Prey* 119: Ned an' me is goin' to flit right now. **ca*1959 Opie & Opie *Lore & Lang.* 192: Juvenile language is well stocked…with expressions inviting a person's departure,…*flit, float away*, [etc.]. [**1993 Englishman in N.Y.C., age 28 (coll. J. Sheidlower): "Debbie and Dave did a midnight flit" would mean they left the party at midnight. I don't think it could be a verb, though.]

flitsy *adj.* silly; flighty.

1973 N.Y.C. man, age *ca*26: She was one flitsy chick…yeah, *flitsy*. My mother used to use that expression.

fliv *n.* **1.** FLIVVER, *n.*, 2.

1911–12 Ade *Knocking the Neighbors* 53: The Ignition was Punk and the Transmission was a Fliv. **1919** S. Lewis *Free Air* 184: You're right. I'm a fliv. **1919** in Sandburg *Letters* 154: But in literature and matters that have to do with the intellectual, spiritual and artistic honesty of other people, I'm a good deal of a fliv. **1921** Sandburg *Sunburnt West* 55: There was a little fliv of a woman loved one man and lost out. **1923** *N.Y. Times* (Sept. 9) VIII 2: *Fliv*: Same as flop. *Flop:* A failure.

2. FLIVVER, *n.*, 1.a.

1930 Bodenheim *Roller Skates* 31: He puts that on to…get a crowd around his fliv', see?

fliv *adj.* ¶ In phrase: **go fliv** to break down; collapse; fail.

1918 in Sandburg *Letters* 136: In Russia, the Terror is on and all who have issued from the hot breath of it have their nerves gone fliv and can only gibber a disconnected story.

fliv *v.* FLIVVER, *v.*

1917 *N.Y. Times* (Dec. 23) IV 6: They had "flivved." **1920** *Amer. Legion Wkly.* (July 9) 7: There have been plenty of Franco-American hand-books before this one, but they have all F.O.B. Detroited—flivved in other words. **1922** *Sat. Eve. Post* (June 3) 10: Is he going to fliv on you this year?

flivver *n.* [orig. unkn.] **1.a.** a small, cheap, or old automobile, usu. a Ford Model A or Model T. Now *hist.*

1910 in *OEDS*: You stick to me an' you'll be travellin' round the coun-try in a flivver. **1915** *N.Y. Eve. Jour.* (Aug. 4) 16: With all the flivvers on the road burning gasoline I'll soon make it up. **1915** Lardner *Gull-ible's Travels* 3: If we was runnin' a foot race between each other, and suppose I was leadin' by eighty yards, a flivver'd prob'ly come up and hit you in the back and bump you over the finishin' line ahead o' me. **1919** MacGill *Dough-Boys* 20: Half a dozen flibbers swung into the square and swept out, their wheels grazing the wagon drawn by the bul-lock. **1920** in Fitzgerald *Stories* I 211: I haven't seen his silly little flivver in two weeks. **1920** S. Lewis *Main Street* 40: Yep. I get a good time out of the flivver. 'Bout a week ago I motored down to New Wurttemburg.

1930 Pasley *Al Capone* 95: A flivver squad, dispatched from the West Englewood station, was told of this. **1933** Milburn *No More Trumpets* 5: The new flivver got woefully scratched and battered. **1960** H. Lee *To Kill a Mockingbird* 16: One night, in an excessive spurt of high spirits, the boys backed around the square in a borrowed flivver. **1962** Houk & Dexter *Ballplayers* 169: They pay no attention to the old crack about singles hitters riding in flivvers while homerun champions ride Cadillacs. **1968** I. Reed *Yellow Back Radio* 77: Take a spin in the flivver. **1975** T. Berger *Sneaky People* 59: Years back, the late mister had a little flivver.

b. *Navy.* a 750-ton destroyer.

1918 Beston *Full Speed Ahead* 64: Our great destroyer fleet may be divided into two squadrons, the first of larger boats called "thousand tonners," the second of smaller vessels known as "flivvers." **1918** Connolly *U-Boat Hunters* 165: He commanded a *flivver*, which is the service name for the small class of destroyers, the 750-ton ones. **1919** *Our Navy* (Aug.) 61 [ref. to 1914]: The old happy days can be recalled by any of the flivvers of the Navy from the "O'Brien" to the "Shaw," when we used to lay up in Liverpool trying to bum a couple of bunker plates to go over on the ferry.

c. *Av.* a small aircraft.

1926 in *OEDS*: Won't it be amusing when we can…step into our little up-shooting flivvers at the back door? **1944** Mellor *Sank Same* 43: A Piper Cub, the tiny "flivver plane" known to every civilian flying field in America. **1945** Hamann *Air Words*: *Flivver*. A small airplane; a light plane.

2. a failure or disappointment; something inferior, cheap, small, or insignificant. Also attrib.

1914 (cited in Weingarten *Dict. Slang*). **1915** Lardner *Gullible's Travels* 29: If they was all as good as *Carmen*, I'd go every night. But lots o' them is flivvers. **1915** *DN* IV 233: *Flivver*, a hoax; also, a failure. **1918** *N.O. Times-Picayune* (Aug. 29) 9: As a Republican, Ford Was a Flivver, but He Ran a Rattling Race. **1918** *Wadsworth Gas Attack* 8: As a Mixer, Artie was a Flivver. **1918** Stringer *House of Intrigue* 53: A transfer company would deliver it at a flivver address, and Bud would move on as soon as it came. **1919** Darling *Jargon Book* 13: *Fliver*—A failure or mistake. **1927** *Vanity Fair* (Nov.) 132: "Flivver" which is a synonym for a Ford car was first used to describe a show that failed. **1928** Hall & Niles *One Man's War* 347 [ref. to 1918]: But no one is very happy over the Liberty. It has been tried out and found out to be a flivver. **1934** Weseen *Dict. Slang* 335: *Flivver*…anything small, cheap, or insignificant. **1969** Sidney *For Love of Dying* 59: Just turned thirty-four and falling to pieces already. A flivver of a man.

flivver *v.* **1.** to fail; fizzle.

1912 in *OEDS*: If the production flivvers, I'll need that thirty cents. **1916** *Variety* (Nov. 17) 4: Film Flivvers Abroad. **1918** Mayers *A.E.F. Hymnal* (unp.): The motor wouldn't work at all,/The ailerons flivvered too. **1921** Marquis *Carter* 146: You think I do nothing but flitter, flutter, frivol and flivver! **1923** McAlmon *Companion Vol.* 14: We can't begin thinking that way about the proposition or we'll flivver completely. **1948** in *DA*: Plan for Liverwurstless Day flivvered.

2. to ride or drive in a FLIVVER.

1927 in *OEDS*: I was finding the desert a bit flat when you flivvered in. **1930** *Amer. Merc.* (Oct.) 162: A policeman flivvered up. **1947** in *DA*: About 10,000 of them flivvered down to Juniper Grove.

FLK *n. Hosp.* (see quots.).

1968 "J. Hudson" *Case of Need* 311: And in pediatrics is perhaps the most unusual abbreviation of all, F L K, which means "Funny-looking kid." **1972** *Nat. Lampoon* (July) 76: F. L. K. "Funny-looking kid." Usually a mongoloid. **1979** Univ. Tenn. student: My boyfriend in med school talks about *FLK*'s—funny-looking kids. **1981** in Safire *Good Word* 157. **1985** *Maledicta* VIII 117: F. L. K. Funny-looking kid. Said of a child-patient with a strange appearance…but not fitting any particular pattern of disease.

Flo *n. Local.* Florence, S.C.; Florence, Ala.

1984 S.C. woman, age *ca*32: Is she coming back to Flo?

float *v.* **1.** to leave.

1894 in Crane *N.Y.C. Sketches* 33: Well, let's float, then! **1895** Townsend *Fadden Explains* 64: So we floated. *****1935** in *OEDS*: Come on. Let's float.

2. to dispose of by selling; sell.

1899 A.H. Lewis *Sandburrs* 205: I goes to d'chains an' floats ten of 'em at five a chain.

3. *Finance.* to negotiate (a loan). Now *colloq.*

1958 C.M. Kornbluth, in Pohl *Star of Stars* 42: Cursed be the day when I floated a New York loan.

¶ In phrase:

¶ **enough to float a battleship** [or **gunboat**] (of liquor) a large quantity.

1866 G.A. Townsend *Non-Combatant* 187: Drinking like a fish, or, as "Pop" remarked, enough to float a gun-boat. **1901** [Hobart] *John Henry* 16: How dare you trail into my flat with your tide high enough to float a battleship? **1918** in [Grider] *War Birds* 76: Enough champagne to float a battleship. **1932** T. Wolfe *Death* 228: If you took all the rotten old licker they'd poured down their throats since then you'd have enough to float a battleship. **1952** C. Sandburg *Young Strangers* 165: Think of it, and him in his life has drunk enough whisky to float a battleship! **1967** Aaron *About Us* 104: They've drunk enough beer to float a battleship.

floater *n.* **1.** *Police.* a corpse found floating in a body of water.

1890 Riis *Other Half* 230: "Floaters" come ashore now and then with pockets turned inside out. **1932** in *DA*. **1962** D. Hamilton *Murderers' Row* 78: A floater's a stiff that's been fished out of the drink. **1963** J. Mitford *Amer. Way of Death* 83: Floaters…are another matter; a person who has been in the Bay for a week or more…will decompose more rapidly. They used to burn gunpowder in the morgue when floaters were brought in, to mask the smell. **1970** Boatright & Owens *Derrick* 84 [ref. to *ca*1910]: A floater—a dead man—was found in the…Neches River. **1973** P. Benchley *Jaws* 14: "I think we've got a floater on our hands, Chief." "A floater? What in Christ's name is a floater?" "A drowning." **1982** Savitch *Anchorwoman* 63: The grotesquerie of the floater…made my head spin. *a*1991 J.R. Wilson *Landing Zones* 213: He said that's how it was done with "floaters."

2. *Law.* a suspended sentence, esp. with an order to leave a locality at once.

1914 Jackson & Hellyer *Vocab.* 34: *Floater*…A suspended sentence; a mandatory order to quit a community or locality.…"The rap wasn't strong enough, so they took a floater." **1922** N. Anderson *Hobo* 26: Accordingly, the so-called "floater" custom of passing vagrants on to other communities is widespread. **1926** J. Black *Can't Win* 69: I was just after gettin' a six months' floater out of Denver. **1931–34** in Clemmer *Pris. Community* 332: *Floater*, *n.* A release from jail with admonition to leave town immediately. *a*1934 in Lomax & Lomax *Amer. Ballads* 25: The John had a "bindle"—a workers' plea/So they gave him a floater and set him free. **1952** Steinbeck *East Of Eden* 334: If I…admit I'm your wife I'll get a floater out of the county and out of the state. **1968** Spradley *Owe Yourself a Drunk* 36: Next time I took a floater, 90 days suspended.

3. *Sports.* a slow or weakly thrown ball.

1942 *ATS* 652: Slow ball…*floater*. *Ibid.* 664: *Floater*, a slow, wobbling pass. **1984** *TriQuarterly* (Spring) 315: He watches Igor…lob this pathetically feeble floater…[to] second [base].

4. *Narc.* (see quot.).

1972 *Nat. Lampoon* (Oct.) 38: QUAALUDE 300 mg. (floater).

floating batteries *n.pl. Mil.* bits of hardtack broken into coffee or tea. *Joc.*

1871 Schele de Vere *Amer.* 343: The term *Floating Batteries* was…applied in bitter irony to the army-bread issued by the Confederate Government. **1883** Gerrish & Hutchinson *Blue & Gray* 740: "Soup," "floating battery," "pies," dumplings, and even light rolls were made. *****1889** Barrère & Leland *Dict. Slang* I 372: *Floating batteries*…bits of bread broken up and put in the evening tea. When soldiers are under stoppages or otherwise impecunious and unable to buy herrings, bacon, sausages, and other savoury articles for the tea meal, they are compelled to do with floating batteries.

float-out *n. Law.* a suspended sentence and an order to leave town or be sentenced for vagrancy.

1968 Gover *JC* 99: Johnlaw give 'em a floatout an only three came back t' town.

flog *n. Army.* a march; slog.

1983 Beckwith & Knox *Delta Force* 158: It was just a flog, a march from one point to another.

flog *v.* **1.** to defeat; (*also*) to excel; surpass.

1812 in Shay *Sea Songs* 162: It ofttimes has been told,/That the British seamen bold/Could flog the tars of France so neat and handy, oh!/…Could flog the Frenchmen two to one so handy, oh! *****ca*1841 in *OED*: Good cherry-bounce flogs all the foreign trash in the world. *****1847** in *OED*: Of all the brimstone spawn that I ever came across that same she-devil flogs them. **1864** in Bleser *Secret & Sacred* 298: Hood is cut off & Hardee badly flogged at Jonesboro. **1882** A.W. Aiken *Joe Buck* 3: Oh, you're a man-eater then, like the fellow who got flogged s‹

handsomely. **1909** *WNID*: *Flog*…To surpass; excel. *Dial. Eng. or Slang.*

2. (of a male) to masturbate.—usu. constr. with joc. obj., as in **flog the log, flog the bishop,** etc.

1916 Cary *Venery* I 90: *Flogging the Pup*—Masturbation. **1916–22** Cary *Sexual Vocab.*: Masturbate…*flog the dummy*. **1950* Partridge *DSUE* (ed. 4) 1050: *Flog one's donkey*. (Of a male) to masturbate: low (? orig. Cockney): late C. 19–20. Also *flog one's mutton*…Also *flog the bishop*. **1946–51** J. Jones *Eternity* ch. 19 [ref. to 1940]: "Oh, blow it out your ass," he said savagely. "I'm working. What do you think, I'm floggin' my doggin'?" **1966* Partridge *DSUE* (ed. 6) 1124: *Flog*…to masturbate: low Australian: C.20. **1967** *DAS* (Supp.) 684: *Flog the dummy* [or] *meat sausage.* *a*1972 B. Rodgers *Queens' Vernacular* 115: To masturbate…*flog the bishop (donkey, pork)* (rare) **1972** Jenkins *Semi-Tough* 45: There was Bubba…staring at some lovelies on the beach for inspiration—and flogging away. **1973** Overgard *Hero* 168: If I ain't back, tell him to go flog his log—if he's got one. **1972–76** Durden *No Bugles* 107: I flog my dong, First Sergeant. **1980** Spears *Slang & Euph.* 140: *Flog one's meat, flog one's sausage*…to masturbate. **1984** J. Green *Contemp. Slang* 97: *Flog the log* v. to masturbate. **1986** J. Green *Slang Thes.* 107: (To masturbate (male)): Flog one's mutton,—the dolphin,—the dog,—the log. **1980–89** Cheshire *Home Boy* 91: Pounding the pud. Flogging the log. Beating the meat.

3.a. to sell or offer for sale, esp. illicitly.

*1919 *Atheneum* (Aug. 1) 695 [ref. to WWI]: "Flogging" is the illegal disposal of Army goods. **1925* Fraser & Gibbons *Sailor & Soldier Wds.* 96 [ref. to WWI]: *To Flog*. To sell something not the vendors own to dispose of. **1935* in *OEDS*: If a crook disposes of stolen property through a fence he is "fencing," but if it is sold through any other channel it is "flogging." **1951, *1966, *1967* in *OEDS*. **1975** *Oui* (Mar.) 134: Dope dealers…have switched to flogging Quality antique Indian and African jewelry and 17th Century hand-woven Kurta rugs. **1977** Dunne *True Confessions* 13: And those cheap gold-leaf chalices with fake emeralds and rubies that he flogs to parents whose sons are getting ordained. *a*1988 C. Adams *More Straight Dope* 50: A wimp definition that enables them to flog off sterile juice in the place of genuine, raw, unpasteurized cider.

b. to promote the sale of; advertise.

1983 *Morning Edition* (Nat. Pub. Radio) (Nov. 2): To *flog* a book means to promote it in the media.…He was probably out flogging his latest collection. **1985** *Newsweek* (June 17) 72: Nickelodeon, the children's cable channel, is flogging the Yup Pups for all they are worth, which it hopes is a lot. **1989** *Geraldo* (synd. TV series): His new book that he's flogging around the country. **1991** W. Savage *Comic Books* 67: Peddling…breakfast food and flogging decoder rings.

4. to hurry; go at great speed.—constr. with *it.*

1972 Jenkins *Semi-Tough* 108: They usually hop in Big Ed's Firestream Two, his six-seater jet, and flog it in on Saturday night and then flog it back to Fort Worth on Sunday night. **1977** Olsen *Fire Five* 164: We had to flog it, man…That was an important service call we were making.

flogger *n.* an overcoat.

1904 *Life in Sing Sing* 248: *Flogger*. An overcoat. **1915** T.A. Dorgan, in *N.Y. Eve. Jour.* (Dec. 11) 6: What was the matter with the flogger? **1932** D. Runyon, in *Collier's* (Jan. 30) 8: A chinchilla flogger that moves Israel back thirty G's.

flooey *adv.* [orig. unkn.; cf. BLOOEY] awry; askew; to ruin. Occ. as interj. or adj. Also vars.

1905 W.S. Kelly *Lariats* 319: You…bumped your head and knocked your wits "flewey." **1918** Streeter *Dere Mable* 54: Yesterday I spent all afternoon shinin up for guard sos to be the colonels orderly. Then I step out of the tent and flui. The sargent says, "Smith dont you know enuff not to go on guard lookin like that?" **1919** *Amer. Legion Wkly.* (Sept. 19) 13: PHLOOEY OIL STOCK. **1920** Acker *Our Outfit* 127: Hun plans, like those of mice and men, often go "flooey." **1921** Sandburg *Sunburnt West* 62: And the bubble busted, went flooey, on a thumb touch. **1922** Farrar *Jack* 29: If they lamped any dough on you, they'd finish us both. Flooey. (*Snaps his fingers.*) Like that. **1925** Nason *Eyewash* 162: I seen it go flooey off the road while I was duckin' for that shell. **1931** in Woods *Horse-Racing* 67: And this dook's luck is certainly gone flooey. **1932** Berg *Prison Doctor* 234: The railroad had gone flooey and his stock wasn't worth a dime. **1942** in Truman *Dear Bess* 480: Then my store went flooy and cost my friends and Frank money. **1950** O'Brian & Evans *Chain Lightning* (film): 15,000 feet and my heat control goes flooey. **1960** Glemser *Fly Girls* 271: The pressure's gone flooey. It's those damned toilets acting up again. **1983** *New Yorker* (Aug. 8) 23: The director…loses his easy touch and the picture goes flooey.

floof *n.* [of fanciful orig.] a silly fool.

1919 S. Lewis *Free Air* 58: Why, you poor floof, it's one of the best cars in the world. Imported from France.

floogie *n.* [prob. alter. of FLOOZY] **1.** FLOOZY, 1, 2.

1938 S. Gaillard, S. Stewart, & Bud Green *Flat-Foot Floogie (With the Floy Floy)* (pop. song). **1939** in M. Gardner *Casey* 112: A floogie and a frump. **1941** H.A. Smith *Low Man* 217: It is unlikely that Stephen knows the precise meaning of "Flat-Foot Floogie with a Floy Floy." **1945** in *Calif. Folk. Qly.* V (1946) 376: "You're off the beam because you got a sugar report from a flugie."…"You are confused because you received a love letter from a girl." *Ibid.* 385: A well-stacked *flugie*…A comely and curvaceous girl. **1959** Sterling *Wake of the Wahoo* 227: He was pointing at the picture of a girl. "Floogie," he said.

2. a foolish or inconsequential person.

1939 "E. Queen" *Dragon's Teeth* 216: Velie, tell this floogie I'm one of the best people.

floor *v.* **1.** *Stu.* to make a perfect score on (an examination); get through successfully; master (a problem).

*1852 in B. Hall *College Wds.* (ed. 2) 204: To *floor a paper*, is to answer every question in it. **1854** in *Ibid.*: We *floored* the Bien. Examination. **1861* in *OED*: I've nearly floored my little-go work. **a*1889 in Barrère & Leland *Dict. Slang* I 373: "I *floored* that paper," *i.e.*, answered every question on it. "I *floored* that problem," did it perfectly or made myself master of it.

2. to press (a gas pedal) to the floor; (*hence*) to accelerate (an automobile) in this manner.

1951–53 in *AS* (May 1954) 96: Floor it! **1955** in C. Beaumont *Best* 132: I floored the Duesenberg. **1954–60** *DAS*. **1974–77** A. Hoffman *Property Of* 143: José…floored the Mustang. **1977** Caron *Go-Boy* 44: Trembling, I floored the gas pedal and we tore out of there.

floorboard *v.* FLOOR, 2.—usu. constr. with *it.*

1954–60 *DAS*. **1971** Tak *Truck Talk* 62: *Floorboard it*: to accelerate by depressing the accelerator…right down to the floorboards. **1973** Huggett *Body Count* 156: If the convoy was hit, SOP was to floorboard it, go like hell, and fire everything like crazy. **1976** Atlee *Domino* 8: The overhauling vehicle was a pickup.…The driver must have had his vehicle floorboarded. **1980** in McCaulley *Dark Forces* 166: With the windows down, I floor-boarded it across the plains.

floor-timbers *n.pl.* *Naut.* the feet. *Joc.*

1846 Codman *Sailors' Life* 167: When you get down to her floor-timbers, all I can say is, that nature got 'em out neat.

flooze *n.* FLOOZY.

1952 J.D. MacDonald *Damned* 40: And a guy with a girl, even this flooze, would look better than a guy alone. **1966** F. Copley *Catullus* 7: Ya got yerself a flooz. **1987** Levi's 501 Jeans ad (Fox-TV) (Sept. 20): She wasn't a regular flooze. **1986–91** Hamper *Rivethead* 21: The flooze…had tired of his mooching.

floozied up *adj.* gaudily dressed; dressed up.

[**1943* in *OEDS*: There was a tremendous crowd going, all flossied up for a day out!] [**1965* G.W. Turner *Eng. in Austr. & N.Z.* 137: "Flossied up" *sur son trente et un.*] **1978** Univ. Tenn. student theme: How come you're all floozied up?

floozy or **floozie** *n.* [prob. alter. of FLOSSY, *n.*] **1.** a woman or girl.—used derisively. Also vars.

1902 T.A. Dorgan, in *S.F. Bulletin* (Oct. 24) 6: Here comes a couple o dem wise flusies. **1907** *Univ. of Tenn. Volunteer* (unp.): Wouldn't it be funny if?…Bird should desert from the ranks of the "fluzie killers"? **1908** *Univ. of Tenn. Volunteer* (unp.): I saw him with a pretty little fluzie the other day. **1910** *Univ. of Tenn. Volunteer* 55: The "Fluzzies" giggled at the manly voices of the boys. **1911** *DN* III 543: Defined by one contributor as a young woman to whom attention is paid, "John took his floozy to the baseball game"; by another as a term sometimes used of waitresses, or shopgirls, "From which floozy did you get that?" **1914** Jackson & Hellyer *Vocab.* 36: Fluzie…A woman; a questionable female character. [**1945** Mencken *Amer. Lang.* (Supp. I) 508: [Britons occasionally use] Americanisms…in senses that must inevitably give every actual American a start. In 1942…Margaret Louise Allingham, in a book review…described two quite respectable American girl characters as *floosies*.…She was brought to book…by D.W. Brogan.]

2. a tawdry or immoral woman; (*specif.*) a prostitute. Also vars.

1909 Chrysler *White Slavery* 30: Tell that floosie to cut out that yelping. *Ibid.* 176: He don't care for the "cheap floosies"; he's out after a "doll." **1919** Sandburg *Smoke and Steel* 33: Ship riveters talk with their feet/To the feet of floozies under the tables. **1926** Wood & Goddard *American Slang* 18: *Fluzie*. A daughter of joy, a prostitute. **1928** Bodenheim *Georgie May* 38: Sho' looked pretty…the best floosie he'd evah had. **1930** Dos Passos *42nd Parallel* 66: God, I'd have beat up the goddam flousies. **1936** Tully *Bruiser* 145: There's more floozies in this town than cattle in a stockyard…But a bad girl's like a bad fighter, Shane—they always think they're winnin'. **1936** Gaddis *Courtesan* 51: I don't want you to look like a floozy, babe. **1939** Saroyan *Time of Your Life* IV: It's floozies like her that raise hell with our racket. **1942** Davis & Wolsey *Call House Madam* 135: A floozy in a sailors' brothel. **1951** Mailer *Barbary Shore* 50: Who knows what kind of floosies you guys are bringing in. **1952** Uris *Battle Cry* 71: After an hour, a gum-popping floozy took his picture and he hastened to return to the base. **1953** Petry *Narrows* 65: The little floosey you'd picked up over on Franklin. **1956** J.D. Brown *Kings Go Forth* 113: She's not a floosie, some little tramp you picked up in the Negresco Bar. **1963** Horwitz *Candlelight* 12: So walk me home now and let the floozies go. **1980** *Daily News* (N.Y.C.) (Manhattan ed.) (Sept. 6) 5: Jean…once told Wisconsin legislators to keep their "floosies" home and welfare pickets to "get off their duffs and work." **1988** *Daily News* (N.Y.C.) (June 8) 2: The floozy in TV preacher Jimmy Swaggart's life wants to go home to Indiana, get her high school diploma and live the good life as an interior decorator. **1992** *Crain's N.Y. Business* (Mar. 16) 11: Hitching up with one floozie after another.

floozy *adj.* **1.** crazy.
1918 *Radiator* (July 18) 2: Floozie in the filbert? Not a-tall. Just the way some cubist poet might gertrudestein the present brand of weather. **1937** Steinbeck *Mice & Men* 86: You got some floozy idears about what us guys amounts to. You ain't got sense enough in that chicken head to even see that we ain't stiffs.

2. debauched; dissipated.
*ca***1929** *Collection of Sea Songs* 35: Rebecca was a floozy coot/A prostitute of ill repute. **1933** Ersine *Prison Slang* 37: *Floozey, adj.* Dissipated.

flop *n.* **1.** *Stu.* a deception or prank; trick.
1851 B. Hall *College Wds.* 133: A correspondent from the University of Vermont writes: Any "cute" performance by which a man is sold [deceived] is a *good flop*, and, by a phrase borrowed from the ball ground, is "rightly played."

2. *Pol.* a turnaround or sudden change of policy or the like; flip-flop.
1880 in *OEDS:* Mr. Skinner's apparent flop on the railroad question is injuring his chances in the Speakership struggle. **1904** in *DA:* That a flop by the most militant of the unionists is under contemplation has been denied. **1911** H. Harrison *Queed* 230: The editor, instead of seeing in West's letter a spontaneous act of magnanimity,…maliciously twisted it into a grudging confession of error.…So ran the editorial, which was offensively headed "West's Fatal Flop."

3.a. a complete failure; (*broadly,* now *rare*) someone or something that does not or cannot meet one's expectations. [*a**1890–93* F & H III 31: *Flop*…(common).—A collapse or breakdown.] **1919** *Variety* (Mar. 28) 32: One of the coldest flops of the year…"The Love Chase." **1920** *Collier's* (Mar. 20) 39: I hear the Bermuda joint's a flop, anyways. **1921** Witwer *Leather Pushers* 192: Professional strong men are flops as a rule whenever they turn to the ring. **1924** *Sat. Eve. Post* (July 12) 15: *A Flop*—terrible, a hopeless failure. **1925** Stallings *Big Parade* (film) [ref. to 1918]: This war's a flop! **1928** Benchley *20,000 Leagues* 123: The funniest line in the world…if spoken into a vacuum, would sound like the biggest flop in the world. **1938** T. Wolfe *Web & Rock* 366: And if the show is a flop, she gets nothing. **1944** in Mencken *Amer. Lang.* (Supp. I) 452: H.W. Seaman, returning to England after ten years in the United States, has [observed that]…No English drama critic would shrink from writing of a *flop* [although it is an Americanism.]. **1954** Schulz *More Peanuts* (unp.): Boy, are you ever a flop!! You can't do anything! **1965** Karp *Doobie Doo* 51: The music was a flop. She turned it off. **1972** *Penthouse* (Aug.) 78: He decided the band was a waste of time because he knew he was too much of a flop to become a rock 'n' roll star. **1980** Albrecht *Brain Power* 3: The schools have been a spectacular flop. **1988** *N.Y. Post* (June 6) 6: I play a producer who's looking for a flop so he can take a tax write-off. He buys this science fiction picture, and it turns out to be a hit.

b. *Pris.* a denial of parole.
1944 *Pap. Mich. Acad.* XXX 598: *Flop,* a setback in parole, losing good time. **1948** Webb *Four Steps* 45: The guy got a flop today. **1952** Himes *Stone* 113: A convict who'd served twelve long, tough, hard years getting a six months' flop by the parole board for "investigation." **1954** McGraw *Prison Riots* 132: The parole board…will give nothing but three-year flops. *Ibid.* 268: *Flop* or *flop-over:* A term of years designated

by a parole board before which an inmate cannot have another parole hearing. **1973** Goines *Black Girl* 89: They didn't want any trouble over a seat in the damn television room which would cause them to get a flop at the parole board.

4. the act of lying down to receive a man sexually; (*hence*) an act of copulation; LAY.
*a**1890–93* F & H III 32: *To do a flop*…(venery) to lie down to a man. **1937** Steinbeck *Mice & Men* 57: If a guy don't want a flop, why he can just…have a couple or three shots and pass the time…and Susy don't give a damn. She ain't rushin' guys through and kickin' 'em out if they don't want a flop. **1938** "Justinian" *Amer. Sexualis* 21: *Flop*…*n.* An act of coition…"He gave her a quick flop." U.S., C. 20, low coll.

5. *Und.* an arrest; FALL.
1904 *Life in Sing Sing* 248: *Flop.* An arrest. **1915–16** Lait *Beef, Iron & Wine* 161: I was pretty near thirteen before I takes my first flop. **1942–49** Goldin et al. *DAUL: Flop, n.*…An arrest. "Tony the Junker took a flop on a dead-banger (red-handed)."

6.a. a place to sleep, esp. a rented room.
1910 Ranney *30 Yrs.* 70: You can get a bed in a lodging-house for ten cents, or if you have only seven cents you can get a "flop." **1913** E.A. Brown *Broke* 28: "Say, Jack, can you tell a fellow where he can find a free flop?"…"You can flop on the floor up there for a nickel." **1917** Depew *Gunner Depew* 158: It used to remind me of a trial I saw in New York once, where the police had raided a yeggman's flop and had all their weapons in the courtroom as exhibits. **1922** N. Anderson *Hobo* 22: I am going to hunt up a box car for a flop. **1922** J. Conway, in *Variety* (Jan. 13) 7: They hired a flop in a local hotel. **1930** Dos Passos *42nd Parallel* 61: It was too cold to sit down anywhere, and they couldn't find anyplace that looked as if it would give them a flop for thirty-five cents. **1931** Gallagher *Bolts & Nuts* 126 [ref. to 1918]: Why worry about that when they were getting two square meals a day and a flop? **1947** Motley *Knock On Any Door* 163: I ain't got a flop. Can you let me have the price? **1965** Spillane *Killer Mine* 39: I got a flop upstairs over Moe Clausist's hock shop. **1972** Bunker *No Beast* 83: Most of these flops don't even have a carpet. **1972** Poniscan *Cinderella Liberty* 96: They'll remind you of your three squares a day and a flop. **1975** *Sing Out!* (July) 8: Check into a mission, any place downtown where bums go to eat and get a flop.

b. *Hobo.* a cheap lodging house; FLOPHOUSE.
1913 E.A. Brown *Broke* 32: To-day you walk…to Union Street, to Chicago's free "flop." **1915–16** Lait *Beef, Iron & Wine* 221: This ain't no hobo's flop, neither. **1918** *Chi. Sunday Tribune* (Oct. 27) V 3: A "flop" is a lodging house for vagrants. **1920** in DeBeck *Google* 63: Sure—you can hire a bed down on fourteenth street for a dime you know—Hogan's flop. **1922** N. Anderson *Hobo* 39: Flops are unwholesome and unsanitary. Efforts have been made to improve these conditions, but they have not been wholly successful. **1925** Dos Passos *Manhattan Transfer* 121: This is a hell of a lousy stinking flop. **1934** Veil & Marsh *Adventure's a Wench* 9: I took a bunk in a sailors' flop two blocks from the water front. **1980** Bruns *Kts. of Road* 166: Hogan's Flop was perhaps the best known.

c. *Specif.,* a bed, mattress, or the like.
1914 Jackson & Hellyer *Vocab.* 34: *Flop*…A bed; a place to sit, recline, or lie down. **1919** Wadsworth *Gas Attack* 13: Remove your clothes before denting the flop. **1928** Shay *More Pious Friends* 157: Went to sleep on his hall-room flop. *a***1940** in Lanning & Lanning *Texas Cowboys* 47 [ref. to *ca*1900]: The…way we slept out would be to find a small rise and throw the flop right on top of it. **1940** *AS* (Dec.) 450: *Flop.* A bed (to a seaman ashore; aboard ship his bed is a *bunk*). A hotel is a flophouse. **1958** Gilbert *Vice Trap* 22: You know the brass tubing that connects the bed-posts across the top of an old flop? *ca***1977** R. Adams *Lang. of R.R.* 62: *Flop:* a bed.

d. a place to sit down; seat.
1914 (quot. at (c), above). **1928** *N.Y. Times* (Mar. 11) VIII 6: *Grab a Flop*—Take a seat.

e. *Army.* FLOP TRENCH.
1918–19 MacArthur *Bug's-Eye View* 89: It was a strange feeling to be safe—to know that no German was wheeling up a little gun and getting ready to blow you back into the flops. **1928** MacArthur *War Bugs* 166: The cannoneers dug their flops—shovels burning.

7. a sleep; a rest; (*specif.*) *Pris.* a convict's final night before release; WAKE-UP.
1916 *The Editor* (May 6) 487. **1925** *AS* I (Dec.) 138: After a "flop" on his bunk the logger "lets 'er settle," then he "gangs up" to "roll the guff." **1926** *Writer's Mo.* (Dec.) 541: *Flop*—One night left to serve [in prison]. **1928** O'Connor *B'way Racketeers* 59: Many's the good night's flop I had in that joint. **1942–49** Goldin et al. *DAUL:* Two and a flop and I hit the street.

8. *Und.* a helpless or sleeping beggar or derelict; (see also 1927, 1942–49 quots.).

1927 *DN* V 446: *Flops,* n. Legless beggars. **1942–49** Goldin et al. *DAUL* 72: *Flop.*...A term of contempt, usually applied by skillful pickpockets to those who rob drunkards...."Even a flop wouldn't hustle with...that stiff." *ca***1955** in D.W. Maurer *Lang. Underworld* 241: *Flop.*...A person sleeping in a public place. **1959** W. Burroughs *Naked Lunch* 227: The...Dean of Lush Workers...pulls the gold teeth and crowns of any flop [a]sleep with his mouth open.

9. *Und.* (see quot.).

1940 D.W. Maurer, in *AS* (Apr.) 118: *The Flop.* A shortchange racket sometimes worked by con-men when they are short of money.

10. excrement or a piece of excrement; (*hence*) an act of defecation.

1951 in Mailer *Ad. for Myself* 143: A smell...which...meant carabao flop. **1980** *Nat. Lampoon* (Dec.) 12: The sidewalks are lined with Port-O-Lets. No matter where you are...you can take a flop. **1992** *CBS This Morning* (Mar. 2): Anybody can pick up the dog flops and throw 'em in the neighbor's front yard.

¶ In phrase:

¶ **take a flop to** become aware of; TUMBLE TO.

1915–16 Lait *Beef, Iron & Wine* 186: No matter how bad a guy feels...he's gotta wake up an' take a flop to himself.

flop *v.* **1.a.** Esp. *Boxing.* to knock down; (in 1906 quot.) to shoot down.

1846 Neal *Ploddy* 159: She "flopped" her husband...with a shovel applied in its latitude, "broadside on." *1888 in *F & H* III 32: 'E can't flop a bloke. **1903** C.E. Stewart *Uncle Josh* 47: If he indulged in any foolishness with me I'd flop him in about a minnit. **1906** *So. Hist. Soc. Paps.* XXXIV 289 [ref. to Civil War]: I flopped from his horse that was coming after us so savage. **1910** *N.Y. Eve. Jour.* (Mar. 2) 16: If I flop him again, as I did in our other fight, believe me I won't rush in bullheaded to certain defeat.

b. *Boxing.* to feign being knocked out; throw a fight.

1907 Siler *Pugilism* 118: The "nigger," if he was not thoroughly game, would flop to his white opponent. **1910** T.A. Dorgan, in *N.Y. Eve. Jour.* (Feb. 1) 14: I don't think they could give [Jack] Johnson enough money to flop.

c. to throw oneself to the ground for protection.

1918 Woollcott *Command Is Forward* 134: "Flop, everybody!" the captain called out to the men of Company H. **1926** Nason *Chevrons* 180: He was going to be a brave boy an' not flop for the shell. *Ibid.* 46: We heard it coming...and we flopped. **1930** Nason *Corp. Once* 236: If any lights go up near at hand, flop!

2.a. *Stu.* to get through (an examination) or improve (one's marks) by trickery.

1851 B. Hall *College Wds.*: "A man writes cards during examination to 'feeze the profs'; said cards are 'gumming cards,' and he *flops* the examination if he gets a good mark by the means." One usually *flops* his marks by feigning sickness.

b. to manage to achieve (a score on an examination).

1856 B. Hall *College Wds.* (ed. 2) 204: At the University of Vermont, to *flop a twenty* is to make a perfect recitation, twenty being the maximum mark for scholarship.

c. *Und.* to shortchange; FLIMFLAM.

1914 Jackson & Hellyer *Vocab.* 35: *Flop,* verb....Also used by money changers to signify fraud by confusion. Example: "There's a muff in that candy store that can be flopped because she can't count change."

3.a. to fall from rectitude.

*1871** Schele de Vere *Amer.* 603: The [English] slang term to *flop down*...means, to fall suddenly, to collapse, both in the literal and the figurative sense of the phrase. **1879** Campbell *My Partner* 65: NED. You are a Methodist, are you not? BRIT. Yes, in Sacramento. But a fellow can't maintain his grip on Methodism against a clear majority of two hundred Baptists in the district. (*Looks longingly at bottle*) So, I've flopped. **1934** Appel *Brain Guy* 93: I knew that dame in school....Boy, was she the iceberg! N' now she's flopped. They all flop.

b. to prove a complete failure.

1898–1900 Cullen *Chances* 89: The favorite is going to kerflop. **1914** in Pound *Letters* 34: The thing flopped so before, that there has been no use "talking it up." **1917** *N.Y. Times* (Dec. 23) IV 6: His act "flopped" in Boston. **1919** in De Beck *Google* 39: We ain't had a meal outside our home since the Kaiser flopped. **1930** Lavine *3d Degree* 11: I never flopped at an exam yet. **1959** M. Harris *Wake Up* 30: So you might as well know your stunt flopped. **1969** Layden & Snyder *Diff.*

Game 146: Another idea flopped.

c. *Stu.* to fail (an examination); to fail (a student).

1930 *AS* V (Apr.) 305: I'll flop that test as sure as shootin'. As near as I can tell she flopped the boy.

d. *Und.* (see quot.); FALL.

1935 D.W. Maurer, in *AS* (Feb.) 15 [ref. to *a*1910]: To *flop.* To be arrested.

e. *Pris.* to deny parole to.

1948 Webb *Four Steps* 46: They flopped him one year again.

f. *Police.* to reassign (a detective) to the status of patrolman; demote.

1972 J. Mills *Report* 192: Who's got this squad, who's got that squad, who's got the biggest hook, who's movin' up, who's gettin' flopped. **1974** Dubinsky & Standora *Decoy Cop* 27: He can be flopped, reassigned to uniform. **1974** Charyn *Blue Eyes* 51: Before the squad commander flopped him, Arnold provided little amenities for her at the stationhouse. **1974** Radano *Cop Stories* 116: I used to be in the Narcotics Squad...I got flopped. **1975** V. Miller *Trade-Off* 18: I don't care if they flop me back to patrolman. **1984** Caunitz *Police Plaza* 262: I'll flop you out of the Bureau. **1992** Hosansky & Sparling *Working Vice* 143: We had nothing to lose. They had already flopped us back to basic patrol.

4. (of a woman) to lie down to receive a man sexually; (*hence*) (*trans.*) to copulate with; LAY.

*a*1890–93** F & H* III 32: *To flop a judy*—to lay out, or "spread" (q.v.) a girl. **1928** Bodenheim *Georgie* May 30: He didn't lie about women when they wouldn't flop for him. **1930** J.T. Farrell *Calico Shoes* 259: What was she, just one of that abnormal kind that flops for anything in pants? **1938** "Justinian" *Amer. Sexualis* 21: Flop, v. To copulate...The female is always the predicate of this verb which emphasizes her passive role, e.g., "He flopped her." **1963** Coon *Short End* 61: Some of them would come over here, and go into town, and fall in love with the first whore they flopped. **1966** Braly *Cold* 68: They were rich, with two Cadillac automobiles, and beautiful broads flopped for them.

5. to become enamored of; (*also*) to believe foolishly; fall (for).

1905 *Nat. Police Gaz.* (Dec. 16) 3: "Look...she's flopped." "They all begin that way, but she'll know better next time." **1925** in D. Hammett *Continental Op* 199: I might flop for that if I didn't know you. **1930** Lait *On the Spot* 18: The floozies flop for him. It's his America. **1948** Lait & Mortimer *New York* 152: Gotham gals don't flop for saps, simps or retail buyers. **1973** in H. Ellison *Sex Misspelled* 280: No wonder Patricia Mullen flopped for John Smith.

6. to lie down to sleep or rest; (*hence*) to spend the night.

1907 J. London *Road* 107 [ref. to *ca*1893]: "Kip," "doss," "flop," "pound your ear", all mean the same thing; namely, to sleep. *Ibid.*: I climbed a fence and "flopped" in a field. **1916** *The Editor* (May 6) 487. **1918** McBride *Emma Gees* 172: The next night we made our way to billets,...near Renninghelst, where I immediately "flopped" for a straight forty-eight hours' continuous sleep. **1922** N. Anderson *Hobo* 22: Come on, let us hunt up a place to flop till daylight. **1926** Nason *Chevrons* 37: Would you mind tellin' a guy where you expect to flop in these wet woods? **1928** C. McKay *Banjo* 106: You got all the balance a the night foh sweet flopping. **1929** E. Booth *Stealing Through Life* 286: You better come over and flop with Mae and me tonight. **1950** Calmer *Strange Land* 83: They can flop down-cellar on those two extra mattresses in the back, Bill. **1958** Motley *Epitaph* 64: Don't get the idea I'm a whore you can flop with any time you want. **1965** Daniels *Moments of Glory* 79: The rest of you flop.

7.a. to turn or roll over.

1965–68 E.R. Johnson *Silver St.* 22: Wasn't sure until we flopped him, anyway.

b. *CB.* to turn (a vehicle) around.—constr. with *it.*

1977 *Sci. Mech. CB Gde.* 169: I'm going to flop it at Exit 19.

¶ In phrase:

¶ **the way the mop flops** the way things are.

1957 Trosper *Jailhouse Rock* (film): That's the way the mop flops. **1981** Graziano & Corsel *Somebody Down Here* 26: What could I tell you. That's the way the mop flopped.

flop-eared *adj.* stupid. Cf. LOP-EARED.

1863 in *Ark. Hist. Qly.* XLII (1983) 66: The "flopeared Dutch"...were...anxious to fill their pockets. *ca*1865** in Randolph *Ozark Folksongs* III: It was the sixth of March/That we did march away/To fight the Feds an' the flop-eared Dutch/An' hear what they did say.

flophouse *n.* a cheap, rundown lodging house or hotel patronized esp. by tramps, beggars, etc. [1909 quot. seems to denote such an establishment where prostitutes may operate rather than specifically a brothel.]

1909 in Monaghan *Schoolboy, Cowboy* 52: My father was hanged as a horse-thief,/My mother was burned as a witch./My sisters ain't fit f'r a flop house,/I'm a cow-punching son-of-a-bitch. **1919** Darling *Jargon Book* 13: *Flop House*—A hotel or rooming house. **1919** *DN* V 56: *Flop house*. A cheap lodging house where one can sleep for a few cents. Seattle. **1922** J.J. Davis *Iron Puddler* 160 [ref. to N.O., *ca*1895]: This was called a "Five Cent Flop" house. **1922** Anderson *Hobo* 16: The flophouse and the cheap hotel compel promiscuity but do not encourage intimacy or neighborliness. **1929** *AS* IV (June) 340: *Flop-house*. Lodging house wherein many men sleep on cots in a single room. **1929** Milburn *Hobo's Hornbook* 74: St. Peter runs the flop house,/And angels walk the drag. **1937** Kyner & Daniel *End of Track* 157: A "bunkhouse" or "flophouse" where, within the…walls of the big tents, the sagebrush and cactus had been cleared away so that men could spread their bedrolls on the ground. **1948** Wouk *City Boy* 255: "All right, boys…Flophouse reveille for Herbie Bookbinder."…Lennie…and Eddie Bromberg sprang to the ends of Herbie's cot and upset it sideways. The sleeper sprawled to the floor and opened red, bleary eyes. **1958** S.H. Adams *Tenderloin* 10: Rates were…five cents a night at Dirty Dick's flophouse on Hester Street, where typhus fever once wiped out half the temporary populace. **1977** R.S. Parker *Effective Decisions* 12: The only solution was…the flophouse. **1991** C. Fletcher *Pure Cop* 46: An old flophouse at Erie and Dearborn.

flop joint *n.* Esp. *Hobo.* FLOPHOUSE.

1928 O'Connor *B'way Racketeers* 120: Helbig checked out of the side street flop joint. **1929–33** J. Lowell *Gal Reporter* 62: They just have flop joints for men. **1946** J.H. Burns *Gallery* 127: It was like the lobby of a New York flop joint. **1959** Lipton *Barbarians* 15: And the imitation palaces of the Doges became flop joints. **1973** *AS* XLVI 77: Shabby hotel…*flop joint, flop house*. **1980** T. Jones *Adrift* 271: The flop-joints 'r' closin' down.

flop-out *n.* an utter failure.

1974 Charyn *Blue Eyes* 22: After the flop-out at Bummy's, the three bulls drove home to Islip, Freeport, and Massapequa Park.

flopper *n.* **1.** *Pol.* a person who deserts one political party for another.

1884 in *DA:* The kept organ refers to the great masses of the people…who conscientiously oppose Mr. Stevens' election…as a "little band of floppers and kickers." **1905** in *DA:* Assemblyman Rogers is a flopper because he withdrew from the speakership race and re-entered it.

2. *Und.* a short-change swindler.

1914 Jackson & Hellyer *Vocab.* 35: *Flopper*, noun…money changer, flim-flammer.

3. (among mendicants) a beggar who is or who pretends to be crippled.

1918 Livingston *Delcassee* 46: The police cleared the thoroughfares of every class of flopper. **1929** Zombaugh *Gold Coast* 111: The "flopper," too, studies his public.…The flopper is a man or woman who has lost both legs. **1937** Reitman *Box-Car Bertha* 139: The "floppers"…pretend being crippled and sit all day before churches and entrances. **1980** Bruns *Kts. of Road* 91: He had watched "floppers" squatting on sidewalks with pleading hands upraised.

flopperoo or **floperoo** *n. Entertainment Industry.* a notable failure; complete FLOP.

1931 *AS* VII 45: Walter Winchell loves to…[see] terpsichorines…in revusicals which might even turn out floperoos. **1932** Hecht & Fowler *Great Magoo* 138: This town is baggy at the knees with floperoos. **1934** *Journalism Qly.* (Dec.) 350: [Sportswriters' slang:] *Flopperoo*—a failure. **1937** *AS* (Feb.) 18: John Oliver, in the *Richmond News-Leader* for Dec. 26, 1936, terms Georgia Tech the "greatest flopperoo" in football of the sports season. **1940** in *AS* XVII (1942) 13: Most…were spectacular flopperoos. **1941** *N.Y. Post* (June 6) 7: She had a personality-plus part in an outstanding floperoo. **1961** Considine *Ripley* 151: Including the grand floperoo on Broadway. **1978** *New West* (Jan. 16) 44: A ten-minute cameo in the Fox floperoo, *Myra Breckinridge*.

flopping dump *n. Und.* FLOPHOUSE.

1918 Livingston *Delcassee* 19: Disturbances…might have attracted a visitation to the flopping dump by the police agents.

floppings *n.pl.* (among tramps) a place to sleep; sleeping accommodations.

1907 London *Road* 17 [ref. to 1892]: A world of…"bulls" and "shacks," "floppings" and "chewin's." **1921** Casey & Casey *Gay-Cat* 38: "What yer got there?" "Floppin's fur the night." *Ibid.* 53: A bo we shared floppin's with last night.

floppo *adj.* Esp. *Show Bus.* being a complete failure; (*joc.*) dead or unconscious. Also as *n.* & *adv.*

1929 in Perelman *Old Gang* 58: He was found floppo the next day in a deserted lot. **1930** *Bookman* (Dec.) 397: Show looks floppo. **1932** Hecht & Fowler *Great Magoo* 190: Let's get good and drunk. Huh? I mean floppo. **1934** Weseen *Dict. Slang* 140: *Floppo*—A big failure. **1938** *AS* (Oct.) 239: As an adverb *floppo* has been in use for some time. "The show went floppo." **1971** *Business Week* (Nov. 13) 126: The class is a floppo. I don't think these students are going to make it.

floppola *n.* FLOPPEROO.

1984 *N.Y. Post* (Aug. 20) 50: His last was some B'way floppola which lasted an hour.

flop sweat *n. Theat.* nervous perspiration caused by fear of failure before an audience.

1966 Susann *Valley of Dolls* 292: The applause had been deafening on her entrance, but after ten minutes the air was heavy with "flop sweat." **1979** Homer *Jargon* 121: And the *flopsweat* beginning to trickle down neck. **1983** *Harper's* (Feb.) 60: Their shirts turn sticky with flop-sweat as they fret that their audience is straying out the door. **1991** *New Yorker* (Dec. 30) 80: The magician's nervousness makes us squirm: the movie seems drenched in flop sweat.

flop trench *n. Army.* FOXHOLE.

1918–19 MacArthur *Bug's-Eye View* 79: The guns were swung around, flop trenches were dug, ammunition stacked. *Ibid.* 87: Then would follow a debate as to whether we should seek shelter in the main flop trench or remain in our holes.

floss out *v.* to dress up.

1918 Stringer *House of Intrigue* 28: Bud flossed me out with a Bonwit-Teller hand-me-down.

flossy *n.* a young woman. Also **flossie**.

1901 Irwin *Sonnets* (unp.): You tie down the Flossie you can take. **1929** Bodenheim *60 Secs.* 50: No chance to think with the flossies around. **1929–33** Farrell *Young Manhood* 348: Say, Studs, I'll bet some flossie's got you. **1943** Pyle *Here Is Your War* 42: Some Arab women wore white sheets and hoods that covered the face, except for one eye peering out. The soldiers called them "One-Eyed Flossies." **1958** S.H. Adams *Tenderloin* 312 [ref. to 1890's]: Society's darling…[is] an old man's flossie.

flossy *adj.* **1.** impertinent; saucy.

1889 in *DA:* Phil, we have got it in for you if you don't quit being so flossy. **1900** Ade *More Fables* 152: He'd show you if you could get Flossy with a Lady, even though she Works. **1913** *Sat. Eve. Post* (July 5) 44: Them fresh Janes that's so flossy give me a pain.

2. fancy; stylish.

1895 Gore *Stu. Slang* 13: *Flossy*, beautiful, stylish. "The flossiest suit of clothes you ever saw." **1899** A.H. Lewis *Sandburrs* 93: An' you can gamble your socks me friends is a flossy bunch at that. **1903** A.H. Lewis *Boss* 122: He's as flossy a proposition as ever came down th' pike. **1906** *Nat. Police Gaz.* (Apr. 21) 3: The Barton and Guestler vintage of '84, the kind Smithy always orders when he wants to be real flossy. **1914** Graham *Poor Immigrants* 248: My! You have a *flossy hat.* **1920** Ade *Hand-Made Fables* 31: Nymphs who were flossy beyond compare. **1956** G. Green *Last Angry Man* 347: That lousy schoolteacher with the flossy accent! **1981** Wambaugh *Glitter Dome* 45: Flossy fatcats from Brentwood.

flounder *n.* a Newfoundlander. *Joc.*

1908 Sullivan *Crim. Slang* 10: *Flounder*. A person from Newfoundland.

flower *n.* **1.** a homosexual man, esp. if effeminate; PANSY.

1964 *AS* (May) 118: Since…*pansy* is available with reference to a male homosexual, the speaker is at liberty to…refer to the person as simply a *flower*. **1971** *All in the Family* (CBS-TV): That big football player is a *flower?* **1973** *TULIPQ* (coll. B.K. Dumas): Male homosexual…*3-dollar bill, flower.*

2. *pl.* the vulva; in phr. **eat (someone's) flowers** to perform cunnilingus on (someone).

1971 *Ramparts* (Dec.) 23: Then he wants to eat your flowers—go down on you. **1988** Ross & Spielberg *Big* (film): You can see all the way down to her flowers.

flowerpot *n.* a flowery compliment.

1904 in W.C. Fields *By Himself* 27: Had you any strength of mind You wouldn't be chucking flowerpots at Yourself all the time.

flu *n.* influenza. Now *S.E.*

*1839 R. Southey, in *OED* s.v. *flue*: I have had a pretty fair share of the Flue. **1863** in *Jour. Miss. Hist.* XXXIII (1971) 367: A severe attack of the flu...has reduced me a great deal. ***1893** in *OED*: I've a bad attack of the flu. ***1911** in *OEDS*: The "flu" season. **1918** in Truman *Dear Bess* 289: You told me Frank had the "flu." **1925** Z. Grey *Vanishing Amer.* 270: Well, Gakin Yashi is down with "flu." **1965** in A. Sexton *Letters* 259: God, was I sick...Maybe the Flu. **1980** Teichmann *Fonda* 195: Henry Fonda and the "flu" bug met in Philadelphia.

flub *n.* an instance of bungling; a mistake; (*specif.* and *usu.*) *Golf.* a poor shot. Also **flubber.**

1900 in Davies *Golf. Terms* 66: C is the Caddie who carries your Clubs;/He calls you a "Corker" in spite of your "flubs." **1914** *Century Dict.* IV (Supp.): *Flub...n.*...golf, a badly-played stroke. **1970** Scharff *Encyc. of Golf* 417: *Flub.* A poor shot, usually caused by hitting the ground before hitting the ball. **1975** Univ. Tenn. student: Did you see the movie they made from all the flubbers they cut from old *Star Trek* episodes?

flub *v.* to bungle; botch.—also constr. with *up.*

1916 D. Runyon, in Paxton *Sport* 97: And that sounds belittling, especially if it is translated as meaning to flub, or even to dub. **1924** P. Marks *Plastic Age* 122: I have the feeling...that I have flubbed this talk. **1931** in *DA*: A team...flubbed its major assignments horribly. **1959** Cochrell *Barren Beaches* 226: But they might flub the other truck. **1966–80** McAleer & Dickson *Unit Pride* 249: I was afraid I'd flub it. **1981** D. Burns *Feeling Good* 101: I'll probably flub typing this and make a bunch of typos. **1982** Woodruff & Maxa *At White House* 37: He drops his note cards and flubs his remarks. **1987** Univ. Tenn. professor, age *ca*65: I don't think he's going to flub it up.

¶ In phrase:

¶ **flub the dub, 1.** (of a man or boy) to masturbate. Also **flub the dummy.**

1916–22 Cary *Sex. Vocab.*: *Flub the dummy*, to masturbate. **1945** in *AS* (Oct. 1946) 238: *Flubbin' the dub.* Loafing, gold bricking, obscenity. **1945** in Wallrich *AF Airs*: The clap is bad,/But the syph is worse,/So flub your dub/For safety first. **1966** Elli *Riot* 244: I'll be flubbin' my dub in here for the next twenty years. *a***1972** B. Rodgers *Queens' Vernacular* 115: Then I flub my dub. **1980** Former Dallas, Tex., police officer, age *ca*45: One of the guys in the outfit used to flub his dub every night in his bunk.

2. *Mil.* to loaf or evade duty.

1943 Hersey *G.I. Laughs* 200: Wanders from barracks to barracks...generally flubbing his dub. **1945** (*AS* quot. at **(1)**, above). **1944–46** in *AS* XXII 55: *To flub the dub.* To escape assigned duty. **1955** R.L. Scott *Look of Eagle* 191: They don't drink their share of suds,/They just sit and flub their dubs. **1959** [*41st Ftr. Sq. Songbk.*] 7: Drink your drink and flub your dub,/41st Fighter Country Club.

3. *Esp. Mil.* to bungle; make a botch; blunder.

1945 in *Calif. Folk. Qly.* V (1946) 380: Anyone who is *on the ball* is alert, alive, thinking clearly, and performing efficiently. The diametric opposite of this is *to drop the ball* or the more popular *flub the dub.* **1957** Mulvihill *Fire Mission* 12: You had the whole damn day and you flubbed the dub. **1959** "D. Stagg" *Glory Jumpers* 109: The Air Corps flubbed the dub again and scattered the drop. **1974** Lahr *Trot* 197: But John flubbed the dub. He cared for this girl. **1977** Bredes *Hard Feelings* 24: What I began to fear is that I will, as my mother says, flub the dub before I really get started.

flubadub *n.* [var. FLUBDUB; infl. by *Flubadub*, the name of a grotesque marionette character on NBC television's *Howdy Doody Show*] a blockhead; idiot.

1975 *Nat. Lampoon* (June) 56: You were supposed to use the inert glass test tube, flubadub! **1978** Pilcer *Teen Angel* 66: An ugly, crabby, awkward, repulsive, flat-chested flub-a-dub.

flubdub *n.* [of fanciful orig.] **1.** twaddle; foolishness.

[**1866** May *Beadle's Mo.* 393: A fellow...comes in with that hat of yours...and says it fits him so that...it will do first-rate after he tears off those "ribbons and flubdigs."] **1877** Burdette *Mustache* 177: He taught me all the gestures and inflections and flubdrubs. **1888** in Farmer *Amer.*: By swiping out the flub-dub and guff, I guess we'll have room to put in the points. [**1905** in Opper *H. Hooligan* 68: It's the Duke of Flub-dub.] **1911** H.L. Mencken, in *Manuscripts* XXXI (1979) 175: This lecture...will have a certain amount of sociological flub-dub in it. **1916** D. Runyon, in Paxton *Sport* 97: Back in the newspaper offices the copy readers will refer to this as "flubdub"—this crowd stuff. **1918–19** MacArthur *Bug's-Eye View* 69: Squads east and a good deal of other flub-

dub occupied most of our time...for a week. **1929** Bodenheim *60 Secs.* 22: All the rest was flubdub, preachers' lies, covering-up. **1952** in H.S. Truman *Confid.* 127: It is hard for me to stand for "flub-dub," though, which is intended to fool people.

2. a blockhead; idiot.

1909 in O. Johnson *Lawrenceville* 37 [ref. to 1890's]: We don't want you...You're a flubdub and a quitter. **1987** S. Stark *Wrestling Season* 130: How many gallons of ice cream have been lost because one of you flubdubs put the carton back into the bread drawer instead of the freezer?

flubdub *v.* to fool about.

1928 Bodenheim *Georgie May* 108: It would be better to quit flub-dubbing and get down to brass tacks.

flub off *v.* to loaf or evade duty.

1944–46 in *AS* XXII 55: *To flub off.* To escape assigned duty.

flue *n.* **1.** the vagina.

*ca***1888** *Stag Party* 231: For trespassing in his Elizabeth's flue. *ca***1920** in Logsdon *Whorehouse Bells* 148: While you lick out my flue. **1927** *Immortalia* 59: The divil's in the piss-pot and's got me by the flue. **1930** *Lyra Ebriosa* 18: Some buckaroo would monkey with her flue. **1981** *Nat. Lampoon* (Oct.) 26: I'm actually a two-buck whore...who...lets American businessmen stick dollar bills up her flue.

2. the anus; rectum.

1927 Aiken *Blue Voyage* 135: Well, I don't give a damn *what* he said— he can stick it up—the flue. **1936** LeClerq *Rabelais* 15: If you do not believe me, may your vent-peg slip, may your stopper fail your [rectal] organ, your fundament fall and your flue pipe collapse. **1945** Laurents *Home of the Brave* 566: Up your floo, Rockefeller. **1959** Morrill *Dark Sea Running* 85: I took out the whistle and let go again. They came running—but I got it up my flue in time. **1970** E. Thompson *Garden of Sand* 390: I'm going to fuck you in your flue. **1978** Novelty Christmas card, seen in N.Y.C.: Up your flue, Santa!

3. *Und.* (see *ca*1974 quot.); (*also*) a swindle that turns upon the pretended placement of money into an envelope.

*ca***1974** in D.W. Maurer *Lang. Und.* 362: *Flue.* The envelope in which money is placed in any big-con or short-con game. **1987** Mamet *House of Games* (film): And that's a little larceny called "the flue."

¶ In phrases:

¶ **line (one's) flue** *West.* to eat or drink.

1902 A. Adams *Log of a Cowboy* 86 [ref. to 1882]: Lining our flues with Lovell's good chuck. **1936** R. Adams *Cowboy Lingo* 18: Light an' line yo' flue with chuck. *a***1940** in Lanning & Lanning *Texas Cowboys* 62: Plenty of good chuck for lining our flues.

¶ **loose in the flue** demented.

1972 W. Kelly, in *N.Y. Post* (Sept. 23) 31: You'll surely admit that anybody what picks a duel with my big toe is gotta be a little loose in the flue.

¶ **up the flue** in pawn; (*hence*) lost; gone to ruin; dead; *up the spout* s.v. SPOUT.

*1821 *Real Life in London* I 366: Up the spout or up the flue...pledging property with a Pawnbroker. **1882** Peck *Peck's Sunshine* 275: The thing was going up the flue. ******a***1890–93** *F & H* III 34: *In* (or *up*) *the flue*...(common).—Pawned....*Up the flue* (or *spout*)....Dead; collapsed, mentally or physically. **1895** Gore *Stu. Slang* 14: *Go up the flue.* To die. **1926** Finerty *Criminalese* 23: *Flue, up the*—Pawned. **1938** *Amer. Merc.* (Oct.) 248: He has spent lots of money, but it hasn't all gone up the flue.

fluff *n.* **1.** a young woman or young women.—often constr. with *bit of, piece of.*

*1903 in *OEDS*: A bit of fluff was blown up the platform, and, before Webster had had time to send up a petition for a safe journey, it (the fluff) had come to rest on the corner seat opposite him. **1908** McGaffey *Show Girl* 195: Personal friends of every chorus fluff that ever scanned a dope sheet. ***1919** in *OEDS*: Got a little party on, you know, two bits of fashionable fluff. **1929** Perelman *Ginsbergh* 217: The unhappy hubby turns to the blonde fluff who pounds the Remington...or the trim pullet who pretties up his nails. **1934** Berg *Prison Nurse* 29: It ain't often that we get a nifty piece of fluff like that around here. **1936** Duncan *Over the Wall* 249: The one with the red-headed fluff serving hamburgers. **1939** "E. Queen" *Dragon's Teeth* 45: There are a million fluffs who'd give their right arms to be in your shoes. **1953** Chandler *Goodbye* 5: A bit of high class fluff that couldn't stick around. **1954** Collans & Sterling *House Detect.* 24: You can't for the life of you recall this excited bit of fluff who seems so delighted to see you again. **1963** Doulis *Path* 272: What's that town we passed through...? Do you guys ever go there? I mean, has it got any fluff? **1974** Andrews & Dickens *Over the*

Wall 153: This jazzy twenty-one-year-old fluff…is the editor of her institutional paper. **1979** Hurling *Boomers* 204: Some pretty little fluff without a brain in her head. **1991** "R. Brown" & R. Angus *A.K.A. Narc* 208: I'll send…my boys down with a batch of fluff.

2. *Homosex.* (among homosexual women) the usu. passive partner in a lesbian relationship.

1947 (cited in J. Katz *Gay/Lesbian Almanac* 625). **1965** Trimble *Sex Words* 79: *Fluff.* A femme; a passive female homosexual. **1962–68** B. Jackson *In the Life* 126: But now the fluff…'ll just force the butch down at times. **1972** *Anthro. Linguistics* (Mar.) 102: *Fluff* (n.) A female homosexual who has feminine traits; opposite of "butch." **1981–89** R. Atkinson *Long Gray Line* 411: Those considered too feminine by the men were "fluffs"; those too masculine were "dykes."

fluffer *n. Film.* (see 1980 quot.).

1980 *Penthouse* (Dec.) 186: I was on the set as a "fluffer," the term for a person who gets an actor physically aroused. My "client" was Robert DeNiro's stand-in, who was needed for an especially risqué scene. **1986** J.A. Friedman *Times Square* 94: This was an important factor for future "spermathons." Anyone who tries to break Tara's record can't use a fluffer. **1987** *21 Jump Street* (Fox-TV): You used to make…two, three grand a [pornographic] film. Then what? Five hundred? A hundred? Fifty? Then [be a] fluffer? **1991** *Nat. Lampoon* (Feb.) 49: Tuesday's gonna be wetter than the fluffer in a Seka movie.

fluff off *v.* **1.** to dismiss, slight, or reject; BRUSH OFF.

1942–44 in *AS* (Feb. 1946) 33: *Fluff Off,* vt. To snob, slight, or to humiliate. **1948** Manone & Vandervoort *Trumpet* 79: "You can't take these boys out of school just to play for a dance," the teacher told me, trying to fluff me off. **1967** Gonzales *Paid My Dues* 15: He…called himself all kinds of names for "blowing" a hit record by fluffing me off. **1970** S. Ross *Fortune Machine* 130: The one girl I'd made a play for and I was fluffed off. **1981** O'Day & Eells *High Times* 82: Fluffed off by Don, I got right onto the next train and headed for Chicago. *Ibid.* 101: She eventually fluffed him off for someone else. **1986** Clayton & Elliott *Jazz World* 57: George tried to fluff him off but the guy was insistent.

2. to evade responsibility; FLUB OFF.

1962 Butterworth *Court-Martial* 20: The General might think he was trying to fluff off, now.

flugie var. FLOOGIE.

fluid *n.* whiskey. *Joc.*

1843 Field *Pokerville* 130: Won't you take a little of the *fluid?* **1846** in Blair & McDavid *Mirth* 85: Send them along and we'll negotiate for the fluid. **1847** Robb *Squatter Life* 81: All parties gathered into the bar to take a little *fluid.* **1878** Hart *Sazerac* 50: One of the boys was to…get the fluid and a few decks of cards. **1927** Rollins *Jinglebob* 61 [ref. to 1880's]: We's packed along some fluid specially for you.

flujin *n.* [of fanciful orig.] (used as a mild oath or term of comparison); esp. in phr. **cold as (blue) flujins.** Also vars.

1830 N. Ames *Mariner's Sks.* 130: This was "New South Shetland," a group of islands of which I had never before heard, and which certainly showed signs of being allied or adjoining to that part of the world generally known to sailors by the name of "*Blue Flujin*" where it is said fire freezes. **1830** in *DA:* "Oh dad," says he, "I'm making money like flugens." **1835** Longstreet *Ga. Scenes:* Flugens!…What an oversight! **1849** in *DA:* You're a nice chap to run like flugins from a dead man that you killed yourself! **1850** in Blair & McDavid *Mirth* 105: And when I drop this handkercher…you jerk like flujuns. **1886** P.D. Haywood *Cruise* 63: It blew cold as Blue Flugen. **1894** *DN* I 389: Cold as blue flujins. **1898** J.C. Harris *Home Folks* 129: It's colder'n Flujens.

fluke[1] *n.* [cf. dial. E *fluke* 'a guess'] **1.** an accidentally successful stroke in billiards or pool; *(hence)* a chance happening of any kind.—often attrib. Now *colloq.*

*1857 in *F & H* III 35: In playing at billiards, if a player makes a hazard, etc., which he did not play for, it is often said that he made a *crow.…*Another term is, "He made a *flook* (or *fluke*)." ***1860** Hotten *Slang Dict.* (ed. 2): *Fluke,* at billiards, playing for one thing and getting another. Hence, generally, what one gets accidentally, as an unexpected advantage, "more by luck than judgment." ***1869** in *F & H* III 35: Only lost a pony on the whole meeting…And even that was a fluke. **1869** Logan *Foot Lights* 129: A man whose greatest successes must necessarily be "flukes." ***ca1873** in Barrère & Leland *Dict. Slang* I 374: These conditions are not often fulfilled, I can tell you: it is a happy fluke when they are. **1880** *N.Y. Clipper Almanac* 44: *Fluke.*—So said when a horse has won through an accident. Also called a "scratch." **1899** in J. London *Letters* 19: He was afraid it was a fluke and perhaps it would be impossible for me to repeat it. **1899** Cullen *Tales* 47: Everybody agreed

that it was a fluke of the flukiest kind. **1900** *DN* II 35: *Fluke,…*An accident. **1905** Riordan *Plunkitt* 25: Such men may get to be district leaders by a fluke, but they never last. **1906** *Nat. Police Gaz.* (July 21) 6: He is bound to call the winning long-priced things mere flukes. **1909** *WNID: Fluke…*An accidentally successful stroke at billiards or pool; hence, any accidental or unexpected advantage; as, he won by a *fluke. Sporting Cant or Slang.* **1920–21** Witwer *Leather Pushers* 8: Of course it was a fluke win. **1928** Dahlberg *Bottom Dogs* 45: There was a fluke in his own case. **1980** *AS* LV 97: *Fluke…*Chance occurrence, usually beneficial. (Although this word is in the lexicon of American English, it seems no longer a part of the American poolroom vocabulary.) **1984** McInerny *Bright Lights* 45: Totally fluke thing…Senseless death. **1988** *Newsweek* (May 2) 51: The ad was largely the result of a fluke.

2. Esp. *Stu.* a failure.

1895 Gore *Stu. Slang* 3: *Fluke…*a failure to recite. **1900** *DN* II 35: *Fluke, n.…*An utter failure. [Reported from 20 colleges.]. **1909** Krapp *Mod. Eng.* 208: The college boy *flunks* an examination, or *makes a fluke* of a recitation. **1914** *Century Dict. & Cyc.* IV (Supp.): *Fluke.…*A failure, as of a yacht race for lack of wind.

3. a peculiar or eccentric person.

1929–30 J.T. Farrell *Manhood* 293: What the hell kind of a fluke is he?

fluke[2] *n. Whaling.* a hand.

1891 *United Service* (Dec.) 633: Bill…once showed the Markis of Keensberry the right way to put up his flukes.

¶ In phrases:

¶ **cut (one's) flukes out** *Whaling.* (see 1889 quot.).

1870 *Overland Mo.* (Mar.) 237: If you go to cutting your flukes out here, I'll send the whole *posse* of you a whaling, and a precious little good will this gold do you when the voyage is up! **1873** Scammon *Marine Mammals* 310: "He attempted to cut his flukes out," is a slang expression in whaling parlance, when any members become refractory, or attempt in any manner to create disturbance on board. **1889** *Century Dict.: To cut flukes out.…*To become refractory or mutinous; make a disturbance on board ship.

¶ **go up the fluke** [app. orig. an erroneous var. of *go up the flue* or *up the flume* (s.v. FLUE, FLUME)] to come to grief; fail.

1889 Field *Western Verse* 158: Although it broke my heart to see my friend go up the fluke,/We all opined his treatment uv the girl deserved rebuke. **1900** *DN* II 35: "To go up the *fluke,*" to fail in recitation or examination.

¶ **turn flukes** *Whaling.* (see 1889 quot.).

1851 Melville *Moby Dick* ch. iii: It's getting dreadful late, you had better be turning flukes…it's a nice bed. **1889** *Century Dict.: To turn flukes,* in *whaling…*To go to bed; bunk or turn in.

fluke *v.* **1.** to fail, esp. by chance.—usu. constr. with *out.*

1900 *DN* II 35: *Fluke, v.i.* To fail utterly. [Reported from 19 colleges.]. **1942** *ATS* 245: Have bad luck…*fluke out.*

2. to back down; renege.—constr. with *out.* [The sense of the 1864 quot.—not otherwise recorded—is 'to shirk'.]

[***1864** in *F & H* III 35: By Jove! I think I shall *fluke* doing Verses; I should like to see Paddy drive tandem through College.] **1955** Margulies *Punks* 173: You fluke out, you'll never live it down.

3. to die.—constr. with *out.*

1958 Motley *Epitaph* 150: You fluke out. You die. *Ibid.* 161: Another and I flukes out too. **1964** Howe *Valley of Fire* 165 [ref. to 1951]: Rohr fluked out last night.

4. to come by luck or chance.—constr. with *into.*

1984 Heath *A-Team* 18: He fluked into that Pulitzer.

fluked out *adj.* intoxicated by drugs or alcohol. Also **fluked.**

1952 Mandel *Angry Strangers* 127: You're real fluked out, Dinch; take it easy, be cool. **1985** Univ. Tenn. student theme: To be "fluked" means to be inebriated almost to the point of unconsciousness. A variation of this term is "flukey."

fluking *adj.* drunk.

1919 McKenna *Battery A* 187: We'll all be flukin' tonight, pos-i-tively flukin'.

flukum *n.* [perh. pseudo-Latinization of FLUKE[1], *n.*] (among pitchmen) any of various preparations, compounds, or inexpensive items offered for sale by a street hawker. Also vars.

1929 *Sat. Eve. Post* (Oct. 12) 29: *Flukum:* Nickelplate ware. **1934** Weseen *Dict. Slang* 159: Circus and Carnival…*flookum*—A powder containing flavoring and coloring for soft drinks. **1936** *New Yorker* (Sept. 12) 35: The pitchman's general name for oil, glue, or any nonpotable fluid is "flookem." **1943** *Sat. Eve. Post* (Sept. 25) 39: You may be cutting up vegetables or rubbing flukum on tarnished silver. *ca*1947–52 in *AS* (Feb. 1953) 116: Carnie Talk...*Flookum,* n. A windshield preparation, supposed to keep rain off. *Hustlers* frequently work "flookum" during the off season. **1954–60** *DAS: Flukum, flookum, flookem*....Any of various kinds of cheap...merchandise...which are attractive at first sight.

fluky *adj.* **1.** being or resembling a chance occurrence; accidental; atypical; unpredictable. Now *colloq.* [The earliest exx. occur in the context of cricket.]

*1867 in *OEDS:* Playing a very flukey innings. *1879 in *OED:* There was some flukey hitting off Mr. Steele. *1881 in *OED:* Lascelles scored a flukey two in the slips. *1882 in *F & H* III 35: Bonnor got a *flukey* three. *1882 in *OED:* A very fluky etymology. *a1889 in Barrère & Leland *Dict. Slang* I 374: Can describe who's "bowled clean,"/Which a fluky hit's been. **1889** *Century Dict.: Fluky*...obtained by chance rather than by skill. [Slang] **1899** Cullen *Tales* 47: Everybody agreed that it was a fluke of the flukiest kind. **1943** Chandler *High Window* 452: It would have been a very fluky shot, even if he happened to have the camera in his hand.

2. peculiar; markedly strange. Cf. *1882 *OED* quot. at **(1),** above.

1910 Lomax *Cowboy Songs* 249: He was a rookey, so flukey,/He was a Loo Loo you bet. **1929–33** Farrell *Manhood of Lonigan* 197: Something flukey about him all right! **1968** *Rolling Stone Interviews* 64: They loved us. I thought it was flooky. I couldn't understand, man, how could a band play that shitty and have everyone dig them? **1977** Appel *Hell's Kitchen* 45: The redhead was used to the Spotter's fluky way of putting things. **1993** N.Y.C. woman, age *ca*50: Then this fluky sound starts coming from the chimney.

flumbergast *v.* FLAMBERGAST.

1839–40 Cobb *Green Hand* I 267: I'm charmed with both—flumbergasted for life.

flume *n.* ¶ In phrase: **go up the flume** *West.* to die; (*hence*) to go to ruin.

1871 "M. Twain" *Roughing It* 250: One of the boys has gone up the flume. **1872** in Silber & Robinson *Songs of Amer. West* 98: For in his bloom, he went up the flume. **1873** J. Miller *Modocs* 95: If you keep on slinging your six-shooter around loose...you will go up the flume as slick as a salmon. **1874** Carter *Rollingpin* 15: Rescue, my noble Festus, rescue! or all is gone up the Flume! **1881** Nye *Forty Liars* 160: The tyrant's crust is busted...and he...hath scooted up the flume. **1882** in "M. Twain" *Stories* 191: Well, then, *that* idea's up the flume. **1888** Nye & Riley *Railway Guide* 29: He...[yearns] to star in an "Uncle Tom" company, and watch little Eva meander up the flume at two dollars per week. **1888** *Stag Party* 19: God...has...taken our darling up the flume. **1975** Texas woman, age 29: *To canter up a flume* is an old-time Texas expression that means "die." My father uses it.

flummadiddle *n.* [fanciful alter. of *flummery* + DIDDLE] foolishness; foolish items.

1854 in *DAE:* What does she want of any more flummerdiddle notions? **1868** in *DAE:* What's the use of so much "flummy-diddle"? **1882** in *OED:* Directions for...crocheting all sorts of flummediddles. **1889** *Century Dict.: Flumadiddle*....Silly or delusive nonsense; balderdash; flummery. [Slang, U.S.]

flummocky *adj.* muddled; (*also*) eccentric.

1834 Caruthers *Kentuck. in N.Y.* II 215: He's a little flumucky altogether about the head. *1891 in *F & H* III 36: It is a nice solemn dress....There's nothing flummocky about it.

flummox *n.* an embarrassing failure. Also as quasi-adv.

1856 B. Hall *College Wds.* (ed. 2) 205: Any failure is called a *flummux.* In some colleges the word is particularly applied to a poor recitation. At Williams College, a failure on the play-ground is called a *flummux.* **1905** *DN* III 9: *Flummux,* n. A failure. **1907** *DN* III 212: *Flummux, n.* A failure. **1915** *DN* IV 203: *Flummox,* in colleges applied to a poor recitation. "I went *flummox* this morning in German."

flummox *v.* [orig. unkn.; perh. of dial. E orig.] **1.** to ruin, thwart, or do for; (*also*) to confound, confuse, trick, or disconcert.—occ. constr. with **up.** Also vars.

1834 Caruthers *Kentuck. in N.Y.* I 29: Flummuck me if ever I want to be so fixed again. **1836** *Spirit of Times* (Mar. 19) 39: I never tries to *flummox* nobody, beside the *beaks.* *1837 C. Dickens *Pickwick* ch. xxxiii: If your governor don't prove an alleybi, he'll be what the Italians call reg'larly *flummoxed,* and that's all about it. **1839** *Amer. Joe Miller* 81: Flummocks me if I want to be so fixed again. *1840 in *F & H* III 36: So

many of the men I know/Were *flummoxed* at the last great go. *ca*1850 in Barrère & Leland *Dict. Slang* I 375: Fool! fool! You distressed—you ruined—you tortured—you—you—*flummuxed* me! *1889 Barrère & Leland *Dict. Slang* I 374: *Flummocks* (tailors), to spoil. *1890 in *F & H* III 36: I'm fair flummoxed, and singing, "Oh, what a surprise!" *1892 in *OED:* The Unionists appear to be completely flummoxed by the failure of Mr. Balfour's Land act. *a1890–93 *F & H* III 36: *To flummox the coppers*—to dodge the police. **1905** *DN* III 9: *Flummux*...to thwart. *Flummuxed up*...confused. In the expression "to be all flummuxed up." **1909** *WNID: Flummox*....To throw into perplexity; to embarrass greatly; confound. *Slang.* **1944** *PADS* (Nov.) 27: *Flummixed:* adj. Excited, bewildered. **1950** S.J. Perelman, in *New Yorker* (Sept. 30) 23: Fu-Manchu tries to abduct a missionary who has flummoxed his plans in China. **1958** S.H. Adams *Tenderloin* 337: You look flummoxed. Not feeling good? **1975** H. Ellison *Gentleman Junkie* 19: I was going to try flummoxing [them] into buying a book I hadn't written yet. **1984** H. Gould *Cocktail* 54: The poor girl has been flummoxed. **1989** CNN-TV broadcast (May 19): They're a little flummoxed by the fact that we have to play by the book on this.

2. to give up or give in; quail; (*also*) to fail or renege; (*Stu.*) to fail an examination or the like or to recite badly; (*joc.*) to die. Also vars.

1839 D.P. Thompson *Green Mtn. Boys* 256: Well, if he should flummux at such a chance, I know of a chap...who'll agree to take his place. **1843** Field *Pokerville* 73: And prehaps Pokerville didn't wiggle, wince, and finally "flummix" right beneath him! **1849** in *OED:* Men of mighty stomachs,/Men that can't be made to flummux. **1851** B. Hall *College Wds.* 131: *Flummox.* To fail; to recite badly. **1855** in Schele de Vere *Amer.* 603: We regularly *flummuxed,* and after that dared not say a word to our Mexican guards. **1871** Schele de Vere *Amer.* 603: *Flummux*...denotes in America the giving up of a purpose, and even to die. *ca*1877 in Bartlett *Amer.* (ed. 4) 227: I thought I should a *flummuxed!*...I lay down an' rolled till...I thought I should a bust my biler. **1905** *DN* III 9: *Flummux, v.i.* To fail. **1909** *WNID: Flummox*....To fail ignominiously; to collapse; to be thoroughly disconcerted. *Slang.* **1914** *DN* IV 154: *Flummux, v.i.* To back out of a trade.

flunk[1] *n.* **1.a.** *Stu.* a complete failure in a recitation, examination, or course of study; a failing grade.

1842 Strong *Diary* I 179: I'd got through [my jury summation] without any distinct flunk. **1846** in B. Hall *College Wds.* (ed. 2) 205: This 0...meant a perfect flunk. **1849** in B. Hall *College Wds.:* I've made some twelve or fourteen flunks. **1853** Root & Lombard *Songs of Yale* 54: In moody meditation sunk,/Reflecting on my future flunk. **1856** B. Hall *College Wds.* (ed. 2) 205: *Flunk.* This word is used in some American colleges to denote a complete failure in recitation. **1877** in *F & H* III 37: A *flunk* is a complete fizzle; and a *dead flunk* is where one refuses to get out of his seat. **1895** Wood *Yale Yarns* 42: Phil Gardiner [was] out of sorts from recitation after a dead flunk in mathematics. **1900** *DN* II 35: *Flunk, n.* 1. A very poor recitation. [Reported from more than sixty colleges]. 2. A failure. [Reported from Tulane Univ.]. **1904** in *DAE:* Received a flunk in one study and a condition in another. **1909** *WNID: Flunk*....College Cant, a total failure in a recitation or examination. *U.S.* **1948** *Time* (Feb. 16) 94: This time there were twice as many flunks. **1968** Baker et al. *CUSS* 119: *Flunk*...The grade "F".

b. *Stu.* a student who has failed.

1900 *DN* II 35: *Flunk, n.* One who fails. [Reported from more than thirty-five colleges]. **1925** *Lit. Digest* (Mar. 14) 64: A "flunk" is a man who has failed to pass an exam.

2. (see 1889 quot.).

1877 Bartlett *Amer.* (ed. 4) 227: *Flunk.* A backing out. **1888** in Farmer *Amer.:* Riddleberger forced the presidential possibilities of the senate to a complete flunk. **1889** *Century Dict.: Flunk, n.*...A failure or backdown.

3. a shirker.

1890–93 *F & H* III 37: *Flunk*...(American colloquial)....An idler, a loafer.

4. a waiter; flunky.

1899 A.H. Lewis *Sandburrs* 95: 'D' flunk slams down d' consommé in a tea cup.

flunk[2] *n.* [orig. unkn.] *Und.* a strongbox or locked steel compartment within a safe.

1928 Callahan *Man's Grim Justice* 56: It required only two or three minutes to "break down the flunk," jimmy the strongbox loose from its fastenings. **1931** in D.W. Maurer *Lang. Und.* 43: Inside...a top keister and a flunk. *Ibid.* 47: *Flunk,* n. A steel compartment with a thin iron door in a safe.

flunk *v.* [perh. alter. of *funk*] **1.** to give in, back down, quit, or renege, esp. from weakness or fear; show reluctance or cowardice.—also constr. with *out.* [*OED* erroneously dates 1871 quot. as "*ca*1830."]

1823 in B. Hall *College Wds.* (ed. 2) 206: We must have, at least, as many subscribers as there are students in College, or "flunk out." **1834** *Mil. & Nav. Mag. of U.S.* (Nov.) 206: "Why, it won't do, you see, Tremaine," replied Purnly, "for me to appear to flunk, nor I won't, that's flat!" **1837** J.C. Neal *Charc. Sks.* 46: Why, little 'un, you must be cracked, if you flunk out before we begin. **1848** Judson *Mysteries of N.Y.* 27: What's the matter, Charley, you're not going to flunk out, are you? **1849** in B. Hall *College Wds.* (ed. 2) 206: Nestor was appointed to deliver a poem, but most ingloriously *flunked.* **1850** in *DAE:* They were…exposed to the fire of the red-coats…But they didn't flunk a bit. **1855** Burgess *500 Mistakes* 51: "To flunk out" is a vulgar expression for *to retire through fear.* **1871** Hay *Pike Co. Ballads* 18: A keerless man in his talk was Jim,/And an awkward man in a row,/But he never flunked, and he never lied,—/I reckon he never knowed how. **1873** *Slang & Vulgar Forms* 13: Flunk.—"He flunked out" is low. "He sneaked out," or "he backed out," are better expressions to denote a mean or cowardly abandonment of an enterprise. If the act was not mean or cowardly, say "he gave up," "he retired from the enterprise." **1887** Peck *Pvt. Peck* 211: He said he had rather be considered a coward…for if he flunked when a chance come to show his metal, it wouldn't be thought much of. **1889** Barrère & Leland *Dict. Slang* I 375: *Flunk, to* (American), to die out, to give out, to fail, to make a feeble effort and then collapse. **1899–1900** Cullen *Tales* 203: It looked like flunking and playing the baby act to me. *Ibid.* 214: He'll expect you to talk Greek and Latin, and when you flunk on that he'll wonder. **1900** Hammond *Whaler* 326: That's jest what he done—clean flunked….He…left that wheel and climbed head over heels into the mate's boat. **1902** "J. Flynt" *Little Bro.* 181: Besides, he gave me a whole quarter to do the errand, an' he looked…as if he'd kill me if I flunked. **1906** *Nat. Police Gaz.* (May 12) 10: Philadelphia Jack O'Brien has deliberately flunked out of another meeting with Bob Fitzsimmons after having signed articles to do so. **1906** London *Moon-Face* 78: Go ahead!…Don't flunk! **1910** in *DAE:* I don't mean that he's flunking, for he's no coward. **1911** Funston *Memories* 71: We turned him over, but could see no blood. "The damned coward is flunking," yelled Pennie. **1941** H.A. Smith *Low Man* 191: There were twenty-three Jersey cows, and these, in theory, were the wives of Elmer…But he had flunked out.

2.a. to go back on; disappoint; outwit.

1829 in M. Mathews *Beginnings of Amer. Eng.* 106: *Flunkt.* "Overcome, outdone." *Kentucky.* **1841** F. Jackson *Week in Wall St.* 112: What does Swartout mean by being flunked?…That's a Wall-street word, and means that he has been outwitted, in trying to make up the money that he was behind. **1914** Nisbet *4 Yrs. on Firing Line* 81 [ref. to Civil War]: I wooed the fickle goddess too long. I backed the queen to win and the old huzzy flunked me!

b. to shirk or ignore (an obligation). *Obs.* in U.S.

1871 in *DA:* The fine for "flunking" an appointment at a "special meeting" was two dollars. **1915** H.L. Wilson *Ruggles* 263: He flunked a meeting of the Onwards and Upwards Society. *1984 Partridge *DSUE* (ed. 8) 411: At the last moment, he flunked going to the police.

3.a. *Stu.* to fail an examination, recitation, or course of study.—also constr. with *out; (also)* to be expelled for academic failure.—constr. with *out.* Cf. 1823 quot. at **(1)**, above. Now *S.E.*

1837 Strong *Diary* I 69: I've flunked oftener on [Horace]…than on all the rest. **1847** in *DA:* I fear I should have flunked. **1849** in B. Hall *College Wds.* (ed. 2) 206: They know that a man who has *flunked,* because of too much of a genius to get his lesson, is not in a state to appreciate joking. **1856** B. Hall *College Wds.* (ed. 2) 206: The phrase *to flunk out*…was formerly used in some American colleges as is now the word *flunk.* **1871** *Yale Naught-Ical Almanac* 15: It is more honest to flunk than to skin. **1889** *Some Songs* [of Rochester Univ.] (sheet music) 30: When in class you meet your Waterloo, when you flunk three times in every two. **1895** Gore *Stu. Slang* 5: *Flunker*…one who habitually fails in recitations. **1898** *Scribner's Mag.* XXIV 55: And she flunked in her exam. **1900** *DN* II 35: *Flunk, v.i.* 1. To fail in recitation or examination. **1919** Hedges *Iron City* 52: And he flunked out at Yale, too. **1920** Fitzgerald *Paradise* 34: He'll fail his exams…and flunk out in the middle of the freshman year. **1927** S. Lewis *Elmer Gantry* 9: He kept from flunking only because Jim Lefferts drove him to his books. **1977** Newman & Berkowitz *Take Charge* 51: There's the kid down the block who flunked out of school. **1977** Bredes *Hard Feelings* 247: I'm on the verge of flunking out of school. **1978** De Christoforo *Grease* 88: She's gonna quit school before she flunks out.

b. *Stu.* to give (a student) a failing grade; cause to fail. Now *S.E.*

1843 *Yale Lit. Mag.* ix 61: That day poor Fullman was *flunked,* and was never again reinstated. **1891** *Outing* (July) 317: They'll flunk me right and left! **1897** in *DAE:* That almost flunked me at the hour exam. **1915** Poole *Harbor* 46: He "flunked" the worst twenty [students] and let the rest through. **1948** in *DA:* Four teen-agers were accused today of blasting a pretty high school teacher's home with gunfire after a telephoned death threat warning her not to flunk anybody in mathematics.

c. *Stu.* to fail to get a passing grade in. Now *S.E.*

1924 Marks *Plastic Age* 107: I'm going to flunk that exam. **1926** W. White *Flight* 86: He's yanked me out of college 'cause I flunked math and physics again. **1962** in J. O'Hara *Sel. Letters* 386: It embarrasses me to have to report that *I* flunked a test today. **1965** N.Y.C. high-school student: I think I'm going to flunk calculus. *ca*1979 Peers & Bennett *Logical Laws* 84: Better to have flunked your Wassermann, than never to have loved at all.

4. to fail (at anything).—usu. constr. with *out.*

1891 in Alter *Utah Journ.* 191: Our failure, like that of the paper which has flunked out here, does the town more harm than most people suppose. **1895** Gore *Stu. Slang* 5: *Flunk*…To fail in an undertaking; to make a botch of anything. **1900** *DN* II 35: *Flunk, v.i.*…2. To fail in an undertaking. **1905** in *DAE:* We've flunked once, and, no matter how good the reason is, no more big jobs'll come our way. *1975 Witchell *Loch Ness Story* 152: We thought we'd flunked out again…All we had left were the colour films from Doc's camera.

flunkee see FLUNKY, 2.

flunkout *n. Stu.* a student who has failed a course or been expelled for academic failure.

[**1956** *Harper's* (Oct.) 68: Psychiatrists shudder at the high percentage of flunkouts at the end of the first semester.] **1967** Mailer *Vietnam* 40: Thirteen-year-old swivel ass flunkout in classics. **1971** N.Y.C. high-school student: We always used to say McBurney got the flunkouts from Horace Mann and Fieldston and Rhodes got the flunkouts from McBurney. **1974** N.Y.C. copywriter, age 28: He was a flunkout from medical school. **1988** *Lame Monkey* (Univ. Tenn.) (Mar. 21) 2: These 156 students could be disgruntled, lazy flunkouts, for all anybody knows.

flunk under *v.* to give in; knuckle under.

1859 Stowe *Minister's Wooing* 157: You a man, and not stan' by your color, and flunk under to mean white ways?

flunky *n.* **1.** *Stock Market.* an inexperienced investor who may easily be taken advantage of.

1841 [F. Jackson] *Week in Wall St.* 81: Deceived by appearances, [these investors] come into market without any knowledge of it, and generally lose what they invest. These are called *flunkies. Ibid.* 91: I'll help the bulls operate for a rise and draw in the flunkies. **1871** Schele de Vere *Amer.* 603: *Flunky*…in the slang of Wall-street…denotes the unlucky outsider who ventures to speculate in stocks without the necessary knowledge of financial matters. **1893** in *DA:* The lambs that we have in the Street these days were called flunkeys…forty-five or fifty years ago.

2. [sugg. by FLUNK, *v.*] *Stu.* a failing student; a student who has failed. Also **flunkee.** [The *-ee* spelling, based on FLUNK, *v.* + *-ee,* does not represent pronunciation.]

1838 Strong *Diary* I 89: The Flunkies of July. **1854** *Yale Lit. Mag.* XX 76: I bore him safe through Horace,/Saved him from the flunkey's doom. **1924** Marks *Plastic Age* 111: Some of the flunkees took the news very casually. **1959** Morrill *Dark Sea Running* 108: I was booted out like a common flunkee. **1963** *Time* (July 19) 36: Hardly any of the summer students are flunkees trying to catch up.

3.a. a ship's steward; *(also)* a waiter or cook's assistant, esp. in camp.

1883 (quot. at SLUSHY, *n.*). **1884** Symondson *Abaft the Mast* 55: The steward, who is known as the "flunkey," is generally looked down upon by the forecastle hands on account of his many menial and effeminate duties. **1899** Robbins *Gam* 152: Aye aye…that's the chart our flunky sails by, bless his tarry soul. **1914** *Century Dict. & Cyc.* IV (Supp.): *Flunky*…a cabin waiter on a passenger vessel. **1926** Norwood *Other Side of Circus* 58: A waiter was a "flunkey" and those who washed dishes were called "pearl divers." **1929** *AS* IV (June) 340: *Flunkey*—A camp waiter. **1951** *Time* (ad) (Mar. 12) 90: A squad of waitresses, known in woods jargon as flunkeys. **1979** *Edmonton Journal* (Canadian section) 9: "What's a flunky?" "A cook's helper….He sets dishes, peels potatoes and all that."

b. a person who performs menial chores, as a dishwasher, porter, or errand boy.

1926 *AS* I (Dec.) 651: *Flunky*—porter. **1927** *AS* II (Sept.) 506 [ref. to 1920]: *Flunky*—handy-man, menial assistant, dishwasher. **1937–40** in Whyte *Street Corner Society* 102: The corner-boys looked upon those who were closely identified with the settlement as "stooges" or "flunkies" for the social workers. **1948** A. Murphy *To Hell & Back* 6: I became a flunky in a radio repair shop. **1949** A.J. Liebling, in *New Yorker* (Jan. 22) 32: A flunky came into the grill-room of the Hotel Bristol to tell me that I had a long-distance call. **1987** Santiago *Undercover* 22: He uses flunkies for everything.

flunky *adj.* apprehensive; nervous.

1912 in J.I. White *Git Along Dogies* 150: Just to show us flunky punchers he was the wolf of the world.

flush *adj.* **1.** having money, esp. ready cash. Now *S.E.*

1821 Waln *Hermit in Phila.* 29: Let's have a *flyer* if you're *flush*. **1847–49** Bonney *Banditti* 101: They appear to be *flush*. **1865** in "M. Twain" *Selected Shorter Writings* 14: If there was a horse-race, you'd find him flush or you'd find him busted at the end of it. **1888** in *Amer. Heritage* (Oct. 1979) 20: It makes us sigh for days gone by when "flush" with cash were we.

2. broke.

1986 Stinson & Carabatsos *Heartbreak* 52: That's all I got, man. Shit, I swear. I'm flush!

flush *v.* **1.a.** to spoil; waste; ruin.

1958 Gilbert *Vice Trap* 74: Don't flush things for us now. **1969** L. Sanders *Anderson Tapes* 80: He flushed three G's on a free-lancer and got nothing to show for it. *a***1972** B. Rodgers *Queens' Vernacular* 83: *Flush*...to reject; to cancel; to eliminate...."That flushed their relationship." **1978** Diehl *Sharky's Machine* 166: She could blow the whistle...and flush the whole machine.

b. *Stu.* to fail to get a passing grade in.

1964 in *Time* (Jan. 1, 1965): A flunking student has *flagged it, flushed it,* or *tubed it.* **1979** (quot. at TUBE, *v.*).

2. to get rid of (someone), as by discharge; reject; dismiss. Cf. FLUSHOGRAM.

1967 *DAS* (Supp.) 684: *Flush v.t.* To ignore, reject, or dismiss someone, usually socially. **1968** Baker et al. *CUSS* 119: *Flush.* Reject someone for membership in a club, frat., etc. *a***1972** (quot. at **(1.a.)**, above). **1986** *Newsweek* (May 26) 51: The potentially bitter internal competition among newly hired M.B.A.'s—"flourish or get flushed," in the words of one...insider. **1989** Berent *Rolling Thunder* 41: Jones knew he'd be flushed at twenty years of total service.

3. to consider as lost.

1975 V.B. Miller *Deadly Game* 17: And if the Feds lose John "Blue" Andrews, you can take Ben Keller's six months of work and flush them.

4. *Basketball.* (see quot.).

1980 Wielgus & Wolff *Basketball* 43: *Flush (v)* To score.

5.a. *Computers.* (see quot.).

1983 Naiman *Computer Dict.* 60: (To) *flush.* To empty a portion of memory of its contents....*She suggested we flush the buffer.*

b. to quit work at the end of the day; knock off.

1983 Naiman *Computer Dict.* 60: *Flush*...to go home after a day's work. *Six o'clock—time to flush.*

flush-bottom *n. Pol.* a wealthy contributor.

1983 R. Thomas *Missionary* 34: Over the years Replogle had come to specialize in political fund-raising, which he always called "shaking down the flush-bottoms back East."

flushogram *n.* a note of dismissal or rejection.

1956 Hargrove *Girl He Left* 66: I'll just send the girl a flushogram and sacrifice my whole evening.

flute *n.* [**1.** the penis. See also **(5)** and *play the flute,* below, and FLUTER.

****1671** in Adlard *Forbidden Tree* 89: She will handle a flute/Better far than a lute/And make what was hard to grow tender.]

2. [sugg. by syn. *recorder*] *Und.* a local criminal magistrate.

****1698–99** "B.E." *Dict. Canting Crew: Flute*...The Recorder of *London,* or of any other town. ****1725**, ****1785**, ****1797**, ****1807** (cited in Partridge *Dict. Und.* 257). **1867** *Nat. Police Gaz.* (Jan. 5) 2: The "cracks"...have been before the "flute" and convicted.

3. *Narc.* an opium pipe; in phr. **hit the flute** to smoke opium.

1881 in Partridge *Dict. Und.* 334: The foolish...boy...who deems it something smart and clever to "visit a joint" or "to hit the flute."

4. *Und.* a police officer's whistle. *Rare* in U.S.

****1934** (cited in Partridge *Dict. Und.* 257). **1935** Pollock *Und. Speaks: Flute,* a police whistle.

5. FLUTER.

1937 in *AS* (Feb. 1938) 46: *Flute.* A male homosexual. **1941** G. Legman, in Henry *Sex Vars.* II 1166: *Fluter.* A fellator. Among jazz (and other?) musicians, the term is often shortened to *flute.*

6. [perh. sugg. by S.E. *flute* 'a tall, stemmed glass for champagne'] *Police.* a soft-drink bottle filled with whiskey.

1971 *N.Y. Post* (Oct. 19) 28: "We would get a call to bring in a 'flute' for a lieutenant." A "flute," he explained, was a soda bottle filled with whiskey. "We'd go to a bar, and tell the bartender the lieutenant wanted a flute. He needed no explanation. He'd fill the bottle, you'd put it in your pocket and deliver it to the station house." **1973** Maas *Serpico* 60: "Flutes"—Coca-Cola bottles filled with liquor supplied by bars in the precinct. **1974** Charyn *Blue Eyes* 144: He delivered his "flutes" to the captain's man (Coke bottles filled with rye). **1984** Caunitz *Police Plaza* 15: You might as well bring him a flute too—he'll be a little parched by then.

¶ In phrases:

¶ **fix (someone's) flute** to do for; fix.

1840 in Haliburton *Sam Slick* 138: If that critter had raelly been a knowin' one, the name of it wouldn't a-fixed his flute for him.

¶ **play the flute** [fr. **(1)**, above] to perform fellatio.

1916 Cary *Venery* II 47: Playing the Flute—...cock sucking. **1917–20** Dreiser *Newspaper Days* 590 [ref. to 1894]: They go down on you...play the flute. Aren't you on? **1927** [Fliesler] *Anecdota* 43: An old rounder,...tired of the various postures of love, determined on discovering how demure his wife was, to begin by teaching her how to play the flute.

flute-player *n.* FLUTER. *Joc.*

1916 Cary *Venery* I 91: *Flute Player*—A cock sucker. **1972** R. Wilson *Forbidden Words* 106: *Flute Player.* A male homosexual.

fluter *n.* a fellator.

1904 *Life in Sing Sing* 248: *Fluter.* A degenerate. **1930** Irwin *Tramp & Und. Sl.: Fluter*...A degenerate. The reference is apt enough, but impossible to give here, and the term is universal in America. **1932** *AS* VII (June) 332: *Fluter*—a pervert (used only in strict sense). **1935** J. Conroy *World to Win* 64: We'll head that fluter down the line.

flutter *n. Stu.* a party or social dance.

1926 Hormel *Co-Ed* 78: What say to a flutter at Varsity Hall?

fly *n. Und.* FLY-COP, 2.

****1857** in *F & H* III 41: A policeman; a *fly*. **1890** Roe *Police* 227: [He] became a "fly" in the "Big Chief's corps." *Ibid.* 227: Indeed it was chiefly to the ability he displayed when a private "fly" that he owed his public appointment. **1897** in J. London *Reports* 320: Hit a fly on the main-drag for a light piece....on the main street I begged a policeman in citizen's clothes for a small sum. **1912** Berkman *Prison* 127 [ref. to 1892]: The Captain of the night watch is "fierce an' an ex-fly."*...*Fly* or fly-cop, a detective. **1913** *Sat. Eve. Post* (Mar. 15) 37: In about five minutes a couple of flies is goin to make a pinch! **1926** *Flynn's Mag.* (Jan. 16) 639: I know that th' fly was jerry because he gave me th' once over as I was comin' out.

¶ In phrase:

¶ **no flies [on]** nothing slow, dull, or lackluster (about); nothing wrong (with).

****1848** in *OEDS:* "There were 'no flies' about that black bull."...This expression is very common in Australia....Anything particularly good is said by the class of men we are here describing to have "no flies" about it. ****1868** in *OEDS:* To this celebrated pugilist [Deaf Burke] is attributed the old story of the "flies in the gin-and-water," and hence the term "no flies" became prevalent. **1885** *Puck* (June 17) 251: She was a daisy, I'm tellin' yer, and no flies. **1888** Farmer *Amer.:* There are no flies on St. Louis or the St. Louis delegation either. **1888** in *F & H* III 42: There ain't no flies on him, signifies, that he is not quiet long enough for moss to grow on his heels; that he is wide awake. F.H. Smith *Tom Grogan* 63: No flies on them fellers, wuz ther', Patsy? They wuz daisies, they wuz. **1897** Work *Waifs* 65: He is a pretty good man. There are no flies on him. **1899** A.H. Lewis *Sandburrs* 47: There was no flies on us when me an' Mother Worden went fort' to graft. **1902** Dunbar *Sport of Gods* 76: You kin bet your life they ain't no flies on N'Yawk. **1931** Bontemps *Sends Sunday* 71: "Hot damn!" "No flies on Lil Augie." **1948** Erskine *All My Sons* (film): She's got a lot of spunk....No flies on her. **1952** Sandburg *Young Strangers* 311 [ref. to *ca*1890]: There are flies on you,/There are flies on me,/But there ain't

no flies on Jesus. **1975** S. Lee *Son of Origins* 82: Well, ain't no flies on Stan Lee!...I brought out a new strip named *Ant-Man*. **1966–80** McAleer & Dickson *Unit Pride* 152: There were no flies on him, and if there were they were damn well paying rent.

fly *adj.* [app. of dial. orig.] **1.a.** Esp. *Und.* clever; artful; wide-awake; smart. [The *1724 quot. represents a Scots pronun., but later usage as slang is undoubtedly an extension of sense **(b)**.]
*1724 in *EDD* II 432: The malt-man is right cunning/But I can be as flee. *1821 *Real Life in London* II 340: [He] walks out himself, *up to snuff* and *fly.* *1850 in *F & H* III 41: They say the *fliest* is easy to take in some-times—that's the artfullest. *1859 in *EDD* II 432: The brave, wily Turks were too fly for your bait. *1861 in *F & H* III 41: He's...a smart one, too. He's fly, is Harry. **1872** Burnham *Secret Service* 320: Hard-grave was "fly" enough to know he couldn't be convicted, if the stamps were not found upon his person. **1880** Pinkerton *Prof. Thieves & Detective* 183: The wily Howard had been entirely too "fly" for the gentle-men who found themselves so egregiously duped. **1880** in M. Lewis *Mining Frontier* 127: Billy used to be the boss gambler of camp, and warn't afeared to sit in a game with the flyest sport that ever slung a card. *1881–84 Davitt *Prison Diary* I 55: An experienced hand at this game will be "fly" enough not to win continuously when he gets his vic-tim or victims fully engaged in the speculation. **1885** *Puck* (Apr. 8) 83: Quite fly, wasn't he? **1888** in *Amer. Heritage* (Oct. 1979) 21: I've talked me with the highest, the dumbest and the "fly-est." **1891** *Munsey's Mag.* (Dec.) 306: You're fly...but I'm on to you fellers. Tried to swipe a ticket, eh? **1893** *Life* (Feb. 2) 70: Dey're fly enough to know dat. **1894** Gardner *Dr. & Devil* 62: The Doctor was too "fly" to be caught that way. **1895** *Harper's* (Oct.) 778: I heerd Frisco Shorty say oncet you was the fliest bloke in yer line West o' Denver. **1895** Townsend *Fadden* 32: Don't yer know wot a plunk is? W'y it's er case, er dollar. Say, youse ain't as fly as I taut. **1896** Ade *Artie* 49: I was pleadin' with my tall friend to just go right ahead and order anything she wanted. Well, she was fly enough to do that. **1899** Boyd *Shellback* 169: Con-siderable smart—yes, sirree....They're fly, horse, tail, buggy, and all. **1899** A.H. Lewis *Sand-burrs* 134: Now, understan' me! I ain't no crook. I'm a fakir, an' a grafter; an' I've been fly in me time an' I ain't no dub to-day, but I never was no crook, see! **1903** A.H. Lewis *Boss* 272: I'll tell you why it won't be fly to do it. *ca*1910 in Lomax *Cowboy Songs* 150: Oh, Tom is big six-footer and thinks he's mighty fly,/But I can tell you his racket—he's a deadbeat on the sly. **1911** A.H. Lewis *Apaches of N.Y.* 78: Ike couldn't pick th' pocket of a dead man....That's how fly he is. **1951** in J. Blake *Joint* 17: I had planned to get next to the colored maid there, who's pretty hip, but not hip enough to be fly, if you know what I mean.

b. *Und.* aware of what is going on; alerted; informed; in the know.—often constr. with *to.*
*1811 *Lexicon Balatron.*: *Fly.* Knowing. Acquainted with another's meaning or proceeding. The rattling cove is fly; the coachman knows what we are about. *1812 Vaux *Vocab.*: *Fly*: vigilant; suspicious; cun-ning; not easily robbed or duped; a shopkeeper of this description, is called a *fly cove*, or a *leary cove....*I'm *fly* to you. *1821 *Real Life in London* II 60: I am not *fly* to the subject....*Fly*—to be *up* to any thing, to understand, to know, or *be awake*. *1823 in *F & H* III 41: *Jerry*: Char-lies' fiddles?—I'm not *fly*, Doctor. *Log.*: Rattles, Jerry, rattles. *Jerry*: Rattles! You're *fly* now, I see. *1826 "Blackmantle" *Eng. Spy* II 5: You've told the town that you are *fly/*To cant, and rant, and trickery. *1838 Glascock *Landsharks* I 150: I see you're fly to every fakement. **1839** *Spirit of Times* (Mar. 23) 25: It was from "Snaffle"—are you "fly" to that "Artful Dodger?" **1853** in Thornton *Amer. Gloss.* I 64: He is considered "fly" upon all sporting matters. *1851–61 H. Mayhew *Lon-don Labour* II 53: A public-house whose landlord is "fly" to its meaning. **1866** *Nat. Police Gaz.* (Nov. 3) 3: Some well-meaning "bloke" putting him "fly" to the whole thing. **1882** *Frank James on the Trail* 37: I am fly to it all, and your little game, too. **1885** *Puck* (Sept. 16) 93: Yes, b'gosh, boss, but you ain't fly; one on them there plunks are lead. **1895** Foote *Coeur D'Alene* 147: Wan will take you over to my place....Wan is "fly." **1903** A.H. Lewis *Boss* 182: You're fly to some things, an' a farmer on others.

2. sophisticated; stylish; (*hence, Black E.*) attractive; splen-did; superlative.
1879 *Nat. Police Gaz.* (Sept. 20) 15: The young...men about town who think it is awfully "fly" to know tow-headed actresses. **1896** Ade *Artie* 94: They get in with a lot o' cheap skates and chase around nights and think they're the real thing....They think they're fly, but they ain't. **1902–03** Ade *People You Know* 33: Several dignified Gentlemen whom Brad described as Them Fly Eastern Mugs. **1941** in Ellington *Music My Mistress* 179: *Fly...*fine. **1942** *Pittsburgh Courier* (Jan. 17) 13: I'm

next, fly mama. **1950–52** Ulanov *Hist. Jazz* 351: *Fly*: smooth; to describe looks or manner or performance, usually the first two ("he's a fly cat."). **1954** L. Armstrong *Satchmo* 41: When the break [in the tune] came I made it a real good one and a fly one at that. **1954–60** *DAS*: *Fly chick*, n. An attractive, hip girl. **1967** Colebrook *Lassitude* 128: Gee—her hair's done up and everything. She looks fly! **1967–69** Foster & Stoddard *Pops* 115: Grant Cooper wasn't any fly trombone player, but he could play what he saw. **1969** Geller & Boas *Drug Beat* xvii: *Fly...*an adjective meaning "good." **1972** [V.M. Grosvenor] *Thursdays* 12: I was wearing the suit and the shoes. I knew that I was fly. *Ibid.* 13: I wasn't fly (but I wasn't looking scroungy). **1979** in B. Adler *Rap!* 21: All the...fly guys, get high. **1983** Sturz *Wid. Circles* 16: He himself wore nothing but superthreads; he had to look "fly." **1988** *Right On!* (June) 4: Went to the newsstand to buy my fly magazine,/But couldn't believe what I was seein'. **1991** Nelson & Gonzales *Bring Noise* 257: A day in the life of a drug dealer:...flye [*sic*] cars and begging women.

3.a. (esp. of women) characterized by a disregard for restraint in social or sexual conduct; wanton; wild; (*specif.*) of or associated with the demimonde.
1880 Martin *Sam Bass* 20: The woman who made the least secret about the color of her garters, and who was the "flyest of all the mob," was the belle of the place. **1880** Nye *Boomerang* 37: She dreamed that she dwelt in marble halls and kept a girl and had a pretty fly time generally. *1886 (cited in *EDD*). **1888** in *F & H* III 42: I'm just gettin' sick'n tired o' the way 't them fly dames go on, 'n the way 't the fellahs hang round 'em 'n dance with 'em. *1888–90 (cited in *EDD*). *a1890–93 *F & H* III 41: *Fly...*(venery).—Wanton. *Fly-girl, -woman,* or *-dame*—a prostitute. **1922** S. Lewis *Babbitt* 124: Babbitt was not an analyst of women....He divided them into Real Ladies, Working Women, Old Cranks, and Fly Chickens. **1929–33** J. Lowell *Gal Reporter* 66: You don't look like a fly dame to me and it sure must be hell to be...busted. **1937** Reitman *Box-Car Bertha* 198: "Loose" Married Women... "Lonesome" widows and "fly" divorcees. **1959** Murtagh & Harris *Who Live in Shadow* 46: Jimmy was "in a groove" as far as the fly chicks, the prostitutes, and their sweet men were concerned.

b. insolent or impertinent; audacious; brash. Also as adv.
1884 in Miller & Snell *Why West Was Wild* 515: A pair of very "fly" Chicago drummers came down last week bent on doing the "boys" up and painting the town red. **1892** in Spaeth *Read 'Em & Weep* 169: "You've been held up," said the "copper" fly. **1896** Ade *Artie* 25: You won't think I'm too fly if I ask you a question, will you? **1902** Dunne *Observations* 169: Th' American business man is too fly. **1915** in Garrett *Army Ballads* 21: And I'm nursing an eye I got for being fly. **1915–16** Lait *Beef, Iron & Wine* 58: They cops him in a fly job, done good but gone bad. **1928** Fisher *Jericho* 156: I got a picture o' myself lettin' any guy alone that gets fly with my girl. **1928** Dahlberg *Bottom Dogs* 58: We kin show yu what we do with newcumbers who get fly! **1930** Graham & Graham *Queer People* 116: I caught...Bill Holmes, passing a fly crack about "Mr. Bagshaw" one day. **1934** Peters & Sklar *Stevedore* 38: These young fly niggers who get uppity notions. **1944** Quillan & Bennett *Show Business* (film): In Hawai-yah the maidens there are fly-ah! **1988** *Right On!* (June) 52: What kind of girls do you like?...Shy girls, fly girls, and all types of girls.

fly *v.* **1.** to be heavily intoxicated, esp. by drugs; to take psycho-tropic drugs.
1952 "R. Marsten" *So Nude* 10: Man, I'm stoned! Flying...! **1968** "J. Hudson" *Case of Need* 184: We didn't want her to fly for a while after the abortion. **1974** G.V. Higgins *Cogan's Trade* 10: You're gonna be flying and you're gonna go in stoned. **1980** Gould *Ft. Apache* 8: The guy was flying. Downs, or maybe angel dust. **1989** *Geraldo* (synd. TV series): But I like to fly. I like to do acid.

2. to meet with approval or success.
1984 "W.T. Tyler" *Shadow Cabinet* 244: Hey, did I tell you the Arab Emirates package is gonna fly?

¶ In phrases:

¶ **fly light, 1.** Esp. *Naut.* to sail without cargo; (*hence*) to wear or carry little equipment or few belongings.
1859 in C.A. Abbey *Before the Mast* 181: She...is going back *"flying light."* **1883** Parker *Naval Officer* 110: I was "flying light" upon this occasion; instead of being loaded down with arms and ammunition as most of the officers were I had but my dress sword. **1899** Hamblen *Bucko Mate* 37: The old-timers went to sea "flyin' light." They dis-dained, as effeminate, the deep-water sailor who carried a good stock of clothes, bedding, and oilskins. **1911** in Bierce *Letters* 183: I shall leave my...books at home and...be "flying light." *1929 Bowen *Sea Slang* 51: *Flying Light.* The state in which the sailing ship seaman fre-quently joined his ship, possessing nothing but the clothes he wore.

1930 Irwin *Tramp & Und. Sl.: Flying Light*...travelling without any excess impediment such as a "bindle."
2. Esp. *R.R.* to skip a meal.
1926 *AS* I (Jan.) 250: Missing a meal is "flying light." **1930** Irwin *Tramp & Und. Sl.: Flying Light*...Hungry; without food. **1945** Hubbard *R.R. Ave.* 343: *Fly Light*—Miss a meal. *Boomers* often did that.

¶ **fly right** [from title of pop. song *Straighten Up and Fly Right*, by N. Cole & I. Mills, introduced in 1943 film cited below] Esp. *Mil. Av.* to conduct or comport oneself properly.—usu. constr. with *straighten up and.*
1943 Townley & Davis *Here Comes Elmer* (film): Why don't you straighten up and fly right? **1948** *Neurotica* (Spring) 33: The gulls... straighten up and fly right. **1948** Manone & Vandervoort *Trumpet* 239: Make that horn straighten up and fly right. **1949** McMillan *Old Breed* 257 [ref. to WWII]: Calm down, boy, and fly right. **1950** Hemingway *Across River* 208: Wipe the egg off your chin, Jack, and straighten up and fly right. **1956** M. Wolff *Big Nick*. 130: You are grouchy....Why don't you take an aspirin and fly right? **1958** Ferlinghetti *Coney Island* 51: I am waiting/for the American Eagle/to really straighten up and fly right. **1959** Murtagh & Harris *Who Live in Shadow* 54: But I soon got on my rocker and started in flying right again. **1962** Killens *Heard the Thunder* 85 [ref. to WWII]: Why don't you straighten up and fly right, soldier! **1965** Bonham *Durango St.* 137: You'd better straighten up an fly right! **1971** J. Brown & A. Groff *Monkey* 33: I knew I had to snap out of it and fly right.

¶ **go fly a kite** go away and quit being a nuisance!
1927 in *Sat. Eve. Post* (Jan. 7, 1928) 21: Now would you like for mamma to go on reading to you...or would you like to go fly a kite? *1942** in *OEDS:* He suggested...that I go fly a kite! **1942** *ATS* 266: Mind your own business!...*go fly a kite!* **1955** Abbey *Brave Cowboy* 50: Go fly a kite on the moon, you slew-balled old fart. **1962** Perry *Young Man Drowning* 26: Aw, go fly a kite!

flyaway *n.* a runaway; deserter.
1914 Paine *Wall Between* 145: We'll turn this gay flyaway over to the prison guard and good riddance to him. **1930** "D. Stiff" *Milk & Honey* 205: *Fly-away*—A deserter from the army or navy.

flyball *n.* [alter. FLY-BULL] *Und.* a police detective.
1926 *AS* I (Dec.) 651: *Fly-ball*—detective. **1929** Milburn *Hobo's Hornbook* 233: And a fly-ball comes and drags you out,/And fans you with a loaded bat.

fly bob *n.* [perh. abbr. of (unattested) *fly bobby;* see FLY, *adj.;* FLY-COP, *n.*] a police detective.
1901 *Chi. Tribune* (July 28) 38: Fly bobs and rubber shoes walk with soft, cat-like tread and...always say, "Hist! I have a clew." **1942** *ATS* 419: *Fly bob*, a plainclothesman. **1954–60** *DAS: Fly bob*...[has] seen wide hobo use.

flyboy *n.* **1.** a shrewd, brash, or sophisticated fellow. [Orig. as two words.]
1888 *Stag Party* 15: Jim Blake lived in the country, and though a pretty fly boy among the rustics was not up in the ways of the outside world. **1895** Townsend *Fadden* 67: 'E says dat I was er pretty fly boy, an' otter be in polytics. **1896** Ade *Artie* 34: Here comes a whole crowd o' people—a lot o' swell girls and their fly boys. **1921** *Variety* (Jan. 14) 20: A poet, boob, and fly-boy [are] calling on a girl...the homely comedy and business of the "boob" and the roughness of the fly-boy. *1975** (cited in Partridge *DSUE* (ed. 8) 412). **1991** Nelson & Gonzales *Bring Noise* 230: Waging the most savage attack...is flyeboy[*sic*]-sex symbol Shabba Ranks.
2. Esp. *Mil.* an aviator; a member of an air force. Cf. FLY-FLY BOY.
1937 in Galewitz *Great Comics* (Zack Mosley's "Smilin' Jack") 216: "Say, Girls—if anyone here at St. Paul knows where Smilin' Jack is, will you send this letter to him?" "Okay, flyboy." **1944** *Time* (Nov. 13) 10: *Semper fidelis*, "flyboy."*...*Airman. **1946** *AS* XXI 248: Airforce flying personnel are sometimes labelled *bird-men* or *flyboys*. **1946** Bowker *Out of Uniform* 78: As he returned to his prolonged, uncomfortable, unending quarrel with the enemy, it is no wonder that his envy developed into dislike for what he termed the "fly boys." **1951** Sheldon *Troubling of a Star* 21: What's eating you, fly-boy? **1951** VMF-323 *Old Ballads* 38: But you can't blame those fly boys/'Cause they've been all shook up. **1958** Cope and Dyer *Petty Officer's Guide* (ed. 2) 346: *Fly boys:* (Slang). United States Air Force personnel. **1961** Crane *Born of Battle* 54: The flyboys are clobberin' 'em. **1963** Morgan *Six-Eleven* 221: I think flyboy here has some ideas that start with taking the center armrest out of the seat. **1971** Giovanni *Gemini* 3: You...get the feeling of drunken fly-

boys in green airplane hats. **1972–76** Durden *No Bugles* 17: Put some fire in there 'n let the fly boys take care of 'em. **1984** J.R. Reeves *Mekong* 166: I sort of resented the flyboys. *a*1990 Poyer *Gulf* 143: I'll send the fly-boys out for a look. **1992** *Time* (Dec. 28) 23: Have you heard those Air Force flyboys are already building...a PX in Mog?

flybrush *n.* a horse's tail.
1865 Williams *Joaquin* 9: I swan if 'taint my mare Kezi'ah, if 'tis shaved pesky close and the fly-brush docked.

fly-bull *n. Und.* FLY-COP, 2.
1919 *DN* V 41: *Flybull, n.* A detective. **1927** *DN* V 446: *Fly-bull, n.* A detective. Also *fly-mug*. **1935** Pollock *Und. Speaks: Fly bull,* a detective.

fly captain *n.* (see quot.).
1884 Triplett *American Crimes* 135: Holcroft got another vessel, and with Edwards as "fly captain,"* soon set sail....*Slavers sailing from Brazilian ports carried usually two captains and two sets of papers; one American, one Brazilian. The "fly captain" was a mere figurehead, who showed up with the American papers whenever the ship was searched, the other captain being the one mentioned in the Brazilian papers.

flycatcher *n.* (see quot.).
1955 O'Connor *Last Hurrah* 189: The bum was a flycatcher, a scene stealer. He tried to cop the act at his own brother's wake.

fly-chaser *n. Baseball Journ.* an outfielder.
1934 Weseen *Dict. Slang* 209: *Fly chaser*—An outfielder. **1980** Lorenz *Guys Like Us* 25: He had...the hands of a fly-chaser. **1993** N.Y.C. man, age 31 (coll. J. Sheidlower): Anyone who knows baseball would know *fly chaser* for an outfielder, but I wouldn't say it's very common.

fly-cop *n.* **1.** Orig. *Und.* an alert or experienced police officer.
1859 Matsell *Vocab.* 34: *Fly-Cop.* Sharp officer; an officer that is well posted; one who understands his business. **1866** *Nat. Police Gaz.* (Apr. 21) 3: Big Casey endeavored to "work" the crowd at the "go-away's" in Thirtieth street, but was driven away in quick time by the "fly cop." **1872** Burnham *Secret Service* v: *Fly-Cop.* A ready, quick-witted officer or Detective. **1885** *Puck* (Apr. 8) 83: It's a cold day when a fly-cop can give me a tip.
2. a police detective, esp. a plainclothesman.
1866 *Nat. Police Gaz.* (Apr. 21) 3: "Fly-cops" Tyner and Sheehan "pulled" them both. *Ibid.* [He] is well known to the present "fly-cops" there. **1872** Crapsey *Nether Side* 185: You and your fly cops are a set of green suckers. **1872** Burnham *Secret Service* 98: The "fly-cop" who had this koniacker now in hand understood his biz'. **1879** Dacus *Frank & Jesse* 170: With him was a St. Louis "fly cop"...distinguished for his shrewdness and daring, who for the time had assumed the name of Wright. **1882** Pinkerton *Bank Robbers* 91: The "fly cops" were making it hot for us. **1891** Clurman *Nick Carter* 20: He is a fly cop...and he must die. **1899** A.H. Lewis *Sandburrs* 156: In ten minutes every cop an' fly cop is on d' chase. **1900** Willard & Hodler *Powers That Prey* 32: A town as big as this can find its own guns without callin' in private fly cops. **1902** Dunne *Observations* 23: Ye see, [Sherlock Holmes] ain't th' ordh'nary fly cop like Mulcahy that always runs in th' Schmidt boy fr ivry crime rayported. **1908** in H.C. Fisher *A. Mutt* 32: Here comes those fly cops too. **1916** Miner *Prostitution* 3: Fly cops wouldn't have no jobs if it wasn't for us. **1925** Mullin *Scholar Tramp* 218: We knew he was a fly-cop. **1936** Steel *College* 243: The flycops are taking this thing seriously. **1942** Chandler *High Window* 358: Fly cops with granite faces and unwavering eyes. **1944** C.B. Davis *Leo McGuire* 215: Mr. Mills called a fly cop to the stand. **1958** S.H. Adams *Tenderloin* 286 [ref. to 1890's]: The fly-cop set about some preliminary snooping. **1960** Roeburt *Mobster* 15 [ref. to 1920's]: He kept that damned entry book where fly cops could get at it. **1965** in Jackson *Swim Like Me* 102: A fly-cop fell to the floor./The other dick made an exit quick.
3. *Naval Av.* an aviator belonging to a naval antisubmarine patrol. *Joc.*
1918 Kauffman *Our Navy at Work* 133: *Fly-cops* (Hydroaeroplanes).

fly copper *n. Und.* FLY-COP.
1892 Moore *Own Story* 187: While on our way [to jail], the officers tipped us off right and left in true "fly copper" style.

fly-dick *n. Und.* a police plainclothesman.
1924 *N.Y. Times* (Aug. 3) VIII 16: He is the law or a fly dick or an office man if he comes from headquarters. **1927** *AS* (June) 385: A plainclothesman, now called a *fly-dick,* was an *elbow.*

flyer var. FLIER.

fly-fly boy *n. Navy.* FLYBOY. [The 1976 assignment of the term to WWI, though made by a veteran, is perh. anachronistic.]
1949 Morison *WWII* IV 39: Ship recognition comes hard to the "fly-

fly boys" of every nation. **1949** Brown & Grant *Sands of Iwo Jima* (film): Don't forget the fly-fly boys. **1956** *AS* XXXI (Oct.) 192: An airman is a *fly-fly boy* or a *bus driver*. **1956** Lockwood & Adamson *Zoomies, Subs & Zeroes* 76: The Stingray...rescued two...fly-fly boys. **1976** A.W. Moffat *Maverick Navy* 68 [ref. to 1918]: [The] gasoline...is all allocated to the fly-fly boys.

fly-girl *n.* **1.a.** a sexually promiscuous young woman, esp. a prostitute.
*a**1890–93** *F & H* III 41: *Fly-girl*...a prostitute. **1918** *Outlook* (June 26) 346: I played around with the gang and a bunch of fly girls. *Ibid.* 347: What is she, a fly girl? **1957** Hecht *Charlie* 63 [ref. to *ca*1920]: There were trollops galore....There was also a less gaudy pushover type called "fly girls."...They were to be found in honorable surroundings but...were willing to try a dishonorable bed, if...properly approached.
b. an attractive young woman.
1986 Eble *Campus Slang* (Nov.) 4: *Flygirl*—sexy female. **1987** Univ. Tenn. student: A *flygirl* is a cute girl. **1993** *Source* (July) 43: This twentysomething Brooklyn flygirl.
2. an airline stewardess.
1960 Glemser *Fly Girls* 85: Hi, fly-girls. All by yourselves, fly-girls? **1985** *Lady Blue* (ABC-TV): So you is Leo's little fly-girl.

fly-guy *n.* **1.** FLYBOY, 1. [Orig. as two words.]
1893 in Spaeth *Read 'Em & Weep* 166: You've got to be a real fly guy that's wise to the all-night push—see? **1906** *Nat. Police Gaz.* (May 5) 3: They're fly guys there all right...but the flyer they are the easier it is to trim them. **1979** in *Folklore Forum* XVII (1984) 149: She said, "Damn flyguy I'm in love with you/The Casanova legend must have been true." **1989** in *Nat. Lampoon* (Feb. 1990) 62: Rather be a flyguy/Than sit on Mount Sinai.
2. an aviator; FLYBOY, 2. *Joc.*
1951 Grant *Flying Leathernecks* (film): You a fly-guy? **1963** E.M. Miller *Exile* 82: You fly-guys keep bringing back new formulas.

flying *adj.* (used for emphasis with various terms, the whole expression meaning "a curse; the least bit").—usu. constr. with *give*.—usu. constr. in negative.
1946–51 J. Jones *Here to Eternity* [ref. to 1941]: I don't give a flyin' fuck. **1953** Brossard *Bold Saboteurs* 30. They did not give a flying hoot. **1956** H. Ellison *Deadly Streets* 190: Tony didn't give a flying damn. **1967** in H. Ellison *Sex Misspelled* 154: I...don't give a flying *shit* what time you were behind your desk. **1972** N.Y.U. student: I don't give a flying fart. **1973** R.M. Brown *Rubyfruit* 67: I don't give a flying fuck what you do. **1974** Strasburger *Rounding Third* 12: Who gives a flying fuck, Junior? **1975** Univ. Tenn. student: I just don't give a flyin' shit. **1980** Conroy *Lords of Discipline* 297: He wouldn't have given a flying crap about this city. **1984** Ehrhart *Marking Time* 19: Most...weren't worth a flying fuck. **1985** Finkleman *Head Office* (film): He doesn't give a flying shit about Stedman's position.
¶ In phrase:
¶ **[go] take a flying leap at the moon** get away! go to hell! Also vars., some usu. considered vulgar.
[**1899** A.H. Lewis *Sandburrs* 245: I tells Mike to take a run an' jump on himself.] **1926** Nason *Chevrons* 73 [ref. to 1918]: Me, I'd tell 'em to take a flyin' fling at the moon. **1929–30** Dos Passos *42nd Parallel* 271: I hadn't the nerve/to...tell/them all to go take a flying/Rimbaud/at the moon. **1932** Miller & Burnett *Scarface* (film): "They said you could take a flyin'—" "That's enough of that!" **1934** W. Saroyan, in North *New Masses* 93: I didn't obey my mother or my teachers and I told the whole world to take a flying you-know-what. **1935** J. Conroy *World to Win* 64: Go take a flyin' jump at a gallopin' goose for all o' me. **1936** Kingsley *Dead End* 706: Well, go take a flyin' jump at a moose! **1938** in J. O'Hara *Sel. Letters* 140: I say go take a flying fuck at a galloping r——ster. **1939** Appel *Power-House* 165: If this's the *Hamilton Detective Agency* it can take a flyin' trip to the moon. **1941** Brackett & Wilder *Ball of Fire* (film): Tell the D.A. to take a flyin' jump for himself. **1944** Stiles *Big Bird* 105: You can take a flying one at a rolling one. **1949** Bezzerides *Thieves' Market* 122: He can go take a flying frig at himself. **1949** Pirosh *Battleground* (film) [ref. to WWII]: Tell him to take a flyin' leap at a rollin' doughnut. **1952** Himes *Stone* 238: How would you like to take a flying frig at yourself? **1961** Brosnan *Pennant Race* 48: Brosnan, you can take a flying leap at my —. **1962** Killens *Heard the Thunder* 415: And you and your colored problems can take a flying frig at the moon. **1966** "T. Pendleton" *Iron Orchard* 40: You take a flyin' bite at my ass! **1968** Swarthout *Loveland* 169: "Go take a flying jump at a rolling doughnut!" I hollered. **1971** Cameron *First Blood* 119: Why don't you go take a flying fuck at a rolling doughnut? **1972** N.Y.U. student: Go take a flying fuck for yourself. **1972** R. Wilson *Forbidden Words* 107: Take a flying

Philadelphia fuck in [*sic*] a rolling doughnut. **1972** *Rowan & Martin's Laugh-In* (NBC-TV): I told him to go take a flying leap. **1979** Hurling *Boomers* 133: I...just told him to take a flyin' fuck at a rollin' doughnut. **1979** McGivern *Soldiers* 185 [ref. to WWII]: Why don't you take a flying fuck at a rolling doughnut? **1966–80** McAleer & Dickson *Unit Pride* 117: Go take a flyin' fuck at a rollin' doughnut. *Ibid.* 408: You go take a flyin' fuck at the moon. **1983** S. King *Christine* 296: Tell him to take a flying fuck at a rolling doughnut. **1985** Briskin *Too Much* 264: Tell 'em to go take a flying fuck. *a***1986** in *NDAS*: Go take a flying frig. **1988** DeLillo *Libra* 93: Take a flying fuck at the moon.

flying banana *n.* [sugg. by the shape] *Av.* **1.** a Piasecki HRP helicopter. Now *hist.*
1950 *Nat. Geographic* (Sept.) 321: Piasecki Helicopter Corporation [is] maker of the twin-rotor "flying banana." **1961** W.T. Larkins *USMC Aircraft* 136: Piasecki HRP-1..."Flying Banana" 1948. **1980** Millett *Semper Fidelis* 455: Piasecki HRP's, a heavy-lift helo nicknamed "the flying banana." **1984** Apostolo *Encyc. Helicopters* 79: Piasecki HRP-1. The first tandem rotor helicopters built by Frank Piasecki [1947] were nicknamed "flying bananas."
2. a Vertol H-21 Shawnee or CH-21 Ute helicopter.
1957 (cited in Partridge *DSUE* (ed. 8) 414). **1962** Tregaskis *Viet. Diary* 162: "Flying bananas"...were supplying...transportation....In its time, the H-21 was a marvel. **1964** J. Lucas *Dateline* 90: Bolton also asked about phasing out CH-21 "Flying Banana" helicopters. **1984** Doleman *Tools of War* 35: The army's CH-21 Ute "Flying Banana."

flying bathtub *n. Mil. Av.* (see quot.).
1937 Parsons *Lafayette Escadrille* 96 [ref. to 1916]: He was the first one to take across the twin-motored Caudron G-4, scathingly referred to as the "Flying Bathtub."

flying bedstead *n.* **1.** *Army.* an ambulance.
1918 *Collier's* (Jan. 5) 12: The veteran wouldn't do for the Flying Bedsteads, alias the United States Army Ambulance Service. **1918** McNutt *The Yanks Are Coming!* 195: My legs are too bad shot up for the infantry, so I thought I might hook on here with the Flyin' Bedsteads. **1920** *Amer. Legion Wkly.* (July 23) 22: One sunny day in France I was driving my flying bedstead into Toul.
2. *Mil. Av.* a training airplane.
1918 in Crowe *Pat Crowe, Aviator* 76: For instance, how was I to know that "Flying bedsteads" is the name for training planes?

flying boxcar *n.* **1.** *Mil. Av.* a large clumsy multiengine airplane. [Later an industry name for various cargo aircraft.]
1918 in Hall & Niles *One Man's War* 290: The Americans who go to Italy will be doomed to fly the Italian Capronis—those beautiful flying box-cars—those unmanageable crates! **1936** Mulholland *Splinter Fleet* 150: They flew antiquated, lumbering flying boats which we promptly dubbed *Flying Boxcars*. **1942** Nichols *Air Force* (film): I want to get out of this flying boxcar. **1944** E.H. Hunt *Limit* 51: You could crack-up in one of those flying box-cars of yours. *a***1983** Newby *Target: Ploesti* 22: The B-24 had many nicknames, but "Flying Box Car" and "Pregnant Cow" were perhaps the two most descriptive.
2. (see quot.).
1945 *Yank* (May 25) 8: A "flying boxcar," one of the Japs' 320-mortar shells, had just landed.

flying brick *n. Mil. Av.* an ungainly airplane.
1944 Hubler & DeChant *Flying Leathernecks* 94 [ref. to 1942]: The J2F Duck was a crate....The pilots, not too affectionately, called it the "Flying Brick." **1990** G.R. Clark *Words of Vietnam War* 168: F-4 Phantom II...*Flying Brick.* **1991** Foss & Brennan *Top Guns* 7: I named the Spad the "flying brick."

flying chicken-coop *n. Mil. Av.* (see quot.).
1937 Parsons *Lafayette Escadrille* 95 [ref. to 1916]: He inspired confidence to such an extent that they soloed him immediately on the old Caudron G-2, the flying chicken coop, considered as a very speedy ship, and exceedingly difficult to handle.

flying circus *n.* **1.** see CIRCUS, 3.
2. a ridiculous or confused organization. Cf. *Monty Python's Flying Circus*, television series by the English comedy troupe.
1972–76 Durden *No Bugles* 22: What kinda fuckin' flyin' circus is this, anyway?

flying coffin *n.* **1.** a racing car.
1918 O'Brien *Wine, Women & War* 120: Thinks he's Barney Oldfield and the Ford a flying coffin.
2. *Av.* an aircraft that is dangerous to fly. Cf. FLAMING COFFIN.

1918 in Paine *First Yale Unit* II 219: Signor Caproni's Flying Coffins. **1937** Codman *Contact* 53 [ref. to 1918]: Equipped with Liberty Motored D.H.'s (Flying Coffins) which flew at a different speed from our Brequets, they operated independently from us. **1944** Kendall *Service Slang* 23: *Flying coffin*....a PBY Navy patrol bomber. **1944** *Official Guide to Army Air Forces* 368: *Flying coffin*. Dilapidated plane. **1945** in *AS* (Dec. 1946) 310 [AAF]: *Flying coffin*. Used in the Air Corps to describe a B-24 Liberator bomber. Airborne troops called the gliders they used for their operations by this name because the gliders were extremely vulnerable to enemy artillery. **1958** Craven & Cate *AAF in WWII* VII 25: But among ATC pilots the [C-46] Commando was known...as the "flying coffin." **1966** J. Lucas *Dateline* 333: An old DH-4—a two-seater known then and now as the "Flying Coffin." **1983** M. Skinner *USAFE* 114: The F-104 soon gained more grim nicknames—"Flying Coffin" and "Widow Maker." **1988** *Wings* (Discovery Channel TV): B-24's could take very little damage....I lost all my friends in '24's...."Flying Coffins." **1991** Linnekin *80 Knots* 10: The notorious de Havilland D.H. 4—the "Flying Coffin."

flying devil *n. Army.* a kind of German grenade.

> **1928** Wharton *Squad* 299 [ref. to 1918]: Cheap leather equipment, rifles, bayonets in tangled Maxim belts, Potato Mashers, and that type of winged, German grenade which the Americans always called a "Flying Devil."

flying fish *n. Mil. Av.* a pursuit plane.

> **1918** in Crowe *Pat Crowe, Aviator* 120: Behind them, like the playful pup lapping at the heels of the herd, came the "flying fishes," circling, zooming, diving, through the most marvelous gyrations I have ever seen. *Ibid.* 205: It would be lots of fun to "zoom" the old homestead in a little Flying Fish, and make circles around the spire.

flying-fish sailor *n. Naut.* a sailor accustomed to voyages in warm latitudes, esp. in the Indian Ocean or Eastern Asia.— used derisively. Now *hist.*

> **1906** *Yachting Mo.* (Oct.) 452: Packet ship sailors...looked down on other foreign-going seamen as effeminate and dubbed them "flying-fish sailors." **1909** in *Spin* IX (No. 3) (1973) 9: And so I shipped on a China packet,/Just for to be a flying fish sailor. **1918** King *Bk. of Chanties* 3: I'm a flying-fish sailor, just home from Hong Kong. **1939** Linscott *Folk Songs* 129: I'm a flying fish sailor and I come from Hong Kong. **1951** Doerflinger *Shantymen* 327: Capt. Patrick Tayluer said the term [*flying fish sailor*] particularly referred to sailors...whose vessels remained in Indian and Chinese waters. *1961 Burgess *Dict. Sailing* 93: *Flying-fish sailor*. One who selects his ships for his voyages through the tropics, and avoids sailing through the colder climes.

flying-fish weather *n. Naut.* warm, calm weather.

> **1941** Cruse *Apache Days* 279 [ref. to 1900]: But there were no hardships; the Pacific was smooth, and in that "flying fish weather" one day seemed exactly like another. **1943** Coale *Midway* 11: "Flying fish weather"—porpoise, albatross, and sunshine.

flying flapjack *n.* [sugg. by its unique circular configuration] *Av.* the Vought XF5U-1 experimental fighter airplane. *Joc.* Now *hist.* Also **flying pancake.**

> **1953** *ATS* (ed. 2) 708: *Flying flapjack*, a twin-engined circular craft, the XF-5-U-1. **1955** Ruppelt *Report on UFOs* 35: The U.S. Navy and their XF-5-U-1, the "Flying Flapjack." **1991** Linnekin *80 Knots* 259: The F5U "Flying Pancake."

flying foxhole *n.* [sugg. by its unusual twin-boom construction] *Mil. Av.* a Lockheed P-38 Lightning fighter airplane. *Joc.* Now *hist.* Also **flying pancake.**

> [**1945** Hamann *Air Words*: *Flying foxholes*. Fighter planes.] **1961** Foster *Hell in the Heavens* 235 [ref. to WWII]: It could have been a Jap or it could have been a Flying Foxhole (P-38).

flying jib *n.* (see 1908 quot.).

> **1908** Sullivan *Criminal Slang* 1: *A flying jib*—a talkative drunk. **1935** D.W. Maurer, in *AS* (Feb.) 16 [ref. to *a*1910]: *Flying jib*. A drunk man; three sheets in the wind.

flying-jib coat *n. Naut.* a man's frock coat. Now *hist.*

> **1966** Hugill *Sailortown* 320: Their displays would consist of bowlerhats, flying-jib coats, gaff-tops'l hats, caps, nautical-looking blue serge suits [etc.].

flying machine *n. Horse Racing.* a fast horse.

> **1984** *N.Y. Post* (Aug. 16) 68: Tiffany Ice, the gray flying machine...rebounded to win the Sanford at 5-2.

flying pig *n. Army.* any of various high-explosive trench-mortar projectiles. Now *hist.* [Quots. ref. to WWI.]

> **1917** *Infantry Jour.* XIV (Dec.) 461: This is the "flying pig," the British giant trench mortar shell. **1918** Proctor *Iron Div.* 272: The mortar platoons always were close at hand when the infantry stopped, baffled by the mazes of wire, and called for the "flying pigs" to open a path. *1919 Downing *Digger Dial.* 24: *Flying pig*—A heavy trench-mortar shell used early in the war. **1919** Gilder *Def. Democracy* 202: Then the "flying pigs," as big as a good sized ash barrel. **1920** E.A. Edwards *Doniphan* 42: There was constant sniping, frequent use of grenades, artillery fire, and flying pigs. *a*1925 Fraser & Gibbons *Soldier & Sailor Wds.*: *Flying pig*. A name given to a...(9.45 inch) heavy trench-mortar shell. From its corpulent elongated form (2 feet long) and tail with steady vanes which suggested the appearance of a pig in the air. **1925** Taber *168th Inf.* 164: Then a flock of French "Flying Pigs" would go wobbling over to blow it up. **1955** Semmes *Patton* 48: The trench mortar shells were called "Flying Pigs"...[and made] shell holes into which the Renault tanks drove for practice.

Flying Prostitute *n.* [see 1943 quot.] *USAF.* the Martin B-26 Marauder bomber aircraft. *Joc.* Now *hist.*

> **1943** *Yank* (Sept. 24) 4: The Marauder [is] nicknamed the "Flying Prostitute" because, with its short stubby wings, it has no visible means of support. **1945** in *AS* (Dec. 1946) 310: *Flying prostitute*. A B-26 bomber, so called because it seemed to have no visible means of support. Most Air Corps personnel considered it a very dangerous plane. **1968** W.C. Anderson *Gooney Bird* 36: When it was rolled out with its small wings it had been promptly dubbed "The Flying Prostitute"—because it had no visible means of support. **1975** in Higham & Siddall *Combat Aircraft* 11: The stubby wings were responsible for her nickname of "Flying Prostitute"—she had no (or very little) visible means of support. **1984** J. Dailey *Silver Wings* 320: Look at the morale problems we had...over the B-26. They were half scared to fly the damned "Flying Prostitute."

flying saucer cap *n.* [sugg. by its circular crown] *Mil.* a service cap.

> **1971** Army veteran [ref. to 1961–62]: Let's see, there was the "flying saucer," which is that cap that looks like a cop's hat, with a visor and a flattened top. **1973** USAF veteran: The service cap is called the flying saucer. **1980** Cragg *L. Militaris* 170: *Flying Saucer Cap*. The service cap. Because of its circular design. **1981** Hathaway *World of Hurt* 15: He polished the brass emblem that shone above the bill of his flying saucer hat.

flying seven *n. Navy.* a rapid series of seven inoculations given to recruits.

> **1972** Ponicsan *Cinderella Liberty* 79: Prompted by the shot, Baggs dreams of the Flying Seven in boot camp.

flying telephone pole *n. Mil. Av.* an enemy surface-to-air missile.

> **1977** [B.P. Wyatt] *We Came Home* (unp.) [ref. to 1967]: The...aircraft's job was to seek out the guided missile sites, knock them out before they could launch the "flying telephone poles."

flying twenty-five *n. Army.* the first pay installment given to recruits in training. Earlier **flying ten, flying twenty.**

> **1956** Hargrove *Girl He Left* 44: Day after that you'll get your "flying ten." That's a ten-dollar bill to take care of you until you're assigned to your unit. **1960** Bluestone *Cully* 21: "My Flyin' Twenny [has] flown."...But the twenty-buck installment on his pay was all the dough he'd had. **1964** Beech *Article 92* 8: He was a soft touch for a flying twenty the week before payday. **1969** Moskos *Enlisted Man* 56: Every recruit...is tested, issued clothing, receives a regulation haircut, and given a pay advance (the "flying twenty-five") to buy toilet and other personal articles. **1983** Elting, Cragg, & Deal *Soldier Talk* 113: *Flying 25*...The first $25 paid to recruits shortly after their processing at the recruit depot. The money does not last very long.

Flying Whale *n. Mil. Av.* the Consolidated B-24 Liberator bomber or one of its variants. Now *hist.*

> **1961** Forbes *Goodbye to Some* 16 [ref. to WWII]: The airplanes are Liberators...known...occasionally as Flying Whales.

fly-man *n. Police & Und.* a security guard; a plainclothes detective.

> *1851–61 H. Mayhew *London Labour* III 405: Sometimes we used to get nothing shoplifting; the men, perhaps, would notice—the fly-men, as we called them. They used to be too wide-awake for us. **1882** D.J. Cook *Hands Up* 276: The Company sent one of their "fly" men to the place to work up the case. **1894** in Ade *Chicago Stories* 100: Every policeman in uniform and every "fly" man was on the lookout for a murderer. *Ibid.*

117: There is no mistaking the "fly man" from the city hall. **1902** Hapgood *Thief* 44 [ref. to 1883]: I ran up Seventh Avenue, but was caught by a flyman (policeman), and taken to the stationhouse. **1918** Stringer *House of Intrigue* 23: She saw the store "flyman" on her trail.

fly-mug *n.* **1.** (see quot.).
1898 L.J. Beck *Chinatown* 260: Many…would be termed, in Mr. Appo's picturesque lingo, "Fly mugs" (gamblers and sharpers).
2. *Und.* FLY-MAN.
1906 H. Green *Boarding House* 88: The fly mugs. Here's the finish! **1916** *Lit. Digest* (Aug. 19) 53: The minions of the law are also given the following names which are very expressive: "cops," "mugs," "fly mugs," "bulls," "dicks" (an abbreviation for detectives). **1929** Milburn *Hobo's Hornbook* 99: I stayed there and drank till a fly-mug came in,/And he put me to sleep with a sap on the chin. **1930** "D. Stiff" *Milk & Honey* 50: There is the private police force consisting of "fly mugs", "stool pigeons", and "finks". **1931–34** in Clemmer *Pris. Community* 332: Fly mug, *n.* A railroad detective.

flypaper *n.* paper money. *Joc.*
1899 A.H. Lewis *Sandburrs* 82: 'D' bank chucks her a bundle of flypaper big enough to stan' for all her needs until she croaks, for cuttin' in on our play, see!

Flynn *n.* ¶ In phrase: **in like Flynn** quickly or most emphatically in (in any sense).
1945 in *AS* (Dec. 1946) 310: *In like Flynn.* Everything is O.K. In other words, the pilot is having no more trouble than Errol Flynn has in his cinematic feats. **1951** *AS* (May) 99: *In like Flynn.* A phrase describing a [poker] player who calls his bets ahead of a turn. **1953** Eyster *Customary Skies* 43 [ref. to WWII]: So I was in like Flynn. **1956** M. Wolff *Big Nick.* 168: I think your scheme just came in like Flynn. **1959** Murtagh & Harris *Who Live in Shadow* 14: I'm pretty lucky now that I learned to put down the right psychology. I got myself in like Flynn with the coppers and the big boys too. **1966** Jarrett *Private Affair* 28: From then on I was in like Flynn and a convention wasn't complete without Kay Jarrett girls. **1966** Neugeboren *Big Man* 29: Man, I'd be in like Flynn. **1971** Cole *Rook* 161: *Man, when she likes you, you are in like Flynn.* **1971** Sonzski *Punch Goes Judy* 95: I was…in like Flynn [sexually]. **1980** Manchester *Darkness* 181: I wanted to be in like Flynn. **1993** *New York* (Dec. 13) 86: He has no trouble snowing them. Paul flatters their self-esteem, and he's like Flynn.

fly-trap *n.* **1.** the mouth.
*ca1795 M.G. Lewis, in *OED*: The bride shuts her fly trap; the stranger complies. **1839** *Spirit of Times* (Mar. 16) 20: "Look here, Mister, if you don't like the smell of fresh bread, you had better quit the bakery." Well, I tell you, that shut up his fly-trap. **1848** in Blair & Meine *Half Horse* 153: Jest keep that ugly fly-trap o' yourn shut. **1850** in Blair & McDavid *Mirth* 103: So I shut up my fly-trap, and lay low and kept dark! **1882** *United Service* (June) 629: Shut up your fly-trap. **1913** J. London *Valley of Moon* 25: There wouldn't been a peep from my fly-trap. **1919** Darling *Jargon Book* 13: *Fly-trap*—A person's mouth. **1942** Garcia *Tough Trip* 307: I was heard enough of this, now close your fly-trap, Bill. **1977** T. Berger *Villanova* 10: Shut your…flytrap. **1982** Braun *Judas Tree* 40: Close your flytrap and make tracks, or I'm gonna stunt your growth.
2.a. a fly-infested or shabby room, office, or establishment.
1909 "O. Henry," in *OEDS*: Before setting forth to his down town fly-trap. **1922–24** McIntyre *White Light* 23: The tarnished "Flytrap" could not compete with the mirrored elegance of a tea dansant. **1940** Chandler *Farewell, My Lovely* 131: He looked like a waiter in a beachtown fly-trap. **1971** *Go Ask Alice* 70: We took the elevator up to her apartment…After our dirty little fly trap both of us were panting.
b. a dilapidated vehicle.
1944 Ind *Bataan* 284: Our old flytraps are off to cover as far as Lingayen in the northwest.

fly-up-the-creek *n.* a Floridian. [Orig. a name for the green heron; see *DAE*.]
1844 in *DAE*: The inhabitants of…Florida [are called] Fly up the Creeks. **1872, 1888** in *DAE*.

fly wagon *n.* an old or worthless motor vehicle.
1978 Wheeler & Kerby *Steel Cowboy* (film): Do you own four payments on this fly wagon?

FNG *n.* [*fucking new guy*] *Mil.* a newly arrived replacement, esp. in a combat unit. [Quots. ref. to Vietnam War.]
1966 *N.Y. Times Mag.* (Oct. 30) 104: F.N.G. designates a "foolish new guy." **1966** Shepard *Doom Pussy* 217: Major Nails says several FNGs believe it. **1972** T. O'Brien *Combat Zone* 73: Look, FNG, I don't want

to scare you. **1980** M. Baker *Nam* 54: Who the hell was I? This rather quiet, slightly older FNG. **1983** Van Devanter & Morgan *Before Morning* 80: "And what's an FNG?" "What else?…A Fucking New Guy." **1983** Groen & Groen *Huey* 7: Rather than look like FNGs, fucking new guys, including officers, suffered their anxieties quietly. **1985** J. McDonough *Platoon Leader* 65: Despite…his disdain for new guys ("FNGs" he would mutter under his breath),…he was the most respected member in the platoon.

FO *n. & v.* Esp. *Mil.* FUCK-OFF.
1945 *AS* (Dec.) 262: F.O., to avoid work. **1948** *N.Y. Folk. Qly.* (Spring) 20. **1957** E. Brown *Locust Fire* 149 [ref. to WWII]: I'm an R.O., you F.O. **1974** Strasburger *Rounding Third* 132: F.O., Carter. **1978** *UTSQ*: [Go away and stop bothering me] *F.O., get off my case.* **1983** Groen & Groen *Huey* 98: "Just CYA for a few months and then FO." Cover your ass and then fuck off.

foal *n.* an infant. *Joc.*
1972 Wambaugh *Blue Knight* 263: I'm not gonna get involved if you're off somewhere selling your ass in a strange town with a foal kicking around in your belly.

foam *n.* beer; SUDS.
1908 *New Broadway Mag.* (July) 34: I'd rather have foam than bubbles any day. **1916** *Editor* (May 20) 535: *Foam*—beer. **1980** *Nat. Lampoon* (Sept.) 62: The round-trip run to the 7-11 for foam and chips. **1987** D. da Cruz *Boot* 217: Twenty days and I'll be home, drinking foam.

foam domes *n.pl.* a padded brassiere. *Joc.*
1971 Jacobs & Casey *Grease* 29: FRENCHY. I happen to know she wears falsies. SONNY. You oughtta know, Foam-Domes.

foamie *n.* **1.** *Stu.* a beer drinker.
1966 Goldstein *1 in 7* 26: Marijuana users are disdainful of the beer-guzzling element on campus. They call such students "hicks," or "foamies."
2. FOAM DOMES.
1971 Sonzski *Punch Goes Judy* 89: She…frisbeed another of Janet's old foamies.

fob *n.* [fr. *fob* 'to cheat, deceive' < ME *fobben*, cognate with G *foppen* 'to deceive'] a trick or deception.
*1622 in *OED*: Many men would deale more honestly…if these fobs and giggs were not put into their heads by others. ***1654** in *OED*: Such fobbs and cheats are more tollerable…in persons of mean fortunes. ***1698–99** "B.E." *Dict. Canting Crew*: Fob, a cheat, a trick. ***1785** Grose *Vulgar Tongue*: Fob, a cheat, trick, or contrivance. **1848** Judson *Myst. of N.Y.* 62: He come ze fob on some of ze nobilitie.

fob *v.* *Und.* to steal from a fob pocket.
*1889 Barrère & Leland *Dict. Slang* I 377: Fob, to (old cant), to pick a pocket. **1903** in Partridge *Dict. Und.* 260: He declared defiantly that he would learn to "fob" as well as anybody, and he kept his threat. *Ibid.*: "What's fobbin'?" "Switchin' change out o' change pockets." **1930** Irwin *Tramp & Und. Slang*: Fobber. An old pickpocket, or one…able only to steal from outside or fob pockets.

fobby *n.* *Und.* a fob pocket.
1888 (quot. at MOBBY).

fod *n.* [short for *fodder*] food.
1862 in R.G. Carter *4 Bros.* 124: My "fod" (food) had given out in the morning. *Ibid.* 163: We enjoyed that kind of "fod" until our stomachs were not big enough for our eyes.

fodder *v.* to eat; dine.
1836 *Spirit of Times* (Feb. 20) 1: When does the President fodder?

fog *n.* **1.** smoke; (*hence*) steam, as from a locomotive.
*ca1700 in *OED*: Fog, smoke. ***1785** Grose *Vulgar Tongue*: Fog. Smoke. *Cant.* **1937** *AS* (Apr.) 154: Fog. Steam. **1945** Hubbard *R.R. Ave.* 343: Fog—Steam.
2. *Finance.* currency issued by a state bank.
1816 in *DAE*: The secretary of the treasury…permits the debtors in the middle and southern states to discharge theirs in paper "fog," which is depreciated 10 per cent below treasury notes.…southern *fog notes*.
3. foolishness; HOT AIR.
1926 Nason *Chevrons* 125 [ref. to 1918]: "I've got some chewin'," said Jake. "Cigarettes is so much fog."
¶ In phrase:
¶ **pitch a fog** *Black E.* (see quot.).
1945 Drake & Cayton *Black Metropolis* 135: She "pitched a fog" (made a scene). She raved about the fact that I didn't love her and that I played a dirty trick on her. I finally quieted her down and explained things to her.

fog *v.* **1.** *S.W.* to run, gallop, or go at great speed; hasten.—also constr. with *it.*

1893 Wister *Out West* 158: *Texas Vocabulary…To fog* to hurry, to scamper, to go quickly. **1900** *Harper's* (May) 904: Out he comes a-fannin' and a foggin' over the Southern Pacific. **1927–30** Rollins *Jinglebob* 29 [ref. to 1880's]: Here's when they started to fog it. They jumped from a walk right into a run. **1934** Weseen *Dict. Slang* 182: *Fog*—Hasten, as to fog out of bed. **1937** E. Anderson *Thieves Like Us* 14: Stomp it, Chicamaw. Fog right up this line. *a***1949** in Kiskaddon *Rhymes* 29: And you cain't git up to ketch him till he's foggin' down the flat. **1963–64** Kesey *Great Notion* 248: They're foggin' it up the road to beat thunder. **1964** Hill *One of the Casualties* 29: Milton,…you better fog it to town and churn him out. **1973** L'Amour *Ferguson Rifle* 13: A dozen Injuns come foggin' it out of a coulee. **1990** Rukuza *W. Coast Turnaround* 179: The goddam trucker came a' foggin' outta dat fuckin' hospital wit' half the fuckin' town behind him!

2. [cf. SMOKE] *West.* **a.** to fire a weapon.

1904 in "O. Henry" *Works* 832: We fagged [*sic*] 'em a batch of bullets. **1929** *Sat. Eve. Post* (Apr. 13) 54: A man shooting a gun is fogging or smoking. "I fogged away with my heat until I pooped that dummy." **1930** in *DA:* When in doubt they…"came a-foggin'," not waiting for the other party to get into action. **1962** Regan & Finston *Toughest Pris.* 799: *Fog*—To shoot.

b. to shoot (a person).

1913 [W. Dixon] *"Billy" Dixon* 214: The boys opened upon him full blast. They certainly "fogged" him. **1921** A. Jennings *Through Shadows* 64: Marshals in New Mexico fogged us a cargo of lead…as a…salvo of welcome. **1930** *Amer. Mercury* (Dec.) 455: I takes me heat an' fogs 'em. **1946** "J. Evans" *Halo in Blood* 66: She didn't fog him; no.

3. *S.W.* to chase at great speed.

1909 in Monaghan *Schoolboy, Cowboy* 53: I fogged them cattle, an' I fogged 'em hard,/An' I eat sowbelly 'til I shit pure lard. **1914** D.W. Roberts *Rangers* 101 [ref. to 1878]: The robbers…ran into a chaparral thicket and the Rangers kept "fogging" them, until they all quit their horses, and took cover through the thick brush.

4. *Baseball.* to pitch (a fastball).

1942 *ATS* 653: Pitch hard…*fire,…fog.* **1944** F.G. Lieb *Cardinals* 167: Like Dizzy, he could fog 'em through, and make batters look silly. **1946** H.A. Smith *Rhubarb* 26: At such happy moments the opposing pitcher fogged them in, straight down the middle… **1953** in *DAS:* Ole Diz was in his prime then, fogging a fast ball. **1985** Univ. Tenn. instructor, age 37: You remember Ryne Duren? He could really fog 'em in.

5. to subject to hazing.

1947 Motley *Knock on Any Door* 43: Let's fog the new kid.

fogbound *adj.* confused; fuddled; dazed.

1930 *AS* V (Feb.) 238: *Fog-bound:* to be in a dreamy state. "Joe is fogbound most of the time." **1935** E. Anderson *Hungry Men* 105: I'm gettin' fogbound over you, if you want to know. **1941** *Guide to U.S. Naval Acad.* 150: *Fog-bound.* In a daze.

fog-breaker *n.* a bracing drink.

1845 in *DA:* Cold water is his only fog-breaker.

fog-clearer *n.* a bracing drink of liquor.

1844 in *DA:* The farmers up here wouldn't take her ginger-vengeance airly in the morning instead of eye-openers and fog-clearers.

fog-cutter *n.* a bracing drink of liquor. [In modern S.E. use, a type of cocktail made with rum, brandy, gin, orange juice, lemon juice, orgeat syrup, and sherry.]

1832 [M. St.C. Clarke] *Sks. of Crockett* 157: They then take a fog-cutter, [and] eat breakfast. **1835** in *DAE:* Telling him that the internal application of a double fog-cutter, would prove a much more pleasant and effective medicine.

fog dog *n. Naut.* (see quot.). Cf. *S.E. sun dog.*

****1831** (cited in Partridge *DSUE* (ed. 8) 415). **1883** Russell *Sailors' Lang.* 54: *Fog-dog.*—A break in a fog.

fog-driver *n.* a bracing drink of liquor.

1806 in *DA:* I have heard of a *jorum,* of *phlegm-cutter* and *fog-driver.*

fog-eater *n. Av.* a pilot who can easily fly through fog or cloud.

1933 Stewart *Airman Speech* 66: *Fog-Eater.* A pilot good at flying through fog. **1985** Former SP4, U.S. Army: About half-way through my tour in Taiwan [i.e., *ca*1975] I remember Captain Jackson looking out of his helicopter and saying, "I'm a fog-eater; let's get the hell out of here."

fogey var. FOGY.

fog factory *n. Av.* a consistently foggy or cloudy area.

1933 Stewart *Airman Speech* 66: *Fog Factory.* Any sections of the country which are consistent producers of fog.

fogged *adj.* fuddled, as with fatigue or drink; tipsy.—also constr. with *up.*

****1883** in *F & H* III 49: They were all treading on one another's heels, trying to do their best, but hopelessly fogged. ****1887** in *F & H* III: An Australian says that he is bushed just as an Englishman, equally characteristically, declares that he is fogged. **a***1890–93** *F & H* III 49: *Fogged…*(common)….Drunk. **1915** *DN* IV 212: He walks like he might be fogged. **1959** Groninger *Run from Mtn.* 29: I was fogged when I got in bed but I did not want to go to sleep. **1964–70** in *Qly. Jour. Stud. Alcohol* XXXII (1971) 732: *Fogged up.* Intoxicated.

fogger *n. Baseball.* a fastball pitcher.

1937 *N.Y. Daily News* (Jan. 31) (cited in Nichols *Baseball Terminology*). **1939–40** Tunis *Kid from Tomkinsville* 85: Seems to me, Jack, like this fogger out there might turn into something. He seems to have pretty good control for a rookie.

fog goggles *n.pl. Av.* (see quot.). *Joc.*

1945 Hamann *Air Words: Fog goggles.* Radar or terrain clearance indicator.

foggy *adj.* ¶ In phrase: **have the foggiest** to have the least notion.—constr. in negative.

****1917** in *OEDS:* "Wonder who she is."…"Haven't the foggiest." **1961** Kohner *Gidget Goes Hawaiian* 15: "You've no idea?"…"Not the foggiest." *Ibid.* 104: How to *find* him I had not the foggiest. **1979** W. Cross *Kids & Booze* 52: And the next day you haven't the foggiest. **1982** "W.T. Tyler" *Rogue's March* 59: I haven't the foggiest…but I'm sure we'll manage something.

Foggy Bottom *n. Journ. & Pol.* the U.S. Department of State. *Joc.* [Located in Foggy Bottom, a district in Washington, D.C.; as applied to the State Department, the name is employed for its connotations of befuddlement and obscurity.]

[**1947** J. Reston, in *N.Y. Times* (May 25) VI 7: The State Department has moved its principal offices…from Pennsylvania Avenue to Foggy Bottom, which, for the benefit of any cynics, is not an intellectual condition but a geographical area down by the Potomac.] **1950** *Sat. Eve. Post* (July 29) 60: Another reporter asked a taxi driver to take him to Foggy Bottom, as the new State Department Building is known. **1951** *Time* (June 25) 18: Johnson had noted in Foggy Bottom a seeming hostility to Chiang's government. **1955** McGovern *Fräulein* 244: Yet, mused the men of Foggy Bottom unhappily, these were serious times. **1961** *S.F. Examiner* (July 23) 22: He is merely the fall guy of Foggy Bottom. **1968** Safire *New Language of Politics* 150: *Foggy Bottom:* the State Department. **1973** in J.C. Pratt *Vietnam Voices* 280: An area specialist in Foggy Bottom. **1982** in *N.Y. Times Mag.* (Jan. 2, 1983) 15: This philosophy is making for certain changes at Foggy Bottom. *a***1989** R. Herman, Jr. *Warbirds* 72: My contacts over at Foggy Bottom. **1989** Rawson *Wicked Words* 289: *Foggy Bottom…*the U.S. State Department, [was] popularized in 1947 by James Reston of *The New York Times*, but earlier used according to him by Edward Folliard of the *Washington Post.*

foghorn *n.* a tuba or saxophone.

1919 Small *Story of the 47th* 119: Joe extracted his "foghorn" [saxophone] from its unshapely box and proceeded to his place in the ring. **1939** Calloway *Swingformation Bureau:* The fog horn is the…tuba.

fogle *n.* [prob. < G *Vogel* 'bird'; It *foglia* 'leaf' has been suggested (mistranslated as 'pocket'), but it is phonologically unlikely since It /lj/ would not yield E /g/] *Und.* a handkerchief or neckerchief, esp. of silk.

****1811** *Lexicon Balatron.: Fogle.* A silk handkerchief. ****1812** Vaux *Vocab.: Fogle:* a silk handkerchief. ****1820–21** P. Egan *Life in London* 178: Jerry's sneezer was touched with some convulsive efforts so that his *fogle* was continually at work. ****1834** Ainsworth *Rookwood* 178: *Fogles* and *fawnies* soon went their way. ****1837** Dickens *Oliver Twist* ch. xviii: Fogles and tickers…pocket-handkerchiefs and watches. **1842** *Spirit of Times* (May 28) 152: He and all his partizans displayed their silk *fogles* of blue and white spots. **1848** *Ladies' Repository* VIII (Oct.) 315: *Fogle,* A neck handkerchief. ****1857** A. Mayhew *Paved with Gold* 69: Why, they're just made for hooking a fogle out of a clye. **1925** in Partridge *Dict. Und.* 261: *Fogle-getter.* One who steals handkerchiefs or trifles.

fogle-hunter *n. Und.* a handkerchief thief.

*1821 *Real Life in Ireland* 14: They...stuck to him like *fogle-hunters.*
*1827 in *F & H* III 50: The fogle hunters doing their morning fake in the prigging lay. ***1830** in *F & H* III: Who's here so base as would be a fogle-hunter? **1848** *Ladies' Repository* VIII (Oct.) 315: *Fogle hunter,* One who steals handkerchiefs. **1849** [G. Thompson] *Venus in Boston* 43: *Fogle hunters,* (handkerchief thieves). ***1856, *1865** (cited in Partridge *Dict. Und.* 261).

fogmatic *n. & adj.* **1.** *n.* a bracing drink of liquor. Cf. ANTIFOG-MATIC.

   1827 J.F. Cooper *Red Rover* 124: "Bitters," "juleps," "morning drams," "fogmatics," &c.

2. *adj.* tipsy.

   *a***1856** in B. Hall *College Wds.* (ed. 2) 460: We give a list of a few of the various words and phrases which have been in use...to signify some stage of inebriation...high, corned,...fogmatic [etc.].

fogy or **fogey** *n.* [app. of Scots orig.] **1.** a dull or hidebound elderly person.—usu. constr. with *old.* Now *colloq.*

   a*1720** in D'Urfey *Pills* VI 276: I spurr'd my aw'd [*i.e.* old] Nagg *Fogey.* ***1745** in C.H. Wilkinson *King of Beggars* 120: Brush rumley to the Fogy Cull. ***1790** in *OED:* Foggies the zig-zag followers sped. ***1790** in *OED:* Now ilka lad has got a lass,/Save you auld doited fogie. ***1808** Jamieson *Scot. Dict.* II 266: *Foggie, fogie*...Applied, in a general sense, to one advanced in life. ***1828** in *EDD:* Your ne'er-do-weels, your drunken rapscalians, your useless foggies. **1840** *Spirit of Times* (Nov. 21) 446: Your old fogey of a parson. **1847** Strong *Diary* I 303: Such a corps of respectable old fogies. **1854** Doten *Journals* I 190: Let no "old fogy"...turn up his immaculate nose...at what he may term "follies." ***1855** W.M. Thackeray, in *F & H* III 48: And now, a grizzled, grim old fogy, I sit and wait for Bouillabaisse. ***1860** Hotten *Slang Dict.* (ed. 2): *Fogey,* or *old fogey,* a dullard, an old-fashioned or singular person. ***1864** in *F & H* III 48: An old fogey who particularly hated being "*done.*" **1871** Schele de Vere *Amer.* 474: *Fogy*...means, in the United States, mainly an ultra-conservative in politics. It occurs in Scotch as *fogie,* a dull, slow, old man, unable or unwilling to reconcile himself to the ideas and manners of a new generation; in English as *fogey,* a singular, old-fashioned person—popularized by Thackeray. ***1889** Barrère & Leland *Dict. Slang* I 377: *Fogey*...a man becoming stupid with age. **1910** *DN* III 453: He's an old fogy. **1915** *DN* IV 202: *Fogey, fogy, fogay, foggi,* old, eccentric person. "That old fogey is ten years behind the times."

2. *Mil.* a member of a veteran or invalid company, esp. in garrison; (*broadly*) a veteran of long military service.

   *1785 Grose *Vulgar Tongue: Fogey, old fogey,* a nick name for an invalid soldier. ***1808** Jamieson *Scot. Dict.* II 266: *Foggie, fogie*...A term used to denote an invalid, or garrison soldier. ***1812** in *F & H* III 48: My company is now forming into an invalid company. Tell your grandmother we will be like the Castle foggies. **1956** Heflin *USAF Dict.: Fogy, fogey, fogie*...an airman or soldier with long service.

3. *Mil.* a pay increase after a given number of years of service; longevity pay; (see also 1956 quot.). Also (*obs.*) **fogy ration.**

   1879 in *DAE:* Pay...in addition to the fogy ration or longevity ration. **1881** in *DAE: Fogy,* an increase of pay due to length of service. **1891** Kirkland *Capt. of Co. K* 348: This is the height of Mark's ambition...his arm nearly covered with "Service stripes" and his purse overflowing with "fogy rations." **1896** C.C. King *Garrison Tangle* 9: And his pay isn't as big as yours by one fogy. **1907** Moss *Officer's Manual* 243: *Fogey*—Ten per cent increase of pay for each five years' service. **1918** Ruggles *Navy Explained* 61: *Foggy* [*sic*]—Officers, after five years service, receive a bonus from the government of ten per cent in addition to their pay. The bonus is given every five years until 35 per cent is reached. "I have just received my second foggy," an officer might say. **1920** *Am. Leg. Wkly.* (Mar. 26) 2: The old-timer with four fogies to his credit. **1931** Erdman *Reserve Officer's Manual* 436: *Fogey.* An increase in pay after the completion of a period of service. **1943** *Yank* (Feb. 26) 7: Do I pay tax on "Fogey pay" (commission on pay for years of service)? **1956** Heflin *USAF Dict.: Fogy, fogey, fogie*...**2.** an additional amount of money paid for a specified period of service, i.e. longevity pay, also called *fogy pay.* **3.** credit for a specified period of service, as in "He has three fogies." **1963** J. Ross *Dead Are Mine* 269 [ref. to 1944]: A big, fat, loudmouthed topkick drawing plenty of old-fogey pay.

fogy stripe *n. Mil.* a service stripe.

   1956 Heflin *USAF Dict.: Fogy stripe*...a federal service stripe or "hash mark."

folding *n.* paper money; cash. Also **folding stuff.**

   1940 O'Hara *Pal Joey* 161: A handsome wallet stuffed with a liberal supply of folding. **1943** *Billboard* (June 26) 61: She and her husband have been getting folding stuff in large amounts. **1945** *Yank* (Oct. 12) 19: A guy with a bulging pocket of green folding stuff. **1949** R. Chandler *Little Sister* 42: Just put this hunk of the folding back in your saddlebag. **1953** Kramer & Karr *Teen-Age Gangs* 154: And to have fun, you need the folding stuff. **1953** R. Chandler *Goodbye* 88: He must have made plenty of the folding. **1967** Talbot *Chatty Jones* 6: Men...don't mind peeling off a bunch of folding stuff. **1981** Graziano & Corsel *Somebody Down Here* 147: I'm leavin the track after the last race, beat out of all my foldin stuff. **1988** J.S. Young *China Beach* (film): Make the geetus, the folding,...the filthy lucre.

folkie *n.* an entertainer who performs folk music, esp. folk-songs; a devotee of folk music.

   1966 (cited in *W10*). ***1966** in *BDNE* 173. **1968** in *Rolling Stone Interviews* 54: And then there were cats around who were folkies, esoteric folkies, who put blues among other esoteric, ethnic folk music. **1971** *Playboy* (Nov.) 193: The hard-core folkies booed him off the stage. **1983** *Rolling Stone* (Feb. 3) 46: Buckskin folkies like him for *Harvest.* **1988** *Time* (Aug. 29) 73: Rockers always suspected folkies of being sanctimonious. **1990** *Nation* (Oct. 22) 463: A variety of styles, from naive folkie to savvy chanteuse.

folknik *n.* [*folk* + (BEAT)NIK] *Journ.* FOLKIE.

   1958 in *AS* XLI 139: In Greenwich Village...lies the Folklore Center...Invariably, folkniks...are present, for this den is the meeting place and home address for New York's up and coming folksingers and hangers on. **1961** *New Yorker* (ad) (Jan. 28) 81: Everyone is applauding the driving style of these rousing new folknik hipsters. **1961** *N.Y. Times* (Jan. 29) XII 2: This may seem a little tame to those familiar with the frenetic activity of the New York "folkniks." **1963** *Time* (July 26) 39: Peter, Paul and Mary conducting 13,934 folkniks into collective rapture. **1967** Sankey *Golden Screw* 69: The only folkniks at that concert will be standee.

folks *n.pl.* [cf. FAMILY] *Und.* a fellow criminal or criminals.

   1927 *AS* II (June) 385 [ref. to 1880's or 90's]: A gang of yeggs was generally known as *the folks.* Sometimes they were called the *Johnson Boys,* from the "Johnson-bar" the reverse lever of the locomotive of those days; yeggs used a tool somewhat similar to it. **1940** Burnett *High Sierra* 14: Well, keep your baby-blue eyes on him. He's folks.

fongoo var. FUNGOO.

fonk var. FUNK.

fonky var. FUNKY.

foodaholic *n.* a person who overeats compulsively. Orig. *Joc.* Also **foodoholic.**

   1965 in *AS* XLIX 176: Are you a foodoholic suffering from creeping overweight? **1975** *Cosmopolitan* (Aug.) 48: My name is Alan Sues and I am a foodaholic. **1980** *Nat. Lampoon* (Aug.) 41: She is not a foodaholic, he adds, she is a pig. **1987** R. Miller *Slob* 150: She would eventually learn to anticipate the way a foodaholic looks forward to the next banana split.

foodie *n.* a person keenly interested in food, esp. in eating or cooking.

   *1982 in *OED2:* The [colour] supplements encouraged the foodie movement. **1984** L.A. man, age *ca*40: I've never seen so many dedicated foodies. **1987** *RHD2.* **1989** *Psychology Today* (Dec.) 29: Those thick, creamy desserts that foodies scarf down after dutifully taking their greens and mineral water.

fooey var. PHOOEY.

foo fighter *n.* [*foo* (a nonsense word used in the comic strip "Smoky Stover") + *fighter*] *USAF.* any unidentifiable light encountered by aircrews during combat operations in WWII and presumed to be a German secret weapon. Now *hist.* [1969 quot. is applied to an actual jet or rocket plane.]

   1945 *N.Y. Times* (Jan. 2): "There are three kinds of these lights we call *foofighters,*" Lieutenant Donald Meiers of Chicago said. "One is red balls of fire which appear off our wing tips and [others] fly in front of us, and the third is a group of about fifteen lights which appear off in the distance—like a Christmas tree in the air—and flicker on and off." **1945** *Amer. Legion Mag.* (Dec.): The Foo Fighter Mystery....The foofighters simply disappeared when Allied ground forces captured the area east of the Rhine. This was known to be the location of many German experimental stations. **1947** *Houston Post* (July 7): Charles Odom, former B-17 pilot...describes his encounters with "foo fighters" over Germany during the fall and winter of 1944–45....They "looked like crystal balls, clear, about the size of basketballs" and were seen often over Vienna, Munich, and other larger target areas. **1955** Jessup *Case for UFO* 144: Followers of *flying saucers* are well acquainted with the "Foo Fighters" reported so extensively during World War II. **1959** Jung *Flying Saucers* 20: Reports about "Foo fighters," i.e. lights that accompanied the Allied bombers over Germany (Foo = *feu*). *__1964__ *Flying Saucer Review* (Jan.) 16: What appear to be diffuse luminous objects, similar to…ball-lightning, behave as if they were under intelligent control. Classical observations of this type are the so-called "foo-fighters." **1969** Coppel *Little Time for Laughter* 200 [ref. to 1944]: He could hear the wild chatter on the radio. The pilots were saying something about a "foo fighter" and a "jet."

foofoo *n.* **1.** a soft, weak, or effeminate fellow; sissy; (*obs.*) a fool. Also as quasi-adj. Also vars.

1848 Baker *Glance at N.Y.* 16: Them's foo-foos…A foo-foo, or outsider, is a chap wot can't come de big figure. **1850** "N. Buntline" *G'hals of N.Y.* 17: Moll, you're a fou-fou…to go on an' keep us all in this 'ere starvin' way. **1855** Whitman *Leaves of Grass* 46: Washes and razors for foofoos…for me freckles and a bristling beard. **1877** Bartlett *Amer.* (ed. 4) 229: *Foo Foo.* In New York, a term of contempt, nearly equivalent to "small potatoes," a man not worth notice. **1905** Hobart *Search Me* 51: That duck isn't a critic, he's only a Foofoo…A Foofoo is something that tried to happen and then lost the address. *__1929__ Bowen *Sea Slang* 54: *Fu-fu.*…anybody inefficient at sea. **1968** Baker et al. *CUSS* 123: *Fuu-Fuu.* An obnoxious person. **1971** Pvt., U.S. Army (coll. J. Ball): One more week of this shit and I'll go foofoo. The guys will start lookin' good to me. **1988** Knoxville, Tenn., shopkeeper, age *ca*30: You better watch out for them foofoos. "Elbows out, girls!"

2. Esp. *Navy.* cologne, perfume, shaving lotion, etc. Also vars.

1928 *AS* II 453: *Foo foo*—Perfume. **1933** *Leatherneck* (Jan.) 13: "Willie"…Morrison, with a new bottle of fu-fu and a hashmark. **1938** in *AS* (Feb. 1939) XIV 77: *Foo Foo.* Perfume. **1941** Kendall *Army & Navy Slang* 19: *Foo foo*…perfume. **1942–48** in *So. Folk. Qly.* XIII (1949) 204: Liberal application of *fou-fou* (after-shave talc, lotions, pomades, etc.). **1958** Cope and Dyer *Petty Officer's Guide* (ed. 2) 346: *Foofoo:* (Slang). Face lotion or hair tonic. **1961** Davis *Marine at War* 172: The hair oil and lotion which Marines call "foo-foo" and love to smear on themselves. **1984** K. Weaver *Texas Crude* 113: You smell like a French whore with all that foo-foo on.

foofoo band *n.* *Naut.* an impromptu band formed from a ship's crew.

1905 *Bluejacket* (Feb.) 146: [The USS *Tacoma's*] "foo-foo" band of eighteen pieces played. **1913–14** London *Elsinore* 312: A full-fledged "foo-foo" band makes most of the day and night hideous. *__1949__ W. Granville *Sea Slang* 101: *Foofoo band*…A band made up of whatever instruments are possessed by the ship's company.

foofoo powder *n.* talcum powder; (*broadly*) any sort of powder. Also vars. Cf. FOOFOO, 2.

1918 *Stars & Stripes* (Apr. 12) 8: Thuh other day one o' thuh cooks spilt a can o' this here "frou-frou" powder in the cocoa. **1935** *Our Army* (July) 24: Don't ever put that fufu powder on me! *__a1961__ Partridge *DSUE* (ed. 5) 1094: *Foo-foo.* Talcum powder: pejorative: since *ca*1920. *__a1967__ Partridge *DSUE* (ed. 6) 1126: *Foo-foo powder.* Talcum powder, used a great deal by sailors in the tropics…: Naval lowerdeck: since *ca*1930. *a*1972 B. Rodgers *Queens' Vernacular* 84: *Foo-foo dust*…any powder: baby powder, antilouse powder dusted upon new prisoners, chalk powder, etc.

foofoo water *n.* FOOFOO, 2. Also **foofoo juice.**

1923 *Our Navy* (June 16) 21: The salty old bird [was] scented with "foo-foo" water. **1971** Georgia woman, age *ca*40: Gotta put on some foofoo juice. **1974** *Sanford & Son* (NBC-TV): What's that stuff you got on you, that foofoo juice? **1976–79** Duncan & Moore *Green Side Out* xxii: *Foo foo juice*—Aqua Velva aftershave lotion. Standard toiletry for Marines of other times.

foo gas *n.* [folk ety. fr. *fougasse* 'a kind of land mine'] *Army.* a mixture of explosives and gasoline buried in large drums to be detonated in defense of a perimeter. [Quots. ref. to Vietnam War.]

1978 Downs *Killing Zone* 20: Foo Gas was fifty-gallon drums filled with explosives and napalm and buried at strategic places in the perimeter. **1980** M. Baker *Nam* 202: Fu-gas is the best.…You take gasoline and you pour soap into it.…Then…you take a Thermit grenade and…a stick of dynamite.…The dynamite pushes the gasoline up, then the Thermit ignites it.

fool *n.* a person who is excessively dedicated to a given activ-ity.—usu. constr. with prec. ppl.

[**1875** in *DAE*: A Fool for Luck.] **1913–15** Van Loan *Taking the Count* 176: He's the fightin'est little fool 'at ever pulled on a glove. **1918** *Lit. Digest* (Sept. 28) 65: Yanks; you're fighting fools. I'm for you. **1927** *S.F. Examiner* (May 22) 1: Capt. Charles Lindbergh, the intrepid "Flyin' Fool" from St. Louis, Missouri, landed here tonight at 10:22 Paris time. **1929** Shay *Drawn from Wood* 47: Born in the saddle and ridin' fools…we're cut-throats and hellers, we're whoopers and yellers. **1938** "E. Queen" *4 Hearts* 47: He can fly like a fool, and that's a sweet ship he's got. **1953** *I Love Lucy* (CBS-TV): I'm a dancing *fool!* **1987** Zeybel *Gunship* 127: He's a flying fool. Definitely, the best.

fool farm *n.* FOOLISH FACTORY.

1968 "R. Hooker" *MASH* 162: His wife had folded and been placed in a private fool farm.

foolish factory *n.* a psychiatric hospital.

1910 in Blackbeard & Williams *Smithsonian Comics* 56: If we could only be sure Desmond wasn't around, we could enjoy this "foolish factory" more. **1936** Duncan *Over the Wall* 58: The old guys moving…to the foolish factory across the way.

foolish house *n.* FOOLISH FACTORY.

1901 Hobart *John Henry* 17: She hadn't time to decide that I ought to be on my way to a foolish house. **1904** Hobart *Missouri* 68: Where's the medal you got for keepin' out of the Foolish House? **1905** Hobart *Get Next!* 49: If things go on in this way I think this will soon develop into a foolish house! **1907** in "O. Henry" *Works* 212: They took him to the foolish house in August. **1910** Service *Trail of '98* 22: It's that that makes me fit for the foolish house. **1911–12** Ade *Knocking the Neighbors* 200: She is a raving Beetle.…She is a Candidate for Padded Cell No. 1 in the big Foolish House.

foolish powder *n.* *Narc.* powdered heroin or cocaine.

1930 Irwin *Tramp & Und. Sl.: Foolish Powder*…Orginally [*sic*], heroin; more lately, any narcotic which robs the user of his senses and judgment. **1930** *Amer. Mercury* (Dec.) 455: *Foolish powder, n.:* Heroin. "The mutts bang up on foolish powder an' go one the hist." **1934** Weseen *Dict. Slang* 14: *Foolish powder*—Heroin; any drug.

¶ In phrase:

¶ **take a foolish powder** to do something that causes one to act foolishly.

1899 Kountz *Baxter's Letters* 33: She must have taken a foolish powder…just before she left home, as she was clean to the bad. **1901** Oliver *Roughing It* 38: You have taken a foolish powder and no mistake. **1912** Field *Watch Yourself* 226: So don't take a foolish powder kase a preacher workin' at his trade handed ye a few.

foolish ward *n.* *Hosp.* a psychiatric ward.

1907 in H.C. Fisher *A. Mutt* 6: Mr. A. Mutt…Winds Up in Foolish Ward.

foolish water *n.* **1.** champagne.

1907 in H.C. Fisher *A. Mutt* 4: Start cooling another case of "foolish water."

2. [perh. orig. pidgin] *West.* whiskey. Now *hist.*

1936 *Chrons. of Okla.* XIV (Sept.) 331: The Indians' name for whiskey [was] "foolish water." **1976** J. Healey *Buffalo War* 49: The Kiowas and Comanches acquired their "foolish water" mainly from the New Mexican Comancheros.

fool-killer *n.* **1.** (*occ. cap.*) "an imaginary character whose business it is to exterminate fools"—*DA.*—sometimes cap. *Joc.*

1853 in *DA:* What a fool-killer he would make! *a*1860 [J. Jones] *Marie* 19: If I ain't game for the fool-killer, there's no snakes in old Virginny. **1927** in *DARE:* If the Fool killer came along, the town would be empty. **1939** in *DARE:* Whenever he heard of the death of somebody he didn't like, he'd say, "Well, the Fool-Killer's come for so-and-so." **1948** in *DA.* **1974** in *DARE:* During the 1850's, a stout little man…got so tired of the fools in North Carolina that he…got himself a big club. Then, whenever he met up with a fellow saying or doing a silly, foolish thing, he pounded the rascal to the ground. Today there are wise citizens in North Carolina hoping for the Fool Killer to return.

2. something that can kill or injure an unwary person; (*specif.,* in 1902, 1968 quots.) a cigarette.

1902 Swift *Iowa Boy* 298: One minute, laddie, till I light up another fool-killer. **1947** in *DA:* A fool-killer…was a live tree bent over by a fallen one so that when an unwary chopper drove an axe into it the tremendous tension, suddenly released, sent the tree splitting and charging up to catch him under the chin. **1950** in *DARE: Fool killer.* A piece of equipment which is unsafe. **1968** in *DARE: Nicknames for cigarettes*...Foolkillers. **1984** in *DARE: Fool killers*. Dead limbs that can become dislodged when a tree is cut and cause fatal injuries to a careless sawyer.

foop *n.* a stuffy or unpleasant person.

1961–65 M. Howard *Bridgeport* 120: I do have you poor foops scared.

¶ In phrase:

¶ **in one swell foop** [intentional spoonerism] in one fell swoop. *Joc.*

1972 N.Y.U. prof., age *ca*45: You can't do it in just one swell foop. **1980** L.N. Smith *Venus Belt* 128: Figure'd I'd just finish off the list in one swell foop. **1981** *N.Y. Times* (Aug. 23) IV 5: In one swell foop! **1986** R. Zumbro *Tank Sgt.* 114 [ref. to 1967–68]: You have to pull it in, in one swell foop!

foot *n.* **1.** *Sports.* speed or stamina in running.

1842 *Spirit of Times* (Sept. 3) 318: He has plenty of "pluck," lots of "foot."

2. a rejection, dismissal, discharge, etc.—constr. with *the*.

*a***1904–11** Phillips *Susan Lenox* II 119: You've got to have the mon. or you get the laugh and the foot—the swift, hard kick. **1912–14** in O'Neill *Lost Plays* 185: Some nerve to that greaser chicken giving a real white man the foot! **1951** Thacher *Captain* 104: His girl gave him the foot.

3. *Auto Racing.* **a.** (see quot.).

1968 Ainslie *Racing Guide* 467: *Foot—Speed...Early foot—*Good speed at beginning of race.

b. (see quot.).

1980 Pearl *Pop. Slang* 53: *Foot n....*(Sports) a driver of a race car.

¶ In phrases:

¶ **feet dry** *Naval Av.* (of an aircraft) in flight over land. [Orig. radiocommunications code.]

1969 Cagle *Naval Av. Guide* 393: "*Feet Dry*" A report made by a pilot flying from a carrier to the beach when he reaches the coastline. **1984** Cunningham & Ethell *Fox Two* 38: No one broke radio silence as we went "feet dry." **1986** Coonts *Intruder* 4: Devil Five Oh Five is feet dry. **1988** *Supercarrier* (ABC-TV): Roger. Feet dry. *a***1989** R. Herman, Jr. *Warbirds* 230: They were feet dry and in bad-guy land—Iran.

¶ **feet wet** *Naval Av.* (of an aircraft) in flight over an ocean or other large body of water. [Orig. radiocommunications code.]

1966 F. Elkins *Heart of Man* 20: The pilot...struggled to the feet-wet point. **1979** D.K. Schneider *AF Heroes* 20: We are...heading out feet wet. **1984** Trotti *Phantom* 22: Just get on and off target in a hurry and out feet wet (over the ocean) at the coast so you don't get in the way. *Ibid.* 80: Tricky, Boilerplate flight off target heading feet wet. *Ibid.* 168: How about holding feet wet while I find something for you to do. **1988** *World News Sunday* (ABC-TV) (July 3): Flights come feet wet out of Iran very quickly.

¶ **my [or your] foot!** (used to express strong negation or disbelief). Now *colloq.*

1921 "M. Brand" *Black Jack* 41: Standards your foot! *****1923** in *OEDS*: Honest your foot! *****1925** in *Ibid.* It indicates a small mind....Small mind my foot! **1936** "E. Queen" *Halfway House* 9: "That Curry case was a lucky break." "Lucky your foot!" **1980** Sobol *Brown Carries On* 23: A lion on the loose, my foot! **1988** *Larry King Live* (CNN-TV) (July 27): "It's so sad that—" "Sad my foot!"

¶ **pull foot** to start on one's way; get going.

1775 in Whiting *Early Amer. Prov.* 163: The cruisers all pulled foot and harbored. *****1821** *Real Life in Ireland* 309: Pull foot, and make no delay. **1825** in *F & H* III 54: How they pulled foot when they seed us commin'. **1837** *Every Body's Album* II 29: Hurra! Keep a toddling—pull foot for the watch. **1848** in Lowell *Poetical Works* 216: Pomp...jest grabbed my [wooden] leg, an' then pulled foot, quicker an' you could wink. **1854** "Youngster" *Swell Life at Sea* 14: Set *our* royal-studdin'-sails, and sky-sails, Mr. Garnet—we'll pull foot. **1891** Maitland *Slang Dict.* 212: *Pull foot* (Am.), to start off rapidly, to run. **1924** Nason *Three Lights* 28: Go on! Git! Pull foot!

¶ **sure as you're [or I'm] a foot high** most assuredly.

1882 in Sweet *Sweet's Texas* 32: Indian's been here last night, sure's you're a foot high. **1883** Sweet & Knox *Mustang* 78: Dis yere ole darkey knows what he am a talkin' 'bout, sure's yo' a foot high. **1911** *Hampton's Mag.* (Feb.) 189: I'd alienate the party as sure as you're a foot high. **1912** Lowrie *Prison* 95: I'll put you both in the morgue as sure as I'm a foot high. **1952** A. Sheekman *Young Man with Ideas* (film): That's a time bomb as sure as I'm a foot high!

¶ **throw (one's) feet, 1.** to walk or tramp; (among tramps) to go in search of work, food, etc.

1895 (quot. at STIFF, *n.*). **1902** "J. Flynt" *Little Bro.* 199: It was only necessary to tell him that they were nearing the famous "swimming place" to make him "throw his feet" the harder. **1907** London *Road* 51 [ref. to *ca*1894]: I was as good a hustler as ever "threw his feet." **1914** *Sat. Eve. Post* (Apr. 4) 10: He don't have to throw his feet. He can beg coin enough to keep him in booze regularlike. *Ibid.* 11: Got to throw your feet if yuh want scoffin's. **1919** S. Lewis *Free Air* 339: You'd 'a' died laughing to seen him throw my feet for grub. **1925** Mullin *Scholar Tramp* 13: "It's about time to ditch the old bus and throw our feet for breakfast in Toledo," yawned Frisco....Now, when a hobo sallies out to beg food, his peregrinations in quest of it are known on the Road as throwing his feet. Its application is special. A hobo throws his feet for food—and for food only. **1980** Bruns *Kts. of Road* 17: It gave him a legitimate excuse...for "throwing the feet."

2. to dance. Also **shake a foot.**

1863 in *Del. Hist.* XXI (1984) 92: One beating time and singing while the other "shake out de feet." **1927** E.C.L. Adams *Congaree* 2: Time dat nigger hit heben he hit it a throwin' them foots an' shoutin'.

footback *n.* [*foot* + horse*back*] ¶ In phrase: **on footback** on foot. Also as adj.

*****1589** in *OED*: Beggers [have forgot] that ever they carried their fardles on footback. *****a***1625** in *Ibid.*: Like St. George...Running a footback from the furious dragon. *****1630** in *Ibid.*: Footback trotting Travellers. **1846** in *Ill. Hist. Soc. Jour.* (Summer 1953) 152: In a few days we expect to march (on foot back) to Tampico. **1863** in Benson *Civil War Book* 49: When I saw him he was "footback," with no sword and a gun on his shoulder, trying to straighten out the line. **1862–64** Noel *Campaign* 30: Those of us who brought up the rear on "foot back." *a***1867** in G.W. Harris *Lovingood* 59: He...cum tu Knoxville a footback. **1898** Green *Va. Folk-speech* 147: *Footback, n.* On foot. **1907** in "O. Henry" *Works* 1514: Enough of the footback life for me. **1947-53** Guthrie *Seeds* 342: A rather long footback journey it would be.

football *n.* **1.** *Mil.* a cannonball.

*a***1875** Williams *Black Cruiser* 50: A shot from the schooner came flying over our heads...."That ere football was plaguy near," said Tom Harding.

2. *Army.* a fragmentation grenade.

1961 J. Jones *Thin Red Line* 130 [ref. to WWII]: Eggs! Eggs! Footballs! Footballs!

3. *Narc.* a football-shaped tablet or capsule of a psychotropic drug.

1965 Vermes *Helping Youth* 119: Benzedrine drugs...are also known as..."Footballs." **1965–66** in Maurer *Lang. Und.* 301: *Football.* A type of encapsulated amphetamine...or mescaline. **1962–68** B. Jackson *In the Life* 236: And we had cube morphine, footballs, quarter-grains and sixteenths of Dilaudid. **1968** Louria *Drug Scene* 208: *Footballs:* a combination of dextroamphetamine and amphetamine. *a***1969** B. Jackson *Thief's Primer* 57: *Footballs...*Dilaudid (Knoll Pharmaceutical Company brand name for hydromorphine). **1971** J. Brown & A. Groff *Monkey* 58 [ref. to 1940's]: I would shoot those "footballs"—1/2 grain [of Dilaudid]—by the hatful. **1972** Eble *Campus Slang* (Oct. 1972) 2: *Footballs*—biphetamine.

4. *Pol. & Mil.* (see 1968 quot.). [Cf. the use in the 1959 film comedy *The Mouse That Roared* of an actual football, equipped with wire coils, to represent a doomsday weapon.]

1968 Safire *New Lang. of Politics* 151: A new, more ominous use of "football" refers to the small, thirty-pound metal suitcase containing codes that can launch a nuclear attack. It is carried by a military aide to the President and follows the Chief Executive wherever he goes. **1971** *New Yorker* (Jan. 9) 56: Wherever the President travels, he is shadowed by "the man with the football," an individual whose single function is to carry a bag holding a variety of codes that pertain to the release—or recall—of one or more nuclear bombs. **1982** Woodruff & Maxa *At White House* 10: The ever-present military aide with the "football,"...a black bag that contains top secret military and communication codes that follows the President wherever he goes, to be used in the event of a national security crisis. **1982** *Time* (Mar. 29) 18: Their other responsibility: not to drop the briefcase. Hence its irreverent nickname—"the football." **1991** *Newsweek* (Sept. 2) 57: [The] briefcase containing launch codes for Soviet missiles—"the football," as Americans say.

footie *n.* FOOTSIE. Also redup.

1921 Benét *Beginning of Wisdom* 115 [ref. to 1915]: Playing "footie" with the jitney *demi-vierges* of New Haven was a Freshman sport he had always drawn away from with supercilious distaste. **1930** in Perelman *Old Gang* 118: Yet you think nothing of playing footie with the *haut monde*. **1932** Behrman *Biography* 285: Well, if a brilliant and beautiful woman who has played footie with royalty in the capitals of the world loved him, maybe there's a secret charm in him that I've overlooked. **1945** S. Lewis *C. Timberlane* 300: Fellow, you got to do something about Bradd and your wife....They're playing a little too much footie-footie. **1945** *Yank* (Sept. 21) 10: Nothing more serious than a little footie-footie. **1948** J.H. Burns *Lucifer* 387: Buddy and Midgie were sitting close together, playing footie-footie with their loafers.

foot-in-mouth disease *n.* [pun on *hoof-and-mouth disease* and colloq. *put (one's) foot in (one's) mouth*] *Pol. & Journ.* (see 1968 quot.).

1968 Safire *New Lang. of Politics* 151: *Foot-in-mouth disease:* tendency to blunder when ad-libbing; errorprone. **1978** *Business Week* (Jan. 30) 41: A period when foot-in-mouth disease is endemic in the Carter Administration. **1983** L. Wachtel, on WINS Radio News (Dec. 12): A leaning on the part of the administration team on foot-in-mouth disease. **1990–93** M. Moore *Woman at War* 168: I learned a long time ago I have foot-and-mouth disease, so I plan on keeping my mouth shut.

foot juice *n.* [alluding to the trampling of wine grapes to extract the juice] cheap wine.

1925-26 Black *You Can't Win* 153 [ref. to 1890's]: "Foot juice" or "red ink" as the winos called it.

Foot, Leggit and Walker's Line *n. Army.* (used allusively to refer to marching or to the infantry in general). *Joc.* Cf. FOOT'S HORSE.

1891 Kirkland *Captain of Co. K* 89 [ref. to Civil War]: I didn't enlist to be a pack-horse on Foot, Leggit and Walker's Line. *Ibid.* 177: "Foot, Leggit and Walker's line again," they said.

footlocker cocktail *n. Army.* a makeshift substitute for an alcoholic drink.

1944 Kendall *Service Slang* 7: *Footlocker cocktail.*...lemon extract substituting for liquor. **1956** Boatner *Military Customs* 125: *Footlocker cocktail.* A drink concocted by certain desperate soldiers from toilet preparations (after-shave lotion, etc.) and liquid shoe polish (by straining through bread.)

footpad *n.* [fr. the colloq. sense 'highwayman'] *Confed. Army.* an infantryman.

1862-64 Noel *Campaign* 22: The cavalry commands moved off at a brisk pace, followed by the artillery, close behind which came the "foot pads," as they designed to call themselves. *Ibid.* 30: The broken down "foot pad" hove in sight of the noble Rio Grande.

foot-pounder *n. Army.* FOOT-SLOGGER.

1986 R. Zumbro *Tank Sgt.* 245 [ref. to 1967–68]: *Foot-Pounder* Infantry-man (slang).

foot queen *n. Homosex.* (see quot.).

1972 *Anthro. Linguistics* (Mar.) 102: *Foot Queen* (n.): One who derives sexual pleasure from looking at, fondling or using his mouth or tongue on someone else's feet.

foots *n.pl. Theat.* footlights.

1919 *Variety* (Mar. 28) 10: Seated high up above the "foots." **1941** "G.R. Lee" *G-String* 50: Then we get our warning in the foots.

foot-shaker *n. Army.* FOOT-SLOGGER.

1907 *McClure's Mag.* (Feb.) 381: There was a whole regiment of foot-shakers in camp, a battery with one of them old-time Napoleon field-pieces and a Gat, and another big troop of cavalry.

Foot's horse *n.* (see 1890–93 quot.).

*1823 "J. Bee" *Slang Dict.*: To travel by Foot's horse. **1883** in *DAE*: The privilege of taking this trip on "foot's horse." *1890–93 F & H* III 54: To take Mr. Foot's horse...(old.)—To walk; to go by *Shank's mare.*

footsie *n.* ¶ In phrase: **play footsie** [or **footsies**] **[with], a.** to express affection by using the foot to caress another's foot and ankle, esp. surreptitiously, as under a table.

1944 in *OED2*: I played footsie with her during Don José's first seduction by Carmen. **1965–66** Pynchon *Crying* 19: They went to lunch. Roseman tried to play footsie with her under the table. **1966** "Petronius" *N.Y. Unexp.* 6: Secluded footsies, kneesies and thighsies out of the park. **1984** Caunitz *Police Plaza* 38: Marcia caught him playing footsy with the girlfriend under the kitchen table. **1988** *Daily Beacon* (Univ. Tenn.) (Mar. 1) 7: Two drinks, and they're playing "footsie" under the table.

b. to parry arguments without coming to a point; to behave coyly; to waste time.

1951 Bowers *Mob* (film): Let's stop playing footsie with each other. You're a cop working out of the Sixth Precinct. **1953** Petry *Narrows* 279: You been playing footsie with [your job] for months now. **1954** Sherdeman *Them* (film): We're grown up. There's no reason to play footsie with us. In fact, we resent it. **1964** Caidin *Everything But Flak* 136: We were eager to have at it, instead of playing footsy with the customs people. **1974** A. Bergman *Big Kiss-Off* 119: We're sitting around playing footsie. I ask a question and get a tap dance in return.

c. to curry favor or cooperate surreptitiously or shamefully with.

[1935 S. Lewis *Can't Happen* 232: My, my, Doremus, ain't we had fun, Lindy and you, playing footie-footie these last couple years.] **1954** in Rowan *Go South* 20: Mayor Edmond Orgill has been playing "footsie" with Memphis' negro population. **1954** Schulberg *Waterfront* 232: "Accepting bribes," Father Barry explained. "Playing footsie with the boss stevedores." **1966** Susann *Valley of Dolls* 278: Imagine the deals I have to make and the footsies I have to play. **1967** Spillane *Delta* 74: He was playing footsies with the Reds. **1988** M. Maloney *Thunder Alley* 187: The Grays and the Aggressors are playing footsies.

footslogger *n. Mil.* an infantry soldier.

*1894 in *OED2*: Some of the Johannesburg "Foot-Sloggers"...were doing damage in the village. **1918** Penner et al. *120th Field Artillery* 256: They were "our boys"—our own old footsloggers. **1928** Dolph *Sound Off!* 556: Those foot-sloggers out in the Cuartel del España are plain, hard men who like their songs and whisky straight. **1940** Hartney *Up & At 'Em* 34: How sorry I felt for the small detachment of foot-sloggers at one corner of the field, wearily drilling as I had done for so many months. **1955** Post *Little War* 68 [ref. to 1898]: But no one could keep up with those damned staff horses who set the pace for us foot sloggers. **1960** Leckie *March to Glory* 16: In winter the Chinese footslogger wears a heavy quilted cotton uniform over his summer dress. **1961** Joswick & Keating *Combat Cameraman* 120: Those poor devil foot-sloggers ain't got a chance! **1966** Derrig *Pride of Green Berets* 249: What the hell you been doing, Tiny? Making like a footslogger?

footstool *n.* [sugg. by Isaiah 66:1, "Thus saith the Lord, The heaven is my throne, and the earth is my footstool"] the earth. *Joc.*

a1817 in *DAE*: We felt a total superiority to all the humble beings who were creeping on the footstool beneath. **1859** in *Ibid.*: I would give that power to no President—none that has ever stood upon this footstool. **1877** Bartlett *Amer.* (ed. 4) 229: *Footstool.* The earth. An irreverent familiarization of Isaiah lxvi.1. **1877** E. Wheeler *Deadwood Dick, Prince of the Road* 80: Ter be sure ther Lord manyfactered this futstool in seven days. **1879** Tourgee *Fool's Errand* 104: There was never a kindlier...people on the footstool, than those of Verdenton. **1891** in *OED*: I found Mauchline to be the most God-forsaken place on the footstool. **1906** in *DAE*: This New York of ours, regarded by many as the wickedest city on the footstool.

footwarmer *n. CB.* a linear amplifier used with a CB radio.

1973 Montpelier, Vt., man, age 22: A footwarmer is an illegal amplifier used to boost the wattage of a CB. **1975** Dills *CB Slanguage* 34: Foot warmer. Linear amplifier.

foot-wobbler *n. Mil.* an infantry soldier.

*1785 Grose *Vulgar Tongue:* Foot warbler [*sic*]. A contemptuous appellation for a foot soldier, commonly used by the cavalry. **1882** *United Service* (Apr.) 440: Such derogatory epithets applied to the infantry by the cavalry,—as "mud-mushers," "foot-wobblers," etc.

footy *n.* [orig. unkn.] a silly or foolish person; (*also*) an error.

1877 Bartlett *Amer.* (ed. 4) 230: *Footy; fouty.* A mistake; a simpleton; a blunderer; any one slightly valued. Local in Massachusetts. **1889** Barrère & Leland *Dict. Slang* I 379: *Footy* (American and English), a foolish person, a "goose," a "coot."

footy-footy *n.* FOOTSIE.

1935 (quot. at *play footsie* [*with*], c., s.v. FOOTSIE). **1953** in Hemingway *Sel. Letters* 807: I cannot help out very much with the true dope on God as I have never played footy-footy with him.

foozle *n.* [fr. dial. G (see FOOZLE, *v.*); perh. infl. by *fossil*] **1.** a fool, esp. a foolish elderly person.

1855 M. Thomson *Doesticks* 255: Two old foozles in white neckcloths and no collars. *Ibid.* 257: One of the old foozles now wanted to talk spirit. *1860 in *OED*: Have we not almost all learnt these expressions of old foozles? *1867 in *F & H* III 55: Frumps and foozles in Eaton Square. *a1889* in Barrère & Leland *Dict. Slang* I 380: *Foozle* (American), a man who is easily humbugged, a fool. *a*1890–93 *F & H* III 55: *Foozle*…A bore; a fogey; and (in America) a fool. **1898** Westcott *David Harum* 247: He was a slow, putterin' kind of an ole foozle.

2. Orig. *Golf.* a bungled stroke; (*hence*) an error in baseball; a blunder of any kind.

*1869 in P. Davies *Dict. Golfing* 68: Fowls a la Foozle. *1886 in *Ibid.*: The *sclaff,* the *foozle,…*/The ups and downs of this dear game. *1890 in *OED*: On the very rare occasions on which he made a foozle. *1891 in *Ibid.*: A "carry" of a quarter of a mile would be a mere "foozle" to him. **1903** C.E. Stewart *Uncle Josh* 92: I jist whaled away at that durned little [golf] ball, and by gum I missed it, and the boys all commenced to holler "foozle." **1908** in Fleming *Unforget. Season* 43: Nearly everybody contributed a foozle to the lost cause. **1914** Z. Grey *Western Stars* 198: We've gone an' made a foozle right at the start. **1927** *AS* (Feb.) 255: A "*foozle*" [in baseball], as in golf, is a bungled play. **1957** in P. Davies *Dict. Golfing* 68: Lost balls,…*fluffs, foozles*—all the irritations in the book.

foozle *v.* [< dial. G *fusel[n]* 'to work in a slapdash way'] **1.** to act foolishly; fool (around).

1861 Stowe *Orr's Island* II 106: Sally Kittridge may think he's goin' to have her because he's been foozling round with her all summer.

2. *Golf.* to bungle (a stroke); (*hence*) to bungle; botch.

*1888 in *F & H* III 55: Park foozled his second stroke. *1892 in *OED*: You "will" your opponent to foozle his tee shot. **1896** F.P. Dunne in Schaaf *Dooley* 175: Foozled his approach. **1898** Dunne *Peace & War* 27: We foozled our approach at Bull R-run. **1900** Bangs *Acre Hill* 101: Brinley took his eye off the ball to look indignantly upon his wife, and consequently foozled. **1900–01** in R. Glanz *Jew in Early Humor* 90: He don't foozle much in his [business]. **1925** in Mencken *New Lttrs.* 187: If he foozles it I suggest a new firm. **1931** in Robinson *Comics* 39: If I foozle this, the jig is up.

fopdoodle *n.* a blockhead or fop. *Rare* in U.S.

*16.. in *OED*: Bee blith Fopdoudells. *1664 in *OED*: Where sturdy Butchers broke your Noddle,/And handl'd you like a Fop-doodle. *1689 in *F & H* III 55: Come, come, you brace of fop-doodles. **1889** Barrère & Leland *Dict. Slang* I 380: *Fopdoodle* (American), a silly fellow. "Come, don't be such a *fopdoodle.*" This is [also] provincial English. **1938** P. Crawford *Hello, Boat!* 157 [ref. to 19th C.]: Bandy-legged zanies!…Goggle-eyed fop-doodles!

for *prep.* ¶ In phrases: **for it** Orig. *Mil.* facing punishment or other adverse consequences; in trouble. *Rare* in U.S. [Of Brit. army orig.; see *OEDS*.]

*1909 in *OEDS*: "He'll give the whole show away?" "Then, I suppose, we'll all be for it." *1915 in *OEDS*: Then it is that he realises so acutely that if anything happens to his pilot he is "for it," as the current flying phrase is. **1934** Weseen *Dict. Slang* 116: (Soldiers' slang:) *For it—* Ordered into action. **1986** R. Campbell *In La-La Land* 100: Willy got scared his ass was for it.

¶ **for (one's)** for (one's) lot; (*hence*) for (one); as far as (one) is concerned.

1905 in Opper *H. Hooligan* 106: Back to jail for mine. **1905** *Nat. Police Gaz.* (Dec. 23) 3: The one that does the shooting takes it for his up the Bowery. **1914** in J. Reed *Young Man* 102: "Guess I'll re-enlist when I get over the border." "Not for mine." **1927** in Hammett *Knockover* 307: If you go back, it's lights out for yours. **1929** Hammett *Maltese Falcon* 149: She's a tough racket. You can have it for mine.

Ford *n.* [sugg. by *F4D,* the plane's orig. (1954) designation] *Naval Av.* the Douglas F4D (later F-6) Skyray shipboard jet fighter.

1969 Cagle *Naval Av. Guide* 393: Ford. The F-6 "Skyray."

fore-and-aft *n.* FORE-AND-AFT CAP.

*1943 (cited in Partridge *DSUE* (ed. 8) 419). **1973** Krulewitch *Now That You Mention It* 36 [ref. to 1918]: Red…took off his fore-and-aft.

fore-and-aft cap *n.* *USMC & Navy.* an overseas or garrison cap. Also **fore-and-aft hat.**

*1940 in *OEDS*. **1944** Kendall *Service Slang* 36: *Go-to-Hell hat*…garrison cap. Sometimes called the fore-and-aft hat or the over-seas cap. **1947** Heggen & Logan *Mr. Roberts* 417: Doc is between thirty-five and forty and he wears khakis and an officer's fore-and-aft cap. **1959** Cochrell *Barren Beaches* 276: Lt. McGhee…smoothed the limp fore-and-aft cap on his knee and straightened the ornament. **1966** Heinl *Marine Officer's Guide* (glossary): *Fore-and-aft cap.* Garrison cap, also frequently referred to as a "p-scutter." **1980** Manchester *Darkness* 165: Fore-and-aft (overseas) caps down around our ears. *a*1990 Poyer *Gulf* 257: A sweat-stained fore-and-aft cap with scratched lieutenant's bars.

fore-and-after *n.* **1.** *Navy.* an officer's cocked hat.

1839-40 Cobb *Green Hand* II 115: I had the choice…to roll its rim under at the sides and stick it on as a fore-and-after, or reverse the crown. *1867 Smyth *Sailor's Wd. Bk.*: *Fore-and-after,* a cocked hat worn with the peak in front instead of athwart. **1883** Russell *Sailors' Lang.* 55: *Fore and after.*—A cocked hat. *1949 W. Granville *Sea Slang* 101: *Fore-and-after*…An officer's cocked hat worn on occasions of ceremony.

2. *Naut.* a party.

1849 in Doten *Journals* I 8: We had a fore-and-aft-er on the main deck, we danced till we were tired.

fore-and-aft hat *n.* *Naut.* **1.** FORE-AND-AFTER.

1931 *Leatherneck* (Aug.) 25 [ref. to *ca*1880]: Did you ever wear a "fore-and-aft" campaign hat or the old blue overcoat with chevrons on the cuff? **1967** Lockwood *Subs* 196: Thus, when I passed examinations for commander in May, 1933, I had to pay $160 to have my uniforms changed and buy a new "fore-and-aft" full dress hat—but continued to draw the lower pay of a lieutenant commander. **1969** Gallery *Cap'n Fatso* 123: This guy will come aboard in a frock coat, fore-and-aft hat, swabs and a sword.

2. see FORE-AND-AFT CAP.

forecastle lawyer *n.* *Naut.* SEA LAWYER, 2.

*ca1910 in Clements *Manavlins* 84: Come all you focsle lawyers/That always take delight/By brooding o'er your troubles/To set all matters right. **1914** *DN* IV 150: *Forecastle lawyer*…a sailor conversant with the navy regulations. **1965** Schmitt *All Hands Aloft!* 76 [ref. to 1918]: Hank Wilson, a true "fo'c'sle lawyer,"…had great ideas for revising the government and would argue long and loud with anyone who would listen.

forefoot *n.* the hand.

*ca1598 Shakespeare *Henry V* II i: Giue me thy fist, thy fore-foote to me giue. *1811 *Lexicon Balatron.*: Fore Foot, or Paw. Give us your fore foot; give us your hand. **1905** W.S. Kelly *Lariats* 299: And if you think a man is tellin' the truth just because he holds up his right forefoot and [swears]…, your the durndest set of suckers I ever seen.

fore-hatches *n.pl. Naut.* the mouth.

1839-40 Cobb *Green Hand* I 265: If that old fellow isn't puffed up like a bladder when he gets at his journey's end, it won't be because he don't open his fore-hatches wide enough.

forepaw *n.* a hand.

*1785 Grose *Vulgar Tongue* s.v. *paw*: Fore paw; the hand. *Hind paw;* the foot. **1828** Bird *Looking Glass* 44: Avast there, my hearty, or I shall draw my forepaw athwart your hawse. **1837** Bird *Nick of the Woods* 78: Thar's my fo'paw, in token I've had enough of you, and want no mo'. **1859** Matsell *Vocab.* 65: The fore-paw, hand. **1867** G.W. Harris *Lovingood* 156: He sot his fore paws ontu the aidge ove the gourd. **1880** Pilgrim *Old Nick's Camp Meetin'* 192: Broke Joe Simmon's fore-paw, but no harm to speak of. *a*1889 F. Kirkland *Anec. of Rebellion* 242: I want to have a little satisfaction out of them cusses for spiling my fore paw.

foreskins *n.pl. Army & Pris.* creamed chipped beef.—used derisively.

1935 (cited in Partridge *Dict. Und.* 263). **1937** *AS* (Feb.) 74: *Foreskins—* creamed dried beef.

foretacks *n.pl. Naut.* the arms.

1849 Melville *White Jacket* 293 [ref. to 1843]: I'll have you hauled up and riveted in a clinch—both fore-tacks over the main-yard, and no bloody knife to cut the seizing.

foretopsail *n.* ¶ In phrase: **pay with a [flying] foretopsail** *Naut.* to sail away without paying a debt.

*1833 Marryat *Peter Simple* 255: I said, the midshipmen had paid their crockery bill with the fore-topsail. **1849** Melville *White Jacket* 19 [ref. to 1843]: The *middies* were busy raising loans…or else—in the Navy phrase—preparing to pay their creditors *with a flying fore-topsail.* **1875** Sheppard *Love Afloat* 182: They wasn't goin' to let them middies pay with a flyin' foretaupsle. **1883** Russell *Sailors' Lang.* XV: "Up keeleg," "paying a debt with the fore-topsail," namely, sailing away without paying.

forget *v.* Orig. *Black E.* to damn; FUCK, *v.*

1969 *Elementary English* XLVI 495: F'get you, honky! **1983** *Reader's Digest Success with Words* 85: Black English…forget it = "emphatic phrase expressing negation, denial, refutation." **1980–89** Cheshire *Home Boy* 105: Forget you, shit-for-brains. **1990** *Simpsons* (Fox-TV): Forget you, pal! Thanks for nothin'!

fork *v.* **1.a.** *Und.* to pick the pocket (of); (*specif.*) to do so using only two fingers. Cf. FORKS.

*1698–99 "B.E." *Dict. Canting Crew: Let's fork him,* let us Pick that

Man's Pocket. *Ibid.* s.v. *meggs: We fork'd the rum Cull's Meggs to the tune of Fourty...We Pickt the Gentleman's Pocket of full Fourty Guineas.* **1850** in H.C. Lewis *Works:* Fingers which the previous session had never been employed in higher surgery than forking a sleepy chum. ***1889** Barrère & Leland *Dict. Slang* I 381: *Fork...(Thieves)...to pick a pocket by extracting an article with two fingers only. a1955* in D.W. Maurer *Lang. Underworld* 241: *Fork v.t. To pick a pocket with the index and middle fingers, using them as pincers.*

b. *Broadly,* to steal; filch.

1855 in Meserve & Reardon *Satiric Comedies* 140: The towel, silver *fork* and spoon/You *forked* from me.

2. to intrude oneself.—constr. with *into.*

1839 Marryat *Diary* 266: I heard a young man, a farmer in Vermont, say, when talking about another having gained the heart of a pretty girl, "Well, how he contrived to *fork* into her young affections, I can't tell."

3. FORK OVER; FORK OUT.

1877 Wheeler *Deadwood Dick, Prince of the Road* 83: Durned a cent'll I fork! **1884** "Craddock" *Where Battle Was Fought* 37: I won it all! I'll have it all! Fork! With your left hand—mind! **a1889* in Barrère & Leland *Dict. Slang* I 381: "His fee was a tenner. *Fork.*" Master forked. **1915** Howard *God's Man* 15: Fork out. Come on....Fork. **1938* in Partridge *Dict. Und.* 264: I forked him a quid.

4. *West.* to mount or bestride (a horse); in phr. **fork leather** to climb into the saddle. Also *transf.*

1882 Aby *Hoffenstein* 14: Keep off'n that 'ere plug, an' git somebody as knows how to fork 'em to break him in for you. **1882** Baillie-Grohman *Rockies* 192: Beans is pison if you ain't "forking" (riding) a bucking cayuse. **1903** A. Adams *Log of Cowboy* 295: So fork that swimming horse of yours. **1917–20** in J.M. Hunter *Trail Drivers* I 273: Throw your rope, and whatever it falls on, fork him. **1927** Rollins *Jinglebob* 180 [ref. to 1880's]: How good can these blamed tenderfoots fork? **1928** in Davidson *Old West* 86: Forkin' 'em bareback like Injun Piutes. **1931** Z. Grey *Sunset Pass* 6: An' Ash is as bad a hombre as ever forked a hoss. **1931** in Goodstone *Pulps* 86: We gotta fork leather again an' hunt for three missin' hombres. **1933** W.C. MacDonald *Law of .45's* 36: We ought to be forkin' leather to— **1948** J. Stevens *Jim Turner* 5: Think you can fork a cayuse? That's Idyho talk. **1953** Gresham *Midway* 1: To Earl Purtle, for his patience with a guy who had never forked a motorcycle in his life. **1959** L'Amour *Fast Draw* 46: A man forks his own broncs in this country. **1968** S.O. Barker *Rawhide Rhymes* 24: This Buck could fork a bronc, he said, there wasn't any doubt. **1981** Hogan *D. Bullet* 91: Just fork your bronc and get on out of town.

¶ In phrase:

¶ **fork on** (see quot.).

1851 B. Hall *College Wds.* 134: At Hamilton College, *to fork on,* to appropriate to one's self.

forked *adj.* [prob. sugg. by *forked lightning*] remarkable.

1850 in Blair & McDavid *Mirth* 103: The way they did hustle her about...was forked!

fork out *v.* to hand over or give up (usu. money); pay.

*1831 in *OED:* Fork out something better than this. **1836** (quot. at LOCKER). **1839** *Spirit of Times* (June 15) 174: Our *City* subscribers have not been called on to "fork out" for six months or more....I forked a quarter out. **1839** Briggs *H. Franco* I 117: When I want money, I go to the old woman and tell her I want to subscribe to the Missionary Society, and she always forks out. **1863* in T. Taylor *Plays* 212: Now fork out the pictures [i.e., face cards], old boy. **1930** Huston *Frankie & Johnny* 48: All right then, fork out,—hand over. **1973** Haney *Jock* 46: I ended up having to fork out $500 of my own money for her.

fork over *v.* to hand over (usu. money); pay; pay up.

*1820 (cited in Partridge *DSUE* (ed. 7) 1144). **1835** *New Yorker* (May 2) 3: The publishers close [their appeal] with the parting injunction— "Reader fork over." **1839** in *OEDS:* The gambler should fork over his illgotten gains. **1841** [Mercier] *Man-of-War* 234: Fork over that 'ere trifle of chink. **1845** Durivage & Burnham *Stray Subjects* 69: So the lawyer forked over one V and kept the other. **1847** Neal *Charc. Sks.* (Ser. 2) 42: Can a steam-engine fork over the change for a five-dollar note? **1852** Stowe *Uncle Tom* ch. viii: "Here's her shawl."..."That ar's lucky....Fork over." **1858** Elton *Rough & Ready Jester* 89: Come Sam! fork over my money. **1891** Clurman *Nick Carter* 17: Fork over, an' I'll row ye where ye wanter go. **1896** Brown *Parson* 144: Fork over your gold watch...or you're a dead goner! **1897** Fox *Hell fer Sartain* 25: He forks over four mo' dollars. **1898** Westcott *David Harum* 16: He hauled out his wallet an' forked over. **1938** "E. Queen" *4 Hearts* 163: Fork over! **1948** in *DA:* I have to...fork over the final payment of a quarter of a million dollars. **1972** Madden *Bros.* 11: All they could fork over was

the gas money. **1983** *Saturday Contact* (WKGN Radio) (May 14): Donahue should have forked over the information.

forks *n.pl.* *Und.* the index and middle fingers as used in picking pockets; (*broadly*) the fingers. Cf. FORK, *v.,* 1.a.

*1812 Vaux *Vocab.: Forks:* the two fore-fingers of the hand; to *put your forks down* is to pick a pocket. ***1834** Ainsworth *Rookwood* 178: *Forks...*the two fore-fingers used in picking a pocket. **1848** *Ladies' Repository* VIII (Oct.) 315: *Forks,* Fingers. **1859** Matsell *Vocab.* 34: *Forks.* The fore and middle fingers. **1944** Burley *Hndbk. Jive* 138: *Forks*—Fingers.

fork-up *n.* a payment.

1916 in Pound *Pound/Joyce* 67: With the Egoist fork-up I think I have come about to the end of my connections.

fork up *v.* FORK OUT.

1836 in *DA:* "Fork up, and that instantly, or take the contents of this," he added fiercely, as he thrust the cold barrel of the pistol against the supplicant's cheek. **1839** in *DAE:* Well, then, fork up and be quick. **1840** *Spirit of Times* (June 27) 198: $2000...will be "forked up" and delivered out to the winners. **1846** *Nat. Police Gaz.* (June 20) 346: In the St. Louis Recorder's Court...Alexander McManus was fined $5 for stealing wood from the steamer Hannibal, and was asked to "fork up" by his honor. **1855** Simms *Forayers* 139: And now for your son's ransom. What do you say to that? Fork up steady! **1859** Bartlett *Amer.* 160: Jonathan, I've trusted you long enough; so fork up. **1905** *DN* III 9: *Fork up, v.phr.* To pay up. **1916** E. Pound, in *OEDS:* I will fork up the remaining £20 of the fifty promised. **1938–39** Dos Passos *Young Man* 154: Eddy forked up a ten-dollar bill. **1947** in *DA:* Forking up 30¢ a day for dues and the benefit fund. **1988** N.Y.C. woman, age *ca*50: Then they expect you to fork up the money at the last second.

form *n.* one's person as an object of sexual interest; in phr. **warm for (someone's) form** sexually attracted to (someone). *Joc.*

1953 in Cannon *Like 'Em Tough* 54: Didn't know you were still warm for her form, pal. **1964** in Gover *Trilogy* 244: If he so warm for my form why don't he jes *say* so? **1980** Tenn. man, age 27: But that Julie! I'm warm for her form. **1984** Caunitz *Police Plaza* 226: The broad wants my form.

fornicate *v.* to fornicate with. *Joc.*

1924 Wilstach *Anecdota Erotica* 21: It's great to be fornicated with your shoes on. **1977** M. Franklin *Last of Cowboys* 141: He didn't fornicate you?

fort *n.* *Stu.* (see quot.).

1851 B. Hall *College Wds.* 134: At Jefferson and Washington Colleges in Pennsylvania, the boarding houses for the students are called *forts.*

Fort Apache *n.* [ref. to the film *Fort Apache* (1948), about a military post in the Old West] *N.Y.C.,* orig. *Police.* The Forty-first Police Precinct, a crime-ridden area in the South Bronx.

1976 T. Walker *Ft. Apache* 3 [ref. to *ca*1969-70]: "This is Fort Apache."...The name sticks. **1976** R. Daley *To Kill* 233: The 41st Precinct...was called Fort Apache, and was one of the most crime-ridden in the city. **1976** Price *Bloodbrothers* 212: The South Bronx. Fort Apache. The pits. **1980** H. Gould *Fort Apache, the Bronx* (title). **1991** *CBS This Morning* (CBS-TV) (Mar. 14): A fire destroyed a building in a Bronx neighborhood known as Fort Apache. **1993** *N.Y. Times* (June 23) B 2: Many...have a deep ambivalence about Fort Apache and whether the name should carry over into the new era. *Ibid.* Others recall hearing [the name] as early as the late 50's.

Fort Head *n.* *Army.* Fort Hood, Texas.

1968 *N.Y. Post* (July 15) 12: So much pot is smoked and so many other kinds of dope consumed at Ft. Hood that the place is known to many enlisted men and some officers as "Fort Head." **1970** Just *Military Men* 55: The base is known as Fort Head for the quantity of marijuana available and used.

forthwith *n.* [fr. the appearance of the word in the order] *Law.* an order to appear, surrender, etc., forthwith.

1984 Caunitz *Police Plaza* 201: A week later they were given a "forthwith" to report to the [review board].

Fort Lost-in-the-Woods *n.* *Army.* Fort Leonardwood, Missouri; (*broadly*) any remote military post.

1974 Personnel Sgt., U.S. Army (coll. J. Ball): Fort Lost-in-the-Woods. **1980** Cragg *L. Militaris* 173: *Fort Lost-in-the-Woods.* Fort Leonard Wood, Missouri; any remote military post. *a1984* in Terry

Bloods 19: Fort Leonardwood, Missouri. "Lost in the Woods," yeah. **1986** Merkin *Zombie Jamboree* 35: I took my...training at Fort Lost-in-the-Wood, Missouri.

Fort Pricks *n.* [pun on PRICK 'penis'; *Dix* is homophonous with DICKS 'penises'] *Army.* Fort Dix, New Jersey.—usu. considered vulgar.
   1974 Personnel Sgt., U.S. Army (coll. J. Ball): He's getting sent to Fort Pricks, New Jersey. **1980** Cragg *L. Militaris* 173: *Fort Pricks.* A play on Fort Dix, New Jersey.

Fort Puke *n. Army.* Fort Polk, Louisiana.
   1974 Personnel Sgt., U.S. Army (coll. J. Ball): Fort Puke, Lousyanna—Little Vietnam. **1980** Cragg *L. Militaris* 173: *Fort Puke.* A play on Fort Polk, Louisiana.

Fort Shit *n. Army.* Fort Sam Houston, Texas.—usu. considered vulgar.
   1986 Merkin *Zombie Jamboree* 334 [ref. to *ca*1971]: Fort Sam Houston In Texas (Fort S.H.I.T.).

Fort Swill *n. Army.* Fort Sill, Okla.
   1920 *Amer. Leg. Wkly.* (Oct. 29) 7: This is just practice, as held at Fort Swill. **1980** Cragg *L. Militaris* 173: *Fort Swill.* A play on Fort Sill, Oklahoma.

Fort Useless *n. Army.* Fort Eustis, Virginia.
   1974 Lieut., U.S. Army Nat. Guard, age 24: "Fort Useless, Vagina" is Fort Eustis, Virginia. Even Uncle Sam Thinks It Sucks. **1980** Cragg *L. Militaris* 173: *Fort Useless.* A play on Fort Eustis, Virginia.

forty *n.* Esp. *Black E.* a forty-ounce bottle of malt liquor. See also FORTY DOG, FORTY-O.
   1990 "3rd Bass" in B. Adler *Rap!* 103: With a forty in my system. **1991** in *RapPages* (Feb. 1992) 43: Some of us drink a lot of 40's. **1992** *Martin* (Fox-TV): "Whatcha got there?" "Coupla forties." **1993** *N.Y. Times* (Apr. 16) A 1: It gets you pumped up....I feel more comfortable when I'm drinking a 40.
   ¶ In phrase:
   ¶ **like** [or **as**] **forty** (used as an intensive). Cf. *like sixty* s.v. SIXTY.
   1829 in *DA*: Such is Mr. Owen's romance of the social system...; as loving as the Vermonter said, as *forty.* **1843** Oliver *Illinois* 93: I'd have whipped him like forty. *a*1846 in *DAE*: Going it like forty at twenty-deck poker. **1852** Stowe *Uncle Tom's Cabin* 50: I has principles, and I sticks to 'em like forty. **1863** in *Civil War Times Illus.* (July 1968) 40: They fought like demons. **1871** Schele de Vere *Amer.* 313: Boys say, "You have scared me like *forty*," and teamsters boast of a powerful horse, that will *pull like forty.* **1888** Gordon & Page *Befo' De War* 100: An' de niggers was singin' like forty. **1944** in *DA*: This stream...goes like forty.

forty *adj.* fine; satisfactory; O.K. Also as adv.
   1910 *Variety* (Aug. 20) 13: I always stood in forty with the boys around home. **1930** Schuyler *Black No More* 2: Why I thought you and her were all forty. **1931** in D.W. Maurer *Lang. Und.* 40: That will be forty as there will be no beef. **1933** in Clarke *Amer. Negro Stories* 68: He asted me, "Who is dat broad wid de forte [*sic*] shake?" Dat's a new word. Us always thought forty was a set of figgers but he showed us where it means a whole heap of things...."Yessuh, she's forte!" **1934** L. Hughes *Ways of White Folks* 63: He'd got the idea...that he didn't have to give them anything but himself—which wasn't so forty for them little Broadway gold diggers who wanted diamonds and greenbacks. **1926–35** Watters & Hopkins *Burlesque* 18: Bonny. How's tricks, Bozo? *Bozo.* Not so forty. **1949** Shane & Cooper *City Across the River* (film): They don't look so forty to me. **1950** L. Brown *Iron City* 108: Well, that wouldn't have been so forty any time, but on payday night—. **1954** Killens *Youngblood* 153: I don't see where he so forty. **1962** L. Hughes *Tambourines to Glory* 202: You're forty!...You know, forty means fine, O.K., great. And you're great with me.

forty-and-eight *n. Army.* a French boxcar, as used for transporting troops. Now *hist.* [Such cars carried the French railway notice that they were meant to accommodate *Hommes 40* [ou] *Chevaux 8* (40 men or 8 horses).]
   1920 McKenna *315th Inf.* 300 [ref. to WWI]: After a three day train ride in the popular "40 and 8" we arrived in Esnoms. **1939** Callaway *Packs & Rifles* 50 [ref. to WWI]: These small cars were of the "forty and eight" variety. **1943** in Huebner *Long Walk* 15: The officers' car is hardly more comfortable than the 40-and-8s. **1950** Calmer *Strange Land* 52: It was an American train, not the 40 and 8 cattle cars we were on night before last night. **1953–57** Giovannitti *Combine D* 464:

French forty-and-eights from the last war. **1960** Matheson *Beardless Warriors* 8: I remember we was in a forty-and-eight, like sardines. **1970** Ziel *Steel Rails* 221: Fifty or so men jammed into the small French "40 and 8's."

Forty-Deuce *n. N.Y.C.* West Forty-Second Street and the Times Square area. Cf. DEUCE, *n.*, 10.
   [**1975** *N.Y. Post* (July 22) 71: Making a living through shoplifting, mugging, and prostitution on "Forty-Deuce Street."] **1978** Fisher & Rubin *Special Teachers* 3: Tense and restless..., he'd hit Forty-deuce. **1984** *Miami Vice* (NBC-TV): Yo, man. Let's go down to Forty-Deuce. *a*1986 in *NDAS*: Forty-deuce is what its seamy inhabitants call 42d Street. **1986** in B. Adler *Rap!* 45: Peek-show...on the Forty-Deuce.

forty dog *n.* [FORTY + DOG] a forty-ounce bottle of beer or ale.
   1988 *Spin* (Oct.) 47: *Forty dog* n, 40-oz. bottle of Olde English 800 malt liquor. **1989** "LL Cool J" *Big Ole Butt* (rap song): Cold forty dogs.

forty-eight *n. Mil.* a 48-hour pass.
   1942 *Leatherneck* (Nov.) 145: *Forty-Eight.* Two-day leave. **1946** G.C. Hall, Jr. *1000 Destroyed* 72: On subsequent 48s he headed straight for the Jules Club on Jermyn Street. **1966* G.M. Williams *Camp* 16: It keeps you from getting a clear weekend, unless you get a forty-eight.

forty-eleven *adj.* very many.
   1859 Holmes *Prof.* 165: On asking him what was the number of his room, he answered, that it was forty-'leven. **1869** Stowe *Oldtown* 69: They...should come if there were forty-eleven more of 'em than there be. **1885** *Puck* (Mar. 18): 'Bout forty-'leben thousan', Massa. **1905** *Lippincott's Mag.* (Nov.) 581: Forty-'leven Coaches...hammered football into him for eight solid hours. *ca*1912 in Kornbluh *Rebel Voices* 134: And the grub it stunk as bad as forty-'leven skunks. **1934** L. Hughes *Ways of White Folks* 55: Hell of a fine guy, Mr. Lloyd, with his 40-11 pretty gals.

forty-fives *n.pl.* beans. Cf. syns. FORTY-FOURS, BULLETS.
   1930 "D. Stiff" *Milk & Honey* 205: Forty-fives—Moniker for navy beans, givers of energy.

forty-fours *n.pl.* **1.** *So.* black-eyed peas.
   1911 *JAF* (Oct.) 382: I looked on [the] table: "forty fo's" was out. **1929** *Amer. Mercury* (Aug.) 386: If I be camp cook in dugout kitchen, jes' like slingin' slop an' fohty-fohs for shack-rouster in construction camp. **2.** beans.
   1919 Wilkins *Company Fund* 45: Company Expressions: Chow. Punk. Slum. Frog Eyes. Fourty fours [*sic*]. **1958** McCulloch *Woods Words* 132: *Pass the 44's*—Pass the beans. Loggers graded beans according to size as 22's, 30–30's, 44's, etc.

forty-miler *n. Circus & Carnival.* a halfhearted or unseasoned employee, usu. of a small circus or carnival, who is reluctant to travel far from home.
   1935 *Amer. Mercury* (June) 229: Fortymiler: an apprentice to the carnival business: he is afraid to get more than forty miles from home. **1946** Dadswell *Hey, Sucker* 15: Then you'll become a "forty-miler" and go home. **1950** Bissell *Stretch on the River* 37: I seen him. A forty-miler if I ever seen one. By the time we get to Rock Island lock he'll decide he's got to go home. **1951** Mannix *Sword-Swallower* 54: "I ain't no forty-miler," called Lu resentfully over her shoulder.

forty-O *n.* a forty-ounce bottle of beer or ale.
   *a*1990 E. Currie *Dope & Trouble* 244: We start drinking forty-O's of Old English.

forty-rod *n.* [see 1856, 1858 quots.] cheap powerful whiskey or rum. Also *attrib.*
   [**1856** in *DA*: The title is nothing more nor less than "rot-gut whisky," with an addenda about its "killing forty rods around a corner."] [**1858** in *AS* XII 115: *Liquor...warranted to kill at forty rods.*] **1861** in W.H. Russell *My Diary* 114: "40 rod" and "60 rod," as whisky is called [by Confederate soldiers in Mississippi]. **1862** in *Jour. Ill. Hist. Soc.* XVIII (1926) 921: Burnap...passed "forty-rod" around in tin cups. **1869** in "M. Twain" *Stories* 20: Trading for forty-rod whisky, to enable you to get drunk and happy and tomahawk your families, has played the everlasting mischief with the pomp of your dress. **1872** in *DAE*: The chief ingredient was forty-rod rum. **1883** Sweet & Knox *Mustang* 131: The old man had histed in a good load of forty-rod juice that day. **1884** "M. Twain" *Huck. Finn* 31 [ref. to 1850's]: He got powerful thirsty and...traded his new coat for a jug of forty-rod. **1897** Hayne *Klondyke* 91: "Forty-rod whisky"—a facetious allusion to its supposed power of killing at that distance! **1897** in D. Cohen *Airship* 44: Seeing "airships" is a new deal, and must be caused by water diluted forty rod. **1908** Summerhayes *Vanished Arizona* 231 [ref. to 1877]: It was before the days of

the canteen, and soldiers could get all the whisky they wanted at the trader's store; and, it being generally the brand that was known in the army as "Forty rod," they got very drunk on it sometimes. **1921** Casey & Casey *Gay-Cat* 100: What brand o' forty-rod does youse most fill up on? **1936** N. West *Cool Million* 204: The patrons of Powder River Rose usually ordered mountain oysters and washed them down with forty-rod. **1940** F. Hunt *Trail fr. Tex.* 187: Forty rod bug juice. **1942** Garcia *Tough Trip* 144: He...did not refuse a drink of forty rods. **1966** "F. O'Brian" *Bugle & Spur* 24: Forty-rod....Maybe three weeks old. That's *aged* whiskey, Ben. **1968** S.O. Barker *Rawhide Rhymes* 46: He tried Joe Todd/For stealin' a barrel of forty-rod.

forty-yards *n.* FORTY-ROD.
    1876 in *Buffalo Bill* 209: An' a little flask o' likker, as cost fifty cents a horn./Tho' *forty yards* war nowhar, it was finished soon, ye bet.

forward light *n.* usu. *pl. Naut.* an eye.
    1899 Robbins *Gam* 72: Holy Joe on deck with blood in his for'ard lights, b'gawsh! *Ibid.* 88: *Look!* clap yer for'ard lights on *that!*

fotz up *v.* FUTZ UP.
    1963 Rubin *Sweet Daddy* 90: He fotzes up—everyone hates him.

foul *adj. Und.* (discovered) in the act of committing a crime; found out; (*also*) in possession of stolen goods or contraband. Cf. *OED* s.v. *foul, adj.*, 7.b., 'guilty of a charge or accusation; criminally implicated' *a*1300–1621. Cf. syn. DIRTY.
    1846 *Lives of the Felons* 12: As soon as White saw that his accomplice was "foul," he took advantage of the momentary surprise of the store-keeper and his clerks, to...effect his escape. **1852** Hazen *Five Years* 417: Suppose you should be taken foul, as I was in the old Columbus, how would you avoid [the cat-o'-nine-tails]? **1859** Matsell *Vocab.* 84: "The cove pinched a keeler of spread, and was pulled foul"..., the fellow stole a tub of butter and was arrested with it in his possession. **1860* (cited in Partridge *Dict. Und.* 265).
    ¶ In phrases:
    ¶ **run foul of** *Naut.* to meet by chance.
    1864 Fosdick *Frank on a Gun-Boat* 91: We ran foul of some guerrillas out there in the woods, sir. **1887** (quot. at MITTEN). **1918** *DN* V 21: *Run foul of*, to meet. **1933** Witherspoon *Liverpool Jarge* (unp.): Then one day I runs foul of him on the street in London and we goes into a pub for a bit of a gam.
    ¶ **run foul of a snag** *Riverboating.* to get into difficulty.
    1846 Codman *Sailors' Life* 160: That moon and your twister...reminds me...about my running foul of a snag, too—that is, being in love.

foul *v.* ¶ In phrase: **foul (someone's) hawse** *Naut.* to confound, obstruct, or interfere with.
    1899 Hamblen *Bucko Mate* 32: Where ye goin'? Look as if ye'd fouled Connors' hawse.

foul ball *n.* **1.** a worthless person, esp. a troublemaker or misfit; (*also*) an unpredictable or untrustworthy person.
    1925 T.A. Dorgan, in Zwilling *TAD Lexicon* 37: Oh, he's just a foul ball. **1930** Nason *Corporal Once* 91 [ref. to 1918]: "Ain't they a bunch of foul balls!" agreed the One-Eyed Man. **1931** Lorimer *Streetcars* 204: Davey can be an awful foul ball at times. **1929–33** Farrell *Young Manhood* 372: He's the biggest fake in the joint....He's a foul ball! **1937** Weidman *Can Get It Wholesale* 215: So at first I figured maybe I'd picked a foul ball. But then I remembered how attractive she was, and all the guys hanging around her in the showroom. **1939** Polsky *Curtains for Editor* 101: Mr. Francis Cook is opined to be a fairly foul ball. **1942** Breslow *Blondie Goes to College* (film): That about does it, Bumstead! A dog can sense a foul ball the minute he sees one. **1956** I. Shulman *Good Deeds* 84: Are you a bunch of foul balls. **1959** "D. Stagg" *Glory Jumpers* 11: And to beef up these foul balls, they're throwing me some casuals they just got on transfer from the Eighty-second. **1960** Swarthout *Where Boys Are* 3: The Social Chairman of a boys' dorm calls the Social Chairman of a girls' dorm and says he needs some flesh for Friday night, no foul balls, nothing too brainy, all queens and amenable, can she supply. **1962** Quirk *Ribbons* 97: I'm glad that foul ball is gone. **1963** D. Tracy *Brass Ring* 31: He'd better...hope that he hadn't tied himself up with the worst foul ball in Dorset. **1980** McDowell *Our Honor* 185: Some foul-ball Private in Platoon Four-Eighty-Seven went berserk and started threatening everybody with a bayonet. **1982** T.C. Mason *Battleship* 181: Since he was periodically in trouble for such offenses as AOL, failure to obey orders, and lying, and had a disagreeable personality, he was considered the rankest of foul balls. **1987** D. da Cruz *Boot* 7: We don't have time and resources to waste on slackers, incompetents, and foul balls.
    2. *quasi-adj.* incompetent; ill-advised.

1965 Linakis *In Spring* 317: I think this is one hell of a foul-ball operation...I haven't drawn my pay in over a week.

fouled-up *adj.* Orig. *Navy & USMC.* confused, chaotic, or disorganized; (*broadly*) mistaken; (*also*) stupid or worthless. [See note at FOUL UP, *v.*]
    1942 *Leatherneck* (Nov.) 145: *Fouled Up*—Mixed up, confused. **1942** *Yank* (Nov. 11) 4: Navy [Slang]...*Foul,* or *foul up*—Trouble or being in trouble or to get someone in trouble. Thus, if a sailor gets all fouled up with a skirt, he's got babe trouble. **1943** *Sat. Eve. Post* (Mar. 20) 86: Those knuckleheads are all fouled up. **1944** Kendall *Service Slang* 23: *All fouled up*...messed up. **1945** in *Calif. Folk Qly.* V (1946) 390: *Fouled up like an ensign's sea bag* is the commonest [USN simile]. **1940–46** McPeak MS., in IUFA: You're as fouled up as a man overboard in dry dock...as a mess-cook drawing small stores...as a marine at fire drill. **1947** J.C. Higgins *Railroaded* (film): Somebody's all fouled up. **1948** Manone & Vandervoort *Trumpet* 157: Aw, I don't want to go out to ol' Cali-fouled up-ornia and mess with those square people out there. **1949** Grayson & Andrews *I Married a Communist* (film): We're trying to get some sense into a fouled-up situation while there's still time. **1956** Boatner *Military Customs* 125: *Fire Call.* A confused situation or formation. "All fouled up like a Fire Call." **1960** Simak *Worlds* 43: It was all just this side of crazy, anyhow. No matter how fouled up it was, Steen seemed satisfied. **1964** Rhodes *Chosen Few* 57: I've been in this fouled-up place for almost four years straight now and I don't think I can or want to get used to it. **1967** W. Crawford *Gresham's War* 7 [ref. to Korean War]: I called him Goat, for fouled-up like Hogan's goat, which he was. **1968** W.C. Anderson *Gooney Bird* 124: The whole thing is insanity. More fouled up than an Ethiopian fire drill. **1967–69** Foster & Stoddard *Pops* 1: I've always wanted to write down what I know about the times in New Orleans. Some of the books are fouled up on it and some of the guys weren't telling the truth. **1977** R.S. Parker *Effective Decisions* 2: Some cynics might say, "It is all society's fault. That's the real reason our lives are all fouled up." **1981** Ehrlichman *Witness* 21: Wooley earned a reputation for running the most fouled-up ticket and credential operation in modern Republican history.

foul owl *n. So.* a troublemaker or dangerous individual; an obnoxious person; FOUL BALL.
    1964 S. Silliphant *In Heat of Night* (film): There's a foul owl on the prowl. **1984** Knoxville, Tenn., man, age *ca*18: He's a *foul* owl.

foul-up *n.* **1.** Orig. *Navy & USMC.* a blunder leading to a state of confusion or inefficiency; (*also*) a state of confusion brought about by ineptitude or inefficiency; (*also*) a mechanical malfunction. [Freq. regarded as a euphem. for FUCK-UP, *n.*, 2.]
    1943 in Sherrod *Tarawa* 82: Orders...never came because of the radio foul-up. **1944** *Newsweek* (Feb. 7) 61: *Janfu:* Joint Army-Navy foul-up. *Jaafu:* Joint Anglo-American foul-up. **1945** J. Bryan *Carrier* 139: There's been a foul-up. **1958** Hailey & Castle *Runway* 109: There's a foul-up on the phones in the press room. **1959** Fuller *Marines at Work* 143: "That's the history of the rock, doll," she was told. "Always a foul-up somewhere." **1971** Dibner *Trouble with Heroes* 44: The foul-up was especially galling to this bunch because ten days earlier the landing had been smooth and undetected. **1986** F. Walton *Once Were Eagles* 8: There he ran into a bureaucratic foulup: he couldn't get back into the Marine Corps.
    2. Esp. *Mil.* a bungler or misfit. [Freq. regarded as a euphem. for FUCK-UP, *n.*, 1.]
    1945 in M. Chennault *Up Sun!* 136: I know what you foulups were up to. **1954–60** *DAS: Foulup*...A person who makes frequent blunders. **1964** Pearl *Stockade* 70: I should have known better than to trust that foul-up Larkin. **1965** Linakis *In Spring* 293: These foul-ups are kids mostly. **1966** Derrig *Pride of Berets* 144: Even if he is a short-timer we can't afford even one foul-up in the outfit. **1987** D. da Cruz *Boot* 49: You're the worst bunch of foul-ups it's ever been my misfortune to have inflicted on me.

foul up *v.* **1.** Orig. *Navy & USMC.* to bring into confusion; mix up; confound; botch; ruin; in phr. **foul up the detail** *Mil.* to bungle. Now *colloq.* [Freq. regarded as a euphem. for FUCK UP, *v.*, 1.]
    1942 (*Yank* quot. at FOULED-UP, *adj.*). **1943** in Rea *Wings of Gold* 76: I fouled up a navigation quiz completely. **1944** Wakeman *Shore Leave* 21: You know damn well she's in Hartford, making those Pratt-Whitney engines you foul up. **1946** S. Wilson *Voyage to Somewhere* 108: They've just fouled up the mails. I don't doubt she's writing. **1949** Bezzerides *Thieves' Market* 198: She's always fouling us up. **1949** "R. MacDonald"

Moving Target 82: I'm fouled up. Why should I foul you up? **1952** Uris *Battle Cry* 132 [ref. to WWII]: You guys have been fouling up field problems like a Chinese firedrill. **1953** Brackett, Reisch, & Breen *Niagara* (film): It'll be all right if I don't foul it up. **1953** Felsen *Street Rod* 83: We'd clobber the first guy that fouled us up by racing or being reckless on the roads. **1955** McGovern *Fräulein* 170: You're in charge here, and I never try to foul you up. **1957** Myrer *Big War* 150 [ref. to WWII]: Somebody fouled up the detail, that's for sure. **1958** Plageman *Steel Cocoon* 55: A guy like that is a jinx. He could foul us all up. Don't you see that? *Ibid.* 165: He fouled it up!…We almost had it, just perfect, and he fouled it up! **1958** Cooley *Run for Home* 343: The sonuvabitch nearly fouled up the whole detail. **1966** Rose *The Russians Are Coming!* (film): You're gonna foul up the whole detail! **1966** Christopher *Little People* 179: And you're determined to foul it up if you can. **1971** Capaldi *Art of Deception* 95: He might easily fit both categories and hence foul up the classification again. **1971** Keith *Long Line Rider* 91: He put black pepper behin' 'em to foul up the dogs. **1971** Rowe *Five Years* 402: My screwed-up additions to the map had done some good, even if they hadn't fouled Charlie up completely.

2. Orig. *Navy & USMC*. to become confused, esp. to blunder into or cause trouble; fail through confusion or ineptitude; go wrong or awry. [Freq. regarded as a euphem. for FUCK UP, *v.*, 2.]

1944 *New Yorker* (May 6) 26: Look how we fouled up on maneuvers. **1946** S. Wilson *Voyage to Somewhere* 197: Pretty soon all the crew will know that to get a transfer, all they have to do is foul up. **1954** E. Hunter *Blackboard Jungle* 27: They'd come to within a term of graduation, and they…didn't want to get thrown out of school for fouling up at this late stage of the game. **1956** M. Wolff *Big Nick.* 243: You fouled up and the old man came and took the kid. **1958** Schwitzgebel *Streetcorner Research* 21: We want to know why kids foul up and why they do the other things they do. **1964** Newhafer *Last Tallyho* 135: If anything fouls up, he wants to be there. **1965** Linakis *In Spring* 292: I don't like to see a G.I. foul up. **1970** Thackrey *Thief* 295: Only my tipsters had fouled up again. **1978** J. Lee *13th Hour* 21: If anything can foul up, it will. **1972–79** T. Wolfe *Right Stuff* 265: Please, dear God, don't let me foul up.

four-bagger *n. Baseball.* a home run. Cf. TWO-BAGGER, THREE-BAGGER.

1883 (cited in Nichols *Baseball Term.*). **1918** *N.Y. Age* (June 8) 6: Sunday week he made a four-bagger. **1925** in *DA*: Hazel Killian hit a four-bagger as a prophet on that last remark. **1927** *AS* (Feb.) 255: A…"four-bagger" is a home run. **1982** T. Considine *Lang. Sport* 21: *Four-bagger:* a home run.

four-banger *n.* an automotive engine having four cylinders.

1951–53 in *AS* (May 1954) 96: Those four-bangers are more potent than they look. **1955** *AS* XXX 92: *Four banger, n.* A four-cylinder diesel engine. **1970** E. Thompson *Garden of Sand* 155: The car barked with the beat of its little four-banger heart.

four-bit *adj.* costing fifty cents; (*hence*) contemptible or inconsequential; TWO-BIT.

1901 Irwin *Sonnets* (unp.): Well, just watch me try to shake/The memory of that four-bit Scheutzen Park. **1929** in E. O'Neill *Letters* 341: A 4-bit whore. **1932** in *DAS*: To smoke four-bit cigars. **1957** Yordan *Men in War* (film): There's nothing in regulation says a colonel has to talk to a four-bit lieutenant.

four bits see BIT, *n.*

four-deuce *n. Army & USMC.* a 4.2-inch chemical mortar.

1977 Caputo *Rumor of War* 281 [ref. to 1966]: The four-deuces would at least suppress the VC rifle fire. **1985** J.M.G. Brown *Rice Paddy Grunt* 88: The 4.2 (or "four-deuce") Mortar Platoon. **1984–88** in Berry *Where Ya Been?* 113 [ref. to 1950]: Mortars. We called them "four-deuces."

four-eyed *adj.* wearing eyeglasses.—used derisively.

1878 Mulford *Fighting Indians* 102: "That is nothing," said the Major, "[the enlisted men] referred to me as *Four-Eyed-Son-of-a-Gun*." **1896** Ade *Artie* 66: W'y, t'e four-eyed nobs dat sent me out on t'e Sout' Side. **1929–31** J.T. Farrell *Lonigan* ch. iv: And he's tryin' to make a gentleman of that four-eyed kid of his. **1956** E. Hunter *Second Ending* 325: That four-eyed bitch. **1974** Radano *Cop Stories* 30: A four-eyed punk bastard with dark-rimmed glasses.

four-eyes *n.* **1.** a person who wears eyeglasses.—used derisively.

1865 Sala *Diary* II 33: It is wicked to hint that all the fair Bostonians have four eyes [i.e., wear glasses]. **1873 Hotten *Slang Dict.* (ed. 4):

Four-eyes, a man or woman who habitually wears spectacles. **1876** in *N.Dak. Hist.* XVII (1950) 176: Capt Michiales [nicknamed] Four Eyes [by Indians]. **1895** Wood *Yale Yarns* 120: Give me the glass, old four eyes! **1952** Sandburg *Young Strangers* 142 [ref. to *ca*1880]: Their boy Ross blinked his eyes a good deal and wore large spectacles. Some kids thought it smart to call him "Four Eyes." **1961** Terry *Old Liberty* 52: Shove, four-eyes. **1983** S. King *Christine* 109: Who's the four-eyes swamping out the toilet in there?

2. eyeglasses.

1966 Neugeboren *Big Man* 68: First time I see him with four-eyes and it makes him look older.

fourflush *n.* **1.** an incompetent or worthless person; FOUR-FLUSHER. Also attrib.

1896 Ade *Artie* 77: I never see one o' them fellows yet that wasn't a four-flush. **1901** Ade *Modern Fables* 40: So the Job was given to a Four-Flush who posed in Public Places and Frowned and kept one Hand inside of his Coat. **1903** Ade *Society* 121: He said he didn't propose to strain himself being Polite to a lot of Four-Flushes who owed him money. **1905** *Nat. Police Gaz.* (Nov. 11) 3: There is many a fourflush in New York to-day who is getting away with it. **1922** S. Lewis *Babbitt* 99: Who says Mike Monday is a four-flush and a yahoo? Huh?

2. something false or insincere. Often as quasi-adj.

1899 Ade *Fables* 4: But she always saw the same old line of Four-Flush Drummers from Chicago and St. Louis. **1901** Hobart *John Henry* 11: The four-flush call-down makes you back-pedal. **1906** H. Green *Boarding House* 36: The few steps she did were only "fourflush." **1916** MacBrayne & Ramsay *One More Chance* 74: I made…[the check] out myself, but I had never tried to pass it….I simply used it for a four-flush…to make it appear that I could raise money any time I wanted it. **1919** Z. Grey *Desert* 45: Facts have been told showin' a strange an' sudden growth of this here four-flush labor union.

fourflush *v.* **1.** to bluff, esp. by pretending expertise or knowledge.

1896 Ade *Artie* 26: He was four-flushin', I know the brand. **1899** *Nat. Police Gaz.* (Apr. 8) 7: The latter had been "four flushing" around the country as a fighter. **1901** *Chi. Tribune* (July 28) 38: Quitter…One who four-flushes. A person who does not make good. **1905** Hobart *Search Me* 56: He's been fourflushing around for years about the pitiful condition of the "drummer." **1906** H. Green *Boarding House* 61: The four-flushin', cross-eyed slob. **1918** Witwer *Baseball to Boches* 191: I figure he's four-flushin', Joe. **1918–19** MacArthur *Bug's-Eye View* 73: He was plainly moved. So were we, although we four-flushed a bit and pretended it was routine stuff.

2. *Poker.* to bluff on the basis of a worthless four-card flush. [Perh. the orig. sense; but since the noun *fourflush* is attested since 1887 and the figurative senses arose soon afterward, it is possible that this technical use of the verb did not arise until later.]

1948 J. Stevens *J. Turner* 122: He might be…bobtailing or fourflushing. I could only imagine.

fourflusher *n.* a prevaricator; fraud; poseur.

1904 *Life in Sing Sing* 255: Four Flusher. One who poses for effect. **1910** *N.Y. Eve. Jour.* (Feb. 5) 6: He quit like the fourflusher I always said he was. **1911** *DN* III 543: *Four-flusher, n.* Bluffer; one who cannot "make good." **1948** Ives *Wayfaring Stranger* 17: Oh, he's a big four-flusher. I wouldn't vote for him on a bet. **1956** Neider *Hendry Jones* 55: He was just a loud-mouthed fourflusher. **1987** *N.Y. Times* (July 7) A 12: That fraud!…That four-flusher!

four F's *n.* (see 1942, 1986 quots.). Also vars.

[**1934** Berg *Prison Nurse* 29: No one ever got rich letting suckers keep their dough. My motto is "Find them, fool them, and forget them!"] [**1941** Macaulay & Wald *Manpower* (film): You're talkin' to the guy who finds 'em, feeds 'em, and forgets 'em.] **1942** in Hollingshead *Elmtown's Youth* 422: The Five F's—"find 'em, feed 'em, feel 'em, f— 'em, forget 'em." **1953** *ATS* (ed. 2) 325: *The four F's*, high-pressure romancing—find 'em, fool 'em, frig 'em, and forget 'em. **a1961* Partridge *DSUE* (ed. 5) 1096: *Four F method, the.* This is the lower-deck's allusive synonym (C.20) of its sexual motto, *Find, feel, f**k and forget*, itself current since *ca*1890. **1965** *Playboy* (Nov.) 67: The Four F's. **1966** Harris & Freeman *Lords* 30: What a sportsman mean when he say weaving the four F's is—you got to find you chick and you got to fool her and you got to frig her and forget her! **1974** Lahr *Trot* 7: Melish, baby, the Four F's are forever.…Find 'em. Feel 'em. Fuck 'em. Forget 'em. **1978** Kopp *Innocence* 58: I aspired to the macho four Fs of my generation: find 'em, feel 'em, fuck 'em and forget 'em. [**1978** W. Brown *Tragic Magic* 23: He could find them, fool them, feel them, fuck them, and forget them with exceptional agility.] [**1986** Ciardi *Good Words* 118: *Find 'em, fool 'em, fuck 'em, and forget 'em*....I was first drilled to these orders in WWII and received them as essential GI pith.]

four-letter man *n.* [orig. in allusion to *letterman* 'student who has won a varsity letter'] a stupid or despicable fellow who may be described by various words of four letters.
  1923 Manchon *Le Slang* 263: *Shit*...bêtant et spécl un gaffeur. L'euph. est *four letter-man.* *1924, *1927 in *OEDS.* *1936 Partridge *DSUE* 298: *Four-letter man.* A very objectionable fellow...; heard among Army officers as early as 1917....i.e., a *s-h-i-t.* **1936** *Our Army* (Apr.) 41: "I hear that new recruit is a four-letter man." "Yeah! G-O-O-F!" **1952** R. Alexander *Time Out* 15: Oh, your big four-letter man—b-o-r-e. **1954-60** *DAS*: *Four letter man.* A dumb or stupid man....*Some student use. The four letters are "d-u-m-b."*

four-oh *adj.* *Navy.* perfect; most estimable; very well; fine. Cf. FORTY.
  1919 *Our Navy* (Sept.) 8: One of the gobs...should have been marked "4.0 plus" as a "leader of men." **1928** *AS* III (Aug.) 453: *Four-O (4.0)*— A grade of 100 per cent; perfection. **1943** *Newsweek* (Nov. 1) 48: Waves do a 4.0 (perfect) job of inspecting, repairing, and keeping the ships in tip-top condition. **1945** J. Bryan *Carrier* 79: That's a dilly! That's four-oh! **1953** Dibner *Deep Six* 59: "How's the crew?" "Four-oh, Admiral." *Ibid.* 104: Everything's four-oh, Alec. *Ibid.* 149: He's four-oh, boss. *Ibid.* 159: I'm okay. Four-oh. **1968** W. Crawford *Gresham's War* 17: "That's four-oh," James said....We watched Miss Scott at her duties. **1973** Overgard *Hero* 82: That's why when we signed over to the mad Cuban and things got humming, it was 4-O with me. **1978** Diehl *Sharky's Machine* 3: "How ya doin' buddy-boy?" "Four-O." **1982** T.C. Mason *Battleship* 201: That's four-oh with me.

four-on-the-floor *n.* a four-speed, floor-mounted standard transmission, as in a sports car.
  1971 Dahlskog *Dict.* 24: *Four-on-the-floor, n.* A four-speed, floor-mounted, standard automatic transmission. **1982** Del Vecchio *13th Valley* 94: He cranks up his four-on-da-floor.

four-plus *adv. & adj.* *Hosp.* extremely; very; (*also*) absolute; utter. Also as *v.*, to go all-out.
  1961 *AS* (May) 146: *Four plus*, adv. To the utmost degree, extremely, completely. From the method of reporting the results of certain laboratory tests as *negative, one plus, two plus, three plus,* and *four plus.* "That accident case is four plus drunk; I can't get a decent history from him." **1978** Shem *House of God* 333: Jo, angered at the thought of failure, shouted out: "With this kid we're four-plussing it, all the way!" and wouldn't stop. *Ibid.* 333: We're going all out. Four-plus! **1982** Huttmann *Code Blue* 30: "The poor nurse must feel like a four-plus fool." Later I learned that "four-plus" is a term used to refer to extreme amounts....Nurses use it in slang a lot: "Dr. Allen is four-plus nasty today—watch out." *Ibid.* 55: You look...four-plus terrified!

four sheets to the wind var. THREE SHEETS TO THE WIND.

four-star *adj.* [in allusion to hotel and restaurant ratings] superlative; first-class.
  1935 Odets *Waiting for Lefty*: You're a four-star bust! **1936** Gaddis *Courtesan* 18: See here, Dave Esmond, don't be a four-star sap. **1986** *Miami Vice* (NBC-TV): What I got is distribution—first-class and four-star. **1987** *N.Y. Times Bk. Review* (June 21) 13: She...travels to France and eats four-star meals. **1987** Kent *Phr. Book* 159: Sent his neighbors into a four-star swivet. **1991** *Night Court* (NBC-TV): Call one of your four-star girlfriends.

four-striper *n.* [a captain's insignia includes four stripes on the sleeve above the wrist] *Navy.* a naval captain.
  1914 *DN* IV 151: *Four-striper*, captain. **1920** Chambers *Subchasers* 9: A certain four striper (naval captain) on board one of our battleships. **1943** Coale *Midway* 18: The broad shoulders of our Navy four-stripers. **1962** E. Stephens *Blow Negative* 186: The base chaplain is a four-striper. **1983** Curry *River's in My Blood* 252: And there's a four-striper from Washington there with sundry lesser officers. **1984** "W.T. Tyler" *Shadow Cabinet* 243: They put a few more bird colonels or four-stripers out to pasture.

fourteen-carat *adj.* thoroughgoing; utter; genuine.
  1966 Elli *Riot* 39: He must look like a fourteen-carat ass-kisser. *Ibid.* 203: Fletcher's turned into a fourteen-carat phony. **1983** Flaherty *Tin Wife* 251: Groves was a fourteen-carat shit.

fowl ball *n.* a chicken croquette. *Joc.*
  1884 *Life* (Oct. 16) 215: *A Foul-Ball*—a chicken croquette. **1918** Rug-

gles *Navy Explained* 22: Chicken croquettes are "fowl balls."

fox *n.* **1.** (see quots.).
  1845 in *DAE*: The inhabitants of Maine are called Foxes. **1889** in *Ibid.*: The "Imperial Dictionary" informs us that the people of Maine are called "foxes" in the United States. I once lived in that state, yet I never have heard the nickname applied as indicated.
  2.a. [back formation fr. FOXY, 1.b.] Orig. *Black E.* a sexually attractive young woman; pretty girl.
  1961 Brosnan *Pennant Race* 33: So ah says to this cute lil ol' fox—dis is *befoh* ah's married, yuh understand—ah says, "Honey, let's me and you make a little happiness." *Ibid.* 39: So ah start in to sweet-talkin' this lil ol' fox, y' see. **1962** Crump *Killer* 102: "Ain't she tough? A real looker, right?" "Yeah, she's a real fox." **1963** *Time* (Aug. 2) 14: *Fox, flavor.* Pretty girl....A *stone fox*, a very pretty girl. **1963** in Clarke *Amer. Negro Stories* 301: Daddy, she was a real fox! **1964** R.S. Gold *Jazz Lexicon* III: *Fox.*...some currency esp. among Negro jazzmen since c.1958. **1964** Rhodes *Chosen Few* 51: Evahbody is shootin' at that fox. **1966** S. Stevens *Go Down Dead* 16: She one hot number that fox. **1968** Kirk & Hanle *Surfer's Hndbk.* 139: *Fox:* see *beach bunny.* **1969** *Playboy* (Dec.) 304: All these foxes keep me goin'. **1986** P. Markle *Youngblood* (film): She is a fox.
  b. *Pris.* the passive partner in a lesbian relationship.
  1969 in Giallombardo *Impris. Girls* 189: The fox is supposed to iron [her lesbian partner's] clothes and give him [i.e., her] respect.
  3. Esp. *Stu.* a sexually attractive person of the opposite sex. [An extension of meaning that subsumes sense (**2.a.**), above.]
  1976–77 C. McFadden *Serial* 39: Joan thought Spenser was "a fox." **1978** *UTSQ*: (Attractive) young man...*hunk, good-looking, tough, fox, built.* **1981** Univ. Tenn. student: Have you met Jimmy? He's got long hair and he's so cute. **1981** Crowe *Fast Times* 155: The red spotlight hit Mick Stillson, school fox, as he sat...with his guitar. **1982** Eble *Campus Slang* (Nov.) 2: *Fox*—handsome, attractive male: Rick Springfield is a *fox.* **1986** R. Walker *AF Wives* 15: If I had a chance with a fox like Steven, I'd daydream, too. **1987** G. Trudeau *Doonesbury* (synd. comic strip) (Apr. 20): And Sean's like this total fox, okay? But he won't take a blood test. **1987** *21 Jump St.* (Fox-TV): The guy's a fox!
  ¶ In phrases:
  ¶ **crazy like a fox** see s.v. CRAZY, *adj.*
  ¶ **hotter than a fresh-fucked fox in a forest fire** extremely hot (in any sense).—usu. considered vulgar. *Joc.*
  *ca*1950 in Atkinson *Dirty Comics* 197: Betty! This guy's got me hotter than a fresh fucked fox in a forest fire. **1973** *TULIPQ* (coll. B.K. Dumas): Horny...Hotter than a fresh-fucked fox in a forest fire. **1974** E. Thompson *Tattoo* 264 [ref. to 1940's]: It's a bitch down there. Hotter than a fresh fucked fox in a forest fire. **1974** Blount *3 Bricks Shy* 307: I'm hotter than a freshly fucked fox in a forest fire. **1977** S. Gaines *Discotheque* 268: It's hotter in here than a fresh fucked fox in a forest fire. **1980** Ciardi *Browser's Dict.* 41: Hot as a fresh fucked fox in a forest fire.

fox *v. Und.* to watch or follow closely.
  1848 *Ladies' Repository* VIII (Oct.) 315: *Fox,* To follow stealthily and watch closely. *1859 Hotten *Slang Dict.*: *Foxing.* Watching in the streets for any occurrence which may be turned to profitable account.

foxed *adj.* drunk.
  *1611 in *F & H* III 64: They will bib hard; they will be...sufficient fox'd or columber'd now and then. *1661 in *Ibid.*: Ah, blind as one that had been fox'd a sevennight. *1673 in *Ibid.*: But here's my cup...Udsooks, I begin to be fox'd! **1722** B. Franklin, in *AS* XV (Feb. 1940) 103: *Boozy, cogey, tipsey, fox'd, merry, mellow.* *1891 in *F & H* III 64: And so to bed well nigh seven in the morning, and myself as near foxed as of old. *1896 in *OED*: Will Symons had often seen him "foxed," amid the most undignified surroundings. **1978** *Nat. Lampoon* (Aug.) 26: A fellow has to carry three wallets of money to the taproom in order to get foxed.

foxhead *n.* *Ozarks.* moonshine whiskey. Cf. FOXED.
  1933 *AS* (Feb.) 49: *Fox-head*, n. Moonshine whiskey. **1952** Randolph & Wilson *Down in the Holler* 245: *Fox-head*: n., moonshine whiskey. There is a variety of rye known as *fox-head*, and it may be the name is derived from this.

foxhole *n.* *Mil.* a small pit dug usu. hastily for the protection of usu. one or two soldiers from enemy fire. Now *S.E.* [The 1924 quot., ref. to events of 1916, sugg. that the term may have arisen in the British Expeditionary Force before U.S. entry into WWI.]

1918 in Sherwood *Diary* 40: Fox holes, dug by little hand spades, shell holes and natural protection are taken advantage of…against cannon and machine gun fire. **1918** in Rendinell *One Man's War* 123: We were standing in some fox-holes when they asked me. **1919** Hamilton & Corbin *Echoes* 175: The attack…was met with torrents of rifle fire from the American line, from the shell holes, fox holes and brush. **1919** Haterius *137th U.S. Inf.* 162: The "fox holes" on Baulny Ridge are just as the occupants left them. ***1924** Blunden *Undertones* 120: Dead men…flung down by their last "foxholes." **1928** A. York *Sgt. York* 27: I wrote it…in the fox holes and trenches at the front. **1938** Noble *Jugheads Behind the Lines* 108: On a gentle slope across the valley were several hundred American soldiers digging "fox holes."

foxhole pajamas *n.pl. USMC.* (see quot.). *Joc.*
1945 J. Riordan, in *West. Folk. Qly.* (1946) 387: Foxhole pajamas. The overall-coat combination of heavy, water-resistant jungle cloth.

fox-in-the-bush *n. Juve.* a man with a full beard.
1929–31 Farrell *Young Lonigan* 140 [ref. to *ca*1916]: His old man was that sheeny fox-in-the-bush they always saw on Fifty-eighth Street. **1929–33** Farrell *Manhood of Lonigan*: A fox-in-the-bush got his place beside grandma.

fox pass *n.* [intentional folk ety.] a faux pas. *Joc.*
1925 *Collier's* (Sept. 19) 46: I'd pulled a fox pass. **1942** in Truman *Dear Bess* 477: It would be something of a *fox pass* if I address her dear sir. **1977** Univ. Tenn. student: We'll call that a fox pass.

fox paw *n.* [intentional folk ety.] a faux pas. *Joc.*
***1788** Grose *Vulgar Tongue* (ed. 2): *Fox's paw.* The vulgar pronunciation of the French words *faux pas.* He made a confounded fox's paw. ***a1890–93** F & H III 65: *To make a fox paw*…(common).—To make a wrong move; specifically (of women) to be seduced. **1942** *ATS* 194: Fox paw. **1968** Swarthout *Loveland* 109: Ain't this a fox paw!

foxtail *n. Naut.* a small hand brush.
1942 *Leatherneck* (Nov.) 145: *Foxtail*—A small hand dust brush. **1951** "W. Williams" *Enemy* 102 [ref. to WWII]: Daniels was…sweeping dirt with a short-handled brush the men called a "foxtail," into a trash tray. **1964** *Coast Guardsman's Manual* 859: *Foxtail*: a small hand brush, for sweeping. **1964** Hunt *Ship with Flat Tire* 112: The seaman recruit reaches for his dustpan and foxtail. **1972** Ponicsan *Cinderella Liberty* 42: Baggs on the sidewalk…with foxtail and dustpan.

foxy *adj.* **1.a.** (of women) amorous.
1877 in J.M. Carroll *Camp Talk* 75: Glad to know you are feeling so foxy. Shall endeavor to keep you busy at the game. **1977** B. Davidson *Collura* 99: We dropped these Tuies, man, and we jumped in bed, and man, she was as foxy as ever.
b. Esp. *Black E.* stylish and attractive; (*hence,* of women) sexy.
1895 Gore *Stu. Slang* 11: *Foxy*…Stylish, pretty, attractive, showy. "What a foxy dress you have on!"…"That's a foxy drawing." "I believe I handed in some foxy curves." **1900** *DN* II 36: *Foxy,* n.…Well-dressed. [Reported from 13 colleges and universities.] **1913** *DN* IV 21: *Foxy.* Stylish looking, attractive. Usage widespread in Nebraska. "She's a *foxy* looking little lady." ***1926** Walrond *Tropic Death* 92: Why, roared Miss Buckner, stockings could not be bought with that, much more take care of a woman accustomed to "foxy clothes an' such." **1944** Burley *Hndbk. Jive* 32: Studs in frantic duds; and foxy chicks, togged to the bricks. **1957** H. Simmons *Corner Boy* 162: "That yours [*viz.* a Cadillac]?" "Yeh." "It's foxy," Georgia said. **1960** R. Reisner *Jazz Titans* 156: *Foxy:* beautiful. **1963** in Clarke *Amer. Negro Stories* 303: And she was lookin' foxier by the minute. **1964** in Wepman et al. *The Life* 93: Tina, a foxy kind of doll. **1964** in B. Jackson *Swim Like Me* 98: I picked up on your wardrobe and it's foxy, too. **1966** Ward *Happy Ending* 5: One of them foxy, black "Four Hundred" debutantes, you dig! **1966** Braly *On Yard* 237: I used to be a pretty foxy-looking youngster. **1971** *Room 222* (ABC-TV): Now, the gentleman that thinks I'm foxy—what's a yellow dog contract? **1992** *Young & Restless* (CBS-TV): You look foxy! It's a great style on you!
c. (among young women) handsome; attractive (said of young men).
1980 Peck & Young *Little Darlings* (film): I'd advise you to choose a foxy stud.
2. Now esp. *Black E.* splendid; fine.
1900 *DN* II 36: *Foxy*…extremely good. [Reported from Indiana University.] **1940** in Oliver *Meaning of Blues* 320: Then everything will be foxy. **1946** Mezzrow & Wolfe *Really Blues* 86: We…were for making music that was real foxy, all lit up with inspiration and her mammy. *Ibid.* 305: *Foxy:* sly, clever, good.

frabbajabba *n.* [of fanciful orig., partly sugg. by *jabber*] nonsensical talk.
1957 Laurents & Sondheim *West Side Story* 140: Cut the frabbajabba.

fracture *v.* **1.** Orig. *Show Bus.* to delight, esp. to convulse with laughter.
1946 in *OEDS:* This guy Muller fractures me. **1947** *ATS* (Supp.) 4. **1948** M. Shulman *Dobie Gillis* 57: That Walter Pidgeon is so dreamy. I mean he fractures me. **1952** Uris *Battle Cry* 90 [ref. to 1942]: "That guy fractures me," Ski said. "Always trying to make like an Indian." **1956** M. Wolff *Big Nick.* 81: Funny, funny girl. You fracture me. **1960** Kirkwood *Pony* 154: She was beautiful, too, and that ponytail fractured me. **1960** *Twilight Zone* (CBS-TV): Tomorrow we'll fracture 'em! **1972** Kopp *Buddha* 202: The grooviest, most fracturing grass of all time. **1973** *Penthouse* (June) 80: This fractured the boy…He was laughing so hard he had trouble speaking. **1987** R.M. Brown *Starting* 32: What fractures me about most men is that they can't live without male approval.
2. to trounce.
1946 Werris et al. *If I'm Lucky* (film): They'll kill him! They'll murder him! They'll fracture him! **1948** Seward & Ryan *Angel's Alley* (film): Lemme at that guy. I'll fracture him! **1970** Landy *Underground Dict.* 81: *Fracture*…Beat up; clobber.
3. to astonish or disconcert.
1970 Landy *Underground Dict.* 81: *Fracture*…shake up; disturb. **1985** M. Baker *Cops* 188: "Fuck you, you little baldheaded prick," she says. We were positively fractured.

fractured *adj.* intoxicated.
1953 Manchester *City of Anger* 354: She's a drunk…gets fractured every night. **1954-60** *DAS: Fractured.* Drunk. Fairly common since c1940. **1970** Landy *Underground Dict.* 81: *Fractured*…Drunk.

frag *n.* **1.** *Mil.* a fragmentation bomb or grenade. Also attrib.
1943 R. Scott *God Is Co-Pilot* 105: Let's bomb the railroad yards at Laokay with our frags. **1944** *Life* (May 29) 73: He fought for fighters dropping "frag" bombs on bombers. **1951** Jones *Face of War* 7: What kinda grenades we gettin', frag or personnel? **1952** Landon *Angle of Attack* 122: We got to open up to drop frags. **1970** Williams *New Exiles* 299: They told him to throw a frag (grenade). **1972** T. O'Brien *Combat Zone* 76: I learned that…a hand grenade is…a "frag." **1982** Del Vecchio *13th Valley* 31: Hey, L-T. We got any more frags? **1986** Thacker *Pawn* 61 [ref. to 1970]: Jake hefted the frag in his hand like a baseball.
2. *Mil.* a fragment of a shell, grenade, etc.
1966 Marshall *Battles in the Monsoon* 250: One bomb frag smashed the radio of Lieutenant Goodowens' RTO. **1967** in B. Edelman *Dear Amer.* 87: [The] frag went inside and bounced off my bones. **1972** Haldeman *War Year* 28: Here in 'Nam they called them "frags" instead of shrapnel. That's what they were—fragments—like when an artillery shell goes off, the explosive inside shatters the lead casing into hundreds of frags. **1973** Kingry *Monk & Marines* 84: He was wounded in the side by grenade frags. **1983** Van Devanter & Morgan *Before Morning* 99: He held a forcep in one hand, ready to grab the frag. *a***1984** in Terry *Bloods* 112: I got frags in the lower back.
3.a. *Mil. Av.* a fragmentary order.
1962 Tregaskis *Vietnam Diary* 67: I'll go briefly over the frag (short for fragmentary order). **1982** W.R. Dunn *Fighter Pilot* 133 [ref. to WWII]: Let's get to work on this frag. **1984** Trotti *Phantom* 53 [ref. to Vietnam War]: It divvied the missions out to the air groups by means of a missive known as the FRAG—fragmentary combat operations order. **1987** Robbins *Ravens* 399 [ref. to 1960's]: In the Air Force the Frag was the daily plan for the number of fighter-bombers and the type of ordnance they would carry.
b. *Mil. Av.* a mission carried out under a fragmentary order.
1985 Heywood *Taxi Dancer* 187 [ref. to 1967]: I don't want the frag jeopardized for a taxi in friendly territory.

frag *v.* **1.** *Mil.* to assign or transfer by fragmentary order.
1967 in Tuso *Vietnam Blues* 219: But Seventh frags us on the railroad. **1969** Broughton *Thud Ridge* 82: His wingman…had been fragged to carry a cumbersome camera pod. **1970** *17th Wild Weasel Songbk.* (unp.): He frags all the targets and sends us out to die. **1978** J. Webb *Fields of Fire* 91: Frag yourself and get the hell outa here before you crack up. **1983** T. Page *Nam* 17 [ref. to Vietnam War]: You could spend days with one aviation unit fragging missions all over the Corps. *Ibid.* 21: A Huey fragged by PIOs of the 25th Div. **1985** Heywood *Taxi Dancer* 237 [ref. to 1967]: The Eleventh was fragged against the thermal plant and the power station. **1986** Coonts *Intruder* 273 [ref. to Vietnam War]: Lieutenant Cole and I hit the fragged target. **1990** R. Dorr *Desert Shield* 98: Loftus was "fragged" (scheduled to fly) for C-141B Starlifter 64-0627.

2.a. *Mil.* to kill or wound (a disliked superior officer), usu. by means of a fragmentation grenade.

1970 in *OEDS:* "To frag" is a term meaning to use a fragmentation grenade "to cool the ardor of any officer or NCO too eager to make contact with the enemy." **1971** *N.Y. Post* (Jan. 5) 39: Keyes Beech of the Chicago Daily News has reported on the new outdoor sport in Vietnam of "fragging" officers—hitting an officer or a non-com with a fragmentation grenade. **1971** *Newsweek* (Jan. 11) 34: The grunts' word for it is "fragging"—which comes from the fact that the most decisive way to deal with an overtly aggressive officer or noncom is to lob a fragmentation grenade at him. **1971** *N.Y. Times Mag.* (Sept. 19) 66: Goddammit, if no one was looking, I'd frag the sonuvabitch. **1971–72** Giovannitti *Medal* 116: You damn well knew Thomas fragged Doll [with a bullet]. **1975** Kangas & Solomon *Psych. of Strength* 8: The soldier loyal to his comrades and lieutenant fights harder than the one coerced, who may turn against the leader (as in the "fragging" by unmotivated, resentful soldiers in Vietnam). **1975** Wambaugh *Choirboys* 210: The explosion of cheers startled the shit out of Lieutenant Finque who thought he was being fragged. **1976** C.R. Anderson *Grunts* 192: That's it, Man—I'm gonna frag me a lifer some night! **1978** J. Webb *Fields of Fire* 412 [ref. to 1969]: *To Frag:* To wound or kill someone using a grenade. **1986** Stinson & Carabatsos *Heartbreak* 92: He was gonna frag the entire platoon…[with] an AK-47 assault rifle. **1992** *Newsweek* (Nov. 23) 27: "If Clinton…walks on this base, he's dead." No good soldier is going to frag the commander in chief, of course.

b. *Mil.* to direct a fragmentation weapon, usu. a grenade, against (an enemy position). Also absol.

1971 *N.Y. Post* (Jan. 6) 50: Now he has to decide whether to zap Charlie with 20mm cannon or 40mm grenades, spray him with 4000 rounds a minute from his 7.62 minigun, or "frag" him with rockets containing 2500 deadly 1½-inch nails. **1973** Huggett *Body Count* 12: Bunker!…Frag it! **1973** R. Roth *Sand in Wind* 285: Every deserted hootch had a bunker beneath it, and now began the troublesome job of fragging and entering each one. **1985** Dye *Between Raindrops* 43: Frag first and ask questions later.

c. *Mil.* to booby-trap with a fragmentation grenade.

1973 Browne *Body Shop* 121: And we did frag their bodies so their buddies would get fragged when they came to pick up the bodies.

d. to sabotage.

1984 N. Stephenson *Big U.* 31: He was just screwed up enough to frag the System for revenge.

fraggle *v.* [orig. unkn.] to rob.

1859 Bartlett *Amer.* (ed. 2) 161: *To fraggle.* To rob. A word used in Texas.

frago *n. Mil.* a fragmentation order.

1991 in LaBarge *Desert Voices* 148: We got what they called fragos, fragmentation orders.

fragrance-peddler *n.* a skunk. *Joc.* Cf. syn. ESSENCE-PEDDLER.

1882 Baillie-Grohman *Rockies* 369: A defunct "fragrance pedlar" *i.e.* skunk.

frail *n.* [sugg. by *frail sisters* or *frail sisterhood,* a literary euphem. for prostitutes] **1.** a prostitute.

[***1820–21** P. Egan *Life in London* 142: He *merely* "looks in" to see…if any thing "new" appears in the stock of "Frailties"…the frail sisterhood in general.] [***1821** *Real Life in London* I 172: He asks the frail ones…if…he is not a good-looking fellow. *Ibid.* 195: Of frail ones, ten score.] ***1846** (cited in Partridge *DSUE* (ed. 5) 1096). [**1846** *Nat. Police Gaz.* (June 20) 347: A Frail Female in Trouble.…The frail mother was finally removed to the City Hospital.] [**1869** "G. Ellington" *Women of N.Y.* 209: There is an antiquated mansion owned by one of the frail sisters.] [**1890** Langford *Vigilantes* 61: The gambling saloon, cheap whiskey, frail women, and all the evils necessarily flowing from such polluted combinations.] **1916** Cary *Slang of Venery* I 93: *Frail*—A whore.

2.a. a woman; BROAD.—often used disparagingly.

1899 A.H. Lewis *Sandburrs* 80: D' old frail goes round d' place. **1908** H. Green *Maison* 50: Aw, the frails is all the same. **1911** Runyon *Tents of Trouble* 24: I'll drink to your healt' wit' the frail we liked when I git to the Big White Way. **1919** Darling *Jargon Book* 13: *Frail*—A girl. **1926** Dunning & Abbott *Broadway* 237: I thought you was out with one of the frails. **1929** Milburn *Hobo's Hornbook* 193: A dead swell frail came in the place. **1931** C. Ford *Coconut Oil* 148: Hey, Harry, where'dja pick up the frail! **1956** Levin *Compulsion* 131: Hey, drag a frail, we'll make it a real party! Bring that babe of yours, Ruthie. **1957** J.D. MacDonald *Death Trap* 78: I need a frail with a pail. **1963** Dwiggins *S.O. Bees* 151: Son, you've never had a frail till you've had a rosy-cheeked lass from

there. **1967** Talbot *Chatty Jones* 35: That frail's a bitch on wheels. **1982** *World's Finest Comics* (Sept.) (unp.): I wouldn't mind wastin' either of these frails. **1989** *Dream St.* (NBC-TV): And you figure some frail put him up to it?

b. *Pris.* the passive partner in a lesbian relationship.

1958 (quot. at STUD).

frail eel *n. Black E.* a young woman.

1933 in Clarke *Amer. Negro Stories* 66: Y'all pritty lil frail eels don't need nothin' lak dis. **1935** Hurston *Mules and Men* 219: All dese frail eels gittin' skittish. **1942** *Pittsburgh Courier* (July 18) 7: All you frail eels. **1970** Major *Dictionary of Afro-Amer. Slang:* Frail eel: any good-looking woman.

frame *n.* **1.a.** Orig. *Und.* FRAME-UP, 1.a.

1911 T.A. Dorgan, in Zwilling *TAD Lexicon* 37: He can spot a "frame" when they pull it. **1914** Jackson & Hellyer *Vocab.* 35: *Frame.* Noun. General currency. A prearranged plan of action; a secret implying sinister intention; a frame-up:…"What's the frame for putting this one over? The lemon." **1913–15** Van Loan *Taking Count* 118: Didn't you know that you was up against a frame?…Sure you won,…but the way they had it fixed up I was to take a poke on the jaw and go out. *Ibid.* 322: "A frame, eh?"…"He says not. Says the fight has got to be on the level." **1924** Bronson-Howard *Devil's Chaplain* 36: This louse woulda beat us to the frame if I hadn't plugged him. **1931** in D.W. Maurer *Lang. Und.* 42: The prop is in on the frame for the hoist at chow time. **1987** Mamet *House of Games* (film): You'd have to go to a *museum* to see a frame like this!

b. Orig. *Und.* FRAME-UP, 1.b.

1929 Barr *Let Tomorrow Come* 149: I'm here on a frame.…If they can't stick you straight, they'll frame you. **1934** R. Chandler, in *DAS:* The dough was passed to me to make the frame tighter. **1947** Bowers & Millhouser *Web* (film): If it's a frame, there's only one guy can clear you. **1949** "J. Evans" *Halo for Satan* 148: He…wasn't a killer but just the victim of a frame. **1959** Lederer *Never Steal Anything Small* (film): Get lost. This is a frame. **1962** Ragen & Finston *Toughest Pris.* 799: *Frame*—A false accusation. **1980** H. Gould *Ft. Apache* 189: You got us in here on a frame.…You're gonna set us up for that cop killing.

2. a young woman having an attractive figure. Also **frame dame.**

[**1934** Weseen *Dict. Slang* 182: College…*Frame*—A dance partner.] **1945** *Amer. N & Q* (Aug.) 70: Girl with sex appeal—frame dame, blackout girl, ready Hedy. **1946** Boulware *Jive & Slang* 3: *Fine Brown Frame*…Good-looking brown girl. **1955** in *Tenn. Folk. Soc. Bull.* XXII (1956) 28: Any stud or frame who so goofed would see all the hipsters cut out. **1963** Rubin *Sweet Daddy* 157: *Frame:* a woman having an attractive figure. **1979** *AS* LI 22 [ref. to *ca*1950]: *Frame dame* "seductive girl."

frame *v.* **1.a.** to concoct, plan, or contrive, esp. for a sinister purpose.—usu. constr. with *up.* [Except for the typically late-19th C. addition of the particle *up,* this is scarcely distinguishable from the early exx. in *OED2* s.v. *frame,* v., 8.a., quots. for 1514, 1577, 1608, 1682.]

1899 A.H. Lewis *Sandburrs* 187: An' now youse is framin' up a blowout over findin' it! **1904** Limerick *Villagers* 74: They framed up a scheme to bring matrimonial negotiations to a head. **1905** Hobart *Search Me* 28: I've got it all framed up. It's good for a thousand plunks apiece every week. **1911** Bronson-Howard *Enemy to Society* 105: You don't believe that a man who can't write was capable of framing up such a gorgeous robbery? **1914** Spencer *Jailer* 60: They will frame up enough evidence on you, if you plead not guilty, to get you. **1915-16** Lait *Beef, Iron & Wine* 21: He's layin' low, framin' a big job somewhere. **1931** in D.W. Maurer *Lang. Und.* 40: We can frame a pinch for the mope. **1937** Herndon *Let Me Live* 171: We are…thrown into jail on framed charges. **1945** *Calif. Folk. Qly.* IV 250: We framed it up in Alaska. **1956** Ross *Hustlers* 77: You framed this!…You knew! All the time. **1973** N.Y.U. student: We're trying to frame up a good story.

b. to make ready or prepare; set up; put together; fix (a drink, etc.).—also constr. with *up.* Cf. *OED* s.v. *frame,* v., 8.

1901 A.H. Lewis *Croker* 63: There's a kind of good example that prize fighters set that a…banker ain't framed up to offer. **1901** Ade *Modern Fables* 9: Go before a Lawyer and have him frame up an Iron-clad Contract. **1902** Cullen *More Tales* 86: I asked the man to frame me up another [cocktail]. **1902–3** Ade *People You Know* 134: He had framed up a Poker Festival for that Night. **1908** *Hampton's Mag.* (Oct.) 462: The average popular song is usually "ground out" or "framed up", as the *patois* has it, in…a song publisher's office. *a*1909 Tillotson *Detective* 91: *Framed up*—To make complete arrangements. **1911** A.H. Lewis

Apaches of N.Y. 77: I'm there wit' a gatt meself....W'en they sees I'm framed up, they gets cold feet. *Ibid.* 164: He's framed up with a gun. **1911** Bronson-Howard *Enemy to Society* 112: We're framed for him this time....Tell him. **1931** in D.W. Maurer *Lang. Und.* 30: (To) *frame*, v. To prepare, set up, or build anything. "We got up early so's we could frame the joint." **1943** *Sat. Eve. Post* (Sept. 25) 39: This done, [the pitchman] next proceeded to "frame the flash."

c. to dress.

1903 A.H. Lewis *Lion Inn* 77: Dan bein' all framed an' frazzled up...like a Injun medicine man. **1906** H. Green *Boarding House* 30: Is the dames all framed up in decollaty rags?

2. *Sports.* to prearrange (a contest) illicitly.

1908 in H.C. Fisher *A. Mutt* 23: I am leaving the country so the book makers can't shoot me for framing it. **1911** T.A. Dorgan, in *N.Y. Eve. Jour.* (Jan. 10) 14: Abe fought like a novice and either "framed" the go or was saving himself for his bout with Patsy Kline. **1930** Farrell *Calico Shoes* 193: I ain't never had nothin' to do with a framed fight, or a faked boxing match of any kind. **1942** *Amer. Mercury* (Dec.) 678: That's all the bunk about these matches being framed....We mix it up for real. **1970** in P. Heller *In This Corner* 21: They were crooks, they framed fights, and...the poor guy had to follow orders.

3.a. to scheme.

1908 Hopper & Bechdolt *9009* 72: Yes—four of them are framing....There'll be a dozen of them in it by that time. **1918** *Chi. Sun. Trib.* (Mar. 24) V (unp.): We begin to find out which was the guys what was framin' agin honest labor. **1929** Barr *Let Tomorrow Come* 6: You can have a lot of fun framin' with 'em about what you'll do to the screws at Leavenworth.

b. to explain.—constr. with *up*.

1910 Raine *O'Connor* 23: I merely wanted to frame up to you how this thing's going to turn out.

4. to appear; shape up.—constr. with *up*.

1910 Hapgood *City Streets* 320: There's no guy here wat'd get drunk on Christmas Eve if he could help it. Course sometimes dey fall, but every regular tries to frame up good to his folks on Christmas.

5.a. Orig. *Und.* to contrive evidence against (an innocent person); to incriminate or convict falsely. Also **frame up on.** Now *S.E.*

1915 *Report on Colo. Strike* 21: They said that they had "framed up" on him. They...stuck a gun in his pocket and arrested him for carrying concealed weapons. **1919** in E. O'Neill *Letters* 98: I suspect [the drunk]...was being "framed" for a "frisk." **1919** in Partridge *Dict. Und.* 265: I was the chicken-hearted pen-wiper...who had been "framed." **1922** Titus *Timber* 234: So they were after Bryant were they? They were framing him? **1924** Henderson *Keys to Crookdom* 405: *Framed*—Incriminated through false testimony or conspiracy. **1925** *Writer's Mo.* (June) 486: *Frame*—To arrange evidence in perpetrating a crime so as to throw all the blame on a certain person. Sometimes the person "framed" is innocent of any wrongdoing. **1927** McIntyre *Slag* 153: If he does, the bulls might frame us for it. **1927** Murphy *Gray Walls* 38: I did not know why I had been placed in solitary confinement, but I was certain that some stool pigeon had "framed" me. **1929** Sullivan *Look at Chicago* 75: The vice lords...had crossed him up, "framed" him forty ways. **1929** in Mencken *Amer. Lang.* Supp. I 441: I've been framed. **1937** "L. Short" *Brand of Empire* 89: When a man frames another, it's because he wants him out of the way. **1974** Radano *Cop Stories* 30: I never framed a guy, even when I used to make narcotics arrests. When I locked him up it was always because I had caught him with the goods. **1992** *Likely Suspects* (Fox-TV): If I wanted to frame him, why would I give him an alibi?

b. to place in a dangerous or compromising situation; set up.

1925 *Collier's* (Sept. 19) 46: So you framed me, eh? **1930** Sage *Last Rustler* 157: I believed they'd framed me in some way. They'd already drawed their horses and all there was left was a big buckskin. **1930** E. Caldwell *Poor Fool* 98: He framed me. He gave me something that made me dizzy and the other pug knocked me out the window. Now I can't get no more fights. **1932** W. Smith *Lost Sqdrn.* (film): Acid on the control wires! Von Furst's framed him! **1954** Collans & Sterling *House Detect.* 51: So you thought you could frame me for a sucker!

c. to trick; hoodwink.

1926 Norwood *Other Side of Circus* 105: "They're just trying to frame you." The others chuckled. **1936** Miller *Battling Bellhop* (film): Tryin' to frame my kid into takin' a punch at him? **1948** Manone & Vandervoort *Trumpet* 196: So I had to frame him to get my meals free. This was easy, because there would be so many guys sitting in the band, if we put in an order for six, he didn't know which six guys were doin' the eatin'. **1957** *This Is Your Life* (CBS-TV): John Nelson and I *have* kind of framed you—you're on television coast-to-coast!

¶ In phrase:

¶ **frame in** *Und.* to go into partnership for a sinister purpose.

1904 *Life in Sing Sing* 261: *I blew away and beat it back to Chic, and framed in with a couple of guns.*...I parted from them and returned to Chicago. There I met two pickpockets.

framed *adj. Und.* **1.** (of a known criminal) represented by a photograph in a police rogue's gallery.

1904 *Life in Sing Sing* 263: *In making my get-away, the cash got my mug. Pink had me framed....He picked me right....*The cashier saw my face as I fled...and picked my picture from the Rogue's Gallery, where Pinkerton placed it some time ago.

2. being watched by police.

1923 *Atlanta Constitution* (Feb. 1) 12: Th' joint's framed?...There's a lotta dicks outside.

frame dame see s.v. FRAME, *n.*, 2.

frame job *n.* FRAME-UP, 1.b.

1973 R. Roth *Sand in Wind* 436: But how you gonna prove it's a frame job if you don't know all the facts? **1974** Radano *Cop Stories* 30: This is a frame job. You slipped that into my pocket. **1976** "N. Ross" *Policeman* 54: When an addict or pusher gets out of hand, we'll take steps to get him off the street, whether it be surveillance, using our many pigeons, or even a frame job. **1983** *Real Entertainment* (ABC-TV): It was a complete frame job. I was framed.

frame-up *n.* **1.a.** Orig. *Und.* a usu. sinister scheme or plan; conspiracy; a put-up job or prearranged contest; setup.

1900 "Flynt" & Walton *Powers* 141: He could arrange a "frame-up" and relieve "Soapy" of the stolen pocketbook. **1906** *Nat. Police Gaz.* (Dec. 8) 6: Dis frame-up I'm after readin' about where you're goin' t' try t' pickle a bunch o' rum eaters....Does it go? **1907** *McClure's Mag.* (Feb.) 384: They knew something about this frame-up to attack the strikers' camp. **1908** H. Green *Maison* 55: Can't you take a joke?...It's a frame-up. Let him up! **1908** in H.C. Fisher *A. Mutt* 25: We were never divorced. That was just a frame-up with the judge to scare you. **1908** *New Broadway Mag.* (Aug.) 142: It was the finest frame-up I ever went up against. **1908** Beach *Barrier* 100: I'd rather tackle a gang-saw than a man like Poleon Doret. Your frame-up may work double. **1911** T.A. Dorgan, in *N.Y. Eve. Jour.* (Jan. 12) 16: The boxers are either under a pull, out of condition, or in a frame-up. **1912** *Hampton's Mag.* (Jan.) 748: The whole thing's nothing more than a plant, a frame-up...a plan to trap you. **1922** Hisey *Sea Grist* 54: I knew now that it was not a frame up, so braced myself for the worst. **1928** Callahan *Man's Grim Justice* 46: The most important part of the job is the frame up....Always look your mark over carefully before you go up against it. **1928** in Galewitz *Great Comics* 149: That's a frame-up, sure as yer born—but what about? **1930** Sage *Last Rustler* 158: I told him about the buckskin horse and that it looked like a frame-up. **1930** Farrell *Calico Shoes* 194: I'm gonna offer one hunerd dollars...to the man that can prove that this last fight was a frame-up. **1932** in Fortune *Fugitives* 84: The "police" called it a "frame-up,"/Said it was an "inside job." **1971** Simon *Sign of Fool* 138: I ran it down to him, explaining my idea about the city's plot to close 848 with a frame-up between the Health Department and the Fish and Game people. **1987** Mamet *House of Games* (film): Goodbye! You're gettin' into the frame-up!

b. *Specif.,* a fraudulent incrimination of an innocent person.

1908 in H.C. Fisher *A. Mutt* 35: The pinch looks like a "frame up" to annex the reward. **1913** *Vice Comm. Phila. Report* 13: It was a frame-up, then? **1914** in J. Reed *Young Man* 102: I'm wanted for two murder charges—I didn't do it, I swear to God I didn't—it was a frame-up. **1914** *London Jacket* 42: All the treacherous frame-up of Cecil Winwood was news to them. **1916** Griffith *Intolerance* (film): The Musketeer...arranges the old familiar frame-up. **1924** Henderson *Keys to Crookdom* 405: *Frame up*—a conspiracy to incriminate an innocent person. **1928–30** Fiaschetti *Gotta Be Rough* 48: The stratagem I used had been worked more than once, which may account for some of the common stories of frame-ups, railroading and plants. **1930** in *DAS*: I'll prove to you it's a frame-up. **1942–49** Goldin et al. *DAUL* 73: *Frame-up*, n. Conviction and subsequent imprisonment on trumped-up charges, or as a result of any improper—even if legal—procedure. **1963** Loomis *Develop. Arth. Romance* 15: How much of fact and how much of "frame-up" was in the criminal indictments against Sir Thomas Malory? **1981** G. Wolf *Roger Rabbit* 59: This is a frame-up. Somebody is trying to saddle me with Rocco's murder.

c. an arrangement of any sort.

1908 J. London *M. Eden* 141: Here's the frame-up. The wages for two is a hundred and board.

2. *Pris.* a prevaricator.

1908 Kelley *Oregon Pen.* 71: The "frame-up" is a prisoner who tries to get his work in by playing a job....The officers know he will...boost the dump and do any lying they want him to.

3. (among pitchmen) a display of wares; set-up.

1941 in *AS* (Feb. 1942) 91: A good frame-up will work wonders for an energetic pitchman.

frammis *n.* [orig. unkn.] a thing; thingamabob; (*hence*) uproar.

1957 *Newsweek* (July 8) 85: Cocktail-party sports use a "framis" or broomstick to retrieve the Frisbee from under chairs. **1958** J. Thompson *Getaway* 99: He was going to get *something* out of this frammis. **1970** Thackrey *Thief* 319: And that's how the *real* frammis [uproar] started. **1972** R. Barrett *Lovomaniacs* 190: Anyway, there was this frammis with Sam. **1988** *CBS This Morning* (CBS-TV) (June 23): We'll [call] this the frammis, for lack of a better word.

Frank *n. Und.* a German.

1848 *Ladies' Repository* VIII (Oct.) 315: *Frank*, A Dutchman.

frank *n.* **1.** a frankfurter. Now *S.E.*

1925 T.A. Dorgan, in Zwilling *TAD Lexicon* 37: Hot Franks a Dime. **1936** in E.E. Cummings *Letters* 145: Sand there shall be with our franks. **1952–58** Kerouac *On the Road* 7: We had a farewell meal of franks and beans.

2. the penis. *Joc.*

1981 (quot. at CRANK, *n.*).

frankie *n. Mil.* a French franc. Also **franker**.

1918 *Lit. Digest* (Aug. 17) 59: With his hands in his pockets, jiggling "*bokoo frankies.*" **1919** T. Kelly *What Outfit?* 55: For one good ten-spot, American dough, I'd give 'em all the *frankers* they ever printed. **1919** McKenna *Battery A* 159: Frankers. **1920** *Amer. Legion Wkly.* (Aug. 20) 7: Ah's got vink-sank frankies. **1930** *AS* V (June) 383 [ref. to 1917]: *Frankies.* Francs. **1936** Reilly *Americans All* 299: The Alabams took good care of him, however, advancing "frankies" freely.

Frankie Baileys *n.pl.* [see 1962 quot.] *Theat.* attractive legs, esp. of a young woman. Also **Frankies.** Now *hist.*

1921 T.A. Dorgan, in Zwilling *TAD Lexicon* 38: A pair of beautiful "Frankie Baileys" never yet made a champ. **1923** *N.Y. Times* (Oct. 14) VIII 4: *Frankie Baileys*—Commendable legs. **1962** Charters & Kunstadt *Jazz* 14: At Weber & Fields' [theater in N.Y.C. in the 1890's] the shapely legs of Miss Frankie Bailey were so famous that "Frankie Bailey's" became a slang term for pretty ankles. **1971** Faust *Willy Remembers* 25: And so help me if she was not in possession of one of the most outstanding pairs of Frankies I had...ever seen.

frantic *adj. Jazz.* splendid; exciting; CRAZY; WILD.

1934 in M. Starks *Cocaine Fiends* 101: Boy she's really frantic—the wildest chick in town. **1944** Burley *Hndbk. Jive* 138: *Frantic*—Great, wonderful. **1946** Mezzrow & Wolfe *Really Blues* 305: *Frantic*...unusually good. **1946** in R.S. Gold *Jazz Talk* 98: [The tune] jumps, it's exciting or frantic, as the fan would describe it. **1947** *ATS* (Supp.) 4: Teen Talk and Jive Jargon...Excellent; "super."...*frantic*. **1952** J.C. Holmes *Go* 173: Everything before, you see, just last year, was "crazy," "frantic," "gone." **1952** Himes *Stone* 13: "All he needs is a good turning out." "Not if he's a college boy. Them college boys are frantic." **1954–60** *DAS: Frantic.* Exciting; satisfying; wonderful; cool. Wide bop use since *ca*1946. **1959–60** R. Reisner *Jazz Titans* 156: *Frantic:* something of wild beauty. **1960** *Many Loves of D. Gillis* (CBS-TV): Ooh! Frantic!

frap *n.* ¶ In phrase: **the frap** [back formation fr. FRAPPING] (a euphem. for) *the fuck*, 1, s.v. FUCK, *n.*

1992 Eble *Campus Slang* (Fall) 3: What the frap is going on?

frap *v. U.S. Nav. Acad.* to strike or hit. [S.E. until 19th C.; see *OED*.]

1894 *Lucky Bag* (No. 1) 67: Frappe...See "Biff." **1905** *Lucky Bag* (No. 12) 206: Frap...to smear in de mush wid a hot potoot. **1922** Taylor *Nav. Acad. Songbook* 58: I frap the pap three times a day.

frapping *adj. Mil.* (a euphem. for) FUCKING; FRIGGING; dratted.

1968 W.C. Anderson *Gooney Bird* 76: We'll let a whole frapping regiment get away before we'll risk hitting one old lady in sneakers. **1970** *N.Y. Times* (Apr. 19) 1: And finally in desperation: "What's the frappin' altitude?" **1972** W.C. Anderson *Hurricane* 196: And the poor frapping navy! **1973** M. Collins *Carrying the Fire* 334: Yeah, but the frapping thing bombed out again. **1989** Berent *Rolling Thunder* 133: That frapping Dash-K is shooting out our cover as the frapping roots.

frat *n.* **1.** *Stu.* a Greek-letter fraternity.—often attrib. Now *colloq.*

1895 Gore *Stu. Slang* 7: *Frat,* n. 1. A fraternity. **1902** Harriman *Ann Arbor* 78: Ain't it funny he's not to be at his frat. house? **1906** in *OEDS:* I became a Frat man. **1910** Ade *I Knew Him When* 43: He acquired a Frat Pin. **1911** Van Loan *Big League* 70: He saw my "frat" pin one day. **1926** *Ladies' Home Jour.* (Nov.) 12: It's a frat house. **1943** Shulman *Barefoot Boy* 41: Join Alpha Cholera, our swell frat. **1954** in *Social Problems* II (1955) 168: I don't think any frat is going to sacrifice its character for the sake of admitting a Negro.

2. *Stu.* a member of a Greek-letter fraternity.

1895 Gore *Stu. Slang* 7: *Frat...*2. A member of a fraternity. **1934** Weseen *Dict. Slang* 182. **1966** H.S. Thompson *Hell's Angels* 264: They...named Jews, Negroes and Frats (well-dressed students) as hate objects. **1988** Univ. Tenn. instructor: All her boyfriends have been frats.

frat *v. Army.* to engage in fraternization, orig. with German and Austrian women after the end of WWII.

***1945** in *OEDS:* "Fraternization" has become a word denoting sexual intercourse ("frats" and "fratting" are new Army words). **1945** *Yank* (Aug. 31) 5: The endless discussion...added a new word to the vocabulary: frattin'. **1945** Hamann *Air Words: Fratin'.* Fraternization. ***1965** in *OEDS:* He did frat, I mean make friends with the people you're thinking of. **1986** R. Walker *AF Wives* 226: "I can't wait to do a little fratting, can you?" "Fratting?" "Fraternizing."

frat bait *n. Army.* (see quot.).

1945 *Am. N & Q* (June) 40: *Frat Bait:* candy, chewing gum, and cigarets in the pockets of American and British soldiers in [European] occupied zones.

frat-rat *n. Stu.* a member of a Greek-letter fraternity.—used disparagingly.

1958 J. Davis *College Vocab.* 5: *Frat rat*—Fraternity man. **1963** IUFA *Folk Speech: Frat rat*—Someone who lives in a fraternity. **1964** *AS* (May) 118: *Frat-rat* "fraternity man" (contemptuously viewed). **1966** Goldstein *1 in 7* 114: At Shimer, a "frat-rat" is "a guy who's flunked out of another college and comes to Shimer with all the trapping of a fraternity type." **1974** E. Thompson *Tattoo* 384: After consultation one of the frat-rats called back, "OK."

frau *n.* [< G] a wife. *Joc.*

***1821** *Real Life in London* I 119: The lads...tip their *frows** the velvet....*Frows*—Originally a Dutch word, meaning wives, or girls. **1902** (cited in Weingarten *Dict. Slang*). **1911** in Truman *Dear Bess* 55: Pete and his frau will be here to dinner. **1929** Burnett *Iron Man* 190: I ain't got no frau. **1934** Berg *Prison Nurse* 124: I had the letter in my kick and I was just passing it to the frau in the visitors' room when the screw glomed it. **1938** Chandler *Big Sleep* 76: He was sweet on Eddie Mars' frau. **1943–47** in Hodes & Hansen *Sel. from Gutter* 27: His frau was a little bit of a gal. **1963** E.M. Miller *Exile* 226: King Lear put all his blue chips on his daughter's love and Othello put all of his on his frau's fidelity.

frazzle-assed *adj.* frazzled.—usu. considered vulgar.

1953 Brossard *Bold Saboteurs* 24: And I know just what you want, Yogi, my frazzle-assed friend. **1960** C. Cooper *Scene* 179: I'm gonna work you frazzled-assed! **1968** Myrer *Eagle* 175: Plain, frazzle-ass luck, you ask me.

frazzled *adj.* **1.** fatigued; nervous and exhausted.—often constr. with *out.* Now *colloq.* [The phr. *worn to a frazzle* seems always to have been colloq.; see *OEDS.*]

[**1865** in *OEDS:* Tell General Lee, I have fought my Corps to a frazzle.] **1883** in *DA:* We have also in the South the expression *all frazled out,* figuratively used, about equivalent to "used up." **1895** *DN* I 371: *Frazzled out:* tired out. **1897** Norris *Vandover* 506: You look all frazzled out, all pale around the wattles. **1905** *DN* II 80: *Frazzled out, adj. phr.* Worn out, tired out. "I'm completely *frazzled out.*" Common. **1908** *DN* III 312: After this long day's tramp I was completely *frazzled.* **1908** in "O. Henry" *Works* 694: You must have looked pretty well frazzled out to the little hero boy. **1912** in *OEDS:* Many a frazzled-out member of society owes his failure in life to...the mere failure to make connections with his calling.

2. tipsy.

1906 *Army & Navy Life* (Aug.) 93: I takes a little drink, mebbe four or five times an' the first thing you know, ol' Hill's drunk again. But I gets out fo' guard-mount alright. I was feelin' a little bit frazzled, but I—. **1928** *AS* IV (Dec.) 102: The following expressions synonymous with or circumlocutory for "drunk" may interest readers....*frazzled. Ibid.* 103: The writer has not himself encountered..."frazzled."

frazzling *adj. So.* darned.

1906 *DN* III 136: *Frazzlin' thing, n.phr.* Something, anything. "He won't do a *frazzlin'* thing." **1911** *JAF* (July) 278: I ain't goin' give you a frazzlin' thing. **1940** in Wentworth *Amer. Dial. Dict.* 234: I don't like 'em a bit, not a frazzling bit. **1941** in *Ibid.:* Ever frazzlin' cent of it.

freak[1] *n.* **1. a person who is markedly or offensively eccentric in dress or behavior;** WEIRDO.

1895 F.P. Dunne, in Schaaf *Dooley* 165: Th' deluded ol' freak…had me up all las' month. **1895** *DN* I 417: *Freak, n.*…A student who gets high marks. **1896** Ade *Artie* 4: Don't it just kill you dead to see a swell girl…holdin' on to some freak with side whiskers? **1900** *DN* II 36: *Freak, n.*…Fool, blockhead. **1906** Ford *Shorty McCabe* 281: There's too many freaks around 42nd-st. to keep cases on all of 'em. **1919** *DN* V 66: *Freak,* an odd person. Who is that *freak* walking on the other side of the street? New Mexico. **1940** Stout *Where There's a Will* 10: Mr. Hawthorne, who was…my friend, was not a freak. **1952** Mandel *Angry Strangers* 323: I don' like she should be wit them freaks alla time. **1953** Laird *Miracle* 120: That freak? I wouldn't have a date with her. **1956** M. Wolff *Big Nick.* 30: I'm not going to…let you make some kind of a sissy freak out of my kid. **1962** Carr & Cassavetes *Too Late Blues* (film): "This party's a real drag." "Buncha freaks." **1967** "M.T. Knight" *Terrible Ten* 82: This guy's a freak.…Let's go outta here. **1986** P. Welsh *Tales Out of School* 100: Nearby are the "freaks"—kids with punk hair styles and New Wave clothes. **1992** *Beyond Reality* (USA-TV): This is the freak I told you about.

2. an ardent or extreme devotee, practitioner, or enthusiast.—usu. in comb. with prec. noun. See also **(5),** below. [Early quots. are opprobrious and stem directly from def. 1; use of the term became very widespread during the 1960's—seventy-eight exx. collected at the Univ. of Vermont in 1970 appear in *AS* XLIV 307.]

1895 Gore *Stu. Slang* 19: *Freak*…A student who is exceptionally proficient in a given subject. "The philosophy freak did all the reciting yesterday." **1906** in Safire *Stand Corrected* 169: Evidently, from the evidence in this case, he was one of your Kodak freaks.…Wherever they go and whoever they see and whatever place they come to, they have got to have a Kodak along for the purpose of getting pictures. **1914** in Kornbluh *Rebel Voices* 150: So, you tried to imitate Knowles, the Nature Freak, and live the simple life. **1946** in R.S. Gold *Jazz Talk* 98: "I'm a train freak," Duke [Ellington] says. **1958–59** Lipton *Barbarians* 39: He looked more like one of those…Nature Boy health freaks than a real hipster. **1959** Himes *CrazyKill* 90: "Where's he likely to be at this time?" "Acey-Deucey's poolroom. He's a pool freak." **1960** J.A. Williams *Angry Ones* 22: Kit was a "writer's freak"—she associated only with writers, dated them, slept with them. **1963** Williamson *Hustler!* 101: Every time I made a piece of money I always bought me some clothes. I'm a clothes freak. **1966** Braly *On Yard* 12: He was a tireless clean freak who liked the cell spotless. *Ibid.* 13: It was senseless…to degenerate into a neat freak. **1966** Bullins *Goin' a Buffalo* 182: The come freaks, that's who. The queers who buy sex from a woman. **1967–68** T. Wolfe *Kool-Aid* 13: Stewart Brand is an Indian freak. **1969** *Life* (Dec. 5) 14: Musing of a Fireside Map Freak. **1971** *Reader's Digest* (Oct.) 139: I consulted a 15-year-old, fast-food freak I know, who partially confirmed the judgment. **1977** Walton *Walton Experience* 144: There were several exaggerated reports to the effect that my mother, my brother, and I were freaks on the subject of Unidentified Flying Objects. **1978** B. Johnson *What's Happenin'?* 10: A work freak with unchallengeable determination to let nothing pass without notice. **1978** Strieber *Wolfen* 6: She had gotten a neighborhood electronics freak to do the job, a guy with a computer in his living room. **1982** *Time* (July 12) 65: Stores that cater to chocolate freaks. **1986** R. Walker *AF Wives* 472: Krause was a power freak.

3.a. Esp. *Prost. & Pris.* **a person, esp. a homosexual or a prostitute's customer, who habitually engages in unorthodox sexual practices; (usu. in comb.) a sexual fetishist.—often used with neutral force.**

1922 Paul *Impromptu* 333: It was understood that the "heavies," being less in demand, had to entertain the rough men, the freaks, and those that were so drunk they were hard to handle. **1937** Reitman *Box-Car Bertha* 178: The rest of the girls thought nothing of it. Edna said, "The big money is in the 'queer' guys. And what freaks some of 'em are!" **1940** in *Amer. Jour. Socio.* XLVIII (1943) 570: Female impersonators (freaks). **1942** *ATS* 372: Effeminate man or masculine woman; homosexual…*freak.* **1942** Davis & Wolsey *Call House Madam* 280: Some brought women's slippers or stockings with them and played with them like nuts out of their head.…We had to put up with these freaks. **1952** Himes *Stone* 107: Tell him about the trouser freak we had here.…Had

to send him to the insane asylum. **1965** Ward & Kassebaum *Women's Pris.* 99: It usually follows a set pattern unless you get with a freak and they're usually freaky about only one or two things. **1966** Braly *On Yard* 185: That sweet freak in your cell ain't no pig. **1966** "Petronius" *N.Y. Unexp.* 40: Most run-of-the-mill heteros [have] been run out by the freaks. **1969** Angelou *Caged Bird* 266 [ref. to 1940's]: But true freaks, the "women lovers," captured yet strained my imagination. **1973** Schulz *Pimp* 16: The other tricks are crazy…or are piss freaks or shit-eating freaks. **1990** Vachss *Blossom* 29: "He never loved me at all," the freak sobbed.

b. *Black E.* **a sexually passionate or sexy young woman; (specif.) a nymphomaniac.**

1955 *AS* (Dec.) 302: *Crazy freak*…Girl, usu. pretty. **1953–58** J.C. Holmes *Horn* 112: White babies, jazz babies, freaks (as musicians called them) who attached themselves to hornmen. **1962** in Wepman et al. *The Life* 45: [In] came a broad that looked [like] some boss freak. **1965** C. Brown *Manchild* 181: This chick looked like an animal, a natural-born freak.…She had a beautiful shape, jet-black skin, long, jet-black hair, and slanted eyes. *Ibid.* 301: I got a freak up there. You get in bed with this chick one time, and I guarantee you that you'll lose your mind. **1970** Ebert *Beyond Valley of Dolls* (film): "You made me into a whore." "And you dig it, you little freak." **1980** Univ. Tenn. student theme: They got some fine-looking freaks around this college. We talked about this one freak for about one hour. She is so good looking.…She is a bad-looking freak. She is built like a "Brick Shit House." I forget her name but she is a fine freak. **1986** Eble *Campus Slang* (Mar.) 4: *Freak*—a desirable woman, used primarily by males: "Oh man, did you see that freak that walked by?" **1987** *21 Jump St.* (Fox-TV): It's some fresh-lookin' freak. And a gray boy.

4. a beatnik or hippie. [The usual designation among hippies, used with neutral or positive force; cf. **(1),** above.]

1960 Thom *Subterraneans* (film): This neighborhood's filled with freaks—artists and bums. **1967** Bronsteen *Hippy's Handbook* 13: *Freak n.* a complimentary term for a person who wears flowers, beads, etc.; it often appears in the term "beautiful freak." **1967** Yablonksy *Hippie Trip* 199: Wow! Dig all of the beautiful freaks. **1967–68** T. Wolfe *Kool-Aid* 13: All the freaks came and did their thing. **1970** *Playboy* (Aug.) 114: Hey, too much, man. A freak for a priest. I don't believe it. **1971** N.Y.C. high school student: All the freaks hang out there, writer freaks, artist freaks. They're very beautiful people. **1979** J. Morris *War Story* 28: Two…girls, one of whom was the first freak I'd ever seen, outside of Haight Ashbury. **1981** *Chicago Sun-Times* (Oct. 15): The freaks may have the long, hanging ones [*sc.* earrings] with pot leaves.

5. *Narc.* **a person addicted to the use of a drug.—usu. constr. with prec. attrib.**

1967 Wolf *Love Generation* xli: The meth-freaks who took their trips on a needle ran the additional risk of serum hepatitis. **1967** Yablonsky *Hippie Trip* 33: Even some high priests and novices refer to the "new breed" as "Meth" or "speed" freaks. **1970** *Nat. Lampoon* (Aug.) 48: Cynthia Sunflower, scag freak and bottomless cocktail waitress. **1971** *N.Y. Times Mag.* (Sept. 19) 68: I hear they're *all* scag freaks down there. **1972** *N.Y. Post* (Apr. 8) 25: When the heroin would hit 15 minutes after a snort, you would just go out of the world. But it doesn't stay like that too long, you know. The freaks (addicts) warned us about that. **1982** *Compass* (Feb. 28) 11: The Freaks or stoners, who are the real dopers, wiped out all day on pot and pills. **1986** Thacker *Finally the Pawn* 8: Skag freaks. **1990** C.P. McDonald *Blue Truth* 56: Acidheads, PCP freaks, crack smokers.

6.a. FREAK-OUT, *n.*

1967 L. McNeill *Moving* 120: The freak is complete. **1968** "J. Hudson" *Case of Need* 184: She took a couple of down trips, real freaks, and it shook her up.

b. a strong, esp. temporary, interest or enthusiasm; KICK.

1967–68 T. Wolfe *Kool-Aid* 13: The zodiac—that's her freak. *Ibid.* 24: They're off on their own freak.

c. an astonishing thing.

1988 *New Yorker* (Aug. 8) 26: Herbert, a bartender:…Man, though, this is a freak!

freak[2] *n.* var. FREQ.

freak *adj.* Esp. *Prost.* **characterized by or involving homosexuality, fetishism, or other unorthodox sexual practices.—used prenominally.**

1945 Drake & Cayton *Black Metropolis* 610: Prostitution, bootlegging, "freak shows," "reefer dens," and "pads," however, must operate as an "underworld."…"Freak shows"—pornographic exhibitions by sexual perverts. **1952** Ellson *Golden Spike* 71: Yeah, that's freak stuff.…Just say it again and I'll punch you right in the fuckin' mouth! **1965** Ward & Kassebaum *Women's Pris.* 131: Others had participated in "freak shows" but...did not think of themselves as homosexual. **1966** Braly *On Yard* 175: Give your [mouth] a rest so I can read this freak book. **1966** Manus *Mott the Hoople* 122: You think I dig freak sex? **1970** Landy *Underground Dict.* 82: *Freak trick*...Man who buys a prostitute and engages in unusual or deviant sexual activities, eg., masturbating while holding an ice cube. **1972** Hollander *Happy Hooker* 4: A scrawny white hooker...had been the victim of a "freak trick"—a customer who gets his kicks from brutally beating girls. **1980** Gould *Ft. Apache* 273: She wanted to hear about...every freak scene he'd ever been in, so she could be all those women when they made love.

freak *v.* see FREAK [OFF]; FREAK [OUT].

freakazoid *n.* FREAK, *n.*, 1; WEIRDO.
   1984 Eble *Campus Slang* (Fall) 3: *Freakazoid*—person involved in the "new wave" or "punk rock" music. **1984** *Miami Vice* (NBC-TV): Boogaloo Jones...a 350-pound freakazoid. **1990** *In Living Color* (Fox-TV): We're not all freakazoids like you, but we've *all* sinned. **1994** *N.Y. Times* (Feb. 6) VIII 2: I knew that I couldn't compete with those freakazoids who were on drugs.

freaked or **freaked out** *adj.* **1.a.** (orig. among LSD users) under the influence of a hallucinogenic or similar drug.
   1967 Wolf *Love Generation* 172: But he was really freaked alla time. He was on a super acid trip every second. **1967** in H.S. Thompson *Shark Hunt* 448: There is always a sprinkling of genuine, barefoot, freaked-out types on the dance floor. **1970** Della Femina *Wonderful Folks* 15: They think you walk around...freaked out on acid or hash.
   b. elated or ecstatic as though on drugs.
   1968 Tauber *Sunshine Soldiers* 45–46: He tells me he gets stoned behind the PX and then comes in and gets quietly freaked on records that he has stashed in his barracks.
   2. completely crazy; utterly deranged.
   1964-66 R. Stone *Hall of Mirrors* 223: Are we going to sit around here and argue about that freaked out twitch? **1967** Mailer *Vietnam* 133: There are secret freaked-out grope types who dig dental rot. **1967** Kornbluth *New Underground* 270: As everyone who writes for *The Village Voice* seems to know, this country is crazy. Freaked. Out of touch with reality. **1972** Morris *Strawberry Soldier* 10: I had expected some freaked out right-winger. **1973** Browne *Body Shop* 101: They had him in a straightjacket [*sic*]...."They think I'm freaked." **1983** *Batman* (Apr.) 18: You two deserve each other—you're both freaked-out! **1993** *Mystery Sci. Theater* (Comedy Central TV): You freaked-out maniac!
   3. upset, confused, nervous, scared, or angry.
   1969 Crumb *Motor City Comics* (unp.): We can't cope!! We're too freaked out! **1971** Simon *Sign of Fool* 39: When he got back to his pad, Richie became a little freaked. **1978** Diehl *Sharky's Machine* 189: We're all a little, uh, freaked right now. **1980** in *Penthouse* (Jan. 1981) 168: But Jetty's gonna be freaked about losing his fish. **1989** S. Robinson & D. Ritz *Smokey* 86: I was too freaked to look at the audience.
   4. physically exhausted; worn out.
   1971 Glasser *365 Days* 26: Even freaked out, they'd go. **1972** *Playboy* (Feb.) 177: Boy, am I freaked out!

freaking *adj. & adv.* (a euphem. for) FUCKING; FRIGGING.
   1928 Bodenheim *Georgie May* 9: Oh yuh cain't catch o-on to thuh freakin' Mistah Stave an' Chain. *Ibid.* 70: Ah hate the hull, freaking pack uh you. **1955** *Harper's* (Mar.) 35: Open the Freaking Door, Joe. **1961** Garrett *Which Ones Are the Enemy* 16: Not freaking likely. **1965** Hardman *Chaplains* 1: A great big freaking disaster! **1972** C. Gaines *Stay Hungry* 152: He's freaking Superman is who he is. **1972–76** Durden *No Bugles* 9: It's too freakin' late now. **1978** Wharton *Birdy* 276: It's like my freaking body has some kind of controls all its own. **1972–79** T. Wolfe *Right Stuff* 6: It was a struggle to move twenty feet in this freaking muck. **1982** *Flash* (Dec.) 10: Have you gone freakin' bananas? **1989** USN officers, on *Prime News* (CNN-TV) (Jan. 5): "He's got a missile off!" "Freakin' right!"

freakish *adj.* Esp. *Black E.* sexually deviant; suggestive of unorthodox sexuality, esp. homosexuality or nymphomania; (*also*) lustful. Also **friggish**.
   1929 in *AS* VI 158: *Freakish* is used to describe an effeminate man or a mannish woman. **1946** Mezzrow & Wolfe *Really Blues* 305: *Freakish*: homosexual, perverted, weird. **1956** Holiday & Dufty *Lady Sings the Blues* 29: But any kind of freakish feelings are better than no feelings at all. **1963** Charters *Poetry of the Blues* 126: She called me a freakish man, what more was there to do./Just because she said I was strange that did not make it true. **1964** in Wepman et al. *The Life* 90: A cute little nose

and freakish eyes. **1966** in B. Jackson *Swim Like Me* 136: Then you both get friggish and then you pull off every stitch—/You starts to slow jivin', Mike...ain't it a bitch? **1966** Braly *On Yard* 14: I heard yours was freakish for billy goats.

freako *n.* WEIRDO. Also as adj.
   1963 in H. Ellison *Sex Misspelled* 47: Then I tried a freako who made the Sunset Strip scene. **1974** E. Thompson *Tattoo* 401: He's a freak-o all right...Dyin' his hair like that. **1975** in L. Bangs *Psychotic Reactions* 172: The quack doctor who services every freako...on Woodward Ave. **1981** *Film Comment* (May) 27: A close-knit crowd of sixties freakos, living with their parents, ingesting mammoth quantities of drugs. **1986** Merkin *Zombie Jamboree* 196: And the freakos didn't have to be mere Airborne troopers. **1991** Hasburgh *N.Y.P.D. Mounted* (film): The horse went completely freako nutso.

freak [off] *v.* **1.** Esp. *Black E.* to masturbate; (*fig.*) to obtain sexual gratification.
   1954 in Wepman et al. *The Life* 109: Another whore named Grace...Who'd freak off in the good Lord's face. **1963** in Bruce *Essential* 81: Dayaddy! Will yew tawk ta me? Ah'm tahd of freakin' awf with mahself. **1962–68** B. Jackson *In the Life* 207: He just cut off some of the...girl's pubic hair, and he rubs them in his chest and this is the way he freaks off. **1968** Gover *JC* 37: Them em-efs down there steady...freakin off on gunsmoke. **1963–70** in *Paris Rev.* (Nov. 1950) 96: The sight of her dressed like that and freaking like she did was too much disgust. **1974** U.C.L.A. student: I'm tired of freaking off by myself. **1967–80** Folb *Runnin' Lines* 238: *Freak off*...Masturbate.
   2. Esp. *Black E.* to engage in unrestrained or unorthodox sexual activity.
   1966 Braly *On Yard* 272: I love to freak off, but get strung out? That's something else. **1967** Colebrook *Cross of Lassitude* 103: Nothing doing, I'll go freak off with another Jasper. Both of us go for what we know. **1968** Gover *JC* 21: Hey, let's all go up to my room, get high an freak off. **1970** Landy *Underground Dict.* 82: *Freak off*...Engage in any and all sexual activity; engage in unusual or deviant sexual activity. **1971** Goines *Dopefiend* 122: I'll give either one of you half a fourth of dope if you'll freak off with Butch, in front of everybody. **1973** N.Y.C. man, age 25: To *freak off* is to go with some really hot broad and get high and engage in all kinds of far-out sex. **1967–80** Folb *Runnin' Lines* 238: *Freak off*...Engage in unconventional sex...Engage in homosexual relations. **1990** *Nat. Lampoon* (Apr.) 99: Boy, I'd like to fuck you! You look like you know how to freak!

freak-out *n.* **1.a.** a nightmarish hallucinatory experience induced by a drug, esp. LSD.
   *****1966** in *OEDS*: The tape recorder picked up the horrifying moans and shrieks of one man who had made 33 pleasurable "trips" with LSD and was encountering his first "freak-out" or bad LSD experience. **1967** Bronsteen *Hippy's Handbook* 13: *Freak out*...*n.* a bad trip or a bad portion of a trip. **1967** in H.S. Thompson *Shark Hunt* 454: Acid and alcohol can be a lethal combination, causing fits of violence, suicidal depression, and a general freak-out that ends in jail or a hospital. **1968** Cohen *Medical Science* xix 34: Less frequent are the "bum trips" or "freakouts," which are horrendous encounters with madness. **1987** Dusek & Girdano *Drugs* (ed. 4) 105: The bad drug experience, or "freakout" as it once was called, can be triggered by various stimuli.
   b. a sudden attack of madness.
   1983 Univ. Tenn. student: That was about a week after my freak-out.
   c. a shock.
   1973 R. Roth *Sand in Wind* 289: Remember that Gook chick we saw with the napalmed face?...What a freak-out.
   2. a gathering, as of hippies, for the taking of LSD or other hallucinogenic drugs; (*hence*) a rock-music performance or song designed to simulate such a gathering or a FREAK-OUT, 1.a.
   1967 Bronsteen *Hippy's Handbook* 13: *Freak out*...*n.* group environment with rock band and kinetic lights. **1969** N.Y.C. man, age 21: It's like a hippie freak-out. **1969** *Rowan & Martin's Laugh-In* (NBC-TV): How about layin' some bread on me for the freak-out? **1978** *Rolling Stone* (July 27) 54: "Radio Ethiopia," an interminable Sixties freak-out in which Smith performs a guitar solo consisting of her playing one note very fast. **1992** *Rolling Stone Album Guide* 288: The famous acid tests that transformed San Francisco into one large freakout.
   3. a person who has freaked out.
   1967-68 von Hoffman *Parents Warned Us* 225: I've only met creeps, psychos, freak-outs, and dealers. **1981** Hathaway *World of Hurt* 84: I seem to be attracting a lot of freak-outs lately.

freak [out] *v.* **1.** to induce usu. overpowering astonishment, anger, fear, or confusion in; cause to lose composure, sense, or sanity. [*Freak out* is the earlier and more common form; both gained national currency among young people after 1966 as a result of the hippie drug movement.]

1964 in Bruce *Essential* 138: Tomorrow, fix him up mit Dirty Bertha. Freak him out. Start him out right. **1964-66** R. Stone *Hall of Mirrors* 219: "It'll freak him." "Don't freak him….He's about to make a statement." **1967** McNeill *Moving Through Here* 17: It was really strange and it freaked them out. **1969** Mitchell *Thumb Tripping* 112: Twenty of the bikers surrounded his car. Not to stomp him or..; but planning to freak wife, kids and sweet hubby, slowly….Physically safe, but utterly freaked. **1969** *New Amer. Rev.* (No. 6) (Apr.) 215: You want to freak the cats in Mexicali?…You'll dig them choke and turn gray and their knees'll knock together. **1965-70** J. Carroll, in *Paris Rev.* (No. 50) 106: It freaked our minds. **1970** Wexler *Joe* (film): It freaks me out! You know how it freaks me out! **1970** A. Young *Snakes* 62: It freaks customers out when I bring em up here and it's somethin funny goin on. **1970** Williams *New Exiles* 238: Eventually, I came to the conclusion that man was merely nothing more than a pure piece of carbon and water. That freaked me out. **1971** Sanders *Family* 108: Along came Bob Beausoleil, who freaked the group with his throwing of knives. **1976** A. Walker *Meridian* 151: I don't freak myself out, analyzing everything I do. **1983** K. Miller *Lurp Dog* 115: Marvel was there to freak them out with his…goofy smile. **1983** Ehrhart *VN-Perkasie* 403: Man, you musta freaked her right out of her drawers. *a***1984** in Terry *Bloods* 6: That really freaked me out. This little bitty kid smokin' cigarettes. **1985** B.E. Ellis *Less Than Zero* 38: It still freaks me out a little and I step on the gas really hard.

2. Esp. *Prost.* to engage in unorthodox or unrestrained sexual activity. [Prob. the orig. sense; cf. FREAK OFF.]

1966 Bullins *Goin' a Buffalo* 182: Those muscle cats, you know, muscle queens…always wantin' ta freak out on ya. **1981** Men's room graffito, Knoxville, Tenn.: Who wants to FREAK? [Swing] Leave name and number.

3.a. to go crazy or out of control (in the broadest sense); (*esp.*) to go wild with madness, fear, enthusiasm, or excitement.

1966 H.S. Thompson *Hell's Angels* 263: He freaked out and killed a dozen people for reasons he couldn't explain. **1966** "Mothers of Invention" *Freak-Out* (rock song title). **1967** Wolf *Love Generation* 72: Girls are getting stoned on meth and get fucked for a couple of days until they freak out. But that's not sexual freedom, that's sexual compulsion. **1967** McNeill *Moving Through Here* 87: Group Image audiences are bound to freak. **1969** *N.Y. Times Mag.* (May 18) 120: There is a level of action at which the brass freaks and oppresses the anti war movement. **1969** Mitchell *Thumb Tripping* 113: The kitten freaked and ran, too—more excitement than it could handle. **1964–70** J. Carroll, in *Paris Rev.* (No. 50) 102: I thought I would freak out on the spot. **1972** *Nat. Lampoon* (July) 6: He'll absolutely freak [with delight]. **1985** B.E. Ellis *Less Than Zero* 47: Oh man, my mother must be freaking out. **1986** *Newsweek* (June 9) 73: When he shows up on the set, it's all business—no freaking out. **1986** *Campus Voice* (Sept.) 69: Stage fright….I freaked out, and the information just drained away. **1987** Kent *Phr. Book* 159: Naturally the police completely freaked. **1993** *Newsweek* (Jan. 11) 61: Is the guy going to freak out if I mention condoms?

b. (of things) to go out of order; go haywire.

1968 I. Reed *Yellow Back Radio* 98: Then things really started to freak out. **1982** S. Black *Totally Awesome* 45: Your hair freaks out and you get all these split ends and stuff. **1986** Anti-cocaine TV commercial: One night my heart freaked out. I thought I was going to die.

c. to abandon customary or conventional restraints; cut loose.

1967 in *OEDS:* Frank Zappa…answers: "On a personal level, freaking out is a process whereby an individual casts off outmoded and restricted standards of thinking, dress and social etiquette." **1967** Kornbluth *New Underground* 92: That's it, soon as you freak out and have a good time, it's dangerous. **1968** in *Rolling Stone Interviews* 50: They freak out a bit, sort of a not-really-jazz but jazz-oriented on some things. **1980** Wielgus & Wolff *Basketball* 43: *Freak out* (v) When Fly McDuitt is loose on a fast break, with only Sonny Suburban back on defense, this would be the cry to Fly from throughout the park.

4.a. to experience an altered state of consciousness induced by a hallucinogenic drug such as LSD. Also *fig.*

1965 in *OEDS:* Grand Opening!!! Freak with the Fugs!!! The East Side's Most Infinite Hallucination in Person. **1966** *Life* (Mar. 25) 32: I just put a little acid in the kids' orange juice in the morning and let them spend the day freaking out in the woods. *Ibid.* (caption): A user "freaking freely"…gyrates with his own shadow. **1967** *L.A. Times* (May 28) West 17: The most important love symbol is the flower….You can freak freely; flowers don't hurt.

b. to experience nightmarish hallucinations induced by LSD or a similar drug. [The more common of the two nuances.]

1967 Wolf *Love Generation* 86: I would freak out, and have a very bad trip. **1967–68** von Hoffman *Parents Warned Us* 78: A nine-year-old boy was up here freaking out on acid. Maybe you sold it to him. *Ibid.* 96: You can freak trying to act straight [while under the influence of LSD]. **1968** Wojciechowska *Tuned Out* 104: I'm sorry your brother freaked out. Has he come out of it yet? **1969** in *Rolling Stone Interviews* 226: Apparently she had…freaked on heavy drugs or something and either committed herself or someone picked up on her and put her there. **1969** Geller & Boas *Drug Beat* 162: Occasionally a student would "freak out" (have a bad experience with the drug), an incident that would immediately flare into headlines. **1978** Matthiessen *Snow Leopard* 46: On her first drug trip, D freaked out….she saw my flesh dissolve, my head become a skull. **1988** *U.* (Nov.) 29: People can also easily "freak out" after using inhalants. **1990** Stuck *Adolescent Worlds* 90: Angel dust…is pretty potent, you can freak out on that stuff.

freak up *v.* (see quot.).

1970 Landy *Underground Dict.* 83: *Freak up*…Act in a strange and obvious manner to attract attention.

freaky *adj.* **1.** odd or crazy.

1895 *DN* I 417: *Freaky.* Queer, improper. "He does *freaky* things." **1966** Young & Hixson *LSD* vi: But soon it's gonna get pretty freaky. **1970** Williams *New Exiles* 295: That just did it with me, man, I just went freaky! **1971** Glasser *365 Days* 139: He…just got freaky as hell.

2. Esp. *Stu.* delightfully unusual or imaginative.

1968 in *Rolling Stone Interviews* 72: Oh boy, they're freaky! **1969** *N.Y. Post* (Mar. 22) 24: His "freaky" ways.

Fred *n.* an average or nondescript man.

*****1973** in Wilkes *Dict. Austral. Colloq.* 148: Even down where the Freds are browsing in their nocturnal pastures, the herd heroes are largely wasted. *****1975** in *Ibid.:* The average Fred. **1983** *Cheers* (NBC-TV): You're a dink, a wimp, a Fred, a loser. **1992** *L.A. Times* (Aug. 18) E5: *Fred:* An unattractive or unintelligent male.

Fred Astaire *adj.* *Stu.* stylish.

1969 Coppel *A Little Time for Laughter* 294 [ref. to 1940's]: You remember when we used to say things were *Fred Astaire?* Like smoking Virginia Rounds and wearing neckties instead of belts? And brown-and-white shoes.

Freddie *n.* ¶ In phrase: **ready for Freddie** ready and eager; primed.

1952 Himes *Stone* 13: Aw, beat it, gunsel!…Go get ready for Freddy! **1964** Howe *Valley of Fire* 141 [ref. to Korean War]: Thing is now they're ready for Freddie; one push and they'll fall down. **1967** Hamma *Motorcycle Mommas* 93: Really ready for Freddie—double my usual hot pants feeling. **1972** *Nat. Lampoon* (Apr.) 31: Besides, I hadn't gotten petted in about a week and I was ready-Freddy.

Freddie Mac *n.* *Finance.* (see quot.).

1985 *N.Y. Times* (Aug. 15) D 16: The Federal Home Loan Mortgage Corporation, known as Freddie Mac. **1987** J. Green *Jargon* 236.

free *n.* [short for FREE WORLD] *Pris.* the world outside prison.

1966 C. Cooper *Farm* 221: Maybe not for you. Maybe you had somethin goin with her in the Free, and I didn't know about it. **1974** Andrews & Dickens *Over the Wall* 11: We would like to extend heartfelt thanks to those solid-gold folks out there in the free.

free-and-easy *n.* a tavern, cheap music hall, or brothel. Now *hist.* [Cf. earlier colloq. sense, 'a drinking party', in *OED* and *F & H* and reflected in 1853 quot.]

*****1821** in *F & H* III 67: Blew a cloud at a free-and-easy. *****1832** in *OED:* The prisoner was a frequenter of Free and Easys. **1837** J.C. Neal *Charc. Sks.* 27: Why, he would have a song about it, and sing it at the "free and easies." [**1853** in S. Clemens *Twain's Letters* I 31: We have what is called a "free-and-easy," at the saloons on Saturday nights.] **1872** in *DAE:* Druther git drunk at the "free-and-easy" ever' night. *****1880** in *F & H* III 67: The "Medley," in Hoxton, a combination of theatre and music-hall,…serves as a free-and-easy chiefly for boys and girls. **1884** Sweet & Knox *Through Texas* 256: Here is…a dance-house, a restau-

rant, a free-and-easy, a saloon, [etc.]. **1943** J. Mitchell *McSorley's* 126: On some of the side streets there were brothels in nearly every house; Dutch refers to them as "free-and-easies."

freebase *v. Narc.* to heat and inhale freebase cocaine. Also trans. [The noun is a clipping of the pharmacological term *freebase cocaine*; the verb, however, arose among abusers of cocaine.]
1980 *New York Post* (Mar. 10): The latest wrinkle, called Freebasing, involves smoking a raw paste-like form of the drug. **1981** *Time* (July 6) 59: More and more users have sought the deeper ecstatic "rush" that comes from "freebasing," smoking a chemically treated form of the powder. **1981** *N.Y. Times* (June 26) A 10: A cocaine dealer…free-based and smoked an astounding 15 grams a day. **1983** Rovin *Pryor* 192: Freebasing originated in Columbia in the 1930's and takes its name from the freeing of cocaine (i.e. base) from impurities, thus producing a more intense high. **1989** "Capt. X" & Dodson *Unfriendly Skies* 123: A guy in the john was using a blowtorch for free-basing. **1992** *Nation* (Dec. 28) 811: He also liked to freebase cocaine.

freebie *n.* **1.** something given, offered, or performed without charge, esp. a complimentary ticket.
1928 Fisher *Jericho* 300: *Freeby* Something for nothing, as complimentary tickets to a theater. **1946** Mezzrow & Wolfe *Really Blues* 186 [ref. to 1930's]: Always lookin' for a freebie. **1954** L. Armstrong *Satchmo* 92: Maybe because that meal was a freebie and didn't cost me anything but a song. **1959** *Life* (Nov. 23) 45: *Freebie*—plug for a record given without payola. **1959-60** R. Reisner *Jazz Titans* 156: *Freebee:* Something for nothing. **1961** J.A. Williams *Night Song* 26: But they ain't no freebees here. No suh. **1964** Faust *Steagle* 57: Oh, that's all right, sir, I've got freebies and twofers. **1970** Della Femina *Wonderful Folks* 62: TWA was looking for freebies—presentations of agencies' work without paying the freight. **1973** W. Crawford *Gunship Cmndr.* 100: I convince about as easy as a flat-broke hundred-dollar hooker that she ought to lay a freebie on some John. **1977** Butler & Shryack *Gauntlet* 220: The offers of late-night freebies from the whores. **1983** WUOT-FM Radio broadcast (Apr. 23): They sound like freebies, but somebody has to foot the bill. **1987** *Nat. Lampoon* (Dec.) 7: Michael Berman…offered us freebies to *any* Yale football game.
2. *Esp. Prost.* a sexually promiscuous woman who does not charge money for her favors.
1945 Drake & Cayton *Black Metropolis* 595–96: The lower class does, however, distinguish between habitual, professional prostitutes…and casual pick-ups available for a "good time" to lower-class men. Many women of the latter sort are regarded not as prostitutes but as "free-bys"—the passing of money becomes not so much a commercial transaction as a token of appreciation for a "good time." **1957** Murtagh & Harris *Cast the First Stone* 8: Prices are low in Coney Island because competition is too keen ("too many freebies around wanting to give it away"). **1966** S. Harris *Hellhole* 79: But I was never a prostitute…I was a freeby. I never charged any of the boys…a penny. **1967** *N.Y. Times* (Aug. 15) 27: Rhonda…sneers at the "freebies," girls who charge nothing for their favors. **1970** Wambaugh *New Centurions* 172: Lonely broads on the make, you know, just amateurs, freebies.

freebie *adj. & adv.* free of charge.
1971 Rader *Govt. Inspected* 136: Maybe that's why she did it freebee.

freedom bird *n. Mil.* an airliner that flies military personnel who have completed their tours of duty overseas back to the U.S. [Quots. ref. to Vietnam War.]
1971 *Newsweek* (Jan. 11) 37: I warn them that if they balk in combat, the Army will make sure that they miss that "freedom bird" back to the world at the end of their tour. **1971** Jury *Vietnam Photo Book* 82: All they want to do is put in a year and get on board that "freedom bird." **1971** Polner *No Victory Parade* 131: A freedom bird, the kind that brings guys home from Saigon. **1972** T. O'Brien *Combat Zone* 70: I'm not safe till that ol' freedom bird lands me back in Seattle. **1976** C.R. Anderson *Grunts* 74: Now it looked like one's Freedom Bird would never come. **1977** Carabatsos *Heroes* 139: He walked off the Freedom Bird that took him home. **1978** Hasford *Short-Timers* 95: I'll be on that big silver Freedom Bird, flying back to the World. *a***1989** Berent *Rolling Thunder* 143: The G.I.'s had started to call the returning civilian planes the "freedom bird" that would carry them to the "real world."

freedom flight *n. Mil.* a scheduled flight aboard a FREEDOM BIRD.
1986 "J. Cain" *Suicide Squad* 177 [ref. to 1968]: Their freedom flight out of The Nam was canceled without warning.

freehole *n.* a sexually promiscuous woman.

1934 H. Roth *Call It Sleep* 415: G'wan, he said, ye little free-hole, he called me. **1988** Haverford Coll. student, age 18: She's easy. She's a freehole.

freeload *v.* [back formation from FREELOADER] to cadge or sponge. Also trans.
1942–49 Goldin et al. *DAUL* 19: C'mon, we'll go out and free load…some scat. **1956** Resko *Reprieve* 57: Even the Sing Sing guards refused to free-load on the leftovers. **1957** M. Shulman *Rally* 203: In sixty years of freeloading, Manning did not remember such a turnout. **1959** Brosnan *Long Season* 200: Free-loading on one's family is so much more satisfying to one's conscience. **1977** Harnack *Under Wings* 82: I told you to get rid of those free-loading kids. **1982** M. Royko, in *N.Y. Post* (Aug. 26) 35: I can't really blame all these moochers for wanting to freeload at my RibFest.

freeloader *n.* a sponger.
1936 Washburn *Parlor* 22: A little dinner or supper party had no fixed charge. Usually a host would suggest what he had in mind and the number of free-loaders. **1947** *Time* (Mar. 24) 63: And free loaders were no problem; most people bought at least a few beers while they watched. **1942–49** Goldin et al. *DAUL* 74: *Freeloader.* One who freeloads. **1952** H. Grey *Hoods* 104: You know I'm no free loader. I like to pay for services rendered. **1956** Yordan *Harder They Fall* (film): I hope all you freeloaders are enjoying those drinks and dollar cigars. **1961** Considine *Ripley* 169: Doug Ripley called Connolly…a freeloader and ordered him off the premises. **1992** D. Burke *Street Talk* I 146: Man, what a freeloader.

free lunch *n.* something for nothing. [Proverb illus. in 1949, 1966 quots. was popularized by economist Milton Freedman. The 1949 quot. was claimed to be a reprint of "an editorial we published 11 years ago," and the phrase may thus date from 1938.]
1949 W. Morrow, in *S.F. News* (June 1), cited by W. Safire in *N.Y. Times Mag.* (Jan. 23, 1994): There ain't no such thing as free lunch. **1966** R.A. Heinlein *Moon Is Harsh Mistress* ch. 11: There ain't no such thing as a free lunch. [**1974** R.A. Caro, in *N.Y. Times Mag.* (Feb. 14, 1993) 14 [ref. to 1934]: [Mayor Fiorello La Guardia shook] his little fist at its [*sc.* City Hall's] white Georgian elegance and shouted, "*E finita la cuccagna!*" ("No more free lunch!"), a phrase which…the Mayor was using to promise "The party is over! No more graft!"] **1986** Ciardi *Good Words* 121: He thinks life is a free lunch.

free-o *n.* FREEBIE.
*a***1986** in *NDAS:* So he picks up a few free-o's here and there.

Freep *n.* The *Free Press,* a newspaper. [1970 and 1971 quots. ref. to the *L.A. Free Press;* 1989 to the *Detroit Free Press.*]
1970 Landy *Underground Dict.* 83: *Freep*…The *Free Press,* a Los Angeles underground newspaper. **1971** *Playboy* (Apr.) 152: Full-page freak-out ads appeared in the *Freep* (*Los Angeles Free Press* to non-Californians). **1989** Kienzle *Eminence* 33: Lennon had worked at the Freep.

free ride *n.* something obtained without cost or effort; (*specif.*) *Poker.* (see 1949 and 1945–50 quots.). [1899 quot. perh. illus. S.E. sense.]
1899 (cited in *W9*). **1938** *Amer. Mercury* (Oct.) 141: And let's hint that he, himself, had better start managing because *very, very soon the free ride is going to be over.* **1949** Coffin *Winning Poker* 178: Free Ride—Drawing without putting more chips in the pot. **1945-50** in *AS* (Feb. 1951) 98: *Free ride.* A round of cards in stud poker which are dealt without any betting having taken place. The players are given a free ride when everyone checks or when the dealer makes an error in dealing. **1979** *U.S. News & W.R.* (Dec. 31) 22: The virtual free ride to renomination usually accorded sitting Presidents. **1990** *National Review* (Apr. 16) 30: National [health] insurance extends the "free ride" to the middle-class working population.

freeside *n. & adv.* [sugg. by STATESIDE] *Pris.* outside of prison; the world outside prison.
1954-60 *DAS: Freeside*…outside the walls of a penitentiary. **1966-67** P. Thomas *Mean Streets* 244: I wished I could stop thinking about the free side. *Ibid.* 296: Free Side Is the Best Side. **1972** P. Thomas *Savior* 19: I was with her a hundred per cent on staying free-side.

freesies *n.pl.* ¶ In phrase: **for freesies** free of charge.
1982 Del Vecchio *13th Valley* 465: I've a friend at Columbia, so I stay there for freesies.

free ticket *n. Baseball.* a base on balls.
1927 *AS* (Feb.) 255: To receive a base on balls is to have…"a free

ticket." **1982** Considine *Lang. Sport* 21.

freeway sign *n.* [because often given by discourteous drivers] (see quot.). *Joc.*

    1980 Pearl *Pop. Slang* 54: *Freeway sign n.* an insulting gesture made with an erect middle finger and other fingers folded: "the finger."

free world *n. Pris.* the world outside of prison. Often attrib.

    1902 Hapgood *Thief* 196 [ref. to *ca*1895]: I left Auburn penitentiary and went forth into the free world. **1945** Lindner *Stone Walls* 456: In the free world. **1954** Lindner *50-Minute Hr.* 119: His effect on others, too, is less subtle here than it is in the free world. **1962** Crump *Killer* 387: When I was in the free world I had three Caddy's. **1966** Elli *Riot* 44: He didn't give two bits for a ton of the stuff in the free world. **1966** Braly *On Yard* 14: Polished free-world shoes and expensive wrist-watches.

freeze *n.* a snubbing or slighting; cold shoulder.—constr. with *the.*

    1942 *ATS* 332: *Slight; snub—n.*....the cold shoulder,...the freeze. **1946** I. Shulman *Amboy Dukes* 137: For nights that seemed like years the Dukes had given Frank the freeze. **1945–51** Salinger *Catcher in Rye* ch. xi: She gave me the big freeze when I said hello. **1957** Kohner *Gidget* 26: He said "Hi" too but gave me a big freeze otherwise. **1967–80** Folb *Runnin' Lines* 238: *Freeze, the.* The "cold shoulder."

freeze *v.* **1.** to yearn; in phr. **froze for** ardently desirous of.

    1847–48 in Bartlett *Amer.* (ed. 4) 233: This child felt like going West for many a month, being half *froze* for buffalo meat and mountain doins. **1871** Schele de Vere *Amer.* 475: *Freeze, to,* is used in almost all parts of the country as an extravagant term for wishing something ardently. "I tell you I *froze* for meat before the week was gone." **1884** "M. Twain" *Huck. Finn* 130: I'm jist a freezin' for something fresh, anyway. **1889** J. Farmer *Amer.: Freeze*...Another meaning is to become possessed of an intense longing for anything; as I freeze to go back, would be the expression of one thoroughly home-sick. **1894** Lee *Genl. Lee* 109: The South Carolina regiments...were *freezing* for a fight.

    2. to appropriate; *freeze to,* 2, below.

    a*1890–93 *F & H* III 68: *Freeze*...(thieves).—...to appropriate; to steal. **1900 *DN* II 37: *Freeze, v.t.*....To appropriate. **1904** *Life in Sing Sing* (gloss.): *Freeze.*—To retain.

    3. to snub; slight. Cf. FREEZE OUT, 3.

    1900 *DN* II 37: *Freeze, v.t.*....To slight. **1917** in Dreiser *Diaries* 183: A little German girl...tries to flirt with me. Bert freezes her. **1936** Gaddis *Courtesan* 75: For Pete's sake, kid, you didn't have to freeze the guy just because you're feeling low. **1942** *ATS* 332: *Slight; snub...freeze (out).* **1945** *Yank* (Nov. 2) 15: Many's the civvy I myself have frozen. **1954–60** *DAS: Freeze*...To snub.

    4. *Stu.* (see quot.).

    1900 *DN* II 37: *Freeze, v.t.* 1. To do easily. 2. To pass a high rank in examination.

    5.a. to put a stop to; quit; give up.

    1929–33 Farrell *Manhood of Lonigan* 251: Nate...started bawling him out. Studs told him to freeze it. **1962** Crump *Killer* 44: Freeze that action....Forget it—skating, girls, the gang, sports, right now, forget it all.

    b. *Black E.* (see quots.).—constr. with *on.*

    1970 Major *Afro-Amer. Slang* 55: *Freeze on:* to ignore a person or situation. **1967–80** Folb *Runnin' Lines* 238: *Freeze on (something).* Discontinue use of, avoid. **1984** J. Green *Contemp. Slang* 101: *Freeze on* v. to ignore, to snub, to reject...1983.

    ¶ In phrases:

    ¶ **freeze on [to], 1.** to take hold (of); (*hence*) to go to it; pitch in.

    1847 *Yale Lit. Mag.* XII 111: "Now, boys," said Bob, "freeze on," and at it they went. **1864** in C.H. Moulton *Ft. Lyon* 172: I "froze on" to a few balls of the butter and took them to my boarding mistress. **1867** in *DA:* Our men froze on the valises, and took them away. **1918** in *DA:* By freezing on to them, Supply Company often got a day's vacation.

    2. to secure for oneself.

    *a*1889 in Barrère & Leland *Dict. Slang* I 384: There was no more intimacy shown between James and Ann other than might exist between any woman trying *to freeze* on to a boarder.

    3. see **(5.b.)**, above.

    ¶ **freeze [on] to, 1.** to cling or stay close to; stick with, to, or near; (*also*) to grasp or hold firmly or tenaciously; (*hence*) to take a strong liking to.

    1840 *Spirit of Times* (Nov. 21) 447: Freeze down solid to [the oyster].

1848 *Life in Rochester* 67: Well, we shot ahead, like thunder, but I froze to him, like death to a dead nigger. **1851** B. Hall *College Wds.* 135: [At Williams College] We *freeze* to apples in the orchards, to fellows whom we electioneer for in our secret societies, and alas! some even go so far as to *freeze* to the ladies. **1851** M. Reid *Scalp-Hunters* 143: "Now, boys! what say ye?" "I freeze to Kirker." **1855** Wise *Tales for Marines* 154: I rayther guess I'll freeze on to him fer my own private spec. **1859** Avery *Comical Stories* 58: I freeze to a good cigar; I'm one of the smokers. **1871** "M. Twain" *Roughing It* 251: When I know a man and like him, I freeze to him. **1878** Flipper *Colored Cadet* 54: "To freeze to."...To hold firmly. **1882** "M. Twain" *Life on Miss.* 153: So I let the wages go, and froze to my reputation. **1883** in *F & H* III 68: If there was one institution which the Anglo-Indian froze to more than another, it was his sit-down supper and—its consequences. **1889** Barrère & Leland *Dict. Slang* I 384: *Freeze, to* (American), to stick to. **1896** Ade *Artie* 58: She froze to me and steered me through without an error. **1905** in "O. Henry" *Works* 1443: Cut out that blonde, Kid, or there'll be trouble. What do you want to throw down that girl of yours for? You'll never find one that'll freeze to you like Liz has. **1907** in *DA:* So...he'd sneak in an' freeze to a chair by th' door.

    2. to pilfer; take.

    1851 (B. Hall quot. at **(1)**, above). **1888** *Stag Party* 46: A burglar..."I'll just freeze to 'em"/He chuckled with fiendish glee. ***1889** Barrère & Leland *Dict. Slang* I 384: *Freeze*...(common), to *freeze to,* to...take, steal; "Someone has *frozen* to my watch." **1934** Weseen *Dict. Slang* 336: *Freeze on to*—To obtain; to keep.

    3. to acknowledge.

    1865 William *Joaquin* 35: You lie, and you're a coward if you don't freeze to it!

    4. to keep firmly in mind.

    1879 *Puck* (Sept. 27) 451: We've got the boss aristocratic candidate, you jes' freeze to that fact. **1885** in Jerrold & Leonard *Parody* 367: Stranger, you freeze to this—there ain't no kinder gin-palace...lays over a man's own rancho. **1898** Bullen *Cachalot* 3 [ref. to 1875]: I'se de fourf mate ob dis yar ship, en my name's Mistah Jones, 'n yew jest freeze on to dat ar, ef yew want ter lib long 'n die happy. See, sonny.

    ¶ **wouldn't that freeze you?** isn't that amazing?

    1934 L. Hughes *Ways of White Folks* 60: Mr. Lloyd, jealous of a jig! Wouldn't that freeze you?

freeze down *v.* to settle down or in.

    1840 [T. Haliburton] *Clockmaker* (Ser. 3) ch. iii: Freeze down solid to it, square up to it, as if you was a-goin' to have an all-out-door fight of it. **1862** J.R. Lowell, in *DA:* I friz down right where I wus, married the Widder Shennon.

freeze in *v.* to set or fall to; get busy.

    1850 Garrard *Wah-to-Yah* 29: "Hyar's the doins, and hyar's the coon as *savvys* 'poor bull' from 'fat cow'; freeze into it, boys!" And all fall to with ready knives, cutting off savory pieces of this exquisitely appetizing prairie production. *Ibid.* 191: "Freeze into it, boys," said Metcalfe, producing a rial's worth of Mexican soft soap. **1876** in *DA:* Freeze in, and show them snails how to travel.

freeze-out *n.* FREEZE-OUT GAME; (*hence*) a betrayal of associates.

    1875 in *DA:* [In San Francisco] "clean out," "freeze out," are synonyms for rascally operations in business. **1904** in *DA:* The freeze-out will be a fact accomplished. **1905** White *Boniface* 458 [ref. to 1873]: "It's a freeze-out," he gasped to Wilkes. **1974** Radano *Cop Stories* 72: No hatchets were used, just an economic freeze-out.

    ¶ In phrase:

    ¶ **play freeze-out** *West.* to be compelled to endure extreme cold.

    1865 in *Kans. Hist. Qly.* VII (1938) 31: Cold and very stormy....No wood in Post; all playing "freeze out." **1885** Siringo *Texas Cowboy* 89: I...played a single-handed game of freeze-out until morning, not having any matches to make a fire with. **1886** in *DA:* The *Sod House* is doing duty in snug quarters on the Cimarron...playing a game of "freeze-out," as it were. **1894** *Harper's Mag.* (Feb.) 356: Getting up in the night to poke the fire and thaw the stiffening out of one's legs is called by the boys "playing freeze-out."

freeze out *v.* **1.** to exclude intentionally; drive out.

    1861 in *OEDS:* We finally froze him out. **1864** in *DAE:* Jealousy...and an insane fear that Colt would freeze them all out, delayed the erection of this machinery. **1867** in *Iowa Jour. of Hist.* LVII (1959) 214: Those who try to "freeze out" billiard saloons and euchre clubs, and not furnish any substitute, will find that they can't do it. **1869** in *DAE:* Thus "freezing out" the unhappy stockholders. *a*1890–93 *F & H* III 68: To *freeze out*…(American).—To compel to withdraw from society by cold and contemptuous treatment; from business by competition or opposition; from the market by depressing prices or rates of exchange. **1907** in McCay *Little Nemo* 79: Huh! No smoking! Well, that freezes me out. **1926** "Max Brand" *Iron Trail* 100: But tell me, are you figuring on something that freezes me out? **1963** D. Tracy *Brass Ring* 455: You froze me out of the will. **1974** Lahr *Trot* 145: Tell me one thing you said to the shrink. Anything. Don't freeze me out. **1978** B. Johnson *What's Happenin'* 105: I'm gonna get my shots. I showed I can score. These guys ain't gonna freeze me out.

2. to obtain from by trickery.—constr. with *of.*

1883 Peck *Peck's Bad Boy* 197: I must go down to the office and tell Pa I have reformed, and freeze him out of a circus ticket. **1889** Barrère & Leland *Dict. Slang* I 384: *Freeze out, to* (English and American), to…deprive of.

3. FREEZE, 3.

1966 Fariña *Down So Long* 83: Smiling falsely at the two coeds, who froze him right out. **1984** "W.T. Tyler" *Shadow Cabinet* 166: I make a pass at a bar girl, but she freezes me out. **1987** *Wkly. World News* (Sept. 15) 13: She might be warm one day and freeze you out the next.

freeze-out game *n.* a plan or example of deliberate exclusion. **1863** in *DA*: We never before exactly understood the villainous process of the "freeze-out game." **1916** S. Lewis *Job* 50: It's a freeze-out game; editors just accept stuff by their friends. **1947** in *DA*: It was just a freeze-out game, and I let my stock go without paying the assessment.

freezer *n.* a jail; COOLER. *Rare* in U.S.

1929–31, *1942 (cited in Partridge *Dict. Und.* 267). **1953** Chandler *Goodbye* 65: You didn't spend three days in the freezer just because you're a sweetheart.

freight *n.* **1.** *Army.* a heavy artillery shell, esp. one in flight. Also **freight car, freight train.** [Early quots. ref. to WWI.] **1918** Sherwood *Diary* 172: A big freight train (large calibre shell from a Big Bertha)…blew it up into a million bits. **1919** *A Battery, 308th* 16: The Boche "freight cars" and "gas"…kept us on the alert. **1919** J.R. Hinman *In France* 109: Another "slow freight" unloaded with a crash. **1925** Nason *3 Lights* 123: Yeah, but s'pose one o' them freight cars falls short. **1928** Jacks *Service Record* 51: The great shells sounded like enormous trains, "fast freights" our men called them. **1967** McClure *Yankee Doughboy* 200: The Yanks had a big gun somewhere in our rear, for every hour or so we heard a terrible screeching noise. We called it the "Freight Train," and it must have been a very big shell. **1972–76** Durden *No Bugles* 132 [ref. to Vietnam War]: A fast fuckin' freight roared over our heads and exploded about two hundred meters in front of us.…He…told 'em to fire, and another freight slammed over us.

2. cost.

1957 M. Shulman *Rally* 209: Money's no object in the electronics game.…The government pays the freight! **1966** Susann *Valley of Dolls* 421: *You* paid the freight for her at Haven Manor. **1966–67** W. Stevens *Gunner* 76: "What's the freight?"…"Three packs of butts." **1970** Della Femina *Wonderful Folks* 62: TWA was looking for freebies—presentations of agencies' work without paying the freight.

¶ In phrase:

¶ **haul** [or **pull**] **(one's) freight, 1.** Esp. *West.* to get moving; go; leave hurriedly.

1885 Siringo *Texas Cowboy* 8: I spied a large drove on ahead, pulling their freight for the water. **1891** in Davidson *Old West* 131: And he, too, pulled his freight and swore the 7th hard to face. **1895** F. Remington, in *Harper's* (July) 244: [The bear] had discreetly "pulled his freight." **1897** A.H. Lewis *Wolfville* 43: Thar's the stage an' our ponies to pull our freight with when Wolfville life begins to pall on us. **1906** M'Govern *Sarjint Larry* 65: Larry has long since "pulled his freight" to "answer check." *Ibid.* (gloss.): *Pull-My-Freight:* -To get out; to run away; to desert from the army, probably originally from practice of stealing away from a garrison aboard of a freight car. **1919** in Niles *Singing Soldiers* 106: Jackass you bes' haul yo' freight. **1921** in Handy *Blues Treasury* 135: So just pull your freight/I mean for you there's the gate. **1922** Rollins *Cowboy* 19 [ref. to 1890's]: It might be a terse request to…"pull your freight," or to "git." **1926** C.M. Russell *Trails* 9: We decide we'd better pull our freight before we're snowed in. **1936** in R.E. Howard *Iron Man* 195: Well, pull your freight while you're able to. **1944** in *DA*: "About then I hauled freight," Porky admitted. **1952** Hopson *High Saddle* 21: I'll be hauling my freight out of here *muy pronto*. **1961** Steinbeck *Winter of Discontent* 4: Someone near and dear to me is going to get a kick in the pants if she doesn't haul freight. **1966** Olsen *Hard Men* 52: You pull your freight or out you go. **1970** in Earp *Wyatt Earp* 110: I wasn't taking any chances.…I hauled my freight for Mexico.

2. to carry influence.

1896 Ade *Artie* 54: If she ever passes me up it'll be for some guy that hauls a good deal more freight than that Indian does.

French *n.* **1.** *Mil.* FRENCH LEAVE.

1841 [Mercier] *Man-of-War* 127 [ref. to 1839]: I'd no notion/For any girl on *French* to prance. **1863** in Bear *Civil War Letters* 37: Those that deserted and took Frenches are flocking in to their Regts like geese. They dread that Proclamation. **1863** in Geer *Diary* 117: Nearly everyman [*sic*] who drew his money has taken a french. *Ibid.* 119: Many boys returning from home on Frenches. **1906** in S.C. Wilson *Column South* 241 [ref. to Civil War]: Nearly every house contained two or three "graybacks," most of them…on a "French." **1918** Mills *My Story* 131 [ref. to 1871]: But in your case I don't object to your taking a "French," and I don't think your colonel will make any trouble with you if you arrive thirty days late. **1928** *AS* II 453: *French*—A.W.O.L.

2. blunt or offensive language; esp. (in U.S. now solely) in phr. **excuse** [or **pardon**] **my French.**

1865 Sedley *Marian Rooke* 342: Excuse my French. **1895** *Harper's Mag.* (Mar.) 648: Palaces be durned! Excuse my French. ***1909** Ware *Passing Eng.* 171: *Loosing French.* Violent language in English. ***1914–21** J. Joyce *Ulysses* 446: Bad French I got for my pains. **1923** Platt *Mr. Archer* 299: You ought to have heard, not the Latin, but the "French" spoken straight from the shoulder to the horses. **1929** Brecht *Downfall* 39: The dirty sonofabitch. Excuse my French. **1954** E. Hunter *Blackboard Jungle* 22: We are running a school that will teach these kids to be useful citizens of a goddamn fine community, and pardon my French, ladies, but that's exactly the way I feel about it. **1963** N.Y.C. woman, age *ca*45: These were kids who—pardon my French—went to *bed* with girls. **1977** Dunne *Confessions* 328: Not as sorry as I am, Monsignor, and that's no shit, if you'll excuse my French. **1982** C.R. Anderson *Other War* 84: That turd…The goddam line goes dead.…Please pardon my French, eh? **1987** N.Y.C. man, age *ca*27, on *Eyewitness News* (WABC-TV) (July 13): I'd just like to get the hell out of here—excuse my French. **1988** *New Yorker* (Aug. 8) 26: I could not remember the goddam Triple Sec. 'Scuse the French.

3. French Champagne.

1902 in Blackbeard & Williams *Smithsonian Comics* 23: And he wouldn't allow Uncle Bill to pay for the "French."

4. an act of fellatio or cunnilingus; oral copulation; in phr. **speak French** to practice oral copulation.

1916 Cary *Slang of Venery* I 94: *French*—To do the French—Cocksucking; and, inversely, to tongue a woman.…c.1700. An English Toast. Here's to the French/That wonderful race,/Which fights with its feet/And fucks with its face. **1924** Wilstach *Anecdota* 43: Old man marries. Doctor glands him. Told to wire him as to his success, and so: "Flunked in everything except French." **1927** *Immortalia* 157: This pretty wench/Was adept at French,/And said all else was uncouth. **1957** Murtagh & Harris *Cast First Stone* (gloss.): *French, Frenchy,* Fellatio. **1961** Gover *$100 Misunderstanding* 17: Yoo-hoo, pritty baby, you wanna lil french? Haff an haff? How bout jest a straight? **1966** S. Harris *Hellhole* 97: How much for a straight and a French? **1966** S. Stevens *Go Down Dead* 63: Everybody making out with something. Some doing french some double french. **1967** Schmidt *Lexicon of Sex* 372: "For another dollar she speaks French." Used during World War I. **1970** Wambaugh *New Centurions* 176: And hear her offer the guy a French for ten bucks. **1971** *Nude, Blued & Tattooed* 83: She's really a linguist—she's the only girl I know who can speak English and French at the same time. **1973** Schulz *Pimp* 18: The gays don't have to do too much, just a little french and maybe a little ass-fucking. **1976** "N. Ross" *Policeman* 140: "I just want a head job." "Man, I the best French on the street." **1992** Hosansky & Sparling *Working Vice* 94: A straight French.…You know, a blow job.

French *adj.* **1.** sexually indecent; pornographic. [The 1842 *OEDS* ex. seems to refer literally to a novel written in French.]

[***1842** in *OEDS*.] ***1849–50** W.M. Thackeray, in *F & H* III 71: The man…came to barracks and did business, one-third in money, one-third in eau-de-Cologne, and one-third in French prints. **1873** Lening *N.Y. Life* 652: He had published not less than 320 different works…of the most obscene character.…Haines also manufactures the so-called French or fancy playing-cards. **1932** V. Nelson *Prison Days & Nights* 90: He had a large assortment of photographs of women in various stages of undress…including a goodly number of extraordinarily filthy "French" pictures. **1943** Viereck *Men Into Beasts* 79: Sometimes he draws a French picture and passes it over. **1972** in *Penthouse* (Jan. 1973) 113: Vibrators are frequently used and "French films" are popular in some areas.

2.a. Esp. *Prost.* characterized by or involving oral copulation. Also as quasi-adv.

1888 *Stag Party* 95: Common, old fashioned f—k $1.00....Tasting (French) $2.50...French fashion with use of patent balls $3.50. **a***1890–93** *F & H* III 71: *French vice*...A euphemism for all sexual malpractices....First used (in print) in the case of Crawford *v.* Crawford and Dilke. **1934** "J.M. Hall" *Anecdota* 186: "The French way"...Substitution...of mouth for vagina. **1941** G. Legman, in G.V. Henry *Sex Vars.* II 1166: To fellate (or cunnilingue)....*do it the French way.* **1944** E. Caldwell *Tragic Ground* 58: "French or straight?" she asked coldly, shaking him until he opened his eyes. **1956** Levin *Compulsion* 238: This led to jokes about the French way, and McNamara, looking directly at Judd and Artie, said that he had been over there during the war, and some of those frogs were just as expert in the French way as their women. **1966** S. Stevens *Go Down Dead* 22: Other day you had Shirley and Jo Jo down here going french on you and you promise them a dollar each. **1969** Bartell *Group Sex* 82: "French culture" is cunnilingus and fellatio. **1969** S. Harris *Puritan Jungle* 103: "French love," known even to many non-swappers as oral stimulation of the vulva by male or female [is] practiced in swap circles. **1980** in *Penthouse* (Jan. 1981) 172: A nice massage? The French arts? Threesomes? Leather? Your fantasy is our command, Benjamin.

b. preferring, or adept at performing, oral copulation.

1917–20 Dreiser *Newspaper Days* 590 [ref. to 1894]: They're French all right...Don't you know, sport, what people mean when they say *French?*...They go down on you. **1929–31** J.T. Farrell *Young Lonigan* 140: They kidded Andy because he was of French extraction, and Kenny punned the word French. Andy missed the pun and defended the French. **1937** Reitman *Box-Car Bertha* 178: I want a French broad. I don't have to come here for the regular. I can get that at home. **1946** Mezzrow & Wolfe *Really Blues* 29: I'll show you a good time, honey, I'm French. *Ibid.* 30: A reputation as the best French girl in the place. **1952** Viereck *Men Into Beasts* 132: I manage to conceal what's masculine about me. And if they delve too deeply, I tell them I'm a French girl or that I've got the curse.

French *v.* **1.** *Navy.* to go absent without leave; take FRENCH LEAVE.—occ. constr. with *out.*

1894 *Lucky Bag* (No. 1) 67: *Frenching*...Taking French leave. **1900** Benjamin *Naval Acad.* 162 [ref. to *ca*1860]: Its staid dwellers regularly escaped into town, or as they called it, "Frenched." *Ibid.* 178: The process called "Frenching" or "Frenching it." **1907** *N.Y. Times* (Sept. 14) 18: The midshipman recently recommended for dismissal from the Naval Academy for "frenching" from his ship during the late summer cruise. **1912** *Lucky Bag* (No. 19) 394: I in Bancroft Hall will be/Ready to go in every room/And send some "frencher" to his doom. **1944** Maryland WPA *Gde. to U.S. Nav. Acad.* 151: *French Out*—To take unauthorized liberty. **1949** *Sat. Eve. Post* (Jan. 22) 73: I Frenched out last night....I left as soon as I secured Bancroft Hall.

2.a. to perform fellatio or cunnilingus on; BLOW. Also absol. Also (*rare*) **Frenchy.**

1923 *Poems, Ballads, & Parodies* 19: Bartender, he Frenched my Nellie./ He kissed it and stole her away. *a***1927** in P. Smith *Letter from Father* 61 [ref. to 1915]: Women frenching men. By frenching I mean...sucking them off. **1936** Heartman *Blue Book* 31: For two bits we will Frenchy you. **1938** "Justinian" *Amer. Sexualis* 22: *French.* v. To adopt the subordinate position in the act of *penis in ora*....U.S., C. 19-20, low coll. **1940** *Tale of a Twist* 17: "I jazz better after I'm Frenched anyway." "I don't French," Pauline said. **1943** in Legman *Limerick* 74: She'd bugger, fuck, jerk off, and french. **1949** *Gay Girl's Guide* 9: *French:* Another, and quasi-straight, euphemism for "blow" or do. **1955** Caprio *Vars. in Sexual Behavior* 237: She was menstruating and said, "I'll have to French you." **1960** Jordan & Marberry *Fool's Gold* 75 [ref. to 1899]: She would set up headquarters and tack this card on the door: *Frenching Inside.* I would guess that the Lousetown Babe made more money than any other trollop in the North, because of the fast turnover. **1966** S. Harris *Hellhole* 236: Well, I'm a butch now...but...I can French men while having a woman in my mind. **1970** Conaway *Big Easy* 18: You reckon that little fella over there knows how to French? **1973** Toma & Brett *Toma* 19: I French and I got the best pussy in all of Newark.

b. *Prost. & Homosex.* to caress with the tongue.

1967 [R. Beck] *Pimp* 82: His tongue was "frenching" his "chops." **1975** Harrell & Bishop *Orderly House* 44: First I'll French your titties, then I'll...lick your thing. **1975–77** in Fine *With Boys* 172: French my hole.

3. SHORT-SHEET.

[**1906** *DN* III 137: *French sheet, n.phr.* A bed which has been rearranged as a joke.] **1948** Wouk *City Boy* 279: Lennie, I appoint you to make Herbie's bed. And if it's Frenched or tricked up in any way, you'll spend

the next two days on your cot. **1970** in W. Allen *Getting Even* 17: Göering swore he would get even, and it was rumored later that he had special S.S. guards french Speer's bed. **1979** Kunstler *Wampanaki Tales* 39: How about french his bed?

4. FRENCH-KISS.

1955 O'Hara *Ten North Frederick* 152: She...Frenched me. **1970** Wakefield *Going All the Way* 144: It...was much better than just the necking stuff like frenching and getting covered-tit or even bare-tit. **1975** C.W. Smith *Country Music* 253: I kissed her on the mouth, Frenched her. **1988** J. Brown & C. Coffey *Earth Girls* (film): I can't believe you're frenching an alien in front of all these people!

5. *Hot Rodding.* to modify the configuration of (headlights) so as to integrate them with the front fender of a hot rod.

1951–53 in *AS* (Feb. 1954) 96: "Frenched headlights" are headlights whose rims have been welded and smoothed to form an integral part of the front fenders. **1953** Felsen *Street Rod* 63: With frenched headlights. **1982** Sculatti *Catalog of Cool* 116: A chopped, nosed, and decked 1949 Mercury with frenched headlights.

6. FRENCH-INHALE.

1970 A. Young *Snakes* 64: "Ain't yall high yet?...Do *this!*" He took a puff and pinched his nostrils shut with his fingers and then blew into them without letting anything escape. "That's what you call frenching."

French bath *n. Prost.* an erotic act consisting of extensive licking of the partner's body.

1935 in Atkinson *Dirty Comics* 151: The winner shall receive a French bath by three professional French girls who's services have been retained for the occasion.

French blue *n. Narc.* a mixture of a barbiturate and an amphetamine, usu. in capsule form.

1968 Barclay *Sex Slavery* 134: The first *French blue* or *purple heart* (a pep pill of the amphetamine group). **1970** Landy *Underground* 83: *French blue*...Mixture of an amphetamine and a barbiturate, injected. **1972** *Nat. Lampoon* (Oct.) 41: METHEDRINE and AMYTAL (French blue). *****1978** in Partridge *DSUE* (ed. 8) 426.

French cap *n.* a condom.

1976 D.W. Maurer, in *AS* LI 13 [ref. to 1920's]: Euphemisms like...*French cap*...also became taboo.

French deck *n.* a novelty deck of playing cards the face of each of which is decorated with an erotic picture.

[**1873** Lening *N.Y. Life* 652: He had published not less than 320 different works...of the most obscene character....Haines also manufactures the so-called French or fancy playing-cards.] **1963** N.Y.C. high-school student: They sell French decks on Times Square. **1980** W. Sherman *Times Square* 23: "French Decks," fifty-two playing cards with nude women in various positions showing just a hint of pubic hair. **1981** Vincent *Mudville* 159: The advertisements for gambling equipment, love potions, prophylactics, and "French deck" picture cards...were now rare.

French fuck *n.* (see quots.).—usu. considered vulgar.

1938 "Justinian" *Amer. Sexualis* 22: *French Fuck.* n. A form of sexual activity in which the male sits astride the recumbent female and achieves sexual orgasm by rubbing his penis between her breasts, while concomitantly effecting her orgasm by digital stimulation of her vaginal area. Br. & U.S., C. 19-20. **1974** Univ. Tenn. grad. student: A...French fuck is when you rub your dick between her breasts. [Heard in Ark., *ca*1970.].

French furlough *n.* [sugg. by FRENCH LEAVE] *Army.* an instance of desertion or absence without leave. Now *hist.* Also **French pass.** [Quots. ref. to Civil War.]

*ca***1864** in Wiley & Milhollen *They Who Fought* 169: I take a French pass once in a while but haft to look out for the petrolls...Frank...has just got back home from a French furlow. **1865** J. Pike *Scout & Ranger* 253: I took "French furlough," and made a visit to my home. **1890** Goss *Recollections* 139: Eighty thousand men were absent from causes unknown or on "French furloughs,"—"walked off on their cheek," as the boys styled it, and they dared not face the consequences by voluntary return. **1893** Casler *Stonewall* 49: Some six or seven of my company, being very anxious to go home on a visit,...took a "French furlough" and disappeared one night. What we meant by "French furlough" was simply "absent without leave," and was not considered desertion. **1987** J.I. Robertson *Blue & Gray* 133: Unauthorized leaves ("French furloughs," soldiers called them).

French handshake *n. Juve.* (see quot.).

1972 *Nat. Lampoon* (Apr.) 34: You're shakin' hands, right? And one of you tickles the palm with the middle finger. It's a signal the Frenchies use when they got the hots. They go around givin' French handshakes till somebody says yes.

French harp *n. So.* a harmonica.

1883 J.W. Riley *Old Swimmin'-hole* 25: A slice of worter-melon's like a french-harp in their hands. **1884** in Lummis *Letters* 25: They were grouped around a not too harmonious French harp. **1938** in Gelman *Photoplay* 209: His dad stuck a French harp in his little paws and Mickey was in show business. **1946** in *DA*: She would play the organ for me, and I would play my French harp. **1968** J.P. Miller *Race for Home* 113 [ref. to 1930's]: His harmonica, or French harp, and his pocketknife being standard operating equipment, were already in his pocket.

Frenchie var. FRENCHY, *n.*

French-inhale *v.* to puff on a cigarette, exhale the smoke through the nose, and then inhale it again.

1957 Simmons *Corner Boy* 21: He watched the smoke curl into her nose as she french-inhaled. **1965** Cassavetes *Faces* 75: You know how to French inhale? No, no, I mean through one nostril. **1971** Jacobs & Casey *Grease* 19: Yeah, then I'll show ya how to French inhale. **1988** *Kate & Allie* (CBS-TV): Carter's teaching me how to French-inhale. **1990** Bing *Do or Die* 217: When I was a teenager [in 1960's]....We called it French inhaling, and I never did get it right.

French kiss *n.* an open-mouthed kiss in which the tongue of one partner is manipulated in the mouth of the other.

1936 Levin *Old Bunch* 180: She...gave him a long French kiss. **1956** P. Moore *Chocolates* 16: Your first French kiss. **1970** Byrne *Memories* 28: Helene Hanson let her tongue slide slowly into view, as if rehearsing a French kiss. **1974** Lahr *Trot* 16: French kiss 1 pt. Hickie 2. Breast 3. **1983** E. Dodge *Dau* 109: Cajoling her with a series of French kisses.

French-kiss *v.* to give or exchange French kisses. Also trans.

1918 in Lindner *Letters* 119: A sort of liaison between tongues (not to be confused with French kissing). **1928** McKay *Banjo* 292: The fust time I evah French-kiss a he, chappie. **1929–30** Dos Passos *42d Parallel* 336: She taught him how to frenchkiss. **1929–33** Farrell *Manhood of Lonigan* 188: Their mouths opening, french-kissing in public. **1960** Swarthout *Where Boys Are* 112: The only thing suspect about his innocence was his tendency to French-kiss given the slightest opening. **1970** Sorrentino *Steelwork* 48: If a girl French-kisses you, you can fuck her. **1979** Gutcheon *New Girls* 152: Have you ever been French-kissed?

French landing *n. Av.* (see quot.).

1956 Heflin *USAF Dict.* 221: *French landing.* A landing possible with certain airplanes in which the airplane rolls along the ground on its two main wheels, holding the tail in the air as long as possible before coming to a stop. *Slang.*

French leave *n.* [specialization of the S.E. sense 'a departure from a social event without taking leave of one's host'] an escape or flight; (*Mil.*) an instance of absence without leave or of desertion. Also *fig.*

***1771** T. Smollett, in *OED2*: He stole away an Irishman's bride, and took a French leave of me and his master. ***1785** Grose *Vulgar Tongue*: *To take French leave*...: a saying frequently applied to persons who have run away from their creditors. ***1803** in J. Ashton *Eng. Satires on Napoleon* 189: A Knock Down blow in the Ocean, or Bonaparte taking French Leave. ***1805** in *F & H* III 70: One of the French prisoners of war on parole at Chesterfield, took French leave of that place, in defiance of his parole engagement. **1824** in Paulding *Bulls & Jons.* 214: In my retreat I heard the little Frenchman exclaim, "Diable! this is what you call taking French leave, I think!" **1833** *Mil. & Nav. Mag. of U.S.* (Dec.) 218: "And so, you scamp, you were about to take French leave of us," said Mr. Snookes. **1841** [Mercier] *Man-of-War* 174: My new hat...took *French leave*. **1847** Reid *McCulloch's Rangers* 11: Many of them took *French leave*, by scaling the walls of the barracks. **1850** E.G. Buffum *Gold Mines* 68: Merchants closed their stores, lawyers left their clients, doctors their patients, soldiers took "French leave." **1852** Hazen *Five Years* 181: Those worthy officers who were the authors of this wholesale "French leave." **1863** in Theaker *Through One Man's Eyes* 37: Four discharged, and several at home on "*French Leave*." **1873** Sutton *N.Y. Tombs* 199: Just as I was getting ready to take "French leave" I was betrayed by one of my fellow prisoners. **1890** Goss *Recollections* 37 [ref. to Civil War]: As soon as I was relieved from guard duty, I went over on "French leave" to view our enemy's fortifications. **1898** Doubleday *Gunner* 12: It was evidently one of the men taking "French" leave. **1907** Moss *Officers' Manual* 243: *French Leave*—unauthorized

absence. Absent on French leave—absent without authority. **1917** Eddy *In France* 27: As soon as they were paid several months' back salary, some of them took "French leave," and went on a spree and did not come back until they were penniless. **1953–55** Kantor *Andersonville* 74 [ref. to Civil War]: With all that smoke and banging...many in the company might have felt like taking *French leave*. **1963** Cameron *Black Camp* 69 [ref. to WWII]: Pulled three weeks in the stockade...for taking French leave. **1980** Valle *Rocks & Shoals* 132 [ref. to 1828]: The convicted seamen...[stated] that they had only meant to take "french leave" so that they could have an overnight "frolic" ashore.

French letter *n.* a condom.

***a1856** in *OEDS*: French letters...prevent the spread of venereal contagion in casual intercourse between the sexes, and in the marriage state, the increase of the family. ***ca1857**, ***1886** in *Ibid.* ***a1890–93** *F & H* III 71: *French-letter*...A sheath—of india-rubber, gold-beater's skin, gutta-percha—worn by a man during coition to prevent infection or fruition. ***1888–94** in *OEDS*. ***1900** *Horn Book* 148: A well-known check is the use of the French letter, name given to a kind of elongated bag or case made of very thin skin or fine india-rubber. ***1909** in Joyce *Selected Letters* 158: You told me...Holohan...wanted to fuck you...using what they call a "French letter." **1922** *Erotic Appliances* 19: A cundum is likewise known as a French, Italian, or Spanish letter. **1938** "Justinian" *Amer. Sexualis* 22: *French Letters.* n.pl. Cundums....Obsolescent in U.S. **1969** Briley *Traitors* 220: He felt another wave of guilt....because he hadn't used one of the damn French letters Thai had given him. **1977** T. Berger *Villanova* 36: Desiccated French letters discarded by fornicators long dead. **1980** in McCauley *Dark Forces* 482: This wonder condom, first-class special delivery French letter...could fool the inside of a vagina.

French liberty *n. Navy.* an unauthorized liberty; FRENCH LEAVE.

1841 [Mercier] *Man-of-War* 168: The master-at-arms can't possibly have gone ashore for *French* liberty men.

French polish *n.* [alluding to the smart appearance of French vessels] *Navy.* elbow grease.

1841 [Mercier] *Man-of-War* 184: All our guns have got acquainted/ With the *French polish* which we use.

French postcard *n.* an erotic photograph printed on a card or postcard. Cf. FRENCH, *adj.*, 1.

[**1922** Paul *Impromptu* 115 [ref. to 1918]: If anyone [in France] tries to sell you dirty postal cards, look him straight in the face and see who drops his eyes first.] **1926** *Reader's Digest* (Sept.) 288: The appeal of these periodicals is no more nor less than that in the old-fashioned "French picture postcards" which used to be offered for sale at two for a quarter—"mailed to you in a plain envelope." **1929–30** J.T. Farrell *Young Lonigan* 110: Nate said he was getting some new French post cards. **1930** "D. Stiff" *Milk & Honey* 152: At one time, the hobo enjoyed almost exclusively the "French post cards." [**1931** Stevenson *St. Luke's* 261 [ref. to *ca*1910]: Maybe a few of you has heard about these postcards they sell in Paris France for a high price?] **1932** Mahin *Red Dust* (film): Don't you think she's ever seen a French postcard? **1944** in *Best from Yank* 140: He could use the mashed-up goo for pasting French postcards...on his barracks wall. **1951** Mannix *Sword-Swallower* 136: I've got some genuine French postcards here—the kind you hear about but seldom see. **1956** H. Gold *Not With It* 103: Benedict...now pushed French postcards. **1958** Cooley *Run for Home* 349: It was no more than he'd felt when he saw his first so-called "French post-cards" in high school. **1960** Brooks *Elmer Gantry* (film): I have in my pockets—lewd, dirty, obscene...French postcards! **1963** D. Tracy *Brass Ring* 276: We're not exactly in the French postcard business.

French safe *n.* a condom; FRENCH TICKLER. Cf. SAFE, *n.*

1870 in M.W. Hill *Sisters' Keepers* 236: French Imported Male Safes—A perfect shield against disease or conception. **1897** *Science of Generation* 235: The use of various mechanical contrivances, such as French Safes, Condom Sheaths, etc., is also objectionable. **1963** *AS* XXXVII 115: The British term *French letter* is included...while *French safe* is not. **1966–80** McAleer & Dickson *Unit Pride* 184: French safes and whatnot. **1980** Ciardi *Browser's Dict.* 140: *French safe.* A condom.

French 75 *n.* [sugg. by *French 75* 'a French 75-mm gun employed during WWI'] a mixed drink typically consisting of champagne, cognac, lemon juice, and sugar.

***1936** (cited in Partridge *DSUE* (ed. 8) 426). **1942** Epstein, Epstein, & Koch *Casablanca* (film): A French 75! **1963** W.C. Anderson *Penelope* 34: They had met over a punchbowl of French 75's. **1976** *Esquire* (Sept.) 83: *The French 75*, named after a World War I cannon, hit café society like a shot. **1977** Caputo *Rumor of War* 39: The boys'd be down there guzzling those French-seventy-fives.

French tickler *n.* **1.** a condom or (formerly) band for the penis designed to stimulate the vagina during sexual intercourse.

1916 Cary *Venery* II 165: *Tickler*...a band of rubber through which are drawn loops of floss...used for the purpose of exciting the woman while the penis is moved back and forth in the vagina. Sometimes called a French tickler. **1935** J. Conroy *World to Win* 234: To examine the latest French ticklers. **1938** "Justinian" *Amer. Sexualis* 22: *French Tickler. n.* A sharp, delicate protuberance situated at the head of a cundum, which serves to stimulate additional sexual excitement within the vagina during intromission. **1939** C.R. Cooper *Scarlet* 57: French ticklers, manufacture of which is outlawed. **1949** Mende *Spit & Stars* 225: Any of you mugs ever hear of a French tickler? **1968** P. Roth *Portnoy* 195: Her child's hair-raising collection of French ticklers. **1972** Pearce *Pier Head Jump* 59: Stag movies. Dildos. French ticklers. **1981** Raban *Old Glory* 33: The condom...[was] a "French tickler."

2. a mustache.—used derisively.

1968 J.D. Houston *Between Battles* 107: Grab that French tickler he's wearing and rub it in the sawdust!

Frenchy or **Frenchie** *n.* **1.** a French person; (*hence*) a French-Canadian.—often used derisively.

*a***1860** [J. Jones] *Marie* 11: The blasted Frenchies will be down on us like hornets. **1864** in Lyman *Meade's HQ* 204: The General, accompanied by the Frenchies,...paid a grand visit to Butler. ***1883** in *OED*: The squires had begun by calling him Frenchy. **1889** (quot. at ELI). **1891** in *OEDS*: I wouldn't give him for half a dozen of those *parlez vous* Frenchies. **1893** *Century* (Nov.) 100: Canada is left pretty much in the hands of the local vagabonds, who are called "Frenchies." **1966** in *OEDS*. **1976** C.R. Anderson *Grunts* 64: The Frenchies knew how to fight a war. **1976** Simon *Murder by Death* (film): I'm not a Frenchie, I'm a Belgie.

2. **FRENCH**, *n.*, 4.

1957 Murtagh & Harris *Cast First Stone* 248: Four dollars for French. O.K. for four dollars for a Frenchy? **1977** Torres *Q & A* 207: Okay, but only a quick Frenchie.

Frenchy *adj.* **FRENCH**, *adj.*, 1.

1936 Washburn *Parlor* 131: There were pictures of the various [brothel buildings]—nothing Frenchy. But it was 1911; nudist magazines were unknown on the newsstands.

freq /frik/ *n.* an electromagnetic, esp. a radio, frequency. Also **freak.**

1969 Marshall *Ambush* 87: A strange voice came in on the command freak. **1982** Del Vecchio *13th Valley* 231: He'll come up on your freq. **1985** Heywood *Taxi Dancer* 88: If your tanker was listening to the strike freak...he could get underway to meet you. **1990** Rukuza *W. Coast Turnaround* 213: The voices...filled the freq with demands for his immediate surrender.

frequency *n.* a state of complete, usu. mutual, understanding.—usu. constr. with *right, wrong*, etc.

1959 *Swinging Syllables: Not on your frequency*—Don't understand you. **1966** N.Y.C. high-school student: You gotta get on the right frequency with her....I guess you're just on different frequencies. **1968** Ark. State Univ. student (coll. J. Ball): Man, me and you is on the wrong frequency! **1971** Drill Sgt., U.S. Army (coll. J. Ball): The first thing we gotta do is get on the same frequency. *a***1988** C. Adams *More Straight Dope* 186: Am I missing something?...Cecil, what's the frequency?

fresh *n.* *Stu.* a freshman or freshmen.

1827 in *DA*: That awful hour/When Sophs meet Fresh. **1848** in B. Hall *College Wds.* (ed. 2) 210: Listen to the low murmurings of some annihilated Fresh. **1849** in Eliason *Tarheel Talk* 272: The old students have a custom of hollwing at the Fresh when they go out in the Campus. **1859** in *Ibid.*: The Fresh treat came off last Saturday every Fresh has to put in $2.00 apiece to treat to water-mellons. **1899** in *DA*: Here, Fresh, one of you take his suit case upstairs.

fresh *adj.* [cf. G *frech* 'impudent'] **1.** forward; (esp. of children) impudent; (*specif.*, of men) offensively forward in behavior toward a woman. Now *S.E.*

1845 Corcoran *Pickings* 175: A Salt Who was Fresh. **1848** Bartlett *Amer.* 399: *Fresh.* Forward; as, "don't make yourself too fresh here"; that is to say, not quite so much at home. **1859** *Ibid.* (ed. 2) 162: *Fresh, adj.* Forward; bold. **1875** in R.L. Wright *Irish Emigrant Ballads* 595: Old man, you're getting too fresh,/And we'll soon have to put you on the ice. **1877** in Asbury *Gem of Prairie* 134: Lottie Maynard should not

be so fresh with other girls' lovers. **1886** *Chi. Tribune* (Mar. 2) 10: There was another [conductor] that had a little scrap with a fresh woman. **1887** Francis *Saddle & Moccasin* 136: Has Piggy been too "fresh"?*...*Cheeky. *a***1899** B.F. Sands *Reefer* 58: The novelty had worn off for us, and whilst the youngster was "fresh," the "oldsters" were *blasés!* **1902** in *OEDS*: And when she goes out and says that isn't right they tell her she's too fresh. **1905** *Nat. Police Gaz.* (Dec. 23) 3: This fresh guy has insulted me. **1907** J. London, in *DAS*: If he got fresh, two or three of us would pitch on him. **1908** in *OEDS*: That [remark] was pretty fresh, and my only excuse for doing it was that I couldn't think of anything fresher. **1913** J. London *Valley of Moon* 61: You're too fresh to keep, young fellow. **1931** Wilstach *Under Cover Man* 218: Pretty fresh, ain't you? **1937–40** in Whyte *Street Corner Society* 4: I was the tough guy. But he began to get fresh with me. **1942** Pegler *Spelvin* 73: My guy Harold got fresh. **1957** E. Lacy *Room to Swing* 65: Get fresh and I'll give you a [traffic] ticket right now.

2. *Rap Music.* appealing; attractive; nice; **COOL.**

1984 Nakano & White *Body Rock* (film): "I like to look fresh." "Fresh?" "Yeah. *Fresh.*" **1984** Toop *Rap Attack* 158: *Fresh*...good-looking, stylish, or cool...."That new gear my man was wearing was fresh." **1985** Graham & Hamdan *FLYERS* ch. xxviii: *Fresh*...trendy (esp. clothes, songs, etc.). **1986** Cosby *Fatherhood* 112: "Turn that crap down."..."But, Dad, this stuff is *fresh.*" **1986** Eble *Campus Slang* (Mar.) 4: *Fresh*—appealing, attractive, fashionable, socially attractive...."She definitely looks fresh." Also cool, sweet. **1987** *21 Jump St.* (Fox-TV): Man, that girl is totally fresh. I'm gonna get me a slice of that. **1988** *Sonny Spoon* (NBC-TV): I like your hair. It's fresh. **1990** Costello & Wallace *Signifying Rappers* 53: "Fresh" means irresistibly stylish, oft modified by "funky," "crazy," or "stoopid." **1992** Majors & Billson *Cool Pose* 78: The cool guys get the freshest girls. The cool girls.

¶ In phrase:

¶ **fresh and sweet** *Und.* (see quots.) *Joc.*

1970 Landy *Underground* 83: *Fresh and sweet*...Just out of jail. **1970** Horman & Fox *Drug Awareness* 466: *Fresh and sweet*—Out of jail. **1972** Smith & Gay *Don't Try It* 202: *Fresh and Sweet.* Just out of the penitentiary; new to the dope scene. **1975** *DAS* (ed. 3) 701: *Fresh and sweet.* Just released from jail. *Said of prostitutes. Prostitute use.*

fresh fish see s.v. **FISH**, *n.*

freshie *n.* **1.** *Stu.* a freshman.

1847 in *DA*: The freshies were tremendously beat. **1871** Bagg *At Yale* 64: Go it, Freshie! **1900** *DN* II 37: *Freshie, n.* A freshman. **1928** Carr *Rampant Age* 2: How do they fit, freshie? **1929** Bodenheim *60 Secs.* 36: I had him in Alg' when I was a freshie. **1935** J. Conroy *World to Win* 121: Every freshie on the campus. **1958** Motley *Epitaph* 267: I'm a freshie at the University of Chicago.

2. a fresh or forward person.

1908 in "O. Henry" *Works* 697: But he's easy spoken and not a freshy.

fresh meat *n.* **1.** *Mil.* maggots infesting food.

1863 in R.G. Carter *4 Bros.* 357: Our crackers are poor, being filled with *fresh meat.*

2. Esp. *Prost.* a new sexual partner, esp. a virgin.

a*1890–96** *F & H* IV 296: *Fresh meat* = a new piece. **1916** Cary *Venery* I 95: *Fresh Meat*—A virgin; a new piece. ***1940** in Partridge *Dict. Und.* 267: "Fresh meat sales" and the shipping of "young stuff across the Channel." **1958** Talsman *Gaudy Image* 35: Sleepin' with a virg and didn't know it. I told ya I was partial to fresh meat.

3. a new victim; (*hence*) a new or inexperienced young person, (*esp.*) *Pris.* a newly arrived convict; *Mil.* a new recruit or replacement; (*Sports*) a new team member.—often used collectively.

1908 J. London *M. Eden* 313: Here's fresh meat for your axe, Kreis. **1925** *Amer. Legion Wkly.* (Aug. 28) 15: "New man?"..."Yes, fresh meat for the wolves." **1931** Gallagher *Cognac Hill* 148: The Major joined our regiment in July, 1917, and as he came into the barracks...in civilian dress he was greeted with that well-known battle cry, "Fresh Meat." **1934** Weseen *Dict. Slang* 254: *Fresh meat*—A new opponent, especially in prizefighting. **1937** Herndon *Let Me Live* 197: Fresh meat! You son-of-a-bitch! What do you mean by breaking into jail on us? **1948** A. Murphy *Hell & Back* 42: Has anyone ever seen a nicer pack of fresh meat? **1971** H.S. Thompson *Las Vegas* 46: In...[Las Vegas] they love a drunk. Fresh meat. **1968–77** Herr *Dispatches* 22: A sergeant...took one look, called me Freshmeat, and told me to go find some other outfit to get myself killed with. **1984** J.R. Reeves *Mekong* 60: The new sailors were the "fresh meat" he'd been sent to get. **1984** *N.Y. Post* (Aug. 31) 81: Fresh meat in Pittsburgh, a 37 percent roster turnover. **1985** Dye *Between Raindrops* 253: Fresh meat only brought the unit up to fifty percent of normal combat strength. **1986** R. Zumbro *Tank Sgt.* 83: Holt was speculating about who would get the "fresh meat."

frick var. FRIG.

Frick and Frack *n.pl. Black E.* a pair of individuals or items. *Joc.*
1973 *Sanford & Son* (NBC-TV): "Who were they?" "Uh-h-h—Frick and Frack." **1967–80** Folb *Runnin' Lines* 238: Frick and frack. Testicles. **1987** *Miami Vice* (NBC-TV): I forget the names—something like Frick and Frack. **1990** *Sydney* (CBS-TV): Well, if it ain't Frick and Frack.

fricking *adj. & adv.* (a euphem. for) FUCKING; FRIGGING. Also as infix.
***1936** Partridge *DSUE* 982: Fricking. A s. euphemism for f**king, adj.: C.20 On or ex *frigging*, adj. **1970** in P. Heller *In This Corner* 237: That fricking bum. **1975** Univ. Minn. student: I just finished writing a paper. I'm so frickin' tired. **1976** Univ. Tenn. student: That's no frickin' reason. **1976** Rosen *Above Rim* 40: Jesus H. Keerist! What a fricken ball club! **1977** Dowd *Slap Shot* (film): Grab your frickin' gear and get goin'. **1986** *L.A. Law* (NBC-TV): You got a problem with that, you go live in the *frickin'* Soviet Union! **1987** Univ. Tenn. prof., age *ca*65: In Albany [N.Y., *ca*1934] we used *frickin'* a lot. Certainly more than *friggin'*: "That frickin' son of a bitch!" **1989** *CBS Summer Playhouse* (CBS-TV): Who do you think you are? Attila the Hun? Jack the fricking Ripper? **1989** *21 Jump St.* (Fox-TV): Absofrickinlutely! We're talkin' total obliteration.

Friday *n. Naut.* (see quot.). Cf. FISH-EATER.
1965 E. Hall *Flotsam, Jetsam & Lagan* 311 [ref. to *ca*1910]: Fish chowder served aboard Catholic ships on Friday and at any time aboard Protestant ships when fish or clams were available was dubbed by Jack Tar as "friday."

fridge *n.* a refrigerator. Now *colloq.* [Common in U.S. only after WWII.]
***1926**, ***1935**, ***1939**, ***1946**, ***1954**, ***1955**, ***1957**, etc., in *OEDS*.
1962 T. Berger *Reinhart* 212: There's a tuna plate all prepared in the fridge. **1970** L. Gould *Friends* 150: I got a steak in the fridge. **1975** *Wond. World of Disney* (NBC-TV): There's fresh strawberries in the fridge.

fried *adj.* **1.** intoxicated.
1923 in J. O'Hara *Sel. Letters* 6: I celebrated…[and] I got nicely fried. **1927** *New Republic* (Mar. 9) 72: Fried to the hat, slopped to the ears, stewed to the gills. **1927** Mayer *Between Us Girls* 69: I mean they all get fried. **1928** MacArthur *War Bugs* 15: The wastrels got fried. **1929** in Perelman *Old Gang* 70: By the time came for the ceremony he was pretty well fried. **1945** Seaton *Junior Miss* (film): They're out getting fried at some cocktail party. **1952** Bankhead *Tallulah* 92: I have been tight as a tick! Fried as a mink! Stiff as a goat! **1963** Coon *Short End* 229: Well, at least maybe we can get fried—if I don't decide to go into town that night. **1964** Pearl *Stockade* 13: She came staggering in here 'bout fifteen minutes ago, like she was fried to the eyeballs. **1971** Cole *Rook* 275: So there I sat wryly getting slowly fried…on hot sake. **1979** Univ. Tenn. student paper: Synonyms for Drunk…died, fried, and laid to the side. **1987** *Yank* (quot. at SKUNKED).

2. *Stu.* angry; BURNED.
1968 Baker et al. *CUSS* 121: *Fried.* Angry. **1990** *Coach* (ABC-TV): Chances are she's a little fried by now.

3. tired out; FRAZZLED.
1980 Eble *Campus Slang* (Oct.) 3: *Fried*—Absentminded, incoherent, irrational, mentally fatigued because of over-celebration. **1983** Naiman *Computer Dict.* 64: After debugging this crock for 36 hours, I'm completely fried. **1992** *Melrose Place* (Fox-TV): It's late. I'm fried!

4. ruined.
1981 Univ. Tenn. student: My mind is fried. **1983** Naiman *Computer Dict.* 64: I'm afraid your memory-board is completely fried.

fried egg *n.* **1.a.** *U.S. Mil. Acad.* (see 1936 quot.).
1908 *Howitzer* 325: *Fried-egg*, n. Dress-hat ornament. **1936** *Nat. Geographic* 778: A "fried egg" is the U.S. Military Academy insignia worn on the full-dress hat equipped with "feather duster." **1941** *AS* (Oct.) 165: *Fried Egg.* Insignia of U.S. Military Academy. **1988** D.O. Smith *Cradle* 73 [ref. to 1930]: Tall black shakos with plumes and large brass insignia called fried eggs.

b. *Army.* (see quot.).
1945 *Yank* (Sept. 21) 3: GIs…in the [37th Infantry] division…sometimes call it the Fried Egg Division. This is a commentary on the 37th's shoulder patch.

2. *Mil. in Pacific.* the rising-sun emblem of Japan; (*hence*) the Japanese national flag.
1943 Wakeman *Shore Leave* 62: Remember that time, Mac, I came in from a scouting mission and reported spotting two Jap P-Boats? Why they even had fried eggs on them, which was unusual over those waters. **1952** in *DAS*: Morton's *Wahoo* sunk about everything the Japs owned with a fried egg on its masthead. **1981** Rogan *Mixed Co.* 264 [ref. to WWII]: And fluttering above the compound was the Japanese flag—"That fried egg," said Minnie.

3. *Golf.* a lie in which the ball is partially buried in sand.
1960 in P. Davies *Golf. Terms* 71: The ball was half-buried in the sand.…"What we call a fried-egg lie," I told her cheerily. **1970** Scharff *Encyc. of Golf* 420: *Plugged lie.* A "lie" generally in a bunker in which the ball is buried in the sand. Same as a *fried egg*. **1977** in Davies *Golf Terms* 71.

4. a woman's breasts; (*specif.*) small, flat breasts.
1975 *UTSQ: Breasts*…tits, watermelons, fried eggs. **1985** "Blowdryer" *Mod. Eng.* 77: Tits…*fried eggs.* **1992** *Donahue* (synd. TV series): I don't like myself because I've got fried eggs.

fried hole *n.* a doughnut.
1918 I. Cobb *Glory of Coming* 58: There were genuine old-fashioned doughnuts—"fried holes," the Far Westerners call them.

friend *n.* [euphem.] a menstrual period. Also **friends.**
***1889** Barrère & Leland *Dict. Slang* I 366: Menses…"I've got…my friends." ***a1890–93** F & H III 73: *Friend* (or *little friend*)…The menstrual flux,…whose appearance is sometimes announced by the formula, "My little friend has come." **1968** Baker et al. *CUSS* 121: *Friend, get your…Friend, have a visit from a.* Be menstruating. **1971** Jacobs & Casey *Grease* 52: You havin' your friend?…Your friend. Your period. **1974** Verona & Gleckler *Lords of Flatbush* 48: My friend is a month late. **1974** Lahr *Trot* 94: Take your pants off, darling. I've got "my friend." **1978** Pilcer *Teen Angel* 191: I've got my friend and all. **1984** D. Smith *Steely Blue* 41: You got your friend, an operation, or what?

friendly *n.* [sugg. by mil. jargon *friends* 'friendly forces or non-combatants'] *Pol.* a political supporter (of a particular candidate).
1984 WINS Radio News (Sept. 3): President Reagan will begin his campaign in Orange County [Cal.] because, in the words of an adviser, "He wants to kick off his reelection bid with an audience of known friendlies."

friendly *adj.* ¶ In phrases:

¶ **(one's) friendly neighborhood** —— [sugg. by the cliché *your friendly neighborhood grocer*, used in advertising during the 1950's] (used as a jocular and ironic term of reference).
1965 N.Y.C. high-school student: So the natives go see their friendly neighborhood witch doctor. **1970** La Motta et al. *Raging Bull* 27: These guys shooting craps weren't exactly your friendly neighborhood ribbon clerks. **1976** "N. Ross" *Policeman* 54: I don't believe it's too far fetched to imagine the friendly neighborhood CIA agent paying a visit to the dope-maker in Turkey or France saying…"If you insist on working, your fucking brains will be blown out." **1981** *Home Room* (ABC-TV): Hi, I'm…your friendly neighborhood guidance counselor.

¶ **make friendly** *West.* to shoot at or kill (American Indians). *Joc.*
1871 Crofutt *Tourist's Guide* 18: The Indians—"friendlies"—have made several raids of late on the settlers, and have killed a number of miners and ranch men, but were finally driven off by the miners, who *made a few "friendly."*

friendo *n.* friend.
1964–66 R. Stone *Hall of Mirrors* 134: "Friendo," he added hoarsely.

frig *n.* [**1.** an instance of masturbation.—usu. considered vulgar. [App. not attested in U.S.]
***1786** R. Burns, in Farmer *Merry Songs* IV 282: Defrauds her wi' a frig or dry-bob. ***ca1888–94** in *OEDS*: I pulled out my prick and with two or three frigs spent in a spasm of pain and pleasure.]

2. an act of copulation.—usu. considered vulgar.
1888 *Stag Party* 62: What is the difference between a flag and a frig? One is bunting, the other is cunting. **1927** *Immortalia* 44: 'Twas a frig to a finish. **1935** in Randolph & Legman *Roll Me in Your Arms* 376 [song learned *ca*1908]: At every frig I'd fetch a pig.

3. a damn; FUCK, *n.*, 3.a.—usu. considered vulgar.
1954–55 McCarthy *Charmed Life* 66: This is ridiculous.…I don't give a frig about Sinnott's heredity. **1968** Myrer *Eagle* 61: Ain't worth a frig.

4. (a euphem. for) *the fuck*, 1, s.v. FUCK, *n.*
1944 Kapelner *Lonely Boy Blues* 91: And who the frig is Sam Duncan? **1948** Wolfert *Act of Love* 239: Here the frig we go again. **1964** Howe

Valley of Fire 98: Leave him the frig alone. **1978** De Christoforo *Grease* 96: And who the frig are you?

frig *v.* **1.** [a specialization of the obs. S.E. sense 'to rub or chafe'] to masturbate.—usu. considered vulgar.

*1598 J. Florio, in *F & H* III 74: *Fricciare*...to frig, to wriggle, to tickle. *ca1650 in Wardroper *Love & Drollery* 197: And lest her sire should not thrust home/She frigged her father in her mother's womb. *1680 Lord Rochester, in *OEDS*: Poor pensive lover, in this place, Would Frigg upon his Mothers Face. *ca1684 in Ashbee *Biblio.* II 333: All the rest pull out their dildoes and frigg in point of honour. *ca1730 in Burford *Bawdy Verse* 254: *You* know, at fifty-five,/A man can only *frigg* her! *1734 in Legman *No Laughing Matter* III 18: Assembled, and Frigged upon the Test Platter. *ca1716–46 in *F & H* III 74: So to a House of office...a School-Boy does repair, To...fr— his P— there. *1785 Grose *Vulgar Tongue: To frig.* To be guilty of the crime of self-pollution. **1835** in Valle *Rocks & Shoals* 167: *Question.* Did you ever frig Lt. Burns? *A.* Yes— *Q.* How often? *A.* Five or six times. *ca1866 *Romance of Lust* 27: Fortunately, I had never frigged myself. *1909 in Joyce *Selected Letters* 182: You...frigged me slowly till I came off through your fingers. **1940** Del Torto *T.S.*: My finger against his asshole....I pushed it up and began to frig him. **1957** Myrer *Big War* 361 [ref. to WWII]: There'll be no friggin' in the riggin'...and no poopin' on the poop-deck. **1970** Peters *Sex Newspapers* 4: I began frigging myself even harder.

2.a. to copulate; (*trans.*) to copulate with.—usu. considered vulgar. [The earliest quots.—vars. of the same ribald song—involve word play on the obs. S.E. sense 'to move about restlessly; wiggle' and sugg. that the current sense arose as a euphem.; note that as early as *ca1650 the word seems to have been regarded as coarse and to be avoided.]

*ca1610 in Burford *Bawdy Verse* 65: Faine woulde I try how I could frig/Up and downe, up and downe, up and downe,/Fain would I try how I could Caper. *ca1650 in Wardroper *Love & Drollery* 186: Fain would I go both up and down.../No child is fonder of the gig/Then I to dance a merry jig. Fain would I try how I could —. *ca1684 in Cary *Sex. Vocab.* II: You frigg as though you were afraid to hurt. **1888** *Stag Party* 71: Why is the firing of an outhouse like flies frigging? It is arson on a small scale. *ca1889 E. Field *Boastful Yak*: She would have been frigged, but he reneagued. **1918–19** in Carey *Mlle. from Armentieres* II (unp.): The First Division is having a time,/Frigging the Fraus along the Rhine. **1916–22** Cary *Sex. Vocab.* I s.v. *copulation*: Frigging like a mink. To perform with vigor. *frigging like a rabbit.* To have great capacity. **1922** H.L. Mencken, in Riggio *Dreiser-Mencken Letters* II 463: But frigging, as you must know, is invariably unlawful, save under ecclesiastical permit. *1922 in Lawrence *The Mint* 155: [It sounded] like a pack of skeletons frigging on a tin roof. **1927** in E. Wilson *Twenties* 413: Story about the fellow whose girl kept on eatin' an apple all the time he was friggin' her. **1927** *Immortalia* 32: The Khan would rather frig than fight. **1930** *Lyra Ebriosa* 12: We'll go over and do some friggin';/Dollar and a half will pay your fee. **1934** in Randolph *Pissing in Snow* 88: She was better frigging than the other girl, so he diddled her twice. **1938** "Justinian" *Amer. Sexualis* 23: Frig (Frick). v. To copulate with....Often used as euphemistic expletive for the phrase "Fuck it!" **1942** McAtee *Supp. to Grant Co.* 4 [ref. to 1890's]: *Frig*, v., copulate. **1942** in Legman *Limerick* 18: A young wife.../Preferred frigging to going to mass. **1944** in P. Smith *Letter from Father* 426: He would "frig" her himself. **1969** Jessup *Sailor* 6: Better than you, letting him come up here while I'm at work and frigging from morning til night, probably.

b. (used as an expletive); SCREW; to damn; (*hence*) to disregard utterly.—usu. considered vulgar. [Now regarded as a partial euphem. for FUCK, *v.*, 3.a.]

*1879 *Pearl* 103: Two prisoners were brought in....The Sergeant requested orders regarding them. The Major merrily answered: "Oh, take them away and frig them!" *1905 in J. Joyce *Letters* II 104: Cosgrave says it's unfair for you to frig the one idea about love, which he had before he met you, and say "You have educated him too much." **1929–35** Farrell *Judgment Day* 629: Phrigg you, Catherine! **1936** Kingsley *Dead End* 691: Spit. Frig you! Drina...I'll crack you...you talk like that! **1938** O'Hara *Hope of Heaven* 131: Frig dat. **1940** Zinberg *Walk Hard* 133: Aw, frig it, if I hadn't been expecting a fight...it wouldn't of happened. **1946** Gresham *Nightmare Alley* 20: Frig him, the Bible-spouting bastard. **1948** Wolfert *Act of Love* 155: Frig them. *Ibid.* 399: The Navy was still saying, Frig you, Joe, I'm okay. **1949** Bezzerides *Thieves' Market* 23: Frig Mom, let her try to stop me. **1953** Manchester *City of Anger* 116: Frig trouble, I always say. Better frig before it frigs you. **1956** Metalious *Peyton Place* 358: "Frig you," said Kenny hostilely. **1970** Gattzden *Black Vendetta* 102: Let's frig it. **1980**

McAleer & Dickson *Unit Pride* 96: Frig 'em all and their mothers too. All but six and leave them for pallbearers.

c. to cheat.—usu. considered vulgar. [Regarded as a partial euphem. for FUCK, *v.*, 2.a.]

[*ca1684 in Ashbee *Biblio.* II 339: I'll then invade and bugger all the Gods/And drain the spring of their immortal cods,/Then make them rub their arses till they cry,/You've frigged us out of immortality.] **1928** *AS* III (Feb.) 219: *Frig.* To trick, to take advantage of. "They frigged me out of the last bottle of Scotch!" **1935** J. Conroy *World to Win* 209: They'll frig themselves and ever'body elset out of a job. **1945** in Perelman *Don't Tread* 60: I don't use a literary agent, but I probably should, because I have been frigged time and again by publishers. **1952** H. Grey *Hoods* 88: He's the kind of guy who talks through both sides of his mouth and whistles "I frig you truly."

3. to trifle or fool around.—in U.S. now constr. with *with* or *around*.—usu. considered vulgar. [Now usu. considered a euphem. for FUCK, *v.*, 5.]

*1785 Grose *Vulgar Tongue: To frig.*...Frigging is also used figuratively for trifling. **1811** in Howay *New Hazard* 15: Staying jib-boom; loosing and handing sails over; getting boat on the quarter and frigging about all the afternoon. *ca1900 in *EDD*: I can do nothing while you keep frigging about. **1928** C. McKay *Banjo* 241: Don't think I like frigging round officials. I hate it. **1930** Fredenburgh *Soldiers March!* 151 [ref. to 1918]: What the hell do you want, frigging around that echelon? *1933 Masefield *Conway* 211 [ref. to 1891]: *Frig about*, to fool around. **1940** Hemingway *For Whom Bell Tolls* 272: We do not let the gypsy nor others frig with it. **1946** J.H. Burns *Gallery* 301: Untying his shoelaces and frigging with the buckles on his boots. **1949** Ellson *Tomboy* 127: Do you let any punk in the mob frig around with you? **1952** H. Grey *Hoods* 225: No friggin' around. **1954** Schulberg *Waterfront* 11: I worked too hard for what I got to frig around with a cheese-eater. Know what I mean? **1961** A.J. Roth *Shame of Wounds* 34: Now if you was in my gang, we'd fix Nolan for you. He don't frig around with none of us. **1962** Dougherty *Commissioner* 187: You go in there—no friggin' around. **1975** J. Gould *Maine Lingo* 102: *Frig.* A word with four-letter nuance almost everywhere except Maine. Here, it means fiddle around, dawdle, fidget, fuss, fondle idly, putter. A Maine lady of unimpeachable gentility once described her late husband as nervous and ill at ease in public, and said he would sit "*frigging* with his necktie."

¶ In phrases:

¶ **friggin' in the riggin'** *Naut.* loafing on duty.—usu. considered vulgar. Joc. Cf. 1957 quot. at (1), above.

1979 Former supply-man, USN, age 45 [ref. to *ca1955]: *Friggin' in the riggin'* meant loafing. They also had a song that ended, "They're friggin' in the riggin'" on the midnight watch."

¶ **go frig [oneself]!** get away! go to hell!—usu. considered vulgar.

1936 Kingsley *Dead End* 726: Ah, go frig! **1951** Sheldon *Troubling of a Star* 20: Tell the bastard to go frig himself.

frigate *n. Naut.* a handsome woman.

*1675 in Duffett *Burlesque Plays* 68: That every Frigot...you have, shall strike...and receive a man aboard. *1691 in H.E. Rollins *Pepys Ballads* VI 154: I'm a Friggot that's of the First Rate. *1698–99 "B.E." *Dict. Canting Crew: Friggat well rigg'd*, a Woman well Drest and Gentile. **1778** in Connor *Songbag* 128: As I was walking through Francis Street/A lovly Frigate I change [*sic*] to meet. *1785 Grose *Vulgar Tongue*: A well-rigg'd frigate, a well-dressed wench. **1798** *Amer. Musical Misc.* 121: Cried honest Tom, my Peg I'll toast,/A frigate neat and trim. *1833 Marryat *Peter Simple* 122: My little frigate lowered her topgallant sails out of respect....I mean that she spread her white handkerchief...and knelt down upon it on one knee. **1893** Macdonald *Prison Secrets* 68: Isn't she a full-rigged frigate? An' w'at masts!

frigger *n.* (a euphem. for) FUCKER, 2.

1953 Manchester *City of Anger* 145: That bastard...that no good frigger.

frigging *adj. & adv.* contemptible or despicable; damned; (often used with reduced force as a mere intensifier).—usu. considered vulgar. Also as infix. [Perh. orig. abstracted and generalized from opprobrious literal collocations such as *frigging youngster, frigging madman,* etc.; now usu. regarded as a euphem. for FUCKING, q.v.]

*a1890–93 *F & H* III 74: *Frigging...Adj. and adv.* (vulgar).—An expletive of intensification. Thus *frigging bad*—"bloody" bad; a *frigging idiot*—an absolute fool. **1929-30** Dos Passos *42nd Parallel* 55: If people only realized how friggin' easy it would be. *Ibid.* 89: I told 'em I was a friggin' bookagent to get into the damn town. **1943** in P. Smith *Letter from Father* 332: It was a "friggen" swell party. **1944** Wakeman *Shore Leave* 10: It took me three more weeks to get off that frigging island. **1947** Motley *Knock on Any Door* 194: I'm no friggin' good. **1948** Wolfert *Act of Love* 136: On your feet, you friggin' volunteers. **1949** Bezzerides *Thieves' Market* 3: You're frigging right, Pa. **1947-52** R. Ellison *Invisible Man* 192: A frigging eight-day wonder. **1954** F.I. Gwaltney *Heaven & Hell* 264 [ref. to WWII]: That would be oh-friggen-kay with me. **1956** Metalious *Peyton Place* 93: Where's the friggin' bottle? **1957** Mayfield *Hit* 89: "Is he the only one who can drive this friggin' car?" squealed Frank. **1974** Cherry *High Steel* 160: So friggin' what? **1980** J. Carroll *Land of Laughs* 22: I got the friggin' renewal already. **1986** *Newsweek* (July 28) 26: I said, "Give me a break, this ain't no frigging war." **1989** *Tour of Duty* (CBS-TV): There ain't no friggin' justice! **1991** Marcinko & Weisman *Rogue Warrior* 63: I don't frigging believe it. **1992** N. Cohn *Heart of World* 9: Straight off the friggin' boats.

frigging-A *interj.* (a euphem. for) FUCKING-A.—usu. considered vulgar.

1971 Jacobs & Casey *Grease* 13: DANNY. Is that all you ever think about, Sonny? SONNY....Friggin'-A! **1973** W. Crawford *Stryker* 41: You're friggin-A-well right I would have. **1979** McGivern *Soldiers* 139 [ref. to WWII]: "So you know what I'm thinking."..."Frigging A." **1984** in Safire *Look It Up* 120: A euphemism from my adolescence, like "Friggin'-A, I'm going."

friggish var. FREAKISH.

frightened water *n.* tea. *Joc.* Cf. syn. WATER BEWITCHED.

1868 Macy *There She Blows!* 25: Old Jeff swore at tea, called it "frightened water."

frigidly *adv. Navy.* thoroughly; cold.

1877 Lee *Fag-Ends* 68: He'll be frigidly bilged in May.

frig off *v.* **1.** to masturbate to orgasm.—usu. considered vulgar. *Rare* in U.S.

***1909** in J. Joyce *Selected Letters* 191: Do you frig yourself off first? **1979** *AS* LI 22 [ref. to *ca*1950]: *Frig* and *frig off.*

2. to go away; go to hell.—used imper.—usu. considered vulgar. [Regarded as a euphem. for syn. FUCK OFF.]

1961 A.J. Roth *Shame of Wounds* 141: "Go on, frig off," Red's scowl dared him. "See how far you get by yourself." ***1965** in *OEDS*: "Frig off," he said, swinging towards the door.

frig-stick *n.* (see quot.).—usu. considered vulgar.

1976 Univ. Tenn. prof., age *ca*40: In Beaumont, Texas, in the early or mid 1950's, male college-student pool players would refer to a pool cue as their *frig-stick.*

frig-up *n.* (a euphem. for) FUCK-UP, 1. & 2.

***1941** S.J. Baker, in *OEDS: Frigg-up,* a confusion, muddle. **1948** I. Shaw *Young Lions* 542: You're the frig-ups of the Army. **1954** F.I. Gwaltney *Heaven & Hell* 15 [ref. to WWII]: Hell no! I ain't no frigup. *Ibid.* 18: They're frigups, sure, but they ain't jailbirds.

frig up *v.* **1.** (a euphem. for) FUCK UP, 1.

1933 in Dos Passos *14th Chronicle* 428: All my plans for work are frigged up for fair, too. **1937** Weidman *Wholesale* 60: Something's frigged up around here! [***1942** S.J. Baker *Austral. Lang.* 267: It is common in English for *up* to be added in a verbal sense, thus *mess up, rust up, knock up,* and even for certain nounal forms to emerge...Thus we have...*frigg-up* or *muck-up,* a confusion, a row or argument.] **1954** F.I. Gwaltney *Heaven & Hell* 26: When they frigup [*sic*] here, they ain't no place to send 'em except home in a box. ***a1966** S.J. Baker *Austral. Lang.* (ed. 2) 217: *Frig up,* to mar.

2. (a euphem. for) FUCK UP, 2.a.

1953 Paley *Rumble* 257: The Stompers are saying that only a Digger could frig up like that. *a***1981** in S. King *Bachman* 470: No, I frigged up.

frill *n.* [lit. 'trimming, ruffle', by metonymy; cf. SKIRT] a woman.—often used contemptuously.

1927 *Amer. Legion Mo.* (Oct.) 20: He meets a frill. Nice-lookin' kid. **1930** Bodenheim *Roller Skates* 279: Frill...Girl, woman. **1932** Minehan *Boy & Girl Tramps* 208: Met a frill on the loose. **1942** A.C. Johnston *Courtship of A. Hardy* (film): Not that she's a revolting frill or anything like us. **1960** Stadley *Barbarians* 91: Listen, punk, when Rand tells a frill— *Ibid.* 105: We pull out together, cutting off a Ford loaded with frills. **1963** Westlake *Getaway Face* 15: It's a frill....But she's okay.

fringie *n.* a person on the fringe of some group, activity, or the like.

1966 Goldstein *1 in 7* 17: It is true that the long-haired element on campus (those who are variously called "ethnic," "beatnik," "folkie," or "fringie") is often a major source of marijuana. **1967** *Seattle* (Oct.) 59: What are these damned fringies up to, smoking pot and making a religion out of LSD? **1980** *Nat. Lampoon* (Sept.) 31: I would have had to get a job if I'd wanted to stay on as a campus fringie. **1983** *Harper's* (May) 92: His mission: to find out to what extent these "fringies on the right" have affected the nation's political conscience. **1985** "Blow-dryer" *Mod. Eng.* 61: Fringie...Someone on the fringe of the community or gang.

frip *n. & adj. Stu.* (see quots.).

1949 *Time* (Oct. 3) 37: Nothing, teen-agers thought, could be more "frip" than getting down to work in the first weeks of fall....*"Frip" has replaced "lousy" in the South.* **1970-72** in *AS* L (1975) 59: *Frip* n. Person considered dull, foolish, or stupid.

Frisco *n.* San Francisco, Cal. Now *colloq.* [Discussed by P. Tamony, "Sailors Called It 'Frisco,'" *West. Folk.* XXVI (1967) 192–95.]

1849 in O.T. Howe *Argonauts* 82: Made a good passage to 'Frisco. [**1850** in *DA:* The steamers "Noo World" & "Hartford" were going too run to Frisky at from 3 to 5 dolls a tikket.] **1851** in *West. Folk.* XXVI (1967) 193: Frisco. [**1852** in *Ibid.:* S. Frisco.] **1854** in *DA:* You came down to "Frisco" with a "pile," didn't you? **1857** in Dressler *Pioneer Circus* 87: In Frisco...next week. **1869** J.R. Browne *Apache* 182: She had...bobbed around Frisco for the last few years. **1873** Beadle *Undeveloped West* 251: We leave chilly "Frisco" at 4 P.M. **1887** Francis *Saddle & Moccasin* 173: Are you acquainted in 'Frisco, sir? **1901** "J. Flynt" *Graft* 71: Course this berg ain't Chi, an' t'ain't 'Frisco either, but I can hold it down all right. **1911–12** J. London *Smoke Bellew* 36: They'd contracted to 'Frisco bunch for six hundred. **1956** Neider *Hendry Jones* 61: We had been to Frisco and had seen the difference. **1963** S. Plath, in J.P. Hunter *Norton Intro. Poetry* (ed. 2) 60: Big as a Frisco seal. **1970** in P. Heller *In This Corner* 44: I got Dempsey out in "Frisco" the first time. **1978** Maupin *Tales* 164: An aggressive sailor made inane conversation about "Frisco." **1986** C. Freeman *Seasons of Heart* 266: A pretty little Frisco girl.

frisco *v. & n. Police.* FRISK, *v. & n.*

1954 Collans & Sterling *House Detect.* 136: When I had the maid give the guest's room a frisko, enough hotel stationery turned up to circularize the entire membership of the D.A.R. *Ibid.* 219: *Frisco.* To case a guest's room and luggage.

frisk *n. Und.* a search, as of a person or a room.

***1789** G. Parker *Life's Painter* 142: Though we should stand the *frisk* for it. ***1812** Vaux *Vocab.:* To stand *frisk* is to stand search. **1904** *Life in Sing Sing* (gloss.): *Frisk....*A search. **1912** Lowrie *Prison* 25: After a thorough "frisk" I was escorted to the photograph gallery and "mugged." **1930** Lait *On the Spot* 166: You all stand for a frisk. **1946** Gresham *Nightmare Alley* 252: Oh-oh—it's a frisk. **1987** Norst & Black *Lethal Weapon* 181: What about a frisk? They're bound to shake me down.

frisk *v.* [var., infl. by S.E. *frisk,* of earlier *fisk*] **1.a.** Orig. *Und.* to search for booty or contraband; (now usu.) to search (a person), usu. for a weapon, by quickly patting or feeling through the clothing. Now *colloq.* or *S.E.*

[***1724** D. Defoe, in Partridge *Dict. Und.* 246: Desiring him to *Fisk* him.] ***1737** (cited in Partridge *Dict. Und.* 268). ***1788** Grose *Vulgar Tongue* (ed. 2): *Friz,* or *Frisk.* Used by thieves to signify searching a person whom they have robbed. Blast his eyes! Friz, or frisk him. ***1789** G. Parker *Life's Painter* 186: When they take a person up on suspicion [the officers] *frisk* him, that is, search him. ***1812** Vaux *Vocab.: Frisk:* to search; to *frisk a cly,* is to empty a pocket of its contents. **1845** (quot. at TURN UP). **1848** Judson *Mysteries* 61: Vel, sare, the offisaire ave frisk me; he ave not found ze skin or ze dummy, eh? **1849** "N. Buntline" *B'hoys of N.Y.* 32: You may frisk me an' see for yourself. **1859** Matsell *Vocab.* 35: *Frisk.* To search; to examine. **1896** Ade *Artie* 50: Last night I had nine cases. This morning when I frisked myself I couldn't turn up only sixty cents. **1899** Bowe *13th Minnesota* 114: One soldier was "frisking" some of the buffalo carts when Major Bell, seeing him, roasted him to a finish. **1900** Ade *More Fables* 114: She would Frisk his Wardrobe every day or two, looking for Evidence. **1912** Berkman *Prison* 209: The screw's goin' t' frisk* me....*Search. **1914** in C.M. Russell *Paper Talk* 107: I think by frisking his clothes youd find a fiew noisless articals like this. **1918-19** Sinclair *Higgins* 84: He passed his hands over his prisoner, a ceremony known as "frisking." **1921** *Variety* (Sept. 2) 5: I...even frisked his tights. **1925** in Hammett *Knockover* 79: We'll go after her when she's inside. That's our excuse for frisking the joint. **1939** C.R. Cooper *Scarlet* 18: I left the Swing and frisked some cars outside to see what I could find. *1980 T. Jones *Adrift* 194: We were all frisked at the door…for bottles. 1989 D. Sherman *There I Was* 104: Frisk him.

b. *Und.* to rob; steal from (esp. a person who is asleep or helpless).

*1811 *Lexicon Balatron.* s.v. *lob*: To frisk a lob; to rob a till. *1828 in *F & H* III 75: The arms are seized from behind by one, while the other *frisks* the pockets of their contents. 1845 (quot. at DUMMY). 1848 Judson *Mysteries* 40: You're as good a knuck as ever frisked a swell. 1894 in Asbury *Gem of Prairie* 156: He had been "frisked" of 1,500 dollars. 1918 in H.W. Morgan *Addicts* 85: Another "hop head," loaded with morphine, went into a room and "frisked" the sleeping occupant's clothes of six dollars and a half. 1922 Murphy *Black Candle* 300: She robs persons at night—or in her own words "frisks them." 1922 *Variety* (June 30) 6: The cannons…have to wear badges to keep from friskin' each other. 1923 O'Hare *In Prison* 96: I also know the best methods of "raising a bill," "fixing a check," "passing the queer," and "frisking the nobles." 1928 Sharpe *Chicago May* 288: Frisk—search, steal from person. 1928-29 Nason *White Slicker* 159: He's gone out to frisk some stiff. 1956 Sorden & Ebert *Logger's* 15 [ref. to *ca*1925]: *Frisked.* Robbed while drunk. Same as rolled.

c. *Und.* to pilfer.

*1802 (cited in Partridge *Dict. Und.* 268). 1928 MacArthur *War Bugs* 205: As usual we frisked schnapps and iron rations as they passed the guns. 1928 *Amer. Mercury* (Aug.) 435: The old man was frisking a drink of whiskey out of the medicine-closet. 1930 "D. Stiff" *Milk & Honey* 126: And I frisked some spuds and onions/Just to pass the time away.

2. *Und.* to scrutinize; inspect.

1859 (quot. at **(1.a.)**, above). 1927 *AS* (June) 388: To *frisk a drag* is to look it [a freight train] over to find the most logical place to ride.

frisker *n.* *Und.* a pickpocket; petty thief.

*1802 (cited in Partridge *Dict. Und.* 268). 1929 Bodenheim *60 Secs.* 231: Badger-game men and small-time friskers. 1930 (cited in Partridge *Dict. Und.* 268).

frit *n.* [prob. alter. of FLIT] an effeminate male homosexual.—used contemptuously.

1960 Sire *Deathmakers* 44 [ref. to WWII]: How the fuck did we ever get this little queer on the point?…This is a war, frit, you know what I mean? 1967 *DAS* (Supp.) 685: *Frit* n. A homosexual.

Fritz *n.* [G hypocoristic form of *Friedrich* 'Frederick'] *Mil.* **1.** the German armed forces. Also **Fritzie.**

1915 in Roy *Pvt. Fraser* 23: In due time we learned from Fritz what…machine-guns really were. *1915 in *OEDS*: By that time, of course, Fritz had made himself scarce. 1917 in Cowing *Dear Folks at Home* 64: The firing did not seem to bother Fritz. 1917 Depew *Gunner Depew* 159: But the Turks were not as bad as Fritz. 1918 in Dolph *Sound Off!* 162: We'll be over there to get you, Fritzie. 1924 Nason *Three Lights* 22: I guess Fritz must be raisin' hell back along them roads. 1975 Larsen *Runner* 29 [ref. to WWII]: Fritz was some kind of awful. 1985 Westin *Love & Glory* 403 [ref. to WWII]: Maybe old Fritz wants us to think just that.

2. a German, esp. a German military serviceman; (*hence*) a German vessel or aircraft. Also **Fritzie.**

*1916 in *OEDS*: Described by Tommy as "strafing the Fritzes." 1917 in Peat *Legion Airs* 70: Takin' pot shots at the Fritzes with the Tommies and the French. 1918 Beston *Full Speed Ahead* 46: He shoved his periscope and spotted a Fritz on the surface in full noonday. 1918 in Rendinell *One Man's War* 78: We listened to what the Fritzies were doing. 1918 in Loosbrock & Skinner *Wild Blue* 77: The Fritzie nose-dives in flames. 1919 Streeter *Same Old Bill* 18: You can hit a Fritz in the stummick three miles away. 1927 Cushing *Doughboy Ditties* 73: And the fellow I caught—how that poor Fritzie swayed. 1948 Miller & Rackin *Fighter Sq.* (film): No Fritzes up here today. 1955 Puzo *Dark Arena* 78 [ref. to WWII]: Get the rest of the Fritzes loaded. 1962 Houk & Dexter *Ballplayers* 39 [ref. to WWII]: "Let's find out if any Fritzes are hanging around," I told my sergeant. 1966-67 W. Stevens *Gunner* 49: This is The Lone Fritz.

fritz *n.* [sugg. by, rather than the orig. of, *on the fritz*, below] that which is no good.—constr. with *the*, used predicatively.

1932 in Partridge *Dict. Und.* 268: Things is the fritz.

¶ In phrases:

¶ **on the fritz** [or (*obs.*) **fritzer**] [orig. unkn.] **1.** in a bad way or condition; (now usu.) (of a mechanical, electrical, or electronic device) out of working order.

1902 (cited in *W9*). 1903 McCardell *Chorus Girl* 15: They gave an open air [performance] that put our opera house show on the fritz.

1904 *Life in Sing Sing* 248: *Fritzer.* Not good. *Ibid.* 261: I went to the coast, with a mob of paper-layers, but graft was on the fritzer. 1906 H. Green *Boarding House* 3: He'd just put the heat on the fritz for fair. 1911 A.H. Lewis *Apaches of N.Y.* 45: Their domestic affairs was on th' fritz. *Ibid.* 111: I wonder Mollie Squint an Pretty Agnes don't put her on th' fritz. 1911–12 Ade *Knocking the Neighbors* 179: Certain Stiffs…were trying to put the Town on the Fritz. *Ibid.* 204: She married a good man and put him on the Fritz. 1912 in Kornbluth *Rebel Voices* 76: Things are…On the fritz in Kansas City. 1917 in Bowerman *Compensations* 21: My left leg went on the fritz so I didn't enjoy the scenery much. 1918 *Chi. Sun. Tribune* (Mar. 24) V (unp.): They put some o' the machinery on the fritz…put the works outta business for a week. 1920 Ade *Hand-Made Fables* 30: All the cherished plans…were unmistakably on the Fritz. 1922 S. Lewis *Babbitt* 67: Course I don't mean you'd ever do anything that would put a decent position on the fritz but—. 1924 in Galewitz *Great Comics* 139: Gee, the bell is on the fritz and they don't hear me knock. 1926 Dunning & Abbott *Broadway* 229: Holy gee, but the orchestra put that number on the fritz. 1932 L. Berg *Prison Dr.* 19: Cheez, Doc, I ain't been feeling right for a couple of days. My stomach is on the fritz. 1929-33 Farrell *Manhood of Lonigan* 194: His dukes [were] on the fritz. 1935 Pollock *Und. Speaks: On the fritz*…in poor physical condition. 1959 *Lucille Ball-Desi Arnaz Show* (CBS-TV): The plumbing's on the fritz again. 1962 T. Berger *Reinhart* 27: I see you got the car off the Fritz, Carlo, and thank you. 1968 Kirkwood *Good Times* 16: "The [toilet] in there's on the fritz," he said.

2. *Specif.*, destitute.

1905 *Nat. Police Gaz.* (Sept. 23) 6: He found himself on the fritz in San Francisco, and shipped in the navy up at the Mare Island Yard. 1907 Hobart *Beat It!* 70: They are putting all our millionaires on the fritz. 1935 Pollock *Und. Speaks: On the fritz*, without any funds. 1936 Mackenzie *Living Rough* 93: There's so many guys on the fritz that unless you have a good line you can't get a thing.

¶ **to the fritz** *on the fritz*, above.

1903 Hobart *Out for the Coin* 83: I catch your words, Murf, but the meaning is away to the fritz.

Fritz *adj.* *Mil.* German. Also **Fritzie.** [Quots. ref. to WWI.]

1915 in Roy *Pvt. Fraser* 68: There must be a Fritzie sniper behind our lines. 1919 Streeter *Same Old Bill* 24: You'd have thought we got off right in front of the Fritz trenches. 1923 *Amer. Leg. Wkly.* (Feb. 9) 13: How would you like to be in a squad that was being attacked by the whole Fritz army?

fritz *v.* to ruin, spoil, or interfere with; cause to malfunction; (*intrans.*) to malfunction.—usu. constr. with *up* or *out*.

1918 Wallgren *AEF* (unp.): Suffer'n kats—me glims is fritzed. 1926 Finerty *Criminalese* 23: *Fritzed out*—Ruined, put out of business. 1948 in *DAS*: Lightning hit some wires and fritzed the generator. 1948 Cozzens *Guard of Honor* 162: Then he was going to fritz up his firing circuits and claim that about the guns. 1954 in F. Harvey *Jet* 99: The radio's fritzing up. 1969 *Time* (Nov. 28) 18: The television camera fritzed out on the lunar surface. 1978 N.Y.C. man, age *ca*50: A Con Edison switch station fritzed up. 1986 Ciardi *Good Words* 123: That fritzed it. 1986 R. Campbell *In La-La Land* 49: Something fritzed the gates. Goddam things closed on the Rolls before it was through.

fritz around *v.* to fool around; FUTZ.

1963 Cameron *Black Camp* 93: And let's not be fritzin' around with any limey broads on the way.

fritz away *v.* to fritter away.

1966 Brunner *Face of Night* 135: But there can't be any probation on a peddling charge and you fritzed that one away.

Fritzer *n.* *Mil.* FRITZ, *n.*, 2.

1918 in *Forum* (Feb. 1919) 229: Talk about your Fritzers who are aiming for a fall. *a1980 (cited in Partridge *DSUE* (ed. 8) 429).

Fritzie var. FRITZ.

friz *n.* *Stu.* (see quot.).

1976 Eble *Campus Slang* (Nov.) 2: *Friz*—(shortening) frisbee: Let's throw some friz.

'fro *n.* an Afro hairstyle.

1970 *Time* (Dec. 14) 40: The first sergeant…don't like no black man with a 'fro. 1970 in Sanchez *Word Sorcerers* 107: The girls really looked good in their…'fros. 1978 Univ. Tenn. student: She'd just gotten herself a new 'fro and it was kind of hard to miss. 1980 Wielgus & Wolff *Basketball* 69: Gonna mess up my 'fro, man. 1982 Del Vecchio *13th Valley* 130: He…fluffed up his 'fro. 1990 Rukuza *W. Coast Turnaround* 231: Bringing her hands clear of her big, floppy 'fro.

frob *n.* *Computers.* FROBNITZ.

> **1983** Naiman *Computer Dict.* 64. **1983** Steele et al. *Hacker's Dict.*: *Frob*...Any somewhat small thing; an object that you can comfortably hold in one hand.

frob *v.* *Computers.* to manipulate (as a control knob), esp. aimlessly.

> **1983** Naiman *Computer Dict.* 64: Stop frobbing the contrast on that CRT and come play space war with me. **1983** Steele et al. *Hacker's Dict.*: Please frob the light switch.

frobnicate *v.* *Computers.* FROB.

> **1983** Naiman *Computer Dict.* 64. **1983** Steele et al. *Hacker's Dict.*: This word is usually abbreviated to simply "frob," but frobnicate is recognized as the official full form.

frobnitz *n.* [prob. of fanciful orig.] *Computers.* a thing; GIZMO.

> **1983** *Time* (Jan. 3) 39: *Frobnitz* (plural: frobnitzem): an unspecified physical object, a widget. **1983** Naiman *Computer Dict.* 64: Their new printer has this little frobnitz on the side that lets you flush the buffer....The plural—in imitation of Yiddish—is *frobnitzim.* **1987** J. Green *Jargon* 239: *Frobnitz*...a thingummybob....It was originally used...by model railway enthusiasts.

frog *n.* **1.** a contemptible or offensive person. Orig. *S.E.*

> ***ca1330** in *OED:* Formest was sire Gogmagog,/He was most, þat foule froge. ***ca1550** in D. Lindsay *Satyre:* Quhat kynd of woman is thy wyfe,...Ane Frog that fyles the winde. ***1626** in *OED:* These infernall frogs [Jesuits] are crept into the West and East Indyes. ***1652** in *Ibid.*: Neither had I ever wished the charming of those Froggs [the Dutch]. ***1688** Shadwell *Squire of Alsatia* V i: I'll try a Trick of Law, you Froggs of the bottomless Pit. **1868** Baer *Champagne Charlie* 14: Apollo has proved a frog. He has not even the courage of a woman. **1965** (quot. at WIMP, *n.*). **1968** Baker et al. *CUSS* 122: *Frog.* An obnoxious person. **1965–78** J. Carroll *B. Diaries* 81: We never pay the little frog that comes around to collect for it.

> **2.a.** [ref. to the custom of eating frogs' legs] a French person.—used contemptuously.
> ***1772** in *AS* XXIII (Feb. 1948) 216: They [the British] will fly at the French with the stomach of hogs,/And, like storks, in a trice clear the sea of the frogs. ***1778** F. Burney, in *OEDS:* Hark you, Mrs. Frog...you may lie in the mud till some of your Monsieurs come to help you out of it. **1799** in Tyler *Verse* 107: They fought the British Lion,/And tam'd his noble Rage;/And can't we their descendants/A poltroon'd frog engage:/We'll teach poor Monsieur Fricasee [etc.]. ***1803** in J. Ashton *Eng. Satires on Napoleon* 135: "Monsieur Jean Bull, I am come...to present your vone *Ultimatum*..." "Hark ye, Mr. Frog!...I'll shew you the use of my Horns." ***1828** (cited in Partridge *DSUE* (ed. 8) 429). **1835** in Paulding *Bulls & Jons.* 29: With orders not to spare a single soul among all the frogs. **1838** Crockett *Almanac* (1839) 28: Then down comes Mr. Frog again on John Bull. **1840** in Poe *Complete Tales & Poems* 519: That's all no use, Mounseer Frog, mavourneen. *Ibid.* 520: Ye little spalpeeny frog of a bog-throtting son of a bloody noun! **1844** in Haliburton *Sam Slick* 194: Then hear that noisy, splutterin' critter, Bull Frog. He talks you dead about...the beautiful France, and the capital of the world, Paris. ***1845** in *OEDS:* Surely I will always be able, go where I will among frogs or maccaronis, to procure *sucre noir* or *inchiostro nero.* **1868** Williams *Black-Eyed Beauty* 66: Opposite Bella, sat a Frenchman, a fine physical portrait wanting nothing of six feet two, and super-developed in muscle. No "frog" about him. ***a1891** in Barrett *Folk-Songs* 21: They may come, the frogs of France,/But we'll teach them a new-fashioned dance. **1895** Barentz *Woordenboek* 121: *Frog*,...Franschman. **1918** Straub *Diary* (July 11): Some of these "Frogs" are afraid of their own shadows. **1918** in Casey *Cannoneers* 224: Never could believe the Frogs, anyway. **1919** T. Kelly *What Outfit?* 28: She didn't get me....just like a Frog. **1933** "W. March" *Company K* 64: These frogs can beat the whole world when it comes to frying eggs. **1943** Hersey *Bell for Adano* 185: Why the hell do we have to give the Frogs and the Limeys and the Chinks all the stuff we make? **1951** *Amer. Jour. Socio.* LI 436: [In WWII] many Americans formed the habit of calling all British "goddamn Limies" and all French "dirty Frogs." **1956** J.D. Brown *Kings Go Forth* 42: He ain't a *paesano*, ya jerk, said another indignantly,—he's a frog! **1961** Joswick & Keating *Combat Cameraman* 137: We made the Frog signal a change of target. **1987** Robbins *Ravens* 170: Francophobes to a man, [they] all agreed that was about what you could expect from the Frogs.

> **b.** the French language.—used contemptuously.
> **1922** in Hemingway *Sel. Letters* 65: Do you speak frawg? **1936** Reilly *Americans All* 159 [ref. to 1918]: A French soldier saw me and started spitting "frog," which I did not understand. **1954** Faulkner *Fable* 327:

You can speak Frog. **1975** *Atlantic* (May) 43: Gibbering phony frog over the CB. **1984** W. Murray *Dead Crab* 80: You talking frog?

> **c.** *pl.* *USMC.* French-fried potatoes.
> **1922** *Leatherneck* (Apr. 22) 5: *Frogs*: Fried potatoes, especially French fried, from the popular name for Frenchmen.

> **3.** *Und.* a policeman. *Rare* in U.S.
> ***1857** "Ducange Anglicus" *Vulgar Tongue* 9: *Frog*, n. Policeman. *Th*[ieves' slang]. **1859** Matsell *Vocab.* 35: *Frog.* A policeman. ***1886** in *F & H* III 76: A policeman is also called...a "frog,"...because he is supposed to jump, as it were, suddenly upon guilty parties. **1949** *Mo. Hist. Soc. Bull.* V 47 [ref. to St. Louis, *ca*1895]: I found myself deserted by my companions and involved in a foot to foot struggle with the officer, whose objection to the epithet Froggie was...vitriolic in intensity.

> **4.a.** [cf. *muscle* < L *musculus* 'little mouse'] *So.* the biceps, esp. when flexed.
> **1858** in *DAE*: I warnt afeard that somebody was goin to hert me, for I has bonier nuckles than most men and you know the size uv the frog in my arm. **1899** Green *Va. Folk-Speech*: *Frog*...The biceps muscle in the arm when made to move and swell by contraction.

> **b.** *So. Juve.* a swelling of the upper arm caused by a blow with the fist, esp. as a penalty.
> **1911–29** in *PADS* (No. 11) 6: *Frog*, n. A knot on a muscle made by a blow. **1947** Willingham *End As a Man* 77: He offered to bet me a frawg he was. *ca*1970, **1983** in *DARE*.

> **5.** FROGSKIN.
> **1933** (cited in Partridge *Dict. Und.* 269). **1954–60** *DAS*: *Frog.* A one-dollar bill....*Underworld use. Not common.*

> **6.** *Stu.* a freshman; (*hence*) a prospective member of a Greek-letter fraternity.
> [**1851** B. Hall *College Wds.* 226: In Germany, a student while in the gymnasium, and before entering the university, is called a *Frosch*,—a frog.] **1942–44** in *AS* XXI (1946) 33: *Frog*, n. A first-semester freshman. **1958** J. Davis *College Vocab.* 5: *Frog*—Freshman. **1959** Maier *College Terms* 1: *Frogs*—Pledges. **1966** in *IUFA Folk Speech*: *Frog*: freshman. **1971** Dahlskog *Dict.* 25: *Frog*....A fraternity pledge.

> ¶ In phrases:
> ¶ **drop a frog** to give birth. *Joc.*
> **1975** Wambaugh *Choirboys* 66: The Mary Sinclair Adams Home for Girls...."They go in there, drop a frog and cut out."
> ¶ **when I say "frog," you better jump!** I require instant and complete obedience. Also vars.
> **1962** Bonham *War Beneath Sea* 134 [ref. to WWII]: When Casey said "frog," Mr. Ratkowski saw to it everybody jumped. **1965** Bonham *Durango St.* 8: When I say "frog," those cats better jump. **1971** Cameron *First Blood* 12: When I holler froggy, you had best be prepared to jump. **1980** Hogan *Lawman's Choice* 157: They'll hop when I holler frog soon as they see how all this is coming out.

frog *adj.* French.—used contemptuously.

> **1910** T.A. Dorgan, in *N.Y. Eve. Jour.* (Jan. 10) 12: Paris...Harvey has started to grow a goatee since we hit this frog joint. ***1914** R. Brooke, in *OEDS:* The Frog-Art show. **1928** Scanlon *God Have Mercy on Us!* 224: It's a Frog invention. **1931** Dos Passos *1919* 55: Even the dogs looked like frog dogs. **1932** in Hemingway *Sel. Letters* 353: Could take Frog vessel to Suez and board lime juicer for there to Mombassa. **1955** McGovern *Fräulein* 245: I can't go that frog food.

frog *v.* **1.a.** to bound or hurry; (*also*) to march or slog, esp. through mud or shallow water.—also constr. with *it.*

> **1833** J. Hall *Harpe's Head* 152: Then you must *frog it* some. *a*1861 Chamberlain *Confession* 257: My horse...was taken from me and I was obliged to "frog it." **1863** in R.G. Carter *4 Bros.* 224: If we move I do not know whether I shall have to shoulder a gun and "*frog it*" with the company or not. **1889** Cox *Frontier Humor* 25: He appeared frogging up the steps of the dwelling. ***1893** (cited in Partridge *DSUE* (ed. 8) 430). **1903** in *AS* XXXVII (1962) 152: Joel he had to frog it clean down to the ole man's place there. **1903–08** in *AS* XLIX (1974) 62: He frogged to town. **1909** *Sat. Eve. Post* (July 3) 14: Mulhall and Corbett frogged it while the others used the lines and rings. ***1925** Fraser & Gibbons *Soldier & Sailor Wds.* 99 [ref. to WWI]: *Frogging it.* Walking. Marching. **1948** Wolfert *Act of Love* 465: Where the Goddamn hell is Krueger! I'm bleeding to death, and he frogs off somewhere. **1949** in *PADS* (No. 14) 78: *Froggin'* around in the rain. Prowling around in the rain. Hernando County [Fla.]. **1975** J. Gould *Maine Lingo* 102: *Frog it.* To cross a swampy place by jumping like a frog from hummock to hummock. More specifically, to walk a canoe, through water too shallow to float it with a person aboard.

b. to get along.—also constr. with *on.*

*a*1889 in Barrère & Leland *Dict. Slang* I 386: Hey, ho countrymen—how you froggin' on? **1889** *Ibid.*: Frogging on (American), getting on. ***1896** in *EDD*: "How are you froggin'?" is the usual form of greeting at Sutton Coldfield, and in the neighbourhood.

2. [perh. alter. of *flog*] *S.W.* to beat; thrash.

1966 "T. Pendleton" *Iron Orchard* 25: Dendy, you little bastard, you better not use no hot water til I git there, or I'll frog yo ass.

Frog and Toe *n. Und.* New York City. Cf. 1857 quot.

[***1857** "Ducange Anglicus" *Vulgar Tongue*: We will go to *frog and toe.* Thieves coming up to London with plunder.] **1859** Matsell *Vocab.*: *Frog and Toe.* The city of New-York. **1866** *Nat. Police Gaz.* (Nov. 3) 3: Dutch returned immediately to "frog and toe" with a gay set of whiskers, which he had raised in "stur," and a black plug "cady" on his "knob," which gave him the appearance of a superannuated "grabber."

frogbrain *n.* a blockhead.

1977 Stone *Blizzard* 57: Listen, frog-brain, that snowball had a rock in it.

frog-eater *n.* a French person.—used contemptuously.—also attrib.

1812 (cited in *AS* XXIII (Feb. 1948) 214). **1816** Paulding *Letters from So.* I 183: In plays, poems, and romances, the Frenchman was almost always a swindler, a coward, a braggadocio, or a frog-eater. ***1828** (cited in Partridge *DSUE* (ed. 8) 429). **1849** "N. Buntline" *B'hoys of N.Y.* 39: Frog-eater! Vat zat you call me, sare! ***1872** in *EDD*: And lick the English just as they did them frog-eaters. **1883** *Judge* (Jan. 20) 3: Now follows the "frog-eater," a sly Parisian cheater. **1890** *Overland Mo.* (Feb.) 115: Another frog eater! Seems to me they'd orter have had enough of this camp by this time. **1893** C.C. King *Waring* 94: The little "frog-eater"...Lascelles. **1906** London *Moon-Face* 20: The ringmaster called him a frog-eater. **1919** in Truman *Dear Bess* 293: I've had enough *vin rouge* and frogeater victuals to last me a lifetime. **1928** Sharpe *Chicago May* 135: He wanted to get revenge on the frog-eaters. **1930** "D. Stiff" *Milk & Honey* 205: Frog or frog-eater—A Frenchman. **1984** H. Searls *Blood Song* 279: "Hang the Greaser and the Frog-eater," yelled Enoch. "They killed our Johnny-boy."

frog-eating *adj.* French.—used contemptuously.

*1809 in W. Wheeler *Letters* 31: Damn their cowardly eyes and limbs, if it was not for the cursed chain across the harbour, we wood soon make the frog eating sons of Bitches lick the filth off with their tongues. **1816** Weems *Hymen's Recruiting Sgt.* 1: Our *Buckskin* heroes are made of...as good stuff as the *best* of the *beef* or *frog-eating* gentry on t'other side the water. ***1838** Glascock *Land Sharks* II 169: Here's...the rest on us ready to come Trafflygar over the jabberin' frog-eatin' fry. *ca*1840 Hawthorne *Privateer* 259 [ref. to 1813]: Sammy...could take a joke from a Yankee, because, as he said, they were "cousins loike;" but he could not endure it in a frog-eating Frenchman. **1854** Sleeper *Salt Water Bubbles* 203: You are a set of frog-eating b-b-b-b-. **1865** Williams *Joaquin* 37: Damn you for a brace of frog-eating swindlers. **1909** M'Govern *Krag Is Laid Away* 184: A Frenchy—the measly little sawed off, frog-eating pea-soup-and-johnnie-cake guy. ***1933** Witherspoon *Liverpool Jarge* (unp.): There was a tradin' post set in a clearin' cut out of the jungle and run by a gang of Frog-eaters. **1936** *Our Army* (Feb.) 14: This is what's been stopping the frog-eaters and limeys for three years? **1953** *New Yorker* (Feb. 7) 87: That...frog-eating sieve.

frog eggs *n.pl.* tapioca pudding.

1956 Sorden & Ebert *Logger's* 15 [ref. to *a*1925]: *Frog-eggs.* Tapioca.

frogeyes *n.pl.* tapioca pudding. Also **frog's eyes.**

1942 *ATS* 98: *Frog eyes,* tapioca pudding. **1944** *Time* (Dec. 18) 9: A limited list of the more well-known slang terms in common use [in the USMC]: Eggs *Henfruit.* Tapioca pudding *Frog eyes.* ***1945** S.J. Baker *Australian Lang.* 162: *Frog's eyes.* Tapioca.

froggy *n.* [cf. FROG, *n.*, 2.a.] a French person.—used contemptuously.

1865 in J.W. Haley *Rebel Yell* 238: At 4 p.m. had dress parade by General de Trobriand. This conduct on the part of Old Froggy must have been the result of intoxication. **1871** Schele de Vere *Amer.* 82: As when Frenchmen were dubbed Froggies and the like. ***1883** in *OEDS*: The Froggies must answer for Tamatave. **1889** O'Reilly & Nelson *50 Yrs. on Trail* 83: The one-eyed man's rifle...went off...and, by the merest miracle, missed sending Mr. Froggy to glory. **1918** Broun *Army at the Front* 70: The doughboys called him "Froggy" with ever so definite a sense of condescension. **1918** Mayo *Trouping for the Troops* 109: The "Froggies" would get their camions out of line. **1919** Rickenbacker *Fighting the Flying Circus* 139: Suddenly the Froggy leaped headlong

from his perch and clutching his parachute rigging...began a rapid descent to earth. **1927** Ranlett *Let's Go* 112: "Swiped it from the Froggies," he whispered to me. **1927** McKay *Home to Harlem* 12: We was always on the defensive as if the boches, as the froggies called them, was right down on us. **1927** Shay *Pious Friends* 79: Froggie, have you a daughter fine.../Fit for a marine just out of the line? ***1955, *1965** in *OEDS.* **1976** Hayden *Voyage* 246: Yore pretty slick, ain't ya, froggy? **1985** (quot. at EYETIE).

froggy *adj.* **1.** French.—used contemptuously.

1918 in M. Carey *Mlle. from Armentieres* (unp.): My Froggy gal was true to me. ***1936** Partridge *DSUE* 303: *Froggie* or *Froggy.* A Frenchman...Also adj. **1954** G. Kersh, in Pohl *Star of Stars* 32: We stopped the Froggy boats in mid-channel. ***1962** in *OEDS.* **1971** Waters *Smugglers of Spirits* 29: If these Froggie broads are as good as he says, maybe old Goosey will be doing us a favor.

2. [sugg. by JUMP, *v.*] *So. & West.* eager for a fight. Also **froggish.** (*also*) nervous; jumpy.

1939 "L. Short" *Bounty Guns* 7: Anybody else feels froggy, now's the time to hop on. **1970** T. Morrison *Bluest Eye:* Don't get froggy; it be over soon. **1971** Memphis (Tenn.) man, age *ca*17: OK, you feel froggy? Then jump! **1972** Wambaugh *Blue Knight* 81: There were a couple other guys in the group that might get froggy if someone leaped. **1967–80** Folb *Runnin' Lines* 238: *Froggy.* 1. Belligerent. 2. Out of line. **1984** Wilder *You-All* 79: If you want to get froggy, go ahead and jump. **1984** Sample *Racehoss* 60: George, anytime you feel froggish, jes hop! **1985** Former SP5, U.S. Army, age 35: I heard *froggy* [in this sense] throughout the army between 1971 and 1978. Like one drill sergeant used to say, "Any of you feelin' froggy, I'll knock your ass into splinters." Also "He's the froggiest bastard in this whole pond. Stay away from him."

frog hair *n.* **1.** a hairbreadth. Also **frog's hair.**

1958 McCulloch *Woods Words* 68: Frog hair—One frog hair is a very fine measurement in forest surveys. **1981** Hogan *D. Bullet* 108: You came within a frog's hair of getting yourself killed. **1982–84** Chapple *Outlaws in Babylon* 172: He stays only a frog's hair inside the law.

2. *Golf.* short grass that borders the edge of a putting green; apron.

1962 in P. Davies *Golf. Terms* 71: So I put the shot...into the frog hair around the green. **1970** Scharff *Encyc. of Golf* 417: *Frog hair.* Short grass bordering the edge of the green. **1977** *N.Y. Times* (Aug. 8) 33: It landed on the frog hair of the 11th green.

3. money.

1972 (cited in *BDNE2*). **1974** *Time* (Feb. 4) 29: Disturbingly, many of the plaque owners were contractors or architects who stood to benefit from making political contributions—frog hair,* as such funds are known [in Oklahoma]....*Because, as old Sooners say, new money feels "as slippery and smooth as frog hair."

¶ In phrase:

¶ **fine as frog's hair** exceedingly fine (in any sense). *Joc.*

1865 in C. Davis *Diary* 5: I have a better flow of spirits this morning, and, in fact, feel as fine as "frog hair," as Potso used to say. **1905** *DN* III 79: *Fine as frog hair.* Extremely fine. **1942** *ATS* 6: In order, in good condition. *Fine* (or *fit*) *as a frog's hair* (split down the middle). **1948** J. Stevens *Jim Turner* 228: Well, that's fine, finer'n frog hair. **1949** in *PADS* (No. 14) 78: *Fine as frog hair.* Hernando County [Fla.] simile in answer to "How are you?" **1961** L.G. Richards *TAC* 67: The weather was fine as frog's hair. [**1976** Adcock *Not for Truckers Only* xiv: A ton of data you'll need just about as much as a frog needs hair.] **1977** M. Franklin *Last of Cowboys* 90: "How you doin', Nighthawk?" "Fine, fine, fine as frog's hair." **1992** Hosansky & Sparling *Working Vice* 263: "How are you?"..."I'm finer than frog's hair."

Frogland *n.* Esp. *Army.* France.—used derisively.

1919 Russell *151st Field Artillery Brigade* 21: So this is Frogland! **1919** Ashton *F, 63* 75: No, ya herring, I lugged it all over Frogland so's t' make you a present of it. **1952** E. Pound, in Materer *Pound/Lewis* 270: Death of mind in frogland.

Froglander *n.* a Netherlander. Cf. 1652 quot. at FROG, *n.*, 1.

*1698-99 "B.E." *Dict. Canting Crew: Frog-landers,* Dutchmen. **1848** Judson *Mysteries* 111: A Froglander grocery-keeper caught one of 'em with his hands in the money-till. *Ibid* 527: "*Froglander.*" A Dutchman. ***1867** Smyth *Sailor's Wd.-Bk.*

frogman *n.* Esp. *Navy.* an underwater demolitions specialist; (*hence*) any swimmer specially equipped, as with scuba gear and swim fins, for underwater work. Now *S.E.*

*1945 in *OEDS:* The complete apparatus worn by the "frog-men." **1949** *N.Y. Times* (Dec. 25) E 7: "Frogmen," as they are called, wear self-contained breathing apparatus and web-like rubber shoes, used in the war. **1959** Ryan *Longest Day* 42: The five men...wore rubber frogmen's suits. **1967** Weiss & Lawrence *Easy Come* (film): "Frogman"—please! It's "explosive ordnance disposal man." **1978** Gann *Hostage* 409: An ex-Navy frogman. **1984** J.R. Reeves *Mekong* 4: How the hell could they use frogmen in a jungle war, anyway? **1985** *N.Y. Post* (Aug. 12) 3: Trapped Rock Star Rescued by Frogman.

frog-march *v.* [shift and alter. of *frog's march* (not recorded in U.S.), as in 1871, 1873 quots.] Esp. *Police.* to carry (a resisting person) face downward by the arms and legs; (*hence*, now solely) to propel (a resisting person) forward, as by seizing his collar and the seat of his trousers or by pinioning his arms behind his back.
  [***1871** in *OED*: They did not give the defendant the "Frog's March."] [***1873** Hotten *Slang Dict.* (ed. 4): *Frog's march*, the manner in which four or more policemen carry a drunken or turbulent man to the station-house. The victim is held face downwards, one constable being at each shoulder, while the others hold on above the knees. Often...another...officer...beats time...on the recalcitrant hero's posteriors.] [***1884** in *OED*: Deceased was "frog's marched"—that is, with face downwards—from Deal to Walmer.] ***1894** in *OED*: Death was accelerated by the "frog marching." ***1931** in *OEDS*: Caesar slewed him round, and forcing both arms behind his back, got ready to frog-march him to the door. *ca***1935** in R.E. Howard *Iron Man* 136: I hauled him out myself and frog-marched him to the door. **1957** O'Connor *Co. Q* 79: We're going to frog-march you all the way back to Pigeon Run in that fancy night-shirt of yours. ***1969** in *OEDS*: He...took me by the collar and the seat of my pants and frogmarched me the length of the café. **1992** *NewsDay* (CNN-TV) (Dec. 9): Tightly bound and frog-marched away.

frog's hair see FROG HAIR.

frogskin *n.* a U.S. banknote; (*specif.*) a one-dollar bill; (*pl.*) money.
  1902 Jarrold *Mickey Finn* 96: He had to spind "frog skins" to git an eddicashun. **1902** Ade *Girl Proposition* 104: A couple of Frog Skins each Month. **1902** *DN* II 274: *Frog-skins* [is] used in Virginia for paper money or "greenbacks." **1920** Weaver *In American* 39: You draw down what you need, six hundred frogskins. **1921** Wily *Lady Luck* 120: Whah at kin I trade dis frog skin [$10 bill] fo' a ra'r o' licker? **1927** Nicholson *Barker* 102: *Frog-skins*—Greenbacks. **1930** Lait *On the Spot* 201: $1 bill..."Frogskin." **1938** in Gelman *Photoplay* 209: M-G-M had forked out six hundred frogskins for uniforms. **1941** Attaway *Blood on the Forge* 78: One frogskin just like the other when you gamblin'. **1949** Gresham *Limbo Tower* 59: I *seen* guys with a system start with one frogskin and roll it up. **1953** Brossard *Saboteurs* 116: I was able to...slip the old lady a few frogskins. **1973** N.Y.C. man, age 24: A *frogskin* is a dollar bill. **1982** *Swap Shop* (WKGN Radio call-in show): I'm asking five frogskins for it. **1987** *Miami Vice* (NBC-TV): A deal somewhere in the neighborhood of two hundred million frogskins.

frogsticker *n.* **1.** a knife.
  1836 W.G. Simms *Mellichampe* 357: Wait a bit, till I...find my frogsticker, which has somehow tumbled out of the belt. **1850** in *DAE*: I'll knock that frog-sticker out of his hand in no time. **1885** Siringo *Texas Cowboy* 95: My old frog-sticker—an old pocket knife I had picked up a few days before. **1893** *DN* I 230: *Frog-Sticker.* The old blunt-pointed Barlow pocket-knife bought for children. Schoolboys say, "Loan me your *frog-sticker.*" **1906** R. Casey *Parson's Boys* 137 [ref. to *ca*1860]: I jerked out my frog-sticker on the run. **1908** in Botkin *Treas. Amer. Folk.* 469: Got a frog-sticker yer want ter swap? **1928** Dobie *Vaquero* 259: I also killed one wolf with a rock and another with a frog-sticker knife tied on the end of a stick. **1942** Rodgers & Hammerstein *Oklahoma!* 46: I tell you whut I'd like better'n a frog-sticker, if you got one.
  2. *Army.* a sword, lance, or bayonet.
  1862 in *Jour. Ill. Hist. Soc.* XVIII (1926) 910: Whipping out my sabre,...it flashed on my mind that I was playing the fool with only a "frog sticker" in my hand. **1889** *United Service* (June) 578 [ref. to Civil War]: Whin I say soords, ivery mother's son of yez whips out his frog-sticker. **1909** in "O. Henry" *Works* 426: In a week I'll have the eagle bird with the frog-sticker [a lance] blended in so you'd think you were born with it. **1918** Crowe *Pat Crowe, Aviator* 92: We tried to cross a bridge, but we found a French soldier with a four-foot frog-sticker on the end of a rifle guarding it. **1927** J. Stevens *Mattock* 6 [ref. to 1918]: Let the prison guard put the frog-sticker to 'em if they make a false move. **1942** *Sat. Eve. Post* (May 30) 67: *Frog-sticker*: a bayonet. **1965** Fink, Saul, & Peckinpah *Maj. Dundee* (film): They could...finish us off with them ten-foot frogstickers.

frog's tonsils *n.pl.* BEE'S KNEES.—constr. with *the. Joc.*
  1936 Sandburg *People, Yes* 63: He seems to think he's the frog's tonsils but he looks to me like a/plugged nickel.

frog-strangler *n. So.* a torrential rain.
  1942 *ATS* 70: *Frog strangler*, a heavy rain. *ca***1951** in *PADS* (No. 15) 70: *Frog-strangler*, n. A flood rain. **1973** F. Carter *Outlaw Wales* 49: A blinding, whipping rain...."A real frog-strangler." **1986** F. Walton *Once Were Eagles* 31: Now I really understood what the phrases "coming down in buckets," "raining in sheets," and "frog strangler" meant. **1987** Eble *Campus Slang* (Apr.) 3: *Frog strangler*—heavy rainfall.

frog-walk *v.* **1.** *S.W.* (of an unbroken horse) to arch the back and jump forward while being ridden.
  1937 *DN* VI 618: On cold mornings practically all young broncos pitch a little or *frog walk* when first mounted. *a***1940** in Logsdon *Whorehouse Bells* 95: He starts his frog walkin'.
  2. FROG-MARCH.
  [**1954-60** *DAS*: French walk...ejecting a man...forcibly by grabbing the seat of his pants...and the back of his collar...and...forcing him to walk until he reaches the door.] **1977** J. Olsen *Fire Five* 55: He puts her in a tight half nelson and starts frog-walking her to the squad car.

front *n.* **1.** [sugg. by *Front!*, a desk clerk's command to a bellboy] a bellboy.
  1892 Garland *Spoil of Office* 146: He...gave it to the insolent little darky who served as "Front." **1894** *Harper's* (Jan.) 222: "Front!" called the clerk. "Show Mr. Stone up to 313." **1956** N.Y.C. woman, age *ca*70: Tell them to send up the front.
  2. Esp. *Und.* the favorable appearance provided by good clothing; (*hence*) a good suit of clothes.—occ. constr. in pl.
  1899 Cullen *Tales* 18: I had a front and all colors of...[money] in my clothes. *Ibid.* 60: I've got the front—meaning my layout of togs—left anyhow. **1905** in Partridge *Dict. Und.* 269: My own humble $40 front (suit). **1906** H. Green *Boarding House* 190: One needed a "front" to make a hit with the managers, and "fronts" cost money. **1911** Roe *Prodigal Daughter* 76: I'll provide you with a new front and stake you to enough money to get out of town. **1922** N. Anderson *Hobo* 35: When he does buy clothing, either rough clothing or a good "front," he finds his way to places where new clothes are on sale at astonishingly low prices. **1931** Wilstach *Under Cover Man* 45: Just took this front out of camphor. **1935** E. Anderson *Hungry Men* 243: That's a good-looking suit you got on there...I wish I had a good front like that. **1937** Reitman *Box-Car Bertha* 192: With this I got myself a new front, a smart black traveling dress and a hat to match. **1944** Burley *Hndbk. Jive* 138: *Front*—wearing apparel. **1957** H. Simmons *Corner Boy* 83: Hey, I want to show you my new front. **1964** in B. Jackson *Swim Like Me* 91: Joe, you have a short, some fronts, and a fine ticker too. **1967** Bronsteen *Handbook* 48: Have three sets of clothes, including one "front," with which you can go back into the square world for a job. **1967-80** Folb *Runnin' Lines* 238: *Fronts.* Clothes, especially a suit or sports jacket.
  3. *Und.* a watch and chain.
  1902 Hapgood *Thief* 46 [ref. to 1883]: I could "bang a super," or get a man's "front" (watch and chain) as easily as I could relieve a Moll of her "leather." **1904** *Life in Sing Sing* 248: *Front.* Watch and chain. **1915** (quot. at GRIFTER, *n.*). **1924** *N.Y. Times* (Aug. 3) VIII 16: A front is both watch and chain.
  4. *Und.* a bluff; (*also*) self-assurance.
  1903 A.M. Lewis *Boss* 272: Sometimes he'd throw a front an' talk about havin' me fired off the force. **1932** Hecht & Fowler *Great Magoo* 30: He's one of those boardwalk Romeos with a lot of cheap front.
  5. something extended on credit.
  *a***1990** E. Currie *Dope & Trouble* 69: When I was selling [drugs], even the *seniors* in high school would...ask me for fronts.
  ¶ In phrases:
  ¶ **from [in] front** *Black E.* from the very start.
  1956 in R.S. Gold *Jazz Talk* 100: Every musician is a friend of mine from front, we don't need any introductions. **1958-59** Lipton *Barbarians* 104: Sherry McCall is beat from in front, as the bop jive boys of the forties would have put it. *Ibid.* 316: *From In Front*—First. From the beginning. **1960** in R.S. Gold *Jazz Talk* 100: My frame is bent, Naz. It's been bent from in front!
  ¶ **in** [or **up** or **out**] **front, 1.** Orig. *Black E.* in advance; beforehand; first.
  1932 R. Fisher *Conjure-Man* 50: Show me two bucks in front. **1937** in Leadbitter & Slaven *Blues Records* 60: Must Get Mine In Front. **1960** in R.S. Gold *Jazz Talk* 100: I need a little bread out front. **1962** L. Hughes *Tambourines to Glory* 188: In this play, according to the pro-

gram, you might thing [*sic*] I'm Big-Eyed Buddy Lomax—if I didn't tell you in front, no I'm not. **1963** in L. Bruce *Essential* 145: Can I get some bread in front here? **1967** Rosevear *Pot* 159: *In front*: Referring especially to giving money to a person for marihuana. They is given before the exchange takes place, or "in front" of the exchange. **1970** Wexler *Joe* (film): How 'bout a taste up front? **1971** *Night Gallery* (NBC-TV): I tell you this up front. **1989** *Geraldo* (synd. TV series) (May 19): I apologize out front for asking the question, but I'm curious.

2. Orig. *Black E.* free of guile or deception; out in the open; truthful; frank. Also as adv.

1912-43 in *Frank Brown Collection* I 599: *Tell out in front*…To tell one frankly to his face.—Chapel Hill. **1966** Fariña *Down So Long* 140: It's all in front, man, they have a heart thing going for them. **1967** Yablonsky *Hippie Trip* 163: Our association was for the most part direct and "out-front." **1970** *Playboy* (Dec.) 120: First thing I did…was to check the ashtray…just to make sure that the ads are really up front. **1971** *All in the Family* (CBS-TV): Let's be up front with [each] other. **1980** *Nat. Lampoon* (Apr.) 44: Look, I'll be really out front with you. I'm married too. **1980** Algren *Dev. Stocking* 121: He tells her out front she'll go to jail sooner or later.

¶ **in front of** just before.

1970 Thackrey *Thief* 4: Sweating. I'm always like that in front of a score.

front *v.* **1.** *Und.* to conceal the actions of (a pickpocket) by distracting the victim's attention. Also intrans.

*****1879** *Macmillan's Mag.* (Oct.) 503: My pal said, "Front me and I will do him for it." *****1896** in Partridge *Dict. Und.* 269: It commonly took three men to secure a single watch in the open street—one to "front," one to snatch, and a third to take from the snatcher. **1914** (cited in *Ibid.*).

2. Orig. *Und.* (see 1929 quot.); to act as a front (for someone). Now *S.E.*

1929 Beesley & Hotstetter *Racket* 225: *Front*…To protect or act as a screen for anyone in illegal practices or criminal activities; to make a display as a disguise of respectability; to use political influence for someone; *e.g.* "He has a couple of big shots at the City Hall fronting for his racket." **1932** in *OEDS:* You'll have to front for us, knowin' the collegiate racket and all. **1939** R. Chandler *Big Sleep* ch. xxvi: Why should I front for that twist? **1942-49** Goldin et al. *DAUL* 74: You front for us and we'll shake this [abortionist] for a nice buck. **1955** in Maurer *Lang. Und.* 241: *Front*…To serve as a cover for an illicit operation.

3. Esp. *Black E.* **a.** to put up a front of self-assurance; put up a bluff, esp. as part of a confidence game.—also constr. with *off.*

1966-67 P. Thomas *Mean Streets* 112 [ref. to 1940's]: I'm digging maybe you're fronting now, cool Piri. **1987** Mamet *House of Games* (film): What are you gonna do? What are you fronting off for? **1988** T. Logan *Harder They Fall* 30: Maybe you be frontin'.

b. *Broadly,* to posture; show off.

1983 *Reader's Digest Success with Words* 85: Black English…*front* = "to put on airs." **1991** *Fresh Prince* (NBC-TV): You the one frontin' like you all that [i.e., as though you are wonderful]. **1991** *Source* (Oct.) 10: Just because I'm white doesn't mean I'm a devil, frontin' or trying to be Black. **1991** *Yo! MTV Raps* (MTV): Every day frontin' and maxin'.

c. to lie; dissemble.

1988 "Biz Markie" *Vapors* (rap song): The boss fronted,/Said, "Sorry Mr. Lee, but there's no help wanted." **1991** *Houston Chronicle* (Oct. 8) 2D: *Frontin'*—Lying. **1992** "Fab 5 Freddy" *Fresh Fly Flavor* 28: *Frontin'*…Telling lies. **1993** *Source* (July) 50: Trying to front about my situation instead of dealing with it.

4.a. Orig. *Und.* to give in return for a promise of payment; give in advance.

1966 McNeill *Moving Through Here* 51: A few trusted assistants to whom they "front" drugs to sell for a commission. **1971** Simon *Sign of Fool* 11: Richie'd fronted twelve hundred dollars to him and said, "If you're not back here with the dope a half hour from now, someone's gonna die." **1978** *Adolescence* XIII 501: When he wanted to borrow some money, he asked his friends to "front" him. **1986** *Campus Voice* (Sept.) 56: The hash was fronted to him,…no money down, provided he pay his supplier $390 in two days.

b. to hand over; give.

1971 *N.Y. Times Mag.* (Nov. 28) 92: Hey, man, front me a quarter. **1972** *Nat. Lampoon* (June) 52: Look, you don't have to front us nothing, man.

c. *Und.* to show in advance.

1973 Schiano & Burton *Solo* 11: That way, I didn't have to front my money.

d. *Narc.* to purchase (drugs) on credit.

1989 G.C. Wilson *Mud Soldiers* 140: Started frying again on acid. Fronting it (buying it now but paying later).

front burner *n.* a condition or position of top priority.—usu. constr. with *on the.* Also attrib. Cf. BACK BURNER.

1969 *Business Week* (July 5) 49: The team moved up a rank in the organization to become a department unto itself.…Whereupon, [a project] was shifted to the front burner. **1970** *U.S. News & W.R.* (May 25) 30: Some domestic programs are not on the front burner right now. **1976** in *AS* LIV (1979) 110: In dealing with the economy we're going to put jobs on the front burner. **1983** *L.A. Times* (Aug. 28) IV 1: Civil rights is not a front-burner issue today. **1985** Sawislak *Dwarf* 142: We didn't exactly put it on the front burner.

front door *n.* **1.** the vulva or vagina.

*****a1890-93** *F & H* III 77: *Front-door*…The female pudendum…*To have* (or *do*) *a bit of front-door work*—to copulate. **1990** Rukuza *W. Coast Turnaround* 98: She wanted him inside the front door one more time.

2. *CB.* the leading position in a line of vehicles; (*hence*) the vehicle in that position.

1975 Dills *CB Slanguage* 35: *Front door:* first CB vehicle in a line of two or more; e.g. "We got that one Red Pepper running the front door for us." **1976** *Nat. Lampoon* (July) 56: I got yer front door 'n' there's a mess o' giant bugs up here!

front-door name *n.* *Circus.* a nickname.

1961 Clausen *Season's Over* 188 [ref. to *ca*1945]: The origin of a lot of the front-door names I heard tossed around…puzzled me.

front end *n.* **1.** a woman's bosom; (*pl.*) a woman's breasts.

1962 W. Crawford *Give Me Tomorrow* 46 [ref. to 1951]: He quoted statistics till I told him forty-inch front ends was all the numbers I understand. **1965** W. Crawford *Bronc Rider* 172: Did you *see* the front end on 'er? **1980** Univ. Tenn. student: I like babes with big front ends. **1988** *N.Y. Post* (June 6) 6: Front end job. Star magazine reports that Jane Fonda has undergone breast implant surgery to improve her figure.

2. the penis.

1984 W.M. Henderson *Elvis* 106: Now get on back there and grease his front end.

frontispiece *n.* the face.

*****a1625** in *OED:* That fayre frontispeece of yours. *****1754**, *****1772**, *****1821** in *Ibid.* **1842** *Spirit of Times* (May 28) 152: Broome…caught him with the left on his damaged frontispiece. **1845** in Robb *Squatter Life* 120: Judgin' from that stranger's frontispiece…I shouldn't like him fur a near neighbour.

front-loader *n.* (see quot.).

1979 Univ. Tenn. student: A *front-loader* is a brassiere that hooks in the front.

front money *n.* **1.** *Business & Pol.* money paid or raised in advance. Now *colloq.* or *S.E.*

1925 *Collier's* (Aug. 8) 30: Expense money…"front" money. *ca*1928 (cited in *W9*). **1931** in Partridge *Dict. Und.* 270: *Front money,* money advanced to a salesman before commissions are earned. **1935** in *Ibid. ca*1945-50 in Maurer *Lang. Und.* 186: *Front money*…Bankroll money [used by a gambler]. **1961** (cited in Partridge *Dict. Und.* (ed. 2) 821). **1963** J.A. Williams *Sissie* 59: He demanded "front money" (an advance) and was uneasy over "back money" (arrears). *ca*1986 in *NDAS:* In the drive for $4.5 million in "front money."

2. *Und.* (see *ca*1945-50 quot.).

1941 Wald, Macauley, et al. *Navy Blues* (film): Aw, we need front money. If I only had an idea where we could borrow some.…We just want front money. We're not gonna spend a dime of it. *ca*1945-50 in Maurer *Lang. Und.* 186: *Front money:*…Money used to make an impression on suckers.

front office *n.* *Police & Und.* detective headquarters; police headquarters.

1900 "Flynt" & Walton *Powers* 79: The Front Office wanted to know who does that touch in Jersey. **1901** *Chi. Tribune* (Aug. 17) 1: The entire [N.Y.C.] police force, from patrolmen up to the "front office." **1901** "Flynt" *World of Graft* 219: *Front Office,* police headquarters. **1903**, **1915**, **1924** (cited in Partridge *Dict. Und.* 270). **1930** Irwin *Tramp & Und.* 79: *Front Office.* The detective bureau at police headquarters. **1941** in D.W. Maurer *Lang. Und.* 127: The fuzz picked me up…and took me into the front office.

front-piece *n.* FRONTISPIECE.

1836 in Haliburton *Sam Slick* 42: That will take the frown out of her front-piece. **1903** Ade *Society* 188: You cannot iron the Lines of Rugged Character from his Front-Piece.

front porcher *n.* [cf. S.E. *front-porch campaign*, in W. Safire *New Lang. Pol.*, p. 156] *Pol.* a political candidate who is reluctant to campaign widely.

1977 Coover *Public Burning* 432: I like campaign trains, I'm no front porcher, but this was too goddamn much!

frontseater *n. Mil. Av.* the command pilot of an aircraft having fore-and-aft cockpits. Cf. BACKSEATER.

1988 *Supercarrier* (ABC-TV): I'm short a frontseater.

frosh *n.* [< archaic or dial. G *Frosch* 'grammar-school pupil', lit. 'frog'] *Stu.* a freshman; freshmen.

[**1851** Hall *College Wds.* s.v. *frog*: In Germany, a student in the gymnasium, and before entering the university, is called a *Frosch*,—a frog.] **1915** in *DA*: The "frosh" started a "back to nature movement." **1922** *Bomb* (Iowa State Coll.) 400: The Frosh should have won it. **1924** Marks *Plastic Age* 22: Won't I make the little frosh walk. **1931** McConn *Studies* 26: All Frosh have to take English I. **1959** E. Hunter *Killer's Wedge* 101: But some stupid frosh pledge had…forgotten to replenish the dwindling supplies. **1969** *Playboy* (Sept.) 194: Curfew for frosh coeds only. **1981** *Daily Beacon* (Univ. Tenn.) (Oct. 21) 7: Devoe expecting frosh help. **1990** *Newsweek* (Dec. 24) 55: Some frosh…were uncomfortable with ideals foreign to their upbringing.

frost *n.* **1.a.** Orig. *Theat.* an utter failure; (*hence*) a thorough disappointment.

***1885** in *F & H* III 77: He is an absolute and perfect frost. ***1885** in *Ibid.*: The affair…[was] almost as big a frost athletically as it was financially. ***1889** in *Ibid.*: The pantomime was a dead frost. ***1889** Barrère & Leland *Dict. Slang* I 386: *Frost* (society), a failure, a fiasco…"The ball is a *frost* if the Marquis ain't there." (Theatrical), a dead failure; "a *frost*, a killing *frost*." **1889** in Leitner *Diamond in Rough* 168: "Perfect *frost*?" "*Utter fraud?*" "*Game for kids?*" "*Boshiest business I ever saw?*" **1896** Ade *Artie* 51: I can kid all right, but when it comes to makin' a dead serious play I'm a horrible frost. **1899** Cullen *Tales* 87: Going back to your old boyhood home.…It's usually a frost when you…get there. **1901** Ade *Modern Fables* 112: The Lawn Party was the heaviest June Frost ever known in that part of the State. **1904** in W.C. Fields *By Himself* 29: You…explained to all that I would be a bigger frost than the blizzard in 1888. **1906** H. Green *Boarding House* 53: They followed us on the bill, an' was a frost. **1918** *Sat. Eve. Post* (Aug. 24) 9: The whole thing's a frost…with Kennedy in it. **1923** *N.Y. Times* (Sept. 9) VIII 2: *Frost*: A failure. Opposite of a hit. **1933** *Leatherneck* (Jan.) 8: He was a "frost"— not awful enough to be funny, just bad enough to be "rung down." **1955** Shapiro *Sixth of June* 153: We jumped on Adak. What a frost! The Japs skedaddled couple weeks ahead.

b. a boring or unpleasant person.

1934 Wohlforth *Tin Soldiers* 79: Anyway, this bimbo here is kind of a frost.

2. an icy reception; cold shoulder.

1892 Norr *China Town* 38: I don't think she had a heart. I never went up against the frost myself; I don't like light women. *Ibid.* 43: The girl…wouldn't flirt with a sucker to draw him to us, and had given…many good people the "frost." **1896** in S. Crane *Complete Stories* 318: I came here looking for a theatrical job—that's my business— but I don't get a thing but a frost from every manager I strike. **1897** *Harper's Wkly.* (Jan.) 90: To meet with a cool reception is called "getting a frost." **1911** Van Loan *Big League* 61: That's what I call a pretty chilly love letter! Looks like Biff is up against a frost. **1937** in D. Runyon *More Guys* 111: The frost he meets with when he approaches the barber with his sure thing gives him…pneumonia. **1957** M. Shulman *Rally* 270: Grace always replied with such a frost that he finally gave it up.

3. (see quot.).

1906 *DN* III 137: *Frost, n.* An unanswerable hit or retort. "That's a *frost* on him."

¶ In phrase:

¶ **holy frost** (used to express astonishment).

1899 Boyd *Shellback* 364: "Holy frost!" the captain exclaimed.

frost *v.* **1.** to snub, spurn, or jilt; give the cold shoulder.

1896 Ade *Artie* 42: You know—that guy you was goin' to frost. **1899** Ade *Fables*: Little did he suspect that he could be Frosted. **1901** Irwin *Sonnets* (unp.): Nifty Mame has frosted me complete.

2. to astonish or (*usu.*) infuriate. Also in humorous or vulgar vars.

1895 Gore *Stu. Slang* 13: *Frost v.* To surprise. "Wouldn't that frost you!" **1896** Ade *Artie* 66: Wouldn't that frost you, though, Miller? This

is little Bright-eyes that took the note for Hall. **1909** M'Govern *When the Krag Is Laid Away* 96: Wouldn't that frost your Galways? **1913** *DN* IV 10: Wouldn't that frost you? **1947** Mailer *Naked & Dead* 408 [ref. to WWII]: Them men are enough to frost your nuts. **1947** Heggen & Logan *Mr. Roberts* 423 [ref. to WWII]: Won't that frost the Old Man's knockers? **1951** J. Wilson *Dark & Damp* 233 [ref. to *ca*1920]: "Now wouldn't that frost your balls," he grumbled. "I'm runnin' that potlicker in the state trials next week and he's lettin' a spindly-assed pup out-run him!" **1957** E. Brown *Locust Fire* 116 [ref. to WWII]: The snipers were slopies. Now wouldn't that frost your butt? **1958** Frankel *Band of Bros.* 6: What frosts me is we already got the best skipper in the division. **1960** MacCuish *Do Not Go Gentle* 13 [ref. to *a*1940]: Frosts yer ass, eh? **1963** J. Ross *Dead Are Mine* 262: Wouldn't that frost the squareheads. To see some silly son of a bitch barreling hell-bent for election without the lines and find the crazy bastard's so full of hop he doesn't know what he's doing. **1968** W.C. Anderson *Gooney Bird* 185: Wouldn't that frost your balls! **1971** Rowe *Five Years to Freedom* 46: "That ought to frost their balls," Dan chuckled. **1971** *Current Slang* V 12: *Frost, v.* To anger. **1972** Hall & Nordby *Individual & Dreams* 122: It really left him high and dry, really frosted his ass. **1972** *West Village* 30: That really frosts me. **1974** Montpelier, Vt., man: Wouldn't that frost your duck? **1981** *N.Y. Post* (Dec. 14) 32: You know what really frosts me? **1981** *Hill St. Blues* (NBC-TV): Well, that really frosted my flakes. **1985** Yeager & Janos *Yeager* 161: It really frosted me that guys were jealous because I made speeches. **1987** B. Ford & Chase *Awakening* 46: I believe you have to treat VIPs like any other patients…And I think this frosted her. **1989** *Married with Children* (Fox-TV): You know what really frosts my weenie?

3. [prob. sugg. by syn. CHILL] *Mil.* to kill.

1960 MacCuish *Do Not Go Gentle* 217 [ref. to WWII]: Gonna find that stinkin' Jap what nailed me an' frost his ass seven ways to Sunday. *Ibid.* 228: Nice lil ole Jap wantin' to play grab-ass's all, an' you up an' frost 'im!

frostbit *adj.* unlucky.

1985 Boyne & Thompson *Wild Blue* 610: Brown was marked: snakebit, frostbit, unlucky, not to be seen with.

frost call var. FROST NOTICE.

frosted *adj.* **1.** [sugg. by SNOW] under the influence of cocaine.

1951 Fowler *Schnozzola* 122: The Link [was] full of liquor and well frosted with cocaine. **1967** [Beck] *Pimp* 219: I was so frosted with cocaine I felt embalmed.

2. angry.

1956 Hargrove *Girl He Left* 18: She didn't get frosted until the next time, when she played AX and I put the Z in front of it. **1958** Gilbert *Vice Trap* 125: He was frosted good. **1974** *Night-Stalker* (ABC-TV): I shouldn't have gotten so frosted, I guess. **1988** *Crossfire* (CNN-TV) (Aug. 17): I got a report that you were pretty frosted by the treatment of some of our friends on the right.

frost freak *n. Narc.* (see quot.).

1971 Guggenheimer *Narcotics & Drug Abuse* 22: Frost-Freak. freon abuser.

frost notice *n. USMC.* (see quots.). Also **frost call.**

1969 Graham & Gurr *Violence* 460: On a rainy night last June a "frost notice"—a word-of-mouth warning system used by the U.S. Marines to inform personnel of emergency situations—went out to all Marines in and around the Washington, D.C., area. **1983** J. Green *Newspeak* 101: *Frost call*…USMC: a procedure established within a command whereby under certain emergency conditions all officers and other key personnel may be alerted by special notification.

frosty *n.* a cold beer.

1961 Peacock *Valhalla* 46 [ref. to 1953]: We'll be back more skosh.…Let's get some frosties. **1970-72** in *AS* L (1975) 59: *Frosty n.* Beer. **1978** *Adolescence* XIII 495: Let's go cruisin' and drain some frosties. **1979** Gutcheon *New Girls* 117: Give my granny a frosty. **1982** *Nat. Lampoon* (Sept.) 47: Nothing like a sixteen-ounce frosty to round out the corners. **1989** Radford & Crowley *Drug Agent* 116: We popped the tops on the frosties.

frosty *adj.* **1.** very unfriendly. Now *S.E.*

1895 Gore *Stu. Slang* 16: *Give the frosty hand.* To be uncivil, or distant. **1896** Ade *Artie* 19: It was frosty, too. I couldn't see any folks I knew. *Ibid.* 56: This frosty party was doin' the touch-me-not business all day. **1898** Hobart *Many Moods* 54: Jee! but dat guy was frosty!

2. cool; unexcited.

1972 Wambaugh *Blue Kt.* 81: Stay frosty, Sitting Bull.…Here, have a cigar. **1980** Teichmann *Fonda* 17: They call me a frosty son-of-a-bitch, my peers in the New York theater, because I'm not nervous. They're throwing up...and I can't wait to get on. **1990** *Mystery Sci. Theater* (Comedy Central TV): And stay frosty, you two.

3. stylish; COOL.

1986 Eble *Campus Slang* (Nov.) 4: *Frosty*—cool, hip, in vogue: "That's a *frosty* little outfit for only $25."

froze *adj.* **1.** drunk.

1722 B. Franklin, in *AS* XV (Feb. 1940) 103: [Drunkards] are *Almost froze, Feavourish, In their Altitudes, Pretty well entered, &c.*

2. desperate.

1847–48 Ruxton *Far West* (quot. at FREEZE, *v.*, 1.). *Ibid.* 28: "How do you feel?" "Half froze for hair [scalps]. Wagh!" **1851** M. Reid *Scalp Hunters* 30: I'm most froze for a squaw.

frozen *adj.* FROZE, 1.

1737 *Penna. Gaz.* (Jan. 6) 1: He's...Fox'd, Fuddled,...Frozen.

Frozen Chosen *n.* **1.** *USMC.* the Chosin Reservoir, Korea.—usu. constr. with *the.* Usu. **Frozen Chosin.** Now *hist.*

1952 Geer *New Breed* 259: The reservoir was to receive its Marine name—Frozin Chosin. **1960** Leckie *March to Glory* 36: The area which the [American] Marines called "Frozen Chosin" had been no kinder to [the Chinese]. **1971** Flanagan *Maggot* 220: Got that at the frozen Chosin when you were still in high school, sweetheart. **1973** Huggett *Body Count* 229: He'd walked out of the Frozen Chosen with Chesty Puller. **1978** J. Webb *Fields of Fire* 209: Couple gunnies, maybe, who remembered something about the Frozen Chosin in the Freezin' Season.

2. [sugg. by *Chosen* /ˈtʃoˌsɛn/, Japanese name for Korea] *Mil.* Korea during the Korean War. Now *hist.*

*ca*1954 in Wallrich *AF Airs* 158: Frozen Chosen. **1955** Sack *Here to Shimbashi* 30: "Back in Frozen Chosen," he would say, "we never useta sleep in sleepin' bags." **1969** Lynch *Amer. Soldier* 260 [ref. to 1953]: I came all the way from Frozen Chosen to come to some fifty-cent cathouse, man, where they got diseases, man, Washington hasn't even heard of yet. **1969** Cray *Erotic Muse* 144: The police action in Frozen Chosen.

frozen face *n.* an impassive or unfriendly facial expression; (*hence*) an unfriendly reception.

1896 Ade *Artie* 78: You won't get no frozen face at this place that I'm steerin' you against. **1900** Ade *More Fables* 176: Society gave him the Frozen Face. **1906** Ford *Shorty McCabe* 175: She'd got the frozen face ever since she came to town. **1911** A.H. Lewis *Apaches of N.Y.* 37: He would be given the frozen face at the rackets, the icy eye in the streets. **1927** *AS* II 276: *Frozen face*—straight face. **1939** Appel *Power House* 13: No one was getting his goat. He'd show them the old frozen face like a real actor.

frozen front *n.* FROZEN FACE.

1902 Townsend *Fadden & Mr. Paul* 360: So, sir, dis rude poisson, Miles, gets de frozen front.

frozen mitt *n.* [modeled on GLAD HAND; cf. syns. CHILLY MITT, ICY MITT] an unfriendly reception. Cf. 1895 quot. at FROSTY, *adj.*, 1.

*1915 in Partridge *DSUE* (ed. 8) 431: Begging for leave to do [their] bit/ And getting for [their] pains the frozen mit. **1917** *Living Age* (Nov. 10) 379: "To give one the frozen mit"...was a phrase...one heard many years ago. *1918 in Fraser & Gibbons *Soldier & Sailor Wds.* 156: He tried to make up to me but I gave him the frozen mit. **1923** *N.Y. Times* (Sept. 9) VIII 2: *Frozen Mitt.* Uncordial reception. **1929** Bodenheim *60 Secs.* 240: Listen, why'd you slip me that frozen mit the morning 'fore last?

frozen rope *n. Baseball.* a line drive or a hard-thrown ball.

1964 Thompson & Rice *Every Diamond* 140: *Frozen rope:* A line drive base hit. **1973** J. Garagiola, on World Series (NBC-TV) (Oct. 16): He hit a frozen rope. C. Gowdy, on *Ibid.*: What a throw that was! A frozen rope from right field! **1982** T. Considine *Lang. Sport* 21: *Frozen rope.* A line drive.

fruit *n.* **1.a.** baked beans. *Joc.*

1865 Browne *Ward: Travels* 26: Them beans...are a cheerful fruit when used tempritly. **1919** Camp *305th Field Arty.* 347: After saving half a can of "fruit" for dinner, I pulled in a hitch on my belt and prepared for the day.

b. *Restaurant.* a slice of onion. *Joc.*

1928 *New Yorker* (Dec. 8) 24: It was here that we learned that "a piece of fruit" means sliced onion as applied to a hamburger sandwich.

2.a. something delightful; (*hence*) a fine or pleasant person.

1879 Rooney *Conundrums* 85: Their frequent exclamations of delight—such as, "Red hot, you bet!" "Ain't it fruit, though?" "Houp-

la!" etc., plainly indicated that they were enjoying themselves in the best possible manner. **1900** *DN* II 37: *Fruit*, n....A good fellow, a trump. [Reported from three colleges.] **1921** in D. Ford *Pappy* 22: Dear Old Fruit...I am going to keep a sort of [diary] for you about happenings on board.

b. a person who is easily overcome, impressed, or victimized; (*also*) something easy.

1894 Bangs *3 Wks. in Pol.* 32: Thaddeus was what certain politicians call "fruit". He was hanging on a tree ready to be plucked, they thought. **1895** Gore *Stu. Slang* 12: *Fruit*...one who can be easily deceived....An easy course in college. **1899** *Tip Top Wkly.* (Apr. 22) 16: It strikes me that he'd be easy fruit. **1900** *DN* II 37: *Fruit*, n. 1. A person easily influenced. 2. One easy to defeat. 3. An instructor whose course is not exacting....7. A girl whose acquaintance is easy to make....*Fruit*, *adj.* Easy to do or accomplish. **1901** Irwin *Sonnets* (unp.): Hot society was easy fruit! *a*1904–11 Phillips *Susan Lenox* II 72: You'd treat 'em like ladies and they'd treat you as easy fruit. **1927** Thrasher *Gang* 267: *Fruit*—easy mark. **1931** Cressey *Taxi-Dance Hall* 35: *Fruit.*—An easy mark. **1947** in *West. Folk.* VII (1948) 72: Annapolis [slang]...*Fruit:* An easy assignment or quiz, or anything that insults the intelligence.

c. *Specif.*, an easily seduced woman; PUSHOVER.

1900 *DN* II 37: *Fruit*, n...An immoral woman. **1930** Irwin *Tramp & Und. Sl.* 81: *Fruit.* An "easy mark." A girl or woman willing to oblige. **1963** Cameron *Black Camp* 59: Dames are fruit for medals.

3. *Stu.* a worthless or disagreeable person; JERK. Also as adj.

1900 *DN* II 37: *Fruit*...a disagreeable person. [Used at Princeton Univ.]. **1911** O. Johnson *Stover* 6 [ref. to *ca*1900]: "Yes; and the team's going to need ends badly."..."I'll bet we get a lot of fruits."..."Oh, some of them aren't half bad." **1932** *AS* VII (June) 332: *Fruit*—a "no account fellow." **1950** C.W. Gordon *High School* 121: Look at that guy's socks. Is he "fruit"! *Ibid.* 126: Disapproved behavior was "fruit."

4. an effeminate male; a male homosexual.—used derisively.—occ. used collect.

1900 *DN* II 37: *Fruit*, n...An immoral man. [Reported from Tulane Univ.]. **1917** in Fitzgerald *Letters* 320: Oh and that awful little——(a sort of attenuated super-fruit) is still around...and contributes such elevating...generalities as "why I'm suah that romanticism is only a cross-section of reality." **1928** Panzram *Killer* 95 [ref. to 1916]: Then I thought he must be a bit queer sexually. I thought he must be a punk or some kind of fruit. **1931** J.T. Farrell *McGinty* 187: You know what boyfriend....Harry the fruit. **1932** in *AS* (Feb. 1934) 26: *Fruit.* A degenerate. **1929–33** J.T. Farrell *Young Manhood* 197: The guy was fruit, the first one he'd ever met like that. **1939** in Inman *Diary* 949: We call queers fruit. This fruit...looks very sloppy. **1947** Spillane *Jury* 70: She walked with a swagger and he minced his way to the sidewalk holding on to her arm. Fruit. **1950** *Sat. Eve. Post* (July 29) 60: "Fruits," he said, "the whole place is fulla fruits. Fruits and treachers." **1968** Kirkwood *Good Times* 195: Nobody would have ever called them "fruits"—they were attractive, popular, masculine. **1976** Braly *False Starts* 43: The hard definition between a fruit and a punk was that the fruit wanted to where the punk didn't. **1985** Swados & Trudeau *Rap Master Ronnie* 12: Help us to uproot,/Every queer and fruit. **1993** M. Korda, in *New Yorker* (Mar. 29) 44: Surely nobody had used the word "fruit" to describe a homosexual since the thirties.

5. a crazy or silly person; FRUITCAKE, 1. Also as quasi-adj.

1959 W. Burroughs *Naked Lunch* 4. **1960** Kirkwood *Pony* 15: I tried to get her to say that the parrot had gone completely fruit and killed him. **1965** Summers *Flunkie* 111: You guys are just a bunch of fruits. **1978** Alibrandi *Killshot* 35: Or maybe his challenger was just plain crazy. All kinds of fruits wandered into the Y.

fruit *v. Black E.* to play or fool around, esp. romantically.—also constr. with *around*.

1938 in R.S. Gold *Jazz Talk* 101: *Fruiting:* fickle, fooling around with no particular object. **1946** Mezzrow & Wolfe *Really Blues* 73: High-pressure fruiting. *Ibid.* 305: *Fruit:* romance playfully. **1966** in IUFA *Folk Speech: Fruitin' around, goofin' off.* not doing what one is supposed to be doing.

fruitball *n.* a crazy or eccentric person.

1972 W.C. Anderson *Hurricane* 192: Look at some of those fruitballs down there drinkin' beer and wavin' at us.

fruitbar *n.* FRUITBALL; (*also*) FRUIT, 4.

1976 *Nat. Lampoon* (Feb.) 19: Half the pro athletes are pansies. Homos. Fruitbars. **1980** W.C. Anderson *Bat-21* 91: I've seen fruit bars...but you win the cut-glass fly-swatter. **1981** *Nat. Lampoon* (Feb.) 75: Now the docks are overrun with "gays" and other fruitbar types. **1986** *NDAS: Flaming fruitbar*...A male homosexual; queen.

fruit basket *n.* an effeminate male homosexual; FRUIT, 4.— used derisively.

1963 Coon *Short End* 27: Now I'm not saying golf is major-league wrestling or anything like that, and I've seen a few fruit baskets on the links, but if there's anything golf ain't, it's a fag game.

fruit boots *n.pl.* men's shoes of any style believed to be favored by homosexuals.

1960 D. Hamilton *Death of a Citizen* 31: Light-colored, low-heeled, pull-on boots with the rough side of the leather showing that are some-times known locally as fruit-boots, being the preferred footgear of a few gentlemen whose virility is subject to question. **1970** Tamony *Americanisms* (No. 26) 6: Years ago suede shoes were worn only by consenting adults in Britain, and were so known as *fruit boots.* **1971** Jacobs & Casey *Grease* 38: Whataya say, Fruit Boots? **1973** *Oui* (Feb.) 122: Real cute fruit boots today, big boy. **1973** *Nat. Lampoon* (Oct.) 65: Exchanging alligator shirts and loafers for pegged pants and fruit boots. **1974** Univ. Tenn. grad. student: *Fruit boots* meant those Italian pointed shoes in 1962 or '63 [in Memphis]. **1980** McDowell *Our Honor* 10 [ref. to *ca*1952]: Bucks?…They're fruit boots, that's what they are—fruit boots. **1982** Sculatti *Cat. of Cool* 1: He stood there…in stovepipes and fruit-boots.

fruitburger *n.* FRUITCAKE, 1.

1978 Wheeler & Kerby *Steel Cowboy* (film): That old fruitburger!

fruitcake *n.* [sugg. by phr. *nutty as a fruitcake*; see NUTTY] **1.** a crazy, eccentric, or silly person; in phr. **go fruitcake** to go crazy.

1942 in *AS* LI (1976) 215: If you had lost…I guess you would have gone fruitcake. **1945** in *AS* (Oct. 1946) 238: *Fruitcake.* An insane sol-dier; one who is bomb-happy. **1949** Gordon & Kanin *Adam's Rib* 20: "Crazy when you married her?"…"Certainly. A fruit cake." **1949** Shane & Cooper *City Across the River* (film): That fruitcake…ain't got all his marbles. **1954** Schulberg *Waterfront* 191: Terry shook his head in disbelief. "Boy, what a fruitcake you are!" **1958** Heinz *Professional* 120: Man, you're nutty….Real fruitcake. **1972** *Sanford & Son* (NBC-TV): Know what I think? He's a fruitcake. **1976** in *AS* LI 215: The audience is going fruitcake, 'cause they know the answer. **1994** *N.Y. Times* (Jan. 10) D 6: People polarizing the discussion: you're either seri-ous or you're a fruitcake.

2. an effeminate male homosexual; FRUIT, 4.—used deri-sively.

1960 Hoagland *Circle Home* 232: I'm even looking for a fruitcakes' club, to use the sailors that are going to pour in here. **1965** Trimble *Sex Words* 84: Fruitcake…A male Homosexual. **1967** P. Roth *When She Was Good* 208: A real honest to God…fruitcake, just like you hear about. **1971** M. Miller, in *N.Y. Times Mag.* (Jan. 17) 48: Pansy, fairy, nance, fruit, fruitcake, and less printable epithets. **1978** in *Maledicta* VI (1982) 22: Male homosexual…*fruit, fruit puff, fruitcake.* **1992** *Northern Exposure* (CBS-TV): You're not one of them *fruitcakes* are you? **1993** Styron *Tidewater Morning* 36: It wasn't a *she,*…but a *he.* He was a White Russian fruitcake.

fruiter *n.* a homosexual man, esp. a fellator.—used derisively.

*ca*1918 in *Immortalia* 47: When he swore he was a fruiter the king/ Took down his royal pants. **1927** Rosanoff *Manual of Psych.* (ed. 6) 208: *Fruit, fruiter, fairy,* a passive homosexual who practices irrumation. **1928** Panzram *Killer* 157: A face artist is an exceptionally well-experi-enced fruiter. One who knows his bananas better than an amateur. **1941** in Legman *Limerick* 67: No faggot, no fairy, no fruiter. **1966** Elli *Riot* 39: The fruiter stays here. **1973** W. Crawford *Gunship Cmndr.* 100: The American MP had told his Viet pals that Stavros was a fruiter. **1977** Bunker *Animal Factory* 124: The first word I got was that he's a fruiter, but then I found out he isn't, at least not overt.

fruit factory *n.* a psychiatric hospital.

1967 Campbell *Hell's Angels on Wheels* (film): What fruit factory you guys come from?

fruit farm *n.* a psychiatric hospital.

1966 Susann *Valley of Dolls* 354: She was locked in a fancy fruit farm! **1978** *UTSQ*: Insane asylum…*looney farm, crazy house, nut house, fruit farm.*

fruit fly *n.* **1.** *Homosex.* (see quots.).

1966–71 Karlen *Sex. & Homosex.* 160: All sorts of people—fruit flies, drag queens, closet queens, leather freaks. *a*1972 B. Rodgers *Queens' Vernacular* 87: Fruit fly…woman who enjoys the company of gay men. **1972** *Anthro. Linguistics* (Mar.) 102: *Fruit Fly* (n.): A heterosexual female who associated with male homosexuals. **1988** R. Snow *Members of Committee* 3: What do you call a woman who prefers the company of

gay men?…*Fag Hag, Fruit Fly.*

2. an idiot; FRUITCAKE, 1.

1987 *Miami Vice* (NBC-TV): Why should I believe anything a fruitfly like you has to say?

fruithead *n.* a silly or crazy person.

1955 Nabokov *Lolita* 115: The fruithead!…He should have nabbed *you!*

fruit hustler *n. Police.* a man who robs or extorts money from male homosexuals; (*also*) a male homosexual prostitute.

1959 J. Rechy, in *Big Table* I (No. 3) 15: Masculine vagrants— "fruithustlers." **1963** Rechy *City of Night* 92: Male hustlers ("fruihus-tlers"/"studhustlers"). **1969** Whittemore *Cop!* 141: Your former schoolmate, she seems to think that Rudolph James was a fruit hustler (a male prostitute). **1972** Wambaugh *Blue Knight* 31: I stopped by the arcade and saw a big muscle-bound fruit hustler standing there. **1987** J.B. Harris *Cop* (film): It doesn't explain getting kickbacks from fruit hustlers. **1991** C. Fletcher *Pure Cop* 200: You'd refer to him as a male prostitute. We [*sc.* police officers] refer to him as a fruit hustler.

Fruitliner *n. Trucking.* a White Motor Co. Freightliner. *Joc.*

1971 Tak *Truck Talk* 66: Fruitliner: truckese for a White Freightliner tractor. **1976** Dills *CB 1977* 41: Fruitliner: truck made by White.

fruit-loop *n.* [sugg. by *Froot Loops,* a trademark for a sweetened breakfast cereal, and FRUIT, *n.,* 4 & 5] **1.** a crazy or eccentric person; FRUITCAKE, 1; (*also*) an effeminate homosexual man; FRUIT, 4.

1984 Algeo *Stud Buds* 2: An extremely dull teacher…*fruitloop.* **1987** G. Trudeau *Doonesbury* (synd. comic strip) (Feb. 19): If our study of self-esteem is to be taken seriously, we can't afford to be seen as a bunch of fruit-loops. **1987** *Wkly. World News* (May 26) 2: Pansy Preacher's Ghost Haunts Church Picnic…Nobody knows just what the fruit-loop spook was up to. **1989** "Capt. X" & Dodson *Unfriendly Skies* 158: Many of these guys [male flight attendants] have to take a lot of rib-bing…"Great Airborne Fruit Loops." **1993** *Quantum Leap* (NBC-TV): Hey, fruit loop! Where are your tights?

2. FAG-TAG.

1980 Birnbach *Preppy Hndbk.* 219: Fruit loop *n.* Same as fag tag. **1993** (quot. at FAG TAG).

fruit-picker *n.* a man posing as a male prostitute who black-mails or robs homosexual men. Hence **fruit-picking,** *adj.*

1971 Rader *Govt. Inspected* 6: I was detached, like a fruit-picking pro. *a*1972 B. Rodgers *Queens' Vernacular* 87: Fruit picker one who black-mails or robs homosexuals.

fruit ranch *n.* FRUIT FARM.

1985 *Maledicta* VIII 117: Fruit ranch. psychiatric unit.

fruit salad *n.* **1.** *Mil. Av.* easy prey.

1918 *Atlantic Mo.* (May) 691: And if I had been a Hun!…Oh, man! you were fruit salad! Fruit salad, I tell you! I could have speared you with my eyes shut.

2. *Mil.* an array of military service ribbons and decorations, as worn on a uniform.

[**1929** Nordhoff & Hall *Falcons* 228: *Bananas* was the *poilu* word for decorations.] *1943 Hunt & Pringle *Service Slang* 33: *Fruit salad.* A large collection of medal ribbons which runs to three or more rows. **1944** *Reader's Dig.* (Sept.) 76: Any member of the Armed Forces who wears a lot of campaign ribbons on his chest is wearing "fruit salad." **1945** *Collier's* (Oct. 6) 30: Fruit salad. That's what they call [ribbons] in the Army. I had a bunch of those ribbons myself after the last war. **1946** Nason *Contact Mercury* 208: He displayed his…fruit salad of campaign ribbons and decorations, a triple bar, three ribbons to the row. **1952** Cope & Dyer *Petty Officer's Guide: Fruit Salad.* (Slang). Ribbons worn on uniform. **1960** MacCuish *Do Not Go Gentle* 360: An' looka the pretty ribbons. Where'd ya get the fruit salad, cousin? My, my, the Purple Heart, too. **1966** King *Brave & Damned* 36: Any decoration a GI gets, the brass has to get his fruit salad first. **1971** Flanagan *Maggot* 267: Midberry was surprised at how many medals Maguire wore. "Fruit salad," he said, laughing. **1978** in Higham & Williams *Combat Aircraft* 48: A tough little captain with a "fruit salad" on his chest. **1991** K. Dou-glass *Viper Strike* 12: Sam Magruder had racked up an impressive display of fruit salad…including both the Silver Star and the Distinguished Flying Cross.

3. [sugg. by the parti-colored appearance] a random combi-nation of psychotropic drugs in capsule or tablet form. Usu. *Joc.*

1969 Lingeman *Drugs A to Z* 80: *Fruit salad.* Among teen-agers, a game in which each participant takes one pill from every bottle found in the family medicine cabinet. **1972** N.Y.U. student: A *fruit salad* is when you just grab handfuls of pills and don't give a shit what they are. As long as you think they'll get you high. **1975** *DAS* (ed. 3).

fruit shaker *n. Police.* FRUIT-PICKER.

1963 Gann *Good & Evil* 43: A...purse-snatcher, a...junkie...and two large...men known as "fruit shakers."...The last two individuals are con men...[who] prey on perverts by representing themselves as police officers....They tell the victim they'll forget all about everything for a hundred dollars.

fruit wagon *n.* **1.** an ambulance; MEAT WAGON.

1952 *Harper's* (Apr.) 29: "If you squawk, you leave the docks, most likely in the fruit wagon," said one longshoreman. (The "fruit wagon" is the ambulance.)

2. (see quot.).

1989 *Newsweek* (Nov. 6) 8: *Fruit wagon* or *tanker*: The [garbage] truck itself.

fruity *n.* FRUIT, 4.

1953 Brossard *Saboteurs* 120: The fruities' dank, convoluted world.

fruity *adj.* **1.** *Stu.* (see quot.).

1900 *DN* II 37: *Fruity*, adj. 1. Easy, requiring no work. 2. Desirable.

2. crazy.

1929–30 J.T. Farrell *Young Lonigan* 39: He's a sap. I tell you he's fruity. **1949** McMillan *Old Breed* 115: "By then," said a corporal, "everybody was acting fruity." **1958** Bloch *Psycho* (film): You think I'm fruity, don't you? **1960** Serling *Stories from Twilight Zone* 8: This fruity old man....It just never ended and it never got any better. **1970** C. Harrison *No Score* 64: If they really believed it they were both fruity as a nutcake. **1970** Quammen *Walk the Line* 162: Those old dames are driving me batty. Fruity! **1971** Wynn *Glass House* (CBS-TV): He's goin' fruity workin' in that laundry room. **1977** Univ. Tenn. student: He went a little fruity and went out strangling women and quoting Shakespearean lines while he was doing it.

3. homosexual.

1940 Zinberg *Walk Hard* 74: Haven't been near a girl in months. Max and Happy must think I'm fruity 'cause I don't talk about having a girl. **1942** "D. Ormsbee" *Sound of American* 143: He was as fruity as [hell]. **1966** Neugeboren *Big Man* 29: I mean, we got a lot of real fruity guys. **1971** Curtis *Banjo* 172: Top pansy's just as fruity as the bottom one. **1973** W. Crawford *Stryker* 25: You go fruity in the joint. **1978** De Christoforo *Grease* 17: Ya fruity fags.

fry *n.* **1.** [fr. FRY, *v.*, 6] *Black E.* a process by which curly hair is straightened.

1976 Calloway & Rollins *Moocher & Me* 182: Mash me a fin, gate, so I can cop me a fry.

2. *Narc.* the hallucinogen LSD.

*a***1990** E. Currie *Dope & Trouble* 140: PCP...took me higher than...fry.

¶ In phrase:

¶ **get a fry on** to get angry. Cf. FRY, *v.*, 5.

1956 W. Brinkley *Don't Go Near Water* 98 [ref. to WWII]: Listen, Griffin,...don't get a fry on. Don't let Nash make you feel insecure.

fry *v.* **1.a.** to punish or reprimand severely.

1919 V. Lindsay *Golden Whales* 16: Phillips Brooks for heresy was fried. **1954–60** in *DAS*: *Fry*...to chastise or be chastised. **1962** Quirk *Red Ribbons* 197: You know, the other day I got drunk and kicked down the door of the BOQ....They're going to fry my ass for that. **1971** Dahlskog *Dict.* 25: *Fry*...to reprimand severely. **1980** Berlitz & Moore *Roswell* 67: I heard that the brass fried him later on for putting out that press release. **1985** Sawislak *Dwarf* 35: The governor really fried Jimmy McGrath's behind. **1986** *Heart of the City* (ABC-TV): Van Duzer will fry us for this.

b. to be punished or reprimanded severely.

1954–60 (quot. at **(a),** above). **1983** *Good Morning America* (ABC-TV) (Apr. 22): I was the only one in the courtroom interested in the truth. And I fried for it.

2.a. to be executed in the electric chair.

1928 in E. Ferber *One Basket* 331: She can't get away with that with no jury....I bet she fries. **1929** in *OEDS*. **1930** Bodenheim *Roller Skates* 143: Don't fry on that hot seat for nothing. **1935** Saunders *Std. Equipment* 137: I ain't gonna fry just so you rats can take it on the lam. **1954** E. Hunter *Runaway Black* 7: People fried for homicide. **1980** Kotzwinkle *Jack* 76: If they catch us, we'll fry. **1993** *N.Y. Review of Books* (Sept. 23) 3: Boasting that he would see his stepdaughter's killer fry.

b. Esp. *Und.* to execute or cause to be executed in the electric chair.

1933 Ersine *Prison Slang* 38: *Fry, v.* To electrocute. **1931–34** in Clemmer *Prison Comm.* 332: *Fry,* v.t. To electrocute. **1936** in Partridge *Dict. Und.* 270: That scar will fry you, Simon. That and your finger-prints. **1938** in *AS* (Apr. 1939) 90: *Fry him.* Electrocute. "The law is certain to fry him." **1946** "J. Evans" *Halo in Blood* 202: I built up a case against Sandmark. You could probably have fried him with it too. **1950** Rackin *Enforcer* (film): You think Mendoza will let me fry him? **1953** Paley *Rumble* 169: What the hell they going to get if they fry him? **1966** G.L. Rockwell, in *Playboy* (Apr.) 79: No, but we have an electric chair in Sing Sing that's already done a great deed for America by frying the Rosenbergs. **1990** *U.S. News & W.R.* (June 18) 20: Dianne would have fried Willie Horton, personally.

3. to develop or occur; COOK.

1944–49 Allardice *At War* 11: What the hell's fryin' here?

4.a. to ruin (a person); *(also)* to impair (the mind).

1960 C.L. Cooper *Scene* 234: We've really got the thing to fry your ass—photographs. **1971** Dahlskog *Dict.* 10: *Brains fried, get (one's),* to get high on drugs. **1972** West *Village* 204: If we tripped one of those things up at My Hue some night, it would really fry us. **1977** Butler & Shryack *Gauntlet* 171: If Ben said the President of the United States was out to fry his ass, that was good enough for Josie. **1980** Univ. Tenn. student: He fried his mind on dope. **1989** S. Robinson & D. Ritz *Smokey* 220: He'd been frying his brain with coke.

b. *Stu.* to fail (an examination).

1980 *N.Y. Times Mag.* (Sept. 7) 130: We were into some heavy booking [*i.e.* studying] so we wouldn't fry our eccy midterm.

c. to take drugs, esp. LSD; get high.

1989 G.C. Wilson *Mud Soldiers* 140: I started...frying again on acid. *a***1990** E. Currie *Dope & Trouble* 102: I was frying for four *days* one time....Took twenty-six hits of LSD.

5. to infuriate.

1961 Boyd *Lighter Than Air* 10: What fries me is how worried you are that you might fly an hour or two a month more than somebody else. **1982** Knoxville, Tenn., woman, age *ca*40: Now that really fries me to death! **1983** *Special Assignment* (AP Radio Network) (Feb. 27): It just *fries* me that he can get up there and proclaim National Bible Week.

6. [cf. FRY, *n.*, 1] *Black E.* to straighten the hair of.

1968 Halsell *Soul Sister* 67: Black celebrities came regularly to be "shown" (head shaved) or "fried" (the kinks removed).

¶ In phrases:

¶ **fry (one's) mind** to astonish; stun. Cf. 1971, 1980 quots. at **(4.a.),** above.

1972 N.Y.U. student: Man, that really fried my mind! **1980** *N.Y. Times* (Dec. 28) V 6: Howard Siler, American bobsledder, after reading a newspaper story that quoted Willie Davenport, the Olympic hurdler-turned-bobsledder, as saying that all bobsledders were rich and white: "That fried everyone's mind."

¶ **go fry an egg!** mind your own business! Also vars.

*****1841** in *OED*: Fry your eggs, Gandelot, and leave other people to fry theirs. *a***1889** in Barrère & Leland *Dict. Slang* I 387: You vas no goot, go and vry your faces. **1889** in *Ibid.*: Fry your face, go and (American and English), low slang expression addressed to a thin-faced, lean man. **1926** Dunning & Abbott *Broadway* 216: PEARL (*under her breath, as she turns away*). Go fry an egg. **1928** Nason *Sgt. Eadie* 311 [ref. to 1918]: "Fry your face!" howled Eadie. *Ibid.* 365: Fry your ear! **1944** *Slanguage Dict.* 59: *Go fry ice*—get going. **1988** Univ. Tenn. instructor: Tell him to go fry his ass!

FSH *n.* (see 1990 quot.).

1969 in Tuso *Vietnam Blues* 78: Oh, FSH! **1990** in *Ibid.* 251: *FSH*: A fighter pilot war cry, often uttered in exasperation; may mean "Fight! Shit! Hate!"...which were supposed to be the only essential activities for a genuine fighter pilot; or may mean "Fuckin' shit hot!" which can indicate high praise, great joy, or even ironic contempt.

F.T.A. *interj. Army.* "fuck the Army."—usu. considered vulgar.

1958 "Harde" *Lusty Limericks* 44: Marching Song of the F.T.A. (Fuck The Army). **1963** Doulis *Path* 32: "And what does FTA stand for, Specialist?"..."Sir...excuse me....The initials stand for "Fuck the Army." **1969** *N.Y. Times Mag.* (May 18) 122: Some of the blacks gave the closed-fist militant salute and several soldiers shouted "F.T.A."—initials which recruiting sergeants insist stand for "Fun, Travel, and Adventure" but which most soldiers recognize as a suggestion of what should be done to the Army. **1970** Just *Military Men* 67: The slogan is F.T.A., which means Fuck the Army. **1984** Riggan *Free Fire* 109: New helmet covers with none of that FTA stuff written in ballpoint pen on them.

FTG *interj.* [see quot.] TGIF (Thank God It's Friday).

1964 Kaufman *Down Staircase* 54: It's FTG (Friday Thank God). *Ibid.* 67: Another FTG.

FTW *interj.* "fuck the world."—usu. considered vulgar.

1972 R. Wilson *Forbidden Words* 113: F.T.W. A slogan of Hell's Angels...meaning *fuck the world.* **1980** hand-lettered sign in Univ. Tenn. student dormitory window: F.T.W.! **1981** *Easyriders* (Oct.) 68: F.T.W. **1987** *Village Voice* (N.Y.C.) (July 14) 19: F.T.W. on the top [of the tattoo], M.O.D. on the bottom. He reads off, "Fuck The World, Method Of Destruction."

fu *n.* [orig. unkn.] *Narc.* marijuana.

1936 in E.L. Abel *Marihuana Dict.* 40: The drug and cigarettes containing it are known as "fu." **1937** C.L. Cooper *Here's to Crime* 333: It is now being called "fu." **1946** in *DAS.*

FUBAR /ˈfuˌbar/ *adj.* [*fucked up beyond all recognition; sugg. by* SNAFU] **1.** Orig. *Mil.* thoroughly botched or confused. Occas. as n., v. Also **fubar'd.** *Joc.*

1944 *Yank* (Jan. 7) 8: The FUBAR Squadron....FUBAR? It means "Fouled Up Beyond All Recognition." **1944** *Newsweek* (Feb. 7) 61: Recent additions to the ever-changing lexicon of the armed services: *Fubar.* Fouled up beyond all recognition. **1944** in Tobin *Invasion Jour.* 48: The Italian campaign was SNAFU for so long....SNAFU...means, Situation Normal All Fouled Up—with, of course, an unprintable variation in the most common use....To be FUBAR is much worse. It means Fouled Up Beyond All Recognition. **1952** Uris *Battle Cry* 114: Fubar on the nets and you can louse up an entire landing team. *Ibid.* 300: A full-scale fubar'd mess. **1957** Myrer *Big War* 119: What's to this yarn about you being a fubar character from the word advance? **1972** Davidson *Cut Off* 30 [ref. to WWII]: An even stronger superlative was Fubar—Fucked Up Beyond All Recognition. **1982** *Daily Beacon* (Univ. Tenn.) (Feb. 3) 2: Move it, fubar! **1987** *Daily Beacon* (Univ. Tenn.) (Apr. 9) 4: I already have a name picked out for my license plate. ..."FUBAR." Figure it out for yourself. [*Hint*]...beyond all repair. **1990** Rukuza *W. Coast Turnaround* 196: And the situation? FUBAR.

2. thoroughly intoxicated.

1985 Univ. Tenn. student: *Fubar* means drunk. Like, "Man, I was fubar last night." **1991** Eble *Campus Slang* (Fall) 2: *Fubar*—very drunk.

FUBB *adj.* [sugg. by FUBAR] Orig. *Mil.* "fucked up beyond belief." *Joc.*

1952 *Time* (Aug. 18) 6: Snafu and cummfu are a bit old hat in Washington, along with tarfu ("things are really"), fubar ("beyond all realization"), fubb ("beyond belief"). **1979** Homer *Jargon* 162. **1983** K. Weaver *Texas Crude* 40: F.U.B.B. Fucked Up Beyond Belief.

FUBIO *interj. Mil.* (see quot.). *Joc.*

1946 *AS* (Feb.) 72: The final word came after V-J day, FUBIO. Its description of the post-war attitude...meant "F— You, Bub, It's Over."

FUBIS *interj. Army.* (see quot.). *Joc.*

1967 *DAS* (Supp.) 685: *Fubis* Fuck you, buddy, I'm shipping (out). Army use since c1960.

fuck *n.* [see ety. and note at FUCK, *v.*] **1.a.** an act of copulation; (*hence*) a person considered as a sexual partner.—usu. considered vulgar.

***1680** in *OEDS*: Thus was I Rook'd of Twelve substantial Fucks. ***ca1684** in *Ibid.*: A little fuck can't stay our appetite. ***1763** in J. Atkins *Sex in Lit.* IV 154: Then just a few good fucks, and then we die. ***ca1775** *Frisky Songster* 21: She could not get one poor f—k. ***a1850** in Cary *Slang of Venery* I 91: Well mounted as with speed,/Famed for his strength as well as speed,/Corinna and her favorite buck/Are please'd to have a flying f—k. **1860** in Neely *Lincoln Encyc.* 155: When Douglas found his chances were scarcely worth a shuck/He bade his Delegates, go home, to take a little fu—. ***ca1866** *Romance of Lust* 35: I wished to quietly enjoy a fuck. **1867** in Doten *Journals* II 949 [in cipher]: Me & my love have had this far just one hundred good square fucks together. ***1879** *Pearl* 127: Oh! What a nice fuck! **1888** *Stag Party* 42: Adonis...gave her a most systematical fuck. **1899** *Memoirs of Dolly Morton* 249: Here goes for the fust fuck. **1923** *Poems, Ballads, & Parodies* 22: He was working like a son of a bitch/To get another fuck. **1928** in Read *Lexical Evidence* 55: Me and my wife had a fuck. **1934** "J.M. Hall" *Anecdota* 26: Every time you threw a fuck into me I put a penny in the bank. **1934** H. Miller *Tropic of Cancer* 78: He has absolutely no ambition except to get a fuck every night. ***1936** Partridge *DSUE* 305: She's a good f[uck]. **1938** H. Miller *Trop. Capricorn* 104: Into each...one...I throw an imaginary fuck. **1947** Willingham *End As a Man* 240: A fuck for a buck. **1956** in Cheever *Letters* 178: You've just talked yourself out of a fuck. **1972** Rodgers *Queens' Vernacular* 87: Was Tyrone a good

fuck? **1990** L.B. Rubin *Erotic Wars* 75: All she wanted was "a good clean fuck."

b. copulation.—usu. considered vulgar.

***ca1675** in R. Thompson *Unfit for Modest Ears* 49: If giufted [*sic*] Men before now sweare and Rant/(Then surely I for Fuck may Cant). ***1687** in Burford *Bawdy Verse* 179: Half ten Guineas spent in Wine and Fuck. ***a1720** in D'Urfey *Pills* VI 266: She'd dance and she'd caper as wild as a Buck,/And told *Tom the Tinker,* she would have some—. **1918** in Carey *Mlle. from Armentieres* II (unp.): The S.O.S. was sure out of luck,/They stayed behind and got all the—. **1938** H. Miller *Trop. Capricorn* 104: The place is just plastered with cunt and fuck.

2.a. [cf. sim. sense devel. of E ModE *foutre* < MF *foutre* 'to copulate (with)'] a jot; a goddamn.—usu. constr. in phr. of the sort *not worth a* or *not care a.*—usu. considered vulgar. [The *ca*1790 quot. remained unpublished until 1977. Tucker's satirical poem ("The Discontented Student") concerns a collegian who cannot make love to his bride by night because of thoughts of his books, yet cannot concentrate on his studies by day. Sense seems to demand that the excised phrase in its final line be "a fuck." The only plausible alternative, "a *foutre*," though well attested in 18th-C. English and perhaps adequate to the sense, is unlikely to have been considered obscene by a satirist who elsewhere wrote *bum* in full (p. 134).]

*ca*1790 in St. G. Tucker *Poems* 144: Our scholar every night/Thinks of his books; and of his bride by light..../"My wife—a plague!—keeps running in my head/In ev'ry page I read[,] my raging fires/Portray her yielding to my fierce desires."/"G— d— your books!" the testy father said,/"I'd not give — for all you've read." ***1917** in E. Wilson *Prelude* 184: An English soldier on the boat: "I down't give a fuck if the bowt goes dahn, it doesn't belong to me!" ***1929** Manning *Fortune* 48 [ref. to WWI]: They don't care a fuck 'ow us'ns live. **1931** Dos Passos *1919* 200 [ref. to 1919]: The bosun said it was the end of civilization and the cook said he didn't give a f—k. **1934** H. Miller *Tropic of Cancer* 22: Nobody gives a fuck about her except to use her. **1935** T. Wolfe *Death to Morning* 74 [ref. to 1917]: I don't give a f— what ya t'ought. **1936** in Oliver *Blues Tradition* 246: When I first met you I thought I fell in good luck,/Now I know you ain't worth a—. **1946** in J. Jones *Reach* 61: It dont mean a *fuck* to me. **1960** Sire *Deathmakers* 44: They don't give a fuck about you. **1965** Reeves *Night Action* 86: It mattered not a fuck. **1969** N.Y.C. man, age *ca*30: Doesn't that pull on your heartstrings? Or don't you give a rusty fuck? **1969–71** Kahn *Boys of Summer* 107: Rocco's a helluva man, but that don't mean a fuck. **1974** R. Carter *16th Round* 53: What makes you think that I give a fuck about you—or the horse you came to town on? **1972–76** Durden *No Bugles* 9: Nobody gives two fucks. **1977** Dowd *Slap Shot* (film): It don't make a fuck's bit of difference. **1979** D. Thoreau *City at Bay* 36: Who gives a rusty fuck about some wino?

b. anything whatsoever.—constr. in negative.—usu. considered vulgar.

1970 in *Rolling Stone Interviews* 429: They didn't play fuck. **1971** *Nat. Lampoon* (Dec.) 58: That croaker don't know fuck.

c. (used with *like, as,* or *than* as an emphatic standard of comparison).—also constr. with *a.*—usu. considered vulgar.

1938 in Legman *Limerick* 393: The colloquial comparative, "hotter than a Persian fuck." **1976** C.R. Anderson *Grunts* 61 [ref. to 1969]: To them it was still "hotter than fuck and rising." **1980** Whalen *Takes a Man* 272: "You in pain, man?"..."It stings like a fuck." **1983** Thickett *Outrageously Offensive* 60: It's raining like a fuck outside. **1980–86** in Steffensmeier *Fence* 5: You sure as fuck don't go around telling people: I'm a fence! **1988** "N.W.A." in L. Stanley *Rap* 236: I'm sneaky as fuck when it comes to crime. *a*1989 in Kisseloff *Must Remember This* 72: It was no good, that's all, and you suffer like a fuck. **1991** in *RapPages* (Feb. 1992) 67: Lawnge's production is dope as fuck.

d. a bit of difference.—constr. in negative.—usu. considered vulgar.

1984 Sample *Racehoss* 198 [ref. to 1950's]: It don't make a fuck who it is.

3. semen (now *rare*); in phr. **full of fuck** full of sexual desire or (*broadly*) energy.—usu. considered vulgar. Cf. BULL FUCK.

***ca1866** *Romance of Lust* 390: The cunt full of fuck only excited him the more. ***a1890–93** *F & H* III 80: *Fuck*, subs....The seminal fluid. *Ibid.* 85: Like a straw-yard bull, full of fuck and half-starved....A friendly retort to the question, "How goes it?" *i.e.,* "How are you?" **1916** Cary *Venery* I 98: Full of fuck.—Ready to work. **1938** "Justinian" *Amer. Sexualis* 23: *Full of fuck,* amorously potent. **1993** *Farmer's Step-Daughter,* on

USENET discussion group alt.sex.stories: She had thought often about what it would be like to let [him] shoot a full load of his fuck into her face. *Ibid.*: She felt the warm fuck filling her mouth, coating her tongue and draining back toward her throat.

4. a despicable person, usu. a man.—usu. considered vulgar. [See note at **(2.a.)**, above.]

1927 [Fliesler] *Anecdota* 188: You bloomin' fuck. **1927** in E. Wilson *Twenties* 399: You oughtn'ta be a prizefighter, yuh fuck—yuh ought to be a bootblack! **1933** Ford & Tyler *Young & Evil* 40: Take that fuck McAllen. **1934** H. Roth *Call It Sleep* 414 [ref. to *ca*1910]: Yer an at'eist, yuh fuck, he hollers. **1942** in Perelman *Don't Tread* 46: I was that superior fuck who smiled patronizingly and observed…"Recent statistics show that the French have the greatest land army in the world." **1946–50** J. Jones *Here to Eternity* ch. xxxvi: I told you, you dumb fuck. **1958** T. Berger *Crazy in Berlin* 136: Go on, you fuck, or I'll take ya apart. **1967** Hersey *Algiers Motel* 134: Them fucks took my tape recorder. **1968** J.P. Miller *The Race for Home* 294 [ref. to 1930's]: "He said he don't, you dumb fuck," Dawg said. **1970** Byrne *Memories* 117: Come in off of there, you dumb fuck. **1972** B. Harrison *Hospital* 50: I swear I thought that fuck was going to offer me a bribe to save Tessa's life. **1973** Schiano & Burton *Solo* 80: He's the meanest fuck in town. **1973** P. Benchley *Jaws* 191: You lying fuck! **1987** Santiago *Undercover* 63: Don't bother with this fuck. **1991** "Who Am I?" in L. Stanley *Rap* 383: He was a big-ass fuck.

5. an evil turn of events; a cheat of fortune.—usu. considered vulgar.

1972 Pelfrey *Big V* 9: "Regulars by God." Conscripts by fuck. **1984** in Terkel *Good War* 306: Know what they did? They made him a lieutenant colonel and me a captain. Ain't that a fuck?

¶ In phrases:

¶ **flying fuck** see FLYING, *adj.*

¶ **for fuck's sake** for heaven's sake.—usu. considered vulgar.
1961 J. Jones *Thin Red Line* 16 [ref. to WWII]: Don't *talk* like that!…for fuck's sake. *****1966** G.M. Williams *Camp* 94: What'll we call you then for fuck's sake? *****1966** in *OEDS*. **1976** Schroeder *Shaking It* 20: An inmate kicked irritably at an uncooperative piece of machinery and announced succinctly that "the fuckin fucker's fucked, fer fuck sakes!" **1964–78** J. Carroll *B. Diaries* 26: Now he's on tour for fuck's sake. **1982–84** Chapple *Outlaws in Babylon* 191: *Farmers* for fucksakes.

¶ **fuck of** a wretched or splendid example of; hell of.—usu. considered vulgar.
1928 in Read *Lexical Evidence* 55: This is a fuck of a rain. **1942** H. Miller *Roofs of Paris* 121: It would be a fuck of a lot more interesting. **1970** Thackrey *Thief* 230: Oh, wow! What a fuck of a way for a couple hot-rocks like them to go out. **1973** Flaherty *Fogarty* 26: It was a fuck of a country that could scrimmage for souls. **1977** Bartlett *Finest Kind* 20: I'll have a fuckuva time getting back in. **1978** Truscott *Dress Gray* 219: It's gonna be one fuck of a long two months. **1982** C.R. Anderson *Other War* 171: Thanks a lot, Altizer. Thanks a fuck of a lot. **1985** Bodey *F.N.G.* 114: He's lost a fuckuva lot of blood.

¶ **holy fuck!** (used to express astonishment).—usu. considered vulgar.
1945 in Shibutani *Co. K* 202: Holy fuck! We're gonna freeze our ass off. **1967** *DAS* (Supp.) 690. *****1977** T. Jones *Incred. Voyage* 373: "Holy fuck!" I thought, "I've only got a mile of sea-room." **1983** Ehrhart *VN-Perkasie* 138: "Holy fuck," he muttered. **1989** Zumbro & Walker *Jungletracks* 89: Holy fuck, Lieutenant, kill 'em quick!

¶ **the fuck, 1.** (used as an expletive); the hell.—also constr. with *in*.—usu. considered vulgar. [The construction *why* or *what the puck* in *****1864 and *****a*1903 quots. is precisely synonymous with *why the devil* (see *EDD, OED2*); the similarity of both the phonetics and the construction may conceivably have influenced the development of the present usage of *fuck*.]
[*****1864** S. LeFanu, in *OED2* s.v. *puck, n.*: And why the puck don't you let her out?] [*****a*1903** in *EDD* s.v. *puck, n.*: What the puck are you doing?] **1934** H. Roth *Call It Sleep* 281 [ref. to *ca*1910]: An de nex' time watch out who de fuck yer chas— **1936** Levin *Old Bunch* 122: Where the f— you think you're trying to horn in?…Who the f— wants to ride in your robber hacks anyway? **1942** H. Miller *Roofs of Paris* 23: I don't know what the fuck to say. **1943** Tregaskis *Invasion Diary* 45: You f—g eight balls get the f— off this God-damn hill before I rap this rifle-barrel around your neck! **1945** in Shibutani *Co. K* 291: Where in the fuck's that truck? **1951** *Amer. Jour. Socio.* XXXVII 138: But what the f—, that's his business. *Ibid.* 140: Sure, they're a bunch of f—ng squares, but who the f— pays the bills? **1959** W. Burroughs *Naked Lunch* 33: How

in the fuck should I know? **1962** Mandel *Wax Boom* 273: I might blow my top…if people don't start leaving me the fuck alone! **1963–64** Kesey *Great Notion* 6: He don't even the fuck know! **1968** Schell *Military Half* 185: Abruptly, someone called out, "Where the fuck are we?" **1971** in L. Bangs *Psychotic Reactions* 86: Why'n the fuck d'ya think? **1977** Ill. photographer, age *ca*25: What the flying fuck is he talking about? **1979** *Nat. Lampoon* (Dec.) 59: I go to Medicine Hat, way the holy fuck up in fuckin' Alberta, Canada, man. **1966–80** McAleer & Dickson *Unit Pride* 128: "Did you ever see such a screwy bunch?"…"Guess the fuck I ain't." **1990** Bing *Do or Die* 218: What the fuck I want to change for?

2. absolutely not; the hell; like hell.—usu. considered vulgar.
[*****a*1950** Partridge *DSUE* (ed. 3) 1054: F*ck! like.…"certainly not!": low: late C. 19-20.] **1965** Linakis *In Spring* 50 [ref. to WWII]: "They don't keep you locked up."…"The fuck they don't." **1966** Keefe *The Investigating Officer* 184: "This one I happen to remember very well." "The fuck you do." **1970–71** Rubinstein *City Police* 328: "You ain't [arresting] my mother."…"The fuck I ain't." **1974** G.V. Higgins *Cogan's Trade* 4: The fuck you sell driving lessons to people. **1983** P. Dexter *God's Pocket* 65: The fuck I have, you think I'm crazy?

3. daylights; hell.—usu. considered vulgar.
1971 *Rolling Stone Interviews* 448: I even got another guy out of jail, a spade cat they'd…beat fuck out of. **1972** N.Y.U. student: There's only one thing left to do—beat the fuck out of you. **1975** Temple Univ. student: I felt like kicking the fuck out of the [computer] terminal, but I figured it would cost me $2,000. **1989** *Life* (July) 27: "This s---," literally, scares the f--- outta me."…girl, 15.

¶ **the fuck of it** the fun of it; the hell of it.—usu. considered vulgar.
1970 N.Y.U. student: I'd beat him up just for the fuck of it. **1976** Hayden *Voyage* 196: Take a look. Just fer the fuck of it. **1979** Nashville, Tenn., man, age 27: I went down there just for the fuck of it. **1985** Bodey *F.N.G.* 174: Doing it…just for the fuck of it. **1990** Bing *Do or Die* 123: Who's gonna die "for the fuck of it"?

fuck *adj.* describing, depicting, or involving sexual intercourse; pornographic; erotic.—used prenominally.—usu. considered vulgar.
1941 W.C. Williams, in Witemeyer *Williams-Laughlin* 61: You've got to feed 'em the bunk—love and war and all the old fuck stuff. **1942–44** in *AS* (Feb. 1946) 33: F—k Books, *n.* Sexy pulp magazines. **1950** in Hemingway *Sel. Letters* 694: They start writing those over-detailed fuck scenes. **1966** Fry *TS.*: Will show fuck movies. **1967** Mailer *Vietnam* 27: Pretending to write a…fuck book in revenge. **1967** Rechy *Numbers* 105: I got some fuck-movies at home. **1969** in Estren *Underground* 11: The State University will never contain any "fuck books." **1975** T. Berger *Sneaky People* 60: He's got a fuck-book there, too. **1976** "N. Ross" *Policeman* 105: Phil liked to hear fuck stories on stakeouts. **1981** *Nat. Lampoon* (Aug.) 60: Let's turn this solemn occasion into a real fuck party. **1984** J.R. Reeves *Mekong* 12: Bullshitting, kidding, telling fuck jokes. **1987** Zeybel *Gunship* 6: I'd watched the live fuck shows in the Angeles night clubs.

fuck *v.* [E reflex of a widespread Gmc form; cf. MDu *fokken* 'to thrust, copulate with'; dial. Norwegian *fukka* 'to copulate'; dial. Sw *focka* 'to strike, push, copulate' and *fock* 'penis'; the recent forms *fug, fugg* are printed euphem. and do not represent pronun.]

1.a. to copulate with; (*intrans.*) to copulate.—usu. considered vulgar. Also in transf. senses. Hence **fucking,** *n.* [The date of the initial citation may be as early as 1450–75; its orig. form has the E words (from *fuccant*—the -*ant* is a pseudo L third person pl. ending—to *heli*—i.e., Ely, a town in Cambridgeshire) in cipher, sugg. that the word was already taboo. The quot. translates as "They [*sc.* the monks] are not in heaven/because they fuck the wives of Ely." For asterisks in 1848 and *****1854 quots., see note at FUCKING, *adj.* The centuries-old cultural taboo against use of this word has weakened somewhat in recent decades. For general discussions see A.W. Read, "An Obscenity Symbol," *AS* IX (Dec. 1934), 264–78; L. Stone, "On the Principal Obscene Word of the English Language," *Inter. Jour. Psycho-Analysis* XXXV (1954), 30–54.]

*****a*1500** in *Verbatim* (May 1977) 1: Non sunt in celi/quia fuccant uuiuy·

of heli. *ca1500 in W. Dunbar *Poems* 40: He clappit fast, he kist, he chukkit...ʒit be his feiris he wald haif fukkit. *1535–36 in D. Lindsay *Works* I 103: Ay fukkand lyke ane furious Fornicatour. *ca1550 in D. Lindsay *Satyre* 88: Bischops ar blist howbeit that thay be waryit/For thay may fuck thair fill and be unmaryit. *a1568 in *F & H* III 80: Allace! said sche, my awin sweit thing,/Your courtly fukking garis me fling. *1598 J. Florio, in *OEDS: Fottere,* to iape, to sard, to fucke, to swive, to occupy. *ca1610 in Burford *Bawdy Verse* 63: She's a damn'd lascivious Bitch/And fucks for half-a-crown. *ca1650 in Wardroper *Love & Drollery* 187: Had ever maiden that good luck.../O 'twould invite a maid to ——. *1683 in *F & H* III 80: From St. James's to the Land of Thule,/ There's not a whore who f—s so like a mule. *ca1684 in Ashbee *Biblio.* II 337: Then arse they fuck, and bugger one another. *1730 N. Bailey *Dict.: To Fuck*...a term used of a goat; also *subagitare foeminam.* 1766 in Eliason *Tarheel Talk* 185: As to the flesh tho', I cannot say I have occasion for any violent longings, as I have reduced F—n almost to a regular matrimonial system. 1778 in Connor *Songbag* 24: He often times fuck't the old whore in the Night. *1785 Grose *Vulgar Tongue: To f—k.* To copulate. *ca1800 in Holloway & Black *Later Ballads* 223: Jenny cries nay, I won't F—k for a shilling. 1845 in A. Johnson *Papers* I 218: In other words...he was "Chewing drinking & *fucking* his way to the Legislature." 1848 [G. Thompson] *House Breaker* 42: I was going to **** that same little *blowen,* in Boy Jack's *crib.* 1849 Doten *Journals* I 40: There are plenty of girls in Talcahuano and the principal business carried on is—F---ing. *1854 in *AS* IX (1934) 271: [According to the actor David Garrick,] when it was asked what was the greatest pleasure, Johnson answered *******. 1864 in Rable *Civil Wars* 161: Have you any sisters? If you have I should like to read them. That was my business before I came into the service, and now I am fucking for Uncle Sam. 1867 in Doten *Journals* II 949 [in cipher]: The best fucking on the face of the earth. 1877 in Stallard *Glittering Misery* 146: Didn't you ---- that girl yourself? *1879 *Pearl* 203: Can't you just fuck her in the bum? *1882 *Boudoir* 226: She f—d me as dry as a stick, last night. 1888 *Stag Party* 219: Sodom...was the worst place for wild fucking of all descriptions...(barring Chicago). *1909 in Joyce *Sel. Letters* 184: I feel mad to...fuck between your...bubbies. 1916 M. Cowley, in Jay *Burke-Cowley Corres.* 22: He drinks, fucks, swears,...is popular with girls. 1918 in Carey *Mlle. from Armentières* II (unp.): Over the top with the best of luck,/The first over there is the first to ——. 1923 *Poems, Ballads, & Parodies* 47: A bull dog fucked him in the ear. 1938 in J. O'Hara *Sel. Letters* 134: Oh, and Mrs. —— ——, who wanted everybody to get drunk and start fucking. 1940 in T. Williams *Letters* 11: I am taking free conga lessons...and fucking every night. 1947 in Cheever *Letters* 125: I want to write short stories like I want to fuck a chicken. 1964–66 R. Stone *Hall of Mirrors* 194: Is she fuckin' other people? 1968 P. Roth *Portnoy* 145: They have a whore in there, kid, who fucks the curtain with her bare twat. 1982 R.M. Brown *So. Discomfort* 195: Great ladies don't even admit fucking with their husbands. 1985 E. Leonard *Glitz* 88: Iris was fucking *somebody. a1990* E. Currie *Dope & Trouble* 205: You know, they fucked, and everything.

b. (in var. vulgar similes and provs.). See also FOUR-F's.

*ca1677 in Rochester *Complete Poems* 137: My heart would never doubt,/...To wish those eyes fucked out. 1916–22 Cary *Sex Vocab.* I (s.v. *copulation*): *Fucking like a mink.* To copulate frequently. [1928 Benét *John Brown's Body* 99: The whole troop grumbled and wondered, aching/For fighting, fleeing or fornicating/Or anything else except this bored waiting.] 1942 McAtee *Supp. to Grant Co.* 6 [ref. to 1890's]: *Mink*", *"fuck like a,* phr., with the senses of enthusiastically, enduringly, intensively. 1952 in Legman *Dirty Joke* 284: I'm going to fuck you till your ears fly off. 1964 Peacock *Drill & Die* 140: He'd fuck a snake if someone would hold its head. 1965 Linakis *In Spring* 60: The fellow said the fräulein's name was Gertie and she fucked like a mink. 1968 Tauber *Sunshine Soldiers* 117: You know what you look like, Pea-zer, stupid? You look like a monkey trying to fuck a football. 1970 W.C. Woods *Killing Zone* 112: I wish you were here too, so I could fuck your brains out. 1971 S. Stevens *Way Uptown* 241: And 'fore you could fuck a duck they went into the whole white-guilt thing. 1972 in *Penthouse* (Jan. 1973) 116: Emily is fucking like a minx. 1974 Univ. Tenn. student: I'd like to fuck her eyes out. 1975 Wambaugh *Choirboys* 248: You don't look big enough to fight, fuck or run a footrace. 1976 Kalamazoo, Mich., man, age 29: My father used to say, "Now you're ready to fight, fuck, or run a footrace." It meant all ready to go. 1976 Hayden *Voyage* 663: Make or break. Fuck or fall back. 1976 Braly *False Starts* 204: I thought I should have been able to fuck a bear trap if someone had glued a little hair on it. 1977 in Lyle & Golenbock *Bronx Zoo* 17: Jesus Christ! You looked like a monkey trying to fuck a football out there! 1978 Alibrandi *Killshot* 235: These kids today don't know whether to fuck, fight or hold the light. 1979 Univ. Tenn. student: He was mad enough to fuck a duck. 1980 in *Penthouse* (Jan. 1981) 26: By that time she was so hot that she would have fucked a rock pile if she thought there was a snake in it. 1980 Di Fusco et al. *Tracers* 35: Sounds

like...two skeletons fuckin' on a footlocker. 1983 Ehrhart *VN-Perkasie* 14: While every...hippie in Trenton fucked her eyeballs out. 1984 K. Weaver *Texas Crude* 34: That guy tryin' to change a tire looks like a monkey tryin' to fuck a football. 1986 in *NDAS: Fuck like a bunny*...To copulate readily and vigorously. 1988 C. Roberts & C. Sasser *Walking Dead* 143: Everybody said you'd fuck a snake if somebody held its head.

c. (used as an interj. to express dismay, disbelief, resignation, surprise, etc.; often constr. with *it,* occ. elaborated); shit; hell.—usu. considered vulgar. Cf. **(3.a.),** below. [Perh. infl. by the inarticulate sound of disgust illustrated in early bracketed quots.]

[*1681 in Otway *Works* II 102: Fogh, ye Lowsy Red-coat rake hells.] [*1697 Vanbrugh *Provoked Wife* 82: Phugh, pox, sit an hour!] [1915–16 Lait *Beef, Iron & Wine* 10: Fugh— me for the pleasant things of life!] *1929 Manning *Fortune* 160 [ref. to WWI]: A man...uttered under his breath a monosyllabic curse. "Fuck." 1933 in H. Miller *Letters to Emil* 131: Fuck it! I'm starting off bad with my colors. 1934 "J.M. Hall" *Anecdota* 146: "Oh, fuck!" he cried in disgust. 1934 in J. O'Hara *Sel. Letters* 93: My message to the world is Fuck it! 1935 in Oliver *Blues Tradition* 231: Whee...tell 'em about me! Fuck it! 1938 "Justinian" *Amer. Sexualis* 23: Fuck a dead horse! 1945 in Shibutani *Co. K* 301: Fuck, we're gonna be in the army for another year anyway. *a1949 D. Levin *Mask of Glory* 64: Fuck yes. *Ibid.* 80: Fuck no. 1959 Kerouac *Dr. Sax* 40: Ah fuckit, Zagg—helmets is helmets. 1962 in B. Jackson *In the Life* 157: I'm no gambler because if I tried to gamble, fuck, I'd lose my goddamned drawers. 1964–66 R. Stone *Hall of Mirrors* 51: Fuck no, I ain't stoppin' you. 1973 P. Benchley *Jaws* 194: "Fuck!" he said, and he threw the full can into the wastebasket. 1980 Garrison *Snakedoctor* 186: Well, fuck-a-doodle-doo! 1981 Stiehm *Bring Men & Women* 263: One woman officer...told of stopping an activity because a frustrated woman had said, "Oh, fuck." 1982 W.Va. woman, age *ca*27: Well, fuck a snake! Look who's here! 1985 E. Leonard *Glitz* 207: I thought, fuck, the guy's a natural. 1987 Chinnery *Life on Line* 208: Brian...said, "Oh, f***." Then he died. 1990 L.B. Rubin *Erotic Wars* 180: Fuck it, why not? 1993 *New Yorker* (Oct. 6) 185: She was a girl who wouldn't say "Jesus!" but would...say, "Well, *fuck!*"

2.a. to cheat; victimize; deceive; betray.—usu. considered vulgar. Hence **fucking,** *n.* Cf. syns. SCREW and FRIG. [At the 1866 quot., there is a note by the notary public following *fucked* that reads: "Before putting down the word as used by the witness, I requested him to reflect upon the language he attributed to Mr Baker, and not to impute to him an outrage upon all that was decent. The witness reiterated [*sic*] it, and said that it was the word used by Mr Baker."]

1866 in Berlin et al. *Black Mil. Exper.* 789: Mr Baker replied that deponent would be *fucked* out of his money by Mr Brown. 1927 [Fliesler] *Anecdota* 76: It looks like you've fucked yourself out of a seat. 1932 in H. Miller *Letters to Emil* 114: But they fucked me all right. Fucked me good and proper. 1934 H. Miller *Tropic of Cancer* 49: One by one I've fucked myself out of all these free meals which I had planned so carefully. 1935 in E.E. Cummings *Letters* 136: "Fuck" has been changed to "trick" in new [*New English Weekly*] today arriving with editor's comments. 1942 *ATS* 312: Cheat; defraud...*fuck (out of).* 1951 in *Inter. Jour. Psycho-An.* XXV (1954) 39: To "get fucked" is to be made a "sucker." 1954 Yablonsky *Violent Gang* 75: Although I hang with them for protection, I fuck everybody. They try to burn me, I get my blade, I'll get 'em all but good. 1959 W. Burroughs *Naked Lunch* 179: You're trying to fuck me out of my commission! 1960 Sire *Deathmakers* 44: They're out to fuck you. The whole fucking world. So fuck them first. 1961 Baldwin *Another Country* 77: We been fucked for fair. 1965 in J. Mills *On Edge* 8: You thought you were going to get laid, and what you really got was fucked. 1969 Whittemore *Cop!* 27: So it's the Puerto Ricans that fuck the Puerto Ricans. They sell their own people the worst shit. 1972 Halberstam *Best & Brightest* 66 [ref. to 1961]: Carl Kaysen...brought in the news that the Soviets had resumed atmospheric [nuclear] testing. The President's reaction was simple and basic and reflected the frustrations of that year. "Fucked again," he said. 1978 Strieber *Wolfen* 201: But he ain't gonna fuck me. He must think I'm some kind of schoolboy. 1979–82 Gwin *Overboard* 195: As Mick tried to teach me, "Top dog fucks the bottom dog. That's the law of the jungle." 1983–86 G.C. Wilson *Supercarrier* 67: "Being in the Russian military is like being in a chicken coop," Belenko would say in his lectures. "You know you're going to be fucked, you just don't know when."

b. (in vars. implying crueler deception or brutalization).— usu. considered vulgar.

1945 in Shibutani *Co. K* 115: We'd get fucked out of Saturday afternoon though....In this place they always fuck you in the ass when they get a chance. **1965** in H.S. Thompson *Shark Hunt* 114: We read/a newspaper and saw where just about everybody/had been fucked in the face/or some other orifice or opening.../by the time the Chronicle went to press. **1974** R. Carter *16th Round* 257: The cops knew that they were fucking me with a dry dick. **1977** Torres *Q & A* 75: You got ten big ones....We will fuck Reilly in the ass. **1978** R. Price *Ladies' Man* 106: Me? I went to [college]. I got fucked up the ass...I dropped out of school with six months to go.

c. to exploit to one's own benefit.—usu. considered vulgar.
1985 M. Baker *Cops* 282: I'm going to stay here, but I'm going to fuck the job to death. They're not going to get anything out of me.

3.a. (used as an imprecation or oath); God damn; to hell with; curse.—usu. considered vulgar. [Cf. earlier parallel use of BUGGER, *v.*, and **(1.c.)**, above; also FUNGOO, *interj.*; often accompanied by the corresponding gesture described at FINGER, *n.*]
*ca*1895 in Randolph & Legman *Blow Candle Out* 755: Fuck You. [**1905** *Independent* (Mar. 2) 486: "D—n you, Jack, I'm all right," is being gradually adopted by the lords of the forecastle and quarter deck alike in place of the old time motto of generous consideration that was world famous, "Remember Your Shipmates."] *ca*1915 in Brophy & Partridge *Long Trail* 229: Dieu et mon droit./F— you, Jack, I'm all right. *ca*1916 in Gammage *Broken Yrs.* 126: Goodbye and —— you! *ca*1916–18 in *N & Q* (Nov. 19, 1921) 417: —— you, Jack, I'm in the lifeboat. *ca*1918 in Randolph & Legman *Blow Candle Out* 754: Fuck 'em all. *1918 in E. Wilson *Prelude* 213: I've often seen a couple o' chaps bringin' back a wounded prisoner and they get tired of leadin' 'im and one o' 'em says: "Aw, fuck 'im, Jock! Let's do 'im in," and they shoot 'im and leave 'im there. *1914–21 Joyce *Ulysses* 603 [ref. to 1904]: God fuck old Bennett. **1922** Cummings *Enormous Room*: F— it, I don't want it. **1924** in Hemingway *Sel. Letters* 113: I have lost the fine thrill enjoyed by Benj. Franklin when entering Philadelphia with a roll under each arm. Fuck Literature. *ca*1925 in K. White *First Sex. Revolution* 94: Fuck you. **1929** in E. O'Neill *Letters* 341: But I am forgetting our old watchword of the Revolution—F--k 'em all! **1931** Dos Passos *1919* 249 [ref. to WWI]: Hey sojer your tunic's unbuttoned (f—k you buddy). **1934** H. Roth *Call It Sleep* 420 [ref. to *ca*1910]: Yuh crummy bastard....Fuck yiz! **1934** H. Miller *Tropic of Cancer* 280: He was for eating a sandwich. "Fuck that!" I said. **1935** McCoy *They Shoot Horses* 37: "F— you," Gloria said. **1942** Tregaskis *Guadalcanal Diary* (Sept. 1): "F--- you, Mac," he said, indulging in the marines' favorite word. **1947** Mailer *Naked & Dead* 169 [ref. to WWII]: I'm fugged if I'm going to tote a box all the way back. **1949** Van Praag *Day Without End* 215: "Orders be fucked!" he muttered. **1952** Bellow *Augie March* 397: Oh, fuck Oliver! **1961** Peacock *Valhalla* 425 [ref. to 1953]: Eat the apple and fuck the Corps in '54! **1965** Linakis *In Spring* 206: "Are you?" "Fucked if I know." **1966** Fariña *Down So Long* 244: Double-fuck the letter. **1967** Yablonsky *Hippie Trip* 206: I said fuck this shit and moved over here. **1974** 2nd Lieut., U.S. Army, age 24: A big expression is "Fuck 'im if he can't take a joke." It means you don't care what the fuck happens to the guy. **1978** Maupin *Tales* 70: Fuck you very much. **1983** Ehrhart *VN-Perkasie* 55 [ref. to 1967]: Fuckin' ARVN got better equipment than we do. Eat the apple and fuck the Corps. **1976–84** Ettinger *Doughboy* 8 [ref. to 1918]: Fuck you. If you got any sisters, fuck them too. **1985** J. Dillinger *Adrenaline* 102: He drew a few stares in his...Bermudas and...sport shirt. Fuck 'em if they couldn't take a joke. **1990** P. Munro *Slang U.* 85: Fuck you! I did not go out with Dave last night!

b. (also in stronger, more vivid, or more elaborate curses).—usu. considered vulgar.
1940 Del Torto TS: Fuck you where you breathe. **1958** *Stack A Lee* 1: So fuck Billy the Lion in his motherfucking ass. **1962** Mandel *Wax Boom* 72 [ref. to WWII]: I fuck you all where you breathe. **1967** Rechy *Numbers* 68: Fuck you in the ears, muscle-ladies. **1968** Gover *JC* 164: As for the board [of directors], fuck it with a sixpenny nail. **1969** N.Y.C. man, age *ca*45: When we were kids we'd say, "Fuck 'em all, big and small, right up the nostrils!" **1970** Conaway *Big Easy* 94: "*Chinga su madre!*" "Fuck you in the heart," he rejoined. **1970–71** Higgins *Eddie Coyle* 92: Fuck you, lady,...*and* the horse you rode in on. **1971** Selby *Room* 134: You're a rotten lousy son of a bitch and I fuck you where you eat, and your mother too. **1973** Scorsese & Martin *Mean Streets* (film): I fuck you where you breathe! I don't give two shits for you! **1975** S.P. Smith *Amer. Boys* 309: Fuck you in your mouth, Red! **1972–76** Durden *No Bugles* 78: Fuck you...'n' the horse you rode in on. **1977** Bunker *Animal Factory* 117: If she's been a jive-ass bitch, fuck her in her ass. **1978** Truscott *Dress Gray* 370: Yeah? Well, fuck them and their marching orders. **1979** *Nat. Lampoon* (Dec.) 17: Fuck you in the eye. **1980** Gould *Ft. Apache* 51: Fuck them and the horse they rode in on....Fuck 'em all, big and small. **1979–82** Gwin *Overboard* 185: Fuck you in the mouth, kiddo. This job is mine. **1983** S. Wright *Meditations* 297: Fuck you in the ear. **1984** Caunitz *Police Plaza* 254: Fuck 'em where they breathe. **1984** Sample *Racehoss* 217 [ref. to *ca*1960]: Fuck all ya'll rat dead in the ass! **1987** N. Bell *Cold Sweat* 11: So fuck you both in the heart.

c. to cease or abandon, esp. suddenly; ditch.—usu. considered vulgar.
*1925 *Englische Studien* LX 279 [ref. to WWI]: *Fuck it*...meant much the same as *chuck it*, "put a sock in it"—stop talking; or even "clear out." **1965–70** J. Carroll in *Paris Review* (No. 50) 103: No solution coming so I fuck it and start to yell. **1973** R. Roth *Sand in Wind* 150: I got the idea to fuck everything and head for California. **1979** Charyn *7th Babe* 174: Hell...why don't we fuck baseball camp and stay right here? **1984** W. Henderson *Elvis* 8: For two cents I'd fuck this job! Two goddamn cents —.

4.a. to harm irreparably; finish; do for.—esp. in passive.—usu. considered vulgar. Hence **fucking**, *n.* [The *ca*1775 quot. was discovered as this book was going to press; thus, the current definition is not in chronological order. This sense is the earliest figurative sense of the verb known.]
*ca*1775 *Frisky Songster* 37: Hey ho! the wind did blow, down they fell,/Breeches and petticoat into the well./O, says the breeches, I shall be duck'd./Aye, says the petticoat I shall be f--k'd./O, how my old grannum will grumble and grunt,/When she's got ne'er a petticoat to cover her c—t. **1929** Hemingway *Farewell* 206 [ref. to WWI]: "It's all —ed," I said. **1929** in Fitzgerald *Corres.* 226: Now you make them read the word cooked (+ fucked would be bad) *one dozen times*. **1931** Dos Passos *1919* 7 [ref. to *ca*1914]: I guess I'm f—d for fair then. **1934** H. Miller *Tropic of Cancer* 48: We'll take his lousy review and we'll fuck him good and proper....The magazine'll be finished. **1935** L. Zukofsky, in Ahearn *Pound/Zukofsky* 160: Time fucks it. **1937** Binns *Laurels Are Cut Down* 200 [ref. to 1920]: We did all their fighting. Now that we've quit, they're —ed. **1938–39** Dos Passos *Young Man* 257: Less said everything was the matter, American Miners was f—d to hell and back, the boys in Slade County was f—d and now here was this christbitten hellbound party line f—g them proper. **1941** in Hemingway *Sel. Letters* 532: We are fucked in this war as of the first day. **1947** Mailer *Naked & Dead* 206: Even *they* can't fug me this time. **1958** Schwitzgebel *Streetcorner Research* 50: If a kid went and fucked up, you just don't go out and give him a fuckin'. **1967** Mailer *Vietnam* 111: He, Rusty, is fucked unless he gets that bear. **1970** M. Thomas *Total Beast* 137: He was fucking old Sunshine with that knife! **1970** Byrne *Memories* 90: The snowdrifts and slush made darting and dodging impossible. I was, in short, fucked. **1972** Jenkins *Semi-Tough* 159: We got too many ways to fuck 'em. **1984** Wallace & Gates *Close Encounters* 155 [ref. to 1968]: I drew a breath and continued, man to man. "Vietnam fucked you, Mr. President, and so, I'm afraid, you fucked the country." **1984** K. Weaver *Texas Crude* 3: I got you faded, fucked, and laughed at. **1989** S. Lee *Do the Right Thing* (film): I oughta fuck you just for that.

b. to botch; bungle; FUCK UP, 1.—also constr. with *it.*—usu. considered vulgar.
1969 L. Sanders *Anderson Tapes* 43: It might fuck the whole thing. **1973** Karlin, Paquet, & Rottman *Free Fire Zone* 108: Pellegrini, you fucked it again. *Ibid.* 110: Them niggers fucked the roof—built this house so *fast*. **1972–79** T. Wolfe *Right Stuff* 243: Oh, it was obvious...that Grissom had just *fucked it*...that was all.

5.a. to trifle, toy, meddle, or interfere; fool; play; *(hence)* to harass, tease, or provoke; mess.—constr. with *with.*—usu. considered vulgar. [1940 quot. is euphem.; cf. FUCK AROUND, 2, and, semantically, FRIG, *v.*, 3.]
[**1940** R. Chandler *Farewell, My Lovely* 5: I'm feelin' good...I wouldn't want anybody to fuss with me.] **1946** in Shibutani *Co. K* 391: The Boochies won't fuck with him because they don't want to catch shit. **1948** in Hemingway *Sel. Letters* 644 [ref. to *ca*1915]: I learned early to walk very dangerous so people would leave you alone; think the phrase in our part of the country was not fuck with you. Don't fuck with me, Jack, you say in a toneless voice. **1953** M. Harris *Southpaw* 239: Do Not F--- With Me. **1962** Killens *Heard the Thunder* 221 [ref. to WWII]: Why do you fuck with me so much, man? There are millions of other people in the Army. **1965** C. Brown *Manchild* 189: It was practically a twenty-four-hour-a-day job trying to get some money to get some stuff to keep the [heroin] habit from fucking with you. *Ibid.*: If you fuck wit that rent money, I'm gon kill you. **1968** Tauber *Sunshine Soldiers* 169:

No one fucks with chow. You eat when you're supposed to. **1968** Gover *JC* 100: Can't rezist fuckin with him jes one more time. **1970** Thackrey *Thief* 209: Took the carburetor off and soaked it in solvent and put it back on. Fiddled and fucked with it. And finally it seemed to be okay again—running good. **1968–71** Cole & Black *Checking* 113: I...turn around and scream, "Don't fuck with my mind!" **1968–71** Cole & Black *Checking* 198: Stay the fuck away....And if you think I'm fucking with you, try me. **1971** *Playboy* (June) 216: I don't like anyone fucking with my head while I'm doing [a movie]. **1977** Bunker *Animal Factory* 46: "Tony tells me you're good at law." "I used to fuck with it. No more." **1977** L. Jordan *Hype* 230: Them people are fuckin' with us, man! **1981** Crowe *Fast Times* 92: They're just fuckin' with us! **1990** Bing *Do or Die* 122: 'Cause he fucked with my food...took one of my French fries.

b. *Trans.* to trifle or interfere with.—usu. considered vulgar.

1989 S. Lee *Do the Right Thing* (film): Look, don't fuck me, awright?

¶ In phrases:

¶ **fuck a duck, 1.** get out! go to hell!—usu. constr. with *go.*—usu. considered vulgar.

[***1785** Grose *Vulgar Tongue*: Duck f-ck-r. The man who has the care of the poultry on board a ship of war.] [**1932** *AS* VII (June) 332: *Go milk a duck*—"mind your own business."] **1933** in H. Miller *Letters to Emil* 133: Tell her to go fuck a duck! [**1946** Gresham *Nightmare Alley* 47: Go frig a rubber duck.] **1953–55** Kantor *Andersonville* 183: Aw, go fuck a duck. [**1958** Chandler *Playback* 168: Why don't you go kiss a duck?] **1965** Beech *Make War in Madness* 67: Go fuck a duck, Otis. **1973** *TULIPQ* (coll. B.K. Dumas): You mother, go fuck a duck. **1977** in Partridge *Dict. Catch Phr.* (ed. 2) 104: *Go fuck a duck!* "Get lost!" "Beat it!" Current, 1920s [in US], now virtually dead. *a***1990** Poyer *Gulf* 389: Bernard gave him a go-to-hell sneer....He could fuck a duck.

2. to engage in sexual promiscuity.—constr. with *will* or *would.*—usu. considered vulgar.

*a***1930** in Legman *No Laughing Matter* 177: Fuckaduck Films. [**1951** Thacher *Captain* 40: Hambley, as the saying goes, would frake a drake.] **1972** *Nat. Lampoon* (Apr.) 34: You can get anything from an ugly chick....Really foul, but they'll fuck a duck.

3. (used as an interj. to express anger or astonishment).—usu. considered vulgar.

1934 H. Miller *Tropic of Cancer* 36: Well, fuck a duck! I congratulate him just the same. **1954–60** *DAS.* **1972–76** Durden *No Bugles* 234: I looked at Ski. He looked away. Lord fuck a duck. **1976** Hayden *Voyage* 420: Well, now, fuck a duck, whaddaya know about that? **1977** Bredes *Hard Feelings* 250: Operation Rollaway!...Fuck a *duck!* **1990** P. Munro *Slang U.* 85: *Fuck a duck!* Damn!

4. (see 1971, 1979 quots. at **(1.b.),** above).—usu. considered vulgar.

¶ **fucked by the fickle finger of fate** thwarted or victimized by bad fortune.—usu. considered vulgar. *Joc.* Cf. *fickle finger* s.v. FINGER, *n.*

1944–46 in *AS* XXII 56: *Flucked by the flickle flinger of flate* [*sic*]. Doomed by Army snafu. **1957** E. Brown *Locust Fire* 93 [ref. to 1944]: The fickle finger would foul you sure in the end. It would goose you over the edge. Fouled by the fickle finger of fate. **1968** D. Stahl *Hokey* 220: I was being totally and fatally fucked by the fickle finger of fate. **1972** R. Wilson *Forbidden Words* 104: *Fucked by the fuckle* [*sic*] *finger of fate,* (said by those whose plans are thwarted.) **1976** in Partridge *DSUE* (ed. 8) 433: *Fucked by the fickle finger of fate*...Current in U.S. (student) circles at least several years earlier [than WWII]. *a***1986** in *NDAS*: Fucked by the fickle finger of fate.

¶ **fucked [up] and far from home** in a hopeless situation.—usu. considered vulgar. See also *fed up, fucked up, and far from home* s.v. FED UP.

*1936 Partridge *DSUE* 305: *F*cked and far from home.* In the depths of misery, physical and mental: a military [catch phr.]: 1915. ***1950** Partridge *DSUE* (ed. 3) 1054: *F*cked-up and far from home*...dates from 1899. **1972** R. Wilson *Forbidden Words* 117: When the IRS was through auditing my return, I was fucked and far from home.

¶ **fuck 'em all but six** Esp. *Mil.* to hell with them all.—usu. considered vulgar. Also in elaborated and euphem. vars.

1916–17 in *Tenn. Folk. Soc. Bull.* XXI (1955) 100: Cuss 'em all, cuss 'em all,/Cuss 'em all but six! **1932** Nicholson & Robinson *Sailor Beware!* 22: "All but six." "And you can use them for pallbearers." **1931–34** Adamic *Dynamite* 393 [ref. to ca1925]: The motto in a factory where I once worked was: "To hell with 'em all but six; save them for pallbearers!"

1950 Stuart *Objector* 216: "Screw the Army, the whole God-damned Army." "All but six....They'll need pallbearers." **1952** Uris *Battle Cry* [ref. to 1942]: "Fugg you guys and save six for pallbearers," Levin shouted. **1920–54** Randolph *Bawdy Elements* 120: Oh, fuck 'em all but six, and save them for pall-bearers. **1960** MacCuish *Do Not Go Gentle* 116 [ref. to 1941]: Screw all but six and save them for pallbearers. **1972–76** Durden *No Bugles* 7: Dumb bastards. Fuck 'em all but eight. Leave six for pallbearers and two to beat the drums. **1987** *Nat. Lampoon* (June) 14: How about the famous Army saying "Fuck all of them but six and save *them* for pallbearers."

¶ **fuck me!** (used to express anger or astonishment); I'll be damned!—usu. considered vulgar. Also elaborated vars.

*1929 Manning *Fortune* 126 [ref. to WWI]: "Well, you can fuck me!" exclaimed the astonished Martlow. **1943** G. Biddle *Artist at War* 77: Teddy's run of literary allusions is a pleasant relief after the too concentrated diet of "fuck me's" and "fuck you's" of the G.I.'s. **1944–57** Atwell *Private* 64 [ref. to WWII]: F--- me, I'm not hangin' around here! **1958** Talsman *Gaudy Image* 197: Well, fuck me double...if it isn't Aphrodite Schultz in person. **1957–62** Higginbotham *USMC Folklore* 24: Fuck me dead! **1970** Wakefield *Going All the Way* 296: Fuck me in the teeth. What a fuckin piece of luck. **1973** Hirschfeld *Victors* 32: Fuck me blind! That hole ain't half done. **1977** Bredes *Hard Feelings* 293: I'm just trying to talk myself out of being scared shitless because, fuck me, I have to go down there. **1984** K. Weaver *Texas Crude* 28: Fuck me naked!, Fuck me a-runnin'! **1985** Dye *Between Raindrops* 315: Well, fuck me blind. OK, Lieutenant. Got the picture right here.

¶ **fuck (one's) mind** to astonish, intimidate, or befuddle.—usu. considered vulgar.

1966 Goldstein *1 in 7* 113: Mind-fucking is taking advantage of a student who is high on pot—and thus susceptible to suggestion. For instance: "You tell someone who's inhaled pot for a while that he's been holding his breath for twenty minutes, and he's liable to believe you. It really fucks his mind." **1968** Gover *JC* 137: Hey that sure would fuck some minds, huh. **1970** Landy *Underground Dict.* 84: *Fuck someone's mind v.* To persuade forcefully without regard for the feelings of those being persuaded. *a***1974** in *Adolescence* XIII (1978) 467: [Solitary confinement] fucks your mind, you keep saying you want to go home.

¶ **fuck the dog** see s.v. DOG.

¶ **fuck the duck** to loaf; *fuck the dog* s.v. DOG.—usu. considered vulgar.

1968–77 Herr *Dispatches* 57: I met a man in the Cav who'd been "fucking the duck" one afternoon, sound asleep in a huge tent. **1978** Selby *Requiem* 31: Well lets stop fuckin the duck and figure out how we can pick up the bread. **1979** L. Heinemann, in *TriQuarterly* (Spring) 180 [ref. to Vietnam War]: He was taking one of his famous naps—fucking the duck, we called it.

¶ **fuck wise** to act or speak like a know-it-all.—usu. considered vulgar.

1979 Gram *Blvd. Nights* 49: "Don't fuck wise!" shot back Chuco.

¶ **get fucked!** go to hell!—usu. considered vulgar.

*a1950 Partridge *DSUE* (ed. 3) 1054: F*cked!, go and get....mid C.19-20. **1966** Shepard *Doom Pussy* 151: We told him to go ahead and ask. And he did. And *we* said, "Get f-----." **1968** L.J. Davis *Whence All Had Fled* 218: "Get fucked," he said. **1986** Dye & Stone *Platoon* 16: Tell that dipshit to get fucked. *a***1990** Westcott *Half a Klick* 125: Tell him ta get fucked with a mule's dick, I don't care.

¶ **go fuck (yourself)** go to hell! get out! be damned!—usu. considered vulgar. Also vars. with other obj., esp. **go fuck your mother.** [*Go fuck your mother* is universally perceived as the most offensive and idiomatic imprecation in English.]

*ca1730 Haddington *Sel. Poems* 168: Go home and f—. [***1879** *Pearl* 210: He'd been told,/To bloody well bugger himself.] **1897** in Cary *Sexual Vocab.* II s.v. *fuck*: Go, and, f..k yourself....Get out of my cart and go and f..k yourself. [**1905** W.S. Kelly *Lariats* 273: If yer don't like 'em, go and puke yourselfs.] **1920** in Dos Passos *14th Chronicle* 306: As for an intellectual class it can go f— itself. ***1922** T.E. Lawrence *Mint* 99: "Go and fuck rattlesnakes," retorted Garner. **1929** D. Marquis, in Legman *No Laughing Matter* 149: Go fuck thy suffering self. **1931** Dos Passos *1919* 150 [ref. to WWI]: Joe got sore and told him to go f— himself. **1932** Hemingway *Winner* 152: F— yourself. F— your mother. F— your sister. **1933** in H. Miller *Letters to Emil* 126: Tell her to go fuck herself. **1938** R. Chandler *Big Sleep* 60: Go —— yourself. **1942** in D. Schwartz *Journs.* 88: "Then go fuck yourself!" said May, hanging up, enraged. **1947** Mailer *Naked & Dead* 12: Go fug yourself. [**1951** *African Studies* X 32: "Copulate with your mother!" Normally no insult could be more frightful.] **1955** Sack *Here to Shimbashi* 92: Sometimes they toss cigarettes to the MP's on patrol, and sometimes they have been known to shout, "Hey, GI —— your mother!" in English. **1959** N.Y.C. schoolboy, age 13: Aw, go fuck your mother in bed, you little prick! **1961** J. Baldwin *Another Country* 34: Drop dead, get lost, go fuck yourself. **1961** Granat *Important Thing* 80 [ref. to WWII]: You just go f---. [**1965** G. Legman, in *F & H* I (rev.) (1966 ed.) xxxix: Compare the Russian ultimate insult, "*Idy v kibini matri*" ("Go fuck your mother!").] **1967** Mailer *Vietnam* 94: Go fuck, D.J.'s got his purchase on the big thing. **1969** in Girodias *New Olympia Reader* 68: She [was] screaming, "Go fuck your mother." [**1976** C. Amuzie, in *Jour. Black Studies* VI 416: Among the Igbos, one could hear male and very old female adults cursing [in Igbo] as follows: "fuck your mother," "fuck your sister," "may a dog fuck your mother." These curses are perceived by the Igbos as among the worst.] **1976** J. Harrison *Farmer* 28: Oh go fuck yourself. **1973–77** J. Jones *Whistle* 320 [ref. to WWII]: "Appreciate it." "Go fuck." **1980** E. Morgan *Surgeon* 195: "Yeah," screamed the little girl. "Go fuck your cat, fuck your mother." [**1985** J.M.G. Brown *Rice Paddy Grunt* 122: The gook tells him, "*Du Mau, Du Mau*" (to fuck his mother, in Vietnamese).]

fuck *interj.* **1.** see FUCK, *v.*, 1.c.—usu. considered vulgar.
2. [phonological reduction of *fucked*, p.ppl. of FUCK, *v.*, 3] damned (if).—usu. considered vulgar.
1978 Maupin *Tales* 18: Fuck if I know. **1983** Ehrhart *VN-Perkasie* 143: Fuck if I'm stickin' around. **1984** Ehrhart *Marking Time* 123: Fuck if I know.
3. *the fuck*, 2 s.v. FUCK, *n.*—usu. considered vulgar.
1983 S. King *Christine* 147: "Turn out your pockets, Buddy."..."Fuck I will."

fuckable *adj.* **1.** sexually desirable.—usu. considered vulgar.
***a1890–93** *F & H* III 80: *Fuckable...Desirable.* **1938** "Justinian" *Amer. Sexualis* 23: *Fuckable*, sexually desirable (of a female). **1974** Lahr *Trot* 15: "I'd like to dip my wick into that." "Fuckable." **1973–77** J. Jones *Whistle* 233: She was...eminently fuckable. **1986** R. Campbell *In La-La Land* 3: Showing how brave, how manly, how fuckable he was.
2. sexually available.—usu. considered vulgar.
1977 Univ. Tenn. student: What you do is, you just come right out and ask her, "How fuckable are you?"

fuckaholic *n.* [FUCK, *v.*, 1.a. + -AHOLIC] a person who compulsively engages in promiscuous sexual intercourse.—usu. considered vulgar. *Joc.*
1981 Jenkins *Baja Okla.* 246: He's just a fuckaholic, is all he is. **1989** Knoxville, Tenn., man (coll. J. Ball): I'm getting to be a fuckaholic. **1989** Chapple & Talbot *Burning Desires* 294: Both were serious fuckaholics.

fuck-all *n.* **1.** absolutely nothing; the least bit; FUCK, *n.*, 3.a., 3.b.—usu. considered vulgar. Also as quasi-adj.
1918 Noyes *MS.* (unp.): *Fuck-all.*—(1) nothing. "There's not a fuck-all to do this afternoon." ***1919** *Athenaeum* (Aug. 1) 695: There is a very queer phrase denoting "nothing"—"— all!" No record of war slang is complete without it. ***1929** Manning *Fortune* 130 [ref. to 1916]: We all go over the top knowing sweet fuck-all of what we are supposed to be doing. **1939** Bessie *Men in Battle* 133: Nobody's seen fuck-all of 'em. **1941** in Legman *Limerick* 35: The cube of its weight.../Was four fifths of five eighths of fuck-all. *ca*1944 in A. Hopkins *Front & Rear* 54: The officers they know fuck all. *ca*1950 in Cray *Erotic Muse* 116: There was fuck-all else to do. **1961** Forbes *Goodbye to Some* 169 [ref. to WWII]: Nothin'. Absolutely fuckall nothin'. **1961** Hemingway *Islands* 400: But I am not going to put Willie and Ara and Henry into one of those burpgun massacres in the mangroves for fuck-all nothing. **1965** Linakis *In Spring* 74: Didn't a mean fuck-all to the ones that busted you. **1967** Kornbluth *New Underground* 91: The *Daily Mirror* carried thirteen thousand inches of advertising—and fuck-all to read. **1976** Univ. Tenn. student: That ain't worth fuck-all. **1976** Atlee *Domino* 160: They would have fuckall chance against us. **1978** Truscott *Dress Gray* 45: Said the supe...didn't know fuckall. **1979** in L. Bangs *Psychotic Reactions* 283: What have we got! Fuckall! **1980** Univ. Tenn. grad. student, age 31: I know fuck-all about Eliot!
2. (used as an expletive); hell.—usu. considered vulgar.
1938 in Hemingway *Sel. Letters* 466: It's been a fuck all of a six weeks. Nobody's got any social standing at all now who hasn't swum the Ebro at least once. **1958** Cooley *Run For Home* 138 [ref. to 1920's]: Who the fuck-all does he think he is?
3. a damn; a fuck.—usu. considered vulgar.
1958 Cooley *Run For Home* 20 [ref. to 1920's]: I don't give a fuck-all

what you think!

fuck-all *adv.* utterly; at all.
1961 Hemingway *Islands* 336: I feel fuck-all discouraged about things sometimes. **1991** O. Stone & Z. Sklar *JFK* (film): Don't matter fuck-all.

fuck-all *interj.* FUCK, *interj.*, 1.—usu. considered vulgar.
1918 Noyes *MS.* (unp.): *Fuck-all*....(2) Also used as an expression of disgust. "Oh fuck-all!" **1966** Reynolds & McClure *Freewheelin Frank* 29: FUCK ALL! I GOT THE CLAP.

fuckaround *n.* contemptuous treatment.—sometimes constr. with *play*.—usu. considered vulgar.
1970 in H.S. Thompson *Shark Hunt* 101: Well, to hell with it. You don't need publicity and I sure as hell don't need this kind of fuckaround. **1972** in *Ibid.* 123: A gig that was a...fuckaround from start to finish. **1980** Conroy *Lords of Discipline* 394: This is the last night we're going to play fuck-around with that bunch. **1984–87** Ferrandino *Firefight* 39: I'll teach you to play fuck around with me.

fuck around *v.* **1.** to engage in promiscuous sexual activity.—usu. considered vulgar.
1931 in H. Miller *Letters to Emil* 76: I fucked around with this one and that. **1942** H. Miller *Roofs of Paris* 201: Does she know that you've been fucking around with her father? **1951** *Amer. Jour. Socio.* XXXVII 138: Eddie f—s around too much; he's gonna kill himself or else get killed by some broad. And he's got a nice wife too. **1969** Crumley *One to Count Cadence* 100: Yes, I know my wife is fucking around. **1978** Schrader *Hardcore* 39: Your daughter was an absolutely clean girl, she never had rebellious or impure thoughts, she didn't fuck around. **1989** Sorkin *Few Good Men* 36: Don't fuck around with this one, Danny.
2. to play or fool around; trifle; mess.—usu. considered vulgar. [*Fuck about* in ***1922**, ***1929** exx. is the usu. BrE form; perh. cf. syn. *muck about* (***1856** in *OEDS*). 1938 quot. is euphem.]
[***1922** T.E. Lawrence *Mint* 49: I wasn't going to fuck about for those toffee-nosed buggers.] [***1929** Manning *Fortune* 17 [ref. to WWI]: They kept 'em fuckin' about the camp, while they sent us over the bloody top.] **1931** in H. Miller *Letters to Emil* 76: "My dear," she says. "I just couldn't stay away from you. I'm sick of all this fucking around." [*ca*1933 in Sevareid *Wild Dream* 39: What's the difference between a mountain goat and a soda jerk?...The soda jerk mucks around the fountain.] **1935** T. Wolfe *Death to Morning* 73 [ref. to 1917]: What are ya doin' here ya f— little bastards!—who told ya t'come f— round duh hangah? *Ibid.* 74: Don't f— aroun' wit' me, ya little p—. **1936** Dos Passos *Big Money* 313: If you f—k around it'll cost you more. [**1938** R. Chandler *Big Sleep* 66: So all you did was not report a murder that happened last night and then spend today foxing around so that this kid of Geiger's could commit a second murder this evening.] **1942** H. Miller *Roofs of Paris* 260: And here I am fucking around trying to get her to buy a camera. *ca*1944 in A. Hopkins *Front & Rear* 55: They fuck around but they never work. **1947** Mailer *Naked & Dead* 539: We're gonna move out in half an hour, so don't be fuggin' around. **1950** G. Legman, in *Neurotica* (Autumn) 13: I could stop fugging around writing pulp. **1952** Kerouac *Cody* 220: I stayed out all night and fucked around. **1954** Weingarten *Amer. Dict. of Slang* 141: *Stop f--king around.* Common in the street language. **1955** Yablonsky *Violent Gang* 48: We don't fuck around—man, when you want to whip one on, just call....Our boys are always ready. **1971** Torres *Sting Like a Bee* 34: He's just fucking around....He'll be O.K. **1978** *N.Y. Post* (Dec. 9) 13: I won't shoot to kill, but I'll shoot them so they know not to fuck around with me no more. **1981** T.C. Boyle *Water Music* 67: A sandstorm is nothin' to fuck around with.
3. to cheat or treat with contempt; make trouble for.—usu. considered vulgar.
[***a1900** in *EDD* s.v. *frig*: They are not going to frig me about.] **1960** Pollini *Night* 29: Why you fucking me around? **1970** A. Young *Snakes* 144: Big a juicehead as he is, he gon fuck me round over some gauge. **1970** E. Thompson *Garden of Sand* 328: Don't try to fuck me around, old man. **1970** T. Wolfe *Radical Chic* 125: They ripped off the white man and blew his mind and fucked him around like nobody has *ever* done it. **1973** W. Crawford *Stryker* 68: Don't try fucking me around. **1977** Bunker *Animal Factory* 105: "Would he kill somebody over that?" "Oh yeah...quick if he thought the guy was deliberately fuckin' him around."
4. to astonish; bring up short.—usu. considered vulgar.
1978 W. Brown *Tragic Magic* 139: *Sands of Iwo Jima.* That's the one that really fucked me around.

fuckass *n.* a despicable or contemptible fellow.—usu. considered vulgar.

   ca*1960 Partridge *DSUE* (ed. 5) 1099: *F*ck-arse.* A low term of contempt: C.20. **1968 Cuomo *Thieves* 219: LaSala was really a slob, old fuck-ass everybody called him. **1987** Kalamazoo, Mich., man, age 40: Whoever wrote that fuckass's script knew just what he was doing.

fuckass *adj.* contemptible.—used prenominally.—usu. considered vulgar.

   1961 J. Jones *Thin Red Line* 30 [ref. to WWII]: Any man'd leave it layin around's a fuckass soldier anyway. **1979** Univ. Tenn. student: I hate that fuckass course.

fuckathon *n.* [FUCK + mar*athon*] a prolonged period of esp. orgiastic sexual activity.—usu. considered vulgar. *Joc.*

   1968 in *Rolling Stone Interviews* 58: If you were at a fuck-a-thon, you'd have to know when a good fuck went down to know what's happening. **1972** *Anthro. Linguistics* (Mar.) 102: *Fuckathon* (*n.*): Refers to an extended period of sexual activity in which a large number of persons participate. **1982** Del Vecchio *13th Valley* 336: How could he confess to him that he'd been on a fuckathon?

fuck away *v.* to squander or idle away; PISS AWAY.—usu. considered vulgar.

   1975 S.P. Smith *Amer. Boys* 171: The others…fucked their bread away on booze.

fuckbag *n.* DOUCHEBAG; ASSHOLE.—usu. considered vulgar.

   1972 USAF A 1/c Taiwan, age 20 (coll. J. Ball): I wouldn't go out with that fuckbag if she was the last woman on earth.…Listen here, fuckbag. **1977** Univ. Tenn. student: Hi, fuckbag!

fuckboy *n.* a catamite; (*hence*) a man who is victimized by superiors.—usu. considered vulgar.

   [**1954** F.I. Gwaltney *Heaven & Hell* 233 [ref. to WWII]: Grimes loves the army and the army's using him for a screw-boy.] **1971** J. Blake *Joint* 67 [ref. to 1954]: They were known as pussyboys, galboys, fuckboys, and all had taken girls' names like Betty, Fifi, Dotty, etc., and were universally referred to as "she" and "her." **1974** R. Carter *16th Round* 76: A goddamned faggot, a fuck boy. **1973–76** J. Allen *Assault* 124: One or two slip through who aren't so obvious. There's a lot of them we call undercover fuck boys.

fuckbrain *n.* FUCKHEAD.—usu. considered vulgar. Hence **fuckbrained,** *adj.*

   1970 Whitmore *Memphis-Nam-Sweden* 35: Not at all like the lazy fuckbrain before him. *a*1981 Spears *Slang & Euphem.* 149: *Fuck-brained.* stupid. **1986** N. Jimenez *River's Edge* (film): You pot-head fuckbrain!

fucked *adj.* **1.** exhausted.—usu. considered vulgar.

   a*1950 Partridge *DSUE* (ed. 3) 1054: *F*cked,* adj. Extremely weary; (utterly) exhausted; late C. 19-20. **1987 G. Matthews *Little Red Rooster* 201: It's…time for sleep.…I'm totally fucked. ***1990** T. Thorne *Dict. Contemp. Slang* 190: *Fucked*…(of people) completely exhausted.

   2. FUCKED UP, 1.

   1955 in W.S. Burroughs *Letters* 257: The typewriter is fucked again.

   3. FUCKED UP, 2.a.—usu. considered vulgar.

   1965–66 in Maurer *Lang. Und.* 301: *Fucked* or *fucked up.* Stoned. **1970** Landy *Underground Dict.* 84: *Fucked*…Under the influence of a drug. **1972** Smith & Gay *Don't Try It* 202: *Fucked up.* High on heroin (sometimes other drugs): "He was so fucked up he couldn't even drive a car."…Also *fucked around, fucked over,* and just plain *fucked.* **1973** *TULIPQ* (coll. B.K. Dumas): Drunk…fucked to the max. **1976** in L. Bangs *Psychotic Reactions* 195: You're probably so fucked that it doesn't…hurt yet. **1990** P. Munro *Slang U.* 85: *Fucked*…drunk…under the influence of drugs.

   4. lacking in sanity or good sense; crazy.—usu. considered vulgar.

   1970 Landy *Underground Dict.* 84: *Fucked*…messed up; confused. **1975** in L. Bangs *Psychotic Reactions* 180: You're allll [*sic*] fucked.…I can do anything I want. **1978** B. Johnson *What's Happenin'* 64: "He don't care what he says as long as people notice him." "He's fucked, man." *Ibid.* 167: You guys are fucked. You don't even know what you talkin' about. **1981** C. Nelson *Picked Bullets Up* 31: Babich looked at me through jaundiced eyes. "Kurt, you're fucked." **1985** B.E. Ellis *Less Than Zero* 100: Girls are fucked. Especially this girl. **1990** *Nat. Lampoon* (Apr.) 97: They're fucked in the head.

   5. exceedingly bad or offensive; rotten; awful.—usu. considered vulgar.

   1971 in L. Bangs *Psychotic Reactions* 86: Some cat…made a really fucked album. **1973** *TULIPQ* (coll. B.K. Dumas): I had a fucked time last night.…That exam was really fucked. **1975** S.P. Smith *Amer. Boys* 58: Morgan [was] yelling at the top of his lungs about how fucked everything was while Padgett…egged him on. **1976** Schroeder *Shaking It* 121: I mean, like, the last stanza's completely fucked, man! **1978** Maupin *Tales* 92: Your karma is *really* fucked! **1980** Conroy *Lords of Discipline* 311: We're living in fucked times. **1985** J. Dillinger *Adrenaline* 115: "Want to know something fucked?"…"How fucked?" "We're outa gas." **1985** O'Bannon *Return of Living Dead* (film): First, I got a really fucked headache; then my stomach started cramping up. **1990** P. Munro *Slang U.* 85: *Fucked*…unfair. **1986–91** Hamper *Rivethead* 161: Squeezing rivets is fucked!

fucked duck *n.* DEAD DUCK.—usu. considered vulgar.

   1939 Bessie *Men in Battle* 133: If France don't come in now, we're fucked ducks. *Mucho malo.…Mucho fuckin' malo.* **1968** Spradley *Owe Yourself a Drunk* 30: I had twenty-three bucks when booked. Now they tell me I've only got $3.30. I guess I'm a fucked duck—I've got twenty days hanging.

fucked off *adj.* angry; PISSED OFF.—usu. considered vulgar.

   ***1940–45** in Page *Kiss Me Goodnight* 80: Because I'm fucked off, fucked off, fucked off as can be.…Fucked off lads are we. **1971** Dahlskog *Dict.* 25: *Fucked off.*…Angry; irritated; tee'd off. **1973** Pace Coll. student: *Fucked off* means the same as *pissed off.* **1974** N.Y.C. social worker, age 26: I've heard a few people say "He was really fucked off" when they meant "pissed off." This was in the past couple of years. **1977** Univ. Tenn. student: I'm really fucked off!

fucked out *adj.* exhausted from excessive copulation; (*hence*) utterly worn out.—usu. considered vulgar.

   ca*1866 *Romance of Lust* 443: Poor Mr. Nixon was evidently fucked out. **1934 H. Miller *Tropic of Cancer* 225: It is…the dry, fucked-out aspect of things which makes this crazy civilization look like a crater. **1942** H. Miller *Roofs of Paris* 259: She's as drunk as we're fucked out. **1945** in Hemingway *Sel. Letters* 605: Suffer like a bastard when don't write, or just before, and feel empty and fucked out afterwards. **1950** in Inman *Diary* 1480: I guess…Billy was just plain fucked out, the way he looked. **1966** Susann *Valley of Dolls* 121: And what should an ingenue look like? A fucked-out redhead with big tits? **1967** Schmidt *Lexicon of Sex* 42: Sexually exhausted; fucked out. **1969** Girodias *New Olympia Reader* 91: By Christ, you tired old bag, you're asleep. Fucked out. **1973** Roth *Sand in Wind* 239: The ones he had seen didn't have the fucked-out eyes of American prostitutes, and so many other American women. **1975** R.P. Davis *Pilot* 144: They called her the "fucked-out, boozy bitch" or the "FOBB." **1977** Univ. Tenn. student: No more pizza. I'm fucked out. **1977** Sayles *Union Dues* 144: It's a Monday, they're all fucked-out from the weekend. **1978** *Nat. Lampoon* (Oct.) 26: Gertrude was so fucked out that she never wanted to do it with anyone again. **1981** Hathaway *World of Hurt* 162: Must've got so fucked out in two days, you had to come back to rest up.

fucked over *adj.* **1.** FUCKED UP, 2.a.—usu. considered vulgar.

   1972 (quot. at FUCKED, 3). **1973** N.Y.U. student: *Fucked over* can mean very, very drunk. Like I've heard guys say, "I was fucked over last night. Man, I wasn't worth a dime." **1979** Univ. Tenn. student paper: [Drunk:] queezy, fucked over, stewed, zonked.

   2. FUCKED, 5.—usu. considered vulgar.

   1978 Wharton *Birdy* 197: You know,…this is really a fucked-over situation.

   3. FUCKED, 1.—usu. considered vulgar.

   1983 S. King *Christine* 257: You look like a sleepwalker. You look absolutely fucked over.

fucked up *adj.* **1.** Esp. *Mil.* ruined or spoiled, esp. through incompetence or stupidity; botched; chaotic; in difficulty; (*broadly*) messed up.—usu. considered vulgar. Also (esp. *Mil.*) in fanciful similes.

   1939 Bessie *Men in Battle* 133 [ref. to 1937]: The detail's all fucked-up. **1954–60** *DAS: Fucked up*…in trouble. **1961** Forbes *Goodbye to Some* 173 [ref. to WWII]: Their balance is all fucked up too.…They can't stay right side up. **1962** G. Ross *Last Campaign* 36: I never heard of such a fucked-up mess. *Ibid.* 293: The boxes are busted open, see. And the [machine gun] belts are all fucked up with snow. **1963** Doulis *Path* 108: Man, there ain't *ever* been such a fucked-up operation! **1964** H. Rhodes *Chosen Few* 118 [ref. to *ca*1950]: It don't make sense t'get fucked up on a humble. **1972** Pearce *Pier Head Jump* 49: They're as fucked up as a Mongolian fire and lifeboat drill. **1972–76** Durden *No Bugles* 1: Right off I knew things were gonna be fucked up as a picnic in a free-fire zone. **1976** Atlee *Domino* 53: My company has a reputation for quality, but we've been fucked up here like Hogan's goat. **1987** Kent *Phr. Book* 156: As fucked up as a Chinese fire drill.

2.a. heavily intoxicated by liquor or drugs.

*_ca_**1944** in Hopkins _Front & Rear_ 179: There was old Uncle Ned, he was fair fucked up. **1965** in H.S. Thompson _Hell's Angels_ 185: We'll smoke up some weed, get all fucked up, feel no fuckin pain. _ca_**1969** Rabe _Hummel_ 44: Ohhh, you know how much beer I hadda drink to get fucked up on three-two beer? **1970** A. Young _Snakes_ 40: Man, I was fuhhhhhked-up! **1973** _Oui_ (Apr.) 108: God, but I'd love some cocaine....I got so gloriously fucked up the other night. **1973** R. Roth _Sand in Wind_ 148: I was timing myself on every glass. I was getting fucked up but not as fucked up as I wanted to be. **1977** Patrick _Beyond Law_ 144: Either you can sit around here gettin' fucked up and feelin' sorry for yourself, or you can straighten up and solve this God damn case. **1978** Fisher & Rubin _Special Teachers_ 31: He was fucked up on weed. **1979** Hiler _Monkey Mt._ 109: "Eddy!...You fucked up?"..."No, he's not fucked up....He's just crazy." **1967–80** Folb _Runnin' Lines_ 238: _Fucked up._ Excessively _high._ **1985** D. Steel _Secrets_ 48: Sandy's not fucked up again, is she?

b. thoroughly confused; mentally or emotionally ill; crazy.—usu. considered vulgar. Also (esp. _Mil._) in fanciful similes.

1945 in Dundes & Pagter _Urban Folklore_ 108: The returning soldier is apt to find his opinion different from those of his civilian associates. One should call upon his reserve of etiquette and correct his acquaintances with such remarks as "I believe you have made a mistake" or "I am afraid you are in error on that." Do NOT say "Brother, you're really f—d up!" **1946–50** J. Jones _Here to Eternity_ 537: I've even seen a couple of them that clean lost their head and had to actually be carried out finally they got so fucked up. **1961** Peacock _Valhalla_ 385: If he didn't see Chebe-san he would be more fucked up than Hogan's goat. **1965** Linakis _In Spring_ 214: I would even go so far as to say that you're all fucked up from the war, as they do say. **1967** Rechy _Numbers_ 138: It happened long ago, when I was fucked up! **1968** H. Ellison _Deadly Streets_ 103: He wasn't a bad kid, just fucked-up. **1970** in Estren _Underground_ 155: Wow, man, what kind of fucked up trip are _you_ on? **1970** Terkel _Hard Times_ 136: It's the textbooks that are fucked up. **1973** G.C. Scott, in _Penthouse_ (May) 61: Fucked-up kids live in fantasy worlds anyway. **1972–76** Durden _No Bugles_ 31: You're fucked up like a Filipino fire drill. **1976** A. Walker _Meridian_ 178: I know white folks are evil and fucked up. **1978** in Fierstein _Torch Song_ 52: And here you are, more fucked up than ever. _a_**1982** H. Berry _Semper Fi_ 190 [ref. to WWII]: But then again, who was Mr. Hogan and why was his goat any more fucked up than any other goat? **1984** J. McCorkle _Cheer Leader_ 162: You're crazy, Jo, fucked up. **1989** "Capt. X" & Dodson _Unfriendly Skies_ 115: "Aw, hell" said one of the pilots, "now I'm all fucked up here." **1992** in _Harper's_ (Jan. 1993) 23 (cartoon): You're too fucked up—Next patient, please.

c. deeply troubled or upset; distraught.—usu. considered vulgar.

1948 in Hemingway _Sel. Letters_ 648: I was all fucked up when I wrote it and threw away about 100,000 words which was better than most of what I left in. **1951** _Amer. Jour. Socio._ LI 421 [ref. to WWII]: We learn of soldier attitudes to authority by noting the sympathy for those who are not successful in adjusting but are "f—ed up."...It may connote inability or inefficiency. **1962** Riccio & Slocum _All the Way Down_ 68: I ain't hooked. I only use it when I feel all fucked up. **1970–71** Rubinstein _City Police_ 404: He's so fucked up about it he's thinkin' of quittin'. **1966–80** McAleer & Dickson _Unit Pride_ 115: I was gonna change it myself but I was too fucked up at the time. **1983** P. Dexter _God's Pocket_ 158: I got to have this funeral on time....Jeanie's all fucked up over this.

3. contemptible; worthless; miserable; (_hence_) damned; FUCKING.—usu. considered vulgar.

1945 in Shibutani _Co. K_ 124: I never been in such a fucked up place in my life. _ca_**1960** in Abrahams _Down in Jungle_ 130: He throwed me a stale glass of water and flung me a fucked-up piece of meat. **1963** J. Ross _Dead Are Mine_ 269: And you won't worry about Felix and all the other Felixes in the whole fucked-up Army. **1970** _Playboy_ (Sept.) 278: I've met a lot of politicians, and politicians are fucked up everywhere, and they fuck us up because we allow them to. **1974** V.E. Smith _Jones Men_ 103: Shit!...This is fucked up. **1982** D.A. Harper _Good Company_ 76: A half gallon of that old fucked-up wine. **1980–89** Chesire _Home Boy_ 105: They'd go for your ankles and sink their little fucked-up teeth right into you. **1990** "Ice Cube," in L. Stanley _Rap_ 160: Rolling in a fucked-up Lincoln...[with a] leopard interior.

4. utterly fatigued.—usu. considered vulgar.

1979 Gram _Blvd. Nights_ 93: I'm tired man. Fuckin' fucked up.

fuckee /fʌˈki/ _n._ **1.** a person who plays the recipient role in copulation.—usu. considered vulgar. _Joc._

_ca_**1938** in Barkley _Sex Cartoons_ 118: The fuckee does a handstand while

the fucker simply drops it in. **1975** N.Y.C. man, age 27: And who was the fuckee in this transaction?

2. the victim of malicious treatment.—usu. considered vulgar. _Joc._

1971 S/Sgt., U.S. Army (coll. J. Ball): I am one big ugly fucker and I am always on the lookout for fuckees. You _don't_ want to be one of them! **1980** W. Sherman _Times Square_ 23: You're either the fuckee, the fucker, or you're not in any kind of business. **1983** R.C. Mason _Chickenhawk_ 158 [ref. to 1960's]: The Fuckee's Hymn. **1986** Merkin _Zombie Jamboree_ 44: They'd rather be fuckers than fuckees. **1986** Univ. Tenn. instructor: I do recall hearing "He is the fuck_er_ and you is the fuck_ee_" sometime in the '70's.

fuck-else _n._ nothing else.—usu. considered vulgar.

1978 Groom _Better Times_ 33: You mean you got fuck-else to worry about than something happened sixty years ago?

fucker _n._ **1.** a person, usu. a man, who fucks, esp. promiscuously.—usu. considered vulgar.

***1598** J. Florio, in _OEDS: Fottitore,_ a iaper, a sarder, a swiver, a fucker, an occupier. ***1882** _Boudoir_ 239: Such a prince of f—kers as he is. ***1928** D.H. Lawrence _Lady Chatterley_ ch. xviii: I'm not just my lady's fucker, after all. **1973** _TULIPQ_ (coll. B.K. Dumas): I'm a fucker, a fighter and a wild-bull rider!

2. a person, esp. a man, who is despicable, wretched, formidable, etc.; BASTARD; BUGGER.—often used with reduced force.—usu. considered vulgar.

*_a_**1890–93** _F & H_ III 80: _Fucker_...a term of endearment, admiration, derision, etc. ***1918** in _Englische Studien_ LX (1926) 277: We had a sergeant-major/Who never saw a Hun,/And when the Huns came over/ You could see the fucker run. ***1914–21** Joyce _Ulysses_ 600 [ref. to 1904]: I'll wring the bastard fucker's bleeding blasted fucking windpipe! ***1926** _Englische Studien_ LX 279 [ref. to WWI]: The noun _fucker_...the very old term of derision, as well as pity (cp. "that poor blighter!")...was used in the sense of "bloke," "rotter," "blighter," or "bastard," a word which decorated the speech of overseas men and Americans. **1927** _Immortalia_ 159: The dirty old fucker. ***1929** Manning _Fortune_ 146 [ref. to WWI]: Laugh, you silly fuckers! _Ibid._ 150: I'd rather kill some other fucker first. _Ibid._ 208: If any o' us poor fuckers did it, we'd be for th' electric chair. **1945** in Shibutani _Co. K_ 197: Them fuckers piss me off. **1949** Van Praag _Day Without End_ 168: Make your shots count!...Kill the lousy stinking fuckers! **1959** Morrill _Dark Sea Running_ 11: We carry high-octane gas that burns. If I catch any of you fuckers smoking forward of the messroom doors, I'll crack your nobs. **1960** Sire _Death-makers_ 43: You're a mean fucker, Chico. **1961** McMurtry _Horseman, Pass By_ 142: "I used to ride them bulls when I was a young fucker," he said. **1961–64** Barthelme _Caligari_ 43: Oh that poor fucker Eric. **1965–70** J. Carroll, in _Paris Rev._ (No. 50) 107: Her mother [was a] dumb, New Jersey, housewife fucker. **1969–71** Kahn _Boys of Summer_ 96: Gonna get them fuckers....Teach them fuckers to mess with me. **1972** Hannah _Geronimo Rex_ 96: Monroe, you dopey fucker. **1975** Brownmiller _Against Our Will_ 364: I hate that fucker more today than I did when it happened to me. **1976** Univ. Tenn. student: Sorry, you got the wrong fucker. **1981** Gilliland _Rosinante_ 117: The fucker is going to set himself up as _king._ **1992** G. Wolff _Day at Beach_ 127: Only thing to keep the fuckers out.

3.a. an annoying thing; fucking thing; (_hence_) a difficult task.—usu. considered vulgar.

1945 in Shibutani _Co. K_ 155: I don't think I could walk a mile with this fucker on. **1947** Mailer _Naked & Dead_ 10 [ref. to WWII]: Let's stop shuffling the fuggers and start playing. **1958** Berger _Crazy in Berlin_ 186: If you are that close to the end, you can put the fucker aside for fifteen minutes and write me a letter to the wife. **1968** Myrer _Eagle_ 695: And the fucker better work, I'm telling you! **1973** _Penthouse_ (May) 62: Oh my God, I've got to come back tomorrow and do this fucker again. **1976** in Mack _Real Life_ (unp.): Sixteen out of 178 of us got in! It's a _fucker_ isn't it! **1980** in _Penthouse_ (Jan. 1981) 173: He wanted me to wear this schoolgirl rig and shoes—and shine the fuckers first. **1983** Beckwith & Knox _Delta Force_ 176: Are they shitting us? The fucker's real. **1981–85** S. King _It_ 30: Just give me the fucker. **1987** Blankenship _Blood Stripe_ 68: Took me five years to earn that fucker. **1992** G. Wolff _Day at Beach_ 180: You fucking get the fucker up, Dad.

b. a splendid or wretched example.—usu. considered vulgar.

1980 Kotzwinkle _Jack_ 156: She'll burn up the competition....It's one fucker of an engine.

fuckery _n._ [FUCK + treach*ery*] treachery.—usu. considered vulgar.

1978 S. King *Stand* 461: That was an act of pure human fuckery.

fuckface *n.* an ugly or contemptible person.—usu. used abusively in direct address.—usu. considered vulgar.

1961 J. Jones *Thin Red Line* 39 [ref. to WWII]: All right, fuckface! Where's that fucking platoon roster…? [**1967** W. Crawford *Gresham's War* 139: Hey, frickface.] **1968** J.P. Miller *Race for Home* 294 [ref. to 1930's]: "Tell what happened to 'im, fuckface," Dawg said. **1968** Mares *Marine Machine* 5: You come down here with this blade to cut me, fuckface? *Try it!* **1971** T. Mayer *Weary Falcon* 126: I tried giving it to the fuck faces whole, but then they sell it. **1977** Univ. Tenn. student: You'll get some fuckface writin' about ballads. **1983** W. Walker *Dime to Dance* 55: Why don't you mind your own business, fuckface?

fuckfaced *adj.* having an ugly or miserable face; despicable.—usu. considered vulgar. [1940 quot. is euphem.]

1940 Hemingway *For Whom Bell Tolls* 369: Muck my grandfather and muck this whole treacherous muck-faced mucking country. **1973** W. Crawford *Gunship Cmndr.* 24: You fuckfaced animal. Either do something with that or put it away. **1978** *Penthouse* (Apr.) 130: Gradually people file down for breakfast. Totally bleary-eyed and fuck-faced.

fuckfest *n.* an occasion of unrestrained or orgiastic sexual activity.—usu. considered vulgar.

1976 Lee *Ninth Man* 183: They had simply engineered themselves a good old-fashioned fuckfest.

fuckhead *n.* a stupid or contemptible person.—usu. considered vulgar. Hence **fuckheaded,** *adj.*

1962 in Rosset *Evergreen Reader* 467: MANAGER MERCHANT BANKER PROFESSIONAL FUCKHEAD. **1964** in Bruce *Essential Lenny* 97: I mean, it's the fault of the motion pictures, that have made the Southerner "a shit-kickuh, a dumb fuckhead." **1965** Linakis *In Spring* 348 [ref. to WWII]: Go ahead, fuck-head. You'll do me a favor. **1964–66** R. Stone *Hall of Mirrors* 116: You simple-minded fuckhead. **1969** Jessup *Sailor* 389: You're nothing but a dumb fuckhead sailor. **1970** Quammen *Walk the Line* 149: Boss action, fuckhead. **1971** T. Mayer *Weary Falcon* 121: Shut up, you fuckheaded slope. **1980** Kotzwinkle *Jack* 56: How ya doin', fuckhead. **1984** Hammel *Root* 244: Come on fuckhead, get your ass out of the way!

fuckhole *n.* **1.** the vagina.—usu. considered vulgar.

*ca***1890–93** *F & H* III 80: *Fuck-hole*…The female *pudendum.* **1916** Cary *Slang of Venery* I 97: *Fuck hole*—The vagina. **1934** "J.M. Hall" *Anecdota* 23: First you muck up me fuck hole. **1959** in Cray *Erotic Muse* 73: At the fuck-hole of Kathusalem. **1989** *Maledicta* X 58: Flabby cunt…*fuck-hole.*

2. a despicable person.—usu. considered vulgar.

*a***1981** in S. King *Bachman* 621: Goddam…fuckhole! **1985** J. Dillinger *Adrenaline* 54: Unlock my cuffs, fuckhole. *Ibid.* 215: Hey, fuckhole.

fuck-in *n.* (among hippies) a LOVE-IN that includes public copulation.—usu. considered vulgar. Usu. *Joc.*

1967–68 von Hoffman *Parents Warned Us* 211: That was when we had a fuck-in at the White House. **1968** in Estren *Underground* 17: Grand Opening of the Great International Fuck-In and Orgy-Riot. **1971** Le Guin *Lathe of Heaven* 69: And there were the riots, and the fuck-ins, and the Doomsday Band and the Vigilantes. **1971** *Playboy* (Apr.) 184: If you want to get rid of dormitory rules, you have a fuck-in.

fucking *n.* see s.v. FUCK, *v.,* 1.a., 2.a., 4.a.

fucking *adj.* contemptible or despicable; goddamned.—often used with reduced force as a mere intensifier.—usu. considered vulgar. [Perh. orig. abstracted and generalized from opprobrious literal collocations such as *fucking whore* (as in *1882 and 1917–20—which refers to 1893—quots. below); G. Legman's sugg. ety. (from unrecorded ME p.ppl. *fucken) is unsupported by any early evidence. *Fucking* is probably the word intended in 1857 quot.: the number of asterisks is correct for the length of the word (and there are no other seven-letter words of corresponding vulgarity), and any word less vulgar would only be partly rather than entirely omitted by ellipsis (e.g., *damned* was customarily written *d—d* in this period, and cf. representation of *bitch* in the same quot.); cf. identical use of asterisks in clearer contexts from same era in 1848 and *1854 quots. at FUCK, *v.,* 1.a. Cf. FRIGGING.]

1857 *Suppressed Bk. about Slavery* 211: The Dr.…applied the lash. The Woman writhed under each stroke, and cried, "O Lord!"…The Doc-tor…thus addressed her (the congregation must pardon me for repeating his words), "Hush, you ******* b—h, will you take the name of the Lord in Vain on the Sabbath day?" [*1882 *Boudoir* 160: Hurray, hurray, she's a maid no more,/But a f—g wife for evermore!] *a***1890–93** *F & H* III 80: *Fucking…Adj.* (common).—A qualification of extreme contumely. **1915** E. Pound, in Materer *Pound/Lewis* 18: God damn the fucking lot of 'em. **1917–20** Dreiser *Newspaper Days* 233 [ref. to 1893]: A large, Irish policeman…[said] "She's a Goddamned drunken, fucking old whore, that's what she is." *Ibid.* 276: I'm living…with a Goddamned fucking whore. ***1914–21** Joyce *Ulysses* 595: I'll wring the neck of any bugger says a word against my fucking king. *Ibid.* 600: I'll do him in, so help me fucking Christ! ***1921** *N & Q* (Nov. 19) 415 [ref. to WWI]: [*Fucking*] was used adjectivally to qualify almost every noun in the soldier's vocabulary. **1923** McAlmon *Companion Vol.* 51: What in fucking hell do youse think this is, a sunday school picnic, or a teaparty? **1927** *Immortalia* 124: He's a fucking son-of-a-bitch. **1928** in Read *Lexical Evidence* 54: You god Dam fucken fool. **1929–30** Dos Passos *42nd Parallel* 77: Jack, it was a fucking shame. **1934** H. Roth *Call It Sleep* 231 [ref. to *ca*1910]: Didja ever see dat new tawch boinin' troo a goider er a flange er any fuck'n hunka iron? **1935** T. Wolfe *Time & River* 598: I'll kick duh f—kin' s—t outa duh f—kin' lot of yuh, yuh f—kin' bastards, you. **1937** Hemingway *To Have & Have Not* 225: A man alone ain't got no bloody fucking chance. **1938** in Oliver *Blues Tradition* 170: I…don't deny my fuckin' name. **1942** Algren *Morning* 39: Dey ain't a book in da f— place. **1943** Wakeman *Shore Leave* 184: "The f—ing island," Crewson corrected. **1948** Cozzens *Guard of Honor* 561: Said why the f—holy hell didn't they get a boat from Lake Armstrong. **1951** Morris *China Station* 129: You're a fucking liar. **1953–55** Kantor *Andersonville* 224: What?—with this fucking pistol of yours? **1955** O'Hara *Ten North Frederick* 365: I think you're a fucking hypocrite. **1960** in A. Sexton *Letters* 97: My (fucking) book comes out March 1st in case you've forgotten. **1964** Faust *Steagle* 105: I can't ever get a fuckin break. **1972** Capt. John W. Young, on lunar surface, in *Newsweek* (May 1) 24: "I haven't eaten this much citrus fruit in twenty years," he snorted. "And I'll tell you one thing: in another twelve f— days, I ain't ever eating any more." **1992** *Newsweek* (Nov. 23) 32: We're going to blow up your f— building.

fucking *adv.* exceedingly; damned.—often used with reduced force as a mere intensifier.—usu. considered vulgar.

*a***1890–93** *F & H* III 80: *Fucking…Adv.* (common) Intensive and expletive; a more violent form of *bloody.* **1918** in E. Wilson *Prelude* 210: The situation is fucking serious! **1918** E. Pound, in J. Joyce *Letters* II 424: The world is too fucking with us. ***1929** Manning *Fortune* 6 [ref. to WWI]: They can say what they bloody well like….but we're a fuckin' fine mob. **1933** Ford & Tyler *Young & Evil* 31: It's too fucking cold to be running around trying to raise fifty dollars. **1934** in H. Miller *Letters to Emil* 153: I'm getting fucking critical of people. *Ibid.* 156: Maybe I'll get…fucking famous one day. **1942** H. Miller *Roofs of Paris* 250: I'm so fucking mad now that I don't care what she does. **1947** Mailer *Naked & Dead* 10: Pretty fuggin funny. **1956** Chamales *Never So Few* 510: You're asking too fucking much of me. **1963** Hayden *Wanderer* 126: You're pretty fucking dumb, kid, you know that. **1964** in A. Sexton *Letters* 254: It's too fucking hard to write. **1969–71** Kahn *Boys of Summer* 312: "Well, how did you get to play it like that?" "I worked, that's fucking how." **1973** R. Roth *Sand in Wind* 83: STOP! FUCKING STOP! **1977** Caron *Go-Boy* 152: I'll be fucking seeing you later. **1979** Gutcheon *New Girls* 12: "You're very fucking rude, Lisa," said Jenny. **1993** *New Yorker* (Jan. 11) 78: I'm getting out of here, you fucking crazy.

fucking *infix.* (used as an intensifier).—usu. considered vulgar. See also ABSOFUCKINGLUTELY, FANFUCKINGTASTIC.

***1921** *N & Q* (Nov. 19) 415 [ref. to WWI]: Words were split up to admit [*fucking*]: "absolutely" became "abso—lutely," and *Armentières* became "Armen—teers." "Bloody"…quite lapsed as being too polite and inexpressive. **1939** (quot. at FUCKED DUCK). **1952** in Russ *Last Parallel* 13: Reveille goes tomorrow at four o'fuckin' clock. **1961** J. Jones *Thin Red Line* 42 [ref. to WWII]: I guaran-fucking-tee you! **1966** Fariña *Down So Long* 84: He gets himself infuckingvolved. **1968** Mares *Marine Machine* xii: Outfucking-standing, Private Smith! *Ibid.* 30: Forget what you're doing and I guaranfuckintee you, you'll get blown away. **1968** Gover *JC* 158: That's the ee-fuckin'-end of it. **1971** *Playboy* (Mar.) 189: Unfucking-believable! **1971** Sonzski *Punch Goes Judy* 19: Tele-*fucking*-phone for you. **1972** Pearce *Pier Head Jump* 6: It's unfuckin'-believable sometimes. *Ibid.* 156: Six o'fuckin' clock! **1973** Layne *Murphy* (unp.): Do me one more favor, Private. Dis-a-fuckin'-pear! **1974** N.Y.U. student: That was out-fuckin'-rageous. **1975** C.W. Smith *Country Music* 230: How po-fucking-etic! **1978** R. Price *Ladies' Man* 128: Go away. Go afuckin'way.

fucking A *n.* **1.** the least bit.—usu. considered vulgar.

1966 S. Stevens *Go Down Dead* 203: Youth workers. Shit on them. They don't know fucking A about us.

2. a contemptible or despicable person.—usu. considered vulgar.

1980 Rimmer *Album* 75 [ref. to 1967]: LBJ's a fuckin' A.

fucking-A *adv., adj., interj., & infix.* [FUCKING + A (orig. unkn.; perh. abstracted fr. a phr. such as *"you're fucking A-number-one right!"*: cf. 1970 Woods, *a*1982 Berry quots., below; alternatively, cf. A, *n.*)]

1.a. Esp. *Mil.* yes indeed; absolutely (correct); esp. in phr. **[you're] fucking-A**, occas. with elaborations, esp. **fucking-A [well] told.**—usu. considered vulgar.

1947 Mailer *Naked & Dead* 21 [ref. to WWII]: "You're fuggin ay," Gallegher snorted. **1961** J. Jones *Thin Red Line* 137 [ref. to WWII]: "No, I never." "You fucking A you never." **1961** Peacock *Valhalla* 181 [ref. to 1953]: Fucking A. **1967** Crowley *Boys in the Band* 827: Fuckin' A, Mac. **1967** Brelis *Face of S. Vietnam* 29: "It can't be the same kid." "You're fuckin' A, it's the same fuckin' kid." **1969** Briley *Traitors* 273: You're fucking A I had to work. **1969** Sidney *Love of Dying* 146: Fucking-eigh. **1970** Wakefield *Going All the Way* 42 [ref. to ca1950's]: Fuckin-A John Do. **1970** Wexler *Joe* (film): Fuckin' A! **1970** Ponicsan *Last Detail* 171: Fucking-ay-John Ditty-Bag-well-told I don't. **1970** Woods *Killing Zone* 143: Fuckin-A-well-told. *Ibid.:* Fuckin-A-number-one-well-told. **1975** Larsen *Runner* 38: Your fucking A told he is. *Ibid.:* "Fucking A told", Antonino agreed. *a*1982 Berry *Semper Fi* 192 [ref. to WWII]: "Hey, Bull, you going on liberty?" "Fuckin' A doodle de doo." **1985** J. Dillinger *Adrenaline* 199: "You were traumatized." "You're fuckin' A we were traumatized." **1985** N. Kazan *At Close Range* (film): "Looks like a nice gun." "Fucking-A-plus it's a nice gun."

b. (used to express astonishment, dismay, or recognition).—usu. considered vulgar.

1979 Hiler *Monkey Mt.* 103 [ref. to 1972]: "Three pair and…The deuce of spades."…"Fuckin' A!" **1980** J. Carroll *Land of Laughs* 168: Fuck-ing A!…The guy who walked around the world! **1988** Eble *Campus Slang* 4: *Fuckin' A*—exclamation, either positive or negative. "What? A Quiz today?…Fuckin' A!"

c. splendid.—usu. considered vulgar.

1986 Stinson & Carabatsos *Heartbreak* 29: The Night had gone from fucking-A to all-fucked-up in record time. **1986** *NDAS*: We won? Fucking a! **1987** Pelfrey & Carabatsos *Hamburger Hill* 51 [ref. to Vietnam War]: The ham's fucking A, Ma.

2.a. Esp. *Mil.* FUCKING; goddamned.—usu. considered vulgar. [1955 quot. is euphem.]

1955 Sack *Here to Shimbashi* 18: "That was a mighty freaking-A loud sneeze," declared the sergeant major. **1968** Bullins *In the Wine Time* 389: That's right…that's fucken "A" right. **1986** Heinemann *Paco's Story* 20: Guys with their chests squashed flat from fuckin'-A booby-trapped bombs. **1987** B. Raskin *Hot Flashes* 87: "That was too-fucking-A-much," Joanne says tersely.

b. Esp. *Mil.* FUCKING WELL; very well; very.—usu. considered vulgar.

1960 Sire *Deathmakers* 211 [ref. to WWII]: You can fucking-aye say that again. *Ibid.* 262: You fucking-aye have spoken, Captain. **1968** Heard *Howard St.* 72: You fuckin'-A-right! **1970** *Evergreen Rev.* (Apr.) 66: You know fucking-A I deserve it, Krim, now where is it going to be published? **1970** Appleman *Twelfth Year* 89: You hear, I do not fuckin'-aye in*tend* it! **1968–71** Cole & Black *Checking* 215: "You Puerto Rican?" "Fuckin' A-right!" **1972** Ponicsan *Cinderella Lib.* 8: No one knew who first got carried away…and wound up with the melodious invective "Fuckin' aye John Ditty Bag," but since then any number of sailors have gilded the lily and produced things like, "Fuckin' well told aye John Ditty Bag I be go to hell on a forklift!" **1973** Hirschfeld *Victors* 38: Now that is fucking-A important. **1973** "J. Godey" *Pelham* 151: He fucking-aye-right *better* be. **1976** C.R. Anderson *Grunts* 78 [ref. to 1969]: You know fucking A well you can't ask the man no dumbass question like that. **1978** Truscott *Dress Gray* 443: You could fuckin'-A say that again. **1981** Hathaway *World of Hurt* 209: You're my fuckin'-A favorite ridge-runner. *a*1982 Berry *Semper Fi* 192: *Fuckin' A told* or *Fuckin' A right* were everyday expressions [in the Marine Corps during WWII]. **1985** Frede *Nurses* 237: I am fucking-A *ripped*! **1985** Bodey *F.N.G.* 4: Marines. Fuckin'-A filthy.

fucking Able *adv.* [FUCKING(-A) + former mil. comm. alphabet *Able* 'A'] *Mil.* FUCKING-A.—usu. considered vulgar.

1966 Newhafer *No More Bugles* 176: That certainly is tough shit, Da-

nang. You are fucking able right I violated air space.

fucking-A well *adv.* FUCKING WELL.—usu. considered vulgar.

1976 Crews *Feast of Snakes* 83: He fucking-A-well had the words right.

fuckingly *adv.* damned; extremely.—usu. considered vulgar.

1927 in Hemingway *Sel. Letters* 261: Got a sheet to fill out from Who's Who and my life has been so fuckingly complicated that I was only able to answer two of the questions.

fucking well *adv.* very well; absolutely.—often used as an intensifier.—usu. considered vulgar. Cf. 1875 quot. at BLOODY, 1.b. [*Furkin'* in second 1939 quot. is euphem.]

1922 T.E. Lawrence *Mint* 80: She'll stay as she fuckin' well is. *1931 Brophy & Partridge *Song & Slang* (ed. 3) 17 [ref. to WWI]: By adding *-ing* and *-ingwell* [to *fuck*] an adjective and adverb were formed and thrown into every sentence. **1939** Bessie *Men in Battle* 177: God send the—day when we'll—fuckin' well march no more! *1939 in *So. Folk. Qly.* XL 104: Look at the people, furkin' well cryin';/Isn't it nice to be furkin' well dead. **1945** in Hemingway *Sel. Letters* 590: If he doesn't take care of you he better never fucking well run into me. **1952** Kerouac *Cody* 201: You got the whole thing fuckingwell summed up. **1952** in Russ *Last Parallel* 13: I was behind the wheel of a fuckin' Diesel truck before you ever learned to fuckin' well drive… **1965** Friedman *Totempole* 267: You better fucking-well believe it! **1971** Selby *Room* 42: You're fucking well right he did. **1973** Maas *Serpico* 200: Get this fucking-well straight. **1974–77** A. Hoffman *Property Of* 166: I fucking well do not know, all right? **1987** Univ. Tenn. instructor, age 34: You fucking well *better.*

fuckish *adj.* eager for copulation.—usu. considered vulgar.

*a1890–93 F & H III 81: *Fuckish*…wanton;…inclined for coition. **1969** R. Beck *Mama Black Widow* 246: Dorcas is fuckish as hell.

fuck job *n.* an act of victimization; victimization.—usu. considered vulgar.

1973 Sgt., USAF (coll. J. Ball): Someone's always tryin' to do the old fuck job on me. **1988** Knoxville, Tenn., attorney, age 36: I tell you, the fuck job never stops.

fuck-me *adj.* intended to invite sexual advances.—usu. considered vulgar.

1989 P. Munro *UCLA Slang* 41: *Fuck-me boots* mid-calf or higher boots worn under a miniskirt. **1990** P. Munro *Slang U.* 86: *Fuck-me eyes*…flirtatious stares or glances/I'm feeling some serious fuck-me eyes from that guy in the corner. **1992** *Letters to Penthouse* III 63: Her legs ended in a pair of "fuck-me" stilettos.

fuck-nutty *adj.* obsessed with the idea of copulation.—usu. considered vulgar.

1942 H. Miller *Roofs of Paris* 32: Those fuck-nutty kids.

fucko *n.* [prob. infl. by BUCKO] FUCKER, 2.—usu. considered vulgar.

1973 Schiano & Burton *Solo* 76: Hey, fucko, what're you following me for? **1974** Terkel *Working* 582: Hey, fucko, come over here.…You fucker. **1976** Price *Bloodbrothers* 247: No sweat, fucko. **1988** Gallo *Midnight Run* (film): My name's *Carmine*, fucko!

fuck-off *n.* Esp. *Mil.* a person who shirks duties or responsibilities; loafer or shirker; an incompetent.—usu. considered vulgar.

1947 N. Mailer *Naked & Dead* 229 [ref. to WWII]: You think I'm just a fug-off, don't you? *a*1949 D. Levin *Mask of Glory* 22 [ref. to WWII]: Shitbirds,…fuckoffs, get going, get going. **1953** Eyster *Customary Skies* 141 [ref. to WWII]: How come you fuckoffs waited to now to start this fussing? How come you didn't pray none in calm water? **1961** Hemingway *Islands in the Stream* 356: Where you two fuck-offs been? **1968** "J. Hudson" *Case of Need* 271: The radiologist for the night is Harrison. He's a fuck-off. **1969** in *Rolling Stone Interviews* 274: I tell you the whole world is a drop-out. I mean, everybody's a fuck-off. **1978** Wharton *Birdy* 176: I hate to think of going into combat with fuck-offs like these. **1984** J.R. Reeves *Mekong* 76: You fuckoff!

fuck off *v.* **1.** to run away; (*imper.*) get away! get out! go to hell!—usu. considered vulgar.

*1929 Manning *Fortune* 20 [ref. to WWI]: As soon as a bit o' shrapnel comes their way, [they] fuck off 'ome jildy, toot sweet. **1939** Bessie *Men in Battle* 89: No one ever saw him again. He "fucked off" over the border, as the men expressed it. *Ibid.* 91: "You're talking through your hat." "Fuck off." **1943** in *AS* (Apr. 1944) 108: You would say of a man who has absented himself at the approach of some unpleasant job of work, "Oh, he *fucked off.*" **1944** in Bowker *Out of Uniform* 119: Another…use, exclusively intransitive, exists in combination with the preposition "off." In this case, the meaning is "to leave hurriedly." The most frequent usage occurs in connection with a request to stop annoying the speaker. Often it is followed by the words, "—will ya!" added for emphasis. **1948** in Hemingway *Sel. Letters* 640: The opposing characters will fuck off once the column shows. *Ibid.* 647: There is no substitute in English for the phrase "Fuck off, Jack," if you mean it and will make it good. **1961** McMurtry *Horseman, Pass By* 58: "Fuck off," he said. "You ain't got no private milkin' rights." **1966** Manus *Mott the Hoople* 23: Fuck off, and quick. **1967** Aaron *About Us* 183: That wasn't brave. I knew they'd fuck off. ***1971** M.J. Harrison *Committed Men* 24: Oh, fuck off. **1988** Univ. Tenn. student: Tell her to fuck off. **1986–91** Hamper *Rivethead* 21: I...told everyone to fuck off.

2.a. to loaf or evade duty; shirk.—usu. considered vulgar. [1955 quot. is euphem.]

1945 in Shibutani *Co. K* 275: What's the use of being on the ball....May as well fuck off. **1951** *Amer. Jour. Socio.* LI 421 [ref. to WWII]: There is little stigma to the expression "f— off" applied to...acts, such as when a man gets away with something against the Army by evading a detail...or in some other way avoids an Army requirement. **1955** Klaas *Maybe I'm Dead* 327 [ref. to WWII]: Vat are you furkin' off for? **1964** Rhodes *Chosen Few* 65: You missed formation. You fucked off and we don't tolerate fuckoffs. **1968** Maule *Rub-A-Dub* 127: And I personal am gonna see you get logged if you fuck off. **1970** Terkel *Hard Times* 136: If he didn't fuck off those four years in the steel mills, he could've gotten ahead. **1977** Sayles *Union Dues* 57: You let me know he stots fuckin off, right? **1980** Univ. Tenn. prof., age *ca*58: I first heard *fuck off* in 1939 when I was working in the railroad yards [in N.Y. State]. "Quit fuckin' off," they'd say. **1985** B.E. Ellis *Less Than Zero* 33: Don't fuck off. Don't be a bum. **1987** Zeybel *Gunship* 10: I fucked off in Bangkok a few days.

b. to slack off; fail through inattention.

1954–60 *DAS* 204: *Fuck off*...to make a blunder or mistake. **1964** Rhodes *Chosen Few* 225: You were on yo way t'breakin' some kinda record, son, bu'cha fucked off on th' five hundred.

c. to be deprived of through bungling.—usu. considered vulgar.

1972 Bunker *No Beast* 158: It's too late. We fucked off a score because you weren't here.

3. to disregard; brush aside; put off.—usu. considered vulgar.

1962 G. Ross *Last Campaign* 431 [ref. to 1951]: They been trying to retire him for months...but he keeps fucking them off and turning down his retirement and refusing to leave the division.

4. to idle away.—usu. considered vulgar.

1966 Braly *On Yard* 14: The big yard's a cold place to fuck off your life. **1969** *Playboy* (Dec.) 301: You're going to get tired of running around in a pair of dirty Levis, fucking off your time with those other young cats. **1972** in *JAF* LXXXVI (1973) 222: Do you know what an old whore does on her vacation?—She just fucks it off. *a*1979 Pepper & Pepper *Straight Life* 332: I used to get on his case all the time behind his talent, fuckin' off that talent in the pen.

fuck out *v.* **1.** to give out; break down.—usu. considered vulgar.

1978 Univ. Tenn. student: My car fucked out on me. Motor conked. You can't even jump it anymore.

2. to be sexually unfaithful.—usu. considered vulgar.

1984 L. McCorkle *Cheer Leader* 15: "I cannot tell a lie" is important and fucking out on Martha is not.

fuck over *v.* [prob. FUCK (UP) + (WORK) OVER] Esp. *Black E.* **1.** to treat harshly or with contempt; mistreat, victimize, cheat, betray, etc.; damage.—usu. considered vulgar. [1961 quot. is euphem.]

1961 J.A. Williams *Night Song* 155: Eagle ain't even cold yet and you cats are effin' over him already. **1965** C. Brown *Manchild* 98: We couldn't be fucked over but so much. **1966** in IUFA *Folk Speech*: Used to mean that someone or something has been used to the point of abuse. *fucked over*. **1967–68** von Hoffman *Parents Warned Us* 55: My head's pretty badly fucked over by life in general. **1968** Mares *Marine Machine* 93: You fucked over those weapons so much they probably will never fire again for other privates. **1969** Mitchell *Thumb Tripping* 125: He couldn't let this Brylcreamer fuck over his head. He'd have to keep it together. **1969** *New Amer. Review* 6 (Apr.) 103: Fuck over the city. Do them in. **1970** Ponicsan *Last Detail* 17: Don't it sound like somebody's fucking over Meadows? **1970** Whitmore *Memphis-Nam-Sweden* 134: I was refusing to be a part of that country which was fucking over my own people. **1972–76** Durden *No Bugles* 16: It was a weird scene, a

noncom fuckin' over an officer in front of grunts. **1976** in Mack *Real Life* (unp.): Bill, it's a dog eat dog world. They gonna fuck all over you, man! **1974–77** A. Hoffman *Property Of* 221: Something gets fucked over in the store, take it out of her wages. **1979** Coleman Young, mayor of Detroit, in Terkel *Amer. Dreams* 357: I was attracted to this...way of fighting back at the thing that had been fuckin' me over all my life. **1985** Boyne & Thompson *Wild Blue* 453: We can't let these punks fuck over the whole goddamn Air Force! **1991** C. Fletcher *Pure Cop* 282: Don't fuck *over* me!

2. to beat up; WORK OVER.

1970 Landy *Underground Dict.* 84: *Fuck over*...Beat someone up. **1971** T. Mayer *Weary Falcon* 31: The fourth mission I went on was the time they really fucked us over. **1986** Univ. Tenn. instructor, age 35: When I first heard *fuck someone over* in 1966, it meant specifically to beat them up.

fuck-ox *n. Army in Vietnam.* a water buffalo.—usu. considered vulgar. Now *hist.*

1984 Holland *Let Soldier* 239 [ref. to 1967]: Ah, Wolf Lead, do you have that fuck-ox in sight?

fuck-plug *n.* a contraceptive diaphragm.—usu. considered vulgar.

1987 Univ. Tenn. student: My husband uses condoms anyway, 'cause I can't stand those damned fuck-plugs.

fuckpole *n.* FUCKSTICK, 2.—usu. considered vulgar.

1965 in B. Jackson *Swim Like Me* 159: A fuck-pole longer than mine. **1985** "Blowdryer" *Mod. Eng.* 72: Genitalia...Male...*Fuck pole.* **1989** (quot. at FUCKSTICK, 2.).

fuck rubber *n.* a condom.—usu. considered vulgar.

1983 K. Weaver *Texas Crude* 114: She found that fuckrubber under her pillow.

fuckster *n.* FUCKER, 1.—usu. considered vulgar. *Rare* in U.S.

***ca*1675** in Burford *Bawdy Verse* 170: Fucksters,...Have a care. **1930** *Lyra Ebriosa* 20: Nearby there lived a fuckster tall.

fuckstick *n.* [perh. modeled on BrE slang *funk stick* 'a coward']

1. a worthless, contemptible, or despicable person.—usu. considered vulgar.

1958 Talsman *Gaudy Image* 222: There's still the heavenly debasement of the imperturbable fuckstick. Surely that appeals to you. **1968** Baker et al. *CUSS* 122: *Fuck-stick*. A person who always fools around. **1974** N.Y.C. man, age *ca*28: A *fuckstick* is a really foul, ugly prostitute. This was at Ft. Polk and environs in 1969. It's like a *skank*. **1975** Univ. Tenn. student: That guy at the other end was a real fuckstick, too. **1978** Truscott *Dress Gray* 152: Hey, fuckstick, buck up, man. **1980** Conroy *Lords of Discipline* 145: Get your fucking chin in....Rack it in, fuckstick. **1983** S. King *Christine* 362: The fuckstick had parked at the far set.

2. the penis.—usu. considered vulgar. [Presumably the orig. sense.]

1977 Torres *Q & A* 239: My pistol is like my fuck-stick. Don't go nowhere without it. **1981** *Penthouse* (Apr.) 26: I pulled my fuck-stick out of her cunt. **1989** *Maledicta* X 55: Penis...*fuck-stick*...*fuckpole* [etc.].

fuck-struck *adj.* obsessed with copulation.—usu. considered vulgar. Cf. earlier CUNT-STRUCK.

1966 E. Shepard *Doom Pussy* 160: Like a tomcat at a petting party, Alby tried to force two B-girls to sit on his knee. Tors eyed him with distaste. "He's fuck-struck," observed the Swede to no one in particular.

fuck-up *n.* **1.** Esp. *Mil.* a chronic bungler; misfit.—usu. considered vulgar. [The ***1942** quot., collected from Australian schoolchildren, may have resulted from misapprehension of this term.]

[***1942** S.J. Baker *Austral. Lang.* 206: *Fug-up*. A stodgy person, one who prefers a "fuggy" atmosphere to playing out of doors.] [**1944** *Newsweek* (Jan. 24) 68: I am not a messup any more. I like the army.] **1945** in Cheever *Letters* 108: Last night two fuckups were discussing their dissatisfactions [*sic*] with the army. **1947** Mailer *Naked & Dead* 224 [ref. to WWII]: Bunch of fug-ups, lose a goddam gun, won't even take a drink when it's free. **1946–50** J. Jones *Here to Eternity* ch. iv: He's such a fuckup I was afraid he'd shoot somebody on a problem. **1951** in Hemingway *Sel. Letters* 721: To me he is an enormously skillful fuck-up and his book will do great damage to our country. **1954** F.I. Gwaltney *Heaven & Hell* 194 [ref. to WWII]: You're not commanding a fukup company. This is a regiment, and not every man in it is a fukup. **1955** T. Anderson *Your Own Beloved* 8: Whenever he screwed up they knew it. He was a fuckup. **1962** Killens *Heard the Thunder* 39 [ref. to WWII]:

You're nothing but a first-class fuck-up. **1965** C. Brown *Manchild* 145: The cats who had a little bit of sense but who were just general fuck-ups were sent to the Annex. **1967** Kornbluth *New Underground* 14: What stupid fuck-ups men are! **1971** *Playboy* (May) 207: You mean we're gonna let them fuck-ups play on *our* ball diamond? **1979** in Terkel *Amer. Dreams* 396: I'm not a great believer in failure as a sin. A couple of our writers are fuckups. **1980** Kopp *Mirror, Mask* 81: I become…[an] uncomfortably vulnerable fuck-up whose blunder is now exposed to my eyes and to theirs. **1985** E. Leonard *Glitz* 152: I thought maybe I was a total fuckup. *a*1990 E. Currie *Dope & Trouble* 22: I used to be a real fuck-up, you know?

2. Esp. *Mil.* a blunder; botch; FOUL-UP, 1.—usu. considered vulgar. Cf. *1941 quot. at FRIG-UP, *n.*

a*1950 Partridge *DSUE* (ed. 3) 1054: *F*ck-up of, make a.* To fail miserably at; to spoil utterly: low coll.: C.20. **1958 J. O'Hara *From the Terrace* 257: Such a Goddam fuck-up. **1964** Allen *High White Forest* 266 [ref. to WWII]: Two of our divisions got tangled up there…and the Krauts hit them from the slope. What a fuck-up! **1968–71** Cole & Black *Checking* 105: Not only was that a fuck-up of LEAP's name but why the hell did I accept their stealing? **1972** *Metropolitan Rev.* (May) 4: No fuck-up should go unridiculed. **1977** Coover *Public Burning* 455: And now it scared them that somebody might catch them in a fuck-up. **1984** "W.T. Tyler" *Shadow Cabinet* 241: A royal bureaucratic fuck-up, take my word. *a*1986 D. Tate *Bravo Burning* 96: A small…, probably perfectly explainable fuck-up.

fuck up *v.* [cf. syn. BUGGER UP; also infl. by—if not the inspiration for—syn. *muck up* (*1886 in *OEDS*)] **1.** to ruin, spoil, or destroy; (*specif.*) to botch; in phr. **fuck up the detail** *Mil.* to bungle.—usu. considered vulgar. Cf. SCREW UP, FRIG UP.

***1916–29** in Manning *Fortune* 51 [ref. to WWI]: And they'll call up all the women/When they've fucked up all the men. [**1932** Halyburton & Goll *Shoot & Be Damned* 206 [ref. to 1918]: That big tub of sour owl milk will jazz up the detail for all of us. You'd better dust off a court martial for him.] **1942** H. Miller *Roofs of Paris* 248: You and Sid are going to fuck up everything before you're through. **1944** in J. O'Hara *Sel. Letters* 184: I know I fucked up your afternoon schedule. **1951** in *Inter. Jour. Psycho-An.* XXXV (1954) 35: When a man says: "I got my day all fucked up," he is [yet] fully aware of the primary sexual meaning of the word. **1952** in Perelman *Don't Tread* 123: So many bothersome and ridiculous complications with which you'd managed to fuck up your life here. **1953** M. Harris *Southpaw* 143: Them goddam bastards would as soon f— up my ball club as not. **1956** Chamales *Never So Few* 574: They fucked something up when they moved that piece….They're missing us. **1965** Yurick *Warriors* 71: That fucked everything up, Hector thought. **1966–67** W. Stevens *Gunner* 119 [ref. to WWII]: It's not going to do…anybody…any good if you go around fucking up the detail. **1968** Mares *Marine Machine* 29: Mouse, the coffee's cold! You're a Kremlin spy sent here to fuck up my stomach. **1969** Stern *Brood of Eagles* 341: Oh, I would have fucked it up for fair. I know that. **1984** J. Fuller *Fragments* 23: Duds, the drill sergeants would call us….Fuck up a two-car funeral. **1991** "R. Brown" & R. Angus *A.K.A. Narc* 188: They'll fuck this up like they fucked up everything else.

2.a. to blunder badly; (*hence*) to get oneself into trouble of any kind; fail.—usu. considered vulgar. Cf. syn. SCREW UP.

1945 in Shibutani *Co. K* 115: We always fuck up when we march. **1953** M. Harris *Southpaw* 201: The first man that f—s up in this respect is going to get hit in the pocketbook, and hit hard. **1944–57** Atwell *Private* 33: He f—ed up there too, so they sent him down to us in C Company. **1957** Simmons *Corner Boy* 73: People will fugg up. **1961** Forbes *Goodbye to Some* 53: I really fucked up. We were going way too fast. **1961** McMurtry *Horseman, Pass By* 48: "You fucked up," Hermy said. **1963** J. Ross *Dead Are Mine* 87: Keep your nose clean and this will all be forgotten. Fuck up and you're dead. **1964–66** R. Stone *Hall of Mirrors* 271: But in my journalistic opinion they're gonna fuck up. **1971** Meggyesy *Out of Their League* 189: I also watched how Ernie and Larry did and I must admit I was pleased when they made mistakes and fucked up. **1972** Halberstam *Best & Brightest* 281 [ref. to 1963]: Americans in Vietnam…had come up with a slogan to describe the ARVN promotion system: "Fuck up and move up." **1978** Rascoe & Stone *Who'll Stop Rain?* (film): "I've been waiting all my life to fuck up like this." "Well, you've finally made the big time." **1972–79** T. Wolfe *Right Stuff* 221: *Falling behind* put you on the threshold of *fucking up.* **1982** Gino *Nurse's Story* 318: Maybe somebody fucked up.

b. to go awry; malfunction; break down.—usu. considered vulgar.

1980 J. Carroll *Land of Laughs* 90: How many things are going to fuck up before we get this straightened out. **1982** D.J. Williams *Hit Hard*

175 [ref. to WWII]: A-17 gun fucked up. **1985** Sawislak *Dwarf* 193: In case you miss a transmission or the radios fuck up.

3.a. to befuddle or confuse; confound; thwart; interfere with.—usu. considered vulgar.

1945 in Shibutani *Co. K* 133: I bet that fuckin' CO stays awake every night tryin' to think up some new way to fuck us up. **1968** in E. Knight *Belly Song* 15: Perhaps it was just the brother's definition that fucked me up. **1968–71** Cole & Black *Checking* 223: "It will be six months before they use those rooms again.…" "That's cool…I dig fucking up white prejudiced pricks." **1971–72** Giovanitti *Medal* 109: I said what I said because I had nothing else to go on. I ain't changing that story now. And nobody's going to fuck me up. You understand? **1976** Chinn *Dig the Nigger Up* 37: I'd sure like to do it to her!…She fucks me all up! **1978** E. Thompson *Devil to Pay* 156: It was Milt's idea to cook out. "Really fuck up the neighbors, man. They'll think it's springtime."

b. to make intoxicated, esp. on drugs.—usu. considered vulgar.

1971 in H.S. Thompson *Shark Hunt* 147: Five reds, enough to fuck *anybody* up. **1980** DiFusco et al. *Tracers* 46 [ref. to Vietnam War]: There's enough shit here to fuck up the entire squad for at least a week.

4.a. Esp. *Black E.* to injure, esp. severely; mangle; wound.—usu. considered vulgar.

1962 in Wepman et al. *The Life* 23: He romped and stomped, and he fucked up his face. **1965** C. Brown *Manchild* 144: Man, those bullets can really fuck you up. **1966–67** P. Thomas *Mean Streets* 60 [ref. to *ca*1950]: I felt his fist fuck up my shoulder. *Ibid.* 209: Louie, if the motherfucker makes a move, fuck him up good. **1970** Cole *Street Kids* 88: The guy who was on our kid fucked the other guy up. The guy was bleeding from his eye. **1970–71** Rubinstein *City Police* 358: You think it was a gun?…O.K., pal, just relax, at least he didn't fuck you up. **1972** T. O'Brien *Combat Zone* 76: You don't get mangled by a mine, you get fucked up. **1972–74** Hawes & Asher *Raise Up* 84: My man from Harlem had overheard the…hassle…and asked if I wanted him to get some cats to fuck up the bass player. **1975** S.P. Smith *Amer. Boys* 162: A few losers who'd…been fucked up not quite bad enough to be sent home. **1978** W. Brown *Tragic Magic* 152: "Fuck him up!" "Waste his ass!" **1982** Del Vecchio *13th Valley* 22: Some innocent dudes always get fucked up and blown away.

b. *Mil.* to kill.—usu. considered vulgar. Cf. *1916–29 quot. at **(1)**, above.

1967 in Edelman *Dear Amer.* 87: The company lost 5 KIA and about 40 wounded. We fucked up at least two times as many Charlies as far as KIA, but we have more wounded. **1987** Whiteley *Deadly Green* 201 [ref. to Vietnam War]: Fuck them up! Fuck them fuckers up!…Get some!

5. *Black E.* to fool around.—usu. considered vulgar.

1969 Hannerz *Soulside* 62: I earn good money, you know, with those two jobs, and my old lady earns a lot on her job, so actually I don't have to leave too much money at home 'cause she takes care of much of that. So this means I got a lot to spend just fucking up. **1970** A. Young *Snakes* 125: We both need to get away from this old school grind for awhile. Why don't we go out and fuck up tonight? It's Friday, man….Let's go out and party!

¶ In phrase:

¶ **fuck up a wet dream** *Mil.* to be exceedingly clumsy or stupid.—usu. considered vulgar.

1967 Dubus *Lieutenant* 52 [ref. to 1956]: Freeman, you are nothing but a skinny turd and would fuck up a wet dream. **1971** Flanagan *Maggot* 242 [ref. to *ca*1956]: They fuck-up everything. Some of them would fuck-up a wet dream. **1975** Wambaugh *Choirboys* 185: Roscoe Rules could fuck up a wet dream. **1966–80** McAleer & Dickson *Unit Pride* 391 [ref. to *ca*1951]: Billy, I swear you'd fuck up a wet dream. **1984** Caunitz *Police Plaza* 193: That guy could fuck up a wet dream. **1987** D. Sherman *Main Force* 191 [ref. to 1966]: Lewis, you'd fuck up a wet dream. Go back to sleep.

fuckwad *n.* a stupid or contemptible person.—usu. considered vulgar.

1974 *UTSQ*: Motherfucker, fuckwad, sonofabitch, [etc.]. **1986** "J. Cain" *Suicide Squad* 97: I wanna see ID cards on all these fuckwads. **1987** "J. Hawkins" *Tunnel Warriors* 144: That goofy fuckwad. **1990** Rukuza *W. Coast Turnaround* 8: Some fuckwad shootin' up da scenery wit' a machine gun.

fuck-you lizard *n.* [sugg. by a fancied resemblance between the E phr. and the gecko's call] *Mil. in S.E. Asia.* a tokay gecko.

[**1933** Clifford *Boats* 309: A gecko lizard in a nearby papaya tree croaked throatily. "Obscene devils, those," he went on dryly. The colonel laughed.] **1971** *Playboy* (Aug.) 199: From the undergrowth comes the chant of "Fuck you, fuck you" from small lizards, not unexpectedly called fuck-you lizards. **1978** Hasford *Short-Timers* 151 [ref. to Vietnam War]: The fuck-you lizards greet us. **1984** J. Fuller *Fragments* 78: Did you know that if you grab one of those Fuck You lizards by the tail, he just lets go and walks away? **1986** Thacker *Pawn* 133: That's because of the fuck-you lizard. **1987** Lanning *Only War* 253: FNGs were told that the "fuck-you" lizards were NVA taunting us. **1988** Clodfelter *Mad Minutes* 33 [ref. to 1965]: Naturally we labeled these leftovers from the prehistoric past "Fuck You Lizards."

fuck-your-buddy week *n. Mil.* a hypothetical period during which betrayal or exploitation of one's friends is supposedly encouraged.—usu. considered vulgar. *Joc.* Also vars.
[**1952** Haines & Krims *One Minute to Zero* (film): John, this isn't help-your-buddy week. We might need those guys again.] **1960** MacCuish *Do Not Go Gentle* 342 [ref. to WWII]: National American custom of Screw Your Buddy Week. **1962** Crump *Killer* 279: Don't worry about it, weed....This is Frig Your Buddy Week. *ca***1963** in Schwendinger & Schwendinger *Adolescent Sub.* 296: It's fuck your buddy week, fifty-two weeks of the year....If you have a buddy kind and true, you fuck him before he fucks you. *a***1967** in M.W. Klein *Juve. Gangs* 98: It's fuck your buddy week, fifty-two weeks of the year. **1971** *Playboy* (Apr.) 182: That old Army expression, "Every week is fuck-your-buddy week." **1973** W. Crawford *Gunship Cmndr.* 148: The whole army overreacted, filed charges against everybody in sight, good old fuck-your-brother week. **1980** Manchester *Darkness* 156 [ref. to WWII]: The school's shabbiest custom [was] known as "fuck-your-buddy night." Every candidate was required to fill out a form rating his fellows. ****1984** Partridge *DSUE* (ed. 8) 1323: What *is* this?—International Fuck-Your-Buddy Week?...Prob. adopted from the US forces in Korea, 1950-53.

fud *n.* FUDDY-DUDDY. Also **fudd.**
1913 (cited in *W10*). **1942** in *OEDAS* II 104: The first Mrs. Evans was an old Boston fud from the beginning. **1942–45** Caniff *Male Call* (unp.): The liddle man thinks we're phuds. **1949** Bartlett & Lay *Twelve O'Clock High* (film): An old fud like you ought to know better. **1953** *Time* (Sept. 7) 15: Republicans in Congress are acting like "quarreling old women," and a few are "old fuds." **1968** in Rowan & MacDonald *Friendship* 48: To...tell old-fud lies. **1983** C. See, in *L.A. Times* (Aug. 11) V 26: A brittle, acerbic, duty-bound, "silly," "conservative" semi-fudd.

Fudd *n. Mil. Av.* WILLY FUDD.
1971 Windchy *Tonkin* 203 [ref. to 1964]: *Ticonderoga* had three Fudds. *Ibid.* 243: The Fudd found no hostile aircraft.

fuddle *n.* liquor; (*also*) an intoxicated state. Hence **fuddled,** *adj.* drunk.
****1674** in Duffett *Burlesque Plays* 16: They have drunk all the fuddle. *Ibid.* 18: Rhenish wine [is] base fuddle. ****1680** in *OED*: They have taken their dose of Fuddle. ****1698–99** "B.E." *Dict. Canting Crew: Fuddle,* Drink. *This is rum Fuddle,*...this is excellent Tipple. ****1705** in *F & H* III 81: And so...we sipp'd our fuddle...'Till every man had drowned his noddle. ****1733** in *Ibid.*: They have had their dose of fuddle. ****1764** in *OED*: In order to take large Morning Draughts, and secure the first Fuddle of the Day. ****1805** J. Davis *Post-Captain* 163: Caesar was in the high road to get fuddled. **1807** W. Irving *Salmagundi* 61: Got fuddled, and d—d the Professors. **1807** J.R. Shaw *Autobiog.* 129: I got pretty well fuddled. ****1889** Barrère & Leland *Dict. Slang* I 387: *Fuddle* (popular), drink. **1898** Dow *Reminiscences* 394: Those who formerly gathered at such places to get the "fuddle" were no longer drawn thither.

fuddy-duddy *n.* [prob. of dial. orig.] a stuffy, fussy, or foolishly old-fashioned person. Now *colloq.* Also **fuddy-dud.**
1904 in Wentworth *Amer. Dial. Dict.* 236: Fuddy-duddy. **1907** *DN* III 244: He's an awful old fuddy-duddy. **1904–14** *DN* IV 72: *Fuddydud* or *fuddyduddy, n.* Fussy person. **1934** Weseen *Dict. Slang* 337: *Fuddy-duddy*—A fussy person; an effeminate male. **1941** *Time* (Sept. 8) 70: Alexander I & Louis XVIII—a parricide & a fuddyduddy. **1963** Gant *Queen St.* 144: He had me tabbed as an old fuddy-duddy. **1975** J. Gould *Maine Lingo* 103: *Fuddydud.* Maine preference for fuddy-duddy. **1982** Heat Moon *Blue Hwys.* 109: You're a fuddydud! It's all just modalities. **1993** *TV Guide* (Mar. 6) 5: I'm an old-fashioned fuddy-duddy about TV.

fuddy-duddy *adj.* stodgy; fussy; foolishly old-fashioned. Now *colloq.*
1907 *DN* III 204. **1940** in *OEDS*: A great many people...believe its

officer class is caste-ridden and fuddy-duddy. **1977** S. Gaines *Discotheque* 89: Max may have been a bit fuddy-duddy but he was no fag. *a***1986** D. Tate *Bravo Burning* 11: Some of them could still have the old fuddy-duddy notion that turning you into a disciplined fighting...*man* could be of value.

fudge *n.* **1.** nonsense; rubbish.—often as interj. Now *colloq.*
****1766** O. Goldsmith, in *OED*: The very impolite behaviour of Mr. Burchell, who...at the conclusion of every sentence would cry out Fudge! ****1791** A. Radcliffe, in *OED*: That is all fudge to frighten you. **1814** B. Palmer *Diary* [entry for Jan. 12]: The Capt. brings a report that the Presidents frigate is sunk by an English line of Battle Ship./All Fudge/— **1849** in Windeler *Gold Rush Diary* 40: The captain said it belonged to the agent of the ship. But that is all fudge. **1851** W. Kelly *Ex. to Calif.* I 15: Pooh! pooh! gammon! fudge! treachery! **1859** Holmes *Prof.* 49: It's a neat little fiction,—of course it's all fudge. **1859** in Botkin *Treas. Amer. Folk.* 589: Pshaw! fidgetty fudge!...that's nothin'. **1865** in *PADS* (No. 70) 34: A report was circulated...that Gen. Sherman had asked for an armistice...."All fudge." **1879** [Tourgée] *Fool's Errand* 137: Break up the meeting! Fudge! ****1882** in *F & H* III 82: Much that we hear concerning the ways and means of the working classes is sheer fudge.
2. [fr. the brown color] *Homosex.* excrement; in phr. **hold (one's) fudge** to control (one's) bowels, as in the midst of panic; in phr. **pack fudge** to engage in anal copulation.
*a***1972** B. Rodgers *Queens' Vernacular* 88: (Syns. for anal intercourse:) *goose,...pack fudge* ('40s). *Ibid.* 90: *Fudge baby.* turd. **1972** *Anthro. Ling.* (Mar.) 101: *Dipping in the fudge pot...*Performing anal intercourse. **1980** D. Hamill *Stomping Ground* 158: Tell you, wouldn't mind stirring that Connie's fudge some day. **1984** E.M. Rauch *Buckaroo Banzai* (film): I'm scared. I can barely hold my fudge. **1988** R. Snow *Members of Committee* 4: What words do you [male homosexuals] use to describe the physical act of making love?...*Packing fudge.*

fudge *v.* [see FUDGE, *n.*, 2] to foul with excrement.
1986 *NDAS: Fudge one's pants* (or *undies*)...To become frightened...shit one's pants.

fudge *interj.* **1.** see *s.v.* FUDGE, *n.*, 1.
2. (used to indicate disappointment or mild annoyance).
1924 *DN* V 267: *Oh fudge* (vex[ation], disap[pointment]). **1942** *ATS* 195: (Aw) fudge! **1954–60** *DAS.*

fudge factor *n.* an allowance for imprecise calculation; margin for error; (*also, joc.*) a mathematical factor required to convert an incorrect answer to a problem into the correct answer.
1962 (cited in *W10*). **1969** Pendleton *Death Squad* 32: First time I ever blew a safe I added a bit of fudge factor, just in case. **1971** in Susman *Drug Use* 174: You can throw in all the "fudge factors" you want. **1974** N.Y.U. student: The fudge factor is the factor you have to multiply your answer by in order to get the correct answer. **1975** in Higham & Siddall *Combat Aircraft* 134: You always added...another 10 mph or so as a fudge factor. *ca***1979** Peers & Bennett *Logical Laws* 105: If your answer and the prof's answer do not match, you have obviously left out the fudge factor. **1985** Heywood *Taxi Dancer* 5: Setting a wind factor into the window put a fudge factor into the bomb drop.

Fudge Factory *n. Pol.* the U.S. Department of State. *Joc.*
1983 R. Thomas *Missionary* 270: I'm retiring from the fudge factory in exactly two months and nine days. **1986** Former U.S. Asst. Secy. of State B. Kalb (public lecture, Knoxville, Tenn.) (Nov. 18): The building that is known everywhere affectionately as the Fudge Factory.

fudge-packer *n.* a male homosexual anal sodomist.
1985 L.M. Carson *Texas Chainsaw Massacre II* (film): Ahh! You two shits—you fudge-packers—you'll be the death of me yet! **1985** "Blow-dryer" *Mod. Eng.* 74: Homosexual men...*Fudgepackers.* **1986** Eble *Campus Slang* (Nov.) 5: Homosexual man...*Fudge packer.* **1987** W. Georgia Coll. instructor, age 32: A *fudge-packer* is a sodomist. That's a word I learned from some frat guys about two years ago. **1987** Univ. Tenn. instructor: I asked my class about *fudge-packer*—and half of them recognized it immediately. **1988** *Nat. Lampoon* (Apr.) 26: Quoted as demanding "the goods on every fudge packer in town." **1992** N. Baker *Vox* 36: J.M. Barrie was a fudgepacker from way back.

fuel tank *n.* an aluminum beer keg.
1980 Wielgus & Wolff *Basketball* 133 (caption): The Fraternity Look...T-shirt from local watering hole...fuel tank.

fugazi *adj.* [orig. unkn.] (see quots.).
1980 M. Baker *Nam* 50: We didn't know anything was fugazi until we

got to a certain place in the South China Sea. *Ibid.* 321: *Fugazi*—fucked up or screwed up. **1985** Univ. Tenn. instructor, age *ca*35: *Fugazi* means fucked up in the head. I think it's a California expression.

fugle *v.* [orig. unkn.; prob. dial.] to cheat; bamboozle. Cf. HONEYFUGGLE.
     *1719 T. D'Urfey, in *OED*: Who fugell'd the Parson's fine Maid. **1871** in Thornbrough *Black Reconstructionists* 113: By dextrously "fugling" the negro vote, [he] got himself advanced to this high position. *1883 in *OED*: *Fugel*, or *Fugle*, to cheat, deceive, or trick; used actively. **1896** in *DAE* s.v. *fugle man*: I imagine that the gentleman who made the charge is a sort of a fugleman,...but I think he will fugle some before he gets through.

fugly *adj.* [blend of FUCKING + *ugly*] *Stu.* very ugly.
     1984 Mason & Rheingold *Slanguage: Fugly*, adj....fucking ugly. **1988** Eble *Campus Slang* (Fall) 4: *Fugly*—extremely ugly. **1989** P. Munro *UCLA Slang* 41: She's so fugly she makes my mother-in-law look cute.

führer or **fuehrer** *n.* [< G *(der) Führer* (title of Adolf Hitler)] (among U.S. prisoners of war in Germany) a prisoner responsible for a specified duty. Now *hist.* [Quots. ref. to WWII.]
     1955 Klaas *Maybe I'm Dead* 38: You're the room Führer. Start organizing. **1960** Simmons *Kriegie* 105: Well, each combine has a group of fuehrers. I am the bread fuehrer and I issue your bread every morning after breakfast....Pirtle is the coffee fuehrer and he makes all the coffee. Rhinehart is food fuehrer.

FUJIGMO *interj. Mil.* (see 1980 quot.). *Joc.* Cf. FUIGMO s.v. FIGMO.
     1950 *Sat. Eve. Post* (Aug. 5) 89: With him flew Lt. Col. "Pappy" Hatfield, in his famous bomber the "Fujigmo"—translation unprintable. **1953** in Valant *Aircraft Nose Art* 295: FUJIGMO. **1980** Cragg *L. Militaris* 158: FUJIGMO. Fuck You, Jack, I Got My Orders.

full *n. Football.* a fullback.
     1904 in Paxton *Sport USA* 134: Whenever the 'Varsity full kicks...charge him and knock him down.

full *adj.* [cf. Scots *fu'*] drunk; also in extended phr. such as **full as a tick.**
     1844 Porter *Big Bear* 136: My licker gourd full, and I half full. **1883** Peck *Bad Boy* 155: But about Pa. "He has been fuller'n a goose ever since New Year's day." **1887** *Lantern* (N.O.) (Aug. 6) 2: Ed did come home full as an egg. **1888** in *F & H* III 83: When he was *full* the police came and jugged [him]. **1892** *DN* I 210: *Full as a tick,* drunk. **1892** in S. Crane *Stories* 76: "He's full as a fiddler," said the little man. **1899** W. Green *Va. Folk-Speech* 152: Full, adj. Filled with liquor; drunk. **1905** *DN* III 80: *Full as a fiddle (goat, lord, tick)...Badly intoxicated. *1915* in *OEDS*: We both got full as ticks. **1924** Anderson & Stallings *What Price Glory?* 75: He's full to the scuppers. *ca1960 in Partridge *DSUE* (ed. 8) 434: Full as a fiddler's fart.
     ¶ In phrase:
     ¶ **full of it** see s.v. IT.

full barn *n. Poker.* a full house. Also vars.
     1949 Coffin *Winning Poker* 178: *Full Barn* (Shanty, Saloon, etc.)—Colloquial for full house. **1968** F. Wallace *Poker* 216: *Full House, Full Barn,* or *Full Tub*—Three of a kind with another pair.

full bird *n. Mil.* BIRD COLONEL.
     1963 Doulis *Path* 312: Soldiers don't interrupt Full Birds.

full boat *n. Poker.* a full house.
     *ca1969 Rabe *Hummel* 57: Full boat. Jacks and threes. **1978** (cited in T.L. Clark *Dict. Gamb.* 86). **1988** *Supercarrier* (ABC-TV): Read 'em and weep. Full boat, queens over aces.

full bore see s.v. BORE, *n.*

full bull *n. USAF.* a full colonel; FULL BIRD.
     1962 Mahurin *Honest John* 17 [ref. to 1950]: He was now a "full bull." **1966** Panama et al. *Not With My Wife You Don't* (film): See you're a full bull. **1966** Shepard *Doom Pussy* 167: A couple of full-bull colonels passed through Blytheville. **1985** Boyne & Thompson *Wild Blue* 485: That would put me in line to retire as a full bull. **1986** R. Walker *AF Wives* 124: Full bull, eagle on the shoulder.

full chisel *adv. N.E.* at full speed.
     1833 S. Smith *President's Tour* 15: You must...take away all the pine brush and sich like stuff from the door yard so we can drive up in front of your house full chizel and have all Downingville wide awake to meet us. **1846** in J.R. Lowell *Poetical Works* 181: Hosy he cum down stares

full chizzle, hare on eend and cote tales flyin. **1878** in *DA.*

full cob *n.* full speed.
     1968 Coppel *Order of Battle* 117 [ref. to WWII]: P-51's...closing the enemy at full cob.

full cooker *n. Av.* full power.
     1984 Cunningham & Ethell *Fox Two* 78 [ref. to Vietnam War]: Two J-79s at full cooker would have presented a great heat source.

full hand *n.* (see quot.).
     *ca1890–93 *F & H* III 84: *A full hand*...(American waiters'). Five large beers.

full house *n.* **1.** *Poker.* a hand consisting of three of a kind and a pair. Now *S.E.* [The earlier *S.E.* term *full hand* is virtually obsolete.]
     1887 *Puck* (Sept. 7) 21: Noah drew to pairs and got a full house. **1896** Ade *Artie* 14: W'y, that chump had a full house, nines on somethin'. **1899** in *DAE: A Full House, Full Hand,* or *Full.* Triplets and a pair together. **1944** in *DA: Full house,* or *full hand.* Three of a kind and a pair. **1949** Coffin *Winning Poker* 178: Full House—Three of a kind with a pair in hand.
     2.a. (see quots.).
     1942 *ATS* 23: A sufficiency; enough...*full house.* *1949 Granville *Sea Slang* 104: *Full house.* A mixed grill: (Lower deck). **1961** Clausen *Season's Over* 135 [ref. to *ca*1945]: Mary Louise advised us to order "a full house"—everything on the bill of fare. *1976 in Partridge *DSUE* (ed. 8) 434: *Full house*...A general [nautical] term for a complete set of anything [either] particularly pleasant or particularly unpleasant.
     b. *Baseball.* loaded bases.
     1922 (cited in Nichols *Baseball Term.*).
     c. Esp. *Naut.* (see 1942–49 quot.).
     1940 *AS* (Dec.) 450: A sailor contracting several [venereal] diseases at the same time complains of a *full house.* **1942–49** Goldin et al. *DAUL* 75: *Full house.* Simultaneous infection with gonorrhea and syphilis, often accompanied by body lice. **1958** Cooley *Run For Home* 188 [ref. to 1920's]: "I've seen a lot of guys get conned by those snooty 'nice girls' and wind up with a full house!"...He knew that a "full house" meant coincidental cases of gonorrhea and syphilis. *1976 in Partridge *DSUE* (ed. 8) 434: *Full house*...A double dose of V.D., syphilis and gonorrhea together: Merchant (and, I think Royal) Navy: since *ca*.1930.
     d. *Hot Rodding.* (see quots.).
     1951–53 in *AS* (May 1954) 97: *Full house*...An engine fully modified for racing, with "heads," "carburetion," "ignition," "cam," etc. **1962** *AS* XXXVII 269: *Full house,* n. An automobile engine with a full complement of high-speed modifications on it.

full-mooner *n. Journ.* a person who is demented or insane, presumably under the influence of the full moon.
     *a1986 in *NDAS*: In San Francisco, where there are full-mooners on every street corner. *Ibid.*: This issue goes beyond the full-mooners.

full-on *adj. & adv.* all-out; full out; completely.
     1970 Southern *Blue Movie* 174: Why don't we do some full-on S.M.? **1978** Alibrandi *Killshot* 170: You're full-on wacko. **1982–84** in Safire *Take My Word* 241: Other phrases of praise by teens are *tubular, killer,...and *full on.* **1984** D. Jenkins *Life Its Ownself* 57: She would be all-out, full-on...tolerant.

full-out *adj.* extremely keen or enthusiastic.
     1918 in Rossano *Price of Honor* 129: We're both "full-out" for it. *Ibid.* 185: He's a "full-out" old scout, I'll say that much for him. *Ibid.* 189: On the way home I was feeling particularly "full out," so I dove for a very famous...[antiaircraft] battery.

full-rigged *adj. Naut.* fully dressed, esp. in one's best clothing; (*hence*) out-and-out; full-fledged.
     1899 Robbins *Gam* 142: You ought to seen him play it on them full-rig Mohammedans at Johanna. **1900** Hammond *Whaler* 193: "He's full-rigged, and got ev'ry rag set," Jack said on the side. **1906** J.H. Williams, in *Independent* (Apr. 19): Billy...was a full-rigged, respectable, sea-faring goat of the noble "butt in" breed.

full-time *adj.* utter; absolute.
     1965 Capote *In Cold Blood* 248: He was dead against me. Said I was a full-time nobody. **1976** Price *Bloodbrothers* 129: He was a full-time chump if Stony ever saw one.

full tog *n. Navy.* full-dress uniform. Also **full togs.**
     *1834 in Partridge *DSUE* (ed. 8) 435: *Sam.* Our captains also appeared in full uniform....*Ned.* The skippers seldom wear full togs for nothing. *ca1899 B.F. Sands *Reefer* 72 [ref. to *ca*1832]: One...midshipman had

the temerity or vanity to venture an appearance in "full tog."

full-weight *adj.* genuine.

> **1859** Avery *Comical Stories* 57: I'm one of 'em, I'm around, I'm full weight, potato measure.

fully *v.* [sugg. by phr. *fully committed for trial*] *Police.* to commit for trial. *Obs.* in U.S.

> **1849 in OEDS:* The prisoner said…he expected either to be *turned up* or *fully'd*…—those are *cant* expressions, meaning either to be discharged, or committed for trial. **1859** Matsell *Vocab.* 35: *Fullied.* Committed for trial. **1867** *Nat. Police Gaz.* (Mar. 30) 2: Jersey Jimmy…was "fullied" on the attempt at larceny. **1926, *1936 in OEDS.*

Fu Manchu *n. Navy.* a kind of anti-radar device used on board German naval vessels during World War II. Now *hist.*

> **1962** Farago *10th Fleet* 212: The…*Funkmessbeobachtungsgeraet* (or FuMB for short and known as "Fu Man-Chu" to the Americans) worked against radar.

fumblefart *n.* a clumsy or inept person.—usu. considered vulgar.

> [**1940** Goodrich *Delilah* 152 [ref. to 1917]: Listen, fumble-foot, lay off the kid! Get me?] **1963–64** Kesey *Great Notion* 73: Ain't I *tole* you 'bout thisyere fumble-fart an' fallin' *down* all the time.

fume *v. Mil.* to smoke tobacco. Also as *n.*

> **1894** *Lucky Bag* (No. 1) 67: *Fume*…To smoke. **1898** Allen *Navy Blue* 137: "Put out that cigarette, Pete Rollins, or I'll do it for you!" "What's the matter with a quiet little fume?" **1900** *Howitzer* (No. 1) 119: *Fume.*—To smoke. **1906** *Army & Navy Life* (Nov.): *Fume.* to smoke.

¶ In phrase:

¶ **on fumes** Esp. *Av.* with or having little fuel remaining in fuel tanks.

> **1985** Boyne & Thompson *Wild Blue* 226: It was the last run of the day, and I…was running on fumes. **1989** Berent *Rolling Thunder* 285: Give us a snap vector to Da Nang. We're on fumes. **1990** *Twin Peaks* (ABC-TV): Riding on fumes now, gotta tank up soon.

fumigate *v.* to smoke tobacco. *Joc.*

> **1881** A.A. Hayes *New Colo.* 121: "Stranger, do you fumigate?" "If you mean smoke, sir, I do not." **1900** *DN* II 38: *Fumigate*, v.i. To smoke. [Reported from 14 colleges.]

fun *adj.* amusing; enjoyable. Now *colloq.* [The 1862 quot. is remarkably early and may simply reflect a slip of the pen or a typographical error for *funny*; the sense of the 1918 quot. is 'done simply for fun'; cf. exx. discussed by John Algeo, "A Fun Thing," *AS* XXXVII (1962), 158–59. Pre-1950 prenominal uses in *OED2* represent attributive use of the noun.]

> **1862** in Wightman *To Ft. Fisher* 27: This was "never so fun…except when he was drunk." [**1918** in Truman *Dear Bess* 241: This is a fun letter and it is a bad day.] **1950** Hartmann & O'Brien *Fancy Pants* (film): Oh, this is a fun group, isn't it? **1961** *Mad* (July): You're such a "fun" guy. **1961** in *AS* XXXVII 158: This must be one of the most fun ages. **1962** J. Algeo, in *AS* XXXVII 159: The future development of adjectival *fun* needs watching. We can surely expect to find pure intensifiers used with it: a *very fun party* is only a matter of time. We may even anticipate being told that one car is funner than another, and that will be the funnest thing of all. **1980** Ciardi *Browser's Dict.* 142: We had a fun party. It's a fun thing. *a*1986 in *NDAS*: Mickey and his chums introduce each other as "a real fun guy." **1987** *Science News* (Sept. 5) 153: I skydive because it is very fun to fly. **1987** M. Groening *School Is Hell* (unp.): Go for the swings—they're the funnest. **1993** K. Costner, on *Live with Regis & K. Lee* (synd. TV series) (Mar. 9): That was probably the funnest part of it.

fun-bags *n.pl.* a woman's breasts. *Joc.*

> **1965** in *Playboy* (Feb. 1966) 165: Bazooms…fun-bags. **1976** J.W. Thomas *Heavy Number* 1: He did a number on her fun bags you wouldn't believe. **1985** "Blowdryer" *Mod. Eng.* 77: Tits…*funbags.*

Fun City *n.* New York City.—later often used ironically. Also **fun city.**

> **1966** in J. Flaherty *Chez Joey* 3: Why has the Fun Fled Fun City? *ca*1968 W. Klein, in Safire *New Lang. Pol.* 158: As for the origin of "Fun City," I believe that the Mayor [John V. Lindsay] himself originated this term early in 1966, or possibly in late 1965 when he participated in an advertisement for an airline and he was asked about New York. His reply contained the phrase "Fun City." **1972** J. Mills *Report* 70: And if you came into the squad and said your wife had just been beaten and

raped on the sidewalk, he'd laugh, and slap you on the shoulder, and say, "Well, that's fun city, man." **1975** V. Miller *Trade-Off* 24: Not right here in the middle of Fun City! **1977** S. Gaines *Discotheque* 268: This place is about the best time I've had in Fun City. **1989** "Capt. X" & Dodson *Unfriendly Skies* 130: That poor band director was about to encounter "Fun City"—with certain results that would not be too humorous for him. **1989** *Comments on Ety.* (May) 8: [On his first day in office in 1966, Mayor Lindsay was] asked…if he was still glad he'd been elected, and he said, "I still think it's a fun city." I [Dick Schaap]…capitalized [the phrase]…I wrote a regular column in the Herald Tribune…called "What's New in Fun City?"

funeral *n.* one's concern or affair, esp. if likely to be disastrous.

> **1854** in *OEDS:* A boy said to an outsider who was making a great ado during some impressive mortuary ceremonies, "What are you crying about? It's none of your funeral." **1870** in *DAE:* Mr. Painter, then addressing you, said, "This is not my funeral." **1871** Schele de Vere *Amer.* 239: "This is none of your funeral," is heard quite frequently an indirect rebuke for intermeddling. **1882** Sweet *Sketches* 41: Just suit yourself. It's not my funeral. **1888** C.C. King *Deserter* 40: It's none of our funeral, as Blake says. **1891** Maitland *Slang Dict.* 189: *None of my funeral* (Am.), no business of the person using the expression. **1918** Kelland *Highflyers* 11: It wasn't any of your funeral. **1942–43** C. Jackson *Lost Weekend* 44: That was *their* funeral; who cared? **1979** T. Baum *Carny* 155: Don't worry about the girl.…The girl's my funeral. **1980** McDowell *Our Honor* 235: Very well, Krupe, it's your funeral. **1986** Stinson & Carabatsos *Heartbreak* 189: It's their fuckin' funeral. Let's go!

funeralize *v.* to ruin; do for.

> **1882** Baillie-Grohman *Rockies* 9: Guess them dog-garned horses have funeralized us all-fired meanly.

fungo *n.* a stupid or worthless person.

> **1963** E.M. Miller *Exile* 54: What are you fungoes doing here? Aren't you happy at home? **1960–69** Runkel *Law* 139: Manys-a-time I…seen my sister suckin' on some dirty fungo.

fungoo *interj.* [aph. < It *affanculo!* 'I fuck [you] in the ass!'; 1944 and 1962 quots. represent E respellings of the full form] Orig. *Ital.-Amer.* (used as a vulgar insult). [Often accompanied by a corresponding stiffened-arm gesture.]

> **1944** in Olmstead *Yoxford Boys* 82: [Name painted on P-51D Mustang] Ah Fung Goo II. **1962** N.Y.C. schoolboy: Aw, fun*goo*, motherfucker! [**1968** Legman *Rationale* 152: "Fa'n'gul" (dialectal Italian for "I fuck (you) in the ass").] **1980** Pearl *Slang* 56: *Fungoo interj.* euphemism for fuck you. **1988** N.Y.C. woman, age 54: I knew this kid named Gerald Shane who used to say "Fungoo!" all the time. This was in 1948.

fungus *n.* **1.** an offensive person; CREEP. [**1803 quot. is fig. S.E.]

> [**1803 in J. Ashton *Eng. Satires on Napoleon* 227: From a Corsican dunghill this fungus did spring.] **a*1890–93 *F & H* III 87: *Fungus*…(old).—An old man. **1929** "E. Queen" *Roman Hat* 30: Where the average police system falls down…is in its ruthless tracking down of gentlemen who dispose of such fungus as Mr. Monte Field. **1933** Mahin & Furthman *Bombshell* (film): I'll get rid of this fungi. **1960** in IUFA *Folk Speech*: There's a fungus among us. *ca*1965 in *Ibid: Fungus*—similar to a "square." **1980** Cragg *Lexicon* 20: At Ease, Disease, There's A Fungus Among Us. Often merely *At ease, disease.*…I first heard it used in 1958. **1988** Dietl & Gross *One Tough Cop* 253: I won't say, "Oooohh, I'm not going." I won't be a fungus.

2. whiskers; a beard.—used derisively.

> **1925 in *OEDS:* Where did you get the fungus? **1936, *1937 in *Ibid.* **1942** S. Johnston *Queen of Flat-tops* 27: He would not shave his upper lip.…Tonight this fungus had reached gigantic proportions and from constant twirling stuck out on both sides of his face. **1977** Olsen *Fire Five* 24: Get that fungus off your face!

funhouse *n.* a brothel.

> **1962** Crump *Killer* 183: The whoah's in de fun house spread for Crow.

funk[1] *n.* [fr. dial. *funk* 'a stink'; see FUNK[1], *v.*, and *OED2, DARE*] **1.** *Und.* tobacco.

> [**1698–99 "B.E." *Dict. Canting Crew: Funk*…Tobacco Smoak…*What a Funk here is! What a thick Smoak of Tobacco is here!*] **1703 E. Ward (cited in Partridge *DSUE*). **1791** [W. Smith] *Confess. T. Mount* 19: Tobacco, *weed* or *funk.*

2. [back formation fr. FUNKY[2], *adj.*] Orig. *Jazz.* a strongly earthy or bluesy quality in jazz or blues; (*hence*) music having such a quality. Also **fonk.** Now *S.E.*

1953–58 J.C. Holmes *Horn* 27: All [musicians] who comped with funk. **1958** in Tamony *Americanisms* (No. 20) 9: "Funk" became the dernier cri...the drive being sought for was less the far-out swinging drive of Parker and more and more the drive of the New Orleans gutbucket. **1959** in R.S. Gold *Jazz Talk* 101: Miles Davis blowing his sophisticated funk. **1964** *N.Y. Times* (Mar. 22) 2 23: The soul-funk-gospel cliché that is one of the compulsory routines of today's pianists. **1965** Oliver *Conversations with Blues* 6: Today, "funk" means blues, "soul" means blues feeling in the parlance of the modern jazz musician. **1969** *Playboy* (Mar.) 32: It's a fine batch of funk. **1971** S. Stevens *Way Uptown* 138: The box was playing heavy funk and it made me feel trapped. **1978** Truscott *Dress Gray* 129: She...went to rock-and-roll concerts at the Fillmore East to capture a feel for what had become known as "funk." **1984** Toop *Rap Attack* 42: Plenty of far superior funk and disco records. *ca***1986** in *NDAS*: He *is* New Orleans "fonk."

funk² *n.* [prob. < obs. Flemish *fonck*; cf. FUNK², *v.*, attested slightly earlier] **1.a.** a state of fear or panic; fear. [First noted as Oxford Univ. slang, with the above ety.]
*****1743** in *OED*: To be in a funk. *****1765** in *Ibid.*: Poor Todd...is said to be in a violent funk. *****1785** Grose *Vulgar Tongue*: I was in a cursed funk. *****1819** [T. Moore] *Tom Crib* 21: Up he rose in a funk. **1843** *Spirit of Times* (Aug. 5) 266: I was rather in a "funk."...I knew not whether I had commenced aright, and if I had, what course I should next pursue....I had worried myself into a *mal au ventre*. **1847–48** Ruxton *Far West* 13: The mules...was a-snortin' with funk...before the Injuns. **1850** in Bartlett *Amer.* (ed. 2) 164: So my friend's fault is timidity....I grant then, that the funk is sublime. *****1856** T. Hughes, in *F & H* III 87: If I was going to be flogged next minute, I should be in a blue funk. *****1859,** *****1861,** *****1870,** *****1871,** *****1888** in *Ibid.* **1927** in Hammett *Big Knockover* 298: I hope you won't think I'm in a funk...but I'm not an antique murderer like you.
b. a black mood, esp. a state of confusion or depression. Now *S.E.*
*****1820–21** P. Egan *Life in London* 220: I was in a complete *funk*. *****1808–25** Jamieson *Scot. Dict.* II 321: *Funk*...Ill-humour. *In a funk*, in a surly state, or in a fit of passion. **1851** B. Hall *College Wds.*: *Funk*. Disgust; weariness; fright. **1954–60** *DAS*: *Funk*...A mood of idle depression. [Also] *blue funk*. *a***1961** in *WNID3*. **1966** *RHD*: He's been in a funk ever since she walked out on him. **1974** in Rowan & MacDonald *Friendship* 233: I was in a funk. **1980** Freudenberger & Richelson *Burn Out* 146: You're in a funk, and I'd like to help you get out of it. **1982** Trudeau *Dressed for Failure* (unp.): Boy, I wish I could shake this funk. Today I got so depressed I came home from work after lunch.
2. a coward.
[*****1808–25** Jamieson *Scot. Dict.* II 321: *Funkie*...One who shuns the fight.] **1859** Bartlett *Amer.* (ed. 2) 164: *Funk*...a coward. **1867** in Rosa *Wild Bill* 61: He tried to back out of this, but the men raised a row, calling him a funk, and a bragger, and all that. *****1882** in *F & H* III 87: They were neither of them *funks*, of course, but they lost their heads. *****1888** in *OED*: The public opinion among youth would...dub a "fellow" a "funk." *a***1930** in Tomlinson *Sea Stories* 585: There was a pair of funks aboard this craft, eh?

funk³ *n.* PETER FUNK.

funk¹ *v.* [< North F dial. *funquier* 'to give off smoke'] to smoke. [Also in obs. BrE slang 'to blow smoke upon; to annoy with smoke'; see *OED2*.]
*****1699** E. Ward, in Winship *Boston* 51: Their Mouths smell as bad as the Bowl of a Sailers *Pipe*, which he has funk'd in...a whole Voyage to the *Indias*. *****ca**1704** in *OED2*: Since Jove...Gives us the Indian weed to funk. *****1764** in *OED2*: A round dozen pipes they funk. *****1785** Grose *Vulgar Tongue*: *Funk*. To smoke. **1829** in *OED*: *Funk*, to smoke. **1860** Bartlett *Amer.* (ed. 2) 164: *To Funk*. To make an offensive smoke or dust. When the smoke puffs out from a chimney place or stove, we say "it *funks*."

funk² *v.* [fr. FUNK², *n.*, despite the slightly earlier first citation for the v.] **1.a.** to flinch, freeze, or shrink through fear; become afraid.
*****1737–39** H. Walpole, in *OED*: The last time I saw him here, was standing up funking over a conduit to be catechised. *****1785** Grose *Vulgar Tongue*: *Funk*. To smoke, figuratively to smoke or stink through fear. *****1813** in *OED*: I funk before Ellenborough as much as ever. *****1808–25** Jamieson *Scot. Dict.* II 321: *Funk*...to become afraid. *****1827** in *F & H* III 88: Do not go out of your depth, unless you have available assistance at hand, in case you should funk. **1848** J.R. Lowell, in *F & H* III 88: To funk right out o' p'litical strife ain't thought to be the thing.

1854 "Youngster" *Swell Life at Sea* 194: I say, young 'un, you ain't funking, are you? *****1885** in *OED*: I hope you will not think I am funking. **1909** in O. Johnson *Lawrenceville* 38: At the sight of the solid front of bone and muscle ready to sweep him off his feet,...he shut his eyes and funked deliberately and ingloriously. **1910** Stirling *Mid. in Philippines* 120: If that fellow Tillotson hadn't funked...we could have flayed 'em alive. **1935** Algren *Boots* 139: Start funkin', Mexy! Your arse is goin' clean through the floor in a second! **1945** Himes *If He Hollers* 117: I knew she would know I'd funked.
b. to back down or renege.—constr. with *out.*
1837 *Spirit of Times* (May 27) 113: Peter was not the man to funk out of a treat [because of stinginess]. **1859** Matsell *Vocab.* 35: *Funked Out.* Frightened; backed out. **1892** L. Moore *Own Story* 26: Now they have seen you, they have all funked out and don't dare bet. **1903** *Pedagog. Sem.* 380: To eat dirt. To funk out. **1905** *DN* III 10: *Funk out*...To back out in a cowardly manner. **1962** Reiter *Night in Sodom* 112: [He] never funked out! **1968** Johnson & Johnson *Count Me Gone* 46: Me, funking out that way yesterday.
c. to fail; fizzle out.—constr. with *out.*
1841 *Spirit of Times* (Oct. 30) 409: I did fancy we might have a gay winter season, but I am now fearful it will all "funk out." **1961** Kohner *Gidget Goes Hawaiian* 3: His sense of humor funked out.
2. to frighten; scare. Hence **funked,** *adj.* scared.
*****1819** in *OED*: The Frenchman, funked at the superiority of his antagonist. *****1831** Sir W. Scott, in *OED*: Jeffrey is fairly funked about it. **1846** in H.L. Gates, Jr. *Sig. Monkey* 93: De meanin ob de word funked is dat you feel half dead. *****1857–58** A. Mayhew *Paved with Gold* 294: "For," said that bold young vagrant, "perhaps we're only funking ourselves useless, and it mayn't be the farm chaps at all." **1892** in *OED*: The jury, "funked" by the Anarchists, returned extenuating circumstances in the miscreant's case. **1899** Lounsberry *West Point* 22: "To tell the truth, I feel rather 'funked,' don't you?" Harold laughingly acknowledged that he was not altogether at his ease. **1965** Yurick *Warriors* 106: Don't let these Masai coons funk you, because the Blazers have them in control.
3. to shrink from facing; try to shirk or evade.—also constr. with *it.* Now *S.E.* and *rare* in U.S.
*****1836** in *F & H* III 88: And I never funk the lambskin men/When I sits with her in the boozing ken. *****1846** in *F & H* III 88: But as yet no nose is bleeding,/As yet no man is down;/For the gownsmen funk the townsmen,/And the townsmen funk the gown. *****1857** in *OED*: He'll have funked it, when he comes to the edge, and sees nothing but mist below. *****1873** in *F & H* III 88: Come along! don't funk it, old fellow! **1881** H. James *Portrait of Lady* ch. xlv: Not that he liked goodbyes—he always funked them. **1972–79** T. Wolfe *Right Stuff* 328: Having funked it in business of night carrier landings.

funker *n.* *Und.* a petty or unskillful thief; (*also*) a PETER FUNK.
*****1797** in Partridge *Dict. Und.* 272: *Funkers*, idle and disorderly fellows of the lowest order of thieves. **1852** in *DA*: Petronius Funk, Fictitious Auctioneer. Wylie, Bonnett, Associate Funkers. **1859** Matsell *Vocab.* 35: *Funkers*. The very lowest order of thieves.

funkhole *n.* *Army.* a hole or dugout that offers protection from enemy fire. [U.S. quots. ref. to WWI.]
*****1900** in *OEDS*: The Funk Holes which the besieged residents had mined in the river bank. *****1914** in *OEDS*: I am sitting in my "funk hole" lined with straw. **1917** in Roy *Pvt. Fraser* 276: The positions, funkholes, do not offer much protection. **1918** *Sat. Eve. Post* (Jan. 19) 62: These holes are named funk holes and I seen quite a lot of Jocks asleep in them. **1918** *Chi. Daily Trib.* (Oct. 16) 4: Maj. Whittlesey ordered his men to dig "funk holes," which were only large enough to get their bodies below the level of the ground, and prepare to spend the night there. **1919** Camp *305th Field Arty.* 208: The floor of the forest was fairly honey-combed with elaborate funk-holes. **1925** Nason *Three Lights* 173: *Understand für Officiere*—officers' funk-hole. **1926** [O'Brien] *Wine, Women and War* 318: Funk hole. A shelter against shrapnel. **1928** Harrison *Generals Die in Bed* 55: The dugouts here are filled with water and we live in hastily-constructed funk-holes, holes burrowed into the side of the parapet or parados. **1931** Bullard *Amer. Soldiers* 50: Get back into your "funk-holes" you damned fools!

funk out see FUNK², *v.*, 1.a., 1.b., & 1.c.

funk up *v.* *Music.* to suffuse with funk.
*ca***1984** in Toop *Rap Attack* 42: Wants to get funked up.

funky *n.* *Black E.* the rump.—used derisively.
1966 J. Reed *Pall-Bearers* 33: Why don't you get up off your big funkey sometime and pick up a mop?

funky[1] *adj.* [fr. FUNK[2], *n.*] nervous; frightened; timid. Now *rare* in U.S.

> ★**1837** Dickens *Pickwick* ch. xxxi: Mr. Phunky…had a very nervous manner, and a painful hesitation in his speech; it…seemed the result of timidity. ★**1845** in *OED:* I do feel somewhat funky. ★**1863** in *F & H* III 89: The remaining Barkingtonians were less funky, and made some fair scores. ★**1876** in *F & H:* The second round commences with a little cautious sparring on both sides, the bouncing Elias looking very funky. ★**1899** Mackintosh *Course of Sprouts* (unp.): Here my heart began to thump/And no wonder I felt funky,/For the frog with one big jump/Leap'd hisself into a monkey. **1906** A.H. Lewis *Confessions* 206: This cove…is turning funky. **1952** Bellow *Augie March* 358: Is that mighty bird funky? Is he yellow?

funky[2] *adj.* [fr. dial. *funky* 'musty or foul-smelling', fr. BrE dial.; (hence) 'filthy'; see *OED2*] **1.** *Black E.* worthless; rotten; bad; objectionable. Also **fonkey.**

> [**1929** in *AS* VI 158: *Funkey* is used to describe the odor of perspiration, as *"a funkey old man."*] **1964** N. Hentoff, in *New Yorker* (Oct. 24) 86: They looked even funkier than I did, I guess. They weren't dressed right, or something. **1965** C. Brown *Manchild* 244 [ref. to 1950's]: He treats her like she's just an average old funky bitch out there. **1967** [Beck] *Pimp* 95: I been getting funky breaks since I came to this raggity city. **1970** Landy *Underground Dict.* 85: *Funky*…Describes raw (deal). **1971** Goines *Dopefiend* 40: Like we really give a fuck about her funky fifty dollars. *a***1972** B. Rodgers *Queens' Vernacular* 91: *Funky (fonky)*…inferior; in bad taste. **1974** Gober *Black Cop* 35: It ain't easy to come by men who are going to get down and take care of business when the shit gets funky. **1982** Goff, Sanders, & Smith *Bros.* 54: It's funky out here, man.…Like we was out there for eighty-three days before we came in for stand-down. **1986** Merkin *Zombie Jamboree* 275: If you got funky stuff, drop it in the jungle. **1989** S. Robinson & D. Ritz *Smokey* 78: Shit, man…This sure is some funky business. **1992** *In Living Color* (Fox-TV): Such a funky attitude!

2.a. Orig. *Black E.* excellent; deeply satisfying.

> **1939** in A. Banks *First-Person* 257: That'll be a funky fight. **1959–60** Bloch *Dead Beat* 4: The deal was working out perfectly. Or, as the sax [player] would put it, "funky." **1961** Brosnan *Pennant Race* 163: Negro music…You're a college boy and you don't know…what "funky" means! **1968–70** *Current Slang* III & IV 49: *Fonky*, adj. Nice.—Watts. —I had a fonky time at the party last night. **1970** Landy *Underground Dict.* 85: *Funky*…Groovy; with it; in with the times—eg., *She's a funky chick.* **1980** Ciardi *Browser's Dict.* 142: *Funky*…Term of general approval. *We had a real funky time.* **1989** MTV (Sept. 2): Yeah, and some of that funky pasta primavera. **1991** *UTSQ: Funky*—similar to awesome.

b. Orig. *Black E.* (esp. of music) intensely earthy; bluesy; down to earth. Now *colloq.* [Discussed by Peter Tamony, "Funky," *AS* LV (1980), 210-13.]

> **1954** *Time* (Nov. 8) 70: Far-Out Words for Cats…*funky, adj.* Authentic, swinging. **1954** W. Winchell, in Tamony *Americanisms* (No. 20) 4: "Funky."…Real hipsters say it means old-time rickety jazz. **1958–59** Lipton *Barbarians* 74: The occasion seemed to call for funky music. **1959** in *BDNE* 179: In current jazz argot, "funky"…is a term of final approbation meaning earthy, unpretentious and rooted in the blues. **1959** *Social Problems* VII 252: In the last few years there has been a tendency for jazz to move away from the "cool" and toward a more "funky" (earthy) style of expression. **1959–60** R. Reisner *Jazz Titans* 156: *Funky:* earthy. Originally meant an obnoxious smell, a repellent stench. It now refers to music with a basic, down home, hard beat. **1964** Gregory *Nigger* 60: She didn't want to dance to the blues, the gut bucket, the funky songs. **1965** Cleaver *Soul on Ice* 27: Rather, LeRoi is expressing the funky facts of life. **1966** Braly *On Yard* 175: He liked his bitches funky. **1967** Colebrook *Cross of Lassitude* 215: I sure could use some of that funky guitar. **1971** Wells & Dance *Night People* 117: *Funky*…Earthy. Contemporary equivalent of earlier "barrelhouse" and "gutbucket." **1980** Ciardi *Browser's Dict.* 142: Sidney Bechet once explained to me that *ca*1900 *funky* had the sense "back on the plantation," and *funky jazz* now labels primitive…pre-Dixieland jazz. **1984** Toop *Rap Attack* 131: Party people—can't y'all get funky? **1992** "Fab 5 Freddy" *Fresh Fly Flavor* 28: *Funky* or *fonky*…A state of mind, music, clothes or attitude that can come from being totally immersed in black music and culture.

c. unconventionally or unpretentiously appealing or enjoyable, esp. stylishly quaint or eccentric.

> **1969** in *OEDS:* You can't hype kids into buying things they don't want, even with people in funky clothes soft-selling them. **1970** *Time* (Aug. 17) 32: That's a funky jacket. **1972** *N.Y. Times* (Oct. 28) 15: I love funky far-out things with wild colors. **1976–77** C. McFadden *Serial* 66: At the new Saturday Night Movie series in that funky old Odd Fellows Hall on Throckmorton. **1978** Maupin *Tales* 8: The room was supposed to look funky: brick-red walls, revolving beer signs, kitschy memorabilia. *Ibid.* 12: I've found this darling place…on the third floor of the funkiest old building. **1979** Lyle & Golenbock *Bronx Zoo* v: Behind the Daliesque, funky mustache, Lyle was an athlete seemingly without a nervous system. **1993** *CBS This Morning* (CBS-TV) (Mar. 10): A fresh, funky script.

d. strange; odd.

> **1984** Mason & Rheingold *Slanguage* (unp.): *Faunky* [*sic*]…strange…as in a faunky taste…sight, sound, feeling. **1984** in P. Munro *UCLA Slang* 41: *Funky* bizarre.

3. (of a mood or feeling) sad; dejected. [Less prob. belonging to FUNKY[1], *adj.*]

> **1974** Blount *3 Bricks Shy* 252: I fall off into my funky moods.

funky *v.* to play or dance to FUNKY music.

> **1970** Quammen *Walk the Line* 58: Tyrone was still funkying.

funky-butt *n. Jazz.* an obnoxious person.

> [**1954** L. Armstrong *Satchmo* 22 [ref. to *ca*1910]: At the corner of the street where I lived was the famous Funky Butt Hall where I first heard Buddy Bolden play.] **1964** Smith & Hoefer *Music* 167 [ref. to 1920's]: The place finally got overloaded with funky butts*…and Jerry slapped on a cover charge.…*Squares from downtown.

funky-butt *adj. Jazz.* FUNKY[2].

> **1968** Maule *Rub-A-Dub* 11: While the band plays the funky butt blues.

funky-fresh *adj. Rap Music.* very stylish or appealing.

> **1982** "Fearless Four" in L.A. Stanley *Rap* 127: Can't you hear my rhymes are funky fresh? **1988** Eble *Campus Slang* (Fall) 4: *Funky fresh*—neat…with it. **1992** *In Living Color* (Fox-TV): He's the funky-fresh dude that don't have time for sweets.

funky monkey *n. Black E.* (used as an arbitrary symbol of value).

> *ca*1974 in J.L. Gwaltney *Drylongso* 17: I'll bet you a funky monkey and two old maids you would have told me what to do with this food.

funnel *n.* a heavy drinker; in phr. **funnel gang** a group of heavy drinkers.

> **1906** *DN* III 126: Belong to the *funnel gang*, v. phr. To drink intoxicants to excess. "He *belongs to the funnel gang.*" **1923** *Bomb* (Iowa State Coll.) 422: The Sig Eps lead in the funnel gang. **1927** *AS* II (Mar.) 276: *Funnel*…a drinking student.

funny *n.* (see quot.).

> **1972** *New Yorker* (Nov. 11) 66 [ref. to Apollo XIII, 1970]: The INCO told Kranz about a communications "funny"—an aberration that doesn't clear up immediately, as opposed to a "glitch," which is a transitory one.

funny *adj.* **1.** tipsy.

> ★**1756** in *OED:* More brandy was drank, and, Tom Throw beginning to be what is called funny, the house was full of uproar and confusion. ★**1820–21** P. Egan *Life in London* 183: The trio were getting rather *funny.* **1857** in Stacey & Beale *Uncle Sam's Camels* 64: This morning I observed some of our young gentlemen coming into camp with a gait that denoted a slight indulgence in alcoholic stimulants. Subsequently I was informed that the whole party who were in Fort after dark got funny.

2. [sugg. by earlier colloq. sense 'odd, peculiar'] treacherous; deceitful; (hence) impudent; esp. in phr. of the sort **get funny**; in phr. **funny business** [or **work**] deceit; treachery. Now *colloq.*

> **1882** in Nye *Western Humor* 77: Now if we have been the cause of any such funny business as that, we are sorry and ashamed of it. **1884** in Lummis *Letters* 165: This Company…is trying to come the funny business on the public. **1896** Ade *Artie* 63: He had to do all kinds o' funny work to get the nomination. *Ibid.* 68: Some day you'll get too gay an' a guy'll give you a funny poke. [**1897** *Harper's Wkly.* (Jan.) 90: The horseplay of the mountebanks in the variety shows is commonly called "funny business," and the term has now come to be applied to all rough play—frolicking, scuffling, and practical joking—among the masses.] **1898** Norris *Moran* 100: China boy no likee funnee business, savvy? **1899** Garland *Eagle's Heart* 246: You got mixed up in some funny business on the plains and had to take a sneak to the mountains. **1899** "J. Flynt" *Tramping* 370: Don't you try any funny work. **1899** Hamblen *Bucko Mate* 106: I felt now that we could give a good account of ourselves in case the dagoes took a notion to be funny. **1903** A. Adams *Log*

of Cowboy 100 [ref. to 1880's]: No false moves or funny work or I'll shoot the white out of your eye. *Ibid.* 240: Stallings sat up and yawningly inquired "what other locoed fool had got funny." *Ibid.* 249: He might get funny and tip the old man. **1905** *Nat. Police Gaz.* (Nov. 11) 3: Just cut all dis funny business out and leave my gal alone. **1919** Darling *Jargon Book* 14: *Funny Business*—Acts which are not understood and which one feels are being done to fool or deceive him. **1921** Casey & Casey *Gay-Cat* 76: If he tries any funny work, we'll— **1925–26** Black *You Can't Win* 144: Don't try any funny business. **1935** R. Graves *Speed Limited* (film): Don't try anything funny if ya know what's good for ya! **1944** C.B. Davis *Leo McGuire* 63: I never like to get funny with Uncle Sam. Those federal penitentiaries aren't any joke. **1953** R. Chandler *Goodbye* 119: You are in no position to get funny. **1967–80** Folb *Runnin' Lines* 239: *Get funny* 1. Engage in unpredictable or disruptive behavior. 2. Start something dangerous or threatening. **1987** *Perfect Strangers* (ABC-TV): Don't you guys try to pull anything funny or we'll hurt ya.

funny bin *n.* FUNNY HOUSE; LOONY BIN.
  1952 Mandel *Angry Strangers* 34: Don't start calling people crazy or you'll have to put all the citizens in the funny bin. *Ibid.* 367: He's in the nuthouse, a big big funny bin.

funny bunny *n.* a peculiar or ridiculous person or thing.
  1966 *Fact* (June) 42: In the [Women's] Army [Corps] we call the gay crowd "funny-bunnies." **1969** Pendleton *Death Squad* 53: Emilio Giordano would not be any man's funny bunny. Only once…had any man made a monkey out of him. **1975** in D.C. Dance *Shuckin' & Jivin'* 198: Awright, you funny-bunny motherfucker, go pick on somebody yo' own size. **1976** Lieberman & Rhodes *CB* 129: *Funny Bunny*—Disguised police car.

funny cigarette *n.* a marijuana cigarette. *Joc.*
  1949 Algren *Golden Arm* 30: Funny cigarettes ain't all that one pushes. **1968** N.Y.C. man, age 20: I like those funny cigarettes [hippies] smoke, though. **1984** J.R. Reeves *Mekong* 101: From the smell of his smoke, I knew he'd lit up one of his funny cigarettes. **1989** *Donahue* (synd. TV series): No funny cigarettes or anything like that in your background?

funny factory *n.* a psychiatric ward or hospital.
  1944 *Pap. Mich. Acad.* XXX 592: The "funny factory" is a detention hospital [in prison]. **1942–49** Goldin et al. *DAUL* 302: You'll end up in the funny factory (insane asylum). **1967** Colebrook *Cross of Lassitude* 97: You better occupy your mind, honey…or you'll be ready for the Funny Factory. **1972** Andrews & Dickens *Big House* 25: She says there ain't nobody putting her Spiel in the funny factory. **1977** Max Rabinowitz *The Day They Scrambled My Brains at the Funny Factory* (title).

funny farm *n.* a psychiatric hospital.
  1959 Knowles *Separate Peace* 101: You might start to believe it and then I'd have to make a reservation for you at the Funny Farm. **1961** in C. Beaumont *Best* 90: Another few days of this and I'll be ready for the funny farm. **1962** Quirk *Red Ribbons* 89: Like he's a candidate for the funny farm, that's how. **1963** R. Breen, P. Ephron, & H. Ephron *Capt. Newman, M.D.* (film): What makes you think I'd join that big funny farm of yours? **1961–65** M. Howard *Bridgeport* 82: The weekend visit with her husband at the funny farm. **1966** Fariña *Down So Long* 266: Maybe some time at the local funny farm would help. **1968** Moura & Sutherland *Tender Loving Care* 220: What's new at the funny farm? **1970** Sorrentino *Steelwork* 65: They'll send me out to that Long Island funny farm with the loonies. **1977** Caron *Go-Boy* 56: You oughta be on the funny farm, you jerk.

funny house *n.* an insane asylum or psychiatric hospital.
  1906 M'Govern *Sarjint Larry* (gloss.): *Funny-House:*—Insane asylum. **1912** *Adventure* (May) 129: Is this a hotel, or a funny-house for millionaire ginks with twisted tops? **1915** Howard *God's Man* 376: You better can that black smoke…or it'll have you in the funny-house. **1940** R. Chandler *Farewell* 141: Who put me in your private funny house? **1963** Boyle *Yanks* 56: He was a happy-go-lucky spaghetti bender—one of the least likely candidates among us for the funny house.

funny money *n.* **1.a.** counterfeit money; play money; (*hence*) money from questionable or unlawful sources.
  [**1909** in "O. Henry" *Works* 1520: G'wan and get yer funny bill changed yourself. Dey ain't no farm clothes yer got on. G'wan wit yer stage money.] **1938** *AS* (Oct.) 237: Funny money [Kansas state sales-tax tokens] buys nothing but increased burdens of government. **1948** *New Yorker* (Mar. 20) 27: Mr. Scott…calls the present American currency "funny money." **1949** Monteleone *Crim. Slang* 93: *Funny money*…Counterfeit coins. **1950** *Sat. Eve. Post* (Mar. 18) 64: The gamblers paid a tax on slot machines into a "Special Fund" of the [Peoria] city treasury—"funny money," it was called. **1968** Longstreet *Wilder*

Shore 55: The San Francisco merchants, bartenders and cabbies accepted this kind of funny money with a smile. **1975** *Kojak* (CBS-TV): Joe Torre…is gonna be up to his toupee in funny money. **1987** Attorney, age *ca*60, on Headline News Network (Dec. 13): The settlement means cash. It doesn't mean funny money or paper or they'll pay us ten years from now. It means cash on the barrelhead. **1989** *Capital Gang* (CNN-TV) (Aug. 5): We're all gonna do it with funny money. It isn't gonna cost a thing.
  b. *Mil.* military payment certificates; MICKEY-MOUSE MONEY.
  1965 Marks *Letters* 123: We are no longer being paid in green backs, but in Military Pay Certificates (MPC)—we call it funny money. **1966–67** Harvey *Air War* 18: I got a fistful of funny money at the…Naval Base gate. **1969** Crumley *One to Count Cadence* 31: Military Payment Certificates, MPC, Scrip, or Funny Money as it was called. **1970** Gaffney *World of Good* 109 [ref. to WWII]: "Well tell him to serve us more wine," Ost said handing the owner a crumpled ball of our funny-money. **1985** Bodey *F.N.G.* 169: Nineteen days and a wake-up…and this funny money will be greenbacks. **1987** Lanning *Only War* 17: The conversion into what was called "funny money" was to prevent the black market trade in dollars.
  2. *Black E.* deception; funny business.
  1968 Heard *Howard St.* 15: They pulled some funny money now and then.

funny paper *n.* *Mil.* a topographical map.
  1980 Cragg *L. Militaris* 180: *Funny Papers.* Maps. **1982** Del Vecchio *13th Valley* 423 [ref. to Vietnam War]: Any indications of it on your funny papers? **1989** Zumbro & Walker *Jungletracks* 183 [ref. to Vietnam War]: One of the old French roads, marked on your funny paper as number three.
  ¶ In phrase:
  ¶ **see you in the funny papers** (used as a joc. farewell).
  1926 Maines & Grant *Wise-Crack Dict.* 14: *See you in the funny sheet*— A humorous way of saying good-bye. **1928–29** Faulkner *Sound & Fury* 137: Ta-ta see you in the funnypaper. **1947** Goodrich & Hackett *Wonderful Life* (film): So long, George. See you in the funny papers. **1981** G. Wolf *Roger Rabbit* 3: "See you in the funny papers," joked the rabbit.

funny place *n.* FUNNY HOUSE.
  1975 Wambaugh *Choirboys* 294: I'm probably going to shoot myself or go to live with my mom in the funny place!

funny-time *adj.* *Black E.* odd; peculiar; (*hence*) worthless. Also as quasi-adv.
  1954 in Wepman et al. *The Life* 39: You're a funny-time lame. **1968** in Andrews & Dickens *Big House* 13: It was a funny-time cat, wearing a funny-time hat/That must have been five years old. **1970** A. Young *Snakes* 66: Edgar Allan Poe…wrote…some funnytime stuff, man. **1970** in W. King *Black Anthol.* 51: I think the bitch needs bifocals.…Funny time dressin' slut. **1976** Wepman et al. *The Life* 181: *Funny-time, adj.* Odd, ridiculous, disreputable.

funny wagon *n.* a van used to convey patients to a mental hospital.
  1941 J. Thurber, in Paxton *Sport* 300: They're goin' to be sendin' the funny wagon for you, if you don't watch out. **1984** *N.Y. Post* (Dec. 13) 112: Send for the funny wagon.

funny ward *n.* a psychiatric ward.
  1963 J. Ross *Dead Are Mine* 269 [ref. to 1944]: And if you ever admitted it to anyone they'd slap you in the funny ward so fast you'd never know how you got there.

funny water *n.* liquor.
  1974 L.D. Miller *Valiant* 32 [ref. to 1940's]: "I didn't know you had taken up drinking."…"What drinking? This giggly soup?" "What did you call it?" "Giggly soup. Funny water." **1986** La. English prof., age 38: Then he went back to drinking funny water.

funsy *n.* **1.** a prank; a joke.
  1962 Kesey *Cuckoo's Nest* 249: You can take just so many funsies like white mice in your pillowcase and worms in your cold cream and frogs in your bra.
  2. *pl.* fun.
  1965 *N.Y. Times* (Dec. 27) 20: Difficult things (like exams) are ironically "funsies." **1983** in "J.B. Briggs" *Drive-In* 185: Beating each other up for funsies. **1984** R. Salmaggi, on WINS Radio News (Dec. 25): But not to make it a total loss, *Starman* is funsies.

funsy *adj.* providing silly fun; amusing.
  1962 in Algren *Lonesome Monsters* 38: "Funsy," the redhead said. "We

did things like this at the studio."

fur *n.* ¶ In phrase: **fur will fly** violent or noisy conflict will ensue. Also vars.

1814 in *DA*: Smugglers look out, or you will soon see "the fur fly." **1833** Crockett *Autobiog.* ch. ii [ref. to *ca*1800]: My father had been taking a few *horns* and was in a good condition to make the fur fly. **1848** Bartlett *Amer.: To make the fur fly*. To claw; scratch; wound severely. Used figuratively. **1889** "M. Twain" *Conn. Yankee* 65: I am just quietly arranging a little calamity here that will make the fur fly in these realms. *Ibid.* 289: I instructed my boys to be...ready to man the pumps at the proper time, and make the fur fly. **1898** Brooks *Strong Hearts* 66: I reckon you'll see the fur flying pretty soon. **1936** Dos Passos *Big Money* 317: Then when I come back we'll see the fur fly. **1948** Cozzens *Guard* 554: He'll make the fur fly for a couple of hours and then suddenly...find he's hungry. **1979** Terkel *Amer. Dreams* 4: When it came out...that I said Nixon should resign, that he was a crook, oh dear, the fur flew. **1988** *U.S. News & World Rep.* (Jan. 18) 22: Watching the Fur Fly.

furball *n.* **1.** *Mil. Av.* a DOGFIGHT involving several aircraft.

1983 M. Skinner *USAFE* 42: The "fur-ball"—a confused dogfight full of swarming airplanes. **1988** *Nova* (WGBH-TV): Tangling in what is known to pilots as the furball of a conventional dogfight. **1989** J. Weber *Defcon One* 10: With four shooters tagging along, this could turn into a real furball. *Ibid.* 336: Furball: Multiaircraft fighter engagement. **1991** *N.Y. Times* (Jan. 23) A 6: Pilots talk about "fur balls," or particularly tangled dogfights.

2. a small furry animal. *Joc.*

1984 *Night Court* (NBC-TV): [He's a] geek who's in love with his furball. **1990** *Maclean's* (July 2) 57: The cute little fur ball with alarming reproductive habits.

furburger *n.* FUR PIE.—usu. considered vulgar.

1965 Trimble *Sex Words* 85: Furburger...The vagina or entire female genitalia, particularly as an object of cunnilingus. **1970** Landy *Underground Dict.* 85: Furburger...Female's pubic area. **1972** N.Y.U. student: I was out on maneuvers in Louisiana, and I heard these two really stupid guys saying, "Let's go into town and get some of that furburger and hair pie." I thought it was like a hamburger or something. **1972** *Nat. Lampoon* (Nov.) 35: Furburger. This rather eloquent euphemism for the vulva... **1973** TULIPQ (coll. B.K. Dumas): Female sexual organs: cunt, hole,...furburger, pussy. **1982** Rucker *Kafka* 150: Up to her...furburger deluxe.

furgle *v.* [< G *vögeln* 'to screw'] to copulate with.—usu. considered vulgar. *Joc.*

1923 in Cray *Erotic Muse* (ed. 2) 230: They fergie [*sic*] a bull and fill him full,/Those hardy sons of bitches. **1961** Heller *Catch-22* 52: He could never decide whether to furgle them or photograph them, for he had found it impossible to do both simultaneously.

fur pie *n.* the vulva or vagina, esp. as the object of cunnilingus.—also used collectively.—usu. considered vulgar. *Joc.*

1934 "J.M. Hall" *Anecdota* 177: "Eat fur pie,"...otherwise known as "Cleaning the kitchen," "Gobbling the gravy," "Getting down on it," scientifically *cunnilingus*. **1958** Southern & Hoffenberg *Candy* 207: Grindle resumed his fondling of her sweet-dripping little fur-pie. **1983** Ehrhart *VN-Perkasie* 178: But the beach....Fur-pie everywhere.

furschlugginer var. FERSCHLUGGINER.

fur snatching *n. West.* fur trapping.

1889 O'Reilly & Nelson *Fifty Years on Trail* 79: I had always been partial to "fur snatching"—a very paying game.

fur-trapper *n. Police.* a fur thief.

1954 Collans & Sterling *House Detect.* 136: An "undesirable" might have been a shoplifter or a sob-story artist, a fur-trapper or a bagsnatcher. *Ibid.* 138: The fur-trappers were older and bolder.

fusebox *n.* the mind or head.

1946 Mezzrow & Wolfe *Really Blues* 187: His fusebox...blew out long ago. *Ibid.* 305: Fusebox: head. **1979** Crews *Blood & Grits* 55: Something's burned in your fuse box. *a*1990 Westcott *Half a Klick* 143: Buddy had...a few loose wires in his fuse box.

fusel oil *n.* cheap liquor.

1874 Pember *Metropolis* 368: He can drink a whole tumbler of fusel-oil whiskey without blinking an eye. **1879** Rooney *Conundrums* 80: "Fusil oil" is the new name for whiskey, "spondulix" cognomen for pelf. **1892** Norr *China Town* 73: The "dope" and fusel oil dispensed in the neighboring saloons as whiskey. **1904** Ade *True Bills* 122: He would take the Gang down into a Thirst-Parlor and buy Fusel Oil. **1963** Coon *Short*

End 28: I reached out and grabbed that bottle of fusel oil Tomachek put in front of me and took a big pull of it.

fuss *v. Stu.* to flirt or court.

1912 *Lucky Bag* (No. 19) 83: [His] long suit is "fussing." **1912** in Truman *Dear Bess* 101: Aileen is the finest girl to fuss with on Mary's list. **1917** in J. Reed *Young Man* 133: With the school social butterflies I "fussed" girls in the town, and was not laughed at. **1918** *Stars & Stripes* (Feb. 15) 2: Two Ways to Fuss a Nurse. **1922** *Bomb* (Iowa State Coll.) 395: If you fuss a woman from the halls always send up enough rope to reach from her window to the ground. **1924** *DN* V 290: *Fuss*, v.i. To go out with girls. "Jack's out *fussing* tonight."

fussbudget *n.* a fussy, nervous, or meddlesome person. Now *colloq.*

1904 *DN* II 397: *Fuss-budget*...A nervous, fidgety person. **1961** Forbes *Goodbye to Some* 211: Robinson is becoming merely a nervous fuss-budget.

fusser *n. Stu.* a young man who frequently flirts and socializes with young women; ladies' man.

1898 *Portfolio* (Amherst Coll.) 48: Harkness receives 13 votes for our "star-fusser." **1909** in O. Johnson *Lawrenceville* 115 [ref. to 1890's]: "Oh, you fussers!" "You lady-killers!" **1918** *Grindstone* (Baldwin-Wallace Coll.) 215: Improvised Order of Fussers. **1925** Lewis *Arrowsmith* 639 [ref. to *ca*1910]: I wouldn't care a hoot if she fell for the gabbiest fusser in the whole U., and gave me the go-by all evening. **1931** Lorimer *Streetcars* 61: Anybody that knows Hubie could tell you what a fusser he is. **1950** *Time* (Mar. 13) [ref. to *ca*1915]: *Fusser.* A genteel wolf.

fuss-fart *n.* FUSSBUDGET.—usu. considered vulgar. Also as *v.*

1918 Noyes *MS.* (unp.): *Fuss-fart*—a nuisance, a meddler, one who hurries aimlessly about. *To fuss-fart*—to hurry aimlessly about. to fuss, to mooch. Derivation unknown. [**1919** *Amer. Legion Wkly.* (cartoon) (July 11) 11: Jerry Whoozis broke a leg coming from the opera....Pete Fussfut's wife ran away.]

fusspot *n.* FUSSBUDGET.

***1921** in *OEDS*: You *are* a fuss-pot. First you won't and then you will. **1952** Mandel *Angry Strangers* 26: Don't be an old fusspot or I'll pickle you. **1978** Puritan Vegetable Oil TV commercial: And you know what a fusspot he is.

fussy *adj. Stu.* attractive.

1918 in Truman *Dear Bess* 255: Bought me a Sam Brown [*sic*] belt today and I look real fussy in it.

futhermucker *n.* [intentional spoonerism] MOTHERFUCKER.—usu. considered vulgar. *Joc.*

1965 Walnut Ridge, Ark., high-school student (coll. J. Ball): Every one of your Hoxie friends turns out to be a futhermucker if you ask me. **1972** R. Wilson *Forbidden Wds.* 171: Mammy-jammer,...futher-mucker. **1972–76** Durden *No Bugles* 41: Thanks, futhermucker.

futz *n.* **1.** a foolish or unpleasant fellow.

1935 *Bedroom Companion* 79: Some crusty old futz who has had too much to drink starts off on this tangent. **1940** W.R. Burnett *High Sierra* 35: He was an old phutz and a has-been. **1959–60** Bloch *Dead Beat* 84: The old futz inside the loan office gave him a cold eye.

2. (euphem. for *the fuck* s.v. FUCK, *n.*).

1947 Schulberg *Harder They Fall* 104: Nobody knows what the futz you're talkin' about.

futz *v.* [prob. alter. of Yid *arumfartzen*] **1.** to fool or play.—constr. with *around* or *with*. [Often regarded as a euphem. for syn. FUCK, *v.*, 5, or FUCK AROUND.]

1929–30 J.T. Farrell *Young Lonigan* 63: Studs kept futzing around until Helen Shires came out with her soccer ball. **1932** *AS* VII (June) 335: *Phutz around*—to trifle; to interfere; "to horse around." **1936** Levin *Old Bunch* 64: There was a fellow that never wasted time. No fuzzy futzing around. *Ibid.* 249: No more futzing around being a schoolboy. **1941** Brackett & Wilder *Ball of Fire* (film): Why do you think we're futzin' around with these? **1941** in Boucher *Werewolf* 129: There's nothing he likes better than futzing around with the occult. **1944** Liebling *Back to Paris* 113: I mean, have we really started, or are we still futzing around? **1948** Wolfert *Act of Love* 158: What's he futzing around for? **1949** Robbins *Dream Merchants* 14: At least he didn't say a word about my futsing around all those years. **1959–60** Bloch *Dead Beat* 3: "Good crowd," said Eddie, futzing around with his mustache. **1964–66** R. Stone *Hall of Mirrors* 78: To...watch a room full of stooges futz with soap. **1968** P. Roth *Portnoy* 263: I am nobody to futz around with. **1970** C. Harrison *No Score* 55: You futz around in the darkroom all the time.

1973 Schiano & Burton *Solo* 106: All that futzing around with bits of paper. **1984** *USA Today* (Nov. 7) 3A: President Reagan…[suggested] it is time to "stop this futzing around."

2. to treat with contempt.—constr. with *around*.

1966 Brunner *Face of Night* 165: Futz me around a little more and find out.

futzer *n.* FUTZ, 1.

1938 H. Miller *Trop. Capricorn* 30: You poor old futzer, you, just wait.

futz off *v.* to loaf.

1968 Baker et al. *CUSS* 123: *Futz off.* Waste time, not study.

futz out *v.* FRITZ.

1963 Coon *Short End* 254: What happens to you, if you are Halstead…and the whole shooting match futzes out right in your face and lies there?

futz up *v.* to spoil; confound; FUCK UP.

1947 Willingham *End As a Man* 296: I've got her all futzed up. She does everything I tell her. **1948** Wolfert *Act of Love* 293: If you're futzing it up I want to know. **1965** Hardman *Chaplains* 64: Not while you're futzing up the clergy I won't!

fuzz *n.* [orig. unkn.] Orig. *Und.* **1. the police.**

1929 E. Booth *Stealing Through Life* 301 [ref. to 1920]: Don't run, and rank yourself—the fuzz don't know what's doin' yet. **1930** *Liberty* (Aug. 2) 38: I get a good picture in my mind of all the fuzz on the city's force. **1937** Reitman *Box-Car Bertha* 219: The fuzz (the squad)! Ditch the fireworks! **1956** Holiday & Dufty *Lady Sings the Blues* 123: While the Treasury agents knocked, I hollered, "Joe, it's the fuzz, clean up." **1957** Gelber *Connection* 92: The fuzz are coming. We're going to get busted. **1958** Talsman *Gaudy Image* 17: I use it for protection. To keep the fuzz guessin'. **1965** Conot *Rivers of Blood* 54: I'm ready for them fuzz when they come again. **1971** Le Guin *Lathe of Heaven* 96: If the fuzz stops me,…it looks kind of funny in my handbag. **1972** Barker & Lewin *Denver* 62: The fuzz lock it on one of the wheels of a car that has been ticketed three times for overparking without the owner's having paid the fines. **1981** in *West. Folklore* XLIV (1985) 9: We don't mess with the fuzz at all. **1991** "R. Brown" & R. Angus *A.K.A. Narc* 167: You might…have…gone to work for the fuzz.

2. a police officer or detective.

1930 Irwin *Tramp & Und. Slang* 81: *Fuzz.* A detective; a prison guard or turnkey. **1935** *Amer. Mercury* (June) 229: *Fuzz:* officer of the law. **1935** Pollock *Und. Speaks: Fuz,* a police officer. **1936** D. Runyon in *Collier's* (Dec. 12) 7: Lou…is a private fuzz often employed by big insurance companies,…a fuzz being a way of saying a detective. **1964** Tamony *Americanisms* (No. 3) 5: Purists and old timers employ *fuzz* or *Federal fuzz* to denominate only the F.B.I. and such government men now officering the country for "Mr. Whiskers." **1966–67** P. Thomas *Mean Streets* 82: The fuzzes were coming into the alley. **1971** *N.Y. Post* (Jan. 12) 28: A fuzz batted me with a club hitching a ride on a freight train and I was sentenced to a chain gang. **1972–75** W. Allen *Feathers* 36: I'm fuzz, sugar, and discussing Melville for money is an 802. **1977–85** Carmen & Moody *Working Women* 137: That fuzz got some gall. He saw me down at 100 Centre.

fuzzbrain *n.* a foolish person.

1969 Scanlan *Davis* 109: The one-star fuzz-brains who would crush Hitler with cocktails. **1981–85** S. King *It* 336: You're such a fuzzbrain.

fuzzed out *adj.* groggy, as from lack of sleep.

1980 in Safire *Good Word* 216.

fuzzface *n.* a bearded man.—used derisively.

1908 in H.C. Fisher *A. Mutt* 63: Abdul Houdini Fuzzface, Commander in Chief of the Imperial Secret Police. [**1930** Irwin *Tramp & Und. Sl.: Fuzz Face*…A young tramp…one not old enough to raise a beard, but with a growth of fuzz on the face.]

fuzz factory *n.* a police station.

1982 Savitch *Anchorwoman* 61: "Let's go on over to the fuzz factory," he told me.…It turned out, of course, to be the police station.

fuzz sandwich *n. Tennis.* an overhead smash hit directly toward an opponent's face.

1976 *AS* LI 293. **1981** D.E. Miller *Jargon* 244.

fuzz-tail var. FUZZY-TAIL.

fuzz wagon *n.* a police vehicle.

1973 N.Y.C. cabdriver, age 25: A *fuzz wagon* is a police car.

fuzzy *n.* **1.** FUZZY-WUZZY.

***1890** in Kipling *Barrack-Room Ballads* 10: The Fuzzy was the finest o' the lot. **1899** Robbins *Gam* 158: Whatever those fuzzies thought of my seamanship, they evidently held a very low estimate of my diplomacy. ***1926** in *OEDS.*

2. *West.* a wild range horse.

1922 Rollins *Cowboy* 28: Both South and North might betake themselves to slang and talk of fuzzies (Range horses) and broomies or broom tails (Range mares). **1936** R. Adams *Cowboy Lingo* 81: "Fuzzies" were range-horses.

3. FUZZ, 2.

1942 *ATS* 418: *Fuzzy,* a diligent policeman. **1966** *New Yorker* (Dec. 31) 30: The fuzzies…said it was needed for evidence.

4. [sugg. by A*lpha Xi*] *Stu.* a member of Alpha Xi Delta sorority.

1963 Reuss & Legman *Songs Mother Never Taught Me* (unp.): "Fuzzies," Alpha Xi Delta's.

fuzzy-tail *n.* (among tramps) an unpleasant or ignorant fellow. Also **fuzz-tail.**

1918 (cited in Partridge *Dict. Und.* 272). **1924** in Tamony *Americanisms* (No. 3) 11: "You old fuzzy-tail." "You old ding-bat!"…"You old jungle-buzzard."…"You old scissor-bill!" **1925** Mullin *Scholar Tramp* 91 [ref. to ca.1912]: "I hope they aren't the two fuzzy-tails from the good ship *Cuspidor,*" I muttered. **1926** *AS* I (Dec.) 651: *Fuzzy-tail.* a hobo in bad humor. **1927** *DN* V 447: *Fuzzy tail,* n. An ill-humored tramp, so called, possibly, from the fact that certain angry animals bristle at the back and tail. **1930** "D. Stiff" *Milk & Honey* 205: *Fuzz-tail*—Name for an unpopular fellow. **1933** Ersine *Prison Slang* 38: *Fuzzytail,* n. A conceited person, a yap. **1961** Bendiner *Bowery Man* 83: The "fuzzy-tail"—the young boy who stole quietly out of nowhere to the fireside in the "jungle."

fuzzy-wuzzy *n.* a member of any of various dark-skinned ethnic groups who wear their hair in a very thick and full fashion, esp. (in U.S. naut. & mil. use) a Papuan or Fijian.—usu. considered offensive.

***1890** in R. Kipling *Barrack-Room Ballads* 10: So 'ere's to you, Fuzzy-Wuzzy, at your 'ome in the Soudan. ***1940** in *OEDS:* There are Chinks and Japs and Fuzzy-Wuzzies. **1942** in *Yank* (Jan. 6, 1943) 6: Dear Fuzzy-Wuzzy [a Papuan]….Thanks. **1950** Morison *Naval Ops. in WW II* VI 30: Angau was responsible for the loyalty of these "fuzzy-wuzzies" during the Papuan campaign. **1954** L.H. Crockett *Magnificent Bastards* 333: Not a single man out of uniform, well, discounting the fuzzywuzzies. **1962** Quirk *Red Ribbons* 25 [ref. to WWII]: Suva in the Fijis….The Fuzzy Wuzzy drop-kicked an American football sixty yards, barefooted. **1967–68** von Hoffman *Parents Warned Us* 71: A white boy whose curly, uncut hair made him look like a fuzzy-wuzzy. **1968** Myrer *Eagle* 585: I just wish they'd shipped him out here among the snakes and fuzzy-wuzzies. **1970** T. Wolfe *Radical Chic* 5: The…unbelievable Afro [hairstyle], Fuzzy-Wuzzy-scale in fact. **1970** R. Sylvester *Guilty Bystander* 283: I was on a jungle road [in New Guinea] and here came a Fuzzy Wuzzy walking toward me. **1993** *N.Y. Observer* (Jan. 25) 5: Expeditionary actions undertaken by the British…against primitively armed "natives." General Gordon taking on the fuzzy-wuzzies.

G *n.* **1.** [sugg. by syn. GRAND] **a.** Orig. *Gamb.* (one) thousand dollars. Also **gee.**

1928 O' Connor *B'way Racketeers* 182: They had me in the bag for nearly ten G's before I pulled the string and let the joint go blooey. **1929** in Runyon *Guys & Dolls* 70: I am going to stake them to a few G's. **1930** Conwell *Thief* 61: He feels sure the mark is ripe for the take and will go for sixty G. **1934** Jerne & Purcell *Joe Palooka* (film): I'm bettin' ten G's on him myself. Ten thousand. **1936** Duncan *Over the Wall* 21 [ref. to 1918]: A thousand-dollar bill was a Gee. **1936** Steel *College* 314: You'll get your twelve G. **1937** Odets *Golden Boy* 308: I'm giving four to five on Bonaparte tomorrow....Four G's worth. **1941** Schulberg *Sammy* 80: "A little birdie tells me that lunch is going to cost him about ten G's," Sammy said. **1954** Schulberg *Waterfront* 50: "Okay, ask ten G," Johnny said. **1957** Ness & Fraley *Untouchables* 89: I'm betting five gees myself. **1982** Rucker *57th Kafka* 138: Two G advance plus three points gross after turnaround.

b. one thousand.

1938 *AS* (Apr.) 156: *Hit it a G.* To use the 1000 pound pressure press.

c. *Rap Music.* money.

1993 *Youth Break* (WKXT-TV): *G* can mean...money. **1993** Eble *Campus Slang* (Fall) 3: *G...*money: "Give me some G, mom."

2. *Und.* the U.S. government; federal authority.—constr. with *the.* Also attrib.

1935 C.J. Daly *Murder* 14: Get me the check book on the G account. **1936** Dai *Opium Addiction* 199: *G.* The Government. Also called *whiskers.* **1942–49** Goldin et al. *DAUL* 82: *G-joint...*A federal penal institution. **1966** Brunner *Face of Night* 98: Last year a cop's wife had got sore and what did she do? She told the G he was cheating on his income tax, and bango, he was dropped from the force. **1976** "N. Ross" *Policeman* 59: You're going to be pinched for possession of stolen property—state charge—and after that...the "G" will probably hit you with a federal charge.

3. *Gamb.* GAFF³, *n.*—often used in comb.

1946 Dadswell *Hey, Sucker* 73: They specialize in controlled G-wheels and horrifyingly vulgar kooch-shows. **1961** Scarne *Comp. Guide to Gambling* 524: The maker knows very well that the *G* (gaff) will be used most of the time.

4.a. *Rap Music.* guy, fellow, man.—used esp. in direct address.

1989 *Rolling Stone* (Oct. 19) 54: His lyrics were unapologetically macho, contemptuous of "hos" and "g's" and adoring of uniforms, discipline and strength. **1990** *TV Guide* (Oct. 20) 19: Yo, G! Peep this! **1991** Nelson & Gonzales *Bring Noise* 214: That's BULLSHIT G! **1992** *Martin* (Fox-TV): She didn't sound that bad, G! **1993** *Wall St. Jour.* (Mar. 29) B1: Sup G! How ya livin? **1993** *Source* (July) 38: I'm the best, G....none of them niggas can fuck with me. *Ibid.* 50: I'm homeless, G.

b. *Und.,* orig. *L.A.* [sugg. by gangster] a member of a violent street gang.

1990 Bing *Do or Die* 231: A G won't even take a youngster with him when he sets out to grab another G. **1992** *L.A. Times* (Aug. 18) E1: They say, "What's up, G?" (gangster).

c. *Rap Music.* girlfriend.

1991 *Source* (Oct.) 33: Treats his forty dog better than his G. **1991** *Houston Chronicle* (Oct. 8) 2D: What's up, Gee?...Gee...is the equivalent of girlfriend or homeboy.

¶ In phrase:

¶ **up in** [or **to**] **G** [alluding to the key of G in music] superlative; doing very well; at or to a high point.

1884 *Accidentally Overheard* 15: The young lady next door...is up in solos in G. **1894** C. Lawlor & J. Blake "Sidewalks of N.Y." (pop. song) st. 3: Things have changed since those times, some are up in G./Others they are on the hog. **1894** *Harper's* (Dec.) 104: I've got to get a mother; what I mean is, a real way-up-in-G one—I mean to say a mother that's out of sight, m'm. **1895** *Harper's* (Apr.) 786: You get everything way up in G there, with cakes on the side. **1895** Townsend *Fadden* 5: Say, I knowed ye'd be paralyzed wen ye seed me in dis harness. It's up in G, ain't it? Dat's right. **1895** in Dale *Songs of Seventh* 97: The new Q.M. was right in line,/He's higher up than "G." **1902** Wister *Virginian* 75:

The travellers had not seen her, but...Lin McLean had told him she was "away up in G." **1903** Townsend *Sure* 119: De fun was just about up to G when I see...de cop on post! **1924** *Adventure* (Dec. 10) 94: The fact that Matt Downs and Horace C. Manning were bidding for acreage sent prices up in G.

gab¹ *n.* [Scots var. of GOB, *n.*, 1] the mouth; (*hence*) in phr. **shoot (one's) gab off** to speak loudly or out of turn.

*1724 in *OED:* He dighted his gab and pri'd her mou'. ***1725** in *OED:* Bannocks.../Might please the daintiest gabs. ***1785** Grose *Vulgar Tongue: Gab,* or *Gob.* The mouth. *Gab,* or *Gob, String.* A bridle. ***1890** in *F & H* III 94: Clap a stopper on your gab and whack up. **1908** *DN* III 313: Shut up your gab. **1923** McAlmon *Companion Volume* 50: Go into another tent if you want to shoot off your gabs. **1924** P. Marks *Plastic Age* 100: Close your gabs, everybody. **1930** Huston *Frankie & Johnny* 38: Close yer gab. They'll hear ye. **1933** Halper *Union Sq.* 52: Did Comrade Lukotas get up and shoot his gab off? **1935** Coburn *Law Rides Range* 11: You keep your gab shut. **1965–70** in *DARE.*

gab² *n.* [shift of Scots (now S.E.) *gab* 'to talk volubly; prate' infl. by syn. *gabble* and GAB¹] talk, esp. idle conversation or prattle; a conversation; speech; (*also,* as in 1877 and 1885 quots.) language. Now *colloq.*

*1790 in *OED:* Perhaps Rob G—y's auld grey pate/...May join the social gab. ***1811** in *F & H* 94: Then hold your gab, and hear what I've to tell. ***1819** [T. Moore] *Tom Crib* 2: His Lordship...is *flashing his gab**....*Showing off his talk. ***1808–25** Jamieson *Scot. Dict.* II 331: *Gab...*Prating, saucy talking...entertaining conversation. **1833** J. Neal *Down-Easters* I 62: He's a match for gab with any body. ***1839** W.M. Praed, in *OED:* The captain hates "a woman's gab." **1850** Strong *Diary* II 9: His one faculty of unlimited gab. ***1863** in *F & H* III 94: Come stash your gab, my lad. **1872** Alger *Phil* 294: Hould yer gab, Tim Rafferty. **1877** in F. Remington *Sel. Letters* 17: I...am progressing "right bully" in the "Roman gab." **1885** S.S. Hall *Gold Buttons* 3: Negro, meanin' Black, in Greaser gab. **1905** "H. McHugh" *Search Me* 60: Skinski was a warm member with the gab. **1905** *DN* III 10: *Gab, n.* Slang. Prating. **1926–35** Watters & Hopkins *Burlesque* 20: All the rest of this gab is applesauce. **1941** "L. Short" *Hardcase* 18: I don't savvy his gab. **1944** *Pap. Mich. Acad.* XXX 589: "Joint gab," the jargon of the inmates of our penal institutions. **1944–49** Allardice *At War* 38: You two quit your gab. **1953** Paley *Rumble* 85: It was just goin' to be a gab between acemen. **1983** N. Proffitt *Gardens of Stone* 51: The rude and empty gab...had driven him out. **1993** *New Yorker* (Apr. 13) 100: To promote and define its line of gab, CNBC herded its celebrity hosts into a studio at Rockefeller Center.

gabbo *n.* (see 1931 quot.).

1931 *AS* VI (Aug.) 438: *Gabbo.* A talkative person. **1933** Milburn *No More Trumpets* 300: He ought to, the old gabbo. **1942–49** Goldin et al. *DAUL* 76: That gabo [*sic*] is a bitch....Don't crack...to him.

gabfest *n.* a period or occasion of gossiping or other trivial conversation.

1897 in *OEDS:* A Chicago paper speaks of the speechmaking on Andrew Jackson's day as "the Democratic gabfest." **1902–03** Ade *People You Know* 46: There was a Rally and some other Gabfest on the Bills. **1908** *New Broadway Mag.* (July) 32: They were in a gab-fest up to their pompadours. **1910** *N.Y. Eve. Jour.* (Feb. 15) 20: Maggie's givin' a gabfest at th' house tonight. **1921** Casey & Casey *Gay-Cat* 267: We'll have a real honest-to-goodness gabfest up in my room later. **1953** M. Harris *Southpaw* 148: There was a big gabfest...amongst the whole 6 of them. **1982** *Business Week* (May 31) 97: After the elegant gabfest at Versailles is over, U.S. and European leaders will have to come home.

Gabriel *n.* [joc. allusion to the trumpet of the archangel Gabriel] *Logging.* a dinner horn. Also (pron. sp.) **Gaberel.**

1938 Holbrook *Holy Old Mackinaw* 44 [ref. to *ca*1910]: Instead of the human voice, some camps used a conch shell, a tin horn,* or the guthammer....*Often known as the "gaberel." **1956** L.G. Sorden & Ebert *Logger's Words* 15: *Gaberel...*dinner-horn. **1964** in *DARE: Gabriel*—A long tin horn which "cookee" blew to call the shanty boys to their "hash."

gaby *n.* [dial. E; ult. orig. unkn.] a foolish or silly fellow. *Rare* in U.S.

*1796 Grose *Vulgar Tongue* (ed. 3): *Gabey*, a foolish fellow. *1833 Marryat *Peter Simple* ch. xxxiv: The marine officer is a bit of a gaby. *1848 W.M. Thackeray, in *OED*: She is still whimpering over that gaby of a husband. 1873 Such *Fun, Fact & Fancy* 12: At first I was a gaby. *1875, *1885 in *OED*.

gadget *n.* [orig. unkn. but perh. < F *gâchette*] **1.a.** Orig. *Naut.* a comparatively small item or device whose name is unknown or forgotten; contrivance; thingamajig. Now *S.E.*

*1886 in *OEDS*: Even the sailors forget at times, and if the exact name of anything they want happens to slip from their memory, they call it a chicken-fixing, or a gadjet, or a gill-guy, or a timmey-noggy, or a wim-wom—just *pro tem.*, you know. *1898 Bullen *Cachalot* 6 [ref. to 1875]: I had been accustomed to hard words if I did not steer within half a point each way; but here was a "gadget" that worked me to death, the result being a wake like a letter S. *1902 R. Kipling in *OEDS*: Steam gadgets always take him that way. 1910 *Everybody's Mag.* (Jan.) 112: He cast his eyes upon each bright gadget crowded about him—the telescope sights, air-blast, hoist-controller. 1918 Ruggles *Navy Explained* 66. 1921 *Variety* (Feb. 25) 23: If Whelan didn't wear the gadget there wouldn't be a fight. 1922 *Leatherneck* (Apr. 22) 5: *Gadget*: Any little thing without a special name. Any little thing, the name of which is not recalled at the moment. Any little thing which is too much trouble to name specifically. Anything. 1926 *AS* II (Oct.) 62: Every snipe endeavors to impress the poor swabbos with his talk of gillguys, gadgetts [*sic*] and gimmicks, to say nothing of other doohickies. 1927 *Amer. Leg. Mo.* (Sept.) 87: Gadget, that's anything. Punk, that's bread. 1935 F.H. Lea *Anchor Man* 3: The cork gadget got loose. 1941 H.A. Smith *Low Man* 31: A gadget called the "bull market" reached its peak. 1961 de Kerchove *Maritime Dict.* (ed. 2): *Gadget*. Slang term applied by seamen to anything whose name is unknown to them, also to denote makeshift contrivances on board ship. Also called gilguy (U.S.), gilhickey (U.S.), hootnanny (U.S.), gimmick, gismo (U.S. Navy).

b. the penis; (*pl.*) genitals. *Joc.*

1942 *ATS* 147: Genitals...gadgets....Male pudendum...*gadget*. 1972 R. Wilson *Forbidden Words* 118: *Gadget*. The penis. 1986–89 Norse *Memoirs* 116: You don't have the right gadgets.

2. *USAF.* an aviation cadet; (*hence*) fellow; person. Now *hist.*

1944 Kendall *Service Slang* 7: *Flying gadget*...a flying cadet. 1945 *Yank* (Apr. 13) 22: One of the gadgets is flunking the...course. 1945 in *AS* (Dec. 1946) 310: *Gadget*. An Air Force cadet, an inconsequential person. 1951 R.L. Richards *Air Cadet* (film): For every gadget I wash out, there's a dozen who should be. 1959 Montgomery & Heiman *Jet Nav.* 37: "Guess I'm the gadget you're gonna have to bunk with," the new cadet said. 1978 Ardery *Bomber Pilot* 22: I discovered that cadets were called "gadgets" [at Randolph Field, Tex.] and that I had better parade as a visiting easterner rather than a local gadget, since gadgets continually overran the town.

gaff[1] *n.* [orig. unkn., unless obscurely connected with S.E. *gaff* 'an iron hook, etc.'; cf. GAFF[3], *n.*] **1.** *Und.* a fair or (in later use) other place of amusement.

*1753 in *OED*: The first Thing they do at a Gaff is to look for a Room clear of Company. *1797, *1809 (cited in Partridge *Dict. Und.* 273). *1811 *Lexicon Balatron.*: *Gaff*. A fair. *The drop coves maced the joskins at the gaff*; the ring-droppers cheated the countryman [*sic*] at the fair. *1812 Vaux *Vocab.*: *Gaff*: A country fair; also a meeting of gamblers for the purpose of play; any public place of amusement is liable to be called *the gaff*, when spoken of in *flash* company who know to what it alludes. *1821 in *F & H* III 96: We stopped at this place two days, waiting to attend the *gaff*. 1859 Matsell *Vocab.* 35: *Gaff*. A theatre; a fair. *1851–61 H. Mayhew *London Labour* I 40: These places are called by the costers "Penny Gaffs;" and on a Monday night as many as six performances will take place. *Ibid.* 44: They court for a time, going to raffles and "gaffs" together.

2. *Und.* a house, building, or place of business, esp. if illicit; JOINT.

*1932 in *OEDS*. 1935 Pollock *Und. Speaks*: *Gaff*, a place operating unlawfully, gambling, bootlegging, or prostitution. 1940 *AS* (Apr.) 114: I don't want a single one of you starters to round or look up while he is lamping the gaff. 1941 in D. Runyon *More Guys* 383: You cannot keep these cattle in my gaff. 1945 D. Runyon, in *Collier's* (Sept. 29) 11: A meal in a one-arm gaff in West Forty-ninth. 1972 R. Wilson *Forbidden Words* 119: *Gaff*. A house of prostitution. 1981 Graziano & Corsel *Somebody Down Here* 81: A lot of broken-down Broadway actors make his gaff.

gaff[2] *n.* [of Eng. dial. and Scots orig.] foolish or impudent talk; tomfoolery; GUFF, *n.*

*1825 "Blackmantle" *English Spy* I 235: Could *bag* a proctor.../Or stifle e'en a *bull-dog's* [proctor's assistant's] *gaff*. *1877 in *OED*: I also saw that Jemmy's blowing up of me was all "gaff." *1880 in *SND* IV 227. 1909 *WNID*: *Gaff*...talk, esp. of a deceitfully boasting nature; humbug. *Slang*. *1930 in Partridge *DSUE* (ed. 8) 440: The usual gaff about green flares being sent up for danger. 1926–35 Watters & Hopkins *Burlesque* 21: Yeah, but who cares a damn. I can't get steamed up about this Broadway gaff. 1937 Herndon *Let Me Live* 136: Enough of your gaff, young fellow! 1943 *Yank* (Feb. 10) 9: Listening avidly while the old goof shoots his gaff. 1959 Himes *Crazy Kill* 64: Why do all of us have to take the cop's gaff if I know Chink did it? 1959 H. Ellison *Gentleman Junkie* 207: He had talent: not the kind of gaff the Village phonies put out, but the real thing.

gaff[3] *n.* [S.E. *gaff* 'a steel spur for a fighting cock'] **1.a.** *Gamb.* a small hook or spur set in a ring worn by a cardsharp to facilitate cheating.

1843 J. Greene *Exposure of Gambling* 132: For this purpose, the dealer has on the middle finger of his left hand, what is called a *gaff* or *spur*; this is fastened on by cement made for that purpose; it is about an inch and a quarter in length....This gaff has been used against the smartest of gamblers without being detected by them. 1859 Matsell *Vocab.* 112: The gaff is a ring worn on the fore-finger of the dealer...[who] when dealing from a two-card box, can deal out the card he chooses. It is now out of date.

b. *Gamb. & Carnival.* a hook, catch, etc., used to facilitate cheating by the house in any game of chance; (*hence*) a cheating or deceiving device or stratagem of any kind; in phr. **give the gaff** [infl. by *blow the gaff*, below] to cheat, victimize, or betray.

1893 Hampton *Maj. in Washington* 159: There was a fresh, green snoozer...who lost most of the money and he tried to intimate...that we had given him the gaff. I told him that if he reflected on my honor I'd split him like a dried coonskin. 1895 Townsend *Fadden* 50: Wese don't go chasin' roun' tellin' w'en wese gets de gaff, fer ye'd only get de laugh fer it, see? 1915 Howard *God's Man* 75: If he'd given them the gaff he'd just as soon do it to us. 1916 in Partridge *Dict. Und.* 273: *Gaff*. Means of making a player lose or win at will. 1922 *Variety* (June 30) 8: When the gaff is on, he is bound to lose. (The gaff is a secret trick by which the game is controlled.) 1927 Nicholson *Barker* 102: *Gaff*—A dishonest gaming device. 1942 Liebling *Telephone* 11: "Gaff," a synonym for "gimmick," means a concealed device. 1951 *New Yorker* (Jan. 27) 20: The terminology of pitchmen. "The gaff is the trick, or the gimmick." *Ibid.* 21: People start looking for a gaff. 1953 Gresham *Midway* 8: He was the only piper I ever saw who "slipped in a gaff" —to keep from blowing himself silly he had hooked up the mouthpiece of his pipes to a little air pump....You couldn't see where the air was coming from. 1965–72 E. Newton *Mother Camp* 44: The stripper always wears a "gaff" to conceal (strap back) his genitals. 1979 T. Baum *Carny* 42: "The floor...was electrified." "That's right....That was the gaff."

c. *Und. & Carnival.* a fraud.

*1889 Barrère & Leland *Dict. Slang* I 391: (Prison), a *gaff*, a pretence, imposture. 1936 *Esquire* (Sept.) 64: The philosophy of life being a gaff and a gimmick is a heritage from carny lingo. 1942–49 Goldin et al. *DAUL* 76: *Gaff*...(Carnival) A special game or concession crookedly operated. 1953 Gresham *Midway* 8: This was no gaff; the man was a genuine freak, one of the top human-oddity acts in the business. 1966 Braly *Cold* 155: Broads are the biggest gaff on the midway.

d. *pl. Gamb.* (see quot.).

*ca*1945–50 in D.W. Maurer *Lang. Und.* 186: *Gaffs*. Crooked dice of any kind.

e. *Carnival.* a criminal occupation; RACKET.

1979 T. Baum *Carny* 42: You'll lay off the pickpocket gaff.

2.a. punishment or severe treatment; hardship; strain.—usu. constr. with *stand, get,* or *give*.

1899 A. Thomas *Arizona* 124: All we care about now is, will they stand the gaff? 1903 A.H. Lewis *Boss* 151: The question now is, how to give th' Chief th' gaff, an' gaff him deep an' good. 1911 Runyon *Tents of Trouble* 23: He stood the gaff for me in the Third Degree. 1918–19 MacArthur *Bug's-Eye View* 71: We...marched all evening and until the next morning. Forty-five kilometers was the gaff. 1922 Tully *Emmett Lawler* 102: You can stand the gaff like an old-timer. 1927 S. Lewis *Elmer Gantry* 46: I'll be mighty proud of your trusting me to stand the gaff. 1928 Weaver *Collected Poems* 206: You got to be hard-boiled to stand the gaff! 1929 T. Gordon *Born to Be* 11: They were not allowed to rough it like the rest of us boys, so they couldn't stand the gaff. **1936** in R.E. Howard *Iron Man* 191: She has scornt my love!...She has handed me the gaff! **1938** T. Wolfe *Web & Rock* 191: Paul...couldn't stand the gaff! He was eating his heart out...because he couldn't make the Varsity. **1947** W.M. Camp *S.F.* 333: In short, they "took the gaff," and by so doing preserved the life of the Union. **1949** Daves *Task Force* (film): Looks like it'll stand the gaff. **1955** L. Shapiro *6th of June* 57: Fitness reports O.K. and you look like you can stand the gaff. **1958** Drury *Advise and Consent* 710: How do we all stand the gaff?

b. an instance of dismissal or ridicule.—constr. with *the.*

1896 Ade *Artie* 65: Everybody's shakin' him down this spring, and if he gets the gaff he'll be flat on his back. **1903** in "O. Henry" *Works* 137: Did you mean that straight, or was you trying to throw the gaff into me? **1903** Townsend *Sure* 62: De gang gives us de gaff for fair, when dey pipes us in de carriage.

3. the penis.

1963 T.I. Rubin *Sweet Daddy* 90: They just wait there for dough to stuff between their legs see? Even the gaff—same thing. Like they got it coming see? *Ibid.* 157: *Gaff*:...sexual intercourse;...penis.

¶ In phrases:

¶ **blow (one's) gaff** blow (one's) stack s.v. BLOW.

1948 Wolfert *Act of Love* 243: Don't blow your gaff, Lieutenant. Just take it easy.

¶ **blow the gaff, 1.** Orig. *Und.* to reveal a secret, esp. concerning trickery or wrongdoing. Cf. **(1)**, above.

***1812** Vaux *Vocab.: Blow the gaff:* A person having any secret in his possession, or a knowledge of any thing injurious to another, when at last induced...to tell it openly to the world...is then said to have *blown the gaff upon* him. ***1823** "J. Bee" *Slang* 12: To "blow the gaff," or "gaff the blow," is to speak of, or let out the fact. ***1833** Marryat *Peter Simple* 347: I wasn't going to blow the gaff, so I told him, as a great secret, that we got it up with a kite. **1848** Judson *Mysteries* 413: We'll have to clap a stopper on her jaw-tackle, or she'll blow the gaff! as Cooper says in the Water-Witch! **1860** L. Barney *Auraria* 87: Many of these "dupes," who have become familiar with these artifices, to their repentant sorrow, feel disposed to "blow the gaff," but know too well the danger, and so keep silent—hence the game goes on. **1883** Russell *Sailor's Lang.* 16: *Blow the gaff.*—To inform against a man. "He has blown the gaff," he has "split." **1953** Gresham *Midway* 148: It took the Second World War, which blew open so many governmental secrets, to "blow the gaff" on the East Indian snake men. **1976** Hayden *Voyage* 422: Mebbe...[he]'ll see fit to blow the gaff a'tween here and there. **1982** Randi *Flim-Flam!* 71: It was unfortunate that we "blew the gaff" right there on the show.

2. Esp. *Und.* to make a botch.

***1899** Whiteing *John St.* 206: Might ha' been doin' well still, but the gaff was blowed by a set o' fools. **1987** Mamet *House of Games* (film): George, you *blew* the gaff!

¶ **split the gaff** to inform; *blow the gaff*, 1, above; SPLIT, 1.

1887 Davis *Sea-Wanderer* 29 [ref. to 1831]: I'll be bound not one of 'em will split the gaff on a friend of mine.

gaff⁴ *n.* golf. *Joc.* [The 1688 quot. is not relevant to U.S. usage.]

[***1688** in *OED*: Pythus, the first inventer of many Games at Ball: I do not say of Gaff, Tennis or Paille-Maille.] **1900** *Howitzer (No. 1)* 119: *Gaff.*—A synonym for golf. **1905** *Howitzer (No. 6)* 294: *Gaff*—Synonym for golf.

gaff *adj.* *Gamb.* rigged.—used prenominally.

1930 Irwin *Tramp & Und. Slang: Gaff wheel.* A gambling wheel controlled by the foot of the operator. **1933** Ersine *Pris. Slang* 39: *Gaff Joint, n.* A crooked gambling establishment. **1984** *Ripley's Believe It or Not* (ABC-TV): It's a gaff table, a rigged table, of course.

gaff¹ *v.* [orig. Scots dial.] to gab; chaff. *Rare* in U.S.

***1801** J. Hogg, in *SND* IV 227: An useless gauffin tike. ***1808–25** Jamieson *Scot. Dict.* II 333: To *Gaff*...To talk loudly and merrily. Roxb[urghshire]. **1970** Cole *Street Kids* 82: So I was gaffing with a friend sitting next to me until class started.

gaff² *v.* **1.** *Gamb. & Carnival.* to cheat or victimize.

[***1811** *Lexicon Balatron.:* To *Gaff.* To game by tossing up halfpence.] [***1812** Vaux *Vocab.: Gaff:* to gamble with cards, dice, etc., or to toss up.] **1903** A.H. Lewis *Boss* 151: Gaff him deep an' good. **1930** Lait *On the Spot* 203: *Gaff.*...To cheat. **1956** Gold *Not With It* 135: I don't want to cheat you, Stan, I want to play you straight fifty-fifty, not gaff you for fifty-fifty. **1961** *Newsweek* (Sept. 4) 22: I ducked the card mechanic because I didn't want to get gaffed, but I wound up getting taken by a

bust-out man who cackled the dice.

2. *Gamb. & Carnival.* to equip with a cheating device of any kind; rig.

1934 in *OEDS*: He was...putting in slot machines for a racketeer, and "gaffing" them...to increase the house percentage. **1936** *New Yorker* (Sept. 12) 33: Con machines can be "gaffed" or fixed. **1942** Liebling *Telephone* 11: The...Chicago volcano was "gaffed" with steampipes. **1953** Gresham *Midway* 18: Yet the games of the midway [are] heavily weighted by percentage in favor of the operator even if they are not gaffed. **1961** Scarne *Guide to Gambling* 280: The most popular forms of *gaffed* (doctored) dice and the methods for detecting them are described below. **1979** T. Baum *Carny* 78: They gaffed it to look like an Egyptian mummy.

3. to endure.

1971 N.Y.U. student: Sorry, I can't gaff Jane Parker cakes.

gaffer *n.* **1.** a fellow, esp. a youngster.

***1653** in *OED*: The best little gaffer that was to be seen between this and the end of a staffe. **1895** in Mencken *Amer. Lang.* (Supp. II) 252. ***1910** (cited in Partridge *DSUE* (ed. 8) 440). **1932–34** Minehan *Boy & Girl Tramps* 15: The rest of you gaffers...get some grub. **1934** in Fenner *Throttle* 70: "Who the devil's this Bryson?"..."Young gaffer, with a lot against him as I recall." **1939** in A. Banks *First-Person* 202 [ref. to ca1890]: I was a young gaffer in my early teens.

2.a. a master; (*hence*) boss; owner; head workman; manager. [*Obs.* in U.S. except in circus usage and in glassmaking.]

ca1659, *1735, *1876, *1881,** in *OED*. **1894** *DN* I 335: *Gaffer:* one who finishes bottle by putting mouth upon it. **1926** Norwood *Other Side of Circus* 272: A boss —the gaffer. **1931** *Amer. Mercury* (Nov.) 352: *Gaffer*...The circus manager. **1934** Weseen *Dict. Slang* 159: *Gaffer*—A manager (of a circus). **1942** *ATS* 458: *Gaffer*, a glassblower who finishes the necks of bottles. **1961** Clausen *Season's Over* 32: That's how he got to be a gaffer. He can get anybody to do anything. *a1981** H.A. Applebaum *Royal Blue* 66: The "gaffer"...is the most skilled of the [glassblowing] team and...shapes...and blows it into its final form.

b. *Labor.* a foreman; (*specif.*) (now *S.E.*) the chief electrician of a theatrical, motion picture, radio, or television production.

1841, *1856, *1862, *1897,** in *OED*. **1939** Appel *People Talk* 370: The head electrician's called "the gaffer," the assistant electrician's the "best boy." **1942** *ATS* 576: Stage electrician....*gaffer*, the head electrician. **1944** *Pap. Mich. Acad.* XXX 598: *Gaffer*, an inmate who holds a job of some authority. *ca1948** in Mencken *Amer. Lang.* (Supp. II) 699: *Gaffer.* The head electrician [of a motion picture production]. *Ibid.* 718: Telephone and power linemen....A foreman is a *gaffer*. *Ibid.* 761: (Miners' slang.) *Gaffer.* A foreman. **1962** Ragen & Finston *Toughest Pris.* 800: *Gaffer*—A boss, foreman, etc.

3. [a special application of the S.E. sense] one's father; OLD MAN.

1704 S.K. Knight *Journal* 15: Poor Child sais Gaffer. **1929–31** J.T. Farrell *Young Lonigan* 40 [ref. to 1916]: I don't want to go, but the gaffer wants me to. *Ibid.* 80: Mr. O'Brien was different from his own gaffer. *Ibid.* 126: The gaffer was home and he tried to pitch in too.

4. a tobacco pipe.

1927 Cushing *Doughboy Ditties* 77: Now pull the "gaffer" stronger,/'Til gaseous clouds appear.

gaffle *v.* [of dial. orig., perh. alter. of S.E. *gaff* 'to strike (a fish) with a gaff'] **1.** Esp. *Maine.* to seize; take hold of, esp. for oneself; (*hence*) to steal. Also **gaffle onto.**

1900 H. Day *Up in Maine* 24: Gaffled up his britches' slack. *Ibid.* 142: Gaffle up your peavies. **1902** H. Day *Pine-Tree Ballads* 218: Gaffle holt an' gallop for an eight hands round. **1904** H. Day *Kin o' Ktaadn* 51: A big chilly fist had gaffled his reins. **1907** *DN* III 244: *Gaffle up, v. phr.* Possess oneself hastily, or without formality. "I *gaffled on to* that in a hurry." **1914** *DN* IV 73: *Gaffle, v.t.* Take or seize hold of. **1949** Monteleone *Crim. Slang* 93: *Gaffle on to*....To seize; to steal. **1965** J. Gould *Maine Lingo* 105: A group of men *gaffle* or *gaffle onto* a heavy object and all lift together. **1965–66** in Maurer *Lang. Und.* 302: *Gaffel*...To shoplift or steal.

2. *Und.* to take into custody; apprehend.

1954 in Partridge *Dict. Und.* (ed. 2) 822: Someone...who had hung a great deal of paper before getting gaffled. **1965–66** in Maurer *Lang. Und.* 302: *Gaffel*...To arrest. **1966** Braly *On Yard* 234: Jesus, am I glad to see you. I heard they had you gaffled. The goon squad. Someone said they marched you right across the yard. **1991** *Newsweek* (Oct. 28) 10: *Gaffle up.* To arrest.

gaff off *v. Naval Av.* (see quot.).

    1992 Parsons & Nelson *Fighter Country* 157: *Gaff Off.* To ignore.

gaff-topsail *adj. Naut.* (of an article of clothing, esp. a hat) tall or long; remarkable in any way. Also *n.*, a top hat.

    *1840 Marryat, in *OED:* Your mother…with…such a rakish gaff topsail bonnet, with pink pennants. **1849** Melville *Redburn* ch. xv: The legs were quite long, coming a good way up toward my knees….The sailors used to call them my *"gaff-topsail-boots."* **1854** Sleeper *Salt Water Bubbles* 53: His appearance, even when rigged out in his best style, with a bran-new spanker, gaff-topsail, and flying-jib, never caused many heart-burnings among the belles on shore. **1897* J. Conrad *Nigger of Narcissus* ch. iv: He had a square-mainsail coat and a gaff-topsail hat, too. **1899** Robbins *Gam* 144: An' them copper-colored natives, an' their gaff-tops'l turbans. **1929* Bowen *Sea Slang* 55: *Gaff Topsail Hat.* A silk top hat.

gag *n.* **1.** a deception; imposture; trick; *(obs.)* lie.

    *1805 in *OED:* I hate to hear such gag about a Goliath of thirteen. **1813* in *OED:* Whether the Gag come [*sic*] in the shape of a compliment to the Gaggee, or some wonderful story, gravely delivered, with every circumstance of apparent seriousness. **1823* "J. Bee" *Dict. Turf: Gag*,—a grand imposition upon the public; as a mountebank's professions, his cures, and his lottery-bags, are so many *broad* gags. **1843** Field *Pokerville* 118: Leaving the manager with but one alternative—namely, to *"slope,"*…and the company but one hope—a "gag" to enable them to follow him. **1846* in Partridge *Dict. Und.* 274: G was a Gag, which he told to the beak. **1885** *Puck* (Mar. 18) 38: I've called to introduce myself to you, so that you couldn't work the stranger "gag" on me when I come around with that bill you've been owing us for two years. **1894** *Century* (Mar.) 713: Better than any of these tricks is what is called the "faintin' gag." **1896** Ade *Artie* 20: She kept playin' that "pa-pah" gag on me. **1898** Kountz *Baxter's Letters* 8: Teddy worked the old gag that he was showing her how they did it in a play. **1900** Kennedy *Man Adrift* 178: I think the trial was a damned fraud, anyway. The old circumstantial evidence gag, you know. **1912** *Hampton's Mag.* (Jan.) 842: What kind of a gag is this, Breeze? What you putting over? **1919** S. Lewis *Free Air* 22: Oh! So he's still working that old gag! **1927–28** Tasker *Grimhaven* 41: The gag is to find some spot where they won't discover you. **1928** Dahlberg *Bottom Dogs* 117: The foreman was taking no chances…so…Lorry couldn't pull that gag. **1930** *Bookman* (Dec.) 398: Today the gag is growing from the racket stage to a business—and a sweet one at that. **1931** Hellinger *Moon* 215: and the racketeer explained the old gag. **1935** Coburn *Law Rides Range* 108: Well, Klink blows into town wit' 'is newspaper gag. Bull ain't wise, see? **1947** Mailer *Naked & Dead* 280: It's the last time I can pull that gag, he told himself. **1950** Stuart *Objector* 90: Everybody is trying to pull a gag that will either get them out of the Army or a soft racket in it. **1957** J.D. MacDonald *Price of Murder* 80: "What's the last public place, big place, you took a fare to?" "What kinda gag is this?" **1978** Wharton *Birdy* 12: I decide to work this gag on Birdy and write it up just the way it happens.

2.a. *Theat.* remarks of any sort interpolated, often ad lib, into a part by the performer; an ad lib remark.

    1835 *Spirit of Times* (Dec. 12) 4: Theatrical Gag….The President's Message…*would be read from the stage* the moment it was received in town. **1837** *Spirit of Times* (Feb. 25) 12: Dinneford is an enterprising fellow, without half of Hamblin's "gag," and will make money. **1837** *Spirit of Times* (May 27) 113: It is unnecessary to say that this *gag* produced as much noise as any of Finn's jokes upon the removal of the deposites. **1841* in *F & H:* I shall do the liberal in the way of terms, and get up the *gag* properly. **1851–61* H. Mayhew *London Labour* III 126: You see the performances consisted of all gag. I don't suppose anybody knows what the words are in the piece. **1867** *Galaxy* (Dec.) 936: Who cheer the loudest at a melodramatic and high-sounding moral "gag" from an actor's tongue? **ca1871* in Pinto & Rodway *Common Muse* 190: A Ballad from the Seven Dials Press together with "the 'gag' and 'patter' of a man formerly known as "Tragedy Bill."

b. a joke; jest. Now *S.E.* [The nuance in 1840 quot. is, strictly, 'laughingstock'.]

    1840 "S. Slick" *Clockmaker* (Ser. iii) 27: Sam,…they tell me you broke down the other day in the house of representatives, and made a proper gag of yourself. **1863* in *OEDS:* The whole farce [is] crowded full of gags. **1866** W.D. Howells, in *F & H:* I have heard some very passable *gags* at the Marionette, but the real *commedia a braccio* no longer exists. **1869** Logan *Foot-Lights* 368: The "gags" that he repeats and the songs which make you laugh are not funny to him, for he has repeated them in precisely the same tone and with exactly the same inflection for an indefinite number of nights. **1879** Rooney (title): Pat Rooney's Quaint

Conundrums and Funny Gags. **1885** *Puck* (Apr. 22) 116: Gag (written by profess. funny man) $2.00. **1887** DeVol *Gambler* 288: Wilson…had a fondness for "gags," and was ever joking. **1896** Ade *Artie* 7: Then there was a guy called an entertainer, that told some o' the gags I used to hear when my brother took me to the old Academy and held me on his lap. **1906** Kildare *Bailiwick* 145: A state of mind that will be susceptible to…the prehistoric gag, "Why does a chicken cross the street?" **1938** "E. Queen" *4 Hearts* 129: Don't you know a gag when you hear one?

3.a. a variety of action or behavior; practice, business, method, etc.

    1890 Howells *Hazard* 193: The popular gag is to abuse Bevans, and Maxwell is the man to do it. **1899** Kountz *Baxter's Letters* 75: He would do the earnest conversation gag until some one else had made good. **1900** Ade *More Fables* 178: He did the Shoulder-Slap, and rang in the Auld Lang Syne gag. **1902** Townsend *Fadden & Mr. Paul* 95: It comes to gags to make you laugh in one block and pump weeps to your peepers in de next. **1904** Hobart *Jim Hickey* 13: I'm too delicate for this one-night stand gag. I'm going to New York and build a theater. **1906** *Nat. Police Gaz.* (Sept. 22) 6: They're hardened to the gag, and they're fully aware that worrying isn't going to get them anything. **1906** H. Green *Boarding House* 55: You been doin' the Simon Legree gag till I got enough. **1907** Hobart *Beat It!* 85: Jack says he's going to get married some of these days and do that Europe gag himself. **1921** Marquis *Carter* 198: Every new gag that come out the perfesser took up with it, Biddy says; one time he'd be fussing around with gastronomy through a telescope and the next he'd be putting astrology into William's breakfast food. **1925** Weaver *Collected Poems* 124: 'Cause every time I tried out some new gag,/Like bein' sympathetic, or actin' like/A two-year-old, hopin' I wouldn't scare him…/It didn't get me much of anywheres. **1928** Callahan *Man's Grim Justice* 36: She finally persuaded me to cut the dipping gag (quit picking pockets). **1928** McKay *Banjo* 148: What's his gag, pardner? **1929** *AS* IV (June) 340: *Gag*—A means of getting by. **1934** Cain *Postman* 3: I tried some comical stuff, but all I got was a dead pan, so that gag was out.

b. a plan of action or behavior; scheme.

    1901 Hobart *John Henry* 58: Here's the gag. **1908** H. Green *Maison* 282: Here's the gag! **1911** *Hampton's Mag.* (June) 742: I suppose some woman statesman will come tearing in some day and figure out a new gag, hey? **1926** W. Rogers, in C.M. Russell *Trails* xiv: Now I am going to try to talk Nancy out of that introduction Gag to that book. **1926** "M. Brand" *Iron Trail* 100: You try me….What's the gag?

c. an undertaking.

    1917 *Editor* (Feb. 24) 154: *On This gag*— on this job.

4. a thing or object; *(also)* an aspect.

    1908 McGaffey *Show Girl* 48: Dressed up…like a queen…in a low-neck gag. **1915–16** Lait *Beef, Iron & Wine* 159: They's only two gags to it—what youse tallheads calls heredity an' environment. **1933** in D. Runyon *More Guys* 4: That's a gag that looks like a pencil, but it's really a syringe. **1936** Praskins & Kelly *One in a Million* (film): I leaned down to fix one of these gags and he was gone.

gag[1] *v.* **1.** to trick; hoax.

    *1777 in *OED:* I gagged the gentleman with as much ease as my very little ease would allow me to assume. **1819* in *OED.* **1823* "J. Bee" *Dict. Turf.:* He thus *gags* the public. **1873* Hotten *Slang Dict.* (ed. 4): *Gag*, to hoax, "take a rise" out of one; to "cod." **1873** T.W. Knox *Underground* 814: And then I knew how those fellows had been gagging me.

2.a. *Theat.* to ad lib.

    1840 *Spirit of Times* (July 4) 216: Theatrical Adventures in the Country. The Gagging Concern…By a Gagger. **1852* Dickens *Bleak House* ch. xxxix: The same vocalist "gags" in the regular business like a man inspired. **1851–61* H. Mayhew *London Labour* III 141: We only do the outline of the story, and gag it up. We've done various plays of Shakespeare in this way. **1876* in *OED:* They "gag" to such an extent that the author oftentimes does not recognize his own dialect. **1883* in *F & H* III 99: Toole…cannot however play a tendency to gag and to introduce more than is set down for him by the author. **1902** H.A. Clapp *Dram. Crit.* 94: Giving him full leave to "gag;" that is to say, to enlarge and vary his assigned text with new matter of his own interpolation.

b. *Theat.* to tell jokes; jest. Now *S.E.*

    1910 *Variety* (Aug. 20) 12: The "gagging" by Harry Cooper was one big scream. **1931** *Amer. Merc.* (Dec.) 413: Gus is…always gaggin' and clownin'. **1962** Serling *New Stories* 53: You try to gag it up one more time and you'll wind up plucking chickens at a market.

gag[2] *v.* In phrase: ¶ **gag me [with a spoon]!** (esp. among teen-aged girls) (used to indicate disgust or dislike). [Typical of the "Valley Girl" fad of 1982–83.]

1982 S. Black *Totally Awesome* 40: Heavy Make-up. To like hide the zits, gag me! *Ibid.* 58: Cheerleading....Rah-rah, I'm sure. Gag me with a spoon! **1983** Lane & Crawford *Valley Girl* (film): God, gag me! How could you? **1983** *Good Morning America* (ABC-TV) (Sept. 20): *Strange Invaders* does have its share of gag-me-with-a-spoon touches. **1984** N. Stephenson *Big U.* 74: Most fled, hysterically grossed out. "Gag me green!" **1985** *N.Y. Times Higher Ed. Supp.* (Mar. 8): *Gag me.* An emphatic term to express disgust. **1988** Univ. Tenn. student theme: High school slang tended to lean toward California "valley girl" talk such as *gross* and *gag me.* **1993** Kellogg's Corn Flakes TV ad: Nothing but flakes? Gag me!

gaga *n.* **1.** a person who is the object of an infatuation.

1928 McEvoy *Show Girl* 20: And what do you think has happened to my other ga-ga?

2. nonsense; foolishness.

1930 Franklyn *Kts. of Cockpit* 146: I've found out what a sucker I've been to swallow all the ga-ga about liberty and freedom for a race of people that are bein' hog-tied.

gaga *adj.* [< F] **1.** fatuous (in early use, esp. from senility); silly; crazy; (*hence*) (now *esp.*) naïve; infatuated.

1917 R. Kipling, in Birkenhead *Kipling* 275: I expect the poor old bird (who is ga-ga) was worked upon as a "patriot and a statesman" by someone....Brassey, who is also vehemently ga-ga, holds Lansdowne's opinions in advanced form. **1920** in Pound *Pound/Joyce* 173: One grows increasingly gaga with time's attrition. **1920** F.M. Ford, in *OEDS*: The V.G.F. must be gaga! **1925** Dos Passos *Manhattan Transfer* 40: Marco's gaga the old fool. **1927** *Vanity Fair* (Nov.) 132: "He's gah-gah" means he's crazy over her. **1927** Sandburg *Good Morning America* 221: Many polite liars full/of blah, all gah gah. **1927** Mayer *Between Us Girls* 126: She is slightly ga-ga and piquée, which is to say in vulgar parlance, nuts. **1931** Lorimer *Streetcars* 20: All the girls are just ga-ga over you. **1934** in Ruhm *Detective* 116: I want double the salary you offered....I'm ga-ga, am I? **1936** Steel *College* 211: And when I *do* go gaga and give you a job to do, what happens? **1936** Parker *Battling Hoofer* (film): Don't you go getting gaga over that guy. **1938** "E. Queen" *4 Hearts* 31: He's a local character—quite mad...Just gaga. **1939** Saroyan *Time of Your Life* 49: He sees KITTY and goes ga-ga again. **1963** D. Tracy *Brass Ring* 114: Why, I thought you were positively gaga over Vi. **1971** Freeman *Catcher* (film): There's enough ga-ga Callendars around to form our own mental ward. **1983** R. Thomas *Missionary* 211: You claimed that kid of yours was gaga....That he had scrambled eggs for brains. **1987** *'Teen Mag.* (Jan. 1988) 86: To this day...I still have this ga-ga outlook. **1993** *New Yorker* (May 17) 104: Like Koresh, a guru gone gaga.

2. drunk.

1927 Mayer *Between Us Girls* 101: They were actually ga-ga enough to perpetrate anything. **1933** Ersine *Pris. Slang* 39: *Gaga*, adj. Drunk.

gaga *v.* to indulge in sentimental or lovesick reveries; moon.

1930 Franklyn *Kts. of Cockpit* 120: I don't care for that sort of ga-ga-ing!

gage *n.* **1.** [app. directly from the obs. BrE sense 'a quart pot (of liquor); a quart pot full' (see *OED*)] *Und.* cheap whiskey.

1932 in *AS* (Feb. 1934) 26: *Gage.* Cheap whisky. **1944** Burley *Hndbk. Jive* 138: *Gage*—...liquor, intoxicant.

2. *Black E.* marijuana. Also **gauge**. [Cf. the 17th C. sense 'a pipe or pipeful (of tobacco)' in *OED* and Partridge, *Dict. Und.*; the sense given in 1947 quot. is app. local and obs.]

1934 in M. Starks *Cocaine Fiends* 101: She blows her gage—flies in a rage,/Sweet Marijuana Brown. **1938** *New Yorker* (Mar. 12) 36: They are reefers,...gauge- or goofy-butts. **1941** in Garon *Blues* 97: I used to didn't blow gage. **1946** Mezzrow & Wolfe *Really Blues* 145: Sucking on a stick of gauge like it was a hunk of peppermint candy. [**1947** *AS* (Apr.) 121: *Gage.* Any form of tobacco such as cigars, cigarets, or chewing tobacco.] **1948** *Neurotica* (Summer) 37: She smoked like she'd been living on the gage since milk. **1952** E. Brown *Trespass* 106: They could keep all the gauge you could blow in a lifetime. **1960** Himes *Gold Dream* 59: Blowing gage and talking underneath their clothes as if they were hustlers. **1962** L. Hughes *Tambourines* 192: Blow gauge, support the dope trade. **1965** Lurie *Nowhere City* 147: I had my shirt *pocket* full of gage. **1966** L. Armstrong *Self-Portrait* 51: And to me you'd have a better session with gage, as we called it, than getting full of whisky. **1970** A. Young *Snakes* 35: That good gauge'll straighten anybody out in a minute! **1972** *Playboy* (Dec.) 194: "Dynamite," she said. "Jamaican gauge." **1982** D. Williams *Hit Hard* 60 [ref. to WWII]: Bootleg booze, gage, cocaine. **1987** *Nat. Lampoon* (June) 84: Shee, James, this gage *down*, man.

gaged *adj. Und.* intoxicated, esp. by marijuana. Also **gauged**.

1932 in *AS* (Feb. 1934) 26: *Gaged.* Intoxicated. **1957** H. Danforth & J. Horan *D.A.'s Man* 221 [ref. to 1942]: "We'll get you real gauged tonight," he said. This was the term to describe a form of intoxication resulting from smoking the cigarettes and breathing in the stagnant smoke.

gage up *v. Black E.* (see quots.).

[**1932** in *AS* (Feb. 1934) 26: *Get one's gage up.* To become intoxicated.] **1973** *N.Y. Times Mag.* (Dec. 16) 81: They drink whisky and "gage up" (smoke pot).

gaggle *n.* Orig. *Mil. Av.* a group of aircraft in flight; (*broadly*) a group of any vehicles. Now *colloq.*

1942 in C.R. Bond & T. Anderson *Flying T. Diary* 124: Bob Neale and I took a gaggle of P-40s over to Namsang. **1944** *Official Guide to AAF* 368: *Gaggle:* group of aircraft in formation. **1946** G.C. Hall, Jr. *1000 Destroyed* 157: Form up on me by those vapor trails from that big gaggle. *Ibid.* 421: *Gaggle:* A cluster; pack; a gaggle of FWs might range from 10 to 50. **1955** Scott *Look of Eagle* 15: Is that *the* Steve Dallas who'll be spearheading this gaggle? **1960** Caidin *Black Thursday* 220: A big gaggle of Ju-88s had rushed through the formation. **1962** Mahurin *Honest John* 39: A large gaggle of fighter aircraft would be the easiest thing in the world to spot and track. **1968** Coppel *Order of Battle* 111: We did see bandits, about thirty of them, a mixed gaggle of Me-109s and twin-engined Me-110s. **1969** Cagle *Naval Av. Guide* 393: *Gaggle.* A group of planes flying together. *a*1987 Coyle *Team Yankee* 53: Do you see that last gaggle coming down the hill? **1989** T. Blackburn *Jolly Rogers* 120: Rog spotted the enemy gaggles.

gait *n.* one's manner or way of doing things, esp. of making a living or enjoying oneself; (*hence*) behavior, preference, or intention.

1859 Matsell *Vocab.* 35: *Gait.* Manner; fashion; way; profession. "I say, Tim, what's your gait now?" "Why, you see, I'm on the crack," (burglary). **1865** "M. Twain," in *DA*: Preachin' was his natral gait, but he warn't a man to lay back...because there didn't happen to be nothin' doin' in his own special line. **1869** "M. Twain" *Innocents* I 32: She's doing all she can—she's going her best gait. *Ibid.* 33: The watch was "on its best gait." **1885** B. Harte *Snow-Bound* 117: When I say George Lee's a white man, it ain't because I know him. It's his general gait. Wot's he ever done that's underhanded or mean? **1885** B. Harte *Shore & Sedge* 166: You don't seem to suit the climate, you see, and your general gait is likely to stampede the other cattle. **1892** Bunner *Letters* 141: That's your gait, Prof. **1893** Griggs *Lyrics* 27: For such a harum-scarum lot,/ Of course my gait was slow. **1896** Ade *Artie* 46: "Nit," I says, because I knew his gait. **1901** Bull *Flashes* 45: I've struck my *gait* right here on the Midway, and I don't want to see any other for some time yet. **1902** Wister *Virginian* 19: So that's the gait, is it?

¶ In phrase:

¶ **get a gait on** to hurry.

1892 Frye *From Hq.* 161: Well, get a gait on you. **1896** in Crane *Complete Stories* 316: Get a gait on you, will you? Think I want to lie here forever? **1900** Remington *Bark on* 148: Now run along—vamoose—underlay—get a gait on you. **1902** Masefield *Salt-Water Ballads* 14: Get a gait on ye, ye're slower'n a bloody snail! **1903** Jarrold *Bowery* 18: You better get a gait on if you want to see Mag before she passes in her checks.

gal *n.* [orig. dial. pron. of *girl*] girl; woman. Now *colloq.*

ca*1770 in Baring-Gould *Mother Goose* 63: What care I how black I be,/ Twenty pounds will marry me;/If Twenty won't, Forty shall,/I am my Mother's bouncing Girl [*sic*]. **1795 in *OEDS*: Improprieties, commonly called Vulgarisms, [include]...Gal for girl. **1815** in M. Mathews *Beginnings of Amer. Eng.* 58: Gals, girls. **1817** in Royall *Letters from Ala.* 97: This comes o' larnin gals to write! **1827** in *JAF* LXXVI (1963) 293: The...galls wer awl drest up. **1836** *Davy Crockett's Almanack* (1837) 17: I was courting a fine little gal on Swamp Creek, in old Kaintuck. **1838** [Haliburton] *Clockmaker* (ser. 2) 22: Then the galls all have a chance for him. **1843** Field *Pokerville* 159: You'd better *kiver* up till the *gals* undress. **1846** in Harlow *Old Bowery* 191: There's other gals/As beautiful as she. **1847** in Blair & Meine *Half Horse* 102: Galls is galls, and whisky is whisky, an' when they both get into the head at the same time, they're a leetle dust too hot for each other. **1847** Robb *Kaam* 10: I'd a winked that young Ingin gal into a high state of tenderness. **1858** in Rosa *Wild Bill* 25: My gall washed them for me. **1890** E. Custer *Guidon* 31: The "gals," as the Western man calls them, took care of some cows. **1915** C. Harris *Co-Citizens* 149: That gal, she looks damn dangerous seditious. **1916** D. Runyon, in Paxton *Sport USA* 90: No guy is gonnah make hisse'f out a cheap mug in front of his gal. **1961** Grau *Coliseum St.*

34: That makes you a most unusual gal. **1985** L. Iacocca, in *Newsweek* (Dec. 23) 11: These are the guys and gals we should elect in 1986.

gal *v.* to court young women.—constr. with *go*.
> **1838** *Crockett Almanac* (1839) 14: I was a big boy that jist begun to go galling. **1840** [Haliburton] *Clockmaker* (ser. 3) 31: Goin' a-gallin'. **1920** J.M. Hunter *Trail Drivers* 300: Going courtin is "goin' gallin'." **1927** *DN* V 474: *Gal*...To seek feminine society. "Th' boys allus goes a-gallin' of a Sunday."

gal-boy *n.* see GIRL-BOY, *n.*

Galilee *n. Black E.* (see quot.).
> **1954** L. Armstrong *Satchmo* 229 [ref. to *ca*1920]: There was no place for colored people to eat on the trains in those days, especially down in Galilee (the South).

gall *n.* effrontery. Now *S.E.*
> **1882** in *DA*: There is only one word which thoroughly expresses the quality of Dr. Anderson's communication. That word is the strong expression, "gall." **1885** in Lummis *Letters* 229: Then he had the gall to show me that hideously besmeared clothing. *ca*1889 in Barrère & Leland *Dict. Slang* I 393: Well, what do you think he had the *gall* to do to-day? **1896** Ade *Artie* 68: I'd give a t'ousand dollars if I had your gall. **1897** *Critic* (Sept. 13) 153: "Gall," "nerve," "cheek," "sand," "brass" and "face" are...y synonymous terms. **1906** *Variety* (Apr. 7) 12: Ain't that actor got a gall! **1908** in Kornbluh *Rebel Voices* 13: The master class is small/But they have lots of "gall." **1926** in J.M. March *Wild Party* 93: Hasn't she got the gall,/Making a play for you that way! **1942** Pegler *Spelvin* 192: It takes gall to sit down to a typewriter...and presume to tell the people what it is all about.

Gallagher *n.* ¶ In phrase: **Let 'er go, Gallagher!** go ahead! [D. Shulman provides an extensive discussion of the phrase and its origins in *Comments on Etymology* XXII 8 (May 1993), pp. 20ff.]
> **1887** W.W. Delaney, *Hi ho! Let Her Go, Gallagher!* (pop. song) (cited in *Comments on Ety.*, May 1993, 20): Hi! ho! Let her go, Gallagher. That's what I cry when I'm out on a spree. **1893** W.C. Robey *Naughty Doings on the Midway Plaisance* (Chicago: Will Rossiter) (sheet music): Like "Gallagher" they shouted, "Let her go!" **1895** Gore *Stu. Slang* 3: *Let her go Gallagher*. An expression signifying readiness to proceed. **1903** in "O. Henry" *Works* 1013: Let her go...Gallagher. **1905** in Blackbeard & Williams *Smithsonian Comics* 25: [To photographer] Let her go Gallagher. **1931** J.M. Saunders *Last Flight* (film): Well, let 'er go, Gallagher! Who cares? **1933** G. Fowler *Timber Line* 116: A temple of fistiana presided over by Reddy Gallegher, a quondam athlete of Cincinnati, and of whose right fist the saying originated: "Let 'er go, Gallegher!"

gallery *n. Narc.* SHOOTING GALLERY.
> **1968–73** Agar *Ripping & Running* 160: Gallery...shooting gallery. **1992** in Ratner *Crack Pipe* 215: Among older users...the old term "gallery" is used.

galley angel *n. Navy.* a messboy.
> **1835** *Military & Naval Mag. of U.S.* (Jan.) 356: No water? blast that boy! master at arms...send that galley angel of ours here.

galley-growler *n. Naut.* a grumbler.
> ***1867** Smyth *Sailor's Wd.-Bk.*: *Galley-growlers*, idle grumblers and skulkers, from whom discontent and mutiny generally derive their origin. **1883** Russell *Sailors' Lang.* 59: *Galley-growlers.*—Loafing, mutinous grumblers. **1899** Robbins *Gam* 122: Tell us how you proved yourself the fool-hardiest, dare-devilest galley-growler that ever earned a "sailor's blessing!" ***1929** Bowen *Sea Slang* 55: *Galley growlers*. Idle malcontents.

galley-hound *n. Naut. & USMC.* CHOWHOUND; (*also*) a cook or cook's helper.
> **1919** T. Kelly *What Outfit?* 46: Generally, the whole outfit includin' the crew, galley hounds, and even Punkjaw, shot [craps] all mornin' long. **1935** F.H. Lea *Anchor Man* 122: Don't give him too much. It'll make him a galley-hound.

galley news *n. Naut.* a shipboard rumor.
> **1813** B. Palmer *Diary* (Dec. 31): It is rumor'd about that a Cartel is preparing for us to be in readiness in a short time but I'm fearfull it is only Galley news. **1816** Waterhouse *Young Man of Mass.* 145: When discovered to be false, [these rumors] were called *galley news* or galley *packets*. **1883** Parker *Naval Officer* 18: We were to fill up and get off before the arrival of the *Delaware*...at least that was the "galley news."

galley packet *n. Naut.* a shipboard rumor.
> ***1785** in *OED*: Why, sure, Miss,...that must be a galley-packet somebody or other has told you. **1816** (quot. at GALLEY NEWS). ***1829** in Partridge *DSUE* (ed. 8) 442: Unauthenticated rumour; or, as sailors term it, "*a galley-packet.*" ***1929** Bowen *Sea Slang* 55: *Galley packet.* A rumour.

galley-ranger *n. Naut.* a loafer.
> **1852** Hazen *Five Years* 182: "How long have you been in the ship?" "Eleven days, sir."..."Only eleven days, and asking leave of absence. Why you infernal galley-ranger—"

galley sights *n.pl. Naut.* (see quot.).
> **1940** *AS* (Dec.) 450: *Galley Sights*. This term is applied to false reports as to ship's position, the inference being that the unreliable information probably came from the cook, who would know less of where the ship was than anyone aboard. *Shaft-alley sights* has the same meaning.

galley slave *n.* [pun on senses 'shipboard kitchen' and 'type of ancient rowboat'] *Navy.* a mess cook.
> **1961** L.E. Young *Virgin Fleet* 99 [ref. to 1941]: Those galley slaves have a rough time of it....The Officers' cooks are [called] galley slaves. We even refer to the Officers' kitchen as the slave galley. **1992** Jernigan *Tin Can Men* 41: A mess-cook worked from 4:00 AM until 9:00 PM. In fact, they were called "galley slaves."

galley-west *adj.* [alter. of dial. E *colly-west*] awry; askew.
> **1928** Tilton *Cap'n George Fred* 196: It wrecked the tent, tore it all to pieces and slat it galley-west. **1945** Beecher *All Brave Sailors* 122: His nose is completely galley-west, the whole bridge smashed flat.

¶ In phrase:

¶ **knock galley-west, 1.** to knock askew, down, over, or to pieces; (*joc.*) to astonish.
> **1833** Ames *Yarns* 308: Here is one of that bloody Don Dego's shot...knocked all the beef and hot water galley west. **1875** in "M. Twain" *Letters* I 250: Your verdict has knocked what little I did have galley-west! **1881** Nye *Forty Liars* 109: He may be knocked galley west by an old pick handle. *Ibid.* 277: The storm of life beats upon me and the angry billows knock me galley west. **1884** "M. Twain" *Huck Finn* 248: Then she grabbed up the basket and slammed it across the house and knocked the cat galley-west. **1908** in Fleming *Unforget. Season* 249: "Kid" Kroh...knocked six of them galley-west. **1915** Garrett *Army Ballads* 32: I knock them Galley West. **1920** Ade *Hand-Made Fables* 26: Mr. and Mrs. Wilton...read the Letter and were knocked Galley-west. **1933** J. Conroy *Disinherited* 123: A street light burst through the window, knocking a Granger Twist display galley-west. **1967** G. Green *To Brooklyn* 14: Albert expected the whole place to career over, knocked galley-west.

2. to destroy; (*hence*) to surpass completely.
> **1882** "M. Twain" *Life on Miss.* 174: Says enough to knock *their* little game galley-west, don't it? **1887** Francis *Saddle & Moccasin* 199: I'll be darned if this establishment of yours, Huse, don't knock any one of them galley west!...It just dumps the filling out [of] them! **1896** Hamblen *Many Seas* 165: Treating ourselves, and knocking the old man's profits "galley-west" at the same time. *a*1982 in Berry *Semper Fi* 38: Naturally we all thought our Navy was knocking the Japs galley west.

galley wireless *n. Naut.* (see quots.).
> ***1929** Bowen *Sea Slang* 56: *Galley wireless.* News of a merchant ship's destination, etc., which reaches the men from the officers by way of the stewards. **1940** *AS* (Dec.) 450: Ill founded rumors on shipboard are said to have been reported by the galley wireless.

galley yarn *n. Naut.* a hoaxing story; (*also*) a rumor.
> **1835** *Mil. & Naval Mag. of U.S.* (Oct.) 94: Then commenced a series of what are called on shipboard "galley yarns." ***1873** Hotten *Slang Dict.* (ed. 4): *Galley-yarn*, a sailor's term for a hoaxing story. **1885** Clark *Boy Life in USN* 189: I've got a galley yarn for you. **1920** Bishop *Marines Have Landed* 151: From the "galley yarns" flying about the ship, it would not surprise me if we were on our way to Guantanamo in a day or two.

gallopers *n.pl. Gamb.* dice.
> **1919** Wiley *Wildcat* 14: Little gallopers, speak to me! Shoots fifty cents. **1920** in Hemingway *Dateline: Toronto* 35: In their manipulations of the gallopers. **1922** *Bomb* (Iowa State College) 407: He couldn't find the little green Gallopers that he reserved for wear with his Date Clothes. **1926** Finerty *Criminalese* 26: *Galloper*—Dice [*sic*]. **1935** Coburn *Law Rides Range* 49: I took my last fin and ran it up to fifty with a pair of gallopers.

galloping *adj. Med.* (of an illness) rapidly worsening in severity and usu. resulting in death.—used prenominally. [Used orig. of consumption; in recent use app. becoming joc.]

*1785 in Burns *Poems & Songs* I 114: Enthusiasm's…Gane in a gallopin consumption. *ca***1875** Fullerton *Amer. Italy* 7: Dr. Richie…feared he would pass into "galloping consumption." **1877** Bartlett *Amer.* (ed. 4): Galloping Consumption. **1914** in *DARE*: She died of the breast-complaint; some calls it the galloping consumpt'. ***1927** Lowe-Porter, tr. *Magic Mt.* 432: He was told of the "galloping" form the disease sometimes assumed, which made the end an affair of not more than a few months or even weeks. **1942** H. Miller *Roofs of Paris* 22: Syphilis! The galloping kind that carries you off in six months. **1944** Hartman et al. *Up in Arms* (film): He has everything from hoof and mouth disease to the galloping willies. **1956** Childress *Like One of Family* 107: She thought I might give her folks gallopin' pellagra or somethin'. **1988** *Supercarrier* (ABC-TV): You got the galloping stupids.

galloping bones *n.pl. Gamb.* dice. Also **galloping cubes.**
   1920 *Amer. Leg. Wkly.* (Mar. 12) 26 [ref. to 1918]: Bottle of cognac, gallopin' cubes. **1942** Sanders & Blackwell *Forces* 158: *Galloping Bones…Galloping Cubes…*Dice. **1971** Thigpen *Streets* 9: He has/poker and gallopin' bones.

galloping dandruff *n. Esp. Army.* head or body lice. *Joc.*
   1920 Rigg & Platt *Btry. F* 63 [ref. to 1918]: The shacks were rife with "galloping dandruff" and the stables full of filth. **1923** Platt *Mr. Archer* 317 [ref. to 1918]: We used to call the cooties "galloping dandruff" and you'd ought to seen 'em stepping out on the day. **1925** Mullin *Scholar Tramp* 36 [ref. to *ca*1912]: "Once, in Seattle," said Frisco, seating himself elaborately, "I got galloping dandruff so bad I used to jerk along like I had locomotor ataxia; got 'em from a nigger shovel-stiff in a boxcar." **1927** *Am. Leg. Mo.* (Feb.) 35 [ref. to 1918]: Canned willie and goldfish, fleas-lined underwear, inspections, o.d. pills, sign-there-soldier and galloping dandruff [are] out of the running. [**1940** *AS* XV 447: *Crawling dandruff.* Head-lice.] **1974** Millard *Thunderbolt* 83: I hope you catch everything the docs have invented, including galloping dandruff and leaky valves.

galloping dominoes *n.pl. Gamb.* dice. *Joc.*
   1918 Sherwood *Diary* 87: We don't have much carnage as a result of the "galloping dominoes," but occasionally a fight ensues. **1920** in Hemingway *Dateline: Toronto* 33: Galloping Dominoes have at last come into their own. **1920–21** Witwer *Leather Pushers* 53: A exhibition of the gallopin' dominoes, or, to get technical, a crap game. **1922** *Leatherneck* (Apr. 22) 5 *Galloping Dominoes:* Dice. **1923** McKnight *Eng. Words* 46: *Bones* or *galloping horses* or *African golf balls* or *spotted cubes* or *galloping dominoes* for dice. **1933** Deleon & Martin *Tillie & Gus* (film): You were always better at the galloping dominoes. **1936** Reddan *Other Men's Lives* 69: There was nothing to do but…play cards or maybe a little game of "galloping dominoes." **1948** Menjou & Musselman *Nine Tailors* 26: He was an astute student of the…"galloping dominoes." **1952** Lait & Mortimer *USA* 187: The galloping dominoes and whirring slot machines were invested with official approval. **1968** Swarthout *Loveland* 195: "Like dominoes?" "Sure, only galloping. Oy veh." **1969** in *Playboy* (Jan. 1970) 296: Why, I do believe I see a pair of gallopin' dominoes. **1986** F. Walton *Once Were Eagles* 72: It'd be a fair bet that sackhound Mack was at those galloping dominoes.

galloping freckles *n.pl.* GALLOPING DANDRUFF. *Joc.* [Quots. ref. to WWI.]
   1922 *Amer. Legion Wkly.* (July 7) 31: I'm gonna change my style and quit writing about galloping freckles, speckled dominoes, top kickers, gold fish and slum. **1923** *Amer. Legion Wkly.* (Jan. 19) 13: Cooties? We knew not the galloping freckles in the early campaigns.

galloping galley *n. USMC.* (see quot.). *Joc.*
   1922 *Leatherneck* (Apr. 22) 5: *Galloping Galley:* A rolling kitchen.

galloping goose *n.* a locomotive, car, aircraft, etc., that runs poorly.
   1918 in Clover *Stop at Suzanne's* 39: Perhaps that is where the M. Farmon received its name of "Galloping Goose." **1918** in Crowe *Pat Crowe, Aviator* 90: We graduate from "flying Fourposters" to the "Galloping Geese" and if we are good we get one of those cute little Flying Fishes. **1934** Brewer *Riders of the Sky* 50: At last there was flying again—dual control/Twenty-three metre Nieuports, faster by far/Than "Galloping Goose" of Caudron…. **1945** Hubbard *R.R. Ave.* 343: *Galloping Goose*—A shaky section car. **1958** McCulloch *Woods Words* 69: *Galloping goose*—a. Any small steam or diesel locie which does not run smoothly. b. A three- or four-wheeled old time steam traction engine used to pull heavy log carts in the California pine country. c. A loose-jointed speeder or crummy. **1961** in *AS* (May 1962) 133: *Galloping goose, n.* Any steam or diesel locomotive which does not run properly.

galloping horses *n.pl.* dice.

1923 (quot. at GALLOPING DOMINOES).

galloping irons *n.pl.* the connecting rods in an automotive or aircraft engine.
   1942 *ATS* 720: *Galloping irons*, connecting rods. **1945** Hamann *Air Words: Galloping irons.* Pistons and rods. **1951** Shidle *Clear Writing* 94: *Galloping irons…*connecting rods. **1971** Tak *Truck Talk* 69: *Galloping irons:* connecting rods in a motor.

galloping ivories *n.pl. Gamb.* dice. *Joc.*
   1919 *Acotank* 197: Nance Chappy and his galloping ivories. **1931** *Amer. Merc.* (Dec.) 405: Fade them…gallopin' ivories. **1936** Reddan *Other Men's Lives* 156: You guessed it, "Galloping Ivories," the old army game of "shooting craps."

galloping snapshots *n.pl.* motion pictures. *Joc.*
   1922 *Leatherneck* (Apr. 22) 5: *Galloping Snap-shots:* Moving pictures. **1946** Boulware *Jive & Slang* 6: *Pad Of Galloping Snap-Shots…*Theatre.

gallows see GALLUS.

gallstone *n.* a galling person.
   1961–65 M. Howard *Bridgeport* 124: I've had that gallstone up to here.

galluptious *adj.* [of fanciful orig., prob. sugg. by *voluptuous*] delicious; scrumptious; superb; wonderful. Also vars.
   1856 Brougham *Humorous Stories* 193: "Gollopshus!" says Tom. ***1856** in *OED*: Raising the galoptius draught to his lips. ***1862** in *OED*: Cooking for a genteel family, John, it's a goluptius life. ***1864** Hotten *Slang Dict.* (ed. 3): *Golopshus,* splendid, delicious, luscious.—*Norwich.* **1882** Miller & Harlow *9'-51"* 259: Home to kiss galumptious Sally. **1887** Bauman *Lauderbach* 3: Oh! golly, won't we have a golumptious time, though. ***1887** in *F & H* III 107: Four young ladies represented the *galopshus* sum of 20,000,000 dollars. ***1889** in Barrère & Leland *Dict. Slang* I 394: *Galluptious* (popular), delightful. ***ca1890–93** Barrère & Leland *Dict. Slang: Galoptious* or *Galuptious…*(popular).—Delightful; a general superlative. **1895** *DN* I 389: *Galloptious:* Splendid, excellent. Staten Island, N.Y. ***1903** in *OEDS:* She gives you the most galumptious teas. **1909** in "O. Henry" *Works* 1539: Say, girls, it's galuptious. ***1926** Fowler *Mod. Eng. Usage* 164: Goloptius. **1937** in Rawick *Amer. Slave* III (pt. 3) 164 [ref. to *ca*1865]: When I git on de train him always slap me on de head and say: "Well, Bill, how your corporosity seem to sagasherate dis morning?" And I say: "Very galopshous, I thanks you, Captain."

gallus *adj.* [colloq. pron. of obs. *gallows* 'fit for the gallows; wicked'] **1.** splendid; attractive. Also adv. Also **gallows.**
   *1789 G. Parker *Life's Painter* 140: While some their patter flash'd in gallows fun and joking. ***1830** in *F & H* III 106: Ah, Dame Lobkin, if so be as our little Paul vas a vith you, it would be a gallows comfort to you in your latter hend! **1848** Baker *Glance at N.Y.* 21: Say, Lize, you're a gallus gal, anyhow. *Ibid.* 29: He's got to look a little more gallus, like my Mose, afore he can commence to shine. *Ibid.* 31: Ain't he gallus? *ca*1849 in Jackson *Early Songs of Uncle Sam* 56: They are "gallus" bloods indeed. *Ibid.* 57: My name is Jack Romaine, and a bull dog I'm in grain/And a mighty gallus chap, well I am! *Ibid.:* Oh a gallus gang was there. **1850** G.G. Foster *Gas-Light* 106: Well, now, yer'd better *bleeve* we had a gallus time! **1852** in *Amer. N & Q* (Feb. 1944) 168: Ain't the new rig gallus? **1854** in *Calif. Folk. Qly.* I (1942) 276: When first I went to mining, I was uncommon green,/ With a "gallus" rig I went to dig, and claimed a whole ravine. **1854** G.G. Foster *15 Mins.* 110: A dashing bonnet…twice as "gallus" as Madame Lawson's best. **1858** in *Amer. N & Q* (Oct. 1946) 108: "How's yer ice cream?"…"Gallus! How's yourn?"…"Stunning!" **1861** in F. Moore *Rebel Rec.* I 142: A gallus place, that! **1885** *Puck* (Apr. 29) 138: Everything went gallus, and I was always flush. **1894** Henderson *Sea-Yarns* 3: The *Central Park* was one o' the gallusest old hookers wot I ever sailed on. **1900** Ade *More Fables* 145: A dozen other Men, some of them Younger and more Gallus, were after her in Full Cry. **1923** *DN* V 235: *Gallus…*Excellent, very fine. **1947** in Botkin *Sidewalks* 240: "Gallus" meant something like "tip-top."
   2. peculiar; remarkable.
   1869 "M. Twain" *Innocents* II 159: Camels are not beautiful, and their long under-lip gives them an exceedingly "gallus" expression….Excuse the slang—no other word will describe it. **1870** "M. Twain," in R.L. Ramsay *M.T. Lexicon* 91: She has a "gallus" way of going with her arms akimbo. *ca*1946 in Rosa *Wild Bill* 108: The gallus Wild Bill was a feature in the landscape to attract attention.

gallus *adv.* exceedingly; very; awfully. *Rare* in U.S. Also **gallows.**
   1805 *Port Folio* (Aug. 24) 261: 'Tis gallows silly. ***1821** *Real Life in London* I 294: How gallows *lushy* she gets. ***ca1823** in *OED*: Then your Blowing will wax gallows haughty,/When she hears of your scaly mis-

take. *1851–61 H. Mayhew *London Labour* II 225: I yarns my money gallows hard, and requires to support to do hard work. *1869 in *F & H* III 106: Put it on your face so gallus thick that the devil himself won't see through it. 1889 Barrère & Leland *Dict. Slang* I 394: *Gallows* or *gallus* (common), a vulgar word for "very," in use in America and England until it was almost superseded by "awful," and "dreadful."..."I am gallows hard up for capital."

gally v. [dial. < early ModE *gallow* < OE *agælwan* 'to frighten'] *Whaling & N.E.* to frighten or confuse; daze. [Cf. earlier dial. E use in *OED*.]
*1840 Marryat, in *OED*: [Bull whales] are...easily "gallied," that is, frightened. 1851 Melville *Moby-Dick*: That strange perplexity of inert irresolution, which, when the fishermen perceive it in the whale, they say he is *gallied*. 1868 Macy *There She Blows!* 66: Don't let them "gally" you, if they shout in that boat. *Ibid.* 71: The Pandora's crew tried to gally you, didn't they? *Ibid.* 72: This word "gallied" is in constant use among whalemen in the sense of frightened or confused. 1871 *Overland Mo.* (June) 548: *Gallied*...*A whaler's phrase for frightened. 1873 Scammon *Marine Mammals* 68: Among right-whalemen there is a difference of opinion about...[how] to avoid "gallying" it. *Ibid.* 310: The boat-steerer got so gallied he could not strike the whale. 1878 Shippen *30 Yrs.* 288: The majority of the men were so "gallied" by the time the action was over, from enduring so severe a fire without being able to respond...that I doubt whether they could have been got to thus bring off a man whom they knew to be dead. 1896 Hamblen *Many Seas* 243: One...important part of the business is knowing how to go up to [whales], and get "fast" without "galleying" (scaring) them; for nothing can be done with "gallied" whales. 1916 in *DARE*: *Galley*—To frighten, to terrify..."gallied"...applied to a whale when alarmed. 1938 in *DARE*: The boat...was soon outdistanced by the "gallied," or frightened whales. 1968 in *DARE*: *Expressions meaning "confused, mixed up"...Gallied.*

gallyhoot v. [prob. alter. SCALLYHOOT, infl. by *gallivant*] to go on a spree.
1941 *Amer. N & Q* (Dec.) 133: The word "gallihooting"—without the last letter, of course, is current in southern Indiana. It appears to be related to "gallivanting." 1950 *PADS* (No. 14) 18: *Gallihootin, adv.* At high speed. (S.C.) 1968 S.O. Barker *Rawhide Rhymes* 16: But Charlie's saddle's cold tonight, he'll gallyhoot no more.

galoot n. [orig. uncert.; though occ. alleged to be fr. Krio, the authoritative *A Krio-English Dictionary*, ed. Clifford N. Fyle & Eldred D. Jones (Oxford: Oxford University Press, 1980), derives Krio *galut* '(of a person) hefty' directly fr. E] Orig. *Naut.* or *Und.* a person, usu. a man, who is clumsy, unpleasant, stupid, or the like. [In early use often applied by sailors to soldiers or marines, esp. recruits; app. pop. in U.S. during the Civil War.]
[*1812 Vaux *Vocab.*: *Galloot*: a soldier.] *1818 (cited in Partridge *DSUE* (ed. 8) 443). *1835 Marryat *J. Faithful* 313: The tally is right...and four greater galloots were never picked up. *1838 Glascock *Land Sharks* II 24: As for his subs, the greenest of green "galoots," neither had an idea beyond a draught board, button burnisher, or stick of pipe clay. 1859 in C.A. Abbey *Before the Mast* 193: Some *"Gilute"* let go the...sheets before hauling down on the clewlines. 1866 "A. Ward," in *DAE*: Wake Bessy, wake,/My sweet galoot! *1867 Smyth *Sailor's Wd.-Bk.*: *Galoot*, an awkward soldier....A soubriquet for the young or "green" marine. 1871 Hay *Pike Co. Ballads* 19: I'll hold her nozzle again the bank/Till the last galoot's ashore. 1871 "M. Twain" *Roughing It* 252: He could lam any galoot of his inches in America. 1875 *Minstrel Gags* 6: Ax dem galloots if I aint. 1879 Rooney *Conundrums* 80: They call you "galoot" if untutored/In every galoot's knavish tricks. 1883 Sweet & Knox *Mustang* 254: He was the fellow that first put us on the trail of these galloots. 1888 Hawes *Cahaba* 230: See me go through th' galoot. 1905 W.S. Kelly *Lariats* 4: All the local "galoots" assembled on Wilson's ranch to "see him off." 1912 Field *Watch Yourself* 272: Oh you dam Dutch galoot look scared. 1916 *Army & Navy Life* (Nov. 4) 294: They called us "raw recruits," and "rookies" and "galoots."/When first we hit the prairies way down here. 1929 in R.E. Howard *Book* 65: Bat is a handsome galoot who has a way with the dames. 1929–30 Dos Passos *42d Parallel* 55: It's about a galoot that goes to sleep an' wakes up in the year two thousand. 1930 Sage *Last Rustler* 7: Hey, you little big-eared galoot! 1947 Overholser *Buckaroo's Code* 6: The last time I saw you galoots was over on the other side of Bridger Butte. 1956 G. Green *Last Angry Man* 3: Why, you scum! You bunch of galoots! 1968 J. Kerr *Clinic* 17: What are you going to do with a young galoot like this, Miss Winters? 1978 L'Amour *Proving Trail* 4: He was a tall, thin galoot.

1980 D. Hamill *Stomping Ground* 43: You and that other galoot. 1993 *CBS This Morning* (CBS-TV) (Mar. 12): It's about this kind of galoot...in search of fame and fortune.

galvanize v. 1. *Mil.* to administer (to a prisoner of war) an oath of allegiance to the capturing government, usu. to muster him into military service.—usu. as p.ppl. Now *hist.* [Depending on the context, *galvanized Yankee* or *galvanized rebel* could ref. to a former prisoner of either side.]
1863 in Heartsill *1491 Days* 101: There is several lively conversations going on between our men and "galvanized" Yankees. 1864 Northrop *Chronicles* 159: Great activity by Rebels in recruiting; perhaps 100 go out daily to whom the soubriquet of "galvanized Rebels" is attached....If they appear after the act, "Ho, Reb!", "Galvanized Yank!," or "Reb!" greet them. 1865 Edmondston *Jour.* 693: Robbed...by a "Galvanized Yankee," i.e., a Yankee prisoner who has been allowed to take the oath of allegiance to the Confederacy & to serve in the army. 1865 in Springer *Sioux Country* 67: Then I found a Lieut. Jacob Roeswer of Comp. G 6 U.S. Vol. Inft. (galvanized). 1865 in W.C. Davis *Orphan Brig.* 260: We were "galvanized" [by the federal provost in Nashville]. 1868 in Mattes *Indians, Infants, Infantry* 63: Fort Bridger...was garrisoned by three companies of ex-rebel soldiers, who enlisted in our army, when prisoners of war, for duty on the frontier, fighting Indians. These troops are styled officially U.S. Volunteers, but are more generally known as "Galvanized Yankees." 1870 *Overland Mo.* (May) 418: Prisoners who procured their release by taking the oath of allegiance, were called "Galvanized Yankees." 1871 Schele de Vere *Americanisms* 23: The poor Confederate soldier, who succumbed morally to the privations and sufferings of Northern prisons...and...enlisted in the United States Army, was contemptuously called a *galvanized Yankee*—probably by an indistinct association with the worthless galvanized imitations of gold and silver, now so popular with the masses. 1919 Sabin *Pacific R.R.* 158: Ex-bluecoats and "Galvanized Yanks" labored with transit, rod, chain, pick and bar and spade and sledge. 1953–55 Kantor *Andersonville* 183: Who the hell told you I wanted to be galvanized?...As galvanized Rebels they would be suspect for a long time.
2. *Mil.* (of a prisoner of war) to swear allegiance to the capturing government as a condition of release.
1865 in Jackman *Diary* 169: Taking the amnesty oath..."galvanized." 1878 McElroy *Andersonville* 305 [ref. to 1864]: I suppose that five hundred [Union prisoners] "galvanized," as we termed it.

galvanized adj. 1. see GALVANIZE.
2. in disguise; imitation. *Joc.*
1883 Peck *Bad Boy* 246: You would pass in a colored prayer meeting, and no one would know you were galvanized. 1939 Coolidge *Old Calif. Cowboys* 65 [ref. to ca1914]: He [an American]'s a galvanized Mex.

Galway n. [app. in ref. to Galway-style whiskers] (among tramps) a priest, esp. an Irish Catholic priest.
1891 *Contemporary Rev.* (Aug.) 255: The Catholic priest is nicknamed "The Galway." 1893 *Century* (Nov.) 100: The "Galway" [Catholic priest] is perhaps the best friend of the Frenchies. 1897 in J. London *Reports* 320: *Galway*—priest—from the Gaelic. 1899 "J. Flynt" *Tramping* 372: Slim made friends with the Galway (the Catholic priest) who visited the jail. *Ibid.* 384: Y'ole Galway, you, yer an ole hypocrite. 1921 Casey & Casey *Gay-Cat* 54: A Galway named Father John Bresnahan...tole us we oughta put by some money fer a rainy day. 1927 *AS* (June) 387: *Galway*...was applied by vags to Irish Catholic priests; now it is used by old-timers to refer to any kind of priest. 1930 "D. Stiff" *Milk & Honey* 206: *Galway*—A priest.

gam[1] n. [prob. < Polari < It *gamba* 'leg'; but cf. heraldic *gamb* 'the leg of an animal as represented on a coat of arms' < OF *gambe* 'leg'] Orig. *Und.* a leg; (now *specif.*) a young woman's leg, esp. if shapely. [*1789 quots. are erroneously dated "1781" in *OED*.]
*1785 Grose *Vulgar Tongue*: *Gambs*, thin, ill shaped legs; a corruption of the French word jambes. *1789 G. Parker *Life's Painter* 151: If a man has bow legs, he has queer gams, gams being cant for legs. *Ibid.*: Stockings—Gam-cases. *1812 Vaux *Vocab.*: *Gams*: the legs, to have *queer gams*, is to be bandy-legged, or otherwise deformed. *1819 [T. Moore] *Tom Crib* 61: Back to his home, with tottering *gams*. 1837 Neal *Charcoal Sks.* 124: There's a good deal of circumbendibus about Spoon's gams. 1856 Brougham *Humorous Stories* 21: Look at them stockin's, Mary,...flimsy, skimpin things, for a cowld Christian to wear on his *gams*. *1887 W.E. Henley, in J. Farmer *Musa Pedestris* 175: At you I merely lift my gam. 1898 Dunne *Peace & War* 186: Capital is at home

now with his gams in a tub iv hot wather. *a*1909 Tillotson *Detective* 91: *Gam*—A leg. **1925** in Partridge *Dict. Und.* 276: *Gams*...The nether limbs of girls. **1927** *Vanity Fair* (Nov.) 67: "Stems" and "Gams" (legs). **1938** Bellem *Blue Murder* 21: The slugs kicked his gam from under him. **1941** Cain *Mildred Pierce* 190: The gams, the gams! Your face ain't news! **1943** *Newsweek* (Oct. 11) 80: Same Miss Grable, gams still stable. **1945** Himes *If He Hollers* 63: Nice gams. **1953** Dibner *Deep Six* 110: It's going to be a little rough on you...with that bum gam. **1960** in T.C. Bambara *Gorilla* 51: Not to mention your long, lean gams. **1970** Zindel *Your Mind* 46: Her gams were splendid. **1985** C. Busch *Vampire Lesbians* 73: I was always a sucker for a shapely gam. **1988** M. Barrie & J. Mulholland *Amazon Women* (film): Let me see your gams. **1993** *TV Guide* (May 29) 27: The June Taylor Dancer's gams...kicked off *The Jackie Gleason Show*.

gam² *n.* [prob. abbrev. of GAMMON; cf. technical sense 'a school of whales', which is contemporaneous with this sense] Esp. *Whaling*. a social meeting between ships at sea; (*hence*) conversation.

*1826 in J. Farmer *Musa Pedestris* 96: Says I,—"Miss Moll, don't tip this gam." **1846** J.R. Browne *Whaling Voyage* 76: When two whalers meet on any of the whaling grounds, it is usual to have a "gam," or mutual visit, for the purpose of interchanging the latest news...and enjoying a general chit-chat. ***1850** in *OED*: Gam is the word by which they designate the meeting, exchanging visits, and keeping company of two or more whale ships. **1851** Melville *Moby-Dick*: What does the whaler do when she meets another whaler in any sort of decent weather? She has a gam. **1866** C.E. Hunt *Shenandoah* 57: He had come on board of us for a "gam." **1873** Scammon *Marine Mammals* 273: The two captains met during a "gam" off Geographe Bay. **1890** in *DAE*: When the whalemen met on the high seas...they would lay to, sometimes for hours, captains and crews would exchange visits, letters from and for home be delivered, and the story of the voyages told. That was a "gam." **1899** Robbins *The Gam* (title). **1913–14** London *Elsinore* 314: I go on deck to relieve Mr. Pike, who lingers a moment for a "gam," as he calls it. **1945** Colcord *Sea Lang.* 86: Come over after supper and have a gam. **1965–70** in *DARE*: When men out in seagoing boats get together...that's called a...Gam.

gam³ *n.* [clipping of *gambler*] a gambler.

1875 in *DA*: A Hard Place for Gams. **1890** Quinn *Fools of Fortune* 368: I guess you "gams" knows who I is. **1893** Hampton *Maj. in Washington* 92: Next day the old "gams" went back and took a look. **1903** A.H. Lewis *Boss* 291: Them gams took it off him so fast he caught cold. **1903** Ade *Society* 178: He had the Confidence of many of our most celebrated Barkeeps and could give the Hurry-Up to any well-known Gam. **1920** Ade *Hand-Made Fables* 46: He surely knew how to throw a scare into the Gams. **1921** *Variety* (Apr. 8): One of the gams tipped me thinkin it wuz a great joke.

gam *v. Naut.* to engage in a GAM².—also constr. with *it*. Now *hist.*

1849 J.F. Cooper *Sea Lions* 132: I see no reason why we should not be neighborly, and "gam" it a little, when we've nothing better to do. *Ibid.* 137: Gardiner...went a "gamming," as it is termed, on board the other schooner. **1890** in *F & H* III 111: To *gam* means to gossip. The word occurs again and again in the log-books of the old whalers. **1906** in *DAE*: The skipper came over with the boat's crew and gammed with us. **1926** in *DARE*: *Gamming*: Visiting, as practiced between whaleships at sea. **1953** *N.Y. Times* (Jan. 11) VII 7 [ref. to 19th C.]: At many a rendezvous, the wives waited and "gammed" by the hour. **1968** in *DARE*: Come in and gam awhile.

gamahuche *v.* [< F *gamahucher*] Orig. *Prost.* to perform fellatio or cunnilingus upon. Also intrans. Also as *n.*, an act of oral copulation. *Rare* in U.S.

*1865 in *OEDS*: Quick, quick, Blanche!...come and gamahuche the gentleman. ***ca1866** *Romance of Lust* 35: Into a better position for me to gamahuche her. *Ibid.* 148: I and Lizzie mutually gamahuched each other. *Ibid.* 451: Uncle enjoyed a...gamahuche with Ellen. ***1879** *Pearl* (Oct.) 108: I commenced to suck and gamahuche Sophie. ***ca1888–94** in *OEDS*: She gave me a gamahuche for a few minutes. ***1900** *Horn Book* 142: The man's face is thus between the woman's thighs and he gamahuches her. **1916** Cary *Venery* I 102: *Gamahuching*—Tonguing a woman. [**1972** *Nat. Lampoon* (Apr.) 77: *Gamma Hutch: The Playboy Fall-out Shelter*.]

gambolier *n.* a gambler. Also vars. *Joc.*

1858 in Dwyer & Lingenfelter *Songs of Gold Rush* 59: There was a noted gam-ba-lier a living in our camp. **1866** *Night Side of N.Y.* 76: The gay gamboliers would sometimes set four and twenty hours at a stretch.

1867 *Galaxy* (Nov.) 790: A gay young gam-bo-lier stabs himself with the queen of hearts. **1868** Williams *Black-Eyed Beauty* 12: They might be "bold gamboliers" and his pocket might suffer as his fob had. **1874** Carter *Rollingpin* 196: And from a busted gambolier he purchased dice and truck. **1882** A.W. Aiken *Joe Buck* 3: You are a gentle gambolier on the green. **1905** Belasco *Golden West* 319: See here, gamboleer Sid, you're too lucky.

game *n.* **1.** [extension of *game* as a hunting term] *Und.* the victim or victims of sharpers or criminals.

*1698–99 "B.E." *Dict. Canting Crew*: Game,...Bubbles drawn in to be cheated. **1821** Martin & Waldo *Lightfoot* 31: When he thought it was time for the *game* to come along, he gave me my instructions.

2. *Und.* **a.** a criminal or illicit occupation of any kind; in phr. **on the game** practicing one's criminal specialty; engaged in theft or other crime.

*1739 in *OEDS*: I, and others went out again upon the Old Game. ***1811** *Lex. Balatron.*: *Game*. Any mode of robbing. The toby is now a queer game; to rob on the highway is now a bad mode of acting. ***1812** Vaux *Vocab.* s.v. *cadge*: The cadge is the *game* or profession of begging. *Ibid.*: *Game*. every particular branch of depredation...is called a *game*; as, what *game* do go upon? One species of robbery or fraud is said to be a good *game*, another a *queer game*, etc. ***1839** in *OEDS*: On the game, thieving. **1859** Matsell *Vocab.* 36: *Game*. The particular line of rascality the rogue is engaged in; thieving; cheating. ***1898** in *OEDS*: The prosecutrix pestered her to "go on the game," i.e. the streets. ***1911** F. Harris, in *OEDS*: The phrase of the prostitute to-day on the streets of London is: "I'm on the game." **1922** *In the Clutch of Circumstance* 58: After making a big "haul" we would go West to start in the "game" on a large scale. **1928** Sharpe *Chi. May* 43: He put her on the game (had taught her thieving).

b. Orig. *Prost.* prostitution.—constr. with *the*. Cf. GAME, *adj*.

*1898, *1911 (quots. at (a), above). **1932** Reckless *Vice in Chicago* 146: I've been in the game twelve years now. **1936** Mackenzie *Living Rough* 93: The streets were full of street-walkers too—dames on the game. **1945** Drake & Cayton *Black Metropolis* 193: I am not in the "game" any more. You see, all I do now is rent rooms to the girls, and if they cause trouble here, I don't let them rent any rooms. **1956** A.J.V. Levy *Others' Children* 176: She never intended to "stay in the game" after she had accomplished her purpose. **1957** Murtagh & Harris *Cast the First Stone* 125: Sugar asked Lorraine, "Your little friend in the game, honey?" Lorraine said, "Not yet. But she wants to be."

3. calling; business; vocation.

1868 in G.W. Harris *High Times* 190: Hit takes a feller a long time, George, to fine out what his gif' am, his bes' pint, what game he's stronges' on. **1905** Riordon *Plunkitt* 8: Some young men think that the best way to prepare for the political game is to practice speakin' and becomin' orators. **1910** *N.Y. Eve. Jour.* (Feb. 2) 18: "You ticket speculators must make a lot of money don't you?" "Oh about $500 a night — was you thinkin' of gettin' into the game?" **1920–21** Witver *Leather Pushers* 331: Box-fightin' is the only game I know. **1922** in Ruhm *Detective* 6: Crude?—maybe—but then I know my game and you don't. *Ibid.* 12: My game and women don't go well together. **1925** W. James *Drifting Cowboy* 60: He'd been in the picture game too long to quit so sudden. **1928** Dahlberg *Bottom Dogs* 116: Donald had gotten on in the printing game. **1929** T. Gordon *Born to Be* 138: The music game is a hard game, you know. **1931** Hellinger *Moon* 102: I'm going down to Wall Street and get a job in that game. **1931** Armour *Little Caesar* (film): I've been in this game a good many years. **1926–35** Watters & Hopkins *Burlesque* 14: Bonny's the best scout in this game. *Ibid.* 20: Don't you ever want to get ahead in this game? **1945** in Conklin *Sci. Fi. Omnibus* 438: I was in the advertising game for a while. **1954** Matheson *Born of Man & Woman* 137: I'm in the plumbing game. **1957** J.D. MacDonald *Death Trap* 18: "Construction work." "I've got a son-in-law in that game, friend." **1959** M. Harris *Wake Up* 198: I guess that's the writing game for you. **1978** Kopp *Innocence* 41: Spinning flax is my game/and Rumpelstiltskin is my name.

4. (one's) concern or affair; (*also*) attention or interest.

1889 B. Harte *Dedlow Marsh* 102: An ordinary six-shooter...would lay over that...but that ain't your game just now, Don Kosay. You must get up and get, and at once. **1896** Ade *Artie* 4: Say, I like that church, and if they'll put in a punchin'-bag and a plunge they can have my game, I'll tell you those.

5. state of affairs; set of circumstances; situation.

1893 F.P. Dunne, in Schaaf *Dooley* 226: There's somebody runnin' th' game wrong. **1895** Townsend *Fadden* 55: But lemme tell ye wot happened ter put me on de inside [of] der game up ter our house. **1896** Ade *Artie* 51: Don't tell me nothin' about that game. I know just what it'l be. **1899** Cullen *Tales* 96: I had a straight-out talk with him then, and told him the whole game. **1899** Kountz *Baxter's Letters* 50: A woman…will make you jump through, lie down, and roll over.…You show me a man who hasn't been up against such a game and I'll show you a man who lacks experience. **1902–03** Ade *People You Know* 26: Brad was for the Money End of the Game. **1911** A.H. Lewis *Apaches of N.Y.* 134: This is a fine game I'm gettin'! **1913** H. Jackson *Eighteen Nineties* 233: The critics…felt…that they were, to use that language of the street which Kipling turned into literature, up against a new game. **1936** Dos Passos *Big Money* 232: You can't beat the game with that guy. **1982** Neaman & Silver *Kind Words* 251: The pimp may provide such services as *running down the game* (informing her about the presence of police, etc., in her area).

6. *Und.* benefits.—contrasted with *name* 'reputation'.—constr. with *the*.

1894 in J. London *Tramp Diary* 57: The long lean Yankee from Cairo. "May as well have the game as the name." **1934** L. Berg *Pris. Nurse* 66: But they just laughed at him and called him a…punk.…When the wolves…came bearing…prison luxuries—he accepted them and forgot to struggle. After all, he had the name, why not the game? **1952** Himes *Stone* 230: They'll swear you're a fag and keep after you until it breaks you down.…You'll have the name without the game.

7. *Und.* (one's) skill or effectiveness, esp. in criminal activity.

1954 in Wepman et al. *The Life* 39: Do you think your game is stronger than mine? **1967** [Beck] *Pimp* 79: If your game is strong you could play a "hog" outta her ass. **1968** in Andrews & Dickens *Big House* 17: Your record's too long; their game is too strong;/And I can't buy a break nowhere. **1976** Wepman et al. *The Life* 182: *Game n.*…Skill in the activities of the Life (usu. with possessive).

¶ In phrases:

¶ **have (one's) game together** *Black E.* to be appropriately prepared, esp. in terms of intelligence or emotional stability. Cf. *get (one's) act together* s.v. ACT.

1969 Rodgers *Black Bird* 17: Laugh in my face, call me uh/simple Black woman who/ain't got her game togetha.

¶ **jump the game** *Gamb.* to renege; quit; clear out.

1871 Banka *Pris. Life* 83: He became frightened, and "jumped the game" at Jeffersonville, Indiana.

¶ **only game in town** an unsatisfactory situation that one must accept for lack of an alternative.—constr. with *the*.

1942 Sonnichsen *Billy King* 165 [ref. to *a*1900]: "Don't you know they're dealing the best of it? You haven't got a chance to win." "What of it?…It's the only game in town, ain't it?" **1944** *Collier's* (Feb. 12) 70: Maybe the captain is like the old faro bank player who is warned as he is going into a gambling house to beware of the bank game there because it is crooked and who says: "Yes, I know it is, but what am I going to do? It is the only game in town." **1966–67** W. Stevens *Gunner* 123: "How much you want to pay?"…"This is the only game in town, pal. It'll be whatever you want to stick me."

¶ **run** [or **put** or **whip**] **[a] game on** Esp. *Black E.* to take advantage of; hoodwink; fool.

1940 Ellis & Logan *Star Dust* (film): Did you and Mr. Brooke put up a game on me? **1961** H. Ellison *Gentleman Junkie* 149: Stop tryin' to whup the game on me, boy. **1962** H. Simmons *On Eggshells* 202: And if you think they ain't whipping a game on him, Jim, you just ain't bright enough to be alive. **1965** in W. King *Black Anthol.* 305: Ever since Dan and Mac were in the kindergarten together, Mac been putting game on him.…You so square Little Orphan Annie could put game on you. **1971** Goines *Dopefiend* 22: You know I ain't tryin' to put no game on you, man. **1973** Childress *Hero* 48: I cut him off. "Don't run that game on me," I say. **1974** V.E. Smith *Jones Men* 122: You tryin' to run a game on me or somethin'? **1974** C.M. Rodgers *Ovah* 63: Jesus…whipped [a] game on em/though/cause he strutted on up and out/again/after three days. **1977** *Watch Your Mouth* (WNET-TV): "Did you go to jail?" "Naa. We ran some game on 'em."

¶ **tighten (one's) game** *Und. & Black E.* to improve (one's) behavior.

1967 *Lit Dict.* 42: *Tighten Up Your Game*—Get straightened out; change your ways; be cool, not a fool. **1973** Goines *Players* 23: Bitch, if you don't know how to respect a man yet, a couple of well placed punches upside your head will make you tighten your game up so that you'll respect one in the future.

¶ **try (someone's) game** *Gamb.* to get to know (someone).

1896 Ade *Artie* 46: "Did you ever try his game?" "I never heard of him."

game *adj.* **1.** *Und.* whorish; living by prostitution.

[***1698–99** "B.E." *Dict. Canting Crew: Game*…At a Bawdy-house, Lewd Women. *Have ye any Game Mother? Have ye any Whores Mistress Bawd?*] **1788** Grose *Vulgar Tongue* (ed. 2): *Game pullet.* A young whore, or forward girl in the way of becoming one. **1821** in Partridge *Dict. Und.* 276: Two blones [women]…both completely flash, as well as game. **1845** Ingraham *Harefoot* 33: There go two fine women, but they are not game! **ca*1890–93** *F & H* III 109: *Game-woman*—a prostitute.

2. *Und.* corrupt or dishonest; living by criminality.

1805 in Partridge *Dict. Und.* 276: Game lightermen (who conceal and dispose of illicit goods). **1823*, **1828** (cited in Partridge *Dict. Und.*). **1847–49** Bonney *Banditti* 101: "Young tells me that Fox and Birch are game." "They are—no mistake.…They appear to be *flush*." **1889** in Partridge *Dict. Und.* 276: "Game," or corrupted, revenue officers. **ca*1890–93** *F & H* III 109: *Game-cove*—an associate of thieves.

game *v.* Orig. *Und.* to fool or swindle; engage in deceit toward. Also intrans.

[**1944** *New Cab Calloway's Hepster's Dict.* 255: *Gammin'*…showing off, flirtatious.] **1963** in Wepman et al. *The Life* 80: It's time for the kid to game. **1968** Gover *JC* 85: Gonna lowrate your ole lady without even gamin her. *Ibid.* 97: I gamed him for his wristwatch. **1970** Cortina *Slain Warrior* 187: What a naive fool I was…how I gamed myself. **1968–71** Cole & Black *Checking* 26: So they game the hell out of him and his friend with exactly the same games they use on white middle-class social workers. **1972** Eble *Campus Slang* (Oct. 1972) 3: *Game*—to deceive, tease, trick: You can't game me. **1977** Bunker *Animal Factory* 125: But they don't expect Whitey to game back. **1979** T. Baum *Carny* 139: She was lying…She gamed you. **1979** Homer *Jargon* 218: Don't game me, Jack. **1993** H.R. Clinton, on *World Today* (CNN-TV) (May 26): The system is being gamed and ripped off.

game face *n.* Orig. *Sports.* a belligerent or determined expression, as affected by a player during a competition. [Almost certainly older than this evidence attests.]

1983 W. Walker *Dime to Dance* 21: "Put your game face on, boy." It was a favorite expression of Coach Walsh's…in high school.…"When your hat goes on, your game face goes on with it." **1989** Dickson *Baseball Dict.* 175: *Game face*…A look of determination affected for play. **1991** Lott & Lieber *Total Impact* 51: In the locker room before kickoff, Robinson never wore a game face. **1993** *New Yorker* (Feb. 8) 104: Wearing their best game faces, the patrol officers…begin their shifts.

game of fives see s.v. FIVE.

gamer *n.* **1.** *Sports.* a game-winning point or hit. Hence, as adj. a situation requiring a gamer.

1980 in Dickson *Baseball Dict.* 175: Reggie Jackson singled home the gamer. **1982** Luciano & Fisher *Umpire Strikes Back* 54: Yaz coming to bat in a gamer situation…Fenway Park fans were screaming at him. **1984** *N.Y. Post* (Aug. 3) 72: Rick Cerone was the catalyst last night, collecting three hits, including his first gamer this season.

2. *Sports.* an especially tenacious or effective team player.

1982 T. Considine *Lang. Sport* 21: *Gamer.* A "game" ballplayer who plays in spite of injuries. *Ibid.* 143: *Gamer.* A player whose performance in actual games always exceeds the ability he shows in practice. **1984** WINS radio news (Aug. 29): I think he's a real gamer and I think he can help us win. **1986** in Dickson *Baseball Dict.* 175: His…teammates counter that Murray is a "gamer," that he is playing in pain.

gammie *n.* a gambler.

1966 L. Armstrong *Self-Portrait* 14: And all the old gammies and pimps, they'd call for us to sing.

gammon *n.* [perh. through misunderstanding of obs. E thieves' argot, *give (someone) gammon* 'to distract a victim who is being robbed'] talk; chatter; (*usu.*) nonsense; bosh.

1781 G. Parker *View of Society* I 208: I thought myself pretty much a master of *Gammon*, but the Billingsgate eloquence of Mrs. P—…exceeded me. **1789** G. Parker *Life's Painter* 143: What's all this *gammon* and *patter* about? **1805** in *OED*: "Come, come, none of your gammon!" cried one, "tell us where the other black sheep is." **1811** *Lex. Balatron.*: What rum gamon the old file pitched to the flat; how finely the knowing old fellow humbugged the fool. **1812** Vaux *Vocab.*: *Gammon*: flattery; deceit; pretence; plausible language; any assertion which is not strictly true, or professions believed to be insincere. **1824** Paulding *J. Bull in Amer.* 72: O! I *guess* we call it gammon. **1847** Hooton *St. Louis' Isle* 151: "Gammon!" says I. "It's all your wimmin's nonsense." **1848** "Cpl. of Guard" *High Private* 15: You shall share with me—my bed shall be your bed—my food, your food—(gammon!). **1848** *Ladies' Repository* VIII (Oct.) 315: *Gammon*, Lies; idle talk; stories told to deceive. **1849** Melville *White Jacket* 218: It's turned out all gam-

mon, Jack. **1853** Lippard *New York* 93: "I have no cash-box. My cash is all in bank." "Gammon. It won't do. Behind yer seat is yer iron safe." **1862** in Andrus *Letters* 25: That is the kind of gammon the nation has been fed on for the last year. **1870** *Comic Songster* 25: "Gammin!" says she, "get out!" **1873** Small *Knights* 6: "Gammon, my boy, gammon," quoth I. **1878** Pinkerton *Criminal Reminiscences* 232: This is no gammon story. **1909** in "O. Henry" *Works* 1546: Oh, gammon and jalap! **1953** Randolph & Wilson *Down in Holler* 247: *Gammon*...Idle talk, untruths.

¶ In phrase:

¶ **up to gammon** wide awake; alert to trickery.

1845 Corcoran *Pickings* 78: The lapidary...was at once "up to gammon."

gammon *v.* **1.** to deceive or lie to; hoax; cheat.

[***1789** G. Parker *Life's Painter* 158: When one of them [*sc.* criminals] speaks well, they say he gammons well.] ***1812** Vaux *Vocab.*: To *gammon* a person, is to amuse him with false assurances, to praise, or flatter him, in order to obtain some particular end;...to *gammon* a shopkeeper, etc., is to engage his attention to your discourse, while your accomplice is executing some preconceived depredation upon his property. ***1821–26** Stewart *Man-of-War's-Man* I 137: But this, Oliver used to say, was a thing that was all in his eye,—a mere quiz to gammon the flats. **1839** in Strong *Diary* I 116: He has fairly gammoned him out of probably the larger half of an estate of $200,000. **1848** Judson *Mysteries* 66: You've been awfully gammoned. **1866** Brockett *Camp, Battle Field & Hospital* 109: Mrs. Cushman most successfully "gammoned" some of the leading secessionists of Louisville. **1946** in Randolph & Legman *Roll Me in Your Arms* 273 [ref. to *ca*1910]: He gammoned our Nell to run away.

2. to tease.

1843 *Spirit of Times* (Sept. 30) 365: Now olthough I jist wanted to gammon the Jineral, I know'd he warn't a koward.

gander *n.* **1.** a man, esp. away from his home; in phr. **gander party** a party for men only.

1859 Matsell *Vocab.* 36: *Gander*. A married man not living at home with his wife. **1867** J.R. Lowell, in *DA*: Gander-party: a social gathering of men only. **1896** in *War Papers* I 321: This occasion was strictly a "gander party."

2. a look.

1914 Jackson & Hellyer *Vocab.* 36: *Gander*, Noun. General currency. An inquisitorial glance; a searching look; an impertinent gazing or staring. Also the simple act of looking or seeing. **1929** Booth *Stealing Through Life* 257 [ref. to 1918]: It looks like it's going to rain, so we better make the lower yard for a quick gander, then get back and stick near this shed. **1939** R. Chandler *Big Sleep* 86: I go over and take a gander into it. **1947** T. Williams *Streetcar* 58: Now let's have a gander at the bill of sale. **1949** in F. Brown *Honeymoon* 75: "Cut the malarkey," said Professor Winslow, "and take a gander at this." **1958** A. King *Mine Enemy* 121: You may take a gander at it in the rare-book department. **1959** in A. Sexton *Letters* 68: I do not think you will really like...my poetry once you get a real gander. **1964** Faust *Steagle* 47: Weissburg debates two years whether to drop his pencil and cop a gander. **1966** van Italie *I'm Really Here* 37: Doris is getting her first "gander" at...Paris. **1967** Crowley *Boys in the Band* 857: I, however, cannot seem to locate it for a gander. **1987** Norst & Black *Lethal Weapon* 6: Take a gander at yourself. **1989** Kienzle *Eminence* 121: Take a gander at my calf. **1993** *Simpsons* (Fox-TV): We can charge two bits a gander.

gander *v.* [orig. S.E., later dial. E] **1.** to wander; ramble.

*1687 in *OED*: To go a gandering, whilst his Wife lies in, *chercher à se divertir ailleurs* [etc.]. ***1859** in *F & H* III 116: Nell might come gandering back in one of her tantrums. ***1865** in *OEDS*: The deerhounds get between everybody's legs...and gander about idiotically. **1940** *AS* (Apr.) 204: *Gandering*. Visiting or sightseeing. **1946** Boulware *Jive & Slang* 4: *Gander*...To walk. **1972** Grogan *Ringolevio* 318: He...got an urge to go out and gander around the neighborhood.

2.a. to crane one's neck for a look; to look.—used intrans.

*1887 in *OEDS*: *Gonder* [*sic*], to stretch the neck like a gander, to stand at gaze. "What a't gonderin' theer fur?" **1903** in *DA*: *Gander*—To stretch or rubber your neck. **1931** in D.W. Maurer *Lang. Und.* 48: We went gandering for a peterman. **1934** in Partridge *Dict. Und.* 278: To *gander*...is to look. **1936** Twist *We Have to Die* (film): Don't be ganderin' around or you'll get an eyeful of slugs. **1944** Kapelner *Lonely Boy Blues* 7: My girl...ganders at dresses. **1950** in *DAS*: She [an astrologer] had gandered at the stars for him. **1959** De Roo *Young Wolves* 13: I stand in the hall to gander at her when she walks by. **1989** *Harper's* (June) 58: Again and again, I see men gandering at Beargrease.

b. to look at; see.—used trans.

1936 *Esquire* (Sept.) 162: To "gander the gams." **1939** *AS* (Oct.) 239: *To gander*. To examine. **1944** *Pap. Mich. Acad.* XXX 598: *Gander*, to look at. **1942–49** Goldin et al. *DAUL* 77: *Gander*, *v.* To take a gander at. **1949** Monteleone *Crim. Slang* 94: *Gander*...look at. **1968** Beck *Trick Baby* 225: Make sure you turn that bullet wound so he ganders it.

gander-gutted *adj.* scrawny. Hence **gander gut,** *n.*

1839 *American Joe Miller* 75: All legs, shaft, and head, and no belly: real gander-gutted lookin' critter. **1941** in *DARE*: Gander gut, one who is both skinny and awkward. **1959** in *DARE*: Gander gutted...thin. *Rare.*

gander-legged *adj.* having long, thin legs.

1844 in *DA*: He's a monstrous grate, long, gander-legged feller. **1845** J. P. Barnum *Life* 31 [ref. to *ca*1830]: I will put fire to that d—d old gander legged Farrel's house and shed...d—n him. **1970** in *DARE*.

ganderneck *v.* So. RUBBERNECK; GANDER, 1, 2.a.

1976 Univ. Tenn. student: It's a good place to go if you're just ganderneckin' around. **1979** Univ. Tenn. student: Every time there's a wreck you get a bunch of gandernecks.

gander-pluck *v.* (see quot.).

1841 in *DA*: It was said formerly every second man in Kentucky had an eye gouged out, and every third a nose or ear gander-plucked—that is, bitten off.

gandy *n.* GANDY-DANCER. Also attrib.

1925 Mullin *Scholar Tramp* 126 [ref. to *ca*1912]: When I got back to Los, the bright lights looked so good after that hard life with the gandies, I got drunker than a fiddler's bitch, and blowed all my jack. **1930** Irwin *Tramp & Und. Sl.*: *Gandy*...A railroad section hand or labourer [*sic*]....The word was used as far back as the 1860's. **1952** in *Qly. Jour. Studies on Alcoholism* XIV (1953) 478: The alcoholic...may ship out on a "gandy crew" (railroad gang). **1951–59** F. Ramsey *Been Here* 86: The section boss, or "cap'n" of the gandy crew. **1973** Mathers *Riding the Rails* 28: I'm in this boxcar and there're these gandies in the other end.

gandy-dance *v.* to work as a GANDY-DANCER. Also **gander-dance.**

1918 *Independent* (Mar. 2) 382: "Gander-dancin'"....Workin' with pick and shovel. *Ibid.* (May 11) 250: We had been gander-dancing on a new railroad for weeks. **1920** *Amer. Legion Wkly.* (Sept. 3) 8: Brannigan were "gandy-dancin'" up an' down the track,/Jugglin' ties an' fish plates on his bruised an' broken back. **1971** Curtis *Banjo* 63: There's hard times in K.C. I'm lucky to gandy-dance.

gandy-dancer *n.* [orig. unkn.; cf. 1945 Hubbard quot.] **1.a.** R.R. a section hand or track laborer.

1918 *Outlook* (June 26) 326: A "gandy dancer" is a railway worker who tamps down the earth between the ties, or otherwise "dances" on the track. **1918** in *AS* (Oct. 1933) 22: Gandy Dancer. Section hand. **1922** N. Anderson *Hobo* 93: A "gandy dancer" is a man who works on the railroad track tamping tie. **1923** in Holbrook *Mackinaw* 204: Wages: gandy dancers, $3.75. **1925** Mullin *Scholar Tramp* 125 [ref. to *ca*1912]: Last time I tried a long-stake job, I shipped gandy-dancer with a railroad construction outfit. Shovel stiff, y' know. **1930** "D. Stiff" *Milk & Honey* 206: Gandy Dancer—Hobo track laborer, tie tamper and rail layer. **1945** Hubbard *R.R. Ave.* 344: Gandy Dancer—Track laborer. Name may have originated...from the old Gandy Manufacturing Company of Chicago, which made tamping bars, claw bars, and shovels. **1945** Himes *If He Hollers* 100: I used to be a water boy for a bunch of Irish ganny dancers in Arkansaw. **1956** I. Shulman *Good Deeds* 170: Former occupations: gandy dancer and cowboy. **1976** *Sat. Review* (June 26) 58: We danced on the ceiling/And we danced on the wall/ At the Gandy Dancer's ball. **1979** in Terkel *Amer. Dreams* 237: He was a roustabout, gandy dancer, track gang laborer.

b. a member of a road construction crew. Cf. 1918 quot. at GANDY-DANCE, *v.*

1942 *AS* (Dec.) 221: Gandy Dancer. A pick-and-shovel man. **1942** *ATS* 456: *Gandy dancer*....loosely a pick-and-shovel laborer, esp. on railroad or highway construction. **1976** Lieberman & Rhodes *CB* 129: *Gandy Dancer*—Road construction worker.

2. *Und.* a petty criminal.

1920 E. Hemingway, in *N.Y. Times Mag.* (Aug. 18, 1985) 23: You gaudy [*sic*] dancers...better not run in with The Hand. **1933** Ersine *Prison Slang* 39: *Gandy Dancer*. A petty criminal. **1942–49** Goldin et al. *DAUL* 77: *Gandy dancer*. A cheap crook.

3. *Carnival.* (see quot.).

1935 *Amer. Mercury* (June) 229: *Gandy dancer*: grifter who sells novelties.

4. (see quot.).

1942 *Life* (Sept. 21) 44: Last week the nation's needle nuts and gandy-dancers (jitterbugs) were cut to the quick by a WPB official who declared that the wasteful manufacture of "zoot suits" and "juke jackets"...must stop.

5. an active socialite; "man about town."

1992 *Donahue* (NBC-TV): So you were a gandy dancer then. Women were a part of your life.

gandy stick *n. R.R.* a tamping bar.

1942 *ATS* 75: *Gandy stick*, a tamping bar used by railway section workers. **1965** O'Neill *High Steel* 271: *Gandy Stick*: a tamping bar used in railroad work.

gandy stiff *n.* (among hoboes) GANDY-DANCER. Also **gandy hand.**

1918 Livingston *Delcassee* 72: Wabash Dan...confirm[ed] the assertion of the gandy stiff. *Ibid.* 82: He and the gandy stiff went to the barrack of the Salvation Army. **1956** Sorden & Ebert *Logger's* 15 [ref. to *ca*1925]: *Gandy-dancer*, Pick-and-shovel man. Same as road monkey. Same as *gandy-hand*.

gang *n.* **1.** a large amount or number; a lot. [Cf. *OED* def. 8, 'a set of articles such as are usually taken together'.]

1811 in Howay *New Hazard* 11: Commences snow squalls. A gang of water. **1929–32** in *AS* (Dec. 1934) 288: That dog has a gang of luck. **1942** in *Jour. Gen. Psych.* LXVI (1945) 132: A gang of fun. **1948** Manone & Vandervoort *Trumpet* 17: We spent a gang of time "front o' town." **1953** W. Fisher *Waiters* 261: A whole gang of flowers. **1967** in Rowan & MacDonald *Friendship* 26: A whole gang of pressure was brought to bear on me. **1977** Dunne *Confessions* 278: Is that not a gang of giggles? **1988** *Morning Ed.* (Nat. Pub. Radio) (Mar. 1): He earned a gang of Cub Scout badges. **1992** G. Wolff *Day at Beach* 10: I had sure done a gang of writing.

2. *Army.* a military unit; outfit.

1917 in *Sat. Eve. Post* (Jan. 5, 1918) 9: We got this first-division gang beat a mile. **1921** Dos Passos *Three Soldiers* 47: "Oh, it's one o' my gang," came the Sergeant's voice. **1926** *Sat. Eve. Post* (Mar. 6) 154: You're from I Company, aren't you?...Where are the rest of your gang? **1929** L. Thomas *Woodfill* 34 [ref. to 1899]: My gang had the village of Carigara, right on the coast.

3. a group of one's friends.

[**1841** Strong *Diary* I 170: My delightful gang of college classmates.] **1893** W.K. Post *Harvard* 2: Several of Holworthy's "gang"...dropped into the room on their way back to Jarvis Field. **1933–34** Lorimer & Lorimer *Stag Line* 5: "Shut up, gang," Alix said, with a worried look. **1945** in *OEDS*: I thought...we'd go over and meet the gang. **1984** C. Francis *Who's Sorry?* 15: I'm not unpatriotic, but let's face it, gang! My apologies, Mr. Key, but it's a bad song.

¶ In phrase:

¶ **gang of** *Black E.* excellent.

1933 *Fortune* (Aug.) 47: Yeah,...he plays a gang o' horn.

gang *v.* **1.** to attack or kill with or as part of a gang; gang up on.

1922–24 McIntyre *White Light* 22: "Ganging the cop" is a lost art. **1927** in Hammett *Knockover* 308: Vance ganged him in Larrouy's. **1928** in Partridge *Dict. Und.* 278: A traitor had been ganged, that was all.

2. GANGBANG, *v.*, 1.

1933 N. West *Miss Lonelyhearts* 82: The guys on the block got sore and took her into the lots one night. About eight of them. They ganged her proper. **1940** O'Hara *Pal Joey* 186: Like the time we ganged that poor unfortunate mouse. **1967** *N.Y. Times Mag.* (Oct. 29) 27: Then they gang her, 14, 15 of them. **1972 in Partridge *DSUE* (ed. 8) 445: We'll...gang her. **1974** C.W. Smith *Country Music* 287: Let's gang her!

gangbang *n.* **1.** an occasion on which a number of people copulate successively with one person; (*also*) gang-rape; (*also*) a sexual orgy.

1945 in Valant *Aircraft Nose Art* 206: Gang Bang. **1950** (cited in *W10*). **1953** in *OEDS*: "Wonder gear," it developed, is an attractive girl, in Navy lingo, and "gang-bang" is a juicy party involving wine, women and song. **1954** Ellison *Owen Harding* 173 [ref. to 1940's]: Gang Bang, boys—We'll have a smashing Gang Bang. **1956** Fleming *Diamonds* 52: The mob...left the girls alone but had themselves a gangbang with Tiffany. **1957** in J. Blake *Joint* 167: I'm sharing a cell now with a young cat sentenced to the chair for gang-bang. **1958** Motley *Epitaph* 179: And no gang-bang babe for the kid! **1958** Frede *Entry E* 97: SIGN HERE FOR GANGBANG WITH DIANA-SUE. **1959** Farris *Harrison High* 116: He's a juvenile delinquent. I met him on a gang bang. **1961** J. Baldwin *Another*

Country 12: It was to remember the juke box, the teasing, the dancing, the hard-on, the gang fights and gang bangs. **1962** Quirk *Red Ribbons* 156 [ref. to 1940's]: There were four young men and four roundheels from town...."I'm jaded. Let's have a gang bang." **1968** Yglesias *Orderly Life* 40: I did not go for gang bangs. **1972** *N.Y. Times* (Jan. 9) 13: Rossini's "The Thieving Magpie" as background for a gangbang would seem to have very little esthetic value for the victim of such a gathering. **1978** S. King *Stand* 76: He had treated the girl like an old whore on the morning after the frathouse gangbang.

2. *Narc.* an occasion in which a number of individuals use illicit psychotropic drugs at the same time.

1953 W. Brown *Monkey on My Back* 31: A couple of the older boys...wanted to try "a bang." Dave had to give them joints....five or six of the boys...would slip into the woods for a "gang bang" in the afternoons.

3. a confused or chaotic situation, state of affairs, operation, etc.; CLUSTERFUCK.

1964 Howe *Valley of Fire* 74 [ref. to Korean War]: Man, if I ever get out of this gangbang I'll go over the hill before they'd get me a second time. **1978** *New West* (Jan. 1, 1979) 37: See the country as the westerner sees it, urban sprawl mounting urban sprawl, a vast geographical gang-bang of incestuous blight, incestuous problems, incestuous ideas. **1989** Leib *Fire Dream* 18 [ref. to Vietnam War]: Let's get this gang bang on the road.

4. a gang fight; free-for-all; (*Mil. Av.*) a strafing attack, usu. on a target of opportunity, by several military aircraft.

1966–67 Harvey *Air War* 175: There are also times when it is better to skirt a place and leave it for a "gang bang" (a wild pounce by a bunch of free-firing, free-dropping Skyhawks). **1969** Briley *Traitors* 30: But the immediate danger was from another gang bang. **1971** Dahlskog *Dict.* 26: *Gang bang*....A gang or group fight; a rumble. **1978–89** in Jankowski *Islands in Street* 150: I got into a gangbang about two weeks ago.

gangbang *adj.* Esp. *Journ.* involving several persons who must be dealt with in a usu. peremptory manner by a single beleaguered individual.—used prenominally. *Joc.*

1982 Savitch *Anchorwoman* 81: Trying to work my way through a packed room to get to the speaker, a technique known in Houston as the gang-bang interview. **1986** Univ. Tenn. instructor, age *ca*30: Well, it's gangbang conferences week.

gangbang *v.* **1.** to copulate [with] in a GANGBANG.

1949 Monteleone *Crim. Slang* 94: Gang banging....When teen-age girls are forced by teen-age males to have sexual relations. **1961** Reuss *Field Collection* 266: Gang bang all night long./Who we gonna gang bang/When Sportsie's dead and gone? **1964** Faust *Steagle* 59: She's the biggest piece of ass in school. She gang-bangs too. **1966** Elli *Riot* 234: They're not gonna want their ol' ladies gang-banged. **1966** Bullins *Goin' a Buffalo* 208: Remember that time you, me and the guys gangbanged that Pachuco broad? **1970** E. Knight *Black Voices* 107: They would...gang fight, gang-bang the girls, swipe hot cars, and sometimes rob and assault. **1972** Meade & Rutledge *Belle* 114: Nubile young girls...don't care what's good for them...gangbanging a fraternity. **1974** E. Thompson *Tattoo* 246: Think she gangbangs or takes them all three at once? **1982** *Atlantic* (July) 68: Offstage, Cassandra was being gang-banged by the palace guard. **1991** B.E. Ellis *Amer. Psycho* 240: He used to let frat guys...gang bang him at parties.

2. to engage in a gang fight or belong to a violent street gang. Hence **gangbanger** a member of a violent street gang.

1968 in *Trans-Action* VI (Feb. 1969) 27: Quit gang-bangin (fighting, especially as a group). **1969** Whittemore *Cop!* II 178: Drugs aren't involved, not too much among the gang-bangers....because...a drug addict...has no more time for gang activities. **1970** *Newsweek* (May 11) 36: Three years ago, Jose (Cha Cha) Jimenez was just another "gangbanger" prowling Chicago's Puerto Rican barrio—a street-wise kid shooting dope, dodging cops and busting heads any time a white "greaser" gang ventured onto his turf. **1971** *Newsweek* (Mar. 8) 24: I told them I was a little old to be gang-bangin'. **1983** Goldman & Fuller *Charlie Co.* 33: War ain't no big deal....Be like gang-bangin' on the block. **1987** *Newsweek* (Mar. 23) 62: Gang-banging—in Chicago, the term meant gang war, not gang rape....Its solitude made it easy prey to gang-bangers. **1988** *48 Hours* (CBS-TV): If I say, "Well, I don't gang-bang no more," it's like say I'm a punk. **1988** M. Schiffer *Colors* (film): We got over 50,000 gangbangers out there. **1992** *L.A. Times* (Apr. 26) 8: Most unemployed young men would rather work at decent jobs than gangbang or sell drugs.

3. to victimize ruthlessly and repeatedly; to destroy.

1972 Pendleton *Vegas Vendetta* 106: If the movie industry think they're in trouble now, just wait until the mob starts gangbanging 'em. **1982** R. Bradbury, in *California* (July) 89: A phalanx of…gang-banging steam shovels may soon knock the place flat.

gangbanger *n.* see GANGBANG, *v.*, 2.

gangbuster *n. Journ.* a law-enforcement official or officer who is actively and successfully engaged in the breakup of criminal gangs.

1936 *Gangbusters* (CBS radio series) (Jan. 15) (title). **1940** in *AS* XVIII (May 1943) 150: The boys with leather boots who liked to act as a combination of Army, vigilantes, Ku Kluxers, gangsters, gangbusters and defenders of the pure Italian or German way of life. **1941** in *Ibid.*: The release of these gang-buster [motion] pictures…coincided with a trial in New York City which provided the national Republican press new material for publicizing Dewey. **1942** *ATS* 418: *Gang buster*, an officer engaged in breaking up organized crime. **1943** *AS* XVIII (Feb.) 62: *Trust-buster* and *gang-buster* are the pivotal examples of *-buster*, which might be defined as "one who seeks to destroy an organization regarded as undesirable." **1947** Mencken *Amer. Lang.* (Supp. II) 355: *Gang-buster* was launched in 1935 to describe Thomas E. Dewey. **1959** Zugsmith *Beat Generation* 134: "If your gangbusters knew you were here, they'd be all over us," Stan jeered. **1962** Fraley & Robsky *Last Untouchables* 77: We are getting quite a vaunted reputation as fearless gangbusters.

2. *Jazz.* an exciting or remarkable thing.

1946 Mezzrow & Wolfe *Really Blues* 106: A tricky homemade muffler that was a gangbuster.

¶ In phrases:

¶ **do** [or **go**] **gangbusters** *Entertainment Industry.* to be extremely successful.

1978 *N.Y. Times* (Dec. 24) II 11: If a title tests badly and still goes out and does gangbusters, "Well, it would have done even more if it had a better title." **1989** *World News Sunday* (ABC-TV) (Mar. 12): Business…was going gangbusters. **1990** *Early Prime* (CNN-TV) (July 6): I was 45…and I was going gangbusters. **1990** *Live! with Regis and Kathie Lee* (synd. TV series) (Dec. 20): They didn't expect the film to do gangbusters.

¶ **like gangbusters** [ref. to the explosive sound effects (machine guns, police sirens, etc.) at the beginning of each episode of *Gangbusters*, a radio series broadcast between 1936 and 1957] Esp. *Jazz.* aggressively, forcefully, energetically, or without hindrance; (*hence*) excitingly, vigorously, or well.—usu. *come on like gangbusters.*

1940 *Current History & Forum* (Nov. 7) 21: Prison Slang…*coming on like Gang Busters* means doing all right. **1942** Z.N. Hurston, in *Amer. Mercury* (July) 89: Man, I come on like the Gang Busters. **1944** Burley *Hndbk. Jive* 136: *Comes on like Gang Busters*—Doing something in a terrific way. **1946** Mezzrow & Wolfe *Really Blues* 53: We'd come on like gangbusters playing together. **1948** Manone & Vandervoort *Trumpet* 140: I blew back in town the day of my record date, ready to come on like gang busters. **1950** L. Brown *Iron City* 217: Spring really comes on like Gang Busters down here. **1952** Holmes *Boots Malone* (film): This kid rides like gangbusters. **1952** E. Brown *Trespass* 21: Basie was coming on like Gangbusters, with that K.C. stuff. **1952** Mandel *Angry Strangers* 119: I could set you up like gangbusters any time you're ready. **1958** Gilbert *Vice Trap* 101: Don't come on like gangbusters. **1976–77** Kernochan *Dry Hustle* 140: God damn it! I gotta pee like gangbusters. **1983** *Agronsky & Co.* (radio news show) (Mar. 6): I wish with all my heart that things were going like gangbusters.…I'm not at all sure that things are going to continue in gangbuster fashion.

gangbusters *adj.* rousing.—used predicatively.

1984 *World News Tonight* (ABC-TV) (June 18): In purely political terms, said one Presidential advisor, it was gangbusters. **1985** Boyne & Thompson *Wild Blue* 609: But when you add a plate of salami, cheese, and paté, it's gangbusters.

gange *n.* [abbr. of *ganja*] marijuana.

1971 *Inter. Jour. of Add.* VI 357: *Gange.* Marijuana (from the cannabis preparation "ganja" in India). **1975** Hardy & Cull *Drug Lang.* 64: *Gange.* Marijuana. **1988** Univ. Tenn. student theme: In a family inclined to smoking pot, the youth would "get some ganj" and "fire up a big, sappy one." **1988** *N.Y. Times* (June 4) 36: Grass…gange… smoke…[mean] marijuana.

gang-fuck *n.* GANGBANG, *n.*—usu. considered vulgar. Also **gang-screw.**

1941 G. Legman, in G.V. Henry *Sex Vars.* II 1166: *Gang-fuck.* An instance of pedication or irrumation of a single boy or homosexual by two or more men consecutively, and with or without his consent. Also used as a verb, and in both senses heterosexually. **1946–51** Motley *We Fished* 350: The fellows had the girl back behind a stairway. She was willing. It was another gang-screw. *a*1968 in Haines & Taggart *Ft. Lauderdale* 60: Gang fucks. **1972** D. Jenkins *Semi-Tough* 58: Less fun than being next-to-last on a high school gang-fuck.

gang-fuck *v.* GANGBANG, *v.*, 1.—usu. considered vulgar.

1916 Cary *Venery* I 103: *Gang Fucked*—Said of a woman who, willingly or unwillingly, submits to the embraces of the individuals in a crowd of men in succession. **1938** "Justinian" *Amer. Sexualis* 24: A *gang* of boys or young men escorts a girl or young woman to its rendezvous and proceeds to *gang-fuck* her. U.S. vulgarism, C. 20. **1940** *Tale of a Twist* 77: I guess I've been gang-fucked a few times. **1959** W. Burroughs *Naked Lunch* 125: I been gang fucked. **1975** C.W. Smith *Country Music* 84: They'd just as soon gang-fuck you as look at you! **1984** Ehrhart *Marking Time* 66: What kind of person could gang-fuck some poor starving refugee in the middle of a war?

gangplank fever *n. Mil.* fear of going overseas, esp. as exhibited at the time of embarkation. Also **gangplankitis.**

1945 in *AS* (Oct. 1946) 238: *Gangplank fever.* Psychosis, fear of going overseas. **1956** Boatner *Military Customs* 118: *Gangplank fever.* Psychotic tendencies developed by reluctant warriors about the time they are scheduled to ship overseas. **1958** Craven & Cate *AAF in WWII* VII 446 [ref. to 1944]: The approach of overseas movement usually…[brought on] the appearance of an ailment that came to be known as "gangplankitis." Its symptoms ran the gamut from nervous tremors to AWOL and desertion.…But "gangplankitis" normally presented no grave problems. *a*1992 Ambrose *Band of Bros.* 39 [ref. to WWII]: Winters remembered only one case of Gangplank Fever. A medical officer was "just smart enough to know what it takes to be assigned to sick call and miss the voyage."

gang roll *n. Prost.* GANGBANG, *n.*, 1.

1965 Longstreet *Sportin' House* 253 [ref. to 1890's]: Alice…was making trouble in a gang roll in her room with some of the army officers.

gang-screw see GANG-FUCK.

gang-shag *n.* GANGBANG, *n.*, 1. Also **gang-shack.**

1927 Thrasher *Gang* 237: The gang shag includes boys from sixteen to twenty-two years of age. It is a party carried on with one woman by from fifteen to thirty boys from one gang or club. A mattress in the alley usually suffices for this purpose. This number of boys have relations with the woman in the course of a few hours. **1929–30** Farrell *Young Lonigan* 69: Iris…took all kinds of guys up to her house…and let them all have a gang-shag. **1956** I. Shulman *Good Deeds* 101: We're a little too old for a gang shack. And we don't hate her. **1959** Cochrell *Barren Beaches* 151: "Hey, chumps," someone yelled on the balcony, "Gang shag." **1960** Roeburt *Mobster* 118: Get some clothes on your dancer, or there'll be a gang shag any minute. **1963** T.I. Rubin *Sweet Daddy* 9: A gang shack yet—musta been twenty of us—a real gang bang. **1966** C. Ross *N.Y.* 97: Dope,…gang shags, and marijuana parties.

gang-shag *v.* GANGBANG, *v.*, 1.

1929–33 Farrell *Manhood of Lonigan* 195: Ever since the time we gang-shagged that little bitch Iris. **1938** "Justinian" *Amer. Sexualis* 24: *Gang-Shag.* v. See *Gang-fuck.* **1963** Coon *Short End* 63: Boy, if I had me a broad on contract, I sure as hell wouldn't be sitting here while Dawg Company is gang-shagging her.

gang-splash *n.* Esp. *Homosex.* GANGBANG, *n.*, 1.

ca*1966 S. Baker *Austr. Lang.* (ed. 2) 213: *Gang splash*, a heterosexual orgy. **1966 Herbert *Fortune & Men's Eyes* 23: Well don't wait until they give you a gang splash in the storeroom. *a*1972 B. Rodgers *Queens' Vernacular* 92: *Gang-splash*…mass rape. Usually used of prison assaults.…homosexual orgy.

gangster *n.* **1.** *Naval Av.* an enemy aircraft in flight; BANDIT.

1942 S. Johnston *Queen of Flat-tops* 158: He was calling his own carrier from the air to report "a gangster." A few seconds later we heard his voice again identifying the plane as a Kawanishi. *Ibid.* 170: Gangster near the fleet.…It's a Kawanishi snooper.

2. *Black E.* marijuana; a marijuana cigarette.

1960 C.L. Cooper *Scene* 262: Just go on and smoke that gangster and be real cool. Drink that juice and smoke that gangster and keep them needles outta your arm. *Ibid.* 308: *Gangster:* marijuana. **1961** C.L. Cooper *Weed* 12: Gangster (because everybody used to think gangsters smoked it, and found out they didn't, all of them), Weed, Reefer—all the same thing. **1966** "Petronius" *N.Y. Unexp.* 224: Gangster cigarettes…just sniff around, easy to locate. **1967** Rosevear *Pot* 158: *Gangster:* Marihuana. **1970** A. Young *Snakes* 35: We can score for some gangster. **1989** R. Miller *Profane Men* 62: "Some good gangster." He takes a big hit.

gantline *n. Naut.* a gaunt or thin person.
   1901 King *Dog Watches* 127: The mate, a long, wiry gantline, came along just then. **1904** *Independent* (June 23) 1432: At the further end of the bar stood a long, lanky gantline.

gants *n.pl.* [short for *gantlets*, var. *gauntlets*] gloves.
   1835 *Knickerbocker* (Dec.) 562: I…drew my silk *gants* hastily over my hands.

G.A.P. *n.* (see quots.).
   1965 *Life* (Feb. 12) 71: The G.A.P.—the Great American Public—has been given the [wrong] impression. **1981–89** R. Atkinson *Long Gray Line* 411: Many men resented the attention lavished on the women by the media and the GAP, the Great American Public.

gap *n.* **1.** a look.
   1908 T.A. Dorgan, in Zwilling *TAD Lexicon* 38: Take a gap at the stems. **1914** Jackson & Hellyer *Vocab.* 37: *Gap,* noun. General currency. (syn. with **GANDER**, *n.*) Used also as a verb.
   2. the mouth.
   1915 T.A. Dorgan, in *N.Y. Eve. Jour.* (Aug. 2) 10: I won't open my gap. I tell you. **1915** *DN* IV 244: Shut your gap. **1934** Weseen *Dict. Slang* 338. **1958** Swarthout *They Came to Cordura* 139: "Shut yer gap," Chawk advised. **1965–70** in *DARE*.

gap *v.* [prob. dial. pron. of *gape*] to stare; (*hence*) *Und.* to watch.
   1914 (quot. at GAP, *n.*, 1). **1919** Darling *Jargon Book* 14: *Gap*—To look. **1932** in *AS* (Feb. 1934) 26: *Gap.* To witness a crime without taking part in it. **1945** in Galewitz *Great Comics* 125: Well, wot're you yaps gappin' at? **1942–49** Goldin et al. *DAUL* 77: While you're clipping…the joint, I'll gap and stall…any beef.

gape *n.* ¶ In phrase: **give the gapes** to amaze.
   1840 *Spirit of Times* (Nov. 21) 446: But what gave me the gapes was the scenes.

gaper *n. Gamb.* a small mirror or reflecting surface used in a card game by a dishonest dealer.
   1931 in D.W. Maurer *Lang. Und.* 82: Why couldn't he win? He had…a gaper. **1942–49** Goldin et al. *DAUL* 77: *Gaper.* A tiny reflector in the palm of the hand or on a ring, used in card cheating. **1987** T. Clark *Dict. Gamb.* 91: *Gaper.…*a small mirror, often disguised as a coin, cigarette lighter, or some such object, used by a dishonest dealer for seeing the undersides, or faces, of cards as they are dealt.

gaposis *n.* (see 1954–60 quot.); (*hence*) a problem that involves gaps or poor spacing; (see also 1987 Semler quot.). *Joc.*
   1942 *Yank* (July 22) 24: They have dishpan hands, tattletale gray,…and gaposis. **1944** H. Brown *Walk in the Sun* 127: I'm anti-social.…I got gap-osis. **1954–60** *DAS: Gaposis…*a mythical disease, the symptom of which is a customary gap in one's clothing, as between buttons or when one's shirt and trousers or blouse and skirt do not properly meet. *A synthetic commercialism.* **1965–70** in *DARE.* **1970** *Harper's* (Mar.) 84: As sizable and unjustifiable salary gaposis develops between that privileged group and the people who are doing the real work. **1987** N.Y.C. editor, age *ca*50: The typesetter says everything looks OK; they're just having a few minor problems of gaposis in spacing. **1987** Semler et al. *Lang. Nuc. War* 110: *Gaposis* describes the American public's historical sensitivity to claims of U.S. nuclear inferiority…a missile gap, a bomber gap, an ABM gap, and a window of vulnerability.

gapper *n.* **1.** *Und.* a foolish bystander; onlooker; (*hence*) a blockhead.
   1919 *Lit. Digest* (May 17) 50: Every goof you meet is…looking for a job for some poor gapper who is just back from Europe. **1932** in *AS* (Feb. 1934) 26: *Gapper.* One who gaps (q.v.). *Gapper's bit.* A small sum given to one who sees the commission of a crime but takes no part in it. **1942–49** Goldin et al. *DAUL* 77: *Gapper…*One who gaps, especially a bystander who might hinder the execution of a crime.…A kibitzer in a card game; an onlooker.
   2. GAPER, *n.*
   1931–34 in Clemmer *Pris. Commun.* 332: *Gapper,* n. A piece of mirror used as a periscope to watch the guard, used by inmates…when…handling…contraband. **1944** *Pap. Mich. Acad.* XXX 598: *Gapper,* a mirror. **1962** Regan & Finston *Toughest Prison* 800: *Gapper*—A mirror.
   3. a view of the fully exposed vulva.
   1973 *Oui* (June) 13: Here is the *little woman* sitting on a bed throwing a full head-on gapper at me.

4. *Baseball.* a ball hit safely between infielders.
   1980 Lorenz *Guys Like Us* 20: He'd dived into second, stretching a gapper.
   5. the mouth.
   1981 Graziano & Corsel *Somebody Down Here* 96: When she opens her gapper you could see Brooklyn.

gar *n.* [prob. as in 1983 quot.] a black person.—used derisively.
   1962 in *Harper's Mag.* (Feb. 1964) 44: One of the first things the white soldier learns is the "gar glance"—a quick over the shoulder to see if any Negroes are listening. **1970** Landy *Underground Dict.* 86: *Gar.…Negro.* **1975** *Nat. Lampoon* (Sept.) 51: Ever been laid by a gar before? **1983** W. Walker *Dime to Dance* 120: "Gar" was short for "nee-gar."

garage doors *n.pl. Mil. Av.* dive brakes.
   1954 *N.Y. Times Mag.* (Mar. 7) 20. **1955** *AS* XXX 117: *Garage doors,* n. Dive brakes. **1956** Heflin *USAF Dict.* 228: *Garage doors.* Dive brakes. *Slang.*

garb or **garby** *n.* [var. GOB, *n.*] a sailor.
   1917 Depew *Gunner Depew* 15 [ref. to *ca*1910]: Every garby (sailor) who came along would give me or the bucket a kick. *Ibid.* 17: A Limey garb told me it was the same way with them.

garbage *n.* **1.** *Av.* (see 1969 quot.).
   1961 R.L. Scott *Boring Holes* 4: I was already reaching forward with my throttle hand to retract the "garbage." **1967** H.M. Mason *New Tigers* 222: *Garbage:* Extended devices that result in increased, unwanted drag, such as gear, flaps, and speed brakes. **1969** *Current Slang* I & II 37: *Garbage, n.* Hardware on an aircraft which can be retracted, usually including flaps, landing gear, and speed brakes.
   2. *Sports.* weakly made shots, hits, points, etc.
   1978 Alibrandi *Killshot* 150: Barry almost threw his arm into the seats trying to dig out Kritzer's garbage. **1979** Frommer *Sports Lingo* 50: *Garbage Shooter.* A player who specializes in taking and making easy shots close to the basket. **1980** Wielgus & Wolff *Basketball* 44: *Garbage* (n) A loose ball or rebound that results in a lay-up or short jumper. **1980** Pearl *Pop. Slang* 57: *Garbage n.…*(Basketball) an easily scored basket.
   3. /ˈgɑrˈbɑʒ/ garbage; (*specif.*) nonsense. *Joc.*
   1973 *Oui* (Oct.) 46: Do not drop thee gar*bazh* in the *street.* **1981** *Hill St. Blues* (NBC-TV): I thought if I could tell you the details of the case, you'd see what gar*bage* it really is. **1987** Univ. Tenn. student: It's such gar-*bage.*

garbage *adj.* **1.** *Sports.* (of a point or hit) weakly or narrowly made.
   1977 Dowd *Slap Shot* (film): It was a garbage goal. It was a garbage win. **1978** in Lyle & Golenbock *Bronx Zoo* 105: I gave up five straight bloops, chops, and garbage hits. **1984** *N.Y. Post* (Aug. 11) 42: Robertson rebounded a Ewing miss for a garbage bucket. **1986** *NDAS:* She uses a lot of tricky garbage shots to win games and sets.
   2. worthless; inconsequential; pointless.
   1980 W. Sherman *Times Square* 93: He didn't want any "garbage arrests" or phony fanfare. **1986** Coonts *Intruder* 24: Why in hell [do] we keep getting men killed and planes chewed up over garbage targets? **1986** *NDAS:* I call it a garbage movie. *a*1988 D. Smith *Firefighters* 55: Four months out of the fire academy, I had had a lot of garbage runs, you know, smoke scares and pots of food.

garbage can *n.* **1.** a filthy or disgusting person.
   1927 *DN* V 447: *Garbage can, n.…*An old prostitute. **1935** Odets *Till the Day I Die* 141: There's my boy friend, dead tired on the bed, fresh from the jug, and this garbage can won't let him rest. **1961** Parkhurst *Undertow* 153: Girls I took before to flophouses knew the places better than me, they even knew what room to ask for. Garbage cans, that's what they were.
   2. *Army.* a heavy artillery shell in flight.
   1931 Adamic *Laughing* 175 [ref. to 1918]: At night we sat in the trenches and listened to the terrific roar and swish of large projectiles, the so-called "garbage cans," both American and German, sailing over our heads.

garbageman *n. Esp. Ice Hockey.* a player who commonly scores easily made goals.
   1976 *Webster's Sports Dict.* 180.

garbage-mouth *n.* a foulmouthed person; (*occ.*) the mouth of such a person.
   1970 A. Lewis *Carnival* 27: Last year he blew up at a carny they call "Garbage Mouth" because of his foul language. **1971** *Nat. Lampoon*

(Jan.) 27: Be a garbage mouth! **1971** Wells & Dance *Night People* 107: Say, where's Garbage Mouth? **1974** Kurtzman *Bobby* 40: You look here Doyle, you shut your garbage mouth! **1977** Sayles *Union Dues* 89: Bunch of sorry-lookin', garbage-mouth coal miners and he missed them. **1987** Zeybel *Gunship* 138: I was a garbage mouth from way back.

garbage queen *n. Army.* a woman assigned to a trash or KP detail. Now *hist.*

1985 Westin *Love & Glory* 263 [ref. to WWII]: I thought I'd see what I was missing with you lowly garbage queens.

garbonzo *n. & adj.* [prob. sugg. by GONZO] an idiot; BOZO; (hence, as adj.) crazy.

1982 *Fury of Firestorm* (Jan. 1983) 7: What a first class garbonzo! **1989** Sorkin *Few Good Men* 49: What the hell kinda garbanzo nonsense is this?

garbonzas *n.pl.* a woman's breasts. Cf. GAZONGAS.

1982 in "J.B. Briggs" *Drive-In* 10: Herschell Gordon Lewis…put nek-kid garbonzas on the drive-in screen for the first time in 1959. **1983** in "J.B. Briggs" *Drive-In* 142: Bootsie is not just another humongous set of garbonzas. **1987** *Nat. Lampoon* (June) 44: Virginia…puts these little whirlybirds on her garbonzas and starts making a hurricane. **1992** *N.Y. Times Bk. Review* (Dec. 13) 29: More synonyms for breasts—hoot-ers…garbonzas [etc.]—than even this reviewer has heard.

garden *n. Baseball.* the outfield.— constr. with *the.*

1869 (cited in Nichols, *Baseball Term.*). **1908** *Atlantic* (Aug.) 225: The ball will come down in B.…an unguarded region of the "front yard"…or…some defenseless section of "left garden." **1911** in *DA*: Bodie, Brinker, Chovinard and Johnston…are conceded a chance to land in the outer garden. **1926** *AS* I (Apr.) 369. **1967** G. Green *To Brooklyn* 5: He was…patroling the outer garden for the Brooklyn Dodgers.

gardener *n. Baseball.* an outfielder.

1908 *Atlantic* (Aug.) 225: When the ball soars across the blue, and the "gardener" turns his back on it,…Micky relights his pipe.

gargle *n.* liquor; a drink. *Joc.*

[***1871** in E. Lear *Complete Nonsense* 300: There was an old man of the Dargle/Who purchased six barrels of Gargle.] ***ca1889** in Barrère & Leland *Dict. Slang* I 397: Her taste for high-priced gargles could in no way be restrained. ***1889** in *F & H* III 119: We're just going to have a gargle—will you join us? **1902** Cullen *More Tales* 96: He eyed me pretty closely as he shook the gargle together. **1968** W.C. Anderson *Gooney Bird* 115: Let's go have a very large gargle while I tell you my troubles. **1969** H.A. Smith *Buskin'* 6: Glasses filled? Hit the gargle a little more heartily.

gargle *v.* to take a drink; guzzle. *Joc.*

*1889 in *F & H* III 119: We gargled. ***1891** in *F & H*: It's my birthday; let's gargle. **1918** Grider *War Birds* 120: They…were agreeable to gar-gling a little champagne. **1919** *Vanity Fair* (Mar.) 26: These here suds, Gretchen, are, honest to Gawd, the lowest imitation of beer I ever gar-gled. **1929** *Our Army* (Nov.) 15: Brave soldiers gargle bootleg gin. **1936** R. Chandler, in Ruhm *Detective* 144: We'll go to my place and gargle.

garlic *n. Army.* a Spaniard.—used contemptuously.

1898 *Harper's Mag.* (Nov.): "Now we can hold San Juan Hill against them garlics—hey, son!" yelled a happy cavalryman to a doughboy.

garlic-eater *n.* a southern European, (now esp.) an Italian.—used contemptuously.

1865 in R. Mitchell *Civil War Soldiers* 203: [The French are] frog-eat-ers…garlic-eaters. **1942** Sanders & Blackwell "Forces" 160: *Garlic-Eater*…An Italian. **1947** Goodrich & Hackett *Wonderful Life* (film): He's frittered his life away playing nursemaid to a lot of garlic-eaters. **1980** S. Fuller *Big Red* 154 [ref. to WWII]: I'm going to kill every garlic eater I see.

garlic-eating *adj.* Spanish or Portuguese.—used contemptu-ously.

1833 Ames *Yarns* 297: If we are such d—d fools as to let that garlic-eat-ing scarecrow make a prize of us without firing a gun, we shall be sent to the mines for life. **1855** Wise *Tales for Marines* 37: Ye dam kiar Port-ingee garlic eatin' swab, take that! **1908** Paine *Stroke Oar* 98: The gar-lic-eatin' low-browed Pedro Cabañas is deceased for the prisint, anyhow.

garlic-snapper *n.* an Italian. Hence **garlic-snapping,** *adj.*—used derisively.

1942 Sanders & Blackwell "Forces" 160: *Garlic-Snapper.* An Italian.

1963 J. Ross *Dead Are Mine* 5 [ref. to 1944]: That, my garlic-snapping pisan, is none of your business. *Ibid.* 167: Hello, garlic snapper.

garret *n.* the head; mind.

*1788 Grose *Vulgar Tongue* (ed. 2): *Garret,* or *Upper Story.* The head. His garret, or upper story, is empty, or unfurnished; i.e., he has no brains, he is a fool. **1843** "J. Slick" *High Life in N.Y.* 28: A little soft in the garret. **1859** Matsell *Vocab.* 36: *Garret.* The head. **1903** Hobart *Out for the Coin* 79: Isn't it wonderful how he can make people believe that there isn't any furniture broken in his garret? **1904** in "O. Henry" *Works* 1210: Tolstoi?—his garret is full of rats.

garritrooper *n.* [*garri*son + para*trooper*; coined by Bill Mauld-in, Army cartoonist] *Army.* a rear-echelon soldier.—used derisively.

1944 in Mauldin *Up Front* 139: We calls 'em garritroopers. They're too far forward to wear ties an' too far back to git shot. **1946** *AS* XXI 242: *Garritrooper*…while received with amusement, never passed into everyday speech. **1991** Reinberg *In the Field* 91 [ref. to Vietnam War]: *Garitrooper* [sic]…slang for service personnel in the rear who acted as if they were involved in heavy action.

gas *n.* **1.a.** empty, esp. boastful, nonsensical, or flattering talk; conceit; HOT AIR.

1793 in *DAE*: The immense amount raised by political gas could not bring down with it the supporting balloons. ***1821** *Real Life in London* I 107: A learned little Devil, inflated with gas, has suggested a plan for…a Medical-Assurance office. **ca1846** in *DAE*: The boys said that was all gas, to scare them off. **1848** *Ladies' Repository* VIII (Oct.) 315: *Gas,* Bragging talk, boasting. **1848** Baker *Glance at N.Y.* 18: Oh, gas! **1856** Ferguson *Amer. by River & Rail* 319: "Dat's all gas, Massa," was Sam's cool reply,—"gas" in Yankee, being equivalent to our "moon-shine." **1865** Edmondston *Jour.* 699: This we thought was gas. **1872** Brace *Dangerous Classes* 80: One pungent criticism we remember…in the words "*Gas! gas!*" whispered with infinite contempt. **ca1880** Bellard *Gone for a Soldier* 21: Being pretty well supplied with gass he had wormed himself into the friendship of a lawyer. **1881** Small *Farming* 44: Have I been wasting all this gas over a deaf galloot? ***1889** in *F & H* III 122: It went on to state that the petitioner's talk about a divorce was all gas. ***a1890–93** *Ibid.*: *To turn on the gas*…To begin bounc-ing.…*To turn off the gas*…To…cease, or cause to cease, from bouncing, vapouring. **1930** Irwin *Tramp & Und. Sl.: Gas*…Talk; idle chatter. **1958** Talsman *Gaudy Image* 35: You're talkin' gas. **1974** Strasburger *Rounding Third* 6: Murph and Carol and I passed gas for a few minutes or so. **1978** Truscott *Dress Gray* 440: You're too…smart to try and pass that gas. **1980** S. Fuller *Big Red* 75: Don't cloud the air with that intel-lectual gas.

b. verbal abuse; taunting; ridicule.—constr. with *give* or *take.*

*1860 Hotten *Slang Dict.* (ed. 2): "To give a person *gas*" is to scold him or give him a good beating. Synonymous with "to give him Jessie." **1959** Searls *Big X* 143: The White House is on the phone and Con-gress goes into special session and the aircraft company declares bank-ruptcy, and everybody's taking gas when the president calls in the little engineer. **1962** in *AS* (Oct. 1963) 169: To be called to the Dean's office:…*take gas.* **1968** Baker et al. *CUSS* 125: *Give Gas.* Tease or annoy someone. **1969** *Current Slang* I & II 88: *Take gas,* v. To take abuse. Col-lege males. New York. **1970–71** G.V. Higgins *Coyle* 71: I'm giving him a little gas, you know, one thing and another. **1971** Sorrentino *Up from Never* 17: My…teacher…[was] Mr. Goldfart (that name took a lot of gas outside of his ear-reach). **1981** G. Wolf *Roger Rabbit* 180: I try and save this dopey rabbit some grief, and I take gas for it. OK.

2. *Irish-Amer.* fun.

*1914 J. Joyce *Dubliners* 24: He had brought it to have some gas with the birds. **1961** A.J. Roth *Shame* 49 [ref. to ca1938]: Watch the gas. *Ibid.* 51: Man, that was gas all right.

3.a. energy.—usu. in phr. **out of gas.**

1918 *Chi. Sun. Trib.* (Mar. 24) V (unp.): Maddigan…was runnin' her out o' gas tryin' to get her to pay some attention to him. **1926** Nason *Chevrons* 12 [ref. to 1918]: I'm glad we're gettin' there. I'm about outta gas. **1926** Norwood *Other Side of Circus* 106: He was pretty nearly out of gas when he got over here to my tent. **1928** McEvoy *Show Girl* 118: They're running my poor Jimmy out of gas. **1952** Holmes *Boots Malone* (film): Don't hustle this horse too fast. He's liable to run out of gas. **1957** H. Danforth & J. Horan *D.A.'s Man* 54: He's run out of gas, Dan. **1961** *Newsweek* (July 31) 13: Beef up the Civil Defense program. "We're really going to put some gas in this," the President said. **1965** Linakis *In Spring* 108: Listen, I'm slightly out of gas.…I'm fini. I've already had quite enough for one night. **1989** in *Cosmopolitan* (Jan.

1990) 130: You have to stay in the race and keep on running and running, knowing that one day you just might run out of gas.

b. *Specif.* stamina.

1991 D. Anderson *In Corner* 99: This kid's gas is bad. He's no six-round fighter.

4. (esp. among tramps) any dangerous substitute for grain alcohol; adulterated liquor or denatured alcohol; (in later use) homemade liquor; JUNGLE JUICE. Cf. GAS-HOUND, 3.

1927 *AS* (June) 389: Denatured alcohol, wood alcohol and canned heat are known as *gas*....One who drinks gas is a *gas-hound*,—a glorious product of prohibition. **1929** *AS* IV (June) 340: *Gas.* Wood alcohol; doped cider; ether, etc. **1930** Irwin *Tramp & Und. Sl.*: *Gas*...Impure liquor, such as doped cider or wine, "needle beer," "smoke" and the like. *a*1990 Poyer *Gulf* 50: I never refuse gas, but we don't want to drink up that kind of liquor.

5. Esp. *Jazz.* that which is exciting or delightful; thrill; good time.—usu. used with indef. article. Cf. (**2**), above, and GASSER.

*ca*1953 Hughes *Lodge* 94: First kicks on horse are...the biggest gas in life. **1957** H. Simmons *Corner Boy* 47: She's a gas, man, a natural petrol. **1957** J. Baldwin, in *OEDS*: Brand-new pianos certainly were a gas. **1958–59** Lipton *Barbarians* 316: Gas—Supreme, tops, the most. A gasser. **1959–60** R. Reisner *Jazz Titans* 156: His act was a gas. *1962, *1963, *1964, *1967, *1971 in *OEDS*. **1973** Jong *Flying* 27: Well, isn't that interesting?...Isn't that a gas? **1978** B. Johnson *What's Happenin'* 222: We gonna make the playoffs. Ain't that a gas? **1982** Rucker *57th Kafka* 42: Well, it's *all* right now, in fact it's a gas. **1985** *Miami Vice* (NBC-TV): I'm having a gas.

6. *Black E.* a hairstyle that has been gassed (s.v. GAS, *v.*, 3).

1972 Carr *Bad* 50: Stan was a real pretty boy with a bad gas, and all the chicks loved him. **1986** Clayton & Elliott *Jazz World* 47 [ref. to 1930's]: I...got in his chair to get a gas. Gas was another name that we called conk.

7. [sugg. by HEAT] *Baseball.* a fastball or fastballs.

1986 in P. Dickson *Baseball Dict.* 176: He just came in throwing gas.

¶ In phrases:

¶ **cook with gas** see s.v. COOK, *v.*

¶ **pass gas, 1.** [in joc. allusion to flatulence] *Med.* to administer anesthesia. Cf. GAS-PASSER. *Joc.*

1961 (quot. at GAS-PASSER, *n.*). **1964** "Doctor X" *Intern* 233: We had old Tightbelly passing gas for us...and something wasn't right with the anesthesia. **1980** E. Morgan *Surgeon* 58: "I am ready to pass gas any time you guys are ready to cut," said the anesthesiologist cheerfully. **1982** M. Elias & R. Eustis *Young Doctors* (film): Charles Lido—Chicago—anesthesiologist. I like to pass gas.

2. see (**1.a.**), above.

¶ **play to the gas** [alluding to the gaslights used for illumination in 19th-C. theaters] *Theat.* to perform for a nearly empty house.

1923 *N.Y. Times* (Sept. 9) VIII 2: *Playing to the Gas:* A miserably small audience, not sufficient to pay for the lighting. **1929** *Bookman* (Apr.) 150: "Playing to the gas" means giving a performance to an audience not worth lighting up for.

¶ **take gas, 1.** Orig. *Surfing.* to be thrown from a surfboard; (*hence*) to fail or do poorly at anything.

1963 *Time* (Aug. 9) 49: To "take gas" or "wipe out" is to lose a board in the curl of the wave and land in the foamy "soup." **1964** in *AS* XL (1965) 194: *To take gas*..."to do poorly on an examination." *1966 S.J. Baker *Austral. Lang.* (ed. 2) 254: *Take the gas*, (of a surfrider) to get caught in the curl of a wave. **1967** *Lit Dictionary* 39: *Take Gas*—A surfing expression meaning to lose control of one's surfboard; to wipe out; to fall. **1968** Kirk & Hanle *Surfer's Hndbk.* 148: *Taking gas:* losing control; going under; losing board; wiping out; being knocked off board. **1968–70** *Current Slang* III & IV 123: *Take gas, v.* To do badly on anything. To make a poor showing,...New Hampshire. **1979** G. Wolff *Duke of Deception* 238 [ref. to 1960]: Only a couple of friends *took gas*, were [expelled] from Princeton. **1981** in Safire *Good Word* 111: You wiped out. You took gas. **1990** *NBC News Sunrise* (NBC-TV) (Aug. 14): Either we work on the deficit or the dollar is going to take more gas. **1992** *CBS This Morning* (CBS-TV) (Sept. 1): Meanwhile the stock market's taken some gas, dropping 150 points.

2. to commit suicide by any means; die.

1975 Wambaugh *Choirboys* 53: If that whacko bitch wanted to take gas, fuck it, it ain't our fault....Who cares if *all* these rotten motherfuckers take gas...What the fuck's a life anyway, less it's yours?

3. see (**1.b.**), above.

¶ **take the gas pipe** [or (*obs.*) **route**] to kill oneself by asphyxiation; (*broadly*) to commit suicide. Cf. *take the pipe* s.v. PIPE.

1907 in H.C. Fisher *A. Mutt* 6: For 4 bits I'd take the gas route. I'm done. **1951** in W.S. Burroughs *Letters* 78: Yes, I remember...Bozo took the gas pipe. **1956** Hargrove *Girl He Left* 165: I haven't got the tiniest compulsion to save your life. You can save yourself time by taking the gas pipe. **1963** D. Tracy *Brass Ring* 276: Either that or take the gas pipe one of these days. **1977** L. Jordan *Hype* 53: If I don't get something soon, I'm going to take the gaspipe. **1980** Ciardi *Browser's Dict.* 147: *Take the gas pipe.* To commit suicide by inhaling...asphyxiating gas. **1983** State Univ. of N.Y. physics prof., age 36: I was afraid if I didn't pass her she'd take the gas pipe. **1987** W. Allen *Radio Days* (film): If you don't like it, take the gas-pipe!

gas *v.* **1.a.** to talk, esp. emptily or volubly; chat; gossip.

1852 in *AS* XLIII (1968) 96: I have been gassing with travellers generally. **1853** in *DAE*: We were going to gas a little upon our newspaper establishment. **1861** in C.W. Wills *Army Life* 46: We sit and lie in the tent and gas and joke. **1863** in Brobst *Civil War Letters* 16: There are lots of boys in it from Sheboygan that I know, and when I get tired of staying here, I go over there and gas awhile for pastime. **1883** Sweet & Knox *Mustang* 363: An old man who never dries up, but keeps on talking and gassing all day long. **1890** *Overland Mo.* (Feb.) 113: The usual crowd of loungers, card playing, smoking, and "gassing," as the gossip of the chiv's was locally termed. **1893** F.P. Dunne, in Schaaf *Dooley* 332: But whin th' 'ell am I doin' gassin' away about goats an' th' like iv that whin I beggan to tell you about th' fire. **1904** London *Faith* 122: I was gassin' with one of them. **1915** H.L. Wilson *Ruggles* 284: Everybody laughing and gassing back and forth. **1916** in E. Pound *Letters* 87: They all go on gassing about the "deathless voice." **1944** Kapelner *Lonely Boy Blues* 18: The guys in the barracks gas about their girls and I rave about you. **1957** Murtagh & Harris *First Stone* 34: Quit gassing and start working. **1958** Frankel *Band of Bros.* 6: I was gassin' with him back at the CP. **1962** T. Berger *Reinhart in Love* 150: I believe you could stand there and gas all day in this vein. **1965** Spillane *Killer Mine* 78: So he sits here and gases with me. **1968** J.P. Miller *Race for Home* 222: Been gassing with ole Anna, ain't ye? **1968** Young *Apollo* 147: Say, it's late....I really have to stop gassing.

b. to speak insincerely to; hoax; KID. Also intrans.

1847 in *DAE*: Found that Fairspeech only wanted to "gas" me, which he did pretty effectually. **1856** B. Hall *College Wds.* (ed. 2) 226: *Gas.* To impose upon another by a consequential address, or by detailing improbable stories or using "great swelling words"; to deceive; to cheat. **1872** in "M. Twain" *Life on Miss.* 292: I need you...want [weren't] gassing & all the boys knod it. **1874** Alger *Julius* 1: Goin' West? You're gassin'. **1888** in *DAE*: But in all the rest, he's gassin' you. **1917** Oemler *Slippy McGee* 22: When you gas like that I feel like bashing in your brain, if you've got any! **1959** W. Miller *Cool World* 82: Get on the subway and it take me to the ocean? Duke you gassin me? **1960** Barber *Minsky* 60: Don't gas me, kid. **1991** Coen & Coen *Barton Fink* (film): Don't gas me, Fink.

c. to taunt.

1986 Coonts *Intruder* 67: Cowboy's got it in for me because I gassed him in the locker room.

2. Orig. *Jazz.* **a.** to thrill or delight.

1941 *Pittsburgh Courier* (Nov. 15) 7: Dagwood was "gassed" to wash the slate clean this way. **1944** Burley *Hndbk. Jive* 149: *To gas*—To thrill, to overcome, to stir the emotions. **1946** Mezzrow & Wolfe *Really Blues* 165: His friendly relaxed voice...just gassed me. **1947** *Time* (Oct. 6): "To scarf" (to eat), "to fall out" (to sleep), "gassed" (tickled pink). **1948** Manone & Vandervoort *Trumpet* 198: The idea behind "The Gasser" was that this tune won't knock you out or send you. It'll gas you. **1953** Russ *Last Parallel* 90: It, along with "Now the Day is Over," used to gas me (man). *ca*1953 Hughes *Fantastic Lodge* 65: It would just gas me to make phone calls. **1954** L. Armstrong *Satchmo* 123: Just the same the game gassed me. **1955** *Science Digest* (Aug.) 33: They were gassed (favorably impressed). **1956** Holiday & Dufty *Lady Sings the Blues* 11: I remember Pops' recording of "West End Blues" and how it used to gas me. **1958** A. King *Mine Enemy* 121: This piece of news simply gassed me. **1961** Braly *Felony Tank* 171: This is going to gas Marion. **1967** Wolf *Love Generation* 196: I wasn't really that gassed by it in the first place.

b. to astound.

1959 F.L. Brown *Trumbull Pk.* 347: But the thing that gasses me was the slick way this cat came down with that "I'm your friend" crap. **1959–60** R. Reisner *Jazz Titans* 156: *Gas*...to overwhelm. *a*1973–87

F.M. Davis *Livin' the Blues* 85: When I brought in my final grades, including an A in chemistry, they were gassed.

3. *Black E.* to straighten (the hair) by the application of various preparations, esp. gasoline.

1965 Bonham *Durango St.* 38: All of them had the same orange-red hair. "Gassed" was the name for it. You straightened your kinky hair....The next time it started to curl, you soaked it in gasoline to straighten it. Now it was straight again, but it was also red. **1967** Baraka *Tales* 76: Shaking his long gassed hair. **1972–74** Hawes & Asher *Raise Up* 9: Get your hair gassed, brothers,...and play pretty for the white folks. **1986** Clayton & Elliott *Jazz World* 47: So this day I walked in to get gassed, and the barbershop was full of guys.

4. *Narc.* (see quot.).

1970 Horman & Fox *Drug Awareness* 466: *Gassing*—sniffing gasoline fumes.

gasbag *n.* **1.** an observation balloon; (*hence*) a dirigible.

*1852 in *OEDS*: Above us reeled the monster gas-bag like a monster peg-top. **1874** Rudge & Raven *I.O.G.B.* 18: Many...suggested that the transatlantic balloonatics be sent to...Africa in a gas-bag. *1917 in Lee *No Parachute* 73: This afternoon, while we were hanging round the squadron office on standby, we were given an interesting exhibition of gas-bag strafing. **1918** *Nat. Geographic* (Jan.) 83: Airships and balloons are known in the slang of the fighting front as "gas-bags." **1940** Hartney *Up & At 'Em* 261 [ref. to 1918]: We've got to land that gas bag this morning. **1943** Fetridge *Second Navy Reader* 203: Gas Bags on Patrol.

2. an empty or boastful talker.

1862 in J.M. Merrill *Battle Flags* 148: [He is a] gas bag. **1865** in J.W. Haley *Rebel Yell* 250: He was a cheap buffoon and a very prince of gas-bags. **1865** in Dooley *Confed. Soldier* 177: Concluding that this talker is a gasbag, I leave him and go elsewhere for information. **1873** in *DA*: Gas bags were never known to do more than make a noise. **1877** Bartlett *Amer.* (ed. 4) 783: *Gas-Bag.* A person who habitually parades and prates of his own importance on cognate topics. **1891** Maitland *Slang Dict.* 121: *Gas-Bag*, a man who boasts habitually of his own doings and importance. **1925** S. Lewis *Arrowsmith* 19: To work under that gasbag, with his fool pieces about boozers. **1931** Farrell *McGinty* 53: He even forgot that he had ever been called a fat gasbag. **1940** in E. Pound *Letters* 347: Socrates a distinguished gas-bag in comparison with Confucius. **1953** Rodgers & Hammerstein *Me & Juliet* 514: I'm talking to you, you big gas bag. **1977** Coover *Public Burning* 95: Those fatuous Dixie gasbags. **1979** in Raban *Old Glory* 127: Don't pay no attention to that old gasbag. **1988** *21 Jump St.* (Fox-TV): Can you believe this gasbag?

gas-bagger *n.* a balloonist.

1874 Rudge & Raven *I.O.G.B.* 6: Staner, an importunate gas-bagger.

gash[1] *n.* **1.** the mouth.

1852 H. Stowe *Uncle Tom's Cab.* ch. xxxviii: Shut your old black gash, and get along in with you. **1878** H. Stowe *Poganuc People* 122: Ef Zeph Higgins would jest shet up his gash in town-meetin'. **1899** Boyd *Shellback* 237: Shet your baboon's gash and get to loo'ard. **1904** *Life in Sing Sing* 248: *Gash.* The mouth. **1935** D.W. Maurer, in *AS* (Feb.) 16 [ref. to *ca*1910]: *Gash*...The mouth.

2.a. the vulva or vagina.—usu. considered vulgar.

[**ca*1730 Haddington *Sel. Poems* 34: Feel, Tommy, what a gash is there.] **ca*1866 *Romance of Lust* 15: The pinky gash, with its fleecy hair. **1888** *Stag Party* 24: And why that gash—the female bifurcation. **ca*1890–93 *F & H* III 122: *Gash*...the female *pudendum*. **1916** Cary *Venery* I 105: *Gash...*the vagina. **1927** [Fliesler] *Anecdota* 72: Here's where ah cuts de gash dat nevah heals. **1934** H. Miller *Tropic of Cancer* 225: There is concealed the ugly gash, the wound that never heals. **1962** T. Berger *Reinhart* 401: Her gash run crossways, like they say, and that's no lie. **1968** J.P. Miller *Race for Home* 283: He give 'er the word, she [a cow] 'ow that gash up at ye like a tin cup! **1969** in Girodias *New Olympia Reader* 626: That would mean that excitement would be given to the rim of the "gash," its lips, as it were, to the clitoris. **1971** Hilaire *Thanatos* 56: These goons...'ve needed slaughtering since they slid down the gash. **1987** *Penthouse Letters* (Oct.) 24: I licked her gash harder and deeper. **1992** Madonna *Sex* (unp.): Honey poured from my...gash.

b. a woman considered as an object of sexual gratification.—sometimes collect.—usu. considered vulgar.

1914 Jackson & Hellyer *Vocab.* 37: *Gash*, Noun. General currency. An invidious term for woman; synonymous with *flip*, which see. **1925** Dos Passos *Manhattan Transfer* 238: This guy who's a wellknown lawyer down town was out in the hall bawlin out his gash about something. **1926** Finerty *Criminalese* 24: *Gash*—Fast woman. **1936** Levin *Old*

Bunch 124: It certainly was a cinch to pick up the gash in the new Paige. **1939** *AS* (Oct.) 239: *Gash.* Prostitute. **1950** Bissell *Stretch on the River* 66: You got that St. Paul gash...on your mind. **1951** Robbins *Danny Fisher* 221: The gash jumps like rabbits all through the South. **1958** W. Burroughs *Naked Lunch* 119: Yeah. This gash comes to the door, and I say I want a piece of ass and the double sawski on her. **1961** Sullivan *Shortest, Gladdest Years* 140: Take your gash along. She'll get a charge out of it. **1968** Myrer *Eagle* 676: Isn't he humping that gash? **1974** Quincy, Mass. man, age *ca*25: Ten or fifteen years ago I heard these guys saying, "Aw shit, a gash don't know nothin'." They meant chicks don't know anything. **1966–80** McAleer & Dickson *Unit Pride* 383: Nothing but all them good-looking young gash to stare at.

c. sexual gratification as experienced by a man; PUSSY.—usu. considered vulgar.

1916 (implied by quot. at GASH-HOUND). **1918** in K. White *First Sex. Revolution* 88: I said...there was always a chance of picking up a piece of gash in here. **1931** Farrell *Guillotine Party* 85: You never think of nothing but gash. **1934** H. Roth *Call It Sleep* 412: O'Toole don' have to buy his gash. **1938–39** Dos Passos *Young Man* 83: Hello, buddy, how about some gash. **1954** Schulberg *Waterfront* 216: Specs wore thick glasses and sometimes they kidded him about...the fact that he had to pay for his gash because he wasn't good-looking enough. **1959** Hunter *Matter of Conviction* 76: I think we were talking about gash. **1966** Bogner *Seventh Ave.* 16: Two things he can't say no to, food and gash, but I love 'im. **1985** Baker *Cops* 47: I heard her, for a sum of money, offer this man, you know, some gash.

gash[2] *n.* [fr. Brit. slang *gashions* 'an extra portion', itself prob. of dial. orig.] *Naut.* garbage. *Rare* in U.S.

*1943 in *OEDS*: *Gash*...any surplus or residue. *1953, *1960, *1965 in *OEDS*. **1975** Mostert *Supership* 113: Graham Chalmers collected empty beer cans and took out the "gash."

gash-hound *n.* a whoremonger; lecher.—usu. considered vulgar.

1916 Cary *Venery* I 105: *Gash Hound*—A whoremonger. *Gash Hound's Kennel*—A whore house. *ca*1935 in Holt *Dirty Comics* 87: The strain on poor Snuffy is most terrific as the poetic gash-hound hides the weenie. **1955** Puzo *Dark Arena* 124: How can you stand this gash hound? **1956** H. Gold *Not with It* 17: I...had myself a stable of clappers for the gash-hounds too dumb to do their own howling. **1957** H. Simmons *Corner Boy* 28: Anyway, everybody knew his reputation as a gashhound. **1962** Dougherty *Commissioner* 227: The Great Man Russell, the Honest Gash-hound. **1966** Longstreet & Godoff *Wm. Kite* 120: You're a gash hound tonight and with no subtle nuances. **1969** Coppel *A Little Time for Laughter* 45 [ref. to *ca*1940]: So he told this other guy...that his son—that's me, old sport—was a real gash hound and he bet him twenty bucks that I could make a date for afterward with this B-girl, see?

gashman *n.* GASH-HOUND.

1952 Mandel *Angry Strangers* 294: Come on, gashman, don't go 'way.

gas-hound *n.* **1.** *Army.* a gas sentry.

1919 Mozley *Miracle Battery* 51 [ref. to WWI]: The reply sounded as if the men were talking with their masks on, and the gas corporal, better known as "Gas-hound," continued on his way.

2. a garage or filling-station attendant.

1921 *15th Inf. Sentinel* (Mar. 18) 13: I taken the road cootie of the skipper's over to the M.T.C. and got some gashounds to help me tune it up so it runs good.

3. (esp. among tramps) a habitual drinker of GAS, *n.*, 4; (*broadly*) a low drunkard.

1929 *AS* IV (June) 340: *Gas hound.* A consumer of "gas." **1934** Kromer *Waiting* 14: They are gas hounds...going to get soused on derail. **1942** in M. Curtiss *Letters Home* 139: Many of the men on freighters are gashounds, or as they are known ashore, drunks. **1944** *AS* (Apr.) *Gashound*...rumdum. **1947** Boyer *Dark Ship* 153: A drunk is always a "gas hound." **1980** Allanson *Dr. at Sea* 63: I finally put that old gas-hound to sleep in the cabin.

gas house *n.* **1.** *Mil.* a chemical-warfare training facility.

1918 in Campbell *Diary-Letters* 50: We'll be off on a hike with full packs, rifles, helmets, gas-masks and machine guns, on our way to rifle range, machine gun range, practice trenches or "gas-house." **1918** *Bugler* (Feb. 16) 2: His eyes were still moist an hour after returning from the gas-house. **1941** *AS* (Oct.) 165: *Gas House Gang.* Chemical warfare instructors.

2. [< (or infl. by) G *Gasthaus* 'a small inn or hotel'] a drinking saloon.

1920 Riggs & Platt *Battery F* 22: The greater part of the battery was billeted in a large barn at the village "Gas House." **1941** *AS* (Oct.) 165: *Gas House.* Saloon or beer garden. **1941** Hargrove *Pvt. Hargrove* 84: *Gashouse*—a beer joint. **1954–60** *DAS*: *Gas house.* A beer saloon...*WWII Armed Forces use. Common.*

Gas House Gang *n. Baseball.* the St. Louis Cardinals team of 1934 and years immediately following. Now *hist.* [The 1918 quots. illustrate lit. and fig. uses of the colloq. sense, 'a gang of toughs from a city's gas-house district'.]

[**1918** *Stars & Stripes* (May 10) 4: The bunch all know one another and hang together like a college frat or a gas-house gang.] [**1918** in Niles *Singing Soldiers* 88: About three in the afternoon the Gas-House Gang went to town (Paris) to help celebrate.] **1944** F.G. Lieb *Cardinals* 164: The most colorful, picturesque club of modern baseball was the Cardinal World's Champion outfit of 1934, the famous Gas House Gang....The term...was first used by Frank Graham in the *New York Sun*. And Frankie attributes it to Leo Durocher...."They wouldn't let us play in [the American] league," snapped Durocher...."They'd say we were a lot of gas house ball players." **1952** in *OEDS*: On the mound pitching for the old St. Louis Cardinal gas-house gang. **1975** Durocher & Linn *Nice Guys* 81: The best thing we had going for us, as far as posterity is concerned, was our name. The Gas House Gang. **1993** W. Sheed, in *N.Y. Times* (May 10) C 20: The saga of the Gashouse Gang....The boys fought and sang their way to exactly one world championship and a couple of great pennant races.

gas jockey *n.* a gas-station attendant.

1952 *ATS* (ed. 2) 398: *Gas jockey,* a serve-yourself gas station attendant. **1963** in H. Ellison *Sex Misspelled* 52: "You save Blue Chip stamps?" the gas jockey asked. **1977** *West-Folk.* XXXVI 176: Ranch hand, flunky, ice house worker, and gas jockey. **1977** M. Franklin *Last of Cowboys* 33: What'd he call you back there, the gas jockey? **1982** *Nat. Lampoon* (Aug.) 16: A fellow...tricked a...gas jockey into admitting he had destroyed motorists' battery terminals. **1983** S. King *Christine* 48: From the gas jockey's hurried wheel-balancing.

gasket *n.* a doughnut; (*also*) a pancake.

1942 *ATS* 733: *Blind gaskets*...hot cakes; *gaskets,* doughnuts. **1944** *Slanguage Dict.* 51: *Gasket*—flapjack.

¶ In phrase:

¶ **blow** [or **split**] **a gasket** to become furiously angry; (*also*) to go insane.

1949 R. Smith *Big Wheel* (film): All right, Reno. Don't blow your gasket. **1951** Pryor *The Big Play* 308: He blew a couple of gaskets, but he had to go along. **1952** Uris *Battle Cry* 229 [ref. to WWII]: You look as if you might blow a gasket, Major. Go on, say it. **1954** Freeman *Francis Joins WACs* (film): I'm so mad I could blow a gasket! **1956** Chamales *Never So Few* 551 [ref. to WWII]: I really blew a gasket over this Lewje business. **1958–59** Lipton *Barbarians* 48: I would one day...blow a gasket from sheer anger and frustration. **1961** Rosten *Capt. Newman* 118: Okay, okay, don't blow a gasket. **1962** G. Ross *Last Campaign* 69: Boy, Kelley's going to blow out a gasket. **1965** D. Gallery *8 Bells* 288: They would all split gaskets from frustrated intellectual arrogance. **1966** D. Gallery *Start Engines* 22: In five minutes we can have him crazier than a gooney bird. He'll blow his main gasket and pee in his pants. **1969** H.A. Smith *Buskin'* 97: Her husband blew a gasket. **1970** Rudensky & Riley *Gonif* 149: They must have thought that I had taken a sky pill or had finally blown a gasket.

gaslight *v.* [alluding to the film *Gaslight* (1944), in which a grasping husband, eager for an inheritance, attempts to drive his wife insane so that her murder will be interpreted as suicide] to attempt to frighten or confound in a manner so as to make the victim question his or her own sanity.

1956 *N.Y.C.* woman, age 41: To *gaslight* someone is to play tricks on them to make them think they're crazy. It comes from the movie *Gaslight.* **1965** *Reporter* (Dec. 2) 32: Some troubled persons having even gone so far as to charge malicious intent and premeditated "gaslighting." **1978** Charrell *How to Get Upper Hand* 23: "Gaslighting": The Art of Disorienting Your Antagonist. *Ibid.* 26: The identically turned out "gaslighter"...took his place. *a***1987** in *Nat. Lampoon* (Dec. 1987) 16: You gonna be gas-lighted by dese spooks. **1988** P. Beck & P. Massman *Rich Men, Single Women* 310: She felt as if she were being *Gaslighted.*

gas-man *n.* (see quot.).

1848 *Ladies' Repository* VIII (Oct.) 315: *Gasman,* A braggart.

gas monkey *n.* (see 1934 quot.). Cf. GREASE MONKEY, *n.*

1934 in *AS* (Feb. 1934) 76: *Gas monkeys.* Filling station attendants.

1938 *Amer. Mercury* (Oct.) 248: Did he ever talk with taxi-drivers, gas-monkeys, grease-balls, gandy-dancers, soda-jerkers,...pearl-divers, bindle-stiffs, nut-knockers, or plow-jockeys?

gasoline cowboy *n. Army.* (see quot.). *Joc.*

1941 *Army Ordnance* (July) 79: *Gasoline cowboy....*Member of Armored Force.

gas-out *n. Surfing.* a wipeout.

1976 *Webster's Sports Dict.* 180.

gas-passer *n.* **1.** *Med.* an anesthetist or anesthesiologist. Cf. *pass gas* s.v. GAS, *n.*

1961 *AS* (May) 146: *Gas passer,* n. An anesthetist or anesthesiologist. He is sometimes said to "pass gas on a case." **1968** "R. Hooker" *MASH* 67 [ref. to 1951]: Find the gas-passer and tell him to premedicate the patient. **1981** *Rod Serling's TZ Mag.* (June) 20: And, given enough time to tell the whole story, they would welcome the gas-passers with open arms. **1983** Van Devanter & Morgan *Before Morning* 318: *Gas passer*: anesthetist or anesthesiologist.

2. *Mil. Av.* a boom operator on a tanker aircraft.

1984 USAF veteran, served during Vietnam War: The boom operator was called the *boomer* or the *gas-passer.* **1986** Zeybel *First Ace* 123 [ref. to Vietnam War]: Shame on you, too, gas passer.

gasper *n.* a cheap cigarette or cigar.

1914** in *OEDS*: He prefers the Irish-grown "gasper" to all others. ***1916** in *OED*: Admirals don't smoke gaspers! ***1919** Downing *Digger Dialects* 25 [ref. to WWI]: *Gasper* (n.)—A cigarette. ***1919** *Athenaeum* (Aug. 8) 727: A "gasper" is a cheap cigarette. *a1923** Stringer *Diamond Thieves* 393: Gimme a gasper! **1927** *AS* II (Mar.) 276: *Gasper.* Cigarette. ***1929** Manning *Fortune* 131 [ref. to WWI]: I want some gaspers; they're good enough for the troops. **1938** *AS* (Feb.) 5: *Gasper,* n. Cigar. **1940** in Goodstone *Pulps* 114: Then I set fire to a gasper. **1942** *Time* (May 4) 19: Non-wowser Aussies Scrambling for U.S. Gaspers. **1945** *Life* (Jan. 1) 2: There is nothing cute about a young girl who is continuously stoking a gasper. **1946** Boulware *Jive & Slang* 4: *Gaspers*...Cigarettes. **1952** T. Bankhead *Tallulah* 177: When I'd run out of "gaspers," he'd chug off on his motorcycle to get me cigarettes. **1961** Terry *Old Liberty* 93: He smoked a pack of gaspers just waiting for everybody to arrive. **1979** G. Wolff *Duke of Deception* 183 [ref. to 1950's]: My father begged me to lay off the *gaspers,* though I smoked them anyway.

gas-pipe *n.* **1.** *Mil.* an old or outdated rifle.

***1883** in *F & H* III 122: The old Snider—the despair-breeding gas-pipe of our Volunteers—continues to be used in many of the competitions. **1890** *United Service* (Mar.) 324: The old "gas pipe" had given place to the 45-calibre breech-loader.

2. a blowhard; GAS BAG, 2.

1898 C.H. Crawford *Earlier Days* 96 [ref. to 1860's]: I think you are a regular gaspipe. **1919** *DN* V 65: *Gas-pipe,* one who talks a great deal. "That old fellow is quite a *gas-pipe.*" New Mexico.

3. *Music.* (see quot.).

1932 *AS* VII (June) 332: *Gas pipe*—Slide trombone.

¶ In phrase:

¶ **take the gas pipe** see s.v. GAS, *n.*

gassed *adj.* **1.** intoxicated.—also constr. with *up.*

1919 T.A. Dorgan, in *Chi. Herald & Examiner* (Feb. 9) IV 4: You're gassed now. ***1925** Fraser & Gibbons *Soldier & Sailor Wds.* 103 [ref. to WWI]: *Gassed.* Drunk. **1934** Kromer *Waiting* 21: He is gassed up. **1939** Howsley *Argot* 20: *Gassed Up*—Drunk on wood alki, mixed with gasoline. **1945** Beecher *All Brave Sailors* 124: He's so gassed up he can't climb the Jacob's ladder. **1947** Boyer *Dark Ship* 213: Anyone gassed up...will be fined five dollars and tossed out. *Ibid.* 259: You'd get in cars with guys gassed to the gills. **1951** O'Hara *Farmers Hotel* 71: Let someone get the least bit gassed and he won't go near them. **1954** Schulberg *Waterfront* 55: What he needed was to get gassed somewhere and knock off a little piece. **1957** M. Shulman *Rally* 174: Let's go over to Beer Can Boulevard and get gassed. **1957** H. Simmons *Corner Boy* 137: He stayed gassed on pod and alcohol. **1958** Cooley *Run for Home* 150 [ref. to ca1920's]: Half the time he's gassed up and can't perform the work. **1958** Ferlinghetti *Coney Island of the Mind* 31: Cakewalkers and carnie hustlers/all gassed to the gills. **1961** Brosnan *Pennant Race* 133: Bross,...you were a little gassed on the plane. **1962** Riccio & Slocum *All the Way Down* 67: That bastard is all gassed up. He had two caps today. **1964** Smith & Hoefer *Music* 14: When he was real gassed-up I was turned down flat and went home without him or the pay check. **1970** Hatch *Cedarhurst* 186: Everybody was throwing down those bloody martinis and getting gassed. **1971** Horan *Blue Messiah* 524.

Maxie, who was half-gassed, kept shaking my hand. **1989** *Night Court* (NBC-TV): A bunch of gassed-up yahoos. **1986–91** Hamper *Rivethead* 57: By night's end you'd be totally gassed and ornery enough to punch out your own grandmother.
2. *Jazz.* delighted; thrilled; happy.
> **1958–59** Lipton *Barbarians* 24: He was so grateful the next day, he was just gassed, no recriminations, no criticisms.

gassed-out *adj.* weary; played out.
> **1964** Smith & Hoefer *Music* 21: Today, if they go four rounds with gloves they're gassed-out and ready for the sponge.

gasser *n.* *Jazz.* something or someone that affords great excitement, amusement, or delight.
> **1944** *New Cab Calloway's Hepster's Dict.* 7: *Gasser* (n., adj.): sensational....“When it comes to dancing, she's a gasser.” **1944** Burley *Hndbk. Jive* 139: *Gasser*—Something that is tops, great, excellent, something that thrills or delights, an enjoyable occurrence or situation, that which gives pleasure, a story packed with action. **1944** Joe Davis phono. record JD 779, rec. (Dec. 15) by Wingy Marone and His Orchestra. *The Gasser* (song title). **1946** Mezzrow & Wolfe *Really Blues* 186: Jim, this jive you got is a gasser. **1954** L. Armstrong *Satchmo* 239: Every number on opening night was a gassuh. **1956** Hargrove *Girl He Left* 27: “I'm not your type.”...“That's a gasser....That's *really* a gasser.” **1957** M. Shulman *Rally* 44: Betty Ann Steinberg had this absolute gasser of an idea! **1958** J. Davis *College Vocab.* 13: *Gasser*—A funny joke or incident. **1958** Landau & Yates *Frankenstein—1970* (film): Yeah, a real gasser. **1959–60** R. Reisner *Jazz Titans* 156: *Gasser*: a person or thing that brings forth tremendous enthusiasm. **1967** Hamma *Motorcycle Mommas* 104: The committee has really thought up some gassers. **1979** W. Cross *Kids & Booze* 17: The big kids thought it was a gasser to get me bombed.

gassy *adj.* **1.** given to boasting.
> **1847** (quot. at COVE, *n.*). **1848** *Ladies' Repository* VIII (Oct.) 315: *Gassy*, Given to boasting. **1863** in W. Whitman *Corres.* I 92: I was so in hopes they would take the conceit out of that gassy city. **1875** Whitney *Lang.* 17: We call an empty and sophistical but ready talker *gassy*. **1889** Barrère & Leland *Dict. Slang* I 398: *Gassy*...(American), talkative, bouncing, full of wind. *a***1910** Bierce *Shapes of Clay* 78: We have this little gassy don/Instead.
2. *Orig. Jazz.* exciting or wonderful.
> **1966** Bullins *Goin' a Buffalo* 187: That number's a gassy one, honey. **1970** Landy *Underground Dict.* 87: *Gassy*...Good, great; fantastic.

gas wagon *n.* —an automobile.—used derisively.
> **1914** T.A. Dorgan, in Zwilling *TAD Lexicon* 105: If you're going to spiel about gas wagons—shoot!!! **1917** E.R. Burroughs *Oakdale Affair* 98: She was gassin' 'bout her pals croakin' a guy an' trunin' 'im outten a gas wagon. **1921** in C.M. Russell *Paper Talk* 183: It pleases me plenty to know that thair is so many men and women that will quit a gas wagon...[for] a hoss.

gas work *n.* GAS, *n.*, 1.
> **1854** in Eliason *Tarheel Talk* 273: Dr. Ashe is speaking strongly of going to Alabama, leaving N.C. but I am in hopes it is all gas work.

gat *n.* **1.** *Army.* a Gatling gun. [Despite the evidence of the dates, prob. the orig. sense.]
> **1907** *McClure's Mag.* (Feb.) 381: There was a whole regiment of footshakers in camp, a battery with one of them old-time Napoleon fieldpieces and a Gat. **1923** Platt *Archer* 232 [ref. to *ca*1903]: It was my idea to teach the gats and then make him a sort of top sergeant of the battery.
2.a. *Esp. Und.* a pistol; (*broadly*) a firearm of any sort.
> **1897** in J. London *Reports* 320: *Gat*, gun. **1904** *Life in Sing Sing* 248: *Gatt.* A revolver. **1908** in H.C. Fisher *A. Mutt* 27: You're a Hindoo with that gat [shotgun], Pa. *a***1909** Tillotson *Detective* 91: *Gat*—A gun. **1913** *Sat. Eve. Post* (May 10) 12: You got to dump your gats, then. **1912–14** in E. O'Neill *Lost Plays* 42: Take yer hand away from that gat or I'll fill yuh full of holes. **1915** Braley *Workaday World* 103: “I am!” says Ike, as he draws his gat. **1917** *Editor* (Jan. 13) 33: Army Vernacular...“Gat”—Pistol. **1918** in York *Mud & Stars* 54: There's mud in your gas mask, there's mud in your hat. There's mud in your helmet, there's mud on your gat. **1920** *Hicoxy's Army* 38: Willis attempted to shoot holes through the car roof with his “gat.” **1920** *Amer. Legion Wkly.* (Feb. 9) 13: We gripped our best friend, the old gat. **1927** Blumenstein *Whiz Bang!* 31: We had our gats and rifles with us. **1929** Thomas *Woodfill* 66: He was...as happy-go-lucky a buck as ever juggled a gat in this man's army. **1948** *Reader's Digest* (Aug.) 150: Mickey, our war councilor, packs a gat. **1952** Sandburg *Strangers* 395 [ref. to *ca*1890]:

He said, “This gat comes in handy, boy. It saves you a lot of hard work.” **1961** Joswick & Keating *Cameraman* 162: We're wearing our gats because we're just back from combat. **1981** G. Wolf *Roger Rabbit* 66: A piece, a gat, a rod, a *gun*. **1986** *Morning Call* (Allentown, Pa.) (Aug. 18) D3: *Gat*: Gun.
b. *Und.* a gunman.
> **1928** Anderson & Hickerson *Gods of Lightning* 559: Heine, the Gat did it. **1929** McEvoy *Hollywood Girl* 106: Mike the Rat and Gyp the Gat.

gate *n.* **1.** ejection or dismissal.—usu. constr. with *get* or *give*.
> **1901** A.H. Lewis *Croker* 60: A mug don't go to a theater any more to learn things; he goes to be entertained. That's where Shakspere gets the gate, see! **1911** T.A. Dorgan, in *N.Y. Eve. Jour.* (Jan. 3) 14: The referee...told the Pawtucket gent that if he [butted the opposing boxer with his head] again he would be given the gate. **1911** A.H. Lewis *Apaches of N.Y.* 111: Youse've got to wear 'em at these swell feeds....They'd give youse the gate if you don't. **1916** *Rio Grande Rattler* (Oct. 11) 5: Some “Guy High Up” will give us all the “Gate.” **1916** S. Lewis *Job* 264: I've been fired!...Canned. Got the gate. **1918** Witwer *Baseball to Boches* 143: Give this hick the gate. **1920** O'Neill *Diff'rent* 250: So you're givin' me the gate, too, eh? **1920** Ade *Hand-Made Fables* 26: Not until he began cutting all Recitations did the Authorities make a sign to give him the Gate. **1924** Marks *Plastic Age* 273: I guess his girl has given him the gate. **1928** in Paxton *Sport* 129: “They just won't play your way.” “Then they'll get the gate....I'll get a new line.” **1929** Perelman *Ginsbergh* 185: Speech On Being Given the Gate By The Girl Friend. **1930** Huston *Frankie & Johnny* 51: Ye wouldn't gimme the gate! **1938** Haines *Tension* 122: If you're right you get a raise; if you're wrong you get the gate. **1965–70** in *DARE* [very extensive evidence]. **1984** Ehrhart *Marking Time* 148: I hear the second engineer's gonna get the gate when we get to Bellingham.
2. the mouth. *Rare in U.S.*
> **1936** R. Adams *Cowboy Lingo* 219: If such a person talked too much, he might be told to...“keep yo' gate shut.” ****1936** Partridge *DSUE* 318: *Gate*...The mouth: New Zealanders' (from *ca*1910), esp. soldiers' in [Great War]. ****1955**, ****1963** in *OEDS*. ****1966** in Partridge *DSUE*: Shut your big ugly gate at once.
3. [pop. by Louis Armstrong; see 1936 Armstrong quot. and cf. GATEMOUTH] *Jazz.* a fellow player or devotee of swing music; (*hence*) friend.
> **1936** L. Raymond, W. Bishop & C. Williams *Swing Brother Swing* (pop. song): Come on, swing me, gate! **1936** L. Armstrong *Swing* 77: When I was a kid...they started calling me “Gate-mouth,”...I started calling the other boys “Gate” too. Then...when I got into Kid Ory's band when the boys were all swinging good and hot, I would sing out “Swing it, Gate,”...and now “Gate” is a word swing players use when they call out to one another. **1936** Parker *Battling Hoofer* (film): Come on, gate, what do you need—a blue-print? **1939** Calloway *Swingformation Bu.*: If you meet a fellow hepster at a bar, what is the proper greeting?...“Greetings, gate, let's dissipate.” **1941** *Pittsburgh Courier* (Apr. 19) 24: So long, gate. **1943** *Merrie Melodies* (animation): Greetings gate, let's osculate! **1945** Himes *If He Hollers* 71: See you, gate. See you, Jaxon. See you, stud. **1947** Schulberg *Harder They Fall* 189: Where *you* been, gate? Gimme some skin, man. **1947** Willingham *End As a Man* 183: Gates, I can't take any more. **1948** *Neurotica* (Summer) 40: From then on it's all over and the gates are latching on from everywhere. **1954** L. Armstrong *Satchmo* 221 [ref. to N.O., *ca*1915]: We used such nicknames as Gate, Face and Gizzard when we said hello or good-bye. **1954** Matheson *Born of Man & Woman* 136: He clapped him smartly on the shoulder. “Greetings gate!” said the man. **1958–59** Southern & Hoffenberg *Candy* 116: “Greetings, Gates!” Livia screamed merrily. **1959** Bechet *Treat It Gentle* 76: They've got all that crazy jive-talk, all that stuff about “gate” and “tea” and being real “cool.” **1970** *Playboy* (Aug.) 161: I hear you talking, gate!

¶ In phrases:

¶ **crash the gate** see s.v. CRASH, *v.*

¶ **slam a gate** (among beggars) to beg from a private house.
> **1907** London *Road* 91 [ref. to *ca*1894]: Then there are places like the quarries at Rutland, Vermont, where the hobo is exploited, the unearthed energy in his body, which he has accumulated by “battering on the drag” or “slamming the gates” being extracted for the benefit of that particular community. **1925** Mullin *Scholar Tramp* 13: If he winds up at your back door and asks for something to eat, he is slamming a gate.

-gate *comb. form.* [abstracted fr. *Watergate*] (used as the final element in journalistic coinages, usu. nonce words, that name scandals resulting from corruption and cover-up or other improprieties in government or business). [This has been and continues to be an enormously productive combining form; additional examples of its use in a wide range of contexts may be found in the "Among the New Words" column in *American Speech* LIII (Fall 1978) 3 and LVI (Winter 1981) 4, *OED2*, and elsewhere.]

1973 in *AS* LIII (Fall): There have been persistent rumors in Russia of a vast scandal....Implicated in "the Volgagate" are a group of liberal officials. **1974** in *AS* LIII (Fall): "Watergate" became an international symbol of corruption. (A French vintage scandal became "Winegate"; crooked Southeast Asian unions produced a "Laborgate.") **1977** *U.S. News & W.R.* (Aug. 29) 18: Reactions to "Koreagate." Michel, who is Republican whip in the House, often was asked about the Korean pay-off scandal. **1980** *L.A. Times* (July 28) II 5: Jimmy Carter's proven ability to cut his own throat—most recently by the "Billygate" episode involving his brother's role as a lobbyist for Libya. **1983** *Mother Jones* (June) 6: The squalid Environmental Protection Agency affair some dubbed "Sewergate" has now joined a dozen other larger and lesser "gates" in the nation's scandal archives. **1984** *Time* (Sept. 10) 76: It may now be time to close the -gate. Ten years is a long time for any political fashion....In that decade we have had Watergate, Koreagate, Lancegate, Billygate and now Ferrarogate, with Meesegate and Debategate on temporary hold. **1992** *N.Y. Daily News* (Mar. 18) 18: Rep. Joe Early (D–Mass.), one of the leading House check bouncers, yesterday angrily attacked House Speaker Tom Foley for his handling of "Rubbergate." **1993** *Nation* (Mar. 1) 256: Sessionsgate: Why did F.B.I. Director William Sessions get caught in such a tangled web?

gate-crash *v.* [back formation from GATE-CRASHER, *n.*] to attend or enter without an invitation or ticket of admission. Now *S.E.*

*1927 in *OEDS:* The Committee of the White Rose Ball...dealt severely with a few cases of "gate crashing." ***1931** in *OEDS:* Geoffrey Hayes is giving a party to-night—shall we gate-crash? ***1939** Entwistle *European Balladry* 6: It is not considered possible for unknown young men to gate-crash on kings in this way. **1951** Cowley *Exile's Return* 68: The Liberal Club was forced to yield to a mass demand that was accompanied by threats of gate-crashings and riots. **1981** Raban *Old Glory* 79: I set out to gate-crash the affair. **1993** *N.Y. Times* (Mar. 30) C 16: Every year several hundred uninvited people show up, all dressed up, trying to gate-crash.

gate-crasher *n.* a forward or undesirable person who attends or enters a sporting event, social function, or commercial entertainment without a ticket of admission, invitation, etc. Now *S.E.*

1921 T.A. Dorgan, in Zwilling *TAD Lexicon* 39: The world's champion "gate crasher"...came to grief in trying to "make" the gate at the Vernon arena last night. ***1927** in *OEDS:* "One-eyed Connolly," the champion American "gate crasher" (one who gains admittance to big sporting events without payment). **1929** W.R. Burnett *Iron Man* 17: Gate-crashers and bums...drifted in. **1943** Chandler *High Window* 392: You're not a member....No gate crashers. **1946** *Time* (Apr. 8) 17: Gate crashers schemed to get into UNO meetings with a vigor heretofore reserved for the World Series and heavyweight fights. **1974** Fair *New Nonsense* 50: A man...had been ejected from Casriel's sessions as a gate-crasher. **1981** *Hart to Hart* (ABC-TV): Let's hope your next party has a better class of gate-crashers. **1983** *Nat. Lampoon* (Mar.) 77: This ol' gate-crasher ain't paid to think on such matters.

gate money *n. Pris.* (see 1936 quot.).

1931–34 in Clemmer *Pris. Commun.* 332: Gate money....The ten dollars given a convict upon release. **1936** Dai *Opium Addiction* 199: Gate money. The money given to a prisoner upon release. **1967** Spradley *Owe Yourself a Drunk* 15: Most state pens pay a little and give a man "gate money."

gatemouth *n. Black E.* a person having a large mouth; (*also*) a loquacious person.—usu. as a nickname. Hence **gate-mouthed,** *adj.*

1936 L. Armstrong *Swing* 77: When I was a kid...they started calling me "Gate-mouth." **1944** Burley *Hndbk. Jive* 139: Gatemouth—One who knows everyone else's business. **1945** Drake & Cayton *Black Metropolis* 719: "Gate-Mouth" cut in: "Yeah, me too. I believe when we go oughta take one of 'em with us!" **1983** *Reader's Digest Success with Words* 85: Black English...gatemouth = "gossiper." **1985** Dye *Between Raindrops* 43: Gate-mouthed asshole grinning at me and my camera.

gatling *n.* a revolver; pistol. Also **gatling gun.** Occ. cap.

1880 in *DA:* Every sole kin kerry a gatlin under his cote. **1893** in Dobie *Rainbow* 160: Mr. Loessin got his Gatlin' for to bring me back. *Ibid.* 165: I'll lay my Gatlin' at my head, Babe. **1897** A.H. Lewis *Wolfville* 99: The victim...brings his gatlin' into play surprisin'. **1909** in McCay *Little Nemo* 165: Quick as a flash our determined hero clutched his gatling! *a***1910** in Lomax & Lomax *Amer. Ballads & Folk Songs* 95: You've gone and shot my husband/With a forty-four gatlin' gun. **1915** White *Amer. Negro Folk-Songs* 360: Jones, I got my butcher knife and gatling gun and 't ain't no use for you to run. **1923** *Poems, Ballads, & Parodies* 28: When the groceryman saw what the fly had done,/He went for his trusty gatling gun. **1926** Dunning & Abbott *Broadway* 248: I ain't going to. I don't carry any gatlin' gun. **1933** in Lomax & Lomax *Amer. Ballads & Folk Songs* 107: Underneath the ruffles of her petticoat,/She had a young Gatlin' gun. **1966** in Jackson *Swim Like Me* 48: He said, "I'm gonna give you just one chance to run/before I draw my old Gatling gun.

gator *n.* [orig. dial.] **1.a.** an alligator. Now *colloq.*

1844 in *OEDS:* The 'gator isn't...a han'some critter. **1862** "E. Kirke" *Among Pines* 154: De ole 'gator, quicker den a flash, put a knife enter him. **1894** J. Slocum *Liberdade* 155: Adventures with coons and 'gators. **1895** Coup *Sawdust* 150: Nearly all the larger 'gators' took part in it, springing at each other and locking their jaws. **1921** *Variety* (July 15) 4: Unruly 'Gator. "Alligator Boy" Attacked...By Beast. **1951** Mannix *Sword-Swallower* 92: A ten-foot bull 'gator. **1959** Bechet *Treat It Gentle* 17: A 'gator [was] disturbed by the splash. **1959** L'Amour *Fast Draw* 39: The huge old 'gator locally known as Ol' Joe. **1987** *Sun* (May 5) 3: Mom tells how gator ate her baby daughter.

b. ALLIGATOR, *n.*, 5.

1937 in *DARE:* Members of the athletic teams of the University of Florida...The Gators. **1962** in *AS* (Dec. 1963) 270: Floridians are known as *gators*.

c. *USMC.* an Alligator LVT (a kind of self-propelled tracked landing vehicle).

1944 *Word Study* (May) 3: *Beach the 'Gators*—This is a command meaning "Land the landing barges." **1970** Ponicsan *Last Detail* 14: I was in the 'gator navy, you know, in the Med doing amphibious landings with the marines.

d. *Jazz.* ALLIGATOR, *n.*, 7.

1944 Burley *Hndbk. Jive* 139: *Gator*—Swing music fan. **1944** Breslow & Purcell *Follow the Boys* (film): So listen, all you gators. **1944** in Himes *Black on Black* 204: It was doin' some steps I ain't never seen and I'm a 'gator from way back. **1947** *ATS* (Supp.) 1: Swing enthusiast; "jitterbug."...'gator.

2. Esp. *Black E.* usu. *pl.* a shoe made of alligator leather.

1969 Joseph *Me Nobody Knows* 97: And I will buy me a casmere coat and a pair of gators at the shop and I will run for President. **1971** in Sanchez *Word Sorcerers* 179: They wore...pointed-toe gators and stingy-brim hats. **1972** A. Kemp *Savior* 109: Green and yellow 'gators tipping lightly over the dirty pavement. **1977** Sayles *Union Dues* 182: Help keep the rags on his back and the gators on his feet. **1983** *Reader's Digest Success with Words* 85: Black English...gators = "alligator shoes."

gator bait *n.* ALLIGATOR BAIT.—used contemptuously.

1970 in *DARE:* Derogatory names for Negroes...'gator bait. **1991** *World News Tonight* (ABC-TV) (July 11): "There goes a coon!" "Hey, gator bait!"

gat up *v. Und.* (see quots.).

1926 Finerty *Criminalese* 26: *To gat up*—to hold-up with a gun. **1928** *Amer. Mercury* (May) 81: *To gat up* means to hold up a person or place with a gun. **1933** Ersine *Prison Slang* 39: *Gat up.* To arm yourself. "Gat up and we'll blow."

gauge *n.* **1.** temper. Cf. *get (one's) gauge up,* below.

1942 *Yank* (Dec. 23) 18: The old hepster rose, with his gauge brewing hot.

2. [sugg. by *twelve-gauge shotgun*] a shotgun.

1975 Greer *Slammer* 60: "Hold this," Rhiner said, handing Walsh a shotgun. "They're prone to light out if they don't see a little gauge." *Ibid.* 62: Level that gauge on those men. **1988** M. Schiffer *Colors* (film): He's got a gauge. **1990** Bing *Do or Die* 124: I'm a madman with a fully loaded 'gauge.

¶ In phrases:

¶ **get (one's) gauge up** to excite, invigorate, or stimulate (oneself).

1932 in *AS* (Feb. 1934) 26: Get one's gage up. To become intoxicated. **1942–49** Goldin et al. *DAUL* 79: Get one's gage up. To stimulate oneself by smoking marijuana, or, less frequently, by drinking hard liquor. **1954–60** *DAS: Gage up, get one's...*To become angry....To become emotional....To become drunk. **1971** Wells & Dance *Night People* 21: Maybe you would have a little taste upstairs, but when you got your gauge up and your stomach full, you'd go back and blow some more [jazz].

¶ **wipe the gauge** [applying the emergency brakes causes the air pressure indicator to fall to zero] *R.R.* (see quot.).
1929 *Bookman* (July) 526: Should an engineer "wipe the gauge" or "clean the clock," it means that he has brought the train to a sudden stop by setting the air brakes. **1962** *AS* (May) 132: *Wipe the gauge*...To apply the emergency airbrakes on a locomotive.

gauged *adj.* see GAGED.

Gaul *n. Und.* (see quot.).
1848 *Ladies' Repository* VIII (Oct.) 315: *Gaul*, A Frenchman.

gaunch *n.* [perh. cf. GINCH, *n.*] *Stu.* a gross or obnoxious person, esp. a woman.
1954–60 *DAS: Gaunch.* n. An unpopular girl; a female goon. *Some teen-age use ca1940; never common.* **1976** D.W. Maurer, in *AS* LI 22 [ref. to ca1950].

gawnicus *n.* [prob. elab. of GONEY] *N.E.* a blockhead.
1877 Bartlett *Amer.* (ed. 4) 242: *Gawnicus.* A dolt.

gay *n.* [fr. the adj.] **1.** Orig. *Homosex.* a homosexual person, esp. a man. Now *colloq.* or *S.E.*
1953 (cited in *W10*). **1956** Reinhardt *Sex Perv.* 48: *Gay*—adjective and noun, homosexual. **1958** in *Social Problems* IX (1961) 110: This gay came over and felt me up....Well, my younger brother...told me this gay'd blowed him. **1964** in Gover *Trilogy* 339: He's a gay....some boyfriend...beat him up. **1967** Rechy *Numbers* 64: He's a muscle gay—I mean guy. **1962–68** B. Jackson *In the Life* 379: They call them queens, gays, whatever. **1971** Rader *Govt. Inspected* 187: One of the gays fluttered his eyelashes at my father. **1983** Stapleton *30 Yrs.* 63: The corner was filled with black gays, or fags as they were called [in 1960]. **1993** *Newsweek* (July 26) 59: If gays and lesbians hate one term even more than the crudest epithets hurled at them, it's got to be "lifestyle choice."
2. *Black E.* homosexual practices; homosexuality.
1978 *N.Y. Post* (Dec. 9) 14: I done gay when I was locked up....Some girls don't like gay but if they know they're going to do a long time they get serious.

gay *adj.* **1.a.** living by prostitution. [Orig. euphem., a specialization of the S.E. sense, 'addicted to social pleasures and dissipations' (see *OED*); the 1889 quots. from Chester et al. (the words of a male homosexual prostitute) anticipate but do not seem to illustrate **(b)**, below.]
***1805** J. Davis *Post-Captain* 150: As our heroes passed along the Strand, they were accosted by a hundred gay ladies, who asked them if they were good-natured. "Devil take me!...there is not a girl in the Strand that I would touch with my gloves on." ***1826** "Blackmantle" *Eng. Spy* II 19: She had two sisters, both *gay*, who formerly figured on the *pavé*...; but of late they have disappeared, report says, to *conjugate* in private. **1851** Ely *Wanderings* 16: If they had been gay girls or even of the appearance of courtesans, I should not have wondered so much, but they were all quite respectable people, although quite poor. **1853** G. Thompson *Gay Girls of N.Y.* 21: The landlady and the "gay girl" continue the combat. *Ibid.* 72: Thus...can be seen the manner in which many of the "gay girls of New-York" are manufactured for the market. ***1854** in *F & H* III 126: How long have you been gay? ***1857** in *F & H*: Here in Catherine-street vice is a monster of a hideous mien. The gay women, as they are termed, are worse off than American slaves. ***1851–61** H. Mayhew *London Labour* IV 240: Then for some...ten years, till I was six-and-twenty,—I went through all the changes of a gay lady's life. ***1872** Hotten *Slang Dict.* (ed. 4): "*Gay* woman," a kept mistress or prostitute. **1877** in Asbury *Gem of Prairie* 112: Our Carter has allowed a number of gay damsels to nestle down, and they are rather homely ones at that. **1880** Martin *Sam Bass* 15: He had a "gay girl" to solace his hours, and Sam and Jack Davis had to have one each, too. ***1889** in Chester et al. *Cleve. St.* 52: I am still a professional "Mary-Anne." I have lost my character and cannot get on otherwise. I occasionally do odd jobs for gay people. *Ibid.* 156: I worked hard at cleaning the houses of the gay people—the gay ladies on the beat, but I did not earn much. **1889** Barrère & Leland *Dict. Slang* I 399: *Gay* (common), loose, dissipated; a "*gay* woman" or "*gay* girl," a prostitute. ***ca1888–94** in Rawson *Dict. Euphem.* 120: I saw a woman walking along Pall Mall....I could scarcely make up my mind whether she was gay or not, but at length saw the quiet invitation in her eye, and...followed her to a house in B * * y Street, St. James.

b. [perh. infl. by GAYCAT, 2] Orig. *Homosex.* (esp. of men) homosexual; (*hence*) pertaining to or indicating homosexual interests. Now *S.E.* [The meaning intended in the 1922 quot. from a lesbian author is problematic. See also 1983 quot.]
[**1922** Gertrude Stein "Miss Furr & Miss Skeene," in *Vanity Fair*: They were...gay, they learned little things that are things in being gay,...they were quite regularly gay.] **1933** Ford & Tyler *Young & Evil* 163: Gayest thing on two feet. **1938** Mast *Bringing Up Baby* 99: *Aunt:* But why are you wearing these [women's] clothes? *David:* Because I just went gay...(He leaps into the air as Aunt Elizabeth recoils.)...all of a sudden. **1941** G. Legman, in G.V. Henry *Sex Vars.* II 1167: *Gay.* An adjective used almost exclusively by homosexuals to denote homosexuality, sexual attractiveness, promiscuity...or lack of restraint, in a person, place or party. Often given the French spelling, *gai* or *gaie* by (or in burlesque of) cultured homosexuals of both sexes. **1942** in Legman *Limerick* 94: There was a young belle from Bombay/Who never had thought herself gay. **1944** in J. Katz *Gay/Lesbian Almanac* 594: It is significant that the homosexual's word for his own kind is "gay." **1945** in T. Williams *Letters* 164: Getting us both thrown bodily out of a gay bar last week. **1948** Vidal *City & Pillar* 246: Jim discovered their language, their expressions. The words "fairy" and "pansy" were considered to be in bad taste. It was fashionable to say that a person was "gay." **1948** Lait & Mortimer *New York* 72: Not all New York's queer (or as they say it, "gay") people live in Greenwich Village. **1949** De Forrest *Gay Year* 23: Joe, tell me, are you gay or not? **1950** *Neurotica* (Spring) 37: I had lost all facility with "gay" argot. **1952** in Russ *Last Parallel* 31: "Do you want to go to a gay party?"..."Sure, I'm...not gay myself, but I'd love to come along." **1953** Brossard *Bold Saboteurs* 121: We went one night to the queerest joint in town, a "gay" bar where all the liver-lipped faggots flocked to shriek at each other. **1957** Gutwillig *Long Silence* 93: I mean, you drink, as drunks are O.K....But since you're not gay, you don't want anyone else to be. **1958** Motley *Epitaph* 201: See that the gay guy don't go with no rough trade. **1960** Bannon *Journey* 36: That lousy bitch is gay. I mean, a Lesbian. **1963** Horwitz *Candlelight* 25 [ref. to WWII]: I have the uneasy impression that about 60 per cent of the men in England are gay. **1966** *Time* (Jan. 21) 40: The Gay Subculture...."gay" bars [are] flourishing all over the U.S. **1966** S. Harris *Hellhole* 82: They mostly looked like bulldykes, though there weren't too many gay nurses. **1967** Gonzales *Paid My Dues* 50: "Rubber" was "gay" but he weighed two hundred pounds and was so rough that he got any "guy" he had eyes for. **1972** Friday *Secret Garden* 81: People like me. Lesbians. And I don't like to be called "gay." I'm no faggot. [**1983** J. Katz *Gay/Lesbian Almanac* 315: A reference of 1868 refers to a song titled the "Gay Young Clerk in the Dry Goods Store," by Will S. Hays, a female impersonator. *Ibid.* 405: A three-act farce, "The Gay Young Bride" (1923), included a song of the same title sung by Tom Martelle, "America's Greatest Female Impersonator."] **1985** D.K. Weisberg *Children of Night* 21: During World War II...homosexuals [in San Francisco]...began to speak of themselves and their mores as "gay." **1993** *Jerry Springer Show* (synd. TV series): Being a lesbian means two women who love each other. Being gay means two men who love each other.

c. *Juve.* stupid; foolish; crazy; LOUSY.
1978 G. Kimberly *Skateboard* 41: "It looks terrific on you." "It looks gay." **1982** N.J. highschool students: You must be gay!...That was really gay, Peter! **1987** *Creem Close-Up Presents* (No. 1) 6: Your so-stupid-they're-funny captions are gay. Get into some [real] humor. **1988** Univ. Tenn. student: Making students wait for the light is kind of a gay rule anyway. **1988** Knoxville, Tenn., teenager: Don't get that [Halloween III videotape]. I heard it was really gay. **1988** Huntsville, Ala., high school student: Aw, man! That's gay! Who'd think he'd be that stupid? *a*1990 P. Dickson *Slang!* 217: *Gay.* Not cool; totally stupid.

2. [perh. a dial. survival of early E (ca1470–1593: *OED*); cf. also *OED* defs. 7 & 8] fine; (*also*) safe.
1863 in G. Whitman *Letters* 89: I have a bran new tent and when I get it fixed up to suit me, it will just be gay I tell you. **1863** in Geer *Diary* 113: [They are] gay boys on a tear. **1866** in "M. Twain" *Letters fr. Hi.* 85: Here's hoping your dirt'll pan out gay. ***a*1889** in Barrère & Leland *Dict. Slang* I 27: James Hawes reported to the fourth man that it was *all gay*, which the detective, who was hiding in a garden, understood to mean that no one was at home. ***1890–93** *F & H* III 126: *All gay*....All right; first-rate. *a*1910 Bierce *Shapes of Clay* 217: Tom was my style—that's all I say;/Some others [prizefighters] may be equal gay. ***1914** in Partridge *DSUE* 982: "There, that's all gay," he broke off, pacifically.
3. unruly; impertinent; forward; reckless.—often constr. with *get*.

1893 in S. Crane *NYC Sketches* 21: When a feller asts a civil question yehs needn't git gay. **1895** F.P. Dunne, in Schaaf *Dooley* 204: War…'tis like gettin' gay in front iv a polis station. **1896** Ade *Artie* 68: Some day you'll get too gay an' a guy'll give you a funny poke. **1898** F.P. Dunne *Peace & War* 130: Well," said Mr. Dooley, "th' European situation is becomin' a little gay." **1899** A.H. Lewis *Sandburrs* 173: Well! me Rag lights into this hobo who's got gay wit' d' little goil. **1899** Ade *Fables* 50: He had come very near getting Gay with our First Families. **1899** Garland *Eagle's Heart* 273: You're lately from the East, or you wouldn't get gay with strangers in this country. **1907** S.E. White *Ariz. Nights* 100: "What in hell would we do here?…Collect Gila monsters for their good looks?" "Don't get gay." **1914** Z. Grey *West. Stars* 103: If he gets gay over in Arizona he'll go to the pen at Yuma. **1921** U. Sinclair *K. Coal* 11: Because you're too gay, kid. Didn't you know you had no business trying to sneak in here? **1922** Colton & Randolph *Rain* 68: If that Davidson gets gay with me again, I'll tell him who his mother was. **1940** Zinberg *Walk Hard* 350: You shouldn't be so gay with your mitts. **1953** Chandler *Goodbye* 288: Don't get gay with me, cheapie. **1969** Bouton *Ball Four* 157: The result is that you get gay, throw it down the middle and get clobbered. **1970** Terkel *Hard Times* 73: People got a little too gay on the way up.

gay-and-frisky *n.* [rhyming slang] whiskey. *Rare* in U.S.
   1919 T.A. Dorgan, in Zwilling *TAD Lexicon* 39: Gay an' frisky that's a whiskey. **1961** Franklyn *Dict. Rhyming Sl.*: Gay and frisky Whisky…it has wide currency, both in Britain and in the United States.
¶ In phrase:
¶ **do the gay and frisky** to go out carousing.
   1904 Dunbar *Happy Hollow* 248: Whath the mattah? Up againtht it? You look a little ol' to be doin' the gay an' frithky.

gay boy *n.* a man who is homosexual.—often used derisively.
   [**1903** in *AS* 63 (Summer 1988) 115: He treated us like we belonged to the gayboy bunch—no back room for us; not any.] **1945** in T. Williams *Letters* 167: Goes hog-wild in the presence of gay boys, flitting from one to another. **1952** Lait & Mortimer *USA* 246: We were solicited by gay boys around Henry's. **1958–59** Lipton *Barbarians* 316: Gay Boy—Homosexual. **1963** T.I. Rubin *Sweet Daddy* 31: This great big fruit. One of the gay boys, Doc. **1963** G. Abbott *Mr. Abbott* 70: Around Broadway they will be referred to as "queers" or "gay boys." **1978** in *Maledicta* VI (1982) 22: Male homosexual…*fruitcake, gay, gayboy.* **1989** *Newsweek* (Oct. 9) 31: I have nothing against gays or lesbians. I have lots of gay boys working for me.

gaycat *n.* [orig. unkn.] **1.** *Und.* (among tramps and itinerant criminals) an inexperienced hand having little knowledge or understanding of itinerant life; amateur; newcomer; (*broadly*) a worthless fellow.
   1893 *Century* (Nov.) 106: The gay-cats are men who *will* work for "very good money," and are usually in the West in the autumn to take advantage of the high wages offered to laborers during the harvest season. **1894** *Century* (Feb.) 519: Troy's all right, and it's only a rotten gay-cat that 'u'd say it wa'n't. **1895** *Harper's Wkly.* (Aug. 10) 753: The hobo is an exceedingly proud fellow, and if you want to offend him, call him a "gay cat" or a "poke-outer." **1899** "J. Flynt" *Tramping* 395: Gay-Cat: an amateur tramp who works when his begging courage fails him. **1907** London *Road* 25 [ref. to 1892]: In a more familiar parlance, gay-cats are short-horns, *chechaquos*, new chums, or tenderfeet. A gay-cat is a newcomer on The Road who is man-grown, or, at least, youth-grown. **1910** Livingston *Life* 33 [ref. to 1885]: Chase yourself, you Gay Cat! Go and work for your matches. *Ibid.* 34: A Gay Cat…is a loafing laborer who works maybe a week, gets his wages and vagabonds about, hunting for another "pick and shovel" job. **1914** *Sat. Eve. Post* (Apr. 4) 10: "I ain't no gay-cat that 'ud kick you after makin' friends." *Ibid.* 11: "You old gay-cat, you can't scare me."…A gay-cat is the scum of hoboes….To call a man that is to brand him with the most loathed name a hobo knows. **1916** *Editor* (May 6) 487: Gay-cat. (among tramps a term of contempt) A tramp who degrades himself by working at odd jobs. **1919** *DN*: Hobo Cant…gay-cat…One not to be trusted. **1922** in Partridge *Dict. Und.* 281: Now [gaycat] means a cheap, no-account grafter. **1925** Mullin *Scholar Tramp* 3: I was a gay cat, as the apprentice tramp is universally called on the Road. **1926** in *AS* LVII (1982) 261: Gaycat. Thief who steals only when necessity compels him to raise money. **1926** *AS* I (Dec.) 651: Gay-cat. A tenderfoot in Hobodom. **1933** Ersine *Pris. Slang* 39: Geycat [*sic*]…A pompous person, a *fuzzytail.* *a***1944** in Botkin *Treas. West. Folk.* 572: If you think I'm just a gaycat you're pretty damn dumb. I'm a timber beast from Kokomo. **1944** C.B. Davis *Leo McGuire* 168: "Well thanks, pop," the pimple-faced gaycat said. **1937–50** in *West. Folk.* IX (1950) 117: Gaycat. A newcomer; one who is a fancy dresser. **1952** Sandburg *Strangers* 377 [ref. to *ca*1890]: I

would be a hobo and a "gaycat." I had talked with hoboes enough to know there is the professional tramp who never works and the gaycat who hunts work and hopes to go on and get a job that suits him.
   2. *Und.* a person, typically a boy (often a catamite), who scouts, acts as lookout, or runs errands for a gang of tramps or criminals.
   1902 "J. Flynt" *Little Bro.* 98: I saw him again about a month ago travelin' with a gay-cat from Chi. **1908** Sullivan *Crim. Slang* 11: Gay cat…one who goes ahead to get information. **1918** in Partridge *Dict. Und.* 281: I'd play gay-cat while he dug for glass and junk. **1919** *Amer. Legion Wkly.* (Sept. 12) 8: An old-time gay-cat who had fallen on evil ways. **1921** Casey & Casey *Gay-Cat* 147: This gay-cat spots the fat banks 'n' swell mansions an' draws plans jest how ter rob 'em—*Ibid.* 157: You are a gay-cat for a bunch of circus yeggs yerself, Frisco Red! **1922** Tully *Emmett Lawler* 153: A "gay-cat" is the term used for a day tramp. *ca***1923** Stringer *Diamond Thieves* 86: Marie Deschamps, *alias* Maiden Lane Mary, acting as gay-cat for Parker, unfortunately made her escape! **1932** in *AS* (Feb. 1934) 26: Gay Cat. A boy who acts as runner for a gang. **1933** Ersine *Pris. Slang* 39: Geycat [*sic*]…A homosexual boy. **1936** Duncan *Over the Wall* 75: In the good old days,…our…jobs were always prefaced by a thorough casing of the lay beforehand by our "gay cat."

gaycat *v.* **1.** *Und.* to act as a GAYCAT, 2.
   1918 Stringer *House of Intrigue* 13: He wasn't in need of a gun-moll to gay-cat for him in his established profession of bank-sneak. **1921** Casey & Casey *Gay-Cat* 204: Gay-cattin' fer a bunch o' circus sharpers!
   2. *Black E.* (see 1946 quot.).
   1924 in Handy *Blues Treasury* 144: He ain't gaycattin' round with dicty cats,/Don't go gay cattin' round in buffet flats. **1927** in Leadbitter & Slaven *Blues Records* 323: Gay Catin' [*sic*] Daddy. **1946** Mezzrow & Wolfe *Really Blues* 184: I wasn't working then, and didn't have much money to gaycat with. *Ibid.* 305: Gaycat: have a good time.

gay deceivers *n.pl.* FALSIES.
   1942 in *OEDS*: Her pink sweater…clung properly to the seductive curves of her Gay Deceivers. **1945** T. Williams *Glass Menagerie* 21: They call them "Gay Deceivers." **1968** Swarthout *Loveland* 222 [ref. to *ca*1930's]: No gay deceivers, nothing.

gayola *n.* [GAY, *adj.*, 1.b. + (PAY)OLA] **1.** blackmail, bribes, or extortion paid by a homosexual or by a homosexual establishment.
   1960 *Times* (London) *Literary Supp.* (Nov. 25) 750: The latest San Francisco usage…[is] "gayola," the alleged payment to policemen to protect "gay"—i.e., homosexual—bars. **1966** *Time* (Jan. 21) 41: There is also a constant opportunity for blackmail and for shakedowns by real or phony cops, a practice known as "gayola." **1972** *Sat. Review* (Feb. 12) 23: Homosexual bars, steam baths, restaurants and movie houses…pay "gayola" to crime syndicates and to law enforcement agencies.
   2. a homosexual man.—used derisively.
   1988 *Wkly. World News* (July 5) 23: Mercy knows how many other gayolas are swishing around the plant, too.

gazabe *n.* GAZEBO.
   1899 Kountz *Baxter's Letters* 50: A lot of these handsome gazabes go around looking wise, winning girls out. **1901** Dunne *Dooley's Opinions* 111: A lot iv distinguished gazabs. **1903** Ade *Society* 28: I'm the Gazabe that puts the Shot. **1903** Harriman *Homebuilders* 34: Shut up out there, you gazabes, and git your money ready. **1904** Limerick *Villagers* 33: There was a very glib gazabe who labored under the erroneous impression that what he didn't know…was…unascertainable.

gazabo var. GAZEBO.

gazebo /gəˈzibou/ or /gəˈzeibou/ *n.* [fanciful use of S.E. *gazebo* 'type of pavilion', perh. infl. by Sp *gazapo* 'a shrewd fellow'] **1.** a stupid, loutish, or peculiar person; (*broadly*) a fellow. Also vars., esp. **gazabo.**
   1889 in *DARE*: Gazeebo…Colloquially, it sometimes means a laughing stock.…I think it is Anglo-Irish in its origin. **1893** F.P. Dunne, in Schaaf *Dooley* 54: "What's that?" I says, pointin' out a gazabo with long hair. "That's Gilder.…He's a great pote." **1893** Frye *Staff & Field* 170: Well, he's a dam' chump!…a reg'lar galvanized gazaboo, an' nuttin' else. **1893** in Ade *Chicago Stories* 33: He's an all-round gazabo. **1896** Ade *Artie* 29: Who does I meet comin' out o' the house but a cheap gazabo that was with her the first time I see her. **1899** A.H. Lewis *Sandburrs* 9: An' says this gazeybo for a finish: "This Cleopatra was a wonder for looks." **1899** Cullen *Tales* 130: No less a famous gazebu than William Shakespeare. **1902** Townsend *Fadden & Mr. Paul* 160: I've piped

whole bunches of mugs in me time; wise guys and gillies; fly ducks and gazeaboos. **1907** in H.C. Fisher *A. Mutt* 3: A gazabo who was a stable boy for Jennings. **1910** Roe *Panders* 127: The owner, the head gazaboo, told them that. **1913** J. London *Valley of Moon* 134: She's a wise gazabo. **1921** Marquis *Carter* 195: You can never tell what one of them long gazaboos is going to do. **1923** Ornitz *Haunch, Paunch* 73: Al Wolff, one wise gazabo. **1927** S. Lewis *Elmer Gantry* 19: And I get so sick of that gosh-awful Weekly Bible study—all about these holy old gazebos. **1938** Baldwin & Schrank *Case of Murder* (film): Give me the ugliest and toughest little gazebo you got. **1964** in *DARE*: They're not our sort, Frank, the gazebos who go in for that. **1971** in *DARE*: *Gazabo*...an uncomplimentary term applied to a person. **1984** *All Things Considered* (Nat. Pub. Radio) (May 14): I'm as American as the next /gǝˈzeibou/. **2.** the mouth.
1909 M'Govern *Krag Is Laid Away* 119: It ain't the funeral of no enlisted men like us, with three and four parchments to our record, who ain't supposed to open our gazabos but do just what the officers commands us, whether they know the Regulations or not.

gazee *n.* GAZEBO.
1927 Shay *Pious Friends* 96: Us two was pals, the kid and me;/'Twould cut no ice if some gayzee,/As tough as hell jumped either one,/We'd both light in and hand him some.

gazeeka box *n.* [orig. unkn.] *Burlesque.* a stage prop used in comedy acts which takes the form of a large box from which beautiful girls emerge, supposedly endlessly. Now *hist.*
1941 "G.R. Lee" *G-String* 75: Furniture and props that would be found only in a burlesque theater. A gazeeka box. **1960** Barber *Minsky's* 214: The Fabulous Gazeeka Box! I am willing to part with it because you *are* my friend, and let you have the Fabulous Gazeeka for one hundred dollars cash.

gazelle *n.* a person, esp. a young woman. *Joc.*
1871 Hay *Pike Co. Ballads* 24: So, my gentle gazelles, thar's my answer. **1903** Ade *Society* 84: His Glad Raiment carried him right into Sussiety, and he began to meet Gazelles that suited him, so he figured on the Probable Expense of Keeping House. **1929** McEvoy *Hollywood Girl* 39: One of those little Main Street gazelles. *ca*1940 in Weinberg et al. *Tough Guys* 465: "Dan...!" the gazelle wailed faintly.

gazer *n. Und.* a federal narcotics agent.
1931 *AS* IV (Aug.) 438: *Gazer, n.* A government narcotic agent. **1959** Murtagh & Harris *Who Live in Shadow* 8: He is one man sure to attract all the gazers, all the whiskers and uncles, all the narcotics agents who are on the make today. *Ibid.* 201: *Gazer.* A federal agent in search of narcotics.

gazongas *n.pl.* [orig. unkn.; but cf. BAZONGAS] a woman's breasts. Cf. GARBONZAS
[**1968** Baker et al. *CUSS* 123: *Gajoungas.* The female breasts.] **1978** C. Miller *Animal House* 75: Look at those gazongas! **1979** Univ. Tenn. student: I first heard *gazongas* in 1975. **1983** *Nat. Lampoon* (June) 41: Is this an excuse to print another picture of me with my gazongas hanging out? **1986** Merkin *Zombie Jamboree* 24: Enormous gazongas. **1992** *Daily Beacon* (Univ. Tenn.) (Sept. 4) 4: Seeing the terms "gazongas" and "hooters" in one article was enough.

gazoo¹ *n.* GAZOOK.
1960 Jordan & Marberry *Fool's Gold* 221 [ref. to *ca*1900]: What do you think of that big gazoo?

gazoo² *n.* var. KAZOO, *n.*

gazook *n.* [orig. unkn.] GAZEBO, 1. Also **gazoop.**
1901 Irwin *Sonnets* (unp.): Then I shall strive and be the great main squeeze,/The warm gazook, the only on the bunch,/The Oklahoma wonder, the whole cheese. **1911–12** Ade *Knocking the Neighbors* 177: There lived a blue-eyed Gazook named Steve. **1912** *DN* III 550: *Gazook,* vaguely uncomplimentary epithet, about the same as "gazabo." **1918** *DN* V 24: *Gazook-strap, n.* A leather thong attached to a handle, used to punish rule-breakers in "frat" houses. Washington State College. **1918** in Braynard *Greatest Ship* I 154: That may sound all right to a naval gazoop, but take it from me. **1919** *DN* V 69: *Gazook,* a gawky person. "There comes the old gazook again." New Mexico. **1921** Sandburg *Sunburnt West* 37: If any such noisy gazook stands up and makes himself/heard—put him out—tie a can on him—lock him up. **1928** Levin *Reporter* 133: He is...reciting his experience to a bearded old gazook who was an eyewitness. **1928** McEvoy *Show Girl* 171: Daughter of the big gazook who own the Evening Tab. **1931** Haycox *Whispering Range* 210: Now I wonder what that gazook has done gone and lost himself? **1936** J.T. Farrell *World I Never Made* 153: That's why he ain't got gray in his head like this gazook here. [**1938** T. Wolfe *Web & Rock*

342: "I got frightened and gazooky," she said comically. "What's gazooky?" "You know—the way you feel when you are looking down from a high building."] **1942** *ATS* 396: [Terms of disparagement:]...*gazoop, geek.* **1969** in *DARE*: *A person who tries to appear important*...*Head gazook.*

gazookus *n.* [orig. unkn.; cf. GAZOOK] **1.** thing; in phr. **the real gazookus** the genuine article.
1924 H.L. Wilson *Professor* 109: Do it with real acting so the hicks...will think they're getting the real gazukus.
2. GAZOOK. Also **gazoopus.**
1924 *Our Navy* (Dec. 15) 30: What are you two gazzookuses doing here? **1932** in Sagendorf *Popeye* 128: I'm one tough Gazookus/Which hates all Palookas. **1932** Nicholson & Robinson *Sailor Beware!* 66: The boys want you to ditch gazoopus, here, and come on over.
3. the vagina.—usu. considered vulgar.
1976 Selby *Demon* 43: Right up the old gazoo, the moist and hungry gazookus.

gazooney *n.* [alter. Hiberno-E *gossoon,* Ir *garsuin* 'boy, lad' + *-ey* (dim. suff.)] **1.** a boy or lad; an inexperienced youth; (*hence*) a foolish, ignorant, or eccentric fellow; GAZEBO.
1914 Jackson & Hellyer *Vocab.* 37: *Gazuny,* Noun. Current in ultra slang circles. A man. **1918** Stringer *House of Intrigue* 213: All you gasoonies think just because I'm a woman I haven't the nerve to put a half ounce of lead through your ribs! **1933** Ersine *Pris. Slang* 39: *Gazooney, n.* A lad. "Send the gazooney after a couple of pints." **1937** *Our Army* (May) 10: I have never in all my time run into a screwier gazooney than this James Grover. **1940** *AS* (Dec.) 451: *Gazooney.* An ignoramus. **1943** in Dickson *Baseball Dict.* 177: "Gazoonies" is probably the most modern nickname for..."rookies." **1948** J. Stevens *Jim Turner* 120 [ref. to *ca*1910]: By God, let the gazoony play....His money is as good as anybody's to me. **1964** Tamony *Americanisms* (No. 3) 4: Older bums imposed rites of passage on embryos, punks and gazoonies. **1986** R. Campbell *In La-La Land* 20: Oh, for Christ's sake,...this gazoony was going to talk like the character in the show. **1987** A. Parker *Angel Heart* (film): Don't be a gazoony, fellow.
2. (among tramps and convicts) a catamite.
1918 in *AS* (Oct. 1933) 27: *Gazooney.* Catamite. **1927** *AS* (June) 387: The man is called a *wolf* or a *jocker;* the boy has many names,—*punk, gazooney, guntzel,* and *bronc.* Punk, guntzel and gazooney are also used to refer to any sort of green lad. **1935** Pollock *Und. Speaks: Gazooney,* youthful male companion of a sexual pervert. **1970** L.D. Johnson *Devil's Front Porch* 115: This type [of homosexual] is commonly called "punk," "brat," "gazooney," "singer," and "dancer."

gazoop var. GAZOOK.

gazoopus var. GAZOOKUS, 2.

gazump *n.* [orig. unkn.; cf. GAZUMPH, *v.*] a dolt.
1919 Sandburg *Smoke & Steel* 45: Fix it, you gazump, you slant-head, fix it. **1925** in Spectorsky *College Years* 254: Helen Gazump....Her chum.

gazumph *v.* [orig. unkn.; cf. David L. Gold, "On the Supposed Yiddish Origin of the English Verb *gazump,*" *Jewish Linguistic Studies* I, 1989, pp. 26–34] to swindle, esp. by unfairly raising the price of an item, now usu. a house or automobile. Also vars. *Rare* in U.S.
*****1928** in *OEDS*: "Gazoomphing the sarker" is a method of parting a rich man from his money. An article is auctioned over and over again, and the money bid each time is added to it....I "gazoomphed" a friend of mine with complete success last night. *****1934** in *OEDS*: "Gezumph"...means to cheat or overcharge....*Gezumpher,* a swindler. **1936** *AS* XI 374: *Gazoomph, gazoomphing.* *****1961** in *OEDS*: M.P.s had admitted that they had been "gazoomphed" by fast-talking racketeers. *****1971** in *OEDS*. **1972** *Business Week* (May 27) 70: The best way to avoid getting "gazumped" is to stick with big, reputable homebuilders. **1979** Homer *Jargon* 23: *Gazumphing*...boosting the price of an item (often a house) after the deal has already been made.

G.B. *n.* [grand B(OUNCE)] a usu. forcible ejection or expulsion; dismissal.—constr. with *the.*
1880 in *OEDS*: Well, I've got the g.b....I've been fired! **1885** Siringo *Texas Cowboy* 52: Mr. Wiley got the G. B. at once. **1900** *DN* II 38: To get the *G.B.,* i.e. grand bounce, "to be expelled." **1911** Roe *Prodigal Daughter* 63: The fracas most always ends in the woman getting the "G.B." out of the house. **1914** *Amer. Lumberman* (Apr. 25) 33: He come to camp expectin' he/Would get from Bunyan the G.B. **1919** Darling *Jargon Book* 14: *G.B.*—Grand bounce.

G.B.F. *interj.* (see quot.). Cf. TGIF.

1917 *DN* IV 357: *G.b.F.* God bless Friday: among teachers.

G.D. *n.* GODDAMN, *n.*

1920 in Cummings *Letters* 71: We didn't give a good g.d. what they gave us to do. **1989** *CBS This Morning* (CBS-TV) (Nov. 30): Because we have a President who doesn't give a G.D. about AIDS.

G.D. *adj. & adv.* GODDAMNED, *adj. & adv.* Also **G.d., g.d.**

1846 in *Utah Hist. Qly.* V (1932) 50: I will shoot that G.d. mule. **1863** in A. Cook *Armies of Streets* 95: Piper then said he had been drafted and that all the G.D. drafted men would have to turn out and resist the draft. **1864** in Bensill *Yambill* 148: He informed the Detail…"not to pull a G—d oar." *ca***1865** O.W. Holmes, Jr., in M.D. Howe *Shaping Yrs.* 106: Well Harry I'm dying but I'll be G.d'd if I know where I'm going. **1904** Miles *Breeze* 60: It's only three animals in this world what works./That's horses, mules, and G.D. fools. **1917** *DN* IV 357: *G.d.* God damn. **1918** in Cummings *Letters* 54: When a man comes to Fort Jay, the first thing they do is give him a g.d. fine beating. **1935** F.H. Lea *Anchor Man* 138: Look where you're going, you g.d. fool! **1951** Longstreet *Pedlocks* 85: The biggest g.d. engine in the West comin'. **1963** Uhnak *Policewoman* 108: I want the whole g.d. mess drawn up again. **1967** P. Roth *When She Was Good* 49: He had caught up on all the rest he had lost on the g.d. bed. **1970** Gattzden *Black Vendetta* 54: You're a G.D. liar. **1972** Madden *Bros.* 94: Shut your g.d. mouth.

G.D.F. *n.* (see quot.). Cf. D.F.

1917 *DN* IV 357: *D.f.* Damn(ed) fool. Also *G. (God) d.f.*

G.D.I. *n.* [*goddamned independent*] *Stu.* a student who is not a member of a Greek-letter fraternity or sorority.

*a***1961** Boroff *Campus U.S.A.* 24: The GDI…Goddamned Independents…provide the soldiery of dissent on campus. **1961** Terry *Old Liberty* 8: The GDIs…lived in the middle floors between. **1964** *AS* (May) 119: *G.D.I.*, or "God-damned independent," a term used by the "Goddamned independents" themselves. **1980** *Daily Beacon* (Univ. Tenn.) (Dec. 2) 2: If you were an avowed GDI, greeks were snotty, hypocritical, dishonest. **1983** Univ. Tenn. freshman theme: The G.D.I.'s—kids not in the Greek system. **1990** in *Texas Mo.* (Jan. 1991) 163: GDIs ("goddam independents," or non-sorority women).

gear *n.* **1.** Now *Naut.* stuff. [Orig. S.E.; cf. the various senses (from *ca*1200) in the *OED*.]

*****1415** in *OED*: Our fadres medled no thyng of swich gear. *****1489** W. Caxton, in *OED*: A drinke myxte with suche manere of gere that aftre they had taken hyt they were alle dronken. ***ca*1529** J. Skelton, in *OED*: For drede ye darre not medyll with such gere. *****1608** in Wardroper *Love & Drollery* 162: Tobacco…Never was Better gear Than is here. *****1665** R. Head *Eng. Rogue* 36: Double-brewed beer was sold, notable humming gear. *****1700** J. Dryden, in *OED*: For priests with prayer and other godly gear,/Have made the merry goblins disappear. *****1821–26** Stewart *Man-of-War's-Man* I 171: Don't stand preaching there…we've had plenty of that there gear already. **1900** Cullen *Tales* 392: It's the same old gear. **1902** Cullen *More Tales* 23: And all this gear stacked up around here is now for sale? *****1925** in Fraser & Gibbons *Soldier & Sailor Wds.* 103 [ref. to WWI]: *Gear:*…Also used as a colloquial term for anything giving satisfaction—*e.g.*, "That's it, that's the gear!" **1942** *Leatherneck* (Nov.) 145: *Gear*—Stuff. *****1954** in E.L. Abel *Mar. Dict.* 43: [Marijuana] may [be called]…"dope," or "kif," or "charge," or "gear," or "tea." **1967** W. Crawford *Gresham's War* 129: This is good gear [food].

2.a. Now esp. *Naut.* the male or (*obs.*) female genitals. Orig. S.E.

*****1598** J. Florio, in *F & H* III 127: A woman's geere or cunnie. *****1611** in *OED*: *Chaud-colle*, saltnesse, leacherousnesse, geere[-]itch. ***ca*1650** in Wardroper *Love & Drollery* 186: If any of you chance to fear/That I am too young, pray look you here./Few maids can show you so much —. *****1672** *Covent Garden Drollery* 83: Such geer I think thou ne're did see. *****1675** in *OED*: To the dogs to eat they threw his gear. *****1698–1720** in D'Urfey *Pills* IV 61: The Brewer…takes his Maid by the Geer. ***ca*1790** in Farmer *Merry Songs* V 222: Gird hame your gear, gudeman. *Ibid.* 223: Ye [were] weel girt in my gear. **1930** *AS* V (June) 393: *String of gear*, n. phr. Sexual equipment. *ca***1972** B. Rodgers *Queens' Vernacular* 152: The genitals…*business,*…*gear* ("He lost half of his gear in the first world war"). **1978** Hasford *Short-Timers* 10: You queer for Private Cowboy's gear?

b. *Naut. & Pris.* a person or persons regarded as objects of sexual, often homosexual, gratification. Cf. GEARED, *adj.*

1933 Ersine *Pris. Slang* 39: *Gear, adj.* [*sic*] Homosexual. **1951** Thacher *Captain* 52 [ref. to WWII]: He was short,…almost plump (behind his

back the crew called him "tender gear"). **1951** W. Williams *Enemy* 130 [ref. to WWII]: I been shacked with too many women that had husbands gone. When I get married I want to keep my eye on the gear. **1953** *S.F. News* (Oct. 14) 23: "Wonder gear"…is an attractive girl, in Navy lingo. **1962** Maurer & Vogel *Narc. & Narc. Add.* (ed. 2) 302: *Gear.* A sexually perverted person, usu. a male. **1962** McKenna *Sand Pebbles* 301: I bet some of them young [women] are real tender gear. **1967** W. Crawford *Gresham's War* 17: "She's something." James licked his lips, spaced teeth showing. "Like dreams. Strictly officer's gear." *ca***1972** B. Rodgers *Queens' Vernacular* 17: *Ace gear* (mid '60s) sexually talented homosexual. **1977** Langone *Life at Bottom* 201: All them nice tender gear that'd never been here before.

3. an important or influential person; WHEEL.

1955 *AS* XXX (May) 120: *Wheel; brass; gear, n.* Important person. **1967** Mailer *Vietnam* 12: Dallas matrons complain about the sexual habits of their husbands, all ex hot rodders, hunters, cattlemen, oil riggers, corporation gears and insurance finks, zap!

¶ In phrases:

¶ **get in[to] gear** to get going; get busy.—usu. (*vulgar*) **get (one's) ass in gear.** Also vars.

1914 Patten *Lefty o' the Bush* 40: He's just a bit shaky to start with, but he'll git into gear soon. **1929** Jimmy Rodgers "High-Powered Mama," on *Train Whistle Blues* (RCA Victor LPM-1640 A) (sound rec.): High-powered mama, get yourself in gear. **1947** Mailer *Naked & Dead* 240: [ref. to WWII]: Corps…told Cummings to get his ass in gear. **1951** Mailer *Barbary Shore* 118: Oh, Lordie, I'll never get in gear. **1952** Uris *Battle Cry* 44 [ref. to WWII]: Hey, you guys, how about getting your ass in gear? We got to shave too. **1961** H. Ellison *Memos* 140: Right now I should get my can in gear. **1964** Howe *Valley of Fire* 71: So shove off, get in high gear. **1966** King *Brave & Damned* 40: Domingo, Konrad, get your asses in high gear. **1966** Garfield *Last Bridge* 43: Then God damn it, quit jaw-assing over this telephone and get your balls in gear. **1969** L. Gardner *Fat City* 73: Shape up and get your ass in gear or you can spend all day in the bus. **1970** C. Harrison *No Score* 109: Before he could get his mouth in gear. **1971** Meggyesy *Out of Their League* 13: Yes, you.…Get your ass in gear if you want to make this football team! **1971** *Batman* (Aug.) 4: *Will* you get it in gear? This joint gives me the creepy-crawlies! **1973** Hirschfeld *Victors* 15: Put it in gear, Garfinkel, I ain't got all day! **1975** V.B. Miller *Deadly Game* 15: Then get your butts in gear and start making this city safe for all the nice people. **1977** Schrader *Blue Collar* 15: Well, get your rear in gear! **1980** *U.S. News & W.R.* (Jan. 14) 60: Nurses have got to be in gear every single minute.

¶ **pack the gear** *USMC.* to have the necessary ability or authority; to meet standards or requirements.

1957 Barrett *D.I.* (film): You just don't pack the gear. **1958** Frankel *Band of Bros.* 25 [ref. to 1950]: You pack the gear. You're the captain. **1971** Flanagan *Maggot* 40: It was obvious the boy was not a marine, that he simply didn't pack the gear. **1974** former L/Cpl., USMC, age 26: At Parris Island [in 1967] the DI's used to say, "You don't pack the gear, boy!" **1978** Hasford *Short-Timers* 5: My orders are to weed out all non-hackers who do not pack the gear so I can serve in my beloved Corps.

¶ **slip (one's) gears** to lose (one's) sanity.

1963–64 Kesey *Great Notion* 228: My dear old daddy is slippin' his gears. **1972** N.Y.U. student: I thought he'd finally slipped his gears.

gear *adj.* [sugg. by GEAR, *n.*, 1, in phr. *the gear*] *Stu.* stylish; attractive; wonderful. [Chiefly Brit. teenagers' slang, introduced into U.S. by the public relations campaign surrounding the first U.S. tour of The Beatles (1964); by 1966, rarely heard.]

*****1951** in *OEDS*: If a guy is "gear," as they call a smart boy, he will dress in a single-breasted…drape jacket. *****1963** in *OEDS*: They're gear! The Beatles leave for London after a triumphant tour of Sweden! **1964** *N.Y. Times* (Nov. 1) B 100: For what 17's like, their current vocabulary includes "fabulous," as well as "gear" and "tuff." **1965** *N.Y. Times* (Dec. 27) 20: Daddy-O…had no sooner added "gear" and "Sam" to his vernacular when he discovered that "wig" and "boss" have [also] come to mean…"great." **1967** W. Murray *Sweet Ride* 75: Choo Choo, you're boss! Fab! Gear! Bitchin'! **1969** Ricks & Marsh *Patterns in English* 48: The current slang expressions of today's teenagers, *gross, tough, gear,* and *put-on,* for example, are hardly comprehended by the older generation (those twenty-five or over) who remember *neat* and *square* with nostalgia! **1974** *Nat. Lampoon* (Dec.) 54: Like these "gear" love beads.

gear-bonger *n. Trucking.* (see quot.).

1971 Tak *Truck Talk* 70: *Gear bonger:* a trucker who heedlessly grinds gears while shifting.

gear-dropper *n. Av.* an airplane copilot.

1957 E. Brown *Locust Fire* 25 [ref. to 1944]: "You the pilot?" the captain asked him "No, the gear-dropper."

geared *adj.* **1.** *Pris.* homosexual.—also constr. with *up.* Cf. GEAR, *n.,* 2.b.

1935 Pollock *Und. Speaks: Geared,* sexually perverted. **1962** in J. Blake *Joint* 316: A very lewd shrewd dude, geared, that I had known in Raiford. **1963** Gann *Good & Evil* 27: There would be a...gay party when he came out and every single person there would be geared. **1966** Elli *Riot* 228: You'll never get another chance to see a buncha geared-up freaks like that in action. **1967** Kolb *Getting Straight* 3: He's so goddam queer he scares other fairies. No kidding, there was a cat in my class so geared I wouldn't sit near him, but after he listened to Willhunt for a while he started dating girls. **1970** L.D. Johnson *Devil's Front Porch* 115 [ref. to 1940's]: These stories gain momentum, and before long it is a foregone conclusion that so-and-so is "geared," and this sticks to the innocent man. **1976** G. Kirkham *Signal Zero* 163: He's geared....You know—a fruit, a fag.

2. intoxicated.—constr. with *up.*

1939 Howsley *Argot* 20: *Geared Up*—Drunk. **1965–71** in *Qly. Jour. Studies on Alcohol* XXXII (1971) 733: Moderately intoxicated...*half-geared-up.*

3. very excited; eager.—usu. constr. with *up.*

1944 *Life* (July) 71: I'm all geared up ahead of everyone else around me, I'm looking for a slowdown. *ca***1986** in *NDAS:* A sexy rock star, and he got the audience so geared. **1990** *Teenage Mutant Ninja Turtles* (CBS-TV): I haven't been feeling too geared up lately.

gearhead *n. Stu.* a student majoring in engineering or a related subject; *(also)* an engineer or a person skilled in mechanics.

1974 Hendrix College student: A *gearhead* is an engineer. **1974** Univ. Tenn. student: A *gearhead* is a computer man or an engineer or a mathematician. They're also called *slide rules.* **1987** Univ. Tenn. student theme: A word for engineering students...is *gearhead.* **1990** *Newsweek* (May 7) 8: *Gearheads:* Engineers who maintain equipment. When things break you call a gearhead. **1986–91** Hamper *Rivethead* 140: Do any of these gearheads look like readers of leftist literature? **1992** O. Kelly *Brave Men* 242: In each boat, he had a "gearhead," who could keep the engine running no matter what.

gearie *n.* GEAR-JAMMER, 1.

1976 *Nat. Lampoon* (July) 56: How 'bout those weary gearies?...Can ya copy?

gear-jammer *n.* **1.** *Trucking.* a driver of trucks or other large motor vehicles.

1929 in *AS* (Oct. 1931) 22: *Gearjammer*—bus driver. **1936** in *AS* (Feb. 1937) 75: *Gear jammer*—truck driver. **1938** *AS* (Dec.) 307: *Gearjammer.* Any driver, regardless of skill. **1971** Tak *Truck Talk* 71: *Gear jammer:* 1. a driver who usually clashes gears....2. generally speaking, any truck driver. **1976** *N.Y. Post* (June 19) 27: The "gear jammers" have been reborn as existential folk heroes. **1978** Wheeler & Kerby *Steel Cowboy* (film): I believe I know these gear-jammers. **1993** CBS *This Morning* (CBS-TV) (Apr. 23): Did you crash any trucks, gear-jammer?

2. *Petroleum Industry.* (see quot.).

1972 Haslam *Oil Fields* 103: *Gear-Jammer, n.* A driller who is not smooth in his driving of the rig. Also, a rotary driller (called this by cable-tool workers).

gear job *n.* [sugg. by GEAR, *n.,* 2.b.] *Pris.* a homosexual.

1971 Hilaire *Thanatos* 174: He's been acting like he was a gear job since his diapers came off.

gear jockey *n. Trucking.* GEAR-JAMMER, 1.

1977 Corder *Citizens Band* 17: I got a gear jockey stuck on Seventy-three and I can't raise him.

gedunk *n.* [orig. unkn.; perh. related to *dunk,* in allusion to the ice cream being put into a soda] Esp. *Navy.* **1.** ice cream or an ice-cream soda; candy or sweets; *(broadly)* a snack. Also **gedonk, geedunk.**

1927 in Galewitz *Great Comics* 53: The remains of seven gedunk sundaes. **1931** *Leatherneck* (Oct.) 20: Smith, what is the meaning of gedunk? **1942** Casey *Torpedo Junction* 10: *Gee-Dunk.* A double scoop of ice cream. **1944** Kendall *Service Slang* 23: *Gedunk*....Ice cream sodas, etc. **1944** Olds *Helldiver Squadron* 8: A gedunk was a one-man portion of what the carrier's ice-cream-making machine turned out daily. Every afternoon and evening Bob was near when the gedunk stand opened. **1944** in Rea *Wings of Gold* 124: Mis-

cellaneous pogey bait and geedunks. **1956** Wier & Hickey *Naval Social Customs* 102: *Gedunk.* Candy, ice cream, soda, etc. Also, anyplace where these are sold. **1964** Hunt *Ship With Flat Tire* 69: Is this the only kind of geedunk you can find to stock, Mr. Westbridge? **1967** Dibner *Admiral* 71: "How about the gedunk, Cap'n?" "Tell 'em to try Schrafft's." **1969** Bosworth *Love Affair with Navy* 59: In some ways it saddens me to report that Navy hammocks are no more, and that bunks have been installed in warships along with such things as "gedunk bars," or soda fountains. **1974** Former L/Cpl., 5th Mar. Div., age *ca*27: *Gedunk* or *pogie bait* was candy, ice-cream. **1982** T.C. Mason *Battleship* 166 [ref. to WWII]: My offer of a gedunk was also rejected with barely disguised horror. "Tea?" he asked.

2. *Navy & USMC.* a place where gedunk is sold; *(hence)* a restaurant, esp. on shipboard.

1956 (quot. at (1), above). **1962** Mandel *Mainside* 11: Gedunk—that was what one called an ice-cream stand aboard ship. **1970** Ponicsan *Last Detail* 167: Maybe they have a gedonk there where he can get some candy, I don't know. **1972** Ponicsan *Cinderella Liberty* 6: The crew has an hour...to...pick up a supply of skin books and cellophane-wrapped sandwiches at the little gedonk at the end of the pier. **1974** Stone *Dog Soldiers* 49: The United Seaman's Service geedunk took up one wing of the old Legion barracks. Converse located the bar...and bought a gin and tonic with...his military scrip. **1980** in Safire *Good Word* 215 [ref. to USMC, 1962]: *Gedunk* (store, or canteen, where you can buy pogy bait). **1987** D. Sherman *Main Force* 84: Then he took him to a geedunk, where the big sergeant stuffed himself on the first American hamburgers and french fries he had seen in months.

gedunk sailor *n. Navy.* a soft, inexperienced sailor.—used derisively.

1982 T.C. Mason *Battleship* 70 [ref. to 1941]: "Goddam gedunk sailor!" they sneered, turning to their joe pots.

Gee *n.* var. GUEE.

gee[1] /dʒi/ *n.* see G.

gee[2] /gi/ *n.* [perh. imit. of F *Guy* (male given name) in place of *guy;* perh. infl. by GEEZER] man; guy. Also **ghee.**

1907 *McClure's Mag.* (Feb.) 380: Here's a gee hungerin' to slip us two bucks a day and all found, and you hams standing around with wrinkles in your bellies sidestepping like a bunch of mules in the road. **1915** Howard *God's Man* 143: The big gees who're running the game ud soon get sore. **1921** J. Conway, in *Variety* (Mar. 4) 9: She reminds me of a wise crackin' gee I met last week. **1921** Casey & Casey *Gay-Cat* 103: I wanted to git to thet big gee fer mebbe a thousand more. **1922** in Hemingway *Sel. Letters* 64: Show the Ghee the screed. **1927–28** Tasker *Grimhaven* 11: You ought to see what *some* of these gees are doing. **1929–30** J.T. Farrell *Young Lonigan* 39: Nobody is gettin' away with anything on this gee. **1932** *AS* VII 332: Gee (hard "g")—a fellow. **1933–35** D. Lamson *About to Die* 104: It was easy to imagine him working over a gee with a piece of rubber hose—or being the gee worked over. **1939** *Hell's Kitchen* (film): Mr. Crispy, you're an O.K. ghee. **1940** Baldwin *Brother Orchid* (film): You're a funny ghee. **1941** "G. R. Lee" *G-string* 18: Did you see the old Gee that sends me the perfume? **1946** in Clarke *Amer. Negro Stories* 140: He may be awright to you, but I heard about that ghee—plenty. **1947–48** J.H. Burns *Lucifer* 72: But these gees were heckling one another and passing girls in bandannas and bobbysocks. **1951** Mannix *Sword-Swallower* 54: After you swallow a few torches, some gee is bound to yell out that it isn't real fire. **1956** in Algren *Lonesome Monsters* 196: In fact, this ghee could scarcely remember one day to the next where he'd lain the night before. **1973** Schiano & Burton *Solo* 42: Show the Ghee. The Big Gees, the big gangsters,...never lifted a finger in honest work. **1981** Graziano & Corsel *Somebody Down Here* 25: All kind of ghees come up to me an wanna be my manager. **1988** H. Gould *Double Bang* 85: He's the main gee in the garment center.

gee[3] /gi/ *n.* [see 1981 quot.] *Narc.* gum opium as prepared for smoking; *(broadly)* narcotic drugs.

1936 Dai *Opium Addiction* 199: *Gee.* Drugs in general. Also called *stuff, junk, gow, hocus,* or *smeck.* **1938** *AS* XIII 184: *Gee*...smoking opium, especially refined or reworked opium....*Gee-stick.* An opium pipe. **1981** D.W. Maurer *Lang. Und.* 10: *Gee* /gi/ [gum opium] is probably [better] spelled *ghee* since it seems to be derived from the Hindustani *ghee* (dark-colored butter).

gee /dʒi/ *v.* [fr. *gee!,* a command to make a horse turn right or go faster] to suit, go, work, etc.; *(hence)* to behave as desired; get along well.

*****1698–99** "B.E." *Dict. Canting Crew: It won't Gee,* it won't hit, or go.

*1719 in *OED:* If Miss prove peevish, and will not gee. ***1785** Grose *Vulgar Tongue:* It won't gee, it…does not suit or fit. ***1803** in *OED:* They do not Ge well together. ***1850** in *OED:* "It don't seem to gee!" said Isaac, as he was trying to adjust the stove. **1889** *Century* (Dec.) 225: Me and the president didn't gee. He hadn't no fault to find with me; but I didn't like his ways, and I quit. **1914** Atherton *Perch* 207: But don't put weird ideas into my head, Ora. They don't gee with Butte. **1922** *Sat. Eve. Post* (July 29) 76: They just don't gee. They been battling around for a month. **1938** in Rawick *Amer. Slave* III (Pt. 4) 211: But some women…the devil gets in 'em. Get so they won't "Gee" nor "Haw."

gee /dʒi/ *interj.* [short for *Jesus, Jerusalem, Jehoshaphat*] (used to express surprise, disappointment, vexation, enthusiasm, or simple emphasis).—also in extended vars.

[**1851** M. Reid *Scalp-Hunters* 176: Gee-zus! ef thur ain't that d—t—n [i.e. damnation] dog!] **1895** *DN* I 376: Gee buck! See all them bees drownded in the honey! **1895** Townsend *Fadden* 13: Holy gee! it hits some mug plunk on 'is nut. **1905** *DN* III 61: *Gee,* or *gee holliken, whilliken, whizz, buzz, interj.* Exclamations of surprise, etc. **1915** C.P. Gilman *Herland* 14: Gee! Look, boys! **1918** *N.Y. Age* (Mar. 30) 1: Gee, they look fine. **1926** Watters & Hopkins *Burlesque* 9: Gee, I forgot me monocle. **1955** NYC schoolboy: Gee, that's funny. **1961** *AS* XXXVI (Feb.) 40: *Holy God* is softened into *holy gee* [in Canada]. **1978** S. King *Stand* 263: Holy gee, mister! **1982** Trudeau *Dressed for Failure* (unp.): Wow…Gee…What a breakthrough.

geech *n.* [alter. GEETS] money.

1967 Lit *Dictionary* 17: *Geech*—Money, gelt.

Geechee *n.* [Gullah dial., perh. fr. *Ogeechee* River, Ga.; see Holm & Shilling, *Dict. of Bahamian Eng.*] **1.a.** *So.,* Esp. *Ga. & S.C.* a Gullah-speaking black person; *(hence)* a black speaker of any unfamiliar or hard-to-understand dialect of English; *(also)* (used contemptuously) a poor, uneducated black person of the rural South.

1905 in D.J. Waters *Strange Ways* 360: The Negroes inhabiting the tide-water section of Georgia and South Carolina are so peculiar in their dialect, customs, and beliefs that the term Geechee, which means a rough, ignorant, and uncouth person, is applied to them. **1917** *DN* IV 345: *Geechee, n.* A negro from the Islands, as from the Bahamas. **1919** *Jour. Amer. Folk.* XXXII 378: Among the Geechee of the Florida Keys. **1940** E. Caldwell, in *OEDS:* He sounds like one of those Geechee niggers.…That breed'll do anything to keep them from working. **1945** M.K. Rawlings, in *New Yorker* (Sept. 8) 20: (Creecy was a Geechee,…blacker than the soot in the fireplace. **1946** Mezzrow & Wolfe *Really Blues* 305: *Geechee:* Southerner from Georgia. **1950** *PADS* XIV (Nov.) 31: *Geechee, geechy…n.* A low country [South Carolina] term for a Negro. **1954** Himes *Third Generation* 103: He was of a curious racial mixture of Negro, Indian and Spanish, whom the people in that section called "geechies," and spoke a patois of these native tongues combined with English. **1954–60** *DAS: Geechee…*A Southern American Negro.…Used derisively.…Most often used in eastern Ala., Ga., and the Carolinas. **1962** Maurer & Vogel *Narc. & Narc. Add.* (ed. 2) (glossary): *Gee-chee.* A Negro from the Sea Islands. **1971** B.B. Johnson *Blues for Sister* 28: In Geetchie country they have big feeds after. **1967–80** Folb *Runnin' Lines* 239: *Geechie, geech…*Black person who speaks in the Gullah dialect.…Any black person whose speech is peculiar or unintelligible to the hearer. ca**1982** Holm & Shilling *Dict. Bahamian Eng.* 86: *Geechee…*A rustic Black American from the South: *A Geechee is what you could call a Merican who's work field.* (Nassau). **1984** C. Fuller *Soldier's Story* (film): Come on, Geechee! ca**1986** in *NDAS:* Obsessed with hatred for the "geechees," those he feels are holding back the race.

b. *S.C.* (see 1951 quot.).

1951 *AS* XXVI (Feb.) 14: *Geechee* is commonly used, with mildly insulting connotations, by up-country South Carolinians as a nickname for any low-countryman, especially one from the Charleston area. **1959** A. Anderson *Lover Man* 83: Everybody calls me Geechie.…I'm from…Rock Hill, South Carolina. **1974** Clemson Univ. student: Folks from Charleston are called Geechees.

2. *Naut. & Mil.* any dark-skinned foreign national.

1940 *Life* (Oct. 28) 99: Native girls [are referred to] as *Geechies* (from Geishas). **1952** Landon *Angle of Attack* 14 [ref. to WWII]: The geechees (Italians) are comin' with the stone tomorrow. *Ibid.* 26: He was probably shacked up with some geechee pig all last night.

Geechville *n.* [GEECHEE, *n.,* 1.b. + *-ville*] *Naut.* Charleston, S.C.

1964 Hunt *Ship with a Flat Tire* 74: Westbury…shifted into civvies and went over to give Saturday night in Geechville a try.

geed-up *adj.* [orig. unkn.] **1.** incapacitated; crippled; *(hence)* worn-out or old; broken down; in disorder.

[**1903** *Enquirer* (Cincinnati) (May 9) 13: Gee—Spoil.] **1920** Murphy *Gray Walls* 21: He is all geayed up.…crippled. **1927** *AS* (June) 390: Say, mister! Ye ain't got a rusty old geed-up dime ye c'n let a feller have? *Ibid.* 391: A cripple is said to be *geed up.* **1936** *AS* (Apr.) 121: *Geed up.* Down and out. Applied to…an addict who has gone boots-and-shoes. **1962** Maurer & Vogel *Narc. & Narc. Add.* (ed. 2) (glossary): That was a geed up joint. **1966** Adams *West. Wds.* 125: *Geed-up*—A cowman's term for lame or out of commission.

2. *(rare)* keyed up; excited; *(also)* heavily intoxicated by drugs or alcohol; *(also)* *(rare)* angry.

1921–26 Sentee *Men* 118: Last night's sign…still keeps me geed up some. **1936** Dai *Opium Add.* 199: Full of drugs…high,…geed up, loaded, polluted. **1939** in *OEDS:* She fell from the doorway…on account of being so geed up. **1944** *AS* (Apr.) 104: Gassed up, gas-hound, gheed-up, rumdum…are cognate and self-explanatory. **1942–49** Goldin et al. *DAUL* 77: *Geed-up.* Intoxicated; under the influence of drugs; (rare) angry. **1972** Pearce *Pier Head Jump* 11: But after layin' around in there for most of the afternoon, I'm gettin' pretty well geed up.

gee-gaw *n.* GEE-GEE[1].

1928 O'Connor *B'way Racketeers* 84: Folks…followed the gee-gaws for a thrill. **1930** Lait *On the Spot* 203: Gee-gaws…Race horses (Var.: Bangtails).

gee-gee[1] *n.* [redup. of *gee!*, a command to a horse; orig. a nursery word] a horse.

*1869 in *OED:* The "great Gee-Gee"—as all the small ones entitled me. ***1886** in *OED:* To carry two heavy boys…on his back, pretending that he was a gee-gee. ***1889** in *F & H* III 127: He knows as much about gee-gees as a professional trainer. **1902** Wister *Virginian* 208: There's a great market for harmless horses. Gee-gees, the children call them. **1908** McGaffey *Show Girl* 223: The gee-gee I intended betting on didn't even start. **1911–12** Ade *Knocking Neighbors* 52: To…save the Expense of keeping a Gee-Gee he purchased a…Runabout. **1918** McNutt *Yanks* 165: I watched one poor gee-gee get cut apart and sewed together again for appendicitis. **1936** Gaddis *Courtesan* 23: Only a fool bets on the favorite—and barely breaks even if the gee-gee romps home ahead.

gee-gee[2] *n.* [orig. unkn.] the rectum; *(also)* the vagina.

1954–60 *DAS: Gee-gee…*The vagina.…The rectum. **1974** *Nat. Lampoon* (Nov.) 20: They were supposed to graduate last June but they copied each other's papers for Rem Eng and took a royal doucheroonie up the gee-gee.

geek *n.* [dial. E var. of obs. *geck* 'a fool'; see *OED*] **1.a.** a doltish, clumsy, peculiar, or offensive person. [Spelling in *1611 quot. is most likely an error for *gecke,* obs. form of *geck* (as in *Twelfth Night* V i).]

[***1611** Shakespeare *Cymbeline* V iv: To become the geeke and scorne o' th' others vilany.] ***1876** in *OED:* Gawk, Geek, Gowk, or Gowky, a fool; a person uncultivated; a dupe. **1908** in H.C. Fisher *A. Mutt* 62: A geek who spends his spare time making Czar-removers was slammed into the city cooler. *Ibid.* 73: That kid of mine is certainly a handsome-looking geek. **1911** A.H. Lewis *Apaches of N.Y.* 23: "What was that shooting?" "Oh, a couple of geeks started to hand it to each other." **1911** *DN* III 544: *Geke, n.* Awkward fellow, guy. "Isn't that fellow a queer, crazy geke?" **1915** *DN* IV 199: *Geek, geke,* person lacking animation. "That *geek* won't jump at all. Just backs off!" **1921** Benét *Beginning of Wisdom* 297: The geeks on the other side'll be just as scared. **1929** Milburn *Hobo's Hornbook* 259: At last he looked up and he says to us geeks,/"I think it's time dat youse mugs beat yer sneaks." **1953** W. Brown *Monkey on My Back* 111: Harlem roofs are infested by derelicts, drug addicts, geeks, fags, and muggers. **1957** in Rosset *Evergreen Reader* 51: I tried to convey to the geek back of the counter what I wanted. **1965** Cleaver *Soul on Ice* 30: The "frustration" of fat-assed American geeks safe at home worrying whether to have bacon, ham or sausage with their grade-A eggs in the morning. **1969** *Playboy* (Mar.) 218: All these geeks live around here…on their estates. **1972** R. Barrett *Lovomaniacs* 14: Who's that geek? **1977** Filosa *Surf. Almanac* 186: *Geek…*A beginner who is always in the way of experienced surfers. **1977** M. Franklin *Last of the Cowboys* 181: Why don't you go back to Jupiter, you geek? Get off my case. **1979** Frommer *Sports Lingo* 193: Geek. An unskilled or clumsy skateboarder. **1979** *S.F. Examiner & Chronicle* (Apr. 1) 12: *Geek, n.* A repulsive person.…*dildo, nerd, freak.* **1983** Breathed

Bloom Co. 121: You insensitive geek!

b. *Specif.* (*Stu.*) an unsociable or overdiligent student.

1967–80 Folb *Runnin' Lines* 239: Geek…Studious person. **1984** Algeo *Stud Buds* 3: A studious classmate…geek. **1987** *Campus Voice* (Winter) 10: Once a math-team geek at the University of Washington, Seal is postponing his schooling to become an MTV veejay.

2. *Carnival.* a sideshow performer, usu. billed as a "wild man," who performs sensationally morbid or disgusting acts, as biting the head off a live snake or chicken.

1928 *AS* III (June) 414: Geek. A snake charmer. **1931** D.W. Maurer, in *AS* (June) 331: Geek, n. A freak, usually a fake, who is one of the attractions in a pit show. The word is reputed to have originated with a man named Wagner of Charleston, W. Va., whose hideous snake-eating act made him famous. **1935** *Amer. Mercury* (June) 229: Geek: a degenerate who bites off the heads of chickens in a gory cannibal show. **1942** *AS* XVII 91: Geek. An alleged savage or snake-eater. **1942** *ATS* 621: Geek show, a snake or freak show, esp. a cannibal show where performers bite off the heads of pigeons, snakes, etc. **1953** Gresham *Midway* 16: Yet during World War II, a friend of mine, stationed in Florida, saw a geek tear a live chicken apart and eat the entrails like spaghetti. **1956** Algren *Wild Side* 87: There were stage shows and peep shows, geeks and freaks. **1970** A. Lewis *Carnival* 298: An ordinary geek doesn't actually eat the snakes, just bites off chunks of 'em, chicken heads and rats. **1972–75** W. Allen *Feathers* 6: She ran off to Finland with a professional circus geek. **1979** T. Baum *Carny* 100: Frankie…is the only human carnival attraction in a cage, not counting a geek. **1985** Dye *Between Raindrops* 3: I could…remember the geeks and the headless chickens. **1986–91** Hamper *Rivethead* 8: Like some…circus geek. **1993** *New Republic* (Sept. 13) 11: Today, there was an agricultural fair.…"Maybe they got some pretty hogs!…or a geek!"

3. *Mil.* GOOK.

1963 S.L.A. Marshall *Battle at Best* 73 [ref. to 1951]: Colonel…the geeks had a bunch of Mongolian ponies staked out on that hill. **1986** Spears *Drugs & Drink* 215: Geek…Most current use is as a derogatory term for an Oriental.

geek *v. Carnival.* to work as a GEEK, 2.

1946 Gresham *Nightmare Alley* 6: How do you ever get a guy to geek?…I mean, is a guy born that way—liking to bite the heads off chickens? **1953** Gresham *Midway* 15: And the next night when you throw in the chicken—he'll geek. **1961** Forbes *Goodbye to Some* 83: Geek? Sure mister, I'll geek, till something better comes along.

¶ In phrase:

¶ **geek it** *Carnival.* to quit or give up; back down; give out. Also **geek out.**

1935 Pollock *Und. Speaks:* Geek it, to quit on a job; lose nerve. **1937** in D. Runyon *More Guys* 219: And my guy geeks it the first good smack he gets. **1952** Holmes *Boots Malone* (film): Ya gonna get up? Or are ya gonna lay there and geek it? **1956** H. Gold *Not with It* 22: My legs were coming rubbery and I geeked out the first time: "Grack, I can't make it." *Ibid.* 25: What if I went and geeked out on you? What about this here fever I had?

geek up *v.* to make jittery; frighten.

1984 *Knoxville* (Tenn.) *Jour.* (Oct. 6) B2: It always used to geek me up when we were facing third-and-one or first-and goal, and they would send me in to get it. It's at those times now that I miss being out there the most.

geeky *adj.* being or resembling a GEEK; obnoxious or stupid.

1981 (quot. at PORKER, n.). **1988** *It's Garry Shandling's Show* (Fox-TV): A chaperone? Isn't that just a little geeky? **1990–93** M. Moore *Woman at War* 222: It looks very geeky when you put it on.

geep *n.* [perh. alter. of GEEK] an offensive, obnoxious, or unpleasant person; lowlife. Also **geepo.**

1940 S.J. Perelman, in *New Yorker* (Sept. 14) 19: Hesitating…lest her suppliant turn out to be a geep, or a wolf.…A drunken geep.…He retains two geeps to…trip up his inamorata and…humiliate her. **1942–49** Goldin et al. *DAUL* 77: Geepo. A person, often with the implication that he is an informer, a policeman [etc.]. *Ibid.* 293: Person, slow-witted or inept…geepo. *Ibid.* 294: Person, suspicious-looking…geepo. **1952** *Harper's* (Apr.) 31: Then there's the ship-jumpers. They call them "geeps." They jump ship and get jobs as longshoremen. **1990** *Harper's* (Mar.) 71 [ref. to ca1950]: We got this big influx of Italians from the Old Country—geeps. They're not like us. *Ibid.* 74: The kids we used to call "geeps."

geerus *n.* [orig. unkn.] (see quot.).

1894 *DN* I 389: Geerus. Policeman. (Heard in N.Y.C.)

geesefeathers *n.pl.* snow. *Joc.*

[**1912** in Truman *Dear Bess* 73: The heavenly geese are certainly shedding feathers around this neighborhood this morning.] **1926** Nichols & Tully *Twenty Below* 19: The room'll be full of geese feathers in a minute. Shut that *god-dam door.*

geets *n.* GEETUS, *n.*

1951 H.S. Becker, in *Amer. Jour. Socio.* 144: The following are synonyms for money [among dance musicians]: "loot," "gold," "geetz," and "bread." **1959–60** R. Reisner *Jazz Titans* 156: Geets: money. **1960** in R.S. Gold *Jazz Talk* 105: I'm spendin' my hard-earned geets. **1968–70** *Current Slang* III & IV 54: Geets, n. Money.—University of Kentucky. **1971** Mingus *Underdog* 189: The underworld moves in and runs it strictly for geets.

geetus *n.* [orig. unkn.] money. Also vars.

1926 Finerty *Criminalese* 25: Geetus—Bankroll. **1935** Pollock *Und. Speaks: Gheetus,* money. **1936** Duncan *Over the Wall* 113: I wanted some cash, geetas, dough-ra-me, a bunch of the green fodder that makes the world go round. **1938** Bellem *Blue Murder* 35: I need some quick geetus. **1943** *Billboard* (June 26) 61: Shekels, long green,…kale,…and geedus. **1943** in Botkin *Sidewalks* 267: As soon as you have them laughing, you know it will be easier to get that geedus out of their pokes. **1951** S.J. Perelman, in *New Yorker* (June 30) 21: Promoting the geetus for your celluloid [debut] has tested us tads to the utmost. **1961** Forbes *Goodbye to Some* 81 [ref. to WWII]: And you pushed out a little gietus? **1966** Westlake *Busy Body* 23: There's a nice bonus in it for you, plus the geetus for rubbing Willy. **1993** *N.Y. Press* (Nov. 24) 16: You always lose. The old timers call it getting the geetus from the poke. *Ibid.* 17: The frat boy slumps away, his geetus gone.

gee whilliken *interj.* GEE, *interj.* Also vars.

1851 in *DA:* Jewhilliken, how he could whip er nigger! **1856** in *DA:* Gee-whitaker! What a kurchy she made. **1859** in Eliason *Tarheel Talk* 273: Geewhilekins! how it did rain. **1890** *DN* I 61: Gee Whittaker! an exclamation of surprise. **1902** in *DA:* Gee whittakers! **1904** *DN* III 134: Gee-whillikins, geewhilligins, geewhiz, interjections. **1924** *DN* V 267: Gee whillicats. **1944** *AS* (Dec.) 243: Gee-whillikins, gee-whittaker. **1954** N.Y.C. woman, age 39: Gee whiskers!

gee-whiz *adj.* intended to astonish; amazing; (*also*) naive in approach.

1934 (cited in *W10*). **1941** *Pittsburgh Courier* (Nov. 22) 7: A nice murder or some other Gee-Whiz story. **1954** Huff *Statistics* 60: The Gee-Whiz Graph. *Ibid.* 72: The same issue of the magazine contained a truncated, or gee-whiz, line graph. **1977 Holroyd *Psi* 40: And there are too many books published about parapsychology that adopt a breathless "Gee whiz!" approach and rest their case on wonder. **1986** Zeybel *First Ace* 20: The gee-whiz electronics inside the cockpit. **1991** *CBS This Morning* (CBS-TV) (Jan. 23): All of the information is transmitted to the pilot's gee-whiz seeing-eye helmet.

gee whiz *interj.* GEE, *interj.* Also vars.

1876 Cody & Arlington *Life on Border* 42: Sloat: (*Looking at cards.*) Gee-wees!…I'll bet one hundred dollars on that hand! **1878** Mulford *Fighting Indians* 7: Gee Whiz! **1885** in *DA:* Gee wiz. **1891** *Outing* (Nov.) 106: Gee whizz! boys, how she goes! **1893** *Life* (Mar. 16) 170: Jee Whizz! Only one hunter in two weeks! **1894** Henderson *Sea-Yarns* 24: Gee-whizz!—the way we went through the water fur a minute or two! **1906** in McCay *Little Nemo* 58: Gee whiz! can swim fine wid dis tail on me! **1909** in Thornton *Amer. Gloss.* I 358: "Gee whiz!" said the cook, "but ain't that nice?" **1924** *DN* V 267: Gee whiz. **1982** M. Mann *Elvis* 88: Gee whiz, Mr. Presley, we forgot to ask you for your autograph.

gee-whizly *adv.* [cf. JESUSLY] to an extent that "gee whiz!" is the expected reaction.

1884 in Lummis *Letters* 73: Fix up your darned old world to suit yourselves, if you're so gee-whizzly smart.

geez *n.* GEEZER, 1.

1977 Bredes *Hard Feelings* 344: The driver…was a gray-haired geez named Mel.

geez *interj.* var. JEEZ, *interj.*

geeze *n.* [short for GEEZER, 2.b.] *Narc.* an injection of heroin or a similar drug; (*hence*) an illicit narcotic, such as heroin, that is injected, esp. intravenously.

1967 Maurer & Vogel *Narc. & Narc. Add.* (ed. 3) 358: Geez…An injection of drugs. **1975** Wambaugh *Choirboys* 221: You can leave a litle geez for me hidden away sometimes when you rip off a doper's pad. **1976** Braly *False Starts* 241 [ref. to ca1960]: Do a little geeze and lay back to dig the sounds.

geeze *v. Narc.* to inject heroin or a similar drug, esp. intravenously. Also trans.

1966 Reynolds & McClure *Freewheelin Frank* 51: Which you use to geeze amphetamine drugs with. *Ibid.* 58: A person who geezes…cannot relax. *Ibid.* 105: Geezing their arms full of crystals and opiates. **1967** Wolf *Love Generation* 14: If you're on smack, geezing up in the kitchen, you generate a certain type of energy. *Ibid.* 278: *Geezing.* Take drugs intravenously. **1967–68** von Hoffman *Parents Warned Us* 114: She started geezing (shooting) when she was twelve. **1969** Geller & Boas *Drug Beat* xviii: *Geeze:* To inject a drug intravenously. **1975** Wambaugh *Choirboys* 222: When he's geezing and on the nod, he'll burn himself half to death when he's smoking cigarettes. **1967–80** Folb *Runnin' Lines* 239: *Geeze.* Inject drugs (usually refers to heroin).

geezed *adj.* [sugg. by GEEZER, 2] intoxicated by alcohol or narcotic drugs.—also constr. with *up.*

1928 *AS* IV 102: "Drunk"…*geezed.* **1934** Weseen *Dict. Slang* 15: *Geezed up*—Under the influence of a narcotic. **1954–60** *DAS* 211: *Geezed, all geezed up*…Under the influence of narcotics. **1984** *UTSQ:* Drunk…*geezed.*

geezer *n.* [prob. dial. pron. of *guiser*] **1.a.** an offensive or dull-witted old person, esp. a man. [The only sense now in common use in U.S.]

***1885** in *OED:* If we wake up the old geezers we shall get notice to quit without compensation.…The two geezers, as Sandy styled the landlord and his wife. ***1886** in *F & H* III 128: This frizzle-headed old geezer had a chin on her as rough…as her family. **1893** F.P. Dunne, in Schaaf *Dooley* 227: Googin wint down to see th' old geezer. ***1894** in *EDD:* Tell the old geezer I'll be going to chapel reg'lar. **1914** *DN* IV 201: The old geezer wouldn't let us play ball in his pasture. **1951** Robbins *Danny Fisher* 120: All we had to do was coldcock the geezer and snatch the dough. **1956** Neider *Hendry Jones* 4: Fifty old geezers…walked in from the deserts or hills claiming to be the Kid himself. **1963–64** Kesey *Great Notion* 202: Some old motheaten geezer. **1980** W.C. Anderson *Bat-21* 184: A beat-up old geezer twice my age. **1988** *Wkly. World News* (Oct. 18) 37: Good news for geezers—aspirin may be miracle cure for senility.

b. *Broadly,* an odd or unusual fellow; blockhead; (*hence*) (*obs.*) chap.—also used affectionately.

1893 in Ade *Chicago Stories* 11: Like a great, big geeser I only puts on ten. Well, I win twenty-five. **1896** Ade *Artie* 10: The geezer was settin' there lookin' into three kings all the time. **1896** in Isman *Weber & Fields* 204: "The Geezer" [title of musical comedy]. **1899** Cullen *Tales* 45: The good-natured geezer…bought me a three-dollar seat. *Ibid.* 331: "Yep," said I. "I'm the geezer." **1898–1900** Cullen *Chances* 7: I found him to be a pretty decent sort of a young geezer. **1904** *Life in Sing Sing* 248: *Geezer.* A fellow. **1910** in O. Johnson *Lawrenceville* 48: Goodbye, old geezer! **1911** A.H. Lewis *Apaches of N.Y.* 164: Makin' more row than some geezer fallin' down stairs with a kitchen stove. **1911–12** J. London *Smoke Bellew* 101: Hell is…cluttered with geezers that played systems. *Ibid.* 333: He's the top geezer. **1912** D. Runyon *Firing Line* 80: I know 'em as pretty good geezers. **1913** J. London *Valley of Moon* 228: If he ain't got a couple of knuckles broke…I'm a geezer. **1917** Stange & Mears *Seventeen* 11: But I can remember when you were a skinny geezer. **1918–19** Sinclair *Higgins* 60: That's what you geezers are sweating for! **1922** Tully *Emmett Lawler* 298: Every geezer who does anything at all has to fight. **1957** Ness & Fraley *Untouchables* 126: The other one was a tough-lookin' little geezer who looked like he might use a stiletto on you. **1972** Cleaves *Sea Fever* 135 [ref. to 1920's]: Us geezers on the afterfalls let the line go too fast. **1977** Coover *Public Burning* 111: The other geezers, the…Phantom's boys.

c. *Prizefighting.* weakness of character, esp. cowardice.

1947 Schulberg *Harder They Fall* 325: I think he's full of geezer tonight.…He's had the trots all day. **1954** Schulberg *Waterfront* 203: Terry was on his guard because he could feel all their eyes watching him for sign of geezer. How tough was the tough kid now? their eyes were asking. **1958** Heinz *Professional* 285: I always know that boy got some geezer in him.

2.a. *Und.* a drink of whiskey or other liquor.

[***1866** in *EDD: Geezer,* n.…(Lincolnshire) a state of inebriety.] **1914** Jackson & Hellyer *Vocab.* 37: *Geezer,* Noun. General circulation. A drink of liquor. **1931** *AS* VI (Aug.) 438: *Geezer,* n. A drink of any high-powered booze. **1944** *Pap. Mich. Acad.* XXX 598: *Geezer,* a drink of whisky.

b. *Narc.* an injection or small dose of morphine, heroin, or a similar drug.

1929 Booth *Stealing Through Life* 282 [ref. to ca1920]: "That's a lot of guff!" Dan said, sharply. "I take a geezer once in a while myself. It never hurt me—but you gotta use judgement." **1935** Pollock *Und. Speaks: Geezer,* a shot or injection of morphine. **1936** Dai *Opium Addiction* 199: *Geezer.* A shot of drugs. **1970** Horman & Fox *Drug Awareness* 466: *Geezer*—a narcotic injection. **1970** Landy *Underground Dict.* 87: *Geezer*…small quantity of narcotics.

c. *Narc.* an addict who injects heroin or a similar drug.

1967–68 von Hoffman *Parents Warned Us* 29: Now the Haight is a freak show, a street of poisoners, killers, geezers, burn artists, sadists, beggars and thieves.

geezle *n.* [orig. unkn.] (at The Citadel, Charleston, S.C.) a newly enrolled cadet; (*also*) GEEZER, 1.

1856 in *Law Citadel Cadets* 80: At Kingsville I met several Cadets, E. White, Calhoun and Manget and several obstreperous young "Geezles" whom we took in hand and gave a good session in military politeness. *Ibid.* 89: As usual, we did little but supply the "Geezles" with guns, beds, etc., a part of which devolved on me. *Ibid.* 175: In the afternoon several "geezles" came in, and we had to fix them up. All…looked like good additions. [**1931** *AS* VI 438: *Geezo,* n. A convict.] **1954–60** *DAS: Geezle.* A man. *Not common.*

gehuncled *adj.* [prob. < G **gehunkelt* (p.ppl. of **hinkeln* 'to limp, hobble', dim. of *hinken*), with *-t* reinterpreted as E *-ed*] incapacitated; crippled.

1927 *AS* (June) 391: A cripple is said to be *geed-up* or *gehuncled.* **1966** Kenney *Caste* 80: When you're gehuncled, you're gehuncled for keeps!

geister *n.* [< G *Geist* 'ghost' + E *-er,* or < G *Geister* 'ghosts' reinterpreted as a sing.] *Und.* (see quot.).

1798 in J. Greene *Brothers* 114: The word THIMBLE means Watch, crome, clock…The word GEISTER means An extra thief.

gel *n., v.* see JELL.

gelt *n.* [orig. resp. of G *Geld* or Du *geld* 'money' (the *-d* of each of which is pronounced /t/); fr. 19th C. onward, also < Yid *gelt* 'money'] money. Orig. *S.E.*

***ca1529** J. Skelton, in *OED:* That nothynge had There of theyr awne,/ Neyther gelt nor pawne. ***1591,** ***1629,** ***1648,** ***1658** in *OED.* ***1698–99** "B.E." *Dict. Canting Crew: Gelt,* money. There is no Gelt to be got. ***1815** Sir W. Scott *Guy Mannering* ch. xxxiii: All the gelt was gone. **1821** Waln *Hermit in Phila.* 26: Rouse out your gelt. ***1892** in *OEDS:* Fourteen *Shtibbur's* a lot of *Gelt.* **1910** T.A. Dorgan, in *N.Y. Eve. Jour.* (Jan. 3) 10: He's going to get a fine chunk of gelt before he lets them go, too. **1920** Ade *Hand-Made Fables* 112: He wanted his Gelt for himself. **1953** Brossard *Saboteurs* 132: This was Roland's latest scheme for picking up a little extra gelt. **1967** *Lit Dictionary* 17: *Geech*—Money, gelt. **1971** Horan *Blue Messiah* 338: I ain't quittin' any job until I see the gelt. **ca1985** *A-Team* (NBC-TV): If you got the gelt, you don't give it away cheap.

gen *n.* **1.** *Army.* general officer.

1918–19 MacArthur *Bug's-Eye View* 63: The gen suffered from an impediment of speech.

2. [orig. RAF slang, prob. fr. official phr. "for the *general* information of all ranks," infl. by *genuine*] *Mil. Av.* authentic significant information; LOWDOWN; (*also*) gossip. [Quots. ref. to WWII.]

***1940** in *OEDS:* Operations room, where I got my "Gen" (R.A.F. for information, or instructions). **1946** G.C. Hall, Jr. *1000 Destroyed* 421: *Gen:* Information; the dope. **1946** Hamann *Air Words* 26: *Gen.* Information, usually rumor. **1955** Klaas *Maybe I'm Dead* 12: This gen is top secret until the Old Man says to pass it out in the morning. *Ibid.* 13: What's the gen? **1968** Westheimer *Young Sentry* 58: Now before I take you to the colonel I'll give you guys the gen. The dope. ***1970** in *OEDS:* A vast amount of "gen" is included, and this will be invaluable for settling arguments.

general *n.* the penis.

1961 Gover *$100 Misunderstanding* 36: His lil ol genrill still up an lookin peppy.

General Jackson *interj.* (used as a mild oath).

1925 Bailey *Shanghaied* 148 [ref. to 1899]: And Jehu General Jackson, what laughter! **1944** *Stars & Stripes* (Rome) (Nov. 21): Admiral Carney's favorite cuss-word is "Holy Jumping General Jackson."

general's car *n. Army.* a wheelbarrow or other vehicle used for the hauling of trash or the like.—constr. with *the. Joc.*

1941 *AS* (Oct.) 165: *General's Car.* A wheelbarrow. **1944** *Slanguage Dict.* 50: *Drive the General's car*—drive the garbage truck.

gen out *v.* [GEN, *n.*, 2 + (DOPE) OUT] to figure out; DOPE OUT.
  1946 in Hemingway *Sel. Letters* 610: Can't gen out yet exactly how or when to take Mary to Ketchum.

gent *n.* gentleman; (*broadly*) a man, fellow.
  1780 in *N.Y. History* LI (1970) 67: The unhappy young Gent. whose fate is the tragedy of the day. *1789 G. Parker *Life's Painter* 133: So nobles and gents, lug your counterfeits out. **1829** in A.T. Hill *Voyages* 1: I have a gent passenger going to Charleston. He is a stranger to me but appears to be a very pleasant man and very much of a gent. **1841** [Mercier] *Man-of-War* 266: There's one certain gent…still on mischief bent. **1847** Robbs *Squatter Life* 15: In the course of their conversation the old gent learned John's history. **1851** W. Kelly *Ex. to Calif.* II 23: It was good fun to see those "gents" nibbling at the useless soil. **1851** Ely *Wanderings* 95: I am still solicited to introduce my friends to some of these gents. **1854** G.G. Foster *15 Mins.* 47: The "gent" frowns sublimely at him. **1865** Harte *Sk. of Sixties* 34: A Perfect Gent got up from his seat and said: "Take my seat, dear Beauty." **1867** Alger *Ragged Dick* 257: "Morning, gents," said he, sociably. **1868** Bache *Vulgarisms* 51: Gents…is inadmissible in the language of good society. **1873** Miller *Modocs* 227: You gents will be the last men on earth to mention it. **1892** Bierce *Beetles* 241: Gents…shall exhume them later,/In the dim and distant future. **1905** Riordon *Plunkitt* 45: But if they mean that the Tammany leaders ain't got no education and ain't gents they don't know what they're talkin' about. **1907** in H.C. Fisher *A. Mutt* 20: Be a little gent and use your spoon. **1922** Rollins *Cowboy* 71: In all affairs of ceremony every white male above sixteen years of age was a "gent" unless the matter were one of icy coldness. **1933** West *Miss Lonelyhearts* 102: I thought he was a gent, but…he…wouldn't even give me money for an abortion. **1936** in R.E. Howard *Iron Man* 158: I'm always a gent. I never socked a lady in my life. **1947** D. Owen *Golden Empire* 75: They're probably a couple of gents that Travers hired…for his dirty work. **1954** in Marx *Groucho Letters* 131: You are a fairly migratory gent. **1958** J. Ward *Buchanan* 118: Luther wants to treat you like a real gent, so don't you go spoilin' the fun. **1967** Schaefer *Mavericks* 69: Mean-lookin' gent. **1971** T.C. Bambara *Gorilla* 3: Just a nice ole gent from the block that we all know. **1981** *N.O. Times-Picayune* (Apr. 6) IV 1: "Those things will kill you," said the balding gent in his green Hibernia top. **1984** Tiburzi *Takeoff!* 38: Those men were gents. **1990–93** M. Moore *Woman at War* 61: Gents, we're going to Saudi Arabia.

gentleman *n.* *Und.* a crowbar.
  1807 Tufts *Autobiog.* 292 [ref. to 1794]: Gentleman…a crow bar. *ca1890–93 F & H III 130: Gentleman…(thieves').—A crowbar.

gents' *n.* [abbr. *gents' room*] a men's lavatory.—constr. with *the.*
  1954–60 *DAS*. **1963** in Marx *Groucho Letters* 179: Freedom of speech is one thing, but these gents are overdoing it. And when I say "gents," this is where most of them should be doing their act. **1977** Dunne *True Confessions* 30: They do it in the gents', is where they do it.

Geordie *n.* Esp. *Naut.* a Tynesider; (*broadly*) a North Country Englishman or vessel.—sometimes attrib. *Obs.* in U.S. exc. in ref. to BrE.
  1855 Nordhoff *Man-of-War Life* ch. vi: The sailors belonging to the ports on the northeastern coast of England are called Jordies. They are a peculiar set, known as great growlers and excellent sailors. **1871** *Overland Mo.* (Feb.) 166: I was apprenticed…to the skipper of an old "Jordy" brig, carrying coals to London. **1894** J. Slocum *Liberdade* 71: As the "Geordie" would say. **1898** Stevenson *Cape Horn* 310: He isn't fit for a geordie brig, much less a clipper ship.

George *n.* **1.** *Mil. Av.* an automatic pilot system.
  [**1916** T.A. Dorgan, in Zwilling *TAD Lexicon* 105: [He] visits his home town, hires a car and calls it a *bus* and the driver *George.*] *1931 in *OEDS*: "George" is the automatic pilot about which there has been so much talk lately. **1943** R. Scott *God Is Co-Pilot* 88: We…turned the ship over to the automatic pilot—Old Iron George, we call it. **1945** on *Twentieth Century* (CBS-TV, 1958): I'll look after George, the automatic pilot. **1956** Heflin *USAF Dict.* 231: *George, n.*…An automatic pilot. *British slang.* **1958** Cope & Dyer *Petty Off.'s Gde.* (ed. 2) 347: *George.* (Slang). Automatic pilot. **1961** L.G. Richards *TAC* 235: She's got an automatic pilot that is really automatic.…You can just sit there and watch George do the work. **1975** in Higham & Siddall *Combat Aircraft* 44 [ref. to 1945]: To ease the strain on the pilots until George (the automatic pilot) could be engaged. *Ibid.* 45: Master switch off, George off, and cross-feed off. **1978** in *Ibid.* 103: The Starlifter's "George," or Automatic Flight Control System (AFCS), is an immensely capable friend.
  2. (used as a form of address to a Pullman porter).
  1939 in Paxton *Sport* 320: I couldn't have been more surprised if a Pull-

man porter had turned to me and called me George. **1974** Terkel *Working* 108: When I was first employed, the [Pullman] porter status was very low. Everybody called him George.
  3.a. [fr. the portrait of *George* Washington on the bill] a one-dollar bill. Also **George Washington.**
  1948 Manone & Vandervoort *Trumpet* 40: It griped us jazzmen…to have to go hungry, or get paid off in George Washingtons. [**1962** T. Berger *Reinhart* 122: I'll tell all I know for a picture of George.] **1970** Cannon *Brewster McCloud* (film): Look at that! Two big Georges right there! **1984** E.L. Abel *Dict. Drug Abuse* 67: *George*…One dollar.
  b. *Pris.* (see quot.).
  1975 Hardy & Cull *Drug Lang.* 66: *George.*…one of anything…a one-year prison sentence.
  ¶ **let George do it** let someone else do the task.
  1910 in *DA.* **1911** in Kornbluh *Rebel Voices* 117: Oh Let George Do It…George can't do it all. **1918** Rowse *Doughboy Dope* 25: The worst of it is…that the mysterious George, who did the things you didn't do yourself on the outside, doesn't seem to have enlisted in this man's army. **1926** *Jour. Applied Psych.* X 255: *Let George do it* means…Pass the buck. **1936** Mulholland *Splinter Fleet* 146: There was no such expression in the Splinter Fleet as "Let George do it." **1947** Kuttner *Fury* 22: Let George do it.

George *adj.* **1.** *Und.* in the know; WISE; HEP.
  1917 *Editor* (Feb. 24) 152: Be George or hep—to be wise. "Hello, George," said when meeting a bo is tantamount to saying, "I'm a bo, too." **1925** in *AS* (Jan. 1926) 251: Be George—to understand, to be jerry, to be wise. **1927** *DN* V 438: *Be George, v.* To be versed in the lore of the underworld. Also *be Jerry.*
  2. excellent; fine.
  1930 Stiff *Milk & Honey* 208: Jake or George—The same as *hunkydory.* **1950** C.W. Gordon *High School* 126: Approved behavior was "rite," "neat," "george," and "okay." **1952** in *DAS:* That's real george of you to lend a hand like this. **1953** W. Brown *Monkey on My Back* 15: "George." "What's that mean?" "The squares say okay." **1955** Archibald *Av. Cadet* 41: Think I'll buy me a pair of those cowboy boots.…They're really George. **1955** Salter *Hunters* 182: He was a george guy. **1956** in Marx *Groucho Letters* 120: I thought your piece on "I Love Lucy" was real George. **1956** E. Hunter *Second Ending* 314: How clever, how George, these hopheads sure know how to put things, hey! **1958** Gilbert *Vice Trap* 5: George—O.K., fine. **1960** C.L. Cooper *Scene* 151: Thanks, my man.…That was real George. **1970** Landy *Underground Dict.* 87: *George adj.* All right; O.K. [**1972** in Fromkin & Rodman *Intro. to Lang.* 273: "Tom" and "George" were signals casino employees used to describe a player. "Here comes George" meant a good tipper or "live one." "Tom" meant an approaching player was a poor tipper, a "stiff," a wiseguy, or possibly an irate husband.]

George *v.* [var. of GEORGIA, *v.*] *Black E.* (see quots.).
  1960 C.L. Cooper *Scene* 51: Trick, was he? A trick to be georged and then told on? *Ibid.* 31: One of the girls georged him…just to see if he was as good a producer as a braggart. *Ibid.* 308: *Georged:* Lured into sexual activity by a woman.

George Spelvin *Theat.* [app. coined by the actor Edward Abeles for the Broadway production of *Brewster's Millions* (premiered Dec. 31, 1906); see B. Alsterlund and W. Pilkington, "The Spelvins on Broadway," *Amer. N & Q* (Oct. 1947), pp. 99–103] (an alias used by actors to disguise their identity in a small role).
  1908 *N.Y. Telegraph* (Oct. 15) (cited in *Amer. N & Q* (Oct. 1947) 103). **1936** in *Amer. N & Q* (Oct. 1947) 100: For years (including the present one) I have never had a program that did not have George Spelvin's name in it. **1942** Pegler *Spelvin* 12: George Spelvin, American. **1943** *Amer. Mercury* (Nov.) 588: Anyone associated with the show-shops during the past generation has taken for granted…[that] an actor who had a mere "walk-on" rôle was likely to be listed on the program as George Spelvin [and that] any actor who played more than one rôle in one show made his second appearance disguised as George Spelvin on the play bills. **1943** *Newsweek* (Nov. 22) 103: "George Spelvin" is the traditional handle for an actor doubling in a minor role. **1968** Safire *Lang. of Politics* 73: *George Spelvin.* The name a hungry actor accepts as a pseudonym when he accepts a role so minor that playing it under his own name would hurt his reputation.

George Washington see s.v. GEORGE, *n.*, 3.a.

Georgia *n.* *Und.* any of various crude swindles, esp. the cheating of a prostitute. Also **Georgia scuffle.**
  1942–49 Goldin et al. *DAUL* 78: *Georgia scuffle*…(Carnival) A very

crude and often rough handling of swindle victims who are too dull-witted to be subtly prepared for the theft. **1967** [R. Beck] *Pimp* 82: She was setting me up for the "Georgia." **1970** Winick & Kinsie *Lively Commerce* 127: I can tell when a guy wants to pay instead of waiting for a "Georgia" (sexual access without pay).

Georgia *v. Und.* to swindle (esp. a prostitute); hoodwink.
1960 Himes *Gold Dream* 54: "He Georgiaed me," the girl told Dummy hysterically. "He sent me to Georgia."…He knew she meant that a man she had taken to her room had shown her some money, but afterwards had refused to pay her. **1967** Colebrook *Cross of Lassitude* 329: She'd…been "Jonah'ed," played-on, "Georgia'd." **1968** I. Reed *Yellow Back Radio* 77: When she georgiaed me, you had to follow. **1971** S. Stevens *Way Uptown* 173: She woulda too but some stud georgia'd her outta the buck one night. **1972** R.A. Wilson *Forbidden Words* 136: The sonofabitch georgiaed me and went out the window. **1973** Andrews & Owens *Black Lang.* 120: *Georgian* [sic]—Getting something for nothing.

Georgia buggy *n. So.* a wheelbarrow. *Joc.*
1918 *DN* V 18: *Georgia-buggie,* a wheelbarrow. N.C.; S.C. **1928** Callahan *Man's Grim Justice* 105: Now let's see if y' can cause a riot with one o' them "Georgia buggies" (wheelbarrows). **1941** *Pittsburgh Courier* (Mar. 22) 21: Something else besides pushing the "Georgia buggy" (wheelbarrow). **1952** Himes *Stone* 32: The snow had softened and was slushy and the wheelbarrows churned it into heavy muck. Rolling those "Georgia buggies" was a killing job. **1965–70, 1986** in *DARE*.

Georgia ice-cream *n. So.* hominy grits. *Joc.*
1941 Hargrove *Private Hargrove* 83: Hominy grits are glamorized into *Georgia ice cream.* **1941** Kendall *Army & Navy Sl.* 6: *Georgia ice cream*….grits. **1972** in *AS* XLIX 91: Grits is…sometimes known as "Georgia ice cream." **1976** Conroy *Santini* 34: The South ain't produced nothin' to defend. Except grits. Georgia ice cream or screwed-up Cream of Wheat. **1984** Wilder *You All* 83.

Georgia overdrive *n. Trucking,* esp. *So.* the neutral gear position of a motor vehicle as used for coasting. *Joc.*
1971 Tak *Truck Talk* 71: *Georgia overdrive:* the neutral gear position; used…going downhill. **1976** Lieberman & Rhodes *CB* 129: *Georgia Overdrive*—Neutral gear position used in going downhill.

Georgia skin *n.* [short for *Georgia skin game;* see SKIN GAME] *Black E.* a kind of card game.
1930 in Leadbitter & Slaven *Blues Records* 510: Georgia Skin. **1947** in *DARE: Georgia skin*…Basically, it is an adaptation of Faro. **1954** *Ebony* in *DARE:* I tried to pick up extra dough shooting craps or playing Georgia Skin. **1967** [R. Beck] *Pimp* 25: Steve blew it in a "Georgia-skin" game within a week after we got to Chicago. **1979** in Terkel *Amer. Dreams* 356: Down the street, there was black jack and Georgia skin.

gerbil *n. Juve.* a foolish or obnoxious person.
1988 Cherbak *Broken Angel* (film): Shut up, you gerbil. **1986–91** Hamper *Rivethead* 119: Hell yes that squat little gerbil loves me.

Germ *n.* [clipping of *German,* with allusion to *germ* 'disease-producing microorganism'; cf. GERM] a German.—used derisively. Also **Germy, Germo.**
*1915 in Partridge *DSUE* (ed. 8) 455: Germs. **1936** Traven *Death Ship* 185: Germy. **1975** Stanley *WWIII* 184: He had been the only member of his U.S.-Germo infantry company to emerge from a Chinese flanking attack.

germ *n.* an insignificant or contemptible person.
1942 *ATS* 368: Contemptible person…cur,…dead beat,…germ [etc.]. **1970** Gattzden *Black Vendetta:* "In the county jail."…"Where you belong, germ." **1976** "N. Ross" *Policeman* 61: Listen, germ. If you ever mention money in front of me again, I'll bust your ass. **1965** in J. Mills *On the Edge* 2: Degenerates, perverts and lawbreakers—to Barrett, "germs." *Ibid.* 11: Hey, germ!…Come here!

German goiter *n.* a fat belly caused by excessive beer drinking. *Joc.*
1935 Pollock *Und. Speaks: German goitre,* a beer drinker with a big belly [sic]. **1941** *AS* (Feb.) 22 (Indiana): *German goitre.* A large stomach. **1943** *AS* (Feb.) 67: *German goitre* (a large stomach) S.C., N.C. **1950, 1965–70** in *DARE.*

Geronimo *n.* **1.** [fr. the *interj.*] *Army.* a paratrooper.
1947 Rapport & Northwood *Rendezvous* 807: The smooth farmland over which his little Geronimos moved on toward Arnhem/Lies flooded. **1959** Sabre & Eiden *Glory-Jumpers* 34: Now get these Geronimos…back to the operations tent. **1962** Tregaskis *Viet. Diary* 314: Maj.…Peters…is a real Geronimo sort with lots of airborne experience.

2. *Narc.* a barbiturate capsule; (*also*) alcohol mixed with barbiturates.
1950 *Time* (Aug. 28) 4: A goof ball is a…Geronimo…or any other barbiturate sleeping pill. **1969** Lingeman *Drugs A to Z* 244: *Wild Geronimo*…a drink consisting of barbiturates dissolved in an alcoholic beverage. **1971** Guggenheimer *Narc. & Drug Abuse* 23: *Geronimo.* alcoholic drink plus a barbiturate. **1977** Wesson & Smith *Barbiturates* 122: *Geronimo.* Alcohol mixed with barbiturates.

Geronimo *interj.* [orig. alluding to a leap made by a character in the film *Geronimo* (1939); see 1946 quot.] Orig. *Army.* (a cry shouted by paratrooper trainees in jump training; later in more extended use as a battle cry).
1941 *Nat. Geo.* (July) 16: As each man's chute opens, he yells "Geronimo!" **1944** Huie *Can Do!* 24: As rambunctiously American as "Yea team!" or "Geronimo!" **1944** Ruskin et al. *Andy Hardy's Blonde Trouble* (film): Geronimo! We're gonna get away with it! **1946** Hamann *Air Words* 26: The practice of yelling "Geronimo"…originated at Fort Benning, Georgia, with members of the 505th Battalion, U.S.A., who attended a motion picture portraying the life of the famous Indian warrior and chieftain before their first jump. **1971** Cameron *First Blood* 31: He did not think…to shout "Geronimo!" **1974** *Police Woman* (NBC-TV): Geronimo! **1978** B. Smith, Jr. *Chick's Crew* 8 [ref. to WWII]: If one [paratrooper] yelled "Geronimo," their war cry, all the others came running to join the ruckus. **1983** Ehrhart *VN-Perkasie* 160: All around me, Marines shouted, "Gung ho!" "Get some!" "Geronimo!" **1986** Watterson *Calvin* 65: See, I'll…make a parachute!…Geronimo!! [**1987** Nickelodeon Network TV spot (Sept. 6): I had a turtle and his name was Geronimo…because he'd walk around on the edge of the table and fall off all the time.]

gertrude *n.* [perh. orig. a joc. allusion to radio and TV character actress *Gertrude Berg,* noted for calling "Yoo-hoo!"] *Navy.* (see quot.).
ca1984 T. Clancy *Red Oct.* 302: "You have a gertrude, sir?" "Gertrude?" "Underwater telephone, sir, for talking to other subs."

gestapo *n.* the police; a policeman.—constr. with *the.*
1953 Manchester *City of Anger* 127: We just got to be careful, take care of the gestapo better, is all. *Ibid.* 210: He knows more than the gestapo, which is nothing. **1965** in *AS* XLI (1966) 72: Teen-Gang Talk…*Gestapo,* n. A highway patrolman. **1967** Grefé *Wild Rebels* (film): It's the gestapo! **1978** Pici *Tennis Hustler* 223: The sneaking gestapos! **1967–80** Folb *Runnin' Lines* 239: *Gestapo(s).* Police.

gesundheit starter *n. Trucking.* (see quot.). *Joc.*
1971 Tak *Truck Talk* 71: *Gesundheit starter:* an air-powered starter; named for the "sneezing" noise a tractor makes when its air starter is activated.

get *n.* Esp. *Und.* GETAWAY, *n.,* 2. Also **gets.**
*1898 in *OEDS:* Their inquisitiveness…compelled Jim to…do a timely "get." **1902** Hapgood *Thief* 97 [ref. to ca1880]: Patsy was too large to squeeze himself through the opening, but "stalled" for Johnny while the latter "made his gets." *Ibid.* 116: I made my "gets" out the window. ***1914** in *OEDS:* I must make a git. So-long. **1931–34** in Clemmer *Pris. Commun.* 332: *Get,* n. An escape or a get away. **1949** in *Harper's* (Feb. 1950) 74: The wheel-man's other major responsibility is the layout of the get, or getaway route.
¶ In phrase:
¶ **from the get** *Black E.* from the start.
ca1974 in J.L. Gwaltney *Drylongso* 19: I know that he is a asshole from the git. **1978** Sopher & McGregor *Up from Walking Dead* 186: I dug Frank right from the git. **1986** *Miami Vice* (NBC-TV): Our snitch must have given us up because they had us made from the get. **1988** H. Gould *Double Bang* 57: Most of whom are stoned from the get anyway.

get *v.* **1.a.** to victimize by cheating or trickery; trick. Now *colloq.*
1851 B. Hall *College Wds.:* In Princeton College, when a student or any one else has been cheated or taken in, it is customary to say, he was *got.*
b. to puzzle or perplex; nonplus. Now *colloq.*
1864 in Bensill *Yamhill* 132: Turpin says, "Every Veteran had a brass watch and wore 'revolving shirts.' This last article gets me." **1868** *Overland Mo.* (Sept.) 268: Thirty or forty high! Well, that's what gits me! **1868** in *OEDS:* Scratching his head a minute, Benjamin F. replied: "Well, I confess your Honor's got me there!" **1870** Duval *Big-Foot* 87: That gets me! I have been in a good many "scrimmages" with the Indians, but I never saw them "snake off" their dead in that way before. **1878** B. Harte *Drift* 60: Ole Daddy must use up a pow'ful sight of

wood....But what gets me is, that the pile don't seem to come down. **1886** *Lantern* (N.O.) (Sept. 22) 4: That's where you got us, darling. **1902** *N.Y. Eve. Jour.* (Dec. 4) 16: "When did you work last?" "You got me, boss." **1960** N.Y.C. high school students: "What the heck's that mean?" "You got me."

c. to worry, exercise, or annoy. Now *colloq.*

1867 B. Harte, in *OEDS:* To have let bigger things go by, and to be taken in by this cheap trick,...is what gets me. **1885** B. Harte *Snow-Bound* 145: I'll tell ye whot got me, though! That part commencing, "Suckamstances over which I've no controul." **1914** Atherton *Perch* 174: Wouldn't that come and get you? Just listen. **1985** Univ. Tenn. instructor: Life's tough, but you can't let it get you.

2. (as a command to a team of animals) get up! get going!; (*hence*) (usu. *imper.*) to get out or be off; clear out; run away. Often **git.**

1854 in H. Nathan *D. Emmett* 419: Now "git up an' git!" **1861** Wilkie *Iowa First* 84: Crows, buzzards, rabbits, and everything else with legs and wings "get up and *git*" the very instant an Iowa man comes in sight. **1862** in Allan *Lone Star Ballads* 54: But the Texans made them everlastingly "git!" **1863** in R.G. Carter *4 Bros.* 353: But soon "hard times will come knocking at the door," saying in our own language, "*get up and git!*" **1863** in Heartsill *1491 Days* 144: At 2 o'clk the Feds plant a battery opposite our camp and open on us quite lively and they make us "git" for awhile. **1864** in C.H. Moulton *Ft. Lyon* 201: We...soon compelled them to "git up and git." **1864** *Harper's Mag.* (Oct.) 565: George, after belaboring the mules till he was tired, and telling them to "git" till he was hoarse, would lean back in his seat and think. *ca*1867 in G.W. Harris *Lovingood* 56: He minded ove a durned crazy ole elephant...jis' *gittin* frum sum imijut danger ur tribulashun. **1875** Daly *Pique* 285: Take my advice and git. **1881** Field *Yankee Duelist* 5: Come, get out!...What, git, vambozzle? **1884** in *OED:* He presented a cocked revolver and told them to get, and they got. **1887** F. Francis *Saddle & Moccasin* 83: A captain and a full company appeared, but this brave man "made them get." **1922** Rollins *Cowboy* 19: The proof of legal ownership...might be a terse request...to "git."

3. to do for; wound; (*specif.*) (and *usu.*) to succeed in killing (a person), esp. in retribution. See also *get it*, 1.a., below. Now *colloq.* or *S.E.*

1862 in R.B. Hayes *Diary* II 238: The enemy retreated, leaving four dead, four mortally [wounded], four more dangerously. All these we *got. Ibid.* 240: Five enemy killed, nine badly wounded that we *got.* **1864** in O.J. Hopkins *Under the Flag* 159: Old Marmaduke is a mean old sneak and a *Gorrilla*, and we are going up to "git him." **1865** in S.C. Wilson *Column South* 271: The general issued orders for a hundred cavalry to go out...and "get" them. They "got" them, killing many. **1866** Dimsdale *Vigilantes* 90: They told him that they were armed, and if they were attacked they would make it a warm time for some of them; at any rate they would "get" three or four of them. *ca*1866 in Heaps *Singing Sixties* 391: Three hundred thousand Yankees lie stiff in Southern dust;/We got three hundred thousand before they conquered us!/...I wish it was three million instead of what we got! **1887** F. Francis *Saddle & Moccasin* 138: They'll get you one of these days, Colonel, when you are driving around in your wagon. **1922** Rollins *Cowboy* 52: Incidentally, the sheriff, elected to "get" him, loaded a weapon and "got" him. **1927–28** in R. Nelson *Dishonorable* 184: Somebody got Johnson. **1959** L' Amour *Fast Draw* 154: They got Bob Lee....The Peacocks ambushed him.

4.a. to understand; fathom (now *colloq.*); *specif.* (usu. interrogatively) to grasp the intentions and resolve of (the speaker) without error or uncertainty.

1907 in *OEDS:* "I don't get her," she murmured, as if Leonora was a telephone number. **1911–12** J. London *Smoke Bellew* 287: We dissolve pardnership there an' then. Get me? **1912–14** in E. O'Neill *Lost Plays* 42: If you bother this goil again I'll fix yuh and fix yuh right. D'yuh get me? **1914** Paine *Wall Between* 241: Do you get me, Sergeant? **1922** in H. Miller *Letters to Emil* 4: Get me, Steve? **1929–30** Dos Passos *42nd Parallel* 31: Sure, I get you. **1930** *Variety* (Jan. 8) 123: Justices of the Peace, get me, will take anything from a red hot stove to a cross on a church. **1935** Lindsay *She Loves Me Not* 38: "You use your eyes to see with and for nothing else"...."I gotcha." **1936** Steel *College* 318: You wanta wake up inna morning...so you wanta be onna level. Get me? **1939–40** Tunis *Kid from Tomkinsville* 19: I getcha. **1944** Brooks *Brick Foxhole* 103: Gotcha, Hank. Gotcha. What's her name? **1954** Chessman *Cell 2455* 66: "Got ya," Tim said. **1963** Gant *Queen St.* 135: We form at the south edge of [the] open square. Get me? **1992** Strawberry & Rust *Darryl* 237: I wouldn't "get it" until five years later—I certainly didn't see it that morning.

b. to pay close attention to; appreciate the import or irony of; (*also*) to look at.—used imperatively.

1911–12 Ade *Knocking the Neighbors* 129: Get me!...Pipe the lid! **1918** E.E. Rose *Cappy Ricks* 43: Says he's going into business—get that, Skinner—...going into business! **1919** in De Beck *Google* 44: Get the beads of perspiration on his brow!! **1927** H. Miller *Moloch* 15: Now get this! **1934** Cain *Postman* 6: Well, get this. I'm just as white as you are, see? **1949** *Gay Girl's Guide* 10: Get You!: Who do you think you're kidding! ("Get..." is used in an infinite number of phrases). **1980** Berlitz & Moore *Roswell* 15: And get this—they're saying something about little men being on board! **1992** L. Johnson *My Posse* 69: Get her, man. She's trying to use child psychology on us.

5. to get even with; take vengeance on. Now *colloq.*

1918 *DN* V 24: I've been laying for him for years; to-day I *got* him. **1919–21** Chi. Comm. Race Rel. *Negro in Chi.* 55: They went down Forty-seventh Street with firearms...in autos...and shouting as they went, "We'll get those niggers!" **1922** S. Lewis *Babbitt* 141: I'm going to *get* those guys, one of these days, and I told 'em so. **1932* in *OEDS* (s.v. *gotcha*): "Gotcher!" It was Jiggs' triumphant voice. **1942–49** Goldin et al. *DAUL* 78: *Get...*To fulfil a threat of vengeance upon. **1957** H. Danforth & J. Horan *D.A.'s Man* 247: Rodriguez muttered that some day he would "get" Ramos. **1986** P. Welsh *Tales Out of School* 67: Another boy...threatened to "get me" when I asked him to stop talking to the girls around him. *Ibid.* 152: The kids describe those teachers as "frustrated," "unhappy," "out to get us." **1988** M. Bartlett *Trooper Down!* 22: I just wish the public realized we're not out there to "get" anyone.

6. *Bodybuilding.* to build up the muscles of (part of the body).

*ca*1984 in *AS* LIX (1984) 199: *Get—v phr* Of a body part, develop that part more, as in "get arms."

¶ In phrases:

¶ **get any** see s.v. ANY.

¶ **get away with** to overcome; get the better of; take advantage of. Cf. S.E. sense 'to do (something) without consequent punishment'.

1878 Beadle *West. Wilds* 41: More'n once the robbers would tackle some gritty man that was handy with his "barkers" [pistols], an' he'd get away with two or three of 'em. *a*1881 G.C. Harding *Misc. Writings* 136: He was mighty wide...between the shoulders, an' I wasn't altogether clear in my own mind that he wouldn't git away with me. **1883–84** Whittaker *L. Locke* 151: Are you going to let that kid get away with you? **1884** in *DAE:* The Moorheads will have to play for all they are worth to get away with them. **1885** in Guerin *Mountain Charley:* There were certain young bloods in the camp who seemed to have an idea that it would be an easy matter to "get away" with her. **1887** in *OED:* The boys got away with the...road agents. **1893** *Confed. War Jour.* (May) 16: A Johnny Reb got away with me entirely one day after we captured him at Resaca. **1896** in J.M. Carroll *Benteen-Goldin Lets.* 240: Stanley got drunk, so the game was thrown into Custer's hand, and thus he "got away with Stanley." **1908** *DN* III 314: You can't get away with me. **1913** J. London *J. Barleycorn* 93: Letting an old man like French Frank get away with him.

¶ **get behind** to enjoy or appreciate. Cf. BEHIND, *prep.*

1976–77 McFadden *Serial* 166: He said he...[disliked] raw fish. So what's the problem. I can't get behind sushi, either.

¶ **get down** see s.v. DOWN, *adv.*

¶ **get hat** see s.v. HAT, *n.*

¶ **get into** see s.v. INTO, *prep.*

¶ **get it, 1.a.** to be shot or wounded; esp. to be killed. Cf. (3), above.

1844 Porter *Big Bear* 131: *Bang!* Oh, dam you! you've got it! I *know* you is! you aint shakin' that tail for nothin'! Yes, thar's blood on the snow! **1847** Scribner *Volunteer* 61: Our captain was the next to fall, exclaiming "I've got it, boys!" **1863** in H.L. Abbott *Fallen Leaves* 209: Ropes & Mason...got it badly. **1878** in W.A. Graham *Custer Myth* 263: I heard the soldier cry out as he fell, "Oh! my God, I have got it." **1881** in Miller & Snell *Why West Was Wild* 501: "Good God, Mike, are you hit?"..."Yes; tell my wife I have got it at last." **1890** Langford *Vigilante Days* 99: "He has got it" (meaning his death wound), "and I guess he can stand it." **1898** Norris *Moran* 226: I think he's got it through the lungs. **1899** Marshall *Rough Riders* 197: Once in a while one of them would "get it." Sometimes—when a man was hit in an outstretched arm, or the extreme center shoulder—he would whirl part of the way around before he fell. **1900** Reeves *Bamboo Tales* 112: I've Got It! I've Got It!...What the Wounded Say and Do. **1909** Irwin *Con Man* 72:

Ten men are killed by them to one that gets it from the big cats. **1917** Empey *Over the Top* 26: Always remember that if you are going to get it, you'll get it, so never worry. **1918** *Lit. Digest* (Oct. 5) 64: It seems that every one of the pals I had got bumped off. Lindsey got it about the hottest part of the fighting. **1925** Thomason *Fix Bayonets!* 124: But before he got it, he knew that we were winning. **1936** "E. Queen" *Halfway House* 192: So this is the dump where he got it, eh? **1943** Pyle *Brave Men* 167: There were so many ironic cases of men "getting it" on their last flight that the leaders were as nervous about it as the pilots. **1960** Roeburt *Mobster* 34: Where and how would he get it, he wondered. **1964** *Combat!* (ABC-TV): That's when North and Whitcomb got it. **1970** *Adam-12* (NBC-TV): If you try to follow us, the lady gets it, understand? **1982** R.A. Anderson *Cooks & Bakers* 146: Hey, did you hear about Riley getting it? **1982** Goff et al. *Bros.* 7: I saw a lot of guys get it.

b. *Mil. Av.* (of an aircraft or aircrewman) to be shot down.
1953–57 Giovannitti *Combine D* 48: He got it over Munich three days ago and now he's here.

2. to take punishment. Now *colloq.*
1851–61** H. Mayhew *London Labour* III 387: When we were both at the same hospital after the flogging, and saw each other's backs, the other convicts said to me, "D—it, you've got it this time." ***1872** in *OED*: The German Emperor, Bismarck, and Earl Granville, also "got" it, but not quite so hotly. ***ca1890–93** F & H III 135: *Get it*...To be punished, morally or physically. **1899** Ade *Fables* 13: The Fable of the Good Thing with the Lorgnette, and why She Got it Good. *a1909** Tillotson *Detective* 92: *Got it all*—Life imprisonment.

3. to go at great speed.
1942 *Pittsburgh Courier* (Sept. 14) 15: *Jump, Get it*—Work fast. **1973–76** J. Allen *Assault* 114: So I tell JoJo to *get it*, and when I say, "Get it!" JoJo immediately pulls out of the traffic onto the sidewalk.

4. to be pleasing or satisfactory; do.—usu. in negative contexts.
1968–70 *Current Slang* III & IV 54: *Get it, v.* To be attractive or pleasing.—University of Kentucky. "That house really gets it." **1972** in *Penthouse* (Jan. 1973) 128: Man. Them shoes jes ain't gonna git it. **1974** E. Thompson *Tattoo* 3: There was nothing to say. "Sorry" would not get it. **1976** C.R. Anderson *Grunts* 41 [ref. to 1969]: Now that's the kind of shit, gentlemen, that don't get it in this Company. **1993** Knoxville, Tenn., attorney: That kind of stuff just ain't gonna get it.

¶ **get it all** *Baseball.* to hit a pitch squarely, esp. for a home run. See also *a*1909 quot. at *get it*, 2, above.
1974 Blount *3 Bricks Shy* 113: When a batter hits a baseball on the nose he says, "I got it all."

¶ **get it on** see s.v. GET ON.

¶ **get it up, 1.** to get an erection of the penis. Also **get one up.**—usu. considered vulgar.
1943 in P. Smith *Letter from Father* 239: The men looked as if they could never get "it" up again. **1953–55** Kantor *Andersonville* 537: I said he was too blame small. Couldn't get it up— **1959** W. Burroughs *Naked Lunch* 15: He can't drink. He can't get it up. **1962** T. Berger *Reinhart* 424: Even in a brothel...you are required at the minimum to *get one up*. **1962** Kesey *Cuckoo's Nest* 66: Could you get it up over her...if she...had the beauty of Helen? **1965** in Sanchez *Word Sorcerers* 1961: I can't quite git it up to perform. **1968** Coppel *Order of Battle* 144: Imagine Ray Porta so stoned he couldn't even get it up. **1971** in L. Bangs *Psychotic Reactions* 62: Maybe the poor schmuck cares *too much* to get it up. **1982** Del Vecchio *13th Valley* 490: You ever not been able to get it up? **1982** Kinsella *Shoeless Joe* 43: Why should I stick around you, you can't even get it up anymore.

2. to become sufficiently enthusiastic.
1970 in H.S. Thompson *Shark Hunt* 197: The liberals simply can't get it up. **1976** *Esquire* (Sept.) 69: Now, I've never been able to get it up for most conservative visions of American History. **1978** E. Thompson *Devil to Pay* 56: Women...did not have to "get it up and get it on" daily, as men were absolutely required to do. **1980** in Safire *Good Word* 289: I found myself invited to cover a particular event—to which I replied, "I can't get it up." This is odd, for two reasons: 1. I'm a woman. 2. I never use crude or sexual vernacular....I hope you can get it up to discuss this in your column. **1984** Univ. Tenn. student (female): I just couldn't get it up for this assignment.

¶ **get left** see s.v. LEAVE, *v.*

¶ **get lost** [despite popular belief, not fr. Yid; see *Jewish Linguistic Studies* 2, 1990, p. 218] to get out of sight or out of someone's way; (*hence*, as imper.) get away! get out! [The imperative form has been common only since the 1940's.]

1902 Cullen *More Tales* 40: If I made any effort whatsoever to get lost until...he was through...he'd...send out a general alarm for me. **1939** S. Herzig *They Made Me a Criminal* (film): Get lost, will ya? **1943** Holmes & Scott *Mr. Lucky* (film): Awright, boys. Get lost! **1948** Seward & Ryan *Angel's Alley* (film): Aah, git lost. **1950** Jacoby & Brady *Champagne* (film): In the ridiculous idiom of your [radio] profession, "Get lost!" **1955** Graziano & Barber *Somebody Up There* 307: Get lost, ya creep. **1959** in Cannon *Nobody Asked* 147: The beat generation, let them get lost forever. **1971** *Odd Couple* (ABC-TV): O.K. I'll get lost. **1966–80** McAleer & Dickson *Unit Pride* 435: "Get lost," Dewey said, the scorn in his voice surprising even me. **1984** *Daily Beacon* (Univ. Tenn.) (Apr. 13) 8: "Get lost!"...scram. **1992** *Time* (Dec. 28) 14: The show of force was meant to tell armed looters: You can't match our firepower, so get lost.

¶ **get lucky** see s.v. LUCKY.

¶ **get next** see s.v. NEXT, *adj.*

¶ **get off** see GET OFF, *v.* for all forms.

¶ **get on** see GET ON, *v.* for all forms.

¶ **get (one's), 1.** to receive (one's) due punishment.
1905 T.A. Dorgan, in Zwilling *TAD Lexicon* 39: Ed Martin got his in two rounds with Johnson. *ca*1910 in "O. Henry" *Works:* Oh, yes, it was rum that did it. He backslided and got his. **1912** Lowrie *Prison* 410: Some of the men were reported at the office for infractions of the rules and then they "got theirs." **1956** N.Y.C. woman, age *ca*65: You'll get yours some day! You wait! **1974** Millard *Thunderbolt* 82: But when this job is over, don't think you aren't going to get yours, but good.

2. *Esp. Mil.* to be killed.
1909 Irwin *Con Man* 172: Two days later Soapy got his. ***1913** R. Kipling in *OEDS*: He'd got *his*. I knew it by the way the head rolled in my hands. **1914** Paine *Wall Between* 261: It was the toughest kind of luck that Captain Ramsay had to "get his," they said, as they talked among themselves, but anyhow, he had lived long enough to see them make good. **1916** in Clark *Letters* 28: Poor Barb got his, night before last. **1919** Roosevelt *Average Americans* 197: Do you remember how we got that machine-gun nest? That was where McPherson got his. **1924** T. Boyd *Points* 26: Well, he got his trying to take a machine-gun nest single-handed. **1928** Wharton *Squad* 103: Jim got his. **1928** Santee *Cowboy* 122: For a puncher knows he's apt to get his any time when a pony turns over on him. **1929** Tully *Shadows of Men* 273: In many a jungle it was told how the marshal "got his'n." **1944** (quot. at ETO). **1974** Gober *Black Cop* 201: "I may get mine tonight but you're going to get yours now." He raised the .45 to firing position. **1981** G. Wolf *Roger Rabbit* 58: Dead as a doornail. He got his. **1986** Heinemann *Paco's Story* 21: Ka-blamo, some poor fuckin' fool would get his eating breakfast.

¶ **Get out of town!** [elab. of colloq. *get out of here!*] *Stu.* (used to express disbelief.)
1984 Eble *Campus Slang* (Sept.) 4: *Get out of town*—a response made to an unbelievable claim. **1988** *Charmings* (ABC-TV): "Eric and I had a fight." "So?" "So we've never fought before." "Get out of town!" **1988** *Supercarrier* (ABC-TV): "I've seen you play poker." "Get outa town!" **1992** D. Burke *Street Talk* I 7: "You're kidding"...*Get outa town!* **1993** *Oprah* (synd. TV series): Get out of town! [That] happens every day....Get out of town, girl!

¶ **Get some!** *Mil.* (a cry of encouragement, esp. to attacking aircraft). [Quots. ref. to Vietnam War.]
1978 J. Webb *Fields of Fire* 412: *Get Some:* a common exhortation to kill the enemy. **1985** Dye *Between Raindrops* 93: Get Some, mourners. *Ibid.* 149: Now it's personal. Get Some, Captain. **1986** J. Hawkins *Tunnel Warriors* 332: Get some. Kill someone.

¶ **get (someone) wrong** to hold erroneous beliefs about (someone); misunderstand.
1911–12 Ade *Knocking the Neighbors* 203: You've got me wrong, Steve....I used to be a Depraved Character, but now I am the Big Hero. **1913–15** Van Loan *Taking the Count* 93: Nix, doc; nix!...You got him wrong. **1936** in Ruhm *Detective* 175: You got me wrong, mate. **1936** West *Klondike Annie* (film): Charity? Sister, you got me wrong. **1952** in C. Beaumont *Best* 18: Now don't go getting me wrong, kid. It ain't me. **1952** Bruce & Essex *K.C. Confidential* (film): You got me wrong! **1963** Holzer *Ghost Hunter* 8: Don't get me wrong—these people understand who I am. **1989** *U.S. News & W.R.* (Dec. 18) 19: Don't get me wrong, I'm happy to help....But this was getting a bit out of hand.

¶ **get there** see THERE, *adv.*

¶ **get with** see s.v. WITH, *prep.*

¶ **You got it!** Yes; I agree; (*also*) I will.
1968 Craig *Anzio* (film): "O.K....Keep me in your sights." "You got it." **1972–76** Lynde *Rick O'Shay* (unp.): Fishin'!? You *got* it, pard!

get-along *n.* one's gait; (*hence*) (*pl.*) the legs. *Joc.*

1930 Sage *Last Rustler* 39: Every one had a cheerful twitch in his git-along. **1941** *AS* (Feb.) 22 (Indiana): *Get-alongs.* Legs. "Get up/on your get-alongs." **1965–70** in *DARE.* **1987** R. Miller *Slob* 243: It was either blood pressure, the dropsy, the whim-whams,...a severe hitch in the gitalong, or one of those cases of spofus sporium you read about.

getaway *n.* **1.a.** a sudden dash, as the breaking of a fox from cover or the breaking of racehorses, etc., from the starting line. Now *S.E.*

***1852** in *OED:* The quick find, the quick get-away. [**1880** *N.Y. Clipper Almanac* 44: Turf Directory....*Get away.*—To rush from the score [starting line].] **1904** in Paxton *Sport USA* 16: The man with the ball...was swerving now to the right, now to the left, meditating a get-away. ***1923** in *OEDS:* No one failed to start, although in general the getaways were not so fast or neat as in the case of the trade riders.

b. the very start.—constr. with *the.*

1896 Ade *Artie* 55: A little slow on the get-away, but I made a Garrison finish. **1900** Ade *More Fables* 186: That was only the Get-Away. **1908** in Fleming *Unforget. Season* 180: So he was available when Ames blew up at the getaway.

2.a. *Und.* a railroad train or other vehicle that may be used for an escape; a method or avenue of escape.

1859 Matsell *Vocab.* 36: *Getaway.* A locomotive; railroad train. **1926** *N.Y. Times* (Oct. 10) VIII 20: "Get-away" was originally the name given by the burglar brotherhood to a locomotive or railway train in the early days of steam transportation. **1937** Reitman *Box-Car Bertha* 184: Make for the get-away, kid. **1961** in Himes *Black on Black* 96: That's their get-away. He's gonna take her right after it's over.

b. *Orig. Und.* an escape or means of escape, as from confinement or from the scene of a crime; (*hence*) a hurried departure. Now *colloq.*

***1890** in *OED:* There is some get away, if anything broke, short of your neck. **1892** L. Moore *Own Story* 172 [ref. to 1870's]: He was instructed...to be sure to have his team fresh and in good condition...as we might be forced to make a quick "get away." **1896** in Alter *Utah Jour.* 196: Making his getaway; he left the country for good. **1902** "J. Flynt" *Little Bro.* 196: S'pose you steal something, and want to make a get-away. **1907** in C.M. Russell *Paper Talk* 59: Every time I try an make my git-away he invites me up to have crackers an milk. **1908** in H.C. Fisher *A. Mutt* 97: Escape of Pete and Felix Recalls Other Famous Get-Aways. **1912** in Truman *Dear Bess* 91: If we hadn't made a hurried get-away. **1913** *Sat. Eve. Post* (Mar. 1) 50: Knocked me out an' made his getaway! **1914** Callison *Bill Jones* 356: He had made a complete get-away. **1916** Scott *17 Yrs.* 18: Each act is...measured only by dollars and cents, and the opportunity for a clean "getaway." **1921** Casey & Casey *Gay-Cat* 61: No screw or warden shook *my* fin when I made my gitaway from thet stir. **1925–26** Black *You Can't Win* 302: You've got to stand them off and dash out. Where? Why, nowhere. There's no getaway here. **1928** MacArthur *War Bugs* 226: We paused in our get-away to see his epic end. **1931** Bontemps *Sends Sunday* 51: Gonna pack up ma trunk an' make ma get-away. **1931** Burdick *J. Goodall* 17: On several occasions Goodall made "getaways" from hostile Indians.

getaway bag *n. Baseball.* first base.

1907 Lajoie *Official Base Ball Guide* 110 (cited in Nichols *Baseball Term.*).

getaway car *n. Orig. Police.* a car used by criminals in making an escape. Now *colloq.*

1930 Lavine *Third Degree* 129: The stolen get-away Cadillac car. **1949** in *Harper's* (Feb. 1950) 74: The procurement of the getaway car is one of his responsibilities. ***1968** in *OEDS:* You...provided the get-away car. **1979** in Terkel *Amer. Dreams* 247: A young boy came forward with the license number of the getaway car.

get-away day *n. Horse Racing.* the final day of a series of horse races.

1891 in *DA:* Track talk. Get-away-day. **1899–1900** Cullen *Tales* 236: I'd probably have owned the track on get-away day. **1908** in H.C. Fisher *A. Mutt* 82: I will be back in time to get a bet down on get-away day. **1935** Pollock *Und. Speaks:* Get away day, the last day of a race track meeting.

getaway money *n. Orig. Horse Racing.* money sought on GET-AWAY DAY to enable owners to move on to another race elsewhere; (*hence*) a usu. nominal payment given to participants at the conclusion of a semiprofessional entertainment event.

[**1895** in *DA:* Last Day at Morris. Get-Away Purses are Divided.] **1923** in *DA:* All the burglars at the track will be levelling for the get-away money. **1981** O'Day & Eells *High Times* 41: Then Hal asked everyone connected with the fiasco to line up along the bleachers and he passed out "getaway" money.

get down *v.* see s.v. DOWN, *adv.*

get-go *n.* Esp. *Black E.* the very beginning. Cf. colloq. *from the word "go."*

1966 in T.C. Bambara *Gorilla* 42: I knew Dick and Jane was full of crap from the get-go. **1970** D.L. Lee *We Walk* 31: From the get-go she was down, realdown. **1971** Woodley *Dealer* 102: It was his bust from the git-go. **1976** H. Ellison *Sex Misspelled* 27: False and untenable rules...had been the order...from the git-go. **1980** *Oui* (Aug.) 92: He's kind of a fun guy from the get-go. **1985** Baker *Cops* 99: If I caught it right from the get-go, there'd still be people out there in the street. **1986** *L. A. Law* (NBC-TV): Like I told you from the get-go, honey. **1986** *Larry King Live* (CNN-TV) (Oct. 14): And that's why the President's position is a nonstarter from the get-go. **1987** *21 Jump St.* (Fox-TV): They gotta believe you from the get-go. **1988** *Beauty and the Beast* (CBS-TV): So the search was illegal from the get-go. **1992** Hosansky & Sparling *Working Vice* 131: Right from the getgo.

get-off *n.* **1.** a beginning.

1843 "J. Slick" *High Life in N.Y.* 41: I've made a good git-off this time.

2. a joke.

1895 Sinclair *Alabama* 43: He opened the conversation in a facetious vein, recently adopted, and which he seemed to nurse as a pretty good "get off."

3. *Jazz.* (see quot.).

1937 *New Yorker* (Apr. 17) 27: The musical phrases which constitute a swing style are called *licks, riffs,* or *get-offs. Ibid.* 30: He...launched the band into a real hunk of get-off.

get off *v.* **1.** to utter or tell, esp. a joke or anecdote. Now *S.E.*

1849 in *DA:* There is the writing of one who tried to "get off," as the boys said, something comic on every occasion. **1882** in Francis *Saddle & Moccasin* 22: Brown then "got off" his last tale or joke. **1911** H.S. Harrison *Queed* 15: Miss Miller applauded the witty hit. "Oh, it ain't mine," said Mr. Klinker modestly. "I heard a fellow get it off at the shop the other day." **1929–32** in *AS* (Dec. 1934) 290: *Get your stuff off....*To say what you have to say; to tell your story.

2.a. to induce orgasm in.—usu. considered vulgar. Cf. OFF, *adv.*

1867 Doten *Journals* II 954 [In cipher]: She mounted me & fucked till she got us both off. **1961** Gover *$100 Misunderstanding* 33: Git yer ass upstairs an git them tricks off an git yer ass back downstairs. **1967** Hamma *Motorcycle Mommas* 54: He liked it, I could tell, but I couldn't get him off.

b. to achieve orgasm.—usu. considered vulgar.

1867 Doten *Journals* II 959 [In cipher]: She didn't get off at all—Too much in a hurry. **1970** Landy *Underground Dict.* 88: *Get off...*Have a climax (sexual). **1977** C. McFadden *Serial* 252: Heavy-duty erotic art; Bill practically got off on the invitation. **1977** *Rolling Stone* (Dec. 1) 58: You tip the girl, and we see that you...get...off [ellipses in original]. **1981** Spears *Slang & Euphem.* 160: *Get off...*to ejaculate.

3. to steal.

1872 in "M. Twain" *Life on Miss.* 292: I hadn't no more than got it off when i wished i hadn't done it.

4. *Black E.* to achieve success; obtain one's object.

1929 in Oliver *Blues Tradition* 221: I got a gal she's got a Rolls-Royce,/ She didn't get off by usin' her voice.

5. *Orig. Jazz.* to play or improvise jazz or other popular music skillfully and imaginatively, esp. in solo.

[**1932** in R.S. Gold *Jazz Talk* 107: There is an abundance of trumpet-playing of the first order from the local "get-off" man.] **1933** *Fortune* (Aug.) 47: Trombonist Brown...can *get off* (...syncopate to beat the band). **1936** *Harper's* (Apr.) 571: Thus it is not the purpose of the jazz soloist who is "getting off" merely to distort. **1936** in R.S. Gold *Jazz Talk* 107: *Getting off.* Really swinging. **1937** *AS* (Oct.) 181: After a change, when one musician rises from his seat and plays a solo chorus with accompaniment by...the...orchestra, he is said to "get off" or "take off." **1946** Mezzrow & Wolfe *Really Blues* 73: Musicians get keyed-up...when a brother of the same school drops in to hear them get off. *Ibid.* 305: *Get off:* express yourself, render a good performance. **1964** R.S. Gold *Jazz Lexicon: Get off.* To improvise skillfully. **1968** in *Rolling Stone Interviews* 48: You got to look at the other cat and get off right there. **1971** Wells & Dance *Night People* 8: In those days we played blues, but we played a lot of pop numbers, too. Those guys could really get off on tunes like that....They could play just about anything, in whatever key you wanted, but they played it like they felt it.

6. to stop criticizing, plaguing, or harassing (someone).—often constr. with *of.*

1943 *AS* (Apr.) 154: *Get off me.* "Stop criticizing me." [**1946** Boulware *Jive & Slang* 6: *Off Me*...Don't annoy me.] **1958** N.Y.C. schoolboys: "Get off me!" "Get offa him, Bobby!" **1973** Childress *Hero* 45: You get off my kids!

7. *Black E.* to release one's hold on; hand over; provide; impart.—usu. constr. with *up.*

1951 in W.S. Burroughs *Letters* 92: I have to get up off $200. **1961** in Himes *Black on Black* 70: Harlem is full of rich Johns who'd get off a C-note for her. **1965** C. Brown *Manchild* 215: People who have a gun in their face will get up off money in a hurry. **1966** Braly *Cold* 91: You better get off the five bills and save yourself some jail. **1970** A. Young *Snakes* 42: A lot of em still dont wanna get up off no trim. **1971** in Sanchez *Word Sorcerers* 119: Well I might give a broad a good time, but I don't get up off no head....If you ever accuse me of cuntlapping again, I'll punch you in the mouth. **1978** W. Brown *Tragic Magic* 19: One way or the other, somebody will be getting up off of *something. Ibid.* 38: He never gets up off too much talk.

8. *Narc.* to begin to feel the effect of a narcotic, psychotropic, or hallucinogenic drug.—also *trans.*; (*hence*) to take illicit drugs.—often constr. with *on.*

[**1936** *AS* (Apr.) 121: *Get the habit off.* To indulge in narcotics; to satisfy a desire intensified by abstinence.] **1952** H. Ellson *Golden Spike* 92: I'm dying to get off. **1954** Maurer & Vogel *Narc. & Narc. Add.* (gloss.): At that time I was getting off on H and speed balls. **1962** Larner & Tefferteller *Addict in the Street* 85: All I can think about is getting off, getting my fix. **1967–68** von Hoffman *Parents Warned Us:* They'll get ya off, I guess....They're not a burn. **1968** Heard *Howard St.* 15: That woman knew he hadn't got off since six this evening. **1969** Mitchell *Thumb Tripping* 184: "Wow, you're getting off!" he applauded. **1970** Cain *Blueschild Baby* 5: Flow, get my things out, Georgie's going to get off. **1976** in *High Times* (Jan. 1977) 9: It takes a huge joint to get one person off. **1967–80** Folb *Runnin' Lines* 239: *Get off.* Begin to feel the impact of a particular drug or substance.

9. *Orig. Black E.* to enjoy oneself; **get off on** to derive intense pleasure from; become excited or enthusiastic about; enjoy.

1952 Himes *Stone* 210: I passed two colored convicts...rocking from side-to-side and singing a repetitious chant....It was just an emotional outlet, just a substitute for sex. Just getting off, I thought. **1971** N.Y.U. student: I don't get off on Dante. **1974** V.B. Miller *Girl in River* 12: I'm told they really get off on vice jobs. **1974** U.C.L.A. student: Some people really get off on this stuff. *ca*1976 in *6,000 Words* 82: For a long while, if I heard somebody play a piece that was really hard to play, I got off more on that than on the melody. **1977** C. McFadden *Serial* 75: Martha...seemed to get off on laying bad trips on people. **1977** *N.Y. Times* (Sept. 15) (Home Sec.) 25: A lot of people get off on getting into a loft. **1978** *Saturday Night Live* (NBC-TV): They're the lowest form of life, but they really get off. **1984** *Miami Vice* (NBC-TV): You're diggin' on me and him at the same time. Really gettin' off on it. **1986** Spears *Drugs & Drink* 217: *Get off on*...to become stimulated by anything including academic subjects. **1992** L. Johnson *My Posse* 24: Teachers...get off on rules.

10. to thrill or delight.

1970 in *Rolling Stone Interviews* 403: It really gets me off. I love it. **1976** *Dallas Times Herald* (Dec. 12) 2F: A great singing performance gets me off more than a great guitar solo. **1977** *Rolling Stone* (May 5) 23: A boogie concert where you just try to get everybody off.

¶ In phrases:

¶ **get 'em** [or **it** or **one**] **off** (orig. of a man) to reach orgasm; copulate; (*hence*) to derive great pleasure.—usu. considered vulgar.

1930–31 Farrell *Grandeur* 140: I'd get 'em off on these hot days, sitting in my white flannels with some rich jane on the veranda of a club like that, sipping my liquor. **1934–35** in Farrell *Guillotine Party* 272: Me, I'd like to go to a can house. I feel the imminent need of getting 'em off. **1943** Farrell *Days of Anger* 132 [ref. to 1925]: "Let's go to Twenty-two and get laid." "Dopey, you're too drunk to get 'em off." **1965** Trimble *Sex Words* 88: *Get it off.* To achieve Orgasm in the male; to cause Ejaculation. **1972** R. Wilson *Playboy's Forbidden Words* 123: *Get it off*...is to achieve orgasm. **1975** Harrell & Bishop *Orderly House* 80: He either gets on top or puts me up there and we get it off very big. **1975** Nat.

Lampoon (Sept.) 52: So. Never gotten one off with a garette before, eh? **1977** B. Davidson *Collura* 60: I guess getting it off with a chick was part of the high. **1983** Flaherty *Tin Wife* 176: She gets it off embarrassing anyone who won't adhere to her party line. **1992** *Donahue* (NBC-TV): Your wife's getting it off with other men!

¶ **get off it!** stop talking nonsense!—sometimes constr. with *up.*

*1923 (cited in Partridge *DSUE* 325). **1962** Killens *Heard the Thunder* 15 [ref. to 1943]: If he ain't no sergeant, you sure ain't no corporal, so get up off it, you bubble-eyed punk. **1970** Quammen *Walk the Line* 150: Aw shit, get off it, Book. Don't play that game. **1978** Wharton *Birdy* 6: Ah, come on, Birdy. Get off it, huh? **1992** D. Burke *Street Talk* I 128: Oh, *get off it*...Oh, *stop talking nonsense.*

¶ **get off the natural** *Narc.* to get high.

1966 Elli *Riot* 44: If a guy wanted to get off the natural in a zoo like this, he didn't have much choice.

¶ **get (one's) rocks** [or **nuts** or **balls**] **off, 1.** to ejaculate or experience orgasm; engage in copulation. Also trans.—usu. considered vulgar. [Usu. said of men, but the form with *rocks* is now occ. applied to women also.]

1941 G. Legman, in Henry *Sex Var.* II 1167: *Get one's nuts off.* To ejaculate; to experience sexual relief. **1945–48** *Marianas Coll.* (unp.): Marines get rocks off every night,/Three thousand dollars brings great delight. **1953** Manchester *City of Anger* 370: "In a glass house I wouldn't get my rocks off, if I was you." "The poor man's Milton Berle." **1965** C. Brown *Manchild* 165: I'd gotten my nuts off about six times. **1967** Mailer *Vietnam* 149: The climax within Alaska is yet to come—you will get rocks off you thought were buried forever. **1967** [Beck] *Pimp* 688: Some broad is going to lay out five-hundred frog skins to get her rocks off. **1969** Tynan *Oh! Calcutta!* 39: You know how men are, honey. They just gotta get their rocks off in different places. So I says to him, "What about me, I got rocks to get off, too!" **1970** *Playboy* (Nov.) 244: I thought it was ugly the way a guy would just grab a naked girl, throw her to the ground and get his rocks off. **1970–71** Rubinstein *City Police* 321: Let him get his rocks off before you pull him out of the car. **1971** *Nightsounds* (Jan. 8) 5: If you want to get your balls off.... **1966–80** McAleer & Dickson *Unit Pride* 244: Just watchin' her is almost enough to get your rocks off. **1980** in *Penthouse* (Jan. 1981) 38: He told her she was copping out—getting her rocks off and leaving him to his own devices.

2. to derive intense or perverse pleasure; (*broadly*) to enjoy (oneself). Also trans.—usu. considered vulgar. [See note at **(1)**, above.]

1948 *AS* XXIII 249: *Get your rocks off.* An expression used to denote extreme enjoyment. **1959** Cochrell *Barren Beaches* 146 [ref. to WWII]: You'll never get your rocks off this way. What's the matter with you? **1963** J. Ross *Dead Are Mine* 269 [ref. to WWII]: Let's face it. You get your rocks off up there. You bitch about the rain and the mud...but you like it. **1968** Myrer *Eagle* 476: That's a good one....If there's anything that gets my rocks off it's an officer with a sense of humor. **1971** S. Stevens *Way Uptown* 103: That's how they get their rocks off. Yeah, they're sick. **1972** Wambaugh *Blue Knight* 64: You got your rocks off once by [arresting] me, Morgan. **1973** Gent *N. Dallas* 32: That little honey...really gets her rocks off over football. **1973** Flaherty *Fogarty* 144: Go get your rocks off over someone else's life. **1974** Radano *Cop Stories* 30: I'd work him over. Not because I get my rocks off. I never beat on a guy unless he gave me a reason to do it. **1978** Diehl *Sharkey's Machine* 217: You get your balls off thinking about all the people you control.

¶ **tell** [or **show**] **where to get off** [perh. in allusion to *get off (one's) high horse*] to rebuke for one's presumption; scold.

1900 Ade *More Fables:* He said he was a Gentleman, and that no Cheap Skate in a Plug Hat could tell him where to Get Off. **1904** Ade *True Bills* 109: My Children...tell me every Day where to get off. **1908** McGaffey *Show Girl* 84: I told them where to get off, and don't you forget it. **1913–15** Van Loan *Taking the Count* 22: I want to show these knockers where to get off. **1918** McNutt *Yanks* 208: What do you want to get your disposition all run down at the heel for, trying to show me where I get off? **1919** Bates *Fighting to Win* 71: I'll just tell 'em where to get off. **1920** in Fitzgerald *Stories* 105: Come through, Bernice....Tell her where to get off. **1930** Dos Passos *42nd Parallel* 18: A cop tried to stop me, but I told him right where to get off. *1932, *1953, *1963, in *OEDS.*

¶ **where does (someone) get off?** where does (someone) get the effrontery or impudence?

1908 in H.C. Fisher *A. Mutt* 61: Where would Joe Gans get off if

Beany had focused his powerful mind upon the Queensberry game? **1908** H. Green *Maison de Shine* 2: Where does Maggie de Shine get off at? **1915** T. Dreiser, in Riggio *Dreiser-Mencken Letters* I 197: Yet if they can pick things like…"The Spoon River Anthology" and things of that sort, and you can't or don't, where do you get off? **1925** Hemingway *In Our Time* 74: Where the hell do you think you get off? **1948** Lay & Bartlett *Twelve O'Clock High* 24: "You're right, Keith," he said finally. "Where do I get off lecturing you?" **1963** D. Tracy *Brass Ring* 32: Where does he get off makin' me do his work for him while he plays tennis with some girl? **1988** Lambert *Liberace* (film): Where do you get off telling me that stuff?

get-on *n. Und.* (see quot.).
1930 Conwell *Professional Thief* 42: A cannon mob may be working a get-on (place where many people enter streetcars) and beat the first man just before he steps on the car.

get on *v. Narc.* to get high; use psychotropic or hallucinogenic drugs; TURN ON.
1961 Russell *Sound* 15: But let's all get on first. *Ibid.*: You get on, don't you Bernie?…You know, man—pot. Like, get high! **1963** Braly *Shake Him* 70: I can't get on with this, not even if I shot the whole piece at once. **1964** Anslinger & Gregory *Protectors* 229: *Get on.* to take drugs either for the first time or to maintain the habit. **1982** E.L. Abel *Marihuana Dict.* 43: *Get on.* Various meanings including smoking marihuana.

¶ In phrases:
¶ **get it on, 1.** to get the better of.
1906 T.A. Dorgan, in Zwilling *TAD Lexicon* 105: To night [*sic*] the boys are going to the ring with the idea of getting it on the other fellow a bit.

2. to get started; get going; get busy; go to it; (*hence*) to perform or work with energy or enthusiasm.
1956 Ross *Hustlers* 63: Let's get going. Get it on! *Ibid.* 107: "Yah," said Mambo. "Let's get it on." **1962** B. Jackson *In the Life* 156: You think you slick with cards and I think I'm slick with cards, so let's get it on. **1966** I. Reed *Pall-Bearers* 112: Tell us when we gone get it on. **1968–70** *Current Slang* III & IV 55: *Get it on…*Get started. **1970** Fonda, Hopper & Southern *Easy Rider* (film): Let's get it on. **1970** *Time* (Aug. 17) 32: *Get it on:* to pull yourself together ("Get it on, Max; the fuzz is outside.") **1970** T. Wolfe *Radical Chic* 110: You can't get it on and bring thirty-five people walking all the way from the Mission to 100 McAllister and then just turn around and go back. **1970** Grissim *White Man's Blues* 51: He doesn't give the audience two seconds to comprehend before he gets it on with some great Cajun fiddling and a magnificent gap-toothed smile. **1971** Meggyesy *Out of Their League* 81: Once the fight was on in earnest Randy really got it on. **1971** J.D. Simmons *Blues* 20: Git it on, God/let it rain. **1976** Rosen *Above Rim* 159: "What's really happening on the team? Anything unusual? Everybody getting it on?" "Sure. All together. Harmony." *ca*1986 in *NDAS*: And they overlay their daring with pure joy. They're getting it on. **1987** *RHD2*: A rock group really getting it on with the audience. **1993** *News Hour* (CNN-TV) (Mar. 8): We are ready.…Let's get it on.

3. *Orig. Black E.* to start or engage in a fight, brawl, or altercation.
1959 A. Anderson *Lover Man* 101: I got you on two counts, so…let's git it on! **1961** Braly *Felony Tank* 51: You want to get it on? Is that it? You want to have it out right now? **1962** in *AS* (Dec. 1963) 276: In a potential fight situation, one boy can indicate his willingness to have a fight by saying "Get it on." **1968** Gover *JC* 22: Out front a this hotel, them wind-up toy [police] is gettin it on. Rat-a-tat-tat. **1970** in Sanchez *Word Sorcerers* 107: It was Red Beans who had snatched the key and Sonny knew they were going to get it on. **1973** in H.S. Thompson *Shark Hunt* 84: By half time the place was a drunken madhouse, and anybody who couldn't get in anywhere else could always…try to get into…[the] "Men's Room" through the "Out" door; there were always a few mean drunks lurking around to punch anybody who tried that.

4. to copulate.
1970 Landy *Underground Dict.* 88: *Get it on…*Have sexual intercourse. **1971** B.B. Johnson *Blues for Sister* 31: She gripped him with her legs and they got it on. **1972** Wurlitzer *Quake* 79: Would you make it with her if you could?…Would you get it on with her? **1973** *Atlantic* (Dec.) 81: I think you and Eldorado ought to git it on. There ain't a better lookin' dude. **1978** *Rolling Stone* (Nov. 16) 65: Yeah, I met her, we almost got it on but…her old man was hangin' around, keepin' an eye on her. **1984** W. Murray *Dead Crab* 63: I didn't tell him we got it on, stupid. **1992** *Sally Jessy Raphaël* (synd. TV series): We don't allow people to get it on on their front lawns.

¶ **get one on, 1.** to get angry.
1929–30 Farrell *Young Lonigan* 17: All right, don't get…a…don't get so excited!…That was a narrow escape. He'd almost told his sister not to get one on, and then there'd have been sixteen different kinds of hell to pay around the house.

2. to have an erection of the penis.
1973 Eble *Campus Slang* (Mar.) 2: *Get one on*—applied to males, to become sexually aroused.

get out *n.* **1.** the utmost degree.—used in comparisons, now usu. constr. with *all*. Now *colloq.*
1838 Neal *Char. Sks.* 12: We look as elegant and as beautiful as get out. **1866** G.A. Townsend *Non-Combatant* 172: My regiment…give 'em "get out!" ***1869** in *OEDS*: As common as get out. (Cornish proverb.) ***1884** "M. Twain" *Huck. Finn* ch. xxxviii: We got to dig in like all git-out. *ca*1890 *F & H* I 33: *All-Get-Out…*(American).—That beats *all-get-out*, is an old retort to any extravagant story or assertion. **1904** Ade *True Bills* 60: What in the Name of all Get-Out do you find to talk about? **1941** "G.R. Lee" *G-String* 233: Stingy as all get-out. **1948** J.H. Burns *Lucifer* 220: Ya gettin aggressive as all get-out, the coach said. **1953** Bradbury *Fahr. 451* 23: I'm hungry as all-get-out. **1976** Calloway & Rollins *Moocher & Me* 128: But I was angry as all get out. **1979** Gutcheon *New Girls* 15: She sure looked chic as all get-out. **1987** *RHD2*: Once his mind is made up, he can be stubborn as all get-out.

2. *Und.* GETAWAY, 1.
***1899** in *OEDS*: I ask you, was there ever a better get-out? **1949** in *Harper's* (Feb. 1950) 74: Certain [cars are] widely known as "dogs on the get-out," which is to say that they accelerate slowly from a standing start.

get over *v.* **1.a.** Now *Black E.* to seduce or copulate with (a woman). Also *intrans.*
ca*1890–93 *F & H* III 135: *To get over…*To seduce, to fascinate, to dupe. **1916 Cary *Venery* I 107: *Getting Over*—To seduce a girl. **1971** Dahlskog *Dict.* 27: *Get over (someone). vulgar.* To have sexual intercourse with someone. **1994** N. McCall *Wanna Holler* 39: He had "gotten over" on some broad he'd been working on.
b. Now *Black E.* to impress favorably, esp. through insincerity or manipulation.—also *intrans,* constr. with *with.*
ca*1890–93 (quot. at (a), above). **1971 H. Roberts *Third Ear* (unp.): *Get over v.* to maneuver oneself into a more favorable position with another. **1967–80** Folb *Runnin' Lines* 137: To *get over*—essentially to win over another with your words and actions. **1984** *Miami Vice* (NBC-TV): Mr. Taylor, you trying to get over with my woman? **1986** *NDAS:* He did everything he could think of, but still couldn't get over her.
c. *Black E.* to get the better (of).—constr. with *on.*
1982 Del Vecchio *13th Valley* 87 [ref. to 1960's]: They say, "gotta get over on them cause they gettin over on us." **1988** *Spin* (Oct.) 24: It's the Great American…Novel of Godless human flotsam all trying to get over on one another. *a*1990 E. Currie *Dope & Trouble* 7: One lady try to get over, you know?…tryin' to get over on people.

2. [orig. short for *colloq. get over the footlights* (trans. of F *passer la rampe*), as in first 1915 quot.; cf. GO OVER, 2] **a.** *Orig. Theat.* to achieve success, as with an audience; (*hence*) to achieve one's object; (*broadly*) (*Black E.*) to get by.
[**1915** in *DA* 694: Shaw was generally considered altogether too wild to stand a chance of getting over the footlights.] **1915** *Variety* (June 4) 4: Sketch Gets Over.…"The Call" went over big this weekend. ***1920** in *OEDS:* "The Rose of America"…had apparently got over. **1922** *Variety* (Sept. 8) 17: "Hairy Ape" Gets Over—Mixed Notices for "Blue Kitten." **1928** Callahan *Man's Grim Justice* 281: The average writer spends ten or twelve years…before he gets over. **1929** Booth *Stealing Through Life* 304 [ref. to *ca*1920]: "If you hadn't let that guy get away, we could have weeded the chip and got over worth while." He was still regretting the escape of the customer, which had prevented us from rifling the vault. **1934** Duff & Sauber *20 Million Sweethearts* (film): This is his chance for a comeback. If this doesn't get over he might as well sign up with a burlesque show. **1984** J. Green *Dict. Contemp. Slang* 111: *get over v.* (US Black use) to achieve a given goal. **1988** *Morning Edition* (Nat. Pub. Radio) (Sept. 16): I'd say, "Do I look like an Irishman or a Scotsman to you?" And that's how I'd get over!
b. *Theat.* to make (a dramatic work or the like) successfully appealing.
***1916** in *OEDS:* Uses…bits of business to "get his plays over." **1933** in E. O'Neill *Letters* 411: The new plays will be difficult to "get over" and they will need all the breaks possible.
3. *Esp. Black E.* to improve one's status or condition; suc-

ceed in life; (*broadly*) to do very well.

1968 in [V.M. Grosvenor] *Thursday* 16: We got 7 servants helpin' us to get over. **1968–70** *Current Slang* III & IV 55: *Get over*, v. To cross barriers; to make it; to be functioning in the White World.—John wasn't able to *get over*...v. To do well.—I *got over* on the exam. **1971** H. Roberts *Third Ear* (unp.): Get over, *v*....to make oneself better. **1977** Smitherman *Talkin & Testifyin* 72: All black groups speak of *gittin ovuh*, overcoming strife and pressures of oppression and thus being in a continuous state of *happiness* and *highness*. *Ibid.* 73: "How I Got Ovuh." **1967–80** Folb *Runnin' Lines* 239: *Get over*...1. Succeed in life. 2. Acquire status.

4. *Mil.* to get along by holding a soft assignment; have things easy; loaf.

1969 in Lanning *Only War* 16: Talked to Lt in club—Has some easy job in Saigon—Proud he is "getting over"—SOB. **1972** Ft. Campbell Ky. Drill Sgt. (coll. J. Ball): You trainees think once you're out of BCT you'll be getting over all the live-long day. **1974** U.S. Army PFC (coll. J. Ball): All any soldier cares about is just getting over. **1978** U.S. Army Spec. 6 (coll. J. Ball): What's it like at [Ft.] Lewis? I bet you get over like a mother fucker.

5. Esp. *Und.* to take advantage of; impose upon.

1978–79 in E.M. Miller *Street Woman* 165: I've learned how to get over banks, how to get over people.

-getter *comb. form. Und.* a thief.

1880 Pinkerton *Pro. Thieves* 59: Working in silk robberies, or, in criminal parlance, among "swag-getters." **1901** "J. Flynt" *World of Graft* 220: *Prop-getters*, thieves who make a specialty of "lifting" scarf-pins. **1904** *Life in Sing Sing* (gloss.): *Stone-getter*—Thief who steals diamonds or any other precious stone from the person. **1926** *N.Y. Times* (Dec. 26) VIII 3: A "keister getter" is a baggage thief who works around railroad stations particularly. "Damper getter" means till tapper.

get-there *n.* ambition or energy.

1898 in *DA*: He hain't got much "git there" in his make-up.

getting-over *adj. Mil.* conducive to loafing; soft.—used prenominally.

1982 Del Vecchio *13th Valley* 8 [ref. to Vietnam War]: Dude, I had one gettin-over job....We didn't have to pull guard duty or have any details.

get-up *n.* **1.** energy; spirit.

1841 in *OED2*: It flats right down, and stays there, like a junk of dough—no get up up to it. **1863** in *DAE*: In vain I tried to convince him that there was some "get-up" in the animal. **1864** in C.W. Wills *Army Life* 280: Of several hundred factory girls I have seen,...they...lack "get up." **1873** Beadle *Undevel. West* 74: If you...have any "get-up" about you, and can and will work, there's a show for you in rural Nebraska. **1905** W.S. Kelly *Lariats* 85: The only one that's got any brains or "get-up" in the whole crew. **1909** in *DAE*: The' ain't a chance for a man with get-up on this place. **1918** *Chi. Sun. Tribune* (Feb. 17) V (unp.): Now there's a girl with...a lot o' getup an' pep. **1946** Steinbeck *Wayward Bus* 147: He's young, and he's got lots of get-up, and he's got ideas. **1947** in *DA*: Therein lies the answer to any charge that he hasn't any "git-up" to him. **1965–70** in *DARE*.

2. costume. Now *colloq.*

***1847** in *OED*: He is just like Lord Combermere in face, figure, and get-up, but a little bigger. ***1856** in *F & H* III 137: Is that killing *get up* entirely for your benefit, John? ***1866** "G. Eliot," in *F & H*: The graceful, well-appointed Mr. Christian...sneered at Scales about his *get up*. **1881** Trumble *Man Traps of N.Y.* 8: Society belles are not in the habit of making acquaintants in this way, however much the gorgeous get-up of the sirens in question may incline you to the contrary belief. **1900** Dunbar *Gideon* 124: Some of the jockeys laughed at his get-up. ***1908** Chesterton *Man Who Was Thursday* 94: That's a good get-up of yours. **1920** S. Lewis *Main St.* 333, in *DARE*: Wasn't that the darndest get-up he had on? **1974** Dubinsky & Standora *Decoy Cop* 118: Most times it's a great getup, but not today.

3. *Pris.* the final morning of a prison term.

1918 in *AS* (Oct. 1933) 27: *Get-up*. The morning of one's release. "Boy, I only got sixty-seven more days an' a get-up." **1932** Lawes *20,000 Years in Sing Sing* 239: He is going home soon. It's so close he is counting the days. So many days and a "get-up." **1935** (cited in Partridge *Dict. Und.* 285).

get-up-and-git *n.* energy, spirit; ambition; get-up-and-go.

1870 in R.W. Paul *Mining Frontiers* 123: There is not that "git up and git" that can be seen in the mining districts of Nevada especially. **1884** Peck *Boss Book* 183: The adjutant...felt his position demanded a horse that had some git-up-and-git. **1888** in *DAE*: More vim and more "git-

up-and-git." **1889, 1892, 1902** in *DAE*. **1949** *Time* (Mar. 7) 63: There was plenty of farm news if someone only had the get-up-and-git to go after it.

G.F. *n. Stu.* girlfriend.

1926 Lardner *Haircut* 59: A G.F., that's a girl-friend, and a B.F. is a boyfriend. I thought everybody knew that. **1928** McEvoy *Show Girl* 45: Well by this time the G.F. is pretty dizzy. **1932** *AS* VII (June) 332: *G.F.*—girl friend.

GFO *n.* [general *fuck-off*] *Mil.* a lazy individual. *Joc.*

1948 *N.Y. Folklore Qly.* 20 [ref. to WWII]. **1957** Myrer *Big War* 213 [ref. to WWII]: Snap-to, you pitiful gutless GFO!

GFU *n.* [general *fuck-up*] *Mil.* an incompetent individual. *Joc.*

1942 *Yank* (Nov. 25) 21: G.I. Jones...was the GFU of Bat. B 66th CA (AA). **1944** in *AS* XX 148: *G.F.U.* General foul up; a soldier who does not do the work he is supposed to do. **1945** *Sat. Rev. of Lit.* (Nov. 3) 7: He had better learn. Otherwise he will be known as a GFU...and that would be just TS. **1945** *AS* (Dec.) 262: *G.F.U.*, "a soldier who never does anything correctly." **1962** Killens *Heard the Thunder* 208 [ref. to WWII]: Sad sacks and GFUs and...goldbricks. **1991** Reinberg *In the Field* 93 [ref. to Vietnam War]: *G F U* abbr. for General Fuck-Up, usually referring to specific persons.

G-girl *n.* (see quot.). Cf. G-MAN.

1962 *AS* XXXVII 178: *G-girl* "government girl," a term commonly applied during the 1930s to a woman employee of the Federal government.

G-guy *n.* G-MAN, *n.*, 1.

1932 D. Runyon, in *Collier's* (June 11) 7: It seems that these G-guys are members of a squad that comes on from Washington, and...do not know that Good Time Charley's joint is not supposed to be busted up. **1935** S. Miller *"G" Men* (film): I don't want to get tangled up with you G guys.

g'hal *n.* [alter. of GAL on analogy with B'HOY] a young working-class woman, the counterpart of a B'HOY.

1850 [Judson] *G'hals of New York* (title). **1855** in Dwyer & Lingenfelter *Songs of Gold Rush* 25: We've got a few unmarried g'hals.

G-heat *n. Und.* pressure or trouble from federal law enforcement agencies; (*also*) federal law enforcement agents.

1937 Hoover *Persons in Hiding* 114: You're hot. It's G heat! We don't want to lay eyes on you! **1940** Longstreet *Decade* 357: He chalked out a momser, and the coppers...and G-heat are on him. **1949** in *Harper's* (Feb. 1950) 74: The G-heat may assume it has been stolen and enter the case on that basis. **1955** E. Hunter *Jungle Kids* 102: Also he was getting G-heat because...he transported some broads into Connecticut for the purpose of prostitution. **1966** Longstreet & Godoff *Wm. Kite* 277: No G-heat on you?

Ghee *n.* var. GUEE.

ghee[1] *n.* var. GEE[2].

ghee[2] *n.* var. GEE[3].

ghetto blaster *n.* a large portable stereophonic combination radio and tape player. [These devices, played very loud in public, were a fad among many inner-city youths, esp. *ca*1978-81.]

1981 *L.A. Times* (Apr. 2) I 26: Whites, who once disparaged the "boxes" with such nicknames as "ghetto blasters" and "third world briefcases" are flocking to buy the units. **1983** Eble *Campus Slang* (Mar.) 3: *Ghetto blaster*—larger portable radio or tape player. Also *ghetto box, jam box.* **1983** Wambaugh *Delta Star* 23: He also had a ghetto blaster strapped around *his* neck. **1984** McInerny *Bright Lights* 150: A kid...turns down the volume on his ghetto-blaster. **1986** Stinson & Carabatsos *Heartbreak* 47: A ghetto blaster wailed in a corner. **1987** *Daybreak* (CNN-TV) (Dec. 18): Here's a letter from a kid in Colorado that says, "Dear Santa: I would like a ghetto blaster." **1992** Majors & Billson *Cool Pose* 84: Ghettoblasters playing earsplitting music.

ghetto box *n.* GHETTO BLASTER.

1983 (quot. at GHETTO BLASTER).

ghetto guitar *n.* GHETTO BLASTER. *Joc.*

1984 D. Smith *Steely Blue* 114: One with a ghetto guitar, tuned to a Motown screeching station.

ghinny *n.* see GUINEA, *n.*

ghinzo *n.* see GINZO, *n.*

ghost *n.* **1.** a photograph.

1864 in H. Johnson *Talking Wire* 131: Al showed me his [sweetheart's] *ghost*. It looks quite natural, I think, all the boys that saw it think it is splendid.

2.a. a writer, artist, or other skilled individual who does work for someone else, who then takes public credit. Now *S.E.*

*1884 in *OED:* Plaintiff said he had heard of the expression "A sculptor's *ghost*"…a few months ago, and understood it to mean that a person who was supposed to do a work did not do it. ***1889** in *OED:* The only persons who make no secrecy about their ghosts are American millionaires, one of whom in…advertising once for a private secretary stated that the chief duties of the post would be to issue all his invitations and write all his speeches. ***1892** in *F & H* III 138: Would not the unkind describe your "practical man" as a *ghost*? **1927** in Paxton *Sport* 150: Special articles are prepared by ghost writers. **1935** in Paxton *Sport* 203: I was Dizzy's "*ghost*" in the 1934 World Series. Virtually all ball players who write for the newspapers have ghosts who take the athletes' thoughts…and transcribe them into articles for the public prints. **1942** *ATS* 491: *Ghost*, one who does literary work for which another takes credit. **1954** *AS* XXIX (Oct.) 189: When [Maurice] Dekobra speaks of a writer who follows "la profession de ghost," one immediately recognizes an Americanism. *ca***1961** in *WNID3:* It is his lot to serve as ghost for successful comic-strip artists. **1988** *New Republic* (Apr. 18) 19: The division of labor between ghost and "author."

b. a person who substitutes for another.

1945 Hamann *Air Words* 26: *Ghost*. A person who participates in an aircraft flight as a substitute for someone else.

c. a fictitious employee, student, etc., fraudulently given official status, esp. for the purpose of manipulating funds or the like; *(also)* a person for whom a place has been reserved who fails to appear.

1952 in *AS* XXXIX (May 1964) 145: Mississippi "*ghost*" students cost millions. **1959** in *AS* XXXIX (May 1964) 145: If even Harvard has "ghosts" (admitted applicants who do not show up on registration day), the smaller colleges must expect to be roundly haunted, and they are. **1978** *Business Week* (July 24) 179: A ghost…is a false bidder in the rear of the hall whose "bid" is used by the auctioneer to remove an item from sale if the coming knockdown price is too low. **1981** *L.A. Times* (June 13) I 3: The three…tricked the movie companies into paying the salaries of persons who did not work, known as…"ghosts" who did not exist. **1983** Sturz *Wid. Circles* XIII: Many of them are "ghosts" on the Board of Education rolls. **1989** *CBS This Morning* (CBS-TV) (May 31): A no-show or ghost employee situation.

3. [sugg. by phr. *the ghost walks*, below] a treasurer, paymaster, or cashier.

1901 Oliver *Roughing It* 167: The ghost had his money and papers in readiness. **1926** *AS* I 437: *The ghost*—The [theater] company treasurer. **1928** *N.Y. Times* (Mar. 11) VIII 6: *Ghost Window*—Cashier's window where pay checks are issued.

4. *Journ.* a ghost-written article; ghost job.

1961 Considine *Ripley* 36: Walsh is generally credited in sports with being the inventor of the press-box ghost, the by-lined story of an athlete about a contest in which he is participating.

5. (see quot.).

1961 *PADS* XXXVI (Nov.) 28: *Ghost, n.* A semi-humorous appellation for a carpenter, painter, or other workman wearing a white uniform.

6. *Black E.* a white person.—used contemptuously.

1971 Wells & Dance *Night People* 117: *Ghost, n.* A white person. **1982** "J. Cain" *Commandos* 334: The man spotted the "white ghost" following him and darted down a driveway. **1988** Poyer *The Med* 370: The man sends you out there, the ghost officers.

¶ In phrases:

¶ **great Caesar's ghost**! see s.v. CAESAR.

¶ **the ghost walks** Orig. *Theat.* salaries are about to be disbursed.

*1833 R. Dyer *9 Yrs. of Actor's Life* 53: If I played with applause, it was a matter of indifference whether "the ghost" walked on Saturday or not. ***1853** in *OED:* When no salaries are forthcoming on Saturday, *the ghost doesn't walk.* ***1873** Hotten *Slang Dict.* (ed. 4): *Ghost,* "the ghost doesn't walk," a theatrical term which implies that there is no money about, and that there will be no "treasury." ***1883** in *F & H* III 138: An Actor's Benevolent Fund box placed on the treasurer's desk every day when the ghost walks would get many an odd shilling or sixpence put into it. *ca***1889** in Barrère & Leland *Dict. Slang* I 405: A new play called "The Skeleton" has been produced at a Vaudeville matinée. It isn't likely to be in much esteem with the actors, owing to a natural defi-

ciency of "fat," although, on the other hand, it may certainly be expected to offer a favourable opportunity for the *ghost to walk*. ***1889** Barrère & Leland *Dict. Slang* I 405: *Ghost walking*…(commercial) in large firms, when the clerk whose duty it is goes round the various departments paying wages, it is common to say the *ghost walks*. **1898** *American Soldier* (Manila) (Nov. 12) 3: The Ghost walked on Monday. **1899** in Gatewood *Smoked Yankees* 155: The paymaster is in town and the boys are anxious to see the "ghost" walk, which is the camp name for the paymaster. **1901** Oliver *Roughing It* 162: The "ghost not having walked" since the latter part of July, when we were in Tampa, the majority of the troopers were unable to buy bananas and eggs. **1906** Beyer *Amer. Battleship* 82: "The ghost walking"—pay day. **1920** Herr *Co. F* 21: It is worth mentioning that the "Ghost walked" in Bouquemaison for the first time since leaving Camp Lee. Beaucoup Francs were handed out to everyone. **1927** *AS* III 24: On payday "the ghost walks" or it is "Christmas." **1942** H. Miller *Roofs of Paris* 24: I have to live on credits until the ghost walks again. **1946** Sevareid *Wild Dream* 28: The ceremony of the "ghost walking" with the pay envelopes on Saturday afternoon was merely one of the more delightful moments of the week. **1952** Sandburg *Young Strangers* 165 [ref. to Illinois, 1880's]: Like grown men, on a payday we said, "This is the day the ghost walks." **1959** Hecht *Sensualists* 100: One hundred dollars per week and I shall be content to remain your negligible and invisible husband for as long as the ghost walks. **1974** Sann *Dead Heat* 19: How about a ball-park figure of ten down and twenty after the ghost walks?

ghost *v.* **1.** to write or create (a work) for someone else who takes public credit. Also intrans. Now *S.E.*

*1922 in *OEDS:* "A certain general," for whom he did some "ghosting." **1925** in *OEDS:* A very distinguished person's wife once asked me if I would care to edit or "ghost" her husband's diary. **1929** McEvoy *Hollywood Girl* (title page): Worked up from Ghosting on a tabloid to writing dialogue for Rin-Tin-Tin. **1934** Forrest *Behind Front Page* 321: "Ghosted" somewhat by Stowe, Noville's story was cabled as follows. **1934** Weseen *Dict. Slang* 341: *Ghost*—To write articles or speeches used by another person. **1952** in *DAS:* I "ghosted" my wife's cookbook. **1988** *New Republic* (Apr. 18) 19: Hyman ghosted books and articles for Senator Jacob Javits. **1993** *Newsweek* (July 26) 4: Los Angeles writer Mel White ghosted books for Pat Robertson, Jerry Falwell and Billy Graham.

2. (see quot.).

1980 Pearl *Pop. Slang* 59: *Ghost v.* to share lodging with another without the knowledge of the proprietor of the hotel, motel, etc., and without paying any additional charge.

3. *Mil.* to avoid duty; loaf; malinger. [Quots. ref. to Vietnam War; cf. GHOST TIME.]

1982 Goff et al. *Bros.* 87: You never wanted to be lagging, what we called half-stepping or ghosting. Ghosting was kicking back in the rear. **1982** Del Vecchio *13th Valley* 87: Only dude yo gettin over on in the boonies ef yo ghostin is yoself. *Ibid.* 232: He's sittin back ghostin with 3d Plt. **1991** L. Chambers *Recondo* 225: I needed to do some serious ghosting.

ghost job *n.* **1.** *Publishing.* material that has been written by a ghostwriter.

1950 G. Legman, in *Neurotica* (Autumn) 12: A Broadway play, ten novels, a slick serial, two ghost jobs. **1985** J. Dillinger *Adrenaline* 214: An as-told-to sort of thing, although a ghost job isn't out of the question.

2. *Mil.* an easy, esp. non-combat, assignment.

1991 L. Chambers *Recondo* 185 [ref. to Vietnam War]: I would extend my tour and try to get a ghost job in the rear.

ghost-man *n. Naval Av.* (see quots.).

1945 *Newsweek* (July 30) 36: *Spook Suit:* The fluorescent-striped suit and paddles of a carrier's signal officer glow in the dark like a skeleton as he directs night fighters to a safe landing. Pilots call him the "ghost man." **1945** in *Calif. Folk. Qly.* V (1945) 378: A *ghost-man*, the carrier's flight-deck signal officer…dresses in a fluorescent *zootsuit* at night.

ghost suit *n. Army.* (see quot.).

1944 Kendall *Service Slang* 8: *Ghost suit*….white uniforms of Ski Troops.

ghost time *n. Mil.* time that is or may be spent in loafing or off duty.

1967 in B. Edelman *Dear Amer.* 88: When a guy is not *seriously* wounded it's time for laughs etc. because he knows he's in for a rest and "ghost time." **1983** K. Miller *Lurp Dog* 114 [ref. to Vietnam War]: Ghost time, baby, good ghost time. **1990** G.R. Clark *Wds. of Vietnam War* 200: *Ghost time*…GI slang for free time or off duty.

ghost turds *n.pl.* accumulations of lint found under furniture.—usu. considered vulgar.

1965–70 in *DARE.* **1980** Cragg *L. Militaris* 196: *Ghost Turds.* A name for the small clumps of dust which collect underneath beds and furniture in the barracks. **1981** *AS* (Summer) 145: *Dust bunnies*...one of my students reported *ghost turds* [as a synonym]. **1986** *NDAS.*

ghoul *n.* **1.** *Police.* (see quots.).

1859 Matsell *Vocab.* 36: *Ghouls.* Fellows who watch assignation-houses, and follow females that come out of them...and...threaten to expose them to their husbands, relatives, or friends if they refuse to give them not only money, but also the use of their bodies. **1927** *DN* V 447: *Ghoul,* n. A blackmailer who follows a woman as she leaves an assignation house.

2.a. *Med.* a morgue attendant; (*hence*) a medical examiner.

1938 in Partridge *Dict. Und.* 285: *Ghoul*...convict in charge of morgue. **1978** Strieber *Wolfen* 33: Come on, ghoul. **1984** Caunitz *Police Plaza* 39: How's my favorite ghoul?

b. *Mil.* (see quot.). Cf. GREEN GHOUL.

*a***1986** Muirhead *Those Who Fall* 66 [ref. to WWII]: "The ghouls will be with you as soon as they confirm the casualties." By "ghouls" Jim meant the people who were required to collect and seal all the effects of anyone killed or missing in action.

3. an unpleasant person; (*specif.*) *Stu.* an unattractive person of the opposite sex.

1940 in Cheever *Letters* 57: Some other ghoul has been given Brown's job. **1943** A. Scott *So Proudly We Hail!* (film): She's just naturally a frozen-faced ghoul. **1950** Gordon & Gordon *FBI Story* 10: Gotta hang up. A couple of ghouls just came in. **1956** I. Shulman *Good Deeds* 76: Don't you mention again the ghouls Phil fixed us up with. **1963** *Harper's* (Feb.) 93: There is a disagreeable ritual, known as the "ghoul pool," in which boys put money in a pool to be won by the cadet with the ugliest date. **1965** Hersey *Too Far to Walk* 47: Which one?...Talking to those two ghouls?—with two guys, yes! You see her? **1969** *Current Slang* I & II 40: *Ghoul,* n. Unattractive female.—Air Force Academy cadets. **1971** Dahlskog *Dict.* 27: *Ghoul,* n. An ugly girl. **1972** M. Rodgers *Freaky Fri.* 76: And here I'd been expecting the school ghoul.

ghoulie *n.* *Film.* a low-budget horror film which is composed primarily of graphic depictions of extraordinary violence or cruelty.

1967 A. Knight & H. Alpert, in *Playboy* (June) 187: Dave Friedman has contributed to this far out field an unholy trilogy of films—*Blood Feast, Color Me Red,* and *Two Thousand Maniacs*—in which nudity is minimized but violence runs riot; they're aptly called "ghoulies" in the trade. **1974** Turan & Zito *Sinema* 19: Other exploitation movie makers were turning to hard, crude, sex-and-violence pictures—lowbrow items known in the trade as Ghoulies, Roughies, and Kinkies....Limbs are hacked off [etc.]. **1985** *California* (Mar.) 52: Ever-so-artful compositions that emphasize blood slowly oozing out of a bullet hole here, elegantly flowing from a nose there—a tedious...homage to venerable 1960s ghoulies like *Blood Feast* and *Two Thousand Maniacs.*

GI *n.* **1.** *Army.* GI CAN.

1918 in Bliss *805th Pioneer Inf.* 221: There's about two million fellows, and there's some of them who lie/Where eighty-eights and G.I.'s gently drop. **1919** Cober *Trail of Battery D* 38: The fourgons moved to a clump of trees to the left of the position but after a few G.I.'s landed close to the place, orders were given to move to another place. **1920** Crowell *313th Field Arty.* 47: Just as we were passing near the position Jerry threw over one of those GI's, which hit and damaged one of the guns and also got a man. **1920** Riggs & Platt *Battery F* 20: After we had made sure that Heiney was not fooling us and that no more G.I.'s were coming over, we policed up our clothes, took baths, and found a house that had a roof over it to sleep in. **1923** *Amer. Leg. Wkly.* (Mar. 16) 22: They would run out, some G.I.'s would drop and they would dodge back again.

2.a. [abbr. *GI soldier*] *Army.* (orig. among officers) an enlisted man in the U.S. Army; (*broadly*) Esp. *Journ.* a common soldier of any army. Now *colloq.* or *S.E.*

1939 *Bugle Notes* 92: *G.I.,* n. An enlisted man. **1942** *Yank* (June 17) 3: Covering practically every situation in the life of a G.I. **1942** *Good Housekeeping* (Dec.) 11: He's just an ordinary soldier, but how do all his buddies refer to him? Regular—G.I.—Chicken—Doughboy. **1943** *Newsweek* (Oct. 18) 46: Even in Germany the [captured] G.I.'s have to line up for chow. **1943** *Newsweek* (Nov. 29) 24: All G.I.'s consider themselves to be long-suffering creatures, but Chinese soldiers have special reasons for thinking so. **1944** in Stilwell *Papers* 244: He had the nerve to make a speech at our headquarters but he doesn't fool our GIs

much. **1946** G.C. Hall, Jr. *1000 Destroyed* 345: Two Russian officers...ran up and dragged the nonplussed Russian G.I. off. **1953** Michener *Sayonara* 17: We were passing a corner at which a half a dozen enlisted men—we had orders not to call them G.I.'s any more—were loafing. **1960–61** Steinbeck *Discontent* 3: And those Roman G.I.'s thought it was an execution. **1962** *Newsweek* (Nov. 5) 63: The Vietnamese GI abhors U.S. K-rations. **1965** Linakis *In Spring* 283: I got on the lousy business...of an officer making a G.I. dig his foxhole for him. **1968** P. Roth *Portnoy* 300: But what a battle she gave me, this big farm cunt! This ex-G.I.! This mother-substitute! **1968** W.C. Anderson *Gooney Bird* 70: The North Vietnamese have learned the truth and tried to convince their GI's that it's no mysterious demon coming to get them. **1987** Zeybel *Gunship* 74 [ref. to Vietnam War]: He drives like one of our GIs. Oops, sorry gunners.

b. usu. *pl.* a person in or veteran of U.S. military service, regardless of rank or branch. Now *S.E.*

1943 in Sevareid *Wild Dream* 293: Designed to teach G.I.'s how to get along in China. **1944** in Stiles *Big Bird* 25: When you left, G.I. [i.e., lieutenant], it seemed as though all the fun of life had also left. **1945** in *Calif. Folk. Qly.* V (1946) 388: The *G.I.* may be a soldier, marine, or sailor, though in using the term one usually means the soldier. **1947** *AS* (Apr.) XXII 114: The next step, which seems to have taken place late in 1943 or early 1944, found *G.I.* designating all the enlisted men of the Army, Navy, and Marine Corps, together with their feminine adjuncts. **1949** Davies *Happens Every Spring* (film): He was a G.I. He had it rough. **1953** Russ *Last Parallel* 332: I think I understand why so many G.I.s return with Japanese wives. **1953–57** Giovannitti *Combine D* 15: I just had a crazy idea that when the GI's got here we'd tear down the barbed wire and run all over the place. **1957** Mulvihill *Fire Mission* 39: Haven't you ever heard about guys getting shot at by mistake and the Air Corps bombing G.I.'s? **1968** Tiede *Coward* 355: Ten dead GI's, including Lieutenant Price, had been found and air-lifted back to base camp. **1970** *Playboy* (Apr.) 53: Some people in the U.S. are giving us GIs in Vietnam a terrific pain....I'm a recon Marine. **1974** L.D. Miller *Valiant* 83: There were few people shopping, and more G.I.s than civilians.

c. Esp. *USMC & Navy.* an army soldier.

1945 (quot. at 2.b., above). **1951–52** Frank *Hold Back Night* 78: The offensive...had been bloodily thrown back by the GI's, and the Marines. **1954** Crockett *Magnificent Bastards* 16 [ref. to WWII]: He could see two Americans—GI's, no Marines. **1967** Ford *Muc Wa* 203: "When I think what we could do with a couple divisions of U.S. Marines—" "Or GIs." **1980** Manchester *Darkness* 315: The GIs began to move in step with the Marines.

3. *pl. Army.* U.S. Army uniform.

1942 in *Best from Yank* 64: Dressed in regulation GIs...he looks inches smaller than in his tailored pinks. **1947** *AS* (Apr.) XXII 113: One's G.I.'s were one's uniforms and, most frequently, the heavy field shoes or combat boots. **1956** in Harvey *Air Force* 56: He felt crumby in his wet GI's. **1973** Hirschfield *Victors* 103: "You look terrific in civvies."..."I wouldn't be caught dead in GIs again."

4. *pl.* [prob. abbr. GI SHITS] Orig. *Mil.* diarrhea or dysentery.

1943 Pyle *Brave Men* 87: A couple of days after getting back to normal I was hit with the "GIs," or Army diarrhea. **1943** *Yank* (Sept. 3) 7: He had the "GIs." **1945** in *Calif. Folk. Qly.* V (1946) 388: *To get the G.I.'s* is to contract diarrhoea from polluted drinking water; but this is an abbreviation of gastrointestinal. **1945** Nurre *534th AAA* 17: Any man who didn't suffer the agonies of dysentery (GI's) is eligible for the DSC. **1946** J.H. Burns *Gallery* 96: I had the GI's because I'd neglected to scald my mess gear with one soapy and two clear. **1944–48** A. Lyon *Unknown Station* 102: I had to drop out because of another sneak attack of GI's. **1951–52** Frank *Hold Back Night* 67: "I don't feel too well,"..."The GI's?" In Korea...diarrhea was always possible. **1961** Rubin *In the Life* 82: What a case of the GI's. **1974–77** Heinemann *Close Quarters* 26: Cures heartburn, jungle rot, the Gee-fucken-Eyes, all them things. **1978** Wharton *Birdy* 275: I've got the GI's all the time.

5. *Mil.* G.I. SHOWER, *n.,* 1.

1974 (quot. at G.I. SHOWER, *n.*).

GI *adj.* **1.a.** *Army.* entirely typical of the U.S. Army, esp. its requirements, customs, or practices. Now *S.E.* [*G.I.* was by 1907 a semiofficial army abbr. of "galvanized iron," used esp. in inventories to describe iron cans, buckets, etc.; by 1917 it was also interpreted as an abbr. of "government issue," and used in such collocations as *G.I. shoes* and *G.I. soap.* The present fig. sense followed quickly though it did not become common until the 1920's. Early quots. ref. to WWI.]

[**1917** in Lahm *Diary* 10: [The U.S. Army Acceptance Depot at Lympe, England] is a large depot where machines are delivered for forwarding to France. 12 large hangers [*sic*], brick, G.I., about 75 ft wide by 150 ft long.] **1918** *La Trine Rumor* (Dec.) (cartoon): A G.I. Christmas. **1926** *Sat. Eve. Post* (May 1) 18: Harry was not really a common, or G.I., dog-robber. **1926** *Sat. Eve. Post* (July 17) 154: I'd say he had a real old G.I. bun on. **1929** *Our Army* (Oct.) 14: Then Sgt. Elbert Funnel...went to live in a G.I. igloo. **1930** Nason *Corporal* 159: Well, he...was in for one good old G.I., Old Army bawling-out now anyway. **1931** *Our Army* (Feb.) 16: 2 dog tags and one G.I. soldier. **1944** Tobin *Invasion Jour.* 11: The G.I. soldier and the privileged guest must take some of each meal....But for the G.I. soldier down in the hold...eating is a bulky problem. **1947** Matthews *Assault* 122: Our leaders whipped us into a semblance of a GI advance. **1974** former 2d Lieut., U.S. Army, age 77 [ref. to 1918]: In our medical unit at Gondrecourt we had nurses and a few WAACS. We called them *G.I. women.*

b. *Mil.* (of aspects of military life) contemptible; bad.

1947 *AS* (Apr.) XXII 114 [ref. to WWII]: *G.I.* is tantamount to *It's lousy* (i.e., no good). **1956** Heflin *USAF Dict.* 232: GI situation, a snafued situation.

2. Orig. *Army.* punctiliously observant of or conforming to official regulations.

1929 *Our Army* (Mar.) 19: The Old Man felt G.I.! Fine! That would mean Jay Company would come dragging its spent strength back to barracks along about 11 o'clock. *Ibid.*: I'm making inspection this morning, I tell ya, and I'm gonna make it G.I. **1944** in *Best from Yank* 95: I'm not a stickler for rules and regulations nor do I believe in being too GI. **1947** Matthews *Assault* 72: The lieutenant...had been too GI—a stickler for spit and polish. **1949** Van Praag *Day Without End* 134: You're the GI'st, Fort Sam, dress-parade sergeant I ever did see! **1952** Uris *Battle Cry* 90: "This place is too damned GI," Danny said. **1956** J.D. Brown *Kings Go Forth* 13: He was a little too GI, too snappy. **1965** Koch *Casual Company* 97: And Captain...the Colonel desires all personnel to wear their service ribbons. Thought I'd better warn you. He's pretty G.I. about some things. **1972** Wambaugh *Blue Knight* 107: We're too GI to permit mutton-chops or big moustaches. **1982** T.C. Mason *Battleship* 137: Your trouble, Mason, is that you're too goddam GI.

GI *v.* **1.** Orig. *Army.* to scrub or clean vigorously and completely, as for a military inspection.

1944 in Kluger *Yank* 217: Who would *guess* that my undies were GI'ed 30 times! **1945** *Yank* (Apr. 20) 20: We GId the floor on our hands and knees. **1947** *AS* (Apr.) XXII 114 [ref. to WWII]: *To G.I.,* as in *G.I. the barracks!,* indicates "to clean thoroughly." **1967** Stevens *Gunner* 104: Say something about GIing the ward. **1968** Tauber *Sunshine Soldiers* 239: We are told that we must "GI" the barracks and clean our weapons. **1969** Lynch *American Soldier* 103: We're going to G.I. the tent, everything outside. **1983** Sturz *Wid. Circles* 40: Unless this group wants to G.I. (scrub) this building forever.

2. to field-strip (a cigarette).

1968 Heard *Howard St.* 208: Jackie nervously G.I.ed his cigarette.

GI *interj.* (see quot.).

1837 *Spirit of Times* (May 27) 113: All at once, he heard from every quarter of the office, the mysterious exclamation—"G.I.!" "What does 'G.I.!' mean," inquired Peter Spike—"Great Indulgence!" replied one of the hands; "and you must treat the office!"

giant *n.* *Constr.* GIANT POWDER, *n.*

1948 (quot. at COYOTE HOLE).

giant-killer *n.* whiskey.—constr. with *the.*

*****1930** (cited in Partridge *DSUE* (ed. 8) 462) [ref. to WWI]. **1936** in Hemingway *Short Stories* 6: Let's have a spot of the giant killer. **1940** Hemingway *For Whom Bell Tolls* 467: I'll take a good spot of the giant killer.

giant powder *n.* [orig. a trade name] a kind of blasting powder.

1871 in *DAE*: Mr. Cassell...has introduced Giant powder and the single-hand drill. **1880, 1887** in *DAE*. **1895** Foote *Coeur D'Alene* 209: I think dynamite and Giant powder are tolerably promiscuous. **1926** C.M. Russell *Trails* 79: Bedrock Jim...puts some giant powder in with the pie to thaw it out. The powder...cuts loose and scatters the cabin for miles up and down the gulch. **1940** Dempsey & Stearns *Round by Round* 75: Sticks of dynamite or "giant powder." **1948** J. Stevens *Jim Turner* 80 [ref. to ca1910]: I've been watchin' how handy you are with giant powder.

GIB *n.* [guy *i*n *b*ack(seat)] *Mil. Av.* a radar operator in a two-cockpit aircraft; photo- or weapons-system officer. Also **GIBS.**

1967 *Time* (June 2) 16: He and his "gibs" (guy-in-the-back-seat, or copilot) spotted 15 slower...MIG-17s. **1968** W.C. Anderson *Gooney Bird* 225: The huge, fast, two-place fighter bomber with its GIB (Guy In Back) was built like an airborne destroyer. **1977** [B.P. Wyatt] *We Came Home* (unp.): I...was sent to Udorn AFB on the 4th of July 1972 as a Photo Systems Operator (GIB) RF4C Phantom. **1978** in Higham & Williams *Combat Aircraft* 114: In October 1963 we headed to Mac-Dill AFB, Florida, to become GIBs, "guys in back." *****1979** in Partridge *DSUE* (ed. 8) 462: *Gibs. Guys in the Back Seat* (Navigators). **1985** Boyne & Thompson *Wild Blue* 382: His GIB—guy in the back seat—was twenty-four years old, bitter not to be in the front seat.

Gib *n.* *Naut.* Gibraltar.

*****1822** in Wheeler *Letters* 242: At Gib. we took in an old Jew, a native of Jerusalem, he could not spake a word of any European language. *****1838** Glascock *Land Sharks* II 143: The Little Liner "left Gib," as Darcy termed it. **1853** in McCauley *With Perry* 41: Still a little more like Gib. *****1904** Kipling *Traffics* 294: Not much adventure at Malta, Gib, or Cyprus. **1922** (quot. at CONSTAN). *****1933** Witherspoon *Liverpool Jarge* (unp.): We was passin' Gib.

G.I.B. *adj.* [coined by Wendy Leigh in 1977 quot.] "good in bed."

1977 W. Leigh *What Makes a Woman G.I.B.?** (*Good in Bed*). (title). **1977** *Nat. Lampoon* (July) 56: His satisfied sigh, followed by a deep, consuming sleep, is a sure sign that he, and you, are "G.I.B." **1980–83** Claire *Dangerous English* 59: G.I.B....Having the qualities of a desirable sexual partner. **1986** *NDAS.*

G.I. banjo *n.* *Army.* a shovel; BANJO, 2.

1956 Hargrove *Girl He Left* 170: I'm supposed to learn soldiering, not how to play a GI banjo.

G.I. bath *n.* *Mil.* the rough, forcible scrubbing of a trainee's person, usu. administered by barracks mates as a punishment for bodily uncleanliness. [Quots. ref. to WWII.]

1943 *Yank* (Mar. 26) 6: They don't call it a G.I. bath here...but the general effect is just as brutal. **1952** Uris *Battle Cry* 112: I'll tell you men, if I ever get my meathooks on that bastard, I'll rip him open from asshole to appetite. I'll give him a GI bath. *ca*1979 Pepper & Pepper *Straight Life* 55: They tore our clothes off and threw us in the shower. They gave us a "GI bath" with strong brown soap with lye in it and scrubbed us with big brushes made out of wood sticks. We were hollering and fighting.

gibroney *n.* [alter. JIBONEY] an Italian.—used contemptuously.

1964–66 R. Stone *Hall of Mirrors* 316: We are not strutting maniacs like the gibroney and the greaseball!

gibs see s.v. JIB.

Gibson Girl *n.* [after the *Gibson Girl,* idealized American girl of 1890's; see 1945 quot.] *Mil. Av.* a small radio transmitter (SCR-578) designed to send a distress signal. Now *hist.*

1943 *Yank* (Sept. 17) 7: He brought out the yellow "Gibson Girl" emergency radio. **1943** *Newsweek* (Oct. 4) 88: With this hourglass-shaped radio transmitter, popularly named "The Gibson Girl", they can blanket a 150,000-square-mile area with an SOS signal merely by turning a crank. **1945** Hamann *Air Words*: Gibson girl...An emergency radio transmitter...capable of sending an automatic SOS over an effective range of 100,000 square miles....Because of its hour-glass contour, the transmitter was nicknamed "Gibson girl" during its development by Bendix Aviation, Ltd., of North Hollywood, Calif. **1956** Lockwood & Adamson *Zoomies* 127: Our staffs went to work on "Gibson Girls" (hand-powered transmitters for little rafts). **1958** Craven & Cate *AAF in WWII* VII 491: The first portable radio transmitter for this purpose was the SCR-578, widely known as the Gibson Girl. By July 1942 this transmitter was being carried in bombers and transport planes leaving for combat theaters. **1975** J.W. Spencer *Limbo* 38 [ref. to 1948]: Each life raft was equipped with a survival kit which included a "Gibson Girl," a small hand-cranked radio designed to be held between the knees. **1975** Ebon *Bermuda Triangle* 37: What about the automatic Gibson Girl radio transmitter? That's the kind that you hold between your knees. Turn a crank and it belts out its own coded signal.

G.I.C. *n.* *Army.* GI CAN, *n.*

1919 Hamilton & Corbin *Echoes from Over There* 164 [ref. to 1918]: We crossed the river on a span of a sunken bridge that was struck by a G.I.C. (galvanized iron can).

GI can *n.* [sugg. by *GI can* 'galvanized iron trash can'; see note at GI, *adj.*] *Army.* a heavy artillery shell; (*also*) an aerial bomb. [Quots. ref. to WWI.]

1918 in Casey *Cannoneers* (Sept. 24): At 11 o'clock he started to drop G.I. cans into our woods. *Ibid.* (Nov. 1): A G.I. can full of mustard. **1918** in Ellington *Company A* 23: Our first air raid was experienced last night....Several G.I. cans were dropped at Royaumeix. *Ibid.* 113: *G.I. Cans*—Large Aviation Bombs; German. **1918** Rendinell *One Man's War* 161: Their artillery sent over shot after shot of G.I. cans. **1919** Hamilton & Corbin *Echoes from Over There* 184: As we drew nearer the lines a "Gi can" came threateningly near us. **1919** Morrow *58th Inf.* 66: More terrifying, a number of "G-I cans"—large caliber trench mortar bombs, which were hurtled through the air from emplacements at Bazoches. **1919** Farrell *1st U.S. Engineers* 88: After dark that night, old Fritz came over and started dropping those famous G.I. cans. **1919** Law *2nd Army Air Service* (unp.): Al they sent some plains over Colombey where we was and dropped some G.I. cans (thats slang for ariel bums) on the flying field. *Ibid.* (unp.): One evening about supper time Fritz appeared and, opening his tail-gate, dumped out ten G.I. cans. **1919** Piesbergen *Aero Squadron* 53: The hum of the motor.../ Was mingled with the report of the G.I. can. **1920** *304th Field Sig. Bn.* 162: He'd been duckin' G.I. cans and fightin' "the Hun." **1922** Jordan *Battery B* 60: Fritz heaved over a few G.I. cans. **1924** Nason *Three Lights* 113: A few of those G.I. cans had burst near enough to throw dirt on him. **1926** Nason *Chevrons* 101: The G.I. cans were showerin' down like rain. **1928** Wharton *Squad* 222: I'm beginnin' to jump every time I hear the wheeze o' one o' them goddam G.I. cans. **1931** Ottosen *Trench Arty.* 240 [caption]: A 240mm Bomb (G.I. can) in a Shot Galley.

gick *n.* GUCK, *n.*

1959 W. Burroughs *Naked Lunch* 56: They are stained with some sticky, red brown gick.

giddyap or **giddyup** *n.* **1.** a racehorse.

1922 T.A. Dorgan, in Zwilling *TAD Lexicon* 106: A bloke who has a system to beat the giddyaps but has nothing but holes in his shoes. **1937** in D. Runyon *More Guys* 98: Unser Fritz...is following the giddyaps since the battle of Gettysburg.

2. force; energy.

1986 *N.Y. Mets. vs. Phila. Phillies* (WOR-TV) (Sept. 12): That ball had some giddy-up on it.

¶ In phrase:

¶ **from the giddyap** from the outset.

1974 R. Carter *16th Round* 36: I knew from the giddy-up they were cops. **1984** Caunitz *Police Plaza* 320: I'm telling you right from the giddyap that we know all about your hit team for the rich.

gidget *n.* [by alter.] GADGET.

1944 *Life* (July 3): I can't handle these little gidgets and gadgets. **1954–60** *DAS*. **1993** *Jerry Springer Show* (synd. TV series): All the little gidgets and gadgets were in the car.

gidgy *n.* [alter. of *kitchie*-kitchie-coo, syllables uttered when one is chucking an infant's chin] a chucking or tickling under the chin; (*broadly*) romantic caressing.

1952 Bellow *Augie March* 86: So...don't play with your dummy...And don't play gidgy with your little girl friends. It don't do you or them any good. **1969** *Rowan & Martin's Laugh-In* (NBC-TV): What would you say to a little gidgy?

gietus *n.* var. GEETUS, *n.*

GIF *n.* [guy *in front*] *Mil. Av.* the pilot of a two-cockpit aircraft.

1975 former USAF navigator [ref. to 1971]: The guy in the back of a 105 is the *gib* and the pilot is the *gif,* "guy in back" and "guy in front." ***1979** in Partridge *DSUE* (ed. 8) 462: *Gifs.* Guys *in the Front Seat* (Pilots).

gig[1] *n.* [orig. unkn.] **1.** the vagina.

***1698–99** "B.E." *Dict. Canting Crew: Gig,*...a Nose; also a Woman's Privities. ***1698–1720** D'Urfey *Pills* V 109: And then I went to her, resolving to try her....I told her I'd give her a Whip for her Gig. **ca*1775 *Frisky Songster* 31: Come bodder [*sic*] my gig with your Shawnbree. **a*1850 in J. Atkins *Sex in Lit.* III 209: I broke the main-spring of her gig. **1954–60** *DAS: Gig*...The vagina....*Not common.*

2. the anus. Cf. GIGGY, *n.*

1954–60 *DAS: Gig*...The rectum....Used euphem. by some children, as part of their bathroom vocabulary....Used by some male adults (taboo) as a euphem. for "ass" in such expressions as "up your gig."

gig[2] *n.* [arbitrary application of *gig* 'a two-wheeled, one-horse carriage'] (in policy gambling) a set of usu. three numbers

played by a bettor; (*broadly*) a policy bet.

1847 in *DAE*: I make it 4, 11, and 44; and a very good gig it is, too. **1872** Crapsey *Nether Side N.Y.* 106: A "flat gig" is three numbers played for all three to be drawn. **1875** *Chi. Tribune* (Nov. 21) 13: The "gig" is the most popular form of play. A gig may consist of three, four, or five numbers. To win on a gig, if it be one of three numbers, all the numbers must be drawn from the wheel. In a five-number gig, three numbers must be drawn from the wheel in order for the player to make a hit. **1882** McCabe *N.Y.* 551: Three numbers make a "gig," and win from $150 to $225; four numbers make a "horse," and win $640. **1887** *Courier-Journal* (Louisville) (May 8) 12: He...thought he could increase his income somewhat by selling Louisiana lottery tickets and policy gigs. **1890** in *DAE:* The "washerwoman's gig"—4-11-14—[is] the chance that these three, or any other three numbers, will, in any order, be the first three numbers out of the thirteen taken from the wheel. **1910** in *DA:* Three numbers make a "gig" and win $150 to $225.

gig[3] *n.* [cf. GIG[1], *v.*] **1.a.** an instance of goading, gibing, or reproving.—usu. constr. with *the.*

1901 Ade *Modern Fables* 170: The Old Gentleman was very rough on Wallie. He gave him the Gig at every opportunity, for he had no sympathy with Puppy Love and he hated a Dude. **1942–49** Goldin et al. *DAUL* 80: *Gig*...a renewal of pressure; a final effort to swindle a difficult victim...."Give him the gig, but heavy."

b. a trick or swindle.

1970 in *DARE: To...play tricks or jokes on people: He's always*...Pulling a gig. *ca*1986 in *NDAS:* It ain't no gig, lady, and I don't really care what you think.

2. Esp. *Army.* an instance of being placed on disciplinary report; demerit. Now *S.E.*

1930 in D.O. Smith *Cradle* 62: I'm riding well with only six gigs so far this month. **1941** *AS* (Oct.) 166: *Gig.* Unfavorable report. *Gig getter.* A rifle which...fails to pass inspection. **1942** *Randolph Field* 130: *Gigs*—Demerits given for misdemeanors. **1955** Archibald *Aviation Cadet* 9: Aviation Cadet Mercer...continued to establish something of a record at Hondo for gigs. **1973** Droge *Patrolman* 52: We were given "gigs," or delinquent points as used in high schools. **1986** P. Welsh *Tales Out of School* 183: Postponing the courses would have resulted in a "gig"—a demerit—from the Virginia Department of Education.

gig[4] *n.* [perh. alter. of GAG, *n.* 3, infl. by GIG[2], *n.*] **1.a.** business; affair; state of affairs; (*hence*) undertaking or event.

1907 *McClure's Mag.* (Feb.) 379: What's this gig about militia? **1957** in J. Blake *Joint* 167: Some fatass got stuck and blew the gig. **1958** in *DAS:* Life is a Many Splendored Gig. **1966** H.S. Thompson *Hell's Angels* 247: The hippie drug scene was a brand-new dimension—a different gig, as it were. **1971** Dahlskog *Dict.* 27: *Gig*...Any thing, situation or happening, as: We saw that the whole *gig* was bad, so we dropped out. **1971** Sonzski *Punch Goes Judy* 13: And we do the whole gig, right? Build a fucking nursery upstairs. Buy fucking booties and carriages. **1972** P. Barrett *Lovomaniacs* 198: Who else *could* help with a gig like this one? **1973** in H.S. Thompson *Shark Hunt* 21: I would bet that Nixon will resign...within the next six months. It will be a nasty gig when it happens. **1980** M. Baker *Nam* 11: My guy dies, it's no big gig to me. I tag him, book him and bag him. **1980** Lorenz *Guys Like Us* 168: Laughing at the crazy gig they were into. **1984** Heath *A-Team* 171: Good as we are, we can't crack this gig by ourselves. **1985** Dye *Between Raindrops* 95: What we have here is your classic romance-adventure gig....Just want to be *in* on a gig of this magnitude. **1987** D. Sherman *Main Force* 154: I was beginning to hope maybe your friends in the NVA wasted you for fucking up their gig so badly. **1988** Norst *Colors* 199: A whispering gig...was still in progress....Danny sensed that they were talking about him.

b. (one's) preference or special interest.

1965 in H.S. Thompson *Shark Hunt* 470: Social radicals tend to be "arty." Their gigs are poetry and folk music, rather than politics. **1967** Bronsteen *Hippy's Handbook* 14: Gig *n.* someone's "bit" or "thing"; a jazz term. **1970** Landy *Underground Dict.* 89: *Gig*...Interest; hobby. **1971** Dahlskog *Dict.* 27: *Gig,* n. One's field of endeavor or interest; one's thing or bag, as: Skiing's not my *gig.* **1972** W.C. Anderson *Hurricane* 37: I could get a job [flying] passengers around, pinching stewardesses,...but it's not my gig.

c. practice or action; routine.

1970 *Playboy* (Sept.) 90: Jack Nicholson was born in New Jersey and does a different gig. **1973** in H.S. Thompson *Shark Hunt* 300: That's an old Hell's Angels gig, dragging people down the street. **1985** D. Killerman *Hellrider* 15: Roadblocks, searches—you know the gig. **1990** C.P. McDonald *Blue Truth* 69: I'm getting kinda tired of this whole gig.

d. intent, plan, or design.

1982 "J. Cain" *Commandos* 397: Come on, boys—level with me. What's the gig? **1987** *21 Jump St.* (Fox-TV): "I don't understand his gig. What does he want with high-school kids?" "Sounds like Lancer wants to be God."

2.a. a job; occupation. [In current use infl. by **(b)**, below.]

1908 H. Green *Maison de Shine* 48: "What's your game?" the Property Man's tone was rather unpleasant. "I'm champion paper-tearer of the West," said Charlie. "I pass....What kind o' gig is that?" *ca*1953 Hughes *Fantastic Lodge* 82: I had been working at this record store where they did not have a cash register....I wish I had that gig back again though, man! **1958** Gilbert *Vice Trap* 9: I've got a steady gig. **1958–59** Lipton *Barbarians* 25: That godawful car-selling gig. **1963** in L. Bruce *Essential* 269: He's doing your gig and he's a second class citizen. **1965** Lurie *Nowhere City* 86: I have to be at the gig at two. **1965** C. Brown *Manchild* 300: Man, I got to...find me a gig. **1966** Liebow *Tally's Corner* 59: Talk about jobs is generally limited to isolated statements of intention, such as "I think I'll get me another gig." **1973** Duckett *Raps* 5: Man, I'm tired of my gig. *a*1979 Pepper & Pepper *Straight Life* 45: I got the gig for the Club Alabam. **1982** *Morning Line* (WKGN radio) (July 9): Milking goats in Afghanistan—that's quite a gig.

b. *Specif.*, an engagement, esp. for a single evening, to perform jazz, rock, or other popular music.

*1926 in R.S. Gold *Jazz Talk* 108: One popular "gig" band makes use of a nicely printed booklet. **1927* in *OEDS*: This seven-piece combination does many "gigs" in S.E. London, but is hoping to secure a resident engagement...in the near future. **1929** T. Gordon *Born to Be* 192: We were engaged to sing by one of the middleaged hostesses who entertain the four hundred. These gigs came through our manager. *Ibid.* 236: Gig—Entertaining with music. **1944** Micheaux *Mrs. Wingate* 174: You always tried to get him to go out on a gig over the week-end, to pick up some extra money. **1948** Manone & Vandervoort *Trumpet* 58: After playing some gigs around the Windy City I landed with Charlie Straight at the Rendezvous. **1950–52** Ulanov *Hist. Jazz* 50 [ref. to *ca*1907]: He...always knew where a "gig," a one-night job, could be found. **1954** L. Armstrong *Satchmo* 221 [ref. to *ca*1918]: As a rule we would meet on a gig, or one-night stand, and we would play so well together that one would swear we had been working in the same outfit for months. **1961** J.A. Williams *Night Song* 24: Once he wondered where Eagle was but decided perhaps he had a gig that night and would not be in. **1964** R.S. Gold *Jazz Lexicon*: Gig....According to jazzman Eubie Blake, bandleader James Reese Europe used the term in its jazz sense as early as *ca*1905; widely current since *ca*1920. *ca*1979 Pepper & Pepper *Straight Life* 45: When I got the gig for the Club Alabam he was one of the first people I thought of. **1988** *Rage* (Knoxville, Tenn.) (Sept.) 35: They decided to start playing their own gigs as a country band.

c. *Und. & Police.* a criminal undertaking; JOB, 1.

1953 E. Hunter *Jungle Kids* 21: He'd picked me for the gig, and I knew it was an important one. **1955** in Wepman et al. *The Life* 78: Now I've got a gig, and it's going to be big,/But just keep it under your hat. **1982** L. Cohen *Serpent* (film): The whole gig will take three and a half minutes, in and out. **1987** *21 Jump St.* (Fox-TV): Burglary says it smacks of an inside gig. **1978–89** in Jankowski *Islands in Street* 41: I would make more money if I could do more gigs (various illegal economic ventures) on my own.

d. *Esp. Black E.* a jazz party or jam session; party.

1954 in Wepman et al. *The Life* 109: She spoke of a gig that would last for weeks. **1954** L. Armstrong *Satchmo* 141: Kid Ory had some of the finest gigs, especially for the rich white folks. **1959** De Roo *Young Wolves* 160: Let's go to the Cubbyhole, Cliff....For a gig. **1964** R. Kendall *Black School* 216: Daddio says he wants to take her to a jig [*sic*]. **1965** Bonham *Durango St.* 165: Don't see why we can't throw a gig, too. **1966** in *Trans-action* IV (Apr. 1967) 8: The perpetual search for the "gig," the party. **1968** Sebald *Adolescence* 252: Gig—a Saturday night party.

3. an example or instance.

1976 in H.S. Thompson *Shark Hunt* 560: The only bet I could get was a $5 gig with Jody Powell, Carter's press secretary.

gig⁵ *n.* [sugg. by GIG LAMP, *n.*, 1] an eye.

1924 Hecht & Bodenheim *Cutie* 12: The way our hero lost his gig was like this.

gig⁶ /dʒɪg/ *n.* a gigolo.

1926 Finerty *Criminalese* 24: Gig—A dance hall sheik, dude. **1930** Lait *On the Spot* 203: Gig...Gigolo.

gig¹ *v.* [prob. sugg. by *gig* 'to spear with a gig'] **1.** to cheat; take dishonest advantage of.

1914 *DN* IV 163: Say, didn't you gig me a little on the price of that room? **1935** J. Conroy *World to Win* 109: He knows damned well he gigged me out of a dollar. **1942** *ATS* 457: Swindle; cheat; defraud...*gaff*,...*gig*, *gyp*. **1962** Quirk *Red Ribbons* 213: I wonder how Mata Hari felt sleeping with the guy she was gigging.

2. Esp. *Army.* to place on disciplinary report; administer official punishment to. Now *colloq.* or *S.E.*

1930 in D.O. Smith *Cradle* 60: I'll have to be on my toes continually for it's an easy soiree to get gigged on. **1942** in Cheever *Letters* 73: I forgot to snap the trigger on my rifle so I was gigged along with a dozen other men and we spent the...evening scrubbing baseboards. **1944** *Stars & Stripes* (Rome) (July 1): I got gigged because I was a few minutes late for 5:30 reveille. **1948** Cozzens *Guard of Honor* 331: And that lug right behind you is Lieutenant Edsell, who now gets gigged, as I believe they said at OCS, for being eleven minutes late. **1961** Rosten *Newman, M.D.* 51: You could gig me, sir. You could send me to the guardhouse. **1968** Moura & Sutherland *Tender Loving Care* 93: Box-Body says they like to open them and gig you if they find any dirt inside. **1971** Sloan *War Games* 117: The sociology major, with his rusty weapon gigged, is standing next to the one recruit who happens to have cleaned his weapon, for no reason, the night before. **1974** Kingry *Monk & Marines* 43: They want to gig obvious users on other charges, not on charges of use of marihuana.

gig² *v.* [shift of GIG⁴, *n.*, 2] **1.** Orig. *Jazz.* to play single engagements as a jazz musician or (later) other entertainer; (*hence*) to have employment. Occ. trans.

1939 in *OEDS*: To gig around meant to play for small parties, weekend engagements, and the like. **1947** in R.S. Gold *Jazz Talk* 108: At present he is "gigging around," a musician's term for those who take casual dates whenever they can find them. **1950–52** Ulanov *Hist. Jazz* 227: A well-trained New York musician, he had the usual Gotham gigging beginning. **1955** in R.S. Gold *Jazz Talk* 108: Gig: to work one-night jobs. **1957** H. Simmons *Corner Boy* 44: They got into a jam with the locals last place they gigged, so you got to play it chilly. **1959–60** Bloch *Dead Beat* 116: He'd been a bellhop...gigging band dates on his time off. **1961** J.A. Williams *Night Song* 85: What you need with bread, Background? You giggin' steady. **1962** Carr & Cassavetes *Too Late Blues* (film): Tell me where you guys were giggin' when I picked you up. **1971** S. Stevens *Way Uptown* 87: I hadda lay that on most of the studs that were gigging for me. **1972–74** Hawes & Asher *Raise Up* 11: Hey, Hamp, I didn't know your old man was still gigging. **1983** *Reader's Digest Success with Words* 85: Black English...*gig around* = "to work at a number of jobs."

2. to provide employment for.

1971 Curtis *Banjo* 195: How come you giggin' that elevator hop?

giggle *n.* **1.** something that is amusing or fun; in phr. **for giggles** for fun.

*1936 in *OEDS*: It's no giggle being in the nick. **1958*, **1959*, **1963*, **1966*, **1968* in *OEDS*. **1977** *Nat. Lampoon* (Aug.) 9: But, hey, I don't hate life. I think it's a giggle. **1979** *L.A. Times* (Sept. 2) (Calender) 87: At the very least, the affair would be a giggle. **1989** *Cops* (Fox-TV): You got sixteen-year-old kids shootin' the first person they see, just for giggles. **1992** *Herman's Head* (Fox-TV): He's a giggle, isn't he?

2. GIGGLE-WATER, *n.*

1952 in *DAS*: But I never lifted the curfew or brought out a giggle bottle. **1974** U.S. Army Sgt. Major., USACC-Taiwan (coll. J. Ball): Keep away from the giggle! That's for the officers!

3. GIGGLE-SMOKE, *n.*

1972 U.S. Army Pvt., Ft. Jackson, S.C. (coll. J. Ball): God, I'd give anything for a lungful of giggle right about now.

gigglebox *n.* a child, esp. a little girl, who giggles easily.

1962 H. Simmons *On Eggshells* 58: You're just an old gigglebox. **1963** Junior High School student, Walnut Ridge, Ark. (coll. J. Ball): I can't stand her—she's a real giggle-box.

giggle dust *n. Narc.* cocaine.

1993 *New Yorker* (May 17) 106: The choking dread is mixed with giggle dust.

giggle-juice *n.* GIGGLE-WATER, *n. Joc.*

1939 Howsley *Argot* 20: Giggle Juice—Champagne. **1940** in Goodstone *Pulps* 112: For one thing, ghosts don't imbibe giggle-juice. **1951** *West. Folk.* X 80: Give me a shot of...giggle juice. **ca*1966 S.J. Baker *Austral. Lang.* 232: Giggle juice...wine.

giggle smoke *n.* a marijuana cigarette; (*also*) marijuana. Also **giggle stick.** *Joc.*
   1937 in E.L. Abel *Marihuana Dict.* 43: They are spoken of as "giggle smokes." **1943** *Time* (July 19) 54: Cigarets made from it are...giggle-smokes, or reefers. **1944** Burley *Hndbk. Jive* 122: A lone giggle stick. **1971** Guggenheimer *Narc. & Drug Abuse* 23: *Giggle smoke.* marijuana. **1971** U.S. Army S/Sgt., Ft. Campbell, Ky. (coll. J. Ball): Private, you haven't been fooling with the giggle-smoke, have you? **1972** U.S. Army Pvt., Ft. Jackson, S.C. (coll. J. Ball): Man, he fucked up on giggle-smoke!

giggle-soup *n.* intoxicating liquor. Also **giggly-soup.** *Joc.*
   1933 J. Conroy *Disinherited* 215: "Drunk again." "Yes! The giggle soup." **1941** *Slanguage Dict.* 17: *Giggle soup*—intoxicating liquor. **1942** *Yank* (Sept. 9) 9: A bottle that once contained giggle soup. **1912–43** *Frank Brown Collection* I 544: *Giggle-soup,* n. Strong drink.—Chapel Hill. **1974** L.D. Miller *Valiant* 32 [ref. to 1940's]: "I didn't know you had taking up drinking."..."What drinking? This giggly soup?" "What did you call it?" "Giggly soup. Funny water." **1982** W.R. Dunn *Fighter Pilot* 68: Every eye was on the depth of giggle soup in the mug.

giggle-water *n.* intoxicating liquor, esp. Champagne. *Joc.*
   1926 Finerty *Criminalese* 15: That which produces intoxication [is] called "giggle water." **1928** in E. Wilson *Twenties* 436: Poe couldn't hold his giggle-water. **1931** *AS* VII (Oct.) 45: Intoxicating beverages he [Walter Winchell] calls *giggle water, whoopee water, silly milk,* and *laughing soup.* **1937** *AS* (Feb.) 75: *Giggle-water*—gin. *1949 Granville *Sea Slang* 108: *Giggle-water.* Cocktails, overindulgence in which makes the girls giggle. **1950** *West. Folk.* X 80: Give me a shot of...giggle water. **1971** U.S. Army Staff Sgt., Ft. Campbell, Ky. (coll. J. Ball): You get you a clean mama, a room at the Ramada Inn, and a $3.00 bottle of giggle-water and you think that's class. **1974** U.S. Army Sgt., USACC-Taiwan (coll. J. Ball): Give me the best! Fuckin' bubbly! Giggle-water! Champagne! **1980** L.N. Smith *Venus Belt* 208: *I'll* get the champagne, okay?...I stuck my tongue out, and started nursing gigglewater from a wall-tap.

giggle weed *n.* marijuana. Also **giggle-grass.** *Joc.*
   1937 in Starks *Cocaine Fiends* 103: We tried Tony's giggle water, let's try his giggle weed. **1951** in E. L. Abel *Marihuana Dict.* 44: Before that, it was marijuana, which we call "giggle weed." **1954–60** *DAS: Giggle weed.* Marijuana. *Addict use. Never common.* **1972** Pearce *Pier Head Jump* 13: Then I lights up another stick of giggle grass. **1964–78** J. Carroll *B. Diaries* 28: Wow, this is some fine weed, giggle weed, man.

giggling academy *n.* LAUGHING ACADEMY. Also **giggle academy.**
   1942–49 Goldin et al. *DAUL* 80: *Giggle academy.* A hospital for insane or mentally defective delinquents. **1980** *Daily Beacon* (Univ. Tenn.) (Oct. 10) 2: He was previously committed to the state giggling academy.

giggly-guts *n.* GIGGLEBOX, *n.*
   1972 N.Y.U. student: A *giggly-guts* is a giddy person.

giggy *n.* [cf. GIG[1], *n.,* 2] the anus. Also in fig. senses corresp. to those at ASSHOLE, *n.*
   1953 Eyster *Customary Skies* 9 [ref. to WWII]: Aw, up your giggy with a wire brush. **1955** Klaas *Maybe I'm Dead* 373 [ref. to WWII]: Up your giggi. **1958** T. Berger *Crazy in Berlin* 187: World, you got twenty-eight years from me, you can keep all the rest and stick them up your giggy. *ca*1961 Partridge *DSUE* (ed. 5) 1107: *Giggy.*...Anus; low Canadian: C.20. **1961** Brosnan *Pennant Race* 236: That's the way to shove it up their old giggies, Broz! **1962** Quirk *Red Ribbons* 70 [ref. to 1940's]: Up your giggy, Mandel. **1967** Kolb *Getting Straight* 101: I will personally stuff those fish up your gigi. **1971** Cole *Rook* 145: "Up your giggy," I said. **1974** V.B. Miller *Girl in River* 10: We've got cases up the giggy, Captain. **1975** Univ. Tenn. student: He's living with a guy and getting bumfucked in his giggy.

G.I. gin *n. Mil.* cough syrup having a high alcohol content.
   1964 R. Moore *Green Berets* 133: I reached...for the bottle of GI gin....80 proof terpin hydrate elixir. **1974** Winek *Drug Abuse* 136: Terpin hydrate and codeine elixir...contains 43% alcohol. That's 86 proof! This is the stuff called "GI Gin." It...is popular among addicts during dry spells of heroin. **1979** J. Morris *War Story* 91: Bill, dose these men with GI gin. We can't have any coughing. **1980** D. Cragg (letter to J.E.L., Aug. 10) 4: *GI gin.* I first heard this while being trained as a medic at Ft. Sam Houston [late 1958]. "I got some GI gin for my cold." **1985** Former SP5, U.S. Army, (served 1971–78): One way they'd malinger was to take one of them bottles of GI gin and drink it all up. **1991** Standifer *Not in Vain* 200: It was terpine hydrate with codeine, a

clear liquid that we called "GI gin" [in WWII]...40 percent alcohol.

gig-lamp *n.* **1.** *pl.* spectacles; eyeglasses. *Obs.* in U.S.
   *1853 in *OED:* "Looks ferociously mild in his gig-lamps!" remarked a third, alluding to Mr. Verdant Green's spectacles. **1859** Matsell *Vocab.* 37: *Gig-Lamps.* A pair of spectacles. **1865** Sala *Diary* II 33: Some men had a passion for seeing "gig-lamps" on the nasal bone of those they admire. **1871** Bagg *Yale* 45: *Gig-lamps* and *goggles,* eye-glasses. **1886** McAfee *Kentucky Politician* 229: From behind his screening "gig lamps," resting lightly upon his proboscis. *ca*1890–93 F & H III 142: *Gig-lamps* (certainly a university term. I first heard it in 1848 or 1849, long before Mr. Verdant Green was born or thought of). **1898** Green *Va. Folk Speech* 159: *Gig-lamps, n.pl.* Spectacles. **1913** *Sat. Eve. Post* (Mar. 1) 18: She pulls a pair of gold an' di'mond gig-lamps on me. **1925** Mullin *Scholar Tramp* 239 [ref. to *ca*1912]: "Hey, youse with the gig-lamps!" bellowed a hobo a few paces behind me. "Are ye deaf?" *1980 Leland *Kiwi-Yank. Dict.* 45: *Gig-lamps*...the glasses you wear...on the end of your...nose.
   2. an ostentatious gemstone.
   1896 in S. Crane *Complete Stories* 318: How's that for a gig-lamp?

gig-line *n. Army.* a straight alignment of the buttons of a shirt and jacket, the belt buckle, and the fly of the trousers.
   1970 W.C. Woods *Killing Zone* 35: He pulled his pants up [and] squared away his gigline. **1976** Univ. Tenn. student: My father calls that the *gig-line.* When your shirt lines up with your fly. You get gigged at inspection if it's not lined up. **1978** De Christoforo *Grease* 144: He kept straightening things out on both of us—collar, cuff, crease, gig-line, knot. **1981** Rogan *Mixed Co.* 194: A trim "gig-line"—the line made by jacket edges and trouser seams when everything is correct. **1983** N. Proffitt *Gardens of Stone* 91: "I wish we could see what was going on down there," Webber said, straightening his gig line.

GIGO /'gaɪˌgoʊ/ *n.* [garbage *i*n, garbage *o*ut] *Computers.* the axiom that faulty data fed into a computer will result in distorted information.—often used attrib. Also *transf.*
   1964 in *OEDAS* II 114. **1966** Gallery *Start Engines* 177: "They better allow for the GIGO factor," said Willy. "What's that?" "Garbage In—Garbage Out." **1974** Widener *N.U.K.E.E.* 156: They're still computers, and they function on the same old GIGO principle. **1980** *Business Week* (Jan. 21) 73: If the model is not accurate and the operating data are incomplete, [it] can result in a phenomenon well-known to computer users called GI-GO. **1991** Raymond *New Hacker's Dict.* 177: *GIGO*...Also commonly used to describe failures in human decision making due to faulty, incomplete, or imprecise data.

gigunda *adj.* [alter. of *gigantic*] gigantic; oversize. Also vars.
   1972 N.Y.U. student: *Gigunda* means gigantic and huge. **1972** N.Y.U. student: Yeah, *gigunda* means really big and massive. **1973** N.Y.U. student: *Gigumbo* is really tremendous. It's gigantic and jumbo. **1974** N.Y.U. student: *Gigundo, gigundus, gigunda*—they're all the same, very big. They were in use in Pittsburgh and Maryland in 1970.

GI Jane *n.* [sugg. by GI JOE] *Mil.* a female member of the armed forces, esp. the army.
   1944 *N.Y. Times Mag.* (Sept. 17) 32: *G.I. Jane.* A member of the WAC. **1945** *House Beautiful* (Jan.) 32: G.I. Jane Will Retool with Ruffles. **1947** Mencken *Amer. Lang. Supp.* II 779: *GI Joe,* for the soldier himself, and *GI Jane* for his female comrade-in-arms, followed inevitably. **1974** U.S. Army Master Sgt. (coll. J. Ball): That's all we need—another G.I. Jane to get knocked up and bounced out. **1985** Westin *Love & Glory* 205 [ref. to WWII]: My magazine wants me to write an article about GI Janes with the Eighth Air Force. **1991** *NewsDay* (CNN-TV) (June 23): Do GI Janes deserve a place on the battlefield?

GI Jesus *n. Army.* a military chaplain of the Christian faith.
   1944 Kendall *Service Slang* 7: *The GI Jesus....*the Chaplain. **1944** in *AS* XX 147: *GI Jesus,* "chaplain." **1961** Crane *Born of Battle* 135 [ref. to Korean War]: There's a flock of newsmen outside...and a GI Jesus. You're going to be best man at a wedding.

GI Joe *n.* an American soldier, esp. an enlisted man. [Pop. by the cartoon *G.I. Joe,* by David Breger, which first appeared in 1942.]
   1935 *Our Army* (Oct.) 46: G.I. Joe wants to know if steel wool comes from hydraulic rams. **1942** *Yank* (June 6) 24: G.I. Joe by Corp. Dave Breger. **1944** in Inman *Diary* 1244: G.I. Joes wearing holly sprigs in their helmets. **1955** F.K. Franklin *Combat Nurse* 221 [ref. to WWII]: Hey, you GI joes!...The krauts have quit! **1958** Camerer *Damned Wear Wings* 127: He knows the GI Joe when he sees one. **1977** Caputo *Rumor of War* 84: We're All-American good-guy GI Joes. **1982** Del Vecchio *13th Valley* 80: The number one GI Joe of Attack Company

Seven. **1983** *New Yorker* (Aug. 8) 27: Smiling campesinos talking with G.I. Joes in pidgin English. **1990** *Newsweek* (Jan. 29) 23: [General Noriega] didn't want to end his life being shot by some GI Joe from Missouri.

Gila Monster Route *n. Hobo & R.R.* railway lines of the desert Southwest.

*ca*1920 Hobo College *Hobo Songs* (unp.): He was ditched on the Gila Monster Route. **1922** N. Anderson *Hobo* 194. **1976** Hayden *Voyage* 528: Blacker'n the heart of a shack on th' Gila Monster Route.

gilgadget *n.* a gadget. Also **gillgadget.**

1934 Weseen *Dict. Slang* 338: Gadget...Gilgadget is a variant. **1941** Kendall *Army & Navy Sl.* 19: Gilgadget....a gilhickey or a gimmick or a gadget. **1954** *PADS* (No. 21) 28: Gillgadget...a thingumbob, a dingus.

gilguy *n.* [see 1867 quot.] *Naut.* a gadget.

[***1867** Smyth *Sailor's Wd. Bk.*: Gilguy.—a guy for tracing up, or bearing a boom or derrick. Often applied to inefficient guys.] **1882** *United Service* (Feb.) 223: Go below, Mr. Marline, and take off all those gill guys. **1883** Russell *Sailors' Lang.* 62: Gilguy.—A term applied by seamen to anything they forget the name of. **1918** *Literary Digest* (Sept. 28) 50: A full line of gilguys and gadgets. **1918** Kauffman *Navy at Work* 194: You know, in the Marines, when we can't think of the generic name for anything, we call it a "gadget" or a "gilguy." **1922** *Am. Leg. Wkly.* (Sept. 28) 9: Nobody gave a left-handed gillguy about what happened to us fellows, any way. **1926** *AS* II (Oct.) 62: Every snipe endeavors to impress the poor swabbos with his talk of gillguys, gadgetts [*sic*] and gimmicks.

gilhickey *n.* [prob. *gilguy* + doo*hickey*] *Naut.* a gadget.

1922 *Leatherneck* (Apr. 22) 5: Gil-hickey: A gadget. **1942** *ATS* 74.

gill *n.* [< ScotGael *gille*, Ir *giolla* 'lad'] *Und.* a fellow; (*also*) a fool; gull. Also **gil.** [Later U.S. usage infl. by GILLY, *n.*]

*1797 in Partridge *Dict. Und.* 585: *Rum gill.* A gentleman who appears to have money that is meant to be robbed. ***1812** Vaux *Vocab.*: Gill: a word used by way of variation, similar to *cove, gloak,* or *gory;* but generally coupled to some other descriptive term as a *flash-gill,* a *toby-gill.* ***1812** in *OED*: Come list ye all, ye fighting Gills and Coves of boxing note, sirs. ***1834** Ainsworth *Rookwood* 172: High Pads and Low Pads, Rum Gills and Queer Gills. **1923** Revell *Off the Chest* 210: One from Daniel Burns, an old circus man, read: "Here's hoping the day is near when you will be able to take the gils on a high pitch." **1923** Witwer *Fighting Blood* 141: I've tried everything *I* know to get this gil to fight us. **1925** *Collier's* (Sept. 19) 7: This gil told the authorities that me and Barbara was mixed up in the bootlegging ring. **1928** (cited in Partridge *Dict. Und.* 286). **1934** Weseen *Dict. Slang* 16: Gill—An easy prey; a gullible person. **1936** Fellows & Freeman *Big Show* 119 [ref. to 1890's]: Circus folk stigmatized the townsmen...[as] "gillipins" or "gills," "jays," and "saps."

Gilligan hitch *n.* **1.** *Naut.* an unusual or hastily tied knot.

1919 *Our Navy* (Aug.) 51: It must be an orful temptation to a hard boiled gob to take a couple of extra gilligan hitches around Clarence's neck and string him up to a chandelier. **1941** Kendall *Army & Navy Sl.* 19: Gilligan hitch....an imaginary knot in an imaginary rope. **1958** Cope & Dyer *Petty Officer's Guide* (ed. 2) 347: Gilligan hitch: Any clumsy, unseamanlike knot. **1983** K. Weaver *Texas Crude* 94: Gilligan hitch. Name used for any method of binding with a chain. "Hell, throw a Gilligan hitch on it and let's go."

2. *Und.* a stranglehold. [Cf. substance of 1919 quot. above.]

1933 Ersine *Pris. Slang* 39: Gilligan, Gilligan Hitch. (From Mr. Gilligan, an old time strong-arm actor.) A strangle-hold used by robbers. The strangler, attacking from the rear, slips the crook of his elbow under the victim's chin and throttles him. *ca*1955 in Maurer *Lang. Und.* 241: Gilligan hitch...A stranglehold (West Coast).

gills *n.pl.* the high corners of a stand-up collar; a stand-up collar.

*1826 in *OED:* Your shirt collars should be loose round the neck, and the gills low. **1828** in B. Hall *College Wds.* (ed. 2) 228: Far worse than dust-soiled coat are ruined "gills." ***1852** in *OED:* He wore no gills. ***1859** in *F & H* III 143: With a red face,...with gills white and tremendous, with a noble white waistcoat. ***1873** Hotten *Slang Dict.* (ed. 4): Gills, overlarge shirt collars. ***1884** in *OED*.

¶ In phrase:

¶ **to the gills** completely.

[**1847** in Peskin *Vols.* 22: If the water didn't get up to my gills as it was.] **1918** E. O'Neill *Straw* 63: I was pickled to the gills myself when I arrived here. **1927** *AS* III (Feb.) 221: *Stewed to the gills,* adj. phr.—Superlatively drunk. **1929** *AS* IV (Aug.) 440: Words and expressions

for "drunk"...lit to the guards...up to the gills. **1938** "E. Queen" *4 Hearts* 23: Hypochondriac to the gills, they say. **1941** *Pittsburgh Courier* (Nov. 15) 7: Secretly thrilled to the gills. **1960** *AS* XXXV (May) 115: *Stewed to the gills, phr.*....Thoroughly intoxicated. **1965** Reagan & Hubler *Rest of Me* 18: Keep her stuffed to the gills with old green cheese. **1967** Wolf *Love Generation* 53: He'll just be fed up to the gills with plastic. **1985** Heywood *Taxi Dancer* 3: The guns were sandbagged to the gills and well concealed. **1987** E. Spencer *Macho Man* 113: I'm...pissed to the gills. **1986–91** Hamper *Rivethead* 19: Stoned to the gills on...mescaline.

gilly *n.* [prob. dim. of GILL, *n.*] *Circus & Carnival.* a yokel or ignorant countryman; simpleton; fool.

[***1796** Grose *Vulgar Tongue* (ed. 3): *Gilly Gaupus.* A Scotch term for a tall awkward fellow.] **1882** *Judge* (Dec. 9) 7: Want to scoop the gillies for enough to go to Europe next year. **1888** Nye & Riley *Railway Guide* 25: We managed to *use* him, though,—/Coddin' the gilley along the rout'. **1889** Farmer *Amer.*: Gilly.—A fool. **1895** Coup *Sawdust* 28: I am glad to know that the circus man who speaks of his patrons as "gillies," and who endeavors to obtain his wealth by fair or foul means, is becoming more and more rare. **1895** Townsend *Fadden* 49: Say, she must take me fer er worse gillie dan I am. **1895** Townsend *Fadden Explains* 114: Dere ain't no gilly like a old gilly. **1896** Ade *Artie* 55: Say, you must think I'm a prize gilly to set around here and give up my insides to you about her. **1902** Mead *Word-Coinage* 165: "A yap" and "a jay" are synonymous with "farmer" and "gilley." **1905** in "O. Henry" *Works* 1520: The Central Office must be bughouse to send you out looking like such a gillie. **1911** *DN* III 544: He's a *gillie,* he doesn't know beans. **1912** Field *Watch Yourself* 250: We can easily get rid of Jake, he's a "gilly." **1920** Conklin & Root *Circus* 26 [ref. to 1870's]: That's good 'nuff fer them "gillies" and "rubes." **1939** in W.C. Fields *By Himself* 327: You have made me a gilly.

gillyclicker *n.* [of fanciful orig.] *Arkansas.* the vulva or vagina.

1973 Gwaltney *Destiny's Chickens* 1: There was a plodding balls-and-pecker quality to Poppa and an equally plodding gillyclicker-and-tits to Momma. *Ibid.* 59: So Arvajean couldn't help with the old gillyclicker.

gilpin *n.* [prob. fr. *gilpin,* a kind of apple, sugg. by APPLE, *n.,* 2.b.] a stupid person; sucker. Also **gillipin.**

1934 Weston & Cunningham *Old Fashioned Way* (film): Didn't you hear me tell those gilpins I'd arranged for 100 extra seats? **1936** Fellows & Freeman *Big Show* 108 [ref. to 1890's]: We only want the...leathers (pocketbooks) from the gillipins (townsfolk) during the parade downtown. **1938** in W.C. Fields *By Himself* 307: Whipsnade works in the box-office [and]...short-changes the...gilpins. **1939** Wald *Roaring Twenties* (film): What a first-class gilpin I turned out to be!

gilt *n.* [a devel. of the S.E. sense; not fr. Yid or G] money; GELT. Orig. *S.E.*

*1598 in *OED:* So that some guilt may grease his greedy fist. ***1608** in *OED:* Though guilt condemnes, tis gilt must makes vs glad. ***1637** in *OED.* ***1708** in *OED:* And from thence conducted (provided he has Gilt) over the way to Hell. ***1857** "Ducange" *Vulgar Tongue* 9: Gilt, n. Money. ***1873** Hotten *Slang Dict.* (ed. 4): Gilt, money. ***1885** in *F & H* III 144: Disputatious like mobs grouped together to discuss whether Charrington or Crowder had the most *gilt.* **1891** Maitland *Slang Dict.* 123: *Gilt,* money. **1899** Cullen *Tales* 105: We all had on buck privates' uniforms, but when we flashed the gilt on him and paid...in advance he had to stand for the uniforms. **1899** Ade *Fables* 80: He'd often wished he could close in on enough to the Gilt to buy him a nice piece of Land. **1898–1900** Cullen *Chances* 71: Part o' the...gilt...'ll belong to you. **1908** in H.C. Fisher *A. Mutt* 56: 50 slices of the gilt on Gemmell. **1910** T.A. Dorgan, in *N.Y. Eve. Jour.* (May 3) 20: He sure did hate to part wid de gilt. **1918** Ruggles *Navy Explained* 102. **1940** Baldwin *Brother Orchid* (film): Say, there's good gilt in that.

gimix *n.* GIMMICK, *n.*

1926 Norwood *Other Side of Circus* 197: Like as not, you'd overlook some gimix or other. *Ibid.* 272: A small machine or tool—gimix. **1942** *ATS* 74: Contrivance; indefinite object; "gadget."...gilguy,...gimix.

gimme /ˈgɪmi/ *n.* [colloq. pron. of *give me*] **1.** *pl.* a reliance on or a demand for the generosity of others; acquisitiveness.—constr. with *the.*

1918 *Wadsworth Gas Attack* 15: That old disease has returned which is called the "gimmies" and Joe Fitzpatrick is very ill with it. **1920** Weidman *312th M.G. Bn.* 55: The French were badly smitten with that awful disease commonly known in the U.S.A. as the "Gimmes." **1923** T.A. Dorgan, in Zwilling *TAD Lexicon* 39: I had three of them wife things and they all had the gimmes. **1923** H. Pease *Me No Speaka Good*

English (sheet music) 4: She soon got the "gimmies." **1932** Miller & Burnett *Scarface* (film): You can hide behind…politicians with the gimmies. **1935** S. Lewis *Can't Happen* 91: Every guy in the country with a bad case of the gimmes comes to see me!

2.a. *Golf.* a short putt that is conceded to an opponent.

1929 in P. Davies *Golf. Terms* 74: Bill carelessly tapped his ball toward the hole, following the usual custom of considering a putt of that short distance a "gimme." **1964** in P. Davies *Golf. Terms* 74: There are no "gimmes" on the pro tour. **1970** Scharff *Encyc. of Golf* 417: *Gimme.* A putt so short that it will most likely be conceded by an opponent. **1976** *Webster's Sports Dict.* 181. **1982** Considine *Lang. Sport* 189.

b. *Baseball.* a player who is easily put out; an easy out.

1978 K. Jackson *ABC-TV Monday Nt. Baseball* (July 3): Remy at .263 is no gimme at the plate.

c. an easy victory; (*Sports.*) a contest that is easily and decisively won.

1986 Zeybel *First Ace* 128: They…went into a flat spin.…Real gimmes. **1987** *Academe* (July) 56: "Our first game is against a freshman team called the Rabbits."…"This is a gimme!"

3. a bonus; gift.

1974 Strasburger *Rounding Third* 157: Carter…was allowed the same 10% reduction from absolutely perfect behavior. This was his "gimme" for the week.

¶ In phrases:

¶ **a handful of gimme and a mouthful of much-obliged** *So.* an expectation or demand for generosity coupled with insincere or minimal gratitude or acknowledgment.

1923 in Handy *Blues Treasury* 143: These men up north, they surely do make me tired./They've got a mouthful of "gimme,"/Handful of "much obliged." **1930** Botkin *Folk-Say* 338: You got a handful of gimme, a mouthful of much obliged. **1978** Wheeler & Kerby *Steel Cowboy* (film): All anybody comes up with's a hand full of gimme and a mouth full of much-obliged.

¶ **on the gimme** seeking or accepting bribes; on the take.

1981 *Hill Street Blues* (NBC-TV): I know you think he's a little rough around the edges, but La Rue is too smart a cop to be on the gimme.

gimme cap *n. S.W.* a baseball cap bearing the name or trademark of a business and usu. distributed as part of an advertising promotion.

[**1941** in *DARE*: Sam bought…a can of dime tobacco and some gimme papers for himself.] **1978** *Texas Monthly* (Oct.) 141: The basic Texas head will likely be topped off with a new headdress, whose first advantage is that it probably arrived free of charge.…I give you the Gimme Cap. **1978** in *Texas Monthly* (Jan. 1979) 143: Anglers in gimme caps advertising machine shops or bait stands. **1983** *Newsweek* (Dec. 12) 98: You will not see his cowboys fixing a baler or wearing the increasingly common "gimme" caps. **1986** in *Atlantic* (Mar. 1987) 100: He received…an armadillo hat, a purple sweatshirt…and several gimme caps. **1987** *CBS News Special Report* (CBS-TV) (Oct. 16): That orange and white cap is the kind they call a *gimme cap* in Texas. **1990** L. Nieman *Boomer* 13: The walls are lined with "gimmie caps" bearing local industrial logos.

gimmick *n.* [orig. unkn.] **1.a.** a hidden mechanical device used dishonestly to control a game of chance; (*also*) the mechanism that creates the illusion in a conjurer's trick; a hidden or secret method.

1922 *Variety* (July 21) 9: Lolita…tips the gimick on the joint. **1925** *Collier's* (Aug. 29) 26: Here was the second gimmick I had met. **1926** Maines & Grant *Wise-Crack Dict.* 8: *Gimmick*—device used for making a fair game crooked. **1928** *AS* III (June) 414: *Gimmick.* The brake, tip-up, or other device used on games of chance to make them crooked or unfair to the towner who plays them. **1929** *Sat. Eve. Post* (Oct. 19) 26: *Gimmick:* Secret of work. **1933** Ersine *Pris. Slang* 40: *Gimmic.* Any cheating device. **1934** *WNID2*: *Gimmick*…Any small device used secretly by a magician in performing a trick. **1949** *AS* XXIV (Feb.) 40: Somewhere between 1928 and 1932 the word *gimmick* came to magic and filled a conspicuous vacancy in the language. The word is used to describe any article secretly brought into play during a trick.…*Gimic, gimmik,* and *gimick* all appear…but anything other than *gimmick* is now considered to be a misspelling.

b. a trick or stratagem, esp. as used in swindling.

1930 *Variety* (Jan. 8) 123: [Con men] aren't bad—the gimmick is all they know. And the scratch is such short money that it never hurts anyone much. **1930** Lait *On Spot* 203: *Gimmick*…Any contrivance to make a fair transaction or contest unfair. **1930** *Bookman* (Dec.) 398: A gim-

mick that is illegal if worked through mail solicitation. ***1951** in *OEDS*: Washington has suspected that a political "gimmick" might be wrapped up in the Malik offer. **1952** H. Grey *Hoods* 89: The gimmick is this.…Pipy pulls a switcheroo. **1953** *AS* XXVIII (May) 116: *Gimmick, n.*…any device used to misrepresent merchandise.

c. a concealed, usu. devious, aspect of something; catch.

1942–49 Goldin et al. *DAUL* 81: *Gimmick*…The trick; the catch; the deceptive element, whether concrete or abstract. **1956** Kubrick & Thompson *Killing* (film): I figure'd there'd be a gimmick. **1956** G. Green *Last Angry Man* 247: Must everything have a gimmick, Ben, a windup? **1975** Mahl *Beating Bookie* 47: That's the gimmick, how do you know what the true-risk odds should be?

d. Esp. *Adver.* a clever feature or idea that will lure customers, attract notice or the like. Now *colloq.* or *S.E.*

1946 Dadswell *Hey There Sucker!* 102: *Gimmick*…a special idea or scheme in connection with concession or show operations. **1952** McCarthy *Academe* 70: It would have no selling-point, no gimmick, as they said in advertising. **1965** Reeves *Night Action* 11: Club proprietors stay up nights thinking up new gimmicks. ca**1966** Barth *G. Goat-Boy* XXV: You've thought up some gimmick for your dissertation. **1972** B.J. Minsky *Gimmicks Make Money in Retailing* (title). **1977** Kleinberg *Live with Computers* 21: The speed at which a computer works is not just a gimmick.

2.a. any small article or device; gadget.

1926 *AS* II (Oct.) 62: Every snipe endeavors to impress the poor swabbos with his talk of gillguys, gadgetts [*sic*] and gimmicks. **1928** *N.Y. Times* (Mar. 11) VIII 6: *Gimmick*—Word for anything. **1931** D.W. Maurer, in *AS* (June) 331: Where's the gimmick that turns on this fan? **1936** in *OEDS*: The word *gimac* means "a gadget." It is an anagram of the word "*magic*" and is used by magicians the same way as others use the word "thing-a-ma-bob." **1942** Algren *Morning* 259: Slip a gimmick in his [boxing] glove now, Doc! **1951** *AS* XXVI (Feb.) 17: Some current favorites are *gadget,* now high in popularity, *gimmick, gismo.* **1951** W. Miller *Hong Kong* (film): I put the gimmick [a jeweled statuette] back in the safe. **1972–75** W. Allen *Feathers* 32: Joy buzzers—those little fun gimmicks that give people a shock when they shake hands.

b. the penis.

1966 Kenney *Caste* 19: She shifted my gimmick from side to side, like it was a piece of salami.

c. usu. *pl. Narc.* a hypodermic needle or syringe; equipment used to inject drugs.

1967 J.B. Williams *Narc. & Halluc.* 112: *Gimmicks*—The equipment for injecting drugs. **1966–70** J. Carroll, in *Paris Rev.* (No. 50) 113: Two sets of gimmicks…in the plastic cup. **1972** Grogan *Ringolevio* 270: He was shouting that he found an outfit, a set of gimmicks. **1975** Sepe & Telano *Cop Team* 151: You must have gotten him…for possession of "gimmicks." **1976** Chinn *Dig Nigger Up* 240: *Hypodermic needle:* point, spike, gun, gimmick, etc.

3. a foolish, peculiar, or eccentric person.

1926 *Sat. Eve. Post* (Oct. 23) 129: There's an interpreter there, a gimmick with a khaki uniform and a sphinx on his collar. ca**1928** in Wilstach *Stage Sl.* (unp.): "Gimick" is a lame man. **1930** (cited in Partridge *Dict. Und.* 287). **1935** Pollock *Und. Speaks: Gimmick,* a person who has been mulcted by cults, healers, fortune tellers or mystics.

gimmick *v.* **1.** to equip with or add a gimmick or gimmicks; arrange or alter dishonestly or deceptively; rig. Also constr. with *up.*

1922 *Variety* (Aug. 18) 8: Games that were on the level are "gimmicked" (fixed with a mechanical or electric pinch). Even the ball games…can be instantly gimmicked. **1928** (cited in *W9*). **1946** Gresham *Nightmare Alley* 135: With this house, I can gimmick it up from cellar to attic. **1961** Scarne *Comp. Guide to Gambling* 279: All he needs is a circle of suckers and a pair of gimmicked dice. **1963** D. Tracy *Brass Ring* 371: He had to gimmick records, pay blackmail. **1967** Spillane *Delta* 19: The bathroom mirror was gimmicked the same way and that particular invasion of privacy I didn't like at all. **1977** in Terkel *Amer. Dreams* 338: How am I gonna gimmick this [political issue] up so I can go back home and not get in trouble? **1993** *Sally Jessy Raphaël* (synd. TV series): We wanted to do this right, so I gimmicked it up a little bit.

2. *Und.* to cheat or swindle.

1925 *Collier's* (Aug. 29) 26: She had a whole inch of advantage. Her beau had been gimmicked again.

gimmick around *v.* to fool around.

1936 Moffitt & Solkow *Murder with Pictures* (film): The photogs were gimmicking around.

gimp[1] *n.* [orig. unkn.; cf. GIMPY[1], *adj.*] energy; spirit; vim;

determination. [The *a*1919 quot. may have been written as early as 1863.]

1893 Frye *Field & Staff* 84: But he was some lackin' in sperrit. O-ho! he cert'nly *was* lackin' o' gimp. **1901** *Munsey's Mag.* XXIV 567: Sort of took the gimp out of you, didn't it? **1903** Ade *Society* 76: At 6:30, when the Producer showed up for Dinner, he was a Faded Flower, and had about as much Gimp as a Wet Towel. *****1906** in *OEDS*. **1911–12** Ade *Knocking the Neighbors* 121: The fond Parents had…robbed him of all his Gimp. *a*1919 J.W. Haley *Rebel Yell* 106: This seemed to take all the gimp out of them. **1925** Cobb *Many Laughs* 182: Padre, I ain't lost my gimp and I wouldn't hang back if Uncle Sam wanted me to help mop up anybody. **1926** Carter *Old Sgt's. Story* 19 [ref. to 1870's]: The swiftly moving mass of fleeing Indians had taken nearly all the "gimp," snap, and live wire spirit out of our hitherto bold Fourth Cav. warriors. **1931** Stevenson *St. Luke's* 26 [ref. to *ca*1910]: "What does *gimp* mean?"…"Sand, sir, grit, sir." **1936** in Botkin *Treas. Amer. Folk.* 216: It seems that being straightened out sort of took the gimp out of the river. **1939** *Chi. Tribune* (Jan. 22) (Graphic Sec.) 9: *Gimp*—courage, guts. **1958** P. Field *Devil's R.* 106: There ain't a sign of gimp in that hairpin. **1968–69** in *DARE*.

gimp² *n.* [cf. G *Gimpel* 'simpleton'; perh. related to GIMP³] a stupid obnoxious person; GINK, *n.*, 1. Also **gimpy.** Cf. GIMP, *adj.*, 1.

1924 Hecht & Bodenheim *Cutie* 22: A gimp like you takes my appetite away for a week. *****1942** S.J. Baker *Austral. Lang.* 130: Fools of one kind and another have carved a considerable niche for themselves in Australian speech…: *lardhead,…nit,…drip,…gimp.* **1959** Murtagh & Harris *Who Live in Shadow* 55: The gimpies told me no, I couldn't have my license. *Ibid.* 201: *Gimpy:* a mocking term for people beneath one's notice. **1971** H.S. Thompson *Las Vegas* 63: Some doom-struck gimp who couldn't handle the pressure. **1972** Hannah *Geronimo Rex* 48: What kind of a gimp did you think I was? **1979** Gram *Foxes* 148: "God, what a gimp," grumbled Annie. **1990** P. Dickson *Slang!* 218: *Gimp* A loser.

gimp³ *n.* [perh. related to GIMP²] **1.a.** a person who is lame or unable to walk; cripple.—used derisively. Also **gimpy.**

1925 Mullin *Scholar Tramp* 187 [ref. to *ca*1912]: He was crippled in one leg, which fact accounted for his moniker, for on the Road a lame man is a gimpy; even as a one-armed man is a wingy. **1929** *New Yorker* (Feb. 9) 38: He'd…kick a gimp in the good leg and leave him lay in the sawdust drumming upon the floor with his wood instrument. **1940** W.R. Burnett *High Sierra* 113: It's because she's a gimp, I guess. **1941** Macaulay & Wald *Manpower* (film): I saw you duckin' out with that gimp. **1949** Foreman *Champion* (film): Look out, gimp. **1958** McCulloch *Woods Wds.* 70: *Gimpy*—A lame man. **1959** Lipton *Barbarians* 17: The jerk, the drip, the half-wit and spastic, the hare-lip and gimp. **1967** *N.Y.P.D.* (ABC-TV): And this one—a gimp to boot. **1968** Cuomo *Thieves* 289: They…were either all gimpies or else a little stir-bugs, too. **1970** Thackrey *Thief* 77: The guy was a gimp. Had a big, deep limp on his right side. **1978** Alibrandi *Killshot* 275: Who is this gimp, Coldiron? **1982** in *Nat. Lampoon* (Feb. 1983) 8: Well, the damn gimps…just *rolled* twenty-six miles. **1983** Eilert *Self & Country* 163: Do you want your girl saddled with a gimp?

b. a limp.

1925 in *OEDS*: *Gimp*, a lame leg. **1929–31** D. Runyon *Guys & Dolls* 160: She walks with a gimp in one leg, which is why she is called Madame la Gimp. **1965** Herlihy *Midnight Cowboy* 128: First, I'll have to walk a lot, and with this gimp, it takes time and it's no picnic. **1970** Sorrentino *Steelwork* 80: The kid couldn't run so well, he had a slight gimp. **1983** Beckwith & Knox *Delta Force* 122: Because of a…leg wound…, on cold damp days Dick would walk with a slight gimp.

2. a twist.

1966 H.S. Thompson *Hell's Angels* 189: The O. Henry gimp in the plotline gives it real style.

gimp *adj.* **1.** inferior; second-rate.

1877 *Puck* (May) 5: "Snide," "gimp," "tart," and all similar condemnatory slang phrases are suspended. The latest vestibule neologism is "dire."

2. GIMPED.

1976 Hayden *Voyage* 38: The pervert with the gimp leg. **1982** in "J.B. Briggs" *Drive-In* 23: His leg might be gimp.

gimp *v.* **1.** to limp.

1929–31 D. Runyon *Guys & Dolls* 90: She…goes gimping away. **1944** D. Runyon, in *Collier's* (Mar. 18) 12: He enters…walking with a cane and gimping slightly. *a*1966 Barth G. *Goat-Boy* 5: The buck…set me gimping down the road I travel yet. **1972** Hannah *Geronimo Rex* 276:

He gimped downstairs. **1979** J. Morris *War Story* 61: Gimping along using their carbines like canes. **1992** J. Garry *This Ol' Drought* 15: He…was gimping around on crutches.

2. to lame; cripple.

1962 *Untouchables* (ABC-TV): I'm an old-time fisherman that gimped his leg when the *Mary Jo* went down. **1965** in H.S. Thompson *Shark Hunt* 472: His revolutionary zeal is gimped by pessimism.

gimped *adj.* crippled; disabled; lame; halting.—usu. constr. with *up*.

1948 McCulloch *Woods Words* 9: An old codger too gimped up to log any more. **1972** in H.S. Thompson *Shark Hunt* 122: A first, gimped effort in…"The New Journalism." **1983** Eilert *Self & Country* 213: Hell, I'm all gimped up. **1987** Robbins *Ravens* 214: I can't go home all gimped up like this.

gimper¹ *n.* [GIMP¹, *n.* + -*er*] a spirited, reliable fellow.

1918 *Lit. Digest* (Aug. 24) 36: [Lieut. Edward Rickenbacker] explains,…"A gimper is…a scout who does everything just a little better than he has to…I got the word from a mechanic…in the racing game.…In this man's life there were two kinds of people—gimpers and bums."

gimper² *n.* [GIMP², *n.* + -*er*] **1.** GIMP³, *n.*, 1.a. Also **gimpster.**

1974 *Coq* (Apr.) 46: Gimpsters. Effin' crips can't fuck nobody. **1988** Knoxville, Tenn., woman, age 23: A handicapped person is a *gimper*.

2. *Journ.* (see quot.).

1989 *Newsweek* (Sept. 4) 8: *Gimper:* A human interest "sob" story about an incurable disease, loss of life, severe injury.…"Let's do this gimper. It's got a wheelchair case in it."

gimp stick *n.* a crutch or cane.

1939 Howsley *Argot* 20: *Gimp stick*—a crutch, a cane.

gimpty *adj.* GIMPY², 2.

1934 H. Roth *Call It Sleep* 420: Aaa! Who touched yer hump, yuh gimpty fu—. **1953** Paley *Rumble* 100: That crazy gimpty bastard shot somebody. **1973** N.Y.U. student: My grandmother says *gimpty*, not "gimpy."

gimpy¹ *adj.* sprightly; energetic.

1877 Bartlett *Amer.* (ed. 4) 245: *Gimpy.* Sprightly, active; as, "a *gimpy* horse." **1941** in *DARE*: Lively, spry…gimpy.

gimpy² *adj.* **1.** lame; unable to walk; crippled.

1929 Barr *Let Tomorrow Come* 151: An' old stiff wid a gimpy leg. **1930** G. Irwin *Tramp & Und. Sl.* 85: *Gimpy.* Lame; crippled. **1944** C.B. Davis *Leo McGuire* 44: I've got a gimpy leg. **1962** B. Davis *Lonely Life* 175: You gimpy-legged monster! **1968** Ainslie *Racing Guide* 468: *Gimpy*— Of a lame, sore, "ouchy" horse. **1979** C. Martin *Catullus* 36: Gimpy Vulcan.

2. inferior; second-rate; LAME.

1970–72 in *AS* L (1975) 59: We paid for a gimpy job.

gimpy *n.* see GIMP², *n.*

gin *n.* *Black E.* a street fight; brawl.

1963 *Time* (Aug. 2) 14: *Gin time.* Time to fight. **1976** Wepman et al. *The Life* 182: Gin (*n* and *vi*) "fight."

gin *v.* *Black E.* get it on s.v. GET ON, *v.*

1940 in Leadbitter & Slaven *Blues Records* 461: Can't You Roll Up And Gin? **1963** in Wepman et al. *The Life* 84: The whore/Took sick and couldn't gin. **1976** (quot. at GIN, *n.*). **1986** *NDAS*.

gin barrel *n.* a drunkard.

1865 Blake *Potomac* 257: Here comes the old gin barrel!

gin blossom *n.* a red nose or red blotches on the face caused by alcoholism. Cf. RUM BLOSSOM.

1931 Hellinger *Moon* 237: Beautiful blossoms have replaced the gin blossoms. **1993** The Gin Blossoms [name of rock group].

ginch *n.* [orig. unkn.] **1.** a young woman or women, esp. considered as sources of sexual gratification; copulation with a woman.

1936 *AS* (Oct.) 280: *Ginch* Any girl. **1961** Coon *Meanwhile at the Front* 76 [ref. to Korean War]: When criminals start throwing ginch around, that's pretty low. **1962** E. Stephens *Blow Negative* 38: In…California, surrounded by snatch, ginch and sunshine. **1963** Coon *Short End* 50: This boy ain't tryin' to take your ginch. **1963** Doulis *Path* 220: What a stupid ginch. **1964** Howe *Valley of Fire* 104 [ref. to Korean War]: So this little ginch gets me all squared away, see? **1966** H.S. Thompson *Hell's Angels* 169: There was not going to be any strange ginch either. **1971** Cole *Rook* 88 [ref. to late 1940's]: "Everybody saturated with ginch," he said sourly. **1972** R. Wilson *Forbidden Words* 123: A new woman may be known as "the new ginch" until a better name is found for her. **1977** Olsen *Fire Five* 43: Plummer's specialty is ginch, not food. **1986** Heinemann *Paco's Story* 152: There is some strange ginch in that town, don't ask me how come. *a*1990 Westcott *Half a Klick* 47: How do you like this guy? Pays some ginch to cut him.

2. the vulva or vagina.

1973 *Penthouse* (May) 78: Ginch. Gash. Where Auntie got hit with the ax.

ginchy *adj.* *Stu.*, Esp. *West Coast.* **1.** wonderfully good or attractive.

1959 I. Taylor *Kookie, Kookie, Lend Me Your Comb* (pop. song): You're the ginchiest! **1966** IUFA *Folk Speech*: Ginchy—Anything great. **1967** in H. Ellison *Sex Misspelled* 177: "Everything groovy?"..."Ginchy." **1986** Merkin *Zombie Jamboree* 162: I just thought it was the ginchiest hiding place I'd ever seen. **1990** *Mystery Sci. Theater* (Comedy Central TV): Aw, she's the ginchiest.

2. [perh. of independent origin] anxious; jumpy; ANTSY.

1970 C. Harrison *No Score* 53: I got very ginchy about being left alone with Aileen, very hopeful and very anxious both at once.

ging *n.* JING, *n.*

ginger *n.* spirit; energy; temper; (*also*) (*obs.*) a spirited horse. Now *colloq.*

*1825 in *OED*: If you want to splash along in glory with a ginger. **1838** [Haliburton] *Clockmaker* (Ser. 2) 24: The...beast was ginger to the backbone. **1843** in *OED*: Talk Yankee to him, and get his ginger up. *1859 in *F & H* III 146: A *ginger* is a showy fast horse. **1888** in Farmer *Amer.*: Considerable ginger is departing from your resolution. *1891 in *F & H* III 147: I'll take the ginger out of him in short order. **1894** in Somers *Sports in N.O.* 262: To use a slang expression, the boys have gotten more ginger in them. **1894** *Harper's* (Dec.) 107: It ain't great, but it's got the ginger in it; and it shows I'm on to curves. **1905** in Paxton *Sport USA* 26: To display "ginger" on the field, he must "keep away from people" and not dissipate thoughts, hopes and emotions. **1907** in Fleming *Unforget. Season* 2: He said that the umpires would not let him get out on the coaching lines and "pump ginger" into his players. **1910** *N.Y. Eve. Jour.* (Mar. 9) 14: Simon Legree,...with his...whip could not have hammered ginger in the Yankee ball players this morning. **1910** in O. Johnson *Lawrenceville* 257: I'll scatter a little ginger around all right. **1919** Dreer *Immed. Jewel* 1: Be serious, but not too serious. Get some ginger into you. **1942** in *DA*: Ginger, n. Temper. "She's got her ginger up this morning." **1945** in *DAS*: A...redhead...imbued with an effervescent quality that used to be called "ginger." **1965–70** in *DARE*: Ginger...somewhat old-fash...28 of 33 inf[ormant]s old.

gingerbread *n.* Orig. *Naut.* carved and gilded ornamentation on a sailing vessel; (*hence*) fancy, tasteless, or unnecessary trimmings of any kind. Also *adj.* Now *S.E.*

*1748 T. Smollett *Rod. Random* ch.iii: Lookee...if you come athwart me, 'ware your gingerbread-work. *1804 in *OED*: As the sailors term it, there is an abundance of gingerbread work. *1833 C. Lamb, in *OED*: What can make her so fond of a gingerbread watch? **1851** M. Reid *Scalp-Hunters* 74: One of "them ar gingerbread guns"...[with] an ornamented stock. **1875** "M. Twain" *Old Times* 38: A fanciful pilothouse, all glass and "gingerbread," perched on top of the "texas" deck. **1903** *Independent* (Nov. 26) 2792: There was no trashy gingerbread work or useless adornment about the "Besant." **1945** Monks *Ribbon & Star* 123: He tells a good story, but doesn't waste his great store of energy on emotional ginger-bread. **1969** Bouton *Ball Four* 159: That's because our uniforms look so silly with that technicolor gingerbread all over them. **1969** *Playboy* (Mar.) 44: Slim, functional beauty with no ugly gingerbread popping out all over the place.

ginger-peachy *adj.* excellent.—usu. used ironically.

1950 in M. Daly *Profile of Youth* 228: Smooth tunes are "fine like wine"; Western songs are "ginger peachy". **1952** Englund *Never Wave at a WAC* (film): That's just ginger peachy! **1957** Laurents & Sondheim *West Side Story* 153: Ad libs: "Oh, ginger peachy," etc. **1970** Gattzden *Black Vendetta* 108: That's real ginger-peachy.

ginger up *v.* [earlier *S.E.* *ginger* 'to treat a horse with ginger'; see *OED*] to inspirit or stimulate; enliven. Also *intrans.*

*1849 B. Disraeli, in *OED*: Whether they were gingered up by the articles in the "Times" or not I can't say. **1893** Hampton *Maj. in Washington* 13: As soon as I can lay eyes on Hoke Smith I'm goin' to ginger him up a little. **1910** *N.Y. Eve. Jour.* (Apr. 6) 15: Ginger up; show some pepper.

gingery *adj.* spirited; lively.

1902–03 Ade *People You Know* 84: You write a good gingery Skit for me.

ginhead *n.* a gin alcoholic; drunkard. Hence **gin-headed**, *adj.*

1927 C. McKay *Home to Harlem* 31: She was called Gin-head Susy. **1929–31** Runyon *Guys & Dolls* 89: A busted romance made her become a ginhead. **1940** Zinberg *Walk Hard* 122: I bet you're a regular gin-head. **1956** Algren *Wild Side* 132: The little ginhead's demented skip-and-hop step was lost in the brainless titter of the rain. **1963** D. Tracy *Brass Ring* 28: He was...finished covering for the gin-headed bastard any longer. **1963–64** Kesey *Great Notion* 156: That damn ginhead. **1992** *Homefront* (ABC-TV): When is that no-account ginhead gonna hit the road?

gink *n.* [orig. uncert.] **1.** an odd, eccentric, or stupid fellow; (*broadly*) a person; character.

1906 *Nat. Police Gaz.* (May 5) 3: The gink that knows it all thinks he's so damned smart. **1910** in McCay *Little Nemo* 258: Pipe the face on him, kids! He's a gink! Hello, gink! **1910** *N.Y. Eve. Jour.* (Feb. 4) 14: You're a clever gink, eh? Well take this. **1911** A.H. Lewis *Apaches of N.Y.* 75: Do youse take any stock in them ginks who claims they can skin a deck of cards...an' then put you next to everyt'ing that'll happen to you in a year? **1911–12** Ade *Knocking the Neighbors* 196: We have rounded up a tough bunch of Ginks. **1912** in Truman *Dear Bess* 78: I suppose the gink who wrote *Beautiful Snow* has received a genteel sufficiency of it today. **1913** *Sat. Eve. Post* (Mar. 15) 6: I've walloped many a fresh gink that was bigger'n him. **1914** London *Jacket* 72: "Ain't they the crazy ginks, these college guys," Captain Jamie snorted. **1915** Braley *Songs of Workaday World* 103: Honestly, boys, I'm the ca'mest gink, With the softest heart an' the kindest ways. **1918** Paine *Fighting Fleets* 63: Knock on wood, you gink. **1918** McNutt *Yanks* 91: He was just a long, lean country gink,/From away out West where the hop-toads wink. **1919** T. Kelly *What Outfit?* 38: A gink, the manager, I guess, blew out on stage between acts. **1930** Irwin *Tramp & Und. Sl.*: Gink...A generic term for man, rather slighting in its use. **1934** Appel *Brain Guy* 81: I was tellin' Schneck what ginks we are. *1957 in *OEDS*: Hughie was a heel or a gink or anything you liked to call him. **1963–64** Kesey *Great Notion* 110: He's made a good-sized gink, bigger than any of us would ever of expected. **1967** Moorse *Duck* 71: A wild-eyed gink with a goldfish bowl over his head...appeared asking to be taken along to Mars. **1976** Hayden *Voyage* 528: Thet tall gink on th' poop looks like he was made outa plaster. **1979** Charyn *7th Babe* 173: Who is that gink?

2. an East Asian; CHINK; GOOK.—used contemptuously.

1948 in *DA* s.v. *Guinea*: The Hunkeys, the Spicks, the Guineas and the Ginks are down on the rest of the family. **1951** Mailer *Barbary Shore* 215: Reds and gooks and...ginks, we've got 'em all to fight. *ca*1970 in Brownmiller *Against Our Will* 106: He was advised that "some gink grabbed a rifle and shot one of the nurses." **1971–72** Giovannitti *Medal* 94: "Shit, sarge, we're here to find ginks, ain't we?" "Yeah. Only we ain't sure he's a VC." **1973** Former Sgt., U.S. Army: A *gink* is the same as a *gook*. I heard it used that way in 1967. **1980** Cragg *L. Militaris* 198: *Gink*...a Vietnamese.

3. *Police.* (see quots.).

1970–71 J. Rubinstein *City Police* 43: Taking the risks of being branded as a "gink," a spy. *Ibid.* 61: A hidden camera used by the department's internal inspection unit, the ginks, to conduct secret investigations of complaints against policemen.

ginky *adj.* of or resembling a GINK.

1968–70 *Current Slang* III & IV 56: Ginky, adj. Out of style.—High school females, Ohio. **1972** *Playboy* (Apr.) 84: He felt that the guy was kind of ginky-looking.

gin mill *n.* an unsavory establishment where hard liquor is sold; saloon.

1866 *Nat. Police Gaz.* (Nov. 3) 2: Passing the gin mill on the corner of Grand and Crosby streets. **1866** *Night Side of N.Y.* 95: This gin-mill is one of the cheapest...gates to ruin in the city. **1867** S. Clemens, in *Twain's Letters* II 36: The scenes of my beer-hood,...the station-house, gin-mill, and deep-tangled railroad. **1869** Carleton *Kaleidoscope* 18: He used to keep a bully good gin-mill. **1882** Campbell *Poor* 17: I got strength...to...save my money...instead o' givin' it to gin mills. **1885** Harte *Shore & Sedge* 45: Don't you worry about that gin-mill and hash-gymnasium downstairs. **1891** Clurman *Nick Carter* 14: He was standing idly before the door of a "gin-mill" leisurely picking his teeth. **1896** F.P. Dunne, in Schaaf *Dooley* 253: If money was plenty enough for him to get some without wur-rukin' he'd open a ginmill. **1908** McGaffey *Show Girl* 70: Going to a gin-mill. **1939** Goodman & Kolodin *Swing* 233: We were playing...in the honky-tonks and ginmills. **1943** J. Mitchell *McSorley's* 30: At night he sings ballads in Irish gin mills on Third Avenue. **1976** S. Lawrence *Northern Saga* 19: Clara'll be in some

gin mill. 1992 M. Gelman *Crime Scene* 20: I hustled out to some nearby gin mill to get a coffee cup filled with scotch.

ginned *adj.* **1.** fatigued.—constr. with *out.*

1841 *Spirit of Times* (Oct. 2) 367: I went into the St. Charles…and "so help me, Bob"…if I wasn't perfectly "ginned out."…I can tell you the yellow *fever* has *hardly* begun.

2. intoxicated with gin; drunk.—usu. constr. with *up.*

[*ca**1811** in J. Farmer *Musa Pedestris* 78: They ginned themselves at jolly Tom Cribb's.] **1900** in *DA*: This man Shewman got pretty well ginned up. **1924** Marks *Plastic Age* 213: Hold me up, kid; I'm ginned. **1929–31** Runyon *Guys & Dolls* 89: She is…generally somewhat ginned up. **1963** Horwitz *Candlelight* 21: The gin hit her, as gin can. I was ginned up myself.

3. (see quot.).—constr. with *up.*

1927 *AS* II 276: *Ginned up*—dressed up.

Ginnie Mae *n. Finance.* the Government National Mortgage Association or one of its securities. Cf. FANNIE MAE.

1975 in *BDNE3*: "Ginnie Mae" has been more active than ever before, particularly in the area of "pass-through" securities. **1982** WINS radio news (Dec. 10): Ginnie Mae is a securities [*sic*] backed by the Government National Mortgage Association. **1986** Chase Manhattan Bank Brochure: This fund invests primarily in Government National Mortgage Association Certificates, or "Ginnie Maes."

ginny *adj.* GINNED.

1928 McEvoy *Show Girl* 81: I know this sounds ginny but there is nothing stronger than aspirin on the baby's breath. **1929** McEvoy *Hollywood Girl* 36: I'm a little ginny.

gin-slinger *n.* a bartender.

1887 in *DA*: Saloon-keepers and white-aproned gin-slingers stood in the doors of the saloons. **1891** McCann & Jarrold *Odds & Ends* 34: He hates gin-slingers worse'n my boss hates the Excise law. **1894** in *DA*: Last Saturday the wife of Mayor Bogg sloped with a gin-slinger at the El Dorado saloon.

gin-soak *n.* a gin alcoholic; drunkard.

1939 M. Levin *Citizens* 226: This ginsoak declared how could Cleveland be anything but a thief. **1981** T.C. Boyle *Water Music* 35: Ned's mother was a second-generation ginsoak.

gin up *v.* **1.** LIQUOR UP, *v.*

1887 F. Francis *Saddle & Moccasin*: They were ginning her up, that's a fact. **1894** in *DA*: As for jags, he held that he can gin up when he likes.

2. to prepare; make ready; (*hence*) to engineer; (*also*) to enliven; excite.

1973 in J.C. Pratt *Vietnam Voices* 569: Ginned up 17+ F-111 targets. **1983** in Safire *Look It Up* 98: Secretary of State George Shultz was asked if the United States had stimulated requests of Caribbean nations to rescue Grenada. He replied…"We haven't been trying to gin up anything." **1989** Brooks & Pinson *Working with Words* 119: *Gin up*…to enliven. **1992** Cokie Roberts, on *This Week in Washington* (ABC-TV) (Mar. 15): Voters ginned up by the revelations [will vote congressmen out of office]. **1993** *N.Y. Times Mag.* (Feb. 14) 40: Too crippled or drunk or hungry to gin up much enthusiasm for the celebration. **1993** *New Republic* (July 12) 12: His staff…ginned up a sixty-five-page report.

gin-wrangler *n. West.* a bartender.

1971 *Gunsmoke* (CBS-TV): Ask that gin-wrangler. He'd know.

ginzo *n.* [prob. alter. of GUINEA; *-zo* prob. of expressive orig., cf. BOZO] **1.a.** an Italian or person of Italian descent; (*hence*) any foreigner.—used contemptuously.

1931 *Amer. Merc.* (Dec.) 413: He's a Roumanian or some kinda guinzo. **1934** Appel *Brain Guy* 10: The two ginzos were gabbing with fat Bobbie. **1936** in D. Runyon *More Guys* 165: He is nothing but a ginzo out of Sacramento. **1943** Tregaskis *Invasion Diary* 55: Those Ginzos just went crazy when the bombs went off. **1946** J.H. Burns *Gallery* 9: I suppose you've got a fidanzato? A little Ginzo who's a P/W in Africa. **1952** Brossard *Darkness* 240: The people in this country think there is no such thing as a decent Italian. They're wops and ginzoes. **1955** O'Connor *Last Hurrah* 46: You take guys like…that little ginzo Camaratta. **1956** G. Green *Last Angry Man* 275: Any man who cured five ginzos in one house—. **1963** Cameron *Black Camp* 108: Well, you can't say the Ginzos haven't been pushing their luck. **1977** Sayles *Union Dues* 246: The word he gets from the local is keep those ghinzos under control. **1983** Flaherty *Tin Wife* 86: A lot of the old-time ginzos were like that.

b. a foreign language spoken by a GINZO.—used contemptuously.

1969 Moynahan *Pairing Off* 150: You would see her there talking

French or ginzo with some big spender in from South America and you wouldn't know what to make of her.

2. a peculiar or worthless fellow; character.

1938 O'Hara *Hope of Heaven* 139: That guinzo over there. He had it. **1949** R. Chandler *Little Sister* 178: Then I meet this ginzo with her doorkey in his hand. **1958** J. Thompson *Getaway* 11: You got a lot of guts, Jackson.…A real gutsy ginzo, that's you.

ginzo red *n.* DAGO RED.—used contemptuously.

1969 NYC man: That was a lot of ginzo red talking.

gip *n., v.* var. GYP.

GI party *n. Army.* an enforced scrubbing and cleaning of a barracks by its residents.

1942 *Yank* (Nov. 18) 16: A G.I. party…turned out to be scrubbing the barracks on our hands and knees. **1947** *AS* (Apr.) XXII 114: *G.I. party night* denotes the evening on which the soldiers clean their quarters. **1956** Hargrove *Girl He Left* 51: A little GI party…for you young soldiers—that's a party where I bring the soap and you bring the elbows. **1963** Fehrenbach *This Kind of War* 463: The new platoon sergeant told his men the barracks needed cleaning, but if everyone would cooperate, each man clean his own area each day, he could get a few men off detail to clean the common areas, and there need be no GI parties. **1969** J. Shepherd, in *Playboy* (Jan. 1970) 180: Friday was the day of the dreaded "GI party," an insane orgy of crawling around on the barracks floor with brushes, soap, sand and hot water that lasted far into the night, getting ready for the Saturday inspection. **1970** Woods *Killing Zone* 31: He won't have to help with the GI party. **1971** *Playboy* (May) 210: Immediately following chow, we will have a company GI party. We will clean every inch of this area.

giraffe *n. Mining.* (see quot.).

1876 W. Wright *Big Bonanza* 171: In this groove winds the cable as the incline-car ("giraffe") is let down into or drawn up out of the mine.

¶ In phrase:

¶ **come** [or **play**] **the giraffe over** [perh. orig. alluding to an anecdote like that referred to in *1959 quot.] to get the better of; hoodwink.

1844 in *DA*: "No you don't," said the watchman, "you don't come the giraffe over me that way." *ca***1845** in *DA*: But our animal know'd how to come the giraffe over *him*. **1867** J. Edwards *Shelby* 135: Blackwell rode up to one party of eleven Federal cavalry…and, having dressed his detachment in blue overcoats and pantaloons, determined to play the "giraffe" over them—a kind of bluff game only known to soldiers. [*1959 G. Durrell, in Heuvelmans *Unkn. Animals* 18: You feel that the people who adopt this argument would, on being presented with a hand-tame abominable snowman in a wrought-iron cage, remark—like the Irishman on seeing the giraffe for the first time—"I don't believe it."]

giraffe *v.* to hoodwink or humbug.

1840 in *DA*: We can never be humbugged or Giraffed long.

girdle *n. Mil. Av.* a G-suit.

1955 *AS* XXX 117: G-suit, girdle.

girl *n.* **1.a.** (used derisively in direct address to a man, without homosexual implication).

1906 in A. Adams *Chisholm Trail* 165: "Now, girls," said Baugh, addressing Carter and the stranger, "I've made you a bed out of the wagon sheet." *Ibid.* 195: I gave him as mean a look as I could command, and said tauntingly, "Now, look here, old girl."

b. *Esp. Pris.* an effeminate male homosexual, esp. a catamite.

1912 (quot. at SALLY, *n.*). **1931** B. Niles *Strange Bro.* 288: All of the girls were put to work in the [prison] laundry. **1934** Kromer *Waiting* 26: A girl can't even have a decent date without the goddam cops breaking in. **1942** in T. Williams *Letters* 30: All the soldiers in town are ugly.…The "girls" are much more attractive. **1949** *Gay Girl's Guide* 10: Girl: As a vocative, synonymous with *darling.* Also used loosely by homosexuals with reference to themselves and their friends. **1957** H. Danforth & J. Horan *D.A.'s Man* 3 [ref. to *ca*1926]: He's got a new girl. His "wife" went home last week. **1958** Talsman *Gaudy Image* 58: He rolled queers, called them "his girls." **1965** Capote *In Cold Blood* 156: Those kind of girls, they can give you an evil time. **1967** Baraka *Tales* 27: Open up, faggots!…Hey, let us in, girls! **1979** D. Milne *Second Chance* 130: There's gonna be a lot of "girls" where we're goin' now.

c. *pl. Mil.* (used derisively in direct address to male recruits in training).

1943 Horan & Frank *Boondocks* 5: Well, girls, here they come. **1967** Johnston & Peters *Beach Red* (film): Awright girls, don't let 'em step on your tender little hands. **1973** Layne *Murphy* (unp.): My name is Briant, girls. I'm your mother now. **1978** J. Webb *Fields of Fire* 124: Un-fucking-military, girls. Get that shit off today. Understand? **1980** McDowell *Our Honor* 36: I don't want to hear one word out of you girls. **1985** Dye *Between Raindrops* 253: Is that clear, girls? It's clear, sir.

2. *Narc.* cocaine.—also constr. with *the*. Cf. BOY, 4.

1953 Anslinger & Tompkins *Traf. in Narc.* 309: The girl. Cocaine. *ca*1953 Hughes *Lodge* 97: We had...a couple of cans of pot and a few caps of heroin and maybe some girl once in a while, too. **1959–60** R. Reisner *Jazz Titans* 156: Girl: Cocaine. **1960** C. Cooper *Scene* 58: They call cocain girl because it gives 'em a sexual jab when they take a shot. **1971** S. Stevens *Way Uptown* 131: Girl, what they call coke downtown, is dynamite stuff but only if you stay on top of it. **1968–73** Agar *Ripping & Running* 60: Like throw in a little girl with it, man. **1989** R. Miller *Profane Men* 51: A new car loaded with fifteen years worth of girl stashed in some...parking lot.

3. *Cards.* a queen of any suit.

1954–60 *DAS.*

girl-boy *n.* Now esp. *Pris.* a girlish boy or homosexual young man; sissy.—used derisively. Also **gal-boy.**

*1589 in *OED:* Girle-boyes, fauoring Ganimede. *1598 M. Drayton, in *OED:* That girle-boy wanton Gaueston. **1877** Bartlett *Amer.* (ed. 4) 237: Gal-Boy. A girlish boy. **1884 in *OED:* My father used to call him the girl-boy. **1899** in S. Crane *Complete Stories* 608: In consequence, a small contingent of blue-eyed weaklings were the sole intimates of the frail sex, and for it they were boisterously and disdainfully called "girl-boys." **1925** Dos Passos *Manhattan Transfer* 97: "That's enough, Herfy's licked." "Girl-boy...Girl-boy." **1937** Herndon *Let Me Live* 211: "Gal-Boy" parties were frequently given....The little boys wore girl's pink bloomers. **1942–49** Goldin et al. *DAUL* 76: Gal-boy. (Gulf State area prisons) A passive pederast or a male oral sodomist. **1952** Himes *Stone* 185: They transferred the fag to the girl-boy company on 5-4. **1969** Hopper *Sex in Prison* 94: If a young prisoner is forced into a homosexual relationship, he may be known as a "gal-boy." **1971** J. Blake *Joint* 67 [ref. to 1954]: They were known as...galboys,...and all had taken girls' names. **1972** Pearce *Pier Head Jump* 142: We got one of them girl-boys on board? *a*1988 in *AS* LXIII (Summer 1988) 133: *Gal-boy n.* Flagrantly effeminate passive homosexual partner.

girlesk *n.* burlesque that features stripteasers or the like. *Joc.*

1942 *ATS* 581: Burlesque show...girlesque. **1946** Dadswell *Hey, Sucker* 71: Of all the "girlesk shows" we exhibited...the most popular...was Lottie Mayer's Disappearing Water Ballet.

girlfriend *n. Narc.* GIRL, 2.

1979 Homer *Jargon* 197: Cocaine...a.k.a....*girlfriend.*

girlie *n.* a girl or young woman.

*1860, *1877 in *OED* (in sense "a little girl"). **1882** C.C. King *Colonel's Daughter* 201: Don't sob so, girlie; *don't* sob so. **1908** McGaffey *Show Girl* 27: Say, girlie, you're all right. **1919** S. Lewis *Free Air* 107: Gee, did I touch you, girlie? Why, that's a shame. **1926** Dunning & Abbott *Broadway* 216: You went into that step off the beat, girlie. **1937** Walt Disney's *S. White* (film): "Really?" "Yes, girlie." **1966** Guerin, Labor, et al. *Hndbk. Crit. Appr. to Lit.* 53: To His Coy Mistress..."make hay while the sun shines, girlie." **1974** Terkel *Working* 50: It's not what it's cracked up to be, girlie. **1978** Maggin *Superman* 125: Whatcha got there, girlie? **1986–91** Hamper *Rivethead* 80: The girlies would come fallin' out of the trees.

girlie *adj.* featuring or depicting nude or scantily clad young women.—used prenominally. Now *colloq.*

1921 *Variety* (Nov. 25) 23: The Adams act...is of the girly variety. **1950** Spillane *Vengeance* 33: I came up with a handful of girlie mags that were better than the postcards you get in Mexico. **1962** T. Berger *Reinhart* 419: Heroic girlie posters rose before the large tent. **1963–64** Kesey *Great Notion* 112: A lonely mountain cabin full of girlie books. **1974** Stone *Dog Soldiers* 25: A girlie bar off Tu Do Street.

girl-san *n.* [*girl* + *-san*, Japn honorific] *Mil.* an East Asian girl or young woman.

1967 Sack *M* 114: Girlsan, I no dinky dow! **1971** Cole *Rook* 260 [ref. to Korean War]: All the girlsans speak mighty fine English. **1973** Karlin, Paquet & Rottmann *Free Fire Zone* 161: Lai Dai, girl-san. **1966–80** McAleer & Dickson *Unit Pride* 243 [ref. to Korean War]: Give girl-san bra, Joe. **1980** Di Fusco et al. *Tracers* 10 [ref. to Vietnam War]: Girlsan. Boysan. Mamasan. Papasan. Babysan. **1981** C. Nelson *Picked Bullets Up* 316: I decided to try a new story, "Little Girl-san Who Is Half Fish."

G.I. shits *n.pl. Mil.* diarrhea or dysentery contracted by military personnel.—usu. considered vulgar.

1944 in *AS* XX 147: GI Shits, "diarrhea." **1951** *Amer. Jour. Socio.* 51:411 [ref. to WWII]: Diarrhea (the "G.I. s—"). **1972** Palfrey *Big V* 110: In the morning I had the dry heaves and GI shits.

G.I. shower *n.* **1.** *Mil.* G.I. BATH.

1956 Hargrove *Girl He Left* 102: That most effective of all trainee gestures—a GI shower, with yellow soap and brushes. **1974** former L/Cpl, USMC, age *ca*28 [ref. to 1967]: In boot camp—they'd take a guy who was really dirty and filthy and they'd grab him and rub him down with a wire brush. That was called giving him a *GI shower* or a *GI.* **1989** Sorkin *Few Good Men* 33: The men in his squad would give him a GI shower....Scrub brushes, brillo pads, steel wool.

2. *Mil.* an application of deodorant.

1983 Eilert *Self & Country* 116 [ref. to 1968]: I gave myself a GI shower with a little can of deodorant.

gism *n.* see JISM, *n.*

git *n.* [dial. var. of E *get* 'a bastard child'; see *OEDS* s.v. *get, n.,* 2b; see also *DARE* s.v. *get, n.,* 2] a worthless person; good-for-nothing. *Rare* in U.S.

1929 Haycox *Chaffee* 86: You no-count Pi-ute git. *1946 in *OEDS:* Chalky! You idle git! *1960, *1967 in *OEDS.*

gitbox *n. Esp. So. & West.* a guitar.

1937 *AS* (Oct.) 181: Gitbox. Guitar. **1939** Calloway *Swingformation Bureau:* A git-box or a belly fiddle is a...guitar. **1946** Mezzrow & Wolfe *Really Blues* [gloss.]: Git-box: Guitar. **1974** in *DARE.*

git-bucket *n. S.W.* a guitar.

1983 K. Weaver *Texas Crude* 113: Gitfiddle, or gitbucket. A guitar.

git-fiddle *n. So. & West.* a guitar.

1935 Z.N. Hurston, in *DARE:* De git fiddles was raisin' cain over in de corner. **1935** Pollock *Und. Speaks:* Git fiddle, a guitar. **1942** *Yank* (Nov. 18) 17: The twang of a git-fiddle. **1945** Hubbard *R.R. Ave.* 195: My voice, plus the "git-fiddle," was as good as a meal ticket. **1957** M. Shulman *Rally* 228: Ah brought muh git-fiddle. **1962** L. Hughes *Tambourines to Glory* 216: Hum-mmm, you got a pretty gitfiddle, boy. **1967** Grefé *Wild Rebels* (film): Dig the cat at the bar. The one with the git-fiddle. **1972** P. Thomas *Savior* 81: All four had git-fiddles. **1975** J.I. White *Git Along Dogies* 191: He packed up his "git-fiddle." **1983** K. Weaver *Texas Crude* 113: Gitfiddle, or gitbucket. A guitar.

Gitmo *n. Mil.* Guantanamo Bay, Cuba, site of a U.S. Navy base.

1959 Herbert L. Pugh *Navy Surgeon* 87 [ref. to 1917]: "This ain't nothing but "Gitmo' Bay," said a boatswain. Some of the crew guessed that we must have ducked in to evade or outfox a German submarine that had been stalking us. **1962** *Life* (Nov. 9) 44: At Gitmo And Havana, Guns at Ready. **1962** *Time* (Dec. 14) 19: The Pentagon hoped to have all the dependents returned to Gitmo by Christmas. **1965** Gallery *Eight Bells* 53 [ref. to 1921]: What happened was that they gave us a lousy load of coal in Gitmo just before sailing. **1971** WINS radio news (Mar. 20): They call it Gitmo, the sprawling, strategic Guantanamo Naval Base in Cuba. **1976** Conroy *Santini* 243: At 0600, squadron 367: will break a day and deploy twenty planes to Gitmo. **1984** T.K. Mason *Cactus Curtain* 13: Gitmo, as they call this outpost of America. **1987** Nichols & Tillmann *Yankee Sta.* 9: "Gitmo" was frequently the site of live-fire exercises. **1989** Sorkin *Few Good Men* 93: We only use it down at Gitmo, sir.

G.I. trots *n.pl.* G.I. SHITS. Also **G.I. runs.**

1943 Hersey *Bell for Adano* 96: That *vino's* murder, Captain, it'll give you the GI trots every time. **1945** O'Rourke *E Co.* 78: Half of Company E ate something that gave them all a...severe case of the GI trots. **1944–48** A. Lyon *Unknown Station* 145: I'll bet half the company's got the GI trots. **1966–67** W. Stevens *Gunner* 201: That gave him the GI trots. **1969** in B.E. Holley *Vietnam* 102: I'm hot, and I've got the GI trots. **1986** F. Walton *Once Were Eagles* 35 [ref. to WWII]: Dysentery ("GI runs") was common.

give *v.* **1.** (of a young woman) to consent readily to and engage in sexual intercourse; PUT OUT.—also constr. with *out.*

1935 *Esquire's Bedroom Companion* 100: She can do what the current vernacular expresses in an only partially accurate word as "give." **1949** Ellson *Tomboy* 27: "Only she don't give out," Lucky said. *a*1968 in Haines & Taggart *Ft. Lauderdale* 31: Girls...give out in Florida like it was just kisses. **1973** Lucas, Katz & Huyck *Amer. Graffiti* 41: And screw around—I hear college girls really give out. **1990** L.B. Rubin *Erotic Wars* 28: The whole game was to get a girl to give out.

2.a. to tell, esp. to confess.—used imper.

1936 "E. Queen" *Halfway House* 21: Tell me everything that's hap-

pened, Mr. Queen....Give, Mr. Queen. **1947** Schulberg *Harder They Fall* 237: Well, what happened? Give. **1954** in Farrar *N.Y. Times Crosswords* 14 12: Provide information: Slang...GIVE. **1956** E. Pound, in *OEDS:* Thazza a good tough start. Give.
b. *Horse Racing.* to give a tip on (a racehorse).
1935 in R. Nelson *Dishonorable* 230: Hey, Mike, I told you the guy that gave me that horse was plenty smart.
3. to give in; give up; surrender.
1956 N.Y.C. schoolboys: Do you give? **1975** Hinton *Rumble Fish* 27: "You give?" I sat back on his gut and waited. **1976** *S.W.A.T.* (NBC-TV police series): Aw, we give!
¶ In phrases:
¶ **give five** see s.v. FIVE, *n.*
¶ **give good** [or **great**]—— (followed by sing. count noun treated as mass noun) to be notable for ——; to be notable for the use of or abilities with ——. [Used to generate usu. joc. nonce phr., all reminiscent of (and patterned after) *give head* s.v. HEAD, *n.*]
1971 W. Murray *Dream Girls* 49: Now look at Tony! He gives good belt! **1979** C. Higgins *Silver Streak* (film): "How do you keep your job?" "I give great phone." **1981** Jenkins *Baja Okla.* 186: "What do you think about Arizona State?"..."I hear they give good cactus." **1982** in *AS* LVIII (1983) 96: When she finished, the artist said, "You give great studio." *Ibid.:* "She gives great telephone." **1988** *TV Guide* (Mar. 19) 27: Miami does give good sushi but Japanese...are nearly as rare there as Eskimos. **1991** *Time* (Sept. 23) 65: Rush [Limbaugh] gives great spiel. **1994** *New York* (Jan. 31) 22: His fans marvel...at his...salesmanship. "He gives great phone."
¶ **give it to** [a specialization of the S.E. sense, 'to make an energetic physical or verbal attack upon'; see *OED* s.v. *give,* 46] to kill or murder.
1823 [J. Neal] *Errata* I 165: I have come to give it to you. I have born [*sic*] your insolence, long enough. **1833** J. Neal *Down-Easters* I 54: Hurra for you!...give it to him Gage! **1843** [W.T. Thompson] *Scenes in Ga.* 35: Give it to him, Spotty! **1863** in Harwell *Confed. Reader* 153: Give it to the rascals! **1873** in Rosa & Koop *Rowdy Joe* 82: Now all you sons of bitches keep away from me for I am liable to give it to any of you. **1945** Dos Passos *Tour* 332: Two krauts with a burp gun...gave it to him. **1957** H. Danforth & J. Horan *D.A.'s Man* 87 [ref. to 1938]: He knows too much. I'll give it to him tonight. **1959** Horan *Mob's Man* 5: Two guys came in and gave it to him in the head. **1973** *Playboy* (Sept.) 213: They were trigger happy as hell and really wanted to give it to me.
¶ **give it to (someone) hot** to scold or punish severely.
1868 Williams *Black-Eyed Beauty* 46: If Nathan excused him for a couple of nights, and kept quiet, away from Matty, she "gave it him hot" the next time they met. **1872* in *OED:* The Commander-in-Chief has given it to the offenders rather hot.
¶ **give it up, 1.** *Black E.* (of a woman) to agree to engage in copulation.
1974 Piñero *Short Eyes* 70: But if you're gonna give it up...I want some. **1967-80** Folb *Runnin' Lines* 240: *Give it up* Agree to have sexual intercourse. **1994** N. McCall *Wanna Holler* 44: He was gonna go off on her if she didn't give it up.
2. *Entertainment Industry.* to applaud.—used imper.
1990 *Spring Break* (MTV) (Mar. 17): Give it up for Tanya!...Give it up! **1990** *In Living Color* (Fox-TV): Everybody give it up for my very good friend Marion Barry. **1990** *Kid 'n Play* (NBC-TV): Give it up for the rapping of Kid 'n Play!
¶ **give ten** see s.v. TEN, *n.*
¶ **give with** to perform or provide.
1940 O'Hara *Pal Joey* 186: I give with the vocals. **1951** in *DAS:* He wouldn't give with the information.
¶ **what gives?** [trans. of G *Was gibt's?*] what's happening? what's going on? (often used as a simple greeting).
1940 J. O'Hara *Pal Joey* 133: What gives, I asked her. **1962** L'Engle *Wrinkle in Time* 32: What gives around here?...I was told you couldn't talk. **1969* in *OEDS:* What gives with this sheilah? **1990** *U.S. News & W.R.* (Aug. 6) 18: The overwhelming response to George Bush's Supreme Court nomination of...David Souter was a giant "What gives?"

give-a-shit *n.* one's sense of motivation, enthusiasm, or concern.—usu. considered vulgar. Also **give-a-fuck.**
1976 Univ. Tenn. student: That's not a question of talent; it's a question of *give-a-shit.* *ca*1985 in K. Walker *Piece of My Heart* 127 [ref. to 1970–71]: The frontal lobe—what one of the corpsmen, and shortly

after that everybody, called the "give a shit" lobe, because once you lose it you don't give a shit about anything. **1985** Dye *Between Raindrops* 235 [ref. to Vietnam War]: Feel like all my give-a-fuck drained out. *Ibid.* 237: I can't seem to work up a good give-a-shit about it. *ca*1987 in K. Marshall *Combat Zone* 140 [ref. to *ca*1970]: Like that kid I told you about; he lost his frontal lobe—it was what the corpsmen used to call the "give a shit" lobe because in an adult if you took out the frontal lobe, they didn't give a shit about anything.

give away *v.* *Und.* to inform on or turn over to the authorities.
1872 Burnham *Secret Service* v: *Given away,* to turn one over to the law, or to officers. *Ibid.* 351: Hart turning on him and "giving him away" this time, out of revenge. *Ibid.* 360: These Detectives got an old coney man...to "give her away." **1878** *Scribner's Mag.* XV 812: Ye went back on her, and shook her, and played off on her, and gave her away—dead away. **1887** Flinn *Chicago Police* 386: Murray "gave away" Andrews and they both went to the penitentiary.

give out *v.* see GIVE, 3.

give-up *n.* *Und.* a payment, esp. one made under duress.
1970 Terkel *Hard Times* 183 [ref. to 1930's]: Those were pretty big give-ups in those days.

give up *v.* **1.** *Und.* to tell what one knows.
1894 *Harper's* (Dec.) 107: I'm a sure loser whenever I try to give up to a lady like you. I get way off my base. **1930** *Amer. Mercury* (Dec.) 455: *Give up, v.:* To turn informer. "One sock in the puss and he'd give up."
2. *Und.* to pay money, esp. under duress; COUGH UP.
1902-03 Ade *People You Know* 111: When he arrived at the Track he gave up for a Badge and a Dope-Sheet. **1904** *Life in Sing Sing* (gloss.): "*Giving up.*" Paying for protection. **1904** in Partridge *Dict. Und.* 289: An English Moll...had to "give up" [pay bribe money] heavily. **1906** H. Green *Boarding House* 59: Sam...blows his coin like a sport. I never see Pugnose give up. **1942-49** Goldin et al. *DAUL* 82.
3. *Und.* to inform on, betray, or disclose to the authorities. Cf. earlier S.E. senses in *OED* s.v. *give,* 64 a (*b*), 64 g.
1942-49 Goldin et al. *DAUL* 82: That creep...gave up a lot of good people...so he wouldn't burn. **1979** Alibrandi *Custody* 211: You don't give us up and we don't give you up. **1988** H. Gould *Double Bang* 27: Somebody...would give up his hideout for a twenty-dollar bill.
¶ In phrases:
¶ **give it up** see s.v. GIVE.
¶ **give up (one's) insides** to tell all (one) knows.
1896 Ade *Artie* 55: Say, you must think I'm a prize gilly to set around here and give up my insides to you about her.

giz *n.* **1.** *USMC.* GIZMO, 1.
1952 *Leatherneck* (Nov.) 74: Gizmo [or] "giz." **1957** Myrer *Big War* 171 [ref. to WWII]: We'll get blown a mile in the air with all this high-powered giz under our butts. **1962** S. Smith *Escape from Hell* 90 [ref. to WWII]: Mackay fiddled with the focus giz. **1966** Heinl *Marine Officer's Guide* 593: *Giz.* Diminutive for "gizmo."
2. the vagina.
1975 Wambaugh *Choirboys* 59: Guy tried to shove a...bottle in his wife's giz after he caught her stepping out on him. **1983** Wambaugh *Delta Star* 127: Saying his mouth was as dry as Rose Bird's giz.

gizmo or **gismo** *n.* [orig. unkn.; not fr. Yid, as sometimes thought] **1.** Orig. *Navy & USMC.* **a.** a gadget or device; whatchamacallit; (*also*) stuff.
1942 *Leatherneck* (Nov.) 145: Gizmo—When you need a word for something in a hurry and can't think of one, it's a *gizmo.* **1942** *Yank* (Nov. 4) 15: Leathernecks...even have a name for a whatsis. They call it a "gizmo." **1943** *Sat. Eve. Post* (Mar. 20) 86: "Gizmo" is any object whose proper name does not come immediately to mind. **1943** *Time* (July 19) 69: Gizmo..."gadget," "stuff." **1948** I. Shulman *Cry Tough* 65: And some cream for that gismo of yours. **1950** Wouk *Caine Mutiny* 113: Why, he can work these damn decoding gismos ten times faster than anybody in the wardroom. **1952** Bellow *Augie March* 71: This or that commodity, engine, gizmo, sliding door, public service. **1957** M. Shulman *Rally* 58: The square on the hypotenuse of a right triangle is equal to the gizmo on the rillera of my blue suede shoes. **1958** Landau & Yates *Frankenstein—1970* (film): After you finish this show, you won't want to fool around with atomic gizmos. **1960** Tucker *Canaveral Monsters* (film): What is that gizmo you use in those restraints? **1967** Dibner *Admiral* 228: Ain't the gizmo hurts. It's my goddam *foot.* **1972** Madden *Bros.* 23: He steals a check-making gizmo. **1979** in Raban *Old Glory* 185: See this little gizmo? That measures the exact moisture of the grain as I'm cutting it. **1993** *TV Guide* (Apr. 24) 103: Gadgets and gizmos.

b. the vulva or vagina; *(also)* the penis.

1942–48 in *So. Folk. Qly.* XIII (1949) 205: *Gizmos...*(sometimes used particularly in reference to parts of the female anatomy—definitely old Navy). **1951** Thacher *Captain* 87 [ref. to WWII]: He's worried about his gizmo—his mommie always told him to stay away from them foreign women. **1985** Univ. Tenn. grad. student, age 35: He was in the toilet trying to twist the head off his gizmo.

2. *Esp. Navy.* a foolish or inconsequential fellow.

1942 *Leatherneck* (Nov.) 141: Down the red lead, Gizmo, and knock off the shortstop. **1945** J. Riordan, in *Calif. Folk. Qly.* V (1946) 376: Let's sack out, you gismos. *Ibid.* 385: Hey,...Gismo,...how about a little haba-haba? **1946** *Amer. Legion Mag.* (Feb.): *Gizmo*—person whose proper name you don't know. **1956** *AS* XXXI (Oct.) 193: Gizmo [is] often applied to a person whose name is unknown or difficult to pronounce.

gizzard *n.* **1.** the human digestive tract, esp. the stomach. [1668 quot. is primarily fig.]

*1668 S. Pepys, in *OED*: I find my wife hath something in her gizzard that only waits an opportunity of being provoked to bring up. ***1672** in *OED*: There was some grumbling of the Gizard. **1827** in *JAF* LXXVI (1963) 290: Yeud split yure gizerd laffin. **1846** in Botkin *Treas. Amer. Folk.* 29: I had a sore gizzard for two weeks arterward. **1846** in Harris *High Times* 65: Darn yer little snakish gizzard. **1847** Robb *Squatter Life* 34: The storekeeper swore that John must "eat the other fellar's gizzard." **1859** "Skitt" *Fisher's River* 126 [ref. to 1820's]: Feelin' considd-ible qualmy 'bout my gizzard. **1927** in Mencken *New Ltrs.* 210: I have a sturdy gizzard, and have never had a headache in my life. **1927–30** Rollins *Jinglebob* 2 [ref. to 1880's]: I needs coffee in my gizzard. **1931** Buckingham & Higgin *Painted Desert* (film): What have we got to feed his gizzard?

2. essential strength or spirit; *(hence)* courage; GUTS.

1838 [Haliburton] *Clockmaker* (Ser. 2) 44: A farm...that's had the gizzard taken out of it. **1860** in *Ala. Hist. Qly.* XLIV (1982) 104: Mills is a man who has neither heart, soul, nor gizzard. **1872** *Myself* 69: A feller's got no gizzard if he don't...let 'em have it back jest as good as they send! **1908** *DN* III 315: *Gizzard*...the seat of one's courage. **1930** Lait *On the Spot* 76: Kinky didn't have the gizzard to croak one o' his boys.

3. the throat.

*1974 P. Wright *Lang. Brit. Industry* 111: Windpipes and pharynxes can be [called by patients] *throats, guzzles,...*or *gizzards*. **1983** Van Devanter & Morgan *Before Morning* 204: Ain't no snake gonna wrap itself around my gizzard. **1984** J.R. Reeves *Mekong* 73: He cut the man from bellybutton to gizzard.

¶ In phrases:

¶ **bust my gizzard!** (used as a joc. oath).

1862 C.F. Browne *Art. Ward* 164: Bust my gizzud, but its grate doins.

¶ **fret (one's) gizzard** to worry (oneself).

*1755 S. Johnson, in *OED*: He *frets his gizzard*, he harasses his imagination. **1843** *Spirit of Times* (Jan. 7) 531: Don't fret your gizzard, stranger....I can't take your money. **1857** in Barnum *Letters* 96: Fret not thy gizzard.

¶ **save (one's) gizzard** to save (oneself).

1875 *Minstrel Gags* 97: Can't keep still to save their gizzards. **1894** *Atlantic* (Sept.) 323: I got all-fired sleepy, 'n' ter save me gizzard I c'u'dn't keep me eyes open.

gizzum, *n.* var. JISM, *n.*

G-joint *n.* [gaff + JOINT] *Carnival.* a concession where a rigged gambling game is set up.

1946 Dadswell *Hey, Sucker* 160: The device has a control button that is easy to gaff so the sucker never knows he's up against a G-joint. **1961** Scarne *Comp. Guide to Gambling* 459: A gaffed or G-joint is a [carnival] game that can be operated dishonestly.

glad *adj.* impudent; saucy.

1899 Cullen *Tales* 117: "Don't get glad with me," said the cop, "or I'll rough-house you up some."

glad bag *n. Esp. Mil.* [fr. *Glad Bags,* a trademark used for plastic sandwich bags] a body bag.

1983 Van Devanter & Morgan *Before Morning* 88 [ref. to Vietnam War]: Dead bodies in Glad bags were lined up outside the ER doors. *Ibid.* 318: *Glad bag:* slang term for a bag used to wrap a dead body. **1983** *War: A Commentary* (KCTS-TV): You want to send him home in a glad bag to his mommy. **1984** Ehrhart *Marking Time* 13: No more American boys coming home in Glad Bags. **1985** former U.S. Army Spec. 4: *Glad Bags* were body bags. [Heard *ca*1974.]

glad duds *n.pl.* GLAD RAGS.

1912 Berkman *Prison* 242 [ref. to 1894]: Put on your glad duds, Kate.

glad eye *n.* a look of intense interest or invitation; *(occ.)* a knowing glance or wink.—usu. constr. with *the.*

1903 Townsend *Sure* 3: Some of de goils de Duchess gives me a knock down to passed me out a glad eye. ***1917** *Living Age* (Nov. 10) 379: In recent American slang no phrase has conquered the English-speaking world...as "the glad eye." It is a masterpiece of vulgar genius. **1919** Piesbergen *Overseas with Aero Squadron* 32: Say, Gus, you oughta seen the mamoselles giv us the glad eye. **1922** Farrar *Jack* 21: That cop on the corner has been givin' us the glad eye for months. **1928–30** Fiaschetti *Gotta Be Rough* 79: Give him the glad eye and get him to shine up to you. **1941** "G.R." Lee *G-String* 9: Moey, the candy butcher, was the only man...she hadn't given the glad eye to. **1942** Garcia *Tough Trip* 110: They all start in to give me the glad eye, which said come on let us kiss and make up. **1951** Elgart *Over Sixteen* 150: A traveling salesman was about to check in at a hotel when he noticed a very charming bit of femininity giving him the so-called "glad-eye." **1953** Brossard *Young Saboteurs* 153: A nice-looking guy had lately been giving her the glad eye in church. **1956** in Woods *Horse-Racing* 48: I gave Frank the glad eye as I said, "Gambler, poet, and lover." **1958** Kerouac *Subterraneans* 3: I tried to shoot her the glad eye. **1977** Sayles *Union Dues* 67: Cheats my husband out of a job then keeps on givin me the glad-eye ever time we pass. **1984** Sample *Raceboss* 40: She wasn't so slow about giving him the glad-eye.

gladeye *v.* to eye eagerly or invitingly.

1938 *AS* (Oct.) 195: Denominative Verbs...*glad-eying.* **1968** Gover *JC* 97: Now he's hangin round gladeyein me.

glad hand *n.* **1.** a hand extended in welcome; *(hence)* a hearty or effusive greeting, esp. if insincere.—usu. constr. with *the.* Also *(obs.)* **glad mitt.**

1895 Gore *Stu. Slang* 16: *Give the glad hand.* To welcome. **1895** *DN* I 417: *Glad hand*...To welcome with the *glad hand.* **1896** Ade *Artie* 4: She meets me at the door, puts out the glad hand and says: "Hang up your lid and come into the game." **1897** Siler & Houseman *Fight of the Century* 22: I've been getting the glad hand so often...that it is a pleasure to shake the hand of a man who has no financial or other gains in view. **1902** Mead *Word-Coinage* 167: "The glad hand" means a real or simulated warmth of greeting. **1903** A. Adams *Log of Cowboy* 188: Every rascal of us gave old man Don the glad hand as they drove around the herd. **1904** *Life in Sing Sing* 255: Glad Mitt.—Warm welcome. **1908** Whittles *Lumberjack* 197: There...is an extra one for the glad hand you gave the Sky Pilot yesterday. **1917** Empey *Over the Top* 50: Arriving at our section, the boys once again tendered us the glad mitt, but looked askance at us out of the corners of their eyes. **1921** "M. Brand" *Black Jack* 105: Say, kid, ain't you got a glad hand for me? **1959** *Time* (Aug. 3) 52: A man with a muscular glad-hand and a sharp tongue. **1970** Gattzden *Black Vendetta* 53: Ignoring the glad-hand.

2. *Trucking.* (see quots.).

1956 *AS* (May) 150: *Glad hand*...An air hose coupling. **1971** Tak *Truck Talk* 73: *Glad hand:* an air-line connection between the tractor and the trailer. **1971** in *AS* XLIV 204: *Glad hands* Connections for the air brake system between the tractor and the trailer. **1993** Wash. State man (coll. J. Sheidlower): Any trucker can tell you that a *glad hand* is a device for connecting the airlines between the tractor and trailer.

glad-hand *v.* to greet or welcome effusively and usu. insincerely, as by shaking hands.

1895 *DN* I 417: *Glad hand*...To welcome with the *glad hand.* **1904** Ade *True Bills* 18: Standing around the front Doorway and glad-handing the Yaps. **1912** Livingston *Curse* 20: On turning about I "glad-handed" him. **1920** Ade *Hand-Made Fables* 119: He had to glad-hand them out of the Gate. **1929–33** Farrell *Young Manhood* 321: Fat Malloy arrived and glad-handed all the boys. **1951** *N.Y. Times* (Feb. 25) VI 10: They could have been glad-handed into the abandonment of ideological principles. **1962** *Time* (Aug. 31) 55: Darting into showrooms to glad-hand buyers. **1973** Walkup & Otis *Race* 37: Just a new president, wanting to gladhand everybody. **1972–79** T. Wolfe *Right Stuff* 124: He had to glad-hand and shoot the breeze and trade the small talk with all these Congressmen. **1980** *Newsweek* (Feb. 4) 37: There was no trudging through snowdrifts to glad-hand farmers, no rhetoric to inflame passions. **1984** Riggan *Free Fire* 17: I just didn't want O'Neill to have any illusions about...Smith's gladhanding. **1993** *New Yorker* (July 26) 31: The great middleweight Emilio Griffith was also glad-handing [with the audience].

glad-hander *n.* a person, often a politician, who greets others effusively and usu. insincerely; one who seeks self-aggrandizement through flattery and feigned cordiality.

1918 in Clover *Stop at Suzanne's* 134: Well, this…[fellow] is a glad-hander, besides being a mighty clever man. **1929** Merriam *Chicago* 275: One type [of politician] is the good fellow, the mixer, the "joiner," the glad hander, whose chief reliance is the cultivation of the personal friendship of individuals and the acquaintance with all sorts of groups and societies of a non-political nature. **1934** Weseen *Dict. Slang* 342: *Glad hander*—A person who is always very friendly and cheerful. He is often suspected of ulterior motives. **1963** Gant *Queen St.* 156: He was a glad-hander,…a tinhorn politician. **1972** Hannah *Geronimo Rex* 108: In their ranks were the hard-lipped scowlers for Jesus and the radiant happy gladhanders for Jesus. **1986** *New York* (Dec. 15) 36: Reagan…is the glad-hander most at home at the ceremonial functions other politicians abhor.

glad rag *n.* **1.** *pl.* formal or fancy clothing.

1899 Cullen *Tales* 69: I had…enough glad rags to stock a second-hand store. **1902** [E.M. Gilmer] *Fables for Elite* 72: All the Females Assembled in their Glad Rags and proceeded to go through their particular Stunts for his Benefit. **1907** in H.C. Fisher *A. Mutt* 16: A. Mutt…spends a few rubles for glad rags. **1908** Paine *Stroke Oar* 31: An appalling wreckage of "glad rags." **1910** in McCay *Little Nemo* 255: Let's put on our glad rags. We will soon be in the big city! **1912** Lowrie *Prison* 302: The officer came to dress Smoky in his "glad rags," and a few minutes later he…passed out of the front gate. **1916** S. Lewis *Job* 31: Very haughty urbanites who knew all about "fellows" and "shows" and "glad rags." **1930** Irwin *Tramp & Und. Sl.: Glad Rags*…One's best clothes, or those worn on occasions of recreation or to give an air of prosperity and wealth. **1952** E. Brown *Trespass* 140: I be damn if I get into my glad rags just to go all the way downtown to some midnight session. **1976** (quot. at GLAD WEEDS). **1993** *New Yorker* (Feb. 22) 43 [ref. to 1925]: He was…accustomed to wearing a top hat, white tie, and tails…unlike…Harold Ross, who…was suspicious of what were then slangily called "glad rags."

2. *Narc.* a rag soaked with an intoxicating chemical substance whose fumes are then inhaled.

1967 J.B. Williams *Narc. & Halluc.* 112: *Glad rag*—A piece of cloth saturated with glue or gasoline, usually a sock. **1970** Horman & Fox *Drug Awareness* 466: *Glad rag*—cloth material or handkerchief saturated with the chemical.

glad weeds *n.pl.* GLAD RAGS, 1.

1976 *N.Y. Folklore* II 240: Dress clothes are called *glad rags* or *glad weeds*.

glam *n. Entertainment Industry.* glamour. Also as adj., v.

1937 *AS* (Oct.) 242: Loretta Young—does that girl know how to *glam*! *ca***1961** Partridge *DSUE* 1109: *Glam.* glamour: film-world hangers-on: since *ca*1940. **1980** in *Barnhart Dict. Comp.* I (1982) 61: A champagne reception before the awards had the glitz and glam the Genies needed. **1981** *Daily News* (N.Y.C.) (July 23) 59: To look like this I adore but I am not naturally a glam dame…I really naturally am a sloppy joe. **1986** *Eyewitness News* (WABC-TV) (Sept. 16): Glitz and glam [in fashion] is back. **1989** *TV Guide* (Aug. 26) 36: Mud wrestling and metal music….They're both very "glam." **1991** D. Weinstein *Heavy Metal* 104: The early-1970s glam rock following…coalesced around David Bowie. **1993** *New Republic* (July 12) 9: The glamming of [beer] closely follows the upscaling of wine in America in the 1960s and '70s.

glammy *adj.* glamorous.

1936 O.O. MacIntyre, in *AS* (Apr.) 192: The glammiest of the glamour girls—Tallulah Bankhead.

glamour boy *n.* a glamorous fellow, esp. if conceited, shallow, or the like.—usu. used derisively.

1939 *Life* (July 31) 18: Political Glamor Boys: Dewey and Murphy compete for crime-busting honors. ****1939** in OEDS: People do him a great injustice by calling him a glamour boy. **1942** *Time* (Jan. 5) 54: The Glamor Boys…Errol Flynn, Prince David Mdivani, "Prince Mike" Romanoff. **1944** Huie *Can Do!* 26: All the glamour boys—the Marines, the PT captains, the Commandos, the submariners, and the hot pilots. **1946** Sherwood *Best Years of Our Lives* (film): It isn't so easy for those air force glamour boys when they get grounded. **1947** Carter *Devils in Baggy Pants* 193: Oh, I wish I were a paratrooper!…You guys are the glamour boys of the damned army….Hell, I see you loafing about Naples most of the time. **1948** Wolfert *Act of Love* 432: Piet was the glamour boy, but the Major was the horse Piet rode into battle. **1955** Graziano & Barber *Somebody Up There* 289: You take this glamour boy back to his dance hall and get me a fighter—quick! **1958** J. King *Pro Football* 129: There were quite a few glamor boys available.

1959 Searls *Big X* 113: How's it going, glamour boy? Christ, you look awful. **1964** Kaufman *Down Staircase* 28: Glamor boy of Eng. Dept. Unpublished Writer…He'll woo you with rhymes. **1973** Sesar *Catullus* xxxvii: High society glamor boys. **1985** Sawislak *Dwarf* 70: Reporters are the glamour boys and gals. **1988** Barrow & Munder *Joe Louis* 58: If you want to be a champion boxer, you can't be a glamour boy as well. **1993** *USA Today Baseball Wkly.* (Aug. 4) 6: Key…wasn't one of the glamour boys [but the] Yankee manager…was happy to have him.

glamour girl *n. Journ.* a glamorous young woman, esp. a model or film star. Now *S.E.*

1935 in *OEDS*: Horrible grimacing pictures of the Glamour Girl. **1936** (quot. at GLAMMY, *adj.*). **1941** H. A. Smith *Low Man* 113: The press agent…described her as Great Britain's chief glamor girl. **1945** Crow & Crow *Teen-age* 140: Then began Jane's attempts to change her mother into a "glamour girl." **1947** in Botkin *Sidewalks* 429: "Glamor girl"…[was] coined by [society columnist] Maury [Paul]. **1956** in *DAS*: She was a beautiful thing when she started her career as a glamor girl and she still retains her basic figure and good looks.

glamour-puss *n.* [*glamour* + PUSS] a glamorous person, esp. a woman.—usu. used ironically.

1941 *Sat. Eve. Post* (June 14) 22: We called them superswoopers instead of glamourpusses. **1947** Schulberg *Harder They Fall* 206: I'd better rescue him from that glamour-puss. **1952** J.D. MacDonald *Damned* 137: One year of starch and laundry work will turn me into a glamour-puss for sure. **1955** Stern *Rebel Without a Cause* (film): Hey, glamour-puss! ****1963** *Time* (Mar. 1) 26: A spokesman for the Old Lady of Threadneedle Street…came up with "She's a glamour puss. We are really with it." **1984** D. Young, in *N.Y. Post* (Aug. 2) 82: Mark Breland [is the] glamorpuss of the USA boxing team. **1987** *Wkly. World News* (July 21) 13: Some chauffeurs make $1,500 a week for driving the [Hollywood] glamor-pusses to & from work.

glands *n.pl.* **1.** the testicles.

1916 Cary *Venery* I 111: *Glands*—The testicles. **1925** H.L. Mencken, in Riggio *Dreiser-Mencken Letters* II 546: You will freeze your glands if you start on a Northward walking tour in this weather.

2. a woman's breasts.

1974 Strasburger *Rounding Third* 43: Toba Morton *did* have a rather sizable pair of glands. **1987** *Daily Beacon* (Univ. Tenn.) (Aug. 7) 6: Here they sit, beers in hand, lustfully leering at glands. **1988** *Sonny Spoon* (NBC-TV): I like American girls—they have such nice glands.

glass *n. Und.* diamonds.

1918 Stringer *House of Intrigue* 29: He specialized in glass or ice, which same means simply diamonds. **1935** Pollock *Und. Speaks: Glass*, diamonds. **1940** W.R. Burnett *High Sierra* 13: The safety-deposit boxes are lousy with glass.

glass *adj.* [cf. GLASS ARM] *Boxing.* (of a part of the body) exceptionally vulnerable to a knockout blow; unable to withstand a blow.—usu. used prenominally.

1917 T.A. Dorgan, in Zwilling *TAD Lexicon* 40: Those glass jawed champions go just so far…and then back to the hod and the overalls. **1920–21** Witwer *Leather Pushers* 162: The glass-jawed bimbo…can't take it. **1922** Tully *Emmett Lawler* 295: He's got a glass jaw. **1930** in Sagendorf *Popeye* 48: He must have a glass chin—I didn't pop him very hard. **1937** Odets *Golden Boy* 240: Looka, kid, go home, kid, before I blame Kaplan's glass mitts on *you*. **1947** Overholser *Buckaroo's Code* 7: I'm gonna have the supreme pleasure of taking a punch at Red Donahue's jaw. I think it's glass, and boys, I'd sure love to bust it. **1955** Graziano & Barber *Somebody Up There* 286: But he had a glass jaw. **1960** Hoagland *Circle Home* 130: Today's the day we see if this [chin] is glass. **1960** Roeburt *Mobster* 29: Ginnis is soft as mush, and he's got a glass jaw. **1970** La Motta, Carter & Savage *R. Bull* 174: He had two big weaknesses as a fighter: he didn't have a punch and he had a glass head. **1970** Thackrey *Thief* 61: Stupid bastard was slow. And he had a glass gut from drinking so much. Took me just one minute to land him on his ass for good. **1971** Torres *Sting Like a Bee* 165: Had a reputation of having a glass chin. **1974** Millard *Thunderbolt* 45: He had a glass head….In fact, all of these big guys are pretty much alike. Glass heads. **1991** D. Anderson *In Corner* 38: God created…some with a…glass jaw.

glass arm *n. Baseball.* a pitching or throwing arm that is weak, sore, or easily injured; a sore arm.

1892 in Nichols *Baseball Term.* 29: Glass arm. **1898** (cited in *Ibid.*). **1899** Ade *Fables* 11: If you asked him who played Center for Boston in 1886 he could tell you quick—right off the Reel. And he was a walking Directory of all the Glass Arms in the Universe. **1908** *Atlantic* (Aug.) 223: Murphy, not O'Toole, is to pitch, O'Toole having doubtless a temporary "glass arm." **1922** *Sat. Eve. Post* (June 3) 11: What have dreams to do with that guy's glass arm? **1929** *AS* (Oct.) 49: *Glass arm*—stiff arm, telegrapher's cramp. **1937** I. Shaw *Sailor Off Bremen* 106: Then you're the one man in the United States that don't know Cooney got a glass arm. **1982** T. Considine *Lang. Sport* 21.

glass blowing *n. Hobo.* commercial ice-cutting.

1930 (quot. at DIAMOND-CUTTING, *n.*).

glass eye *n.* ¶ In phrase: **bully boy with a glass eye** see s.v. BULLY, *adj.*

Glass House *n.* [because housed in a building having an exterior largely of glass] **1.** *L.A.* the Los Angeles County Jail.

1966 Cohen & Murphy *Burn* 214: Every entrance to the "Glass House" was covered by weaponry. **1967** Yablonsky *Hippie Trip* 52: Last week I was in jail, in the glass house, the city jail. **1969** Bullock *Watts* 151: I get a toothache and they take me downtown to the glass house. **1972** Wambaugh *Blue Knight* 55: "I'm not drunk," he repeated all the way to the Glass House. **1974** Gober *Black Cop* 28: From his office window in the *Glass House*, the downtown LA police department and jail, he could see the lights of the city.

2. the world headquarters of Ford Motor Co. in Dearborn, Mich.

1982 Abodaher *Iacocca* 11: It is appropriately known as the Glass House. *Ibid.* 135: The imposing Glass House had been dedicated [in 1956].

glass jaw *n.* see s.v. GLASS, *adj.*

glass stomach *n.* (see quot.).

1983 L. Frank *Hardball* 69: A player [tells] an umpire that "You have your head up your ass!" or, equivalently, "You have a glass stomach!" (through which his head, which is up his ass, can see).

glassy eye *n.* a blank or disdainful look.—constr. with *the.*

[**1901** Irwin *Sonnets* (unp.): Say, will she treat me white, or throw me down,/ Give me the glassy glare, or welcome hand.] **1908** Kelley *Oregon Pen.* 100: When I…commenced speaking to Lee he gave me the glassy eye. **1916** A. Stringer *Door of Dread* 53: Seein' Kestner and yuh'd told me the feds had ev'rything fixt, I give him the glassy eye. ***1916** (cited in Partridge *DSUE* (ed. 8) 470).

glaum *v.* var. GLOM, *v.*

glaze *n. Und.* a window or pane of glass; (*also*) glass.

*1698–99 "B.E." *Dict. Canting Crew: Glaze*…the Window. ***1720** in Partridge *Dict. Und.* 290: *Look slily into the Glaze.* That is, look privately into a Window. ***1781** in Partridge *Dict. Und.* 290: Glaze is cant for glass. ***1788** Grose *Vulgar Tongue* (ed. 2): *Glaze*—A window. **1807** Tufts *Autobiog.* 293 [ref. to 1794]: *Glaze*…a square of glass. **1871** Banka *Pris. Life* 493: Window…Glaze.

gleef *n.* GLEEP.

1963–64 Kesey *Great Notion* 145: This gleef should of known better. *Ibid.* 155: That gleef in bar in Colorado.

gleep *n.* [perh. intended to represent a Chinese speaker's pron. of CREEP, *n.*] *Stu.* an odd, obnoxious, or worthless person.

1947 *ATS* (Supp.): Unpopular Person; "Drip"…*gleep.* **1960** Serling *Stories from Twilight Zone* 28: I go back to being a manager of nine gleeps so old that I gotta rub them down with formaldehyde. **1963** *Twilight Zone* (CBS-TV): I'm…talking about this and that, when this funny gleep gives me a stop-watch. **1969** *Current Slang* I & II 40: *Gleep, n.* A clod; backward person.—High school students, both sexes, California. **1979** Pa. man, age 46: A *gleep* is a worthless individual. I heard that in 1953. **1987** *Car & Driver* (July) 26: I found myself suddenly wishing I had hung around with the gleeps on my high school's debating team.

gleep *v.* [orig. unkn.] to steal; swipe.

1953 Paxton *Wild One* (film): I didn't win it. I just gleeped it. But I gleeped it off of a guy who didn't win it either. **1966** IUFA *Folk Speech: Gleep*—This word is used in place of steal.

gleet *n.* [earlier in sense 'slimy matter', < Old F *glette*] **1.** a purulent discharge from the urethra; urethritis. Orig. *S.E.*

*1718 in *OED*: Old Gleets, that proceed more from Debility than any malignity. ***1813** in *OED*: Similar to the inner surface of the urethra, when it is forming the discharge commonly called a gleet. **1863** in Boyer *Naval Surgeon* I 162: The rest [of the venereal cases] are all well, except one or two cases, who still complain of gleet. ***1878** in *OED*: Gleet may be the result of some stricture or local urethral disease, such as an ulcer. **1927** *Immortalia* 60: My balls are all covered with gleet. **1934** "J.M. Hall" *Anecdota* 114: Sometime it's the clap and/Sometimes

it's the gleet. **1943** in J. O'Hara *Sel. Letters* 173: Gleet, brother, is a horrid word, but its worse on the end of your cigar, take it from one who knows.

2. (see quot.).

1979 Charyn *7th Babe* 250: "A person would swear I gave you the gleet." "What's the gleet?" "The syph and the clap rolled into one."

glide *n. Und.* a skiff.

1848 *Ladies' Repository* VIII (Oct.) 315: *glide*, A skiff.

glim *n.* [prob. fr. GLIMMER, *n.*; but cf. *OED*] **1.a.** Orig. *Und.* fire (*obs.*); (*hence*) a candle, match, lantern, or lamp; a light of any kind; in phr. **douse the glim** to put out the light.

*1676 (cited in Partridge *Dict. Und.* 291). ***1698–99** "B.E." *Dict. Canting Crew: Glim*…a Dark-Lanthorn used in Robbing Houses…*Glimfenders*…Andirons. *Rum Glimfenders*, Silver Andirons. *Glimflashy*…angry or in a passion…*Glimstick*, a Candle-Stick. **1745** (cited in *AS* (Oct. 1940) 231). ***1785** Grose *Vulgar Tongue: Glim.*—A candle, or dark lantern, used in house-breaking; also fire. **1798** in J. Greene *Secret Band* 114: The word *Thimble* means Watch, crome, clock…the word *Glim* means Light. **1807** Tufts *Autobiog.* 292 [ref. to 1794]: Glins [*sic*]…the stars. *Ibid.* 293: Douse the glin…put out the light. ***1831** B. Hall *Voyages* I 188: These "glims" yielded but little light. **1848** *Ladies' Repository* (Oct.) 315: *Glim*, A lamp or candle; a window or door; light in general. **1848** Judson *Mysteries* 37: And then old Jack bade Harriet trim the glim. *Ibid.* 527: *Glim.* A light, or lantern. **1851** Melville *Moby Dick* ch. iii: "Come along here, I'll give ye a glim in a jiffy"; and so saying, he lighted a candle. **1854** "Youngster" *Swell Life* 226: Dowse the glims, boys! **1861** in *Civil War Hist.* vii (1961) 433: It is time for my light to be out and I must "douse the glim." **1862** in Browne & Browne *Navy* 54: The sailor's phrase, "douse goes the glim," means out goes the light and is the common expression among us. **1871** Banka *Prison Life* 492: Light,…Glim. **1874** Pember *Metropolis* 266: Mr. Casey "doused the glim" (put out the lamp). **1883** Flagg *Versicles* 16: Who doused—that glim? **1895** Taylor *Frontier & Indian Life* 203: His dread of a multitude of uninvited, undesirable guests…caused him to "douce [*sic*] the glim" with such alacrity. **1899** A.H. Lewis *Sandburrs* 6: Stand by wit' that glim now! **1906** Wooldridge *Hands Up* 417: I saw her coming down Wabash Avenue Sunday smoking cigarettes like a college dude. She spotted me and doused the glim. **1908** in Kornbluh *Rebel Voices* 40: In a short time a glim (lantern) appears and the brakeman jumps into the car. **1914** Jackson & Hellyer *Vocab.* 37: *Glim*…a match. **1919** Bates *Fighting to Win* 27: "Shall I douse the glim?" asked Franz. **1928** *New Yorker* (Nov. 3) 94: Taxicab Words…*Glims*—Headlights. **1928** Callahan *Man's Grim Justice* 19: Red put the "glim" (flash light) up against the keyhole and peered into it. **1938** Korson *Mine Patch* 48: Now quit your grumbling an' give me a glim,/To go down, down, down. **1963–64** Aiken *Limericks* 7: It's time to make love: douse the glim.

b. Orig. *Und.* gonorrhea.—usu. constr. with *the.*

*1812 Vaux *Vocab.* s.v. knap: To *knap the glim*, is to catch the venereal disease. ***1889** Barrère & Leland *Dict. Slang* I 411: *Glim*…(common), the *glim*, gonorrhea. **1916** Cary *Slang of Venery* III 52: *Glim.* A venereal disease.

2. a look; glimpse.

*ca1620 in *OED*: If the way might be found to draue your eie…to take a glim of a thing of so mean contemplation. **1899** Green *Va. Folk-Speech* 198: *Glim*…glimpse, glance. **1935** in *DARE*: Can't git a glim of the light from down here. **1958** S.H. Adams *Tenderloin* 147 [ref. to 1890's]: Pipe the country jay…Take another glim. **1961** Sullivan *Shortest, Gladdest Years* 181: It's the Biltmore for us and a quick glim to see what's waiting to be had.

3.a. an eye.

*1789 (cited in Partridge *Dict. Und.* 292). ***1794** in Holloway & Black *Broadside Ballads* 30: A cartridge burst, and douted/Both my two precious glims. ***1796** Grose *Vulgar Tongue* (ed. 3): *Glimms.* Eyes. ***1820** in Egan *Grose's Dict.*: His glims I've made look like a couple of rainbows. **1832** *Spirit of Times* (Feb. 4) 1: Douse his glims; shiver his mizen. **1841** [Mercier] *Man-of-War* 44: He was…beetle-browed, with his starboard glim shut up. **1859** Matsell *Vocab.* 37: *Glims.* Eyes. **1900** J.F. Willard & Hodder *Powers That Prey* 174: The captain asked him what in the name of things unprintable "his glims were for." **1906** *DN* III 138: *Glims. n.pl.* Eyes. "I didn't get my glims on it." **1910** T.A. Dorgan, in *N.Y. Eve. Jour.* (Apr. 7) 16: He ups with his right and bounces one off my glim. **1920–21** Witwer *Leather Pushers* 28: The kid sees…the bleedin' gash under the glim. **1922** in Cummings *Letters* 95: COURAGE he said and pointed to his GOGGLELESS GLIMS!!! **ca1927** Sandburg *Good Morning* 20: Since the city hicks and the hicks from the sticks go to the/ latest Broadway hit hoping to fix their glims on a/birdie with her last feather off in a bathtub of booze. **1936** Duncan *Over the Wall* 173: My glims were only a couple of puffed slits. **1943** in Ruhm *Detective* 358: He stops and looks at me out of that one glim he's got. **1944** in Himes *Black on Black* 201: I raised my neck and skinned my glims. **1958** Appel *Raw Edge* 78: Not even a pair of straight glims in his head. **ca***1979** (cited in Partridge *DSUE* (ed. 8) 470).

b. *pl.* spectacles; eyeglasses.

*****1846** (cited in Partridge *Dict. Und.* 292). *****1873** Hotten *Slang Dict.:* *Glims*, spectacles. **1904** in *DARE*: They might have these "particular" pugs wear colored glims. **1914** Jackson & Hellyer *Vocab.* 37: *Glims, Noun.* General currency. A pair of spectacles or nose glasses. **1919** *DN* V 41: *Glims, n.pl.* Spectacles. **1926** Maines & Grant *Wise-Crack Dict.* 9: *Glims*—Pair of spectacles. *ca***1928** in Wilstach *Stage Sl.* (unp.): "Glims" are spectacles. **1937** *Lit. Digest* (Apr. 10) 12: *Glims*. A pair of spectacles.

glim *v.* **1.** *Und.* to light; illuminate.

1914 Jackson & Hellyer *Criminal Slang* 37: *Glim*...Also used as a verb, signifying illuminated. Example: "Go and take a pike [peek] at the dump and see if it's glimmed." **1928** Callahan *Man's Grim Justice* 80: As a precautionary measure, we glimmed up [flashed our light around] the interior of the bank...We cut out the glimming and waited.

2.a. to look (*obs.*); catch sight of; see.

*****1893** in Partridge *Dict. Und.* 292: Glimming at bank-business. **1912** T.A. Dorgan, in Zwilling *TAD Lexicon* 40: He brought a friend up with him to slant at the new masterpiece. The friend glimmed it. **1921** Casey & Casey *Gay-Cat* 189: I was afeard them shacks had glimbed me. **1931** Nash *Free Wheeling* 57: You will lose your lunch/When you glim an Amurrican joke in *Punch*. **1943** *Billboard* (June 26) 61: A pitchman glimmed the law and did a fade-out. **1967** [Beck] *Pimp* 51: Just to "glim" him and you know he's rough.

b. to realize. Cf. devel. of GLOM, 2.

1959 Murtagh & Harris *Who Live in Shadow* 5: Cat, do *you* glim what happened to George? *Ibid.* 201: *Glim.* To see; look at; sometimes, to know.

glimmer *n.* **1.** Orig. *Und.* GLIM, *n.*, 1.

*****1566** in Partridge *Dict. Und.* 183: These Demaunders for glymmer be for the moste parte women; for glymmar, in their language, is fyre. *****1608** in Partridge *Dict. Und.* 292: For *Glymmer* (in canting) signifies fire. *****1610** in Partridge *Dict. Und.* **1665** in *OED*: *Glymmer*, fire. *****1698**–99 "B.E." *Dict. Canting Crew*: *Glimmer*,...Fire. *****1725** *New Canting Dict.*: Oh! thy Glaziers shine, As Glymmar by the Solomon. *****1785** Grose *Vulgar Tongue*: *Glimmer.*—Fire. *Cant.* **1859** Matsell *Vocab.* 37: *Glimmer.* The fire. **1871** Banka *Pris. Life* 492: Match...*Glimmer.* **1940** *Railroad Mag.* (Apr.) 44: *Glimmer*—Locomotive headlight. **1946** Mezzrow & Wolfe *Really Blues* 305: *Glimmer:* electric light. **1964** *AS* (Oct.) 281: *Glimmer, n.* A kerosene lamp.

2.a. an eye.

*****1814** in *OED*: Get out of my way, you booby, or I'll darken your glimmers for you...Come, my lad, close your glimmers, and I'll apply a plaster. *****1821** *Real Life in London* I 72: By sewing up one of his *glimmers*. **1901** Irwin *Sonnets* (unp.): Weeps were in my glimmers when I tried. **1915** Lait *Gus* 19: The minute I swung my glimmers on your noble feacher's [*sic*] I knew life never would be the same after that. **1928** O'Connor *B'way Racketeers* 50: Eventually he was referred to as "The bird with the trick glimmer." **1930** Lait *On the Spot* 203: *Glimmer*...A black eye. **1931** Harlow *Old Bowery* 537: To-day, if you get a "shanty on your glimmer," you just step down the street to a barber shop whose sign promises, "Black eyes made natural." **1932** Pagano *Bluejackets* 99: I'll give him a forty-five between the glimmers and wreck this joint to boot! **1943** *Yank* (Oct. 1) 18: Keep both glimmers on the joint. **1952** Holmes *Boots Malone* (film): How are the glimmers?...Read that. **1954** Wertheim *Innocent* 112: Now his *other* glimmer, Pete! **1968** I. Reed *Yellow Back Radio* 18: Eyes were bulging and we stood there with our glimmers hypnotized.

b. *pl.* eyeglasses.

1935 Pollock *Und. Speaks*: *Glimmers*, eyeglasses. **1964** *AS* (Oct.) 281: *Glimmers, n.* Reading glasses.

3. a cut gem.

1915–17 Lait *Gus* 53: If dey ketches me wit' dis here glimmer on me, I goes to stir.

glimpse *n.* an eye; GLIM.

1910 Hapgood *Types from City Streets* 54: She put her glimpses on me sharp-like, and, sez she, "Are you Chuck Connors?"

gliss *n.* *Music.* glissando.

1953 *Pop. Science* (Feb.) 158: Beginners could give out "gliss" tones, or slur notes. **1982** A. Shaw *Dict. Pop/Rock* 141: *Gliss.* An abbreviation of *glissando*.

glisten *n.* *Und.* a diamond or diamonds.

1839 *Spirit of Times* (June 8) 159: He did not, as a Cuffee said, "shine like any glissen." **1848** Judson *Mysteries* 34: He...is as daring a cove as ever cracked a crib, touched a dummy, or palmed a glisten. *Ibid.* 527: "*Glisten*" A term used by thieves for diamonds.

glitch *n.* [< G *glitschen* 'to slip, make a slip'; Yid *gletshn*] **1.** Esp. *Electronics.* a malfunction or difficulty in a system, esp. a brief or sudden interruption or surge in voltage in an electric circuit.

1962 J.H. Glenn, Jr., in *We Seven* 159: Another engineering term we used [in Project Mercury] to describe some of our problems was "glitch." Literally speaking, a glitch is a spike or change in voltage in an electrical circuit which takes place when the circuit suddenly has a new load put on it...A glitch...is such a minute change in voltage that no fuse could protect against it. **1962** Graf *Dict. Electronics* 124: *Glitch*—Low-frequency interference in a television picture. It is seen as a narrow bar moving vertically. **1972** *New Yorker* (Nov. 11) 66 [ref. to Apollo XIII, 1970]: The INCO told Kranz about a communications "funny"—an aberration that doesn't clear up immediately, as opposed to a "glitch," which is a transitory one. **1979** *Time* (Apr. 9) 8: A minor glitch somewhere in the complex system. **1980** WINS Radio News (June 5): The military admits that there was a glitch at Colorado Springs that led to the momentary belief that a missile attack was on the way. **1981** W. Safire, in *N.Y. Times Mag.* (June 7) 12: A "glitch," or niggling breakdown in technology, is from the Yiddish [*sic*] verb *glitschen*, "to slip." **1984** L. Christie & J. Christie *Encyclopedia of Microcomputer Terminology*: *Glitch:* Low-frequency interference that appears as a narrow horizontal bar moving vertically through a CRT screen. Also an extraneous voltage pip, that moves along the signal on an oscilloscope screen. **1987** J. Rosenberg *Dict. Computers* 258: *Glitch:* a pulse or burst of noise; often reserved for the types of noise pulses which cause crashes and failures. **1989** *CBS This Morning* (CBS-TV) (Mar. 14): In spite of a small glitch in the Shuttle's electrical system.

2. a difficulty, error, or mishap, esp. if minor or unexpected; slip; snag; hitch.

1962 in *OEDS*: *Glitch...slang*—a hitch. **1965** *Time* (July 23) 37: "Glitches" (a spaceman's word for irritating disturbances). **1968** *Time* (Mar. 1) 52: Goofs and glitches always creep into the early blueprints for any new aircraft. **1980** *N.Y. Post* (Mar. 19) 29: [Pres. Carter] apologized for what he called a "glitch" in his failure to have understood full implications of the U.N. vote. **1981** T. Randall, in Safire *Good Word* 90: The first time I heard the word "glitch" was in 1941...at WTAG (Worcester, Mass.). When an announcer made a mistake...that was called a "glitch" and had to be entered on the "Glitch Sheet," which was a mimeographed form. The older announcers told me the term had been used as long as they could remember. **1982** *N.Y. Times* (Aug. 29) V 1: There were glitches but no serious hitches...The guerrillas then continued to Tunis. **1983** *Rolling Stone* (Feb. 3) 10: None of them can seem to find all those glitches. **1983** Neaman & Silver *Kind Words* 310: One may also describe a military mess-up still more euphemistically as a *glitch*. **a***1984** J. Green *Newspeak* 107: *Glitch* meaning a slight and unexplained error is used throughout technology, incl. TV, radio, radar, motor racing,...space flight, and more. **1987** B. Ford & Chase *Awakening* 146: She really looks forward to living each day, whatever glitches occur don't put her in a negative attitude. **1988** *New York* (Aug. 29) 40: Actually, the Quayle announcement was only the most noticeable of a host of glitches affecting the Republicans.

glitch *v.* *Electronics.* to malfunction or cause to malfunction; (*hence*) to interfere with; snarl up.

1979 Homer *Jargon* 144: Also, *glitch* can be used as a verb to characterize the mess caused by an unexpected problem [with a computer]. *****1979** in Partridge *DSUE* (ed. 8) 471. **1982** *L.A. Times* (Sept. 22) V 14: Greed can glitch even the most sophisticated science. **1987** Zeybel *Gunship* 85 [ref. to Vietnam War]: TV glitched, Ed. Stand by.

glitter *n.* diamonds or other cut gems.

1977 *Kojak* (CBS-TV): We got enough glitter here to double our money.

glitterati *n.pl.* [blend *glitter* and *literati*] *Journ.* wealthy, fashionable, publicity-conscious people.

1940 (cited in *W9*). **1956** *Time*, in *OED2*: A passel of New York glitterati. **1979** *Time* (May 7) 27: Celebrities...the glitterati. **1983** *Time* (Feb. 28) 58: For weeks the glitterati have been jockeying for gilded invitations. **1989** *TV Guide* (Feb. 18) 26: Bona fide member of the media glitterati. **1993** *CBS This Morning* (CBS-TV) (Mar. 12): In Hollywood the glitterati turned out in force.

Glitter Gulch *n*. Fremont Street and the downtown casino and entertainment area of Las Vegas, Nev.

1953 O. Lewis *Sagebrush Casinos* 188: The eight-mile long Las Vegas Strip was living up to its nickname of "Glitter Gulch." **1972** Pendleton *Vegas Vendetta* 128: Just the same, there was a noticeable apprehension all along the Strip and in the city's Glitter Gulch—wherever games were played in that valley. **1977** Laxalt *Nevada* 120: It is business as usual along the Las Vegas Strip and in that dazzlingly lighted downtown casino area known as Glitter Gulch. **1983** Glass & Glass *Touring Nevada* 179: Downtown Las Vegas, "Glitter Gulch," is the original site of the development of southern Nevada's tourist attraction. **1988** *Spin* (Oct.) 18: Suzanne…and her buddies…came roarin' through "Glitter Gulch" on three scarlet Harleys.

glitz *n*. [back formation from GLITZY] flashy, esp. meretricious, splendor; showiness.

1977 in *OED2*. **1978** *Houston Chronicle* (Mar. 5) IX 5: Sable…rubbed shoulders with black leather and sleazy glitz in…designer Billy Falcon's spring-summer show. **1980** *N.Y. Times Bk. Review* (Dec. 28) 10: Elsewhere we read of musical "glitz" or "zap." **1981** Alan Cartnal *California Crazy* (dust jacket): The flash and trash, the glitz and glitter of L.A.! **1983** *Newsweek on Campus* (Dec.) 9: Far removed from showbiz glamour and glitz.

glitz up *v*. to make glitzy.

1956 *New Yorker* (Nov. 3) 43: All glitzed up with diamonds. **1981** *L.A. Times* (Dec. 24) V 14: Television came along to glitz up the holidays. **1990** *Time* (July 9) 64: The survey may give news executives a further excuse to…glitz up their products to try to woo the young.

glitzy *adj*. [< G *glitzig*, Yid *gletzik* 'glittering'] flashy; showy; dazzling.

1968–70 *Current Slang* III & IV 56: Streisand was really glitzy in *Funny Girl*. **1973** *Playboy* (Mar.) EA2: People were communicating like crazy in a speedy, glitzy lingo. **1973** Chandler *Captain Hollister* 70: Why should a man going out to the Smokehouse want to bring along something glitzy? **1976** *N.Y. Times Mag.* (Mar. 21) 111: "Glitzy"…comes directly from the German *glitzen*, and means "sparkling," or dazzlingly meretricious. **1980** *N.Y. Daily News* (Aug. 20) 3: It was Hoving, with his glitzy box office sensibility, who helped turn the museum into the city's number one tourist attraction. **1980** *WCBS-TV Evening News* (Dec. 25): That's just another of the film's glitzy effects. **1981** *N.Y. Times* (July 19) 40: And she herself, dressed in a glittering, glitzy swirl of pink and orange, is a bouncing, bumping embodiment of disco lights. **1984** *All Things Considered* (Nat. Public Radio) (May 30): It was one of those glitzy, "only-in-Los-Angeles" events.

Globemonster *n*. *USAF*. the C-124 Globemaster cargo and transport plane. *Joc*.

1961 L.G. Richards *TAC* 222: [C-124] Globemonsters, as the pilots affectionately call them.

globes *n.pl*. a woman's breasts.

1889 Barrère & Leland *Dict. Slang* I 411: *Globes* (American), a woman's breasts. **1954** in *DAS*: I'd even feel Elena's soft globes through her nighty. **1983** Neaman & Silver *Kind Words* 19: *Globes*…is somewhat more literary than the vulgar *knockers*.

glom *n*. **1.** a stupid or worthless fellow.

1930 *Amer. Merc.* (Oct.) 161: A guy don' wanna wuyk, so he tuyns into a glom. **1942–49** Goldin et al. *DAUL* 82: That glom screwed up the detail. **1970** Gattzden *Black Vendetta* 68: What the hell are you gloms doing in my room? **1972** J. Mills *Report* 90: And you feel, you know, really like Joe Glom. *Ibid*. 99: You know who resents you?…The gloms. The do-nothings. **1973** Schiano & Burton *Solo* 76: "Yeah, man," he says. "I know a dude who's got a lot of stuff, good stuff." He thinks I'm a real glom. **1974** Charyn *Blue Eyes* 16: Who's the glom with the stick in his hand? **1979** Homer *Jargon* 122: A difference best to be appreciated by the *geeks* and *gloms* themselves.

2. a hand.

1938 *AS* (Apr.) 156: *Glom*. A hand. **1942** *Leatherneck* (Nov.) 145: *Gloms*. Hands. **1966–68** in *DARE*.

3. a look.

1941 in D. Runyon *More Guys* 302: Then take a glaum at Johnny One-Eye here. **1944** D. Runyon, in *Collier's* (Jan. 15) 49: Well, then I get a good glaum at the gee.

glom *v*. [Scots *glaum at* 'to snatch at' < ScotGael *glàm* 'to grab'] **1.a.** *Und*. to steal.

1897 in J. London *Reports* 320: *Glam*, steal. **1907** London *Road* 33 [ref. to *ca*1894]: "Where'd ye glahm 'em?" I asked. "Out of an engine-cab,"

he answered. **1914** Jackson & Hellyer *Vocab*. 38: Glom this short and drop of two blocks below. **1918** Wagar *Spotter* 56: From…"nickel grabbers" to "quarter glommers." **1919** *DN* V 41: *Glaum*…To steal. **1925** Mullin *Scholar Tramp* 27: Just before I arrived, he had lounged into the waiting-room of the station and had glommed (stolen) a generously filled lunch-box which someone had carelessly left unguarded. **1927** *DN* V 448: *Glom* v. To steal. Also pronounced "glaum" and "glam." **1929** in Hammett *Knockover* 38: I glaumed that stuff last week. **1962** Riccio & Slocum *All the Way Down* 52: I glommed the watch from a drunk the other night. **1976** Hayden *Voyage* 212: He and a few hustlers glommed a shanty boat.

b. to seize; grab; (*hence*) to apprehend; place under arrest.

1911 Bronson-Howard *Enemy to Society* 293: The "dicks" rushed in and glomed him. **1917** Livingston *Coast to Coast* 32: Jack London was "glommed" at Niagara Falls…where he drew down a sentence of thirty days. **1919** *DN* V 41: *Glaumed, to be*, to be arrested. **1927** *AS* II (Mar.) 276: *Glomm*—seize greedily. **1927** *DN* V 448: *Glaumed, to be* v. To be shanghaied, strong-armed, or arrested. **1928** Callahan *Man's Grim Justice* 57: I've…never served a day, never even been glommed (arrested). **1929** Barr *Let Tomorrow Come* 40: I try to lam for the sticks, but he gloms me. **1937** Reitman *Box-Car Bertha* 33: The railroad dicks will glom you sure. **1940** R. Chandler *Farewell, My Lovely* 127: Hell, he ain't there…Somebody must have glommed him off. **1981** Ballenger *Terror* 8: He glommed my house and my car and the money we had in the bank. **1992** *Sally Jessy Raphaël* (synd. TV series): They glom onto each other as a way of helping each other.

c. to manage to obtain; get; take.—now usu. intrans., constr. with *onto*.

1915 Bronson-Howard *God's Man* 129: Wish I could glom a dame who could dance. **1936** Duncan *Over the Wall* 112: Who does this loot belong to and where did you glom on to it? *Ibid*. 143: Those people glommed a good look at your mug. **1937** M. Mooney *You Can't Buy Luck* (film): Glom onto these groceries and go sneak a gander at yer grandma. **1941** *Slanguage Dict*. 18: *Glom on to*…take; seize; snatch; steal. **1971** B.B. Johnson *Blues for Sister* 126: As a switchboard operator, you will glom on to a lot of salient facts. **1974** Millard *Thunderbolt* 71: Then you oughta be able to glom onto a couple extra bucks.

d. *Hobo*. to harvest by hand; to pick (crops).

1921 Casey & Casey *Gay-Cat* 48: He's a hop-glomer and sorter like a hobo himself. **1922** N. Anderson *Hobo* 93: A "cotton-glaumer" picks cotton, an "apple-knocker" picks apples and other fruits. **1927** *DN* V 443: *Cotton-glaumer, n*. A cotton picker. **1930** "D. Stiff" *Milk & Honey* 206: *Glauming*—Refers to crop gathering. We have *berry glauming, apple glauming…, cherry glauming*, etc. **1944** *PADS* (No. 2) 54: *Berry-glaumer*.—A person who can pick strawberries very rapidly. "A real *berry-glaumer* never eats a berry while picking berries." **1980** Bruns *Kts. of Road* 189: Working as fruit glommers in the Northwest.

e. to steal a ride on (a train).

1925 Mullin *Scholar Tramp* 21 [ref. to *ca*1912]: We'll stick on the main line here and glom a through freight at that grade up yonder, ahead.

f. to eat, esp. fast or greedily.

1937 E. Anderson *Thieves Like Us* 27: T-Dub pointed at the…table…"You want to glom?" **1966** in *DARE*: "He —— ice cream."…*Glommed*. **1971–72** in Abernethy *Bounty of Texas* 205: *Glom*, v.—to eat fast. **1993** *Donahue* (NBC-TV): A man will *glom* in public.

g. to seize upon.—intrans., constr. with *onto*.

1972 *N.Y. Times* (Oct. 28) 21: I think it's too easy to glom onto an idea just because it's contemporary.

2. to look at; catch sight of; see; (*hence*) realize; "get wise to."—also intrans., constr. with *on(to)*.

1916 S. Lewis *Job* 194: She kept her eyes glommed onto you all the time. **1918** *Chi. Sun. Trib*. (Mar. 24) V (unp.): Her eyes lit on Fancy Frank…When a woman gloms a man…an' she begins droppin' tin plates ev'ry time her eyes meet his'n, then it's like hangin' out a banner. **1930** *Liberty* (Aug. 2) 38: I'm waiting my chance to glom the size of the pile without giving myself away. **1931** *N.Y. Eve. Post* (Apr. 10) 22: I was…sitting in the blues…glomming the kinkers. **1936** Sandburg *The People, Yes* 130: Jeez ja see dat skirt/did ja glom dat moll. **1943** W.C. Fields *By Himself* 484: I went over to "glom" the infant the other day. **1951** Robbins *Danny Fisher* 341: "Glom that."…I picked it up and looked at it. **1956** Ross *Hustlers* 90: She glommed me some more, then remembered something. **1957** Myrer *Big War* 44: Look at that.…Just glom on to that. **1963** D. Tracy *Brass Ring* 4: In these…games there would be kids who were really good and they'd glom him; he'd wind up being the last kid picked on the team. **1966** "Petronius" *N.Y. Unexp*. 60: The guests are still the craziest looking and acting…and worth a cover charge just to glom. **1968** Swarthout *Loveland* 76: Glom that tube?

1974 Nims *Western Wind* 69: That Dursey!.../If Charon ever gloms on to her.../Ghost or not,/That dirty ol' man's gonna jump her! **1975** C.W. Smith *Country Music* 27: Glom on that tac, that rolled headliner! Here, I'll crank her up for you. **1990** Rukuza *W. Coast Turnaround* 199: By the time they glommed onto the scam, he'd be long gone.

3. to stick; to become stuck or entangled.—constr. with *up* or *together*.
1980 *TV Guide* (May 10) 48: Grappling dimly with yards of plastic hopelessly glommed together. **1985** N.Y.C. woman, age *ca*50: Then it all begins to glom up....It gets all glommed up.

gloom bug *n.* a chronically gloomy person; pessimist.
1923 T. Boyd *Through Wheat* 38: Come out of it, you gloom bug.

glooms *n.pl.* a mood or fit of depression.
***1914–22** J. Joyce *Ulysses* 763: I'm not going to think myself into the glooms about that any more. **1954** J.D. MacDonald *Condemned* 52: I got the glooms again when I rejoined the group and tried to figure out some way to work on Wilma. **1968–70** in *DARE:* To feel depressed or in a gloomy mood...*He has the glooms today.*

Gloomy Gus *n.* [the name of a comic-strip character created by F. Opper] one who is chronically sad, gloomy, or pessimistic.
1904 in Opper *Happy Hooligan* 3: Happy Hooligan Gets Another Job. Against the Advice of His Brother, Gloomy Gus, He Accepts a Position as a Sandwich Man. **1920** Witwer *Kid Scanlan* 19: The noble beast got gamely to its feet at the word from Gloomy Gus. **1928** MacArthur *War Bugs* 43: A lot of Gloomy Gusses they were, too, shaking their heads sadly. **1934** Berg *Prison Nurse* 9: That's just "Gloomy Gus's" way of putting you in your place. **1942** in Stilwell *Papers* 51: Magruder said, "Isn't that a hell of a looking country?" Gloomey Gus. **1949** Robbins *Dream Merchants* 115: Stop being a gloomy Gus. **1955** O'Connor *Last Hurrah* 365: But he's such a Gloomy Gus anyway. **1956** G. Green *Last Angry Man* 162: Gloomy Gus, that's you. **1981** Wolf *Roger Rabbit* 153: No more Gloomy Gus?

gloop *n.* [alter. GOOP, *n.*] *Mil.* napalm.
1953 W.L. White *Down the Ridge* 13: If they could just plaster the back side of the ridge with enough gloop, some of it would leak down into the crevasses and burn the Chinese out.

glooper *n.* (see quot.).
1981 D.E. Miller *Jargon* 244: *Glooper.* Also *glue pot.* A player who seems stuck to the playing surface, hoping the ball will come right to him.

gloopy *adj.* ICKY, *adj.*
1965 Karp *Doobie Doo* 161: Now you're getting gloopie and mean.

glop *n.* [coined (1933) by cartoonist Elzie Segar as a meaningless sound uttered by the infant character Swee'pea in the comic strip "Popeye"] **1.a.** a thick viscous liquid or semiliquid material; GOO. [Often applied derisively to an unappetizing food mixture.]
1945 *N.Y. Times Mag.* (Nov. 4) 12: [Among U.S. prisoners of war in Germany] "glop" [meant] any food mixture. There are two opinions as to its derivation, one faction claiming that it is the sound made by the spoon stirring the thickening mass, the other that it is the sound made when gulping it. **1963** *Harper's* (Sept.) 68: Pouring some rubber-like glop over the inside of the scar. **1970** W.C. Woods *Killing Zone* 139: Goddam plastic glop. **1971** *Newsweek* (Sept. 25) 67: A blasting cap embedded in the glop provided the coup de grace. **1971** Capon *3d Peacock* 15: Primeval matter, *Urstoff* or original glop which God...was simply stuck with. **1975** Cohen *Monsters, Giants, Little Men* 61: A huge lump of pinkish organic glop was washed up at St. Augustine Beach, Florida, in 1896.
b. *Av.* heavy overcast.
1972 W.C. Anderson *Hurricane* 37: Mostly just flying around in the glop.
2. silly nonsense; drivel.
1952 in *DAS:* That is very dull. I hate glop. **1954** J.D. MacDonald *Condemned* 51: He lined up a tame seal to do the rewrite, and between us we took all the sting out of it and stuck in some of the usual glop. **1960** Wohl *Cold Wind* 198: You can hardly expect him to be talking a lot of glop into the phone. **1962** Harvey *Strike Command* 53: Not a bunch of dull glop!...Some real thrilling stuff! **1971** Dahlskog *Dict.* 27: *Glop*...insincere nonsense, as: Don't hand me that *glop.*

glorioski *interj.* [*glorious* + Slavic suffix *-ski*] (used to express astonishment).
1972 N.Y.U. student: Glorioski!...I think that comes from [the comic

strip] "Little Orphan Annie." **1978** WINS radio (June 27): Gloriosky! The Yankees win it 6 to 4 in the bottom of the fourteenth! **1986** Merkin *Zombie Jamboree* 138: "I could use some reefer."..."Glorioski." **1992** *Eek the Cat* (Fox-TV): Glorioski, children! We're saved!

glork *n.* [of fanciful origin; cf. GORK] *Stu.* thing, idea, whatchamacallit, etc.
1983 Naiman *Computer Dict.* 66: *Glork*...A generic name for just about anything...[It] isn't restricted to physical objects.

glory boy *n. Mil.* **1.** a conceited man who recklessly seeks glory.
1951 Thacher *Captain* 291 [ref. to WWII]: "You glory boys."..."If that's all you've got to say, you can get the hell off of this ship." **1956** Chamales *Never So Few* 380 [ref. to WWII]: That other guy...He's a real glory boy. **1958** Frankel *Band of Bros.* 47 [ref. to 1950]: Don't think you're going to pull some damn' gloryboy trick on me. **1972** Grogan *Ringolevio* 231: Only the glory boys escaped, but home wasn't the same for them either. **1988** M. Maloney *Thunder Alley* 26: Remember my name, glory boy.
2. *Specif.*, a man who is a member of the U.S. Marine Corps or U.S. Air Force.—used derisively.
1942–51 MSU *Army Jargon:* 29 *Glory Boy*—Marine. **1963** W.C. Anderson *Penelope* 135: My daughter has been exposed to the glory boys long enough. It is time she became acquainted with the Navy way of life. **1971** G. Davis *Coming Home* 167: "No, I'm a pilot."..."Oh, shit, a glory boy."

glory hallelujah *n.* something extraordinary.
1898 Norris *Moran* 7: I've got a stand of horns for you, Ross, that are Glory Hallelujah. **1899** Norris *Blix* 147: Isn't it glory hallelujah?

glory hog *n.* GLORY HOUND, *n.*
1985 Westin *Love & Glory* 343: One of those glory-hog flyboys.

glory hole *n.* [dial E. *glory hole* 'a place for the storage of odds and ends'] **1.** *Naut.* shipboard quarters for stewards and stokers; (*Navy.*) chief petty officers' quarters.
1889 Meriwether *Tramp at Home* 210: There are twenty men that sleep in the "glory hole" of the *Queen of the Pacific.* **1896** Kelley *Ship's Company* 20: The "glory hole"...a den sacred to the...stewards. ***1897** in *OEDS.* ***1902** Masefield *Salt-Water Ballads* 23: You're aboard the R.M.S. "Marie" in the after Glory-Hole. **1919** Hawke *E. Battery* 6: We've slept in the glory-hole, hung on a hook,/We've pounded our ears on the floor. **1923** Bellah *Sketchbook* 138: In the Glory Hole [steward's quarters] he washed his hands and lay down on his disordered bunk. **1936** Healey *Foc's'le and Glory-Hole* 48: Here also are the stewards' sleeping quarters, which are known to all seafaring men as the "glory hole." (The origin of the name is lost.) **1943** P. Harkins *Coast Guard* 197: The glory hole—the lower berth deck where Pete stored...his sea bag in a locker. **1947** Boyer *Dark Ship* 123: He would persecute the glory hole (quarters for the stewards) unnecessarily. **1950** Riesenberg *Reporter* 26: Upward past the "Glory hole"—the stewards' living quarters. **1961** E.B. White, in *New Yorker* (Mar. 25) 70: The much juicier fraternity of pantrymen and cooks, denizens of the glory hole in the stern of the ship. **1983** Elting et al. *Soldier Talk* 357: *Glory hole* (Navy)...The chief petty officer's quarters aboard ship.
2. the vagina.
*ca***1930** G. Legman, in *F & H* (rev.) (1966 ed.) lxxi: One cried Hosanna up her Glory-hole. **1935** in Atkinson *Dirty Comics* 155: Both cat and dog are still stageing a bloody war for the supremacy of the glory hole. *a***1969** J. Kimbrough *Defender of Angels* 68 [ref. to 1920's]: My glory hole ain't for sale.
3.a. *Homosex.* a hole for the penis used for anonymous sexual encounters, esp. made in a partition between toilet stalls in a public lavatory; (*broadly*) a peep-hole.
1949 *Gay Girl's Guide* 10: *Glory Hole:* Phallic size hole in partition between toilet booths. Sometimes used also for a mere peep-hole. **1959** W. Burroughs *Naked Lunch* 75: Glory holes in a toilet wall closing in on the Last Erection. **1966** "Petronius" *N.Y. Unexp.* 107: The "glory Hole" in the...john has won citations. **1967** Humphreys *Tearoom Trade* 65: If there is a "glory hole" (a small hole, approximately three inches in diameter, which has been carefully carved, at about average "penis height," in the partition of the stall), it may be used as a means of signaling from the stall. **1970** Wambaugh *New Centurions* 179: He spots a brand-new glory hole between the walls of the toilets. **1976** G.V. Higgins *D. Hunter* 99: We're supposed to grab the guys at the glory holes. **1981** *Film Comment* (May) 23: He is in a downtown cruise john seated on the can...fondling genitals thrust at him through a "glory hole." **1985** J. Dillinger *Adrenaline* 89: Nick looked down and saw...a glory

hole about the size of a fist. **1992** *New York* (June 8) 38: Makeshift alleys with their glory holes (punched to facilitate anonymous encounters).

b. a bar or similar establishment that caters to a male homosexual clientele.

1966 C. Ross *N.Y.* 86: Most lesbians and homosexuals,…at times, frequent the same "gloryholes" and bars in the Village and in Harlem. **1979–82** Gwin *Overboard* 244: The Vision…looked…much like the homo glory holes of the L.A. Strip.

4. *Av.* a patch of clear sky in an overcast.

1987 Robbins *Ravens* 209 [ref. to 1970]: The weather was bad, so he decided to try working glory holes (isolated openings in an overcast sky where a Raven could rendezvous with fighters and lead them…onto a target).

glory hound *n.* Esp. *Mil.* one who seeks personal glory.—used derisively.

1945 *Yank* (Sept. 28) 15: "Glory hound," he muttered. **1945** O'Sheel & Cook *Semper Fidelis* 215: It poked fun at the "glory hounds" that many thought the Marines were. **1956** Poe *Attack* (film): Hero! Gloryhound. **1958** *AS* XXXIII (Oct.) 182: *Glory-hound.* Not a smokejumper's term, but a "ground pounder's" derisive word for a smokejumper. **1966** Newhafer *No More Bugles* 57: One moment, you glory hounds. **1968** G. Kelly *Unexpected Peace* 8: He's not a glory hound. **1980** McDowell *Our Honor* 57: Or don't you glory-hounds think Marines get killed? **1983** S. Wright *Meditations* 11: I'm not gonna get killed for a bunch of crazy glory hounds. **1987** *Academe* (July) 34: The bottomless money-pit of the glory-hound, acerebral gridiron warriors.

glory pole *n. So.* the penis. *Joc.*

1950 in Randolph *Pissing in Snow* 113: "That's the glory-pole," says he.

Glory Wagon *n. USAF.* a Boeing B-17 Flying Fortress bomber. *Joc.*

1965 Jablonski *Flying Fortress* 37 [ref. to WWII]: Pilots sometimes referred to it sardonically as "The Glory Wagon," in acknowledgement of the wide publicity it was given.

glove *n.* a condom.

1958 R. Wright *Long Dream* 30: "He found a glove for his bat," Sam giggled. **1973** *TULIPQ* (coll. B.K. Dumas): Glove (condom). **1982** Tesich *World According to Garp* (film): Where's your thing? Your glove? **1992** *N.Y. Observer* (Apr. 20) 12: A night full of love,/Just you, me, and a glove.…No glove, no love!

glover *n.* (see quot.).

1854 in Thornton *Amer. Gloss.* I 364: I have always found [President Franklin Pierce] a very kind and agreeable man,—what the "rounders" in New York would term a "glover."

glow *n.* ¶ In phrase: **have a glow on** to feel happy or relaxed, esp. from the use of alcohol or drugs.

1942 *ATS* 121: Drunkenness…*glow-on.* **1958** Motley *Epitaph* 279: I think I'll get a glow on. **1954–60** *DAS: Glow*…a state of moderate intoxication. Usu. in the phrase, "have a glow on." **1962** (quot. at PISS AND VINEGAR, *n.*).

glow boy *n.* [prob. pun on DOUGHBOY] *Nuclear Industry.* a male technician trained to service a nuclear power plant after a dangerous leakage of radiation.

1986 in *Barnhart Dict. Comp.* IV 134: "Glow boys" are "hot stuff."…Their work is deep inside a nuclear power plant, an atmosphere so radioactive the glow boys absorb intense bursts of radiation and can only stay for minutes.

glue *n.* **1.** money.

1896 in Rose *Storyville* 127: Kate Soaked the Sloan Diamonds to Raise the Needful—Florrie Davis Will Help the Partners to Raise More Glue. **1941** Kendall *Army & Navy Sl.* 6: *Glue*…money.

2. beer. Cf. GLUED.

1945 *Yank* (Nov. 9) 15: I gotta…get myself a few pails of glue before the bars all shut down.

3. *Av.* heavy clouds, fog, overcast, etc.

1946 Haines *Command Decision* 111: We tested without parachutes, we flew the mail through solid glue. **1966–67** Harvey *Air War* 9: They can…"punch down through the glue" (penetrate the cloud cover) and hit by surprise.

¶ In phrases:

¶ **full of glue** worthless or contemptible.

1928 Levin *Reporter* 52: This old-fashioned amateur detective idea of snooping around trying to scoop the other guy is full of glue.

¶ **in the glue** in trouble.

1965 Gary *Ski Bum* 15: They were dangerous because you could easily fall for them, and then you were in the glue all right. **1988** T. Harris *Silence of Lambs* 192: Are you in the glue? Can Senator Martin do anything to you?

glue *v. Und.* to pilfer; (*hence*) to seize or apprehend; place under arrest.

1925 (cited in Partridge *Dict. Und.* 293). **1929** Milburn *Hobo's Hornbook* 150: Now I was feelin' salty and I glued Squire Grimes' hat. **1934** in Partridge *Dict. Und.* 293: A copper glued me, backed me up against a wall, and frisked me. **1942–49** Goldin et al. *DAUL* 83: Glu [*sic*] it quick. **1962** Maurer & Vogel *Narc. & Narc. Add.* (ed. 2) 304: Arrested…*glued,…snatched.* **1971** Guggenheimer *Narc. & Drug Abuse* 23: *Glued.* arrested.

¶ In phrase:

¶ **glue to** *West.* to remain seated on (a bucking horse or bull).

1927 Rollins *Jinglebob* 231 [ref. to 1880's]: Ain't nobody here can glue to that geezer for more'n five jumps.

glued *adj.* [cf. GLUE, *n.*, 2] drunk.

1957 Gutwillig *Long Silence* 133 [ref. to 1951]: We'll both get glued to the eyeballs. **1968** Baker et al. *CUSS* 126: *Glued.* Drunk.

glue-foot *n.* a slow runner.

1906 Ford *Shorty McCabe* 30: I have done a little track work myself, and Leonidas didn't show up for any glue-foot.

gluehead *n.* a person, usu. an adolescent, who habitually sniffs fumes from model-maker's glue so as to become intoxicated.

1972 Wambaugh *Blue Knight* 299: I ain't a gluehead. It makes guys crazy.

glueneck *n.* (see quot.). Hence **glue-necked,** *adj.*

1927 *DN* V 448. *Glue neck, n.* A filthy prostitute. **1976** Hayden *Voyage* 43: Some blowsy glue-necked whore.

gluepot *n.* **1.** [fr. the use of horse carcasses in glue making] *Horse Racing.* an old, slow or worthless horse.

1924 Isman *Weber & Fields* 252 [ref. to *ca*1900]: And that galloping glue pot isn't home yet. **1949** Cummings *Dict. Sports* 176. **1952** in *DAS:* The Starting Price bookmakers only pay the old gluepot rates when he toes the line. **1966** Westlake *Busy Body* 13: If Engel's father's imperfection happened to be throwing his money away on a lot of gluepots, it could have been worse.

2. *Und.* a post office.

1925 *Collier's* (Aug. 8) 30: A post office is a "glue pot."

3. *Und.* (see quot.).

1927 *DN* V 448: A filthy prostitute…*glue pot.*

gluey *n.* GLUEHEAD, *n.*

1967 J.B. Williams *Narc. & Halluc.* 112: *Gluey*—Glue-sniffer. **1970** Horman & Fox *Drug Awareness* 467: *Gluey*—glue sniffer.

glug *n.* a big swallow.

1977 Bredes *Hard Feelings* 262: Rocky takes a glug from his can. **1981** Wolf *Roger Rabbit* 55: I swigged down a healthy glug. **1986** *NDAS.*

glunk *n.* GUNK, *n.*

*a*1967 Bombeck *Wit's End* 73: Use a spreckentube to clean out the glunk.

glutes *n.pl. Bodybuilding.* the glutei; buttocks.

1984 *L.A. Times* (Oct. 11) V 25: Layin' on your gluts [*sic*] inhalin' [beer] is not workin' out. **1986** *Equalizer* (CBS-TV): My glutes are disintegrating. **1987** *RHD2.* **1989** *U.* (Spring Break Issue) 26: Got a yearning for bulging biceps, washboard abs and gorgeous glutes?

G.M. *n.* [good *m*orning] A.M.; morning. *Joc.*

1901 Irwin *Sonnets* (unp.): Since ten o'clock, G.M. *1901 in *OEDS:* Merely referring to it as such-and-such an hour G.M. **1902–03** Ade *People You Know* 218: Uncle Jabe would yank him out at 4:30 G.M. **1906** Ford *Shorty McCabe* 118: I had to lift him out at four G.M. **1920** Ade *Hand-Made Fables* 36: This thing of squaring up every G.M. to the same old Lay-Out…was beginning to pall on him. **1922** *Sat. Eve. Post* (Aug. 26) 6: I didn't hit the hay until about three G.M. **1929** S. Lewis *Dodsworth* 341: I bet I never went to bed before three G.M. once. **1936** Steel *College* 146: Well, about three G.M. this morning somebody calls up Singleton and tells him about those four slugs in the wall. **1948** Manone & Vandervoort *Trumpet* 41: I woke up St. Louis, in the early G.M. (Good Morning).

G-man *n.* [government *man,* first applied (*a*1917) to political detectives in Ireland; see *OEDS*] **1.** a special agent of the Federal Bureau of Investigation.

1930 Pasley *Al Capone* 33: He offered a G man (government agent) ten gran' to forget it. **1935** Pollock *Und. Speaks:* G. man, federal officer. **1935** R. Graves *Speed Limited* (film): I think they're G-men. **1935** *G-Men* (NBC radio series) (July 20) (title). **1942** Boucher *Werewolf* 20: Anybody can marry an actor or a G-man; but a werewolf—. **1949** *N.Y. Times* (May 1) IV 2: G-Men Act. **1952** Himes *Stone* 116: It took the G-men to get Sid in here. **1957** H. Danforth & J. Horan *D.A.'s Man* 41 [ref. to *ca*1935]: Do you want the G-men raiding the joint! **1974** Bernstein & Woodward *President's Men* 184: The G-man paused for another 30 seconds or so. **1977** *N.Y. Post* (Aug 5) 1: Godfather picked up by FBI...The move by G-men cast him back into his usual image as a racketeer. **1981** *Time* (Nov. 9) 39: The pilot was a hit with G-men, at least. At a screening at the bureau...the show won knowing nods and murmurs. **1993** *Newsweek* (July 26) 29: J. Edgar Hoover hung on for decades as the nation's G-man by collecting damaging information on his employers.

2. a garbage man. *Joc.*

1941 Kendall *Army & Navy Sl.* 6: *G man*...a garbage man. **1944** in *AS* XX 148 *G-Man.* Soldier attending to garbage on K.P. **1970** Wambaugh *New Centurions* 180: "I can tell all my friends I'm a G-man," Ranatti muttered. "G for garbage." **1974** Terkel *Working* 103: They call you G-man, or "How's business, picking up?"

gnarly *adj.* **1.a.** Orig. *Surfing.* dangerous or difficult; tough.

1977 Filosa *Surf. Almanac* 186: *Gnarly.* [South African] Big, hairy surf. [American] Challenging surf, but ridable and fun. **1988** *China Beach* (ABC-TV): We're looking for a particularly gnarly dude. **1992** *Northern Exposure* (CBS-TV): Was [the trail] as gnarly as you remembered it?

b. Esp. *Stu.* unpleasant; awful; disgusting; unattractive.

1978 G. Kimberly *Skateboard* 119: Right on the eye. That's pretty gnarly. **1981** *Nat. Lampoon* (Oct.) 46: It was bitchin' gnarly, having to watch children with third-degree burns over 95 percent of their bodies do improvisational dance. **1981** *Nat. Lampoon* (Oct.) 46: Most of them are the sons and daughters of Hollywood stars, so you can imagine how gnarly they are on the inside and all. **1981** Wambaugh *Glitter Dome* 271: It seemed better than going back to those gnarly massages. **1981** Jenkins *Baja Okla.* 269: We're not talking about a lame chick and a gnarly guy. We're talking about a couple of far-out dudes. **1982** L. Glass *Valley Girl* 29: *Gnarley:* disgusting. **1985** "Blowdryer" *Mod. Eng.* 13: Fuck, man, I got a gnarly bruise on my elbow. **1988** *Nat. Lampoon* (Apr.) 12: God, this will like totally ruin my weekend! How totally gnarly! **1988** M. Barrie & J. Mulholland *Amazon Women* (film): I just saw this old guy in the hallway with these gnarly scabs all over his body—gross me out!

2. *Stu.* splendid; wonderful; attractive.

1982 S. Black *Totally Awesome* 42: Stylish belt. It looks totally gnarly. **1982** A. Lane & W. Crawford *Valley Girl* (film): It's totally gnarly birth control. **1984** Algeo *Stud Buds & Dorks:* Very good...*narly, knarley.* **1986** Calif. man, age *ca*19, on *Story of English* (PBS-TV): That was gnarly. **1986** *New Gidget* (synd. TV series): Why don't you try some of the...paté. It looks really gnarly. **1988** *Sonny Spoon* (NBC-TV): Gnarly car, man! Bitchin' wheels, dude! **1993** Kool-Aid TV ad: It's the gnarly new flavor from Kool-Aid Burst soft drinks!

gnat *n.* ¶ In phrase: **gnat's eyelash** [or **eyebrow** or **heel** or (*vulgar*) **ass**] the slightest amount or degree; hair; **fit to a gnat's eyelash** to fit or suit perfectly; **to a gnat's heel** with perfect accuracy.

1840 *Spirit of Times* (May 9) 109: You must learn to march fust....Well fellas, you went that lock-step to a nat's [*sic*] heel. **1893** Hampton *Maj. in Washington* 156: I told him he had expressed my views to a gnat's heel. **1903** *DN* II 315: "I fitted to a gnat's heel," that is, perfectly. **1911** H.B. Wright *Barbara Worth* 107: "I voices yer sentiments correct, pard?"..."To the thrim av a gnat's heel." [**1930** in Weaver *Collected Poems* 232: And what/Anybody could seem to ever learn him,/You could write very big on a gnat's eyebrow.] **1937** Parsons *Lafayette Escadrille* 271: They had my range to a gnat's eyebrow. **1956** in Loosbrock & Skinner *Wild Blue* 101: McCook engineers had figured the T-2's performance under load to a gnat's eyelash. **1972** R. Barrett *Lovomaniacs* 196: It...fitted Buddy's life to a gnat's eyelash. **1979** Hiler *Monkey Mt.* 17: If anything's just a gnat's ass off, it blows their minds. **1982** Del Vecchio *13th Valley* 146: It don't make a gnat's ass [of] difference. *a*1990 R. Herman, Jr. *Force of Eagles* 372: Rupe had our fuel figured to a gnat's ass.

gnome *n.* an inconsequential person; (*also*) a usu. industrious lower-level employee.

1959 *AS* (May) 154: The opposite of a *B.M.O.C.* is a *loser, gnome, mullet,* or *spook.* **1969** *Current Slang* I & II 41: *Gnome, n.* A campus employee, especially ground keepers, janitors, and kitchen help...College students...Texas. **1986** N.Y.C. book editor, age *ca*50: Pat can get the gnomes in the computer department to work something up.

G-note *n.* Orig. *Und.* a $1000 currency note.

1930 D. Runyon, in *Sat. Eve. Post* (Apr. 5) 4: They all have big coarse G notes in their hands. **1935** in Thompson & Raymond *Gang Rule in N.Y.* 352: I want that G-note. **1961** in Cannon *Nobody Asked* 358: They all backed up from the Greek when the keister was loaded with G-notes. **1987** N.Y.C. woman, age *ca*50: Well, if you've got a G-note you're not using, you can spend it on a parrot. **1988** H. Gould *Double Bang* 90: Maybe a G-note.

go *n.* **1.** fashion; rage.—constr. with [*all*] *the.* Now *S.E.* and *rare* in U.S.

*ca***1787** (cited in Partridge *DSUE*). *****1793** S.T. Coleridge, in *OEDS:* Have you read Mr. Fox's letter to the Westminster electors? It is quite the political go at Cambridge, and has converted many souls to the Foxite faith. *****1800** in *OEDS:* He is quite the thing; the *go* in every respect. *****1811** *Lexicon Balatron:* Go, The. The mode. He is quite the go, he is quite varment, he is prime, he is bang-up, are synonimous expressions. **1840** in *F & H* III 160: Whatever is the *go* in Europe will soon be the cheese here. **1843** in G.W. Harris *High Times* 23: At the present time preaching thrives and matrimony is all the go. *****1846** in *F & H* III 160: Where muffins are the go. **1899** Green *Va. Folk-Speech* 65: Broad-brim hats are all the go.

2.a. a drink, usu. a gill, of liquor.

*****1796** Grose *Vulgar Tongue* (ed. 3): *Go-shop.*—The Queen's Head in Duke's-court, Bow street, Covent-garden...where gin and water is sold in three-halfpenny stools, called Goes. *****1799** in *OED:* (1) drank four *goes* of brandy and water. *****1835** C. Dickens, in *F & H* III 159: Chops, kidneys, rabbits, oysters, stout, cigars, and *goes* innumerable. *****1841** in *F & H:* Waiter, a go of Brett's best alcohol. **1842** *Spirit of Times* (Sept. 10) 326: Waiter—a go of gin. **1866** Locke *Swingin Round* 34: I called for a go uv gin. *****1883** in *F & H* III 159: Two half-goes of rum hot and a half-pint of beer. **1946** Steinbeck *Wayward Bus* 170: Here's a go, kid. Your health, kid.

b. *Narc.* (see quot.).

1936 Dai *Opium Addiction* 196: *Bindle.* A very small quantity of drugs done up in paper. Sometimes referred to as...*a deck, a go,* or *a cap.*

3. a bargain; agreement. Now *colloq.*

1878 B. Harte, in *DA:* Then it's a go! **1911–12** J. London *Smoke Bellew* 55: "It's a go," said Kit, as his hand went out in ratification. **1914** in *DA.* **1930** Rogers & Adler *Chump at Oxford* (film): It's a go. **1930** M. West *Babe Gordon* 135: One-third on everything....Is it a go?

4. a fight, esp. a prizefight; match. Now *S.E.*

1890 in *OEDS:* Lost me five dollars the other day to see the tamest kind of a go. There wasn't a knockdown in ten rounds. **1896** Ade *Artie* 3: I'll...get a couple o' handy boys and put on a six-round go for a finish. **1905** J. London *Game* 18: The go with O'Neil cleared the last payment on mother's house. **1921–25** J. Gleason & R. Taber *Is Zat So?* 8: I never meant to lose that go tonight. *****1959** in *OEDS.*

go *adj.* [orig. aerospace jargon] **1.** Esp. *Mil. & Pol.* ready or favorable, esp. for action.

1962 in *DAS* (Supp.) 704: As the astronauts say...all signs are go in the National League. **1965** Hardman *Chaplains* 14: Men...First Battalion, 16th Marines, is a go outfit. We go. *Ibid.* 14: In this outfit,...everything that's right is [called] go. **1972–79** T. Wolfe *Right Stuff* 210: His system was "go." **1985** Ferraro & Francke *Ferraro* 109: As far as the Zaccaros are concerned, it's all go.

2. stylish; sophisticated and energetic.

1962 in *Time* (Jan. 4, 1963) 48: Not so...for beatniks, whose heavy black turtleneck sweaters had never looked particularly go with white tennis socks. *****1964** in *OEDS:* I am not a go person.

go *v.* **1.** to bet; (*hence*) to accept the challenge or offer of.

*****1635** J. Shirley *Lady of Pleasure* V i: The rooks...went their smelts [half guineas] upon his hand. **1827** in *JAF* LXXVI (1963) 291: I'le go 50. **1831** in *DA:* Well,...what will you go now? **1842** *Spirit of Times* (Apr. 9) 67: They "went their entire pile." **1860** in *DARE:* The main or drinking-room was also occupied...as a gambling-hall, and their incessant clamor of "Who'll go me twenty?" **1875** "M. Twain" in *DARE* s.v. *fill, v.* 2: His last acts [*sic*] was to go his pile on "Kings" [etc.]. **1908** J. London *M. Eden* 141: "I'll go you," Martin announced, stretching out his hand.

2. to experience a sexual orgasm. See also GO OFF, *v.*

*****1749** (cited in Partridge *DSUE* (ed. 8) 473). **1974** L.D. Miller *Valiant* 56: I went twice! I never thought a man could make me feel that way again...ever!

3. to endure or withstand; put up with; tolerate; stomach.—usu. in negative constructions.

1830 in *DA:* "I can't go it, sir!" replied the dandy, strutting up and down. **1833** J. Hall *Soldier's Bride* 112: I can't go it, sir!…never slept in a room with any body in my life, sir! **1843** Field *Pokerville* 141: I'll go the naked truth, by thunder! **1852** Hazen *Five Years* 27: "What do you think of it, Hatfield?"…"Can't go it!" was the reply. **1858** in *N. Dak. Hist.* XXXIII (1966) 142: Some could not "go it" [buffalo meat], pronouncing it horrible. **1864** *Battle-Fields of So.* 250: I know you can't "go" rye-coffee. **1912** Mathewson *Pitching* 214: I cannot "go" young ball-players who attempt to become the bootblacks for the old ones. **1934** Burns *Female Convict* 47: I just can't go the stuff. **1946** in *DA:* I can drink milk, coffee and pop, but I can't go tea. **1965–70** in *DARE:* An unexplainable dislike…"I don't know why, but I just can't *go* him."…34 Inf[ormant]s. **1970** Gattzden *Black Vendetta* 111: If you can't go that cold slop, I'll clear it away.

4. to master or accomplish.

1830 in *DAE:* These low Virginians cannot go the letter *r.* **1843–45** T.J. Green *Tex. Exped.* 101: By God, general, me and the whole of my company will go it!

5. to accept, like, or believe in.

1835–37 in *DA:* I love the Quakers, I hope they'll go the Webster ticket yet. **1845** in Oehlschlaeger *Reveille* 127: That's *too* [hard to believe]—I can't go it. **1849** G.G. Foster *Celio* 51: "A Mesmerist." "Oh, I go animal magnetism." **1855** H. Greeley, in *OED:* He…tells everybody he is connected with the Tribune, but doesn't go its isms. **1961** Gover *$100 Misunderstanding* 181: I tell her I don' go that crap, but I guess he jes tryin' to set up a weekend. **1966–80** McAleer & Dickson *Unit Pride* 113: I sure do go that kind of water [cognac] to put in your canteen.

6.a. to be permissible, acceptable, or tolerated; (now *esp.*) to be acceptable without hindrance or interference. Now *S.E.* [App. fr. S.E. sense '(of coins or banknotes) to be acceptable as currency', as in bracketed *1805 quot.]

[*1805 J. Davis *Post-Captain* 52: Joes are golden coins, that go in the West Indies; and would, I presume, go anywhere.] *1879 G. Meredith, in *OEDS:* Everything goes on the stage, since it's only the laugh we want on the brink of the action. **1890** Quinn *Fools of Fortune* 401: His was an administration which might fairly be described as one under which "everything went." *Ibid.* 514: The "wide open" "everything goes" policy prevailed there. **1895** Townsend *Fadden* 19: Say, if she wants ter string me, it goes. **1895** in J.I. White *Git Along Dogies* 66: That verse shows…that no monkeying goes for a minute. **1903** A. Adams *Log of Cowboy* 191 [ref. to 1880's]: Don't ever get the impression that you can ride your horses into a saloon, or shoot out the lights in Dodge; it may go somewhere else, but it don't go there. **1906** *Nat. Police Gaz.* (May 5) 3: I'm game; does a check go? **1907** in *DAE:* This one is goin' to be called "No Creek" "Lee Creek" or I fight. Does it go? **1914** Atherton *Perch* 194: "May I call her Ora to you?"…"Ora goes." **1964** in "Malcolm X" *By Any Means* 155: We've got some new rules, and these rules mean anything goes, *anything goes.* **1968** Lockridge *Hartspring* 138: Some things go in a war that don't go on the outside.

b. (of words, demands, actions, etc.) to be valid; count; (*hence*) to carry authority or require compliance; be final; **go for** to express the opinion of.

1890 Quinn *Fools of Fortune* 213: I'm a capper for the house and my play doesn't go. **1891** in Leitner *Diamond in Rough* 155: His judgment is right and it "goes." **1892** Bunner *Letters* 139: However, he is a BOY, and anything he does, goes. **1895** Townsend *Fadden* 12: "Dat goes, Miss Fannie."…Dat goes, says I, fer what she says goes if I have ter lick de biggest mug on eart' to make it go. See? **1898** Brooks *Strong Hearts* 48: But what the big chief says goes, you see. **1905** *Variety* (Dec. 16) 9: Gee, say, you won't believe this, but it goes. **1908** in H.C. Fisher *A. Mutt* 21: Whatever she says goes double for me. **1909** in O. Johnson *Lawrenceville* 23: That's what I said, and what I say goes—and that's what I say now. **1910** in O. Johnson *Lawrenceville* 197: "My friend…here's setting up."…Stover…advanced saying, "That goes." **1911** A.H. Lewis *Apaches of N.Y.* 14: No Discussion of Politics or Religion Allowed. This goes! **1939** Goodman & Kolodin *Swing* 99: What goes for Jimmy goes for me too. **1944** Inks *Eight Bailed Out* 56: Rank don't go in a situation like this.

7. to begin acting in a manner reminiscent, suggestive, or typical of ——; esp. **go Hollywood; go ape** (see s.v. APE, *adj.*).—constr. without article. [Cf. orig. Brit. colloq. (now S.E.) go native where the complement is adverbial in function but ambiguously adjectival or nominal in form.]

1917 in Dos Passos *14th Chronicle* 71: Don't think that I've gone militarist or believe in conscription. **1929** McEvoy *Hollywood Girl* 102: I thought he was the one who had gone Hollywood. Pictures in the paper, guest of this and that. It's a wonder you notice me, I told him. **1930** *Amer. Merc.* (Dec.) 456: He goes stool for a [pardon]. **1931** *Amer. Merc.* (Nov.) 352: *Gone Sunday-school:* said of a circus that has abolished the grift. *a*1940 in Fitzgerald *Notebooks* 333: They go ostrich about their faults—[and] magnify their virtues. **1941** *Slanguage Dict.* 18: *Go*…to acquire the characteristics of, as *go* Hollywood. **1947** Blankfort *Big Yankee* 127: And so, after graduation, he went "society."…He made his protocol calls, joined the Army and Navy Club [etc.]. **1948** Lait & Mortimer *New York* 55: Not all who "go Park Avenue" are fakes and phonies. **1962** Tregaskis *Viet. Diary* 149: Some of the VNAF pilots have sort of gone Hollywood. **1963** D. Tracy *Brass Ring* 311: Don't try to go hero on me. **1964** Thompson & Rice *Every Diamond* 210: The phrase "going Hollywood" was vaporously defined. *a*1987 Bunch & Cole *Reckoning* 23: Don't be a showboat…don't go Hollywood on me. **1988** Univ. Tenn. instructor: All we need is for a U.S. reactor to go Chernobyl. **1992** *CBS This Morning* (CBS-TV): (Mar. 20): Even with all their success, they've never gone Hollywood.

8. to develop or demonstrate an exclusive preference for (in a manner deducible from context); to choose, esp. to become a member of.

1926 in *AS* III (1927) 276: *Go frat* or *go the Row*—join a fraternity. **1934** Weseen *Dict. Slang* 143: *Go vaude*—To change to vaudeville. **1941** *Slanguage Dict.* 18: *Go*…to become a member of, as *go Deke.* **1942** Liebling *Telephone* 146: The local playhouse was "going Shubert." **1973** advertising in rpt. of Haycox *Whispering Range* (255): "Go Warner Paperback Library Westerns." **1975** US Navy recruiting poster: Go Navy!

9. Orig. *Juve.* to say; (*hence*) to think to oneself.—used in narration. [Extended from S.E. sense (see *OED* def. 10) 'to make a sound that may be imitated as' (e.g., *a clock goes "tick-tock"; a cow goes "moo"*), often used colloquially (see *OEDAS* II 119) of inarticulate human utterances (*I took one look at that mess and I went ugghh!*) and to preface the reenactment of movement or gestures (often followed by *like*): *So he goes (like)* [e.g., hand waved in gesture of rejection, often with accompanying utterance]; discussed by R.R. Butters in *AS* LV (1980), pp. 304–07; L. Schourup, *ibid.* LVII (1982), pp. 148–49; and W. Safire, *I Stand Corrected*, pp. 185–87.]

1942 in *Jour. Genetic Psych.* LXVI (1945) 132: *Go*…to say. "He goes, 'Well, what did you do?' and I go, 'I didn't do nothing.'" **1966** C. Ross *N.Y.* 86: "Do you know what that dame's gonna pay our friend?" Jill asked. "She looks so correct—that dame," went Gladys. **1975** in *AS* LV (1980) 304: And she goes, "No, I had them bound in front of me." *a*1977 in S. King *Bachman* 125: Ted goes to me, "I'll be right back." *1984 Partridge *DSUE* (ed. 8) 473: "He goes, 'I don't want to.'"…I heard this usage in the Channel Islands, mid-1970s, and later, in England, among teenagers. *a*1985 in Walker *Piece of My Heart* 143: We started getting patients from another company. I was going, "Oh, shit, how long is this going to go on?" *Ibid.* 240: I ended up getting straight A's, and now I'm going, "How did I ever do that?" **1987** in *Black Teen* (Jan. 1988) 10: Then once in a while I'll go, "Honey, I can't get any further with this, would you help?"

10. to develop; happen; go on.—used interrogatively.

1944–48 A. Lyon *Unknown Station* 268: Hey, what goes? **1953** *New Yorker* (Mar. 7) 52: What goes?…It ain't rained in a week. **1954** MacDonald *Condemned* 27: What goes, Steve? What the hell is up?

¶ In phrases:

¶ **go down** see GO DOWN.

¶ **go for, 1.** to be very enthusiastic about; to like, enjoy, or be enamored of. Now *colloq.* [In earlier political use, 'to support or vote for (a piece of legislation or the like)'; see *OEDS.*]

[1874 Clark *State St.* 12: Their lady-loves/…"went for them," and laughed to see/Those left go mad in misery.] **1918** in Rossano *Price of Honor* 206: The wife thinks the idea is fine, but the husband doesn't go for it. **1930** *Amer. Mercury* (Dec.) 456: *Go for*, v.: To have implicit confidence in. "I go for that gee. He's a righto." **1931** Cressey *Taxi-Dance Hall* 98 [ref. to *ca*1926]: You know, all the Filipinos go for blondes. **1936** March *Sudden Death* (film): I could go for a shot [of liquor]. **1936** Dai *Opium Addiction* 141: She used to go for me in a big way, and I was the only one that she had ever loved in her life. **1940** Fitzgerald *Last Tycoon* 11: We don't go for strangers in Hollywood. **1941** H.A. Smith

Low Man 97: Does he go for the girls!...And do the girls go for him! **1950** in *OEDS:* I could go for you in a big way, kid. **1966** Kenney *Caste* 18: You go for her, Mike?

2. to believe or accept, esp. readily.

1930 *Amer. Mercury* (Dec.) 457: We rib the sap that it's McCoy and he goes for it. **1962** in *OEDS:* The people will never go for that guff. **1988** G. Trudeau "Doonesbury" (synd. cartoon strip) (Oct. 27): Hee, hee! Not a bad rap. I'm going to go for it, young lady.

¶ **go for it, 1.** to die; fail.—usu. in past tenses.

1845 Clarke & Clarke *Sufferings* 113: "Will he die?" "O yes! surely gone for it, now." **1865** J.K. Hosmer *Bayonet* 239: We thought we were gone for it...when you made that charge. **1877** Bartlett *Amer.* (ed. 4) 250: *Go for (it),* to fail; to die.

2. to go ahead eagerly, esp. in a risky or challenging situation; do it.—often used imper.

1978 Alibrandi *Killshot* 29: Yeh. Go for it. **1979** Univ. Tenn. students (shouted at "monster" character in film): Go for it! **1981** D.E. Miller *Jargon* 231: "I'm thinking of entering; what do you think?" "Go for it." **1982** Pond *Valley Girl Gde.* 57: *Go for it*—It's like, um, do something. **1982** Corey & Westermark *Fer Shurr* (unp.): *Go for it*...exclamatory expression implying boundless optimism about life's possibilities. **1982** Trudeau *Dressed for Failure* (unp.): Hey, babe! Hope you're having a nice day! Let's go for it! **1983** E. Drew *Campaign Jour.* 183: "Go for it" and "Thumbs up" are part of the [Sen. John] Glenn lexicon. **1985** J. Ferrell & M. Lichter *Vixens* (film): You gonna go for it, man? **1989** *Beachin' Times* 6: Ridin' the wild surf, shootin' the curl and really goin' for it. Gnarly, dude.

¶ **Go it, boots!** see s.v. BOOT.

¶ **go it strong on** to favor strongly.

1869 J. Browne *Apache Country* 379: I am disposed to go it strong...on the many-ledge theory.

¶ **go south** see s.v. SOUTH, *adv.*

¶ **go the entire** [sugg. by *go the whole hog* s.v. HOG] to go all the way or all-out.

1839 *Spirit of Times* (Oct. 26) 397: They go the *entire*, and with them it is, if you love me, you must love my horse, my dog, and every thing that is old Kentucky.

¶ **not go much on** to dislike.

1865 in H. Johnson *Talking Wire* 218: Some of the boys like it, but I don't "go much" on it.

¶ **Way** [or **how**] **to go!** Well done!

[**1940** R. Buckner *Knute Rockne* (film): That's the way to go, Pete!] **1955** Goethals *Chains of Command* 187 [ref. to WWII]: Well, Jack, hear you got promoted. How to go, kid! **1958** N.Y.C. schoolboys: Way to go! Way to go! **1978** *Muppet Show* (CBS-TV): Way to go, guys! **1981** *Rod Serling's Mag.* (Sept.) 39: "I'm on it." "Way to go, Skeet." **1987** Blankenship *Blood Stripe* 46: Roper was genuinely impressed. Way to go. **1988** *Superboy* (synd. TV series): Way to go, Lex! **1993** *New Yorker* (June 14) 78: Way to go, Sandy.

goak /gouk/ *n.* [orig. intended to represent an illiterate spelling of *joke*] a joke. *Joc.*

1862 C.F. Browne *A. Ward* 79: Extry charg fur this larst remark. It's a goak.—A.W. **1894** in Dreiser *Jour.* I 222: It 'ud have been a goak, then, wouldn't it?

goal *n.* ¶ In phrase: **knock** [or **bump**] **for a goal** [or **gool** or **ghoul**] to astonish; dazzle (an audience). [The forms *gool* and *ghoul* reflect a dial. pron.; cf. Bartlett, *Amer.*, 1877, p. 254: "*Gool* for *Goal* is universal with New England boys, the same as *Loom* is *Loam.*"]

1915 T.A. Dorgan, in *N.Y. Eve. Jour.* (Aug. 2) 10: If you make any cracks I'll knock you for a ghoul. **1918** Noyes (unp.): *I'll knock you for a ghoul!*...I'll knock hell out of you...der[ivation] unknown. **1919** Cambio *301st Engrs.* 192: I'll knock you for a goal. **1920** Weaver *In American* 40: Well, sport, we sorter knocked 'em for a gool. **1921** "M. Brand" *Black Jack* 104: They say you bumped old Minter for a goal. **1922** Rice *Adding Machine* 126: You were on one of the triremes that knocked the Carthaginian fleet for a goal. **1923** Ornitz *Haunch, Paunch, and Jowl* 74: I'm gonna show them a new combination step that's gonna knock them for a gool. **1924** P. Marks *Plastic Age* 36: Would he hit Math I in the eye? He'd knock it for a goal. **1925** McAlmon *Silk Stockings* 76: Get to hell out of my way or I'll knock you for a goal. **1935** Coburn *Law Rides Range* 64: An editorial that will knock the populace for a goal.

goal *v.* to knock down or out; (*hence*) to defeat decisively; (*also*) to stun; floor; dazzle. Also **gool, ghoul** [see note at GOAL, *n.*].

1921 *Variety* (Feb. 4) 29: However, if he keeps goalin' them [opposing fighters] I should worry, for I have him tied up to a Shubert contract. **1920–21** Witwer *Leather Pushers* 303: Knock him dead, goal the big stiff! **1921** in Hemingway *Sel. Letters* 60: I brew a rum punch that'd gaol [*sic*] you. **1925** *Collier's* (Sept. 19) 7: Barbara's proposition goaled me. **1929** *Bookman* (Apr.) 150: The actor..."wows 'em," "panics" or "gooles" them. **1930** Lait *On the Spot* 203: *Ghoul*...To defeat. Perversion of "Goal." **1932** Hecht & Fowler *Great Magoo* 74: I'll gool 'em. **1942** Pegler *Spelvin* 75: President Spelvin Swings on Russian Ambassador and Is Goaled by Left to Chin. **1970** S.J. Perelman, in *New Yorker* (Oct. 17) 41: The picture...goaled all the critics.

go-ashores *n.pl. Naut.* good clothing to be worn by a sailor while on shore. Hence **go-ashore,** *adj.* Now *hist.*

1834–40 Dana *Two Yrs.* ch. xvi: Go-ashore jackets and trousers [were] got out and brushed. ***1867** Smyth *Sailor's Wd.-Bk.:* Go-Ashores.—The seaman's best dress. **1961** Burgess *Dict. Sailing* 102: Go-Ashores. The seaman's...shore-going apparel.

goat *n.* **I.** Senses referring to people, esp. derisively.

1. a lecherous or lascivious man or (*rarely*) woman.—now usu. constr. with *old.* Orig. S.E.

1675** in *OED:* When a covetous man doteth on his bags of gold...the drunkard on his wine, the lustful goat on his women...they banish all other objects. ***1698–99** "B.E." *Dict. Canting Crew:* Goat, a Lecher, or very Lascivious Person. ***1717** in *F & H* III 166: At the tea-table I have seen the impudent goat must lusciously sip off her leavings. ***1773** H. Kelly *School for Wives* 146: Our old goat of a General. **1929** Hotstetter & Beesley *Racket* 226: *Goat*...an amorous individual. **1951** Pryor *The Big Play* 124: She did not tell Brock that she had endured a pinch on the fanny and a surreptitious feel of her breast from the bald-headed old goat. *a1958** in *WNID3:* The doctor is...an old goat and has ideas about spiriting his lovely client off to a little hideout. **1961** Braly *Felony Tank* 151: You're a regular goat boy, aren't you? **1985** Univ. Tenn. student theme: The word *goat* is applied to a female who is sexually active to an excessive degree.

2.a. a fool.

***1675** in Duffett *Burlesque Plays* 64: Pry'thee old Goat, tye up thy Clack. **1793** Brackenridge *Mod. Chiv.* 188: No doubt, we are but goats...Compar'd with you...you son of a gun. **1841** [Mercier] *Man-of-War* 103: Some simple, hot-brained editorial goat/For want of more has set this yarn afloat. ***1879** in *OEDS:* Don't be actin' the goat. **1911** in O. Johnson *Lawrenceville* 440: "Of all the fools!" "Goats!" "Asses!" "Idiots!" **1913** in Thompson *Youth's Companion* 124: "What war?" asked Ransom, vaguely. "The Civil War, you goat!" **1946** (cited in Partridge *DSUE* (ed. 8) 479). **1947** in *OEDS:* Don't be a goat.

b. *U.S. Mil. Acad.* the cadet who is last in his graduating class; (*also*) (*obs.*) the junior commissioned officer in a battalion, regiment, etc.

1900 *Howitzer* (No. 1) 120: *Goat.*—A Cadet in the lowest section; formerly called an "Immortal." **1909** J. Moss *Officer's Manual* 283: *Goat.* Junior officer in post, regiment, etc. **1972** *CBS News* (June 7) (CBS-TV): And ending 800 names later with the class goat—the last cadet to graduate. **1978** Truscott *Dress Gray* 374: Three years in the bottom ten in the class...considered a likely contender for Goat. *a***1987** Bunch & Cole *Reckoning* 40: "Went to the Point. Class of '38." "Where he was the goat?"

c. an offensive old person, usu. a man.—usu. constr. with *old.*

1943 Holmes & Scott *Mr. Lucky* (film): Go on, show the old goat [woman] your hands. **1946** Diamond & Kern *Never Say Goodbye* (film): Your mother...The old goat butted you right into Reno. **1947** Helseth *Martin Rome* 54: The D.A. acted more like some pompous old goat in a mystery melodrama. **1963** *Travels of J. McPheeters* (ABC-TV): They're goin' to string you up by the neck, you old goat! **1965** Petrakis *Pericles* 4: I don't have to take that stuff from an old goat like you. *Ibid.* 5: What a goat. **1982** I.M. Hunter *Blue & Gray* (NBC-TV movie): John Brown. I want a portrait of that fierce old goat. **1987** *Golden Girls* (NBC-TV): Your mother's a stubborn old goat.

3. *Pol.* (see quot.).

1855 in *Kans. Hist. Qly.* vii (1938) 413: *Goats*...Free Soilers in Kansas are so designated.

4. a scapegoat; butt. Now *colloq.* or *S.E.*

1894 in *DAE:* I was in for no less a scheme than actually smuggling a cargo into New York!...for no other reason than "to be the goat" (as Jim Stern had it) to prove a theory. **1910** T.A. Dorgan, in Dickson *Baseball Dict.* 181: No more for me, I've quit being the "goat." **1921** in Dreiser *Diaries* 377: In order to make him the goat and joke of the party. **1923** *WNID* (Addenda): *Goat, n.* A scapegoat; one bearing burdens or blames for others; as, they made him the *goat. Slang*. **1931** Haycox *Whispering Range* 30: I hate to see old Jake Leverage the goat. **1936** S.I. Miller *Leathernecks Have Landed* (film): It's big money because you're the goat if anything happens. **1948** in *DA:* But like in all ball games there is sometimes a goat for the fans to hop on and chose their target as Smith. **1953** Paul *Waylaid* 39: Meanwhile, Mr. Finke, you are what Americans term "the goat." **1958–65** Alfred *Hogan's Goat* 32: I was the goat for fair.

5. *Local.* a Welshman.—used derisively.

1922 J.J. Davis *Iron Puddler* 68 [ref. to Sharon, Pa. *ca*1885]: A Frenchman is a "frog," a negro a "coon" and a Welshman a "goat."

6. (see quot.).

1952 Sandburg *Strangers* 392 [ref. to *ca*1890]: "I think I'll try the goat in this town," said one [hobo] and I learned the goat in a town is the Catholic priest.

7. *Stu.* (see *a*1961 quot.). Cf. GOAT ROOM, *n.*

*a*1961 *WNID3: Goat...slang...*one who is being initiated into a fraternity or sorority. **1968–70** *Current Slang* III & IV 57: *Goat, n.* A fraternity pledge.

II. Other senses.

8. *West.* a pronghorn antelope.

1759 in *DA:* I have lately been reading Hennepin's *Travels*...He often mentions they were sustained by killing *goats*. **1789** in *DAE:* He had killed 500 goats by running them down. **1826** in *DAE:* The pronghorn is usually called a goat by the Canadians. **1851** M. Reid *Scalp Hunters* 25: Did you come across the "goats"? **1860–61** R.F. Burton *City of Saints* 75: The prong-horn antelope...[is] called "le cabris" by the Canadian, and "the goat" by the unpoetic mountain man. *ca*1902, **1948, 1982** in *DARE.*

9. a goatee.

1856 in *DAE:* His special admirers saw great merit in...his long shaggy *goat.* **1876** in *DAE:* The...Esquimaux, with his slight sprinkling of a moustache and "goat," was also exhibited.

10. a slow or worthless horse; (*derisively*) a horse.

1898–1900 Cullen *Chances* 71: Let a kid take care o' your two goats and the caloosh. **1904** Ade *True Bills* 80: It seems that Lou Perkins was commonly regarded as a crippled Goat,...the Price running as Long as 275 to 1. **1907** in H.C. Fisher *A. Mutt* 16: He could not leave well alone and had to dally with the other goats. **1918** McNutt *Yanks* 225: Seeing horses they had looked upon as mere goats...flashing around the first turn. **1920** Ade *Hand-Made Fables* 45: He had a line on the performances of every Goat from the cradle up. **1926** Nason *Chevrons* 109: The Johns don't know how to take care o' their goats, d'yuh see? **1928** MacArthur *War Bugs* 241: We thought we knew all about horses, but these goats...must have escaped from a reform school. **1928** Santee *Cowboy* 70: An' it took a lot of strong-arm stuff to learn them goats to rein. **1951** *Sat. Eve. Post* (Apr. 21) 10: He had a hot tip on some goat. **1951** Hunt *Judas Hour* 56: One of my goats paid off at Tropical yesterday. **1957** Townley *Up in Smoke* (film): That goat hasn't got a chance against a mule.

11. *pl. Police.* rural police precincts.—constr. with *the.*

1911 Bronson-Howard *Enemy to Society* 294: Kneebreeks ferget all about this, or you to "the goats."

12. *R.R.* a yard locomotive or switch engine.

1916 *Editor* (Mar. 25) 343: *Goat.* yard engine. **1918** *DN* V 25: *Goat, n.* A switch engine at a roundhouse. Eastern Washington and northern Idaho. **1931** *Writer's Digest* (May) 41: *Goat*—A yard engine. **1934** *AS* (Feb.) 73: *Goat.* Switch engine. This type of engine butts cars around the yards. **1939** Attaway *Breathe Thunder* 216: The "goat" then had just cut out a few cars was chugging in a cloud of steam on a siding. **1958** McCulloch *Woods Words* 71: *Goat...*a switch engine. **1990** Niemann *Boomer* 251: *Midnight goat* Switch engine on the midnight job.

13. *Mil.* mutton.

1918 K. Morse *Letters* 148: The boys are living on a diet of what they call "goat's meat" at present;—whenever it is time for a chow line to form you can hear a chorus of bleats and baas half across the camp. **1919** *Acotank* 43: English mutton didn't suit an army used to good beef. It was popularly alleged to be "goat" and many claimed to be developing horns as a result of frequent doles of this unsavory article. **1942–46** MSU .GF2.1: Army: Jargon, in IUFA: 29 "*Goat*"—Mutton, which so many soldiers disliked.

14. (see quots.).

1971 Tak *Truck Talk* 74: *Goat:...*a small truck, used to gather fruit, that has a hoist to lift the body to the height of the fruit and to tilt the body for discharging the fruit. **1985** Baker *Cops* 219: They have these things called goats which are vehicles they use in orange groves. It's usually

some old chopped up vehicle like a flatbed truck. Sometimes it has a little crane on the back of it to lift pickers up into the trees.

15. [sugg. by the initialism] *cap.* a Pontiac GTO.

1983 Goldman & Fuller *Charlie Co.* 26: His pet Goat, the '66 Pontiac GTO he bought practically the moment he came of driving age.

¶ In phrases:

¶ **been to three county fairs and a goat-roping** [or (*vulgar*) **goat-fucking**] *So.* seen many astounding sights. *Joc.*

1974 Univ. Tenn. student: I been to three county fairs and a goat-fuckin' and I ain't never seen the like of *that.* **1981** B. Bowman *If I Tell You* 98: "I've been to three county fairs, two goat-ropings and a 'tater digging." I know what's going on; I've been around. **1984** K. Weaver *Tex. Crude* 30: I've seen a goat-roping, a fat stock show and a duck fart under water, but if that don't beat any damn thing I've *ever* seen, I'll put in with you!! **1988** Dye *Outrage* 16: Colonel, you and me been to three county fairs and a goat-fuckin' contest and I ain't seen you hit by nothin' heavier than shrapnel.

¶ **burn (someone's) goat** [BURN, *v.* + *get (one's) goat,* below] to anger (someone).

1949 Gordon & Kanin *Adam's Rib* 12: The kind of thing that burns my goat!

¶ **get (someone's) goat** [despite several attempted explanations, the inspiration behind this phrase remains unknown] **1.** to anger or annoy (someone).

1904 *Life in Sing Sing* 248: *Goat.* Anger. **1908** in Fleming *Unforget. Season* 184: The supreme contempt shown...evidently got the "goat" of Mr. Frederick Clarke. **1908** in H.C. Fisher *A. Mutt* 46: To have one's goat is to have one buffaloed or the Indian sign on one's contemporaries. **1908** *Atlantic* (Aug.) 223: A little detraction will "get their goat." **1914** Knibbs *Outlands* 46: Says I, "Then let's be on the float; you certainly have got my goat." **1914** Lardner *Al* 29: I guess I must of got Walsh's goat with my spitter because him and I walked back to the hotel together and he talked like he was kind of jealous. **1928** Scanlon *God Have Mercy* 217: I was tired, and the climb up and down those steps...was a goat-getter. **1950** Felsen *Hot Rod* 11: Don't let Walt Thomas get your goat, Bud. **1953** in "T. Sturgeon" *Unicorn* 47: And don't let 'em get your goat. **1958** Cooley *Run* 132: Why don't you drop it, Spots? He's tryin' to get yer goat! **1982** Associated Press Network News (June 26): No one on Capitol Hill will comment publicly about what got Haig's goat. **1985** MacLaine *Dancing* 299: He certainly knew how to get your goat, didn't he? **1990** Costello & Wallace *Sig. Rappers* 84: Does it get your goat when "postmodernism" is tossed around as if everyone agreed on what it meant?

2. to have an unsettling effect upon (someone).

1911–12 J. London *Smoke Bellew* 184: "Your turn," he called. "But just keep a-coming and don't look down. That's what got my goat." **1918** *Chi. Sun. Tribune* (Feb. 17) V (unp.): Now there's a girl with a swell figger, an' hair jus' the color that gets my goat, an' a lot o' getup an' pep to her style. **1959** Wurthman & Brackett *Rio Bravo* (film): That got my goat. I can't stand to watch.

¶ **ride the goat** (see *a*1890–93 quot.).

*a***1890–93** F & H III 166: *To ride the goat...*To be initiated into a secret society. [From the vulgar error that a live goat, for candidates to ride, is one of the standing properties of a Masonic lodge.] **1904** in *DA:* Congressman Harrison "rode the goat" last night at the monthly meeting of the Tammany Society. Two other new members were initiated.

¶ **shining like a diamond** [or **dime**] **in a goat's ass** *So.* shining brightly.—used derisively.—usu. considered vulgar.

1980 Cragg *L. Militaris* 357: It shines like a diamond in a goat's ass. **1984** K. Weaver *Texas Crude* 22: He keeps that thing shinin' like a dime in a goat's ass. **1985** Masters & Johnston *Sassy Sayin's* 27: He came out of that deal shining like a diamond in a goat's ass.

goat *v.* [sugg. by phr. *get (one's) goat,* s.v. GOAT, *n.*] (see quot.).
1904 *Life in Sing Sing* 248: *Goat...*to exasperate.

goatee *n.* ¶ In phrase: **get (someone's) goatee** to *get (someone's) goat* s.v. GOAT, *n. Joc.*
1930 Sage *Last Rustler* 89: That country around there would get a man's goatee.

goat-feeder *n. R.R.* the fireman of a yard engine.
1940 *R.R. Mag.* (Apr.) 45: *Goat feeder*— Yard fireman.

goat fuck *n. Mil.* a fiasco; mess.—usu. considered vulgar. Also (*euphem.*) **goat screw, goat rope.**
1971 T. Mayer *Weary Falcon* 15: "What a goatfuck," I said. **1986**

NDAS: Goat fuck. **1990** Ruggero *38 N. Yankee* 80: There seemed to be some order creeping into Barrow's "goat screw." **1991** Marcinko & Weisman *Rogue Warrior* 199: It had been one humongous goatfuck. *a***1991** Kross *Splash One* 34 [ref. to Vietnam War]: What's a guy like you doing in a goat rope like this?

goat horns *n.pl. Trucking.* (see quot.).

1971 Tak *Truck Talk* 74: *Goathorns.* twin exhaust stacks that are curved at the top.

goat locker *n. Navy.* chief petty officers' quarters, as on shipboard.

*a***1990** Poyer *Gulf* 311: I'm in the goat locker. **1991** Marcinko & Weisman *Rogue Warrior* 55: He would have taken grief in the chiefs' goat locker, so to keep the peace he reamed us out.

goat-mauler *n. R.R.* the operator of a yard engine.

1945 Hubbard *R.R. Ave.* 327: The goat mauler throws the Johnson bar in the corner and pulls the latch out over the apron.

goat room *n.* [sugg. by *ride the goat* s.v. GOAT, *n.*] *Stu.* a room where fraternity initiations take place.

1924 Marks *Plastic Age* 133: Then they marched up-stairs to the "goat room." Once there, the president mounted a dais.

goat-roper *n. West.* an unsophisticated rustic.

1968–70 *Current Slang* III & IV 57: *Goat roper,* n. An agriculture student. New Mexico State. **1973** *TULIPQ* (coll. B.K. Dumas): Cowboys: shit kickers and goat ropers. **1978** Wheeler & Kerby *Steel Cowboy* (film): How are ya, y'old goat-roper? **1980** *AS* (Fall) 200. *a***1984** in Beaty & Hunter *New Worlds* 704: For me, Norco [Calif.] High consisted of the goat ropers, the dopers, the jocks, the brains, and one quiet Iranian.

goat's nest *n.* a dirty or disorderly place; BOAR'S NEST.

1951 Algren *Chicago* 58: Old soaks' goat's nests, backstreet brothels, unlit alleys and basement bars.

goaty *adj. Army.* **1.** (see quot.).

1907 J. Moss *Officer's Manual* 243: *Goaty.* Awkward, ignorant.

2. exasperated; annoyed.

1918 Noyes (unp.): *Goaty.* meaning "exasperated" or "annoyed." Derived from the expression "to get one's goat." One gets "goaty" when one is knocked down by a bicycle on Broadway, or when a messenger boy with a dirty face...slips into the seat, on a subway train, that you are in the act of giving to a fair maid. **1971** Gallery *Away Boarders* 100: Well, then the King began to get a bit goaty with this whippersnapper who was lousing up a formal palace ceremony. But he kept his temper as best he could.

3. amative; lustful; HORNY. Cf. S.E. *goatish.*

1918 Noyes (unp.): *Goaty*...may also express the feelings one has on being contiguous for a length of time with said maid. **1946** Steinbeck *Wayward Bus* 198: Oh, he's all right...He's just a little goaty. Most kids are like that.

go-away *n. Und.* (see 1859 quot.). Cf. GETAWAY, *n.,* 2.b.

1859 Matsell *Vocab.* 38: *Goaways.* Railroad trains. "The knuck was working the goaways at Jersey City"...The pickpocket was busy in the cars at Jersey City. **1866** *Nat. Police Gaz.* (Apr. 21) 3: Big Casey endeavored to "work" the crowd at the "go-away's."

go-away gear *n. Trucking.* (see quot.).

1971 Tak *Truck Talk* 74: *Go-away gear:* the highest gear or combination of gears in the gearbox.

gob[1] *n.* [ME *gob* 'a lump'] a great quantity or number. Orig. S.E.

*****1542** in *OED:* Some good goubbe of money. *****1566** in *OED:* A gubbe of goulde. *****1574** in *OED:* Many gubs of gouldde. *****1593** in *OED:* Tenne good gobbs...Of golde or siluer. *****1598, *****1655, *****1692** in *OED.* **1839** *Spirit of Times* (May 11) 115 (cited in Weingarten *Amer. Dict. Slang*). **1864** in Bensell *Yamhill* 137: "Gobs" of news. **1865** in C.W. Wills *Army Life* 364: All seemed to take "gobs" of comfort from Lee's declaration. **1887** in Bunner *Letters* 124: Give me gobs of time to do it in and I will spread myself. **1911** *Adventure* (Apr.) 953: I bet big money. If your dope is on the level, I'll bet a gob. **1924** in C.M. Russell *Paper Talk* 190: We are meeting gobs of folks and things look O.K. so far. **1928** in Tuthill *Bungle* 101: Spending gobs of money. **1934** Faulkner *Pylon* 44: A gob of cotter keys in her mouth like they tell how women used to do with the pins and needles. **1967–74** in R. Rosenthal et al. *Diff. Strokes* 207: I have—oh, gobs and gobs of phone numbers. **1983** Van Riper *Glenn* 257: Labor gave him gobs of money. **1986** N.Y. State Lottery ad, WINS radio (Mar. 20): I'm talkin' major mazuma!...Gobs o' gold!

gob[2] *n.* [ScotGael & Ir *gob* 'beak, mouth', infl. by *gab*] the mouth. Orig. dial.

*****a***1550** in *OED:* Quhair thair gobbis wer ungeird. *****a***1605** in *OED:* Ile dryt in thy gob. *****1674–91** in *OED:* A Gob, an open or wide mouth. *****1698–99** "B.E." *Dict. Canting Crew:* Gob, the Mouth. *****1785** Grose *Vulgar Tongue:* Gob. The mouth...Gift of the gob; wide-mouthed, or one who speaks fluently, or sings well. *****1819** [T. Moore] *Tom Crib* 18: Home-hits in the *bread-basket,* clicks in the *gob.* *****1833** in *OED:* I thrust half a doubled-up muffin into my gob. **1859** Matsell *Vocab.* 38: Gob. The mouth. **1877** Wheeler *Deadwood Dick, Prince of Road* 84: I smacked him in the gob...for calling me a liar. *****1890–93** *F & H* III 167: Shut your gob! **1929–30** Farrell *Young Lonigan* 17: He was going to walk out...when they blew their gobs off. **1967** in *DARE:* He had a gob full of feed and nevertheless he kept right on talking.

¶ In phrase:

¶ **sluice (one's) gob** to drink liquor heartily.

*****1788** Grose *Vulgar Tongue* (ed. 2): *Sluice your Gob,*—Take a hearty drink. *****1819** [T. Moore] *Tom Crib* 35: We well had *sluiced* our *gobs*...Had drunk heartily. *****1821** *Real Life in London* I 119: The old song, "The Christening of Little Joey," formerly sung by Jemmy Dodd, of facetious memory: "And when they had *sluiced* their *gobs* [etc.]." **1866** *Nat. Police Gaz.* (Apr. 21) 3: After "sluicing" their "gobs" several times, [they] resolved to...[rob] him.

gob[3] *n.* [short for *gobby* or GOBSHITE, *n.*; see *****1890 quot. below] a bluejacket; naval sailor. Also (*obs.*) **gobby.** [App. never restricted in U.S. to the usu. Brit. sense 'coastguardsman'.]

*****1890** in *F & H* III 168: When a meeting takes place the men indulge in a protracted yarn and a draw of the pipe. The session involves a considerable amount of expectoration all round, whereby our friends [coastguardsmen] come to be known as *gobbies.* **1909** in *Our Navy* (Jan. 1910) 19: A nod, a look, a glance of an eye,/And some poor "gob" is money shy. **1910** *Our Navy* (June) 16: The sailor...should properly be called a "bluejacket" or a "man of warsman." "Jacky" is uncalled for and cheapening. Also the use of the slang words "gob" and "gobshite" and "jackshite" is to be deplored. **1914** *DN* IV 150: Gob. n. A bluejacket. **1918** *Camp Meade* (Md.) *Herald* (Feb 1) 3: Any man in the navy is known as a "gob" or "gobbie." He is also known as "flat-foot." **1919** *Our Navy* (Dec.) 31: Secretary Daniels has issued an order to all recruiting stations that the term "gobs" shall no longer be applied to boys in the U.S. Navy. In his order, the name is designated as "ugly." **1928** Scanlon *God Have Mercy* 301 [ref. to 1918]: Beyond Sainte-Menehould we passed quite a few long-range naval guns, manned by gobs. **1929** Bowen *Sea Slang* 58: Gobby. In the British Navy, a coastguard, or in the old days a quarterdeckman. In the American, any bluejacket. **1935** Harbord *Army in France* 294 [ref. to 1918]: This ravine was called Gobert on the maps but the Marines shortened it to Gob Gully. **1938** in W. Burnett *Best* 500: I knowed other gobs before that was O.K. **1939** "E. Queen" *Dragon's Teeth* 163: He's been spending that million Cole left him like a gob on shore leave. **1942** Casey *Torpedo Junction* 21: Below decks the gobs...paid no attention to the seriousness...of the present situation. **1951** [VMF-323] *Old Ballads* 21: 10,000 gobs lay down their swabs just to whip one sick Marine. **1956** in Loosbrock & Skinner *Wild Blue* 200: Honolulu would be crowded with fun-seeking GI's and gobs. **1962** W. Robinson *Barbara* 43 [ref. to WWII]: "Read it and weep, you guys!" the white-hatted gob had yelled. **1962** Quirk *Red Ribbons* 156: He wasn't going to be a lousy gob saluting officers. **1974** A. Marx *Everybody* 104: A man in a gob's suit.

gob *v.* to expectorate (usu. tobacco). *Obs.* in U.S.

1872 *Galaxy* (Jan.) 144: What can be the meaning of a sign that a year or two ago stood...in the Bowery..."Gobbing in the Rear"? *****1881** in *OEDS:* Gob, to spit out; expectorate. *****a***1890–93** *F & H* III 168: Gob...(common).—To expectorate. *****1953** D. Thomas, in *OEDS:* And they gob at a gull for luck.

gobble *n.* **1.** *Golf.* (see 1970 quot.).

*****1857** in P. Davies *Golfing Terms* 74: His only chance lies in a bold put—a rapid gobble over level ground. **1893** in P. Davies *Golfing Terms* 74: *Gobble.*—A rapid straight "putt" into the hole, such that, had the ball not gone in, it would have gone some distance beyond. **1970** Scharff *Encyc. of Golf* 417: *Gobble.* A boldly hit putt that unexpectedly finds the hole.

2. food.

1982 Univ. Tenn. instructor, age 34: Let's get some gobble.

gobble *v.* **1.a.** to grab; seize hastily or eagerly; (*hence*) to steal or make off with.

1825 in *OED:* He...sprang up—gobbled on the clothes...and set off. **1826** T. Jefferson, in *DAE:* Not to have [my property] gobbled up by speculators to make fortunes for themselves. **1850** in B. Hall *College Wds.* (ed. 2) 228: Upon that night, in the broad street, was I by one of the brain-deficient men *gobbled*. **1851** B. Hall *College Wds.*: *Gobble*. At Yale College, to seize; to lay hold of; to appropriate; nearly the same as *to collar*. **1860** in S. Clemens *Twain's Letters* I 104: If they were to die, their administrators would "gobble up" everything you've got. **1861** in C.W. Wills *Army Life* 34: We gobbled up all the loose plunder we could find lying around,...and marched back. *Ibid.* 40: Every horse or mule that showed himself was gobbled instanter. **1863** in Rowell *Artillerymen* 58: Boys went out foraging and gobbled some hogs, plenty of fresh meat now. **1868** Aldrich *Bad Boy* 190: There wasn't nothin' honest I wouldn't have turned a hand to; but the 'longshoremen gobbled up all the work, an' a outsider like me didn't stand a show. **1872** Burnham *Secret Service* 80: The go-between...brings five $20's like the first, which Jake Buck readily gobbles. **1878** in "M. Twain" *Sketches* 387: Any private mine may be "gobbled"...by the baron if it has not been worked during five years previously. **1890** *Overland Mo.* (May) 541: The greasers will gobble your mules some night while you are eating supper. **1898** *Cosmopolitan* 217 [ref. to Civil War]: Hey, you—what you spooking around at this hour for? Want to gobble a blanket or overcoat? **1909** H.L. Mencken, in Riggio *Dreiser-Mencken Letters* I 27: We had only one professional philanthropist in Baltimore...and New York gobbled him a few years ago. **1966** in *DARE: Before anyone else gets it, I'm going to*...Gobble on to it.

b. to win.

1853 in B. Hall *College Wds.* 228: Then shout for the hero who gobbles the prize.

2.a. to catch or apprehend (a person).

1849 in B. Hall *College Wds.* (ed. 2) 228: Alas! how dearly for the fun they paid/Whom the Proffs *gobbled* and the Tutors too. **1864** in C.W. Wills *Army Life* 231: He...mounted on it all the offenders against discipline he could "gobble." **1906** *Army & Navy Life* (Nov.): *Gobbled*. Being caught in a scrape. **1914** Jackson & Hellyer *Vocab.* 38: *Gobbled*...Arrested.

b. *Mil.* to capture or take prisoner. Now *hist.*

*ca***1859** Chamberlain *My Confession* 89 [ref. to Mexican War]: More volunteer cavalry gobbled up! **1861** in *Century Dict.*: Nearly four hundred prisoners were gobbled up after the fight, and any quantity of ammunition & provisions. **1863** in Connolly *Army of Cumberland* 46: We hope to surprise a rebel camp and "gobble" a bunch of prisoners. **1863** in R.G. Carter *4 Bros.* 277: Danger of being gobbled by gorrils, you know they have a way of paroling 'em by running a knife across the wind pipe. **1864** in Connolly *Army of Cumberland* 200: I might possibly be gobbled (that's a standard word in the army), and [if so] address me Major James A. Connolly, Libby Prison, Richmond, VA. **1864** in Hough *Soldier in W.* 219: If our forces are worsted, we here have a "smart" chance of being gobbled. **1890** Goss *Recollections* 59: Uncle Robert...is goin' to gobble up the Yankee army and bring 'em to Richmond. **1892** Cox *5 Yrs.* 20 [ref. to 1873]: It was the special object of "Major Walker's Black Hills Expedition" to keep an eye on this big party [of gold-seekers] and to "gobble" them when they should attempt invasion of the sacred lands of the reservation. **1953–55** Kantor *Andersonville* 88 [ref. to Civil War]: Sixty-odd men gobbled by the Rebs in less time than a heifer'd take to switch her tail. **1957** O'Connor *Co. Q* 3 [ref. to Civil War]: We'll gobble up their sentries and ride through their bivouac.

3. *Mil.* to vanquish, rout, or destroy.

1864 in Andrus *Letters* 87: About eleven o'clock P.M. the Straglers from the flight come up with us & reported the whole thing gobbled up and the Reb cavalry following close behind them. **1864** Fosdick *Frank on a Gun-Boat* 185: I hope to thunder that you will be gobbled up. **1865** in Norton *Army Letters* 253: When this was done, the 20,000 was to break through our line on the right and gobble us all up. **1877** Bartlett *Amer.* (ed. 4) 249: *Gobble up*...to rout; to scatter; to vanquish. Much used in the late Civil War, and, in somewhat modified applications, is still sometimes used.

4. to copulate orally with.—also constr. *with off*.

*a***1927** in P. Smith *Letter from Father* 98: I could hardly go a day without gobbling her. **1927** [Fliesler] *Anecdota* 188: I'm always a Goblin under de sheets. ***1928** N. Douglas *Some Limericks*: There was an old buggar of Como/Who suddenly cried "Ecce Homo!"/He tracked his man down/To the heart of the town/And gobbled him off in the duomo. *ca***1935** in Barkley *Sex Cartoons* 76: I'll gobble for nix...A man with a prick like you've got must save his money. **1968** J.W. Wells *Taboo Breakers* 68: He saw Marcia...getting herself gobbled.

5. [sugg. by TURKEY, *n.*] *Entertainment Industry.* (see quot.).

1971 Dahlskog *Dict.* 27: *Gobble, v.* To fail or bomb, as a theatrical production that closes after one or two performances.

¶ In phrase: **gobble the goop** [or **goo** or **gook** or **goose**] to perform fellatio or cunnilingus.—usu. considered vulgar.

1918–19 in Carey *Mlle. from Armentières* I (unp.): Oh, Mademoiselle from Niedermendig/Gobbled the Goop for fünfzehn pfennig." *Ibid.* II (unp.): The Mademoiselle from Bar-le-Duc/Taught the Yanks to gobble the goop. **1941** G. Legman, in G. Henry *Sex Vars.* II 1167: *Gobble the goo.* To practice fellation. Also: *gobble the goop* and *gobble the goose*. **1957** in *AS* XXXIV (Feb. 1959) 44: Let me enlighten you on the true meaning of the word [*gobbledygook*]...Gobble (eat) Dy (the) Gook (penis). The phrase originated in Chicago's once notorious "Levee" in the 1890's and was used up to the start of the "Depression"...It is not a word, but a three word phrase...[signed] An Old Rounder. **1969** Girodias *New Olympia Reader* 631: But I have experienced cases where the girl was perfectly willing to be sucked, but did not actually care to risk the loss of her dignity gobbling the goo. **1973** *Zap Comix* (No. 6) (unp.): Gobble the goop, mama. **1974** *Nat. Lampoon* (Oct.) 36: Discreet semaphores to your fellow goop-gobblers. **1974** Loken *Come Monday Mornin'* 50: Who was down gobblin' my gook three seconds [later]? **1974** E. Thompson *Tattoo* 188: She got right down in broad daylight standin outside the car, me layin back in the seat and gobbled the goop. **1984** H. Gould *Cocktail* 10: Another night of goose gobbling. This Lit Major was taking her orals the hard way. *a***1973–87** F.M. Davis *Livin' the Blues* 36 [ref. to Kans., *ca*1920]: Fellatio was beyond our ken, but we all knew what happened when a person "gobbled the goo."

gobbledygoo *n.* [alter. of phr. *gobble the goo* s.v. GOBBLE, *v.*] **1.** *Pros.* (see quots.). Also **gobblegoo.**

*a***1938** in D.W. Maurer *Lang. Und.* 116: *Gobblegoo.* A prostitute who prefers intercourse through the mouth. **1941** G. Legman, in G. Henry *Sex Vars.* II 1167: In prostitutes' slang a fellatrice is called a *gobbledegoo*.

2. GOBBLEDYGOOK, *n.*

1963 S. Plath, in J.P. Hunter *Norton Intro. Poetry* (ed. 2) 61: I have always been scared of *you*,/With your Luftwaffe, your gobbledygoo.

gobbledygook *n.* [cf. GOBBLEDYGOO] pretentious or deceptive nonsense; MALARKEY; (*specif.*) language characterized by pomposity, circumlocution, or jargon. Now *S.E.* [Introduced in its specific sense by Maury Maverick, chairman of the Smaller War Plants Corp., early 1944.]

1944 *Amer. N & Q* (Apr.) 9: *Gobbledygook talk:* Maury Maverick's name for the long high-sounding words of Washington's red-tape language. **1944** *Time* (Apr. 10) 57: Maury Maverick, fluent, fiery but literate Texas talker, railed against what he called Washington's "gobbledygook" language..."Anyone using the words 'activation' or 'implementation' will be shot." **1944** M. Maverick, in *N.Y. Times Mag.* (May 21) 11: Gobbledygook...People asked me how I got the word. I do not know. It must have come in a vision. Perhaps I was thinking of the old bearded turkey gobbler back in Texas. **1945** in *OEDS*: The explanations sound like gobbledegook to me. **1956** Heinlein *Door* 32: Skipping the gobbledegook—like all lawyers, Miles was fond of polysyllables.—Miles wanted to do three things. **1957** in Sandburg *Letters* 513: He knew gobbledygook but didn't talk it. **1958** Frankel *Band of Bros.* 51 [ref. to 1950]: Everybody's got his own kind of gobbledygook. *a***1962** in Morris & Morris *Dict. Wd. & Phr. Orig.* I 156: I can report...[having learned the word *gobbledygook* from] Mess Sergeant Bacher, Co. F, 112th U.S. Engineers, at Camp Sheridan, Montgomery, Alabama, in August 1917:...When I order beef, I get corned Willie! When I order spuds, I get beans! And when I holler at them, all I get is a bunch of *gobbledygook!* *a***1962** in *Ibid.*: *Gobbledygook*...I first heard this word [long before 1944] when I was a schoolboy in northwestern Pennsylvania and it had the same meaning—confused, meaningless words—that it has today. **1968** Mackey *Family Meeting* 233: Speeches, tears, glorified tributes, dressed-up gobbledygook. **1972** J. Pearl *Cops* 11: Tony had been appalled by the gobbledygook on the police frequencies,...The seemingly inane and unintelligible prattle. **1972** *Life* (Oct. 27) 26: English to Creole to gobbledygook. **1992** L. Johnson *My Posse* 103: He was chanting some goobledygook [*sic*]. **1993** Sachar *Let Lady Teach* 57: This was gobbledygook, word soup!

gobble pipe *n. Music.* a saxophone. *Joc.*

1935 *Vanity Fair* (Nov.) 71: *Gobble pipe* for saxophone.

gobbler *n.* **1.** a performer of fellatio or cunnilingus.

*a***1927** in P. Smith *Letter from Father* 78: She was some gobbler. **1932** in *AS* (Feb. 1934) 26: *Gobbler.* A degenerate. **1942–49** Goldin et al. *DAUL* 83: *Gobbler.* A male oral sodomist. **1975** C.W. Smith *Country Music* 216: Ginger? A...gobbler? Would wonders never cease?

2. *Entertainment Industry.* (see quot.).

1971 Dahlskog *Dict.* 27: *Gobbler*...Something that fails; a turkey.

gobble-up *n. Army.* a capture.

1864 Gilbert *Confed. Letters* 36: Now he talks of…"gobble ups."

gobby *n.* see GOB³, *n.*

goblin *n. Navy.* a Soviet submarine.

1962 Farago *10th Fleet* 308: Black diamond-shaped markers indicate the "goblins" on a wall-to-wall map. They are Soviet submarines presumed to be at large in specific ocean areas.

goblin juice *n.* whiskey. *Joc.*

1969 H.A. Smith *Buskin* 117: When he was ready to drive to the battlefield, he concealed a flask of goblin juice on his person.

goboon *n.* [*gob* + spitt*oon*] a spittoon.

1931 *Amer. Merc.* (Dec.) 408: Spittoons, goboons. **1931** J.T. Farrell *McGinty* 40: McGinty stumbled over and overturned goboon. **1936** Washburn *Parlor* 99: The gold gobboons, too, came in for a bit of heralding. **1942** in Botkin *Sidewalks* 209: The brass "gaboon" on the tiled floor. **1944** in J.I. White *Git Along Dogies* 112: He makes his biscuits in a goboon.

gobshite *n.* **1.** *Navy.* an enlisted seaman; bluejacket; GOB³. Also **gobshike.**

1909 in *Our Navy* (Jan. 1910) 20: It came to pass, a charming lass,/Sat bravely down and wrote/A young "Gob-shyte" she met one night,/A cunning little note. **1910** *Ibid.* (Mar.) 21: You can imagine all the feelin's/In a foolish "gobshite's" breast. **1910** (quot. at GOB³, *n.*). **1914** *DN* IV 150: Gobshite. *n.* = gob [bluejacket]. **1916** *Our Navy* (Apr.) 33: Little matter of a Gob-shyte's duds going up in smoke. **1918** Ruggles *Navy Explained* 10: Gobshike. **1919** *Our Navy* (June) 48: Take beware also honorable gobshite.

2. [prob. GOB² + *shite* (dial. var. of SHIT, *n.*); cf. *1890 quot. at GOB³] an expectorated wad of chewing tobacco; expectorated tobacco juice. [Presumably the earlier sense.]

1918 Noyes (unp.): Gob. = sailor. derived from the term "gob-shite" or excretion from chewing tobacco.

gob-stick *n.* **1.** usu. *pl.* a spoon; an eating utensil.

*1789, *1792, *1797, *1809, *1846, *1848 (cited in Partridge *Dict. Und.* 296). **1859** Matsell *Vocab.* 38: Gobsticks. Silver forks or spoons. *ca*1890–93 F & H IV 169: Gob-stick…(nautical), a horn or wooden spoon.

2. a clarinet; (*also*) a fife.

1923 McKnight *English Words* 45: Gob stick, silver sucker (clarinet). **1926** Norwood *Other Side of Circus* 236: Then we call a clarinet a gob stick. **1939** Calloway *Swingformation Bureau*: A stick or gob stick is a…clarinet. **1953–55** Kantor *Andersonville* 618: He said that sometimes musicians referred to their fifes as gob-sticks; again, he didn't know why.

go-cart *n.* an automobile. *Joc.*

1915 Bronson-Howard *God's Man* 198: Who wouldn't, with a little ten-thousand-dollar go-cart sent around afternoon to ride her around again, Willie. **1961** Heinlein *Stranger* 145: Get your go-cart out of my flower beds.

gock *n.* GUCK, *n.*

1970 in *Barnhart Dict. New Eng.* 189. **1973** N.Y.C. schoolteacher, age 27: It's all covered with gock.

God *n.* ¶ In phrases:

¶ **by guess and by God** Orig. *Naut.* without a set course; (*hence*) by reliance on common sense or intuition rather than on knowledgeable technique. Also vars.

1909 in *OEDS* s.v. *Godfrey*: If ever a craft was steered by guess and by godfrey, 'twas that old hooker. **1929** Hammett *Maltese Falcon* 52: You've got to convince me…that you're not simply fiddling around by guess and by God, hoping it'll come out all right somehow in the end. **1934** Binns *Lightship* 235: On deck, things were done by guess and by God. **1934** Cunningham *Triggernometry* 393: Drummond took charge of one of the ancient Spanish muzzle-loaders which was trained "by-guess-and-by-God" out toward the Nicaraguan vessel. **1943** in *DA*: No more job training "by guess and by God." **1984** Kagan & Summers *Mute Evidence* 193: It was necessary to use a "guess and by golly" system of estimation when administering [a drug] to an animal.

¶ **God's teeth** [or **guts**]! (used to express amazement).

1927 Saunders *Wings* 116: God's teeth! What the 'ell are you doing in 'ere? **1930** in Farrell *Calico Shoes* 34: God's guts, she's used to it. **1937** Odets *Golden Boy* 264: God's teeth! Who says you have to be one thing? **1943** Hersey *Adano* 188: "God's teeth," said Lieutenant Commander Robertson, "that's the first Army man I ever saw that was willing to give the Navy credit."

¶ **God's zounds!** (used to express amazement).

1778 Connor *Songbag* 25: God's zounds says the people that live in that place.

god-awful *adj. & adv.* tremendous (*obs.*); (*also*) terrible; extraordinarily bad. As adv., terribly; extraordinarily. Now *colloq.*

1877 Beadle *West. Wilds* 611: Went to work with a hurrah…to make a God-awful crop. **1897** in *DAE:* Ellis is such a God awful fool. **1938** Bellem *Blue Murder* 53: She got me in one God-awful mess. **1945** *Reader's Digest* (June) 42: They said there was the most god-awful crash when the car plunged off the track and turned over. **1951** Pryor *The Big Play* 239: It's God-awful hot. **1952** "E. Box" *Fifth Position* 114: It was godawful today. **1957** Hecht *Charlie* 184: Godawful crap. **1960** Bannon *Journey* 36: They did a godawful job. **1966** Olsen *Hard Men* 58: That is a godawful way to punish a man. **1967** J. Kramer *Instant Replay* 142: It is one of the most Godawful things I've seen in a long time. **1982** Heat Moon *Blue Hwys.* 17: Sitting full in the moment, I practiced on the god-awful difficulty of just paying attention. **1988** *N.Y. Post* (June 6) 6: I hated the god-awful lecturing and group therapy.

god-blessed *adj.* (a euphem. for) GODDAMNED.

1980 Conroy *Lords of Discipline* 14: You god-blessed fellow traveler Leninist.

godbox *n.* **1.** a church.—used derisively.

*1917 *Living Age* (Nov. 10) 380: On one occasion we ourselves fell in with an atheist who persistently referred to churches as "god-boxes." *1928 J. Galsworthy, in *OEDS*: This great box—God-box the Americans would call it—had been made centuries before the world became industrialised. **1980** Manchester *Darkness* 159 [ref. to WWII]: They…drank hair tonic…and never went to chapel ("the God-box").

2. Esp. *Jazz.* an organ. *Joc.*

1937 *AS* (Oct.) 181: Godbox. Organ. **1942** *Time* (Mar. 2) 80: "Godbox" is given for church but not [as a word] for organ. **1960** A. Shaw *Belafonte* 311 (quot. Thomas "Fats" Waller): First Mr. Dupré played the God-box and then I played the God-box. **1980** S. Fuller *Big Red* 15: The first church we find that has an organ, I want you to play on the god-box for the French.

goddamn *n.* a damn (used as a symbol of worthlessness). Also **goddam.**

1847 in Peskin *Vols.* 127: I don't care a God damn how you cook. **1876** J.M. Reid *Old Settlers* 143 [ref. to 1847]: "General, what do you think of it?"…Not worth a G—d d—n!" **1899** J.S. Wise *End of Era* 382 [ref. to Civil War]: They don't know, and don't care a —— —— about that! **1905** in A. Adams *Chisholm Trail* 119: That little fellow…is the only man in my outfit that is worth a —— ——. [**1908** in Fleming *Unforget. Season* 113: Nobody seemed to give a gosh darn.] *a*1921 in W.D. Lane *Civil War in W. Va.* 60: Don't matter a God damn, you get off of this river on that noon train in the morning. **1921** R. McAlmon *Hasty Bunch* 277: They…don't give a goddam. **1925** *AS* I (Dec.) 135: I don't give a good God dam. **1929** E. Caldwell *Bastard* 32: Flo ain't worth a good God-damn! **1934** H. Miller *Tropic of Cancer* 124: He wasn't worth a good goddamn. **1935** T. Wolfe *Time & River* 487: Do you think I care one good God-damn now for all the courts and laws that ever were? **1950** Bissell *Stretch on the River* 52: She did not give a good goddamn what kind of hat the girl at the next table had on. **1953** R. Wright *Outsider* 103: I don't give a good goddamn *what* you've done! **1971** T. Robbins *Roadside* 9: I do not give a rusty goddamn what these butterflies are called in Greek. **1976** Arble *Long Tunnel* 138: It don't make a goddam how smart you are. **1983** S. Wright *Meditations* 7: Now I know the majority of you could give a good goddamn about the welfare of these people. **1986–91** Hamper *Rivethead* 56: They really don't give a god-damn.

goddamn *adj. & adv.* see GODDAMNED.

goddamn *interj.* (used to express anger, astonishment, pain, disappointment, etc.). Also **goddam.**

*1832 B. Hall *Voyages* (Ser. 2) II 235 [ref. to 1812]: Johanna man like English very much. God d—n!…Very fine day. **1845** Corcoran *Pickings* 172: I say no, G—d d—n. [**1851** M. Reid *Scalp Hunters* 72: The "sacre" and the English "God-dam" were hurled at everything Mexican.] **1858** in C.A. Abbey *Before the Mast* 153: Guess he thought "G-d d--n." **1898** in *OEDS*: Before I could say "Goddam"…they would be fired. **1905** Sinclair *Jungle* 250: The first time that the little rascal burst out with "God damn," his father nearly rolled off the chair with glee. **1935** Odets *Waiting for Lefty*: Maybe get killed, but goddamn! We'll go ahead! **1946** Steinbeck *Wayward Bus* 103: But she had beautiful eyes, he thought. God-damn, she was a looker! **1967** Baraka *Tales* 14: Ow, goddamn. **1978**

Univ. Tenn. student: Well, goddamn! What's he gonna do?

goddamn *infix.* (used as an intensifier).

1924 Anderson & Stallings *What Price Glory?* 118 [ref. to 1918]: Toot sweet—toot sweet—toot God damn sweet. **1927** Niles *Singing Soldier* 46 [ref. to 1918]: The drivers of army motor vehicles were said to be "ambigodamdextrous" and knew the roads besides… **1927** in E. Wilson *Twenties* 414: Who told yuh yuh could be so indegoddampendent? **1954** F. Hunt *MacArthur* [ref. to 1917] 68: How these proud bucks enjoyed answering the inevitable question, "Where you from, Buddy," with their standard reply, "We're from Alagoddambam." **1955** Semmes *Portrait of Patton* 261: He stated that he didn't want to be under any "obli-goddam-gations" to the Russians. **1963** Coon *Short End* 141: I guarangoddamnedtee you you'll get one hell of a lot worse from me. **1965** Herlihy *Midnight Cowboy* 42: And one young soldier, who claimed he was from Cinci-goddam-nati, had this remarkable system of fitting cusswords into unexpected corners of his talk. **1972** Pearce *Pier Head Jump* 138: O-kay. O-god-damn-kay. **1982** Heat Moon *Blue Hwys.* 97: Selma, everlovin' Alagoddamnbama. **1986** E. Weiner *Howard the Duck* 138: Microgoddamscopic baby zucchini! **1987** S. Martin *Roxanne* (film): I can be effergoddamnvescent.

goddamned or **goddamn** *adj. & adv.* **1.** accursed; most damnable.—freq. with weakened force as a mere intensive.—usu. considered vulgar. [Unquestionably older than the available citations suggest; Burton's remark in 1860–61 quot. indicates that he believed this modifier to be an Americanism.]

[*1697 D. Defoe, in G. Hughes *Swearing* 209: *God Damn ye*, does not sit well upon a Female Tongue.] [*1723 *Comical Pilgrim* 63: Up nimbly, Boys, G— d— you, all together.] [1816 in J.K. Williams *Vogues in Villainy* 15: A villain overtook me…and said you *God dambd Brasington* and…gave me a blow…on my left cheek.] **1844** in R.F. Burton *City of Saints* 599: He opened and read a number of the documents himself, and as he proceeded, he was frequently interrupted by "that's a lie, that's a God damned lie," "that's an infernal falsehood," "that's a blasted lie," &c. **1847** in Peskin *Vols.* 22: I'm God damned if I care. *Ibid.*: I was so God damned drunk. **1856** *N.Y. Times* (Jun. 26) 6: I have heard Brigham Young say in the pulpit…[that Elder John] Taylor was a G—d d—d son of a b—h, and he wished he was rotten in hell. **1853–60** Olmsted *Texas* 438: We've concluded that you are a God damn'd abolitionist. **1860–61** R.F. Burton *City of Saints* 18: The owner addresses to the clumsy-handed driver the universal G— d—, which in these lands changes from…expletive…to an adjectival development. **1861** in F. Moore *Rebel Rec.* I P78: It was finally decided to hang the "God damned spy." **1864** in Redkey *Grand Army* 54: We will never forget the cry of "Kill the G—d d—n s—s of b—s," when the 54th Massachusetts went into the fight. **1873** in R.H. Dillon *Shanghaiing Days* 150: It serves me goddamned right. *1894 in *OED* (s.v. *God, n.*, def. 8): I'll burn every God-damned house I come to. **1914** W.H. Fink *Ludlow* 25: Your God damn right I did. **1918** O'Brien *Wine, Women & War* 29: I'll be the same God damned crab I was when I went away. **1917–20** Dreiser *Newspaper Days* 233 [ref. to ca1893]: She's no Goddamned good. **1922** in Hemingway *Sel. Letters* 62: Joyce has a most god-damn wonderful book. **1924** Marks *Plastic Age* 237: You can goddamn well bet that I'm not going to leave until I get them back. **1928** J.M. March *Set-Up* 34: And be goddamned thankful. **1929–31** Farrell *Young Lonigan* 59 [ref. to 1916]: Studs Lonigan was one pretty Goddamn good physical specimen. *Ibid.* 100: It made him Goddamn sore. *Ibid.* 150: They're goddamn different from Iris. **1931** in Fitzgerald *Corres.* 261: I miss you so Goddamn much. **1931** E. Pound, in Ahearn *Pound/Zukofsky* 88: It is god damn well time for some agitation. **1936** Farrell *World I Never Made* 67: Well, it's too goddamn bad about her. **1938** Bezzerides *Long Haul* 155: You God damn near went over. **1940** Zinberg *Walk Hard* 7: That was one goddam good left hook. **1942** Hurston *Dust Tracks* 30: He remarked that I was a God-damned fine baby. **1946** Steinbeck *Wayward Bus* 103: But he was angry at the blonde. The goddamned hustler. **1978** in Lyle & Golenbock *Bronx Zoo* 125: Roy White is probably the nicest Goddamn guy on the club. **1979** Kienzle *Rosary Murders* 38: It was one of the most goddam satisfying moments I've ever had.

2. extraordinary or exasperating.—used in superlative only.

1847 in J.M. McCaffrey *Manifest Destiny* 80: This is the G—d damnedest shot of work I ever saw yet. ca1863 in Wiley & Milhollen *They Who Fought* 30: We run under some of the god dames [*sic*] hills. [1884 "M. Twain" *Huck Finn* ch. xiv: He had some er de dad-fetcheds' ways I ever see.] **1917–20** Dreiser *Newspaper Days* 344 [ref. to 1890's]: You…are the Goddamnedest man I ever knew. **1939** Appel *People Talk* 316: That was the God-damnest fire I ever did see. **1944–49** Allardice

At War 43: This is the God-damndest outfit I ever saw. **1952** Bissell *Monongahela* 8: Ain't this here Blue Beetle the goddamnedest? **1954** N.Y.C. man, age *ca*70: Ain't that the goddamnedest thing you ever heard? **1956** M. Wolff *Big Nick.* 39: She's the goddamnedest woman I ever knew, that's what she's like!

Godfrey *n.* God.—used in mild oaths.

1853–60 Olmsted *Texas* 14: By Godfrey,…you ought not to have missed that. **1868** in *AS* 63 (Summer 1988) 115: By Godfrey, them thet's got luck kin hev anything else. **1963–64** Kesey *Great Notion* 7: I'll by godfrey say he changed his plans. **1977** Coover *Public Burning* 79: By Godfrey Daniel, we ain't been knocked outa this ballgame yet!

God-hopper *n.* a very religious person, esp. an evangelist.—used derisively.

1942 *ATS* 416: *God-hopper*, a religious person. **1953** in Hemingway *Sel. Letters* 807: I have…never been a cane brake God hopper.…Never trust a God-hopper either North or South of the Macy-Dixie line.

go down *v.* **1.** *Und. & Police.* to be arrested, convicted, and imprisoned; go to prison.

*1906 in *OEDS*: "Going down," as it is termed, for seven or fourteen days…The same youth will "go down" time after time, and become more reckless and indifferent with every repetition. **1915–16** Lait *Beef, Iron & Wine* 35: He went down for burglary. **1925** in Handy *Blues Treasury* 161: Rock Pile Blues…Went down for stealin' 'cause I didn't have a dime./ Nothing will relieve me but the thing called father time. **1927–28** in R. Nelson *Dishonorable* 170: And since Beauty went down you've been singin' at Wieberg's. **1942–49** Goldin et al. *DAUL* 83: We go to bat [stand trial] tomorrow. I still figure we're going down. **1968** "H. King" *Box-Man* 102: Two or three box-men…went down the same way. **1984** *Miami Vice* (NBC-TV): When he goes down, he goes down hard! **1992** *CBS This Morning* (CBS-TV) (May 1): I think all four cops should've gone down.

2.a. to perform fellatio or cunnilingus.

1916 Cary *Venery* I 112: *Going Down*—To tongue a woman, or suck a man. **1917–20** Dreiser *Newspaper Days* 590 [ref. to 1894]: They go down on you…play the flute. Aren't you on? **1927** [Fliesler] *Anecdota* 67: A notorious cock-sucker was once caught going down on one of the midgets. **1929** in E. Wilson *Twenties* 524: She started to go down on me but stopped and wouldn't finish. *ca*1929 *Collection of Sea Songs* 11: Though you went down on me/In days that used to be/I live in pregnancy among my souvenirs. **1930** *Lyra Ebriosa* 24: Every night at half-past eight they'd go down on each other. **1944** Micheaux *Mrs. Wingate* 51: The Negro said that Frank *went down* on women. **1949** *Gay Girl's Gde.* 10: Go Down On: A quasi-straight term for…"blow." **1951** Mailer *Barbary Shore* 47: He goes down on her and everything. **1956** Chamales *Never So Few* 538: The Doc asked him if he had ever gone down on a woman. **1970** *Nat. Lampoon* (Apr.) 58: They knew that women get to the top by "going down!" **1990** *Cosmopolitan* (May) 340: If she gets up, leans over, and goes down on you just thank your lucky stars and rest assured it's worth doing the same to her.

b. (of a woman) to engage readily in sexual intercourse; PUT OUT.

1968 Lockridge *Hartspring* 113: I've got a…pal says there isn't a girl in the world won't go down with somebody. **1970** Standish *Non-Stand. Terms* 14: Go Down also refers to a female's submission to the male's desire for coitus, as in "She went down for him." **1971** Dahlskog *Dict.* 27: Go down, v. *Vulgar.* Of a girl, to have sexual intercourse…as: She *goes down* only for him. **1974** Strasburger *Rounding Third* 66: Isn't it enough that she's willing to go down for you? **1983** Neaman & Silver *Kind Words* 234: Promiscuous…*She goes down!*

c. to copulate.

1978 Sopher & McGregor *Up from Walking Dead* 22: The brothers had a broad up on a rooftop. Everyone was invited to go down on her.

3. Orig. *Black E.* to happen; take place.

1946 Mezzrow & Wolfe *Really Blues* 186 [ref. to 1930's]: Sure it ain't nothin' freakish goin' down 'tween you two? *Ibid.* 305: *Go down:* happen. **1947** *Time* (Feb. 10) 12: Help us pick up on what's going down. **1956** Holiday & Dufty *Lady Sings the Blues* 157: In view of what went down later, who can say? **1961** in J. Blake *The Joint* 281: I know immediately what's going down. **1965** C. Brown *Manchild* 286: They couldn't be aware of…what was going down. **1968** Heard *Howard St.* 35: Rosemary said that you seen what went down with my brother last night. **1968** Brautigan *Pill vs. Springhill* 44: That's the way it's going down. **1968** in *Rolling Stone Interviews* 56: You gotta know what's going down. **1976** *S.W.A.T.* (NBC-TV): What's going down between you and Beau? **1978** *Rolling Stone* (Mar. 23) 11: He told me…about what's been going down in your life and career. **1993** *As World Turns* (CBS-

TV): No matter what went down with Scott and Neil that night.

4. *Und.* to attack or fight, as with a rival street gang.—constr. with *on.* Also absol.

[**1954** *Harper's Mag.* (Nov.) 38: One gang will "come down" on another or "turn it on."] **1958** *Life* (Apr. 14) 127 [ref. to *ca*1950]: Man, when we goin' down? **1958** Salisbury *Shook-up Generation* 33: Let's go down! I'm going to get me a guinea. **1959** W. Miller *Cool World* 34: Rod say. "We shoulda gone down on the Wolves right away after they beat up on you. We shoulda revenged you." **1962** Larner & Tefferteller *Addict in the Street* 228: When the Maros asked us to go down on another club, we went. **1966** Samuels *People vs. Baby* 38: A dozen Dragons "went down" on the Vikings that week with bats, blades, and a sawed-off shotgun. **1966–67** P. Thomas *Mean Streets* 227 [ref. to 1940's]: He had been alone and he still had gone down; cool stud, hard stud. **1974** Gober *Black Cop* 180: How do you expect to stay alive when we go down against the big boys if you can't deal with one man.

5. *Police.* to sleep on duty.

1973 (quot. at HUDDLE, *v.*).

God squad *n.* **1.** a group of religionists; (*Mil.*) a chaplain and his assistants.—usu. used derisively.

1965 Matthiessen *Fields of Lord* 14: Oh, yeah…The God Squad, huh? **1968–70** *Current Slang* III & IV 57: *God squad,* n. Any religious organization on campus.—College students, both sexes, Minnesota. **1971** J. Shepherd, in *Playboy* (May) 110 [ref. to WWII]: God Squad Gorman, our nearsighted battalion chaplain, had been trying to get transferred himself for over a year. **1971** Dahlskog *Dict.* 27: *God squad,* n. Those in the ministry; the chaplains in the armed services. **1973** Browne *Body Shop* 50: We called ourselves God Squad Six. **1976** C.R. Anderson *Grunts* 56 [ref. to 1969]: This member of the general's "God Squad" was actually going to hump with them. **1978** Cleaver *Soul on Fire* 223: The God Squad—a nickname of an organization called Follow-up Ministries. **1983** "J. Cain" *Dinky-Dau* 55: They trucked sixth platoon down to the post chapel and introduced them to the "God Squad." **1984** Riggan *Free Fire* 224: They all wear their caps, all the members of the God Squad.

2. *Pol.* the Endangered Species Committee, a cabinet-level committee authorized to reduce the protection of a species under the Endangered Species Act to benefit business. [The committee was formed in 1978.]

1991 *Time* (Dec. 9) 72: Interior Secretary Manuel Lujan Jr. announced he would convene the so-called God Squad, a Cabinet-level committee that can override the Endangered Species Act in the regional or national interest. **1992** *Nation* (Mar. 30) 417: This allows the President to convene a panel, dubbed the "god squad," to exempt protected species from coverage of the act. **1992** *New Republic* (Aug. 10) 4: Examples include the Endangered Species Act God Squad reducing protection of the Olympic Forest and Spotted Owl.

godunk *n.* [orig. unkn.] *Av.* (see quot.).

1933 Stewart *Airman Speech* 68: *Godunk.* A person who will fly anywhere if he can go free.

Godzilla shot *n.* [sugg. by *Godzilla,* dinosaurlike monster in the film *Godzilla* (1955)] *Tennis.* (see quot.).

1976 *AS* LI 293: *Godzilla shot.* Rising backhand smash on the volley.

godzillion *n.* [*Godzilla,* film monster + ZILLION] an unimaginably great number.

1982 Univ. Tenn. instructor, age 33: The guy's got godzillions [of dollars]. **1986** *Morning Edition* (Nat. Pub. Radio) (May 14): America can turn out godzillions of [top] athletes.

go-easter *n. West.* a valise or traveling bag.

*ca*1888 (quot. at BABY HERDER). *a*1890–93 *F & H* III 170: *Go-easter*…(American cowboys').—A portmanteau. **1922** Rollins *Cowboy* 264: "Boughten" bags of carpet or of imitation leather…the punchers often termed "go-easters." **1927–30** Rollins *Jinglebob* 14 [ref. to 1880's]: Their "go-easters"…in other words, leather traveling bags.

go-fasters *n.pl.* USMC. (see quot.).

1987 D. da Cruz *Boot* 300: *Go-fasters.* running shoes.

gofer *n.* [resp. of *go for,* punning on *gopher*] a usu. submissive subordinate who is typically required to run routine errands and do other menial tasks; errand boy; lackey. Also **gofor, gopher.**

1930 *Amer. Mercury* (Dec.) 456: *Gofor,* n.: A dupe. "Listen monkey, don't be a gofor all your life." **1946–51** Motley *We Fished* 439: And…the voters knew that Don was strictly a "go-for." **1963** Morgan *Six-Eleven* 257: Sometimes they turn into glorified gophers—"Go for

the script in the car…go for some coffee…go for the make-up." **1964** Larner & Tefferteller *Addict* 99: Or you can tell a fellow you're a gopher. You know the pusher and you'll gopher narcotics. **1964** *Outer Limits* (ABC-TV): My loyal, faithful gofer going to turn fink on me? **1968** Safire *New Language of Politics* 166: *Gopher.* One who will "go for" coffee and run errands in a political headquarters. **1970** *Playboy* (Nov.) 254: They sent one of the studio "go-fers" to a nearby market. **1971** Horan *Blue Messiah* 23: A gofer was usually an old drunk or a young kid on the docks who did nothing but go for coffee in the morning, sandwiches at noon, and containers of beer in the afternoon. **1972** *Playboy* (Aug.) 73: I was a go-fer, a stagehand. I swept out studios. **1972** T.C. Bambara *Gorilla* 88: Aunt Gretchen…was the main gofer in the family. **1983** *Minding Your Business* (Mutual Radio Network) (Apr. 12): Treating his assistant as a problem-solver one minute and a gopher the next. **1993** *N.Y. Times* (July 1) D 1: A few gofers eager to learn a thing or two between errands.

gofer *v.* to be a gofer; run errands.

1964 (quots. at GOFER, *n.*). **1971** Horan *Blue Messiah* 23: Tom…told me between gofering.

go-getter *n.* a remarkably effective person or thing; *specif.,* an energetic, ambitious, enterprising person. Now *colloq.*

1910 in E. Rhodes *Novels* 76: He was a regular go-getter. *ca*1880–1914 in *DN* IV 107: *Go-getter*…A thing productive of results. **1921** S. Ford *Inez & Trilby* May 26: Think you're one of these go-getters, do you? **1922** in *OEDS.* **1924** H.L. Mencken, in Riggio *Dreiser-Mencken Letters* II 517: He talks and acts like a Rotary Club go-getter, but he prints many good books. **1926** Nason *Chevrons* 129: Oh, this is going to be a tough fight! Oh, this is going to be a go-getter of a battle! **1932** *AS* VII 258: A rustler was the type of man we call a *go-getter* today. **1933** Weseen *Dict. Slang* 342: *Go-getter*—An aggressive person who is full of vitality. **1947** Blankfort *Big Yankee* 102: Now, he became the go-getter, the smart, jump-to-your-feet, prompt, efficient, think-ahead young man. **1970** *Nat. Lampoon* (Aug.) 44: She's a mean motor scooter and a bad go-getter. **1992** Hosansky & Sparling *Working Vice* 155: He was a hard worker.…A go-getter.

goggle-eyed *adj.* wearing spectacles.

1881 Nye *Forty Liars* 16: They have sunk beneath the fire-waters of the goggle-eyed Caucasian. **1906** in Botkin *Sidewalks* 225: Being "goggle-eyed" (i.e., wearing glasses).

goggles *n.pl.* **1.** the eyes.

***1710** in *OED:* Whose dim Goggles cou'd not bear the Rays of the Sun. *a*1763 in *OED:* When on a fair day he fixes his Goggles. *1815 in *OED:* Villains…glare with their goggles. *1821–26* Stewart *Man-of-War's-Man* II 185: Well, Jack, I always thought your goggles were in better trim than I find them are now. **1846** in H.L. Gates, Jr. *Sig. Monkey* 95: De organ ob sight…called de "blinkers," de "goggles," de "peepers," [etc.]. **1972** Andrews & Dickens *Big House* 32: Your goggles have been constantly exploring my woman's aphrodisiac loveliness.

2. spectacles.

1871 Bagg *Yale* 45: Gig-lamps and goggles, eye-glasses. **1884** "M. Twain" *Huck Finn* 12: Her sister, Miss Watson, a tolerable slim old maid, with goggles on, had just come to live with her. **1898** Green *Va. Folk-speech* 163: Goggles…Spectacles. **1920** *Am. Leg. Wkly.* (Feb. 13) 17: Gertie, hand me your goggles before he gets here. **1926** MacIsaac *Tin Hats* 42: Take yer spectacles off. It's ag'inst the law to hit a man with goggles. **1927** Mayer *Between Us Girls* 32: Odd-looking girls with large-sized horn-rimmed goggles.

goggle-box *n.* a television set; television.

*1959 in *OEDS:* Switch the goggle-box on at 10 a.m. *1967 in *OEDS:* Mr. Wilson was…so good at television appearances, that he had convinced himself that he, single-handed, could "win elections with the help of the goggle box." **1981** *TV Guide* (Dec. 12) 21: One summer night I was sitting in front of the goggle box, waiting for a ball game to come on.

go-go fund *n. Finance.* (see quot.).

1983 Pessin & Ross *Words of Wall St.* 100: *Go-go fund.* Popular name for investment companies that specialize in highly speculative ventures.

gohicle [*go* + ve*hicle*] a vehicle. *Joc.*

1858 J.C. Reid *Tramp* 108: A corporal's guard…drew up by the side of our "gohicle."

go in *v.* to die.

1865 C.F. Browne *Ward: Travels* 79: Informing them, in a hoarse whisper, that their "old man had gone in."

going *adj.* beaten (*obs.*); (*also*) baffled, confused, fooled, excited, or angry.—constr. after *have* or *get*. Now *colloq.*

1900 Patten *Merriwell's Power* 58: You've got 'em going! They're cracking! **1906** H. Green *Boarding House* 109: I got him goin', yunno, 'cause I cud show the letters tuh his family. **1911** Van Loan *Big League* 165: You've let the knockers get you going. **1925** Cohan *Broadway* 60: They had me "going," all right, but I pretended not to mind the banter. **1928** Dahlberg *Bottom Dogs* 75: A sure enough dictionary of wicked words, a string of earthy words that had the bible going. **1931** Rouverol *Dance, Fools, Dance* (film): You've got me going, sister—in a big way! **1953** Essex *It Came from Outer Space* (film): I hear they got you goin', John!...Don't let 'em ride you too much. *a*1970 *Webster's New World Dict.* (ed. 2) 600: *Get one going* (Slang) to cause a person to be excited, angry, etc.

goin'-home hole *n. Trucking.* the highest gear position. Also **goin'-home gear.**

1971 Tak *Truck Talk* 74: *Goin' home gear...goin' home hole:* the highest gear or combination of gears in a truck's transmission. **1976** Bibb et al. *CB Bible* 62: With the precision of a driver shifting all the way from granny to goin-home gear. **1976** Lieberman & Rhodes *CB* 129: *(The) Going Home Hole*—The highest gear allowing trucks to go as fast as possible.

go-juice *n.* automotive or jet fuel. Also redup.

1951–53 in *AS* XXIX (1954) 97: I'm running on 29-cent go juice. **1955** *AS* XXX (May) 118: *Juice; Go juice* J.P. 4, n. Jet fuel. **1959** Montgomery & Heiman *Jet Nav.* 196: We drop down for more go juice. **1961** L.G. Richards *TAC* 165: The briefing had called for six tankers...so...there would be plenty of go-juice for all. **1966–67** Harvey *Air War* 142: They need all the go-juice they can get, so a couple of 450-gallon drop tanks are hung on the wings. **1975** Dills *CB Slanguage* ('76 ed.) 36: *Go juice* or *go-go juice:* gas; fuel. **1983** LaBarge & Holt *Sweetwater Gunslinger* 57: Our go-juice is getting low.

G.O.K. *Esp. Hosp.* "God only knows." Hence **Gok's disease,** *n.*

1915 in *DN* IV 246: *G.O.K.* God only knows: doctors' term. ***1918** in Sullivan *Our Times* V 328: *G.O.K.:* God only knows. An abbreviation used by English physicians at dressing stations to indicate that they have not had time to make a satisfactory diagnosis. **1918** McBride *Emma-Gees* 141: The medical officers use a Greek name for this fever, which, translated, means "a fever of unknown origin," but the colloquial designation is "G.O.K.," (God only knows). It is rarely, if ever, fatal. I never heard of anyone dying of it. **1969** Hicken *Amer. Fighting Man* 207: The World War I equivalent of SNAFU...was GOK (God only knows). **1983** Naiman *Computer Dict.* 66. **1984** Wilder *You All* 203: *Gok's disease:* God only knows [the proper diagnosis]. **1992** *National Geographic* (PBS-TV): This is what we call a GOK [/gɑk/] pile—G-O-K for "God only knows" [where the artifacts came from].

gold *n. Esp. Black E.* money; DOUGH.

1940 in Oliver *Meaning of Blues* 319: Mama meant me twist it to the slammer and let me cut my throat,/I been throwed in the hole, black baby, ain't been able to dig no gold. **1947** Schulberg *Harder They Fall* 172: I need more gold, Eddie. **1948** Manone & Vandervoort *Trumpet* 145: If I don't collar a sample of your fine gold within a set of seven brights, I'm gonna get mighty salty. **1952** E. Brown *Trespass* 14: A man got so much gold...he can't be straight. **1952** Brossard *Darkness* 10: Can you lend me some gold? **1956** Ross *Hustlers* 14: I had to dig in and give her almost all my gold. **1961** Wolfe *Magic of Their Singing* 26: Prosp, listen, where's the gold from yesterday's lessons? **1970** Baraka *Jello* 20: Now where's the gold, man? **1972** Wambaugh *Blue Knight* 43: The doper was moving fast like a hype with gold in his jeans. **1977** Langone *Life at Bottom* 65: He's going to sell it back in the States and make a bundle, beaucoup gold. Call his transport system the Shit Ships, man can make a big mother of a living.

goldang *v., adj., adv., interj.* [euphem. alter. of GODDAMN, GODDAMNED] GOLDARN. [Usu. assoc. with rural speakers.]

1877 Wheeler *Deadwood Dick, Prince of the Road* 77: Thar's them gol danged copper-colored guests uv ther government. **1974** Blount *3 Bricks Shy* 61: And he's so gol-dang smart he'll make a believer out of you.

goldarn *v., adj., adv., interj.* [euphem. alter. of GODDAMN, GODDAMNED] darn; darned. Also vars. [Usu. assoc. with rural speakers.]

1832 in *DA*: We have..."*Gaul darn you*" for G— d— you...and other like creations of the union of wrath and principle. **1840** *Spirit of Times* (Sept. 26) 360: Gawl darn ye, quit that ye tarnal cus! **1846** Codman *Sailors' Life* 106: Gaul-darn-ye. **1849** in *DA*: I'll be gaul-durned ef I

deu. **1856** Olmsted *Slave States* 312: Seems to me them gol-durned lazy niggers ain't a goin' to come over arter you now. **1885** in *DA:* You're a goldarn liar. **1888** in Farmer *Amer.:* I've broken my goldarned neck. **1940** M. LeSueur *Salute to Spring* 153: And these here [debt] collectors it's got so you can't move the hay in your barn to feed a cow without uncovering a goldarn collector! **1948** *Reader's Digest* (Mar.) 128: Another great story ruined by a goldurned eyewitness. **1964** in L.B. Johnson *White House Diary* 183: The farmer said..."Well, I'll be goldurned—the salesman...said it was Harry Truman in his ceremonial Masonic clothes!"

goldbar *n.* [in allusion to the insignia of rank] *Army & USMC.* a second lieutenant. Also **goldbars.**

1921 *Amer. Legion Wkly.* 17 [ref. to WWI]: And what's more we had a goldbars who said he didn't give a hoot what the skipper or the major thought of him so long as the bucks had a good opinion. **1957** Herber *Tomorrow to Live* 6: If them leaves ride in the back, you know hell for certain gold bars ride in the back. **1991** *Daybreak Saturday* (CNN-TV) (Jan. 12): Every officer from four-star to goldbar.

Goldberg *n.* [regarded as a typical Jewish family name] *Esp. Black E.* a Jew or Jews.—used contemptuously.

1965 C. Brown *Manchild* 295: "Goldberg is never gonna get over me with the whip."..."Who's Goldberg?" "You know, Mr. Jew....Goldberg's just as bad as Mr. Charlie." **1966** Harris & Freeman *Lords of Hell* 136: Shitman, I seen colored men all my life working they lifes away in Goldberg's factories and then when they gets old, they got nothing to show for it. **1968** P. Roth *Portnoy* 169: Calling you Goldberg in the bargain, [they'll] send you on your way. **1973** Schulz *Pimp* 27: My Goldberg don't like bein' called in the middle of the night, but I pay him good money and he likes that. **1977** Sayles *Union Dues* 154: At least three different poems and articles...have some mention of "offing Goldberg" or "wasting the kikes." **1984** T. Wolfe, in *Rolling Stone* (Aug. 2) 19: *Yo, Goldberg!...*Goldberg is the code name for Jew. It's insolent!—outrageous!—that anybody throws this word in the face of the Mayor of New York City!

gold braid *n. Esp. Navy.* commissioned officers, esp. senior commissioned officers; BRASS; *(also)* a commissioned officer.

[**1899** Thomas *Arizona* 103: Ma don't care a heap about leather, but she loves gold braid...She fixed up Estrella's match with the Colonel.] **1937** Parsons *Lafayette Escadrille* 95 [ref. to WWI]: With his customary tact, he soon convinced the gold braids that they were losing an unparalleled opportunity by not letting him pilot. **1939** Howsley *Argot* 21: *Gold Braid*—a commissioned officer; an official; a higher up. **1940** Goodrich *Delilah* 438 [ref. to 1917]: As he neared the building...there arose the familiar warning shout: "Gold braid!" **1941** Kendall *Army & Navy Slang* 19: *The Gold Braid...*Commissioned officers. **1942** *American Neptune* (Apr.) 165: In the meantime, a lot of "Gold Braid" had come aboard with interpreters. **1943** in Rea *Wings of Gold* 73: Have had a number of days of perfect inspection, and the gold-braid really likes that stuff. **1943** in P. McGuire *Jim Crow Army* 73: In fact all of the Gold Braids at Hampton treat you like a human being and not like a dog. **1944** Klaw *Camp Follower* 7: I hope those gold braids [lieutenants] are going a long way....They'll get mighty uncomfortable sitting like that. **1959** W. Anderson *Nautilus* 128: At the same time, legions of engineers, workmen, and high Navy gold braid came aboard to grapple with our most serious problem. **1960** Hardy *Wolfpack* 75: The first night he met Lisa he had been the only lieutenant (jg) in a room full of gold braid. **1967** Dibner *Admiral* 131: That morning we had enough goldbraid off duty to run a coronation ball on Haliewa alone. **1978** *N.Y. Post* (Dec. 6) 36: It's far too late for the current gold braid in Washington to recapture lost youth. *a*1990 Poyer *Gulf* 6: The crew waited, quieted by the gold braid in the front row.

goldbrick *n.* **1.** a brick of base metal that appears to be made of gold; *(hence)* a fraudulent or worthless thing; in phr. **sell a gold brick** to swindle or cheat. Orig. as two words.

1881 in *OEDS:* The gold brick swindle is an old one but it crops up constantly. The bar, or brick as it is called,...is really of base metal. One corner, however, is of gold. **1887** in *DA* 709. **1897** Work *Waifs* 178: Speaking of that Maryland farmer that they sold the gold brick to last month. **1900** S.E. White *Westerners* 94: Bunco men can clean him out in a gambling joint, but whoever heard of their selling him a gold brick? **1901** A.H. Lewis *Croker* 64: Take me when I'm tankin' up, I'm that easy a baby could sell me a gold brick. **1903** A.H. Lewis *Boss* 97: I've got no great use for a church...I never bought a gold brick yet that wasn't wrapped in a tract. **1909** Munro *N.Y. Tombs* 253: When these fellows try to sell you a "gold brick" or borrow money from you, the best thing to do is to "drop them." **1909** Irwin *Con Man* 160.

That...was about eighteen hundred and ninety-five. The gold-brick game was getting too well known for safety. "Gold brick" had already become slang for a bunco game; and when that happens you might as well quit. **1911** in O. Johnson *Lawrenceville* 450: German measles is most pleasant, but real measles isn't what we're looking for. What's to guarantee us we get what we pay...for and not a gold brick? **1911** B.T. Washington *My Larger Ed.* 292: In many cases, the diploma that the student carries home...is nothing less than a gold brick. It has made him believe that he has gotten an education, when he...actually [has not]. **1912** in Truman *Dear Bess* 86: Then they'll beef around worse than if they'd been sold a gold brick. **1925** Dos Passos *Manhattan Transfer* 209: And for God's sake don't buy any more Blue Peter Mines on a margin without asking me about it. I may be a back number but I can still tell a goldbrick with my eyes closed. **1931** Dos Passos *1919* 171: This whole goddam war's a gold brick, it ain't on the level. **1937** Hecht *Nothing Sacred* (film): New York...where the slickers and know-it-alls sell gold bricks to one another. **1940** Asbury *Gem of Prairie* 151: Reed Waddell [was] inventor of the gold-brick fraud. **1943** in P. Smith *Letter from Father* 225: Paris was...the goldbrick for the sucker. **1944** Botkin *Treas. Amer. Folk.* 361: Many swindling dodges, such as selling a greenhorn gold bricks. **1946** W.A. White *Autobiog.* 354 [ref. to 1904]: Roosevelt...cried, "Well, by George, I almost bought a gold brick!" **1952** Lait & Mortimer *USA* 5: Rural America is changing too...No longer do they buy gold bricks. **1952** Knight *Psychoanalysis* 12: Perhaps Dr. Goldschmidt had been sold a gold brick [by Freud] in Vienna. **1966** Farrar *N.Y. Times Crosswords* xiv 47: Worthless thing passed off as valuable...goldbrick. **1975** N.Y.C. woman, age 86: To *sell someone a goldbrick* means you've taken advantage of them, you've fooled them or sold them something that's no good. It's the same as to sell someone a lemon. If a car is no good, for example, you say, "He sold me a goldbrick," or "That car is a goldbrick." That's a very old expression. I can remember that from way back.

2. *U.S. Nav. Acad.* an unattractive or unpleasant young woman.

1906 *Army & Navy Life* (Nov.) 497: *Femmes* is the word constantly used for the ladies in common conversation, and *Peaches* designates the fairest of the fair sex, and a *Gold Brick*, according to the authority of the "Lucky Bag of 1903," a publication annually made by the midshipmen, is a girl who can neither talk, dance, nor look pretty. **1918** in *Pap. Mich. Acad.* X (1929) 305.

3. *Army.* an incompetent officer having had only minimal training.

1914 *DN* IV 107: *Gold-brick*, n. Applied to army lieutenants appointed from civil life. "The gold-bricks are overbearing." **1917** (quot. at WAR-BABY, *n.*).

4. Orig. *Army.* a malingerer, loafer, or shirker. [Early quots. ref. to WWI.]

1918 in Casey *Cannoneers* 168: Any spy who comes in here will probably break his neck tripping over telephone lines and gold bricks, looking for quiet places in which to sleep. **1919** Davis *Battery C* 61: Remember?...The scarlet fever goldbricks at Camp Mills? **1922** Paul *Impromptu* 162: I'm goin' to give some of these gold bricks a chance to do something. **1923** LaBranche *Amer. Battery* 104: A fellow without cooties was either a "gold brick" as the "soft job" soldiers with cozy berths were called, or they had just come to us as replacements. **1926** Nason *Chevrons* 260: Me and Baldy hollered, "Hey, goldbrick!" down every dugout between here and Sivry-la-Perche and when you didn't answer, we thought you were gone for good. *Ibid.* 275: I think you're a goldbrick. You don't look as if you're wounded the slightest bit. **1930** E. Colby, in *Our Army* (Jan.): *Goldbrick*—A soldier on special duty, as in the military police detachment, at the Post Exchange, or officially absent from "straight duty" with a line organization. **1930** *Our Army* (Aug.) 15: God pity the gold-brick and faker when the Top had him up on the mat. **1932** Halyburton & Goll *Shoot and Be Damned* 175: He was a crook in office back home and a goldbrick at the front. **1941** Hargrove *Pvt. Hargrove* 32: "Goldbrick," they muttered as they passed me...I brushed them away disdainfully and sat down to read a comic book or two. **1959** Cochrell *Barren Beaches* 291: A whole flock of goldbricks returned to duty. **1960** Duncan *If It Moves* 38: As far as I'm concerned, you are a goldbrick. All of you are goldbricks...Would you rather be transferred to the infantry? **1987** D. da Cruz *Boot* 254: If the D.I.'s had been allowed to drop the gold-bricks and the sea lawyers, they'd have cut the platoon in half. **1991** *New Yorker* (Sept. 16) 96: Hardworking Amos and goldbrick Andy, disparate buddies, were nearly universal characters.

goldbrick *adj.* **1.** swindling; fraudulent; false.—used prenominally.

[**1900** *Blue Book* (unp.): Don't be misguided by touts or gold brick masons but look for whatever you desire in this book.] **1909** Munro *N.Y. Tombs* 254: It is the commonest thing in the world for a crook to ask the assistance of a lady missionary to get him out of prison, and present a "gold brick" story that is nothing but deception and fabrication from first to last. **1915–17** Lait *Gus* 95: You can operate your gold brick game...all you like.

2. conducive to loafing.—used prenominally.

1936 Duncan *Over the Wall* 43: He recommended that I be placed in charge of the regimental canteen, a gold-brick job of no little importance.

goldbrick *v.* **1.** to swindle or befool, orig. by means of a fraudulent gold brick.

1902 H.L. Wilson *Spenders* 328: He'll be gold-bricked if he wears...[whiskers]...around this place. **1906** Ford *Shorty McCabe* 163: I've been gold-bricked so much lately that I'd almost suspect my own grandmother. **1907** *Reader* (Aug.) 254: "I have been gold-bricked!" gasps Tolma. **1908** in Fleming *Unforget. Season* 150: I shall strive to show New Yorkers they were not "goldbricked" when they got me. **1914** in *OEDS*: Well, look out they don't gold-brick you, sonny. **1919** Wadsworth *Gas Attack* 37: He strove to goldbrick the evacuation officer into marking him "Blighty." **1929** Springs *Carol Banks* 182: If you think it's hard to bluff the dean out of a cut, try to goldbrick Kismet. **1988** *Reporters* (Fox-TV) (Dec. 3): He felt that she'd been goldbricking him.

2. Orig. *Army.* **a.** to malinger or evade duty; loaf. [Early quots. ref. to WWI.]

1918 Casey *Cannoneers* 123: Gold bricking is frowned upon in war time. **1926** Nason *Chevrons* 71 [ref. to 1918]: "Where's Ham and the machine gunners?" asked Eadie. "Over in the field, goldbricking." *Ibid.* 39: I was just this minute wishing you were here and thinking you were somewhere in hospital goldbricking your time away. **1926** *Sat. Eve. Post* (Nov. 6) 132: He checks up on ambulances comin' and goin' to see who's drivin' an' who's gold-brickin'. **1927** *AS* II (Mar.) 281: *Goldbrick*—To feign illness or any excuse to avoid doing assigned work. **1928** Harlin *Company A* 30: Dr. Tibbets treated many cases at sick call at the infirmary, some serious and some just "goldbrickin". **1928** Wharton *Squad* 208 [ref. to 1918]: He'll have the Medical Officer send ambulances up in th' mornin'. But no gold brickin'! **1930** Barkley *No Hard Feelings?* 179: What you doin' in here? Gold-bricking? **1930** Fredenburgh *Soldiers March!* 131 [ref. to 1918]: Mr. Duryea goldbricked in the stable while the rest of the outfit manhandled wagons in the rain and muck. **1931** *Our Army* (Dec.) 12: He's just a gold-bricking duty-dodger. **1941** Hargrove *Pvt. Hargrove* 20: We finished the job in an extremely short time to impress the corporal. This, we found later, is a serious tactical blunder and a discredit to the ethics of goldbricking. The sooner you finish a job, the sooner you start on the next. **1942** *Leatherneck* (Nov.) 145: *Gold Brick*—To dodge work. **1942** Kahn *Army Life* 104: Gold-bricking consists in not doing something and not being caught at it. **1959** Cochrell *Barren Beaches* 313: "Leeper's goldbrickin' for sure this time," he said. **1966** "T. Pendleton" *Iron Orchard* 45: That'll be better than reportin' sick, because they'd figure you couldn't take it and were gold-brickin'.

b. to shirk (duty or responsibility).

1918 *Stars & Stripes* (Sept. 13) 4: What are you trying to do, goldbrick it? **1924** *Amer. Leg. Wkly.* (Nov. 7) 18: I gold-bricked the detail and slunked to a side street.

c. to force (someone) to take responsibility for one's shirking or malingering.

1962 Mandel *Wax Boom* 232 [ref. to WWII]: That's fine, gold-bricking us like a couple of recruits. Everybody has to pull guard for you.

goldbricker *n.* **1.** a swindler who offers for sale a fraudulent gold bar; (*hence*) a professional swindler.

1902 Cullen *More Tales* 85: He was the top-notch gold-bricker of his own or any other age—a man that made nearly $1,000,000 out of the brass billets. *Ibid.*: Tom O'Brien, the most notorious of the gold-brickers.

2. Orig. *Army.* a malingerer or shirker; loafer. [Early quots. ref. to WWI.]

1919 Duffy *G.P.F. Book* 297: As a gold-bricker, well, far be it from him to boast. **1920** Riggs & Platt *Battery F* 3: By order, we were given twenty-four hours off duty, which started many a "Goldbricker's" career. **1926** H. Allen *Toward the Flame* 65: A few of them later dropped out and went to hospital. Some of these, of course, were "gold-brickers" and some were really in bad shape. **1928** Scanlon *God Have Mercy* 144: Back of the lines there's a bunch of gold-brickers that run around with a stretcher and look wise. **1932** *Our Army* (Jan.) 18: The owly·

eyed gold-bricker! **1937** Parsons *Lafayette Escadrille* 239: I'm going out and show you goldbrickers something. **1939** Callaway *Packs & Rifles* 98: Go wan, you darned goldbricker. **1952** Malamud *Natural* 45: We don't need any more goldbrickers or four-flushers or practical jokers around. **1952** Uris *Battle Cry* 100: Joe Gomez was the biggest thief, liar, and goldbricker in the Marine Corps. **1961** Rosten *Newman, M.D.* 94: Throw that no good gold-bricker in the guardhouse. **1968** Moura & Sutherland *Tender Loving Care* 133: We were goldbrickers, as far as she was concerned. **1989** *21 Jump St.* (Fox-TV): He is nothing but a gold-bricker.

goldbug *n. Pol.* a plutocrat (*obs.*); (*also*) a person in favor of the free circulation of gold; a gold speculator.
   1878 *Harper's Wkly.* (Feb. 23) 156: Bloated Bondholder. Gold Bug. **1878** in *DA*: [Our forefathers] carried on business in gold…In short, they were "goldites," "gold-bugs," and "gold-sharps." **1878** in Sperber & Trittschuh *Amer. Pol. Terms* 172: The "gold bugs"—in the elegant language of Western statesmen—have the power to squeeze the debtor by making gold scarce at the time of payment. **1890** in Sperber & Trittschuh *Amer. Pol. Terms:* The gold bugs of the East and the silver kings of the West have come to an understanding. **1893** Hampton *Maj. in Washington* 50: That's the trouble with them gold-bugs…They scared the country a leetle too much. **1896** F.P. Dunne, in Schaaf *Dooley* 129: Misther Hinnissy here…was jus' tellin' me th' advantages iv th' free coinage iv silver. Misther McKenna is a gould bug. **1903** T.W. Jackson *Slow Train* 87: You take President Roosevelt. He is a big gold bug. **1973** *Business Week* (May 19) 70: Dr. Franz Pick, outspoken currency expert, devout chrysophile (gold bug), [etc.]. **1976** Hayden *Voyage* 366: Them bloomin' gold bugs'll spend the rest of their lousy lives tryin' to undo the scramble. **1976** *Business Week* (Aug. 23) 42: A $70 price for gold is a far cry from the $300 that the goldbugs widely predicted. **1980** *ABC Network News* (ABC-TV) (Sept. 17): A handful of so-called "goldbugs" claim that gold is the only real money and advocate a return to the gold standard. **1981** Wambaugh *Glitter Dome* 96: The two old geezers were goldbugs from Spring Street…[who] had been buying and hoarding gold in their store.

gold-buttons *n. R.R.* (see quot.).
   1923 McKnight *Eng. Wds.* 44: To the vocabulary of railroad men belong such words as…*gold buttons* or *brains* for "conductor."

gold-dig *v.* to behave like a GOLD-DIGGER, 1; to prey upon (a man) for his wealth.
   1923 (quot. at PULLET, *n.*) **1925** McAlmon *Silk Stockings* 108: They had money to drink on…rather than gold-dig off foreigners. **1926** S. Lewis *Mantrap* 148: Aside from calling me a fool and a rotten housekeeper, and saying I gold-dig you for all the money I can get. **1931** Farrell *Calico Shoes* 112: Their fondest dream was…to be laid in a taxicab…or else to find and gold-dig some chump for all he was worth. **1946** Steinbeck *Wayward Bus* 255: I'll bet maybe she never loved him at all…I'll bet she just gold-dug Eddie. **1994** N. McCall *Wanna Holler* 272: Them gold-diggin' bitches go for it every time.

gold-digger *n.* **1.** a woman who associates with or marries a man solely for his wealth.
   1915–16 Lait *Beef, Iron & Wine* 77: Now don't get me wrong. I'm no gold digger. **1918** Guttersen *Granville* 156: The same way that other girls are classified as "Gold-diggers," or "Dinner hounds," or "Bricks." **1925** Weaver *Collected Poems* 152: I didn't want Mr. Kirby to think I was tryin'/Any gold-digger tricks. I ain't that kind. **1926** Dunning & Abbott *Broadway* 234: ROY (*contemptuously*). A gold digger. **1926** Springs *Nocturne Militaire* 232: She always considered all our other friends black-mailers, dope fiends, gold diggers, and octogenarians, but was seldom specific in her charges. **1927** *AS* II (Mar.) 276: *Gold digger*. A woman student who gets the maximum amount of entertainment at maximum expense from a man student. **1931** Cressey *Taxi-Dance Hall* 100: The first thing in being a successful "gold-digger" is to choose the right fellow. **1941** in A. Gray *Arf* (unp.): You're a billionaire. She's a little gold-digger. It's a perfect set-up. *ca*1954 in Oliver *Blues Tradition* 145: My baby must be a gold digger, she got all my pockets clean. **1957** Bergler *Psych. Gambling* 13: He was engaged to a girl whom he suspected of being a gold-digger. **1983** Ephron *Heartburn* 65: Amelia was much too good-hearted to have been a gold digger. **1988** T. Babbes *Dreams* (film): She's just a little gold-digger, can't you see that?
   2. a prostitute.
   1916–22 Cary *Sexual Vocab.* II s.v. *female*: *Gold digger*. A mercenary harlot. **1923** T. Boyd *Through the Wheat* 54 [ref. to 1918]: The conversation turned upon decent prostitutes and honest gamblers…"You betcha there can be decent gold-diggers. And honest gamblers, too." "A woman gets married. And then she leaves her husband…Well, she

marries another guy and then another. Now, how is she any better than a regular gold-digger?" **1929** Gill *Und. Slang:* Gold diggers—Women of vice.

golden *adj.* **1.** Esp. *Stu.* perfect; fine, esp. comfortable, safe, or secure.
   1958 J. Davis *College Vocab.* 9: *Golden*—Really great, the best. **1962** W. Robinson *Barbara* 312 [ref. to WWII]: "Nothing but a golden go up here," said Lee. "A golden go." **1961–63** Drought *Mover* 128: It's not your goddamn golden luck that tees me off. **1968** Moura & Sutherland *Tender Loving Care* 139: "One more take, Slate baby, and we'll be golden." To appease Hardman, Penner had lapsed into what he considered Hollywood dialogue. **1971** *Current Slang* V 12: *Golden*, adj. Assured of success, to have it "made." **1972–73** in M.J. Bell *Brown's Lounge* 76: Two of the best barmaids in West Philly. Both of them are just golden. **1974** Beacham & Garret *Intro 5* 65: Age around fortyish—and that's golden. **1975** H. Ellison *Gentleman Junkie* (ed. 2) 13: One cannot write three hundred stories in three years and not come golden at least a few times. *Ibid.* 141: I was golden. Every time those dice hit that…wall…they read heavenly. **1977** Sayles *Union Dues* 167: In fact, you get on with us, you're golden. *Golden.* **1977** Univ. Tenn. instructor: I came out golden on that deal. **1984** Heath *A-Team* 217: I would have thought you'd know this monster has a reserve tank. We're golden. **1983–86** G.C. Wilson *Supercarrier* 5: Once you go above [the clouds], you're golden and it's terrific. **1986** *USA Today* (Aug. 1) 1 C: She took the plunge and came up golden.
   2. very lucrative.
   1985 *Harper's* (Nov.) 26: There are always promising [new opportunities for funded research]. Two years ago, you never heard of Alzheimer's. Today it's golden.

golden BB *n. Mil. Av.* a shell or missile that, fired from the ground, brings down an attacking aircraft.
   *ca*1969 in Tuso *Vietnam Blues* 229: A damned golden BB met up with my plane. **1975** in Higham & Siddall *Combat Aircraft* 107: Some of the Nellis crews, who was hit by a "golden BB" in December [1968], told of the Communist prison guard who…said, "You F-111…Whoosh!" **1977** [B.P. Wyatt] *We Came Home* (unp.): On 18 October 1965…a "golden B-B" from an enemy machine gun sent my F-4C "Phantom II" out of control. **1987** Robbins *Ravens* 60 [ref. to Vietnam War]: It was just one of those things. His plane took the golden BB. *Ibid.* 399: *Golden BB.* The single bullet with the pilot's name on it, destined to kill him. **1987** Zeybel *Gunship* 207 [ref. to Vietnam War]: A Golden BB—one shot directly on the nailhead.

golden boy *n. Police.* a gold-shield detective.—used disparagingly.
   1974 *Kojak* (CBS-TV): Detectives aren't exempt from the rules, no matter *what* you golden boys seem to think.

golden chair *n. Mil. Av.* the front seat of a two-place aircraft.
   1929 *Sat. Eve. Post* (Apr. 6) 190 [ref. to WWI]: I'd have to side-slip to get in, and riding in the "golden chair," as we called the front seat, made it look doubtful to me.

golden doughnut *n.* the vulva and vagina. *Joc.*
   *1972 in Wilkes *Austr. Colloq.* 482: We'll be in like Flynn…We'll thread the eye of the old golden doughnut—no worries. **1974** Lahr *Trot* 216: Don't think women aren't attracted to me. I've threaded the eye of the Golden Doughnut many times.

golden handcuffs *n.pl. Business.* attractive financial benefits that an employee will lose in the event of his or her resignation.
   1976 D.W. Moffat *Economics Dict.*: *Golden handcuffs:* Benefits provided by employers in such a manner as to make it costly for employees to change jobs. **1982** in *AS* LVIII (1983) 177: Most corporations have been compelled to expand the concept of "golden handcuffs"—perks that will keep valued employees locked in. **1983** *Business Week* (Mar. 21) 121: One result of Cap Cities' "golden handcuff" philosophy is low management turnover.

golden handshake *n. Business.* the giving or offering of very generous severance pay, as to a business executive, often as an incentive to early retirement; (*hence*) such payment itself.
   *1960 in *OEDS*: There is little public sympathy for the tycoon who retires with a golden handshake to the hobby farm. *1960 in *Ibid.*: On the financial side, Cyprus receives its golden handshake of over £14 m. **1972** *Business Week* (Feb. 5) 58: Trafalgar paid more than $600,000 in "golden handshakes"—severance pay—to get rid of the unwanted executives. **1981** in *AS* LVIII (1983) 176: Wood talks of the "golden hand-

cuff," the "golden handshake," and the "golden parachute." **1984** *Wall Street Journal* (radio ad) (May 19): Voluntary early retirements...According to an article in *The Wall Street Journal*, these golden handshakes aren't cheap. **1986** P. Welsh *Tales Out of School* 174: The only way to move them out is with the "golden handshake" of a few years' pay. **1987** *Your Money* (CNN-TV) (July 18): A quarter-million dollar golden handshake isn't all that unusual these days.

golden key *n. Mil. Av.* (see quot.).
1967 H.M. Mason *New Tigers* 222: *Golden key:* The parachute arming lanyard anchor, a solid brass ring attached to...seat belts. In case of ejection, the golden key ensures that the automatic opening of the parachute after seat separation will begin.

golden oldie *n. Entertainment Industry.* a formerly popular phonograph recording, motion picture, or the like that is still regarded affectionately.
1966 *Time* (Dec. 2) 46: The platter...promises to become what the deejays call a "Golden Oldy." **1967** *Sat. Eve. Post* (July 15) 71: Their teen-age scream has become a Golden Oldie. **1967** *Time* (July 21) 38: He intones such golden oldies as *A Visit from St. Nicholas* and *Silent Night.* **1970** *Atlantic* (Dec.) 97: DJ's with great golden oldie collections draw regretful blanks looking for his singles. **1972** J. Morris *Strawberry Soldier* 66: He turned on the radio and got some asshole announcer blathering about a golden oldie from out of the past. **1973** in *DAS* (ed. 2): A golden oldie like "Honeysuckle Rose" by the immortal Fats Waller. **1976** Rosen *Above Rim* 123: I just saw that in a John Wayne golden oldie, you dig? **1981** *N.Y. Times Mag.* (June 21) 26: A hit in the morning, a golden oldie in the afternoon. Quality was out. **1984** Hindle *Dragon Fall* 107: Obviously, the girl had seen the same golden oldie once. **1985** E. Leonard *Glitz* 73: I do three golden oldies for every *one* I want to play. **1993** *N.Y. Times* (June 28) B 5: He spends an hour or so working out...while golden oldies play on the radio.

golden parachute *n. Business.* an employment contract that guarantees the uninterrupted continuation of an employee's salary and benefits even in the event of the company's takeover by another firm and the loss of the employee's position; (also) GOLDEN HANDSHAKE. Now *S.E.*
1981 (quot. at GOLDEN HANDSHAKE, *n.*). **1982** in *AS* LVIII (1983) 177: Usually such "golden parachutes" don't open until a third party gains actual control, or 51% of a company's stock. **1982** *N.Y. Times* (June 9) D 1: $15 million in "golden parachute" severance benefits that the ousted board members are scheduled to receive. **1984** *Business Week* (June 11) 45: So-called golden parachutes, or lucrative severance payments for management approved after a tender offer has begun. **1986** *L.A. Law* (NBC-TV): You'll be able to negotiate some cushy golden parachutes for your client. **1994** *N.Y. Times* (Jan. 13) B 12: If they give Taylor a golden parachute, they would have to give other longtime Giants...the same when they leave.

golden rivet *n. Naut.* (see 1945, 1973 quots.). Also **gold rivet.**
1945 Trumbull *Silversides* 97: He...could get Royal to do for him the distasteful job of cleaning the bilges, by telling Royal that somewhere in the bilges he would find "the gold rivet"—the mythical gold rivet which, they tell the green hands, was the first rivet put in the ship. **1942–48** in *So. Folk. Qly.* XIII (1949) 202: *Pogey*...had a lascivious connotation...There are two old Navy phrases with a similar connotation: "to go below to see the dead marine" or "to go below to see the golden rivet." *****1959** Behan *Borstal Boy* 42 [ref. to *ca*1940]: Any old three-badge stoker ever shown you the golden rivet? **1973** *Penthouse* (Mar.) 24: *Golden rivet:* Fictitious central structural part of a ship alleged to have been used by homosexual sailors to lure new recruits down into the hold of the ship to see the rivet, where they could then be assaulted without fear of interruption. The phrase is sometimes used by homosexuals as a slang term for the penis. **1973** H. Beck *Folklore of the Sea* 11: It is highly possible that the memory of this act [the fastening of a gold coin to the keel of a newly built ship for luck] has been retained in a kind of horseplay inflicted on green hands in American naval ships who are sometimes told to go below and "polish the golden rivet" located in the most inaccessible part of the keel.

golden shower *n. Pros. & Homosex.* an act of being urinated upon as a method of masochistic sexual excitement; a stream of urine.
1943 in T. Williams *Letters* 111: You should have told Margo only thing I really enjoy is a "golden shower" from a black cloud. **1950** G. Legman, in *Neurotica* (Spring) 3: Urine-drinking..."the golden shower." **1965** Trimble *Sex Wds.* 91: *Golden Shower*...A urolagniac act...*Golden Shower Queen*...A passive male homosexual urolagniac.

1970 Landy *Underground Dict.* 91: *Golden shower boy*...One who obtains sexual gratification by ingesting urine. **1971** Rader *Govt. Inspected* 168: "Piss on me," he whispered, his voice hoarse...But I held back and grew angry. Golden shower queen. **1972** *Anthro. Linguistics* (Mar.) 103: *Golden Shower* (n.): Urine. **1972** R. Barrett *Lovomaniacs* 289: I dig that Golden Shower routine sometimes. **1977** T. Berger *Villanova* 95: He was here for more than a golden shower from some hooker. **1980** *Nat. Lampoon* (Apr.) 42: He requests golden showers, heavy bondage, dogs, and lots of Greek culture. **1987** *New Republic* (Sept. 28) 15: She...leaned over the edge, and gave the first row an unexpected, but much deserved, golden shower (ruining one photographer's Nikon). **1992** Hosansky & Sparling *Working Vice* 132: The older man...[requested] "A golden shower."

golden twenty-five *n. Army.* twenty-five years of service required for retirement.
1970 Gattzden *Black Vendetta* 159: You've done your golden twenty-five.

goldfinch *n.* **1.** *Und.* a wealthy man, esp. as the target of thieves.
*****1698–99** "B.E." *Dict. Canting Crew: Goldfinch*...He that has alwaies a Purse or Cod of Gold in his Fob. *****1735** in Partridge *Dict. Und.* 297: I fancy the goldfinches are not yet flown. *****1822** D. Carey *Life in Paris* I 15: The deuce is in it if the *goldfinches* won't sing now. **1848** Judson *Mysteries* 37: Was the swell a gold-finch? *Ibid.* 527: "*Gold-Finch.*" A man with plenty of money about him.
2. a gold coin.
*****1785** Grose *Vulgar Tongue: Goldfinches;* guineas. **1821** Waln *Hermit in Phila.* 26: Out with your *goldfinches.* **1836** *Spirit of Times* (July 16) 170: You might meet with a "mob of swells"..."well breeched" into the bargain, with lots of *goldfinches* to make the "wisit pleasant."

goldfish *n.* **1.a.** *Mil.* canned salmon. Now *rare* and *hist.*
1900 Mabey *Utah Batteries* 92: They made comments, too, not at all flattering to the bill of fare, about "gold fish" and "slum-gullion." **1906** M'Govern *Sarjint Larry* s.v. [gloss]: *Gold-fish:* Canned Salmon. **1911** Moss *Officer's Manual* 306: *Gold Fish*—Salmon. **1918** Crowe *Aviator* 74: The hated Bully Beef and canned Goldfish and Army Punk. **1918** O'Brien *Wine, Women & War* 13: Got "ration issue" in morning, by looting freight car—canned goldfish, pickles & what not. **1928** Scanlon *God Have Mercy!* 36: There were a few cans of bully beef, goldfish, and beans lying around, and these were quickly snatched up. **1942** Herman *42nd Foot* 32 [ref. to 1898]: "Gold Fish" was the disrespectful name of a really good component of the ration but earned its bad name by its over-frequent appearance on the company bills-of-fare. That was the canned salmon, of which the Commissary Department of the Army loaded up the scandalous amount during the period of, and immediately following, the Spanish-American War. **1942** *Leatherneck* (Nov.) 46: *Goldfish*—canned salmon. **1944** Ind *Bataan* 238: We just ate fast, lest it should turn into "goldfish." **1956** *AS* XXXI (Oct.) 192: *Goldfish* is canned salmon.
b. sliced peaches, as served in a cafeteria.
1940 (quot. at SALVE, *n.*). **1946** Boulware *Jive & Slang* 4: *Gold Fish*...Sliced peaches.
2. [cf. GOLDFISH BOWL, 1] *Police.* (see quot.).
1930 Lait *On the Spot* 203: *Goldfish*...Prisoners in the police line-up where detectives and potential witnesses may observe them without being themselves observed.
3. *Police.* a beating administered to a prisoner so as to extract a confession; (also) a length of rubber hose used in such a beating.
1926 Finerty *Criminalese* 24: *Goldfish.* Third degree. **1928–29** Nason *White Slicker* 199 [ref. to WWI]: Let's just show this young Jerry here the goldfish. **1930** in Partridge *Dict. Und.* 297: The closet held certain lengths of rubber hose technically known as "goldfish" in underworld jargon. **1930** C. Shaw *Jack-Roller* 147 [ref. to *ca*1920's]: Prisoners are herded and kicked and cuffed and razzed like brutes. This is called "showing the goldfish" or the "third degree." **1931** *Amer. Merc.* (Dec.) 418: They took him in the goldfish room and went to woik on him with the hoses. **1932** *Writer's Digest* (Aug.) 47: A "gold fish"...is a piece of rubber hose used to inflict punishment without leaving marks on the body. **1938** C. Shaw *Brothers in Crime* 213: The Goldfish was their term for taking me into a fairly large room where I was questioned and beaten—mostly beaten. **1947** Motley *Knock on Any Door* 351: "Are you ready to talk?" Nick didn't answer. The sergeant said, "Take him upstairs to see the goldfish."

goldfish bowl *n.* **1.** *Police.* an interrogation or lineup room in

a police station, typically furnished with a one-way mirror.
1930 Lait *On the Spot* 79: There was a small back room which was known to every crook in the city. The "goldfish bowl." **1961–62** in *AS* XXXVII (1962) 269: *Goldfish bowl*...An interrogation room in a jail or detention station.

2. *Mil. Av.* a manned gun turret.
1943 Mears *Carrier* 90: In the TBF there are two crew members besides the pilot, namely, the turret gunner, who squeezes himself into the small gun turret, the "gold-fish bowl," sitting above the tail, and the radioman-bombardier, who sits in the bombardier's compartment in the belly of the ship behind the torpedo or bomb load.

goldie *n.* [in allusion to the Gold Record Award of the Record Industry Association of America] *Recording Industry.* a phonograph recording that has sold a million copies.
1985 Sawislak *Dwarf* 163: I've heard them even do some oldies and goldies. **1989** Martorano & Kildahl *Neg. Thinking* 39: An old song—not necessarily a goldie.

gold-sharp *n. Pol.* GOLDBUG, *n.*
1878 (quot. at GOLDBUG).

gold star *n.* [in allusion to the detective's gold badge] *Police.* a gold-shield police detective. Also **gold shield, gold tin.**
1965 Horan *Seat of Power* 61: You've got to have a lot of pull to take care of a gold star that big. **1978** Strieber *Wolfen* 127: For some unknown reason this gold shield had been allowed to live. **1990** P. Dickson *Slang!* 85: To "get the gold tin" is to be promoted to detective.

gold-stripe *n. Navy.* a commissioned officer.
1917 Depew *Gunner Depew* 16 [ref. to *ca*1910]: There was a gold stripe (commissioned officer) on the bridge and I knew that if anything was wrong, he would cut in.

golfball *n. Mil. Av.* an antiaircraft tracer shell.
1946 G.C. Hall, Jr. *1000 Destroyed* 160: The orange golf balls began criss-crossing their course. **1951** Sheldon *Troubling of a Star* 156: As Ronsdale began his shallow dive, the bright golf balls began to stream up from the ground. **1956** Lasly *Twin Tiger Loose* 21: The flak position was hosing up golf balls with frantic urgency.

golf lawyer *n.* [sugg. by SEA LAWYER] *Golf.* a contentious golfer who frequently disputes the interpretation or application of the rules.
*1922 in P. Davies *Golf. Terms* 77: If there's one thing that gives me a pain...it's a golf-lawyer. **1949** in P. Davies *Golf. Terms*: One of the familiar types is the Golf Lawyer, or Rulebook Demon.

goll *interj.* GOLLY.
1829 in Jackson *Early Songs of Uncle Sam* 48: I wonder, by goll, what's the matter. **1973** *TULIPQ* (coll. B.K. Dumas): Goll, that was a ballbuster! **1979** Gram *Foxes* 72: Gol, Annie, don't say that.

golly *interj.* [euphem. for *God*] (used to express astonishment).—also constr. with *by.* Now *colloq.*
*1775 in *OEDS*: Golly, a sort of jolly kind of oath, or asseveration much in use among our carters, & lowest people. **1827** J.F. Cooper *Red Rover* 39: Golly! I like to see Dick, without a foot-rope, ride a colt tied to the tree. **1828** Bird *Looking Glass* 40: Golly! Mr. Bolt is satirical. **1833** A. Greene *Nullifiers* 31: Two hundred dollars!...By gauly, what a price! **1851** M. Reid *Scalp-Hunters* 95: Great Gollys! we will be froze in half the time. **1864** in *Civil War Hist.* XXVIII (1982) 332: Good golly! How the lead whistled through our hair! **1916** *Sat. Eve. Post* (Feb. 12) 9: By golly, why didn't I lay for the little rat and choke him to death? **1929–31** J.T. Farrell *Young Lonigan* 19: Golly, it would be great to be a kid again! **1970** Boatright & Owens *Derrick* 38: By golly, they certainly deserve a lot of credit.

gollywhopper *n.* a very large or otherwise remarkable specimen.
1839 *Spirit of Times* (Dec. 28) 512: For you never *hear* the creturs *put out* 'ceptin' they're hit; and he's a golly whopper too. **1933** in *DARE*: The cat[fish] that is dyin' on the gravels is shore a golly-whopper. **1938** in *AS* (Apr. 1939) 90: The fish which Sam caught was a gollywhopper. **1953** in *DARE*: I fixed me up a gollywhopper of a speech. *a*1975 in *DARE*: A "gollywhopper" means a big one.

gollywobbles *n.pl.* COLLYWOBBLES.
1942 *ATS* 157: Stomach-Ache...collywobbles, gollywobbles. **1968** R. MacLeish, on WINS radio (July 28): It's enough to give the Republicans the green gollywobbles. **1991** Univ. Tenn. student: The *gollywobbles* are fear or trembling.

gomer *n.* [fr. TV yokel character *Gomer Pyle*; see GOMER PYLE;

the ety. in *a*1982 quot. does not merit consideration, and acronymic etymologies lack early attestation] **1.** *Hosp.* a patient, esp. if elderly, who is dirty, undesirable, or unresponsive to treatment, esp. a poor or homeless man who habitually seeks emergency-room treatment for minor or imaginary complaints.
1964 (cited in *JAF* XCI (1978) 571). **1972** *Nat. Lampoon* (July) 76: *Gomer.* A senile, messy, or highly unpleasant patient. **1978** Shem *House of God* 38: Gomer is an acronym: Get Out of My Emergency Room—it's what you want to say when one's sent in from the nursing home at 3 A.M. *Ibid.* 424: *Gomer*...a human being who has lost—often through age—what goes into being a human being. **1978** *JAF* XCI 571: On the east coast of the United States, gomer is explained as an acronym for "Get Out of My Emergency Room." On the west coast, the interpretation more usually advanced is "Grand Old Man of the Emergency Room." **1979** *AS* (Spring) 37: The patient will become a *gomer* "unresponsive patient" within a short period of time. *a*1982 in W. Safire *Good Word* 156: The noun "gomer" comes from the Hebrew root G-M-R which means "to finish"...A patient who is a gomer...is in the process of finishing his existence on the face of this earth. **1982** Medved *Hospital* 215: *Gomers* are old pathetic patients, and in any decent, life-respecting society they'd be allowed to die gracefully. The *gomers* are so sick, their lives are so miserable, that we're not doing them any favors by keeping them alive. **1983** *Lang. in Society* 175: *Gomer*...in intensive care units...a person who is critically ill for an extended period of time and shows no sign of improvement. **1987** *60 Minutes* (CBS-TV): These doctors even use acronyms like GOMER to describe their patients...GOMER: Get Out of My Emergency Room. **1987** *Discover* (Nov.) 30: Hospitals have a reputation for...crude jargon: the difficult patients labeled gomers (Get Out of My Emergency Room), the doctors referred to as 007s (licensed to kill). **1992** *Doctor Dean* (synd. TV series): There's another term we use, *gomers*, which stands for "Get Out of My Emergency Room."

2. a clumsy or stupid fellow (often applied by noncommissioned officers to military trainees); GOOF, 1.
1967 *DAS* (Supp.) 687: *Gomer, gomar*....A first-year or naive Air Force cadet. *Air Force use.* **1973** D. Barnes *See the Woman* 126: Hey, Gomer. Come on. **1980** Cragg *L. Militaris* 200: *Gomer.* A trainee; any dull or stupid person.

3. *Mil. Av.* a person in Vietnamese Communist military service; an enemy soldier or airman; (*also*) a flier's adversary in air combat training.
1980 W.C. Anderson *Bat-21* 9 [ref. to 1972]: If the Birddog pilot had homed in on his parachute beeper...chances are the gomers had too. *Ibid.* 70: The gomers were more determined than ever to get him before the Americans did. *a*1982 in Safire *Good Word* 159: In Southeast Asia in 1969...the term "gomer" meant a North Vietnamese or Vietcong soldier and supposedly was the acronym of "guy on motorable enemy route."..."These are six gomers on route nine charlie at delta thirty-seven." **1984** Cunningham & Ethell *Fox Two* 3: The Gomers, as someone had nicknamed the North Vietnamese early in the war, meant business. *Ibid.* 78: I could see the little Gomer inside [the cockpit] with his beady little Gomer eyes, Gomer hat, Gomer goggles and Gomer scarf. **1986** Coonts *Intruder* 24: There's got to be some better targets in gomer country. **1987** Zeybel *Gunship* 172: Some non-Christian Gomers who didn't speak English/Were shooting at us with a Communist gun. **1987** G. Hall *Top Gun* 74: Guest Gomers of all stripes are invited to fly to Yuma and jump in. *Ibid.* 95: *Gomer.* Slang for a dogfight adversary, the usage presumably stemming from the old Gomer Pyle television show. **1988** *Supercarrier* (ABC-TV): That gomer's got some real moves on him. *Ibid.*: OK, gomer, talk fast. **1989** J. Weber *Defcon One* 6: The fighter pilots['}...mission was to...confront the unknown gomers. **1991** K. Douglass *Viper Strike* 60: There you'll be, off on the frontier with gomers and alligators for playmates.

4. [short for GOMER PYLE] an enlisted man in the U.S. Marine Corps; marine.—used derisively.
1984 Ganz et al. *Splash!* (film): Up yours, gomer—I'm waitin' for a fare! **1991** Reinberg *In the Field* 95 [ref. to Vietnam War]: *Gomer* army nickname for a marine.

Gomer Pyle *n.* [the name of a comic yokel character played by Jim Nabors on *The Andy Griffith Show* (CBS-TV, spring 1963 through summer 1964) and *Gomer Pyle, U.S.M.C.* (CBS-TV, fall 1964 through summer 1970); cf. GOMER]
1. an enlisted man in the U.S. Marine Corps.—used derisively.

1982 "W.T. Tyler" *Rogue's March* 68: Up yours too, Gomer Pyle.

2. a yokel or dolt.

1987 Nichols & Tillman *Yankee Sta.* 81: A good driver in a clunker can beat a Gomer Pyle in a hotrod.

gon[1] *n.* GUN, *n.*, 1.

1911 A.H. Lewis *Apaches of N.Y.* 131: He joined out wit' that mob of gons Goldie Lovie took to Syracuse last fall. **1933** Ersine *Pris. Slang* 40: *Gon, Gonif*, n. (From the Hebrew). A thief.

gon[2] *n. R.R.* a gondola car.

1934 *Louisville & Nashville* (Dec.) 27: Big gon of coal. **1970** *Current Slang* V 5: *Chip gon*, n. A high sided gondola car used in hauling wood chips.

gon[3] *n.* gonorrhea.—also constr. with *the.*

1935 E. Anderson *Hungry Men* 194: "Have any of you guys ever had the syph?"..."I've had the gon." **1939** C.R. Cooper *Scarlet* 105: If a girl likes a fellow and she catches the "gon" from him, and her parents find out about it, she'll blame everybody else before she'll put the finger on the boy she likes. **1963** Packer *Alone at Night* 72: In charge of syph and gon.

gonads *n.pl.* **1.** the testicles; in phr. **have by the gonads** to have in a helpless position.

1919 H.L. Mencken, in Riggio *Dreiser-Mencken Letters* II 350: Be sure to keep the X-rays off your gonads. **1957** Rowan *Go South* 26: If the mob responds slowly, kick it where it thinks—in its collective gonads—by playing upon its sexual fears. **1962** Quirk *Red Ribbons* 140: That's the word, the jockeys will not violate air-safety rules on penalty of having their gonads smashed with a wooden mallet. **1966** Derrig *Pride* 30: And that's where the Major has you right by the gonads. **1966** Shepard *Doom Pussy* 166: We've got 'em by the gonads. Why don't we squeeze? **1978** in *Maledicta* VI (1982) 23: Testicles...gonads. **1989** "Capt. X" & Dodson *Unfriendly Skies* 124: I had a guy on board wearing pants with no crotch seams in them. I had to...tell him to cover his gonads.

2. courage; (*also*) effrontery; nerve.

1972 R. Barrett *Lovomaniacs* 299: That creep...Pure brass gonads! **1973** Overgard *Hero* 52: I can shape your boys up, put 'em on the boat and wave bye-bye, but from there on it's God and gonads.

gondola *n.* usu. *pl.* a large clumsy shoe.

1929–31 D. Runyon *Guys & Dolls* 76: He only thinks the old gondolas are a little heavy to shove around this night. **1971** Sorrentino *Up from Never* 102: Will ya watch where ya step wid those gondolas.

gone *adj.* **1.** drunk.

1929–33 Farrell *Young Manhood* 225: You were pretty gone last night. **1961** Terry *Old Liberty* 19: He was a little gone.

2. *Jazz.* **a.** superlative; delightful; wonderful.—often constr. with *real.*

1946 Mezzrow & Wolfe *Really Blues* 306: *Gone*: out of this world, superlative. **1947** *Time* (Oct. 6): "Gassed" (tickled pink), "to be nowhere" (to be broke), "you're gone" (you're great). **1949** Flesch *Readable Writing* 4: "Give me a double hunk of that gone apple pie!" "Gone"...means good—tops—out of this world. "Real gone" means absolute tops. **1950** *Neurotica* (Spring) 33: Thrashing out the differences between "gone pot" and "nowhere pot." **1950** *Neurotica* (Autumn) 46: And if'n you cats wanna make it back later on...like that's gone. **1950–52** Ulanov *Hist. Jazz* 351: *Gone*: superlative, may be further qualified, such as "real gone." **1952** Ellson *Golden Spike* 138: That's a gone coat. **1955** O'Connor *Last Hurrah* 131: He gimme one of them *real* gone keys! Crazy crazy! **1956** E. Hunter *Second Ending* 278: "You asleep?"..."No." "Gone. Try some of this, man." **1962** Killens *Heard the Thunder* 159 [ref. to 1943]: Worm was a real gone [jitter] bug. **1966–67** P. Thomas *Mean Streets* 24: Musicians pound out gone beats on...conga drums and bongos.

b. extraordinary; (*also*) complete or thoroughgoing.—used prenominally.

1955 Ellson *Rock* 123: He's a real gone stud. You don't know what he'll do next. **1959** Zugsmith *Beat Generation* 137: This is a real gone drag. **1959** in Cox *Delinquent, Hipster, Square* 35: The most useless occupation in this whole gone world. **1964–66** R. Stone *Hall of Mirrors* 75: Where did you get that pitch about how you were a gone juicehead and...you see the light? **1971** Cameron *First Blood* 103: But you are a real gone dingbat, Marvin.

¶ In phrase:

¶ **gone on, 1.** disgusted with.

1873 Small *Douglass & Mule* 20: "I'se clean gone on dat yer dam mule. He's de cussedest knowing mule dat ebber I seed," said Fred, rubbing for repairs.

2. infatuated with; enamored of.—often constr. with *dead.* Now *colloq.*

*1887 in *F & H* III 176: He was a fine fellow...And was gone on Lady Lorrimor. **1890** *Puck* (Feb. 19) 437: Why, she's just dead gone on music. *1890 in *F & H* IV 176: He must have been terribly gone on this woman. **1891** Maitland *Slang Dict.* 90: *Dead gone* (Am.), infatuated. A girl is "dead gone" on a man or *vice versa.* **1896** Ade *Artie* 53: Oh, but they was gone on each other. **1899** Dunne *Hearts of Countrymen* 73: I've heerd that th' president is dead gawn on him. **1908** in "O. Henry" *Works* 1315: I tell you, old man—there's a dandy girl in that old house next door that I'm dead gone on. **1923** Ornitz *Haunch, Paunch & Jowl* 60: I am dead gone on Gretel. **1942** Breslow *Blondie Goes to College* (film): Is she that gone on the drip? **1948** Manone & Vandervoort *Trumpet* 27: My papa...got tired of me being so gone on music.

gone *adv.* surpassingly; extraordinarily.

*a1867 in G.W. Harris *Lovingood* 40: She...tole me I wer gwine tu hev "the gonest purty shut [i.e. shirt] in that range."

gone beaver *n. West.* GONE GOOSE.—used collect.

1847 Ruxton *Far West* 46: From that moment he was "gone beaver"; "he felt queer," he said, "all over, like a buffalo shot in the lights." **1857** in *DA*: We are "gone beaver," sure—the whole of us!

gone bird *n.* GONE GOOSE.

1889 Barrère & Leland *Dict. Slang* I 417: He is a "gone case," a "gone goose," a "gone coon," "gone bird," or a "goner."

gone chicken *n.* GONE GOOSE. Also **gone chick.**

1834 W.G. Simms *Guy Rivers* 171: Yes—I thought myself a gone chick under that spur, George. **1835** in *DA*: I really believe I'm assassinated—I'm a gone chicken! *ca1863 in *JAF* V (1892) 277: And, if you chance to miss, why, you are a poor, gone chick. **1864** *Battle-Fields of So.* 110: If you hadn't dodged so much, you was a gone chicken long ago.

gone coon *n.* GONE GOOSE.

1837 *Spirit of Times* (June 10) 132: If they didn't do something for him, he was a *gone coon*. **1839** *Spirit of Times* (July 27) 247: There is no getting around a widder, when one takes a hankering arter a feller he's a gone coon. **1839** Marryat *Diary* 266: "I'm a *gone coon*" implies "I am distressed—or ruined—or lost." **1845** in Thornton *Amer. Gloss.* I 373: The acquisition of Canada...is put down on all sides as a gone coon. **1850** Garrard *Wah-to-Yah* 163: Sez I, hyar's a gone coon ef they keep my gun. **1853** "P. Paxton" *In Texas* 309: If he onst gits thar he's a gone coon. *a1889 in Barrère & Leland *Dict. Slang* I 417: I knew, in the language of the States, that I was a *gone* coon. **1889** Meriwether *Tramp at Home* 95: If you blow on us, you're a gone coon. **1894** S. Crane *Red Badge* 26: I'm a gone coon this first time. **1931** Lubbock *Bully Hayes* 58: Of course the sheriff's...a gone coon. **1968, 1970** in *DARE.*

gone gander *n.* GONE GOOSE.

1848 Bartlett *Amer.* 160: In New York it is said, "He's a *gone gander*," i.e. a lost man.

gone goose *n.* a person or thing that is doomed beyond all hope or saving; [a] gone goose with (*obs.*) the end for.

1830 in Thornton *Amer. Gloss.* I 373: You are a gone goose, friend. **1831** in *DAE*: The Huntonites see how 'twas gone goose with 'em. **1836** in Haliburton *Sam Slick* 72: I guess it's a gone goose with him. He's heavy mortgaged. **1838** [Haliburton] *Clockmaker* (ser. 2) 22: It's gone goose with them arter that. **1840** *Spirit of Times* (Oct. 24) 398: I am up a tree, you may depend. It's gone goose with me. **1845** in *DAE.* **1849** Mackay *Western World* I 149: I soon discovered that there were two sorts of candidates, the "winning horses" and the "gone geese." **1850** G.G. Foster *Gas-Light* 43: Everyone who goes there is likely to turn out a "gone goose." **1864** in Horrocks *Dear Parents* 105: The Southern Confederacy is a gone goose. **1866** in Thornton *Amer. Gloss.* I 373: That house is a gone goose [in the flood]. *1867 Smyth *Sailor's Wd. Bk.* 343: Gone goose.—a ship deserted or given up in despair (*in extremis*). **1930** Raine *Valiant* 93: You're a gone goose if you go foolin' around the lady. **1958** Burns & Allen (CBS-TV): If Bonnie Sue sees them spooning around the house, I'm a gone goose.

gone gosling *n.* GONE GOOSE.

1837 Neal *Charc. Sks.* 179: Me and the whole on 'em is little better nor a flock of gone goslings. *a1859 in Bartlett *Amer.* (ed. 2) 174: The poor greenhorn who falls into the clutches of the sharpers upon arriving in the metropolis may regard himself as a *gone gosling.* **1906** *DN* III 138: *Gone goslin*, in phr. "He's a gone goslin." Doomed. **1918** *Sat. Eve. Post* (Nov. 23) 54: He's a gone gosling, marching to the calaboose with steel jewelry on his wrists. **1919** *Am. Leg. Wkly.* (Oct. 24) 23: "Is there any gas here, lieutenant?"..."I don't know, but if there is I'm a gone goslin." **1957** Willingham *Strange One* (film): Those freshmen talk, and we're gone goslin's. **1970** L.D. Johnson *Devil's Front Porch* 13: If a man collapsed from fright…he was a gone gosling.

gone in *adj.* done for; played out; (*hence*) tired out; (*also*) broke.
1863 in Dwyer & Lingenfelter *Songs of Gold Rush* 160: I wake to find that I am "done gone in." **1871** in M. Lewis *Mining Frontier* 28: The "Camp" of 1870 is quiet, sleepy, shrunken, poor, "gone in," "gone up." *ca***1880** Bellard *Gone for a Soldier* 54: We thought we were gone in sure this time. **1897** Norris *Vandover* 506: But you *do* look gone-in this morning, sure.

goner *n.* a person or thing that is dead, lost, or past recovery; GONE GOOSE.
1847 Robb *Kaam* 6: Take jest anuther smell and you're a goner. **1850** G.G. Foster *Gas-Light* 55: If the stranger is not fully aware of the character of those among whom he has fallen, he is a "goner." **1853** in *AS* (Oct. 1951) 225: Or you're a goner, as far as this country is concerned. *a***1859** in Bartlett *Amer.* 174: You are a goner, now, for sartin! *a***1864** in J.I. Robertson *Blue & Gray* 104: More men die of homesickness than all other diseases, and when a man gives up and lies down he is a *goner*. **1872** "W. Dexter" *Young Mustanger* 12: We're goners, Jack, sure's "guldy." **1903** A. Adams *Log of Cowboy* 129: Then he's a goner. **1940** F. Hunt *Trail fr. Tex.* 71: Looks like he's a goner. **1951** Pryor *The Big Play* 6: If he ain't a goner, he ought to be. **1975** J. Gould *Maine Lingo* 112: "My motor's a goner; crankshaft snapped."…"He's a goner; Doc gives him three months." **1978** Strieber *Wolfen* 68: I think I would have been a goner.

gone sucker *n.* GONE GOOSE.
1833 in Botkin *Amer. Folklore* 274: I wouldn't risk a huckleberry to a persimmon that we don't…get treed and sink to the bottom like gone suckers. **1840** *Spirit of Times* (June 13) 174: But for their "stealings in," they would be "gone suckers." **1841** in Thornton *Amer. Gloss.* I 373: I tell'd 'em you and the boy was gone suckers. **1851** in Thornton *Amer. Gloss.*: I feared that I should lose my way, and then I knew I was a gone sucker. **1868** "L. Legrand" *Dime Dial.* 91: I'm sorry for you—you're a gone sucker! **1873** Badger *Two-handed Mat* 67: Fight like devils or we're gone suckers!

gone under *adj.* see GO UNDER, *v.*

gone up *adj.* see GO UP, *v.*

goney *n.* [of dial. E orig.] Esp. *N.E.* a simpleton; dolt. Cf. GOONEY, *n.*
*ca***1580** in *OED* s.v. *gony:* & yet the gray-beard gonnie daunceth, praunceth, & skippeth friskoioly. **1836** in Haliburton *Sam Slick* 62: There's a proper goney for you to go and raise such a buildin'. **1838** [Haliburton] *Clockmaker* (Ser. 2) 41: That goney…is like a gun that goes off at half cock. *****1857** in *F & H* III 176: But the lark's when a goney up with us is shut,/As ain't up to our lurks, our flash patter, and smut. **1859** Bartlett *Amer.* (ed. 2) 174: *Goney* or *Gony.* A great goose; a stupid fellow. New England.

gong[1] *n.* [app. short for GONGER, *n.*] *Narc.* an opium pipe.
1915 Bronson-Howard *God's Man* 393: Come, lie 'round and join in the fun;/With the aid of "the gong"/We will quit the mad throng,/For the Land of the Pure Li-um. **1922** J. Conway, in *Variety* (May 5) 12: She's one of them curious kind that you've met around the gong who knock over the lamp tryin' to roll their own pills and then want a history of the grease from the time it was a poppy seed in China. **1933** D.W. Maurer, in *AS* (Apr.) 27: The [opium] pipe is a *gong*, a *gonger*, or a *stem*.

¶ In phrases:

¶ **hit** [or **beat**] **the gong** *Narc.* to smoke opium.
1933 D.W. Maurer, in *AS* (Apr.) 27: When the opium addict is smoking he is said to be *hitting the gong, kicking the gonger, kicking the gong around*, or *lying on his hip.* **1936** D.W. Maurer, in *AS* (Apr.) 118: *Beat the gong.* To smoke opium.

¶ **kick** [or **boot**] **the gong** [around], 1. *Narc.* to smoke opium or (*less freq.*) marijuana.
1928 Callahan *Man's Grim Justice* 26: We can lay off for a few days and "kick the old gong around." **1931** L. Zukofsky, in Ahearn *Pound/Zukofsky* 109: Not that I expect to…kick the gong around. **1931** *AS* VI (Aug.) 439: *Kickin' the gong.* A drug addict expression meaning "charged up." **1933** in W.F. Nolan *Black Mask Boys* 203: Took 'er down to Chinatown; showed 'er how to kick the gong aroun'. **1936** Kingsley *Dead End* 719: Dis is a swell pipe-dream I'm havin'! I'm Minnie de Moocher kickin' a gong aroun'! **1942–49** Goldin et al. *DAUL* 116: *Kick the gong around*…To smoke marijuana. **1952** H. Grey *Hoods* 26: "I would like to smoke a pipe of that stuff sometimes"…"That's what they call kicking the gong around." **1956** Longstreet *Real Jazz* 144: It certainly has put

a lot of new chords into jazz when you're kicking the gong around. **1957** H. Danforth & J. Horan *D.A.'s Man* 75 [ref. to 1938]: The room seemed to be the magnet for visiting mobsters, who stayed for the night, drinking and smoking opium—"kicking the gong around" as the old-time mobs called it. **1957** Hecht *Charlie* 139: Our boy was incommunicado, kicking the gong.

2. to fool around; cut up.
1945 Seaton *Junior Miss* (film): Are you sure your father's serious? Maybe he's just kicking the gong around. **1956** *All Hands* (Apr.) 58: The sailor's been to Hong Kong/And kicked the gong around./He's sailed the whole world over/And one thing he has found:/His ship is…still his home. **1976** *N.Y. Times Bk. Review* (Sept. 12) 8: To watch him, impeccably dressed in white tails and shiny patent-leather shoes, gyrate and jump, shout his "hi-de-hos" and generally kick the gong around in front of that superb group of…musicians.

3. to gossip, chat, or talk, esp. idly.
1945 Dos Passos *Tour* 106: This bitchin' don't mean a thing. If the boys didn't get it up their nose sometimes an' kick the gong around a little, they'd get the Asiatic stare. **1969** Moynahan *Pairing Off* 151: My regulars'd hang in here a while and then go across the street and kick the gong around in Margarite's house until the small hours. **1981** L. Wachtel, on WINS radio (July 6): So with monetary strategists in Washington set to kick the gong around today….

gong[2] *n.* **1.** *Mil.*, esp. *USAF.* a medal.
*****1921** *N & Q* (Nov. 12) 384 [ref. to WWI]: Gong. A medal. *****1941** in Wiener *Flyers* 46: Collect a gong. Be awarded a medal. **1941** Kendall *Army & Navy Slang* 3: Chest hardware…medals, also called gongs. **1944** D. Runyon, in *Collier's* 70: The only person present is a big guy in uniform with a lot of gongs on his chest, which is a way of saying medals. **1946** G.C. Hall, Jr. *1000 Destroyed* 83: Their medals accumulated systematically on their tunics and photographers were there to snap the "gong" ceremony. **1948** Lay & Bartlett *Twelve O'Clock High!* 117: Congratulations…on the gong. **1951–52** Frank *Hold Back Night* 189: And I want to put him in for a gong, sergeant. **1963** Ross *Dead Are Mine* 14 [ref. to WWII]: Maybe I'll play hero again and pick up another medal. Or gong, as the Limeys say. **1965** LeMay & Kantor *Mission with LeMay* 35: I number now among my intimate friends a man who is now entitled to wear a pretty good gong or two among his ribbons. **1966** Shepard *Doom Pussy* 52: The most recent had been a celebration when Smash received a gong, the Distinguished Flying Cross. **1967** Taggart *Reunion of the 108th* 111: "What was that one decoration, Chappie—Distinguished Service Order?" "Some gong, I scarcely recall." **1980** S. Fuller *Big Red* 202: The general'll hang a gong on you. **1987** Robbins *Ravens* 225: Take the gongs but keep your hands off my ass.

2. *Boxing.* the chin.
1922 J. Conway, in *Variety* (Mar. 3) 42: I knew we had a chance if Tomato could cop him on the button.…He let his right drive and socked this big clam digger right on the gong.

3. the penis.
[**1916** Cary *Venery* I 113: Gong Beater—The penis.] **1967** Mailer *Vietnam* 174: Whoever said your gong was not a magnet? **1968** Baker et al. *CUSS* 127: *Gong.* Male sex organ.

gong *v. Mil.* to award a medal to.—used passively.
1951–52 P. Frank *Hold Back Night* 65: I told you I'd put you in for the Silver Star, and promotion. You're getting gonged okay, but no promotion.

gonger *n.* [orig. unkn.] *Narc.* an opium pipe; in phr. **kick the gonger** to smoke opium. Also (*obs.*) **gongerine**.
1914 Jackson & Hellyer *Vocab.* 38: *Gonger*, Noun. Current amongst opium smokers and drug fiends. An opium pipe. Also used in the diminutive form of "Gongerine." **1931** in D.W. Maurer *Lang. Und.* 48: *Gonger*, n. An opium pipe. **1936** Dai *Opium Addiction* 199: *Gonger.* Pipe for smoking opium. Also called *the stick* or *log.* **1936** D.W. Maurer, in *AS* (Apr.) 123: *To kick the…gonger.* To smoke an opium pipe.

gonicles *n.pl.* [gonads + testicles] testicles. *Joc.*
1958 Gilbert *Vice Trap* 127: He's got you by the gonicles.

gonies *n.pl.* [alter. of GONADS] testicles.
1970 Ponicsan *Last Detail* 132: My goddam gonies are frozen. **1972** Ponicsan *Cinderella Liberty* 23: You better pray the doctor don't slip and lop off your gonies.

gong-kicker *n. Narc.* an opium smoker. Also **gong-beater.**
1934 in Partridge *Dict. Und.* 298: Gong-kicker. **1953** Anslinger & Tompkins *Traf. in Narc.* 309: *Gong kicker.* An opium addict. **1955** in *OEDS*: *Gong beater*, one who smokes opium. **1970** Landy *Underground Dict.* 91: *Gong beater*…Opium smoker.

gonk *n.* [orig. unkn.] *Theat.* (see quot.).

1942 Liebling *Telephone* 171: They prefer the word "gonk" to "hokum." *Ibid.* 182: Drinking coffee and devising new bits of gonk.

gonnif *n.* [Yid *ganef* 'thief'] **1.** *Und. & Police.* a thief; (esp. in early use) a pickpocket. Also vars.

*1839 Brandon *Poverty & Crime* 164: *Gonnoff*,—A thief. **1846** *Lives of Felons* 82: He yet lives in New York...and is still surrounded by the most celebrated "cracksmen" and "gonnaufs" of the country. *Ibid.* 94: "Is that man a *gonnauf*", charley?"..."Thief. **1848** Judson *Mysteries* 61: He next...became a "gnof" or pickpocket. *Ibid.* 527: "Gnof." Pronounced *gonof*, a gipsy and slang term for pickpocket. *1852 C. Dickens *Bleak House* 265: I am obliged to take him into custody. He's as obstinate a young gonoph as I know. **1859** Matsell *Vocab.* 38: *Gonnoff*. A thief that has attained the higher walks of his profession. **1860–61** R.F. Burton *City of Saints* 299: A Hindu "gonnoff" would soon "pike" out of a "premonitory" like this. **1871** Banka *Pris. Life* 493: A Retired Rogue,...Gonoff. **1911** A.H. Lewis *Apaches of N.Y.* 15: He used to be a gonoph, and had worked the rattlers and ferries in his youth. But he got settled a couple of times and it broke his nerve. No pickpocket is good after he passes forty years. **1951** D. Wilson *My Six Convicts* 73: Where they pickin' up these type gonifs? **1954** Schulberg *Waterfront* 15: A D.A. might enjoy the hospitality of Tom McGovern and go easy on the waterfront, but he wasn't an out and out goniff like Donnelly. **1972** Wambaugh *Blue Knight* 9: What's the matter, you old gonif? **1986** R. Campbell *In La-La Land* 11: The rain had washed...the gonifs and petty grifters off the [street]. **1987** *Nat. Lampoon* (Dec.) 33: The Double-Dealing Gonif or Two-Faced Chiseler. **1991** Stoppard *Billy Bathgate* (film): Like the lowdown fuckin' gonnif that he is.

2. (with reduced force) a rascal; scoundrel; good-for-nothing. Also vars.

*a1889 in Barrère & Leland *Dict. Slang* I 418: "Produce the infant."..."This is it," said...the proud father..."An ugly red-faced gonoph like that." **1935** *Amer. Mercury* (June) 229: Goniff: fool. **1939** *AS* (Oct.) 239: *Gonnof.* Unpleasant guest.

gonnif *v.* to steal.

*1857 C. Dickens, in *F & H* III 177: From the swell mob, we diverge to the kindred topics of cracksmen, fences,...designing young people who go out gonophing, and other "schools." **1867** *Nat. Police Gaz.* (Mar. 23) 2: As he is generally called by the "gonoffing" fraternity. *a1889 in Barrère & Leland *Dict. Slang* I 418: He invested all that he'd gonophed from his poor old father in di'mond shares.

gon-moll *n.* var. GUN-MOLL.

gonsil *n.* var. GUNSEL.

gonus *n.* [alter. of GONEY, *n.*] a blockhead; fool.

1842 in *DAE*...A stupid fellow, a dolt, a boot-jack, an ignoramus, is called [at Dartmouth College] a *gonus.* **1848** in *DAE*: Future gonuses will swear by his name. **1856** B. Hall *College Wds.* (ed. 2) 229: *Gonus.* A stupid fellow...The word *goney*, with the same meaning, is often used.

gonzel *n.* var. GUNSEL.

gonzo *n.* **1.** a wild, aggressive, or eccentric person.

1977 in Ayto & Simpson *Oxf. Dict. Mod. Slang*: To make sure I wouldn't make too big a gonzo of myself. **1984** Heath *A-Team* 187: Give this gonzo a haircut. **1993** Evans & Gunter *Journey to Center of Earth* (film): Seven type-A gonzos [make up the crew].

2. *Journ.* eccentricity or craziness.

1978 *Rolling Stone* (Apr. 6) 8: A flash of gonzo from Dr. Thompson. **1978** *Rolling Stone* (May 4) 13 [caption]: Ted Nugent treats the crowd to a dose of live gonzo.

gonzo *adj.* [introduced by Hunter S. Thompson in *Rolling Stone* (Nov. 11, 1971) to characterize his own style of subjective, creative, hyperbolic, strongly satirical journalism; perh. ult. sugg. by It *gonzo* 'simpleton']

1. wild, eccentric, or out of control; crazy; (*hence*) highly intoxicated. [The term is discussed by P. Tamony in *AS* LVIII (1983), 73–75.]

1971 H.S. Thompson, in *Rolling Stone* (Nov. 11) 38: But what *was* the story? Nobody had bothered to say. So we would have to drum it up on our own...Horatio Alger gone mad on drugs in Las Vegas...pure Gonzo journalism. *Ibid.* 40: My name is Doctor Gonzo. Prepare our suite at once. **1973** *Atlantic* (July) 100: Gonzo Journalism supplements the techniques of the novelist with the techniques of the lunatic. **1978** *Nat. Lampoon* (Oct.) 4: Blotto, wigged, wired, gassed, wacked out of your skull, gonzo, gone, wasted, shit-faced. **1982** in "J.B. Briggs"

Drive-In 13: The Reaper turned gonzo and knifed her in the stomach. **1984** *TriQuarterly* (Spring) 311: She has to go be this big gonzo sucker you gotta look up just to look at her. **1986** *Campus Voice* (Sept.) 43: Topping this year's list of celebrated parties: a political rally gone gonzo. **1987** *Campus Voice* (Winter) 25: Here's who's responsible for the gonzo gimmickry that makes a band. **1988** D. Clements *Vampire* (film): The guy's completely gonzo.

2. [elaboration of *gone*] gone; finished.

1974 Andrews & Dickens *Over the Wall* 86: Caddy and all—/gonzo!/ (*Laughs softly*). **1987** *Crossfire* (CNN-TV) (May 7): He predicted that by Friday, Gary Hart would be gonzo. **1987** *Miami Vice* (NBC-TV): "The girl?" "Gonzo. She didn't even come down to check his pulse." **1989** Leib *Fire Dream* 287: This is a serious problem, but if we handle it just right, old Mendoza is gonzo.

gonzoed *adj.* highly intoxicated.—also constr. with *out.*

1979 in *AS* LVIII (1983) 74: All gonzoed out on nitro poppers. **1984** Algeo *Stud Buds* 6: To be drunk...gonzoed.

Gonzo Station *n.* *Navy.* the Indian Ocean and Persian Gulf.

1980 *Newsweek* (June 16) 38: "Gonzo Station," the irreverent nickname weary U.S. sailors have given the Indian Ocean. **1982** *U.S. News & W.R.* (Feb. 22) 32: The *Constellation* is one of about 20 U.S. ships patrolling sea-lanes leading to the Strait of Hormuz, gateway to the gulf—an area known by the Americans posted here as "Gonzo Station." **1983** M. Skinner *USAFE* 48: Navy Tomcat drivers out on Gonzo Station in the Persian Gulf.

goo *n.* [orig. uncert.; perh. clipping of *burgoo* 'a type of stew'; cf. 1915 quot.] **1.** an oozy, sticky, or viscous substance; muck. Now *colloq.*

1900 *DN* II 30: *Cream de goo, n.* Milk toast. *Ibid.* 38: Goo, n. 1. Any liquid. 2. Anything sticky. 3. Dirty moisture. **1915** H.L. Wilson *Ruggles* 55: A stew...which Cousin Egbert declared was "some goo." **1918** *Sat. Eve. Post* (Oct. 5) 38: There is...real American cake with what the gob calls goo between the layers—goo being a generic term for any soft, sweet, sticky ingredient such as jam or jelly. **1918** Penner et al. *120th Arty* (Nov. 11): I saw men actually fall in to their waists in the glimy goo. **1941** G. Legman, in G. Henry *Sex Vars.* II 1167: "Goo" refers to the viscid semen. **1941** in Bond & Anderson *Flying T. Diary* 24: A pail of horrid-smelling goo that was shaving cream. **1962** T. Berger *Reinhart* 40: Powder and lotion and scalp-goo. **1972** in *Penthouse* (Jan. 1973) 126: Out there in the drizzle, ankle-deep in the goo. **1981** Gahan Wilson, in *Rod Serling's Mag.* (July) 8: What could be more pleasant than to see such a thoroughly nasty fellow turn into slimy goo, even as we watch? **1981** Story *UFOs & Science* 99: It was speculated that the eerie goo might have come from outer space. **1991** Marcinko & Weisberg *Rogue Warrior* 5: I was about to splatter myself into strawberry-colored goo.

2. maudlin sentimentality or sweetness.

1901 Irwin *Sonnets* (unp.): Coax her to think that I'm no gilded pill,/ But rather the unadulterated goo. **1943** in T. Williams *Letters* 73: The poem is by no means "goo" nor do I find it unoriginal or imitative. **1961** Terry *Old Liberty* 58: Full of advice and sickening goo, I'm sure.

3. *Av.* heavy fog or overcast.

1966 F. Elkins *Heart of Man* 61: It was all milk and goo and high overcast. **1969** Cagle *Naval Aviation Guide* 393: Goo. Fog, "soup." **1986** Coonts *Intruder* 186: Get out of the goo and try again.

goob *n.* GOOBER, 1.a. [The word seems to have acquired wide currency in the early 1980's.]

1919 Cortelyou *Arizona to the Huns* 88: [He] was a great big awkward "Goob." **1923** *Bomb* (Iowa State College) 428: They are the gang that used to have Nutts Satchel, and that goob Sessions hangs around there too. **1987** Univ. Tenn. student theme: [Being called a] *twit, goob, geek,...dip* or *sap* is definitely an insult. **1988** *Lame Monkey* (Univ. Tenn.) (Mar. 21) 6: [The professor] is a goob who couldn't teach an ape to scratch his ass. **1988** Eble *Campus Slang* (Spring) 5: What a goob— he's even wearing a pocket protector.

2. [perh. a fanciful coinage of indep. origin] GOOBER, 4.

1970–72 in *AS* L (1975) 59: *Goob, n.* Pimple, skin blemish. **1976** Eble *Campus Slang* (Nov.) 3: *Goob*—an acne pimple. **1976** Conroy *Santini* 16: Jesus,...you must cure my brother of his maggot face...cure Ben Meecham, the boy whose face is one big goob. **1981** Spears *Slang & Euphem.* 168: *Goob* a pimple. **1981** Eble *Campus Slang* (Mar.) 3: *Goob*— an acne pimple: "I've got an awful goob on my chin."

goober *n.* [dial. *goober* 'peanut', of African orig.] **1.a.** *So.* a yokel; foolish bumpkin; (*also*) a simpleton or (now esp.) a silly person.

1862 in W.C. Davis *Orphan Brig.* 77: The Lt....was such a "goober" !

don't believe he knew which road to take. **1946** Bill *Beleaguered City* 227: There was an up-country "gouber" who had vowed not to have his hair cut until the war was won. **1981** D.E. Miller *Jargon* 244: Goober. A loser. **1987** *Cheers* (NBC-TV): Hey, goober! How about pourin' us another round?

b. Esp. *Confed. Army.* a native of North Carolina or Georgia.

1863 in *DAE*: Conscripts by the dozen…Some from Mississippi state and "Goobers" from Tar river. **1871** *Schele de Vere Americanisms* 57: *Peanuts* [are]…known in North Carolina and the adjoining States as *Goober* peas, so that during the late Civil War a conscript from the so-called "piney-woods" of that State was apt to be nick-named a *Goober*. **1914** Giles *Rags & Hope* 168 [ref. to Civil War]: They filled their haversacks with snow-ball cartridges and filed off up the valley, so as to take the innocent and unsuspecting "goobers" from the rear. **1937** in *DARE*: *Goober*…Used some way in poking fun at the CCC boys who came from the "goober country," Georgia or Alabama.

2. *So.* the penis. *Joc.*

1952 *AS* (Feb.) 157 [ref. to 1920's]: *Goober* had formerly been identified with the distinctive organ of young boys. **1952** Randolph & Wilson *Down in the Holler* 101: Goober and goober-pea are names for peanut, but are not favored by the ultra-refined because they also designate the male genitals. **1965** Trimble *Sex Words* 91: *Goober*…The Penis. Cf. the joke, "Why can't a peanut have sex?" "Because he can't get his goober out!" **1979–82** Gwin *Overboard* 119: Gobble my goober, you animal.

3. a gob of phlegm.

1966–70 J. Carroll, in *Paris Rev.* (No. 50) 112: Spitting a giant goober all over the…door. **1972** Carr *Bad* 136: He coughed up a big yellow goober. **1978** Wharton *Birdy* 54: Not big goobers or anything gross, just a fine spray kind of spit. **1983** K. Miller *Lurp Dog* 189: He hawked and let fly with a real goober. *a***1987** in K. Marshall *Combat Zone* 139 [ref to *ca*1970]: And you'd squirt saline down into [the patients'] trach and they'd cough and the phlegm would come out in big clumps. We had goober contests, they were called goobers. It's like who could hit the wall farthest. The patients were unconscious, they didn't know what was going on.

4. *Stu.* a large pimple, esp. on the face. Cf. GOOB, 2.

1972–79 T. Wolfe *Right Stuff* 130: Zits,…whiteheads, blackheads,…goobers. **1981** Spears *Slang & Euphem.* 168: *Goober*…a pimple. *Ibid.* 175: Gubers acne; facial pimples.

¶ In phrase: **hang a goober** to kiss.

1927 Mayer *Between Us Girls* 17: In Pɪᴛᴛsburgh they call a little light sᴍᴀᴄᴋing "ʜᴀɴɢing ɢᴏᴏʙᴇʀs"—can you ʙᴇᴀʀ it, my dear?

gooberbrain *n. So.* PEABRAIN, *n.*

1968 J.P. Miller *Race for Home* 170 [ref. to 1930's]: The same must work for climbing chicken shacks, he knew: foot in crotch of chinaberry tree, up and onto roof of shack before those rows of goober-brains could even cluck a what-was-that… **1987** graffito, Univ. Tenn.: Billy is a goober brain!

goober-grabber *n.* **1.** *So.* a poor white farmer, esp. a lowlander of Georgia or Arkansas; a yokel.—used derisively. Also vars.

1869 *Overland Mo.* (Aug.) 129: A Georgian is popularly known in the South as a "Gouber-grabbler." **1877** Bartlett *Amer.* (ed. 4): Goober-Grabbers. In Georgia and Alabama, backwoods people. **1878** McElroy *Andersonville* 271 [ref. to Civil War]: "So yer Yanks, air ye?" said the venerable Goober-Grabber (the nickname in the South for Georgians). **1881** A.A. Hayes *New Colo.* 93: I struck a kind of a colony of *goober-grubbers* from Georgia… **1908** *DN* III 316: *Goober-grabber, n.* A Georgian. Sometimes used of any backwoodsman. **1936** *AS* (Oct.) 315: *Goober-grabbers, n.* People of southern Arkansas, as distinguished from the hillbilly. **1966** in *DARE*: A rustic or countrified person…*Goober-grabber.*

2. *So.* (see quot.).

1952 Randolph & Wilson *Holler* 101: Some people use *goober grabber* to mean a lowlander as distinguished from a mountain man…But there are many settlements in Arkansas and Missouri where *goober-grabber*…means a wanton, lascivious woman.

good *n.* liquor or psychotropic drugs of high quality.—constr. with *the.*

1843 in G.W. Harris *High Times* 28: Each party should…treat: a quart of the *good.* **1976** *Deadly Game* (ABC-TV): I got five keys of the good.

¶ In phrase: **on the good** *Und.* satisfactory; perfect.

1904 *Life in Sing Sing* 263: Everything was on the good, when we got a blow.

good *adj. Mil.* (of one of class of enemies) dead.—used prenominally. Orig. *Joc.*

1868 in *DA*: I like an Indian better dead than living. I have never…seen a good Indian…except when I have seen a dead Indian. **1884** in *DA*: On the frontier, a good Indian means a "dead Indian." **1890** in *DAE*: Good Indian: a dead Apache. **1928–29** Nason *White Slicker* 265 [ref. to WWI]: "Any Boche in these woods?" "Not now…Only good ones." **1930** Irwin *Tramp & Und. Sl.*: *Good*…Dead, when applied to a criminal. **1930** in *DA*: He was apt to pay with at least two "good Indians" shot from his dusty ranks. **1970** former SP3, U.S. Army, age *ca*25: You know the old saying, "The only good Indian is a dead Indian"? In Vietnam you'd hear, "The only good gook is a dead gook."

¶ In phrase: **get good** to get drunk.

1897 Ade *Pink* 173: I neveh couldn' 'splain to huh 'bout 'at night I got good on gin an' honey.

good buddy *n.* **1.** Esp. *So.* a male friend.—used esp. in direct address; (*hence*) (*CB*) a fellow CB radio operator.

1956 Algren *Walk on Wild Side* 170: Why, then *lead* me, goodbuddy, *Ibid.* 171: There's a deal, goodbuddy. **1964–66** R. Stone *Hall of Mirrors* 92: Waal, goodbuddy,…WUSA is a well planned out business operation. **1975** Dills *CB Slanguage*: *Good buddy*: salutation originally by truckers but now used by most highway CBers. **1976** *N.Y. Times Mag.* (Apr. 25) 64: Aaay, we definitely thank you for that info, good buddy. **1989** Leib *Fire Dream* 361: Bombs away, good buddy.

2. a homosexual.

1985 in Safire *Look It Up* 150: It is apparent that you haven't used your CB radio for some time, since the term *good buddy* has for several years been used as a derogatory synonym for the more pejorative terms applied to homosexuals. **1988** *New Yorker* (Sept. 19) 78: "What you don't want to do…is call someone 'good buddy.' No, definitely not." It turns out that the most famous term in the CB vocabulary, which used to mean "friend" or "fellow-driver," has become slang for "homosexual."

goodbye *interj.* ¶ In phrases:

¶ **Goodbye, John!** (see quot.).

1889 Barrère & Leland *Dict. Slang* I 418: *Good-bye, John!* (American), equivalent to all is gone, lost, or over.

¶ **kiss goodbye** to leave or lose permanently; be rid of; (*also*) regard as lost.

1904 Ade *True Bills* 119: The Mark…has kissed good-bye to his Shekels. **1921** *Variety* (Feb. 11) 7: I kissed my dough good-bye after the first round, for it was a foregone conclusion. **1929** Burnett *Iron Man* 211: "I'm going to bet two grand on O'Keefe." "Kiss that good-bye." **1929–30** Farrell *Young Lonigan* 11: Well, I'm kissin' the old dump goodbye tonight. **1939–40** O'Hara *Pal Joey* 18: I guess you kissed that fifty goodbye but that isn't the way I do things. **1940** Hartman & Butler *Rd. to Singapore* (film): I must be so careful/Or I'll kiss my heart goodbye.

good enough *n. West.* (see 1968 quot.).

1967 Edson *Fast Gun* 51: A "good-enough" doesn't often fit this well, no matter how good the man that puts it on. **1968** R. Adams *West. Words* (ed. 2) 128: *Good-enoughs.* Horseshoes purchased by the keg in various sizes, ready to put on a horse's feet cold.

good fellow *n. Stu.* (see quot.).

1856 B. Hall *College Wds.* (ed. 2) 230: *Good fellow.* At the University of Vermont, this term…indicates a soft-brained boy; one who is lacking in intellect, or…"an epithetical fool."

good guy *n.* usu. *pl. Mil.* a member of U.S. or friendly armed forces; a friendly aircraft.

1969 Spetz *Rat Pack Six* 37: The smoke grenade was the standard method of marking friendly positions on the ground so the Air Force could tell where the "good guys" were. **1978** L. Davis *MiG Alley* 50: We two were the only good guys in the area. **1981** C. Nelson *Picked Bullets Up* 59: The coastal fortifications…belong to us good guys. **1988** D. Howard, U.S. Dept. of Defense spokesman (CNN-TV) (July 5): Our good guys we are certainly able to identify—we can certainly identify our own friendly aircraft. **1991** LaBarge *Desert Voices* 194: We were still in good guy country.

good head *n.* Esp. *Und.* an admirable, reliable, or trustworthy person; good fellow.

1927 *DN* V 448: *Good head,* n. A kind-hearted person, one charitably disposed to tramps. **1933** Ersine *Pris. Slang* 40: When you call a criminal a goodhead, you pay him the greatest compliment. **1949** *Time* (Oct. 3) 37: In San Francisco a nice guy is a "good head." **1966** Elli *Riot* 90: Both goodheads, I've known 'em for years.

goodie *n.* a hero, as in a motion picture.

   *1951 in *OEDS* s.v. *baddy:* We got shouted to the pictures...where we cheered the goodies and booed the baddies. **1980** M. Baker *Nam* 41: You see the baddies and the goodies on television and at the movies.

goodied up *adj.* (see quots.).

   1971 Tak *Truck Talk* 75: *Goodied up:* a tractor with many driver luxuries, such as an air conditioner, stereo and a television in the bunk. **1976** Lieberman & Rhodes *CB* 129: *Goodied Up*—Said of a fancy truck.

goodies *n.pl.* **1.** extra or additional features, items, or accessories, esp. those necessary for automotive high performance; (*also*) ingenious or effective devices.

   1951–53 in *AS* (May 1954) 97: *Goodies,* n. Outside accessories on an engine to make it look good or "souped up"; speed accessories. **1957** *Life* (Apr. 29) 140: *Goodies*...Hot-rod accessories. **1962** Tregaskis *Vietnam Diary* 116: He'd drop all his bombs and goodies on time. **1972** R. Barrett *Lovomaniacs* 37: They put these little goodies in the airplane for intelligent pilots to use. **1974** Stevens *More There I Was* 75: Basically a good design, the '39 was loaded down with "goodies" at the expense of performance. **1975** in Higham & Siddall *Combat Aircraft* 4: The latter models had such goodies as more nosewheel tread..., larger escape hatches, Holley carburetors, relocated feathering buttons [etc.]. **1984** Trotti *Phantom* 23: Crammed to the teeth with electronic goodies, it was able to ferret out and jam enemy radar sites. **1991** Marcinko & Weisman *Rogue Warrior* 4: Other goodies: flash-bang grenades...strobes and light-sticks.

   2. the genitals (*occ.* as sing.); (*also*) a woman's breasts or nude figure; (*also*) copulation.

   1958–59 Southern & Hoffenberg *Candy* 216: Snapping his wig like that on account of my tight slick goodie. **1961** L.E. Young *Virgin Fleet* 22 [ref. to 1941]: I feel sorry for the poor swabbies cooped up on this Island without any way of getting their goodies, except for the...cat houses. **1967** Hamma *Motorcycle Mommas* 35: This time I stopped at the goodies and she spread her legs to help me. **1974** Strasburger *Rounding Third* 22: I always have this picture of Smokey Robinson singing while some girl is grabbing his goodies. **1978** Ponicsan *Ringmaster* 62: A genuine hermaphrodite whose goodies you could see for an extra two bucks. **1967–80** Folb *Runnin' Lines* 240: *Goodies*...vagina. **1983** *Night Court* (NBC-TV): What kind of guy wants his entire bowling team to know what his wife's goodies look like? **1991** *Simpsons* (Fox-TV): I'm not asking you to put yourself in a position where I can touch your goodies.

   3. (used ironically).

   1958 J. Davis *College Vocab.* 11: *Goodies*...undesirable tasks. **1978** Univ. Tenn. instructor: The military-industrial complex has all sorts of goodies up its sleeve.

good-looker *n.* a good-looking person, esp. a young woman. Now *colloq.*

   1894 *Harper's Mag.* (Mar.) 498: "What sort of a girl is she?"..."She's a good-looker." **1896** Ade *Artie* 81: How about her bein' a good looker? **1897** Ade *Horne* 167: Is she a good-looker? **1901** Ade *Modern Fables* 20: "But we are not Orientals," said the Good-Looker, proudly. **1902** Wister *Virginian* ch. ii: She's a good-looker. **1920** S. Lewis, in *DA:* Doc Kennicott's new bride, good looker, nice legs.

good night *interj.* (used to indicate or comment on a disastrous conclusion); also used to indicate surprise or exasperation).—also constr. with *nurse, Irene.*

   1889–90 Barrère & Leland *Dict. Slang* I 228: *Carry me out!* (American)...often preceded by "oh, good night!" **1898** Brooks *Strong Hearts* 46: If it had gone the other way, it would have been "good-night, John!" for you and Young Wolf, too. **1911** Van Loan *Big League* 17: If he ever gets within reaching distance of a fly ball—good night! **1914** *Collier's* (May 16) 11: I was to be married a week from tomorrow, but now—good *night!* **1917** Appleton *With the Colors* 17: Stickin' for the Big Show! Will it ever start? When it does, Good night, Irene! **1917** *Camp Meade Herald* (Sept. 23) 4: But, good night, I came up with nary a spavin. **1918** *Ladies' Home Jrnl.* (Feb.) 1: I felt like jumping off the trestle. Good night! **1918** *Independent* (June 22) 472: When he draws a bead on one, it's good night nurse. **1925** Ranck *Doughboys' Book* 20 [ref. to 1918]: Holy smoke! Look at that shell! If one of them things ever hit you, kid, it would be a case of "good night, nurse!" **1929** Benchley *Chips* 186: "Good night!" said Mr. Hertz. "What a layout!" **1973** Boyd & Harris *Baseball Card* 204: When the demon elbow begins its mordant, mournful throb, it's good night, Irene.

good numbers *n.pl.* *CB.* best wishes.

   1975 Dills *CB* 37: *Good numbers:* best wishes..."We'll be putting the

good numbers on you and yours." **1984** *Daily Beacon* (Univ. Tenn.) (Oct. 5) 9: Ten-four and good numbers to ya, good buddy.

good-o *interj.* excellent; fine.

   [***1916** in *OEDS:* The rain came down good-oh.] ***1926** in *OEDS:* "Goodo!" said Dal. **1927** McKay *Home to Harlem* 118: Good oh Jake! **1955** L. Shapiro *Sixth of June* 179: Good-o. So would I. **1956** Hargrove *Girl He Left* 52: "Nobody lost." "Good-o." **1965–66** Pynchon *Crying* 144: Oh, goodo...No nightmares any more?

goods *n.pl.* **1.** a prize.—constr. with *the.*

   1852 in Thornton *Amer. Gloss.* I 373: I'm going to take three chances at the match, and if I win the goods, I'll give them to you.

   2. stuff; (*also*) (*obs.*) **a.** a racehorse or an athlete considered as to ability.—used with prec. adj.

   *1873 Hotten *Slang Dict.* (ed. 4): *Goods,* in the sporting world, men or horses. A horse or man of exceptionable quality is called "good goods," and a backer will speak of either as being..."best goods," as compared with others in the race. **1880** Hayes *New Colo.* 103: The mariner heard an expert, who was chipping away at the wall with a little hammer, remark, "That's good goods." ***1886** in *F & H* III 177: He was a nice young man for a small tea party, and rather good goods at a Sunday school treat. ***1889** Barrère & Leland *Dict. Slang* I 418: *Goods* (sporting), men or horses. Termed "good goods," or "bad goods" according to quality. **1905** in Spalding *Base Ball* 257: This little...Japanese is the goods. He pitches every day, never seems to weaken. **1915–18** *Coll. Kans. State Hist. Soc.* XIV 306: I said I had not seen any [who were]...drunk, but they were all supplied with the necessary "goods." **1929** *N.Y. Times* (June 2) IX 2: "Stuff" is a pitcher's also called...his "stock" and his "goods." **1963** *Travels of J. McPheeters* (ABC-TV): Well, how much share of the goods [Aztec gold] would you want?

   b. exactly what or who is required; (*hence*) a fine person or thing.—constr. with *the;* in phr. **there with the goods** meeting expectations or requirements; estimable.

   1899 Ade *Fables* 1: Reverence—well, when it comes to Reverence, you're certainly There with the Goods! **1904** in *OEDS:* I'll agree to make it 25 [dollars] at the end of 60 days if you are the goods. **1905** *Nat. Police Gaz.* (Nov. 11) 3: "Who was that lady who was singing as we came in?" "Little Melba; she's there with de goods all right, ain't she?" **1906** *Variety* (Jan. 6) 9: If they haven't got the goods, the audience will know it. *Ibid.* 10: I liked those fellows...They're the goods. **1906** *Blue Book* (unp.): She also has a lot of jolly good girls who are the "goods" as one would term them. *Ibid.* Everyone who knows to-day from yesterday will say that my Blue Book is the goods right from the spring. **1907** in H.C. Fisher *A. Mutt* 22: I knew you were the goods as soon as you breezed in. **1911–12** J. London *Smoke Bellew* 70: Them dogs of ours is the goods. **1914** Ellis *Billy Sunday* 29: I bought a suit of clothes...I thought I was the goods. **1914** Kreymborg *Edna* 17: Edna...squeezed his arm a little harder and exclaimed: "You're the goods." **1918** *N.Y. Eve. Jour.* (Aug. 10) 9: You certainly look the goods in a uniform. **1927** C. McKay *Harlem* 123: "Is she the goods?" "She's a wang, boh. Queen o' Philly, I tell you."

   3. confidential or special information; (*hence*) facts or truth, esp. of a damaging or incriminating nature.—constr. with *the.*

   1877 Pinkerton *Maguires* 143: The next thing was the instruction of the new member in the passwords and signs—or secret work—commonly called "the goods" of the society. **1901** Hobart *John Henry* 16: It isn't poetical...but it's the goods. **1909** in O. Johnson *Lawrenceville* 128: Trouble is, they've got the goods on me—dead to rights. **1916** H.L. Wilson *Somewhere in Red Gap* 177: No one ought to talk that way about any one if they ain't got the goods on 'em. **1933** Ersine *Pris. Slang* 40: The bulls have enough *goods* on Ike to send him to the chair. **1946** H.A. Smith *Rhubarb* 10: Why don't you get the goods on him? **1962** T. Berger *Reinhart* 303: Now I don't care what the other side gave you for the goods on me. **1964** *Twilight Zone* (CBS-TV): That's the goods. It's an illusion.

   4. conclusive proof of guilt; in phr. **catch with the goods [on]** to catch in possession of stolen articles or other proof of guilt; to catch in the act.

   1900 Ade *More Fables* 136: I have Caught him with the Goods. **1902** Townsend *Fadden & Mr. Paul* 98: It looked like I was caught wit de goods on me. **1903** A.H. Lewis *Boss* 98: Sheeny Joe must get th' collar, an' I want him caught with th' good, d'ye see? **1903** McCardell *Chorus Girl* 54: I caught them with the goods on. **1908** in H.C. Fisher *A. Mutt* 25: If you were ever caught with the goods you know how it is. **1918** Stringer *House of Intrigue* 54: But they had him with the goods on. **1947**

Beloin & Rose *Fav. Brunette* (film): A busy day pinning the goods on assorted thugs, toughs, and murderers. **1970–71** Rubinstein *City Police* 168: He closes in quickly to "get the goods" before they are consumed.

¶ In phrases:

¶ **deliver the goods** to do what is required or expected; to come up to expectations. Now *colloq.*

1879 in *DAE*: There are men in the North who walk around...saying, "...I will take you to victory." They cannot deliver the goods. **1903** in *DAE*: Jones...promised Lucas County to Johnson. If he is able to "deliver the goods," he will add five votes to the Democratic-Independent combination. **1912** in *DAE*: Joan of Arc...delivered the goods. **1917** in *DAE*.

¶ **straight goods, 1.** the truth.—also as interj.

1892 O. Wister, in *Harper's Mag.* (Dec.) 138: I'm givin' yu' straight goods, yu' see. **1895** Tisdale *Behind the Guns* 14: Give him the straight goods, but cut it short. **1899** A.H. Lewis *Sandburrs* 188: That's straight goods, see! **1902** "J. Flynt" *Little Bro.* 99: "Ain't that straight goods?"...Several nodded and grunted their assent. **1910** in O. Johnson *Lawrenceville* 362: "Honest?" "Straight goods!" **1918** O'Neill *Straw* 86: Say, Steve, what's this bull about the Doc lettin' yuh beat it if yuh gain today? Is it straight goods? **1919** Z. Grey *Desert of Wheat* 8: "It's straight goods," he declared. **1942** R. Chandler *High Window* 335: That straight goods about your owing Morny twelve grand? **1967** W. Crawford *Gresham's War* 171: This is straight goods, No bull, no way. **2.** an honest or admirable person.

1908 *DN* III 376: *Straight goods*...1. The truth, a true statement. 2. A perfectly honest person.

good thing *n.* Orig. *Und.* a person who may easily or profitably be swindled or exploited.

1909 Irwin *Con Man* 42: I was kept in reserve to skin good things—rich Easterners with a roll, usually. **a1984* (cited in Partridge *DSUE* (ed. 8) 487).

good-time Charlie *n.* a convivial fellow.

1927 T.A. Dorgan, in Zwilling *TAD Lexicon* 41: A flock of good time Charlies...chat about the loves of other days. **1930** D. Runyon, in *Collier's* (Feb. 1) 8: Drinking after hours in Good Time Charley's speakeasy. **1930** J.T. Farrell *Calico Shoes* 275: There had been others,...stray good-time Charlies. **1938** Shaw *Brothers in Crime* 147: He was known as a free-spender, a good-time Charlie. **1939** Polsky *Curtains* 14: Erstwhile good-time Charlie, playboy of the western world. **1944** *Slanguage Dict.* 59: *Good Time Charlie*—a playboy. **1951** Leveridge *Walk on Water* 95: He loved the world, the traditional good-time Charley. **1953** R. Wright *Outsider* 85: "What do they call you?"..."Charlie, just Good-Time Charlie," he said, laughing. **1962** Perry *Young Man Drowning* 86: I have a little place down in the Village where a bunch of free-loaders hang out because they know I'm a good-time Charlie. **1969** *Atlantic* (Nov.) 88: A royal-style good-time Charlie,...akin to Edward VII.

good-time Jane *n.* a convivial, usu. sexually promiscuous, woman.

1943 *Life* (Dec. 20) 102: Soldiers and sailors call them..."roundheels,"..."chippies," "good-time Janes," and..."Victory Girls." **1960** Carpenter *Harlot* 89: She was heartless, a goodtime Jane, with everything for a laugh.

goody locker *n. Mil. Av.* a locker for spare parts.

1984 Trotti *Phantom* 176 [ref. to Vietnam War]: We had learned to live with it by the creation of "goody lockers" and hangar queens. *Ibid.* 177: They'll...build their own goody lockers.

goody two-shoes *n.* [through misapprehension of archaic *goody* 'goodwife' in the name of the title character of the nursery tale *The History of Little Goody Two-Shoes* (1765)] a prudish or self-righteous person; goody-goody.

1934 (cited in *W10*). **1942** S.J. Perelman, in *New Yorker* (Nov. 21) 17: The next thing I knew, Miss Goody Two-shoes had sealed the door. **1973** R.M. Brown *Rubyfruit* 73: Carolyn was the school's Goody Twoshoes. **1979** Strasser *Angel Dust* 38: Fran Jamison, the most perfect, most all-around-goody-two-shoes-brown-nosed president-of-everything...in the class. **1982** Hayano *Poker Faces* 11: Now, go play in some of these private games with some of these goody two-shoes, and see how you come out. **1988** Lewin & Lewin *Thes.* 299: *Prude*...bluenose,...goody-goody, goody two-shoes. **1991** D. Gaines *Teenage Wasteland* 91: Goody-two-shoes were busy sucking up to teachers.

gooey *adj.* [GOO, *n.* + *-ey*] **1.** viscid or sticky. Now *colloq.* or *S.E.*

1903 *DN* III 351: *Gooey*...Sticky, not easily handled. **1919** in *OEDS*: In gooey substances. **1923** H.L. Foster *Beachcomber* 333: See, that gooey

part there. **1934** Kromer *Waiting* 42: Messy and gooey. **1963** Gant *Queen St.* 9: I felt the tar soft and gooey.

2. mawkishly sentimental. Now *colloq.*

*1935 in *OEDS*. **1958** Chandler *Playback* 88: Nobody goes all gooey over a character like me.

goof *n.* [prob. alter. of Scots and N. Irish *coof*, or dial. E and Scots. *guff*, var. obs. *goff*] **1.a.** a simpleton; clumsy fool; (*also*) a silly person.

1916 R. Lardner, in *Sat. Eve. Post* (Feb. 19, 1917) 37: It ain't the same show, you goof!...They change the bill every day. **1919** *Blackhawk Howitzer* 50: Say, you big goof up there! **1921** in E. Ferber *Gigolo* 3: Or Gertie the goof? **1926** Upson *Me and Henry* 132: You ain't such a goof as you look. **1927** Faulkner *Mosquitoes* 120: "You poor goof," the nephew said. **1976** Schroeder *Shaking It* 108: You know what I do to guys what call me a goof? **1988** N.Y.C. woman, age *ca*50: Lucy, you're such a goof!

b. *Broadly*, a man, esp. if peculiar or loutish; character; GUY.

1915–16 Lait *Beef, Iron & Wine* 95: This goof...made a play for me in the rest'rant. **1918** Ruggles *Navy Explained* 113: To cope with the situation, some goof ashore made a salt water soap. **1920** Weaver *In American* 38: Dick Finch, he was a goof like what I mean. **1923** McKnight *Eng. Words* 62: Noncommittal in general are: *dude, goof,...guy, kid.* **1925** Mullin *Scholar Tramp* 286 [ref. to *ca*1912]: A big goof he was wid a slouch-down mustash, cowboy hat, coupla guns strapped on im— **1931** *AS* VI (Aug.) 438: *Goof.* A prison salutation; used as "Buddy" is on the outside. **1952** Sandburg *Young Strangers* 390 [ref. to 1890's]: I heard panhandlers talk about "how to work Main Street," what kind of faces to ask for a dime or a quarter. "Never mooch a goof wearing a red necktie." I heard.

c. a crazy person; lunatic.

1927 Tully *Circus Parade* 87: I had to...listen to this poor goof rave. **1928** Segar *Thimble Th.* 17: Good night! Are all the goofs in the world running loose around here! **1929** Hammett *Dain Curse* 250: But even your goof must have a motive. *ca*1953 in Hammett *Knockover* 262: I don't know how the shell shocks (goofs in our language) made out. **1957** Thornton *Teenage Werewolf* (film): You keep the man in the white coat for the goofs.

2.a. *Narc.* psychotropic drugs, esp. marijuana or barbiturates. Cf. GOOFBALL, 1.

1941 Kendall *Army & Navy Sl.* 7: A goof burner...smokes marihuana. **1944** in Mencken *Amer. Lang. Supp. II* 682: Goof pill [Pentobarbital]. **1942–49** Goldin et al. *DAUL* 285: Marijuana, smoke cigarettes containing...*hit the goof.* **1952** J.C. Holmes *Go* 101: He gave me the address of a guy that peddles goof balls, though, but kee-rist, who wants to get hungup that way? Hell, no, man, none of that goof for me! Not any more! **1952** Mandel *Angry Strangers* 362: You're a baseball man, not a goof popper. **1960* in *OEDS*: "Goof" pills were sold openly.

b. wine or other liquor.

1964 Allen *High White Forest* 179 [ref. to WWI]: Give him a drink. Where's the jug of goof?

3. a blunder; mistake.

1954 in *Britannica Bk. of Yr. 1955* 814: *Goof, n.* A mistake. **1955** L. Shapiro *Sixth of June* 208: This is your last goof, Dan. Next time...court-martial. **1956** G. Green *Last Angry Man* 17: It looks like their fellahs are trying to blame our fellahs for their own goof. **1962** Dougherty *Commissioner* 146: Sounding off when he ought to be out trying to rectify his own goof. **1971** N.Y.U. professor: It looks as if I've made a desperate goof. **1990** *U.S. News & W.R.* (Mar. 12) 83: Until the goof is corrected, they will have paid too much tax.

4.a. a source of surprise or fun, esp. a joke or prank; fun; (*often*) a lark.

1958 Kerouac *Subterraneans* 21: The *Pierre*-of-Melville goof and wonder of it. **1965** in Thompson *Hell's Angels* 254: Is it you & Tiny's personal goof, or really what you all *want*? **1967** in McNeill *Moving Through* 19: The Sweep-In on Saturday was a success because it was a goof. **1967** A. Hoffman *Revolution for Hell of It* 50: Jail is a goof. Easiest jailing of all time. **1969** Mitchell *Thumb Tripping* 18: These strange people, their weird goofs; he both could and could not dig it. **1965–70** J. Carroll, in *Paris Rev.* (No. 50) 106: "Pretty great, huh?" "What a goof." **1971** *N.Y. Times Mag.* (Nov. 28) 94: As a goof, Jumper puts the make on a whore at 50th Street, but she turns away. **1987** *RHD2*: We short-sheeted his bed just for a goof. **1990** *New Republic* (Nov. 12) 46: The [Teenage Mutant Ninja] Turtles were a kind of charming goof on the superhero ethos.

b. *pl.* fun; amusement.

1977 N.Y.C. reporter, age 24: So we took the ride just for goofs.

5. something painfully unpleasant.

1962 H. Simmons *On Eggshells* 162: He got drafted for that goof they called police action in Korea. **1971** N.Y.U. student: Man, what a goof this is!

¶ In phrase:

¶ **on the goof** *Narc.* drowsing from the effect of a depressant drug, esp. heroin.

1959 Murtagh & Harris *Who Live in Shadow* 8: Most of them sit slumped in their chairs, more than half asleep, on the goof, on the nod. *Ibid.* 201: *On the goof.* Drowsy, dreamy, relaxed; under the influence of a narcotic drug; on the nod.

goof *v.* **1.a.** to clown; engage in horseplay; play or fool around.—now usu. constr. with *around*.

1929–31 Farrell *Young Lonigan* 14 [ref. to *ca*1916]: He always ran them off the grass when they goofed on their way home from school. *Ibid.* 60: He goofed around for a while in the vacant lot. *Ibid.* 136: Kenny and Davey goofed over a cigarette butt. **1947** Motley *Knock on Any Door* 28: School started again. But they still goofed around. **1948** in R.S. Gold *Jazz Talk* 112: Just Goofin'. **1952** Kerouac *Cody* 150: We'll just goof, you understand, like a string quartet. **1957** Shulman *Rally* 119: No jumping through windows, no cutting up, no goofing. **1958** Motley *Epitaph* 87: Don't goof with no goof-balls…You goof with them and pretty soon you're riding the Horse. **1961** McMurtry *Horseman* 21: I would rather go to the Thalia and goof around…than listen to his old-timy stories. **1962** L'Engle *Wrinkle in Time* 24: You just goof around in school and look out the window and don't pay any attention. **1966–67** W. Stevens *Gunner* 53: The crew traditionally goofed after a lengthy [bombing mission]. **1970** Knight *Black Voices* 78: I'm in a hurry…done wasted too much time already…goofing with you. **1970** R.N. Williams *New Exiles* 136: We used to goof a lot. This is the only way to stay sane…Make it into a travelogue of idiocy. **1977** B. Davidson *Collura* 98: Carlos and another Puerto Rican boy named Pedro, did a lot a huddling together and were on a "goofing bag," giggling and fooling around. **1986** *Time* (June 23) 72: Goofing and jamming together. **1988** *Wkly. World News* (May 3) 20: I know he goofs around with other girls, but I can't let go.

b. to play with (a ball).

1919 Wilkins *Company Fund* 30: He sure was some pitcher and he had a real team goofing the onion in the pasture.

2.a. to tease, taunt, or attempt to fool; KID; JIVE.—sometimes intrans.

1929–31 Farrell *Young Lonigan* 78 [ref. to 1916]: They goofed Three-Star about the elevated incident. *Ibid.* 88: "Sure, I got an autographed ball from him." "Don't goof me. You're too young to have got it." **1930–31** Farrell *Grandeur* 148: Don't goof your grandpa! I remember the time you broke down and told me what you thought of her. **1952** Ellson *Golden Spike* 162: I was only goofing in the first place. I didn't want it. **1968** Baker et al. *CUSS* 127: *Goof.* Tease or annoy someone…To deceive someone. **1970** Cain *Blueschild Baby* 38: And the hole, she be goofing this sucker too, laughing and pulling my dick. **1968–71** Cole & Black *Checking* 286: They goofed him, never maliciously, as they often goofed the homosexuals on the block. **1974** E. Thompson *Tattoo* 90: "Goin to the Navy tomorrow, Ron."…"No goofin, man?" "You know it." **1979** G. Trudeau *Doonesbury* (synd. cartoon strip) (Mar. 20): You're goofing [jesting] on me, right? **1982–84** Chapple *Outlaws in Babylon* 45: And so he starts goofing.

b. to talk foolishly.

1939 Appel *Power-House* 171: What're you goofing about now?

c. to mistreat; ill-use; victimize.—also constr. with *around*.

1959 F.L. Brown *Trumbull Pk.* 347: Some of the Negroes I know would goof you ten times faster than some whites. **1966** Brunner *Face of Night* 192: I'll change the shape of his head when I find him. Nobody goofs me around like that.

3. to gawk; become absorbed in watching.—constr. with *at* or *on*.

***1940** in *OEDS*: Go quickly to your shelter or refuge room: suppress your curiosity and don't "goof." **1952** in *DAS*: I'm goofing at all the things I can have. **1970** Landy *Underground Dict.* 92: *Goof on someone v.* Become absorbed in watching another person.

4.a. *Narc.* to be in a dazed or stupefied state from the use of drugs or liquor; to nod off in a drugged state; (*hence*) to be inattentive; (*broadly*) to use drugs.

1951 Kerouac *Cody* 6: Bums…grimly read the papers to show that tonight they are not goofing in no alleys with rotgut. **1950–52** Ulanov *Hist. Jazz* 351: *Goof* or *goof off:* to wander in attention…; in musical performance, to play without much attention, to miss coming in on time,

etc. **1952** Mandel *Angry Strangers* 29: He likes I should play when he's goofin. *Ibid.* 438: Take about four of them'n you'll goof awright. **1956** E. Hunter *Second Ending* 276: "You goofing?"…"Mmm." **1958** Gilbert *Vice Trap* 5: *Goof, Goofing*—to take drugs, be on drugs. *Ibid.* 23: If you didn't goof heavily, you could make yourself come off it. But those needle scratches didn't go. **1960** in Rosset *Evergreen Reader* 277: You don't *swing* with you heavy gage, you jest *goof*…that's what you call that. **1966** J. Mills *Needle Park* 126: I generally, if I'm not goofing, I get on the phone and make some calls and arrange to have some dates for the evening. **1970** Cole *Street Kids* 10: Kids in basements with glue bags and in playgrounds with half-filled wine bottles. Goofing.

b. to loaf or idle; waste time.

1953 Paley *Rumble* 23: The gang had gone torpid…He…got ready to yell down into number one hold and give them hell for goofing. **1953** Hughes *Lodge* 75: We'd screw around like that sometimes and just goof in bed, saying nothing, doing nothing. **1957** in Algren *Lonesome Monsters* 131: After a while you'll learn how to goof so they can't see it. **1958–59** Lipton *Barbarians* 45: I'd go away where nobody knew me and just goof for a while. **1961** J. Baldwin *Another Country* 97: I…just walk around or go to the movies by myself or just read or just goof. **1967** Kornbluth *New Underground* 40: Let's go down there and goof. **1968** Wojciechowska *Tuned Out* 14: Mostly I just goof with the other guys and some girls who hang around the Wigwam, which is a place we have where we just sit around and drink Cokes. **1970** N.Y.U. students: "Now what are you doing?" "Just goofing."

5. *Orig. Jazz.* **a.** to blunder.—used intrans.

1944 in Huebner *Long Walk* 23: I really goofed when I volunteered in 1938. **1952** *Life* (Sept. 29) 67: Bop Vocabulary…*Goof:* to blow a wrong note, or make a mistake. **1954** *Time* (Nov. 8) 70: These are the terms currently most often used by modern jazz addicts:…*goof, v.* Make a mistake. **1955** *Walt Disney's Comics* (Apr.) 13: I'll catch him, Pop! But I hope I don't goof! **1955** R.L. Scott *Look of Eagle* 24: Then I goofed…I…pressed the salvo switch instead and so dropped two perfectly good full tips. **1955** Ruppelt *Report on UFOs* 154: The majority of the visitors thought that the Air Force had goofed on previous projects. **1956** Hargrove *Girl He Left* 28: It's just a wrong number, and I'm the one who goofed. **1958** J. Davis *College Vocab.* 14: *Goof*—Make a mistake. **1960** Sire *Deathmakers* 190: We're all jumpy. Probably just one of our guards goofed off a burst. **1961** Plantz *Sweeney Squadron* 195 [ref. to WWII]: Somebody goofed. **1962** Killens *Heard the Thunder* 35: He had been given responsibility and he had goofed and he would suffer the consequences. **1962** Shapiro & Henning *Lover Come Back* (film): You goofed. If it wasn't for me, those Vip commercials wouldn't be on the air right now. **1965** Hentoff *Jazz Country* 28: Where did I goof, Moses? **1972** Kopp *Buddha* 138: I told him how recently I had goofed anew. *a***1979** Pepper & Pepper *Straight Life* 205: I almost stopped, but then I goofed again.

b. to botch; bungle; GOOF UP, 2.—used trans.

1952 Ellson *Golden Spike* 32: I goofed my shot. **1956** G. Green *Angry Man* 113: He's goofed every television job he's had. **1958** Gilbert *Vice Trap* 48: That liquor store man goofed your [license] number. **1961** Schulz *Peanuts Every Sunday* (unp.): Yeah, well, I remember *last* year…you almost goofed the whole program. **1971** Hirschfield *Power* 31: Okay, buddy. So our science people goofed a space shot. *a***1986** in E. Knight *Essential* 47: We goofed the whole thing.

6. to malfunction.

1966–67 Harvey *Air War* 62: The damned igniters must have goofed. **1972** Bunker *No Beast* 153: The chlorine machine is goofing and the pool is like poison gas.

¶ In phrases:

¶ **goof on, 1.** to make fun of; taunt; laugh at.

1956 H. Gold *Not with It* 241: I stood…while this goof goofed on us. **1969** Geller & Boas *Drug Beat* xviii: Goof (on): To *play with someone's head*, that is, to *put him on* in an attempt to break down his reserve or find out what kind of person he is. **1970** Cole *Street Kids* 38: Before the girls went up we started goofing on one part of the movie that seemed very funny. **1970** R.N. Williams *New Exiles* 137: I goofed on that too. **1968–71** Cole & Black *Checking* 6: We sat in the car wisecracking, goofing on everything that moved. **1971** N.Y.U. student: "Don't goof on me, man!" It means "don't make fun of me." Like you could say, "Let's go down to the bar and goof on all the drunks." **1978** Price *Ladies' Man* 22: I mean, you know, like, you don't know who you're goofin' on over here. **1992** *Roc* (Fox-TV): I was just goofin' on ya, son.

2. to victimize; undermine.

1959 F.L. Brown *Trumbull Pk.* 322: I don't want to hear a damn thing you got to say to me. You goofed on me!

¶ **goof oneself** to get into trouble.—constr. with *with*.

1957 Ellison *Web of the City* 70: Look, don't goof yaself with nobody.

goof around *v.* see GOOF, *v.*, 1.a., 2.c.

goofball *n.* **1.** [fr. GOOF, *n.*, 2.a.] *Narc.* **a.** a pill containing a barbiturate or other depressant drug; (*also*, in 1938 quot.) marijuana. ['Marijuana' is a possible meaning of GOOF, *n.*, 2.a., but 1938 def. may still be erroneous.]
1938 *AS* XIII 185: *Goof-ball.* Marijuana. **1939** C.R. Cooper *Scarlet* 351: *Goof balls*—barbital. I gave them to her but they didn't quiet her. **1945** *Reader's Digest* (June) 109: Goof-balls, small white knockout pills, are bought through bootleg drug connections or from shady pharmacies. Slipped into a drink, they dope the prospect within an hour. **1950** *Time* (Aug. 28) 4: A goof ball is a...barbiturate or sleeping pill. **1952** Viereck *Men into Beasts* 41 [ref. to 1940's]: If an inmate was lucky he might get hold of some "goof balls." **1953** R. Chandler *Goodbye* 219: Goofballs are one of the barbiturates laced with benzedrine. **1954** Arnow *Dollmaker* 428 [ref. to 1945]: Wotta they given you? Goof balls a some kind. **1959** Trocchi *Cain's Book* 160: Moe, Trixie, catatonic under goofballs. **1966** J. Mills *Panic in Needle Park* 32: He wasn't drunk, but he certainly wasn't sober either. He was high on barbiturates, goofballs, GB's. **1980** Whalen *Takes a Man* 219: Their friends sometimes bought cheap "goofballs." *ca***1986** *Diff'rent Strokes* (ABC-TV): I got red devils, yellow jackets, and goofballs.
b. a pill containing an amphetamine or a similar stimulant.
1952 J.C. Holmes *Go* 101: He gave me the address of a guy who peddles goof balls, though. **1970** Cortina *Slain Warrior* 76: But my brother he wuzn't usin' redbirds...he wuz tryin' goof balls...them is the amphetamines. I usta take them and go half crazy behind them. **1970** *Nat. Lampoon* (Apr.) 37: Then she swallowed a handful of amphetamines or "goof-balls," as the jet-set calls them... **1990** *Mystery Science Theater* (Comedy Central TV): A bright young singer who's hopped up on goofballs right now.
2.a. a GOOFY individual, esp. a silly or amusingly eccentric person; GOOF, 1.
1944 in Inks *Eight Bailed Out* 32: Dig this goofball. **1954** Schulberg *Waterfront* 258: There's no room for goof-balls in this business. **1955** Ellson *Rock* 13: She's got a build, but she looks like a goofball. **1956** Ross *Hustlers* 19: Then the goofball came by, Little Pancho. **1957** Simmons *Corner Boy* 89: He was going to screw up, and in this business you can't afford to have no goof balls. **1960** Bluestone *Cully* 79: Mad at all the goofballs like himself who'd broken the marching symmetry. **1966** Neugeboren *Big Man* 27: Some kids think I'm a real goofball the way I go on talking about things like this. **1971** Keith *Long Line Rider* 26: These goofballs in taverns and bars don't really look closely at anything. **1974** Charyn *Blue Eyes* 61: Leaves names and dates with the operator...I'm not getting down with those goofballs for less than seventy-five. **1981** *Film Comment* (May) 16: Randy Quaid. Bringer of humanity to goofball roles. **1989** *CBS This Morning* (CBS-TV) (Jan. 12): It was such a relief after having so many grim goofballs running around the White House.
b. an insane person.
1961 Rosten *Capt. Newman* 112 [ref. to WWII]: I ain't one of your goof-balls you know. **1966** Gallery *Start Engines* 178: Like the time the goofball got loose in the bug house, raped one of the nurses and escaped. **1967** W. Murray *Sweet Ride* 104: If those goofballs in Washington want to fight their nasty, stupid, meaningless war over there, let them.

goofball *adj.* silly; crazy; GOOFY.—used prenominally.
1956 in Harvey *Air Force* 50: It was probably a goofball rumor. **1962** in *OEDS*. **1978** Wharton *Birdy* 92: Birdy and I did some goofball things. **1983** *Time* (June 27) 78: The stunt wedding has a certain goofball exhibitionist charm.

goof-butt *n. Narc.* a marijuana cigarette. Also **goofy-butt.**
1938 *New Yorker* (Mar. 12) 36: Marijuana cigarettes are...sticks, reefers,...or goofy-butts. **1938** *Call-Bulletin* (San Francisco) (Mar. 19): The cigarettes are variously called sticks, reefers, tea, gyves, Mary Anns and goofy butts. **1939** in E.L. Abel *Marihuana Dict.* 45: "Reefers" or "goof-butts" as the marijuana cigarettes are called. **1943** *Time* (July 19) 54: Cigarets made from it are...goof-butts,...giggle-smokes, or reefers...Commonly they blast the goof-butt collectively.

goof camp *n. Navy.* BOOT CAMP. Also **goofy camp.** *Joc.*
1919 *Our Navy* (Dec.) 8: With "three and a butt" to do the young Texan just into "goofey camp" is given the old "raspberry" by the young Iowan who has been in three whole weeks. **1923** *Our Navy* (Apr. 15) 3: Clean up the goof camp yard again/And line up for your stew.

goofed *adj.* **1.a.** *Narc.* under the influence of marijuana or a barbiturate; HIGH.—often constr. with *up* or *out.*
1944 *AS* (Apr.) 104: There is some allusion in sailors' language to the use of drugs...*Gassed-up*...and *goofed-up* are cognate and self-explanatory. **1952** Kerouac *Cody* 154: When you answer you're goofed. **1952** Ellson *Golden Spike* 116: You can't go up to the house like this. You're goofed out. **1953** Anslinger & Tompkins *Traf. in Narc.* 309: *Goofed-up.* Drug-exhilarated. **1953** W. Brown *Monkey on My Back* 33: When he was goofed, he could listen to the radio for hours, particularly to the disc jockeys who played hot jazz. *Ibid.* 52: Flattie must have been goofed up plenty. **1956** Ross *Hustlers* 38: You a junkie, too? Ever take horse, get goofed, smoke weed? **1962** Riccio & Slocum *All the Way Down* 76: Riccio, can you tell when I'm goofed up? **1970** Horman & Fox *Drug Awareness* 467: *Goofed up*—under the influence of barbiturates. **1977** S. Foote *September September* 113: "Goofed up. Zonked." "Looks like fun."
b. drunk.—constr. with *up.*
1941 Kendall *Army & Navy Slang* 26: Swacked...crocked, binged, boiled, goofed up, mellow, bleary-eyed, stinko, rummed up, oiled, jagged, half-seas-over, inebriated, drenched, saturated or even intoxicated.
2. crazy; (*hence*) infatuated; (*also*) bewildered.—also constr. with *up.*
1952 Mandel *Angry Strangers* 51: "Let her rave with her goofed-up morality." "Goofed-up, is it?...Any sound concept of living is *goofed-up.*" **1955** Ellson *Rock* 32: Yeah, if he goes down there, he's really goofed. **1956** Heinlein *Door* 23: I was as goofed up about Belle as is possible for a man to be. **1957** Simmons *Corner Boy* 60: That babe goes for you, and you're goofed behind her. **1959** F.L. Brown *Trumbull Pk.* 76: That damned Gardner Building—that's what had me goofed. **1962** T. Berger *Reinhart in Love* 198: You talkin' goofed, man. **1966** Brunner *Face of Night* 13: Boy, am I goofed up! I forgot all about it. **1975** Univ. Tenn. *Daily Beacon* (Dec. 4) 3: What gives?! Are you goofed up?!

goofer *n.* **1.** a clumsy fool; lout; GOOF, 1. Also vars.
1918 *Lit. Digest* (Aug. 24) 36: They're promoted to goopher standing. Then...they have to prove themselves gimpers. **1920** Fitzgerald *This Side of Paradise* 73 [ref. to *ca*1916]: Don't be a critical goopher or you can't go! *Ibid.* 90: "Oh, Isabelle," he reproached himself, "I'm a goopher." *Ibid.* 96: If you don't pass it, you're the world's worst goopher. **1926** Dunning & Abbott *Broadway* 242: I wouldn't stay and entertain your gang of goofers if you kissed my foot in Macy's window at high noon. **1927** C.F. Coe, in Paxton *Sport* 147: He...crosses his right to this bimbo's chin. Down goes the goofer like a window shade. **1930** Lait *On Spot* 5: You don' mean we're gonna let them West Side goofers get away with this? **1981** D.E. Miller *Jargon* 244: *Goofer*...A loser.
2. *Narc.* a habitual user of psychotropic drugs, esp. marijuana or barbiturates.
1952 Mandel *Angry Strangers* 430: The talkers and the goofers were packed around coffee-drenched tables. **1967** J.B. Williams *Narc. & Halluc.* 112: *Goofer*—One who drops pills.
3. *Narc.* GOOFBALL, *n.*, 1.
1966 Elli *Riot* 37: Give us some goofers. **1969** Fort *Pleasure Seekers* 236: Doriden Goofers. **1972** Smith & Gay *Don't Try It* 202: *Goofers.* Barbiturates, hypnotics, sedatives. **1974** Hyde *Mind Drugs* 154: Goofballs...goofers...sedatives.

go-off *n.* start.—constr. with *the.*
1833 in *DAE*. **1851** Melville *Moby Dick* ch. iv: The first go off of a bitter cold morning. **1899** Cullen *Tales* 88: It sounds too much like beery ballads from the go-off. **1906** *Nat. Police Gaz.* (May 5) 3: Play close to your skin at the go-off.

go off *v.* to experience a sexual orgasm. Cf. GO, *v.*, 2.
ca*1866** *Romance of Lust* 66: I went off and spent with a scream. **1916** Cary *Venery* I 112: *Going Off*—To achieve emission. Said of either sex. **1918** in *Lyra Ebriosa* 11: Hurrah for the Corporal that went off in his pants! **1927** [Fliesler] *Anecdota* 28: Three old maids went off on a tramp in the woods. The tramp died. ***1928** D.H. Lawrence, in *OEDS*: You couldn't go off at the same time as a man, could you? **1953–57** Giovannitti *Combine D* 152: It makes every inch of your body jump until you're frantic to go off. **1971** *Coming, Dear!* 51: The chaperone thought one couple was dancing so vulgarly that they should be put off the college dance floor...little did she know that before the dance was over they went off by themselves. **1978** Shem *House of God* 188: She moved around on me slowly,...and then, starting to go off, bent down to me. **1986** Zeybel *First Ace* 6: He...had to go off or go crazy.

goof hat *n. USMC.* (see quot.).
1983 Elting et al. *Soldier Talk* 357: *Goof hat* (1930s; Marines)...A cotton khaki overseas cap, with *RD* (Recruit Depot) stenciled in black on both

sides. It was worn by boots…until they were issued their uniforms.

goofies *n.pl.* [orig. unkn.; any relationship to GOOF, *n.* is obscure] *Juve.* (see quot.).

1905 *DN* III 81: *Goofies on*…The promise of. "He's got *goofies on* the woolly."

goofing *adj. Jazz.* fine; wonderful.

1958 Gilbert *Vice Trap* 127: You figure he's a real goofing fuzz because he balled with that knocked-out Lona.

goof-off *n.* **1.** Orig. *Mil.* a person who is habitually inattentive to duty; loafer; idler; blunderer.

1945 *Yank* (Apr. 20) 20: You, you goof-off! **1949** in Brookhouser *Our Years* 221: Maniac directors and goof-off actresses. **1952** Uris *Battle Cry* 173 [ref. to 1942]: In true Marine tradition, I found my platoon were first-class goof-offs. **1947–53** Guthrie *Seeds* 35: I'm the careless, reckless rambler, th' don't-give-a-damn feller…The goof-off. **1954** Matheson *Born of Man & Woman* 180: He's s'posed to work…but he's a goof-off. **1957** Myrer *Big War* 194: There's going to be enough…sweating around as it is without some goof-off getting blasted all for nothing. **1957** Mulvihill *Fire Mission* 7: The senseless routine was…making laggards and goof-offs of good men. **1960** Bluestone *Cully* 134: If I send over some of the goof-offs,…maybe you'll help them out. **1961** *Atlantic Mo.* (Apr.) 42: The students who were most successful were a bit rebellious, a bit offbeat, though not entirely "goof-offs." **1962** Killens *Heard the Thunder* 40: The one kind of person in the world he had no use for was a goof-off, a slacker, a goldbrick, who expected others to carry his weight. **1968** Hawley *Hurricane Yrs.* 183: Some goof-off on the production line had missed putting in a vital cotter pin. **1971** Hammer *Calley Court-Martial* 125: A pot-smoker, a goof-off, a coward, and a liar. **1973** Browne *Body Shop* 100: There are enough goof-offs over there who might have got killed and didn't. **1986** *New York* (Dec. 15) 109: Who could have watched a sober report on these two goof-offs stumbling into the grave.

2. a blunder; mistake.

1961 Considine *Ripley* 173: Naturally, a goof-off of such proportions by…Ripley…formed the basis of a humorous story. **1979** Kienzle *Rosary Murders* 129: It was no goof-off. You were doing what you should've been doing.

3. GOOF, *n.*, 4.a.

1968 I. Reed *Yellow Back Radio* 123: Da whole shebang would be one big goof off from coast to coast, everything would be boss.

goof off *v.* **1.** Esp. *Mil.* to blunder; fumble; GOOF, *v.*, 5.a.

1941 Hargrove *Pvt. Hargrove* 84: *Goof-off*—to make a mistake. **1941** *Saturday Review* (Oct. 4) 11: *Goof off.* To make a mistake in drill. **1944** in *Best from Yank* 186: But his heart was heavy at the thought of having goofed off. **1951** Algren *Chicago* 74: We all make mistakes, fellas…We all goof off, we're all human—it's what I done, I goofed off too. **1952** Ellson *Golden Spike* 244: *Goof-off*…also, to do something in the wrong manner, to fumble. **1957** *Phil Silvers Show* (CBS-TV): Somebody goofed off…Didn't I tell you to get nylons?

2. Esp. *Mil.* to shirk or loaf; fool around. [Early exx. ref. to WWII.]

1943 *Word Study* (Feb.) 5: He will *goof off* with finesse, so that his absence will be unnoticed. **1943** *Yank* (Oct. 22) 3: He was just goofin' off. **1948** A. Murphy *Hell & Back* 90: When the old man with the sickle gives you the nod, it's one detail you can't goof-off on. **1948** Vidal *City & Pillar* 198: Hi…Goofing off? **1948** Wolfert *Act of Love* 487: He had had enough of taking orders for a while. It was time to goof off. **1951** Thacher *Captain* 80: He's got a job to do, and he can't have any guys goofing off. **1952** Uris *Battle Cry* 27: All right, you people. We have a long row to hoe tonight so I don't want to see anybody goofing off. Drop your gear and follow me. **1953** *I Love Lucy* (CBS-TV): Has Fred goofed off? **1955** *Science Digest* (Aug.) 34: To "goof off"…means to waste time, or to fail in any project on purpose. **1961** Rosten *Captain Newman, M.D.* 21: Snap out of it, Buster! Quit goofing-off. **1970** R. Vasquez *Chicano* 127: You think I was just goofing off,…without any plan? **1977** Johnson & Williamson *Whatta Gal* 60: Well, that girl, she was just goofin' off and blowin' the game. **1981** *Time* (Nov. 16) 58: Things were running so far ahead of schedule, in fact, that most workers…would have time for "goofing off." **1988** *Boys Will Be Boys* (Fox-TV): When you start school I want you to pay attention and not goof off. **1992** M. Gelman *Crime Scene* 24: The editors would think we'd been goofing off.

3. *Narc.* to nod under the influence of a sedative or hypnotic drug; to be under the influence of a drug; (broadly) to nod off; sleep.

1950 *Time* (Aug. 28) 4 [ref. to WWII]: By goofing off or going on the nod they entered a state ranging from mild intoxication to complete unconsciousness. **1951** Kerouac *Cody* 121: You were all high in the livingroom, and all high, goofing off real high. **1952** Mandel *Angry Strangers* 362: Don't be goofing off on me, man…Listen to my story next time. **1952** Ellson *Golden Spike* 3: He could have been goofing off with a load of stuff. *Ibid.* 41: He thought of the girl whose couch he'd burned while goofing off the night before. *Ibid.* 244: *Goof off*—to nod. **1968** Johnson & Johnson *Count Me Gone* 53: Sleeping in my heap.…I used to…goof off in the garage.

4. to ignore.

1971 Wells & Dance *Night People* 14: If you tried to shake up the likes of Benny Carter, Hawk, Don Redman, or Buster Bailey, they would just goof you off, and you wound up angry, not them.

goof out *v.* to startle by means of a prank; play a trick on.

1980 *Nat. Lampoon* (Dec.) 57: He liked to…"goof people out." He liked to put pet-store turtles in cafeteria soup.

goof-proof *adj.* foolproof. *Joc.*

1970 N.Y.U. student: There was some product that used to be [in the 1960's] advertised as *goof-proof.* **1982** *Popular Computing* (May) 50: It will be as easy to use as a television and totally goofproof. **1990** *Bicycling* (Oct.) 92: The…derailleurs and…shifters offered goof-proof changes over the wide…gearing range.

goof trap *n. Army.* a military booby trap.

1918–19 MacArthur *Bug's-Eye View* 64: The French [engineers]…were clipping the wires of the goof-trap.

goof-up *n.* **1.** a blunder; FOUL-UP.

1956 in *OEDS:* His embarrassment is assuaged by past goof-ups among English men of letters. **1962** G. Ross *Last Campaign* 4: He worried only lest events, goof-ups beyond his power to control, might obscure his status. **1966–67** Harvey *Air War* 3: One little goof-up can snowball…into a major catastrophe. **1973** Overgard *Hero* 113: If there's a goof-up, then you'll be the first to know. **1981** D. Burns *Feeling Good* 40: You exaggerate the importance of…your goof-up or someone else's achievement. **1993** *N.Y. Times* (Mar. 26) A 29: Nobody out there knew what they were doing. It was one big goof-up.

2. a blunderer; bungler.

1957 M. Shulman *Rally* 208: You must be a bigger goof-up than I was! **1960** Bluestone *Cully* 123: He's a goof-up. **1969** Linn & Pearl *Masque of Honor* 150: I can think of a few other gallant goof-ups who'll get hurt if you kill Adam March's brainchild. **1972** N.Y.C. dentist: Everywhere you go you're surrounded by goof-ups…I heard that during World War II when I was in the Army. **1981** D. Burns *Feeling Good* 133: Or you might label yourself a "total goof-up."

goof up *v.* **1.** to blunder; cause trouble for oneself; GOOF, *v.*, 5.a.

1943 Hersey *G.I. Laughs* 130: Okay! Okay! Who goofed up? **1959** O'Connor *Talked to a Stranger* 112: Most of the guys that I figured would go straight: they're right back in jail again. I couldn't figure that out, except that they just goofed up along the way again. **1964** *Dick Van Dyke Show* (CBS-TV): A lot of funny things could happen, like goofing up in the kitchen. **1968** Schell *Military Half* 156: One shows a North Vietnamese soldier goofing up—falling into a canal, and that kind of thing. **1969** *Playboy* (Dec.) 112: One of the 11 guys on the field would miss the play or goof up. **1979** Strasser *Angel Dust* 76: You like to blow off steam by goofing up in class. **1984** *Time* (Aug. 27) 17: He will inevitably have more impromptu encounters with the press—and thus more chances…to goof up.

2. to bungle, botch, or spoil; (hence) to injure.

1938 Macaulay & Wald *Brother Rat* (film): Why did Bing goof up Garrison Review? **1954** Schulberg *Waterfront* 22: Now get on it. And don't goof it up. **1959** Farris *Harrison High* 26: I really goofed things up. **1964** Smith & Hoefer *Music* 18: My mother goofed up my appearance. The way she dressed me. **1966** Jarrett *Sex Is a Private Affair* 183: I'm an expert at goofing myself up with the wrong people. **1971** *Smith Family* (ABC-TV): You sort of goofed it up. **1971** Rhinehart *Dice Man* 23: I keep goofing up real opportunities. **1992** D. Burke *Street Talk* I 5: I goofed up my leg skiing.

goofus *n.* a fool; idiot.

1917 *Wadsworth Gas Attack* 19: Joe Goofus, of the 105th Infantry, was a Wise Guy. **1917** in Niles *Singing Soldiers* 5: Why, Oley, you rumbefuddled goovus, I'll bet you don't remember your orders. **1918** *N.Y. Eve. Jour.* (Aug. 10) 9: Well, well, if it ain't ole Joe Goofus. **1919** Mowry *R.U. 307* 18: Pvt. Goofus, Co. Z, Umpty Steenth Squad. **1926** Wood & Goddard *Amer. Slang* 21: *Goof, goofus.* Dumbell; silly person. **1929** Tully *Shadows of Men* 246: They're allus kind to a goofus when he gits old in the pen. **1929** in Segar *Thimble Th.* 104: Say, do you know what a "goofis" is? **1930** in Perelman *Old Gang* 112: The big goofus of a husband of hers. **1964** Hill *One of the Casualties* 308: Kooks and nuts and goofuses and comedians. **1969** Bouton *Ball Four* 209: That's the old Rufus Goofus. **1987** M. Groening *School Is Hell* (unp.): You may be a budding genius...or you may be a budding goofus. **1988** *New Yorker* (Mar. 28) 16: He crinkles his face in the grin of a goofus.

goofy *adj.* stupid or crazy; silly; infatuated; (*hence*) dazed.
   1919 *Our Navy* (May) 55: Writes a goofy gob—"What is the correct plural for 'Jack Tar'?" **1920** *Amer. Leg. Wkly.* (Dec. 24) 16: They are the goofiest of all "goofs". **1921** in Murphy *Black Candle* 212: That is why I smashed the door of the police station on the South Side. I had a craving and was "goofey." **1920–21** Witwer *Leather Pushers* 252: "Fried!" says Knockout with a goofy grin. *Ibid.* 303: A right smash to the head drove him against the ropes, goofy. **1922** in *DN* V 147: I'm goofy about Jack. **1928** McEvoy *Show Girl* 109: She's just a little bit goofy about me. **1931** Hellinger *Moon* 48: Besides all that, I'm goofy about you. **1932** Hawks *Crowd Roars* (film): Don't let those goofy signs go to your head. **1953** Brackett et al. *Niagara* (film): I feel goofy after what happened. **1957** Russell *Permanent Playboy* 138 [ref. to 1920's]: The goofy girls were wonderful. They used to have names like Flip and Bootsie, they said things like, "You tell 'em, kid, I stutter." **1960** Bannon *Journey* 52: She's goofy and she's pure trouble. **1971** Glasser *365 Days* 139: Nobody makes it through six months as a field medic and then goes goofy unless somebody pushes him, does he? **1980** Lorenz *Guys Like Us* 156: The guy went goofy...You saw him shoot the mud puddle. **1981** G. Wolf *Roger Rabbit* 35: Of course Roger's a touch goofy. He's a *cartoon rabbit*.

goofy butt *n.* var. GOOF-BUTT.

goofy-foot *n. Surfing.* a person who surfs with the right foot forward. Also **goofy-footer.** Also adv.
   ***1962** in *OEDS: Goofy foot*, a very good [surf] rider who reverses the usual way of standing by putting right foot in front of left. **1965** *N.Y. Times* (Aug. 22) VI 73: With practice, he can...coast "goofy foot" (the right leg in front of the left leg). ***1965** in *OEDS:* A goofy footer. **1968** Kirk & Hanle *Surfer's Handbk.* 36: You will be known...as a "goofy-footer," but that's hardly a dirty word. Southpaws have done pretty well in the sports world. *Ibid.* 139: *Goofy-foot:* a right-foot-forward surfer, as opposed to the usual left foot forward. **1976–79** Milius & Coppola *Apocalypse Now* (film): Mike Kilgore. I'm a goofy-foot.

goofy grape *n.* [sugg. by *Goofy Grape*, trademark for a purple powdered soft drink] *Army.* a signaling grenade that emits violet or purple smoke. [Quots. ref. to Vietnam War.]
   1968–90 Linderer *Eyes of Eagle* 64: The...pilot radioed that he had identified goofy grape. *a*1993 Leninger *Time Heals* 312: *Goofy grape:* Purple smoke grenade.

goog[1] *n. Mil.* GOO-GOO[1], *n.*—usu. used contemptuously. Cf. GOOK[2].
   1923 *Our Navy* (Oct. 15) 20 [ref. to *ca*1918]: Bigger men and bigger horses than the googs had ever dreamed of. **1971** Tuchman *Stilwell* 127 [ref. to 1930's]: Wops for Italians, chinks or chinos for Chinese, googs for Filipinos.

goog[2] *n.* [sugg. by GOO-GOO EYES, *n.*] **1.** *pl.* (esp. among pitchmen) eyeglasses.
   1924 Henderson *Crookdom* 404: Eyeglasses—*googs, glims.* **1929** *Sat. Eve. Post* (Oct. 12) 29: *Googs:* Eyeglasses. *Glims:* The same. **1933** Ersine *Pris. Slang* 40: *Googs, n.* Spectacles which are often used as a disguise. *ca*1947–53 in *AS* XXVIII (1953) 116: Carnie Talk...*Googs, n.* Glasses or sun glasses.
   2. an eye blackened by a blow.
   1929 in Hammett *Knockover* 56: "You might start back with the night you gave her the goog."..."I hadn't ought to hit her in the eye, that's a fact." **1930** Irwin *Tramp & Und. Sl.* 88: *Goog.*—A black eye....usually an eye injured in a fight, rather than...through an accident. **1933–34** Lorimer & Lorimer *Stag Line* 164: We don't want any googs handed out around here.

google-eyed *adj.* goggle-eyed.
   1902–03 Ade *People You Know* 106: The men were all google-eyed. **1920** Ade *Hand-Made Fables* 104: You will be google-eyed after you have studied some 200 Masterpieces. **1973** *Oui* (Apr.) 26: Some other google-eyed moron.

googobs *n.pl. Black E.* lots; GOBS.
   1970 in *DARE.* **1974** R. Carter *16th Round* 58: Googobs of uncontrolled fists began flying every which-a-way. **1978** W. Brown *Tragic*

Magic 122: Goo-gobs of chicks started inviting him over. **1994** N. McCall *Wanna Holler* 279: Goo-gobs of historic landmarks that kept me in wide-eyed awe.

goo-goo[1] *n.* [prob. sugg. by *goo-goo* (a representation of baby talk), in ref. to various unfamiliar languages] **1.a.** Orig. *Mil.* a Filipino or other islander of the South China Sea or adjacent areas.—usu. used contemptuously. Also **gugu.** Now *hist.*
   [**1873** B. Harte *Mrs. Skaggs's Husbands* 186: His repetition of the word "goo-goo"...when taken in conjunction with his size in my mind seemed to indicate his aboriginal or Aztec origin.] **1898** *Oregon in Philippines* (Aug.) 12: Words added to the regimental vocabulary, "Manana," Googoo, Adios. **1899** Bowe *13th Minn.* 77: The goo-goos shot into the town for a couple of hours. **1900** Reeves *Bamboo Tales* 41: The unanimous opinion [was] that the "gugus" did not and never would know when they were "licked." **1900** Baker *30th Inf.* 43: As we advanced down the hill the googoos held their fire. **1901** Sonnichsen *Among Filipinos* 366: The soldier laughed and called him a "goo-goo," whatever that may be. **1906** *Independent* (Feb. 8) 333: It was hoped that Miss Roosevelt would not be seen dancing with any "gugu"—the American term of contempt for the Filipino. **1910** Stirling *Midshipman* 13: They don't know anything, these gugus. **1918** Abbot *Soldiers* 294: And they've had a few scraps with the little Brown Japs/And with Gugus way out in Samar. **1929** Thomas *Woodfill* 42 [ref. to 1899]: I don't know why we called 'em goo-goos, but all the soldiers did. **1933** Clifford *Boats* 110: Those goo-goo carpenters hammering away for a peso a day. **1936** Mackenzie *Living Rough* 35: I got in wrong with the Goo-goo's (Philippinos) in this cannery. **1937** Steinbeck *Mice & Men* 58: But Susy's [brothel] is clean and she got nice chairs. Don't let no goo-goos in, neither. **1946** *Amer. Leg. Mag.* (May) 26: Pacific Islanders were "gugus." **1958** Cooley *Run for Home* 295 [ref. to 1920's]: If that steward don't send one of them goo-goos back here with...that...coffee, I'm gonna go up and get it myself. **1969** Searls *Hero Ship* 46 [ref. to WWII]: That goo-goo wardroom chief'll never handle him any better than he could Joe Louis.
   b. a dark- or yellow-skinned foreigner; GOOK[2], 1.a.—usu. used contemptuously.
   1921 *Ohio Doughboys in Italy* 89: It was not that we had anything against the cabbies [in Italy], who were merely petty thieves, it was, I really believe, that every man who swung a fist that night saw before him, not a fat-faced bewhiskered, patent-leather-hatted goo-goo, but a lean-faced, square-jawed man with a star on his shoulder. **1934** (quot. at GOOK[2], *n.*, 1.a.). *ca*1943 in L'Amour *Over Solomons* 65: To the devil with these gugus [Brazilian Indians]. **1960** Leckie *March to Glory* 69 [ref. to 1950]: The Goo-Goos [Chinese soldiers] are late. *Ibid.* 105: Hello, Arson One Four. The Goo-Goos are fouling up the detail. They're unloading their own WP. **1972** Swarthout *Tin Lizzie* 219 [ref. to 1916]: Well, well, if this ain't a fine band of goo-goos [Mexicans].
   2. any language other than English spoken by GOO-GOOS.—used contemptuously.
   1972 Swarthout *Tin Lizzie* 232: He might as well have been talking goo-goo.

goo-goo[2] *n.* [sugg. by phr. *good government*, infl. by *goody-goody*] *Pol.* an idealistic supporter of political reform.—used derisively.
   1895 in T. Roosevelt *Letters* I 466: The Goo-Goos, and all the German leaders...have attacked me. *Ibid.* 483: And those prize idiots, the Goo-Goos, have just played into their hands by...nominating an independent ticket of their own. **1909** in O. Johnson *Lawrenceville* 150: Down with the Goo-Goos...Rally to the Federalists and Down the Dickinson Goo-Goos. **1912** (cited in *W9*). **1931** Steffens *Autobiog.* 255 [ref. to 1890's]: The reformers called goo-goos after their Good Government clubs. **1938** Adamic *My America* 24 [ref. to 1912]: Mayor Alexander...ran on the Good Government League ("Goo-Goo") ticket. *Ibid.* 26: The "Goo-Goos"...had only one more card to play. **1958** S.H. Adams *Tenderloin* 364: The goo-goos haven't got a look-in. *a*1984 Formisano & Burns *Boston* 147 [ref. to 1903]: Their electoral attempt did produce a reputation for arrogant self-righteousness and their nickname of Goo-Goo. **1988** *Newsweek* (May 16) 27: [The] Chicago electorate [is] so inured to influence-peddling and other political shenanigans that good-government types are derided as "goo-goos." **1988** *McLaughlin Group* (synd. TV series) (Sept. 4): It's going to hurt him with the googoos—the good government crowd. **1992** *New Republic* (Dec. 14) 23: The goo-goos should know better, because the budget deal didn't even work on its own anti-political terms.

goo-goo[3] *n.* GOO-GOO EYES, *n.pl.*

1901 Hobart *John Henry* 13: Throwing a goo-goo at me that settles everything. **1904** Hobart *Eppy Grams* 43: Vimmen may be flirts, but...dey doan'd brag abouid it like dem male Goo-Goo Givers. **1906** H. Green *Boarding House* 146: Mignon...made goo-goos at Mr. Sinclair. **1944** Micheaux *Mrs. Wingate* 31: I've seen her giving you the goo goo two or three times.

goo-goo⁴ *n.* GOO, *n.*, 1. Also attrib.

1903 Townsend *Sure* 107: He digs out...a bottle of claret, some goo-goo stuff dat Duchess calls patty, and some cheese sandwiches. **1918** Casey *Cannoneers* (Oct. 29): There's a gas shell busted down at the battery position...An' I got a lot of the goo-goo on my hands an' it burns a little. **1969** Miss. man, age *ca*55: There's googoo grease on it.

goo-goo⁵ *n.* a silly fool.

1931 Uhler *Cane Juice* 243: "Oh, you're just a goo-goo!" Marcia said contemptuously.

goo-goo *v.* to cast amorous glances at. Also absol.

1901 Ade *Modern Fables* 111: She put her Chin on his shoulder and Goo-Gooed him and he lost the Power of Speech. **1908** H. Green *Maison de Shine* 190: Never mind goo-gooin' Birdie Trippit. **1912–14** in E. O'Neill *Lost Plays* 174: Some one of these Mexican dolls you're googooing at will carve her initials on your back with the bread knife some one of these days. **1944** Micheaux *Mrs. Wingate* 254: He...made goo goo eyes at her, and she goo-gooed back at him.

goo-goo eyes *n.pl.* foolishly sentimental, romantic, or amorous glances.

1897 Ade *Horne* 172: She'd had a lot o' them cigarette children over in the corner, makin' goo-goo eyes at 'em an' "talkin'" 'em to a standstill. **1900** F. Queen & H. Cannon *Just Because She Made Dem Goo-Goo Eyes* (pop. song). **1902** Townsend *Fadden & Mr. Paul* 53: Remember de Wily Widdy...what used to make goo-goo eyes at Whiskers. **1906** H. Green *Boarding House* 11: The ingenue made goo-goo eyes at him during her second song. **1908** in "O. Henry" *Works* 1262: It is goo-goo eyes or "git" when he looks toward a pretty girl. **1919** Small *Story of 47th* 24: But Doc and Stockie and Crowley were wise,/So went to the theatre and made goo goo eyes. **1930** in Perelman *Old Gang* 111: If I ever catch Phyllis...making goo-goo eyes at my Fred again I will make it hot for her. **1941** Hargrove *Pvt. Hargrove* 75: We made the rounds here together, went to Charlotte together, made goo-goo eyes at the same waitress in Fayetteville. **1950** Hartmann & O'Brien *Fancy Pants* (film): That earl was makin' googoo eyes at her. **1960** Jordan & Marberry *Fool's Gold* 20 [ref. to 1899]: She seemed to think Florrie was making goo-goo eyes at me. **1962** T. Berger *Reinhart* 408: She made simple-minded googoo-eyes at him. **1987** *Wkly. World News* (Aug. 25) 13: Dolph Lundgren...was spotted making goo-goo eyes with a leggy lovely at a London hotspot. **1991** *TV Guide* (May 18) 4: In Love, complete with sighs and moony goo-goo eyes.

googy eyes *n.pl.* GOO-GOO EYES.

1919 MacGill *Dough-Boys* 170: You go mooning after a girl, making googy eyes at her.

gook¹ *n.* [perh. dial. var. of obs. *gowk* 'cuckoo, simpleton'] **1.** Orig. *Und.* a slovenly or offensive woman, esp. a prostitute; (hence, disparagingly) a woman; BROAD.

1859 Matsell *Vocab.* 38: Gooh [*sic*]. A prostitute. *a*1890–93 *F & H* III 181: *Gook*...(American).—A low prostitute. **1951** Sheldon *Troubling of a Star* 56: "White gooks don't show me a thing. Not a goddam thing," said Goff. **1957** Myrer *Big War* 315 [ref. to WWII]: A good gook is hard to snag,/You can always get a mean old bag.../Just when you think you've copped a nice big feel/You'll find she's giving you a double deal. **1966** S. Harris *Hellhole* 161: Molly still designates [underworld characters]...by the names with which she first learned to identify them [*ca*1910]: "cats" or "gooks"—the small-time madams...; "bats" or "owls"—streetwalkers who work at night.

2. a foolish or peculiar person; GINK.

1911 T.A. Dorgan, in Zwilling *TAD Lexicon* 41: Packey had the softest time of his life trimming the Gotham gooks. **1919** *Camp Knox News* (Oct. 18) 4: Some of them gooks...wants to live in...luxury. **1923** *Bomb* (Iowa State College) 426: Rutter is the only gook in the house that ever had a date in his life and with his Daniel Boone sideburns he makes quite a striking figure. **1935** Pollock *Und. Speaks*: Gook, a boob; easy mark; hick. **1959** H. Ellison *Gentleman Junkie* 86: He wasn't a gook like Leon, who wore *his* on his beanie. **1963** T.I. Rubin *Sweet Daddy* 1: I'm not like a lot of the gooks here making with this head shrinker talk and all. *Ibid.* 158: *Gook*: a fool, [also] a foreigner. **1970–72** *AS* L (1975) 59: *Gook*...Person regarded as dull, foolish or stupid. **1987** *21 Jump St.* (Fox-TV): 'Cause a few gooks accidentally exploited a weakness in our strategy?

gook² *n.* [prob. fr. GOO-GOO¹, infl. by GOOK¹, 2] **1.a.** Orig. *Mil.* a dark- or yellow-skinned foreigner; native; (often *specif.*) a native of the Philippines, the Southwest Pacific and adjacent areas, Central America, Japan, North Africa, southern Europe and the eastern Mediterranean, Korea, or Indochina; (now *esp.*) an East Asian person of any nationality; (*broadly*) any usu. non-European foreigner.—usu. used contemptuously.—usu. considered offensive. Often attrib.

1920 *Nation* (July 10) 36: The Haitians in whose service the United States Marines are supposedly in Haiti are nicknamed "Gooks," and have been treated with every variety of contempt, insult and brutality. I have heard officers...talk of "bumping off" (i.e. killing) "Gooks" as if it were a variety of sport like duck hunting. **1921** *15th Inf. Sentinel* (Tientsin, China) (Jan. 14) 10: McDonald, the vegetable dieter, wants to go to Gook Land [the Philippines] on this boat. **1927** Shoup *Marines in China* 73: These "gooks" [Filipinos] are very able seamen. **1927** in Thomason *Marines and Others* 202: Can't see why she conked. I'm certain those Gooks [Nicaraguans] never hit the motor back there. **1928** in *Our Army* (Jan. 1929) 26: Even the gook [card-]sharks over in Manila learned about deck-flipping from Red. **1934** Mencken *Amer. Lang.* (ed. 4) 296: The Marines in Nicaragua [1912–33] called the natives *gooks*. Those of Costa Rica are sometimes called *goo-gooks*. **1935** *AS* (Feb.) 79: *Gook*. Anyone who speaks Spanish, particularly a Filipino. **1935** *Our Army* (May) 34: So you came on here to Oahu/Where the gooks make more than you do. **1940** Goodrich *Delilah* 75 [ref. to 1916]: Did you see any of these gooks [Filipinos] up north with a book that the Americans, English, or Spaniards didn't bring? **1944** Kendall *Service Slang* 24: *Gooks*...South Sea natives. **1944** Pyle *Brave Men* 211: To Muncy and his tentmates all Italians were "gooks." It wasn't a term of contempt at all, for Muncy loved the Italians and they loved him. **1945** *Yank* (July 27) 22: The Italian storekeeper said something in Italian....The gunner...asked me, "You know what this gook is saying?" **1945** *Yank* (Nov. 9) 2: The Japanese...[are] known among GIs as "gooks," the GI name for all natives in the Pacific. **1946** J.H. Burns *Gallery* 284: These Eyeties...ain't human beins. They're just Gooks, that's all. **1947** Matthews *Assault* 125: That valley...is lousy with Gooks [Japanese troops]. **1947** *N.Y. Herald Trib.* (Apr. 2) 28: The American troops...don't like the Koreans—whom they prefer to call "Gooks." **1950** *Time* (Aug. 21) 21: "Gook" is the universal G.I. word for any and all Koreans. **1951** *Sat. Eve. Post* (Jan. 27) 117: The guys said they were stompin' over frozen dead gooks [Chinese Communist soldiers] all the way up. **1951–52** P. Frank *Hold Back Night* 116: What the hell was happening, when a bunch of gooks [Koreans] and Chinks could lick the United States? **1952** J.D. MacDonald *Damned* 34: The gook [Mexican] prisoners can do handicraft stuff and sell it and get the extra pesos. **1952** Landon *Angle of Attack* 150 [ref. to WWII]: What the hell do you care, they're only gooks [So. Europeans]. **1954** Crockett *Magnificent Bastards* 84: Half a dozen gooks [Melanesians] squatted on the ground near by, their bare black skins gleaming in the rain. **1958** Camerer *Damned Wear Wings* 38 [ref. to WWII]: If the colonel has to bail out over enemy territory [Romania or Yugoslavia] those gooks will think the High Lama dropped in. **1959** Cochrell *Barren Beaches* 39 [ref. to WWII]: Gook money...Two shillings, six pence. *Ibid.* 42: These gooks [white New Zealanders] are fine people. *Ibid.* 44: The railroad tracks...were real gook narrow gauge. **1959** W. Burroughs *Naked Lunch* 82: Hassan...Uppa your ass, you liquefying gook. **1960** Morrison *Hellbirds* 83 [ref. to WWII]: What difference does it make?...He's only a gook [native of India]. **1962** Gallant *On Valor's Side* 258 [ref. to WWII]: It's a gook sub...it ain't ours for sure. **1963** Boyle *Yanks Don't Cry* 16 [ref. to 1941]: I've been through these gook wars before...This one...[is] bound to be bigger and better than Nicaragua. **1965** Koch *Casual Company* 5 [ref. to WWII]: Scratch a gook [New Zealander] and you find an army. **1965** Karp *Doobie Doo* 97: A gook in the purest sense is anybody what ain't American. **1967** Reed *Up Front* 37: The gooks [Vietnamese] opened up with a machine gun. **1970** S.J. Perelman, in *New Yorker* (Oct. 17) 41: So the gooks [natives of India] head for me. **1970** Poniscan *Last Detail* 48: When they landed the marines at Lebanon they had to dodge the swimmers and when they got on the beach there was a gook there to sell 'em a cold Coke. **1974** former LT, USAF, age 29: [In Turkey, 1965] we used to call the Turks *gooks*....We didn't like them. **1983** Van Devanter & Morgan *Before Morning* 135: Like thousands of Americans, I began calling the Vietnamese—both friendly and enemy—"gooks." **1984** in Terkel *Good War* 63 [ref. to WWII]: "There's an old gook woman. Got a bad wound." This is what we called the natives in the Pacific. **1985** Boyne & Thompson *Wild Blue* 434: A damn gook [Guamanian], a foreigner. **1988** Coonts *Final Flight* 338: The gooks [Arabs] had thrown the grenades.

b. *Mil.* an enemy soldier or sympathizer (as distinguished from a friendly or neutral inhabitant).—*usu.* used contemptuously. [Contextually specific, but not contrastive with **(a).**]

1950 *Sat. Eve. Post* (Aug. 19) 27: I also saw my countrymen take a vigorous mauling from a Soviet-directed raggety-tag army that they had nicknamed "Gooks." **1951** Jones *Face of War* 12: The gooks are coming...get the hell out! **1964** R. Moore *Green Berets* 220: Guess you couldn't snatch a Chicom for us, eh?...It would square whatever action we take if we could prove that the gooks [Vietnamese Communists] are here [in Laos]. **1971–72** Giovannitti *Medal* 93: Go around to the other side of this group [of Vietnamese] and keep your eyes open....If that's a gook, we'll take him quietly. **1978** J. Webb *Fields of Fire* 99 [ref. to 1969]: She [a Vietnamese] could have been a gook....Look twice and you're dead, Senator. **1987** Lanning *Only War* 56 [ref. to 1969]: Collier dragged a middle-aged man out of his hooch and accused him of being a VC...."He's a fucking VC! Only gooks have mustaches."

2. *Mil.* any language other than English spoken by GOOKS.—used contemptuously.

1952 Haines & Krims *One Minute to Zero* (film): Don't let him hear any gook talk or he'll get up fighting. **1953** *ATS* (ed. 2) 188: Foreign language...*gook.* **1965** Friedman *Totempole* 292: He even tried to learn their language and *speak* gook [Korean]. **1967** W. Crawford *Gresham's War* 122 [ref. to 1953]: None of us speak gook [Chinese or Korean]. **1968** *Newsweek* (Jan. 29) 32: The gook was babbling away in gook [Vietnamese]. **1972** Pelfrey *Big V* 126: Can you talk gook, sir? **1981** Wambaugh *Glitter Dome* 161: They talked a few words of gook [Vietnamese].

gook[3] *n.* [perh. blend of GOO and *muck*] **1.a.** viscid matter of any kind, esp. slime or oozy or sticky dirt; (dysphemistically) unpleasant or unhealthful food. Also **guck.**

1942 *ATS* 72: Viscid or thick fluid...*gook.* *Ibid.* 97: Syrupy types of food...*goo, gook.* **1950** *Sat. Eve. Post* (May 6) 42: The company...sells shaving guck. **1956** in *DAS:* "Glim" gets the gook off! **1961** Scarne *Comp. Guide to Gambling* 536: Most [playing] cards are still made from two thicknesses of paper glued together with a black paste called *gook.* **1965** LeMay & Kantor *Mission* 247: The guck...interfered...with visibility. **1968** C. Victor *Sky Burned* 86: Like putty, harmless, pliable gook. **1970** Della Femina *Wonderful Folks* 192: They dip this thing into a vat of guck. **1972** Buell *Shrewdale* 28: Then they heaved guck at the windshield. **1973** *Penthouse* (Aug.) 14: I got...sick of rolling over into a blob of that guck. **1982** *N.Y. Post* (Sept. 2) 28: That creamy gook will add an inch to your waistline. **1985** M. Carducci *Neon Maniacs* (film): I heard forensics found this slimy guck all over the place. **1987** *RHD2*: She looks ridiculous with all that gook [makeup] around her eyes. **1993** *CBS This Morning* (CBS-TV) (July 28): But the mud and guck didn't come.

b. (see quot.).

1985 Eble *Campus Slang* (Oct.) 5: *Gook*—anything gross, worthless. "This homework is a bunch of gook!"

2. *Av.* heavy clouds or fog.

1957 E. Brown *Locust Fire* 122 [ref. to 1944]: And how much time do the rest of us flying worms have to log even for a cruddy air medal? How much at night? Or in the gook?

gook boots *n.pl. Mil. Av.* fancy flying boots affected by some aircrewmen.—*usu.* considered offensive.

1957 Wallrich *A.F. Airs* 51: The fly-boy type, with his hundred-mission-crush hat, his gook boots, parachute silk scarf [etc.]...walked into the pages of history in World War II.

Gookland *n. Mil.* a country inhabited by GOOKS, as the Philippines or Vietnam.—used contemptuously.—*usu.* considered offensive. Cf. GOONEYLAND.

1921 *15th Inf. Sentinel* (Tientsin, China) (Jan. 14) 10: McDonald, the vegetable dieter, wants to go to Gook Land [the Philippines] on this boat. **1982** Del Vecchio *13th Valley* 14 [ref. to 1967]: The Americanization of Gookland. **1986** Thacker *Pawn* 35 [ref. to 1970]: It turns brown in a week; no scabs in gookland. **1986** D. Tate *Bravo Burning* 172: He leans out and gives all of Gookland the big finger.

gook-legged *adj. Mil.* cross-legged.—*usu.* considered offensive.

1966 R.E. Alter *Carny Kill* 14: The orchestra sat gook-legged on a Persian rug and they were dressed to look like Malay pirates I guess.

gook sores *n.pl. Mil.* ulcerous sores resulting from fungal infection of the skin.—*usu.* considered offensive. [Quots. ref. to Vietnam War.]

1989 D. Sherman *There I Was* 129: The immersion foot and gook sores

most of us had. **1990** G.R. Clark *Wds. of Viet. War* 204: *Gook Sores*...Ulcerous sores common among GIs who spent extended periods of time...in the boonies.

Gooksville *n. Mil.* GOOKLAND; (*USAF*) North Vietnamese air space.—*usu.* considered offensive. Now *hist.* Also **Gookville.**

1967 D. Ford *Muc Wa* 6: Same place we're all going, sooner or later...Gooksville. **1985** Heywood *Taxi Dancer* 89 [ref. to 1967]: He'd come out of Gookville plenty of times sucking wind.

gook wagon *n. Hot Rodding.* (see 1960 quot.). Also **gook car.**

1951–53 in *AS* XXIX (1954) 97: "Hot Rod" Terms...*gook wagon*, n. A car which is primarily "stock" with an abundance of cheap accessories like flapping skirts and chrome adornments. **1953** *New Yorker* (Mar. 7) 23: We furnished most of the soup-up and doll-up accessories for this car. You'll notice it's not a gook car. **1953** Felsen *Street Rod* 149: I think it's a gook wagon. All show and no guts. **1960** in *West. Folk.* (Jan. 1962) 30: *Gook wagon*—an automobile which has been overly ornamented with chrome and accessories or altered in some manner not currently in vogue among hot rod enthusiasts...."Gook" is synonymous with gawdy decoration.

gooky /ˈgʊki/ or /ˈguki/ *adj.* sticky, viscous, etc.; (*also*) difficult; awkward.

1961 Kohner *Gidget Goes Hawaiian* 90: That was one of those gooky misunderstandings. **1966** Susann *Valley of Dolls* 262: Her hair was sticking out at all angles and gooky. **1983** Nelkin & Brown *Workers* 29: I once spent two days cleaning out brushes...[that were] all hard and gooky.

gool var. GOAL, *n., v.*

goola[1] *n.* [orig. unkn.; cf. GOOLA BOX] *Jazz.* a piano.

1944 Burley *Orig. Hndbk. Harlem Jive* 11: Those gams...are like the props on a goola. **1975** R.S. Gold *Jazz Talk* 112: *Goola*, n....according to jazzmen, term had some currency c.1917–c.1940...piano.

goola[2] *n.* [< It *culo*; cf. GOUL, *n.*] the anus.

1949 Mende *Spit & Stars* 175: Up your goola, Mr. Bick.

goola box *n.* [cf. GOOLA[1]] *Black E.* a jukebox.

1938 *AS* (Dec.) 316: A *goola-box* is Omaha [Black] slang for a nickarola.

goolie chit *n.* [GOOLIES + *chit*] *Mil. Av.* (see quot.). Now *hist.*

***1945** (cited in Partridge *DSUE* (ed. 8) 489). **1968** Westheimer *Young Sentry* 15 [ref. to 1943]: Several months earlier they had been briefed meticulously on evading capture, finding assistance and getting back to Allied lines. They had been issued detailed maps on silk handkerchiefs and printed messages promising cash rewards to those who assisted them. But the maps were of Egypt, Libya and Tunisia and the messages, called "goolie chits," were in Arabic.

goolies *n.pl.* [prob. < Hindi *golí* 'ball'] the testicles. *Rare* in U.S.

***1929** Aldington *Death of a Hero* 249 [ref. to WWI]: At 'is stummick an' goolies, Point! ***1966, *1967** in *OED2.* **1969** in Legman *No Laughing Matter* 456: Well, pop it again—you've got me caught by the goolies! ***1971** in *OED2.*

goombah *n.* [< a dial. pron. of It *compare*] **1.** Orig. *Ital.-Amer.* a close or trusted male friend. Also vars. [Pop. by Rocky Graziano, U.S. prizefighter and actor, on the *Martha Raye Show* (NBC-TV).]

1955 R. Graziano, on *Martha Raye Show* (NBC-TV): Hey, goombah! **1957** R. Graziano, in Blumgarten *Mr. Rock & Roll* (film): Hey, goombah! Break it up [a romantic embrace]! **1969** Salerno & Tompkins *Crime Confed.* 9: And in the summer of 1939...he overheard the manager make the same judgment: "Don't let him lock the back door. He'll leave it open and let his goombahs in." *Ibid.* 52: Don't get snide with me, goombah. **1970** *Harper's* (June) 78: The cops had collared a big gumbah of Frank Costello's and made a deal with him. **1972** J. Pearl *Cops* 45: She thought of Sean as "Pat's lad" and Tony as her "goomba." **1973** Layne *Murphy* (unp.): We can improvise, baby, we can improvise. C'mon, gumbaah! **1974** Sann *Dead Heat* 155: Don't knock yourself out tryin' to find my goombah. **1979** V. Patrick *Pope* 103: He's my *goombah*, Charlie. I still call him uncle. **1981** Sann *Trial* 39: I did indeed, goombah. **1987** *ALF* (NBC-TV): Of course I care! He's my Willy—my goombah!

2. a mafia boss; mafioso. Also vars.

1969 M. Puzo *Godfather* 55, in *OEDAS* II 121: I don't care how many guinea Mafia goombahs come out of the woodwork. **1972** R. Barrett *Lovomaniacs* 11: That's how gumbahs do it....The gumbahs. The *pad-*

rone. **1972** Grogan *Ringolevio* 96: He was a mean, cruel, brutal heavy-weight of a goomba. **1977** Torres *Q & A* 121: And who's them other two guys…? Them is gumbas. **1987** R. Miller *Slob* 92: Some ancient leftover of whatever the goombahs are calling Cosa Nostra these days. **1992** *L.A. Times* (Mar. 25) E1: "Gangland," the city's first gossip column for gangsters.…[has] become must reading for Mafia voyeurs, *goombahs* on the run and the district attorneys pursuing them.

3. a stupid person.

1952 Mandel *Angry Strangers* 158: Cleanimup good…muhfookagoombah! **1988** B. Breathed *Bloom County* (synd. comic strip) (Aug. 31): Keep those flat-footed goombahs in Washington out of my hair. **1992** B. Breathed *Outland* (synd. comic strip) (Nov. 22): Mankind's stupidest expressions.…They'll start sayin' [them] and sound like real goombahs!

goom-bye *interj.* [imit. of an Italian accent] good-bye. Also **goon-bye.** *Joc.*

1900 Belasco *Madame Butterfly* 15: Goon-bye, sayonara, Butterfly. **1929** McEvoy *Hollywood Girl* 202: Goom bi, slaves. **1942** Swerling & Mankiewicz *Pride of Yankees* (film): I'm master of ceremonies, so goombye. **1956** Gold *Not with It* 18: We'll say goombye to the habit together, kid. **1960** Wohl *Cold Wind* 12: He had left her mother when Iris was ten. Bingo! Goom-by. **1965** Pollini *Glover* 255: Well, goombye then.

goomer *n.* [cf. GOMER] **1.** GOOF, 1.

1966 *Beverly Hillbillies* (CBS-TV): He sure is a funny-lookin' goomer. **1967** *Ibid.*: Get out of my kitchen, ya hairy little goomer! **1974** Univ. Tenn. grad. student: Who's that big goomer she's always with? **1981** D.E. Miller *Jargon* 244: *Goomer.* Also *goomer…goofer,* and *goober.* A loser. **1988** Eble *Campus Slang* (Spring) 5: Look at that guy wearing his boxers *over* his shorts. What a goomer. **1986–91** Hamper *Rivethead* 73: Unemployed factory goomers.

2. *Mil.* GOONER; GOMER, 3.

1978 *Nat. Lampoon* (July) 67 [ref. to 1972]: *Goomers, V.C., Charlie…*Our enemies.

3. *Hosp.* GOMER, 2.

1986 *NDAS: Goomer…*A hypochondriac (fr. *get out of my emergency room*).

goon *n.* [app. introduced as a nonce term by Frederick Lewis Allen (see 1921 and first 1948 quot. below), perh. ult. fr. GOONEY, *n.* Allen's sense, "a stolid, usu. unimaginative person, esp. a writer or public figure," seems to have been evanescent: no independent exx. are known. All later senses of the word appear to have been inspired by "Alice the Goon," a fantastic, dull-witted, muscular character who appeared in E.C. Segar's popular comic strip "Thimble Theater, featuring Popeye," beginning in 1933.]

1.a. a stupid person.

[**1921** F.L. Allen, in *Harper's Mag.* (Dec.) 121: The Goon and His Style.…A goon is a person with a heavy touch as distinguished from a jigger, who has a light touch. While jiggers look on life with a genial eye, goons take a more stolid and literal view. It is reported that George Washington was a goon, whereas Lincoln was a jigger. Gladstone seems to have been a goon, Disraeli a jigger. *Ibid.* 122: A goonish style is one that reads as if it were the work of a goon. It is thick and heavy…It employs the words "youth" and "lad," likes the exclamation "lo!" [etc.].] **1938** *Life* (Nov. 14) 6: The word "Goon" was first popularized by college students who used it to mean any stupid person. **1941** *AS* (Oct.) 166: *Goon.* Soldier who falls in lowest [intelligence] category in Army classification. **1942** Freeman & Gilbert *Larceny, Inc.* (film): Cut it, cut it, you goon. **1943** *Newsweek* (Feb. 8) 52: If a ship's motor failed and a pilot had to bail out in that country he was a "gone goon." **1944** Kapelner *Lonely Boy Blues* 80: They walked like goons to a table. **1945** Seaton *Junior Miss* (film): Aw, don't be a goon. **1948** Mencken *Amer. Lang. Supp. II* 776: *Goon…*Frederick L. Allen…tells me that it was used in his family before [Dec. 1921], and may either have been picked up elsewhere or invented. **1948** J.H. Burns *Lucifer* 111: Pop's a good old goon once you know how to handle him. **1950** Spillane *Vengeance* 25: Did he think I was some goon with loose brains and stupid enough to take it lying down? **1952** Malamud *Natural* 52: Lay off of that, you goon. **1953** Harris *Southpaw* 305: Henry…you are a stupid goon. **1958** Cooley *Run for Home* 352: What kind of a goon is this guy, anyway? **1959** Trocchi *Cain's Book* 19: They won't…run the risk of having some irresponsible goon send for a doctor! **1962** E. Stephens *Blow Negative* 312: You mean those two goons out there actually have the intelligence to—. **1969** Zindel *Hamburger* 32: Right in the auditorium you said he looked like a goon. **1971** *Go Ask Alice* 24: It seems like

every family has to have one goon.

b. a big, muscular fellow.

1980 Lorenz *Guys Like Us* 20: "Can you slug [a softball]?" "I'm no goon but I'll get my share."

c. a crazy person.

1980 Grizzard *Billy Bob Bailey* 210: A goon shot Patricia Barry dead [on the street].

2.a. a ruffian, esp. one hired to do violence; thug.

1938 *AS* (Oct.) 178: [In Seattle] a goon is a member of a labor-union's beef-squad…who can be depended on to cow and frighten recalcitrant union-members and to injure those who displease the union hierarchy. The term…first gained common currency…a year ago. **1938** in Tamony *Americanisms* (No. 34) 5: The word "goon," used to express a labor racketeer, thug or beatup man, was given legal sanction…during the trial of Al Rosser, former Portland teamster head. **1947** Schulberg *Harder They Fall* 51: A couple of goons were waiting for him,…anxious to convince him of his mistake. **1958** Roberts *Understanding English* ix: To others he [the linguistic scientist] is a goon madly bent on the destruction of literacy everywhere. **1967** J. Harris *Freedom Rd.* 38: The false rumor spread that "goons"…were to prevent Negroes from boarding the buses. **1970** J. Freedman *Old News* 126: Can you…lynch it with ropes,…scare it with goons? **1970–71** Rubinstein *City Police* 320: It was a rough place…They were real goons, truckers, and the kid was terrified. **1981** Gilliland *Rosinante* 81: You think you need company goons…or the union would maybe take over the place? **1982** *World's Finest Comics* (Oct.) (unp.): Don't try it, King! You're no faster than your goon! **1986** Sliwa *Attitude* 39: Many goons dress the way they do to inspire fear in normal, hard-working citizens.

b. (among POWs in Germany during WWII) a German prison-camp guard; a German. Also *attrib.* Now *hist.*

1945 *N.Y. Times Mag.* (Nov. 4) 12: "Goon" (German soldier or guard). ***1945** in *OEDS:* I think it was an Australian who first called the Germans "Goons." **1955** Klaas *Maybe I'm Dead* 13: Yeah. If the goons just don't move us. *Ibid.* 141: A goon soldier in combat gets only six. **1953–57** Giovannitti *Combine D* 17: That goon [radio] commentator sounded nervous. **1960** Simmons *Kriegie* 100: If at any time a "goon" enters the barracks we will be signaled by the call "Tallyho."…By the way, "Tallyho" is used at any time any German enters any barracks. **1965** *Hogan's Heroes* (CBS-TV): They figure if you can't find it, the goons can't. **1968** Westheimer *Young Sentry* 216: "Latrine," Hartman explained. "The Goons call it the abort." "Goons?" said Lang. "Germans," Augustine said.

3. *Av.* a Douglas DC-2 or DC-3 airplane; GOONEY BIRD, *n.*, 2.

1937 in Tamony *Americanisms* (No. 34) 6: The old Ford transport plane…was a *tin goose,* while the sleek DC-2 of today is referred to as a *goon.* **1938** *AS* (Apr.) 156: GOONS. Transports or sleepers on T.W.A. Lines. [Douglas Aircraft plant, Santa Monica] **1959** R.L. Scott *Flying Tiger* 117 [ref. to WWII]: We climbed as high as the lumbering old goons would go. **1962** Harvey *Strike Command* 43: They'll probably be rocking in the Old Pilots' Home before the Goons are through flying. **1963** E.M. Miller *Exile* 114: And tell Sergeant Jonas I said to get the Goon ready. **1973** *Playboy* (Apr.) 45 [ref. to Vietnam War]: On one lobster run, the goon was badly damaged in an accident. **1975** in Higham & Siddall *Combat Aircraft* 56: I have ridden through crow-hop landings that would do credit to the old "Goon." **1987** Zeybel *Gunship* 6: Travel…was by C-47, the old Goon.

4. a black person.—used contemptuously.—usu. considered offensive.

1942 in Mencken *Amer. Lang. Supp. I* 633: In the [U.S.] Virgin Islands…the blacks are called *goons* or *goonies.* **1947** Willingham *End As a Man* 78: And he commenced to choke the goon…and after a while the nigger agreed he was a nigger.

5. *Mil.* GOONEY, *n.*

1951–52 Frank *Hold Back Night* 33: Who picked out this goddam icebox full of fleas and gooks and goons and Chinks in uniforms that look like those old-fashioned comforters they used to put on beds?

6. *Narc.* a form of phencyclidine (PCP).

1977 (cited in Spears *Drugs & Drink* 227). **1978** Petersen & Stillman *PCP Abuse* 1: Some of the street names for phencyclidine include: angel dust…crystal…goon. **1979** Feldman et al. *Angel Dust* 124: PCP…street names…*crystal…hog…goon* [etc.].

goon box *n.* (among POWs in Germany during WWII) a German sentry box atop a guard tower. Now *hist.*

1948 *AS* XXIII 218 [ref. to WWII]: A *goon-box* was one of the guard towers along the fences around the camp. **1955** Klaas *Maybe I'm Dead* 21 [ref. to 1944]: This time machine guns are set up at the four corners of the parade ground in addition to the goon-box guns. **1968** West-heimer *Young Sentry* 235 [ref. to WWII]: The guard towers, called goonboxes by the prisoners, were…set high on heavy timbers the size of telephone poles just outside the wire. Each mounted a machine gun and had a telephone.

goon-child *n. Stu.* a silly fool.
  1942 Breslow *Blondie Goes to College* (film): Looks like you're doin' all right, goon-child! **1943** *AS* XVIII 154: *Goon child.* A dumb or simple person. **1975** Univ. Tenn. student: She's such a goon-child.

gooned *adj.* very intoxicated.—also constr. with *out.*
  1968 Moura *Tender Loving Care* 146: They were both gooned…Penner then saw the window and vibrated his head to clear up his alcoholic vision. **1966–69** Woiwode *Going to Do* 28: "Swacked?" "Smashed, gooned, juiced, bombed, stoned, zorched, my head wedged." **1983** *Nat. Lampoon* (Aug.) 40: Janice [was] gooned-out on amaretto and milk. **1983** Wambaugh *Delta Star* 17: I think he's gooned out most a the time. On ludes or somethin.

gooner *n.* [prob. alter. of GOONEY, *n.*] *USMC.* a Communist Vietnamese soldier; (*broadly*) GOOK[2], 1.a. Now *hist.*
  1969 Austin *Grunt's Little War* (WCCO-TV Minneapolis): The goon-ers are picking up and using some of our rounds. **1976** C.R. Anderson *Grunts* xiv: The Vietnamese were almost always referred to in the most derogatory terms—*gooks, gooners, zipperheads* or *zips, slopes, dinks,* and *slanteyes. Ibid.* 111: Fucking tankers can't even tell the difference between us and gooners. **1978** J. Webb *Fields of Fire* 2: Ahhh, Lieutenant…More gooners than I ever seen. *Ibid.* 125: How're they gonna *walk* through all this wire, if there's gooners hitting the compound? **1984** Trotti *Phantom* 5: Oh, well, ain't nobody up that way but gooners, no how. **1989** D. Sherman *There I Was* 54: Those little gooners done bugged out on us.

gooney *n.* [var. of earlier dial. & colloq. *goney*] **1.** a stupid or silly person.
  *****1872** in *EDD* s.v. *gawney:* Wheedled and coax'd un and miade un a gooney. **1896** *DN* I 418: Don't be such a gooney. [Maine.] **1904** *DN* II 425: Cape Cod Dialect…*gooney, n.* A stupid fellow. "You great *gooney,* don't you know anything?" **1935** Pollock *Und. Sp.: Gooney,* a chump; boob. **1945** *Yank* (Nov. 23) 9: Come sit beside me, you old gooney! **1966** King *Brave & Damned* 164: The bird-brained Ridge Runner…the goonies Double Ugly and Butcher. **1984** Heath *A-Team* 32: They were parked out in front of my place like a buncha goonies at a supermarket opening.
  2. *Naut.* any of various albatrosses or similar seabirds. [The earlier form *goney* is S.E.]
  1856 in C.A. Abbey *Before the Mast* 47: 2 "*gooneys*" and 5 "Cape hens." *****1895** in *OED:* A goonie (a sea-bird…second only in size to the albatross). **1929** in Williams *One Whaling Family* [ref. to *ca*1870's]: The end of this incident was a relief to the older members of the crew who believed it would bring bad luck to the ship to kill a booby, or gooney as it may have been. **1942** Casey *Torpedo Junction* 226: The gooneys have left us or maybe have left the gooneys. **1945** O'Sheel & Cook *Semper Fidelis* 278: The gooney, which is an albatross, is one of the most graceful of all birds in flight. **1967** Lord *Incredible Victory* 51: A kind of large albatross, the gooneys were a graceful delight in the air, but a clumsy absurdity on the ground. **1993** *Natural World* (Discovery TV): The Laysan albatross, more commonly known as the gooney.
  3. *USMC.* a dark- or yellow-skinned native, esp. in enemy military service; GOOK[2], 1.a.; (in Korean War) a Chinese Communist soldier, esp. as distinguished from a North Korean.
  1927 in Thomason *Marines & Others* 180: No firing except by order…Don't want to kill any of these poor gooneys [Nicaraguans]. *Ibid.* 238: This battle, now….Any casualties? These goonies got any special ideas about fightin'? **1943** W. Simmons *Joe Foss* 115: Those goonies [Japanese] are going to pay. **1944** Kendall *Service Slang* 24: *Gooney gals….*young native girls. **1944** *AS* XIX 172: In the Virgin Islands…the blacks are called *goons* or *goonies.* **1953** in Russ *Last Parallel* 101: "Get down! 'Goonies!'" (Chinese) "Heave all the grenades you got!" *Ibid.* 199: The goonies have probably spotted him, too. **1958** Frankel *Band of Bros.* 8: If I was a goonie, you'd be buzzard bait by now. **1961** Coon *Meanwhile at the Front* 262: They figure if we stopped patrol actions we might tip our hands to the goonies. **1963** *Sat. Post* (July 27) 25: Joseph Stalin is dead, but the enemy is still called "Joe," the name he acquired right after the armistice when the command started discouraging the use of "gook" and "gooney." **1964** Peacock *Drill & Die* 10: Would it make any difference if you got shot by a Goony or a Limey or one or your own men? *Ibid.* 18: You could go up

to the Goony side of the DMZ. **1969** Lynch *Amer. Soldier* 121: The goonies have been in these mountains a long time. They have no rotation system. The Chinese stay here until they die. **1971** Cole *Rook* 245: The goonies are gone now, aren't they?
  4. *Av.* GOONEY BIRD, *n.*, 2.
  1957 E. Brown *Locust Fire* 84 [ref. to WWII]: The gooneys weren't built for the hump, son. **1958** *Airman* (Aug.) 19: They fished the "Gooney" out easily enough.

gooney bird *n.* [elab. of GOONEY, *n.*, 2] **1.a.** *Naut.* GOONEY, 2. Now *colloq.*
  1942 *Life* (Nov. 2) 62: Unperturbed gooney bird preens his fluffy grey feathers before smoke-blackened remains of a hangar. **1942** Casey *Torpedo Junction* 189: Dark brown gooney birds—a small edition of the northern albatross—were romping about us. **1943** Coale *Midway* 157: The only ladies here are female goonie birds. **1960** Leckie *Marines!* 1: Up in the roof of the jungle I could hear the birds clucking and rustling while they bedded down for the night, and right through a big hole top-side I could see one of those big scavenger birds—"goony birds" we called them—gliding along on an air current like it was being towed. **1967** Lockwood *Subs* 224 [ref. to 1940]: We encountered a problem at Midway in the form of the Laysan albatross, better known as the gooney bird…The gooneys did not…move. **1991** *Nature* (WNET-TV): Affectionately known as the "gooney bird," it has become the symbol of Midway Island.
  b. *Navy.* chicken, as served at mess. *Joc.*
  1959 Sterling *Wake of the Wahoo* 193 [ref. to WWII]: In the messroom I met an aroma of stewed chicken and dumplings. There were a good many…requests of "Pass the gooney-bird."
  2. *Av.* a Douglas DC-3 passenger and cargo plane or any variant thereof, esp. the military C-47 or naval R4D; (*occ.*) the Curtiss C-46 military transport plane. Cf. GOON, *n.*, 3.
  1942 in C.R. Bond & T. Anderson *Flying T. Diary* 207: Twenty-one of us got aboard the old gooney bird and left Kweilin. **1951** *Sat. Eve. Post* (Jan. 27) 118: Our two-motored "gooney bird"—C-47. **1955** R.L. Scott *Look of Eagle* 165: What about the Curtiss gooney-bird that's going to land at Sinuiju day after tomorrow? **1957** E. Brown *Locust Fire* 84 [ref. to 1944]: "The old dependable gooney bird," I said. **1962** Harvey *Strike Command* 43: The first Gooney Bird was the old reliable DC-3, or C-47 in USAF terminology. **1963** Dwiggins *S.O. Bees* 47: Harry Masters stood in the door of the Gooney Bird. **1965** LeMay & Kantor *Mission with LeMay* 335 [ref. to 1945]: Sent him up in a Gooney Bird (C-47) with all the radio equipment which would be needed. **1969** Garfield *Thousand-Mile War* 19: Obsolete B-18 gooneybirds that had been hastily redesigned from DC-3 cargo planes. **1971** Tuchman *Stilwell* 292 [ref. to 1942]: The transports were unarmed…C-47s…which the pilots…called "gooney birds" for a species said to fly backward to see where they came from.
  3. *Mil.* a person in Japanese, Chinese or North Korean military service. Now *hist.* Cf. GOONEY, *n.*, 3.
  1942 Tregaskis *Guadalcanal Diary* (Aug. 18): "Oh, look, they've got a couple of goonie birds," said one of the marching marines. The Japs looked particularly abject. **1969** Lynch *Amer. Soldier* 80 [ref. to 1953]: You'd do ten years in Leavenworth, Paterson said. I'd rather take my chances with the goonie birds.
  4. Esp. *Mil.* a blockhead, esp. an untrained recruit.
  [**1953** Taradash *Eternity* (film): You march like a drunken gooney bird!] **1956** H. Ellison *Deadly Streets* 41: I've wanted to be your drag before this but that goony-bird you've been in the way. **1963** J. Ross *Dead Are Mine* 15 [ref. to 1944]: Is this little gooney bird implying that I should tell Blair to hit it too? If he is, he's taking a lot for granted. **1968** Safire *New Language of Politics* 149: *Gooney bird.* Week-end Air Force reservist flying around for practice. **1969** in Foley & Burnett *Best Stories 1970* 290: "What are you looking at, gooney bird?" said the CID man to Frazer. **1980** McDowell *Our Honor* 120 [ref. to Korean War]: Suppose he broke down, the way those other two gooney birds broke down and had to be sent to Simple City? **1994** *Newsweek* (Jan. 17) 45: First baseman Wally Joyner was hit by a knife thrown from the upper deck of Yankee Stadium. "There's quite a few gooney birds out there," Joyner says.

gooney-bird stare *n. USMC.* THOUSAND-YARD STARE.
  1962 Gallant *Valor's Side* 349 [ref. to 1942]: Guadalcanal developed…the Gooney Bird Stare. This symptom of mental breakdown was named on Guadalcanal….A Marine with the Gooney Bird Stare appeared…utterly exhausted, his eyes blank and without expression.

gooneyland *n. Mil.* territory occupied by Communist Chinese or North Korean forces. Now *hist.*

1953 in Russ *Last Parallel* 210: The words "goonie" and "goonyland" are used exclusively around here. I have never heard the words "Reds" or "Commies" used by anyone but Army men. *Ibid.* 217: We turned left and moved north, into the gradual slope that leads eventually into the vast rice paddy down there in goonyland, with its network of trenches. **1953–60** in *AS* XXXV (May 1960) 120 [ref. to Korean War]: The enemy were sometimes *goons* or *goonies*, and their territory, north of the parallel, was *goonyland*. **1964** Peacock *Drill & Die* 3: None of us here volunteered to go over to Goonyland to get a goddam red lantern.

goon gun *n. Army.* a 4.2-inch mortar.
1944 *Army & Navy Register* (Apr. 22). **1945** *Yank* (July 13) 12: One great blessing to GIs fighting on Okinawa was the "goon gun" or mortar. **1961** Kirk & Young *Great Weapons of WWII* 268: The medium U.S. 4.2-inch mortar made a tremendously effective showing in Italy and throughout the fighting which followed the landings in France in 1944. The weapon was known to its users as the "goon gun."

goonhead *n.* GOON, 1.a.
1982 in "J.B. Briggs" *Drive-In* 94: Here's the goonhead…tossing out coins to these kung-fu masters.

goonland *n.* (among POWs in Germany during WWII) Germany.
1955 Klaas *Maybe I'm Dead* 118 [ref. to 1944]: Even the kids in this God-damned goonland go around shooting people.

goon platoon *n. Army.* any small unit regarded as being composed primarily of dolts and misfits.
1978 Groom *Better Times* 228 [ref. to Vietnam War]: Thurlo had made Brill's outfit sort of a "goon platoon," filling it with misfits and malcontents who did not perform well elsewhere. **1980** Cragg *L. Militaris* 203: *Goon Platoon.* A platoon (or any unit) filled with awkward, misfit and malcontent soldiers who are all put in one place to control them better and keep them out of everybody else's way. **1982** "J. Cain" *Commandos* 21 [ref. to Vietnam War]: Membership in this new, "elite" goon platoon was voluntary.

goon shot *n. Softball.* a powerfully hit home run.
1980 Lorenz *Guys Like Us* 51: Launching goon shots into parking lots. *Ibid.* 79: A tremendous goon shot over the scoreboard and into…a vacant field.

goon squad *n.* a group of hired thugs; (*hence*) any group of muscular or aggressive individuals.
1937 *Nation* (Sept. 4) 239: The goon squad, as it is commonly called, consists of at least twenty picked thugs and ex-convicts. **1937** in Tamony *Americanisms* (No. 34) 5: On Thursday morning the Teamsters beef squad…proceeded to call the men all sorts of names and proceeded to rip the ILA buttons off the men. He was of course, accompanied by his goon squad. **1938** *AS* (Oct.) 178: *Goon* and *goon-squad*…were not used here [in Seattle] generally until a year ago. **1944** *Amer. N & Q* (Nov.) 117: *Goon Squad:* [Police] Squad formed for the purpose of making especially dangerous apprehensions. Also called "coffin squad." **1947** W.M. Camp *S.F.* 342: Dynamite, tear gas, bullets, brickbats, strikebreakers, "goon squads," the police, and the state militia. **1969** Ellis *Alcatraz* 18: The goon squad was made up of the biggest and meanest guards in the prison. **1979** Coleman Young, Mayor of Detroit, in Terkel *Amer. Dreams* 358: At that time [1937] Ford had a goon squad. **1990** *National Review* (Dec. 3) 24: When House Republicans rejected the pro-tax budget package, the Administration sent in the goon squad.

goony *adj.* being or resembling a GOON, 1.a.; stupid; silly; foolish.
1939 *Merrie Melodies* (animated cartoon): I'm so goony, loony tuney, tetched in the head. **1944** *Slanguage Dict.* 59: *Guy-goony*—a boy-crazy chick. **1961** Dillon *Judi* 18: I can't imagine anyone goony enough to ask you. **1970** in *Rolling Stone Interviews* 416: They *are* all goony. **1971** Giovanni *Gemini* 17: Three goony girls. **1971** Sorrentino *Up from Never* 13: The Ungraded Class…kept breaking into goony laughter. **1972** M. Rodgers *Freaky Fri.* 16: A big, gooney smile all over his dumb face.

goony bin *n.* a psychiatric hospital; LOONEY BIN.
1963 Boyle *Yanks Don't Cry* 225: This place looks like a damn goony bin!

goop¹ *n.* [coined in 1900 by Gelett Burgess to designate fantastic creatures that somewhat resembled mischievous children] a simpleton.
[**1900** G. Burgess *Goops & How to Be Them* (title).] **1915** in O'Brien *Best Stories of 1915* 89: You're getting as pale and skinny as a goop. **1925** Nason *Three Lights* 32: Now these poor goops that joined yesterday don't know what they're doin' here. **1929** J.T. Farrell *To Whom It May*

Concern 140: Billy was a goop, and he hated him. **1931** Stevenson *St. Lukes* 192 [ref. to ca1910]: Didn't you know that, you poor goop? **1932** Lorimer *Streetcars* 30: Listen, you goop. **1939** "E. Queen" *Dragon's Teeth* 103: Don't be a goop. a1954 J. Cheever, in Grassi & DeBlois *Comp. & Lit.* 299: All the American transcendentalists were goops. **1959** in A. Sexton *Letters* 68: I must have sounded like a goop to say I didn't know your work. **1963** in Asimov et al. *Sci. Fi. Short Shorts* 110: Newton's Three Laws…[are] all goops like you can understand. **1966** "Petronius" *N.Y. Unexp.* 46: Who needs to be reminded about the group goops that sign up or join anything? **1970** E. Thompson *Garden of Sand* 39: What do you think about a hare-brained goop like that? **1984** R. MacLeish, on *Morning Edition* (Nat. Pub. Radio) (Oct. 22): Mr. Mondale tried to prove that the President is too much of a goop to be allowed much responsibility.

goop² *n.* [prob. var. GOO, *n.*, with excrescent *p*] **1.** any thick, sticky, or unpleasant liquid or, usu., semiliquid substance; GOO, 1. Now *colloq.*
1918–19 in Carey *Mlle. from Armentières* I (unp.): Oh, Mademoiselle from Niedermendig/Gobbled the goop for fünfzehn pfennig. **1935** *AS* (Oct.) 235: *Goup*…is not only a name for the liquid (usually chocolate) that is poured over ice-cream at soda-water fountains, but it is a term current in beauty shops also. In the latter it is a sticky gelatinous fluid used to keep the hair moist while the operator works in a finger wave. **1941** G. Legman, in Henry *Sex Variants* II 1167: *Goop*…refers to the viscid semen. **1958** McCulloch *Woods Words* 71: *Goop*…Any dirty, sticky, smelly, messy stuff. **1959** "W. Williams" *Ada Dallas* 82: She called the hotel drugstore and they sent up a sprayer and some goop, but it didn't work. **1962** G. Olson *Roaring Road* 58: Injectors sucked in a lot of goop. **1971** *Playboy* (May) 227: There won't be as much goop in the air, either. **1973** Overgard *Hero* 169: You got a sunburn! Why don't you let me put somethin' on it? I got some great goop Carmen gave me. **1982** *Flash* (Dec.) 15: That blazin' heat-shield of his is turnin' our bullets to goop! **1987** Blankenship *Blood Stripe* 91: A large dab of prairie dog goop was stuck firmly to the bottom of one of her…boots. **1986–91** Hamper *Rivethead* 159: With a canister of goop aimed…at her…mass of tresses.
2. Orig. *Mil.* napalm or a similar incendiary substance; (*hence*) a plastic explosive.
1944 *Army & Navy Register* (Apr. 22). **1945** *Newsweek* (Mar. 19) 34: The 500-pound "goop" bomb is made of clusters of 6-pound bombs packed with jellied oil and magnesium. **1946** *AS* XXI: *Goop*…the mixture in an incendiary bomb…The name goop arose from its sticky character. **1946** *Britannica Bk. of Yr.* 832: *Goop Bomb.* The M-76 incendiary bomb. (1944). **1955** Reifer *New Words* 94: *Goop. n.* A greasy jelly, also called Pyrogel, which contains magnesium powder and is used as an incendiary agent. **1958** McCulloch *Woods Wds.* 71: *Goop*…Petroleum jelly used for starting slash fires. **1969** Pendleton *Death Squad* 31: How much goop did you use, Boom? **1972** Pendleton *Boston Blitz* 100: A pound and a half of "goop"—plastic explosives. a1981 in S. King *Bachman* 532: He wanted explosives…I sold him the goop.

goop *v.* **1.** [sugg. by *gobble the goop* s.v. GOBBLE, *v.*] to perform fellatio or cunnilingus.
1967 DeCoy *Nigger Bible* 80: In this strange bewilderment, she "gouped," guiding his Head clear back, to the bottom or pit of her throat. *Ibid.* 118: The two famous "Goupers": LIVER TONGUE LOUIS and BLUE TONSILS MOORE.
2. to cover or smear with goop.—also constr. with *up.*
1965–70 in *DARE.* **1976** J.W. Thomas *Heavy Number* 39: It was merely gooped up with dirt. **1985** Frede *Nurses* 145: Goop the paddles.

goopus *n.* (see quot.). Cf. GOOFUS.
1966 IUFA *Folk Speech: Goopus*—A drip or dope. (Nevada.)

goopy *adj.* like or suggesting a GOOP¹; (*esp.*) silly.
1955–57 Felder *Collegiate Slang* 2: *Goopy*—anything overdone, such as a too elaborate dress. **1962** in Rosset *Evergreen Reader* 459: Goopy creepy families with elephant guns so that nobody [can] take refuge with them. **1965** Karp *Doobie Doo* 159: Imbedded in the goopy mind of man…is the bitter inclination. a1990 E. Currie *Dope & Trouble* 220: French, ballet, all that goopy stuff.

goose *n.* **1.** [sugg. by *cook (someone's) goose* s.v. COOK, *v.*] (one's) well-being, life, reputation, etc., (when threatened).
1887 Andrews *Mountebanks* 5: Ronald Davenport once in his father's house, and my goose is dished. **1957** J. Jones *Some Came Running* 64: She had discreetly saved his goose with his wife when that lady called the store for him and he was gone.
2. [perh. sugg. by *goose* 'a tailor's smoothing iron with a*

curved handle', in allusion to the many Jews who were tailors before the mid-twentieth century] a Jew.—used contemptuously.

1898 in Thompson *Youth's Companion* 364: You know how it is when "the geese"—the East Side Jews—get a scare trun into 'em! **1904** *Life in Sing Sing* 248: Goose. A Hebrew. *Ibid.* 259: *Rousting a goose for his poke.* Jostling a Hebrew so that the pickpocket may steal his purse. **1905** *Nat. Police Gaz.* (Dec. 16) 3: Well, she'll get hers all right if she sticks to that fresh goose. **1924** Wilstach *Stage Slang* 26: A Hebrew impersonater [*sic*] is a "goose" or a "Yid." **1935** *AS* (Feb.) 16 [ref. to *a*1910]. *ca*1938 in D. Runyon *More Guys* 195: This is most disrespectful, like calling Jewish people mockies, or Heebs, or geese. **1940** O'Hara *Pal Joey* 149: I also like them zoftick as some goose in the band says.

3. the neck.

1902 T.A. Dorgan, in *S.F. Bulletin Mag.* (Apr. 19) 12: Even the gripman has his "goose" out for the news in your paper.

4. a sudden prod in or between the buttocks, as with the thumb. Cf. GOOSE, *v.*, 1.a.

1938 (quot. at GOOSE, *v.*, 2.a.). **1941** in Legman *Limerick* 106: There was a young lady named Spruce/Whose favorite thrill was a goose/Just the sight of a thumb/Made her tokus all numb,/And her bowels got excited—and loose. **1943** in *Best from Yank* 36: He'll give you no more than a chuck in the ribs or an American "goose" he's learned to administer. **1958** Elgart *Over Sexteen 6* 44: Let us mention the fowl tale of the butcher who opened a new establishment and rewarded his first twenty women customers with a free goose. **1964** J. Thompson *Pop. 1280* 71: I gave the horse a goose and made him jump. **1967** Mailer *Vietnam* 190: Like a businessman copping a goose on a bare-ass nightclub waitress, yum! **1977** S. Gaines *Discotheque* 187: I don't...think ass pinches are endearing gestures...Not even tweaks or gooses.

5. an incitement to action, esp. the act of sharply accelerating a motor vehicle; a prodding.

1938–43 Stegner *Rock Candy Mtn.* 328: He shifted into second and gave it a good goose before shifting back. **1959** in A. Sexton *Letters* 69: They need more *goose* left in to take away my breath. **1983** *Rolling Stone* (Feb. 3) 34: Spurred on by inflation and given an added goose by generous labor settlements. **1983** Flaherty *Tin Wife* 324: The Mayor's polls remained stagnant. They could use a goose. **1985** Frede *Nurses* 79: I'll give X-ray a little goose on your behalf, okay?

¶ In phrases:

¶ **cook (someone's) goose** see s.v. COOK, *v.*

¶ **gobble the goose** see s.v. GOBBLE.

¶ **loose as a goose** extremely loose (in any sense).

1930 Botkin *Folk-Say* 106: There, she's loose as a goose. *ca*1944 in Kaplan & Smith *One Last Look* 119: [The women] are loose as a goose...and outspoken about what they will give you for gum or candy. **1952** Randolph & Wilson *Down in the Holler* 178: *Loose as a goose* refers to diarrhea. **1953** Manchester *City of Anger* 383: "You loose?"..."As a goose." **1957** Myrer *Big War* 322: I'm a sort of citizen of the world, you know? Loose as a goose. **1961** Brosnan *Pennant Race* 236: Hutch isn't exactly loose as a goose...It's tougher on the manager in some ways than it is on the players. **1966** "T. Pendleton" *Iron Orchard* 111: That old Pluto water is still giving me a fit, Ort...I been loose as a goose all week. **1970** Wakefield *Going All the Way* 50: Loose as a goddam goose, nothing to tie you down. **1992** *Good Morning, America* (ABC-TV) (Oct. 12): I liked his style last night. He was loose as a goose.

¶ **milk a goose** to engage in idle or pointless activity; loaf.

1935 J. Conroy *World to Win* 218: What 're you doin' here then? Milkin' a goose?

¶ **skin the goose** (of a man or boy) to masturbate.

1973 *Zap Comix* (No. 6) (unp.): Skin my *goose!*

¶ **sound** [or **right**] **on the goose, 1.** (among proponents of slavery in Kansas) strongly supporting the issue of slavery; (*hence*) sound in one's adherence to any specific orthodox belief.

1862 M.V. Victor *Unionist's Dtr.* 40: What do you suppose brought him 'way down to Nashville to volunteer, if he wasn't sound on the goose? **1871** Schele de Vere *Americanisms* 267: Now, *sound on the goose* means simply to be stanch on the party question, whatever that may be for the moment. **1872** *Galaxy* (Mar.) 430: Our theologians are sound on the goose. **1889** Cox *Frontier Humor* 332: He was sound on the goose, he was. **1893** Hampton *Maj. in Washington* 138: He's sound on the Southern goose and know's where he's "at."

2. thoroughly satisfactory or dependable.

1863 in H. Nathan *D. Emmett* 398: 'Tis all "OK," I say and right upon

the goose. *ca*1890 Averell *10 Yrs.* 254 [ref. to 1861]: "If anybody happens to ask you what my business is, you can tell him you don't know." The driver...gave a knowing wink and said emphatically, "All right here on the goose."

¶ **work the goose** to fetch beer from a tavern in a pail.

1895 Townsend *Fadden* 141: I knowed I'd find a Avenue A gang what would rather scrap dan work de goose—rush de growler, I mean.

goose *v.* **1.** [cf. Eng. rhyming slang *goose-and-duck* 'an act of copulation' in *F & H* III 182 (*a*1893), and GOOSING SLUM, *n.*]

a. to copulate with.

***1879** Pearl* 257: I don't like to see vulgar girls in the town/Pull their clothes up and stand to be goosed for a crown. ***a**1890–93 F & H* III 182: *Goose...Verb...*To possess a woman. *a*1896 in *Immortalia* 8: Lil was the best our camp perduced;/And of all the gents what Lillian goosed,/None had no such goosin', nor never will,/Since the Lord raked in poor Lady Lil. **1969** Jessup *Sailor* 203: The old man who owns the place is crippled or something. Kolb gooses his wife once in a while.

b. to copulate with anally. Also intrans.

***1881** in Ackerley *Father & Myself* 200: It's the commonest thing possible in the army. As soon as (or before) I had learned the goose-step, I had learned to be goosed. **1943** Doshay *Boy Sex Offender* 75: Sodomy...Vulgarisms frequently applied to the practice are "buggery" and "goosing." **1965** Trimble *Sex Words* 92: *Goose...*vt. To perform genital-anal intercourse. **1973** *Oui* (Feb.) 32: The Godfather gets goosed...*Last Tango in Paris...*still, if you like...allusive goosing, Bertolucci's your boy...When Brando growls for anal sex, the earthy colors and music flush a bloody red.

2.a. to startle by poking or (*rarely*) pointing; (*specif.*) to poke (someone) in or between the buttocks so as to startle, tease, or harass (see also first 1943 quot.); (*broadly*) to prod from behind. Cf. GOOSE, *n.*, 4.

1906 *DN* III 138: *Goose...*to create nervous excitement in a person by pointing a finger at him or by touching or tickling him and making a peculiar whistle. **1908** *DN* III 316: *Goose, v.tr.* To punch or motion to punch (a person) with the finger, making at the same time a short smack or hiss. Some persons are said to be *goosey*, and they jump spasmodically when *goosed*. **1926** W. James *Smoky* 96: How quick he could leave the earth if anything "goosed" him. **1928** Hecht & MacArthur *Front Page* 450: Them alienists make me sick. All they do is goose you and send you a bill for five hundred bucks. **1930** Franklyn *Kts. of Cockpit* 65: Somebody goosed somebody else and they let go to bust out laughin'! **1932** L. Berg *Prison Doctor* 69: Don't you dare "goose" me, you nasty thing. **1938** "Justinian" *Amer. Sexualis* 24: *Goose.* v. To prod or jerk one's thumb into another's buttocks in an unexpected and vulgar manner. n. The act described above. U.S., 1925– , low coll. **1942** McAtee *Supp. to Grant Co.* 5 [ref. to 1890's]: *Goose, v...*means specifically to poke in the anus, an action usually accompanied by a lip-sucking sound. [**1943** in Mencken *New Ltrs.* 529: Fishbein suggests that the verb may come from an old custom of testing a goose by feeling of the fat in the anal region.] **1943** M. Shulman *Barefoot Boy* 99: A playful lab assistant goosed her. **1956** Neider *Hendry Jones* 113: This old coot sneaked up and goosed the Kid's girl again. **1966** Manus *Mott the Hoople* 144: Ever been goosed from behind by another car while doing sixty mph? **1967** G. Green *To Brooklyn* 14: Sometimes a real tough guy like Zetz would sneak behind Jimmy and goose him. **1971** LeGuin *Lathe of Heaven* 42: Orr stood upright as if he had been goosed. **1975** C.W. Smith *Country Music* 162: He sent his hand down to goose the inside of her thigh. **1985** Sawislak *Dwarf* 190: Real woodsy fella. Folks say he can sneak up and goose a bear. **1993** *New Yorker* (Feb. 8) 102: A curvy brunette bends over to pick up a phone, and a giant ant gooses her.

b. (in coarsely joc. similes).

1961 Coon *Meanwhile at Front* 50 [ref. to Korean War]: I saw those two miserable bastards leap into the ditch like goosed gazelles. **1969** Stern *Brood of Eagles* 185: Johnny Marrel has it better: it was like trying to goose a ghost—all you get is a handful of sheet. **1970** Thackrey *Thief* 65: I slammed my foot down on the accelerator, and that car took off like a goosed deer. **1972** *Moneysworth* (May 29) 1: Even without the backing of the renowned Linus Pauling, guru of the Vitamin C craze...Vitamin E has taken off like a goosed gazelle. **1979** Hurling *Boomers* 70: Runs like a goosed rabbit. **1986** Zeybel *First Ace* 40: Dobbs went up like a goosed kangaroo for a tip-in.

c. (see 1973 quot.).

1960 N.Y.C. junior high school students: "Watch out for Eliot in the lockers. He likes to goose people." "What do you mean?" "He'll grab your balls from behind. He thinks it's funny." **1973** *Penthouse* (March) 24: *Goose, to:* Slang term for...the grasping of another person's genitalia from behind.

3.a. to prod into action; spur; goad; provoke.—also constr. with *up*.

1934 L. Berg *Prison Nurse* 42: That makes me one up on you! I "goosed" him first that time! **1941** H.A. Smith *Low Man* 45: I like to goose the people a little and see how they'll react. **1947** Schulberg *Harder They Fall* 161: That gives you plenty of time to goose the people, doesn't it, lover? **1948** Lay & Bartlett *Twelve O'Clock High!* 111: "We send guys home on the next boat for goosing our British Allies." Pamela's eyes opened wide. "What an extraordinary expression!" she exclaimed. "You know," explained Savage. "It means *needling*." "Try me again," she said. "Ribbing." "One more chance?" "Riding." "It's no use." **1948** Wolfert *Act of Love* 465: Keep moving, and I'll goose Neale up to make contact with you later. **1948** Guthrie *Born to Win* 135: And I'll josh and joke and tease them/And I'll rib and razz and goose them. **1955** Klaas *Maybe I'm Dead* 261: They'll goose us out of here with guns. **1956** Gold *Not with It* 290: I was pounding on the cabbie's window and he was saying how he didn't care about the tip, I had better just quit goosing him or he'd throw me out right where he was. **1957** Ellison *Web of the City* 39: It was goosing him more and stronger every second. **1959** E. Hunter *Matter of Conviction* 178: I guess your beating finally goosed the police into action. **1961** Gover *$100 Misunderstanding* 157: You just goose that old Imp's accelerator. **1983** L. Barrett *Gambling with History* 458: Reagan asked Meese what was taking so long. "Don't we have to goose them a bit?" the President asked. **1993** *Newsweek* (Oct. 25) 76: Vedder doesn't possess a bottomless bag of vocal tricks, but [the] guitarists goose him along.

b. to feed fuel to (an engine or vehicle) in brief, irregular spurts; to cause to accelerate in this manner.—also constr. with *up*.—occ. absol.

1940 Hartney *Up & At 'Em* 257 [ref. to 1918]: A lone Spad came in with the pilot goosing his engine and causing a terrific racket. **1942** *AS* (Apr.) 103: *Goose It*. To feed gas in irregular spurts. **1955** T. Anderson *Beloved Sons* 43: Outside sounded the gasket-tearing whine of a jeep being started and goosed. **1958** Whitcomb *Corregidor* 80: Goose that thing up a little down there, bombers coming in from toward Manila! **1966** Gallery *Start Engines* 84: Curly goosed his jets. **1969** Thompson *They Shoot Horses* 146: How about goosin' it a little? **1971** Tak *Truck Talk* 75: *Goose it*: to choke the engine, to feed it a richer fuel-to-air mixture. **1973** Lucas et al. *Amer. Graffiti* 160: Falfa…gooses the Chevy. **1974** Millard *Thunderbolt* 19: The…salesman handed me the key, told me to goose it up good. **1980** L.N. Smith *Venus Belt* 12: I reprogrammed the Neova and goosed up to a safe and proper hundred and ten. **1986–91** Hamper *Rivethead* 22: I got back in the car and goosed it.

c. to increase; raise.—also constr. with *up*.

1949 G.S. Coffin *Winning Poker* 179: Goose—To raise [a bet]. **1952** Landon *Angle of Attack* 25: Were they really goosing the odds, jacking up the vigerage, cutting an extra round for the house? **1975** *Business Week* (Oct. 20) 91: Congress decides to goose up the housing industry. **1977** *Baa Baa Black Sheep* (NBC-TV): Nobody changes wingmen to goose up his victory tally. **1992** *CBS This Morning* (CBS-TV) (Apr. 23): The salaries go up and up as bosses goose up their own pay.

d. to enliven.—also constr. with *up*.

1970 Terkel *Hard Times* 188: I thought, to goose up the magazine, I would take photographs of people at my own home. **1978** G. Trudeau *Doonesbury* (synd. cartoon strip) (July 20): "What are you putting in the Gatorade, sir?" "I'm just goosing the juice with a few steroids."

gooseberry *n.* **1.** a chaperon. *Obs.* in U.S.

*1837 in *OED: Gubbs*, a go-between or gooseberry. ***1870** in *OED:* Gooseberry I may be…but, at all events, I won't be instrumental in making myself so. ***1881, *1889** in *OED*. **1901** *DN* II 141: *Gooseberry*, n. A person *de trop*; the third person who makes a "crowd." **1914** Atherton *Perch* 187: "Don't leave me for a moment." "I won't, although, believe me, the rôle of gooseberry is no cinch." ***1952** Frank O'Connor, in *New Yorker* (Sept. 13) 44: She coaxed Kitty to come with her. "Ah, I'm too old a hand to play gooseberry," said Kitty.

2. (among tramps and thieves) a piece of laundry hung out to dry that may be easily stolen; (*also*) a clothesline with laundry; in phr. **gooseberry lay** [or **trick**] the stealing of laundry that has been left out to dry.

1848 *Ladies' Repository* (Oct.) 315: *Gooseberry Lay*, To steal clothes hung out to dry. **1859** Matsell *Vocab.* 38: *Gooseberry-Lay*. Stealing wet clothes from clothes-lines or bushes. **1904** *Life in Sing Sing* (gloss.): *Gooseberry*.—A line of clothes. **1914** Jackson & Hellyer *Crim. Slang* 38: *Gooseberry*, Noun. Current amongst yeggs, hobos and meanders. A clothesline; laundry hung up to dry. Example: "He prowled the gooseberry for a skin." **1926** *AS* I (Dec.) 651: *Gooseberry*. A clothesline. **1929**

Hammett *Maltese Falcon* 107: How long have you been off the gooseberry lay, son? **1930** "D. Stiff" *Milk & Honey* 206: Gooseberries are the garments that adorn the line in the moonlight. **1933** Ersine *Pris. Slang* 40: The boys are out picking gooseberries. **1937** *Lit. Digest* (Apr. 10) 12: *Sniping a clothes-line*. Stealing off a clothes-line. **1950** J. Lardner, in *N.Y. Herald Tribune Bk. Review* (Dec. 24) 6: I always liked a phrase given me by a retired New York detective of the 1890's, "the gooseberry trick," for stealing washing off a clothesline.

3. a bullet.

1849 Melville *White Jacket* 302 [ref. to 1843]: Among their shrouds…our marines sent their leaden peas and gooseberries, like a shower of hailstones in Labrador.

4. a fool.

*a1890–93 F & H III 182: *Gooseberry*…(common)…A fool. **1918** *N.Y. Eve. Jour.* (Aug. 8) 18: Is that so?…you poor gooseberry. **1942** *ATS* 390: Silly person…*gooseberry*.

5. a bit of excrement clinging about the anus; DINGLEBERRY.

1944 in Legman *Limerick* 227: Pants pigeons flew/Where her gooseberries grew.

gooseberry *v.* (among tramps and thieves) to steal clothes that have been left out to dry. Also trans. Now *hist.*

1925 (cited in Partridge *Dict. Und.* 300). **1927** *AS* (June) 389: A *gooseberry* is a loaded clothesline; to rob one is to go *gooseberrying*. **1929** *AS* IV (June) 340: *Gooseberrying*. Stealing clothes off the line. **1936** Mencken *Amer. Language* (ed. 4) 582: To steal washing off the line is to *gooseberry* it. **1960** *Tenn. Folk. Soc. Bull.* XXVI 117: To steal washing off a line was to *gooseberry* it.

gooseberry bush *n.* (among tramps and thieves) a clothesline from which items of clothing may be purloined.

*ca***1894** in *Independent* (Jan. 2, 1902) 28: They get their underwear and shirts off from somebody's cloths line—the H.B.'s call it "picking a gooseberry bush." **1927** *DN* V 448: *Gooseberry bush*, n. A clothesline. Also *grapevine*. **1930** "D. Stiff" *Milk & Honey* 206: *Gooseberry bush*— The clothes line. **1943** in *AS* XIX (1944) 103: A clothesline ripe for the taking is a *gooseberry bush*.

gooseberry-eyed *adj.* bleary-eyed from drink.

1821 Waln *Hermit in Phila.* 28: A little *goose-berry eyed or so*.

gooseberry pudding *n.* [pun on GOOSE and PUDDING] (see quots.).

*1857 "Ducange" *Vulgar Tongue* 9: *Gooseberry-pudding*, n. Woman. *Th*[ieves' slang]. **1930** Irwin *Tramp & Und. Sl.* 88: *Gooseberry Pudding*.—A wanton, especially one not too clean or neat in appearance or dress.

gooseberry ranch *n.* [sugg. by GOOSING RANCH] a brothel.

1930 Irwin *Tramp & Und. Sl.* 88: *Gooseberry Ranch*.—A brothel.…the origin [probably] lies in the verb "to goose," meaning to tickle. **1971** Altman & McKay *McCabe & Mrs. Miller* (film): You think I'm gonna let some goddam chippy come up here and tell me how to run a gooseberry ranch?

goosebrain *n.* GOOSEHEAD, *n.*

1908 (quot. at BIRDBRAIN, *n.*).

goose-bumper *n.* *Film Journ.* a horror or suspense movie.

1987 *TV Guide* (Oct. 24) 22: *Poltergeist II*…the dead take no pity on the living in this goose-bumper.

Goose City *n.* *Mil.* Tegucigalpa, Honduras.

1986 G. Trudeau *Doonesbury* (synd. comic strip) (Nov. 20): Gotta head back to Goose City to grease Contra Command and assorted locals.

goosed *adj.* intoxicated.

1979 Gram *Foxes* 15: "She came in goosed."…"From what?" "Quaaludes, beer, wine, some other thing, too." **1986** Univ. Tenn. student theme: Goosed, ripped or plastered [syns. for *drunk*]. **1986–91** Hamper *Rivethead* 133: The steering gear man showed up absolutely goosed to the gills.

goose-drownder *n.* *So. Midlands.* a heavy and prolonged rainstorm. Also **goose-drowner.**

1929 *AS* V (Oct.) 18: *Goose-drowner*: A very heavy rain, a cloudburst. **1933** *AS* (Feb.) 49: *Goose-drowner*, n. A very heavy rain, a cloudburst. Lesser showers are called *fence-lifters* or *gully-washers*. **1938** in *AS* (Apr. 1939) 90: *Goose Drownder*. A terrific rainstorm. **1950** *PADS* (No. 14) 32. **1954** in *DARE*: "Goose drownder"…an unusually heavy rain. **1965–70** in *DARE*. **1983** in *DARE*: *Goose drownder*…a rain heavier than a *gulley washer*.

goose egg *n.* **1.a.** Esp. *Baseball.* the numeral zero, as in a score.

1866 in *DA*: At this stage of the game our opponents had fourteen runs—we had five large "goose eggs" as our share. **1867** in Dickson *Baseball Dict.* 183: The Buckeyes in this inning were treated to a goose egg. **1874** *Chi. Inter-Ocean* (July 1) (cited in Nichols *Baseball Term.*). **1891** Maitland *Slang Dict.* 128: *Goose-egg* (Am.), when a man scores a nought or "round O" at any game he makes a "goose-egg." **1900** *DN* II 38: *Goose-egg*, n. 1. Cipher, as in score of foot-ball, or base-ball. 2. Zero, as in marks or other connection. **1902** Fulbright *Baylor U. Round-Up* 145: The goose-eggs that patient Profs. on the Record-books inscribe. **1904** in "O. Henry" *Works* 40: 'Tis one of them Yale lads celebratin' the goose egg they give to the Hartford College. **1914** Patten *Lefty o' the Bush* 105: Shut 'em out without a tally, gave 'em nine beautiful goose eggs. **1934** *Journalism Qly.* (Dec.) 352: Goose Egg, n. (general)—a "0" score. **1951** in Clarke *Amer. Negro Stories* 187: Score one goose egg for Jane. **1976** Conroy *Santini* 135: One to goose egg, sportsfans. **1976** Woodley *Bears* 131: Amanda threw nothing but goose-eggs. **1978** in Lyle & Golenbock *Bronx Zoo* 244: We had all those goose eggs up there on the scoreboard. **1984** *Good Morning America* (ABC-TV) (June 26): I just put some young pitchers out there and they keep throwing those goose eggs.

b. nothing; *(hence)* that which is completely unproductive. **1935** Maltz *Black Pit* 34: I pretty near get a goose egg at the end of the month. **1939** Appel *Power-House* 198: Ajax Restaurant came through with three hundred…But one goose egg from *B+Z*. **1963–64** Kesey *Great Notion* 347: Then at least the trip wouldn't been a *complete* goose-egg. **1978** Diehl *Sharky's Machine* 259: What do I get out of it? Sore feet and a fuckin' goose egg, that's what. **1988** *Miami Vice* (NBC-TV): "Anything, anything—you got anything?" "Goose egg."

2. a large lump raised by a blow, esp. on the head. **1953** in *DARE*: That goose egg on your head.…Ye're not the first boy that ol' pony has throwed. **1961** N.Y.C. woman, age 73: He wound up with a big goose egg on his head. **1966** *RHD*. **1985** in Safire *Look It Up* 163: A lump that comes up on your head when you get a sharp blow or knock…*goose egg*.

goose-egg *v.* Esp. *Baseball.* to keep scoreless in a game; to give a score of zero to.
1895 C.C. King *Trooper Ross* 124: You are "goose-egged" by the Kid Nine. **1910** *N.Y. Eve. Jour.* (Mar. 15) 12: The sod-busting volunteers goose-egged the stars by 3 to 0. **1952** Malamud *Natural* 118: Fowler goose-egged the Cubs in the last of the ninth. **1952** Sandburg *Strangers* 185 [ref. to *ca*1895]: Galesburg had picked the best nine in the town to meet them and the word was that maybe Galesburg would "goose-egg" them. **1967** Decker *To Be a Man* 127: We goose-egged you because you were coasting with your left foot when you brought…[the bucking horse] out.

goosefoot *n.* a detective; FLATFOOT.
1915 Bronson-Howard *God's Man* 129: So, with a lot of heavy-headed goose-feet on my trail, I'm gonna lay low.

goose grease *n. West.* smooth or flattering talk.
1931 in E.M. Rhodes *Best Novels* 239: What was all that goose grease Elmer was giving us?

goosehead *n.* a dolt.
1885 *Puck* (Jul. 1) 275: If you should say Nantucket,/You're told you are a goose-head. **1902** Hobart *Back to Woods* 94: Th' ould goosehead.

gooser *n.* **1.** [alludes to GOOSE, *v.*, 1] the penis.
***a*1890–93** *F & H* III 184: Gooser…The penis. **1971** *Nude, Blued & Tattooed* 70: The size of your gooser/Is slightly obtuse, sir.
2. an automobile ignition.
1928 Carr *Rampant Age* 65: With hands that trembled he worked the "gooser."

goose's jacket *n.* an application of tar and feathers. *Joc.*
1838 [Haliburton] *Clockmaker* (Ser. 2) 109: Many a man has had a goose's jacket lined with tar here…and a tight fit it is too.

goose tracks *n.pl.* awkward handwriting.
1871 Wood *Scrap Book* 255: My "goose-tracks" did the cadets grieve, I'm Chaplain in the Army. **1894** C.C. King *Cadet Days* 225: Benny's performances the first few weeks won high marks, while Geordie's "goose-tracks" were rewarded with nothing above 2. **1954** in *DARE*: Goose tracks…illegible handwriting. **1968** in *DARE*: Handwriting that's hard to read…Goose tracks.

goosey *adj.* jumpy, nervously excitable, esp. due to the threat of a GOOSE, *n.*, 4.
1906 *DN* III 138: Goosy…used of a person who is susceptible to nervous excitement when a finger is pointed at him, or when he is hardly touched or tickled. **1908** *DN* III 316: Goosey, adj. Extremely nervous or ticklish. **1928** C. McKay *Banjo* 88: Bugsy made a sharp noise with his mouth and snapped his fingers, and the flute boy started apprehensively. "Hi, but you sure is goosey," laughed Banjo. **1933** *AS* (Feb.) 31: Goosey. Nervous; touchy. **1933** J.V. Allen *Cowboy Lore* 60: Goosy, Very nervous touchy man. **1938** in *AS* (Apr. 1939) 90: The boy is goosey. **1942** McAtee *Supp. to Grant Co.* 5 [ref. to 1890's]: Goosey, adj. susceptible to goosing. **1959** Bechet *Treat It Gentle* 85: And he was goosey; if you just pointed your fingers at him goose pimples would jump out on him and run wild. **1980** *N.Y. Daily News* (Sept. 5) 22: A recent issue of the Journal of the American Medical Association carries an article, "Are the Jumping Frenchmen of Maine Goosey?"

goosing ranch *n. Und.* GOOSING SLUM.
1927 *DN* V 448: Goosing ranch, n. A brothel. **1930** Irwin *Tramp & Und. Slang* 88: A brothel…Goosing Ranch.

goosing slum *n.* [cf. GOOSE, *v.*, 1] *Und.* a brothel. Now *hist.*
1859 Matsell *Vocab.* 38: Goosing Slum. A brothel. ***1865** in *Comments on Ety.* XVII (No. 1) 4: "Brick-topped Slavey Shake," lately "grafting" in George Green's "goosing-slum"…for her "chuck." **1866** *Nat. Police Gaz.* (Nov. 3) 2: The "cops" know her as a "stall lifter," "bludget," and "goosing slum" keeper, which is quite an extensive *repertoire* to choose from. **1877** in Asbury *Gem of Prairie* 133: The Sutherlands (Jet and Ida)…keep a "goosing-slum" on North Clark Street. **1955** Kantor *Andersonville* 223: Doubtless a whore from a goosing slum on Water Street.

go out *v.* [cf. colloq. sense 'to lose consciousness'; cf. G *ausgehen* '(of plants) to die', lit. 'to go out'] to die.
***1888** in R. Kipling *Under the Deodars* 107: I thought the man had gone out long ago—only—only I didn't care to take my hand away. *Ibid.* 108: "Not going out this journey," whispered Bobby Wick gallantly. "Bravo!" said the Surgeon-Major. "That's the way to look at it, Bobby." **1938** J. Swerling *I Am the Law* (film): He had to go out some way—we both knew that. **1956** Neider *Hendry Jones* 79: They're aiming to hang you…and not to let you go out with a hot bullet. **1971** Capon *3d Peacock* 35: Too many scoundrels died in their beds and too many saints went out in agony ever to permit such a notion to be advanced realistically. **1977** Caron *Go-Boy* 116: The government had him hanged not long afterwards. We read in the paper where he went out like a real champ. **1980** M. Baker *Nam* 245: This guy is really *fucked up*. I think he's going out. **1980** McAleer & Dickson *Unit Pride* 31: If I'm gonna die, I'd rather go out fighting. **1982** Gino *Nurse's Story* 15: There are only two of us on [duty], and a cystic kid went out. **1988** Lambert *Liberace* (film): I want to go out while I'm still on top.

go over *v.* **1.** *Und.* to be sent to prison.
1872 Burnham *Secret Service* vi: Gone Over, sent to the Penitentiary, or other prison. **1929** Barr *Let Tomorrow Come* 153: 'E was goin' over anyway, so why shouldn' 'e cop?
2. Orig. *Theat.* to be successful with an audience; be received. Now *S.E.* Cf. GET OVER, 2.
1910 *Variety* (Aug. 20) 13: It went over immense. **1915** *Variety* (June 4) 4: Sketch Gets Over.…"The Call" went over big this weekend. **1923** Witwer *Fighting Blood* 281: These synthetic actors…are going over big with their parents. **1934** Weseen *Dict. Slang* 142: Go over big—To make a decided success.

goozle *n.* [var. GUZZLE] the throat; *(also)* the Adam's apple. Also **goozle pipe**.
1883 J.C. Harris, in *DARE*: Some'rs down in de neighborhoods er de goozle. **1902** *DN* II 235: Goozle…the larynx. **1917** in Johnston *Prison Life* 316: Just shove it down your "goozle." **1940** in Pyle *Ernie's Amer.* 310: I got him by the goozle. **1954** in *DARE*: I heard tell o' windpipe. We allus call it goozle. **1969** Beck *Mama Black Widow* 219: Fo Ah stick mah shank en you goozul pipe. **1980** Garrison *Snakedoctor* 12: Got hit in the goozle with a baseball bat…He'd talked with a squeak ever since. **1984** Wilder *You All* 55: Adam's apple: goozle.

goozler *n.* GOOZLE.
*ca*1969 *Gunsmoke* (CBS-TV): You ever see that blamed thingamajig old Doc jams down your goozler?

goozlum *n.* [orig. unkn.] gravy or syrup; any unidentified fluid.
1911 *DN* III 544: Goozlum, googlum, n. Used of syrup, molasses, etc. at table. "Pass the goozlum for these flapjacks." **1918** McNutt *Yanks Are Coming* 165: Dobbin gets his little squirt of goozelum to protect him against glanders. **1925** *AS* I (Dec.) 135: Gravy is "goozlum" or "sop." **1950** in *DARE*: Goozlum: a thin custard sauce for puddings or fluffs.

gopher *n.* **1.** [alluding to the *gopher* tortoise] **a.** an Arkansan.
1845 in *DA*: The inhabitants of…Arkansas [are called] Gophers.

b. a Floridian.

1869 *Overland Mo.* (Aug.) 129: A Floridian is called a "Gopher."

c. a Minnesotan.

1871 in *Harper's Mag.* (Jan. 1872) 317: Nicknames given to the States and people of this republic…Minnesota, Gophers. **1873** Beadle *Undevel. West* 706: In May, 1859, I first became a "Gopher,"—practical Western title of the Minnesotians. **1962** Killens *Heard the Thunder* 411: He was mild-faced and bow-legged and blue-eyed and medium-sized and corn-fed and Midwestern Yankee. A Minnesota gopher maybe. **1976** Berry *Kaiser* 375: These Gophers loved having a Kansas man come in as one of their officers—just like poison they did. **1981** Ehrlichman *Witness* 28: Mr. and Mrs. Ed Gopher of St. Paul.

2. a kind of plow.

1854 *Spirit of Times* (Nov. 4) 447: Dad and me goes to the field, I…a-totin' the gopher plow…I hitched him onto the gopher, and away we went. **1868** in *DAE:* Then there is the "scraper," the "half-shovel," "shovel," "gopher," and other peculiar forms of implements. **1894** in *DAE:* The gopher is an iron plow. **1954** in *DARE: Gopher*….A primitive plow.

3. a louse.

1864 in Northrop *Chronicles* 106: Lice…crawl in droves over the sick, herd in his ears, gnaw him, shade in his hair…Talk about "gophers" in the army, no name for this! They sap the life of the strongest.

4. *Army.* a person who builds or takes refuge in a dugout or GOPHER HOLE, 1; *(joc.)* an infantryman.

1866 Shanks *Per. Recol.* 47: [During the March to the Sea] the soldiers called each other "gophers" and "beavers," and "gopher holes" were more common in the armies' track than were campfires.

5. an offensive, uncouth, or stupid person; *(also)* a SUCKER.

1865 Williams *Joaquin* 85: Give in, you dod-rotted gopher! The woman's sold you! **1884** *Life* (Jan. 24) 51: Go yourself, you old gopher. *ca*1940 in Mencken *Amer. Lang. Supp. II* 733: [Barbers' slang:] *Gopher.* A man who has not had a haircut in a long time. **1943** Snell & Marks *In Brooklyn* (film): Save your breath you—you—gopher! **1963** Gann *Good & Evil* 105: There was a high school from which every student emerged lighting a cigarette…To be seen carrying a book was regarded as being a gopher and therefore inviting a beating. **1967** Maurer & Vogel *Narc. & Narc. Add.* (ed. 3) 360: *Gopher.* One who accepts unpleasant circumstances apathetically. "Yes, I'd call a gopher a 'lame'…[or] a 'chump.' **1969** B. Beckham *Main Mother* 46: A gopher—a man who would always go for [believe] anything. **1971–72** in Abernethy *Bounty of Texas* 205: *Gopher*…one lacking in intelligence.

6. *Und.* a bank vault; *(also)* a safe or strongbox.

1871 Banka *Prison Life* 492: Safe…*Gofer.* **1882** Pinkerton *Bank-Robbers* 91: "The gopher was cracked"* again last night…*The bank was robbed. **1904** *Life in Sing Sing* 248: *Gopher.* A safe. **1914** Jackson & Hellyer *Vocab.* 38: *Gopher*, Noun. Current amongst yeggs chiefly. A safe; a strong box. **1926** in *AS* LVII (1982) 262: *Gopher.* Small safe. **1931** in D.W. Maurer *Lang. Und.* 48: He punched the gopher open.

7. *Und.* GOPHER MAN.

1891 Maitland *Slang Dict.* 128: *Gopher* (Am.), in police language, a young sneak-thief or associate of burglars, who is passed into a room through a transom or window. **1903** A.H. Lewis *Boss* ch. xii: Darby the Gopher. **1928** Sharpe *Chi.* May 287: *Gopher*—one who tunnels to steal. **1928–30** Fiaschetti *Gotta Be Rough* 67: She was hooked up with a mob that did strong-arm work…and her boy friend was a gopher.

8. [see 1927 quot.] *N.Y.C.* a member of a notorious West Side street gang of the 1890's and after; *(broadly)* a thug. Now *hist.*

1927 Asbury *Gangs of N.Y.* 253: The Gophers were lords of Hell's Kitchen [in the 1890's], their domain running from Seventh to Eleventh avenues and from Fourteenth street to Forty-second street. They were fond of hiding in basements and cellars, hence their name. **1930** Lavine *3d Degree* 103: The youths were tough West Side "gophers" who wouldn't hesitate to use a gun…if they happened to take a dislike to a victim. *Ibid.* 109: The "gopher" appeared and asked for the booze in his best Tenth Avenue language. **1930** Irwin *Tramp & Und. Sl.: Gopher*…A gangster or other hard character.

9. *Logging.* (see quot.).

1958 McCulloch *Woods Wds.* 72: *Gopher*—a. A digging tool used to scrape a hole under logs which were hauled by big wheels. This made it easier to pass a chain under the logs…b. A small power shovel.

10. see GOFER, *n.*

¶ In phrase:

¶ **choke the gopher** (of a man or boy) to masturbate. Cf. *choke the chicken* s.v. CHICKEN. *Joc.*

1978 Alibrandi *Killshot* 220: Just like choking the gopher…Jacking off.

gopher *v. West.* to burrow like a gopher; *(hence) Mining.* (see 1889 quot.); dig energetically; *(also,* in 1870 quot.) to employ underhanded methods.

1870 in *DA:* In California, a man who practices deception, or acts in an underhanded manner, is sometimes called a "gophering fellow." **1889** *Century Dict.: Gopher*…To begin or carry on mining operations at haphazard, or on a small scale; mine without any reference to the possibility of future permanent development. Such mine openings are frequently called *gopher-holes* and *coyote-holes.* (Pacific States). **1909** *WNID: Gopher*, *v.i. & t.* To mine in irregular holes comparable to the burrows of gophers; to burrow. **1927** C.M. Russell *Trails* 129: This old boy is a prospector and goes gopherin' 'round the hills, hopin' he'll find something. **1927–30** Rollins *Jinglebob* 27 [ref. to 1880's]: "Boys, start gopherin' for wire." A search through the wagon produced a considerable amount of the desired article. **1966** in *DARE:* Gophering is just going along a vein 'n' finding a likely place that might be some ore.

gopher ball *n.* [pun on *go for*] *Baseball.* a pitched ball which is easily hit for a home run.

1932 *Baseball Mag.* (Oct.) 496 (cited in Nichols *Baseball Term.*). **1939–40** Tunis *Kid from Tomkinsville* 114: The pitcher threw two wild ones, and on the next pitch Swanson hit a "gopher ball" out of the park. **1959** Brosnan *Long Season* 109: Not as far as that gopher ball, I think. **1983** L. Frank *Hardball* 108: "Gopher ball"…is synonymous with "home run."…A fielder had to "go for" a ball that was hit past him. **1989** P. Dickson *Baseball Dict.* 184: *Gopher ball*…Hy Turkin reports that it was coined by Lefty Gomez when he pitched for the Yankees (1930–42).

gopher hole *n.* **1.** *Army.* a deep hole, often roofed with earth and timbers, dug in the ground for protection; dugout; *(also)* FOXHOLE; fighting hole.

1846 *Spirit of Times* (June 6) 176: Almost every man has a "gopher" hole dug to jump into to escape the explosion of the shells. **1864** in Hough *Soldier in W.* 213: Almost every house [in Atlanta] has what we call a "gopher hole" attached to it, that is a large hole made in the yard, then covered with timber and the earth…thrown over the timber, with a small entrance to it on the *south* side. **1864** in Rowell *Artilleryman* 229: The yards of all the houses had "gopher holes" dug in them where the citizens took refuge from the firing. **1882** Watkins *Co. Ayteh* 158: Soon we had every "gopher hole" full of Yankee prisoners. *Ibid.* 201: The old citizens had dug little cellars, which the soldiers called "gopher holes," and the women and children were crowded together in these cellars, while Sherman was trying to burn the city over their head. **1887** Hinman *Si Klegg* 603: Behind the fortified lines they dug "gopher holes" in which they slept, to avoid the plunging shot from the enemy's cannon. **1890** *Overland Mo.* (May) 506: The enemy's skirmishers…were sheltered in "gopher" holes, extending in a straight line some twenty yards apart…the gophers being large holes dug in the ground four or five feet deep, and large enough for seven or eight men, more or less, to stand in while firing. *a*1894 in *War Papers* I 159 [ref. to Civil War]: They would dive into their "gopher holes" for safety. **1901** in *Civil War Times Illus.* (Feb. 1986) 17 [ref. to 1863]: We dug holes with our bayonets and tin cups—"Gopher holes" which were a good protection. **1919** J.H. Smith *War with Mex.* I 176: But by this time the Americans had bomb-proofs and "gopher holes." **1942** in *Best from Yank* 180: Even the cunning Jap gunner in his steep gopher hole must have doubted his sentences.

2. *Mining.* (see 1889 quot. at GOPHER, *v.*).

1889 (quot. at GOPHER, *v.*). **1941** in *DARE:* Piles of weathered rock…mark the shafts of abandoned "gopher hole" mines. **1943** in *DARE:* Small mines variously called "country banks,"…"gopher holes" [etc.].

gopher-hunter *n. Baseball.* a hard-hit ground ball.

1874 *Chi. Inter-Ocean* (Aug. 9) (cited in Nichols *Baseball Term.*).

gopher job *n.* [GOPHER, *n.*, 5] *Und.* a bank robbery.

1906 *Nat. Police Gaz.* (Mar. 31) 3: I thought you always went up against those gopher jobs.

gopher man *n.* **1.** [GOPHER, *n.*, 5] *Und.* a burglar, esp. a bank burglar, who crawls, bores, or tunnels to reach his objective; *(also)* a safecracker.

1899 A.H. Lewis *Sandburrs* 77: He's a bank woiker, what d' fly people calls a "gopher man"; he's a mug who's onto all d' points about safes an' such. **1901** "J. Flynt" *World of Graft* 220: *Gopher-men*, safe-blowers. **1904** *Life in Sing Sing* 255: *Gopher Man.* Safe blower or burglar. **1925–26** Black *You Can't Win* 12: Famous "gopher men," who tunneled under banks like gophers and carried away their plunder. **1954** in *West.*

Folklore XIV (1955) 135: *Gopher man.* A burglar.

2. *Logging* (see quot.).

1958 McCulloch *Woods Words* 72: *Gopher man*—a. Powder man, particularly one who blew holes under logs for chokers. b. Man who dug a hole under logs which were to be hauled by big wheels.

go pill *n.* a pill, tablet, or capsule containing a stimulant drug.
1957 (cited in Spears *Drugs & Drink*). **1961** L.G. Richards *TAC* 49: These red capsules...are go pills—dexedrine, dextroamphetamine sulphate...They do for the human machine what the afterburner does for the jet engine. **1962** Harvey *Strike Command* 7: They get by on nervous drive and "go pills." **1967** [Beck] *Pimp* 206: Those "go" pills she had taken.

gore *n.* [prob. sugg. by *gory details*] interesting gossip; scandal.
1926 Hormel *Co-Ed* 67: Hello, Bab? What's the gore? [**1927** *AS* II (Mar.) 276: *Gory Talk.* braggadocio.] **1931** Lorimer *Streetcars* 102: Sylvia started handing me a lot of gore about a cute Frenchman...she'd met in Paris.

gorill *n.* a guerrilla; (*also*) GORILLA, 1.a. Also **gueril.** [Lines in bracketed 1864 quot. are intended to rhyme.]
1863 in R.G. Carter *4 Bros.* 277: Danger of being gobbled by gorrils. **1864** in C.W. Wills *Army Life* 224: To...clean out a nest of "guerils." [**1864** in *Mid-Amer. Folk.* XIV (Fall, 1986) 2: And by the Bushwhackers—the Missouri guerrillas [*sic*],/Led by the ruffian, Captain Quantrill.] **1929–31** in D. Runyon *Guys & Dolls* 107: You will never figure them to be gorills, even from St. Louis. *Ibid.* 111: I never care to be around gorills when they are drinking. **1940** O'Hara *Pal Joey* 172: These gorills come and ask me to work for them.

gorilla *n.* **1.a.** a brutish, powerful, or ugly man; ruffian; (during the Civil War) a guerrilla; (*often*) a violent criminal; thug. [The obs. form *guerrilla* in 1903, 1928 quots. and the nuance indicated in the second 1910 quot. show the influence of that word; cf. GUERRILLA.]
1861 in *DA*: He was long detained in Washington, having interviews with Abe [Lincoln], the Gorilla. **1862** Strong *Diary* III 204: [Lincoln] is a barbarian, Scythian, Yahoo, or gorilla, in respect of outside polish (for example, he uses "humans" as English for *homines*). **1862** M.V. Victor *Unionist's Dtr.* 157: We'se 'fraid to stay dar, after dem gorillas found us out. **1869** *Galaxy* (Jan.) 94: Not far off is Mr. Garroter...He is the gorilla of Crime Land. **1869** "M. Twain" *Innocents* I 20: Who is that spider-legged gorilla yonder with the sanctimonious countenance? **1885** McClellan *Own Story* 152: [Secy. of War Stanton] never spoke of the President in any other way than as the "original gorilla." **1893** Casler *Stonewall* 275 [ref. to Civil War]: Three of you "gorillas" are to be hung tomorrow. **1903** Kildare *Mamie Rose* 78 [ref. to *ca*1885]: Capt. B—, of Hoboken, a notorious "guerrilla" chief, was a frequent employer. **1904** *Life in Sing Sing* 249: *Gorilla.* A thief who uses violence in committing crimes. **1907** in McCay *Little Nemo* 102: Why, if that gorilla had his way, none of us would get in. **1910** Hapgood *City Streets* 20: I know a common loafer, or "bum," or "gorilla," as they call such on the Bowery, who in his spoken language has the elements of literature. **1910** in *DA*: The "gorilla," the strong-arm highwayman,...holds up people on the roadside and relieves them of their valuables. **1921** E. O'Neill *Hairy Ape* 256: I seen lots of tough nuts dat de gang called gorillas, but yuh're de foist real one I ever seen. **1928** Hammett *Harvest* 96: Dutch Jake Wahl, a guerrilla. **1930** Lavine *3d Degree* 5: Strong-arm men, *gorillas*, and tough gangsters. **1931** Adamic *Laughing* 58: The "easy one" was an Irish gorilla...a stevedore used to rolling barrels on the docks ten hours a day. **1938** "E. Queen" *4 Hearts* 38: Alec's gorillas told him what happened. **1939** Saroyan *Time of Your Life* IV: What kind of gorilla is this gorilla Blick? **1940** Baldwin *Brother Orchid* (film): Don't let them two gorillas go back to Chicago. **1965** C. Brown *Manchild* 213: People started saying that he was a gorilla, that he was going around shaking down people. **1973–76** J. Allen *Assault* 102: A gorilla pimp just whup a broad all the time, and they fear him. **1978** Severin *Brendan* 70: At least our two "gorillas," as we cheerfully called the muscle squad, had room to stretch out full length, and stow their gear. **1978** Truscott *Dress Gray* 73: You listened to the gorillas over in OPE, anybody who couldn't do more than ten pull-ups was the...enemy. **1987–91** D. Gaines *Teenage Wasteland* 62: He used to beat the boys. He was a gorilla.

b. *Stu.* a very unattractive, usu. overweight, young woman.
1971 Jacobs & Casey *Grease* 39: Jesus, is she a gorilla!

2. a shaggy sweater.
1939 West *Locust* 328: He wore a long-haired sweater, called a "gorilla" in and around Los Angeles, with nothing under it.

3. [sugg. by MONKEY] *Narc.* a severe dependency on a drug, esp. heroin.
1956 E. Hunter *Second Ending* 315: And it costs a lot of money to feed this gorilla of mine...If you have a gorilla, I guarantee that you will steal...You will do anything to feed that gorilla because he is the boss and not you. **1971** *Inter. Jour. Addictions* VI 11: I was hooked in my mind. Then after that I got a chippy, then after that a monkey going towards a gorilla. **1973** Schiano & Burton *Solo* 162: He's got a monkey on his back that's more like a gorilla. **1979** in J.L. Gwaltney *Drylongso* 213: It starts off like a monkey...Then you start doing it so much it gets to be a gorilla. **1993** *Donahue* (NBC-TV): This is more than a monkey on your back! It's a gorilla! **1994** N. McCall *Wanna Holler* 358: That shit [*sc.* crack] will knock your socks off in a minute and put a *go-rilla* on your back.

4. [sugg. by a conundrum, Q.: "Where does a five-hundred-pound gorilla sleep?" A.: "Anywhere he wants to." The riddle featured in a frequently broadcast TV commercial in the early 1970's] a person or thing that offers an irresistible advantage or that poses or causes extraordinary difficulties.—constr. with *five-hundred-pound, six-hundred-pound*, etc.
[**1978** *Saturday Night Live* (NBC-TV): Where does a five-hundred-pound gorilla sleep?] *a*1986 in *NDAS*: She is a 600-pound gorilla...She can intimidate anybody. **1986** *Daily Beacon* (Univ. Tenn.) (Oct. 16) 2: "We've got a 500-pound gorilla on our side at the moment," said [Sen. Daniel] Evans [R.–Wash.]. **1990** *Time* (Jan. 29) 21: The N.R.A. went up against Texas police groups...."They're an 800-lb. gorilla with no finesse....Every issue isn't the Alamo." **1990** *N.Y. Times* (Nov. 18) E 18: This guy...helped bring in this 300-pound gorilla named Prop 140. **1991** *New Republic* (May 20) 19: Cuomo is the 900-pound gorilla....He could easily win the nomination, but he can't win the election.

5. *Sales.* an exceedingly popular and profitable product, esp. a new item whose sales are continuing to increase.
1982 A. Shaw *Dict. Pop/Rock* 143: "Gorilla." A new record and music biz term meaning a monster of a bestseller. *a*1986 in *NDAS*: It is very simple to create the appearance of a "gorilla," a product with a lot of momentum.

gorilla *v.* [cf. GUERRILLA, *v.*] **1.** *Und.* to bully; coerce with violence; assault. Also **gorill.**
1922 J. Conway, in *Variety* (May 5) 12: He is gorillin' all the other stokers and handlin' things to suit himself. **1959** Horan *Mob's Man* 70: We began guerrilla-ing cons—making them pay protection with food and other items. **1959–60** R. Reisner *Jazz Titans* 157: *Gorilla:* To gorilla someone means to strong-arm the person. **1965** C. Brown *Manchild* 265: If you let somebody gorilla you out of some money...you got your ass beaten when you came back home. **1967–80** Folb *Runnin' Lines* 240: *Gorilla* v. 1. Severely beat. 2. Rape. **1980** Gould *Ft. Apache* 51: Murphy grabbed him by the shoulder and spun him around..."Don't gorilla me, Murphy," he said, balling his big fist. **1985** Baker *Cops* 103: These guys are punks...They'll gorilla you, maybe, but they're not tough guys.

2. *Und.* (see quot.).
1970 *Current Slang* V 8: *Guerrilla*, v. To take over; to appropriate.

gorilla biscuit *n. Narc.* GORILLA PILL.
1972 (cited in Spears *Drugs & Drink*). **1984** H. Gould *Cocktail* 115: Drinking beer and eating gorilla biscuits. *Ibid.* 286: They've taken a few "downs," or "gorilla biscuits" as they're called because they make you extremely violent.

gorilla dunk *n. Basketball.* a slam dunk.
1978 *Wash. Post* (May 9) D5: I don't think Larry Wright is going to survive in the NBA with a steady diet of gorilla dunks. **1992** Majors & Billson *Cool Pose* 77: Darryl Dawkins....His "gorilla dunks" were so named because of his enormous strength.

gorilla juice *n. Sports.* (see quots.).
1984 *ABC World News Tonight* (July 24): Growth hormones...from cows and monkeys [are] known [by athletes] as *gorilla juice*. **1986** *U.S. News & W.R.* (Nov. 3) 59: "Gorilla juice," steroids used by body builders.

gorilla pill *n. Narc.* a pill or capsule containing a strong stimulant or depressant.
1969 Lingemann *Drugs A to Z*: *Gorilla pills.* Barbiturates or other sedative pills. **1972** *N.Y. Post* (Feb. 2) 5: Is there any credible reason why children in the seventh grade trade pills—reds, greens, blues, uppers, downers, golfballs [*sic*], gorilla pills—the same way kids of a decade ago swapped baseball cards?

gork *n.* [perh. fr. GOK] **1.** *Hosp.* a patient who is brain-dead or in an irreversible coma. Also as *v.*

1964 "Dr. X" *Intern* 275: This drainage tube business could give Mary the chance of years of fruitful life, while if it isn't done, she will slowly turn into a gork and then die in a year or two. **1972** *N.Y. Times Mag.* (Jan. 16) 30: It's funny, because I had just started my internship then and I had a patient with the same problem—he was basically a gork*— and the program was very real....*Medical slang for a completely unresponsive person. **1974** Hejinian *Extreme Remedies* 77: He'd wake up. But in another week he'd gork again. **1974** *N.Y. Times Bk. Review* (Aug. 4) 4: Within the brain ward vegetable patients are referred to unfeelingly as "gorks." **1979** *NBC News* (Mar. 6): I only pulled the plug on the gorks. **1980** E. Morgan *Surgeon* 137: The gork in that room has the "O" sign, did you notice? **1983** Van Devanter & Morgan *Before Morning* 318: *Gork:* a slang expression for a patient who is brain-dead. *a***1985** in K. Walker *Piece of My Heart* 123: One Quonset hut was all intensive care-type patients that were..."gorks," we used to call them...missing part of their brains or had spinal cord injuries and were never going to walk again. *a***1987** in K. Marshall *Combat Zone* 137 [ref. to 1970]: All our patients were either unconscious or awake but basically retarded. Vegetables, really. We called them gorks—gorks because they'd lost part of their brain.

2. *Stu.* a stupid or offensive person. Cf. DORK.

1968–70 *Current Slang* III & IV 58: *Gork,* n. A dupe.—New Mexico State. **1981** R. Feldman *Hell Night* (film): Until finally she delivered a little gork named Andrew. Andrew never spoke a word in his first fourteen years.

gorked *adj.* Orig. *Hosp.* in the condition of a GORK; stupefied; (*hence*) mindless; stupid.—also constr. with *out.*

1973 *AS* XLVIII 205: *Gorked* "stupefied from anesthetic." **1974** Hejinian *Extreme Measures* 8: He's half paralyzed anyhow, and a bit gorked. **1981** in Safire *Good Word* 153: Leaves you "gorked"—stupefied, as if by an anesthetic. **1981** R. Feldman *Hell Night* (film): [He left] the cruellest punishment of all to his fourteen-year-old, gorked out son Andrew.

gorky *adj.* being or resembling a GORK.

1964 "Dr. X" *Intern* 274: Viral encephalitis...often leaves the patient gorky.

gorm *v. Stu.* (see quots.).

1856 B. Hall *College Wds.* (ed. 2) 232: *Gorm.* From *gormandize.* At Hamilton College, to eat voraciously. **1964** *AS* (Oct.) 281: *Gorm,* v.i. To overeat.

go-see *n. Fashion Modeling.* a job interview.

1986 Sliwa *Attitude* 49: At job interviews—or "go-sees" as they're called—...models wait in a room to show themselves and their portfolios to prospective employers. **1991** *Donahue* (NBC-TV) (Oct. 8): A go-see [is fashion] model lingo for go see a photographer about a possible job....I had a few go-sees.

gosh *interj. & n.* [euphem. alter. of *God*] (used as a mild oath, now esp. to express surprise). Now *colloq.*

*****1757** in *OED:* Then there's highest—and lowest, by gosh. **ca***1804** in *OED:* I promise, by Gosh (which is the most elegant and classical oath imaginable). **1838** [Haliburton] *Clockmaker* (ser. 2) 36: By gosh! there goes the dairy cows! **1843** Field *Pokerville* 102: I'll shoot you, by gosh! **1855** Wise *Tales for Marines* 264: Gosh! Miss Maggaret, don't git riled. **1864** J.R. Browne *Apache Country* 45: Oh, Gosh!...Oh, Jeeminy Gosh! **1966** Farley *Fog Man* 47: My gosh, I'm so glad you came to visit. **1979** Kiev *Courage to Live* 30: Gosh, I feel great now that I'm no longer depressed.

goshawful *adj.* GODAWFUL.

1902–03 Ade *People You Know* 168: Love's Young Dream was handed several goshawful Whacks about the Time that they started in to get a line on each other.

gosh-fired *adj.* ALL-FIRED.

1868 "W.J. Hamilton" *Maid of Mtn.* 56: It was a gosh-fired nice little 'un tew.

gosling *n.* **1.a.** a young, inexperienced person; child. Orig. *colloq.*

*****1607** Shakespeare *Coriolanus,* in *OED:* Ile never Be such a Gosling to obey instinct. *****1766** T. Gray in *OED:* You are a green gosling! I was at the same age (very near) as wise as you. *****1824** in *OED:* What a gosling you are, child,...you know nothing. **1868** M. Reid *Helpless Hand* 13: She ain't a goslin' any more—*she* ain't.

b. *Army.* a newly commissioned officer.

1891 Bourke *Border* 153: On the plains these two classes of very excel-

lent gentlemen used to be termed "coffee-coolers" and "goslings."

2. *Stock Market.* a broker or investor unable to pay his obligations. Cf. GONE GOSLING.

1870 Medbery *Wall St.* 136: *Gosling.* A Lame Goose. **1885** *Harper's Mag.* (Nov.) 842: [A broker caught by worthless securities] runs the risk of classification as a "gosling," or a "lame duck," who cannot meet his engagements, or a "dead duck," who is absolutely bankrupt.

gospel bird *n.* Esp. *Black E.* a chicken; chicken. Also **gospel fowl.** *Joc.*

[**1902** Corrothers *Black Cat* 214: You know chicken is a preachah's diet. De Laud made 'em 'specially foh minister's o' de gospel. An' when dey kin eat a whole chicken at one settin', people calls 'em "D.D.'s"—which mean "desp'ut devourers," I reckon.] **1935** Hurston *Mules & Men* 32: "Come on, heart-string, have some gospel-bird on me." [Note:] Chicken. Preachers are supposed to be fond of them. **1946** in Mencken *Amer. Lang. Supp.* II 232: *Gospel-fowl,* a chicken. **1973** Wagenheim *Clemente!* 127: Outfielder Willie Stargell bewildering waiters in restaurants, ordering "gospel bird" (fried chicken) and "jungle plum" (watermelon). **1976** *N.Y. Folklore* II 238: Well known is the term *gospel bird* for chicken. **1978** W. Brown *Tragic Magic* 94: Your hands don't make me no nevermind as long as I get me a piece of this gospel bird.

gospel mill *n.* a church.—used derisively.

1871 "M. Twain" *Roughing It* 249: Are you the duck that runs the gospel mill next door? **1874** Carter *Rollingpin* 219: He ground out sum light from his own "gospel mill." **1948** McIlwaine *Memphis* 77: Parson Smith...had set up a "gospel mill" in Memphis.

gospel-peddler *n.* a Christian evangelist; (*hence*) a sanctimonious person.—used derisively.

1900 Fisher *Job* 9: There was no clergyman. The "Gospel Peddlers," as the miners called them, had not yet come to the hills to stay. **1927** S. Lewis *Elmer Gantry* 21 [ref. to 1902]: Good Lord! You ain't going to help a gospel-peddler!

gospel-pipe *n.* [perh. pun on *organ*] the penis.

1916 H.L. Mencken, in Riggio *Dreiser-Mencken Letters* I 283: As absurd as the man who fights for the right to walk down Broadway naked, and with his gospel pipe in his hand. **1920** H.L. Mencken, in Riggio *Dreiser-Mencken Letters* II 389: One [hive] even showed today on my gospel-pipe.

gospel-pusher *n.* GOSPEL-PEDDLER.—used derisively.

1922 S. Lewis *Babbitt* 98: But there was opposition from certain Episcopalian and Congregationalist ministers, those renegades whom Mr. Monday so finely called "a bunch of gospel-pushers with dishwater instead of blood."

gospel shark *n.* a Christian clergyman; preacher; (*hence*) (*Stu.*) a sanctimonious person.—used derisively.

1889 Barrère & Leland *Dict. Slang* I 421: *Gospel shark* (Canadian), a parson. *****1899** Whiteing *John St.* 63: I ain't a-goin' to sit along with no sinners, not me, to be talked down to by a gospel shark. **1900** *DN* II 38: *Gospel-shark,* n. A preacher, a goody-goody, or sanctimonious person. **1901** J. London *God of His Fathers* 287: All gospel sharks and sky pilots. **1908** Whittles *Lumberjack* 14: The gospel sharks are in the tall timber. **1910** in O. Johnson *Lawrenceville* 407: Not the high markers and the gospel sharks? **1932** in *AS* (Feb., 1934) 26: *Gospel Shark.* A preacher.

gospel sharp *n.* a Christian clergyman; preacher.

1871 "M. Twain" *Roughing It* 250: What we want is a gospel sharp. See? **1876** G. Miller *First Fam'lies* 173: Send for a gospel sharp all to once, Jake. **1885** Harte *Shore & Sedge* 55: You understand they aren't asking you to run in opposition to that Gospel sharp—excuse me— that's here now. **1885** S.S. Hall *Gold Buttons* 3: Es true es ary word a gospel-sharp ever slung. **1887** Peck *Pvt. Peck* 68 [ref. to Civil War]: We have broken up a nigger funeral and captured the gospel sharp. **1899** A.H. Lewis *Sandburrs* 232: I was dead strong on patter in them days, an' puts it up I'm a gospel sharp from Hamilton. **1942** *AS* XVII 213: Jack contracted pneumonia, and someone brought the local "gospel sharp" to his bedside.

gospel shop *n.* a church or chapel.

*****1782** in *OED:* From Whitfield and Romaine to Pope John range;/ Each gospel shop ringing a daily change. **a***1791** in *OED:* My next enquiry was for Mr. Wesley's Gospel-shops. *****1811** *Lex. Balatron.: Gospel Shop.* A church. **1848** Judson *Mysteries* 35: I knows of a Gospel-shop w'ere they takes in their Sunday dimes on silver plates, and serves up their goodies on the same sort o' stuff. *Ibid.* 527: *Gospel-shop*—A Church. **1850** J. Greene *Tombs* 100: That coon over there...looks like one o' them gospel-shop men. **1865** S. Fleherty *Our Regt....102nd Ill. Inf.* 132: There goes your d—d old gospel shop. *****1873** Hotten *Slang*

Dict. (ed. 4): *Gospel shop*, an irreverent term for a church or chapel of any denomination. Mostly in use among sailors. **1891** Riis *How Other Half Lives* 17: The Street Arab…attending at the "gospel shop" on Sundays. **1891** McCann & Jarrold *Odds & Ends* 49: Up t'de Gospel shop on de Bowery. **1906** Buffum *Bear City* 86: How about the gospel shop? There is a chap fresh from the States who holds forth tonight. **1908** Whittles *Lumberjack* 40: You'd make us as welcome in the gospel shop as we made you in the bunkhouse. **1909** *DN* III 411: *Gospel shop*…A church [in Maine]. **1966** Kenney *Caste* 101: You sound just like a buck in a gospel shop.

gospel-slinger *n.* a Christian minister, esp. an evangelist.
1877 *Puck* (Aug. 8) 7: The inhabitants…referred to the reverend gentlemen as "gospel-slingers." [**1880** in M. Lewis *Mining Frontier* 128: Bill is goin' to stand in an' sling gospel for the boys as well as he can.] **1880** Pilgrim *Old Nick's Camp-Meetin'*: Taint no use fur any other gospel-slinger to put in his jaw. **1987** *Legends* (CNN-TV) (Jan. 19): His career from [being] an obscure gospel-slinger on the revival trail.

goss[1] *n.* [prob. as in 1944 quot.] severe treatment, esp. punishment or a severe scolding; a thrashing; "hell."—constr. with *give*, *get*, or *catch*.
1840 *Spirit of Times* (Mar. 21) 25: Everybody should read the article, for the Notion pedlar being mad as a wet hen, the way he gives us "goss" is equal to cats-a-fighting. **1840** in *DAE*: Offences trivial—loafing and drunkenness. Some of them got *gos*, and some got nothing. **1843** Field *Pokerville* 114: Old Sol was going to get goss, sure. **1844** in *DA*: I incurred…the displeasure of the proprietors of that house, and was informed…that I should catch goss, on the first suitable opportunity. *a***1846** in *DAE*: Two-thirds of the foot-lights were at once kicked over, while shouts of "Fair play," "Turn 'em out," "Give him goss," "No gouging," were heard on all sides. **1847** Robb *Squatter Life* 33: When giving "perticular goss" to the lower town editor and his abettors. **1862** in F. Moore *Rebel. Rec.* V D534: "You're right, Major—they are Yankees, and you may give them goss." Austin then poured in a deadly fire. **1864** *Battle-Fields of So.* 283: Give 'em goss! show 'em a taste of ole Alabamy! **1888** in J.A. Applegate *Cow Column* 60 [ref. to 1840's]: He…charged…at the top of his speed, and…leaped up from the ground (the boys yelling, "Give her goss, Andy!"). **1899** Green *Va. Folk Speech*: If you do, he'll give you goss. **1944** in *DARE*: To give (a person) goss = to give a person a whipping. [He] said that this expression, used in his area, contains the regional pronunciation of *gorse*, and that "to give one goss" means to whip a person with a gorse branch.

goss[2] *n.* [short for *gossamer hat* 'a light silk hat'] a silk hat; hat.
*****1848** in *OED*: When you carry off a 26*s.* beaver be careful to leave a 4*s.* 9*d.* goss in its stead. **1871** Schele de Vere *Americanisms* 208: The English use of *beaver* for a hat has entirely ceased, giving way to "gossamer," or in modern slang, "goss."

gotcha *n.* [fr. *gotcha!*, pron. spelling of *got you!*] **1.** a sudden discomfiture or humiliation, or that which causes it; (*specif.*) *Stu.* the act of suddenly exposing one's buttocks or genitals as a crude prank.
1964 in Reuss *Field Collection* 185: Old Vodka…makes you lay a gotcha. **1965** in Reuss *Field Collection* 185: "Gotcha"…either means "beaver" (female genitalia or pubic hair) or a "vertical smile" (a girl sitting down with legs and skirt wide apart.). **1974** Lahr *Trot* 116: Angie drops his pants….He's standing in the headlights' glare with his bare ass to the driver…"Gotcha!" Angie yells. **1979** Gutchen *New Girls* 65: "Well, I've never seen anybody throw a Gotcha."…So he leaped on the table…and he pulls down his pants. **1984** *Knoxville Journal* (Oct. 8) A6: Walters wondered whether Wallace was more puppet than journalist. Wallace called that a "gotcha" question. "It became a gotcha only because I handled it badly," Wallace said. **1985** Boyne & Thompson *Wild Blue* 502: There was a grim "gotcha" satisfaction in failing someone on a check ride. *a***1986** in *NDAS*: "This is a gotcha," Johnson allegedly told Jaffee.
2. a jolt or minor injury.
1983–86 G.C. Wilson *Supercarrier* 179: Then came the "gotcha" yank everybody who ejects prays for. *Ibid.* 223: The "gotcha" yank told me the wire had caught our plane. *a***1986** in *NDAS*: "Remember the gotchas you got from that worn old wrench?"

go through *v.* **1.** to thrash; (*intrans.*) to suffer; be defeated.
1836 *Davy Crockett's Alm.* (1837) 3: I'll go through the Mexicans like a dose of salts. **1855** in Dwyer & Lingenfelter *Songs of Gold Rush* 60: They were going through at Monte, though they pungled down the dust. **1868** "W.J. Hamilton" *Maid of Mtn.* 18: If ye don't stop p'intin' that thing at my weskit, I shill feel called upon tew go threw yew like a lizard in an eel-trap. **1908** in Fleming *Unforget. Season* 280: Matty…will go through the Phillies like a rifle bullet through a cigar box.
2. *Und.* to rob (a person), esp. with thoroughness.
1865 *Rogues & Rogueries of N.Y.* 42: A short time ago a fashionable method of pocketpicking was to first render the victim insensible by means of chloroform and then "go through" him or her at leisure. **1866** *Beadle's Mo.* (Feb.) 147: He…took the opportunity to "go through" (as pickpockets say) several of our shanties. **1872** Burnham *Secret Service* 202: His observant companions at No. 61 Bowery "went through" him. **1877** in Asbury *Gem of Prairie* 134: May Willard, the pocket-book snatcher,…went through a granger on the West Side lately. **1879** Rooney *Conundrums* 80: Robbing they call "going through you." **1880** *Harper's* (July) 195: The road agents had "gone through" all the passengers of the stage. **1887** Francis *Saddle & Moccasin* 71: The gentlemen had lately "gone through" the coaches with great regularity. **1891** in F. Harris *Conklin'* 79: The robber pocketed the watch and money, and told him he might tell Sheriff Johnson that Tom Williams had "gone through" him. **1893** Casler *Stonewall* 268 [ref. to Civil War]: I told them they could find nothing on me after those "Jessie Scouts went through me…worse than a dose of salts." **1896** in Harlow *Old Bowery* 383: In the front lobby we met a man whom somebody had just "gone through." **1914** D.W. Roberts *Rangers* 126: The robbers "went through" the passengers, then cut open the mail sacks. **1930** "D. Stiff" *Milk & Honey* 205: But train crews also *go through* the hobos.

go-to-hell *adj.* disregardful of or exceeding the conventional bounds of good taste or behavior; cocky; wild; (of apparel or hair) jaunty, nonchalant, or extreme in style. [In 1941 quot., as *n.*]
1918 (quots. at GO-TO-HELL CAP). **1921** (quot. at GO-TO-HELL HAT). **1937** E. Anderson *Thieves Like Us* 91: He tried on the powder-blue, but it was just too much of a go-to-hell suit for him. **1941** in Grayson *New Stories* 33: I'd be feeling like a real go-to-hell, an adventurer. **1945** Hubbard *RR Ave.* 344: "Go-To-Hell Signal"—Signal given with violent motion of hand or lantern. **1945** *AS* 226 (AAF): *Go-to-hell buggy.* A Cushman [motor] scooter, used by dispatch riders. **1946** Howard & Whitley *One Damned Island* 221: These men were members of a 318th Squadron called the "Bar Flies," a go-to-hell bunch of pilots and maintenance personnel. *Ibid.* 222: Wood and the others didn't feel so "go-to-hell" that night, however. **1948** Mencken *Amer. Lang. Supp. II* 745: *Go-to-Hell collar* (Catholics). An ordinary men's collar, sometimes worn by priests on holiday. **1948** McHenry & Myers *Home Is Sailor* 94: I'll be go-to-hell. **1954** F.I. Gwaltney *Heaven & Hell* 255: They had me try on one of those go-to-hell air corps hats. **1960** J.D. MacDonald *Slam the Big Door* 67: But I can't be as go-to-hell as she is. **1973** P. Benchley *Jaws* 136: It's not every night we throw a no-kidding, go-to-hell dinner party. **1976** Univ. Tenn. student: Something that's described as *go-to-hell* is something that's outrageous or unusual—and if anybody doesn't like it, you tell them to go to hell. Like David Bowie has a go-to-hell haircut. And I've heard of go-to-hell jackets, go-to-hell hats, go-to-hell pants, anything like that. **1972–79** T. Wolfe *Right Stuff* 41: As dilapidated and generally go-to-hell as [the place] actually was. *Ibid.* 230: Ban-lon shirts and…go-to-hell pants. **1980** Birnbach *Preppy Hndbk.* 193: Occasionally a go-to-hell blazer may be worn with plain pants.

go-to-hell cap *n. Mil.* **1.** an overseas or garrison cap.
1918 in J.D. Lawrence *Fight. Soldier* 160: In the afternoon we are issued overseas caps…These caps are known as the "go-to-h—l" caps. **1918** in Truman *Ltrs. Home* 50: Captain's bars, go-to cap [*sic*], Samuel Brown belt and everything. **1941** Kendall *Army & Navy Sl.* 7: Go-to-Hell caps…over-seas caps. **1944** Wakeman *Shore Leave* 12: They wore…garrison, or go-to-hell caps, as the marines called them. **1946** Michener *S. Pacific* 60: He was wearing shorts, only one collar insigne, and a little go-to-hell cap. **1969** Searls *Hero Ship* 47 [ref. to WWII]: He removed the tiny shield-and-eagle pinned to his go-to-hell cap.
2. a fatigue hat.
1943 Colby *Army Talk* (ed. 2) 226: Go-To-Hell Caps…Also used for the "fatigue hat."

go-to-hell hat *n. Mil.* **1.** GO-TO-HELL CAP.
1921 Benét *Beginning of Wisdom* 305 [ref. to WWI]: They had their overseas outfits, "go to hell hats" and all. **1942** *Leatherneck* (Nov.) 146: *Go-To-Hell Hat*—Garrison cap. Also known as overseas cap and fore-and-aft-hat. **1952** Cope & Dyer *Petty Officer's Guide* 437: *Go to Hell Hat.* (Slang). An overseas or garrison cap. **1961** Plantz *Sweeney Squadron* 10 [ref. to WWII]: As much a part of being a fighter pilot as the sagging ungrommeted "go-to-hell" hat on his head.
2. a wide-brimmed jungle hat.
[**1962** Tregaskis *Vietnam Diary* 110: Thanh…wore a rakish campaign hat in the best go-to-hell style (one side of the brim pinned up).] **1966**

E. Shepard *Doom Pussy* 1: I wore…an Australian Go to Hell bush hat. **1966** Baxter *Search & Destroy* 30 (caption): This war has spawned a new generation of American fighting men. They have their own slang and their own nonregulation gear such as a "go-to-hell hat." *a***1987** Bunch & Cole *Reckoning* 63 [ref. to Vietnam War]: Still more booths had…go-to-hell hats [for sale],…the pinned-back Aussie hat.

Gotrocks *n.* [*got* + ROCK 'dollar' + *-s*] a wealthy individual.—used as a surname.

1938 T. Wolfe *Web & Rock* 303: This is Mr. Maecenas Gotrox speaking. **1941** *Great Guns* (film): Listen, Mr. Gotrocks, what'd I tell you about that dark room? **1954** in D. McKay *Wild Wheels* 93: You could be Mr. Got-rocks or Joe Blow. **1962** G. Olson *Roaring Rd.* 144: It'd serve ol' Hardin Gotrocks right. **1969** Stern *Brood of Eagles* 135: And who…holds the other three quarters?…Mr. Gotrocks.

gouge *n.* **1.a.** a method of defrauding or swindling. [The 1845 quot. illus. an earlier colloq. sense, 'the act of cheating, extorting, etc.']

[**1845** in Bartlett *Amer.* (ed. 2) 176: There is a clean plain *gouge* of this sum out of the people's strong box.] **1859** Bartlett *Amer.* (ed. 2) 176: *Gouge.* A cheat, fraud, robbery. **1887** in *DA*: Another "gouge" was to charge the women a nominally [*sic*] cost price per spool for the thread furnished them.

b. a cheat or swindler.

1877 Burdette *Rise of Mustache* 298: Billinger says he knew he would get the law on the old gouge if he held on long enough.

2. Esp. *U.S. Nav. Acad.* an illicit aid such as a list of correct answers used by students while reciting, taking exams, or the like; answer key; CRIB SHEET.

1882 Miller & Harlow *9'-51"* 279: The Professor forgot what he wanted to say, but with commendable presence of mind thrust his hand into his coattail pocket and brought forth a "gouge" from which he read the remaining stanzas with a reassuring smile. **1894** *Lucky Bag* 67: *Gouge*…An "aide memoire." Any little artifice whereby anyone receives unauthorized assistance in the recitation room. **1918** "Commander" *Clear the Decks!* 78: Where is your gouge, you sneak? **1928** *AS* III (Aug.) 451: *Gouge*—The correct answers to questions. **1944** in Rea *Wings of Gold* 198: "The gouge" is a copy of the answers to a test. **1945** *Calif. Folk. Qly.* V (1946) 383: The key or correction sheet for Navy tests is the *gouge*.

3. *Navy.* authentic or inside information; (*hence*) information or news.—usu. constr. with *the.*

1947 in *West. Folk.* VII (1948) 73: Annapolis [slang]…*Gouge*…a solution to a problem "that even a professor can understand." **1983–86** G.C. Wilson *Supercarrier* 85: "I got the gouge" (navalese for hot information), enthused one of the pilots from the air wing. *a***1987** J. Green *Dict. Jargon* 258: *Gouge*…(US) (Business)…is information, which may be "good gouge" or "bad gouge." **1987** G. Hall *Top Gun* 95: *Gouge.* The latest information. Also the poop, the skinny. **1988** *Supercarrier* (ABC-TV): Hello, mate. What's the gouge?

gouge *v.* Esp. *U.S. Nav. Acad.* to cheat on an examination, in reciting, or the like.

1877 Lee *Fag-Ends* 41: "Gougers" trembled in their boots, fearing detection. **1886** in *DA*: Of all academic vices, "gouging" is the most despised and most severely punished. **1903** Clapin *Amer.* 210: *Gouging*—At the Naval Academy of Annapolis, dishonesty in work, as for instance the copying as one's own of a theme written by another. **1944** in Rea *Wings of Gold* 198: "Gouge"…is a naval term meaning to cheat, crib, copy, etc. **1949** *So. Folk. Qly.* XIII 204 [ref. to 1920–24]: To be caught "gouging" or "cheating" was an occasion for dismissal.

gouge game *n.* a swindle.

1862 C.F. Browne *Art. Ward* 49: The clerks tried to cum a Gouge Game on me.

goul *n.* [var. GOOLA[2], *n.*] the anus.

1969 Lynch *Amer. Soldier* 67 [ref. to 1953]: "Airborne, the man shouted from the porch, all the way." "Yeah, right up your goul."

goulash *n.* **1.** nonsense; rubbish; confused information.

1921 in Kornbluh *Rebel Voices* 86: It sounds like hokum and goulash and swill. **1928** Dahlberg *Bottom Dogs* 63: He was a lot of goulash anyway, and full of bull. **1928** *AS* III (Feb.) 255: *Goulash.* False information. **1942–49** Goldin et al. *DAUL*: *Goulash.* Misleading information to thieves; a garbled tip.

2. a dolt.

1928 Dahlberg *Bottom Dogs* 66: Sic 'em, goulash!

¶ In phrase:

¶ **know (one's) goulash** to know (one's) business thoroughly.

1926 Dunning & Abbott *Broadway* 233: Well, maybe you know how to handle gorillas—you know your goulash. She don't. **1928** Dahlberg *Bottom Dogs* 82: Doc sure knows his goulash.

go under *v.* **1.** to die. Hence **gone under** dead. [The S.E. sense 'to go out of business' presumably developed from this.]

1847–48 Ruxton *Far West* 4: Thar was old Sam Owins—him as got "rubbed out" by the Spaniards at Sacramenty…He "went under."*…*Died…[term] adapted from the Indian figurative language. *Ibid.* 14: Seven of us went under, and the Pawnees made a raise of a dozen mules, wagh! **1855** Kendall *Santa Fé Exped.* II (ed. 7) 440: A majority…have departed for California or some other new range, or else have "gone under."…This is a common way of saying that a man is dead in our western borders. *a***1861** Chamberlain *Confession* 293: He is a white man…and I'll be d—d if he shall go under in that fashion! **1872** G. Gleason *Specter Riders* 14: I hope he's not gone under, 'cause…thar ain't a better hoss on the plains. **1876** Cody & Arlington *Life on Border* 27: I'll stick to you till I'm gone under, by jingo. **1885** B. Harte *Maruja* ch. vii: What with old Doc. West going under so sudent. **1888** in *F & H* III 165: Whether Jim lived or had gone under. **1907** *DN* III 213: *Go under*…To perish. *ca***1960** in *DARE*: *Go under*…Fail or die.

2. *Police.* to go undercover.

1986 *Miami Vice* (NBC-TV): They decided I still looked young enough to go under.

go up *v.* **1.** to go to ruin; meet with or end in disaster; fail or go bankrupt; be disposed of. Hence **gone up** finished; done for.

1849 in *Calif. History* LXIII (1984) 316: His Woman's in the straw, and instead of going off he'll have to go up. **1862** in Jackman *Diary* 17: Such conduct as was then exhibited would cause us to "go up." **1862** in Geer *Diary* 51: The general impression prevailed that the 20th & 30th [regiments] were gone up except the skedaddlers. **1863** in R.G. Carter *4 Bros.* 340: If we do not stay here for at least four days, I am *gone up*. **1864** in R.G. Carter *4 Bros.* 388: I believe my *coat* will have to *go up*, for I cannot wear it during the warm weather. **1864** "E. Kirke" *Down in Tenn.* 95: I mus' git 'em, Leftenant, or we's gone up. **1864** Hill *Our Boys* 139: I found about one-half the tents *non est*, in fact, gone up. Fortunately, my own had stood firm. **1864** in *F & H* III 164: Soon after the blockade, many thought we should go up on the salt question. **1865** in W.C. Davis *Orphan Brig.* 252: We knew then…that we had "gone up." **1866** Dimsdale *Vigilantes* 203: "Jules, I am going to kill you;" to which the other replied, "Well, I suppose I am gone up; you've got me now;"…Slade immediately opened fire and killed him with his revolver. **1867** Clark *Sailor's Life* 80: If he deserts us, we are all gone up. **1867** Duke *Morgan's Cavalry* 338: I wished to avoid every thing which might warm the affair up into a hot fight, feeling pretty certain that when that occurred, we would all, guns and men, "go up" together. **1872** Burnham *Secret Service* 185: Poor fellow. King's gone up!…The "Knights" are after him! *Ibid.* 379: McCabe…was soon disposed of, in a manner similar to that whereby Kopf had "gone up." **1874** Carter *Rollingpin* 153: We're gone up, Bill. **1878** in *OED*: Oh, they are all going to pieces…I should not be surprised to hear of their going up at any moment. *ca***1885** Stearns *Co. K* 144 [ref. to Civil War]: "Good by…You are gone up now." At Antietam, all the color guard but one was either killed or wounded, and judging from that, they thought my turn had come. *ca***1890** Averell *10 Yrs.* 255: Stranger…I just thought you was gone up. They were four of the cussedest cut-throats in Arkansas. **1890** in L. Stillwell *Common Soldier* 50 [ref. to Civil War]: How did you feel…when they broke our lines…and it looked like the whole business was gone up generally? *****1892** in *OED*: We've rather bad news for you…your firm's gone up. **1898** Bullen *Cachalot* 191 [ref. to Civil War]: I've a great respect for the English, and consequently I'll let you go this time. But if I ever catch you again, you're gone up. As for those d—d Dutchmen, they'll be strung up inside of five minutes. **1899** Lounsberry *West Point* 65: Great Scott! We are gone up now! **1914** H.L. Mencken, in Riggio *Dreiser-Mencken Letters* I 155: You will lose nothing, even if we go up—which now seems improbable. **1980** M. Harris *Why Nothing Works* 14: It's all going up…It's too late for anything.

2. to die or be killed.

1863 in F. Moore *Rebel. Rec.* VI P33: Doctor, you've done all you could do, but I'm just a going up. **1864** in R.G. Carter *4 Bros.* 431: Then it was that we lost Baxter, Walton, and Steele, and your humble servant came near "going up" (pardon the expression). **1864** Kirke *Down in Tenn.* 259: Good by. If you do not see us within ten days, you will know we have "gone up." **1867** in *F & H* III 165: Unruly citizens are summarily hung on a cotton tree, and when any question is asked about them, the answer is briefly given, *gone up.* **1869** in Rosa *Wild Bill* 148: Threats as: "I shall kill someone to-night just for luck," or "some one will have to go up to-night," etc. **1871** *Galaxy* (May) 692: Hello, Captain! I thought you'd gone up!

3. to wear out or break down; become useless.

1863 Connolly *Army of Cumberland* 121: My boots with huge shiny legs but soles "gone up." **1873** [De Witt] *Dundreary* 21: Oh, that's played out…I mean 'ter say, it's gone up. **1980** in Safire *Good Word* 288: Could you drive? My car has gone up.

4. *Und.* to be sent to prison. [1849 quot. at **(1)**, above might belong to this sense.]

1872 Burnham *Secret Service* 149: Clark gone up! Pierce arrested and ruined! Carpenter secured! **1974** Gober *Black Cop* 183: If I get busted down, I'm going to spill my guts.…I'm not going up by myself. **1977** *Kojak* (CBS-TV): Fellows go up or go free depending on how we book 'em. **1982** Castoire & Posner *Gold Shield* 206: He'd have gone up for twenty-five years.

5. to become furiously angry.

1929–33 Farrell *Young Manhood* 346: Fran would be sore and go up, Jesus, like a balloon.

6. [short for colloq. *to go up in (one's) lines*] *Theat.* to forget one's lines while on stage; (*hence,* among musicians) to make a mistake while performing.

1964 in Redfield *Let. from Actor* 41: What the hell do you say if you go up?…Which means forget your lines. **1970** Landy *Underground Dict.* 91: *Go up*…Make a mistake in playing…music. *a***1988** J. Green *Dict. Jargon* 254: *Go up*…to forget one's lines.

7. (esp. among hippies) to take a psychotropic, esp. hallucinogenic, drug.

1967 *DAS* (Supp.) 687: *Go up.* To become high on narcotics…*Addict and student use.* **1969** Gustaitis *Turning On* 59: But only ten of us are "going up," as it's put. **1970** Landy *Underground Dict.* 91: *Go up*…become high.

gourd *n.* **1.** the head or mind; in recent phr. **out of (one's) gourd** insane.

*****1829** Marryat *Mildmay* 203 [ref. to *ca*1810]: Thinks I to myself, "If ever I saw "lodgings to let, unfurnished," it is in that cocoa-nut, or pumpkin, or gourd of yours. **1844** in *AS* (Feb. 1937) 75: Her brother would…tell him not to show his damned old gourd. **1848** Baker *Glance at N.Y.* 9: If you don't get off de hose I'll hit you over de gourd wid my trumpet! **1874** Carter *Rollingpin* 188: With a movement of his feet he—/Lifted off the top of Patrick's gourd. **1893** Hampton *Maj. in Washington* 91: From that time on, he said, no fly had ever lit on his old gourd. **1919** Darling *Jargon Book* 15: *Gourd*—The head. **1942** Horman & Corley *Capts. of the Clouds* (film): All he did was nick his gourd! **1961** in C. Beaumont *Best* 94: I'm going to go off my gourd, I know it! **1963** Braly *Shake Him* 144: Dino must be out of his gourd. **1963–64** Kesey *Great Notion* 61: You out of your gourd? **1964** Howe *Valley of Fire* 103: Head, gourd, skull! **1966** Garfield *Last Bridge* 134: Once a guy cracks up, you'd have to be out of your cotton-picking gourd to trust him again, sir. **1966** E. Shepard *Doom Pussy* 53: The troublemaker's gourd had been caught in a bucket of tequila all afternoon and he was about nine feet tall. **1970** Southern *Blue Movie* 38: Nothing that a kick in the gourd won't fix. **1975** Wambaugh *Choirboys* 309: I took out my sap and hit him upside the gourd. **1976** Conroy *Santini* 466: Have you lost your gourd? **1981** *N.Y. Daily News* (Jan. 1) 30: I always seem to start the New Year the same way: with a throbbing gourd. **1978–86** J.L. Burke *Lost Get-Back Boogie* 51: Something to expand that jaded gourd of yours.

2. a blockhead.

*a***1867** G.W. Harris *Lovingood* 69: The *wais*' yu durn oninishiated gourd, yu!

¶ In phrases:

¶ **flip** [or **lose** or **blow**] **(one's) gourd** to go crazy.

1970 *N.Y. Times* (Jan. 25) II 21: Women lose their gourd over John. **1973** N.Y.U. student: *Blow your gourd* means go crazy, *wig out.* **1977** Olsen *Fire Five* 209: Looks like everyone in town is flipping his gourd. **1977** in *Bugs Bunny* (Feb. 1978) (unp.): You've flipped your gourd for sure!…Trees can't really talk!

¶ **saw gourds** to snore loudly.

1859 "Skitt" *Fisher's River* 261: What the devil are you arter here? a-sawin' gourds…breakin' the stranger ov his rest? **1906** R. Casey *Lar-*

son's *Boys* 314 [ref. to 1860's]: Sawin' gourds, I reckon. **1908** in "O. Henry" *Works* 1363: Stop sawing gourds…and sit up and take notice.

gourd-head *n.* a large, empty head; (*hence*) a blockhead.

1858 in G.W. Harris *High Times* 90: Softsoaping the two old spectacled gourd heads about their intelligence and profound legal ability. **1926** Thomason *Red Pants* 12: Haven't got flat noses an' gourd-heads like a cawn-fiel' nigger down South. **1948** A. Murphy *Hell & Back* 33: Okay, gourd-head. Get that cotton-picking butt off the ground and give us a hand. **1969** Stern *Brood of Eagles* 276: Just because you fly airplanes is no reason for you to sound like one of Johnny's gourd-head mechanics.

gory-eyed *adj. West.* having eyes that are bloodshot or bleary, usu. from drink.

1942 *ATS* 122: Drunk…*gory-eyed.* **1942** Garcia *Tough Trip* 298: Both of them were gory-eyed and drunk as boiled owls.

gov *n.* **1.** a state governor.

1846 J.H. Ingraham *P. Fenning* 81: I live at the Gov's. **1867** S. Clemens in *Twain's Letters* II 115: Remember me to the Gov. **1928** W. Rogers *Chews to Run* 33: They nominated Gov, or Senator Jasbo. **1942** *ATS* 787: Gov, guv…governor. **1984** *N.Y. Daily News* (Aug. 10) 10: Top lottery winner checks in with gov.

2. GOVERNOR, 1.

1861 in H.L. Abbott *Fallen Leaves* 36: The gov. thinks I had better not go.

3. GOVERNOR, 2. *Obs.* in U.S.

1883 Peck *Bad Boy* 88: Hellow, Gov., how's your liver?

government straight *n. Mil.* military rations.

1898 in McManus *Soldier Life* 80: It is believed that our grub during the voyage will be "government straight" for every meal. It consists of hard-tack, coffee and potatoes, with either beef or salt pork or slum gullion.

government watch *n. Army.* a ball and chain. *Joc.*

1863 in H. Johnson *Talking Wire* 72: Those prisoners…are wearing what the boys call government watches, that is a twelve pound cannonball chained to their left leg.

governor *n.* **1.** (one's) father. Now *rare* in U.S.

*****1827** in *OED*: I was accompanied on this occasion by my Governor. **1836** Strong *Diary* I 31: I amused myself…greatly to the dismay of my "governor." **1837** *Spirit of Times* (May 13) 99: But the gov'nor, the old un, he drink'd down his sorrow. **1851** W. Kelly *Ex. to Calif.* II 254: Here's a line from your guvnor. **1854** G.G. Foster *15 Mins.* 76: Young men…scattering the "governor's" allowance. **1855** in B.C. Mitchell *Paddy Camps* 103: They…pay their own board. They either live with the "boss," "governor," or "old man," or elsewhere, as they please. *****1858** A. Mayhew *Paved with Gold* 380: Rum old fellow, my governor. **1866** Williams *Gay Life* 8: Harry Callow and Frank Dutton, having obtained the necessary consent…from their "governors," go with him. **1869** Carleton *Kaleidoscope* 18: Billy, how's your governor? **1871** *Yale Naught-Ical Almanac* 6: The Governor chances on the Field of Battle. **1872** McCabe *New York Life* 155: "The Governor," as he patronizingly terms his father. **1905** Sinclair *Jungle* 279: Thass my guv'ner—hic—hard as nails, by Harry! **1910** Livingston *Life* 92: I could…show the "governor" as I called father, "a trick or two." **1939** A.C. Johnston et al. *Hardys Ride High* (film): My governor won't let me. **1981** Sann *Trial* 45: "All *goniffs,*" the Governor shot back.

2. sir; fellow.—used in direct address. Now *rare* in U.S.

*****1844** C. Dickens, in *OEDS*: "My youngest died last week." "I'm sorry for it, governor, with all my heart," said Mark. *****1860** Hotten *Slang Dict.* (ed. 2). **1861** Berkeley *Sportsman* 169: Hallo, guv'nor, so you're a going to the plains, and I guess I'll go along with you. **1868** *Overland Mo.* (Aug.) 163 [ref. to 1854]: Say, Guv'ner, be you the ferry man? **1875** Daly *Pique* 315: No fear, governor! We are alone here, you and me. **1883–84** Whittaker *L. Locke* 146: I say, governor, I've got a favor to ask of you. **1886** E.L. Wheeler *N.Y. Nell* 2: You're mighty sharp at guessin', Governor. **1888** Pierson *Slave of Circumstances* 24: "Drop that, governor," exclaimed the other, in a hoarse whisper. **1931** Bontemps *Sends Sunday* 198: Where you goin', governor? **1968–70** *Current Slang* III & IV 58: *Governor,* n. False title given to anyone. "You've got it, *governor.*"—Watts. **1974** Blount *3 Bricks Shy* 55: Hold *on* to that egg, guv'nor. **1974** Piñero *Short Eyes* 56: Looks like you made the wrong move there, governor.

gow[1] *n.* HOOSEGOW.

1908 in H.C. Fisher *A. Mutt* 125: I sentence you to ten days in the gow. **1940** in Goodstone *Pulps* 115: He…wanted to take me down to the gow on an assault charge.

gow² *n.* [prob. < Chinese *yao-kao* 'opium'] **1.a.** *Narc.* opium, morphine, or heroin. Cf. GOWED, *adj.* Also **ghow.**

1922 *DN* V 182: Opium...Gow. **1923** *DN* V 236: *Gow, n.* Opium. **1925–26** J. Black *Can't Win* 159 [ref. to 1890's]: You're in with what "gow" [morphine] I've got. Let's bang it up before they come in. **1933** *AS* VIII 27: When one has contracted the habit...he is...hitting the gow. **1931–34** in D. Clemmer *Pris. Community* 332: *Gow joint*...A place where opium is smoked, or any place where any narcotic is sold. **1936** in D.W. Maurer *Lang. Und.* 90: *Gow.* Dope in general, especially dope used hypodermically; probably of Chinese origin, but no longer restricted to opium. **1954** in *West. Folklore* XIV (1955) 135: *Gow.* Morphine. **1972** Bunker *No Beast* 80: You got some ghow [heroin]? **1972** Smith & Gay *Don't Try It* 202: *Gow.* Heroin.

b. a thrill of pleasure, as caused by a drug.

1948 Lait & Mortimer *New York* 119: White women learned where they could get a "belt," a "jolt," or a "gow."

2. *Hot Rodding.* high speed or fast acceleration in a hot rod. Also quasi-*adj.*

1944 in Loosbrock & Skinner *Wild Blue* 334: He was risking his neck as a "gow" driver back on the flat desert race tracks of California. **1955** *AS* (Oct.) 237: *Gow* (a noun, meaning fast acceleration, pep, liveliness) does not seem to be used in Southern California.

3. *Pub.* CHEESECAKE; spicy commercial artwork. Cf. GOW JOB, 2.

1957 *Pub. Wkly.* (Apr. 8) 18: As yet, the record people haven't invented a trade word to describe this type of artwork, which in the newspaper field is called "cheesecake" and in the paperbooks field is "gow."

4. *Pris.* sauce.

1966 Braly *On Yard* 187: It was some of that gow you smear all over our good state food.

gowed *adj.* [GOW², *n.* + *-ed*] **1.** highly intoxicated by drugs or liquor.—usu. constr. with *up.*

1917 Ruggles *Navy Explained* 70: When a man is gowed up he has had too much liquor or other intoxicating drink. It is a purely sailor slang word and I have never heard where it originated, neither have I ever heard it outside of a circle of navymen. **1931–34** in Clemmer *Pris. Community* 332: *Gowed up*...under the influence of a narcotic. **1936** Duncan *Over the Wall* 209: We were all gowed up on "merry" constantly. **1936** *AS* (Apr.) 121: *Gowed.* Having too much dope. **1940** Chandler *Farewell, My Lovely* 75: What must have happened was that some gowed-up runt they took along for a gun-holder lost his head. **1940** E. O'Neill *Iceman* 134 [ref. to 1912]: Put fresh peanut oil in the lamp and cook the Lieutenant another dozen pills! It's his gowed-up night! **1957** Campbell *Cry for Happy* 20: He was all gowed-up on gin and sake.

2. *Hot Rodding.* modified for speed and high performance.—constr. with *up.*

1942 *ATS* 682: *Hopped-up,...gowed-up,...souped-up*...speeded up by special equipment.

gowhead *n. Narc.* a drug addict.

1936 Dai *Opium Addiction* 199: *Gow heads.* Addicts who use hypodermic needles. Also called *junkies, needle fiends, hypo smeckers.* **1938** in D.W. Maurer *Lang. Und.* 103: *Gow-head.* Originally an opium addict, but now generalized to include all forms of addiction except marijuana.

gow job *n.* [sugg. by GOWED, 2] **1.** *Hot Rodding.* an automobile that has been modified for high performance; hot rod.

1941 *Collier's* (July 26) 14: Gow Jobs; Youth's Newest Hobby: Jalopy Racing. **1942** *ATS* 682: *Gow job...hopped-up job* [etc.]...a racing car that has been speeded up by special equipment.

2. *Stu.* (see quot.).

1944 *Life* (May 15) 68: A "gow job" (flashy girl) wears at least two [hair clasps].

gowster *n. Und.* a habitual user of opium, heroin, marijuana or the like.

1936 *AS* (Apr.) 121: *Gowster.* A narcotic addict, especially one who uses heroin, morphine, or cocaine. **1936** Dai *Opium Addiction* 199: *Gowster.* One who smokes opium. Also called *smoker, pipe fiend, pipies.* **1946** *Amer. Mercury* (Feb.) 225: Thus *gowsters* or underworld addicts are made. **1948** Lait & Mortimer *New York* 119: Reefer smokers are called "gowsters." **1967** [Beck] *Pimp* 130: He's a crazy "gowster" if he thinks he'll con me into banging any "H."

GOYA *Navy.* "Get off your ass." *Joc.*

1966 Noel *Naval Terms:* GOYA. Slang: "Get Off Your Tail [*sic*]."

gozzle *n.* [var. GOOZLE] the throat.

1906 *DN* III 138: *Gozzle*...Throat. **1958** S.H. Adams *Tenderloin* 282 [ref. to 1890's]: If I could get my hands on that...bitch's gozzle. **1965–70** in *DARE:* Some food got stuck in his...*Gozzle.*

gozzle *v.* [var. GUZZLE] Esp. *Und.* to strangle or throttle.

1942 Liebling *Telephone* 73: Really, the Clutch is a gozzler...a fellow who gozzles people—chokes them in order to rob them. The gozzling business cannot be very good, because Marty is customarily...broke. **1954** Collans & Sterling *House Detect.* 47: This is an ugly customer who may combine any or all of the traits of sneak thief, burglar and gozzler.*...*A throttler, one who gozzles his victim by choking, sometimes to death.

G.P. *n.* general principles.

1942–44 in *AS* (Feb. 1946) 33: *G.P., n.* General Principles. **1969** Bullock *Watts* 138: If they stopped you for a traffic violation, you'll never know it. They just stopped you on GP [general principles]. **1973** *TULIPQ* (coll. B.K. Dumas): Justification for anything *G.P.* (comes from "general principles.") **1974** Matthews & Amdur *Race Be Won* 32 [ref. to *ca*1960]: They were going to mess with you just for "G.P.," as they liked to call it—general principle. **1982** Luciano & Fisher *Umpire Strikes Back* 83: I almost threw him out of the game right there for...G.P., or general principles. **1994** N. McCall *Wanna Holler* 4: And THIS is for G.P.—General Principle—just 'cause you white.

GQ *adj.* [abbr. of *Gentleman's Quarterly*, a men's fashion magazine] Esp. *Stu.* (orig. of a man) extremely fashionable; attractive.

1983 Eble *Campus Slang* (Mar.) 3: *GQ*—dressed like an ad in the *Gentleman's Quarterly:* He looks GQ with his designer shirt and pants and his cowboy boots. **1984** Gottlieb et al. *Dr. Detroit* (film): Look a little GQ, would you? **1984** *Miami Vice* (NBC-TV): You don't understand, Mr. GQ man. **1985** Eble *Campus Slang* (Apr.) 4: *GQ*—good-looking, stylish, fashionable. **1987** Univ. Tenn. student theme: A good-looking guy who dresses neatly and attractively is said to be *G.Q.* **1987** Lipper *Wall St.* 35: Another GQ couple stepped out behind their host. **1990** P. Dickson *Slang!* 218: Teen and high-school slang...*G.Q.* Nice clothes [*sic*]. **1992** D. Burke *Street Talk* I 26: He's *very* GQ: He's very handsome.

grab *n.* **1.** *Und. & Police.* an arrest or seizure.

*1753 in Partridge *Dict. Und.* 302: For Fear of a Grab, that is, for Fear of being taken; and if so, the others will rescue him. **1962** Perry *Young Man Drowning* 149: The Bug calls these pick-ups "token grabs" or "the nuisance pinch." **1969** Whittemore *Cop!* II 117: This afternoon he had tried to pick up the seventeen-year-old boy, Donald, who was wanted for five shootings, hoping to "make the grab" on his own time. **1990** C.P. McDonald *Blue Truth* 66: He *did* come up with the felony grabs.

2. a theft.

*1841 in Partridge *Dict. Und.* 302: He...yelped to the grab. **1866** *Nat. Police Gaz.* (Nov. 17) 3: Dutchy has made another "grab." **1889** Barrère & Leland *Dict. Slang* I 423: *Grab*...In the United States means a robbery or "a steal." **1932** Fort *Wild Talents* 6: The indications were of one wide grab, and the girl's intention to set the house afire, to cover it. **1972** Grogan *Ringolevio* 262: He was going to be in real trouble if someone could place him at the scene of any other grabs. **1976** G.V. Higgins *D. Hunter* 136: Arthur goes out one night on a medium grab.

3. Esp. *Und.* a constable or police officer. *Rare* in U.S. Cf. syn. NAB.

*1821 *Real Life in Ireland* 15: The *grabs* were emptying his own [house, for debt]. ***1823** in *OED:* When bailiffs and grabs hunt us up in the East. ***1849** in *OED:* Do you want to...have the grabs point at us as swindlers? **1958** *AS* (Oct.) 225: Less frequently used [terms for policeman] among nonmusicians...are...*shamus, fuzz, grab.*

4. a try or move.

1872 Beidler *Delegate* 67: I was once as much opposed to African voting, but I found that was the grab to make if we intend to carry the South for our party. *Ibid.* 71: We'll make our best grab, we have everything fixed to turn out...the votes.

5. a hand.

1901 Irwin *Sonnets* (unp.): The pastor...slipped a sixteen K on Mamie's grab. **1939** M. Levin *Citizens* 617: Look at those grabs on him, big as steam shovels.

6. *Circus & Carnival.* a snack or quick meal; in phr. **grab-stand** a snack stand. Cf. earlier GRAB JOINT.

1917 *Editor* (Feb. 24) 154: Grease-*Joint*—A restaurant where one gets a grab. **1918** *Chi. Sun. Trib.* V (Apr. 21) (unp.): [You] could stand for a grab in a joint where Java is 4 cents a cup an' a wafer o' roast beef is retailed on the block for 'leven c's. **1970** A. Lewis *Carnival* 52: Most of these [concessions] are completely legitimate like those clean grab-stands run by local churches and the Girl Scouts. These places are great; they give the customers more than their money's worth. **1972** *Playboy* (Feb.) 180: Get yourself something to eat at a grabstand.

7. *Gamb.* profits; TAKE.

1943 Holmes & Scott *Mr. Lucky* (film): Our grab oughta be over two hundred grand.

¶ In phrases:

¶ **put the grab on** to steal or kidnap; (*also*) to arrest.

1968–70 *Current Slang* III & IV 99: Someone put the grab on my tape recorder. **1978** *Go Go Globetrotters* (NBC-TV): Strogonoff just put the grab on von Brain. **1990** *Cops* (Fox-TV): Let's put the grab on her.

¶ **up for grabs** into the air for anyone to seize; (*hence*) no longer certain or secure; potentially the prize of anyone who makes energetic effort. Now *colloq.*

1928 MacArthur *War Bugs* 145: His monocle was tossed up for grabs [as the result of a blow]. **1930** Farrell *Grandeur* 213: Fogarty is plenty tough…[but] Barlowe threw him up for grabs. **1944** *Slanguage Dict.* 61: *Up for grabs*—a girl who is easy to date. **1978** *Muppet Show* (CBS-TV): I don't understand you people! Immortality is up for grabs! **1984** "W.T. Tyler" *Shadow Cabinet* 194: Like everything was up for grabs and I was the guy to see. **1988** Univ. Tenn. instructor: Once Dukakis lost that 17-point lead in the polls, the election was up for grabs.

grab *v.* **1.a.** to seize by force of law, esp. to place under arrest or take into custody.

*1753 in Partridge *Dict. Und.* 302: We all resolv'd, if *Brown* was grabb'd, that is, taken, to rescue him. **1800* in *OED*: Agreed to grab about a dozen old acquaintances. **1811* *Lex. Balatron.*: *The pigs grabbed the kiddey for a crack*: the officers seized the youth for a burglary. **1812* Vaux *Vocab.*: *Grab*: to seize; apprehend; take in custody…*Grab'd*: taken, apprehended. **1818* in *F & H* IV 191: Tramp it, tramp it, my jolly blowen,/Or be grabbed by the beaks we may. **1829* in J. Farmer *Musa Pedestris* 108: They grabbed me on the prigging lay. **1859** Matsell *Vocab.* 39: *Grabbed*. Arrested. **1851–61* H. Mayhew *London Labour* III 386: I was grabbed for an attempt on a gentleman's pocket by St. Paul's Cathedral. **1900** Doughty *Bradys & Girl Smuggler* 18: That will be the time for us to grab them. **1914** Jackson & Hellyer *Vocab.* 38: *Grab*, Verb. General currency…arrest. **1969** Whittemore *Cop!* I 50: It's only a matter of time before he gets grabbed again.

b. to take prisoner; capture, abduct, or kidnap.—also constr. with *off.*

1928–29 Nason *White Slicker* 124 [ref. to WWI]: The first thing you know someone's liable to grab us off! How can a man tell where his own Front line is? **1942** *ATS* 460: Kidnap…*grab.* **1971** H.S. Thompson *Las Vegas* 146: We had a case where they grabbed a girl right out of a McDonald's hamburger stand. **1971** E. Tidyman & J. Black *Shaft* (film): You know were she is…Somebody grabbed her. **1988** *Daily Beacon* (Univ. Tenn.) (Feb. 18) 1: Unknown assailants grab Marine officer in Lebanon.

2. to get or obtain for oneself, esp. to one's advantage or chagrin; earn or receive; in recent phr. **grab some bench** (of an athlete) to sit on the bench, esp. after a reprimand or removal from a game.—also constr. with *off.*

*1819 [T. Moore] *Tom Crib* 37: *Grab* the bit…To seize the money. **1821* *Real Life in London* I 89: *Grab'd*—Took, or stole. **1848** [W.T. Thompson] *Jones's Sks.* 68: Keep a eye on my plate, and [don't] let anybody grab it off. **1899** A.H. Lewis *Sandburrs* 10: Dey grabs off a garret in d' Astorbilt tenement, an' does t' keepin' house. **1913** T.A. Dorgan, in Zwilling *TAD Lexicon* 41: I'm going up to Newport—Maybe I can grab off an heiress up there. **1918** Witwer *Baseball* 286: I have grabbed off a lotta friends there now. **1921** Woolston *Prostitution in U.S.* I 146: In other cities, prostitutes pick their men, for fear they might "grab" a policeman. **1922** in Ruhm *Detective* 12: I grabbed many a good laugh. **1927** Shay *Pious Friends* 97: And knock this bucko for a row,/And grab a wagon load of dough. **1937** Weidman *Wholesale* 114: Then how come nobody grabbed her off yet? **1939** Wald et al. *Roaring Twenties* (film): Aw, grab yourself some sense. **1969** Bouton *Ball Four* 272: If you want to tell a guy to go sit down, it's *go grab some bench.* **1978** Gann *Hostage* 62: We both grabbed five demerits for dust under the radiator.

3. to excite the interest of; make a strong, usu. favorable, impression upon; in phr. **How does that grab you?** What do you think of that? Now *colloq.* [The "1942" quot. may be a later interpolation.]

a1915 in [Swartwood] *Choice Slang* 35: How does dat grab yer? **1921** *Variety* (Dec. 30) 4: They tell me to go and get a new act and I would have no trouble grabbin' the New York houses [vaudeville theaters].

1942 in C.R. Bond & T. Anderson *Flying T. Diary* 119: An English breakfast was something new to me…The tea just didn't grab me. **1958** J. Davis *College Vocabulary* 1: "How does that grab you?"—How do you feel about it? **1959** Farris *Harrison High* 238: How does that grab you? **1961** Anhalt & Miller *Young Savages* (film): How does that grab you, Mr. Bell? **1962** T.F. Jones *Stairway to Sea* 76: Isn't it beautiful?…Doesn't it grab the hell out of you? **1964** Redfield *Let. from Actor* 37: Then he gets bored…and wants to change it again. How does that grab you? **1971** *Adam-12* (NBC-TV): How does that grab you? **1975** in Terkel *Amer. Dreams* 28: Doesn't interest me. That stuff doesn't grab me.

4. to catch (a train, taxicab, or other conveyance). Now *S.E.*

1922 F.L. Packard *Doors of Night* 229: Spend this on the first taxi you can grab. **1926** in Lardner *Best Stories* 96: I'm going to grab the eleven-something train for Jacksonville. **1929** Milburn *Hobo's Hornbook* 30: The flier's due, when she pulls through/I'll grab her and I'll blow. **1968** N.Y.C. man, age 20: I'll just grab a cab and meet you there.

5. to comprehend; grasp.

1959 Morrill *Dark Sea Running* 11 [ref. to WWII]: When I blow my whistle, don't stand around like a flock of old whores at a fish fry. *Move*, grab me? **1961** in Cannon *Nobody Asked* 143: He's nothing but a high-class lawyer. You grab what I mean? **1962** T. Berger *Reinhart* 399: I don't know what's so hard to grab about that.

6. to irritate; GRIPE.

1961 Kanter & Tugend *Pocketful of Miracles* (film): Hey? What's grabbin' her? **1963** E.M. Miller *Exile* 266: "What's grabbing you, Dad?" Turk asked, a little annoyed.

7. to make (a turn in a motor vehicle).

1971 Sanders *Family* 271: They grabbed a right and proceeded to the house on the hill. **1978** Univ. Tenn. instructor: Grab a left up here.

¶ In phrases:

¶ **grab a root** to hold on tight; (*also*) to get busy; to go ahead vigorously.

1865 in Upson *With Sherman* 148: His mule lost his footing and some one yelled to him to grab a root and the boys took it up and you could hear "Grab a root" in evry direction. **1882** Baillie-Grohman *Rockies* 60: Every man "grabbing a root," *i.e.* helping himself to his own. **1899** J.N. Opie *Reb. Cav.* 54 [ref. to Civil War]: Jump down and grab a root, we are going to bust a cap! **1907** *Lippincott's Mag.* (Mar.) 385: Grab a root if you see yourself goin'. **1925** Mullin *Scholar Tramp* 211: Grab a root, dah, yo fo-eyed bastahrd! **1963–64** Kesey *Great Notion* 490: Grab a root an' dig.

¶ **grab sky** to put one's hands in the air.

1990 *Cop Rock* (ABC-TV): Grab some sky! **1992** *Daily Beacon* (Univ. Tenn.) (Nov. 23) 7: Believing it was…another mugging, Tom grabbed some sky.

grab-ass *n. Mil.* rough horseplay; (*hence*) foolish behavior; in phr. **play grab-ass** to indulge in rough horseplay; fool around.—usu. considered vulgar. [Early quots. ref. to WWII.]

1947 Heggen & Logan *Mr. Roberts* 430: By God, that's the rankest piece of insubordination I've seen. You've been getting pretty smart playing grab-ass with Roberts here…but now you've gone too far. **1951** W. Williams *Enemy* 180: Looks like we're really going to play some grab-ass with Them this time. **1952** Uris *Battle Cry* 114 [ref. to 1942]: Andy, knock off the grab ass and pay attention. **1952** Geer *New Breed* 273: "Knock off the grab-ass," Jaskilka yelled back. **1959** Morrill *Dark Sea* 200: You've been playing grab-ass with the Legion wives for a year and a half. **1959** E. Hunter *Killer's Wedge* 30: We can't fool around here. We can't go playing grab-ass because nitroglycerin is very potent stuff. **1963** Boyle *Yanks Don't Cry* 15 [ref. to 1941]: A salty, professional Marine, Frankie was all business, and it was plain that he was in no mood for the usual grab ass. **1963** J. Ross *Dead Are Mine* 254 [ref. to 1944]: I'm sick of stiffs. I am damned tired of playing grabass with a bunch of dead people. **1964** Rhodes *Chosen Few* 37: No noise, no laughing, no grab-ass. **1968** Spradley *Owe Yourself a Drunk* 57: Those punk cops are busy playing grab-ass—they're all queer. **1969** Hopper *Sex in Prison* 59: My men know I won't put up with any grab ass about anything. **1975** S.P. Smith *Amer. Boys* 327: Now quit playin' grab-ass and get this tent up. **1977** Caputo *Rumor of War* 44: Knock off the grabass, Glen. **1984** Caunitz *Police Plaza* 231: The Chief of Op is not the kind of man you play grab-ass with. **1990** Ruggero *38 N. Yankee* 24: The "grab-ass" was louder here for the benefit of the soldiers in other companies.

¶ In phrase:

¶ **mass** [or **organized**] **grab-ass** *USMC.* calisthenics or athletics.

a1949 D. Levin *Mask of Glory* 23 [ref. to WWII]: "Mass grab-ass," the

DI ordered. **1956** *AS* XXXI 194: *Organized grabass*, n. Athletics.

grab-ass *v.* **1.** Esp. *USMC & Navy.* to indulge in rough horse-play.
  1957 Myrer *Big War* 100 [ref. to WWII]: Squabbling, grab-assing around. **1958** Frankel *Band of Bros.* 53 [ref. to 1950]: Grabassing with a subordinate. **1964** Peacock *Drill & Die* 13: Quit grab-assing…and check your fucking gear. **1965–66** Pynchon *Crying* 58: The Paranoids were…grabassing around, trying to push each other over the side. **1967** Dubus *Lieutenant* 65: That Corporal was grab-assing as much as anybody else. **1977** Langone *Life at Bottom* 179: Well, man, we had guys grab-assing around with that one, I'll tell you. **1982** Downey *Losing the War* 49 [ref. to WWII]: You damn little people got that much energy to grab-ass?

2. to grab at and squeeze the buttocks of.—usu. considered vulgar. Also absol.
  1958 Gardner *Piece of Action* 107: Here's this married fellow Lowshak, with *children* yet, and he still grab-asses around, still goes after other [women]. **1963** Gant *Queen St.* 116: I saw one of the girls muss up his hair and he grab-assed a couple of them as they went by. **1974** *Playboy* (Mar.) 202: Grab-assing the waitresses. **1988** DeLillo *Libra* 264: This guy like grab-assed one of the waitresses.

grab-ass bug *n. Army.* any large flying or stinging insect.—usu. considered vulgar. *Joc.*
  1978 Groom *Better Times* 226 [ref. to Vietnam War]: They were pestered relentlessly by bugs, the most annoying of which was a fierce winged insect known as the "grabass bug."

grabber *n.* **1.** *Und. & Police.* a thief.
  1846 *Nat. Police Gaz.* (Jan. 3) 160: Jack Gibson! Jack Gibson! Come out of your den?/"*Clyfaker*" and "*Grabber*"—of all the "*Crossmen*." **1866** *Nat. Police Gaz.* (Nov. 3) 3: Dutch returned immediately…with a gay set of whiskers…which gave him the appearance of a superannuated "grabber."

2. *pl.* hands; clutches.
  1859 Hotten *Slang Dict.*: *Grabbers*, the hands. **1889–90 Barrère & Leland *Dict. Slang* I 423: *Grabbers* (popular), the hands. **1946 Mezzrow & Wolfe *Really Blues* 139: New Orleans had put her grabbers on them like a powerful magnet. **1970** Major *Dict. Slang* 61: *Grabbers*: the hands.

3. *R.R.* (see 1945 quot.).
  1931 *Writer's Dig.* (May) 41: *Grabber*—Conductor. **1939** *Sat. Eve. Post* (Apr. 15) 26: The grabber told the ground hog he'd never get the rocking chair on the Indian Valley Railroad. **1945** Hubbard *R.R. Ave.* 345: *Grabber*—Conductor of a passenger train. (He grabs tickets.)

4. something that seizes the attention.
  1966 H.S. Thompson *Hell's Angels* 25: The national news media had a guaranteed grabber on their hands. **1966–67** W. Stevens *Gunner* 89: Someone came up with a grabber, a clincher. **1968** Seaton & Pirosh *What's So Bad About Feeling Good?* (film): Now here comes the real grabber! **1987** S. Stark *Wrestling Season* 106: When a new client came in, he needn't have cash, but his story had to be a grabber.

grabble *v.* to seize or steal; grab.
  1781 in Partridge *Dict. Und.* 302: *Grabbles* all his *Bit* [takes all his money]. **1788 Grose *Vulgar Tongue* (ed. 2): To *Grabble*. To seize. *To grabble the bit*; to seize any one's money. *Cant.* **1859 Matsell *Vocab.* 39: *Grabble* To seize. "You grabble the goose-cap and I'll frisk his pokes," you seize the fool, and I'll search his pockets. **1893** (cited in Wentworth *ADD*).

grabhooks *n.pl.* hands or fingers.
  1913 Light *Hobo* 45: Back in New York…they don't use their palms for tips any more—their "grab-hooks" hold a hat. **1933** W.C. MacDonald *Law of .45's* 55: It might be a good idea to stick yore grab-hooks up in the air. **1946 in *OEDS*: Royal Navalese…Grabhooks*, fingers.

grab joint *n.* a cafeteria; (*hence*) a lunch counter, snack bar, or small cheap restaurant.
  1904 in *New Yorker* (Aug. 1, 1988) 41: [*The Restaurant Bulletin* described cafeterias as] "grab joints," where heaven helps those who help themselves. **1922** *Variety* (Aug. 4) 8: "Grab-joints," "juice-joints," cookhouses and refreshment stands. **1926** Finerty *Criminalese* 27: *Grab joint*—Sandwich stand. **1931** *AS* VI (June) 332: *Grab-joint*, n. A restaurant or eating stand. **1935** *Amer. Mercury* (June) 229: *Grab joint*: hamburger stand. **1961** Clausen *Season's Over* 143: The white-jacketed concession men…worked the "juice" and "grab" joints. **1970** A. Lewis *Carnival* 30: I'm runnin' a goddamned grab-joint now…That's a food stand where there ain't no place for the marks to sit down; they have to eat on the fly. **1979** T. Baum *Carny* 43: He…start[ed] across the infield to the grab joint.

grab-stand *n.* see GRAB, *n.*, 6.

grad *n. Stu.* a graduate. Now *colloq.*
  1871 Bagg *Yale* 45: *Grad*, abbreviation for *graduate*. Not common. **1928** Dahlberg *Bottom Dogs* 139: It was no job for a high school grad.

grade *n.* ¶ In phrase: **make the grade, 1.** to do what is required or come up to the proper standard. Now *colloq.* or *S.E.*
  1908 Whittles *Lumberjack* 58: "Do you think I'll make the grade?"…"Yes, you can make the grade, Will, but you will have to look for help.…Lord Jesus Christ. Every man he has helped has made the grade." **1921** S. Ford *Inez & Trilby* May 168: Three days! I doubt if she can make the grade. **1927** *AS* (June) 390: To *make the grade* or *connect* is to get the amount of money one is after. **1927** C.F. Coe, in Paxton *Sport* 147: I don't want him to let that ham get started after the count. But the goofer makes the grade. He's up at seven. **1928** Farrell *Guillotine Party* 22: And Jill. He hadn't made the grade there. **1927–30** Rollins *Jinglebob* 3: He couldn't make the grade. Sent his regards an' a heap o' messages. Was mashed by a bronc, but'll be O.K. in a week. **1933** in R.E. Howard *Iron Man* 83: None of my other boys quite made the grade.

2. to succeed in a seduction.
  1930 Farrell *Calico Shoes* 48: Well, now, I think that Monk Sweeney made the grade with her over on the Jackson Park golf course one night. **1931** Farrell *McGinty* 255: He'd be making the grade with a ritsy jane. **1929–33** Farrell *Manhood of Lonigan* 185: He knew he'd be able to pick her up and make the grade.

grade A *n.* an order of milk, as at a lunch counter.
  1953 A. Kahn *Brownstone* 214: One down, make it two…Grade A…the CB's mine. **1993** N.Y.C. man, age 57 (coll. J. Sheidlower): When I worked as a soda jerk in the late 1940's, you would say "Gimme a grade A!" for a glass of milk.

grade A *adj.* highest-quality; (*hence*) first-class, thoroughgoing.
  1938 in Loosbrock & Skinner *Wild Blue* 179: Grade-A, sea-level air. **1953** M. Harris *Southpaw* 81: When you are a top-flight grade-A ballplayer you will not go around telling everybody. **1974** Dubinsky & Standora *Decoy Cop* 61: I'm in a grade-A lousy mood. **1978** S. King *Stand* 554: A grade-A case of the creeps. **1981** Sann *Trial* 49: My own brand of Grade-A nonbelief. **1982** in "J.B. Briggs" *Drive-In* 72: Told me I was a grade-A jerkola. **1991** K. Douglass *Viper Strike* 28: They'd been treating the guy like a genuine grade-A hero.

graft *n.* **1.a.** *Und.* a criminal enterprise or occupation; racket; a dishonest or devious scheme.
  1865 *Nat. Police Gaz.* (July 8) 1: 'Twas handy that we were so related, as, when about a "graft," or "doing stur," both sisters could keep each other company. **1886 in *OEDS*: This "Guide" cannot work this "graft" alone, for he has to have a good supply for stock, a bag of "snide" or base coins. **1887** DeVol *40 Yrs. a Gambler* 25: We had a great "graft," before the war, on the Upper Mississippi. **1899** Garland *Eagle's Heart* 237: You're here for no man's good—you've got a "graft." **1899** A.H. Lewis *Sandburrs* 9: Billy's graft is hangin' round d' Bowery bars, layin' for suckers. **1899–1900** Cullen *Tales* 212: I told him he was about right, and then he sprung his graft. **1902** Hapgood *Thief* 268: Two of my new pals were safe-blowers, and we did that graft, and day work. **1905** Brainerd *Belinda* 74: Cleverest shop-lifter in the graft. **1907** Corbin *Cave Man* 320: Your blackmailing graft is played out. **1908** Train *Crime Stories* 10: At breakfast the girl inquired of her companion what his particular "graft" was, to which he replied that he was an expert "second story man." **1918** *Chi. Daily Tribune* (Oct. 16) 9: Many "seers," believing the "lid" was off, had come to Chicago to share in the lucrative "graft."

b. *Und.* thieving or swindling; criminal activities.
  1879 *Snares of N.Y.* 66: Some of them look after graft but more of them for cops. **1901** "J. Flynt" *World of Graft* 4: "Graft"…is a generic slang term for all kinds of theft and illegal practices generally. **1902** Hapgood *Thief* 31 [ref. to ca1880]: We had learned our first practical lesson in the world of graft. We had seen a pickpocket at work.

c. a soft job; a position of ease, comfort, or influence; sinecure.
  1893 in Partridge *Dict. Und.* 303: *Grafts*, in con slang, are special quarters occupied by sinecurists (favoured convicts doing no or little work). **1899–1900** Cullen *Tales* 299: All I had to do was walk up and down in front of the place…Nice graft, eh? **1903** *Independent* (Dec. 31) 3104: Here we found assembled a motley crowd of both races and both sexes—mostly mixed-ale tanks of the genus *bum*, all eagerly waiting for

a drink, a racket or a graft. **1904** *Life in Sing Sing* 248: *Graft.*—Something easy. **1915** Braley *Songs of Workaday World* 51: Though I know it there's lots of fellers that considers the position/Is a mighty easy sinecure, a graft. **1921** Dos Passos *Three Soldiers* 14: The corporal…is from New York, an' all the New York fellers in the company got a graft with him. **1931** Stevenson *St. Luke's* 59: He's got a stinking graft with Faraday. **1941** Halliday *Tickets for Death* 5: Damned if you haven't got a sweet graft, Mike.

2. an undertaking of any kind.

*1873 Hotten *Slang Dict.* (ed. 4): "What *graft* are you at?" What are you doing? **1896** Ade *Artie* 4: Where? Well, that's a good thing. To the church show—the charity graft. **1916** L. Livingston *Snare* 85: You moosed in and now are trying to spoil the graft.

3.a. labor or the action of laboring; work.

*1888–90 in *EDD:* "Well, I've got some graft to do now." Often heard in and about Sheffield. ***1889–90** Barrère & Leland *Dict. Slang* I 424: *Graft* (prison and popular), work; to *graft*, to work. ***1890** in *OED:* It is when hard graft has to be done…that they're troubled a bit. ***1904** *Athenaeum* (Apr. 30) 560: In Australia the slang word for work of any sort or kind, from that of the head of a State to that of a crossing sweeper, is "graft." All sorts and conditions of people use the word in this connexion. **1907** in H.C. Fisher *A. Mutt* 7: Guess I'll have to go back to hard graft. *Ibid.* 114: I never thought you'd fall for hard graft. **1908** J. London *M. Eden* 298: That beats hard graft. **1908** Kelley *Oregon Pen.* 81: He tried to beat the moulding room, for it was a hard graft. **1925** Bailey *Shanghaied* 63 [ref. to 1898]: Get up, ye moke, an' look fur graft.

b. occupation, trade, or calling; line of work or business.

*a1890–93 F & H III 192: *Graft*…(common).—Work; employment…*e.g.* What *graft* are you on now? **1896** in *DAE:* Fargo boasted of having a printers' ball nine worthy of a better "graft" than sticking type at thirty-five cents per thousand. **1896** *Pop. Sci. Mo.* (Dec.) 255: The roadster proper is distinguished from the tramp by having a "graft," or in other words a visible means of support. **1897** Ade *Horne* 168: I s'pose the book graft was slow. **1899** Cullen *Tales* 108: He…asked us what our graft was. **1899** Ade *Fables* 1: Is the Graft played out?…Is Science up against it or what? **1905** *Nat. Police Gaz.* (July 1) 12: The silhouette man of Coney Island, whose graft is cutting portraits out of black cardboard with a pair of scissors. **1906** London *Moon-Face* 53: "You are a newspaperman, I understand."…."That's yer *graft.* Work it," Slim prompted. **1908** Beach *Barrier* 53: He's made and lost a bank-roll…in the mining business, but it ain't his reg'lar graft. **1911** Bronson-Howard *Enemy* 37: Learn some good, square graft and stick to it. **1915** T.A. Dorgan, in *N.Y. Eve. Jour.* (Nov. 15) 12: Well—who are you and whats your graft anyway? **1929** Bodenheim *60 Secs.* 227: This isn't the only graft on earth. **1929–30** Dos Passos *42d Parallel* 150: Sailoring's a pretty good graft with this war on. **1931** J.T. Flynn *Graft in Business* 40: These gentry [pitchmen, gamblers, etc.] referred to their special callings as "grafts." A man's graft was his special and peculiar device for making a living on the fringes of the [circus].

4.a. Orig. *Und.* profit, esp. illicit profit.

1892 Norr *China Town* 62: What a graft the gang'd had if you'd stacked up against 'em instead o' me. [***a1890–93** F & H III 192: *Great graft* = profitable labour; good biz.] **1898** *Amer. Soldier* (Nov. 26) 2: The tendency of the average American youth is distinctly commercial and the prospect of good "graft" is enough to awaken the keenest enthusiasm. **1909** Munro *N.Y. Tombs* 94: Every week when I divided the graft, we had a big roll of bills each. **1914** Ellis *Billy Sunday* 55: He asked the bum what graft he got out of this. **1917** Oemler *Slippy McGee* 118: But why do they do it? Where's the graft?

b. Orig. *Journ. & Pol.* personal advantage, gain, or profit obtained through corrupt political or commercial practices, esp. money paid for bribes or protection; commercial and political corruption in general. Now *S.E.*

1901 "J. Flynt" *World of Graft* 4: The Under World has had occasion to approach him for purposes of graft and found him corrupt. *Ibid.* 12: The City Hall people want their graft just as much as I do. **1905** Riordan *Plunkitt* 3: Everybody is talkin' these days about Tammany men growin' rich on graft, but nobody thinks of drawin' the distinction between honest graft and dishonest graft. **1907** in "O. Henry" *Works* 1449: You know, Mac…they're trying Inspector Pickering on graft charges. **1911** H.B. Wright *Barbara Worth* 213: I mean…the way these four-flushers…attempt to work their graft right under our eyes. Did you hear about this man Worth getting that franchise out of the council? **1914** *Century Dict.* (Supp.): The word *graft*…came suddenly into extensive use in the political and journalistic language of the United States about 1901, as a new term more convenient in some respects than the equivalent terms bribery, corruption, dishonesty, blackmail,

"boodling," all of which it connotes and of which it is a succinct synonym. **1917** in W.A. White *Letters* 180: I wasn't jawing at Joe for exposing graft. **1929** T. Gordon *Born to Be* 36: His wife put the sheriff on Louie and he was run out of town; that necessarily cut our graft again. **1929–30** Farrell *Young Lonigan* 12: His old man kicked about paying for [a certificate] because he thought it was graft. **1931** J.T. Flynn *Graft in Business* 37: The characteristic vice of business today is graft. *Ibid.* 39: Graft is, I believe, comparatively recent as a term for describing a certain form of parasitic profit. **1937** Reitman *Box-Car Bertha* 78: They say that she pays a big graft…for protection. **1952** in Bradbury *Golden Apples* 91: We have to pay big graft to keep our franchise. **1955** Q. Reynolds *HQ* 329: No one blamed the citizens who did not hesitate to pay out graft to avoid traffic tickets.

graft *v.* [dial. E *graft* 'to dig'] **1.a.** *Und.* to pick pockets; to engage in theft or swindling of any kind.

1859 *Nat. Police Gaz.* (May 14) 3: Liz Thompson and her husband…do not intend going out to "graft" until the summer season sets in. **1859** Matsell *Vocab.* 39: *Grafting.* Working; helping another to steal. ***1863** in *OEDS:* I expect Poll and Bob will be able to go out with me and graft (pick pockets) in a few days. **1865** in *DA:* The granting of licenses (payable monthly) to "graft" on the City Railways is a great accommodation. **1866** *Nat. Police Gaz.* (Apr. 21) 3: They "graft" on the greenhorn "lay," which does not create much suspicion. **1866** *Nat. Police Gaz.* (Nov. 24) 3: The whole crowd…[was] scared to "graft" there. **1868** *Detective's Manual* 149: When Fred and Jack worked together, Fred thought he had got to kingdom come when he was allowed to "graft" with him. **1872** Burnham *Secret Service* vii: *Graft*, or *work*, to operate secretly; "Work a job," &c. **1877** Bartlett *Amer.* (ed. 4) 260: To *graft*…To pick pockets. A slang term.…"Scotch Moll is making out good grafting in the 8th Avenue cars." **1892** Norr *China Town* 47: It was great grafting, and the gang was in clover. **1896** Ade *Artie* 64: He's better 'n any o' them shell-workers that used to graft out at the gover'ment pier. **1901** *Chicago Tribune* (Aug. 25) 3: Thieves…started for the cemetery to "graft" in the Sunday crowds. **1902** Hapgood *Thief* 42 [ref. to ca1880]: Zack and I were grafting, buzzing Molls.

b. Orig. *Und.* to rob or steal; exploit unethically for money.

1900 Willard & Hodler *Powers That Prey* 49: I was a little shaver sellin' papers and graftin' molls. **1904** in "O. Henry" *Works* 335: We've grafted a dollar whenever we saw one. **1932** Lorimer *Streetcars* 164: This is my girl and no guy can graft any time with her. **1936–37** Kroll *Share-Cropper* 220: He was grafting the niggers with his cheap jewelry, and we were grafting them with photographs.

c. to cadge or sponge. Also *trans.*

1901 Irwin *Sonnets* (unp.): A schooner can be purchased for a V/Or even grafted if you're fierce at bumming. **1914** S. Lewis *Our Mr. Wrem* 61: I do not want to live on you. I always did hate to graft on people. **1917–20** Dreiser *Newspaper Days* 232 [ref. to 1890's]: Several struggling artists…"grafted on them," as the phrase then went.

d. *Jour. & Pol.* to acquire money, gain, or advantage through the practice of political corruption, esp. bribery or extortion.

1901 "J. Flynt," in *McClure's* (Apr.) 572: I'd like to see this town run by thieves once more. Course they'd graft…but not any more'n the police do. **1901** "J. Flynt" *World of Graft* 4: A "grafter" is one who makes his living, and sometimes his political fortune, by "grafting." He may be a political "boss," a mayor, a chief of police, a warden of a penitentiary, a municipal contractor, a member of the town council, [etc.]. **1905** D.G. Phillips *Plum Tree* 61: Politics is on a money basis now…I don't see how those in politics that don't graft, as they call it, are any better than those that do. **1909** in O. Johnson *Lawrenceville* 155: Turn the Robbers Out. No More Grafting. **1910** in Asbury *Gem of Prairie* 267: Hell, they all graft. There is not a policeman around here that doesn't hold us girls [prostitutes] up.

2. to work (at any business, trade, or occupation). *Obs.* in U.S.

*1859 Hotten *Slang Dict.: Graft.*—To go to work. **1859** Matsell *Vocab.* 39: *Graft.* To work. ***1873** Hotten *Slang Dict.* (ed. 4): "Where are you *grafting*?" *i.e.,* where do you work? ***1878** in F & H III 192: Perhaps in a generation or two Paddy will fail us. He will have become too refined for hard grafting. ***1888–90** in *EDD:* He'd graft away all night if they'd let him. ***1890** in *OED:* "You graftin' with him?" "No, I'm with Johnson." **1906** London *Moon-Face* 75: You ain't graftin' for a paper, are you? ***1936** in *OEDS.* **1958** S.H. Adams *Tenderloin* 25: Back in the 1880's…the verb *graft* was rogue's jargon for *work.* ***1958, *1966** in *OEDS.*

¶ In phrase:

¶ **graft onto** to obtain by dishonest or devious means.

1903 A. Adams *Log of a Cowboy* 194: He had a card or two…up his sleeve, by which he expected to graft onto some of the coin of the realm from the Wayfaring man.

grafter *n.* **1.** *Und.* a pickpocket, thief, or swindler; crook. *Obs.* in U.S.

1866 *Nat. Police Gaz.* (Nov. 3) 3: This "jug" "grafter"…was "copped" in Philadelphia. **1892** Norr *China Town* 48: George was a petty-larceny grafter and I had no use for him. **1896** in *DAE*: Most of the "grafters" have left the town and not many of them will remain here. **1899** "J. Flynt" *Tramping* 394: *Grafter:* a pickpocket. **1901** *Chicago Tribune* (Aug. 25) 3: The "guns"…tell them when some outside grafter comes into the city to work. **1901** "H. McHugh" *John Henry* 49: No more swell Sandwich Salons for me where the grafters want to butt in all the while. **1902** Hapgood *Thief* 28 [ref. to *ca*1880]: The result was I grew to think the career of the grafter was the only one worth trying for. **1902** Cullen *More Tales* 131: Spark grafters, porch-climbers and yeggs. **1908** in H.C. Fisher *A. Mutt* 77: Tobasco is busily engaged trying to bull a rich native into prosecuting the Ping Pong grafters. **1909** W. Irwin *Con Man* 13: Grafter…We mean by it any one who uses skin games as a vehicle for stalling through life. **1916** Miner *Prostitution* 14: I went with that grafter to a hotel. **1931** Haycox *Whispering Range* 177: This always was a lousy joint, run by penny-ante grafters. **1967* in *OEDS*.

2. *Orig. Journ. & Pol.* a person, esp. a politician or official, who takes advantage of his position to gain money or property unethically or illegally, as by taking bribes, levying extortion, diverting funds, etc. Now *S.E.*

1901 (quot. at GRAFT, *v.*, 1.d.). **1903** in *DAE*: Every member of the union knew the exact character of Parks, that he was a "grafter." **1904** F. Lynde *Grafters* 298: You were to crush the grafters in this railroad struggle…and climb to distinction yourself on the ladder from which you had shaken them. **1914** Atherton *Perch* 58: Butte…has her pestilential politicians, her grafters and crooks. **1953** Pohl *Star of Stars* 48: It was an informal club for goldbricks and staff grafters who caroused within.

gram *n.* a telegram.

1891 in *OEDS*: I…sincerely hope the 'grams reached you safely. **1928, *1960* in *OEDS*. **1962** in H. Ellison *Sex Misspelled* 93: I put Kantor and his…'gram out of my mind.

grampus *n.* Esp. *Naut.* a blusterer; a blustering fool.

1823 J.F. Cooper *Pilot* 158: Pshaw! you grampus, do you turn braggart in your old age? **1823** J.F. Cooper *Pioneers* 253: How should you know, you lubber?…How should you know, you grampus? **1851** M. Reid *Scalp Hunters* 47: The blustering old grampus of a governor is to honor the ball with his presence. **1855* Brougham *Chips* 362: It's halterin' hevery day, you grampus. **1861** Guerin *Mountain Charley* 26: Go it, young grampus.

¶ In phrase:

¶ **blow** [or **tip**] **the grampus** *Naut.* to drench someone, as a sailor caught sleeping on watch, with a bucket of water, or to hold one's head under water as a prank or form of punishment.

1804 *Port Folio* (Aug. 4) 246: Six A.M. Bonypart lands (that is, if he can); then we begin to blow the grampus; seven A.M. Bonypart in a pucker. **1829* Marryat *Mildmay* ch. iv: The buckets of water which were…poured over me by the midshipmen, under the facetious appellation of "blowing the grampus"…could [not] rouse my dormant energies. *a*1867 Smyth *Sailor's Wd. Bk.: Blowing the grampus.*—Sluicing a person with water, especially practised on him who skulks or sleeps on his watch. **1883** Russell *Sailor's Lang.* 148: *Tipping the grampus.*—Ducking a man for sleeping in his watch on deck.

grand *n.* **1.** *Orig. Und.* the sum of one thousand dollars. [The pl. form *grands* is now obsolete.]

1915 Bronson-Howard *God's Man* 212: This fellow was wise and asked for a hundred grands to get the letters back. **1917** T.A. Dorgan, in Zwilling *TAD Lexicon* 41: I refused a "grand" a week to play—yep, 1000 bucks. **1920–21** Witwer *Leather Pushers* 174: Fifteen one-thousand-buck notes, or "grands." **1922** *Variety* (June 30) 6: The sap had about five grand ridin'. **1924** in Lardner *Haircut* 181: Even 25 grand is a big bunch of money and if a man could only turn out one hit a year and make that much out of it I would be on Easy st. **1925** E. Hemingway *Men Without Women* 137: You know what I'm betting on him? Fifty grand. **1926** Maines & Grant *Wise-Crack Dict.* 8: *Grand*—Thousand dollars. *Ibid.* 12: *One-half grand*—Five hundred dollars. **1928** Callahan *Man's Grim Justice* 54: We ought to get ten gran. *Ibid.* 119: I borrowed

two gran (two thousand dollars). **1930** in R.E. Howard *Iron Man* 33: I'm going to get a hundred grand for this fight. **1931** C. Shaw *Delinquent Career* 162: They talked of "grands" and "C notes" as though they were familiar with them. **1936** "E. Queen" *Halfway House* 56: Don't tell me an outfit like the National Life can't stand paying out three hundred grand. **1958** in C. Beaumont *Best* 207: He got at least five hundred grand a year out of his lumber business. **1970** R. Vasquez *Chicano* 109: They got about two grand in wages coming. **1976** J. Harrison *Farmer* 31: It'd take fifty grand in equipment to even get started. **1992** *Amer. Detective* (ABC-TV): Made fourteen hundred to two grand a day.

2.a. one thousand (of anything).

1946 G.C. Hall, Jr. *1000 Destroyed* 413: One Grand…Stewart's group blasted 1,016 Nazi planes.

b. *Av.* one thousand feet of altitude.

1955 R.L. Scott *Look of Eagle* 47: Forty-nine angels in radio phraseology, almost fifty grand above the level of the sea. **1980** W.C. Anderson *Bat-21* 8: I'm the parachute at about twelve grand. **1987** Zeybel *Gunship* 172: I started my bomb pass from twenty-one grand.

c. one thousand pounds.

1971 Tak *Truck Talk* 64: *Forty grand:* a payload weighing forty thousand pounds. **1986** Coonts *Intruder* 61: If that would squeeze another grand or two of gas into the tanks. **1989** J. Weber *Defcon One* 85: "How much gas you have left?" "Bout four thousand pounds."…"I'll take two grand."

grand bounce *n.* see s.v. BOUNCE, *n.*

grand-daddy *n.* the largest, most remarkable, or best known example (of all). Now *colloq.*

1907 S.E. White *Ariz. Nights* 133: Speakin' of snakes…I mind when they catched the great-granddaddy of all the bullsnakes…in the Black Hills…He was more'n a foot thick. **1956** *AS* XXXI 255: This is known as the "grandaddy" of all [radio] bloopers. **1963** Robertson & Skarstedt *Slime People* (film): Oh brother, this must be the granddaddy of all storms. **1979** Cassidy *Delta* 194: Well, here was the granddaddy of all targets.

grandkid *n.* [*grand*child + KID] a grandchild. Now *colloq.*

1927 (cited in *W10*). **1948** J. Stevens *Jim Turner* 218 [ref. to *a*1910]: I got the dam'est grandkids. **1982** Heat Moon *Blue Hwys.* 151: I give…most to my grandkids. **1983** Flaherty *Tin Wife* 325: Some worthless medallion to trot out for the grandkids.

grandma *n.* **1.** the menses. Cf. syn. GRANNY, *n.* Cf. GRANNY RAG.

[**a*1890–93 *F & H* III 193: *To see* (or *have*) *one's grandmother…with one…*(common).—To have the menstrual discharge.] **1952** Randolph & Wilson *Down in the Holler* 106: But the expression reminded people of *old grandmaw's coming*, which refers to menstruation. **1969** *Current Slang* I & II 43: *Grandma George*, n. Menstruation.— College females, Mississippi.

2. Esp. *S.W.* lowest gear, as of an automobile.

1941 *AS* (Oct.) 166: *Grandma.* Low gear. **1966** "T. Pendleton" *The Iron Orchard* 5: Come on, ye wore-out ol' sonofabitch! Take a country mile t'git you outa grandma! **1968** J.P. Miller *Race for Home* 4 [ref. to *ca*1930's]: Forcing the abused and protesting gearbox from third into second and from second into low and from low into lowlow, or "grammaw." **1973** Gwaltney *Destiny's Chickens* 10: He throwed'er into Grandmaw. **1983** K. Weaver *Texas Crude* 9: "Grandma" is the lowest, therefore the slowest, gear in a truck transmission.

grandma turn *n. Av.* a very wide, flat, slow turn, as in an airplane.

1929 *N.Y. Times* IX 10: The Texas lads were droning their way in "grandma" turns and slow circles over the flat Texas plain.

grandmother *n.* ¶ In phrases:

¶ **my grandmother!** (used to indicate surprise).

1834 Caruthers *Kentuck. in N.Y.* I 27: Oh! my grandmother! what a smashin rage he flew into.

¶ **Tell it to your grandmother!** I don't believe you.

1929–33 J. Lowell *Gal Reporter* 65: He again demanded to know my name. "Jane Hoyt." "Tell that to your grandmother. How old are you?"

¶ **your grandmother!** (used, esp. postpositively, to indicate disbelief or ridicule). Cf. similar expressions at GRANNY, *n.* Also vars.

*1821–26 Stewart *Man-of-War's-Man* I 173: "Is the fid out?" again resounded from the deck. "Is your grandmother out?" muttered Dennis impatiently. **1868** Aldrich *Bad Boy* 83: "Phil, do you think they

will—*hang us?*" "Hang your grandmother!" returned Adams impatiently. **1870** in "M. Twain" *Stories* 47: "If they had sent a boy up to shake the tree—" "Shake your grandmother! Turnips don't grow on trees!" **1884** "M. Twain" *Huck. Finn* 72: "Watchman your grandmother," I says: "there ain't nothing to watch but the taxes and the pilothouse." **1884** F.R. Stockton *Lady or Tiger?* 68: "But we try to do it in the proper way." "Proper grandmother!" he exclaimed. **1894** Henderson *Sea-Yarns* 35: "Did you hit her?" "Hit your grandmother's sneeze!…No." **1897** *Harper's Wkly.* (Jan. 23) 86: "You'd set the place afire, with all this loose hay about." "Set yer gran'mother afire! Gimme a lucifer!" **1914** Paine *Wall Between* 93: "Would you have had me degrade my rank by engaging in a fist fight with an enlisted man?" "Degrade your great-grandmother's cat!" gustily answered Captain Ramsay. **1914** London *Jacket* 139: "He didn't feel anything. He's paralysed." "Paralysed your grandmother," sneered the warden. **1926** Norwood *Other Side of Circus* 90: "Siam, your grandmother!" **1927** Barry *Paris Bound* 272: *Mary (overcome).* Why Richard—*Richard.* Why, your grandmother. **1928** C. McKay *Banjo* 182: "Enough you' grandmammy!" cried Banjo. **1947** Willingham *End As a Man* 40: So your grandma says!

grand quay *n.* [perh. sugg. by *dock*] *Und.* a state prison.
 1848 *Ladies' Repository* (Oct.) 315: *Grand Quay,* Penitentiary. **1871** Banka *Pris. Life* 492: State Prison…*Grand Quay.* **1919** Darling *Jargon Book* 15: *Grand Quay*—State prison.

grandstand *n.* [sugg. by GRANDSTAND PLAY] actions taken to impress onlookers.
 1925 *Adventure* (Dec. 10) 90: Some more grandstand!…I could break you in two and you know it.

grandstand *adj.* [sugg. by GRANDSTAND PLAY] intended to impress onlookers.
 1902 Cullen *More Tales* 113: There was no grandstand finish to my desertion of the Sierras either. **1912** Raine *Brand Blotters* 162: That grandstand escape of Mr. Boone's.

grandstand *v.* **1.** to conduct oneself or perform showily or ostentatiously in an attempt to impress onlookers; show off.
 1900 in *OEDS*: [Kentucky will go for McKinley] if Teddy can only be secured to do some "Grand Standing." **1925** *Adventure* (Dec. 10) 85: Any flyer could do that who was crazy enough. Just grandstanding! **1927** Nicholson *Barker* 132: I ain't grandstandin' an' I'm tellin' you what I'm goin' to do. **1927–28** in R. Nelson *Dishonorable* 182: No little wop's goin' to…grandstand around about what he's goin' to do to me. **1934** W. Smith *Bessie Cotter* 189: Just grandstanding, that's what it was. **1963** Uhnak *Policewoman* 129: I will warn you to take all necessary precautions. In other words…no grandstanding. **1970** Hersh *My Lai 4* 122: "I was in a position to have grandstanded on this for several months if I wanted to," Udall said later. **1975** Kangas & Solomon *Psych. of Strength* 9: Heroics, or grandstanding, are for personal gain. Nathan Hale…stands in contrast to the grandstander like the show-off who sky-dives into the football stadium at half-time.
 2. to accomplish or perform (something) in an ostentatious manner.
 1930 Lait *On the Spot* 62: If I let this girl out, after the way I grandstanded her arrest, I'd be laughed out of the city limits.

grandstand play *n.* Orig. *Baseball.* a fielding play executed so as to impress the audience in the grandstand; (*hence*) any action taken showily or ostentatiously so as to impress others. [In 1928 quot., used collectively.]
 1893 in *DA*: They all hold on to something or clasp their knees tightly—to faint or fall over would be a grand-stand play. **1900** Ade *More Fables* 121: This was his Chance to make a Grand-Stand Play. **1900** *DN* II 39: *Grand-stand,* adj. 1. Done for exhibition, as a "grandstand play" in baseball. 2. Showy. **1905** Phillips *Plum Tree* 166: It was as good a political "grand-stand play" as ever thrilled a people. **1912** Mathewson *Pitching* 68: It wasn't to make a grand-stand play I did this, but because this was baseball. **1915** Raine *S. Yeager* 8: Corking chance for a grandstand play. **1928** Lake *Earp* 38: I would shun flashy trick-shooting—grandstand play—as I would poison. **1941** Schulberg *Sammy* 50: I had the feeling that this was more a grandstand play for me than kindness toward Miss Goldbaum. **1952** Uris *Battle Cry* 25: I'm not trying to make a grandstand play. **1956** Gruber *Big Land* 87: That was a damnfool grandstand play! **1962** E. Stephens *Blow Negative* 328: It's a grandstand play on his part…He thinks it's his one chance for glory now. **1974** Strasburger *Rounding Third* 1: This is no grandstand play for sympathy. **1984** *All Things Considered* (Nat. Pub. Radio) (July 27): I think appointing Geraldine Ferraro was a grandstand play.

grandstand player *n.* one who GRANDSTANDS; show-off. Also **grandstand artist, grandstand jockey.**
 1888 in *OEDS*: It's little things of this sort which makes the "grand stand player." They make impossible catches, and when they get the ball they roll all over the field. **1942** *ATS* 646: *Grandstand player,* a "show-off." **1948** Lay & Bartlett *Twelve O'Clock High!* 106: I can't be expected to run a big show…if my commands are ignored by a grandstand artist. **1965** Harvey *Hudasky's Raiders* 28: I am not interested in grand-stand players. **1978** Dills *CB* 48: *Grandstand jockey:* driver who is careless or shows off.

granger *n.* [generalized from *Granger* 'a member of the Patrons of Husbandry (a farmers' organization)'] a farmer or countryman.—usu. used derisively.
 1877 in Asbury *Gem of Prairie* 134: May Willard, the pocket-book snatcher,…went through a granger on the West Side lately. **1877** Burdett *Mustache* 11: We have always pictured Adam as a funny-looking granger who would sigh fifty times a day. **1889–90** Barrère & Leland *Dict. Slang* I 424: *Granger*…The word is now generally used to mean a countryman, a rustic, or "a gentleman from the rural districts." **1909** Irwin *Con Man* 28: The granger came back with no winnings. *Ibid.* 37: The Swede figured on going from fair to fair, cleaning up the grangers and making a million.

granny *n.* **1.** an old woman.
 ***1698–99** "B.E." *Dict. Canting Crew: Granny,* an old Woman, also a Grandmother. **1970–71** Rubinstein *City Police* 366: Patrolmen dress up cab drivers, drunks, drifters,…and even old ladies, called "grannies." **1974, 1976** (quots. at GRANNY-DODGER).
 2. [perh. sugg. by the head of Liberty which formerly appeared on dollar coins] a dollar.
 1865 Duganne *Camps. & Pris.* 420: "Fifteen dollar fur dis yer, an' ten dollar fur dat dar"…. "Dry up, old cotton-head!" "Fifteen grannies!" "What's Confed. money worth?"
 3. the menses.—constr. with *the.* Also pl. Cf. syn. GRANDMA. Cf. GRANNY RAG.
 1929 Millay *Against the Wall* 322: "Menstruation."…She could have called it "granny" and nobody would have raised an eyebrow. **1942** McAtee *Supp. to Grant Co.* 5 [ref. to 1890's]: *Grannies, n.* menses. **1968** Baker et al. *CUSS* 129: *Granny's here for a visit*…Be menstruating. **1976** D.W. Maurer, in *AS* LI 14 [ref. to ca1930]: To have the grannies.
 4. the lowest gear of a vehicle. Cf. syn. GRANDMA. [1992 quot. ref. to a bicycle.]
 1975 *Nat. Lampoon* 51: Down in the corner…Granny gear. **1976** Bibb et al. *CB Bible* 62: With the precision of a driver shifting all the way from granny to going-home gear. **1979** J. Morris *War Story* 89: The trucks were put in double-low, four-wheel granny, and just by God went up the side of the mountain. **1990** Rukuza *W. Coast Turnaround* 39: He cruised around the lot in granny low. **1992** Donahue (NBC-TV): The granny gear is about 7.9 inches.
 5. GRANNY LANE.
 ¶ In phrases:
 ¶ **Shoot (one's) granny** to blunder.
 1858 [S. Hammett] *Piney Woods* 40: "Barkin up the wrong tree,"…"shootin' yer granny,"…"finding a mar's nest"…hit's all the same I reckon in the long run.
 ¶ **your** [or **my**] **granny!** not at all!—used postpositively as a sarcastic retort. Cf. similar phrs. at GRANDMOTHER.
 1837 J.C. Neal *Charc. Sks.* 35: "Any fool might know that it was a sign of war." "War!" ejaculated the party; "Oh, your granny!" **1863** in *DA*: "Repose, your granny," answered Addie, who, when vexed never stopped for elegant phrases. **1876** "M. Twain" *Sawyer* 154: "Do they hop?" "Hop?—your granny! No!" **1926** Nason *Chevrons* 157: "Counterattack my granny!" scoffed the officer. **1927** C. McKay *Harlem* 36: Know her mah granny. You knows her just like I do, from the balcony of the Lafayette. **1938** T. Wolfe *Web & Rock* 551: Healthy iron, your granny! **1942** McAtee *Supp. to Grant Co.* 6 [ref. to 1890's]: *Granny, n.,* rump, ass; "Aw yer—", exclamation of disagreement or disbelief.

granny bar *n. Mining.* (see quots.).
 1919 *DN* V 56: *Granny bar.* A huge crowbar used in quarries that takes several men to work. Probably because it is the grandmother of crowbars. **1965** O'Neill *High Steel* 271: *Granny Bar.* A big crowbar.

granny-dodger *n. Black E.* a contemptible fellow; (*also*) *Pris.* a raper of elderly women. Hence **granny-dodging,** *adj.*
 *a***1969** J. Kimbrough *Defender of Angels* 179 [ref. to 1920's]: These granny-dodgin' peckerwood laws. **1974** A. Murray *Train Whistle Gui-*

tar 23: Goddamn granny-dodging son-of-a-bitching motherfucking motherfucker. *Ibid.* 48: Some of them...bony-butt granny-dodgers don't back up off nobody when it come to shooting a goddamn rifle. **1976** Braly *False Starts* 236: His victims were all over fifty. We had all heard of granny dodgers...but they were seldom really encountered. *a*1973–87 F.M. Davis *Livin' the Blues* 67 [ref. to Kans., *ca*1925]: Listen at this grannydodger.

granny dumping *n.* the abandonment of an elderly person, esp. a relative, in a nursing home, hospital, or the like.
1991 *AARP Bulletin* (Sept.) 1: "Granny dumping:" new pain for U.S. elders. **1992** *N.Y. Times* (Mar. 29) E 16: 70,000 elderly Americans were abandoned last year by family members unable or unwilling to care for them or pay for their care. Social workers call this phenomenon "granny dumping." **1992** *Time* (Apr. 20) 75: The fraying of family and community is visible in homelessness and granny dumping and children shooting other children. **1993** *N.Y. Times* (nat. ed.) (Apr. 18) 26: The case focused national attention on the problem of "granny dumping," the abandonment of the elderly by their children.

Granny Howland *n.* [orig. unkn.] *Naut.* (a personification of the sea); in phr. **Granny Howland's** [or **Granny's**] **washtub** the bottom of the sea; DAVY JONES' LOCKER.
1899 Robbins *Gam* 72: *Granny Howland!* what a crew these here heathen Chilenos be! *Ibid.* 73: Them pulparees is the sartin road to Granny Howlan's washtub. *Ibid.* 89: That there *Ganges*, that's jest naow a-bunkin' in Granny's wash-tub.

granny lane *n. CB.* the right or rightmost traffic lane on a highway. Also **granny**.
1978 Dills *CB Slanguage* (ed. 4) 48: *Granny lane:* right lane; slow lane. **1980** Motorist on L.I. Expressway over CB radio: They've got the middle and the granny lanes closed. **1986** N.Y. fireman, age *ca*40 (coll. J. Sheidlower): The three lanes on a typical highway are the *hammer lane*, the *sandwich lane*, and the *granny lane.* **1994** Motorist in White Plains, N.Y., over CB radio (coll. J. Sheidlower): There's a down four in the granny at 8W.

granny rag *n.* a menstrual cloth. Cf. GRANDMA; GRANNY, 3.
1976 D.W. Maurer, in *AS* LI 14 [ref. to 1920's]: The strongest taboo word in this area, never used in mixed groups, was *granny rag.*

grape *n.* **1.** [short for GRAPEVINE] *Army.* gossip; rumor.
1864 in *Ark. Hist. Qly.* XII (1953) 362: "Grape" is dull. News from our armies good. **1864** in D.R. Hundley *Pris. Echoes* 104: The prison is greatly agitated tonight with a fearful "grape" from Atlanta. **1865** in *So. Hist. Soc. Pap.* III (1877) 56: Plenty of "grape," *i.e.* rumors afloat of a speedy general exchange. **1865** in *Ibid.* XIX (1891) 41: Occasionally a startling "grape"* is seen on the board...*Grapevine telegram.* **1885** Cannon *Where Men Only* 236 [ref. to 1865]: This sort of talk got the name of "grape," and an idle or incredible rumor was dismissed with the remark, "Oh, that's grape!" **1971–72** in Abernethy *Bounty of Texas* 205: *Grape,* n.—news or rumors: to hear some grape.
2.a. wine.—often constr. with *the.* Also (*Black E.*) pl.
1898 Kountz *Baxter's Letters* 17: When you are cutting into the grape at four dollars per, you always want to say Mr. Bartender. **1908** in H.C. Fisher *A. Mutt* 155: Can you blame him for dallying with the grape? **1910** T.A. Dorgan, in *N.Y. Eve. Jour.* (Mar. 25) 20: The general opinion last night was that Steve had been at the grape too often. **1911** Van Loan *Big League* 63: He ought to be fined for this! And cutting into the grape, too! **1928** O'Connor *B'way* 22: Another bottle of grape was uncorked. *Ibid.* 252: *Grape*—Champagne. *Ibid.* 66: We went into an all-night joint and I called for some grape. **1944** Burley *Hndbk. Jive* 139: *Grape cat*—Male devotee to wine. *Grape chick*—Female devotee to wine. **1971** Goines *Dopefiend* 85: There's a wine store, baby, let's chip in and get a couple bottles of grapes. **1975** S.P. Smith *Amer. Boys* 99: Like he couldn't get enough wine and shit...He had to suck up that grape. **1983** *Reader's Digest Success with Words* 85: Black English... *grapes* = "wine."
b. a wine drunkard.
1977 Bunker *Animal Factory* 14: The wino was snoring lustily, spittle drooling from his toothless mouth. In jail vernacular he was a "grape."
3. *pl.* hemorrhoids.
1942–49 Goldin et al. *DAUL* 86: *Grapes.* Hemorrhoids. ***1965** S.J. Baker *Australian Lang.* (ed. 2) 153: *Grapes,* haemorrhoids.
4. *Navy.* a member of the Aircraft Fuels Division on board an aircraft carrier.
1986 *Reader's Digest* (Aug.) 187: Men wearing purple jerseys—called grapes —fuel the planes. **1990** R. Dorr *Desert Shield* 17: Mike Nevatt is a "grape," or fuel chief,...aboard the carrier USS *Dwight D. Eisenhower.*

1993 *How'd They Do That?* (CBS-TV): [Specialists in] purple jerseys, known as "grapes," fuel the planes.

grape-cutting *n.* [sugg. by GRAPEVINE, *n.*, 2] *Army.* a rumor.
1864 in C.W. Wills *Army Life* 305: I just thought I would give you a sample of the "grape cuttings" that accompany a march.

Grapefruit League *n. Baseball.* major-league baseball teams holding spring training in Florida. Also (*obs.*) **grapefruit loop.**
1934 Weeseen *Dict. Slang* 211: *Grapefruit loop*—A schedule of exhibition games played before the official opening of the baseball season. **1949** Cummings *Dict. Sports* 184: Grapefruit League. **1953** in *DAS:* The Cards dropped a 5-2 grapefruit league decision to the...Yankees. **1962** Houk & Dexter *Ballplayers* 86: But we were a poor last in the Grape Fruit League. **1989** *CBS This Morning* (CBS-TV) (Feb. 28): Where's Mark this morning? Isn't he in the Grapefruit League?

grape juice *n.* wine.
***1837** in *OEDAS* II 124: Let topers of grape-juice exultingly vapour. **1887** DeVol *40 Yrs. a Gambler* 24: The party were all full of grape juice. **1906** *Nat. Police Gaz.* (Jan. 6) 7: The liquor refreshment board...where several quarts of cold grape juice awaited me. **1928** MacArthur *War Bugs* 30: Little feet had to be careful where they led us after a quart of grapejuice and six or eight *bières terribles.* **1972–76** Durden *No Bugles* 161: It wasn't Dago red, but that's about all I know about grape juice.

graper *n. Petroleum Industry.* (see quot.).
1944 Boatright & Day *Hell to Breakfast* 140: One of the less offensive names for a man who plays up to his boss for special favors is a "graper," who is held in very low esteem.

grape up *v. Petroleum Industry.* to curry favor.—constr. with *to.*
1966 "T. Pendleton" *Iron Orchard* 7: He grapes up to Drum and Drum grapes up to Bruner, an' you gonna grape up to the three of 'em if you git in *that* gang, or they'll run yo' ass off fo' you make a payday.

grapevine *n.* [short for GRAPEVINE TELEGRAPH] **1.a.** any informal or unofficial method of relaying important or interesting information, esp. by word of mouth; the means by which gossip or rumor travels. Also quasi-adj., (of a report) learned confidentially. Now *S.E.*
1862 in Connolly *Army of Cumberland* 25: We get such "news" in the army by what we call "grape vine," that is "grape vine telegraph." It is not all reliable. **1863** in Sperber & Trittschuh *Amer. Pol. Terms* 179: A despatch came from Richmond "via grapevine." **1864** in *War of the Rebellion* (Ser. II) VII: They pretended to have "grapevine" intelligence that [the raiders] were up as far north as the Missouri River. **1891** *Century Mag.* (Mar.) 713: The "grape-vine" spoke...of little else. **1928** Benét *John Brown's Body* 41: And the grapevine whispered its message faster/Than a horse could gallop across a grave. **1929–33** Farrell *Young Manhood* 327: Down there at that express company they find out about everything a guy does. They got the best grapevine in the world. **1939** Appel *People Talk* 30: They passed the word by the grapevine through all the bars on Columbus. **1944** Botkin *Amer. Folk.* xxii: Folklore...in its purest form is associated with the "grapevine" and the bookless world. **1952** "M. Roscoe" *Black Ball* 78: "You plugged Verzallia, didn't you?" "You have a good grapevine." **1953** Breihan *Jesse James* 78: The Confederate grapevine was functioning perfectly, and from his mother Jesse learned of the dispatch of this garrison from Plattsburg. **1959** W. Williams *Ada Dallas* 74: The grapevine said he wrote out a check for $100,000 for the nomination. **1972** Buell *Shrewsdale* 242: This'll get on the community grapevine. **1982** "J. Cain" *Commandos* 91: Word had reached them through the GI grapevine. **1984** Kagan & Summers *Mute Evidence* 381: And he had a good grapevine for information.
b. gossip, rumor, or news; (*also*) a rumor. Also quasi-adj., being of the nature of an untrustworthy rumor.
1863 in Connolly *Army of Cumberland* 48: It is "grape vine" that Grant's and Burnside's armies will unite within the next month. **1863** in F. Moore *Rebel. Rec.* VI P33: It is just another *grapevine.* **1867** Duke *Morgan's Cavalry* 185: A straggler captured at Glasgow gave us some "grape vine" intelligence which annoyed us no little. **1887** Hinman *Si Klegg* 460 [ref. to Civil War]: I'll bet you a day's ration o' hardtack that it's only 'nother o' them grapevines. *Ibid.* 581: Camp rumors were "grapevines." **1888** McConnell *Cavalryman* 17 [ref. to 1866]: The human mind runs in ruts, anyhow, and isolate a few hundred men in a military camp, the items of real interest being scarce, the imaginary, or, as they called them at Carlisle, "grapevine" stories multiply. **1890** in *DAE:* [The newspaper dispatch was] what we used to call a "grapevine." **1899** Biederwolf *161st Ind.* 134 [ref. to Civil War]: The men spent the next day lounging about camp making "pipes" and "grape-

vines" on the next move. **1905** E.F. Langdon *Cripple Creek* 143: I had set three "galleys"...and my husband and brother-in-law had "gotten up" all the "grape vine" before the raid. **1937** Johnston *Prison Life* 35: Any grapevine on the board meeting? Are they gonna loosen on paroles? **1942** Casey *Torpedo Junction* 185: "Scuttle butt"...means the same as bull, grapevine, gossip. **1958** S.H. Adams *Tenderloin* 322: What's this grapevine about Brockholst Farr?

2. (among tramps) a clothesline.
[**1843** in Sperber & Trittschuh *Amer. Pol. Terms* 178: Mrs. C. made an extemporary screen by hanging...[a sheet or garment] on a rope or grape vine stretched near our quarters.] **1925** Mullin *Scholar Tramp* 172 [ref. to *ca*1912]: Subsequently I learned that stealing clothes from a clothes-line is expressed in Hoboland by the hilarious phrase, "glomming the grape-vine." *****1934** (cited in Partridge *DSUE* (ed. 8) 495).

grapevine *v.* to transmit (news) by the GRAPEVINE, 1; rumor.
1932 L. Berg *Prison Doctor* 106: At least so it was "grapevined." **1976** *Nat. Lampoon* (June) 26: It has been grapevined that [they] have been denounced...as mere university wits.

grapevine cinch *n.* an absolute certainty.
1891 (quot. at CINCH, *n.*).

grapevine dispatch *n. Army.* a rumor.
1864 in C.W. Wills *Army Life* 305: The "spring or grapevine" dispatch said that Hardee's headquarters were in Marietta. **1864** in T. Jones *Letters* 164: Grapevine dispatches are plenty. **1868** in *DA*: Major-General Thomas is no sensationalist; he is not given to grape-vine despatches. **1887** Hinman *Si Klegg* 460 [ref. to Civil War]: "Grapevine dispatches" was the name given to the wild, sensational rumors that were always circulating through the army.

grapevine telegram *n. Army.* GRAPEVINE DISPATCH.
1865 (quot. at GRAPE, 1).

grapevine telegraph *n.* **1.** GRAPEVINE, 1.a.
1852 in Sperber & Trittschuh *Amer. Pol. Dict.* 178: By the Grape Vine Telegraph Line...we have received the news. **1862** (quot. at GRAPEVINE, *n.*, 1.a.). **1886** Johnson *Soldier's Reminiscences* 50: The post sutler received the same information by the "GrapeVine Telegraph." **1889–90** Barrère & Leland *Dict. Slang* I 425: During the [Civil] war exciting accounts of battles not fought and of victories not won were said to have been conveyed by *grape-vine* (or clothesline) *telegraph*..., but the term was in earlier use, meaning news conveyed in a mysterious manner. **1901** B.T. Washington *Up from Slavery* 32 [ref. to Civil War]: These discussions showed that they understood the situation, and that they kept themselves informed of events by what was termed the "grape-vine" telegraph. **1914** Wyeth *Sabre & Scalpel* 144: The open platform in front of the doctor's drug-store...served...as the post-office and headquarters of the "grapevine telegraph." **1932** Daly *Not Only War* 59 [ref. to 1918]: "Damn! Whar'd yo' get that frum boy?" asked the sergeant enthusiastically. "Grape-vine telegraph." **1941** Cruse *Apache Days* 172: His Indians were in touch with Apache affairs by a sort of grapevine telegraph, and they would talk to him. **1970** L. Johnson *Devil's Front Porch* 59: It might be said that I was a roving reporter for the miner's edition of the "grapevine telegraph."

2. *Army.* GRAPEVINE, 1.b.
1864 in Chamberlayne *Virginian* 255: Rumours the soldiers call grapevine telegraphs and canteen dispatches.

grapevine wireless *n.* GRAPEVINE TELEGRAPH, 1.
1930 Lavine *3d Degree* 173: The grapevine wireless usually informed the inspector how the political boss stood in with...the powers that be.

grapey *adj.* [orig. unkn.] irritated or annoyed.
1866 *Night Side of N.Y.* 74: If a ball...was advertised when Dick was obliged to use crutches, it made him decidedly "grapey."

graph *n. Journ.* a paragraph.
1974 in H.S. Thompson *Shark Hunt* 391: And in the first graph of the story he sees the name of E. Howard Hunt...and a few graphs lower...is Gordon Liddy's name. **1978** Hamill *Dirty Laundry* 98: Keep all the stories to three graphs. **1982** in "J.B. Briggs" *Drive-In* 67: Wait until you hear the last two graphs. **1983** P. Dexter *God's Pocket* 217: "Gimme two paragraphs."..."Okay,...two graphs." **1983** R. Thomas *Missionary* 98: Second graph: "A member of the Office of Strategic Services in World War II [etc.]." **1985** Sawislak *Dwarf* 2: "Insert a graf"..."hold for release." **1993** *Village Voice* (Aug. 24) 9: The story broke nationally last week...(*The Washington Post* ran a 19-graph story on August 12th).

grapnel *n.* usu. *pl. Naut.* a finger.
1851 Melville *Moby Dick* ch. ii: With anxious grapnels I had sounded my pocket, and only brought up a few pieces of silver.

grapples *n.pl.* the hands; clutches.
1866 Williams *Gay Life in NY* 13: The next time you come to town, keep your own grapples on your baggage! *****1877** in *F & H* III 195: Anything she once put her grapples on she slipped inside.

grappling *n. Naut.* GRAPPLING HOOK.
1904 *Independent* (June 23) 1432: I seized his eager, outstretched grappling and we shook. **1921** in J.H. Williams *Blow the Man Down* [ref. to 1880's]: I...vowed that if ever I got my grapplings on him again I would make short work of him.

grappling hook *n.* usu. *pl.* a finger or hand.
*****a1890–93** *F & H* III 195: The fingers...*grappling-hooks.* **1901** *Univ. of Tennessee Volunteer* 189: Shall I take up each upstart fish and wring his neck with these two grappling hooks of mine...? **1905** Dey *Scylla* 61: Warp up alongside an' throw out your grapplin' hooks.

grappling irons *n.pl.* **1.** the fingers, hands, or arms; clutches.
*****1826** "Blackmantle" *Eng. Spy* 185: Seizing fast hold of my single fin with both of his grappling irons. **1845** Corcoran *Pickings* 113: He is sure to lay his grappling irons on me and take me...to the watch house. *****1860** Hotten *Slang Dict.* (ed. 2): *Grappling irons,* the fingers.—*Sea.* **1969** *Current Slang* I & II 43: *Grappling irons,* n. arms.—Air Force Academy cadets.

2. *West.* spurs.
1922 Rollins *Cowboy* 116 [ref. to *ca*1890]: Each spur, or "grappling iron," as slang often dubbed it.

grass *n.* **1.** green vegetables; salad. *Joc.*
*****1867** Smyth *Sailor's Wd. Bk.* 347: *Grass.*—Green vegetables. *****a1890–93** *F & H* III 195: *Grass*...(Royal Military Academy)...Vegetables. **1935** Pollock *Und. Speaks: Grass,* vegetables. **1935** in *AS* (Feb. 1936) 43: *Grass.* Lettuce. **1942** *Leatherneck* (Nov.) 146: *Grass*—Salad. Also known as rabbit food. **1943** Hersey *G.I. Laughs* 171: *Grass,* salad. **1942–46** Michigan State Univ. folklore archives 29: "Grass or hay"—Lettuce or salad.

2. the hair of the head; (*also*) the pubic hair; in phr. **cut the grass** to cut or trim hair or whiskers. *Joc.*
*****1919** Downing *Digger Dialects* 56 [ref. to WWI]: *Grass*—Hair. **1928** in Read *Lexical Evidence* 56: And on her belly I'de put a sign/Keep off the grass the hole is mine. **1938** "Justinian" *Amer. Sexualis* 22: *Grass.* n. The pubic hair, usually of the female. **1944** Burley *Hndbk. Jive* 139: *Grass*—short hair. **1960** *Perry Mason* (CBS-TV): Come in, I'll cut the grass. **1963** Walnut Ridge, Ark., teenager (coll. J. Ball): Guess I'll go cut the old grass. **1969** Pharr *Numbers* 114 [ref. to 1930's]: God sure gave me a break when he passed out the grass. **1970** Winick & Kinsie *Lively Commerce* 87: One of the New York prostitutes had the inscription "Keep Off the Grass" [tattooed] above her pubic hair.

3. *Narc.* marijuana.
1938 (cited in Spears *Drugs & Drink* 231). **1943** *Time* (July 19) 54: Marihuana may be called...grass. **1946** Mezzrow & Wolfe *Really Blues* 183: He picks up on some good grass. **1952** in W.S. Burroughs *Letters* 136: I had asked him to keep the grass. **1957** Margulies *Punks* 182: How you like we smoke some grass, Juan? **1958** Gilbert *Vice Trap* 11: There wasn't time to eat the grass Lona and I were smoking. **1961** B. Wolfe *Magic of Their Singing* 38: I've got to let them know we're coming. So they'll have some of that good and gassifying grass waiting for us. **1963** Braly *Shake Him* 95: But why waste grass? **1972** Singer *Boundaries* 127: She was...getting stoned on grass every weekend. **1977** in Mack *Real Life* (unp.): Shmuck! Can't you tell good grass when you smell it? **1983** *Time* (Jan. 3) 26: Staff brainstorming sessions were fueled with generous quantities of grass. **1993** *Village Voice* (N.Y.C.) (June 22) 30: As habits go, grass is a pet jones.

¶ In phrases:

¶ **ass is grass** see S.V. ASS, *n.*

¶ **go to grass, 1.** to be knocked down or sent sprawling.
*****a1625** Beaumont & Fletcher, in *OED*: Away, good Sampson; you go to grass else instantly. **1859** Holmes *Prof.* 279: He tripped and "went to grass." **1878** [P.S. Warne] *Hard Crowd* 10: The Red Hand went to grass like a thousand o' brick! **1893** *Small Comic History* 22: During this preparatory scrimmaging, King Philip and several other big Injuns went to grass and gave up the business of fighting entirely. *****1894** in *OED*: I naturally went to grass through having too much steam on to be able to pull up in time. **1899** Hamblen *Bucko Mate* 52: I shoved a Norwegian through the door, and as he went to grass, I sprang lightly out.

2. to go to the devil; (*hence*) go away; get out.—usu. imper.
1807 in Thornton *Amer. Gloss.*: Now he will have to go to grass, as the saying is. **1821** Waln *Hermit in Phila.* 25: Now you may *go to grass*.

1843 in *DAE*: Go to grass, Thimbles! I wish't you hurry on with that. **1848** Durivage & Burnham *Stray Sub.* 95: A gentleman…declared that he might go to grass with his old canoe, for he didn't think it would be much of a shower, anyhow. **1848** in *AS* (1935) 42: Go to grass. Be off. **1859** Hotten *Slang Dict.*: *Go to grass!*, a common answer to a troublesome or inquisitive person. **1877** Bartlett *Amer.* (ed. 4) 256: *Go to Grass!* Be off! Get out! "Stop your nonsense,—tell that to the marines." **1903** *Pedagog. Sem.* X 371: Rebuke to Pride…"Go to grass." **1905** Belasco *Girl of Golden West* 361: You go to grass. **1928** Bodenheim *Georgie May* 24: Oh, let him go to grass—ah'm not begging from no man. **1938–43** Stegner *Big Rock Candy Mtn.* 79: "Oh, go to grass," Ella said. **1958** P. Field *Devil's R.* 33: "Oh, go to grass!" the little man growled.

¶ **hunt grass** to be knocked down.
1871 "M. Twain" *Roughing It* 252: When you get in with your left, I hunt grass every time.

¶ **push up the grass** see s.v. PUSH, *v.*

¶ **send to grass** *Boxing.* to knock down; send sprawling.
1868 *Galaxy* (Oct.) 557: Mulhalbully came up groggy, and was caught by the Little 'Un with a nasty one on the right peeper, which sent him to grass. **1870** *Putnam's Mag.* (Mar.) 301: Knocking the unfortunate knocker off his pins…to say nothing of…sending him to grass. **1875** A.F. Hill *Sanctum* 49: He "squared away" at his assailant and…"sent him to grass." **1887** DeVol *40 Yrs. a Gambler* 10: He hit me another lick in the nose that came very near sending me to grass. *ca*1888 *Stag Party* 174: An Irishman, watching a game of base-ball, was sent to grass by a foul.

grass *v.* **1.** *Orig. Boxing.* to knock down; throw to the ground; (*hence*) to astonish; floor.
1814 in *OED*: A terrific blow on the mouth, which floored or grassed him. **1819** [T. Moore] *Tom Crib* 57: The shame that aught but death should see him *grassed.* **1818** in *F & H* III 195: He had much the worst of it, and was ultimately grassed. **1848** C. Dickens *Dombey* 597: He was severely fibbed and heavily grassed. **1864** in *OED*: He…fell head foremost into the pit of Professor Sharp's stomach, grassing him at once. **1870** *Putnam's Mag.* (Mar.) 301: I couldn't have been more completely grassed.*…*Prostrated. **1877** Burdette *Mustache* 261: He struck her on the head…dropping her; "grassed the old lady", Master Bilderbeck afterward explained to his sister. **1906** *Nat. Police Gaz.* (Oct. 6) 7: The supreme bliss of "grassing" an opponent.
2. *Hunting.* to bring down with a shot; kill.
1871 in *OED*: The excitement of grassing blue rocks. **1881** in *F & H* III 195: The Doctor had killed twenty out of twenty-five, while his opponent had grassed seventeen out of the same number. **1889** O'Reilly & Nelson *Fifty Years on Trail* 81: I killed and scalped my first Ute in one of these scrimmages. I had frequently grassed Indians before, but my fancy had never taken the form of scalp-lifting.

grass-clipper *n.* GRASS-CUTTER, 1.
1868 in *DAS*: Wright goes to first base on his short grass-clipper to center field.

grass-cutter *n.* **1.** *Baseball & Golf.* a hard-hit ball that skims the top of the grass.
1887 (cited in Nichols *Baseball Term.* 31). **1908** in Fleming *Unforget. Season* 247: Devlin…was forced at second by McCormick's grass cutter. **1952** Malamud *Natural* 178: Allie Stubbs chopped a grass cutter through a hole in the infield for a single. **1970** Scharff *Encyc. of Golf* 417: *Grasscutter.* A hard-hit ball, traveling low and skimming the grass.
2. *Mil.* (see 1930 quot.). Cf. DAISY-CUTTER.
1925 Bullard *Personalities & Reminiscences* 188 [ref. to 1918]: His "grass-cutters"—a light bomb for use against men and animals—could be heard crashing far and wide over the sector as our wagons and men moved to the forward positions at night. **1930** Brophy & Partridge *Songs & Slang* 128 [ref. to WWI]: Grass-cutters.—Small bombs dropped by aeroplanes on camps and bivouacs behind the lines, bursting on hitting the ground and scattering shrapnel pellets at low level, i.e. to kill rather than to destroy material things. **1942** *Leatherneck* (Dec.) 54 [ref. to 1918]: They were low,…so they threw over a few "grasscutters" (contact bombs).

grass-cutting *n. Av.* (see quot.).
1956 Heflin *USAF Dict.* 234: *Grass cutting.* Flying just above the ground and following the contours of the earth…*Slang.*

grass-eater *n. Police.* a police officer who engages in petty graft of any kind. Cf. MEAT-EATER.
1972 *N.Y. Times Mag.* (Dec. 17) 42: According to the Knapp Commission, there are two kinds of crooked cops: "grasseaters," who take what minor graft comes their way but don't make any particular effort to get

it, and "meat-eaters," who go all out for the buck. **1974** *N.Y. Post* (Oct. 3) 1: The grasseaters are…cooperating fully….The meateaters are going to get the full blame. **1986** Philbin *Under Cover* 102: In this precinct comprising psychos, drunks, other grass-eaters, a few meat-eaters, old guys, and guys who had just angered the brass. **1990** Murano & Hoffer *Cop Hunter* 186: "Grass eaters"…take whatever freebies…come their way…."meat eaters"…actively seek ways to make extra cash with little or no regard for legal and moral implications.

grass-eating *n. Police.* the solicitation or acceptance by a police officer of petty bribes; petty graft of any kind by a police officer.
1986 Philbin *Under Cover* 37: Edmunton…had been assigned there for "grass-eating"—petty thievery that couldn't be proved.

grasshead *n.* a habitual user of marijuana.
1968 H. Ellison *Deadly Streets* 103: He was a righteous grasshead. **1971** *Playboy* (Dec.) 14: Grassheads should be left alone to toke up in peace.

grasshopper *n.* **1.** *Av.* (see 1956 quot.).
1941 in *Pop. Science* (Jan. 1942) 63: Grasshoppers…that's what the army calls its new odd-job planes. **1942** *Yank* (Aug. 12) 2: "Grasshopper"…small, low-powered observation planes. **1952** Geer *New Breed* 13: Two days later Valentine was back flying his "grasshopper" armed with "twin thirty-eights"—thirty-eight caliber pistols he and his observer carried. **1956** Heflin *USAF Dict.* 234: *Grasshopper*…any small, light, cabin monoplane used for observation, liaison, or training. **1961** Crane *Born of Battle* 113: At daylight, we'll send a grasshopper up to look for them.
2. *Narc. & Police.* a habitual smoker of marijuana.
1948 (cited in Abel *Marihuana Dict.* 46). **1963** Braly *Shake Him* 27: What's shaking, Daddy-O? You catch yourself some poor grasshopper? **1967** Rosevear *Pot* 158: *Grasshopper:* An obsolete word for a marihuana smoker. **1971** S. Stevens *Way Uptown* 131: I been a grasshopper a long time now. **1973** Wambaugh *Onion Field* 67: He became a stone grass-hopper.
¶ In phrase:

¶ **knee-high to a grasshopper** see s.v. KNEE-HIGH.

grassie *n. Firefighting.* a grass fire.
1983 Stapleton *30 Yrs.* 186: He's got a couple of grassies down there, maybe he can call them in to Fire Alarm.

grass sandwich *n.* an act of copulation on the grass in a secluded spot.
*ca*1915 in Turan & Zito *Sinema* 4: The Grass Sandwich. **1942** Sanders & Blackwell *Forces* 164: *Get a Grass Sandwich:* To copulate. **1952** Sandburg *Strangers* 168 [ref. to *a*1920]: They told of a young fellow saying to his girl, "Let's go to the picnic and after sundown we'll have a grass sandwich."

grassville *n. Und.* rural areas.
1859 Matsell *Vocab.* 39: *Grassville.* The country.

grating *n.* ¶ In phrase: **dance a grating hornpipe** *Navy.* to be flogged at a ship's grating.
1841 [Mercier] *Man-of-War* 127: If I'd got catched, my doom was certain—/They'd make me a *grating hornpipe* dance.

graum *v.* to worry; complain. Cf. GRAUMS.
1956 in *DAS*: All a bookmaker graums about is they don't drop a [*sic*] atom bomb on top of New York and kill all the horse players. That's all a bookmaker worries about.

graums *n.pl.* [orig. unkn.] low spirits; blues.—constr. with *the.*
1952 *Park East* (Sept.) 20: O.L. was in Nicky's with the graums last night. **1971** in Cannon *Nobody Asked* 198: Soldiers never talk about the graums a chick gives them…Overseas, every chick is Raquel Welch.

gravedigger *n. West.* a dangerous horse.
1922 Rollins *Cowboy* 146: From the side-lines came…comments such as "froliceome little beast," "real hunk o' death," and "cutey, little grave-digger."

gravel *n. Esp. Pris.* granulated sugar available at a mess table. See also GRAVEL TRAIN, 3.
1926 *Writer's Mo.* (Dec.) 541: *Gravel*—Sugar.
¶ In phrases:

¶ **get gravel for (one's) goose** *So.* to engage in copulation.
1938 in Randolph *Pissing in Snow* 11: There was a drummer wanted some gravels for his goose, but he couldn't find nothing only a girl named Lizzie that worked in the tavern. **1952** Randolph & Wilson *Down in the Holler* 110: Many expressions and allusions link the noun

gravel with sexual contact. Ask a hillman where he is going and he replies, "To git some *gravels* for my goose," meaning that he is in search of sexual satisfaction. **1959** in IUFA *Folk Speech*: To want "some gravel for your goose" is to want to engage in sexual intercourse. **1976** Univ. Tenn. student: Gettin' any gravel for your goose?…I mean, gettin' laid. That's a colloquial expression. **1984** Wilder *You All* 97: Get gravel for *your goose*: Satisfy sexual appetite.

¶ **scratch** [or **dig** or **throw**] **gravel** to go or leave at top speed; hurry; (in 1898 quot.) to work hard for a living.
1834 in *DA* s.v. *scratch*: I thought I'd go home—and so I *scratched gravel* for Tennessee. **1861** E.S. Ellis *N. Todd* 57: They've got to dig gravel fast to overtake me in this race. **1875** Sheppard *Love Afloat* 351: Now, sah, we got to scratch grabbel. **1887** Hinman *Si Klegg* 100: Ye wants ter scratch gravel, 'cause the comp'ny is formin'. **1898** Westcott *David Harum* ch. xxv: Till I was consid'able older'n you be I had to scratch grav'l like all possessed. **1908** Raine *Wyoming* 89: If y'u take my advice, you'll throw gravel lively. **1909** in McCay *Little Nemo* 167: Keep right on scratchin' gravel! **1914** Ellis *Billy Sunday* 206: While you are scratching gravel to make one lap, your boy makes ten. **1967** Lit Dictionary 51: *Scratch Gravel*—Split quickly. **1972** Madden *Bros.* 155: I scratched gravel to catch up with Mr. French.

gravel agitator *n. Army.* an infantryman.—used derisively.
1898 in Tisdale *Behind the Guns* 277: The "gravel agitators" [soldiers] nursed the thought all the way out here that we were unable to do anything until they came to show us how. **1910** Runyon *Tents* 86: Gravel agitators on a long, hard hike—/Hep! **1919** Witt *Riding* 159: Gravel-agitators, fall in. **1933** *Winners of the West* (Feb. 28) 4: It might be of interest to the Comrades of the Indian Wars to learn of a most wonderful turkey dinner provided for the "Old Canary Birds" and their gravel agitator comrades… **1945** Rossen *Walk in the Sun* (film): All right, you gravel-agitators, let's go. **1945** Hamann *Air Words* s.v.: *Gravel agitator.* Infantryman; non-flying person. *Synonyms:* Ground gripper, dust eater, paddlefoot, blisterfoot. **1968** W.C. Anderson *Gooney Bird* 140: Don't they teach you gravel agitators nothin' in the Special Forces school?

gravel-cruncher *n. Mil. Av.* a person in military service who is not an aviator.—used derisively. Hence **gravel-crunching**, *adj.*
1929 *Our Army* (Feb.) 6: I might as well just pack myself off to some gravel-crunching doughboy outfit. **1945** in *AS* (Dec. 1946) 310: *Gravel cruncher.* A desk officer in the Air Corps. **1958** Camerer *Damned Wear Wings* 66: He was being cut out for…a gravel cruncher in the Air Force. **1976** Conroy *Santini* 439: You're not bad for a gravel cruncher, Captain. **1985** Yeager & Janos *Yeager* 52: Those damned gravel-crunchers back at the base already had their lunch. **1988** Hynes *Flights of Passage* 208: Our own Marine infantrymen were…called Gravel-crunchers or Crunchies.

gravel-crusher *n. Army.* an infantryman.—used derisively.
[***1889** Barrère & Leland *Dict. Slang* I 426: *Gravel-crusher* (military), a soldier compelled to tramp about a square at defaulter's drill.] **1918** W.R. Jones *Fighting the Hun* 123: Good old "gravel crushers," we were…proud of you that day. *Ibid.* 170: "Hello, you gravel crushers," we called to them. **1928** Harrison *Generals Die in Bed* 232 [ref. to 1918]: God, who would've thought that plain gravel-crushers like us would ever get rich pickin's like this. **1930** *Our Army* (Jan.) 47: Gravel-crushers. **1942** Colby *Army Talk* 95: *Gravel crushers*…long used in both British and American armies, especially by mounted troops. **1991** Reinberg *In the Field* 96 [ref. to Vietnam War]: *Gravel crusher*…infantryman.

gravel-grinder *n. Army.* an infantryman; (hence) USAF. a non-aviator.—used derisively.
***a1890–96** *F & H* IV 374: An infantryman…*gravel-grinder*. **1942** Colby *Army Talk* 147: Close to the plain gravel grinder where heavier guns never go,/You will find us, the one-pounder section, taking our part in the show. *ca*1964 K. Cook *Other Capri* 46 [ref. to WWII]: I'd like to see that paddlefooted gravelgrinder fly an airplane.

gravel-pounder *n. Army.* an infantryman.—used derisively.
1980 S. Fuller *Big Red* 52 [ref. to WWII]: It could fit any gravel pounder in the First Division.

gravel-pusher *n. Army.* an infantryman.—used derisively.
1955 F.K. Franklin *Combat Nurse* 120 [ref. to WWII]: The town's full of…MP's just waiting to spoil a gravel-pusher's fun! *Ibid.* 167: Gravel-pushers come a dime a dozen.

gravel-rattler *n. Army.* an infantryman.—used derisively.
1972 Meade & Rutledge *Belle* 162: "Gravel rattlers," Wheelright said derisively, with the age old contempt of the airman for the foot soldier.

gravel-scratcher *n. Army.* an infantryman.—used derisively.

1969 Cray *Erotic Muse* 147: A gravel-scratcher's specific protest against the indignities of war.

gravel train *n.* **1.** (see quot.).
1863 in *Ala. Review* X (1957) 149: The trip was…refreshing to us who were accustomed to travel on the "gravel train" as the boys term the Virginia turnpike roads.
2. *Und.* (see quot.).
1908 Sullivan *Crim. Slang* 11: *Gravel-train*—The go-between of lobbyists who buys up legislators.
3. [fr. GRAVEL, *n.*] a sugar bowl. Also **gravel wagon**.
1935 E. Levinson *Strikes* 179 [ref. to 1916]: The sugar bowl was "the gravel wagon." **1936** *AS* (Feb.) 43: *Gravel train.* Sugar bowl.

gravel-walloper *n. Army.* an infantryman.—used derisively.
1907 *McClure's* (Feb.) 379: I recollect the time you first took on—Plattesburg, '97, wasn't it? I had an idea then that you came from the state gravel wallopers.

grave rat *n. Stu.* a medical student.
1850 in H.C. Lewis *Works* 121: I was sauntering over the city and amusing myself with the many strange sights which pass unnoticed by the denizens, yet have such an attraction for the "grave rat" just emerged from the country.

graveyard *n.* **1.** GRAVEYARD SHIFT. Also as adj., adv.
1908 (quot. at GRAVEYARD SHIFT). **1918** *DN* V 25: *Graveyard,* n. The shift that goes into the tunnel at midnight or at two o'clock. "The *graveyard* hasn't gone in yet." Coeur d'Alenes. **1938** Smitter *Detroit* 174: It got started on the graveyard—last night. **1972** Haslam *Oil Fields* 104: *Graveyard,* n. A seldom used expression for the shift from midnight to 8 a.m. Also [called]…Hoot Owl. **1978** Alibrandi *Killshot* 8: Walt on graveyard had been robbed twice in six months. **1978** Diehl *Sharky's Machine* 201: The graveyard man takes over from ten to six in the A.M. **1978** Strieber *Wolfen* 157: I'm not on duty. I'm graveyard tonight. **1979** Hiler *Monkey Mt.* 230: I'm on graveyard, remember? **1980** in McCauley *Dark Forces* 226: You can't get his truck until morning. Ron's working graveyard tonight. **1982** Kingsport, Tenn., man, age 28: I'd work the day shift for a week, then get two or three days off and come back and work graveyard. **1988** *Larry King Live* (CNN-TV) (July 27): I was a working mother…I worked graveyard.
2. *Bowling.* a lane or set of lanes that consistently yields low scores.
1949 Cummings *Dict. Sports* 185: *Graveyard*…A defective (therefore difficult) alley. **1980** Pearl *Pop. Slang*: *Graveyard* n. [Bowling] a lane in which it is difficult to score. **1982** Considine *Lang. Sport* 88.
3. the least desirable, usu. least used seats in a restaurant.
1984 T. Wolfe, in *Rolling Stone* (Aug. 16) 18: Do you have any idea where they would put "Mrs. Bradshaw" and her party…? Back there in the graveyard, by the kitchen.

graveyard juice *n.* whiskey. *Joc.*
1947–53 Guthrie *Seeds* 383: You deserve another…slug…of graveyard juice.

graveyard shift *n. Labor.* a late-night work shift beginning about midnight and continuing until about 8 a.m. Also adv.
1907 in *DA*: It was the graveyard gamblers' shift…The small hours of the morning. **1908** in Butterfield *Post Treasury* 92: A month later he and his fellows went on "graveyard" shift. "Graveyard" is the interval between twelve midnight, and eight in the morning. **1920** *DN* V 82: *Graveyard shift.* A shift in the shipyards from midnight to seven a.m. **1923** in Kornbluh *Rebel Voices* 92: Andy and I came on the Graveyard shift together. **1926** *AS* II (Nov.) 88: The miner's working day is divided into three eight-hour shifts, known respectively as "daylight," "four o'clock," and "graveyard." **1928** Wharton *Squad* 82: Comin' off de graveyard shift back at de mines. **1930** "D. Stiff" *Milk & Honey* 206: *Graveyard shift*—Night work, usually in the small hours. **1933** J. Conroy *Disinherited* 112: The "graveyard" shift from midnight till eight in the morning. **1936** R. Adams *Cowboy Lingo* 114: The "graveyard shift" came at one A.M. **1974** *Playboy* (Feb.) 60: I worked for Bethlehem Steel on the graveyard shift, in front of a furnace. **1977** Garrity *Canal* 17: The first time I heard the expression "graveyard shift," it was from canal men [*ca*1910]. **1981** *N.Y. Daily News* (*Tonight*) (June 18) M3: Liz and I worked graveyard shift at the Bagel. **1984** Kagan & Summers *Mute Evidence* 86: The graveyard radio shift was not new to either of us. **1985** *WINS Radio News* (Dec. 21): A sanitation spokesman says the graveyard shift is making sure that all streets are salted and sanded. **1992** *Melrose Place* (Fox-TV): I've got the graveyard shift tonight.

graveyard stew *n.* (among tramps) warm milk and toast.
1911 *DN* III 544: *Graveyard stew*…Bread and milk stew. **1930** "D

Stiff" *Milk & Honey* 206: *Graveyard stew*—Hot milk and toast. **1958** *Sing Out!* (Summer) 30: Hamhocks and bumblebees…Graveyard stews and stacks of wheats.

graveyard tour *n.* Esp. *Petroleum Industry.* GRAVEYARD SHIFT.
1928 in Botkin *Amer. Folklore* 225: The word [*sc. tour*] is pronounced "tower" [in Texas], and means a shift of men…The tower that goes on at midnight is the "graveyard tower." **1942** *ATS* 259: *Graveyard tour*: a shift from midnight to 8 A.M. **1966** "T. Pendleton" *Iron Orchard* 91: Now it just so happens that yours truly is acquainted with a roughneck on the graveyard tour on that well.

graveyard watch *n. Naut.* the midnight watch.
1895 in Tisdale *Behind the Guns* 28: I am to stand the first lookout in the graveyard watch. **1930** Buranelli *Maggie* 57 [ref. to 1918]: The graveyard watch is not so bad if you have someone to talk to. **1932** Pagano *Bluejackets* 85 [ref. to 1926]: The twelve to four watch, termed by us the "Graveyard watch." **1976** Hayden *Voyage* 174: Last night, in…the graveyard watch. **1992** Oringer & Torme *Intruders* (CBS-TV): I was standing the graveyard watch at the back of the base.

gravy *n.* **1.** the male or female sexual discharge.
***a*1796** R. Burns *Merry Muses* [1965 ed.] 68: Again he wan atweesh my thies,/And, splash!, gaed out his gravy. ***a*1890–93** *F & H* III 198: *Gravy*…The sexual discharge; the *spendings* (q.v.) both male and female….*to give one's gravy*, to spend. **1934** "J.M. Hall" *Anecdota* 177: "Gobbling the gravy,"…*cunnilingus*. **1938** "Justinian" *Amer. Sexualis* 24: *Gravy.* n. The sexual discharge of either sex. ***1978** in Partridge *DSUE* (ed. 8) 497: *Going down for the gravy*…Fellatio or cunnilingus.
2. *Theat.* an easy role, esp. in low comedy. [The precise sense of the 1864 quot. is unclear.]
***1864** in *OEDS*: The farce…was gone through with equal rapidity—of course, all the "points" were carefully given, "cartfuls of beefsteaks and bucketsful of gravy" especially. **1923** *N.Y. Times* (Sept. 9) VIII 2: *Gravy*: Easy lines to get over; surefire hokum. *Ibid.* (Oct. 7) VIII 4: *Gravy*—Comedy with a suggestion of the improper. ***1952** W. Granville *Theat. Terms* 92: *Gravy.* Easy laughs from a friendly audience. (2) Good lines, or business, in a farce or comedy.
3. *Boxing.* blood, esp. from the nose.
1870 *Putnam's Mag.* (Mar.) 301: The combatants struck each other…upon…the nose…drawing the blood, the claret,…the gravy. **1885** S.S. Hall *Gold Buttons* 7: He might give a signal that would spill our gravy.
4. a person or thing of excellence; the best.—usu. constr. with *the.*
1908 in "O. Henry" *Works* 272: He is some gravy on delivering himself of audible sounds relating to matters and conclusions. *ca*1921 Sandburg *Sunburnt West* 7: Tell each other you're all to the mustard—/ You're the gravy,…tops. **1942** *ATS* 22: Most superior; the best…*the dandy,… gravy,…tops. Ibid.* 30: Something excellent…*gravy,…peach.*
5.a. profit or benefit, esp. if unexpectedly or easily obtained. Cf. GRAVY TRAIN.
1910 *Sat. Eve. Post* (July 30) 13: Stick him for all you can. You're a hard worker, and you mustn't let somebody else git the gravy. **1917** in Clover *Suzanne's* 224: If I can only get in at the first I can "hop the gravy" for fair. The gravy being a good commission and the better chance for promotion. **1923** Ornitz *Haunch, Paunch & Jowl* 55: He's been getting the gravy out of all their jobs. ***1927** Shay *Pious Friends* 56: It's the rich what gets the grivy,/Aynt it all a bleedin' shime? **1929** W.R. Burnett *Iron Man* 39: It'll cost us like hell and Mike'll take all the gravy. **1931** Dos Passos *1919* 151: What do you think of that for the gravy, Joe? **1933** Halper *Union Sq.* 172: You'll be making gravy from both ends then. **1940** Hartney *Up & At 'Em* 108: But not everything was "ham and gravy." **1950** F. Brown *Space on Hands* 105: Sector Two gets all the gravy and Sector Three gets all the work. **1952** Ephron *What Price Glory* (film): Now you're fightin' for the Navy,/And the sailors get the gravy. **1972** Kopp *Buddha* 116: The results turned out to be spectacular, but that was just gravy as far as I was concerned. **1992** N. Cohn *Heart of World* 15: All the rest be gravy.
b. money, esp. if easily or illicitly obtained.
1930 Irwin *Tramp & Und. Sl.*: *Gravy*…Any unearned, easily acquired money. **1932** in *OEDS*: Sixty grand…was pretty good gravy. **1934** *Journalism Qly.* (Dec.) 349: *Gravy*—money. **1933–35** D. Lamson *About to Die* 201: Why should he be a sucker…when there's all that gravy goin' around? **1944** Kapelner *Lonely Boy Blues* 45: I wonder what will happen to that blonde and her pooch when her lovers run out of gravy? **1951–52** Frank *Hold Back Night* 37: "Milt, he stayed in the reserve. Maybe he wanted that Navy gravy." The Marine Corps reservists got their checks from the Navy Department. **1955** Puzo *Dark Arena* 71: I

guess everybody in the occupation has a little hunk of gravy. **1979** Crews *Blood & Grits* 109: It was heavy gravy, at least a couple of hundred thousand dollars worth of boxcar.

¶ In phrases:

¶ **by gravy!** by heavens!—used as a mild oath. Also (esp. in recent use) **good gravy!**
1831 in *DA*: By gravy! I'll get up early to-morrow morning! **1847** in G.W. Harris *High Times* 71: No, by gravy! *a*1855 in *DA*: Good gravy, but don't they? **1860** E. Ellis *Bill Biddon* 55: I'm sick of this, by gravy! ***1892** in Partridge *DSUE* (ed. 8) 497: By gravy! **1928** Levin *Reporter* 196: Good gravy! Were all of them insensible! **1929** "E. Queen" *Roman Hat* ch. xv 164: Good gravy, are you dumb or what? **1959** in *DARE*: By gravy!…Rare. **1962** T. Berger *Reinhart in Love* 176: Good gravy, I've got to be home by twelve. **1966–70** in *DARE*. **1986** N.Y.C. woman, age *ca*50: Good gravy!

¶ **ride the gravy** ride the gravy train s.v. GRAVY TRAIN.
1917 in Bowerman *Compensations* 26: Hap, Ted, and Van Doran…left for Paris to join Section 64…they may "ride some gravy." **1918** in Rossano *Price of Honor* 146: Who accused Bob of riding the gravy? **1921** Benét *Beginning of Wisdom* 86 [ref. to 1914]: I've been ruined all my life by my friends' riding [the] gravy. **1967** E. Wilson *Prelude* 125 [ref. to 1916]: Ride the gravy.

gravy *adj.* **1.** (of a job or the like) easy; CUSHY.
1917 in Bowerman *Compensations* 27: I…spend the whole day unloading wooden barrack sections from a freight car…It wasn't exactly a "gravy" job. **1919** *Our Navy* (May) 41: And you can tell the world it wasn't gravy making a twenty-one-day one-way trip in the winter of 1917 with the watch four on and four off. **1919** *307th Field Arty.* 140: This detail was "gravy," according to all reports. **1931** Springs *Carol Banks* 35: It ought to be gravy to shoot 'em down. **1932** L. Berg *Pris. Doctor* 262: A lot of us are sick of watching guys like that grafting politician grab off the gravy jobs while we sit around on our tails waiting for our time to finish. **1938** *AS* (Apr.) 156: *Gravy job.* A cinch. **1944** in *Amer. Jour. Socio.* LVII (1952) 431: Willie commented on my gravy job. **1963** Dwiggins *S.O. Bees* 181 [ref. to WWII]: Blackburn joined Killefer and Hogan on the "gravy run"—flying freelance top cover. **1965–68** E.R. Johnson *Silver St.* 19: He was an old-time cop, but one out of the gravy beats. Residential beats, where…major crime [was rare]. **1983** Flaherty *Tin Wife* 312: The gravy days of giving them a chance to [be let off easily]. **1990** Rukuza *W. Coast Turnaround* 19: That locks you out of most of the gravy jobs.
2. profitable or advantageous.
1937 in D. Runyon *More Guys* 219: The one-two…is considered quite a gravy punch if properly put on.

gravy boat *n.* GRAVY TRAIN.
1943 Lees & Rinaldo *Crazy House* (film): You will have to pay me a fee for letting you ride the gravy boat. **1948** Menjou & Musselman *Nine Tailors* 141: Once you get on the Hollywood gravy boat, it is no trick to make money…Imagine actors making $1,000, $5,000, $10,000 a week! **1966** "T. Pendleton" *Iron Orchard* 135: I already told you, you're wasting your time. Your girl friend's got the gravy boat. I got no money. **1981** *N.Y. Post* (Aug. 15) 3: Elvis' manager is kicked off the gravy boat.

gravy-eye *n. Naut.* (see quot.). Cf. GRAVEYARD SHIFT and related terms.
[***1889–90** Barrère & Leland *Dict. Slang* I 426: *Gravy eye*…a term rather loosely and unmeaningly applied as a derisive epithet—"Oh! you *gravy eye!* How much gravy does your mother put on your 'taters'?"] **1896** Hamblen *Many Seas* 41: The trick at the wheel from four to five A.M. is called the "gravy eye" because of its notorious tediousness…It is looking forward to this hot drink…that makes the "gravy eye" seem so awfully long….I do not know how the name "gravy eye" originated.

gravy-eyed *adj.* bleary-eyed.
***1785** Grose *Vulgar Tongue: Gravey eyed,* blear eyed, one whose eyes have a running humour. **1821** Waln *Hermit in Phila.* 27: A *hanger-on* to *bracket-faced, carrotty-pated, gravy-eyed ape-leaders!*

gravy hop *n. Mil. Av.* (see quot.).
1944 in Rea *Wings of Gold* 217: Yesterday I got in a "gravy hop," that is an extra flight.

gravy list *n. Sales.* a list of affluent potential customers.
1985 Univ. Tenn. grad. student, age 35: When I was a Bible salesman in West Virginia [in 1970], they had us make what they called *gravy lists.* A *gravy list* was a list of families who weren't home when you rang the doorbell. That suggested they both worked and had money to spend. You'd put them on the list and call again.

gravy-rider *n.* a person holding an easeful but profitable position.

1922 *Amer. Leg. Wkly.* (Oct. 6) 29: Even if the Chief was a boot and a gravy-rider, he was handy with his dukes. **1982** USAAF veteran, age *ca*60 [ref. to WWII]: *Gravy-riders* were nonflying support personnel, or anyone with a soft job and little responsibility.

gravy street *n.* a condition of ease, success, or profit; EASY STREET.

1977 *N.Y. Post* (Mar. 19) 3: This is gravy street for them.

gravy train *n.* a source or condition of excessive, esp. undeserved, ease, advantage, or profit; sinecure; in phr. **ride the gravy train** to exploit a source of easy profit or advantage.

1914 in Handy *Blues Treasury* 86: On Easy Street I felt no pain/But I fell off o' the gravy train. **1917** in Rossano *Price of Honor* 38: For once I'm riding the gravy train. **1918** in Clover *Suzanne's* 132: Those who weren't on a "gravy train" of any kind had to drill and stand guard or clean up. **1924** *Adventure* (June 20) 158: Now, if you want to ditch the gravy train, just fire a clip or two. **1926** *Sat. Eve. Post* (May 1) 125: Now this bird will sit down with us an' show off how he can talk French and the gravy train goes for a gool. **1926** Nason *Chevrons* 107: If the top comes along and sees us, he's liable to throw the gravy train in the ditch. **1927** *AS* II (Mar.) 276: *Gravy train*. Sinecure. **1933** *AS* (Feb.) 32: *Ride a gravy train*. To continue to receive more than one's deserts. **1943** Stuart *Pvt. Tussie* 55: Look what he makes from the state! He's on the gravy train! **1947** in *West. Folk.* vii (1948) 73: *Gravy train:* A rich girl friend. **1948** Lait & Mortimer *New York* 63: When the war ended, the "cheap-John" gravy train was over, too. **1949** Foreman *Champion* (film): We're in. We're on that gravy train and it's makin' no stops. **1961** *Twilight Zone* (CBS-TV): A sad-faced perennial punching-bag who missed the caboose of life's gravy train. **1964** Thompson & Rice *Every Diamond* 149: Should the gravy train be derailed, their plushy assignments would be finished. **1983** *Rolling Stone* (Feb. 3) 34: The Hollywood gravy train hasn't derailed. **1993** *CBS This Morning* (CBS-TV) (May 6): Why did the gravy train stop before it got to me?

gray *n. Black E.* a white person.—used contemptuously.

1944 Burley *Hndbk. Jive* 139: *Grey*—A white person, Nordic....*Grey who wouldn't play the game like it should be played*. **1944** (quot. at SPOOK, *n.*). **1950** L. Brown *Iron City* 107: Here comes this gray tipping up on me and he wants to know where he can get some trim. **1959–60** R. Reisner *Jazz Titans* 157: *Gray:* a white person. **1963** in Clarke *Amer. Negro Stories* 300: She asked one of the greys in the settin' room. **1970** A. Young *Snakes* 42: Some of these simple-ass grays. **1975** S.P. Smith *Amer. Boys* 101: And then a splib and a gray to it outside the post gate on New Year's Eve. **1967–80** Folb *Runnin' Lines* 240: *Gray*. White person.

gray *adj. Black E.* racially white.—used contemptuously. See also GRAYBOY, *n.*

1944 Burley *Hndbk. Jive* 139: *Grey*...Nordic. **1965** C. Brown *Manchild* 163: I came up to the cab, and he had two gray bitches in it. **1967** in T.C. Bambara *Gorilla* 69: I'm sitting in the storefront which is this gray lady, Miss Ruby, who came...to get us in jobs and stuff like that. **1969** B. Beckham *Main Mother* 160: I was married to a gray girl—Jewish. **1994** N. McCall *Wanna Holler* 40: As much as we claimed to hate white folks, we lived for the chance to bone a gray broad.

grayback *n.* **1.** (see quot.).

1829 in *DA:* [Professed Christians] have a number of names here [in Pennsylvania] as in other states, "Grey-backs, Round-heads, &c."

2. a louse.

1840 *Crockett Almanac 1841* 24: You'll find gray-backs enuff up in the Kalibuse. **1847** in Peskin *Vols.* 103: I had gotten a number of big grey backs [body lice] on my person. **1855** in Dwyer & Lingenfelter *Songs of Gold Rush* 72: I used unguentum once or twice,/But could not kill the grey-backs. **1862** in Davidson *Old West* 15: Graybacks brought the wearers to the scratch. **1862** in R.G. Carter *4 Bros.* 82: Vermin...the genuine and unmistakable "greyback." **1863** Hollister *Colo. Vols.* 28: Finding two hundred grey-backs on his shirt at one time. **1866** *Beadle's Mo.* (Oct.) 284: Certainly,...that is if you haven't any graybacks about you! **1885** Siringo *Texas Cowboy* 3: We boys...made an iron-clad rule that whoever was heard swearing or caught picking grey backs off and throwing them on the floor without first killing them should pay a fine of ten cents for each and every offense. **1899** Garland *Eagle's Heart* 93: They ain't got the sense of a grayback louse. **1901** Freeman *Soldier in Philippines* 22: These belligerents were known as "gray backs." *ca*1910–18 Hoyt *Buckskin Joe* 63: Here they washed us, gave us clean clothes, and got rid of our graybacks. **1930** "D. Stiff" *Milk & Honey* 203:

Lice...*gray backs* and *seam squirrels*. **1937** Steinbeck *Mice & Men* 20: Then how come he got graybacks? **1965–70** in *DARE:* Joking names for a head louse, or body louse...*Grayback.*

3.a. *Army.* a Confederate soldier. Now *hist.*

1862 in G. Whitman *Letters* 142: We could see the greybacks leaving there [*sic*] works and running through the woods. **1863** Galwey *Valiant Hours* 177: "Yank, why the hell didn't you charge yesterday?" "Go to hell, you Grayback S—s of B—s, you're damned glad we didn't." **1863** in Connolly *Army of the Cumberland* 77: Our men were hungry, and the broiled fish, fried eggs, broiled chickens, onions, warm biscuit &c, that the marauding "graybacks" had stolen from union citizens, soon disappeared. **1864** in Horrocks *Dear Parents* 80: The cry of our troops is like a regular English shout, but the Greybacks (or Rebels) make a noise like the howl of...a thousand dogs, or...the war-cry of so many Indians. **1864** Hill *Our Boys* 319: Old boy, I killed one d—d grayback! **1864** in Lyman *Meade's HQ* 94: "Ya-as, sir," said grey-back, and was marched to the rear. **1865** in *Civil War Hist.* IV 24: Graybacks were scarce as greenbacks from Atlanta to the sea. **1866** Brockett *Camp, Battle Field & Hospital* 169: I hadn't more'n got up fore a dirty grey-back, drunker'n a member uv Congress, staggered inter the tent. **1908** in J.I. Robertson *Blue & Gray* 142: It was no uncommon sight, when visiting the picket posts, to see an equal number of "graybacks" and "bluebellies," as they facetiously termed each other, enjoying a social game of euchre. **1957** O'Connor *Co. Q* 3: Charge down on them graybacks with all we've got.

b. *So.* a Union soldier.

1864 in *Ark. Hist. Qly.* XLII (1983) 139: Gen. Price at last became alarmed...as the graybacks seemed to be in earnest about making us a visit. *Ibid.* 140: Dr. Parham has run from the graybacks. *Ibid.* 158: Mrs. Cooksey rushed in before sunrise to say the town was full of graybacks. **1865** in *Ibid.* 165: The rivers are too high for mail or graybacks.

c. a messenger boy who wears a gray uniform.

1885 in *DA:* The employés...include about fifty pages, called "graybacks," from the color of their uniforms.

d. *USMC.* a German soldier.

1933 *Leatherneck* (Dec.) 56 [ref. to 1918]: Greybacks!...Heinies!

4. *Whaling.* a California gray whale.

1873 Scammon *Marine Mammals* 25: "Gray-back" is indicative of its color. **1884** in *DA.*

5. [sugg. by *greenback*] *Finance.* a Confederate treasury note.

1875 in *DA:* We printed a partial history of the issue, decline, and fall of the grayback. **1897** in *OED:* The depreciation in the purchasing power of "graybacks," as we call the rebel treasury notes, is so rapid.

Graybar Hotel *n.* prison or jail.—constr. with *the*. *Joc.* Cf. GRAYSTONE COLLEGE.

1970 Landy *Underground Dict.* 93: *Greybar hotel*...Jail. **1981** Wambaugh *Glitter Dome* 74: The Greek...certainly didn't want to share accommodations at the graybar hotel with a Turk. **1990** C.P. McDonald *Blue Truth* 78: He faced many years in the graybar hotel.

graybeard *n. Naut.* (see quot.).

1986 Wilbur *Tall Ships* 19: Fifty-foot waves, the Cape Horn greybeards, made the Cape passage hazardous indeed.

grayboy *n. Black E.* a white man or boy.—usu. used contemptuously. Cf. GRAY, *n.* and *adj.*

1951 Algren *Chicago* 83: Find them out for yourself, greyboy. **1962** in *OEDS.* **1970** Landy *Underground Dict.* 93: *Greyboy*...White male. **1967–80** Folb *Runnin' Lines* 240: *Gray boy.* White male. **1987** *21 Jump St.* (Fox-TV): You got a real good sense of humor for one of the stupidest grayboys I ever met.

grayhog *n. & adj. U.S. Mil. Acad.* (see quots.).—used derisively.

1978 Truscott *Dress Gray* 133 [ref. to 1960's]: Jesus, there wasn't anything more...gray-hog than this. *Ibid.* 276: He becomes a regular grayhog. That's like a super-straight cadet. **1987** D.O. Smith *Cradle of Valor* 256: *File boner*—overly conscientious cadet. (Now called a "grey hog.")

graymail *n.* [sugg. by *blackmail*] *Journ. & Law.* a method of preventing prosecution, as for espionage, by threatening to reveal or subpoena classified government information in court.

[**1964** *Newsweek* (Aug. 24) 32: Political blackmail is becoming...a commonplace...Perhaps there should be gradations of the term..."white-mail" and "graymail," for starters.] **1973** (cited in *BDNE3*). **1979** *N.Y. Times,* in *BDNE3:* Secret proceedings would not eliminate graymail. **1984** *Time* (Nov. 19) 115: The CIA's worries were rekindled when Boyce threatened "graymail": the introduction of sensitive information in his testimony. **1987** Levinson & Link *Terrorist* (film): *Graymail*—the threat to reveal classified information in court. **1990** *Newsweek* (Jan. 1) 19: Noriega's lawyers are already saying they will require reams of classified material for their defense. U.S. officials say the graymail problem isn't insurmountable.

gray matter *n.* intelligence. *Joc.*
    1899 Ade *Fables* 13: When it came to the Gray Matter, May Wright Sewall...Pulled up Lame. **1908** Train *Crime Stories* 14: Mabel, you've got the "gray matter" all right.

gray mule *n.* corn whiskey or gin. Cf. MULE; WHITE MULE.
    1906 M'Govern *Sarjint Larry* 34: The Chino at the market-place just t'other side of the outpost had laid in an uncommonly big supply of "gray-mule." *Ibid.* (gloss.) s.v.: *Gray-Mule:*—whisky. **1919** (quot. at WHITE LIGHTNING, *n.*).

Graystone College *n.* *Und.* a prison. Also **Graystone Hotel, Gray-Rock Hotel.** *Joc.* Cf. GRAYBAR HOTEL.
    1933 Ersine *Pris. Slang* 41: *Graystone College,* n. Any prison. **1962** Crump *Killer* 198: I nodded to the County Jail. "There's the Graystone Hotel," I said. **1967** Rose *Flim-Flam Man* (film): I figured you'd change your mind after you got a taste of the Gray-Rock Hotel over there.

grease *n.* **1.** rancid butter; (*hence*) butter or margarine.
    *1788 in *OED*: *Grease,* rancid butter, of the lowest degree. **1874** in *AS* (Oct. 1933) 82: A western paper says dealers in butter classify it as wool grease, cart grease, soap grease, variegated, tesselated cow grease... [etc.]. *1919 *Athenaeum* (Aug. 8) 727 [ref. to WWI]: When..."grease" was asked for at mealtimes,...butter (?) was meant. **1930** Irwin *Tramp & Und. Slang*: Grease. Butter. **1935** E. Levinson *Strikes* 179 [ref. to 1916]: Butter was "grease," meat was "horse," milk was "cow," the sugar bowl was "the gravel wagon," and the pudding concoction was "paste." **1943** *AS* (Apr.) 154: *Skid the grease.* Pass the butter. **1942–44** in *AS* (Feb. 1946) 33: *Grease,* n. Butter. **1944** Kendall *Service Slang* 24: *Grease down...*table etiquette for pass the butter.
    2. bribe money.
    [**1797** in *DAE:* Cash...is a necessary article in their business, and without daily application of this specific grease their Wheels must roll heavily on.] **1801** in *DAE*: When the American flag-staff comes down, it will take a great deal of grease (meaning money) to get it up again. *1823 "J. Bee" *Dict. Turf: Grease.*—A bonus given to promote the cause of any one. **1859** Matsell *Vocab.* 39: *Grease.* A bribe. "Grease the copper in the fist, and he'll be as blind as your mother," put money in the officer's hand, and he will not watch you. **1921** in McArdle *Collier's* 230: Original cost, per case, $20; boat transportation, per case $5; car transportation, per case, $1; "grease" for officials, per case, average $10. **1929** Merriam *Chicago* 64: The payment of graft to city officials whether as blackmail...or as "grease" in an undertaking that cuts the corners of the law. **1930** *Amer. Mercury* (Dec.) 456: *Grease, n.*: Money paid for protection. "With all these new monkeys on the river the grease's too stiff." **1960** *Untouchables* (ABC-TV): A little bit of grease goes a long way. **1967** Spillane *Delta* 31: A little grease helps out when you got a warrant on you. **1971** Horan *Blue Messiah* 479: That's a lot of grease, Pepe. Are you going to pay it? **1983** R. Thomas *Missionary* 37: Not if it's against the law in the country where you hand out the grease. *a*1988 in *N.Y. Times Mag.* (Feb. 7, 1988) 13: There's enough grease to fry a dinosaur.
    3. *Theat.* (see quot.).
    1853 C. Hill *Scenes* 52 [ref. to 1820's]: The "Grease," as the lamplighter was termed in stage vocabulary.
    4. flattery; suave talk. Cf. GREASE JOB, 1.
    *1877 in *OED*: *Grease,* flattery. "I should like him a vast sight better if he hedn't so much of his grease." *a1890–93 F & H III 200: *Grease...*(common).—Fawning; flattery. **1904** in *Army & Navy Life* (Nov. 1906) 500: All things come to him who waits, provided he uses *grease* discriminately. *Ibid.* 498: *Grease* means a bootlick. **1951** Wouk *Caine Mutiny* 252: Is that a man-to-man promise, Steve, or are you just applying the grease?
    5. *Narc.* opium.
    1922 *Variety* (May 5) 12: They...want a history of the grease from the time it was a poppy seed in China. **1938** in D.W. Maurer *Lang. Und.* 103: *Grease.* Smoking opium before it is rolled into pills.
    6. Esp. *Und.* nitroglycerine.
    1924 Henderson *Keys to Crookdom* 407: *Grease.* Nitroglycerine. **1927** *AS* II (Mar.) 282: *Soup, grease*—Nitroglycerine. **1928** Callahan *Man's Grim Justice* 69: We knew that "grease" (nitroglycerine) was exploded by concussion. **1929** Tully *Shadows of Men* 76: Nitro was a past master at boiling dynamite in water. He would pour off the water and retain the oily substance which remained at the bottom of the vessel. This was called "grease" or "soup." Nitroglycerine was its proper name. **1968**

"H. King" *Box-Man* 34: We used grease: nitroglycerin that we cooked ourselves. **1970** Rudensky & Riley *Gonif* 80: If you really want to get good as a touch man, you got to study grease and explosives for a couple of years.
    7. political influence; PULL.
    1941 *Guide to Naval Acad.* 151: *Grease.* Pull or influence. **1980** Gould *Ft. Apache* 155: Hey, Murphy, your brothers have a little grease downtown, don't they?...Do you think they could pull me a transfer?
    8. *Black E.* food, esp. short-order food; a meal.
    1959–60 R. Reisner *Jazz Titans* 157: *Grease:* food. **1961** J.A. Williams *Night Song* 64: Look, man, can we take off our things and get some grease? **1967** Baraka *Tales* 14: So get away from my grease. **1970–72** in *AS* L (1975) 60: *Grease* n. Meal, dinner. "Let's go to grease." **1972** Pfister *Beer Cans* 12: I hastily proceeded back to the table (slid to the greeze).
    9.a. *Black E.* GREASER, 1.a.
    1963 Parks *Learning Tree* 131: "Git them greases!"..."Watch that grease!"
    b. GREASER, 2.
    1967 Hinton *Outsiders* 23: I'm a grease, same as Dally. **1970** Grissim *Country Music* 249: True, he did once belong to the Sigma Alpha Epsilon fraternity ("back in 1962 you were either frat or grease") but he was not kicked out for growing long hair and joining the Beatnik crowd. **1983** K. Rowell *Outsiders* (film): Dally's my buddy—I'm a grease, too.
    10. *Mil.* GREASE GUN.
    1965 Adler *Vietnam* 95: I carry a .45 caliber submachine gun; some call it a "grease" because it looks like one. **1976** R. Daley *To Kill* 7: "What about the grease?"..."It's under the laundry."
    ¶ In phrases:
    ¶ **get the grease** *Mil.* to be killed by gunfire.
    1968–77 Herr *Dispatches* 30: Like the corpsman at Khe Sanh who said, "If it ain't the fucking incoming it's the fucking outgoing. Only difference is who gets the fucking grease, and that ain't no fucking difference at all."
    ¶ **in the grease** in serious trouble. Cf. S.E. *in hot water.*
    1929 McEvoy *Hollywood Girl* 21: We call it the *Pan American* because we're always putting somebody in the grease. **1930** *Liberty* (July 5) 25: *Put me in the grease*—Put me in trouble. **1938** Bellem *Blue Murder* 184: He might spill something to put me in the grease. **1963** in Robinson *Comics* 141: Don't use logic on me. *I'm* the one who's in the grease.
    ¶ **shoot through the grease** Esp. *Black E.* to deceive or victimize (someone).
    1967 Lit *Dictionary* 24: *I wouldn't shoot you through the grease*—It's no lie; I'm telling it like it is. **1967** [R. Beck] *Pimp* 194: Kid, your map sure looks like that bullshit bitch you got is been shooting you through hot grease. **1968** Baker et al. *CUSS* 196: *Shoot through the grease.* Lie. **1986** *L.A. Law* (NBC-TV): Don't shoot me through the grease, kid. I was a P.D. for too long.

grease *v.* **1.a.** to bribe (someone). *Occ. absol.*
    *1528 in *OED*: With rewardes they must him greace. *1648 in *OED*: While pluralities greas'd them thick and deepe. *1707 in *OED*: I greas'd the Gaoler...with three Pieces of Eight. *1785 Grose *Vulgar Tongue: To Grease.* To bribe. **1839** *Amer. Joe Miller* 174: Popularity is like soap, it hardly stiffens before it runs back to lye and grease again. **1866** (quot. at BOBBY). **1882** C. Morris *Shadow Sam* 5: Catch me greasin' them rich car companies. I've got better investments than that. **1904** *Life in Sing Sing* 249: *Grease.* To pay for protection. **1935** McCoy *They Shoot Horses* 95: It just means we'll have to grease somebody. **1936** Washburn *Parlor* 154: Preachers got to be greased the same as bulls. **1940** Asbury *Gem of Prairie* 274: She was an exceptional strumpet who...refused to "grease" the police. **1951** in J. Blake *Joint* 27: It was the guard I greased. **1967** Gonzales *Dues* 100: The only guy he had to grease was the doorman. **1970** S.J. Perelman, in *New Yorker* (Oct. 17) 41: I got hold of the concierge, greased him with a few hundred lire. **1980** Gould *Ft. Apache* 92: You try to grease me again, and I'll turn your head like a doorknob. **1983** O. Stone *Scarface* (film): How do I know that you're the last cop I'm gonna have to grease?
    b. to cooperate upon payment of a bribe; be amenable to bribery.
    1971 in J. Blake *Joint* 14: It isn't as hard as it might seem, because one of the guards will grease for twenty-five bucks.
    c. to prearrange illicitly; FIX.
    1947 Schulberg *Harder They Fall* 231: Do you want the whole town to know what round we got it greased for?
    2. to get away; clear out.
    1854 *Crockett Almanac* (unp.): Now what would you do—keep the tree

from the bear...or grease and slope? ***1984** Partridge *DSUE* (ed. 8) 497: *Grease*...In WWI army usage, it = "to get away" (esp. by running).

3.a. *Stu.* (see quot.).

1900 *DN* II 39: *Grease*, v.t. To pass a student by giving a slightly higher grade than was deserved.

b. to slip; progress smoothly.—constr. with *through*.

1900 *DN* II 39: *Grease through*...To be passed by being greased. **1959** *AS* (May) 156: To *grease*...*through* is to pass by the skin of one's teeth. **1973** M. Collins *Carrying the Fire* 338: It greased on through channels and won final approval. **1990** Tuso *Vietnam Blues* 6: To..."grease through" Operational Readiness Inspections.

c. to schedule, prepare, or arrange for imminent action; arrange; expedite.

1927–28 in R. Nelson *Dishonorable* 148: But you are greased for a suspension. **1984** Hammel *Root* 39: Mead's request was "greased" by Fleet Marine Force, Atlantic, and all the additional personnel arrived... within thirty-six hours. **1989** *Tour of Duty* (CBS-TV): Look, man, I got it all greased.

d. *Av.* to land (an airplane) smoothly.—constr. with *in* or *on.* Occ. intrans.

1943 Ford *Short Cut to Tokyo* 61: Down we went, a beautiful approach; he "greased" it in. **1945** Hamann *Air Words: Grease 'er in, to.* To make a smooth landing. **1951** Sheldon *Troubling Star* 158: Ronsdale bounced twice and Tindle greased his own ship in. **1958** in Harvey *Air Force* 44: He...greased the X-15B onto the dry lake. **1961** L.G. Richards *TAC* 96: Lorentzen greased her in for a smooth landing. **1966** Gallery *Start Engines* 206: Then he greased his Banshee in for an eggshell landing, and taxied up to the line. **1973** Overgard *Hero* 98: The yacht merged with the dock as imperceptibly as a jet greasing onto a runway at Kennedy International. **1975** in Higham & Siddall *Combat Aircraft* 17: A pilot could..."grease" her in on landing with a featherlike touchdown time after time.

4. to flatter or curry favor with.—also constr. with *down.*

1935 *Amer. Mercury* (June) 229: *Grease:* to bribe; curry favor. **1942** *ATS* 296: Flatter...*blarney,*...*grease.* **1988** *Sonny Spoon* (NBC-TV): Stop greasing me down, Salvatore. I can see through you like a pane of glass.

5.a. Esp. *Black E.* to eat.—also constr. with *down.*

1944 Burley *Hndbk. Jive* 139: *Grease*—to eat. **1959** *Swinging Syllables: Grease*—Eat. **1965** in Sanchez *Word Sorcerers* 195: He sho cud grease. **1969** C. Brown *Mr. Jiveass* 32: I wanna grease. **1968–70** *Current Slang* III & IV 59: *Grease down,* v. To eat.—College males, Iowa. **1974** R. Carter *Sixteenth Round* 9: There was nothing wrong with my stomach, and I was ready to grease. **1977** Bunker *Animal Factory* 126: I go grease in the kitchen every night. **1980** D. Hamill *Stomping Ground* 296: Let's go greeze. **1985** Ky. man, age *ca*20: Man, when do we grease down?

b. to serve food to.

1981 Hathaway *World of Hurt* 102: Come on, Cookie, grease the troops.

6. *Mil.* **a.** to kill by gunfire or explosion; (*also*) to shoot (a person). Cf. GREASE GUN.

1964 R. Moore *Green Berets* 29: I don't want to get myself greased any more than you do. **1966** Garfield *Last Bridge* 39: I don't aim to get greased...not after all the crap I been through. **1969** Maitland *Only War We've Got* 160: We're goin' after the Cong, an' I want you to be around when we grease their asses. **1973** Karlin et al. *Free Fire Zone* 85: Tripped a booby trap and got himself greased. **1972–76** Durden *No Bugles* 64: Last one he had, and the one before that, got greased. One dead, one fucked up. **1977** Caputo *Rumor of War* 302: He's makin' a break, grease the motherfucker. **1982** Del Vecchio *13th Valley* 419: I saw at least ten of em get greased.

b. to shell or bombard heavily; destroy.

1971 Sheehan *Arnheiter* 191: They'll grease us right out of the water with six thousand rounds a minute. **1980** M. Baker *Nam* 62: Called in artillery and really greased the fuckers. **1988** M. Maloney *Thunder Alley* 225: Nice job greasing that Gray artillery base.

¶ In phrases:

¶ **grease (one's) gills** to eat.

*a***1890–93** F & H III 201: To *grease one's gills*...To make [*sic*] a good or luxurious meal. **1929** in J.I. White *Git Along Dogies* 108: Yew razorbacks! Come an' git yo' stuffin'!...Grease up yo' gills.

¶ **grease (one's) throat** [or **tonsils**] to take a drink of liquor.

1874 Rudge & Raven *I.O.G.B.* 51: Whiskey and brandy, to grease throats with. *1916** in O Lochlainn *Irish Street Ballads* 129: So take off your coat and grease your throat/With the real old mountain dew.

1975 Swarthout *Shootist* 73: From a pocket he slipped a pint bottle, offered it to Books. "Time to grease your tonsils, too."

¶ **grease (someone's) hide** to whip someone.

1880 J.C. Harris *Uncle Remus* 260: You better go an' git yo' hide greased.

¶ **grease the rails** [or **track**] *Hobo.* to be crushed to death by a railroad train.

1911 in Tamony *Americanisms* (No. 19) 9: I came to the conclusion that Overland Slim...had "greased the rails." **1912** in *Ibid.*: The uncountable other victims of the "Wanderlust" who fell under the wheels and had "greased the tracks." **1918** Livingston *Delcassee* 88: Almost everyone of his original enemies either had "greased the rails"...or come to a premature death by diseases. **1927** *DN* V 448: *Grease the track,* v. To be run over by a train. **1930** Irwin *Tramp & Und. Sl.: Grease the Track*— To commit suicide by leaping in front of a train; to be run over. **1960** *Jour. Amer. Folk.* LXXIII 207: *Greasing the Rails.*...heard...orally from...a former Wob, in Occidental, California, on 20 April 1958. It refers to the death of a worker under the train wheels after he was deliberately thrown there by yeggs and hijackers.

¶ **grease the skids** see s.v. SKIDS.

greaseback *n.* *Naut.* a ship's engineer.

1917 in Curry *River's in My Blood* 144: Tyler Rowe, the old engineer of the *Menomonie,* was a humorous old grease-back.

greaseball *n.* **1.** a filthy or unsavory person; one having an oily or greasy appearance.

1917 (quot. at COMET, *n.*). **1921** *Variety* (Feb. 11) 7: The grease ball...said in my ear, "I thought so." **1927** *AS* (June) 387: *Greaseball* is a contemptuous name for a filthy vag. **1927** *DN* V 448: *Grease ball,* n. A low class tramp. **1927–28** Tasker *Grimhaven* 146: The greaseball wins his name for an obvious reason, for the woolly texture of his clothing absorbs an unlimited amount of grease and dust. **1928** O'Connor *B'way Racketeers* 252: *Grease-Ball*—A derelict of Racketland. **1929** *AS* IV (June) 340: *Greaseball.* A dirty beggar. **1933** Ersine *Pris. Slang* 41: *Greaseball,* n. A filthy person. **1933** "W. March" *Company K* 69: These whores are refined, sensitive girls. They wouldn't even unbutton their drawers for a bunch of grease-balls like you. **1990** C.P. McDonald *Blue Truth* 44: A...greaseball, shithead, spitball, and just plain rotten puke.

2. *Army & USMC.* a mess cook or cook's assistant.—used derisively.

1918 *Marine* (Parris I.) (Sept. 20) 4: "Cap." Smith and his "trained greaseballs" are doing good work...handing us the chow. **1919** *Amer. Leg. Wkly.* (Aug. 22) 6: I looked up under one of those strange bonnets into a pair of shifty eyes and a nice pistol that would have brought 200 francs from a greaseball. **1919** Hamilton & Corbin *Echoes* 160: Our field kitchen went astray and was lost for a few days, along with our mess sergeant and the rest of the "greaseballs." **1919** Lincoln *Company C* 32: The fellows soon came to call the latter "Grease Ball Sam." Things did not run very smoothly in the kitchen. **1923** T. Boyd *Through the Wheat* 129: These damned yellah grease balls ain't got any sense. **1928** Scanlon *God Have Mercy* 7: We hadn't seen the cook or his greaseballs since we left Chaumont-en-Vexin. **1930** Fredenburgh *Soldiers March!* 260: Whaddaya say, ole grease balls, how about some chow for the army? **1931** *Amer. Mercury* (Nov.) 352: *Grease ball*...A hamburger cook. *a***1934** in Lomax & Lomax *Amer. Ballads* 559: Our greaseball is a goddam dirty bum.

3. an ignorant or offensive white person of Mediterranean or Latin-American birth or descent.—used contemptuously.—usu. considered offensive. Cf. GREASER, 1.a.

1922 *DN* V 147: *Grease ball*—a foreign cake-eater or bun-duster. **1927** in E. Wilson *Twenties* 426: But when this greaseball came along, she was just wild about 'um. **1931** *Amer. Merc.* (Dec.) 414: You cheap grease-ball so-and-so. **1931** Grant *Gangdom's Doom* 25: Genara and Anelmo. Couple of tough greaseballs, them fellows. **1934** Appel *Brain Guy* 53: He whispered groggily something about the glory that was Greece, not these greaseballs, the ancient Greece with all her glories. **1937** Weidman *Wholesale* 18: You guys are all Americans! You don't want to have anything to do with Unions! Why, that stuff is only for grease balls! **1945** Mencken *Amer. Lang. Supp. I* 610: *Grease-ball* is most often applied in the United States to Greeks. **1946** Michener *So. Pacific* 369: Called hard-working young DeVito a grease ball. **1957** Laurents & Sondheim *West Side Story* 218: Even a greaseball's got feelings. **1961** Kohner *Gidget Goes Hawaiian* 89: Why...did you get mixed up with that guitar playing greaseball? **1969** Gardner *Fat City* 102: To hell with these greaseballs. They don't know who their real friends are. **1977** Torres *Q & A* 51: You ain't talkin' to no greaseball here. I know my rights. **1978** T. Sanchez *Zoot-Suit* 63: You got a Spanish name around here,...they figure you a greaseball wetback. **1981** Gilliland *Rosinante* 6: I ain't never going to help no...greaseball tear down the Alamo.

4. a person who greases or lubricates machinery; mechanic.

1930 Irwin *Tramp & Und. Sl.: Grease Ball*...a garage or machine-shop assistant....A term of derision when applied by one mechanic to another. **1937** Lay *I Wanted Wings* 331: *Greaseball*. A mechanic (mech). **1938** (quot. at GAS MONKEY). **1941** in *AS* XVI 240: *Grease Ball*. Chassis lubricator. **1941** *Amer. Mercury* (Mar.) 347: Greaseballs (mechanics) repaint it. **1945** Hamann *Air Words: Grease ball*. An assistant mechanic or handyman; also a plane washer and oiler. **1967** Baraka *Tales* 81: To be wheeled close to a hangar by the grease balls.

greaseburger *n.* a greasy hamburger.

1961 H. Ellison *Gentleman Junkie* 143: It was just as easy to take strychnine as eat his greaseburgers. **1985** Heywood *Taxi Dancer* 84: I'll stick with greaseburgers. *a***1991** Kross *Splash One* 111: Let's go get a greaseburger.

grease-burner *n.* a cook.—used derisively.

1927 *AS* (June) 392: A cook is a *grease-burner, stew-builder*, or *mulligan-mixer*. **1963** J. Ross *Dead Are Mine* 134 [ref. to 1944]: As soon as you grease-burners get settled, drag Bell over...and we'll have a little game now and then. **1969** Pharr *Numbers* 18: "Now hear this, you grease burner," Blueboy said. "We traveling waiters are cosmopolites, and the ward's best is none too good for us."

grease call *n. Mil.* mess call.

1973 Huggett *Body Count* 208: "Chow call, grease call, garbage call," they chanted in unison.

greased *adj.* drunk; OILED.

1928 *AS* III (Feb.) 219: *Greased*. Somewhat intoxicated. Cf. *oiled*. **1938** in *AS* (Apr. 1939) 90: *Greased*. Partly drunk. "Bob's greased." **1958** Frankel *Band of Bros.* 225 [ref. to 1950]: I am not tight or plastered, polluted, greased, blind, sozzled, ossified, or atomized.

greased lightning *n.* [elab. of LIGHTNING, infl. by colloq. phr. *quick as greased lightning*] (see 1942 quot.).

1936 Reddan *Other Men's Lives* 284 [ref. to 1918]: Once in a while some soldier would break loose and indulge a little too freely in "greased lightning," Vin Blanc. **1942** *ATS* 112: Strong liquor...*greased lightning*.

grease gun *n. Mil.* a .45-caliber submachine gun.

1945 *Yank* (Mar. 2) 4: We never did have any trouble with "grease guns." **1945** in *Calif. Folk. Qly.* V (1946) 380: Marines [call a machine pistol] *grease gun*. **1945** Hamann *Air Words: Grease gun*. The M-5 machine gun. **1944–48** A. Lyon *Unknown Station* 279: He had a knapsack flung over his shoulder and a grease gun in his hand. **1953** T. White *Down the Ridge* 16: As his weapon, Eddie had picked a grease gun, so called because it looks like one, but it is really a tanker's weapon—a compact submachine gun which shoots 30 .45 slugs at a loading. **1962** Tregaskis *Vietnam Diary* 104: There was also a grease gun, a .45-caliber submachine gun. **1963** *Sat. Eve. Post* (Mar. 23) 35: Jones carried a grease gun (submachine gun), Jasper a sawed-off pump shotgun. **1965** Bryan *P.S. Wilkinson* 11: The truck driver carried the submachine guns—M8 "grease guns" which Wilkinson admired. **1971** Rowe *Five Years to Freedom* 78: The M-3 "grease gun," a submachine gun of simpler design. **1979** Cassidy *Delta* 3: The Colt .45 pistol and its machine-gun counterpart, the famous grease gun. **1982** R.A. Anderson *Cooks & Bakers* 137: Two carried carbines and one had a grease gun.

greasehound *n.* a motor mechanic; GREASE MONKEY.

1920 Norton *639th Aero Squadron* 52 [ref. to 1918]: Grease hounds. **1942** *ATS* 458.

grease job *n.* **1. an instance of flattering; deceptive flattery.**

1942 *ATS* 296: Flatter...*give a grease job*. **1951** in Mailer *Ad. for Myself* 127: You should have seen the grease job I gave to Carter. I'm dumb, but man, he's dumber. **1959** Morrill *Dark Sea* 28: Quit stalling. If I want a grease job I'll go down to the engine room. **1985** *A-Team* (NBC-TV): So why don't we just cut through the grease job here.

2. an act of coitus or anal copulation.

*ca***1950** in Barkley *Sex Cartoons* 90: Hold still while I really give this stick a hot, fast grease job. **1958** W. Burroughs *Naked Lunch* 174: I'll bet she needs a grease job worst way. **1973** N.Y.C. man, age *ca*25: A *grease job* is up the ass with Vaseline.

3. *Av.* a smooth landing made under difficult conditions. Also as v.

1961 R.L. Scott *Boring Holes* 291: This last landing had to be a "grease job." **1968** W.C. Anderson *Gooney Bird* 53: What a grease job! **1974** former SAC navigator, age 32: A *grease job* or a *greaser* is a smooth landing. Even under favorable conditions it's hard to land smoothly in a '52.

1975 in Higham & Siddall *Combat Aircraft* 56: The tricycle gear configuration permitted "grease jobs" of a quality previously unheard of. **1989** "Capt. X" & Dodson *Unfriendly Skies* 3: When the pilot brings the plane in on one of those smooth-as-glass, I-hardly-even-felt-us-touch-the-ground grease jobs. *Ibid.* 164: I grease-jobbed that landing. It was the smoothest damn touchdown in history.

grease joint *n. Orig. Carnival.* a cheap eating place, (*specif.*) a hamburger or hot-dog stand; (*derisively*) a restaurant.

1917 *Editor* (Feb. 24) 154: *Grease-Joint*—A restaurant where one gets a grab, such as a cup of Java or some sinkers or doughnuts. **1921** Casey & Casey *Gay-Cat* 62: Five-cent grease joints fur coffee...thet's bin my limit. **1922** *Variety* (Oct. 27) 8: Framing up their juice, grab, and grease joints. **1926** Finerty *Criminalese* 27: *Grease joint*—Hamburger stand. **1927** in Hammett *Big Knockover* 285: They took us to all the hangouts in San Francisco, to cabarets, grease joints, pool rooms, saloons, flophouses, hockshops, gambling joints, and what have you. **1928** *AS* III (June) 413: *Grease joint*. A hamburger or hot dog concession. The term is also applied to the cook-house on some shows. **1933** D. Runyon, in *Collier's* (Feb. 11) 8: Hot Horse Herbie...and me are in a little grease joint...putting on the old hot tripe a la Creole. **1951** Henderson & Taplinger *Circus Doctor* 177: She had seen him...at the "grease joint." **1961** Clausen *Season's Over* 150: Louie, the proprietor of the back-yard grease joint, was handing out coffee and hamburgers right and left. **1967** *Lit Dictionary* 49: *Grease Joint*—A restaurant.

grease monkey *n.* a mechanic, esp. one who works on automobiles or airplanes.

1928 Gravatt *Pioneers* 251: All the way down the line...from skilled draftsmen in a polished office to the "grease monkeys" with blackened faces and smeary over-alls. **1931** Post & Gatty *Around World* 61: He looked like a "grease-monkey." **1933** Stewart *Speech of the American Airman* 68. **1940** Wexley *City for Conquest* (film): He was just a grease monkey in a junkyard garage. **1941** *AS* (Oct.) 166: *Grease Monkey*. Air mechanic's assistant. **1943** Arnold & Eaker *Flying* 191: *Grease monkeys*...—good mechanics—account for my being alive today. **1945** Peeples *Swing Low* 18: There was the painter's assistant, the grease monkey and the railroad fireman—each bearing the odor and the stain of his trade. **1947** Brooks *Brute Force* (film): We're gonna make all you grease monkeys famous. **1949** B. Manning & T. Hovey *That Midnight Kiss* (film): Johnny talks to [him]...like some kinda grease monkey. **1956** Heflin *USAF Dict.* 235: *Grease monkey*. A mechanic or other member of a ground crew. *Slang*. **1956** J. Brown *Kings Go Forth* 67: I was just an ordinary grease monkey, filling tanks and airing up tires and wiping windshields. **1958** P. O'Connor *At LeMans* 7: From grease monkey to businessman in four not-so-easy lessons. **1962** Olson *Roaring Road* 100: Dave Falconer, Boy Grease Monkey. **1980** Manchester *Darkness* 46: I was working as a grease monkey in a machine shop at thirty-five cents an hour. **1980** *Ford's Insider* (Nov.): Be Your Own Grease Monkey. **1991** W. Chamberlain *View from Above* 221: They didn't get their reputations from being "grease monkeys."

grease pot *n.* a cook.—used derisively.

1914 *DN* IV 150: Navy Slang...*Greasepot, n.* A cook. **1942** *ATS* 417: *Grease pot*...a camp or prison cook. **1967** *Lit Dictionary* 49: *Grease Pot*—A cook.

grease-pusher *n.* **1.** *Theat.* a makeup artist.

1928 *N.Y. Times* (Mar. 11) VIII 6: *Grease-Pusher*—A make-up man.

2. GREASE MONKEY.

1951 Sheldon *Troubling Star* 35: The grease-pushers in the 66th didn't have half the work with jets that Braith had.

greaser *n.* **1.a.** a Mexican; (*hence*) a Hispanic person of any nationality; (*occ.*) any person of southern European birth or ancestry.—used contemptuously.

1836 in G.A. McCall *Letters* (Apr. 23) 298: The pervading sentiment among the defeated and disorganized "Greasers" was, "*sauve qui peut.*" **1846** in *Ill. State Hist. Soc. Jrnl.* (Summer 1953) 166: They would (the greasers) raid and massacre all the Yankees. **1847** McClellan *Mexican War Diary* 69: The "Greasers" had it all in their own way. **1858** J.C. Reid *Tramp* 36: Mexicans...are called "Greasers," their females "Greaser Women." **1858** in Dwyer & Lingenfelter *Songs of Gold Rush* 31: When you get to Panama,/Greasers want a back-load. **1859** Bartlett *Amer.* (ed. 2) 179: *Greaser*....A term vulgarly applied to the Mexicans and other Spanish Americans. **1866** in "M. Twain" *Letters from Hawaii* (Mar. 19): Balboa...like any other greaser over any other trifle...shouted in his foreign tongue and waved his country's banner. **1866** *Night Side of N.Y.* 32: A Portuguese sailor took her away from the man she was dancing with—a South American greaser, I guess. **1874** J.G. McCoy *Sks. Cattle Trade* 375: The "Greasers" are the result of

Spanish, Indian and negro miscegenation. **1887** E. Custer *Tenting* 144: A Mexican driver (a greaser). **1894** *Harper's* (Jan.) 222: I've seen Dagoes you could tie to, and sometimes a greaser, now and then. **1898** *Chicago Record's War Stories* 41: Their frequently expressed wish is to "kill ten d—d greasers for every one of the boys blown up in the Maine." **1904** *Life in Sing Sing* 249: Greaser.—Italian or Mexican. **1905** Belasco *Girl of Golden West* 326: Heads a crew of greasers and Spaniards. **1906** *DN* III 139: *Greaser land, n.phr.* New Mexico or any other region where "greasers" (Mexicans) live. "You don't want to get swallowed by the land sharks of *greaser land.*" **1922** Rollins *Cowboy* 106: Along the Mexican border, some men, principally "Greasers," wore the huge straw hats of Mexico. **1927** Thrasher *Gang* 310: A gang of about fifteen boys, twelve to fifteen years old, all of whom are Jewish with the exception of two Italians who are known as the "Greasers." **1928** Dobie *Vaquero* 44: On another occasion he killed a "greaser" across the Rio Grande from Eagle Pass. **1943** Whyte *Street Corner Society* xviii: Even the Italian family has been broken into two separate generations. The Italian-born are known to the younger generation as "greasers." **1946** J.H. Burns *Gallery* 207: That fellow is what I'd call a greaser…Italo-Americans of the first generation. **1956** Neider *Hendry Jones* 31: They're already saying I got no business keeping a greaser on this job. **1962** T. Berger *Reinhart* 398: In South America…nothing a greaser won't do for a Gigantic Flameburst Straight Eight. **1968** P. Roth *Portnoy* 196: Perched like some greaser over his bongo drums. **1977** Bartlett *Finest Kind* 22: A "greaser" is [among Italian-American fishermen] a fisherman who was born in Sicily. **1982** "W.T. Tyler" *Rogue's March* 64: All you wetback greasers.

b. *Naut.* a ship of a Hispanic country.

1872 Thomes *Slaver* 142: "She looks like a greaser"…The man meant that she was a Spanish ship.

c. any language, usu. Spanish, typically spoken by a GREASER, 1.a.—used contemptuously.

1907 J.R. Cook *Border & Buffalo* 297 [ref. to 19th C.]: I could now talk a little "Greaser" and make understandable signs.

2.a. a coarse, unkempt, or unsavory person.

1864 in *DN* VI 305: In the frontier settlements…there are a set of *greasers*, poachers, men that will not live by industry, but by Rob Roy practices. **1865** in Glatthaar *March to Sea* 180: Sherman's Greasers…Slouch Hats…Swamp Angels…Thieves. **1904** *Life in Sing Sing* 263: *What does the greaser do but flash his rod and bark away*…What does the fellow do but draw his pistol and shoot. **1925** (cited in Partridge *Dict. Und.* 306). **1966** in IUFA *Folk Speech: Greaser:* an unkempt person.

b. a rowdy, usu. working-class, white youth, esp. a member of a hot-rod or motorcycle club, or of a juvenile gang.

1964 in *OEDS:* The boy distinguished…"the Surfers"…from less-favored individuals called "Greasers," who indulge in…drag-racing, putting grease on their hair, smoking marijuana and dancing the Twist. **1967** Hinton *Outsiders* 6: Greasers are almost like hoods; we steal things and drive old souped-up cars…and have a gang fight once in a while. *Ibid.* 50: You know what a greaser is?…White trash with long hair. **1968** Kirk & Hanle *Surfer's Hndbk.* 139: *Greaser:* non-surfer; an outsider. **1972** Eble *Campus Slang* (Oct. 1972) 3: That guy over there with the white socks and the Budweiser shirt is a real greaser. **1973** *Oui* (Feb.) 85: Surfin' became the California greaser thing to do. **1974** Terkel *Working* 224: Until a couple of months ago, I was a greaser. My hair was slicked back. **1978** DeChristoforo *Grease* 40: Finn was one of the few greasers who played sports. **1987** Univ. Tenn. prof., age *ca*65: In 1963 or '64 I went into a diner in Sterling, Colorado, and I noticed a sign that said, "No Greasers Allowed." When I asked the woman who seemed to own the place if she had something against Mexicans, she didn't know what I was talking about. She protested that a *greaser* just meant a dirty teenager on a motorcycle! **1987** *Village Voice* (N.Y.C.) (July 14) 17: In another age they'd be greasers or hippies.

3. *Naut.* a second or third mate.—also constr. with *second* or *third.*

1858 in C.A. Abbey *Before the Mast* 137: The 2d Greaser has been laid up for two days. *Ibid.* 139: Third greaser made himself very obnoxious. *Ibid.* 141: The "*greaser*"…[is] detested by all hands. **a***1888** in L.A. Smith *Music of Waters* 38: And who do you think was second greaser? **1899** Hamblen *Bucko Mate* 36: The "greaser," as the second mate is disrespectfully called, *behind his back.* **1901** King *Dog-Watches* 129: It was Mr. Kane, the second mate, "a bluenose bucko greaser." **1908** *Independent* (Apr. 23) 905: I ain't no mister nor yet a "greaser" on board ship. **1925** Riesenberg *Under Sail* 34 [ref. to 1898]: Weighed on a rusty scales by the second greaser each day.

4. a hot, humid day or night.

1869 Logan *Foot Lights* 106: Then p'raps you'll have a blazing midsum-

mer night—a regular "greaser"—when the house in front feels as hot as a brick-kiln.

5. *Naut.* a ship's oiler; (*broadly*) any member of a ship's engineering division.

1870 in *DA: Greaser*…An assistant to the fireman of a steam-boat; one who oils the machinery.—N.Y. **1894** *Lucky Bag* (U.S. Nav. Acad.) (No. 1) 67: *Greaser*…Anyone in the Engineer Corps. **1906** *Army & Navy Life* (Nov.) 498: *Greaser* was long since given as a term of derision to the Engineer Corps of the Navy by the midshipmen of the line. *****1909** Ware *Passing Eng.* 147: *Greaser* (Navy 1860–82), a scornful way of describing naval engineers. **1918** Kauffman *Our Navy at Work* 9: From sun to sun the stokers shovel and the "greasers" oil. **1936** Healey *Foc's'le & Glory-Hole* 28: The next step in the engine room is that of "greaser" or oiler. **1943** J. Mitchell *McSorley's* 156: He…worked his way to New York as a greaser on a freighter.

6. *Mil.* GREASE GUN.

1965 Yordan & Sperling *Battle of the Bulge* (film): Take the greaser. **1991** Reinberg *In the Field* 96: *Greaser*…M-3…[or] M3A-1 .45 caliber submachine gun.

7. *Av.* GREASE JOB, 3.

1972 R. Barrett *Lovomaniacs* 52: The landing was a real greaser. **1974** (quot. at GREASE JOB, 3). *****1980** (in Partridge *DSUE* (ed. 8) 498).

greaserita *n.* [GREASER + señor*ita*] *West.* a señorita.

1849 in *AS* XLIII 98 (1968): *Como no,* or *quien sabe,* as the fair *greaserita* said.

grease stop *n.* a stop for food during a bus or automobile trip.

1982 N.Y.C. woman, age 28 (WINS Radio, Jan. 3): We're going to have to be taking a few grease stops so people can get something to eat.

grease trough *n.* a lunch counter; diner. Also **grease-trap.**

1942 *Sat. Eve. Post* (June 13) 27: The linguist wishing to broaden his grasp of Americanese might well drop into the "grease trough"—lunch counter to you—in any railroad yard. **1984** C. Parker, A. Debevoise & G. Scaife *Breakin'* (film): All I know is you're slavin' away in this grease-trap.

grease-wagon *n.* **1.** a lunchwagon; (*obs.*) *Army.* a rolling kitchen. [Quots. ref. to WWI.]

1920 *Amer. Leg. Wkly.* (May 14) 10: Put him on the grease wagon until he gets his commission. **1920** *Amer. Leg. Wkly.* (Sept. 24) 9: Let's hope we see [in war movies]…the old greasewagon, the line-up at the alleged pail of hot and sparkling water, with two hundred and fifty slum satiated hopefuls trying to dip their eating irons.

2. a cheap eating place; mess hall.

1983 Ehrhart *VN-Perkasie* 143 [ref. to 1967]: "Hasn't been to the mess-hall yet."…"Can't say I blame him for avoiding the grease-wagon."

greasy *adj. Whaling.* good or profitable in terms of whaling. Now *hist.*

1868 Macy *There She Blows!* 34: Prophesying a short voyage and "greasy luck" to the Arethusa. **1912** R.C. Murphy *Logbook for Grace* 37: The Old Man was once officer in a ship when most of its water had been used up, toward the end of a good, greasy voyage.

greasy grind see s.v. GRIND, *n.,* 5.

greasy guts *n. Juve.* a fat person.

1947 Willingham *End As a Man* 83: Look here, greasy guts.

greasy Mac *n.* a fast-food restaurant.

1983 Eilert *Self & Country* 18: Why couldn't I be home cruising the greasy Macs.

greasy spoon *n.* a small cheap restaurant or lunch counter, esp. one specializing in short-order fried foods.

1918 Mayo *Trouping for the Troops* 88: At the foot of the hill…was a little black "lean-to" called "The Greasy Spoon." **1925** *Writer's Mo.* (June) 486: *Greasy spoon*—A low-class restaurant. **1943** J. Mitchell *McSorley's* 74: For a time Gould haunted the all-night greasy spoons in the vicinity of Bellevue Hospital. **1948** Chaplin *Wobbly* 68: The rancid smell of beer and frying hamburgers from a nearby "greasy spoon" eating joint did things to my stomach. **1958** Cooley *Run for Home* 80: Eat in one of the greasy spoons, but don't waste any time. **1959** J.H. Griffin *Black Like Me* (Nov. 21): All the honors in the world cannot buy them a cup of coffee in the lowest greasy-spoon joint. **1961** Himes *Pinktoes* 115: Shortly afterwards two truck drivers came out of an all night greasy spoon. **1975** V.B. Miller *Deadly Game* 61: The Variety Luncheonette, the closest greasy spoon in the neighborhood. *****1980** T. Jones *Adrift* 183: I made for an all-night greasy spoon. **1989** Kienzle *Eminence* 197: I'd be washing dishes in some greasy spoon.

great *adj.* excellent; wonderful. Now *S.E.*

*1803 in Wetherell *Adventures* 41: Six dozen lashes on his bare posteriors. Great. **1809** W. Irving, in *OED2*: She [a ship]…was particularly great in a calm. **1818** in Royall *Letters from Ala.* 181: Doctor Crab is goin to have a great barbacue [*sic*]…and there's to be the greatest doins that ever was heard on. **1837** in M. Mathews *Beginnings of Amer. Eng.* 119: *Great* horse…a horse of good qualities…*great* plantation, a fertile one. **1857** in *Calif. Hist. Soc. Qly.* IX (1930) 151: Had a great time. **1859** in Hafen & Hafen *Reports from Colo.* 194: The danseuse…is not very good as a reader, but she is great on the "toe and heel." **1863** in J.M. Merrill *Battle Flags* 279: This glorious…news. It is great, Mr. Welles, it is great. **1897** Kipling *Capts. Courageous* 97: Say, this is great!

¶ In phrases:

¶ **great Caesar's ghost** see s.v. CAESAR.

¶ **the greatest** Orig. *Jazz.* something or someone that is unusually exciting, pleasing, amusing, or gratifying. Now *colloq.*

1946 in R.S. Gold *Jazz Talk* 113: "Duke's the greatest" is certainly the easiest cliché tossed around swing circles. **1954** *Time* (Nov. 8) 70: A term of high approbation in the swing era…is "the greatest." **1956** in R.S. Gold *Jazz Talk* 113: Lips is the greatest. Farther out than J.J. **1964** in *OEDS*: Baby, you're the greatest. **1965** N.Y.C. high school student: Man, ain't this the greatest? **1970** S.J. Perelman, in *New Yorker* (Oct. 17) 39: Everything about this broad spelled class, crème de la crème, *Social Register*; she was the greatest.

great gun *n.* an individual who is celebrated, prominent or preeminent, esp. for influence or ability; BIG GUN.

*1815 in *OED* s.v. *gun*: None of the great guns were at Madame de Coligny's. **1821** Martin & Waldo *Lightfoot* 10: All this money was spent in my favorite haunts of vice, and being so *flush* I was always the *great gun* of the company. *1825 "Blackmantle" *Eng. Spy* I 72: Joe Cannon…'s a *gun*.*…*A Gun*—"He's a great gun," a good fellow, a knowing one [at Eton]. *1825 in *OED*: A worthy clergyman, one of the great guns, as they call them. **1843** Haliburton *Attaché* 265: The great guns, and big bugs. *1858, *1870 in *OED*. *a1890–93 *F & H* III 202: *Great gun*…(common)…A person of distinction; a thing of importance.

¶ In phrases:

¶ **[like] great guns** violently or loudly (esp. in ref. to gale winds); (*hence*) energetically, successfully, or effectively.—often constr. with *blow*. Also vars. Now *colloq.*

*ca1780 in Holloway & Black *Broadside Ballads* 21: It curls like great guns to the sight. **1800** *Amorous Songster* 7: Great guns, let it blow high, blow low. *1826 "Blackmantle" *Eng. Spy* II 158: What time has a sailor to palaver about creeds when it blows great guns. **1827** J.F. Cooper *Red Rover* 187: Blowing great guns from the northward and the eastward the time. *1829 in *OED*: It blew great guns. **1836** *Naval Magazine* (Jan.) 35: Soon after this it came to blow great guns. **1838** [Haliburton] *Clockmaker* (Ser. 2) 116: It blows like great guns. **1860** Shipley *Privateer's Cruise* 11: Blowing great guns and marline-spikes. **1866** in "M. Twain" *Letters from Hawaii*: I just know it's going to blow great guns for *me* today. **1867** Smyth *Sailor's Word-Book*: Great guns and small arms, The general armament of a ship. Also, a slang term for the blowing and raining of heavy weather. **1888** Gordon & Page *Befo' De War* 56: 'Twas a wile March mont', an' de win' was blowin'/Blowin' great guns, de sailors say. **1945** in Truman *Dear Bess* 522: We have been going great guns the last day or two. **1966** Susann *Valley of Dolls* 439: We've got Joey Kling going great guns. **1973** Herbert & Wooten *Soldier* 82: The Ranger department [was] going great guns. **1993** *N.Y. Times* (July 8) C 8: "The Fifties" is going great guns, currently No. 2 on the…best-seller list.

¶ **no great guns** not of outstanding ability or appeal; ordinary.

1864 in Ransom *Diary* (entry for Nov. 19): While he is no great guns, seems quite a sensible chap and a decided improvement on many here to mess with.

great shakes see s.v. SHAKE, *n.*

greeby *adj.* [perh. alter. of *grubby*] *Stu.* (see quots.).

1947 *ATS* (Supp.) 5: Teen talk…Unsatisfactory; displeasing…greeby. **1954–60** *DAS*: Greeby…Terrible. *A teenage fad word, c1945. No longer common.* **1968–70** *Current Slang* III & IV 60: *Greeby*, adj. Ugly; nasty-looking.—College females, New Hampshire.—"My shoes are *greeby* looking."

greedhead *n.* [coined by Hunter S. Thompson] an avaricious person.

1970 in H.S. Thompson *Shark Hunt* 184: Dead-end the highway, zone the greedheads out of existence. **1971** H.S. Thompson *Las Vegas* 188: What kind of a greedhead are we dealing with?…Last night it was four hundred. **1982** Trudeau *Dressed for Failure* (unp.): You descended into the valley of the greedheads and returned in one piece.

greedy-gut *n.* a glutton. Also **greedy-guts.**

*1550 in *OED*: Disceitful Merchauntes, couetous greedyguttes, and ambicious prollers. *1579 in *OED*: Euerie one of vs woulde…play the greedie guts without all measure. *1613 in *OED*: A glutton or greedy gut. *1736 in *OED*: Lurco, a glutton…a greedygut, a great eater. *1811 *Lexicon Balatron.*: Greedy Guts. A covetous or voracious person. **1899** Green *Va. Folk-Speech* 205: Greedy gut…A glutton. *ca1940 in Botkin *Treas. Amer. Folk.* 537: Greedy-Gut Gus was born a twin. **1946** *Calif. Folk. Qly.* V 241: Don't be a Greedy-gut. *1950, *1959 in *OEDS*. **1970** in *DARE*. **1993** *Frasier* (NBC-TV): Don't be a greedy-guts. Let's have a look.

greefa *n.* [< MexSp *grifa* 'marijuana' (rel. to MexSp *grifo, grifa* '[male/female] drug addict')] *Narc.* marijuana. Also vars.

1931 *AS* VI (Aug.) 438: *Griffa*, n. Marijuana, a narcotic herb. **1933** *Jour. Crimin.* XXIII 1091: The Mexican beet-field workers have introduced…marihuana or grifo. **1934** in Partridge *Dict. Und.* 306: *Greefo.* **1936** in *Ibid.*: *Griefo.* **1938** in *Ibid.*: *Grifo.* **1938** *Amer. Jour. Med. Sci.* CXV 351: The drug is known by many different names such as…"greefo." **1946** Mezzrow & Wolfe *Really Blues* 85: The grefa they pushed around Detroit was like the scrapings off old wooden bridges. **1953** Anslinger & Tompkins *Traff. in Narc.* 309: *Griffo.* Marihuana. **1956** Longstreet *Real Jazz* 144: The Negro hornman or drummer is often on…grefa. **1962** Maurer & Vogel *Narc. & Narc. Add.* (ed. 2) 304: Smoking griefo is my idea of nothing to do. **1974** Angelou *Gather Together* 43 [ref. to 1945]: "Let's have a little grifa before dinner.…You like grifa?" "Yes. I smoke." **1988** Norst *Colors* 114: It was nothing like *grifa* by itself, this smoldering sherm.

Greek *n.* **1.** a clever, cunning, or wily individual, esp. a professional gambler or swindler.—usu. considered offensive. Also attrib. Orig. *S.E.* [The pronun. in 1960 quot. may reflect Russ *Grek* 'Greek', ref. to the time when Alaska was part of the Russian Empire, *a1867*.]

*1528 *OED*: In carde playing he is a goode greke. *1568 in *OED*: A cowle for such a Greek/Were fitter for to wear. *1664 in *OED*: Giles Musgrave was a Guileful Greek. *1794 in *OED*: The waiter pillages the greek,/The greek the spendthrift fleeces. *1821 *Real Life in London* I 193: A Greek should be a man of some personal courage, never shrink from a row, nor be afraid to fight a duel. He should be able to bully, bluster, swagger and swear…[and] not object even to assassination. *1823 in *F & H* III 204: Play will begin—some of the pigeons are here already, the Greeks will not be long following. *1834 Ainsworth *Rookwood* 247: Jerry was a *Greek* by nature, and could *land* a flat as well as the best of them. *a1845 N. Willis *Dashes* 117: "Greeks" and blacklegs are convertible terms. He thought you were more *au fait* of the slang dictionary. **1873** Scammon *Marine Mammals* 268: Aye, aye, sir; I've killed the bloody Greek [a whale] seven times, but he won't turn up. *1873 Hotten *Slang Dict.* (ed. 4): Greek, a wide-awake fellow, a sharper. *1889 Barrère & Leland *Dict. Slang* I 428: Greeks…sharpers. **1909** in "O. Henry" *Works* 975: The Swell "Greek." Half of the mysterious term was a tribute to his cool and gentleman-like manners; the other half denoted, in the language of the brotherhood, the leader, the planner, the one who…secured the information upon which they based their…desperate enterprises. **1942–49** Goldin et al. *DAUL* 87: *Greek bottom.* The crooked dealer's technique of dealing the second card from the bottom of the deck. **1949** G.S. Coffin *Winning Poker* 179: Greek—A crooked player. **1960** Jordan & Marberry *Fool's Gold* 188 [ref. to 1899]: A [card] cheat in Alaska was called a hustler or a philosopher, or a Greek, always pronounced "Greck."…A Greck in the States could make a handsome living by manipulating the cards, but he found it far more difficult to rook people in the North. **1968** F. Wallace *Poker* 216: Greek—A cardsharp.

2. an Irish person.—usu. used contemptuously. Also as *adj.*

*1823 "J. Bee" *Dict. of Turf*: Greek—Irishmen call themselves *Greeks*—none else follow the same track to the east; throughout this land, many unruly districts are termed Grecian. **1848** *Ladies' Repository* (Oct.) 315: *Greek*, An Irishman. *1851 H. Mayhew *London Labour* I 226: We had the Greeks (the lately arrived Irish) down upon us more than once. **1858** in Bartlett *Amer.* (ed. 4) 262: In some of our Atlantic cities, the men of foreign birth, especially those in vulgar style called *Greeks*, constitute…nearly a majority. *1859 Hotten *Slang Dict.*: Greeks, the low Irish. **1867** *Galaxy* (Mar. 15) 634: John Ryan, otherwise known as "Johnny the Greek,"…a stalwart young Irishman…a most dexterous pilferer of watches. **1870** in M. Keller *T. Nast* [plate 112]: The Greek Slave [cartoon depicting Irishman enslaved to Tammany Hall]. ***1872** in *F & H* III 204: The Greek element...*Greek*, as some of your readers are aware, is colonial slang for "Irish." ***1889** Barrère & Leland *Dict. Slang* I 428: *Greeks*...a name given in derision to the low Irish in London who spoke Gaelic.

3. *Stu.* a member of a Greek-letter fraternity or sorority.
1934 Weseen *Dict. Slang* 184: *Greek*—A member of a fraternity. **1956** I. Shulman *Good Deeds* 142: Grover Stillwell, a junior and hot-shot Greek. **1975** Univ. Tenn. student: *Greeks* are frat guys. **1989** *U.* (Spring Break Issue) 19: A newfound liability awareness strikes Greeks.

4. a person, esp. a male homosexual, who engages in anal copulation; (*hence*) anal copulation.—often considered offensive.
1938 "Justinian" *Amer. Sexualis* 24: *Greek.* n. A homosexual; a male pervert of a subordinate type. Very popular U.S. euphemism, 1929–. **1941** G. Legman, in G. Henry *Sex. Vars.* II 1168: *Greek.* A pedicator, the term perpetuating an ancient libel on the Greek race. **1949** in D. Schwartz *Journs.* 339: Are you a Greek?...Oh, a rear admiral! **1953** Brossard *Bold Saboteurs* 122: Ace later explained to me that men who went in for his sort of pleasure were known as Greeks. *a***1972** B. Rodgers *Queens' Vernacular* 100: *Greek*...the active pederast. **1975–76** T. McNally *Ritz* 57: Get your hands off me, you goddamn Greek. **1989** Chapple & Talbot *Burning Desires* 8: Advertising for a couple interested in Greek, French, or B & D.

Greek *adj. & adv.* being or involving anal copulation; willing to engage in anal copulation.
1931–34 in Clemmer *Pris. Comm.* 269: His chances of turning to the ancient "Greek love" for gratification are excellent. **1937** Reitman *Box-Car Bertha* 178: If you're going to hustle in any kind of a joint you've got to learn to be French, and maybe Greek. **1965** Trimble *Sex Words* 93: *Greek culture* or *Greek love* or *Greek way*...Genital-Anal intercourse or pederasty. **1967** Hamma *Motorcycle Mommas* 130: I met up with a fellow who liked to ball it greek as much as I. **1969** Tynan *Oh! Calcutta!* 33: Interested in French and Greek culture. Discretion assured. **1971** S. Stevens *Way Uptown* 39: She'd make French love turn Greek over night. *a***1972** B. Rodgers *Queens' Vernacular* 100: *Greek love,...way*...anal intercourse. **1980** in *Penthouse* (Jan. 1981) 173: She's dying to take it Greek from any guy.

¶ In phrase:

¶ **go Greek, 1.** *Stu.* to join a Greek-letter fraternity or sorority.
1975 Univ. Tenn. student theme: Many students "go Greek" at least for a year or so. **1987** Univ. Tenn. student theme: The decision to join a sorority or fraternity is commonly referred to as going greek.
2. to engage in anal copulation.
1982 in *Nat. Lampoon* (Feb. 1983) 25: Maybe you want to go Greek!...Bend over!

Greek *v.* to engage in anal copulation.—also constr. with *it*.
*a***1972** B. Rodgers *Queens' Vernacular* 100: *Greek*...to practice anal eroticism. *Ibid.* 88: He'd rather greek than freak. **1973** *Best from Screw* (No. 4) 25: Sort of like...getting greeked by your own condomed pinky. **1975** *DAS* (ed. 3) 706: *Greek* v.i., v.t. To have heterosexual anal intercourse. **1980** Ciardi *Browser's Dict.* 161: *Greek it.* To practice anal sex.

green *n.* **1.** GREENHORN, 3.
[***1825** in *OEDS*: It appears that George Charteris...had been "doing" the *green*, and taking in the "deep ones," quite in the gull-catching style.] ***1837** C. Dickens, in *OEDS*: "Well, well," said the Dodger..."That hasn't got anything to do with young Green here." ***1840** in *Ibid.*: I then with my comrade stole from a green twelve shirts...and some stockings. **1841** *So. Literary Messenger* vii 54: I lost at euker/Nine thousand dollars; and being out of means,/I knifed a flat-boat Hoozier—took his lucre—/Went up the country—rifled twenty *greens*. ***1859** (cited in Partridge *DSUE* (ed. 5) 1118).
2. money.
1898–1900 Cullen *Chances* 182: All three of them had gobs of the green. **1901** in "O. Henry" *Cabbages & Kings* 275: They're hanging men and women now,/For lacking of the green. **1943** in Kluger *Yank* 114: Too often dogfaces will part with the good green for a fancy bauble. **1948** in Galewitz *Great Comics* 280: Then he started the countin' of the green. **1953** Kramer & Karr *Teen-Age Gangs* 155: And how's he going to do that without the green? **1953** Brossard *Bold Saboteurs* 73: She must have stashed away quite a bundle of the good old green. **1961** Gover *$100 Misunderstanding* 18: Ain you got no green? No loot? **1969** S. Harris *Puritan Jungle* 52: Money, Mann. *Dinero.* If you got green, you can buy your own acid. **1970** Zinberg *Walk Hard* 97: And I'll have

the green. **1970–71** Rubinstein *City Police* 399: There's no green there, just good, hard police work. **1973** Gwaltney *Destiny's Chickens* 70: Orval hauled out his wad and paid, green on the line, for a brand new rig. **1974** J. Rubin *Barking Deer* 199: There's always more green. **1981** Sann *Trial* 10: How much green you say was in that wallet? **1988** Kienzle *Marked for Murder* 131: She's not gonna service him until she sees some green.

3. *Narc.* (see 1952–58 quot.).
1957 Gelber *On Ice* 192: I've got hold of some crazy green. **1952–58** Kerouac *On Road*: He got hold of some bad green, as it's called in the trade—green, uncured marijuana. **1959–60** R. Reisner *Jazz Titans* 157: *Green*: marijuana.

green *adj.* Esp. *Stu.* (of actions or beliefs) ridiculously or contemptibly unsophisticated. Cf. the related S.E. sense, applied to individuals only.
1845 in B. Hall *College Wds.* (ed. 2) 241: For instance, when a man rushes to chapel in the morning at the ringing of the first bell, it is called green. ***1850** in *F & H* III 205: Have I done anything particularly *green*, as you call it?

¶ In phrase:

¶ **See anything green [in my eye]?** Do you think I'm a fool?
***1820–21** P. Egan *Life in London* 189: Asked..."if he saw anything *green* about him?" **1848** [W.T. Thompson] *Jones's Sks.* 77: Do you see anything green,...eh, hos? What do you think of me now, eh? ***1859** Hotten *Slang Dict.*: "Do you see any green in my eye?", ironical question in a dispute. **1882** C. Morris *Shadow Sam* 5: "Jist look here, Sam, and see if there's anything green 'bout my optics." And he pulled down the corners of his eyes significantly. ***1889** Barrère & Leland *Dict.* I 326: *Do you see anything green in my eye?* (popular), Do you think that I am to be taken in or gulled? **1929–33** J.T. Farrell *Manhood of Lonigan* 217 [ref. to *ca*1920]: "See anything green?" asked Paulie. **1936** Farrell *World I Never Made* 392: "See anything green?" the fellow sneered, coming toward Jim. **1967–79** in S. King *Bachman Bks.* 235: "See anything green?" Garraty asked irritably.

green *adv.* to the point of disability; thoroughly.
1912 in Truman *Dear Bess* 104: That Galt guy ran out...and nearly scared me green. **1924** *Adventure* (Dec. 10) 107: I'll say you was scared pea-green. **1936** Farrell *World I Never Made* 35: Come on, you White Sox, skunk them green! *Ibid.* 36: Come on Matty, sock it green! *a***1981** "K. Rollins" *Fighter Pilots* 214: He's scared green of the Old Man.

green apple *n.* a foolish, inexperienced person; (*also*) a novice.
1961 H. Ellison *Purgatory* 34: I stopped pickin' green apples like you when I was twelve. **1963** N.Y.C. man [ref. to WWII]: Our lieutenant was kind of a green apple. **1976** Whelton *CB Baby* 101: She was a green apple for sure.

green-apple quickstep *n.* diarrhea. Also **green-apple trots, green-apple two-step.** *Joc.*
1950 in *DARE*: Diarrhea or looseness of the bowels...Green-apple two-step...Green-apple quickstep. **1963** E.M. Miller *Exile* 41: I was up all night with the green-apple trots. **1973** Gwaltney *Destiny's Chickens* 58: Cramps, green-apple quickstep, or sprained back. **1975** *Nat. Lampoon* (Sept.) 94: They eat so much they get the green apple quickstep. **1985** in *DARE* [ref. to *ca*1920]: Sometimes we ate them too early and got the "green apple trots" as the result of our impatience. **1987** in *DARE*: Had the green apple two step, was keeping the bathroom busy.

green-ass *adj. & n.* inexperienced; raw; green; (*hence*, as n.) an inexperienced or raw person.—usu. considered vulgar.
1949 N. Algren *Golden Arm* 51: I spent thirty-four months havin' green-ass corporals chew me up. **1958** J. Davis *College Vocab.* 7: *Green ass*—An inexperienced member of a group whose actions seem foolish to older members. **1970** Wakefield *Going All the Way* 29: Watched us run around chasing our tails, a bunch of greenasses. **1973–77** J. Jones *Whistle* 33: Like a green-ass recruit, he had fainted dead away across his makeshift desk.

greenback *n.* a frog.
*a***1889** *Century Dict.* III 2617: *Greenback*...A frog (Anglers' slang). ***a1890–93** *F & H* III 209: *Green-back*...(common).—A frog. **1932** in *DARE*. **1967–70** in *DARE*.

greenback *v.* to pay, esp. as a bribe.
1979 Homer *Jargon* 162: You wanna get out of KP, all you gotta do is greenback the Mess Sergeant.

green bag *n.* *USAF.* a green flight suit.
1987 Zeybel *Gunship* 179 [ref. to Vietnam War]: "And all three were

wearing"—I flicked…my flying suit—"…green bags." *a*1990 R. Herman, Jr. *Force of Eagles* 30: And get the hell out of that green bag.

greenbean *n.* GREEN APPLE.

1958 J. Davis *College Vocab.* 7: *Green bean*—One who is inexperienced as a member of the group and acts accordingly thus seeming foolish in the eyes of older members. 1959 Maier *College Terms* 5: *Greenbean*—stupid character. 1985 Boyne & Thompson *Wild Blue* 98: You'll be the low-time green bean in [your] job.

green beanie *n.* **1.** *Army.* the green beret worn as part of the uniform of the U.S. Army Special Forces.

1963 Doulis *Path* 270: Good to see you. Even with the green beanie. 1982 "J. Cain" *Commandos* 101: Worked hard for this green beanie.

2. *Mil.* a member of the U.S. Army Special Forces (Green Berets).

1966 E. Shepard *Doom Pussy* 53: Those Green Beanie guys are overrated. Too lazy to work, too nervous to steal. 1970 *Just Military Men* 113: The Special Forces…are dismissed as "green beanies" by the Army establishment. 1972–76 Durden *No Bugles* 46: This was more like I woulda expected from Special Forces, the green beanie boys. 1978 Hasford *Short-Timers* 38: We watch John Wayne leading the Green Beanies. 1983 N. Proffitt *Gardens of Stone* 247: The only people halfway fighting this war the way they should are the green beanies, the Special Forces.

greenbelly *n.* **1.** GREENHORN, 3.

1955 "W. Henry" *Wyatt* 124: What that greenbelly doesn't know about poker, Hoyle could be lynched for.

2. *Navy.* (see quot.).

1981 former USN yeoman: *Greenbelly* was a Stateside term referring to Army soldiers. I heard it in Norfolk, Va., in 1964. It wasn't used in Nam because we all wore green fatigues there.

green-boy *n.* a greenback. Cf. YELLOWBOY.

1926 Finerty *Crim.* 25: *Green-boys*—Paper money.

green death *n.* Esp. *Stu.* an illness that causes diarrhea.

1968 Baker et al. *CUSS* 129: *Green death.* Have a minor illness, feel sick. 1971 *Current Slang* V 12: *Green Death*, n. Diarrhea and nausea resulting from eating university cafeteria food.

green dragon *n.* *Narc.* a green capsule containing a strong stimulant or depressant.

1970 Landy *Underground* 93: *Green dragon*…Amphetamine; an upper. 1972 *Nat. Lampoon* (Oct.) 41: *Desbutal* (green dragon). 1975 Hardy & Cull *Drug Lang. & Lore* 71: *Green dragons.* barbiturates.

greener *n.* **1.** [fr. GREENHORN; not, as occ. claimed, fr. Yid or G] GREENHORN, 1, 2.

1875 Lloyd *Lights & Shades in S.F.* 207: Other country chaps may be greeners. *1888 in *OED:* The master sweater gets hold of a new hand, a greener, as he is termed, and pays him a shilling a day. *1890, *1892, *1893 in *OED* 1893 W. James *Mavrick* 137: Those cattle are the remnant of old stock that fellow has been working off on greeners for sometime. 1898 Cahan *Bridegroom* 148: Feive is a *greener* to take such a match into his head! 1929 Hostetter & Beesley *Racket* 226: *Greener*—An immigrant; or, one who has just come to the city from the country. 1931 Adamic *Laughing* 66: Everybody in the saloon…knew that I was a "greener," and there was no end of laughing at my expense. *a*1940 in Lanning & Lanning *Texas Cowboys* 55: In those days a greener would be stood off for his pay by some of the ranchmen. 1949 Algren *Golden Arm* 113: He's over there shakin' down the greenhorns 'n the biggest greener on the beat is his own brother. 1966–70 in *DARE.*

2. a greenback, esp. a dollar bill.

1942 *ATS* 535: *Greeners*…paper money, esp. greenbacks. *Ibid.* 537: Dollar bill…*greener.* 1978 Groom *Better Times* 54: "What's the ante—dollar?" "A greener to you, Lieutenant."

green ghoul *n.* usu. *pl. Army & USMC.* a member of a graves registration unit.

1978 Hasford *Short-Timers* 73 [ref. to Vietnam War]: The green ghouls from graves registration stuff Winslow into a body bag. *Ibid.* 126: I get the map coordinates of a mass grave from some green ghouls.

Green Giant see JOLLY GREEN GIANT.

green goods *n.pl.* **1.** *Und.* counterfeit greenbacks; (*also*) (*obs.*) counterfeit or worthless securities.

1887 in Partridge *Dict. Und.* 306: He informs his prospective victim that he has a large quantity of "green goods" (counterfeit money) of different denominations. 1889 in *DA:* James T. Holland…[was] decoyed to New York to buy "green goods."…The "green-goods" dealer drops

him [the small investor] from the list [of "suckers"]. 1891 R.H. Davis *Gallegher* 130: Green goods is the technical name for counterfeit bills, and the green-goods men send out circulars…offering to sell $5000 worth of counterfeit money for $500. 1897 Townsend *Whole City Full* 164: Mike Golden's place was a headquarters for "green-goods" swindlers. 1899 F.P. Dunne, in Schaaf *Dooley* 368: They'd be sthrong enough to do business in spite of th' polis, they'd have no throuble in bein' incorpyated in New Jarsey, where th' green goods comes from. 1908 Sullivan *Crim. Slang* 1: *A green-goods man*—One who sells worthless securities to farmers and swindles poor people. 1910 Hapgood *City Streets* 160: That bloke over there asleep on the table is Jerry N—, a green-goods man, and one of the best in the country. 1932 Lawes *Sing Sing* 165: He has sold gold bricks and "green goods." 1933 Ersine *Pris. Slang* 41: *Green Goods.* A piece of counterfeit money. *Green-Goods Merchant.* A counterfeiter.

2. money.

1913 Light *Hobo* 76: Didn't you see that yegg man…brighten up when I produced the green goods? 1960 Barber *Minsky's* 319: Give the judge the greengoods.

green handshake *n.* a gift of money given as a tip, bribe, bonus payment, or the like. Cf. GOLDEN HANDSHAKE.

1975 Lichtenstein *Long Way* 34: Women's tennis had changed since the bad old days when players got paid with a "green handshake" and everyone was called an amateur.

green hat *n.* *Army.* a member of the U.S. Army Special Forces; Green Beret. Cf. GREEN BEANIE.

1979 J. Morris *War Story* 116 [ref. to Vietnam War]: Get that, Jim. They specified they want green hats.

greenhorn *n.* [one ME occurrence of this form is known, curiously applied to a horse (see *MED* and *OED*); present senses gained force fr. colloq. or S.E. *green* 'raw or inexperienced']

1. *Mil. & Naut.* a raw recruit (*obs.*); a novice in any profession or undertaking; TENDERFOOT.—usu. used derisively. Now *S.E.*

*1650 in *OED:* The Scotch king, being upon the castle-hill to see his men, which he called his Green Hornes, beaten. *1682 in *OED:* *Tyrones*, fresh-water Souldiers, or new levyed; Greenhorns: also it signifieth novices in any profession. 1832 Wines *2½ Yrs. in Navy* I 13: "Green-horn" is a term applied on shipboard to all who have never been to sea before. 1839 Olmsted *Whaling Voyage* 69: The crossing of the line, is considered an important event in a "greenhorn's" life. 1858 in *N. Dak. Hist.* XXXIII (1966) 147: I have escaped the usual fate of "Greenhorns" in being "bled" & enticed into foolish doings. 1859 H. Greeley, in *OED:* The chances for "big strikes" in the mines are few, and greenhorns cannot share them. 1861 in C.W. Wills *Army Life* 24: We are now drilling about six hours a day, but the greenhorns act as though they think it fun. 1865–67 De Forest *Miss Ravenel* 77: Both sides fought timidly…just as greenhorns naturally would do. 1884 Blanding *Sailor Boy* 52: "Greenhorns" who had never been to sea. 1893 Hill *20 Yrs. at Sea* 15: You Jim! come here and take this greenhorn down into the steerage and show him his chest. 1929 Bowen *Sea Slang* 59: *Greenies.* The American abbreviation, particularly in whalers, of greenhorns, or men going to sea for the first time. 1945 Colcord *Sea Lang.* 89: A green-horn…is a person making his first voyage. 1958 C. Funk *Horse Feathers* 186: The *greenhorn*…is a novice or ignoramus in any given trade, line or profession. 1966 Elli *Riot* 20: I'll be damned if I'll wait for that greenhorn in there to get done makin' his rounds. 1989 *Cheers* (NBC-TV): I told the supervisor to send the greenhorn down here so I could size him up.

2. a raw countryman, esp. when in the city; (*hence*) a recently arrived European immigrant.—used derisively.

*1753 in *F & H* III 211: A slouch in my gait, a long lank head of hair and an unfashionable suit of drab-coloured cloth, would have denominated me a *greenhorn*, or in other words a…very green [countryman]. *1790 in *OED:* Overseers are glad to get green-horns, because they can impose hardships on them. 1873 Lening *N.Y. Life* 251: Strangers in the city or "greenhorns." 1900 Greenough & Kittredge *Words & Ways* 65: A *greenhorn* is one who knows nothing of city life. 1917 Cahan *Levinsky* 93 [ref. to 1880's]: "Green one" or "greenhorn"…a contemptuous quizzical appellation for a newly arrived, inexperienced immigrant…stung me cruelly. 1923 Ornitz *Haunch, Paunch & Jowl* 2: Yiddish, the lingo of greenhorns, was held in contempt by the Ludlow Streeters. 1949 Algren *Golden Arm* 39: Don't call me "Zosh," I ain't no greenhorn, I wasn't born in Slutsk, I was born on eart' on Awgoosty Boulevard. 1983 Flaherty *Tin Wife* 25: A cop…who mocked the "greenhorn"...to reinforce his own Americanization.

3. a naive person who is easily taken in; unsophisticated fellow; dupe.

1805 Weems *Hymen's Sgt.* 34: This is the end of many *a green-horn*, who runs into bad company and ruin, for want of a beloved wife. ***1815** Sir W. Scott, in *F & H* III 211: Why, wha but a crack-brained green-horn wad hae let them keep up the siller that ye left at the Gordon-Arms? **1821** Waln *Hermit in Phila.* 27: A *blue greenhorn.*—A frequenter of *hot-water conventicles.* ***1821** *Real Life in London* I 161: A *Green-horn*...to whom you sell it for twice its value. **1846** in *Ill. State Hist. Soc. Jour.* (Summer 1953) 156: I don't think I have made much of a *green-horn* of myself in coming to Mexico. ***1849** in *F & H* III 211: A green-horn of a son. **1929** "M. Brand" *Last Showdown* 87: But he preferred to take on the tenderfeet, and the greenhorns, and the poor drunk cattlemen.

green hornet *n.* [sugg. by *The Green Hornet*, NBC radio series, 1936–52; ABC-TV series, 1966–67; arbit. ref. to color green] **1.** *Narc.* a green pill containing a strong stimulant or depressant.

1942 in Mencken *Amer. Lang. Supp.* II 682: *Green hornet*, sodium pentobarbital. **1975** Hardy & Cull *Drug Lang. & Lore* 72: *Green hornets.* the stimulant dextroamphetamine sulphate and amobarbital in combination.

2. *Army.* an Army Commendation Medal.

1982 W.E.B. Griffin *Lieuts.* 335 [ref. to 1946]: The Army Commendation Medal, called the Green Hornet.

3. *Mil.* (see quot.).

1951 *Time* (July 2) 17: The endlessly flowing paper [in the Pentagon] is controlled by colored tags...One "rush-rush" marker is known as "the green hornet."

4. [from the former color scheme of dark green, black, and white] *N.Y.C.* a police patrol car. Now *hist.*

1969 Salerno & Tompkins *Crime Confed.* 5: Even kids could spot it three blocks away and yell, "Here comes a Green Hornet!"

greenhouse *n. Av.* a glassed-in enclosure on an aircraft, as a gun turret, bombardier's compartment, or large cockpit.

*1941 *Life* (Mar. 24) 85: In the slang of the Royal Air Force man, the cockpit...is the "pulpit" or "office," the glass covering over it the "greenhouse." **1942** R. Casey *Torpedo Junction* 10: The transparent turret on a bomber. **1943** Tregaskis *Invasion Diary* 10: I crawled through the narrow tunnel to the bombardier's compartment in the nose, the "greenhouse," where he operated his machine gun and bombsight. **1944** Hubler & DeChant *Flying Leathernecks* 127 [ref. to 1942]: The five-and-a-half ton plane, with its steel-hooped greenhouse and gunner in the turret top, its stinger radio gunner under the plane... **1944** *Off. Guide to AAF* 368: *Greenhouse.* Glass enclosure, usually bombardier compartment. **1952** Cope & Dyer *Petty Officer's Guide: Green-house.* (Slang) An airplane cockpit enclosure. **1968** *Airman* (Feb.) 7: He kind of dreads climbing into that hot "greenhouse." **1970** Corrington *Bombardier* 115: Teaching us to drop from forty to forty-five thousand, using this new sight, up front in the greenhouse of the B-29. **1971** Cameron *First Blood* 16: I'll be up in the greenhouse, if and when he ever arrives.

greenie *n.* **1.a.** GREENHORN, 1.

1848 Judson *Mysteries* 262: Any body would know that these was took by a *greeny*. **1860** E. Ellis *Bill Biddon* 32: Whar'd you sight yourn, Greeny? **1862** in Dodge *Army & Other Tales* 213: What am I doing, greeney? Why, I'm huntin'! **1867** Eno *Twenty Years* 167: Instead of a Greely he has shown himself a *greeny* or a Granny. **1868** Macy *There She Blows!* 21: They ridiculed us as "greenies." **1878** Mulford *Fighting Indians* 29: When the Sergeant dismisses us from drill, we greenies take a bee-line for the sutler. **1884** Blanding *Sailor Boy* iii: Tricks played upon the "Greenies." ***1898** Bullen *Cachalot* 4 [ref. to 1875]: As night fell, the condition of the "greenies," or non-sailor portion of the crew was pitiable. **1900** Kennedy *Adrift* 16: That way, Greeny. **1905** White *Boniface* 106: Blather all you want, greeny; we're going to stay right here till night comes. **1926** Norwood *Other Side of Circus* 48: Don't tip yourself off as a greeny by taking the top slice. **1938** Ashley *Yankee Whaler* 100 [ref. to 1904]: You greenies have got just a week to box the compass and learn the ropes. **1956** H. Gold *Not With It* 134: You're just a greenie in the business. **1981** Pietropinto & Congress *Clinic* 50: I suppose he didn't want her to wind up with one of the "greenies,"...though practically everyone we'd picked up was on his or her first job. **1982** P. Michaels *Grail* 92: Two greenies, first week on the beat. **1986–91** Hamper *Rivethead* 34: A greenie like me.

b. GREENHORN, 2.

1861 E.S. Ellis *N. Todd* 107: When I first knowed you I used to call you "Greeny." **1878** McElroy *Andersonville* 128: He spoke with a slightly rustic twang that was very tempting to a certain class of sharps to take him up for a "lubberly greenie." **1900** Ade *More Fables* 97: "You go slow there in the City."..."I ain't no Greeny." **a1904–11** Phillips *Susan Lenox* I 257: She's going pretty good with these greenies...But I've my doubts whether city people'll care for anything so milk-like. **1948** Lait & Mortimer *N.Y. Confid.* 220: A greenie in Gotham. **1953** in Cannon *Like 'Em Tough* 97: He wants to know how to get to Forty-seventh and Broadway...so I figure him for a greenie. **1964** Faust *Steagle* 63: Give me a greenie right off the boat. **1973** Haney *Jock* 113: Talk about a greenie. I remember getting out of the cab in front of Belmont Park and being terrified.

c. GREENHORN, 3.

1854 St. Clair *Metropolis* 59: The aristocracy of Boston are not such "greenies" as had been supposed. **1863** Hollister *Colo. Vols.* 89: Two gamblers colleagued to *do* a greeny. **1865** Barnum *Humbugs* 125: Clergyman said he would take further advice...thought he wouldn't be shown up as a "greeny" in the police reports. **1865** *Rogues & Rogueries of N.Y.* 60: She *is* exerting all her arts to entice "greeny" into her net. **1873** Badger *Two-handed Mat* 15: You fellers go by the books you read—that's why you're sech blessed greenies. **1885** Siringo *Texas Cowboy* 45: Mr. "Shanghai" had the fun of selling them over again, to some other greeny, may be. **1892** Cox *5 Yrs.* 48: Those fellows think they have a "greeny" in tow. **1895** W.N. Wood *Big I* 131: There was sitting on the fence, in appearance, a regular "greeny" of a young man. **1902** "J. Flynt" *Little Bro.* 50: The poor little greeny. **1905** W.S. Kelly *Lariats* 183: I never saw a greeny in my life but what was a moralist. **1931** Bisbee *Four Wars* 79: There were certainly a lot of "greenies" aboard with gullible appetites for wealth. **1960** *Twilight Zone* (CBS-TV): It was your idea to give it to that little college greenie! **1976** Knapp & Knapp *One Potato* 86: "Greenies are afraid to make out," "a person who's never been kissed by a boy," "someone who's shy in front of girls."

2.a. a greenback.

1942 *ATS* 535: *Greenies*...paper money, esp. greenbacks. **1958** S.H. Adams *Tenderloin* 258 [ref. to 1890's]: I still got that fifty-dol greenie, Dan. ***1980** in Partridge *DSUE* (ed. 8) 501: A brutal lunge at the greenies in your wallet.

b. a nickel.

1942 Algren *Morning* 22: "Borrow me a greenie now 'n I'll show you the machine." Bruno found a nickel in his pants pocket.

3. a green capsule containing a stimulant or a depressant.

1966 "Petronius" *N.Y. Unexp.* 171: Amies, Cheracol, Terpin Hydrate, greenies, [etc.]. **1967** Colebrook *Cross of Lassitude* 312: Thank God I took the "greenies." **1969** Bouton *Ball Four* 81: Greenies are pep pills—dextroamphetamine sulfate—and a lot of baseball players couldn't function without them. **1970** Horman & Fox *Drug Awareness* 467: *Greenies*—green, heart-shaped tablets of dextroamphetamine sulfate and amobarbital. **1973** Gent *N. Dallas* 230: "Jesus, how strong were the hearts?"..."He didn't say. I think they were greenies." **1985** *N.Y. Times* (Aug. 21) A 23: Conversations...centered on how common it was for players to use amphetamine pills, known as "greenies."

4. *pl.* envy.—constr. with *the*.

1966 Herbert *Fortune & Men's Eyes* 47: It's Catso-Ratso, your old gearbox buddy, who's got the greenies.

5. *pl.* green vegetables.

1976–77 McFadden *Serial* 235: The *point* is I've gotta have a place for greenies.

6. *Juve.* a small mass of expectorated phlegm.

1985 Bodey *F.N.G.* 55: He hawkers...a greenie.

Greenland *n.* Ireland. Hence **Greenlander** an Irishman. *Joc.*

*1873 Hotten *Slang Dict.: Greenlander*...Sometimes an Irishman. **1882** in Foner *Labor Songs* 239: I am a roving Irishman,/I sailed from Greenland's shore.

¶ In phrase:

¶ **from Greenland** gullible; ignorant.

*1838 C. Dickens *Oliver Twist* ch. viii: "A new pal," replied Jack Dawkins, pulling Oliver forward. "Where did he come from?" "Greenland." **1848** *Ladies' Repository* VIII (Oct.) 315: From Greenland, A man who is not initiated, or does not know much. **1848** Pry *Life in Baltimore* 13: The verdant youth from "Greenland"...is invariably taken in. ***1889** Barrère & Leland *Dict. Slang* I 429: "He comes from *Greenland*," he is unsophisticated.

green-light *v.* Now esp. *Film.* to give approval to proceed to (a person or project).

1943 in Loosbrock & Skinner *Wild Blue* 214: Now we can green light the big shots. **1952** *Sat. Eve. Post* (June 28) 19: The Americans felt that an "agreement in principle," among allies, green-lighted the whole project. **1961** *Harper's* (Sept.) 6: I hope that President Kennedy will read it carefully before green-lighting any more idiotic *Putsches.* **1990** *Cosmopolitan* (Mar.) 222: Development hell is the term for the period when you work on movies before they're "greenlighted." **1992** *N.Y. Observer* (July 13) 3: The man empowered to green-light movies. **1993** *L.A. Times* (Feb. 15) F1: Mike Medavoy, the chairman of TriStar Pictures…has green-lighted or been closely associated with seven best picture winners.

Green-light Hotel *n.* a police station; jail. *Joc.*
   1951 Yordan & Wyler *Detective Story* (film): "What do you want, room service?" "Well, it's the Green-light Hotel, ain't it?"

Green Machine *n.* *Mil.* the U.S. Marine Corps or U.S. Army.—constr. with *the.*
   1969 *N.Y. Times* (Aug. 31) IV 5: They fall victim to the stern rule of the "Green Machine," as some soldiers call the military. **1971** *Newsweek* (Jan. 11) 30: There is a widespread determination to thwart the "Green Machine" and many troops…merely go through the motions when they are off on their own. **1973** *Oui* (Feb.) 96: Addicts took their final furlough from the "green machine" under pressure. **1973** R. Roth *Sand in the Wind* 79: You're gonna be Marines—little green machines that make up the Big Green Machine. **1978** Hasford *Short-Timers* 122: Green Marines in the green machine have liberated a cherished past. **1982** Del Vecchio *13th Valley* 22: Fuck the Army. Fuck the green machine. *Ibid.* 87: There's a lot of crazy…dudes in this battalion…[who] think they're gettin over on the green machine. **1983** "J. Cain" *Dinky-Dau* 59: There's rules and regs everywhere the Green Machine goes. **1983** Eilert *Self & Country* 210: What they were going to do once they got out of the Green Machine. **1989** D. Sherman *There I Was* 59: That's all this goddam Green Machine ever does.

greenmail *n.* *Finance.* the practice of buying a large block of a company's stock, usu. as part of a takeover attempt, in the expectation that shareholders of the target company will buy back the stock at a premium to forestall the takeover; (*hence*) the funds used in greenmail.
   1983 in *OED2*: Those professional investors who practice "greenmail"—putting pressure on a company to get a buy-out for cash. **1984** *Newsweek* (Apr. 30) 66: Shareholders…are up in arms about the rash of corporate "greenmail." **1984** *N.Y. Times* (June 13) 29: Greenmail…refers to the pressure management feels to buy back shares that may be used in hostile takeovers. **1986** *NewsWatch* (CNN-TV) (Dec. 5): They said no greenmail would be paid or accepted. **1986** *Money Line* (CNN-TV) (Dec. 5): *Greenmail* is a premium paid to dissident shareholders. **1987** G. Trudeau *Doonesbury* (synd. cartoon strip) (Mar. 6): The arbs will jack up the price, I'll bail, and you take greenmail. What do you think?

greenmail *v.* *Finance.* to threaten or employ GREENMAIL against. Hence **greenmailer.**
   1984 *Time* (July 30) 89: St. Regis has been greenmailed twice. **1986** *Moneyline* (CNN-TV) (Oct. 20): What did they do? They greenmailed them! **1987** Weiser & Stone *Wall St.* (film): You're a two-bit pirate and a greenmailer. **1993** *New Republic* (Oct. 18) 22: Though their desire to purchase companies (with borrowed money) was sincere, they seemed relegated to the role of small-time greenmailers.

Green Monster *n.* *Baseball.* the high left-field wall in Fenway Park, Boston.
   1982 Luciano & Fisher *Umpire Strikes Back* 94: Oliva…swatted it over the Green Monster, the wall in left field. **1989** P. Dickson *Baseball Dict.* 189: The "Green Monster"…was painted green in 1947.…[previously] it was covered with advertisements. **1993** N.Y.C. man, age 31 (coll. J. Sheidlower): The *Green Monster* is the left-field wall in Fenway Park. It's been called that forever—anyone who knows the slightest thing about baseball knows it.

green motherfucker *n.* *Army & USMC.* the U.S. Army or U.S. Marine Corps.—usu. constr. with *this.*—used opprobriously.—usu. considered vulgar. Also vars. [Quots. ref. to Vietnam War.]
   1968 Stuard TS. (unp.): I'll be out of this "green thing" in another year. **1973** Karlin et al. *Free Fire Zone* 137: Plan on getting out of this green amphibious motherfucker. **1976** C.R. Anderson *Grunts* 146: How did you ever get in this green mother anyway? **1978** J. Webb *Fields of Fire* 210: The Corps…I *love* this green motherfucker. **1982** R.A. Anderson

Cooks & Bakers 116: They talked about how much they hated Vietnam and the Marine Corps—"the Crotch," "the Green Motherfucker." **1983** Ehrhart *VN-Perkasie* 54: The Army buys…jeeps that work. But the Green Mother spend money for good equipment? **1985** Dye *Between Raindrops* 144: Could have gotten *out* of this green motherfucker and been set, man.

green one *n.* a dollar bill; dollar.
   1928 Nason *Sgt. Eadie* 8 [ref. to 1918]: Every pay day I invested ten nice clean green ones, cryin' aloud that I could roll three sevens in a row.

green pea *n.* a naïve or inexperienced person; GREENHORN.
   1912 in P. Dickson *Baseball Dict.* 189: You're the green pea of the American League. **1924** T.A. Dorgan, in Zwilling *TAD Lexicon* 41: He's gotta look out for celler [*sic*] smellers you know because he's new here—He's just a green pea—Ain't hep to the reg'lars as yet. **1935** Pollock *Und. Speaks: Green pea,* a boob, sucker, chump. **1944** M. Hart *Winged Victory* (film): I hope we don't get one of them stuck-up green peas for a pilot. **1977** J. Olsen *Fire Five* 154: She's a green pea and she's got to be handled like one.

Green River *n.* ¶ In phrases:
   ¶ **send up Green River** to kill. Hence **go up Green River** to die.
   1871 Schele de Vere *Amer.* 200: A very odd expression, confined, however, mainly to the mountaineers in the wilder parts of the Southwest, is quite expressive; they say they send a man *up Green River,* when they have killed him. **1945** in *DA:* Four early expressions for [railroad] conductor—*superintendent, pilot, captain,* and *master of the cars*—have gone up Green River.
   ¶ **up to the Green River** (among trappers) to the maximum extent or degree; "to the hilt." [1850 quot. is literal.]
   1848 Ruxton *Life in Far West* 189: A thrust from the scalp-knife… seldom failed to strike home—up to the "Green River" on the blade.…The knives used by the hunters and trappers are manufactured at the "Green River" works, and have that name stamped upon the blade. Hence the mountain term for doing anything effectually is "up to the Green River." [**1850** Garrard *Wah-to-Yah* 163: I…socks my big knife up to the Green River, first dig.]

greens *n.pl.* **1.** copulation.
   1888 *Stag Party* 40: For Sairy gets her Bottomfelt,/John Henry gets his Greens. *1889 Barrère & Leland *Dict. Slang* I 429: *Greens* (common), "to have one's greens," to have sexual intercourse. *a1890–93 F & H III 206: *To get, have, or give one's greens*…To enjoy, procure, or confer the sexual favour. Said indifferently of both sexes. *1963 in *OEDS:* Section A make a study of the kind of greens the big shots go in for. *1967 in *OEDS:* She's not getting what I believe is vulgarly called her greens. **1983** in *Harper's* (Jan. 1984) 76: This sounds like a sexual metaphor—think of the expression "getting one's greens."
   2. money; cash.
   1904 Hobart *Missouri* 94: It cost our candidate a smart bundle of greens. **1924** Wilstach *Stage Slang* 21: *Greens:* Money. **1925** in Partridge *Dict. Und.* 306: *Greens,* paper currency; banknotes. **1969** Pendleton *Death Squad* 15: Just any guy with a sudden hungering for a large chunk of greens.
   ¶ In phrase:
   ¶ **for greens** *So.* for no particular reason; for fun. Cf. GRIN, *n.*
   1848 in *F & H* III 209: I've made up my mind to make a tower of travel to the big North this summer, jest for greens, as we say in Georgia, when we hain't got no very pertickeler reason for anything, or hain't got time to tell the real one. **1861** "Citizen" *So. Chivalry* 15: Long ago, at New Orleans,/You whipt the British "just for greens."

greenseed *n.* *Army.* GREEN APPLE. [Quots. ref. to Vietnam War.]
   1988 F.C. Berry *Chargers* 157: *Greenseed*—New arrival. **1990** G.R. Clark *Wds. of Viet. War* 207: *Greenseed*…New troop.

green stamp *n.* **1.** a dollar bill; (*pl.*) money.
   1956 Hargrove *Girl He Left* 20: Why should you sit around screaming about forty bucks? It's just a handful of green stamps. **1976** Whelton *CB Baby* 16: Green stamps are money. A Green Stamp Highway is a toll road. **1976** Adcock *Not Truckers Only* 45: Not much in the way of green stamps, this trip. **1976** *Sci. Mech. CB Gde.* 171: I fed Smokey some green stamps. **1976** Bibb et al. *CB Bible* 79: 25 green stamps.
   2. *CB.* a green traffic summons.
   1975 *Atlantic* (May) 42: Might be a Bear wants to give us some green

stamps. **1976** Whelton *CB Baby* 98: What do you say, Super Trooper, you pulling in the green stamps today? **1977** Dills *CB Slanguage* (ed. 4) 49: *Green stamps*—speeding tickets.

green stuff *n.* money.

1887 DeVol *Gambler* 207: Bill…reached the wharf-boat with a large roll of the good green stuff. **1897** Ade *Pink* 114: Boy, wheah you get 'at green stuff? **1908** T.A. Dorgan, in Zwilling *TAD Lexicon* 107: He…will carry a wad of the green stuff with him. **1915** Howard *God's Man* 216: A chunk of perfectly good green stuff. **1950** Gordon & Gordon *FBI Story* 12: He pulled out a wallet and started fingering the…green stuff. **1953** W. Brown *Monkey on My Back* 14: Yeah, green-stuff, money to you.

green tuxedo *n.* USAF. a green flight suit. *Joc.*

1985 Heywood *Taxi Dancer* 165: Nuclear nice guys in starched green tuxedos.

green up *v. Mil. Av.* (of an aviator) to arm (ordnance) electronically. [Quots. ref. to Vietnam War.]

*a*1981 "K. Rollins" *Fighter Pilots* 252: Green 'em up, Panther. *a*1991 Kross *Splash One* 8: "Lance, green 'em up." And the…pilots armed their bombs.

green weenie *n.* **1.a.** Esp. *Mil.* an instance of discomfiture or victimization, esp. if unpredictable or undeserved; a damaging or finishing action.—usu. in phr. **get** [or **have had**] **the green weenie**; in phr. **eat the green weenie** to be killed. Also vars.

1944 Kendall *Service Slang* 24: *Green weinie*…anything bad. **1959** Brosnan *Long Season* 242: "Now let's watch Purkey slip the green weenie past Banks."…"Where in the world did you pick up an expression like that, Ellis?" "That's an old baseball term…I've been using it for years." "Sure, but what does it mean?" "Oh, I don't know…I guess it means give the batter something he doesn't like." **1968–70** *Current Slang* III & IV 56: *Give the green weeney* v. To break a date or to "break up."—University of Kentucky. **1971** B.B. Johnson *Blues for Sister* 11: But before Frank could get his national distribution set…he was really given the green wienie by Luke. **1971** Sorrentino *Up from Never* 238: Ah'm puttin' you yardbirds on notice. You have had the green wienie. [**1973** Wagenheim *Clemente!* 128 [ref. to *ca*1966]: Announcer Bob Prince…conspired with Danny Whelan (then the team trainer [of the Pittsburgh Pirates]) to invent the "Green Weenie," a huge plastic hot dog that would put the "whammy" on opposing players.] **1980** Garrison *Snakedoctor* 140: "Danner just gave me the Great Green Weenie." "A reprimand or what?" "Suspension." **1986** Univ. Tenn. instructor, age *ca*33 [ref. to *a*1970]: When my father used to throw things out that were broken he'd say, "Well, *that's* had the green weenie." **1986** Merkin *Zombie Jamboree* 93: I see the world as something that arbitrarily sticks the green, raspy weenie up my butt when it feels like it. *a*1987 Bunch & Cole *Reckoning* 203 [ref. to Vietnam War]: Willie had been doomed. Guys who were shiny-new or mossbacked-short always ate the green weenie.

b. *Army & USMC.* fate in general; (*also*) the military regarded as a victimizing agent. [Quots. ref. to Vietnam War.]

1976 C.R. Anderson *Grunts* 92: The green weenie strikes again, eh, Lieutenant? **1979** Hiler *Monkey Mt.* 280: That's what he gets for shippin' over. The Green Wienie'll do it to you every time!

2. *Mil.* gonorrhea.—constr. with *the*. *Joc.*

1972 U.S. Army Spec. 5, U.S. Army Comm. Command—Taiwan (coll. J. Ball): Whatever you do, don't order tea at the clubs—the girls will figure that means you got the green weenie. **1972** U.S. Army PFC, U.S. Army Comm. Command—Taiwan (coll. J. Ball): Mack got the weenie, the weenie, the greenie, greenie weenie, to match his olive drab!

3. *Army.* the Army Commendation Medal. *Joc.*

1975 *Playboy* (Nov.) 160: This morning's is to be an awards parade, but—it being peacetime—the awards will be neither green weenies nor M.C.M.s nor Silver Stars. **1980** Cragg *L. Militaris* 206: *Green Weenie.* The Army Commendation Medal. **1991** Reinberg *In the Field* 97 [ref. to Vietnam War]: *Green weenie*…Army Commendation Medal.

greet *n.* a greeting; (*pl.*) greetings!

1908 in Fleming *Unforget. Season* 226: This is Mr. Marquard come to pitch for you. Grant him a little greet. **1986** Merkin *Zombie Jamboree* 155: Greets…Didn't know you were in the neighborhood.

grefa var. GREEFA.

gremlin *n.* [orig. unkn., but prob. infl. by *goblin*] **1.** Orig. *Mil.*

Av. a small gnomelike being humorously postulated as the cause of unaccountable occurrences, esp. engine trouble or other mechanical mishaps aboard an aircraft in flight; (*broadly*) any recurrent or unidentified cause of trouble or difficulty. [In 1929 quot., figuratively used to denote junior officers regarded by their superiors as troublesome or insignificant.]

***1929** Aeroplane* (Apr. 10) 57: All Officers below the rank of Squadron Leader…They are but a herd of gremlins,/Gremlins who do all the flying,/Gremlins who do much instructing. ***1941** in OEDS:* As he flew round, he wished that his instructor had never told him about the Little People—a mythological bunch of good and bad fairies originally invented by the Royal Naval Air Service in the Great War…Those awful little people, the Gremlins, who run up and down the wing with scissors going "snip, snap, snip," made him sweat. **1942** *Newsweek* (Sept. 7) 24: First reports of the "Gremlins" reached the United States last week. Gremlins are exasperating pixies, often clad in caps, ruffled collars, tight breeches and often spats, who delight in raising hell in Allied planes…The great-granddaddy of all "bloody Gremlins" was born in 1923 in a beer bottle belonging to a Fleet Air Arm pilot whose…plane was cursed with perpetual engine trouble. **1942** *Time* (Sept. 28) 10: During the winter of 1922…[a weather forecaster at LeBourget Airport] was asked by a worried pilot, en route to England, for the weather conditions in the English Channel. He announced solemnly "*Gremlins sur la Manche*," and left it at that. Further efforts by the pilot to get an explanation were met by…silence. ***1942** in OEDS:* They called them Gremlins, "on account of they were the goblins which came out of Fremlin beer bottles." They were the genii loci of the R.A.F. messes in India and the Middle East, where Fremlin's beer bottles were plentiful. **1943** Pyle *Here Is Your War* 227: We have gremlins in the infantry too. And the meanest gremlin is the one who moves mountains. We start for a certain hill in the dark, we check everything carefully as we go along, and then when we get there some gremlin has moved the damned mountain and we can't find it anywhere. **1944** *N.Y. Times Mag.* (June 4) 12: Another name for [AAF] rest homes is Gremlin Grange. This has its origin in RAF gremlin mythology. Anyone who begins seeing gremlins is ready for Gremlin Grange. **1944** *AS* XIX 280: Now the gremlin seems to be extending its sphere of operations, so that the term can be applied to almost anything that inexplicably goes wrong in human affairs. **1945** G. Frank et al. *Seawolf* 79: If there are sea gremlins, they were certainly having a time with us. *a*1966 in *World Bk. Dict.* 872: Our biggest gremlin was rust. **1977** *N.Y. Times Bk. Review* (Dec. 25) 15: Around this time [1941] he [Roald Dahl] also wrote "The Gremlins," his first book for children. "The Gremlins," a name he invented, were tiny men who lived on fighter planes and bombers and who were responsible for all the airplane crashes during the war. **1979** G. Wolff *Duke of Deception* 67: North American had given my father the title of Assistant Chief Designer, and the responsibility to work gremlins out of the RAF's new Mustangs. **1981** D.E. Miller *Jargon* 195: When data is transmitted across a connecting wire, or *line,* parts of it sometimes turn up missing—lost to noise or signal drift, or, when there's no other handy explanation, line gremlins. **1982** Basel *Pak Six* 56: That Thud had gremlins, bad ones…it went crazy on nearly every mission—usually at a critical point. **1988** Dye *Outrage* 93: I'd say this damn high-tech…system is full of gremlins, sir. **1989** T. Blackburn *Jolly Rogers* 14: That [plane's] gremlins…were legion.

2.a. *Surfing.* a young person, often a nuisance or troublemaker, who frequents a surfing beach but does not surf; (*also*) an inexperienced surfer.

1961 *Life* (Sept. 1) 51: The toddler…will be a "gremlin" in a few years, running errands for older surfers. ***1965** in OEDS: Gremmie* or *gremlin,* a young inexperienced surf enthusiast to whom nothing counts in life but surf-board and water. Also, an uncomplimentary term applied to those who hang around the beaches for reasons other than surfing. **1968** Kirk & Hanle *Surfer's Hndbk.* 139: *Gremlin, gremmy, gremmie:* pseudo-surfer; young or beginning surfer; also an objectionable type, often rowdy.

b. *Skateboarding.* an inexperienced skateboarder.

1979 Cuddon *Dict. Sports & Games* 379.

gremmie *n.* **1.** GREMLIN, 2.

***1962** in OEDS: Gremmies,* young poor mannered surfers. **1963** Rusoff *Beach Party* (film): Where the gremmies and the hodads never go. **1963** *Time* (Aug. 9) 49: The true surfer is scornful of the "ho-daddies" (a gibe of undetermined origin) and "gremmies" (gremlins, usually girls), those hangers-on who may never get wet behind the ears as far as surfing goes but like to immerse themselves in the dense jargon of the ii.

group. **1966** *Sat. Eve. Post* (Nov. 19) 32: I used words like woodie (a station wagon with a wooden body) and a gremmie (an onlooker). But I didn't surf. **1967** *New Yorker* (June 17) 24: A lot of gremmies come out just to impress girls. **1967** W. Murray *Sweet Ride* 7: I inched in between two wagons full of surfboards and blue-looking gremmies sitting in their cars and warming up on coffee. **1981** *New West* (May) 93: Murphy, Rick Griffin's characterization of a typical gremmie, made his debut in 1961 in the second issue of *Surfer* magazine. *a***1985** Schwendinger & Schwendinger *Adolescent Sub.* 316: Some surfers…denigrate their surfing competitors by calling them "Gremmies."

2. a Gremlin automobile.

1972 *Motor Trend* (Oct.) 40: Both Gremmies are handy cars.

Greta Garbo *n. Yachting.* (see quot.).

1961 Burgess *Dict. Sailing* 104: *Greta Garbo.* Yachtsman's name for a large quadrilateral jib worked by a sheet on each clew.

grette *n. Stu.* a cigarette. Cf. RET.

1968 Baker et al. *CUSS* 129: *Grette.* Cigarette. **1969** *Current Slang* I & II 43: *Grette,* n. Cigarette.—College students, both sexes, Minnesota.

grid *n. Jour.* GRIDIRON, 2.—also attrib. Now *colloq.*

1928 in *DA:* Law…to Lead Irish on Grid in 1929. **1940** Ellis & Logan *Star Dust* (film): He's a grid star at ATI. **1946** in *DA:* Thirty-Four Out for Grid Practice. **1970** R. Angell, in *New Yorker* (Oct. 3) 34: You grid fans are just going to have to buckle down, Moe.

2. *Mil.* a general location, esp. on a battlefield; place.

1978 *Nat. Lampoon* (July) 67 [ref. to 1972]: *Hot grid* A location where an enemy force is suspected. *Ibid.* 96: They opened up with those miniguns and lit up the entire motherfuckin' grid, man.

gridder *n. Sports Journ.* a football player.

1934 Weseen *Dict. Slang* 227: *Gridder*—A football player. **1982** Considine *Lang. Sport* 144: *Gridder:* A football player.

gridiron *n.* **1.** *Naut. & Mil.* the Stars and Stripes.—constr. with *the.*

1812 in *OEDS:* The masts from which they flew, went over the side, while Hull's four "*gridirons*" floated in the air triumphant. **1833** Ames *Yarns* 206: The whiteness of her canvass, and her bright-varnished sides, sufficiently indicated her to be a Yankee, without the trouble of hoisting the gridiron. **1843** Leech *30 Yrs. from Home* 211 [ref. to 1815]: We longed to get once more where the "old gridiron" floated in fearless triumph. **1857** Nordhoff *Merchant Vessel* ch. xiii: For a moment I felt my heart sink, and longed to be back on my old ship, with the *gridiron* overhead. **1860–61** R.F. Burton *City of Saints* 276: There is only one "Yankee gridiron" in the town. **1861** in W.H. Russell *My Diary* 14: The great gaudy stars and stripes, or as one of the Secession journals…styles it, the "Sanguinary United States Gridiron." **1862** in Heartsill *1491 Days* 89: Sorrel Top look at that d—m big grid Iron (flag). **1863** in *Kans. Hist. Qly.* VII (1938) 100: We also in our enthusiasm gave a few cheers for the old "Gridiron." **1863** in Norton *Army Letters* 159: Give me the Confederate flag. I don't want none o' yer gridirons about me. **1864** in *Civil War Times Illus.* X (Apr.) 13: The flag was insulted, called the United States gridiron & they threaten'd to arrest one of our men. **1871** Schele de Vere *Americanisms* 258: Sailors…seeing it hoisted, say "There goes the *gridiron.*" **1879** *Scribner's Mo.* (Feb.) 534: The alternate red and white stripes of the Yankee "gridiron." **1891** *United Service* (Feb.) 209: But now he floated the Gridiron and now he flaunted the Jack. **1949** Pei *Story of Lang.* 300: Canadianisms… [include] "The Gridiron" for "Old Glory."

2. *Football.* a football field. Now *S.E.*

1896 in *OED:* Gridiron…is the technical name applied to an American football field. **1900** *DN* II 39: *Gridiron*…foot-ball field. **1903** in "O. Henry" *Cabbages & Kings* 110: His right elbow laid out the governor man on the gridiron. **1906** *Independent* (Nov. 29) 1260: Now, this is the gridiron. **1930** in D.O. Smith *Cradle* 79: There are 3 complete gridirons with 6 goal posts. **1929–33** Farrell *Manhood of Lonigan* 247: And if any of you birds are carried off that gridiron, cold, don't expect to break down and weep for you.

grief *n.* trouble or annoyance. Now *colloq.*

1897 Hamblen *General Mgr.* 181: He could stand more grief than the old engine herself, and thrive on it, too. **1925** in Hammett *Big Knockover* 155: Don't be foolish and poke your nose into a lot of grief. **1933** Nason *Trumpets* 117: Hello, Penrose!…What's the grief now? **1938** Bezzerides *Long Haul* 14: That's not my grief…We can't hang around here all morning. **1948** Lay & Bartlett *Twelve O'Clock High!* 41: I'd like to settle without bothering the colonel. He's got enough grief. **1965** O'Neill *High Steel* 271: *Grief.* caustic criticism from a boss.

griefer *n.* [see GREEFA] *Narc.* (see quot.).

1936 Duncan *Over the Wall* 21 [ref. to 1918]: The griefers were habituated to marijuana or Mexican hemp.

griever *n. Labor.* a member of a grievance committee.

1952 *ATS* (ed. 2) 720. **1961** Kalisher *R.R. Man* 77: The griever is the grievance committeeman. **1979** in Terkel *Amer. Dreams* 238: I ran for griever when I was twenty.

griff *n.* var. GRIFT, *n.*

griffin *n.* **1.** *Naut. & Mil.* a white person from Britain or North America who has recently arrived in Asia.

***1793** in *OED:* You must, I presume, be a perfect griffin. ***1794** in *OED:* I am little better than an unfledged Griffin, according to the fashionable phrase here [Madras]. ***1807** in *OED:* Every arrival from Europe…as soon as he touches terra-firma is a griffin. ***1816** in *OED:* Young men, immediately on their arrival in India, are termed griffins, and retain this honour until they are twelve months in the country. ***1836** in *OED:* Griffin means a freshman or freshwoman in India. ***1883** in *F & H* III 214: Many a youngster has got on in his profession…by having the good fortune to make a friend of the old Indian who took him in as a griffin or a stranger. **1942** *Leatherneck* (Nov.) 146: *Griffin*—Man on duty in Asiatics less than a year (Just a boy!). **1946** Sawyer *Gunboats* 8 [ref. to *ca*1899]: We younger officers were "griffons," newcomers to the coast of Asia. **1967** *AS* XLII 26: Not only…the *griffins* but…the *old China hands* as well. **1982** R.H. Williams *Old Corps* 43 [ref. to 1930's]: A foreigner on the China coast, like a China pony, was called a "griffin" for his first year.

2. (see quots.).

*a***1889** *Century Dict.* III 2623: *Griffin*…(Anglo-Ind.)…A racing pony or horse that runs for its first time. ***1889** Barrère & Leland *Dict. Slang* I 430: *Griffin*…(Anglo-Chinese), a horse fresh from the wilds. ***a1890–93** *F & H* III 213: *Griffin*…(Anglo-Chinese) = an unbroken horse. **1936** in Thomason *Stories* 299: A griffin, out there [Peking], is a new pony that has never faced the starter's flag.

grift *n.* [perh. orig. in phr. *on the grift,* based on GRIFT, *v.* (cf. *on the make, on the lam,* etc.); perh. alter of GRAFT, *n.,* infl. by *drifter*]

1.a. Orig. *Und.* unlawful activity, esp. swindling, pickpocketing, and unlawful or crooked gambling; in phr. **on the grift** engaged in such activity.

1914 Jackson & Hellyer *Vocab.* 39: *Grift,* Noun. General usage. Graft; an opportunity for plying criminal talents. Example: "How's grift on the shorts in the winter?" "Crow. Too many togs." **1918** *Chi. Sun. Trib.* (Apr. 7) V (unp.): But for guys in our line o' graft an' grift it's soup bones an' hard tack. **1922** *Variety* (July 7) 10: Internal Evils of Carnival Management Come Out…Less Grift this Summer. *Ibid.* (Aug. 18) 8: And so a clean show is transformed into a "grift" outfit. **1928** Callahan *Man's Grim Justice* 128: Don't tell her anything about Danny being on the grift. **1928** *AS* III (June) 413: *Grift.* The circus and carnival equivalent of the uglier word "graft." "Grift," and the "grifters," the men who ply it, have nearly disappeared from outdoor show life. **1930** Lait *On Spot* 204: *Grift*…Thievery. **1931** *Amer. Mercury* (Nov.) 352: *Grift show*…a circus that permits crooked gambling. **1946** Dadswell *Hey, Sucker!* 237: In the first place "grift" is now more the exception than the rule [in carnivals]. **1951** Mannix *Sword-Swallower* 63: [When] the word is passed to lay off the grift,…the [gambling] joint men don't pay off in cash but with slum. **1975** McKennon *Horse Dung Trail* 57: In spite of the weather, and the "grift," the big show prospered. **1982–84** in Safire *Take My Word* 160: The audiences, never having been on the grift, took it to mean something less recondite. **1992** *Melrose Place* (Fox-TV): We were on the grift! Stealing from the rich!

b. *Und.* a criminal profession; (one's) racket.

1914 Jackson & Hellyer *Vocab.* 44: "What's his grift?" "He's on the hoist." **1925** in Hammett *Big Knockover* 221: Her friends…were a mixture of bookies, con-men and the like. I couldn't find out what her grift was. She talked a thieves' slang and high-school English. **1931** C. Ford *Coconut Oil* 88: That's our grift: we're puttin' this African big-game hunting racket on a sound Chicago basis. **1938** H. Miller *Trop. Capricorn* 112: They were carnival people who worked "the griffs and the grinds," as he put it. **1938** R. Chandler *Big Sleep* 47: Got a grift, brother—or just amusing yourself? **1940** D.W. Maurer, in *AS* (Apr.) 118: *Grift*…A racket or criminal profession. Often used where *grifter* would not be used in a strict sense. "I've been on the grift all my life." **1949** R. Chandler *Little Sister* 66: He had some kind of a grift, but he don't have the looks or personality to bounce checks.

c. business; profession. *Joc.*

1929 Hammett *Dain Curse* 155: "How's the literary grift go?" I asked.

2. *Und.* GRIFTER.

1915 Bronson-Howard *God's Man* 133: An old-time Mississippi riverboat cheater could clean him, let alone a couple smart young grifts like us. **1964** in B. Jackson *Swim Like Me* 108: I can show any pennyweight thief or grift any kind a game they try to play. **1966** S. Harris *Hellhole* 161: Molly still designates [underworld characters] by the names with which she first learned to identify them [*ca*1910]:…"griffs"—young thieves.

3. *Und.* a location where grifting may be practiced.

1921 *Variety* (July 22) 7: They were in the softest grift in the racket and…they worked under protection. **1927** H. Miller *Moloch* 79: Eking out a precarious living "playing the grifts and the grinds."

4. money obtained through bribery, swindling, or extortion.

1929 Hotstetter & Beesley *Racket* 227: Grift—Graft; money accepted as a bribe; money dishonestly obtained through the influence of official position. **1931** *Amer. Mercury* (Nov.) 352: *Grift*, n. Graft; proceeds from short-changing, crooked gambling, etc. **1953** Manchester *City of Anger* 110: By morning no grift for the judge himself on that run. **1956** Algren *Walk on Wild Side* 168.

5. a cheating aspect.

1972 R. Barrett *Lovomaniacs* 241: There's a grift—a joker—in this scam somewhere.

grift *v.* **1.** Orig. *Und.* to engage in swindling or petty theft as an occupation; (*trans.*) to obtain by swindling or petty theft, esp. pickpocketing.

1915 Bronson-Howard *God's Man* 263: Grifting ain't what it used to be. **1930** Conwell *Pro. Thief* 13: There are many business maxims and rules, which may be illustrated by the rule, "Never grift on the way out." **1933** Ersine *Pris. Slang* 41: Grift, *v.* To steal. **1934** Appel *Brain Guy* 30: He…had grifted ten bucks in ten minutes. **1935** *Amer. Mercury* (June) 229: *Grift:* euphemism of *graft;* to swindle. **1937** Reitman *Box-Car Bertha* 106: They had grifted for a week in Chicago. **1982** (quot. at DUNNIGAN).

2. *Und.* to practice grifting in (a location).

1930 Conwell *Pro. Thief* 5: A cannon (pick-pocket) mob was grifting (stealing in) an "L" station in Boston. **1937** Reitman *Box-Car Bertha* 103: The conversation quickly switched to the next spot they would grift.

3. *Carnival.* to create in a specious or fraudulent manner.

1951 Mannix *Sword-Swallower* 141: I supposed the old man's [sideshow] routine was "grifted"—which is carny slang for faked.

grifter *n.* Orig. *Und.* a small-time swindler, crooked gambler, or pickpocket, esp. one preying upon the patrons of a circus or carnival; (*broadly*) petty criminal; crook.

1915 Bronson-Howard *God's Man* 366: We grifters had a damn good right to nick a Front or peel a poke so long as Wall Street and Washington were picking everybody's pockets. **1915–16** Lait *Beef, Iron & Wine* 36: The grifters was more entertaining in the old days. **1917** *Editor* (Feb. 24) 153: *Grifters*—short change swindlers, or swindlers of small caliber. **1926** *AS* I (Feb.) 282: *Grifter.* The old time gamblers and short-change artists who followed the circus in days gone by. **1928** *Variety* (Oct. 24) 59: If a grifter's wife…is alleged to have "talked" too often, the "mob" settles those scores in a manner typical of the fate meted out to squealers or stools. **1928–30** Fiaschetti *Gotta Be Rough* 185: Just a couple of two-cent grifters. **1932** *Writer's Digest* (Aug.) 48: *Grifter*, a card cheat. **1935** *Amer. Mercury* (June) 229: *Grifter:* agent of a flat or strong joint; confidence man. Obviously derived from combining the two words, *grafter* and *drifter.* **1939** *AS* (Oct.) 239: *Grifter.* Small time crook. **1947** Mailer *Naked & Dead* 480: It's a pretty small grifter who fugs around for twenty-one bucks. **1952** Holmes *Go* 102: The place looked like some strange social club for grifters, dope passers, petty thieves. **1959** Bonner *Villon* 171: Cops, all grifters themselves,/string up five or six at once. **1971** *N.Y. Times Mag.* (Nov. 28) 94: A "grifter" is any kind of street hustler. **1982** Braun *Judas Tree* 36: He might have been a grifter or a thimblerigger or a robber. **1983** *Newsweek on Campus* (Dec.) 5: Rourke has made grifters and mystics equally appealing. **1990** *The Grifters* (film title).

grik *n.* a Greek.—used contemptuously.

1971 Faust *Willy Remembers* 133: Hollywood is controlled by yids and griks. **1987** *Miami Vice* (NBC-TV): Ah, the grik—bearing gifts, no doubt.

grill *n.* Esp. *Black E.* the face.

1980 "Grandmaster Flash & Furious Five" in L.A. Stanley *Rap* 146: Mama say to break down and dull my grill. **1990–91** *Street Talk!* 3: You

got a messed up grill. **1993** *Source* (July) 58: B-Real has a puzzled expression glued to his grill.

¶ In phrase:

¶ **on the grill** Esp. *Police.* under close interrogation. [Exact sense of initial quot. is not clear.]

[*a*1904–11 Phillips *Susan Lenox* II 188: If he ever found out I had a lover— somebody—anybody that didn't pay—why, it'd be all up with me. Little Maud would go on the grill.] **1925** in Hammett *Big Knockover* 64: I didn't pretend to believe her. But my feet weren't solidly enough on the ground for me to put her on the grill. **1927** "Van Dine" *Canary Case* 266: When we put him on the grill last night, he said he changed his name after the Brooklyn racket. **1928** in *OEDS.* **1981** Sann *Trial* 194: I'm on the grill…in another indictment.

grill *v.* to subject to intense and prolonged questioning; interrogate. Now *S.E.*

*1894 G. Meredith, in *OEDS:* She comes to-day and she shall be grilled. **1910** *Harper's Wkly.* (Mar. 5) 17: The "I forget" and the "I do not remember" answers of certain heads of corporations undergoing a legal grilling. **1913** in Truman *Dear Bess* 143: I suppose Mamma and I will have to be present at Aunt Susan's grilling. **1924** in D. Hammett *Continental Op.* 60: The neighbors had to be grilled. **1929** "E. Queen" *Roman Hat* 41: The girl is caught in the gang's hangout and is being grilled by the villain. *Ibid.* 49: You know you ain't got no right to grill me this way, don't you, Inspector? **1930** *Liberty* (Aug. 23) 33: A guy never knows how to rate himself as a thief until he finds he can hold out against a fourteen-hour grilling and beating. **1940** R. Wright *Native Son* 169: They'll grill you about me and you, you drunk fool, you'll tell! **1941** *Slanguage Dict.* 19: Grill…to question; to give the third degree to. **1947** Motley *Knock on Any Door* 350: Seventy-two hours they could grill him. For three days they could give him the third degree. **1949** Hollingshead *Elmtown's Youth* 76: Such a "grilling" is part of the Elmtown ritual of becoming acquainted. **1969** Crichton *Andromeda Strain* 28: Just a minute, son…This isn't a grilling. Just tell it naturally. **1973** Flaherty *Fogarty* 144: That's how they grill people. **1977** A. Patrick *Beyond Law* 16: Pull in a few *capos* for a grilling.

grimbo *n.* [orig. unkn.] *Stu.* a jerk; loser; DORK.

1984–88 Safire *Language Maven* 21: Those who fail to attract…are scorned as *grimbo* [or] *dork.* **1989** Ebbitt & Ebbitt *Index to Eng.* (ed. 8) 238: Goof, geek, goober, grimbo, nerd, wonk.

grin *n.* a source of amusement; (*pl.*) fun; in phr. **for grins** for fun. Cf. **for greens** s.v. GREENS.

1966 in IUFA *Folk Speech*: It could be grins: something could be fun. **1973** Eble *Campus Slang* (Mar.) 1: *Ain't life a grin?*—expression used when everything is going wrong. **1977** Texan man, age 32: We're just playing for grins. **1981** Safire *Good Word* 80: You head for a party to *get some grins.* **1983** Univ. Tenn. instructor: Come on. It'll be a grin. **1987** *Cheers* (NBC-TV): It's been a lot of grins, but we both knew it wasn't gonna last forever.

grind *n.* **1.** Esp. *Stu.* monotonous, oppressive, or fatiguing labor, esp. hard or close study; an instance of such labor; drudgery; in phr. **the old grind** the oppressive, everyday routine. Now *S.E.*

1850 in B. Hall *College Wds.* (ed. 2) 242: I must say 'tis a *grind*, though. *1852 C. Kingsley, in *OED:* We lost him [the fox] after sunset, after the fiercest grind I have had this nine years. **1856** B. Hall *College Wds.* (ed. 2) 241: Students speak of a very long lesson which they are required to learn, or of anything which it is very unpleasant or difficult to perform, as a *grind.* *1857 T. Hughes, in *OED:* "Come along, boys," cries East, always ready to leave the grind, as he called it. **1867–71** Bagg *Yale* 48: *Grind*, a hard and unpleasant task. *1880 A. Trollope, in *F & H* III 215: Isn't it a very great grind, sir? *1887 in *OED:* "Hadn't we better take the overcoats?"…"Oh, no—they're a frightful grind to carry. *1889 Barrère & Leland *Dict. Slang* I 431: *Grind* (university)…A tedious piece of academical work. *a1890–93 *F & H* III 215: *Grind*…(common).—Daily routine. **1900** *DN* II 39: *Grind*, n…A disagreeable task. **1926** T.A. Dorgan, in Zwilling *TAD Lexicon* 41: Well, it's the old grind till next October. **1963** NYC teenager: Back to the old grind. **1990** *Cosmopolitan* (Nov.) 210: People who regularly inject some variety into their lives…are far more content than those who stick to the same old grind.

2.a. an act of copulation. *Rare* in U.S.

*1870 in Legman *Limerick* 100: Sir, I find/You a very good grind. *a1890–93 *F & H* III 215: *Grind*…an act of sexual intercourse: e.g., "to do a grind." **1962** Perry *Young Man Drowning* 168: The trim, the grind, the scratch…the pussy! **1966–71** Karlen *Sex. & Homosex.* 447: Among experienced lesbians…genital apposition (a grind or rub job)…[had been practiced] by more than half. **1993** *N.Y. Perspectives* (Jan. 29) 13: Fantasies of future sex...typically conjure up doing the groin-grind in zero gravity.

b. a sensual rotation of the hips, as in an erotic dance, esp. as part of a striptease. Cf. BUMP, *n.*

1938 in Botkin *Sidewalks* 303: Girls were certainly doing shimmys, quivers, and grinds when your old man was a kid. **1942** *Time* (Dec. 14) 72: *Bump:* a sudden forward projection of the pelvic region; *grind:* an unabashed rotation of the same.

3.a. a swindle; a method of swindling.

1867–71 Bagg *Yale* 45: *Grind*...an imposition, a swindle. **1927** H. Miller *Moloch* 79: Eking out a precarious living "playing the grifts and the grinds."

b. *Esp. Stu.* a joke.

1878 Flipper *Colored Cadet* 53: "A gag," "Grin," "Grind."—Something witty, a repartee. **1895** *Harper's* (Nov.) 966: It would be an awful grind on you if this ever became known. **1895** Wood *Yale Yarns* 16: I was awfully sorry then that I had put up the grind on him. **1898** Norris *Moran* 86: Oh, me, but that's a good grind. **1900** *DN* II 39: *Grind*, n...A joke or take-off, usually personal. **1901** Ade *Modern Fables* 119: A Husband worked up many Grinds on the Better Half. **1904** *Howitzer* (U.S. Mil. Acad.) (No. 5) 221: *Grind*—Something humorous, a joke. **1906** *JAF* XIX 24: The sailor is happy when he can get a "grind" on the "skipper." **1930** in D.O. Smith *Cradle* 33: There are a lot of good wisecracks or "grinds" when the fellows are free.

c. *Stu.* (see quot.).

*a***1889** *Century Dict.* III 2625: *Grind*...A satirist: an inveterate jester. (College slang.)

4. a foot race. [Earlier at Oxford Univ., 'a steeplechase'; see *OED*.]

*****1872** in *F & H* III 215: Joe Rullock,...the hero of a hundred grinds. **1936** Levin *Old Bunch* 81: The Wop offered to train him and maybe get him into the next Chicago grind.

5. *Stu.* an excessively diligent, usu. unsociable, student; drudge; WONK.—often **greasy grind.** Now *colloq.* or *S.E.*

*a***1889** *Century Dict.* III 2625: *Grind*...One who studies laboriously or with dogged application. (College slang.) *****1889** Barrère & Leland *Dict. Slang* I 431: *Grind* (university)...A plodding student who keeps aloof from the usual sports and pastimes. **1893** in *DAE:* Go over to the Law School and look at those grinds, each one working night and day to get ahead of the rest. **1895** Townsend *Fadden Explains* 243: Although he had more to do with the literary set than any other, he was anything but a grind. **1895** Wood *Yale Yarns* 1: Even the "greasy grinds" hardly felt it in their hearts to begin the evening's cram. **1900** *DN* II 39: *Grind*, n....A student who confines himself to persistent study...A person who is tiresome. **1903** *Some Songs* (No. 46): Away with the books of the greezy grind! **1909** in O. Johnson *Lawrenceville* 90: Don't be a grind, Smithy. *Ibid.* 142: Hickey, you are getting to be a greasy grind. **1911** Spectorsky *College Yrs.* 147: And such grinds...They take notes all the time and read all the references and learn them by heart. **1924** Marks *Plastic Age* 80: No one except a few notorious grinds studied that night. **1931** McConn *Studies* 30: Herb is only a greasy grind any way. **1931** Stevenson *St. Luke's* 25 [ref. to *ca*1910]: Don't be a greasy grind. **1958** Drury *Advise & Consent* 572: "Guess we have to have at least one grind," one of his older brethren, a football player, had remarked. **1960** in Horowitz *Campus Life* 142: We don't pride ourselves on having "greasy grinds" in our [fraternity] house. **1974** (quot. at WONK, *n.*). **1983** *Daily News* (N.Y.C.) (Mar. 25): Teentalk Glossary...*grind*—a bookworm. **1985** Briskin *Too Much* 220: The bright guys were never pre-med, just the grinds.

6. *Circus & Carnival.* the largely rehearsed public sales talk of a barker.

1926 *AS* I (Feb.) 282: *Grinder*—A man who gives his spiel or grind in front of the kid show calling attention to the various attractions pictured on the banners. **1933** Ersine *Pris. Slang* 41: *Grind*, n. A long sales talk, a *spiel.*

grind *v.* **1.a.** to copulate or copulate with. Also (of men only) in phr. **grind (one's) tool.**

*****1647** in *OEDS:* Digbie's Lady takes it ill,/That her Lord grinds not at her mill. *****1811** *Lexicon Balatron.:* Grind. To have carnal knowledge of a woman. *****ca***1835–40** in Speaight *Bawdy Songs* 33: He'll never grind again. *****1851** in D.R. Cox *Sex. & Vict. Lit.* 137: [The whores] can...grind the piano—and that is not the only slum [thing] they can grind. *****1880** *Pearl* 258: A married man grinding another man's wife. *****a***1890–1903** *F & H* VI 159: *To grind one's tool* = to copulate. **1911** *JAF* (Oct.) 352: Went down to de depot track,/Beggin' my honey to take me back./She turn

'roun some two or three times,/"Take you back when you learn to grind." **1916** Cary *Venery* I 117: *Grinding One's Tool*—To copulate. Said of men. *ca***1925** in Longstreet *Real Jazz* 52: I'm busy grindin' so you can't come in. **1934** H. Miller *Tropic of Cancer* 130: Coupled like a pair of goats and grinding and grinding away for no reason except the fifteen francs. **1935** in Oliver *Meaning of Blues* 153: I will roll your jelly and also grind you deep. **1961** J.A. Williams *Night Song* 98: Why, baby, you'd think it'd be harder to grind one o' them gray broads. **1962** Killens *Heard the Thunder* 11: Any old fool can stop a bullet, but how many men can grind like Jody Grinder? **1994** N. McCall *Wanna Holler* 47: She acted like she didn't even wanna grind when I got on.

b. to rotate the hips in a sensual or erotic manner, as during a burlesque dance. Cf. BUMP, *v.*

1928 Bodenheim *Georgie May* 80: Sometimes finding a man that knew how to grind and looked handsome. **1936** *New Yorker* (Sept. 12) 13: I make no suggestive motions...No grinding, no bumping, no tasseltossing. *a***1948** in Mencken *Amer. Lang. Supp.* II 693: The argot of burlesque...*Grind*, *v.* To revolve the backside. **1968–71** Cole & Black *Checking* 118: He was holding onto this girl and grinding with her and wouldn't let her go. He was still teaching her how to grind while they were playing "I Heard It Through the Grapevine." **1979** (quot. at BUMP, *v.*).

2. *Stu.* to apply oneself to close study, orig. under the direction of a tutor. Occ. *trans.*

*****1815** in *OED:* Perhaps when Tom leaves Oxford...we may contrive some gainful grinding scheme between us. *****1835** in *OED:* I am obliged to "grind"...that is, undergo a private examination with an authorized teacher or tutor. *****1849** in *OED.* **1852** in B. Hall *College Wds.* (ed. 2) 242: The successful candidate enjoys especial and excessive grinding during the four years of his college course. **1867–71** Bagg *Yale* 45: *Grind*...to give close application to a study, especially to a distasteful one. *a***1889** in *Century Dict.* III 2625: He's a fellow that *grinds*, and so he can't help getting some prizes. **1900** Flandrau *Freshman* 159: Oh, I wasn't grinding; I was just glancing over these notes. **1900** *DN* II 39: *Grind*, v.i....To devote an unreasonable amount of time to study, with or without commensurate results. **1904** *Independent* (Apr. 14) 860: Ideal Schedule as the Faculty Would Have It...Study...Work...Grind. **1951** Longstreet *Pedlocks* 299: Peter and Ike and Stinky were...a solid trio who did not grind their studies or act longhair.

3. *Stu.* (see quots.).

*a***1889** *Century Dict.* III 2625: *Grind*...To satirize severely; make a jest of. (College slang.) **1900** *DN* II 39: *Grind*...To ridicule or satirize.

4. *Circus & Carnival.* (see quots.).

1930 Irwin *Tramp & Und. Sl.:* *Grinder*—The man who "grinds." **1934** Weseen *Dict. Slang* 160: *Grind*—To shout the praises of a circus or a show in an effort to draw patronage. **1935** *Amer. Mercury* (June) 229: *Grind:* to spiel at a concession.

grinder[1] *n.* **1.** usu. *pl.* a tooth. [In earlier S.E., a molar.]

*****1676** in Partridge *Dict. Und.* 308: *Grinders*,...Teeth. *****1698–99** "B.E." *Dict. Canting Crew:* *Grinders*, Teeth. *The Cove has Rum Grinders*,...The Rogue has excellent Teeth. **1804** in *So. Folk. Qly.* XIX (1955) 172: Nation to me if I don't shoot out your two remaining old grinders. **1841** [Mercier] *Man-of-War* 142: Their white *grinders* forming an elegant contrast to their...ebony skin. **1847** Robb *Squatter Life* 138: I war carfully reachin' fur Jess' ear with my grinders. **1852** in Chittick *Roarers* 30: His grinders made a noise jest as if all creation war sharpening cross-cut saws by steam-power. **1882** *Harper's* (Oct.) 808: Where once my unthinned grinders grew,/What dismal gaps at fifty-two! **1962** Kesey *Cuckoo's Nest* 84: Hey there, old buddy, what's my chance of gettin' some toothpaste for brushin' my grinders?

2.a. *Stu.* a private tutor.

*****1813** in *OED:* Put him into the hands of a clever grinder or crammer, and they would soon cram the necessary portion of Latin and Greek into him. **1870** *Galaxy* (Feb.) 268: A "coach" is a private tutor who prepares pupils...for public examinations...The worst species of coach is sometimes called a "grinder," a term which originated in the London medical schools.

b. *Stu.* GRIND, *n.*, 5. *Rare* in U.S.

*****1852** in *OEDS:* The difficulty is great enough to discourage any but a real "grinder" at such work. *****a***1890–93** *F & H* III 215: A plodding student, *i.e.* a *grinder*. **1945** (quot. at BRAIN BOX).

3. *pl. Hobo.* the wheels of a locomotive or railway train.

1909 Warner *Lifer* 39: The big "grinders" would have crushed out my heart.

4.a. *Circus & Carnival.* a barker who works continuously in front of a single show.

1926 *AS* I (Feb.) 282: *Grinder*—A man who gives his spiel or grind in front of the kid show calling attention to the various attractions pictured on the banners. **1931** *Nat. Geo.* (Oct.) 514: *Grinder* applies to the announcer in front of the side-show ballyhoo line. **1953** Gresham *Midway* 22: I started in with Joe Ferrari's Wild Animal Show as a grinder—that's the fellow that keeps talking, trying to "build a tip" and hold them until the show outside is over and the outside talker comes back to the bally platform.
b. *Adver.* an actor hired to give a sales pitch in a commercial.
1979 Homer *Jargon* 91: *Grinder*…was first used to describe the quack doctors who toured with medicine shows and now describes an actor posing as a member of any profession.
5.a. *USMC & Navy.* a drill field or parade ground.
1944 *N.Y. Times Mag.* (Sept. 17): *Grinder*—Spar drill field. **1944** Kendall *Service Slang* 53: *The grinder*…drill field. **1959** Sterling *Wake of the Wahoo* 187: We straggled down to a large cement square, called a "grinder." **1968** Mares *Marine Machine* 56: While there was still light, the drill instructors usually had the platoon out on the "grinder" practicing drill. **1972** Ponicsan *Cinderella Liberty* 163: The wind sliced across the grinder. **1975** *Playboy* (Nov.) 160: The parade ground is of the type known at Parris Island as a grinder, gravel over macadam. **1982** T.C. Mason *Battleship* 31 [ref. to 1940]: Fall in on the Grinder! **1986** L. Johnson *Waves* 40: She stood watching from the far side of the grinder.
b. *Mil.* an obstacle course.
1968 *Airman* (Jan.) 43: Students go through Eglin's "grinder," a series of run, jump, climb and crawl obstacles used to harden muscles for additional training.
6. esp. *N.E. & N. Midland.* a hero sandwich. Now *colloq.*
1954 in *DARE*. **1954–60** *DAS*: *Grinder*…A very large sandwich…on a long roll, [etc.]…c1945. **1967** *AS* XLII 282: Submarine Sandwich…*Grinder* [term used in] Des Moines, Hartford, San Francisco, Providence, Akron, Cleveland, Chester, Philadelphia. **1982** Flexner *Listening to Amer.* 477: The Italian Hero sandwich…[is] called a *grinder*…in Boston.
7. *Burlesque.* a stripteaser.
1954–60 *DAS*: *Grinder*…A stripper; a burlesque dancer. **1963** (quot. at TAKE-OFF, *n.*). **1981** E. Keyes *Double Dare* 38: A nonstop fare of "exotic" grinders wearing only G-strings.
8. *Police.* a computerized system that provides arrest records or other information about suspects.—constr. with *the.*
1970 Conaway *Big Easy* 189: Delaverne reminded himself to check up on old Jesus—run his name through the grinder; you never knew.
9. *Surfing.* a heavy or dangerous breaker.
1981 in Safire *Good Word* 111: A three-foot close-out grinder pounding on dry reef. *a***1984** in Safire *Stand Corrected* 202: There's a hairy ten-foot grinder coming at you.

grinder[2] *n.* [< dial. *griner, greiner,* vars. G *Krainer* 'a Slovenian inhabitant of Carniola in Austria-Hungary'] *Midwest.* a Slovene.—usu. used contemptuously.
1976 J.F. Kess, in *AS* LI 295: Slovenes have been known as…*grinders* in a number of large industrial cities, particularly Cleveland, Ohio.

grind joint or **grind house** *n.* **1.** an establishment, as a carnival concession, casino, or burlesque theater, that employs a GRINDER[1], 4.a., to solicit customers; (*hence*) an establishment, as a burlesque house or motion picture theater, that provides continuous shows throughout the day and all or most of the night.
1929 *Sat. Eve. Post* (Oct. 12) 29: *Grind joint.* To work continuously [*sic*]. **1930** in Perelman *Old Gang* 104: The hip wavers in the grind houses. **1937** *New Yorker* (Aug. 7) 19: The "grind joints," as they are called in the jargon of the [auction] racket, know…that they can trade only with strangers. **1969** S. Harris *Puritan Jungle* 20: In New York, I went to one grindhouse paying three dollars for the privilege—grindhouse prices are not cheap—that smelled like a Bowery flophouse, pungent with the odor not only of plain, unwashed manhood but also of urine lingering in the air. **1973** Overgard *Hero* 7: Happy Tufts, better known in the grind houses as the Mammary Marvel, uncorked an eye from last night's mascara. **1974** Turan & Zito *Sinema* 5: Annually released and rereleased a few pictures each to the so-called grind houses that would play them. **1978** Skolnick *House of Cards* 40: Downtown casinos…are called in the trade "grind joints," a term suggesting a larger number of less affluent bettors…and heavy slot machine action. *a***1986** in *NDAS*: He dragged me to the Times Square grind-house to which it had been relegated.

2. a brothel.
1962 Perry *Young Man Drowning* 156: It's the snazziest grind joint you ever heard of. **1982** Flexner *Listening to Amer.* 452: *Grind house,* a low brothel,…about 1910.

grind show *n. Circus & Carnival.* a show that runs the same performance or performances continuously throughout its period of operation.
1927 Nicholson *Barker* 103: *Grind show*—One having a continuous performance. **1931** *AS* (June) 332. **1953** Gresham *Midway* 162: These are…"grind shows" in which the ticket seller grinds out over and over a sales talk on the exhibits inside, sometimes "ding" shows in which the customer, at the exit, makes a voluntary contribution of what he thinks the show is worth.

grinning bear *n.* the vulva.—usu. considered vulgar. *Joc.*
1961 Peacock *Valhalla* 180 [ref. to 1953]: I…woulda sworn…I was starin' that old grinnin' bear right in the face.

grinny bin *n.* LOONY BIN.
1975 *Nat. Lampoon* 5: Definitely get life and then turned over to the grinny bin, so no hope for parole.

grip *n.* **1.** (see quot.).
1872 in "M. Twain" *Life on Miss.* 292: I saw the leather [purse] was a grip (*easy to get*).
2. *Theat.* a stagehand. Now *S.E.*
1888 in *DAE*: Meanwhile the "grips"…have hold of the side scenes ready to shove them on. **1918** in Gelman *Photoplay* 10: Actors, extra men, grips, electricians, cameramen, etc. **1925** *AS* (Oct.) 36: "Grips" shift the scenery about and give orders grandly to "that flunkey" who is not on the regular crew. **1941** in Botkin *Sidewalks* 491: *Grips* are property men. *a***1948** in Mencken *Amer. Lang. Supp. II* 697: *Grip.* One who assists the carpenter and…carpenter's chief assistant. **1950** in *DAS*: Crowded with assistant directors, character actors, movie stars, grips and electricians. **1961, 1965, 1967** in *OEDS.*
¶ In phrases:
¶ **get a grip** to regain or retain one's composure; get a grip on oneself.
1971 H.S. Thompson *Las Vegas* 92: Of course. Get a grip. [*1974 in Partridge *DSUE* (ed. 8) 505: *Get a grip!*…dating from late 1940s…is a common Army…exhortation…"Put some effort into what you're doing!"] **1981** Eble *Campus Slang* (Oct.) 4: *Get a grip*—pay attention, come down from the clouds: Today's Monday, not Friday—and hardly a time to celebrate. Get a grip! **1986** E. Weiner *Howard the Duck* 9: Gotta get a grip.…Can't panic. **1988** *Daily Beacon* (Univ. Tenn.) (Jan. 25) 4: The new president will…not use the job as a political base. Get a grip. Who's supposed to believe that?
¶ **lose (one's) grip** to lose one's sanity, composure, or good sense.
1875 J. Miller *First Fam'lies* 246: Lost my "grip" as they say, didn't have any "snap" any more. **1894** "M. Twain" *Pudd'nhead Wilson* ch. xx: Come, cheer up, old man; there's no use in losing your grip. **1920** Weaver *In American* 32: I'm losin' my grip, I tell you. **1931** Dos Passos *1919* 330: He's a very brilliant man…but I'm afraid he's losing his grip. **1935** Anderson *Winterset* 32: Maybe I lost my grip there just for a minute. That's all right. **1940** Lawes *Murderer* 123: I'm sorry I lost my grip, Warden. **1942** in Truman *Dear Bess* 474: I…even went to a picture show yesterday afternoon…so you know I'm losing my grip. **1948** Cozzens *Guard* 429: Tired? Can't he take it? Losing his grip? Bucking for Section Eight?

gripe *n.* **1.** a tedious or vexatious person or thing.
1928 *AS* III (Feb.) 219: *Gripe n.* Something worthless, stupid, uninteresting. "That course in Public Finance sure is a gripe."
2.a. a complaint; in phr. **gripe session** an opportunity for the candid airing of complaints.
1929–33 Farrell *Young Manhood* 330: It was like losing all the gripes that had been piling up within him. **1934** Appel *Brain Guy* 154: As if he were the weariest bloke, sick of kids among other gripes. **1940** *AS* (Apr.) 211: Gripe session. **1942** in C.R. Bond & T. Anderson *Flying T. Diary* 70: Just a lot of petty gripes. **1944** *Time* (Oct. 2) 6: I have a gripe. Its crux is the problem of returning servicemen. **1948** B. DeVoto, in *Harper's* (Jan. 1949) 61: I want to clear my desk of various matters, mostly gripes. **1954** *WNID2* (Add.) CX: *Gripe*…Vexation; complaint. **1959** Farris *Harrison High* 63: I sort of miss those gripe sessions we used to have on the back porch. **1964** "Doctor X" *Intern* 34: This is supposed to be a gripe session, with Dr. Case there is all sweetness and light to hear our troubles and find solutions to our problems. **1968** L. Downe *She-Devils* (film): Even though we got a gripe, we gotta be fair.

1979 Kunstler *Wampanaki Tales* 15: The Sloth's big gripe this year was that he was going to be the oldest kid in the whole camp. **1992** *Time* (Dec. 28) 22: But missing Christmas is their biggest gripe. **1993** *N.Y. Times* (Apr. 5) A 18: They had previously told him, at a gripe session..., that they felt he was not discussing the issues of most concern.

b. *Av.* a pilot's written identification of a repair to be made on an aircraft. Also **gripe sheet.**

1986 Coonts *Intruder* 43 [ref. to 1972]: He read each discrepancy, or "gripe," that had been written for the last ten flights. Serious problems...were "down gripes" and had to be repaired before the machine could be flown again. Less serious problems, or "up gripes," would be repaired as the opportunity presented itself. **1990** R. Dorr *Desert Shield* 42: Major L.W. Crane wrote in the "gripe sheet"...that the aircraft had mechanical problems needing attention.

3. a mood of ill-temper; GROUCH.—constr. with *on.*

1938–40 W.V. Clark *Ox-Bow* 19: But with his gripe on he wasn't taking his winning right.

gripe *v.* **1.a.** to sicken or disgust. Cf. earlier S.E. sense 'to grieve, afflict, or distress' (*OED*, def. 7).

1905 Beach *Pardners* 29: It gripes me to hear a man cry. **1927** *AS* II (Mar.) 276: *Gripes*—Disgusts.

b. to anger or annoy.

1927 Mayer *Just Between Us Girls* 230: I mean they honestly *gripe* you. **1928** *AS* III (June) 435: At the University of Colorado I have heard "gripe" used often as a verb: "It gripes me," "It gives me a pain;" "Don't gripe," "Don't complain." **1930** *AS* V (Apr.) 282: *Gripe.* A new verb meaning to annoy or harass. "It gripes me." "He griped me." It is especially used by the young as a term of resentment to criticism. **1931** Lorimer *Streetcars* 18: Some things in life sort of gripe a person. **1941** Cain *Mildred Pierce* 188: What's griping him is that he can't do anything for the kids. **1941** Schulberg *Sammy* 15: If he gripes you that much why don't you can him instead of wanting to hand you a raise? **1966** Shepard *Doom Pussy* 109: It gripes me that we're supposed to care so much for world opinion. **1974** Hejinian *Extreme Remedies* 56: That's what gripes me. **1993** N.Y.C. woman, age *ca*55: It really gripes me when people track dirt into the house.

2. to complain; grumble. Hence **griper.**

1928 (quot. at (**1.b.**), above). **1930** E. Caldwell *Poor Fool* 114: She's always griping about something. **1931** Uhler *Cane Juice* 48: The Puritans would gripe like hell. **1932** *AS* VII (June) 332: *Gripe*—v.—to complain. **1934** Wohlforth *Tin Soldiers* 316: Don't tell me you're griping about this? **1935** E. Anderson *Hungry Men* 4: I gripe out on the road about having to go through all this red tape for a bowl of soup. **1937** E. Anderson *Thieves Like Us* 80: But what are you gripin' about, man? **1937** *AS* XII 315: Radio lacks a word to describe the disgruntled listener...Griper is not precise enough. **1942** in *Jour. Gen. Psych.* LXVI (1945) 132: We started griping about the rules. **1946** Dadswell *Hey, Sucker* 101: Language of the Carnival...*gripe*...complain. **1947** Blankfort *Big Yankee* 134: The men and officers griped like hell. **1954** *WNID2* (Add.) CX: *Gripe*...To grumble; bellyache. **a*1961 Partridge *DSUE* (ed. 5) 1119: *Gripe*...To complain, as in "What are you griping about?"...since *ca*1910, within my own knowledge. **1973** Haring *Stranger* 59: You gripe about being behind the times. **1988** D.S. Smith *Down-Home Talk* 17: You'd gripe [even] if they hung you with a new rope.

¶ In phrase:

¶ **gripe (one's) soul** Esp. *Stu.* to anger or disgust greatly. Also vars., some vulgar. [The sense in the 1593 quot. is 'to afflict or grieve the soul'; see *OED*, s.v. *gripe, v.*, 7; mod. slang usage may stem from exposure to the phr. in literature.]

[**1593 Shakespeare *3 Henry VI* I iv: How inly Sorrow gripes his Soule.] **1931** *AS* VI 205: *That gripes my soul:* that annoys me. **1947** *ATS* (Supp.) 5: Displeasure...*gripe one's cookies.* **1954–60** *DAS*: *Gripes my middle kidney.* Gripes me extremely. Common c1945. **1966** King *Brave and Damned* 187: It gripes my pee the way you're always bitching. **1966** Shepard *Doom Pussy* 212: It gripes my very soul to think about you and your women. **1978** Selby *Requiem* 39: Jesus Krist they gripe my shit the rotten bastads. *Ibid.* 164: It just gripes my shit is all. **1986** *NDAS*: Gripe one's ass...balls...butt...left nut [etc.].

griped *adj.* angry.

1928 in J. O'Hara *Sel. Letters* 37: They're griped with nice young Rosenbergers-Frankers who made D.K.E. at Yale. **1934** Appel *Brain Guy* 8: He pulled up his coat collar, griped with himself for being groggy. *Ibid.* 48: No wonder the kid's griped. **1953** Eyster *Customary Skies* 272: "You're griped because I beat you out of Second class,"

Averag retorted. **1966** Gallery *Start Engines* 20: He does it because he's griped about not making our team.

griper *n.* **1.** an annoying or nettling thing.

1781 in Silber *Songs of Independence* 137: Come—is not this a griper...That...'Tis you must pay the piper.

2. see GRIPE, *v.*, 2.

grit *n.* **1.a.** competitive or combative spirit; tenacity; strength of character; (*also*) an individual having such qualities.—often (*obs.*) in phr. **clear grit.** Cf. (**b**), below.

1808 in *DAE*: The prude doats on beauty, the bully on *grit.* **1825** in *DA*: A chap who was clear grit for a tussle, any time—any where. **1830** in *DAE*: "You are grit," said he of Rockingham to Nine-eyes. **1835** *Spirit of Times* (Dec. 12) 2: Their...candidate...had just finished a stump speech..."He's a screamer."..."He's bottom."..."He's grit to the back bone." **1838** [Haliburton] *Clockmaker* (ser. 2) 24: The...beast was...all clear grit. **1846** in J.R. Lowell *Poetical Works* 181: The parson wuz dreffle tickled with 'em as I hoop you will Be,/And said they wuz True grit. **1851** *Spirit of Times* (July 19) 266: That 'ere hoss of mine is clear grit—a hull race-cose. **1852** Stowe *Cabin* 40: Besides, you're a right brave gal. I like grit, wherever I see it. **1855** in Whitman *Leaves of Grass* 70: You there, impotent, loose in the knees, open your scarfed chops till I blow grit within you. **1871** Banka *Prison* 225: Bring him up and I'll try his grit. **1875** Daly *Pique* 312: Ain't true grit like true gold? **1876** Cody & Arlington *Life on Border* 36: He has grit. He gives all his pay to the lost scout's family. That's true grit. **1876** Hayes *Diary* 39: I shall show a *grit* that will astonish those who predict weakness. **1877** Pinkerton *Maguires* 81: He's the true grit from head to toe! **1878** Wheeler *Deadwood Dick on Deck* 1: The gal's got honor left w' her grit. **1883** Hay *Bread-Winners* 115: Well, I'll be hanged if you ain't the best grit of any fellow I know. **1888** Gordon & Page *Befo' De War* 45: All de men/O' dat family's been/Purty good grit. **1891** Campbell, Knox & Byrnes *Darkness & Daylight* 627: Nobody need starve in New York if he's got any grit about him. **1900** Hammond *Whaler* 396: He has hardly the grit to slap a fly. **1937** Parsons *Lafayette Escadrille* 129: Will power and pure grit were the only things that kept them going. **1958** Talsman *Gaudy Image* 202: So the old girl finally ran out of grit. **1972** *Playboy* (Feb.) 74: Grit counted more than money. **1993** *Reader's Digest* (May) 96: The people...have, in a word, grit.

b. in phr. **the clear** [or **true**] **grit** the genuine article.

1832 J. Hall *Legends of W.* 38: These Mingoes...*ain't* the *raal true grit*, no how. **1839** *Spirit of Times* (Nov. 9) 423: I hab ebery cent...all in de clar grit—de raal specier! [**1891** Maitland *Slang Dict.* 68: *Clear grit.* (Am.), decided; honest.]

c. a bracing alcoholic quality; KICK.

1842 *Spirit of Times* (July 16) 231: He always liked liquor that had a grit in it.

2. land; property. Cf. *OED*, def. 3.

1846 in G.W. Harris *High Times* 65: I never vierlates the law of horspitality at this house, nur on my grit. **1859** "Skitt" *Fisher's R.* 26 [ref. to 1820's]: Josh is the only joyful man on the "grit." The rest are all melancholy. *Ibid.* 52: Here's at you, sir. What bizness have you on my grit? *Ibid.* 90: I piked off to Skull Camp to smash up a few bucks on that grit.

3. usu. *pl. Black E.* food. [The British Army ex. cited by Partridge is app. unrelated to U.S. usage.]

*1943 (cited in Partridge *DSUE* (ed. 3) 1067). **1959** L. Hughes *Simply Heavenly* 136: Ain't you gonna help me carry the grits? **1962** *N.Y. Times Mag.* (May 20) 45: *Grit.*—Food. **1964** R.S. Gold *Jazz Lexicon* 130: According to jazz dancer Leon James, the term [*grit*] was introduced into jazz speech by Southern Negro musicians c.1940. **1966–67** P. Thomas *Mean Streets* 140: She got some good grit waiting for me...Like greens, an' black-eye peas. **1972** Eble *Campus Slang* (Oct. 1972) 3: *Grits*—food: Jigger's granny sure do serve some good grits. **1976** Calloway & Rollins *Moocher & Me* 241: I had a barbecue for some of my black friends from the track...They were dressed to kill and it took them about an hour to get out of their neckties and jackets and really get down to the grits. **1987** Univ. Tenn. student theme: Throw up...*spit grits* or *barf.*

4.a. *Black E.* a white person.—used derisively.

1964 in Gover *Trilogy* 343: Got other people takin care a you grits worries pretty good, huh. *Ibid.* 344: Whoever boss over the grits...wanna *stay* boss.

b. a white southerner, esp. REDNECK.—used derisively.

1966 in IUFA *Folk Speech*: A grit—A southerner or any person who lives in the south. **1967** Mailer *Vietnam* 17: One professor at Harvard, first Texas professor they ever had..."You clammy Have-it grit." **1973** R. Roth *Sand in the Wind* 91: Isn't that right, grit?...Isn't that right, red-neck? **1976** Crews *Feast of Snakes* 93: Trying to imitate their grit voices. **1976** Conroy *Santini* 46: Ah, the grits who put up the road signs in the South never got past second grade. **1978** J. Webb *Fields of Fire* 238: He's a goddamn grit, I tell you. **1972–79** T. Wolfe *Right Stuff* 231: The Hardiest Cracker, the Aboriginal Grit. **1979** Crews *Blood & Grits* 1: Grits don't take to long-haired freaks wearing packs in their bars.

c. *Stu.* a working-class white student, esp. a rowdy.
1986 P. Welsh *Tales Out of School* 98: A preppy wouldn't be caught dead hanging around with a "grit," a type that dresses down in T-shirts and jeans.

¶ In phrase:

¶ **hit the grit, 1.** to go on the road as a tramp.
1904 Ade *True Bills* 82: I never caused a Book-Maker to hit the Grit. **1924** Tully *Beggars of Life* 268: How long you been hittin' the grit, Red?

2. *R.R.* (of a tramp) to jump from a moving train; (*hence*) to get going; run or go rapidly; (*imper.*) get out!; hit the road!
1905 *DN* III 83: Hit the grit, *v.phr.* To leave; to walk away. "I guess I'll *hit the grit*, seein's I've got fired." **1906** *Army & Navy Life* (Nov.): Grit, Hit The: To hurry up. **1907** London *Road* 37 [ref. to ca1894]: Hit the grit, you son of a toad! Hit the grit! **1908** *DN* III 320: *Hit the grit*...To go, especially at a rapid pace. "I made him *hit the grit*." **1925** Mullin *Scholar Tramp* 182: I hit the grit until out of sight of the marshall. **1930** "D. Stiff" *Milk & Honey* 207: *Hitting the grit*—To be forced off a fast moving train. **1932** V. Fisher *In Tragic Life* 220: So hit the grit! *ca*1940 in Botkin *Treas. Amer. Folk.* 535: The roadmaster would have fired the Boomer and told him to hit the grit...and never come back again. **1941** "L. Short" *Hardcase* 16: Hit the grit. Get out of here.

grit *v. Black E.* **1.** to eat.—also trans., also constr. with *it* or *down.*
1966 in *IUFA Folk Speech*: Grit down—In other words eat! **1966–67** P. Thomas *Mean Streets* 286 [ref. to 1940's]: Damn, you look funny. Something you gritted, eh? **1967** in T.C. Bambara *Gorilla* 73: I likes to grit...I grit back, I won't lie. **1968** Baker et al. *CUSS* 130: Grit. Eat. **1969** *Current Slang* I & II 44: *Grit it*, v. To eat—College females, Minnesota.— Let's *grit it*. **1970** *Current Slang* III & IV 60: *Grit*, v. To eat.— College males, South Dakota.

2. (see quot.).
*ca*1970 in D. Rose *Black Street Life* 183: *To grit on*...to stare uncivilly [at].

gritch *v.* [prob. blend GRIPE + BITCH] *Stu.* to complain. Also as n.
1968 Baker et al. *CUSS* 130: Gritch. Constantly complaining and irritable [*sic*]. **1970–72** in *AS* L (1975) 60: All my mother ever did was gritch. **1983** Naiman *Computer Dict.* 67: Gritch...A complaint.

gritchy *adj. Stu.* (see 1968 quot.).
1968 Baker et al. *CUSS* 138: Constantly complaining and irritable. *Gritchy.* **1970–72** in *AS* L (1975) 60: God, is she ever gritchy!

grit out *v.* [alludes to idiom *grit (one's) teeth [and bear it]*] to endure through toughness of character.
1982 W. Wharton *Midnight Clear* 13: So I was more or less prepared to grit it out again in the army. **1981–89** R. Atkinson *Long Gray Line* 154: Most simply gritted out whatever ailed them.

gritty *adj.* **1.** courageous; tenacious. Now *S.E.*
*ca*1829 in Silber *Songs of Independence* 54: It was the year of Seventy-three,/And we felt really gritty. **1835** *Spirit of Times* (Dec. 12) 2: Hurrah, stranger, that's gritty. **1841** [Mercier] *Man-of-War* 245: Her crew were strong and gritty. **1845** in Robb *Squatter Life* 106: Thur never was a grittier crowd. **1868** Mrs. James *Rob Ruskin* 11: She's as gritty as her dad, every bit! **1873** Bunner *Letters* 17: But why don't you say something of my own plucky, gritty little Columbia? **1919** Kelly *What Outfit?* 118: Docs claim he was the grittiest man they'd seen in some time. **1950** *N.Y. Daily News* (Oct. 1): And they'll talk about the gritty five-hitter by the 24-year-old Whiz Kid named Robin Roberts.

2. angry.
1843 in *DA*: Darn her! it makes me gritty only jest to think on it.

griz *n.* a grizzly bear or bears. Also **grizzer.**
1967 Mailer *Vietnam* 114: Big Luke had known grizzers all his life. *Ibid.* 116: Going for griz in the morning. **1972** Milius & Anhalt *Jeremiah Johnson* (film): I hunt griz—grizzly bears...You know how to skin griz? **1992** *Those Incredible Animals* (Discovery TV): This little griz is named Koba.

grizzly *n.* a fierce or tough man.
1863 "E. Kirke" *So. Friends* 57: Hit 'im agin! Smash his mug! Pluck the grizzly! Hurrah for Smith! **1872** G. Gleason *Specter Riders* 72: "Hyur's

a grizzly's claw on that, youngster," said the trapper earnestly as he extended his hand.

groan box *n.* a musical instrument or radio regarded as a source of unpleasant sound.
1919 Wiley *Wildcat* 55: "See kin you find me a Memphis Blues in de groan box."...Cinnamon snatched a handful of melody from his guitar. **1928** *N.Y. Times* (Mar. 11) VIII 6: *Groan Box*—Portable organ on a picture set. **1929** McEvoy *Hollywood Girl* 59: A little fiddle and a groan box or organ. **1935** Pollock *Und. Speaks*: *Groan box*, a piano. **1937** *AS* (Oct.) 184: *Groan Box.* Accordion. **1941** *Slanguage Dict.* 19: *Groan box*...an accordion. **1944** Kendall *Service Slang* 7: *Groan box*...radio. **1951** *West. Folk.* X 170: Barroom Slang from the Upper Rio Grande...*Groan box*:...Juke box. **1955** in *West. Folklore* XV (1956) 203: *Groan box* means radio.

groaner *n.* **1.** *Und.* (see 1859 quot.).
*1797 in Partridge *Dict. Und.* 309: *Groaner* and *sigher*, wretches hired by methodists and others to attend their meetings for the purposes of fraud. **1809, *1848* (cited in Partridge *Dict. Und.*). **1859** Matsell *Vocab.* 39: *Groaners.* Thieves who attend at charity sermons, and rob the congregation of their watches and purses, exchange bad hats for good ones, steal the prayer-books, etc. etc.

2. a bad pun that elicits groans.
1985 *N.Y. Times* (May 2) 14: Then, Mr. Morgan offered a groaner. **1988** *Supercarrier* (ABC-TV): Please, not that old groaner.

groatable *adj.* drunk.
1722 B. Franklin, in *AS* XV (Feb. 1940) 103: [Drunkards] are *boozy, cogey, fox'd,...groatable*, [etc.].

groceries *n.pl.* **1.** food of any sort, esp. when prepared for eating.
1871 Thomes *Whaleman* 370: It's the only way to save the groceries. Mount your hoss and be off. **1929** in Blackbeard & Williams *Smithsonian Comics* 106: Do you mind if I join you and pack in a few groceries? **1930** Pasley *Al Capone* 242: He learned to talk the argot...Victuals were groceries. **1930** Sage *Last Rustler* 133: How I did tuck the groceries out of sight! **1959** *Swinging Syllables*: Groceries—Food or meal. **1962** in *AS* (Oct. 1963) 176: To eat...*to gobble groceries.* **1966** "T. Pendleton" *Iron Orchard* 57: You better eat some groceries and come on back into camp. **1971** *Western Horseman* (May) 45: This type of country seemed to fit some wild horses, but the lack of groceries produced a stunted animal.

2. the genitals, breasts, or buttocks, considered as erogenous areas.
1965 Trimble *Sex Words* 93: Groceries...The Penis or Vagina as objects of Oral Intercourse. **1971** Rader *Govt. Inspected* 7: The score is down on me lapping the groceries. *a*1972 B. Rodgers *Queens' Vernacular* 100: *Groceries*...genitalia. **1983** in "J.B. Briggs" *Drive-In* 116: This bimbo pops open a raincoat and flashes her groceries. *Ibid.* 210: A lot of the guys get kicked in the groceries.

grody *n. Hosp.* a filthy patient, esp. in an emergency room.
1984 in *Maledicta* VI (1985) 15: Ten grodies scratching...*Grodies*, street people, often infested with lice (pediculosis).

grody *adj.* [prob. alter. of GROTTY or GROTESQUE] *Stu.* offensive, dirty, or disgusting.
1965 in *OEDAS* II 130: *Groaty*, adjective meaning bad in appearance. **1967** *DAS* (Supp.) 688: *Groaty*...Slovenly; ugly. **1969** *Current Slang* I & II 44: *Groady*, adj....unkempt or untidy.—College students...South Dakota. *Grody*, adj. Overly concerned with girls.—Air Force Academy cadets. **1972** N.Y.U. students: "What about *grotty?*" "*Grody* is the proper way to say it. It means dirty, disgusting, scuzzy." **1982** S. Black *Totally Awesome* 42: It...hides the grody baby fat. **1982** Eble *Campus Slang* (Nov.) 3: *Grody to the max*—disgusting. **1982** A. Lane & W. Crawford *Valley Girl* (film): You know, Tommy's going to look really good after six grody bus rides in the Hollywood [bus]. **1982** Corey & Westermark *Fer Shurr* (unp.): It's like so *grody*, the Styrofoam is melting in the tea. **1983** *Daily News* (N.Y.C.) (Mar. 25): Teentalk Glossary...*grody*—ugly, disgusting,...gross.

grog *n.* [long asserted to derive from *Old Grog*, nickname (allegedly ref. to his habit of wearing a grogram cloak) of Edward Vernon (1684–1757), Brit. admiral, who in 1740 ordered that diluted spirits replace the straight rum formerly served to seamen]
1. Esp. *Naut.* spirits, esp. rum, diluted with water. Now *S.E.*
1754 in Breslaw *Tues. Club* 453: Hearty pulls of Grog. **1768** in *DAE*: Rum ne'er shall meet my lips (cry'd honest Sam)/In shape of toddy, punch, grog, sling, or dram. **1770* in *OED*: Groggy; this is a West

Indian phrase; Rum and Water, without sugar, being called Grogg. *1773 in *OED*: *Grog* (arrack mixed with water.). *a*1775 in *DN* VI (1933) 356: At night *hot-suppings*, at mid-day, *groggg*. *1781 in *DN* VI: A mighty bowl on deck he drew,/And filled it to the brink;/Such drank the Burford's gallant crew,/And such the gods shall drink./The sacred robe which Vernon wore/Was drenched within the same;/And hence his virtues guard our shore,/And Grog derives its name. 1792 Bracken-ridge *Mod. Chiv.* 10: A pint...of grog. *1796 Grose *Vulgar Tongue* (ed. 3): *Grog.* Rum and water. Grog was first introduced into the navy about the year 1740, by Admiral Vernon, to prevent the sailors intoxicating themselves with their allowance of rum or spirits. 1807 W. Irving *Sal-magundi* 58: Stage drivers love grog. *1835 Marryat *Jacob Faithful* ch. xii: Do put a little drop of stuff in mine, it's seven water grog. 1837 W. Irving, in *DAE*: Captain Bonneville...ordered a free allowance of grog to regale them. 1884 Blanding *Sailor Boy* 60: I think it was in the month of October, 1862, that Congress passed a law abolishing grog in the army and navy. *a*1889 *Century Dict.*: *Grog*...Originally, a mixture of spirit and water served out to sailors, called, according to the propor-tion of water, *two-water grog*, *three-water grog*, etc. 1897 in *DAE*: Steaming glasses of potent, soul-inspiring grog. *a*1900 in Doerflinger *Shantymen* 15: Here comes the cook with the whiskey can,/A glass of grog for every man.

2. *Broadly.* alcoholic liquor of any kind; (now esp.) beer.
1805 Weems *Hymen's Sgt.* 33: It was all soon squandered on frolicking and grog. 1813–18 Weems *Drunk. Looking Glass* 85: I mean a *grog-shop*. 1836 Strong *Diary* I 40: The soldiers disposed of the books...for grog. *a*1889 *Century Dict.*: *Grog*...Strong drink of any kind; used, like *rum*, as a general term in reprobation. 1914 Ellis *Billy Sunday* 106: I go into a grog-shop and throw down my dollar. 1919 in Hemingway *Sel. Let-ters* 27: You won't take any chances bringing the grog up as I don't believe that cars are searched at all. 1920 Ade *Hand-Made Fables* 6: Not one trickle of Grog could be uncovered. 1920 in Hemingway *Dateline: Toronto* 40: How long are they going to be able to ship grog out of Can-ada? 1944 in Himes *Black on Black* 197: Fo' bucks for a half-pint grog. 1954 Himes *Third Generation* 241: We're going around the corner to buy some grog. 1963 W.C. Anderson *Penelope* 186: Then break out the grog. We've got time for a short one before we get to the motel. 1961–64 Barthelme *Dr. Caligari* 136: Is that a flask of grog you have there? 1972 Claerbaut *Black Jargon* 67: *Grog, n.* beer. 1986 restaurant sign, N.Y.C.: Food & Grog.

3. a groggy condition.
1930 M. West *Babe Gordon* 117: When the hell are you snappin' out of your grog?...Where's your common sense?

¶ In phrase:

¶ **stop (someone's) grog** *Navy.* to punish or do violence to; do for; kill.
*1805 J. Davis *Post-Captain* 114: "Messmate, are you much wounded?" "I fear...my grog is stopped." *ca*1816 in Dolph *Sound Off!* 442: They first attacked and thought to crush/Our gallant little navy;/But Yankee tars soon stopped their grog,/And sent 'em to old Davy! 1827 J.F. Coo-per *Red Rover* 493: "Give it to 'em, right and left, Guinea," cried Fid; "here is one who will come in as a backer, as soon as he has stopped the grog of the marine."

grog *v.* **1.** Esp. *Naut.* to drink grog or other liquor.
1824 in Eliason *Tarheel Talk* 275: Groging...he gets grogey. *1833 in *OED*: Captain Ross...has dined and grogged with messmate William at Windsor. 1887 in *OED*: I ordered all hands to grog and turn in.

2. Esp. *Naut.* to provide with grog or other liquor.
*a*1900 in Doerflinger *Shantymen* 15: I'll treat my crew in a decent way/I'll grog them all three times a day.

Grogans *n.pl.* [fr. the Irish family name *Grogan*] muttonchop sidewhiskers.
1906 T.A. Dorgan, in *N.Y. Eve. Jour.* (Jan. 3) 10: Jim Corbett with "Grogans." 1912, 1916, 1927 (all T.A. Dorgan, cited in Zwilling *TAD Lexicon* 107).

grog blossom *n.* a red facial blemish caused by hard drinking; (*hence*) a drunkard's red nose. Cf. syn. RUM BLOSSOM.
*1796 Grose *Vulgar Tongue* (ed. 3) *Grog-blossom.* A carbuncle, or pim-ple on the face, caused by drinking. 1813–18 Weems *Drunk. Look. Glass* 124: A...Grog-blossom on your learned snouts is enough. *1821 [P. Egan] *Real Life in Ireland* 74: Witness the pimples on his nose, vul-garly called *grog blossoms*. 1824 in Paulding *Bulls & Jons.* 189: The peo-ple exhibit a ruddy complexion...but...the roses will be found to be nothing more than what are called grog-blossoms. 1883 Russell *Sailors' Lang.* 62: *Grog-blossom.*—A nose reddened by drink. Also a pimple due to drink. 1898 Green *Va. Folk-Speech* 169: *Grog-blossom, n.* A redness or

an irruption of inflamed pimples on the nose or face of a man who drinks ardent spirits to excess. *1961 Burgess *Dict. Sailing* 105: *Grog blossom.* A red nose, the colour being attributed to rum. 1992 G. Wolff *Day at the Beach* 91: Florid noses ("grog blossoms" we called them).

grogged *adj.* drunk.—now also constr. with *up* or *out.* Cf. 1753 quot. at GROGGY, 2.
[*1796 Grose *Vulgar Tongue* (ed. 3): *Grogged.* A grogged horse; a foun-dered horse.] *1821 *Real Life in London* I 287: With lads and lasses, prim'd and grogg'd for bang-up fun and glee. 1932 D. Runyon, in *Col-lier's* (June 11) 7: She can fight like the dickens when she is grogged up. 1985 *UTSQ*: Sloshed, hammered,...grogged-out.

groggery *n.* a disreputable saloon.
1822 in *DAE*: Consisting of warehouses, low taverns, groggeries, dens of prostitution, and gaming-houses. 1840 Strong *Diary* I 151: Mass-meetings are held in every groggery. 1884 in *DAE*: Lumley had to pass more than one groggery on his way to the mountains. 1889 in C. Fan-ning *Dunne & Dooley* 14: Behind a groggery.

groggy *n.* a grog-seller or opponent of prohibitionism.
1893 in *DAE*: We said...that the "groggies" of Iowa were bigger fools than we ever knew them to be.

groggy *adj.* **1.** drunk.
*1770 in *OED*: [Intoxicated] *Groggy*; this is a West-Indian phrase. *1785 Grose *Vulgar Tongue*: Groggy, or *groggified*; drunk. 1807 J.R. Shaw *Autobiog.* 54: Mr. H. one night at home got very groggy,...in a very ill humour. 1818 in *DN* V (1925) 383: *Groggy* for intoxicated. 1824 in Eliason *Tarheel Talk* 275: Groging...he gets grogey. *1826 "Blackmantle" *Eng. Spy* II 187: May I never get groggy again, if I couldn't have forgiven her freely. *1829 in *F & H* III 220: Make him groggy, then press him off to sea. *1863 in *F & H*: A certain Mrs. Thunder...was fined twelve shillings for being...groggy. *1872 in *F & H. a*1889 *Century Dict.*: *Groggy*...Overcome with grog, so as to stagger or stumble; tipsy. (Slang.)

2. staggering or unsteady, esp. from exhaustion or blows; dazed and weakened; PUNCHY. Now *S.E.*
[*1753 in Partridge *Dict. Und.* 309: Horses that...have the...Grogs....Grog'd is founder'd.] *1828 in *OED*: A rare shaped thor-oughbred horse, very groggy. *1831 in *F & H* III 220: Long journeys at a fast pace will make almost any horse groggy. *1833–34 Marryat *Jacob Faithful* ch. iv: He is what is termed *groggy*, from the constant return of blows on the sides of the head. 1842 *Spirit of Times* (Sept. 3) 322: Bell came up groggy, and scarcely able to see. *1854 W. Thack-eray, in *OED*: My poor old governor is exceedingly shaky, very groggy about the head. 1859 Matsell *Vocab.* 127: *Groggy.* Not able to stand erect from punishment received. *1873 Hotten *Slang Dict.* (ed. 4): When a prize-fighter becomes "weak on his pins," and nearly beaten, he is said to be *groggy.* *1888 in *F & H* III 220: In the tenth Thompson, who had been growing groggy, to the surprise of Evans began to force the fighting. *a*1889 *Century Dict.*: *Groggy*...In *pugilism*, acting or mov-ing like a man overcome with grog; stupefied and staggering from blows and exhaustion. *1889 Barrère & Leland *Dict.* I 432: *Groggy* (common), unsteady like a drunken man, generally applied to horses when they become weak and unsteady from age and overwork. 1930 in D.O. Smith *Cradle* 59: Unless I keep moving I always feel groggy. 1945 Colcord *Sea Lang.* 90: Among shore people...groggy means dizzy and staggering. 1965 Harvey *Hudasky's Raider's* 158: Don...was too groggy to take it in. 1986 Ciardi *Good Words* 137: The challenger took a right to the jaw that left him groggy.

grog-mill *n.* GIN MILL.
1949 "J. Evans" *Halo in Brass* 33: No grog-mill cuties with peekaboo blouses.

grog watch *n.* (see quot.). *Joc.*
1898 Green *Va. Folk-Speech* 170: *Grog-watch, n.* A watch fast and always ahead of time so that the hour for taking a drink will come quicker.

groid *adj. & n.* [fr. *negroid*] *Stu.* Negro; black.—used derisively or contemptuously.
1970–72 in *AS* L (1975) 60: *Groid, n.* Negroid, black (derogatory white use). 1973 Eble *Campus Slang* (Mar.) 2: *Groid*—a derogatory term for a black: "Look at the size of the Afro on that groid." 1974 *Nat. Lampoon* (Nov.) 84: Get...the groid chick from "Star Trek."...My old man gets mugged by some groid. 1975 *Nat. Lampoon* (Aug.) 79: The big groid started to smell something cheesy.

grok *v.* [introduced as a term from the "Martian" language by Robert A. Heinlein in his science-fiction novel *Stranger in a Strange Land* (1961)] *Stu.* to perceive or understand thoroughly; to feel complete empathy with; (*hence*) to appreciate; enjoy.

1961 Heinlein *Stranger* 10: Smith had been aware of the doctors but had grokked that their intentions were benign. *Ibid.* 17: There was so much to grok, so little to grok from. **1967** *Lit Dictionary* 19: *Grok*—West Coast expression meaning to dig something. **1968** *Playboy* (June) 80: "Sure I grok you," she said. **1969** Gustaitis *Turning On* 79: Heinlein wouldn't do it…But his admirers grok the story. **1970** in *Nat. Lampoon* (Feb. 1971) 26: I really *grok* Libras! **1971** E. Sanders *Family* 103: They walked barefoot as they cleaned out the…barn, shovels in hand, grokking the fullness of the green horsemush between their toes. *Ibid.* 180: Gypsy supposedly at first was extremely hesitant to have affairs with the Satans, but grew to grok it. **1972** *Nat. Lampoon* (July) 6: Really grokked your issue with the David Cassidy cover! **1985** Knoxville, TN, financial consultant, age *ca*38: I'm really grokking this. **1986** *Cheers* (CBS-TV): "I don't like to be touched!" "Hey, I can grok that." **1987** M. Groening *School Is Hell* (unp.): I'm getting bad vibes from you. The rest of the class groks what is going on—why can't you? **1992** *Harper's* (June) 31: Try to grok the notion of so many people throughout the world enjoying themselves. **1993** *Village Voice* (N.Y.C.) (June 22) 28: A sign of the need to grok.

grommet *n.* Esp. *Naut.* the vagina or anus.

*1889 Barrère & Leland *Dict. Slang* I 435: *Grummet* (low), *pudenda muliebris.* **1935** Pollock *Und. Speaks: Knight of the golden grummet*, a male sexual pervert whose complex is boys. *ca*1942 in A. Hopkins *Front & Rear* 177: Mrs. Black had a very tight grommet.

gronked *n. Stu.* ill or exhausted; sound asleep; very drunk.—often constr. with *out*.

1968 Baker et al. *CUSS* 130: *Gronked.* Drunk and passed out. **1972** Ariz. man, age *ca*20: Man, I was really gronked out [i.e., asleep]. **1983** Naiman *Computer Dict.* 67: *Gronked*…very tired or sick.

gronk out *v.* **1.** *Computers.* CONK OUT.

1983 Naiman *Computer Dict.* 67: This bletcherous keyboard just gronked out again!

2. *Computers.* to quit work.

1983 Naiman *Computer Dict.* 67: *Gronk out*…to go home and/or to sleep.

grooby *adj.* GROOVY.

1943 *Time* (July 26) 56: You, too, can get on the grooby side. **1966** B. Dylan *Tarantula* 34: Oh great grooby foxeyes,/Lead me to the garbage.

groove *n.* **1.a.** *Baseball.* an imaginary line between the pitcher's position and the center of the strike zone; ALLEY.

1908 in Fleming *Unforget. Season* 164: Donlin sent a chopper down the groove. **1910** *Amer. Mag.* (May) 224. **1912** Mathewson *Pitching* 285: But that straight one looked awful good to me coming up the "groove." **1976** *Webster's Sports Dict.:* *Groove*…The middle of the strike zone.

b. *Baseball.* a batter's vulnerability to a pitched strike; (*hence*) a weakness.

1912 Mathewson *Pitching* 1: His "groove" was a slow curve over the outside corner, and I fed him slow curves over that very outside corner with great regularity. *Ibid.* 6: He was new to me and I was looking for his groove. *Ibid.* 252: His one "groove" was massages and manicures. *Ibid.* 277: He was caught [off base] time and again…It was his "groove."

c. *Av.* the path that an aircraft must take for a perfect landing, esp. aboard an aircraft carrier.

1942 Casey *Torpedo Junction* 350: The first plane switched on its riding lights and came slowly into the groove to land. **1944** Olds *Helldiver Squadron* 86: The Captain sent word to Catwalk that he should permit no further landings unless pilots made "in the groove" approaches. **1945** Hamann *Air Words* 28: *Groove, into the.* Making a perfect landing in the middle of a runway or on the deck of an aircraft carrier. **1965** Harvey *Hudasky's Raiders* 6: Soon they were astern of the ship coming up the groove.

2. *Jazz.* category; style, esp. of performing; (*hence*) predilection; preference. Cf. syn. BAG, 11.

1935 in *OEDS:* The Boswells are not in the hot groove. **1936** in *OEDS:* His first chorus is really in the right groove. **1939** Goodman & Kolodin *Swing* 119: I guess I was in kind of a bad groove mentally at the time. **1940** in R.S. Gold *Jazz Talk* 115: Has a sax-unison melody somewhat in the Tuxedo groove. **1942** Bullock & Englund *Springtime in Rockies* (film): It's that mellow groove that sends me. **1958** in R.S. Gold *Jazz Talk:* Romance? No, bruz, that's not my groove. **1959–60** R. Reisner *Jazz Titans* 157: *Groove:* category. A person's predilection. **1965** C. Brown *Manchild* 314: On Saturday night, there is something happening for everybody in Harlem, regardless of what his groove might be. **1994**

N. McCall *Wanna Holler* 37: I was just getting into the party groove, and was more defiant than any of my brothers.

3. Esp. *Black E.* the vagina.

*ca*1936 in Atkinson *Dirty Comics* 81: I can see I ain't the first one ever dropped it in your groove. **1963** Charters *Poetry of the Blues* 124: In the 1930's the expression "in the groove" became popular, with its obvious reference to a man's delight as he joins a woman, as he "…gets in the groove," but its meaning quickly was obscured, probably because many Negroes weren't inclined to explain it to anyone. **1969** Tynan *Oh! Calcutta!* 119: I mean,/The size of my groove? *a*1973–87 F.M. Davis *Livin' the Blues* 67 [ref. to *ca*1920]: A few got in the groove real early.

4. Orig. *Jazz.* **a.** something intensely enjoyable; a delight.

1946 Treadwell *Big Book of Swing* 124: *A groove:* swell, good to hear. **1958–59** Southern & Hoffenberg *Candy* 141: Aren't they a *groove?* They're so funny! **1959** *Swinging Syllables: Groove*—A good scene. **1963** in H. Ellison *Sex Misspelled* 42: Rooney was…loving me with her eyes, which was a groove. **1966** Fariña *Down So Long* 134: She's a real groove, baby. **1967** *Sat. Eve. Post* (Sept. 23) 30: You're a groove. **1967** Welles *Babyhip* 128: I adore older men, they're a groove. **1967** Yablonsky *Hippie Trip* 23: For people fully tuned-in, sex is "free," plentiful, and, from all reports, "a groove" (great) in the hippie world. **1969** Mitchell *Thumb Tripping* 3: Isn't that thing a groove? **1971** B.B. Johnson *Blues for Sister* 104: She ain't a bad groove, when you can reach her. **1976** J.W. Thomas *Heavy Number* 29: It's a groove if *we* decide to be Mr. or Mrs. Clean.

b. rhythm; beat.

*ca*1969 J. Joplin, in *Wilson Qly.* (Summer 1993) 23: Young white kids have taken the groove and the soul from black people and added intensity. **1979** "Sugar Hill Gang" *Rapper's Delight* in L.A. Stanley *Rap* 318: And me, the groove, and my friends are gonna try to move your feet. **1991** B.E. Ellis *Amer. Psycho* 136: This is laid down with a groove funkier and blacker than anything Prince or Michael Jackson…has come up with. **1993** *CBS Sunday Morning* (CBS-TV) (Aug. 22): In the bassist's vernacular, "We've got a good groove."

5. *Rock Music.* a phonograph record or cassette recording, esp. of rock music; (*broadly*) a song. Also pl.

1965 Yurick *Warriors* 19: And now, for all the boys and girls of the Paradise Social and Athletic Club, these grooves…it's *los* Beatles, boys and girls… **1983** *Rolling Stone* (Feb. 3) 35: Read this and forget about those guys who charge $13+ for European grooves. **1990** Costello & Wallace *Sig. Rappers* 18: James Brown's ageless groove "Funky President."

¶ In phrases:

¶ **hit the groove** to hit one's stride.

1971 Meggyesy *Out of Their League* 216: With my injury healed, I was beginning to hit the groove and looked forward to finishing strong the last part of the season.

¶ **in the groove** Orig. *Jazz.* performing or doing exceptionally well; splendid; HIP; in phr. **back in the groove** back to being one's self again.

1932 in *OEDS:* Having such a wonderful time which puts me in a groove. **1933** in *OEDS:* The jazz musicians…got a burn from playing in the groove. **1936** Bluebird phono. record BB6616, rec. by Wingy Manone and His Orchestra: *In the Groove* (title). **1936** in R.S. Gold *Jazz Talk* 115: He's in the groove tonight. **1939** "E. Queen" *Dragon's Teeth* 163: And finally, with a grunt of satisfaction, he said to himself, "It's in the groove." **1939** in A. Banks *First-Person* 232: If they are right and in the groove you can tell immediately. **1942** Boardman et al. *Pardon My Sarong* (film): I want all you hepcats and jitterbugs to come on up here and get in the groove. **1944** *Slanguage Dict.* 59: Get out of the rut and into the groove—get on the beam. **1945** Fay *Be Poor* 23: Or, to use the vernacular of today, it was "double in the groove"—plus. **1945** Hartman & Shavelson *Wonder Man* (film): He added in-the-groove improvements. **1946** Heggen *Mr. Roberts* 191: Last night he was batting his head against the wall. Tonight he's right back in the old groove. **1946** in Clarke *Amer. Negro Stories* 140: "Are you in the groove, Smooth?"…"Yeah, man. Groovie as a ten-cent movie." **1948** Manone & Vandervoort *Trumpet* 104: When a guy took a chorus, the rest of the boys in the band would turn around and look at him, to let him know he was in the groove. **1953** Paul *Waylaid* 17: Jellyroll got into what jazz addicts call "the groove," that is, he lost himself in his improvisations, and felt inventiveness and spontaneity take possession of his mind and flow through his arms and fingers. **1973** N.Y.U. student: It takes time to get back in the groove [after being ill]. **1985** Swados & Trudeau *Rap-Master Ronnie* 2: We're in a groove now. Ow. **1992** *Roc* (Fox-TV): We must have been in some groove, sweet thing.

¶ **slide the groove** *West.* to follow easily a clearly blazed trail.

1922 Rollins *Cowboy* 317 [ref. to 1890's]: The trail might be...clearly blazoned. Then its pursuit was so facile as to amount to no more than, in the scout's vernacular, "sliding the groove."

groove *adj. Black E.* GROOVY.

1969 Bullock *Watts* 90: That is not too groove goin' to jail, I know it is not too groove.

groove *v.* **1.** *Baseball.* to pitch (a baseball) fast and straight.

1911 Van Loan *Big League* 170: He "grooved" the first ball, and Hardy "pulled" it down the first-base line like a flash of light. **1912** *N.Y. Tribune* (Apr. 21) 10: Rucker grooved a beauty, waist-high. **1918** *Stars & Stripes* (Feb. 22) 1: He's just about to groove it toward a ducking Fritzy's bean. **1939–40** Tunis *Kid from Tomkinsville* 50: "You grooved that ball for Allen."...That was a bad mistake. **1976** *Webster's Sports Dict.: Groove*...To throw a pitch right over the middle of the plate. **1993** N.Y.C. man, age 31 (coll. J. Sheidlower): He *grooved* it right in there.

2. *West.* to wound (with a bullet).

1927 Rollins *Jinglebob* 163 [ref. to 1880's]: O' the nex' two shots,...one killed Gimcrack an' one grooved Jackson.

3. *Jazz.* to record (a piece) phonographically.

1935 *Vanity Fair* (Nov.) 38: That's the third date we've grooved half a dozen schmaltzy tunes for that wand-waver with never a swing item in the list.

4. *Orig. Jazz.* to play jazz or rock music in an exciting or emotional way.—also trans.—also constr. with *it.*

1937 *AS* XII 182: Men who can...groove it. **1939** in A. Banks *First-Person* 231: Boy, we used to groove real holes out there. **1945** in Bechet *Treat It Gentle* 229: Groovin' the Minor. **1963** J.A. Williams *Sissie* 52: Figure about three numbers. Introduction, you come on in, we groove. **1994** *Showbiz Today* (CNN-TV) (Feb. 16): You can have all the technique in the world. But if you don't groove, you'll get nowhere.

5.a. *Orig. Jazz.* to enjoy oneself intensely.—occ. constr. with *it* or *out.*

1950 *Neurotica* (Autumn) 46: Man we came to...groove a little. **1958** A. King *Mine Enemy* 84: We really grooved it from the start. **1959** "D. Stagg" *Glory Jumpers* 97: Grooving with it, dad? **1960** *Mad* (Sept.): We figured it was just another of Harry's wild kicks, and we all grooved it. **1964** Rhodes *Chosen Few* 23: To groove or not to groove, that is the question. **1966** Goldstein *1 in 7* 125: Marijuana became plentiful, and almost anyone could "groove" on pot. **1967** Kornbluth *New Underground* 39: Let's put the budget books in the archives for future history freaks who wish to groove on the past. **1967** *Zap Comix* (Oct.) 11: I groove in this desert. **1968–70** *Current Slang* III & IV 61: *Groove out*, v. To dance.—College students, both sexes, California.

b. to like or appreciate.—also constr. with *on.*

1966 in *DAS* (ed. 1975) 707: They see the spade cats going with ofay chicks and they don't groove it. **1992** *N.Y. Observer* (June 15) 25: If you groove on...gadgetry.

6. *Orig. Jazz.* to make happy or ecstatic; delight; thrill.—occ. constr. with *out.*

1952 J.C. Holmes *Go* 198: This enabled him to get enough morphine to keep him "grooved" for several weeks...small amounts were sufficient in the beginning. **1959** [Sabre & Eiden] *Glory Jumpers* 94: Cool it, kid. When that junk hits, it'll groove you out. **1959** in R.S. Gold *Jazz Talk* 115: To groove someone means to provide them with enjoyment. Example: Her singing grooved me. **1966** H.S. Thompson *Hell's Angels* 89: It didn't groove them at all. They...were genuinely offended. **1991** Nelson & Gonzales *Bring Noise* 159: This jam grooved the dancers.

7. to get along; get on, esp. well.

1960 Swarthout *Where the Boys Are* 21: What the company is most interested in is how well a guy will groove, how well he'll adjust to the job and the togetherness. **1967* in *OEDS: Groove*, make good progress, co-operate. **1988** *USA Today* (June 8) 1: Consumer mood groovin', best since '69.

8. to be intensely enjoyable.

1965 Elder *Dark Old Men* 107: It is not ridiculous! It works! It grooves! It moves! It soothes the soul! It upends! It transcends! It deliberates! It copulates!

groove ball *n. Baseball.* a baseball pitched squarely into the strike zone.

1915 Lardner *Haircut & Others* 158: He whales the groove ball to the fence in left center and gets round to third on it.

groover *n.* **1.** *Baseball.* GROOVE BALL.

1911 Van Loan *Big League* 209: He whipped in a "groover" with...his powerful arm.

2.a. *Esp. Stu.* a hippie; (*hence*) a person, esp. a teenager, who apes the styles and attitudes of the drug culture of the late 1960's; a would-be hippie.—used derisively.

1967 *Time* (July 7) 20: The "groovers," graduates of the 16-to-19 mod-togged teeny-bopper school, who take drugs mostly for libidinous kicks. **1970** Landy *Underground Dict.* 93: *Groover*...Person who likes acid-rock music and psychedelic things...[or] who gets high on drugs. **1979** Homer *Jargon* 197: *Groovers* are teenagers into "kiddy kicks," *i.e.*, sniffing glue, drinking soda pop laced with aspirin, inhaling nail-polish remover, etc. **1987** *Rage* (Knoxville, Tenn.) I (No. 2) 22: Only went out with this guy because I felt sorry for him. He brought me a flower, took me to a groover hang out. So I got wasted.

b. a shallow or uninteresting person who attempts to be fashionable.

1983 Eble *Campus Slang* (Mar.) 3: *Groover*—person who tries to be cool, usually a male. **1985** Eble *Campus Slang* (Apr.) 4: *Groover*—a person who tries to be in style with the latest fashions but just can't make it: "The new fraternity is full of groovers"....—a male who continuously and unsuccessfully tries to woo females: "The groover in the polyester suit keeps bothering me."

groovy *adj.* [sugg. by *in the groove* s.v. GROOVE, *n.*] **1.** *Orig. Jazz.* "in the groove"; splendid; delightfully exciting; fine; attractive; well. Also *adv.* [Now usu. associated with the hippie movement of the 1960's and often used in derisive reference to attitudes popularly associated with that period.]

1937 *AS* XII 46: *Groovey.* Name applied to state of mind which is conducive to good playing. **1941** *Pittsburgh Courier* (Nov. 15) 7: Love is Groovie. **1941** in Leadbitter & Slaven *Blues Records* 426: Boy! It's solid Groovy! **1945** Himes *If He Hollers* 151: You sound groovy. **1946** Mezzrow & Wolfe *Really Blues* 180: Warm air came out of the fan, too, so things were groovy. **1946** in Clarke *Amer. Negro Stories* 140: You jus' g'wan an' sell yo' li'l bit a whiskey, an' ev'vything's gonna be groovy. **1947** *Time* (Feb. 10) 12: *Groovy*—solid. **1948** in M. Shulman *Dobie Gillis* 92: "I pitched a no-hit game last summer"..."Hey, groovy," said Sally. **1948** Manone & Vandervoort *Trumpet* 210: So we used one of my groovy instrumentals. **1950** *Neurotica* (Autumn) 46: This shit is groovy. **1947–52** R. Ellison *Invisible Man* 368: You like the groovy music on the juke? **1950–52** Ulanov *Hist. Jazz* 351: *Groovy*: applied to a good swinging beat (earlier, "in the groove"). **1952** Brossard *Darkness* 81: They're groovy, aren't they? *ca*1953 Hughes *Fantastic Lodge* 66: Everything tastes groovy. **1958** A. King *Mine Enemy* 166: This was surely the grooviest moment I'd had in many years. **1959** L. Hughes *Simply Heavenly* 129: Just feeling a little groovy that's all. **1959** Zugsmith *Beat Generation* 86: She was groovy. She could really be hip. **1962** in Bruce *Essential Lenny Bruce* 50: Then they keep building—Janet Leigh, Grace Kelly, to Marilyn Monroe, Audrey Hepburn, just really groovy-looking chicks. **1962** Carr & Cassevetes *Too Late Blues* (film): Groovy, baby. **1965** in H. Ellison *Sex Misspelled* 340: Oh, revenge, thy taste is groovy. **1969** Bullock *Watts* 58: I thought, "Wow, this is the grooviest," but looks like later I found out different. **1970** in B. Edelman *Dear Amer.* 244: What a groovy family we're going to have! **1972** R. Barrett *Lovomaniacs* 139: Feeling absolutely *groovy*. **1979** *Buck Rogers* (NBC-TV): Groovy! Get down! **1989** Ramis & Aykroyd *Ghostbusters II* (film): "How do you feel?" "Groovy." **1989** *California Raisins* (CBS-TV): [It's] a groovy place to eat. **1992** *CBS This Morning* (CBS-TV) (Dec. 16): I don't like when my mother uses words from the '60's like *groovy* and *neato* and stuff. It's *so* embarrassing! **1993** *New Yorker* (May 17) 36: He spoke a kind of hip sixties patois...."Oh, groovy....I dig New York."

2. stylish; fashionable. [See note above.]

1941 in Ellington *Music My Mistress* 179: *Groovy*...in the know. **1944** Burley *Hndbk. Jive* 53: To be really groovy, Stud Hoss,...ease into your racket-jacket with the mellow drag. **1968* in *OEDS*: There are a lot of guys going round with groovy hair styles. **1984** J. McCorkle *Cheer Leader* 53: A colorful "groovy" language that I did not know nor have any desire to learn. **1989** *TV Guide* (Feb. 18) 22: People often think it's some groovy kind of actor's spelling, but it's not.

grope *n.* a fondling of someone's genitals, breasts, etc.

1946 J.H. Burns *Gallery* 132: You weren't allowing yourself a free grope from these putains. *a*1972 B. Rodgers *Queens' Vernacular* 101: Give somebody a grope.

grope *v.* to handle, feel, or caress the breasts, buttocks, or genitals of; FEEL UP. [Orig. S.E.; erroneously labeled "Obs." by *OED.*]

*13.. in *OED:* þow gropedest þe wif aniȝt to lowe. **a*1380 in *OED:*

Heo lay stille a luytel whil, þen heo groped him atte laste. ***1611** in *F & H* III 221: Groping of a wench. ***1664** in *OED:* Kissed her and groped her and felt her brests. ***1719** in *F & H* III 221: Smoking, toping,/Landlady groping. **1925** in Armitage *Held* 23: If you care to keep your collegiate standing, never stage a groping party until you break fifty-five an hour. **1933** Ford & Tyler *Young & Evil* 161: The first thing I knew she was groping me. **1936** Le Clercq *Rabelais* 37: May the drunkard's pip rot your guts if the little lecher wasn't forever groping his nurses upside-down, arsey-turvey. **1939** Bessie *Men in Battle* 270: I don't need a guard, except from Rusciano; he gropes me in his sleep. **1945** in T. Williams *Letters* 163: I met Nims...and *groped* him just to get *rid* of him—and *did!* **1949** *Gay Girl's Guide* 10: *Grope:* To feel someone's penis (usually with reference to semi-public conditions where one must remain more or less clothed). **1953** Brossard *Bold Saboteurs* 122: A lot of groping going on here tonight...That's queer talk for feeling up. **1959** Hecht *Sensualists* 125: "The ladies of the house," said Liza, "would catch their husbands groping me. And file a complaint." **1973** P. Benchley *Jaws* 14: A vision that he was back in high school groping a girl on a stairwell. **1992** *This Week with D. Brinkley* (ABC-TV) (June 28): If they groped those women, they should go to *jail.*

gross adj. **1.** *U.S. Mil. Acad.* (of a plebe) clumsy or awkward in drill; stupid. Cf. *OED* s.v. *gross, adj.,* 13 & 14.

1833 *Mil. & Naval Mag. of U.S.* (Oct.) 85: My drill master, a young stripling, told me I was not so "gross" as most other plebis, the name of all new cadets. **1900** *Howitzer* (U.S. Mil. Acad.) (No. 1) 120: *Gross.—* Awkward, clumsy, stupid. **1905** *Howitzer* (U.S. Mil. Acad.) (No. 6) 294: *Gross—*Asinine, wooden, stupid. **1936** Monks & Finklehoffe *Brother Rat* 112: You're gross. You're gross as hell....you haven't got enough brains to pour rain out of a boot. **1988** D.O. Smith *Cradle* 53 [ref. to 1930's]: A "gross" plebe was mentally or emotionally incapable of coming up to standard.

2. *Stu.* disgusting; sickening; (*hence*) unpleasant; unfortunate; displeasing.—often as interj. Also adv. [The "complimentary" application of the term alleged in second 1959 quot. must be regarded as idiosyncratic.]

1959 N.Y.C. junior high school students: It smells gross in here!...Those big cockroaches are gross....Pickin' his nose in class. Gross! **1959** *AS* (May) 155: [Univ. Fla. slang:] *Gross,...neat,* and *tremendous* are either complimentary or derogatory, depending on how they are said. **1964** Walnut Ridge, Ark., high school teacher (coll. J. Ball): When I was growing up, "gross" meant 144. Now it means "nasty." **1968–70** *Current Slang* III & IV 61: The fight was gross. **1970** N.Y.U. student: The trains were late and I had to walk into class half an hour late. She just stopped lecturing and looked at me and said, like, "Class begins at nine sharp. Be here on time or not at all." It was so gross! **1974** Univ. Tenn. student: I know I did gross on that exam. **1976–77** C. McFadden *Serial* 59: Like Joan's, Marlene's entire range of expression was pretty much limited to "far out," "super," and "gross." **1979** Norwood *Survival of Dana* (film): It seems pretty gross to be punished for telling the truth. **1979** Gram *Foxes* 9: "Don't be gross," said Madge. **1989** Univ. Tenn. instructor: *Gross* was a common term when I was in high school in Chicago in 1958—in daily use.

grossed adj. *Stu.* (see quot.).

1968 Baker et al. *CUSS* 130: *Grossed.* Disgusted.

grossed-out adj. *Stu.* disgusting.

1976 Knapp & Knapp *One Potato* 132: Forty-nine kids! The girls called that "grossed out!" **1984** R. Reed, in *N.Y. Post* (Dec. 27) 23: She was pursued by a grossed-out midget called "The Geek."

grosser n. *Stu.* a GROSS or unattractive person.

1979 Gutcheon *New Girls* 183: I'd be embarrassed...to...see real grossers representing Miss Pratt's.

gross-out n. Orig. *Stu.* a revolting thing, action, idea, etc.; (*also*) (see 1969 quot.). Also attrib.

*a***1968** in Haines & Taggart *Ft. Lauderdale* 11: A real gross-out. **1969** *Current Slang* I & II 44: *Gross out,* n. A sort of competition at being gross.—College students, both sexes, Minnesota. **1972** *Nat. Lampoon* (Apr.) 31: "Gross-out, gross-out," they kept saying. **1972** *Nat. Lampoon* (Dec.) 33: A "Deke" House complete with "gross-outs" and "brew blasts." **1979** Gram *Foxes* 98: Angel's having a gross out and he wanted you there. **1981** *Film Comment* (May) 28: Hard-core gross-outs were abandoned for good after *Pink Flamingoes,* once their attention-grabbing purpose had been served. **1985** *Time* (Apr. 15) 103: Some Hollywood people worry that the day may come when there will be one gross-out too many. **1986** *New Yorker* (Dec. 8) 28: The film provides a visually sophisticated form of gross-out humor. **1989** Spears *NTC Dict. Slang* 163: What a gross-out day this has been! **1991** Nelson & Gonza-

les *Bring Noise* 26: It's one gross-out after another.

gross out v. **1.** *Stu.* to shock and disgust; revolt.

1965 Walnut Ridge, Ark., high school student (coll. J. Ball): What are you trying to do—gross me out? **1966** in IUFA *Folk Speech: Gross out:* repulse with crude language. *a***1968** in Haines & Taggart *Ft. Lauderdale* 11: When you want to gross out a girl. **1968** "J. Hudson" *Case of Need* 117: She was always trying to gross you out. **1968** Baker et al. *CUSS* 130: *Gross out.* To disgust someone. **1970** N.Y.U. student: Did we ever gross him out! **1971** Sonzski *Punch Goes Judy* 132: I wouldn't want to gross you out. **1971** N.Y.U. student: I saw an exhibitionist on the subway last night. Was I ever grossed out. **1970–72** in *AS* (1975) 60: Those things he kept saying really grossed me out. **1978** Pilcer *Teen Angel* 119: It totally grossed him out.

2. to become overcome with disgust.

1976 C. Schultz *Peanuts* (synd. cartoon strip) (Dec. 19): I think if I don't get everything I want for Christmas this year, I'm gonna gross out. **1980** *Daily Beacon* (Univ. Tenn.) (May 6) 2: And we all stared. And grossed out. And kept waiting for the mass suicide. **1981** Wambaugh *Glitter Dome* 214: I almost grossed out.

¶ In phrase:

¶ **gross me out!** *Stu.* I'm disgusted! That's terribly disgusting!

1980 Birnbach et al. *Preppy Hndbk.* 220: *Gross adj.* Disgusting....Also, "gross me out." **1982** Univ. Tenn. student: Eeuugh! Gross me out! **1983** in Thom *Letters to Ms.* 17: I have several feelings at once. Here are a few of them. 1. Gross me out! 2. I don't believe it. **1989** C.T. Westcott *Half a Klick* 121: Hairy pits, huh? Gross me out! **1992** D. Burke *Street Talk* 7: Susan and Bob are going together! Gross me out!

grotty adj. [alter. of GROTESQUE] ugly, dirty, or offensive; displeasing; disgusting.

*1964 in *OEDS:* "I wouldn't be seen dead in them. They're dead grotty." Marshall stared. "Grotty?" "Yeah—grotesque." ***1964** in *OED:* Called the [hockey] match "grotty" which seemingly means disappointing. ***1966, *1967, *1970** in *OEDS.* **1968–70** *Current Slang* III & IV 61: *Grotty...*Grotesque...shocking. **a***1970** Partridge *DSUE* (ed. 7) 1178: *Grotty...*(Very) inferior; bad....Popularized by The Beatles and, by 1962, fairly gen. among teenagers. **1971** N.Y.U. student: *Grotty* is halfway between *grotesque* and *cruddy.* **1979** *Film Comment* XV 49: Purists...will tell me that *Planet X* isn't strictly a horror film at all, but science fiction, and a grotty specimen at that. *a***1988** C. Adams *More Straight Dope* 305: When I was a grotty child I used to crack...my toe joints. **1988** M. Maloney *Thunder Alley* 141: They're grotty. **1989** *Village Voice* (Apr. 11) 48: You'd go, ew, grotty, you know?

grouch n. [prob. back formation fr. GROUCHY] **1.** a fit of illtemper or sullenness; (*occ.*) a grudge or complaint.—esp. in phr. **have a grouch on.** Now *colloq.*

[**1805** Brackenridge *Mod. Chiv.* 546: Slouch vs. Crouch...[and] Grouch.] **1895** *DN* I 418: To go on a *grouch,* "to become a little out of sorts." Also, "to get on (or have) a *grouch.*" **1895** Gore *Stu. Slang* 9: *Grouch...*A fit of ill humor. "You've got a grouch on today." **1899** Norris *McTeague* 120: You've got a grouch about something. *Ibid.* 195: You two fellahs have had a grouch at each other for the last year or so. **1900** Ade *More Fables* 113: Papa would get a Grouch and hide in the Corner. **1900** Willard & Hodler *Powers That Prey* 15: It's the second time 't he's had a grouch on. **1902** "J. Flynt" *Little Bro.* 222: He and me's got a grouch on. **1908** in H.C. Fisher *A. Mutt* 22: I don't blame you for having a grouch. **1909** *WNID: Grouch...*A fit of ill temper or sulkiness. *Slang.—grouchy...Slang.* **1909** *DN* III 397: *Grouch,* n. A fit of ill-humor; a dislike; cause for complaint. **1913** J. London *Valley of Moon* 175: Hey, Bill, you seem to think I've got a grouch. **1917** U. Sinclair *K. Coal* 65: What's that? Got a grouch on them mules? **1927** *AS* II (Feb.) 260: Everybody in those days seems to have had a grouch on. **1928** *Amer. Mercury* (Aug.) 434: The day's cares, worries and grouches of a million tired business men. **1933–34** "Max Brand" *Mt. Riders* 39: He's on a grouch this morning. **1971** J. Brown & A. Groff *Monkey* 51: I got up in a grouch one morning.

2. a sullen or ill-tempered person. Now *colloq.*

1900 (cited in *OEDS*). **1902–03** Ade *People You Know* 90: One was a Gusher and the other a Grouch. **1918** W.A. White *Henry & Me* 290: That measly bunch of grouches. **1919** in *DA:* In the section across from us was a fifty-five-year-old male grouch...who had been snarling at everyone that came near him ever since the train left New York. **1920** in *Ibid.:* We pity poor old Carlyle, a crabbed, grumbling grouch all his life long. **1924** B. Conners *Applesauce* 21: You've been married to an old grouch for eight years. **1926** in Rhodes *Novels* 4: You never were a grouch back home. **1957** *Sat. Eve. Post* (Aug. 17) 27: Gee, what a grouch! **1981** Sann *Trial* 43: This old grouch didn't like too many people. **1986** E. Weiner *Howard the Duck* 180: He became a grump, a grouch, a crab.

grouch *v.* to sulk or grumble. Now *colloq.*

1916 in *OEDS: Grouch*, to mope; to grumble. **1917** U. Sinclair *K. Coal* 381: Get the hell out of here, you old groucher! **1925** in *DA:* The tourists...grouched all the way home. **1925–26** J. Black *You Can't Win* 90: "Oh, sure," he grouched, "Everything's all right." **1930** in D.O. Smith *Cradle* 105: Shoot square and don't grouch. **1932** Hecht & Fowler *Great Magoo* 117: Oh, now don't you start grouching. **1982** D.A. Harper *Good Company* 95: Stop grouching! **1992** N. Cohn *Heart of World* 224: "But they're everywhere," she grouched.

grouch bag *n.* (esp. among traveling performers) a small pouch or bag worn esp. beneath clothing and containing emergency funds; (*broadly*) such funds themselves.

1908 McGaffey *Show-Girl* 152: I have met gentlemen who threw the lid of their grouch bag in the gutter. **1914** Jackson & Hellyer *Vocab.* 39: *Grouch bag*, noun. Current amongst yeggs and western thieves. A place, as a pocket or receptacle, for concealing money or valuables; a reserve fund held in secret to the exclusion of fraternists. Example: "He's under cover with a grouch bag." **1927** W. Winchell in *Vanity Fair* (Nov.) 134: "The Grouch bag" or "boodle bag" is the purse that actors wear pinned to the underclothing. **1927** Tully *Circus Parade* 30: Some of the men had a few dollars in their "grouch bags" which were made of chamois skin and tied about their necks. **1928** O'Connor *B'way Racketeers* 218: The sucker was reaching for his grouch bag. **1941** "Gypsy Rose Lee" *G-String* 12: She unpinned a grouch bag from her G-string and took out a five-dollar bill. **1956** Algren *Wild Side* 16 [ref. to *ca*1930]: He could tell carnie hands and circus roustabouts because they took their money out of grouch-bags, pouches drawn by string, like tobacco pouches. **1961** Clausen *Season's Over* 189: Circus people are free spenders and anyone who saved was considered a grouch, so that chamois money bags worn around the neck or waist were called grouch bags. **1966** R.E. Alter *Carny Kill* 12: How's the grouch bag holding? **1971** Roberts *Shoot Out* (film): She had a nice roll in that grouch bag. **1966–72** Winchell *Exclusive* 15: Her bank was what vaudevillians called "the grouch bag," pinned to her chemise. **1974** *Socio. Symposium* XI 31: The [peddlers]...carry small pouches known as "grouch bags" in which they deposit the money and make change. **1984** *L.A. Times Bk. Review* (Feb. 19) 6: He was a serious poker player who carried his money in a "grouch bag."

grouched *adj.* annoyed; angry.

1913 J. London *Valley of Moon* 173: Aw, what's the use of gettin' grouched?

grouch money *n.* [cf. GROUCH BAG] (see quot.).

1941 Coldewey *Lady Gangster* (film): All she's got left is her grouch money....That's what show people call their savings for a really rainy day.

grouchy *adj.* [prob. palatalized var. of obs. dial. syn. *grouty*, perh. infl. by *grudge* or obs. dial. var. *grutch*] ill-tempered; irritable; grumpy. Now *colloq.*

1861 in *AS* 63 (Summer 1988) 115: The only exploit he was ever guilty of, except of playing *grouchy* at Bull's Run, was in Mexico. [**1865** Dennett *South as It Is* 79: He's the one at fault, he's so grouty.] [**1890** *DN* I 61: Notes from Cincinnati...*grouchy*, adj. stingy. (Connected with *grudge?*).] **1895** Gore *Stu. Slang* 9: *Grouchy*...Gloomily irritable; cross. "Go away from me, I'm grouchy." **1902** in *DA:* Thus we may learn which of them, in the opinion of his fellows, is...the slouchiest, the biggest fusser, the "grouchiest." **1909** (quot. at GROUCH, *n.*, 1). **1909** *DN* III 397: *Grouchy*...In a bad humor. Quarrelsome; disagreeable. **1917** in Dreiser *Diaries* 165: Marion is very grouchy, principally because they are broke, I think. **1931** in *DA:* Garden City...is grouchy because children shouted so loudly at a municipal band concert...that the music was drowned out. **1931** *DN* VI 308: *Grouchy*. Ill-tempered, sulky. Slang. **1934** Weseen *Dict. Slang* 345: *Grouchy*—Sulky; ill-tempered.

ground *n.* ¶ In phrase: **hit the ground** *Pris.* to be released from custody.

1962–68 B. Jackson *In the Life* 94: "Well, you're not getting out of jail anymore, I bet you." On Friday I hit the ground.

ground *v.* [broadened from the aviation sense] **1.** *Labor.* to suspend (a driver or similar employee) from work.—usu. as p.ppl. *grounded.*

1939 M. Levin *Citizens* 43: Ladislas Wyznowieki, craneman, why was he grounded? **1942** *AS* (Apr.) 103: *Grounded*. License [to drive a commercial vehicle] revoked. **1968** Ainslie *Racing Guide* 468: *Grounded*—Of

a jockey, suspended from competition for infractions of rules.

2. to punish (a young person) by forbidding him or her to engage in dating or other social activities.—usu. as p.ppl. *grounded.*

1950 Felsen *Hot Rod* 74: It didn't matter about his being grounded. **1959** Gault *Drag Strip* 16: I told my dad about that race I had with you and he's grounded me for two weeks. **1961** *Leave It to Beaver* (ABC-TV): Gee, Dad, you mean I'm grounded for a whole week? **1969** *Fred MacMurray Show* (ABC-TV): You're grounded! **1971** *Smith Family* (ABC-TV): You make one teenage crack about "the fuzz" when your father comes home, and 15 years old or not, I'm going to ground you for a year! **1972** *Nat. Lampoon* (July) 6: Grounded for a whole week. **1973** *Oui* (Apr.) 28: Rumbles, draft notices, the service, alienation, going steady, getting grounded. **1973** Giallombardo *Impris. Girls* 129: To speed up the process, the cottage would be "grounded"...that is, all the inmates were confined to the cottage. **1983** WINS News (WINS radio) (Dec. 12): I can't go out Saturday night. I'm grounded.

ground apple *n.* GROUND NUT.

1931 *AS* (Oct.) 52: "Ground apples" are rocks in the "sawing woods."

grounder *n.* **1.** a cigarette that is picked up from the ground and smoked.

1930 *AS* V (Feb.) 239: *Grounder*. A used cigarette, picked up nonchalantly. "Jim has been reduced to using grounders."

2. *Av.* a nonaviator.

1961 Forbes *Goodbye to Some* 82 [ref. to WWII]: Prime despises him and all other "grounders."

3. *Police.* a police call that demands or results in relatively little investigative effort.

1984 Caunitz *Police Plaza* 3: We caught a few grounders, but nothing heavy. *Ibid.* 19: If it's just a grounder, clean it up and forget it. **1986** Philbin *Under Cover* 20: Most of the killings were...what cops call "grounders"—cases where the perp is known and is collared quickly, or cases where the killer...will never be known.

4. *Narc.* a barbiturate or similar depressant drug.

1978 N.Y.C. man, age 30: He was selling coke, smack, uppers, downers, grounders—everything...Grounders are the same as downers. **1989** R. Miller *Profane Men* 167: Reds, ludes,...grounders.

ground flying *n. Av.* (see 1926 quot.).

1919 Yarwood *Overseas Dreams* 108: Meanwhile, we did considerable "ground flying." **1920** Hall & Nordhoff *Lafayette Flying Corps II* 257: "Ground Flying" at the Chatham Bar. **1926** *Writer's Monthly* (Nov.) 395: *Ground flying*—Conversation about flying, usually indulged in by those who cannot, or do not, fly. **1927** Lindbergh *We* 41: "Ground flying" is the term used to designate the exchange of flying experiences among airmen.

ground-gripper *n.* [sugg. by *Ground Gripper*, a trademark for a kind of shoe] *Mil. Av.* a nonaviator.

1944 Stiles *Serenade* 2: Spaugh...checked out later as a toggleer-bombardier, when they tried to make a ground-gripper out of him. **1944** *AAF* 368: *Ground-gripper*. Non-flying [Air Force] personnel. **1945** in *Calif. Folk. Qly.* V (1946) 384: Aviators...exhibit scorn for those who do not spread their wings by stigmatizing them as *groundgrippers*. **1945** Hamann *Air Words: Ground grippers*. Non-flying personnel of the Air Force; also anyone who doesn't fly. **1958** Camerer *Damned Wear Wings* 19 [ref. to WWII]: This ninety-day wonder...this ground gripper with a pilot's jargon and the military bearing of a clown. **1966–67** W. Stevens *Gunner* 40: He was in intelligence or Operations, a ground-gripper. **1968** Coppel *Order of Battle* 154 [ref. to WWII]: Remember....These guys are ground-grippers....These foot soldiers are going to ask the impossible now and then. *Ibid.* 171: General Jurika wants our FAC to have enough rank to impress the ground-grippers. **1968** W.C. Anderson *Gooney Bird* 74: Grunts. Ground grippers. Army troops. **1983** Kaplan & Smith *One Last Look* 15 [ref. to WWII]: The "ground grippers"...didn't fly but labored with little recognition to keep the air crews flying.

groundhog *n.* **1.** a sausage; frankfurter; hot dog. *Joc.*

1911 *DN* III 544: *Groundhog, n.* Sausage. "Give us that there groundhog. **1935** in *AS* (Feb. 1936) 43: *Groundhog*. Frankfurter sandwich. **1956** Malden, Mo., man (coll. J. Ball): I told him we were having groundhog and he like to shit.

2.a. *Av.* a nonaviator, esp. a nonflying air force officer.

1918 in Grider *War Birds* 135: The groundhog captain at London Colney finally got his wish and killed himself in a Pup. **1928** *Pop. Science Mo.* (May) 72: A "kiwi" is a "groundhog" or pilot who does not like to fly. **1929** Niles et al. *Songs* 163: The Ki-Wi Song (Making merry with the ground hogs)...In the third verse, the Ki-Wi...is a non-flying aviation officer, sometimes called a ground-hog. **1933** Stewart *Airman Speech* 68: *Groundhog*. One who doesn't enjoy flying. **1944** *Slanguage Dict.* 51: *Ground-hog*—member of air force in nonflying status.

b. a telephone-line repairer's assistant who remains on the ground.

1919 Darling *Jargon Book* 15: *Ground Hog*—A lineman who does ground work only. **1920** *304th Field Signal Bn.* 188: One of our reliable "ground hogs." **1948** Mencken *Amer. Lang.* Supp. II 718: A lineman's helper...who never leaves the ground is a...*groundhog*.

c. *R.R.* a brakeman.

1926 *AS* I (Jan.) 250: Brakeman, "shack," "ground hog," "fielder," and "car catcher." **1930** Irwin *Tramp & Und. Sl.: Ground Hog*...A railroad brakeman.

3. *Labor.* a person who customarily works underground, esp. a miner or caisson worker.

1926 *AS* I (Dec.) 651: *Groundhogs*. Men who work in compressed air at caisson work. **1927** *DN* V 449: *Groundhogs*, n. Caisson workers. **1939** Howsley *Argot* 22: *Ground Hog*—miner. **1939** in A. Banks *First-Person* 82: You can't keep a groundhog out in the sun long. **1951** Wilson *Dark & Damp* 228 [ref. to ca1920]: I know you goddam ground-hogs are all alike! I know you're always bellyachin' about a contract—.

4. *Sports.* a groundskeeper.

1971 Coffin *Old Ball Game* 56: *Groundhog* (groundskeeper).

5. (*cap.*) *USAF.* the Republic F-84 Thunderjet fighter aircraft. Cf. HOG.

1991 *Wings* (Discovery Channel TV) [ref. to Korean War]: Many fliers called it the Groundhog, because of its unsatisfactory takeoff characteristics. [The name] was shortened to Hog.

groundhog case *n. West.* a desperate or inescapable situation.

1885 Siringo *Texas Cowboy* 125: Dangerous to cross. But the wagons being over made it a ground hog case. **1887** J.W. Nichols *Hear My Horn* 19: It was a ground-hog case and I knew...he was bound to have watter or die before morning. **1907** *DN* III 231: *Ground-hog case, n. phr.* An unavoidable situation. **1908** *DN* III 317: *Groun(d)-hog case, n. phr.* An extreme case, no other alternative. **1914** in W. Camp *Custer* 136 [ref. to 1876]: He would say, "Men, this is a groundhog case; it is live or die with us." **1926** C.M. Russell *Trails* 88: But sizin' up the hoss under me, it's a groundhog case—climb the tree or the dog'll get you. **1928** L.C. Roberts *Reminiscences* 20 [ref. to 1875]: Boys, this is a ground hog case; we have to camp. **1942** Garcia *Tough Trip* 123: I was going to try to get rid of him on the square, but if it came a ground-hog case I was going to do it crooked. *Ibid.* 133: It was a ground-hog case and I had good luck finding them so close. **1956** Neider *Hendry Jones* 237: I killed him...because it was a groundhog case of him or me.

groundhogging *n. Football.* (see quot.).

1971 Meggyesy *Out of Their League* 25 [ref. to ca1950's]: Coach Vogt had us doing this drill we called "ground-hogging." Two players would get down on their hands and knees facing each other—you could only use your head and had to keep your hands and knees on the ground. The object of the drill was to butt the other player on his back, and the lower you got to the ground the better leverage you had for tipping him over.

groundie *n. Tennis.* a ground stroke.

1981 D.E. Miller *Jargon* 245.

ground loop *n. Av.* a state of excitement or confusion; SPIN.

1943 Wakeman *Shore Leave* 63: How can I go into a ground loop over a woman I've spent exactly four weeks with? **1947** *ATS* (Supp.) 34.

ground nut *n.* a stone.

1833 Ames *Old Sailor's Yarns* 272: He would try which was the hardest, a Spaniard's scull or that "ground nut," as he designated the stone he held in his hand.

ground-pounder *n.* **1.** *Army & USMC.* an infantry soldier.

1942 *Yank* (Aug. 5) 15: One time...a fellow spoke up for the ground pounders...the Infantry. **1951** Sheldon *Troubling Star* 14: He'd thought a typical ground pounder would be a cool, fearless Daniel Boone kind of character. **1964** Crane *Sergeant & Queen* 91: No flyboy could be tempted into being a ground-pounder in combat. **1965** Twist & Susaki *None but the Brave* (film): Didn't he tell you he used to be a ground-pounder? **1966** Adler *Vietnam Letters* 153: He was a non-combatant type ground-pounder in World War II. **1967** in *Air Classics* (May) 47: Our mission was solely to get the ground pounders on the ground in one piece. **1969** Crumley *One to Count Cadence* 22: All I need now is a swimming pool and a spot of sunshine to be a real recruiting-poster ground pounder. **1969** Lane *Conversations with Americans* 215: I

was in Vietnam three months as a grunt, which is, you know, regular ground-pounder, an infantryman. **1984–88** Hackworth & Sherman *About Face* 38: I & R Platoon was a groundpounder unit.

2. *Mil. Av.* a person in military service who is not an aviator.

1945 in *AS* (Dec. 1946) 310 [AAF]: *Ground-pounder*. Non-flying personnel in the Air Force. **1957** Wallrich *A.F. Airs* 69: Flying personnel, as well as groundpounders, were discharged from the AAF as fast as they could be...sent home. **1958** *AS* XXXIII (Oct.) 182: *Ground-pounder*. A derisive name for a conventional firefighter [who is not a parachutist]. **1962** Mandel *Mainside* 263: Remind the ground-pounders that somewhere...Naval aviators fly airplanes. **1966–67** Harvey *Air War* 148: The flight mechanics and other ground-pounders...think very highly of the pilots whose planes they service. **1969** *Current Slang* I & II 45: *Ground pounder*, n. A non-flying USAF officer. **1976** *Dict. Amer. Hist.* (Rev.) 302: Nonflying [USAF] officers were "ground pounders." **1985** Boyne & Thompson *Wild Blue* 524: That's why they trained a groundpounder like me to fly in the back seat.

3. (see quot.).

1990 Lightbody & Poyer *Complete Top Gun* 253: *Ground-pounder*: Attack planes [*sic*] that operate close to the ground.

ground-pounding *adj. Mil. Av.* nonflying.

1945 in M. Chennault *Up Sun!* 104: We got a young ground-pounding first lieutenant. **1985** Heywood *Taxi Dancer* 63: Two ground-pounding lieutenants.

ground rations *n.pl. So.* copulation on the ground. *Joc.*

1942 Hurston *Dust Tracks* 63 [ref. to ca1915]: I got to have my ground-rations. If one woman can't take care of it, I gits me another one. **1984** Wilder *You All* 97: *Ground rations*: sexual intercourse on a leafy bower in a bosky dell retreat.

ground seed *n.* GROUND NUT.

1871 Schele de Vere *Amer.* 554: I took up a ground-seed (stone) and threw it at a he-biddy (cock).

groundside *n.* [*ground* + *-side* as in STATESIDE, MAINSIDE] *Mil. Av.* the ground; a ground assignment. Also attrib. & adv.

1976–79 H.G. Duncan & W.T. Moore *Green Side Out* 79: Being a "ground side" Marine, I have known only a few Marine airplane drivers. **1985** Heywood *Taxi Dancer* 149 [ref. to Vietnam War]: Maybe flying wasn't so glorious as it seemed from groundside.

ground squirrel *n.* **1.** *Av.* GROUNDHOG, 2.a.

1918 in Sullivan *Our Times* V 328: *Ground squirrel:* A man in the Aviation Corps whose duties do not require him to fly. **1972** Carpentier *Flight One* 225: The bonehead ground squirrels left the safety off the oil sump cap.

2. *Horse Racing.* STOOPER.

1943 *New Yorker* (Oct. 23) 74: Several of the professionals, sometimes referred to as ground squirrels, don't do at all badly.

grouper *n. USAF.* a group commander.

1963 E.M. Miller *Exile* 132: He was a light colonel and "grouper," group commander of one of the eastern seaboard units.

group grope *n.* **1.a.** *Navy.* a maneuver or training exercise involving numerous vessels or aircraft. *Joc.*

1945 in Rea *Wings of Gold* 296: This morning I had the lead of VBF on our pre-dawn strike, or "group grope" as we call it. **1962** E. Stephens *Blow Negative* 270: Well, we are going to go out there in the middle of the Atlantic Ocean and have a group grope...That is where we all take our ships...and...grope around trying to find each other and not run each other down. **1966** Noel & Bush *Naval Terms* 168: *Group grope:* Full deck launch of a carrier air group for a specific mission. **1987** Rea *Wings of Gold* 289 [ref. to 1945]: Squadron exercises were generally pointless....These "group gropes" made men wonder just how we were fighting the war—and winning. **1991** Linnekin *80 Knots* 88 [ref. to 1940's]: It was a squadron "group grope" on some target or other.

b. uncertainty or lack of direction among individual elements.

1970 *N.Y. Times* (June 3) 43: Harvard will re-establish an independent department of sociology, ending 24 years of inter-disciplinary group-grope...under the "social relations" umbrella.

c. *Business.* a usu. confused business meeting or similar occasion at which the participants subtly attempt to ascertain one another's ideas or intentions.

1980 Pearl *Pop. Slang* 64: *Group grope*...(Business) mutual appreciation within a group of creative business people, sometimes including stealing each other's ideas. **1987** *Miami Vice* (NBC-TV): So they gonna make my meeting with Guzman a group grope?

2. a session of nude encounter-group therapy that includes reciprocal touching or massage; (*also*) a gathering of people for the purpose of simultaneous sexual activity; orgy.

1967 *Time* (July 7) 19: Making love, however and with whomsoever they can find (including "group grope"), that "feels good and doesn't hurt anybody." **1967–68** von Hoffman *Parents Warned Us* 182: Everybody takes off their clothes and has a group grope. **1970** J. Howard *Please Touch* 247: "Nudie group gropes" and "touchie-feelie encounters." **1971** Adelman *Generations* 74: The sexual expression of the group-grope hardly expresses total emotional involvement. **1971** *Current Slang* V 5: *Group grope*, n. An orgy. **1972** *Playboy* (Dec.) 148: A thing you might start off with…is one of the group-grope places. **1977** D. Morris *Manwatching* 207: In the 1960's the United States saw the growth of a number of group-therapy cults which introduced into their procedures various rituals of mass body-touching. These "group-gropes," as they were called, revealed the underlying need for body contact. **1980** *Daily News* (Aug. 18) (Tonight) (Manhattan) 12: The one-night stands, the group gropes, the wife-swapping, bed-hopping frenzy of orgasmic pursuit. **1981** *Penthouse* (Mar.) 43: We had engaged in several lovely threeways with one of my boyfriends, and she was saying we should try a group grope with a whole lot of people. **1992** *Village Voice* (N.Y.C.) (Feb. 28) 44: Suddenly the dance floor calls to mind a seminar at Esalen, as if '60s group-grope had been filtered through two decades of doomful shit culture and resurfaced as dance.

groupie *n.* an ardent fan of a rock musician or group, typically a teenage girl, esp. one who follows them on tour, often in hope of achieving sexual intimacy; (*hence*) any ardent fan or devotee.

*1967 in *OEDS: Groupy*, a girl who follows the pop groups. ***1968** P. Townshend, in *Rolling Stone Interviews* 119: You can sense professional groupies because they're at ease. **1968** in H. Ellison *Deadly Streets* 102: She was button cute, the way all groupie teenies are cute. **1970** *Playboy* (Apr.) 23: A 14-year-old groupie…was painted up as a lady of the evening. **1970** *N.Y. Times Mag.* (Nov. 29) 13: As it happens, "Groupies" is a film that treats girl camp followers of rock groups as if they (the girls) were geeks. And not only the girl camp followers but the even more pathetic pansy male groupies of San Francisco. **1970** Grissim *Country Music* 258: In fact in the broad sense of the word, groupie may also be used to describe the men who pile on Merle Haggard's bus as soon as it arrives in town, who sprawl in the aisles and generally cling to their idol's presence. They are the hangers-on who crowd about a celebrity…gaining stature from reflected glory.…In most frequent usage, however, the groupie…refers to the women who simply like to chase entertainers into bed. **1973** Gent *N. Dallas* 139: He's a hard-core football groupie. **1974** *Playboy* (Feb.) 70: Don't you [Clint Eastwood] have groupies pursuing you? **1975** Lichtenstein *Long Way* 173: Women pros didn't yet have groupies the way men tennis players…did. **1981** C. Nelson *Picked Bullets Up* 141: Baseball groupies…baked cookies and boiled fudge. **1983** Flaherty *Tin Wife* 224: She's a…cop groupie. **1986** R. Walker *AF Wives* 347: There's groupies everywhere, just itching to keep the flyboys happy. **1989** Kienzle *Eminence* 105: Good old boys out in search of…naughty nautical groupies.

grouse¹ *n.* [fr. the bird name; cf. CHICK, F *poule*, etc.] a young woman; (*hence*) copulation. Cf. GROUSE, *v.*, 2.

1864 in Wiley & Milhollen *They Who Fought* 192: You can get a plenty of Grous [*sic*] here but you will get wounded nine times out of ten, not with the clap but with something worse. [***a1890–93** F & H III 222: *To go grousing*…To quest, or to run down, a woman.] *a***1989** Spears *NTC Dict. Slang* 163: Who's the grouse I saw you with last night?

grouse² *n.* [fr. GROUSE¹, *v.*] a complaint.

*1917 Nettlingham *Tommy's Tunes*: Now every subaltern had a big grouse/And a very big grouse had he:/"We do all the work," said the subalterns. ***1918, *1923, *1927** in *OEDS.* **1952** Bellow *Augie March* 107: He didn't make a heavy grouse; his observations were casual and dry.

grouse¹ *v.* **1.** Orig. *Mil.* to grumble. Now *colloq.*

*1885 in *OEDS:* Impossible to do anything at all entirely to the satisfaction of a certain class of individuals. This…body of men is commonly designated by their comrades as…the "grousers." ***1887** in Kipling *From Sea to Sea* II 396: "That's the only thing as 'ill make the Blue Lights stop grousin' and stiffin'. It should be explained…that "grousing" is sulking, and "stiffin'" is using unparliamentary language. ***1917** Empey *Over the Top* 33: This decision elicited a little "grousing," but quiet was finally restored. **1917** *Wadsworth Gas Attack* 16: We do a lot of grousing in the 27th Division. "Grousing" is British slang for grumbling and for cursing out the life military. **1917** in Grider *War Birds* 33: He said he had heard that we were grousing because we had

to go to Ground School again. **1918** *Sat. Eve. Post* (Oct. 5) 35: I have heard sailors grousing interminably about their petty officers. **1919** *Century* (Nov.) 1: And yet you'll hear 'em grousing. ***1927** Whall *Sea Songs* 5: "Grouse" (to growl) was a common sea word in those days [1861–72], as it still is in the army. **1929** Panzram *Killer* 212: You know in my letters to you I have been grousing about my job here. **1936** Anderson *High Tor* 58: What are you grousing about? **1944** Ind *Bataan* 156: Show me a bunch of pilots without imagination enough to grouse about the airplanes they've got, and I'll show you a squadron dead on its feet. **1962** *Time* (Nov. 2) 16: Khrushchev…groused about the continuing "violation" of Cuban airspace. **1962** T. Berger *Reinhart in Love* 205: His own dear companion never groused. **1969** Moynahan *Pairing Off* 26: If you want me to co-sign a small bank loan I'll do it. But quit grousing. **1972** *Life* (Oct. 27) 63: "No wonder they got us out here," he groused. **1977** C.A. Owen *Canterb. Tales* 104: His initial impulse is to grouse a little about the story. **1993** *Newsweek* (July 26) 8: Grousing that her dumb clothes compromised her popularity.

grouse² *v.* to engage in lovemaking. Cf. GROUSE¹, *n.*

1958 Southern & Hoffenberg *Candy* 83: Humping under the bed! Grousing in the goodie! *a***1989** Spears *NTC Dict. Slang* 163: They stopped grousing in order to come up for air.

grovel *v. Stu.* to engage in lovemaking, esp. petting. Also quasi-*adj.*

1987 *Rage* (Knoxville, Tenn.) I (No. 2) 32: Did this girl…really disgrace your house by a little innocent grovel session? *a***1989** Spears *NTC Dict. Slang* 163: They spent the whole time in the back seat groveling.

Grover *n.* (see quot.).

1984 D. Jenkins *Life Its Ownself* 163: There was nothing Big Ed couldn't handle with Grovers. Grover Clevelands. Thousand-dollar bills.

growl *n.* **1.** *Naut.* a grumbler.

1841 [Mercier] *Man-of-War* 37: A long line of the *awkward squad* was drawn up the whole length of the starboard gangway, and amongst them many of our *ship's growls*, old customers who had spent their lifetimes on board a man-of-war, and who of course consider the privilege is allowed them of venting their peevish spleen on all around, and which they put in force on every occasion, however trifling. **1847** Downey *Portsmouth* 52: Our ship had her full quantity of Growls and Psalm Singers, nor was she at all deficient in the Wag Line. **1859** in C.A. Abbey *Before the Mast* 215: He is the biggest growl & loafer…aboard. **1875** Sheppard *Love Afloat* 88: What are you talkin' about me for, you old growl? **1903** *Independent* (Nov. 26) 2795: "Old sailor, old growl" is a nautical truism.…And "growl you may but go you must."

2. a complaint or cause for complaint.

1850 in O.T. Howe *Argonauts* 144: And if there was a civil growl, 'twas settled in a trice. **1861** in H.L. Abbott *Fallen Leaves* 75: We never hear an oath or a growl. **1863** in Wightman *To Ft. Fisher* 106: A general growl has followed the new appointment. **1926** Nason *Chevrons* 75 [ref. to 1918]: "You've got no growl," said Eadie.

3. *Navy.* a radio communications transmission.

1962 S. Smith *Escape from Hell* 120 [ref. to WWII]: "Give him a growl," the Admiral said tersely. "Tell him we'll supply fighter cover."

growler *n.* **1.** a cannon.

1860 Shipley *Reefer* 77: See how our old growler will pick off her fancy yards—there goes one now!

2.a. a pail, can, or pitcher used for carrying beer; in phr. **rush** [or **roll**] **the growler** to purchase beer in a growler.

1885 *Puck* (May 13) 165: The old, old story. A happy home, loving parents, the growler, the fall and ruin. **1888** Farmer *Amer.*: To fetch beer for them, or in other words to rush the growler. **1889** Bailey *Ups & Downs* 15 [ref. to 1871]: English Jim sent the "growler" out for beer, and told the girls to drink me good luck. **1889** Pierson *Vagabond's Honor* 100: The "growler," a huge stone pitcher, almost as large as the boy, was dragged out of a corner. **1889** *Scribner's Mag.* (Dec.) 662: He…carries the "growler" for beer. **1891** *Contemporary Rev.* (Aug.) 255: Liquor drinking [is called] "rushing the growler." **1894** F.P. Dunne, in Schaaf *Dooley* 155: He…had to r-roll th' growler f'r a pint in a handbag. **1895** Townsend *Fadden Explains* 31: I always upsets the growler just when it's full. **1897** *Harper's Wkly.* (Jan.) 90: A "growler"…is any vessel—pail, pitcher, or can—that is sent to the corner saloon for the family supply of lager beer. **1900** Greenough & Kittredge *Words & Ways* 75: Not long ago the very vulgar slang phrase "rush the growler" was quoted in a dignified and irreproachable article in a daily newspaper.…A score of such references might make the reader forget that this most objectionable expression ever was slang, or had any offensive associations. **1902** Mead *Word-Coinage* 167: "Chasing the can," or the "duck," "rolling the rock," and "rushing" or "working the growler" all mean sending the tin can to the corner barroom for beer. **1902–03** Ade *People You Know* 126: Etruscan Growlers and Antique Jugs. **1903** Kildare *Mamie Rose* 24 [ref. to *ca*1875]: At these visits the most frequently used utensil was the "can" or "growler"….Children of both sexes were employed until late in the night…to "rush the growler" for their seniors at home. **1910** in McCay *Little Nemo* 217: Stop rushing the growler and put some coal on the fire. **1914** S. Lewis *Mr. Wrenn* 18: I'd…pawn it for ten growlers of Dutch beer. **1943** J. Mitchell *McSorley's* 174: We carried tin growlers and shouted, "We want beer!" **1949** *N.Y. Times* (Apr. 10) I 40: It is more than likely that only regular customers will be able to buy a glass of beer….For the occasional drinker and the floater it will be wines, whiskies or water….Put that growler away for a while. **1980** Gould *Ft. Apache* 18: Little boys "rushing the growler,"…taking home a bucket of beer for their fathers.

b. (see quots.).

1942 *ATS* 438: *Growler*…a [cell] chamberpot. **1970–72** in *AS* L (1975) 60: *Growler. n.* Toilet.

c. jail.—constr. with *the.*

1981 Graziano & Corsel *Somebody Down Here* 136: [The police] take 'im in for a night in the growler.

3. *Naut.* a small iceberg.

***1912** in *OED2*: The growler was an iceberg with very little protruding above the water. **1931** Lubbock *Bully Hayes* 62: The old man's as cool as a Labrador growler. **1934** *WNID2.* **1959** *New Yorker* (July 4) 46: I asked him what a growler is. "A small piece of glacial ice that has broken from a berg," he said. **1970** *U.S. News & W.R.* (Feb. 9) 73: The really dangerous type of glacial ice, or iceberg, is the growler—the small chunk of ice that can still weigh thousands of tons. **1992** G. Wolff *Day at the Beach* 194: I wasn't dodging growlers, icebergs and pirates.

4 a. *Navy.* a public-address system.

1945 in *Calif. Folk. Qly.* V (1946) 378: Because they more or less distort the human voice, the electronic public address and intercommunications sets aboard a ship are styled *squawk boxes* or *growlers.* **1986** Univ. Tenn. grad. student, age 35: A *growler* is an intercom. They growl in the morning when they crank 'em up.

b. a siren.

1961 H. Ellison *Gentleman Junkie* 43: It was the revolving angry red eye of a police growler. **1965** in H. Ellison *Sex Misspelled* 320: The approaching growlers of the police prowl cars.

growly *n.* [orig. unkn.] *U.S. Mil. Acad.* ketchup.

1900 *Howitzer* (U.S. Mil. Acad.) (No. 1) 120: *Growley.*—A mess-hall dish, packed in red bottles labelled "Ketchup."—it is sometimes used in drowning the taste of hash. **1905** *Howitzer* (U.S. Mil. Acad.) (No. 6) 294: *Growley*—Tomato Ketchup. **1942** Hersey *On Bataan* 72 [ref. to 1899]: "Pass the growly, please", for catsup because of its ring of fermentation bubbles. **1973** Jackson *Fall Out* 416 [ref. to 1918]: Did somebody drop a can of growley on you?

grub *n.* **1.** food; provisions; a meal; (*hence*) *Mil.* mess.

***1659** in *OED*: Let's joyne together; Ile pass my word this night/Shall yield us grub, before the morning light. ***1691** in *OED*: To get him some grub,…and a little good bub. ***1725** *New Canting Dict.*: Grub, to Eat, to Dine, &c. also Victuals. ***1781** in *F & H* III 225: How did you procure your Grub and Bub? **1807** Tufts *Autobiog.* 293 [ref. to 1794]: *Grub*…victuals. ***1813** in *OED*: The boys…finished the evening with some prime grub, swizzle, and singing. **1837** Strong *Diary* I 56: Being two-thirds famished, we stopped to get some grub in the Bowery. **1839–40** Cobb *Green Hand* I 189: I have my grub to get at eight bells. **1848** J. Scott *Encarnation* 72: The manner in which the "grub" was served…was more discordant to our feelings. **1854** in McCauley *With Perry* 82: After grub we had a smoke and a palaver with our hosts. **1861** Berkeley *Sportsman* 14: Every jolly fellow would give them a bit of "his grub" whenever he had any himself. **1862** in Wightman *To Ft. Fisher* 28: Let me stop to go to grub. **1863** in G. Whitman *Letters* 88: We can buy plenty of fish, and oysters, and butter, or almost anything else in the way of grub. **1867–71** Bagg *Yale* 45: *Grub*, food, meals, board. A very common word, both as noun and verb. **1875** Sheppard *Love Afloat* 49: He takes his grub regular, sir. **1884** Blanding *Sailor Boy* 65: When the boatswain pipes for grub to-night. **1887** M. Roberts *W. Avernus* 82: They told me that the "grub" was good. **1892** Garland *Spoil of Office* 21: Say, Brad, don't you want some grub? **1893** Riis *Nisby* 7: This one'll have to do for me grub. **1904** in Opper *H. Hooligan* 55: What kind of grub do they have? **1905** W.S. Kelly *Lariats* 5: A pine "grub box." **1911** H.B. Wright *Barbara Worth* 11: A well-stocked "grub-box." **1928** Nason *Sgt. Eadie* 75: I ain't no chow hound nor no grub grabber, but

would you mind tellin' me…what the hell this stuff is? **1935** H. Cobb *Paths of Glory* 8: We'll start out so as to catch up with them in time for evening grub. **1943** J. Mitchell *McSorley's* 68: It's the only grub I know of that's free of charge. **1958** Hailey & Castle *Runway* 11: I'm starving. When do they bring round the grub? **1976** J.W. Thomas *Heavy Number* 28: There's grub in the fridge.

2. *Stu.* an excessively diligent student.

1847 in B. Hall *College Wds.* (ed. 2) 243: A man must not be ashamed to be called a "grub" in college, if he would shine in the world. **1856** B. Hall *College Wds.* (ed. 2) 243: Our real delvers, midnight students, are familiarly called Grubs. **1887** in *DAE*: The reputation of a "grub" is hardly a desirable at the present day. **1900** *DN* II 40: *Grub*, n. = grind, q.v. **1966–68** *Current Slang* I & II 45: *Grub*, n. One who studies very hard.—College students,…New York, Arizona. **1973** Jong *Flying* 48: Just because you were a grub and a grind and did well in school. *a***1982** Safire *Good Word* 300: Other replacements of "grind" are…"pencil geek"…and "grub."

3. Now Esp. *Stu.* a slovenly person, esp. a child; (in recent use) an offensive, obnoxious, or unattractive person. [Various other contemptuous senses, as in 1807 quot., are considered S.E. by *OED2*, cited from *a*1400; see *OED2* def. 2.]

[**1807** W. Irving *Salmagundi* 50: The grubs, the flats, the noddies are pointing their empty guns at us.] ***a*1845** T. Hood, in *OED:* The Cook's a hasher—nothing more—/The Children noisy grubs. ***1888** in *OED:* A dirty little child is called "a young grub." ***a*1890–93** *F & H* III 225: *Grub*…(colloquial).—A dirty sloven; generally used of elderly people. **1966** IUFA *Folk Speech*: *Grub*—A real mean person. **1966–68** *Current Slang* I & II 45: *Grub*, n. An untidy person….Someone who is gross in manner. **1968** Baker et al. *CUSS* 131: *Grub.* An obnoxious person. **1972** Hannah *Geronimo Rex* 36: The only boy who ever asked her out was an absolute grub. **1973** *Urban Life & Culture* III 155: He was labeled "grub" and "hodad" surfer by his contemporaries. **1980** Rimmer *Album* 29 [ref. to 1965]: What a grub.

4. *pl. Stu.* old, comfortable clothing, esp. a T-shirt and jeans. Also **grubbies.**

1968 Sebald *Adolescence* 223: In California in 1966, a preference for battered-looking sneakers evolved…they…were called…"grubbies" by teen-agers. **1969** *Current Slang* I & II 45: I can hardly wait to get out of this dress into my grubs. **1974** Dohan *Our Own Words* 299: *Grubs* are ragged, short-cut blue jeans. **1983** Wambaugh *Delta Star* 217: They wore cut-offs and jeans and grubbies of all kinds. **1990** *Sally Jessy Raphaël* (synd. TV show): Some leftover time when you put on your grubbies.

¶ In phrase:

¶ **ride the grub line** *West.* to travel about looking for work, esp. odd jobs.

[***1785** Grose *Vulgar Tongue: To ride grub,* to be sullen or out of temper.] [***1840** in *OED*: "To ride grub," is to be out of temper, morose.] **1899** in Davidson *Old West* 74: Cow punchers…didn't ride the grub line, like/You see 'em do now days. **1915** *DN* IV 244: Stone's never worked and were [*sic*] always *on the grub line.* **1940** F. Hunt *Trail fr. Tex.* 110: He didn't want to face Felicia as a dead-broke grub-line rider. **1941** in *DA*: Cowboys hired for the season saddle up and "ride the grub line" from ranch to ranch, looking for another job. **1952** Overholser *Fab. Gunman* 55: Slade had mistaken him for a grub-line rider. **1958** Bard & Spring *Horse Wrangler* 225 [ref. to *ca*1905]: Cowboys that were out of work just rode the grub line from one ranch to another,…staying until they thought their welcome was running out. **1964** L'Amour *Hanging Woman Cr.* 24: I never did like riding the grub line in snow country.

grub *v.* **1.a.** to eat a meal or meals; dine.—now also constr. with *up, out,* or *down.*

***1724** in J. Farmer *Musa Pedestris* 41: Frisky Moll…Wou'd Grub in a bowzing ken. ***1725** (quot. at GRUB, *n.,* 1). ***1812** Vaux *Vocab.:* To *grub* well, is to eat with an appetite. ***1819** [T. Moore] *Tom Crib* 28: What with *snoozing,* high *grubbing,** and *guzzling like Cloe.…*Feeding. ***1839** in *OED*: I found some twenty-five gentlemen grubbing in solemn silence. **1847** Downey *Portsmouth* 7: A General Dive was now made for the Berth Deck and Grubbing was the order of the Day, between mouthfuls of which the different merits of the two vessels were discussed. **1847** in G.W. Harris *High Times* 70: I'll grub right *thar,* or die on this dung-hill. **1873** Jewell *Among Our Sailors* 174: You must "bunk" and "grub" in the forecastle with the other sailors. **1889** O'Reilly & Nelson *Fifty Years on Trail* 153: We all grubbed in the rooms of the wife who was in power for the week. **1900** *Harper's* (May) 898: Oh, let's grub first. **1910** in O. Johnson *Lawrenceville* 362: I'd like you to come over and grub with us. **1954–60** *DAS: Grub out*…To eat a meal. **1970–72** in *AS* L (1975) 60: Let's go grub up. **1978** UTSQ: [Eat]…*munch down, get some chow, grub down.* **1982** Eble *Campus Slang* (Nov.) 3: *Grub out*—to eat. **1989** *Rage* (Knoxville, Tenn.) (Mar.) 8: Since you're probably tired, go ahead and grub. Get him/her to buy you dinner.

b. to provide with food; feed.

*1812 Vaux *Vocab.*: To grub a person, is to diet him, or find him in victuals. *1837 C. Dickens *Pickwick Papers* ch. xxii: The red-nosed man…wasn't the sort of person you'd like to grub by contract. *1883 in *F & H* III 225: They are not bound to grub you, don't you know,…and they try the starving dodge on you sometimes. **1886** in Herdegan & Beaudot *At Gettysburg* 77: A man called Dutcher had the contract for "grubbing" us. **1889** O'Reilly & Nelson *Fifty Years on Trail* 279: The Deadwood stage coach always stopped at it to change horses and grub the passengers. **1901** J. London *God of His Fathers* 123: I'm goin' to unrig the dogs an' grub 'em. **1902** *DN* II 236: *Grub yersef, v. phr.* To eat. Used facetiously.

2. *Stu.* to study hard.—also trans., constr. with *out.*

1848 *Amherst Indicator* I 223: I can grub out a lesson in Latin or mathematics as well as the best of them. **1851** B. Hall *College Wds.: Grub.* To study hard; to be what is denominated a *grub*, or hard student. **1900** *DN* II 40: *Grub, v.i.* Equivalent of to bone or to grind. **1966–68** *Current Slang* I & II 45: *Grub, v.* To study intensively. *a*1982 Safire *Good Word* 300: He's in the library grubbing for a history exam.

3. to beg or borrow; cadge; to beg from.—used trans.

1887 *Lantern* (N.O.) (Feb. 19) 3: They ketch a feed when they grub somebody fur it. *a*1890–93 *F & H* III 225: *Grub*…(old).—To beg; to ask for alms, especially food. **1900** *DN* II 40: *Grub, v.t.* 1. To borrow. 2. To obtain. **1908** McGaffey *Show Girl* 152: Me grub, and I got money in the bank? Sure I do. I got to keep in training somehow. **1971** N.Y.U. student: Could I grub a cigarette? **1986** Gilmour *Pretty in Pink* 131: He stops by to clean out the refrigerator, grub money, and change his boots.

4. *Stu.* to neck and pet; MAKE OUT.

1966–68 *Current Slang* I & II 45: *Grub, v.* To kiss; to pet; to have sexual intercourse.—High school students…Alabama. **1980** Eble *Campus Slang* (Oct.) 3: *Grub*—Kiss, hug, etc.: "I couldn't believe they were grubbing right there on the dance floor." **1987** Univ. Tenn. student theme: [To] *grub*…is a word which describes extremely hard kissing and necking but nothing further than that. **1990** Univ. Tenn. student theme: I totally grubbed with this hot guy last night.

grubbed up *adj.* dirtied; dirty.

1961 *Leave It to Beaver* (ABC-TV): We won't get all grubbed up at recess.

grubber *n.* **1.** *Stu.* an overly diligent student.

1881 Palmer *Jeannette's Cistern* 11: Any old grubber, with lots of good marks, can get the valedictory.

2. a beggar.

1904 *Life in Sing Sing* 249: *Grubber*—A beggar.

3. [this sense infl. by or directly < E Yid *grober* 'coarse or rude person'] a person who is coarse, ignorant, or offensive.

1941 Kendall *Army & Navy Sl.* 7: *Grubber*….lowest ranks in the army, even one grade below a yardbird. **1970–72** in *AS* L (1975) 60: *Grubber,* n. Person considered to be disgusting.

grubbies *n.pl.* see GRUB, *n.,* 4.

grubbins *n.* **1.** GRUB, 1.

1847 Downey *Cruise of Portsmouth* 159: He…would never rise except to get his Grubbins, which having swallowed, he would down again, and sleep till next meal time.

2. (among tramps) (see quot.).

1917 *Editor* (Feb. 24) 153: *Grubbing* [*sic*]—money, but not in large quantity.

grub boss *n. Army.* (see quot.).

1899 Young *Reminiscences* 432: The grub boss, that's the quartermaster sergeant, comes around next morning.

grubby *n. Stu.* (see quots.).

1942 Hollingshead *Elmtown's Youth* 218: Sleepy's a "grubby," I don't know whether he's dumb or just not interested in school. *Ibid.* 221: "Grubbies" are set off from the other students for many reasons.…Boys and girls identified as grubbies are "nobody" in the eyes of non-grubbies. To be rated a grubby is comparable to being blacklisted.

grub-choker *n.* a camp cook.

1879 (quot. at POT SLINGER).

grub hook *n.* usu. *pl.* a finger or hand.

1923 *Poems, Ballads, and Parodies* 54: I could hear the dull buzz of the bee/As he sunk his grub hooks into me. **1924** Tully *Beggars of Life* 29: If I'd a stretched out my arms any they'd o' been on the rails, an' I'd a been a bum wit'out grub-hooks. **1959** N. Nye *Long Run* 59: He fastened one of those grub-hooks into the front of Howlett's jacket…and pulled. **1987** Thain *Cold as a Bay St. Banker's Heart* 77: Keep your grub hooks off my things.

grub line *n.* see *ride the grub line* s.v. GRUB, *n.*

grub-liner *n. West.* (see 1936 quot.).

1912 in *DARE:* He was no booze-fighting grubliner. **1936** McCarthy *Mosshorn* (unp): *Grub-liner, n.* One who travels from ranch to ranch for meals. Sometimes referred to as an itinerant cowboy who is able to make his living without working. **1959** in *DARE:* Like giving my grub-liner friends a handout when they stop in at all hours.

grub-mill *n.* the mouth.

1880 Pilgrim *Old Nick's Camp Meetin'* 110: I…kin say off the very words what rolled outn'n his grub-mill.

grub-pile *n. West.* a meal. Also interj.

1871 Crofutt *Tourist's Guide* 142: Teamsters on the plains call a meal a "grub pile." **1876** in Vaughn *Reynolds* 53: To the inspiring cry "Grub pile," "Yars yer hash," "Sup-pah," etc., the…packers press forward to the festive board. **1882** Baillie-Grohman *Rockies* 19: Why I'll be darned if you wasn't the only cuss who said thank ye when the grub pile was trundled over to yer side. **1887** [C.C. Post] *10 Yrs. Cowboy* 454: The word is given, "Grub pile." **1892** in *Dict. Canad.*: "That means 'grub pile,' that does."…We were anxious…[to] parade our guests before the "grub pile" which had been provided for the occasion. **1899** Garland *Eagle's Heart* 253: *Grub-pile! All down for grub!* **1915–18** *Coll. Kans. State Hist. Soc.* XIV 283 [ref. to Civil War]: I was kindly told that "grub pile" had been called, and so I pitched in with the rest. **1927–30** Rollins *Jinglebob* 8 [ref. to 1880's]: Grub pi-i-ile! Come an' get it! **1935** Coburn *Law Rides Range* 71: When you've wrapped yourselves around this grub pile, go out and buy a shave apiece.

grub-rider *n.* [sugg. by *ride the grub line* s.v. GRUB, *n.*] *West.* GRUB-LINER.

1920 in *DA:* All "grub riders" (cowpunchers out of a job) have always been sure of a meal and a place to sleep at his ranch or any of his camps. **1922** in *Dict. Canad.*: For the masters to be bearded by a humble grub-rider was incredible. **1962** in *Dict. Canad.*

grub-slinger *n.* a cook.

1912 R.C. Murphy *Logbook for Grace* 6: "Griddlecakes?" inquired our Dutch West Indian, black grub-slinger, "what's them?"

grub-spoiler *n.* a cook.

1883 Keane *Blue-Water* 35: These "water-whelps," as we called them, are properly called "dough-boys," but our "grub-spoiler"—pet name for ship's cook—called them "swimmers," probably because they were such heavy sinkers. **1903** *Independent* (Nov. 26) 2794: The victualing department was presided over by two heathen grub spoilers, who, according to Spike Riley, could not boil water without burning it. **1936** McCarthy *Mosshorn* (unp.): *Greasy Belly, Gut Robber,* or *Grub Spoiler.* A cook. *1950 Granville *Sea Slang* 114: *Grub spoiler.* A naval cook.

grubstake *n. West.* **1.** money, supplies, or equipment supplied, esp. to a prospector, on condition of the supplier participating in the profits of a particular undertaking. Now *S.E.*

1863 in *DA:* A grub stake is what we are after…and it is one hundred and fifty dollars in good dust. **1879** in *DAE:* It has grown to be a custom for merchants to hire impecunious persons to go prospecting for them, furnishing tools, arms, blankets and rations for a given time. This advance is termed a "grub-stake," in return for which the capitalist receives an interest in whatever may be discovered. **1881** Crofutt *Grip-Sack Guide* 24: It would be well to provide ourselves with a "grub-stake" before starting. **1922** Rollins *Cowboy* 34: A "grub-stake"…required its recipient to pay to its donor an agreed share of whatever profit might accrue from the enterprise on which the recipient was about to embark. **1929** "M. Brand" *Last Showdown* 49: The Duster gave that old-timer fifty dollars,…but he wouldn't look on that as a grubstake. **1951** Mailer *Barbary Shore* 8: I was driven with the ambition that I should be a writer, and I was grubbing…for a grubstake.

2. *Broadly,* money or provisions.

1881 Crofutt *Grip-Sack Guide* 52: Keep out of the lawyers' hands. They…are always hunting a fat "grub-stake." **1900** Wister *Jimmyjohn* 212: Me and my grubstake—provisions, ye know. **1922** Rollins *Cowboy* 34: A "grub-stake"…[might also] denote one's food-supply, no matter how obtained.

grubstake *v. West.* to provide with a grubstake.

1879 in *DA:* Judge Pendary...has been grub-staking a party of miners. **1881** A.A. Hayes *New Colo.* 82: He even showed some inclination to "grub-stake" some men. **1884** in Lummis *Letters* 52: He "grub-staked" a dead-broke miner, advancing him about $7 worth of provisions from his little grocery. **1888** Gunter *Miss Nobody* 101: You're an honest man and I'll grub-stake you. **1927** in J. O'Hara *Sel. Letters* 25: Suffice it to say I couldn't get a job, or I'd have stayed long enough to have saved sufficient dough to grubstake myself on a trip farther west. **1937** Kyner & Daniel *End of Track* 184: They were forced, periodically, to stop work on their tunnel in order to earn enough to "grubstake" them for a time. **1963** R.W. Paul *Mining Frontiers* 98: Some local merchant, professional man, or mining speculator was always ready to "grub-stake" him in return for a large share of any discoveries made. **1967** Spillane *Delta* 39: They were starving artists who needed rent and refrigerator money and I liked their work enough to grubstake them.

grub-trap *n.* the mouth.

*1887 (cited in Partridge *DSUE*). ***1889** Barrère & Leland *Dict. Slang* I 434: *Grub-trap* (popular) the mouth. **1938** E.J. Mayer et al. *Buccaneer* (film): Shut your grub traps!

grub wagon *n.* a chuck wagon.

1917–20 in J.M. Hunter *Trail Drivers* I 80 [ref. to 1879]: We were two miles from the grub wagon when the run was over.

gruel *n.* punishment.

*1797 in *OED:* My pupil talked of nothing but of returning to Devizes, to "give the ostler his gruel" for having taken him in. ***1815** Sir W. Scott, in *OED:* He shall have his gruel! ***1823** Byron *Don Juan* cnt. XI: I've got my gruel! ***1837** in *F & H* III 226: He that was mildest in mood gave the truculent rascal his gruel. **1886** F. Whittaker *Pop Hicks* 22: What's the use of whining, Pop? Take your gruel like a man.

gruesome *adj.* very unpleasant, unattractive, or displeasing.

1932 Hecht & Fowler *Great Magoo* 117: Maybe it's those pajamas....They make you look kind of gruesome. **1940** Clemmer *Pris. Community* 75: The sight of 1,200 men stoically eating in silence is gruesome. **1942** A.C. Johnston *Courtship of A. Hardy* (film): She's not genuinely gruesome. She's just a little—different. **1944** in Galewitz *Great Comics* 50: How long is this sad sack, Curly, gonna impose his gruesome presence...? **1949** H. Ellson *Tomboy* 89: "Yeah, tall, dark and gruesome," Margie said. **1971** Sorrentino *Up from Never* 29: All my friends considered books a gruesome drag. **1982** in *Barnhart Dict. Comp.* IV (1985) 29: Omigod, Mom, like that's totally beige...I mean grody to the max, just gruesome. **1991** B. Adler *Rap!* xv: The music was positively middle-aged....Gruesome.

gruesome twosome *n.* a disliked or unattractive pair of individuals or things; *(hence)* a pair of sweethearts. *Joc.*

1941 "G.R. Lee" *G-String* 19: Let's wrap the old one up like a Christmas present and give it to the Gruesome Twosome. **1944** *Slanguage Dict.* 59: *Gruesome twosome*—couple going steady. **1946** J.H. Burns *Gallery* 147: Why don't you bring one of your Warm Sisters with you and make a gruesome twosome? **1955** *AS* XXX 303: *Gruesome twosome, n.* Couple who go steady. **1972** *N.Y. Post* (Sept. 30) 28: Irreverent non-Communists referred to the bodies of Lenin and Stalin as "the gruesome twosome" and "the cold cuts." **1978** J. Webb *Fields of Fire* 221: Him and the Sergeant Major would make a gruesome twosome. **1966–80** McAleer & Dickson *Unit Pride* 331: Hal and Murph....Now wouldn't that be a gruesome twosome? **1990** *Simpsons* (Fox-TV): My wife's sisters. Or as I call 'em, the gruesome twosome. **1992** *Donahue* (NBC-TV): They are a gruesome twosome on the side.

grumper *n.* [orig. unkn.; perh. rel. to Brit. and Austral. E slang *grummet* 'female genitals'] the buttocks.

1972 R. Barrett *Lovomaniacs* 29: Some chicks lead with the boobs....This chick leads with the grumper.

grumpus *n.* a grumpy or bad-tempered person.

1986 *Cheers* (NBC-TV): Who's Miss Grumpus?

grunge *n.* [perh. back formation fr. GRUNGY; perh. alter. (infl. by *grime*) of GUNGE[1]] **1.** *Stu.* a slovenly or offensive person.

1965 *N.Y. Times* (Dec. 27) 20: "Wimp"..."grunge"..."dip"..."spook." All are bad. **1966–68** *Current Slang* I & II 45: *Grunge,* n. Someone who is sloppy in dress.—Air Force Academy cadets. **1968** Kerdisen *Write It Right* 11: Like, the show was a gas, man, but my date was a real grundge. **1968** Baker et al. *CUSS* 131: *Grunge.* An obnoxious person.

2. grease, grime, or filth; *(also)* anything nasty or inferior.

1968–70 *Current Slang* III & IV 62: *Grunge,* n. A bad, unpleasant thing, especially food.—University of Kentucky.—Did you see the *grunge* we had for supper? **1970–72** in *AS* L (1975) 60: There's grunge in the bottom of my Dr. Pepper bottle! **1976** *Nat. Lampoon* (Feb.) 28: More sex grunge about the Canadian Parliament. **1978** Eble *Campus Slang* (Apr.) 2: *Grunge*—something dull or unappealing: The work for the course was a real grunge. **1987** *RHD2*: He didn't know good music from grunge.

grunged-out *adj.* filthy; GRUNGY.

1986 Stinson & Carabatsos *Heartbreak* 152: What a pathetic, grunged-out little whorehouse.

grungehole *n.* a filthy or disreputable place.

1986 E. Weiner *Howard the Duck* 27: The owners and managers of these grungeholes were pros at one thing only.

grungy *adj.* [prob. fr. SCRUNGY] **1.** dirty; shabby; grimy; disreputable; unpleasant.

1966 in IUFA *Folk Speech: Grundy* [*sic*]—old and dirty. **1966** Idaho teenager: *Grungy* means absolutely filthy and disgusting. **1970** N.Y.U. student: My shoes are beginning to look all grungey. **1970** N.Y.U. student: This is the grungey middle of Central Park where all the teenagers hang out. **1970** N.Y.U. professor: They told grungey stories about monks and nuns. **1972** *WCBS Evening News* (WCBS-TV) (Nov. 1): We had a grungey day today. **1970–72** in *AS* L (1950) 60: We'll wear grungy clothes on the hayride. **1972** *Nat. Lampoon* (June) 52: My last buy had been negotiated on a grungy stairwell with two twitching spades. **1973** Lucas et al. *Amer. Graffiti* 51: You grungy little twerp. **1968–77** Herr *Dispatches* 60: The other guy just ate rice and a few grungy fish heads. **1977** *N.Y. Times* (June 19) X 1: Tropical Eden or grungy Gomorrah? **1980** H. Fonda, in Teichmann *Fonda* 190: Those whores looked grungy. **1981** *Film Comment* (May) 4: The grungy, landlord-green wall of his apartment. **1979–82** Gwin *Overboard* 176: Scouring out every grundgy corner of the boat. **1987** in K. Marshall *Combat Zone* 60: You know, you had on grungy uniforms again and everything was very recognizable and you were with people you felt truly comfortable with. **1987** *TV Guide* (Oct. 24) 24: A typical fictional private investigator—tough, broke and grungy.

2. inferior; poor; dismal.

1969 *New Yorker* (July 19) 20: Real people are pretty grungy actors when you come right down to it. **1985** Boyne & Thompson *Wild Blue* 577: The Pentagon was a grungy place, even for major generals.

grungies *n.pl. Stu.* soiled laundry.

1987 *America:* Nissan (Fall) 15: Bring a complete change of clothes for after the trip as well as a garbage bag to carry your grungies in.

grunt *n.* **1.a.** a slice of ham or bacon; *(also)* pork. Cf. earlier GRUNTER, GRUNTLING.

1925 *AS* I 139: And he goes forth to eat of "cackleberries and grunts (eggs and bacon)." **1931** *AS* (Oct.) 51: [Among lumberjacks] Pork is "forbidden fruit" or "grunt." **1933–34** Lorimer & Lorimer *Stag Line* 166: What'll it be: grunt and a couple of cacklers? **1948** J. Stevens *Jim Turner* 238 [ref. to ca1915]: Grunts and cackleberries and slabs are on the griddle. **1981** (quot. at CLUCK).

b. usu. *pl. Stu.* food, esp. snack food. Cf. **(5),** below.

1968 Baker et al. *CUSS* 131: *Grunts.* Food. **1972** Claerbaut *Black Jargon* 67: *Grunt, n.* A meal; dinner. **1972** Nilsen *Slang at UN1* 2: *Grunts:* Snacks consisting of potato chips, pop, and/or a twinkie served during final exam week, or at a mixer. **1979** Gutcheon *New Girls* 198: You get in line for the grunts...and we'll belly up to the bar. **1983** *Reader's Digest Success with Words* 85: Black English...*grunt* = "meal, dinner."

2.a. (among telephone- and power-line repairers) a line repairer's assistant; *(also)* a mechanic's or an electrician's helper.

1926 *AS* I 659: He must, in order to become a good lineman, start as a "grunt" (ground man)...."Shorty,...you can have Hay and Jabs for grunts."..."Stubby, you take the grunts and frame, roof, and set this pole." **1935** in Mencken *Amer. Lang.* (ed. 4) 587: [A movie] electrician's helper is a *grunt.* **1938** *AS* (Feb.) 70: *Grunt.* An inexperienced workman in the [line-repairing] gang. **1938** Haines *Tension* 48: We put the best of them to work as grunts and second-class linemen. *Ibid.* 79: But he'd be wasted as a grunt. He's a right good mechanic. **1941** *AS* (Oct.) 166: *Grunt.* Electrician's helper (Signal Corps). **1945** Hamann *Air Words: Grunt.* A mechanic's helper. **1945** Hubbard *R.R. Ave.* 345: *Grunt* may also be a lineman's ground helper. **1958** in *AS* (Feb. 1959) 78: *Grunt*...an electrician's helper in the lumber mill. *a*1984 in Safire *Stand Corrected* 319: "When I was employed by a public (N.J.) utility in the late 1930s, the term 'grunt' was used to refer to an electric lineman's helper or a mechanic's helper."..."In 1937...I was hired by the Western Colorado Power Co. as a 'grunt.'"...[This] usage began...before...1918."

b. any person doing menial or routine labor. Cf. GRUNT WORK.

1970, 1978 (quots. at GRUNT WORK). **1982** *Hill St. Blues* (NBC-TV): The last thing I need is a couple of pushy, midlevel grunts telling me my business. **1985** *Campus Voice* (Apr.) 13: Try to stick to entry-level grunts like yourself. **1986** M. Paseornek & B. Kesden *Meatballs III* (film): So you're the grunt we've been waitin' for. **1987** *Campus Voice* (Spring) 30: Drummer Anders Johanson asked the concert load-in crew if they knew any players. "[Yes]," said "grunt" Mario Sepe. **1988** T. Harris *Silence of Lambs* 66: You were a grunt in the lab. **1992** G. Wolff *Day at the Beach* 192: I was no yachtsman; I was a grunt laborer.

c. *Stu.* GRIND, 5.

*a***1986** S. King, in *NDAS*: A grunt is a student who gives a shit about nothing except his sheepskin.

3. *R.R.* a locomotive engineer; HOGHEAD.

1939 *Sat. Eve. Post* (Apr. 15) 26: He asked the grunt to keep an eye on the paddles and use the company notch plenty. **1942** *Sat. Eve. Post* (June 13) 27: The traveling engineer is the "traveling grunt." **1948** Mencken *Amer. Lang. (Supp. II)* 713: A locomotive engineer is a...*grunt.*

4. excrement; (*also*) daylights; "stuffing."

1947 Willingham *End As a Man* 274: I'll mash the grunt out of them. *a***1988** M. Atwood *Cat's Eye* 246: What color is their underwear? Grunt color.

5. a bill, usu. for food or drink; tab.

1951 W. Pegler, in *DAS*: No evidence that El Twirpo ever bought a drink or picked up the grunt for a party. **1965** Pei *Story of Lang.* (ed. 2) 188: There is an entire terminology for drinking and its consequences..."grunt"...the "check." **1974** Sann *Dead Heat* 35: Now pick up the grunt and we'll go. **1981** Sann *Trial* 45: I never stopped paying the grunt for...the annual care.

6.a. *Mil.* an infantryman; (*broadly*) an ordinary combat soldier; (*pl.*) ground troops, esp. infantry. Cf. 2.a., 2.b., above. [**1961** R. Crane *Born of Battle* 19: Or will it be Sergeant James R. Saxon, RA 6299593, who will get it in this gigantic cesspool, only a tiny grunt among the roistering swine in this grim, comedy-of-errors [Korean] war?]. **1962** Tregaskis *Vietnam Diary* 68: He [a USMC pilot] had been in the Marines for eight years, "seven years in the grunts," as he said, meaning he had spent that long as a ground pounder. *Ibid.* 99: Clark was more of a "grunt" than an aviator. **1966** *N.Y. Times Mag.* (Oct. 30) 102: An infantryman is a "grunt" and, unless he is also a paratrooper, a "leg." **1968** Stuard TS.: I was on a [USMC] helicopter crew. A "grunt" is an infantryman. **1968** Schell *Military Half* 106: The pilots...often spoke disparagingly of the Army, compared to the Air Force; they called Army men "grunts." **1968** W. Anderson *Gooney Bird* 74: Grunts. Ground grippers. Army troops. **1969** *Esquire* (Sept.) 154: The old hostility between Grunt and Marine Air became total on [Hill] 861. **1969** Spetz *Rat Pack Six* 181: Sure, but you always can bet that the guys getting the extra trips are the clerks in Division Headquarters, not the Grunts out in the field. **1972** *Playboy* (Apr.) 61: I'm writing this letter in behalf of the many grunts still in Vietnam. **1972** Haldeman *War Year* 30: You grunts, you infantrymen, are going to have Charlie so close you'll be able to smell his BO. **1973** R. Roth *Sand in the Wind* 18: You both grunts, riflemen? **1976** Conroy *Santini* 485 [ref. to 1962]: The grunts of the world could not enter into the language of aviators. **1976** C.R. Anderson *Grunts* 27 [ref. to 1969]: They call them grunts, you know, the guys from the bush in Nam, and they're supposed to be the gungiest mothers around. **1977** Caputo *Rumor of War* 180 [ref. to 1966]: "Goddamned grunts are all crazy," said a headquarters clerk next to me. **1979** Former USAF mech.: I heard *grunts* on Okinawa in '63 from a couple of Navy troops I palled around with. It meant a Marine infantryman. **1980** *AS* LVI 308 [ref. to Vietnam War]: A *grunt* was a common soldier, distinct from an NCO or an officer. **1985** Dye *Between Raindrops* 281: Got to stick together in the grunts. *a***1989** C.S. Crawford *Four Deuces* 64 [ref. to Korean War]: An FO is one of our guys who goes up...with the grunts, the infantrymen. *Ibid.* 231: At that moment I realized exactly why it was that all infantrymen were called "grunts."

b. *Navy.* a member of the U.S. Marine Corps.

1968 in Hayes *Smiling Through Apocalypse* 778: It was the same smile I saw later when a sniper's bullet tore up the wall two inches above his head inside the Citadel. Odd cause for merriment in anyone but a Grunt. **1970** Poniscan *Last Detail* 15: Listen, us guys are goddam saints compared to the grunts. **1970** *Current Slang* V 16: *Grunt*, A United States Marine. **1981** former Navy yeoman [ref. to 1970–72]: A *grunt* meant a Marine, regardless of assignment. When I was in Vietnam, that's the way I heard it—as far as I know, the only way. **1981** C. Nel-

son *Picked Bullets Up* 29: A grunt is a marine, as a soldier is a doggie....and a sailor is a squid. **1982** "W.T. Tyler" *Rogue's March* 72: I'm talking about dependents,...not a few old grunts like us. **1984** T.K. Mason *Cactus Curtain* 111: What do they see in those grunts?

c. *USAF.* a nonflying officer.

*a***1981** "K. Rollins" *Fighter Pilots* 235 [ref. to 1960's]: "Goddamned grunts down at Seventh [Air Force Headquarters] ought to have their...heads examined."..."You don't like grunts?" *Ibid.* 236: They hate the grunts who will survive.

7. a stupid, unpleasant, or contemptible person.

1977 New Brunswick, N.J., editor, age 24: You're turning into a real grunt. **1984** Eble *Campus Slang* (Sept.) 4: *Grunt*—a dull, clueless student, usually male. Characterized by lack of participation in class except for exclamations like Huh? **a***1987** J. Green *Dict. Jargon* 266: *Grunt*...a derisive term used by those who write "men's magazines" for the frustrated men who buy their product. **1987** Univ. Tenn. student: I hate that little grunt. **1988** *21 Jump Street* (Fox-TV): In a couple of years these *grunts* are gonna be fat ex-jocks talking about the good old days.

grunt *v.* **1.** *Labor.* to work as a menial assistant or GRUNT, 2.a.

1938 Haines *Tension* 104: Good? A guy that's just good couldn't grunt for him at the piano. **1945** Hubbard *R.R. Ave.* 345: *Grunting* is working as a lineman's helper.

2. to defecate.

1967 *DAS* (Supp.) 688: *Grunt*...To defecate. **1968** Baker et al. *CUSS* 130: *Grunt*. Defecate.

grunter *n.* **1.** a hog; (*hence*) pork. Cf. GRUNTLING.

*****1703** E. Ward *London-Spy* 373: The Buying of...*Grunters Muns*, and the like. **1805** *Port Folio* (Aug. 24) 261: No gruner's truer to his sty. **1850** in K.E. Olson *Music & Musket* 32: He should visit...Cincinnati and take lessons in killing and packing the grunters. **1867** Macnamara *Irish Ninth* 209: Considerable attention was paid to the "grunters," many of which squealed their own...requiem. **1887** Davis *Sea-Wanderer* 290 [ref. to *a*1860]: Beef is generally salt horse....Pork was grunter, and mutton, when we had any, was simply mutton.

2. *Journ.* a professional wrestler.

1936 *Esquire* (Sept.) 160: A grunter is Varietyese for wrestler.

grunt horn *n. Music.* a tuba. Also **grunt iron.**

1926 Norwood *Other Side of Circus* 236: The cymbals are the pot lids, and the tuba is the grunt horn. **1935** *Vanity Fair* (Nov.) 71: *Grunt iron* for bass horn.

gruntling *n.* a hog. *Joc.* Cf. GRUNTER.

*****1686** in *OED*. *****1726** A. Smith *Mems. of J. Wild* 179: She us'd much of the canting Language, saying, *Take Coach, take Horse*, and *mill the Gruntling*, by which she...meant, *Cut a Throat, take a Purse*, and *steal a Pig*. **1726** in *William & Mary Qly.* (Ser. 3) XXXVIII (1981) 291: The ill-got Gruntling.

grunt work *n.* drudge work typically performed by a menial. Cf. GRUNT, *n.,* 2.

1970 *Current Slang* V 16: That's grunt work. **1978** Strieber *Wolfen* 202: Now assign a...grunt-work department so all these officers don't get their hands dirty. **1984** N.Y.C editor, age 32: It's grunt work but it's got to be done. **1984** McInerny *Bright Lights* 162: I'm going to hire out some grunt work. **1987** Waldron *Billionaire Boys* (NBC-TV): Chris is working down in the warehouse doing grunt work. **1989** *Daily Beacon* (Univ. Tenn.) (Apr. 7) 7: Why do I always get stuck with the grunt work?

G-shot *n.* [perh. *G* for GEEZE] *Narc.* (see quots.).

1969 Smith & Gay *Don't Try It* 109: The small amount of heroin he is given (known as a *G shot*). **1970** Cortina *Slain Warrior* 199: "I went for G-shots." "Skin popping, is that what you mean?" "For a little while, then I mained." **1971** *N.Y. Post* (Jan. 13) 41: My friend's old man asked me if I wanted a g-shot. A small amount of heroin.

G.T. *adj.* (see quot.). Cf. syn. G.T.T.

1839 in *OEDS*: G.T.—This is said to be a common mode of making sheriff's returns in the South West. It means "Gone to Texas."

G.T.H. *interj.* (see quot.).

1917 *DN* IV 357: G.t.h. Go to hell.

G.T.T. *adj.* "Gone To Texas" to avoid paying debts; absconded. Now *hist.*

1839 in *OEDS*: G.T.T.—General Nathaniel Smith...has fled to Texas, with...$70,000...in his pocket. **1840** in Haliburton *Sam Slick* 136: "I believe I must hang out the G.T.T. sign." "Why, what the plague is that?"..."Gone to Texas." **1847** Hooton *St. Louis' Isle* 15: It has become almost a proverb...that when a runaway debtor is not to be found,...or a murderer has contrived to elude justice, he has chalked upon his house door "G.t.T."—*Gone to Texas.* **1853** "P. Paxton" *In Texas* 1 [ref. to 1838–39]: The three ominous letters G.T.T., done in white chalk by mischievous urchin or suspicious creditor, would stare him full in the face. **1853–60** Olmsted *Texas* 124: "G.T.T." (gone to Texas) was the slang appendage, within the reader's recollection, to every man's name who had disappeared before the discovery of some rascality. **1864, 1944, 1949** in *DA.* **1988** *Daily Beacon* (Univ. Tenn.) (Nov. 17) 4: The term "G.T.T."...meant "Gone To Texas." But it didn't literally mean "Gone To Texas." When you said that someone was "G.T.T.," you meant that he had gotten out of town in a hurry, usually because the police were after him.

G-2 *n. & v. Army.* (see quots.).
  1941 *AS* (Oct.) 165: *G-2.* Inquisitiveness. **1943** in Tregaskis *Invasion Diary* 30: "General, I haven't talked to you since this Mussolini thing. How do you G2 that?" "I G2 it this way." **1944** in Litoff et al. *Miss You* 129: It is all right for you to guess, and I think you are pretty good at the G-twoing. **1946** *AS* XXI (Dec.) 251: *G-2.* Used as a verb, this is roughly the equivalent of "to case"—i.e., to size up a situation before deciding on a course of action. G-2 is, of course, the staff division responsible for intelligence. **1947** *AS* XXII (Apr.) 109: *G-2,* a designation for the super-secret Army Counter Intelligence Service, meant colloquially at first "inquisitiveness," then "to dope out," and finally "to prophesy." **1974** former Army lieut., age 26 [ref. to 1970]: "He's got a lot of G-2" means he's smart, he's got a lot of intelligence.

Guadal *n. Mil.* Guadalcanal. Now *hist.*
  1944 E.H. Hunt *Limit* 130: So the boys on Guadal can have filets? **1945** *Yank* (Sept. 21) 3: After Guadal, bingo, they shoved off for Bougainville. **1951** Wouk *Caine Mutiny* ch. XX: We ferried a bunch of marines along the coast...at Guadal.

Guam *n.* ¶ In phrase: **for Guam** *Naut.* for some port unknown.
  ***1881** in *OEDS:* Having...docked the steamer...they cleared out "for Guam." ***1898** in *OEDS:* Sailed for Guam. **1961** de Kerchove *Maritime Dict.* (ed. 2): *Bound for Guam.* Idiomatic phrase which means in nautical slang: bound for no specific place.

guarandamntee *v.* to guarantee absolutely. Also (vulgar) **guaranfuckingtee.** [1948 quot. is a nonce euphemism.]
  1948 Manone & Vandervoort *Trumpet* 180: I guaran-(fussin')-tee you, when we got the place fixed up it was real pretty. **1954** LeMay *Searchers* 122: Not the Texas legislature, I guarandamtee. **1973, 1975** *AS* 55 (1980) 173: Guarandamntee. **1986** Stinson & Carabatsos *Heartbreak* 14: I'll guaranfuckintee you. **1989** Univ. Tenn. employee, age *ca*30: That I'll guarandamntee you!

guardhouse lawyer *n. Army & USMC.* a contentious or insubordinate enlisted soldier who claims to be an expert on military regulations or law.—used derisively.
  1888 McConnell *Cavalryman* 197 [ref. to 1868]: Such a chap frequently becomes a nuisance to the officers, and is usually known in camp as a "guard-house lawyer." **1893** Putnam *Blue Uniform* 184: He had heard the so-called "guard-house lawyers" clumsily advance similar views. **1895** C.C. King *Fort Frayne* 69: "Another guardhouse lawyer," said the first sergeant...disgustedly. **1907** J. Moss *Officer's Manual* 243: *Guardhouse Lawyer.* A soldier with a smattering knowledge of regulations and military law; quite loquacious and liberal with advice and council to men in the Guard House or other trouble. **1918** O'Reilly *Roving & Fighting* 80 [ref. to 1899]: He was a sneak-thief and a "guard-house lawyer," always in trouble and always dodging duty. **1918** in O'Brien *Wine, Women & War* 59: But the guardhouse lawyers yapped back and forth. **1924** Anderson & Stallings *Glory* 84: You can't play guardhouse lawyer in this country. **1930** Waldron *Old Sergeant* 107: Some guardhouse lawyer is the ring leader and the rest are following along like sheep. **1962** Downey *Indian Wars* 217: It mattered nothing that "guardhouse lawyers" occasionally got around him. **1982** D.J. Williams *Hit Hard* 260: I saw the crafty grin...and knew that he was a guardhouse lawyer.

guardhouse rat *n. Army.* BRIG RAT.
  1956 Packer *7th Cavalry* (film): The name of every scrounger, no-good, guardhouse rat and shirk in the outfit. **1980** Univ. Tenn. *Film Advocate* 38: Led by straight-laced [*sic*] Captain Douglas...and guardhouse rat Cyril Leech...the mercenaries are an unsavory lot.

guardo *n.* [fr. *guard*ship + *-o*] *Navy.* **1.** a receiving ship.
  ***1821–26** Stewart *Man-of-War's-Man* I 7: Why the devil don't he keep a tender for his own use, like any other guardo. **1841** [Mercier] *Man-of-War* 280: If they send me aboard a *guardo* to finish my time. **1847** Downey *Portsmouth* 1: A tarry of one year had sickened me of "life in a

Guardo." **1849** Melville *White Jacket* 293 [ref. to 1843]: Oh, I know the moves, sir. I have been on board a *guardo.* **1867** Clark *Sailor's Life* 171: We were on the "Guardo." **1871** Willis *Forecastle Echoes* 16: I did find myself bundled aboard of the Guard-ho. **1878** Willis *Our Cruise* 8: The old guardho's decks wore a lonely and deserted appearance. **1884** *United Service* (Mar.) 237: The receiving-ship, still popularly termed the "guardo." **1884** Blanding *Sailor Boy* 49: During the Rebellion, the government maintained three receiving ships, commonly called Guardos by the sailors; one at the Charlestown navy yard, the "Ohio"; one at the Brooklyn navy yard, the old "North Carolina"; and a third in Baltimore, the "Alleghany." **1899** Boyd *Shellback* 168: We've got no prisoners....This isn't the "Guardo." **1906** Beyer *Amer. Battleship* 74: A receiving-ship is known as the "guardo," and is nothing more or less than a sailors' boarding house. **1926** *AS* II: Perhaps you will find some old-timer who when he was young was shipmates with the old plank-owners and guardo-stiffs.
  2. a sailor serving aboard a receiving ship.
  1865 Smyth *Sailor's Word-Book* 353: *Guardo.* A familiar term applied equally to a guard-ship or any person belonging to her. It implies "harbour-going;" an easy life.

guardo move *n. Navy.* a trick or stratagem used by a sailor. Now *hist.*
  1849 Melville *White Jacket* 292 [ref. to 1843]: From...familiarity with the *guardo moves* and *manoeuvres* of a frigate, the master-at-arms and his aids can almost invariably tell when any gambling is going on by day. **1980** Valle *Rocks & Shoals* 328 [ref. to *a*1860]: *Guardo moves.* Slang. tricks or stratagems used by berth-deck gamblers and clandestine drinkers to avoid detection by the master-at-arms.

guck /gʊk/ or /gʌk/ *n.* see GOOK³, *n.*

gudgeon *n.* a fool or dupe; SUCKER. Orig. *colloq.*
  ***1584** in *OED:* They would doo no harme, were it not to make fooles, and catch gudgins. **ca*1600 in *F & H* VI 268: Now mine host...gudgeon! ***1657** in *OED:* They will not swallow this Impostors principles of knavery, which none but fools and gudgeons will. ***1698–1720** in D'Urfey *Pills* III 126: And Lawyers Fish for Gudgeons. ***1727–28** in *OED.* ***1785** Grose *Vulgar Tongue: Gudgeon.* One easily imposed on;...from the fish of that name, which is easily taken. **1821** Waln *Hermit in Phila.* 25: O! you haven't...caught a gudgeon;—I'm no flat. **1839** *Spirit of Times* (Mar. 30) 43: With the exception of some purchases of *gudgeons* and *flat-fish* by certain [dishonest] club-house-keepers, there was nothing else of consequence done. **ca*1830–50 in Holloway & Black *Broadsides* II 310: Pike off, says she,/You don't catch me,/For Joey I'm no gudgeon. **1853** "Tally Rhand" *Guttle & Gulpit* 9: We're a bound to Wall Street, where gudgeons swarm and sharks prey. **1873** Beadle *Undeveloped West* 93: The..."cappers"...have borne their part in the game and "hooked a gudgeon." **1881** Trumble *Man Traps* 9: The female blackmailer hooks many a rich gudgeon from the living tide. *Ibid.* 15: The "gudgeon" usually calls and finds his friend comfortably quartered in...an aristocratic hotel. **1882** C. Morris *Shadow Sam* 5: Him nab a burglar!...A high old gudgeon of a burglar that must have been! **1898** L.J Beck *Chinatown* 259: McNally...employed this man to impersonate a rustic "gudgeon." **1922** *Sat. Eve. Post* (Mar. 4) 108: He is the biggest gudgeon in the universe. **1928** Sharpe *Chicago May* 101: We had been under heavy expense landing the gudgeon.

Guee /giˈ/ *n.* [< Portu*guee*] *Naut.* a Portuguese person.—often used contemptuously. Also **Gee, Ghee.**
  1856 H. Melville, in *Harper's Mo.* (Mar.): The 'Gees...The word 'Gee (*g* hard) is an abbreviation, by seamen, of *Portugee,* the corrupt form of *Portuguese.*...In short, by seamen the abbreviation 'Gee was hit upon in pure contumely. **1868** Macy *There She Blows!* 25: He was ably seconded by Burley...and the two Ghees. **1894** *DN* I 389: Gees. For *Portuguese.* **1896** Hamblen *Many Seas* 240: These poor 'Gees...are easily captured and carried off whaling. *Ibid.* 242: He was a 'Gee. **1912** R.C. Murphy *Logbook for Grace* 7: The Old Man, however, vows that the iron hoops, which encircle and protect the masthead, encourage drowsiness among the "mokes" and the "geez" (Portuguese). The words are his own complimentary terms for West Indians and Cape Verde Islanders, respectively.

Guee jacket *n. Naut.* (see quot.).
  1856 H. Melville, in *Harper's Mo.* (Mar.): Sailors...often call a monkey-jacket a 'Gee-jacket [because the style presumably originated in Cape Verde].

Guee jockey *n. Naut.* an agent or crimp who procures sailors from among the Portuguese of Cape Verde. Cf. NIGGER JOCKEY.

1856 H. Melville, in *Harper's Mo.* (Mar.): Taking convenient advice from a 'Gee jockey. By a 'Gee jockey is meant a man well versed in 'Gees.

guerrilla *n.* **1.** *Gamb. & Und.* a crooked gambler; swindler; (*also*) one who pockets unclaimed bets. Cf. GORILLA, *n.*, 1.a.
1859 Matsell *Vocab.* 39: *Guerrillas.* This name is applied by gamblers to fellows who skin suckers where and when they can, who do not like the professional gamblers, but try to beat them, sometimes inform on them, and tell the suckers that they have been cheated. **1882** in Sonnichsen *Billy King* 60: You are a [gambling] "check guerrilla," and...your system consists in taking "sleepers." **1890** Quinn *Fools of Fortune* 584: A "guerilla" is a species of the genus "scalper"...and makes a specialty of dealing in stocks and commodities.
2. var. GORILLA, *n.*, 1.a.

guerrilla *v.* *Army.* to make a guerrilla raid upon. Cf. GORILLA, *v.*
1863 in Hough *Soldier in W.* 90: The Rebs..."guerrillaed" a train from here to Nashville last week.

guess *n. & v.* ¶ In phrases:
¶ **by guess and by God** see s.v. GOD.
¶ **I guess yes!** yes, indeed!
1870 Coes *Didymus* 5: L. Oh, I guess not. G. Oh, I guess yes. **1894** in Ade *Chicago Stories* 33: Who? Billy, here? Well, I guess yes. **1897** Norris *Vandover* 299: "Well, I guess yes," she answered. "You Harvard sports make a regular promenade out o' Washington street." **1899** Ade *Fables* 1: Courage? I guess yes!

guesser *n.* *Sports.* a judge, umpire, or referee.
1921 *Variety* (Mar. 25) 4: Tomato...was arguin' with the guesser. **1921** *Variety* (Aug. 26) 7: Rigler, Klem, and Evans, and all the rest of the big league guessers. **1943** *Yank* (Oct. 8) 23: *Guesser.* An umpire.

guess-stick *n.* (see quot.). [See *DARE* for logging sense.]
1937–41 in Mencken *Amer. Lang. Supp.* II 724: *Guess-stick.* A slide-rule.

guesstimate *n.* Orig. *Statistics.* a rough estimate that is in part guesswork. Now *colloq.*
1934 Weseen *Dict. Slang* 346: *Guesstimate*—...an estimate or opinion formed without sufficient evidence. **1936** in *OEDS:* "Guesstimates" is the word frequently used by the statisticians and population experts. **1954** Coleman *Relativity* 88: The best "guestimates"...conclude that the sun will die out and disappear in from fifteen to thirty billion years. **1958** McCulloch *Woods Wds.* 139: Used by logging engineers in making guesstimates.

guesstimate *v.* Orig. *Statistics.* to estimate very roughly. Now *colloq.*
1934 Weseen *Dict. Slang* 346: *Guesstimate.*—To make a hasty conjecture. **1942** *ATS* 201: Guess [v.]...*guesstimate*, blend of "guess" and "estimate." **1983** K. Miller *Lurp Dog* 223: Wolverine could only guesstimate the body count.

GUF *n.* *Mil. Av.* (see quot.). Cf. GIF.
1978 in Higham & Williams *Combat Aircraft* 115: While the GIB is setting up his systems and computers, the GUF, "guy up front," is getting ready to start the right engine.

guff *n.* [prob. < Scots *guff* 'a puff (of wind)'] **1.** insolent or impertinent talk; (*broadly*) (*obs.*) advice.
1879 *Puck* (Sept. 27) 451: Now don't you go to givin' us no aristocratic guff. **1883** Hay *Bread-Winners* 254: Here's your money, and when I want any of your guff I'll let you know. **1899** Garland *Eagle's Heart* 31: I was just givin' him a little guff, and he up and lit into me with a big claspknife. **1906** A.H. Lewis *Confessions* 206: Don't hand me any of your guff. **1938** I. Shaw *Sailor Off Bremen* 181: He stands there, takin' guff from a kid with holes in his pants. **1952** Sandburg *Strangers* 170 [ref. to *ca*1890]: My guff to you is you beat it in the hay tonight. You been lickin it up and throwin it in too fast. **1958** "R. Traver" *Anatomy of Murder* 414: I am sorry for the explosion but I won't sit and take that kind of guff from anyone. **1966** T.V. Olsen *Hard Men* 42: I'd rather starve by my lonesome than take another man's guff. **1971** Contini *Beast Within* 69: I've put up with a lot of guff from you. **1987** L. Cohen *Maniac Cop* (film): They didn't take no guff....They were the law! **1991** *Newsweek* (Mar. 11) 34: When I insisted on this deception plan...I got a lot of guff.
2. empty talk; nonsense; in phr. **roll** [or **punch**] **the guff** (*obs.*), to gossip or converse.
1884 in Lummis *Letters* 18: A little guff about Kansas City. *Ibid.* 134:

The natives take malicious pleasure in filling them with guff. **1885** *Life* (Aug. 20) 108: She is indulging the Concord philosophers in what is known to the vulgar as "guff." **1888** in *OED:* I tell you all this talk is guff, and it just comes down to the money. **1893** Hampton *Maj. in Washington* 228: I had heard that old guff before. **1894** Bridges *Arcady* 156: But that's a lot of guff he's been a-givin' ye. **1902–03** Ade *People You Know* 92: I know it's Guff,...but my Stars! He can ladle out that Soothing Syrup and never spill a Drop! *a*1904–11 Phillips *Susan Lenox* II 161: Don't listen to their guff about wanting to see you again. **1915** Poole *Harbor* 51: Was love really what it was cracked up to be, or had the novelists handed us guff? **1925** *AS* I (Dec.) 138: After a "flop" on his bunk the logger "lets 'er settle," then he "gangs up" to "roll the guff." Until these last years the logger talk heard in these bunkhouse nights was usually about work in the woods or "blow-ins" along the skid-roads in town. **1930, *1936* in *OEDS.* **1939** Trumbo *Sorority House* (film): "Membership in the international democracy of culture."...It isn't guff! **1940** *AS* (Apr.) 117: *To Cut Up Old Scores.* To gather together and talk over old times. Also *to punch the guff.* **1952** Sandburg *Strangers* 163 [ref. to *ca*1890]: When you didn't believe a fellow you might tell him, "Don't hand me that guff," or "I've heard that guff before." It was slang and "guff" was chatter and you were "spreading it on too thick." **1953** R. Chandler *Goodbye* 31: Shove it, Jack....Keep that guff for the juvenile bureau. **1960** Bannon *Journey* 61: He told me a lot of guff. I think he was just tight. **1980** *N.Y. Times* (June 22) II 27: Good background, otherwise guff. **1984** Hindle *Dragon Fall* 25: "I had a dream about you last night." "No guff." **1988** W. Wicket & G. Kaplan *Seventh Sign* (film): Sounded like a bunch of guff to me.

guff *v.* to gossip; chat.
1890 *Overland Mo.* (Feb.) 182: Go long wi' yer guffin now, John Goggin....I'd 'ave none o' yer guffin w'en the girls are haround. **1899** Cullen *Tales* 109: He guffed with me for a while, asked me if I ever drank.

guffy *n.* [prob. alter. dial. E *guffin* 'clumsy fellow'] *Naut.* a lubberly seaman; (*hence*) a soldier.
1856 in C.A. Abbey *Before the Mast* 81: We have got a regular "*Guffy*" crew. **1860** in C.A. Abbey *Before the Mast* 270: Every other man one meets [on St. Helena Island] is a soldier ("Regular Guffies"). **a*1890–93 *F & H* III 229: *Guffy*...(nautical).—A soldier. **1902* Masefield *Salt-Water Ballads* 8: It's a...guffy's yarn. *Ibid.* (gloss.): *Guffy.*—A marine or jolly.

gugag var. HEWGAG.

guido *n.* [fr. *Guido*, an Italian male given name] (see 1991 quot.).—used disparagingly. Also (of women) **guidette.**
1989 *Nat. Lampoon* (June) 91: Think of all those grubby-fingered guidos you had to wait on. **1989** in *Harper's* (Mar. 1990) 73: The "Guidos"...have "sixty chains and hair spray in one hand and a mirror in the other." *Ibid.* 74: The kids Gina Feliciano calls "Guidos." **1990** *Village Voice* (N.Y.C.) (Feb. 20) 16: These are bridge-and-tunnel people. Guidos! A Guns N' Roses crowd. **1987–91** D. Gaines *Teenage Wasteland* 91: Preppies, J.A.P.'s, buppies, and guidos are stereotypes based on combinations of ethnicity and class culture. *Ibid.* 161: How could I wear my leathers with a guido haircut? **1991** *N.Y. Newsday* (Mar. 22) 67: "Guidos" are guys who usually have brushes in their pockets, drive expensive American muscle cars, wear Bugle Boy jeans, like dancing...and are mostly Italian. **1992** *Village Voice* (N.Y.C.) (Feb. 28) 43: It's better than the other places with the guidos and guidettes. **1993** Univ. Tenn. professor: I heard the word *guido* for the first time in New Jersey in 1988. All the students seemed familiar with it.

guilt *v.* GUILT-TRIP, *v.*
1989 *Night Court* (NBC-TV): I was guilted into it.

guilt trip *n.* a state of mind characterized by unwarranted feelings of guilt, esp. when imposed by someone else.
1972 Rossner *Any Minute* 200: I want to make it clear that nobody's sending me on any guilt trip over my money. **1976–77** McFadden *Serial* 282: You must have been on an *incredible* guilt trip. **1978** Selby *Requiem* 147: You start laying guilt trips on me and I don't need it. **1981** *Harper's* (Feb.) 6: I read Peter Marin's exquisitely revolting guilt trip down memory lane to the war in Vietnam. **1982** Basel *Pak Six* 109: A guilt trip struggled in my gut. **1982** *Flash* (Dec.) 10: First he offs a cop, then he tries to lay a guilt trip on Flash to keep him off the streets. **1986** *Kate & Allie* (CBS-TV): Don't put on that innocent face with me. I recognize a guilt trip when I'm being put on one. **1986** Philbin *Under Cover* 112: It's a guilt trip, Barbara....You're just feeling guilty about being alive and happy. **1988** Univ. Tenn. instructor, age *ca*50: He put a big guilt trip on me....He made me feel so guilty that I wouldn't drive over there.

guilt-trip *v.* to attempt to instill a feeling of guilt or responsibility in; to play upon the guilt feelings of.

1980 in *Penthouse* (Jan. '81) 162: How come you're always guilt-trippin' me? **1989** P.H.C. Mason *Recovering* 428: So your family isn't always guilt-tripped by how much you do for them. **1993** *New Republic* (July 12) 12: A guilt-tripped male Senate falling over itself to demonstrate gender sensitivity.

guinea *n.* [short for *Guinea Negro* < Guinea, W. Africa] **1.** a black person, usu. a slave, of West African origin or ancestry; (*contemptuously*) a person of Creole or mixed black, white, and Indian ancestry.—usu. considered offensive.

[**1748** in *AS* XXVII (1952) 283: Run-Away, a likely well-made Guiney Negro Man, named Toney.] [**1765** in Windley *Runaway Slave Advs.* IV 9: RUN AWAY…a NEW NEGROE FELLOW named WILL, Guiney born, speaks little or no English.] [**1767** in Windley *Runaway Slave Advs.* IV 23: A GUINEY NEGROE FELLOW, named JULY.] [**1769** in Windley *Runaway Slave Advs.* IV 36: Sarah, a tall Guiney wench, with her country marks down each side of her face.] [**1789** in *DAE*: He talks as crooked as a Guinea niger.] **1823** J.F. Cooper *Pioneers* 327: But damn the bit of manners has the fellow any more than if he was one of the Guineas, down in the kitchen there. [**1825** in Thornton *Amer. Gloss.*: He's a Guinea nigger, fresh out.] **1848** [G. Thompson] *House Breaker* 6: Guinea Bill, (the negro) lost no time. *Ibid.* 42: As for you, Guinea, you can take the Captain's little *blowen*. **1861** in Lowell *Works* 226: Ner 'tain't quite hendy to pass off one o' your six-foot Guineas/An' git your halves an' quarters back in gals an' pickaninnies. **1877** in J. Haskins *Pinchback* 236: Ah, then it's you Caesar Alligator,…you made yourself a Guinea cock. **1887** *Courier-Journal* (Louisville, Ky.) (May 11) 2: I am a Guinea negro and I belong to the old-time negroes of Africa. My father was a Guinea negro and my mother was a Guinea. **1934–41** in Mellon *Bullwhip Days* 228 [ref. to *ca*1860]: Den somebody holler, "Guinea Jim!" I looks and I didn't see him. **1946** *Social Forces* XXIV 442: Guineas of West Virginia and Maryland…Word "Guinea" said to be an epithet applied to anything of foreign or unknown origin. Other names applied locally…[include] "Guinea niggers."…Originally a mixture of white and Indian types to which Negro has been added.…Italians…are also called "Guineas" in this area. **1947** *AS* XXII 84: An English nobleman—so the story goes—went to the Guinea coast of Africa and married a native woman, the half-breed children of which union crossed to America and became Guineas. **1967** Maurer & Vogel *Narc. & Narc. Add.* (ed. 3) 361: *Guinea*.…2. A Creole. 3. A bright-skinned Negro. [*a*1989 Kisseloff *Must Remember This* 277: I was born in Elizabeth City, North Carolina, in 1897.…They used a term in regard to my grandfather, called "Guinea niggers," which is a term the colored people assumed from the whites.]

2.a. an Italian; (*occ.*, as in 1910, 1965–70 quots.) a central or southern European.—usu. used contemptuously.—usu. considered offensive. Often attrib. Also vars.

1890 *Harper's Wkly.* (Oct. 16) 817: The lower "sporting" element in the poorer quarters of New York call them "Guineas" and "Dagoes." **1894** C. Lawlor & J. Blake *Sidewalks of N.Y.* (pop. song) st. 1: While the Ginnie played the organ on the sidewalks of New York. **1895** Townsend *Fadden Explains* 203: She…took up with a Guinny here in Mulberry Bend. **1904** *Life in Sing Sing* 249: Ginny. An Italian. **1906** in "O. Henry" *Works* 33: I knew he was a Guinea. His name's Tony Spinelli. **1908** *Hampton's Mag.* (Oct.) 529: There's less Jews in the jails than there is ginnies. **1910** Fitch *Steel Workers* 147: "Ginny" seems to include all the "Hunkies" with the Italians thrown in. **1915** Poole *Harbor* 113: Only don't try to talk to those little Guineys. **1927** Wylie *Heavy Laden* 17: Wops (they're guineas in Ohio). **1953** Q. Reynolds *Sutton* 116: Whenever they grabbed a group of suspects you'd hear some cop say, "We'll work over the Guineas first." **1960–61** Steinbeck *Discontent* 15: It's the first time in history a Hawley was ever a clerk in a guinea grocery. **1965–70** in *DARE* [as "Italian," "Greek," "Portuguese," etc.]. **1971** *Harper's* (May) 56: On the Exchange floor, as one of them remarked, "you meet an awful lot of guineas." **1980** Gould *Ft. Apache* 143: Served him right for getting involved with these mountain guineas.

b. a Hispanic.—used contemptuously.—usu. considered offensive.

1911 A.H. Lewis *Apaches of N.Y* 97: Does he think a two-cint Guinea from Sout' Ameriky can bluff a full-blown Mick? **1911** L.J. Vance *Cynthia* 183: I guess it's only what was comin' to me for trustin' a ginny like Perez. **1912** Stringer *Shadow* 184: And you'd better give the *guinney* [a Latin-American] a ten-dollar bill for his trouble. **1938** R. Chandler, in *Dime Detective* (Jan.): Ybarra [a Mexican-American]….said…"The

word guinea.…I don't like it applied to me." **1946** I. Shulman *Amboy Dukes* 35: How do you think he feels about you guineas [Puerto Ricans] coming into Brownsville and marking up our shuls?

c. the Italian language.—used derisively.

1953 A. Kahn *Brownstone* 78: Jew talk and guinea, that's all you hear at the yard.

3. a usu. foolish or no-account fellow; MUG.

1902 T.A. Dorgan, in *S.F. Bulletin* (Jan. 31) 7: The wise guinea from Chicago is "on" Root. *Ibid.* (Mag. Section) (Feb. 16) 12: Ah here comes that wise guinea. Ah!! Johnny Wise comes. **1904** *Life in Sing Sing* 261: Ginny…speaking in the first person. *Ibid.* 261: *I was patting this ginny on the hump.*…I was congratulating myself. **1907** *McClure's Mag.* (Feb.) 380: They gives this employment guinea orders to pick up all he can. **1910** Service *Trail of '98* 17: These guinneys took me for a jay. **1911** T.A. Dorgan, in *N.Y. Eve. Jour.* (Jan. 4) 14: "Moe is a noisy guinea." "Moe who?" "Motor." **1912** D. Runyon *Firing Line* 13: Every ginney's lovely in his/Pants! Pants! Pants! **1914** Jackson & Hellyer *Vocab.* 39: *Guinea*, Noun. General usage. In the sense of a man it is synonymous with "gazebo," "gink," and "mark." **1935** Pollock *Und. Speaks*: Ginney, no-account man; a moron. **1954** Boatright et al. *Texas Folk* 217: That guinea's not worth his salt.

4. *Mil.* (see quots.).—usu. considered offensive.

1944–46 in *AS* XXII (1947) 55: Gooks. Japs, or any natives.…*Guineas*. Same as *gooks*, above. **1954–60** *DAS*: *Guinea*…A native islander of New Guinea.…*WWII Army use.*

5. [prob. fr. (**1**) or (**2.a.**), above] *Horse Racing*. a groom or stable hand.

1949 Cummings *Dict. Sports* 190. *a*1951 in Maurer *Lang. Und.* 214: *Guinea n.* 1. A rub-down man for racehorses. 2. A black employed at the stables. **1955** *AS* XXX 24: An English antecedent has been sought for our practice of calling a groom a *guinea*. **1968** Ainslie *Racing Guide* 468: *Guinea*—Stablehand, because winning British owners used to tip the groom a guinea. **1968** M.B. Scott *Racing Game* 72: For every three horses stabled at the track, there is one groom (or "guinea" as he is frequently called), who typically sleeps in the barn area attached to the horses' stalls. **1984** W. Murray *Dead Crab* 203: Buckingham's string of about thirty horses…was stabled opposite the guinea stand, near the five-eighths pole.

Guinea Cadillac *n. Constr.* (see quot.).—usu. considered offensive. *Joc.*

1974 Cherry *High Steel* 47: You know what a Guinea Cadillac is?…It's a concrete buggy.…power tricycle for taking the concrete from the hopper to wherever they're pouring the floor.

guinea football *n.* Orig. *Army.* a Mills grenade; (*hence*) a bomb used by gangsters.—usu. considered offensive. Also **Italian football.** *Joc.*

1918 Palmer *Amer. in France* 187: Give us an extra bandolier of cartridges apiece and some of them guinea Footballs (hand grenades) and let the Bushes come. **1919** Duffy *Father Duffy* 93: Guinny foot-balls (hand grenades). **1928** *AS* III (Feb.) 255: *Guinea Football*—Bomb. **1930** *Amer. Mercury* (Dec.) 456: *Italian foot-ball*, n.: A bomb. "He gets out of line, so they kick an Italian football round his dump." **1942–49** Goldin et al. *DAUL*: *Guinea Football*. A crudely made bomb, especially a time bomb.

guinea red *n.* inexpensive Italian red wine; DAGO RED.—usu. considered offensive.

1933 West *Miss Lonelyhearts* 127: The first thing she put on the table was a quart bottle of guinea red. **1952** H. Grey *Hoods* 125: We still call it Guinea red. **1971** Cole *Rook* 14: Together also they discovered…Guinny Red. **1971** Faust *Willy Remembers* 147: They drink guinea red all day.

guinea stinker *n.* a cheap cigar.—usu. considered offensive.

1956 I. Shulman *Good Deeds* 50: He…begged Frank Pelleri to get lost with his ginney stinker. **1965–70** in *DARE* s.v. *guinea*. **1970** N.Y.U. student: A *guinea stinker* means a smelly cigar. *a*1989 Kisseloff *Must Remember This* 165 [ref. to 1920's]: The Italian old guys used to smoke what we called Guinea Stinkers, cigars. They were strong.

guitar-pulling *n. Country Music.* (see quot.).

1984 Bane *Willie* 73: We'd gather down at the Orchid Lounge and have a guitar pullin', you know, a jam session. Sing each other our songs.

Guitar Town *n.* Nashville, Tenn.

1975 Dills *CB Slanguage*: *Guitar Town*: Nashville, Tennessee. **1977** *Sci. Mech. CB Gde.* 171: I'll catch Guitar Town on the flip-flop.

gulch *v.* DRY-GULCH.
  1959 N. Nye *Long Run* 84: When those two fellers was being gulched, I was...twenty miles away. **1954–60** *DAS*.

gull *n.* var. SEAGULL.

gully *n.* the vulva or vagina.
  a*1890–93** F & H III 223: *Gully*...The female pudendum. *ca***1935** in Barkley *Sex Cartoons* 66: Down in the gulley he went.

gully-gut *n.* Now *Black E.* a glutton. Orig. *colloq.*
  ******1542** in *OED*: The bealyes of gully-guttes (that can naught dooe, but eate & drynke, and slepe). ******1548** in *OED*: *Lurco*...a gullygutte. ******1599**, *a***1625**, ******1629**, ******1694** in *OED*. **1937** *AS* (Oct.) 241: The obsolete noun *gully-gut* (a glutton)...is still heard among negroes. **1973** Andrews & Owens *Black Lang.* 99: *Gully gut*—someone who is a glutton.

gully-jumper *n.* *So. Midland.* **1.** a small cart or other vehicle.
  1933 Milburn *No More Trumpets* 5: He was getting the gully-jumper up around twenty-five miles an hour regularly. **1952** in *PADS* (No. 46) 26: *Gully-jumper*...A two-wheel cart. **1968** in *DARE*.
  2. a person from the backwoods.
  1936 *AS* (Dec.) 317: Hillbilly, ridge-runner, gully-jumper, [etc.]. **1938** in *AS* (Apr. 1939) 90: We're just poor gully jumpers. **1951**, **1967** in *DARE*.

gully washer *n.* a heavy rainfall.
  1903 in *DARE*: Send us, not a gentle sizzle-sozzle, but a sod-soaker, O Lord, a gully-washer. **1912**, **1937**, **1950**, **1965–70**, **1975** in *DARE*. **1986** D. Tate *Bravo Burning* 85: Between gully washers, the sun switched on fiercely. **1993** *CBS This Morning* (CBS-TV) (July 14): Yesterday here we had a gully-washer of a thunderstorm.

gully-whumper *n.* a forceful or extraordinary example. *Joc.*
  1955 Blackburn *Crockett* (film): You're gonna hear a real gully-whumper.

gulpin *n.* [orig. unkn.] Esp. *Naut.* a gullible person; fool; simpleton; oaf.
  ******1802** in *OED*: There might be a few gulpins who would fire. ******1821** *Real Life in Ireland* 48: She went home without a *gulpin*, and a dirty wardrobe to boot. *a***1867** Smyth *Sailor's Wd. Bk.*: *Gulpin.*—An awkward soldier; a weak credulous fellow. ******1867** *N & Q* (Ser. 3) XII 78: In the days of evil antipathies...a marine was called a gulpin by the sailors; that is a person who would swallow anything told him. ******1886** in *OED*: Go then, for a brace of gulpins! **1941** Kendall *Army & Navy Sl.* 19: *Gulpin*....someone you don't like. **1982** J. Hunter *Grey Fox* (film): I reckon she's already made a gulpin out of you.

gum[1] *n.* impertinent or abusive talk; JAW; LIP.
  ******1751** T. Smollett, in *OED*: Pshaw! brother, there's no occasion to bowse out so much unnecessary gum. ******1785** Grose *Vulgar Tongue*: *Gum.* Abusive language. Come, let us have no more of your gum. **1815** in M. Mathews *Beginnings of Amer. Eng.* 59: *Gum*, foolish talk, nonsense. **1815** in *DN* VI 310: I know what I du mean; and I won't hear nun of your *gum*. **1824** in *OED*: Come, none of your gum—now you are but an underlin'.
  ¶ In phrase:
  ¶ **bump (one's) gums** *beat (one's) gums* s.v. BEAT, *v.* Also vars.
  1941 Hargrove *Pvt. Hargrove* 72: "Quit popping your gums, laddie," I told him, "That's no grind for you." **1944** in *Best from Yank* 122: Pretty soon they were weary of hacking their gums. **1945** Rossen *Walk in the Sun* (film): What are you batting your gums about? **1945** in *Calif. Folk. Qly.* V (1946) 387: Beating his gums, slapping his gums, or woofing. **1947** *ATS* (Supp.) 7: *Bump the gums*...to talk or complain. **1953** *Mr. & Mrs. North* (CBS-TV): Aah, I was just bumpin' my gums. **1957** Herber *Tomorrow to Live* 190 [ref. to WWII]: You ain't just fanning your gums. **1964** Faust *Steagle* 55: Talk....Flap your gums. Give out. Express. **1974** Univ. Tenn. student: Meanwhile I'm just sitting there bumping my gums. **1983** S. King *Christine* 18: You're prepared to run your gums the way Pavlov's dogs were prepared to salivate. **1985** C. Busch *Vampire Lesbians* 74: What are you flapping your gums about? **1987–91** D. Gaines *Teenage Wasteland* 63: Telling stories, throwing the bull, smackin' your gums.

gum[2] *n.* **1.** a trick or deception; in phr. **come the gum over** to hoodwink. Also **gummation.**
  1832 in B. Hall *College Wds.*: As poor "Fresh," we soon found ourselves subject to all manner of sly tricks and "gummations" from our predecessors, the Sophs. **1842** *Dartmouth* IV 117: *Gum* is another word they have here...To say, "It's all a gum," or "a regular chaw," is the same thing. **1848** in *AS* X (1935) 40: He tried to *cum the gum over* him, but, By

Golla! Lijah was up & dressed. Ready—not to be taken in.
  2. *Und.* GUMSHOE, 1.b.
  1925 in Partridge *Dict. Und.* 312: *Gums*...Gumshoe individuals; sneaks. **1934** (quot. at GUMSHOE, *adj.*, 2).

gum *v.* **1.a.** to trick, cheat, or befool.
  1840 *Spirit of Times* (Sept. 5) 324: You are attempting to gum us with these pretended expenses. **1840** in *OEDS*: You are always right as a book and nobody can gum you. **1848** in Lowell *Poetical Works* 216: You can't gum *me*, I tell ye now, an' so you need n't try. **1849** in Thornton *Amer. Gloss.*: He was speaking of the "moon hoax," which gummed so many learned philosophers. **1859** in F & H III 234: I began to think...he was quizzing me—"gumming" is the proper Transatlantic colloquialism. **1865** *Rogues & Rogueries of N.Y.* 113: People were "stuck" and "gummed" in making change. ******1875** in F & H III 234: To "gum-tree" is to elude, to cheat, and this again is shortened into "to gum," as the phrase, "Now don't you try to gum me." **1876** in *DAE*: That'll bring out the truth, if he's tryin' to gum us. **1952** in *PADS* (No. 46) 30: "Don't try to Jew, nor mess, nor gum" means "don't haggle."
  b. *Stu.* (see quot.).
  1851 B.J. Hall *College Wds.*: *Gum.* At the University of Vermont, to cheat in recitation by using *ponies, interliners*, &c.; e.g. "he *gummed* in geometry."
  2. to spoil, botch, or interfere with.—usu. constr. with *up*. Also in phrs. **gum the game** (*obs.*), **gum [up] the works** to spoil everything.
  1901 *Chi. Tribune* (July 28) 38: He will gum up the cards and holler about a misdeal. **1901** in *DA*: The plot that was gummed. **1910** in O. Johnson *Lawrenceville* 255: Well, he's rotten. He gums the whole show. **1911** L.J. Vance *Cynthia* 174: You've just about gummed things up good and plenty. **1912** Mathewson *Pitching* 303: I guess I was "gumming" the inside stuff. **1918** *Sat. Eve. Post* (Jan. 19) 66: If you don't obey orders eggsactly, you will only gum the game. **1918** *Scribner's* (May) 567: Oh, my God! Christ! That forsaken —— gumming up a perfec'ly good comp'ny. **1918–19** MacArthur *Bug's-Eye View* 95: It was explained to him...to sneak through the intervals. Characteristically, he got it gummed up some way. **1920** *Variety* (Dec. 24) 5: Cuthie's wife gummed everything up by bawling the guy out. **1920–21** Witwer *Leather Pushers* 194: That clout in the ribs gummed up the works a bit. **1922** *Variety* (July 28) 5: One of them...is liable to drop dead from old age...and the whole works will be gummed. **1923** Riesenberg *Under Sail* 96: The lubbers "gummed up" their action whenever the least chance was afforded them. **1927** Rollins *Jinglebob* 164 [ref. to 1880's]: Look here, Bill, you's got to help us by not gummin' the game. **1927** Coe *Me—Gangster* 200: An' the get-away has gotta depend on our not gummin' the works. **1928** Bodenheim *Georgie May* 135: That damn Johnny gummed up the wuhks. **1929** Hammett *Maltese Falcon* 186: I'm in this with you and you're not going to gum it. Talk. **1931** in Blackbeard & Williams *Smithsonian Comics* 121: I'll find out at the office why they sent me out with a bill like this with the name all gummed up. **1934** in Fenner *Throttle* 60: He was so scared he gummed things up. **1943** Crowley & Sachs *Follow the Leader* (film): Yeah, they'd gum the whole works up. **1946** in F. Brown *Angels & Spaceships* 28: Those saps at Earth Center shipping department gummed things up again. **1947** Willingham *End As a Man* 295: I just wish you hadn't gummed up this whole thing. **1956** Lee & Bradley *Passed for White* 104: I wasn't trying to gum up your future. **1958** S.H. Adams *Tenderloin* 171 [ref. to 1890's]: Suppose we could catch one of 'em with his pants down. Would that gum the game! **1966** Elli *Riot* 133: A rumble with Fletcher could gum up the works.
  3. to talk idly.—also constr. with *it*.
  1932 *AS* (June) 332: *Gum*, v. to talk nonsense. **1967** in T.C. Bambara *Gorilla* 70: I couldn't see the point of all that gumming and wearing out the teeth smiling and all. **1974** Univ. Tenn. student: Meanwhile, he's just gumming it.

gumbah see GOOMBAH, *n.*

gumball *n.* the flashing roof-beacon of a police car or other vehicle; (*hence*) a police patrol car having such a beacon. Also **gumball light, gumball machine.** Cf. BUBBLEGUM MACHINE.
  1971 in *AS* XLIV 204: *Gumball machine*...Rotating warning light on top of an emergency vehicle. **1976** Whelton *CB Baby* 130: I...hit the siren and red gumball lights. *a***1986** in *NDAS*: Don't believe in gumballs. I kinda like to sneak around, you know. **1990** Rukuza *W. Coast Turnaround* 144: Audrey saw a police car....But wait...there were no gumballs on the roof. **1992** *Donahue* (NBC-TV): Did you see the gumball machine in your rear-view mirror?

gum-beat *n.* a chat. Also as v.

1942 *Yank* (Sept. 23) 14: To…gumbeat her a bedtime fable. **1944** Burley *Hndbk. Jive* 128: He'll gumbeat to himself that ancient fable. **1945** J. Bryan *Carrier* 120: We drifted down to his room and into a gum-beat. **1958** Hughes & Bontemps *Negro Folklore* 484: Gumbeat. To talk a lot, gossip. Women are always gumbeating.

gum-beater *n.* a voluble talker or complainer.

1942 Z.N. Hurston, in *Amer. Mercury* (July) 95: Gum beater—a blowhard, a braggart, idle talker in general. **1942** *ATS* 381: Loquacious person; idle chatterer…*gum-beater*. **1943** in *AS* XIX (1944) 105: We have some great gum-beaters [on shipboard] still. **1954** Schulberg *Waterfront* 95: "Christ, what a gum-beater," Terry said irritably. "Yatata—yatata." **1959** Morrill *Dark Sea* 130 [ref. to WWII]: This big gumbeater, George White, started hollering at Leroy Budzik, the crew mess. **1960** Leckie *Marines!* 10 [ref. to WWII]: A regular gum-beater. **1973** N.Y.U. student: *Gum-beaters* are guys who're always complaining.

gum-beating *n.* idle talk, esp. complaints.

1945 Monks *Ribbon & Star* 126: There was plenty of gum-beating that night. **1946** J.H. Burns *Gallery* 16: The gum-beating of topkicks. **1946** Mezzrow & Wolfe *Really Blues* 143: Gumbeating is just a waste of energy. **1950** in Leckie *March to Glory* 192: There'll be no gum-beatin', we're glad we're retreatin'/So cheer up me lads/Bless 'em all! **1953** Paley *Rumble* 21: And he wasn't like his mother, taking his father's blows and gum-beating all the time. **1957** Myrer *Big War* 3: Now let's not have any gum-beating about it.

gum-boot *n.* **1.** [-*boot* is E *boot*, not G *Boot* 'boat'] *Army.* a gunboat. *Joc.*

1891 Kirkland *Capt. of Co. K* 176 [ref. to Civil War]: Well, he took Fort Henry the other day with a hurrah, after the gum-boots had tramped it all out of shape.

2. see GUMFOOT.

gumbrain *n.* a dolt. Also **gumhead**.

1956 H. Ellison *Deadly Streets* 80: A real gumbrain. **1980** Kotzwinkle *Jack* 203: I'm alone with these two gum-heads.

gumby *n.* [after *Gumby*, a clay figure in animated films] *Stu.* a foolish or ineffectual person.

[**1968–70** *Current Slang* III & IV 63: Gumbies, n. Black tennis shoes.—University of Kentucky.] *a*1986 in *NDAS*: You can become a gumby…by wearing the wrong plaid stretch pants. **1986** *Head of the Class* (ABC-TV): I'm still stuck in here with these gumbies. **1989** Univ. Tenn. students: "A *gumby* is a guy who isn't exactly a studso he-man." "A *gumby* is someone who hasn't really got it."

gumdrop *n. Narc.* a capsule or tablet containing a psychotropic drug.

1967–80 Folb *Runnin' Lines* 241: Gumdrop. 1. Seconal (secobarbital), barbiturate. 2. Any kind of drug in tablet or capsule form.

¶ In phrase:

¶ **goody [goody] gumdrops** *Juv.* good! delightful.—used as interj., often ironically.

1956 N.Y.C. schoolchildren: Well, goody goody gumdrops! **1964** W. Beech *Article 92* 116 [ref. to 1940's]: Oh goodie gum-drops. *1979* T. Jones *Wayward Sailor* 179: Oh, goody gumdrops.

gumdrop *adj.* sweet and silly; sissified.—used prenominally. [The intended meaning in 1882 quot. is prob. 'resembling a gumdrop.']

[**1882** *Puck* (Dec. 12) 230: Next year *Punch* will probably bring out some alleged "comics" on the late Rebellion and work in the stock picture of John Bull in his gum-drop Derby.] **1896** Ade *Artie* 98: If you ever went out to the Carrolls and spring that gum-drop talk the old man wouldn't do a thing to you. **1902** in *DA*: A measly little gum-drop name like Percival.

gumfoot *n.* GUMSHOE, 1.a.—used derisively. Also as v. Also **gumboot, gumheel.**

1927 *AS* II (Mar.) 282: Flat foot, slapman, gumfoot—Plain clothes man. **1938** in Partridge *Dict. Und.* 312: Gum-heel. **1942** *ATS* 419: Detective…gumboot. Ibid. 463: Gumboot, gumfoot…to shadow. **1947** (cited in Partridge *Dict. Und.* 799): Gumboot. **1950** in *DAS*: Still gumheeling?

gumfudgeon *n.* [fanciful coinage] nonsense; foolishness.

1835 *Spirit of Times* (Dec. 12) 2: Come, none of your gumfudgeon to us.

gum game *n.* a trick, swindle, or (*occ.*) prank; foolery or trickery.

1840 in *AS* XVI (1941) 299: I've come the gum game over you. **1846**

Codman *Sailors' Life* 160: There's a good deal of ceremony and gum game both sides in that business. **1852** Furber *Ike McCandliss* 11: You can't come the gum game over me, any how. **1859** Bartlett *Amer.* (ed. 2) 185: Opossums and raccoons, when pursued, will fly for refuge to a Sweet Gum tree, in preference to any other. This is called "coming the *gum game*" over the hunter. **1869** in *F & H* II 162: You can't come that gum game over me any more; I've been to the land-office and know all about the place. **1871** Bagg *Yale* 45: Gum game, a trick, a swindle. **1878** Flipper *Colored Cadet* 55: "Gum game."—A joke. **1882** A.W. Aiken *Joe Buck* 3: No gum-game…now; no dealing from the bottom of the pack. **1910** *DN* III 442: Gum-game, n. A trick; a scheme to deceive. "You can't work any *gum-game* on me." **1977** Coover *Public Burning* 106: Moonshine! Chicanery! The ole gum game!

gumhead var. GUMBRAIN.

gumjob *n.* BLOW JOB.

1980 W. Sherman *Times Square* 11: They can give ya a gum job for two bucks.

gummer's mate *n.* [pun on *gunner's mate*] *Navy.* (see quot.). *Joc.*

1984 Elting et al. *Soldier Talk* 357: Gummer's mate (Navy)…A dental technician.

gummy *n.* **1.** a simpleton.

1839–40 Cobb *Green Hand* I 84: Why deacon,…you don't suppose I'm such a gummy, as to jump over here. **1882** in P.M. Ryan *Tombstone* 69: She and I…parted at last—she in search of some other gullible "gummie." *1889* Barrère & Leland *Dict. Slang* I 437: Gummie (popular), a simpleton, a dull-headed fellow.

2. any adhesive substance offered for sale by a pitchman.

1929 *Sat. Eve. Post* (Oct. 12) 29: Gummy: Glue. **1936** (quot. at RAD, *n.*). **1943** *Billboard* (June 26) 60: Holding down an ace doorway [selling] gummy.

gump[1] *n.* [of dial. orig.] **1.** a dolt; blockhead.

1722 in *DARE*: We have such a poor careless, lazy, gump-headed…Post-Master. *1825* in *OED*: Gump, a numskull; a term most generally applied to a female, conveying the idea of great stupidity. **1825** in *OED*: He's sort of…a gump, hey? **1833** A. Greene *Duckworth* 176: It's in the West, to be sure, you gump you. **1846** in A. Johnson *Papers* I 341: His…first expression was, that they were "gumps"—what did they know? **1846** in Lowell *Poetical Works* 182: An' it makes a handy sum, tu,/Any gump could larn by heart. **1865** Byrn *Fudge Fumble* 35: I knew Dick was a great gump, as a general thing. **1873** *Slang & Vulgar Forms* 13: Gump, for simpleton, blockhead. **1885** *Puck* (Aug. 19) 394: G'way, you gump! **1891** Maitland *Slang Dict.* 133: Gump, a foolish fellow; a dullard. **1900** Hammond *Whaler* 271: The brig's over here, you gump! **1905** *DN* III 62: What a *gump* she is. **1912–14** in E. O'Neill *Lost Plays* 63: You ought to be ashamed of yourself, you big gump, you, goin' round with girls at your age and spendin' money on them. **1919** *DN* V 66: Gump, a silly, stupid fellow. You are a *gump* if you sign that paper. New Mexico. **1926** Tully *Jarnegan* 182: The poor little gump. **1929** *Variety* (Oct. 30) 76: The poor gump did not know, apparently. **1936** Levin *Old Bunch* 15: Oh, don't be a gump. **1966** "Petronius" *N.Y. Unexp.* 90: Popular with the gobs and gumps.

2. (among tramps) a chicken.

1899 Young *Reminiscences* 432: Should a soldier inform a civilian that his bunkie was "baked by a bull for jumpin' a gump"…his meaning would be that his tent mate had been arrested by the provost guard for stealing a chicken. **1910** in Kornbluh *Rebel Voices* 74: Wherefore we gave him gump mulligan and much good advice. **1914** Jackson & Hellyer *Vocab.* 39: Gump, Noun. Current amongst yeggs, hobos, and peripatetics generally. A chicken; a fowl. Example: "We're going down in the jungle and have a gump stew." *ca*1920 *Hobo Songs* (unp.): Not a hen-house there to frisk for a gump. **1925–26** Black *You Can't Win* 64 [ref. to 1890's]: I've got a gump in my bindle. **1927** *DN* V 449: Gump, n. A chicken. **1929** Milburn *Hornbook* 29: "Slip'ry Slim" and "Bashful Tim" croaked gumps for our menu. **1933** Ersine *Pris. Slang* 41: Gump Glommer. A chicken thief, petty thief. **1937** Reitman *Box-Car Bertha* 84: "Gump stew" (stolen chicken) was the chief dish. **1976** Braly *False Starts* 131: He told me chickens were called gumps because they were as chinless as Andy Gump in the Sunday funnies. **1980** Algren *Dev. Stocking* 38: A gump was a sick or dying chicken [given away by poultry handlers].

3. nonsense; GUFF, 1.

1913 J. London *Valley of Moon* 415: There are a million boys…swallowing the gump of canal boy to President.

gump[2] *n.* GUMPTION. *Rare* in U.S.

1920 in *OEDS*: If they weren't so sure of getting me, they would have had the gump to wait a few days till the court adjourns. **1941** Cain

Mildred Pierce 235: In this, Monty may have detected a smug note, an allusion to what *she* had done with a little gump. ***1968** in *OEDS*: A phoney who hasn't the gump to feed and exercise properly.

gump *v.* (see quot.).
   1946 Dadswell *Hey, Sucker* 159: Ever do any gumping?…My gumping outfit was a fishhook on a fifteen foot cord.…We'd put a fish-worm on the hook and throw it into the chicken yard.…The worm wiggled, a chicken snatched, and pretty soon we'd have gump stew.

GUMP check *n. Av.* (see quot.).
   1985 Boyne & Thompson *Wild Blue* 21: Before you took off in a trainer, you ran a GUMP check: gas, undercarriage, mixture, propeller.

gump light *n. Mining.* a miner's carbide light.
   *a***1948** in *West. Folk.* IX (1950) 46: And the tag book and gump light went down the skip chute.

gumption *n.* [Scots] **1.** intelligence, esp. common sense. Now *colloq.*
   *1719 in *OED*: They're but unlearned clerks,/And want the gumption. ***1786, ****ca***1812** in *OED*. **1815** in M. Mathews *Beginnings of Amer. Eng.* 59: *Gumtion,* sense, understanding, intellect. **1816** Pickering *Vocab.* 102: *Gumption.* A low word, which is sometimes heard in conversation, and signifies *understanding,* or *capacity.* **1821** Waln *Hermit in Phila.* 25: "I'm no flat."…"Poh! you've no *gumption!*" **1838** [Haliburton] *Clockmaker* (Ser. 2) 58: That critter may want ginger…but he don't want for gumption. **1861** in A.M. Stewart *Camp. March* 77: Judgment, tact— *gumption* is, perhaps, the best designation. **1878** O. Coomes *Red Rob* 10: That dorg has a mortal sight o' man gumption. **1899** Ade *Fables* 72: They hoped that if she ever Married again she'd pick out Somebody that wuzn't afraid to Work, and had Gumption enough to pound Sand into a Rat-Hole. **1902–03** Ade *People You Know* 97: He told him that he didn't have as much Business Gumption as a Belgian Hare. **1940** Faulkner *Hamlet* 31: When He give me an eye for horseflesh He give me a little judgment and gumption with it.
   2. spirit; initiative; determination.
   *1825 in *OEDS*: *Gumption,* common sense, combined with energy. **1840** Strong *Diary* I 150: A great deal may be made out of the sovereign Public by a combination of humbug and gumption. **1843** in *DAE*: It was the only sign of gumption she had made for a hull day. **1851** M. Reid *Scalp-Hunters* 177: Ef they only hev the gumshin' to go about it. **1862** Browne *A. Ward* 213: I like…your enterprise, gumpshun, &c. **1898, 1903** in *DAE*. **1924** Woollcott *Aisles* 75: But lacking the gumption…to make that response, I set to pondering. **1965–70** in *DARE*: Of *a very able and energetic person*…Gumption…57 Inf[ormant]s. **1981** D. Burns *Feeling Good* 110: I don't have the gumption to jump in on my own like the other kids.
   3. (see quot.).
   1881 in *DA*: Everybody [in 1810] had barrels of cider in their cellars and cider-spirits called "gumption."

gumshoe *n.* [short for *gumshoe man,* etc.; see GUMSHOE, *adj.,* 1]
   1.a. a plainclothes police officer or (now *usu.*) a private investigator; a plainclothes or covert investigator. [1907 quot. is ambiguous; perh. actual gumshoes are meant.]
   [**1907** T.A. Dorgan, in Zwilling *TAD Lexicon* 42: It was a swell raid, the gumshoes worked to perfection and the sports were done to a turn.] **1908** in H.C. Fisher *A. Mutt* 49: Rudolph Tobasco, the great gumshoe comedian in…"How I Captured Mutt." *Ibid.* 103: Surrounded by gumshoes in Idaho. **1913** *Sat. Eve. Post* (July 12) 9: Every gumshoe and flat-foot in the department. **1914** Jackson & Hellyer *Vocab.* 39: *Gum Shoe*…General Currency. A detective; a silent trailer. **1918** Stringer *House of Intrigue* 47: A federal gum-shoe pushed in through the crowd. **1927** in Hammett *Knockover* 278: A yarn designed to get a dollar out of a trusting gumshoe. **1928** Hammett *Harvest* 21: So you're a gum-shoe. **1952** W. Brown *Sox* 98: It will take a thousand gumshoes to prove anything. **1969** Bouton *Ball Four* 279: That's why I'm very upset to find out that you think I've been a detective with this club, a gumshoe. **1973** Toma & Brett *Toma* 48: If [a police officer] ducks into a warm spot to grab a smoke, there's always the possibility that a gumshoe will spot him and make a complaint. **1983** *N.Y. Post* (Aug. 25) 18: Gumshoe Paul Bird, who works for Mutual of New York Life Insurance Co., tailed his man for six months waiting for a fatal slip-up. **1988** *N.Y. Newsday* (June 20) II 6: An apprentice gumshoe staking out cheating spouses.
   b. *Und.* a professional sneak thief or prowler.
   1934 (quot. at GUMSHOE, *adj.,* 1).
   2. *Mil.* an intelligence officer or spy. *Joc.*
   1929 in *Our Army* (Jan. 1930) 47: *Gumshoes*…used with respect to members of the Intelligence Section. **1962** Farago *10th Fleet* 88: Those

"gumshoes" of the ONI had information that [certain naval secrets]…had reached the German Intelligence Service. **1981** *N.Y. Times Mag.* (Aug. 30) 32: Don't go by the K.G.B. gumshoes. The bureaucracy…are past masters at dissimulation.
   3. a police officer; FLATFOOT.
   1926 *AS* (Jan.) 243 [ref. to WWI]: *Gumshoes.* members of the military police. **1968–70** *Current Slang* III & IV 63: *Gum shoes,* n. Policemen.— Watts [L.A.].

gumshoe *adj.* [in allusion to the stealth supposedly afforded by *gumshoes* 'sneakers'] **1.** (of persons) being a stealthy or surreptitious thief or tracker (*obs.*); (now *specif.*) being a plainclothes police detective or, usu., a private investigator.— used prenominally. [Displaced almost entirely by the n.]
   1899–1900 Cullen *Tales* 296: "You and this gum-shoe sleuth of yours are up in the air," I said to the desk sergeant. **1902** Hobart *Back to the Woods* 44: You will play Spike Hennessy and I'll be Gumshoe Charlie. **1906** *Nat. Police Gaz.* (Nov. 17) 3: He had no badge nor credentials of any kind to show he was a gum-shoe man. **1906** A.H. Lewis *Confessions* 198: Cull, you're d'gum-shoe guy I was waitin' fer, see! **1908** Sullivan *Crim. Slang* 11: *Gumshoe worker*—A private detective; a spotter. **1908** in H.C. Fisher *A. Mutt* 66: Detachment of gentlemanly gumshoe men, bodyguard for Tobasco. **1934** D.W. Maurer in *AS* (Feb. 1935) [ref. to *a*1910]: *Gum, gumshoe* or *gumshoe worker.* 1. A burglar or sneak thief. 2. A stool pigeon. (Obs.). **1935** Pollock *Und. Speaks: Gum shoe man,* a detective. **1944** Mauldin *Up Front* 78: These "gumshoe so-and-so's" worked in the comfort and safety of the city [Naples]. **1946** Ruskin & Busch *Postman* (film): He used to be a dick. Now he's my gumshoe man. **1942–49** Goldin et al. *DAUL* 88: *Gumshoe-worker.* n. (Obsolete) A sneak thief. **1958** S.H. Adams *Tenderloin* 170 [ref. to 1890's]: Your gumshoe boys…think nobody is on to them.
   2. (of actions or activities) carried out stealthily or surreptitiously (*obs.*); (*specif.*) [infl. by GUMSHOE, *n.*] involving or pertaining to investigation by a private or plainclothes detective; undercover.—used prenominally.
   1901 *Chi. Tribune* (July 28) 1: The organizers…admit that they are making a "gumshoe" agitation. They are working so secretly, so softly, that not a matron in all Chicago is expected to know whether her roof is sheltering a union girl until the time comes. **1904** in *DA*: No gumshoe democratic campaign in Nebraska. **1907** in H.C. Fisher *A. Mutt* 8: I'm an old hand at this gum shoe stuff. **1907** in *OEDS*: He…was forced to accomplish his ends by main strength rather than by gumshoe methods. **1913** *Sat. Eve. Post* (Jan. 4) 24: Well, if they ever make me Chief I'll break you for your gumshoe work in this doormat job. **1944** Smith & Zurcher *Dict. Amer. Pol.* 149: *Gumshoe campaign.* Unobtrusive efforts to secure the support of political leaders and delegates to a political convention. **1954** Johnson *Black Widow* (film): What's the reason for all this gumshoe work? *a***1991** Kross *Splash One* 83: Not eyewash, real gumshoe intell.

gumshoe *v.* **1.** to come or go stealthily; sneak.
   1902 Dunne *Observations* 231: Their idee is that a German fleet might gumshoe up th' harbor in th' dark iv th' moon. **1902** [Hobart] *Up to You* 15: I…gumshoed away like Raffles. **1904** [Hobart] *From Mo.* 44: It seemed that everyone in the community…gum-shoed after the Two Candidates. **1910** *N.Y. Eve. Jour.* (May 6) 21: I bet he goes gumshoeing around with a record of births in his hand and looks them over in the cradle. **1918–19** MacArthur *Bug's-Eye View* 36: Officers gumshoed here and there, whispering and adding up long columns of figures. **1922** Colton & Randolph *Rain* 69: I saw him gumshoeing down the road this morning. **1953** Petry *Narrows* 247: Dey gumshoe in, through the door. **1966** King *Brave & Damned* 66: Slewfoot gumshoed in.
   2. to work as a plainclothes detective or (now *usu.*) private investigator; (*also*) to conduct a covert investigation.
   1908 in H.C. Fisher *A. Mutt* 135: Yes, it is true I have had Rudolph Tobasco gumshoeing for my lost quadruped. **1927** in Hammett *Big Knockover* 284: So Jack came to the Agency. He thought gumshoeing would be fun. **1943** B. Halliday *Mummer's Mask* 104: That gives you a pretty definite stake in my gumshoeing. **1951** J.D. MacDonald *Murder for Bride* 52: You ready to give up gumshoeing and get back on the job, boy? **1953** "L. Short" *Silver Rock* 88: I'm going to do a little gumshoeing myself. **1983** *Agronsky & Co.* (Mutual Radio news show) (Mar. 13): The FBI is gumshoeing all over town on this. **1989** *Village Voice* (May 9) 8: Dowd was identified by the *Voice*…for the gaybaiting gumshoeing of Koch that year.

gumshoe artist *n.* one who goes about stealthily, esp. a covert investigator.

1930 in *OEDS*: That eminent political gum-shoe artist. **1931** Wilstach *Under Cover Man* 61: He looks like a gumshoe artist to me. *a***1935** in E. Levinson *Strikes* 245: The gum-shoe artist of fiction. **1984–88** Hackworth & Sherman *About Face* 172: Some gumshoe artist was fiddling around and suddenly our numbers were on the vehicle.

gumshoer *n.* a plainclothes or covert investigator.

1909 "O. Henry" *Works* 1514: You must be one of the Central Office gumshoers. **1971** Horan *Blue Messiah* 254: The latest news of the "gumshoers"—the Police Commissioner's Confidential squad, that…was despised as deeply as the FBI.

gumsuck *v.* to employ flattery or deception.

1889 Barrère & Leland *Dict. Slang* I 438: *Gumsuck, to* (American), to humbug or deceive. **1926** Lewisohn *Mr. Crump* 242: You didn't talk that way I notice when you came gum-sucking around me.

gum-sucking *n.* amorous kissing.—used derisively.

*ca***1873** Schele de Vere, in *DA*: *Gumsucking* = kiss[ing] in Ky. and Tenn.; coupled with *neck-sawing*. **1877** Bartlett *Amer.* (ed. 4) 271: *Gum-Sucking*.…A friend informs me that he first heard it at Princeton College, in 1854. *****1911** O'Brien & Stephens *Australian Sl.* 69: *Gum-sucking* /slang/ kissing or courting.

gum-tickler *n.* a drink of liquor.

1810 in *DA*: A *gum-tickler* is a gill of spirits, generally rum, taken fasting. **1862** in *F & H* I 317: Visitors may indulge in "juleps," "cock-tails," "cobblers," "rattlesnakes," "gum-ticklers," "eye-openers," [etc.]. **1869** J.L. Peyton *Over Alleghanies* 35: American drinks…from the "gum tickler" to the "eye opener."

gun[1] *n.* **1.** the penis. See also *get (one's) gun [off]*, below.

*****1675** in Duffett *Burlesque Plays* 83: [She] storms the Fort in private with a Leathern Gun [i.e., masturbates with a dildo]. *****1699** in Burford *Bawdy Verse* 196: Poor Whores may be Nuns/Since Men turn their *Guns*/And vent on each other their passion. **1907** S.E. White *Ariz. Nights* 201: For that gun it shoots high,/And that gun it shoots low,/And it wabbles about/Like a bucking bronco! **1916** Cary *Venery* I 119: *Gun*—The penis. **1918** in Carey *Mlle. from Armentières* I [unp.]: Oh, farmer have you a daughter young,/Fit for a soldier with a long gun? *Ibid.*: A little Marine is coming to France,/His gun on his shoulder and one in his pants. **1938** in Randolph *Pissing in Snow* 11: She give several loud yells too, but the fellow stayed right in there till his gun went off. **1952** Uris *Battle Cry* 53 [ref. to 1942]: "Private Jones, unbutton your fly." "Yes sir." "That's your gun." "Yes sir." He led Jones through the entire tent area. At each street he blew his whistle and a platoon of boots came flying from their tents. Jones then stood there holding his "gun" in his right hand and his rifle in his left and recited: "This is my rifle,/This is my gun,/This is for fighting,/This is for fun." **1962–63** in Giallombardo *Soc. of Women* 204: *Gun*. The penis; to have sexual intercourse. **1968** Tauber *Sunshine Soldiers* 46: A mnemonic device is introduced to break us of the habit of calling rifles guns. It seems that a rifle is a rifle, and a gun is between your legs. "This is my rifle, this is my gun. One is for killing, one is for fun." **1970** Byrne *Memories* 56: If only a girl could have seen her way clear to open her arms and legs to me and let me shoot off my gun without let or hindrance! **1971** Sloan *War Games* 117: This is my rifle, and/This is my gun./One is for shooting,/The other for fun. **1992** Jernigan *Tin Can Man* 91: His gun was showing.

2. *Und.* a scrutinizing look.

*****1812** Vaux *Vocab.*: *Gun*. a view; look; observation; or taking notice; as, there is a strong *gun* at us, means, we are strictly observed. **1914** Jackson & Hellyer *Vocab.* 40: "There's a dick on the corner gunning us." "He's giving us a gun."

3. *Narc.* a hypodermic syringe.

1899 A.H. Lewis *Sandburrs* 26: I shoots into him wit' a dandy little hypodermic gun. **1906** H. Green *Boarding House* 272: She watched him…jab the "gun" into his flesh. **1909** Chrysler *White Slavery* 40: He drops the…"gun" into his pocket. **1915** Bronson-Howard *God's Man* 39: "Guns"—that is, "hypos," hypodermic syringes. **1917** in H.W. Morgan *Addicts* 137 [ref. to 1900]: I bought a gun and began to use two quarter-grain tablets a day. **1922** E. Murphy *Black Candle* 241: Dope "guns" are more destructive to the world than heavy artillery. **1936** Washburn *Parlor* 83: Cocaine addicts would congregate in the drug stores and use the "gun" (hypodermic needle) openly. **1968–73** Agar *Ripping & Running* 53: Although some *junkies* use a *gun*, most do not.

4. BIG GUN.

1903 Kildare *Mamie Rose* 142: Every man, who has lived all his life on the Bowery, as I have, knows that "gun" means an important personage. A millionaire is a "gun", so is a prominent lawyer, or a politician, or a famous crook. **1912** Stringer *Shadow* 59: You call yourself a

gun!…A gun! Why, you're…a broken down bluff. **1986** *NDAS*: He's quite a gun around there now.

5.a. a throttle; power provided by a throttle.—usu. constr. with *give* or *cut*.

1918 in Bowerman *Compensations* 68: We…gave old Lizzie the gun. **1918** Crowe *Pat Crowe, Aviator* 19: They were scared to death when I "gave 'er the gun," and the wind blew their hats off. **1919** in Faulkner *Early Prose* 43: You cut your gun and sit up there like a blind idiot. **1925** L. Thomas *World Flight* 110: Then signaling to Erik and Leigh we all "gave her the gun" together. **1928** *Writer's Mo.* (Feb.) 123: He *cuts* the motor, or *cuts the gun*. **1929** Springs *Carol Banks* 117: He gave it the gun and…away he went. **1930** *AS* V (May) 290: *Cut the gun*, v.phr. To shut off the motor. *Give her the gun*, v.phr. Accelerate the motor. **1937** in Loosbrock & Skinner *Wild Blue* 193: And with full gun. **1939** R.A. Winston *Dive Bomber* 92: I jammed on full gun. **1954** W.G. Smith *South Street* 8: But when we got on the straight-away I gave it the gun and the cat couldn't even see me! **1960** J. Miles, in Kennnedy *Intro. Poetry* 46: Give her the gun, Bud, he needs a taste of his own bumper. **1970** Lincke *Jenny Was No Lady* 41: When you closed the throttle (cut the gun, to be more picturesque)…

b. an all-out effort.

1968 Ainslie *Racing Guide* 468: *Gun*—All-out effort by jockey. **1971** Sorrentino *Up from Never* 279: Timmy Kelly was applying himself full gun at St. John's law school.

6. a usu. hired gunman. Cf. GUN[2], *n.* [The phr. *hired gun*, popularized by westerns, is now *S.E.*]

1920 E. Hemingway in *N.Y. Times Mag.* (Aug. 18, 1985) 61: You know we can't bump him. We ain't guns. **1921** in Hemingway *Dateline: Toronto* 66: Most of the guns were Wops.…Most gunmen were Wops, anyway. **1927–28** in R. Nelson *Dishonorable* 151: A driver for his own car, his personal barber…and five or six of his "guns." **1933** Ersine *Pris. Slang* 42: *Gun*…A gunman, torpedo. **1950** Rackin *Enforcer* (film): Maybe he stuck a gun in a cop's uniform. **1950** Bowers & Sellers *Gunfighter* (film): That's what you always wanted [to be]—top gun of the West. **1953** in Cannon *Like 'Em Tough* 121: She figured I was the gun. **1955** "W. Henry" *Wyatt* 63: He knew the Pima politician was not a gun. He carried one and that was all. **1975** Kennedy *Train Robbers* (film): I told you to get me two guns that could take orders. *Ibid.*: That's the trouble with young guns. **1983** Helprin *Winter's Tale* 33: Guns (marksmen in the gang wars…held in low regard because they could pick neither pockets nor locks).

7.a. *Photog.* a camera, esp. a movie or television camera.

1928 *AS* III 365: [Movie] camera…"gun." **1964** *Newsweek* (July 27) 51: ABC's camera gun: Locomotion. **1978** P. Rizzuto on *N.Y. Yankees Baseball* (WPIX-TV) (June 17): I wish we had a gun on Guidry right now.

b. a surveyor's transit; *(also)* a level.

1935 O'Hara *Butterfield 8* 74: He could not use a transit, but among engineers he could talk about "running the gun." **1942** *AS* (Dec.) 280: *Gun*. A surveyor's transit. **1958** McCulloch *Woods Words* 75: *Gun*…A name for a transit, or for a level. *a***1981** H.A. Applebaum *Royal Blue* 85: He had to walk out on the steel and hold a rod for the man on the "gun."

8. *Orig. Baseball.* a strong and accurate throwing arm; *(pl.)* arms; biceps.

[**1911** Van Loan *Big League* 56: He's peggin' 'em down to second like they was shot out of a gun!] **1929** *N.Y. Times* (June 2) IX 2: A player's arm is his "gun" or his "wing." "A good gun" means that the possessor has a strong arm. **1973** Andrews & Owens *Black Lang.* 79: *Guns*—The biceps and triceps part of the arm. (Where potential firepower lies). **1978** P. Rizzuto on *N.Y. Yankees-Boston Red Sox* (WPIX-TV) (June 27): Boy, he's got a gun! **1980** F. Healey & B. White on *N.Y. Yankees vs. A's* (WWS radio) (June 20): "Willie Randolph is the ideal lead-off batter. He hasn't got big guns but he's strong enough." "What are guns?" "Arms." **1984** *N.Y. Post* (Aug. 3) 66: "Did you see the rightfielder throw?…His gun reminds me of Skoonj"—meaning Carl Furillo. **1989** *Married with Children* (Fox-TV): Does he have guns like *these?*

9. *Surfing.* (see quots.).

1967 *DAS* (Supp.) 688: *Gun*…A long, heavy surfboard. **1968** Kirk & Hanle *Surfer's Hndbk.* 13: *Guns*…are basically big-surf boards—long, narrow, fairly sharp-nosed, relatively heavy, and fast. *Ibid.* 136: *Big gun*: board for big-wave conditions. **1976** *Webster's Sports Dict.*: *Gun*…a large heavy surfboard used especially for riding heavy surf.

10. *pl.* a woman's breasts.

1967–80 Folb *Runnin' Lines* 241: *Guns*. Breasts.

¶ In phrases:

¶ **blow [big] guns** to blow a gale. Cf. *[like] great guns* s.v.
GREAT GUN.
 *1833 in *OEDS:* It rains every night & the wind has blown guns. **1884**
Bruell *Sea Memories* 30 [ref. to 1840's]: It blew big guns, and we had to
send down all the upper yards and spars. *Ibid.* 60: It was "blowing great
guns" from the north. **1884** Kingston *Frolic* 307: It was blowing big
guns and small arms. *1920 in *OEDS:* It's blowing guns to-day.

¶ **get (one's) gun [off]** [fr. (1), above] **1.** (esp. of a man) to
ejaculate; to experience orgasm.—usu. considered vulgar.
Occ. trans. [*1823 quot. refers to actual guns.]
[*1823 in Ludlum *Shooting Stories* 215: A wet day…no jackanapes could
get his gun off.] **1867** Doten *Journals* II 954 [in cipher]: First time I ever
got my gun off in that way in my life. *Ibid.* 957 [in cipher]: She got her
gun off twice to my once. *a*1888 *Stag Party* 177: So I quickened my
motions and got off my gun. **1916** Cary *Venery* I 107: *Getting Off One's
Gun*—To achieve emission. Said of men only. **1927** in Randolph *Pissing in Snow* 137: But the big half-wit has got his gun off by this time.
1942 McAtee *Supp. to Grant Co.* 6 [ref. to 1890's]: *Gun,* penis; *get one's
gun off,* have an ejaculation. **1956** Chamales *Never So Few* 84: This
whorehouse of tonight…sitting around with the other fellows knowing
how badly they wanted to get their gun off and him not needing to.
1958 Plagemann *Steel Cocoon* 64: "I just want to get my gun," he said
reasonably. "I don't want to get mixed up in none of this old love stuff."
1961 Gover *$100 Misunderstanding* 16: She guess she gonna git his gun
wiffout hardly no work. *Ibid.* 42: An he git him his…ten dollar gun. At
las'! **1962** E. Stephens *Blow Negative* 154: "You get undressed?"…"I
didn't even get my tie off." "I didn't even get my gun off." **1967** W.
Crawford *Gresham's War* 173: All kinds of weird stuff…and they got
their gun. **1971** *Coming, Dear* 93: Davy Crockett didn't kill a b'ar when
he was three like a lot of people claim…he didn't GET HIS GUN till
he was twelve! **1976** *Nat. Lampoon* (July) 77: If a Southern male fails to
"get his gun," he looks for positive ways to sublimate those frustrations.
1976 J.W. Thomas *Heavy Number* 87: Strange boys inside her got their
guns off and left her the same.
2. to delight.
1947 Schulberg *Harder They Fall* 31: I got a little project for you that
will really get your gun off.

¶ **get the gun** to be shot to death.
1905 *Nat. Police Gaz.* (Nov. 18) 3: The dirty yellow cur quit like a rat;
he ought to get the gun.

¶ **jump the gun** Orig. *Sports.* to begin a race before the
starting pistol; (*hence*) to start or act hastily or prematurely.
Now *colloq.*
1942 *ATS* 11: *Jump the gun,* to make a false start. **1954–60** *DAS.* **1964**
Newsweek (July 27) 45: I think we're both jumping the gun in talking
about his chances. **1967** J. Kramer *Instant Replay* 165: We jump the gun
almost imperceptibly. **1972** Madden *Bros.* 13: But now I had to jump
the gun. **1974** L.D. Miller *Valiant* 71: We could be jumping the
gun. **1976** Trudeau *Inalienable* [unp.]: Governor? Duke, don't you think
you're kind of jumping the gun? **1989** *CBS This Morning* (CBS-TV)
(Apr. 27): Other scientists warned against jumping the gun.

¶ **on the gun** [cf. (2), above and GUN, *v.,* 1] *Und.* on the
lookout. Cf. *on the gun* s.v. GUN[2], *n.*
1933 Ersine *Pris. Slang* 42: *Gun, n.* The state of being on guard. "Get
on the gun!"

¶ **ride the gun** [sugg. by *ride shotgun* s.v. SHOTGUN] (see
quot.).
1978 *Adolescence* XIII 499: "Riding the gun" meant riding in the passenger seat of the car.

¶ **under the gun** under pressure to take action, esp. in solving a problem or meeting a deadline; (*Cards.*) sitting to the
left of the dealer or eldest hand. Now *colloq.*
1898–1900 Cullen *Chances* 246: The bank president was under the
gun, as they say out there of the man who's to the left of the dealer of
a jackpot. **1902** Cullen *More Tales* 90: Four plainclothes men stepped
in and put O'Brien and his pal under the gun. **1905** *Nat. Police Gaz.*
(July 1) 3: The boss…opened the pot under the gun. **1906** Beyer *Amer.
Battleship* 84: "Under the gun"—one sitting next to the dealer in a
friendly game of draw. **1927** *Amer. Leg. Mo.* (Jan.) 34: Sitting next to
the dealer is called "under the gun." **1956** Poe *Attack* (film): I'm under
the gun? **1968** F. Wallace *Poker* 61: For example, a good player is sitting under the gun (on the dealer's left). **1970** Della Femina *Wonderful
Folks* 169: Creative people…work best under the gun. **1983** B. Taggert
Unkn. Origin (film): I think he's putting me under the gun on purpose.
1985 Sawislak *Dwarf* 149: Grace wants a long piece on the band
and…I'm going to be under the gun.

gun[2] *n.* [clipping of GONNIF, spelling infl. by *gun* 'firearm'; cf.
GUN[1], *n.,* 6] *Und.* a professional criminal, esp. a thief or pickpocket.
 *1857 "Ducange" *Vulgar Tongue:* Gun. A thief. *1858 A. Mayhew
Paved with Gold 70: You ain't a-going to make a gun (thief) of this here
young flat. **1859** Matsell *Vocab.* 39: *Gun.* A thief. **1866** *Nat. Police Gaz.*
(Apr. 21) 3: What is Willy Kay running after "guns'" interests so much
for, of late? Are there any "supers" that have had their "monekers"
"rung" that he has a percentage on? **1868** *Detective's Manual* 149: Had
Lyons any hand in that $21,000 bond affair, in "smashing" them for the
"guns"? **1872** Hotten *Slang Dict.* (ed. 4): *Gun,* a magsman or street
thief. Diminutive of gonnuf or gunnof. **1900** Willard & Hodler *Powers
That Prey* 14: It was soon noised about among the guns that there was
to be a round-up at the Front Office. **1901** *Chicago Tribune* (Aug. 25) 3:
Where the crowd goes is where they are most likely to find the "guns."
1904 A.H. Lewis *President* 429: Dan's a first-class gun and hold-up
man. **1908** Train *Crime Stories* 10: He…proceeded to indulge his imagination in accounts of bold robberies in the brown stone districts and
clever "tricks" in other cities, which left Mrs. Parker in no doubt but
that her companion was an expert "gun" of long experience. **1912**
Hampton's Mag. (Jan.) 842: He…had a speaking acquaintance with
every old hobo and gun that made that part of the country. **1912**
Berkman *Prison* 161 [ref. to 1893]: You see, pard, I'm no gun.*…*Professional thief. **1914** Jackson & Hellyer *Vocab.* 39: *Gun…*A pickpocket.
1921 Casey & Casey *Gay-Cat* 58: The new gun—what's he doing here?
Ibid. 60: A "gun"…means a criminal. **1922** *Variety* (Aug. 11) 8: The
pickpockets carried by carnivals…are known in the open-air vernacular
as "the gun mob." **1923** Ornitz *Haunch, Paunch & Jowl* 48: As good as
any Gun what ever snatched a poke. **1929** *Sat. Eve. Post* (Oct. 12) 82:
The fancy of some gun, carrying that thing around with him.
¶ In phrase:
¶ **on the gun** engaged in theft. Cf. *on the gun* s.v. GUN[1], *n.*
1908 Sullivan *Crim. Slang* 17: *Out on the gun*—Stealing. **1915** Bronson-
Howard *God's Man* 264: I was jest a little sucker to keep on the gun
when there was no jobs like this one laying around loose. **1934** D.W.
Maurer, in *AS* (Feb. 1935) 18: *To be on the gun.* To practice thievery. In
modern parlance this phrase is restricted to pickpockets.

gun[1] *v.* **1.** Esp. *Und.* to watch; examine; look at; look (for); eye;
be on the lookout.
 *1812 Vaux *Vocab.:* To *gun* any thing, is to look at or examine it. *1823
P. Egan *Vulgar Tongue: Do you not see we are gunned?* an expression used
by thieves when they think they are being watched. **1859** Matsell *Vocab.*
39: *Gun.* To watch; to examine; to look at.…"The copper gunned me
as if he was fly to my mug." **1904** *Life in Sing Sing* 249: *Gunning.* On
the lookout. **1914** Jackson & Hellyer *Vocab.* 40: *Gun,* Verb. General
usage. To watch; to scrutinize. Example: "There's a dick on the corner
gunning us." "He's giving us a gun." **1928** *New Yorker* (Dec. 8) 58: I
gun both sides of the street and nobody's giving me a rumble. **1933**
Ersine *Pris. Slang* 41: *Gun, v.* To be on guard, watch warily. "Gun for
the cop while I grab this heap." **1946** Mezzrow & Wolfe *Really Blues*
96: I gunned the kid—I'd never seen him before in my life. *Ibid.* 117:
The house dick began to gun us. **1966** Braly *On Yard* 205: Why are you
gunning me? **1974** Kurtzman *Bobby* 2: Harv's…eyeing her in that black
bathing suit,…gunning her. **1981** Graziano & Corsel *Somebody Down
Here* 106: She spots some…wise guys gunnin' her from other tables.
2. *Finance.* (see quot.).
1870 Medbery *Wall St.* 136: *Gunning a stock,* is to use every art to produce a [decline in value] when it is known that a certain house is heavily
supplied, and would be unable to resist an attack.
3. to seek out, usu. with the intention of settling a
grudge.—constr. with *for* or (*obs.*) *after.* Now *colloq.*
1878 *Nat. Police Gaz.* (June 1) 5: Gunning for a Lecherous Parson.
1882 in *DA:* The Senator from Kentucky…went gunning after the
Senator from Vermont…on account of some unguarded declarations
he made. *a*1893 W.K. Post *Harvard* 189: That bull mick Shreedy is
gunning for me…and if my mother knew I owed money to a prizefighter she would never get over it. **1908** U. Sinclair, in *DAE:* Mrs.
Vivie wished to go home, and asked him to find her escort…for whom
her husband was gunning. **1913** J. London *Valley of Moon* 198: They're
sure gunning for trouble. **1925** Robinson *Old Wagon Show* 122: He
went "gunning" for brother.…Father pulled him out and started to
give him a licking. **1932** Lorimer *Streetcars* 114: She's gunning for this
Felton person. **1932** Farrell *Guillotine Party* 192: You bastard, I've been
gunning for you for three weeks. **1929–33** Farrell *Young Manhood* 224:
Man Bleu is gunning for you, and promises he['ll]…lose his fists in
your…puss. **1958** Talsman *Gaudy Image* 173: I knew they were gunnin'
for a fight. **1976** Price *Bloodbrothers* 22: I heard ol' Three-Fingers is

gunnin' for you. **1981–85** S. King *It* 430: You got one bad black man gunning for you, old hoss.

4. to shoot with a gun.

1898 in *DAE:* I'll gun you if you do that again. **1916** H.L. Wilson *Somewhere in Red Gap* 35: Wilfred went pasty…thinking his host was going to gun him. **1925** in Hammett *Big Knockover* 215: Shall I gun this la-ad now,…or will we wa-ait a bit? **1925** in Partridge *Dict. Und.* 313: *Gun*…to shoot. **1938** Chandler *Big Sleep* 51: So she says I gunned him, eh? **1941** D'Usseau & Collins *Lady Scarface* (film): He knows Slade gunned that guy. **1951** Twist *Ft. Worth* (film): Now you only have to gun Britt. **1969** *Gunsmoke* (CBS-TV): I should've gunned him and saved him his frettin'. **1978** T. Sanchez *Zoot-Suit* 213: We thought we might have gunned the wrong guy.

5. to advance the throttle of (an engine, aircraft, motor vehicle, power boat, etc.) sometimes repeatedly, to increase speed or to apply full power. Occ. intrans. Now *S.E.*

1920 in Loosbrock & Skinner *Wild Blue* 84: Not having room to "gun" the tail down, I cut the switches. **1930** *AS* V (May) 290: *Gun the motor,* v.phr. Accelerate the motor. **1938** Bellem *Blue Murder* 14: I gunned past a traffic light just as it turned from amber to red. **1938** Chandler *Big Sleep* 33: The man in overalls gunned his motor. **1945** Hamann *Air Words* 28: Gun the motor. **1953** Gresham *Midway* 65: Okay, Charley, gun her up on the straight for one lap and then down again. **1956** Heflin *USAF Dict.* 241: *Gun*…To move fast and in a straight line, as in "he gunned across the runway."…To gun an engine, to advance the throttle; hence to apply full power. **1974** N.Y.C. man: You know those hotrod movies where the guys sit at the stop light gunning their engines? **1972–79** T. Wolfe *Right Stuff* 20: He was instructed to touch down and gun right off. **1993** *Smithsonian* (July) 58: You don't gun a Coddington hot rod.

6.a. to throw hard. See also GUN DOWN, 2.

1973 *World Series* (NBC-TV) (Oct. 14): He guns it to second and that's out number two.

b. *Basketball.* to make many shots; (*trans.*) to score (points); in phr. **gun and run** to play aggressively. Also fig.

1967–80 Folb *Runnin' Lines* 241: *Gun*…shoot a basketball an unnecessary number of times during a game (suggests missing shots). **1986** WINS radio news (Apr. 1): The game was billed as "gun and run"— both Duke and Louisville preferring to rely on speed to run away with a win. **1988** ABC-TV spot ad. (Jan. 24): They're slamming and jamming—gunning and running in a college basketball bonanza. **1989** Headline News Network (Mar. 5): Jackson gunned down 55 [points]. **1989** *Rage* (Knoxville, Tenn.) (Mar.) 24: Philosophy in life: Run and gun, work hard, play hard, live long.

gun[2] *v.* [fr. GUN[2], *n.*] *Und.* to engage in theft.

1867 *Nat. Police Gaz.* (Apr. 6) 2: Mo.…swore, might he be blind, stiff, and lame, if ever Pete Tracey had another red of the "sugar" that he "gunned" for. **1899** Willard *Tramping* 388: "To gun," to do "crooked work." **1902** Hapgood *Thief* 92 [ref. to *ca*1888]: He began to "gun," which means to pickpockets [*sic*], an occupation which he found far more lucrative than "swagging" copper from the docks. **1928** Callahan *Man's Grim Justice* 195: "But wait until she gets hep that you're 'a gun.'" "There isn't going to be any more 'gunning,' Jimmy."

gun-ape *n. Army.* GUN-BUNNY.

1988 Clodfelter *Mad Minutes* 26 [ref. to 1965]: A gun ape from Bravo Battery.

gun artist *n.* a western gunfighter.

1929 Haycox *Chaffee* 87: That gent…looks like a gun artist.

gunbird *n. Mil.* a helicopter gunship. [Quots. ref. to Vietnam War.]

1972 Beckham *Runner Mack* 162: I hear the gunbirds. **1973** Browne *Body Shop* 115: They sent the gun bird down and it took fire. **1985** M. Brennan *War* 27: We're going in. Two ships. The gunbirds took fire from that valley. *a***1986** D. Tate *Bravo Burning* 193: The gunbird swoops over us, burping fire.

gunboat *n.* **1.** Orig. *Army.* a large or clumsy boot or shoe; (*hence*) a big foot.

1862 in R.G. Carter *4 Bros.* 183: He has drawn a pair of government brogans (gun-boats). **1864** in Wightman *To Ft. Fisher* 166: We…planted "our gunboats" on an enormous bed of stupendous bivalves. **1880** J.M. Drake *Fast & Loose* 254 [ref. to Civil War]: I saw the old man climb out of that pair of "gun-boats," as Lewis wickedly called them. **1887** Hinman *Si Klegg* 170 [ref. to Civil War]: The shapeless "gunboats" scraped the skin from their feet. **1906** Beyer *Amer. Battleship* 211: Don't judge people by the gunboats on their feet. **1919** *DN* V

69: *Gunboats,* the feet. Keep your *gunboats* out of my way. New Mexico. **1927** H. Miller *Moloch* 154: He…stuck his gunboats up on the front of the car. **1941** Schulberg *Sammy* 68: So get those gunboats out of dry dock and get the hell over here. **1946** Mezzrow & Wolfe *Really Blues* 38: Hobnailed, high-topped gunboats weighing about ten pounds each. **1952** Sandburg *Strangers* 368: A few wore what we called "gunboats"— thick leather spread east and west under a man's foot soles. **1961** G. Forbes *Goodbye to Some* 134: No chintzy Jap is gonna steal my pet gunboats. **1970** in P. Heller *In This Corner* 34: Some sailor named me "The Gunboat" because I was supposed to have big feet. **1976** Conroy *Santini* 80: I'm gonna give you one more chance to answer that simple question before I stick this big ol' gunboat of yours into your left ear. **1982** R.M. Brown *So. Discomfort* 123: "Gunboats"…[was her] judgment on Blue Rhonda's not very delicate feet. **1987** *ALF* (NBC-TV): I could shoot the rapids in one of her gunboats!

2. *West.* a heavily armed stagecoach.

1878 Mulford *Fighting Indians* 66: The new Black Hills stages, or gunboats…consist of a very heavy and large stage with a 2-pound Mountain Howitzer on top. They also have twelve Winchester repeating rifles inside, with plenty of ammunition in little pockets near the windows, or rather portholes. These stages are run from Bismarck to the Black Hills, and despite all their arms and caution, are very frequently held up.

3. (esp. among tramps) a pail or similar vessel, usu. for carrying water.

1929 *AS* IV (June) 340: *Gunboat.* An empty gallon-size tin can. **1930** Irwin *Tramp & Und. Slang: Gunboat*….An empty tin can, used in the "jungles" for cooking, carrying water or liquor, or for boiling the clothes. **1965–66** Pynchon *Crying* 46: Guy in the scullery…in charge of all the heavy stuff, canner kettles, gunboats, Dutch ovens. **1976** Braly *False Starts* 115: We were supplied with a gunboat of water.

4. *R.R.* (see quots.).

1930 Irwin *Tramp & Und. Slang: Gun Boat*….A steel coal car. **1942** *ATS* 727: *Gunboat,*…a steel freight car.

5. a riverboat that serves as a brothel. Now *hist.*

1948 Mencken *Amer. Lang. Supp.* II 683: The Alexandria (Mo.) *Commercial,* June 22, 1876, reported the hanging of Bill Lee for the murder of Jessie McCarty, one of the crew of a Mississippi *gun-boat.*

gun boss *n.* **1.** a leader of a band of western gunmen.

1946 N. Nye *Chaparral* 26: This man was a gun boss. **1947** Overholser *Buckaroo's Code* 108: The gun boss was in no shape to make trouble.

2. *Navy.* a weapons officer.

1971 Windchy *Tonkin* 99 [ref. to 1964]: The weapons officer or "gun boss."

gun-bull *n. Pris.* a guard who is armed with a rifle and stationed on the prison wall.

1927–28 Tasker *Grimhaven* 42: Besides the gun-bulls in the sentry-boxes on the wall, there's a living chain of coppers around the whole place. **1933** Guest *Limey* 261: "Gun bulls" (guards who patrol the walls themselves). **1966** Braly *On Yard* 151: A gun bull…stood [by] the rail that ran along the top of the east block.

gun-bunny *n. Mil.* an artillery crewman; artilleryman.

1980 Cragg *L. Militaris* 208: *Gun Bunny.* An artilleryman. **1980** Cragg (letter to J.E.L., Aug. 10) 4: Current during Vietnam…."He's got it made in as a gun bunny." **1982** Del Vecchio *13th Valley* 399 [ref. to Vietnam War]: His words…set the FDC and the gun bunnies scurrying. **1986** *NDAS.* **1988** Clodfelter *Mad Minutes* 36 [ref. to 1965]: The gun bunnies' bunkers.

gun-bus *n.* [orig. the proper name of a British Vickers airplane of WWI] *Mil. Av.* an AC-47 or similar aircraft used to concentrate heavy gunfire on ground targets; gunship.

1966 Baxter *Search & Destroy* 34: A gun-bus is pictured below….These planes are used when a heavy concentration of VC is located, or a fortified hamlet is about to be overrun….They call their plane "Puff, the Magic Dragon."

gun-coop *n. Navy.* a gundeck.

1918 "Commander" *Clear the Decks* 82: Below him and scattered through the great bowels of the "gun-coop" were nearly a hundred men braced and waiting to feed the huge steel breeches with powder and shell.

gundeck *adj. Navy.* consisting of false show or fakery; intended to deceive.

1923 Southgate *Rusty Door* 110: All this gun-deck talk! Give an ear now and I'll be addin' to your eddycation. *a***1951** Wouk *Caine Mutiny* 200:

Try to see why Willie has written a perfect report whereas yours is a phony gundeck job. **1964** Howe *Valley of Fire* 33 [ref. to Korean War]: Greaves was a shit-artist…trying to work some kind of a phony gundeck deal back at battalion headquarters.

gundeck *v. Navy.* **1.** to bluff or fake, esp. to write up (a report) or fill out (forms) on the basis of guesswork or careless procedure. Hence **gundecker.**

1933 in *U.S. Naval Inst. Proc.* (Jan. 1934) 22: Every ship has a few incorrigibles, "ship's louses," A.O.L.'s, non-regs, skylarkers, gun-deckers, etc. *a*1951 Wouk *Caine Mutiny* 236 [ref. to WWII]: The Navy!…nothing but phony kowtowing and gun-decking and idiot drills. **1951** Morris *China Station* 168: This cavalier treatment of paperwork was known as "gundecking" and was more or less common throughout the fleet. There were too many reports required to cope with them all properly. **1971** Noel & Bush *Naval Terms* 134: *Gundeck:* Slang: to fake or falsify something, such as a report. To pretend to be drunk. **1976–79** H.G. Duncan & W.T. Moore *Green Side Out* 143: When confronted with gross stupidity…don't get excited. Gundeck the damn thing and give them an answer. Never do it with something important. **1988** Poyer *Med* 15: This always happens when the goddamn BMs gundeck their maintenance. **1990** G.R. Clark *Wds. of Viet. War* 212: *Gundecking* Falsification of operational reports.

2. *Specif.* to pretend to be drunk or drunker than one actually is; SMOKESTACK.

1941 *Guide to U.S. Naval Acad.* 151: *Gundeck.* To feign intoxication. **1944** Kendall *Service Slang* 24: *Gundecking*….pretending intoxication. **1962** McKenna *Sand Pebbles* 448 [ref. to 1920's]: The deckforce called it "gundecking." It was a thing kids did. They came off liberty pretending to be drunker than they really were….They would…curse the navy and the officers and all the petty officers they didn't like. They could get away with it because they were drunk. **1971** (quot. at **(1)**, above).

gundeck savage *n. Navy.* (see quot.).

1918 Ruggles *Navy Explained* 66: *Gundeck savage.* A gun deck mess cook, probably better known as a gun deck slusser. In civil life, a waiter.

gun doctor *n. Navy.* a gunner's mate.

1914 *DN* IV 150: Navy Slang…*Gun doctor*…Gunner's mate. **1941** Kendall *Army & Navy Slang* 20: *Gun doctor*….a gunner's mate.

gun dog *n. West.* a gunman, esp. a gunfighter.

1947 Overholser *Buckaroo's Code* 139: The two others were strangers, more gun dogs Abernethy had brought in. **1953** R. Chandler *Goodbye* 126: I've been…a nice, faithful, well-behaved gun dog all day long. **1959** Conquest *Granite Hendley* 26: I remembered the remarks people had made after he'd gotten Barney —"hoodlum," "gundog," "killer."

gun down *v.* **1.** to spurn; reject; *(hence)* refute completely.

1968 Baker et al. *CUSS* 132: *Gunned down.* Turned down when asking for a date. **1972** Univ. Wisc. students: He asked her out twice and she gunned him down twice. **1989** *USA Today* (Feb. 22) 4A: President Bush said the FBI report "gunned down" allegations about Tower.

2. *Baseball.* to throw out (a runner).

1976 *Webster's Sports Dict.*: *Gun down*…To throw out a player especially when he is attempting to steal, [etc.]. **1977** P. Rizzuto on *N.Y. Yankees Baseball* (WPIX-TV) (Aug. 24): Munson gunned him down. **1978** *N.Y. Post* (June 28) 110: The Red Sox rightfielder…gunned down Reggie Jackson at the plate. **1983** L. Frank *Hardball* 92: A player who has been thrown out on the bases…is said to have been "gunned down" or "wiped out."

gun dummy *n. Mil.* GUN-BUNNY.—used derisively.

1988 Dye *Outrage* 113 [ref. to 1983]: Them…gun dummies is gonna *get some* in a minute.

gun-fanner *n. West.* a person who wears and uses a pistol, esp. a gunfighter. Now *hist.*

1903 in *DA*: They were glad to chip in…for the right gun fanner [marshall]. **1931** Haycox *Whispering Range* 154: Another slick-eared gun fanner from other parts.

gunflint *n.* (see quot.).

1845 in *DA*: The inhabitants of…Rhode Island [are called] Gun Flints.

gunge[1] *n. Narc.* GUNGEON; *(also)* heroin.

[**1883** *Harper's Mag.* (Nov.) 945: Gunjeh (the dried tops and leaves of the hemp plant) for smoking. *Ibid.* 946: The dried shrub is known here [N.Y.C.] as *gunjeh*.] **1972** *Prison Poetry* 35: Heroin…called… horse…dope…gunge. *a*1979 Pepper & Pepper *Straight Life* 67 [ref. to *ca*1945]: Every now and then I'd run into some pot. They had what they called Gunje, which was black. **1985** Univ. Tenn. student theme: Marijuana [is referred to as]…*hemp, herb, gunge,…smoke* [etc.].

gunge[2] *n.* **1.** GRUNGE, 1.

***1965** (cited in Partridge *DSUE* (ed. 8) 513). **1971** E. Sanders *Family* 104: And there was no hesitance…to get down and grovel in the gunge of large bins of rotting animal and vegetable matter in order to sort out the good from the less good. ***a*1987** in *World Bk. Dict.*: They call this solid material tholin…but it seems likely that chemists will continue to call this rather familiar material "gunge."

2. (see quots.).

1984 Elting et al. *Soldier Talk* 142: *Gunge*…(Vietnam)…A mythical tropical disease, generally described as a venereal infection that made a man rot "from his genitals outward." *a*1989 Spears *NTC Dict. Slang* 164: *Gunge*…a skin irritation in the groin.…Said of males.

gungeon *n.* [alter. *ganja*] *Narc.* potent marijuana. Also **gungion.**

1944 LaGuardia Comm. *Marihuana* 9: "Gungeon" is considered by the marihuana smoker as the highest grade of marihuana. **1962** Crump *Killer* 276: Pot—weed—gungion—Mexico joints. **1970** Major *Afro-Amer. Slang* 62: *Gungeon*…potent marijuana…from Africa or Jamaica.

gung-ho *n.* [functional shift of *Gung Ho*, motto (interpreted to mean "Work together!") of U.S. Marine Corps Second Raider Battalion, introduced 1942 by Lt. Col. Evans F. Carlson; < Mandarin *kung*[1]*-ho*[2] 'Industrial Cooperatives', erroneously analyzed as an imper. sentence formed from *kung*[1] 'work' + *ho*[2] 'peace, harmony'; see full discussion by A.F. Moe, *AS* XLII (1967), 19–30] Orig. *USMC.* a spirit of teamwork, courage, and wholehearted dedication.

1942 *Yank* (Sept. 23) 20: The Marine commandos have a new battle cry, "Gung Ho!" It's Chinese for "Work Together." **1942** *N.Y. Times Mag.* (Nov. 8) 13: Borrowing an idea from China, Carlson frequently has what he calls "kung-hou" meetings. "Kung-hou" means cooperation. **1943** E.F. Carlson, in *Liberty* (Nov. 10) 67: Believe me, the farther we got into the jungle and hand-to-hand battle, the more we leaned on *gung ho.* [**1943** Hubbard *Gung Ho* (film): The Chinese have a word for it: "gung," to work; "ho," in harmony. *Gung ho.*] **1947** Blankfort *Big Yankee* 28: "Training and Gung Ho is everything," they heard…[Lt. Col. Carlson] say over and over again. *Ibid.* 33: He preached Gung Ho until the phrase became part of their living. Men loading a truck would yell to a Raider passing by, "Hey, Mac. How about a little Gung Ho on the box?" *Ibid.* 299: The civilians had some of our Gung Ho. **1952** *Marine Corps Gaz.* (Nov.) 74: *Gung-Ho*…Aggressive esprit de corps. **1956** in *AS* XLII (1967) 22: This was *gung ho* in practice. **1965** in *Ibid.* 25: Despite nine years as middle traffic cop in the linebacking division, Huff is still full of gung-ho. **1968** Safire *New Lang. Pol.* 178: *Gung ho.* enthusiasm undampened by experience, often shown by a political volunteer. *a*1987 in *World Book Dict.*: When the Corps was born, there was…much gung ho about reforming the world.

gung-ho *adj.* **1.** Orig. *USMC.* exemplifying or imbued with the qualities of teamwork, courage, and wholehearted dedication. [The 1942 quots. may be later interpolations to the original diary.]

[**1942** in C.R. Bond & T. Anderson *Flying T. Diary* 98: Bob is a gung-ho guy. *Ibid.* 127: A clever little insignia. Of course it is a cross of a tiger shark…, the Asian tiger, and the tiger spirit of a gung-ho American fighter pilot.] **1943** E.F. Carlson, in *Life* (Sept. 20) 58: My motto caught on and they began to call themselves the *Gung Ho* Battalion. When I designed a field jacket to replace the bulky and orthodox pack they called it the *Gung Ho* jacket. And they named every new thing *Gung Ho.* **1943** E.F. Carlson, in *Liberty* (Nov. 20) 67: Finally we adopted *gung ho* as a yardstick. Any action was *gung ho* or it wasn't. To help a man out of a tight spot, to jump in and do anything that needed doing without asking whose turn it was to do it—that was *gung ho.* **1947** Blankfort *Big Yankee* 21: But no one became Gung Ho in a day or a week or in months. *Ibid.* 33: His ambition was to be a Gung Ho citizen even after the war. *Ibid.* 300: One son-of-a-bitch wasn't Gung Ho. **1958** Frankel *Band of Bros.* 5 [ref. to Korean War]: Real gung-ho gyrenes. **1962** in *AS* XLII (1967) 25: This is the best bunch of guys [baseball players] I've ever been with. Talk about spirit, man, we're really some sort of Gung-Ho. **1975** *N.Y. Times Mag.* (June 15) 4: There's a gung-ho spirit in the army now. **1975** in Higham & Siddall *Combat Aircraft* 34: Most crews were gung ho. **1976** *N.Y. Times* (Sept. 12) 23: The Brooklyn-born police officer…was described as a "gung ho cop" who had participated in the dismantling of many explosive devices. **1987** *N.Y. Times* (July 7) A 27: A young, gung-ho marine colonel, an energetic worker in the N.S.C. vineyard.

2. *Mil.* offensive or obnoxious, esp. ardently or offensively

warlike or confident; (*also*) ultrazealous or perfervid, esp. in the carrying out of orders or the enforcement of regulations.
1952 *Marine Corps Gaz.* (Nov.) 74: Gung-Ho…sometimes sardonically employed to characterize cocky indiscipline or contempt toward orthodox procedures and regulations. **1953** in Russ *Last Parallel* 68: I was surprised to hear the phrase "gung ho" used seriously. Although it is the unofficial battle cry of the Corps, it is almost always used sarcastically. **1955** *AS* XXX 117: [U.S. Air Force slang] *Gung ho, adj.* eager to adhere to the letter of the regulation. **1956** *AS* XXXI 191: An individual—usually an officer—who is overly zealous about performing duties in strict accord with prescribed regulations is disgustedly described as *gung ho*. **1956** Hargrove *Girl He Left* 76: I've seen some gung-ho outfits in my day…but this one is the worst. I stood out there and listened to those people, and my lower lip was hanging down to here. **1960** Bluestone *Cully* 56: Hey, Powers, you goin' gung-ho? **1965** Bryan *P.S. Wilkinson* 8: Jesus Christ what a time to call an alert!…What kind of gung-ho chickenshit is this now? **1966–67** Harvey *Air War* 87: I'm not a bit gung-ho and I like to go on patrols that are exciting but safe. **1967** *AS* XLII 24: As early as the latter part of 1942, Marines other than those in the Second Raider Battalion used *gung ho* as a term of disparagement to describe anyone whose conduct was obnoxious or offensive. **1968** Spooner *War in General* 24: The gung-ho bastard.
3. *Broadly*, very eager or enthusiastic.
1955 *AS* XXX 117: [U.S. Air Force slang] *Gung ho, adj.* Enthusiastic. **1957** Gutwillig *Long Silence* 143: He seems like a nice enough guy, maybe a little *gung-ho*. **1958** J. Davis *College Vocab.* 9: *Gung ho*—Full of feeling and zest for a certain subject. **1959** *AS* (May) 155: *Gungho*…means that the person has gone overboard about something—his car, his girl, a course, anything. **1960** Swarthout *Where the Boys Are* 55: If you are gung-ho and shoot for A's, that puts you in the grind category. **1961** Gover *$100 Misunderstanding* 105: Prof. Wilbur…[is] all gung-ho about current events. **1965** in *AS* XLII (1967) 24: Are any of you gentlemen really gung-ho for Bold Lad [a racehorse]? **1965** in *Ibid.* 25: Some brothers are…*gung-ho* about changing certain fraternity traditions. **1967** in Safire *New Lang. Pol.* 178: People are getting a bit gung ho for the City of New York, which is good. **1979** C. Freeman *Portraits* 272: Boy, you're a real gung-ho character. **1980** M. Baker *Nam* 28: Hospitals aren't too gung-ho to hire you if you don't have a master's degree or experience of any kind.

gung-ho *adv.* vigorously and successfully.
1987 *RHD2*: The business is going gung-ho.

gung-ho *v.* Orig. *USMC.* to behave or perform in a GUNG-HO manner.
1958 Frankel *Band of Bros.* 73 [ref. to Korean War]: We're going to have to gung-ho up there. *Ibid.* 83: We gotta go gung-hoin' again. **1959** *Sat. Eve. Post* (Jan. 24) 68: I'd rather expected him to *gung-ho* his way, headfirst into danger. *a*1987 in *World Book Dict.*: His son intended to gung ho for the Peace Corps.

gung-ho cap *n.* *USMC.* a garrison cap. Cf. first 1943 quot. at GUNG-HO, *adj.*, 1.
1967 W. Crawford *Gresham's War* 35 [ref. to 1953]: I nodded and pinned the third bar on my gung-ho cap, centered under the faded black globe and anchor emblem.

gung-ho jacket *n.* *USMC.* a field jacket of a design introduced by Lt. Col. Evans F. Carlson.
1943 (quot. at GUNG-HO, *adj.*, 1).

gungy[1] /ˈɡʌŋi/ *adj.* *USMC.* GUNG-HO, 1, 2.
1961 Peacock *Valhalla* 19 [ref. to 1953]: "Was that why you shipped over?"…"I'm a gungy bastard." **1964** Peacock *Drill & Die* 188 [ref. to Korean War]: But he's only a corporal, and he's too goddam gungy. Thinks this Crotch is God. **1969** M. Lane *Conversations* 135: Lieutenant Johnson was a really blue lieutenant. Very gungy. **1976** C.R. Anderson *Grunts* 39 [ref. to 1969]: If someone is "gungi," he's all right, it's good to have him on our side, he's afraid of nothing, he never gets tired, he can be counted on to help in any tight situation, and he's probably a little crazy. The gungi individual also likes to kill a little more than is necessary. **1978** J. Webb *Fields of Fire* 270: Baby Cakes was too gungy….He could live without Baby Cakes' boasts and bravado. **1979** Hiler *Monkey Mt.* 7: He…does this neat little about-face and scoots his gungy butt outta there!

gungy[2] /ˈɡʌndʒi/ *adj.* dirty; grimy; SCUNGY; sticky; (*hence*) poor; inferior.
*1962 in *OED2*: This policy was rewarded by five sixes [in cricket, the equivalent of a home run] (two of them at least rather gungy ones). **1971** E. Sanders *Family* 260: Charlie was attired in gungy blue jeans.

1975 V.B. Miller *Deadly Game* 27: Six stories of brick, gungy windows, and peeling paint. **1979* T. Jones *Wayward Sailor* 76: With his gungy seaman's cap at a swashbuckling angle. [**a*1984 Partridge *DSUE* (ed. 8) 513: *Gungey* = "second-rate, inferior, spoiled," was current in [English] theological collegs, 1960s.]

gun hand *n.* **1.** a western gunman; gunfighter.
1956 Overholser *Desperate* 19: Runyan's got a couple of gun hands with him. **1971** G. Wilson *Lawman* (film): Choctaw's a gun-hand. He's fast and likes his work. **1976** L'Amour *Long Grass* 9: Gunhand…or cowhand? **1991** "R. Brown" & R. Angus *A.K.A. Narc.* 112: Especially you being a gunhand and all that.
2. *Racquetball.* the hand that holds the racquet.
1979 Frommer *Sports Lingo* 175.

gun-happy *adj.* [gun + -HAPPY] relishing or given to the shooting of firearms; (*often*) TRIGGER-HAPPY.
1951 Thacher *Captain* 21 [ref. to WWII]: The bastard's so gun-happy, he can't stay off the deck, hopin' for action. **1951** Bowers *Mob* (film): Claig's a little gun-happy isn't he? **1963** Gant *Queen St.* 104: Some gun-happy punk. **1974** R. Novak *Concrete Cage* 165: You gun-happy ape. **1979** Jenison *Kingdom in Sage* 20: You tamed down that gun-happy bastard at the bar. *a*1986 K.W. Nolan *Into Laos* 105: So gunhappy that they…fired their rifles like toys. **1987** D. Sherman *Main Force* 207: You boys must be real gun happy, the way you're running around killing water boo and chickens and burning down hootches.

gunhawk *n.* GUN-SHARP.
1946 N. Nye *Chaparral* 139: Tune and Jack's gun hawks shooting it out? **1947** Overholser *Buckaroo's Code* 36: Now mebbe you can tell me why you've been paying fighting wages to gunhawks like Harriman's crew. **1964** in Jackson *Swim Like Me* 65: Now this wasn't no talk to a deadly gunhawk. **1972–76** Lynde *Rick O'Shay* (unp.): Make your play, gunhawk. Hit it! **1983** "J.R. Roberts" *Silver War* 65: The young gunhawk…thrust his Colt into its holster.

gunk *n.* [fr. *Gunk*, a trademark for liquid soaps and degreasing solvents (patented 1932)] **1.** thick, viscous, sticky or messy matter; (now *esp.*) thick grease or dirt, or smelly or repulsive matter.
1938 in Conklin *Sci. Fic. Omnibus* 11: Oliveira got a bunch of hairless Chihuahua dogs and tried assorted gunks on them, but nothing happened. **1945** in *Calif. Folk. Qly.* V (1946) 381: Dehydrated vegetables [are] known [in the Navy] as *gunk* or *garbage*. **1946** in Legman *Limerick* 108: The ship was sunk/In a wave of gunk/From mutual masturbation. **1949** in *OEDS*: You can actually see the gook and gunk that drains out with your [motor] oil. **1954** J.D. MacDonald *Condemned* 94: Not making people smell better, not selling more gunk, not kidding the public with phony art. **1956** Metalious *Peyton Place* 144: She looks cheap in that sleazy red dress, and she's wearing gunk on her eyelashes. **1956** Hargrove *Girl He Left* 155: Well, go clean that gunk off you. **1961** Sullivan *Shortest, Gladdest Years* 241: Will one of you rub some of this gunk on my back? **1961** Gover *$100 Misunderstanding* 157: Just take it out for a spin…and blow the gunk out of its huge engine. **1968** *Newsweek* (Nov. 11) 107: He watches red gunk being spewed into a river. **1972** Meade & Rutledge *Belle* 119: An invisible shield like they used to have on television to keep gunk off your teeth. **1976** W. Johnston *Sweathog Trail* 24: We don't want to buy an apple pie that's all pastry and gunk and no apples. **1979** *AS* (Spring) 37: A patient…may *fill up with* "accumulate" *gunk* "greenish secretions." **1982** Rucker *57th Kafka* 64: The gunk was gone anyway.
2. nonsense.
1946 J.H. Burns *Gallery* 345: I could always tell you nearly any ole gunk that came into my head. **1968** in *OEDS*: It was a drag to listen big-eyed to that tired gunk and say Oh and Ahh.

gunkhole *n.* [gunk (orig. unkn.) + hole] *Naut.* a small, sheltered cove.
1908 in *OEDS*: Only a two-cent little dead-and-alive gunk-hole of a place. **1927* in *OEDS*. **1939** Willoughby *Sondra* 83: When a big school works into some sheltered gunk-hole. **1958** in *OEDS*.

gunkholer *n.* *Naut.* a person who engages in GUNKHOLING.
1976 *Webster's Sports Dict.* 196.

gunkholing *n.* *Naut.* shallow-water sailing along a coastline in a small boat.
1965 Pearson *Lure of Sailing* 313: Gunkholing. Shallow water sailing. **1976** *Webster's Sports Dict.* 196.

gunk up *v.* to foul with GUNK.
1961 Granat *Important Thing* 157: Goddamn gun goes right in

the…mud, gets all gunked up with crap. **1966–67** Harvey *Air War* 39: On one corner…were some very beatup-looking twin-engine airplanes, gunked up with a film of something or other. **1984** "W.T. Tyler" *Shadow Cabinet* 192: All gunked up with tar and oil.

gunky *adj.* being, covered with, or resembling GUNK.

1976 W. Johnston *Sweathog Trail* 50: Gunky cereal, gunky pie, gunky soda, gunky gunk.

gun-maker *n.* [fr. GUN², *n.*, punning on the S.E. term] *Und.* (see quot.).

1904 *Life in Sing Sing* 355: *Gun-maker.*—A Fagin; instructor of young thieves. **1934** D.W. Maurer, in *AS* (Feb. 1935) 16 [ref. to a1910]: *Gun-smith* or *gun-maker.* One who trains young criminals, especially pickpockets.

gunman *n.* (see quot.).

1951 Shidle *Clear Writing* 93: *Gunmen*…Electric welders.

gun moll *n.* [orig. GUN², *n.* + MOLL; later uses reflect var. senses of GUN¹, *n.*] **1.** *Und.* a woman who is a professional thief or criminal, esp. a pickpocket; (*later*) a woman who carries a gun, esp. a female gunman.

1908 Sullivan *Crim. Slang* 2: *A gun-moll*—A woman thief. **1910** *Nat. Police Gaz.* (Dec. 31) 3: The professional woman thief…is known to the denizens of the underworld as a gun moll. **1913** Kneeland *Prostitution in N.Y.C.* 40: The most successful prostitutes who solicit for these hotels are "gun mols," that is, pickpockets. **1915** Bronson-Howard *God's Man* 126: What…did the arrival of any mere "gun moll," no matter how proficient in her profession or attractive in her person, mean in his young life? **1918** Livingston *Delcassee* 44: *Gun Moll*…A dangerous woman tramp. **1925** in Partridge *Dict. Und.* 314: *Gun Moll*…A woman who carries a revolver. **1927** *DN* V 449: *Gun moll*, n. (1) A *lady-yegg.* (2) A female tramp of non-criminal proclivities who merely carries a gun as insurance against the courtesy of train crews and yard dicks. **1928** Sharpe *Chicago May* 286: *Gun Molls*, or *Trips*—women who steal from men in the street, or carry guns. **1930** Conwell *Pro. Thief* 44: The term "gun" is still used to refer to pickpockets, and the female pickpocket who operates upon men is called a "gun-moll." **1932** L. Berg *Prison Doctor* 215: She was a gun moll for Big Tony's mob. Furs were their racket. **1942–49** Goldin et al. *DAUL* 88: Some red-headed gun-moll is heisting…all the little jugs…out West with two punks. **1949** in *DA*: Teen-age gun molls—more vicious than their male companions—are reported operating in Brooklyn. **2.** the mistress or female accomplice of a gunman, thief, or gangster.

1928 O'Connor *B'way Racketeers* ix: One brushes by the fur-robed gun moll, leaning on the arm of her boy friend, the key-man in a pay-off mob. **1930** Lait *On the Spot* 204: *Gun-moll*…A thief's woman. (Not a woman who carries a revolver!) **1930** Irwin *Tramp & Und. Slang: Gun Moll*…A crook's consort. **1933** Ersine *Pris. Slang* 42: *Gun-moll*…A gunman's woman. She sometimes carries his *rod.* **1948** Mencken *Amer. Lang.* Supp. II 670: During the Golden Age of the Dillingers the newspapers took to calling a racketeer's girl a *gun-moll*, but this was an error. **1948** in M. Shulman *Dobie Gillis* 19: "You thought about becoming a gun moll?" I asked. **1979** Gutcheon *New Girls* 248: Their girl friends sat like gun molls on the passenger seats. *a***1988** C. Adams *More Straight Dope* 19: *Mary Burns, Fugitive*, a 1935 gun-moll story directed by William K. Howard.

gunner *n.* **1.** *Stu.* one who aggressively seeks attention, affection, or sexual involvement.

1926 Maines & Grant *Wise-Crack Dict.* 8: *Gunner*—Girl out for conquest. **1959** Maier *College Terms* 4: *Gunner*—[socially] active guy. **1968** Baker et al. *CUSS* 132: *Gunner.* A sexually expert male. **2.** *Craps.* the player whose turn it is to roll the dice; shooter.

1930 D. Runyon, in *Sat. Eve. Post* (Apr. 5) 5: Who is the gunner? **3.** *Basketball.* an aggressive player who shoots frequently.

1966 Neugeboren *Big Man* 100: What's the matter, you afraid I'm too good for you? Don't worry, I'm not a gunner. I'll pass off to you, so you can be the star. **1972** N.Y.U. student: *A gunner* is a guy who always gets his shot in the basket. **1980** Wielgus & Wolff *Basketball* 45: *Gunner* (*n.*) A player who enjoys shooting. Connotes some degree of success. **1981** Univ. Tenn. prof., age *ca*35: I can recall *gunner* as a basketball term being used in Pittsburgh as early as 1960. **1988** Frazier & Offen *W. Frazier* 71: When Dick McGuire was the Knick coach, Barnett was his designated gunner. **1989** *Rage* (Knoxville, Tenn.) (Feb.) 15: But let's leave the three pointers to the gunners, all right? **1991** W. Chamberlain *View from Above* 162: It is assumed that if you are a great scorer you must be a gunner.

4. *Stu.* a student who competes aggressively for high marks.

1972 Eble *Campus Slang* (Oct.) 3: *Gunner*—one who really works for grades in school. **1980** Santoli *Everything* 114: I can criticize people today, like at law school…, for being so competitive.…They were called "gunners," would do things just to make sure they got a better grade. **5.** *USMC.* a warrant officer.

1976–79 H.G. Duncan & W.T. Moore *Green Side Out* xxiii: *Gunner*—Misused term of affection for all warrant officers.

gunner's daughter *n. Navy.* a deck gun over which a ship's boy or a sailor may be flogged.—usu. constr. with *kiss* or *marry.* Now *hist.*

*****1785** Grose *Vulgar Tongue: To kiss the gunner's daughter:* to be tied to a gun and flogged on the posteriors, a mode of punishing boys on board a ship of war. **1803** in Whiting *Early Amer. Provs.* 189: Marry him to the gunner's daughter. **1836** *Naval Mag.* (Nov.) 517: Reader! thou beholdest in the picture, the spar-deck of a sloop-of-war, part of the main rigging, a couple of belaying pins to throw the bight of this yarn over, and "No. 6," or "the Gunner's daughter," whom many a lad has kissed to his sorrow. *****1873** Hotten *Slang Dict.* (ed. 4): The method of punishing boys in the Royal Navy [is] by tying them securely to the breech of a cannon, so as to present the proper part convenient for the cat, and flogging them. This is called "marrying" or "kissing" the *gunner's daughter.* **1883** Russell *Sailors' Lang.* 63: *Gunner's daughter.*—The gun to which boys were lashed for punishment. *ca***1890** Melville *Billy Budd* ch. xii: "Such sneaks I should like to marry to the gunner's daughter!" by that expression meaning that he would like to subject them to disciplinary castigation over a gun. **1896** Hamblen *Many Seas* 219: By the time he is "married to the gunner's daughter," he is in condition to enjoy every stroke of the cat. *Ibid.* 228: He was married hard and fast to the gunner's daughter, with his bare back turned up to the wintry sun.

gunny¹ *n.* **1.** a gunman or gunfighter.

1926 Finerty *Crim.* 23: *Gunie*—A crook who will kill. **1932** (cited in Partridge *Dict. Und.* 799). **1950** Bowers & Sellers *Gunfighter* (film): I want you to see what it means to have to live like a big tough gunny. **1958** J. Ward *Buchanan* 53: For all the rep you're supposed to have, I never saw a more cautious gunny. **1966–67** W. Stevens *Gunner* 219: Range instructors strutting around like cowtown gunnies. **1967** in S. Lee *Son of Origins* 76: Iron Man is mopping the place up with the Big M's gunnies! **1979** Jenison *Kingdom in Sage* 62: Brett…watched his gunnies beat up a poor homesteader that didn't have a chance. **2.** *USMC.* a gunnery sergeant; (*hence*) a technical sergeant.

1931 *Leatherneck* (Oct.) 20: Good Luck, "Gunny!" **1942** *Leatherneck* (Nov.) 146: *Gunny*—Gunnery Sergeant. **1957** Herber *Tomorrow to Live* 12: The Gunny was talking. **1961** Coon *Meanwhile at the Front* 54: The gunny may be old but he's not dead. *ca***1930–73** E. Mackin *Suddenly Didn't Want to Die* 235 [ref. to 1918]: Gunny Johnston said, "…Nevuh mind the goddamn souvenirs." **1982** R.A. Anderson *Cooks & Bakers* 91: The gunnies were like right-hand men, older and more experienced. *a***1989** C.S. Crawford *Four Deuces* 15: Most technical sergeants were called "Gunny," a…holdover from an earlier time when there was such a rank in the marines. **3.** *Shooting.* (see quot.).

1957 *AS* XXXII 193: *Gunny.* A gun enthusiast. **4.a.** *Mil.* a member of the crew of a helicopter gunship.

1980 Cragg *L. Militaris* 209: *Gunnie.* An aviator who pilots a gunship. **1984** Holland *Let Soldier* 19 [ref. to 1967]: Not a bad landing for a gunnie. **1987** "J. Hawkins" *Tunnel Warriors* 17: The "Void Vicious"—as many gunnies called the hostile rain forest. **b.** *Mil.* a helicopter gunship.

1983 Groen & Groen *Huey* 78 [ref. to 1970]: Gunnies, Charlie-model gunships, stayed aloft, providing covering fire for troop carriers. **1989** R. Miller *Profane Men* 11: A lethal gunny out of the armed chopper company at Quang Tri.

gunny² *n.* [GUN(GEON) + -y] *Black E.* potent marijuana, esp. from Africa or the Caribbean.

1968–70 *Current Slang* III & IV 63: They were caught with gunny in their possession. **1972** in Dillard *Lexicon* 96: *Gunny* [is] an old word which identifies a particularly strong form of marijuana found in Jamaica and Africa. **1967–80** Folb *Runnin' Lines* 241: *Gunny.* Marijuana.

gun-oil gravy *n. Army.* unappetizing gravy. *Joc.*

1898 in McManus *Soldier Life* 85: Regulation potatoes boiled in jackets, coffee, bread, beef and "gun-oil" gravy.

gun-plumber *n. Mil. Av.* an aircraft armorer.

*a*1989 R. Herman, Jr. *Warbirds* 153: The crew chief punched out a gun-plumber for not inspecting the cannon.

gunpoke *n.* [sugg. by COWPOKE] a gunman or gunfighter. Also **gunpoker**.
1905 *Nat. Police Gaz.* (Dec. 9) 7: That law murderin' gunpoker. **1938** R. Chandler *Big Sleep* 92: He lets you win a lot of money and sends a gunpoke around to take it back for him.

gunpowder *n. Black E.* (see quot.).
1983 *Reader's Digest Success with Words* 85: Black English...*gunpowder* = "gin."

gunpowder tea *n.* gunfire.
1865 Byrn *Fudge Fumble* 51: "Old Hickory" was giving the British gunpowder-tea in real "Yankee style."

Guns *n. Mil.* gunner; gunnery officer; gunner's mate.—usu. as a nickname in direct address.
***1896** R. Kipling, in *OED:* There was no one like 'im, 'Orse or Foot/ Nor any o' the Guns I knew. ***1916** in *OEDS:* Gunnery...lieutenant..."Guns." **1945** in *Calif. Folk. Qly.* V (1946) 384: *Guns* (gunner's mate). ***1950** Granville *Sea Slang* 116: Oh, Guns, will you make up a party for bridge tonight? **1967** Dibner *Admiral* 96: Thanks, Guns. Label 'em Target B and C. **1974** former USAF officer [ref. to WWII]: A [B-17] gunner was usually called "Guns." **1976** S. Lawrence *Northern Saga* 152: "What you say, Guns?" The gunner's mate drew coffee.

gunsel *n.* [prob. < Yid *gendzl* 'gosling', with vowel fr. a blend with E *gun* in slang or S.E. senses] **1.a.** (esp. among tramps) a boy; raw youth.—used derisively.
1910 Livingston *Life* 64 [ref. to *ca*1885]: Reform? None of such wise talk from a little "Gunsel" (young boy) like you. **1914** Jackson & Hellyer *Vocab.* 40: Gunshel, Noun. Current among yeggs chiefly. A boy; a youth; a neophyte of trampdom. **1918** Livingston *Delcassee* 44: Gonsil...Youth not yet adopted by jocker. **1919** Hinman *Ranging in France* 99: Our first casualty was Private Marousek, better known as "Gunsel." **1921** Casey & Casey *Gay-Cat* 209: The foxy varmint, the slick little gunsel! **1927** *AS* II 387: Guntzel...any sort of green lad. **1929** Hammett *Maltese Falcon* ch. xi: Keep that gunsel away from me. **1967** Decker *To Be a Man* 170: Besides, all that gunsel can do is put a fast rein on a horse. **1980** Ciardi *Browser's Dict.* 155: Gonzel kid...A young punk [worthless youth]. William Decker, an editor of Viking Press, reports its use in this sense by an old Oregon cowhand in 1930.
b. (among tramps and convicts) a catamite; (*hence*) a usu. young homosexual man.—usu. used derisively.
1918 in *AS* (Oct. 1933) 27: Gonzel. Catamite. **1928** Panzram *Killer* 157: A gunsel is a punk and a punk is a poofter and a poofter is a pratter and a pratter is similar to a fruiter. The only difference between the two is that one likes to "sit" on it, and the other likes to "eat" it. **1931–34** in Clemmer *Pris. Commun.* 332: Gunsel, *n.* A young, male homosexual. **1934** Berg *Prison Nurse* 64: Why, that hussy has become the worst gonsil in the place. There isn't anything "she" won't do. **1935** Algren *Boots* 187: Ah ain't seen mah gonsil since. **1939** *AS* (Oct.) 240: Guncel. Male homosexual. **1966** Herbert *Fortune & Men's Eyes* 13: He means Gunsel's Alley. Too bad all the queers don't make it there. **1980** Bruns *Kts. of Road* 96: But begging was not the only mission of the yegg gunsel.
2. a stupid or contemptible fellow. [The folk etymology sugg. in first 1974 quot. likens the word to pronuns. such as *fores'l* 'foresail', *mains'l* 'mainsail', etc.]
1932 *N.Y. Times* (Mar. 27) 28: Gunsel—Either a stupid or a treacherous person. It apparently comes from the Yiddish word "gantzel," a gosling. **1935** *Amer. Mercury* (June) 229: Gunzel: fool; inaccurately spelled *gunsel* occasionally. *Ibid.* 231: Case that gunzel with the gray hat. **1967** Maurer & Vogel *Narc. & Narc. Add.* (ed. 3) 361: Gunsel. A disgusting person. **1974** Retired ship's captain, age *ca*70, N.Y.C.: We called a stupid sailor a *guns'l*—because a gun has no sail. **1974** N.Y.C. barmaid: My girlfriend's father calls everybody he doesn't like a real gunsel—it means a creep.
3. [sense infl. by GUN, *n.*, 6, GUNSLINGER, etc., and prob. is a misunderstanding of bracketed 1941 quot., which attests (**1.a.**), above] a gunman; thug.
[**1941** J. Huston *Maltese Falcon* (film): Let's give them the gunsel. He actually did shoot Thursby and Jacoby, didn't he?] **1943** B. Halliday *Mummer's Mask* 46: The back of the gunsel's head thumped against the wall. **1951** S.J. Perelman, in *New Yorker* (Mar. 3) 26: The lives of the pair...are forever being sought by scores of hoodlums, gunsels, [etc.]. **1953** in Cannon *Like 'Em Tough* 100: Was the pin-striped gunsel one of your boys? **1957** Hall *Cloak & Dagger* 143: Those six gunsels would have killed him in a minute if they'd known he was a plant. **1961** Anhalt

& Miller *Young Savages* (film): I went to school with some of the worst gunsels in town. **1981** Sann *Trial* 111: The reformed gunzl took a quick gander around. **1981** O'Day & Eells *High Times* 260: He'd arranged for the bouncer to send over two gunzels....Each wore a .45 in a holster.

gun-sharp *n. West.* a person, esp. a gunfighter, who is expert in the use of a pistol. Also **gun-shark**.
1902 in Kipling *Traffics & Discoveries* 6: You are not a gun-sharp? **1934** Cunningham *Triggernometry* 203: They claim that they knew many a gun-sharp the equal of Wild Bill Hickock. *a*1944 R. Adams *West. Words: Gun shark.* One expert in the use of a gun. **1980** Hogan *Lawman's Choice* 7: Looks more like a gun-shark to me.

gunslick *n.* GUN-SHARP; GUNSLINGER.
1932 (cited in Partridge *Dict. Und.* 799). **1947** Overholser *Buckaroo's Code* 21: All that time you've had Keno Harriman and his gunslicks on the pay roll. **1956** Overholser *Desperate* 29: This is the first time he ever brought a gunslick like Sammy Blue. **1966** Purdum *Bro. John* 20: Meanest bunch of gunslicks in the Territory!

gunslinger *n.* **1.** a western gunfighter; gunman. Now *S.E.*
1928 (cited in *W10*). **1931** Haycox *Whispering Range* 160: You're one of Redmain's imported gunslingers. **1932** Z. Grey *Robbers' Roost* 43: Stud Smith...is somethin' of a gun-slinger. **1932** (cited in Partridge *Dict. Und.* 799). *a*1936 in R.E. Howard *Bear Creek* 8: You may be accounted a fast gunslinger down in the low country. **1942** Sonnichsen *Billy King* 16: Gamblers, pimps, claim jumpers, gun-slingers—and their women. **1946** N. Nye *Chaparral* 121: He had beckoned a couple of his handiest gun slingers. **1954** Gruber *Bitter Sage* 41: I'll fight any man with my fists, but I'm no gunslinger. **1956** Overholser *Desperate* 21: He's a gunslinger. **1961** *Gunslinger* (CBS-TV). *a*1979 Gillespie & Fraser *To Be* 16: Sometimes he got killed, but he was a good...gunslinger. **1989** *Diamonds* (USA-TV): We're detectives, not gunslingers.
2. *Finance.* a manager of a high-risk, high-performance mutual fund.
1971 *Playboy* (Aug.) 22: The mutual-fund gunslinger runs with the pack....The banker, by his conservatism, wastes nest eggs.

gunsmith *n. Und.* (see quots.).
***1868** in *F & H* III 235: Returned to his old trade of *gunsmith, gunning* being the slang term for thieving. **1934** D.W. Maurer, in *AS* (Feb. 1935) 16 [ref. to *a*1910]: Gunsmith or *gun-maker.* One who trains young criminals, especially pickpockets.

gun talk *n.* thieves' argot.
1926 J. Conway, in *Variety* (Dec. 29) 5: The guy who knows all the gun talk.

gun-thrower *n. West.* GUNSLINGER. Hence **gun-throwing**, *adj.*
1912 Z. Grey *Purple Sage* 10: Thieves an' cut-throats an' gun-throwers an' all-round no-good men. **1914** Z. Grey *Pecos Co.* 63: Boss rustlers...gun throwers. **1928** Lake *Earp* 41: Such a move...could be made faster than the eye could follow a topnotch gun-thrower. **1930** Mulford *Eagle* 20: A...half dozen of th' damnedest gun-throwing hombres of th' West. **1932** Z. Grey *Robbers' Roost* 14: But he's a gun-thrower himself....He's done for I don't know how many ambitious-to-be killers. **1946** N. Nye *Chaparral* 183: The role of...gun thrower... **1958** Constiner *Gunman* 57: All right, gunthrower. You've got one, use it.

gun-tosser *n.* GUN-THROWER.
1951 Longstreet *Pedlocks* 111: Pontdue is bringing in bad hombres, gun tossers, and we're having trouble getting men to work for us.

gun-toter *n.* a western gunman or gunfighter.
1925 in *DA:* This opened up the field for the renegade white man...the gun-toter [etc.]. **1932** Z. Grey *Robbers' Roost* 14: Cow-punchers, range-riders, gun-toters. **1934** Cunningham *Triggernometry* 10: Any gun-toter who ever stood on The Law's left hand.

guntz *n.* [clipping of GUNSEL] a worthless person.
1980 Grizzard *Billy Bob Bailey* 110: They applaud even when some guntz hits a good shot.

gun-wadding *n.* soft bread.—also constr. with *bread.*
1919 Darling *Jargon Book* 16: Gun wading [*sic*]—White bread. **1936** R. Adams *Cowboy Lingo* 147: Light bread was "wasp-nests" or "gun-waddin' bread." **1952–53** in *PADS* (No. 29) 11: *Gun wadding*...A disparaging term for bread.

guppy *n.* [sugg. by the shape] **1.** *Mil. Av.* a radar plane.
1952 in *Britannica Bk. of Yr.* (1954) 752: Guppy, *n.* Nickname of an airplane with a radar set in its belly. **1955** Reifer *New Words* 97: *Guppy. Mil. Slang*...A radar plane. **1966** Gallery *Start Engines* 180: Since the

guppy plane is a lot slower than the fighters and bombers, Willy headed in by himself. **1969** Cagle *Naval Av. Guide* 394: *Guppy.* An AEW aircraft distinguished by a large bulbous dish which encloses a radar antennae. Also known as Willy Fudd (E-1A), Super Fudd (E-2A), and Hummer (E-2A). **1980** *Air Classics: Air War over Korea* 81 [ref. to 1953]: Three Marine Composite (VMC) squadrons operated the "Guppy," as the AD-5W and its similarly modified predecessors were called. **1991** Linnekin *80 Knots* 236: This was the "guppy" version with the big overgrown bulge under the forward fuselage.

2. *Av.* a Boeing 737 airliner.

1988 *Time* (May 16) 62: The stubby and squat Boeing 737…the "guppie" has become the bestselling jetliner in history.

guppy-gobbler *n.* MACKEREL-SNAPPER. *Joc.*

1964 *PADS* (No. 42) 34: The Catholic is identified…[as] *guppy-gobbler.*

gush *n.* **1.** a great number or amount.

1849 in *DAE*: Shese a powerful big boat, and kin tote a gush of pork. **1853** "Paxton" *Yankee in Tex.* 44: We've got a gush of peaches.

2. maudlin sentimentality, effusive flattery, or the like; BOSH.

1863 in J.W. Haley *Rebel Yell* 112: I must indulge in a trifle of "gush" over the natural beauty of this place. *1866 in *OED*: Some romantic nonsense, born of gush and the circulating library. *1869 in *OEDS*: The book altogether is silly, and full of gush and twaddle. **1872** O.W. Holmes, in *OEDS*: He didn't go in "for sentiment.…Gush was played out." **1887** *Lantern* (N.O.) (Jan. 29) 5: About Gogan gettin' dat gun from Weideman is all gush. **1893** W.K. Post *Harvard* 126: Brought on by overdoses of gush. **1899** Cullen *Tales* 87: There's been…too much sentimental gush at these experience meetings lately. **1913** in Truman *Dear Bess* 118: She never heard of such gush. **1922** in Ruhm *Detective* 5: Con men are full of that kind of gush. **1980** Grizzard *Billy Bob Bailey* 41: A lot of gush about how much I loved him.

gussie *n.* [fr. *Gussie*, given name] a weak, effeminate, or foolish fellow.

[**1895** J.L. Williams *Princeton* 162: Gussie Thompson was an angel-faced child with pretty ringlety hair, and he had come to college from a strict boarding-school.…People…considered Gussie disgustingly good.] **1901** Ade *Mod. Fables* 46: In his Opinion the Husband that she had set up as a Shining Example was a feather-brained Gussie…who carried a Pocket Handkerchief inside of his Cuff, and chatted about Dress Goods. *1901 in *OEDS*: I'm not a booby that will fall in love with every gussie I see. **1928** MacArthur *War Bugs* 88: Were these the Gussies that dived in the Luneville abris whenever a shell fell a mile away? *Ibid.* 144: Why, these German gussies were rookies. Who ever told *them* they were soldiers? Their mothers? Etc. **1930** *AS* V (Feb.) 238: They made gussies of themselves at the banquet. *1941 S.J. Baker *Austral. Slang* 33: *Gussie*…an effeminate or affected man.

gussy up *v.* to dress up; ornament; make fancy. Cf. GUSSIE, *n.*

[**1928** Hecht & MacArthur *Front Page* 118: Hello, Turkey…How's your gussie mollie?] **1952** in *DAS*: When I get all gussied up, somebody says, "Pull in your pot." **1958** Drury *Advise and Consent* 112: The men encased in tuxedoes…, the women gussied up fit to kill. **1965** D.G. Moore *20th C. Cowboy* 109: We…headed to the San Tan Barber Shop to get "gussied" up. **1969** Furnas *Americans* 603: The thoroughly gussied-up parlor of the high General Grant era. **1976** Hayden *Voyage* 616: Town's all gussied up. Today's election day. **1984** C. Francis *Who's Sorry?* 197: If she thinks she's gonna gussy up my beautiful "God Bless America" with—

gusto *n.* **1.** [sugg. by Schlitz beer advertisements (1966) featuring the slogan "You only go around once in life, so grab for all the gusto you can!", later shortened to "Schlitz. Grab for the gusto!"] Schlitz (brand of) beer.

1970–72 Claerbaut *Black Jargon* 67: *Gusto*…beer. **1977** Schlitz beer ad (CBS-TV): You wanna take away my *gusto?* **1978** *N.Y. City News* (Aug. 28) 110: I don't use no chemicals, only thing is sleep and a little gusto (beer).

2. *Black E.* money.

1984 Toop *Rap Attack* 158: *Gusto:* money, cold cash, dinero.…"Hey man, it's Monday. Where's my gusto?"

gut *n.* **1.a.** also *pl.* the belly; stomach; (now *esp.*) a fat belly; **stuff (one's) gut** to eat gluttonously. Orig. *S.E.* [Regarded as vulgar slang throughout the 19th C., this term has reasserted itself as colloq. in the mid-20th.]

*1393 W. Langland, in *OED*: Al is noȝt good to þe gost þat þe gut/Askeþ. *1535 in *OED*: Dame Avarice, with as greedy a gut…as the best.

*1616 in *OED*: To putt Scraps…in thy half starvd gutt. **1666** G. Alsop *Maryland* 26: Armes all akimbo, and with belly strut,/As if they had *Parnassus* in their gut. *1693 J. Dryden, in *OED*: For his own Gut he bought the stately Fish. *1798 in J. Ashton *Eng. Satires on Napoleon* 59: Oh curse his Guts, he'll take a chop at us next. *1803 in Wetherell *Adventures* 120: My guts are burnt out for want of water with my brandy. **1841** [Mercier] *Man-of-War* 266: I'll stuff your guts with first rate cheese. **1851** M. Reid *Scalp-Hunters* 175: I'll make that niggur larf till his gut aches. **1862** in *Ark. Hist. Qly.* XVIII (1959) 62: Hungry guts are plenty. **1865** in Springer *Sioux Country* 27: I fetched or catched what the old proverb says; hunter's luck, a wet posterior and a hungry gut. **1931** N. West *Balso Snell* 36: He hit Miss McGeeney a terrific blow in the gut and hove her into the fountain. **1932** Hecht & Fowler *Great Magoo* 64: Suck that gut in. **1934** *WNID2*: *Gut…pl. Slang*…Belly; stomach. **1934** Wohlforth *Tin Soldiers* 198: Ram your neck in! Suck up your gut! **1934** Faulkner *Pylon* 128: A gut full of food on top of the drinks. **1942** McAtee *Supp. to Grant Co.* 4 [ref. to 1890's]: "What luck did you have?"…"Fisherman's luck, a wet ass, and a hungry gut." **1944–48** A. Lyon *Unknown Station* 143: What's wrong with stuffing your gut when you can? **1953** Paul *Waylaid* 64: He replied by touching what he called "the old gut." **1956** I. Shulman *Good Deeds* 25: That's politer than saying I've a gut. **1962** McKenna *Sand Pebbles* 27: I got a cast-iron gut. **1975** *UTSQ*: Eat…*stuff your gut.* **1984** Nettles & Golenbock *Balls* 123: Oscar's got a bit of a gut on him.

b. usu. *pl.* a fat, gluttonous, or boorish person. *Rare* in U.S.

*1596 Shakespeare *I Henry IV* II iv: Thou Clay-brayn'd Guts. *1698–99 "B.E." *Dict. Canting Crew: Gutts*, a very fat, gross Person. **1863** Hollister *Colo. Vols.* 75: He was a fine fellow.…The others were what is emphatically termed *guts*, and no one is sorry they are gone. *1869 in *OED*: March, march, old guts! *1896 in *OED*: *Guts*, a glutton. *1959 Opie & Opie *Lore & Lang.* Schoolchildren 168: The unfortunate fat boy…is known as…guts. **1968** in *DARE*: *If somebody always eats a considerable amount of food, you say he's a…Gut.*

c. *pl.* (among tramps) (see 1914 quot.).

1914 Jackson & Hellyer *Vocab.* 41: *Guts.* Noun. Amongst yeggs and others familiar with clandestine railroading, "guts" signifies the various constructive parts underneath a car, or the hidden essentials of rolling stock. Example: "We'll ride the guts tonight over this division." i.e., the gunnels, rods, brake-beams, trucks. *a1922 in N. Anderson *Hobo* 195: So he grabbed the guts of an east-bound freight. **1927** *AS* (June) 388: *Riding the guts* means riding underneath [a railroad car]. **1930** "D. Stiff" *Milk & Honey* 206: *Gunnells* or *guts*—The *rods* or *trucks* of the train where hobos ride. **1936** Duncan *Over the Wall* 29: My berth [was] the guts of a dining car on a transcontinental limited.

d. *Av.* the belly of an aircraft.

1944 Stiles *Big Bird* 92: Ball-turret to pilot.…We got a couple of holes in the gut.

2. *pl.* **a.** insides; (now *esp.*) inner parts; contents. Now *colloq.*

*1751 in *OED*: I will dry them [gourds] next time with the guts in. **1826** in Commager *Spirit of '76* 83: One member of the company told me, many years since, that…he gave [the British] "the guts of his gun." **1827** in *JAF* LXXVI (1963) 294: The pirat…noks a hole…in…her [sc. a ship's] guts. **1841** [Mercier] *Man-of-War* 169: He'd let the *guts* out of your bag just as quick. *1863 in *OED*: The whole "guts" of the ships had to be torn out for the passage of the shaft. **1902** in J. London *Short Stories* 164: Watches with broken guts. **1938** Steinbeck *Grapes of Wrath* 281: They ain't nothin' I love like the guts of a engine. **1958** Gardner *Piece of the Action* 16: I ripped the guts out of an old Victrola. **1972** *All in the Family* (CBS-TV): Where's the guts to my TV?

b. (used hyperbolically with *out*).

1852 Ely *Wanderings* 197: Most ship masters would have hauled their ship up two or three points…keeping the ship steady and easy. But instead of that we have as the sailors say, "Almost rolled her guts out," kept two men constantly at the wheel, and strained the ship in every joint. [**1918** in Hemingway *Sel. Letters* 15: The stretcher bearers had to go over lots because the road was having the "entrails" shelled out of it.] **1975** N.Y.C. woman, age 86: Why must you work your guts out for her? **1984** in "J.B. Briggs" *Drive-In* 293: Excuse me if I…laugh my guts out. **1990** C.P. McDonald *Blue Truth* 185: Working our guts out all those years.

c. also *pl.* the source of one's deep and true feelings; **at gut level** at the level of deep feeling. Now *S.E.*

1893 in Bunner *Letters* 146: The *Scribner* article is written straight out of my guts, so to speak. **1964** in T.H. White *Making of Pres. '64* 328: In your gut you know he's nuts. **1965** in Wilner & Kassebaum *Narcotics* 202: My opinion carries a lot of weight in this house. Get that [at] gut level. **1978** Univ. Tenn. instructor: It's a book written from the gut

1981 Sann *Trial* 52: I'm talking from my guts. **1989** *Star Trek—Next Generation* (synd. TV series): Because your gut tells you so?...But you can't always count on your gut, either. **1990** *N.Y. Times* (Dec. 30) I 10: "My gut tells me that he will get out of there," the President said of the Iraqi leader. **1992** M. Gelman *Crime Scene* 63: Hamill's writing also seemed like it came right from his gut.

d. *pl.* the entire contents of the stomach (in reference to the act of vomiting).

1948 A. Murphy *Hell & Back* 10: "Are you sick, soldier?" "No sir. I'm just spilling my guts for the hell of it." *a*1981 in S. King *Bachman* 553: I'll probably heave my guts.

e. *pl.* all one knows that could be of interest, often to police or other authorities, and esp. when abjectly divulged.—constr. with *spill, cough up*, etc., and possessive; in phr. **hold** [or **keep**] **(one's) guts** to remain silent.

*1879 in Partridge *DSUE* (ed. 3) 1069: Workman [accused of burglary] asked me to...tell her that he had been about Maudsley's job, and she must keep her "guts," what she knew about it. **1912** Berkman *Prison* 164 [ref. to 1893]: Think I'd open my guts to Lord Bighead. [**1915** Bronson-Howard *God's Man* 379: Gamblers don't go spilling their insides out to girls.] **1926** *AS* I (Dec. 12) 653: *Throw-your-guts*—telling everything. Not trustworthy. **1927** Coe *Me—Gangster* 78: Throw him out and have him spill his guts about the whole gang? **1928** Hecht & MacArthur *Front Page* 464: I had to give it to Jacob; before he'd cough up his guts. **1928** O'Connor *B'way Racketeers* 65: Without even bein' asked to, he spits up his guts and spills the works. **1929** Milburn *Hornbook* 26 [ref. to 1890]: Each 'bo throwed his guts while the other mutts/ Laid back and lent an ear. **1929** *AS* IV (June) 345: *Spill one's guts*: Tell everything you know. **1935** Odets *Paradise Lost* 204: Hold your guts a minute! **1935** Coburn *Law Rides Range* 25: Bill Clanton and his coyote sons will spill their guts when they come up for trial. **1946** Gresham *Nightmare Alley* 168: You...listen to the chumps puking their guts out day after day for peanuts. **1954** Schulberg *Waterfront* 212: I didn't ask him to go spill his guts to those stinkin' investigators. **1957** Hall *Cloak & Dagger* 47: What if I'd spilled my guts? **1958** Drury *Advise and Consent* 399: "Oh. Arly's no problem," Senator Munson said. "After he's spilled his guts to the press he'll settle down and be all right for the long haul." **1975** McCaig *Danger Trail* 54: Somebody gets drunk,...spills his guts, and our whole venture is wrecked. **1985** M. Baker *Cops* 103: I would like to snap the girl up first, hoping that she's going to puke up her guts. **1988** *Throb* (synd. TV series): Blow your guts to me....I'm your psychiatrist.

3. *pl.* substantial contents; substance. [In early use almost exclusively in obs. prov., *to have (some) guts in (one's) brains* 'to have some real intelligence' (1721 quot. plays upon this phr. for humorous effect).]

*1663 S. Butler, in *OED*: Truly that is no Hard Matter for a Man to do, That has but any Guts in 's Brains. *1666 in Tilley *Dict. Provs.* 278: A meer brute, an Animal, to have no guts in ones brains....To have some Logick in his pate, to have some guts in his brains, to be no fool. *1694 in Tilley *Dict. Provs.* 278: One without Guts in his Brains, whose Cockloft is unfurnish'd. [**1721** in Whiting *Early Amer. Provs.* 189: For your Works declare, your Guts are in your Brains.] *1738 J. Swift, in Tilley *Dict. Provs.* 278: The fellow's well enough, if he had any guts in his brains. **1972–76** Durden *No Bugles* 114: The guts of it was that intelligence reports...confirmed the absence of...NVA troops.

4. *pl.* energy, power, or vigor in performance or execution. Now *colloq.*

*1821–26 Stewart *Man-of-War's-Man* II 222: You've left the guts out of 'em [songs]. *1889 Barrère & Leland *Dict. Slang* I 439: "No *guts* in it." The expression is pretty general, but it is more especially used by artists to announce their opinion that there is nothing in a picture. **1890** in F. Remington *Sel. Letters* 98: A half dozen litterary ducks have run over your letter and say that it is plumb full of guts. *1892 R.L. Stevenson, in *OED*: It's got life to it and guts, and it moves. *1890–93 *F & H* III 237: *Guts*...(artists', and colloquial).—Spirit; quality; a touch of force, or energy, or fire: e.g., a picture, a book, an actor *with guts*....Put your *guts* into it (aquatic) = Row the very best you can. **1908** J. London *M. Eden* 282: It's guts, and magazines have no use for that. **1915** in Pound *Letters* 51: I think it has some guts, but am perhaps still blinded by the fury in which I wrote it. **1918** E. O'Neill *Moon* 48: Play us a dance, ye square-head swab!—a rale, Godforsaken son av a turkey trot wid guts to ut. **1929** Barr *Let Tomorrow Come* 37: Round we go, men; give 'er guts! **1958** Kerouac *Subterraneans* 100: The first novel...has guts but has a dreary prose to it. **1970** Major *Afro-Amer. Slang* 62: *Guts* (1930's–50's) emotional and spiritual honesty coming from the very bottom of the self; earthiness.

5.a. *pl.* strength of character; moral stamina; courage or fortitude; (now *esp.*) boldness and independence of spirit; in phr. **on guts** through courage or determination alone. Now *colloq.* or *S.E.* [In early use chiefly in negative contexts.]

1891 in *War Papers* I 141 [ref. to Civil War]: The slang phrase in regard to the soldier who was discharged, was "He hasn't got the guts to stand it." The marches were long, the water poor,...the weather torrid, and the rations oftentimes of poor quality. **1892** Frye *From Hqs.* 164: Jus' youse look at 'em sometime, an' see what a peepy-looking lot dey is. Huh! dey ain't got no guts at all! *1890–93 *F & H* III 237: He...has *no guts* in him... = He...is a common rotter.*1900 in *OEDS*: If you have what are, at Cambridge, vulgarly but expressively called "guts." **1914** London *Jacket* 181: You are a stinking coward, and you haven't got the backbone and guts to carry out the dirty butcher's work you'd like to do. **1922** Rollins *Cowboy* 66: Some wise old Westerner defined a cowboy as "a man with guts and a horse." **1928** Barry *Holiday* 499: You've got twice the looks, and twice the mind, and ten times the guts. **1929** Ferber *Cimarron* 90: They won't have the guts to come out in the open. **1934** Appel *Brain Guy* 12: Even Bobbie had no guts for this, her rouge a mask plastered on pallor. **1935** Fortune *Fugitives* 162: There's not a pair of cops in the whole country with guts enough to come after Clyde Barrow alone. **1935** Odets *Waiting for Lefty*: That Wop's got more guts than a slaughter house. **1938** "E. Queen" *4 Hearts* 172: "No guts," jeered Ellery. **1938** Lawes *Invisible Stripes* 101: Being a man of religion don't mean you ain't got guts. **1947** Beloin & Rose *Fav. Brunette* (film): You've got what I call guts. **1951** Pryor *The Big Play* 160: Depends on the size of your guts. **1957** Evans & Evans *Dict. Contemp. Usage* 211: *Guts* is...now used metaphorically for courage and fortitude. Even so, it is felt to be a strong or manly or deliberately rough word and is avoided by the refined. *a*1967 Bombeck *Wit's End* 127: I don't have Grandma's guts in the traffic or her cunning. **1967** Gries *Penny* (film): Why, you got more guts than a man could hang on a fence. **1970** Libby *Life in Pit* 55: I got 'em on guts. **1972** Emrich *Folklore* 30: One may crudely say that the strong verbs are strong because they have independent guts of their own. **1978** Sonnichsen *Hopalong to Hud.* 104: The only trait which every fictional hero had to have was just plain guts. **1989** *USA Today* (Feb. 22) 9A: American liberty first of all is a matter of guts. **1990** *CBS This Morning* (CBS-TV) (Apr. 3): There's a fine line between all guts and no brains.

b. (rarely in *sing.*).

1935 Algren *Boots* 169: Mebbe ah ain't seen so much—but ah sure got gut! Ah'm *all* gut! Ah'm a Texas hell-roarer! **1961** H. Ellison *Gentleman Junkie* 133: You come on out to the chickie-run tonight, and we'll see you got gut enough to be a Prince.

c. *pl. Poker.* a form of draw poker in which bets are made without an opening requirement or with more than one or two hole-cards dealt to each player.

1932 *AS* VII 435: In poker, the various games are called...seven-card stud,..."guts," [etc.]. **1949** G.S. Coffin *Winning Poker* 179: *Guts*...Draw poker with no opening requirement. **1950** *Neurotica* (Spring) 11: Draw poker (also called "guts"). **1977** Univ. Tenn. grad. student: Have you ever played guts?

6. *pl.* effrontery; brazenness.

1919 in Cornebise *Amaroc News* 25: Germany says: "Maybe we'll sign, but before we do...we present the proposals of peace as we wish them." Some guts! **1927–28** Tasker *Grimhaven* 109: You've got a lot of guts standing there and telling us we don't know anything. **1930** in D.O. Smith *Cradle* 104: Yale is cocky. She's got too much guts and has the insolence to think she is just as good as we are. **1931** Farrell *McGinty* 174: You got the guts to stand here and tell me such a goddamn lie and think I'm gonna be fool enough to flop for it? **1929–33** Farrell *Young Manhood* 314: He sneered, thinking that the goddamn niggers had their guts, invading a white man's neighborhood, and sooner or later they'd have to be run out. **1933** Ersine *Pris. Slang* 42: *Guts, n.*...Effrontery. **1934** Appel *Brain Guy* 47: They got guts bitchin'. We could've borrered a couple Duffy's kids for half the dough. **1945** in Shibutani *Co. K* 133: He's got a lot of guts trying to blame it all on us. **1961** Heinlein *Stranger* 75: Anyhow, damn her guts, he wasn't going to let her push him around. **1962** B. Evans *Comfortable Words* 186: In American slang *guts* is widely used for *impudence* ("He's got his guts, coming in here without being asked!"). **1979** Jenison *Kingdom in Sage* 77: You better take it kinda easy." *Kinda easy!* Of all the guts!

7. *pl.* physical or mechanical power.

1928–29 Nason *White Slicker* 24 [ref. to 1918]: About every tenth bullet didn't have guts enough to work the gun. **1953** Felsen *Street Rod* 62: When your car has the guts mine has, I'll be ready. **1966–67** Harvey *Air War* 141: The F-105 is powered by a Pratt & Whitney J-75 (P + W is hard to beat for rugged get-you-home guts). **1980** *Easyriders* (May) 27: The old switch of putting 80 flywheels into a knuck for more guts is pretty well known, right? *a***1988** Gulf (brand of) gasoline slogan: Gulf. The gas with guts.

8.a. a good fellow.

1864 in Bensell *Yambill* 161: Boys on the fort ate well and hearty....Doc Chase is a "gut."

b. certainty; CINCH. Also attrib.

1925 in Hammett *Big Knockover* 227: If it happens that the Circle H.A.R. riders trail you here and take us unawares, it's a gut that you're in for a lynching. **1929** Hammett *Dain Curse* 215: The other employees probably don't really know anything, though it's a gut they could make some good guesses. **1976** Price *Bloodbrothers* 242: Nah, the job's a gut, no sweat.

c. *Stu.* an academic course that is easily passed without much application or study.

1916 in E. Wilson *Prelude* 125: Gut course; hop a gut. **1934** Weseen *Dict. Slang* 184: Gut course—An easy course; a pipe. **1951** in *DAS:* Eco...was a gut course if I ever saw one. **1963** *Time* (Sept. 27) 55: "Mickey Mouse" guts like driver education. **1965** Hersey *Too Far to Walk* 56: Geol 20...boring but the definitive gut. **1966** Fariña *Down So Long* 27: Couple of guys in the house took that one-o-one course for their science requirement, said it was a real gut. **1978** T.H. White *In Search* 44: Government I was a "gut" course, and the student underground passed the word that no one ever failed in Government I. **1983** *Newsweek on Campus* (Dec.) 2: I was deeply disturbed by your inclusion of his course in your list of great "guts". **1988** *Newsweek on Campus* (Apr.) 27: He doesn't care if people call his course a gut.

9. (among tramps) sausage.

1916 *Editor* (May 6) 487: *Gut.* Bologna sausage. **1922** N. Anderson *Hobo* 24: Now and then as at breakfast someone will shout asking if anybody wants some spuds or a piece of punk or a piece of "gut" (sausage). **1926** *AS* I (Dec.) 652: *Punk and gut*—Bread and sausage. **1929** *AS* IV (June) 340: *Gut.* Sausage. **1956** Sorden & Ebert *Logger's* 17 [ref. to *a*1925]: *Gut*, Bologna.

10.a. a main street; in phr. **shoot** [or **drag**] **the gut** to drive up and down the main street. Cf. *OED* def. 5c, "a narrow passage or lane of any kind."

[****1948** Partridge et al. *Forces' Sl.* 89: *The Gut,* a notorious street in Malta.] **1961** Braly *Felony Tank* 43: Ardilla was one-gutted....When they tried to drive out of town a few hours later they were trapped on a single road. **1969** *Current Slang* I & II 46: Gut, n. Main street of town.—High school males, Kansas.—They really dragged the *gut* last night. **1971** Dahlskog *Dict.* 54: *Shoot the gut,* to drive down the main street; to cruise the main drag. **1976** Braly *False Starts* 86: The old thieves would have called this part of the state one-gutted—there was only the one road, and no way off it.

b. *Football.* the middle of the line of scrimmage; in phr. **up the gut** straight up the field.

1975 R. Hill *O.J. Simpson* 16: I reversed my field and shot up the gut...[for] a touchdown. **1976** *Webster's Sports Dict.:* Carried the ball right up the gut. **1990** *N.Y. Post* (Jan. 2) 51: McGuire simply ran up the gut past McCants for Miami's first TD. **1992** *Sports Close-Up* (CNN-TV) (Nov. 2): A touchdown rush...up the gut.

c. *Baseball.* the middle of the strike zone.

1986 *TV Guide* (July 26) 15: [The fastball] was...traveling down the gut.

¶ In phrases:

¶ **bust** [or **break**] **a gut, 1.** to strain or work very hard, esp. to hurt oneself through straining.—usu. used derisively. [For first quot. (literal) cf. **1672 quot. at *split a gut*, 3, below.]

****1698–1720** in D'Urfey *Pills* III 44: He drank whole Butts 'till he burst his Guts. [**a***1720** in D'Urfey *Pills* II 2: Our Crew may crack their Gutts,/They ne'er will win ye.] **1912** *DN* III 572: *Bust a gut*...to make a supreme effort. "Just bust a gut now and see if we can't lift this log." **1925** Nason *Three Lights* 152: He's gonna break a gut! **1932** E. Caldwell *Tobacco Road* 24: Ellie May's straining for Lov, ain't she?...She's liable to bust a gut if she don't look out. **1935** Algren *Boots* 250: They'd get even if they had to bust a gut to get even. **1937** Steinbeck *Mice & Men* 8: That means we'll be buckin' grain bags, bustin' a gut. **1940** N. Johnson *Grapes of Wrath* (film): You're about to bust a gut till I let you know. **1943** in Inman *Diary* 1195: And it's not like I didn't bust a gut trying to please you. **1950** Maddow & Huston *Asphalt Jungle* 22: I'll have it for you tomorrow or bust a gut. *****1966** G.M. Williams *Camp* 32: Well, I wouldn't bust a gut about what he wants. **1992** *World Today*

(CNN-TV) (Oct. 2): He is either going to do it or bust a gut trying.

2. to hurt oneself by laughing too hard; to laugh very hard. [***1888 quot. is quoting ***1750 source; Ebworthy's inaccurate transcription introduces the *bust* form for the first time.]

****1750** *Exmoor Scolding* 9: Ched a most a borst ma Guts wi' laughing. ****1888** F.T. Ebworthy *W. Somerset Word-Book* 305: Chad a most a bust my *guts* wi' laughing.—*Ex. Scold.* I.151. **1929–33** J.T. Farrell *Young Manhood* 183: People nearly busted their guts laughing. **1947** Mailer *Naked & Dead* 189: Caldwell almost bust a gut laughing. **1950** in *DARE:* I thought I would bust a gut [laughing]. **1954** in *DARE:* Bust a *gut*...to laugh very hard. **1955** B.J. Friedman, in *Antioch Rev.* XV 382: You'd bust a gut laughing. **1957** Evans & Evans *Dict. Contemp. Usage* 211: *Gut*...is a slang word, a facetious back-formation from *guts* (as in *I thought I'd bust a gut laughing at his antics*).

3. to explode with anger; hurt oneself through the force of one's anger.

1946 I. Shulman *Amboy Dukes* 40: Take it easy, Feivel...or you'll strain a gut. **1949** Shane & Cooper *City Across the River* (film): My old man's gonna bust a gut. **1950** in *DARE.* **1954** J.W. Ellson *Owen Harding* 31: I thought he would bust a gut. **1953–57** Giovannitti *Combine D* 201: Man, when the Major finds us all lying in the sack, he'll bust a gut. **1975** *UTSQ:* The boss'll bust a gut when he hears about this.

¶ **cut a gut** to make an embarrassing mistake; to make oneself look foolish.

1923 *DN* V 234: *Cut a gut*...To make a mistake, or to fail in a task. (From dressing an animal). "Oh, yes, he said he'd do it, and then he cut a gut." **1933** *AS* VIII 48: *Cut a big gut*...To do something foolish, to make oneself ridiculous. **1939** *AS* XIV 90: He cut a big gut at the dance. **1969** in *DARE.* *ca*1970 in *Ibid.*

¶ **fret (one's) guts to fiddle-strings** to agonize.

1772 in Whiting *Early Amer. Provs.* 189: Mr. Aston has fretted his Guts to Fiddle strings about Mr. Lucas's Pranks.

¶ **hate (someone's) guts** to hate intensely. Now *colloq.* [The 1901 quot., in a letter to Vice-Pres. Theodore Roosevelt, is clearly euphemistic.]

1901 in W.A. White *Letters* 43: Take the case of Quay: I hate his intestines. It seems to me that there is no man in American politics that I have such an utter loathing and contempt for. **1917** in Grider *War Birds* 9: Every infantry officer on board hates our guts because we have the same privileges they do. **1918** in O'Brien *Wine, Women & War* 140: Hate his guts! **1925** Hemingway *Men Without Women* 154: By the time they'd gone five rounds he hated Jack's guts. **1941** Schulberg *Sammy* 299: You hate my guts, don't you? You hate my guts just like all the rest of them. **1949** *Life of Riley* (CBS-TV): I hated his guts. **1954** Lindner *Fifty-Minute Hour* 97: I hate your guts. **1961** J.A. Williams *Night Song* 93: You hated my guts. **1989** Wittliff *Lonesome Dove* (CBS-TV): He hates their guts and livers.

¶ **have more guts than brains, 1.** to be controlled by one's appetites rather than by the intellect; be inordinately foolish.

****1678** in Tilley *Dict. Provs.* 278: He has more guts than brains. [**1742** in Whiting *Early Amer. Provs.* 189: Gutts can sometimes do more than brains.] **1749–50** in Breslaw *Tues. Club* 180: Because that each of us Contains,/a great deal more of guts than brains. ****1785** Grose *Vulgar Tongue:* More guts than brains; a silly fellow. He has plenty of guts, but no bowels; said of a hard, merciless, unfeeling person. *****1828** in *EDD:* He's mair guts ner brains. **a***1900** *EDD* II 768: *More guts than brains,* foolish and greedy, thinking more of the appetite than of the intellect.

2. to be foolhardy.

1965 Harvey *Hudasky's Raiders* 6: That boy's got more guts than brains.

¶ **not fit to carry guts to a bear** (of a person) utterly contemptible.

****1659** in Tilley *Dict. Provs.* 278: He is not worthy to carry guts to a bear. **1789** in Whiting *Early Amer. Provs.* 189: Just fit to carry guts to a bear. ****1829** Marryat *Frank Mildmay* 228: You may go to hell, and be d—d, Sir!...you are not fit to carry guts to a bear! **1833** J. Neal *Down-Easters* I 81: He...ain't fit to carry guts to a bear. **1877** Bartlett *Amer.* (ed. 4) 103: He ain't fit to carry guts to a bear. **1967–68** in *DARE* I 550.

¶ **pop a gut** *bust a gut,* 3, above.

1952 Lamott *Stockade* 45 [ref. to WWII]: The Lieutenant would pop a gut....He just doesn't stand for that sort of stuff. **1974** Radano *Cop Stories* 66: The surgeon sounded like he was going to pop a gut.

¶ **shovel guts** to perform menial, hateful tasks.

1966–67 W. Stevens *Gunner* 111: The Army's got more guys than i[t] knows what to do with. Let somebody else take a turn shoveling guts, I had enough of it.

¶ **spill (one's) guts, 1.** see **(2.d.),** above.

2. see **(2.e.),** above.

¶ **split a gut, 1.** bust a gut, 2, above.

1936 M. Levin *Old Bunch* 174: The Jew…laughs till he nearly splits a gut. **1939** M. Levin *Citizens* 140: And that gang…split their guts laughing. **1956** Resko *Reprieve* 49: The rest of us…think it funny, and wait…for the…Negro to split his gut. **1957** Leckie *Helmet for My Pillow* 133 [ref. to 1943]: I nearly split a gut when I saw you tear-ass up them stairs.…I couldn't keep from laughing. **1958** H. Baker *King Creole* (film): We been laughin' at you ever since it happened. We been splittin' a gut. **1958–59** Lipton *Barbarians* 48: I would one day split a gut laughing. **1969** Hughes *Under a Flare* 199: Rog split a gut as he told Charley and me, "That's how it's been going ever since we got up here." **1979** Gutcheon *New Girls* 66: I thought I was going to split a gut laughing. **1991** L. Chambers *Recondo* 182: He was so funny, I almost split a gut!

2. bust a gut, 3, above.

1943 *Yank* (Aug. 6) 10: I lak to split a gut when I found we'd only staked a claim…here. **1961** H. Ellison *Memos* 100: "He'll be really sore."…To be sure, Pooch would split a gut.

3. bust a gut, 1, above [For *1672 quot. (literal), cf. *1698–1720 quot. at bust a gut, 1, above.]

[***1672** *Covent Garden Drollery* 35: He drank whole Butts/And split his Gutts.] **1953–58** J.C. Holmes *Horn* 156: He's split a gut like that every night for years.

¶ **tub of guts** a grossly obese person.—used contemptuously. Also vars.

1906 *DN* III 162: He's a big *tub o' guts.* **1912** *DN* III 566: *Bag of guts*…A worthless, clumsy fellow, fat and lazy. **1925** Mullin *Scholar Tramp* 306 [ref. to *ca*1912]: As I was sayin' a while ago when I was interrupted by that tub o' guts sittin' over there.…**1930** Thomason, in *Stories* 370 [ref. to 1918]: You won't send a runner, you damn' scuttle of guts, you! You'll go yourself, and you'll go now! **1957** Hall *Cloak & Dagger* 143: Sir, is that bundle of guts one of our men? **1977** *Baa Baa Black Sheep* (NBC-TV): I've seen the guy. He's a tub of guts.

gut *adj.* **1.** *Stu.* easily passed with little application or study.

1916, 1934, 1951 (quots. at GUT, *n.*, 8.c.). **1958** *AS* XXXIII 226: A *snap* course, or what Princeton undergraduates in my day [*ca*1945] called a *gut* course. **1980** Birnbach et al. *Preppy Hndbk.* 91: A Preppy cannot choose a laughably easy or "gut" major.

2. based on one's instincts or emotions; immediately or deeply felt. Now *colloq.*

1951 Kerouac *Cody* 42: Maybe even in the powerful gut feeling I had. ***1968** in *OEDS:* An immediate gut reaction. **1968** *Newsweek* (Dec. 2) 42: No one can accurately predict…Nixon's gut reaction to the play of events. **1968** *College Comp. & Comm.* XIX 287: Gut knowing buried/deep in the womb of/ oppression. **1969** *N.Y. Times Mag.* (Jan. 19) 73: This deep, gut feeling that they want to be part of things. *a*1981 in S. King *Bachman* 594: Although she had given up most religious concepts…some of the gut stuff had stuck with her. **1981** Sann *Trial* 104: I've got a gut feeling that I'm getting to…those guys. ***a1987** J. Green *Dict. Jargon* 267: Gut feeling…"gut" belief in…therapy. **1988** *The Judge* (synd. TV series): I should have followed my gut instinct when I hired you. You can't keep a secret. *a*1989 R. Herman, Jr. *Warbirds* 271: Jack made a gut decision. **1993** *New Yorker* (May 10) 80: Sorry, but I'm still finding it hard to accept gut responses from women.

3. *Pol.* (of a political issue or the like) of fundamental importance; of extraordinary concern to voters, often engendering a visceral reaction.—comparative *guttier*, superlative *guttiest.*

1964 *Newsweek* (Sept. 21) 29: The one issue that the President feels is the "guttiest" of the campaign, and on which he also feels Goldwater is the most vulnerable: peace. ***1964** in *OEDS:* Combined with a concentration on gut issues. **1968** Safire *New Lang. Pol.* 179: A peripheral issue in one campaign can be a gut issue in another. **1969** *Newsweek* (May 26) 48: The gut issues in the forthcoming election are not dramatic ones. ***1970** in *OEDS:* Some gut questions the pacifist must face. **1988** Univ. Tenn. instructor: There aren't any gut issues in this campaign. You call the Pledge of Allegiance a gut issue?

gut bomb *n.* a greasy hamburger; (*broadly*) any food considered to be especially unhealthy. Also **gut bomber.**

1969 *Current Slang* I & II 46: *Gut bombs,* n. Hamburgers.—College males, South Dakota. **1980** Grizzard *Billy Bob Bailey* 27: "Gutbombers," those little hamburgers that used to cost a dime and now cost

thirty-five cents. **1987** Knoxville, Tenn., man, age *ca*30: Let's go for some gut bombs. **1989** J. Weber *Defcon One* 122: Doherty complaining about…"gut bomb" doughnuts destroying his appetite. *a*1990 Poyer *Gulf* 187: Gut bombs and grease sticks.

gutbucket *n.* **1.a.** *Jazz.* jazz played in an especially earthy, bluesy, or robust manner, esp. in barrelhouse style. [Presumably short for *gutbucket jazz*, in allusion to **(2.a.),** below.]

1929 in Charters & Kunstadt *Jazz* 191: Using a mute,…[Louis Armstrong] eschews the tin pail, hat, plunger and other devices of the "gut bucket" player. **1935** *Vanity Fair* (Nov.) 71: *Gut-bucket* music…usually referring to the small hot recording bands and their discs. **1937** *New Yorker* (Apr. 17) 27: The most-used designations, in order of increasing hotness, are *gut-bucket, screwball,* and *whacky.* **1940** *New Yorker* (Sept. 14) 18: The music swings out high, wide, and gutbucket. **1943** Ottley *New World* 63: "Gut-bucket"…is now called boogie-woogie. **1946** Mezzrow & Wolfe *Really Blues* 141: It was real lowdown New Orleans gutbucket. **1950–52** Ulanov *Hist. Jazz* 351: *Gut-bucket:* music of the kind played in barrelhouses; synonymous with "barrelhouse." **1967–69** Foster & Stoddard *Pops* 44: They were gutbucket bands.…They played hot all the time.

b. a jazz or blues musician.

1971 Curtis *Banjo* 220: I got the word about an hour ago from a gutbucket in from Philly. He heard it from a hide-beater hophead.

2.a. *Black E.* a bucket used for food or liquor; (*hence*) inferior liquor, ROT GUT.

1932 R. Fisher *Conjure-Man* 234: Here—git yo'self a pint o' gutbucket. **1939** in R.S. Gold *Jazz Talk* 116: "Gut-bucket" [referred] …originally to the bucket which caught drippings or "gutterings" from the barrels, later to the unrestrained brand of music…played by small bands in the dives. **1954–60** *DAS:* Gutbucket…A pail used to carry beer, food, or water. *ca*1890, *used by Southern chain gangs and laborers, usu. Negro.* **1963** in J.H. Clarke *Harlem* 13: Harlem: A bastard child…baptized in the gut bucket of life, midwifed by oppression.

b. (see quot.).

1942 *ATS* 87: Toilet stool or chamber pot…*gut bucket.*

c. a washtub bass.

1964 *Golden Ring* (Folk-Legacy FSL-16) (LP) (insert p. 17): Herb Nudelman is a Chicago attorney who delights in spending his leisure time "thumping away" on his homemade washtub bass, commonly called a "gut-bucket." **1982** Least Heat Moon *Blue Hwys.* 117: That's DeePaul on the gut bucket.…He's not with the band. **1985** E. Leonard *Glitz* 112: They're beating on everything but a washboard and a gutbucket.

3.a. a grossly fat person.—used derisively.

1938 in *AS* XIV (Feb. 1939) 27: Gutbucket n. A pompous individual, usually corpulent. *a*1989 Spears *NTC Dict. Slang* 165: Harry is getting to be a real gutbucket.

b. the belly; BREADBASKET.

1957 H. Ellison *Deadly Streets* 159: The man was…just ripe for a switch-blade in the gut bucket. *a*1989 Spears *NTC Dict. Slang* 165: Sam poked Tod right in the gutbucket.

4. *Black E.* (see quots.).

1944 Burley *Hndbk. Jive* 139: Gutbucket—A low place, or music. **1957** *AS* (Dec.) 279: *Gut-bucket.* A low dive.

5. *Navy.* an old or unseaworthy vessel; RUST BUCKET.

1989 Cassell *S.S.N. Skate* 328: Escort duty on this twenty-five-year-old gut bucket.

gutbucketing *n.* *Jazz.* playing in GUTBUCKET style.

1936 *Fortune* (Apr.) 570: "Jamming,"…"riffing,"…"gut-bucketing," and all the rest are names for the *hot* performance, which is the…soul of jazz.

gut buggy *n.* an ambulance.

1969 in *DARE* I 437.

gut-burglar *n.* *Logging.* a cook; BELLY-BURGLAR.

1925 *AS* I 137: Cook…"Gut-burglar." **1948** J. Stevens *Jim Turner* 238: Christ, what a gut-burglar! **1965** O'Neill *High Steel* 271: Gut Burglar. Construction camp cook.

gut-burner see GUT-WARMER.

gut-buster *n.* a hilarious joke.

1985 C. Busch *Vampire Lesbians* 52: What keeps me going is a sense of humor…and so far…you're not racking up any gutbusters. **1987** *ALF* (NBC-TV): This one's a gut-buster! **1988** MacHovec *Humor* 101: "Gutbuster"…Hysterical laughter.

gut check *n.* Orig. *Football.* a quick evaluation and reassertion of spirit and resolve, usu. among teammates.

1972 Jenkins *Semi-Tough* 159: He wanted me and Shake to go out in the hall with him and have a "gut check." **1988** *Miami Vice* (NBC-TV): I think it's time for what some football coaches refer to as a "gut check." **1988** *CBS This Morning* (CBS-TV) (Sept. 29): It's really time for a gut check for everyone connected with the space program and at NASA. **1990** *American Gladiators* (synd. TV series): This event has got to be a gut check for you with that sprained ankle. **1993** *N.Y. Times* (June 1) A 14: It was a major gut-check for him to show up....As the Commander in Chief he should be here.

gut course see GUT, *adj.*, 1.

gut-eater *n. West.* a Native American.—used contemptuously. Hence **gut-eating**, *adj.*

1925 Z. Grey *Vanishing Amer.* 129: Your tribe of gut-eaters are too ignorant to see anything, let alone the white man's religion. **1949** Bellah *She Wore a Yellow Ribbon* (film): It was Red Shirt himself, Captain. The black-hearted, gut-eatin' son of a —. **1960** Loomis *Heroic Love* 94: You goddam, gut-eating, calf-butchering Indian! **1965** Fink et al. *Maj. Dundee* (film): Don't look like them gut-eaters was gonna feed 'em very good.

gut-fighter *n.* **1.** an aggressive, usu. undisciplined fighter who delivers rapid powerful punches to the abdomen.

1958 Missouri teenager (coll. J. Ball): Don't go after him. He's a gut-fighter! **1971** N.Y.C. draftsman, age *ca*50: A gut fighter [in the 1940's] meant a fighter who'd go straight for an opponent's stomach and hammer away at it.

2. *Pol.* a candidate or political operative who wages an unusually aggressive uncompromising campaign, especially against a politically stronger opponent.

1962 *Time* (Feb. 23) 62: Brusque, sly and opportunistic, Stanton...was the special blend of gut-fighter and idealist that Lincoln wanted and needed. *a***1968** in Safire *New Lang. Pol.* 179: The people voted for the homely, rumpled, irrational gutfighter, Harry Truman. **1968** *Ibid.*: Gutfighters are at their best dealing with "gut issues." **1984** Univ. Tenn. instructor: I guess the classic example of a political gut-fighter would be Richard Nixon. **1992** *Capitol Gang* (CNN-TV) (July 19): Bill Clinton is very much of a gut-fighter.

gutful *n.* enough to surfeit or disgust one; bellyful.

*****1900** *EDD* II 768: He's hungry [even] when he's got a gutful. **1923** in Hemingway *Sel. Letters* 80: You must either be getting fond of or else have a gutful of Rome by now. *****1960** in *OEDS*: I've just had a gutful, and want to have hell scared out of her.

gut-gouger *n. Logging.* a knot high on the trunk of a tree.

1963–64 Kesey *Great Notion* 179: Watch out those stobs we call gut-gougers.

gut hammer *n. Logging.* a hammer, metal bar, or the like used to strike a dinner gong, triangle, etc.; (*also*) the sound of such a device.

1925 (quot. at STOMACH-ROBBER). **1927** *DN* V 449: Gut-hammer, n. The dinner gong at a construction camp. **1930** *Amer. Merc.* (Oct.) 237: The gut-hammer's *clong, clong* broke the cold, silent darkness outside. **1941** *AS* (Oct.) 233: Guthammer. The musical triangle used for calling the men to mess. **1958** McCulloch *Woods Words* 75: Gut hammer—A short piece of iron used to pound an old saw, an iron triangle, a truck brake drum, or other chunk of metal to make a loud noise indicating when grub is on the table. **1979** Toelken *Dyn. of Folklore* 55: Gut hammer in a logging camp, the dinner bell or triangle.

gut-heater see GUT-WARMER.

gut-hook *n.* usu. *pl.* a riding spur.

1936 R. Adams *Cowboy Lingo* 96: Throw in yo' gut-hooks! *a***1940** in Lanning & Lanning *Texas Cowboys* 65 [ref. to *ca*1900]: We...gave our horses the guthooks and dashed to where the herd was. *a***1940** in Logsdon *Whorehouse Bells* 95: My Garcia gut-hooks are fuckin' his flanks. **1967** Decker *To Be a Man* 134: You don't need to look see if Jerry's using his gut hooks, you can hear him. Too bad he didn't draw a better bronc. **1968** I. Reed *Yellow Back Radio* 44: His reading...was interrupted by the jingle of guthooks mounting the steps. **1988** in *DARE*.

gut horn *n. Logging.* (see 1958 quot.).

[*****1915–25** Fraser & Gibbons *Soldier & Sailor Wds.* 113: Gut's horn, the: The dinner bugle call.] **1958** McCulloch *Woods Words* 76: Gut horn—In the old days, a long tin horn blown by the cook's helper to call a logging crew to eat. **1969** in *DARE*.

gut issue see GUT, *adj.*, 3.

gutless *adj.* cowardly; in phr. **gutless wonder** an abject coward. Now *colloq.*

1900 (cited in *W10*). **1915** in Pound *Pound/Joyce* 45: This deluge of work by suburban counter-jumpers on one hand and gut-less Oxford graduates or flunktuates on the other...bah! **1930** in D.O. Smith *Cradle* 115: Not one man...can be gutless. **1934** Weseen *Dict. Slang* 346: Gutless—lacking in courage or power. **1937** Hemingway *Have & Have Not* 170: Quit stalling, you gutless wonder. **1954** Chessman *Cell 2455* 48: Listen to this punk whine, Charley....I told you he was a gutless wonder. **1956** Poe *Attack* (film): You play the gutless wonder just one more time, I'll come back and get you, Cooney. **1966** *Voyage to Bottom of Sea* (ABC-TV): The gutless wonder just sits there. **1970** Vasquez *Chicano* 76: You, Victorio, are a gutless wonder. **1973** *N.Y. Post* (May 12) 35: I...think you are a gutless wonder for permitting it. **1982** Sen. Jesse Helms (R.–N.C.), on WKGN news (Sept. 23): We don't need any gutless wonders in the United States Senate. **1987** Sen. Orrin Hatch (R.–Utah) (Nov. 9): There are gutless wonders down there who don't back the President when he needs it. **1988** F. Robinson & B. Stainback *Extra Innings* 139: You didn't even have the guts to come close!...You're gutless! **1993** *N.Y. Times* (June 1) A 14: It is an absolute disgrace that this gutless wonder [*sc.* Pres. Bill Clinton] showed up here....He lied and lied and lied again to get out of the draft. He ran away when he had a job to do.

gut out *v.* to endure bravely and tenaciously. Also **guts out.**

1963–64 Kesey *Great Notion* 373: Are you scared to gut it out, Floyd? **1971** *N.Y. Post* (July 8) 68: "Guts," Mike Kekich said. "I gutted it out there tonight." **1973** N.Y.U. student: You'll have to guts it out. **1976** Rosen *Above Rim* 156: We both have to tough it out a little longer...gut it out, know what I mean? *a***1989** R. Herman, Jr. *Warbirds* 241: Right now, though, we have to gut it out. **1993** *N.Y. Times* (June 7) C 2: I had to gut out the head wind up the hill because I knew I would have a tail wind all the way into town.

gut-piece *n.* the abdomen.

1967 D. Ford *Muc Wa* 74: I'm gonna take a bullet through the gut piece and old Toffee is gonna lean over me and say, "Pray, you bastard, pray!"

gut plunge *n.* (among tramps) an attempt to beg meat, as from a butcher shop.—constr. with *on butch.*

1929 Barr *Let Tomorrow Come* 40: I go up on the avenue to make a gut plunge on butch. *Ibid.* 266: Gut—Bologna, or any sausage. To *make a gut plunge on butch* is to beg meat of any kind from a meat-market proprietor. **1935** J. Conroy *World to Win* 57: I made a gut plunge on butch fer a batch o' mulligan meat. **1948** Chaplin *Wobbly* 180 [ref. to *ca*1915]: Ping a couple of clackers when you go broke and make a gut plunge on butch.

gut-punch *v.* to punch in the belly.

1974 Loken *Come Monday Mornin'* 105: He'd'a gut-punched him off that stool.

gut-reamer *n.* (see quot.).

1927 *DN* V 449: Gut-reamer, n. An active pederast. Also *gut-butcher, gut-stretcher, gut-stuffer,* etc. **1930** Irwin *Tramp & Und. Sl.*: Gut Reamer...A vulgarism best undefined.

gut-ripper *n.* **1.** (see quot.).

1865 in *Tenn. Hist. Qly.* XXXV (1976) 305: A strong breast work with a wide ditch...and three rows of gut-ripers [*sic*] in front of that....Gut-ripers are sharp sticks set in the ground close together...to hit a man in the stomach.

2. a knife used as a weapon.

1941 Algren *Neon Wilderness* 56: His own...spring-blade cuts-all genuine...all-American gut-ripper.

gut-robber *n.* BELLY-ROBBER.

1919 Piesbergen *Overseas with an Aero Squadron* 51: The most unpopular man in any organization is the cook...he is "a crab," "a gut-robber," and "a glutton." **1936** McCarthy *Mosshorn* (unp.): Greasy Belly, Gut Robber or Grub Spoiler. A cook. **1942–49** Goldin et al. *DAUL* 299: Prison, cook of a...gut robber...Prison, warden of a...gut robber. **1955** in *West. Folk.* XV (1956) 204: A gut robber is a camp cook. **1956** Sorden & Ebert *Logger's* 17 [ref. to *a*1925]: Gut-robber, A poor cook in a logging camp. **1966, 1967** in *DARE*.

guts *adj.* **1.** requiring or demonstrating courage or fortitude.—used prenominally.

1957 *Newsweek* (July 8) 85: Probably the most exquisite variation of all is the one known to Princeton men as "Guts Frisbee," in which, not a plastic saucer, but a rusty 6-inch circular saw blade is used. **1973** N.Y.U. student: That was a guts move.

2. earthy or spirited.

1962 McDavid *Amer. Lang.* 744: Erroll Garner...*blows* some *guts* piano.

guts ball *n.* a ballgame such as baseball played with great aggressiveness and tenacity; (*hence*) any action or actions requiring or demonstrating fortitude, extreme competitiveness, etc.

1962 Kesey *Cuckoo's Nest* 74: Hey-yah, comin' at you, guts ball from here on out. **1962** Harvey *Strike Command* 11: Want to turn and run?...Or play a little guts-ball and try for the tankers....K.P. Green voted for gutsball. **1965** Harvey *Hudasky's Raiders* 88: "Listen, Buzz— you want to play a little gutsball?" "Gutsball?" "...We'll go in so high he'll never see us on radar." **1977** *Baa Baa Black Sheep* (NBC-TV): Ho boy. Mr. Gutsball, eh?

gutsball *adj.* GUTSY.

1963–64 Kesey *Great Notion* 30: Just like the corny, gung-ho, guts-ball posters that I seen a good thousand of. **1965** Harvey *Hudasky's Raiders* 97: This was real gutsball stuff. **1983–86** G.C. Wilson *Supercarrier* 103: A guts-ball decision.

gut-scraper *n.* a fiddler.

*a1720 in D'Urfey *Pills* II 218: Strike up drowsie Gut-scrapers. **1738** *Vocal Miscellany* (ed. 3) I 215: I still am a merry Gut-Scraper....I can...sing any Tune, but a Psalm. ***1785** R. Burns in *F & H* III 238: Her charms had struck a sturdy Caird,/As weel's a poor gut-scraper. ***1834** Marryat *Peter Simple* ch. xxxi: You may save yourself the trouble, you dingy gut-scraper. **1934** Weseen *Dict. Slang* 143: *Gut-scraper*—A violinist.

gut-shoot *v.* Orig. *West.* to shoot in the belly or abdomen.

1935 Coburn *Law Rides Range* 5: He's out to either gut-shoot or run me outa the country. **1937** Glidden *Brand of Empire* 80: I'll gut-shoot you, sure as hell. **1940** F. Hunt *Trail fr. Tex.* 118 [ref. to 1870's]: Don't believe I'd gut-shoot him if I was you, Ad. **1955** "W. Henry" *Wyatt* 145: In jail for disturbing the peace by gutshooting one Jim Hickey. **1963** *True* (May) 104: Take the safe way and gut-shoot him. **1985** Heywood *Taxi Dancer* 32: He figured they'd come up from below and gut-shoot them.

gut-shot *adj.* Orig. *West.* having been shot in the belly or abdomen.

1848 Ruxton *Life in Far West* 14: Seven Injuns lay wolf's meat, while a many more went away gut-shot. **1878** in *OEDS*: Gut-shot, hit in the belly; wounded but not disabled. **1962** Tregaskis *Vietnam Diary* 86: I've seen 'em gut-shot, head-shot. **1982** I.M. Hunter *Blue & Gray* (NBC-TV movie): You can't help me none. I'm gut-shot.

gut-struggle *n.* a dance in which the partners hold each other as close as possible.

1926 in Leadbitter & Slaven *Blues Records* 196: Gut Struggle.

guts-up *n.* extremely GUTSY; fearless. Also **guts-high.**

1958 Frede *Entry E* 41: Stew Trent...drinker and whorechaser and general guts-high gung-ho aborigine. **1967** W. Murray *Sweet Ride* 183: Denny Maguire? He was guts up, man. **1972** Jenkins *Semi-Tough* 275: Guts up time now. This is a gut check. Gotta have it.

gutsy *adj.* **1.** having a fat belly. Cf. *OED2*, def. 1, 'greedy; voracious'.

1890 in F. Remington *Sel. Letters* 104: Our new general (McCook) "Gutsy" was here.

2. having GUTS; courageous; spirited; plucky; robust.

*1890–93 *F & H* III 237: Gutsy, adj. = having *guts*. **1936** *AS* XL 101: Gutsy folk do not care for much pussyfooting. **1951** in *DAS*: I think he's plenty gutsy. **a1965** in *World Bk. Dict.*: A gutsy singer. **1971** Horan *Blue Messiah* 44: He always was a gutsy guy. **1987** *RHD2*: Gutsy writing; gutsy red wine. **1990** *Regardie's* (Sept.) 27: On the campaign trail, [she] has run a gutsy race.

gut through *v.* GUT OUT.

1975 Greer *Slammer* 111: Tough it out, gut it through, buddy! **1989** Berent *Rolling Thunder* 57: Gutting my way through...Engineering at ASU.

guttersnipe *n.* **1.** *Finance.* (see 1877 quot.).

1856 [M. Thomson & E. Underhill] *Elephant Club* 57: He belongs to a class of beings in New York...known by the ornithological appellation of "gutter-snipes." **1870** Medbery *Wall St.* 136: *Gutter Snipes.* Curbstone brokers. **1877** Bartlett *Amer.* (ed. 4) 272: *Guttersnipes.* A Wall

Street term for brokers who do business chiefly on the sidewalk or in the street, and who are not members of the Stock Exchange. **1885** *Harper's Mo.* (Nov.) 842: A "gutter snipe," or "curbstone" broker,...belongs to no regular organization, has no office where comparisons may be made and notices served..., [and] does business mainly on the sidewalk.

2. *Printing.* (see quot.).

1871 in *OED*: Guttersnipe, a small and narrow bill or poster, which is usually pasted on curbstones.

guttersniping *n.* **1.** *Finance.* operating as a GUTTERSNIPE.

a1877 in Bartlett *Amer.* (ed. 4) 272: A recent ordinance by the Board of Aldermen makes *gutter-sniping* a misdemeanor.

2. (see quot.).

1928 in Wilstach *Stage Slang* (unp.): "Gutter-sniping"...means playing music in the street and passing the hat for money.

gut-twister *n.* *West.* a horse that bucks savagely.

1927 Rollins *Jinglebob* 181 [ref. to 1880's]: Get 'em each a...real gentle, lady's hoss for ridin' now, an' likewise a jubilant gut-twister for when the time's up.

gutty *adj.* GUTSY.

1942 *ATS* 302: Courageous; plucky...gritty, gutty,...spunky. **1952** J.D. MacDonald *Damned* 54: Gutty singing. **1953** in *DAS*: Here come the Guttiest Guys of All. **1958** *Esquire* (Feb.) 35: A good gutty rock number. ***1960** in *OEDS*: I can get gutty characters to play at last. **1962** McDavid *Amer. Lang.* 744: A *gutty* style is replete with a *blue tonality* and a *back beat*. **1968** Johnson & Johnson *Count Me Gone* 149: They're so gutty. **1969–71** Kahn *Boys of Summer* 52: MacPhail was gutty and brilliant and he rebuilt the team.

gut-wagon *n.* **1.** a wagon or truck that hauls the carcasses of dead farm stock.—often in prov. phrs. Also **gut truck.**

1925 Mullin *Scholar Tramp* 109 [ref. to ca1912]: I wuz a-thrapsin' along the sthrate that hungry I wud o' chased a boozzard off'n a gut-wagon. **1930** Botkin *Folk-Say* 110: "You smell like a wet dog."..."You'd stink anybody off a gut wagon." **1930** Randolph *Who Blowed Up the Church House?* 150: She was good looking too, and the boys was all after her like buzzards after a gut-wagon. **1956** Brooks *Last Hunt* (film): Smelled enough to knock a dog off a gut-wagon in a dead faint. **1962** Stone *Ride the High Country* (film): Smellin' bad enough to gag a dog off a gut-wagon. **1966** Braly *On Yard* 11: She was so...homely...she'd come near scaring a dog off a gut wagon. **1975** *UTSQ*: Ugly enough to gag a maggot off a gut-wagon. **1983** K. Weaver *Texas Crude* 41: A "gut truck" is a vehicle used to haul carcasses of dead stock from farms, ranches, etc., to a rendering plant. **1985** Masters & Johnston *Sassy Sayin's* 69: She's ugly enough to scare a buzzard off a gut wagon.

2. *Logging.* (see quot.).

1958 McCulloch *Woods Words* 76: *Gut wagon*—The camp supply wagon.

gut-warmer *n.* a strong or bracing drink of liquor. Also **gut-burner, gut-heater.**

a1944 R. Adams *West. Words*: Gut-warmer. A cowboy's name for whisky. **1958** McCulloch *Woods Words* 75: *Gut heater*—A slug of whiskey. **1976** Rosten *To Anywhere* 321: "Martini." "One gut-burner comin' up!" **1978** *UTSQ*: Splo, gut warmer, shine.

gut-winder *n.* a bullet wound in the abdomen.

1865 in H. Johnson *Talking Wire* 225: [The Indians] fought the boys for half an hour, one of them receiving a "gut winder" which sent him to the "happy hunting ground."

gut-works *n.pl.* the belly.

1974 R. Carter *16th Round* 309: I realized deep down in my gut-works that the...police...hoped—I would...be killed.

gut-wrapper *n.* *Logging.* (see quots.).

1950 *West. Folk.* IX 381: Gut wrapper. A chain or cable that is placed around a half-loaded truck to secure the load better. **1956** *AS* (May) 150: *Gut wrapper*...A piece of chain or cable within a load of logs used to hold together an individual tier. **1962** *AS* XXXVII 269: This chain's specifications and use are defined under the entry for the term *Gut-Wrapper* in the California Vehicle Code. **1967** in *DARE*.

gut-wrench *n.* the penis. *Joc.*

1943 in Legman *Limerick* 129: There was once a mechanic named Bench/Whose best tool was a sturdy gut-wrench. **1983** K. Weaver *Texas Crude* 73: When my old lady gets jumpy, I just give her a little taste of the ol' gutwrench and she settles right down. **1988** Dye *Outrage* 21: I'd like to break her down like a twelve-gauge shotgun and get her with my number-nine gut wrench.

guv *n.* var. GOV.

guv'nor *n.* var. GOVERNOR.

guy[1] *n.* [orig. in allusion to the grotesque effigies of *Guy Fawkes*, leader of the Gunpowder Plot (1605), traditionally displayed in England on Nov. 5, Guy Fawkes Day; sometimes misattributed to Yiddish or Hebrew *goy* 'non-Jew'; see discussion in *Jewish Linguistic Studies* 2, 1990, p. 186]

1.a. a grotesque-looking, ill-dressed, or ridiculous person, esp. an old man; (*hence*) a person who is an object of ridicule or derision; (*broadly*) a fool.

*1820–21 P. Egan *Life in London* 142: The "Old Guy," on the top of the stairs, with his spectacles on, is...inviting her to partake of...wine. ***1823** (cited in Partridge *DSUE* 364). ***1836** in *OED*: The gentlemen are all "rigged Tropical,"...grisly Guys some of them turn out! ***1837** in *F & H* III 240: With her knees to her nose, and her nose to her chin,/ Leering up with that queer, indescribable grin,/You'd lift up your hands in amazement and cry,/"Well!—I never *did* see such a regular guy!" **1840** *Spirit of Times* (Apr. 25) 89: And a precious Guy I looked in it, so the old 'oman said. **1840** *Spirit of Times* (July 4) 216: He was put up for Col. Freelove, proved a forlorn "*guy*," and was hissed from the stage. **1847** in Oehlschlaeger *Reveille* 137: He was not ill-looking, but he was "a guy" in his manners. ***1859** Hotten *Slang Dict.*: Guy, a fright, a dowdy, an ill-dressed person. **1860** in Partridge *DSUE* (ed. 8) 516: Thank God, we have got rid of all those damn drunken guys at last. ***1861** in *OED*: He was such an old guy in his dress. **1869** Logan *Foot Lights* 230: You'd look a pretty guy, wouldn't you, now, after being a good Union woman all along, to go and turn Secesh at the last moment, and just, too, at the very time when their prospects...look most all-fired quisby. **1875** *Minstrel Gags* 5: They were only quizzing you, Mr. Bones....You were the counterpart of a boiling spring, because you was a *guy*, *sir* (geyser). **1879** Campbell *Fairfax* 163: MRS. D. (*Smiling*) Just the same old Guy! GAY. (*Assuming an air of injury*) Now come! I don't think I was ever an old "guy." The crows may have planted their infernal feet in my face, but my heart is still free from the frost, thank heaven! **1884** *Life* (Oct. 1) 185: *She:* What a nonsensical dress for a lady! *He:* And what a guy the man is! **1889** "M. Twain" *Conn. Yankee* 137: They said—"Oh, what a guy!" And hove clods at us. ***a1890–93** *F & H* III 240: Guy...As in the old street cry, "Hollo, boys, there goes another *guy!*" (an abbreviation of Guy Fawkes) = a figure of fun; a fright. ***1893** in *OED*: Little boys were dressed up to look the greatest of guys. **1898** Stead *Satan's Invisible World* 109: The victim, who was known as a "Come on" or as a "Guy," was swindled by a variety of methods. **1901** *Chi. Tribune* (July 28) 38: *Reuben.* A simple rustic....A countryman. A hayseed. A guy. A geezer. **1910** Hapgood *City Streets* 77: Broadway taste, he shows, admits of no such sentiments, for a "softy" and a "guy" are the worst things on earth.

b. a comical or joking fellow; card; (*hence*) a smart aleck.

ca1862 *Dodge's Sketches* 29: Have you ever seen...Ossian E. Dodge, the singer, writer, and punster? He is emphatically a "queer guy," and what he don't happen to *know* about setting a table or a fashionable house in a roar, Hamlet's facetious friend Yorick never could have taught him. **1867** Macnamara *Irish Ninth* 65: One of the many comical characters attached to our regiment was "Balls Hamilton;" and he, indeed, was a comical guy. **1895** in J. London *Tramp Diary* 62: Do I know w'ere dey is? Yer jest bet I do...wot der yer tink I am? A cheap guy? **1913** Jocknick *Early Days* 35: He speedily became a butt of ridicule for all of the "guys" in the Ute nation. **1934** D.W. Maurer, in *AS* (Feb. 1935) 16 [ref. to *a*1910]: Guy. A smart aleck.

c. *Circus & Carnival.* a customer or patron, usu. a man. Cf. similar sense development of MARK.

1878 (quot. at SNIDE, *adj.*). **1886** F. Whittaker *Pop Hicks* 2: Ride... round the tent and whoop up the guys. *Ibid.* 3: I've got a better show...or the guys wouldn't come in as they do. *Ibid.* 11: I don't want to hurt your name before the guys. **1891** Devere *Tramp Poems* 88: "Gawks," "guys" and "Rubes," another day,/When e'er a circus comes your way./And you are spilein' for a "clim,"/Be sure they haven't learned to sing.

2.a. a man or boy; fellow; in phr. **main guy** a man in authority or of importance.—constr. with *the*; in phr. **the Guy upstairs** [and vars.], God. Now *colloq.* [The form *main guy*, common *ca*1885–*ca*1925, is now rare.]

1875 in Miller & Snell *Why West Was Wild* 492: She was finally gathered by a "nabbing guy" [policeman]...under charge of loose and "laskivious" conduct. **1877** in Asbury *Gem of Prairie* [opp. p. 136]: Do you soak your feet in the old guy's barrel of lightning? Hattie says you must, from the smell of your breath every evening. **1882** in Nye *Western Humor* 85: The main guy of *The Boomerang* sanctum was putting some carbolic acid in the paste pot, and unlimbering his genius. **1883–84** F. Whittaker *L. Locke* 178: Skip, cully, skip. Main guy's comin'. **1886** F. Whittaker *Pop Hicks* 3: Go and put the newspaper guy straight. *Ibid.* 9: Who's the guy? *Ibid.* 23: I'll go and see the guy, and find what he means. **1891** Maitland *Slang Dict.* 173: Main guy (Am.), the chief or leader of any organization. **1892** Norr *China Town* 41: Here were these guys going to let a good man go away for a few thousand dollars when Fitz had played in twice the money over their tables. **1893** F.P. Dunne, in Schaaf *Dooley* 54: Lam over with me to th' A-art Institoot...an' see th' big guys in lithrachoor....I asks Tiddy about th' guys above....He ain't no rayporther....He's a lithry guy. *Ibid.* 272: Still she'd be a woman all th' same an' fr th' best lukin' guy in th' race. **1894** in Ade *Chicago Stories* 101: You're the guy that had the fight in that saloon. **1896** Ade *Artie* 56: Tommy Bradshaw—he was the main guy [i.e., the groom], you know. **1897** Work *Waifs* 109: He's de big guy in de Dispatch office. **1898** Dunne *Peace & War* 221: An' he put three or four good faml'ies to wurruk in th' gas-house, where he knew th' main guy. **1899** A.H. Lewis *Sandburrs* 154: Oh! dey was some fly guys locked up in that old coop. **1899** in "O. Henry" *Works* 521: I guess I finds meeself here about de same way as yous guys. **1902** Mead *Word-Coinage* 182: The boss of the [circus] show was called "the main guy." **1902** Wister *Virginian* 23: But a man like that black-headed guy is...need never worry you. **1912** Mathewson *Pitching* 35: That guy, Alexander, is a hard one to beat. **1914** Ellis *Billy Sunday* 183: Oh, but the devil is a smooth guy. **1918–19** MacArthur *Bug's-Eye View* 23: "Red" Langlands was a pretty good guy, even if he was a mess sergeant. **1924** P. Marks *Plastic Age* 192: He is a social leper....He isn't a "regular guy." **1928** *Amer. Mercury* (Aug.) 469: His attempt to be a regular guy was pathetic. **1930–33** T. Wolfe *Time & River* 161: They made a constant and stupefying use of that terrible gray abortion of a word "guy": it studded their speech..., without it they would have been completely speechless. **1935** Fortune *Fugitives* 147: Come here, guy. I want to talk to you. **1935** Marion et al. *Riffraff* (film): These newsreel guys wanna take my picture. **1942** *ATS* 321: God...The Big Guy. **1943** Holmes & Scott *Mr. Lucky* (film): Some of the main guys here don't like gambling. **1947** Kuttner *Fury* 20: I look like an ordinary guy. But I'm not. I'm a trick mutant. **1948** Robinson & Smith *J. Robinson* 75: Actually, I didn't want to know what kind of a guy *he* was—I wanted him to know what kind of a guy *I* was. **1953** W. Brown *Monkey on My Back* 23: Ralph went on to say he wanted his son to be a "real guy," but that his mother was "making a sissy out of the kid." **1954** *West. Hum. Rev.* VIII 273: The millions have seized on *guy* with the proprietary enthusiasm with which they have adopted chewing gum, diners, and comics....It is one of the few words—*okay* is the only other polite one—that *all* Americans feel belong to them. **1957** Evans & Evans *Dict. Contemp. Usage* 211: Guy...must be one of the most frequently used words in America. It is a lazy man's word, reducing all adult males to simulacra among whom there is no need to make a distinction. **1964** W. Stringfellow *My People* 25: Most other guys felt about the same, I think. *a*1979 Gillespie & Fraser *To Be* 48: A blind guy owned the place then. **1981** Graziano & Corsel *Somebody Down Here* 211: The road the Guy up there made me travel. *a*1982 Medved *Hospital* 7: I saw a surgeon, an orthopedist who's a well-known guy. **1987** *Kate & Allie* (CBS-TV): I ran into the delivery guy on the stairs. **1984–88** W.C. Booth *Company We Keep* 319: Total manliness (I'm *that* kind of guy!).

b. a person of either sex regarded as decent, down-to-earth, good company, etc.; (*hence*) (in *pl.*, usu. following *you*) persons of either sex. [The second nuance has become notably common in direct address among young women only since *ca*1940.]

1927 in E. O'Neill *Sel. Letters* 263: She is a "real guy." You'd like her immensely. **1929** Asch *Pay Day* 14: Be a good guy, Ma, and wait a couple of days. **1932** *AS* VII 401: One girl to others: "Come on, guys." **1934** Duff & Sauber *20 Million Sweethearts* (film): She'll understand. She's a great guy. **1934** Burns *Female Convict* 227: There are some mighty hard-boiled guys in here [a women's prison] now...and they're stirrin' up the other convicts. **1935** C.J. Daly *Murder* 175: She was just a regular guy, underneath. **1939** C. Wilbur & F. Niblo *Hell's Kitchen* (film): You're a right guy, Miss Avery. **1939–40** Tunis *Kid from Tomkinsville* 129: Jack MacManus was a real guy. **1942** Wylie *Vipers* 191: Mom, however, is a great little guy. **1942** in *Jour. Gen. Psych.* LXVI (1945) 132: Guy...boy, girl, student, person....One girl to others, "Come on, you guys."..."Guy" is used without regard to age or sex. **1950** Solt *Lonely Place* (film): She's a good guy. I'm glad she's on my side. **1957** Bannon *Odd Girl* 32: Guess I'll hit the sack, you guys [women]. **1962** Carr & Cassavetes *Too Late Blues* (film): Hey, you guys thirsty? **1975** Makkai et al. *Dict. Amer. Idioms* 283: Regular guy...A friendly person who is easy to get along with; a good sport. **1980** Peck & Young *Little Darlings* (film) [one girl speaking to two others]: Guys!…I've got vitamin E and some niacin! **1986** *New Leave It to Beaver* (synd. TV series): For a lady, you're a pretty good guy. **1986** *New York* (Dec. 15) 94: You hear a woman say to two others, "Guys, guys, come on, you guys."

c. (also applied casually to animals, esp. household pets).
1978 Charell *Upper Hand* 28: The poor caged guy [i.e. a dog] would be placed on a conveyor belt, like luggage. **1980** Lorenz *Guys Like Us* 31: Mutant was a big frisky guy who rarely barked.

d. an object; item. *Joc.*
1980 Lorenz *Guys Like Us* 90: "Here," he said, getting another [pastry], "have one of these tasty guys." **1984** Weinberger & Daniels *Lonely Guy* (film): I'll take this guy [a potted plant] here. **1987** *New Yorker* (July 13) 19: These green guys are resistors. These funny little guys are diodes. **1988** *Miami Vice* (NBC-TV): So these guys [bombs] don't know the difference between soldiers and civilians. **1993** *CBS This Morning* (CBS-TV) (July 27): M & M's [candies]. I love these guys.

guy² *n.* [cf. GUY, *v.*] **1.** *Und.* a person who acts as a decoy in a confidence game; (*also*) a petty swindler.
1850 "N. Buntline" *G'hals of N.Y.*: That is the *guy*—…The other…is the victim! **1878** in Miller & Snell *Why West Was Wild* 347: Upon discovering the cheat, Markel caused the arrest of one Harry Bell, the leader of the gang, and a bold and successful guy that sailed under the sobriquet of "Kid."

2. a trick or hoax; prank; jest.
1854 in Dorson *Long Bow* 87: That…was all a *guy*. **1856** "H. Hazel" *Jack Waid* 11: I think the old guys, the tricks, and the dodges vill do 'ere. **1882** in Bunner *Letters* 70: But the idea of putting it into a comic publication is simply absurd. It would be taken for some sort of guy. **1887** in *DN* VI 311: He testified that he swore in his former evidence that he was a democrat, as he says, for a "guy." **1911** in *DA:* I was only joking.…It's a standing guy, you know.

guy *adj.* interesting and fully understandable only to men.—used prenominally. Cf. CHICK, *adj.*
1992 Univ. Tenn. instructor, age *ca*30: It must be a guy thing. **1993** *Funny Times* (Apr.) 16: "The Soviets are working on a mirror in outer space to reflect light back to Earth." "A real guy project." **1993** *Showbiz Today* (CNN-TV) (June 28): A guy movie is *Field of Dreams*. **1993** *New Yorker* (Aug. 23) 62: At last, a real guy movie.

guy *v.* **1.** to ridicule; taunt; bait. Now *S.E.*
*1854 in *OEDS:* "Good gracious! the audience will guy you!"…"Guy me? What do you mean by *guy*?"…"Why, laugh at you, to be sure—and *chaff* you." **1867** *Nat. Police Gaz.* (Jan. 12): He was foolish enough to "guy the cops." **1869** "M. Twain" *Innocents Abroad* I 355: The Roman street-boy who…guyed the gladiators from the dizzy gallery. **1880** in *DA:* They would "guy" the life out of us. **1883** Peck *Bad Boy* 274: They never "guy" me, 'cause I act well my part. **1888** in P. Dickson *Baseball Dict.* 191: They guyed the red stockings and cheered the black. **1890** in L. Stillwell *Common Soldier* 52: That would have given those Indiana fellows a chance to chaff and guy me. **1893** Riis *Nisby* 38: I'll tache ye to come a "guyin'" o' me. **1894** in Dreiser *Journalism* I 229: Welsor, laughing, "guyed" Deputy Skidmore, but declined to give him revenge. He had had enough of checkers. **1898** in S. Crane *Complete Stories* 429: Say, he'll be guyed about this for years. **1907** in "O. Henry" *Works* 1370: The bald-headed fellow was guying him about it the other night after supper. **1908** Fletcher *Rebel Private* 82: The infantry were good at guying the cavalry and thought the boys had little to do but find Yankees for them to fight. **1945** Huie *Omaha to Oki.* 135: The Marines guyed me and said I ought to get a Purple Heart for being shot in the tail with my own canteen.

2. to hoax; PUT ON. Now *S.E.*
1890 E. Custer *Guidon* 117: I was rather incredulous of their stories…as I had been so often "guyed." **1978** T. Berger *Arthur Rex* 87: King Arthur…had begun to suspect that he was being guyed.

guzzle *n.* **1.** the throat or esophagus. Cf. GOZZLE, GOOZLE, GOOZLER.
*1659 in *OED:* A single [cord]…wou'd spoile your drinking, t'wou'd ty up your guzle. **1834** Caruthers *Kentuck. in N.Y.* I 25: I'm told the Yankees always sings a psalm before they go to battle.…A chap would make a blue fist of takin a dead aim…with the butt end of a psalm in his guzle. **1851** R. Burts *Sea-King* 152: I'll beat that binnacle down your guzzle, with a top maul! **1875** in Miller & Snell *Why West Was Wild* 492: A soiled dove got her guzzle full of whisky last Friday. **1905** W.S. Kelly *Lariats* 328: We use ter make a horse swaller medicine by rubbin' its guzzle up and down. **1933** D. Runyon, in *Collier's* (Aug. 5) 8: Somebody

grabs Mr. Justin Veezee by the guzzle. **1986** Univ. Tenn. instructor, age 27: Your throat is your *guzzle*. Or *goozle*.

2. a. liquor.
*1704 in *OED:* Over seal'd Winchesters of three-penny guzzle. ***1709** in *OED:* Drink Porters Guzzle much oftner than Claret. ***1785** Grose *Vulgar Tongue: Guzzle.* Liquor. **1832** in Jackson *Early Songs of Uncle Sam* 258: Heaven ne'er formed a drunker maid,/A maid so fond of guzzle. ***1893** in *OED:* They'd sell ye "guzzle" for next to nothin'. **1936** in *DAS:* No lower guzzle-shop was ever operated in the United States.
b. a drink of liquor.
1879 Rooney *Quaint Conundrums* 80: A drink is a "smile" or a "guzzle." **1975** McCaig *Danger Trail* 5: I figger I should oughta get one guzzle out of you.
3. a fraud.
1852 B.R. Hall *Freeman's Barber Shop* 171: Where information may be had *gratis!* about some great New England North American scheme or—guzzle!

guzzle *v.* **1.** to swindle.
1848 in R.W. Paul *Mining Frontiers* 13: All sham…to guzzle the gullible. **1887** DeVol *Gambler* 278: Them fellers guzzled me out of $1000 in Cincinnati.
2. to seize by the throat, esp. with an armlock; to strangle; (*broadly*) to murder.
*1885 in *OEDS: Guzzle,* to choke violently. **1900** Hammond *Whaler* 249: "I'll be guzzled!"ejaculated Mr. Brown. **1901** King *Dog-Watches* 224: I loudly declared that…I could show some of them…that I could guzzle any one of them. **1930** D. Runyon, in *Sat. Eve. Post* (Apr. 5) 4: Gloomy Gus…is guzzled right at his front door. **1933** in D. Runyon *More Guys* 13: I'd guzzle him like a turkey. **1933** Ersine *Pris. Slang* 42: *Guzzle*…To choke, throttle. "Joe guzzled a drunk and took his roll." **1931–34** in Clemmer *Pris. Commun.* 332: *Guzzle*…To strangle. **1966** S. Harris *Hellhole* 167: He thried to guzzle me like a tiger. I begun crying and he gave me a taste of his fist.
3. *Und.* to arrest.
1936 *AS* (Apr.) 122: *Guzzled.* Arrested. **1937** Reitman *Box-Car Bertha* 107: Anna had just been "guzzled," (that is, arrested).

guzzled *adj.* drunk.
1939 Howsley *Argot* 23: Guzzled—Drunk.

guzzle-guts *n.* a heavy drinker.
*1788 Grose *Vulgar Tongue* (ed. 2): Guzzle Guts. One greedy of liquor. **1942** *ATS* 110: Drunkard…*guzzle-guts.*

guzzler *n.* **1.** *Und.* (see quot.).
1928 Panzram *Killer* 303: It is well understood in the underworld that the worst insulting name that anyone can call another is that he is a muzzler and a guzzler. This means that the man is lost to all decency and is beyond all redemption.
2. Esp. *Wrestling.* a stranglehold.
1972 *Playboy* (Feb.) 126: Swiftly applying a double scissors, a toe hold, a half nelson and a Gilligan guzzler with one hand, he began poking his opponent's eyes out with the other. *Ibid.* 185: Choking each other purple with Gilligan guzzlers.

gweeb *n.* *Stu.* DWEEB; (see also 1982 quot.). Also **gweep, gweebo.**
[**1950** *West. Folklore* IX 158: Goop. Any particularly uninspired hash.…*Gweep.* The same as *goop.*] **1982** *Time* (Nov. 8) 92: In the Hacker's Dictionary, one finds…*gweep* (one who spends unusually long periods of time hacking). **1984** Mason & Rheingold *Slanguage: Gweeb,* n. Intense nerd. **1986** Eble *Campus Slang* (Mar.) 5: *Gweeb*—person entirely lacking style; worse than a geek. **1986** *NDAS: Gweebo*…A tedious and contemptible person. **1988** Univ. Tenn. student theme: A *gweeb* is a guy who does not meet my qualifications.

G-woman *n.* [sugg. by G-MAN] a woman who is an FBI agent.
1984 *N.Y. Post* (Aug. 30) 24: G-Women Mugged. Two female FBI agents having lunch at Central Park's lake were mugged yesterday by two men who stole their guns and handcuffed them together.

gym *n.* a gymnasium. Now *S.E.*
1866–71 Bagg *At Yale* 45: Gym, abbreviation for gymnasium. ***1887** Baumann *Londinismen* 70: Gym-shoes. **1893** in F. Remington *Sel. Letters* 201: New athletic Park and gym. **1910** in O. Johnson *Lawrenceville* 255 [ref. to 1890's]: The old Gym.

gym rat *n.* an athletically inclined person who frequents a gymnasium, as for playing basketball informally.
1978 *Wash. Post* (Apr. 30) D1: He plays volleyball, softball, "gym-rat basketball," and runs. **1987** *60 Minutes* (CBS-TV) (May 11): The new,

approachable face of Notre Dame: President as gym rat.

gynie *n. Med.* gynecology; a gynecologist. Also **gynae.**
*1933 Partridge *Slang To-day & Yesterday* 190: *Gynie,* gynæcology.
1942 *ATS* 513: *Gynae,* gynaecology. *a*1989 Spears *NTC Dict. Slang*
166: My gynie says I'm fine.

gyno *n. Med.* GYNIE.
*a*1967 Partridge *DSUE* (ed. 6) 1161: *Gyno.* Australian...for a gynæcol-
ogist: since *ca*1920 and esp. among medical students. 1985 *Nat. Lampoon*
(Sept.) 82: Who had built up a fanatical following among the gynos.

gyp¹ *n.* [short for *Gypsy*] **1.** (*cap.*) a Gypsy.—usu. considered
offensive.
*a*1840 in *OED:* There was a gip came o'er the land. 1941 in Welsch
Got Yourself a Horse 193: The Gyp paid off the twenty-five dollars.
*ca*1950 in *AS* XXVIII (1953) 116: *Gyp,* n. A Gypsy.
2.a. Orig. *Und.* a thief (*obs.*) or swindler; (now *usu.*) one who
charges an exorbitant price for goods or services; cheat.—
sometimes considered offensive. Also **gip.**
1859 Matsell *Vocab.* 37: *Gip.* A thief. 1880 (cited in *Century Dict.*). 1889
*Century Dict.: Gyp....*A swindler, especially a swindling horse-dealer; a
cheat....slang. 1928 J.M. March *Set-Up* 16: They were cheap [fight]
managers....The perfect gyps. 1932 L. Berg *Prison Doctor* 215: They
worked with the gyp furriers, knocking off lofts for the furs and insurance. 1929–33 J. Lowell *Gal Reporter* 84: We arrived at the agency of
the woman who wasn't a "gyp." 1933 Mahin & Furthman *Bombshell*
(film): Aw, he was a gyp anyway. 1935 in Mencken *Amer. Lang. Supp.*
II 696: *Gyp.* One who charges more than the legal premium on agency
tickets. 1949 W.R. Burnett *Asphalt Jungle* 147: Deal with gyps and
that's what you get. 1954 Collans & Sterling *House Detect.* 188: These
gyps prey on the vanity of out-of-town visitors. 1966 S. Harris *Hellhole*
161: Molly still designates [criminals] by the names with which she first
learned to identify them [*ca*1910]..."griffs"—young thieves, and
"gips"—old ones. *a*1977 S. King *Bachman* 86: "My mother got me a
ring in his store."..."My mother says he's a gyp."
b. an act or method of swindling; a swindle or fraud; (now
usu.) a purchase made at an exorbitant price or the item so
purchased; (*broadly*) an unfair action; a bitter disappointment.
1914 Jackson & Hellyer *Vocab.* 41: *Gyp...*the act of short-changing; a
defrauding by substitution; an action that belies a professed sincerity.
1915–17 Lait *Gus* 95: Don't you start workin' the gyp on him. 1921
Variety (Nov. 18) 7: Some of the lesser orchestra combinations have
gotten wind of this "gyp," and they too spiel the same sob story. 1932
AS VII 401: He won't let me play! That's a gyp. 1936 Washburn *Parlor*
124: So the joint is good for a $5 gyp per chump. 1939 in Botkin *Side-
walks* 389: What a gyp. 1942 in *Jour. Gen. Psych.* LXVI (1945) 132: He
won't let me play. It's a gyp! 1954 Bissell *High Water* 98: The restaurants [were] a big gyp. 1957 N.Y.C. schoolchildren: What a gyp! 1961
Forbes *Goodbye to Some* 223: The whole thing is just one big putrid gyp,
from beginning to end. 1962 L'Engle *Wrinkle in Time* 23: It's a gyp we
missed out on all the fun. 1987 N.Y.C. woman, age *ca*50: What a gyp!
3. *Horse Racing.* GYPSY, 1.
1938 in *DAS:* "Gyp," as applied to horsemen, is...without opprobrium.
Gyp stables try to make a profit. 1939 *Sat. Eve. Post* (Apr. 1) 14:
Autumn finds the gyp heading south through Maryland, Kentucky, or
Arkansas, to winter in Louisiana or Cuba, unless he has a particularly
smart batch of horses....The gyp is in racing as a business. 1940 in
Mencken *Amer. Lang.* Supp. II 769: *Gyp.* A small owner [of race-
horses]....[The term] has no derogatory significance whatever. 1949
Cummings *Dict. Sports* 191. *a*1961 *WNID3.* 1968 M.B. Scott *Racing
Game* 32: Only the gyps...will put you on their plugs. 1970 F.D. Gilroy
Private 32: The elderly "gyp" will go on endlessly about the one stake
horse he owned.

gyp² *n. Mil.* (occ. *cap.*) an Egyptian.—often used contemptuously.—usu. considered offensive. Also (earlier) **gyppie,
gippie.**
*1889 Barrère & Leland *Slang* I 408: *Gippies* (as they call the Egyptian
soldiers here.) *1916 in *OEDS:* Of the "Gyppies" that remained were
picked up seven stretchers full. 1946 Bowker *Out of Uniform* 254:
Americans in uniform went to other countries expecting to dislike
them. As for the people, they were "wogs" or "gyps" or "slopies" or
"wops" or "limies" or "frogs."

gyp or **gip** *v.* **1.a.** to cheat; defraud; charge exorbitantly.—
sometimes considered offensive to the Roma (Gypsies).
Now *colloq.*

1880 (cited in *Century Dict.*). *a*1889 *Century Dict.: Gyp...v.t....*To swindle; cheat. 1908 in H.C. Fisher *A. Mutt* 152: I was gipped for a hundred. 1914 Jackson & Hellyer *Vocab.* 42: *Gyp...*to flim-flam; to cheat by
means of guile and manual dexterity. 1915 in W.C. Fields *By Himself*
61: I can't see what your game is other than to gyp me for $100.00.
1918 *DN* V 24: *To gip...*To fleece someone....General. 1918 *Times-
Picayune* (N.O.) (Sept. 7) "Trench & Camp" Supp. 1: Deny Soldiers
Being Jipped in Alexandria. 1927 in E. Wilson *Twenties* 418: Disagreeable assistant...gypped me on two beers. 1928 in E. Ferber *One Basket*
334: 'Way over to Brooklyn, and then gypped out of his fare! 1928
Dahlberg *Bottom Dogs* 260: Walsh...had just been jipped again. 1934 S.
Anderson *No Swank* 127: Is he trying to gyp us? 1938 *Amer. Mercury*
(Oct.) 247: I've gypped our creditors. 1938–39 Dos Passos *Young Man*
74: Old Spike's a slavedriver like all the employing class but he won't
gyp us. 1943 J. Mitchell *McSorley's* 32: Mazie looks at her dress, fingers
the material, asks how much it cost, tells her she got gypped. 1946
Steinbeck *Wayward Bus* 23: They figure they've been getting gypped
someway. 1953 "L. Padgett" *Mutant* 124: He had a nice little racket
gypping the Hedgehounds. 1956 in Marx *Groucho Letters* 119: I think
you got gypped on that...contract. 1968 de Beauvoir *Force of Circum.*
674: And, turning with an incredulous gaze...I realize with stupor how
much I was gypped. 1975 Zezza *Love Potion* 9: You got gypped.
b. to disappoint.
1928 in E. O'Neill *Sel. Letters* 312: I always found that men and women
knew they could trust me so they never gypped my trust in them.
2. to steal; filch.
1918 *DN* V 24: *To gip...*"to swipe" something.
3. to play truant from (school).
1970 E. Thompson *Garden of Sand* 206: So the very next time you gyp
school, Dan Carrier's going to come get you.

gyp artist *n.* a shortchanger or other swindler.
1935 Coburn *Law Rides Range* 78: That gyp-artist he's ballyhooing for
District Attorney. *1942 (cited in Partridge *Dict. Und.* 288). Gip artist.
1942 *ATS* 425: Swindler...*gyp artist.*

gyp joint *n.* a business establishment that makes a practice of
fleecing customers; (*Navy*) a ship's store.
1927 T.A. Dorgan, in Zwilling *TAD Lexicon* 42: I found a piece of steel
in my chicken soup. Soitenly!! Soitenly!! Spring chicken. This ain't no
gyp joint. 1931 Cressey *Taxi-Dance Hall* 111 [ref. to *ca*1926]: Gee! This
is a "gyp" joint! They sure get your money fast. 1931 Hellinger *Moon*
235: Used to lead a band in the swellest gyp joint on Broadway. 1943
Ottley *New World* 165: There are policemen who—on their off time—
act as "bouncers" in "gyp joints." 1945 S. Lewis *C. Timberlane* 89: I
don't suppose you take her out to that gyp joint...more than three
times a week! 1942–48 in *So. Folk. Qly.* XIII (1949) 202: Our sailor, if
a "regular," will go down to the *gyp-joint* (the ship's store). 1970 Terkel
Hard Times 280: All night long the gyp joints stayed open, where whiskey, dice and women ate up the earnings of the day. 1980 R.L. Morris
Wait Until Dark 51: By 1895 unkempt, sinister-looking clubs, affectionately termed "dives" and "gyp joints"...were the most numerous
saloons found in larger cities.

Gyppo *n.* [alter. of *Egyptian*] *Mil.* an Egyptian.—often used
contemptuously.—usu. considered offensive.
*1916 in *OEDS:* The plagues of the ancient Gyppos. 1944 (quot. at
GYPPY TUMMY). 1985 Boyne & Thompson *Wild Blue* 560: The Gypos
and Syria have mobilized.

gyppo *n.* [*Gypsy* + *-o*] *Logging.* **1.** a small logging or freighting
contractor. Also attrib.
1912 in *Dict. Canad.* 318: There were no "Gyppos" or "wheel-barrow
outfits," as they call the independent freighters. 1923 *Jour. of Political
Economy* XXXI (Dec.) 840: The Gyppo System. 1927 *DN* V 449: *Gyppo,*
n. A piece worker. "A *gyppo's* a goddam skunk what's too goddam mean
to join a union." 1930 "D. Stiff" *Milk & Honey* 206: *Gyppo*—A sub-con-
tractor with poor equipment, but who may be good to work for. 1948
J. Stevens *Jim Turner* 131 [ref. to *ca*1910]: We made miles after a noon
meal at a gyppo camp. 1954 in G. Snyder *Riprap* 8: Only gyps/Run-
ning their beat trucks, no logs on/Gave me rides. 1962 Kesey *Cuckoo's
Nest* 24: I been a bull goose catskinner for every gyppo logging operation in the Northwest. 1963–64 Kesey *Great Notion* 10: Some illiterate
logger with a little gyppo show. 1971 Tak *Truck Talk* 72: *Gippo:* 1. a
trucker who will haul any load anywhere for anyone....2. derogatorily,
another trucker, especially if his rig is in poor shape. *a*1979 Toelken
Dyn. of Folklore 55: *Gypo* (adj.)...used...with the word *outfit* to mean a
small...independent logging company, often run by a single family or
small group of friends. *Ibid.* 66: Them gypo crews. 1978–86 J.L. Burke
Lost Get-Back Boogie 60: A gyppo logger had told me...that I might get

on with a country band in Bonner. *Ibid.* 135: The gyppos...are going to be losing their tractors and everything else.

2. contract work done usu. on a small scale; in phr. **on gyppo** on contract. Also attrib.

1929 *AS* IV (June) 340: *Gypo*—Piecework; being paid on a piecework basis. **1938** Holbrook *Mackinaw* 181: *Gyppo* means piece or contract work. **1939** Appel *People Talk* 291: It's all on the gyppo....On contract. Brown's on gyppo for Winton. The cook's on gyppo for Brown....He buys in big lots and has to make his profit above the gyppo. **1942** *AS* (Dec.) 222: *Gyppo.* Any type of contract work. **1963–64** Kesey *Great Notion* 96: The half dozen or so other gyppo men.

gyppo *v. Logging.* to exploit for one's labor; cheat.—usu. considered offensive.

1925 in *Amer. Mercury* (Jan. 1926) 63: The contract worker is...being unmercifully gyppoed by the boss.

Gyppy *n.* **1.** GYP[2], *n.*

2. GYPPY TUMMY.

1965 LeMay & Kantor *Mission with LeMay* 207: Between these medicaments I was finally over the Gyppy in another three months.

Gyppy tummy *n. Mil.* traveler's diarrhea contracted in Egypt or elsewhere. Also **Gyppo tummy.**

***1943** in *OEDS:* Few set foot in Egypt without contracting "Gyppy Tummy." **1943** in J. Gunther *D Day* 93: Some of his troops in Sicily suffered from "gyppy tummy." **1944** Rock *Field Service* 347: Life's most common ailment—Gyppo tummy (consisting of numerous trips to the latrine and griping gas pains). ***1948** Partridge *Forces' Slang* 89: *Gyppy tummy,* a sharp griping pain, accompanied by diarrhœa, very common in Egypt. **1965** LeMay & Kantor *Mission with LeMay* 206: We became fellow sufferers in the eternal epidemic of Gyppy-tummy. **1978** Ardery *Bomber Pilot* 111: He was stricken with "gippy tummy," more scientifically known as dysentery. **1986** *NDAS.*

gyp sheet *n. Stu.* CRIB-SHEET.

1971 N.Y.U. professor: It was a history gyp sheet.

gyp stick *n. Logging.* a scale rule.

1958 McCulloch *Woods Words* 76: *Gyp stick*—Same as cheat stick.

gypsy *n.* **1.** *Horse Racing.* a small-scale usu. migratory stable owner who trains and races his own horses.

1939 *Sat. Eve. Post* (Apr. 1) 14: Now, "gyp" among horsemen is not a term of reproach. It is just a contraction of gypsy and it means a migratory horseman who aims at a profit. **1949** Cummings *Dict. Sports* 191. *a*1961 *WNID3.*

2. *Trucking.* an independent migratory trucker who owns and operates usu. only a single tractor-trailer; *(hence)* a truck so operated; *(also)* an independent taxicab driver or a taxicab so operated. Now *S.E.*

1953 *ATS* (ed. 2) 716: *Gipsy,* an independent truckman. **1960** *AS* XXXV 240: In truckers' language, a "gypsy" is an owner-driven truck. **1974** Terkel *Working* 208: The owner-operator, we're an outcast,...a gypsy, a fella that everybody looks down on. **1975** Sepe & Telano *Cop Team* 63: A "gypsy" cab is an unlicensed taxi that operates illegally because the driver has not obtained a City of New York medallion license. *Ibid.* 177: He took off in a *gypsy.* **1990** Rukuza *W. Coast Turnaround* 19: You're a gypsy. No really big company will touch you.

3. *Theater.* a chorus dancer; stage dancer.

*a*1978 Cooley *Dancer* 326: In addition to the Kendall Dance Group, there were a number of other gypsies. *Ibid.* 367: The letter went on to say how proud all the "gypsies" were "who knew you and worked with you." **1985** MacLaine *Dancing* 96: Dancers, or gypsies, as we refer to each other, are...exponents of the living body who are in constant pain. **1985** C. Busch *Vampire Lesbians* 68: You'd think I'd never been a chorus gypsy before. **1987** *DayWatch* (CNN-TV) (July 2): The personal struggles of the "gypsies," the dancers trying out for the chorus line. **1987** *Time* (July 13) 66: Still a dance-corps gypsy at heart, Bennett used actual taped recollections by dancers to shape [his play].

gypsy *v. Police.* to assign (a police officer) to duty far away from his usual assignment, usu. as a method of punishment.

1970–71 J. Rubinstein *City Police* 38: Frequently they are "gypsied" to the other end of the district. *Ibid.* 41: The censure can be strengthened by gypsying the man since everyone knows that no sergeant gives away a man he trusts.

gyrene *n.* [orig. uncert.; perh. joc. adaptation of Gk *gyrínos* (whence It *gíríno,* Pg *girino,* L *gyrinus*) 'tadpole, pollywog', infl. by *marine* and ref. to the marine's "amphibious" duties; not, as occ. claimed, alter. of *GI* + ma*rine*; cf. POLLYWOG; discussed by A.F. Moe in *AS* XXXVII (1962), 176–88] Orig. *Navy.* a member of the U.S. Marine Corps; a marine.

1894 *Lucky Bag* (No. 1) (U.S. Nav. Acad.) 68: *Gyrene...*A U.S. Marine. **1898** Allen *Navy Blue* 178: I don't care to have the gyrene report that I said so. **1906** *Army & Navy Life* (Nov.) 498: In the remote period of the origin of [midshipmen's slang]...*gyrene* stood for marine, who was, also, jocosely called a *sea soldier.* **1918** in Cowing *Dear Folks at Home* 222: I think the "jyrenes" must have stopped one hundred tons of machine-gun bullets and shrapnel....in fact, the German fire didn't even slow up the "jyrenes." **1918** Ruggles *Navy Explained* 135: Ah, shove off, peddle your war cry to the jireens. **1919** *Lit. Digest* (Jan. 11) 50: If yo' finds a fellah with a rooster on top of the earth on his hat he's one of dem gyrenes, an' look out—he's a bad man! **1919** *Ladies' Home Jrnl.* (Sept.) 27: The opportunity...arrived in a way to delight the heart of the hardest-boiled "gyrene." **1925** Thomason *Fix Bayonets!* 145: "Don't these 1917 model gyrines talk rough, Mac!" marvelled one old non-com to another. **1926** *Marine Corps Gazette* (Dec.) 241: I thought I'd join the Gyrenes. ***1929** Bowen *Sea Slang* 57: *Gerines.* A name occasionally used for the Royal Marines. **1932** Nicholson & Robinson *Sailor Beware* 34: Well, take my advice, gyrene, and you'll never be lonesome. **1945** in *Calif. Folk Qly.* V (1946) 385: *Girenes...*Marines. There are numerous variants: *Gyrene, gyrine, jirene, jyrene, jyrine,* etc. **1951** Grant *Leathernecks* (film): Them artillery gyrenes came over and claimed they were *their* tents. **1957** Leckie *Helmet* 21: Them Chinese gals...liked Americans best, but you couldn't get them out with a swabby or a dog-face if they was a Gyrene around. **1957** Myrer *Big War* 171 [ref. to WWII]: We're lean-and-mean gyrenes, as you must know by now. **1965** R. Marks *Ltrs.* 63: I...ran into a fellow Gyrene. **1971** Flanagan *Maggot* 208: If the gyrene is the toughest fighting man, then it looks to me like a D.I.'s got to be the toughest of the toughest. **1983** Knoxville, Tenn., woman, age *ca*50: Take it from a gyrene's wife. **1989** D. Sherman *There I Was* 7: Mouse wasn't known as a bad-assed gyrene before then.

gytch *v.* [orig. unkn.] to steal.

1956 H. Ellison *Deadly Streets* 81: I was in the hole for gytching some of the H we had stashed away. *Ibid.* 82: Don't know what...he ever did with all the hubcaps we used to gytch.

This book was edited and composed on Apple Macintosh
computers. It was edited using Microsoft Word 5.1.
It was composed by Electric Ink, Ltd.,
using QuarkXPress 3.2 and FrameMaker 4.0.
The typefaces used throughout this book are from the
Janson family by Adobe. Pronunciation characters are set
in Stone Serif IPA and IPA Alternate, also by Adobe.
The book was printed on Rolland ST Opal
by Rand McNally Book & Media Services, Taunton, Mass.